W9-AUP-727

The Reader's Encyclopedia™
of the
AMERICAN WEST

The Reader's Encyclopedia™
of the
AMERICAN WEST

Edited by

HOWARD R. LAMAR

THOMAS Y. CROWELL COMPANY

New York   Established 1834

FIRST EDITION

Designed by Abigail Moseley

Library of Congress Cataloging in Publication Data
Main entry under title:

The Reader's encyclopedia of the American West.

1. The West—Dictionaries and encyclopedias.
I. Lamar, Howard Roberts.
F591.R38   978'.003   76-17236
ISBN 0-690-00008-1

---

77 78 79 80 81 10 9 8 7 6 5 4 3 2 1

Preface

"Nothing that can be written is so interesting to the casual or constant reader as historical sketches, incidents, actual realities, and occurrences of the new and undeveloped country west of us." These words, penned by the editor of the *Omaha Republican* on July 2, 1869, express a fascination with the American frontier and the American West that has increased rather than diminished in the years since he wrote. That continuing interest would itself be sufficient reason to publish for the first time a comprehensive encyclopedia of the West containing the salient facts about the many real and imaginary Wests that have helped shape American history, literature, and culture.

In 1893 Frederick Jackson Turner stated in his famous essay "The Significance of the Frontier in American History" that the frontier experience had repeated itself in a series of Wests stretching from the Appalachians to the Pacific coast. As every American history student knows, Turner believed that American democracy and, indeed, the American character were products of this unique confrontation of man and the wilderness. In the years since the Turner thesis first appeared, several generations of scholars and popular writers have produced thousands of books and articles on the role of the frontier and the West. Now seems an opportune time to provide in an objective way a critical and topical summary of this immense scholarship along with a guide to the most prominent and most recent literature dealing with westward expansion.

The historical West of Turner, however, has been more than matched by an imaginary West created by an extraordinary range of novelists and poets in the nineteenth century and writers and filmmakers in the twentieth. Building on a literary genre that began with James Fenimore Cooper's *The Pioneers* (1823) and on many subliterary efforts of which the Beadle dime novels were representative, Owen Wister wrote his western novel *The Virginian* (1902). This single volume sold over a million copies in a few years and suddenly elevated the cowboy to the status of a national folk hero.

Wister's success prompted a whole new generation of fiction writers to explore and exploit the history of the trans-Mississippi West. Their efforts were paralleled by Frederic Remington, Charles Russell, and other artists who dramatized western scenes and cowboy life in sketches and paintings. Seldom have the efforts of the historians, novelists, and artists coincided so effectively to create such a distinctive and appealing image of a region and its life-style. Undoubtedly the most obvious reason for publishing *The Reader's Encyclopedia of the American West* is to provide a convenient reference work that includes both those writers who created the fictional West and the real and fictional persons whom they turned into mythic heroes or villians. The editor is persuaded that the deliberate juxtaposition of real and fictional persons and events will provide the reader with a range of information about the West never before available in one volume.

Although Turner thought the westward movement had stopped in 1890 with the end of free land, hundreds of thousands of Americans continued to move to western cities and farms between 1900 and the end of World War I. During the 1930s many thousands more were driven by depression, drought, and poverty out of the Dust Bowl states of the Great Plains to California. Even that movement was dwarfed by the millions of persons who moved west during World War II in search of jobs and a better life. They all had, in a sense, a frontier experience and felt that they were growing up with a new country. Certainly one of the major reasons for writing this volume has been to collect information about the rise of this new, twentieth-century West. While many disciplines have produced compact encyclopedias about a topic or a region, this is probably the first regional-historical volume in an encyclopedia format that combines the story of the older series of real and mythical Wests with an account of the more recent.

Ironically inhabitants of the contemporary West have developed a regional pride in their new home that has in turn led to a consuming interest in the Old West of the nineteenth century. Since 1960, thousands of books and scores of periodicals, both popular and professional, dealing with the West have appeared. The number of college courses in Western history and literature has risen impressively, and professional organizations, research centers, and museums devoted to Western studies and culture now flourish in all parts of the trans-Mississippi West. This academic interest has been complemented by a more subtle and often critical psychological treatment of the West by perceptive writers, artists, and filmmakers. Where possible, the *Encyclopedia* includes entries on both the agencies and critics of this most recent stage of regional self-consciousness.

Historically the term *American West* has meant either any part of the continental United States in its formative or frontier period or the entire trans-Mississippi West from the time of first exploration to the present. The editor has employed both these approaches. Thematically the *Encyclopedia* embraces the story of Indian-white relations; the diplomacy of American expansion; the overland trails experience; the era of the fur trader, the miner, the cowboy, and the settler; and those western subcultures we call Texan and Mormon. As a realm of the imagination the American West encompasses the work of both the romantic and realistic writers and painters of the last two centuries; for the purposes of this volume the term includes work in the fields of music, theater, photography, graphic illustration, film, and television. All of these themes and topics are to be found in the twenty-four hundred entries constituting the *Encyclopedia*. The entries have been prepared by two hundred contributing authors.

When the Thomas Y. Crowell Company first proposed the publication of the *Encyclopedia* nearly a decade ago, writings about the West were undergoing a dramatic change in approach and subject matter. Both the scholars and the general public were in the process of rediscovering the physical West from the perspective of the conservationist and the ecologist. Therefore it seemed imperative to include essays on the environment and the flora and fauna of the trans-Mississippi West along with entries on national parks and monuments. To do this it was necessary to seek the help of scholars from the disciplines of geology, geography, botany, zoology, forestry, and ecology. Specific entries on indigenous animals—and even on that yet unverified man-animal "Sasquatch" or "Big Foot"—add, it is hoped, a new dimension to the environmental history of the West while providing a background for essays on land and water policy, the lumber industry, the national parks and monuments, the conservation movement, and various federal agencies that deal with the West today.

No category in the *Encyclopedia* has proved more exciting and challenging than the compilation of entries dealing with the American Indians, for during the past decade, the American public has rediscovered the Indians of America and writings about them have increased tenfold. The new scholarship demonstrates persuasively that Indian cultures were far more sophisticated and complex than earlier writers have suggested and that the Indian response to whites was both a mixture of necessary resistance and a shrewd, imaginative manipulation of the whites wherever possible. Despite decimation by war and disease, Indians greatly affected Anglo-American life and culture while maintaining distinctive, dynamic cultures of their own. This new scholarship is reflected in the topical and biographical entries concerning Indians. The editor has not attempted to cover Indian prehistory or the historical period exhaustively but has tried instead to provide succinct articles on the historic tribes, with emphasis on those whose contact with whites was both prolonged and significant. Entries on the most important Indian figures (both past and contemporary) and events are supplemented by overview articles on Indian policy, religions and languages, and essays on both Catholic and Protestant Indian missionary activity in the West.

In recent years perceptions of the roles of Spanish and Mexican peoples in the Southwest, of Basques in Nevada, and of the Negro on the frontier and in the contemporary Far West have also undergone revolutionary change. The entries on these important groups, along with biographies of their past and present leaders, provide valuable information for the reader. Other less visible and often neglected minorities who have had an impact on western regions have also been treated: the French in the Mississippi Valley, the Chinese, the Japanese, the Irish, the Jews, and the Italians in the Far West and the German Russians in the Great Plains states.

The attempt to cover new or neglected areas of Western history does not mean the older frontier of the thirteen colonies and the Appalachian region that Tur-

ner wrote about have been ignored. Turner's theory implied that each of the fifty states in the American union was once a West; the editor has honored this concept by including a summary article on the formative period of each state's history from the colonial period onward. These are accompanied by biographical entries on the most important figures associated with the settlement and early development of each state and, for those states west of the Mississippi, biographies of prominent recent and contemporary figures, public men and women, writers, artists, businessmen, and scholars whose lives are integral to the history of the region.

In treating the history of each western state it seemed wisest for the expert on each to determine the major themes and to choose the subjects for the biographical entries. The biographies of persons who contributed most to the development of the states produced some surprising results: rather than unlettered pioneers or the gunfighters, it was the politicians, lawyers, judges, and prominent families who emerged as the local heroes of the formative stage.

There has been no attempt in the *Encyclopedia* to pursue any single interpretation of the western experience, nor have the authors been urged to do so. If there is a revisionist interpretation of a well-known person, real or fictional, or event, the editor asked the author concerned to explain the older interpretation as well. Where the subject is clearly controversial, the author was asked to identify the differing schools of thought. When a person's western career, such as Theodore Roosevelt's, constituted only a portion of his life, no attempt has been made to suggest that that was the most important or influential phase of his life.

To prevent excessive fragmentation and unnecessary repetition, a large number of overview essays on general categories have been included, along with cross-references to related articles. The reader is urged to pursue these references to gain a broader understanding of the given topic. For example, articles on the cattle industry, including the famous trail drives and the exploits of famous cowboys and outlaws, have been supplemented by entries on cowboy clothing, saddles, rodeos, and western music. The persistent reader might then find himself turning to related entries on the horse, the mule, and the sheep ("Sheep Ranching"). Entries on the most famous ranches and ranchers throughout the West add yet another dimension, as do those on Owen Wister, Will James, Zane Grey, and many other novelists who wrote about the cattleman's West. Judicious cross-referencing enables the reader to put together a more wide-ranging account of the factual and fictional society Americans associate with the cattle kingdom.

It also seemed proper—given the concern for the contemporary West in the volume—to supplement accounts of the cattle and mining industries and commercial agriculture with articles on the presently dominant oil, aerospace, and film industries, which have helped revolutionize the economy of the West and urbanize its population. This same approach has been observed in the treatment of western transportation. Traditional accounts of overland stagecoach and railroad routes are complemented by articles on the West's modern roads and highways and its airlines.

The deliberate mixture of the overview essay, the thematic and specific article, and the biographical entry has been pursued in the coverage of most of the general subjects one associates with the West. There are new subject categories, however, that are less easily cross-referenced. There is, as yet, a notable absence of women in general histories of the West. Yet women and families occupied such a central place in the western experience that the old view of a totally masculine West must give way before the facts. Not all readers will find his or her favorite Indian maiden or tough, sharp-shooting heroine, but the entries do include Sacagawea, Annie Oakley, and Belle Starr. They will also find entries on women who were public officials and scholars.

One of the premises of this volume is that the frontier or western experience is nothing less than the story of an evolving American culture. In a selective way the editor has put "tracers" on national institutional and cultural change by looking at the fate of European languages in America. Essays on the English language and the westward movement, Spanish in the Southwest, French in the Mississippi valley, German in Pennsylvania and the Great Plains, pidgin English in Hawaii, the Chinook Jargon in the Pacific Northwest, and the multiple origins of American black English together form a brief but eloquent commentary on the fate of old cultures in new environments and help define the western experience in yet another way.

All major writers of western fiction are included in the *Encyclopedia*. A general essay on the western novel is supplemented by biographical entries on scores of prominent writers, many of whom are associated with a particular region. These in turn bear some relation to entries on actual historical characters such as Daniel Boone, David Crockett, Kit Carson, and Wyatt Earp, whose exploits have become a major source for western fiction. The *Encyclopedia* has made no attempt to cover the thousands of stories and legends we call western folklore, but articles on John Lomax, Mody Boatright, J. Frank Dobie, and Ramon Adams, some of its major interpreters, have been included, along with an essay on frontier humor.

Folklore and legend, while they tell us much about the western cast of mind and ideals, usually obscure the already none too precise historical record, and nowhere more so than in the vague categories of law and order and frontier violence. In a land where no legal institutions had taken root it was possible for yesterday's outlaw to become today's lawman, and so, the editor has been at pains to sort out fact and legend and to include broadly thematic articles that allow a coherent account of an often chaotic situation. Pieces on law and order, vigilantism, and the federal marshal provide the background against which one may read the many entries on individual lawmen and badmen.

Undoubtedly one of the most important aims of the *Encyclopedia* is to provide entries on crucial but less well known aspects of the western experience. There are, for example, articles on the territorial system and the role of the West in the national elections during the nineteenth century. Excellent essays on Indian wars and the Mexican War have been supplemented with entries on the West in the American Revolution, the Civil War, and the Spanish-American War. A series of entries on religious denominations, Peyotism and the Native American Church, and utopian colonies introduce the reader to subjects that are not usually treated in histories of the trans-Mississippi West.

Biographies of standard western figures are here supplemented by pieces that discuss the West as it was seen through the eyes of certain famous Americans not immediately associated with it. For example, a seminal essay on Benjamin Franklin suggests that Franklin, rather than Frederick Jackson Turner, was the real father of the frontier thesis. Interpretive entries on George Washington, Thomas Jefferson, Henry Clay, Abraham Lincoln, and Theodore Roosevelt should prove to be equally rewarding to the reader. The editor has also pursued a conscious policy of including biographies of scholars whose writings and ideas have shaped our perception of western history and given larger meaning to the western experience. By reading the entries on Frederick Jackson Turner, Frederick Logan Paxson, Frederick Merk, and Ray Allen Billington, the student may trace the way in which historians have interpreted the West's role in American life from 1890 to the present.

Generally speaking, the entries do not deal with unprovable abstractions such as the claim that the West was the exclusive inspiration for American democracy, materialism, optimism, or nationalism, nor with the minutiae of the western economy and population movements. The reader will, however, find census figures in the state summaries and valuable statistical information in many individual articles. Undoubtedly many subjects that could have been treated have not been, and for those gaps the editor must take full responsibility.

In addition to the two hundred contributing authors whose scholarship and expertise have made this volume possible, I wish to thank Archibald Hanna, curator of the Yale Western Americana Collection; Earl Pomeroy of the University of California, San Diego; Rodman W. Paul of the California Institute of Technology; and W. Eugene Hollon of the University of Toledo. Each of them in his way contributed to the conception of the project and assisted in its realization. I shall always be grateful for the assistance of Edward Tripp (now with Yale University Press), Patrick Barrett, Nancy Goldner, and Leland Lowther of the Crowell Reference Division for their patience and professional advice during the preparation of the *Encyclopedia*. Finally, I gladly acknowledge the valuable assistance of Robert Schick, Robert Westbrook, Richard Metcalf, Clyde Milner, and Patricia Nelson, five superb historians whose work is evident throughout the volume.

Howard R. Lamar

Yale University
June 1, 1977

Contributors

A.H.	Archibald Hanna	G.D.N.	Gerald D. Nash
A.M.	Albro Martin	G.E.W.	G. Edward White
A.M.G.	Arrell M. Gibson	G.G.S.	G. Gaddis Smith
A.P.N.	A. P. Nasatir	G.H.B.	Gert H. Brieger
A.R.	Andrew Rolle	G.L.	Guy Logsdon
A.W.T.	Allen W. Trelease	G.L.R.	Gary L. Roberts
B.L.F.	Bernard L. Fontana	G.M.	George Miles
B.P.	Betsy Peters	G.P.J.	Gerrit P. Judd
B.P.D.	Bertha P. Dutton	G.R.W.	Gordon R. Wood
B.W.A.	Berten W. Allred	G.T.W.	Gerald T. White
B.W.O.	Bert W. O'Gara	H.A.D.	Harl A. Dalstrom
C.A.M.	Clyde A. Milher II	H.E.M.	Hazel E. Mills
C.B.H.	Charles B. Hunt	H.E.S.	Homer E. Socolofsky
C.B.K.	Carl B. Koford	H.G.W.	Henry G. Waltmann
C.C.	Carol Clark	H.H.D.	Harold H. Dunham
C.C.S.	Clark C. Spence	H.J.D.	Herbert J. Doherty, Jr.
C.H.F.	National Cowboy Hall of Fame and Western Heritage Center	H.J.H.	H. James Henderson
		H.M.	Harold McCracken
		H.P.H.	Harwood P. Hinton
C.H.P.	Clifford H. Pope	H.R.L.	Howard R. Lamar
C.U.	Carl Ubbelohde	J.A.S.	Joe A. Stout
D.A.	Dean Amadon	J.A.W.	John A. Williams
D.A.S.	Duane A. Smith	J.B.	Jen Bilbao
D.B.B.	Daniel B. Botkin	J.B.F.	Joe B. Frantz
D.C.H.	David C. Hunt	J.B.R.	John B. Rae
D.C.S.	Donald C. Swain	J.C.D.	Jefferson C. Dykes
D.H.P.	David H. Price	J.D.	John Dunkel
D.J.	Detlef Junker	J.E.G.	John Edmond Gonzales
D.J.T.	D. Jerome Tweton	J.E.R.	John E. Reinecke
D.L.R.	Daniel L. Racine	J.E.S.	Jane E. Scott
D.L.W.	Dale L. Walker	J.F.	John Faragher
D.M.Q.	D. Michael Quinn	J.F.D.	James F. Downs
D.R.	Don Russell	J.G.	Joseph Giovinco
D.R.R.	Dale R. Roylance	J. Gi.	Jay Gitlin
D.S.	Dorothy Schwieder	J.G.T.	Joseph G. Tregle, Jr.
D.W.C.	Donald W. Chapman	J.H.H.	James H. Hutson
E.A.G.	E. Arthur Gilcreast	J.J.C.	John J. Craighead
E.H.E.	E. H. Eby	J.K.F.	James K. Folsom
E.H.S.	Everard H. Smith III	J.L.D.	J. L. Dillard
E.I.S.	Edgar I. Stewart	J.L.K.	John L. Kessell
E.J.	Erling Jorstad	J.L.L.	John L. Loos
E.M.E.	Emmett M. Essin III	J.N.	Julian Nava
E.P.	Earl Pomeroy	J.O.	Jacob Ornstein
E.R.B.	Edwin R. Bingham	J.P.B.	John Porter Bloom
E.W.K.	Edward W. Kerson	J.P.W.	James P. Walsh
F.A.C.	F. Alan Coombs	J.R.	Jim Reardon
F.C.M.	Frank C. Miller	J.R.V.	James R. Vivian
F.G.M.	Frederick G. Morain	J.S.W.	John S. Whitehead
F.H.	Francis Haines	J.T.	Jonathan Thomas
F.N.	Fred Nicklason	J.T.B.	Jo Tice Bloom
F.P.P.	Francis Paul Prucha	J.T.K.	James T. King
F.R.P.	Frank R. Prassel	J.W.W.	James W. Whitaker
G.B.	Gunther Barth	K.A.M.	Keith A. Murray
G.B.D.	Gordon B. Dodds	K.N.O.	Kenneth N. Owens

K.W.K.	Kenneth W. Keller	R.J.M.	Richard J. Mackie
K.W.P.	Kenneth W. Porter	R.L.	Richard Lowitt
L.B.L.	Lawrence B. Lee	R.M.B.	Richard Maxwell Brown
L.C.K.	Lawrence C. Kelly	R.M.L.	Rudolph M. Lapp
L.D.C.	Leland D. Case	R.N.	Roderick Nash
L.J.A.	Leonard J. Arrington	R.N.E.	Richard N. Ellis
L.L.G.	Lewis L. Gould	R.R.E.	Russell R. Elliott
L.W.D.	Lyle W. Dorsett	R.S.	Robert Schick
M.A.	Majorie Arkelian	R.Sc.	Richard Schickel
M.A.W.	Mitchell A. Wilder	R.V.H.	Robert V. Hine
M.B.	Maxine Benson	R.W.D.	Robert W. Durrenberger
M.B.S.	Morgan B. Sherwood	R.W.F.	Russell W. Fridley
M.F.H.	Michael F. Holt	R.W.L.	Robert W. Larson
M.G.	Mildred Goosman	R.W.P.	Rodman W. Paul
M.G.B.	Merrill G. Burlingame	R.W.W.	Robin W. Winks
M.G.H.	Maurice G. Hornocker	S.B.	Stuart Byron
M.J.P.	Michael J. Pontrelli	S.L.M.	Sandra L. Myres
M.K.	Mark Kelsey	S.N.	Sidney Nathans
M.L.	Marion Love	S.S.	Stan Steiner
M.L.H.	Max L. Heyman, Jr.	T.A.L.	T. A. Larson
M.L.S.	Mary Lee Spence	T.C.H.	Ted C. Hinckley
M.S.	Martin Schmitt	T.D.C.	Thomas D. Clark
M.Si.	Marc Simmons	T.F.A.	Thomas F. Andrews
M.W.	Merle Wells	T.G.D.	Thomas G. Dieterich
M.W.K.	Marc W. Kruman	T.H.B.	Timothy H. Breen
N.M.B.	Natalia M. Belting	T.L.H.	Thomas L. Hall
O.B.F.	Odie B. Faulk	T.R.C.	Thomas R. Cox
O.E Y.	Otis E Young	U.S.L.	Ursula S. Lamb
O.G.C.	O. Gene Clanton	V.H.F.	Victor H. Cahalane
O.K.	Oliver Knight	W.A.D.	William A. Douglass
P.C.	Pedro Castillo	W.B.	Walton Bean
P.C.S.	Philip C. Shelton	W.B.F.	Wilton B. Fowler
P.L.N.	Patricia L. Nelson	W.Bl.	Walter Blair
P.R.M.	P. Richard Metcalf	W.D.W.	Walker D. Wyman
P.S.	Paul Schach	W.E.H.	W. Eugene Hollon
P.W.G.	Paul W. Gates	W.E.P.	William E. Parrish
R.A.B.	Richard A. Bartlett	W.E.W.	Wilcomb E. Washburn
R.A.W.	Robert A. Weinstein	W.H.	Walter Havighurst
R.B.	Richard Batman	W.H.H.	W. H. Hutchinson
R.B.W.	Robert B. Westbrook	W.H.T.	W. H. Timmons
R.D.T.	Richard D. Taber	W.L.B.	Walter L. Brown
R.E.L.	Robert E. Levinson	W.L.R.	Willie Lee Rose
R.F.M.	Ralph F. Meyer	W.R.	Walter Rundell, Jr.
R.H.F.	Robert H. Ferrell	W.R.J.	Wilbur R. Jacobs
R.H.G.	Ralph H. Gabriel	W.T.H.	William T. Hagan
R.I.B.	Robert I. Burns, S.J.	W.T.J.	W. Turrentine Jackson
R.J.L.	Robert J. Loewenberg		

The Reader's Encyclopedia™
of the
AMERICAN WEST

A

A & M colleges. See COLLEGES AND UNIVERSITIES.

Abbot-Downing Company. See STAGECOACH.

Aberdeen, South Dakota. In the spring of 1881 lots were placed on sale for the townsite of present-day Aberdeen. This town, like others in eastern Dakota Territory, grew as the railroads pushed across the land. The Northern Pacific reached Aberdeen in the summer of 1881 and in 1883 the Chicago, Milwaukee and St. Paul Railroad had built to the town.

Aberdeen also benefited from the land boom after the Panic of 1873. As surplus Indian reservation lands were opened to claims in the early part of the twentieth century, still another land boom occurred.

In 1890, a year after South Dakota statehood, Aberdeen had a population of 3,182. Its 1970 population, according to the census of that year, was 26,476.
—D. J. T.

Abert, John James (1789-1863). First commander of the Corps of Topographical Engineers. Abert graduated from West Point in 1811, resigned from the army, and served as a private soldier in the District of Columbia militia at the battle of Bladensburg, Maryland, August 1814. When he rejoined the army later that year, it was with the brevet rank of major and as a topographical engineer. For nearly fifteen years thereafter he was engaged, as an army officer, in civil engineering projects. Then in 1829 Abert was placed in command of the Topographical Bureau at Washington, D.C., and at its creation in 1838, of the Corps of TOPOGRAPHICAL ENGINEERS, with the rank of colonel. He retained this position until his retirement in 1861. In essence, Abert's career and the history of the Topographical Engineers are inextricably connected.

It was Colonel Abert's political sagacity that secured the respected status of the Topographical Engineers in the two decades prior to the Civil War. He was a good administrator, chose excellent personnel, and then inspired them by his own knowledge of the West and enthusiasm for the work of the corps. At the same time he controlled and disciplined his men, criticizing John C. Frémont for taking a cannon along on an expedition and assigning the unpopular Captain John M. Pope to three years of well-drilling on the Staked Plains. The colonel's son, Lieutenant James W. Abert, participated in some of the corps activities.

There is no biography of Colonel Abert. See George W. Cullom, *Biographical Register . . .* vol. I (1868); and William H. Goetzmann, *Army Exploration in the American West* (1959).—R. A. B.

Abilene, Kansas. See CATTLE TOWNS.

Adams, Andy (1859-1935). Novelist and short-story writer. Adams, now remembered as the most articulate spokesman for the authentic "Old West" of the cattle kingdom, was born in Indiana. He ran away from home,

probably in 1874, and drifted west, first to Arkansas and then to Texas. From 1882 to 1893 he lived in Texas, and his experiences there are the basis of practically all his fiction. In 1883 he made the first of many trail drives, accompanying a horse herd from Texas to Caldwell, Kansas; he made many similar drives until 1889. In 1893 rumors of the gold boom at Cripple Creek drew him to Colorado. From Cripple Creek he moved to Colorado Springs, where he settled in 1894 and where, with the exception of two brief periods, he lived until his death.

Although Adams published two stories for juveniles, *Wells Brothers* (1911) and its sequel, *The Ranch on the Beaver* (1927), and left a number of unpublished manuscripts of novels, stories, and plays at the time of his death, his reputation today depends upon the five books he wrote from 1903 to 1907—*The Log of a Cowboy* (1903), *A Texas Matchmaker* (1904), *The Outlet* (1905), *Cattle Brands* (1906), and *Reed Anthony, Cowman* (1907). All of these but *Cattle Brands*, a collection of stories, are novels, though *Reed Anthony, Cowman* has often been misread as an autobiography. In fact, all Adams' writing is autobiographical in format and meticulously researched from the point of view of factual detail. Although ingenious claims have been advanced for Adams as an imaginative writer, he is best noted for his ability as an accurate reporter of a vanished way of life. *The Log of a Cowboy*, by common consent his best book, is typical of his other work as well. It gives a faithful picture of a very particularly conceived trail drive, is anecdotal in focus, and has little plot other than that implied by the journey of a herd of cattle from Texas to Montana. Adams' own desire was avowedly to make his fiction indistinguishable from fact, and in this he succeeds only too well.

See J. Frank Dobie, "Andy Adams, Cowboy Chronicler," *Southwest Review* (January 1926); and Wilson M. Hudson, *Andy Adams: His Life and Writings* (1964), and *Andy Adams: Storyteller and Novelist of the Great Plains* (1967).—J. K. F.

Adams, Charles Francis, Jr. (1835-1915). Writer and railroad executive. Adams was the son of Charles Francis Adams, United States ambassador to England during the Civil War, grandson of John Quincy Adams, and great-grandson of John Adams. Although he studied law after graduating from Harvard, legal practice did not appeal to him. Financially independent, he had barely begun a career as essayist on public affairs when the Civil War intervened.

After serving for three and a half years at the head of one of the Negro regiments raised in Massachusetts, Adams resumed his writing career, now convinced that the most worthy topic in the land lay in the rising problems of railroad finance, management, and regulation.

His incisive study of the unseemly railroad war between Jay Gould and Commodore Vanderbilt, *A Chapter of Erie* (1871), brought him to national attention. Adams consistently advocated full and fair publicity of railroad affairs, rather than rigid regulatory laws, as the most effective method of bringing private gain and public welfare into harmony. As one of the first members and later chairman of the Massachusetts Board of Railroad Commissioners he followed such a policy. Carl Schurz urged him to become one of the government-appointed directors of the UNION PACIFIC in 1878. By 1884, a panic year, the repressive policies that the government had followed since the Credit Mobilier scandal in 1873 had driven the Union Pacific almost to the wall. Recognizing that relations with the government was its chief problem, the major investors in the Union Pacific prevailed upon the prestigious Adams to assume the presidency. After a frustrating six years in which he despaired alike of both the private and the public conscience, Adams was forced to admit defeat in 1890. Three years later the Union Pacific was bankrupt.

Adams' most important writing on the railroad situation of the late nineteenth century, *Railroads: Their Origins and Problems* (1878), reveals a pragmatic, nondoctrinaire approach to a complex problem and an awareness that many of the "abuses" attributed to the railroads originated elsewhere.

Edward C. Kirkland, *Charles Francis Adams, Jr., 1835-1915: The Patrician at Bay* (1965) is a first-rate biography. For a deeper understanding of the situation Adams faced on the Union Pacific, see Robert G. Athearn, *Union Pacific Country* (1971).—A. M.

Adams, Eva B. (1908-   ). Nevada political figure. Born in the small mining camp of Wonder, Nevada, Adams was graduated from the University of Nevada in 1928 and received a master's degree from Columbia University in 1936. She taught at the University of Nevada from 1936 until 1939, when she became Senator "Pat" McCarran's administrative assistant, serving him in that capacity until his death in 1954. She was often called Nevada's "third Senator" because of her influence in Washington, D.C., during those years. Sworn in as director of the United States Mint on October 31, 1961, she held that office until 1969.

See W. K. Bixler, *A Dozen Sierra Success Stories: Twelve Individualists of Our Time* (1964).—R. R. E.

Adams, Hank (1943-   ). Assiniboin-Sioux activist. Adams was born on the Fort Peck reservation in Montana but grew up in Indian communities in western Washington. He was the director of Survival of American Indians Association, an organization based in the Seattle-Tacoma area. It was founded in the early 1960s to help reestablish fishing rights guaranteed to Indians when they signed over Washington Territory to the federal government in 1854.

Before coming to Survival, Adams served in the army and then worked at United Scholarship Service for American Indian and Spanish-American Students, a national organization with headquarters in Denver, which assists students in applying to and attending independent secondary schools and colleges. It offers counseling, grants, and scholarship aid. Later Adams worked as a researcher, writer, and lobbyist for the Congress of American Indians and the National Indian Youth Council in Washington, D.C. Adams became director of

the Quileute tribe's poverty program in the state of Washington and was a leading figure in the Poor Peoples' March of 1968. He made a remarkable showing as a congressional candidate, especially since other obligations kept him off the campaign trail.

The renewed struggle on the riverbanks and in the courts concerning Indian fishing rights has been brutal at times, and early in 1971 Adams was shot point-blank in the stomach after being surprised by two self-styled white vigilantes as he was waiting in his car for a friend to return from checking a fishing net. Despite harassment of this extreme nature, Adams worked on plans for a fishing cooperative and an appeal to the Supreme Court to verify the tribes' rights to fish.

He was editor of Survival's newsletter, *The Renegade,* and a contributor to *Manifesto* (1970) and is featured in a film, *The North American Indian.* He received the Abraham Lincoln Award of the National Education Association in 1971.

Adams and the Survival group have been the subject of articles in *Ramparts* and the *New York Times* (April 1971).—C. C.

Adams, John Quincy (1767-1848). Statesman. A son of President John Adams, John Quincy Adams was preeminently a nationalist during the major portion of his life. It was only in 1831, when he took a seat in the House of Representatives and soon found himself ensnarled in the slavery controversy, that Adams began to look with concern at the increasing expansion of the national territory and the spread of slavery into new areas.

The second presidential Adams was a contentious, assertive, hardworking, and extremely intelligent man. Early in his life he saw that the experience of his boyhood years, the coming of age in Braintree, Massachusetts, outside of Boston, was not a training ground for the understanding of the national concerns of the American republic. Adams quickly became a national man, not a New Englander, and when his own section espoused a position against the embargo in 1807-09 he left the Federalist party and went over to the Republicans. His conversion to Republicanism did not altogether convince President Thomas Jefferson, and for the rest of Jefferson's long life there was uncertainty in the Virginian's mind as to whether Adams was a Federalist in Republican clothing. Despite this doubt by some of the Jeffersonians and their leader, there should have been no question of the New Englander's interests and policies.

As peace commissioner at the Ghent conference in 1814, Adams maintained a strongly national attitude and refused along with his fellow commissioners to allow the conclusion of a peace that would mutilate the territory of the United States. As secretary of state in 1817-25 he militantly defended American rights. Almost alone in the cabinet he defended the actions of General Andrew Jackson in Florida in 1818. Adams would have pressed for the annexation of Texas in the ADAMS-ONIS TREATY of 1819 had he had any support in the Monroe cabinet. In the same treaty negotiations it was his idea not merely to take the Floridas from Spain but to run a boundary of rivers and parallels between Spanish Mexico and the Louisiana Purchase and to take that boundary out to the forty-second parallel and the Pacific. It was Adams who put the noncolonization idea into the Monroe Doctrine in 1823, fearing as he did the encroachments of czarist Russia.

As president, Adams sought an agreement over Oregon through Minister Albert Gallatin in London, and in 1827 obtained an indefinite extension of the "free and open" arrangement then in effect, until the American people could push out to settle that grand territory. In later years he came to fear the slavery issue above all else, and yet he favored the admission of Texas to the Union.

For his national policy see Henry CLAY, Adams' secretary of state.

Adams should be characterized as an expansionist, even though his fears for the extension of slavery sometimes qualified his territorial enthusiasms. He believed in the mission of America to spread republicanism throughout the Western Hemisphere, and that meant the territorial expansion of the United States throughout the American subcontinent, perhaps even to include Cuba (during his presidency he had made an unsuccessful effort to purchase Cuba from Spain). Adams died during the Mexican War, before he could see the territorial additions of that conflict and their deleterious effect upon the sectional balance.

John Quincy Adams' son, Charles Francis Adams, edited the major portion of his father's diary and published it under the title of *Memoirs of John Quincy Adams: Comprising Portions of His Diary from 1795 to 1848,* 12 vols. (1874-77). By far the best biography is by Samuel Flagg Bemis, *John Quincy Adams and the Foundations of American Foreign Policy* (1949), and *John Quincy Adams and the Union* (1956).—R. H. F.

Adams, Ramon F. (1889-   ). A native of Moscow, Texas, and a graduate of Austin College in 1912, Adams was an avid collector of the language of the range, trail, and cow camps for more than half a century. His first two books, *Cowboy Lingo* (1936) and *Western Words* (1944), are valuable contributions to the written literature of the western range, and are widely used by contemporary writers on the West. Adams also gathered an outstanding collection of books and pamphlets about the range livestock industry and western outlaws, which became the basis for his next major contributions to western lore. *Six-Guns and Saddle Leather* (1954) is the first bibliography of the books and pamphlets concerning western outlaws and gunmen. His second important bibliography, *The Rampaging Herd* (1959), lists books addressing all aspects of range life, including cowboys, cattle, cow horses, and cattle trails. The items listed in these two bibliographies were drawn not only from his own collection, but from materials found in libraries and private collections from coast to coast as well. Both bibliographies are widely used by dealers, collectors, and librarians.

In 1964 Adams wrote a lengthy critique, *Burs Under the Saddle,* in which he carefully examines the text of more than four hundred of the most widely read western books, particularly those on outlaws and gunmen. His analysis revealed that some of these popular works, which were often used as source material by other western writers, often omitted factual data and that others contained numerous errors. The reference is indispensable, therefore, for writers who wish to keep the western gunmen records straight.

In addition to these reference works, Adams coauthored *Charles M. Russell, Cowboy Artist* (1948), a

biography; *Come and Get It* (1952), a delightful book on cow-camp and chuckwagon cooks; *A Fitting Death for Billy the Kid* (1960), one of the best books on the little outlaw; *The Old-Time Cowhand* (1961), a thorough treatment on the gear, duties, and code of the real working cowboy; *The Legendary West* (1965), *The Cowman & His Philosophy* (1969), *The Cowboy & His Humor* (1968), and *The Cowman & His Code of Ethics* (1969), each beautifully printed and issued in small numbered and signed editions; and *Wayne Gard, Historian of the West* (1970), vol. 31 in the Southwest Writers Series. He also edited and annotated *The Best of the American Cowboy* (1957), an anthology, which was translated into Italian; and Bob Kennon's *From the Pecos to the Powder* (1965).

Adams was a member of the Texas Institute of Letters, the Western History Association, and the Southwest Writers. In 1968 Austin College awarded him an honorary degree of Doctor of Literature in recognition of his numerous contributions to western history. —J. C. D.

Adams, William Lysander (1821-1906). Writer, editor, farmer, and physician. Adams was born in Plainsville, Ohio, the son of a Great Lakes ship captain and land speculator. After attending Knox College in Galesburg, Illinois, and Bethany College, a Disciples of Christ institution founded by Alexander Campbell, in Virginia, he began teaching school in Illinois. In 1848 Adams, together with his wife and two infant daughters, joined an emigrant train bound for Oregon. A year later, after a profitable foray south to the California gold fields, he bought a farm in Yamhill County, Oregon.

For the next twenty-odd years Adams devoted most of his energies to writing and politics. He wrote a play in verse, *A Melodrama Entitled "Treason, Strategems, and Spoils," in Five Acts by Breakspear,* run serially in the *Oregonian* in 1851 and published in pamphlet form in 1852. In 1855 he established the *Oregon Argus* as a Whig organ and for six years was its editor. Through the newspaper Adams played a significant role in territorial politics first as a Whig and later as a Republican. In 1861 Abraham Lincoln, recognizing Adams' central role in founding the Republican party in Oregon, appointed him collector of customs at Astoria, a post he held until 1867.

In 1868 Adams took a leisurely two-year trip through Central and South America and then went on to the East Coast, where he lectured on Oregon. By 1871 he was back in the Pacific Northwest farming and revising his lectures, later published under the title *Oregon As It Is* (1873). In 1873 Adams again left Oregon to study medicine at the Eclectic Medical College of Pennsylvania, returning in 1874 to begin practicing in Portland. Three years later he moved to Hood River, Oregon, where he resumed farming and operated a hotel and sanatorium.

Although Adams wrote satirical verse for his own as well as other newspapers, his reputation as a political satirist rests largely on *Treason, Strategems, and Spoils.* The satire, an adroit and astringent assault on Asahel Bush, editor of the *Oregon Statesman,* and a handful of other Democratic party leaders known as the Salem Clique, reflects the author's intimate knowledge of territorial politics. Adams portrays the clique as a cluster of alcoholics and pokes barbed fun at their alleged scheme to detach Oregon Territory from the Union, adopt Mormonism, join California, and elevate Brigham Young to rule over a Pacific empire. Because Adams was always free and effective in his use of contemporary slang and colloquialisms, the play remains a reservoir of authentic Americanisms, some of which compete with the earliest citations in nineteenth-century dictionaries of American slang.

Another work, *History of Medicine and Surgery from the Earliest Times* (1888), is a rambling, eccentric account: a combination of scissors-and-paste history on one hand and a sarcastic exposure of the crimes of contemporary quacks and the dogmatism of regular practitioners on the other. From this book it is evident that Adams had left far behind the pious Disciple of Christ and prohibitionist of the 1850s and moved on to free thought and tolerance for topers.

The best treatment of Adams is George N. Belknap's introduction to a modern edition of *Treasons, Strategems, and Spoils* (1968), based on copies of the 1852 pamphlet edition.—E. R. B.

Adams Express Company. Adams and Company, founded by Alvin Adams, first operated in Massachusetts in 1840 and, with the American Express Company, pioneered in the express business. With nine years' experience when the California gold rush began, Adams and Company, on December 1, 1849, opened an office in San Francisco and quickly assumed a commanding position in both express and banking in the state. Two and a half years later, WELLS, FARGO & CO. entered the same businesses in California as a western ally of American Express, Adams' eastern rival. Wells, Fargo & Co. was to operate west of the Mississippi-Missouri rivers and American Express to the east. Fierce competition for the forwarding and banking business of California ensued. In 1854 Adams Express Company was formed in a consolidation of several express and steamship companies and had a capital of $1 million, with Adams as president and William B. Dinsmore as vice-president. Adams and Company's California business was not included in this consolidation, being split off into a separate company in which Adams personally retained an interest. D. H. Haskell, manager of Adams of California, was clever at publicity but unbusinesslike and incautious. A business depression, which began in 1854 in the East, assumed panic proportions in California the following year after the failure of the banking firm Page, Bacon & Company. The major express companies and banking houses in California suspended business on February 23, 1855. Wells, Fargo & Co. was found to be solvent and quickly reopened its offices, but Adams and Company (California) did not reopen. Its collapse was a severe shock to the people and businesses in the state. Mobs stormed its offices in hope of withdrawing their deposits, but the California company went to receivership. Approximately two hundred San Francisco business establishments with liabilities of $8 million were forced to close, and a serious depression was at hand. Wells, Fargo & Co. emerged from the crisis as the dominant organization in the express business in the state. Former employees of Adams and Company attempted to reorganize as the Pacific Express Company, but that firm enjoyed only brief and moderate success.

The credit of the Adams Express Company was not destroyed by the failure of its western affiliate, but the crisis resulted in the resignation of Alvin Adams as president. The Civil War brought prosperity to all the express companies. The Adams Express and Southern Express companies provided the only feasible lines of communication for passengers and mail between the North and South. With the coming of the railroad era, bitter competition developed among the express companies to obtain favorable contracts with railroads controlling strategic terminals, in attempts to establish regional monopolies. Adams Express Company fought with the United States Express Company, primarily for the business between New York and Chicago. By 1886 Adams Express, one of the most powerful of the six express companies that together controlled ninety percent of the nation's business, paid the railroads more than $2 million annually, or one-fourth of the entire amount paid by all the express companies. Its $12 million capital had all been issued as stock dividends accumulated from earnings. Prosperity came to a close during World War I, a crisis period, and the Adams Express Company was the heaviest loser of all the companies involved. As a war measure, Adams Express, American Express, Southern Express, and Wells, Fargo & Co. were merged into the American Railway Express Company, capitalized at $30 million, but supervised by the United States government. Adams Express Company now operates as a closed-end investment company.

Alvin F. Harlow, *Old Waybills: The Romance of the Express Companies* (1934), is the standard account of the express business. A. L. Stimson, *History of the Express Business* (1881), an earlier study, is a valuable reference work, particularly on the early history of the first companies in the East. The California phase of express operations is ably presented in Oscar O. Winther, *Express and Stagecoach Days in California* (1936). The use of stagecoaches by the express companies is noted throughout Ralph Moody, *Stagecoach West* (1967). —W. T. J.

Adams-Onís Treaty (1819). Cession of the Floridas and establishment of the western boundary of the Louisiana Purchase.

The Treaty of San Lorenzo of 1795 which established the boundary between Spanish Florida and the United States at the thirty-first parallel, proved inadequate to contain the frictions and animosities of Spanish-American relations. The fact that the Spanish possessed the Floridas did not prevent the piecemeal occupation of much of West Florida by land-hungry Americans. And with the confusions of the wars of the French Revolution and Napoleon, during which American commerce was jeopardized, it clearly became necessary after the War of 1812 for the two nations to conclude a new treaty arrangement. It was Spain's ill luck, and America's great good fortune, that the secretary of state in President Monroe's cabinet was John Quincy Adams, a fervent nationalist and stickler for American rights in the New World. The resultant treaty of February 12, 1819, was a diplomatic triumph for Adams against his adversary, Luis de Onís, the Spanish minister in Washington.

The diplomacy of the Adams-Onís treaty concerned three major problems, the first of which was the Floridas. (see EAST AND WEST FLORIDA QUESTION). Here Adams simply insisted that the Spanish must cede both East and West Florida—West Florida because it was properly a part of the Louisiana Purchase, and East Florida because of raids by Indians into American territory, the escape of slaves into this Spanish possession, the use of East Florida's ports during the wars of the French Revolution and Napoleon, and the revocation of the right of deposit at New Orleans by the Spanish intendant in 1802. Onís raised as many arguments as possible against cession of the Floridas, but eventually gave in.

The second problem in negotiating the treaty concerned Texas. Adams argued for a Spanish-American boundary that would have included Texas, but he settled for a boundary at the Sabine River, the western boundary of the present-day state of Louisiana. At the time Adams could get support neither from Monroe nor his cabinet. Even General Andrew Jackson, fresh from winning laurels as the conqueror of Pensacola in 1818, was unwilling to see Onís pressed for Texas, deeming possession of the Floridas much more important. And so Adams reluctantly gave up Texas, not knowing that if he had pushed Onís hard enough the Spanish minister would have conceded Texas. When the latter territory became an object of American settlement shortly thereafter, and within fifteen years was ripe for revolution and, as it proved, independence, Adams began to receive an enormous volume of criticism, some of it political but much of it sincere. He vociferously denied that he had lost Texas, although it was difficult for him to make this point thoroughly by showing the lack of support on this issue from Monroe and Jackson. Indeed, it was Jackson's henchmen who were the loudest in criticizing Adams about Texas.

The third and last problem in negotiation of the Adams-Onís Treaty concerned the tracing of a western boundary for the Louisiana Purchase, between the territory of the United States and that of Spain. The purchase of 1803 was never clear in its boundaries, and Napoleon seems to have desired it that way, saying that if an ambiguity did not exist in the treaty it would perhaps be desirable to put one there. The presumption was that the purchase comprised the drainage area of the Missouri and Mississippi rivers west of the latter. Adams and Onís delimited the Spanish-American boundary by a series of rivers and parallels, commencing with the Sabine River, which gave some territory to Spain and some to the Americans but followed roughly the drainage area. In a stroke of genius Adams pushed the boundary line out to the Pacific Ocean at the forty-second parallel, the southern boundary of the present-day state of Oregon. This move strengthened his country's position in what a generation later became the Oregon question. This new boundary brought the United States to within a few hundred miles of New Mexican settlements and presaged the opening of the Santa Fe Trail, as well as a new awareness of Oregon.

After Adams and Onís concluded their treaty, the wily king of Spain, Ferdinand VII, quietly granted most of the public lands in East Florida to three court favorites. Adams had overlooked a proviso in the treaty by which, as it turned out, two of these grants were valid. Two years had to pass until a revolution in Spain enclosed Ferdinand in a constitution. His government annulled the land grants, and the two governments in 1821 ratified the Transcontinental treaty, as it justly should be called.

Philip C. Brooks, *Diplomacy and the Borderlands: The Adams-Onís Treaty of 1819* (1939), is the definitive account; see also Samuel Flagg Bemis, *John Quincy Adams and the Foundations of American Foreign Policy* (1949).
—R. H. F.

adobe architecture. The prehistoric Indians of the Southwest, as well as those in historic times, built single- and multi-storied houses of rock or adobe. Adobe structures were built originally in courses, using fist-size lumps or loaves of clayey loam mixed with water and suitable bonding materials (plant roots, straw, or burned grasses), which were fitted together with thick adobe mortar.

The structures, being hand-fashioned, were of soft and somewhat irregular outline, and consisted of a few contiguous household units built along a common axis. As family needs increased, adjoining chambers were added. Back rooms usually served as storage places. Ells were often built at one or both ends. These, in turn, might have rooms built between the termini, creating a boxlike appearance—hollow on the interior, giving rise to a plaza. Some Indians built their ceremonial chambers in the plaza, others included them among the dwelling rooms. As family size increased, superstructures could be built on any portion of the ground floor units. These were usually terraced back from the front, providing living space out-of-doors.

As the population multiplied, domestic and ceremonial requirements resulted in growth by accretion. The more complex constructions came to be great clusters of rooms, similar to a modern apartment house of stepped outline. Archaeological sites of this nature remain at Aztec and in the Chaco Canyon of New Mexico, at Mesa Verde and other locations in southwestern Colorado and southeastern Utah, and at numerous locations in northeastern Arizona. These great houses are built of sandstone blocks set dry or with adobe mortar, plastered over, inside and out, with adobe plaster. The modern five-storied pueblo of Taos (New Mexico) is an outstanding example of this type of architecture; there the building material is adobe.

When Don Juan de Oñate settled his colonists at Yungue, one of the twin villages of Yunque-Yunque of San Juan Pueblo in 1598, the Indians graciously moved out of their houses, believing that they would be thrown out anyway, and the Spaniards moved in. Bitter complaints immediately arose, as the Spaniards gasped and choked in the smoke-filled, windowless, and doorless houses. The means of entry was through a rooftop hatchway and down a ladder into an interior, where some smoke always seemed to remain. Even after doors and windows were cut, the smoke hung on, and the colonists took to the riverside to sleep. Here they battled mosquitoes and nibbling rodents for months, before they erected the church of San Gabriel and some dwellings.

These early settlers were familiar with adobe construction methods, which had been developed from six to eight thousand years before in the Mediterranean world. The Moors took the system to Spain. (Using this system, a suitable clay is wetted, mixed with the same vegetable litter used by prehistoric Indians, hoed into a mass, trampled with bare feet, then, using wooden molds, shaped into bricks, widely varying in size.)

The Spaniards in New Mexico did not follow the pueblo forms of multi-stories, but used the traditional

Although built as recently as 1939, the Church of Cristo Rey in Santa Fe, New Mexico, typifies the traditional adobe architecture of the Southwest; it is the largest known adobe structure in the world. (New Mexico Department of Development)

Spanish house of one story encircling a court. Their style is nevertheless strongly reminiscent of pueblo dwellings and harmonizes as well with the landscape. Spanish dwellings were, as were those of the Indians, laid out by eye. The average adobe brick measured ten by eighteen by five inches and weighed from fifty to sixty pounds. Walls laid up with these blocks were two feet thick or thicker, and every room, whitewashed inside, opened on the inner court. Usually a *portal*, or porch, ran around all four walls. The portals were supported by round pine or fir posts capped with carved wooden corbels and square beams. The house had few outside openings except a pair of huge, heavy gate-like doors through which horses and carts could go. What windows there were usually looked into the court, or patio. They were very small openings with wooden grills of poles or slats set deeply into the walls. Sometimes they were covered with a parchment of animal skin or a sheet of selenite. These houses were fortresses in times of raids.

Fireplaces were generally of the corner type, essentially a smoke-gathering hood with a tapering flue through the roof. Floors were of hard packed adobe laid somewhat below ground level. Animal blood mixed with ashes was sometimes added to harden the earth and make it water-resistant. Rooms were from thirteen to fifteen feet wide depending upon the length of the *vigas* (beams) and were made larger by increasing their length. A *sala*, or drawing room, used for formal occasions, was sometimes as long as forty feet. Easier to obtain than suitable building stone, wood was nevertheless difficult to obtain, for it meant hauling or dragging logs for many miles. There were no sawmills.

Walls were laid up so as to gradually reduce the width toward the top and thus give greater stability. Corners were rounded. Hands and reveals at the doorways and windows were sculptured. Adobe mixed with straw or minute gravel particles was used as plaster, thus giving a unique texture. Across the ceiling beams either split juniper poles, about two inches in diameter, or willow stems were laid. Over this came a layer of straw, and then adobe dirt from eighteen to twenty-four inches thick. A final coating of mud made a hard surface. Roofs had only enough slope to drain off water to the *canales*, or spouts, which jutted out to carry water away from the walls and foundation.

The next adobe house style was American Territorial. The walls were thinner and carried a burned brick firewall of coping. They were plastered with a lime-sand stucco that was far more satisfactory than the cement stucco of today. House beams were squared, often mill cut or adzed, and split boards were laid over them. A herringbone pattern was achieved in the ceilings by laying the poles and split juniper at an angle to the beam, and alternating their direction. The windows were usually set to the outside face of the wall with the American Colonial (Greek Revival) trim on the outside.

American military forts were built mainly in this style. Actually they were like military villages, for they were not built with defense in mind. They typically included a barracks, officers' quarters, hospital, and quartermaster and commissary storehouses.

Monolithic adobe pueblo missions of New Mexico were built under the direction of the Franciscans, and the proportions are Spanish expressed in Indian character. Their only relation to the California missions built one hundred fifty years later lies in original purpose.

Acoma Pueblo's mission was established by Friar Juan

Ramirez in 1629 and took forty years to complete. Not a vestige of earth was atop the four hundred-foot-high rock of Acoma, and every grain it took to build the prehistoric terraced pueblo and the mighty church had to be carried up a narrow trail. The Acoma mission church is one hundred feet long and forty feet wide. Its front walls are so sloped as to form immense buttresses topped with square towers. Towers had been built by the Indians in ancient times, and all that remains of Spanish embellishment are the carvings on the great *vigas,* forty feet long and one foot square, that had to be transported from a mountain miles away. Whatever Spanish ornamentation occurred on the outside has long ago gracefully eroded away.

Indians in California had no permanent architecture of their own. The Franciscans brought in their own artisans from Mexico or trained the Indians in Spanish methods. They were eager to re-create the elegance of the cathedrals of Spain, their homeland. They had the artisans paint imitation marble on pillars and walls and draw altars, doors, pillars, niches, corridors, and other make-believe on walls in perspective. Elaborate ornamental false fronts were added to plain facades to hide the true low roof lines. Examples of this can be found at Santa Barbara, Santa Ines, and San Miguel.

Those mission churches were built around patios. All of them featured the covered arcades common in Spain and Mexico. The massive pillars, low silhouettes, and overall proportions were due largely to the limitations of the adobe blocks with which most of them were built. To support the heavy tile roof and to be self-supporting, the walls were built four or five feet thick. Wide eaves and covered walkways protected the walls from rain.

Where forges existed, masses of filigreed gates, window gratings, and crosses were shaped to adorn the churches. *Campanarios,* walls that are pierced to hold bells, abounded. Sometimes they are freestanding, as at Pala, and sometimes are an extension of the wall itself, as at San Gabriel. Of California's six-hundred-and-fifty-mile chain of missions, only one, the very first, at San Diego, is modest and plain.

Although they are one hundred fifty years younger than the missions of New Mexico, most of the California missions have had an unhappy history of heavy damage by earthquake, flood, and neglect. Some simply disappeared into weathered mounds, others were sold and razed. The rest have undergone periodic restorations. Owners or vandals removed roof tiles, beams, bells, and even the nails from these structures. Where restoration was possible, concrete and steel were used instead of adobe, often the material of original construction.

San Luis Rey de Francia at San Luis Rey, founded in 1798, is still being restored. The adobe church of San Antonio de Padua, twenty-three miles southwest of King City, founded in 1771, was last restored in 1949. It is the only mission whose surroundings appear as they were originally; the Franciscans rebuilt it as a living monument.

La Purísima Concepción at Santa Barbara, built in 1786-87, is better preserved than most of the existing missions in California. The residence of the Franciscan community, it has not been abandoned since its founding.

Although a temporary church at San Diego was finished in the fall of 1776, the mission structure, as seen today, was not completed until 1813. Deterioration set in about 1824, and the mission was sold in 1846 to a private individual. Not until 1862 were a few acres restored to the Catholic church by Congress. When restoration was begun in 1931, only the church façade and base of the belfry remained. Using these as a guide, the church building and bell tower were built in duplication of the original structure. Later a long portico was added.

A number of buildings survive in California. Casa Covarrubias, the adobe homestead of the Covarrubias family in Santa Barbara, was built in 1817 by Don Diego Carrillo. It was probably constructed by the same Indians who built La Purísima Concepción mission. L-shaped, its sala is fifty-five feet long. Monterey has several colonial adobes: the Old Customs House; the Pacific Building; the Eldorado House; the Escolas House; and the Old Whaling Station. Near Ventura is an old adobe ranch, the Olivas House. The oldest Spanish settlement in California, San Diego still retains the Casa de Bandini, a two-story adobe built in 1829 by Juan Bandini and enlarged in 1869, and the Adobe Chapel, the original church of the Immaculate Conception, built in 1850.

See Kent Baer, *Architecture of the California Missions* (1958); John A. Berger, *The Franciscan Missions of California* (1941); C. C. Cullimore, *Santa Barbara Adobes* (1948); Maynard Geiger, *The Indians of Mission Santa Barbara in Paganism and Christianity* (1960); Charles Steen, "An Archeologist's Summary of Adobe," *El Palacio* (1971). E.C. Sullivan and A.E. Logie, *The Story of the old Spanish Missions* (1927).—B. P. D. and M. L.

aerospace industry. The aerospace industry is concerned with the design and manufacture of aircraft, missiles, and space vehicles, their power plants, guidance systems, and other components. It includes companies that began as aircraft manufacturers, builders of aircraft and rocket engines, and manufacturers of electrical and electronic equipment and components.

Although some important aerospace firms are in the Northeast, the industry is primarily western, with the largest single concentration of firms in southern California. Other centers are in Seattle, Washington; Wichita, Kansas; and Dallas-Fort Worth, Texas. Among the principal western aerospace companies are Boeing, Lockheed, McDonnell-Douglas, the North American Division of Rockwell International, Northrop, and the aerospace activities of General Dynamics.

Western aviation has a long history. John Joseph Montgomery of the University of Santa Clara is credited with having built and flown gliders as early as 1883. In the course of his experiments he developed design features that his heirs later claimed (unsuccessfully) anticipated the wing-warping technique of the Wright brothers. The first successful American dirigible, the *California Arrow,* was built by Thomas Baldwin in Oakland, California, in 1904. It had a Curtiss motorcycle engine weighing sixty pounds and developing ten horsepower. The earliest commercial manufacturer of aircraft in the West was Glenn L. Martin, who opened an airplane factory in Los Angeles in 1912, but Martin moved east during World War I. He had made his first experimental plane three years earlier, and in 1912 he attracted attention by flying one of his models to Catalina Island and back. The Loughead (later Lockheed) brothers, Allan and Malcolm, were close behind Martin in establishing aircraft manufacturing in California. Between 1913 and 1921 they built a number of airplanes at Santa Barbara, assisted by young John K. Northrop. Farther north, William E. Boeing, a successful Seattle lumberman, founded in 1916 the BOEING AIRPLANE COMPANY. From the beginning Boeing had a strong interest in air transport, although at that time commercial aviation was virtually nonexistent.

These were small-scale and essentially experimental operations. The western aerospace industry as a going business began in the 1920s. Donald Douglas, formerly Martin's chief engineer, founded the Douglas Aircraft Company in Los Angeles in 1920, beginning with an order for one plane intended to make the first nonstop flight across the United States (it crashed on a trial and the attempt was abandoned), and then with an order for three torpedo planes for the navy. Douglas selected the Los Angeles area because the climate permitted year-round flying, a significant factor in the location of the aircraft industry. In 1926 Allan Lockheed and Northrop returned to aircraft manufacturing, also in Los Angeles. At the same time T. Claude Ryan in San Diego began building the monoplanes that became famous when Charles A. Lindbergh flew one, *Spirit of St. Louis*, across the Atlantic in 1927. Of these companies Boeing and Douglas were primarily builders of military aircraft, Boeing of fighters for the army and Douglas of army observation planes and a succession of torpedo planes. Lockheed's business was largely transport aircraft.

Meanwhile, Wichita was developing a separate center of aircraft manufacturing, specializing in light private planes. Clyde Cessna built his first plane in Wichita in 1917. Regular commercial production began two years later, with a sequence of small companies coming and going until three emerged as lasting concerns: Cessna, Beech, and Stearman.

These companies did not yet produce significant economic developments for the communities concerned. Employment in the entire American aircraft industry was about two thousand in 1921 and fifty-five hundred in 1927, and the industry was still mainly eastern. Factories were small, with about fifty or sixty employees. The great California boom of the 1920s was based on moving pictures and oil—not aircraft. Yet the bull market of 1928-29 encompassed an optimism about the future of aviation that raised employment to eighteen thousand and produced some ambitious merger schemes. These shriveled in the great crash and were dissolved when the Air Mail Act of 1934 required the separation of manufacturing and transport companies. Even so, employment was still over nine thousand in 1933. Except for Lockheed, which went into receivership in 1932 but remained in business when a syndicate headed by Robert L. Gross bought the company for $40,000, the western aircraft firms survived the great depression in good condition.

They were, in fact, one of the brighter spots in the western economic picture, because at a time of general decline Boeing, Douglas, and Lockheed initiated the steps whereby the American aircraft industry for the first time moved ahead of Europe and established a leadership in the design and production of transport aircraft. This achievement was an outgrowth of competition between airlines and manufacturers, which resulted in the development of the all-metal, low-winged

monoplane, with retractable landing gear and controllable pitch propellers. Boeing started the process with a series of experiments that resulted in the twin-engined 247 of 1932, far superior to any other transport then in service. Since United Airlines had priority on Boeing output, the competitors had to turn elsewhere. TWA (then Transcontinental and Western) turned to Douglas Aircraft, which responded with its DC series; the series was so successful that by the end of the 1930s Douglas planes were carrying ninety-five percent of the nation's civil air traffic and held a commanding international position. Lockheed's recovery was due to the success of a twin-engined transport, the Electra, designed on the same lines as the Boeing and Douglas planes. The design was also applied to military planes. The outstanding contribution of the western aircraft industry to military aviation in this period was the large bomber, introduced by Boeing in 1935 in the form of the B-17, the Flying Fortress.

During the 1930s the western aeronautical industry received substantial accretions. In 1935 Consolidated Aircraft Company moved from Buffalo, New York, to San Diego, California. Since a substantial part of Consolidated's business was building navy flying boats, (the best known being the PBY, the Catalina, of World War II), it seemed advisable to move near a major naval base in a region where flying boats could be tested regularly—not possible on Lake Erie in winter. Consolidated subsequently combined with the Los Angeles-based Vultee Aircraft Corporation to become Consolidated-Vultee, later Convair.

Other newcomers were Northrop and North American, the latter a combination of former eastern companies. By 1940 the Pacific Coast had almost half the airframe manufacturing capacity of the United States, most of it located in southern California. The scale of operations remained small. In 1939 the aeronautical industry ranked only forty-first among American manufacturing industries and accounted for seven tenths of one percent of manufacturing employment, about sixty-four thousand people. Nevertheless, because it was the first major manufacturing industry in southern California (unless oil refining is so classified), the impact of this concentration of aircraft manufacturing on the economy of the region was of considerable long-range significance.

World War II brought major changes. There was a tremendous expansion of production, raising the industry to first place in manufacturing employment. There was also constant pressure for improvement in design and performance. The contribution of the western firms was impressive. The first five producers of military aircraft during the war, in terms of airframe weight, were western: Douglas, Convair, Boeing, North American, and Lockheed. Their aggregate output was sixty percent of the total airframe weight produced. The same five were among the first six in numbers of aircraft built.

Boeing was preeminently a manufacturer of large airplanes, from the B-17 to the B-29 Superfortress. Douglas continued to be a major manufacturer of naval aircraft, plus about 12,000 DC-3s and one thousand of the new four-engined DC-4s, used as troop carriers and military transports. Consolidated-Vultee made the PBY and the B-24 Liberator, North American the twin-engined B-26 Mitchell bomber and the P-51 Mustang fighter, and Lockheed the P-38 Lightning fighter and the Hudson bomber, extremely popular with the Royal Air Force.

The expansion of production required extensive construction of new manufacturing facilities. The government was concerned because eighty percent of the aircraft industry was located within two hundred miles of either the Pacific or the Atlantic seaboard and was considered vulnerable to enemy attack. For this reason new plants were located inland as much as possible; efforts were made also to put them in places where labor and housing were more available than in the existing manufacturing centers. Douglas Aircraft operated factories in Oklahoma City, Tulsa, and Chicago; North American in Dallas and Kansas City; and Convair in Fort Worth. Boeing expanded its Stearman subsidiary in Wichita. Lockheed, alone of the western companies, kept its expansion in the vicinity of its main plant in Burbank, California.

Employment in the aircraft industry reached a peak of 1,345,000 in 1943, making it temporarily the nation's leading manufacturing industry. Boeing became and remained Seattle's largest single employer, and the concentration in southern California converted Los Angeles and San Diego into major industrial centers. The industry absorbed so many of the "Okies" who had swarmed into California during the Depression that they ceased to present a problem. The wartime dispersal of the industry also produced some permanent relocation. Convair retained its Fort Worth facility, and the Dallas plant that North American had operated was occupied afterward by a new aeronautical company, Texas Engineering and Manufacturing, and by Chance Vought when it moved from Hartford, Connecticut, in 1948. The two eventually combined as part of Ling-Temco-Vought (LTV). As a result Texas became the fourth western state (along with California, Washington, and Kansas) to be a major producer of aircraft.

The end of the war brought a sharp decline, but the low point of employment, 237,700 in 1948, was well ahead of the prewar years. The Korean War brought another sharp rise in 1950, which continued upward for twenty years to a level of about 700,000, with about half in western firms. These employment figures reflected a successful response to new technological and economic challenges, whereby the aeronautical industry became the aerospace industry.

First, in the 1950s the piston engine was replaced by the jet, beginning with military aircraft and then in airliners. The western manufacturers, notably Boeing, Douglas, and Lockheed, retained their ascendancy in the world market for transport planes. Then came the introduction of ballistic missiles, a field the aircraft firms entered so successfully that by the early 1960s three fourths of American missile production came from eight aircraft companies, seven of them western: Lockheed, General Dynamics (Convair), Boeing, North American, McDonnell, Douglas (subsequently merged as McDonnell-Douglas), and Northrop. When the space program came into being with the creation of the National Aeronautics and Space Administration (NASA) in 1958, McDonnell Aircraft became the prime contractor for Project Mercury, America's first manned space

flights, and North American for Apollo, through which man reached the moon on July 20, 1969.

The growth of aerospace activities attracted to the production centers a variety of electronic and other companies engaged in providing ancillary services. These include firms producing almost exclusively for the aerospace industry, such as the Garrett Corporation (Los Angeles), which did much of the pioneer work in pressurization for high-altitude flight, and Hughes Aircraft and Hughes Tool (also Los Angeles).

There are also several important companies in California that are not exclusively aerospace but are still important to the aerospace industry, or that are aerospace subsidiaries of other companies: Litton Industries; Lear-Siegler, Inc.; TRW (formerly Thompson-Ramo-Wooldridge); Aerojet-General, a subsidiary of General Tire and Rubber; and Hewlett-Packard, Inc. Honeywell, Inc., of Minneapolis, and Texas Instruments of Dallas are also important.

There are also the Jet Propulsion Laboratory in Pasadena, California, established during World War II under the supervision of the California Institute of Technology; and the Ames Research Laboratory in Sunnyvale, California, also established during the war when the National Advisory Committee for Aeronautics (NACA) needed additional facilities. It is now part of NASA. NASA's Manned Spacecraft Center, which controls manned space flights, is located in Houston, Texas.

Because of the aerospace industry's orientation toward research, the industry is in the unique position of having more salaried and professional employees than production workers. Since the 1950s expenditures on aerospace research and development, by government and industry combined, have constituted about a third of all research and development expenditures in the United States. One consequence has been to produce a high concentration of scientific and engineering personnel in the centers of aerospace activity, especially southern California and the Seattle area, and thereby introduce an important new element into the social pattern of both regions.

The beginning of the 1970s saw a sharp decline in the aerospace industry due to a number of factors, including a reduction in military demand and curtailment of the space program. In a way the industry was a victim of its own success. It designed and produced missiles until further stockpiling of unused weapons appeared to be needless "overkill"; it put men on the moon within the ten-year period prescribed by President Kennedy in 1960 and therefore satisfied the public demand for visible achievements in space to offset the Russian performance; and the jet transports, from the Boeing 707 and the DC-8 to the giant 747 and DC-10, provided capacity in excess of the current demand for air travel. A change in the political climate was also adverse to the industry, which has always been acutely sensitive to public policy because eighty percent of its sales are to the government. As a result it has always had a feast or famine existence. The 1970s ushered in a famine phase because public expenditure shifted from high-level technology to solving ecological problems caused by technology. Not only was the space program reduced, but support was withdrawn in 1971 for the supersonic transport being designed by Boeing. The project was then abandoned, despite the likelihood that two SSTs, the Anglo-

French Concorde and the Soviet TU-144, would be in service in the near future.

The result was that at the beginning of the 1970s the aerospace industry was in a deep depression. Seattle and southern California had the highest levels of unemployment in the United States, with the unusual feature of high unemployment among engineering, scientific, and managerial personnel. This situation offered the disturbing prospect that highly trained design and research groups might be dissolved and their talents irretrievably lost. There was much discussion of putting the skills and capacity of the aerospace industry to work on such problems as pollution and mass transportation, but if this was a remedy either for the problems in question or for the troubles of the aerospace industry, no one had come up with a prescription for applying it. While the discussion continued, both professional personnel and production workers began to move to other parts of the country where job prospects seemed brighter. In addition, the slump in aerospace employment was a major factor in reducing to negligible proportions the influx of people into southern California that had been going on for fifty years at a rate sometimes reaching a thousand a day. In short, in fifty years the handful of glorified machine shops engaged in making quite simple airplanes grew into an industry whose fortunes largely determined the whole economic climate of southern California, Seattle, and Wichita.

See also AIRLINES.

See Richard G. Hubler, *Big Eight* (1966); Douglas J. Ingells, *The Plane That Changed the World* (1966); John B. Rae, *Climb to Greatness: The American Aircraft Industry, 1920-1960* (1968); G. R. Simonson, ed., *The History of the American Aircraft Industry* (1968); and Herman A. Stekler, *The Structure and Performance of the Aerospace Industry* (1965).—J. B. R.

Afro-Americans. See NEGROES IN THE FAR WEST; and NEGROES ON THE FRONTIER.

agrarian movements. Farmers early learned that the way to draw attention to their problems was to work through their friends in state legislatures and in Congress. States were persuaded to subsidize certain crops like wheat and mulberry trees (whose leaves were fed to silkworms), to grant aid to state and county agricultural societies and fairs, to maintain agricultural bureaus, and to collect and publish information of use to farmers. Compensation was even provided for diseased cattle that had to be destroyed to prevent the spread of pleuropneumonia. The federal government sent an expedition abroad to collect disease-free sugarcane plantings to replace defective and weakened American strains, tried to prevent European countries from levying tariff barriers against American tobacco, showed unusual sensitivity about the prospects of American cotton and rice in foreign markets, required American naval vessels to use native-grown hemp, and put raw wool on the protected list. Farm leaders were impressed by the crop data published by the Agricultural Branch of the Patent Office and used their political influence in 1862 to have the Department of Agriculture established and to secure liberal appropriations for it. In the same year agricultural reformers succeeded in getting Congress to pass the Morrill Act for the establishment of agricultural colleges in every state. Thus government at both levels had shown concern for the welfare of farmers but in so doing had not in any way acted against other interest groups.

The first of the farm movements, the National Grange or Patrons of Husbandry, was founded in 1867 by Oliver H. KELLEY not to seek government favors but to provide a meeting ground where farmers could listen to speakers on farm and other problems, enjoy a social hour, and break some of the monotony of their lives. But the Grange was organized at a time when farmers were becoming aware that certain policies of the government and of private industry threatened their well-being, and it became a political center from which they could express their complaints. The contraction of the currency after the Civil War and the move toward the restoration of the gold standard in 1875 had tightened credit, kept interest rates high, lowered farm commodity prices, and made it difficult for debtors to meet their obligations. The Granger movement avoided the monetary question, concentrating instead upon its grievances against RAILROADS—which, it felt, charged much higher rates for services to farmers than to other commercial customers. Grangers also complained that warehouses located on railroad lines not only charged farmers exorbitant fees for storing their grain, but also engaged in monopolistic practices. The movement advocated the creation of state regulatory commissions that would have the authority to establish uniform maximum and minimum railroad charges and sought to minimize the political power of the railroads.

A substantial part of the return from the sale of farm products went to the railroads and warehouses for freight, elevator, and storage charges and for commissions on sales. In the midst of declining prices after the Civil War, and more seriously, after the Panic of 1873, these charges did not decline. Like fixed interest charges and taxes that were not easily subject to reduction, the inflexibility of the cost of these services pinched the farmers during a period of declining commodity prices. Grangers thought they were being gouged by the storage and transportation charges. Also they were convinced that their need for cars to ship their produce was always deemed secondary to the needs of industrial shippers and that the elevators graded their grain as inferior and sold it at top quality prices.

After a slow initial growth between 1867 and 1872, the organization mushroomed in 1873-75 to 21,697 Granges with more than three quarters of a million members. Such spectacular success made it easy for members to obtain reforms, generally through the minority party. In five states—Illinois, Iowa, Minnesota, Missouri, and Wisconsin—later called the Granger states, the movement succeeded in writing into legislation a variety of laws seeking to eliminate unfair and discriminatory practices of the railroads and warehouses and to create state regulatory commissions to enforce these reforms (see GRANGER LAWS). At the same time, state and local Granges were experimenting with farmer cooperatives to pool the purchasing of farm machinery and other equipment and even to manufacture some implements. In the rush to get relief from what they regarded as high commissions and high markups, the Grangers pushed things too rapidly, and the early failure of most of their enterprises lost prestige for the movement. After 1876 much of its membership slipped away, although the Grange was to come back in the twentieth century as a major farm organization.

The railroads took the Granger laws into the courts. Although the United States Supreme Court upheld the right of state legislatures to regulate railroads because they were "clothed with a public interest," officials of the companies refused to abide by the laws, and continued efforts at state regulation were ineffective. However, the Granger movement did much to focus attention upon the railroads, the public gained experience in attempting to regulate them, and the experience thus gained was to be helpful in the forming of the Interstate Commerce Act of 1887 and the drafting of later railroad legislation.

Other farmers' clubs and organizations attempted to emulate the success of the Granger movement. In 1876 it was the GREENBACK PARTY that took the lead in advocating agrarian reforms and in pillorying business leaders and eastern bankers, blaming them for the huge premium which the promised restoration of the gold standard would give to government bondholders. (see BANKING AND CURRENCY). To halt deflation they advocated the reissue of the withdrawn greenbacks and the repeal of the measure providing for the restoration of the gold standard on January 1, 1879. They also called for a federal income tax; the withholding of all public lands, including the reverted railroad land grants, for actual settlers; the banning of alien ownership of land; and government regulation of railroads. The party reached its peak during the mid-term congressional elections of 1878, when it obtained one million votes and won fifteen seats in the House of Representatives.

Two agrarian movements became prominent in the 1880s, the Arkansas Agricultural Wheel and the Farmers' Alliance. They appealed to the antimonopoly feeling of the time and advocated unlimited silver purchase programs. Both were strongest in the South, where the Wheel worked more among tenants and farm laborers as well as small farm owners, and the Alliance centered their attention upon farm owners. Both experimented with farm equipment cooperatives like the Grange and in efforts at pooling their buying and selling.

The southern movements were paralleled by a number of organizations in the midwestern and north central states, which collectively came to be called the Northern Alliance. Smaller in numbers, they were more concerned with railroad issues and reflected discontent among groups from urban and even industrial areas, although the agricultural groups dominated. Politically, the Southern Alliance tried to capture or work within the Democratic party, while the northern groups resorted to a third-party movement. Because of the issues of Negro membership and the Southern Alliance's advocacy of secrecy, the two alliances never formally joined to make a truly national organization.

Farm discontent reached a high point in 1890 when the agrarians working through the political parties scored numerous successes in electing members of Congress and other officials friendly to their objective. Among their victories were the election of "Pitchfork Ben" Tillman as governor of South Carolina, Tom Watson of Georgia and "Sockless Jerry" SIMPSON of Kansas to the national House of Representatives, and William A. PEFFER of Kansas to the Senate. From local elections, members of the Alliances turned to national affairs and

through the organization of the People's party (see POPULISM) found the means to further political successes. High interest charges, the cost of tariff-protected goods they bought, the farm foreclosures brought on by the continued decrease in commodity price levels, the increasing proportion of tenant-operated farms, the iniquities of railroad management, and the widespread engrossment of land by great cattle companies financed by foreign capital all convinced many farmers in the cotton South and the wheat belt of the Missouri valley that it was time for the farmers' influence to be felt through a party free of "Wall Street influence."

Continued depression in the West and South enabled William Jennings Bryan and the Populists to take over the Democratic party on an outright free silver platform in 1896. The result was their inglorious defeat. What may have turned the tide was the recovery of prices of farm staples in the early autumn; that seems to have encouraged many strong bimetallists of the summer to return to their old party affiliations and to accept the gold standard. Though their permanent triumphs were few, the agrarians had pointed the way for many reforms which were to be adopted during the Progressive era (1901-16) and later: the direct election of senators, the federal income tax, effective regulation of the railroads, government farm credit, more enlightened administration of the public lands, downward revision of the tariff, and public works to provide jobs for the unemployed.

Third-party movements had their place in the twentieth century also, with Theodore Roosevelt's "Bull Moose" Progressive party of 1912, the La Follette Progressive party of 1924, and the Wallace Progressive party of 1948. Each deferred to agrarian sentiment and wishes, though none was strictly an agrarian party. Both "Fighting Bob" La Follette, senator from Wisconsin, and Henry A. WALLACE of Iowa tried to bring workers and farmers together, as had the Populists and the Democrats of 1896.

First of the twentieth-century farm movements was the American Society of Equity. Like the Farmers' Alliances and the Patrons of Husbandry, and indeed like so many other organizations that sprang up after 1880, its founders sold charters or chapter organizations and derived their living—if not more—from these concessions, publishing activities, and salaries within the organization. Founders of the society seized upon farmers' grievances and offered as panaceas controlled production and cooperative marketing. Some state equity societies, notably that of Wisconsin, organized cooperative livestock shipping associations and a federation of cheese producers. The North Dakota equity society proposed a state-owned elevator. Other reforms the society favored were corrupt practices legislation, the initiative, referendum, and recall, and conservation of natural resources.

Before the Society of Equity passed out of the picture the Nonpartisan League was established in NORTH DAKOTA in 1915 with the object of remedying farmers' grievances by political means. Virtually a one-crop state, North Dakota was particularly susceptible to the fluctuations of the wheat market. Arthur C. TOWNLEY, the organizer of the Nonpartisan League, had formerly worked with the Socialist party and now in 1915 began a high pressure campaign to build up the league, to which he gave a strongly socialist tinge. Without being very specific about its economic objectives, the league wanted to create a state-owned terminal elevator and a bank; establish state inspection of grain, weights, and measures; and provide for partial exemption of farm improvements from taxation. It also wanted introduced an inheritance tax, women suffrage, and improvements in public education. The league's rise in North Dakota was phenomenal. It won nearly every state office in 1916 and captured control of the state House of Representatives, but the holdovers in the Senate prevented the league from gaining its full objectives. The leaders also carried their organization into Minnesota and other nearby states but not with quite the same overwhelming success.

In 1918 the North Dakota league reelected its state officers and obtained control of the state Senate, thereby assuring adoption of its program, which included an industrial commission to direct the state industries, with the Bank of North Dakota to finance them; construction of an elevator, flour mill, and creamery; and compulsory insurance against damage from hailstorms. At the peak of the league's prosperity personality conflicts rather than disagreement over principles caused defection from its ranks. Charges of disloyalty and mismanagement of state enterprises were directed at some of its leaders, and other reform and farm movements were seeking to replace the league. Defeat in North Dakota by the recall of some of its elected candidates, by constitutional changes, and by the election of opponents brought about the swift decline of the Nonpartisan League.

After World War I the expansion of acreage and the increased yields created marketing difficulties for wheat in an era when other nations were adopting policies of economic nationalism and self-sufficiency and reducing their dependence on foreign or American wheat. The Farmer-Labor party replaced the Nonpartisan League as the spokesman of the wheat farmers, who were angered by the high tariff rates of the Fordney-McCumber Act of 1922 and the dominance of the major parties by eastern conservatives who were unwilling to enact a thorough-going farm-credit program. Victories in Minnesota, Nebraska, Iowa, and Kansas sent a number of outspoken agrarians to the Senate, among them Magnus Johnson and Henrik Shipstead of Minnesota, Smith Brookhart of Iowa, Edwin F. Ladd of North Dakota, and R. B. Howell of Nebraska. Thereafter these men lined up with other western progressives to form the "farm bloc," which exercised on occasion the balance of power in the Senate. By working with the Democrats they were successful in opening the income tax records of wealthy people to public inspection and in achieving some other mildly progressive measures. But the farm bloc's principal objective, summed up in the McNary-Haugen proposals was not gained. The difficulty seemed to be that agrarian radicals found much of their support reverting during presidential elections to Republicanism, and though La Follette won nearly five million votes in 1924, the states that had sent agrarians to the Senate were content to vote for Calvin Coolidge.

McNary-Haugenism was essentially a device to rid the domestic market of the surplus of major farm commodities, principally wheat, cotton, and corn, by using government resources to sell the surpluses abroad at whatever prices they would bring and to peg the American price at a profitable level, thus assuring the farmer fair returns on his crops. Most farm organizations, including the Farm Bureau Federation, the National Grange, the Farmers Union, and the representatives of southern cotton farmers, corn belt farmers, and wheat farmers supported the McNary-Haugen bills. They were passed by Congress in 1927 and 1928 but were vetoed both times by Coolidge. Though the wheat states seemed aflame with discontent they voted in 1928 for Herbert Hoover, who promised aid through a government corporation which would buy up the unwanted surplus. Lacking production controls, the scheme was a failure. Not until the Agricultural Adjustment Administration (AAA) of the New Deal was production control provided to avoid surpluses

The Farm Bureau Federation, like the Grange, included "dirt" farmers of the more substantial sort and others interested for one reason or another in agriculture. Its strength was in the Middle West and the South, though it had a large following throughout the country. In the 1920s it was strongly committed to the McNary-Haugen bills and in 1933 it favored production control through the AAA. Thereafter its conservative leadership veered away from government controls, advocating instead that Congress should let the law of supply and demand control price and, in turn, production. Its most able opposition came from the Farmers Union, which continued to advocate government intervention in controlling production and aid in marketing, and was quite willing to participate in farmers' strikes to win higher prices. Both the Farm Bureau Federation and the Farmers Union became deeply involved in promoting affiliated cooperatively operated enterprises such as insurance, grain processing, marketing and elevator businesses, and farmers' stores. These enterprises have been quite successful in eliminating some of the charges of middlemen and providing better service and, to some extent, quality of goods.

See Christiana McF. Campbell, *The Farm Bureau and the New Deal* (1962); George H. Miller, *Railroads and the Granger Laws* (1971); Theodore Saloutos, *Farmer Movements in the South, 1865-1933* (1960); Theodore Saloutos and John D. Hicks, *Agricultural Discontent in the Middle West, 1900-1939* (1951).—P. W. G.

agricultural expansion. Until the twentieth century, farming was the chief occupation of Americans, but there was always a vast difference between the lordly tobacco, rice, cotton, and sugarcane planter on his extensive plantations where the field work was done by slaves, and the small farmer on a hillside tract, slowly clearing the forest, grubbing out stumps, and for a time growing mostly the essentials for his own use. Demand at home and abroad for southern staples encouraged the move from subsistence to commercial agriculture, and it was these staples, primarily cotton and tobacco, that enabled numerous southern farm families in one or two generations to move into the planter class. The great differences between northern and southern farming were that these two southern staples were grown over wide areas in the upper or lower South by planters on their broad acres and by small farmers—with or without slaves—and that their value was high in relation to weight, whereas in the North, the cultivation of wheat—the major cash crop—was not adaptable to the use of slaves and its value in relation to weight was from one half to one fifth that of tobacco and cotton. Southern staples, needing constant labor the year around from seedtime through harvest, processing, and marketing, were well adapted to the use of slave labor. In contrast, northern agriculture, except for livestock and dairying, required a relatively short season, though there were off-season tasks such as woodcutting and maple sugar making.

Tobacco was the first of the great staples to become well established, first in Virginia and Maryland and later in North Carolina and Kentucky. It was such an important export that the government watched the foreign market for this product with deep concern, protesting when discriminatory regulations or taxes were levied against it. Like other southern staples, tobacco, when continually planted on the same land, encouraged the accumulation of parasites, depleted the soil, and caused erosion, making it necessary for planters to bring new land into cultivation. The need for virgin soil was one of the dynamic factors causing both large and small planters to strike westward, first into the Piedmont, then across the Appalachians into Kentucky.

Large-scale production of cotton was delayed until the perfection of the cotton gin in 1793 so reduced the cost of separating the seed from the lint that cotton fabrics thereafter were the cheapest for clothing. Rarely has an invention so quickly affected farming as did the gin. From 3,000 bales of cotton produced in 1790, the yield jumped to 73,000 in 1800, 335,000 in 1820, and 5,387,000 in 1859. From North Carolina to Louisiana, Arkansas, and Texas, farmers concentrated upon its production. Though it was grown in the antebellum period in practically every county stretching from South Carolina to Louisiana and Arkansas and extensively in North Carolina and Tennessee, the major producing sections where the larger plantations were located were the principal river valleys and the rich delta country of Mississippi and Louisiana. Here in the Black Belt were plantations producing hundreds of bales of cotton worked by some forty to two hundred slaves. In these rich cotton counties, in the sugar area along the lower Mississippi in Louisiana, and in the shore and sea island counties of South Carolina and Georgia where rice was growing, the plantation economy reached its highest state of development.

On these great plantations of the South the ideal was self-sufficiency, that is, the plantation should produce for domestic consumption the hogs and hominy, beef and flour, and—from the point of view of the most ardent regionalists as reflected in *De Bow's Review*—their own osnaburg and other rough cloth needed for the hands. Where the land yielded less than ten bushels per acre of corn or wheat, critics of the PLANTATION SYSTEM could show how ridiculous it was to use expensive slave labor and land much better adapted to cotton, but the regionalists would make no concession. Planters were influenced by the regionalist arguments, but economic arguments prevailed. The lower South continued to buy large quantities of foodstuffs, mostly cereals and meat, from the upper Mississippi valley, which

sent its products south by steamboats, keelboats, and rafts. It was this southern demand that hastened the commercial development of agriculture in the Old Northwest.

Diversity characterized agriculture in the North. Wheat came closest to being its staple but that crop did not do well in New England, its yield in eastern New York was not favorable, and only in the limestone areas of Pennsylvania was it a major cash crop. Pennsylvania Germans were too wise, however, to center their operations wholly around wheat. They rotated their crops, kept sufficient cattle to manure their land regularly, and maintained dairies. They had wheat for sale but also had surpluses of meat and butter. New Englanders may not have been as good farmers, but with some exceptions they had to contend with poorer land, a shorter growing season, and few water routes by which to carry their surpluses to market. Notwithstanding its poorer endowment, New England had the highest ratio of farmers to area—one to 93 acres for Massachusetts, one to 97 acres for Connecticut (and New York), as compared to one to 139 acres for Pennsylvania and one to 226 acres for Maryland. New Englanders preferred, when conditions became crowded, to move into higher elevations and even to take up still poorer land than to move elsewhere.

The higher elevations and the frontier of northern New England could not continue to absorb the expanding population of the older rural areas. Well before the revolution, New Englanders were migrating into New York, others were crossing Long Island Sound to take up land on that island; still others were migrating to the Wyoming valley of northeastern Pennsylvania. In the first half of the nineteenth century they swept across upstate New York, settling in Ohio on the lands of the Connecticut Western Reserve and of the Ohio Land Company, in southern Michigan, and jumping across Indiana, in northern Illinois and southern Wisconsin to create outposts of New England rural culture. They brought with them some capital, experience in New England farming, a strong acquisitive instinct, and a willingness to work hard to create new farms not entirely different from those of their earlier homeland. But diversification gave way to wheat farming in the Genesee valley of New York and in the states beyond. When farmers found that wheat yields declined after a few years of repeated planting, they turned to dairying, selling cheese and butter but still raising much of their own food and fodder. Wherever they settled, the small owner-operated farm, with a comfortable house and barn and fields neatly fenced with stones or rails, were characteristic.

New York, with its Yankee immigrants and descendants of old New Yorkers, was the premier agricultural state from 1850 to 1870. It excelled in the number of farms; the improved acreage in farms; the value of its farms, livestock, and orchard products; the number of dairy cows; the sale of fluid milk; and the production of butter, cheese, hay, potatoes, hops, and maple sugar. Its farmers were innovative, buying the latest machinery, improving their livestock and the methods of making and marketing their cheese and butter, and draining wet areas. Even tenancy, which had earlier existed in the Hudson-Mohawk valley, was largely eliminated, except in the Genesee valley. But competition with farmers on cheap, productive western lands was affecting New Yorkers, impelling them to contemplate moving west, to cease developing their lands, and to give up those at higher elevations where the returns were low. Farm abandonment was beginning. Never again was New York agriculture to be so successful.

Two other great streams of population were flowing westward in the search for land: the first, the southern uplander—from Maryland, Virginia, and North Carolina—where hill farms had become untillable through loss of topsoil; and the second, immigrants from northern Europe ousted by potato blight and other economic catastrophes. The southern uplanders were going in three directions: southwest into Mississippi, Alabama, Arkansas, and Texas; due west to Missouri, Kansas, and perhaps California; and into the southern part of Ohio, Indiana, and Illinois—to get away from slavery; it was sometimes said. The northern Europeans settled in Michigan, southwestern Ohio in the vicinity of Cincinnati, northern Illinois, and southern Wisconsin. Some, of course, remained in eastern cities and others with talents more useful in urban centers sought out Cleveland, Indianapolis, St. Louis, Chicago, and Milwaukee. But the greater number of Germans and Scandinavians looked for land to farm, bringing with them Old World skills and techniques and new strains of seeds and plants that were to contribute their share to the making of the new farm frontier.

Farmers tried wheat in these new areas and found it a profitable crop, with variable returns, depending on the weather and the ravages of parasites and diseases. These factors soon forced the abandonment of wheat as a major crop in western New York, though the Pennsylvania farmers clung to it longer as they had learned to employ it only in rotation. By mid-century the wheat belt was moving westward. The reaper, the thresher, the drill, and improved plows were becoming practical machines, freeing the farmers from depending on numerous hired hands during harvesting and making possible larger operations. In 1859 the chief wheat-producing states were Illinois, Indiana, Wisconsin, and Ohio, respectively. In 1869 Iowa was second, in 1879 Minnesota first. The Red River valley of Minnesota and North Dakota, where spring wheat was widely grown, and Kansas and Oklahoma, where winter wheat was the chief crop, became the principal producers in the twentieth century. The combine (combining reaping and threshing), the gang plow, and the tractor plow all hastened the enlargement of the farm unit in the new wheat belt. High prices for wheat, a cycle of abnormally wet years, the 640-acre stock raising Homestead Act of 1916, and DRY FARMING techniques enabled wheat to be produced in the drier portions of the Great Plains, where grazing on natural grasses had previously flourished. After World War I prices fell, and it became increasingly difficult to sell the surplus wheat abroad. Corn, wheat, and cotton farmers joined in a movement to get the government to aid in marketing their surpluses abroad and at the same time to stabilize domestic prices. President Calvin Coolidge vetoed their desired legislation (the McNary-Haugen bill) in 1927 and 1928. Not until the passing of the Agricultural Adjustment Act of 1933 was relief granted to the distressed farmers.

Corn was important in the farmers' economy almost everywhere because of its high protein yield, large return from the seed, adaptability to various soils, and usefulness as food for both livestock and man, but the modern "corn belt" stretching from Ohio through Indiana, Illinois, Iowa, northern Missouri, and eastern Kansas and Nebraska is the area of its greatest concentration. Production maps show this as early as 1859, with Illinois leading and Ohio and Missouri close behind. Illinois continued as the top corn producer until 1899 when it was displaced by Iowa. Although corn for a long time was a primary diet staple for low-income farmers, it was essentially a grain for livestock and poultry. One of the messages that the agricultural colleges once preached was that farmers should use their corn as feed on their own farms instead of selling it to other feeders, thus assuring themselves two profits instead of one. In the late nineteenth century feeder cattle were brought into the corn belt from the Great Plains for a period of concentrated fattening with corn to put them in the best shape for marketing, after which they were taken to the slaughterhouses in Chicago.

Cotton was king in the delta lands of Mississippi and Louisiana and the Black Belt of Alabama and Georgia in the antebellum years, although the Texas acreage in cotton was showing great possibilities and by 1899 was more than a quarter of the entire American crop. Ravages of the boll weevil which spread into Texas from Mexico in 1892 forced planters to diversify and rotate crops to rid the land of the pest. In later years they began to raise beef and dairy cattle. In the twentieth century, longer, stapled, premium-priced cotton was grown increasingly on irrigated land in California and Arizona where the newly developed cotton picker was widely used, and older fiber-producing sections of the South were hard put to compete. Other innovations such as the tractor and technological inventions like the cotton picker were freeing the planter of dependence on the sharecroppers, who were being forced off the land, as John Steinbeck described in *Grapes of Wrath.* Between 1930 and 1960 the number of sharecroppers in the South fell from 776,278 to 121,037, and the decline in the principal cotton-producing states was much greater.

While land in the Northeast has been going out of cultivation at a rapid rate since 1900, the United States has been pursuing an increasingly liberal land policy in the West to aid people to get new farms under way. The size of the free homesteads obtainable was quadrupled in 1916, beet-sugar production was encouraged by a tariff on sugar imports, and more irrigation land was made available by the Reclamation Service of the Department of the Interior (see RECLAMATION AND IRRIGATION). Eight billion dollars have been invested in giant dams, reservoirs, canals, ditches, generating plants, and transmission lines to provide irrigation water for land still in government hands—though private landowners have been even more benefited—and for water for domestic and industrial purposes for the growing cities of the West. Of the nine million acres irrigated by the federal government and twenty-four million acres irrigated by state and private activity, a considerable part has been high-yielding land with a long growing season and constant sunlight during the day. On these irrigated lands is grown a great part of the country's vegetables and fruits, sugar beets, alfalfa, nuts, dates, and cotton. In 1959 California, the state most intensively developed by irrigation, produced thirty-six percent of the value of all vegetable crops except potatoes, twenty-six percent of the value of all berries and small fruits, and forty-two percent of the value of orchard fruits and nuts. The state ranked first in the value of poultry production and sugar beets, second in the value of its cotton, and third in the value of dairy products. Other states highly developed by irrigation are Colorado, Arizona, Idaho, and Washington.

Partly as a result of this great federal boon to irrigation and cheap electric power for pumping water and other purposes, the vegetable crop—and the seed, nursery, and canning industries—have moved largely to the Pacific Coast, particularly to California. New York State and, indeed, northeastern farmers generally found competition with West Coast producers unprofitable, especially after refrigerated freight cars and fast-through freight trains enabled lettuce, peas, beans, and fruit to get to eastern markets in top condition. Where New York led in 1900 in the production of most vegetables, in 1959 California produced vegetables to the value of seven times those of New York. It also outproduced New York in value of berries and small fruit by eight times and in orchard products by thirteen times. New York farmers gave up, their number diminishing from 226,720 in 1900 to 82,356 in 1960. Sharp but varying declines took place in all the states of the Northeast. In nine northeastern states the number of farms declined in this period by 422,772 while in nine irrigation states of the West the number of farms increased by 101,004.

Dairying was the one agricultural enterprise that flourished wherever there was a market for milk. Urban growth made successful dairy farming possible in every state. The dairy business in the mid-twentieth century, however, was a very different thing from the five- or seven-cow dairies of the earlier years. Electrically operated milking machines; pipelines to carry the milk to the refrigerated bulk tank and from it to the giant tanker trucks; power-driven gutter-cleaners; manure spreaders; huge silos to house the corn and hay silage; power-operated screw machines to transport the silage to the feeding stations; tractor-operated drills; liquid fertilizer and weed-killer distributors; and corn pickers, shellers, grinders, mowers, and balers; herds of forty to eighty highbred cattle, all combined to produce averages of thirty to fifty quarts of milk daily and took large amounts of capital. The dairyman still had to put in long hours of labor and do much bookkeeping, but his many machines had relieved him of the former dependence on numerous hired hands and much hard physical labor. To invest in all this equipment, the dairy farmer needed to operate on a far larger scale than in the nineteenth century and needed a greater amount of land. This is shown by the increase in the average size of farms in New York State from 100 acres in 1900 to 164 in 1959, with sixty-seven percent of the farmland in farms ranging from 180 acres to more than 1,000. (see CORN PRODUCTION; COTTON CULTURE; COTTON PRODUCTION; WHEAT PRODUCTION.)

Among the principal agricultural problems of the twentieth century have been inadequate long- and short-term credit facilities to enable farmers to withhold their crops from market until the most advantageous moment and to plan their operations over a number of years knowing that necessary funds will be available for improvements; overproduction of grain and cotton, heavy storage expenses until markets could be found and, then, often, sale at prices insufficient to cover costs; soil erosion through continued cropping of land without rest or the use of soil-building clover or alfalfa, and without regard to the runoff on steeper slopes; soil exhaustion through failure to use manure and artificial fertilizers; the alarming growth of tenancy in the corn and cotton belts, which with the poverty of the sharecroppers was deplored by social scientists; and corporate or large-scale farming such as that of the Kern County Land Company in California and the Delta and Pine Land Company in Mississippi, which the Farmers Union feared meant the beginning of the end of the small owner-operator.

The Southern Alliance seems to have been the first agrarian group to raise the problem of farm credit as one calling for government action. Crop liens in the South had tied the sharecropper to the land and forced upon him continued planting of cotton, and cotton and wheat growers were obliged to market their crops as soon as they were harvested. The subtreasury plan of the Alliance included government warehouses to house nonperishable crops—cotton, rice, corn, and wheat—for one year, during which time farmers could borrow eighty percent of the value of their deposits at one percent interest. The goods were to be sold within that year and the balance from the sale, after deducting the loan and other costs, would go to the depositor. It was an awkward scheme and, though taken up by the Populists in 1890, its weaknesses were so obvious that it was abandoned for other panaceas. Rising land values in the twentieth century, the limited amount of mortgage credit available on long terms, and high interest rates led to the adoption of the Federal Land Bank System in 1916 and the Intermediate Credits Act of 1923, which broadened the credit available to farmers, but both systems soon fell into difficulties. With the Great Depression and the foreclosure of thousands of farm mortgages, drastic action was necessary. The Emergency Mortgage Relief Act and the Farm Credit Act of 1933 provided both long- and short-term loans and saved thousands of farms from being lost, and for the first time established an adequate system of farm credit.

Overproduction was not new, unmarketable surpluses of cotton and wheat having burdened prices in the 1920s. The domestic allotment feature of the Agricultural Adjustment Act of 1933, by which farmers were induced through benefit payments to reduce their acreage in crops, and subsequent plans such as the "soil bank" have not been altogether successful, in part because farmers learned to withdraw their poorest land from production and to plant only their best land. However, through the establishment of government storage facilities one of the farmers' major needs has been reasonably met.

To check soil erosion, farmers have been encouraged to rotate crops, to resort to strip-cropping interspersed with grass waterways, and, on steeper slopes, to plant soil-binding crops. Lime has been supplied for land deficient in this mineral. Submarginal land has been retired from cultivation, the former owners assisted to settle elsewhere, and the land itself used for reforestation, parks, and wildlife refuges.

Tenancy increased heavily in the 1920s in the upper

Mississippi valley, the mountain states, and the cotton South, the result of chronically low farm commodity prices and high capital needs of the farmer. For the first time, government was asked to take steps to halt the increase and to aid tenants (many of whom were former owners whose mortgages had been foreclosed) in purchasing the farms they rented. Little had been done for the migrant laborer, the croppers, or tenants, who were the most depressed of all rural people. Finally, in 1937 Congress in the Bankhead-Jones, or Farm Tenant, Act authorized modest appropriations as loans to aid tenants in purchasing land, and some aid was provided for migratory laborers through establishing camps for them. These actions were not well supported because of southern objections, and results were small. Yet tenancy diminished after 1935 owing to the adjustment program and other New Deal measures, the beginning of World War II, the abundant credit facilities which permitted former owners to recover their property, and the economic advantages to cotton planters in consolidating their small cropper units. The croppers were thereafter fast disappearing, their proportion as farm operators falling from 12.3 percent in 1930 to 3.3 percent in 1959, and tenant farmers, including sharecroppers, declining from 42.4 percent to 19.8 percent in the same period. Of the hundreds of thousands of sharecroppers thus freed from the land, large numbers went to the northern industrial cities where, being compelled to crowd into the slums, their numbers exacerbated urban problems of race, poverty, educational facilities, taxation, and urban renewal.

Meantime, the soil bank plan, by which farmers agreed to withdraw from commercial use whole farms or substantial acreages, replaced the earlier adjustment program of allotment of acreages in controlled use. In the 1960s there was much concern over the sizable payments to corporate groups and individual owners of large farms—as much in some instances as a million or more dollars—for keeping portions of their land out of cultivation. The Farm Bureau Federation had long since abandoned its support of crop controls, urging that a free market would work much better, whereas the Farmers Union continued to support controls.

Corporate or large-scale farming is not new, but it has troubled the smaller farm owners and their representatives who fear it may mark the doom of the small owner-operator. A recent development is incorporation by individual farmers for the purpose of tax savings.

See Murray R. Benedict, *Farm Policies of the United States, 1790-1950* (1953); and United States Department of Agriculture *Yearbook*, for 1921 and 1922. —P. W. G.

airlines. The airplane era in the United States began on December 17, 1903, when the Wright brothers made their first successful flight at Kitty Hawk, North Carolina. Two years later they made a record flight of 24¼ miles; by 1910, Glenn H. Curtiss flew 142.5 miles between Albany and New York to set a new distance record. Curtiss had already established a speed record of almost 47 miles an hour. In 1911 Calbraith P. Rodgers made the first transcontinental flight from New York to Pasadena, California, a distance of 3,390 miles, in 49 days. His flying time was 82 hours and 4 minutes. By 1914 a plane had also flown over Mount Whitney, in California, attaining an altitude of sixteen thousand feet.

As early as 1908 the United States Army ordered its first plane from the Wright brothers. Aviation played a significant role in World War I. General Billy Mitchell, the first army officer to fly over enemy lines, and Eddie Rickenbacker, an "ace" pilot, became national heroes. When the war came to an end, the army and navy had more than six thousand planes and as many pilots who were eager to continue flying. In 1918 the Post Office Department inaugurated the first air mail service between New York and Washington. At first, army pilots flew the planes, but soon the Post Office Department hired civilian pilots. By 1921 the first transcontinental air mail service had evolved on a route from New York to Chicago, west to Omaha, Cheyenne, Salt Lake City, Elko, and Reno, into San Francisco, thus selecting the lowest crossing of the Continental Divide. In the beginning flights were restricted to daylight hours. The first night flight was made with obliging farmers lighting bonfires to serve as beacons.

In 1925 Congress passed the Kelly Air Mail Act, which turned over the federal air mail service to private corporations. Two years later the contract for delivery west of Chicago was turned over to Boeing Air Transport. Feeder lines to the transcontinental system were also given contracts, including the Western Air Express between Los Angeles and Salt Lake City and the Varney Speed Lines from Elko, Nevada, northwest to Pasco, Washington, a station on the Spokane-Seattle run. In general, only mail and sometimes express were carried by the companies in the West, but the Western Air Express and Pacific Air Transport, flying from Los Angeles to Seattle via San Francisco, also carried passengers.

In 1926 Congress passed the Air Commerce Act to promote air commerce, to regulate it in the interests of safety, and to provide aids in navigation. For a short time the new responsibilities were scattered among various agencies in the Department of Commerce, but amending legislation provided for an Aeronautics Branch in the department. Charles Lindbergh's dramatic transatlantic flight in 1927 produced greater mass enthusiasm for flying than any other event in the history of air transport. This accomplishment gave the struggling young industry the stimulus it needed. Within a year the applicants for pilot licenses increased from 1,800 to 5,500 and the number of licensed planes from 1,100 to 4,700. Between 1926 and 1934 the Aeronautics Branch of the Department of Commerce was expanded and reorganized on several occasions until it became the Bureau of Air Commerce.

Following Lindbergh's flight, the great airlines of the United States were formed, beginning with Transcontinental Air Transport, later to become Trans-World Airlines. This company's line ran from St. Louis to Kansas City, on to Albuquerque, across northern Arizona into Los Angeles. Various airplane manufacturing and air transport companies were combined to engage in the struggle for supremacy on the transcontinental air routes (see AEROSPACE INDUSTRY). William Boeing expanded into the United Aircraft and Transportation Corporation, assimilated National Air Transport, and emerged as United Air Lines. This company's flight west of Chicago was by way of Omaha, Cheyenne, and Salt Lake City into San Francisco, along the route of the earliest transcontinental flights. Universal Aviation Corporation, established in 1929, was to make many mergers before it evolved into American Air Lines. This company originally flew from Cleveland to Fort Worth, Texas, via Kansas City, thence along a route once controlled by Southern Air Transport to El Paso, Texas, and into Los Angeles on a sector once known as the Standard Air Lines. C. M. Keys played a major role in organizing these companies. In addition to sponsoring the establishment of Transcontinental Air Transport and National Air Transport, he was president of North American Aviation Corporation, backed by General Motors. Eastern Air Transport, a component of North American, later became Eastern Air Lines. Thus, the domestic carriers, American, United, Eastern, and T.W.A. became known as the "Big Four," and Pan-American Airways became the largest international operator in the world. In 1930 three transcontinental lines were in operation.

In 1938 the Civil Aeronautics Act created the Civil Aeronautics Authority, a new agency independent of any existing departments in the government, and in 1940 the CAA was placed under the Department of Commerce. A boom in private flying led to the Civilian Pilot Training Program in these same years, whereby more than 435,000 pilots were trained. The Defense Landing Area Program provided 538 airports within the United States and 29 in the United States territories suitable for military operations. These programs laid solid foundations for aviation activities in World War II. To handle the problems and conflicts that grew from the many users of the airways, the Air Coordinating Committee was established in 1945. Three years later the Air Navigation Development Board came into being. Finally, the Federal Aviation Act of 1958 merged all the various governmental bureaus, boards, and committees into the Federal Aviation Agency.

By 1960 one of the more significant developments in the western airline industry was the growth of local service networks, in addition to the transcontinentals, such as: Trans-Texas Lines; Frontier in the Great Basin, the Rockies, and the northern Great Plains; Bonanza in the Southwest; West Coast in the Pacific Northwest; and Pacific Airlines in California.

Among the numerous single-volume histories of the airlines, the following are outstanding: R. E. G. Davies, *A History of the World's Airlines* (1964); Carroll V. Glines, *The Saga of the Air Mail* (1968); Jeremiah Milbank, *First Century of Flight in America* (1943); Henry Ladd Smith, *Airways: The History of Commercial Aviation in the United States* (1942); and E. P. Warner, *The Early History of Air Transportation* (1938). An interesting account dealing exclusively with California as a center of aviation development is Kenneth M. Johnson, *Aerial California* (1961).—W. T. J.

Alabama Territory. Alabama Territory was located between the Tennessee River and the Gulf of Mexico, with Georgia on the east and Mississippi on the west. There were three major points of penetration into Alabama Territory: along the Gulf Coast by way of Mobile Bay, along the Tennessee River, and overland from Georgia. The Gulf coastal area was penetrated first by Spanish and French explorers and then by a mixture of national traders. The territory was occupied by Cherokee, Creek, and Choctaw Indians (see FIVE CIVILIZED TRIBES). The northern Tennessee valley area was acquired in 1806 by treaty with the Cherokee, and these lands were quickly purchased after 1809 by Georgia cotton planters. Settlers pushed up the Alabama River from the South, and after the defeat of the Creek in the battle of HORSESHOE BEND in 1814, the population push into Alabama gained considerable momentum.

Between 1815 and 1819 there was a genuine land rush by settlers seeking new cotton-growing farms and plantations. Most of this immigration came into Alabama across Georgia from the Virginia and Carolina Piedmont, with a few lower Piedmont and tidewater plantation owners included. In Alabama Territory yeoman farmer settlers from the upper Piedmont of the Carolinas became yeoman farmers on their new lands, and large numbers of them settled in the hill sections of the frontier country.

MISSISSIPPI TERRITORY, of which Alabama was a part, before it became a territory also, had a varied political history. The two Florida purchases had added a vast strip of territory to the United States along the Gulf. Georgia had claimed the lands to the west and had created a problem in the Yazoo grants of 1795 in the territory (see LAND COMPANIES). When Georgia ceded her western territory to the United States, the assumption was that the whole territory would ultimately be admitted as a single state as soon as it could qualify for admission. A bill was introduced in the United States Senate to create such a territory, but the old dread of federal court interference with the land claims of the Yazoo grant halted its passage. Too, there was a sharp division of sentiment among the settlers along the Mississippi and in the eastern section of Mississippi Territory. In 1816 a congressional committee considering the Mississippi territorial question favored division with immediate admission of the western half of the territory, but a dispute arose over where the line of division should be drawn. Finally, it was established to run north and south from the Gulf on a southeastward course from an established point on the Tennessee River to the northwest corner of Washington County, and thence southeastward to a point ten miles east of the mouth of the Pascagoula River. With this division line agreed upon, Congress established Alabama Territory on March 3, 1817. Two years later it became a state.

See Thomas Perkins Abernethy, *The Formative Period in Alabama, 1815-1828* (1965); A. B. Moore, *History of Alabama*, rev. ed. (1935); Albert J. Pickett, *History of Alabama* (1900); and Dunbar Rowland, *History of Mississippi*, vol. I (1925).—T. D. C.

Alamo, the. Spanish mission and fortress. As the site of the bloodiest battle in the history of Texas, the Alamo, in San Antonio, has become the most famous symbol of the Anglo-Texan fight for independence from Mexico in 1836. The Alamo began its existence as the Mission San Antonio de Valero, which was founded in 1718 by Father Antonio de San Buenaventura Olivares of the Franciscan college at Querétaro, Mexico. In 1700 Olivares had been assigned to the new, but isolated, mission

The chapel and a portion of wall are all that remain of the Alamo. (Library of Congress)

of San Francisco de Solano on the Rio Grande, but he was soon dreaming of founding a more important mission in south-central Texas that would be a halfway post between the East Texas missions (see SAN FRANCISCO DE LOS TEJAS) and the Rio Grande. In 1709 he and Father Isidro Felix de Espinosa accompanied Captain Pedro de Aguirre's expedition into Texas, during which they visited San Pedro Spring and the beautiful San Antonio River. Impressed by the land and the abundance of water for irrigated farming, Olivares petitioned to move his Solano mission there. His enthusiasm for the area was undoubtedly enhanced by the fact that some of his Indian converts of the Xarames tribe at Solano had come from the region and wanted to return. Finally, in 1716 the Marqués de Valero, viceroy of Mexico, authorized the founding of a new mission. Two years of delay due to the time involved in collecting supplies and herds, as well as to the viceroy's decision to appoint Don Martin de Alarcón governor of Texas and leader of the expedition, kept Olivares waiting impatiently on the Rio Grande until the spring of 1718. Then Alarcón and Olivares, who could not abide one another, took separate routes to the site, bringing with them seventy-two settlers (among them neophytes from the abandoned Solano mission), soldiers, and monks; two hundred cows; one thousand sheep; two hundred oxen; and over five hundred horses.

On May 1, 1718, Olivares dedicated the mission, which he named San Antonio de Valero in honor of the viceroy. Five days later Alarcón established the presidio of San Antonio de Bejar nearby. At first the mission was little more than a set of straw-roofed wood and adobe huts. Sometime in 1719 it was moved from the west to the east bank of the river; it was moved again after a hurricane leveled the mission in 1724. Despite Apache

raids, constant bickering with the military authorities, and the competition of the Zacatecan Franciscans who founded Mission San Jose y San Miguel de Aquayo only a few miles away, San Antonio flourished. It absorbed Indian converts from the abandoned mission of San Francisco Xavier de Naxera in 1726 and recruited among the local Pampoa, Payaya, and Sana Indians. Although the mission population never exceeded 300, over 1,000 persons were baptized and 454 were married at the mission between 1718 and 1761.

A turning point in the history of the mission came in 1731, for that year colonists from the Canary Islands founded the villa of San Fernando (the nucleus of the future city of San Antonio) nearby. At the same time, three new Franciscan missions, San Juan Capistrano, La Purísima Concepción, and San Francisco de Espada, were founded within a six-mile radius of San Antonio de Valero. Almost overnight the community became the most impressive mission center in the borderlands. The concentration created conflicts between the mission population and the presidio soldiers and sailors, however. In 1736 soldiers visiting the mission from the west bank of the river became so abusive and their commander so threatening that the fathers destroyed the river bridge to keep the soldiers from the mission. The missions and settlers were constantly disputing ownership of range cattle and farmlands, the settlers claiming that the missions monopolized Indian labor and glutted the market with food and cattle.

At its peak, San Antonio de Valero, like its neighbor San José, was a thriving enterprise. An inspector in 1745 reported that its three hundred Indians lived in rows of adobe houses on either side of an *acequia* (irrigation ditch). Some tended the mission herds of 2,000 cattle, 1,300 sheep, and 304 goats, and others grew and harvested corn and wheat on irrigated land. The mission also boasted fruit orchards and vegetable gardens. Women were employed in weaving cloth out of cotton and wool. Yet San Antonio began to decline as early as 1778, and by 1790 only forty-eight persons lived at the mission. In 1793 Valero was secularized: the remaining Indians were given land allotments, and the mission's religious functions were assumed by the villa church of San Fernando.

As was the case with the other missions of the area, San Antonio had grown from a set of low-lying adobe and wood buildings to an impressive fortresslike mission. Around the walled plaza could be found the usual mission buildings: a two-story convent for the friars, storage rooms and granaries, weaving rooms, and a blacksmith shop. Corrals for animals were nearby. In 1738 Indian laborers built a new church of limestone, but poor foundations led to its collapse. In 1756 another church was begun with twin towers and a carved doorway that was almost identical to the Tuscan-style church at Mission La Purísima Concepción. Yet it was still incomplete in 1793 and, after secularization, fell into decay. Except for the restored shell of the church and its façade, little remains today to suggest that it was once part of a mission.

Unlike so many other Spanish missions, however, San Antonio de Valero continued to be occupied. A few Indians lived there until 1801, when a flying company of Spanish troops from the pueblo of San José y Santiago del Alamo de Parras were stationed there. It is they who gave the name Alamo to the church in honor of their home town. In 1813, Bernardo Gutiérrez de Lara, leading a motley army of adventurers, occupied San Antonio and the Alamo but were driven out by Spanish forces.

At the outbreak of the Texan revolt against Mexico in 1835, General Cos and his Mexican troops in the Alamo surrendered to the Texan commander, Ben Milam. Then on February 23, 1836, a force of 187 Texans commanded by Colonel William Barret Travis occupied the Alamo and prepared to defend it against attack by the Mexicans. The next day, General Antonio López de Santa Anna, the Mexican dictator, with an army of approximately five thousand men began a thirteen-day siege of the walled mission fortress after Colonel Travis answered a demand for surrender with a cannon shot. As the battle began, Travis dispatched via courier a plea to the Texas government for aid. Signed "Victory or death," this document nonetheless failed to bring reinforcements. On the morning of March 6, 1836, the Mexicans stormed the Alamo. Despite losses estimated at more than fifteen hundred men, Santa Anna's forces breached the walls, and in a short time all of the Texans, including such folk heroes as James Bowie and David Crockett, had been slain. "Remember the Alamo" became a rallying cry as the Texans drove the Mexican forces from their borders the following April. Preserved today as both a Texas and national shrine, the ruins of the Alamo are visited yearly by hundreds of thousands of tourists.

See James W. Burke, *Missions of Old Texas* (1971); H. Bailey Carroll and Walter Prescott Webb, eds., *The Handbook of Texas*. 2 vols. (1952); Carlos E. Castañeda, *Our Catholic Heritage in Texas*, vol. III (1938); Mardith K. Schuetz, *Historic Background of the Mission in San*

Antonio de Valero (1966); Lon Tinkle, "The Alamo," in *Six Missions of Texas* (1965); and Robert S. Weddle, *San Juan Bautista: Gateway to Spanish Texas* (1968). The basic facts of the siege of the Alamo may be found in William C. Binkley, *The Texas Revolution* (1952); Walter F. McCaleb, *The Alamo* (1956); and Lon Tinkle, *13 Days to Glory: The Siege of the Alamo* (1958).—J. B. F.

Alaska. Alaska is in area the largest state of the Union. The arctic and Pacific oceans on the north, west, and south of Alaska and eastern boundary with Canada enclose more than 580,000 square miles. The coastal ranges, the Alaska Range, and the Brooks Range divide the state into geographical provinces as the Great Plains, the Rocky Mountain system, the central plateau, and the Pacific Mountain system do the mainland United States (see PHYSIOGRAPHY OF THE UNITED STATES). The highest mountain of North America is in Alaska (Mount McKinley), one of the continent's largest rivers cuts from east to west across the interior of the state (the Yukon River), and the northernmost town on the continent proper is Point Barrow, Alaska. Volcanoes and glaciers decorate the landscape, and thousands of lakes dot the interior. The flora and fauna of Alaska are, with the landscape, major attractions.

Climate varies. The Arctic region is cold, with long winter nights. Temperatures in the northern interior can go as low as minus seventy degrees Fahrenheit in winter and as high as plus ninety degrees Fahrenheit in the summer. The Aleutian Islands are cool, wet, and windy. Areas of south-central Alaska have the most livable climate in any season. Less than twenty inches of rain is usual for the state's largest city, Anchorage. Farther south and east, in the Alexander Archipelago of Alaska's Panhandle, the weather is mild but extremely wet. Because of Alaska's position in the high latitudes, winters are long and summers are short.

The most ancient known rocks in Alaska are Precambrian, more than 520 million years old. Between 185 million and 520 million years ago, an ocean inundated most of the country; later these seas were disturbed by submarinal volcanic activity and other dislocations of the earth, which produced arched uplifts of land and accompanying troughs. By the early Tertiary Era of geologic time almost all parts of Alaska were above sea level, but not until sometime between 1 million and 30 million years ago did the region come to resemble in a general way the Alaska of today.

Anthropologists seem to agree that all of North America was populated by human migrations moving in both directions across the Bering Strait land bridge, over the Bering Sea platform, and via the Aleutian Islands. Precisely when the migrations commenced is in question. The dates usually given are between 10,000 and 30,000 years ago. Two major groups of indigenous people now occupy Alaska: the Eskimos in the north and west and their cousins the Aleuts of the Aleutian Islands; and the Indians—Athapaskan stocks in the interior and Tlingit (Northwest Coast) in the Alexander Archipelago. The word *Alaska* comes appropriately from an Aleut word meaning "peninsula" or "mainland," which sounded like *A-la-a-ska* to early Russian settlers.

The earliest permanent European contact with Alaska was the culminating voyage of a massive Russian scientific expedition into Siberia and beyond, mounted originally by Czar Peter the Great and supported after his death by successors to the imperial throne. A Dane, Vitus Bering, in command on the *St. Peter,* and Aleksei Chirikov, captain of the *St. Paul,* set sail in 1741 to explore eastward from Siberia. The ships separated. Chirikov sighted land in southeastern Alaska and Bering's first landfall was Cape St. Elias on the Gulf of Alaska. En route home Bering's ship was partially wrecked on an island, in the Komandorskie group, where Bering died in December and which bears his name today.

The crew members who survived returned with sea otter pelts and stories of their abundance. *Promyshleniki,* private fur-hunters, made numerous voyages to the islands and eastward to the mainland, decimating both the otter at sea and the native people on land.

Eventually larger fur companies were formed, and one, the Shelikhov-Golikov firm established a post on Kodiak Island in 1784. In 1799 it received a monopoly charter as the Russian-American Company. The company, a paragovernmental commercial organization like its nearest competitor, the Hudson's Bay Company, prospered under its first general manager, Aleksandr A. BARANOV (1790-1818). He suppressed competition, reestablished SITKA (New Archangel) after the Tlingit Indians destroyed the original settlement, and even founded a company post at FORT ROSS in California. Company affairs were directed from Sitka.

During the late eighteenth and early nineteenth centuries, several Russian and European maritime expeditions were engaged in exploring the coastline. The Russian expeditions included voyages by Joseph Billings (1789-91), Otto von Kotzebue (1816-17), Fëdor P. Lütke (1827-28), and two local captains who stand out, G. G. Izmailov for his wide experience on the coast and G. G. Pribylov for his discovery in 1786 of the seal islands which bear his name. The Spanish sent, among others, Ignacio Arteaga and Juan Francisco de la Bodega y Quadra in 1779, and Alejandro Malaspina in 1791. For the French, Comte de La Pérouse anchored in Lituya Bay in 1786.

The British expedition of Captain James Cook in 1778 had helped to stimulate these European maritime explorations. Cook traced most of what is now the familiar profile of Alaska. Joseph Billings was with Cook, as were Nathaniel Portlock and George Dixon, who sailed to Alaska as English traders in 1786-87. George Vancouver also served with Cook. Vancouver, in 1792-94, mapped the Alaskan coast with remarkable precision from the southern limits north to Cook Inlet. His charts remained in use for more than three quarters of a century.

The disappearance of the sea otter reduced sharply the profits of the company after Baranov's departure. He was succeeded by Russian naval officers, one of whom was the explorer Baron Ferdinand von Wrangell, who served from 1830 to 1835. Under the new managers, Russian influence spread beyond the older communities in the Aleutian Islands, at Kodiak, on Cook Inlet and at Sitka. Wrangell sent M. D. Tebenkov to settle St. Michael, just north of the Yukon River delta, and Alexander Kolmakov established a post up the Kuskokwim River. Nulato, on the Yukon River, was founded in the same decade. During the 1840s the company sponsored some inland explorations, in part to

intercept peltry that might flow eastwardly into British hands, or northwesterly to private Siberian traders. An unsuccessful attempt was made to explore the Susitna River, and Russian explorers went some distance up the Copper River. The latter region was probed again in 1847 by Rufus Serebrennikov; his party was apparently massacred by the natives. An important investigation of the lower Yukon, Koyukuk, Innoko, and Kuskokwim rivers was undertaken earlier in the decade by Lieutenant Lavrenti Alekseev Zagoskin. Before the end of the Russian period in 1867, H. J. Holmberg had completed a pioneer study of the ethnology of the country, I. G. Voznesenskii had studied Alaskan natural history for the Imperial Academy of Sciences, and Peter Doroshin had searched for minerals along the southern coasts.

British explorers representing the Hudson's Bay Company were active in the northeastern part of Alaska. Thomas Simpson traced the northern littoral of the continent from the mouth of the Mackenzie River to Point Barrow in the summer of 1837. Five years later John Bell reached the headwaters of the Porcupine River, which he descended to the Yukon. He recommended that an English post be established at the confluence of the two rivers, a job given to Alexander Hunter Murray in 1847. Though at least one Russian trader had traveled the Yukon's length in Alaska, the river was officially explored and mapped by American parties with the Western Union Telegraph expedition in 1867.

In the meantime, the social character of the country changed in those scattered areas along the coasts where the few Russian posts existed. Russian intermarriage with the native population, particularly the Aleuts, became common. The company relied heavily for technical help upon the so-called Creoles born of these marriages. Creoles worked as navigators, explorers, clerks, traders, and craftsmen; one apparently did the engravings for Mikhail Tebenkov's *Atlas of the Northwest Coast of America.* The Finns were a significant European minority; they also served in the skilled occupations, and they attended their own Lutheran services in Sitka. The older Russian Church established itself at various posts on the Pacific littoral. The scholarly priest Ioann VENIAMINOV became Bishop Innokentii (Innocent) and later the metropolitan of Moscow after a distinguished missionary career in Russian America. On other cultural fronts, some schools were founded, along with a shipyard, a coal mine, and a foundry. Meteorological observations were made at several places, and a modest natural history collection was assembled at Sitka. Such activities were, however, very limited owing to the small Russian population, which did not exceed a few hundred souls.

By the 1860s the Russian imperial government was dissatisfied with the cost of holding Alaska, feared the possible loss of it to Great Britain, and, more important, sought to consolidate Russia's position in Siberia, on the borders of China. Consequently, in 1867, Alaska was sold to the United States for $7 million. United States Secretary of State William Seward promoted the transaction; he possibly recognized the country's geographically strategic position in relation to Asia. A few American newspapers were critical, but most favored the purchase (see ALASKA, PURCHASE OF).

Alaska has been "discovered" five times by the United

States: first, during the Russian period, by New England fur-trading vessels that plied the southern coasts and by whalers operating in the northern Pacific and the Arctic oceans; second, with the purchase itself; third, during the gold rushes north about 1900; fourth, as a militarily significant area during World War II; and fifth, since the late 1950s, with the quickening interest in Alaska's natural resources, particularly timber and petroleum. In between, Alaska experienced an uneven political and economic existence.

Between 1867 and 1877 the territory was ruled by a handful of United States Army troops. The novelty of an American Alaska brought a few hundred people north in the 1860s, mainly to the Panhandle, but the novelty soon wore thin in the damp climate of a distant northern territory without basic industries. The earliest important marks of economic and social permanence were made by the fur business and the missionaries. The new Alaska Commercial Company, with headquarters in San Francisco, bought much of the property of the Russian-American Company and in 1870 the A.C. company obtained a federal lease to exploit the fur-seal rookeries in the Bering Sea. The company soon extended its fur-gathering operations inland. Fur continued to be an important export well into the twentieth century. On the social side the Russian church continued to serve its communicants. The Presbyterian Sheldon Jackson in 1880 encouraged other Protestant churches to divide the country among interested denominations. Missions and schools were established in various parts of the territory. One of these missionaries, John Green Brady, later became an important political figure in Alaska.

When the army was withdrawn in 1877, a few customs collectors and a few small revenue cutters were the only signs of United States authority in Alaska. A threatened Indian uprising at Sitka in 1879 brought the navy to Alaska, and it governed the tiny population until 1884, the year that the territory's first civil charter was granted by Congress. The Organic Act of that year made Alaska a civil-judicial district with an appointed governor and a small number of officials. Criminal and civil codes awaited the national interest aroused by the gold rush, and in 1906 the territory was allowed to send one delegate to the Congress. The post was filled by some able men, including James Wickersham (1909-21), Anthony J. Dimond (1933-44), and E. L. Bartlett (1944-58). But the central political battles were for home rule. The first culminated in the enabling legislation of 1912, which gave Alaska eight senators and sixteen representatives in a bicameral legislature. In 1959, after years of campaigning, Alaska was formally granted statehood. Bartlett, the former delegate, and Ernest Gruening, a former territorial governor (1939-53), were elected to serve as the new state's first United States senators.

Alaska's long wait for home rule, for settlement, and for resident economic development moved some of its historians, most notably Jeannette Paddock Nichols and Gruening, to charge the federal government with mismanagement and neglect. In the early twentieth century, an Alaskan, quoted by Professor Nichols, expressed this sentiment in rhyme:

When you took me, young and trusting, from the
    growling Russian Bear,

Loud you swore before the nation I should have the
    Eagle's care.
Never yet has wing of Eagle cast a shadow on my
    peaks,
But I've watched the flight of buzzards, and I've felt
    their busy beaks.

More recently, revisionist historians have questioned the interpretation. According to them, Alaska's experience did not differ markedly in a negative way from the history of United States western territories; the central government did extend services, some of them historically unique, to the territory; and federal officials were probably neither better nor worse than their counterparts south of the forty-ninth parallel. The revisionists tie Alaska's frontier status to its location, to economic realities, and to the diminished interest of Americans in frontier life.

One activity that the national government pursued with relative vigor was inland exploration. Aside from the Yukon River's course in Alaska, and the lower Kuskokwim regions, the interior was largely uncharted. Army Lieutenant Frederick Schwatka made a reconnaissance of the Yukon in 1883, mapping the upper reaches in Canada. George Stoney for the navy and John C. Cantwell for the revenue marine explored the Kobuk River district in 1884-86. In the summer of 1885 an expedition under army Lieutenant Henry Tureman Allen explored the Copper, Tanana, and Koyukuk rivers. Two federal agencies, the army and the United States Geological Survey, competed for laurels in Alaskan exploration during the gold rush, and the Survey became the major agency for mapping Alaska during the present century.

Population trends reflect the several "discoveries" of Alaska. An estimate for 1840 places the native population at slightly over 40,000 and the nonnative population at 700. There were probably fewer nonnatives by 1860, and their numbers undoubtedly rose immediately after the purchase of the country by the United States, but no reliable figures are readily available for 1870. The 1880 census, conducted by Ivan Petroff, put the native population at 33,000; the number of whites was 430. By 1890 the former figure had slipped to 25,350, and the latter had risen to 4,300. The population remained more or less stable until 1910, with a slight drop in the number of natives and a slight rise in the number of whites, but the census of 1920 revealed fewer nonnatives. Increased spending for military defense brought the figure up again in 1940, and the white population nearly doubled between 1940 and 1950, and doubled again by the census of 1960. The figures for 1960 are 43,081 natives, 150,394 nonnatives, and 32,692 military personnel. Returns for 1970 place the total population at 302,382, over half of whom live in the Anchorage and Fairbanks areas. Despite these urban concentrations the land-man ratio for the whole state is roughly two square miles per person.

During the early American period, the small nonnative population occupied itself mainly in service industries as shopkeepers and traders, or in trapping and prospecting. Though Alaska's fish were a staple in the diet of all native groups, commercial fishing on a large scale did not begin until the 1880s with the establishment of salmon canneries along the southern coasts. By the first years of this century, over sixty plants packed about 1.5 million cases each year. In 1918 the pack numbered 6.5 million cases, then the expanded market of World War I collapsed. After 1920 the size of the catch fluctuated but moved generally upward to a peak in 1936, when some 120 canneries packed 8.5 million cases of salmon. Thereafter, the pack, with some variations in production, dropped alarmingly. Conservationist efforts to halt depletion of the resource were only mildly successful, and absentee fish-canning corporations became the object of political criticism within Alaska both for their hostility to home rule and their operational procedures, particularly the use of fish traps near spawning streams. Although the salmon's decline was not checked during the territorial years, the commercial fisheries (including halibut, crab, herring, and other seafood fisheries) were in 1960 the country's number one resource by value and a major employer among nongovernmental institutions. (See also FISHERIES: ALASKA.)

But it was gold, not fish, that turned the nation's attention north again at the end of the nineteenth century. Traces of the metal had been found before Russia sold the territory, for example, by Doroshin along Cook Inlet and by Western Union Telegraph explorers on Seward Peninsula. After Alaska changed flags, independent miners prospected the Panhandle, on the southern coasts, and along a few of the interior rivers. Two veterans of the Cassiar, British Columbia, diggings found gold at Alaska's future capital, Juneau, in 1880. Nearby, the Treadwell stamp mill soon began to produce sizable quantities from low-grade ore. Miners reached the Yukon River valley over the passes in the northern Panhandle, by ship to the delta, then upstream by riverboat or overland by portage from the east. Three men who were especially influential in the early life of the Yukon came to Alaska overland from Canada. L. N. McQuesten, Arthur Harper, and Al Mayo trapped, traded, and prospected along most of the river's length. Such activities made Alaska an important source of gold even before George Washington Carmack found color on the Klondike River of Canada in 1896. From the Klondike, miners fanned over Alaska. Strikes were made at several locales, most notably at Nome on the Seward Peninsula, and in the Fairbanks region by Felix Pedro in 1902. A literary haze generated in part by the novels and stories of Rex Beach and Jack London, and the rhymes of Robert Service, has obscured the realities of Alaskan life during the gold rushes, and since then. For the vast majority of stampeders and pioneers, discomfort, hard work, and disappointment were the rewards, and it was the ugliness of frontier violence—not its drama—that impressed most observers at the scene.

The federal government contributed importantly to the improvement of transportation and communication, sometimes even in advance of settlement. The United States Geological Survey became the miner's partner, and the army mounted several expeditions to explore and mark the routes northward. When the Survey assumed its mapping functions, the army remained in Alaska to build telegraph lines (and later telephone lines) and roads, the latter maintained by another governmental agency, the Alaska Road Commission. The roadwork was also motivated by the successful comple-

tion of a Canadian narrow-gauge railroad from Skagway in Alaska to Whitehorse on the upper Yukon River.

Alaskans called for an "all-American route," and in Washington, D.C., legislation was passed to permit rights-of-way. Before 1900 some eleven railroad companies filed for permission to build railroads in the interior and into the interior from ice-free ports on the southcentral coast. The Guggenheims financed the Copper River and Northwestern Railroad from Cordova to their rich copper deposits at Kennecott. (The C.R. & N. ceased operation in the late 1930s when the mines closed.) Elsewhere the scramble for routes and coal to stoke the locomotives soon faltered. After a commission appointed by President William Howard Taft recommended a federal railroad, and after President Woodrow Wilson authorized construction, the seventy-mile Alaska Northern from Seward, and the forty-five-mile Tanana Valley Railroad in the interior were purchased. In 1923 the towns of Seward and Fairbanks (milepost 470.3) were linked by rail. A few entrepreneurs, such as "Cap" LATHROP, benefitted from the coming of the railroad, but the Alaska Railroad did not stimulate large-scale development, as its proponents had hoped. However, the city of Anchorage was founded, the A.R.R. served the New Deal's agricultural resettlement project in the Matanuska valley, and the railroad carried tons of military supplies during World War II. During the war, another link in the territory's transportation net was fastened when the army engineers completed the Alaska Highway, which provided Alaska with its first overland connection with the "lower forty-eight" states. Since Alaska achieved statehood and eligibility for more federal highway financing, the state government has tied most of the larger towns together either with new roads or ferry service over water. Airplanes have also played a vital role in Alaska's transportation history since the 1920s.

International and national issues touched Uncle Sam's giant northern stepchild. Pelagic (open-sea) sealing late in the nineteenth century reduced almost to extinction the seals breeding on the Pribilof Islands, and propelled the United States into a disagreement with Canada, Britain, and, later, Japan. The Convention of 1911, between the United States, Russia, Canada, and Japan forbade pelagic sealing and divided the controlled catch on the islands, thus saving the fur seal. Another dispute with Canada, over Alaska's southeastern boundary, was settled in 1903 after the pugnacious intervention of President Theodore Roosevelt. Roosevelt's "Progressive era" also ushered in a vigorous American conservation movement. During his administration, Progressives began to withdraw from exploitation large segments of Alaska's choicest land and natural resources. Political fallout from a conflict of interest dispute over certain Alaskan coal claims, involving Secretary of the Interior Richard Ballinger and chief of the United States Forest Service Gifford Pinchot, affected, among other things, the presidential election of 1912. According to some Alaskan critics, the federal land and resource withdrawals stifled economic development. Historians picked up the indictment, but several recent writers, concerned about environmental quality, consider Alaska's vast public wilderness areas, clean air, and pure water a blessing, and call attention to the effects of the ruthless consumption of natural resources by frontier entrepreneurs in the older American West.

Alaskans in the 1930s worried about fish traps, freight rates, and long winters. Then World War II saw the beginning of massive spending for military defense. The "cold war" with the Soviet Union brought continued expenditures for defense. A slump in the economy was bridged temporarily by the rehabilitation activities that followed the 1964 Alaskan earthquake, which had destroyed large parts of Anchorage, Seward, Kodiak, and Valdez. Later in the decade, expenditures for petroleum exploration (see OIL INDUSTRY) and the construction of related facilities in the Cook Inlet region and on the Arctic Slope buoyed the economy, as did increased tourism and lumbering in southeastern Alaska. Despite recent developments, Alaska still remains America's "last frontier."

See Hubert Howe Bancroft, *History of Alaska, 1730-1885* (1886); Pierre Berton, *The Klondike Fever* (1958); Richard A. Cooley, *Politics and Conservation: The Decline of the Alaska Salmon* (1963); Edwin M. Fitch, *The Alaska Railroad* (1967); Robert A. Frederick, ed. *Frontier Alaska* (1968); Ernest Gruening, *The State of Alaska* (1954); Ted C. Hinckley, *The Americanization of Alaska, 1867-1897* (1972); Jeannette Paddock Nichols, *Alaska . . . During Its First Half Century Under the Rule of the United States* (1963); George W. Rogers and Richard A. Cooley, eds., *Alaska's Population and Economy*, 2 vols. (1962); Morgan B. Sherwood, ed., *Alaska and Its History* (1967), and *Exploration of Alaska, 1865-1900* (1965); and Stuart Ramsay Tompkins, *Alaska, Promyshlennik and Sourdough* (1945).—M. B. S.

Alaska, purchase of (1867). Acquisition from Russia. Secretary of State William H. Seward arranged the Alaska Purchase in 1867 just before the glow of manifest destiny, so evident in earlier years, wore off. For the next generation, the country turned its attention to domestic pursuits, principally the expansion of the national economy.

The treaty was in large part the result of Russian initiative. The privately owned Russian-American Company had fallen upon poor days after the death of its organizer, Alexander Baranov, in 1819, and by the 1860s it was apparent that the czarist government would have to subsidize the company, take it over, or sell it to the Americans. Because there had been some signs of American interest in Alaska even before the Civil War—the Russian minister in Washington, Edouard de Stoeckl, had had conversations on the subject—it seemed sensible to apply to the Andrew Johnson administration and especially to the expansionist secretary of state. The Russians in a meeting in St. Petersburg, attended by Stoeckl, fixed their price at $5 million. The minister then thoughtfully asked for more but allowed the eager Seward to beat him down to $7 million. The negotiators then added the odd sum of $200,000 to the purchase price to recompense the Russian-American Company.

The motives of Seward were obvious enough. It is true that Seward proved so desirous of consummating the sale that, when Stoeckl one evening called upon him and asked what time the secretary would be ready to sign, the latter offered to open the State Department immediately. The two negotiators signed at 4:00 A.M. on March 30, 1867, in a gleam of gaslight. But Seward had arranged a bargain—the purchase of a vast territory of some 591,000 square miles, more than twice the size of Texas, equal nearly to a fifth of the continental United States, at a purchase price amounting to two cents an acre, which was cheap even for ice (if, according to his critics, ice was the only product of Alaska). Moreover, he was concerned about the North's experience during the Civil War when the Confederate raider *Shenandoah* operated in Alaskan waters and burned numerous northern whaling ships. In 1867, Seward also arranged for the appropriation of Midway Island in the Pacific, and there was thought that Alaska and Midway might serve as territorial vestibules to trade with China. Alaska, of course, had figured in the cable schemes of the American promoter P. McD. Collins, who had conceived the project of a telegraph line across Russian America and Siberia to Europe to replace the Atlantic cable that had gone dead before the Civil War; but this calculation was not in Seward's mind by 1867, as Cyrus Field had successfully spanned the Atlantic with a cable the preceding year.

The secretary's reasoning proved insufficient for many of his countrymen, however, who undertook to make jokes about Alaska. There was mention of Seward's folly, of Seward's icebox, of a territory created only for establishment of new political jobs (a polar bears' bureau, a superintendent of walruses). (Senator Charles Sumner, incidentally, in his great Senate speech supporting the treaty, had popularized the name Alaska for what hitherto had been called Russian America.) There also was an uproar when it was discovered that Stoeckl had taken most of the $200,000, which supposedly was to go to the Russian-American Company, and used it as a fund to bribe members of the House of Representatives into supporting the appropriation for Alaska. The House was in the process of arranging the impeachment of President Andrew Johnson and was not above making trouble for Johnson's secretary of state, and it withheld the appropriation for a year. Meanwhile, the American flag was raised at Sitka on October 18, 1867.

See Thomas A. Bailey, "Why the United States Purchased Alaska," *Pacific Historical Review,* vol. 3 (1934); Victor J. Farrar, *The Annexation of Russian America to the United States* (1937); and F. A. Golder, "The Purchase of Alaska," *American Historical Review,* vol. 25 (1919-20). —R. H. F.

Alaska Railroad. See ALASKA.

Albany Plan of Union (1754). The Albany Plan of Union was the response of an assemblage of colonial politicians to the efforts of the French to occupy and control the upper Ohio valley and to make their position there a link in a chain of outposts from Montreal to New Orleans, designed to confine the British-Americans to the eastern slopes of the Allegheny Mountains.

The British Board of Trade was responsible for the conclave that produced the plan. On September 18, 1753, it ordered the governor of New York to convene a conference of commissioners from neighboring colonies to conciliate the IROQUOIS CONFEDERACY, which was suspected of being on the verge of succumbing to French influence, by concluding "one general Treaty" with them, cemented by liberal supplies of presents. Responding to Lieutenant Governor James De Lancey's summons, delegates from seven colonies, including such important politicians as Benjamin Franklin of Pennsylvania and Thomas Hutchinson of Massachusetts, assembled at Albany on June 19, 1754. After a display of truculence, the Indians permitted themselves to be talked into a good disposition and departed with thirty wagonloads of presents, although many were soon in arms against their benefactors.

The important work of the conference was one for which the delegates had not been specifically summoned, the framing of a plan of union, so that the resources of the colonies could be effectively pooled to defeat the French and prevent them from turning the Old Northwest into a Gallic granary. Franklin, who had advocated colonial union for some years, was the principal draftsman of the plan, which the commissioners adopted on July 10, 1754. It proposed that "one General Government" be imposed on the American colonies by act of Parliament. The government was to be administered by a president general, appointed by the crown, and by a Grand Council, appointed by the legislatures of each colony in proportion to the amount of taxes each paid. The General Government's powers were restricted to Indian affairs and defense. It was to conduct all Indian negotiations, purchase all lands from the Indians, regulate all trade with them, and supervise all settlements on property purchased from them. It was also given the power to raise and pay soldiers, maintain vessels of war on oceans, lakes, and rivers, declare war, and conclude peace.

Despite the danger from the French and the advantages of presenting a united front against them, not a single colonial legislature approved the plan. Nor did the British bureaucrats endorse it. So ignominious was its failure that Franklin and other men of broad vision thought that the colonists could never unite. That they did in 1776 seemed little short of a miracle to the veterans of Albany.

The best monograph on the Albany Plan of Union is Robert C. Newbold, *The Albany Congress and the Plan of Union of 1754* (1955). Two careful, although somewhat conflicting, treatments of the plan can be found in Lawrence H. Gipson, *The British Empire Before the American Revolution,* vol. V (1942), and in Leonard W. Labaree et al., eds., *The Papers of Benjamin Franklin,* vol. V (1962).—J. H. H.

Alemany, Joseph (1814-88). Roman Catholic bishop. A Spanish Dominican, Alemany worked in Ohio, Kentucky, and Tennessee from 1840. He became bishop of California in 1850 and was archbishop-metropolitan of post-gold-rush San Francisco in 1853. Active at the Vatican Council in 1870, Alemany retired to Spain in 1885. See John Bernard McGloin, *California's Pioneer Archbishop* (1965).—R. I. B.

Algonquian language. See INDIAN LANGUAGES: *Algonquian.*

Allen, Ethan. See VERMONT, SETTLEMENT OF.

Allen, Henry Tureman (1859-1930). Explorer and soldier. Only a few months of Allen's long service in the United States Army was spent in Alaska, but in those few months Allen led a remarkable journey of discovery that ranks with the great explorations of North America. Allen was born in Sharpsburg, Kentucky, and attended the United States Military Academy at West Point. After graduation in 1882, he was ordered to Washington Territory where he worked as an aide to General Nelson

Miles. Miles, as commander of the army's Department of Columbia, was engaged in organizing a series of expeditions northward to scout the topography, resources, and native populations of interior Alaska. Lieutenant Frederick Schwatka navigated the Yukon River in 1883, and in 1884 William R. Abercrombie was dispatched with a large party to investigate the Copper River. The Abercrombie expedition failed to penetrate the region. In 1885, Lieutenant Allen was given the job.

He arrived in March with two enlisted men, Private Frederick W. Fickett and Sergeant Cady Robertson. Two prospectors were added to the party. Allen and his tiny group explored the Copper River and a tributary, the Chitina, in April, May, and early June, then boated down the Tanana River to the Yukon, which he reached at the end of June. With Fickett, he traveled overland to a tributary of the Koyukuk River, ascending the latter to its headwaters. In canoes the two explorers descended the Koyukuk to the Yukon in August. In one short summer Allen traversed and charted three major river systems, about fifteen hundred miles of wilderness.

The Alaskan achievement was followed by a distinguished military career. Allen taught at West Point, was military attaché to Russia and Germany, organized the Philippine Constabulary, served with the Mexican Punitive Expedition, and became a corps commander in Europe during World War I and commander of American forces in Germany (1919-23).

See Henry T. Allen, *Report of an Expedition to the Copper, Tanana, and Koyukuk Rivers in the Territory of Alaska, 1885* (1887), and Morgan B. Sherwood, *Exploration of Alaska, 1865-1900* (1965).—M. B. S.

Allen, William Vincent (1847-1924). Nebraska Populist politician. A key Populist senator, Allen was an impressive six-footer who established a reputation for himself as a formidable debater and sound thinker. He was an Ohioan by birth, a Union veteran, and a successful Nebraska attorney. First elected to a district judgeship in 1891 by the Populists, he won a seat in the United States Senate in 1893 as a result of the coalition of Populist and Democratic state legislators. He became known for his record fifteen-hour speaking effort as part of a filibuster against repeal of the Sherman Silver Purchase Act. He was a determined advocate of fusion with the silver wing of the Democratic party and a staunch supporter of fellow Nebraskan William Jennings Bryan. After Bryan's defeat in 1896, Allen's voice was influential in urging the Populists to merge completely with the Democratic party. Although defeated in his bid for reelection in 1899, Allen returned to the Senate for two more years by appointment when his successor-elect died. From that time until his death he was a Democrat but relatively inactive in politics. —O. G. C.

Allison, [Robert] Clay (1840-1887). Cattleman and gunfighter. A violent, complicated man who probably suffered from mental disorder, Allison represents a class of men who lived on the fringe of the law and by a code that placed higher value on personal honor than on legal restraints.

His reputation as a bad man was won in Texas and New Mexico, but Allison had humble beginnings on a Tennessee farm. He grew up amidst talk of states' rights and slavery, and when the Civil War divided his native state, young Allison chose the gray. In January 1862 he was discharged for emotional instability resulting from a head injury as a child, but in September he reenlisted and fought the duration of the war as a scout for General Nathan Bedford Forrest.

At war's end Allison and his brothers joined the migration westward. He was soon a cowhand for Texas ranchers Oliver Loving and Charles Goodnight. By 1870 he was ranching in Colfax County, New Mexico, and his reputation for getting into drunken brawls and shooting sprees was spreading. Legend insists that he killed a man named Johnson in a knife duel fought in an open grave that year, but the story has not been verified. In October 1870 he was a leader in a particularly gruesome lynching. Allison reportedly decapitated the victim and displayed the gory trophy in a Cimarron saloon. He was feared by many because of his murderous temper, but not until 1874 are there records to justify his reputation as a gunfighter. In January of that year he killed a hardcase named Chunk Colbert in a gunfight at Clifton House on the Canadian River. That secured his reputation as a man-killer.

Allison's escapades were sometimes tinged with his own peculiar sense of justice and were often followed by embarrassed apologies and efforts to make amends. In 1875, for example, he sided with homesteaders against the ranchers and the stock association in a dispute that logically should have found him on the other side. His sense of what was right dictated that he support the farmers even though he was a rancher himself. Besides, he never learned to like organizations like stock associations.

Clay was also interested in politics, and later that year he found himself immersed in an unsolved murder that had political overtones. New Mexico's politics in the 1870s were dominated by a shifting and nebulous political clique known as the Santa Fe Ring. The ring was made up of politicians, officeholders, and entrepreneurs who sought to extend their influence to the local levels of government in New Mexico and to dominate the economic affairs of the territory. Colfax County was run by men who supported the ring and the patronage and electioneering that went along with it. Allison opposed the ring, partly because its chicanery did not conform to his sense of fair play, partly because the ring was run by northerners who had come to New Mexico after the Civil War as federal officeholders and speculators, and partly because he failed to see eye to eye with the Colfax County politicos.

In the summer of 1875, the Reverend F. J. Tolby wrote a letter to the New York *Sun* criticizing the ring in strong terms, and in September he was mysteriously murdered. The next month an outraged Allison and others seized a Mexican named Cruz Vega, forced him to confess, and then hanged him on a telegraph pole. The lynching of Vega brought Pancho Griego, a well-known man-killer, into Cimarron looking for Allison. He found him, and after a brief chorus of gunfire from Allison's .45, he expired on the saloon floor. Vega had implicated Manuel Cardenas in the Tolby murder. Cardenas was arrested and jailed, but one night a group of men, including Allison, murdered the prisoner in his cell.

Such activities turned many against Allison, including the editor of the Cimarron *News and Press*, who began to editorialize on behalf of the ring. On January 19, 1876, Allison led a mob into the newspaper office and threw the presses into the river. He appropriated the first page of the next edition, which had already been printed, scrawled "Clay Allison's Edition" across the back, and sold them on the streets of Cimarron. Later Allison apologized and paid the firm two hundred dollars for damages.

Allison was basically a racist, harboring an intense dislike for blacks, and the following spring he was arrested for murdering three black soldiers. But the evidence was sketchy, and he was soon on the loose again. Law enforcement officers were noticeably reluctant to arrest him even after warrants were issued against him in the Vega, Griego, and Cardenas cases. The territory even brought charges against him for the killing of Chunk Colbert, but in June 1876 a grand jury refused to return indictments. The year's end found him in Las Animas, Colorado, and under arrest for the murder of a deputy sheriff. Allison posted bond and by March 1877 was a free man again.

Things were quiet for a time after that, but in 1878 he left New Mexico for good. He escorted a herd of cattle to East St. Louis and made the town's newspapers with his brawling. On his return trip west he stopped off at Dodge City, Kansas. There are numerous tales of an encounter with Dodge City Lawmen. These stories are among the most enduring aspects of the Allison legend. Several sources recount how Allison made Bat Masterson and other lawmen "hunt their holes" while he and his men "treed the town." Stuart N. Lake, on the other hand, depicted his hero, Wyatt Earp, forcing Allison to turn tail and run. It may be that Allison did meet with Dodge City peace officers concerning the shooting of a cowboy named George Hoy, but it is clear that no serious altercation or face-down occurred.

Following the Dodge City visit, Allison settled on the Washita River in Hemphill County, Texas. By 1881 age and marriage had slowed him down some, but his reputation was kept alive by reports of peculiar antics. Once, for example, he rode nude through the streets of Mobeetie, Texas. On another occasion he developed a toothache while on a cattle drive in Wyoming. He went to a dentist in Cheyenne who drilled the wrong tooth. Allison angrily left the office, had his dental work done elsewhere, and then returned to the first dentist's office, where he extracted one of the unfortunate doctor's teeth. There was still enough steam in the aging Clay Allison to win him the nickname "the Wolf of the Washita."

Allison was killed in a freak accident. He was thrown from a wagon and a rear wheel rolled over his neck. He was buried in Pecos, Texas.

See Stanley Crocchiola, *Clay Allison* (1956); Harry E. Kelsey, Jr., "Clay Allison: Western Gunman," *Denver Westerners Brand Book* (1957); and Dale T. Schoenberger, *The Gunfighters* (1971).—G. L. R.

Allred, Berten Wendell (1904-   ). Conservationist and writer. Allred was born in Moab, Utah, and grew up on the family ranch. At the age of eight he began helping his father, who also owned a stagecoach line, by lending a hand with the horses. After he had completed his education at Utah State University and the University of Nebraska, Allred ran sheep in the Red Desert in Wyoming and served as an agricultural agent in Colorado.

In 1935 he joined the United States Soil Conservation

Service. First a range conservationist for the Great Plains, Allred transferred in 1953 to Washington, D.C., to serve as a range-planning specialist and, later, as the chief range conservationist. Following his retirement in 1965, he joined the United Nations' Food and Agriculture Organization as a grass and livestock specialist. In 1959 he went into the beef-cattle business on a grass farm in Maryland.

Allred is widely known for his many technical articles and government publications in the field of conservation, including *Range Conservation Practices for the Great Plains* (1946) and *Practical Grassland Management* (1950), which proved to be so useful and popular that it was reissued as a textbook. With Jefferson C. Dykes, he edited and contributed a chapter to *Flat Top Ranch* (1957), the story of the making of a conservation ranch. He also edited the *Dynamics of Vegetation* (1949), the collected writings of the noted ecologist Dr. Frederic E. Clements. Allred was a frequent contributor to magazines read by ranch families, such popular publications as *The Cattleman, The Texas Sheep and Goat Raiser, The National Wool Grower,* and *The Hereford Journal.*

While most of his life's work was devoted to sheep, grass, and cattle, other aspects of the West vied for his attention. He was one of the founders and past president of both the Potomac Corral (one of fifty chapters of the Westerners, an international organization of western history buffs), and the American Society of Range Management. As one of the Old Bookaroos, a group of four men who produce the column "Western Book Roundup" for *True West, Frontier Times, Gold, Old West, American Book Collector,* and *Arizona and the West,* Allred wrote hundreds of reviews of western books. He was a member of Western Writers of America and, using a pen name, supposedly a contributor to the pulps of the thirties.—J. C. D.

Alta, Utah. Mining and resort town. Alta, a prominent winter resort southeast of Salt Lake City, was once a bustling silver mining camp. The wealth of this area of the Wasatch Mountains was first tapped by the soldiers of Colonel Patrick E. Conner in 1864, but the Alta region did not begin to boom until 1869, when J. B. Woodman founded the EMMA MINE. Alta's most productive years were during the 1870s, when over $13 million worth of ore was produced. By the beginning of the twentieth century Alta's mining days began to wane, and when the town was reborn as a ski area in 1937 it was, for all practical purposes, a ghost.

Today Alta is one of the most popular resort areas in the West. The avalanches that imperiled the miners of the nineteenth century have been brought under control, ski tows have replaced bucket trams, and the rock that once formed the miner's buildings has been reshaped into a rustic ski lodge.

See Nell Murbarger, *Ghosts of the Glory Trail* (1956); Duane Smith, *Rocky Mountain Mining Camps* (1967); and Muriel S. Wolle, *The Bonanza Trail* (1953). —R. B. W.

Altube, Pedro (1827-1916). Rancher and Basque leader. Altube, alias "Palo Alto" or "Tall Pole" (he was six feet eight inches tall), the "Father of the Basques in America," was born on a farm near the town of Oñate in the Spanish Basque province of Guipúzcoa. In 1845 Altube sailed from the port of Bilbao to Buenos Aires, where he joined a brother and two stepbrothers who

had established a cattle business. Four years later he paid the passage from Spain to Argentina for his younger brother, Bernardo.

The two brothers, Pedro and Bernardo, were not to remain in Argentina. In 1850 Altube, in the company of other Basques, traversed the South American continent on horseback, shipping out from the port of Valparaiso to participate in the California gold rush. In February 1851 Bernardo and a sizable group of Basques joined him at Sonora Camp in Tuolumne County, California.

With their gold profits the brothers formed a partnership and engaged in the cattle business until 1860, when Altube and two other Basques, Antonio Harispuru and Bernard Ypar, established "Altube and Company," which ran livestock on the range of the Rancho La Laguna (Santa Barbara County). Of the total capitalization of $27,383 to be used for "paying cowboys, leasing lands and other expenses of this sort," fifty percent was advanced by Altube.

In 1870 Altube and his brother Bernardo again pooled their independent resources to purchase three thousand head of cattle in Mexico, driving them to Independence valley near the prosperous mining town of Tuscarora in Elko County, Nevada. While in Nevada the Altubes raised some sheep, but cattle remained their major interest, even after the severe winter of 1889-90 in which their losses approached ninety percent.

Basque sheepherders working with the Altubes in some cases received their salaries in stock; after four or five years such a sheepherder established his own band of sheep. Having acquired in the process a good knowledge of the local pasturages, he simply moved with his band onto new lands and worked for himself. Throughout the decade of the 1890s former Altube herders established themselves as independent sheepmen, first near Jordan valley, Oregon, and subsequently in Boise valley, Idaho. In providing the incentive for this movement Altube gained the reputation of being the "Father of the Basques in America."

Although Altube was never a leader in the Basque community (the Basques were more involved with sheep than with cattle) in the strictest sense of the word, he was widely respected in frontier society as a serious and determined individual. His large stature and outgoing personality made him an impressive figure. He was famous for his horsemanship and noted for his poker playing. He had the reputation of providing employment for his men until their deaths, in many cases long after they had outlived their usefulness.

The Altubes always retained a California residence. Two years after Altube's death, his widow and Bernardo sold the Spanish Ranch (The Palo Alto Land and Livestock Co.) to the firm of H. G. Humphrey, et al. The property at that time consisted of four hundred thousand acres, with sixty-six thousand in meadow and forty thousand under fence. The sale included twenty thousand sheep, twenty thousand cattle and two thousand horses. After the death of Bernardo in Berkeley, California, in 1916, the remainder of the Altube property, called The Taylor Canyon Horse Ranch, was sold by the family.

In 1960 Pedro Altube was inscribed in the Cowboy Hall of Fame, nominee of the state of Nevada.

See William A. Douglass and Jon Bilboa, *Amerikanuak: Basques in the New World* (1975); and Edna

B. Patterson, Louise A. Ulph, and Victor Goodwin, *Nevada's Northeast Frontier* (1969).—J. B.

Alvarez, Manuel (1794-1856). Trader, mountain man, and New Mexico politician. Born in Albegas, León, Spain, Alvarez came to the United States in 1823, probably after a sojourn in Latin America. After living in Missouri for a short time, he entered the Santa Fe trade. He settled in the New Mexican capital and sometime during the mid-1820s became a Mexican citizen.

Besides the Santa Fe trade the great excitement stirring Santa Fe and Taos at this time was the fur trade. Americans, Mexicans, and French traders from St. Louis were scouring the southern Rockies and Great Basin regions for beaver. Alvarez joined the new "fur rush" when he became an associate of P. D. Papin and Company of St. Louis (often called the French Company). Later he worked for the American Fur Company when it absorbed Papin and Company. Although it seems highly unlikely that Alvarez—who has been described as an urbane, hospitable, black-haired gentleman—could transform himself into a mountain man, his career as a free trapper was successful. He operated in the vast region between the upper Missouri and the Yellowstone and in the Green River area. At the famous rendezvous of 1833 on Horse Creek (Green River) he described the fantastic geyser basin of Yellowstone Park to the trappers gathered there. While working in the Rockies Alvarez reputedly married an Indian woman by whom he had three sons. One did not survive beyond early youth, but Alvarez took the other two to Spain to be reared, and he visited them there in 1855.

Alvarez could see that the fur trade was declining. He returned to Santa Fe in 1834, where he established and ran a large store for twenty years. He continued to ship furs and skins to St. Louis, and he made several dangerous trips across the Plains.

Despite the fact that he was not an American citizen, Alvarez was so respected that in 1839 he became the United States consul in Santa Fe and served in that post until 1846. His task was a delicate one, for he had to deal with the political intrigues of Governor Manuel Armijo, whose policies toward Americans changed without warning, and with the 1842 Texas-Santa Fe expedition. Then in 1846 Alvarez helped prepare the way for General Kearney's peaceful occupation of New Mexico. Alvarez appears to have taken seriously Kearney's promise of a democratic government for New Mexico. He served in the General Assembly of 1847 and later that year led a movement to admit New Mexico into the Union. Alvarez was even elected lieutenant governor in an abortive state election. When New Mexico became a territory instead, Alvarez held minor appointive offices until his death at Santa Fe.

Alvarez was articulate and cultivated and a friend of some of the most famous frontiersmen of his time. His papers (housed in the New Mexico State Records Center) throw light on American activity in New Mexico before and after American conquest.

See Robert Glass Cleland, *This Reckless Breed of Men* (1950); Harold H. Dunham, "Manuel Alvarez," in L. R. Hafen, ed., *The Mountain Men and the Fur Trade of the Far West*, vol. I (1965); and David J. Weber, *The Taos Trappers: The Fur Trade in the Far Southwest* (1971).—H. R. L.

Alvord, Clarence W. (1868-1928). Historian. Alvord received his B.A. from Williams College in 1891. He studied history (1893-95) at Friedrich Wilhelm University in Berlin and later went to the University of Illinois, which remained his academic home—first as a student and then as a teacher—until 1920. Next he taught at the University of Minnesota. In 1923 Alvord went to Europe, where he spent the last five years of his life doing research and writing in his chosen field of Anglo-American history.

Beginning in 1905 Alvord spent much of his career as an editor, producing *The Cahokia Records, 1778-1790* (1907) and *The Kaskaskia Records, 1778-1790* (1909). He helped organize the editing of the *Collections* of the state library of Illinois and was a guiding force behind the founding in 1914 of the *Mississippi Valley Historical Review*. From 1914 until 1923 he was an active editor of that journal.

The work for which Alvord is best known is his magisterial *The Mississippi Valley in British Politics: A Study of Trade Land Speculation and Experiments in Imperialism Culminating in the American Revolution* (1917). This two-volume work still stands as the best comprehensive treatment of the subject. Alvord's main argument is stated at the end of the second volume: "If historians would interpret rightly the cause of the American Revolution and the birth of the new nation, they must not let their vision be circumscribed by the sequence of events in the East." As Alvord so clearly understood, arguments about taxation, natural rights, and representation quickly obscured the problem of the western lands. Yet Alvord's studies revealed that when British ministers discussed "the American problem," they did not mean political disturbances in Boston or New York but the development of the vast trans-Appalachian lands acquired from the French in 1763. According to him it was British failure to resolve the hydra-headed problems of western Indian policies, competing colonial land claims, fur trade, land speculation, and imperial interest that led to the American Revolution.

For a complete bibliography of the published works of Alvord, compiled by Solon J. Buck, see the *Mississippi Valley Historical Review*, vol. 15 (1928).—E. W. K.

Amana colonies (Iowa). Utopian community. The Amana colonies consist of seven villages nestled along the Iowa River in eastern Iowa, not far from Iowa City. The colonists were descended from eighteenth-century German mystics and pietists. Their leader, Christian Metz, established the group in New York State in 1842. They purchased five thousand acres near Buffalo, formed a village named Ebenezer, and adopted a communal way of life. Their agricultural and craft operations prospered, and in a short time the group needed additional land. They turned to the western United States, where they could expand and isolate themselves from the outside world. Iowa was selected, and in 1855 the first colonists arrived. Eventually the society purchased thirty thousand acres of contiguous land and established various craft operations along with their agricultural activities. They named their new home Amana, which means "believe faithfully." It is also called the Community of True Inspiration.

In 1932, experiencing severe economic problems, the people voted to abandon their communal life. They organized the colony on a capitalistic basis and each member received stock in the corporation. Today, the

Amana colonies operate a variety of thriving businesses. The major ones are a woolen mill, a refrigeration company, and several handcrafted-furniture factories. Smaller concerns are meat shops, bakeries, and wineries. Visitors to the colonies find a reflection of Old World life as they tour the communal kitchens and blacksmith shops and eat in one of the fine German restaurants.

Two of the most informative books about Amana are *Amana That Was and Amana That Is*, by Bertha M. H. Shambaugh (1932), and *A Change and a Parting*, by a former Amananite, Barbara S. Yambura, in collaboration with Eunice W. Bodine (1964).—D. S.

American Fur Company. In 1808 John Jacob Astor formed the American Fur Company to free him from dependence on Canadian and British markets and suppliers and to enable him to trade in furs on the East Coast, in the Pacific Northwest, and in China (see CHINA TRADE). It became the most powerful of the United States fur companies. In 1811 Astor extended his influence even further when he and the Canadian North West Company agents agreed to divide the trade east of the Rockies in Canada and in the Old Northwest, with Astor becoming the principal investor in a partnership entitled the South West Company. Astor used the abilities of Ramsey Crooks and Robert Stuart as the key men in the South West Company. The American Fur Company continued to operate during the War of 1812 because of his political influence, but the war did put an end to Astor's Pacific Fur Company, which he had founded in 1810. In 1817 Astor obtained full control of the South West Company. He also founded another subsidiary with headquarters at Michilimackinac (later called the Northern Department) to continue his domination of the Old Northwest.

In these enterprises Astor possessed enormous capital, skilled traders such as Crooks and Stuart, and political influence with politicians such as Lewis Cass, the territorial governor of Michigan. Cass aided Astor in his attempts to sabotage the government factory system (see FUR TRADE: *in the United States*) and the statutes regulating the use of liquor in the Indian trade. In 1822, with the aid of St. Louis traders, Astor pressured Congress into repealing the statute establishing the government factories and after 1818 controlled the Indian agents in the Old Northwest. Although after 1822 the use of liquor was prohibited in the Indian trade, the company chose to use it when necessary.

In 1822 the American Fur Company organized the Western Department, which was to exploit the Missouri River trade. It faced competition there from Bernard Pratte and Company and the Columbia Fur Company, headed by Kenneth McKenzie. Disgusted with the inefficiency of his St. Louis partners in the Western Department in the face of these rivals, Astor bought them out. In December 1826 Bernard Pratte and Company became the Western Department of the American Fur Company and in 1827 Crooks persuaded the Columbia Fur Company to ally with the American Fur Company under the name of the Upper Missouri Outfit, which now received its goods and marketed its furs through the American Fur Company. In 1829 American Fur Company trappers invaded the Blackfoot territory, a lush fur country, and in 1830 built a major post called Fort McKenzie at the mouth of the Marias River. Astor's

organizations now seemed supreme both in the Old Northwest and on the upper Missouri, but in the mountains they still had to face the opposition of the ROCKY MOUNTAIN FUR COMPANY and the partnership of William Sublette and Robert Campbell. In 1834 Astor, sensing the impending decline of the fur trade, sold his interests in the fur companies; in the Western Department, Pratte, Chouteau, and Company of St. Louis purchased his interest, while the Northern Department fell to Crooks. In 1836 Chouteau and Company bought out Fontenelle, Fitzpatrick and Company, the successor to the Rocky Mountain Fur Company (see Lucien FONTENELLE). Two years later Pierre Chouteau, Jr., and Company came to control the firm, although the old name was still widely used. A declining supply of furs and the eastward movement of the Hudson's Bay Company forced an end to the fur-trading rendezvous in 1840. Thereafter the American Fur Company concentrated its efforts on the trading posts on the Great Plains and in the Great Lakes region. In 1864 the American Fur Company sold out its holdings to the Northwest Fur Company.

The American Fur Company, greatly feared by its competitors for its enormous capital and its political influence, was one of the earliest examples of corporate monopoly enterprise in United States history. It controlled three fourths of the American fur exports before 1834 and one half after Astor sold out to Crooks and Chouteau.

See Hiram M. Chittenden, *The American Fur Trade of the Far West* (1902); David Lavender, *The Fist in the Wilderness* (1964); Paul C. Phillips, *Fur Trade* (1961); and Kenneth Porter, *John Jacob Astor* (1931).—G. B. D.

American Horse. Name of two unrelated headmen among the Oglala division of the Teton-Sioux Indians. The elder American Horse (?-1876), leader of a northern Oglala band, was usually called Iron Shield by his own people and was the son of Chief Smoke. He fought beside his cousin Red Cloud during the Sioux War of 1866-67 and remained uncompromisingly hostile toward whites even after the treaty of Fort Laramie (1868), refusing to come in to the Red Cloud Agency and continuing a traditional nomadic life in the Powder River country. Soon after participating in the destruction of Custer's regiment at the Little Big Horn (1876), he was killed when his village was attacked by General George Crook's cavalry at the battle of SLIM BUTTES (September 9, 1876).

The younger American Horse (?-1902) was the son of Chief Sitting Bear and was headman of the True-Oglala band. A noted warrior in his youth, he claimed to have personally killed Captain William J. Fetterman. After the 1868 Laramie treaty he followed his father-in-law Red Cloud into the Red Cloud agency and became a factional leader in reservation affairs, usually supporting the white agents. American Horse accompanied Red Cloud on several widely publicized visits to Washington and traveled for a while with Buffalo Bill's Wild West show. In 1889 he helped the government in its fraudulent acquisition of half the remaining Sioux lands, after which the Indian Bureau briefly considered appointing him chief of all the Sioux. His fellow tribesmen were not so appreciative, however, and during the Ghost Dance outbreak the following year his house was pillaged and all his stock run off. In his later years he made a pictographic history of the Oglala, which has often been consulted by scholars.

See Dee Brown, *Bury My Heart at Wounded Knee* (1971); George Hyde, *Red Cloud's Folk* (1937); and James Olson, *Red Cloud and the Sioux Problem (1965)*. —P. R. M.

American party. See KNOW-NOTHING PARTY.

American Revolution (1775-1783). Frontiersmen living on the western edge of settlement from New York to Georgia fought in the American Revolution for reasons that had little to do with the tax on tea, the Boston port troubles, the Intolerable Acts, the theory of natural rights, or the issue of taxation without representation. Beginning with the new imperial policies adopted by the British crown in 1763 (see BRITISH ADMINISTRATIVE POLICY and LAND POLICY: IN THE COLONIES, 1607-1775) American pioneers had been angered by British efforts to hold back settlement, acts that seemed to favor the fur trader, the Indian, and the speculator rather than the settler. But neither these issues nor the unpopular Quebec Act of 1774, which appeared to place the trans-Allegheny West under Canadian jurisdiction, seemed cause for open rebellion. At the outset of the war the back-country settlers of South Carolina were more infuriated by the refusal of the tidewater planters to give them courts and political representation than they were by British injustices.

Once the fighting began at Lexington and Bunker Hill, the frontier settlers feared that the British would form an alliance with the Indians in the Northwest and with the Five Civilized Tribes in the South to devastate the feeble line of settlements scattered along the thousand-mile frontier. American pioneers had good reason to be worried. For more than a decade they had been pushing tribes off their lands, ignoring treaty stipulations, and wantonly murdering individual Indian families. As late as 1774 land-hungry Virginians joined in LORD DUNMORE'S WAR to exact more land cessions on the Ohio and Kanawha rivers. During the spring of 1775 Daniel BOONE had led settlers through Cumberland Gap to Boonesborough, Kentucky, in the heart of a region that the Shawnee and the Delaware considered their hunting preserve. By 1776 Indians both north and south were so distressed at white aggression that the northwestern and southern tribes, long traditional enemies, were talking of forming an alliance to hold back the settlers.

The Americans were further hampered by the fact that the Indians were under the direct control of two fine British superintendents: Sir Guy Johnson and Colonel John Stuart, who were in charge of the tribes of the northern and southern departments, respectively. In 1775-76 both sides so feared Indian atrocities that each labored to keep the Indians neutral. Sir Guy Johnson cleared American missionaries from the Iroquois tribes, while Stuart tried to restrain his southern charges. Meanwhile, the Continental Congress established three Indian departments of its own: a northern one to handle the Six Nations of the Iroquois; a middle department to deal with the Shawnee, Delaware, and other tribes on the Pennsylvania-Virginia frontier; and a southern one to treat with the Cherokee and the Creek. Indian hatred for the Americans was so bitter, however, that efforts to negotiate treaties of alliance or neutrality with the tribes were not very successful.

The British had the potential use of 8,000 Indian allies north of the Ohio and 10,000 south of the river, while the number of Americans west of the Appalachians did not reach 25,000 until 1783. Still, in 1776 there were probably less than a total of 500 British troops in western outposts at Michilimackinac (now Mackinac), Detroit, and Niagara; and when the British approached the Indians, they often found them indifferent, neutral, or interested only in campaigns of their own choice. As a result, British commanders had to take a defensive stand most of the time and confine their activities to raids on settlers and the destruction of supplies. British initiative was also hampered by jealousy between its frontier commanders. Sir Guy Carleton, in charge of Quebec, did not like Captain Henry Hamilton, the able commander at Detroit. John Johnson on the New York frontier did not trust John and Walter Butler, leaders of Tory raiders.

American internal conflicts more than matched those of the British. The back-country settlers of Georgia and the Carolinas were sharply divided between Tory and American loyalties, while the southern Moravians remained passive and neutral. In frontier Virginia and Kentucky, however, the settlers were loyal to the American cause, as were most on the Pennsylvania frontier, although Simon GIRTY and his brothers posed as patriots but actually worked for the Tory cause. In New York State, Tories and Whigs (as the patriots were often called) of all shades could be found, but the German settlers in the Mohawk valley actively supported the American side. Regional jealousies also prevented a united stand against the British. New Yorkers and Pennsylvanians feared that if Virginia troops took Detroit and occupied the Ohio and Illinois country, the Northwest would become a Virginia preserve, while Virginians suspected that any expedition from Fort Pitt to take Detroit was at base a scheme of Pennsylvania land speculators. To make matters worse, Americans had neither treaty goods for the Indians nor sufficient arms for any large-scale western offensive. There was even disagreement over strategy. At the outset of the war Washington thought that the key to the West was Canada and that if Quebec were captured, all other British outposts would fall into American hands. But George Rogers CLARK of Kentucky thought the key to be the important British supply base of Detroit. Unfortunately the Americans never carried out either plan.

Actual fighting on the frontier did not begin until the summer of 1776, when various Cherokee tribes decided to wipe out the Watauga and Nolichuckey settlements in western North Carolina. Warned of the attack, the settlers held their own, and that fall some five thousand militiamen from Virginia, North and South Carolina, and Georgia swept down on the Overhill, Middle, and Lower Town Cherokee; decisively defeated them; and forced them by the treaties of DeWitt's Corner and Long Island (1777) to cede five million acres of land, including much of the rich Tennessee River basin. The militia's prompt action brought two years of relative peace to the southern frontier; in 1778-79 settlers began to pour into Tennessee and in 1780 Nashville was founded.

Conditions on the northern and middle portions of the frontier were in striking contrast to those in the South. Beginning in 1776 New York State became the target of devastating raids led by British officers in alliance with Iroquois tribesmen, among whose leaders could be found the able warrior Joseph BRANT. Tory raiders and Indians, often led by the Butlers, were also active there. When General John Burgoyne began his famous march from Canada down Lake Champlain and the Hudson in 1777 to cut off New England from the rest of the states, British and Indian forces under Colonel Barry St. Leger and John Johnson set out from Fort Oswego to join him. At the same time, Captain Henry Hamilton at Detroit sent raiders south to the Ohio valley to harass the Kentuckians. A stout defense by Americans at Fort Stanwix (renamed Fort Schuyler by the Americans) turned St. Leger's troops back in defeat, but shortly thereafter an American relief column under General Nicholas Herkimer was caught in an ambush at Oriskany, New York, in which two hundred Americans lost their lives. Although St. Leger never reached Burgoyne, who was defeated at the Battle of Saratoga in 1777, British and Tory Indian raids on the Mohawk and Susquehanna valley settlements continued. In the spring of 1778 Chief Joseph Brant attacked settlements and Colonel John Butler led a large Tory-Indian party to Wyoming Valley, Pennsylvania where they killed 360 militiamen and boys at a palisade called Forty Fort. Hard on the heels of the Wyoming Valley massacre, Brant devastated the Mohawk valley and virtually wiped out the settlement of Cherry Valley (November 1778).

By 1779 Washington became so alarmed at the way in which New York's grain regions—a major source of supply for his troops—were being ruined that he mounted a major campaign to crush the Indians: Colonels Goose von Schaick and Marinus Willett at Fort Schuyler were ordered to engage the British, and an expedition under General Daniel Brodhead was ordered north from Fort Pitt to join the campaign. Brodhead's efforts were so half-hearted, however, that he and his troops turned back before reaching their goal. The main body of American troops, commanded by General John Sullivan, slipped up the Susquehanna to central New York, where they joined troops under General John Clinton. Their combined force of four thousand men fought the British and Indians at the battle of Newton (near Elmira, New York) and emerged victorious. The Clinton-Sullivan campaign broke the power of the Iroquois, and members of the tribe began moving to Canada as American troops destroyed forty Indian towns and vast stores of corn. Yet the Americans could not make their victory a lasting one, for they had not dislodged the British at Niagara or Oswego and could not keep a large number of troops on the frontier. British and Indian raiders were soon back in the New York valleys, and even after New York troops under Willett cleared the Mohawk valley of raiders in 1781, sporadic attacks continued. For all practical purposes, the British and the Indians had succeeded in pushing the frontier of settlement back to Albany and Schenectady.

With the exception of the brilliant successes of George Rogers Clark and his Kentucky militiamen in the Illinois country, warfare on the middle frontier was also a disheartening tale of bloody raids, regional jealousies, and eventual stalemate. When the Revolution began, perhaps no more than two hundred men were available

to defend Kentucky, so that when the Shawnee and the Delaware swarmed into Kentucky to drive the whites out in 1777, the settlers were forced to crowd into three forts at Boonesborough, Harrodsburg, and St. Asaph's for protection. Chief Blackfish and his Shawnee warriors so effectively bottled up the Americans at Boonesborough that spring they could not plant crops and might have starved had not Virginia troops under the command of Colonel John Bowman appeared to drive the Indians back across the Ohio. Shortly thereafter, Daniel Boone, who had proved to be an effective leader in the defense of Boonesborough, led a party of about twenty men to the salt spring at Blue Licks to collect much-needed salt for the settlers. The Shawnee captured the party and took the men to Ohio, where Boone was forced to live as the adopted son of Blackfish for nearly a year. After learning of a new plan to attack the Kentucky settlements, Boone escaped in time to warn his fellow frontiersmen.

Chafing under the restraints of Kentucky's defensive policy, Clark visited Governor Patrick Henry and Thomas Jefferson (soon to be governor) in Virginia and secured funds and supplies for an expedition of 350 men to capture the Illinois country as a first step toward taking Detroit. Although Clark was able to assemble only 175 men in the summer of 1778, he marched overland to the French towns of Kaskaskia and Cahokia and captured them, while his emissary, Leonard Helms, persuaded the French inhabitants at Vincennes to accept American rule. Clark also secured the allegiance of a few tribes that had previously supported the British. In the winter of 1778-79, however, Captain Hamilton and a combined force of British and Indian troops recaptured Vincennes. Not to be outdone, Clark marched his men through freezing weather, surprised Hamilton (who had unwisely sent his Indian allies home and had only a few British soldiers with him), captured the fort, and sent Hamilton off to Virginia as a prize war captive. Yet even in victory Clark could not raise enough men and provisions for a march on Detroit.

By 1780 it was the British who took the offensive in the Northwest. British and Indian forces from Michilimackinac attacked the Spanish (now allies of the Americans) at St. Louis and the Americans in the Illinois villages, and although their efforts were not successful, other expeditions swept down on Vincennes and attacked settlers at the Falls of the Ohio. Another expedition under Captain Henry Bird captured two Kentucky stations on the Licking River and persuaded over 350 German settlers there to return with him to the Detroit area. Although more than a thousand fighting men were now available on the Kentucky frontier, they were spread so thinly that in 1782 another British-Indian force ambushed and killed 140 militiamen at Blue Licks and made prisoners of the rest. Clark's retaliation against the Ohio tribes who had participated in the Blue Licks raid was not really effective. Fortunately for the Kentuckians, the British, mindful of impending peace negotiations in Paris, decided to restrain the Indians in the summer of 1782.

The commanders on the Pennsylvania and Virginia frontiers, and especially at Fort Pitt, experienced nearly as many frustrations as Clark and the Kentuckians. The region about Fort Pitt and in present-day West Virginia had more settlers and was better defended than Kentucky. The Indians seemed inclined not to fight in 1776, but in 1777 the frontiersmen themselves ruined the uneasy peace by needlessly murdering a number of Shawnee families as well as Chief CORNSTALK, a lifelong friend of the whites. General Edward Hand, the commandant at Fort Pitt, was so disgusted by frontier behavior that he asked to be transferred.

In the fall of 1778 General Lachlan McIntosh made a feeble attempt to march on Detroit but turned back because of the lateness of the season. In 1779 Pennsylvania forces under General Brodhead failed to aid in the campaign to crush the Iroquois. Racial hatreds were so great that in the spring of 1782 frontier militiamen massacred ninety Indians living peacefully with Moravian missionaries at Gnadenhutten. Campaigns against the Northwest tribes were often mere excuses to seize Indian horses and goods. One such party under Colonel William Crawford set out in May 1782 to raid Shawnee villages on the upper Sandusky, but the Indians, infuriated by the slaughter at Gnadenhutten, defeated the whites, captured Crawford, and—after scalping him—killed him by roasting him over a bed of coals. Tory and Indian raids continued in western Pennsylvania and at Wheeling in late summer of 1782 and only stopped when the British recalled the warriors.

In the final years of the Revolution the center of military action both for the nation and for the frontiersmen shifted south. Having concentrated their troops in campaigns in the northern and middle states during the first half of the war, in 1779 the British decided to force a peace by cutting off the South. After capturing Savannah and Augusta in the winter of 1778-79 and Charleston in 1780, the British persuaded local Tories to join their ranks. Meanwhile, southern commanders of continental troops experienced a series of defeats in the Carolinas, one of the most significant being the defeat at the battle of Camden in the summer of 1780.

As Lord Cornwallis, the British commander, began to cut a swath through the Carolinas on his way to Virginia, he stood a good chance of ending the war on British terms. One of Cornwallis' reasons for mounting a southern campaign had been the belief that back-country Tories would rally to the British cause. During the summer of 1780 Cornwallis sent Major Patrick Ferguson with a crack set of Highland sharpshooters to the western Carolinas to recruit. Instead, Ferguson's presence aroused back-country patriots, who attacked the British at KING'S MOUNTAIN in October 1780, inflicting heavy casualties and killing Ferguson himself. The American victory at Kings Mountain put an end to Tory raiding in the South and allowed the patriots to go west and chastise the Chicamauga Cherokee, from whom they got yet another cession of western land in the second Treaty of Long Island (July 1781).

Yet when the war came to an end with Cornwallis' defeat at Yorktown in October 1781, American claims to the trans-Appalachian region were notably weak, except for lands wrung from the Cherokee. Indian tribesmen were still under British influence; French settlers were outraged by American settlers and land speculators who invaded the Illinois lands and ignored French rights. On the northern border the British still held Oswego, Niagara, Detroit, and Michilimackinac, while to the south they had made allies of the powerful Creek. The revolutionary frontier produced an enduring crop of heroes, among them Daniel Boone, George Rogers Clark, Isaac SHELBY, and John SEVIER, but the trans-Appalachian West was secured for the United States only when John Jay, John Adams, and Benjamin Franklin decided to negotiate directly with the British rather than through the French. The resulting treaty (see PARIS, TREATY OF, 1783) gave the Americans the vast region from the Alleghenies to the Mississippi and from the Canadian border south to the thirty-first parallel. They also won the right to navigate the Mississippi. The British even agreed to evacuate their northwestern posts in return for an American promise to pay war damages to Loyalists whose properties had been confiscated during the Revolution. Undoubtedly American pioneers would soon have occupied the trans-Appalachian West regardless of who governed it, but paradoxically it was British and American diplomats working together who called the first American West into being.

The role of the West in the American Revolution is brilliantly treated in C. W. Alvord, *The Mississippi Valley in British Politics* (1916). Ray Allen Billington, *Westward Expansion* (1974), contains excellent informative chapters on the Revolutionary frontier. The best general coverage is Jack M. Sosin, *The Revolutionary Frontier, 1763-1783* (1967).—E. W. K.

American River. Although not a mighty river by any standard, the American River, by one of those quirks of history, became a notable stream. It was in this stream that gold was first discovered. Had John Marshall chosen to build his lumber mill along the Cosumnes or the Bear, most people would never know that the American River exists. Marshall's discovery of gold was made in the mill race that he had been building to provide power to turn the saw to cut the logs derived from the nearby slopes of the foothills of the Sierra Nevada. It was to the American River that most of the first gold miners came to seek their fortunes.

Like most of the eastern tributaries of the Sacramento, the three forks of the American rise among the snow-covered peaks near the crest of the High Sierra. The waters tumble precipitously down six thousand feet in the first fifty miles or so through narrow canyon walls. The river is almost one hundred miles long and drains a basin of two thousand square miles. It flows through the Sacramento metropolitan area to join the river of the same name.

There is wide variation in runoff, with the main flow a result of snowmelt in the Sierra. The average flow is almost three million acre-feet, but this is frequently exceeded. Giant levees and floodways have been built to confine and control its flow. The waters of the river were among the first to produce hydroelectric power when Folsom Dam was erected in 1895. Power from that dam was delivered to Sacramento twenty-two miles away, a tremendous accomplishment for the time. Additional dams built in recent years store water to be used for the generation of electricity and for irrigating farmlands in the valley below.

For map, see CALIFORNIA.

See S. T. Harding, *Water in California* (1960), and Lawrence R. McDonnell, ed., *Rivers of California* (1962).—R. W. D.

American System. Henry Clay's economic program. Henry CLAY, one of the most charismatic of American statesmen, ran for the presidency three times and failed each time. Partly for political reasons and partly conviction, he developed his American System, borrowing heavily from Alexander Hamilton and Albert Gallatin. It has been described as a planned national economy to be achieved through congressional action. Its major features were a tariff to protect and encourage the growth of domestic industries; a national bank to assure a stable currency and to facilitate commerce between all sections of the country; internal improvements such as roads, canals, and improved waterways; and distribution to the states of the surplus income from the sale of public lands to enable them to build those improvements. To assure considerable income from the public lands for distribution, Clay opposed reducing the price from what western people regarded as the high level established in 1820 and did not favor John C. Calhoun's proposal to cede the public lands to the states in which they were located.

The West, though strongly drawn to Clay for his vigorous nationalism and his support of internal improvements, detested his attitude on price, cession, and distribution and, even more, his opposition to preemption, that is, the right of settlers to take up public land, improve it for a time, and later purchase their tracts at the minimum price. To Clay, "squatters" were mere vagabonds—"lawless rabble"—disdainful of law, squatting on and using public land for a time and then paying not the value of their tracts in competition with others but the minimum price. In the public land states, his condemnation of squatters and his hostility to land reform counted heavily against him in his efforts to reach the presidency. Instead these states supported Andrew Jackson against Clay in 1824 and 1832, and James J. Polk in 1844. In this last election Clay carried only one public land state, Ohio.

Clay's American System, and the constitutionalism on which it was based, contributed much to the economic growth of the United States. The protective tariffs gave entrepreneurs courage to develop their infant industries, and the government loans and land grants to canal companies and the use of the distribution and deposit funds (see INTERNAL IMPROVEMENTS) contributed to interregional trade and had a marked effect in drawing many settlers westward and large amounts of European capital into American development. Clay was defeated on the bank question, but the destruction of the Second Bank of the United States may not have had as serious effects as its advocates feared. With Daniel Webster, John Quincy Adams, John Marshall, and Alexander Hamilton, Clay helped to establish the basis for a more flexible interpretation of the Constitution so that it could meet the needs of a growing country. For a time the Democrats turned the clock back by opposing federal aid or direct appropriations for the improvement of rivers and harbors, railroads, and educational institutions. The Hamilton-Clay American System was to be revived under Abraham Lincoln, in his earlier days a warm admirer of the great Kentuckian.

See Clement Eaton, *Henry Clay and the Art of American Politics* (1957); and Glyndon G. Van Deusen, *The Life of Henry Clay* (1937).—P. W. G.

Ames, Oakes (1804-1873). Manufacturer, politician, and railroad builder. A key figure in the building of the UNION PACIFIC RAILROAD, Ames made one grievous error of judgment and thereby fathered the "robber baron" legend in American history. Born in Easton, Massachusetts, into one of the state's most noted Federalist families, Ames and his brother took over their father's shovel factory and made the Ames shovel famous throughout the world in the era before excavation machinery. Discovery of gold in California greatly stimulated demand for Ames shovels and Oakes, who had been elected to Congress in 1862, was persuaded to take control of the Credit Mobilier, the faltering enterprise that had undertaken to finance construction of the Union Pacific. Having as his purpose, as he later maintained in a speech in Congress, "to connect my name conspicuously with the greatest public work of this century," Ames brought the work to a successful conclusion.

By 1867 the enterprise was faring so well and the profits (mostly on paper) of the Credit Mobilier were so great that Congress began to threaten a stricter policy toward publicly aided railroads. Although there were no hobbling bills before Congress at that time, Ames thought it wise to make key congressmen investors in the Union Pacific; he sold 160 shares on attractive terms "where they will do the most good for us." Almost six years later a disgruntled investor who claimed that he had a valid subscription to buy 25,000 shares of Union Pacific common stock, by then selling at a substantial premium over par, gave the press letters which in tone and substance were sensational. So incriminating were they that leading congressmen such as James A. Garfield barely escaped with their political careers intact, and few congressmen could afford to oppose the censure motion that the Congress adopted against Ames. Brokenhearted and still maintaining his innocence of all wrongdoing, Ames returned to Massachusetts where he soon died of a cerebral hemorrhage.

The CREDIT MOBILIER scandal laid the foundation of the legend of enormous profits in the construction of land-grant railroads and led to the adoption of punitive restrictions which handicapped the Union Pacific and the Central Pacific for the rest of the century. "Rugged, laborious, taciturn, kindly, and shrewd," in the words of historian Allan Nevins, Ames revealed, in his undertaking of the Pacific railroad project and in his fatal error of judgment in selling stock to congressmen, a speculative bent which was out of keeping with the other aspects of his character.

Jay Boyd Crawford, *The Credit Mobilier of America* (1880; repr. 1971), is an early attempt to dispel the myths surrounding the Credit Mobilier affair. Charles E. Ames, *Pioneering the Union Pacific* (1970), is a recent effort. Robert W. Fogel, *The Union Pacific: A Case in Premature Enterprise* (1960), uses the analytical techniques of modern economic history to demonstrate that the profits of the Credit Mobilier were not excessive. The great majority of American historians cleave to the myth as strongly as ever.—A. M.

Amidon, Charles Fremont (1856-1937). North Dakota judge. Amidon, named after John C. Frémont, was born in upstate New York. After graduating from Hamilton College (New York) with Phi Beta Kappa honors, he went to Fargo, Dakota Territory, in 1882 to organize a high school. He read law and was admitted to the bar in 1886. President Grover Cleveland appointed him a federal judge of the United States Circuit Court in 1896, and he served in this capacity until his retirement in 1928.

Judge Amidon was a progressive reformer. He opposed Alexander McKenzie's political machine in North Dakota. He was a friend of the farmer and rendered many decisions in his favor. Among his close friends he counted such men as the Supreme Court justice Louis D. Brandeis, the progressive senator Robert M. La Follette, President Theodore Roosevelt, and the conservationist Gifford Pinchot.

During World War I Amidon went on record as a staunch defender of civil liberties. His interpretation of the Espionage Act was very narrow, and persons accused of committing espionage received a fair and impartial trial in his court.—D. J. T.

Amish, in Iowa. Descendants of Pennsylvania and Ohio Amish, the Amish settled three communities in Iowa. The first Amish families moved to Iowa in the 1840s and settled in the vicinity of Kalona. In 1917 several Kalona families moved to Hazleton to establish a more conservative settlement. Because of their need for additional land, the Amish began a third community near Milton in 1969. The Milton Amish group is rapidly expanding as more Amish families from Iowa communities, as well as from neighboring states, purchase land in the area. Although the Iowa group is generally referred to as Amish, most belong to the Old Order, which is the most conservative faction of the Mennonite church. Other Amish are New Order or Beachy Amish.

The Iowa Amish live much as the eastern Amish, believing in a simple, agrarian way of life. Their activities are dictated by their religious beliefs; they reject worldly conveniences such as electricity, telephones, and automobiles and rely on horses and buggies for transportation. Often called "the plain people," they dress in an Old World manner; the men wear wide-brimmed hats and long, full beards, while the women appear in bonnets and long, dark skirts. Church services are held in the homes. One-room schoolhouses cover the countryside in Amish communities, for the plain people believe that an eighth-grade education is adequate for their children and they strongly resist sending their children to non-Amish schools. Among the Iowa Amish there are some slight variations in beliefs and practices; for example, many Kalona Amish use tractors for field work while the Hazleton farmers use only horses.

The Amish way of life is expertly portrayed in John Hostetler, *Amish Society* (1963). Melvin Gingerich has included several chapters on the Iowa Amish in *The Mennonites in Iowa* (1939).—D. S.

Amon Carter Museum of Western Art. Established in Fort Worth, Texas, under the will of the late Amon G. Carter, the Fort Worth newspaper publisher, the Amon Carter Museum of Western Art opened in January 1961 as a repository for the collection of Frederic Remington and Charles M. Russell paintings and sculpture collected by the founder. The building was designed by Philip Johnson of New York City and was commissioned by the directors of the Amon G. Carter Foundation. It is governed by a board of trustees which includes members of the Carter family.

In 1964 the trustees adopted a policy of expansion, broadening of the original collection to complement and enrich the research and educational program of the museum, whose purpose is "the study and documentation of westerning North America." The painting and sculpture collections currently number approximately 5,158 items, including works of Alfred Jacob Miller, Albert Bierstadt, Thomas and Peter Moran, Peter Rindisbacher, George Caleb Bingham, J. J. Audubon, Carl Bodmer, and the many artists identified with early exploration and travel on the American frontier. Of special interest are significant collections of Currier & Ives prints, lithographic views of American cities in the nineteenth century, and exemplary collections of the pioneer photographers in the West.

Aware of the many interpretations given to the definition of "the West," the museum is also concerned with the work of twentieth-century artists and photographers. The West after 1900 is well represented by works of Georgia O'Keeffe, John Marin, Marsden Hartley, Arthur Dove, Morris Graves, and a collection of prints of the Tamarind Lithography Workshop of Los Angeles (1960-70). Contemporary photography is represented by permanent collections of Ansel Adams; the Westons, Edward and Brett, father and son; Todd Webb; Pirkle Jones; and others. It also has W. Fred Mazzulla's enormous collection of photographs.

Most exhibitions prepared by the museum are the subject of publications, either monographs or complete catalogs. Traveling exhibition units, based upon features presented at the Fort Worth museum, are sometimes available. The museum provides research facilities through a noncirculating library (eleven thousand volumes) and a microfilm archive of American, Canadian, and Mexican newspapers and periodicals of the nineteenth century. A photographic archive (approximately thirty thousand prints, negatives, and slides) complements library and microfilm resources. Research assistance is available through interlibrary loans, a print-out service, and photographs.—M. A. W.

Anderson, John. See GREAT LAKES, MEN OF THE.

Anian, Strait of. See NORTHWEST PASSAGE.

animals. See WILDLIFE.

antelope. See PRONGHORN.

Antrim, William. See BILLY THE KID.

Anza, Juan Bautista de (1735-1788). Soldier, governor, and explorer. Anza deserves to rank alongside Lewis and Clark, John C. Frémont, Kit Carson, and the legion of other publicized pathfinders who opened western North America to settlement. Because Anza was a Spaniard and on the southwestern frontier comparatively early, his extraordinary achievements are not widely known, although much has been written about him. Born and nurtured on the Sonora border, Anza was the son of the captain of the presidio of Fronteras, also named Juan Bautista, who was slain by Apache in 1739. The often repeated assertion that he had a grandfather, also by the same name and also a presidial captain, has no basis in fact.

At age seventeen Anza volunteered for military service and by 1759 had attained the rank of captain and been made commander of the presidio of Tubac (Arizona). Two years later he wed Doña Ana María Serrano. During the next decade he displayed his tactical genius by a series of brilliant campaigns against the Apache, and in 1772 conducted an arduous but successful expedition northwestward to the Pacific Coast, establishing overland communication between Sonora and Upper California. This feat brought him to the attention of the viceroy in Mexico City, and he was commissioned to return to California with a colonizing force. The second expedition resulted in the founding of San Francisco in 1776.

With Anza's appointment as governor of New Mexico in 1777, his theater of operations shifted eastward. At this time the Comanche, Apache, Ute, and Navaho were creating havoc along the Rio Grande, and Anza brought his experience and fitness as an Indian fighter to bear on the problem. His most spectacular triumph was the defeat of the Comanche and the slaying of their powerful chief, Cuerno Verde ("Green Horn"), during late summer of 1779 in south-central Colorado. This was followed in 1786 by arrangement of a lasting peace with the Comanche, which historian A. B. Thomas has called the most brilliant achievement of Anza's administration, if not of his entire career. The governor also forged an alliance with the Ute and Navaho, and with the three tribes waged relentless war on the unconciliatory Apache.

In the first half of 1780, Anza led an expedition to the Hopi villages in northern Arizona. These Indians had remained independent since the Pueblo revolt of 1680 and were now suffering from famine and disease. The governor intended to provide them with material relief and encourage them to submit again to Spanish rule, but his efforts were largely frustrated by the obstinacy of Hopi religious leaders. Later the same year he explored a direct route from New Mexico to Sonora, an attempt to duplicate his earlier success in opening the Sonora-California road. Although he managed to reach Arizpe from Santa Fe, the way was circuitous and deficient in water, so that it never developed as a thoroughfare.

Because of declining health, in 1786 Anza petitioned to be relieved of his governorship. This was granted the following year, and he proceeded to Sonora, where he became provisional commander of the provincial forces and captain of the presidio of Tucson. At the time of his death at Arizpe, Sonora, Anza was Spain's most distinguished soldier in the northern borderlands.

Anza's work in California is covered in Herbert E. Bolton, ed., *Anza's California Expeditions*, 5 vols. (1930). His New Mexican activities receive treatment in Alfred Barnaby Thomas, ed., *Forgotten Frontiers: A Study of the Spanish Indian Policy of Don Juan Bautista de Anza* (1932; repr. 1969).—M. Sí.

Apache Indians. *Apache Indians* is a label that has been used by non-Indians since the first half of the seventeenth century to refer to several tribes and bands of Athapaskan-speaking peoples. In the second half of the nineteenth century the term was even erroneously used to describe Yuman-speaking Mohave, Yavapai, and YUMA Indians, the notion apparently being that almost any Arizona native who wore a breech cloth, rode horseback, and was hostile toward Anglo-American encroachment was an Apache.

Known among themselves as the *N'dé, Indé, Diné,* or closely related terms—all of them meaning "people," depending upon the particular dialect involved—*Apache* may be derived from the Zuñi term for the Navaho, *ápachu,* which translates as "enemy." Spaniards

during much of the sixteenth and seventeenth centuries used a variety of terms to describe these tribes, most prominent among them being *Querechos*.

Although they are linguistically and culturally closely related to the Navaho, the Apache constitute six distinct tribes: the Lipan, which has become extinct as a meaningful social entity; the Western Apache; the Chiricahua; the Mescalero; the Jicarilla; and the Kiowa-Apache. Members of these tribes adhere to internal social, political, economic, and linguistic traditions that make each of them distinct and possessed of an in-group identity.

The Western Apache, the largest tribe, is divided into five major groups, fourteen bands, and six semibands. In the 1800s each of these units occupied contiguous territories within virtually the whole mountainous portion of the eastern half of central Arizona. The various divisions include the White Mountain group, comprised of Eastern White Mountain and Western White Mountain bands; the Cibecue group, with its Cibecue, Carrizo, and Canyon Creek bands; the San Carlos group, divided into Pinal, Arivaipa, San Carlos, and Apache Peaks bands; the Southern Tonto group, composed of six unnamed semibands and the Mazatzal band; and the Northern Tonto group and its Mormon Lake, Fossil Creek, Bald Mountain, and Oak Creek bands. Such peoples as the Pinaleño, Arivaipa, Tonto, and Sierra Blanca were not tribes but subdivisions of the larger Western Apache tribe. *Coyotero* seems to have been a label generally meant for all Western Apache.

In the nineteenth century bands ranged in size from about 60 members to as many as 750. They lacked political unity and were identifiable as cultural units only because band members spoke a common Apache dialect and recognized a common hunting area exclusive of that of other bands. Each band, in turn, was composed of local groups. Local groups, the most basic element of Western Apache society, contained from 35 to 200 people. Each had its own chief, whose job it was to direct virtually all group activities: hunting, gathering, farming, and affairs involving other local groups or outsiders.

The Western Apache were also divided into sixty-two clans, whose members were related through the matrilineal line. Clans were not spatially fixed, and their members were found scattered in various local groups and in all the bands. An Apache could expect food and lodging from a clansman, regardless of band or local group affiliation.

Considerable nonsense has been written about the Western Apache, implying that they were altogether nomadic, marauding, and warlike peoples who lived within no fixed bounds and subsisted almost wholly by preying on innocent neighbors and non-Indian settlers. In fact, each band had well-recognized territorial limits, and local groups within the bands had possessory rights to hunting areas and farming sites. About a quarter of the subsistence of Western Apache in the early and middle 1800s was derived from farming. The rest of their food was hunted, gathered from the local environment, or stolen in enemy territory from herds of cattle or other livestock. Crops were planted in the mountains in early spring and harvested in the fall, activities that necessitated remaining in camp at the farm sites. Hunting for game, gathering wild plants, and raiding cattle herds gave Western Apache their nomad status the rest of the year.

Raiding parties usually consisted of from five to fifteen men of a local group. The sole purpose of Western Apache raiding was "to search out enemy property" or, from the viewpoint of the enemy, to steal cattle and other goods. Warfare, "to take death from an enemy," was quite another matter. Warfare parties were put together to avenge the death of a member of one's family or clan. Stealth and avoidance of the enemy, so important in raiding, gave way to wholesale onslaughts of as many as two hundred warriors bent on doing combat with the enemy. All of one's male clan relatives, whether from the local group or not, were potential members of the warfare party.

Hostilities between Western Apache and Anglo-Americans began in earnest in 1863, when gold was discovered in Tonto territory. They came to a climax with the CAMP GRANT MASSACRE and continued until 1875, when General George CROOK succeeded in defeating these Indians and moving most of them to San Carlos, Arizona, where they were placed under Indian agent John P. CLUM. Subsequently, many Western Apache, such as ESKIMINZIN, served as scouts in the army, helping to track down and defeat Chiricahua and other Apache in Arizona, New Mexico, and Sonora, Mexico.

Although Mexican settlements had been the favored targets of Western Apache raiding and warfare, various local groups had seen fit to molest neighboring Pima, Papago, Navaho, Yavapai, and Anglo-American settlements as well. Fort Whipple, near Prescott, Arizona, was established—in the words of the general order that created the post—"to protect the miners from the Indians," and innumerable military forays were made against Western Apache and Yavapai for the express purpose of making the country safe for prospectors. Fort Apache (originally Fort Ord) was established in 1868 on the White River in the heart of White Mountain and Cibecue Apache territory, and General Crook used the post as a base of his operations to force the surrender of the "hostiles."

The Western Apache now live in several settlements on the Fort Apache (1,664,872 acres) and San Carlos (1,877,216 acres) reservations in Arizona. There are also a few Tonto living on an 85-acre reservation next to Payson, Arizona, and on the Middle Verde and Camp Verde reservations in the same state. There are about twelve thousand Western Apache today, most of whom continue to speak their own language and continue to recognize their band, clan, and local group affiliations. Cattle, timber, and tourism provide modern means of making a living.

Probably the Apache best known to non-Indians, because of their famous leaders, were the nonagricultural Chiricahua. The Chiricahua were divided into three bands: Eastern, Central, and Southern. The Eastern Chiricahua, known variously as the Warm Springs, Ojo Caliente, Coppermine, Mimbreños, or Mogollones Apache, ranged throughout most of western New Mexico from the Rio Grande to the Arizona border and from the Datil Mountains to the Mexican boundary. MANGAS COLORADAS, VICTORIO, NANA, and Loco were some of their leaders. The Southern band, the so-called Pinery Apache, counted Juh, GERONIMO, and, after Geronimo's death, CHATO among their headmen. They hunted,

A wickiup, the typical Apache dwelling, was built of brush and usually covered by blankets or animal hides. (National Archives)

gathered, and raided in northern Sonora and Chihuahua, Mexico, while the Central band, to which COCHISE belonged, ranged throughout southeastern Arizona and southwestern New Mexico. The Chiricahua under Geronimo were the last to capitulate in the Apache wars—and then not until 1886, to Nelson A. MILES. Many of them were deported to Fort Marion, Florida, and then to Mount Vernon Barracks, Alabama. Most Chiricahua ended up either at Fort Sill, Oklahoma, or on the Mescalero reservation in New Mexico. It is in these two places that most Chiricahua live today.

The Mescalero Apache, like the culturally similar Chiricahua, were a hunting-gathering people who lacked clans but whose social organization was founded on strong family ties. A typical Mescalero extended family was made up of an older married couple, their unmarried offspring, their married daughters and sons-in-law, and their daughter's children. It was the custom for a Mescalero man to live in the camp of his wife's family.

A group of ten to twenty families (about one hundred persons) allied themselves under a male leader chosen because of his experience, age, and presumed wisdom to form cooperative resource-exploitation units. Whether properly called "local groups" or "bands," these units, while not strictly attached to a given geographic area, recognized overlapping hunting-gathering regions and were often known by the name of their locale or of their leader. Within the Mescalero range—extending from parts of Chihuahua, Coahuila, and northwestern Texas north to the thirty-fourth parallel and from the Rio Grande eastward beyond the Pecos River—there were perhaps between twenty-five and thirty such bands in the mid-nineteenth century. The band leader best known to whites during this period was Cadete, who was murdered in 1872 by some non-Indians against whom he had testified in a trial for selling whiskey to Indians.

Some Mescalero bands were better adapted to living in the Plains. Some relied on buffalo for big game and lived in conical hide tents ("tepees"), while others, the "edge-of-the-mountain people," lived in the foothills and mountains and used brush-covered wickiups for houses. There was no overall political or military leadership for the entire Mescalero tribe, the band constituting the largest political unit; but taken together, all bands made up the Mescalero entity, a "tribal resource holding corporation" in the words of one investigator, whose members enjoyed a "shared right to exploit a territory common to all."

Hostilities between Mescalero and non-Indians began in the early seventeenth century when the Apache began raiding the Spanish settlement at Jumanos in New Mexico. Spaniards and Mescalero and, subsequently, Mexicans and Mescalero became bound in a cycle of raiding, warfare, and revenge that lasted until the United States took over New Mexico in 1846. Mescalero wasted no time in raiding Anglo-American wagon trains, not bothering to distinguish between foreign ethnic groups or nationalities. By 1852 the governor of Texas described El Paso as "defenseless." Mescalero warfare with American troops led by James Henry CARLETON continued until 1873 when, defeated at last, the Mescalero began to move onto a reservation set aside for them in New Mexico. The Mescalero reservation embodies some 460,000 acres of mountain country and grazing land.

In 1913 the Mescalero were joined on their reservation by Chiricahua from Fort Sill. Today's combined Mescalero-Chiricahua population in New Mexico is a little more than fifteen hundred. The tribe has a cattle industry and a tourism and recreation industry, including a ski lift and resort in the Sierra Blanca ski area.

The native territory of the Jicarilla Apache was northeastern New Mexico, parts of the Oklahoma Panhandle, southeastern Colorado, and some of southwestern Kansas. The Jicarilla hunted on the Plains for buffalo even as they hunted for other game and gathered wild plants in their mountain remoteness. Like the Western Apache and Navaho and unlike the Chiricahua and Mescalero, they were also farmers, raising corn next to streams in the Cimarron area. Also like the Western Apache, the Jicarilla had clearly defined bands (two of them), which were further subdivided into local groups made up of several families. One band was known as the Llanero ("plains people") and the other, Ollero ("sand people"). In the mid-nineteenth century there were six local groups in each band. The Jicarilla joined with the Tiwa in 1680 to help drive the Spaniards out of New Mexico, but after the reconquest of New Mexico by New Spain in 1696 they remained on remarkably good terms with the non-Indian invaders, engaging in considerable trade with them. After 1846, however, when New Mexico became a part of the United States, Jicarilla country began to fill up with American settlers and to be overrun by Anglo trappers and hunters. The result was that Jicarilla began raiding the new settlements. More or less open hostilities continued until the first Jicarilla reservation was proposed in 1873.

Their modern reservation, 722,303 acres in northern New Mexico, dates from 1887. About sixteen hundred Jicarilla live there in an area rich in timber, rangeland, mineral, and tourism potential. The tribe operates innumerable business enterprises of its own.

The Kiowa-Apache have had few connections with Arizona or New Mexico Apache. In all but language, which is Apachean, some of their culture and much of their modern history have been essentially Kiowa. They have lived with the KIOWA INDIANS as part of the tribe's camp circle since the mid-nineteenth century. They were nonagricultural, relying largely on buffalo hunting for their subsistence. According to one student, "Every Kiowa-Apache was literally related by blood or marriage to every other Kiowa-Apache." Like the Kiowa and other Apache, their history of contact with non-Indians through the third quarter of the nineteenth century was marked by raiding and warfare.

Today's Kiowa-Apache live in Caddo County in western Oklahoma in and near Anadarko, Apache, and Fort Cobb. In 1907, when Oklahoma became a state, there were about 150 Kiowa-Apache still living, and they were totally engulfed by white settlers. By 1965, however, their numbers had increased to about 400. Many of them live on trust allotments and receive a small income by leasing their land to white farmers. One or two families have income from oil found on their property, while the remainder live on money earned as unskilled workers or on welfare funds. In spite of the fact that only about a fourth of the Kiowa-Apache still know their Apache language, the people continue to identify themselves as Apache and to maintain an identity distinct from that of the Kiowa.

The Lipan Apache are identified primarily with the history of Texas. Primarily buffalo hunters, Lipan men also went after antelope and, in historic times, after the beefs of Spaniards. They began raiding the hooved larders of European settlers at least as early as the beginning of the eighteenth century, a course of action that led to hostilities between them and whites until the end of the 1800s. Lipan women were in charge of gardens of maize, beans, squash, and pumpkins, but such horticulture among them appears always to have been minor and their crops were raised without benefit of irrigation. In keeping with the hunting basis of their subsistence, Lipan lived in bison-hide tepees in widely scattered camps. In typical Apache fashion, the Lipan extended family involved matrilocal residence (that is, the husband joined the camp of his wife's family). The extended families joined together to form local groups; local groups were often formed in band confederations, the band being the largest unit of political organization.

The combination of their difficulties with traditional Indian enemies, such as Ute, Comanche, and Wichita, and problems of enmity with non-Indians had, by the nineteenth century forced the Lipan southward in the Texas plains along the Pecos River and Edwards Plateau to south of San Antonio and across the border into Mexico. The tribe made treaties with the Texans in 1838 and 1845 and with the United States in 1846. By 1850 their numbers were estimated to be three hundred to five hundred, and continuing difficulties with Texas settlers split the tribe into segments. Some fled into Mexico; others allied themselves with Tonkawa, Kiowa-Apache, or Mescalero people. In 1905 the Mexican Lipan remnant population was put on the Mescalero reservation, the other Lipan having become culturally extinct. By 1940 there were presumed to be about thirty-five Lipan at Mescalero; in 1973 there was one—Delia Treas, probably the last speaker of her language and by then a very elderly person.

See Harry W. Basehart, "Mescalero Apache Band Organization and Leadership," in Keith Basso and Morris Opler, eds., *Apachean Culture History and Ethnology* (1971); Jean Louis Berlandier, *The Indians of Texas in 1830* (1969); Grenville Goodwin, *The Social Organization of the Western Apache* (1969); Grenville Goodwin and Keith Basso, *Western Apache Raiding and Warfare*, (1971); J. Gilbert McAllister, "Kiowa-Apache Social Organization," in Fred Eggan, ed., *Social Anthropology of North American Tribes* (1955); W. W. Newcomb, Jr., *The Indians of Texas* (1961); Morris E. Opler, *An Apache Life-way* (1965), and *Apache Odyssey* (1969); C. L. Sonnichsen, *The Mescalero Apaches* (1958); and H. Clyde Wilson, *Jicarilla Apache Political and Economic Structures* (1964).—B. L. F.

Appalachian Plateaus. See PHYSIOGRAPHY OF THE UNITED STATES.

Applegate, Jesse (1811-88). Oregon pioneer. A Kentuckian, Applegate came to Missouri with his parents in about 1821 and was educated at Rock Springs Seminary, Shiloh, Illinois, where he learned surveying. Between 1828 and 1832 he was a draftsman in the surveyor-general's office in St. Louis, where he had his first taste of the Far West from such fur trappers as Wilson Price Hunt, Jedediah Smith, and David Jackson.

In 1831 Applegate married Cynthia Ann Parker and in 1832 settled in St. Clair County, Missouri, where he farmed, surveyed, acquired more land, and sired thirteen children. He took delight in calling himself "only a farmer, and a rough, slovenly one at that." As an anti-slavery Whig in a county of Democrats and slaveholders, Applegate was neither content nor prosperous. He was attracted by the "Oregon fever" and with his brothers, Charles and Lindsay, and their families joined the Great Migration of 1843. They were among the nearly nine hundred persons who left Independence, Missouri, under the leadership of Peter Burnett, the largest group to set out for Oregon, the first to attempt to take wagons as far as the Columbia River, and the first to take with it a large herd of cattle. The unwieldy size of the company was soon apparent, and it divided into a "light" column under William Martin and a "heavy" or "cow" column captained by Applegate. The experiences of his company were described by Applegate in the essay "A Day with the Cow Column in 1843," a classic description first published in *Overland Monthly*, August 1868.

In November the immigrants arrived at Fort Vancouver, where Applegate was generously treated by John McLoughlin, the chief factor of the Hudson's Bay Company. The Applegates settled on land by Salt Creek, near what is now The Dalles, Oregon.

In 1845 Applegate was elected delegate to the provisional government. He was a leader in the assembly and drafted a memorial and petition to Congress setting forth the "conditions, relations and wants of this country," a plea for territorial government, land donations, public works, mail service, and protection from Indians, all, naturally, at federal expense. He also concluded successful negotiations with McLoughlin, whereby British subjects in Oregon recognized and supported the provisional government.

Applegate's overland journey convinced him that an easier route to the Willamette valley should be found to accommodate wagon trains. In 1846 he explored and opened a difficult but not impossible southern route from Fort Hall, Idaho, via Nevada and northern California. While exploring this route, he noticed the Umpqua valley in west-central Oregon and was impressed with its prospects—fertile land and a navigable river to the ocean. In 1849 he moved there, settling in a valley he called Yoncalla, where he and his brothers benefited from the Donation Land Act of 1850. To settle the region he helped organize the Umpqua Townsite and Colonization Company, but the venture was not profitable.

Though Applegate was busy farming and surveying, he was particularly industrious as a writer. He wrote letters to the territorial newspapers and to Oregon's political figures about government. He was a Whig, then a Republican, and then a Union party supporter, but on individual issues he recognized no party. He was particularly adamant on slavery, holding that "whoever is against the extension of slavery is of my party."

On his reputation as a literate man of principle, Applegate was elected delegate to Oregon's constitutional convention in 1857. However, when his parliamentary maneuvers intended to bury the slavery issue failed, he left the convention in disgust. Though he was later active in organized politics and aspired to be a candidate for governor on the Union ticket in 1861, he remained "a political man without the arts of a politician." From his Yoncalla farm he continued writing letters of censure and advice; there he was consulted by legislators and was visited by travelers who wished to test his reputation as a sage. He rendered public service willingly, notably on the commission to settle claims of the Hudson's Bay Company, but was never elected to major public office. Nor did he benefit from appreciated land values, as did so many of his contemporaries. Instead, his personal and political fortunes declined simultaneously. Applegate was, nonetheless, highly respected as a public person, "sometimes uncouth and impractical," but always the conscience of his generation of politicians.

Major collections of Jesse Applegate papers are in the Western Americana Collection, Yale University Library; the Library of the Oregon Historical Society; the Bancroft Library, University of California; and the University of Oregon Library.—M. S.

Arapaho Indians. See CHEYENNE AND ARAPAHO INDIANS.

archaeology of North American Indians. Most historical accounts of North American archaeology begin with a discussion of Thomas Jefferson's efforts, discussed in his *Notes on Virginia* (1782), to excavate scientifically a prehistoric Indian mound in order to interpret its history. Jefferson's efforts were not the first, however. Peter Kalm, a professor of economy from Swedish Finland, wrote in his *Travels in North America* (1772) that "there have been found a few marks of antiquity, from which it may be conjectured that North America was formerly inhabited by a nation more versed in science and more civilized than that which the Europeans found on their arrival here."

The great prehistoric earthworks of Ohio aroused the curiosity of everyone who visited the area, and in the 1770s the Reverend David Jones described the external appearance of some in detail. Caleb Atwater, an Ohio lawyer and legislator who was commissioner of Indian Affairs under Andrew Jackson, published the results of his careful surveys of Ohio mounds in the first volume of the *Transactions of the American Antiquarian Society* (1820), and Edwin James, botanist and geologist on Major Stephen H. Long's expedition to the Rocky Mountains (1819-20), described, measured, and speculated about several Indian grave mounds near St. Louis. Ephraim G. Squier, writer, diplomat, and self-trained archaeologist, and Edwin H. Davis, an Ohio physician, reported on mounds in the Mississippi valley in the initial volume of the *Smithsonian Contributions to Knowledge* (1848). Their book was heralded by a Swiss archaeologist to be "as glorious a monument of American science as Bunker Hill is of American bravery."

In 1853, the second article of volume 8 of the *Contributions* was S. H. Haven's 168-page study, "Archaeology of the United States," the first summary of its kind. From this point forward archaeological efforts intensified.

Scientific excavations got a helping hand from Mrs. Mary Hemenway, a wealthy Boston philanthropist, who in 1886 sponsored the Hemenway Southwestern Archaeological Expedition in Arizona and New Mexico led by ethnologist Frank Hamilton CUSHING. Prehistoric sites were uncovered in the Salt River valley near Phoenix, Arizona. In 1889 anthropologist Jesse W.

FEWKES took charge of the expedition. In a short time this and other expeditions (see Adolph BANDELIER) began to disclose the incredibly rich historical heritage of the Indians of the Southwest.

In the Northwest, Franz BOAS began to study the native people in 1883. Between 1897 and 1902, members of the Morris K. Jesup North Pacific Expedition worked to establish the relationships between Indians of the North Pacific and natives on the adjacent Asian mainland. Jesup, a New York banker and philanthropist, was one of the incorporators of the American Museum of Natural History (1868). The anthropological campaign whose costs he underwrote carried out work in the archaeology, linguistics, ethnology, and physical anthropology of British Columbia and the northern Pacific Coast.

In the first half of the twentieth century American Indian archaeology blossomed as an established science. In the Southwest, pioneers such as Fewkes, Neil Judd, and Frederick Webb HODGE turned their shovels and talents to the task, soon to be followed by A. V. KIDDER, Edgar Hewitt, Edward Holland SPICER, Earl Morris, Emil Haury, E. B. Sayles, Harold Gladwin, Harold Colton, Florence Hawley Ellis, Eric Reed, Charles DiPeso, Albert Schroeder, and a host of others. They outlined the Hohokam, Mogollon, Anasazi, and early-man cultures of this arid region.

Working elsewhere in the West were Mark Harrington in Nevada, Malcolm Rogers in the Great Basin and southern deserts, and Luther Cressman in Oregon and the Great Basin. Robert Heizer and R. K. Beardsley reconstructed the prehistoric framework for California; Jesse Jennings directed his attention to the Great Basin; and W. C. McKern, Frank H. H. Roberts, Jr., William Duncan Strong, and Waldo Wedel labored in the Plains.

In 1934 the Society for American Archaeology held its organizational meeting and in the following year the first issue of *American Antiquity*, the society's journal, came off the presses. The society and *American Antiquity* continue to be concerned almost solely with the prehistory of American Indians.

In 1916 Nels C. Nelson demonstrated through his work at Tano Ruins, New Mexico, that geographical distribution and archaeological stratigraphy had a definite connection. In other words, he established correspondences between chronological layers of particular sites and specific prehistoric cultures as these were distributed over space. Nelson was able to show, for example, that people whom he called Basket Maker Nomads, whose artifacts he found in the lowest strata of his diggings, lived in widely scattered sites throughout the Four Corners region of the Southwest. More trained archaeologists entered the field, and archaeological techniques and methodology became increasingly refined. In the Southwest, Dr. A. E. Douglass, an astronomer, discovered that certain kinds of trees that add an annual growth ring could be valuable tools in dating Pueblo Indian and other ruins. Archaeologists devised new ways of classifying and studying the artifacts and architectural remains they found.

By the 1970s American archaeologists were using dozens of scientific tools to enable them to date changes in the cultural habits of human beings, climate, environment, and virtually everything else. Radiocarbon dating has almost become a household word. Other techniques include palynology (fossil pollen analysis), paleomagnetism, thermoluminescence, fission track dating, hydration-rind dating, and the dating of trace elements and oxygen isotopes. Archaeologists began discovering clues concerning matrilocal residence, matrilineal descent, and the historical interrelationships of families, local groups, and tribes. Properly studied, artifacts are capable of imparting to the analyst a kind of mental and cultural template of the men, women, and children who fashioned, distributed, used, and discarded them.

The prehistory of the West began either from 20,000 to 40,000 years ago or about 13,000 years ago. Most archaeological data gathered thus far stack up in favor of the more conservative estimate. It is believed that the first people in the New World arrived via the Bering Strait land bridge from Siberia to America and that they were hunters who made distinctive kinds of stone tools, shaping them by essentially flint-working techniques.

Many of these earliest westerners were big-game hunters, as evidenced by several types of fluted and other kinds of lanceolate projectile points that have been found, some of them sticking in the bones of extinct mammals such as the mammoth and Pleistocene bison. Presumed cultures of the "big-game-hunting tradition" are exemplified by Clovis fluted points, originally discovered in eastern New Mexico and made from 10,000 to 12,000 years ago; Sandia points, also found in New Mexico and possibly as old as Clovis points; and Folsom fluted points, found throughout eastern New Mexico, eastern Colorado, eastern Wyoming, and the adjacent areas of adjoining states, dating from about 9,000 to 11,000 years ago. More recent tools are Plano points (including Plainview and Midland forms and Scottsbluff, Eden, Cody, Angostura, and Agate Basin types), dating from 6,000 to 9,000 years ago.

The "Old Cordilleran tradition" is based upon the wide distribution of a carefully chipped bifacial stone point made in the shape of a willow leaf. Stone knives and edge-ground cobbles are also characteristic of this cultural tradition, distributed throughout the Pacific Northwest and California from 9,000 to 11,000 years ago. Unlike the big-game hunters, the people who made these tools are presumed to have depended on a wider source of food, including fish, large and small game animals, and plants.

Indians who tended to collect food followed the "Desert tradition." With surviving material culture characterized by basketry (from dry caves) and the flat milling stone, these people are pictured as nomads who lived in small, extended family groups numbering no more than twenty or thirty people. They wandered on a cyclic basis in search primarily of edible vegetables. Evidences of such a cultural tradition dating all the way from 2,500 to 10,000 years ago have been found in widely scattered sites in Utah, Oregon, Nevada, southeastern California, Arizona, and New Mexico. Indeed, the Desert tradition seems to have survived into the historic period among, for example, the Paiute Indians.

Other early-man traditions, dating from about 7,000 years before the present, include the Northwest Coast tradition, the Plateau tradition, and the California coast and valley tradition. There is also the Plains Archaic tradition dating from about 7,000 B.C., carried on by Indians who relied on hunting small game, fishing, and collecting wild plants.

What separates all these early Americans from most subsequent groups of prehistoric Indians is the fact that they produced no food of their own. They relied on their abilities to hunt, fish, or gather wild plants or edible animals, including insects, from their various environments, and the kinds of artifacts they left and did not leave behind—notably the absence of pottery—are all indicative of this fact.

Although some cultivated corn appeared in the Southwest as early as 3,000 B.C. (at Bat Cave in west-central New Mexico), it was about 500 B.C. before agriculture became widely important in the economic and cultural traditions of Indians of the region. Important southwestern prehistoric agricultural societies include the Mogollon, centered in the mountainous areas of southeastern Arizona and southwestern New Mexico and famed for its fine Mimbres pottery; the Hohokam of the southern Arizona desert, best known for its vast irrigation systems and monumental architecture; the Anasazi of Arizona, New Mexico, Utah, and Colorado, the Basket Maker Pueblo peoples who were the ancestors of today's PUEBLO INDIANS; and the Patayan (or Hakatayan) of the lower Colorado River area, some of whose descendants are likely among today's YUMA INDIANS of the same region. Strangely enough, there is a gap in our knowledge of many of these prehistoric cultures such that it cannot be said with certainty what happened to many of them after about A.D. 1450. The dawn of history in the Southwest breaks with the coming of Fray Marcos de Niza and the Coronado expedition in 1539-42, and a comparison between the archaeological and subsequent documentary record makes it appear that there were serious upheavals in southwestern Indian societies between the prehistoric and historic periods.

The close of the Archaic period in the Plains coincided roughly with the time of the birth of Christ. The Archaic period was followed by what archaeologists have called the Woodland period (c. A.D. 1 to 1000), a tradition characterized by the presence of pottery and a small amount of maize agriculture. This period, in turn, was followed by the development of the Plains village tradition, which appeared about A.D. 1000. It saw the successful foundation of economies based on maize, beans, and squash agriculture in addition to hunting and gathering, especially in the eastern portions of the Plains. These prehistoric developments culminated in the historic period (c. the 1500s) in the Blackfoot and Crow cultures of the northwestern area, the Pawnee and Omaha tribes of the central area, the Comanche and Kiowa tribes of the south, the Mandan and Arikara of the middle Missouri region, and the various Siouan tribes of the northeastern Plains.

Elsewhere in the West, such as in the Northwest Coast, California, the Interior Plateau, and the Great Basin, agriculture never became a significant activity in the cultural inventory of the prehistoric cultures. But here, as elsewhere throughout the West, at least 13,000 years of prehistory witnessed the growth of Indian populations and the increasing complexity of their cultures. Village settlements became larger and more stable, and people were better able to exploit their environments. This meant a corresponding increase in the numbers and kinds of artifacts that marked the material inventory of particular cultural groups (see INDIANS OF

THE NORTHWEST COAST and INDIANS OF CALIFORNIA).

To sum up, as a result of the efforts of archaeologists it is now reasonably sure that man has lived in the New World for at least 13,000 years; that beans, corn, and other food plants were domesticated from 5,000 to 7,000 years ago and on the eve of Columbus' arrival most North American Indians were farmers or horticulturalists; that man first entered the New World from Asia, but subsequently and before A.D. 1492 there were additional migrations; and that as many as nine million people may have inhabited what are now the United States and Canada, speaking more than two hundred distinct INDIAN LANGUAGES and living in crowded urban centers as well as in scattered bands.

Virtually all knowledge of the first 13,000 or more years of western prehistory is based on the efforts of archaeologists. It is true that there are many surviving and otherwise recorded oral traditions of Indian groups that bespeak their own prehistory, but these are difficult to interpret or to evaluate in terms of non-Indian concepts of historical "truth." For example, few non-Navaho would agree that the Navaho emerged from various levels of the underworld, but the Navaho conception of their origins is culturally as valid as the Christian belief that man originated in the Garden of Eden. Archaeologists insist that the Navaho and other southwestern Athapaskan-speaking Indians moved into their present region well after A.D. 1000, but migrations are very difficult to discern archaeologically.

Because the historian deals with documents and most archaeologists deal with prehistory, these two disciplines had very little to do with one another until recent times. Beginning in the 1960s, increasing numbers of archaeologists began to turn their attention to Indian sites of the historic period and, subsequently, to non-Indian sites as well. The First International Conference on Historic Archaeology was held in Dallas, Texas, in January 1967, and it resulted in that year in the formation of the Society for Historical Archaeology. Its membership includes archaeologists and documentary historians as well as archaeologists whose academic training is in history rather than in anthropology. As more archaeology is done in historic sites, the greater will be the cooperation between those who interpret human history on the basis of artifacts and those who rely on the written word.

See C. W. Ceram, *The First Americans* (1971); Panchanan Mitra, *A History of American Anthropology* (1933); and Gordon R. Willey, *An Introduction to American Archaeology* (1966).—B. L. F.

Argonauts, trails of the. See FORTY-NINERS, TRAILS OF THE.

Arikara campaign (1823). During William H. Ashley's second expedition on the Missouri in search of furs, his men were assailed by Arikara Indians on June 2, 1823. Fifteen of Ashley's expedition were killed. To punish the tribe Ashley dispatched an expedition commanded by Colonel Henry Leavenworth and composed of six companies of soldiers, Ashley and his men, and Joshua Pilcher and employees of the Missouri Fur Company. The expedition, comprising about eight hundred men, left Council Bluffs on June 22, 1823, and because of Leavenworth's incompetence, fought an indecisive battle with the Arikara at their villages on August 9-11. The treaty that followed failed to establish permanent

peace with the tribe. The campaign led to Ashley's momentous decision to reach the Rockies by the more efficient overland route rather than the dangerous Missouri.

See Hiram M. Chittenden, *The American Fur Trade of the Far West* (1902); and Dale L. Morgan, ed., *The West of William H. Ashley* (1964).—G. B. D.

Arikara Indians. The Arikara were a small, semisedentary Caddoan tribe whose earth lodge villages were located along the Missouri River near the northern border of present South Dakota, when American explorers first reached that area in 1804. They had migrated into that area from the southwest and were an offshoot of the Pawnee Indians. They were close neighbors with the Mandan, and resembled them in culture. Provoked by early trappers and traders, they soon became hostile toward whites and jeopardized travel and settlement on the upper Missouri for many years. But an accumulation of factors—their defeat by the Leavenworth expedition in 1823, their inability to check white expansion, and, especially, their exposure to epidemic white diseases in the 1770s and 1830s, which reduced their population from more than two thousand to fewer than one thousand, thereby making them more vulnerable to the belligerent Sioux—caused them to change their disposition in the 1850s. Indeed, the Arikara eventually became more than friends of the United States, for scores of them served as army scouts in critical Indian campaigns in the 1870s.

While peaceful, Arikara-white relations after 1860 were not without complications. In 1862, after a twenty-four-year stay near Fort Clark in central North Dakota, the Arikara were assigned to an agency at Fort Berthold, farther up the Missouri. But the treaties they signed in 1851 and 1866 went unratified, so the reservation they finally shared with the Mandan and Hidatsa was not officially established until the 1880s. Meanwhile, the Arikara's aggressive neighbors, inadequate resources, natural disasters, and loyalty to their own culture impeded the Indian Bureau's efforts to mold and assimilate them. Largely because of secessions from the tribe, only about four hundred Arikara remained at Fort Berthold to receive land allotments and citizenship in 1900. Today the Arikara have merged with the Mandan and Hidatsa on the reservation and are culturally extinct.

There is no standard work on Arikara history, and scholars have given little systematic attention to Arikara-white relations. Some noteworthy observations on the life and activities of these people in the first half of the nineteenth century are included in Edwin T. Denig, *Five Indian Tribes of the Upper Missouri* (1961), edited by John C. Ewers. Another informative, although brief, discussion of this tribe is found in Frederick W. Hodge, ed., *Handbook of American Indians North of Mexico* (1907-11), vol. I. An example of Arikara military aid to the United States Army is examined in John S. Gray, "Arikara Scouts with Custer," *North Dakota History* (Spring 1968). Other historical material is in the annual reports of the commissioner of Indian affairs.—H. G. W.

Arizona: *Spanish and Mexican Arizona (to 1846).* Arizona, the Grand Canyon State, contains 113,956 square miles and is bounded on the north by Utah, on the east by New Mexico, on the south by the Republic of Mexico, and on the west by California and

Nevada. Lying on the western slope of the Rocky Mountains, Arizona has two geographical provinces: a northern plateau province, bounded on the south by the Mogollon Rim, and a southern subhumid basin and range province. On the plateau the streams feed the Little Colorado, which runs northwest through eroded country to the COLORADO RIVER; the streams below the plateau drain into the GILA RIVER, which flows west to the Colorado. The plateau province is characterized by extensive forests, lofty mesas, and open grasslands; the basin and range province below the Mogollon Rim is a near-desert country with elongated mountain ranges.

Human habitation in Arizona can be traced back more than twelve thousand years. By A.D. 1 the Anasazi Indians were flourishing in the plateau country above the Rim, while in the Gila valley the more advanced Hohokam were building extensive irrigation works and trading with central Mexico. The first Europeans found a majority of the Indians living in four areas: the Moqui (possibly a remnant of the Anasazi) and the NAVAHO living north of the Little Colorado; the Walapai, Havasupai, Mohave, and Yuma (see QUECHAN INDIANS) along the Colorado; the Yavapai and APACHE in the interior and eastern mountains; and the Pima and the Papago (possibly descendants of the Hohokam) in the central river valleys (see PIMA INDIANS).

Spain became interested in Arizona during the 1530s when stories began circulating about golden cities beyond the northern frontier (see EXPLORATION, SPANISH). Following Alvar Núñez Cabeza de Vaca's report on his trek from Texas to northern Sonora, Viceroy Antonio de Mendoza in 1539 dispatched Fray Marcos de Niza, a Franciscan, and Estevanito, a Moor who had been with Cabeza de Vaca, to investigate the stories. Traveling down the San Pedro River through eastern Arizona, they eventually reached the Zuñi villages in western New Mexico, where Estevanito was killed. Returning to Mexico City, Fray Marcos filed a glowing report. In 1540 Francisco Vásquez de Coronado marched north with a large military force, captured the Zuñi pueblos, and sent parties to contact the Moqui and explore west to the Grand Canyon. In the meantime, Hernando de Alarcón reached the Colorado River with Coronado's supply ships and visited the YUMA vicinity. After crossing the Texas plains to the Republican River in Kansas, Coronado returned to Mexico, his expedition having exploded the myth of the golden cities. In the following decades several Spanish expeditions entered Arizona from the Rio Grande valley. Antonio de Espejo in 1583 visited the Moqui and discovered copper outcroppings in central Arizona; about twenty years later Juan de Oñate inspected Espejo's mines, traveled to the Colorado, then returned to the Rio Grande.

By 1690 Jesuit missionaries were laboring in southern Arizona. Father Eusebio Kino introduced agriculture to the Piman-speaking Indians, explored the Santa Cruz and San Pedro valleys, and carried the Christian witness along the Gila to the Colorado. In 1736 a rich silver discovery at the rancheria of Arizonac, near Nogales, drew prospectors north into the Santa Cruz drainage. Then in 1752, following a rebellion by the Pima Indians, Spain located a presidio, San Ignacio de Tubac, on the Santa Cruz. With the expulsion of the Jesuits in 1767, Francisco Garcés, a Franciscan, took station at the SAN XAVIER DEL BAC mission and explored extensively in western and northern Arizona. He also accompanied Juan Bautista de Anza, commanding at Tubac, on expeditions to California. In late 1775 the garrison at TUBAC was moved north to TUCSON. A presidio-mission also was constructed on the Colorado at Yuma Crossing, on the California side, with Garcés in charge, but in 1781 Spanish colonists invaded the Indian fields and the Yuma massacred the settlers. During the waning years of Spanish rule, northern Sonora (Arizona) prospered. Presidial soldiers from Tucson and elsewhere quieted the troublesome Apache, mines were discovered, land grants were issued at the Sonoran capital at Arizpe, and substantial church structures were erected at San Xavier and Tumacacori.

Following the Mexican revolution of 1810, the Santa Cruz settlements were considered a separate district in Sonora, with Tubac the equivalent of a county seat. Sonora was soon wracked by political turmoil; counterfeiting flourished, taxes went uncollected, and the Apache paralyzed commerce and agriculture. Also, American trappers began prowling the Gila valley. To protect their northern provinces, the Mexicans sent state armies and scalp hunters against the Apache and projected military colonies on the frontier line. However, the successful revolution in Texas and growing American penetration of New Mexico made it obvious that the Mexican borderland could not be defended.

Arizona Territory (1846-1912). In May 1846 the United States declared war on Mexico. By the early fall General Stephen Watts Kearny had occupied Santa Fe, established a provisional government, and attached New Mexico to the Union. As the area north of the Gila River was a part of New Mexico, his actions marked the beginning of American control over present-day Arizona. Kearny then marched west along the Gila with a dragoon detachment, and sent Captain Philip St. George Cooke, with a battalion of Mormons, to blaze a wagon road along a southern route through Tucson to California. The Mexican War ended in 1848, and territorial rule was initiated in New Mexico two years later. In 1853 the United States, because of boundary differences and the desire for a railroad route, purchased the Gadsden Strip (northern Sonora) from Mexico and joined it to New Mexico. Since western New Mexico (Arizona) was an unknown region, the army soon marked wagon and railroad routes along the thirty-fifth and thirty-second parallels and explored the drainage of the Colorado River. To protect travelers from Indians, the federal government built several forts: Fort Yuma at the Colorado-Gila junction; Fort Buchanan near Tubac; Fort Breckinridge on the San Pedro; Fort Defiance in the Navaho domain; and Fort Mohave on the Colorado.

In August 1856 the Sonora Exploring and Mining Company of Ohio reopened the silver mines at Tubac. The population of the district soon soared to more than five hundred, and a newspaper, the Tubac *Weekly Arizonian*, was founded. Complaining of the lack of representation at Santa Fe, the citizens of Tubac, Tucson, and Mesilla, the political seat of Dona Ana County, created in 1860 the provisional Territory of Arizona and a year later cast their lot with the Confederacy. Confederate cavalry occupied Arizona briefly in 1862, but retired to the Rio Grande upon the arrival of Union forces from California. In Washington, a powerful mining lobby pushed a bill through Congress to create the Territory of Arizona, and President Abraham Lincoln signed it into law on February 24, 1863. The territorial party—Governor John N. Goodwin of Maine, Secretary Richard C. McCormick of New York, Chief Justice William Howell of Michigan, and others—reached Walker's Diggings in the central part of the territory early in 1864 and located the capital nearby at Prescott. A census was taken (4,187 whites), a legislature and a congressional delegate elected (Charles D. Poston won), four counties were designated, and a court system was established. The first legislature adopted the Howell Code as the basic law.

Mining dominated Arizona history during the ensuing decades. Rich gold and silver discoveries were made along the Colorado and in the mountains in the interior. Because the influx of prospectors and settlers disturbed the Indian population, the army launched campaigns and drove the hostile tribes onto reservations. The silver bonanza at Tombstone in 1877 stimulated large eastern and foreign capital investments in Arizona, and the Southern Pacific Railroad laid track from Yuma through Tucson to El Paso. In the northern part of the territory the Atlantic and Pacific Railroad completed a line from the Rio Grande west along the thirty-fifth parallel to the Colorado, where it connected with the Southern Pacific. Within a decade north-south branch lines joined these transcontinentals. A prosperous livestock industry arose. The San Raphael Ranch near the Mexican border and the Empire Ranch east of Tucson flourished, as did the ranches of William Flake, Henry Clay Hooker, John H. Slaughter, and the Babbitt family. Above the Mogollon Rim, the Aztec Land and Cattle Company monopolized a princely domain. The sheep industry also boomed; in 1891 five million pounds of wool were marketed from 700,000 animals.

Settlements took root in the central valleys. On the Salt River, Phoenix came into existence to supply the markets at neighboring Fort McDowell, expanded rapidly as large-scale irrigation projects were started, and in 1889 became the territorial capital. On the Gila River, Florence, Safford, and other towns became supply centers for mines, forts, and reservations. To the north the Mormons founded colonies along the Little Colorado River. Between 1870 and 1880 the population of the territory increased from 9,658 to 40,440 inhabitants. Father Jean Baptiste Salpointe revitalized the Roman Catholic witness and became the first bishop of Arizona; and Methodist, Baptist, and Presbyterian congregations were organized in the major towns.

By the late 1880s copper mining surpassed silver and gold production in value. The mines at Ray, Jerome, Globe, Clifton-Morenci, Bisbee, and Ajo became heavy producers, the major companies being W. A. Clark, Phelps Dodge, and the Arizona Copper Company, Ltd. The copper companies built towns, constructed shortline railroads, stimulated the spread of banking, and with the railroads dominated local and territorial politics. In 1902 the Arizona statehood issue was debated in Congress, but an enabling act was not passed until 1910. A convention at Phoenix drafted a state constitution and submitted it, as required, to Congress and the president, who approved it after the recall provision was eliminated. On February 14, 1912, President William H. Taft proclaimed Arizona a state of the Union.

Confederate Arizona. In March 1861 citizens of Mesilla and Tucson declared in public meetings their allegiance to the Confederacy. In the early summer a Confederate column from El Paso, Texas, led by Lieutenant Colonel John R. Baylor brushed aside a token resistance by Union forces on the Rio Grande and occupied Mesilla. On August 1 Baylor declared himself military governor of the Territory of Arizona. To meet this threat the federal government abandoned all the forts in western New Mexico (Arizona) and rushed most of the garrisons to the Rio Grande. At Fort Craig, north of Mesilla, Lieutenant Colonel Edward R. S. Canby concentrated all available men, and on February 21, 1862, he crossed the Rio Grande and at a place called Valverde attacked Brigadier General Henry H. Sibley, who had arrived from Texas with two thousand five hundred Confederates. Canby's force was defeated and driven from the field. Sibley then moved north and seized Santa Fe. In the meantime Captain Sherod Hunter and a cavalry company had entered Tucson on February 28; and Colonel James Reily, who accompanied him, left a few days later on a fruitless mission to secure recognition and supplies in Sonora. Hunter sent a detachment south to the Patagonia mine and obtained supplies from its owner, Sylvester Mowry, and then he went north to the Pima villages to gain information about Union forces on the Colorado. In March at Glorieta Pass, east of Santa Fe, Sibley was defeated by Colorado Volunteers and began a precipitous retreat down the Rio Grande into Texas. On the Gila, Hunter encountered advance units belonging to the Union army of Brigadier General James H. Carleton, who was leading about eighteen hundred men across Arizona. After skirmishing on April 15 at Picacho Pass, forty miles north of Tucson, with a Union detachment, the Confederates withdrew from Tucson and returned to Rio Grande. On May 20 Carleton marched into Tucson, paused for several weeks, and then moved east. In September 1862 he succeeded Canby as commander in New Mexico. The Civil War in the Southwest was over.

Arizona since statehood. The economic progress of Arizona during the first half of the twentieth century paralleled to a large degree the general growth pattern in the United States. Both industry and agriculture reflected sharply the impact of two world wars and the great depression that came between. World War I spurred copper, cotton, and beef production. Copper companies expanded their operations and modernized their plants as metal prices soared. The Goodyear Tire and Rubber Company established two cotton-farming communities in the Salt River valley to raise Pima cotton, which rose to $1.25 per pound. Livestock producers found ready markets for beef cattle and sold horses and mules for farm power and military purposes. During the period 1910-20 farm acreage in Arizona increased almost 400 percent and the value of farm property tripled. In another vein, the war brought labor unrest and strikes in the mines. In July 1917 local law enforcement officers, at the urging of company officials, deported striking miners at Jerome and Bisbee to adjoining states.

During the early 1920s the economic boom ended and there was a sharp fall in prices. More than one half of the banks in Arizona failed, many being absorbed by larger financial institutions; most of the copper producers shut down their mines, and agricultural production dropped. On the bright side, railroads, chambers of commerce, and booster clubs began promoting resort and tourist areas in Arizona, and the spreading use of the automobile stimulated large-scale road building in the state. Interest in developing water storage and power facilities along the Colorado River found expression in a conference at Santa Fe in 1922, where six states compacted to seek federal funds for large power-irrigation projects (Arizona refused to participate). Arizona Governor Thomas Campbell, a Republican, had done much to promote the conference, but a Democratic victory in 1922, generated by groups who depended on the Salt River Valley Project and feared the loss of water rights under the compact, turned Arizona toward isolation. The Arizona legislature, because of power emergencies during World War II, finally voted in 1945 to join the compact states and draw on Hoover Dam, which had been completed on the Colorado a decade earlier.

During the depression of the 1930s, Arizona received large amounts of federal relief and recovery aid. The tariff on silver encouraged copper producers (silver was a by-product) to reopen mines, new irrigation projects were launched, and various federal agencies inaugurated public works on Indian reservations, in parks and forests, and at educational institutions. Although an estimated fifty thousand people (principally from mining towns) left Arizona, monetary relief did much to halt the exodus and provide support for thousands of families. The effect of the hard times of the 1920s and 1930s was reflected in the population growth. In the decade before 1920, the population had doubled; from 1920 to 1940, the total increased from about 335,000 to 500,000.

World War II brought renewed prosperity to Arizona. The military services established a number of camps in the state for desert and air warfare training, for prisoners of war, and for displaced Japanese-Americans from the West Coast. Processing and assembly plants associated with the war effort were built, and meat, cotton, and copper again found excellent markets. During these years the Democratic party, largely controlled by conservative mining, railroad, and agricultural interests, heavily influenced state legislation. However, population growth (749,587 in 1950 to 1,772,482 in 1970), the changing nature of the state economy, and increased urbanization gave rise to a two-party system in Arizona by the 1950s. During the ensuing decade the Republicans captured the governorship (four-year term), steadily gained votes in the state legislature (thirty senators and sixty representatives from fourteen counties), and won control of Arizona's seats (two senators and four representatives) in Congress. The rise of Barry Goldwater of Phoenix as a national figure did much to encourage Republican party growth and influence in Arizona.

By 1970 Arizona was squarely in the mainstream of American life. Phoenix, the capital, was the largest city with more than 580,000 people; Tucson ranked next with about 260,000. The state was nearly 80 percent urban. The population breakdown (1970) showed 91 percent white and 9 percent nonwhite (Indians, 5.4 percent, and Negroes, 3 percent). Nineteen Indian reservations covered 25 percent of the state; the largest

was the Navaho in northeastern Arizona. The government also operated seven national forests, from which 180 million board feet of timber annually was cut; state and private lands yielded another 100 million board feet. Altogether, the federal government owned about 72 percent of the total area of Arizona. The growth of manufacturing and tourism, continued agricultural and mining prosperity, and the population increase focused more and more attention on Arizona's water resources. The state legislature adopted laws concerning well drilling and stream water rights and inaugurated watershed programs. At the national level, Arizona congressmen, with help from representatives of the Colorado Basin states, pushed through the Central Arizona Project Bill, which will direct water from the Colorado River overland to the Phoenix-Tucson areas. The completion of this project should assure the future growth of the state.

See Hubert H. Bancroft, *History of Arizona and New Mexico, 1530-1888* (1889); Martin H. Hall, *Sibley's New Mexico Campaign* (1960); Howard R. Lamar, *The Far Southwest, 1846-1912: A Territorial History* (1966); James H. McClintock, *Arizona: Prehistoric, Aboriginal, Pioneer, Modern,* 3 vols. (1916); Edward H. Peplow, *History of Arizona,* 3 vols. (1958); B. Sacks, *Be It Enacted: The Creation of the Territory of Arizona* (1964); Valley National Bank, *Arizona Statistical Review* (1970); and Jay J. Wagoner, *Arizona Territory, 1863-1912: A Political History* (1970).—H. P. H.

Arizona Historical Society. In January 1884, at the urging of government official Charles D. Poston, a group of pioneers met in Tucson and organized the Society of Arizona Pioneers, patterning their constitution after that of the Society of California Pioneers. Membership was restricted to men who had arrived in the territory before January 1, 1870, and their male descendants. Former Tucson mayor William S. Oury was chosen the first president, and William J. Osborn the historical secretary. The organization held monthly meetings in rented quarters downtown and began acquiring books, magazines, and artifacts. In 1897 the Arizona legislature designated the Tucson group a territorial agency, renamed it the Arizona Pioneers' Historical Society, and appropriated money for its support. All the territorial institutions in Arizona were asked to send copies of their publications to the society. The historical secretary became the most important officer, acting as business manager, curator, correspondent, and field worker. In 1916 the organization accepted its first female member. After being housed in a variety of places, the society in 1955 moved into its own building on land adjoining the University of Arizona. Membership categories were expanded to include territorial (arrived before 1912), historical (thirty years' residence), and participating. The society constructed an elaborate museum depicting Arizona's past, inaugurated an educational program for schoolchildren, and launched *Arizoniana* (now the *Journal of Arizona History*). The name of the institution was changed in 1971 to the Arizona Historical Society, and local chapters and affiliates were organized. The library contains more than 40,000 books and pamphlets, 6,000 biographical files, 2,500 maps, 250,000 photographs, and 800 collections of individual, family, and institutional papers and records. In April 1975 the society opened an elaborate museum depicting the mining and processing of copper.

See Charles C. Colley, ed., *Documents of Southwestern History: A Guide to the Manuscript Collections of the Arizona Historical Society* (1972); and Sybil J. Ellinwood and A. Tracy Row, *The Arizona Historical Society Today* (1973).—H. P. H.

Arkansas. Lying on the west bank of the Mississippi River, immediately west of Tennessee and north Mississippi, the land that became the state of Arkansas was acquired by the United States as part of the Louisiana Purchase in 1803. It was first explored in 1541-42 by de Soto, whose expedition left the first historical records of the land and its Indian inhabitants. Parties led by the Frenchmen Marquette and Jolliet (1673) and La Salle (1682), left additional historical accounts and claimed the area for France. La Salle's trusted associate, Henri de Tonti, had a fur-trading post built near the mouth of the Arkansas River in 1686 while he was in search of La Salle, who had brought an expedition from France and had landed in Texas.

Tonti's post, called Arkansas Post, was the first permanent French settlement in the lower Mississippi valley and became an important link between the French settlements in Louisiana and those in Canada and the upper Mississippi. John Law's Mississippi Company, a French banking and trading company, established a colony of German farmers near Arkansas Post in 1720-21, but the colony failed after Law's financial schemes ended in the bursting of the "Mississippi bubble" in France in 1720. The post itself continued as a fur-trading station, an army garrison, and a Jesuit mission during French supremacy.

In 1762, when France ceded Louisiana to Spain, Arkansas Post remained as a fort and trading center. After the United States won its independence in 1783, Spain, fearing American encroachment, practiced a vacillating policy toward the United States. It refused to recognize the thirty-first parallel as the United States boundary, interfered with American navigation on the Mississippi River, incited Indian attacks against American settlements in the Old Southwest, intrigued to create dissent between Americans in the area and the American government, bribed American officials such as General James Wilkinson, and granted land to Americans in an apparent attempt to win American friends for defense of its border against possible United States encroachment. However, fewer than a thousand persons lived in Arkansas at the time of the Louisiana Purchase in 1803. Under United States rule, Arkansas was a part of the District of Louisiana and in 1812 part of the Territory of Missouri. The Territory of Arkansas was created in 1819 with the capital at Arkansas Post, the law making it a slave territory in a period of heated sectional controversy over Missouri's admission as a slave state. In 1821 the territorial legislature moved the capital to Little Rock, a new town on the Arkansas River, some eighty miles above the Post.

Torn by political factionalism and the turbulent conditions of the frontier, Arkansas won a not undeserved reputation as the "Toothpick State." Albert Pike described it in 1835 as being within "a mile or two of sunset." James Bowie's famous knife had been made by an Arkansas blacksmith named James Black, and according to common belief in the East every man in Arkansas went armed with a bowie knife, or an "Arkansas toothpick." To be sure, there were enough knife fights, duels, lynchings, and shootings reported from Arkansas to sustain its reputation in the East.

When Arkansas was admitted to the Union in 1836 as a slave state, its frontier exuberance hardly subsided. Indian Territory was set up on its western border, and through the state came the Cherokee, Choctaw, Chickasaw, Creek, and Seminole tramping their "Trail of Tears" (see FIVE CIVILIZED TRIBES). They were harmless enough, but Arkansas politicians, with their eye out for federal aid, demanded and got a military garrison at Fort Smith to protect the state from the "savages" on their border. There Arkansas's second largest town, Fort Smith, developed as an adjunct to the garrison and as a base for the federal Indian Service.

Politically, Arkansas was dominated until 1860 by a Democratic party family clique known as the Conway dynasty. Elias CONWAY and James CONWAY were governors, their first cousin Ambrose SEVIER was Arkansas's first United States senator, and Sevier's brother-in-law Robert Ward JOHNSON, a nephew of Vice-President Richard Mentor Johnson, was a congressman and United States senator. The Whigs, urged on by Arkansas's renowned newspaper editor, lawyer, poet, and soldier, Albert PIKE, were almost powerless in Arkansas, whose settlers were largely from Democrat Andrew Jackson's Tennessee. Yet these Tennesseans, who flocked especially to the mountainous northwest half of the state, opposed immediate secession in 1861. They controlled the convention that met in March 1861 and rejected secession but agreed to a referendum on whether to cooperate with the border states or to secede. When Lincoln, after the fall of Fort Sumter, called on Arkansas for volunteers to help coerce the seceded states, the convention met again on May 6, 1861, and voted to secede and join the Confederacy.

With the Indian country on its western frontier and Missouri on its north, Arkansas felt its safety from Federal invasion depended on a Confederate alliance with the slaveholding Five Civilized Tribes and on Confederate recognition and support of the secessionist government in Missouri. Pike accomplished the Indian alliance in the summer of 1861, and Arkansas's General Benjamin McCulloch adopted the strategy of preventing invasion from Missouri. However, McCulloch and General Sterling Price, the Confederate leader in Missouri, failed to agree on the importance of delivering the "Show Me State" from the bluecoats, and by early 1862 Price had been driven into northwest Arkansas. Confederate President Jefferson Davis sent Major General Earl Van Dorn, a fellow Mississippian, to command McCulloch and Price, and on March 6, 7, 8, 1862, the dashing Van Dorn led them to a disastrous defeat at Pea Ridge, where McCulloch was killed.

The battle of Pea Ridge assured Federal control of Missouri and, after Van Dorn took his army east of the Mississippi to support sagging Confederate defenses against General Ulysses S. Grant, Arkansas was left almost defenseless. The Federals, led by Samuel R. Curtis, the victor of Pea Ridge, marched across north Arkansas and occupied Helena on the Mississippi. Protests by Governor Henry RECTOR caused General Thomas HINDMAN to be sent to defend Arkansas. His harsh methods and substitution of military law for civilian law, together with his rash attack on a superior Federal army and defeat at Prairie Grove on December 7, 1862, resulted in his transfer back to Mississippi.

Meanwhile, General Thomas H. Holmes had replaced Van Dorn as commander of the trans-Mississippi department, of which Arkansas was a district. Holmes was indecisive and incompetent, and early in 1863 was superseded by General Edmund Kirby Smith, who nevertheless left Holmes in command of Arkansas. Holmes was repulsed at Helena July 4, 1863, the day Vicksburg surrendered to Grant. Two months later, on September 10, 1863, Little Rock fell to General Frederick Steele, and early in 1864 a Union state government under Isaac Murphy, the only delegate who had refused to vote for secession in May 1861, was established. Yet the Confederate state government, which had fled to Washington in southwest Arkansas, continued until the final Confederate surrender in May 1865. General Steele in the spring of 1864 invaded southwest Arkansas in an attempt to join forces with General Nathaniel Banks, who was moving up the Red River in Louisiana in an assault on Kirby Smith's Shreveport headquarters. When Banks was crushed in Louisiana, Kirby Smith directed his forces against Steele, driving him out of Camden, Arkansas, and chasing him pell-mell back to Little Rock. At Jenkins Ferry on the Saline River, April 24-25, Steele was brought to bay but, in a brilliant rearguard action, got his men safely across to the road to Little Rock. That ended military action in Arkansas, except for General Sterling Price's Missouri expedition in the late summer of 1864, which was launched from north Arkansas. It ended in disaster for the Missourian.

The Union state government installed in 1864 had met President Lincoln's terms for Reconstruction, freeing the slaves, repudiating Confederate war debts, and operating a loyal state government. In 1866-67 the legislature, controlled by ex-Confederates, passed repressive measures against Negroes and sent former rebels to claim seats in Congress. It was these unwise actions, duplicated by the other ex-Confederate states, that impelled the radical Republicans in Congress to substitute congressional for presidential Reconstruction. Arkansas was the first state admitted under the radical plan. In 1867 the Federal military commander in the state, carrying out the radical terms, registered voters and, in the fall, held an election for a constitutional convention. Negroes voted for the first time in this election, which was carried by the newly organized Republican party. In 1868 the convention drew up a constitution enfranchising and extending citizenship to Negroes, providing for public schools, and calling for a state election. The Republicans carried the election, the legislature met and ratified the Fourteenth Amendment to the United States Constitution, and a full congressional delegation was sent to Washington. On June 22, 1868, Arkansas was readmitted to the Union over President Andrew Johnson's veto, and the congressional delegation was permitted to take their seats.

Republicans maintained control of the state government until 1874. They accomplished much that the previous Democratic administrations had not. They established tax-supported free public schools, founded Arkansas Industrial University that later became the University of Arkansas, set up a school for the deaf, warred on the lawless Ku Klux Klan, protected the rights of Negro citizens, encouraged immigration, made provisions for paying the state's debt, and extended state aid to the building of levees and railroads. Later Democratic administrations denounced the Republicans for plunging the state into debt, accused them of pocketing money intended for the building of levees and railroads, and charged them with maintaining themselves in power by fraudulent political practices—disfranchising white enemies, multiple voting, and dishonest counting. The debt problem resulted largely from the Panic of 1873 and the ensuing depression. How much, if any, money was stolen was never proved. And it is pretty obvious the Republicans were not alone in their use of corrupt politics; Arkansans were familiar with the practice, though they may have learned from radical Republicans some new techniques in the art.

A split in Republican ranks in 1872-74 permitted the Democrats under Augustus H. GARLAND to win control of the state in 1874, draw up the present constitution, and set up a new state government. These Democratic "redeemers" repudiated the Republican state debt for levees and railroads; severely cut back expenditures for state services, public schools, and the University of Arkansas; and maintained themselves in power by ruthless political methods. They preached white solidarity to encourage Arkansas's farmers to continue supporting the corrupt Democratic party, became the paid servants of railroad and business interests, and acclaimed Arkansas's future in a "new South," which they described as throbbing with progress—railroads, factories, sawmills, and mines.

The 1880s and 1890s found the farmers organizing into the Brothers of Freedom and the Agricultural Wheel, and merging with the Farmers' Grand Alliance. They forsook the Democratic party and came close to overwhelming it, but the entrenched interests were too powerful to be driven from control. In 1900, however, after the agrarian protesters returned to the Democratic party, Jeff DAVIS came upon the scene to lead them in overthrowing control of the party by business interests. Adopting the old Populist ideas and methods, Davis led the "sun-burned sons of toil," the "one-gallus" Democrats, to six glorious years of power. Attacking the railroads, the trusts, and the insurance companies, and ridiculing the men who represented these new interests, Davis was denounced as a demagogue. Yet he achieved political and penal reforms, collected unpaid taxes from the railroads, regulated business, secured needed labor legislation, and paid most of the state's bonded indebtedness.

With the passing of Davis the Democratic party fell again under the sway of the conservative propertied classes, and there it remained. Since Arkansas has been traditionally a Democratic state, the chief characteristic of politics in the twentieth century has been pure one-party rule with Democrats vying against each other, chiefly on the basis of personalities, for office. In the late 1960s Winthrop Rockefeller of the famous New York industrial-financial family, who had moved to Arkansas in 1953, led the Republican party to victory for two terms (1967-71) but was defeated in a bid for a third term by a young, dynamic Democrat, Dale Bumpers.

Whether the Republican party is to furnish Arkansas a viable two-party system hereafter remains to be seen.

Rockefeller's victory in 1966 was due in part to the twelve-year scandal-ridden administration of Orval E. Faubus. Elected in 1954, Faubus led the massive resistance to the federal government's efforts to enforce school integration at Little Rock in 1957-58, became the hero of segregationists, and was undefeatable from 1958 to 1964. Choosing not to run in 1966, allegedly because of scandals in connection with the state prison and with the financial dealings of some of his political friends, he left the Democratic party badly divided. In 1966, for the first time since Reconstruction, a Republican was elected governor.

The development of RAILROADS in the late nineteenth century sparked economic growth. Between 1870 and 1900, the population grew from less than 500,000 to more than 1.3 million. Railroads sought farmers from other states and from foreign countries to settle on their lands, and they were successful. In the thirty years ending in 1900 over 9 million acres of Arkansas's forests and prairies were turned into farms. Cotton remained the major crop, but after the turn of the century rice, soybeans, fruit, livestock, and poultry became important. Railroads also gave impetus to the growth of the timber industry, rendered coal and bauxite mining profitable, and, after 1921, furnished transportation for the oil industry in south Arkansas.

The coming of the automobile in the decade before World War I found Arkansas, like most other states, unable to cope with the need for good roads and highways. It experimented with local road-building districts, failed to establish a highway system with good standards, and permitted the local districts to run up fantastic debts. The state government, assuming these district road debts on the eve of the Great Depression and issuing state bonds to fund and pay off the debts, found itself almost bankrupt by 1933. But with the aid of the federal government, especially the Reconstruction Finance Corporation, it refunded the debt and brought it within its means to pay.

The years of the Great Depression found the rural, agricultural state hard hit by falling farm prices and unemployment, especially as fewer farm workers were needed once federal crop controls became effective. Increased farm mechanization and the coming of World War II, which opened jobs to Arkansans in industrial cities of the country, resulted in an outward migration of the state's people and sharp declines in its population. This trend continued after World War II, resulting in the state government's establishing an industrial development program to bring the jobs to its displaced farm workers. By the 1960s the program brought results, so that by 1970 its population of 1,923,295 was within a few thousand of the previous largest figure of 1940 (1,949,387).

Since the 1930s, as the state has moved increasingly from a rural-agricultural economy to an urban-industrial one, its chief problems have been those of finding funds to support the state services which it is agreed should be furnished but which many are reluctant to pay taxes to support. Its fiscal difficulties result in part from the low per capita income of its citizens, the large number of welfare recipients, and the presence of large geographical areas (Ozarkia-Ouachitaia) plagued by chronic poverty. But the state's chief fiscal difficulty stems from the conservative class's unwillingness to permit a genuine reform of the tax laws. Constitutional and statutory changes that would have made tax reform feasible have been rejected in recent years.

Arkansas's population of 1,923,295 in 1970 was divided almost evenly between rural and urban dwellers. The increase in urban population followed a trend that began at the time of World War II. Whites made up about eighty percent of the population, Negroes about twenty percent, and Indians and Orientals less than one percent. Its largest cities in 1970 were LITTLE ROCK (132,483), North Little Rock (60,040), FORT SMITH (62,802), PINE BLUFF (57,389), Hot Springs (35,631), and FAYETTEVILLE (30,729). (See also HOT SPRINGS NATIONAL PARK.)

See Walter L. Brown, *Our Arkansas* (1969).—W. L. B.

Arkansas River. The Arkansas rises in central Colorado near Climax, Colorado. It flows southward for sixty miles along the Sawatch Mountains before turning toward the east near Salida, Colorado. Below this point the river has cut a trench more than 1,100 feet deep in the Precambrian granites of the Front Range of the Rockies. In this portion of its course the river tumbles precipitously through a spectacular canyon known as Royal Gorge before reaching the edge of the Great Plains near Pueblo, Colorado. It has dropped more than 6,600 feet in barely 150 miles since leaving its headwaters high in the Rockies. At Pueblo the stream is still clear and still flowing in a narrow canyon. However, it soon becomes a typically muddy, changeable stream much like most of the western tributaries of the Mississippi. It drops to an elevation of 1,300 feet at Wichita, Kansas, and meanders toward the Mississippi, descending to 698 feet at Tulsa, Oklahoma. Through the Ouachita Mountains it again flows as a clear stream in a confined valley near Fort Smith, Arkansas, thence past Little Rock at 233 feet and finally into the Mississippi River at an elevation of about 100 feet. The length of the river is 1,459 miles.

The river and its principal tributaries, the Purgatoire, Canadian, Neosho, and Cimarron rivers, drain an area of 160,645 square miles. Above Pueblo, Colorado, the terrain through which it flows varies from the tundra landscapes on the slopes of nearby Mount Elbert (14,420 feet) and Mount Lincoln (14,300 feet) to the semiarid brush-covered slopes of the Colorado Front Range. Its upper valley draws water from forested slopes around Leadville, Colorado, in a relatively broad valley. Royal Gorge, through which it flows in making its way out of the Rockies, is one of the nation's most spectacular canyons. Most of its tributaries head up on the eastern slopes of the Front Range or in the High Plains areas of Colorado and Kansas. From the eroded, undulating surface of the Great Plains the stream and its tributaries reach the Central Lowland Province and flow in broad valleys. Here the streams meander slowly along sandy floodplains when the flow is low or pour over their banks after a large storm has centered over the basin. Because of the great geographic diversity of the basin and the climatic conditions that prevail, there are great variations in the amounts of available water.

In the mountains most of the winter precipitation in the form of snow, and the melting snow in the spring, brings large volumes of water into the river. Summers

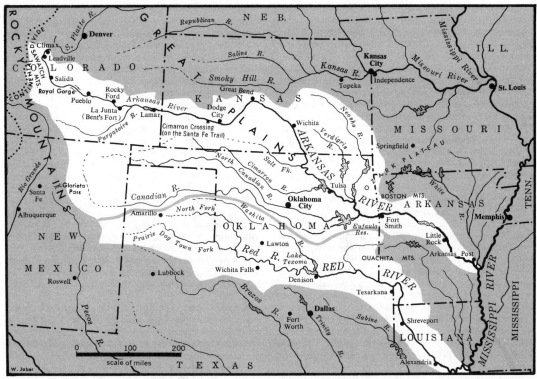

Arkansas River and Red River of the South.

are relatively dry, however, and unless thunderstorms drop their loads of moisture in the right places the streamflow is small. If summer thunderstorms are too intense or too frequent, floods occur. On an annual basis, the upper mountainous part of the basin and the lower part of the basin are well supplied with moisture, the middle portion of the river, between the Front Range and Arkansas, needs stored or supplemental water most of the time. This need has been recognized by the formulation of a river compact between the states of Colorado and Kansas, dividing the flow of the stream in those states.

The river's name is derived from that of the Indians living in the area. Though both Coronado and de Soto reached the stream in their search for wealth west of the Mississippi, we know little about the river or its basin as a consequence of their explorations. Coronado crossed the stream near the Colorado-Kansas border in the summer of 1541 and continued his search for gold on the plains of Kansas. De Soto reached it about the same time, found no gold, and moved on. The first recorded identification of the Indians and the region is that in Louis Jolliet's *Journal* (1673). The name appeared as Arkansea. The French explorers who followed gave it a number of different spellings and pronunciations. This problem persists today. It was first spelled Arkansas by Sieur Bernard La Harpe early in the eighteenth century, but Zebulon Pike in his famous journey across the Great Plains spelled it Arkansaw, and that is how it was spelled in the federal act creating the territory. This is the way the people of Arkansas and Oklahoma pro-

nounce it, but once one crosses into Kansas one finds that it is a different river—a Kansas one, named the *Ar-Kansas*. This pronunciation and spelling also holds among many Coloradans.

The early French and Spanish explorers found the Arkansas more of an impediment than an aid. Across the Plains it generally had too little water in it to be used by boats and after a severe thunderstorm was too wild to ford. Near its mouth it was navigable but, again, its flow was highly undependable. However, it was here near the mouth of the Arkansas that the first French settlement west of the Mississippi was made, in 1686 by one of La Salle's lieutenants, Henri de Tonti. His *Poste Aux Arkansas* (Arkansas Post) remained as a permanent settlement during much of the early period of settlement and today is a state park. The river was also reached by a British trader, Thomas Welch, who traveled overland from the Carolina settlements to reach the mouth of the stream. The British thought of using the Tennessee as a route to the Arkansas and thence to the Spanish settlements on the Rio Grande. Distances proved too great, but the French continued to pursue the idea of connecting their inland empire of Louisiana with the Santa Fe settlement. In the spring of 1739 Pierre and Paul Mallet finally succeeded in reaching the Spanish settlements on the Rio Grande. For a time it looked as though French-Spanish trade might develop over the route from St. Louis and the Arkansas Post, but it was not for some years that the Santa Fe trade was finally established, and then by Americans.

The first major attempt at settlement occurred in

1720 when a group of Alsatians and their slaves were brought to the vicinity of the Arkansas Post in an attempt to establish an agricultural settlement. It was abandoned a year later, and the settlers moved down the Mississippi to settle near New Orleans. It was not until after the purchase of Louisiana by the United States in 1803 that settlers began to move up the river to settle. Many of these pioneer settlers came from southern origins and brought their slaves with them to grow cotton and rice. Upstream, in the High Plains, settlement was delayed by the less desirable nature of the environment; an arid climate, rough and dissected land, and warlike Indians posed problems for individuals or small groups of settlers. However, those spearheads of American penetration of the West, the fur trappers, found their way through this country to the homes of the beaver in the mountain streams of the Rockies.

Thus, the first permanent American settlement in the basin of the Arkansas was associated with the fur trade. Bent's Fort, completed in 1833 near the juncture of the Arkansas and Purgatoire, was one of the most sturdy trading posts in the West. Its adobe walls were seven feet thick at the base, reached a height of fifteen feet, and were topped by lookout posts thirty feet tall, strong enough to resist even the most ferocious Pawnee or Comanche raids. After the 1840s the streams were trapped out and beaver hats went out of style. The old mountain men turned to other pursuits, but Bent's Fort remained a way-stop for trade on the northern branch of the Santa Fe Trail and each year saw caravans of goods destined for the Mexican settlements.

The principal trade route led from Independence or Westport on the Missouri to the northernmost part of the Great Bend of the Arkansas and thence through difficult country along the north bank of the Arkansas. In this section the tributaries enter the main stream in channels cut twenty to thirty feet deep into otherwise flat terrain. Finally, at the Cimarron Crossing, four hundred miles from Independence, the wagons turned south to cross the half-mile-wide bed of the Arkansas. This was always a trying experience. From here the route lay across the Cimarron Desert, up Cimarron River, thence across the headwaters of a number of streams, and across Glorieta Pass to Santa Fe.

Troops under General Kearny marched along the Arkansas to Bent's Fort on their way to subjugate New Mexico and California in 1846. They were followed by those forty-niners taking the southern routes to the gold fields of California. In 1858 discovery of gold on the headwaters of the South Platte diverted a part of this flow up the Rocky Mountain Front to Denver, and the Pikes Peak gold and silver rush was on.

Settlement in the Arkansas basin to the east of the Rockies was fostered by the railroads and based on supplying the needs of the cattle ranchers and railroad men. Irrigational agriculture in Colorado east of the mountains dates from 1874, with the founding of the oasis of Rocky Ford watered by diversions from the Arkansas. The rangeland away from the streams supported beef cattle but was considered too dry for crops until dry-farming practices were developed about the beginning of World War I. High prices for grain led to the breaking of the grass-covered soil, bonanza wheat farming, and eventually disaster in the form of accelerated erosion. This was a part of the "dust-bowl" phenomenon, a region of farm-abandonment and poverty. The scars of mistreatment of the soil are only now beginning to disappear.

Travel along the lower Arkansas reached a peak between 1840 and 1870, when eighteen steamers plied the river as far as Little Rock. With the completion of the transcontinental railroads, river traffic began to wane. But interest in navigation on the river continues to the present, and the building of dams to control the river from Tulsa, Oklahoma, to its mouth has turned the once turbulent stream into a series of elongated lakes along which barges and pleasure craft move.

See Clyde B. Davis, *The Arkansas* (1940).—R. W. D.

Armijo, Manuel (1792?-1853). Governor, soldier, and trader. Armijo ruled as governor of New Mexico three times (1827-29, 1837-44, and 1845-46) in the turbulent period prior to the Mexican War. During his several terms he earned a reputation for dishonesty, vindictiveness, and cruelty unmatched by any of his contemporaries on the southwestern frontier. Most of his ill fame arose from accounts by Anglo-Americans who suffered harshly at his hands, and probably an unbiased study of his career would reveal him less of an ogre and despot than was usually represented by his enemies.

Armijo was born of a humble family near Albuquerque and spent his youth tending sheep. According to tradition he amassed considerable wealth through theft of livestock, and by the early 1820s was a man of some prominence. His initial term as governor, beginning in 1827, was lusterless, while his second term commenced with his seizure of power during the rebellion of 1837. In 1841 he directed operations resulting in the capture of members of the Texan-Santa Fe expedition, who sought to annex New Mexico to the Republic of Texas, for which he was decorated by the Mexican government. About the same time, Armijo became an active participant in the Santa Fe trade, using his powers of office to hurt Anglo competitors and favor friends and relatives associated with him in business. He broadened his financial interests by issuance of a number of huge land grants in which he retained a silent partnership. With the appearance of an American army in 1846, the governor made motions of defending the province, then fled south with his troops without firing a shot. For this he was charged with treason by the Mexican government, but in a trial at Mexico City he was acquitted. Later he returned to New Mexico and engaged in business and ranching until his death at Lemitar, south of Albuquerque.

Readers should consult Daniel Tyler, "Gringo Views of Governor Manuel Armijo," *New Mexico Historical Review*, vol. 45 (1970).—M. Si.

Armstrong, Moses Kimball (1832-1906). Dakota Territory politician and writer. Armstrong, a surveyor, settled in Yankton in 1859 and remained active in the politics and promotion of Dakota Territory most of his life. His letters to the Sioux City *Register* chronicled the events of the early legislatures, and as a delegate to Congress he championed the territory's interest. His book *History and Resources of Dakota, Montana, and Idaho* (1866) served as a guide to prospective territorial residents. In 1901 he published *Early Empire Builders of the Great West.*

A company of the 5th Infantry in front of its barracks at Fort Keogh, Montana, in 1877. (National Archives)

Although important in politics—he was the leader of the territorial Democratic party—Armstrong is better known for his prolific and colorful writing, which played a significant role in territorial development. He is credited as being the first literary promoter of Dakota.—D. J. T.

army on the frontier. When in September 1789 Congress legalized the regular, or standing, army inherited from the Confederation government, the authorized strength was 840 men, although only 672 were actually in service. The tiny military establishment under the supervision of the Department of War, reflected the American faith in the citizen soldier and the widespread fear of a standing army, although experience had demonstrated and would continue to demonstrate the superiority of the regular army, especially on the frontier. The American practice, however, was to authorize a standing army that was barely sufficient to meet minimum needs. In addition, the Constitution provided guarantees against military despotism by making the army responsible to both the executive and legislative branches of the government and by dividing military power between the federal government's regular army and the states' militia system. The result, therefore, was a dual military system of a professional army and a citizen soldiery.

The colonial and Revolutionary war experiences had demonstrated the limited effectiveness of the militia, but the United States continued to rely heavily on it as well as volunteer soldiers. During the colonial period the weakness of the militia system ultimately caused Great Britain to dispatch regulars to America, and it was the regular army that bore the brunt of the fighting and won the final victory against the French and their Indian allies in the French and Indian War (see COLONIAL WARS). The militia was seldom well organized, disciplined, or trained, and simply was not suitable for long offensive campaigns. Rarely were militiamen effective except when an immediate threat to their security developed. The fact that the militia reflected frontier attitudes also made it ineffective in maintaining peaceful Indian-white relations. Therefore, although the regulars were often augmented by the militia during times of crisis on the frontier and volunteer soldiers or militia manned the western posts during the Civil War, it was the regular army, tiny as it was, that provided protection for frontier settlements (see FORTS).

The regular army owed its existence to the frontier. Until the effective settlement of the West in the 1890s, at which time the census bureau announced the end of the frontier, its duties were largely determined by western needs rather than by foreign dangers. In 1789 the United States not only faced Indian opposition, especially in the Old Northwest, but also had to maintain its sovereignty in the vast unsettled territory acquired in the Treaty of Paris in 1783. Spain to the south and Great Britain to the north exercised influence over the Indians, and, in addition, the British still occupied military posts on American soil.

Regardless of the wisdom or justice of United States Indian policy in the Ohio country (see INDIAN-WHITE RELATIONS: *United States Indian policy, 1775-1860*), the army was entrusted with the execution of this policy (see INDIAN WARS: 1789-1865) and in so doing suffered two major reverses. The first expedition of the fledgling army was in 1790, when General Josiah HARMAR led an expedition of 1,453 men (320 regulars) against the Ohio tribes. It resulted in a series of defeats and only encouraged the Indians. In 1791 Arthur ST. CLAIR attempted to conquer the same tribes. His mixed force of regulars and militia suffered a disastrous defeat in which some 900 men were killed and wounded. Congress reacted to this defeat by increasing the army, and President George Washington appointed General "Mad" Anthony WAYNE to command. Wayne raised a force of regulars and militia, trained and disciplined them, and defeated the Indians at FALLEN TIMBERS on August 20, 1794. As a result, most of Ohio was ceded to the Americans.

While the army continued to play an important role in protecting the lives and property of travelers and settlers on the frontier, it also was constructive in the development of the West. President Thomas JEFFERSON desired a utilitarian army led by intelligent and educated officers. The United States Military Academy at West Point, New York, founded in 1802 during Jefferson's administration, became the leading institution of engineering and scientific education in the United States. Jefferson set the army to work building roads and exploring the interior of the continent, tasks that engaged the army throughout most of the nineteenth century.

The LEWIS AND CLARK EXPEDITION, dispatched by Jefferson in 1803, was a military expedition that brought back a wealth of knowledge about the area and the inhabitants included in the Louisiana Purchase. Other army officers also explored the West. In 1805 General James Wilkinson sent young Lieutenant Zebulon PIKE up the Mississippi to explore and counteract British influence among the Indians. In 1806, when relations between the United States and Spain were tense, Pike was sent to explore the southern boundary of the Louisiana Purchase. Pike, an ineffective explorer who was captured and then released by the Spanish, was but one of several men active along the border.

During the WAR OF 1812 the army suffered a number of reverses in the West as Mackinac, Fort Dearborn, Detroit, and other posts fell to the British and Indians. TECUMSEH, a Shawnee chief whose followers had been defeated by Governor William H. HARRISON at TIPPECANOE in 1811, provided dynamic leadership until his death at the battle of the THAMES in 1813. In the South, volunteers under Andrew JACKSON defeated the hostile Creek at HORSESHOE BEND in March 1814 and won a remarkable victory over the British at NEW ORLEANS in January 1815, ending the war on a successful note. American setbacks in the West, however, led to changes in the American defense system, especially under Secretary of War John C. CALHOUN (1817-25).

Calhoun formulated a far-reaching defense policy for the western frontier by which a chain of forts well beyond the frontier settlements would watch over the Indians and counteract British influence among the tribes of the upper Missouri. Calhoun's proposals, however, were not carried out, and the Yellowstone expedition was halted by Congress. As a result, the scientific party under Major Stephen H. LONG was sent to explore the Platte, Arkansas, and Red rivers in 1820. The expedition wrote reports of the Great Plains, calling it the Great American Desert.

Probably the most famous army explorer of the period was John C. FREMONT of the Corps of TOPOGRAPHICAL ENGINEERS, which was created in 1838 and whose guiding force was Colonel John James ABERT. Frémont's 1842 and 1843 expeditions attracted national attention and stimulated western emigration, and his controversial third expedition in 1845 took him to California, where he participated in the Bear Flag Revolt and the conquest of California. Important also were military reconnaissances by Colonel Henry Dodge, Major Stephen Watts KEARNY, and other dragoon officers during the 1830s and 1840s, and Lieutenant Abert's exploration of the Comanche country in 1845.

The army also speeded the development of the West

by making a physical attack upon the wilderness. Soldiers built forts that provided markets and often stimulated urban developments. They cut lumber, built sawmills, quarried stone, grew crops, and, above all, built roads (see NATIONAL ROADS). Indeed, they became as adept with the broadax as with the bayonet, so that Zachary Taylor complained that soldiers were more familiar with the ax, pick, saw, and trowel than with the cannon, musket, or sword. Military roads opened areas to settlement and were as important to civilians as to the army.

During the period before 1849 the military was also deeply involved in the development and implementation of federal Indian policy. The conduct of Indian affairs fell under the Department of War and the military was entrusted with the task of protecting the rights of the Indians and enforcing the Trade and Intercourse Acts. Neither task was crowned with success, however, largely because Congress refused to take the necessary steps to ensure enforcement of these laws. The Bureau of Indian Affairs, created in 1832, remained under the secretary of war until transferred to the newly created Department of the Interior in 1849 (see INDIAN AFFAIRS, BUREAU OF). This divided jurisdiction between the War and Interior departments caused bitter controversy until the 1890s. The military was also responsible for removing the eastern tribes to the West after the passage of the Removal Act in 1830, and this policy contributed greatly to the BLACK HAWK WAR in 1832 and the second SEMINOLE WAR (1835-42). Both conflicts stimulated the debate over the relative merits of regulars and volunteers, but neither war glamorized soldiering in the wilderness.

Army life was unattractive to most Americans, and observers frequently commented on the low intelligence, loose morals, and habitual drunkenness of enlisted men. A private's pay was $5 a month and rose to $8 a month by the time of the Mexican War. Salary did little to attract quality recruits; in addition, discipline was extremely harsh and frontier life was hard. As a result, the army relied heavily on aliens. In the 1840s some forty-seven percent of the recruits were immigrants, and many could not speak English. Those conditions that hindered recruitment also caused high desertion rates. Desertion totaled about one half of the enlistments in 1825 and 1826 and equaled about one quarter of the strength of the army in 1831. Conditions were little better for officers, for in 1842 a second lieutenant received only $42 a month, and prospects for promotion were dismal. Resignations by officers were all too common.

The regular army grew slowly over the years, numbering only about 6,000 officers and men during the 1820s. Army strength grew to 12,449 in 1837 during the height of the Seminole War, but during times of crisis, such as the Seminole War and the Black Hawk War, the government relied heavily upon volunteers. In 1845, on the eve of the Mexican War, the regular army totaled only 8,509 officers and men. In 1846 the army was still largely armed with flintlock weapons, but it had begun to adapt to new conditions with the use of mounted troops in 1832. The experience of infantrymen who escorted freight wagon trains along the Santa Fe Trail, a practice that began intermittently in 1829, and demands from western states and territories brought the establishment of the First Dragoons in 1833. They became the symbol of American authority in the trans-Mississippi West.

Following the Mexican War in 1848 the army was reduced to approximately its prewar size (10,744 in 1849). Nevertheless, it was responsible for the maintenance of peace and American sovereignty in the vast area acquired from Mexico and also in the Oregon country, where a boundary settlement had recently been reached. Despite the necessity of protecting the forty-niners seeking gold, the unwelcome task of dealing with civil disturbances in Kansas, and the exigencies of the Mormon War in 1857-58 (see LATTER-DAY SAINTS: BRIGHAM YOUNG PERIOD), the army remained small. It attained a maximum size of only 17,678 in 1858 and numbered only 16,215 on the eve of the Civil War. Manpower limitations, however, did not restrict military activity in the West, and the accomplishments of the army, especially under the energetic Secretary of War Jefferson Davis, were remarkable.

In addition to occupying the newly acquired territory and conducting expeditions against tribes throughout the West, the army was associated with the Mexican boundary survey (see BOUNDARY COMMISSIONS) and continued its exploration and road-building activities. The discovery of new routes, especially in the Southwest, became a primary objective of the Topographical Corps. Captain Randolph Barnes MARCY and Lieutenant James Simpson traversed the Canadian River route from Arkansas to New Mexico, and Marcy investigated the country between El Paso and Fort Smith, Arkansas, while Simpson remained to explore the Navaho country. Captain Lorenzo Sitgreaves was active in the Southwest; Lieutenant Nathaniel Michler and others worked in Texas; Lieutenant George Derby explored the San Joaquin valley and the lower Colorado River; and Captain William Warner investigated northern California. Lieutenant Gouverneur Kemble WARREN and Captain William Raynolds (see RAYNOLDS EXPEDITION) conducted the most important surveys on the northern Plains. Road building, a task shared with the Department of the Interior, was also important, and the Topographical Corps constructed thirty-four separate roads in the West between 1850 and 1860, while assisting in the work on others. Artesian wells were also dug in the Southwest. Secretary of War Davis' interest in western transportation can also be seen in the CAMEL EXPERIMENT, which was terminated by the sectional crisis despite its apparent success, and by his interest in TRANSCONTINENTAL RAILROAD SURVEY. Under the provisions of the Pacific Railroad Survey Act of 1853 four routes were investigated: the 47-49th parallel by Isaac I. Stevens, the 38th parallel by Captain John W. Gunnison, the 35th parallel by Lieutenant Amiel W. Whipple, and the 32nd parallel by Lieutenant John G. Parke and Captain John Pope. Again, however, the sectional crisis negated their efforts.

With the outbreak of the CIVIL WAR the regulars were withdrawn from the frontier. Volunteer and militia troops manned the posts, guarded the roads, turned back the Confederate invasion of New Mexico, and battled Confederates and bushwackers in Missouri, Arkansas, Kansas, and Indian Territory. It was also the volunteers who confronted the western tribes as hostilities developed during the latter years of the Civil War. The

Galvanized Yankees, Confederates who agreed to serve on the frontier rather than remain in Union prisons, also served on the northern Plains. The volunteer regiments varied greatly in quality. Some regiments, such as the California troops in New Mexico, were well disciplined and fought hard; others fled at the first sight of the enemy; still others were guilty of atrocities against the Indians (soldiers stationed along the Oregon Trail used passing Indians as targets for artillery practice). The SAND CREEK MASSACRE, an attack by Colorado Volunteers under Colonel John Chivington against a Cheyenne village in 1864, shocked the nation with its brutality and caused damaging retaliatory attacks by the Indians.

Although the size of frontier army commands during the Civil War was determined by the needs of the Union army, the western army was, nevertheless, larger than ever before. About 4,200 men, for example, were available for a campaign against the Sioux in 1864. Problems increased, however, in 1865. Although the end of the Civil War released thousands of men for service in the West, they had no desire to fight Indians, and hundreds deserted. Others demanded their discharge, and entire regiments mutinied. As a result, the massive POWDER RIVER INDIAN EXPEDITION of 1865 against the Sioux and Cheyenne Indians ended in failure.

Following the Civil War the army again faced west, and although the rapid growth of western settlement intensified hostilities with the Indians, the army was reduced abruptly to about 57,000 men in 1866, about 37,000 in 1869-70, and between 24,000 and 29,000 from 1871 and 1890. The postwar army did include four Negro regiments—two cavalry and two infantry—which served continuously in the West. The "buffalo soldiers" of the ninth and tenth Cavalry in particular compiled excellent records in the Indian campaigns (see NEGROES ON THE FRONTIER).

The army guarded settlements, roads, survey parties, and railroad construction crews; campaigned against Indians and attempted to protect the tribes in Indian Territory from the activities of the "Boomers," settlers who tried to occupy land there in the 1880s; continued to explore the trans-Mississippi West and Alaska; and administered Yellowstone National Park, created in 1872. The primary task of the army, however, was the maintenance of peace on the frontier. Conflict was inevitable because of demands for the Indians' land, and although many officers were humane men with a concern for the welfare of the Indians, soldiers were representatives of Anglo-American culture and reflected the prevailing view that the Indians could not block the advance of American civilization. The period from 1865 to 1890, therefore, was an era of conflict that saw the final defeat of the western tribes (see INDIAN-WHITE RELATIONS: *United States Indian policy, 1860-present* and INDIAN WARS: *1865-1891*). Indian fighting was difficult and frustrating, and both the cavalry and infantry found the lack of mobility a major hindrance in guerrilla warfare. As one soldier wrote, in a campaign against Indians "the front is all around, and the rear is nowhere." Army dealings with the Indians pleased neither aggressive westerners nor eastern humanitarians; as General William T. Sherman remarked, the army "gets the cuffs from both sides."

Attached to each of the western military departments

were engineers who accompanied military expeditions, led exploring parties, surveyed routes for new roads, and compiled maps of the region. The army also sponsored major surveys such as those of Lieutenant George WHEELER and Clarence KING. The King survey, which took several years, covered the fortieth parallel from California to the Great Plains. In 1874 Lieutenant Colonel George Armstrong CUSTER also led a reconnaissance of the Black Hills, which stimulated the gold rush and increased the difficulties with the Sioux. Except for Alaska, major military explorations terminated in 1879 with the consolidation of western surveys under King, director of the United States Geological Survey.

The enlisted man's life had improved little by 1865. Discipline was harsh; rations were often inedible (bread baked and dated in 1861 was issued to troops in 1867); venereal disease was prevalent and drunkenness common; weapons were often inferior to those in the hands of the Indians (the army did not adopt a magazine rifle as standard issue until 1892); and the pay was terrible (a private's salary was $13 a month, although it had been $16 a month during the Civil War). Soldiers deserted in wholesale numbers (about one-third of the army deserted in 1871) despite serious efforts to solve this problem. Many men, however, devoted most of their adult lives to the army.

By the 1890s and the end of the frontier, the army had accomplished the tasks the nation had set before it. The Indian tribes had been defeated. The West had been explored and settled and had become an integrated part of the nation. The army that had faced westward and dealt with internal problems soon would enter a new era as the United States became more active in the world arena.

See William Goetzmann, *Exploration and Empire* (1966); Francis Paul Prucha, *Sword of the Republic* (1969); Robert Utley, *Frontiersmen in Blue* (1967), and *Frontier Regulars* (1973); and Russell Weigley, *A History of the United States Army* (1968).—R. N. E.

army territorial commands. Beginning in 1813 the United States Army was organized on a territorial basis. The nation was divided into geographical units, variously called divisions, departments, and districts. Each territorial command had a headquarters with a commanding officer and staff and had supervision over the army forts and operational units within its area.

The boundaries of the commands and the terminology used to designate the areas changed frequently. Not only were there periodic rearrangements of the whole system, but there were also additional changes in the boundaries of the commands. The shuffling and reshuffling of the geographical divisions within which the army operated during its frontier activities in the nineteenth century is indicated in the following summary form.

March 19, 1813, to May 17, 1815

On March 19, 1813, the United States was divided into nine military districts.

Military District No. 1—Massachusetts and New Hampshire. Military District No. 2—Rhode Island and Connecticut. Military District No. 3—New York from the sea to the Highlands on the Hudson River near West Point and New Jersey. Military District No. 4—Pennsylvania from its eastern limits to the Alleghenies and Delaware. Military District No. 5—Maryland and

Virginia. Military District No. 6—North Carolina, South Carolina, and Georgia. Military District No. 7—Tennessee, Louisiana, and Mississippi Territory. Military District No. 8—Kentucky, Ohio, and Indiana, Illinois, Michigan, and Missouri territories. Military District No. 9—Pennsylvania from the Alleghenies to its western limit, New York north of the Highlands, and Vermont.

On July 2, 1814, an additional jurisdiction was carved out of Military District No. 5, as follows:

Military District No. 10—Maryland, District of Columbia, and Virginia between the Rappahannock and Potomac rivers.

May 17, 1815, to May 17, 1821

On May 17, 1815, the military districts were abandoned, and the country was divided into a division of the North and a Division of the South, each with subordinate military departments.

Division of the North: Military Department No. 1—New York above the Highlands and Vermont. Military Department No. 2—New Hampshire, Massachusetts, Rhode Island, and Connecticut. Military Department No. 3—New York below the Highlands and the northern counties of New Jersey. Military Department No. 4—Pennsylvania, Delaware, Maryland, and the southern counties of New Jersey. Military Department No. 5—Ohio and Michigan and Indiana territories.

Division of the South: Military Department No. 6—Virginia, North Carolina, and District of Columbia. Military Department No. 7—South Carolina and Georgia. Military Department No. 8—Louisiana and Mississippi Territory. Military Department No. 9—Tennessee, Kentucky, and Missouri and Illinois territories.

May 17, 1821, to May 19, 1837

On May 17, 1821, the Division of the North and the Division of the South were abolished and in their place was established a new twofold division of the country. A line was drawn between Cape Sable, Florida, and Fond du Lac at the western tip of Lake Superior. The Western Department embraced the area west of the line and included all of Kentucky and Tennessee. The Eastern Department embraced all of the country east of the line, except for Kentucky and Tennessee.

May 19, 1837, to July 12, 1842

On May 19, 1837, the country was divided into a Western Division and an Eastern Division by a line beginning at the mouth of the Mississippi, extending up that river to Cassville in Wisconsin Territory, and then north to the Canadian border. Each division had subordinate departments.

Western Division: Military Department No. 1—The country north of the thirty-seventh parallel and west of the Mississippi and the line drawn from Cassville north to Canada. Military Department No. 2—The country south of the thirty-seventh parallel and west of the Mississippi.

Eastern Division: Military Department No. 3—Kentucky, Tennessee, Mississippi, Louisiana east of the Mississippi, Alabama, Georgia, and Florida Territory. Military Department No. 4—North Carolina, South Carolina, and Virginia. Military Department No. 5—Maryland, Delaware, Pennsylvania, New Jersey, and New York. Military Department No. 6—Connecticut, Rhode Island, Massachusetts, New Hampshire, Vermont, and Maine. Military Department No. 7—Ohio, Michigan, Indiana, Illinois, and Wisconsin Territory east of the line dividing the two divisions.

On September 1, 1841, Military Department No. 7 was transferred from the Eastern to the Western Division, and on March 29, 1842, the part of Louisiana east of the Mississippi was transferred from the Eastern to the Western Division.

July 12, 1842, to April 20, 1844

On July 12, 1842, the Western and Eastern Divisions were discontinued, and the United States was divided into nine independent departments. The numbers of the departments in this arrangement pertained to quite different areas from those in the previous enumeration of departments.

Military Department No. 1—West Florida, Alabama, Mississippi, Louisiana, Tennessee, and Kentucky. Military Department No. 2—The country west of the Mississippi, north of Louisiana and Texas, and south of the thirty-seventh parallel. Military Department No. 3—Missouri north of the thirty-seventh parallel, Illinois, Iowa Territory, Wisconsin Territory west of the ninetieth meridian, and the Indian country north and west of the line indicated. Military Department No. 4—Indiana, Ohio, Michigan, Wisconsin Territory east of the ninetieth meridian, and the Indian country north. Military Department No. 5—Pennsylvania, New York, Vermont, New Jersey, Connecticut, and Rhode Island. Military Department No. 6—Massachusetts, New Hampshire, and Maine. Military Department No. 7—Delaware, Maryland, and Virginia. Military Department No. 8—North Carolina, South Carolina, and Georgia. Military Department No. 9—East and middle Florida.

April 20, 1844, to August 31, 1848

On April 20, 1844, the Eastern and Western Divisions were reconstituted, to be divided again by a line from Cape Sable to Fond du Lac on Lake Superior.

Military Departments Nos. 1, 2, and 3 were included in the Western Division; Military Departments Nos. 5, 6, 7, and 8 were placed in the Eastern Division; Military Departments Nos. 4 and 9 were independent.

Western Division—the country west of the Cape Sable to Fond du Lac line, embracing Wisconsin Territory west of the line, Iowa Territory, Illinois, Missouri, Kentucky, Tennessee, Arkansas, Louisiana, Mississippi, Alabama, West Florida, and the Indian country west of the Mississippi.

Eastern Division—New England, New York, New Jersey, Pennsylvania, Delaware, Maryland, Virginia, North Carolina, South Carolina, and Georgia.

Military Department No. 4—Ohio, Indiana, Michigan, and the part of Wisconsin Territory not contained in the Western Division. Military Department No. 9—East and middle Florida.

On September 14, 1845, Military Department No. 9 was discontinued, being absorbed by Military Departments Nos. 1 and 8. On June 1, 1844, Rhode Island was transferred from Military Department No. 5 to Military Department No. 6. On November 3, 1846, two new departments were created, as follows:

Military Department No. 9—To embrace so much of the Mexican Province of New Mexico as has been or may be subjected to the arms or the authority of the United States. Military Department No. 10—to consist of the

Territory of Oregon and so much of the Mexican provinces of the two Californias as has been or may be subjected to the arms or the authority of the United States.

August 31, 1848, to October 31, 1853

On August 31, 1848, a new arrangement of Eastern and Western Divisions with nine subordinate departments and two independent departments was instituted. The numbers of the departments were again thoroughly shuffled.

Eastern Division—The country east of a line drawn from Cape Sable to Fond du Lac on Lake Superior, including Indiana and Georgia, but excluding Illinois, Kentucky, and Tennessee. Military Department No. 1—New England. Military Department No. 2—Michigan, Wisconsin east of the Cape Sable to Fond du Lac line, Ohio, and Indiana. Military Department No. 3—New York, New Jersey, Pennsylvania, Delaware, and Maryland. Military Department No. 4—Virginia, North Carolina, South Carolina, Georgia, and Florida east of the Cape Sable to Fond du Lac line.

Western Division—The country west of the Cape Sable to Fond du Lac line, excluding Indiana and Georgia, but including Illinois, Kentucky, and Tennessee.

Military Department No. 5—Alabama, Louisiana, Mississippi, Tennessee, Kentucky, and Florida west of the Cape Sable to Fond du Lac line. Military Department No. 6—Wisconsin west of the Cape Sable to Fond du Lac line, Iowa, Illinois, and Missouri north of the thirty-seventh parallel. Military Department No. 7—The country west of the Mississippi, south of the thirty-seventh parallel, and north of Louisiana and Texas. Military Department No. 8—That part of Texas south and east of a line drawn from a point on the Rio Grande south of El Paso, at 32 degrees north latitude, to the junction of Choctaw Creek with the Red River, and down the Red River to Arkansas. Military Department No. 9—New Mexico Territory and the country north and west of the line marking Military Department No. 8. Military Department No. 10 (independent)—California. Military Department No. 11 (independent)—Oregon Territory.

On October 10, 1848, Departments Nos. 10 and 11 were assigned to a newly created Pacific Division. The general arrangement underwent a number of modifications before it was replaced.

October 31, 1853, to the Civil War

The system of divisions and numbered departments was abandoned on October 31, 1853, and a system of departments with descriptive names was set up in its place. In this period there were no divisions; each department reported directly to the headquarters of the army.

Department of the East—The country east of the Mississippi River. Department of the West—The country west of the Mississippi River and east of the Rocky Mountains, except the Departments of Texas and New Mexico. Department of Texas—Texas south of the thirty-third parallel. Department of New Mexico—New Mexico Territory east of the 110th meridian. Department of the Pacific—The Country west of the Rocky Mountains, except Utah Territory and the Department of New Mexico.

This simple division into five departments was soon changed, both by the creation of new departments carved out of the original ones, and by repeated changes in the boundaries between the various departments. Changes in the department arrangement were as follows:

Department of Florida created (March 27, 1856)—Florida except that part west of the Chattahoochee and Apalachicola rivers. Department of Utah created (January 1, 1858)—Utah Territory. Department of the Platte created (March 27, 1858)—The line of communication to the west through Nebraska Territory. Department of Florida discontinued August 1,1858)—Merged into the Department of the East. Department of California created (September 13, 1858)—The country west of the Rocky Mountains and south of Oregon and Washington territories, including the Rogue River and Umpqua districts, and excluding Utah east of the 117th meridian and New Mexico east of the 110th. Department of Oregon created (September 13, 1858)—Oregon and Washington territories, except Rogue River and Umpqua districts. Department of the Platte discontinued (May 16, 1859)—Merged into the Department of the West. Department of the Pacific revived (January 15, 1861)—Formed by the consolidation of the Departments of California and Oregon.

Civil War Period

The Civil War upset the normal military command situation. Although the frontier areas still presented serious defense problems and special arrangements had to be made to provide for crises—for example, the creation of a separate Department of the Northwest as a result of the Sioux outbreak of 1862—most of the additions and changes in the territorial departments had to do with the war against the Confederacy. There were ninety changes between April 1861 and the rearrangement of divisions and departments that took place in August 1866.

August 6, 1866, to July 3, 1891

On August 6 and 11, 1866, a new organization of territorial commands was established, reflecting in part the post-Civil War needs in the South and East and in part the frontier situation in the West. The arrangement originally consisted of two divisions with subordinate departments and seven independent departments.

Division of the Missouri: Department of Arkansas—Arkansas and Indian Territory. Department of the Missouri—Missouri, Kansas, and New Mexico and Colorado territories. Department of the Platte—Iowa and the territories of Nebraska, Utah, Dakota west of the 104th meridian (which became the Territory of Wyoming on July 25, 1868), and so much of Montana as lay contiguous to the road from Fort Laramie to Virginia City. Department of Dakota—Minnesota, Dakota Territory east of the 104th meridian, and Montana Territory, except that part contiguous to the road from Fort Laramie to Virginia City.

Division of the Pacific: Department of California—California, Nevada, and Arizona Territory. Department of the Columbia—Oregon and the territories of Washington and Idaho.

Department of the East—New England, New York, New Jersey, and Pennsylvania. Department of the Gulf—Florida, Louisiana, and Texas. Department of the Lakes—Ohio, Michigan, Indiana, Illinois, and Wisconsin. Department of the Potomac—Virginia, except the counties of Alexandria and Fairfax, and West Vir-

ginia. Department of the South—North Carolina and South Carolina. Department of the Tennessee—Kentucky, Tennessee, Georgia, Alabama, and Mississippi. Department of Washington—Delaware, Maryland, District of Columbia, and Alexandria and Fairfax counties of Virginia.

This general setup continued through the period, but with a good many variations as new divisions and departments were created. There were also numerous minor changes, sometimes no more than the switch of a single post from one department to another for convenience of administration. On March 11 and 12, 1867, the departments of the Gulf, Potomac, South, Tennessee, and Arkansas were discontinued. The areas belonging to the discontinued departments were reconstituted into five military districts established for Reconstruction purposes and a new Department of the Cumberland. The military districts, however, were soon abandoned and replaced by the reconstitution of old departments or the erection of new ones.

Aside from the military occupation of the South, the focus of attention after the Civil War was on the Indian regions of the West. Here, as in the East, there were many changes in the organization and boundaries of the territorial commands. In addition to the Departments of the Missouri, the Platte, Dakota, California, and the Columbia, which continued in existence throughout the whole period, the following new departments were created.

Department of Alaska—Established on March 18, 1868, and discontinued on July 1, 1870, merging into the Department of the Columbia. Department of Texas—Established on March 31, 1870 (Louisiana and Texas). Department of Arizona—Established on April 15, 1870 (Arizona Territory and California south of a line from the northwest corner of Arizona to Point Conception). Department of Arkansas—Reestablished from December 18, 1880, to May 6, 1881 (Arkansas, Louisiana, and Indian Territory), then merged into the Departments of the Missouri and of the South.

July 3, 1891, to March 11, 1898

On July 3, 1891, the remaining military divisions (Atlantic, Missouri, and Pacific) were discontinued. The following military departments were retained, the commanders of which reported directly to the major general commanding the army.

Department of the East—New England, New York, New Jersey, Pennsylvania, Ohio, Delaware, Maryland, Virginia, West Virginia, North Carolina, South Carolina, Georgia, Florida, Louisiana, Mississippi, Alabama, Kentucky, Tennessee, and the District of Columbia. Department of the Missouri—Michigan, Wisconsin, Indiana, Illinois, Missouri, Kansas, Arkansas, Indian Territory, and Oklahoma Territory. Department of the Platte—Iowa, Nebraska, Colorado, South Dakota south of the forty-fourth parallel, Wyoming (except Fort Yellowstone), Idaho east of a line formed by the extension of the western boundary of Utah to the northeastern boundary of Idaho, and Utah Territory. Department of Dakota—Minnesota, North Dakota, South Dakota north of the forty-fourth parallel, and Fort Yellowstone, Wyoming. Department of Texas—Texas. Department of California—California north of the thirty-fifth parallel and Nevada. Department of Arizona—Arizona and New Mexico territories and California south of the thirty-fifth parallel. Department of the Columbia—Oregon, Washington, Idaho west of a line formed by the extension of the western boundary of Utah to the northeastern boundary of Idaho, and Alaska Territory.

On June 30, 1893, the Department of Colorado was created (Colorado and the territories of Arizona, New Mexico, and Utah), and the Department of California gained the part of the state south of the thirty-fifth parallel. The Department of Arizona was thus discontinued, being absorbed by the Departments of Colorado and California. On July 20, 1895, the Department of the Platte gained the part of South Dakota lying between the forty-fourth and forty-fifth parallels west of the Missouri River. By that time the frontier aspects of the territorial commands were over.

A complete listing of changes in territorial commands with references to the pertinent military orders is in Raphael P. Thian, *Notes Illustrating the Military Geography of the United States* (1881). A manuscript revision of this work, which carries the data to 1904, is in Record Group 94 of the National Archives.—F. P. P.

Arrington, Leonard J. (1917-   ). Historian. Born in Twin Falls, Idaho, Arrington spent his youth in the Rocky Mountain area, where he received much of his schooling. He attended the University of Idaho and the University of North Carolina. During World War II he worked for the federal Office of Price Administration as a price analyst and in 1946 joined the economics department at Utah State University in Logan.

During these years Arrington's interests shifted to western economic history. By 1958 he had completed a massive and comprehensive work on Mormon economic development to 1900, *Great Basin Kingdom: An Economic History of the Latter-day Saints, 1870-1900.* This study, an analysis of the Mormon church's varied business ventures (from irrigation projects to general stores), established Arrington as a foremost authority not only on Mormon history but on the history of economic growth in the trans-Mississippi West.

During the 1960s Arrington and his students pioneered in exploring aspects of western economic expansion in the twentieth century. Among the short monographs they published were *The Richest Hole on Earth: a History of the Bingham Copper Mine* (1963), *The Changing Economic Structure of the Mountain West, 1850-1950* (1963), and *Federally Financed Industrial Plants Constructed in Utah during World War II* (1969).

Arrington was also a popular teacher and lecturer; he was a Fulbright professor in Italy during 1958-59, and a visiting professor at the University of California at Los Angeles in 1966-67. An active participant in professional organizations, Arrington served as president of the Western History Association from 1968 until 1969 and as president of the Agricultural History Society in 1970.—G. D. N.

Arthur, Gabriel (fl. second half of seventeenth century). Explorer. Arthur, a Virginia indentured servant of trader Abraham Wood, was sent with James Needham in 1662 to explore the western Indian country south of the headwaters of the James River. They wandered up the Yadkin valley where Needham was murdered by an Occaneechi Indian known as "John," who had been hired to secure safe passage through the tribes. Arthur was taken prisoner and just barely es-

caped burning at the stake. He was taken by his captors, perhaps Catawba, southward into Spanish country, and then back through Cumberland Gap in 1674 to visit the Moneton Indians on the Kanawha River. Arthur was captured by the Shawnee near the mouth of the Scioto, but was released to return home on the promise that he would send traders to the Shawnee. Perhaps Arthur was the first white man to see Cumberland Gap.

See Clarence W. Alvord and Lee Bidgood, *The First Explorations of the Trans-Allegheny Region by Virginians, 1650-1674* (1912); and W. E. Connelley and E. M. Coulter, *History of Kentucky*, vol. I (1922).—T. D. C.

Articles of Confederation. Western land problems played a decisive role in the adoption of the Articles of Confederation and were a major concern of the Confederation government throughout its brief existence (1781-89). When Congress presented the articles to the state legislatures in November 1777, they contained extremely modest proposals for the creation of a national government for the United States. The Confederation was to have sovereignty over foreign and Indian affairs, the currency, the waging of war and the making of peace, the settlement of disputes between the various states, the postal system, and a system of standard weights and measures. The states, each of which had a single equal vote in Congress, retained for themselves their "sovereignty, freedom and independence, and every power, jurisdiction and right" not clearly delegated to the Confederation Congress. This meant that since the Confederation could not tax the states and could not regulate foreign commerce, it had to depend for the most part upon money contributions from the states as its chief source of funds.

The articles also declared that the United States had no right to deprive any state of its western lands, a proviso that almost prevented the new government from coming into being. The landless states of Maryland, Pennsylvania, New Jersey, and Delaware argued that the efforts of all the states during the Revolution had secured the western region between the Alleghenies and the Mississippi for the nation rather than for particular states and that, thus, all states should benefit from the disposal of this vast western resource. Maryland's argument sounded patriotic, but it was prompted by speculators who stood to gain if Congress assumed control of western lands.

Those states whose original charters gave them "sea-to-sea" claims to western lands—Massachusetts, Connecticut, Virginia, North and South Carolina, and Georgia—naturally opposed the Maryland view. The problem was further complicated by the fact that many of the landed states' claims overlapped or conflicted with those of land companies or powerful individuals. For example, the area of present-day West Virginia was claimed by the Indiana Company (one of whose shareholders happened to be the governor of Maryland), on the basis of a grant the company had received from the Six Nations at the Treaty of Fort Stanwix in 1768, and by the Ohio Company, many of whose members came from Virginia. If Virginia's charter claim were valid, the Ohio Company stood a better chance than the Indiana Company of having its claim validated.

Resolution of the conflict was not easy. Maryland refused to ratify the articles until the major western land claimant, Virginia, agreed to give up her lands north of the Ohio. In 1781, at the prodding of Thomas Jefferson, Virginia finally did so, but with the understanding that the region would be divided into states and admitted to the union. Yet the question was far from resolved, for Virginia also insisted that it would not cede its lands unless all land purchases from Indians in the region were considered void, an obvious strike at the land companies and speculators of the landless states. Virginia and the companies struggled over the issue in Congress for three years before the Virginians won out. They won in part because the Confederation was badly in need of the revenue that it could get from the sale of lands. Revolutionary soldiers were also waiting to be paid for their services, either in cash or in land warrants, and settlers wanted some military protection and form of government on the frontier to protect them from the Indians. Meanwhile, other states followed Virginia's example: between 1781 and 1802, when Georgia finally ceded her western lands, all other states relinquished their western claims.

Having become the owner of a national domain, the problems of how to dispose of it and how to govern it remained. Congress's answer came in a series of notable acts: the Ordinance of 1784 (see TERRITORIAL SYSTEM), drafted by Jefferson, proposed to create republican states in the West and to admit them into the union on an equal basis with the original thirteen. Jefferson's ordinance was never enacted but its principles were later included in the NORTHWEST ORDINANCE of 1787, which established a territorial system of government over western holdings. Another ordinance, passed in 1785, provided for the survey and sale of public lands (see LAND POLICY: 1780-1896). The procedures formulated by Congress between 1784 and 1787 for settling and governing new territories continued to be used with success throughout America's history of expansion.

Other frontier and western problems continued to plague Congress. Great Britain refused to give up her posts in the Old Northwest, violating the spirit, if not the letter, of the Treaty of Paris (see PARIS, TREATY OF, 1783). Furthermore, Congress was unable to make the states cooperate in the collection of British debts. On the southwestern frontier Spain made a concerted effort throughout the Confederation period to force the United States to give up Kentucky and Tennessee. When Spain closed New Orleans and the lower Mississippi to American commerce in 1784, prominent men in Kentucky and Tennessee—among them James Robertson, John SEVIER, and General James WILKINSON—began to consider seceding from the United States and declaring allegiance to Spain in order to better their fortunes. Meanwhile, settlers in eastern Tennessee, unsure as to whether they were under the jurisdiction of North Carolina or were part of the national domain, formed the independent state of Franklin in 1784. The new state soon succumbed, however, the victim of contending politicians who sought to rule it. In 1785-86 westerners were especially incensed by the news that John Jay, secretary for foreign affairs in the Confederation government, appeared willing to give up the use of the Mississippi for twenty-five years in return for Spain's granting of most-favored nation trading privileges to eastern merchants.

The problem of Indian relations also occupied much of the Confederation government's time. Congress was so anxious to remove the Indians from western New York and Pennsylvania and the Ohio country to facilitate white settlement that between 1784 and 1786 they sent a number of commissioners west to make treaties with the tribes. Summoned to Fort Stanwix on the New York frontier in 1784, Iroquois leaders signed over their tenuous claim to the Ohio country. Early in 1785 representatives from the Delaware, Wyandot, Chippewa, and Ottawa tribes ceded more lands when they signed the Treaty of Fort McIntosh. Before the Indian commissioners could treat with the most important tribe of all, the Ohio Shawnee, who had the most legitimate claim to the region, news of the treaties of Fort Stanwix and McIntosh sent land-hungry pioneers swarming into eastern Ohio. The Confederation government ordered General Josiah Harmar to throw the squatters out, but his efforts were not very successful. Under such conditions a treaty of cession extracted from the Shawnee at Fort Finney in 1786 proved to be a dead letter, for tribes all over the Northwest began to repudiate treaties and to demand that the Indian-white line be pushed all the way back to the Pennsylvania border. Nor were the tribes intimidated when two military expeditions, led by George Rogers Clark and Colonel Benjamin Logan, unsuccessfully tried to cow them in 1786. Aware that Indian-white relations were deteriorating, Congress created an Indian Department, modeled in part on the old British system, that same year.

In its final years the Confederation's western policy was dictated by three realities: a pressing need for hard cash from land sales, the pressure of settlers and land companies for new lands, and the inevitability of Indian hostility to white encroachment. Congress responded by surveying and opening to sale the "Seven Ranges of land which lay between the western border of Pennsylvania and the Falls of the Ohio." And when early land sales proved disappointingly small, Congress agreed to sell large tracts to speculators and land companies at bargain prices. In the summer of 1787 over six million acres of land were sold to the Ohio Company and the Scioto Company; the former was made up of New England businessmen, revolutionary officers, and an indefatigable lobbyist, Reverend Manasseh Cutler; the latter was largely the creation of William Duer, secretary of the Treasury Board, who wanted to speculate in Ohio lands. It was in response to the need of the Ohio Company settlers for a system of government that the Congress passed the Northwest Ordinance. In swift succession other companies founded settlements at Cleveland in northern Ohio and at Losantiville (soon to be Cincinnati) in southern Ohio.

As the Confederation period drew to a close, Americans were busy countering British plans to unite the Northwest tribes in a confederacy to resist American expansion. The Americans also built new forts as settlement moved along the Ohio rivers, some of these destined to be bases in the series of Indian wars that broke out in the Old Northwest in the next decade. Although hampered by limited powers and resources, the Confederation government pursued a western policy that was, despite Indian troubles and threats of defection to Spain, more effective and successful than its diplomatic and economic policies.

Stimulating discussion of these problems is found in several works by Merrill Jensen: "The Cession of the

Old Northwest," *Mississippi Valley Historical Review,* vol. 23 (June 1936); "The Creation of the National Domain," *ibid.*, vol. 26 (December 1939); *The Articles of Confederation* (1940); and *The New Nation* (1950).—E. W. K.

artists of the western surveys. Some of the nation's foremost artists participated in government-sponsored surveys of the West and contributed significantly to subsequent reports.

A majority of them were draftsmen with surveys financed by the War Department or the Department of the Interior. Others accompanied private sporting parties or traders' caravans. Samuel Seymour, an English-born scenic designer from Philadelphia, was probably the first to venture west of the Mississippi when he accompanied Major Stephen Long's expedition from Pittsburgh to the Rocky Mountains in 1819-20. His *View of the Rocky Mountains on the Platte* is considered as the earliest to have been made from firsthand observation and was one of eight sketches used to illustrate the reports of Long's expedition as compiled by botanist Edwin James in 1823.

By far the largest number of Indian pictures produced at this time are by artists commissioned by the federal government. James Otto Lewis (1799-1858) was so employed for nearly fifteen years and produced many portraits that later appeared in his *Aboriginal Portfolio.* He also produced pictures for Indian Bureau director Thomas L. McKenney's *Sketches of a Tour to the Lakes* (1827); but his efforts to follow up the initial success of his *Portfolio* with editions in New York and London proved a failure, his work largely overshadowed by that of Charles Bird KING and the reproduction of King's then-famous Washington gallery of Indian portraits in McKenney and James Hall's three-volume *History of the Indian Tribes of North America* (1837-44).

The Indian also engaged the attention of artists such as George CATLIN and Carl BODMER, whose works were acclaimed in Europe, as well as lesser-known illustrators whose acquaintance with the West was relatively brief, and pictures correspondingly few. American Alfred Jacob MILLER and European traveler Rudolph Friedrich KURZ had only passing experiences in the West, although they managed to produce important collections of paintings. Miller in particular produced a surprisingly large volume of western scenes in his later years as a result of his one excursion to the Rockies in 1837.

Several military officers stationed on the frontier managed to record their private observations in occasional sketches and watercolors. Alfred Sully (1820-79), son of portraitist Thomas Sully, left a number of views of western army life in the 1840s, as did Sergeant E. K. Thomas of Detroit, and West Point graduate Seth EASTMAN, who with explorer-artist Edward KERN furnished the illustrations for Henry R. Schoolcraft's lengthy report entitled *Statistical Information Respecting the History, Condition and Prospects of the Indian Tribes of the United States* (1851-60). Also familiar with the western wilderness were John Woodhouse Audubon, son of naturalist John James Audubon, and Titian Ramsay Peale, son of painter Charles Willson Peale. The younger Peale (1799-1885) served as artist-naturalist at the outset of Stephen Long's expedition to the upper Mississippi in 1821, and again was in the West with fellow artists Alfred T. Agate and Joseph Drayton on Charles Wilkes's expedition to the Pacific in 1838-41. Peale later settled in Washington, D. C., where he worked in the Patent Office. Although Peale never achieved the recognition accorded his more famous father or brothers, he is to be counted among those artists of the first half of the nineteenth century who viewed the vast country beyond the then-untamed frontier.

In 1853 Congress appropriated $150,000 to finance a series of exploratory surveys to discover the most practical route for a proposed transcontinental railroad. Six primary surveys were carried out between 1853 and 1854, and extensive investigations were made of the interior of the country. The several teams involved in this effort were composed of a variety of technical and scientific personnel, including surveyors, civil engineers, geologists, botanists, zoologists, astronomers, meteorologists, draftsmen, and topographers. Preliminary reports were released from time to time, and the results of all surveys were compiled and published by the government in twelve illustrated volumes between 1855 and 1861. Reproduced in these reports was the work of more than a dozen contributing artists, among them William P. Blake, Albert H. Campbell, James G. Cooper, Richard Kern, Charles Koppel, Heinrich Balduin Möllhausen, Carl Schuchard, Gustav Sohon, John Mix STANLEY, John C. Tidball, and John J. Young. Another artist, Solomon Nuñez Carvalho (1815-1894), was attached to an independent survey under John C. Frémont, who was then anxious to prove the feasibility of a central route. Frémont's reports were not published at the time, but information concerning this expedition was included in Carvalho's *Incidents of Travel and Adventure in the Far West,* published in 1859.

Tidball, Campbell, and Möllhausen (1825-1905), who had toured the West with Prince Paul of Wurttemberg in 1851, accompanied Lieutenant Henry Whipple's survey along the thirty-fifth parallel from Fort Smith, Arkansas, through Indian Territory, New Mexico, and Arizona. Koppel and Blake (1825-1910) were with R. S. Williamson's California surveys, and John Young (1830-1879) with Williamson's and H. L. Abbot's California to Oregon branch survey. Albert Campbell (1826-1899) was with Lieutenant John Parke's survey of a connecting route between Los Angeles and San Francisco, and also illustrated Parke's Fort Yuma-Rio Grande reports. Carl Schuchard (1827-1883) joined an independent extension of the Parke survey along the thirty-second parallel under the command of A. B. Gray, and thirty-two of his sketches illustrated Gray's published reports in 1856.

Richard Kern (1821-1853) went with Captain J. W. Gunnison on the central route survey out of Westport, now a suburb of Kansas City. Having earlier accompanied brothers Benjamin and Edward on Frémont's fourth expedition to the Colorado Rockies in 1848-49, Kern lost his life in a Paiute Indian attack in Utah while with the Gunnison survey. His sketches were retrieved and later prepared for publication by John Mix Stanley. Yet another artist, F. W. von Egloffstein (1824-1898), who also had been with Frémont's expedition in the fall of 1853, accompanied Lieutenant E. G. Beckwith's survey out of Salt Lake City. Egloffstein's views of that part of the country appeared in Beckwith's reports, as well as those later documenting Joseph C. Ives's survey of the Colorado River in 1858.

Governor Isaac Stevens of Washington Territory was placed in charge of surveying the proposed northern route from St. Paul, Minnesota, to Seattle. Artists Stanley, Sohon, and Cooper (1830-1902) accompanied this expedition and prepared its reports following the party's return to the East in 1854. Sohon (1825-1903) again ventured into the West in 1858-62 as an interpreter and guide for a military roadbuilding operation, returning to Washington to assist in the preparation of the reports for this latter expedition. He is considered one of the more important artists who participated in the railroad surveys, as is Möllhausen. His drawings appeared in Whipple's *Report Upon the Indian Tribes* (1855) and Ives's *Report Upon the Colorado River of the West* (1861). Möllhausen was better known as a writer of western fiction in later years.

These reports and illustrations created a great deal of political and commercial interest at the time of their publication. Meanwhile, the government turned its attention to other matters, financing additional surveys to ascertain its international boundaries with Canada and Mexico. Geological expeditions to the Rockies and to the Pacific Coast also were sponsored, and many of those who had contributed to the earlier surveys returned to the West to continue their explorations.

Among the several artists active in the government's initial border surveys was Arthur Schott (1813-1875), trained as an engineer, physician, and draftsman. Schott served as first assistant surveyor with Major William H. Emory's United States-Mexican Boundary Survey between 1849 and 1855, and prepared some 226 drawings for publication in Emory's reports. An ardent naturalist, Schott later resided in Washington, D. C., and was a frequent contributor to the Smithsonian Institution's reports 1856-66 on the Rio Grande country of Texas. He is chiefly remembered, however, for his bird prints and Indian portraits appearing in the Emory reports, issued in three volumes between 1857 and 1859. The first dealt with a general account of the survey itself, and the last two with descriptions of the botany and zoology of the regions traversed.

The first of these volumes alone featured 108 illustrations, primarily the work of Schott and John E. Weyss (1820-1903), who served for many years with western surveys under the War Department. Other artists contributing to the Emory survey were William H. Dougal, John H. Richard, Paulus Roetter, and A. de Vaudricourt, who served as head of the party traveling from Indianola to El Paso, Texas. The first volume of Emory's report, prepared under the direction of the secretary of the interior, featured several illustrations by de Vaudricourt, including a colored lithograph of "The Plaza and Church of El Paso," believed to be the earliest published view of this locale.

Initial expeditions to the Yellowstone country in 1869 and 1870 employed no professional artists or photographers. The first pictures of this area to receive national attention appeared in *Scribner's Monthly* in May and June of 1871 as woodcuts rendered largely from the imagination of Thomas MORAN, with some assistance from descriptions and rough sketches by members of these explorations. Under the sponsorship of the Northern Pacific Railroad, Moran accompanied Profes-

sor F. V. Hayden's geological survey to the Yellowstone later in 1871. Also with Hayden was Omaha photographer William Henry JACKSON.

Another artist, Henry W. Elliott, who had previously accompanied Hayden on western expeditions, was a member of the 1871 survey, along with two other photographers: J. Crissman of Bozeman, Montana, whose camera was lost over a cliff during the Yellowstone trip; and T. J. Hine of Chicago, who subsequently lost all his negatives in the Chicago fire of 1871. Sanford R. Gifford (1823-1880), landscape and portrait painter, and a National Academician since 1854, also accompanied this survey; but what he may have contributed was largely forgotten in the subsequent flurry of publicity attending the work of Jackson and Moran.

Officially and unofficially, artists continued to venture westward throughout this period. A lively sense of history-in-the-making is apparent in the pictures of those artist-correspondents who, following the completion of the transcontinental railroad in 1869, joined the influx of newspapermen and photographers to the western sectors of the nation. The government did not employ artists for its exploration of the United States-Canadian border in 1872-75, although a military draftsman by the name of Downing reputedly did some field sketches during a part of this time. At the invitation of Major J. W. Twining, chief astronomer for the United States Northern Boundary Commission, illustrator William de la Montagne CARY joined the survey party on its return to Bismarck, North Dakota, in 1874, and later produced a number of pictures based upon this experience.

Surveys to the upper Columbia River in 1881 and the Harriman Alaska expedition of 1899 employed some photographers, including Edward S. CURTISS, but the illustrations featured in the reports of these expeditions were not held to be as important as in earlier surveys. John E. Weyss, who earlier had contributed to the Emory reports, remained to the last a government survey artist, and in 1889 prepared for publication the *Report Upon United States Geographic Surveys West of the 100th Meridian* for First Lieutenant George M. Wheeler of the United States Army Corps of Engineers.

See Orrin H. Bonney and Lorraine Bonney, *Battle Drums and Geysers* (1970); John C. Ewers, *Artists of the Old West* (1965); and Robert Taft, *Artists and Illustrators of the Old West, 1850-1900* (1953).—D. C. H.

Ashley, William Henry (1778-1838). Fur trader and politician. Ashley organized the brigade-rendezvous system that established the United States fur trade in the Rockies and fostered the rise of the colorful free trapper or "mountain man" as a dominant figure in the trade. In addition, either he or his men rediscovered the South Pass, discovered Salt Lake, and opened the central overland trails to California and Oregon.

Born in Virginia, Ashley moved to Missouri shortly after the Louisiana Purchase of 1803 made that province American territory. He settled first in Ste. Genevieve but soon joined Andrew Henry in the manufacture of gunpowder and lead, two enterprises particularly profitable during the War of 1812. From the start, however, Ashley had political ambitions. He was a popular officer in the territorial and state militia and by 1822 had risen to the rank of general, a title he used for the rest of his life. When Missouri was admitted to the Union in 1821, Ashley was elected lieutenant governor.

In 1822 he and Henry advertised for a number of "enterprising young men" to undertake a fur-trading expedition to the upper Missouri. The famous party included young Jedediah Smith, Mike Fink, the almost legendary river man, and a dozen others whose explorations would soon uncover the geographic mysteries of the American West. Although Ashley and Henry succeeded in building a post (Fort Henry, later Fort Union) on the Yellowstone River, the expedition encountered the determined hostility of the Arikara Indians, who wanted to retain their role as middlemen in the river trade. The next year the Arikara not only ambushed Ashley's second expedition, but killed more than a dozen of his men. Even the punitive ARIKARA CAMPAIGN led by Colonel Henry Leavenworth later in 1823 did not succeed in opening the river.

After this fiasco Ashley decided to send two parties overland from Fort Kiowa to the Rockies, thereby avoiding the treacherous river route. This act, born of desperation, actually revolutionized the fur trade by mounting the trappers on horseback and sending them forth in small parties that would be hard to detect. At the same time the increased mobility allowed for wider ranging hunts. Andrew Henry's party traveled across present-day Nebraska and the Dakotas to reach Fort Henry on the Yellowstone. The second party, led by Jedediah Smith, went in a more westerly direction to the Black Hills and into the Wind River region. In February or March 1824 they rediscovered South Pass, the key to the central Overland Trail to California and Oregon. Equally important for the fur trade, Ashley's men discovered the fur-rich streams west of South Pass in the Green River valley.

Starting late in the fall of 1824 Ashley had to fight the snows and storms to take supplies overland by pack trains and wagons to his trappers in the mountains. (The wagons had to be abandoned in this pioneering attempt.) Arriving in April 1825, he divided his own party into small groups to explore and trap and agreed to meet them at a rendezvous on the Green River in the summer. Ashley's own party then sailed down that dangerous river in buffalo-skin boats and actually passed beyond the mouth of the Uintah River before returning to the famous first rendezvous held twenty miles north of Henry's Fork on the Green (see FUR TRADE: *in the United States*). Ashley and his men could boast that in addition to other firsts they were the first white men to navigate the Green. After attending a second rendezvous in 1826, Ashley sold out to Smith, Jackson, and Sublette and returned to St. Louis to pursue banking and mercantile interests, but he continued to furnish expeditions with supplies and to market their fur catch.

Ashley was now wealthy enough to take up politics again. Although he failed in attempts to win the governorship and to secure a seat in the United States Senate, he was elected to Congress for three terms (1831-1837), where, understandably, he defended western interests.

Unlike the rough mountain men who worked for him, Ashley was of slight build and had the manners of a Virginia gentleman. He maintained an elegant mansion in North St. Louis and enjoyed his stays in Washington, D. C. Yet, all acknowledged his bravery and leadership

in the field, and most understood that it was he who had found a way to exploit the fur trade at minimal expense through the devices of the fur brigades of free trappers, the rendezvous system, and the use of horses to penetrate the wilderness. His system also permitted a frontier town like St. Louis to supply the necessary financial backing without having to borrow from the East or Europe. Under Ashley the fur trade became a pioneer rather than a colorful enterprise from which St. Louis reaped full benefit. Again, it was Ashley's men who, in their efforts to get supplies to the mountains, pioneered the Platte River route of the Overland Trail. Meanwhile, other mountain men explored the West free of charge and found the central overland routes to California and Oregon that were to be used by pioneers in the American occupation of the West.

See Dale L. Morgan, ed., *The West of William H. Ashley* (1964).—G. B. D.

Aspen, Colorado. Mining and resort town. Once one of Colorado's most prosperous silver mining towns, Aspen is today a year-round resort, noted throughout the world for its well-equipped ski areas. The town sprang up following the discovery of silver in 1879 by prospectors from Leadville, Colorado. They ignored the threat posed by the rampaging Ute and explored the beautiful and rich mining country on the western side of the Sawatch Mountains. News of the strike soon reached Leadville, and miners poured down the Roaring Fork River to exploit the riches of the virgin mountains. Railroad men also scrambled to develop the Aspen area, and by 1888 the town was served by both the Denver and Rio Grande and the Colorado Midland railroads.

Aspen prospered throughout the 1880s, and by the end of 1892 it was the largest silver camp in the world with a population of eleven thousand. Annual silver production stood at $10 million, and the town sported electric lights, six newspapers, and a fashion-conscious elite who relished the beauty as well as the productivity of the surrounding mountains. The boom came to an end in November 1893 with the repeal of the Sherman Silver Purchase Act, which ruined the city's millionaires and sent Aspen into hibernation until it was revived as a recreation area.

During the summer, Aspen is a cultural as well as a resort center. The annual Aspen Summer Festival features prominent scholars and artists in a series of concerts, recitals, lectures, and panel discussions. The city has retained its capacity for attracting a diverse and colorful population and is as exuberantly bourgeois today as it was in the 1880s.

See Phyllis Dorset, *The New Eldorado* (1970); and Rodman Paul, *Mining Frontiers of the Far West* (1963). —R. B. W.

Assing, Norman (fl. mid-nineteenth century). Chinese leader. Assing figured prominently in the public affairs of San Francisco, although his iron-hand rule of his countrymen went mostly unnoticed by the public. In August 1850 Assing thanked the mayor of San Francisco for inviting the Chinese to the ceremonies commemorating the funeral of President Zachary Taylor. In the same year he directed the Chinese delegation in the festivities on the occasion of California's admission into the Union. During the first reported Chinese New Year celebration in the United States, in 1851, Assing gave a reception for Chinese and Americans at his home. In the Fourth of July parade of 1852 he led a large number of Chinese merchants in carriages and on horseback. The San Francisco *City Directory* of 1854 listed Assing as Chinese representative among the foreign consuls of the city. This was the only time a Chinese representative was listed until 1879, when the name of the first regular official appeared in the directory's pages.

See Gunther Barth, *Bitter Strength: A History of the Chinese in the United States, 1850-1870* (1964).—G. B.

Assiniboin Indians. The Assiniboin Indians are a Siouan tribe that formerly occupied the plains of the northern United States and Canada, centering around the valleys of the Assiniboin and Saskatchewan rivers and extending as far south as the upper Missouri River. They are believed to have originated from the Wazikute band of the Yanktonai Sioux (Dakota) some time before 1600, when the Sioux were inhabiting the region immediately west of Lake Superior. The Assiniboin spread northwestward and allied with the Algonkian Plains Cree and Ojibwa, becoming bitter enemies of their own southern relatives. In historic times the Assiniboin were typically nomadic Plains buffalo hunters, although they also harvested large amounts of wild rice from the lake regions of their country.

During the late eighteenth century the Assiniboin separated into two regional clusters: a northern group in Canada generally known as the Stoney Indians, and a southern group roaming the Montana tributaries of the Missouri. The tribe's total population in that period has been estimated as upward of 20,000, making them among the most numerous of Plains tribes. Along with their Cree associates, the Assiniboin early became middlemen for trade of white goods to tribes farther west, and the introduction of firearms into the northern Plains was generally through their hands. At the same time they warred with the very tribes with which they traded: the Blackfoot, Crow, Atsina, and Sioux. Their relations with whites, however, were uniformly friendly except for occasional isolated thefts or killings. American traders and visitors to the upper Missouri considered the Assiniboin to be the epitome of the Plains Indian, and many wrote detailed descriptions of their customs.

During the 1780s and again in the 1830s the Assiniboin were ravaged by smallpox, reducing their population to around 4,000 by 1843. In subsequent years the tribe slowly degenerated through other diseases and the effects of trade liquor. The surviving American Assiniboin were in 1885 placed on combined reservations with the Atsina and Sioux at Fort Belknap and Fort Peck, respectively. Those in Canada were gathered under the Battleford, Edmonton, and Assiniboin agencies at Moose Mountain and the Stoney Reservation. In 1960 the Assiniboin population was estimated at about 2,600 in the United States, with an approximately equal number in Canada.

See Edwin T. Denig, *Five Indian Tribes of the Upper Missouri,* ed. John C. Ewers (1961); M. S. Kennedy, ed., *The Assiniboines* (1961); and R. H. Lowie, *The Assiniboine* (1909).—P. R. M.

Astor, John Jacob (1763-1848). Fur-trade entrepreneur. Born in Waldorf, Germany, Astor migrated to Great Britain and then came to the United States in 1784 to dispose of a cargo of flutes. On the advice of a chance

John Jacob Astor. (N.Y. Public Library)

acquaintance he became interested in the fur business. After the British evacuated the Old Northwest in 1796 Astor moved into the area and also traded with the fur companies in Montreal. In 1808 he organized the AMERICAN FUR COMPANY and in 1810 the Pacific Fur Company (see FUR TRADE: *in the United States*). When the latter company's operations at Astoria at the mouth of the Columbia River failed in the War of 1812, Astor shifted his fur-trading interests to the Northwest, where in 1811 he had helped form the South West Company. He obtained control of this company in 1817 and through it came to dominate the trade of this region. Through the device of a powerful lobby, he persuaded Congress to abolish government fur posts in 1821, leaving the field open to private companies. Building upon this base, Astor opened fur-trading operations on the Plains and Rockies in 1823, establishing the Western Department of the American Fur Company. In 1826 he added Bernard Pratte of St. Louis to the American Fur Company, for although Astor's firm dominated the western trade, St. Louis interests were always hostile to Astor.

Sensing the decline of the beaver fur trade, Astor opportunely left the business in 1834 and spent his remaining years in New York City. His extensive realty investments there, plus his profits from the War of 1812 and the fur trade, made Astor the wealthiest man of his time.

See Hiram M. Chittenden, *The American Fur Trade of the Far West* (1902); and David Lavender, *The Fist in the Wilderness* (1964).—G. B. D.

Astoria. See FUR TRADE: *in the United States.*

Atchison, David Rice (1807-1886). Missouri politician. Born at Frogtown, Kentucky, Atchison attended Transylvania College in Lexington, Kentucky, and was a classmate of five others who would later serve with him in the United States Senate. Following the study and practice of law in Kentucky, Atchison moved to the Missouri frontier in 1830 and established a law office at Liberty. Among his early clients were the Mormons, who had recently been driven from their homes in Jackson County.

Following two terms in the state legislature and one as circuit judge, Atchison was appointed to the United States Senate as a Democrat in October 1843 upon the death of Lewis F. Linn. Here he continued the work of his predecessor to extend United States protection to the Oregon settlers and was one of the leaders in the unsuccessful movement for 54°40'. He did prodigious work as chairman of the Committee on Indian Affairs, upholding the treaty rights of the various tribes and attempting to see that they received fair treatment from the government.

In the late 1840s Atchison became a disciple of John C. Calhoun. Following the South Carolinian's demise, he became a leader of the southern ultras in the Senate and served as president pro tempore much of the time between 1846 and 1854. Breaking with his colleague Thomas Hart Benton over the issue of slavery extension in the territories, Atchison led the fight that resulted in Benton's defeat for reelection to the Senate in 1850.

Atchison played a major role in securing repeal of the Missouri Compromise through the Kansas-Nebraska Act and then led the struggle by Missourians to make Kansas a slave state. When this proved unsuccessful, he retired in 1857 to a farm in Clinton County.

Atchison supported the Confederacy and played a major role in securing its acceptance of the pro-southern state government of Claiborne Jackson. After the battle of Pea Ridge, he retired to Grayson County, Texas. He returned to his Clinton County farm in 1867, where he spent the remainder of his life in retirement.

The standard biography is William E. Parrish, *David Rice Atchison of Missouri: Border Politician* (1961). —W. E. P.

Atchison, Topeka and Santa Fe Railroad. The Atchison, Topeka and Santa Fe, the leading transcontinental railroad in the southwest, until 1909 was the only railroad running on its own rails all the way from Chicago to the Pacific coast. Chartered in 1859 under the leadership of Cyrus K. Holliday, it was planned to run from Topeka, in the new state of Kansas, to Santa Fe, New Mexico, the most important point in westward movement over the historic Santa Fe Trail. Construction did not begin until 1868, and despite a generous land grant Congress had voted in 1863, progress was slow. Emporia was reached in 1870; Las Animas, Colorado, in 1875; and La Junta and Pueblo, Colorado, in 1876. Announcing the inevitable celebration, a Pueblo newspaper predicted, "The biggest drunk of the present century will occur here on the 7th of March."

The Santa Fe had reached Kansas City in 1875 via a leased line. But in the railroad age the town of Santa Fe was to prove a mere backwater, for the route westward from that point was unsuitable for a railroad. The main line was run to the south of Santa Fe via Albuquerque, and the first train, operating over a branch line, did not reach Santa Fe until 1880. The search for a pass through the formidable mountains of Colorado and New Mexico brought the Santa Fe into repeated clashes with the DENVER AND RIO GRANDE WESTERN RAILROAD, especially at Raton Pass in New Mexico and in the narrow Royal Gorge of the Arkansas River in Colorado. Legal battles degenerated into bloody warfare before the issues were resolved.

The Santa Fe finally became a transcontinental railroad by cooperating with and ultimately absorbing the Atlantic and Pacific Railroad. Although it had joined with the SOUTHERN PACIFIC at Deming, New Mexico, in 1881, thus completing the nation's second transcontinental route, the Santa Fe's ambition was to form part of the originally projected thirty-fifth parallel route through northern New Mexico and Arizona. The St. Louis-San Francisco ("Frisco") Railroad had undertaken to build the Atlantic and Pacific over this route. In 1880 Thomas Nickerson of the Santa Fe agreed to construct the line (already completed from Pacific, Missouri, to Vinita, Indian Territory) from Albuquerque to the Pacific Coast in a joint venture with the Frisco. The eastern segment of the route would consist of the Santa Fe, from Albuquerque to Wichita, and the Frisco, from Wichita to St. Louis. Collis P. Huntington and Jay Gould, gaining control of the Frisco, stopped the Atlantic and Pacific in 1882 at Needles, Arizona, where a connection to the coast was made with the Southern Pacific. But the doughty people of fast-growing San Diego demanded an outlet to the East independent of the "Octopus," as the Southern Pacific was nicknamed, and built their own line to the Atlantic and Pacific at Needles and into San Bernardino, California, in 1883. The Southern Pacific, bowing to the inevitable, cooperated with the Santa Fe. Having absorbed the Atlantic and Pacific and the Frisco, the Santa Fe reached Los Angeles in 1885 and San Francisco in 1900. Meanwhile, the Santa Fe had taken over the Gulf, Colorado and Santa Fe, which built through Indian Territory (the Indians having been properly indemnified) to Galveston, Texas, in 1887.

Finding itself unable to work out what it considered an equitable division of freight with other lines at Kansas City, the Santa Fe was determined to acquire its own line to Chicago. The logical solution was to buy the Chicago and Alton Railroad—a line whose chilly, independent attitude would eventually bring it to grief—but the smug management of that highly profitable line refused to name a reasonable purchase price. The Santa Fe thereupon undertook one of the most efficient railroad building operations in history. Under a heavy cloak of secrecy to keep land acquisition costs low, the company surveyed and acquired a right-of-way from Kansas City via Fort Madison, Iowa, to Chicago, featuring long straight sections across the prairie and a bridge across the Mississippi at Fort Madison. In 1887 the first Santa Fe train rolled into Chicago.

After 1890 the Santa Fe's weak financial constitution was over-strained by bad management by both the operating executives and its New York bankers. Reorganized in 1895, the Santa Fe divested itself of the Frisco albatross, absorbed the Atlantic and Pacific except for the central division, which went with the Frisco, and entered upon an intensive development program under skilled new management, with Victor Morawetz serving as chairman and Edward P. RIPLEY as president. In the prosperous decades after reorganization the Santa Fe was virtually rebuilt; by 1908, when it opened the Belen cutoff in New Mexico and Texas, thereby acquiring an entirely new low-gradient freight line, the Santa Fe was among the nation's strongest railroads. One of the earliest to convert to diesel motive power, the road had pioneered fast, comfortable passenger service, based in no small part on the Fred Harvey organization, which operated its dining-car service and a number of luxury hotels along the route. In 1890 the Santa Fe, extending over nine thousand miles, had been the longest railroad in the world, and until the mergers of the 1960s the thirteen thousand-mile line remained the longest railroad in the United States. In 1972 it was still a strong independent railroad untouched by the merger movement, although the combination of rising costs and subsidized competition made its future uncertain.

The romantic Santa Fe has been written about and photographed frequently. Two of the best accounts of its history are James L. Marshall, *Santa Fe, the Railroad That Built an Empire* (1945); and Lawrence L. Waters, *Steel Trails to Santa Fe* (1950), an excellent, scholarly study.—A. M.

Athapaskan language. See INDIAN LANGUAGES: *Athapaskan.*

Athearn, Robert Greenleaf (1914-   ). Historian. Athearn was born in Kremlin, Montana, near Havre. As a youth he spent time on his grandfather's isolated ranch on the Missouri, vacationed in a log cabin in Glacier National Park, and watched Charles Russell paint western scenes. He recalls having experienced a West "that never really emerged from the pioneer period." After attending schools in Montana he went to the University of Minnesota, where he received his B.S. (1936) and master's (1938) degrees. He began work on his Ph.D. at Minnesota under the tutelage of the prominent western historian Ernest S. Osgood, who became his lifelong friend. After serving in the Coast Guard (1943-45), Athearn received his Ph.D. in 1947 and began his teaching career at the University of Colorado that same year. He was made a professor at Colorado in 1956.

Athearn's scholarly writings focused on Montana history, reflected in his biography of a Montana politician, *Thomas Francis Meagher: An Irish Revolutionary in America* (1949), and *Forts on the Upper Missouri* (1967); narrative and social history, as seen by contemporary travelers, in *Westward the Briton* (1953); the role of military men, in *William Tecumseh Sherman and the Settlement of the West* (1956); and railroad history. Out of the latter came *Rebel of the Rockies: The Denver and Rio Grand Western Railroad* (1960) and *Union Pacific Country* (1971), both based on extensive research in previously unavailable company records.

Athearn also published a thoughtful and highly readable general history, *High Country Empire: The High Plains and Rockies* (1960), which made the point that this portion of the West would always have a limited potential in terms of economic resources and development. He was co-author with Carl W. Ubbelohde of *Centennial Colorado* (1959); with others to produce the *American Heritage New Illustrated History of the United States.* (1963); and with Robert Riegel to revise the latter's popular text *America Moves West* (1971).

In 1954 Athearn received a Ford Foundation Fellowship and in 1960 was a Fulbright Fellow at University College, North Wales. He was president of the Western History Association in 1965. Four of his books won scholarly prizes. A witty teacher at Colorado, his course in western history was popular, and his presence made that university a strong center in western history. He has also written western novels and mysteries.

See Athearn's autobiographical essay, "A View from the High Country," *Western Historical Quarterly* (April 1971).—H. R. L.

Atherton, Gertrude (1857-1948). Novelist. Atherton, born in San Francisco, was a lifelong resident of that city. She came to authorship after the death of her husband in 1888. A prolific and successful writer, she concerned herself primarily with feminist themes and with historical novels based upon the early history of California. On her ninetieth birthday she was presented a gold medal in honor of her service to California letters by the city of San Francisco.

Time has dealt rather harshly with Atherton's reputation as a writer of fiction, and today the body of her work is relatively unknown. An unwilling prisoner within the conventions of the sentimental historical novel, she transcends the limitations of the genre only rarely, as in two excellent novels of California life, *Doomswoman* (1892) and *The Californians* (1898). Ironically, her autobiographical reminiscences—notably *Adventures of a Novelist* (1932) and *My San Francisco* (1946)—to which she turned in later life, remain the freshest of Atherton's works and the ones that the curious reader in western Americana will find most rewarding.—J. K. F.

Atherton, Lewis E. (1905-   ). Historian. Born in Bosworth, Missouri, Atherton grew up in the atmosphere of small town mid-America, which served as the subject for perhaps his best-known work, *Main Street on the Middle Border* (1954). Atherton's merchant family occupied his attention in his two earliest books: *Pioneer Merchant in Mid-America* (1939; revised and enlarged, 1971) and *The Southern Country Store, 1800-1860* (1949). Both volumes give excellent insights into the problems of these frontier entrepreneurs. Atherton's fourth book, *The Cattle Kings* (1961), is an authoritative study of the operations of cattle barons on the Texas frontier.

In 1936 Atherton joined the history department of the University of Missouri, his alma mater, and remained until his retirement in 1973. Distinguished for his teaching as well as his writing, he was honored in 1969 by former students and friends through the establishment of the Lewis Atherton Research Fund to aid doctoral candidates in history at the University of Missouri. In 1951 Atherton helped organize and served as the first director of the Western Historical Manuscripts Collection, one of the largest such bodies of materials in the Midwest, housed in the University of Missouri library. He was a Guggenheim Fellow in 1941-42 and a Newberry Library Fellow for Mid-Western Studies in 1950-51.—W. E. P.

Atkin, Edmund (1707-1761). British superintendent of southern Indian affairs, Atkin was a leading Charleston merchant, a member of the South Carolina Council, and an expert on colonial Indian affairs. In 1755, soon after the start of the French and Indian War, Atkin submitted a long report to the Board of Trade concerning the Indians in the southern colonies. In this essay he urged the British to "protect" the southern tribes from French encroachment by building a series of frontier forts and by appointing an Indian superintendent for the region. English administrators were impressed by the plan, and, although no one knew much about Atkin's ability, he became southern Indian superintendent in the spring of 1756.

But some English officials, such as Henry Fox and George Halifax, were suspicious of Atkin and noted that he seemed more eager to increase his salary than to discuss plans for the southern tribes. These doubts were well founded, for Atkin turned out to be an ineffectual administrator, indeed, fourteen months passed before he arrived at his post. Governor Dinwiddie of Virginia observed caustically that Atkin was "very slow in all his Affairs," and George Washington complained that the Indian superintendent constantly delayed sending supplies to the soldiers on the frontier. Atkin's jealousy of other officeholders and his tendency to put private business ahead of public affairs also contributed to his failure. A charitable biographer, Wilbur Jacobs, has explained that Atkin's "slow, meticulous labors in organizing his department of Indian affairs constitute a significant chapter in early frontier history, and his plan for Indian management, the first comprehensive one submitted to the Board of Trade, was an outstanding achievement."

See Wilbur Jacobs, *Indians of the Southern Colonial Frontier, The Edmund Atkin Report and Plan of 1755* (1954).—T. H. B.

Atkinson, Henry (1782-1842). Soldier. One of the most active participants in the conquest of the trans-Mississippi West, Atkinson was born in North Carolina. He entered the army in 1808 and rose rapidly through the ranks. In 1819 he was given command of the Yellowstone expedition, an ambitious plan laid out by Secretary of War John C. Calhoun, to take an army of 1,100 men to the mouth of the Yellowstone River as a warning to the Indians and British fur traders. Although the main force never proceeded past Old Council Bluffs in present-day Nebraska, exploratory parties led by Major Stephen H. LONG and Captain Matthew J. Magee were dispatched to Pikes Peak and the mouth of the Minnesota during the summer of 1820. Promoted to brigadier general in 1820, Atkinson went to St. Louis to assume command of the right wing of the Western Department.

In 1824 Congress authorized another expedition to the mouth of the Yellowstone with Atkinson and Major Benjamin O'Fallon in command. They and 476 soldiers left Council Bluffs on May 16, 1825. This expedition succeeded in reaching its objective, and General Atkinson was able to negotiate treaties with several of the Indian tribes he encountered on the journey. In October 1825 he returned to St. Louis and selected the site for Jefferson Barracks, located ten miles south of the city. The barracks subsequently became his home and base of operations.

Early in 1827 Atkinson dispatched Colonel Henry Leavenworth to choose a site for a new post on the Kansas frontier—a mission that resulted in the establishment of Fort Leavenworth. General Atkinson was in general command of the troops in the Black Hawk War of 1832 and led the fighting at Bad Axe on August 2, when the Sauk forces were almost annihilated. In 1840

he supervised the removal of the Winnebago from Wisconsin to Iowa, where Fort Atkinson was established on May 31. The remainder of his life was spent at Jefferson Barracks.

See Roger L. Nichols, *General Henry Atkinson: A Western Military Career* (1965).—R. B. W.

Atlantic and Gulf Costal Plains. See PHYSIOGRAPHY OF THE UNITED STATES.

Atlantic and Pacific Railroad. See ATCHISON, TOPEKA AND SANTA FE RAILROAD.

atomic test site. See NEVADA PROVING GROUND.

Atoy (fl. mid-nineteenth century). Prominent citizen and madam of San Francisco's Chinatown. Her style of life and her beauty made Atoy the toast of the town and earned her the title of the "Chinese Aspasia" in early San Francisco. As legal counsel for other Chinese girls, she secured the immunity of her clients against the charges of Chinese merchants by exposing in court the plaintiffs' reluctance to pay "debts of honor" and their extortion rackets to tax Chinese prostitutes. Like the Chinese merchants, Atoy took advantage of the liberating influences of the California scene and broke away from the confines of the Chinese world as she enjoyed the favor of the gold-rush society.

See Gunther Barth, *Bitter Strength: A History of the Chinese in the United States, 1850-1870* (1964).—G. B.

Atsina Indians. See GROS VENTRE OF THE PRAIRIE.

Auburn, California. Ghost town. Auburn, in Placer County, is built in three stories. At the lowest level is the site of the first gold strike, made in May 1848. Of this original site little is left today save some half-hidden foundations. On the middle level is Auburn's picturesque Old Town, one of the best-preserved ghost towns in California. Here many of the buildings from Auburn's heyday in the 1850s are preserved, including a firehouse and the office of the *Placer Herald,* founded in 1852 and one of the oldest continuously published newspapers in California. Half a mile above the Old Town lies modern Auburn, the capital of one of the largest fruit-growing and shipping areas in the West.

See Remi Nadeau, *Ghost Towns and Mining Camps of California* (1965); and Muriel S. Wolle, *The Bonanza Trail* (1953).—R. B. W.

Audubon, John James (1785-1851). Wildlife painter and naturalist. Audubon is believed to have been born at Les Cayes, Santo Domingo (now Haiti), the son of a French merchant and a Creole woman by the family name of Rabin or Rabine. Reared and educated in France, where it is said that he received some instruction in art from the celebrated Jacques Louis David, Audubon came to the United States in 1803. He settled in Louisville, Kentucky, following his marriage in 1808 to English-born Lucy Bakewell, daughter of a Pennsylvania planter. In Louisville, Audubon attempted to establish himself in business but his preoccupation with natural history dominated all other interests. Upon the failure of various commercial schemes in Kentucky, he moved in 1819 to Cincinnati, Ohio, and found employment as a taxidermist with a private museum. In 1820 he made his first excursion on the Mississippi River between Cincinnati and New Orleans to collect wildlife specimens, and from this time on he seems to have devoted himself almost exclusively to the pictorial documentation of America's native birds and animals. Influenced by an earlier association with the Scottish-

John James Audubon.

American naturalist Alexander Wilson, Audubon determined to publish engraved copies of his work. In 1826 he went to England and by the following year had obtained enough subscribers to begin production of his now famous *The Birds of America*, which upon its completion in 1838 consisted of 435 colored plates depicting 1,055 life-size figures of wild birds. William MacGillivray assisted Audubon in writing the text to accompany this folio, which appeared at Edinburgh in five volumes between 1839 and 1841 under the title *American Ornithological Biography.* During the publication of these works, Audubon divided his time between Great Britain and America, undertaking expeditions to various parts of the United States and Canada in search of additional material. In 1842 he purchased an estate on the Hudson River (now Audubon Park, New York), where he resided until his death, making one more western excursion to the headwaters of the Missouri River in 1843.

In 1844 Audubon published a smaller American edition of *The Birds of America* and also began a new work, *The Viviparous Quadrupeds of North America,* in collaboration with the Reverend John Bachman, Carolina naturalist. Its publication was begun in New York in 1845. Until he died, Audubon was assisted in this effort by his two sons, Victor Gifford Audubon and John Woodhouse Audubon. The *Quadrupeds* was completed in 1848 by John Woodhouse, younger of the brothers and an artist in his own right, who traveled to Texas and California to gather material for his father's animal folio and later married one of Bachman's daughters.

The value of the *Quadrupeds* has been overshadowed

by the enduring popularity of Audubon's *The Birds of America,* despite the fact that subsequent numerous reproductions have all but obliterated the quality of the original illustrations. American editions of either work dating from the 1840s and 1860s can be identified as the production of lithographers J. T. Bowen or Julius Bien. First-edition Havell engravings, although sometimes mistakenly referred to as Audubon "originals," are today highly prized as collector's items.

See Stanley Clisby Arthur, *Audubon: An Intimate Life of the American Woodsman* (1937); and Alice Ford, ed., *Audubon's Animals: The Quadrupeds of North America* (1951).—D. C. H.

Augusta, Treaty of (1763). The Treaty of Augusta, negotiated at the so-called Augusta Congress, was one of the most significant joint agreements in southern Indian history. The French and Indian War (1754-63) and the Cherokee War of 1759-61 had left the Indian situation dangerously unsettled on the southern colonial frontier. Consequently, the British secretary of state ordered district Indian superintendent John Stuart and the governors of Georgia and the two Carolinas to hold a congress with representatives of all the southern tribes. At issue were the reestablishment of the interrupted Indian trade, the pacification of the still restive Cherokee, Indian acceptance of British control in regions previously held by the French and Spanish, and the prevention of a general Indian war such as Pontiac was fomenting in the North. The colonial leaders also saw a chance to cultivate friendships with the Indians opposed to the troublesome Creek and to open parts of Georgia to further expansion.

At first there was contention over the meeting place. The governors wished to meet at Dorchester, South Carolina, but finally accepted Augusta, Georgia, where the congress opened on November 5, 1763. Besides superintendent Stuart, governors present were John Boone, Arthur Dobbs, and Francis Fauquier. Most prominent among the assembled Cherokee, Creek, Choctaw, Chickasaw, and Catawba were Attakullakulla, Paya Mattaha, and a Catawba chief called Colonel Ayres. A series of preliminary agreements were negotiated, and the main general treaty was concluded on November 10. Included were several boundary settlements, a system for punishing murderers, trade agreements, and an announcement of mutual trust and perpetual peace among all concerned, although there was no mention of the already existing British forts in the Indian territory. All parties involved were very pleased with the Augusta treaty, but it solved no problems permanently. The Creek remained resentful of British dominion, and regulation of Indian trade was always difficult. Still, the feared general Indian war was avoided and for a while a new attitude of Indian-white cooperation existed on the southern frontier. Five years later, in 1768, the Treaty of HARD LABOR was negotiated.

See John R. Alden, *John Stuart and the Southern Colonial Frontier 1754-75* (1944); Charles C. Royce, "Indian Land Cessions in the United States" in Bureau of American Ethnology, *Eighteenth Annual Report, 1896-97* (1899); and State of Georgia, *A Digest of the Laws of the State of Georgia* (1800).—T. D. C.

Aurora, Nevada. Ghost town. Aurora was once a prosperous silver-mining camp. It was born in August

1860 when prospectors found large deposits of silver on the nearby California-Nevada border. The discoveries at Aurora began the eastward movement of the mining frontier from California. By 1869, however, the town was well on its way to an early grave, for the mines of the Golden City of the Dawn were extremely shallow. By 1880 most of its miners had moved on to the neighboring diggings at Bodie, California.

Unlike most mining camps, Aurora was built chiefly of brick, which was shipped around the Horn via Sacramento. Today only fragments of the original buildings remain, for the bricks were too valuable to be invested in a ghost town. Many of the town's larger structures were torn down and their bricks sold in Reno.

See Nell Murbarger, *Ghosts of the Glory Trail* (1956); and Muriel S. Wolle, *The Bonanza Trail* (1953). —R. B. W.

Austin, Mary Hunter (1866-1934). Novelist and journalist. Austin wrote twenty-seven books of fiction, as well as eighty-five articles, stories, and poems published in fifty-seven leading popular magazines. Born in Carlinville, Illinois, she graduated from Blackburn College in Carlinville in 1888. Later in the year she and her family moved to the southern Joaquin valley, California, and homesteaded there.

In 1891 Mary Hunter married Stafford Wallace Austin, and both taught school. That same year her first story, "The Mother Felipe," was published by *The Overland Monthly*. It was about rural scenes and people and written with striking simplicity. Having struggled on a droughty homestead, Austin learned the importance of climate on local living conditions, especially the need for thrift. From this appreciation came the background for one of her outstanding books, *The Land of Little Rain* (1903). In *The Flock* (1906) and in her other early writings, she revealed her sensitive descriptive power and deep interest in mysticism and religion, which dominated her writing thereafter.

The Land of Journey's Ending (1924) was published the year Austin moved to her final home in Santa Fe, New Mexico. Here she wrote her memoirs and continued to write busily until her death.

See "Mary Hunter Austin, Independence, California, Centennial 1608-1968," a pamphlet published by the Mary Austin Home, Independence, California; Donald P. Ringler, "Mary Austin, Kern County Days, 1888-1892," *Southern California Quarterly* (March 1963); and J. W. Lyday, *Mary Austin,* Southwest Writers Series (1968).—B. W. A.

Austin, Moses (1761-1821). Merchant, mine owner, and colonizer. Austin was born in Durham, Connecticut. He and his brother were successful in expanding a Philadelphia general merchandising business, and, after opening a branch in Virginia, Austin moved his family there. Interested in lead mining, he obtained from the Spanish government in 1798 a league of land in Missouri on which he established a mine, smelting furnaces, and the town of Potosi. He became a prosperous and influential Missouri citizen, but the general depression following the War of 1812 brought financial ruin.

Austin considered establishing a colony in Texas. In 1820 he traveled to San Antonio de Bexar to request a land grant from the Spanish governor, was rebuffed at first, and then had his petition approved. He was notified in March 1821 that he had received 200,000 acres of Texas land on which to settle three hundred families. However, before arrangements could be completed, Austin died, and the responsibility of colonization fell to his son, Stephen.

See Eugene C. Barker, *The Life of Stephen F. Austin* (1925).—J. B. F.

Austin, Stephen Fuller (1793-1836). Colonizer. Born in Virginia, the son of merchant and colonizer Moses Austin, Austin was educated at Yale College and Transylvania University. Moving to Missouri with his family, he helped manage his father's lead-mining business, served as a militia officer, and was a member of the Missouri territorial legislature from 1814 to 1820. When his father died in 1821 before completing arrangements for an Anglo-American colony in Texas, Austin assumed the responsibility.

Austin selected a site for the colony on the lower reaches of the Colorado and Brazos rivers and negotiated terms of the contract with the Spanish governor in San Antonio. Colonists began arriving in December 1821. When the provisional government established after Mexican independence refused to recognize the Spanish grant, Austin traveled to Mexico City and, using skillful diplomacy, managed to extract a new law favorable to the colonists. The law set forth the details of the EMPRESARIO SYSTEM. Because of periodic upheavals in the Mexican government, the law was continually being altered, necessitating Austin's vigilant negotiations in behalf of the colonies. As empresario Austin was responsible for establishing a law-enforcement system and court procedure; setting up a land system with accurate surveys and recorded deeds; arranging a trade agreement with the United States; encouraging construction of schools, saw mills, and cotton mills; and attracting new settlers to the area. Because Austin received payment primarily in the form of land, he was continually short of funds to cover operational expenses.

Concerned by the increasing number of Anglo-American settlers (by 1832 approximately eight thousand people lived in Austin's colonies) and rumors of United States annexation, the Mexican government passed a law in 1830 limiting further immigration. Although Austin found a legal loophole and arranged to continue expanding his colonies, sentiment among the settlers was strong for repeal of the law, establishment of a separate state government in Texas (it was then linked to the state of Coahuila), and redress of various grievances. At the San Felipe Convention in 1833 a constitution was framed for the proposed state of Texas and Austin was presented a list of demands that he was to carry to Mexico City. President Antonio López de Santa Anna repealed the law of 1830 but refused to grant separate statehood. Austin was imprisoned in Mexico in August 1835, on suspicion of trying to incite insurrection. Upon release, he found the colonists on the verge of revolt and finally abandoned his long-held hope for an Anglo-American state within the boundaries of Mexico. When war erupted in Gonzales, Texas, on October 1, 1835, Austin was placed in command of troops attacking the Mexican forces in San Antonio. In November he was selected commissioner to the United States, a position that took him to Washington to seek United States recognition of the Republic of Texas.

Returning to Texas in June 1836, Austin was defeated in a bid for the presidency by Sam Houston. He served as secretary of state until his death.

Austin's life has been treated in a distinguished biography by Eugene C. Barker, *The Life of Stephen F. Austin, Founder of Texas, 1793-1836* (1925). Barker also edited *The Austin Papers* (1919-1926). A more recent biography is Carleton Beals, *Stephen F. Austin* (1953). —J. B. F.

Australian frontier. See FRONTIER, AUSTRALIA.

Autry, Gene. See MUSIC, WESTERN.

B

Babbitt family. Arizona pioneers. Educated in Jesuit schools and successful in grocery and hardware enterprises in Cincinnati, Ohio, the Babbitts in the early 1880s became interested in ranching in the West. They investigated possibilities in Montana and Wyoming but decided to settle at Flagstaff, Arizona, near the newly constructed Atlantic and Pacific Railroad. In 1886 David H. (1858-1929) and William (1863-1930) purchased a herd of steers, bought a 160-acre tract in neighboring Clark valley, and originated the C-O (Cincinnati, Ohio) brand. David and George (1860-1920) opened a mercantile store, while William and Charles J. (1865-1956) managed the ranching interests. By 1889 the Babbitt Brothers Trading Company had been formed. In the following decades, the firm expanded into real estate, sheep raising, ice and meat-packing plants, and bought the remnant herd of the famous Aztec Land and Cattle Company (Hashknife brand). Store branches were established along the A & P Railroad at Holbrook, Winslow, Williams, and Kingman; and Indian trading posts were started at Red Lake, Willow Springs, and Tuba City. In 1918, when the company was incorporated, the Babbitts also owned automobile dealerships in Phoenix, Tucson, and El Paso. The Babbitt brothers not only were resourceful businessmen, but also took an active interest in civic undertakings and local politics. As a Democrat, George was the first treasurer of Coconino County, mayor of Flagstaff, and a county supervisor. David also was mayor of Flagstaff; and Edward J. (1868-1943), an attorney, was probate judge and territorial legislator. In 1960 the Babbitt empire included a chain of Thriftway Supermarkets, seven Indian trading posts, four cattle ranches, and numerous other enterprises.

See James H. McClintock, *Arizona: Prehistoric, Aboriginal, Pioneer, Modern.* vol. III (1916-18); and Edward H. Peplow, *History of Arizona*, vol. III (1962).—H. P. H.

Baby Doe. See Horace Austin Warner TABOR.

Baca, Elfego (1865-1945). Gunman, deputy sheriff, and lawyer. Baca was the leading participant in one of the most sensational gunfights of the Old West. As a youth in his native Socorro County, New Mexico, he received scant formal education but learned well the hard lessons of survival on a virtually lawless frontier. In 1884 at the age of nineteen he was employed by merchant José Baca of Socorro. At that time Baca's brother-in-law, who was deputy sheriff of Frisco (now Reserve) in western New Mexico, arrived complaining of crimes committed by cowboys in his district. Most were Texans, employees of the huge J. B. Slaughter ranch. In one instance they had prankishly castrated a Mexican in a public saloon and had used another man for target practice when he tried to intervene, wounding him in four places. Indignant over the recital of these and other misdeeds, young Baca borrowed the lawman's badge and as a self-made deputy rode west to set affairs straight in Frisco.

On arrival he found the populace cowering in fear. Several cowboys were riding the streets popping at anything that moved: dogs, cats, chickens, or townspeople. When one of the rollicking crew took off Baca's hat with a well-placed shot, he was promptly arrested and the noise subsided. But on the following day eighty cowboys converged on the town to liberate their comrade and make an example of the self-styled deputy. After placing all women and children in the church, Elfego Baca stood in the open to receive his adversaries. Shooting began almost immediately and he sought cover in a small shack of poles chinked with adobe. During the ensuing siege of thirty-six hours, an estimated four thousand shots were poured into the building. Baca killed four of his attackers, wounded eight others, and himself came through unscathed. When two regular lawmen appeared, the cowboys withdrew and Baca was arrested and taken to Socorro. Later charged with murder in connection with the fight, he was tried in Albuquerque and found innocent.

The courage Baca displayed made him overnight a champion of his people and launched him on a political career that lasted for half a century. In later life he practiced law and operated a detective agency (his business card read "Discrete Shadowing Done") in Albuquerque, where he was a familiar fixture until his death.

Baca's own story was dictated to Kyle Samuel Crichton and published as *Law and Order, Ltd., The Rousing Life of Elfego Baca of New Mexico* (1928; repr. 1970). See also V. B. Beckett, *Baca's Battle* (1962); and William A. Keleher, *Memoirs, 1892-1969* (1969).—M. SI.

Bacon, Nathaniel. See BACON'S REBELLION.

Bacon's Rebellion (1676-77). Anti-colonial revolt. Bacon's Rebellion, which took place in Virginia, is one of those events that is difficult to interpret. Was young Nathaniel Bacon, the leader of the rebellion against

Virginia's imperious colonial governor, Sir William Berkeley, a "torchbearer of the Revolution," or was he a ne'er-do-well rabble-rouser who sought to vent his anger and frustration on defenseless Indians? Interpretations of the rebellion, from the time of its occurrence to the present day, have varied between these extremes.

Certain facts are not in dispute. A series of incidents along the Potomac River frontier, in which both colonists and Indians were killed, brought tensions to the ignition point in the fall of 1675. After a number of Susquehannock chiefs living north of the Potomac were murdered while under a flag of truce, by a mixed force of Virginia and Maryland militia, the Indians killed a number of planters in Virginia. The Virginia Assembly of March 1676 reacted by ordering the erection of forts and providing for rangers to cover the spaces between them. Young Nathaniel Bacon, a newly arrived planter and member of the Council of State of the colony by virtue of his family connections, expressed dissatisfaction with the actions taken by the governor and Assembly. He urged a punitive and aggressive policy against all Indians in general, in defiance of the Assembly's careful distinction between hostile and friendly Indians. When Governor Berkeley refused to authorize such a policy, Bacon raised a body of frontier planters to fight the Indians. They marched first to the island fortress of the Occaneechi Indians near the present border of Virginia and North Carolina. They were received in a friendly manner and aided, but during an ensuing controversy Bacon cut down many of the Occaneechi before withdrawing. The attack was condemned by Governor Berkeley and the Council, which attempted to prevent a reoccurrence. But while the June 1676 Assembly was writing legislation to control such unauthorized expeditions by volunteers and preparing other legislation of a reformist cast, Bacon and his men besieged the Assembly and demanded a formal commission for their leader to battle with the Indians. The intimidated Assembly acceded to the request and Berkeley, under duress, agreed. Shortly afterward, however, Berkeley denounced Bacon's commission and attempted to raise troops against him. Bacon quickly moved his force to Middle Plantation (Williamsburg) and the governor, sensing the inadequacy of his forces, retired to the eastern shore of Virginia across the Chesapeake Bay. Bacon, triumphant, drew up a "Declaration of the People" on July 30, 1676, denouncing Berkeley's administration, and then went off in search of further glory. Meanwhile, Bacon's lieutenant, Giles Bland, failed in his attempt to capture Berkeley on the eastern shore, and the governor was able to sail back across the bay and occupy Jamestown. Bacon then turned on the capital, Jamestown, with his volunteers and once again forced Berkeley to flee to the eastern shore.

On October 26, 1676, Bacon died of a disease described as the "bloody flux," and his movement began to fall apart. Berkeley returned again and soon reestablished his authority among the people. The Indian war subsided with the cessation of expeditions against them.

While Berkeley was attempting to restore order, one thousand troops under the command of Colonel Herbert Jeffreys and a royal commission of investigation, dispatched in the fall of 1676 after receipt of news of the events of the spring and summer, belatedly arrived in February 1677 to put down the reported rebellion and to investigate its causes. Now followed a comedy of errors in which the commissioners reproved Berkeley for his severity against the defeated rebels, whose grievances they now attempted to collect and redress. Berkeley vigorously protested what he regarded as an unauthorized challenge to his authority, and in May 1677 returned to England (when Jeffreys unilaterally proclaimed himself governor) to plead his case before Charles II. He died a broken man, before seeing the king, on July 9, 1677, thirty-six years after having first been appointed governor of Virginia by the king's father. Berkeley's loyal followers proved intractable to the new governor as well as to Jeffreys' successor, Thomas, Lord Culpeper. The bitterness engendered by the rebellion did not soon disappear.

Wilcomb E. Washburn, *The Governor and the Rebel: A History of Bacon's Rebellion in Virginia* (1957), is a frontal assault on the "democratic reform" interpretation of the episode by Thomas Jefferson Wertenbaker, in his *Torchbearer of the Revolution: The Story of Bacon's Rebellion and Its Leader* (1940). Interpretations have swung between these two poles, with textbooks sometimes uncertain as to which "authority" to follow. Wesley Frank Craven, *The Southern Colonies in the Seventeenth Century, 1607-1689* (1949) and *The Colonies in Transition, 1660-1713* (1968), contain the best brief accounts of the rebellion.—W. E. W.

Badin, Stephen T. (1768-1853). Roman Catholic missionary. An *émigré* from France, Badin was the first priest ordained in the United States (1793). He was vicar-general for the Old West from Kentucky to Michigan from 1793 to 1811 and worked with the Potawatomi Indians. He is buried at Notre Dame University.

See J. H. Schauinger, *Stephen T. Badin* (1956).—R. I. B.

Bahía, La. See NUESTRA SENORA DEL ESPIRITU SANTO DE ZUNIGA.

Bailey, Margaret Jewett (c. 1812-1882). Pioneer and writer. Bailey was born in Saugus, Massachusetts, as Margaret Jewett Smith. Most of what is known of her life comes from her transparently autobiographical *Grains, or Passages in the Life of Ruth Rover with Occasional Pictures of Oregon, Natural and Moral* (1854), the first novel printed on the Pacific Slope.

In 1837 she severed her engagement to a gentleman of Boston to join a ship's party that had been organized to reinforce Jason Lee's Oregon Methodist mission to the Indians. While on the long voyage to the Pacific Northwest Coast she alienated the Reverend David Leslie, leader of the group, by lecturing him on his moral shortcomings and collecting what she considered to be damaging evidence to present to Jason Lee. However, Lee took Leslie's side, and Margaret was denied the status among the missionaries she thought she deserved, although she was permitted to teach for a time in the mission school.

In 1838 Smith and William H. Willson, a lay bachelor attached to the mission, became engaged, but she broke the engagement on learning that her betrothed had commitments to a lady in Boston. Willson, in retaliation, confessed that he and Smith were guilty of fornication. She vehemently denied the charge, but under pressure from Leslie, her pastor, she signed a confession that was supposed to remain secret. Later, when she had agreed to marry Dr. William J. Bailey, Leslie and Willson insisted that the doctor be told of the affair. Bailey believed her innocent, and they were married in 1839.

With the launching in February 1846 of the *Oregon Spectator* as the first newspaper on the Pacific Coast, Mrs. Bailey became a regular contributor of poetry and prose. Meanwhile, her marriage was eroding as Bailey resorted to the bottle and brooded over the question of his wife's prior chastity. She procured a divorce in 1854 and began to spill her rancor, loneliness, and despair into a novel. Published in two parts in 1854, *Ruth Rover* was greeted savagely in the Portland *Oregonian* by a reviewer, who signed himself "Squills" and made no effort to fight his antifemale prejudice. The same reviewer, commenting acridly on the second volume, proposed that the author be prosecuted under the territorial law governing indecent and obscene publication. Actually, the book deserved a fairer reception than it received. Stylistically it is on a par with popular fiction of its day, and its sensitive and candid treatment of frontier domestic life entitles it to more than mere antiquarian interest.

Margaret Bailey weathered two more unsuccessful marriages and died in poverty in Seattle.

The only known complete copy of *Ruth Rover* is in the William Robertson Coe Collection in the Yale University Library. The Oregon State Library in Salem has only Part II. For an account of the circumstances leading to the writing of Mrs. Bailey's novel, see Herbert B. Nelson, "Ruth Rover's Cup of Sorrow," *Pacific Northwest Quarterly* (July 1959).—E. R. B.

Baker, James (1818-1898). Fur trapper, guide, and pioneer. Baker typified the popular image of the rough mountain man. Tall and lean with long reddish hair and piercing eyes, he preferred a garb of moccasins and leggings to "store clothes." He drank, gambled, and spoke the mountain man's dialect. More than once he promised to "sculp" or "raise the har" of an enemy.

When Baker ran away from his childhood home in Belleville, Illinois, to trap for the American Fur Company, the fur trade was already in decline. Nevertheless, he joined the famous Oregon train of 1838, which was led by Thomas Fitzpatrick and included as one of its members John Bidwell, the California pioneer. Baker broke away from the train to trap on the Green River. After visiting his home in 1840-41, he returned to the mountains and trapped for Jim Bridger and others until 1859. During the time he was trapping among the Bannock tribes of the Shoshoni, he married an Indian princess, Flying Dawn, who is supposed to have borne him fourteen children.

Baker also served as a guide and interpreter, most notably to the Utah expedition of 1857. After General A. S. Johnston assumed command in 1858 he sent Captain Randolph Marcy on a perilous winter trip from eastern Utah over the Rockies to New Mexico for supplies and horses. Baker led the detachment through snowy passes and down to Taos. Later Baker operated a store at the Green River crossing of the Mormon Trail. When gold was discovered in the Pikes Peak region, he set up a store in Denver, built a toll bridge over Clear Creek, and ran a ranch. Then in 1865 he served as a guide and interpreter to the Ute Indian agency, impressing his superiors with his ability, his kindness, and his basic honesty.

Baker finally moved to a log home in Wyoming just north of the Colorado border, where he lived until his death. Fond of telling stories about his exploits, the battle-scarred old veteran could truthfully boast of a fight with grizzlies, an Indian ambush, drinking bouts, and the thrills of the hunt. Since many travelers and reporters interviewed him, Baker's exploits are often mentioned in accounts of the fur trade.

See Nolie Mumey, *The Life of Jim Baker, 1818-1898, Trapper, Scout, Guide and Indian Fighter* (1931). —G. B. D.

Bancroft, Hubert Howe (1832-1918). Historian and publisher. Bancroft was born and educated in Granville, Ohio. At the age of sixteen he went to Buffalo, New York, to work for his brother-in-law, a bookseller.In 1852 he went to California in charge of a shipment of books. After a few months of working in the mines, he took a job as a bookkeeper and then until 1855 was proprietor of a book and stationery store in Crescent City. In 1856 he opened the firm of H. H. Bancroft & Company, a mercantile business, in San Francisco. Increasing profits, aided by inflation during the Civil War, enabled Bancroft to expand operations, including manufacturing departments in enlarged quarters that he built in 1869-70. Having become interested in collecting books on the history of California as early as 1859, he began systematically in the 1860s to assemble the materials on the history of Mexico and western North America that ultimately became the Bancroft Library (see COLLECTORS AND COLLECTIONS OF WESTERN AMERICANA).

At first planning an encyclopedia of the Pacific states, Bancroft decided in 1871 to prepare a series of histories. A staff of assistants indexed his library, took notes, and wrote drafts of parts and whole volumes of the histories, which ultimately included *Native Races* (5 vols., 1874-75), *History of Central America* (3 vols., 1882-87), History of *Mexico* (6 vols., 1883-88), *History of the North Mexican States and Texas* (2 vols., 1884-89), *History of Arizona and New Mexico* (1889), *History of California* (7 vols., 1884-90), *History of Nevada, Colorado, and Wyoming* (1889), *History of Utah* (1889), *History of the Northwest Coast* (2 vols., 1884), *History of Oregon* (2 vols., 1886-88), *History of Washington, Idaho, and Montana* (1890), *History of British Columbia* (1887), *History of Alaska* (1886), and supplementary topical volumes on *California Pastoral* (1888), *California Inter Pocula* (1888), and *Popular Tribunals* (2 vols., 1887). He also added, in the same format, *Works of Hubert Howe Bancroft, Essays and Miscellany* (1890), and *Literary Industries* (1890). Bancroft himself wrote nearly all of the topical volumes and essays but probably no more than an aggregate of four of the thirty-three principal volumes, though he often added rhetorical flourishes. The principal authors of the western American volumes were Henry L. Oak (1844-1905), his librarian, whose work included the first five volumes on California and the volume on Arizona and New Mexico; and Frances Fuller VICTOR, who wrote the volumes on Oregon, Washington, Idaho, Montana, Nevada, Colorado, and Wyoming, as well as parts of other volumes.

Dispatching a corps of salesmen, Bancroft sold by subscription more than six thousand sets of the thirty-nine-volume work. He also sold by subscription the seven-volume *Chronicles of the Builders of the Commonwealth . . .* (1891-92); furthermore, the subjects of the biographical sketches in it, which amounted to more than two fifths of the set, paid substantial subsidies to Bancroft. Bancroft continued in business, using the name Bancroft Company after fire destroyed his business building in 1886, until 1898. He continued to write on historical and contemporary topics after selling his library to the University of California in 1905.

Helped by solicited testimonials that he distributed in a vigorous promotional campaign, Bancroft received generally favorable reviews. Although he paid fulsome compliments to subscribers, he antagonized partisans of the Bear Flaggers of California and the Protestant missionaries of Oregon. The Society of California Pioneers canceled his honorary membership in 1894. Both Oak and Mrs. Victor protested because he had failed to acknowledge their authorships; Oak published a general indictment of Bancroft's methods and a response to Bancroft's account of them in his *"Literary Industries" in a New Light* . . . (1893).

Organized chronologically and prodigiously detailed, most of Bancroft's histories have been important for reference on matters of fact rather than popular as narrative, despite contemporary praise of him—Wendell Phillips called him "the Macaulay of the West." They remain indispensable authorities on most parts of the Far West; subsequent research confirmed some of the more controversial judgments. Bancroft was less antiquarian than many of his successors, extending his narrative closer to the present and taking vigorous interest in contemporary developments. He was a pioneer in the use of interviews and newspapers, but his failure to consult archives in Spain, Mexico, and the West Indies limited his work on Mexico.

John W. Caughey, *Hubert Howe Bancroft, Historian of the West* (1946), supersedes all previous work. Henry R. Wagner, ed., "Albert Little Bancroft: His Diaries . . . ," *California Historical Society Quarterly*, vol. 29 (1950), presents material on Bancroft's business affairs. See also Harry Clark, *A Venture in History: The Production, Publication, and Sale of the Works of Hubert Howe Bancroft* (1973).—E. P.

Bandelier, Adolph Francis Alphonse (1840-1914). Anthropologist and historian. Bandelier, the founder of anthropology in the Southwest as a scientific discipline, was born in Berne, Switzerland. Although he later made much of his European origins and insisted on the French pronunciation of his last name, Bandelier was raised in the midwestern farming community of Highland, Illinois. In spite of the fact that he had little formal schooling, he read his way—in four languages—into becoming the principal scholar of the native cultures of New Spain and of the Spanish conquest.

Bandelier's interests and expertise brought him into contact with Lewis Henry MORGAN, a wealthy New York attorney whose own immediate interests lay in Iroquois studies. Morgan was also the leading exponent of the idea of unilineal cultural evolution. It was under Morgan's influence and the auspices of the Archaeological Institute of America that Bandelier arrived in Santa Fe, New Mexico, in 1882. He surveyed the archaeological ruins of Pecos and plunged into a study of church archives. He also got himself thrown out of Santo Domingo Pueblo by the Indian village governor, who objected to his questions on esoteric matters.

Bandelier spent more than a decade working in New

Mexico and Arizona. This resulted in a 1,400-page manuscript written for Pope Leo XIII on the history of northern Mexican and New Mexican missions, published in 1969 as *A History of the Southwest*; a novel on Pueblo Indian life, *The Delight Makers* (1890); the *Final Report of Investigations among the Indians of the Southwestern United States* (1890-92); and voluminous journals only now being published (1966 and 1970). *Historical Documents Relating to New Mexico, Nueva Viscaya and Approaches Thereto, to 1773,* collected by Bandelier and his wife and edited by Charles Hackett, was published in three volumes in 1923-37.

Bandelier might also be thought of as the founding father of ethnohistory. *Upstreaming* and *ethnographic analogy,* two terms he never used, are modern concepts revealed in his assertion that "to proceed from the known to the unknown, step by step, is not always sure to yield striking results very rapidly, but it is certain to yield *positive* results." In working with living peoples, documents, and archaeological remains as a single exercise, Bandelier was truly a pioneer in his time.

See Bernard L. Fontana, "A Dedication to the Memory of Adolph F. A. Bandelier, 1840-1914," *Arizona and the West,* vol. 2 (1960); and Leslie A. White, *Pioneers in American Anthropology: The Bandelier-Morgan Letters, 1873-1883* (1940).—B. L. F.

banking and currency. Westerners "on the make," and not uncommonly in debt as they sought to develop farms or establish newspapers, law practices, or real estate agencies on the frontier, tended to have a different attitude toward banking and currency problems, creditors and usury laws, greenbacks and silver, from that of people in older and better established communities. At times this difference created a form of sectionalism, though always there were to be found easterners thoroughly in sympathy with western ideas, and westerners as "sound" in their policies as Daniel Webster himself. Sometimes southerners were aligned with the West, as on the issue of the First and Second Banks of the United States, not because these banks were "monopolistic" or because they exerted political influence, but because as strict constructionists they believed Congress did not have the power to charter them.

One of the earliest economic issues to cause sectional division within the country was the proposal to recharter the First Bank of the United States. Alexander Hamilton had persuaded Congress to establish the bank in 1791 for a twenty-year period. It had rendered considerable service to the young nation in the trying early days, but strict constructionists and others, disliking the power it exerted, prevented a renewal of its charter when it expired in 1811. Financing the War of 1812 proved to be difficult, however, without a strong central bank, and in 1816 opinion in Congress had changed sufficiently to permit the establishment of the Second Bank of the United States, likewise chartered for twenty years. Under Nicholas Biddle's able management it served a useful purpose as a central bank by exerting indirect control over the issues of state-chartered banks and at the same time providing a reasonably flexible currency and system of credit. New York City banks were antagonized by the power the Second Bank of the United States exerted over them, and western banks detested its policy of promptly presenting their notes for

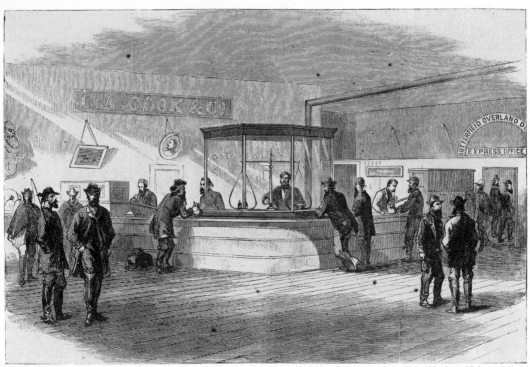

This 1866 Harper's Weekly *engraving of a banking house in Denver, Colorado, shows miners bringing in gold dust. (Library of Congress)*

redemption. Andrew Jackson and other opponents of the bank accused it of making loans for political purposes to politicians and editors, and condemned it because of the large amount of its foreign-owned stock. Because of its ability to affect the economy of the country by expanding or contracting credit, the bank was regarded as too powerful. In Jackson's rhetorical words, the bank was a "monster" that threatened democratic government. Though there was much support for the bank, even from such westerners as Henry CLAY, its reluctance to hold the notes of western state banks and its Whiggish views made it unpopular. Congress voted to recharter it in 1832, but President Jackson vetoed the move and the bank, after a short period of operation under Pennsylvania law, had to close because of bad management.

Government sales of land in the West and resales by absentee investors of land that had earlier been acquired for speculation tended to strip the new states and territories of a circulating medium. Federal annuities and other payments to Indians for their land cessions and expenditures in the territories for surveying, military operations, and the salaries of public officials offset this tendency only slightly. Barter and exchange of labor were common, but the West wanted some generally acceptable medium of exchange and experimented with state banking laws that permitted stockholders and directors of banks to make their subscriptions for stock in the form of mortgages on their property instead of in money. The note issues of these banks were excessive, and their gold reserves were minimal. Large loans were

made to officers of banks on little or no security, and loans were made to customers on property just acquired at $1.25 an acre but valued at $5.00 to $10.00 an acre. Land speculation rather than development seemed to be the objective of the borrowers. In three successive periods, 1817-19, 1834-37, and 1849-57, there occurred this "wildcat" banking, urged on by the craze to purchase land whether one had capital to develop it or simply to carry the investment for a time, and a willingness to push government at different levels into costly internal improvements that would take long years to liquidate. The wildcat banking and craze for land speculation in the 1830s was accelerated by Jackson's deposits of federal money in the state-chartered "pet banks," by John C. Calhoun's Deposit Act of 1836 by which excess federal funds would be distributed among the states in accordance with population, by huge expenditures for internal improvements with funds from abroad, and by the removal of restraints on the issue of bank paper previously exercised by the Second Bank.

Western attitudes toward land speculators and banks were ambivalent. Eastern banks and absentee speculators in land were looked upon unfavorably, while local residents who owned large tracts and improved them were tolerated, even favored. Local banks were preferred, but outside capital was welcomed if it went into financing internal improvements or the building of cities. The West experimented with usury laws, with laws against alien ownership of property, with occupancy laws that placed absentee owners at a disadvantage in litigation with occupants having some color of title, and with suspension of payments on and even repudiation of public debts—which were largely held in the East or abroad. Though western states favored government aid for building railroads, they later sought to regulate the lines and to lower their rates.

During the Civil War the United States suspended specie payments and issued a large quantity of paper dollars known as greenbacks. Until 1879 it was off the gold standard. Silver was demonetized in 1873 as a result of its scarcity.

In the post-Civil War period of deflation when agricultural prices fell, western farmers, faced with mortgage debts they could not pay and fearing the loss of their property through foreclosure, opposed the return to the gold standard and the withdrawal of the greenbacks from circulation, which would mean further deflation. Some channeled their discontent in the ELECTION OF 1868 and later through the GREENBACK PARTY; others urged the remonetization of silver (see SILVER ISSUE). Again, in the 1880s and 1890s, the West sought relief from the declining price level of their commodities through an enlarged silver purchase program and in 1896 called for the free and unlimited purchase of silver by the government to restore the earlier ratio of silver to gold at sixteen to one.

The West's role in American political life was growing but the section did not always act as a unit. By the mid-1840s, Ohio, once a center of radical reform, had become so well developed that it frequently voted with the East against its sister states in the West, and, in the 1890s, Illinois, Wisconsin, and Iowa—where the Granger movement had centered two decades earlier—favored hard money. Despite this tendency for the older public land states to become assimilated to the eastern point of view, the West scored notable reforms. Congress had lowered the price of land to $1.25 an acre and in 1862 it offered free land under the Homestead Act. Western states had experimented with the regulation of railroads and the establishment of maximum rates by state railroad commissions, and when these measures were stripped of their effectiveness by federal court decisions the western states were then influential in securing the beginning of federal regulation by the Interstate Commerce Act of 1887. They secured the adoption of the Bland-Allison Act of 1878 and the Sherman Silver Purchase Act of 1890 under which large purchases of silver were made by the Treasury, though these measures did little to reverse the deflation under way at the time. The West contributed to the movement for the Sherman Anti-Trust Act of 1890. These and other measures were obtained partly because the West, disillusioned with old-line parties, had given support to the Granger movement and the Greenback and Populist parties. When conditions began to improve and the prices of major western commodities recovered, these political movements subsided and westerners retreated into the old parties with which they had earlier been affiliated.

In the twentieth century the mining states of the West, particularly Nevada, continued to favor silver-purchasing by the government during periods of deflation. They were responsible for the passing in 1933 and 1934 of a number of measures authorizing and finally requiring unlimited government purchasing of silver.

The policy did little to bring about inflation and was an expensive subsidy to the silver mining industry.

See Bray Hammond, *Banks and Politics in America* (1957), on the banking question; and Fred A. Shannon, *The Farmer's Last Frontier, Agriculture, 1860-1897* (1945), and Chester McArthur Destler, *American Radicalism* (1945), on agrarianism.—P. W. G.

Bank of America (California). See Amadeo Peter GIANNINI.

Bannack, Montana. Ghost town. Bannack was the site of the first significant gold strike in Montana. During the summer of 1862 a party of prospectors on their way from Colorado to Idaho stopped to pan Grasshopper Creek and made the discovery that touched off Montana's first gold rush. A year later, the handful of miners' log cabins had grown into a town of more than three thousand residents. Most notable of Bannack's early citizens was Henry PLUMMER, who managed to serve both as chief law enforcement agent for the town and as the head of a gang of road agents and murderers.

When Montana Territory was created in May 1864, Bannack became its first capital. This distinction was short-lived, however, for the town lost both the seat of government and much of its population to its rapidly growing neighbor, Virginia City. Mining activity continued sporadically around the town in the late nineteenth century and was given a boost in the 1890s when dredges began to tear into the bed of Grasshopper Creek. Today Bannack is a ghost town that features some well-preserved relics of the past. Chief among these are the jail built by Plummer, the Masonic Hall, the schoolhouse, and the Methodist church.

See William Carter, *Ghost Towns of the West* (1971); Nathaniel P. Langford, *Vigilante Days and Ways* (1890); Virginia R. Towle, *Vigilante Woman* (1966); and Muriel S. Wolle, *The Bonanza Trail* (1953).—R. B. W.

Bannock Indians. The Bannock Indians are a branch of the Northern Paiute who, in historic times, inhabited the southeastern corner of Idaho. They belong to the Shoshonean branch of the Uto-Aztecan linguistic group, and the tribe's history, particularly after the coming of the white man, is closely intertwined with that of the SHOSHONI INDIANS. The Bannock have persistently clung to their tribal identity though their population probably never exceeded two thousand. In the eighteenth century they acquired the horse and developed a culture much like that of the Plains Indians.

The first white men to come in contact with the Bannock were fur trappers and explorers like Jim Bridger. These men soon learned to avoid the Bannock, whom they described as a "predatory race" given to murder and thievery. The establishment of Fort Hall in 1834 brought increased white penetration into the heart of Bannock country. Subsequently, overland travel channeled thousands of emigrants through southern Idaho, impoverishing Indian pasturelands. The white man also brought disease to the Bannock, and in 1853 the tribe was decimated by smallpox.

In retaliation, Bannock warriors became the scourge of the overland trails, ranging from Fort Bridger to Humboldt Sink. In 1863 a combined force of Bannock and Shoshoni was defeated at Bear River by General Patrick Conner's California Volunteers. By 1869 the tribe had been rounded up and placed on the Fort Hall

Reservation under the provisions of the Treaty of Fort Bridger of 1868.

From 1869 to 1877 the Bannock lived a quiet existence on the reservation. The continuing encroachment of white settlement on their lands and the failure of the buffalo herds, however, produced a powderkeg of discontent which was ignited by the hysteria of Chief Joseph's NEZ PERCE WAR. What followed was the short-lived Bannock War of 1878. The rebellion was swiftly suppressed by the army under the leadership of General Oliver Otis Howard. The Bannock were returned to the reservation, where they were officially merged with the Shoshoni by the commissioner of Indian Affairs. There are still Bannock in southern Idaho, but they are no longer distinguished from the rest of the Fort Hall reservation group.

See Brigham D. Madsen, *The Bannock of Idaho* (1958).—R. B. W.

Bannon, John Francis (1905-   ). Clergyman, author, and historian of Latin America and the American Southwest. Bannon was born in St. Joseph, Missouri, "within smelling distance of the old Pony Express stables on Patee St." He grew up in Kansas City, Missouri, and entered the Society of Jesus in 1922, living for a time in Kansas, on the edge of the Great Plains. He received his B. A. (1928), M. A. (1929), and S.T.L. (1936) degrees from St. Louis University and was ordained a priest in 1935.

Bannon's early training was in medieval history and in languages. Entering the University of California for graduate work, he came under the influence of Herbert E. BOLTON and developed an interest in the Jesuit materials of the Mexican and Spanish archives. Under Bolton's direction, he wrote *The Mission Frontier in Sonora, 1621-1687* (1955).

Bannon began his teaching career as an instructor in history and Romance languages at St. Mary's College in Kansas in 1929 and moved to Regis College in Denver in 1931. After receiving his Ph.D., he returned to St. Louis University, where he taught colonial North American and Latin American history. He was made a professor in 1949 and served for eighteen years as chairman of the Department of History (1943-71).

Bannon was a visiting member of the faculty at Marquette University, the University of San Francisco, Mount St. Mary's College, the University of Colorado, the University of California at Santa Barbara, and the University of New Mexico. He served as president of the Jesuit Historical Conference (1947-48), chairman of the Conference on Latin American History (1955), and director of the Institute on Foreign Trade of the Export Managers Club of St. Louis. He was a member of the American Historical Association, the American Catholic Historical Association, the Organization of American Historians, the Catholic Commission on Intellectual and Cultural Affairs, and the Academy of American Franciscan History. In 1965-66 he was president of the Western Historical Association and, from 1962 to 1969 he was a member of its executive council.

Bannon's earliest publications were *Epitome of Western Civilization* (1942) and *Colonial North America* (1946). With Peter Masten Dunne, he coauthored *Latin America: An Historical Survey* (1947) and a two-volume *History of the Americas* (1952; rev. ed. 1963). He also wrote monographs on particular topics in Latin American history, among them *Indian Labor in the Spanish Indies* (1966). His *Bolton and the Spanish Borderlands* (1964) clarifies Bolton's historical views and contributions. His most interesting work for historians of the West is *The Spanish Borderlands Frontier* (1970), which provides a comprehensive narrative of Spanish settlement and development in the Southwest, demonstrating similarities and contrasts with the Anglo-American frontier. The borderlands frontier was, Bannon wrote, "historically on a collision course with the more aggressive and more successful Anglo-American westward movement." Bannon's book provided the background to make that collision intelligible.

In his busy career, Bannon acted as editor for *The Historical Bulletin* from 1943 to 1950 and in 1962 became editor of the American West Series. He served on the editorial boards of the *Hispanic American History Review* (1954-60) and the St. Louis Archdiocesan Bicentennial Series (1964-65). He became a member of the editorial boards of *Manuscripta* in 1957 and *Arizona and the West* in 1959.

A self-described "borderlander," Bannon was one of the most distinguished of Bolton's students. Like his mentor, he saw the American West in a larger perspective by considering Spanish and French New World experiences in conjunction with the Anglo-American experience. His work is reliably objective, balanced, scholarly, and readable.

See John Francis Bannon, "A Western Historian— How He Got that Way," *Western Historical Quarterly* vol. 1.—P. L. N.

Baptists. The "people called Baptists" emerged as a recognizable group in the period of the Reformation. They appeared in the German states but principally in the British Isles in the seventeenth century. Certain basic principles rather than formal organizations united the Baptists. They accepted the Scriptures as the expression of Divine and inerrant truth and the norm both of faith and practice. They affirmed the competency of the individual under God in all matters of religion and refrained from elaborate ritualism in public worship. They rejected the infant baptism of the Church of England and baptized by immersion only persons who had reached the age when they could make considered choices. Their affirmation of the responsibility of the individual person before God carried with it the principle of religious liberty. They demanded the separation of church and state and affirmed its corollary, the autonomy of the local church. They were democrats at a time when, in the stratified and hierarchical society of England, democracy was a dangerous radicalism. The basic principles unifying the people called Baptists did not impose uniformity in all theological matters. By far the larger number accepted the Calvinist teaching but some joined the ranks of the Arminian adversaries of Calvinism.

Persecution in England drove many Baptists to the American colonies. Some of those who came to New England suffered persecution at the hands of the Puritan establishment. Many of them made their homes in Rhode Island, where Roger Williams had written religious liberty into the law. In the southern colonies, where the Church of England was the established church, and especially in Virginia, many Baptists suffered persecution. During and after the American Revolution

Baptist families joined the movement of pioneers to the frontier west of the Appalachian Mountains. They left behind as a kind of anchor for a growing denomination the Philadelphia Baptist Association, which had been created by autonomous local churches in 1742 in a colony where religious liberty had prevailed from the beginning.

With the Great Revival of 1800 and the spirit of RE-VIVALISM, the advance of the Baptists west of the Appalachians got under way. The story of their progress in the lower Mississippi valley, where the denomination had great success, illustrates most of the factors that in time brought a very large church into being. As powerful Indian tribes were forced west across the Mississippi River, migrants from the eastern states south of the Mason-Dixon line moved into Kentucky (see CHURCHES, TRAVELING), Tennessee, Alabama, and Mississippi. Most were farmers, usually poor and illiterate, who sought to make a new start on the frontier. Some were planters with their slaves, fleeing the worn-out land in the old settlements and hoping to acquire fortunes through the exploitation of the rich virgin soils of the Old Southwest. Among these frontiersmen were many Baptists. Inevitably they found one another in the new settlements and organized tiny autonomous congregations that represented quite a different cultural level from that of the urban association of Philadelphia.

Usually a preacher assisted in bringing the congregation into being. Some preachers came from the eastern states, but as the decades advanced they came mostly from the frontier itself. Men of little and sometimes of no education, they preached because they believed they had a call from God. They received their ordination through a call from a local church. The Baptist preacher throughout the frontier period supported himself as a farmer, or a blacksmith, or by some other occupation. He preached on Sundays and sometimes served in successive weeks three or four congregations, which often required long journeys on horseback over primitive roads or forest trails. He preached in equally primitive log structures which struggling congregations erected as soon as they could. Reverend John Davis, for example, a soldier from the American Revolution who had wintered at Valley Forge, came to northern Alabama. He called himself "Club Ax" Davis, the metaphor suggesting the ax that roughed out the log for building before the adz gave it its final and smoother shape. He preached with a combination of ridicule, sarcasm, exhortation, denunciation, pathos, humor, and zeal. His hearers knew that he stood ready to back his words with physical force, if necessary. Club Ax Davis labored in the earliest Alabama settlements. A few decades later the Reverend Basil Manly, president of the young University of Alabama, became a tower of strength among the rapidly increasing Baptists of the state.

Dogmatism—for the great majority the dogmatism of Calvinism—characterized the faith of the frontier Baptists of the Old Southwest. Dogmatism led to disputes because of the value the denomination put on the liberty of the individual believer and of the local congregation. At one time an argument raged as to whether the Bible required or merely suggested the ritual of the footwashing of the saints. More serious was the dispute between those who would send missionaries to the heathen and unchurched frontier farther west and those who objected to the practice. The opposition insisted that God in his wisdom and providence would secure the salvation of such men as he desired; if men could not be saved, it was because God had ordained their destruction from the foundation of the world. The controversy emphasizes the fact that the primary objective of Baptist preaching was conversion and the salvation of the individual soul.

In spite of disputation the Baptists maintained an overall unity. From the beginning of the frontier advance it became the custom for a group of four or five neighboring congregations to form an association, each with its own name. The association did not possess significant authority. Its chief function was to further a sense of unity by bringing preachers and "messengers" from the member churches together for business of a limited character and by offering an opportunity for a social occasion, after the business was concluded.

About their central doctrine, baptism by total immersion, the church members did not dispute. In the Old Southwest Baptists built their churches usually beside or near streams. The baptismal ceremony in the open drew crowds, some of whom came to scoff, but most of whom came to join in the hymns and to hear the prayers of the preachers. Singing provided a most important element in the worship of the frontier church. In the early days the preachers lined out the hymns for the congregation to follow. When books became available, such as *Kentucky Harmony* and the *Sacred Harp,* singing, not only in Sunday worship but at other gatherings, became an outstanding item in the folk culture of the Old Southwest.

The anti-missionary Baptists did not prevail. Among the men of religion who carried Protestantism to the western edge of settlement, the Reverend John Mason Brown, a Baptist preacher, ranked with the greatest. After experiencing a childhood of poverty on a Connecticut farm, he was licensed to preach in 1811. In 1817 he established with James Welch the western mission in St. Louis, the old French-Spanish river town. As a missionary of the Massachusetts Baptist Missionary Society, he made his base in Illinois. For years he rode his horse constantly through Indiana, Illinois, and Missouri, keeping up with his reading as he rode. He organized Baptist churches, distributed Bibles and tracts, and kept notes on the country through which he passed. He helped to found the Rock Spring Seminary for the training of teachers and ministers. He became editor of the *Western Watchman.* Through his *Guide for Emigrants* (1831, 1836, and 1837) and *Gazetteer of Illinois* (1834), with its detailed description of the terrain of the state, Brown made a substantial contribution to the westward movement. At the time of his death in 1858, the Baptist denomination was firmly established in the upper Mississippi valley.

The desire for independence on the part of local churches in a denomination without a powerful central governing body and under a national constitution guaranteeing religious liberty caused throughout the nineteenth century the emergence of many diverse associations using the name Baptist. In 1970 fourteen organized groups had a separate existence. Most of them had small memberships. The American Baptist Association, formed in 1905, reported something more than 745,000 members. The American Baptist Convention, formerly the Northern Baptist Convention, counted a membership of just under 1,455,000. The Southern Baptist Convention, which dates from 1845, counted on its rolls in 1870 something more than 11,140,000 people.

See Sidney E. Ahlstrom, *A Religious History of the American People* (1972); O. K. Armstrong and M. M. Armstrong, *The Indomitable Baptists* (1967); W. B. Posey, *The Baptist Church in the Lower Mississippi Valley, 1776-1845* (1957); W. W. Sweet, *Religion on the American Frontier*, vol. I: *The Baptists* (1931).—R. H. G.

Baraga, Frederic (1797-1868). Catholic missionary. Born in Carniola, Austria, Baraga came to the United States in 1830 and spent four years as missionary among the Ottawa Indians of Michigan, then went to La Pointe, Madeline Island, in Lake Superior among the Ojibwa (Chippewa). He mastered the Ojibwa language and published *Practical and Theoretical Grammar of the Otchipewe Language* (1850) and *Dictionary of the Otchipewe Language* (1853). He then established L'Anse mission in the upper peninsula of Michigan in 1843 and spent the rest of his life in that region. He was made bishop in November 1853. His work is responsible for the strength of Catholicism among the Chippewa of the Lake Superior region.

See C. A. Verwyst, *Life and Labors of Bishop Baraga* (1900).—W. D. W.

Baranov, Aleksandr Andreevich (1747-1819). Manager of fur company in Alaska. Baranov was born at Kargopol, Russia, the son of a shopkeeper. At the age of fifteen he traveled to Moscow where he clerked for a German businessman, associated with foreign merchants, and by extensive reading sought to educate himself. A decade or so later, an unhappy marriage in Kargopol and wanderlust drove him to Irkutsk in Siberia. He built a glass factory and distilleries in Irkutsk, and entered the fur business with a trading post in the Anadyr country. Chukchi natives plundered his northern enterprise, forcing him into bankruptcy. At Okhotsk, he discussed his situation with Grigori Shelikhov, head of the prosperous Shelikhov-Golikov fur company with headquarters at Kodiak, Russian America. Shelikhov named Baranov the Alaskan manager of the firm, with a five-year contract containing terms that lifted the unfortunate entrepreneur out of debt.

Baranov, a stout, balding, industrious little man, sailed for Alaska in 1790. Once established at Kodiak, he introduced rigid discipline, successfully met the competition of the Lebedev-Lastochkin Company in Cook Inlet, and organized exploring and hunting expeditions in search of the valuable sea otter. The vexatious problem of supplying the distant colony he solved in part by contracting with foreign traders. Social problems within his empire were equally taxing. A contingent of churchmen, too many of whom had neither the training nor the temperament for life in a hard country, tested Baranov's patience constantly. (He had regularized but not formalized the relationships between Russian males and Indian women, and had taken a Kenaitze wife himself.) Furthermore, junior naval officers often refused to cooperate with him. And worse still, SITKA, a major post Baranov had founded, was overrun by Tlingit Indians.

That year, 1802, Baranov learned that Shelikhov's heirs had been granted a monopoly in Alaska, that he had been awarded the Order of Vladimir, appointed chief manager of the new Russian-American Company, and given shares worth 25,000 rubles. Sitka was retaken in 1804, and Fort Ross in California was established by his close associate, I. A. Kuskov, a few years later. The attempt by a Russian adventurer to extend the company's influence to the Hawaiian Islands failed. Baranov's new headquarters at Sitka (New Archangel) was soon a miniature city on the earliest northwestern American frontier. Between 1799 (the date of the monopoly charter) and 1819, Alaska exported furs valued at 35 million rubles. Baranov was relieved in 1818, after twenty-eight years of service in Russian America. He died en route home by ship and was buried at sea in the Indian Ocean.

See H.H. Bancroft, *History of Alaska* (1886); Hector Chevigny, *Russian America* (1965); K. T. Khlebinkoa, *Baranov*, trans. by C. Beame and ed. by Richard Pierce (1973); and Helen Shenitz, "Baranov, Empire Builder," *Alaska Sportsman* (July 1961).—M. B. S.

barbed wire. As the frontier farmer moved away from the forested hills of the East into the prairie plains of the West, he encountered the seemingly insurmountable problem of fencing his farm without a readily available source of timber. In the East, where trees were plentiful, the fences were made of wooden rails; in parts of New England, stone walls were patiently erected. However, when the frontier advanced onto the plains neither timber nor stones were to be found.

Faced with the fencing problem, the earliest prairie farmers simply avoided the open land—despite the fact that it was often the most fertile—and planted their fields near streams where sufficient wood could be procured for fences. By the 1870s, however, the West was filling up rapidly and the pressure on the meager fencing resources of the prairie was overwhelming. The issue became paramount in the regions where the agricultural frontier met the cattlemen's domain; they were accustomed to open range for their stock. The cattleman demanded that the farmer fence his crops against cattle, and the farmer maintained that the cattleman should assume the trouble and expense of fencing in his stock.

The Department of Agriculture came to realize that the fencing problem had made a sham of the Homestead Act of 1862, for after a farmer had fenced his land it cost almost as much as good land in a humid region. The cost of fencing in the arid Great Plains was from sixty to three hundred percent higher than in other regions. In 1871 the department released a report revealing that "for every dollar invested in livestock, another dollar is required for the construction of defenses to resist their attacks on farm production." The farmers, in self-interest, began to experiment with new fencing methods.

Of the early substitutes for wooden fencing, hedges were the most prominent. The most popular hedging material was the osage orange plant because it was readily adaptable to a variety of soils and could survive the adversities of a Great Plains winter. However, before hedging could become firmly established on the Plains it was superseded by barbed wire.

The inventor of the type of barbed wire that was ultimately adapted on a large scale was Joseph Farwell

Glidden, a farmer in De Kalb, Illinois. While attending the De Kalb county fair in 1873 with two of his neighbors, Isaac Ellwood and Jacob Haish, Glidden saw an exhibit of a type of barbed wire invented by Henry M. Rose. After some ingenious tinkering, Glidden developed an improved form of barbed wire and applied for a patent on October 27, 1873. Meanwhile Glidden's friend Haish had developed his own improvement; shortly after Glidden made his application, Haish filed for a patent and challenged the priority of Glidden's invention. The court, however, ruled in Glidden's favor, and he was granted the patent.

The important feature of Glidden's barbed wire was that its spur wires were held in place by two wires that were twisted around them. This type of wire proved to be highly effective and was readily adaptable to mass production. In 1874 Glidden began to manufacture barbed wire in De Kalb. The next year Glidden and Ellwood formed a partnership; Glidden then sold his half-interest to the Washburn & Moen Manufacturing Company of Worcester, Massachusetts, in an agreement that included the payment of $60,000 and royalties.

Washburn & Moen bought up as many of the competing patents as they could and developed the power machinery necessary to produce the wire in large quantities. Production increased from 2.84 million pounds in 1876 to 80.5 million pounds in 1880. Every man connected with the business prospered, and Washburn & Moen developed into one of the largest industrial concerns of the Gilded Age.

At first the prairie farmers were skeptical of the new fence, but its practical advantages soon made it *the* fence for the farms of the Great Plains. Barbed wire, the farmers discovered, "takes no room, exhausts no soil, shades no vegetation, is proof against high winds, makes no snowdrifts, and is both durable and cheap."

The effect of barbed wire on life in the Great Plains was momentous. Its advent was an important factor in the decline of the cattle kingdom. It brought about the disappearance of the open range and turned "range country" into "big-pasture country." With barbed-wire fences the rancher could isolate his cattle and breed the blooded stock he desired.

Barbed wire put an end to the "long drive" and gave the railroads a boost in their drive to enlist the trade of the cattlemen. Wars broke out between those who accepted the fence and those who refused to relinquish the open range. Fence-cutters were enlisted by the latter group, and the conflict raged wherever barbed wire was thrown up around previously free land and grass. Often damage was done to stock by barbed wire. A horse could cut a foot on the barbs or severely damage the tendons of the foreleg in such a way as to render him worthless. In addition, water holes sometimes were fenced in, wire was stretched across main roads, and fences built enclosing vast areas by men who did not own the land.

State legislatures soon recognized the seriousness of the situation and passed laws against fence-cutting and against the construction of fencing under certain circumstances. The no-fence men had lost the fight; with barbed wire *and* railroads, the cowboys' days were numbered.

Probably the most important positive effect of barbed wire was that it revolutionized land values and opened the Great Plains to homesteaders by providing a cheap means of fencing, which enabled the farmers to stake out free homesteads. Without barbed wire the homesteader would have been unable to protect his farm from grazing herds, and the Great Plains would have stagnated as an agricultural unit.

See Jack Glover, *"Bobbed Wire": an Illustrated Guide* (1966); Henry D. McCallum, *The Wire That Fenced the West* (1965); and Walter P. Webb, *The Great Plains* (1931).—R. B. W.

Barela, Casimiro (1847-1920). Colorado politician. Barela, born in Embudo, New Mexico, obtained his early education under Archbishop Jean Baptiste Salpointe. Moving with his family to southern Colorado in 1867, he became interested in merchandising and stock-raising enterprises. In 1871 and 1873 he was elected to the Colorado territorial House of Representatives and in 1875 was chosen a delegate to the convention that drafted the state constitution. Elected to the first state Senate in 1876, he was reelected to that office so often that he earned the nickname "The Perpetual Senator." He became a leader of the Democratic party in southern Colorado and was a strong political force in Las Animas County. For a time Barela also served as consul for Mexico and Costa Rica in Denver. Recognizing his contributions to Colorado, Barela's colleagues in the Senate passed a resolution in his honor on the occasion of his birthday in 1907 "as a testimonial of our respect and continued brotherly affection."

A biography of Barela, in Spanish, is *Cuarenta Años de Legislador* (1911), by José Fernandez. A short sketch appears in Wilbur F. Stone, ed., *History of Colorado*, vol. III (1918).—M. B.

Barnard, Kate (1874-1930). Reformer and politician. Barnard was born at Geneva, Nebraska, and raised in Oklahoma Territory, where her father had staked a claim near Newalla and practiced law in nearby Oklahoma City. Barnard's first exposure to poverty came when she was still a child, living near the Oklahoma City slums.

In 1905 she organized the United Provident Association in Oklahoma City and worked at raising funds for charity, turning her home into a center for distributing food and clothing to the poor. One of her appeals for aid to the poor brought in ten thousand garments. After this drive she clothed four hundred children, bought them books, and sent them to school. In a three-year period she provided care for three thousand destitute families and placed five hundred children in the city schools. Her dedicated work and success in succoring the poor brought her public notice across Oklahoma Territory and the Southwest. In 1906 she appeared before the Oklahoma constitutional convention, urging the delegates to adopt provisions providing for compulsory education, an eight-hour day, abolition of child labor, and creation of the office of commissioner of charities and corrections. British ambassador to the United States James Bryce commented that the Oklahoma constitution was "the finest document of human liberty written since the Declaration of Independence, and no little credit for making it such is due to the activities of a single woman—Kate Barnard."

In the first Oklahoma election in 1907 Barnard filed as a Democrat for the office of commissioner of charities and corrections and won, running ahead of her ticket by six thousand votes. She investigated jails, prisons, and asylums, commenting that "hell has reigned here twenty years undisturbed." Her findings led to substantial reform of conditions in public institutions, particularly in the area of child welfare. In one case, where Oklahoma Indian orphans had been deprived by unscrupulous guardians of estates valued at over $2 million, she prosecuted the guardians and won restoration of the property to the children.

By 1910 Barnard's success in social reform in Oklahoma had brought her national recognition. She was awarded membership in the American Academy of Social and Political Science; regularly lectured at Bryn Mawr, Columbia University, Cooper Union, and the League for Political Education; and was an American delegate to the International Prison Congress in Rome in 1911 and American delegate to the International Tuberculosis Congress in Copenhagen in 1913. One admirer commented that Barnard was a "humanitarian, politician, and stateswoman, the first woman to create a state department, write sections of the state constitution, and the first woman elected to public office in Oklahoma."—A. M. G.

Barnum, Phineas Taylor (1810-1891). Showman. Barnum, born in Bethel, Connecticut, grew up as a farm boy with a Yankee shrewdness for making money and a liking for practical jokes and hoaxes. He clerked in a store; he founded a newspaper; and in 1835 he entered show business by employing for exhibit Joice Heth, a Negro woman said to be 161 years old and to have been the nurse of the infant George Washington. Lavish use of posters and advertising put over his exhibit. He next employed two rival jugglers and traveled with them in a circus. Returning to New York in 1841, he contracted to buy Scudder's American Museum. As Barnum's American Museum, its collection of curiosities was augmented by a "lecture room," where melodramas and variety shows were given. Also on view were a model of Niagara Falls, dioramas of the Deluge and a fairy grotto, living statuary, and many other novelties.

As the museum succeeded P. T. Barnum widened his promotional activities. In Bridgeport, Connecticut, he employed Charles S. Stratton, a midget then only five years old, and dubbed him General Tom Thumb. Two years later, in 1844, Tom Thumb toured Europe and was presented to Queen Victoria, King Louis Philippe of France, and King Leopold of the Belgians. Tom Thumb proved a lasting attraction, and his marriage in 1863 to Lavinia Warren, also a midget, was an international sensation. But Barnum could promote culture as well as curiosities. In 1850 he signed Jenny Lind, "the Swedish nightingale" and the foremost singer of her day, for a series of one hundred concerts. The tour was one of Barnum's greatest successes.

At the time he was managing the Jenny Lind tour and also his American Museum, Barnum joined with Seth B. Howes in promoting a traveling show billed as Barnum's Great Asiatic Caravan, Museum, and Menagerie. He had sent an expedition to Ceylon to get ten elephants, and the show was on the road from 1851 to 1854. Barnum then sold out but retained one elephant to plow a Connecticut field—only when passenger trains came by. When a farmer challenged the drawing power of the elephant in comparison with oxen, Barnum answered that the elephant could draw the attention of twenty million Americans to his museum.

When the museum was destroyed by fire in 1865, Barnum quickly rebuilt on a larger scale. After a second disastrous fire in 1868 he decided to retire from show business, but Dan Costello and William Cameron Coup interested Barnum in organizing a large circus and menagerie. It went on the road in 1871 and became so large the following year that it was moved by railroad exclusively. His main rival was the Cooper, Bailey & Hutchinson show. When an elephant was born on their lot, the first native American elephant, Barnum offered $100,000 for it. They turned him down and used his offer in advertising. Barnum then proposed a merger. In 1881 he began his association with James A. Bailey, eventuating in the 1887 partnership in Barnum & Bailey's Greatest Show on Earth.

In 1882 Barnum bought Jumbo from the Royal Zoological Gardens, London, for $10,000. Protests by the British public added greatly to the fame of this largest of elephants (twelve feet high, fourteen feet long). A white elephant from Burma was the 1884 attraction. In the winter of 1889-90 Barnum accompanied his circus to London. He was then eighty years old.

Although Barnum's name has been retained by a circus since his death, the traveling circus was but a small part of his enterprises. He was an unsuccessful candidate for Congress but served four terms in the Connecticut legislature. Much of his fortune was spent in improvements in his hometown of Bridgeport. Speculation in a clock company resulted in bankruptcy, but he cleared all debts in 1857. He also probably owned a cattle ranch near Pueblo, Colorado. He delivered as many as seven hundred lectures on such subjects as "The Art of Money-getting" and "The Humbugs of the World" and exhibited such fakes as the "Fejee mermaid" and the Cardiff giant. While he did not connive in manufacturing humbugs, he defended their exploitation, for in bringing the public to see them they also saw his other less sensational educational exhibits. He insisted on clean and moral entertainment.

In his search for curiosities from far places Barnum did not neglect the American West, which then seemed quite as romantic and inaccessible to easterners as did the Asia of the Siamese twins or the Africa of the hippopotamus, an animal first shown in America by Barnum. Many of his exhibitions were precursory of Buffalo Bill's Wild West show, the rodeo, and the western of stage, film, fiction, and television. One of his first displays at his museum was a band of Indians from Iowa doing war dances and other ceremonies. In 1843 a herd of buffalo was exhibited at the celebration of the completion of Bunker Hill Monument. Barnum brought the herd to Hoboken, New Jersey, and advertized a free "Grand Buffalo Hunt." The catch was that Barnum had leased all ferry boats for the day, the only transportation to the arena.

Barnum's greater contribution to the legendry of the West, however, was his partnership with James Capen Adams, known as Grizzly Adams in dime novels, after Adams brought his California Menagerie to New York in 1860. In the parade down Broadway Adams was mounted on one grizzly bear while he held two others by chains, all of them on top of a platform wagon without bars. It is safe to say that this feat was never duplicated and few have ever attempted to tame grizzly bears.

Adams had been previously so badly mauled and injured by the bears that he barely survived the ten-week tour arranged by Barnum.

Barnum himself toured the West as well as Europe, and in 1870 enjoyed a buffalo hunt with a party of ten. An escort of fifty troopers was provided by none other than General George A. Custer at Fort Hays, Kansas.

Barnum's autobiography, *Struggles and Triumphs*, has appeared in many editions, beginning in 1855. An annotated two-volume edition (1927), edited by George S. Bryan, contains most of the material from the variant editions. Biographies include Harvey W. Root, *The Unknown Barnum,* (1927); Irving Wallace, *The Fabulous Showman* (1959); and M. R. Werner, *Barnum* (1923).—D. R.

Barrow, Clyde. See BONNIE AND CLYDE.

Bartlett, John Russell (1805-1886). Boundary commissioner, artist, and ethnologist. Bartlett was born in Providence, Rhode Island, and lived in Kingston, Ontario, Canada, until the age of eighteen, when he returned with his family to Providence. In 1836 he moved to New York, where he opened a bookstore. The shop specialized in literature and science, and through it Bartlett became friends with a variety of important figures including the aging Albert Gallatin and Edgar Allan Poe.

In these years Bartlett published his *Progress of Ethnology* (1847) and *Dictionary of Americanisms* (1848). He helped form a number of learned clubs, such as the American Ethnological Society and the Providence Athenaeum. Though he had no formal education beyond high school, Brown University awarded him an honorary M.A. in 1848. Because of health and because he needed more income, he accepted the post of Mexican boundary commissioner in 1850.

The border between the United States and Mexico had been rather vaguely determined in the Treaty of Guadalupe Hidalgo (1848) following the Mexican War. Details were to be worked out by a joint commission empowered to make the final determinations in the field. Three successive commissioners—Ambrose Sevier, John B. Weller, and John C. Frémont—had preceded Bartlett but only a fraction of the work had been accomplished. Bartlett was appointed on June 19, 1850. After a summer of frantic preparation, he arrived in El Paso where he was to meet the Mexican commissioner, General Pedro Garcia Conde, in early November. For three years he struggled with the problems of the boundary. The chief difficulty was to determine the initial point where the line would leave the Rio Grande to go due west. Bartlett, a Whig, conceded the Messilla valley and was therefore accused by the Democrats of giving up an area essential to a southern route for the transcontinental railroad. The region eventually became part of the United States as the Gadsden Purchase (1853).

During the survey, Commissioner Bartlett took two excursions into Chihuahua and Sonora and spent several months in California following a bout with typhoid. In May 1852 he resumed his command of the survey, moving from San Diego along the Gila, then south to Tucson and Chihuahua and back to El Paso. Squabbles within the staff had reached gigantic proportions and finances were increasingly critical, especially when Congress, piqued over the initial point decision, suspended funds. Bartlett in anger returned to Washington where the new

administration of Franklin Pierce was unfriendly. Thus he was finally suspended on February 16, 1853.

Throughout his commissionership, Bartlett took every opportunity to advance the interests of science, and he used his artistic skill to document the events and locale of the boundary region. His journal, published in 1854, provided astute insights into the history, archaeology, and ethnology of the areas he visited.

Bartlett married twice and had seven children by his first wife. He was a tall, thin man with dark brown hair and full beard. He spent the later part of his life as Rhode Island's secretary of state (1855-72) and as librarian and bibliographer for John Carter Brown's collection of early Americana, now at Brown University. Bartlett's own papers and drawings are included in that collection.

See John R. Bartlett, *Personal Narrative of Explorations and Incidents Connected with the United States and Mexican Boundary Commission*, 2 vols. (1854; repr. 1965); and Robert V. Hine, *Bartlett's West: Drawing the Mexican Boundary* (1968).—R. V. H.

Barton, David (1783-1837). Missouri politician. Born in Greene County, North Carolina (now part of Tennessee), and educated at Greenville College in that county, Barton emigrated to St. Charles, Missouri, with two lawyer brothers just prior to the War of 1812.

After brief wartime service as an Indian ranger, Barton moved to St. Louis, where he practiced law until appointed attorney general of Missouri Territory in 1813. He was made the first judge of the St. Louis circuit court two years later. In 1818 he resigned to take a seat in the territorial legislature, where his popularity gained him the speakership. He presided over the Missouri constitutional convention of 1820 and played a major role in drafting the state's first charter.

Undoubtedly the most popular political figure in Missouri, Barton easily obtained election in 1820 as one of the new state's United States senators. In Washington he followed the nationalist doctrines of Henry Clay and actively supported both the protective tariff and federally financed internal improvements. In the disputed election of 1824, he urged John Scott, Missouri's lone representative, to cast the state's ballot for John Quincy Adams even though the legislature had instructed him to vote for Andrew Jackson after Clay, Missouri's original choice, had been dropped from the race. This aroused great criticism among Barton's constituents and enabled Senator Thomas Hart Benton, his chief rival for political power in the state and a staunch Jackson supporter, to supplant him in popular favor. Barton voluntarily retired from the Senate in 1830. He served briefly thereafter in the state senate and as a circuit judge in Boonville, where he was residing at the time of his death.

Barton's role in the Missouri constitutional convention of 1820 and his election to the United States Senate are detailed in Floyd C. Shoemaker, *Missouri's Struggle for Statehood* (1916). A more complete biographical sketch may be found in John T. Scharf, *History of St. Louis City and County,* vol. II (1883). William E. Foley, "The Political Philosophy of David Barton," *Missouri Historical Review* (April 1964), offers an insight into Barton's philosophy.—W. E. P.

Bartram, John (1699-1777). Botanist and frontier

traveler. Born of Quaker parents in Darby, Pennsylvania, Bartram was orphaned at an early age by the death of his mother and the migration of his father and stepmother to North Carolina. He grew up on his uncle's farm under the care of his relatives and his fellow Quakers of the Darby Meeting. In 1728 he purchased a farm of his own along the Schuykill River, near enough to the scholarly resources of Philadelphia to provide Bartram with what was, for the most part, a self-education in the natural sciences. Here he laid out the most famous botanical garden in America and began what were probably the first American experiments in hybridization.

The origin of Bartram's fascination with botany is uncertain, but the traditional story, popularized by Crèvecoeur in his *Letters from an American Farmer,* (1782) is suggestive. According to this legend, Bartram was busy plowing his fields when he spied a daisy. Plucking the flower from the ground he was struck by a thought that awakened his curiosity and redirected his life: "What a shame, said my mind, that thee shouldst have employed so many years in tilling the earth and destroying so many flowers and plants, without being acquainted with their structures and uses."

In the early 1730s Bartram began his celebrated correspondence with Peter Collinson, the English botanist and fellow Quaker. According to Collinson's biographer, the Englishman "practically made Bartram as a Botanist." Collinson adopted an almost paternalistic attitude toward his American friend and provided him with books, equipment, and encouragement. Through Collinson, Bartram's plants found their way into the greenhouses of such English notables as Dr. John Fothergill and Lord Petre. These men in turn provided the needed financial support for Bartram's research. Bartram's work soon came to the attention of scientists on both sides of the Atlantic; Linnaeus thought him the greatest "natural botanist" in the world.

In order to gain a better understanding of the flora of America, Bartram often traveled to the frontier to gather seeds, roots, and bulbs for transplantation in his garden. These excursions included a trip over the Blue Ridge Mountains and an extended journey to upstate New York and Lake Ontario. In 1755 he explored the Catskill Mountains with his son William. Bartram also made trips to western Pennsylvania and the Carolinas in the early 1760s. In 1765 Bartram's efforts earned him the position of botanist to King George III. Shortly after his appointment, Bartram set sail for the Carolinas and from there moved inland into Georgia and East Florida. This journey proved to be one of his most fruitful and was marked by his discovery of a new species, the royal palm.

His travel journals provide valuable insights into the social as well as the natural history of the early frontier. The always-observant botanist commented on the customs and habits of both the Indians and white settlers he encountered. Bartram had distinctly un-Quakerlike sentiments regarding the Indians. He resented the obstacle which the red man presented to his botanical expeditions and feared the savages' "revengeful devouring jaws."

Bartram was probably the first to propose a great western survey trip, an idea he suggested to Benjamin Franklin. (His suggestions bear a marked resemblance to Thomas Jefferson's instructions to Lewis and Clark.) Due partially to his Quaker background, Bartram was also one of the earliest advocates of the abolition of slavery. He not only freed his own slaves, but also taught them how to read and write.

Bartram is memorialized by Bartram's Garden, owned and preserved by the city of Philadelphia, and by *Bartramia,* a genus of mosses. Perhaps more importantly, he founded a virtual dynasty of American naturalists that included his sons, John and William, and his nephew, Thomas Say.

See John Bartram, *Observations on the Inhabitants, Climate, Soil, etc. . . . made by John Bartram in his travels from Pennsylvania to . . . Lake Ontario* (1751) and *Description of East Florida, with a Journal by John Bartram of Philadelphia* (1769); Raymond P. Stearns, *Science in the British Colonies of America* (1970); William Darlington, *Memorials of John Bartram and Humphrey Marshall* (1849); and Ernest Earnest, *John and William Bartram: Botanists and Explorers* (1940).—R. B. W.

Bascom Affair (1861). Incident leading to Apache wars. The theft of rancher Johnny Ward's cattle and abduction of his small son by Apache in October 1860 triggered an army-Indian altercation at Apache Pass, Arizona, in 1861. An inexperienced second lieutenant, George N. Bascom, and sixty men were ordered to use force, if necessary, in apprehending the thieves and returning the boy. Some thought the friendly Apache chief Cochise and six braves to be guilty of the theft. Without suspecting arrest, Cochise and braves approached Bascom's tent near Apache Pass for a talk. The lieutenant invited them into his tent. When Bascom tried to arrest Cochise, the chief slit a hole in the tent and escaped, but his six braves were captured. Army investigations were not thorough enough to determine the true identity of the thieves. Embittered, Cochise captured three Americans and offered to exchange prisoners, but Bascom refused. Angry Apache later tortured and killed sixteen Americans and Mexicans between February 4 and 11. Bascom's men hanged the six Apache captives on February 11.

The Bascom Affair was followed by nearly a dozen years of army-Apache warfare. Cochise himself launched terrific wars of retaliation against all whites until Major General O. O. Howard was able to arrange a peaceful settlement with him in 1872.

See Edwin Corle, *The Gila* (1951); Joseph Miller, *The Arizona Story* (1952); Benjamin H. Sacks, "New Evidence on the Bascom Affair," *Arizona and the West* (Autumn 1962); Cornelius C. Smith, Jr., *William Sanders Oury—History-maker of the Southwest* (1967); and Robert M. Utley, "The Bascom Affair: A Reconstruction," *Arizona and the West* (Spring 1961).—B. W. A.

Basin and Range Province. See PHYSIOGRAPHY OF THE UNITED STATES.

Basques. Within the everyday parlance of the West, to say Basque is to say sheepherder. The very success of the Basques in establishing for themselves an unqualified reputation as the most conscientious and dedicated of all open-range sheepherders remains the primary reason for this stereotype of the group.

The Basque homeland straddles the present-day French-Spanish border, where the western range of the Pyrenees brushes the Cantabrian seacoast. The Basques first came to the New World over four centuries ago, occupying key commercial, military, and administrative posts for the powerful Spanish empire. Although the independence movement in the early 1800s terminated the old pattern of elitist Basque emigration, the new Latin American nations realized that lenient immigration policies were necessary in developing their vast potential. By the 1830s the new pattern was established with the Basques settling primarily the Río de la Plata nations of Uruguay and Argentina. These new settlers were persons of modest means who, on arriving in the New World, engaged in the most menial of occupations. In the Río de la Plata this meant work in the *saladeros* ("meat-salting plants") or employment as sheepherders in the pampas. By the 1840s several thousand Basques were involved in the sheep industry, either as herders or small-scale independent operators, in the hinterlands of Buenos Aires and Montevideo.

The discovery of gold in California attracted many Basques, including a number of sheepmen from Argentina and Uruguay. After initial successes and failures in the California mines, a few Basques, notably those with South American experience, perceived a new economic opportunity. Although the growing populations of the mining districts and servicing centers of California presented a ready demand for meat products, the traditional stockraisers of California, the famed California Dons, were neither organized nor in some cases disposed to enter upon large scale commercial production.

By the early 1850s Basques were tending large flocks of sheep in Los Angeles County. This initial foothold of several hundred Basques was expanded rapidly through the 1860s and 1870s to well over one thousand due both to a rapid increase in wool values on the world market and to the Basque sheepman's propensity to attract to his side other Basques, in most cases kinsmen or fellow villagers from the Old World. A pattern developed in which the new arrival would work for his patron for three or four years, taking part of his wages in ewes, which he would continue to run alongside those of his employer. Once his own flock was large enough to support him, the employee would break away, seeking his own range either by leasing from private landowners or by moving out to the margins of civilization, where unclaimed rangeland was available for the taking. (An example of one of the earliest Basques to initiate this chain migration was the cattleman Pedro Altube.) In this fashion small-scale itinerant or "tramp" (to their detractors) Basque-owned sheep outfits spread throughout the great central valleys of California. Many developed a pattern of transhumance wherein flocks were removed to the high Sierra during the summer months.

Increasingly heavy demands on available range land, caused by the rapid proliferation of sheep bands and exacerbated by the agricultural land boom of the 1880s, forced the itinerant Basque sheepmen, now numbering over two thousand in Los Angeles County alone, to roam farther afield, penetrating the Great Basin region. By the 1890s Basque sheep interests were established throughout western and northern Nevada. By the turn of the century there were possibly some ten thousand Basques in the West. By 1910 this base was extended to include parts of southern Oregon, most of southern Idaho, and pockets of Wyoming, Colorado, and Montana. The Basques had become the most prominent ethnic group within the sheep industry of the West, but largely at the level of herder and small-scale itinerant sheep operator.

It was this latter identification that was to set the tenor of relations between Basques and non-Basques, to the detriment of the former. While legally the itinerant sheepmen had as much right to the open range as other livestock interests, the land-owning ranchers despised and opposed what they regarded as foreign interlopers. Harassments were devised, ranging from imposing local taxes on the "tramps," labeling them pejoratively "Black Bascos," and discriminating against them socially, to out and out violence. These troubles provided copy for newspapers, litigation in the courts, and substance to the sheepmen-versus-cattlemen legends. It was not until the passing of the Taylor Grazing Act in 1934, closing public lands to itinerant operators, that the prime source of irritation between Basques and others was removed.

While the Taylor Grazing Act may have hurt many individual Basques economically, it did remove the major source of a negative evaluation of the Basques by the wider society. Thereafter, Basques were appreciated as the most dedicated followers of the essentially lonely and thankless occupation of sheepherding. Further, it was evident that the restrictive immigration laws of the 1920s, removing the source of Old World Basque herders, had provoked a labor crisis in the sheep industry. Throughout the 1940s and 1950s some 383 Basques were able to gain permanent residency status in the United States by jumping ship, making their way to relatives in a sheep-raising state, and then having their status normalized by introduction of a private bill in the United States Congress by a representative of that area. This approach proved to be inadequate to meet the growing demand for herders. In 1950 a law was enacted permitting 250 herders into the country, and in 1952 an additional 500 were authorized. In 1957 the sheepmen of the West organized the Western Range Association, which continues to moderate a program under which Basques come to the United States on three-year sheepherder contracts. Through June 1970, 5,495 herders had entered the West under the plan.

Although there are areas where Basque sheepherders continue to operate in considerable numbers (e.g., Kern County, California; Elko County, Nevada; southern Idaho; Johnson County, Wyoming), the passing of time has produced a degree of erosion in the Basques' maintenance of ethnic identity and ties; second- and third-generation Basque Americans are in most cases no longer involved in the sheep business. However, there are two respects in which Basques still contribute color and variety to contemporary life in the West. The first is the continued existence of Basque hotels and boardinghouses, which were first developed to serve the needs of a sheepherder clientele but today depend primarily upon the fame of their ethnic cuisine and informal, family-style atmosphere to attract a non-Basque clientele. California still has several in San Francisco, Stockton, Los Banos, Fresno, Bakersfield, Chino, and La Puente. Nevada, too, retains a number of these old inns in Reno, Gardnersville, Winnemucca, Elko, and Ely. And Idaho has one at Mountain Home.

The second aspect is the persistence of Basque festivals, held annually in several communities of the West: in California, near Chino, Los Banos, and San Francisco; and in Nevada, near Reno, Elko, and Ely. The larger festivals attract as many as three thousand spectators, who are treated to Basque cooking, athletic events (stone lifting and woodchopping), and folk dancing.

See William A. Douglass and Jon Bilbao, *Amerikanuak: Basques in the New World* (1975); and Robert Laxalt, *Sweet Promised Land* (1957).—W. A. D.

Bass, Sam (1851-1878). Outlaw. Bass was born in Mitchell, Indiana. He left home at eighteen and headed for Texas. For a time he worked as a teamster and hired hand near Denton, but in 1874 he fell in with a ne'er-do-well and small-time bad man named Joel Collins. In 1876 Bass and Collins drove a herd of cattle north to the Black Hills and stayed on to rob stages. Discouraged by poor results, they started south in 1877, and, in company with four others, robbed a Union Pacific train of $60,000 in gold coin at Big Springs, Nebraska. Back in Texas, Bass launched a somewhat less lucrative and highly amateurish career of crime as a train robber. But despite his lack of success the public demanded action. When the Texas Rangers, under the leadership of Major John B. Jones, turned out to run Bass to earth the press dubbed the chase the "Bass War." Bass led them a merry chase through Texas for nearly four months. Once, he seemed to vanish, but he spent stolen gold too freely, which brought the Rangers out again. Then Bass made a fatal mistake: he returned to his old haunts in Denton County. He and his gang were soon on the run again, but this time they blundered into a Ranger company and a fight that disenchanted Bass's followers. Abandoned now except for two companions, Bass eluded the Rangers again. The remnants of the gang were now joined by a sometime cronie named Jim Murphy whose true purpose was to betray Bass to the Rangers.

Bass planned to rob the bank in Round Rock, Texas, in July 1878. Murphy tipped off the Rangers, and on July 21, 1878, Bass's twenty-seventh birthday, Bass was mortally wounded in the attempt. He tried to escape, but the Rangers found him outside of town. With "the world bobbing all around," Bass died, and a legend was born.

That is the strangest part of all. His career as an outlaw was far from spectacular, but he has ridden through the pages of western legend as a brigand chief, a good-natured Robin Hood who, like Jesse James, was betrayed by a friend. "A kinder-hearted fellow, you'd scarcely ever see," a popular song said. "The Ballad of Sam Bass" was soon a standard song among cowboys, and when Charles Lee Martin published *A Sketch of Sam Bass the Bandit* anonymously, in 1880, the legend was assured.

See Helena Huntington Smith, "Sam Bass and the Myth Machine," *American West* (January 1970); and Wayne Gard, *Sam Bass* (1936).—G. L. R.

Bates, Edward (1793-1869). Missouri politician. Bates was born in Goochland County, Virginia. After seeing local service in the War of 1812, he joined his brother Frederick, then secretary of Missouri Territory, in St. Louis in 1814 and began the study of law under Rufus Easton, one of the first territorial judges. Two years later he began his own practice and became interested in territorial politics.

Bates participated in the constitutional convention of 1820 and became a leader of those forces in Missouri that ultimately became identified with the Whig party. Although he served one term in congress (1827-29) and on numerous occasions in the state legislature, the dominance of the Jacksonians in Missouri made any significant political career there an impossibility.

Bates attracted considerable national attention through his stands on the controversial political and economic questions of the 1850s. These led him into the Free-Soil wing of the Whig party and caused a strong but unsuccessful movement for his nomination to the presidency at the Republican national convention in 1860.

Bates served as attorney general under President Abraham Lincoln throughout the Civil War; but by opposing the extraconstitutional limits to which Lincoln went in suppressing subversion, he failed to exercise the influence of some of his less conservative colleagues. He retired from the cabinet in November 1864 and returned to St. Louis, where he led an unsuccessful fight against ratification of a new state constitution promulgated by Missouri Radicals in 1865. His health broke soon after, and he never again resumed active participation in law or politics.

The standard biography is Marvin R. Cain, *Lincoln's Attorney General: Edward Bates of Missouri* (1965). Bates's wartime diary, edited by Howard K. Beale, constitutes the fourth volume of the *Annual Report of the American Historical Association for the Year 1930.*—W. E. P.

Bayfield, Henry W. See GREAT LAKES, MEN OF THE.

Baylor, John Robert (1822-1894). Texas soldier. Born in Paris, Kentucky, Baylor arrived in Texas in 1840 after attending a university in Cincinnati. Settling near LaGrange, he farmed, fought Comanche Indians as a Texas Ranger, served in the state legislature, and was admitted to the bar in 1854. He became an agent to the Comanche reservation in 1855, but resigned the post because of his hatred for Indians. He next led Texan volunteers in the fight to have the Indians removed to reservations in Oklahoma; he then became a rancher near Weatherford.

As a delegate to the Texas secession convention in January 1861, Baylor voted to remove Texas from the Union and then accepted a commission as lieutenant colonel in the Second Regiment of Texas Mounted Volunteers. Assigned to capture Fort Bliss at El Paso, he exceeded his commission by marching to Mesilla, New Mexico, where he defeated the Union soldiers nearby at Fort Fillmore and proclaimed the Confederate Territory of Arizona (all of present Arizona and New Mexico south of the thirty-fourth parallel). As self-proclaimed governor (later confirmed by President Jefferson Davis), he fought federal soldiers and Apache Indians until he was driven out of the territory by General James H. Carleton and the California Volunteers. Davis later stripped him of his rank of colonel and governor because of his policy of exterminating the Apache where possible. In 1863 Baylor was elected to the Confederate Congress, a position he held until the end of war.

In 1865 he returned to Texas, living for a time at San Antonio and then moving to Montell in Uvalde County. There he ranched and defended his life, property, and honor, by fighting a duel in 1881, killing his opponent.

He died at his ranch at Montell, still a self-reliant, strong-willed, and determined frontiersman.

See George W. Baylor, *John Robert Baylor: Confederate Governor of Arizona* (1966).—O. B. F.

Beadle, Erastus. See DIME NOVELS.

Beadle, William Henry Harrison (1838-1915). Dakota Territory official. Beadle came to Dakota Territory in April 1869 and later served as private secretary and adviser to Governor William A. Howard. He was appointed territorial superintendent of public instruction in 1879 and held the office of surveyor general in 1881. Beadle is considered to be the founder of the South Dakota school system and was a promoter of the statehood movement. His "Dakota plan," which assured sufficient funding for public education, became a part of both the North and South Dakota constitutions. —D. J. T.

Beale, Edward Fitzgerald (1822-1893). Surveyor and Indian agent. Beale began his official career in the navy, serving as courier for Commodore Robert F. Stockton in 1846. On December 8, 1846, he, Kit Carson, and an Indian scout crawled through the enemy lines that surrounded General Stephen Watts Kearny at San Pasqual, reached the naval contingents at San Diego twenty-nine miles away, and thus brought relief and victory to General Kearny. In the next few years Beale made several journeys across the continent.

Later he was appointed Indian agent for all of California and Nevada, primarily through the influence of Senator Thomas Hart Benton of Missouri. In 1853, again aided by Benton, Beale conducted an independent railroad survey, that is, one not connected with the official Pacific railroad surveys of that year, along the thirty-eighth parallel. With the aid of a press agent named Gwin Harris Heap, he publicized the thirty-eighth parallel route as the best and shortest railroad route to California. Beale also surveyed a wagon road from Fort Defiance in New Mexico to the Colorado River and was the instigator of the army's CAMEL EXPERIMENT.

Beale deserves a new biography. See Stephen Bonsal, *Edward Fitzgerald Beale* (1912); and William H. Goetzmann, *Army Exploration of the American West* (1959). —R. A. B.

Bean, Roy (1825?-1903). Saloonkeeper and justice of the peace. Bean, self-proclaimed "law west of the Pecos," dispenser of hard liquor and harder justice, was a legend in western Texas in his own lifetime. His career yielded an endless array of anecdotes and humorous tales, not all of them true. His biographers are convinced that the irascible Bean was an active and jovial promoter of his own reputation.

Born in the hills of Mason County, Kentucky, Bean visited New Orleans as a teen-ager, got into trouble, and quickly returned home. In 1847 he left home for good with his brother Sam and headed for Mexico, where he led a rogue's life until he shot a man in a barroom brawl and was forced to flee. He showed up next in San Diego where Joshua Bean, another brother, was *alcalde* and merchant. Roy played the role of dashing *caballero* there until a personal quarrel with a man named Collins over which was the best shot resulted in a duel that landed Bean in jail. He escaped and headed for Los Angeles. There he joined Josh, who had departed San Diego before him. Tradition has it that Josh ran afoul of Joaquin Murietta, California's legendary bandit, over a woman; at any rate, Josh was murdered. Roy took over Josh's prosperous saloon, which he operated successfully until he quarreled with a Mexican officer over a girl. He killed the Mexican in a duel but was hanged by the officer's friends. Fortunately the rope stretched enough to keep him alive until the girl he had fought over cut him down. Bean bore the mark of the rope for the rest of his life and was unable to turn his head.

The attraction of California paled after that, and he was soon en route to New Mexico, where he found Sam and moderate success in business. During the Civil War Bean operated with Confederate irregulars until General Henry H. Sibley withdrew from New Mexico. After the New Mexico campaign he operated out of San Antonio, Texas, as a blockade runner. With his ingenuity and cunning, it proved to be a profitable enterprise. Bean prospered and by 1866 was well established in San Antonio, in spite of a few legal fights regarding his business practices. He spent the next sixteen years there, married, and worked more or less respectably.

In 1882 Bean drifted west across the Pecos River, dispensing whiskey from a tent. There, in the harsh environment of southwestern Texas, he finally made his mark. He plied his trade as a saloonkeeper, first at a place called Eagle's Nest on the Rio Grande and finally beside a new railroad through Dead Man's Canyon in West Texas. He dubbed his saloon the Jersey Lilly and called the spot Langtry (after Lily Langtry, the actress). By then he was established as a justice of the peace who dispensed justice and beer from the same bar, frequently interrupting court to serve liquor. He knew little law or court procedure, but the Texas Rangers accepted his common-sense approach to law enforcement. Bean's handling of cases was often humorous, sometimes bizarre. Once, he reportedly fined a dead man forty dollars for carrying a concealed weapon. But when a friend of Bean's was arrested on the same charge, his verdict was somewhat different. Bean reasoned that if a man was standing still when arrested he was not carrying a weapon. On the other hand, if he was walking or riding, he was traveling, and travelers could legally carry guns. On another occasion he threatened to hang a lawyer for using profane language in court, for the lawyer had informed the judge that he intended to *habeas corpus* his client. In one memorable trial, Bean freed a man accused of murdering a Chinese railroad worker because he could not find any law that made it a crime "to kill a Chinaman." His antics became so widely known that passengers on the train through Langtry often stopped to take a look at the "law west of the Pecos." These visits sparked more tales, which sparked the judge to hand down more "decisions," such as the time he found a dead Mexican with a bullet in his forehead. The judge's verdict: "This gent met his death at the hands of a doggoned good pistol shot." Bean's reputation took another jump in 1896 when he staged a boxing match between Bob Fitzsimmons and Peter Maher. Boxing was illegal in Texas, but Bean arranged to have the fight take place on an island in the Rio Grande not far from the Jersey Lilly while the Rangers watched from the Texas side of the river.

During his last few years Roy Bean dispensed justice only rarely. He spent more of his time worshiping Lily

Judge Roy Bean presides over the trial of a horse thief in 1900. (National Archives)

Langtry, following her career and hoping that she would visit the little community named in her honor. By then he was already a national celebrity. In March 1903 he visited San Antonio but cut his visit short because he was not feeling well. His illness worsened, and on March 16, 1903, he died quietly in his quarters at the Jersey Lilly. Papers all over the country carried his obituary, which would have made him proud, but the crowning touch to Bean's legend came ten months later when Lily Langtry visited Roy Bean's town.

C. L. Sonnichsen, *Roy Bean: Law West of the Pecos* (1948), is the best biography.—G. L. R.

Bear Flag Rebellion (1846). Anglo revolt against Mexican rule in California. The political situation in California immediately before the Mexican War (1846-48) was highly unsettled. With the United States government pressing for annexation of California, the Mexican authorities were suspicious of the intentions of Anglo residents in that Mexican province, and the Anglos, stirred by rumors of approaching war, were fearful of attack. In March 1846 a military "exploring party" led by John C. FRÉMONT had been forced from California by the Mexican commander José Castro. On his way toward Oregon, Frémont was overtaken by Lieutenant Archibald Gillespie of the Marine Corps, who had been acting as a secret agent for President Polk and the American consul in California, Thomas O. Larkin. What instructions, if any, Gillespie brought to Frémont is still hotly debated, but Frémont evidently felt that the situation with regard to Mexico had deteriorated to a point where his presence in California was necessary to the national interest. When Frémont returned to the vicinity of Sutter's Fort in May, supposedly on secret orders from the United States government, the rougher element of the American population in the region decided that patriotism demanded firm action.

A group of roving hunters, trappers, and runaway sailors, who had gathered under the leadership of Ezekiel Merritt, heard rumors that a herd of horses was being driven to the Mexican militia for use in a campaign against Anglos. With the tacit approval of Frémont, Merritt's followers intercepted the herd on June 10 and drove them to Frémont's camp. Four days later Merritt and another local American leader, William B. Ide, took thirty armed men and descended on the village of Sonoma, surrounded the home of retired Mexican colonel Mariano Vallejo, and informed him he was a prisoner of war. Vallejo, one of the stanchest Mexican supporters of the United States's desire to annex California, was most courteous, although puzzled. He invited Merritt and several others into his home for a drink while discussing surrender terms. After several hours passed, Ide, who had remained outside on guard, had to go in and complete the capture for his comrades, who had become sidetracked by the colonel's brandy. Vallejo and his family were taken to Sutter's Fort, where Frémont vented his anti-Mexican hostility by confining them in bare cells.

While at Sonoma, Ide and his associates declared themselves a republic and devised a flag from a sheet of unbleached cotton and some red paint. In the upper left corner was a lone red star and facing it a representation of what was intended as a grizzly bear. "California Republic" was lettered beneath in black ink. This pattern, neatened considerably, has since become the official California state flag. Declaring Sonoma their capital, the Americans prepared to defend their cause against a small force of Mexicans that Castro was sending north from San Francisco. In a brief skirmish on June 24 that was later called the battle of Olompali, two Americans were killed, but the Mexicans, who were not really interested in fighting, withdrew. With this victory Frémont could no longer restrain himself and officially took command of the Bear Flaggers. He marched his unruly force south, killing an occasional Mexican along the way, and on July 1 entered the long-ungarrisoned presidio of San Francisco. After spiking the old Spanish cannon, which had been hopelessly rusted for half a century, Frémont prepared a Fourth of July celebration and organized the California Battalion of American volunteers with himself as commander and Gillespie as adjutant. On July 7, however, the triumphal progress of the rebellion abruptly halted when Commodore John D. Sloat bloodlessly captured Monterey and officially raised the American flag over California. The California Republic quietly melted away, and the Mexican hostages were released. The rebellion's only substantial accomplishments were to unnecessarily embitter relations between Californians and Americans and to generate a still-enduring historical debate over the respective roles of its participants.

Brief accounts of the rebellion are in Walton Bean, *California: An Interpretive History* (1968); Bernard De Voto, *The Year of Decision: 1846* (1942); and A. F. Rolle, *California: A History* (1963). The Frémont controversy is examined in J. A. Hawgood, "John Charles Frémont and the Bear Flag Revolution: A Reappraisal," *Southern California Quarterly* (1962); George Tays, "Frémont Had No Secret Instructions," *Pacific Historical Review* (June 1940); and E. A. Wiltsee, *The Truth About Frémont: An Inquiry* (1936). See also Allan Nevins, *Frémont* (1939).—P. R. M.

Beaubien, Carlos [Charles Hipolyte Trotier, Sieur de] (1800-1864). Pioneer merchant and judge. The life of Beaubien was exemplary of the successful career carved out by many French-Canadians in the trans-Mississippi West. Born in Trois-Rivières, Canada, he went to St. Louis as a boy, worked for fur trader Auguste Chouteau, and in 1823 joined another fur trader, Antoine Robidoux, on a journey to New Mexico. Becoming a Mexican citizen, Beaubien operated a profitable business in Taos, where he wed Paula Lobato in 1827. Forming a partnership with Guadalupe Miranda, he received from Governor Manuel Armijo a large tract of land that later became famous as the Maxwell Land Grant. After the American occupation of New Mexico in 1846, General Stephen W. Kearny named Beaubien as one of the first judges of a newly created superior court. In this capacity he presided at the trial of the Taos rebels who had slain his own son Narciso, Governor Charles Bent, and others in the abortive uprising of January 1847. The verdict sentencing the leaders to be executed was hardly impartial. In the years prior to his death, "Don Carlos" enjoyed immense popularity and had great influence among the people of northern New Mexico.

A brief biography of Beaubien appears in Ralph Emerson Twitchell, *The History of the Military Occupation of New Mexico from 1846 to 1851* (1963). Also see Lawrence R. Murphy, "Charles H. Beaubien," in LeRoy R. Hafen, *The Mountain Men and the Fur Trade of the Far West,* vol. VI (1965).—M. Si.

Beaumont, William. See DOCTORS.

beaver. The beaver (*Castor canadensis* Kuhl) has been called the greatest single stimulus for exploration of North America. If this be true of the continent as a whole, then it is doubly true of the American West, for the fur trade reached its greatest intensity in the early nineteenth century as the Great Plains and Rocky Mountains were being conquered by Europeans. North American Indians used beavers for fur and food long before white men appeared, but their needs were not great and no significant effect on beaver populations can be ascribed to the Indians before trading with the settlers made beaver hunting lucrative.

Felt hats, made from beaver underfur, came into great favor in Europe about 1600. Beavers were scarce in Europe by this time, but the North American source was just being discovered. From then until about 1850, when silk replaced beaver fur for hat making and supplies of beavers began to fail, the search for beavers was practically synonymous with the exploration of North America. The mountain men, who dominated western history for the fifty years following Lewis and Clark, were beaver hunters and trappers.

In the early days beavers were taken by any convenient means—shooting, snaring, draining ponds, and clubbing the helpless animals. Sewall Newhouse, son of a New York blacksmith, invented the steel trap in 1823, but its use was widespread only during the waning years of the fur trade.

The best estimates of numbers of beavers taken in North America during the height of the trading era, 1800 to 1850, are in the range 100,000 to 500,000 per year. During this time and for the remainder of the century, the pelts came from increasingly remote areas. By 1900 the catch was a small fraction of the former take, and most of it came from Canada.

In the United States intense competition between trading companies eliminated any possibility of a controlled harvest, but in Canada the Hudson's Bay Company held a strong monopopy and at times urged its trappers to use restraint so as not to exterminate the resources. The success of this policy probably was not great by modern game management standards and the remoteness of the Canadian wilderness probably had more to do with the survival of beavers than did the policy of the company.

Shortly after 1900 most western states and the provinces of Canada began protecting their few remaining beavers from further exploitation. Numbers have increased steadily since, not only in the West and North but also in the eastern and southern states, where the species had been widely exterminated. Beavers respond well to protection and to stocking programs carried out by conservation agencies. They do not require wilderness areas, but thrive in any situation that provides adequate food and proper aquatic habitat, even close to human habitation. All states and provinces except Florida now have populations of beavers. In settled areas they frequently make a nuisance of themselves by persistently damming culverts, flooding roads and crops, and cutting shade trees. Most states and provinces practice closely controlled harvests. The annual catch from the

United States and Canada now equals that at the height of the fur trade in the last century.

The beaver is the only living member of the family Castoridae. Several other species, including some as large as small bears, lived during late Tertiary and Quaternary time throughout the Northern Hemisphere. North American and Eurasian beavers are recognized as separate species on the basis of minor morphological differences, but their habits are very similar.

Adult beavers commonly weigh thirty-five to fifty pounds and specimens up to one hundred pounds have been reported. The short, thick body forms a smooth profile, an adaptation for minimizing resistance to water. Other adaptations for aquatic life include modifications of the hind feet and tail for propellers and rudder, respectively. The hind feet are as large as a woman's hand and fully webbed between the toes. The tail is flattened dorsoventrally, reaching a length of a foot and breadth of six inches in large specimens. The hair is well oiled and kept groomed by a comb modified from a claw on the hind foot. The ability to dive and work underwater for up to fifteen minutes results largely, as in other aquatic mammals, from their ability to tolerate high concentrations of carbon dioxide in the blood. In addition, the beaver has fleshy valves that automatically close the ears and nostrils underwater, and valves behind the huge front teeth so that the animal can gnaw under water without opening its mouth.

Beavers require relatively large bodies of water for protection from predators and for transporting food material. Natural lakes and large streams serve well when available, but most beavers have to supply their own aquatic environment by damming small streams with sticks, stones, and mud, and by extending waterways by digging canals. Most ponds cover only a few acres, but larger ones are not rare. Dams usually vary from a few feet to a few hundred feet long, but one Montana dam was more than two thousand feet long. Although flooding kills some timber, the ponds provide habitat and food for waterfowl, moose, muskrats, and fish.

Beavers live in bank burrows or in large houses built in the pond or against the bank. The construction habit appears to have evolved from bank burrows through an intermediate step in which the animals repaired caved-in bank dens by piling sticks and mud over them. Entrances to living chambers are underwater.

Beaver intelligence is frequently overstated. Most of their behavior is innate, that is, as the animals mature they are able to build dams, cut trees, and so on without previous experience. The seeming ability to fell trees toward water results from the natural lean of trees growing close to water rather than from beaver intelligence.

A beaver colony normally consists of a pair of adults and litters of three to five young each from the current and immediately past year. When the new kits are born in the spring, the two-year-olds, now two thirds grown, leave or are driven from the colony, so that the total number in the colony remains unchanged. If unoccupied territory is available, these young animals may establish new colonies. But more often good habitat is unavailable and the dispersing beavers wander widely, living in marginal habitat where food may be scarce and where they are much more vulnerable to such predators as wolves, coyotes, dogs, or lynxes than beavers in estab-

lished colonies. Young beavers are often said to bear their first litter when they are three years old, but recent studies indicate that more often the animals are at least four years old before they begin breeding.

During the summer beavers eat a variety of herbaceous plants, including aquatic or semiaquatic plants growing in and around their ponds. The adult female brings food to her kits for several weeks before they are able to forage on their own.

As winter approaches beaver activity intensifies. They reinforce their dams and houses with sticks and mud and turn to the bark of woody species for food. In the northern states and Canada quaking aspen and white birch, which grow abundantly after logging and fires in coniferous forests, provide ideal beaver food. In the western mountains quaking aspen and willows constitute important food items. On the plains cottonwoods and willows are staples. In newly occupied habitat with abundant trees beavers waste food by cutting far more than they can eat, but as trees become scarce efficiency of use increases. In the northern part of the continent where ponds freeze over in winter beavers store large piles of limbs in deep water near their houses so that food can be reached easily after freeze-up. Food is not usually stored in southern latitudes, where the water stays open all winter.

See Hiram M. Chittenden, *The American Fur Trade of the Far West*, vol. I and II (1954); Bernard De Voto, *Across the Wide Missouri* (1947); William H. Longley and John B. Moyle, *The Beaver in Minnesota* (1963); Lewis H. Morgan, *The American Beaver and His Works* (1868); Paul C. Phillips, *The Fur Trade* (1961); and William H. Rutherford, *The Beaver in Colorado: Its Biology, Ecology, Management and Economics* (1964).—P. C. S.

Becker, Joseph (1841-1910). Illustrator. Becker received his first job as an errand boy on New York publisher Frank Leslie's staff about 1859. Leslie, himself a skilled engraver, encouraged Becker in this line of endeavor and by 1863 had employed him as a full-time artist. Assigned to observe life with the Army of the Potomac during the Civil War, Becker followed its campaigns from Gettysburg to Appomattox, and many of his war drawings were reproduced at this time in *Leslie's Illustrated Newspaper*. In October 1869 he made his first trip westward to picture events along the route of the newly completed transcontinental railroad. His views of the trip began appearing in Leslie's paper with the November 13 issue of that year. From about 1875 to 1900 he was head of the firm's art department.

Becker produced a few oil paintings of doubtful artistic merit and is best known today for his newspaper illustrations, particularly those that depict the activities of the Chinese railroad workers in California, who became the subject of his special study.

See Robert Taft, *Artists and Illustrators of the Old West, 1850-1900* (1953).—D. C. H.

Becknell, William (c.1790-1865). Explorer and trader. Becknell is believed to have been born in Kentucky. He came to Missouri at an early age, but little is known of his career prior to 1821. That summer he organized an expedition "for the purpose of trading for Horses and Mules and catching Wild Animals of every description" in the southern Rockies. It left Franklin on August 18, stopped briefly at Fort Osage, then crossed to the Arkansas River. The group reached the mouth of the Purgatoire River on October 21, followed it into the mountains, and then turned south toward Raton Pass, where they encountered a troop of Mexican soldiers, who informed them of the recent overthrow of Spanish rule. Though the New Mexico trade had been closed since the Pike expedition more than a decade earlier, Becknell now learned that Santa Fe would welcome outside goods. He and his men hastened on to become the first Americans to arrive there after independence; they traded their goods for a nice profit. Arriving two weeks ahead of the James expedition, they thus gained the distinction of reinaugurating the Santa Fe trade.

By January 1822 Becknell was back in Franklin planning a new and larger expedition to take advantage of the new opportunity. He headed west that spring with three wagons added to his pack train, thirty men, and $5 thousand in merchandise. It marked the first time wagons had been used on the trail to Santa Fe. Seeking to shorten his route and time and allow easier travel for the wagons, Becknell blazed the Cimarron River crossing just west of Dodge City—not without great suffering from heat and thirst. Having left the Arkansas, he followed the Cimarron up its south fork and over the divide to the forks of the Canadian River and thence across the mountain pass to San Miguel. The Missouri trader thus laid the foundation for what became the Santa Fe Trail, over which hundreds of caravans and hundreds of thousands of dollars worth of goods would flow in the 1820s and 1830s.

Becknell apparently continued in the Santa Fe trade for several years, although records of his subsequent exploits are scarce. In 1824 he took a small party from Santa Cruz to the Green River valley in Colorado, where they spent a severe winter. By 1828 he had settled at Arrow Rock, where he established a ferry across the Missouri River. Following two terms in the Missouri General Assembly, (1828-32) he caught the "Texas fever" in 1835 and settled near Clarksville in Red River County. He participated in the Texas War for Independence the following year. After that, little is known of his career, save that he apparently lived out his life at Clarksville, where he died just as the Civil War was coming to a close.

Becknell's journals of his Santa Fe and Green River trips, as edited by Francis A. Sampson, are in the *Missouri Historical Review* (January 1910).—W. E. P.

Beckwourth, Jim [James Pierson] (1800?-?1866). Black mountain man. Beckwourth was born in Virginia, probably Frederick County, the son of Sir Jennings Beckwith (a descendent of minor Irish aristocrats) and a mulatto slave woman. By nature a sportsman and a wanderer, Beckwith senior moved to Louisiana Territory in 1810 and eventually to St. Louis. It has been suggested that he migrated West so that his mulatto offspring might have more opportunities. Whatever the motive, it appears that Beckwith manumitted his slave son when the youth reached manhood in Missouri.

Jim Beckwourth's handsome mulatto features led Francis Parkman to call him a French half-breed; others, impressed by his black, gently waving hair, said that he resembled an Indian. But Beckwourth's first jobs indicate that he was regarded as a *free* black man, because he was able to move as he pleased. In 1822 he joined the rush to the new Fever River lead mines and

soon thereafter traveled to New Orleans, probably as a roustabout.

Beckwourth's rendezvous with destiny came in the fall of 1824 when he accompanied General William Ashley's famous supply expedition to fur trappers in the Rocky Mountains, which initiated the famous Green River fur-trading rendezvous in the summer of 1825. Beckwourth's exaggerated account of his role in the party conceals the fact that he was merely a combination groom, blacksmith, and body servant for Ashley. He did turn to trapping, however, and soon became known as a mountain man. He wintered with Jedediah Smith in Cache valley in 1825-26 and was in the famous "fight in the willows" between the Blackfoot and Robert Campbell's party of trappers on their way to the 1828 rendezvous. Beckwourth may have been one of the two men who saved the whites from disaster by making a daring charge through Indian lines to summon a rescue party.

Beckwourth worked for various Rocky Mountain Fur Company partners until 1828, when he appears to have been adopted into a tribe of Crow Indians after Caleb Greenwood, a fellow trapper, persuaded Chief Big Bowl that Jim was the chief's long-lost son who had been captured by the Cheyenne as a child and sold to whites. Beckwourth joined in the deception, lived with the Crow for at least six years, and married a series of Blackfoot, Snake, and Crow women. His own version of his life as an Indian suffers from exaggeration, for he describes himself as an important chief and superb warrior who took part in many raids. While he was undoubtedly a leader among the Crow and may have engaged in the raids and killings he describes, it also seems probable that his alliance with them was a stratagem to get furs for his new employer, Kenneth McKenzie of the American Fur Company. In any case, the experience did leave its mark, for thereafter Beckwourth affected braids, moccasins, and Indian costume.

Beckwourth's contract with the American Fur Company was not renewed in 1837, however, and he next appeared in Florida as a muleteer with a Missouri volunteer company recruited to fight against Indians in the Seminole War. Returning to Missouri, Beckwourth became a trader on the Santa Fe Trail for Andrew Sublette (the younger brother of William Sublette) and Louis Vasquez. Then, after serving as a wagon leader at Bent's Fort and a trader in Taos, he and a group of trader-squatters settled at the present site of Pueblo, Colorado, in 1842.

Yet two years later Beckwourth was off to California, where he intrigued against Governor Manuel Micheltorena and is reputed to have become a horse thief. After the American conquest of California in 1846-47 he was a guide and messenger for the American forces and later a mail rider in the Monterey area. At some point he was back in New Mexico, for Lewis Garrard, author of *Wah-To-Yah and the Taos Trail*, states that Beckwourth was running a saloon in Santa Fe soon after the American occupation of that province in 1846.

The discovery of gold in California in 1848 brought Beckwourth to the Sierra mining camps. Joining in the popular craze to find new and better routes through the rugged Sierra, Beckwourth formed a company to lay out a wagon road or trail from Bidwell's Bar through the mountains in 1851. His route was moderately successful, and for a few years he operated a ranch, trading post, and hotel for immigrants at the summit of Beck-wourth Pass through which the trail ran. Travelers all agree that he was an impressive host full of fascinating stories. In 1854 Thomas D. Bonner, a New Englander who had been a justice of the peace in the gold region, interviewed Beckwourth at his Sierra hotel and in 1856 brought out *The Life and Adventures of James P. Beck-wourth, Mountaineer, Scout, Pioneer and Chief of the Crow Nation*. It was Bonner who changed the spelling of Jim's name from "Beckwith" to the presently accepted "Beckwourth."

Beckwourth went east to St. Louis in 1858, but upon learning of the discovery of gold in the Pikes Peak region, went to Colorado as a supplier and storekeeper for his old friend Louis Vasquez. Subsequently he served as a guide for E. L. Berthoud of the Second Colorado Infantry, tried unsuccessfully to trap on the Green River, and joined the Colorado troops, probably as guide and interpreter, who were responsible for the infamous attack on the Cheyenne camp at Sand Creek in 1864. Beckwourth's precise role in the SAND CREEK MASSACRE is disputed. Later he worked for the army at Fort Laramie. Beckwourth appears to have died on a hunting trip during a visit to the Crow Indians in 1866. Some sources suggest that he may have been poisoned by the Crow since he was suspected of bringing smallpox, perhaps deliberately, to the tribe in 1837. Other sources indicate that he may have died near Denver in 1867.

Until recently Beckwourth's published account of his extraordinary adventures has been regarded as exaggerated, inaccurate, and egotistical; he has been called, in fact, "a gaudy liar." Now research indicates that Beckwourth's basic narrative is true. For many years he was accused of fabricating the story that General Ashley nearly drowned on his historic trip down the Green River in 1825. Ashley's diaries now reveal that the incident is true, although Jim's claim that he helped rescue Ashley is not.

Although Beckwourth recounted his *Adventures* in the vein of a raconteur determined to amuse his fellow trappers, the narrative also records the way in which a black man succeeded in the dangerous and demanding life of the Far West between 1825 and 1865. His firsthand acquaintance with the greatest of the fur trappers, Ashley, Smith, McKenzie, Vasquez, and others, and his life with the Crow make him a useful source for the fur-trade period. The epithet "gaudy liar" no longer seems applicable.

In 1892 Charles G. Leland ("Hans Breitman") published a new edition of Bonner's *Beckwourth*, and in 1931 Bernard De Voto published a still newer edition. Beckwourth's career as a mountain man may be followed in Dale Morgan, *Jedediah Smith and the Opening of the West* (1953). Elinor Wilson, *Jim Beckwourth: Black Mountain Man and War Chief of the Crows* (1972) is oversympathetic but the fullest biographical study.—G. B. D.

Bedichek, Roy (1878–1959). Naturalist. Bedichek was born in Cass County, Illinois. When he was six his parents moved to Falls County, Texas, where he was educated in rural schools and at Bedichek Academy, established by his father. As a student in the University of Texas he worked for the university's registrar, John A. Lomax, who later became famous as a folklorist. Bedichek received his B.S. degree from the University of Texas in 1903 and an M.A. degree in 1925.

After working as a reporter for newspapers in Texas and New Mexico and teaching high school in Houston and San Angelo, Bedichek moved to Austin as secretary of the Young Men's Business League. After a year as city editor of the San Antonio *Express*, he returned to Austin in 1917 to become director of the University of Texas Interscholastic League. This position occupied him until his retirement in 1948.

Bedichek's work as coordinator of athletic and debating contests demanded that he visit schools all over the state. He disdained hotels and rooming houses, preferring always to camp out. Frequently he took along companions and observed and read voraciously about wildlife, particularly birds. As he grew older his reputation as a regional sage increased, with the result that in 1946 J. Frank Dobie and Walter Prescott Webb virtually forced him to take a year's leave of absence, seclude himself on Webb's Friday Mountain ranch, and come back from his isolation with a book. The result was *Adventures with a Texas Naturalist* (1947), which brought him international acclaim from both book reviewers and naturalists. He followed with *Karankaway Country* (1950), *Educational Competition, The Story of the Interscholastic League of Texas* (1956), and, posthumously, *The Sense of Smell* (1960).

Of the Texas triumvirate of Bedichek, Dobie, and Webb, Bedichek was considered the senior member in knowledge of outdoor life. He usually rose about three o'clock in the morning, read the classics in the original Latin or Greek, and only then turned to the morning newspaper, since in his words, "I now have my perspective." From early spring to late autumn he could frequently be found on a rock at Austin's Barton Springs, known as Bedi's Rock, where older men like Dobie and young students ringed about him as he discoursed on problems of environment and competition. He died while sitting on the front porch of his Austin home waiting for his wife to finish baking cornbread for lunch.

See Ronnie Dugger, *Three Men in Texas: Bedichek, Webb and Dobie* (1967); and William A. Owens, *Three Friends: Roy Bedichek, J. Frank Dobie, Walter Prescott Webb* (1969).—J. B. F.

Beecher's Island, battle of (1868). Major George A. Forsyth and fifty frontiersmen who had been recruited to assist the pursuit of depredating Cheyenne marched up the Arikaree fork of the Republican River, Colorado, in September 1868. On the morning of September 17 they were attacked by Sioux and Cheyenne and took refuge on the small Beecher's Island. Three massed Indian charges were broken by the rapid fire of the scouts' seven-shot Spencer carbines, and the Indians lost many of their bravest men, including Roman Nose. But the white command faced annihilation, for by evening twenty-two were dead or wounded, and the remaining twenty-nine were surrounded by an estimated six hundred Indians. Jack Stilwell and Pierre Trudeau managed to get through the Indian lines, however, and on September 25, Negro troopers from the Tenth Cavalry came to the rescue.—R. N. E.

Benavides, Fray Alonso de. See NEW MEXICO MISSIONS.

Benjamin, Judah P. (1811–1884). Louisiana politician. Born in Christiansted, St. Croix, Virgin Islands, of Sephardic Jewish parentage, Benjamin moved with his family in early youth to Wilmington, North Carolina, and eventually to Charleston, South Carolina. Entering Yale at the age of fourteen, he was forced to leave her halls in his junior year because of some unexplained offense, and in 1828 he made his way to New Orleans. There he studied French and the law, married into a Louisiana family, and rose quickly into prominence as a leader of the bar and one of the major spokesmen of the Whig party. A power in the state legislature and the state constitutional conventions of 1845 and 1852, Benjamin went to the United States Senate in the latter year, where he remained until the secession crisis and before which he delivered a forceful defense of the southern cause on December 31, 1860. With Louisiana's secession from the Union in January 1861, he lent his considerable talents to the Confederacy in a variety of assignments: as attorney-general until November 1861; as secretary of war from then until March 1862; and as secretary of state from that point until the end of the Civil War. His performance in the war office suffered from his basic unfamiliarity with military concerns, and he was severely criticized for reverses such as the loss of Roanoke Island, but he won the lasting gratitude of Jefferson Davis for his assumption of blame that might otherwise have centered on the president. The grand objective of his diplomacy as secretary of state, recognition of the Confederacy by England and France, was never attained. With the collapse of the Confederacy, he fled via Florida and the West Indies to England, where his legal talents were to give him a wholly new career as an eminently successful barrister, honored as Queen's Counsel in 1872. He retired in 1883 and was buried in Paris.

See R. D. Meade, *Judah P. Benjamin* (1943); B. J. Hendrick, *Statesmen of the Lost Cause* (1939); and Rembert Patrick, *Jefferson Davis and His Cabinet* (1944). —J. G. T.

Bennett, Robert L. (1912-   ). Oneida government official and lawyer. Bennett was born in Wisconsin. He graduated from Haskell Institute, a school for Indians, and worked his way through Southeastern University Law School. He began working for the Bureau of Indian Affairs before he finished school and served in the bureau for more than thirty years. Soon after his graduation, Bennett was appointed superintendent of the Navaho reservation. Following service in the marines (1943-45), he directed a program designed to enable Indian veterans to receive GI benefits. Returning to the bureau, he was assigned to the Aberdeen (South Dakota) area office, where he helped develop an Indian employment program in cooperation with state employment officials. The Partition Act for Ute and Southern Ute Tribal and Family Plan Program were also developed with Bennett's assistance. He was area director for the bureau in Alaska when President Johnson appointed him commissioner of Indian affairs in 1966. After he resigned in 1969, Bennett became director of the American Indian Law Center at the University of New Mexico.—C. C.

Bent brothers. Fur traders and businessmen. The four Bent brothers were the sons of Silas Bent, a native of Rutland, Massachusetts, who moved with his family to St. Louis in 1806. Although Bent's sons are usually seen as frontiersmen and mountain men, he himself was an educated man who served first as deputy surveyor for Louisiana Territory and later as a justice on the supreme court of Missouri Territory.

Charles (1799-1847), the eldest, was born in Charleston, Virginia (now in West Virginia). Caught up in the excitement of the expanding fur trade as a young man, he joined the Missouri Fur Company in 1822 and became a partner of Joshua Pilcher, head of the company, in 1825. Little is known of his years on the Missouri River or in the mountains, but the failure of the Missouri Fur Company and the ruinous competition of the American Fur Company probably caused him to turn instead to the Santa Fe trade. As the captain of a trade caravan, he started down the trail in 1829, accompanied by his brother William. Charles tried oxen as draft animals for the trail and daringly took the Cimarron cutoff to Santa Fe, on which he experienced a serious attack by several hundred Kiowa warriors.

In 1830, with Ceran St. Vrain, Charles formed BENT, ST. VRAIN AND COMPANY, which became the largest mercantile firm in the Southwest, with outlets at Taos and Santa Fe. As a mark of the firm's success BENT'S FORT, an adobe stronghold, was built on the north bank of the Arkansas River near the Purgatoire in 1833 to handle the Indian trade. Since its construction was supervised by his younger brother, William, it was commonly called Fort William and later Bent's Old Fort. An extraordinary trade nexus developed by which Bent and St. Vrain collected and sold blankets from Mexico and buffalo robes from the Plains, drove New Mexican sheep to Missouri, and traded in horses and mules, all while deeply engaged in the fur and Indian trade. The firm established Fort St. Vrain on the South Platte in 1837, and in 1842 Charles made peace with the Kiowa and Comanche tribes, thus enabling him to establish a post on the Canadian River.

Charles' interests centered increasingly on New Mexico, however. Sometime during the 1830s he moved to Taos, married Maria Ignacia Jaramillo, and became a political associate of Manuel Armijo, governor of New Mexico (1837-46). Charles helped persuade Armijo to award to friends large land grants in which he had a secret interest. Nevertheless, when the Mexican War broke out, Charles welcomed American conquest of New Mexico. Since he was one of the most prominent Anglo-Americans in the Southwest, Kearny appointed him to be the first American governor of the province. But Bent, a strong-willed person with a sarcastic tongue, had enemies. His running feud with the powerful Martinez family of Taos and his trade relations with the enemies of the Taos Indians combined with resentment of the conquerors and fear of land seizure to produce the Taos rebellion of January 1847, in which Bent was killed and scalped.

William (1809-1869) was born in St. Louis and was trapping on the upper Arkansas as early as 1824. He became a partner of his brother Charles and of St. Vrain and was the virtual manager of the extensive operations at Bent's Fort. In 1846 he guided Kearny's American troops from Bent's Fort to Santa Fe, and in 1849 he became the sole owner of the firm when St. Vrain retired. That same year, disgusted at the low price the government had offered for his fort, he blew it up and built a new post thirty-eight miles downstream. In 1857 he built a stockade (which he enlarged in 1860) at the mouth of the Purgatoire River, gathered settlers, and thus founded what was to be the first permanent Anglo-American settlement in Colorado. In his final years William lived at Westport, Kansas, where the famed mountain men Jim Bridger and Louis Vasquez were his neighbors.

William was undoubtedly more affected by frontier life than Charles. He liked trading with the many tribes. Each of his three marriages was to Indian women. But he witnessed the collapse of his frontier empire when the Pikes Peak gold rush of 1859 unsettled Indian relations. Although he worked first as an Indian agent and later as a private citizen to ease tensions, conflicts between the Plains tribes grew into open warfare. When Colorado troops marched to Sand Creek in 1864, the officers posted guards to prevent William from warning the Indians of an impending attack on the Cheyenne encampment on Sand Creek, and his half-breed son, Robert, was forced to lead Colonel Chivington to the site.

George (1814-1847) was born in St. Louis and by 1837 had become a partner in Bent and St. Vrain, and in that year constructed Fort St. Vrain on the South Platte River. He held important positions before dying of "fever" at Bent's Fort.

Robert (1816-1841), was also born in St. Louis. He spent the years 1832-41 in the West, living at Bent's Fort and having occasional charge of it. He was killed by the Comanche.

See Leroy R. Hafen, ed., *The Mountain Men and the Fur Trade of the Far West*, vols. II (1965) and IV (1966); and David Lavender, *Bent's Fort* (1954).—G. B. D.

Benteen, Frederick W. (1834-1898). Soldier. Born in Virginia of a family with distinct southern sympathies, Benteen was disowned when he fought on the side of the North during the Civil War. He joined the army in 1861 as a lieutenant in the Tenth Missouri Cavalry and after compiling a distinguished record, mostly in the western theater, was mustered out as its lieutenant colonel. He served briefly as colonel of a Negro regiment and in July 1866 was appointed a captain in the newly created Seventh Cavalry. He served in all of that regiment's Indian campaigns until 1882.

Benteen had very high standards as a soldier and was uncompromising in his judgment of others. His animosity toward George Armstrong Custer is well known. He was senior captain of the regiment at the battle of the LITTLE BIG HORN and during the siege of Reno Hill practically took command, although not formally, from Major Marcus A. Reno, who was indecisive. Benteen's prompt and decisive actions are generally credited with having saved the regiment from even greater disaster there. Although his opinion of Reno was apparently not of the highest, he sided with the major in the later controversy over Reno's actions, possibly from the belief that much of the criticism was in the nature of malicious persecution. In 1882 Benteen was appointed major of the Ninth Cavalry and soon afterward retired from the army.

See F. W. Benteen, *The Custer Fight*, ed. by E. A. Brininstool (1933); and C. G. Du Bois, *Kick the Dead Lion; A Case Book of the Custer Battle* (1954).—E. I. S.

Benton, Thomas Hart (1782-1858). Missouri politician and advocate of the West. Benton was born near Hillsboro, North Carolina. His father, Jesse Benton, was a well-educated Englishman who provided his family with an aristocratic plantation of nearly fifteen hundred acres in North Carolina, plus claims for thousands of acres in Tennessee. His speculations, however, left a debt-ridden estate at his death in 1791. As the oldest son in a family of eight children, young Thomas assumed paternal responsibilities as he and his capable and pious mother struggled to redeem the estate. In the process Benton developed an iron will and determination that characterized his whole life.

Benton's early life established for him a reputation consistent with the image of westerners as violent men. At the age of sixteen he enrolled at the University of North Carolina and almost immediately got into an argument with a fellow student. Drawing his pistol, Benton prepared to settle the dispute with finality, but was restrained by a professor. After Benton was expelled from the university in 1799 for petty theft, the Benton family moved to Tennessee, apparently to escape the embarrassment of his youthful disgrace. In Tennessee Benton was admitted to the bar in 1806 and distinguished himself sufficiently as a lawyer and occasional political journalist to be elected to the state senate in 1809. Nevertheless, his quick temper and pugnacious sense of honor brought him notoriety during the War of 1812 when, after unsuccessfully challenging one officer of the Tennessee volunteers to a duel, Colonel Benton became embroiled in a bitter personal dispute with his friend and mentor, General Andrew Jackson. The quarrel ended in a hotel brawl in Nashville, in which Benton shot Jackson and in turn was stabbed five times by Jackson's cohorts. His career in Tennessee was eclipsed by this encounter with the state's military hero, and Benton moved to Missouri. There, in 1817 he became involved in another affair of honor in which he fought with the same man on two occasions, killing him in the second duel. This incident caused Benton so much anguish that, despite many insults and challenges during his subsequent career, he refused to engage in dueling. Even so, the reputation of his temper and violent past dogged Benton for the rest of his life. Ironically it was probably Benton's almost idealistic sense of honor rather than his frontier upbringing that precipitated the duels in his life.

Benton gained a national reputation as a spokesman for the West only after he was elected to the United States Senate from the new state of Missouri in 1821. It was through that forum that the public came to know him as an outspoken, fearless, and often pompous spread-eagle orator. Actually his crusade in the interests of the West antedated his Senate career by more than a decade. In the Tennessee Senate session of 1809, Benton successfully sponsored a preemption law to allow settlers the option of purchasing land upon which they had settled, but for which they had no title. That concept was later expressed in the national Pre-Emption Act of 1841. Throughout his life Benton did all he could to provide legal encouragement for the settlement of western lands, yet he voted against a bill that would allow reimbursement to persons who had settled and made improvements on lands legally belonging to others. Benton's land views laid the basis for the famous Homestead Act of 1862.

Despite his identification with free land and western development, Benton also believed that a country's greatness was determined by its commerce, and that the great empires of the world had been built on trade. Like other national figures of his time, he was obsessed with the belief that trade with the Far East would make the United States a world power. Indeed, Benton's statue in St. Louis is inscribed with his words: "there is the East; there lies the road to India!" Writing both as prophet and expansionist at the beginning of the War of 1812, Benton (in a letter from "Americus") publicly urged the federal government to raise an army to liberate Mexico and Cuba from European control and to consider building a canal through the Isthmus of Darien, so that "the rich commerce of the east would then flow by our own doors."

In Missouri Benton's westward outlook attained a popularity and intensity that eventually made him one of the West's most important spokesmen. Moving to St. Louis in 1815, he soon came into association with William Clark, August Chouteau, and others whose interests centered in the exploitation and development of the West. With proselytizing zeal Benton wrote the governor of Virginia in 1819:

Look back to what we were thirty years ago; see what we are today; tell what we must be in 1830. From that day the west will give the law to the Republic; and those who have views beyond that period will plant themselves on the waters of the West.

That same year Benton assumed editorship of the St. Louis *Enquirer*, and used the newspaper as a forum to urge the development of Missouri, a system of national roads and canals connecting East and West, the sale of federal lead mine resources to private groups, the acquisition of Cuba, the independence of Mexico, the occupation of Oregon, and the establishment of trade with India through the Missouri and Columbia rivers. He remained editor of the *Enquirer* until 1826, but his manifest destiny ideas continued to be expressed by other editors and especially by his protégé, William Gilpin, in the *Missouri Argus* during the 1830s.

Elected as one of the first senators from the new state of Missouri, Benton took his seat on December 6, 1821. Thus began his thirty-year career as the Senate's western gadfly. In 1822 he began a crusade to obtain confirmation of land claims deriving from Spanish and French grants, but it was not until 1829 that a law provided for a commission to settle the claims. Believing that the Rocky Mountain fur trade held the key to American control of the western regions and thus to the Far Eastern trade, in 1822 Benton successfully argued for the abolition of the government factory system (see FUR TRADE: *in the United States*). For the fur entrepreneurs this meant an economic windfall, but for Benton it also meant American penetration toward the Pacific. Benton went on to urge that United States troops be sent to the upper Missouri River and even to the Columbia River to protect the American fur traders and America's national interests. While his colleagues failed to support this proposal, in 1825 the Senate did establish a government-protected road from St. Louis to Santa Fe, despite the fact that the road passed through hundreds of miles of Mexican territory. On another occasion Benton urged the building of a toll-free wagon road to Oregon so that ordinary settlers would be encouraged to go there.

Benton also began a campaign for cheap land in the West, arguing for graduated prices of public lands to decrease annually until they reached the level of twenty-five cents an acre, at which time the balance of public lands would be given away. Benton's so-called Graduation Act did not become law until 1854, but his annual efforts in its behalf endeared him to westerners. As chairman of the Committee on Indian Affairs Benton was also instrumental in obtaining the cession of Creek lands in Georgia and in inaugurating the removal of Indian tribes from the path of land-hungry Americans.

Benton's influence upon national policy for the West became all the more notable when he and Andrew Jackson became reconciled in 1825. Thereafter Benton was an ardent (though not servile) Jacksonian during and after Old Hickory's presidency. He supported Jackson's attack on the Second Bank of the United States, and his advocacy of hard currency gave him the nickname of "Old Bullion" Benton, although his support for silver may have been determined by the fact that Missouri imported Mexican silver over the Santa Fe Trail. As the perpetual propagandist for westward expansion and exploitation, Benton was aided by his son-in-law, John C. Frémont, whose government explorations he fostered.

Increasingly overshadowing western settlement, however, were the sectional conflicts between North and South. Although Benton himself was a slave-owning aristocrat, he rejected John C. Calhoun's sectional views. So devoted was he to national unity that he refused to allow even his western interests to become the source of national schism. Thus, while he had publicly urged the peaceful acquisition of Texas from Mexico in 1830, in 1836 he opposed any discussion of Texas annexation because of the slavery controversy connected with it. Again in 1843 he opposed Calhoun's plan for annexation on the grounds that it might lead to war with Mexico. As the territories of Oregon and Mexico became the focus of national debate in 1844 and thereafter, Benton refused to support the Democratic party's slogan of "Fifty-four Forty or Fight." Rather he argued for peaceful settlement of the Oregon question with Britain.

Benton's insistence that slavery was a specious question with regard to western territories led him to be increasingly isolated from his southern colleagues and from his constituents. Senators who turned a deaf ear to Benton's advocacy of a national transcontinental railroad and highway were nevertheless willing to risk national fragmentation over the question of extending slavery into areas physically unsuited for it. Eventually this disparity of views made Benton unpopular, and in 1851 he was defeated for reelection to the Senate.

Benton then served Missouri in the House of Representatives from 1852 to 1854. While his eloquence never dimmed, he was in the twilight of his life; it was an age that was increasingly hostile to the sectional moderation he advocated. Having spurned offers of nomination to the presidency during the years of his ascendancy, Benton was now defeated in his 1856 campaign for the governorship of Missouri, the state he had served so well. Undaunted by the disappointments of his old age, Benton wrote during the last years of his life a two-volume history of the national government, from 1820 to 1850; a sixteen-volume abridgment of congressional debates, 1789 to 1856; and finally a legal refutation of the Dred Scott decision.

At his death Benton was survived by four daughters, having been preceded in death by his wife, Elizabeth McDowell Benton, and their three sons.

Benton's life is well treated in Elbert B. Smith, *Magnificent Missourian: The Life of Thomas Hart Benton* (1958), and William N. Chambers, *Old Bullion Benton: Senator from the West* (1956). His western views are brilliantly summarized in Henry Nash Smith, *Virgin Land* (1971).—D. M. Q.

Bent, St. Vrain and Company. Largest United States business firm in the Southwest. Charles Bent and Ceran St. Vrain formed their partnership in 1830, first known as Bent and St. Vrain and later as Bent, St. Vrain and Company. By 1833 the company had stores at Taos and Santa Fe and in that year it built Bent's Fort (also called Fort William) on the Arkansas River, a large and secure structure. It also had a post at St. Vrain's Fort on the South Platte, begun in 1837. The company dealt in general merchandise for Indians, Mexicans, and white trappers, and in robes and furs, horses and mules, and supplies for United States government exploring and military expeditions. Bernard Pratte gave the firm its original financial support, and Robert Campbell was a principal early supplier of goods. William and George Bent were partners in the firm, and Robert Bent and Marcellin St. Vrain (Ceran's brother) may also have been partners. The firm was well organized and honestly conducted, and the partners were highly respected.

See David Lavender, *Bent's Fort* (1954).—G. B. D.

Bent's Fort (Colorado), also frequently known as **Fort William.** Bent's Fort was built by Charles Bent and Ceran St. Vrain in 1833 twelve miles upstream from the confluence of the Purgatoire and Arkansas on the north bank of the Arkansas. Strategically located on the north-south trade axis between the Platte River drainage and Santa Fe and on the east-west route of the Santa Fe Trail, it became a center for Indian trade, the collecting of furs, stock raising, and other enterprises. After he became owner of Bent, St. Vrain and Company, William Bent offered to sell the adobe fort to the United States, but the government's price was too low; angered, he blew it up in 1849 and in 1853 built a new Bent's Fort thirty-eight miles downstream, which he leased to the government in 1860. One of the most famous posts in the Southwest (as well as the largest), it was familiar to Indian, trapper, military man, and explorer.

See David Lavender, *Bent's Fort* (1954).—G. B. D.

Bering, Vitus. See ALASKA.

Bernhisel, John Milton (1799-1881). Mormon leader and Utah politician. Reared on a farm in Pennsylvania, Bernhisel studied medicine for several years, set up a practice in Trenton, Ohio, and then in 1825 resumed his studies at the University of Pennsylvania, graduating in 1827. He practiced in Philadelphia until 1836, at which time he moved to New York.

Just when Bernhisel became a Mormon is difficult to substantiate, but by 1841 he was a bishop in New York City. Corresponding with Joseph Smith, he bought land in the Mormon community of Nauvoo, Illinois, and moved there in 1843. Almost immediately he became an intimate of Smith and helped the Mormon prophet organize the Council of Fifty in 1844.

Bernhisel stayed in Nauvoo between 1844 and 1846, and went with a group of Mormons to the Salt Lake valley in 1848. There he helped organize the University

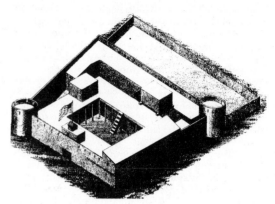

Bent's Fort as it appeared in 1845. (Library, State Historical Society of Colorado)

of Deseret (1850) and became a regent. Bernhisel functioned as a marshal from December 1848 until May 1849, when he was sent to Washington with a petition for statehood, giving Congress the option of granting territorial status. He returned to the Salt Lake valley in July 1851 in company with the first federal appointees to Utah Territory. One month later he was on his way back to Washington as Utah Territory's first delegate to Congress. After four terms (1851-59) he returned to Utah. He went back to Congress for one term (1861-63) and then decided to retire from public life.

In 1864 Bernhisel opened a medical office in Salt Lake City but continued to play a major role in the government of the church.

See Andrew Jenson, *Latter-day Saint Biographical Encyclopedia*, vol. 1 (1901).—L. J. A.

Berninghaus, O[scar] E[dmund] (1874-1952). Painter. Born in St. Louis, Missouri, Berninghaus studied at the St. Louis School of Fine Arts at Washington University and later became an associate of the National Academy of Design, New York City. He worked as a commercial artist in St. Louis and first visited the Southwest as part of a commission from the Santa Fe Railroad to produce illustrations for promotional pamphlets on western rail travel, arriving in Taos, New Mexico, in 1899. Becoming one of the founders of the Taos Society of Artists in 1912, he returned to Taos frequently and in 1923 made it his permanent residence. In later years he was on the advisory board of the School of Fine Arts at Washington University. His works are widely represented in collections at the City Art Museum of St. Louis, the Fine Arts Gallery of San Diego, the Los Angeles County Museum, the Thomas Gilcrease Institute of American History and Art, Tulsa, Oklahoma, and the Stark Museum of Art, Orange, Texas.

See Van Deren Coke, *Taos and Santa Fe: The Artist's Environment* (1963); and Mabel Dodge Luhan, *Taos and Its Artists* (1947)—D. C. H.

Berthrong, Donald J. (1922-   ). Historian. Berthrong was born in LaCrosse, Wisconsin. After army air corps service during World War II, Berthrong completed his education at the University of Wisconsin. He taught for a year at the University of Kansas City. In 1952 he joined the history faculty at the University of

Oklahoma, where he remained until 1970, when he became department chairman at Purdue University.

Berthrong was sensitive to some of the ideas and concepts developed by anthropologists and ethnologists concerning American Indians and attempted to incorporate them in historical research. He edited a diary, *Joseph Reddeford Walker and the Arizona Adventure* (1956), but established himself in his field in 1963 with *The Southern Cheyennes*, which soon became an authoritative work on the subject. Berthrong amplified his views on federal Indian policies in various articles and as a consultant on Indian land claims for the United States Department of Justice between 1957 and 1964. During 1965-66 he was a Fulbright lecturer at the University of Hong Kong.—G. D. N.

Bessey, Charles Edwin (1845-1915). Botanist and educator. Born and reared in rural Ohio, Bessey graduated from Michigan Agricultural College in 1869. A month after his graduation he began teaching botany and horticulture at Iowa State College of Agriculture.

In 1884 Bessey became professor of botany and dean of the Industrial College at the University of Nebraska (Lincoln). As one of the fathers of his discipline, he made the University of Nebraska a center of great importance in botanical scholarship. A prolific writer, he wrote three textbooks and a vast number of scholarly treatises. In 1911 he was president of the American Association for the Advancement of Science.

Bessey was a persistent exponent of the practical applications of science, particularly in agriculture. He assisted in drafting the Hatch Act of 1887, which provided federal support for agricultural experimental work. A firm believer in the relevance of higher education to farm life, he worked vigorously to induce the youth of rural Nebraska to attend the university. In the 1890s Bessey and Lawrence Bruner, a University of Nebraska entomologist, worked with the federal government in a tree-cultivating experiment on the barren plains. In 1901 Bessey induced the government to undertake a forestation project in Nebraska's Sandhills, an endeavor that resulted in the creation of the Nebraska National Forest. Bessey's major contribution in botany was his development of a system of plant classification based upon evolutionary relationships. He also gave much attention to describing the flora of the Great Plains, for he saw that region as a unique botanical area.

See Robert N. Manley, *Frontier University (1869-1919)* (1969); Raymond J. Pool, "A Brief Sketch of the Life

Through Hostile Country *by O. E. Berninghaus. (Thomas Gilcrease Institute)*

and Work of Charles Edwin Bessey," *American Journal of Botany* (December 1915), and "Fifty Years on the Nebraska National Forest," *Nebraska History* (September 1953); and Thomas R. Walsh, "Charles E. Bessey and the Transformation of the Industrial College," *Ibid.* (Winter 1971), and "The American Green of Charles Bessey," *Ibid.* (Spring 1972).—H. A. D.

Bidwell, John (1819-1900). California pioneer, politician, and rancher. Bidwell was born in Chautauqua County, New York, but moved with his family first to Pennsylvania and later to Ohio, where he was educated. After a winter of teaching school he decided that real opportunity lay in the West, and in 1839 he established a land claim of 160 acres near Weston, Missouri. But the next summer, because he was still a minor, he lost his land to a claim-jumper. Not wishing to return to Ohio in disgrace, Bidwell decided to make the trip to California. He spent the winter of 1840-41 enlisting members in his newly formed Western Emigration Society, and by early spring he had promises from five hundred persons to make the trek westward. However, the anti-California propaganda of Missouri merchants and a discouraging report from the leader of an earlier expedition to Oregon combined to reduce the size of Bidwell's party to sixty-nine persons.

None of the members of the party was experienced in western travel, nor did any of them know the trail west. "We only knew that California lay to the west," Bidwell wrote. Fortunately they were joined by a group of experienced mountain men led by Thomas Fitzpatrick, who guided them as far as the Bear River in Idaho. Here the party divided, about half the emigrants turning toward Oregon with the trappers, while the remainder, including Bidwell, continued on to California.

The California party suffered almost unbelievable hardship on their journey. They wandered aimlessly over vast stretches of desert, abandoned their wagons, and struggled over icy mountain trails. The greatest hardship, however, was hunger, and Bidwell wrote that they were forced to eat their pack animals "half roasted, dripping with blood," or nothing at all. Finally on November 4, 1841, the pioneers reached their destination, the first emigrant train to make the journey from the Missouri over the California Trail.

Bidwell found work at Sutter's Fort as Sutter's chief clerk, and in 1844 he received a grant of land. With the outbreak of the Bear Flag Revolt, he joined the rebels and attained the rank of major. After the peace treaty ending the Mexican War (1846-48) was signed, Bidwell returned to Sutter's Fort and tried his hand at prospecting. In 1849 he acquired a 22,000-acre ranch, the Rancho Chico, in northern California. Bidwell devoted a large part of the remainder of his life to developing his land, and he was to become the most famous agriculturist in California.

Bidwell's other passion was politics and he was active on both the state and national levels. He was elected to the House of Representatives in 1864 and ran unsuccessfully for governor three times. In 1892 he was the Prohibition party candidate for president. After his defeat he spent his remaining days supervising his landholdings. An active man to his dying day, Bidwell died of a heart attack after overexerting himself while chopping down a tree.

See John Bidwell, *Journey to California* (1842; repr.

1937); Ray Billington, *The Far Western Frontier* (1956); and Rockwell D. Hunt, *John Bidwell: Prince of California Pioneers* (1942).—R. B. W.

Bieber, Ralph Paul (1894-   ). Author, editor, and historian of the West. Bieber was born in Hellertown, Pennsylvania. He received his B.A. degree from Muhlenberg College (1914) and his M.A. (1915) and Ph.D. (1918) from the University of Pennsylvania. He returned to his undergraduate college as an instructor in history in 1918 and the next year joined the Washington University history faculty, where he served as department chairman in 1950-52.

In 1940 Bieber was awarded a Social Science Research Council grant-in-aid and, in 1952, a Rockefeller Foundation Fellowship. He was a member of the American Historical Association, the American Antiquities Society, the Royal Historical Society, and the Organization of American Historians. In 1947 he was president of the Mississippi Valley Historical Association.

Bieber's interest in colonial history early revealed itself in *The Lords of Trade and Plantations* (1919) and *British Plantation Councils of 1670 and 1672* (1921). His primary interest, however, lay in trails and travelers of the Southwest. From 1931 to 1943, working with the Arthur H. Clark Company, he edited the Southwest Historical Series—"documents hitherto unpublished or inaccessible, depicting social and economic conditions in the Southwest during the nineteenth century"—which includes such works as *Adventures in the Santa Fe Trade*, by J. J. Webb, and *Frontier Life in the Army*, by Eugene Bandel. A sensitive editor, Bieber paid close attention to detail without losing his sense of the work's context and larger significance.—P. L. N.

Bienville, Jean Baptiste Le Moyne, Sieur de (1680-1768). Founder of New Orleans and governor of Louisiana. Born in Ville-Marie, Montreal, Bienville was the younger brother of Pierre Le Moyne, Sieur d'Iberville. As a midshipman of sixteen, Bienville fought under his brother's command against the British on Hudson's Bay, and in 1698 accompanied Iberville on the colonizing expedition to Louisiana. In the absence of Iberville after 1702, Bienville acted as commandant of the colony from his post at Mobile, continuing in this position after his brother's death in 1706. His administration was beset by disease, a shortage of supplies, internal dissension, and neglect occasioned by French preoccupation with the War of the Spanish Succession, but he kept the colony alive through these "times of trouble." In 1712, however, Louisiana was granted as a concession by the crown to Antoine Crozat, a wealthy French merchant, who conferred the governorship of the colony upon Antoine de la Mothe Cadillac, a pompous and incompetent boor, with Bienville as second in command. Friction between the two men was intense, perhaps complicated by an unclear relationship between Bienville and the governor's daughter. Cadillac's assignment of dangerous and onerous tasks to his lieutenant only provided Bienville with opportunities to demonstrate his mastery of relationships with the Indians, as in his establishment of Fort Rosalie in 1716 in the midst of the Natchez tribe, a major factor in the pacification of that nation.

When John Law and the Company of the West assumed control of Louisiana in 1717, Bienville's accomplishments were recognized by his appointment as governor, a position that allowed him to realize his dream of establishing a settlement at the Indian "portage" between the Mississippi and Lake Pontchartrain. Here in 1718 he planted NEW ORLEANS, which became the capital of Louisiana in 1722 largely through his insistence. He was instrumental in the 1724 promulgation of the *Code Noir*, which regulated the status of slaves and persons of color in the colony and provided a base for comparable legal definitions in this area through Louisiana's history down to the Civil War. But his intense and driving personality involved him in renewed internal dissensions, leading to his recall in 1725. In Paris he continued to yearn for Louisiana, and when the Natchez War of 1729-30 finally led to surrender of its concession by the Company of the West, Bienville was sent out to his old command as royal governor in 1733. Obsessed with the determination to punish the Chickasaw for giving refuge to escaped remnants of the destroyed Natchez, Bienville exhausted his energies in two hapless campaigns against the Tennessee strongholds of his enemies in 1736 and in 1739-40. Crushed by the failure of his efforts and weary with the weight of his sixty-two years, he asked to be relieved of his responsibilities, and in 1742 he departed Louisiana forever. As late as 1763, however, he joined in Paris with delegates from New Orleans in an unsuccessful protest against the Treaty of Fontainebleau, which transferred Louisiana to Spain. Bienville died in Paris.

See Grace King, *Jean Baptiste Lemoyne, Sieur de Bienville* (1892).—J. G. T.

Bierce, Ambrose [Gwinett], (1842-1914). Short-story writer. Bierce was born of poor parents in an Ohio log cabin at the time when that state was just emerging from the pioneer stage of its history. He joined the United States Army in the Civil War and, after the cessation of hostilities, moved to San Francisco. There he drifted into newspaper work and gradually rose to the position of literary mentor of the West Coast. In 1897 he returned to the East and in 1913, lured by the promise of adventure, went off to fight in the Mexican Civil War. He was killed in Mexico.

Although he spent most of his adult life in San Francisco, Bierce was not primarily a western writer, although his "Prattle" column in the San Francisco *Examiner* afforded him tremendous local power in the literary world of that city. His nonfictional work is characterized by cutting sarcasm and acid wit in the grand American iconoclastic tradition of the crackerbarrel philosopher. The marvelous aphorisms of his *Devil's Dictionary* (assembled 1906) are characteristic of his mordant humor.

Bierce's fictional work consists of often superb but equally often clichéd stories of the supernatural, the best of which are collected in *Can Such Things Be?* (1893); and of superb tales of war, as in *Tales of Soldiers and Civilians* (1891), later retitled *In the Midst of Life.*

Bierce collected his works in an elaborate twelve-volume edition (1909-12), which is not absolutely complete. The reader interested in running down his fugitive works should consult Vincent Starrett's admirable *Ambrose Bierce, A Bibliography* (1929). His writings may be supplemented as well with his collected *Letters* (1922).

Most biographers have been too much concerned with the romance of Bierce's life and the mystery surrounding his death, and too little concerned with his literary significance. C. H. Grattan, *Bitter Bierce* (1929), and Franklin Walker, *Ambrose Bierce, the Wickedest Man in San Francisco* (1941), are two of the best early biographies, both concentrating perhaps too much on Bierce's misanthropy.

Richard O'Connor, *Ambrose Bierce: A Biography* (1967), is the best recent biography.—J. K. F.

Bierstadt, Albert (1830-1902). Landscape painter. Bierstadt was born at Solingen near Düsseldorf in the German Rhineland and brought by his parents to New Bedford, Massachusetts, in 1831. Determining at an early age to become a painter, Bierstadt returned to Düsseldorf in 1853 to study art at its famed academy, where he developed a taste for the grandiose so characteristic of his later work. After returning to America, he accepted in 1858 an invitation to join a military expedition under the command of General Frederick W. Lander to survey a wagon road from Fort Laramie to the Pacific. Bierstadt spent the summer of 1859 sketching in the Laramie and Wind River regions and in 1860 exhibited the first of his Rocky Mountain landscapes at the National Academy of Design in New York City, winning almost immediate acclaim and an election to that body. Encouraged by his success, he ventured westward in 1863 and again in 1866 to make more studies, laying the foundation for a score of large-scale canvases painted in subsequent years.

Bierstadt's work became enormously popular during this period and brought record prices. Successful both critically and financially, he built a palatial studio on the Hudson River at Irvington, New York. During his travels in Europe he was decorated by several foreign governments. In 1872 he made another excursion to California, staying on his return at the Colorado ranch of the earl of Dunraven. In 1882 his studio at Irvington burned and he opened another in New York City. During the next few years he painted several more landscapes for the Capitol in Washington and in 1885 began a series of paintings depicting the wild animals of North America. By the early 1880s, however, styles in art had begun to change. Galleries at home and abroad exhibited less and less of Bierstadt's panoramic views, preferring works after the French manner then coming into vogue, and his mountain landscapes sold at considerably reduced prices. He died in New York, an almost forgotten man among his contemporaries.

Bierstadt was one of the first to present a new and scenic image of the Far West to the American public of his day. He was a romanticist who loved large and dramatic views, and he used color, contrast, and form chiefly to produce the most dramatic and inspiring impression of his subject. Examples of his work are widely scattered, but some of the best are in the collections of the Buffalo Fine Arts Academy in Buffalo, New York, the Corcoran Gallery of Art in Washington, D. C., and the Thomas Gilcrease Institute of American History and Art in Tulsa, Oklahoma. (See illus. p. 94.)

See Harold McCracken, *Portrait of the Old West* (1962); Paul Rossi and David C. Hunt, *The Art of the Old West* (1971); and James T. Soby and D. C. Miller, *Romantic Painting in America* (1943).—D. C. H.

Big Bend National Park. Big Bend National Park is situated in western Texas. It contains a stunning array of wilderness areas—desert plains, deep arroyos, canyons carved by the Rio Grande, and forested mountains.

Last of the Buffalo *by Albert Bierstadt. (Thomas Gilcrease Institute)*

Alvar Núñez Cabeza de Vaca and his party probably passed through the area in 1535, becoming the first Europeans to see it. In the eighteenth century Comanche roamed from the Persimmon Gap country southward to the Rio Grande. During the late nineteenth century the Chisos Mountains, one of the central features of the park, were an Apache stronghold. Pancho Villa crossed the Rio Grande in 1916 to raid American settlements now encompassed by the park. Vestiges of prehistoric Indian cultures, archaeological sites, and petrified trees may also be found in the park.

Texas set aside much of the area now in the national park as Texas Canyons State Park in 1933. Congress authorized the establishment of Big Bend National Park in 1935 but specified that new lands should be added to the existing preserve. The Texas legislature set up a special commission to purchase the necessary lands and in 1941 appropriated $1.5 million for this purpose. The park in its present form includes 708,221 acres. It was officially established on June 12, 1944.—D. C. S.

Big Hole, battle of (August 9-10, 1877). The battle of Big Hole was one of the four major battles of the NEZ PERCE WAR, the other three being White Bird Canyon, Clearwater, and Bear Paw Mountains. Having crossed into Montana in their flight from Idaho, the Nez Percé went into camp in the Big Hole Basin on August 7. Colonel John Gibbon attacked at 3:30 A.M. on August 9 with 183 men (17 officers and 132 enlisted men of the Seventh Infantry plus 34 civilians); the Nez Percé may have had about 250 warriors. The troops charged on foot, raked the lodges with rifle fire, and took the village in about twenty minutes, only to find themselves suddenly under counterattack. Startled from their sleep, Nez Percé had fled in all directions. From con-

cealed positions, warriors engaged troops in a fire fight for about five hours. Gibbon then withdrew to a wooded hill, where some of the warriors besieged him from about 8 A.M. of August 9 until about 11 P.M. of August 10. Meantime, the remainder of the band moved the village to another campsite about twelve miles away. Gibbon remained in place until relieved by Brigadier General Oliver Otis Howard on August 11. Casualties: army, 29 killed, 40 wounded; Nez Percé, 89 dead by army body count, most of whom were women and children. The battle dealt the Nez Percé a serious, though not crippling, blow.

The Nez Percé War has attracted many writers, but for the battle of Big Hole a reader can best consult Merrill D. Beal, "*I Will Fight No More Forever*": *Chief Joseph and the Nez Percé War* (1963); and Alvin Josephy, *The Nez Percé Indians and the Opening of the Northwest* (1965), which is the better researched.—O. K.

Billington, Ray Allen (1903-   ). Historian. Born in Bay City, Michigan, Billington received his B.A. degree from the University of Wisconsin in 1926. He then entered the University of Michigan and took his M.A. degree in American history, married Mabel Ruth Crotty in 1928, and five years later received a Ph.D. degree from Harvard University. His interest in western America resulted from a seminar with Frederick Merk, although Arthur M. Schlesinger at Harvard directed his dissertation, the "Social Backgrounds of the Know-Nothing Party." This study was later expanded and published in book form under the title *The Protestant Crusade* (1938).

Billington began his teaching career at Clark University, where he was assistant professor from 1931 to 1937. During the next seven years he was on the staff at Smith

College, engaged in teaching and publishing and preparing what would become his most successful work, *Westward Expansion* (1949). He moved to Northwestern University in 1944 as William Smith Mason Professor of History and remained there until retiring from formal teaching in 1963. By this time Billington had won a reputation as one of the foremost authorities in the United States on the American frontier and the West.

Among his many honors was the prestigious appointment to the Harold Vyvyan Harmsworth Professorship at Oxford University (1953-54). He was awarded honorary degrees by Oxford University, Bowling Green University, Park College, and the University of Toledo.

He held numerous visiting professorships and was editorial consultant to the Dryden Press, Holt, Rinehart, and Winston, *American Heritage*, and *Encyclopedia Americana*.

Billington was a charter member of the Western Historical Association and served two terms as its first president (1961-63). He also was president of the Mississippi Valley Historical Association (1962-63) and the American Studies Association (1959-61), a director of the Social Science Research Council (1953-55), and belonged to many other professional organizations.

He resigned from Northwestern University in 1963 to become senior research associate at the Henry E. Huntington Library, San Marino, California. Much of his activity there centered on the Frederick Jackson Turner Papers and on the writing of a comprehensive biography of the man whose influence upon the teaching of western history perhaps exceeds that of any other individual.

Billington's publications include fourteen books, dozens of scholarly articles, and hundreds of book reviews. Through his voluminous writings and lectures, Billington greatly enhanced the prestige of western history as a scholarly discipline. Equally important among his many contributions was the patient encouragement and counseling to colleagues in the field, especially graduate students and young instructors, in various institutions throughout the nation.—W. E. H.

Billy the Kid (1859?-1881). Outlaw. The conspicuous place Billy the Kid occupies in American folklore almost defies explanation. Even before his death at the hands of Pat Garrett, his name was legendary in New Mexico and had been introduced to a broader audience via the *National Police Gazette*. He was dead scarcely three weeks when the first "biography" appeared, and more followed in quick succession. Those early tomes, including Garrett's *Authentic Life of Billy the Kid* (ghosted by Garrett's friend Ash Upson), almost always portrayed him as a swaggering, cold-blooded killer. But gradually a more congenial myth emerged. In 1926 Walter Noble Burn's *The Saga of Billy the Kid* provided the classic statement of a carefree youth forced into a life of crime by evil men. As an American Robin Hood, Billy the Kid still moves through the literature of the West, defying all efforts to understand the historical figure hidden in the gunsmoke of legend.

Indeed, scholars still quarrel over his name. Although most now contend that he lived under the name Henry McCarty as a child, there is some evidence that he was born William H. Bonney, as the legend insists. His childhood was spent in Indiana, Kansas, and New Mexico,

where his mother married William Antrim (hence one of his aliases). In 1874 his mother died, and the next year he got into trouble with the law for the first time. He was arrested for stealing clothes from two Chinese residents of Silver City, although it appears that he was simply the tool of an older prankster who actually stole the clothes and left young Henry literally holding the bag. At any rate, Henry escaped from the Silver City jail and headed for Arizona, working as a farmhand, teamster, and cowboy under the name of William Antrim. His age and size won him the nickname "Kid."

In the little settlement of Bonito near Camp Grant he killed his first man in August 1877. Frank P. Cahill, the local blacksmith, took pleasure in bullying the boy, and one afternoon the usual exchange of insults was followed by a fist fight. Cahill was giving him a sound thrashing when the Kid put a bullet into him. "Kid Antrim" was again arrested and again made his escape. He fled to Mesilla, New Mexico, where he assumed the name William H. Bonney. From there he drifted into Lincoln County, New Mexico. For a time he enjoyed the hospitality of John Chisum, the cattle baron. Chisum was then challenging the economic dominance of Lawrence G. Murphy and Company over government contracts in New Mexico, and Billy the Kid became more directly involved in the struggle when he went to work for John Tunstall, a young Englishman allied with Chisum against the Murphy crowd. In the months that followed, relations between the rival factions worsened, until Tunstall was murdered on February 18, 1878. Billy Bonney watched the murder helplessly from a nearby ridge. After that he gave his full support to Dick Brewer, Tunstall's foreman, and Alexander McSween, Tunstall's attorney and partner, in their feud with Murphy. After the Tunstall murder the LINCOLN COUNTY WAR raged, with Billy in the thick of it. He rode with a group called the Regulators (see VIGILANTISM), which had a cloak of legality because Brewer was appointed constable. In March the Regulators captured two of Tunstall's murderers. Brewer insisted that they be jailed in the town of Lincoln, but before they reached town, both men were killed, probably by Billy the Kid. This gave the Murphy crowd another weapon against the McSween faction. Later, Billy the Kid was among the group that murdered Sheriff William Brady and George Hindman from ambush on the main street of Lincoln. On April 4, 1878, the Kid was involved in the celebrated fight at Blazer's Mill, where a determined partisan of Murphy named A. L. "Buckshot" Roberts shot it out with the Regulators. Roberts fought gamely even though mortally wounded. Billy the Kid and several others were wounded, and they quit the field entirely when Roberts put a bullet in the brain of Dick Brewer. Gradually Billy Bonney moved into greater prominence as a leader of McSween's men. In July 1878 Billy participated in the "five-day battle" in Lincoln. McSween was killed there, but Billy the Kid and others escaped from the burning McSween home. Until then Billy and his friends had been restrained by men of some integrity, who believed that they were justified in their actions. But once McSween was killed their status changed. The "House of Murphy" had won—or so it appeared—and the power structure in New Mexico endorsed the victory and condemned the opposition. In the absence of a leader, the

McSween partisans continued the fight. In August Billy the Kid was present when Morris J. Bernstein, clerk at the Mescalero Indian agency, was killed. After that Billy stayed at the Chisum ranch for a time. When New Mexico governor Samuel B. Axtell was replaced by Lew Wallace, the new chief executive issued a general pardon, but it did not apply to Billy the Kid because of his involvement in the murder of Sheriff Brady. Nevertheless, in February 1879 a truce was called. It lasted only until members of the Murphy faction killed a lawyer named Chapman. Wallace now sought to end the troubles once and for all. He arranged a meeting with the Kid and promised a full pardon for all the charges against him in exchange for his testimony against the murderers of Chapman. When Billy was certain that his own life would not be endangered, he agreed. Billy and Tom O'Folliard were arrested by prearrangement and jailed in Lincoln, but Chapman's killers escaped. Billy the Kid remained in custody until the spring session of court in 1879, when many of the cases arising from the Lincoln County War came before the court. By arrangement with the governor Billy was allowed considerable freedom, but the pardon he hoped for was stalled. Growing impatient, he told his guards that he was tired of waiting, walked away from the store where he was being held, mounted a horse, and left Lincoln as his guards watched.

Billy was free for several months after that. He figured that someone owed him wages for his services to the McSween-Tunstall group, and he tried to collect them from John Chisum. Chisum refused to pay the five hundred dollars demanded by Billy. The young outlaw told him that he would collect in some other way. From that time on, Billy helped himself to Chisum's cattle and horses. In January 1880 Billy killed a saloon braggart named Joe Grant after Grant's gun misfired. By then, Billy the Kid and his gang were the bane of cattlemen. He was almost captured at White Oaks, a little town northwest of Lincoln, in a melee in which a man named Jim Carlyle was killed. Billy was blamed for that, and the new sheriff of Lincoln County, Pat Garrett, made catching the Kid his first priority. He caught up with Billy and some of his followers at Stinking Springs, twenty-five miles from Fort Sumner. After a brisk gunfight, Billy was captured. He was first charged with the murder of Buckshot Roberts, but when that charge was quashed, he was brought to trial for murdering Sheriff Brady and was convicted. Before he could be hanged, he killed two deputies and escaped. Garrett went after him again. On the night of July 14, 1881, he caught up to the Kid at the ranch of Pete Maxwell. Garrett was in Maxwell's darkened bedroom when Billy the Kid stepped into the open door. Garrett recognized his voice, fired twice, and killed him. Billy the Kid died without knowing who shot him.

The Billy the Kid legend is examined in Kent L. Steckmesser, *The Western Hero in Legend and History* (1965), and Ramon F. Adams, *A Fitting Death for Billy the Kid* (1960). The historical Billy the Kid is treated by a mass of students, including Maurice Garland Fulton, Robert N. Mullin, Philip J. Rasch, Frazier Hunt, Jeff C. Dykes, William A. Keleher, Waldo E. Koop, and Frederick W. Nolan.—G. L. R.

Biltz, Norman H. (1902-1973). Nevada financier and politician. Born in Bridgeport, Connecticut, Biltz went to Nevada in the late 1920s and soon amassed a fortune by promoting land development at Lake Tahoe and Reno and in other parts of western Nevada. He brought a number of millionaires to Nevada through a campaign that emphasized the conservative fiscal policy of the state, using the slogan "One Sound State." Biltz, with his partner Johnny Mueller, became a political power in Nevada in the 1940s and 1950s, forming what many observers believed was another bipartisan machine like the earlier one dominated by Nevada politician George Wingfield. Biltz was one of the strongest supporters of Senator "Pat" McCarran but lost interest in Nevada politics when McCarran died in 1954.

See W. K. Bixler, *A Dozen Sierra Success Stories: Twelve Individualists of Our Time* (1964); and Freeman Lincoln, "Norman Biltz, Duke of Nevada," *Fortune* (September 1954).—R. R. E.

Bingham, George Caleb (1811-1879). Painter. Bingham was born in Augusta County, Virginia, and moved with his family to central Missouri in 1814. Largely self-taught, he did study briefly at the Pennsylvania Academy of the Fine Arts in 1837. Once back in Missouri, he gave his attention to genre and landscape painting. In 1845 he sold four pictures to the American Art Union of New York, including his memorable *Fur Traders Descending the Missouri*. A year later he painted three more Missouri River scenes and through the purchase, exhibition, and distribution of his work by the Art Union gained the public notice he might otherwise have been slow to win. Between the years 1856 and 1859, he studied intermittently in Düsseldorf, Germany. Returning to the United States, Bingham thereafter resided in Kansas City, Missouri, where he became known as a prominent figure in politics as well as in art, painting portraits, historical subjects, and genre scenes relating to American rural and political life. In 1877 he was made professor of art at Missouri University, Columbia, Missouri.

Bingham exhibited at the Pennsylvania Academy and the National Academy of Design in New York City during his lifetime, and examples of his work also survive at the Metropolitan Museum of Art in New York City and the Missouri State Historical Society in Jefferson City, Missouri.

See Maurice Bloch, *George Caleb Bingham—The Evolution of an Artist* (1967), and John Francis McDermott, *George Caleb Bingham, River Portraitist* (1959). —D. C. H.

birds. The pioneers who set out across the Mississippi for the Far West, following the Oregon Trail or other routes, encountered birds in a profusion that probably was matched in few parts of the world. The variety of species was also remarkable. The tall prairie grass, interspersed with frequent ponds and sloughs, provided ideal living space for this abundance of birds, as well as for the great herds of buffalo and antelope, which at first were more obvious to the pioneer.

Two species of grouse, the prairie chicken and the sharp-tailed grouse, were prized as food. Many of the lonely settlers supplemented their diets with these and other game birds. In the spring the males of these grouse gather on community courting grounds, or leks, where they perform remarkable courtship dances. The prairie chicken struts around while two tufts of long stiff feathers on the sides of the neck are projected straight upward above the head. At the same time, two yellow sacs, one on each side of the neck, become distended with air. This air is suddenly released, producing a low booming sound. At the same time, the bird stamps its feet rapidly on the ground. The Plains Indians incorporated some of the attitudes and motions of this bird into their dances.

Meanwhile, each spring the prairie was enlivened with the songs of smaller birds. Like many species that inhabit open country where there are no conspicuous singing perches, these birds hover high in the air while singing, like their Old World counterpart, the skylark. One of them, now called Sprague's pipit, was in the early days named the Missouri skylark. The first specimen was collected by the celebrated naturalist John James Audubon in the early 1840s near Fort Union, North Dakota. A plainly colored little bird, the pipit circles high in the blue, pouring out its sweet song. A more conspicuous bird, the black and white lark bunting, springs upward some ten or fifteen feet into the air with fluttering wings to utter its little song, which ends with a peculiar buzzing note. The colorful yellow-breasted western meadowlark, whose rich warbling song is so much more melodious than that of its eastern cousin, pours out its song from any low perch or rock.

Not all of the prairie birds, of course, are good songsters. The buffalo-bird, or cowbird as it is now called, walked about among the grazing bison, snapping up insects disturbed by the large beasts. The cowbird is a plainly colored black bird with a brown head. The song of the male is a ludicrous wheezing sound. This cowbird is the only species of bird in the United States that is a true "brood-parasite." The female lays her egg in the nest of some other bird and it is hatched and reared by the foster parent. Though the young cowbird is thus reared in complete isolation from its own species, an unerring instinct drives it to the nearest flock of cowbirds once it has left its foster parents.

Some of the prairie shorebirds also whistle their songs on the wing. The upland plover soars high in the air uttering a long mournful whistle. Its cousin the long-billed curlew, which is the largest of all American shorebirds, whistles melodiously as it sails around over its nesting grounds on the prairies of eastern Colorado and other western states. The numerous bodies of water and swamps and marshes that dotted the prairie in the days before the plow and drainage ditch harbored vast throngs of waterfowl. Ducks, geese, swans, and cranes nested in profusion, and each spring and fall their numbers were increased by hordes of migrants passing to and from their nesting grounds farther north, either in Canada or Alaska. Among these waterfowl were several species common to the New and Old World, such as the mallard (the ancestor of most of our domestic ducks), the gadwall, the shoveler, and the pintail. Others, however, were peculiar to the North American continent, among them the splendid canvasback, which after fattening on wild rice in the fall becomes the delight of epicures. Geese, too, nested commonly, though in the nesting season only the Canada goose is to be seen. Each fall, however, vast throngs of an arctic nesting species, the snow goose, migrated through the west as they headed toward their winter home on the Gulf Coast or in the central valleys of California. They made their migrations in a few long stages, stopping, in immense flocks, at a few chosen areas in South Dakota and elsewhere.

The cranes of North America are only two in number, the commoner being the bird known as the sandhill or brown crane. Some nested in the prairie marshes, while others passed on farther north to nest even into the arctic. Unlike any duck or swan, the cranes, while paused on their migratory flight, would sometimes circle high into the air, soaring about and uttering their rolling bugle-like calls. Fewer in number, but among the finest of all North American birds, was the great white whooping crane, with black pinions and a red mark on its head. An early naturalist in Kansas, Colonel W. S. Goss, wrote that the whooping cranes, "as a rule, travel in single file, following their leader in a wavy line, croaking as they go, like hounds upon a cold trail." Standing about five feet high, the tallest bird on the continent, the wary whooping crane was not even then a match for the settler's rifle, and soon began its long decline in numbers. Today only a small colony survives.

All life begins with grass, it has been said, and certainly the many birds and animals feeding on the grass of the prairie, and its seeds and flowers, attracted predators. The duck hawk, or peregrine falcon as it is now called, nested in the sharp cutbanks along the Missouri and other rivers, from which it ranged out in swift flight to intercept the migrating shorebirds and waterfowl. Golden eagles ranged far into the prairie, nesting on isolated cliffs or wherever a little groundwater had allowed a few cottonwood trees to grow. Swallowed up in the big sky of Montana, the eagle sometimes looked surprisingly small as it plunged to strike a jackrabbit or prairie dog. Along the rivers, the bald eagle occurred, more plentifully in winter, feeding especially on stranded fish and crippled waterfowl. Smaller hawks and falcons were abundant too. Swainson's hawk and the ferruginous hawk nested in trees along the rivers and ranged out in search of ground squirrels and gophers. The little sparrow hawk, or kestrel, fed upon prairie grasshoppers and locusts, but probably did little to control their periodic outbreaks. At night the great horned owl uttered its muffled hoots from the cottonwoods along the streams. But the most remarkable of the western owls was the burrowing owl. Almost restricted to the colonies of that curious rodent known as the prairie dog, pairs of these little owls nested in abandoned prairie dog burrows. Often they could be seen sitting on the mound at the entrance to the burrow, bobbing up and down in their peculiar way. Among the true scavengers, the turkey vulture, ranging with its graceful, effortless flight over enormous areas, followed the migrating or wandering bison. Its wing quills were sometimes used by the prairie Indians to feather their warbonnets, but were much less desirable than the splendid white tail quills of the adult bald eagle or the white and brown quills of the golden eagle, which also served for headdresses.

Across the mountains were the endless deserts and arid scrublands of the Great Basin. Here the open country birds were often somewhat different from those of the lush prairies. Mountain plover ran across the gravelly flats, and horned larks, the only species of true lark on the continent, occurred everywhere. Like its European cousin, it often sings high in air, but it does not compare in musical quality. Vast areas are covered with sagebrush. Here the pompous sage grouse performs its ludicrous dances.

The isolated ponds and marshes in this area, often overgrown with rushes known as tules, were precious to water birds because of their infrequency. In some of the larger marshy areas in a desert setting, such as the Malheur marshes in eastern Oregon, which was later to become a federal bird sanctuary, the number of water birds was often astonishing. Among their number was one of the largest and most spectacular of the North American species, and one seldom seen farther east, the white pelican. Often a flock of these great white birds with flashing black wing tips would circle high in the air, cutting graceful pirouettes. Closer at hand they appeared somewhat ungainly, but it was always interesting to watch several cooperate to drive fish into shallow waters where they could be scooped up in the pelicans' huge bills and pouches. Sometimes the nesting pelicans would sail away to other lakes twenty-five or thirty miles away to secure food for their young.

Farther south in the deserts of the Southwest, the blistering heat of summer discouraged many birds. A few of the desert sparrows and thrashers are so specialized for this environment that they can survive for long periods without drinking water. Sensitively tuned to the environment, these desert birds may soon begin nesting if rains occur, taking advantage of the sudden flush of vegetation and insects. One of the most characteristic denizens of this hostile, cactus-covered land is the roadrunner, a kind of terrestrial cuckoo. Dashing around on the ground at high speed, using its long tail as a brake or rudder, it snatches up the fleet desert lizard. After immobilizing it with a snap or two of its powerful bill, the roadrunner swallows the reptile whole. Many legends grew up around the *paisano*, as the Mexican-Americans dubbed it, and the famed Texas folklorist J. Frank Dobie wrote a book on the subject. Like the rattlesnake and the coyote, the roadrunner epitomizes the animal life of the desert. Although it is a cuckoo, unlike its European relative it is not a nest parasite. It builds a nest of twigs and grass in a thorny bush and its young compete eagerly for the large insects and small lizards that their parents bring them.

In the deserts of the extreme Southwest, the so-called Lower Sonoran zone of southern Arizona and Mexico, the vegetation, though consisting chiefly of various spiny plants such as cacti and ocotillo, is more varied. The same is true of the bird life. The curve-billed thrasher sings from the tops of the bushes and builds its nest in the almost impenetrable cholla, or "jumping" cactus. Brilliant vermilion flycatchers and hooded orioles flash through the air. Gambel's quail scurry across the ground, their handsome little topknots weaving. Although less colorful than their western cousins, the California quail, they add a charming note to the desert. The Gila woodpeckers are named after the same river as the country's only poisonous lizard, the Gila monster. These woodpeckers' nesting burrows, dug in the giant cactus, or saguaro, are often taken over by the tiny elf owl.

A little higher on the dry rocky slopes other species of birds are found, among them the curious Montezuma quail, with its bizarre head markings. Scott's oriole, named after a pioneer Arizona naturalist, flits among the colorful yuccas. The zone-tailed hawk, one of several species of this family that enter the country only along the Mexican border, soars gracefully over the hillside in a manner resembling that of a turkey vulture.

One of the most striking features of the birds and other wildlife, as well as the plants, of the Southwest is the fact that one passes through several different life zones in ascending the mountains. First the lower or Sonoran desert, then the higher brushy zone just described, then a belt dominated by piñon pine and juniper. In the last, one of the characteristic birds is the piñon jay, which sweeps over the country in flocks, searching for areas in which there is a good crop of piñon nuts, which form one of the staples in its diet, as they also do in that of the local Indians. Clark's nutcracker, a striking black and white bird, named after William Clark of the Lewis and Clark expedition, is also attracted to the piñon forest. It is found much higher in the mountains, however, and often is to be seen around tourist areas begging for food along with chipmunks and ground squirrels. In the higher mountain zones of the Rockies and Sierras, dominated by pines, fir, and spruce, the birds are very different. Steller's jay flashes through the trees. A German explorer and naturalist in the employ of the Russians, Georg Steller recognized this bird when he set foot in Alaska from a Russian boat in July 1741. He had seen a picture in Mark Catesby's *Natural History of Carolina* of the blue jay, and from the similarity of the birds, he knew that he was on the continent of North America.

Along the mountain torrents one encounters that curious bird the water ouzel, or dipper. Though lacking webbed feet or any particular adaptations for an aquatic life, it plunges fearlessly into mountain streams and walks around on the bottom searching for the larvae of various aquatic insects. Its round nest of moss is often placed on a rock in midstream, where it is frequently drenched with spray. One of the most prevalent birds in all these western areas is the raven. It is at home in the rocky areas among the pine trees on the mountains, but also in the bleakest desert of the lowlands.

Finally, in ascending the mountains one reaches timberline, and here yet another group of birds is to be found. Many of them are characteristic of the tundra, which extends southward in the high mountains in this alpine habitat. Among them is the white-tailed ptarmigan, which turns snow white in winter. Feeding on the dwarf vegetation on windswept ridges it can survive even the furies of the winter. Other denizens of that zone, such as the rosy finches and the pipits, descend to lower altitudes or migrate during the winter. A few hawks and other birds migrate southward along the alpine meadows and ridges, but perhaps because of the greater elevations there are not so many moving by this route as along the Appalachian crests in the east.

Traveling on to the West Coast itself, the bird life is in some areas swallowed up in the very vastness of the giant forests of redwood and Douglas fir. Chickadees, kinglets, and creepers lisp their notes high in these trees, but only the bird watcher will detect them. Farther south, in the live-oak country of California and the desert to the south, bird life again becomes more prominent. The lovely white-tailed kite glides about, almost resembling a gull, while the California, or acorn, woodpecker tirelessly drills holes in fence posts in which to store acorns.

Hummingbirds of three or four species buzz about gathering nectar from the flowers.

At the other extreme of the avian size spectrum, one may occasionally see a great California condor sailing majestically overhead. These huge birds can cover miles and miles during a single day in their search for carrion. Today only forty or fifty of them still exist, and their future is precarious. In colonial times the California condor probably ranged north to the Columbia River. Subfossil remains show that during the Pleistocene period it ranged east to the Southwest and even to Florida. The California condor survived the upheavals in climate at the end of the Ice Age, but the decline or the disappearance of many of the great mammals characteristic of that period, such as the saber-toothed tiger and the giant bison, undoubtedly led to a decrease in the numbers of this scavenger. To the California Indians the condor was the "thunderbird." Perhaps this name arose from the noise of the air rushing through its pinions as it plunged earthward, but again the Indians may have admired the aerial feats of this great bird as it soared before an approaching thunderstorm.

This brief survey of the birds of the West has portrayed, to some extent, the conditions as they existed at the time of the Old West. What is the situation today? Most of the prairie has been plowed and the marshes drained. This includes hundreds of thousands of acres in country that is so arid and receives rain so unpredictably that it is more suitable for grazing than for farming. As a result, the water birds especially have undergone a tremendous diminution. During unusually arid periods, such as those of the 1930s in the "great dust bowl," there is reason to fear that some species of waterfowl might become extinct. When the decline in natural habitat is accompanied by overhunting, the existence of such species as the whooping crane or the prairie chicken is threatened. To be sure, in recent years sanctuaries have been established, such as those in the Bear River marshes in Utah, in the Malheur marshes in Oregon, and along the Lower Souris in North Dakota. It is still possible to see flocks of some of the birds that characterized the Old West, but only in a few restricted areas.

The situation is especially deplorable when, as not infrequently happens, one branch of the government is working against another. At the very time when conservationists are trying to save marshes, a federal bureau is urging farmers to drain marshes and potholes in the prairies, and indeed subsidizing them to do so. What makes this conflict even more unfortunate is the fact that the part played by such small bodies of water in maintaining the water table in these semiarid parts of the country is far more important than the few acres of land that may be reclaimed by draining them.

Birds of prey form another group that has suffered badly at man's hand and decreased greatly in number. This is largely the result of shooting, either for sport or by those who believe these birds to be responsible for decreases in game. Actually, the predators keep game birds and mammals at a peak of efficiency and are responsible for those very traits of fleetness of foot or of wing prized by the sportsman. Today a public awareness of the beauty and value of birds of prey is beginning to arise, but this is somewhat offset by the detrimental effect resulting from the use of DDT and other pesticides. Today's system of agriculture in which vast areas are planted with a single crop is also detrimental to most kinds of wildlife. One wonders whether the opportunities thus provided for plant diseases and plant pests to run rampant will not lead to a resumption of seemingly less efficient, but in the long run more desirable, forms of agriculture.

A healthy environment for man is a healthy environment for birds and wildlife too, and one may hope that the western landscape will be nurtured in a way that will permit its potentially rich bird life to exist in something approaching its former abundance.

See Roger T. Peterson, *A Field Guide to Western Birds* (1941); Allan Phillips, Joe Marshall, and Gale Monson, *The Birds of Arizona* (1964); and Ivan T. Sanderson, *The Continent We Live On* (1961).—D. A.

Bismarck, North Dakota. In 1873 the town of Bismarck was officially registered with the United States Post Office Department. Previous to that date the area had been known as The Crossing, Camp Greeley, Camp Hancock, and Edwinton. Officials of the Northern Pacific Railroad bestowed the name of Otto von Bismarck on the settlement as a compliment to German bond holders who had aided the railroad.

The first train, which arrived in Bismarck on June 5, 1873, brought the printing press for Dakota Territory's first newspaper, the Bismarck *Tribune*. Ten years after it was enrolled with the postal department, Bismarck became the capital of Dakota Territory. In 1889, when the territory was divided, it became the capital of the new state of North Dakota.

The population was estimated at 3,167 in 1885. After the migration out of the state following the land boom of the 1880s, the town declined to 2,186 in 1890. In the twenty years following, it doubled in size to 5,433. The 1970 census showed a population of 34,703.—D. J. T.

bison. See BUFFALO.

Bixby, Horace. See RIVERMEN.

Black Bart. Nickname of **Charles E. Boles** (1830-?1917). Stagecoach robber. Black Bart baffled Wells Fargo agents and California lawmen for years, and his eventual capture was as unlikely as his *modus operandi*. From 1875 until 1882, his order to "Throw down the box!" brought results. Wearing a duster and a flour-sack mask, he robbed twenty-seven stages (out of twenty-eight attempts) with an empty shotgun. After each stick-up, he would stroll away on foot across the California countryside with his loot in a valise. Twice, he left behind doggerel verse. His most famous offering was the following: "I've labored long and hard for bread / for honor and for riches / But on my corns too long you've tred / You fine haired Sons of Bitches." The poem was signed, "Black Bart, the Po-8." His poetic offerings provided evidence of his disdain for the authorities but no clues to his identity. Wells Fargo detectives were unable to find any leads. Then, on his last job, a passenger took a shot at him. As Black Bart scurried away, he dropped several items including a handkerchief that yielded the single clue to his name and location. A laundry mark led authorities to Charles E. Boles, a dapper little drifter from New York. He was a Civil War veteran and had a family in Illinois. He had lived in San Francisco under the name Charles E. Bolton for several years.

The "Po-8" went to prison. Four years and two months later he was released. A reporter inquired if he intended to write more poetry. "Young man," he said, "didn't you just hear me say I will commit no more crimes?" After that, Boles disappeared from public view and reportedly died in New York.

See Richard H. Dillon, *Wells Fargo Detective* (1969). —G. L. R.

Black Belt. The Black Belt of southern Alabama and northeastern Mississippi is a crescent-shaped area containing approximately four million acres of land. It was characterized in the early period by its largely treeless condition and the rank growth of coarse grass. The soils are black in color, highly calcareous in chemical content, and fertile. Here it was that a profitable plantation system was developed from the earliest beginnings of cotton culture in the lower South. Many poor migrating farmers from the Carolinas and Georgia were able to develop respectable plantations in this region. It was also here that slavery had one of its most concentrated pockets. An early southern aphorism had it that wherever you found rich black-belt soil you found a bale of cotton with a Negro sitting on it, and nearby was a planter in a silk hat propounding Whig political doctrines.

The Black Belt is drained by the Alabama, Black Warrior, and Tombigbee rivers and was closely bound to Mobile on the Gulf Coast because of this fact. It was directly in the line of the first great migration southwestward to open the cotton belt, and was a major stimulus to the westward movement in this region. It was here also that rapid soil exhaustion by faulty methods of cultivation forced cotton farmers in time to turn to other forms of planting.

See Clement Eaton, *A History of the Old South* (1949); Frank L. Owsley, *Plain Folk of the Old South* (1949); A. E. Parkins, *The South: Its Economic-Geographic Development* (1938); and Rupert, B. Vance, *Human Geography of the South* (1932).—T. D. C.

Black Elk (Hehaka Sapa) (1863-1950). Holy man of the Oglala Sioux Indians. Black Elk was born near the Little Powder River in northeast Wyoming and was a cousin of the famous Crazy Horse. He fought as a young teenager in the battle of the Little Big Horn (1876) and grew to manhood during the era of his people's greatest cultural crises, experiencing the defeat and fragmentation of Sioux (Dakota) society and the confinement of the survivors upon the South Dakota reservations. At the age of nine, while suffering from a severe illness, he experienced a powerful mystic vision, which he later interpreted as a commission from the creators to preserve the purity of Sioux traditions and to help the Sioux regain their spiritual well-being. Black Elk believed that the cause of his people's tragedy was that they had fallen away from a life of harmony with nature and had become too concerned with material things. His youth was spent in fasting and prayer, and he achieved quiet renown as a healer and spiritual guide among the Sioux during the early reservation period of the 1880s.

From 1886 to 1889 Black Elk traveled through the United States and Europe with Buffalo Bill's Wild West show. The experience affected him deeply, and he began to suspect that white men were also in need of the message of his vision. The suspicion became belief after he returned to South Dakota in time to witness the army's brutal suppression of the Sioux and their Ghost Dance religion at the Wounded Knee Massacre (1890). For the rest of his life he remained quietly on the reservation, preserving the traditions and practices in which he believed and waiting for the opportunity to share this spiritual heritage with the wider world.

In 1930 he was visited by the Nebraska poet John G. Neidhardt, who took down Black Elk's oral autobiography and published it as *Black Elk Speaks* (1932). This book is impressive on two levels: first, as a rare view of the inside of the mind and life of a culture now gone; and second, as a moving plea for harmony among the brotherhood of man and between man and the universe. In 1947 Black Elk, then the last living Sioux to possess full knowledge of the metaphysics and practices of the Sioux religion, agreed to save this knowledge from loss by detailing for anthropologist Joseph E. Brown the form and meaning of the most important ceremonials. These accounts were published as *The Sacred Pipe* (1953), which is an anthropological and religious work of much value. In recent years Black Elk's story has gained increasing popularity among both modern Indians and whites, which is as it should be, for his message transcended all bounds of race or ethnicity. —P. R. M.

black English. Like other participants in the population movements involved in settling the United States, the African victims of the slave trade faced complicated language problems, which they solved by the use of a lingua franca. Some of the enslaved Africans learned the European languages of their owners, but most of them used a pidginized version of either Portuguese, French, or English as a lingua franca. These pidgin languages, with vocabulary accretions from such sources as Standard English and the West African languages, became the native languages of black speech communities. (In the linguist's terminology, the pidgin languages "creolized.") A variety of English constituted in this way became dominant in black communities in all parts of the United States except Louisiana, where "Gombo" French Creole remains to this day, and New York and New Jersey, where, as in some of the Virgin Islands, vocabulary was borrowed from Dutch to the extent that the language was regarded as Dutch Creole. Use of pidgin English was commonplace in the New World in the eighteenth century; language creolization was in progress in the same century.

Being a practical language with no concern for the rules of books, pidgin adapted itself to contact with other languages to a degree that is only beginning to be appreciated. Travel writer John Hanson Beadle, in *Western Wilds* (1877), wrote of a "Hoosier language," which was "the result of union between the rude translations of 'Pennsylvania Dutch,' the Negroisms of Kentucky and Virginia, and certain phrases native to the Ohio Valley." The use of "Negroisms" is an (almost unintentionally) apt one: Beadle recorded verbal auxiliary forms with *bin* ("been") as a grammatical indicator that the action of the verb took place in the remote past, one of the most reliable indicators of the pidgin/Creole varieties.

The Negroisms soon spread impressively. Black exslaves joined the Indians (notably the Seminole in Florida), learned the Indian languages in addition to their Creole English, and often acted as interpreters in dealings with whites (see NEGROES ON THE FRONTIER). In the case of the Seminole, it is quite clear that pidgin English was transmitted from black to Indian. Mixed-blood speakers migrated as far as Oklahoma and Eagle Pass, Texas, in the early nineteenth century. In the latter area, a black dialect still shows traces of the Creole. Because of their experience, however grim, in language contact, the blacks were in a sense the unacknowledged leaders in frontier communication.

In the Delaware valley, long considered a source area for the westward-migrating populations, pidgin English established itself in the early eighteenth century. There are accounts of direct importation of slaves from the West Indies to Philadelphia and some records of their speech. Benjamin Franklin recorded a passage beginning

Boccorora [*buckra* "white man," a known Africanism] makee de horse workee . . .

The presence of a Creole or of a formerly creolized variety that had changed to become more like the standard language, throughout the nineteenth century, is attested. It undoubtedly went with those who migrated westward through the midlands.

In the South, black influence was especially great. Children of plantation owners learned the peer group dialect—black English in the Creole stage—from black playmates. Boys went away to school and became bidialectal (or suppressed the plantation dialect), but girls, as reported by geologist Sir Charles Lyell, Charles Dickens, Anthony Trollope, and many others, retained it all their lives. Despite desperate—and oftentimes ludicrous—attempts at eradication, the black influence became entrenched in southern English. In the nineteenth century, a major tradition of sentimentalizing that influence, considered as being due to "Mammy" rather than to her children, grew up. Black and white show the influence of African language in the words *jazz, voodoo/hoodoo, goober/pinder* (peanut), *pinto* (coffin), *tote* (carry)—some of these words, of course, ultimately spread throughout the West in the speech of whites. There is less direct African influence probable in *big eye* (greed), *evening* (any time after twelve noon), or *carry* (conduct). David Dalby, a specialist in Creole and West African languages, claims African origin for *O.K.*, known as the most widespread Americanism.

These and other Negro-influenced southernisms early extended as far as Texas, and thus came into the language of the cattle trade. Many Negroes also worked among the cowboys. Pidginisms like *savvy* and Africanisms like *buckra* (blended with Spanish *vaquero* to form *buckaroo*) enlarged the vocabulary of the cowboys, who of course took a great deal of their lexicon from contact with Mexican Spanish. Words like (*kit and*) *caboodle* and *galoot* have a purely western sound to American ears, but they are paralleled in Krio of Sierra Leone and must have been part of the Afro-Portuguese pidgin, which the Africans and Europeans used in their first efforts to communicate.

The black population itself migrated west earlier than is usually supposed, and they had close contact with other minority groups (Indians and Chinese, especially) who utilized pidgin English. While records, kept by whites, are scanty, it is very likely that creolization remained a major factor in these contact situations.

Black American English today, in California and elsewhere, retains a few vocabulary items like *humbug* (in the sense of "a fight, an altercation"), which parallel pidgin English of West Africa. In Watts and in Oakland's ghetto today, black children speak a dialect strikingly like that of Harlem or of Washington's Adams-Morgan community. One may hear, "Dis de bes'es' candy you ever ate" and "Sometime Daddy be drivin' he call people names—'Bitch!'" The zero copula (*Dis de bes'es'* rather than *Dis is de bes'es'*) and *be*-durative (*Daddy be drivin'* signals a longer period of driving than *Daddy drivin'*) contrast are described in studies made on the East Coast, in the Midwest, and in Texas.

For further reading on black English, see J. L. Dillard, ***Black English in the United States*** (1972). For the influence of black English on United States white English and southern dialect, see David Dalby, ***Black Through White*** (1970). For black-Indian influence, see Dillard, chapter 4; Ethan Allen Hitchcock, ***Fifty Years in Camp and Field*** (1960); and Kenneth Wiggins Porter, "Negro Guides and Interpreters in the Early Stages of the Seminole War," ***Journal of Negro History*** (1950) and "The Seminole Negro-Indian Scouts," ***Southwestern Historical Quarterly*** (1952). For Creole and pidgin in cowboy language, see ***The Negro Cowboys*** (1965); Julian Mason, "The Etymology of ***Buckaroo***," ***American Speech*** (1960); and Philip Ashton Rollins, ***The Cowboy*** (1922). For frontier and western contact languages, see John Beadle, ***Western Wilds and the Men Who Redeem Them*** (1877); Hitchcock; and James F. Rusling, ***Across America*** (1875). For pidginized American Indian languages and black Dutch, see J. Dyneley Prince, "An Ancient New Jersey Indian Jargon," ***American Anthropologist*** (1902) and "The Jersey Dutch Dialect," ***Dialect Notes*** (1910). For black English in northern colonies and states, see Dillard, ***Black English*** and "Black English in New York," ***English Record*** (1971).—J. L. D.

Blackfoot Indians. The Algonquian-speaking Blackfoot tribes—the Piegan, Blood, and Northern Blackfoot—were early nomadic, buffalo-hunting inhabitants of the upper Missouri-Saskatchewan River region. Although their total population probably never exceeded eight thousand after the 1830s, they were long regarded as some of the most powerful and warlike Indians of the northwestern Plains and were feared by rival tribes and whites alike.

Recurrent hostilities between the Blackfoot and the United States began in 1806, when a Piegan was killed by a member of the Lewis and Clark expedition. In conflicts that lasted for more than sixty years, the Blackfoot repeatedly drove trappers and missionaries from their country before signing their first peace treaty in 1855. In the 1860s, as inept administrators and ineffective negotiations failed to keep trespassing miners and settlers off their reservation in northern Montana Territory, many of them resumed their guerrilla attacks. But there were no further major hostilities after the tragic Massacre of the Marias of January 1870, in which federal troops slaughtered about 170 disease-infected Piegan.

In 1877 a majority of the Blackfoot settled permanently in Canada. Many of the Piegan who remained in the United States starved to death in 1883-84 because of the disappearance of the buffalo, crop failures, and insufficient federal aid. The two thousand survivors were eventually confined to a smaller reservation in northeastern Montana, where, in time, some of them became self-sufficient, primarily as ranchers.

The most complete historical treatment of the Blackfoot Indians is John C. Ewers, *The Blackfeet: Raiders on the Northern Plains* (1958). Ewers uses the reminiscences of elderly Indians, as well as a wide range of published and unpublished sources, to analyze the social, cultural, economic, and military factors that conditioned the tribe's relations with whites and other tribes. He has also published a more specialized work, *The Horse in Blackfoot Indian Culture: With Comparative Material from Other Western Tribes* (1969). Valuable insights on the effects of Catholic and Protestant efforts to reform Blackfoot society are offered in Howard L. Harrod, *Mission Among the Blackfeet* (1971). A less analytical book of special interest to those interested in the Indians' point of view is James Willard Schultz, *Blackfeet and Buffalo* (1962). A concise historical resumé on the Blackfoot (Siksika) also appears in Frederick W. Hodge, ed., *Handbook of American Indians North of Mexico* (1907-11), vol. II, and further information is included in the reports of the Blackfoot agents in the annual reports of the commissioner of Indian affairs.—H. G. W.

Black Hawk (1767-1838). Sauk warrior. Known by the Indians as Ma-ka-tai-me-she-kia-kiak, Black Hawk was born at the permanent Sauk village of Saukenuk on Rock River (Illinois), a short distance above its confluence with the Mississippi. As a young man he was frequently engaged against the Osage in the intertribal fighting over hunting grounds and won a reputation for bravery. After his father was killed, he fell heir to the powerful tribal "medicine bag" traditionally guarded by his forefathers.

In the War of 1812, Black Hawk and his band joined the British and fought at Frenchtown, Fort Meigs, and Fort Stephenson before abandoning their allies to return home. As the passing years brought the hated American settlers closer to his village and cornfields with the inevitable misunderstandings and conflicts, he brooded more and more over the injustice of the treaty of 1804 whereby representatives of the Sauk and Fox Indians had ceded the whole of their territory east of the Mississippi River to the United States. He claimed that it was entered into by chiefs who had gone to St. Louis for other reasons and who were inebriated. But in 1816, the year that the army erected Fort Armstrong on Rock Island, near his haunts, Black Hawk "touched the goose quill to the Treaty" which confirmed the old cession, not knowing, he said, that by that act he consented to give away his village.

Under pressure from the Indian agents, the peaceful group of Sauk under KEOKUK moved in 1829 to the west side of the Mississippi and established a village on the Iowa River. Encouraged not only by the principal chief of his own Sauk band, Napope, but also by the teachings of Wabokieshiek, the Winnebago prophet who dreamed of a renascence of native civilization, Black Hawk tried to weld the discontented Sauk into a confederacy. So convinced was he that the British would send supplies from Canada in the event of an armed conflict with the Americans that he returned to Illinois on April 5, 1832, after having judiciously withdrawn his band to the west side of the Mississippi. The result was the BLACK HAWK WAR, which ended in tragedy for the Indians and Black Hawk's own capture. He was incarcerated for a brief

time in Fortress Monroe, Virginia, and then brought to Iowa by way of the principal eastern cities and placed under the supervision of his old foe, Keokuk.

For a new edition of Black Hawk's autobiography, which has become an American classic since its first publication in 1833, see Donald Jackson, ed., *Black Hawk: An Autobiography* (1955)—M. L. S.

Black Hawk War (1832). The underlying cause of the Black Hawk War was the refusal of a faction of the Sauk and Fox Indians led by BLACK HAWK to recognize the validity of the treaty of 1804 (and subsequent confirmation treaties) whereby representatives of the two tribes had ceded to the United States for a pittance the whole of their territory east of the Mississippi River, comprising northwestern Illinois, southwestern Wisconsin, and part of eastern Missouri. The Indians had been left undisturbed until that area was opened to white settlement following the War of 1812. Black Hawk attempted to form an Indian confederation to curb the heavy influx of whites and to maintain possession of the lands. In 1831, however, American settlers began occupying Black Hawk's home village, a part of present-day Rock Island, Illinois, and Black Hawk prepared for forcible resistance. But when General Edmund P. Gaines on an armed steamboat along with a force of regulars and Illinois militia appeared, Black Hawk moved his band to the west side of the Mississippi. However, on April 5, 1832, near the mouth of the lower Iowa, he recrossed with a large band of warriors, women, and children and moved up Rock River to the Winnebago village of his ally White Cloud (also called the Prophet) "to make corn." A heavy force of volunteers and regulars under General Henry Atkinson started in pursuit, and Black Hawk, realizing there was no assistance forthcoming from other Indians or the British, attempted to surrender at Stillman's Run, but one of his truce bearers was killed. War then ensued with Black Hawk winning a bloody skirmish on May 14 and demoralizing the Americans. The conflict lasted until August 2, when the band was practically annihilated at the mouth of the Bad Axe River in Wisconsin as it attempted to escape across the Mississippi. Casualties in the fifteen-week war numbered approximately 70 settlers and soldiers and from 442 to 592 Indians, including those killed by the Sioux, who attacked the pitiful survivors of Bad Axe near the trading post at the Red Cedar River.

As the price of peace the Sauk and Fox Indians had to cede to the United States a fifty-mile-wide tract of land in Iowa, running along the Mississippi from the southern boundary of the neutral ground to the Missouri line, with the exception of a four-hundred-square-mile tract astride the Iowa River, which was reserved for KEOKUK, leader of the peaceful Sauk, and his followers. On her part, the United States assumed $40,000 of the Indians' debts and agreed that for thirty years she would pay an annuity of $20,000 in specie, maintain blacksmith and gunsmith facilities, and deliver forty barrels each of tobacco and salt. The treaty was negotiated by Governor John Reynolds of Illinois and General Winfield Scott—whose troops had been unable to take part in the war as many of them were infected with cholera—and was signed by nine Sauk and twenty-four Fox.

The standard sources include Donald Jackson, ed., *Black Hawk: An Autobiography* (1955); Frank E. Stevens, *The Black Hawk War* (1903), which is unfriendly to Black

Hawk; and the Black Hawk War Collection in the Illinois State Historical Library, part of which was edited by Ellen M. Whitney and published as *The Black Hawk War, 1831-1832* (1970).—M. L. S.

Black Hills. See VEGETATION: *mountains.*

Blackrobes. See ROMAN CATHOLIC MISSIONS AND THE INDIANS.

Blair, Francis Preston, Jr. (1821-1875). Missouri politician and soldier. Blair was born at Lexington, Kentucky. After completing his education at Princeton University and Transylvania Law School, Lexington, Kentucky, in 1842 Blair began practicing law in St. Louis with his brother Montgomery. St. Louis would remain the principal seat of his political operations for the remainder of his career. He accompanied George Bent to New Mexico in the Mexican War and served briefly as attorney general for that territory in 1847.

Resuming his law practice in St. Louis in the fall of 1847, Blair soon plunged into the leadership of the Free-Soil movement in Missouri. Although a slaveholder himself, Blair believed the institution doomed to ultimate extinction and urged the South to accept gradual emancipation coupled with deportation and colonization.

Throughout the 1850s Blair's political career was closely entwined with the declining fortunes of Thomas Hart Benton, although the two did not always agree on issues relating to slavery. After serving two terms in the Missouri General Assembly (1852-56), Blair was elected to the United States Congress on the Free-Soil ticket (the only one from a slave state) in 1856. Thereafter he was in the forefront of Republican party organization both locally in Missouri and nationally.

Anticipating the Civil War long before others realized its inevitability, Blair worked among the Germans of south St. Louis to perfect a strong Union organization in the midst of a sea of southern sympathizers. When war came, his "Home Guards" were prepared to fill Missouri's quota in the federal ranks after Governor Claiborne F. Jackson refused to do so. With Captain Nathaniel Lyon, Blair thwarted whatever attempts at secession Governor Jackson might have had in mind in a series of maneuvers, political and military, in the spring and summer of 1861.

Thereafter Blair played an active role—in state affairs, in Congress, and on the battlefield—in the struggle to preserve the Union. He rose to the rank of major general and served as one of Willian T. Sherman's corps commanders in the 1864-65 campaign. Returning to Missouri after the war with his financial affairs in disastrous straits, he attempted to recoup his losses through cotton operations in Mississippi, and when that failed he returned to his first love—politics. He moved rapidly to the forefront of those opposing the newly dominant Radical Union party in Missouri. But that group relentlessly used the test oath and other means to put down opposition until 1870, and through an alliance with congressional Radicals thwarted even President Johnson's attempts to help Blair with federal appointments.

As a Johnson supporter Blair worked hard to resuscitate the Democratic party in the belief that the Union needed speedy and complete reconciliation. And as a political opportunist he did not overlook his own chances for advancement. The Democrats nominated him for vice president in 1868 on the ticket headed by Horatio Seymour of New York, but he hurt his own ticket's chances with his intemperate remark that Seymour, if elected, should seize power from Congress and restore the South outright.

In the wake of the Liberal Republican triumph of 1870 in Missouri, Blair went to the United States Senate to fill a vacancy. Because of failing health and internecine party politics, he did not stand for reelection in 1873. The remaining two years of his life were spent in retirement at St. Louis, where he held, by appointment, the nominal position of state superintendent of insurance.

No biography has been written of Blair, but he is well treated in William E. Smith, *The Francis Preston Blair Family in Politics,* 2 vols. (1933).—W. E. P.

Blair, Walter. See RIVERMEN.

Blanchet, François Norbert (1795-1883). Roman Catholic missionary. Blanchet founded the Pacific Northwest church. As Quebec's vicar-general to the Oregon country's French and Indians beginning in 1838, Blanchet persuaded Rome to organize it as America's second province in 1846 under himself as metropolitan, with his brother, Magloire, and Modeste Demers as fellow bishops. For forty years he worked for the Indians' interests.

See Mary Letitia Lyons, *Francis Norbert Blanchet and the Founding of the Oregon Missions* (1940).—R. I. B.

Bland, Richard Parks (1835-1899). Missouri politician. Born near Hartford, Kentucky, Bland moved to the Missouri Ozark frontier when he was twenty but departed the following year for the mining camps of the West. During the next ten years he prospected, taught school, and studied law in California, Colorado, and Nevada.

Returning to Missouri after the Civil War, Bland opened a law office in 1869 at Lebanon, where he retained his home for the rest of his life. In this Ozark community he became well acquainted with the problems of the small farmers struggling to carve out an existence on this difficult frontier and their need for cheap currency in the face of ever-present debt. Coupled with his western mining experiences, this background prepared him for the struggle that would consume most of his energies in the last half of his life—the bimetallism issue.

First elected to the United States Congress on the Democratic ticket in 1872, Bland served continuously—save for one term (1895-97)—until his death. In the wake of the Panic and "Crime of '73," in which the silver dollar was dropped from the list of United States coins, he led the West's crusade against the demonetization of silver. As chairman of the Committee on Mines and Mining and later the Committee on Coinage, Weights, and Measures, whenever the Democrats controlled the House, he sought to secure adoption of the bimetallic standard of currency and thereby earned the sobriquet "Silver Dick," in which he gloried. He secured passage of the Bland-Allison Act in 1878, over the veto of President Rutherford B. Hayes. While not providing the unlimited coinage of silver at the sixteen to one ratio he wanted, it did remonetize silver with the secretary of the treasury authorized to purchase two million to four million dollars' worth of silver each month at the market price and issue silver dollars, which were made legal tender.

A logical presidential candidate for the Democrats in their 1896 campaign, Bland yielded to William Jennings Bryan after leading on three ballots but failing to secure the required vote. Bland subsequently turned aside attempts to nominate him for vice president and governor. He returned in triumph to Congress, where he had been turned out two years earlier by a Populist split in his district. While not blind to the disadvantageous side effects of free silver, he believed that a unilateral stand by the United States would force international agreement on bimetallism and, in the long run, work to the advantage of the "producing classes," whose champion he sought to be.

Bland's life is thoroughly covered in W. V. Byars, *An American Commoner* (1900), and W. R. Hollister and H. Norman, *Five Famous Missourians* (1900).—W. E. P.

Bleeding Kansas. See John BROWN; KANSAS; and KANSAS-NEBRASKA ISSUE.

Blizzard, Warren Lale (1888-1954). Animal husbandman and educator. Blizzard was born in McPherson, Kansas. After a brief farming experience he returned to his alma mater, Kansas State College, as an assistant in animal husbandry. In 1915 he joined the faculty of Oklahoma State University, where for the next thirty-eight years he exerted a tremendous influence on the range cattle industry as a livestock judge, scientist, and teacher.

Blizzard judged practically every important livestock show in America and coached many champion judging teams at Oklahoma State. He upgraded the quality of the college's own cattle to such a degree that it is the only college or university ever to win the fat-steer grand championship in all three breeds at the International Live Stock Exposition. Blizzard's expertise was widely recognized by stockmen, and he helped select foundation stock for many purebred herds throughout the nation.

Blizzard received many awards in his long career; in 1950 he was named one of ten persons who had had the most impact on Oklahoma history in its first fifty years and in 1958 was named to the National Cowboy Hall of Fame.—R. B. W.

Bloom, John Porter (1924-   ). Historian. Born in Albuquerque, New Mexico, Bloom was the son of Lansing Bloom, a professor at the University of New Mexico who specialized in southwestern history. After service during World War II, Bloom studied history at the University of New Mexico, George Washington University in Washington, D.C., and Emory University in Atlanta, Georgia. His interests embraced the Spanish borderlands and the trans-Mississippi West. While completing his graduate work, he embarked on a teaching career at various colleges, including North Georgia College in Dahlonega, Brenau College in Gainesville, Georgia, and the University of Texas at El Paso.

In 1960 he joined the National Park Service, where he worked on the opening of the Jefferson Memorial in St. Louis, Missouri. He also served as book review editor of *Arizona and the West* during this period. In 1964 he joined the National Archives staff in Washington, D. C., as senior specialist in western history. At the same time he was appointed editor of the *Territorial Papers of the United States,* succeeding the late Clarence E. Carter. As director of this major undertaking, Bloom prepared to publish more than a dozen volumes in ensuing years,

beginning with the twenty-seventh volume, published in 1969.

In addition to these activities, Bloom made important contributions to western history as one of the organizers in 1961 of the Western History Association. He served as its secretary between 1962 and 1967 and guided it during its first uncertain and crucial years. By 1967, when his duties in the National Archives forced him to relinquish his post, the association had become an active, vibrant organization with more than two thousand members.—G. D. N.

Bloom, Lansing Bartlett (1880-1946). Historian and minister. Bloom was born in Auburn, New York, the son of an old New England family that traced its lineage back to the *Mayflower*. Besides Williams College, he attended Auburn Theological Seminary from 1904 to 1907. Ill health led him to New Mexico, where, in 1907, he married the daughter of John F. McFie, associate justice on the territorial supreme court. Bloom then moved to Saltillo, Mexico, to become a Presbyterian missionary. Later he was transferred to a church at Jémez Pueblo, where his delving into the traditions and past of the Pueblo people increased his fascination for southwestern history. In 1917 he exchanged his ministerial duties for a position in the School of American Research and Museum of New Mexico in Santa Fe, and in 1929 he became a member of the department of history at the University of New Mexico, where he remained until his retirement in 1945. Being very active in the New Mexico Historical Society, he was associate editor of the historical journal *Old Santa Fe* and editor of the *New Mexico Historical Review* from its founding in 1926 until his death.

Bloom was a diligent research scholar whose extraordinary competence was recognized when he was sent at state expense on several long research trips to gather material pertinent to New Mexico's historical heritage in Spain, Italy, France, and Mexico during the late '20s and '30s. On one of these trips he took thirty thousand microfilms, including photographs of the famous "Sahagún," a manuscript on the Aztecs by Friar Bernardino de Sahagún, which was lost for two centuries and found in the Laurentine Library in Florence. Despite the treasure-house of material he consulted and photographed, Bloom was disappointed because he was unable to find any documented evidence on the founding of Santa Fe. He was interested in the often neglected Mexican period of the city, and his article "Mexican Administration in New Mexico," published in the maiden issue of *Old Santa Fe*, was a pioneering effort. His study of the Franciscan missionaries of New Mexico was published after his death.

Bloom's son, John Porter BLOOM, carried on his father's tradition by becoming editor of the *Territorial Papers of the United States.*

For a good biographical tribute to Bloom, see Paul A. F. Walter, "Lansing Bartlett Bloom," *New Mexico Historical Review* (April 1946).—R. W. L.

Blount, William (1749-1800). Land speculator and North Carolina and Tennessee politician. Blount was one of many figures who played a leading role in westward expansion following the end of the revolutionary war. Born in Bertie County, North Carolina, he grew up in his father's trading business. As a young militiaman he marched to Hillsboro against the backwoods Regulators in the Alamance taxpayers' rebellion (1771), but in 1776 went over to the Whig cause. He was active with the Committee of Safety, served as paymaster with the Third North Carolina Battalion of Continental Troops, and became official commissary to General Horatio Gates. With his election to the North Carolina legislature in 1781, Blount began a long political career in both the legislature and the Congress of the Confederation and as a delegate to the Constitutional Convention in 1787.

Blount was intensely obsessed with land speculation in the West, especially the lands around the great bend of the Tennessee River and Muscle Shoals. In and out of office, Blount manipulated legislation in favor of the western land speculators. In time he and his brothers, with John Sevier and others, secured claims to hundreds of thousands of acres. He also signed as a witness at the negotiation of the Hopewell treaties with the Cherokee and Choctaw in South Carolina in 1784 and 1785.

On June 8, 1790, Blount was appointed governor of the SOUTHWEST TERRITORY, and upon the organization of the state of Tennessee he was elected to the United States Senate. The latter office brought him only grief, however. He was expelled from the Senate for becoming involved in the international incident centered around the Chisholm and Romayne scheme to encourage an attack upon Spain by Britain rather than let Louisiana and the Floridas fall into French hands. Blount was of his times, however harshly some historians may have judged him in the past.

See William Masterson, *William Blount* (1954); J. G. M. Ramsey, *The Annals of Tennessee* (1853); and Samuel Cole Williams, *History of the Lost State of Franklin,* rev. ed. (1933).—T. D. C.

Blue Eagle, Acee (1907-1959). Painter and teacher. Born Alexander Che-bon-ah-bee-la McIntosh on the Wichita Indian reservation near Anadarko, Oklahoma, Acee Blue Eagle was educated at various local schools and later studied philosophy and Indian crafts at Bacone College near Muskogee, Oklahoma. Encouraged to develop professionally as an artist, he adopted as a pseudonym his mother's family name, Blue Eagle, coupling it with a nickname derived from his given initials (and a personal tribal name, "Ah-say", which he chose to spell "Acee." Promoted abroad with several other young American Indian painters in the 1930s, Acee received his B.F.A. degree from the University of Oklahoma in 1933 and in 1935 lectured on Indian art and culture at Oxford University in England. He received recognition at home when some of his paintings were included in a show at the Grand Central Art Galleries in New York City in 1938.

Commissioned to paint a mural for the library of the U.S.S. *Oklahoma*, sunk at Pearl Harbor in 1941, Acee produced other murals in his native state and was later appointed art teacher at Bacone, a post he resigned to serve with the army during World War II. Following the war, he married a Balinese dancer named Devi Dja in 1946 and joined the art staff of the Oklahoma State University Technical School in Okmulgee, where he was in residence at the time of his death. Today his paintings are represented in various private collections, the largest number owned by the Thomas Gilcrease Institute of American History and Art and the Philbrook Art Center of Tulsa, Oklahoma. His book, *Oklahoma Indian Painting-Poetry* (1960), was published shortly after his death.—D. C. H.

bluegrass regions. There are two bluegrass regions on the old frontier: one in central Kentucky and one in middle Tennessee. The Kentucky area is located on an eroded limestone dome ranging upward to more than a thousand feet elevation. It covers an area of approximately eight thousand square miles. The area in Tennessee is considerably larger. Both regions are enriched by a constantly decaying limestone base, by numerous springs, and by streams that flow almost on the surface of the land. Soil conditions in these regions are conducive to the growth of the hardy grass *Poa pratensis.* No

Creek Women Making Sofke *by Acee Blue Eagle. (Thomas Gilcrease Institute)*

one will ever be certain whether bluegrass is indigenous to these limestone areas or not. In 1754 Thomas Pownall, the geographer and surveyor, said that he saw bluegrass in the Ohio valley.

Because of the presence of bluegrass in these areas and the existence of fertile soils, settlers were attracted to these lands at the outset of white occupation. Some of the earliest towns on the trans-Appalachian frontier sprang up in the bluegrass areas. Among them were LEXINGTON, Danville, Richmond, Frankfort, and Georgetown; in Tennessee, NASHVILLE, Gallatin, Columbia, and Franklin. The first major land surveys made in Kentucky were in the Bluegrass, and it was here that the Ohio and the Transylvania land companies located parts of their claims.

See Harriet Arnow, *Flowering of the Cumberland* (1963); Thomas D. Clark, *A History of Kentucky* (1937); Lewis Collins, *History of Kentucky*, 2 vols. (1874); Robert S. Cotterill, *History of Pioneer Kentucky* (1917); and W. H. Perrin, ed., *History of Fayette County, Kentucky* (1882). —T. D. C.

Blue Ridge. See PHYSIOGRAPHY OF THE UNITED STATES.

Blumenschein, Ernest Leonard (1874-1960). Illustrator and painter. Blumenschein was born in Pittsburgh, Pennsylvania, grew up in Dayton, Ohio, and at the age of eighteen gave up the study of music to follow a career in art in New York City. He later studied at the Académie Julian and the Ecole des Beaux-Arts in Paris, returning to the United States to become an illustrator for *McClure's* magazine. One of his assignments took him in 1897 to New Mexico and Arizona, where he was captivated by the country and its people. Following another period of study abroad, Blumenschein returned to establish his studio at Taos, New Mexico, living among those Indians who became the focal point of so many of his paintings. He was one of the six charter members of the Taos Society of Artists.

Blumenschein's honors were many during his lifetime. He was made an associate of the National Academy of Design in New York City in 1910 and a full member in 1927. His pictures are noted for their strongly expressive design, vivid coloration, and imaginative, almost mystical, attitude toward the American Indian. To the last, he was an enthusiastic exponent of the Southwest in general and the Taos school of painters in particular.

See Mabel Dodge Luhan, *Taos and Its Artists* (1947); Joaquin Ortega, ed., *New Mexico Artists* (1957); and Jeanne O. Snodgrass, *American Indian Painters: A Biographical Dictionary* (1968).—D. C. H.

Boas, Franz (1858-1942). Anthropologist. Born in Westphalia, Boas took his doctorate in physics in 1881 at Kiel. After his interest shifted to cultural geography, he lived briefly among the Eskimo in Baffin Land in 1883 and 1884, and in 1885-86 he met the Bellacoola Indians from the Pacific Northwest who were "on display" in Berlin. The result was a field trip to the Northwest Coast in 1886 and the beginning of Boas' long dominance in the study of Indian cultures of that area. Subsequently he taught at Clark University in Massachusetts, was chief assistant in anthropology at the World Columbian Exposition in Chicago, and held curatorial positions at the Field Museum in Chicago and at the American Museum of Natural History in New York City. His nearly lifelong

association with Columbia University began in 1896.

Boas is perhaps best remembered for his work on the languages and traditional literature of Northwest Coast peoples, such as; the Kwakiutl, Bellacoola, Bellabella, Haida, Tlingit, and Tsimshian. He also worked for a short time among the Zuñi, Cochiti, and Laguna Indians in New Mexico.

Boas published more than seven hundred books, articles, and reviews concerning anthropological subjects. Regarded by many as the founding father of American anthropology as a scientific discipline, he was the Columbia University and Barnard College mentor of a host of successful students, including Alfred L. Kroeber, Robert Lowie, Margaret Mead, Elsie Clews Parsons, and Edward Sapir, to name but a few.

See Walter Goldschmidt, ed., "The Anthropology of Franz Boas," *Memoir of the American Anthropological Association*, no. 89 (1959); A. L. Kroeber, Ruth Benedict, et al., "Franz Boas, 1858-1942," *ibid.*, no. 61 (1943); and Leslie A. White, "The Ethnography and Ethnology of Franz Boas," *Bulletin of the Texas Memorial Museum*, no. 6 (1963).—B. L. F.

Boatright, Mody Coggin (1896-1970). Teacher, folklorist, and editor. Boatright once wrote to a friend that he was "saturated from infancy with the traditions of the range and ranch." Born on a ranch in Mitchell County, Texas, and growing up on another in Nolan County, Boatright became a competent, if not expert, cowboy. Completing army service in 1918, he attended West Texas State and the University of Texas, and, from 1923 until 1926, taught at Sul Ross State College at Alpine, Texas. He then returned to the University of Texas where, with the exception of a brief stay in El Paso, he remained until his retirement in 1963.

Boatright became interested in the folklore of Texas ranching and the oil industry. He contributed numerous articles to the Texas Folklore Society publications and in 1937 joined J. Frank Dobie in editing the society's annuals. In 1943 he succeeded Dobie as secretary-editor of the society, a post he held for twenty-one years. Some of the best of the society's publications were issued during his period of service.

In addition to his contributions to the society, Boatright wrote many articles for various professional and literary journals and a number of books, including: *Tall Tales from Texas Cow Camps* (1934); *Gib Morgan, Minstrel of the Oil Fields* (1945), a valuable contribution to the folklore on the oil industry; and *Folk Laughter on the American Frontier* (1961).

See Clarence L. Cline, Harry H. Ransom, and Mody C. Boatright, *Mody Boatright, Secretary and Editor, 1943-64* (1965); and Ernest B. Speck, *Mody C. Boatright*, Southwest Writers Series No. 38 (1971).—J. C. D.

Bodie, California. Ghost town. Bodie was once known as one of the toughest and most lawless goldmining camps in the West. Gold placers were first discovered there in 1859, but its isolated position on the eastern slope of the Sierra Nevada kept it from booming. A much larger rush occurred in the late 1870s, when the discovery of amazingly rich lodes brought some ten thousand people to the area. The diggings around Bodie yielded almost $100 million in ore during its boom period in the 1870s and 1880s. By the end of the century the town was fading slowly into a ghost,

although mining operations continued there until
World War II.

Until 1932, when a fire destroyed two thirds of the
business district, Bodie was one of the best-preserved
wooden ghost towns in the West. Today several buildings still remain in various states of arrested decay.

See Nell Murbarger, *Ghosts of the Glory Trail* (1956);
Remi Nadeau, *Ghost Towns and Mining Camps of California* (1965); and Muriel S. Wolle, *The Bonanza Trail*
(1953).—R. B. W.

Bodmer, Carl or **Karl** (1809-1893). Swiss draftsman
and watercolorist. Born in Switzerland, Bodmer came to
tour America in 1832 with Prince Maximilian of Wied
Neuwied. In 1833 Maximilian set out on the Missouri
River from St. Louis aboard the American Fur Company steamer *Yellowstone* to Fort Union, where he spent
the winter. Maximilian collected zoological and botanical specimens along the way and kept a journal, which
he later published as *Travels in the Interior of North
America*. In the introduction to the 1843 English edition
of this narrative, translated by H. Evans Lloyd, Maximilian explained the principal reasons for his journey
into the American wilderness, mentioning with respect
to Carl Bodmer that

in my description of the voyage up the Missouri, I
have endeavored to avail myself of the assistance of an
able draughtsman, the want of which I so sensibly felt
in my former travels in South America. On the

present occasion I was accompanied by Mr. Bodmer,
who has represented the Indian nations with great
truth, and correct delineation of their characteristic
features. His drawings will prove an important addition to our knowledge of this race of men, to whom so
little attention has hitherto been paid.

Schooled in the European tradition of fine
draftsmanship, Bodmer indeed showed remarkable
skill with both pencil and brush in depicting the flora,
fauna, and aboriginal population of the Missouri frontier. Returning to Europe in 1834, he translated many of
his sketches into colored engravings for the atlas that
accompanied the 1839 German edition of Maximilian's
Travels and subsequent editions in French and English.
Bodmer did not repeat his American experience, but
resided in France, for the most part in Paris and Barbi-
zon, until his death. The 427 original watercolors executed at the time of the expedition and shortly afterward were discovered at Neuwied Castle following
World War II and now form the basis of the Maximilian-
Bodmer Collection at the Joslyn Art Museum in Omaha,
Nebraska.

See John C. Ewers, *Artists of the Old West* (1965);
Harold McCracken, *Portrait of the Old West* (1962); and
Paul Rossi and David C. Hunt, *The Art of the Old West*
(1971).—D. C. H.

Boeing Airplane Company. The Boeing Airplane
Company was organized by William E. Boeing (1881-
1956) as the Pacific Aero Products Company. It was

Interior of the Hut of a Mandan Chief *by Carl Bodmer. (Thomas Gilcrease Institute)*

given its present name in July 1916. From small beginnings during World War I, this corporation grew to be the largest employer in the Puget Sound area, Washington, by the 1960s; during its peak period it employed directly more than 100,000 workers and was responsible for thousands of other jobs in related industries. Its founder, a graduate of the Scheffield Scientific School of Yale University, was taught to fly by Glenn L. Martin. He served for a time in the naval reserves, but his main contribution was in aircraft production. Boeing was also the founder of United Airlines, but this association between manufacturer and user was forbidden by the antitrust division of the government.

Boeing aircraft held many "firsts" in design and performance, including the first international airmail flight. During World War I the company built fifty Model C planes for the navy and in 1920 delivered two hundred pursuit planes. In 1934 the staff of engineers and technicians completed Project 299, which was the prototype of the Flying Fortress heavy bomber of World War II. Two years later the army air corps placed an order for thirteen heavy bombers, which were delivered in August 1937. At the outset of World War II, production increased dramatically, creating a demand for electrical dams on the Columbia River to produce aluminum that in turn could be used for the bombers. At the end of 1944 the larger B-29 was used in increasing numbers in the South Pacific. A Boeing-built airplane dropped the atomic bombs on Japan.

When the war ended, the Boeing Airplane Company turned to jet-powered civilian aircraft. Its various models, called 707, 727, 737, and 747, are used by airlines throughout the world.

In 1971 work on the Boeing supersonic transport plane (SST) was abruptly halted by congressional action because of fears of environmental pollution. In spite of other Boeing-built products, such as the "Lunar Rover" used in the Apollo-XV moon exploration and rocket-propelled missiles for the Department of Defense, the loss of the SST caused a drastic reduction in the Boeing labor force and a consequently high rate of unemployment of engineers and skilled aircraft production workers in the Seattle area.

See Peter M. Bower, *Boeing Aircraft Since 1916* (1968); C. R. Roseberry, *The Challenging Skies* (1966); and George H. Tweney, *Air Transportation and the West* (1968).—K. A. M.

Boles, Charles E. See BLACK BART.

Bolton, Herbert Eugene (1870-1953). Historian and educator. Bolton was born on a farm near Wilton, Wisconsin. He taught school in 1889-90, received a teaching certificate in 1891 at the State Normal School at Milwaukee, and after two more years of teaching entered the University of Wisconsin. After graduating with a bachelor of letters degree in 1895 he taught school again for a year and then entered graduate school at the university in 1896. Accepting a fellowship in 1897, he moved to the University of Pennsylvania, where he worked with John B. McMaster and received his doctorate in 1899, writing his thesis on "The Free Negro in the South Before the Civil War." After teaching for two years at Milwaukee, he taught medieval history at the University of Texas and soon substituted a course in Spanish colonization for modern European history. During 1907-08 he was on leave in Mexico, preparing

the *Guide to Materials for the History of the United States in the Principal Archives of Mexico* (1913) for the Carnegie Institution of Washington. In 1909 he moved to the Leland Stanford Junior University and in 1911 to the University of California at Berkeley, which had approached him after failing to attract Frederick Jackson Turner to its staff.

At Texas, Bolton had shared teaching the history of the Southwest with others; at Berkeley, he dominated the western and Latin American fields. He succeeded Henry Morse Stephens as chairman of the history department when Stephens died in 1919, and replaced Stephens' course in the history of western civilization with a course in the history of the Americas; he also became director of the Bancroft Library. Until 1928 the department had only one specialist in the history of the United States, but by the time Bolton retired in 1940 three of his students were teaching with him and four others joined the faculty while he was still active. Bolton customarily taught the big class in the history of the Americas, which had more than nine hundred lower-division students, an advanced class in the history of colonial North America, and a seminar that often had a double row of students around a large table. By 1944 he had directed 105 graduate students to doctorates at Berkeley, well over half the department's total (to 1935, over three fourths). Although retired in 1940, he taught at Berkeley again (1942-44) and later taught part-time at San Francisco State College and Mills College. He was president of the American Historical Association during 1931-32.

Bolton began to publish on the Spanish Southwest in 1902, the year of his first foray into Mexican archives. Before he left Texas he had defined his two major interests: the Spanish frontier in New Mexico and Texas, which led to *Texas in the Middle Eighteenth Century* (1915) and one of his last books, *Coronado, Knight of Pueblos and Plains* (1949); and the Jesuit occupation of northern Sonora, southern Arizona, and Lower California. This second interest centered around the work of Father Eusebio Kino (1644-1711), whose *Historical Memoir of Pimería Alta* he found in 1907 and published in 1919, and whose biography he published as *The Padre on Horseback . . .* (1932) and *Rim of Christendom . . .* (1936). On moving to California, Bolton edited narratives of the occupation of Upper California by Fages, Palóu, Crespi, and Anza, and he served on the historical commission for the beatification of Fray Junípero Serra.

Soon after he went to Berkeley, Bolton spoke of writing about the Spanish Southwest as Francis Parkman had written about French Canada, but the nature of Spanish expansion, his responsibilities as a teacher, and his own taste for exploration suggested other emphases. His great physical energy and his enthusiasm for the achievements of the pioneers of New Spain sustained him during long excursions to the archives and along the trails of explorers and missionaries as well as during legendarily long hours at his desk. Like Walter P. Webb, he spoke of moving with his students to a framework of history broader than Turner's, but he was less interested in deterministic theories than either Webb or Turner, more in re-creating the experiences and visions of the pioneers from the sources and from the physical setting. As a lecturer he held undergraduates by conveying a sense of his own involvement in his subject.

Two festschriften include bibliographies and lists of Bolton's students: *New Spain and the Anglo-American West* (1932) and *Greater America* (1945). See also John F. Bannon, ed., *Bolton and the Spanish Borderlands* (1964) and "Herbert Eugene Bolton: Western Historian," *Western Historical Quarterly* (July 1971), and a memoir by his brother, Frederick E. Bolton, "The Early Life of Herbert E. Bolton," *Arizona and the West* (Spring 1962). His papers are in the Bancroft Library.—E. P.

bonanza farming. *Bonanza farming* is a term applied to the large wheat farms that came into being in western Minnesota and eastern North Dakota in the late 1870s and early 1880s, many of them in the valley of the Red River of the North. When the Northern Pacific Railroad went bankrupt after the Panic of 1873, portions of its 50-million-acre land grant could be purchased by turning in its depreciated bonds at face value for land—a cash outlay of from $.37 to $1.65 an acre. In 1874 George W. Cass, president of the Northern Pacific, and Benjamin Cheney, a director of that railroad, purchased 13,440 acres near Casselton, North Dakota, paying an equivalent of $.40 to $.60 an acre. They hired Oliver Dalrymple to manage their bonanza under a contract by which he could acquire title to a part of the land.

Other purchases followed. For example, the Grandin brothers, bankers from Tidioute, Pennsylvania, bought over 75,000 acres; the Amenia and Sharon Land Company of Sharon, Connecticut, bought 58,350 acres; and Charlemagne Tower of Potsville, Pennsylvania, bought 36,877 acres. Many bonanzas ranged from 15,000 to 50,000 acres; in all, there were ninety-one over 3,000 acres, a minimum for such a farm.

Cheap land; the flat, treeless and stoneless prairie, ideal for large-scale operations made possible by the new farm machines just coming on the market; good rains; and the new milling process that created a demand and good prices for hard spring wheat, all helped along the rise of the bonanza wheat farms.

The managers (among whom was John Miller, first governor of North Dakota) divided the bonanzas into divisions of 5,000 acres under superintendents and these into subdivisions of 1,200 acres under foremen. They used a transient labor force—many for seeding, fewer for plowing and haying, more for the harvest, and still more for threshing. The men came from cities like Chicago or St. Paul, from the lumber camps of Minnesota and Wisconsin, and from neighboring homesteads. In the harvest rush they worked thirteen hours a day, eating five meals from breakfast at 5:00 A.M. to supper at 7:30 P.M. Wages ran from $16 to $25 a month during the crop season with board, room, and washing. In 1884 Dalrymple, the best-known bonanza farmer, had a thousand men in the harvest fields operating two hundred self-binding reapers pulled by eight hundred horses. Such operations attracted national attention and stimulated a rush of settlers to the Red River valley.

Primarily land speculators, the bonanza owners thought such farming a temporary operation, although some large holdings persisted for many years. Rising land taxes led to the breakup of some; rising land values tempted others to sell out. The Amenia and Sharon Land Company, incorporated with a capital of $92,600

in 1875, dissolved in 1922 with a net worth of $2,819,165. The Dalrymple family sold its holdings in 1917 but repossessed them in the farm depression of the 1920s and went back into farming. While it lasted, bonanza farming was most profitable.

See Hiram Drache, *The Day of the Bonanza* (1964); and Stanley N. Murray, *The Valley Comes of Age* (1967). —D. J. T.

Bonga, George (c. 1802-?). Fur trader. The son of a black fur trader and an Ojibwa woman, Bonga spoke Ojibwa, English, and French. Bonga worked in various capacities in the fur trade, first as a *voyageur*, or canoeman, for the American Fur Company. In 1820 he was interpreter for Lewis Cass, then governor of Michigan Territory, at an Indian council at Fond du Lac in present Minnesota. He also was interpreter for government agents when the Ojibwa land treaty was signed at Fort Snelling in 1837. Bonga became well known as a trader, maintaining posts for the American Fur Company at Lac Platte, Otter Tail Lake, and Leech Lake. He later became an independent trader with his own establishment.

See "Black Men in the Fur Trade with the Indians," in *Gopher Historian* (Winter 1968-69).—R. W. F.

Bonneville, Benjamin Louis Eulalie de (1796-1878). Soldier, explorer, and fur trader. Bonneville is best remembered as the redoubtable hero of the third of Washington Irving's books about the West, *The Adventures of Captain Bonneville* (1837). Although the contrast between Irving's adventurous Captain Bonneville and the inept mountain man known to the Indians as "the bald chief" is striking, there can be little doubt that this energetic Frenchman was one of the most colorful figures in the history of the exploration of the trans-Mississippi West.

Bonneville was born near Paris during the middle of the French Revolution. His father was a radical journalist and a close friend of Lafayette, Condorcet, and Thomas Paine. With the rise of Napoleon, the family migrated to America in 1803. After graduating from West Point in 1815, Bonneville served in some of the New England garrisons until 1820, when he was transferred to a force constructing a military road in Mississippi.

During the 1820s he served at various army posts in Arkansas, Texas, Indian Territory, and Missouri, and was able to observe the rapid expansion of western exploration and the growth of the fur-trading industry. By 1830 he had formulated plans for his own expedition to the West.

After a short trip to New York in the fall of 1830, where he gained financial backing for his expedition from a former participant in John Jacob Astor's Astorian enterprise, Alfred Seton, Bonneville requested and was granted a two-year leave of absence.

On May 1, 1832, Bonneville left Fort Osage, Missouri, with a force of 110 men. Their destination was the region surrounding the Green River, which Bonneville thought offered the most fertile ground for exploration and exploitation of furs. Here he built Fort Bonneville, a fortification with no military utility, known as "Fort Nonsense" to veteran trappers. Although Bonneville spent more than three years in the mountains, his efforts were futile, for he could not compete successfully with his more knowledgeable competition. His only accomplishments were to prove the feasibility of taking loaded wagons across South Pass and to dispatch Joseph Walker on his path-finding expedition to California. In July 1835 he gave up the struggle and began the return journey to Missouri.

Upon reaching Independence, he was informed that he had been dropped from the army for overstaying his leave of absence. He went to Washington to fight for reinstatement, finally succeeding in April 1836. During this period Bonneville was befriended by Washington Irving, to whom he sold the manuscript of his account of the expedition for a thousand dollars.

Irving's *Captain Bonneville* is a reasonably accurate account of the expedition despite the fact that he wrote from Bonneville's manuscript narrative rather than from the original journal Bonneville kept on the expedition. The narrative, written in Washington during the fall and winter of 1835-36, is also colored by Bonneville's fight for reinstatement. Irving's Bonneville is an idealistic and high-minded explorer. Little is said about the thinly veiled commercialism of the venture or Bonneville's naïveté in the face of the cutthroat competition for furs. It is Bonneville the adventurous explorer we see in Irving's account, not Bonneville the disappointed fur trader.

After reinstatement, Bonneville served at various frontier posts, fought in the Mexican War, and served in the recruiting service during the Civil War. He eventually attained the rank of brevet brigadier general in 1865. Bonneville spent the remainder of his life at Fort Smith, Arkansas.

See H. M. Chittenden, *The American Fur Trade of the Far West* (1902); and Washington Irving, *The Adventures of Captain Bonneville* (1961).—R. B. W.

Bonney, William H. See BILLY THE KID.

Bonnie [Parker] (1910-1934) **and Clyde [Barrow]** (1909-1934). Outlaws. Two of the most notorious outlaws in the annals of American crime, Bonnie and Clyde cut a wide swath across the Southwest during the Depression, leaving a wake of empty banks and dead peace officers. These two desperadoes are known to have killed at least twelve persons in their heyday between 1932 and 1934—nine of these officers of the law. Bonnie and Clyde operated in a wide circle of territory extending from Dallas, Texas, to Joplin, Missouri, to Louisiana, and back to Dallas.

Born in Teleco, Texas, Clyde Barrow was one of eight children of an illiterate field hand. He left school in the fifth grade and began a life of crime that reached its high point in 1930, when he met Bonnie Parker, the diminutive daughter of a Texas bricklayer. Unlike Clyde, Bonnie was an honor student. The two fell in love at first sight, just in time for Bonnie to smuggle a gun into Clyde's Huntsville Prison cell and aid in his escape. Following this break, Bonnie and Clyde began the criminal rampage that earned them national notoriety.

The state of Texas, determined to end the exploits of crime's most dynamic duo, put one of the last of the great Texas Rangers, Frank Hamer, on the case. Hamer trailed Bonnie and Clyde for four months, and on May 23, 1934, outside of Plain Dealing, Louisiana, he and his assistants brought the short career of Bonnie and Clyde to an end with a barrage of rifle fire.

The memory of these two bandits was revived in 1967, when their misadventures formed the basis of one of the most powerful motion pictures of recent years, *Bonnie and Clyde*.

See H. Gordon Frost and John H. Jenkins, *I'm Frank Hamer: The Life of a Texas Peace Officer* (1968). —R. B. W.

Boomers. See OKLAHOMA.

boom towns. Since the earliest history of the United States, urbanization has been a recurrent phenomenon. Beginning with the initial Spanish and English settlements and moving to the rapidly mushrooming suburbs of Los Angeles or Denver, the frontier West has witnessed the birth and, frequently, the death of urban centers. The western historian Hubert H. Bancroft wrote in his *California Inter Pocula* (1888), "Twenty lifetimes might be spent and twenty volumes written before the story of one mining-camp in all its ramifications could be told. The story of one mining-camp was the story of mankind. . . ." Bancroft need not have limited his statement to mining camps, because it was true of each community.

Scattered throughout the trans-Mississippi West, from the Rio Grande to the Canadian border and from the Great Plains to the Pacific Coast, are the remains of settlements that once nurtured the ambitions of promoters and settlers. They were CATTLE TOWNS such as Caldwell, Kansas; farming towns such as De Witt, Nebraska; company towns such as Colstrip, Montana; short-lived colonies of which Green City, Colorado, is an example; Bear River City, Wyoming, a railroad town; a lumber town such as Mabel, Oregon; and an army-created community such as Mohave, Arizona. Their many purposes were limited only by man's imagination. The sites varied as much as the purposes, from deserts to high mountain valleys. The numbers of persons involved ranged from a hopeful few to thousands. But they all shared a common fate: an erosion from their peak numbers to only a small remnant of residents or complete abandonment.

These settlements appeared rapidly (most in the latter half of the nineteenth century), served a purpose, and died when they had outlived their usefulness. Atlantic City, Wyoming, grew in the 1860s to a population of more than three hundred, but by the census of 1890 had declined to zero. Silver Reef, Utah, peaked at better than a thousand in the 1880s and then underwent a gradual decline, which eventually led it to the same fate as Atlantic City. Caribou, Colorado, completed its entire life cycle as a mining camp between 1870 and 1905. Other towns were born and died in a decade, the majority never growing to more than a few hundred inhabitants at best.

Despite the prospect of such a melancholy eventuality, each of these communities made some contribution to western history and played a role in the area's settlement. Seeing them today, one might question why they ever existed and what could have been their significance. Some ruins and other visual evidence littered about a site do not speak convincingly of any contribution. To find this, one must look at the historical record.

Each was born of expectation; it would be only a short while, the forecasters prophesied, before a new commercial, ranching, or mining center would be established. Mark Twain, in his delightful account of his Nevada experiences, *Roughing It*, tells of the town of Unionville, where he and his partners built a cabin and set to mining. "Meantime the camp was filling up with people, and there was a constantly growing excitement about our Humboldt mines. . . . We were stark mad with excitement—drunk with happiness—smothered under mountains of prospective wealth. . . ." Regardless of the time or place, similar experiences were repeated, similar hopes expressed, and within a few frantic weeks the wilderness could be transformed, instantly it seemed, into the semblance of a town.

Haste characterized the initial efforts—haste to gain the best lots, build the first building, secure the needed merchandise, open the store, and make a profit before competition appeared. And great profit was there to be gained by the skillful and the lucky. Haste also prevailed in building homes. Initially, any shelter would do while its owner searched for wealth or worked at the occupation that had attracted him hither. City planning was generally nonexistent; the settlement merely grew along a main street, branching out from there. A few ghost towns vaguely recall a planner's stillborn dream. In the initial rush of settlement prices for land and buildings soared, mirroring current optimism and speculation. Lots that had been sagebrush only a season before leaped in value to hundreds, even thousands, of dollars, as prospective owners frantically bid for a choice site on the main street or in the business district.

As more people rushed to the site, more opportunities opened. All types of businesses, as well as the professions, were needed, and the needs did not go unmet. In the mining camps, where self-sufficiency did not prevail, the opportunities for providing services amazed observers. In the early boom days residents were willing to pay almost any price to secure desired services, whether it was freighting or dentistry. Out of this excitement grew a town, its life expectancy reflecting the wisdom in selecting its site, the wealth of the surrounding natural resources, and the ambition of its leading citizens.

In the process of settlement in the trans-Mississippi West, the conflicting forces of frontier and urbanization converged. This was exemplified most dramatically in the mining districts. No longer was the individualistic frontiersman or the army the only cutting edge of the frontier; now they shared the responsibility of settlement with towns, a circumstance that uniquely affected both urbanization and the course of settlement. One example is the rapid confrontation brought about between Indians and whites in the Black Hills. A completely different example of the impact of urbanization is the highly developed railroad system, such as the one built in Colorado in the 1870s and 1880s.

To illustrate the effects of urbanization, a hypothetical mining camp will be briefly analyzed. (The largest single segment of western ghost towns was the mining community.) One of the first issues to be faced was law and order (see GOLD AND SILVER RUSHES and MINING LAW). The problem was compounded by the large numbers of people and the existence of easy money, which attracted all types of unsavory characters. Gunfighting or the carrying of weapons was atypical. Rather robbery, rowdiness, public nuisances, and the prevalance of GAMBLING, PROSTITUTION, and the SALOON worried the citizenry the most. But it was difficult to organize a populace so diverse and so transitory to effect the needed control and improvement. If the situation warranted action, leadership emerged and with it, generally, a move to organize a city government.

City government as conceived was simple, the primary requirement being that it remain within financially acceptable bounds. A typical example would be simply a mayor and council, which appointed a marshal and whatever other officials seemed necessary. A perennial shortage of funds reflected a common disenchantment with taxes and the fluid tax base. An equitable property tax was impossible when the values changed overnight. The obvious answer lay with a license fee; even when tried, however, city fathers chronically complained of a lack of money. This lack evidenced itself in many ways, from poor streets to a planned, but never completed, water system. The voters, though, never failed to let the council know when the sidewalks needed to be repaired or the mud holes filled. Fire was an ever-present menace to all mining camps, but only a few made adequate preparations, while many suffered the consequences. Here again, lack of funds and even public apathy handicapped the attempts at control and prevention. The usual expedient, a volunteer fire company, was only as good as its members and water supply. Sanitation and the concomitant problem of a safe water source received much press comment and council debate but little action, as some of the cemeteries pointedly testify. The camp residents polluted their surroundings to appalling degrees: Outhouses were unregulated, waste was dumped into streams, and the stench of decaying garbage fouled the air. Once more the aforementioned factors, compounded by the community's newness, stifled initiative, although older eastern cities often had little better luck in handling the same issues.

The camp's governing leaders aspired to transform the early crudeness into respectable stability and passed a multitude of ordinances to speed the program. Many of these remained dead letters on the statute books and all required enforcement, which was not always forthcoming. The local government was not the only group to foster a growth toward stability; to this end merchants, church members, and other "respectable" people joined together. Nor should the impact of the coming of wives, mothers, and sweethearts be overlooked as an agent for polishing the rough edges of a previously masculine world. Few frontier towns preferred to stagnate at a primitive level. Their inhabitants longed to imitate as much as possible the prosperity and refinements of their eastern counterparts.

Within the typical mining camp, life ebbed and flowed, reflecting the vicissitudes of the industry and the often taxing physical environment. The camp's reason for existence was to provide services and entertainment, and this it did, from the red-light district to the opera house. In a sense the town existed in two worlds, one centered around relaxation and the other the everyday struggle to make a living. For the inhabitants it was a new way of life into which they sought to bring remembered refinements. Churches and schools were built as evidence of the importance of religion and education and served as indicators that the town was becoming "civilized." Literary and debating societies, stone and brick construction, and drives to raise funds for civic improvements indicated the same trend. Better transportation was demanded, particularly the railroad. Local issues would surge to temporary importance, then quickly fade. The issue of whether to remove prostitutes from town or force them into a defined area, for example, could arouse heated debate.

Full of adventures both in town and out, camp life offered intriguing vistas for the children and provided a liberal education in all aspects of life, much to parental dismay. Women faced a continuing round of work, interrupted only by social visiting, parties, church activities, and whatever else was deemed socially acceptable. For men, relaxational opportunities proved much more numerous, but their working life meant long hours and, in many occupations, was physically hard. Nor was the pay high, except in those early flush days, when the cost of living forced everything to amazing heights. Few men made great fortunes, more made a modest living, and the rest made simply enough to manage themselves and their families.

The newspaper, one of the more important influences in the life of a mining community, served as civic spokesman, gadfly, promoter, reformer. A camp that did not have one despaired, since it was considered a vital element for insuring success and future growth.

Future growth was the great American dream to which all towns aspired. Few, however, achieved the goal. The location and the one-sided exploitative mining economy limited their lives to a few years or decades. Boom, gradual decline, and finally abandonment were their inevitable fate. But during the years that life flickered, the hopes and dreams of the community were acted out. The lure was essentially the same: come start a new life. Opportunity unlimited awaited the bold, the chance of success beckoned the skillful. If one town failed, another would soon open. Nor is this phenomenon limited to the nineteenth century; throughout the West in the twentieth century towns such as Rhyolite and Goldfield, Nevada, and Quincy, Kansas, have boomed, declined, and died. The coming of the automobile doomed some and the decline of the railroad others, while the shift from the rural areas to the larger urban centers terminated the life of many small farming hamlets. Being bypassed by a modern highway system can be as deadly today as being missed by the railroad was a hundred years ago. Nor is it any easier now to admit defeat and move on than it was then.

Many once-promising communities have disappeared or drastically declined. The Colorado Rockies, Nevada, and the Great Plains states are dotted with them. Each contributed to western settlement by transmitting social, cultural, political, and economic institutions. For a while these towns were centers of trade and commerce, encouraging surrounding settlement. In the case of mining camps a more varied economy was the result, Colorado and Montana serving as examples. Because of their economic potential, transportation networks reached out to tap them, and many of these lines are still being utilized.

With varying degrees of success the camps and towns served as an important element in the Americanization of the immigrants who lived there. Without question the new towns also helped advertise the West, both favorably and unfavorably. The larger mining camps—for example, Deadwood and Lead in South Dakota; Leadville and Cripple Creek in Colorado; Tombstone, Arizona; Virginia City, Nevada; Bannack and Virginia City in Montana—were front-page news for years

in the East. Every little village, however, tried to advertise its attractions and those of the neighboring countryside, not only to bring in money and settlers, but also to initiate the lucrative tourist trade. Finally, they served as home for several generations of Americans whose aspirations were tied closely to their community's fate. Urbanization on the frontier was not new, but the sweep of it beyond the Mississippi was greater than that witnessed in the seventeenth and eighteenth centuries. These people and their settlements were as much a part of the frontier as the fur trade, although recognition of that fact has been tardy and only recently forthcoming.

Today "ghost towns" stand as testimonials to the optimism, the expectation, and the lure that were the vital ingredients in the frontier saga. Some of these old towns have become prime tourist attractions, but what hits the eye is often only one aspect of the whole story; too often it is the image of what the visitor, long familiar with westerns, conceives the era to have been. An old-timer once said about the West, "Wouldn't it be fun to tear it all down and start again." For the urban West this was a long-standing recital, one that is still being repeated with vim and vigor.

In addition to the large towns, former mining boom towns turned tourist attractions include: Gila City, Jerome, Silver King, and White Hills in Arizona; Auburn, Bodie, Calico, Coloma, Columbia, Downieville, Grass Valley, Nevada City, Old Shasta, Panamint City, Placerville, Randsburg, Sonora, Weaverville, and Yreka in California (see also Gold-Rush Towns of California); Aspen, Central City, and Silver Plume in Colorado; Aurora, Goldfield, Rhyolite, and Tonopah in Nevada; Dolores, Elizabethtown, Golden, Hillsboro, Kelly, Mogollon, and White Oaks in New Mexico; and Alta, Ophir, and Silver Reef in Utah.

An increasing amount of history is being written about western communities. See James Allen, *The Company Town in the American West* (1966); Robert Dykstra, *The Cattle Towns* (1968); Duane Smith, *Rocky Mountain Mining Camps* (1967); and Kenneth Wheeler, *To Wear a City's Crown* (1968).—D. A. S.

Boone, Daniel (1734-1820). Frontiersman. Boone has become the symbol of American pioneering, having wandered during his lifetime from Berks County, Pennsylvania, where he was born, to western Missouri and the Platte River valley. Boone's parents were Quakers, but in time they were to have difficulties with the Friends over the marriages of their daughters outside the faith. This and the rising fever over western lands caused the Boone family to move down through the Valley of Virginia to the Yadkin valley of North Carolina.

In 1753 Daniel's brother, Squire, purchased a farm in Davidson County, North Carolina, and it was from this location that Daniel Boone became deeply interested in western adventures. He had the most rudimentary education and could only scrawl a half-literate note and sign his name in a bold, freehand style. His consuming interest being the woods and hunting, Boone became an expert marksman, was well versed in woods lore, and was an able pathfinder. He married Rebecca Bryan, a neighbor girl in the Yadkin valley, on August 14, 1756. This marriage, however, was to be anything but the

Fort Boonesboro in 1775.

conventional mating in which a frontier couple devoted themselves to a placid, domestic way of rural life.

Boone had the wanderlust, fanned by Yadkin settlers who frequently became long hunters. Two preliminary ventures led Boone to the St. Johns River of Florida, and in 1767 on a long hunt to the eastern Appalachian area of Kentucky. But it was the great venture into Kentucky in May 1769 that was to bring Boone notoriety. Going with his old friend John Finley and a party of four companions, they crossed through Cumberland Gap into the upper reaches of the south fork of the Kentucky River and wandered down to near the mouth of Station Camp Creek. For the next two years Boone wandered about central Kentucky, most of the time alone. During this time he experienced some Indian troubles and some loneliness, but he had an excellent opportunity to view the land. He and his brother, Squire, returned to North Carolina in March 1771, though they were robbed of their cache of skins and furs near Cumberland Gap.

Boone's activities until 1773 are shrouded in some mystery. In 1773 he undertook to lead his family and others to Kentucky to begin settlement, a venture that was thwarted by an Indian attack in Cumberland Gap. Boone was in Kentucky in 1774 as a messenger for Governor Dunmore to the surveyors at the Falls of the Ohio (present-day Louisville, Kentucky). In March 1775 he began opening the Boone's Trace, or Wilderness Road, from Cumberland Gap to the south bank of the Kentucky River for Richard Henderson's Transylvania Company. At the latter place he located and helped to construct Fortress Boonesboro, seat of the Transylvanians.

Between 1775 and 1778 Boone was much involved in the Indian conflict in Kentucky. Near a salt camp on Licking River in February 1778, he was taken prisoner by the Shawnee and for the next three months lived the life of an Indian. Overhearing Chief Blackfish and the British officer DeQuindre discuss plans to raid Boonesboro, he made his escape and rushed home to help defend the fort. This he did successfully but not without being charged with duplicity. Between March 7 and September 20, British and Indians besieged Boonesboro, but the fortress held out. This was Daniel Boone's great moment, and the successful defense of Boonesboro was of major importance to western settlement.

Boone was subjected to the embarrassment of a court-martial because of his capture at the Blue Licks on the Licking River, and he lost his Kentucky lands because of improper registry. In time other misfortunes befell him, although he did serve for a brief time in the Virginia general assembly from western Virginia. In September 1799 he moved with his family from western Virginia by dugout canoe to Missouri, where he trapped, hunted, and dreamed of going on even farther west until his death in 1820.

John Filson's "Boone autobiography" (1784) helped to make Daniel Boone a legend in the West, and Lord Byron in *Don Juan* gave him international literary fame. In time there was to be an enormous amount of sympathy generated for him because of the multiplicity of land squabbles that deprived him of his property. Boone was an able woodsman, a diplomat in Indian dealings, a man of courage, and a thoroughgoing pioneer.

See John Bakeless, *Daniel Boone, Master of the Wilderness* (1939); W. H. Bogart, *Daniel Boone, and the Hunters of Kentucky* (1854); Archibald Henderson, *The Conquest of the Old Southwest* (1920); William Stewart Lester, *The Transylvania Colony* (1935); and Reuben Gold Thwaites, *Daniel Boone* (1902).—T. D. C.

Boone, William Judson (1860-1936). Idaho educator. A graduate of Wooster College and of Western Theological Seminary in Pittsburgh, Boone came to Caldwell, Idaho, on November 9, 1887. He organized a Presbyterian church there in the spring of 1888 and started the College of Idaho in 1891, serving as president of Idaho's first college for more than forty-four years. He specialized in botany and made a botanical survey of the region in a time before grazing and other new conditions transformed plant life in Idaho. He also maintained a long-term study of botanical changes that came with expansion of reclamation and stock raising after Idaho became a state. During his long term of leadership, he developed a liberal arts college with special strength in biological sciences.

Based upon Boone's extensive diaries, Herbert H. Hayman's *That Man Boone: Frontiersman of Idaho* (1948) is a full-length biography.—M. W.

Boone and Crockett Club. Conservationist organization. In December 1887 Theodore Roosevelt, then twenty-nine, entertained a group of wealthy sportsmen at his residence in New York City. After the elegant dinner Roosevelt proposed that the guests become the nucleus of an organization of "American hunting riflemen." The members of the Boone and Crockett Club, as it was christened, were to collect information on their far-flung travels and use it to campaign for the protection of big game and its wilderness habitat. Another aim was to encourage "energy, resolution, manliness, self-reliance, and a capacity for self-help," qualities that wilderness hunting allegedly fostered. Prerequisites for membership in the Boone and Crockett Club were the highest caliber of sportsmanship and the achievement of killing "in fair chase" trophy specimens from several species of North American big game. High social standing and a well-padded bank account did not hurt a man's candidacy.

Founded at a time when American consciousness of wilderness values was in its infancy, the Boone and Crockett Club quickly established itself as a force for environmental protection. With Roosevelt, George Bird Grinnell, and Owen Wister leading the way, it supported the national park and forest reserve movement, helped create a system of national wildlife refuges, and lobbied for the protection of threatened species, such as buffalo and antelope. Club members traveled to the outposts of world civilization, and some, such as Charles Sheldon, made lasting contributions to exploration and natural history. In recent years the Boone and Crockett Club has assumed the responsibility of defining, ranking, and recording record heads of game, but its dominant concern remains wildlife conservation.

James B. Trefethen, *Crusade for Wildlife* (1961), is actually a history of the Boone and Crockett Club. Additional material may be found in Paul Russell Cutright, *Theodore Roosevelt: The Naturalist* (1956); and George Bird Grinnell, ed., *Brief History of the Boone and Crockett Club* (1910).—R. N.

boots. See COWBOY CLOTHING.

Borah, William Edgar (1865-1940). Idaho politician. A native of Illinois who became an attorney in Kansas, Borah sought his fortune farther west. Within a few months after he settled in Boise, Idaho, in the fall of 1890, he rose to a position of community leadership. By February 15, 1892, he had become Republican state chairman. Responding to his guidance, Idaho's Republicans suddenly departed from their traditional anti-Mormonism in time to focus upon national issues in Idaho's initial presidential campaign that fall. When, by declining to endorse the silver standard in 1896, the national Republican party ruined any prospects of success in Idaho, Borah ran for Congress as a Silver Republican. Losing to a Populist-Democratic candidate, he returned to the Republican fold by 1900. He organized a progressive Republican election victory in 1902, but a conservative Republican combine managed to deny him election to the United States Senate. From then on, he regularly battled against the party organization but refrained, after his Silver Republican experience in 1896, from leaving the party.

In 1906 Borah led the Republicans to another Idaho victory, this time with the party committed in advance to his election to the United States Senate. By now, he had a decidedly successful law practice; immediately after his election to the Senate, he gained a national reputation as an attorney for the state in its unsuccessful prosecution of William D. Haywood, who, along with another official of the Western Federation of Miners, was charged with conspiracy in the assassination in 1905 of a former governor, Frank Steunenberg. Borah showed his independence in the Senate by upholding the cause of organized labor and consistently opposing business mo-

nopoly, although as an attorney he had numbered important corporations among his clients.

In the Senate, Borah continued to enhance his national reputation through his exceptional oratorical skills. He sponsored two progressive constitutional amendments—direct election of United States senators and the federal income tax—as well as the creation of the children's bureau and finally the United States Department of Labor. On these issues he strongly supported President Theodore Roosevelt, but when Roosevelt left the Republican party Borah took a neutral position in the presidential election of 1912. Overwhelmingly returned to the Senate, Borah continued to show his independence during World War I, firmly supporting civil liberties at a time when freedom of speech was not popular. He strongly endorsed a tax on corporations' excess profits and upheld the Wilson administration against party obstructionism in conducting the war. Partly in response to this and partly under the influence of Idaho Democrat Fred Thomas Dubois, Wilson privately endorsed Borah's candidacy for reelection to the Senate in 1918, but that did not deter Borah from leading the fight against ratification of the Treaty of Versailles in 1919.

With his interest turning increasingly to international issues after 1919, Borah continued to oppose the 1919 Paris treaties as dangerously imperialist. He regarded the League of Nations simply as a device to maintain an unjust peace and disparaged the World Court as an instrument of the league. He championed unpopular causes, such as recognition of Russia, along with popular ones, such as arms limitation. As chairman of the Senate Committee on Foreign Relations from 1924 to 1933, he had an influential voice in the campaign for renunciation of war. But unlike the isolationists, he felt that the United States should pursue an active, independent international policy for revision of the Paris treaties in order to promote world peace. In domestic matters, he was too independent to join the farm bloc in 1921, but he worked for some decidedly liberal measures to aid the farmer during the 1920s, when agriculture was afflicted while the rest of the nation prospered. He also led the Republican Senate insurgents in a close fight against the Hawley-Smoot Tariff Act in 1930, and in 1932 he could not support Herbert Hoover for reelection as president.

During the New Deal, Borah endorsed banking reform, monetary adjustment for gold and silver, and social security and criticized other important measures including the National Industrial Recovery Act, which violated his antimonopoly principles. His bold opposition to some major features of the New Deal made him a leading presidential contender early in 1936. Fortunately he was spared that nomination. Instead, Idaho returned him to the Senate for a sixth term that year by a vote exceeding Franklin D. Roosevelt's total in the state. During his final Senate term, Borah quietly and effectively worked to defeat Roosevelt's proposal to enlarge (and hopefully, to reform) the United States Supreme Court, because he thought the independence of the judiciary at stake. He also continued to support measures to keep the United States out of European wars, which he had warned against so often. He was still around to witness the collapse of the Paris treaties with Hitler's expansion in Czechoslovakia and Poland in

1938 and 1939, but he did not not survive long enough to see the unexpected defeat of France in 1940.

Even though Senator Borah addressed himself to national issues, he was able, through his exceptional prestige, to serve Idaho as well as the nation. Major reclamation projects expedited the state's economic development, and before the end of his first term, construction began on the world's highest dam just above his home town of Boise. Other projects followed, and Idaho benefited substantially from having an international celebrity serving so many terms in the Senate.

Of the vast literature on Borah, four books are of special use: Claudius O. Johnson, *Borah of Idaho* (1967), a reprint of the 1936 edition with a valuable new introduction by the author; M. C. McKenna, *Borah* (1961); Robert James Maddox, *William E. Borah and American Foreign Policy* (1969); and John Chalmers Vinson, *William E. Borah and the Outlawry of War* (1957). —M. W.

Borein, Edward (1873-1945). Genre painter and etcher. Borein, born in San Leandro, California, made his living as a cowboy in southern California and Mexico and became thoroughly acquainted with all aspects of ranching life. Turning to art for his livelihood, he established a studio in Oakland, California, about 1902 and made frequent sketching trips into the surrounding area. Noted today for his illustrations of the American cowboy, especially as represented in numerous etchings, Borein taught in the 1920s in the department of art of the University of California in Santa Barbara and maintained a studio at Santa Barbara until his death. —D. C. H.

Borglum, Solon Hannibal (1868-1922). Sculptor. Born in Ogden, Utah, of Danish Mormon parents, Borglum eventually moved with his family to Omaha, Nebraska, where his father purchased a ranch and practiced medicine. Young Borglum worked for a time as a ranch hand and foreman, but the urge to become an artist predominated, and in 1893 he joined his elder brother, Gutzon, in California. Renting studio space in Santa Ana, Borglum made his first studies among the Indians and Mexicans of the Santa Ana Mountains. After exhibiting his work locally, Borglum studied at the Cincinnati Academy of Art beginning in 1895. Fascinated with horses, he sketched mounts at the nearby United States Mail Stables in Cincinnati and modeled a clay figure of a horse that received the praise of Louis Rebisso, head of sculpture at the academy, who thereafter allowed Borglum to use his studio. Study at the Académie Julien in Paris followed. While in Paris, in 1898, Borglum married and began producing western horse sculptures that were widely exhibited and acclaimed. Prompted to produce some pieces of this type for the Paris Exposition of 1900, Borglum returned to the American West to obtain further studies of horses and Indians. He arrived at the Crow Creek Reservation in South Dakota in 1899. With the help of an Episcopalian missionary, Borglum obtained many models among the Indians and also acquired considerable knowledge of Indian customs and ceremonials. Borglum and his wife finally settled in Silvermine, Connecticut, in 1907, and there established a studio. Although his reputation was overshadowed by the spectacular sculptures of the presidential heads at Mount Rushmore designed by his brother Gutzon, Solon created numerous lifesize pieces

for expositions and many civic monuments expressive of the characters and the spirit of the pioneer West.

His work is represented by important civic sculptures at Prescott, Arizona; Atlanta, Georgia; and New Rochelle, New York. Among his most memorable works, found in collections throughout the United States, are *One in a Thousand, Lassoing Wild Horses, Stampede of Wild Horses, On the Trail, On the Border of White Man's Land*, and *The Sun Dance*. Borglum organized the School of American Sculpture in New York and was its director until his death.

See Phil Kovinick, "South Dakota's 'Other' Borglum," *South Dakota State Historical Society Quarterly* vol. I, no. 3 (1971)—D. C. H.

Borland, Solon (1808-1864). Arkansas politician, soldier, and doctor. Borland was a Virginia doctor who settled in Little Rock, Arkansas, in 1843. He practiced medicine, edited a Democratic newspaper, and served as a major in the Arkansas regiment under Archibald Yell during the Mexican War, during which he was held a prisoner by the Mexicans for seven months. Returning to Little Rock, he was appointed to the United States Senate and won a full term in 1848 over Arkansas's powerful Ambrose Sevier. He resigned in 1853 to become minister plenipotentiary to Central America, and while there caused an international incident by ordering the shelling of Greytown, Nicaragua. From 1854 to 1861 he practiced medicine in Little Rock. The latter year he occupied Fort Smith with Arkansas troops, entered Confederate service, and rose to the rank of brigadier general. Bad health forced his resignation from the military service.—W. L. B.

Bouchard, James (1823-1889). Roman Catholic priest. Bouchard was the first Indian ordained a Roman Catholic priest in the United States. His Indian name was Watomika (Swift Foot). The son of Delaware chief Kistalwa and Monotowan, a French woman captured by the Comanche when a child, Bouchard converted to Presbyterianism after the Sioux killed his father in battle in 1834, studied briefly for the ministry in Ohio, then became a Catholic in 1846 and two years later a Jesuit in Missouri. Ordained in 1855, he was prominent from 1861 in San Francisco and the Far West as lecturer, preacher, missioner to miners, and anti-Chinese agitator.

See John Bernard McGloin, *Eloquent Indian* (1949). —R. I. B.

Boudinot, Elias (c. 1803-1839). Cherokee leader. Boudinot, a full-blooded Indian, was educated at the Moravian school at Salem, North Carolina, and at the Cornwall Foreign Mission School at Cornwall, Connecticut. In 1828 he became the first editor of the *Cherokee Phoenix*, a weekly newspaper published in Cherokee and English. In 1833 he wrote and published *Poor Sarah or the Indian Woman* in Cherokee using characters devised by Cherokee leader Sequoyah. From 1833 until his death he was joint translator, with the missionary Samuel A. Worcester, of several of the Gospels. In 1831 he lectured in the North to raise funds for the *Phoenix*.

As editor, Boudinot opposed the policy of Georgia to extend by force in the absence of a treaty its laws over that large portion of Cherokee territory that lay within the borders of the state. When Congress passed the Removal Act of 1830, when President Andrew Jackson did not act to enforce the decision of the Supreme Court in WORCESTER V. STATE OF GEORGIA, and when, as a consequence, Georgia began dividing Cherokee land into parcels that were distributed by lot to white settlers, Boudinot became convinced that the Cherokee faced utter demoralization unless they removed to the West. He resigned as editor when the censorship of Principal Chief John Ross prevented him from expressing views opposing the official tribal policy, which was not to remove.

Boudinot and his cousin John Ridge, also educated at Cornwall, signed treaties of removal in 1832 and 1835 that provided the legal basis for the later "shotgun removal" of the tribe to Indian Territory in 1839. Both acted as patriots to save their people, whom they felt had been kept in ignorance of the dire consequences of Georgia's aggressive action by Ross's censorship. Both were assassinated in the West by a faction that, without the knowledge of Principal Chief Ross, had decided to execute the old law of blood against persons who signed treaties alienating tribal lands.

Boudinot is still regarded today as a traitor by the Cherokee of North Carolina. He was one of the first of a succession of Indian and white people who understood the extent of Indian demoralization possible from face-to-face contact between a dominant and ruthless white majority and an Indian minority in which tribal cohesiveness had been destroyed, and who attempted to cope as individuals with American society. He was the forerunner of those who in the twentieth century opposed the policy of "termination."

See Ralph H. Gabriel, *Elias Boudinot, Cherokee, and His America* (1941), and Grace Steele Woodward, *The Cherokees* (1963).—R. H. G.

boundary commissions (1848-1855). The parties assigned to survey the Mexican-United States boundary after the Mexican War and the Gadsden Purchase. Article V of the Treaty of Guadalupe Hidalgo (February 1848), which terminated the Mexican War, specified that both governments should appoint a commissioner and a surveyor to meet in San Diego one year from the date of the ratification of the treaty, and from there run the boundary line to the eastern terminus of the mouth of the Rio Grande.

Complications involving the Topographical Engineers, civilian commissioners, and some civilian employees, the change of administrations in Washington, and the desire of certain American members to guarantee that the boundary would insure a possible railroad route in United States territory, along with the rough terrain, vast distances, and sudden appearance of ragtag contingents of California-bound gold-seekers, all slowed the work of the commission.

President Polk first named Ambrose Sevier as commissioner; he died within a month and was replaced by another politician, John B. Weller. In June 1849 Weller and a civilian, Andrew B. Gray, along with officers William H. Emory and Amiel Weeks Whipple of the Topographical Engineers, began operations at San Diego. Weller was subsequently removed and John C. Frémont was appointed as his replacement; but Frémont resigned before assuming the task, and a scientist, artist, and bibliophile, John Russell BARTLETT, became the commissioner in May 1850. He made an agreement with the Mexican commissioner, General Conde, that placed the boundary several miles north of the location

where Emory and many others believed it should have been. Opposition in Congress ended the Bartlett portion of the survey as of December 1852. Then in May 1853 General Robert Blair Campbell, aided again by Major Emory, was commissioned to complete the survey, which was essentially accomplished by September 1853.

The Gadsden Treaty of December 1853 necessitated a new survey. This time Major Emory was appointed Commissioner, and the new boundary line was successfully run by October 1855. With minor changes, it has remained the same to the present time.

Three quarto volumes under the general heading of *Report of the Mexican Boundary Survey* (1856-59) include numerous scientific reports. See also William H. Goetzmann, *Army Exploration in the American West* (1959); Robert V. Hine, *Bartlett's West* (1969); and Edward S. Wallace, *The Great Reconnaissance* (1955). —R. A. B.

Bouquet, Henry (1719-1765). British soldier. Born in Switzerland of French parentage, Bouquet began a career as a professional soldier in 1736, enlisting as a cadet for the States General of Holland. During the War of the Austrian Succession (1740-48) he fought for the Prince of Orange and in 1755 entered the British service as a lieutenant colonel in the Royal American Regiment. He left for North America with this regiment in 1756, and in 1758, promoted to colonel, served as second in command under Brigadier General John Forbes in the expedition against Fort Duquesne. Bouquet remained on the frontier under the command of generals John Stanwix, Robert Monckton, and Jeffrey Amherst through the closing years of the French and Indian War.

Following the outbreak of Pontiac's Rebellion, Bouquet achieved his most renowned field victory at the battle of Bushy Run in August 1763, when he crushed a large force of Delaware and Shawnee Indians by superior tactics and the rapid, well-drilled movement of his forces. The same year, at the suggestion of Amherst, he sent smallpox-infested blankets among the Northwest Indians from Fort Pitt. In 1764 he led a strong expedition through the upper Muskingum River valley, gaining the submission of the Delaware and allied tribes as part of the general peace ending Pontiac's Rebellion. Although his foreign birth had earlier blocked his promotion to higher command, in 1765 he was publicly honored by the king and made brigadier general. In this new rank he received command over the southern district of the American colonies, but at Pensacola in September of that year he died of a fever.

A serious, studious man, Bouquet showed great talent both as a military administrator and as a field commander. Called the most brilliant leader of light infantry of his day, he perceived before any of his contemporaries the advantages of rapid troop movement and massed firepower in wilderness warfare. A strict disciplinarian, he sought to combine in his troops the precision of the European drill field with the tactical maneuverability demanded by American frontier conditions. Though little appreciated by his fellow officers, Bouquet's methods in warfare gained him the fearful respect of his Indian enemies.

Bouquet's American career is documented in S. K. Stevens and D. H. Kent, eds., *The Papers of Colonel Henry Bouquet*, 19 vols. (1940-41). An excellent sketch by Stanley Pargellis appears in the *Dictionary of American Biography.*—K. N. O.

Bourke, John Gregory (1846-1896). Soldier and ethnologist. Bourke was born in Philadelphia of Irish Catholic descent and broadly educated by his father. At sixteen he left home to join the Fifteenth Pennsylvania Cavalry and served with it as a private throughout the Civil War. He then obtained an appointment to West Point, graduating in 1869. Assigned as a second lieutenant to the Third United States Cavalry in the Southwest, Bourke became aide-de-camp to General George S. Crook in 1872, retaining that post for many years and rising to the rank of captain. He participated in most of the campaigns against the Apache and in the 1876-77 war against the Sioux and Cheyenne. Bourke spent his spare time methodically recording the customs of the Indians he observed, and Crook arranged for him a year's special duty (1880-81) to study the Navaho, Pueblo, and Apache.

Detailed to Washington in 1886 to review and formulate his notes, Bourke published ten careful ethnological papers about the southwestern Indians and completed his important *Medicine Men of the Apache* in 1892. He also produced *An Apache Campaign* (1886), *Mackenzie's Last Fight with the Cheyenne* (1890), *On the Border with Crook* (1891), and *Scatologic Rites of All Nations* (1892), the last a product of Bourke's lifelong fascination with the ceremonial uses of human waste. One of the last in the tradition of humanist-scientific military officers who recorded the American West, Bourke's historical work is vivid, observant, and humorous, and his ethnological studies remain invaluable to modern scholars.

See L. B. Bloom, "Bourke on the Southwest," *New Mexico Historical Review*, vols. 8-13 (1933-38) and 19 (1944). J. Frank Dobie wrote an introduction to the 1958 edition of Bourke, *An Apache Campaign.*—P. R. M.

Bowie, James (1795-1836). Soldier and Texas frontiersman. Bowie ranks alongside Davy Crockett as one of the Texas legends. Born at Elliot Spring, Tennessee, he settled on Bayou Boeuf in Rapides Parish, Louisiana, when he was about nineteen. Legends about Bowie abound, and one is that as a youth he roped and rode alligators and worked with the pirate Jean Laffite to smuggle and sell Negro slaves.

It is no legend that he designed what has come to be known as the notorious bowie knife. The knife has a nine-to-fifteen-inch blade sharpened only on one side to the curve of the tip and then sharpened on both sides to the point. It has a handguard of brass to permit its user to parry or thrust and to slide his hand down over the blade as necessary. The handle is made of wood (usually walnut or hickory), bone, or antler. The knife became famous as a fighting weapon, not for killing game. As a weapon of the southwestern frontier, it fills the chronological gap between the coming of the Anglo-American and the development of the revolver. It was mobile, durable, and easy to use in fights in close quarters.

In 1828 Bowie moved to Texas, where unlike most Anglo-American settlers he became thoroughly Mexicanized. He was baptized into the Roman Catholic Church in Bexar (now San Antonio) and married Ursula Maria de Veramendi, daughter of vice-governor Juan Martin Veramendi. He searched for what has come to be known as the Lost Bowie Mine, named for him and

his brother Rezin, in the San Saba River country and in 1830 became a colonel in the Texas Rangers. He fought in the battle of Nacogdoches (August 2-3, 1832), which occurred when the Mexican commandant there, José de las Piedras, ordered the citizens to surrender their arms. The commandant was captured and removed from East Texas, which must have encouraged the Texans later when they considered full-scale revolt. Bowie also fought against the Indians. In September 1833, while he was away from home, his wife and two children died of cholera, a loss from which he never fully recovered psychologically.

Since the Mexicans in both Texas and Mexico proper fully accepted Bowie's conversion to Mexican citizenship, they were much surprised when Bowie joined the Texans in the revolution against Mexico. A leader in the early battles at Mission NUESTRA SENORA DE LA PURISIMA CONCEPCION DE ACUNA and in the Grass Fight (so called because Bowie and about a hundred men captured part of a Mexican pack train in a field of grass outside Bexar), he was involved in the siege of Bexar and the capture of General Martín Perfecto de Cós in 1835-36. When Bexar finally fell in December 1835, Cós and his troops were freed on condition that they fight no more against the Texans. Cós broke his pledge and commanded a column for Santa Anna at the Alamo.

In late February 1836, Bowie was commanding a small volunteer force in San Antonio when William Barret Travis arrived with regular Texas army troops. Shortly thereafter the groups shared in the defense of the Alamo, but the divided leadership turned Davis and Bowie into undisguised enemies. Bowie's volunteer force would not accept Travis as its leader, while Travis and his "regulars" complained that Bowie was always drunk and most unmilitary in the command of his volunteers. During the siege of the Alamo, Bowie was stricken with typhoid pneumonia and spent his last eleven days alternating between chills and fever on a cot. When the final massacre came on March 6, 1836, Bowie, again according to legend which in this case seems reasonably authentic, fought fiercely with his famed knife from his cot before the Mexicans cut him down. Certainly the Mexican soldiers who killed him paid tribute to his courage. Bowie's status as a frontier hero began with stories of his early fighting prowess in the Mississippi-Louisiana frontier area, followed him to Texas, and enlarged to, and past, the moment of his death. He was the stuff of which heroes are made, a man of huge passions and appetites, a "big dealer" who liked to plunge against long odds, and a natural candidate for folklore. Once when he was drunk, he stormed into the Bexar jail and in a wave of generosity turned all the prisoners loose. That is the kind of man that people talk about, and they have.

Santa Anna wrote that Bowie died like a craven coward, but many of the lesser Mexican leaders and enlisted men who reminisced for history averred that he fought like a madman. Texas witnesses, admittedly biased, claimed that a pile of bodies around his cot attested to his heroism. Since he attracted worshippers, he also attracted detractors.

See Mody C. Boatright and Donald Day, eds., *From Hell to Breakfast* (1944); and Claude L. Douglas, *James Bowie: The Life of a Bravo* (1944).—J. B. F.

Bowman, [Lewis] Ed[ward] (1886-1961). Rancher

and rodeo contestant. Born at Brownwood, Texas, Bowman spent his childhood on his grandfather's ranch in Weed, New Mexico. Bowman bought ranches in Arizona and Colorado and was a highly respected cattleman, but it was as a rodeo contestant that he earned his name as a prominent western figure.

As a roping contestant and relay rider, Ed Bowman followed the rodeo trail until he was forty-four years old. He retired undefeated as the greatest "strap and cinch" relay man after competing in the event for nine years. While recuperating from a broken leg, Bowman developed the first rope-working mount in the game of calf-roping. In 1945 Bowman moved to Colorado. At the same time he became interested in cutting horses (see COWBOY), eventually riding his prize mount, Sonny Boy, to a National Cutting Horse Association championship.

Bowman remained associated with rodeo and cutting-horse competition until his death. He was a member of several cattlemen's associations and served as the first president of the Western States Cutting Horse Association. In 1962 he was elected to the National Cowboy Hall of Fame.—R. B. W.

Bozeman Trail. The Bozeman Trail was mapped out by John M. Bozeman in 1863-65 as the shortest and easiest route for emigrants to the Virginia City (Montana) gold fields. Beginning at Julesburg, Colorado, on the South Platte, the trail continued past Fort Laramie to the Powder River Crossing at Fort Connor. From here, it continued beyond the Big Horn Mountains to the Yellowstone River and westward to Virginia City and the Montana gold fields.

The first caravan used the trail in the summer of 1863. The SIOUX INDIANS resented the invasion because it pierced the heart of their hunting preserve, and when forts Reno, Phil Kearny, and C. F. Smith were established for the protection of the emigrants, they went on the warpath. Red Cloud's War, one of the few successful campaigns launched by the Indians, was the result. By 1868, the trail had been abandoned.

Following the suppression of the Sioux in 1877, the Bozeman Trail became an important route for cattle moving from Texas northward.

See E. A. Brininstool and G. R. Hebard, *The Bozeman Trail* (1922).—R. B. W.

Brackenridge, Hugh Henry (1748-1816). Novelist. Brackenridge came to America from Scotland as a boy, settling with his parents in the frontier county of York, Pennsylvania. About 1768 he entered the College of New Jersey (later Princeton University), where his classmates included the future American president James Madison and Philip Freneau, the soon-to-be-renowned American poet. With Freneau, Brackenridge collaborated on a commencement poem, *The Rising Glory of America* (1771). In 1781 he moved to Pittsburgh, then a frontier city, and in 1801 he moved to Carlisle, Pennsylvania, where he resided until his death.

Although Brackenridge dabbled in poetry and wrote two Revolutionary war plays—*The Battle of Bunker's Hill* (1776) and *The Death of General Montgomery* (1777)—he is remembered primarily for his satirical picaresque novel *Modern Chivalry*, which appeared in various installments from 1792 to 1815. The first literary work published in the West, *Modern Chivalry* is sometimes erroneously interpreted as an attack upon democracy rather than what it truly is, an attack upon democracy's excesses. Despite its derivative form, the novel was the first example of "western humor," a genre that later flowered in the anecdotes of Thomas Bangs Thorpe and the sardonic tall stories of Mark Twain.

See C. M. Newlin, *The Life and Writings of Hugh Henry Brackenridge* (1932).—J. K. F.

Bradbury, John (1768-1823). Naturalist. A Scot by birth and an Englishman by education and early residence, Bradbury's contact with the West began in the summer of 1809 when the Botanical Society at Liverpool commissioned him to conduct investigations of the flora on the frontier. A fellow scientist, Thomas Jefferson, received Bradbury warmly and suggested St. Louis as a starting point for his work. In 1810 Bradbury made numerous trips of up to two hundred miles from that city. The following year he traveled with the John Jacob Astor fur-trading expedition eighteen hundred miles up the Missouri. Captivated by the experience, Bradbury departed from his botany long enough to make accurate and detailed observations of the environment as a whole and of the Indian way of life. His journals added substantially to the information gathered by Lewis and Clark.

Bradbury intended to sail for England following his Missouri River trip, but the War of 1812 between the United States and England delayed his departure for four years. Making good use of the time, Bradbury traveled widely in the Ohio valley, and in his journals he recorded extensive observations of the social, political, and economic conditions he found there. When Bradbury finally returned to England in 1815 he arranged for the publication of his journals under the title *Travels in the Interior of America in the Years 1809, 1810, and 1811*. The book immediately became one of the most widely used sources of information about the American West. In later years Bradbury returned to the United States and eventually made his home in St. Louis.

The most complete references are H. W. Rickett, "John Bradbury's Explorations in Missouri Territory," *Proceedings of the American Philosophical Society*, vol. 94 (1950); and Rodney H. True, "A Sketch of the Life of John Bradbury, Including His Unpublished Correspondence with Thomas Jefferson," *Proceedings of the American Philosophical Society*, vol. 68 (1929). —R. N.

Braddock's Road. In 1752 the Ohio Company cut a road from Will's Creek, near Fort Cumberland (now Cumberland), Maryland, to a point on the Youghiogheny River; two years later George Washington pushed the road to within six miles of present-day Uniontown, Pennsylvania. The road, however, takes its name from Major General Edward Braddock, whose ill-fated expedition employed and extended it.

Starting from Fort Cumberland, on June 10, 1755, Braddock set out to conquer French-held Fort Duquesne in western Pennsylvania. Between the two forts lay one hundred miles of dense, swampy forest and mountains. Braddock and his twenty-five hundred men traveled northwest near what is now U.S. Route 40 with three hundred axmen and carpenters in front of them clearing a twelve-foot path and building sturdy bridges. The pace was slow. Washington, who accompanied Braddock, commented disgustedly that "they were halting to level every mole hill and to erect bridges over every brook—by which means we were four days in getting twelve miles."

By July 9 Braddock was less than ten miles from Fort Duquesne. But in a fierce battle that day, the English, who did not know which way to turn, were roundly defeated by French and Indian forces. Braddock himself was killed, and nearly one thousand of his men were killed or wounded.

Braddock's Road did not, however, go unused. By the 1780s Americans tramped along it in their migration westward from Pennsylvania, Virginia, and Maryland. In the 1780s Pennsylvania and Maryland improved the road sufficiently to enable wagons to use it.

A thorough discussion of Braddock's Road is in Lawrence H. Gipson, *The British Empire Before the American Revolution*, vol. VI (1946).—E. W. K.

Bradley, Alva. See GREAT LAKES, MEN OF THE.

Bradley, Lewis R. (1806-1879). Cattleman and Nevada politician. Born in Virginia, Bradley began his adult life as superintendent of a farm at eighty dollars a year, then became a horse and mule buyer. After spending a year in Kentucky, in 1844 he went to Missouri, where he was engaged in stock raising until 1852, when he trailed a herd of cattle to California. The success of this venture prompted Bradley to return to Missouri, where he bought horses, mules, and sheep and drove them west.

By 1862 he had settled in Nevada and become a rancher and stock raiser, acquiring the nickname Old Broadhorns. He was a county commissioner and treasurer of Elko County and was elected to the first of two terms as governor in 1870. His administration was marked by the founding of the state university and by fights with the Comstock interests over the "net proceeds of mines" tax laws. Although the competition called him "our boss lunatic," the Supreme Court later upheld the law.

Bradley was reelected governor in 1874 but was defeated four years later when he sought a third term. —R. B. W.

Brady, John Green (1848-1918). Alaskan politician. Brady was born in New York City. From an impoverished home, he became a Manhattan street orphan at the age of eight and never again saw his family. Through the Children's Aid Society, Brady was sent to the country town of Tipton, Indiana, where he was adopted by Judge John Green. After obtaining his B.A. in 1874 at Yale, Brady studied for the ministry at New York's Union Theological Seminary for three years, supporting himself by work in various New York City street missions. Because of his own youthful deprivations, the freshly ordained minister determined to begin a school for disadvantaged boys somewhere out west. When such a plan in Texas fizzled, he accepted an offer to serve the Presbyterian Board of Home Missions as a missionary teacher in Sitka, Alaska.

Brady arrived at Sitka in 1878. Sheldon Jackson, a famed field superintendent for the Board of Home Missions, had selected him to teach Christianity to Alaska's Northwest Coast Indians. Although Brady separated himself from the Home Board after it chose not to support his ideas for a native industrial school, he remained a lifelong friend of Jackson's.

In 1881 Brady began a business career in Sitka and by the next decade had become prosperous. To enable native youths to acquire skills that could be utilized in Alaska's changing economy, he employed graduates of Sitka's Presbyterian school (today's Sheldon Jackson College) in his lumber mill and store. When the District of Alaska received its Organic Act in 1884, Brady, an acknowledged Republican, was appointed by President Chester Arthur as a United States commissioner and ex-officio registrar of the land office at Sitka, the District of Alaska's capital. His subsequent success as magistrate, businessman, and public-spirited citizen resulted, in 1897, in his appointment as governor of the District of Alaska by President William McKinley.

Soon after he began his governorship, Alaska began to reel from an influx of miners, but the Klondike phenomenon did little to prosper Brady's own town of Sitka. He futilely opposed the movement of the capital to the more central, if more bawdy, Juneau. Sitka's eclipse by Juneau ended a territorial tug of war waged since the early 1880s. At boom town Juneau considerable power rested with the miner-saloon keeper element. Sitka had been the capital of Russian America; it reflected tradition, social stability, and law and order.

Alaska's aboriginal population, eager to possess the bric-a-brac of white society and lacking the cultural insulation to protect itself against commercial exploitation, suffered both physical and psychological damage. Brady struggled to see that the natives got equal justice in the courts, equal schooling, and equal job opportunities in order to hasten their assimilation. He opposed the importation of a reservation system, convinced it would make the natives dependent on, not independent of, the whites. The territory-wide prohibition against alcoholic drink, a vain effort to try to keep liquor from the Indians, had become a farce. Brady sought a more reasonable solution: high license. Although attacked by missionary friends and smuggler enemies alike, he succeeded in achieving his middle course. A large portion of the license revenue went for public education in Alaska.

Brady discussed the problems of Alaska's aboriginals before the Lake Mohonk conferences; he encouraged native enrollment in Captain Richard Pratt's Carlisle, Indian School; and like his mentor, Jackson, he took advantage of every opportunity to laud and exhibit the indigenes' arts and skills, as at the St. Louis Louisiana Purchase Exposition in 1904. At other expositions as well and by his numerous lectures, official reports, and popular writings, Brady did his best to publicize Alaska's needs and potentials.

Reappointed governor by President McKinley and again by President Theodore Roosevelt in 1905, Brady repeatedly labored to arouse Congress on Alaska's behalf. He concurred with David Starr Jordan's opinion that the Great Land seemed to be "a colony of the United States." Alaska's geographic isolation from the mainstream of American development abetted this. Certainly Brady's constant pleas paralleled those of other Far West territorial governors for improved mail facilities, more efficient law enforcement, railroad development, territorywide suffrage, and more effective representation in the nation's capital. Brady's reiterated demands for a district legal code helped produce the unique Carter Civil and Criminal Code. He early appreciated Alaska's strategic position in America's Pacific defense system and urged expanded military bases there. Likewise, he foresaw the inevitable Canada-Alaska boundary squabble and while governor had the satisfaction of seeing that matter adjudicated, but without his significant involvement as some accounts have claimed.

Because of his defense of the native peoples, his close working relationship with Jackson, and his advocacy of responsible settlement instead of unchecked exploitation, Governor Brady was lumped with "the Presbyterian hierarchy." By 1906 the booster class viewed him as too conservative, while his superior in Washington, Secretary of the Interior Ethan Allen Hitchcock, had grown impatient with his ceaseless requests. When Brady slipped and publicly endorsed a mining company whose activities he sincerely believed in the best interests of Alaska, enemies of the Presbyterian hierarchy demanded his recall. Brady chose to resign. Doubly humiliating was the disastrous outcome of the Reynolds Mining Company. Brady lost most of what he possessed and thereafter tried to reimburse those whom his mistaken enthusiasm had drawn into the Reynolds speculation.

Brady's postgovernorship years were divided between Boston, New York City, and Sitka where he died. Alaskan natives conducted his funeral.—T. C. H.

Brainerd, Erastus (1855-1922). Seattle publicist. Brainerd was born in Middletown, Connecticut, and attended Harvard University. After working at the Boston Museum of Fine Arts and on the editorial staff of a number of eastern newspapers, he moved to Seattle, Washington, in 1890. He was appointed secretary to the advertising committee of the Seattle Chamber of Commerce during the Klondike gold rush of 1898-99. His wide acquaintance in publishing and political circles permitted him to flood the nation's news media and post offices with publicity that successfully established Seattle as the gateway to the Yukon-Alaska gold fields. Seattle's growth of almost five hundred percent in a dozen years was largely the result of his activity. Following his promotion of the Klondike area, Brainerd became editor of the Seattle *Post-Intelligencer* and president of the Seattle Bank of Commerce. He was also Paraguayan consular representative in the Pacific Northwest in 1919.

See C. Brewster Coulter, "John L. Wilson, Erastus Brainerd, and the Republican Party of Washington," *Idaho Yesterdays* (Summer 1960); and Jeannette P. Nichols, "Advertising and the Klondike," *Washington Historical Quarterly* (January 1922).—K. A. M.

Branch, E. Douglas (1905-1945). Historian. Branch was born in Houston, Texas. He secured his education at the University of Texas, Ohio State University, and the State University of Iowa. He began teaching English in 1925 at Oklahoma A. & M. College and served during 1926-27 at Louisiana Polytechnic Institute. Between 1929 and 1932 he became an editor in the P. F. Collier encyclopedia division and taught briefly at Purdue University. From 1933 to 1935 he taught English and history at the University of Montana. He then accepted a position as professor of history at the University of Pittsburgh, where he remained for the next eight years. In 1944 he returned to the West and taught at Montana State College at Bozeman until his death.

Branch was a popularizer and synthesizer of western history rather than a research scholar. His books were designed for the general reader, although he was a frequent reviewer for professional historical journals. His first work was *The Cowboy and His Interpreters* (1926), a well-written analysis of major western writers, such as Owen Wister. He followed this volume with *The Hunting of the Buffalo* (1929), designed mainly for the popular market, in which he advanced the thesis that the demise of the buffalo provided a key to an understanding of the frontier and its disappearance. In the following year appeared his *Westward: The Romance of the American Frontier*, a colorful synthesis about the history of the West. His last book, *The Sentimental Years, 1836-1860* (1934), focused on social development on the frontier and was concerned with the middle-class aspirations of Americans during this period and how these were related to the westward movement.—G. D. N.

Brand, Max. Pen name of **Frederick Schiller Faust** (1892-1944). Short-story writer and motion-picture writer. Brand was born in Seattle, Washington, and died in Italy of wounds sustained during an Allied offensive he was covering as a war correspondent. From an impoverished boyhood in the San Joaquin valley of California, he grew to become one of the most successful and prolific of western writers. His total lifetime literary production, not all by any means "westerns," has been estimated at thirty million words. He wrote under at least nineteen pen names, of which Max Brand is the best known to readers of western stories. Author of *The Untamed* (1919), *Trailin'* (1920), and the famed *Destry Rides Again* (1930), he was also the creator of Dr. Kildare, who, together with Destry, made a successful transition from the printed page to the motion-picture screen and, later, to television. *Max Brand's Best Stories* (1967), a good collection of his shorter work, includes the first tale of Dr. Kildare, "Internes Can't Take Money" (1936). A book of poems, *The Village Street* (1922), and *Notebooks and Poems of Max Brand* (1957) give a representative sampling of the serious literature Brand always hoped to write and somehow never got around to.

See Robert Easton, *Max Brand: The Big "Westerner"* (1970).—J. K. F.

brands. See CATTLE BRANDS.

Brannan, Samuel (1819-1889). Pioneer California capitalist. In 1846 Brannan led a party of more than two hundred Mormons who sailed from New York around Cape Horn to San Francisco Bay. As an elder of the Mormon Church he flagrantly diverted tithe money for his own investments in merchandising and real estate; and when Brigham Young sent a deputation from Salt Lake City to recover "the Lord's money," Brannan was alleged to have replied that he would turn it over when he got a receipt signed by the Lord. Such practices led to his expulsion from the church; they also led to his becoming California's first millionaire. Learning of the gold discovery early in 1848, he cornered all the available supplies of mining necessities and then trumpeted the news that started the gold rush. He was the principal founder of the vigilance movement to suppress crime in San Francisco, but was soon expelled from the movement's leadership. In 1851 he led an unsuccessful filibustering expedition to the Hawaiian Islands. He acquired huge amounts of California land, but heavy drinking contributed to his ultimate ruin and he died in poverty in rural San Diego County.

Paul Bailey describes his career in *Sam Brannan and the California Mormons* (1953).—W. B.

Brant, Joseph (1742-1807). Mohawk chief and military leader. Like most of his tribe, Brant, or Thayendanegea, was strongly influenced by the British and became a convert to the Anglican Church. His sister Molly was the common-law wife of Sir William Johnson, superintendent of Indian affairs and the most powerful figure on the New York frontier. Brant's own career owed much to this connection. He accompanied Johnson on a military campaign in 1755, was sent by him to an Indian school in Connecticut from 1761 to 1763, and served as interpreter for a missionary working among his tribe. Both early and late in life he engaged in church affairs and translated religious texts into Mohawk. After Johnson's death in 1774, his successor, Guy Johnson, made Brant his secretary.

Brant remained loyal to the British during the American Revolution, but his primary commitment was to his own tribe. After visiting England just before the Revolution, where he was received at court and painted by the English artist George Romney, he returned home to participate in some of the bloodiest frontier fighting in American history. A brilliant tactician and master of the arts of border warfare, he led or participated in countless British-Tory-Mohawk raids on frontier settlements, including the Cherry Valley Massacre of November 1778, which he led. He was also a leader in the fruitless Iroquois resistance to the SULLIVAN-CLINTON CAMPAIGN the next year. He opposed a separate Iroquois-American peace until the end of the war, and after the American victory he fled with his followers to Canada. There they settled on lands along the Grand River allotted them by the British government. Brant remained active in the political and religious affairs of his tribe until his death.

See Harvey Chalmers, *Joseph Brant: Mohawk* (1955); J. W. Jakes, *Mohawk: The Life of Joseph Brant* (1969); and Dale Van Every, *A Company of Heroes* (1962).—A. W. T.

Bratt, John (1842-1918). Nebraska rancher and politician. Born in Staffordshire, England, the son of a Methodist minister, Bratt was apprenticed at age twelve to a merchant and at seventeen was in business for himself. He came to America at the age of twenty-one, and after spending some time in Chicago, he invested in goods to be sold in New Orleans. The ship with Bratt and his goods was wrecked in the Gulf of Mexico, and he lost his property. After a near-starvation period in New Orleans he worked on the levee and later on a riverboat.

In 1866 Bratt went to Nebraska City in Nebraska Territory, where he hired out as a bullwhacker freighting to Fort Kearney. At the fort he was employed by Coe and Carter, contractors, freighters, and sutlers; he operated a road ranch and stage station until 1867. In 1869 he became a partner of Coe and Carter in the cattle business under the name of John Bratt and Company. In 1870 he established a ranch with headquarters near North Platte.

Bratt's cattle ranged between the Platte River, Medicine Creek, and Willow Creek, west of Fort McPherson and east of O'Fallon's Bluffs, one of the largest and best known ranches in that area.

Bratt was active in the organization of Frontier County after statehood and was one of the first county commissioners. In 1877 he organized the North Platte

Guards for protection against Indian raids. Much of his life and times was put into his memoirs, *Trails of Yesterday* (1921).—R. B. W.

Bridger, James (1804-1881). Mountain man, fur trader, and guide. Bridger was born in Richmond, Virginia, but soon thereafter his family settled near St. Louis, Missouri. When Bridger was fourteen, both parents died and he was apprenticed to a blacksmith in St. Louis. He accompanied Ashley on his first expedition to the Rockies in 1822. In the following year he and John Fitzgerald, while on an overland journey to the mountains in Major Andrew Henry's party, were assigned to care for Hugh GLASS after he had been seriously wounded by a grizzly bear. Believing that Glass would die, they abandoned him, but Glass survived. In the fall of 1824, or early in 1825, Bridger saw the Great Salt Lake and was perhaps the first white man to do so. Upon tasting the waters he is supposed to have remarked, "Hell, we are on the shores of the Pacific." After Ashley retired from the mountain trade in 1826, Bridger was employed first by Jedediah SMITH, David Jackson, and William Sublette's company and later by the ROCKY MOUNTAIN FUR COMPANY, of which he was a partner from 1830 until its dissolution in 1834. Bridger was wounded in the battle with the Gros Ventre at Pierre's Hole in 1832 and carried part of an Indian arrow in his back until 1835, when Dr. Marcus Whitman removed it. Later (1838) Bridger went to work for the American Fur Company. In the twenty-one years that he was in the fur trade Bridger came to know the vast area from the Canadian boundary to the northern border of New Mexico.

In 1843, seeing that the fur trade had begun to decline, Bridger went into partnership with Louis Vasquez. The two built Fort Bridger (in present-day southwestern Wyoming) on the Black Fork of the Green River. The post became an important way station for migrants to Oregon and California. In 1853 he sold his share in the fort to the Mormons. Meanwhile, Bridger's services as a guide were constantly sought. In 1850 he guided Captain Howard Stansbury's expedition, which was searching for a passage through the Wasatch and Rocky mountains and found Bridger's Pass and Cheyenne Pass. He served the Englishman Sir George Gore on his elaborate big-game hunt in 1851. When the so-called Mormon war of 1857-58 broke out, Bridger, who claimed that the Mormons had driven him from his fort in 1853, was an eager guide for Colonel Albert Sidney Johnston's federal soldiers, who had been sent to Utah to resolve the conflict. Shortly thereafter he accompanied Captain William V. Raynolds' exploring expedition to the Yellowstone region in 1859-60. In 1861 he joined the Berthoud party in its attempt to find a short route over the mountains from Denver to Great Salt Lake. Although troubled by failing eyesight, Bridger served as the guide for the Powder River expedition of 1865-66 and in the latter year measured the length of the Bozeman Trail for the government. He also assisted Granville M. Dodge in the Union Pacific Railroad Survey. Suffering from ill health and approaching blindness, Old Gabe, as his friends called him, purchased a house at Westport, Missouri, close to those of William Bent and Louis Vasquez in 1866 and retired from the field in 1868. While living in the West he had married three Indian women, a Flathead, a Ute,

Jim Bridger, best known of the mountain men. (Montana Historical Society, Helena)

and a Snake, but upon their deaths had sent his children east to Missouri to be educated.

Bridger's fame as a trapper, guide, and scout would be difficult to exaggerate. So vast and accurate was his knowledge of western geography that Bernard De Voto has called him "an atlas of the West." Others commented on the fact that although he was illiterate, he possessed a keen intelligence. Bridger's exploits are nevertheless well known, because so many prominent explorers, military men, and writers gave accounts of him. Journalists interviewed him, and E. C. Z. Judson ("Ned Buntline") fictionalized episodes of his career. Thus, Bridger, in addition to his very real accomplishments, has come to be a popular symbol of the mountain man—illiterate but intelligent, superstitious but shrewd, rough but sensitive, a spinner of yarns in dialect, who knew the West like the back of his hand and hated cities.

See J. Cecil Alter, *James Bridger* (1925); Bernard De Voto, *Across the Wide Missouri* (1947); Dale L. Morgan, *Jedediah Smith and the Opening of the West* (1953); and Stanley Vestal, *Jim Bridger, Mountain Man* (1946). —G. B. D.

Bridges, Harry Renton (1901-   ). Labor leader. A native of Australia who was nurtured in its radical labor tradition, Bridges came to America in 1920, was briefly a member of the Industrial Workers of the World (IWW), and settled down to work on the San Francisco docks, where he became a skilled longshoreman. In 1934 he emerged from the anonymous laboring ranks to take control of the Pacific Coast drive of the International Longshoremen's Association to establish the union hiring hall. This movement evolved into a broad Pacific Coast longshore and maritime strike, which came to a climax with the San Francisco general strike of July 15-19, 1934. Later in the year a federally arbitrated settlement was reached favoring Bridges' nascent Longshoremen and Sailor's Union. By the end of 1934 Bridges was the most powerful labor leader in the West and a figure of national and international note. Not since the days of the early twentieth century, when IWW leader William D. Haywood was in his prime, had the West known such a forceful, charismatic union chief, and like Haywood, Bridges attracted intense hatred (by capitalists and antiunion members of the middle class) and hero worship (by workers).

Bridges was sympathetic to the Communist party but never became a member. In 1945 the United States Supreme Court finally quashed a long-term attempt to deport him to Australia. Meanwhile, Bridges had broken away from the American Federation of Labor (AFL) in 1937 and had taken his renamed International Longshoremen's and Warehousemen's Union (ILWU) into the Congress of Industrial Organizations (CIO). In 1950 the ILWU was expelled from the CIO for allegedly following the Communist line in an era when anti-Communist, anti-Soviet Union passions were inflaming the nation. Independent status scarcely hampered the ILWU. With the signing of the 1960 Mechanization and Modernization agreement with management, which brought lasting stability to the Pacific Coast docks, Bridges and the ILWU entered their phase of greatest success and power. In terms of tangible gains for workers won, Bridges stands as the greatest labor leader in the history of the West.

See Irving Bernstein, *Turbulent Years: A History of the American Worker, 1933-1941* (1970), and Charles P. Larrowe, *Harry Bridges: The Rise and Fall of Radical Labor in the United States* (1972).—R. M. B.

Briggs, Harold E. (1896-   ). Historian. Briggs was born in Byron, Minnesota, and educated at the University of South Dakota and the State University of Iowa. By the time he had completed his graduate work in 1929, Briggs had already served as a school superintendent in the South Dakota schools and in 1928 had begun teaching at Culver-Stockton College in Missouri. In 1935 he joined the history department at the University of Miami and in 1945 moved to Southern Illinois University, where he remained until his retirement twenty years later.

Briggs was one of the first frontier historians to focus on social and cultural developments. In a variety of articles he addressed topics concerning cultural phenomena in the Missouri valley, much of which became part of a more comprehensive work, *Frontiers of the Northwest: A History of the Upper Missouri Valley* (1940). In the work Briggs emphasized the economic and social development of the region, encompassing the Dakotas, Montana, Wyoming, and parts of Idaho and Colorado. Based on original research in contemporary newspapers, diaries, and other primary sources, the book made a useful contribution. Using the Turnerian approach, Briggs wrote of a succession of frontiers, those of the miner, the buffalo hunter, the cattleman, the sheepman, the settler, and the farmer.—G. D. N.

Brigham Young Express & Carrying Co. Between 1851 and 1856 all efforts to maintain a regular and satisfactory mail service between the Missouri frontier and Salt Lake City had failed. Samuel H. Woodson made a pioneering effort between 1851 and 1852, followed by W. M. F. Magraw in 1854-56. The Mormons who lived in Salt Lake City were eager to establish an adequate mail and express route, and Brigham Young even toyed with a plan for an express service from the Missouri River to the Pacific Coast. He was apparently among the first to recognize the importance of the stagecoach in delivering express and mail and at the same time providing passage for travelers. The earliest mails had been delivered by men on horseback or mules on the assumption that they were swifter. Moreover, the first wagons used had broken down in rough terrain or had become stuck in the snow, and delays were encountered in repairing them. To make travel easier, Young and his associates planned for way stations along the proposed stage route.

The upshot of these proposals was the organization of the Brigham Young Express & Carrying Co. (the B. Y. Express Company) in 1856. The company's agent, Hiram Kimball, was awarded a government contract for a monthly mail service between the Missouri River and Salt Lake City for $23,000. He had carefully specified in his bid that he might use horses or mules, wagons or carriages in fulfilling the contract. Kimball was unable to perform the service upon the date provided in his contract, and it was annulled by the government. Men awarded a special contract to meet the emergency made only one trip eastward from Salt Lake to Missouri. Meanwhile, the B. Y. Express Company had been working to improve the trail and build stations. One of its agents made a trip from Salt Lake City to Independence in fifteen days and commenced his return journey with several wagonloads of mail.

The plans of the B. Y. Express Company were abruptly terminated by the outbreak of the Mormon War in 1857, which culminated the long power struggle and feud between federal government and church officials in Utah Territory. Among the federal officials in Utah Territory who criticized the Mormons and helped bring about this war was W. M. F. Magraw, Kimball's unsuccessful predecessor as mail carrier, who aggressively sought the federal government's patronage. For a short period all communication with Salt Lake City was shut off. The mail, delivered under contract, went only as far as Fort Bridger. When service was resumed the contractor was required to use coaches drawn by four horses, as originally proposed by the Mormons, during the summer months, although he could revert to pack mule service in winter.

See Alvin F. Harlow, *Old Waybills: The Romance of the Express Companies* (1934); and J. V. Frederick, *Ben Holladay, the Stagecoach King* (1940).—W. T. J.

British administrative policy (1763-1775). The Treaty of Paris (1763) brought the Seven Years' War to an end. England had overwhelmed the French and had more than tripled the size of the British empire. In the wake of this military success, however, came perplexing administrative problems as English leaders were forced to formulate a policy to deal with the vast, newly conquered possessions. Should they make new colonies out of Canada and the American West? How should they

govern the eighty thousand French settlers still living in North America? Even before the conclusion of the war, the Bute ministry (1762-63) decided to leave a large number of British troops in the New World to maintain security. This crucial decision generated additional difficulties. How, for example, would England pay for an expensive American army, especially considering that the Seven Years' War had already created a national debt of nearly £130 million? Where would the regiments be located? What would be their duties? Would the colonists contribute toward the cost of an army? And lastly, English politicians had to consider the Indians, many of whom had assisted in the COLONIAL WARS against France. Was there anything imperial officers could do to reduce tensions along the frontier? These were the problems that British ministers tried to solve in the years between 1763 and 1775. Unfortunately, the chaotic state of English politics, the leaders' embarrassing ignorance about conditions in America, and their tendency to place private ends above the public welfare made it difficult to establish an effective western policy.

One of the first English ministers to put forward a comprehensive western plan was the earl of Egremont (Charles Wyndham), secretary of state for the southern department from 1761 to 1763. In this work Egremont was assisted by the young and capable Lord Shelburne (William Petty), who served as president of the Board of Trade. These two men drew to a great extent on the precedents set during the Seven Years' War. Before the start of that conflict, Britain had allowed each of her colonies complete freedom in the management of its Indian relations, fur trade, and land grants. However, during the course of the war, English officials found it necessary to exercise some control over these affairs. In 1754 the ALBANY PLAN OF UNION tried to consolidate government, and the next year officials appointed two Indian superintendents who were responsible to the commander-in-chief of the British forces in America. One historian has written, "The imperial Indian superintendents were commissioned in 1755 to do what the colonies had failed to do; that is, maintain the British interest among the Indians by pursuing a uniform and consistent policy toward them." The superintendent for the region north of Virginia was Sir William JOHNSON, while the southern district was administered first by Edmund ATKIN and after 1762 by the more famous John STUART. These imperial agents quickly learned that the Indians wanted guarantees that the colonists would neither settle on their hunting grounds nor cheat them in the fur trade. British ministers who were anxious to find allies in the war against France urged that Indian lands be protected. An important step in this direction was taken when the northern tribes and the government of Pennsylvania signed the Treaty of Easton (1758), an agreement prohibiting white settlement west of the Alleghenies. In 1761 the Board of Trade forbade colonial officials to grant lands in areas that might arouse the Indians' jealousy.

Basically Egremont's policy represented a synthesis of the *ad hoc* measures taken during the war. Above all, he wanted to cut government expenditures and was convinced that England's only hope of averting a costly Indian rebellion lay in the careful regulation of trade and settlement along the American frontier. The secretary believed that the interior garrisons should be maintained "for the security of the Indian Trade." Egremont also warned that "granting lands hitherto unsettled and establishing Colonies upon the Frontiers before the claims of the Indians are ascertained appears to be a measure of the most dangerous tendency." His ideas were contained in a letter submitted to the Board of Trade in the spring of 1763.

Historians have long argued over the relative importance of Shelburne and Egremont in the formation of western policy. Clarence Alvord, for example, claimed that Shelburne "exercised greater influence on the development of western America than any other British statesman." More recently, however, R. A. Humphreys and Jack Sosin have stressed Egremont's originality, pointing out that he had worked out the details of his plan before Shelburne was ever consulted. Whatever the case may have been, both men were out of office before the crown acted upon their recommendations. Egremont died suddenly, and Shelburne resigned as part of a complicated political maneuver.

News of a general Indian uprising along the entire northern frontier gave a sense of urgency to the debate over a western policy. Pontiac, an Ottawa chief, led the assault on Fort Detroit, and by the summer of 1763 the Indians had captured almost every British garrison west of Fort Pitt. The man who was probably most responsible for PONTIAC'S REBELLION was Sir Jeffrey Amherst, commander-in-chief of all English forces in America. Amherst had aroused the Indians' jealousy by allowing illegal settlements to be established at Niagara and Sandusky Bay. Not only did the general ignore Indian land claims, but he also refused to grant the tribes the gifts that had become a traditional part of frontier diplomacy. Spurning the advice of the Indian superintendents, he declared, "as to purchasing the good behavior either of Indians, or any Others . . . I do not understand; when men of what race soever behave ill, they must be punished but not bribed." Before returning to England, the unscrupulous Amherst urged his troops to give the Indians blankets that had been used by smallpox victims. The colonial leader William Livingston was correct when he wrote that Pontiac's Rebellion was the result of Amherst's "blundering and disdainful Conduct toward the distant Tribes." Within a year the hostilities had subsided, but it was not until 1766 that Sir William Johnson made a formal peace at Oswego, which generously allowed Pontiac's followers to go unpunished for their uprising.

In September 1763 the earl of Hillsborough (Wills Hill) took over Shelburne's duties as president of the Board of Trade. Although George III claimed he did "not know a man of less judgement than Lord Hillsborough," the new president saw the necessity of issuing some formal statement that would guarantee the integrity of the Indian lands, and in October the famous Proclamation of 1763 received the royal signature. This document contained most of the ideas that Egremont and Shelburne had discussed during the summer. The proclamation established three new colonies—Quebec and East and West Florida. Americans were encouraged to emigrate to these provinces with the stipulation that no settlers were allowed to cross a line that ran roughly along the crest of the Appalachian Mountains. According to one British official, the vast American in-

terior was to be kept "as open and Wild as possible for the Purposes of Hunting." The western area was under military jurisdiction, and apparently out of ignorance, no civil government was provided for the French colonists living in the Illinois country. While the proclamation made it illegal for private citizens to purchase land directly from the Indians, the English did not regard the line of 1763 as a permanent barrier to American expansion. In fact the British crown explained that the western lands should be reserved only "for the present, and until our further Pleasure be known." Another provision opened the Indian trade to anyone who obtained a license from a governor or military commander. In the fall of 1763 the British ministers argued that the proclamation would protect the Indians from dishonest traders as well as from aggressive land speculators. The English reasoned that with these grievances removed the chances of a new frontier uprising would be greatly reduced. On their part the Americans considered the proclamation a temporary measure, and men such as George Washington advised their friends to survey land west of the line in anticipation of its opening.

A report prepared by the Board of Trade entitled "A Plan for the Future Management of Indian Affairs" represented the next step in the formulation of a British western policy. According to Alvord, "the main purpose of these regulations was to secure the protection of the Indians from traders, settlers, and land speculators." The board advocated the creation of an autonomous Indian Department, and two superintendents—one for the North and one for the South—were to be responsible for regulating the Indian trade. The report also stated that this commerce could be conducted only in certain specified towns and forts along the frontier. Unfortunately this plan would have required more than £20,000 to put into effect, and Parliament was in no mood to authorize the necessary funds. In the absence of financial support the ministry simply instructed the Indian superintendents, Stuart and Johnson, to carry out the program as best they could. Their assignment, however, was clearly impossible. Colonial leaders often refused to cooperate with the superintendents, especially when the aims of the imperial agents clashed with those of local land speculators. Moreover, in some of the northern garrisons British army officers harassed honest Indian traders, while carrying on a flourishing, but illegal, fur business themselves.

For several years following the failure of the Indian plan, English ministers paid little attention to the problems of the American West. George Croghan, one of the colonies' most successful Indian traders, reported from London with disgust, "Nothing has been don Respecting North America—the pople hear Spend thire Time in Nothing butt abuseing one another & Striveing who shall be in power." But Croghan's observation was not completely fair. To be sure, during this period English politics was in a constant state of flux, and no one knew for certain who would be in the ministry from month to month. However, most of the leaders within the British government were greatly concerned about the growing tension between the colonies and the mother country. They were especially worried about the Americans' refusal to pay parliamentary taxes or to contribute toward the cost of maintaining an English army in the New World. In the decade before the American

Revolution these constitutional problems influenced the character of British western policy.

In 1766 Shelburne became the secretary of state for the southern department. It was clear as soon as he entered this office that he intended to re-examine the measures that England had taken in the American West and to offer new programs wherever necessary. But Shelburne was under many pressures that severely limited his freedom in this task. For example, Viscount Barrington (William Wildman), secretary of war, formulated a western policy that was antithetical to Shelburne's intentions and that, furthermore, enjoyed wide popularity among English politicians during this period. Barrington saw no reason to maintain scattered military units throughout the American interior, which the Proclamation of 1763 "professedly intended to be a Desert." He observed that the army had been able neither to regulate the fur trade nor to stop white settlement on Indian lands. With this failure in mind, Barrington argued that it would be much cheaper to station the troops in the East. While the secretary of war recognized that such a move might increase the risk of an Indian uprising, he considered the retrenchment of military expenses as more important than manning the western posts. Shelburne did not support Barrington's plan, which essentially advocated the abandonment of the American West. Nevertheless, he was fully aware that no alternative policy would have a chance of being accepted unless it reduced the cost of the American army.

Shelburne was also influenced during this period by American land speculators who steadfastly opposed Barrington's scheme. The most powerful of these lobbies was the Illinois Company, founded in 1766. Its impressive membership included George CROGHAN, Sir William Johnson, Governor William Franklin, Samuel Wharton, and Joseph Galloway. The partners decided to keep Johnson's role in the venture secret, since they felt that his advice as Indian superintendent would carry more weight in London if he appeared to have no personal stake in the enterprise. Benjamin FRANKLIN soon joined the company and promised to do all he could to convince the British government to establish a new colony in the Illinois country. Franklin, who was then living in England, constantly reminded Shelburne of the many arguments that favored the Illinois project. At the same time, Croghan wrote from America warning that the withdrawal of British troops from the West would result in an Indian rebellion that would in turn allow the French to take control of the fur trade. Moreover, the leaders of the Illinois Company counseled Shelburne not to worry about the expense of maintaining the western forts, since the settlers in the new colony would be able to supply the soldiers at a greatly reduced rate.

In August 1767, after much procrastination, Shelburne presented his proposed western policy to his fellow ministers. His recommendations reflected at once the need to cut expenses and the influence of the American land speculators. First, Shelburne argued that the control over Indian affairs should be returned to the individual colonies, which he believed possessed a far better knowledge of local conditions than did the British politicians. Second, his plan called for the abandonment of all but a few of the western forts and the immediate

reduction of the North American army from fifteen to four battalions. And third, the secretary urged that England create two interior colonies—one in the Illinois country and another at Detroit. He maintained that these new settlements would not become an additional burden on the British treasury, since the colonists would be required to pay quitrents to meet administrative and military costs. These three recommendations appeared to solve the western problem, but according to Sosin, "The program which Shelburne proposed . . . was based on assumptions which were unrealistic and impractical to anyone acquainted with conditions on the frontier since 1754." The secretary should have realized, for example, that England had never been successful in collecting quitrents in America. Moreover, in the years before the French and Indian War, the colonial governments had demonstrated neither compassion nor foresight in dealing with the Indians, and there was no reason to expect that they would act with greater wisdom in 1767.

While the ministry accepted Shelburne's report, the Board of Trade balked at the notion of forming new colonies and abolishing the imperial Indian Department. The board did agree with Shelburne on one point, that a new boundary line, west of the 1763 line, should be surveyed as soon as possible. By the time that any of these proposals were put into action, however, Shelburne had lost control over colonial affairs.

Early in 1768 English leaders established a new post to handle colonial business, the secretary of state for the American Department. After some political maneuvering George III gave this important office to the earl of Hillsborough, whose views on the American West differed from those of Shelburne. In a report issued in March 1768, Hillsborough came out in favor of abandoning all the frontier garrisons except Niagara, Detroit, and Mackinac. He planned to station the English troops in areas where they could be used effectively to meet emergencies in either the East or the West. He estimated that this move would save the British treasury several hundred thousand pounds. The new secretary also recommended giving the colonies responsibility for the regulation of the Indian trade. The two Indian superintendents, however, were still empowered to make alliances and land purchases. In fact, Stuart and Johnson negotiated a new boundary line in 1768 that ran along the Allegheny and Ohio rivers to the mouth of the Kanawha and then south to the Savannah River. The Indian tribes consented to this line in a series of treaties, the most famous of which were the treaties of FORT STANWIX (1768) and HARD LABOR. Where Hillsborough broke most clearly from Shelburne's plan was in his opposition to the formation of new colonies in the American interior. Such settlements, he argued, would anger the Indians, endanger the supply of furs, and require expensive military assistance. Hillsborough insisted that the colonists had ample room for expansion in the region to the east of the 1768 boundary line. The western scholar Clarence Alvord has written, "The British ministry looked upon the western problem during the years after 1768 as practically settled, and for that reason there was relatively little discussion of its various phases: the far West beyond the Indian boundary line was to be maintained temporarily as a vast reservation for the aborigines, and the near West, the upper Ohio

Valley, was supposedly opened by the establishment of the Indian boundary line to immediate settlement."

While the appointment of Hillsborough disappointed American land speculators, they still thought that the British government could be persuaded to create a new interior colony. They based their hopes on the negotiations that had taken place at Fort Stanwix. At that conference Sir William Johnson had disobeyed his official instructions by allowing the Six Nations, or Iroquois confederacy, to give up a huge tract of land west of the 1768 boundary line. The English ministers were reluctant to accept the Iroquois' generosity, especially since the territory in question seemed to belong to other tribes. But the American speculators were determined not to let this opportunity slip away. Samuel Wharton, one of the most energetic promoters, rushed to London to lobby in behalf of the Indiana Company, which wanted to purchase the entire Fort Stanwix cession. Wharton countered Hillsborough's influence by distributing shares in the company among England's most prominent leaders, including three members of the Privy Council. In 1769 this impressive group formed the Walpole Associates or the Grand Ohio Company and petitioned the crown for a grant of twenty million acres. The company also urged the king to declare the region a proprietary colony. Hillsborough dragged his feet at every step, but he could not overcome the political power that his opposition had amassed. After it became clear in 1772 that the Privy Council would support a grant to the Walpole Associates, Hillsborough resigned from the ministry, and the earl of Dartmouth (William Legge) took his place as the colonial secretary. It appeared that Wharton's efforts had at last been successful, for Dartmouth enthusiastically backed the plans for a new colony, which was to be called Vandalia. But to everyone's surprise the Crown Law Officers, bitter over Benjamin Franklin's dealings with the Boston patriots, refused to issue the final charter, and before anything could be done to save Vandalia, the American Revolution turned the ministry's attention to other problems.

By 1773 British administrators realized that much of Hillsborough's western policy had been unsound. The individual colonies had made almost no effort to regulate the Indian trade or to contain the spread of white settlement beyond the boundary line. On the eve of the Revolution, therefore, the northern ministry decided to restore some of the imperial controls that had been discarded earlier in an effort to cut expenses. In April 1773 the Privy Council ordered colonial governors to cease granting land until further notice. After a year of study, the council laid down a new land policy that may well have been the model for the land system later adopted by the United States. Under the 1774 plan no grants could be made until an area had been surveyed and divided into lots of one hundred to one thousand acres. After these lots had been carefully numbered on a map, they were to be sold at a public auction to the "best bidder." Moreover, the governors were prohibited from making free grants in the future. All these provisions worked against the speculators and the political favorites who had previously been able to amass great western tracts at little or no charge. Had this land reform been instituted earlier, it might have removed some of the inequities that had characterized the colonial frontier.

In June 1774 Parliament passed the Quebec Act. This controversial statute attempted to correct some of the mistakes that had been made both in Canada and the American West following the Seven Years' War. The backers of this bill hoped to appease the French majority in Quebec by returning French civil law to the province, by granting the Roman Catholics full toleration and legal rights, and by placing the legislative power in an appointed governor and biracial council. The Quebec Act also reflected England's concern over the confused conditions in the Ohio valley. The measure extended the boundaries of Quebec to include the area north and west of the Ohio and Allegheny rivers. It was argued that this change would at last bring order to Indian affairs. The government of Quebec was expected to regulate the fur trade and to prevent the colonists from seizing Indian lands. In other words the British had returned to the policy first advanced in 1763; the West would be an Indian reservation open only to carefully controlled white settlement. The Quebec Act also provided civil government for the French communities in the Illinois country, which since the Treaty of Paris had been under military jurisdiction.

The Quebec Act raised a storm of criticism in the American colonies. The patriots incorrectly associated the bill with the "Intolerable Acts," which Parliament had passed in order to punish Massachusetts for the Boston Tea Party. The New Englanders—always wary of the spread of Popery—condemned Britain's toleration of the Canadian Catholics. The Virginians protested the extension of Quebec into an area that they had long claimed as theirs. Thomas Jefferson, who was not personally involved in western land speculation, claimed in his *Summary View of the Rights of British America* (1774) that the land in America neither belonged nor ever had belonged to the king of England. Jefferson advised his readers, "It is time . . . for us to lay this matter before his majesty, and to declare that he has no right to grant lands of himself."

Scholars have long debated to what extent British western policy was a cause of the American Revolution. No doubt Clarence Alvord was correct when he observed in 1917, "If historians would interpret rightly the cause of the American Revolution and the birth of the nation, they must not let their vision be circumscribed by the sequence of events in the East." After all, it was in their search for revenues to support the army that British politicians first decided to tax the colonists. This move raised a score of difficult constitutional issues, and by 1774 many Americans had come to challenge the supremacy of Parliament. But the influence of the West in these events should not be exaggerated. The land speculators who were rebuffed in their attempt to form an interior colony represented only a small group within the American population. Moreover, many leading speculators, such as Patrick Henry and Benjamin Franklin, attacked British taxation on constitutional, not economic, grounds. Had the restrictions on western settlement been successfully enforced, they might have become a major grievance along the frontier, However, the various proclamations and instructions sent from London did little to stem the flood of colonists onto Indian lands. Therefore, a fair assessment would be that British western policy was a contributing, but not a major, factor in the growth of tension between the colonies and the mother country.

There are many excellent works on this topic. The best are Thomas Perkins Abernethy, *Western Lands and the American Revolution* (1937); Clarence W. Alvord, *The Mississippi Valley in British Politics*, 2 vols. (1917); and Jack Sosin, *Whitehall and the Wilderness* (1961). See also Clarence W. Alvord, "The Genesis of the Proclamation of 1763," Michigan Historical Society, *Collections* (1907); Ray A. Billington and James B. Hedges, *Westward Expansion: A History of the American Frontier* (1949); Bernard Donoughue, *British Politics and the American Revolution: The Path to War, 1773-75* (1964); R. A. Humphreys, "Lord Shelburne and the Proclamation of 1763," *English Historical Review*, vol. 8 (1921-22); Charles Metzger, "An Appraisal of Shelburne's Western Policy," *Mid-America*, vol. 19 (1937); John Shy, *Toward Lexington: The Role of the British Army in the Coming of the American Revolution* (1965); and George Olien Virtue, *British Land Policy and the American Revolution*, University of Nebraska Studies, vol. 11 (1955).—T. H. B.

British Indian policy. See BRITISH ADMINISTRATIVE POLICY (1763-1775); and INDIAN-WHITE RELATIONS: *British Indian policy, 1763-1775*.

Broadwater, Charles Arthur (1840-1892). Montana businessman. Born and raised in Missouri, Broadwater was by 1860 engaged in a mercantile enterprise in the Colorado gold fields. In 1862 he went to Bannack, Montana, and in company with John Y. Pemberton was soon laying out the townsite of Deer Lodge City. He became superintendent of the Diamond R. freighting company, the largest in the territory. He then took contracts to build Fort Assiniboine and Fort Maginnis, to recondition Fort Benton, and to supply these forts. In 1882 he organized the Montana National Bank in Helena. By agreement with railroad builder James J. HILL he built the Montana Central Railway to link the Great Northern at Great Falls with Helena and Butte. Broadwater's business empire included banks, railroads, mines, forests, flour mills, and cattle ranches. A consuming interest was his "spa," the elaborate Broadwater Hotel and Natatorium west of Helena. A Democrat in politics, he worked closely with Samuel T. HAUSER, William A. CLARK, and Marcus DALY as one of the "Big Four," who, when they agreed, virtually controlled the state.

See *Progressive Men of the State of Montana* (1901). —M. G. B.

Brocius, "Curly Bill" [William C.]. Alias **Bill Graham** (?-?1882). Cowboy and outlaw. Brocius was probably a Texan, but he made his reputation in Arizona. He arrived there in 1878 with a trail herd for the San Carlos Indian reservation. He soon appeared in the Tombstone area, where he worked for the McLaury brothers, Frank and Tom. He was believed to be involved in rustling and smuggling operations along with N. H. "Old Man" Clanton and his sons, Ike, Finn, and Billy. These practices were common on the Mexican border at the time and went virtually unnoticed until Tombstone was established. Thereafter increasing complaints prompted federal investigation of the problem, and Brocius was clearly identified with the illegal activities even though he was never arrested for any crime.

The arrival of the EARP BROTHERS in Tombstone signaled the beginning of the cowboys' difficulties. The cowboys were mostly southerners, Democrats, and used to having their own way in the region. The Earps were northerners, Republicans, and made their living gambling with folks like the cowboys. Too, the Earps were ambitious politically. As law enforcement officers Wyatt and Virgil Earp frequently encountered the cowboys. One evening in 1880 Tombstone's marshal, Fred White, called on the Earps to help him arrest a group of rowdy cowboys. Moments later White was mortally wounded when he tried to take Brocius' gun. Brocius was promptly "buffaloed" (struck on the head with a pistol) by Deputy Sheriff Wyatt Earp and hauled away to jail. Although the dying marshal swore the shooting was accidental, the incident is often cited as the origin of bitterness between the cowboys and the Earp Brothers.

In the spring of 1881 Brocius was wounded in the neck in a brawl. Some old-timers insist that he left Arizona after that, but he was seen at the McLaury ranch as late as October 1881. The Earps believed that Curly Bill was involved in the vendetta that left Morgan Earp dead and Virgil Earp crippled for life. Wyatt Earp claimed to have killed Brocius in the spring of 1882 at Iron Springs in the Whetstone Mountains. The assertion has often been disputed by persons who claim Brocius lived to a ripe old age in Montana, but evidence collected by John D. Gilchriese, Earp's most assiduous student, tends to confirm the Earp claim.—G. L. R.

Broderick, David Colbreth (1820-1859). California politician. Raised in New York, Broderick moved to California in 1849. Through ownership of a private mint and speculation in waterfront real estate, he became a power in San Francisco and built a powerful political machine patterned on his experiences in Tammany politics. Elected to the Senate in 1857, he engaged his colleague William M. GWIN in heated contest for control of federal patronage and the state Democratic party machinery. But as leader of the Free-Soil opposition to Gwin's majority, proslavery wing of the party, Broderick went hungry. In 1859 he was killed in a duel with David S. Terry, a leader of the proslavery forces. After his death, Broderick was canonized by Free-Soil politicians as the "Pacific Coast Lincoln."

See L. E. Fredman, "Broderick: A Reassessment," *Pacific Historical Review*, vol. 29 (1960); Donald E. Hargis, "The Issues in the Broderick-Gwin Debates of 1859," *California Historical Society Quarterly*, vol. 32 (1953); and David A. Williams, *David C. Broderick: A Political Portrait* (1969).—J. F.

Brodie, Alexander Oswald (1849-1918). Soldier and Arizona politician. While commanding the first squadron of ROUGH RIDERS in the action at Las Guásimas, Cuba, on June 24, 1898, Major Brodie, whose utter contempt of the Spanish soldier was matched only by that of his friend and fellow Prescott, Arizona, officer Captain William O. "Buckey" O'Neill, was wounded in the forearm by an enemy Mauser bullet. Cradling the shattered arm, Brodie sat down under a tree and phlegmatically smoked a cigar. Later, walking back from the battle zone and weakening from loss of blood, he encountered his commanding officer, Colonel Leonard Wood. As if suddenly realizing what had happened to him, Brodie shouted, "Great Scott, Colonel! They've *hit* me!"

The man characterized by Theodore Roosevelt as "a soldier by taste as well as training" was born in Edwards, New York, and educated at St. Lawrence University and the United States Military Academy (class of 1870). Fort Apache, Arizona, was his first assignment after receiving his commission. The twenty-one-year-old second lieutenant quickly became one of General George Crook's most intrepid scouts in the Tonto Basin and other Apache strongholds in eastern and northern Arizona.

In 1874, Brodie was promoted to first lieutenant and sent with the First Cavalry to Fort Colville, Washington, where he participated in the last campaigns against the Nez Percé Indians of Idaho. In 1877, shortly after the death of his wife, he resigned his commission. After several years in the cattle business in Kansas, a one-year return to the service with the Sixth Cavalry under the command of Captain Adnah R. Chaffee, and mining in the Dakota and Arizona territories, Brodie settled in Prescott, Arizona. Between 1887 and 1890 he was chief engineer and superintendent of the Walnut Creek Dam on the Hassayampa River, north of Wickenburg. In 1891 the governor of Arizona Territory appointed Brodie the first commander of the Arizona national guard. Shortly after resigning this post, Brodie became county recorder for Yavapai County.

Even before war was officially declared against Spain in April 1898 Brodie, with the help of Buckey O'Neill, mayor of Prescott, and James H. McClintock of Phoenix, began petitioning the territorial governor for permission to raise a regiment of volunteers. While the troopers were being screened and signed up, Brodie (considered the military backbone of the regiment) was named a major of volunteers. His Arizonans became part of the First United States Volunteer Cavalry Regiment, later, the Rough Riders, under the command of Colonel Leonard Wood and Lieutenant Colonel Theodore Roosevelt.

Las Guásimas, where Brodie was wounded, was the first land action of the Cuban campaign. When he had recovered sufficiently to return to the regiment, he was promoted to lieutenant colonel, succeeding Roosevelt, who had assumed the colonelcy.

After the four-month war ended, Brodie returned to Prescott. On July 1, 1902, President Roosevelt appointed him governor of the territory, an office he filled until February 4, 1905, when he resigned to go to Washington as assistant chief of the Records and Pension Office, with the rank of major of the regular army.

Later in 1905 Brodie was promoted to lieutenant colonel and became military secretary and adjutant general of the Department of Visayas, the Philippines. He returned to the United States in 1907. From 1907 until 1911 he was adjutant general of the Department of the Dakotas. For the last two years of his army career, he held the rank of colonel and served with the Department of California in San Francisco. He retired in 1913.

Brodie spent his last years in Haddonfield, New Jersey, with his second wife and two sons. When he was buried in Haddonfield, a sprig of Scottish heather was placed in his clasped hands.

Jay J. Wagoner, *Arizona Territory 1863-1912* (1970), contains a good capsule biography and a full account of Brodie's governorship. See also Charles Herner, *The Arizona Rough Riders* (1970).—D. L. W.

Bronson, Ruth Muskrat (1897-   ). Cherokee government official. Bronson was born in Grove, Oklahoma, and was reared on a farm in that state. She was one of very few women to attend the University Preparatory School at Tonkawa, Oklahoma, a state-run boarding

high school. She went on to the University of Oklahoma for two years and then transferred to Mount Holyoke College in Massachusetts. During her summer vacations in 1925 and 1926, she was sent by the YMCA to the Mescalero Apache reservation as a playground instructor. After graduation she began a long career with the Bureau of Indian Affairs as a teacher at the Haskell Indian School in Kansas, a boarding school for Indians.

After her marriage in 1928, Bronson moved to Washington, D. C. About this time, the Merriam Report, on which much Bureau of Indian Affairs policy was based, was being completed. In 1930 the Brookings Institution commissioned Bronson to do a study on college opportunities for Indians because the Merriam Report had little information in that area. Her study led to the creation of the higher education "desk" at the bureau and to greatly expanded services and scholarships to students through the bureau. Bronson worked in that office, between 1931 and 1943. In 1933 she was chosen to represent American Indians by the Student Christian Federation and took time off from bureau work to attend the federation's international conference in Peiping.

In 1943 Bronson resigned from the bureau to raise and adopt the daughter of a close friend from Laguna Pueblo, who had died. Although she held no paying job for many years, she was executive secretary of the National Congress of American Indians (NCAI) between 1946 and 1949. While in office she was awarded a grant by the Robert Marshall Foundation to make a survey of Indian conditions in Alaska, which she did during 1947. Actually, that meant she was "out of the office," because the NCAI office was located on the first floor of the Bronsons' Georgetown home, with the mimeograph machine in the basement! In 1957 she went back to work for the Bureau of Indian Affairs as a community worker in health education on the San Carlos Apache reservation. In 1962 she was named the head of health education for Nevada, but she had to resign after three months because her husband became ill. Bronson then became a consultant for the Save the Children Foundation.

Her *Indians Are People, Too* was published in 1947. —C. C.

Brooks, Juanita (1898-   ). Historian. Brooks was born in Bunkerville, Nevada, and taught there. After her husband of a year died in 1920 of throat cancer, she attended Dixie Junior College in St. George, Utah, and returned to teaching, meanwhile helping to support a younger sister who was serving on a Latter-day Saint proselyting mission. By 1925 she had received a bachelor of arts degree from Brigham Young University and then taught English and speech at Dixie Junior College. In 1933 she married William Brooks, sheriff of Washington County, Utah.

Her interest in history and the preservation of records began in 1930. She and her assistants collected, transcribed, and typed many diaries and other documents. By 1934 these were the basis of a statewide program. "Close-up of Polygamy" appeared in *Harper's* in 1934, and "The Water's In" in 1941. In 1942 she published *Dudley Leavitt*, a biography of her grandfather.

From 1944 to 1951 Brooks was a field fellow for the Henry E. Huntington Library and in 1950 published *The Mountain Meadows Massacre*. In 1955 she coauthored (with Robert Cleland) a two-volume work, *A Mormon Chronicle: The Diaries of John D. Lee.* In 1961 she edited *On the Mormon Frontier: The Diary of Hosea Stout.* More recent biographies include *John Doyle Lee: Zealot, Pioneer Builder, Scapegoat* (1961); and *Uncle Will Tells His Story* (1970), the latter a biography of her husband.

Brooks, William L. (1849-1874). Stagecoach driver, lawman, and horse thief. Brooks was born in Ohio, but Kansas tradition picks him up in Hays City in the late 1860s. It is said he killed several men there, although no real evidence survives to support the claim. In 1870 he drove a coach for the Southwestern Stage Company between El Dorado and Wichita. The next year he was transferred to the run between Wichita and Newton, the "Swiftest Town in Kansas." After a difficult cattle season in 1871, Newton hired Brooks as marshal in April 1872. He held the position only briefly, resigning after being wounded in a gunfight. He was later at Ellsworth and Dodge City. In Dodge, he was involved in several violent encounters and apparently held an unofficial position as marshal or assistant marshal. Early in 1873 a buffalo hunter named Kirk Jordan tried to kill Brooks. Soon afterward, Brooks left Dodge. He turned up in Caldwell in 1874, again in the employ of the Southwestern Stage Company. That year, it lost its mail contract to a rival company. On June 29, 1874, a number of the rival's mules were stolen. Late in July Brooks and several others were arrested for the thefts, and on the night of July 29, 1874, Brooks and two other men were lynched. From testimony taken later, it appears that the thefts were misguided efforts to recover the mail contract for Brooks's employers by crippling their rival.

See Nyle H. Miller and Joseph W. Snell, *Why the West Was Wild* (1963).—G. L. R.

Brotherhood of Penitents. The Brotherhood of Penitents, in New Mexico and southern Colorado, is a religious society founded for pious ends and aid to the sick, the poor, the dying, and the dead. There are still small groups of the brothers in the foothills and river valleys who practice their religious convictions with great fervor and quietly give help where it is needed. Except for the custom of flagellation, their religious services are based upon those of the Roman Catholic Church, and the organization's rules appear to be a survival of those of the Third Order of St. Francis of Assisi founded in 1218 for the laity who wished to take certain modified vows.

Holy Week services are held in the Penitente *moradas* (chapels) as well as in the village churches. The processions start at the moradas and wind to the church, along the Way of the Cross or back into the hills. On Shrove Tuesday the *sangrador* (bleeder) cuts long crosses in the backs of the *penitentes*, those who have vowed to flagellate themselves as the Roman soldiers lashed Jesus on the road to Golgotha. Some of the brothers voluntarily drag crosses in imitation of Christ. The sangrador's cuts help the blood to flow freely without great pain or welts when the *disciplinas* (yucca cactus whips, which are soaked in salted water) are applied by the hand of the penitent.

The Holy Week processions from Ash Wednesday through Good Friday are led by the *Hermano Mayor* (Head Brother). Accompanying him is the *rezador* (reader) reciting prayers from a *cuaderno* (copybook),

written and copied by generation after generation. The flagellants follow with a fully clad *compañero* (companion) on either side to help each if he stumbles on the rocky road. A *pitero* blows a wild piping note on his *pito* (flute).

The flagellants wear only *calzones* (thin white cotton trousers) and black hoods to conceal their identities against thoughts of vainglory. One or more of the penitents may drag a heavy wooden cross, and one may drag the *carreta del muerto* (death cart) by coarse horsehair ropes tied around his shoulders and across his chest. Low, heavy, and made of wood, this cart moves on solid wooden wheels. In it sits the skeleton figure of Death dressed in black. Her obsidian eyes are set deep in her white skull face and she carries a drawn bow with its arrow stretched for flight.

On Maundy Thursday and Good Friday nights, by lantern and moonlight, a procession of penitents goes to the church to conduct *Tinieblas* (darkness, hell) and the villagers join them. Doleful *alabados* (hymns), written down in fifteenth- or sixteenth-century Spanish, as are the rezador's prayers, are sung. Candles in the *tenebrarios* (candlesticks) on the altar are pinched out one by one as the Hermano Mayor reads the ritual until, at last, the church is in utter darkness. Silence. Then, suddenly, a ratcheted *matraca* (noisemaker) is whirled, the pito wails, chains clank, and the shrieks and howls of souls in torment fill the blackness above the slap and thud of whips on bloody backs. The names of all who have died recently are called out and prayers are recited for their repose. Then candles and lanterns are again lighted and the penitents back out of the church.

From 1349 on the church has forbidden severe penance, but certain cults throughout Europe persisted in inflicting bodily punishment. These customs prevailed in Spain and Mexico when New Mexico was first settled and continued on much later. The first report of penitent rites publicly performed in New Mexico is that of Captain Gaspar Pérez de Villagrá in his epic poem *Historia de la Nueva Mexico*, written in Alcala, Spain, in 1610. Villagrá tells of Don Juan de Oñate, his colonists, soldiers, and priests stopping beside a stream to observe Holy Thursday on March 20, 1598. They built a temporary chapel in which they set a replica of the Holy Sepulcher.

Here in the evening the priests and all the officers and men came and devoutly, on their knees, with tears in their eyes, begged forgiveness for their sins.

The night was one of prayer and penance for all. The women and children came barefoot to pray at the holy shrine. The soldiers, with cruel scourges, beat their backs unmercifully until the camp ran crimson with their blood. The humble Franciscan friars, barefoot and clothed in cruel thorny girdles, devoutly chanted their doleful hymns, praying forgiveness for their sins.

Don Juan, unknown to anyone except me, went to a secluded spot where he cruelly scourged himself, mingling bitter tears with the blood which flowed from his many wounds. This continued throught the camp till early morn. . . . Gerónimo and I took example from these worthy ones and underwent like punishment. What lessons we learned from what we observed that day!

Obviously, Villagrá would not have reported this to the king of Spain unless he believed that the monarch would be pleased to hear it.

The early far-flung Franciscan missions of New Mexico were great teaching centers where the Indians were converted and the Spaniards catechized. The Spanish men were given handwritten books of prayers and alabados and were taught to conduct lay services.

The clergy were supervised laxly from Durango, Mexico, several months' journey away. As the years passed, the Franciscans moved into the towns, and visited remote villages and pueblos when time and weather permitted. The men, possibly of the Third Order of St. Francis, took over the church rites in the isolated foothills and valleys. In 1828 the Franciscans left, and the new French secular priests visited the people of the outposts even more infrequently than had the Franciscans. Left to their own devices, the villagers followed the only religious leaders they had.

See Fray Angelico Chavez, "The Penitentes of New Mexico," *New Mexico Historical Review* (April 1954); Alice Corbin Henderson, *Brothers of Light: The Penitentes of the Southwest* (1962); and Marta Weigle, *The Penitentes of the Southwest* (1970).—B. P. D. and M. L.

Brouillet, John (1813-1884). Roman Catholic missionary. Active in Pacific Northwest Indian missions from 1847, Brouillet founded the Umatilla mission. When the Cayuse Indians in 1847 massacred Marcus Whitman and his family, Brouillet's reward for warning Henry Harmon SPALDING of the attack was vilification for many years as the instigator of the uprising. The issue became a national controversy, becoming part of the backwash of the United States' takeover of Oregon. Brouillet was eventually exonerated. From 1872 he helped evolve the Bureau of Catholic Indian Missions in Washington, D. C. (see ROMAN CATHOLIC MISSIONS AND THE INDIANS).

See Peter J. Rahill, *Catholic Indian Missions and Grant's Peace Policy* (1953).—R. I. B.

Brown, Albert Gallatin (1813-1880). Mississippi politician. Brown was born in South Carolina and migrated at an early age with his parents to Copiah County, Mississippi. Reared in poverty, he identified himself with the masses in the south Mississippi area east of the Natchez District and was a lifelong supporter of his own class, the farmer or small slaveholding class. He was an ardent Jacksonian Democrat. In 1835, at the age of twenty-three, he was elected to the Mississippi House of Representatives and held public office almost uninterruptedly until 1865 without ever losing an election. In addition to being state representative he was United States representative, judge of circuit superior court, governor, and United States and Confederate senator. He held no official position after the Civil War.

Brown appreciated the necessity of education in a democracy and in his gubernatorial election campaign of 1843 promised that public schools would be provided. (White Mississippians supported private elementary and secondary schools.) While governor (1844-48) he tried in vain to establish a sound public school system. A legislative act in 1846 was the state's first serious move to establish public schools. The results of this and subsequent acts were plenty of school laws, but the schools existed only on paper. The University of Mississippi was chartered in 1844, but it was 1848 before the institution

opened its doors and it grew very slowly before the Civil War.

Brown was a secessionist. He also was a strong supporter of southern nationalism. Like Jefferson Davis, he opposed the extreme states'-rights faction in the Confederacy and supported Davis' position of the Confederacy first. The pro-Confederate lawyer Reuben Davis, in his *Recollections of Mississippi and Mississippians* (1899), recalls Brown as "the best-balanced man I ever knew."

See M. W. Caskey, *Speeches, Messages and Other Writings of the Hon. Albert G. Brown* (1859), and James B. Ranck, *Albert Gallatin Brown, Radical Southern Nationalist* (1937).—J. E. G.

Brown, Dee [Alexander] (1908-   ). Librarian and historian. Brown was born in Louisiana and educated at George Washington University and the University of Illinois. He was librarian at the Department of Agriculture in Washington from 1934 to 1942, at the War Department from 1945 to 1948, and then became librarian at the University of Illinois College of Agriculture.

Brown's writings about the West, though scholarly, are intended for the reading public and skillfully strip the mythological overlay from many controversial events without sacrificing that element of adventuresome interest that modern Americans seem to require of the vanished frontier. His most noted work is *Bury My Heart at Wounded Knee* (1971), which recounts the Indian wars of the trans-Mississippi West in the words, and from the point of view, of the Indian participants. Appearing at a time when popular interest in the Indian past was increasing, the book became a best-seller and served to heighten public awareness of the inequities and atrocities committed upon the Indians by white men.

Among Brown's other works are *Grierson's Raid* (1954), *Yellowhorse* (1956), *Cavalry Scout* (1957), *The Gentle Tamers: Women of the Old West* (1958), *The Bold Cavaliers* (1959), *They Went Thataway* (1960), *Fort Phil Kearny: An American Saga* (1962), *The Galvanized Yankees* (1963), *The Girl from Fort Wicked* (1964), *Showdown at Little Big Horn* (1965), and *The Year of the Century: 1876* (1966).—P. R. M.

Brown, Henry Newton (1857-1884). Lawman and outlaw. Brown grew up on a farm near Rolla, Missouri. His youthful wanderings gave him experience as a cowhand and a buffalo hunter. In the late 1870s he drifted into New Mexico, where he was employed by the firm of Lawrence G. Murphy, a powerful entrepreneur who dominated government contracts in that area. After a quarrel with Murphy, Brown shifted his loyalties to John Chisum, a cattle baron and Murphy's rival. In the months that followed, Brown became involved in the events remembered as the LINCOLN COUNTY WAR. After Chisum's associate John Tunstall was murdered, Brown rode with Billy the Kid in support of Alexander McSween, who assumed leadership of the Tunstall faction. Brown was present at several shootings, and his name appeared on several murder warrants.

He survived the Lincoln County troubles, however, and in 1880 drifted into Tascosa, Texas, with Billy the Kid and other Lincoln County partisans. Brown said good-bye to the Kid, and hired on as a deputy sheriff in Oldham County and as a constable in Tascosa. He proved to be an efficient officer, but some questions were raised about his methods as a policeman. Suspicions that he might be too quick to use his guns may have led to his departure from Tascosa in 1882. His wanderings now led him to the Indian Territory and finally to Caldwell, Kansas. Brown joined Caldwell's police force, which, considering the town's record of violence, was an unenviable position. He won the respect of the community and within a year was the town's marshal.

Caldwell's heyday as a cowtown came late, but its history had been particularly violent. Several lawmen had been murdered there, and its proximity to the Indian Territory attracted a substantial floating population of desperate character. Brown put the lid on Caldwell through quiet, efficient law enforcement. The number of killings was reduced and quasi-legal professions such as gambling and prostitution, which had been the source of many of the killings, were controlled. His record was so impressive that the citizens presented him with a gold-plated Winchester. In 1883 he killed a drunken Indian in a general store when the Indian tried to pull a gun on him. Later he killed a gambler named Newt Boyce in a gunfight on the streets of Caldwell. His reputation survived these incidents, and his marriage to Maude Levagood convinced the citizenry that the best marshal Caldwell ever had was there to stay. A month later, with three accomplices, including his assistant marshal at Caldwell, Brown robbed the bank at Medicine Lodge, Kansas, and killed two men. The bank robbers fled but were captured and returned to Medicine Lodge. There a lynch mob hanged Brown's accomplices and killed him as he tried to escape.

Caldwell was stunned. Why had Brown so changed? That was the question the people of Caldwell asked, and it has never been adequately answered. Some speculated that the Caldwell job was merely a front for illegal activities. Others suggested that Brown had a flaw of character that made him susceptible to the influence of his associates. In his last letter to his wife, Brown wrote that he had done it for her.

For further reading, see Nyle H. Miller and Joseph W. Snell, *Why the West Was Wild* (1963).—G. L. R.

Brown, John (1800–1859). Abolitionist. Territorial Kansas abounded in controversy, and no more controversial figure appeared than John Brown. Historical accounts of Brown are generally extreme and treat him either as a vicious fanatic, maniac, and horse thief, or as the greatest abolitionist hero of all time.

Born in Connecticut, the third of six children of God-fearing Calvinist parents, Brown was reared with stringent discipline. In a "magic journey" when he was five years of age, the family moved by ox wagon to Ohio near Cleveland. There his mother died three years later and young, thin, sober John could never fully accept his father's second wife. He helped his father drive cattle to the Detroit vicinity during the War of 1812 where he gained his first unfavorable impressions of Negro slavery. He hated the "peculiar institution" and his abolitionist sentiments echoed the feelings found in his section of Ohio.

After the war Brown attended New England schools for a short time to prepare for college and the ministry, but finances and eye troubles forced abandonment of that goal. Back in Ohio, the austere, tense, humorless, bashful teen-ager worked in his father's tannery, where he had some business success. Before he reached manhood he arrogantly regarded himself as a businessman of unimpeachable credentials. He married and prided himself on his increasing family and his growing business reputation. Something of a go-ahead "plunger," however, and unwilling to accept advice, he suffered through fifteen business failures in four different states by 1852. Tragedy also stalked his family; he buried one wife and nine of his twenty children during the same period. By then, broken financially and physically and plagued by the guilt of his missteps, Brown obtained the assistance of a wealthy landowner and reformer, Gerrit Smith, to aid in Negro resettlement near North Elba, New York.

In the meantime, the passage of the Kansas-Nebraska Act in 1854 (see KANSAS-NEBRASKA ISSUE) renewed a fever of interest in the older states concerning the West. The reopening of the question of slavery in the trans-Missouri region created a "save-Kansas" campaign in the North, and free-soil emigrants were aided in their quest by northern interests with the purpose of seeing that Kansas voted itself a free-soil state (see KANSAS). Five of Brown's sons departed for Kansas in the winter of 1854-55 and located claims near Brown's Station, some thirty miles south of Lawrence. Brown's eldest son sent appeals to him for assistance against the harassment of Missouri border ruffians. Descriptions of a conspiracy to make Kansas slave territory soon caused Brown to abandon his North Elba project to go to his sons in Kansas with a wagonload of guns and swords.

Brown arrived in Kansas in October 1855, and during the final four years of his life he spent about twenty months in the territory with which his name is indelibly associated. His contribution to the era of "Bleeding Kansas" is significant. In fact, it has been suggested that without John Brown there might have not been a "Bleeding Kansas."

Shortly after his arrival, Brown went heavily armed to a local free-state election to oppose an anticipated proslavery invasion, which did not materialize. Brown probably did not cast a vote in this or any other such election in the territory, because at no time did he regard himself as a Kansas citizen. Tensions were increasing over proslavery-free-state issues and Brown was certain that a massive conspiracy existed to drive free-staters out of the territory. He and his boys responded quickly to the threat of the "Wakarusa war" at Lawrence, an action involving free-state and pro-slavery forces but no fighting. While there, he caused dissension in free-state ranks because of his uncompromising views and his opposition to a peaceful alternative to the expected hostilities. Almost every item of news in early 1856 added to his view that free-soil men, who were trying to organize under a free-state constitution, were facing forced removal from the territory.

Along Pottawatomie Creek, to the south of Brown's Station, local proslavery men abusively threatened free-state settlers with violation of the proslavery-inspired laws passed by the territorial legislature, called "bogus" laws by free-staters. Settlers' meetings were held and local pseudo-military organizations were created, such as the Pottawatomie Rifles headed by John Brown, Jr. In late April an assassin wounded the proslavery sheriff of Douglas County, near Lawrence, and rival newspaper editors inflamed partisan readers. Urgent calls for protection from a proslavery army went out from Lawrence on May 21 and the Pottawatomie Rifles set out at once. Brown went along with them although he continued to brood over the "slave hounds" and other supporters of the "black laws" along the Pottawatomie. News of the brutal beating of Senator Charles Sumner following his "crime against Kansas" speech aroused in Brown a strong desire for revenge, and he led a small party south on a secret mission to "regulate matters" along the Pottawatomie. During the night of May 24, 1856, Brown and his group murdered five proslavery men, including three from one family, whom they took from their cabins along the Pottawatomie.

This Pottawatomie massacre shocked most free-state settlers and was unanimously condemned by proslavery Kansans. Brown was now "totally and irrevocably" engaged in war against proslavery forces. He invariably said that he had not killed the men at Pottawatomie but he approved of it. Crisis followed crisis in southeastern Kansas; 1856 was the worst year for violent deaths in the territory. Brown was sought but only his sons were apprehended. A column of Missourians under Captain Henry C. Pate was captured by Brown only to be released a few days later by United States troopers who did not arrest Brown for his actions. His guerrilla-style "holy war" continued through the summer. Brown justified every action—assassination, distortion, lies, terrorization, and plundering—as for the good of the cause. He finally left Kansas in October 1856 and toured New York and New England, where he was acclaimed for his stalwart opposition to slavery. Nevertheless his efforts to raise money for fighting the war in Kansas were frustrated by the hard times brought on by the Panic of 1857. Actually, Brown's need for money did not come from anything involving Kansas; rather he had long been developing plans for freeing all the slaves in the South.

In October 1857 free-state men won control of the Kansas territorial legislature. Shortly thereafter Brown, wearing a beard for disguise, set out for the territory again to keep his name associated with Kansas and to divert suspicion away from any of his other plans. In late 1858 he led his first raiding party into Missouri and liberated eleven slaves whom he conducted out of Kansas early the next year. During the first part of 1859, Brown refined his plans for capturing the federal arsenal at Harpers Ferry, Virginia. On a rented farm nearby he assembled a small band of raiders and in mid-October they seized the arsenal. The slaves of Virginia did not respond as he had expected and Brown's force was quickly killed or captured. Virginia courts acted hastily; Brown was found guilty of treason on October 31 and hanged December 2.

Brown's raid on Harpers Ferry produced an exaggerated alarm in the South. His behavior during the trial helped to make him a saint and martyr to many northern abolitionists. His goal of freeing the slaves and the manner of his death made him a hero to the North during the Civil War. Until Lincoln was cut down by an assassin's bullet in 1865 Brown had no serious rival.

Extensive material on Brown is found in Richard O. Boyer, *The Legend of John Brown* (1972); James C. Malin, *John Brown and the Legend of Fifty-six* (1942); and Stephen B. Oates, *To Purge This Land with Blood: A Biography of John Brown* (1970).—H. E. S.

Brown, John Mason. See BAPTISTS.

Browne, John Ross (1821-1875). Adventurer, author, artist, and government agent. Browne was considered to be one of the most widely traveled and versatile writers of his time. A tolerant, friendly, democratic man, with a current of comedy pulsing through him, he saw the world when traveling was often difficult and risky.

Born in a hamlet near Dublin, Ireland, Browne grew up close to the Ohio River in the United States. When eighteen he learned shorthand and got a job as a reporter in the Senate in 1841. Eight years later he was paid $10,000 to report the proceedings of California's constitutional convention in 1849, published in 1850. Known for his energy and honesty, the Treasury Department made him a confidential agent in the West with orders to survey the customs houses and mints, report on irregularities, and look into Indian and Land Office affairs. He became an authority on Indian affairs, mining statistics, and engineering. Appointed United States minister to China, he served only a short time before being recalled, but this and other sojourns in the Orient apparently made a lasting impression, for when he finally settled in Oakland, California, he built an elaborate house, Pagoda Hill, which combined the art and architecture of many Eastern and Mediterranean cultures.

A prolific writer of books and articles, Browne illustrated many of his works with his own pencil or pen-and-ink sketches and watercolors. Much of his art bore his trademark style of satire.

A product of his funny-bone is quoted from his *Crusoe's Island . . . with Sketches of Adventures in California and Washoe* (1864). A sailor had made him a grotesque suit of clothes from goatskins, and Browne described them by writing, "He made them according to a pattern of my own, which I intend some day or other to introduce to fashionable circles. I stowed them carefully away in my berth, but rats took such a fancy to them that by the time I reached California, there was nothing left but the tail of one goat upon which to hang a portrait." Browne's sketch of himself, robed in the goatskin suit, resembles current cartoons of the Abominable Snowman.

Other interesting books by Browne are *Adventures in Apache Country* (1869) and *Report of J. Ross Browne on the Mineral Resources of the States West of the Rocky Mountains* (1868).

John Ross Browne, His Letters, Journals and Writings (1969) is edited by Lina Fergusson Browne. In her excellent introduction she suggests that Mark Twain borrowed from Browne when he wrote *Innocents Abroad* and further states that the illustrations in Herman Melville's *Moby Dick* are strangely similar to Browne's etchings of a whaling cruise.—B. W. A.

Browning, John Moses (1855-1926). Inventor of firearms. Born in Ogden, Utah, the son of a talented gunsmith, Browning invented more than eighty complete and distinct firearm models. In the process, he was granted 128 patents. In a realistic sense, he was the "father of modern firearms."

Browning's guns have been manufactured in the United States under the names Winchester, Colt, Remington, Savage, and many others. Because of this he has remained literally unknown in a nation that thrives on his modern weapons. In Europe, on the other hand, where his automatic pistols have been produced by Fabrique Nationale, a Belgian firm, Browning's name has been stamped on each firearm. This practice has given his name such widespread usage that in the French language *browning* is a common noun, a synonym for pistols of all kinds.

Browning's first patent, in 1879, was a single shot, which later became Winchester's Single Shot Model of 1885. A lever-action repeating rifle was patented in 1884 and appeared as Winchester's Model 1886. Known for its lever-action weapons, Winchester asked Browning to design a lever-action shotgun. It was constructed along the same lines as the rifle and was placed on the market as Winchester's Lever Action Shotgun, Model 1887. Browning was convinced that a pump-action shotgun would be more advantageous for the hunter, however, and so designed and received the patent for a pump model in 1888. In 1890 it appeared as Winchester's Model 1890.

In sporting arms, Browning developed many variations of his basic designs in lever actions, pumps, and single shots. Examples of these variations are the popular .22-caliber pump with the exposed hammer (1890 Winchester), the shotgun pump with a concealed hammer (1904 Stevens), and his .22-caliber single shot (1900 Winchester), a gun produced to corner a specific market.

Browning's greatest invention, however, was to discover how to use expanding gases and recoil from exploding ammunition to eject, reload, and fire weapons automatically. This came about at a local competition when Browning noticed that reeds between the man firing and the target were blown vigorously by the gases escaping from the gun. His first experiments took place in 1889, and by 1892 he was given a patent on a crude automatic weapon that captured gases at the muzzle. In 1895 he completed an automatic machine gun that diverted the necessary gases from a hole drilled in the back of the barrel. By 1897 he had a patented semiautomatic pistol in production, and by 1911 his .45-caliber semiautomatic pistol was accepted by the United States government as its standard military sidearm. This weapon is still used by the United States military. In 1917 his .30-caliber machine gun was mass produced for use in World War I. Likewise, his Browning Automatic Rifle was also manufactured for use on the battlefront. He began work on a .50-caliber machine gun in 1917, but it was not used until World War II and the Korean conflict.

Browning's inventive genius was equally evident in the development of sporting arms. He applied the principle of automatic weaponry to shotguns, the weapon that took the longest time and was the most difficult to perfect. But through perseverance and hard work, he received four patents for variations of that weapon. His last invention was the superposed, over-under shotgun, invaluable to today's game hunter and trapshooter.

By the mid 1960s, approximately 30 million modern weapons of Browning design had been manufactured, and no fundamental changes have appeared in the firearms industry since his death in 1926.

See John Browning and Curt Gentry, *John M. Browning, American Gunmaker* (1964); Browning Arms Company, *John M. Browning Armory* (1959); and Harold F. Williamson, *Winchester: The Gun That Won the West* (1952).—L. J. A.

Browns Valley Man. See MINNESOTA MAN AND BROWNS VALLEY MAN.

Bruce, Louis R. (1906-   ). Mohawk-Dakota businessman and government official. Bruce was born on the Onondaga reservation in upstate New York, where his father was a professional baseball player, one of the first American Indian dentists, and a Methodist minister. Bruce worked his way through Syracuse University, where he was a pole vaulter and track star. Between 1935 and 1941, he was New York State director of Indians and in that capacity gave special attention to the development of Indian welfare and youth programs. The successful operation of a large New York dairy farm was another important area of interest and achievement for Bruce. As president of the Dairymen's League, he organized young farm people.

In 1957 Bruce helped organize the first National American Indian Youth Conference in Washington, D. C., and has participated in White House Conferences on Youth since 1940. In 1969 President Nixon appointed him commissioner of Indian affairs. His most important accomplishment as commissioner was the return of the sacred Blue Lake area to the people of Taos Pueblo in New Mexico.—C. C.

Bryan, William Jennings (1860-1925). Politician. The son of a well-to-do farmer and politician of Salem, Illinois, Bryan was educated at Whipple Academy and Illinois College. After graduation he spent two years at the Union College of Law in Chicago and was an attorney in Jacksonville, Illinois, from 1883 to 1887. At the urging of friends he moved to Lincoln, Nebraska, in 1887, where he began to win a reputation as a promising young man and powerful orator in Democratic politics.

Bryan ran successfully for Congress in 1890 and won reelection in 1892. During four years in the House of Representatives he became a spokesman for western views on the silver issue. Westerners wanted the federal government to buy silver without limitation as a basis for the currency. Vigorous speeches in opposition to Grover Cleveland's antisilver policy in 1893 earned him national prominence but also helped to defeat his bid for a Senate seat in 1895. This setback did not dismay the ambitious Bryan; he already had a more prestigious office in mind.

From 1895 he labored doggedly to strengthen the silver sentiment within the Democratic party. In the process his letters and speeches built an informal network of potential supporters for his presidential candidacy. Bryan was thus fully prepared for the opportunity that came at the 1896 Democratic national convention. In fact he told friends he was "the logic of the situation" and expected to be nominated. Speaking on behalf of a silver plank in the party's platform, he articulated the wounded feelings of the protesting West in his "Cross of Gold" speech. The people of the frontier, he said, "are as deserving of the consideration of our people as any people in the country." The speech galvanized the delegates and led to nomination on the fifth ballot.

"The Boy Orator of the Platte" made a spirited campaign in the ELECTION OF 1896. He stumped personally, traveled some eighteen thousand miles, and buoyed up the Democratic cause with his rhetorical energy. But his candidacy never went beyond an evangelistic espousal of silver. While he captivated the West and held on to the normally Democratic South, he could not make his ruralistic appeal attractive to voters in the Northeast and industrial Middle West. The Republicans and William McKinley won a decisive victory.

Bryan ran for president again in 1900 and 1908 with similar results, but he remained a power in his party until his death. His weekly newspaper, the *Commoner*, gave him a regular forum from which he reached thousands of like-minded citizens. Lectures and appearances on the Chautauqua circuit brought a substantial income and enabled thousands more of his intellectual constituents to hear him. In the 1912 Democratic convention he aided the candidacy of Woodrow Wilson, a contribution that led to appointment as secretary of state. He resigned in the *Lusitania* crisis of 1915 and devoted his last decade to such causes of rural America as antimilitarism, prohibition, and religious fundamentalism. After assisting the prosecution in the Dayton, Tennessee, trial of John T. Scopes for teaching evolution, Bryan died of diabetes, fatigue, and old age.

Throughout a long career Bryan championed the values of the rural America he had known as a young man. He believed that the simple, individualistic society in which he matured was superior to the new industrial nation. On the stump, at conventions, and in voluminous writings, Bryan argued that the country should adhere to Christianity, majority rule, and agrarian mores. This philosophy, and his ability to enunciate it in comforting rhetoric, gave him unparalleled influence in the South and West between 1890 and 1925. Not simply a reactionary or a reformer, Bryan embodied within himself the contradictory trends of progress and obscurantism that swirled through rural society in the early twentieth century.

See the Bryan Papers, Library of Congress; Paolo Coletta, *William Jennings Bryan*, 3 vols. (1964-69); and Lawrence W. Levine, *Defender of the Faith: William Jennings Bryan: The Last Decade, 1915-1925* (1965). —L. L. G.

Bryant, Sturgis and Co. A Boston firm that became the most important company engaged in the exchange of New England manufactured goods for California cowhides. The trade began in 1822 when its agent, William A. Gale, arrived at Monterey on the ship *Sachem*. The company gained such a large share of the hide trade that the United States was commonly known in Mexican California as "Boston." In turn, the existence of California became widely known in the United States largely because of the hide trade, and particularly after Richard Henry Dana sailed to California and back on Bryant, Sturgis ships between 1834 and 1836 and published his classic *Two Years Before the Mast* in 1840. —W. B.

Bryce Canyon National Park. Bryce Canyon National Park was named after Ebenezer Bryce, one of the Mormon settlers who homesteaded near the present park in the 1870s. It was not until 1919 that the legislature of Utah proposed setting aside the area as a scenic preserve. President Warren G. Harding proclaimed the pink-columned amphitheater a national monument in 1923. A year later, Congress authorized the establishment of a national park but specified that all privately owned lands in the proposed park should first be acquired by the federal government. This was to be Utah National Park. By 1928 the privately owned property within the park's boundaries had been purchased, new

federal lands had been added to the park, and its name had been changed to Bryce Canyon. The park was officially established on September 15, 1928.

The outstanding feature of the park is the gently curving amphitheater eroded out of the Paunsaugunt Plateau, which extends through southern Utah. There is a large display of eroded stone spires and pinnacles, brilliantly colored and gracefully shaped. Trails lead down from the rim into the amphitheater itself. Excellent views of the pink cliffs may also be seen from the rim drive. Much of the park, which contains 36,010 acres, is above eight thousand feet elevation. It is located in south-central Utah.—D. C. S.

Budd, Ralph (1879-1962). Railroad executive. Born near Waterloo, Iowa, Budd was graduated from college as a civil engineer. After working on some of the last through railroad extensions in the United States, Budd went to Panama as the twenty-eight-year-old chief engineer of the Panama Railroad. There he supervised the reconstruction of that suddenly important line across the Isthmus during the digging of the canal. Returning to the United States, Budd caught the eye of James J. Hill, builder of the Great Northern Railway, who made him his assistant. In 1919 Budd became president of the Great Northern—the youngest man ever to head a major American railroad system.

After rebuilding the system, which, like most American railroads, had suffered from the deferred maintenance policy followed during government wartime control, he supervised construction of a new main line through Washington's Cascade Mountains. At the site of the new eight-mile-long Cascade tunnel, the longest in the western hemisphere, Budd was impressed by the economy and dependability of the stationary diesel engines being used. Elected president of the Burlington lines at the beginning of the Depression, he introduced stringent economies and daring innovations, including the first diesel-powered streamlined train, while other major midwestern railroads were going into bankruptcy. At dusk on May 26, 1934, after a record-breaking run from Denver, the Pioneer Zephyr rolled to a stop on the stage of the railroad pageant at the Chicago World's Fair. The train, one of Budd's most significant innovations, was an immediate success and began the conversion to diesel power throughout the industry.

Budd served as railroad advisor to the Soviet government in 1930 and as the president's commissioner of transportation in 1940-41, laying the foundations for the American railroads' spectacularly successful war effort. Retiring at age seventy, he played an important role in organizing the Chicago Transit Authority out of a number of predecessor units. At the end of his career he spoke and wrote about the radical changes needed in public railroad policy.

In the 1920s Budd had been nearly successful in merging the Great Northern and the Northern Pacific. This was finally accomplished in the BURLINGTON NORTHERN RAILROAD merger of 1970.

Richard Overton, *Burlington Route, A History of the Burlington Lines* (1965), tells Budd's story as part of the history of the railroad he headed.—A. M.

Budge, William (1828-1919). Idaho Mormon leader. After his conversion to Mormonism in Scotland in 1848, Budge spent nine years (1851-60) as a missionary in England, Switzerland, and Germany. In 1860 he came to Utah, where he spent ten years prior to his assignment to Paris, Idaho. There he served as the Mormon Bear Lake stake president until 1878, when he went to Europe for two years on a mission. Eventually he was recognized as spokesman for Idaho's large Mormon population, and when Idaho was admitted to the Union in 1890 with an anti-Mormon constitution, Budge led the opposition to constitutional restrictions that prevented the Saints from voting, holding office, or serving on a jury.

Before Mormons were excluded from politics in 1884, Budge had had legislative experience in the territorial council to which he was elected in 1880; after the Saints were readmitted to public life, he was chosen a Bear Lake County senator in 1898. In 1906 he became president of the Logan Temple.

One of his sons, Alfred Budge, was district judge and on the Idaho supreme court; and one of Alfred's sons, Hamer Budge, represented Idaho in Congress before he was appointed chairman of the Securities and Exchange Commission.—M. W.

buffalo. When the first bands of primitive hunters arrived in Alaska by way of the land bridge from Asia and crossed the Rocky Mountains to the northern Great Plains, they found all the western grasslands teeming with large game animals, including several species of large bison (*Bison taylori and Bison occidentalis*), commonly known in the American West as buffalo. They were too large and tough to be attacked in the open by hunters armed with crude spears, but sometimes they could be stampeded by fire into running over cliffs or into swamps. Once the animals had been crippled or bogged down, they became easy prey. Later migrations from Asia brought improved weapons, the dart and throwing stick and the bow and arrow, both capable of seriously wounding an animal at a distance of several yards and hence effective from ambush against the large buffalo.

A gradual warming of North America, beginning about twenty-five thousand years ago, slowly melted the last ice sheet from the upper Mississippi valley. Several thousand years later the American Southwest and northern Mexico became arid and covered with desert scrub. The large grass eaters moved northward toward what is now Canada to the new pastures uncovered by the retreating ice, but for some unknown reason, several species disappeared entirely. They included the horse, camel, and several species of large bison. Only the smallest of the bison, the American buffalo (*Bos bison americanus*) of historic times, survived, along with the elk, deer, and antelope. Fossil remains of this species of bison are common in parts of northern Mexico.

Although the surviving buffalo was smaller than its extinct relatives, it was still a formidable animal. An adult bull stood about seven feet tall at the shoulder and in good condition weighed up to two thousand pounds. The cows were much smaller, standing about five feet tall and weighing seven hundred to nine hundred pounds. The buffalo breed from mid-July to the end of August. The gestation period is approximately nine and a half months.

About ten thousand years ago, probably as a result of the climatic changes, the small buffalo moved out of Mexico, across the Rio Grande, and gradually increased in numbers until they filled the Great Plains and spilled over into other areas. They prospered for several thousand years, reaching their peak number of about forty million by the seventeenth century. They roamed the Great Plains from the Gulf of Mexico to the Canadian woods, and from the Rocky Mountains to the timbered belt along the Mississippi. Some herds crossed the Mississippi into the Ohio valley and spread on through Kentucky, northern Tennessee, and the tidewater country in Virginia and the Carolinas.

Although many of the Plains tribes depended on the buffalo for their main food supply, their success in hunting the animal was limited until they acquired horses. Some small hunting bands followed the herds from early spring until late fall, killing an animal now and again but often going hungry for days at a time. Many other Indian bands settled in little farming villages along the fringes of buffalo country, going out each summer and fall to follow the herds and secure dried meat for winter and hides to tan into robes.

The advent of the HORSE had a profound effect on buffalo hunters. Although most tribes first used horses for pack animals, they soon learned that a hunter mounted on a fast, well-trained horse could, with a little luck, kill enough buffalo to feed the whole camp, and that buffalo could be successfully hunted from horseback at almost any time of the year. Periods of real hunger became rare indeed, and in some bands "starving time" came to mean a period when the people had to subsist for several days on stores of dried meat until the hunters could make a fresh kill.

The new, efficient method of hunting left the men with a great deal of leisure time but greatly increased the work load of the women. It required the services of four or five women to care for the meat and hides provided by one good hunter. Hence, the many women widowed by war or hunting accidents found ready welcome in the tepees of daughters and nieces, and the surplus young women became the second or third wives of the better hunters.

The steady, ample supply of good food caused a rapid increase in the population and built up the fighting strength of the tribes to formidable proportions. As the hunting bands grew larger the men found that buffalo could be hunted more efficiently by a group of thirty or forty men than by the same number of men divided into several smaller groups. The larger group could also protect the camp better.

Once they had horses, several Indian tribes became true nomads, following the buffalo herds the year around. The Comanche furnish a good example of this. They came out of their little canyons and narrow valleys in the Colorado foothills to take over a large part of the southwestern Plains and sent raiding parties deep into Mexico. Along a similar pattern, the Blackfoot moved south from a small area in central Alberta until they held hunting grounds as far south as Sun River in Montana; the Sioux moved west from the Minnesota lake country, partly attracted by the buffalo hunting, partly pushed from their permanent villages by the better armed Cree and Chippewa.

On the eastern edge of the buffalo country, the tribes living along the woodland fringe raised corn as their staple food and usually made two hunting excursions each year to secure buffalo meat and hides. Even after they secured horses they continued to live in permanent

Forty thousand buffalo hides stand piled in Rath & Wright's hide yard in Dodge City, Kansas (1878). (National Archives)

farming villages and to raise corn, but they expanded their buffalo-hunting season. Since these people left most of their possessions in their villages when they went hunting, they needed fewer horses than did the nomadic tribes. Examples of these tribes are the Osage and Pawnee.

After the small fishing tribes in the Columbia Basin secured horses, they made long hunting excursions across the mountains into central Montana to hunt buffalo. Their hunting was greatly hindered by the hostile Blackfoot from 1807 to 1837, when a fortuitous smallpox epidemic greatly reduced the fighting capacity of that tribe. The Flathead, Nez Percé, and Coeur d'Alene tribes were the most successful hunters of the Columbia Basin. About a third of each tribe became seminomadic, spending two or three years at a time east of the mountains; the major food source for each tribe, however, was still the salmon.

Explorers, fur traders, and travelers from the eastern settlements found a dependable meat supply in the buffalo herds. Then the fur trading posts along the Missouri River developed a market for tanned buffalo robes, transporting them to market by boat down the river. On the whole the Plains tribes welcomed these people, but they became alarmed when the covered wagons began to roll in long trains westward along the trail to Oregon and California in the 1840s. The California gold strike in 1848 brought a horde of travelers the next year, and succeeding gold strikes attracted thousands more. The numerous wagon trains and the many small trail herds pastured off the grass on a wide strip all the way to the mountains, while the travelers killed off or drove away the buffalo. The trains also

brought diseases that each year killed many of the Indians along the trail.

Finally, the trail divided the buffalo country into northern and southern segments. No longer did the herds roam freely from Kansas to the Dakotas. The continued invasion and the increasing settlements in the Colorado foothills stirred the tribes to active resistance and brought on a period of bloody fighting that did not end until the buffalo had been exterminated, the fighting powers of the tribes broken, and the remnant Indians herded onto reservations.

The buffalo met its final disaster, however, during the period from 1870 to 1883, when cheap transportation provided by the new railroads into Kansas increased the market for buffalo hides. Eastern tanners bought the hides by the million, and thousand of eager hunters swarmed over the Plains to supply the new demand. After the last large kill, in 1883, all but a few of the herds had vanished, leaving only piles of weathered bones to be gathered up by poverty-stricken farmers and shipped east for fertilizer or to be used in the making of bone china.

As long as the buffalo herds had remained, stockmen and farmers had been barred from the Plains. No range cattle or horses nor any field crops could survive the presence of these trampling herds. As soon as the buffalo and the Indians had been driven from the Plains, however, farmers plowed up the valleys and cattlemen grazed their herds on the rolling grassland.

In the period 1883-1900, a few scattered buffalo were protected and preserved by western ranchers. All the wild buffalo had been killed except for a wild herd in the woods of northern Alberta. Then several groups of people interested themselves in the preservation of the species. The Canadian government bought up a few hundred of the scattered animals and placed them on protected ranges. They also tried for many years to develop a successful cross of buffalo with cattle, but failed.

The United States government finally started preserving small buffalo herds, one on the National Bison Range in western Montana and another in Yellowstone Park. In the ensuing years other herds have been placed in government parks and preserves, and several states now have bison herds. Surplus stock from many of these herds became available to anyone interested in raising buffalo. On the protected ranges the buffalo increased rapidly. After twenty years of the Canadian government program, it was evident that the number of buffalo that could be raised was limited only by the amount of pastureland devoted to their use.

See E. Douglas Branch, *The Hunting of the Buffalo* (1929); Wayne Gard, *The Great Buffalo Hunt* (1959); and Francis Haines, *The Buffalo* (1970).—F. H.

Buffalo Bill. See "Buffalo Bill" CODY.

Buffalo Bill Historical Center. Located in Cody, Wyoming, the Buffalo Bill Historical Center offers paintings by western artists and historical memorabilia of "Buffalo Bill" Cody, Annie Oakley, the participants in Cody's Wild West show, and such notable Indian chiefs as Sitting Bull, Red Cloud, and Chief Joseph. A complex consisting of the Whitney Gallery of Western Art, the Buffalo Bill Museum, and the Plains Indian Museum, the museum is under the single roof of a native stone building on a forty-acre plot of ground beside the main highway into Yellowstone National Park. It is devoted to western Americana and regionally restricted to the Northern Plains and adjoining Rocky Mountain region. The extensive exhibits encompass the whole story of the Old West as it was.

The Whitney Gallery of Western Art is a family memorial to the late Gertrude Vanderbilt Whitney, sculptor and patron of American art. She created the equestrian statue *Buffalo Bill, the Scout* and gave it along with the forty acres for the development of the Buffalo Bill Historical Center. The Whitney Gallery was opened to the public in spring 1959. Ten years later the building was enlarged by more than three times to accommodate the forty-three-year-old Buffalo Bill Museum and a new Plains Indian Museum of ethnology and archaeology. The present building is one of the largest and most imposing in Wyoming.

The Whitney Gallery is devoted to the works of the early documentary artists of the Old West. Frederic Remington and Charles M. Russell are particularly well represented in the museum. In addition to the Remington oils, watercolors, and bronzes is a unique display of his Studio Collection, consisting of the entire contents of his spacious working studio at the time of his death in 1909 on his estate near Ridgefield, Connecticut. A museum in itself, the Studio Collection includes 110 oil sketches made on various trips to the West, large unfinished paintings on which he had been working just prior to his demise, painting materials, and an extensive and important assemblage of paraphernalia and colorful articles of dress and memorabilia of frontiersmen, cowboys, and Indians, which Remington had collected on his numerous western trips from 1880 to shortly

before his death. All his life an avid "collector," Remington used these articles to achieve authentic representation in his paintings. His on-the-spot field sketches were used for the same purpose. In contrast to his representational work, some of his later small oils, done strictly for personal pleasure and relaxation, show an unmistakable leaning toward impressionism, The Remington Studio Collection was acquired from the Remington estate and Art Memorial and was the first major acquisition of the Whitney Gallery.

Charles M. Russell, the Montana cowboy artist, is represented in the Whitney by more than 375 works of art—one of the largest assemblages to be found anywhere. In addition to his paintings, formal drawings, and bronzes are fifty-four original wax models used for the casting of some of his best-known bronzes as well as a number that have never been reproduced. The collection of wax models came directly from the Russell estate.

The Russells assembled in the William E. Weiss Collection include 185 oils and watercolor paintings, illustrated letters, and 98 pen-and-ink and pencil sketches from the Russell estate. Several of the large paintings are considered among the finest works of this artist. Among these are *Roundup on the Musselshell, Smoke Signal, Single Handed, When Law Dulls the Edge of Chance, The Stranglers,* and *Roping the Grizzly.* The last belonged to President William H. Taft and hung in the White House during his tenure. Among the other outstanding Russell paintings are: *Where Great Herds Come to Drink, His Heart Sleeps, Waiting for a Chinook* (large version of the earlier postcard-size picture), *Return of the Warriors, In Enemy Country,* and *Trail's End.*

Next in respect to number and importance is the collection of paintings by Albert Bierstadt. Among the forty-eight oils are *Last of the Buffalo*—a similar version to one in the Corcoran Gallery, Washington, D.C., although evidence indicates that the Whitney one is the earlier. It is accompanied by two of the original sketches. Others are: *Indian Encampment in the Rockies*—a similar version to one in the Metropolitan Museum of Art, New York—*Wind River, Wyoming; Yellowstone Falls;* and *Majesty of the Mountains.*

Among the earliest on-the-spot painters of the West were George Catlin and Alfred Jacob Miller, both of whom are well represented in the Whitney. There are seventy-two Catlin oils, all of the Northern Plains Indian tribes, on indefinite loan. One other, on loan, is the historically important portrait that Catlin painted from life in 1830 of General William Clark, co-leader of the Lewis and Clark expedition.

Alfred Jacob Miller is represented by twenty-two oils and watercolors of his journey in 1837 into present-day southwestern Wyoming. They are the earliest paintings on record of the region. and some are quite large.

Probably the most famous single picture in the Whitney is the Rosa Bonheur oil painting of Colonel William F. Cody on his favorite horse, done while Buffalo Bill was in Paris in 1889 with his Wild West show.

Some of the less widely known but important artists represented are Charles Schreyvogel, J. H. Sharp, Louis Maurer, William Jacob Hayes, Irving R. Bacon, Edgar S. Paxson, Olaf Seltzer, W. R. Leigh, N. C. Wyeth, Henry Farny, and James E. Fraser.

The Buffalo Bill Museum displays more than twenty-five hundred items of personal memorabilia of Cody and many of his associates during all periods of his life. The collection also includes another twenty-five hundred items reserved for historical reference and research.

The Plains Indian Museum displays more than thirty-five hundred ethnological items representing every phase of peace and war of all the Northern Plains tribes before their culture was ruined by the white man. The archaeological section displays cultural materials representing more than nine thousand years of prehistoric occupation of the immediate area, including the mummified body of a Stone Age caveman of the nearby Rocky Mountains. These exhibits are the result of excavations carried on by the museum's staff.—H. M.

buffalo grass. See VEGETATION: *prairies.*

"buffalo soldiers." See NEGROES ON THE FRONTIER.

Buley, Roscoe Carlyle (1893-1968). Historian. Buley was born in Georgetown, Indiana, and attended local schools until entering Indiana University in 1910. He received his bachelor's degree in American history four years later and his master's in 1916. Before obtaining his doctorate from the University of Wisconsin in 1925, Buley taught for seven or eight years in high schools in Indiana and Illinois.

Buley returned to the University of Indiana as an assistant professor of history in 1925 and continued his association with the Bloomington campus for more than four decades. During his last four years (1964-68) he was professor emeritus. An interest in state and regional history resulted in numerous articles before he won the Pulitzer Prize in 1951 for his most significant work, *The Old Northwest* (two volumes, 1950). His next major publication, *The American Life Convention: Study in the History of Life Insurance* (two volumes, 1953), won the Elizur Wright Award for 1953.

Although he wrote several other volumes and articles on life insurance, Buley's scholarly interest related primarily to the American frontier. His unsparing efforts to impart his deep feeling for history to graduate students earned him a reputation as an outstanding lecturer and critic.—W. E. H.

Bunyan, Paul, myth of. The real Paul Bunyan—if indeed he ever was an actual person—is lost in the mysteries of time and of the oral traditions of American lumberjacks. The character first appeared in print in 1910 in the pages of the Detroit *News-Tribune* as boss of the logging crew in a famous and often reprinted tall story, "The Round River Drive." The same story was repeated in doggerel verse in *The American Lumberman* in 1914, in which year W. B. Laughead also produced a promotional pamphlet for the Red River Lumber Company with Paul as hero. Laughead christened Paul's blue ox "Babe," and his much expanded and often rewritten *The Marvellous Exploits of Paul Bunyan* (1922) firmly established Paul's place as a modern American folk hero. Another popularizer, James Stevens, in *Paul Bunyan* (1925) and *The Saginaw Paul Bunyan* (1932), spread his fame still further. Stevens gave the hero a spurious ancestry, reporting him to have been in real life a French-Canadian who fought in the Papineau rebellion of 1837. After Stevens, Bunyan books became solely juvenile books, which they remain today. At present Bunyan's memory is very much alive, and statues of him and his blue ox are thriving in Bemidji, Minnesota.

The Bunyan myth grew out of the earlier Davy Crockett tradition of frontier humor and was coupled rather oddly with nineteenth-century tales of Yankee shrewdness. As Bunyan's fame spread, his peculiarly localized attributes as a lumberjack developed into the less specific qualities of a general American mass hero. Originally an occupational hero of the lumberjacks, he became a patron saint of the oil fields and was also featured as a cowboy and farmer in many stories. His various avatars include not only the predictable giant nature god, but the less expected captain of industry and successful entrepreneur.

See Daniel Hoffman, *Paul Bunyan, Last of the Frontier Demigods* (1952).—J. K. F.

Burbank, Elbridge Ayar (1858-1949). Painter. Born in Harvard, Illinois, Burbank studied at the Art Institute of Chicago and with Paul Nauen in Munich, where he developed his technique in life drawing and crayon portraiture. At first specializing in American Negro subjects, he turned to Indian portraiture about 1897 when commissioned by his uncle, Edward E. Ayar, first president of the Field Columbian Museum of Chicago, to do a series of portraits of prominent Indian chiefs in Oklahoma, New Mexico, and Arizona. Traveling also to California, Burbank produced more than twelve hundred oil, watercolor, and crayon studies, now in the Newberry Library, Chicago. Other collections of his work are in the Smithsonian Institution in Washington, D. C., and the Thomas Gilcrease Institute of American History and Art in Tulsa, Oklahoma.—D. C. H.

Burdick, Usher Lloyd (1879-1960). North Dakota politician. Usher L. Burdick, a native of Minnesota, spent his entire life in the throes of North Dakota politics from the day he entered the state legislature in 1906 until his death. One historian has said that no man in North Dakota history lost more primaries than Usher Burdick. During the 1920s he helped organize the Farmers Union and became president of the organization. During the 1930s he was associated with the farm-holiday movement, and in 1948 a coalition of the Farmers Union and the Nonpartisan League elected him to the House of Representatives. He served in the House throughout the 1950s and in 1958 campaigned for his son Quentin, a Democrat, for his seat in the House. Quentin Burdick became the first Democrat from North Dakota ever elected to the House of Representatives.

Burdick wrote articles, pamphlets, and books on western and North Dakota history. He was also a rancher and lawyer.

The Usher L. Burdick papers are in the Orin G. Libby Manuscript Collection at the University of North Dakota.—D. J. T.

Burke, John (1859-1937). North Dakota politician. In 1888 Burke, the son of Irish immigrants, moved to North Dakota. This struggling young lawyer eventually built up a large practice at Devils Lake. He served in the state legislature and in 1906 was the Democratic candidate for governor, opposing the candidate of the Alexander McKenzie political machine. Burke conducted a vigorous campaign that paid off at the polls, but although he was elected, the rest of the state Democratic ticket was defeated.

The date of Burke's election is generally cited as the end of McKenzie's control of North Dakota politics, for his machine controlled only the state senate at this point.

Progressive legislation such as a direct-primary law, a constitutional amendment authorizing the initiative and referendum, and laws to enforce prohibition were passed. Burke was reelected in 1908 and again in 1910, when both houses of the state legislature were dominated by reform elements from the two parties. —D. J. T.

Burke, Thomas (1849-1925). Washington lawyer and railroad promoter. Burke was born in Clinton County, New York, and was admitted to the bar in 1873. Two years later he moved to Seattle, Washington, where he served as judge of the territorial probate court (1876-80) and as chief justice of the Washington territorial supreme court (1888-89). His attempts to win political office in Congress, however, were unsuccessful.

Known as the man who "built Seattle," Burke promoted construction of the Seattle, Lakeshore and Eastern Railway in 1885. He showed his faith in Seattle after the great fire of 1889 by building the largest office building in the city at that time with his personal funds. But his main claim to fame rested on his association with railroad magnate James J. Hill and the merger of several small railroads in the Puget Sound area that brought the Great Northern Railway into Seattle. He was accepted as Hill's agent in the Northwest and became involved in townsite promotion in the Wenatchee valley and promotion of the apple industry around Wenatchee.

See Charles T. Conover, *Thomas Burke, 1849-1925* (1926), and Robert Nesbit, *He Built Seattle* (1961). —K. A. M.

Burke Act (1906). Law to delay citizenship to Indians. The Burke Act provided that the Indians allotted land under the DAWES SEVERALTY ACT of 1887 would not become citizens of the United States until the end of a twenty-five-year trust period—subject to shortening by the secretary of the interior—or until they received full title to their land. It amended section six of the Dawes Act, which granted citizenship at the time of allotment of land even though the Indian Bureau held the land title in trust for twenty-five years.

In 1905 the Supreme Court had decided (*In the Matter of Heff*) that the Indian Bureau and the courts could not prohibit the sale of whiskey to Indian allottees, on the ground that they were citizens. The Supreme Court thus affirmed that Indians allotted land were indeed citizens, rather than wards, of the nation. The Burke Act, by postponing the Indians' claim to citizenship, circumvented that decision.

In a larger sense, the Burke Act marked the demise of the theory that citizenship and proprietorship would inevitably civilize and assimilate the Indian. The conflict between the Indian's free exercise of his citizenship and the Indian Bureau's application of restrictions to protect him from himself and from the white man had become apparent in the 1890s. It had been resolved, to the Indians' detriment, by the rapid growth of the Indian Bureau and its increased scope of authority. The Burke Act sanctioned its solution and reaffirmed a policy of governmental paternalism that survives to this day. —E. A. G.

Burleigh, Walter Atwood (1820-1896). Indian agent and Dakota Territory politician. As agent to the Yankton Indians from 1860 to 1864 Burleigh demonstrated boundless energy and ability but unscrupulous political methods. Active in politics during the first decade of

Dakota Territory, the 1860s, he aligned himself with Dakota's first governor, William Jayne, and was elected delegate to the United States Congress over John B. S. Todd. He led the opposition to Governor Newton Edmunds because of the governor's Indian peace policy. Because of Burleigh's influence, President Andrew Johnson replaced Edmunds with Burleigh's father-in-law, Andrew J. Faulk. In 1868 Burleigh was defeated for reelection by Republican S. L. Spink.—D. J. T.

Burlingame, Merrill G. (1901-   ). Historian. Born in Boone, Iowa, Burlingame was educated at the University of Iowa. After teaching high school history in Minnesota in 1927 and in Nebraska in 1928, he joined the history department at Montana State College at Bozeman in 1929, where he remained until his retirement in 1967.

Burlingame explored various aspects of Montana's historical development in a number of articles and books. He investigated the career of trailblazer John Bozeman and brought his knowledge to bear in a *History of Montana* (1956), which he co-authored. He also edited an anthology of essays on Montana history, *From Wilderness to Statehood* (1957), and wrote *History of Montana State University* (1968).—G. D. N.

Burlington Northern Railroad. The Burlington Northern Railroad was created on March 3, 1970, a month after a unanimous decision of the United States Supreme Court upheld the Interstate Commerce Commission's approval of a proposed merger of the Burlington; the Northern Pacific; the Great Northern; the Spokane, Portland and Seattle; and the Colorado and Southern railroads. By so doing, the Court ratified a de facto "community of interests" that had existed since the formation of the Northern Securities Company in 1901. The merged lines, with subsidiaries, operate nearly twenty-six thousand miles of track radiating from Chicago and Minneapolis-St. Paul to the Pacific Northwest, through the agricultural heartland of the Midwest to Denver, and south through Texas to the Gulf of Mexico. It is the longest railroad under a single management in North America.

The oldest line was the Chicago, Burlington and Quincy. It was chartered in Illinois in 1849 as the Aurora Branch Railroad to connect several thriving agricultural communities thirty miles southwest of Chicago with the Galena and Chicago Union Railroad (later the Chicago and Northwestern), which was building west from Chicago. The original twelve-mile line began service September 2, 1850, reducing the round trip between Aurora and Chicago from three days to seven hours. In the next decade the Aurora Branch blossomed into a major midwestern trunk line under the direction of James F. JOY, a Detroit lawyer who had persuaded financier John Murray FORBES and other Bostonians to infuse eastern capital into the ailing Michigan Central Railroad in 1846. Responding to Joy's argument that the midwestern roads would be essential feeders to their eastern property, the Forbes group bought into the Aurora Branch in 1855. By acquiring the Northern Cross, Central Military Tract, and Peoria and Oquawka railroads, the group formed a through line from Chicago to the Mississippi River at Burlington, Iowa, and Quincy, Illinois.

The major properties west of the Mississippi that eventually made the Burlington the strongest of the midwestern carriers were the Hannibal and St. Joseph Railroad, which was chartered in Missouri and reached the Missouri River in 1859 and the Burlington and Missouri River Railroad, which, although it became the Burlington's chief link between Illinois and the trans-Missouri country, did not reach the river until 1869. Beyond Council Bluffs, Iowa, the Burlington continued west via a subsidiary, the Burlington and Missouri River Railroad in Nebraska, which prospered under the skillful management of Charles E. Perkins. A junction with the Union Pacific at Kearney, Nebraska, was made in 1872. Disaster was avoided during the 1870s depression by the intervention of Forbes, who took over the presidency at a time when Joy was under a cloud for acting both as a railroad official and construction contractor to the company. During the heyday of railroad building in the 1880s the Burlington was extended to Denver and to Minneapolis-St. Paul, where it quickly became an important Chicago link for the Northern Pacific and the Great Northern. At the depth of the 1890s depression the Burlington built a line northwestward from Omaha to a junction with the Northern Pacific and Great Northern at Billings, Montana; when connected with the Colorado and Southern Railroad and the Fort Worth and Denver City Railroad, both acquired early in the twentieth century, it became a valuable new link between the Northwest and Southwest. By 1901 Forbes and his successor, Perkins, had made the Burlington the strongest and most profitable railroad in the Midwest. Perkins' retirement in that year and the purchase of a controlling interest by J. P. Morgan and James J. HILL brought the carrier's independent history to an end. For seventy years thereafter the Burlington was operated harmoniously with the other Hill lines, the Northern Pacific and Great Northern.

Of the two transcontinental roads that joined the Burlington Northern merger, the Northern Pacific had reached the Pacific Coast first, although a predecessor of the Great Northern had begun operating trains in Minnesota in 1862. Chartered by Congress in 1864 and given a huge land grant, the Northern Pacific made little progress in its early years. The original management, headed by banker Jay Cooke, was toppled by the depression of the 1870s, and portions of the fifty-million-acre land grant were sold off in large lots that gave rise to many Minnesota and North Dakota wheat farms and BONANZA FARMING. Not until 1883, when Henry VILLARD joined the Northern Pacific with the line he had been building eastward along the Columbia River (the Oregon Railway and Navigation Company), did the Northern Pacific actually become a transcontinental railroad. On the eve of the 1890s depression the Northern Pacific was in receivership, and it was time for Cooke's financial excesses and Villard's poor cost control to be replaced by more effective measures. Morgan, in concert with Hill, secured a controlling interest in 1898 and shortly thereafter acquired virtually all of the Burlington stock, setting the stage for the celebrated confrontation with Edward H. HARRIMAN.

The third element in the Burlington Northern, the Great Northern Railway, was primarily the creation of Hill, a prosperous steamboat agent, merchant, and fuel dealer who had settled in St. Paul in the 1850s. Hill had long been impressed by the fertility of the grain-growing areas of the Red River valley between St. Paul and Winnipeg, Manitoba. In 1878 he persuaded three Canadian friends to form a syndicate with him to buy the decrepit St. Paul and Pacific Railroad (incorporated by the territorial legislature of Minnesota in 1856) from the bankrupt Northern Pacific and build it into an all-rail link between Winnipeg and St. Paul, with a branch to Duluth on the Great Lakes. Hill invested most of his savings in the venture and thereafter devoted his energy to improving and expanding the road, the name of which was changed to the St. Paul, Minneapolis and Manitoba. Hill's policy was to use profits to build extensions of the main line, and branch-line feeders where needed; he insisted that his engineers locate them on the best possible routes so that his operating costs would always be lower than those of his principal competitor, the badly built and poorly managed Northern Pacific. In 1889 the Manitoba changed its name to the Great Northern Railway Company and began an extension from Montana to the Pacific Coast, which it reached in 1893.

By 1901 Morgan and Hill controlled both northern transcontinentals and the Burlington, which gave both lines the entrance into Chicago that they had always lacked. But their Burlington takeover did not go unchallenged. Harriman, having reorganized and rebuilt the Union Pacific, was as eager for a Chicago link as Hill, since the Union Pacific always had to turn over its eastbound freight to connecting lines at Council Bluffs and Kansas City. Having failed to outbid Morgan and Hill directly for the Burlington, Harriman almost took it by quietly buying into the Northern Pacific, through which the Burlington was controlled. He acquired a majority of the preferred stock, which had voting rights, but since Morgan and Hill had a majority of the common, a stalemate ensued. Meanwhile the extraordinary demand for Northern Pacific stock had dried up the supply of shares available for trading on the stock exchange and the price rose to more than one thousand dollars a share; the ruin of many Wall Street traders was imminent. Under heavy criticism for having precipitated a brief but disquieting panic, Hill and Harriman agreed to pool all of their Northern Pacific and Great Northern stock (and, therefore, the Burlington), in a gigantic new holding company with a nominal capitalization of $400 million. Challenged as a violation of the Sherman Anti-Trust Act of 1890, the Northern Securities Company was dissolved by the United States Supreme Court in 1904. The decision was of no economic significance, as Justice Oliver Wendell Holmes pointed out, but its great popularity encouraged "trust-busting" under Presidents Theodore Roosevelt and William Howard Taft.

Under the efficient direction of the Hill organization and benefiting from the prosperity of the first three decades of the twentieth century, the Hill lines were developed intensively until they were physically and financially among the strongest in the nation. While making large profits, the Great Northern had decreased freight rates from an average of 2.88 cents per ton-mile in 1881 to 0.77 cent in 1907. The rising demand for agricultural products, population growth, and continued development of iron and copper mines enabled the companies to develop the strength that brought them through the Great Depression without resort to receivership. Dieselization and automatic train control were introduced beginning in the 1930s, and further development continued after World War II. The advantages of a merger of the Great Northern and Northern Pacific in the 1920s had been appreciated by Ralph Budd, president of the Great Northern and later the Burlington, but by the 1960s it was obvious that a much more intimate coordination of the plant and equipment of the three companies, such as could be accomplished only through legal merger, would be required if operating costs were to be held under control in an era of rising wages and prices. After lengthy investigations by the Interstate Commerce Commission, which supported the merger, and the Anti-Trust Division of the Department of Justice, which opposed it, and after lengthy litigation by other railroads, who feared for their historical share of freight interchange with the three roads, the merger was finally approved in 1970. John M. Budd and Louis M. Menk, former heads of the Great Northern and the Northern Pacific became chairman and president, respectively, of the new company. All 47,000 employees of the merged lines joined a growing elite group of workers who, by reason of court-adjudicated mergers of railroads, are guaranteed employment for the rest of their lives, although the number of people actually needed to run the new system will be much smaller. Labor savings, therefore, will be realized gradually through attrition, while wage rates continue to rise rapidly. Advanced management practices, a rising demand for the railroad's services due to better service anticipated on the merged lines, heavy capital investment, and liberalization of government regulatory policy were expected to make the Burlington Northern a success.

The Burlington railroad is the subject of a superb business history: Richard C. Overton, *Burlington Route, A History of the Burlington Lines* (1965). J. B. Hedges, *Henry Villard and the Railways of the Northwest* (1930) is a scholarly discussion of West Coast port rivalries. Hill's creation of the Great Northern is narrated in Joseph G. Pyle's inadequate biography, *James J. Hill*, 2 vols. (1917).—A. M.

Burnet, David Gouverneur (1788-1870). Texas politician. Burnet was born in Newark, New Jersey, the youngest of eight children. After attending a Newark academy, he took a position in the New York counting house of Robinson and Hartshorne. When he lost his savings in an attempt to rescue the company from bankruptcy, he joined Francisco Miranda's 1806 expedition to aid the Venezuelan uprising against Spain. He is supposed to have commanded the launch that fired the first shot for South American independence.

In 1813 Burnet opened a trading post at Natchitoches, Louisiana, but a bout with tuberculosis stopped that activity. He wandered west into the area of Comanche Indians, who nursed him back to health over a two-year period. From 1819 to 1825 Burnet alternately studied and practiced law in Ohio and lived in Louisiana and Texas. In 1826 he, along with Lorenzo de Zavala and Joseph Vehlein, received an empresario contract from the Mexican government in Saltillo, but soon disposed of his interest to become a plantation owner near the mouth of the San Jacinto River in Texas (see EM-PRESARIO SYSTEM).

Burnet first made his appearance in Texas politics as a delegate to the San Felipe Convention of 1833, for which he drew up the resolution for separating Texas from Coahuila. In 1834 he was made judge of the department of the Brazos. When the Texas convention of 1836 met to consider the problems of the revolution against Mexico, Burnet was elected president of the interim government. His eight months as president were marked by much dissatisfaction with his leadership, undoubtedly intensified by the travails through which Texas was passing as it moved into independent status. Many members of the Texas army felt that he was too lenient in his peace terms with Mexico, and one group even tried to arrest him. But Burnet doggedly saw Texas through the transition period and then called an election in which Sam Houston was elected president of the Republic of Texas. Burnet himself refused to be a candidate. In November 1838 he was elected vice-president, and in the middle of December 1841 he briefly filled out the unexpired presidential term of Mirabeau B. Lamar, who had resigned.

In 1846 Burnet became secretary of state for the new state of Texas. After 1848 he became a farmer once more and dropped from sight. During the Civil War he opposed the secession of Texas from the United States. In 1866 he was elected United States senator from Texas, but was never allowed to serve because of Texas' status as an unreconstructed former slave state.

In 1852 Burnet County, Texas, was named in his honor.—J. B. F.

Burnett, Samuel Burk (1849-1922). Cattleman. Burnett was born in Bates County, Missouri. After his parents' home was destroyed by raiders during the turbulent years on the Kansas-Missouri border in the late 1850s, the family moved to Denton, Texas, where young Burnett learned the cattle business at an early age. He took part in his first trail drive at nineteen; by the time he was twenty-five he had acquired a small herd of his own. In the winter of 1874 Burnett bought a herd of steers to hold and fatten for market, setting a precedent among Texas cattlemen—the real beginning of the steer-buying and -feeding business. Then in 1875 Burnett drove his herd to Wichita County in North Texas and started the Burnett Ranch between the Red River and the Big Wichita.

Perhaps his greatest contribution to Texas cattle-raising was his role in securing grazing lands in Indian Territory. In the mid-1880s he went into the Kiowa-Comanche reservation to lease three hundred thousand acres of pastureland. Here he met Indian leader Quanah Parker, who was to become a lifelong friend. Because of his friendship with Quanah and with the tribes generally, Burnett was able to negotiate grazing rights to more than a million acres of land for himself and other Texas cowmen. When the federal government demanded that the cattlemen vacate their leases in preparation for the opening of Indian Territory to homesteaders, Burnett took Parker with him to Washington to appeal the order. Assisted by Senator Joseph Bailey of Texas, they were able to persuade President Theodore Roosevelt to grant a two-year stay, which the cattlemen wanted in order to make an orderly adjustment to the changing situation.

Burnett was a charter member and treasurer (1900-1922) of the Cattle Raisers' Association of Northwest Texas, founded in 1877, which became the Texas and Southwestern Cattle Raisers' Association. He was also an organizer of the National Feeder and Breeders Show and an ardent advocate of better livestock marketing practices. Burnett was also active in civic affairs in Fort Worth, Texas, to which he gave a public park.—R. B. W.

Burns, Tom. See RIVERMEN.

Burr conspiracy. The Burr conspiracy to take over the Old Southwest is difficult to establish because of the complex issues, numerous personalities, and diverse territory involved. It was, in fact, an ever-expanding scheme that at times was little more than a dream and a set of rumors. The numerous personalities and complexity of partisan politics gave it a broad base. Rivalries within the Jefferson administration, the purchase of Louisiana, and frontier irritations made the Spanish territory west of the Sabine River and the American territory within Louisiana highly vulnerable to audacious and expansive schemers.

Aaron Burr and James WILKINSON, the two key personalities in the conspiracy, had been friends since they served together as young officers in the St. Lawrence-Quebec campaign of the American Revolution. In the later years, when Burr was vice-president, the two met frequently in Philadelphia. How clearly the idea of venturing into this territory was developed between Burr and Wilkinson or with others cannot be stated precisely.

The fatal duel between Aaron Burr and Alexander Hamilton on July 11, 1804, ended Burr's political career. He was now faced with the problem of making a new beginning. In the winter of 1804-05, Burr and Wilkinson were studying maps of the Floridas and Louisiana. In New Orleans there were stirrings among the adventurers of that city. Daniel Clark and others were engaged in speculative activities. At this juncture Wilkinson was appointed governor of Upper Louisiana, and Dr. Joseph Browne, Burr's brother-in-law, was made secretary. Burr then sought a half-million dollars from Britain, and hoped for naval support of his scheme.

The drama of the Burr conspiracy really opened with the ex-vice-president's departure from Washington on April 10, 1805, ostensibly for a visit to the West. By this time there had developed a considerable network of intrigue, and there were numerous ambitious participants in what seemed to be a plan to take over the Old Southwest. Burr's journey to Pittsburgh and then down the Ohio River in an elaborately furnished flatboat was dramatic and reflective of his own impracticality. On the way down the river he stopped by Blennerhassett Island, where he visited with Mrs. Blennerhassett, and then passed on to Ohio, Kentucky, and Tennessee. On June 26 he reached New Orleans, where he visited with Spanish, Mexican, and American schemers. He worked with Daniel Clark and the Mexican Association, made up of traders and adventurers, and otherwise furthered his plans.

In the middle of July Burr moved north by way of Nashville, Louisville, Frankfort, and Lexington, and then went to St. Louis. In the latter place he again conferred with General Wilkinson. During this time there were inquiries about the Old Southwest, preparations were in the formative state for a military expedition, and there was much communicating with agents of one sort or another. This activity attracted the attention

of Thomas Ritchie of the Richmond, Virginia, *Enquirer* and other publishers.

Public disclosure of Burr's western activities soon made him a marked man. Even the opportunist Wilkinson became cool toward him. Back in Washington after a visit with Wilkinson in St. Louis, Burr conferred with both Anthony Merry, his British contact, and Thomas Jefferson in an attempt to set the president's mind at ease. The tenor of Jefferson's conversation discouraged him. In Philadelphia Burr conferred with General William Eaton, Jonathan Dayton, and French and Spanish officials, again being somewhat discouraged. By 1806 it became clear that Wilkinson was less than enthusiastic, for he was now in command of the military forces that would be charged with putting down any attempt to snatch the southwestern territory from the United States and Spain.

Burr went westward again in August 1806. After again visiting with numerous persons along the way, including a second call at Blennerhassett Island, he made arrangements for a later rendezvous of his forces at that place and then proceeded downstream to visit in Kentucky and Tennessee. In the latter state he told General Jackson that an attack by the Spanish on American soil was imminent. (Burr was so uncertain about his objectives that most people were deceived about his ultimate aims.) Jackson volunteered the services of the Tennessee volunteer militia forces to President Jefferson and gave Burr $3,500 in support of his cause. Other westerners were generous with contributions. In the meantime Burr purchased half of the shadowy Bastrop land claims of approximately 350,000 acres in Kentucky and the Louisiana Purchase area.

Rumors of land speculation, an attack on Mexico, and other activities were afloat in the communities along the Ohio. Burr's friends, especially Harman Blennerhassett, were talkative. By October 1806, word of Burr's scheme had reached President Jefferson. In Kentucky a group of Federalists, headed by Federal District Attorney Joseph Hamilton Daviess, were highly suspicious, but Daviess had been unable to stir Jefferson to action. Nevertheless, stories and editorials appearing in Joseph M. Street and John Wood's *Western World* created a stir. In back of all this was the militant old Federalist Humphrey Marshall. On November 5, 1806, Daviess swore out an affidavit against Burr charging him in fact with treason. In a subsequent examining trial Burr was cleared of Daviess' charges, but by now his cause had suffered serious exposure.

Following his arraignment in Kentucky, Burr's supporters had begun to assemble men and supplies along the Ohio. Agents were busy enlisting an army to accompany the expedition. There was a high degree of anticipation over the forthcoming journey down the Mississippi. Again the talkative Irishman Harman Blennerhassett gave Republican agents of the federal government too much information about Burr's scheme. Governor Edward Tiffin of Ohio, after receiving legislative authority to act, sent a militia force under Generals Gano and Findley to block the Ohio at Cincinnati. On December 9, Judge Return J. Meigs and General Buell intercepted ten of Burr's boats and forced the abandonment of Blennerhassett Island. Only a remnant of Burr's forces actually got down the Ohio, and there was every indication that most of these were in reality prospective settlers bound for the Red River country. At the Cumberland, Burr had only two partially loaded flatboats and a force of approximately 103 men.

From that point on, the Burr expedition was a highly desultory adventure. At Bayou Pierre in Mississippi Territory, Judge Peter Bryan Bruin showed Burr a newspaper clipping that revealed the fact he had been deserted by General Wilkinson. On January 16, 1807, Burr was arrested by civil authorities of the territory. He surrendered with the belief that he would be tried in the territorial court, and on February 2 he appeared at Natchez for trial before Judges Thomas Rodney and Peter B. Bruin. In the opening of the trial George Poindexter, federal attorney, refused to bring an indictment against Burr on the ground that the territorial court was not competent to try the case because of its appellate jurisdiction. Burr escaped Natchez by jumping bail on February 6 and was declared to be a fugitive by Governor Robert Williams. He attempted to reach East Florida and Pensacola; but he was arrested near Fort Stoddard in the lower Alabama Territory and was started on the long overland journey to stand trial in the federal court in Richmond, Virginia. Burr's dream of an empire in the Old Southwest had by now turned into a nightmare.

On May 22, 1807, Burr's trial commenced before Chief Justice John Marshall. In September the jury brought in a verdict of innocence on the charge of treason. After attempting to press other international schemes unsuccessfully, Burr returned to the practice of law in New York, in 1812.

See Thomas Perkins Abernethy, *The Burr Conspiracy* (1954); Walter F. McCaleb, *The Aaron Burr Conspiracy* (1936); and Nathan Schachner, *Aaron Burr* (1937). —T. D. C.

burro, wild. Remnants of releases of desert prospectors, wild burros have built to an estimated eight thousand animals in the southwestern deserts. The highest concentration is around Death Valley National Monument, California, and on both sides of the Colorado River in Arizona and California. These animals are extremely controversial in that they are claimed to be competitors with wildlife and vicious killers of young livestock. Yet many consider the wild burro representative of the heritage of the exploration of the desert and to many they are aesthetically pleasing. When burros were killed as target animals in California, the public reaction was so intense that very protective legislation resulted. Furthermore, some of the few studies on burros indicate they may not be the problem species their reputation indicates.

Efforts to protect wild burros are often tied to wildhorse protection efforts, since they are in the same need of federal jurisdiction and the establishment of a base from which to manage the populations. Wild burros are now afforded federal jurisdiction by Public Law 92-195, passed in December 1971. (See also MULE.)—M. J. P.

Bursum, Holm Olaf (1869-1953). Rancher and New Mexico politician. Born near Fort Dodge, Iowa, Bursum was orphaned at the age of eleven, while the family was living in Colorado. Two years later he moved to New Mexico, where he found a job with his uncle, A. H. Hilton, father of hotelman Conrad Hilton. Soon he went into business for himself, hauling supplies for the United States government from Wingate to Fort Wingate and acting as railroad agent at Wingate. With the arrival of the railroad in the area, Bursum sold his freighting outfit for twelve hundred sheep, which he parlayed into a profit. He then invested in two ranches, inaugurating a career in ranching that lasted until his retirement; he became one of the most prominent ranchmen in New Mexico, raising both sheep and cattle.

Bursum began his political career as sheriff of Socorro County in 1894. In 1899-1900 he served in the territorial senate, where he was chairman of the Appropriations and Finance Committee. In 1899 he was appointed warden of the New Mexico State Penitentiary, a post he held for seven years. Although Bursum also served as mayor of Socorro from 1906 until 1918, his most important work was within the Republican party itself. He was chairman of the Republican territorial central committee from 1905 to 1911 and represented New Mexico at the Republican national conventions in 1904, 1908, 1912, and 1928. As delegate to the 1908 convention, Bursum was largely responsible for the Republican plank advocating statehood for New Mexico. He worked vigorously to achieve statehood during the next four years and was chairman of the New Mexico constitutional convention of 1910, which wrote a conservative document very much to his liking. In 1919 he was made a member of the Republican National Committee representing New Mexico and was reelected the following year.

Twice, in 1911 and 1916, Bursum was defeated in bids for the governor's office (partly because of his association with the old Santa Fe Ring), but he achieved major office in 1921 when he was appointed to the United States Senate seat vacated by Albert Fall. He was subsequently elected for the unexpired term at a special election on September 29, 1921. Although he only served in the Senate until 1925 he was active as chairman of the Senate Committee on Pensions, where he proved a staunch friend of servicemen, old soldiers, and war widows. His attempt to reduce the size of Pueblo landholdings in New Mexico by federal act ran into determined opposition and was unsuccessful.

During the years in which he was politically active it was evident that Bursum was a master politician. His control over the Republican party in New Mexico between 1900 and 1925 was impressive and suggests that he was the center of the highly sophisticated Santa Fe Ring, a group of political leaders, sometimes from both parties, whose activities extended far beyond the usual range of politics.—H. R. L.

Bush, Asahel (1824-1913). Oregon politician and newspaper editor. Bush went to Oregon Territory as a young man of twenty-six to seek his political fortune. A lawyer who had been admitted to the Massachusetts bar in 1850, and with some experience in journalism, Bush was typical of other professional men who were eager for a turn at political power and who saw opportunities in the new and underpopulated territories of the West. Eighteen years later, in 1868, Bush had won and lost a political fortune and was embarked, with William Ladd, on a banking career where his extensive talents for organization and leadership were put to less exacting and less flamboyant uses than during the territorial period when he marshaled men and votes for Oregon's Democrats.

As owner and editor of the *Oregon Statesman*, which

he established in 1851, Bush was the leading spirit in organizing Oregon's first party apparatus. At a time in American history when national politics was growing more personalized and sectionalized, Bush represented the countervailing tendency toward party government, insisting that "public offices belong to no individual whose position may enable him to control them. They belong to the Democratic party and the people whom the officer serves." By 1852 the Salem Clique, as Bush's enemies called the party in control at the capital city, held almost all local elective and appointive offices, and they had sent Joseph Lane to Washington, D.C., as Oregon's territorial delegate. Six years later (1858) the Oregon Democrats were divided, along with the national party, between Douglas Democrats and Buchanan Democrats. The situation made a mockery of Bush's organization as much as it did of his principles. Following a split with the Buchanan-Lane wing of the party in the state elections of 1859, the Democratic party organization came to a shattering, unorthodox end in 1860, when Clique men in the legislature were forced to trade votes with Republicans, electing one Democrat, James W. Nesmith, and one Republican, E. D. Baker, to the United States Senate. Bush's political career was over.

Collections of Bush papers include those at the Oregon Historical Society in Portland and at the State Library at Salem. There is no biography of Bush. The best assessments of his role in territorial politics are found in James E. Hendrickson, *Joe Lane of Oregon Machine Politics and the Sectional Crisis, 1849-1861* (1967); and Robert W. Johannsen, *Frontier Politics on the Eve of the Civil War* (1955).—R. J. L.

Bush, George Washington (1791-1867). Farmer and Washington pioneer. Bush, a mulatto, was born in Louisiana. He worked as a free-lance trapper in the Rocky Mountains as a youth and from 1814 to 1829 as a fur trader with the Robidoux brothers on the Mexican Pacific Coast and in the Columbia valley of Washington. While in the Northwest he was employed by the Hudson's Bay Company. Removing to Missouri in 1830 as a free black, he farmed there until 1843. In that year he led a party of thirty-two white Americans across the Great Plains to The Dalles, Oregon. Because local regulations prohibited blacks from remaining in OREGON, the Bush party moved north of the Columbia River and became the first American settlers in what is now Washington State. In spite of Hudson's Bay Company policy to discourage American settlement, Bush and his friends were allowed to stay since he had once been a company employee. He cleared and farmed a field south of Olympia on what is still called Bush Prairie and planted his field with wheat. This supplied Olympia's flour mill, and Bush became modestly wealthy from his efforts. Grain from his farm won the Centennial Fair prize for the best wheat from anywhere in the world in 1876. Bush's success with farming and the high regard his neighbors had for him and his family contributed to pioneer "respect for color" in the Northwest, which tempered somewhat the racial prejudices of the day. His son participated in Washington's constitutional convention and was also an elected member of the first state legislature in 1889.

See Alfred Apsler, "George Bush, Negro Pioneer," Portland *Sunday Oregonian* (March 15, 1953); John Edwin Ayer, "George Bush the Voyageur," *Washington Historical Quarterly* (January 1916); and E. S. Meany, "First American Settlement on Puget Sound," *ibid.* (April 1916).—K. A. M.

Butterfield, John (1801-1869). Businessman. Butterfield was born in Berne, near Albany, New York. From early boyhood he demonstrated an interest in horses and transportation. At nineteen he obtained his first job as a stagecoach driver in Albany and later in Utica. Soon, after buying a small stable, he went into the livery business himself. In 1822 he married Malinda Harriet Baker and the couple opened a boardinghouse in conjunction with the livery business to augment their income. His promotional activity gradually increased until he held a controlling interest in most of the important mail and passenger lines in northern and western New York. He invested in packet boats on the Erie Canal, steamers on Lake Ontario, and post roads. Always concerned for his residence, Utica, he originated the first street horse railway system and also constructed the first local steam railroad there. In 1849 he organized the Butterfield and Wasson Express Company and the following year merged his interests with those of Wells and Company and Livingston, Fargo and Company to form the American Express Company. He also turned his attention to the telegraph, and with Henry Wells and Crawford Livingston organized the New York, Albany and Buffalo Telegraph Company. Butterfield was also a highly successful real estate promoter, erecting both the Butterfield House and the Gardner block in Utica; he became a director of the Utica City National Bank. In 1856 he was elected mayor of Utica as a Republican.

The outstanding achievement of Butterfield's career was his role in founding and organizing the OVERLAND MAIL COMPANY and in serving as its president from 1857 to 1860. In his enthusiasm for the project, he traveled on the stagecoach carrying the first mailbags as far as Fort Smith, Arkansas. A man of great energy, who responded to competition, he made plans to establish a daily, rather than a semiweekly, mail service, and proposed the establishment of the Pony Express service to compete with that on the central route. In 1860 a conflict developed between Butterfield and his codirectors of the Overland Mail Company, mainly over the large financial losses incurred by the tremendous undertaking in spite of a $600,000-a-year subsidy from the federal government. The majority were unwilling to consider expansion of the service to include a pony express. At one juncture, Wells, Fargo & Co. threatened to foreclose and take over the Overland Mail Company because of unpaid loans. A compromise was negotiated whereby Butterfield was removed from the presidency and William B. Dinsmore was elected by the board of directors.

Already past the average retirement age for the time, Butterfield withdrew and remained in seclusion for more than two years. His personal fortune was secure, but while recovering from total exhaustion he engaged in various business enterprises in New York City. In October 1867 he suffered a stroke, was removed to his home in Utica, and died there two years later.

See Roscoe P. Conkling and Margaret B. Conkling, *The Butterfield Overland Mail, 1857-1869* (1947). —W. T. J.

Byers, William Newton (1831-1903). Colorado newspaperman. Born in Madison County, Ohio, Byers accompanied his parents to Iowa in 1850. In 1851 he was named deputy United States surveyor for Iowa and the next year signed on with a party going to the Northwest, subsequently engaging in survey work in Oregon and Washington. In 1854 he moved to Omaha, Nebraska, where he was again named a deputy surveyor. He also served as a member of the first territorial assembly of Nebraska Territory in 1854-55. When word came of the 1858 mineral discoveries in the Pikes Peak region of Colorado, Byers decided to set out for the gold fields and establish a newspaper. He arrived in Denver in spring 1859 and issued the first newspaper April 23, 1859. Printed on a handpress in the attic of "Uncle Dick" Wootton's Auraria saloon, Byers' *Rocky Mountain News* beat the rival *Cherry Creek Pioneer* by about twenty minutes. (In early settlements there was often a rush to see who would have the honor of printing the first newspaper.) From that date until his death in Denver, few men were more closely identified with the development of Colorado.

A staunch Republican, Byers supported early statehood efforts as chairman of an 1859 statehood convention and as a member of the assembly that drafted a constitution in 1864. Byers remained editor and publisher of the *News* until 1878 (his partner, John Dailey,

sold his interest to him in 1870), promoting the interests of Colorado and urging the development of agriculture as an economic base in addition to mining. As he told his readers when he sold the paper: "Not educated as a journalist, I have not been confined to the straight and narrow path of the profession. My feelings have been those of personal championship for a state in which I have felt a deep personal interest."

Although he is primarily known as an editor, Byers was active in other areas as well. He was instrumental in organizing the company that established Colorado's first telegraph line from Denver to Santa Fe; we are told that he walked the entire distance between the two towns, selecting the position for every pole. He served as postmaster of Denver from 1864 to 1867 and again from 1879 to 1883, was president of the Denver Chamber of Commerce, and was an organizer and officer of the Denver Tramway Company. He is also remembered as a member of the first party to reach the top of Longs Peak in 1868.

No full-scale biography of Byers exists. See Robert L. Perkin, *The First Hundred Years: An Informal History of Denver and the Rocky Mountain News* (1959); and files of the *Rocky Mountain News* during the period of his editorship.—M. B.

C

Cabeza de Baca, Ezequiél (1864-1917). New Mexican politician. Cabeza de Baca was born in Las Vegas, New Mexico. He was the great-grandson of Luis Maria Cabeza de Baca, the recipient in the early nineteenth century of the land known as the Las Vegas Grant. Cabeza de Baca attended Las Vegas College from 1878 to 1882. As a young man he taught in public schools and worked as a store clerk, deputy county clerk, and deputy assessor. In 1900 he was a delegate to the Democratic National Convention and in 1904 was one of the founders of the Martinez Publishing Company, which published *La Voz del Pueblo*, a Spanish-language newspaper. In 1913 Cabeza de Baca ran second to Albert B. Fall in the state legislature's voting for United States senator.

Elected lieutenant governor of New Mexico in 1911, Cabeza de Baca served in that office until being inaugurated in 1917 as the state's first Spanish-speaking governor. A Democrat from San Miguel County, one of the state's largest counties, he was supported by Octaviano A. Larrazolo, an influential spokesman of Spanish-Americans who had campaigned for about two years seeking to elect more natives to state offices. Cabeza de Baca, however, was seriously ill and died within a few weeks of assuming office. The incumbent governor, W. E. Lindsey, chosen as his lieutenant governor, succeeded him, and Democrats were thus accused of intentionally choosing an ailing Spanish-American for governor to keep Lindsey in the statehouse.

See Jack E. Holmes, *Politics in New Mexico* (1967). Biographical references are contained in R. E. Twitchell, *The Leading Facts of New Mexican History* (1912).—J.R.V.

Cabeza de Vaca, Alvar Núñez, (c. 1490-c. 1557). Spanish explorer and conquistador. Cabeza de Vaca was the most important survivor of the ill-fated expedition led by Pánfilo de Narváez, in which about three hundred men lost their lives. After serious misfortunes in north Florida in 1528, the survivors headed out to sea in five poorly constructed boats. Storms, thirst, starvation, and hostile Indians (when they went ashore) reduced the party to about eighty or ninety survivors, who were then shipwrecked on the low-lying, sandy islands off the Texas coast. Cabeza de Vaca's boat was probably wrecked on Galveston Island.

Within two or three years the survivors of the shipwreck had been reduced to just four—Alonso del Castillo Maldonado, usually called Castillo; Andrés Dorantes de Carranca; Estevanito, an Arab slave who is often incorrectly called a Negro; and Cabeza de Vaca. For nearly four years Cabeza de Vaca lived as a trader among east Texas tribes; then, in 1532, he joined the other three survivors and they began an odyssey across present Texas, New Mexico, Arizona, and the present

Mexican states of Chihuahua, Durango, Sonora, and Sinaloa. For another two years, until about October 1534, they were virtual slaves of the Indians. Finally Cabeza de Vaca, a man of tenacity, courage, and intelligence, won their freedom by building a reputation as an esteemed medicine man and a man of peace. Eventually, on April 11, 1536, they met Spanish slave hunters near the town of Culiacán, in present Sinaloa.

From this incredible adventure, which was first described as part of a viceroy's report to the crown and later in Cabeza de Vaca's own narrative, *La Relación* (in later editions entitled *Los Naufragios*, "The Shipwrecked"), the Spanish derived a more accurate view of the east-west extent of North America. Activity was stimulated toward probing the "northern mystery." The journey of Estevanito and Fray Marcos into the southwest desert in search of the supposedly wealthy Seven Cities of Cíbola, as well as Coronado's great expedition, were a direct result of the interest that was generated by Cabeza de Vaca's adventure. In addition, anthropologists are intrigued by his amazing accounts of the stone age people who lived between the southern limits of the buffalo range and the Gulf of Mexico.

See Cyclone Covey, *Cabeza de Vaca's Adventures in the Unknown Interior of America* (1961); Cleve Hallenbeck, *Alvar Núñez Cabeza de Vaca* (1940); Frederick W. Hodge, ed., *The Narrative of Alvar Núñez Cabeza de Vaca* (1907, 1959); and Buckingham Smith, ed. and trans., *Relation of Núñez Cabeza de Vaca* (1871, 1966)—R. A. B.

Cabrillo, Juan Rodríguez (?-1543). Explorer of the Pacific coast. Cabrillo, a Portuguese in the employ of Spain, commanded an expedition charged with sailing up the coast from Mexico in search of an elusive strait leading from the Pacific to the Atlantic, often called the Strait of Anian. (See NORTHWEST PASSAGE.) Leaving on June 27, 1542, Cabrillo discovered San Diego Bay, Santa Catalina and San Clemente islands, Santa Monica Bay, the Santa Barbara Channel, and the islands of Santa Cruz, Santa Rosa, and San Miguel. He missed the Bay of Monterey and the Golden Gate, but did discover Drake's Bay. Turning south, Cabrillo landed at San Miguel Island, and there he died.

Bartolomé Ferrelo, his chief pilot, assumed command and traveled north again, to a few miles above the California-Oregon boundary. On April 14, 1543, Ferrelo returned to Puerto de Navidad (about twenty miles above present Manzanillo), nearly eleven months after leaving the same place.

The accomplishments of the Cabrillo-Ferrelo expedition in exploring the broken coastline of the Pacific, with its variable winds and treacherous currents, were substantial, though they never found the mythical Strait of Anian.

See Herbert Bolton, *Spanish Explorations in the Southwest, 1542-1706* (1930); and Henry R. Wagner, *Spanish Voyages to the Northwest Coast of America in the Sixteenth Century* (1929).—R. A. B.

Caine, John Thomas (1829-1911). Mormon leader and Utah politician. Born on the Isle of Man, Caine arrived in Utah in 1852, having spent the years since his conversion to Mormonism in 1847 assisting the Perpetual Emigrating Company in the eastern states. His acting ability popularized his name among his fellow communicants. He served a mission to Hawaii (1854-56) and following his return to Utah became a private clerk in the office of Brigham Young. During the "Utah War"

difficulties, which began a year later, he joined the staff of Daniel H. Wells as a military secretary, attaining the rank of lieutenant colonel. He became ecclesiastically prominent in the Latter-day Saint (LDS) church as a counselor in the Salt Lake Stake, 1868-76.

Caine's public service in Utah began in 1856 when he was appointed assistant secretary and later secretary to the territorial legislature. He became editor of the Salt Lake *Herald* in 1871, and the following year was elected to the constitutional convention.

As he closed his ecclesiastical service in the Salt Lake Stake presidency in 1876, Caine began a career that was to lead to national prominence. From 1876 to 1882 he was Salt Lake City recorder and a member of the board of regents for the University of Deseret. Having worked against the antipolygamy Cullom bill in 1870, he then assisted Utah delegate George Q. Cannon in Washington, D.C., 1880-81. When it became apparent that Cannon would be expelled from Congress in 1882, Caine was elected territorial delegate as a candidate from the LDS church-sponsored people's party. Although Caine was also of foreign birth and like Cannon had been absent from America doing foreign missionary work, Caine was not a polygamist and therefore served without congressional opposition from 1882 to 1894. During this time he worked incessantly to block the anti-Mormon legislation introduced in Congress. In 1890 the Mormon church gave up its position on polygamy, which signaled the end of federal-Utah hostilities. Caine worked toward achieving a rapprochement, even assisting in the election of non-Mormon Joseph L. Rawlins as delegate to replace him. In the first election in the state of Utah, Caine was the Democratic candidate for governor, but was narrowly defeated by Republican Heber M. Wells. In 1896, he was elected to the Utah state senate.

See Andrew Jenson, *Latter-day Saint Biographical Encyclopedia* (1901).—L. R.

Calamity Jane (1852-1903). Calamity, whose real name was Martha Canary, was born near Princeton, Missouri, the daughter of Robert and Charlotte (?) Canary, about whom almost nothing is known. Apocryphal stories about her childhood and the source of her nickname are nearly as numerous as those about her supposed love affair with Wild Bill HICKOK. Legend has it that while moving west to settle in Salt Lake City in 1865, both of Martha's parents died and the children were farmed out to various Utah families. Some writers claim that the sad fate of her family led to the name "Calamity." Martha herself is supposed to have become a dishwasher at Fort Bridger, a construction worker on the Union Pacific, a uniformed Army scout for General Custer and other army officers, and a bullwhacker, or teamster, who freighted supplies to the mining camps of Montana and Dakota. Virtually all of these claims remain unproven.

What records exist of her activities tell us instead that in 1865 her family moved to the gold-rush town of Virginia City, Montana. There she matured into a tall, muscular, big-boned girl who learned to ride and shoot, wore men's clothes, and enjoyed the company of men. Sometimes she took in washing; at other times she cared for sick families, although the sobriquet "angel of mercy" used by some biographers hardly seems accurate. In 1875 she accompanied the scientific expedition of Dr.

Walter Jenney to the Black Hills, probably as a camp follower rather than as a hired teamster. She was in the Black Hills from 1876 to 1880 at the height of the gold-rush excitement. She lived with a succession of men and on occasion turned to prostitution to survive.

Careful studies by her biographers have established that she traveled back and forth across Montana, Wyoming, and Kansas between 1880 and 1895. In the latter year she returned to Deadwood to live. At some point, she formed an alliance with Clinton Burke, a native of Texas who worked as a hack driver in the Black Hills, but no record of a formal marriage has yet been found. Nevertheless she identified herself as Mrs. M. E. Burke, the name carved beneath the larger name "Calamity Jane" on her tombstone in Deadwood, South Dakota.

One thing is certain: Calamity Jane had a taste for the theatrical. She boasted of wild exploits, such as scouting for Custer. She frequented saloons and often went on drunken sprees. On one occasion she rode a bull down the main street of Rapid City. By 1896, although suffering from alcoholism, she joined the amusement firm of Kohl and Middleton and appeared on stage at Minneapolis and, in 1901, at the Buffalo Pan-American Exposition. Everywhere she went she peddled a brief autobiography, notoriously inaccurate, for a few cents.

The legend has persisted that she was secretly married to Wild Bill Hickok, despite all evidence to the contrary. The seemingly infinite variations of this and other legends generally assert that while in Kansas, she and Wild Bill were secretly married by a Methodist minister. A daughter, Janey, was supposedly the issue of this unlikely union. Stories about the daughter are legion. One states that she was given to Mr. and Mrs. James O'Neil, an English couple visiting in the West, who subsequently reared her in England as their own daughter. A woman calling herself Jean Hickok McCormick came forward in 1941 claiming to be the long-lost daughter of Wild Bill and Calamity. Mrs. McCormick produced a diary supposedly written by Calamity Jane as proof of her claim, but neither the diary nor Mrs. McCormick's relation has been authenticated. There remains the intriguing fact, however, that some years before her death Calamity appeared in the Black Hills with a young girl and placed her in a Catholic academy in Sturgis. Whether the girl was Calamity's daughter or Burke's child by another woman is not known.

Careful investigations by Hickok's biographers have failed to establish any association whatever between the Kansas lawman and Martha Canary. The famous photograph of Calamity Jane posing before Hickok's grave in Deadwood in the summer of 1903 can be seen both as a final act of showmanship and evidence that she had come to believe stories of her own fabrication. Troubled in mind and body, she seems to have tired of the role she had created. Two years before her death she exclaimed that she wished they would "leave me alone and let me go to hell my own route."

Two brief, but excellent, biographies are J. Leonard Jennewein, *Calamity Jane of the Western Trails* (1965); and Roberta B. Sollid, *Calamity Jane—A Study in Historical Criticism* (1958). See also Joseph G. Rosa, *They Called Him Wild Bill* (1974).—H. R. L.

Caldwell, Kansas. See CATTLE TOWNS.

Calhoun, John C. (1782-1850). Statesman. Few politicians in the experience of the United States have sur-

passed Calhoun in exercising influence over the nation's affairs. So important was his role that Frederick Jackson Turner believed that a biography of the man would constitute the political history of the United States from the War of 1812 through the Compromise of 1850. To Turner, and to other western historians, Calhoun has been especially interesting as the spokesman of the South, the suitor of the West, and the dialectician of the relationship of sections to one another. Somewhat less obviously Calhoun also emerges as a specimen of that Turnerian type, the frontiersman.

Calhoun was born in Abbeville district, South Carolina, on the edge of the frontier. His childhood homestead was ground cleared from a Cherokee forest by his Scots father, who had achieved considerable standing among his neighbors as an Indian fighter, the organizer and captain of a peace-keeping force of "rangers," an accumulator of land, and one of the men who pried out of the Charleston-dominated legislature the right of representation for western South Carolinians. As Calhoun grew up, he saw remnants of Indian life as he traveled the road (itself initially a buffalo path) that took him to the backwoods "log college," where he made an acquaintance with formal learning. At age twenty, with the financial backing of an older brother, Calhoun went off in 1802 to Yale College to prepare for the practice of law. It is unlikely that his father, had he still lived, would have approved; not many years earlier he had indicated his regard for attorneys by offering to "gie a poond" for any lawyer's scalp brought to him.

Calhoun, however, did not stray far from another of his father's antipathies, the one to Hamiltonian federalism. At Yale and subsequently at the Litchfield (Connecticut) Law School he found himself in a defensive minority as a supporter of President Jefferson's policies. At Litchfield, "so much agitated by party feelings," he felt acutely isolated as one of the very few men from "our end of the Union." Consequently, he returned to the pro-Jefferson atmosphere of South Carolina in 1806 with a well-developed brief against Great Britain and Federalists, and it was only natural that when the people of Abbeville met to protest the British attack on the American warship *Chesapeake* in 1807 Calhoun was chosen to speak their grievance. Thereafter the young lawyer rode the wave of anti-British feeling to election to Congress in 1811, where he joined Henry Clay to lead the war hawks, a group conspicuous for its youth and western origin. So vigorous and single-minded was Calhoun's urging of war that he quickly drew the fire of Virginia's splenetic John Randolph, who observed that the new congressman "had not been educated in Connecticut for nothing. He united to the savage ferocity of the frontierman all the insensibility of the Yankee character in a compound most marvelously offensive to every man having pretensions to the character of a gentleman."

Marvelously offensive or not, Calhoun worked himself to exhaustion on behalf of James Madison's administration, in whose eyes he became the "young Hercules who carried the war on his shoulders." As a reward, Madison's successor, James Monroe, appointed Calhoun secretary of war, giving him direct responsibility for the defense of the frontier and for all Indian matters. In executing these responsibilities he was guided by lessons drawn from the war just ended. To Calhoun, the

Treaty of Ghent was merely an armistice that permitted the United States time to prepare for the next round of hostilities with Britain. Accordingly, from 1817 to 1825 he strove to organize the war department into efficient bureaus, maintain a substantial standing army, construct roads adequate for rapid deployment, and remove the possibility of further collusion between the British and the Northwest Indians. The Yellowstone expedition of 1819 and Major Stephen H. Long's expedition to the Rocky Mountains were products of Calhoun's policy. Although Congress failed to appropriate all the funds requested by Calhoun—particularly after the economic crisis of 1819—much of his coordinated program became reality. Surveys and patrols pushed farther up the tributaries of the Missouri and Mississippi rivers, impressing the Indians and erecting fortifications, and throughout the country soldiers built military roads. By 1820 the character of the army's operations under the Calhoun regime could be discerned in the complaint of an army officer named Zachary Taylor: "The ax, pick, saw & trowel, has become more the implement of the American soldier than the cannon, musket or sword." As for Indian affairs, Calhoun's chief contribution was to supervise a detailed study (conducted by the Indian bureau he created) that resulted in the recommendation, made to Congress by President Monroe, that unassimilated Indian tribes in the East be persuaded to remove to a "sufficient tract of country west of the state of Missouri and Territory of Arkansas." It was left to President Andrew Jackson several years later to implement this recommendation and to substitute coercion for persuasion.

In his use of the army to build roads and to open up the frontier, Calhoun seemed to have outgrown some of his Jeffersonian scruples regarding the amassing of power by the central government. He supported the tariff as a means of paying for roads and other internal improvements and tended to dismiss opposition to such measures as impractical: "I am no advocate for refined arguments on the constitution," he said in 1817. Yet, by 1832, after a series of dizzyingly complicated political developments, Calhoun had resigned as Jackson's vice president (he had held office since 1825) and emerged as a senator from South Carolina and the foremost champion of state sovereignty, restricted federal power, and an almost theological adherence to the text of the Constitution. Calhoun and South Carolina aimed their "nullification" at the tariff, but perceived that the real threat was to slavery. A federal government powerful enough to impose a ruinous tariff on a state against its wishes could also impose laws interfering with slavery; the anticipated danger must be met at the threshold. From the mid-1830s onward, Calhoun later remembered, the defense of slavery was his main purpose. To a critic he became a "monomaniac consumed by a single idea."

Calhoun's single idea was, however, a structure of several compartments if not of many mansions. For instance, it certainly could accommodate both his extreme sectionalism and his continuing ambition for the presidency (which was not completely abandoned until 1847). And it permitted him to favor federal subsidies to the West so long as these could be argued to be constitutional and seen to bind the West to the South rather than to the North. Calhoun, in fact, tried repeatedly to in-

gratiate himself and his sectional cause with the West. The culmination of such efforts came in 1845, when he agreed to preside over the Memphis Railroad Convention, whose promoters promised to connect the Mississippi valley to Charleston by rail. It was understood at Memphis that Calhounites would work for the reduction of the price of public lands and for federal funding of improvements to western harbors, rivers, and roads; in exchange western politicians would support the southern objective of low tariffs. Although the bargain was realized only partially, it demonstrated Calhoun's adroitness in the juggling of constitutional principles. He was now able to sanction federal expenditures for improvements on western waterways, because, he maintained, they touched more than one state and formed an "inland sea."

Another means of appealing to the West was to champion the annexation of additional territory. If the territory was also likely to develop into a slave state, so much the better. Not surprisingly, then, Calhoun spoke out for the annexation of Texas immediately after the battle of San Jacinto in 1836 and continued his advocacy through the following years. His chance for action came in 1844, when President John Tyler appointed him to the suddenly vacated position of secretary of state. Calhoun quickly completed a treaty with Texas, by which the latter would be transformed from an independent republic into a state in the Union. Unfortunately, action on the treaty was deferred in the Senate long enough for the publication of an indiscreet communication from Calhoun to the British foreign secretary, in which Calhoun asserted that the United States was obliged to annex Texas in order to save it from the clutches of international abolitionism. This statement helped defeat the treaty in the Senate, whereupon Calhoun and Tyler hit upon the expedient of a joint resolution of Congress to accomplish the same end. So, under the auspices of Calhoun, the strict constructionist, Texas was joined hurriedly to the United States by a procedure of dubious constitutionality.

Calhoun later contrasted the Texas question with the contemporaneous one of Oregon: "In the case of Texas, time was against us—in that of Oregon, time was with us; and hence the difference in my course of policy in reference to them." When, in the middle of both questions, James Polk took over the presidency he not only failed to invite Calhoun to stay on at the State Department, he also ended Calhoun's "masterly inactivity" regarding Oregon. Calhoun was sure that Polk's apparent insistence on the acknowledgment of 54°40' as the northwest boundary would produce war with Britain. When it did not, Calhoun simply turned his fire toward the aims and conduct of the conflict that Polk did produce, the Mexican War. Unlike many southerners, Calhoun did not want "all Mexico." Rather, he declared that "Mexico is to us the forbidden fruit," by which he meant, among other things, that the North would never permit the organization into slave states of so vast an area, despite its location south of the Missouri Compromise line.

Calhoun's dread of a sectional contest over the disposal of lands acquired from Mexico was well founded. The dispute consumed the remaining years of his life. He answered the Wilmot Proviso, which proposed the complete exclusion of slavery from the new territories, with resolutions that though never enacted were similar to the Supreme Court's Dred Scott decision a decade later. Calhoun argued that not only would the proposed Wilmot Proviso violate the Constitution, the Missouri Compromise had already done so. In short, according to Calhoun, far from possessing the authority to exclude slavery from a territory, Congress, in fact, was required to open all territories to settlement by any American citizen regardless of the kind of property—slave or not—that he might bring with him. This deadlock over the territories, which delayed the admission of California to statehood, continued in full force into 1850. In March of that year death removed Calhoun as an obstacle to agreement, and after a decent time interval the Compromise of 1850 was achieved.

As a young congressman Calhoun had told the House that, "We are greatly, and rapidly—I was about to say fearfully growing. This is our pride and our danger; our weakness and our strength." In retrospect, it appears that this growth, this ever advancing frontier, was a major factor in the spoiling of Calhoun's once brilliant prospects for the presidency. It became increasingly difficult and finally impossible for someone who could not compromise on the slavery question to participate in the sectional trade-offs required for the construction of a national political coalition. Calhoun at last had nothing to offer the West except unwanted slavery.

See Gerald M. Capers, *John C. Calhoun, Opportunist: A Reappraisal* (1960); Margaret L. Coit, *John C. Calhoun, American Portrait* (1950); Robert L. Meriwether et al., eds., *The Papers of John C. Calhoun* (1959); August O. Spain, *The Political Theory of John C. Calhoun* (1951); and Charles M. Wiltse, *John C. Calhoun*, 3 vols. (1944-51). —W. B. F.

Calico, California. Ghost town. Calico flourished between 1881 and 1896 as a booming silver town. During this period between $67 million and $86 million in silver was mined. In 1895 the price of silver dropped, the mines quit producing, and the town was soon abandoned and fell into ruin.

Today the town has been restored by Walter Knott of Knott's Berry Farm and thrives as a tourist attraction.

See Remi Nadeau, *Ghost Towns and Mining Camps of California* (1965); and Muriel S. Wolle, *The Bonanza Trail* (1953).—R. B. W.

California. The first Californians were Indians whose ancestors probably came from Asia about 15,000 to 30,000 years ago, across the ice that connected Asia and Alaska during the last Ice Age. Before the coming of the white man, nearly a third of all the Indians in North America north of Mexico lived in California, with its benign climates and its rich natural food supplies—especially acorns, fish, and game. California Indian society remained static—at the Stone-Age level—for many thousands of years because the Pacific on the west and the vast stretches of mountain and desert to the east and south effectively sheltered it from contact with the rest of humanity. This extreme geographic isolation also protected the California Indians from European conquest for so long that California was one of the last areas of the Western Hemisphere to be colonized. After the Spaniards founded their first settlement on the Pacific Coast—in 1519 at Panamá—250 years elapsed before the founding of their first settlement in Alta (Upper) California at San Diego. (See INDIANS OF CALIFORNIA.)

The original "California" was a gold-rich island of Amazons, "on the right hand of the Indies" and "very near to the terrestrial paradise," as described in a Spanish novel written about 1500 by García Ordóñez de Montalvo. The name was first applied, probably in the 1530s, to what the Spanish would later call *Baja California* (Lower California), which they first supposed to be an island. Juan Rodríguez CABRILLO disproved this theory when he discovered and partially explored the coast of Alta California in 1542. In 1602-03 Sebastián Vizcaíno named and charted many prominent features of the coast, including the Bay of Monterey, where he unsuccessfully proposed the founding of a settlement as a port of call for the annual merchant galleons passing southward on their way from Manila to Mexico. But the prevailing winds and currents made it so difficult to sail northward from Mexico that the project for a settlement in Alta California was virtually forgotten for another century and a half, until José de Gálvez revived it during his tempestuous career as visitor-general of New Spain.

The traditional explanation of the founding of Alta California is that it was a measure of defensive expansion to forestall a supposed Russian project for a settlement there, from which Russia or some other power might advance on the mines of northern Mexico. But this fanciful idea served mainly as a rationalization for Gálvez, who was intensely ambitious and who wished to make it appear that New Spain was flourishing and expanding as a result of his political genius. He did make excellent choices for the leadership of the "sacred expedition." Captain Gaspar de Portolá commanded the military part of it, and Father Junípero SERRA became the founder of Upper California's long chain of Franciscan missions.

Actually the Spanish empire was already declining. New Spain lacked the population and resources for the development of a colony on its outermost frontier, and the mission system was an attempt to make Spanish colonists out of the native Indians in the long coastal strip of California that Spain weakly held. But although there were ultimately twenty-one missions, from San Diego to Sonoma (with only four presidios and three pueblos), the system was not really successful. Indian deaths far exceeded births within the mission walls. The missions were fairly effective as agricultural communities based on forced labor; but the ostensible goal of ultimate "secularization" of the missions, or their transition into self-governing communities of converted Indians, was considered impractical, and the padres made no serious attempt to accomplish it. Under Mexico, which secured its independence from Spain in 1821, a form of secularization was finally carried out, but it was merely a process of turning over the mission lands and herds to a new class of Mexican-Californian ranchers (see CALIFORNIA RANCHO SYSTEM). California politics under the Mexican republic consisted mainly of maneuvers by coalitions of *ranchero* families to obtain vast land grants from the governors.

The only substantial commercial enterprise in Mexican California was the export of tallow and cowhides, pioneered by BRYANT, STURGIS AND CO., and McCULLOCH, HARTNELL and COMPANY. The trade was classically described in Richard Henry Dana's *Two Years Before the Mast*. "In the hands of an enterprising people," Dana wrote, "what a country [California] might be!" As America's destiny of expansion to the Pacific became

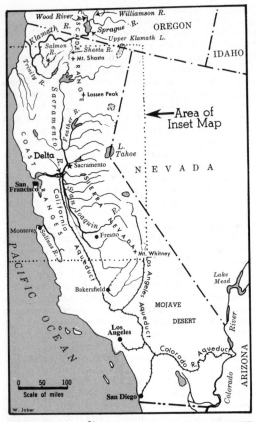

California Streams

manifest, it was also clear that Mexico could not hold California for long (see BEAR FLAG REBELLION). In 1820, after fifty years of Spanish rule, the population of California other than native Indians was about two thousand. On the eve of the American conquest, after twenty-five years under Mexico, it was no more than seven thousand. Overland immigration on the CALIFORNIA TRAIL began with the John BIDWELL train in the first half of the 1840s, encouraged by articles written by John MARSH, an Anglo rancher. WARNER'S RANCH and Sutter's Fort, owned by Anglos, were popular rest stops. Although immigration was still small, its continuation and gradual increase would have made a transition to American sovereignty inevitable within a few years if the Mexican War had not hastened the process.

Mexico ceded California to the United States in the Treaty of Guadalupe Hidalgo. When that document was agreed to on February 2, 1848, its signers were unaware that gold had been discovered nine days earlier, on January 24, on property claimed by John A. SUTTER near his mill at COLOMA on the south fork of the American River. Had that discovery not occurred, several decades might have passed before California reached the sixty thousand population required for statehood. The gold rush, however, increased the population by more than that number in the year 1849 alone. Partly because of the swiftness of its growth and partly because the national Congress deadlocked over the question of the future of slavery in the Mexican cession, California never passed through the formal territorial stage of its political development. A convention at Monterey drew up a state constitution in the autumn of 1849. It prohibited slavery, not for humanitarian reasons but because most of the gold miners, whether they came from the North or the South, feared that slaves would be used to compete with white miners in the diggings. After long and bitter debate, Congress finally accepted this free-state constitution and admitted California to the Union as a part of the Compromise of 1850, on September 9 of that year. Indian civil rights, championed by Hugo REID, were not granted in the constitution, however. In the late 1850s the slavery question broke out again within the Democratic party, with David C. BRODERICK leading the Free Soilers and William M. GWIN leading the pro-southern wing. During the CIVIL WAR California proved to be invaluable to the Union cause.

The gold rush was one of the most colorful adventure stories in human history (see MINING, METAL; GOLD AND SILVER RUSHES; MINING LAW; and GOLD-RUSH TOWNS OF CALIFORNIA). It produced a remarkable outpouring of memoirs and was later much romanticized in fiction by such writers as Bret Harte. But in reality gold mining was excruciatingly hard labor. Most of the gold that individual prospectors could find in the banks and beds of the streams was soon gone, and placer mining gave way to quartz and hydraulic operations that required considerable capital. The cost of food and other supplies, primarily purchased in SACRAMENTO, was cruelly high, and the net earnings of the miners soon fell so low that most of the population of California was made up of bitterly disappointed men who had to remain there because they had no money for transportation back to their homes. Consequently there was a high crime rate and much violence and disorder, but also the beginnings of the western LABOR MOVEMENT. During the 1850s lynch mobs in the mining camps and more formal "committees of vigilance" in SAN FRANCISCO and other towns took the law into their own hands. Gross miscarriages of justice often resulted. Nonwhites in particular were shamefully mistreated. In the mining areas, mainly the mother lode country in the western foothills of the Sierra Nevada, Indians were often slaughtered for sport and Mexicans were driven out of the mines by threats of mass murder. Chinese miners were later permitted to work on claims that white miners had abandoned, provided they paid a heavy "foreign miners' license tax."

Gold production declined after reaching its peak in 1852, but the discovery of huge silver deposits in the Comstock Lode in western Nevada in 1859 revived the mining industry of the region, and San Francisco capital largely financed the Comstock mines. Manufacturing in California developed slowly, and early American agriculture in the state was severely hampered by the long and expensive court battles over land claims based on Mexican land grants. But wheat growing began to flourish in the 1860s, particularly in the Sacramento and San Joaquin valleys, which together form the great Central Valley. The wine industry grew rapidly in the 1860s in the coastal valleys of northern California, and in the following decade the growth of the citrus industry in southern California was phenomenal.

The completion in 1869 of the CENTRAL PACIFIC, the western section of the first transcontinental railroad, was a remarkable achievement made possible by huge loans and land grants from the federal government and by the employment of thousands of Chinese laborers. Theodore JUDAH, the brilliant young engineer who conceived the project, died in the early stages of the work. Four Sacramento businessmen of limited means, Leland STANFORD, Collis P. HUNTINGTON, Mark HOPKINS, and Charles CROCKER became the "Big Four" of California by reaping enormous profits from their very small original investments in the railroad. The SOUTHERN PACIFIC, as it was later called, became the dominant power not only in the economy of California but also in the state's government and politics. By gaining control of the river and coastal steamship companies along with its control of railroad facilities, the Southern Pacific enjoyed a virtually complete monopoly of transportation. By manipulating freight rates and politics in order to prevent any effective governmental regulation of the rates, and aided by the pre-railroad sentiments of Supreme Court Justice Stephen J. FIELD, it had the power to make or break almost any farmer, manufacturer, or miner in the region. Frank Norris' novel *The Octopus* presents a brilliant description of some of the railroad's practices.

"The terrible seventies," as the writer Gertrude Atherton called them, were a decade of depression and social turmoil, climaxed by the brief but spectacular appearance of the Workingmen's party of California. The San Francisco labor unions, still small and struggling for survival, did not trust the party and did not support it; it was made up, therefore, largely of the unemployed and the unorganized. Under the demogogic leadership of Denis KEARNEY, a self-educated Irish immigrant, the movement was vaguely anticapitalist and explicitly anti-Chinese.

California's second constitution, ratified in 1879, was the product of a convention in which workingmen from San Francisco were a large contingent of the delegates, though a hasty fusion of Republicans and Democrats kept them from having a statewide majority. Because of the prevailing distrust of elected legislatures, the new constitution covered matters that are properly the responsibility of a legislature. Still in force nearly a century later, it has required hundreds of amendments and is the longest written constitution in the world with the exception of those of India and Louisiana.

For nearly half a century the Southern Pacific's political machine had more control over the government of California than the state had over the railroad. William F. Herrin, the able chief counsel of the Southern Pacific who also headed its "political department" for nearly two decades after 1893, often exercised the power to select governors, legislators, and judges through a system of alliances with local political bosses. Anthony CAMINETTI was an early critic of the railroads, and a statewide rebellion against this corrupt system began in 1906 with a graft prosecution in San Francisco against the political machine of "boss" Abe RUEF, a brilliant but cynical lawyer whose Union Labor party was not actually more representative of labor than Denis Kearney's party had been. At the same time a "good government" movement gained control of Los Angeles. In 1907 the leaders of these two reform movements joined with other California progressives in a coalition to capture the statewide Republican party. The San Francisco leaders wished to name the statewide reform organization after President Theodore Roosevelt, whom they intensely admired, and who had personally intervened to help the San Francisco graft prosecution by arranging to lend it the services of federal prosecutor Francis J. Heney and federal detective William J. Burns. The southern California progressives, considerably more conservative, preferred the name of Lincoln. A compromise produced the name of the Lincoln-Roosevelt Republican League, and under this banner the California progressives secured the nomination and election of Hiram W. JOHNSON as governor in 1910, along with a progressive majority in the legislature.

Johnson then fulfilled his campaign promise to "kick the Southern Pacific Railroad out of politics," with such favorable results that even Herrin, in a remarkable address to the American Bar Association, concluded that "no railroad manager would agree to dispense with government regulation at the cost of returning to the old conditions." The remarkable body of reforms that Johnson pushed through the legislature of 1911 included not only effective regulation of railroads and other public utilities, but also the first state budget system, a workmen's compensation act, and a series of devices for greater popular control of politics and legislation. The progressives, borrowing partly from the ideas of the Populism of the 1890s, believed that government should be taken out of the hands of party bosses and given directly to the people. The direct primary system, adopted in 1909, had already taken the nomination of party candidates for state office away from state party conventions and given it directly to the voters. The initiative, the referendum, and the recall, approved in 1911, gave the voters the power to pass or repeal legislation independent of the legislature, and to remove elected officials. The cross-filing system, permitting a candidate to run for the nomination of more than one party, was established in 1913. A side effect of these measures was a weakening of the power, prestige, and responsibility of political parties in California politics, and this continued to be true even after the repeal of the cross-filing system in 1959. Moreover the success of Republican progressives in establishing the Republicans as the party of reform was a factor in the long series of defeats for the Democrats, which for decades made California almost a one-party state and thus further weakened its party system.

The twentieth century brought a great surge of population growth in California. Until the great earthquake and fire of April 18, 1906, San Francisco had been the undisputed metropolis with about one fourth of the state's population. But LOS ANGELES was growing rapidly, as southern California's warm winter climate and year-round sunshine became famous throughout the country. By 1920 the population of the Los Angeles metropolitan area surpassed that of the cities around San Francisco Bay.

The romantic lure of motion pictures also attracted many people to southern California. The first movie in southern California was made late in 1907 when a production of *The Count of Monte Cristo*, begun in Chicago but stalled by the approach of winter, was completed in Los Angeles. The Nestor Film Company set up the first studio in the neighboring village of Hollywood in 1911. For several years a number of independent studios violated the camera patents held by a "movie trust," and the nearness of the Mexican border was a great advantage when the independents needed to rush their cameras out of reach of the trust's lawyers and process servers. Within a few years the great majority of all motion pictures were being made in Hollywood (see MOTION PICTURE INDUSTRY).

Another major element in California's growth was the OIL INDUSTRY. Oil has been called "California's other mineral," and indeed the state's "black gold" became far more valuable than its yellow gold had ever been. Edward L. Doheny discovered rich deposits of oil in Los Angeles in 1892. In the early years of the twentieth century great new fields were brought into production in the San Joaquin valley. Still larger fields were discovered in the Los Angeles basin area in the early 1920s, at Huntington Beach, at Santa Fe Springs south of Whittier, and at Signal Hill in Long Beach. Another vast deposit was discovered at Wilmington in 1937. The oil from these fields proved extraordinarily suitable for the production of gasoline, and thus great quantities of this fuel became available in southern California at the very time and in the very region where the use of the automobile was spreading more rapidly than anywhere else in the world. By 1970 California had produced more than one sixth of the nation's oil.

The growth of urban population, industry, and agriculture resulted in a tremendous need for water, and this need created some of California's most controversial problems. San Francisco found its principal water supply in Hetch Hetchy, a beautiful valley within the boundaries of Yosemite National Park. But John Muir, founder of the Sierra Club and leader of the movement for the conservation of the natural beauty of the wilderness, carried on a bitter fight against the Hetch Hetchy dam project from 1908 to 1913 and delayed its construc-

tion for many years. Los Angeles reached out to the Owens valley, east of the Sierra, and completed an aqueduct from the Owens River in 1913, but the farmers of the Owens valley resisted even to the point of dynamiting the aqueduct. Southern California's insatiable thirst also led to several projects for supplying water from the Colorado River, such as the creation of the IMPERIAL VALLEY AND THE SALTON SEA. Hoover Dam on the Colorado, finished in 1936, provided flood control and hydroelectric power. The great Central Valley Project, built by the federal Bureau of Reclamation, was begun in the 1930s.

Beginning with the Newlands Reclamation Act of 1902, federal reclamation laws had limited to 160 acres the amount of land for which a single owner could purchase irrigation water from projects constructed by the federal government. Larger units of land were characteristic of California agriculture, and this became increasingly true as the twentieth century progressed. Huge government projects could provide water at a relatively low cost; but Congress refused to remove the 160-acre limit on "federal water," and the United States Supreme Court upheld the constitutionality of the limitation. This was a major factor in the decision of the state government to undertake its own vast project in order to provide water for larger farms, and incidentally also for domestic consumption and industrial use. In 1960, at the urging of Governor Edmund G. ("Pat") BROWN, the voters of California approved a $1.75 billion bond issue for the Feather River project, designed to bring water from the northern Sierra to the western San Joaquin valley and to southern California via the SACRAMENTO RIVER. This was by far the largest single project of any kind that an American state had ever undertaken, and it was intended as only the first of many projects in a huge state master plan for water development. But increasing resistance began to appear—from northern Californians who opposed the removal of their water to the south and from conservationists who feared damage to the natural environment.

The Great Depression of the 1930s, the worst and longest in American history, affected California even more severely than the nation as a whole. Oranges and other relatively expensive luxury food crops, in which California agriculture specialized, were the first to be dropped from stringent family budgets throughout the country. In 1932 California farm income was little more than half of what it had been in 1929, and the number of building permits was hardly more than one eighth of the peak figure of 1925. By 1934 nearly one fifth of the whole population of California was dependent on public relief. But no mere statistics can convey the real meaning of the Great Depression. Its meaning was in the suffering, anxiety, and grief of the millions whose lives it blighted. Elderly people suffered because it was especially difficult for them to find employment. Hundreds of thousands of old people had moved to southern California to retire, and had now lost their life savings in bank failures. In the 1920s most of them had been conservative, although many had become followers of religious evangelists such as Aimee Semple MacPherson. Now their interest shifted to political messiahs, notably Dr. Francis E. Townsend, an unemployed physician of Long Beach with a plan for "revolving pensions" that would give everyone over sixty years of age $200 a month that had to be spent within thirty days.

Most Californians, like most Americans, laid the blame for the depression on the Republican party, and in the election of 1932 the incumbent president, Herbert Hoover, was humiliatingly defeated not only in his home state of California but even in his home county of Santa Clara. Thus it was almost incredible that California failed to elect a Democratic governor in 1934. But radicalism ruined the chances of reform—as it has so often and typically done—by alarming and alienating the middle-of-the-road voters. Upton SINCLAIR, a famous novelist and pamphleteer who had previously run for governor on the Socialist ticket, captured the Democratic nomination in the primary election of 1934 with a plan called "End Poverty in California" (EPIC). Though he asserted that this plan of production "for use" rather than for profit would work within the capitalist system, it was so radical that it frightened many Democrats into voting for the conservative Republican candidate, Frank F. Merriam, who gained still other supporters by a flirtation with the Townsend Plan. Not until 1938 did California elect a New Deal governor, Culbert L. Olson, the first Democratic governor of California in the twentieth century.

During World War II the federal government spent nearly $400 billion, nearly one tenth of it in California alone, largely for ship-building and the AEROSPACE INDUSTRY. These great federal expenditures not only revived California's economy but launched it into a period of unprecedented growth that has continued for decades without a serious interruption. But the war also brought a tragic blunder. This was the forced evacuation of all persons of Japanese ancestry, regardless of whether they had been born in the United States and were American citizens. On the premise that they were liable to be disloyal and might commit acts of sabotage, the federal government confiscated the property of more than ninety-three thousand Japanese-Americans in California and imprisoned them behind barbed wire in "relocation" camps in interior states.

From 1943 to 1953 California's governor was Earl Warren (1891-1974), a progressive Republican who admired Hiram Johnson and sought to revive and continue the Johnson tradition in California politics. Warren was well aware that a majority of the state's registered voters had become Democrats during the depression, and had remained so. His policies were "nonpartisan" and liberal, and his support from voters of both parties was so great that he became the first governor of California to be elected three times. In 1953 President Dwight D. Eisenhower appointed him Chief Justice of the United States. By 1969, when he retired from that position, Warren had led the Supreme Court in an extraordinary series of pioneering decisions in the fields of civil rights and civil liberties. The most important of these was the unanimous decision of 1954, in *Brown* v. *Board of Education of Topeka*, that racial segregation in the public schools was unconstitutional. This ruling was particularly remarkable because Warren, as attorney general of California in 1942, had vigorously demanded the evacuation of Japanese-Americans. In this his opinion had reflected the historic anti-Oriental racism of many Californians. But in the intervening years he came to regard the decision as a mistake, considering the

"Japanese relocation" as completely unjust and racially discriminatory in general.

In 1958 a split in Republican leadership made possible the election of a Democratic governor, Edmund G. Brown. William F. Knowland, who had succeeded Robert A. Taft as Republican minority leader of the United States Senate, decided to run for governor of California on a platform of a state "right-to-work" law, outlawing the closed and union shops. This was a bitter blow to Knowland's fellow Republican Goodwin J. Knight, who had succeeded Earl Warren as governor and had hoped to run for another term. It was also a frontal assault on the power of organized labor, and the California labor unions rallied for the most intense and successful political campaign in their history, against both "right-to-work" and Knowland.

Brown's administration, from 1959 to 1967, was even more liberal than Warren's. The state continued to grow and prosper. In 1963 it passed New York as the most populous state, with a population nearly one tenth of the whole country's. The United States Census Bureau projected the state's population at nearly 25 million in 1975 and nearly 40 million in the year 2000. In annual production and income California ranked sixth among the *nations* of the world in 1965, after the United States, Russia, West Germany, Britain, and France, and slightly ahead of Japan. But in the later 1960s the state's rate of economic and population growth slowed down. Much of this growth had been the result of federal spending, especially in the aircraft, aerospace, and electronics industries. Much of the vastly expensive equipment that would finally send men to the moon had been developed in California laboratories and factories; but in the late 1960s the federal government sharply curtailed its expenditures not only for the space program but for the construction of intercontinental missiles as well. The opportunities that had attracted many scientists, engineers, and technicians to California suddenly gave way to mass unemployment in these fields.

Climate, as well as economic opportunity, had long been one of California's attractions. But the problem of smog, first noticed in Los Angeles in 1943, gradually became so severe that it resulted in a virtual change in the climate. With the rapid increase in the number of automobiles and trucks, smog eventually covered not only every metropolitan area but even moved into the interior valleys. Water pollution, urban and suburban sprawl, and overcrowding became chronic, not only in the cities but even in such places as Yosemite National Park and Lake Tahoe during the summer seasons. Such measures as the creation of the Point Reyes National Seashore and the Redwood National Park failed to keep pace with the steady encroachments upon California's cherished wilderness. In the California system of values, growth had been the greatest good. Suddenly it seemed to have become an evil.

Race relations were another major problem. The Japanese-Americans made a remarkable recovery from their wartime disaster and achieved a high degree of social advancement. But Negroes (see NEGROES IN THE FAR WEST) and Mexican-Americans remained severely oppressed. Before World War II, black people had numbered less than two percent of the state's population. But the wartime demand for labor in the shipyards and other war industries resulted in a tremendous migration of Negroes to California, mainly from the rural South. By the 1960s the proportion of Negroes had risen to about six percent; and instead of being spread throughout the state they were concentrated in all-black neighborhoods in the cities of Los Angeles, San Francisco, Oakland, Berkeley, Richmond, and Vallejo. The United States Supreme Court decision of 1954 had little meaing in the face of the de facto segregation in neighborhood schools. One of the liberal measures supported by Governor Brown was a law of 1963, introduced by Negro Assemblyman Byron Rumford of Berkeley, which tried to limit racial discrimination in housing. This measure produced a sharp "white backlash." In 1964 the California Real Estate Association sponsored Proposition 14, an initiative measure amending the state constitution to ban all laws that might attempt to limit the "right" of the owners of property to discriminate on racial grounds in its rental or sale. Although the United States Supreme Court later declared this measure unconstitutional, the white majority of the state's voters approved it overwhelmingly. Resentment against Proposition 14 played an important part in the riot that occurred in the Negro ghetto of Watts in southern Los Angeles in August 1965. In turn, white fear of Negro riots played a major part in turning white majority sentiment against the liberal policies of Governor Brown.

The Mexican-Americans were by far the largest ethnic minority in California. They formed about one tenth of the state's population in the middle decades of the twentieth century, and there were more persons of Mexican descent in Los Angeles than in any other city in the world except the capital of Mexico itself. Mexican-Americans in Los Angeles were concentrated in the eastern part of the city, almost to the degree that the Negroes were concentrated in the southern part of it. But unlike the Negroes, many Mexican-Americans worked in the rural areas as agricultural laborers and lived in rural slums that were often worse than the urban *barrios* or ghettos. Hope for improvement of their condition appeared in the 1960s when Cesar CHAVEZ, a leader of the CHICANO LIBERATION MOVEMENT, formed the first successful labor union in the history of California agriculture.

A long series of mass disorders on college and university campuses, beginning with the "free speech movement" at the University of California at Berkeley in the autumn of 1964, and usually led by radical students, alarmed and alienated a great many voters and contributed to a strong conservative reaction in state politics. Public resentment against student unrest interacted with a growing public rebellion against increased taxes. Many taxpayers resented the use of their money to support public colleges and universities for the education of students who tried to shut them down. Ronald Reagan, a well-known motion-picture actor and television personality, emerged as the leader of California conservatism and became the Republican candidate for governor in 1966. Although he had never before held public office, Reagan's promises to "cut, squeeze and trim" the costs of government, and to deal vigorously with campus disorders, had great appeal to voters of both parties, and led to an overwhelming victory in his campaign against Governor Brown. For his political philosophy and program Reagan adopted the name "the Creative Society," to stress his belief that private

enterprise with the greatest possible freedom from government control was the most important creative force in America. In practice, this was a matter of degree, and partnership between government and private industry continues to characterize the economic development of California.

Recent one-volume histories include those by Walton Bean, *California* (1968); and John W. Caughey, *California*, 3rd ed. (1970).—W. B.

California Indians. See INDIANS OF CALIFORNIA.

California missions. See list at MISSIONS, CALIFORNIA.

California rancho system. The rancho system, introduced by the Mexicans after 1820, divided California's vast arable spaces into immense tracts of pastoral land, devoted to the production of cattle hides. This was Mexico's plan to develop its northern province and protect it against possible Russian or Anglo-American encroachment. By the 1820s it had become clear that the mission system, Spain's approach to the same problem, was a failure at establishing decisive control of the area. The missions had developed, however, a profitable system of cattle production that provided the economic basis of the ranchos. With secularization of mission lands after 1834, Mexico moved swiftly to convert to the new system. In 1820 only twenty ranchos existed in California; by 1840 the number had jumped to over six hundred.

Ranchos existed as near-feudal fiefs, distinct social and political units, each controlled by a dominant ranchero family. Grants of land in San Diego County to Pio and Andres Pico totaled 100,000 acres. The Nieto family was granted 200,000 acres in 1841 on which was built the largest adobe house (Rancho Los Cerritos) in southern California in 1844. Among their other holdings, the Carillo family owned all of Santa Rosa Island, which was operated as a sheep ranch. Grants of similar size were made along the coast and in the area of San Francisco Bay. Labor was provided by former mission Indians, now concentrated in small rancherias. These Indians were bound to the rancho, as they had been to the missions, in a peonage very close to slavery. This feudal system lacked any real central authority. Separated by hundreds of miles of desert, the government of Mexico was able to exert only minimal influence over California politics, which in the void consisted mainly of a series of feuds between rancheros.

The ruling class, the *gente de razón*, was by no means isolated from the rest of the world, however. The production of hides demanded access to world leather markets. Unable to meet this need itself, Mexico granted a lucrative trading concession to hungry Yankee traders. In return for hides, Yankees supplied the rancheros with needed commodities and the amenities that helped to create the ranchero life-style. Rancho California was in this sense a society in an international set; maritime commerce created pastoral California just as the ranchos helped in the accumulation of New England capital. The integration of such Anglo-Americans as Abel Stearns, Thomas O. LARKIN, and John T. Warner (see WARNER'S RANCH) into California society was a consequence of this dialectical relationship. The seeds of American acquisition were sown in the trading concessions of the 1820s.

In northern California, where as a consequence of the gold rush Anglo penetration was most profound, the rancho system rapidly gave way to more urban, industrial, or agricultural patterns of land use. But in southern California the system extended past 1850. The federal land act of 1851 set up a commission to determine the validity of ranchero land claims, and through the workings of the commission most California landholders were replaced by Anglos by the late 1850s. This was a clear violation of the spirit, if not the letter, of the Treaty of Guadalupe Hidalgo's guarantee of full rights of liberty, property, and religion to all Mexican-Americans. This change notwithstanding, the basic social and economic patterns of preconquest California remained in the south. Land use remained basically pastoral, and while free labor made steady inroads, Indians and mestizos continued to be attached to the ranches, supplying cheap, essential labor. Consequently, while formally controlled by Anglos, southern California retained its dominant Hispanic culture well into the second half of the century.

The gold-rush years were the golden years for the new Anglo ranchers. As mining and urban growth opened new markets in the north, the ranches shifted to production of beef cattle. The early 1850s saw huge cattle drives up the coast or through the Tehachapi Mountains, thus predating the Texas drives so fixed in American romantic memory. But these northern markets were soon invaded by competitors from the East. They eventually out-priced the southern California cattlemen, who continued to rely on old Mexican styles of operation better suited to an earlier, less capitalistic age. Too, the prolonged drought of the early 1860s virtually destroyed the operation of many of the southern ranches.

The post-Civil War years were the ones of great change for California. Massive numbers of immigrants poured into the state, many settling in the south. Coming on the heels of the disastrous drought, the influx prompted many ranches to sell out and others to diversify their holdings. Few were as successful at keeping their lands intact as was the consortium of capitalists who combined several coastal ranchos into the huge IRVINE RANCH. Most grants were broken up, giving way to new agricultural and urban patterns of development. With the demise of the pastoral way of life, there was little need for a peonage system, and Hispanic influence, carried by the integration of Indians and mestizos into the political economy, began to fade. Modern California was born with the final collapse of the rancho system.

See Robert Glass Cleland, *Cattle on a Thousand Hills* (1951); C. Alan Hutchinson, *Frontier Settlement in Mexican California* (1969); and Leonard Pitt, *The Decline of the Californios* (1966).—J. F.

California Trail. In 1841 an emigrant party led by John Bartleson left the Oregon Trail at Soda Springs, Idaho, headed southwest to the Humboldt River, followed this stream to its sink, thence along the Carson River to the Walker River, and across the Sierra Nevada between the headwaters of the Walker and the Stanislaus River. They had traveled, in part, a route that was later to be known as the California Trail. Unlike the typical emigrant party, this group was composed almost wholly of young men; only one wife and her child were present. They had meager funds and were ignorant of the geography of the West. Their lack of preparation for the journey had not been apparent on the trip to

Soda Springs because to that point they were supervised by an experienced mountain man, Thomas Fitzpatrick, as guide, and accompanied by Pierre De Smet, a Jesuit missionary, both of whom went on to Oregon. Once the California-bound party was on its own, however, inexperience and a lack of leadership led to dissension. Bartleson and a select group of horsemen abandoned the main party for a time, and John BIDWELL assumed command. Thirty-three persons finally arrived in California, the first settlers to make the overland journey.

No emigrant parties started for California in 1842. Joseph B. Chiles, a member of the Bartleson-Bidwell party, went east to lead the migration of the following year. The company of 1843, approximately thirty men and a number of women and children, was unusually well equipped, carrying household belongings in wagons instead of on pack animals, but flour and other provisions that they had expected to purchase along the trail were not available. The situation was critical. At Fort Hall, Idaho, the company divided, with Chiles leading a group of thirteen men on horseback to Fort Boise, thence westward along the Malheur River. They were attempting to work their way into northern California via the Pit River Canyon, thus outflanking the Sierra. At the outset they had hoped to travel rapidly and procure relief for the main party, but their journey was too time-consuming. The wagon train was placed in charge of Joseph Reddeford WALKER, who followed the Humboldt River route and on to the Walker River. Rather than attempt the crossing made in 1841, he led the emigrants southward through the Owens valley and through the pass bearing his name into the southern part of the San Joaquin valley. They had found it necessary to abandon their wagons and resort to pack horses.

In 1844 the Stephens-Murphy party, upon reaching the sink of the Humboldt River, elected to cross the Sierra as directly westward as possible. They thereby opened up the Truckee River route, to be used extensively by future emigrants as a trail, by rail and by highway. This party also had the distinction of being the first group to bring their wagons into California, having mastered the crest of the range via Emigrant Gap into Bear valley. One student of the California Trail has suggested that up to this point the story emphasized the struggle of man against nature, but by 1845 it was man against man. Five or six parties, involving 250 individuals, reached California that year. The largest group, approximately one hundred, led by William B. Ide, experienced brutality and violence. Solomon P. Sublette led a well-equipped and fast-moving party of fifteen men into Sutter's Fort. Thirteen young men, known as the Swasey-Todd party, also crossed the Sierra by the Truckee route into the Sacramento valley. James Clyman, who had been with the Bartleson-Bidwell party of 1841, brought a party of approximately forty into California by a long route to the Willamette valley of Oregon and then southward. The season of 1845 was also notable for two horseback parties on the trail led by two famous explorers, John C. Frémont and Lansford W. Hastings.

The pioneers who came west in 1846 were in a new category, for the war with Mexico had broken out and by the time the settlers reached California the American flag was flying over the land. There were at least two hundred wagons on the trail that year headed for

California, bringing between one thousand and fifteen hundred men, women, and children. Most famous of all the parties was that led by George and Jacob Donner (see DONNER PARTY). This group, electing to follow the Hastings' Cutoff to the south and west of the Great Salt Lake rather than stay on the regular California Trail to the north of the lake, became stranded in the salt flats and lost their way and valuable time. Finally reaching the eastern slope of the Sierra late in the season after the first fall of snow, chronic indecision delayed their crossing the summit. A snowstorm blocked the crest of the mountains and the party was forced to make winter camp. Incredible suffering resulted, with forty of the eighty-nine members of the party perishing. Some of those determined to survive apparently resorted to cannibalism, living off the dead and dying. News of the Donner tragedy resulted in diminished travel along the California Trail and across the summit of the central Sierra.

Four men have left records of their migration along the Truckee River route in 1847, and three of them were members of the discharged Mormon Battalion of Mexican War fame, traveling in a west-east direction to join their families in the Great Basin. There are no known diaries of migration by the Truckee route in 1848. With the discovery of gold in California, this route became a favorite of the Argonauts, who continued to pour into the state during the years 1849-52.

George Stewart, *The California Trail* (1962), is the standard work on pioneer migration to California between 1841 and 1846; his popular and dramatic account of the Donner party is *Ordeal by Hunger* (1960). The first serious investigation of this incident was made by Charles F. McGlashan, whose useful work *History of the Donner Party* was republished in 1947. Dale Morgan, in *Overland in 1846* (1963), has examined every extant account of the migration on the trail during this single year, tabulated and cross-referenced the journey of each party, and published several new diaries.—W. T. J.

Call, Richard Keith (1792-1862). Soldier and Florida politician. Born near Petersburg, Virginia, Call moved at an early age to Kentucky with his widowed mother and three brothers. In 1811 he enrolled in Mt. Pleasant Academy near Clarksville, Tennessee, and was studying there when the War of 1812 broke out. In 1813 he joined a Tennessee militia unit as a third lieutenant and under the command of Andrew Jackson fought in the campaigns against the Creek Indians in 1813 and 1814. After Jackson was commissioned in the Regular Army Call was made a first lieutenant in the Forty-fourth Infantry Regiment and took part in Jackson's expulsion of the British from Pensacola and the battles of New Orleans in December 1814 and January 1815. Soon after, he was promoted to captain. Remaining in the army, he participated in Jackson's 1818 invasion of Florida and was a minor functionary in Jackson's temporary government in Pensacola.

When Jackson was designated to receive Florida from Spain in 1821, Call accompanied him as an aide. This began Call's lifelong association with Florida. He opened a law practice in Pensacola and became a member of the town council. After Congress established territorial government in 1822, Call served in the first and second Legislative Councils. In 1823 President James Monroe commissioned him brigadier general of the West Florida militia and later in the year he was elected for a two-year term as territorial delegate to Congress. The following year he married Mary Kirkman of Nashville in a ceremony at the Hermitage. Settling in Tallahassee in 1825, he became receiver of public monies at the federal land office and held that position until President Jackson appointed him governor of Florida in 1836. During this period he invested in extensive landholdings, practiced law, and headed a corporation that built a railway south from Tallahassee to St. Marks. When he became governor, he was entrusted with command of the United States forces in Florida, succeeding Winfield Scott. An unsuccessful campaign resulted in his being relieved in favor of General Thomas S. Jesup. Call was critical of government war policy during the Van Buren administration and associated himself with a group that eventually became known as the Whig party. Accordingly, he was removed from the governorship in 1839. Becoming an ardent Whig, he campaigned for William Henry Harrison and was reinstated as governor by him in 1841. After being defeated in 1845 for the governorship in the first election under the state government, he retired to his plantation and did not seek office again. He was active in the Whig party, however, and after its demise he went with many Whigs into the short-lived American party in 1855. His later days were spent fighting sectionalism and defending the Union. Though he favored Stephen A. Douglas for the presidency, after the Democratic split in 1860 he joined the Constitutional Union party. Bitter over the secession of Florida, he went into seclusion in 1861 and died a year later in Tallahassee.

See Herbert J. Doherty, Jr., *Richard Keith Call, Southern Unionist* (1961); and Ellen Call Long, *Florida Breezes: or Florida, New and Old*, reprinted in the Floridiana Facsimile and Reprint Series (1962).—H. J. D.

Camden, Johnson Newlon (1828-1908). Industrialist and West Virginia politician. Born near Weston, (West) Virginia, to a politically prominent family, Camden held a local office at the age of seventeen and in 1847 won an appointment to West Point. But he abandoned military life in 1849 in favor of the family avocations of land, law, and politics. After a brief apprenticeship as the appointed prosecuting attorney of Braxton County, he was elected to the same office in Nicholas County in 1852 but changed course again to take up new opportunities in banking and land speculation at Weston.

His interest in land led him in 1859 into the newly opened Burning Springs oil field near Parkersburg, which marked the beginning of Camden's transition from speculator to industrialist. Moving rapidly through the landowning and production phases of the industry, he organized a refining company in 1866. In 1875 he joined forces with the Standard Oil Company and became its principal manager in the Ohio valley fields and Baltimore market while developing extensive coal and timber properties of his own in northern and central West Virginia. Meanwhile he returned to politics in 1868 and with another industrialist, Henry G. Davis, developed a powerful Democratic organization based on public and private patronage and domination of the party press and organizational machinery. Elected United States senator in 1881 and again in 1893, Camden was a controversial but determined spokesman for the oil and coal industries and remained influential in West

Virginia politics until the onset of his final illness in 1906.

Festus P. Summers' *Johnson Newlon Camden: A Study in Individualism* (1937) is a comprehensive and readable scholarly treatment, but it fails to place Camden's political career in the context of the political and social changes wrought by industrialism in the Appalachian region. In the absence of published work of comparable quality, Summers' study must be supplemented by the extensive collections of papers of Camden, Henry G. Davis, Stephen B. Elkins, A. B. Fleming, and other political and business leaders in the West Virginia Collection, West Virginia University Library, Morgantown. —J. A. W.

camel experiment (1855-1900). In 1855 the army assembled about seventy-five camels at Camp Verde, near Bandera Pass, Texas, to test their usefulness as pack-train animals. When Secretary of War Jefferson Davis left office in 1857, interest declined; and although camels were found useful and practical, the experiment was finally terminated. Camels were also used in the mines of the American Northwest and even in British Columbia.

See Lewis Burt Lesley, *Uncle Sam's Camels: The Journal of May Humphreys Stacey* (1929), and William S. Lewis, "The Camel Pack Trains in the Mining Camps of the West," *Washington Historical Quarterly* (October 1928).—R. A. B.

Caminetti, Anthony (1854-1923). California politician. Caminetti was born in the mother lode town of Jackson, Amador County, California. The son of Italian immigrants who had come to California in search of gold, Caminetti worked his way through school and established a law practice in Jackson. In 1877, at the age of twenty-three, he was elected district attorney of Amador County and was reelected in 1879.

The young and energetic county prosecutor was elected as a Democrat to the state assembly in 1882 and to the state senate in 1886. In the legislature, Caminetti became noted as a reformer and ardent opponent of machine-dominated politics. He authored the amendments that established the first state-owned railroad in California, thereby thwarting the plans of the Southern Pacific Railroad for control of the San Francisco waterfront. In educational matters, Caminetti secured amendments that provided additional school facilities for California's rural regions. He is considered the "father" of the California junior college.

In 1890 Caminetti was the first native-born Californian of non-Mexican heritage to be elected to Congress. During his two terms in office he was actively involved in mining and river issues. In 1893 he secured the passage of the Caminetti mining act, which provided for the resumption of hydraulic mining in California and the establishment of the California Debris Commission for preventing damage to the rivers and improving their navigability. In other matters Caminetti introduced legislation calling for federal government operation of the Union Pacific and Central Pacific railroads between Omaha and Sacramento, and he participated actively in a successful fight against a railroad funding bill.

Following defeat for reelection to Congress in 1894, Caminetti returned to California and resumed his law practice before being reelected to the state assembly in 1896. Between 1906 and 1913 Caminetti was in the state senate. He sponsored many progressive political and economic measures and continued to be a thorn in the side of the railroad interests. Caminetti's staunchly pro-labor attitude, his fear that the white workingmen could not compete with inexpensive Asian labor, and his desire to make political capital out of this issue for his party, led him to become one of the legislature's leading exponents of anti-Asian immigration legislation.

In 1913 President Woodrow Wilson appointed Caminetti commissioner-general of immigration. He served in that capacity throughout the Wilsonian period, gaining notoriety for his illiberal position on immigration matters. His fear of radicalism in any form led him to deport the noted anarchist Emma Goldman and to play a major role in the famous "Red scare" roundup and deportation of suspected alien radicals. As a friend of organized labor, Caminetti lent his support to the movement for general immigration restriction legislation, which culminated in the laws of 1921 and 1924. After his retirement from national office, he returned to California and practiced law.—J. G.

Campbell, Alexander. See DISCIPLES OF CHRIST.

Campbell, Robert (1804-1879). Mountain man and merchant. Campbell was born in Tyrone County, Ireland, but came to St. Louis in 1824. Suffering from lung disease, he joined General William H. Ashley's 1825 fur-trading expedition to recover his health. A capable, highly intelligent, fair-minded young man, Campbell soon became a brigade leader. He counted as his close friends James Bridger, Thomas Fitzpatrick, William Sublette, and Jedediah Smith. He admired Bridger so much that at various times he cared for Bridger's children. In turn, Smith held Campbell in such great respect that he named Campbell his executor. An even stronger friendship developed between Sublette and Campbell, who as partners in a supply firm dominated the carrying goods trade to the mountains.

Although Campbell claimed that he did not really care for the wilderness life, he was a remarkable success as a trapper and trader. His expeditions took him over the Northern Plains and Rockies and as far west as the Great Salt Lake. On the way to the 1828 rendezvous he and his men were attacked by Blackfoot at the "fight in the Willows," but the timely arrival of a rescue party saved their lives. In 1829 he trapped in Crow country but returned to St. Louis after that to engage in supplying traders and trappers in the field. He visited his native Ireland in 1830-31. In 1832 he carried goods to the fur-trading rendezvous of that year on his own account. He fought the Blackfoot in the battle of Pierre's Hole (1832) and is credited with saving Sublette's life when the latter was wounded. In December 1832, Campbell and Sublette became partners in the supply trade, a business that produced a fortune for both men. The firm's success was undoubtedly aided by the fact that Campbell's brother, Hugh, lived in Philadelphia, where he was able to buy needed supplies and dispose of furs. Sublette's brother, Milton, was also active in the mountains.

So ambitious were Campbell and Sublette that in the spring of 1833 they decided to challenge the supremacy of the American Fur Company on the upper Missouri by building an "opposition" post, Fort William, only four miles from the American Fur Company's Fort Union. It was Campbell who manned the post in 1833-34 and who countered the efforts of the brilliant Kenneth McKenzie at Fort Union to ruin the Sublette-Campbell enterprise. While McKenzie and the American Fur Company eventually won the contest, Sublette and Campbell persuaded the American Fur Company to stay out of the mountain trade for a year in return for their own withdrawal from the river trade. In 1834 Sublette and Campbell built Fort Laramie (also called Fort William in its early days) in southeastern Wyoming on the Laramie River, an impressive log stronghold that rivaled Bent's Fort in size. But after a short time Laramie, too, became the property of the American Fur Company. Although Campbell ended his formal partnership with Sublette in 1842, they remained friends.

Campbell devoted the rest of his life to the mercantile business in St. Louis. A man of great wealth, he was president of both the State Bank of Missouri and the Merchants' National Bank and owned a hotel. In 1851 Campbell was appointed a commissioner to the Laramie Indian conference that his old friend Thomas Fitzpatrick, now agent to the Plains tribes, had called to effect a general peace and to mark territorial boundaries between tribes. At the request of President Grant, Campbell served on a second Indian treaty-making commission in 1869.

Better educated and more articulate than most mountain men, Campbell left a number of papers and letters covering the years 1825-79; they are located in the Missouri Historical Society (St. Louis). Some of these appear in Robert Campbell, *The Rocky Mountain Letters of Robert Campbell* (1955), and Stella M. Drumm and Isaac H. Lionberger, eds., "Correspondence of Robert Campbell, 1834-1845," *Glimpses of the Past*, vol. 7 (January-June 1941). See also Hiram M. Chittenden, *The History of the American Fur Trade in the Far West* (1902); Dale L. Morgan and Eleanor T. Harris, eds., *Rocky Mountain Journals of William Marshall Anderson* (1967); and John E. Sunder, *Bill Sublette, Mountain Man* (1959).—G. B. D.

Campbell, Thomas. See DISCIPLES OF CHRIST.

Campbell, Walter. See Stanley VESTAL.

Camp Grant massacre. By the 1870s, the "Apache menace" in southern Arizona had reached its peak. The population of non-Indian settlers, including miners, ranchers, and cattlemen, was on the increase. United States military efforts had not yet brought the various bands of Chiricahua and Western Apache to terms. As competition for land and resources intensified, so did Apache practices of raiding and warfare and non-Indians' habit of "punishment" killings.

To avoid the many problems and dangers of fighting, early in 1871 the Arivaipa band of the San Carlos group of Western Apache—a semisedentary farming, hunting, and gathering group—sought and received asylum within five miles of Camp Grant, a United States military post near the junction of Arivaipa Creek and the San Pedro River in southern Arizona. Their leader was Hackibanzin, better known to whites as ESKIMINZIN; the commander of the post was First Lieutenant Royal Emerson Whitman, Third Regiment, United States Cavalry. The year 1871 saw the United States in the midst of President Grant's "peace policy" toward Indians, but uncertain that he had authority to grant the Apache asylum next to his post, Lieutenant Whitman wrote the department commander, General George Stoneman, for clear instructions. What he got in reply

was a message that his communication was not in the correct military form: the contents of the letter had not been summarized on the outside flap. In disgust, Whitman chose to continue to offer asylum and to act on his own discretion.

In a short time nearly five hundred Arivaipa bandsmen were living at Camp Grant. And also in a short time, unknown Apache attacked a baggage train in the Pinal Mountains and killed a man and kidnapped a woman at Tubac, more than fifty miles from Camp Grant. There were another half-dozen raids and killings in March 1871 that were blamed on the Apache by the Tucson *Citizen*, a local newspaper. Eskiminzin's people became the suspects.

Without warning, on the morning of April 30, 1871, the Tucson Committee of Public Safety, composed of six Anglos, including William Sanders Oury, and forty-eight Mexicans, including Jesus María Elias, the expedition commander, descended on the sleeping Apache camp. The committee's allies, who seem to have done most of the work, were ninety-four Papago Indians, traditional enemies of the Apache. When it was over, about a hundred Apache men, women, and children lay dead. Indeed, of those buried by the army a day later, an old man and a "well-grown" boy were the only adult males; the others were women and children. Twenty-seven captive Apache children were sold into slavery or given away to Papago families. Only six of them were ever returned. None of the attackers were killed.

Tucsonans had the temerity to call for the removal of Lieutenant Whitman for having given the Apache asylum in the first place. Whitman was ordered to stand trial in a court-martial, but the proceedings were dropped. A storm of protest in the East over the massacre finally forced a courtroom trial of the perpetrators, including the Papago, in December 1871. The trial, which was held in Tucson, lasted five days. The verdict of acquittal was rendered in nineteen minutes.

Coming, as it had, only six years after the Sand Creek massacre, the Camp Grant massacre convinced many eastern Americans that westerners had an undying hatred for all Indians. President Grant characterized the attack as one of "purely murder," and it served as an additional impetus in the long, slow climb toward a humane federal Indian policy.

See James R. Hastings, "The Tragedy at Camp Grant," *Arizona and the West*, vol. 1, no. 2 (1959); and Don Schellie, *Vast Domain of Blood* (1968).—B. L. F.

camp meeting. See REVIVALISM.

Canadian-American problems. A host of problems have plagued Canadian-American relations for many years, and it was not until after the turn of the twentieth century that the two peoples separated by a highly artificial boundary line learned at last to live in peace. From the very beginning of American history there had existed a feeling in some people that Canada and the British colonies along the Atlantic coast should properly be under one administration, and there was strong colonial support for the mother country during the Anglo-French wars of the eighteenth century. The Quebec Act of the period just before the American Revolution, which liberally provided for the governance of Canada under Britain and seemed a bid for Canadian support against American independence, was a factor inspiring many Americans to revolution; and one of the first acts of the revolutionary colonists was to attempt to seize Canada and make it the fourteenth state. Strong sentiment for annexation existed all through the nineteenth century, and there was considerable sentiment for the same on the Canadian side until the British provided for Canadian self-government after the American Civil War.

Meanwhile other issues were arising between Americans and Canadians. The boundary was set out in treaties with the British government in 1818, 1842, and 1846, with a final rectification by the German emperor in 1872. The War of 1812 and the Civil War raised the old desire for annexation, and in the Civil War there were border incidents that made the North feel that the Canadians under British sponsorship might be unduly encouraging the southerners. An armed raid by a Canadian-based southern party into the Vermont town of St. Albans incensed the North, and there was strong talk of retaliation. In the years after the Civil War the old fisheries question, which had agitated British-American relations ever since the end of the Revolution, rose to prominence again. The Americans sought to adjourn it in the Treaty of Washington of 1871, which, although devoted primarily to arranging the arbitration of the *Alabama* claims, also arranged for the Americans to have inshore fishing privileges for a period of at least ten years, for a cash equivalent of $5.5 million. During the agitation of the *Alabama* issue in the United States, the question of annexation reappeared, albeit indirectly. It was raised by Senator Charles Sumner, who in a notable Senate speech considered that the depredations of the Confederate raiders had doubled the length of the war and that the sum owed to the United States from Great Britain was so large that only a huge act of indemnity would suffice. The fisheries article of the Treaty of Washington expired in 1885, and the fisheries dispute, thus reopened, continued intil it was arbitrated in 1910.

The last of the major problems between Canadians and Americans turned out to be the boundary of Alaska, which created a diplomatic stir at the turn of the twentieth century. When gold was discovered in the Canadian Klondike in 1896, Canadians raised the issue of the uncertain boundaries of the panhandle, boundaries that traced back to the geographical uncertainties of the Anglo-Russian treaty of 1825. The intent of that treaty was clear: the Russians were seeking to exclude the British from the sea, down to the parallel of 54°40', and the British were agreeing to this. The Canadians sought to reinterpret the arrangement, and by taking the issue to arbitration had at least some chance of getting additional territory. President Theodore Roosevelt, incensed at this maneuver, arranged a mock arbitration in 1903 before a board of six members he carefully denominated a tribunal, not an arbitral tribunal. He appointed three American partisans and thus had assurance that the United States could not lose, and if one of the three British-Canadian members budged he might well win. That is what happened, although in the decision of that year the tribunal, so as to give the appearance of compromise, awarded a slight amount of territory to the Canadians.

Since the boundary controversy, the relations between the United States and Canada have improved dramatically, partly because of cooperation in two world wars and the uneasy peace following the second. Today there is general harmony between the two peoples. This is not to say that there are not continuing difficulties that demand negotiation and arrangement. The problem of air defense of the North American continent has bothered and concerned the Canadians, for much of that defense, presumably against Soviet Russia, has required the use of Canadian soil or airspace. With Canadian cooperation, the United States during the early 1950s constructed across Canada's northern reaches the Distant Early Warning (DEW) line, a costly network of radar warning stations against incoming Russian planes. That network quickly became obsolete when the superpowers largely replaced their planes with missiles. Defense against incoming Russian missiles thereupon required the detonation of American anti-missile missiles over Canadian airspace. Would the American government ask the Canadian government for permission in advance? Would there be time? Statements by American officials, civil and military, about the operation of air defenses in Canada's airspace have sometimes raised a furor in the Canadian press and even in government circles.

The single most important contribution to the study of Canadian-American relations is a cooperative series of twenty-five volumes for the Carnegie Endowment for International Peace under the editorship of James T. Shotwell, capped by John Bartlet Brebner, *North American Triangle* (1945). For its special subject, see Robin W. Winks, *Canada and the United States: The Civil War Years* (1960).—R. H. F.

Canadian frontier. See FRONTIER, CANADA.

Canadian Shield. See PHYSIOGRAPHY OF THE UNITED STATES.

canal era. The canal era opened in 1817 when New York State, under the leadership of Governor DeWitt Clinton, undertook to construct a canal from the Hudson River through thinly settled territory to Lake Erie. Large parts of upstate New York were thus accessible for settlement and, equally important, trade between the interior of America and New York was opened. Though the course to be followed by the Erie Canal was not quite a "water level route"—as the New York Central Railroad with its substantially parallel line was later to advertise—it was the lowest route into the interior between the St. Lawrence waterway and that around the southern Appalachians, a truly natural route, as the highest point was only 650 feet above the Hudson at Albany. At the same time, New York adopted the plan to connect Lake Champlain with the Hudson by canal.

Even for New York it was an enormous undertaking to build a 363-mile waterway with eighty-three locks and eighteen aqueducts, the more so because efforts to obtain federal aid were unavailing. Wealthy landowners, such as the investors in the Holland Land Company, John Greig, and managers of the Pulteney estate, were among its principal advocates; merchants, bankers, and residents along the route also supported it. Some enthusiasts were persuaded to grant land for the enterprise, but essentially it had to be supported by the state. Funds were forthcoming, at first from locally interested people, but later John Jacob Astor and New York City banks made large subscriptions. Construction was pushed forward and by 1825 the entire canal was completed and in operation. Well before 1825 stretches of the canal were opened for use, and traffic was astonishingly large.

The Erie Canal was a brilliant success in every way. It was a training ground for engineers and contractors who were to build other canals and, later, railroads. It opened upstate New York to settlement and made possible a transformation from subsistence farming to commercial agriculture. It stimulated the founding and growth of cities all the way from Albany to Buffalo and enabled New York City to outstrip all Atlantic competitors in the struggle for domination of the transatlantic trade. It began the reversal of trade routes by shifting a part of the flour, wheat, and other exports from New Orleans at the mouth of the Mississippi to New York at the mouth of the Hudson. The Erie Canal and other canals and, later, railroads, by bringing in the cheaply produced wheat and flour of the West, made agricultural changes necessary in the Northeast; diversified farming, with increasing emphasis upon dairying, took the place of wheat growing. The great volume of freight and passenger traffic on the canal, the large income from tolls, and the swift rise of cities along the way, all brought home to Americans the energizing effects of canals. Everywhere along the Atlantic seaboard there was a demand for canals to tap the rich trade New York was enjoying. In the trans-Appalachian area, the demand was for canals to provide access to the Great Lakes and to the Ohio and the Mississippi rivers.

New York itself took the lead in projecting branch canals to parallel the Black, the Seneca, the Genesee, the Chemung, the Chenango, and the Susquehanna rivers. Pennsylvania undertook to connect the Susquehanna River with the Allegheny River by way of the Juniata and a portage over the crest of the Alleghenies, and also planned to bring the trade of southern New York to Philadelphia by a canal along the east branch of the Susquehanna to Waverly at the New York line and through the Union Canal to the "City of Brotherly Love." Maryland planned the construction of the Chesapeake and Ohio Canal to parallel the Potomac River from Georgetown to Cumberland, the eastern point of the National Road at that time. Virginia came forth with a plan for the construction of the James River and Kanawha Canal, which might by some miraculous way manage to breach the mountains and gain a share of the western trade. Ohio began a canal to connect the Ohio River at Portsmouth with Lake Erie at Cleveland, and other ventures were adopted by Indiana and Illinois. At the same time, Albert Gallatin's plan for building canals across the headlands on the Atlantic was taken up and three of his proposals were carried to completion: the Chesapeake and Delaware Canal, the Delaware and Raritan Canal, and the Dismal Swamp Canal connecting Chesapeake Bay with Albemarle Sound. Before the canal era had passed, every state east of the Mississippi had experimented with canals.

Pennsylvania and New York, the wealthiest states, were left to build their own improvements, but most other major projects were subsidized to some extent by the federal government. Congress was persuaded to permit surveys for canals to be made by the Corps of Engineers and to subscribe to the stock of the Chesapeake and Delaware, the Chesapeake and Ohio, the Dismal Swamp Canal, and the Louisville and Portland Canal around the falls of the Ohio at Louisville. There was another way to give aid, however, which strict constructionists found more acceptable than stock subscriptions: to give a broad right-of-way through the public lands plus alternate sections of land for a distance of five miles on each side of the routes. Since reserved sections within the ten-mile strip were doubled in price on the assumption that construction of the canal would enhance land values, the government would derive from its reserved sections as much as it might have received from all without the grant. In 1827 and 1828 Congress granted public land on this alternate-section basis to Indiana, Illinois, and Ohio for the building of canals to connect Lake Erie with the Wabash River, Lake Michigan with the Illinois River, and to extend to Lake Erie the Miami Canal, which the state of Ohio was building from Cincinnati to Dayton. Little progress was made on them, however, until the craze for internal improvements reached its high point in the mid-1830s.

Canal construction was pushed forward rapidly in the 1830s during the period of inflation, caused by the easy credit policies of the Bank of the United States and the banks of most western states, whose charters permitted them to expand their note issues liberally. Legislatures heady with dreams of the continuation of easy credit and additional federal deposits in state banks adopted huge programs of internal improvements to be carried out either wholly or in part by the states. Among the projects thus undertaken were the Miami extension canal; the Wabash and Lake Erie Canal from present Toledo, Ohio, to Evansville, Indiana; and the Illinois and Lake Michigan Canal from Chicago to LaSalle on the Illinois River. In addition to these canals, numerous projects were adopted by the states for the construction of thousands of miles of railroads and highways. Andrew Jackson's "specie circular," which required that only specie, not paper money, could be used in the purchase of public land, drastically slowed the craze for speculation in land and for the building of internal improvements by casting doubt on the note issues of banks. The Panic of 1837 forced the suspension of numerous banks, credit dried up, and canal and railroad construction abruptly halted. Pennsylvania, Indiana, Illinois, and some other states were not able to meet the interest on the obligations they had incurred in these construction programs and had to suspend payment. Some compromises were made with bondholders, many of whom had managed to purchase their securities at well below their par value; repudiation was finally avoided by most states although some interest was never paid. With the revival of confidence in the 1840s, the canals were brought to completion, but state railroads generally remained uncompleted until they were sold to private interests. The canals were soon paralleled by railroads and enjoyed fair returns from tolls for only a few years.

By 1850 there were 3,698 miles of canals in the United States, of which 1,757 were in New York and Pennsylvania, 792 in Ohio, 214 in Indiana, and 100 in Illinois. Next to New York, the states most favorably affected in their economic development and population growth in the canal era were Ohio, Indiana, and Illinois, twenty-two percent of the population expansion of the United

States between 1820 and 1850 occurring in these three states. Canals were by no means solely responsible for this flow of population to the West, but the employment they offered during construction, the comparative ease of getting to many sections of these western commonwealths by the canals, the facilities they provided for hauling goods in and produce out, and the lands they opened to settlement all proved attractive to people of older and better developed areas. The canals also contributed to the establishment and rapid growth of numerous small towns and cities along their routes, ranging all the way from such important centers as Cleveland, Columbus, Cincinnati, Toledo, and Chicago, to Fort Wayne, Lafayette, and Evansville, Indiana, and many other smaller communities which became county seats and marketing centers with warehouses, stores, gristmills, post offices, and land offices. Buyers at these towns along the canals purchased the wheat, pork, beef, potash, and lumber and shipped them to Cleveland, Buffalo, or New York, if those markets were nearer, or to Cincinnati, Evansville, Louisville, Memphis, or New Orleans if they seemed to offer better prices. An increasing volume of farm produce was flowing north and east by the canals, though the downriver commerce continued to be large for another decade.

In 1846, just as the canal era was passing, Congress was persuaded by self-seeking real-estate owners to make two generous land grants, one for the building of a canal to connect Green Bay with the Wisconsin River by way of the Fox River and the other for the improvement of the Des Moines River. Badly drafted, these measures produced much vexation and ridiculous losses to the government without any commensurate return. In 1852 Congress granted three quarters of a million acres for the building of a canal to enable vessels to pass from Lake Superior to Lake Huron. Through the locks of the Soo Canals, today, in normal times, more tons of freight pass than through any other canals except the Panama.

See Carter Goodrich, *Government Promotion of American Canals and Railroads, 1800-1890* (1960); Harry N. Scheiber, *Ohio Canal Era* (1969); and Donald R. Shaw, *Erie Water West* (1966).—P. W. G.

Canary, Martha Jane. See CALAMITY JANE.

Cannon, George Q. (1827-1901). Mormon leader. Born in Liverpool, England, Cannon came with his parents to America in 1842. He learned the printing business from his uncle, John Taylor, who edited the Mormon *Times and Seasons* in Nauvoo, Illinois. Crossing the Plains to Salt Lake City, Utah, in 1847, Cannon remained there only two years before going on a mission to California (1849) and Hawaii (1850-54), where he translated the Book of Mormon into the Hawaiian language. Upon his return to America, he became an assistant to the editor of the Mormons' San Francisco paper, *The Western Standard* (1854-57). At Brigham Young's direction, Cannon went east in 1858 to help solve United States-Mormon difficulties. He became an apostle in the Latter-day Saint (LDS) church in 1859 and the next year went to England as a missionary, where he was editor of the *Latter-day Saints' Millennial Star* (Liverpool) from 1860 to 1864.

In Utah once again, Cannon helped organize Mormon sunday schools and founded the *Juvenile Instructor* (Salt Lake City, 1866-70). When the *Deseret News* (Salt Lake City) became a daily in 1867, Cannon was named its editor. He went to Washington, D.C., in 1871 to fight against anti-Mormon legislation and the next year was elected Utah's delegate to Congress, where he served four terms (1872-82).

Cannon served as an executor of Brigham Young's will, 1877-79. The estate was complicated by the fact that, to protect church properties from confiscation (as provided in the 1862 Morrill Act), Young had combined church accounts and properties of his own. When some of the dissatisfied heirs filed suit against the executors, Cannon and the other executors were temporarily imprisoned for refusing to increase their bonds above $300,000. In 1881 Cannon was refused a certification of election victory by territorial governor Eli Murray, who objected to Cannon's ecclesiastical power, his plural marriages, and his foreign birth. In 1882, Congress refused to seat Cannon, declaring the delegate's seat vacant.

Cannon was always in high leadership positions in the church in his later years, serving as assistant counselor to Brigham Young (1873-77) and as first counselor to presidents John Taylor, Wilford Woodruff, and Lorenzo Snow (1880-1901). While he was in hiding during the "raid" on polygamists, a $500 reward was offered for his arrest. He was apprehended in 1886, forfeited bail, but later surrendered in 1888. In his adult years he was an executive of many corporations, including the Union Pacific Railroad Company, Utah Sugar Company, Zion's Co-operative Mercantile Institution, Bank of Deseret, Zion's Savings Bank & Trust Company, George Q. Cannon and Sons Company, Brigham Young Trust Company, and Utah Light and Power Company. Cannon was often regarded as the most influential man in the LDS church during the last decades of the nineteenth century.—L. J. A.

Canton, Frank M. (1849-1927). Lawman. Canton was born Joseph Horner near Richmond, Virginia. His father died in the Civil War and following the end of the war, the family moved to Texas, where he and his brother, John, became cowboys. In 1871 he was a guard at the trial of the Kiowa chiefs Satanta and Big Tree at Jacksboro, Texas. In 1874 he killed a soldier in a saloon brawl and during the next several years was apparently involved in a variety of criminal activities. In 1877 or 1878 he left Texas for Nebraska, where he changed his name to Frank M. Canton.

In 1880 Canton settled in Johnson County, Wyoming, and became sheriff. Although he was a small rancher, he sided with the big cattlemen in their growing controversy with smaller farmers and settlers and accepted a position with the Wyoming Stock Growers Association, which represented the interests of rich cattlemen. In 1892 Canton and Frank Wolcott led an invasion force of cattlemen and hired guns into Johnson County, precipitating the violent climax of the JOHNSON COUNTY WAR.

Later he showed up in Oklahoma, where he was a lawman during the troubled heyday of Oklahoma outlawry. In 1897 he moved to Alaska as a deputy United States marshal. By 1900 he was back in Oklahoma, still wearing a badge; in 1907, when Oklahoma became a state, he was appointed its first adjutant general. In 1916 he retired from the office and later worked for the Texas Cattle Raisers' Association. In his last years he was formally pardoned by Texas for the crimes of his youth.

Canton wrote his own story, *Frontier Trails* (1930), edited by Edward Everett Dale. See also William Gardner Bell, "Frontier Lawman," *American West* (Summer 1964); and Helena Huntington Smith, *The War on Powder River* (1968).—G. L. R.

Capitol Freehold Ranch. See XIT RANCH.

Capitol Syndicate Ranch. See XIT RANCH.

Capper, Arthur (1865-1951). Publisher and Kansas politician. The first native-born governor of Kansas, Arthur Capper rose to statewide prominence through his successful newspaper publishing empire. Born in Garnett, he graduated from high school there in 1884. He then became a printer in Topeka and worked for others in journalism until he bought a weekly newspaper in 1893. This paper and the subsequent acquisition of the Topeka *Daily Capital* led to an extensive publishing empire, including magazines and featuring a long list of state agricultural journals and *Capper's Farmer*, which concentrated on midwestern agriculture. Circulation of all his publications was about five million at the time of his death.

Politics played a prominent role in Capper's publishing career and he was active in Republican party organizations. He did not seek elective office until 1912, when he lost the race for governor by twenty-nine votes. He served two terms as governor beginning in 1915 and began five consecutive terms in the United States Senate in 1919. His ability to gain reelection was considered phenomenal even in predominantly Republican Kansas. He was active in the Congressional "Farm Bloc" and was on the Senate District of Columbia, Agriculture, and Foreign Relations committees. Because of his agricultural publications, many regarded him as the Senate's spokesman for agriculture.

Capper was unassuming, modest, soft-spoken, hardworking, interested in people and their ideas, and a natural politician. His Quaker upbringing stayed with him throughout life; he was a leading pacifist. His wife was Florence Crawford, the only daughter of Kansas' third governor. Most of Capper's wealth was accumulated prior to his full-time public service and his philanthropies were primarily centered on the Capper Foundation for Crippled Children.

The only full-scale biography is Homer E. Socolofsky, *Arthur Capper: Publisher, Politician, Philanthropist* (1962).—H. E. S.

Captain Jack (Keintpoos) (c. 1840-1873). Modoc leader. Keintpoos, or Captain Jack, as he was called by whites, was born in the lake country that straddles the California-Oregon border. During the turbulent decade that followed the opening of an emigrant road through Modoc country in 1846, Jack's father, a leader of a small band of Modoc, was killed in a massacre staged by white settlers. Jack took control of the band on his own initiative, for Modoc leadership was not acquired hereditarily. Jack advocated peaceful coexistence with whites and made friends among the settlers who were moving into the Lost River Valley. By the late 1850s and early '60s his Modoc were carrying on a friendly and profitable trade with the mining town of Yreka, California. A treaty signed in 1864 called for the removal of all Modoc to a reservation with the Klamath in Oregon, but Jack stayed there only briefly. Extremely ambitious and

prestige-conscious, he resented the reservation agent's preference for Old Schonchin as Modoc headman and would not tolerate the Klamath's condescending attitude toward the reservation Modoc. He accordingly led his band of some 150 people back to the Lost River valley, not only because it was his home but also because it was the one place where both whites and Indians respected his authority. He hoped to have a reservation established there, but the Indian Office ruled against the proposal, and in late 1872 an ill-managed attempt to arrest him brought on the MODOC WAR.

Jack's predilection for keeping peace with the whites suddenly made him unpopular in the eyes of some of his followers, who had reason to believe that they would be hanged if Jack surrendered the band. Nevertheless, they needed his support and protection because of his status. This war faction appealed to Jack's responsibility as leader to protect them, and they threatened to replace or kill him if he refused. Jack was unable to resist and agreed, with extreme reluctance, to participate in the planned murder of the federal peace commissioners. After the murder, the war faction betrayed Jack to the whites, and he was hanged, along with three other Modoc, on October 3, 1873, at Fort Klamath, Oregon. He died bitterly resentful that his betrayers were, as a result, given clemency for their parts in a war they had forced him to fight. Ironically, Captain Jack was by then famous in the East as a "hostile" Indian. His body was stolen and taken to Washington, D.C., where it was said to have been held on display before being acquired by the surgeon general and placed in his museum.

Details on Captain Jack's adult life, particularly his role in the Modoc War, are in Keith A. Murray, *The Modocs and Their War* (1958). Jeff C. Riddle, *The Indian History of the Modoc War and the Causes that led to it* (1914), more a folk history than a strict military account of the war, offers valuable material on Jack's background and some insight into his character.—J. E. S.

captivity narratives. See INDIAN-CAPTIVITY NARRATIVES.

Carey, Joseph Maull (1845-1924). Wyoming politician. Born in Milton, Delaware, Carey was educated at Union College and the University of Pennsylvania law school. The young lawyer campaigned for the Republican party in 1868 and was rewarded with an appointment as U.S. Attorney General for the newly organized Wyoming Territory. From his arrival in Cheyenne in 1869 until his death Carey made Wyoming his home and served his state in many capacities. He was advanced to the territorial Supreme Court in 1872, but party feuding cost him this seat in 1876. He continued in politics, however, and was twice elected mayor of Cheyenne and chosen territorial delegate to the national Congress in 1884, 1886, and 1888.

Meanwhile Carey had begun his private business career, supplementing and finally supplanting his law practice with ranching and real-estate investments. His cattle company became one of the larger operations in the state. As a rancher Carey helped form the Wyoming Stock Growers Association and served as its president. He was one of the originators of the Wheatland colony, a private venture, which successfully irrigated several thousand acres. Carey regularly reinvested his capital in Wyoming.

As delegate to Congress Carey worked closely with

Governor Francis E. Warren in securing Wyoming's admission to the Union. Carey introduced and pushed the bill that earned him the title "Father of Wyoming Statehood." The Wyoming legislature responded by electing him the state's first senator along with Warren in 1890.

The major legislation Carey proposed while senator was the CAREY ACT. The senator's stand against free silver lost him much of his support at home. At the same time, Carey and Warren, once friends and co-workers, became estranged. Political machinations cost Carey his senatorial seat in the 1895 election and resulted in his removal as a Republican national committeeman.

Excluded from Republican inner circles, Carey took little part in politics until 1910 when he announced as a candidate for governor. Unable to get the Republican nomination because of machine control of the party, Carey accepted the Democratic nomination but called himself a Progressive Republican. Elected overwhelmingly, Carey proposed a program similar to that advocated by the national Progressives. He was only partially successful in securing this program during his four-year term, but his two legislatures enacted the direct primary, the secret ballot, a bill permitting cities to adopt a commission form of government, a corrupt practices act, and an amendment that paved the way for workmen's compensation and ratified the federal amendments for the direct election of senators and the income tax. Carey also instituted needed penal reform and secured the establishment of a boy's industrial school. He did not press for labor or regulatory legislation.

The governor supported Theodore Roosevelt and the Progressives in 1912 and opposed the reelection of Warren. Warren was victorious and Carey's influence was weakened. He chose not to run again and supported the Democratic candidate, John Kendrick, for governor in 1914. Two years later Carey supported Kendrick for the Senate and Woodrow Wilson for the presidency.

In political philosophy Carey was a conservative Republican but one heavily touched with a concern for political reform. His leaning toward Progressivism was circumscribed by his conservative economic philosophy and by his disposition toward states' rights in opposition to a strong federal government. Thus he could support measures of direct democracy but could not advance into the broadened philosophy of Progressivism that necessitated a strong federal government serving as regulator of the nation's economic and social institutions.

See T. A. Larson, *History of Wyoming* (1965); and the Joseph M. Carey Administrative Papers, Wyoming State Archives Department, Cheyenne, Wyoming. —B. P.

Carey Act (1894). The Carey Act, sponsored by Wyoming senator Joseph Maull CAREY, granted up to a million acres of federal public lands to each of ten arid states or territories, subject to the proviso that such land be reclaimed by the state or its agent and sold to actual settlers in tracts not exceeding a quarter section or 160 acres. A time limit of ten years attached to the land was granted, so that 20 acres out of each quarter section had to be reclaimed within that time. Subsequent amendments to the statute eased the ten-year rule and strengthened the authority of the state governments in dealing with irrigation companies and in preventing speculative interference.

Carey's interest in irrigating Wyoming land stemmed from his large investment in the state's future economic development. His most influential business associate and political ally was Francis E. Warren, owner of the largest mercantile enterprise in Wyoming and future Republican nabob for Wyoming. This political alliance, characterized by the expression, "Me and F. E.," endured from 1884 until 1895. The J. M. Carey and Brother livestock firm was one of the first big outfits to run Texas longhorn steers and Herefords on the Wyoming plains. Carey was also one of the insiders of the all-powerful Wyoming Stock Growers Association, was its president for two terms, and represented this predominant economic interest on all occasions. His Wyoming Development Company secured water rights in 1883 and started the reclamation of 50,000 acres for the Wheatland Colony, which was planned as a model for a new era of irrigation-based agriculture. He sought to proffer federal aid to his Wheatland Colony and similar projects, and also to add voter strength to his faltering senatorial campaign.

Senator Carey designed his irrigation bill so as to meet congressional criticism of suggested previous arid-land legislation, and thus the measure passed into law in 1894 with little national attention. Wyoming's engineer, Elwood MEAD, the most prominent advocate of state-controlled reclamation projects at that time, drafted legislation in Wyoming, and his statute was adopted in Colorado, Utah, and Idaho as well, providing for the administration of Carey Act land grants.

The Carey Act, its provisions still operable today, proved very early to be a disappointment. Although a million acres of desert land were granted each of the so-called arid states and territories, the Panic of 1893 had dried up sources of private capital and prevented state credit from being advanced for reclamation projects. The homestead settlement proviso and the ten-year requirement for completing reclamation caused concern.

Wyoming was the first to apply under the Carey Act and was the only state that had patented land when the Newlands Act, a federally controlled reclamation program, went into effect in 1902. Some states continued Carey Act projects even after the federal Bureau of Reclamation largely preempted the reclamation effort. By midcentury Wyoming was second to Idaho in Carey Act acreage. It constituted approximately a fifth of the million acres of federal land given to the states under the 1894 act. The Carey Act provided a viable alternative to national reclamation for those states that took advantage of it and was by no means the failure depicted by historians of the reclamation movement, whose vision has fastened on the sensational big-dam construction feats of the federal Bureau of Reclamation.

Paul W. Gates, *History of Public Land Law Development* (1968), describes the inception of the Carey Act and assesses its importance in national reclamation. T. A. Larson, *History of Wyoming* (1965), includes irrigation development in the state and notes the role of the Carey Act. Neil J. Meredith, "A Forgotten Alternative: Reclamation by the States," *Idaho Yesterdays* (Winter 1965-66), tells how Idaho was one of the leading states to make the most effective use of Carey Act reclamation land grants. George W. Paulson, "The Congressional Career of

Joseph Maull Carey," *Annals of Wyoming* (April 1963), discusses the legislative history of the Carey Act and its implementation in Wyoming.—L. B. L.

Carleton, James Henry (1814-1873). Soldier. Born in Maine, Carleton was a lieutenant in the Maine militia in 1838, during the Maine boundary dispute with Canada known as the Aroostock War, before becoming a lieutenant in the regular army in 1839. He served on the frontier until the Mexican War (1846-48), when he became aide-de-camp for General John Wool; during the 1850s he served in New Mexico Territory.

With the outbreak of the Civil War, Carleton became brigadier general in the California Volunteers, commanding the California Column and replacing General Edward R. S. Canby as departmental commander in New Mexico in 1862. He turned immediately to the Indian problem, sending Kit Carson and other subordinates against the Mescalero Apache and later the Navaho. Carleton prohibited councils with the Indians and ordered that "the men are to be slain whenever and wherever they can be found." The Mescalero were placed on a new reservation at Bosque Redondo in the Pecos valley in 1862. The troops then invaded the Navaho country and, by destroying the crops and maintaining a constant pursuit, forced the tribe to surrender. Some eight thousand Navaho were taken on the Long Walk to Bosque Redondo, where Carleton planned to Christianize and civilize them. The experiment failed, however. The Mescalero fled, and the cost of maintaining the Navaho convinced the government to allow them to return to their homeland.

Carleton's policies by this time had become a major source of dispute in New Mexico politics. Carleton was arbitrary, tyrannical, and at times a cruel disciplinarian, his maintenance of martial law in New Mexico only antagonizing the citizens. He was, however, successful in defeating two tribes with a minimum of bloodshed despite a policy of killing all male Indians, and while he failed to civilize the Navaho, the psychological impact of Bosque Redondo terminated warfare with that tribe. After the Civil War Carleton served briefly in Texas.

See Aurora Hunt, *Major General James Henry Carleton, 1814-1873* (1958).—R. N. E.

Carlisle Indian School. Carlisle, the first of the Indian boarding schools, established by the government, was opened in the former military barracks at Carlisle, Pennsylvania, in October 1879. The school was almost entirely the creation of Lieutenant Richard Henry PRATT, who had experimented with methods of Indian education at Fort Marion, Florida (with men who had been exiled and imprisoned for crimes committed in Indian Territory), and at Hampton Institute, Virginia. His success persuaded Secretary of the Interior Carl Schurz and Secretary of War George McCrary to allow him to open Carlisle pending congressional approval, which came belatedly in July 1882.

Although Congress showed less than routine interest in the new Indian school, it was Carlisle that established the pattern Indian schools were to follow for the next two decades. It gave training in both academic subjects and industrial arts, the former at the grammar school level, and the latter in skills such as printing, blacksmithing, and carpentry.

Carlisle's most famous innovation was the outing system. The students, usually in the second year of their five-year stay, were sent for the summer to live and work with white families in the agricultural counties surrounding Carlisle, in return for room, board, and a nominal wage. Those who did well in the summer program were allowed to spend the entire next year on outing, where they attended local public schools with white children. The system was designed to promote intensive contact between *individual* Indians and the *best* white families, to immerse Indian children in civilization and to keep them there. Although the outing system operated smoothly at Carlisle under Pratt's rigorous supervision, it was not successfully adopted in any other Indian school, and never tried at most of them. Moreover, to Pratt's great sorrow, nearly all of his students returned to their former homes, and some even resumed their native cultural life. This was perhaps due less to any inadequacy of a Carlisle education than it was to a governmental policy that offered inducements to Indians who stayed on the reservations.

Carlisle opened with eighty-two Sioux children from Dakota Territory. By the turn of the century enrollment had reached one thousand, which represented thirty-nine tribes from throughout the country. After Pratt's dismissal by the Interior Department for insubordination in 1904, Carlisle declined in efficiency and reputation, killing the already remote possibility that Congress might add more eastern Indian schools. In 1918 the army reclaimed the barracks for use as a hospital for the wounded of World War I, and the unique experiment in the education of a deprived minority was abandoned. —E. A. G.

Carmel Mission. See SAN CARLOS BORROMEO.

Carrington, Henry Beebee (1824-1912). Soldier. Carrington was born in Connecticut and graduated from Yale College. He moved to Columbus, Ohio, in 1848, where he established a law practice. He was adjutant general of the Ohio State Militia at the outbreak of the Civil War. Although appointed colonel of the eighteenth Infantry in 1861 and later promoted to brigadier general of volunteers, he saw no field service, his entire career during the war consisting of raising, organizing, and training troops. At the end of the war he was mustered out of the volunteer service and joined the regiment, which, because of the growing menace of the Sioux, was ordered to the Great Plains in 1865.

In 1866 this regiment was ordered to open and guard the Powder River Road to the Montana mines. However, his expedition up the Platte River upset the carefully prepared plans of the government to negotiate a treaty with the Sioux for the peaceful use of this route. Carrington also built and garrisoned Forts Reno, Phil Kearny, and C. F. Smith to protect travelers over the Bozeman Trail. None of these forts had an adequate garrison, and supplies, especially ammunition, were insufficient. Indian attacks were almost incessant, culminating in the FETTERMAN MASSACRE of December 21, 1866. It effectively terminated Carrington's military career, in that he never again was given an important command, although he was later post commander at Fort McPherson and Fort Sedgewick. As a result of a wound suffered in the line of duty, he retired from active service in 1870. Later, Carrington was professor of military science and tactics at Wabash College.

See Dee Brown, *Fort Phil Kearny: An American Saga* (1962).—E. I. S.

Carson, Kit [Christopher Houston] (1809-1868). Mountain man, scout, soldier, and Indian agent. Kit Carson lived and did his work in an age that still respected individual achievement, lauded personal courage and self-sufficiency, and believed in and revered the authentic hero. Today the career of Carson, no matter how faithfully and accurately drawn, seems more the stuff of legend than of fact. Nor has his case been strengthened by the vast body of unhistorical literature, beginning with the popular dime novels, that has obscured the real man in a cloud of untruth.

The mountain men, contemporaries of Carson's, have been termed "symbols of anarchic freedom," and while it is true that many trappers imposed no curb on their baser impulses once they removed to the wilderness, others, of whom Carson was the leading example, showed themselves men of fiber. For in refusing to surrender to these same impulses, they symbolized more strongly the triumph of civilization over barbarism.

Tom Tobin, a taciturn frontiersman and Carson in-law, who claimed to have "et many a beaver tail with him," and whose words may be given credit, spoke of the character of Carson in these terms: as to his reputed fearlessness, "Wasn't afraid of hell or high water"; in his private life, "Clean as a hound's tooth"; on his veracity, "Kit Carson's word was as sure as the sun comin' up"; regarding his language, "Kit never cussed more'n was necessary." A more sophisticated estimate of the man's life and character issued from the pen of W. W. H. Davis, who met Carson briefly early in the 1850s: "There is nothing like the fire-eater in his manners, but, to the contrary, in all his actions he is quiet and unassuming. He has endured all imaginable hardships with a steady perseverance and unflinching courage."

The son of Lindsey and Rebecca Carson, Carson was the descendant of hardy frontier stock who had pioneered the North Carolina and Virginia mountains before settling in Kentucky. From his birthplace near Richmond, Kentucky, the Carsons moved to a Missouri farm in mid-1812. The boy was apprenticed to a saddle maker, David Workman, at age fourteen but fled from this employment in 1826 and joined a caravan bound for New Mexico. Following a brief visit in Santa Fe he traveled to Taos, which proved more congenial to his adventurous nature since it was headquarters and resort for the mountain men. From 1828 to 1831 the youth accompanied the famed trapper Ewing Young through southern Arizona to California and back, learning the difficult trade of harvesting beaver. During the next several years, in pursuit of furs, he wandered up the spine of the Rockies and throughout the Far West, gaining extensive knowledge of frontier trails. In company with Jim Bridger, Carson attended the fur trading rendezvous in 1835 on the Green River. Here he vanquished in a celebrated duel the belligerent French trapper Shunar. During these years he took successively two Indian wives. The first, an Arapaho girl, died, and the second, a Cheyenne, may have divorced him Indian style by casting his belongings outside the teepee.

For a brief period (1841-42) Carson was employed as

Kit Carson (standing) with his friend John C. Frémont. (Kit Carson Memorial Foundation)

a hunter at Bent's Fort on the Arkansas River. In 1842, on a trip to Missouri to visit relatives, he encountered by chance John C. Frémont, who was preparing to launch the first of his western expeditions. In need of a guide, Frémont engaged the then unknown mountain man and over the next several years had ample reason to be grateful for his choice. On three separate expeditions Carson piloted the "Pathfinder" through the central Rockies, the Great Basin, Oregon, and California. Between the first and second of these excursions, on February 6, 1843, he married fifteen-year-old Josefa Jaramillo of Taos.

It was Carson's service with Frémont that first brought him to public attention. Frémont's *Memoirs of My Life* (1897), ably edited by his wife, Jessie Benton, acclaimed Carson's prowess as a scout and skillfully portrayed him as a man of loyalty and courage. His exploits captured the popular imagination and within a short time made him a national hero.

On Frémont's third expedition to California (1845-46), Carson became caught up in the swift-moving events attending the onset of the Mexican War. He engaged in a conflict that led to the establishment of the Bear Flag Republic, performed valuable courier service for Frémont, and guided the army of General Stephen Watts Kearny from New Mexico to California. With the conclusion of hostilities he returned to Taos and in the spring of 1849 took up ranching at Rayado (east of Taos) in company with Lucien Maxwell. In 1853 the two men drove a large flock of sheep to California and realized a handsome profit. Late in the same year Carson was appointed Indian agent for the tribes of northern New Mexico, a position in which he served creditably until 1861.

With the opening of the Civil War, Carson became colonel of the First New Mexico Volunteer Infantry. He saw action at the battle of Valverde on February 21, 1862, and for his service was breveted brigadier general. In the winter of 1862-63 General James H. Carleton sent him to Fort Stanton in southeastern New Mexico to wage war on the Mescalero Apache. When that tribe was defeated, he was ordered to bring hostile Navaho under control by a campaign through western New Mexico and Arizona. Destroying crops and livestock and invading the Indian stronghold at Canyon de Chelly, Carson obliged some eight thousand Navaho to surrender by the summer of 1864. In spite of his success over both Mescalero and Navaho and over the Kiowa later the same year, Carson was a reluctant campaigner. He possessed solid sympathy for the Indians and, although he had suffered at their hands, he understood their situation better than most of his fellows.

After serving briefly as commander of Fort Garland in southern Colorado, Carson settled with his family at Boggsville (near Las Animas, Colorado). His wife died there in April 1868, and Carson succumbed to a hemorrhage the following May 23 at nearby Fort Lyon. The next year his remains and those of his wife were removed to Taos and buried in a small cemetery near his old home.

The definitive biography of Kit Carson remains to be written. A seminal work by Harvey Lewis Carter, *Dear Old Kit: The Historical Christopher Carson* (1968), contains a new edition of the Carson memoirs, as well as thoughtful essays that strip away much legend and misinformation. Lawrence C. Kelly, *Navajo Roundup: Selected Correspondence of Kit Carson's Expedition Against the Navajo, 1863-1865* (1970), shows that Carson's success against the Indian was more the result of perseverance than military ability. Now outdated, but useful in part, is Edwin L. Sabin, *Kit Carson Days: 1809-1868*, 2 vols. (rev. ed., 1935). Serious readers should avoid Stanley Vestal, *Kit Carson, The Happy Warrior of the Old West* (1928).—M. Si.

Carter, Clarence Edwin (1881-1961). Historian and editor. Carter took his bachelor's degree at Illinois College in his home town of Jacksonville, his master's degree at the University of Wisconsin, and his Ph.D. at the University of Illinois. He began his teaching career at Illinois College; in 1910 he accepted an appointment at Miami University in Oxford, Ohio, and in 1931 was named editor of the TERRITORIAL PAPERS OF THE UNITED STATES.

His first important published work was *Great Britain and the Illinois Country, 1763-1774* (1910). In collaboration with Clarence W. Alvord, Carter published a collection of documents relating to Illinois from 1763 to 1769 in the Collections of the Illinois State Historical Society (1915, 1916, and 1921). He was editor of *The Correspondence of General Thomas Gage*, the first volume published in 1931 and the second in 1933. He also produced numerous articles and reviews.

He is best known for his work as editor of the Territorial Papers, a position he held for thirty years. He was responsible for the publication of twenty-six volumes

relating to three territories west of the Mississippi River —Missouri, Arkansas, and Louisiana—and to all the territories east of the Mississippi except for Wisconsin, which was under way at the time of his death.

Carter revealed his approach to the profession of historical documentary editing in his presidential address to the Mississippi Valley Historical Association, published in the *Mississippi Valley Historical Review* in June 1938, and in *Historical Editing* (National Archives Bulletin 7, 1952). He was devoted to "the principle of accuracy," which included matters of format and style, as he explained in a letter in 1953. He felt that within "such circumstances as the limits of typography, the necessity for clarity and the like," the printed page should be a reproduction of the original document. He reproduced archaic forms of abbreviation and punctuation and avoided insertion of editorial brackets, because "to follow with some literalness the writer's style is to place it in the era in which the document was produced." His approach to scholarship is perhaps also reflected in a statement by Frederick Jackson Turner, written to Carter in 1908: "My own idea about editorial work is that the satisfaction of the editor must chiefly lie in the joy of finding and making available material for use. There is little personal advantage."

See Philip D. Jordan, "Clarence E. Carter, a Tribute," and Harold W. Ryan, "Clarence E. Carter, a Memoir," both in *Prologue, the Journal of the National Archives* (Winter 1969).—J. P. B.

cartography. Since "west" in the language of geographers is but a cardinal direction with regard to the earth's poles, or toward sunset, it is obvious that the "West" as an area of the United States must be bounded by historical limits. For purposes of systematic geographic reconnaissance, this limit is most conveniently the time when the young republic of the United States was contained by a common frontier, or roughly by the trans-Mississippi West. In 1796 Thomas Jefferson pointed out to the members of the American Philosophical Society in Philadelphia the great lack of reliable information concerning the lands to the west. Subsequent to the Louisiana Purchase in 1803 Jefferson, then president, obtained the first congressional appropriation for a scientific reconnaissance expedition that would be well prepared and equipped. His accomplished personal secretary, Meriwether Lewis, and Captain William Clark set out on their historic trek from the upper Missouri River at Fort Mandan, reaching the mouth of the Columbia River at the Pacific coast on December 5, 1805. Clark produced two famous maps based on the data gathered in 1810 and in 1814. Subsequent to the feat of the LEWIS AND CLARK EXPEDITION, military exploring parties left almost annually on missions to the West. One of the oldest surveying agencies, created on March 3, 1813, was the Corps of Topographical Engineers, which was made responsible for "planning of construction of works" in addition to mere reconnaissance. Attempts to make a systematic survey of the country, especially needed for the security of settlements in the western territories, resulted in the Coast Survey being given responsibility for inland topographic mapping. On June 20, 1878, it was renamed the Coast and Geodetic Survey, and since 1903 it has operated under the Department of Commerce. The survey of lands west of the one hundredth meridian and the exploration of the fortieth parallel became increasingly important with the movement of the population, and so, a new agency, the United States GEOLOGICAL SURVEY, was founded on March 3, 1879, and put under the Department of the Interior. This purely civilian agency was charged with classifying public lands and with examining the "geological structure, mineral resources and products of the national domain." Eventually responsible for the entire country, the Geological Survey founded to map the West, took over the bulk of topographic mapping and is now coordinating the work of over twenty government agencies which had engaged in gathering data and incorporating it on maps. The maps of the Geological Survey are at present published in sheets drawn to three sets of scales, in order of the importance of detail required and of the area mapped. An additional large scale of one inch to nearly two miles is used for the desert regions of Arizona and New Mexico.

It was the fate of the Spaniards to be lured into just those unpromising regions in search of mineral resources and the legendary rich Seven Cities of Cíbola (New Mexico) and the golden Quivira (Kansas), but no accurate maps resulted. Later, in 1776-77, two notable cartographers of the West, Fathers Escalante and Dominguez, accompanied Captain de Miera y Pacheco's troop on a search for a land route from Santa Fe to California. They reached the Utah Basin and returned via the present-day Zion National Park and Zuñi lands. Their work was used by Alexander von Humboldt in his *Essay on New Spain* and by Lewis and Clark, as well as by their contemporary Zebulon PIKE, who sighted Pikes Peak in central Colorado in 1806.

The work of military reconnaissance was paralleled by that of mountain men, to whom it was left to clear up some major errors in the location of, as well as the respective distance and direction between geographic features and to verify the extent of the vast area called the West. Geographic information from such remarkable men as Jedediah Smith and Jim Bridger reached the public through Missouri newspapers. Among mistaken assumptions even after the Lewis and Clark expedition were the common origin or close proximity of the sources of the great rivers the Rio Grande, Colorado, and Yellowstone; the true formation of the Rocky Mountains, pictured as one single ridge (see PHYSIOGRAPHY OF THE UNITED STATES); and the extent of the Great Plains and of the entire area of the Far West. The latter had been vastly underestimated by Lewis and Clark, who found their journey to cover over a thousand miles more than estimated. The enormous area of the Great Plains was characterized by Zebulon Pike as the American Sahara. Stephen H. LONG called it the Great American Desert on his map of 1821, and the name was to remain on maps for nearly fifty years.

In the Far West, knowledge was gathered by the explorers of the Hudson's Bay Company, especially by David THOMPSON, who crossed the mountains to trace the Columbia River system. It remained for Peter Skene OGDEN to become the first to cross the West from south to north, from the Gulf of California to Vancouver. Famous maps of this middle epoch were those of A. H. Buré published in Paris in 1833; of Aaron Arrowsmith and Sons of London, particularly one of 1834; and the map made in 1839 by H. Burr containing information of the Salt Lake Basin.

By 1832 the Indian tribes of the West had been encountered, beaver streams located, and native trails were mapped. The map by Joseph NICOLLET of "The Hydrographic Basin of the Upper Mississippi River" was about to pave the way for his appointment as cartographer in charge of mapping the entire trans-Mississippi West when he died suddenly in 1843. His ninety thousand instrument readings constituted the bridge to consistent scientific mapping, and his most distinguished disciple, John Charles FREMONT, continued the work in the Far West. A trailblazer as well as a surveyor, Frémont built on the data gathered by Jedediah SMITH and had his work amended by George Gibbs of Oregon. The resultant famous Frémont-Gibbs-Smith map of 1845 portrayed the "fur-trader's West at the moment of climax." Charles PREUSS, a distinguished cartographer, accompanied Frémont on his second expedition and produced a map described as "a monument of western cartography."

The scientific orientation of the mid-nineteenth century resulted in the age of the great surveys. George WHEELER worked west of the hundredth meridian, surveying about 359,000 square miles; F. V. HAYDEN surveyed areas in Colorado, New Mexico, Utah, Wyoming, and Idaho; Major J. W. POWELL covered the Rocky Mountain area in Wyoming, Utah, and Arizona, some 67,000 square miles; and Major Clarence KING was in charge of exploring and mapping the fortieth parallel. Their surveys were based upon extensive networks of triangulation projected from fixed points and measured base lines. After the Civil War the great transcontinental arch of triangles from Atlantic to Pacific joined the problems of mapping the East to those of the West.

The art of printing maps came to America only in the nineteenth century. The Colton family and H. S. Tanner and his disciple Samuel Augustus Mitchell printed excellent and famous maps. Techniques of engraving on copper and steel resulted in incredibly fine lines, and with the use of hachures the delineation of mountains became a distinctive feature. These maps compare with the best published in Europe. American maps also included ample geographic data and lithographic illustrations. Wax engraving coarsened the process but lowered the cost of publishing maps, as did the photoengraving process. Air photography has been particularly appropriate for exact mapping of difficult terrain of desert and mountain and has cut the time of data-gathering enormously. The demand for ever higher precision can now be met with satellite pictures capable of high resolution. The area of the West may be mapped topographically as it has not been before, though the estimate of coverage satisfactory for modern requirements is still put at under fifty percent.

See William H. Goetzmann, *Exploration and Empire: The Explorer and the Scientist in the Winning of the American West* (1960); Henry R. Wagner, *Cartography of the North West Coast of America to the Year 1800* (1937); and Carl I. Wheat, *Mapping the Trans-Mississippi West, 1540-1861*, 5 vols. (1957-63).—U. S. L.

Cartwright, Peter (1785-1872). Methodist circuit-rider. Cartwright was reared with almost no education in the backwoods of Kentucky. In 1801 under the preaching of John Page, he was converted from his gambling ways to revivalist, camp meeting religion. The

Methodists licensed him in 1802, at the age of seventeen, first as a regular exhorter and some months later as a traveling preacher to form a circuit in the region about the mouth of the Cumberland River. The "Kentucky Boy," powerful in build, self-reliant, with a quick sense of humor, and ready with both tongue and fist, became a popular figure and an effective worker in the vineyard in several circuits on both sides of the Ohio River. William McKendree, a Methodist preacher, taught him grammar and laid out for him a course of theological reading. Bishop Francis Asbury ordained him a deacon in 1806. Cartwright's dislike of slavery led him to request to be moved to Illinois. In that territory and state he served for half a century as presiding elder.

In his *Autobiography* (1857) he recounted the adventures of his earlier years, narratives not distinguished for understatement. Like Daniel Boone, the backwoods hunter, and Mike Fink, the Mississippi riverman, Cartwright, the hard-riding preacher of emotional religion who, when occasion required, could leave the pulpit to beat up roughs come to disturb, belongs in the gallery of romantic heroes of the early nineteenth century of forest and prairie.—R. H. G.

Carver, Jonathan (1710-1780). Explorer and author. Carver was born in Weymouth, Massachusetts, grew up in Connecticut, where he became a shoemaker, and served with provincial troops (1746-63). When Major Robert Rogers came to garrison the post at Mackinac Island, Michigan, in 1766, he sent Carver to map the rivers of Wisconsin and Minnesota. Traveling via Green Bay, the Fox-Wisconsin rivers, and the Mississippi, he spent the winter of 1766-67 near the Falls of St. Anthony (St. Paul, Minnesota) and the next summer went to Grand Portage on the north shore of Lake Superior, expecting to find supplies sent by Rogers for the planned exploration of a river route to the Pacific. Not finding the supplies, he returned to the East and then went to London in 1769. There he wrote the first book on the Wisconsin-Minnesota region, *Travels Through the Interior Parts of North America* (1778). The book was an immediate success on both sides of the Atlantic, eventually went through at least sixteen editions, and made Carver the best-known author on eighteenth-century America.

When Carver died in poverty, Dr. John Lettsom helped issue a third edition in order to help Carver's common-law wife and two children in London. In the preface he described a deed to 10,000 square miles of land in northwestern Wisconsin and eastern Minnesota that two Dakota Sioux chiefs had given Carver. Heirs on both sides of the Atlantic sold the claims to speculators, and for many years Congress was approached for confirmation that never came. A "Carver Deed," one of several presumed fraudulent deeds in existence, appeared in northwestern Wisconsin as late as the 1950s.

See E. G. Bourne, "The Travels of Jonathan Carver," *American History Review*, vol. II (1906); William Browning, "The Early History of Jonathan Carver," *Wisconsin Magazine of History*, vol. 3 (1920); and M. M. Quaife, "Jonathan Carver and the Carver Grant," *Mississippi Valley History Review*, vol. 7 (1920).—W. D. W.

Cary, William de la Montagne (1840-1922). Painter. Cary was born in Tappan, New York. When in his teens,

a natural ability in art led to his apprenticeship to an engraver. At the age of twenty, he and two youthful companions journeyed into the Far West via the Missouri River and overland to the Pacific, returning by boat from California to Panama and through the Caribbean to New York at about the time of the outbreak of the Civil War. Following the war, Cary returned to the scenes of his first adventure, visiting Fort Riley, Kansas, in 1867 and the Missouri River country again in 1874. He was then invited by a friend to join the federal government's northern boundary survey of 1874. Cary arrived in time only to accompany the survey party on its return voyage to Bismarck, North Dakota. Not an official member of the survey team, he made nevertheless many sketches of its activities. A large canvas, painted years afterward in his New York studio and depicting the return of the northern boundary surveyors, is included in the collection of the Thomas Gilcrease Institute of American History and Art in Tulsa, Oklahoma, along with numerous other oil paintings and pencil sketches illustrating life in the West. Cary's work was featured regularly in *Harper's Weekly* and other illustrated magazines throughout the 1860s and 1870s.

See Paul Rossi and David C. Hunt, *The Art of the Old West* (1971); and Robert Taft, *Artists and Illustrators of the Old West, 1850-1900* (1953).—D. C. H.

Cascade Range. See PHYSIOGRAPHY OF THE UNITED STATES.

Cass, Lewis (1782-1866). Soldier and politician. Born in Exeter, New Hampshire, Cass decided to seek a career in the West. In 1799 he crossed the Alleghenies and established a law practice on the Ohio frontier. At the age of twenty-four he was elected to the Ohio legislature, the youngest member of that body. An ardent Jeffersonian, Cass opposed the separatist schemes of Aaron Burr by drawing up resolutions of loyalty to Thomas Jefferson. Jefferson rewarded his loyalty by appointing him federal marshal for Ohio.

Like so many young western politicians, Cass welcomed the War of 1812 and, as commander of the Third Ohio Regiment, took part in General William Hull's expedition against Detroit. He was sorely disappointed with Hull's surrender and, following his own release in January 1813, returned to the thick of battle, fighting with distinction at the battle of the Thames. His loyalty to the new nation again did not go unnoticed; in 1813 he was appointed governor of the Territory of Michigan, a post he held for eighteen years. His administration was highly successful in solving the traditional territorial problems of land settlement and Indian affairs. Cass himself was remarkably adroit in his dealings with the Indians; he even was able to take away their lands without resorting to the persuasive power of liquor, a practice he deplored. During his tenure of office, he also acquired enough real estate for himself to amass an ample personal fortune.

In 1831 Cass became Andrew Jackson's secretary of war. He continued to be an effective force in the effort to drive the Indians beyond the Mississippi River, prosecuting the Black Hawk War (1832) with cool efficiency and supporting Georgia in its litigation against the Cherokee.

In 1836 Cass was appointed minister to France, which

enabled him to give full vent to the deep anti-British prejudice he had developed during his frontier years. Following a dispute with his old Exeter classmate, Daniel Webster, over Britain's attempt to secure a quintuple treaty legalizing the right of search, Cass resigned and returned home in 1836 to take part in national politics. His return also was motivated in part by a concern with the issues of manifest destiny, for he was little short of an imperialist. Realizing that expansion was the critical election-year issue in 1844, the opportunistic Cass wrote the Hannegan Letter, strongly urging the annexation of Texas. When this ploy failed to secure him the Democratic nomination for president, he contented himself with a Senate seat from Michigan.

In the Senate (1845-48, 1849-57), Cass continued to press for territorial expansion, demanding that the United States secure the whole of the Oregon country and pressing for the occupation of Mexico. He opposed the Wilmot Proviso and anticipated Douglas' concept of "popular sovereignty," a position that opened the way for his nomination for the presidency in 1848. He lost the election to General Zachary Taylor.

Following his defeat, Cass continued to think in terms of national expansion, subordinating all sectional issues, including slavery. He supported the Compromise of 1850 and defended the fugitive-slave bill. In 1851 Michigan again elected him to the Senate. Between 1857 and 1860 Cass served as Buchanan's secretary of state, scoring important diplomatic victories over Great Britain and Paraguay. He resigned in protest over the decision not to reinforce the Charleston forts.

Cass returned to Michigan and devoted his remaining years to scholarly interests. He was an avid reader, and his articles on early Western history, as well as his essays on French politics, were of high caliber.

See Andrew C. McLaughlin, *Lewis Cass* (1899); and Frank B. Woodford, *Lewis Cass: The Last Jeffersonian* (1950).—R. B. W.

Cassidy, Butch. Assumed name of **Robert Leroy Parker**, alias **George Leroy Parker** (1866-1911? 1937?). Outlaw. Parker was born near Circleville, Utah, to Mormon parents and was raised on his father's remote ranch. As a teen-ager he fell under the influence of a rustler named Mike Cassidy. He got his first taste of the outlaw life under the tutelage of Cassidy and later followed his mentor out of Utah into Colorado in 1884. For nearly two years thereafter Parker worked for a mining company at Telluride, Colorado, but then fell into bad company again. Within a short time Parker was riding with the McCarty gang and participating in train robberies and bank jobs, including the First National Bank in Denver and the San Miguel Bank at Telluride. In 1892, after a lull in his criminal activities, he worked briefly in a butcher shop at Rock Springs, Wyoming, and picked up the nickname "Butch," to which he tacked "Cassidy" in honor of the old rascal that led him into a life of crime. With a new identity he was soon involved in rustling again, and in 1894 he was sent to prison in Wyoming. He was released in 1896 on the promise that he would "never worry Wyoming again." At least that is the story his biographers tell.

Cassidy then turned up in the rugged area known as Brown's Hole, a haven for desperadoes that lies at the junction of Wyoming, Utah, and Colorado. Here, and in the Hole-in-the-Wall, a region that slashes across northern Wyoming, he cultivated associates among a variety of criminal types. Eventually this loose band of outlaws was dubbed the Wild Bunch. Kid Curry, Harry Longbaugh (remembered best as the Sundance Kid and as Parker's closest associate), Ben Kilpatrick (the Tall Texan), Harry Tracy, Elza Lay, Deaf Charley Hanks, Harvey Logan, Blackjack Ketchum, and others of equally unsavory reputation formed a criminal operation that spread its activities into states and territories from South Dakota to New Mexico. In time the Wild Bunch even had its own lawyer, and railroad detectives and Pinkerton agents joined lawmen in pursuit of Cassidy's men.

Beginning with the robbery of the Pleasant Valley Coal Company at Castle Gate, Utah, in 1897, Cassidy's control of the gang was undisputed. In the next few years the group robbed trains and banks in Colorado, Utah, Wyoming, Montana, Nevada, and New Mexico and defended their remote strongholds from all efforts to dislodge them. Gradually, however, the authorities closed in on them, and in 1901 Butch Cassidy and the Sundance Kid left the United States for Latin America, accompanied by a girl named Etta Place. They lived quietly in the backcountry of Brazil near the Chilean border for a while. Then, in 1906, Etta Place became ill and returned to the United States accompanied by the Sundance Kid. He soon rejoined Cassidy, and Etta Place vanished into obscurity.

The two American desperadoes then launched a series of bank and railroad robberies, although for a while they worked for a mining company in Bolivia. The crime wave came to an end in the village of San Vincente, Bolivia, in 1911, when Cassidy and the Kid were killed by Bolivian troops.

The families of both men continue to insist, however, that the two escaped the deathtrap at San Vincente, pointing out that positive identification was never made and even providing the names of the two men who were killed there. They claim that both Butch Cassidy and the Sundance Kid slipped out of South America and quietly reentered the United States. Cassidy is supposed to have visited his family in 1929 and to have died in 1937 at Spokane, Washington, where he lived under the name William K. Phillips. Longbaugh reportedly married Etta Place and lived until 1957. He is allegedly buried at Casper, Wyoming. Whatever the truth, such stories lend an aura of romance to the exploits of Butch Cassidy.

See Pearl Baker, *The Wild Bunch at Robbers Roost* (1965); James D. Horan, *The Wild Bunch* (1958); and Charles Kelly, *The Outlaw Trail* (1959).—G. L. R.

Cataldo, Joseph (1837-1928). Jesuit missionary. Born in Italy, Cataldo was active among Nez Percé, Coeur d'Alene, and Spokane from 1865 to 1877. He founded Gonzaga University in Spokane, Washington, in 1883, was superior of the Pacific Northwest missions from 1877 to 1893, and was then missionary to Alaska and the Northwest. He is noted as a peacemaker in the Nez Percé war (1877) and as an Indian linguist.

See Robert I. Burns, *The Jesuits and the Indian Wars of the Northwest* (1966).—R. I. B.

catamount. See MOUNTAIN LION.

Catawba Indians. The Catawba Indians were an eastern Siouan people who inhabited the Piedmont country of the Carolinas, centering around the Catawba River. Along with more than twenty other small Siouan and linguistically unrelated tribes and parts of tribes, they formed what is known as the Catawba Nation or Confederacy. Among these were the Cheraw, Sugaree, Waxhaw, Woccon, and Tutelo. The Catawba proper evidently occupied the area from early prehistoric times, having migrated from the Ohio valley region. They were sedentary agriculturalists, differing little in culture from the other southeastern woodland Indians. During the period of white exploration and colonization, the Catawba warred bitterly with surrounding Iroquoian and Algonquian tribes who were pressing upon them from the north and west.

Hard-pressed by these enemies, the Catawba initially welcomed the English colonists as allies and suppliers of weapons, and in 1711-13 assisted them during the Tuscarora War. Disturbed by white settlement expanding into the Piedmont, however, they briefly joined in the Yamasee uprising of 1715 but were quickly subdued and remained at peace with the whites ever after. Further resistance would have been impossible in any case, for during the first half of the eighteenth century the Catawba were ravaged by white diseases, including a plague of smallpox in 1738, which reduced their population from nearly five thousand to less than a thousand by 1750. They had no choice but to appeal to the whites for protection and patronage, and through the mediation of the South Carolina government a treaty of peace was made between the Catawba and Iroquois at Albany in 1751. Other tribes, primarily the Shawnee, continued to prey upon the Catawba and killed their noted chief, King Haigler, in 1763. These attacks and a second epidemic of smallpox in 1759 further reduced the tribe to less than four hundred by 1770. The dwindling remnant settled on a fifteen-mile-square tract in South Carolina that had been guaranteed them in the Treaty of Augusta (1763).

To supplement their meager agricultural incomes, the Catawba leased portions of their reservation to white settlers, and by 1840 the Indians retained less than five hundred acres. Seeking a new beginning, they sold their title to South Carolina and joined the remaining eastern Cherokee, petitioning the federal government for permission to remove to Indian Territory in present-day Oklahoma. The government was amenable, but old intertribal animosities interfered, and the bulk of the Catawba returned to their South Carolina homeland, where they were regranted an eight-hundred-acre reserve. In subsequent years some Catawba families did join the Choctaw and Cherokee in Oklahoma, and others moved to Colorado and Utah. During the 1880s Mormon missionaries converted the entirety of the South Carolina group to that faith. In 1944 trusteeship of the Catawba reservation was transferred from South Carolina to the Bureau of Indian Affairs, which had not previously recognized the Catawba as a tribe. Federal administration was terminated in 1962, in which year the Catawba population was reported as 353.

See D. S. Brown, *The Catawba Indians: The People of the River* (1966); C. J. Milling, *Red Carolinians* (1940); and J. R. Swanton, *The Indians of the Southeastern United States* (1946).—P. R. M.

Cather, Willa [Sibert] (1873-1947). Novelist and short-story writer. Cather was born in Virginia and moved to Red Cloud, Nebraska, in 1883. She did not attend regular school until high school and graduated from the University of Nebraska in 1895. An accidental meeting with Stephen Crane in 1894 cemented her desire to be a writer. Previously she had flirted with the notion of becoming a doctor, though since 1891 she had been active in college journalism. Upon graduating from college she worked in Pittsburgh as a journalist and high school teacher; after a brief trip to France she went to New York, where, from 1906 to 1912, she was an editor for S. S. McClure, the publisher of *McClure's Magazine*. During these years she wrote a book of poems, *April Twilights* (1903), and a collection of short stories, *The Troll Garden* (1905), both of which are memorable primarily because they contain almost no mention of Nebraska, which was to become the world of her later fiction and with which she is today almost totally identified.

In New York Cather met the local-color writer Sarah Orne Jewett, who told her to forget the East and "find your own quiet center of life and write from that." Though Cather's first novel, *Alexander's Bridge* (1912), ignored this excellent advice, a trip she and her brother made to the Southwest in 1912 turned her imagination toward the West as a possible fictional world. She had already resigned her position with *McClure's*, and was determined to support herself by writing, which she did for the rest of her life. Her next novel, *O Pioneers!* (1913), was the first to be placed in a Nebraska setting, and was followed by the less successful *Song of the Lark* (1915) and the justly famed *My Antonia* (1918). Her other western writings include *Death Comes for the Archbishop* (1927), *Lucy Gayheart* (1935), and a number of short stories. Cather was awarded a Pulitzer Prize in 1922 for *One of Ours*, the French Prix Femina Americaine in 1933 for *Shadows on the Rock*, and elected in 1938 to the American Academy of Arts and Letters.

Cather's western fiction has always been something of a puzzle to critics, who have more or less openly demanded of it that it fall into one of two fairly simplistic and easily recognizable cliches. Most have thought that her literary achievement would have been much greater if the romantic elements in her writing had not been allowed to run riot. They have been disappointed that Cather's fiction is not a brutally naturalistic treatment of the privations of life on the frontier, and they have censored her for not being true to the facts of pioneer existence on the Great Plains. Ironically, critics on the other side have condemned her for painting pioneer life too harshly. Both sets of critics wish an unequivocal social statement on Cather's part either that frontier life was good or bad; each fails to realize that Cather is optimistically dedicated to the process of pioneering itself, without necessarily being forced into any criticism or affirmation of a particular aspect of the process. Indeed, of Alexandra Bergson, the heroine of *O Pioneers!*, Cather says approvingly: "A pioneer should have imagination, should be able to enjoy the idea of things more than the things themselves."

Cather's fictional world is dominated by faith that the present hardships of pioneer life will somehow be resolved happily in the future. When seen in this light her three best western novels are remarkably consistent in

Red Cloud, Nebraska, Willa Cather's home from 1884 to 1890, supplied the background for many of her writings.

their basic concerns. *O Pioneers!* and *My Antonia* are both biographies of people who succeed because their faith in the future enables them to overcome the hardships of the present. If one's faith in the future is not sufficiently strong, present hardships will inevitably overcome one, as they do Mr. Shimerda in *My Antonia*, who commits suicide because he is overwhelmed by the deprivations of Nebraska life. Cather's other major western novel, *Death Comes for the Archbishop*, is often criticized as a romantic escape from the harsh realities of Nebraska life, probably because it is on one level an adulatory fictionalized autobiography of Bishop Jean Baptist Lamy, the first archbishop of New Mexico. However, the novel may equally well be interpreted as a summary statement of Cather's typical theme, that after surmounting innumerable hardships the archbishop may die peacefully in the desert that his faith has made to blossom like a rose.

See E. K. Brown and Leon Edel, *Willa Cather: A Critical Biography* (1953); Willa Cather, *Novels and Stories*, 13 vols. (1937-41); David Daiches, *Willa Cather: A Critical Introduction* (1959); John H. Randall, *The Landscape and the Looking Glass* (1960); and Elizabeth Shepley Sergeant, *Willa Cather: A Memoir* (1953). —J. K. F.

Catlin, George (1796-1872). Painter and writer. Born in Wilkes-Barre, Pennsylvania, Catlin studied law but abandoned that career to paint. With little formal training, he developed skill as a portrait painter, later becom-

ing the first artist of any importance to document the culture of the American Indian in pictorial terms. His introduction to the subject of his lifelong endeavor is said to have occurred when a group of western chieftains paid a visit to Charles Willson Peale's museum of natural history in Philadelphia in the 1820s. Resolving afterward to dedicate his life to the portrayal of what he felt to be a vanishing race of men, he made his first studies among various eastern reservation tribes. He began his work on behalf of the western tribes in 1830 through an association with the explorer William Clark, who at that time was superintendent of Indian affairs for Missouri Territory in St. Louis. In 1832 Catlin boarded the American Fur Company's steamer *Yellowstone* on its maiden voyage to the waters of the upper Missouri and in 1834 crossed the prairies west of Leavenworth to join a mounted company of dragoons out of Fort Gibson, Indian Territory, on an expedition into Pawnee and Comanche country. Catlin also traveled extensively in Wisconsin and Minnesota territories and was the first white man to visit the ancient quarry in southwestern Minnesota, which for centuries had been the source of the soft red stone utilized by many tribes in the making of their tobacco pipes. This mineral later was designated as "Catlinite" in honor of the artist.

Following his western adventures, Catlin exhibited in the East and in 1839 sailed for Europe, where he exhibited and lectured for a period of eight years. Finan-

Portrait of George Lowry, Cherokee, *by George Catlin.* *(Thomas Gilcrease Institute)*

cial troubles finally forced him to part with much of his collection, but not before he had succeeded in publishing several volumes devoted to his experiences among the Indians in America. He made subsequent trips to South America and spent the latter part of his life making duplicates of many of his earlier works.

Although a financial failure at the time of his death in Jersey City, New Jersey, Catlin is regarded today as having made an invaluable contribution to our knowledge of Indian and frontier life. His style is essentially graphic or descriptive. An accomplished watercolorist, he painted with less success in oil and did not overly concern himself with the more technical aspects of perspective or the rendering of form in action. The most important collections of his pictures are found at the Smithsonian Institution, Washington, D.C., the Joslyn Art Museum, Omaha, Nebraska, the Thomas Gilcrease Institute of American History and Art, Tulsa, Oklahoma, and the American Museum of Natural History, New York.

Catlin's published works include the two-volume *Notes to the Manners, Customs and Condition of the North American Indians* (1841), illustrated with more than three hundred engravings; *North American Indian Portfolio* (1844); and *Eight Years Travel and Residence in Europe* in two volumes (1848). A later narrative, entitled *Last Rambles Amongst the Indians of the Rocky Mountains and the Andes,* was published in America in 1868.

See Lloyd Haberly, *Pursuit of the Horizon* (1948); Harold McCracken, *George Catlin and the Old Frontier* (1959); and Paul Rossi and David C. Hunt, *The Art of the Old West* (1971).—D. C. H.

Catron, Thomas Benton (1840–1921). New Mexican politician and businessman. Of German ancestry, Cat-

ron was born on a farm near Lexington, Missouri; was graduated from the University of Missouri; and as an officer fought for the Confederacy at the battles of Carthage, Wilson's Creek, Pea Ridge, Corinth, and in other engagements. In 1866 he moved to Santa Fe and the following year was admitted to the bar. In association with his close friend Stephen B. Elkins, Catron maintained a law practice and engaged in a wide range of business activities, including banking, mining, and land speculation. With his appointment as United States attorney for New Mexico in 1872, he began his climb to prominence in territorial politics. In subsequent years he served as mayor of Santa Fe, president of the New Mexico Bar Association, and with statehood in 1912 became one of the first United States senators from New Mexico, the other being Albert B. Fall, his longtime political foe.

Catron maintained his influence and furthered his business interests through ironfisted control of the Republican party machinery in New Mexico. An inner circle of his cronies, known as the "Santa Fe Ring," exercised control over both government and the economy and was not above resorting to violence and fraud. The ring was deeply involved in the Colfax War and LINCOLN COUNTY WAR of the late 1870s and in the manipulation of papers relating to ownership of old Spanish and Mexican land grants (see MAXWELL LAND GRANT COMPANY). Toward the end of the century, Catron's monarchical hold began to slip, but he still held enough strength to realize his lifelong ambition of a Senate seat. When he died in Sante Fe, he left a reputation as the most pugnacious and resourceful of those Americans who profitably exploited New Mexico in the later territorial years.

Catron's career is covered in William A. Keleher, *The Fabulous Frontier: Twelve New Mexico Items* (rev. ed., 1962). For reference to his involvement with the Santa Fe Ring, consult Howard R. Lamar, *The Far Southwest, 1846–1912* (1966); and Simeon H. Newman, III, "The Santa Fe Ring," *Arizona and the West,* vol. 12 (1970). —M. SI.

cattle associations. The post-Civil War boom in the cattle industry brought the cattleman problems as well as profits: the incursion of other men's cattle on his grazing lands, heavy losses to cattle thieves, and the lack of coordination of roundup activities. The need to solve such problems as these, as well as to advance the welfare of the industry generally, prompted the formation of cattle associations in all of the major western grazing areas. The associations on the northern ranges had the additional problem of coping with TEXAS FEVER brought north by the Longhorns; each therefore worked—successfully—for the extension of quarantine lines into its territory.

In Texas there were several associations formed during the 1870s; probably the best known was the Northwest Texas Cattle Raisers' Association formed at Graham in 1877. By 1883 this organization had set up a system of cattle inspection and was holding annual conventions to discuss the difficulties encountered by the industry. By 1895 the organization's membership had broadened considerably, and therefore its name was changed to the Cattle Raisers' Association of Texas. Several years later the name again was changed, this time to the Texas and Southwestern Cattle Raisers'

Association. This association divided the area from the Colorado River to the Red River into districts, each of which had a resident member who watched for, and returned, stray stock. Originally, the association appointed brand inspectors and others to oversee the ranges.

Cattle organizations wielded considerable influence over state legislators, obtaining protective legislation in areas where necessary. The Texas cattle associations, like those in other areas, became an extremely significant force for resolving the problems of cattlemen. The associations in the earlier days defended cattle and ranchers against hostile Indians; later, committees and members were appointed to stop cattle thieves, to watch roundups for mavericks and brand changes, and to inspect cattle for diseases such as Texas fever.

In Colorado the cattlemen's biggest problem, and the one that united them, was the intrusion of Texas herds on the ranges of the territory. In 1867 the Stock Growers' Association (known as the Colorado Cattle Growers' Association after 1876) was formed to seek legislation protecting local cattle; it hired detectives to deal with rustlers, oversaw the branding of cattle, and pressed for the establishment of a regional livestock commission.

Wyoming's cattlemen made their first move toward large-scale organization in 1871 with the formation of the Stock Grazers' Association; but the largest and most successful of the territory's cattle associations was the Stock Association of Laramie, founded in 1873 and renamed the Wyoming Stock Growers' Association in 1879. By 1885 the Stock Growers' Association had acquired four hundred members—who collectively owned at least two million head of cattle—and had taken control of the territorial legislature. The association oversaw the branding, sale, and entrainment of millions of head of cattle; petitioned for lower freight rates on rail lines and against revision of federal land-grant policies; and became extraordinarily effective in combating crime on the range (see JOHNSON COUNTY WAR). The special status accorded the association by its power in the Wyoming government made it extremely vulnerable to attacks by homesteaders, whose interests were seldom served by procattle legislation. Until the demise of the range-cattle industry in the late 1880s the Wyoming cattle association was the most powerful in the West.

Drawing on the experiences of the Wyoming cattlemen, Montana's stockmen organized the Montana Stock Growers' Association in 1884. Unlike earlier Montana cattle groups, the new association was able to set up a stable organization that took in the whole territory. Since Montana Territory had its Board of Live Stock Commissioners (also dating from 1884), whose duties included supervision of the branding and shipping of cattle, the association's power, although great, was circumscribed.

The first New Mexico association, the Cattle Theft Association, organized in 1865, was instituted primarily to combat rustlers. In January 1881 the Southwestern Stockman's Association was formed at Silver City, and in April 1884 the Central New Mexico Cattlegrowers' Association was established at Albuquerque. Growth was rapid for most associations: at the annual meeting of the Northern New Mexico Stock Growers' Association in 1884, there were 125 members owning approximately 400,000 head of stock. All these organizations were orig-

inally established to protect against thieves who were taking a ruinous toll of the New Mexico stockmen's property. In May 1886 the Sierra County Cattle and Horse Protection Association was organized at Hillsboro; several other smaller organizations existed at different times. Later, the Grant County and Southwestern Cattle and Horse Protective Association became the New Mexico Cattle and Horse Protection Association and, in 1929, the New Mexico Cattle Growers' Association; it remained the largest and most effective of its kind in the state.

Designed to promote the welfare and business interests of the cattlemen, these organizations provided the unity necessary for the survival of the industry. Most of the major associations cooperated with their counterparts in other areas in matters controlled by the federal government, especially on legislation affecting the public domain. These associations have continued to the present day because cattlemen still recognize the need for collective action to achieve their individual goals.

See E. Everett Dale, *The Range Cattle Industry* (1930); and Ernest S. Osgood, *The Day of The Cattleman* (1929).—J. A. S.

cattle brands. The practice of branding cattle, burning into an animal's hide a distinctive and permanent mark of ownership, was an established Old World custom when the Spanish brought the first cattle to North America. Branding spread from Mexico northward, where it became the accepted method of determining legal ownership. By 1848 Texas law required that each brand be registered with the county clerk, and brands were sometimes advertised in newspapers. In the northern cattle states the various cattle associations maintained brand books, in which all brands within their purviews were to be registered, and usually supervised the branding process.

Before barbed wire came into being in the 1870s, unbranded cattle belonged to those industrious enough to rope and brand them on the open range (see CATTLE INDUSTRY). Consequently, a herd owner had to keep his animals well marked. One of the main purposes of the traditional spring roundup was to brand unmarked stock, usually calves born in winter and early spring. After the cattle had been gathered, those to be marked were cut out of the herd, roped, tied, branded, tallied by age and sex, and released to rejoin the herd. The brand was usually placed on the left hindquarters, where it could be read easily by a right-handed roper.

Brands were infinite in their variety. Convention led to the use of numerals and letters as the most common elements of brands (6666 and XIT), but symbols that represented objects were also used (Pitchfork and Spur). The addition of a quarter circle under a brand caused it to be "rocking" (Rocking A). Curved strokes added at the top made a "flying" brand (Flying M). A diagonal mark before a letter was called a slash (Slash S). Letters whose sharp angles were rounded were "running" letters. An element of a brand could be set in an irregular position: the letter P, for example, tilted to the right (or left) was said to be a "tumbling right (or left) P"; P set backward was a "reverse P"; an upside-down P was a "crazy P"; and P set horizontally, in either direction, with either side uppermost, was a "lazy left up P," "lazy left down P," and so on. A brand could take the form of an acronym, as in the case of the XIT brand; XIT reputedly stood for "Ten in Texas" because the ranch covered all or part of ten Texas counties.

Rocking A	Flying M	Slash S	Running M
Tumbling right P	Tumbling left P	Reverse P	Crazy P
Lazy left up P	Lazy left down P	Lazy right down P	Lazy right up P

Earmarking was another form of brand. A distinctive cut was made in the animal's ear, and this cut was often registered with the side brand.

The practice of branding, while still in use, has somewhat diminished. Today most purebred stock is marked by a tattoo in the ear or by a metal tag, although many commercial cattle are still branded. Purebred stock is raised strictly for show or breeding; commercial cattle are marketed for their meat and other parts (commercial cattle may be purebred, but not necessarily). —J. B. F.

cattle industry. The wilderness environment of the New World provided ample forage for successful livestock farming. Cattle were first imported in 1611, to Jamestown, Virginia. By 1623 cattle were being brought in limited numbers to new communities. Although the cattle population was swelled by the importation of stock from Sweden, England, Denmark, and the Netherlands (thirty-three percent of which died on the arduous crossing), the largest increase came from the unhindered breeding of free-roaming cattle in America. A byproduct of such random mating was the predominance of hybrid offspring; descriptions of cattle in the colonial era were therefore made on the basis of color and size rather than type. Turned loose to forage, the animals thrived during the warmer months, but during winter many became scrawny or died. For example, it has been estimated that fifty thousand head died during the cold spell in Maryland during 1694-95.

So many cattle ran wild by the beginning of the eighteenth century that the annual roundup became a widespread practice. By the middle of the century some attempts were being made to improve breeding and thereby the quality of milk, butter, and cheese. Healthier cattle also produced more milk, and therefore the temperate middle colonies became the center of the fast-growing dairy industry. Proliferation of herds led some large farming operations to maintain as many as two hundred head; however, most herds numbered about twenty head.

So plentiful were wild grasses and other vegetation that many colonial pioneers naturally became herdsmen. This was especially true in the South, described as a "lush and verdant land, peculiarly fitted for grazing livestock." From North Carolina to Texas, in the Allegheny, Cumberland, and Ozark mountains, extending inland for nearly two hundred miles at some places, were excellent ranges for cattle and other stock. As more farmers moved into the areas, the herdsmen pushed steadily west in search of new pastures. Livestock grazing was a major occupation in colonial America as long as there were large sections of public domain on which to graze the stock. Moreover, the large quantities of wild stock in the southern colonies provided stockmen a boundless source of wealth.

Until the late eighteenth century the Piedmont, the Great Appalachian Valley, and other areas nearby were devoted almost exclusively to grazing livestock. Herds were fattened on the public domain and, when ready, were driven to Baltimore, New York, or other eastern markets to be slaughtered. But inevitably the herdsmen were forced to push west, where they found that, because of sparser grass, more land was needed to feed the cattle; they also learned that additional cattle could be kept under surveillance in open grassland country. Thus, the size of herds and profits increased with the westward movement.

By 1800 cattle were grazing on the lower reaches of the Mississippi River in Louisiana, and by 1820, on the prairies of southwestern Louisiana and the Red River district of Arkansas. One contemporary New England missionary recorded that the graziers on the Louisiana frontier had as many as fifteen thousand head of cattle in a single herd. By 1840 the farmers had crowded onto the available grazing lands in the eastern states and had interfered with the grazing practices of the open range; thus, graziers had almost disappeared from those areas as a result of increased population.

As herds moved westward, they met wild herds of Spanish origin that were rangier and better adapted to the aridity of the Plains. Although at first glance the cattle in the West appeared similar, in that both were horned, there were actually four distinct western types: the wild, mealy-nosed brown cow, marked with a light stripe down its back and wide-spreading blue horns; the multicolored Longhorn of the Texas variety; the small-boned Spanish cow; and, finally the sturdily built curly-haired, or chino, breed. Trail herds were generally comprised of these breeds.

Cattle raising in the Southwest began in Texas, where after 1716 the Spanish raised cattle at their missions; by 1770 the ranches of Mission La Bahía del Espíritu Santo, near Goliad, contained as many as forty thousand head. Cattle soon made missions wealthy, and private citizens who invested in herds made profitable long drives from Texas to Louisiana and into northern Mexico. Some sheepherding developed in southern Texas also but did so more slowly than cattle because of the heavily wooded terrain and the shortage of trained shepherds.

The Spaniards also introduced cattle into California, Arizona, and New Mexico. Juan de Oñate brought cattle to New Mexico in 1598. In the Pueblo revolt of 1680 most of the cattle herds were killed or dispersed; but during the reconquest by Diego de Vargas cattle were reintroduced, and thereafter their numbers steadily increased. In 1846, when American occupation began, cattle were a means of exchange and provided much of the property assets. During both the Spanish (1770-1811) and Mexican (1811-1848) periods cattle provided the basis of the economy in California but were of less significance during the American period (1848 on) or during the development of the cattlemen's empire elsewhere in the West.

During the Mexican War, Texas cattlemen sold their beeves to the military and even sent some to New Orleans, from whence the cattle were eventually shipped east. This might have been considered the origin of the range cattle trade, but by the beginning of the Civil War

A Montana ranch, photographed by William H. Jackson in 1872. (National Archives)

the Anglo-American cattle industry in the Southwest had begun for certain. Nevertheless, not until after the war did the cattlemen's empire become the folkloric phenomenon portrayed in the pages of popular periodicals of a later era.

During the war the union blockade of the South had prevented drives eastward from Texas, and so, the Longhorns ran wild on the Texas prairies and increased to an estimated five million head by 1866. Confederate veterans returning to an economically devastated Texas found that there was little they could do to earn a living other than to round up wild cattle and trail them to market. Incentive was provided by the price of cattle (only four dollars a head in Texas but forty or fifty dollars a head at eastern markets) and the ready markets of the East, whose cattle population had been decimated by the war, and of the North and West, where army outposts, Indian reservations, mining towns, and understocked ranges vied for Texas cattle.

The cattlemen's empire of the post-Civil War period began in the area bounded by San Antonio, Corpus Christi, and Laredo, which was naturally conducive to cattle raising, for grasslands abounded, water was plentiful, and predatory animals were few. The cattle industry soon spread rapidly to other areas, for all the stringy Longhorns needed to survive—and even gain weight—was sufficient water and food during cold spells.

Although a few landowners of the Northern Plains had long before entered the cattle business, it was the

Texas cowboys who were to push the cattle empire northward, making the "long drive" over the great cattle trails (see COWBOY). At first, expansion was onto areas in the public domain—land owned by the federal government. Open and uncontrolled lands, where laws were evaded, ignored, and unenforced, provided a haven for graziers. As the buffalo of the Plains were decimated and the Indians were crowded onto reservations, free grass and water (collectively known as free air) were used by cattlemen to fatten their herds and grow rich. Many a cattle baron started with little more than a few cowhands, a branding iron, and a herd rounded up on the prairie and nurtured in the public domain.

Although the long drive had been used before the war, it was only between 1866 and 1885 that it became the most widespread and important means of transport for the cattle industry. The great cattle trails tended to follow Indian or pioneer trails, always depending, of course, on the availability of grass and water along the way. In 1866 Charles Goodnight and his partner, Oliver Loving, cut out the 700-mile Goodnight Trail from west of Fort Worth, Texas, to Fort Sumner, New Mexico; from there Loving moved north to Colorado on what became known as the Goodnight-Loving Trail. Within the year 260,000 head had been driven north to the railheads and ranges of the Great Plains.

The near-legendary Chisholm Trail, from San Antonio, Texas, to Abilene, Kansas, was laid out by the enterprising cattleman Joseph McCoy along an old

The cattle industry of the last half of the nineteenth century centered on the Texas Longhorn. (National Archives)

trading trail marked by Jesse Chisholm. From 1867 until 1871 it was the major artery of the rapidly growing system of trails, with 1.5 million head moving through the yards at the terminus of the Kansas Pacific Railroad. But the proliferation of cattle trails and the westward crawl of the railroads soon ended Abilene's importance as a "cow town" (see CATTLE TOWNS).

Several other cattle trails were opened during the days of the great cattle drives. The Eastern Trail, begun in 1867, originated from several places, the largest drives over the trail being those from the King and Laureles ranches of Texas; sizable drives were also organized at Austin, Waco, and Fort Worth. Ex-Confederate soldiers drove the first cattle over this route to Abilene. The trail, which occasionally merged with the Chisholm Trail, crossed the Washita River near present-day Anadarko, Oklahoma, and ran through the Cherokee Strip to Abilene.

The Western Trail, running from San Antonio to Dodge City, was an outgrowth of the efforts of Lucien MAXWELL. During May 1877, Maxwell and his partner drove cattle north from Matamoros along the Chisholm Trail; at Belton, Texas, they left the well-traveled road and pioneered a new route. They traveled northwest to Fort Griffin; then north to Doan's Store on the Red River; and on through Dodge City, Kansas, to Ogallala, Nebraska, along the so-called Jones and Plummer Trail.

There were several other trails used less frequently during the days of the great cattle drives. In 1882 Jim Stimson, who managed the New Mexico Land and Cattle Company, drove twenty thousand head of cattle from west central Texas to the Estancia Valley, New Mexico, entering the state at Salt Lake and Las Portales Springs. Thereafter, Texas cattlemen drove several thousand head of cattle over Stimson's Trail, which ultimately was extended to the Arizona border.

Two cattle trails frequently used in the Northwest were the Oregon and Northern trails to Montana. Granville Stuart, soon after establishing a large ranch in Montana in the late 1860s, pioneered a route from Oregon to Montana. In 1870 cattle began reaching Montana in considerable numbers by way of a trail that ran east of Lewistown, through Monida Pass, to Baker City, and the Grande Ronde valley. Cattlemen soon discovered that livestock bringing only eight to twelve dollars in Oregon were valued at almost one hundred dollars in Montana. The route actually followed the old immigrant trail; it cut away from the old trail after crossing Big Camas Prairie but returned to it near Fort Hall.

The Northern Trail at times paralleled the Oregon Cattle Trail for many miles. For example, the two routes ran parallel about fifteen miles apart as they crossed through the Boise region and continued to do so almost through Idaho. Cattlemen heading for Wyoming along the Northern Trail crossed the Oregon Cattle Trail and the Montana-bound herds at Big Lost River and then turned toward South Pass. Although no accurate records were kept, perhaps as many as a quarter of a million cattle moved over these trails between 1869 and the end of the drives from Oregon in 1875. And although the Wyoming-Montana trails seem inconsequential in relation to the number of cattle moved from Texas during this time, the lessons learned from the raising of cattle in these areas may have had greater effect on cattle growing in the United States than that in any other area.

By 1871 the ranges of the Northern and Central Plains had become well stocked, with three hundred thousand head moving into them in that year alone. The 1858 Colorado gold rush had early made the area a market for Texas cattle, and when the railroads reached the eastern edge of the territory in the late 1860s, the future of the cattle industry in Colorado was secure; it has been estimated that by 1869 a quarter of a million cattle were grazing within the territory's borders.

The cattle frontier had moved into Wyoming as early as the 1830s, when William Sublette and Jedediah Smith took cattle into the area. The influx of cattle was abetted by pioneers, among them the Mormons, who brought breeding cattle to Wyoming in 1847. Perhaps as many as seventy-one thousand cattle were grazing in Wyoming by 1870.

In MONTANA the pattern was similar: Granville STUART drove sixty head of cattle to the area in 1858. By 1863 cattle raising was a significant enterprise near Alder Gulch, and within seven years, more than one hundred thousand head of cattle were grazing in Montana. In what is now South Dakota, stock raising was bringing high returns on investments by the early 1870s.

While thousands of head of Texas cattle were shipped to Chicago for processing, the livestock industry was not new to Illinois. The state had enjoyed significant status as a beef-producing area. During the early 1860s it had been second only to Texas in the production of cattle. Awareness of the value of the cattle markets, and the fact that Chicago was quickly becoming the major railhead distribution center for eastern markets, prompted investors to move quickly to capture the meat-processing industry. Thus, the Union Stockyards opened in 1865, large meat-processing plants were quickly established, and the city concentrated its efforts to obtain shipments of Texas cattle. Moreover, the development of the refrigerator car in the 1870s also increased market potential for the Chicago livestock industry.

The increased movement of Texas cattle northward to the slaughterhouses of Chicago, St. Louis, and other cities was countered by demands for higher quality beef. The demand was to be met in two ways: by feeding cattle on Middle West corn crops and by introducing greater numbers of "American breeds" of cattle—Shorthorn, Devon, Hereford, Angus, called American to distinguish them from the Longhorns, which were of Spanish or Mexican origin—to the ranges of the Plains. American cattle, whose meat was preferred even by Texas cowmen, had been thriving in Oregon ever since their introduction to the Northwest by settlers in the 1840s. Following the Panic of 1873 and the consequent constriction of local markets (the price per head dropped from twenty-three to twelve dollars), Oregon cattlemen began to move their surplus stock eastward to the Plains. The movement was facilitated by the ever-diminishing distance between railheads and the Pacific Coast, for the American cattle, heretofore handicapped by being less hardy than Texas Longhorns, could now make the relatively short drive to market across the Oregon Trail and onto the ranges of Nevada, Utah, Idaho, Montana, and Wyoming. American cattle had a further advantage over the Longhorn: they matured in about six years, whereas the Longhorn matured in about ten years.

Long trail drives persisted long after the arrival of railroads into the cattle-producing areas of the West. Cattlemen were skeptical about the efficiency and dependability of the railroads and suspected that many of the railroads charged rates that were too high and inconsistent. Moreover, every cattleman knew that railroad cars were usually too small and poorly designed for shipping cattle. Animals were jammed into the cars, and bad roadbeds and the continued use of link-and-pin coupling resulted in the cattle being jolted and injured en route to market. In addition, cattlemen believed that many of the railroad companies were cooperating with stockyards and meat-packing companies to control the supply and price of beef. There had also been some incidents in which trains had run over cattle that grazed freely on the open ranges. In fact, this situation became so serious that several states passed laws forcing the companies to pay for any cattle injured or killed in this manner. Thus, the cattleman's general attitude precluded his immediate and total acceptance of rail transportation for his beeves.

The mass movement of huge herds of animals across the American landscape (between 1865 and 1890 an estimated ten million head were driven out of Texas alone) inevitably met with opposition from those not dependent on the cattle industry, and even from some

The roundup begins. (National Archives)

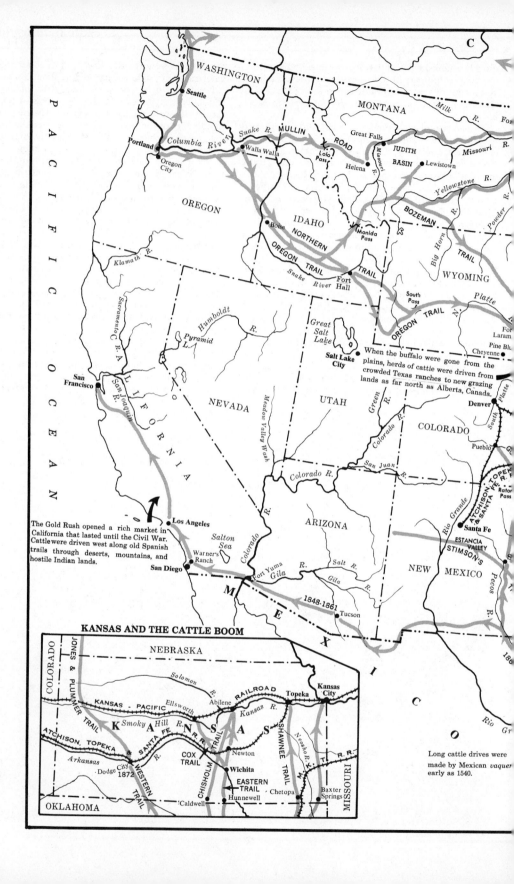

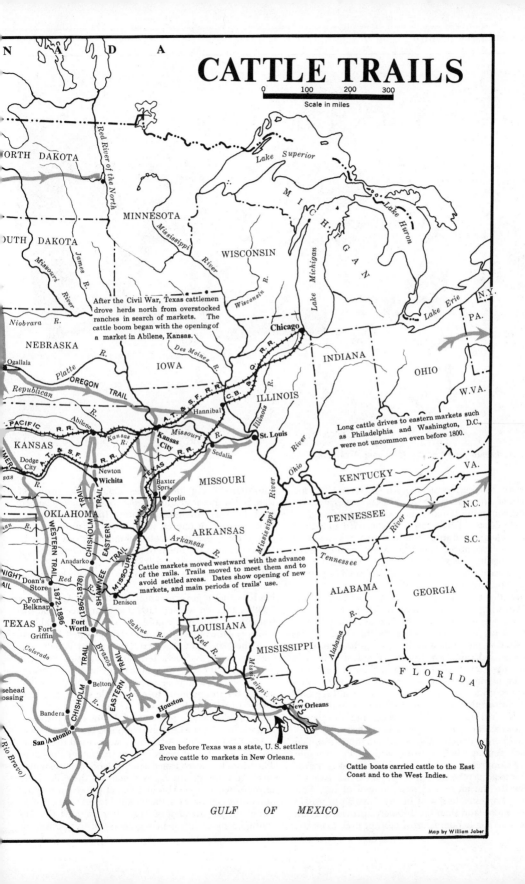

CATTLE TRAILS

0   100   200   300
Scale in miles

Map by William Jaber

After the Civil War, Texas cattlemen drove herds north from overstocked ranches in search of markets. The cattle boom began with the opening of a market in Abilene, Kansas.

Long cattle drives to eastern markets such as Philadelphia and Washington, D.C., were not uncommon even before 1800.

Cattle markets moved westward with the advance of the rails. Trails moved to meet them and to avoid settled areas. Dates show opening of new markets, and main periods of trails' use.

Even before Texas was a state, U.S. settlers drove cattle to markets in New Orleans.

Cattle boats carried cattle to the East Coast and to the West Indies.

A steer is downed for branding. (National Archives)

who were. Northern cattlemen, who suffered heavy losses of their American cattle from TEXAS FEVER carried by the fever-immune Longhorns, everywhere pressed for quarantine laws. Texas cowmen who tried to make a break through quarantine lines in turn lost many of their own cattle at the hands of an outraged citizenry. And so, cattle drives, which had at first been made mostly toward the East, were slowly pushed onto trails further and further west.

When the Consolidated Land, Cattle Raising, and Wool Growing Company, operating in New Mexico and Colorado, was incorporated in 1872, becoming the first of the large cattle companies in the area, it was capitalized at ten million dollars—an indication of the sheer size and rapid growth of the industry, both of which characteristics prompted legislative response. Cattle branding, for example, obviously became a necessity where it was not a convenience; state and regional laws required that all brands within their purview be registered in a brand book. Texas had a branding law on the books as early as 1848 (see CATTLE BRANDS).

Cattlemen were often able to turn to their advantage laws not seemingly helpful to the industry. For example, in 1873 Congress passed the TIMBER CULTURE ACT in an attempt to adjust the eastern-oriented HOMESTEAD ACT of 1862 to the more arid environment of the West. Because homesteaders west of the Mississippi usually needed more land than the 160 acres provided by the Homestead Act to operate profitably or even to make a

subsistence living, the Timber Culture Act provided that if the homesteader planted trees on unclaimed land, he could homestead another 160 acres. The idea did not work: it tended to be used by ranchers to increase their already sizable holdings but did not adequately answer the needs of new homesteaders. The act therefore was repealed in 1891.

Cattlemen opposed much of the land legislation that was suggested, for they wanted to continue using public lands without governmental regulation. As early as 1899, cattlemen wanted laws that guaranteed that the immediate users of the public domain would be able to control all the public grazing land they wished. The next year the National Cattlemen's Association actually lobbied in Congress for a federal land-leasing bill that would allow them to control the rangelands. Significantly, during 1900 a conservation and leasing policy had begun for the national forests. While some cattlemen favored such a policy, many still opposed any change that would increase governmental control of the open ranges. In 1902 the cattlemen opposed bitterly the NEWLANDS RECLAMATION ACT, which was passed to encourage the use of arid lands. Three years later President Theodore Roosevelt called a public-lands commission to meet, and that group exposed many of the evils of the unregulated range. Also in 1905, at the recommendation of the commission, the national forests were placed under the Department of Agriculture, a move that encouraged more stringent regulation of the public domain within the national forests. By the end of 1912 the cattlemen realized that the government was going to play an increasingly important role in managing the public domain. Exponents of a general leasing system for the public domain continued to lobby for new laws, but many of the cattlemen firmly rejected any such changes. In 1928 one experiment in the Mizpah-Pumpkin Creek region of Montana was established and functioned well, but the administration of Herbert Hoover paid the experiment little heed. Moreover, cattlemen opposed bitterly Hoover's one attempt to solve the range-abuse dilemma when he attempted to give the eleven western public-land states all the lands within their boundary so that they could better regulate grazing. However, miners and even some cattlemen opposed this plan, for Hoover insisted that the federal government retain title to all subsoil minerals.

It was left to the administration of Franklin D. Roosevelt to inaugurate new and sweeping grazing laws. Roosevelt and Secretary of the Interior Harold L. Ickes wanted close supervision of the public domain; therefore, they initiated a plan to place all the public grazing lands under close regulation. In March 1933, Representative Edward T. Taylor of Colorado introduced the bill that would revolutionize the American philosophy of land policy, the Taylor Grazing Act. The act repre-

sented the last in a series of measures that completely reversed traditional American land and agricultural policies. Although many cattlemen vigorously opposed the passage of this bill, even more realized that something had to be done at once to preserve the public lands. After considerable debate and lobbying by cattle, mining, and other interests, the bill finally became law before the end of 1934. Virtually all public land outside of Alaska has been placed under regulated grazing. Since 1946, the task of controlling these grazing lands has been delegated to the Bureau of Land Management.

About 1880 the range-cattle industry entered a boom period that in many ways was similar to those of the gold strikes. The prospect of quick wealth in the new country attracted capitalists not only from the East, but from Canada, Australia, and the British Isles; these men raced to the American West to invest in huge land purchases or great herds of Longhorns. In England a parliamentary committee in 1881 reported a thirty-three percent return to stockowners, and this sent even more Britishers to the New World. Thus, British capital helped to finance the great cattle industry just as it had helped finance some of the railroads built in the United States. In fact, the largest cattle companies operating in the country during this period were owned by British or Scottish financiers.

Cattle are "dipped" in chemicals to rid them of disease-carrying parasites such as mites and lice. (National Archives)

Entrepreneurs from the industrial East of the United States invested heavily in the cattle business. In a single year it was reported that twenty corporations, aggregately capitalized at more than twelve million dollars, were organized under Wyoming laws. Fortunes were made and lost quickly, and the industry had its share of swindlers and stock manipulators. Men in New York invested in herds that they never saw—herds that often did not exist. No accurate system of tallying the cattle obtained during this period, for when a rancher sold his herd, the number of steers often was simply estimated.

Many enterprising men made fortunes in the cattle industry. Granville Stuart journeyed to Montana before the Civil War and organized a large and successful cattle ranch; Conrad Kohrs, a butcher in Bannack, Montana, opened his own shop in Helena and quickly joined the ranks of the "cattle kings"; John W. ILIFF established the largest and most successful cattle ranch in the West and operated in Colorado and Wyoming; and Alexander H. SWAN founded in the 1880s the great Swan Land and Cattle Company of Wyoming. These were but a few of the great cattle barons about whom so much has been written.

The range-cattle industry changed quickly: by 1884 the rancher who had expected the coming of BARBED WIRE to ruin the industry had begun to use the new fencing to his own advantage. Many of the ranchers had by this time illegally erected fences around territory that was still in the public domain. Fence wars caused violent disagreements over just who owned land and water.

Still, with all the difficulties plaguing the industry, the demand for cattle to stock the northern ranges increased during the 1880s. During 1884, Texas drovers pointed approximately 416,000 head of cattle northward, more than any other year since 1871. It was thus only a matter of time before the number of cattle increased so much that the range was overstocked and the range industry was faced with the problem of overgrazing of the lands. The marginal lands were already overcrowded, no new lands were available, and the arid country of the Northern Plains was hit hard by winter blizzards; yet profits were so great during the first half of the 1880s that cattlemen took these losses in stride. But there were too many factors militating against the continued success of the open-range industry. Hard winters and the invasion of sheepherders and homesteaders signaled the end of the open range.

The summer of 1886 was extremely dry on the northern ranges in Wyoming and Montana as well as other regions. The ensuing winter was the worst on record; snow, icy winds, and subzero temperatures took a high toll of cattle stranded on the ranges. From November to April a series of storms sent the herds drifting aimlessly with no food or water; huddled in masses, the livestock died by the thousands. It was clear that better procedures for caring for the stock had to be made, agriculture had to be included in the range industry, new and better breeds of cattle had to be introduced, and the open range had to be fenced in.

See Harold E. Briggs, *Frontiers of the Northwest* (1940); E. Everett Dale, *The Range Cattle Industry* (1930); J. Frank Dobie, *The Longhorns* (1941); Henry S. Drago, *Great American Cattle Trails* (1965); Maurice Frink, W. T. Jackson, and A. W. Spring, *When Grass Was King*

(1956); Wayne Gard, *The Chisholm Trail* (1954); J. Marvin Hunter, *Trail Drivers of Texas* (1925); Joseph G. McCoy, *Historic Sketches of the Cattle Trade of the West and Southwest* (1939); Ernest S. Osgood, *The Day of the Cattleman* (1929); Frank L. Owsley, *Plain Folk of the Old South* (1949); Louis Pelzer, *The Cattlemen's Frontier* (1936); and Jimmy M. Skaggs, *The Cattle Trailing Industry: Between Supply and Demand* (1973).—J. A. S.

Cattle Kate. Nickname of **Ella Watson** (1862?-1888). Outlaw. Cattle Kate Watson was a notorious prostitute who prospered by establishing a bawdy house in Sweetwater, Wyoming, where cattle was the medium of exchange. She also washed and ironed for the cowboys. Kate and her partner, Jim Averill, eventually branched out into the cattle-rustling business, an enterprise that led to their execution at the hands of irate ranchers.

Weighing in at about 170 pounds, Cattle Kate was a central figure in the feud between the small ranchers of Wyoming and the powerful cattle barons of the Wyoming Stock Growers Association. Averill and his confederates used Kate's corral as headquarters for their rustling forays on the herds of the large ranchers. Kate took an active hand in this business, for she was known to be good with guns and a pro with a branding iron. The lynching of Cattle Kate and Averill was one of several incidents that ignited the JOHNSON COUNTY WAR.

See James D. Horan and Paul Sann, *Pictorial History of the Wild West* (1954). For a hostile account, see John Clay, *My Life on the Range* (1924).—R. B. W.

cattle towns. The great cattle towns of the quarter-century following the Civil War were born of the massive cattle drives from Texas to northern railheads, where cattle were fattened on surrounding ranges before entrainment to eastern markets. At the end of the war, rail lines reached only as far as Kansas, and so, the state became the meeting ground for western cattlemen and eastern buyers and speculators.

Each cattle town followed the same simple pattern of development: Someone, usually a land speculator, would sell small parcels of land in an isolated area; as the new owners moved in and a community began to develop, local businessmen would entice the railroads to their town, with the hope of attracting the profitable CATTLE INDUSTRY; the community would thrive generally, but local farmers would lose their crops to free-grazing Texas cattle and therefore press for an end to the town's cattle trade, usually successfully. In every case the town's prosperity brought with it hordes of outlaws, gamblers, and "soiled doves" to prey on the footloose cowboy and the unwary businessman, to the dismay of a small, but growing, number of respectable citizens.

The towns' lawmen became famous: Wyatt Earp, the best known of the EARP BROTHERS; Wild Bill HICKOK; Bat MASTERSON; Michael MEAGHER, Thomas James SMITH, and William Matthew TILGHMAN. And so, too, the outlaws and those who operated on both sides of the law: Luke SHORT, William L. BROOKS, Joseph LOWE, Henry Newton BROWN, David MATHER, and Benjamin F. THOMPSON. These men became notorious or famous because each town had its era of violence, albeit grossly exaggerated in story and film. For example, Ellsworth, Kansas, full to the brim with itinerant liquor dealers and other riffraff, experienced eight homicides during its first year as a cattle center. Dodge City had nine

Newton, Kansas, in 1872 looked much the same as other cattle towns. (Kansas State Historical Society, Topeka)

homicides during its first year of existence. Efforts were feeble at first to control the problems. Caldwell had a lynching spree, as did some of the other western cattle towns. Yet in the early days of the cattle trade in each of the towns, there seemed no systematic way to suppress violence. This especially obtained when a town was created just as the cattle trade began. However, in cases such as Wichita, where the town had been organized two years before the advent of the Texas drovers, a better system of control was established. And, in some instances, such as in Abilene and Ellsworth, the Texas drovers were segregated in suburban brothel districts organized to entertain the tired and thirsty cattlemen. Abilene drafted a civil code in 1870 to govern cowboys, and most later cattle towns followed the pattern established. Abilene hired a marshal who controlled the entire police force of the town, who made rounds, routine arrests, and generally kept the town peaceful.

In cases where the towns soon decided that they had to have some form of law enforcement, there usually was disagreement between factions wanting a law-abiding and ordinary citizen as sheriff or a reputed "gunslinger" who feared little. A few men earned reputations; yet still more of the so-called lawmen of the West enjoyed legends that pulp writers of their day and later created for them. In truth, few men were actually killed by lawmen of any type, and while many legendary bad men traveled through the towns, most did not "draw down" on anyone. Lawmen such as Wild Bill Hickok killed just two men—and one was by mistake. Wyatt Earp, the famous gunfighter-marshal, wounded only one cowboy; Bat Masterson lived for a year in and around Dodge City and killed no one.

All society in the cattle towns was not violent, for there were soon ordinary, law-abiding citizens who migrated west from the eastern cities and countryside. Churches were quickly organized, and schools were provided for

by bond issues. For example, during 1881-82 Caldwell established a school system replete with a brick building and permanent fixtures; other cities likewise quickly thought of educating their children and making their towns places where permanent settlers could live happily. As the cattlemen were forced west, so were their hangers-on. And so, by repetition of the pattern, the cowboy gave way to the farmer, the outlaw to the solid citizen, and the West to the East.

In the 1850s Abilene was little more than a campsite. No settlement took root until the arrival in 1860 of Charley Thompson, who surveyed the townsite the following year and gave it its name. The aspiring village had no certain future, for the Civil War was raging and the Texas cowboys had not yet begun their legendary cattle drives. When Joseph G. McCoy, a newcomer to the West, visited Abilene in 1867, seeking to promote a town designed to capture the Texas cattle trade, he described it as a "small, dead place, consisting of about one dozen log huts." He searched the area for the best place to locate a railhead and, with the help of Charley Thompson and Governor Crawford of Kansas, began his enterprise.

McCoy bought about 250 acres for a stockyard—the Kansas Pacific Railroad by 1867 had stretched into the fledgling cattle town—and in August of that year the Texas cattle began to arrive. Soon, nearby towns attempted to organize protective associations to keep the Texas cattle—known to carry the feared Texas fever, which devastated northern cattle—out of the region. Nevertheless, Abilene boomed in 1867 when thirty-five thousand head of cattle arrived, with hundreds of hopeful businessmen, bankers, and land speculators close behind. By 1870 farmers were vying with graziers for the rich lands surrounding Abilene, heralding the beginning of the end of Abilene's heyday as a cattle town. Farmers alone could not have ended the cattle boom; it took an alliance with townspeople, who were tired of the gambling and corruption of the Texans, to do that. Real estate speculators wanting to clear lands of Texas cattle formed the militant nucleus of the anticattle movement.

During 1871 the Texas cattle, allowed to graze freely on the ranges near Abilene, destroyed hundreds of acres of crops. Early in 1872 the farmers of the area formed the Farmers' Protective Association of Dickinson County. Hastily they printed circulars calling for the end of the cattle drives. Still, livestock spent that winter on the plains near Abilene, but with growing pressure and the cooperation of some business interests in Abilene, an effective blockade of the cattle trade soon was set up. Thus, 1871 proved to be Abilene's last year as a rip-roaring cattle town. Abilene was the one Kansas cattle town where the moral reformers, rural dissidents, and urban businessmen effectively worked together to end the local cattle trade.

Abilene had become a full-fledged town by the time the cattle trade ended, and every aspect of its business had prospered, from the brothels to the village churches; but as the stock trade declined, the region became more and more dependent on agriculture.

Even before the end of the cattle-shipping business at Abilene, efforts were under way to create another cattle town. Ellsworth was located sixty miles southwest of Abilene along the railroad tracks heading west. During the 1850s frontiersmen sometimes stopped near the future townsite; the first cabin was constructed and inhabited sometime during the decade. Indians were still the masters of the area, however, and drove off any would-be settlers. Union soldiers were occasionally stationed in the vicinity, but not permanently until the erection of Fort Harker in 1865. Once the army arrived, settlement increased.

In 1866 civilians and soldiers drew up townsite plans. In May 1867 Ellsworth was founded with great hopes, but Indian raids, floods, and cholera struck with such savagery that many people died or left. Ellsworth had prospered briefly because it was an "end-of-the-line town" during 1867, but when the Kansas Pacific Railroad passed beyond the village, it appeared that the town would be abandoned. In the face of impending economic disaster, the businessmen of Ellsworth chose the cattle trade to save their investments. Thus, during the winter of 1868-69 they planned how they could lure the cattle trade away from Abilene.

Ellsworth entrepreneurs used their influence in the Kansas state legislature to lay out a cattle trail from Fort Cobb in the Indian Territory to their town. Along this pathway the Texans would be catered to and would be immune from the fast-spreading quarantine laws, forbidding the trailing of Texas cattle. By the summer of 1871 the Kansas Pacific Railroad, which had been promoting the idea of Ellsworth as a cattle town, realized a measure of success. With optimism the town opened the trailing season of 1872, and the Texans arrived. Yet even while the future of Ellsworth looked bright as a cattle center, movements already were under way that would end all hope of its becoming a permanent cattle departure point.

The winter of 1871-72 had been harsh, and the Texas cattle wintering on ranges near Ellsworth had foraged local crops, broken down fences, eaten baled hay, and generally created strong anticattle feeling among the quickly growing farm population. Thus, as in Abilene, the farmers determined to stop the cattle drives and therefore organized into protective associations in the fall of 1872. By early 1874 overcrowding of the local ranges had made the extension of the quarantine laws inevitable. The cattle trade in Ellsworth would have been doomed in any case, for the railroads drew the business westward in their wake; and so, Wichita became the new haven for cattlemen.

During the Civil War the Wichita Indians settled briefly in an area eighty-five miles south of Abilene that allegedly belonged to the Osage tribe. The Wichita left in 1867, and immediately thereafter land speculators became interested in the area because it lay outside the quarantine region. After considerable trouble over land titles, the government recognized agreements between the Osage tribe and land speculators. Noting the potential of the area, much of which could be granted homesteaders who met the provisions of the HOMESTEAD ACT, William Greiffenstein, a trader, preempted a claim and shortly thereafter platted the townsite of Wichita, Kansas.

By 1869, even with land titles uncertain, between two hundred and three hundred people had moved into the area. The next year the citizens voted a bond issue to attract railroads. When no railroad company immediately responded, the citizens set about organizing their own company. Before they had gotten very far, a director of the Santa Fe line decided to extend the line's rails to the fledgling village. By 1872 the railroad was completed, and the stage was set for Wichita's heyday as a cattle town. In the first year seventy thousand head were shipped east from Wichita.

Initially the opposition to the incoming Texans and their fever-carrying Longhorns was insignificant. However, as with earlier cattle towns, discontent soon developed. Although herd laws ratified by the legislature in 1871 made unrestricted and uncontrolled grazing of the steers illegal, quarantine laws had not been extended to the area. William S. White, a Wichita settler and later a journalist, insisted that the cattle trade really helped no one. After the Panic of 1873 White and many of the anticattle people softened their attitudes about the Texans. Yet by late 1874, with economic recovery beginning, the opponents of the cattle trade found renewed strength.

In April 1875 the Grangers and other anticattle men vowed to act themselves when the legislature refused to extend the quarantine line to Wichita. Ultimately the supporters and the opponents of the cattle trade signed an agreement whereby the Texas drovers were to supervise the herds closely and not allow them to graze freely. This did not wholly placate the anticattle forces, who in early 1876 secured a more stringent herd law that included Wichita's environs. Once again the end of a cattle town was imminent. During 1876, the last year of any significant cattle drives to Wichita, only 12,380 head were entrained there. Railroad authorities had anticipated a change in attitude toward cattle among the power structure in Wichita and, planning well in advance, had already begun to switch the cattle-shipping business to Dodge City. After 1877, Wichita's economy, like those of earlier cattle towns, was forced to become agricultural. Another chapter in the history of cattle towns was completed.

In 1872, while the Santa Fe Railroad was building westward across Kansas, two itinerant liquor dealers opened a saloon alongside the work line a few miles from Fort Dodge and the Santa Fe Trail. Army troops had visited the area only briefly early in 1865 and later that year had established the fort to protect citizens from Indian raids. In August 1872, a few people living about half a mile within the Osage territory joined with army officers to form the Dodge City Company, hoping to develop a town. Negotiations concerning land titles led to an agreement with the Osage tribe.

During Dodge City's first winter (1872-73), only buffalo hides were shipped east—nearly two hundred thousand of them. This provided a temporary boom, yet both townspeople and railroad men knew that the immediate future of Dodge City lay in capturing the Texas cattle trade. The Santa Fe Company constructed cattle pens in Dodge City before 1876, but during that year only 9,540 head of cattle were shipped east. In 1876-77 settlement south of Dodge City posed no threat to the flow of cattle, and therefore the prospects for the future looked bright. In 1877, 22,940 cattle were shipped east, and for a short while Dodge monopolized the cattle trade along the Santa Fe line. Nevertheless, rural agitation against the cattle trade had begun almost as soon as Dodge City became a cattle-trading and -shipping center.

The drought of 1879-80 slowed the migration of farmers into the area, but during late 1882 the number increased and with it attempts to extend the quarantine line. The cattlemen fought back by forming the Western Kansas Cattle Grower's Association, but their efforts to forestall restrictions on the shipping industry were unsuccessful: the governor of Kansas quarantined the entire state against Texas cattle in 1884, by which time farmers had fenced much of the land through which the cattle had been driven. As if to strike the cattlemen a fatal blow, prices for cattle decreased during the year. Dodge City's change from a cattle economy to one supported by crops was inevitable. The next—and last—of the great cattle towns was to be Caldwell.

The town of Caldwell, fifty miles south of Wichita, on the Chisholm Trail, dates from January 1871, when Charles H. Stone, a land speculator, and James H. Dagner, a liquor dealer, surveyed and sold the land. There was then no railroad to the site, but the promoters hoped to induce some line to build from Wichita. The ubiquitous farmers arrived just behind the promoters and by early 1874 were numerous enough to organize effective resistance to the cattlemen. The agricultural depression of 1874 temporarily slowed the growth of the anticattle forces, but by early the following year the farmers were again pressing for extension of the quarantine law to their region and eventually succeeded.

Throughout Caldwell's early history the promoters and speculators sought railroad connections to the town. During the winter of 1874-75 local businessmen financed an independent line. In September 1878 the president and chief engineer of the Kansas City, Burlington and Southwestern Railway arrived at Wellington to express an interest in building south to Caldwell if local subsidies could be obtained. Other companies were moved to advance the same idea. Soon thereafter the citizens of Caldwell voted approval of subsidies by a comfortable margin. However, the Santa Fe Railroad, to whom the subsidies were to go, was not interested in building as quickly as the people wanted. Another vote was taken, and the eager citizens agreed to subsidize yet another railroad promising to build immediately to Caldwell. Taking up the challenge, the Santa Fe Railroad built quickly to Caldwell. On June 1, 1880, the first Santa Fe train reached the city, providing the long-desired transportation for the cattle business. Unfortunately the Kansas City, Lawrence, and Southern Railway, seeing that it had lost the race to Caldwell, built toward another point on the border of the Indian Territory, enabling the town of Hunnewell to siphon off part of the cattle trade from Caldwell.

Just as in other areas, the cattle boom would be short-lived, for by 1883 ranchers had contracted illegally with the Arapaho and Cheyenne tribes to ranch the area just below Caldwell in the Indian Territory. Some of these areas were fenced, making cattle drives through the Indian Territory almost impossible. The extension of the quarantine line to all of Kansas did not hurt Caldwell, for it was on the state line and the town's actual ranching activity occurred across the border in Indian Territory. The cattle trade at Caldwell declined after 1886, as Texans tired of fighting trail difficulties began to utilize the railroads crisscrossing their state. The day of the cattle town was over by 1889, when David Payne and the Boomers (see OKLAHOMA) settled the Indian Territory, thereby blocking cattle drives north from Texas.

While the Kansas cattle towns were a unique product of open-range ranching and the long drives from Texas, wherever open-range ranching thrived in the West, whether in eastern Oregon, Montana, Wyoming, Colorado, the Dakotas, Nebraska, or New Mexico, many established local towns went through similar cattle-town experiences. Certainly Lincoln and Silver City, New Mexico, and Medora, North Dakota, deserved to be called cattle towns during the 1880s, while Helena, Montana; Cheyenne and Laramie, Wyoming; and various Nebraska towns felt the impact of the cattleman and cowboy and catered to their wants. In short, the cattle-town experience occurred in so many areas that it was an integral part of the history of the entire American West.

See Robert R. Dykstra, *The Cattle Towns* (1968); and Floyd B. Streeter, *Prairie Trails and Cow Towns* (1936).—J. A. S.

Caughey, John Walton (1902-   ). Author and historian of the West. Caughey was born in Wichita, Kansas. He received his B.A. degree from the University of Texas in 1923. Before attending graduate school, he was an instructor at Schreiner Institute in Kerrville, Texas, for two years. Studying at the University of California, he earned his M.A. and Ph.D. degrees in 1926 and 1928, respectively. He taught for a year at San Bernardino Junior College, and then, in 1930, he became an instructor at the University of California at Los Angeles, where he later became an assistant professor (1932-39), an associate professor (1939-46), professor (1946-70), and department chairman (1945-47).

Caughey served as both an associate editor (1937-46) and managing editor (1947-68) of the *Pacific Historical Review*. He was general editor of the Chronicles of California series (1946-52), a regional editor of *Ameri-*

can Heritage (1954-58), and literary editor of *Frontier* (1956-67).

Caughey's work has earned him national consideration. He has been a Native Sons of the Golden West Fellow (1928), a Rockefeller Foundation Fellow (1950-53), a Benjamin D. Shreve Fellow at Princeton (1955-56), and an American Council of Learned Societies Scholar (1951-52). He was a member of the executive council of the American Historical Association from 1961 to 1964 and president of the Pacific Branch in 1958. He served as president of the Organization of American Historians in 1964-65. In 1947, he used his academic and administrative skills in a somewhat novel way—as a technical director for Paramount Pictures.

Caughey's publications are extensive, including biographies, surveys of California and American history, and discussions of contemporary social concerns. His biographical studies include *Bernardo de Galvez in Louisiana* (1934), *McGillivray of the Creeks* (1938), and *Hubert Howe Bancroft* (1946). Caughey is at once one of the most prominent and prolific writers on California and the Pacific Coast, his major works in the field being *History of the Pacific Coast* (1933); *California* (1940); *Gold is the Cornerstone* (1948); *The Pueblo Water Rights of Los Angeles* (1969); and with his wife, Laree, *California's Own History* (1963) and *Windows on the Pacific* (1963). Caughey's reflections on the West after a long and prolific career are presented in *The American West: Frontier and Region* (1969), a collection of addresses, essays, and lectures. Caughey's broad view of what constitutes a region has led him to comment on the danger of confining western history to the frontier phase.

Caughey's general works on American history include *America Since 1763: A Survey* (1955); *A History of the United States* (1964), with Ernest May; and *Land of the Free* (1965), with May and John Hope Franklin. Caughey has edited J. E. Ware's 1849 *Emigrant's Guide to California* (1932); *Seeing the Elephant: Letters of R. R. Taylor, Forty-Niner* (1951); and B. D. Wilson's 1852 report *The Indians of Southern California*. His *Their Majesties the Mob* (1960) is an important critical study of vigilantism and mob violence.

Several of Caughey's survey histories are addressed to youthful readers, reflecting his concern with all levels of education. That concern, shared by his wife, has inspired two local studies of education, *School Segregation on Our Doorstep: The Los Angeles Story* (1966) and *To Kill a Child's Spirit: The Tragedy of School Segregation in Los Angeles* (1973).

Caughey has never confined his energy and attention to the academic world. His service on the California Landmarks Approval Committee (1944-50), his work as consultant to the California State Lands Commission (1949-50), and his book *In Clear and Present Danger: The Crucial State of Our Freedoms* (1958) all attest to his concern with contemporary, as well as historical, issues. In the California loyalty oath controversy, Caughey opposed institution of the oath, considering it a threat to academic freedom.—P. L. N.

Cayuga Indians. See IROQUOIS CONFEDERACY.

Cayuse Indians. About five hundred years ago the Cayuse Indians, of Penutian stock, moved from south-central Oregon into the upper drainage of the Umatilla and Walla Walla rivers on the west slope of the Blue Mountains in northeastern Oregon. From the first they

were on friendly terms with their Shahaptian-speaking neighbors, the Umatilla, Walla Walla, Palouse, and Nez Percé. As the years passed and the Cayuse intermarried extensively with their larger neighbors, they allowed their own dialect to lapse into disuse except for some important religious rites and adopted the dialects of their neighbors. During this period the traditional enemies of the Cayuse were the Shoshoni bands who lived on the east slope of the Blue Mountains and along the Snake, Payette, and Boise rivers.

About 1725 the Cayuse acquired horses either from the Nez Percé or the Shoshoni and began raising large herds on their good pasturelands, with a surplus to trade to other tribes. Their chief food was salmon, supplemented with roots, berries, and game.

When the first missionaries came to the Columbia Basin in 1836 they were cordially invited to settle among the Nez Percé. One couple, Dr. Marcus Whitman and his wife, Narcissa, founded their mission about twenty-five miles up the Walla Walla River from old Fort Walla Walla, a Hudson's Bay post. This mission site was on Cayuse lands, although the tribe did not want it there.

Starting in 1843, covered wagon trains moved each year along the Oregon Trail and through Cayuse lands. The Whitman mission served as a way station for the white travelers and offered shelter and food to the destitute. In addition a few children of the mountain men by Indian wives were sent to school there. In a few years the mission was a small village with a resident population of about eighty people, in addition to the Cayuse living nearby.

While the Cayuse disliked so much travel through their lands, they were willing to trade fresh horses to the travelers to supplement their tired teams. So many Cayuse horses reached the Oregon settlements in this way that the term "Cayuse horse" or later just "cayuse" became the common term for western range horses.

Each year the wagon trains brought in white man's diseases, especially measles and scarlet fever, and many of the Cayuse died from them. Dr. Whitman nursed and tended both Indians and whites when they became ill at the mission. Usually the whites recovered, but usually the Indians died. This led the Cayuse leaders to believe that Whitman was killing the Indians with poison administered as medicine.

Following an unusually severe winter in 1846-47 and excessive deaths among the weakened Indians in 1847, a few of the Cayuse leaders on November 29, 1847, killed Marcus and Narcissa Whitman and twelve of the men working at the mission. Several men escaped death, and fifty-three women and children taken prisoner were later rescued by the Hudson's Bay manager at Fort Walla Walla.

Settlers in the Willamette valley raised a volunteer force and harried the Cayuse tribe until six of them surrendered voluntarily to save the rest of their people from further attacks. The six were taken to Oregon City and hanged after the formality of a hasty trial.

Greatly weakened by disease and white attacks, most of the Cayuse tribe wasted away. A remnant joined their immediate neighbors, the Umatilla, on the reservation set up in 1855 for that tribe on the Umatilla River. Other individuals scattered to other tribes, especially to the Nez Percé and Yakima, where they had blood relatives.

See R. I. Burns, *The Jesuits in the Indian Wars of the Northwest* (1963); and Dorothy Johansen and Charles M. Gates, *Empire of the Columbia* (1957).—F. H.

Cazier, Henry Hallowell (1885-1963). Nevada rancher. Born in Nephi, Utah, Cazier moved with his parents in 1887 to Toano, Elko County, Nevada. (His father ran the freighting station and hotel at Toano, while building up a fine herd of cattle.) After graduation from the University of Nevada at Reno in 1906, he worked in San Salvador for two years as an engineer before returning home to manage the family ranch.

In 1910 Cazier began his own ranching operation with some steers from his father's herd plus some purebred Herefords. In 1915 his family formed the John H. Cazier and Sons Company, a firm specializing in cattle breeding. When it was dissolved in 1926, Henry Cazier retained the home ranch, still famous for its purebred Herefords.

Cazier was a civic-minded stockman who took a great deal of interest in public education in Nevada. He was also an active promoter of electric power development in the state; in 1927 he planned and organized the first completely automatic hydroelectric system in Nevada and the first rural electrification system. He was president and manager of the Wells Power Company from 1927 to 1960.—R. B. W.

Central City, Colorado. Ghost town. Central City was the site of the first important gold discovery in Colorado. On May 6, 1859, John Gregory discovered "the richest square mile on earth," and by September miners were extracting $50,000 a week in gold from the area's placers and lodes. In its boom days the population of the city ranged between 10,000 and 15,000, and in the early 1860s Central City rivaled Denver as Colorado's leading city. By the middle 1860s the placers and surface diggings were exhausted, and mining came to a standstill. However, with the introduction of new and improved reduction processes, mining once again picked up, and the 1870s and 1880s were Central City's best years. By 1914 the region's mines were depleted, and the town settled into quaint somnolence.

One of the major attractions of the city in its heyday was its opera house, which drew to its stage some of the finest talent in the country, including Sarah Bernhardt, Otis Skinner, and Edwin Booth. In 1932 the building was restored, and every summer hence the Central City Festival has seen nationally prominent entertainers perform in this historic theater. Other attractions for visitors include the Coeur d'Alene Mining Museum, the Central City Historical Museum, and the Teller House, where the town's citizens received President Grant in 1873 by temporarily paving the front walk with thirty solid silver bricks imported from Caribou, as a protest against inflation.

Central City, Colorado, in the 1880s. (Denver Public Library, Western History Collection)

See Caroline Bancroft, *Gulch of Gold* (1958); Phyllis Dorset, *The New Eldorado* (1970); Lambert Florin, *Ghost Town Trails* (1963); Frank R. Hollenback, *Central City and Blackhawk: Then and Now* (1961); Rodman Paul, *Mining Frontiers of the Far West* (1963); and Muriel S. Wolle, *The Bonanza Trail* (1953).—R. B. W.

Central Lowland. See PHYSIOGRAPHY OF THE UNITED STATES.

Central Overland California and Pike's Peak Express. Upon the discovery of gold in the Pikes Peak region, freighter William H. Russell was convinced that a stagecoach express route would be so profitable that a federal subsidy would not be essential. Russell's partners in the freighting business, William B. Waddell and Alexander Majors, opposed the venture on the grounds that it could not succeed without federal aid and was, in general, too risky. Russell therefore formed a partnership with another experienced freighter, John S. Jones, and Jones, Russell & Company organized the Leavenworth and Pike's Peak Express Company. The first travelers to Pikes Peak and the Cherry Creek diggings at Denver had either traveled along the Santa Fe Trail to Bent's Fort and then taken the upper Arkansas River to Pueblo and on north, or they had followed the Oregon Trail to the mouth of the Platte River and then followed the South Platte. Jones and Russell decided to locate a new route between the two and sent out a surveying party between the Republican and Smoky Hill forks of the Kansas River with instructions to build twenty-seven stations about twenty-five miles apart. When the project was completed, 108 men had been stationed along the 680-mile route, and 800 mules were in corrals along the way. Fifty new Concord coaches valued at $2,500 each were ordered from Abbott-Downing Company of Concord, New Hampshire, and placed on the route. Daily service was begun between Leavenworth and Denver on April 18, 1850.

In May 1859 Jones, Russell & Company purchased the contract of J. M. Hockaday & Company to transport the United States mail from St. Joseph, Missouri, to Salt Lake City. The Hockaday contract provided for a mail service along the Oregon Trail by way of Fort Kearny and Fort Laramie into Salt Lake City once each week. Jones and Russell now abandoned their route along the Smoky Hill and Republican rivers and operated along the mail line. From Julesburg, on the South Platte River, a branch line continued along the South Platte into Denver.

By the end of summer 1859, Jones, Russell & Company was deeply in debt. Receipts from passengers and express were far less than anticipated because of the collapse of the Pikes Peak boom and the excessive costs of maintaining a regular and efficient schedule. Russell's partners in the freighting company were forced to come to his financial aid or risk the downfall of their own firm, and in October 1859 they bought out the bankrupt concern. The Leavenworth and Pike's Peak Express Company continued to operate stages and deliver the mails into Denver and Salt Lake City. In February 1860 the concern was reorganized under a Kansas charter as the Central Overland California and Pike's Peak Express Company. Soon thereafter the mail contract between Salt Lake City and Placerville, California, held by George Chorpenning, was annulled for failure to perform the service, and a new contract was made with

Russell for a semimonthly delivery. This gave to the C.O.C. and P. P. Express Co. control of the entire semimonthly mail service on the central route to the Pacific. Stages on a branch line into Denver carried passengers and express, but the company had no contract with the United States for mail service at this time. Financial losses continued to mount and employees were not paid on time; one of them transformed the well-known initials of the company to read "Clear Out of Cash and Poor Pay." Russell and his partners continued their enterprise with determination, hoping to obtain authorization and subsidy for a daily overland mail. In this hope they were disappointed. In 1861, when the transcontinental overland mail contract was awarded to the Overland Mail Company, the latter subcontracted to the Central Overland California and Pike's Peak Express Company to carry the stage and Pony Express mail on that part of the route east of Salt Lake City. The company continued to operate at a deficit, became heavily indebted to Ben Holladay, and in 1862 the latter bought the property at auction.

See Raymond W. Settle and Mary L. Settle, *War Drums and Wagon Wheels* (1966).—W. T. J.

Central Pacific Railroad. The Central Pacific Railroad, the western half of the first transcontinental railroad, was built from Sacramento, California, across the Sierra Nevada to Promontory Point, Utah, where a junction with the UNION PACIFIC was made on May 10, 1869. The railroad's pioneer advocate was Theodore D. JUDAH, an engineer who had considerable experience in building early eastern railroads and whose efforts were primarily responsible for the Pacific Railroad Act of 1862. The willingness of four California businessmen to invest in the early stages of the project and see it through to completion was necessary, however; when Judah

Snow sheds on the Central Pacific in Placer County, California. (Library of Congress)

A snow plow on the Central Pacific. (Library of Congress)

died, Collis P. HUNTINGTON, Charles CROCKER, Leland STANFORD, and Mark HOPKINS, the "big four," continued the work. (For a discussion of the events leading to the construction of the first transcontinental route see RAILROADS.)

Construction was supervised by Crocker, who expended enormous energy in achieving daily construction records. In order to complete as many miles as possible before meeting the Union Pacific to maximize benefits under a subsidy and land grant, the Central Pacific was pushed rapidly across the mountains—despite harsh winter weather. High in the Sierra the project was brought nearly to a standstill by mountainous snowdrifts. Pressing on down the eastern slope, the builders lavished huge sums of money on snow shields, which proved to be the key to filling in what threatened to be embarrassing gaps in the mountains. When a shortage of labor threatened to halt progress, Crocker hit upon the idea of importing Chinese to do the work and made the happy discovery that Chinese laborers were even more effective than the Union Pacific's burly Irishmen (see CHINESE IMMIGRATION). The most complex job, however, was Huntington's. From a bare office in New York he procured vast quantities of materials and arranged for their shipment via Cape Horn, while struggling to realize as much cash as possible from the government "subsidy" bonds. Meanwhile, Hopkins kept the books, and Stanford maintained good relations with the California legislature.

Like the Union Pacific, the Central Pacific was built by construction companies (organized by the promoters), who defrayed their costs with the sale proceeds of bonds received from the company and took their "profits" in Central Pacific stock, which would have no value until the railroad was established and making money. The years Huntington spent in dogged efforts to keep the railroad solvent, therefore, are critical in understanding its history. The promoters eventually became very wealthy men, but the project had been risky, and western railroads were not firmly established until late in the nineteenth century.

The Thurman Act of 1878, by which Congress sought to guarantee that the Pacific railroads' indebtedness would be paid when due, proved a fatal drag on the Union Pacific's development after 1878. The act also applied to the Central Pacific, requiring the road to immobilize a large part of its profits in a sinking fund at the same time they were needed for further expansion. As a result Huntington and his associates turned their attention to the development of the SOUTHERN PACIFIC RAILROAD, which maintained control of the Central Pacific. By 1895 the Central Pacific's future was gravely in doubt; millions of dollars were due the government for "subsidy" bonds received in the 1860s. When all other proposals failed to satisfy government requirements, Huntington placed the credit of his thriving Southern Pacific behind a refunding plan, thereby achieving the distinction of having seen the Central

Pacific through from its inception to final independence from the government.

The anomalous arrangements whereby the Central Pacific, although obviously the western segment of a through overland route from Omaha to San Francisco, remained separate from the Union Pacific was corrected when Edward H. HARRIMAN gained control of both the Union Pacific and the Southern Pacific in 1900. Although the Union Pacific was ordered to relinquish control of the Southern Pacific and the Central Pacific in 1913, the harmonious relations Harriman introduced have continued. The Central Pacific's route was paralleled after 1900 by George Gould's Western Pacific. Today this historic railroad is only one of many transcontinental routes.

Stuart Daggett, *Chapters on the History of the Southern Pacific* (1922; rep. 1966), is the best financial and economic history of the Central Pacific. Oscar Lewis, *The Big Four* (1938), is a satisfactory account of the five men who built the Central Pacific.—A. M.

Chaffee, Jerome Bonaparte (1825-1886). Colorado politician and mining entrepreneur. Chaffee, born in Niagara County, New York, moved with his parents to Michigan and later settled in St. Joseph, Missouri, where he engaged in banking. He went to Colorado in 1860 and subsequently developed interests in numerous mining properties. With Eben Smith he established a stamp mill in Gilpin County, and he became the largest stockholder in the prosperous Bobtail Lode and Tunnell Company. His other mining investments included gold and silver lodes in Boulder, Gilpin, and Clear Creek counties, and he was an organizer and a principal stockholder of the famed Little Pittsburg Consolidated Mining Company near Leadville. In 1865 he joined with others in purchasing Clark, Gruber & Company, Denver's pioneer bank and mint, and organized the First National Bank, which he served as president from 1865 until 1880. In 1870 he became an owner of the MAXWELL LAND GRANT COMPANY and used his political clout to further the interests of that empire-building company.

He was elected to the house of the territorial legislature in 1861 and 1863, serving as speaker in 1864, and was named territorial delegate to Congress in 1871. He worked tirelessly for statehood until Colorado was admitted to the Union in 1876. A Republican, he became one of the first two United States senators from the new state, serving from 1877 to 1879, at which time he declined to stand for reelection because of health.—M. B.

Chandler, Alexander John (1859-1950). Arizona irrigation engineer and town builder. Born in Coaticook, Canada, Chandler received a doctor of veterinary science degree at McGill University in 1882, worked briefly as a livestock inspector for the Dominion government, and then established a private practice in Detroit, Michigan. In 1887 he came to Arizona as veterinarian for the newly created Livestock Sanitary Board. Impressed by the problem of water use, Chandler made a thorough study of the irrigation possibilities in the Salt River valley and visited the water districts in California, where he noted the high price paid for irrigable land. With financial backing from the D. M. Ferry Seed interests and others in Detroit, Chandler organized the Consolidated Canal Company and by the late 1890s had constructed a modern irrigation system on the Salt River south of

Tempe. He developed extensive farms, where he raised cattle and sheep, alfalfa and grains, and experimented with American-Egyptian cotton strains, which were the forerunners of the famous Pima variety. He dug wells, placed electric pumps in use, promoted interest in a storage dam on the Salt, and was on the first board of governors of the Salt River Valley Project. In 1909 he sold his canal system to the federal government for $187,000. With the completion of the Roosevelt Dam, Chandler subdivided his lands, founded the town of Chandler, and encouraged the Arizona Eastern Railroad to build a line into town. He organized the Bank of Chandler, was the town's first mayor, and built the plush San Marcos Hotel, which was his residence until his death.

See Robert C. Stevens, *A History of Chandler, Arizona* (1955).—H. P. H.

chaparral. See VEGETATION: *broad-sclerophyll woodlands.*

chaps. See COWBOY CLOTHING.

Charbonneau, Jean Baptiste (1805-1866). Mountain man, guide, and goldseeker. Charbonneau lived a life the most romantic adventurer would envy. He was born on the Lewis and Clark expedition, the son of Toussaint CHARBONNEAU and his Shoshoni Indian wife, SACAGAWEA, who accompanied the explorers as interpreters. On February 11, while the party was encamped in Montana, William Clark reported that "one of the wives of Charbono was delivered of a fine boy." Clark, who had developed an overwhelming affection for the lively, dark-skinned child and nicknamed him "Pomp," persuaded the Charbonneaus to let him educate Baptiste in St. Louis at a Catholic academy.

When young Prince Paul of Wurttemberg came West in 1823 on a scientific expedition, he found young Charbonneau living in a trader's village on the Kansas River. The prince was impressed by the handsome youth's excellence as a hunter and horseman and shared with him a deep love of the wilderness. He persuaded Charbonneau to return with him to Europe to further his education and to travel. For the next six years Charbonneau lived at Paul's castle, located a short distance from Stuttgart, where he learned French, German, and Spanish—a routine broken by hunts in the Black Forest and trips through Europe and North Africa. In 1829 the two returned to the states and went on an expedition up the Missouri River. Charbonneau remained in the West, becoming a mountain man in the employ of the American Fur Company. Over the next three years Charbonneau worked with the Robidoux fur brigade in the Idaho-Utah region, traveled with Joe Meek and Jim Bridger, and attended the great fur rendezvous of 1833 on the Green River.

As the beaver declined, Charbonneau—like other mountain men—sought employment at trading posts or served as an overland guide. In 1839-40 he helped Louis Vasquez and Andrew Sublette establish Fort Vasquez on the South Platte. The catch he took down the Platte for his employers in the spring of 1840 represented the end of an era, for his boats were loaded with buffalo robes and smoked tongues as well as with beaver skins. In 1843 Charbonneau accompanied Sir William Drummond Stewart, a Scottish nobleman, on a pleasure trip to the Rockies via South Pass to the Green River and then north into the Yellowstone country. Later he caught antelope and bighorn sheep, which were shipped to Sir William's estate in Scotland.

Charbonneau's skill as a guide became well known; one contemporary observer called him the "best man on foot on the plains and in the Rockies." He accompanied Lieutenant J. W. Abert on a government exploration of the Canadian River, and when the Mexican War began, he served as a guide for Colonel Philip St. George Cooke's Mormon Battalion on its trek from Santa Fe to San Diego.

Charbonneau served as *alcalde* for the mission of San Luis Rey, but the fact that he was a half-breed led some Americans to suspect that he planned to join the discontented mission Indians in a mutiny. Undoubtedly hurt by the unjust charge, he left for the new California gold fields on the American River, where he met his old friend Jim Beckwourth and others he had known in the mountains. After living in the gold regions for at least a decade working at various jobs, he became attracted by the new gold strikes in Montana. While en route to the new fields, he died on the Owyhee River of an illness variously described as mountain fever and pneumonia.

Although Charbonneau impressed everyone with his education and charm, he was also completely at home on the frontier. He fought Indians, refereed a fight between mountain men with obvious satisfaction, and became extremely excited on the hunt. Unlike most halfbreeds of his time, Charbonneau lived well in two worlds, while witnessing the unfolding drama of American expansion.

See Ann W. Hafen, "Jean Baptiste Charbonneau," in L. R. Hafen, ed., *The Mountain Men and the Fur Trade of the Far West*, vol. I (1965).—H. R. L.

Charbonneau, Toussaint (c. 1759–c. 1840). FrenchCanadian trader and interpreter for the Lewis and Clark expedition. The early life of Charbonneau, born in Canada, is obscure. In 1793 he was a trader with the North West Company at Pine Fork on the Assiniboine River. Subsequently he lived among the Hidatsa and Mandan Indians along the Missouri River and was employed for a short time at least by the American Fur Company. In 1803 Meriwether Lewis and William Clark found him living among the Mandan with three Indian wives, the youngest of whom was SACAGAWEA. The explorers engaged him as interpreter for the expedition, and he, Sacagawea, and their infant son accompanied the party to the Pacific Ocean and back. He served a total of nineteen months with the expedition, for which he received $500.33. His contributions on the expedition were cautiously summed up by Lewis in his journals: "a man of no particular merit, [Charbonneau] was useful as an interpreter only, in which capacity he discharged his duties with good faith."

Clark, who had grown much attached to Charbonneau's son, Jean Baptiste CHARBONNEAU (nicknamed Pomp or Pompey), tried to induce father and son to settle at St. Louis with his family. After a brief trial, however, Charbonneau returned to the upper Missouri, leaving his son behind in Clark's care. Subsequently he worked for both Manuel Lisa and the American Fur Company, accompanied the expeditions of H. M. Breckinridge and Prince Maximilian of Wied on their travels, and served also as government interpreter among the Mandan from the 1820s until the nearextinction of that people by smallpox in 1837. A year later he married a young Assiniboin girl at Fort Clark, and in 1839 Charbonneau made his way to St. Louis to claim overdue pay from the government.—K. N. O.

Charless, Joseph (1772–1834). Publisher. Born in Westmeah, Ireland, of Welsh ancestry, Charless fled his homeland in the wake of the Irish rebellion of 1795 and came to the United States the following year by way of France. Unable to find work in New York, he took employment in a Philadelphia print shop, where he became imbued with the principles of Jeffersonian Republicanism.

Charless came to frontier St. Louis in 1808 after stopovers at Lexington and Louisville. There on July 12, he launched the *Missouri Gazette*, the territory's first newspaper, and made it into an important and influential frontier journal that subsequently supported the developing national policies of Henry Clay and his American System to create a self-sufficient United States.

In the struggle for Missouri statehood, Charless condemned the United States Congress' attempts to restrict slavery in the new state. But when the election for delegates to the constitutional convention occurred in the wake of the compromise, his paper alone (of all Missouri papers) favored the gradual abolishment of the institution by Missourians themselves, a position that proved as unpopular as restriction had earlier.

Shortly after this campaign Charless sold the *Gazette* in 1820 to James C. Cummins, recently arrived from Pittsburgh. Although his son Edward repurchased the paper the following year, Charless had no further interest in it. Rather he went into the drug business, which engaged his attention for the remainder of his life.

Charless' contributions to journalism are highlighted in James Melvin Lee, *History of American Journalism* (1917).—W. E. P.

Chatillon, Henri (1816–1875). Mountain man and guide. Chatillon might have been lost to history had not Francis Parkman made him the symbol of a noble hunter and guide in his book *The California and Oregon Trail* (1849). During the years 1842–46 he was employed by P. Chouteau and Company in the West and had just returned to St. Louis when he agreed to lead Parkman and his party on a tour of the Plains. Leaving St. Louis in 1846, the guide led his eastern neophytes first to Independence and then to Fort Leavenworth. From there they crossed the Plains to the Platte and followed that stream to Fort Laramie. Turning south, they visited Bent's Fort on the Arkansas before returning to Missouri over the northern route of the Santa Fe Trail.

Parkman was overwhelmed by Chatillon's mastery of the wilderness, his excellence of character, and his qualities of natural leadership. Rugged and handsome, Chatillon was, in Parkman's words, "the most striking combination of strength and symmetry I have ever seen"—an image made all the more dramatic by the fact that Chatillon dressed as a mountain man in drooping felt hat, fringed deerskin leggings, and moccasins and carried both a rifle and a knife. Thus Chatillon became the symbol of a primitive man made noble by nature. While pursuing his career as a trapper-hunter, Chatillon married Bear Robe, daughter of a Sioux chief. After her death he married a white woman and spent his last years in or near St. Louis.

See Wilbur Jacobs, "Henri Chatillon," in L. R. Hafen, ed., *The Mountain Men and the Fur Trade of the Far West* (1965); and Francis Parkman, *The California and Oregon Trail* (1849) or a later edition edited by Mason Wade (1943).—H. R. L.

Chato (1860?-1934). Indian warrior. Chato was a member of the Southern Chiricahua band of Apache under Juh and GERONIMO. His ascendancy to the role of a charismatic leader began after the death of Victorio in 1880, when he tried to insinuate himself as a leader of the Eastern Chiricahua, or Warm Springs Apache. He carried out successful raids against Anglo and Mexican settlers in 1882. In 1884 he was forced to surrender and was taken to San Carlos, Arizona, by Lieutenant Britton Davis. He subsequently became a scout for the United States Army against his fellow Apache, and when Geronimo and Nachez fled the reservation in 1885, Chato persuaded at least three-fourths of the Apache to remain behind. Geronimo allegedly had earlier attempted to have Chato murdered.

Chato was with a delegation of Apache who visited President Grover Cleveland and other federal officials in Washington, D.C., in a vain attempt to prevent the deportation of Apache to Florida from Arizona and New Mexico. In spite of the fact that Chato and his band of Indian scouts were credited by General Crook with the eventual capitulation of Geronimo, Chato too was imprisoned at Fort Marion. Like Geronimo, he was eventually shipped to Fort Sill, Oklahoma, having been given the non-Indian name Alfred Chatto. Unlike Geronimo, he lived to settle at last on the Mescalero reservation in 1913; there he died in an automobile accident.

See Britton Davis, *The Truth About Geronimo* (1929); and F. Stanley, *The Apaches of New Mexico, 1540-1940* (1962).—B. L. F.

Chaves, José Francisco (1833-1904). Soldier and New Mexican politician. Born in Los Padillas, New Mexico, Chaves was the son of Mariano Chaves, a leading political and military figure of the Mexican period. In the early 1840s his father sent him to St. Louis to be educated with the admonition "The heretics are going to overrun all this country. Go and learn their language and come back prepared to defend your people." The inexorable rush of events was to render defense of New Mexico impossible, but young Chaves at least profited from his knowledge of English, since he served General Stephen Watts Kearny as interpreter briefly in 1846. Later he participated in campaigns against the Navaho and during the Civil War in New Mexico fought at the battle of Valverde, winning a lieutenant colonelcy for gallant and meritorious service. Subsequently he helped establish Fort Wingate, which he commanded for several years.

In later life Chaves served three terms as New Mexico's delegate to Congress and was elected to the territorial legislature from Valencia County for the period 1875-1905, during which he served eight times as president. Of his abilities as a presiding officer, Governor Miguel A. Otero declared, "I doubt if he had many superiors in the whole United States in handling a legislative body or convention of any kind." Chaves was widely admired for his courtly and aristocratic manner and for his vigorous persecution of criminal elements in the territory. That he had enemies became tragically clear when he was felled by an unknown assassin at the village of Pinos Wells. Colonel Chaves has been called the foremost citizen of Spanish ancestry in New Mexico during the nineteenth century.

See Paul A. F. Walter et al., *Colonel José Francisco Chaves*, Publications in History, No. 31, Historical Society of New Mexico (1926).—M. Sɪ.

Chávez, Cesar [Estrada] (1927-   ). Farm labor organizer. Chávez knew the life of the migrant farm worker from personal experience at an early age. One of five children of Librado and Juana Chávez, who were Mexican immigrants, Chávez was born in Yuma, Arizona, a United States citizen. When he was ten his father lost his small Arizona farm and the family became migrant laborers, following the crops from Arizona to California and back. At the age of nineteen he first joined a farm labor organization, the National Agricultural Workers' Union. During 1944 and 1945 Chávez served in the navy.

After marrying Helen Fabela, a native of Delano, California, in 1948, Chávez spent two and a half years as a sharecropper, primarily working in strawberry fields. In 1952, living in the Sal Si Puedes barrio in San Jose,

Chato, a leader of a Chiricahua band of Apache. (National Archives)

Chávez became acquainted with the farm labor movement through a local priest. He joined the Community Services Organization (CSO) and soon became chairman of CSO's voter registration drive in the barrio, one of the earliest efforts to register Chicanos. In two months he had registered more than four thousand persons. He also worked in CSO's program helping Mexican immigrants to gain United States citizenship.

Chávez was given his first paid position with CSO at $325 per month. After six months in San Jose, he became head of the Decoto CSO; later he was sent to Oakland as an organizer. These were formative experiences during which Chávez learned the organizing techniques he was later to employ in Delano. While with CSO, Chávez also learned to read and write. He had attended more than thirty primarily segregated schools while a migrant laborer with his family, but had not gone past the seventh grade.

After starting CSO chapters in Madera, Bakersfield, and Hanford, California, Chávez became general director of the CSO national organization in 1958. His commitment was to organizing the poor, and he became uncomfortable when middle-class professionals entered CSO. His resignation from CSO was precipitated in March 1962, when the CSO convention failed to approve his proposal for a farm workers' union.

Returning to Delano, where his brother was living, Chávez applied his organizational experience in traveling across the valley talking to farm workers. The first meeting of the National Farm Workers' Association, which Chávez founded and heads, was held in Fresno in September 1962; by August 1964 the NFWA claimed a membership of more than one thousand families. A year later Chávez and his staff had added another seven hundred families.

Chávez first used the word *union* to describe the NFWA in May 1965, during the first strike in behalf of rose grafters. Four months later, despite misgivings that the NFWA was not sufficiently well organized for a major, effective strike, Chávez and the NFWA decided on a strike against the grape growers around Delano. NFWA action had been spurred by a walkout on September 20 by the Filipino members of the Agricultural Workers Organizing Committee. A year later Chávez' NFWA merged with the AWOC, forming the National Farm Workers' Organizing Committee, which became affiliated with the AFL-CIO.

In March 1966, Chávez led a 300-mile Easter march from Delano to Sacramento to dramatize the cause of the farm workers. A day earlier, he had testified before the Senate Subcommittee on Migratory Labor, which held hearings in Delano. Chávez then, and subsequently, belittled the importance of such investigations into the problems of farm workers.

As early as 1967, Chávez expressed a fear that the militancy of some forces in *la raza* ("the race") would be divisive, separating the poor into ethno-racial groups. A constant, ardent advocate of nonviolence, Chávez drew his political philosophy in part from his Catholic religion and in part from the lives of Gandhi, St. Paul, and Thoreau. On February 14, 1968, Chávez began a twenty-five-day fast as an expression of penitence for the militancy of some members of his union and of his commitment to nonviolence. He had fasted twice previously for periods of four and ten days.

On March 11, Chávez ended his fast, breaking bread with Senator Robert F. Kennedy, who was then campaigning for the presidency in the California primary. Kennedy unequivocally endorsed Chávez that day at a rally in Delano, and Chávez was selected as a Kennedy delegate to the Democratic National Convention after successfully registering many Chicano voters. After Kennedy's death in June 1968, Chávez decided against attending the convention.

Suffering from painful muscle spasms in his back, apparently worsened by fasting, and hospitalized during the winter of 1968-69, Chávez continued to work for *la causa* as it became nationally known through his grape boycott campaign, begun in spring 1968. Although grape pickers had been in active protest since 1965, it was the boycott tactic that was most effective; by mid-1970 about two-thirds of California grapes were under UFWOC contract.

When UFWOC contracts expired in 1973, many California grape growers signed new contracts with the Teamsters Union. UFWOC membership, which reached a peak of 72,000 in 1972, dropped precipitously during UFWOC competition with the Teamsters Union for representation of grape pickers. Chávez declared that court injunctions limiting pickets were unconstitutional, and mass arrests followed his order that followers defy the injunctions. As UFWOC strikes spread across the entire San Joaquin valley, Chávez stated that the UFWOC was in a struggle for its existence. In an effort for the UFWOC to remain the sole representative of farm workers, Chávez again turned to the national boycott technique. After a speech in Washington, D.C., he received overwhelming support from the American Federation of Teachers. The National Student Association also joined in the boycott. When during the crisis two UFWOC members were killed and others were injured, Chávez went on a three-day fast to demonstrate a continuing commitment to nonviolence.

John Gregory Dunne, *Delano* (1967), provides an account of the NFWA through 1966. Dunne has assembled a biographical sketch of Chávez from interviews, some of which were tape-recorded for *Ramparts Magazine*, "The Tale of the Raza," by Luis Valdez (July 1966). Peter Matthieson, *Sal Si Puedes*, provides a more journalistic and often first-hand account of the movement and Chávez to 1969. See also *So Shall Ye Reap* (1970) by Joan London and Henry Anderson.—J. R. V.

Chávez, Dennis (1888-1962). New Mexican politician. Born in Valencia County, New Mexico, Dennis Chávez (christened Dionicio) was the third of eight children of David and Paz (Sanchez) Chávez. At age seven he moved with his family to the Barelas section of Albuquerque and attended a Presbyterian and a Catholic school, but he was forced to leave school and take a job before finishing the seventh grade. He studied engineering and surveying at night and worked in construction as an apprentice and later in his own business.

Active in politics for several years before New Mexico's statehood, Chávez married Imelda Espinosa in November 1911, immediately after the state's first elections. Two of his three children were born by the time he moved to Belen in 1914. After working for a weekly newspaper and as a court interpreter, he returned to Albuquerque as an engineer. In 1917 Chávez went to

Washington to take a job as assistant executive clerk of the Senate, a position obtained for him by Senator A. A. Jones of New Mexico. Passing a special admission exam, Chávez entered Georgetown University Law School, where he studied at night. He was graduated in 1920 and returned to Albuquerque to establish a law practice.

Chávez ran successfully in 1922 for the New Mexico state legislature and was elected as the Democratic candidate for Congress in 1930, during which term he served on many committees. Renominated by acclamation, he was returned to Congress in 1932 and became chairman of the Committee on Indian Affairs. He was defeated in the Senate race of 1934, but after Senator Bronson Cutting was killed in May 1935, Chávez was appointed by Governor Clyde Tingley to fill the vacant Senate seat. In the 1936 election he retained the remaining four years of Cutting's term and was successful in each reelection bid before his death. Without doubt, he became the most important Spanish-American senator to date.

A liberal, schooled in the era of New Deal politics, Chávez was instrumental in improving higher educational facilities in New Mexico. He was also highly concerned with the natural resources of his state and with its agricultural prosperity. To that end he was an active supporter of legislation benefiting the state's farmers and was protective of New Mexico's share of the waters of the Colorado River. He sponsored many bills affecting both the franchisement of Indians and their economic, agricultural, medical, and educational well-being.

Cautious on the question of foreign aid, Chávez generally supported organizations that sought international cooperation. He was pro-labor and vigorously opposed the passage of the Taft-Hartley Act. He was a committed supporter of war veterans and a diligent servant to the people of his state, who sought his help. He traveled widely in the Americas to the South, was centrally involved in the Pan American highway system, and was a frequent advocate of the good-neighbor policy. In 1952 he received the Vasco Núñez de Balboa decoration in Panama and later received Mexico's highest honor, the Order of the Aztec Eagle, First Class. From 1950 to 1954 he was a member of the Democratic National Committee.

After a long illness, during which he conducted the affairs of his Senate office from a hospital bed, Chávez died in Washington, D.C. The people who lined the route of his funeral procession through the low-income sections of Albuquerque attested to the extent to which he was respected and revered by the poor people of his state.

On March 31, 1966, the state of New Mexico placed a bronze statue of Chávez in the rotunda of the Capitol, making him the first individual to be so honored by his state.

Statue of Dennis Chávez (1966) and *Dennis Chávez, Late a Senator from New Mexico: Memorial Addresses Delivered in Congress* (1963) are compilations of the public statements of Chávez' contemporaries after his death. Pat Munroe, "The Chávez Story," *Albuquerque Journal* (January 7-January 18, 1962), a series of biographical articles, is based on interviews with the senator a year before his death.—J. R. V.

Cherokee Indians. See FIVE CIVILIZED TRIBES.

Cherokee Nation v. State of Georgia (1831). The suit *Cherokee Nation* v. *State of Georgia* was brought before the United States Supreme Court by the Cherokee Indian Nation against Georgia for an injunction to prevent the execution of Georgia's persecutory laws against the Cherokee. The Indians of the Cherokee Nation, living in the southern Appalachians, were remarkably proficient in learning and adopting the white men's culture. In 1827, the tribe put in force a written constitution modeled on that of the United States and established a government based on it. The Cherokee had become literate, using the characters that Sequoyah had invented for their language, and were a prosperous agricultural people. Their extraordinary economic and political progress caused Georgia to fear that the Indian nation might become strong enough to exclude whites from settling in their desirable territory, a considerable portion of which lay within the boundaries of the state. In 1928, Georgia began the adoption of a series of laws designed to break up the Cherokee Nation, take its lands, and ultimately push the Indians west of the Mississippi River. To make matters worse, gold was discovered within the Cherokee domain in 1829. The state urged on Congress the policy of the removal of all tribes in the Old Southwest across the Mississippi, and Congress passed the Removal bill in 1830.

The Cherokee retained the famous William Wirt of Baltimore as attorney and in March 1831 sued Georgia in the United States Supreme Court for an injunction to prevent the execution of Georgia's laws. The suit was brought under the constitutional provision giving the Court jurisdiction over cases between a foreign nation and a state of the United States. The Cherokee Nation based their case on the premise that they were a foreign nation, having had negotiated treaties with the United States, and on the fact that they had neither sold nor ceded the land demanded by Georgia.

Chief Justice John Marshall wrote in the opinion of the Court that the Indians were not a foreign nation in the sense of the Constitution but, in part because they resided within the boundaries of the United States, the Indians were "domestic dependent nations," and thus could not sue as a foreign nation before the Court. And although the opinion expressed sympathy for the cause of the Indians, the Court denied the injunction. The following year, however, in the case of WORCESTER V. STATE OF GEORGIA, the Court ruled on behalf of the Cherokee Nation.—R. H. G.

Cherokee War (1759-61). The Cherokee Indians were allied to Britain through a treaty concluded by Sir Alexander Cuming in 1730, and despite occasional friction over trade regulations and intrigues by French agents, relations between the Indians and the English colonists remained generally peaceful for nearly thirty years. In 1757 Fort Loudon was built on the Tennessee River to protect the Cherokee country from attack during the French and Indian War, and Cherokee warriors fought on the British side, assisting in the capture of Fort Duquesne in 1758.

The latent hostility between Cherokee and colonist erupted soon after, however, when the Cherokee force returning from the Duquesne campaign was fired on (perhaps mistakenly) by settlers along the Virginia and Carolina borders. In a series of sharp skirmishes several were killed on each side. Rumors of a Cherokee uprising abounded, and when several chiefs went to Charlestown to settle the dispute they were roughly treated by the governor, William H. Littleton. An armed colonial force was sent out to quell the "uprising" but quickly retired after taking a few prisoners, when it became apparent the Cherokee really were angry enough to fight. Soon afterward, some whites murdered the hostages, and the Cherokee seized Fort Loudon on August 8, 1759, killing most of the captives they took. The two Carolinas then mounted a combined campaign against them, and two years of protracted skirmishing interspersed with negotiations ensued, marked by perfidy on both sides. When white fire-raids finally took serious toll of the Cherokee croplands, the Indians sued for peace, which was proclaimed by treaty on December 22, 1761.

See J. R. Alden, *John Stuart and the Southern Colonial Frontier, 1754-1775* (1944).—P. R. M.

Cheyenne and Arapaho Indians. Many Great Plains tribes paid dearly for their militant opposition to white expansion in the nineteenth century, but few, if any, fared worse than the closely allied Cheyenne and Arapaho Indians. The Cheyenne, in particular, lost not only warriors but whole villages in some of the bloodiest, most notorious conflicts of the 1860s and 1870s. Indeed, the fate of these two tribes fueled many incendiary public debates over the comparative efficacy of coercive and noncoercive Indian policies.

Although they stubbornly resisted the United States' initial efforts to convert them into sedentary farmers on limited reservations, neither of these Algonquian tribes had always followed the roving, buffalo-hunting existence they sought to preserve. Both the Cheyenne and Arapaho, who numbered about 3,500 and 3,000 respectively in 1780, originally raised crops and inhabited permanent villages in present northwest Minnesota. But during the eighteenth and early nineteenth centuries, largely because of Dakota incursions, they gradually migrated westward across the Missouri River, then southwestward to the upper Platte country. In the process, they perpetuated their confederation, fought mutual Indian foes, and turned to nonagricultural pursuits.

The period between 1830 and 1840 was significant for the Cheyenne and Arapaho, not in their dealings with whites, which were still limited, but in their intertribal relations. In these years they began to form two permanent geographic divisions, with the Northern Cheyenne and Northern Arapaho continuing their unincorporated affiliation in Wyoming, while the Southern Cheyenne and Southern Arapaho carried on their association in southeastern Colorado. Simultaneously, each group became embroiled in internecine warfare with other tribes that contested their usurpation of new hunting grounds, notably the Sioux in the north and the Kiowa, Comanche, and Kiowa-Apache in the south. Remarkably, though, these struggles resulted in peace agreements that facilitated later alliances between the contending tribes.

Having established their western domain with great difficulty, the Cheyenne and Arapaho were predictably inhospitable toward white invaders. Their uneasiness over the hundreds of emigrants who passed through their country en route to Oregon and California in the 1840s was only temporarily allayed by the Treaty of FORT LARAMIE (1851), which affirmed their claim to the

area between the North Platte and Arkansas rivers in Colorado. For the rapid settlement of Kansas and Nebraska territories after 1854 and the Colorado gold rush of 1859 soon compromised this understanding and produced sporadic fighting. Consequently, in 1861, federal commissioners induced several southern division chiefs to sign an agreement at Fort Wise, Kansas, ceding all Cheyenne and Arapaho lands except a small reservation southeast of Denver. But most of the northern Indians and many of their southern kinsmen repudiated this pact and remained openly belligerent.

Neither side showed restraint in the ensuing CHEYENNE AND ARAPAHO WAR of 1864-65, but the ruthlessness with which white militia avenged the Indians' raids was particularly reprehensible. In the spring and summer of 1864, while most federal troops were preoccupied in the East, Cheyenne and Arapaho war parties terrorized southwestern Nebraska and northwestern Kansas, killing about fifty whites. However, their attacks were overshadowed by the infamous SAND CREEK MASSACRE that followed on November 29 near Fort Lyon, Colorado. Surprising a Southern Cheyenne village under the leadership of Chief Black Kettle, who had sued for peace, Colorado volunteers, commanded by Colonel John M. CHIVINGTON, slaughtered and savagely mutilated at least 150 Indians, including many women and children. This atrocity was repeatedly cited by policy makers who later opposed the War Department's bids to take charge of Indian affairs. Immediately, though, it provoked widespread Indian uprisings before some of the Cheyenne and Arapaho leaders agreed to an armistice in October 1865.

The next decade brought further strife and misery to the southern confederation. The Treaty of MEDICINE LODGE, which they concluded with the renowned United States peace commission in 1867, assigned them to a new reservation between the Cimarron and Arkansas rivers in northern Indian Territory. But subsequent dissension over this site and other stipulations of the treaty delayed their resettlement and prompted TALL BULL, ROMAN NOSE, and their followers to join the Kiowa and Comanche on the warpath in 1868. Again the Cheyenne bore the brunt of a crushing defeat. On November 27, while snowed in near the Washita River, southwest of their reservation, Chief Black Kettle and 102 other survivors of the Chivington attack were killed by Colonel George Custer's Seventh Cavalry in the battle of the WASHITA. This blow, another losing battle at Summit Springs, Colorado, in 1869, and the issuance of a presidential proclamation shifting their reservation westward persuaded most of the southern group to move to present Oklahoma by 1870. Yet some of their most militant dog soldiers, mainly Cheyenne, did not abandon their nomadic ways until they had been decisively conquered in the bloody RED RIVER WAR of 1874-75.

Meanwhile, the northern tribes remained defiant toward the government's attempts to confine them to a designated area and joined forces with the hostile Sioux. In the four years after the Chivington incident, while maintaining base camps on the tributaries of the Yellowstone River, their war parties clashed with settlers and troops on a broad front, sometimes in conjunction with their southern brethren. Many were involved in key battles in the POWDER RIVER INDIAN EXPEDITION in

1865-66, including the heralded FETTERMAN MASSACRE of December 1866. The following year, after the HAN-COCK CAMPAIGN burned a Cheyenne and Sioux encampment near Pawnee Fork, in Kansas, they spurned peace proposals and made further assaults on wagon trains and military units. In May 1868 leaders of the northern tribes finally signed a treaty with the peace commission at Fort Laramie, receiving the option of going to Indian Territory or living on the Sioux reserve in Dakota. Accordingly, most of their people moved to the vicinity of the Red Cloud Sioux Agency, where about 1,200 Cheyenne and 1,100 Arapaho received annuities in 1874. Still, until 1875, they retained off-reservation hunting privileges, and this, among other things, produced continuing collisions with whites.

The climactic phase of the northern Indians' struggle came between 1876 and 1879. Cheyenne and Arapaho warriors aided the Sioux in the dramatic battle of the ROSEBUD and the battle of the LITTLE BIG HORN of June 1876, and some remained allies of Crazy Horse until he capitulated to the army in 1877. Soon afterward the government transferred more than nine hundred of the humbled and destitute Northern Arapaho to the eastern half of the Shoshoni Wind River Reservation in Wyoming and sent most of the defeated Cheyenne to the Cheyenne-Arapaho Reservation in Indian Territory. But in September 1878, because of the hardships they encountered in the South, LITTLE WOLF, DULL KNIFE, and more than three hundred other Northern Cheyenne began an unauthorized northward trek, known as "Dull Knife's Raid." Dozens of Indians and whites died in skirmishes during their dash to Fort Robinson, Nebraska, where a majority of them surrendered and were imprisoned. In January 1879, at least thirty more Cheyenne were killed trying to escape from the fort. Four years after this last desperate confrontation, the Northern Cheyenne were permanently moved to a reservation on the Tongue River in Montana.

Thus, by the mid-1880s the Cheyenne and Arapaho had lost their struggle for self-determination and were faced with the difficult task of adjusting to agency life. Acculturation and economic reform came slowly for them, especially for the northern tribes. By 1900 many of the two thousand Cheyenne and one thousand Arapaho at the Cheyenne-Arapaho Agency in Oklahoma were living on allotted lands, were making progress in farming and livestock production, and were sending their youngsters to Indian schools. But the eight hundred Northern Arapaho in Wyoming were not as far along in those matters, while the one thousand four hundred Northern Cheyenne in Montana had not yet begun to divide up their reservation and were generally unenthusiastic about the white man's way of life.

There is an extensive amount of historical and nonhistorical literature on the Cheyenne. George Bird Grinnell, *The Cheyenne Indians* (1962), is a classic treatment of their tribal life, migrations, and other activities, while his *Fighting Cheyennes* (1915) is a moving account of their conflicts with whites and other tribes. Donald J. Berthrong, *The Southern Cheyennes* (1963), utilizes previously untapped materials and challenges some of Grinnell's conclusions with respect to the Cheyenne who inhabited the Central and Southern Plains prior to 1875. Berthrong has also published two instructive articles on Cheyenne-white contacts in the late nineteenth

century: "Cattlemen on the Cheyenne-Arapaho Reservation, 1883-1885," *Arizona and the West* (Spring 1971), and "White Neighbors Come Among the Southern Cheyenne and Arapaho," *Kansas Quarterly* (Fall 1971). In addition, the reminiscences of Cheyenne who lived through the turbulent post-Civil War era and fought against the United States are effectively presented in Mari Sandoz, *Cheyenne Autumn* (1953); and John Stands-in-Timber and Margot Liberty, *Cheyenne Memories* (1967).

The most thorough study of the Arapaho is Virginia C. Trenholm, *The Arapahoes, Our People* (1970), which draws upon both historical and anthropological sources. Two useful articles on Arapaho-government relations are Trenholm, "Arapahoes in Council," *Annals of Wyoming* (Fall 1972); and James C. Murphy, "The Place of the Northern Arapahoes in the Relations Between the United States and the Indians of the Plains, 1851-1879," *Annals of Wyoming* (April 1969). Essays on the Arapaho are in Frederick W. Hodge, ed., *Handbook of American Indians North of Mexico*, 2 vols. (1907-11); and Muriel Wright, *The Indian Tribes of Oklahoma* (1951). Further important information is in the annual reports of the commissioner of Indian affairs.—H. G. W.

Cheyenne-Arapaho War (1864-1865). The Cheyenne-Arapaho War, in the high plains of Colorado, Kansas, and Nebraska, grew out of conditions created by the 1859 rush of gold prospectors into unceded Indian lands in Colorado Territory. Although in the Treaty of Fort Wise (1861) Arapaho and Cheyenne leaders agreed to a huge cession of lands in the present states of Wyoming, Nebraska, Colorado, and Kansas in exchange for a small reservation in present southeastern Colorado, many of the younger tribesmen refused to adhere to the treaty's restrictions, and hunting parties ranging far beyond the new reservation's borders often clashed with whites. By 1864, Colorado's Governor John Evans apparently had become convinced that a general outbreak of hostilities was imminent, and he began preparations for defense and retaliation. The war began in earnest in the spring of 1864, when a series of Indian raids on ranchers' cattle herds brought swift, often indiscriminate, reprisal from the Colorado militia. Columns operating under orders from Colonel John M. Chivington attacked two Cheyenne villages early in May. One, in northeastern Colorado, was believed to have contained some of the raiders, but the other, in western Kansas, was a friendly village headed by Black Kettle, Lean Bear, and Wolf Chief. Lean Bear was killed and, although Black Kettle managed to call his warriors away from that conflict, the young men of the tribe were now determined to carry the war to the whites.

By the end of the summer of 1864, Cheyenne, Arapaho, and allied Sioux warriors had raided throughout the region between the Arkansas and North Platte rivers, and Colorado settlers were demanding a war of extermination. Peace overtures from Black Kettle and several other moderate Cheyenne and Arapaho leaders were rejected in September by Governor Evans, and in November Black Kettle and his people were denied asylum at Fort Lyon. Black Kettle's village was treacherously attacked on November 29, 1864, by Chivington's militia in the SAND CREEK MASSACRE, driving even that peaceable chief into hostility. At the end of the summer of 1865, after a year of the bloodiest warfare in Central

Plains history, Black Kettle, Little Robe, and other Cheyenne and Arapaho leaders accepted the government's invitation to a peace council. In the resulting Treaty of the Little Arkansas (October 14, 1865), the signatory Cheyenne and Arapaho surrendered their old reservation for lands elsewhere, and the war was ended for most of the Indians south of the Platte.

The war is well covered in both Donald J. Berthrong, *The Southern Cheyennes* (1963); and Robert M. Utley, *Frontiersmen in Blue* (1967).—J. T. K.

Chicago and Northwestern Railroad. The Chicago and Northwestern Railroad originated in Illinois in 1836 as the Galena and Chicago Union Railroad. Galena, the ore from which lead is refined, was being mined in considerable quantities near the town of Galena, 165 miles northwest of Chicago, when William Butler Ogden, Chicago's first mayor, led in organizing a railroad to link the two towns. Early policy, typical of pioneer western railroads, called for the raising of all capital by local subscription, to the exclusion of eastern capitalists, and early growth was slow. Strap-iron rail was used, while the first locomotive, Pioneer, was a third-hand bicycle type (an early, unsuccessful design with only two driving wheels) bought from the Michigan Central and originally built eleven years before by Baldwin for the Utica and Schenectady Railroad. The first trip out of Chicago was on Oct. 25, 1848, to what is now the suburb of Oak Park. On the return trip an anonymous farmer, persuaded to transfer a load of wheat from his wagon to the train's lone freight car, became the first person to ship wheat into Chicago by rail.

Since the Illinois Central Railroad beat the Galena to the lead-mining area, the new road decided to build due west toward the Mississippi River. Elgin, Illinois, was reached in 1850; Rockford in 1852; Freeport in 1853; and Fulton, on the Mississippi, in 1855. As the tempo of midwestern railroad building heightened on the eve of the Civil War, the Galena grew rapidly, expanding north of Chicago by absorbing various lines that ran to Fond du Lac and Green Bay, Wisconsin. One of these roads was named the Chicago and Northwestern, to which the name of the merged lines was changed in 1864. A lake shore route north to Milwaukee was absorbed in 1866. Anticipating early completion of the new transcontinental route, the Northwestern pushed construction to Council Bluffs, Iowa, in 1867, in time to become a major link between Chicago and the Union Pacific Railroad. By 1880 the road extended as far west as Pierre, South Dakota, and in 1882 a route to Minneapolis-St. Paul was acquired by merger.

Marvin Hughitt, only in his thirties but already general manager of the Pullman Company, became general superintendent of the Northwestern in 1872. As president of the railroad from 1882 to the eve of World War I, Hughitt developed it into one of the most efficient and profitable carriers in the nation, and became a leading spokesman for the industry. In the 1880s the Northwestern was controlled by the Vanderbilt family, which valued it highly as a western feeder for the New York Central system. Excellent management and the prosperity of the first three decades of the twentieth century made the Northwestern a powerful, independent economic force in the midwestern and western United States, but the Depression drained the far-flung railroad of its strength, and in 1935 it was placed in receiv-

ership. Reorganized in 1944, the ten-thousand mile railroad was intensively improved during the first prosperous postwar decade, but by the 1960s the company had begun to suffer financial erosion as a result of the combination of rising costs and subsidized competition. Under the aggressive management of Ben W. Heineman, a solution to the Northwestern's problems was sought in various merger possibilities, notably with the Chicago, Milwaukee, St. Paul and Pacific.

The story of the Chicago and Northwestern is tightly woven into the history of the westward movement of the American frontier. Robert J. Casey and W. A. S. Douglas, *Pioneer Railroad; the Story of the Chicago and Northwestern System* (1948), is a dependable account from the beginnings through World War II.—A. M.

Chicago, Burlington and Quincy Railroad. See BURLINGTON NORTHERN RAILROAD.

Chicago, Milwaukee, St. Paul and Pacific Railroad. The Chicago, Milwaukee, St. Paul and Pacific Railroad, a leading midwestern railroad and an important link between the trunk lines of the East and the UNION PACIFIC, was the last of the railroads to be extended to the Pacific Coast. Incorporated in Wisconsin in 1847 as the Milwaukee and Waukesha, it began construction over a route Asa Whitney, pioneer promoter of a transcontinental railroad, had surveyed in 1845. Waukesha was reached in 1851; Madison in 1854; and Prairie du Chien, on the Mississippi River, in 1857. In 1867 the railroad was renamed the Milwaukee and St. Paul Railway Company, and in 1874, after various lines south of Milwaukee had been consolidated and connected with Chicago, it became the Chicago, Milwaukee and St. Paul. Through service to Minneapolis-St. Paul, MINNESOTA, was pioneered via Marquette, Iowa, in 1867, almost a decade before direct routes were developed. After the Civil War the railroad expanded rapidly, reaching Omaha in 1882; Kansas City in 1887; Chamberlain, South Dakota in 1881; and Fargo, North Dakota in 1884, where the railhead would remain until the Pacific extension was undertaken in 1906.

Byron Kilbourn, first president of the Milwaukee road, encouraged farmers to become the exclusive source of investment funds for the new venture, which he saw as a means to "ruin this accursed monopoly," as eastern-financed railroads were considered. Inadequate financing resulted in receivership and rescue by eastern capital in 1860, and a decade later the Milwaukee had become one of the bitterest foes of Granger legislation. An innovative company, the road devised one of the earliest Mississippi River crossings, a pontoon bridge at Prairie du Chien; pioneered refrigerator cars in 1874, thus helping to revolutionize the livestock and meat-packing industries; ran its own sleeping cars for a time; and was one of the first railroads to manufacture its own locomotives and rolling stock.

With strong support from such major stockholders as Philip D. Armour and William Rockefeller, the Milwaukee weathered the depression of the 1890s without mishap. But rapid growth of freight traffic after 1897, especially in the Pacific Northwest, placed it at a distinct disadvantage as the only major northwestern railroad without its own line to the Pacific Coast. Efforts to interest the Chicago and Northwestern in a jointly financed extension came to naught.

After long deliberation, during which the opening of

the Panama Canal to commercial traffic and the rise in construction costs due to inflation were seen as sources of trouble, the Milwaukee decided in 1906 to extend its main line from Evarts, South Dakota, to Seattle. Although nearly everybody, including railroad-empire-builder James J. Hill, applauded the decision, the extension never proved itself a sound investment. The cost of the project soared from the original estimate of $60 million to $234 million by time of completion in 1909. Extremely well engineered, the extension included the first long-distance electrification in the nation (650 miles in Montana, Idaho, and Washington), but even this innovation paid off very slowly—had it been delayed fifteen years, the advent of the diesel locomotive would have rendered it permanently unnecessary.

At the height of the 1920s prosperity the Milwaukee went into receivership. It was reorganized in 1927, taking its present name at that time, but the eleven thousand-mile system went under again during the Great Depression. Since its reorganization in 1945, the Milwaukee has been well managed, and its system intensively developed. In common with all American railroads, however, it has suffered financial erosion from rising costs and subsidized competition.

August W. Derleth, *The Milwaukee Road: Its First 100 Years* (1948), is an adequate account of this railroad through World War II.—A. M.

Chicago, Rock Island and Pacific Railroad. The Chicago, Rock Island and Pacific Railroad was the pioneer midwestern railroad, reaching the Mississippi River in 1854. With the Southern Pacific, it eventually formed a route between Chicago and the Pacific Coast. Originally promoted by James Grant and other businessmen of Davenport, Iowa, as a link between Rock Island, Illinois, across the river from Davenport, and LaSalle, Illinois, where it would meet the canal to Chicago, the road was chartered in 1847 as the Rock Island and LaSalle Railroad. By 1851 plans had been made to run the line from Chicago all the way to Rock Island, across the river to Davenport, then westward across Iowa via lines already being projected for that state, and the name was changed to the Chicago and Rock Island.

In 1854 the road reached the Mississippi River. Noting that the first train from the East had entered Chicago barely two years before, the toastmaster began the celebration with the words, "To the 22nd of February, 1854, the espousal day of the Mississippi River and the Atlantic Ocean! May no vandal hands ever break the connection!" Two years later the first bridge ever built across the broad river carried the Rock Island into Davenport. River steamboat interests fought the bridge in and out of the courts as a hazard to navigation, but the railroad, with the help of lawyer Abraham Lincoln, won. Thereafter, the road expanded rapidly. Council Bluffs was reached in 1869, the same year that the Union Pacific was opened. By 1880, when numerous lines were consolidated into one company, the Rock Island was serving thousands of communities from Minnesota to Kansas, and by 1893 it had advanced as far west as Denver, Colorado, and Fort Worth, Texas.

The prosperous, conservatively managed company survived the 1890s depression without trouble, but disaster arrived in 1901, when Daniel G. Reid and William H. Moore, two trust promoters, gained control. Using the blue-chip railroad as a credit base, these men and their associates proceeded to buy such dubious properties as the Choctaw, Oklahoma and Gulf (a sickly railroad that ran through unrelievedly poor country from Memphis, Tennessee, via Little Rock, Arkansas, to a railhead in Indian Territory) and the St. Louis, Kansas City and Colorado (a third-rate line from St. Louis to Kansas City, which the Santa Fe, as badly as it wanted a St. Louis connection, had written off as hopeless). Also acquired were the St. Louis-San Francisco ("Frisco"), never much of a railroad, and the Alton, a once-prosperous road whose smugly independent policies of forty years had finally caught up with it; the purpose of these acquisitions, if any, was never revealed. In receivership by 1915, the looted Rock Island relinquished the Frisco and the Alton.

After reorganization in 1917, the Rock Island made good progress. The line was physically rehabilitated, and its passenger service (the Golden State Limited, operating between Chicago and Los Angeles in conjunction with the Southern Pacific) was popular. The weakest of the major midwestern railroads, however, it preceded much stronger roads into receivership in 1933; it did not emerge until 1948. During the first postwar decade the line made excellent progress. By the 1960s, however, the Rock Island, along with the entire railroad industry, had begun to feel the pinch of rapidly rising wages and subsidized competition. Various merger proposals were discussed, but problems of freight interchange stood in the way.

William E. Hayes, *Iron Road to Empire* (1953), is a good account of the history of the Rock Island.—A. M.

Chicano liberation movement. Unlike the black power and red power movements since the 1960s in the United States, the brown power movement has not spawned a generally acceptable name for its heterogeneous members, who constitute the second largest minority group in the nation. Moreover, as is the case with Negroes and Indians, many members of the minority do not identify themselves with the movement. Nevertheless, since the 1960s there have been many examples of a growing Chicano movement.

In the fall of 1965 the National Farm Workers' Association (NFWA), headed by Cesar CHAVEZ, joined Filipino workers in a major strike against the grape growers around Delano, California. With the advent of a national boycott against table grapes, *la Huelga* ("the strike") grew into *la Causa* ("the cause"); and the plight of California's farm workers received national attention. A Senate subcommittee held hearings on the problems encountered by migrant farm workers, and many national periodicals adopted a sympathetic stance toward Chávez and the NFWA.

Less than two years after NFWA's first major strike, a raid on the Tierra Amarilla Court House in northern New Mexico briefly focused public attention on the Alianza de Pueblos Libres (Confederation of Free City States). Reies TIJERINA and his followers had raised the century-old question of the New Mexico land grants.

Beginning in 1965 "Corky" GONZALES organized in Denver, Colorado, the Crusade for Justice, a militant organization that sought at a conference in March 1969 to foster a national Chicano movement. Dr. Hector P. GARCIA, founder of the moderate G.I. Forum, in 1969 suggested the formation of a new state in southern Texas for the Chicanos residing there. Since the 1960s, and especially since 1967, Chicano students on university and high school campuses have formed numerous organizations, focusing on political as well as academic issues.

These are the prominent, but far from the only, examples of the movement for Chicano liberation. But to speak of a single movement—and to name it Chicano liberation—is in part a rhetorical tool.

The major difficulty in naming this group, the most numerous minority in the Southwest, stems from differences in ancestry. Ninety percent of the total Spanish-speaking population of more than five million in the United States reside in the five southwestern states of Arizona, California, Colorado, New Mexico, and Texas. They comprise about 12 percent of the total population of these states. Some individuals think of themselves as Spanish rather than Mexican. For example, an early census pointed out the fact that many northern New Mexicans considered themselves to be of Spanish, rather than Mexican, descent. Others adopt the opposite point of view. Reies Tijerina, for example, prefers to talk of the people of northern New Mexico as the *new breed* or *Indo-Hispano* to connote their mixed Indian and Spanish heritage.

Most frequently, both inside and outside of the minority, these people are referred to as MEXICAN-AMERICANS, for although the group is one of the oldest in the United States, it is steadily augmented by new immigrants from Mexico. Most members of the group can trace their lineage to Mexico, especially since much of the Southwest was a part of Mexico until the Treaty of Guadalupe Hidalgo (1848). The term *Mexican-American* also correctly differentiates the population from other Spanish-speaking groups, such as Puerto Ricans and Cubans. Nonetheless, there are at least two popular criticisms of the use of *Mexican-American* to describe the minority. First, many object to the hyphenated name; they feel strongly that they are full American citizens. Second, *Mexican* has frequently been used as an abusive expression, invoked by Anglos and Chicanos alike.

Yet many terms are less precise than *Mexican-American*. *Spanish-speaking* blurs the fact that many Chicanos speak better English than Spanish and that many Anglos speak Spanish. *Spanish-surname*, once used in the United States Census, does not include those Chicanos who have typically Anglo names. *Spanish-American*, *Hispano*, *Latin*, and *Latin-American* are even less appropriate names for the minority as a whole. To call the population *native* overlooks the fact that Indians preceded them in the Southwest. Thus, the term *Chicano* (a familiar form of *Mexicano*) appears to be transcending the debate over a name for the minority, an issue to which almost every contemporary author on the Chicano movement must address himself. *Chicano* is a relatively new term and one that is particularly acceptable to the youth. It suggests a positive cultural identity—Mexican, Spanish, and Indian in heritage, but also distinctively American—within a pluralistic society. The Chicano liberation movement, then, seeks to create an historical awareness within the minority while working for social and political justice and better educational opportunities.

The Chicano has deep historical roots in the South-

west. After Coronado's expedition of 1540, Juan de Oñate in 1598 led one of Spain's first attempts to establish colonies in the Southwest (see NEW MEXICO). He founded the colony of San Juan, now part of northern New Mexico, and by 1630 some twenty-five missions had been established from San Juan. Although the Spaniards were driven out by Indians in 1680, Diego de Vargas reconquered the area twelve years later. In 1640 Spain also had colonized Texas and had subsequently colonized Arizona and California. Many present communities in the Southwest date from this early Spanish colonial period, during which the Spanish formed three types of settlements: missions to teach the Indians, *presidios* ("forts") to protect the priests and settlers, and pueblos. Mostly male, the Spanish settlers and soldiers married women of the indigenous Indian population. While their offspring spoke Spanish, they developed a culture that combined aspects of both Spanish and Indian life. Removed both from Europe and the United States until well into the nineteenth century, a distinct culture emerged in the Southwest.

Mexican rule in the Southwest was comparatively short-lived, from Mexican independence in 1821 to the end of the Mexican War and the Treaty of Guadalupe Hidalgo in 1848. The treaty stipulated that "property of every kind" belonging to Mexicans in the ceded territory would be "inviolably respected." However, the treaty made no reference to cultural rights. By 1853 the United States had acquired almost one million square miles of Mexican territory, or half of all Mexico at that time. Thereafter the Southwest witnessed an influx of Anglos and, to the present day, Mexican immigrants as well. For example, between 1960 and 1964 nearly 218,000 Mexicans immigrated to the United States.

Although the total Chicano population in the United States was small until the twentieth century, in some areas it was highly significant. In New Mexico Chicanos represented more than half of the total population until two decades after statehood. Presently, Chicanos constitute varying proportions of the total population of each southwestern state: about 15 percent in Arizona, 9 percent in California and Colorado, 28 percent in New Mexico, and 15 percent in Texas. These figures do not reveal, however, that Chicanos reside primarily in discrete communities. Until the 1940s these communities were predominantly rural. Presently, more than two thirds of Chicanos in the Southwest reside in urban areas, and the movement into urban areas continues. Some rural areas in the Southwest remain primarily Chicano, an example being impoverished north-central New Mexico.

The highly concentrated nature of the Chicano population in urban areas has tended to perpetuate the Chicano's difficulties in participating fully in American life. Chicanos also have the youngest population and the highest birthrate of any group in the nation. For example, in California between 1950 and 1960 the Chicano population increased at almost double the rate of the white population. As is frequently the case with large families, Chicanos have difficulty in finding adequate housing and comprise a high percentage of the urban and rural poor of the Southwest; more than one third of Chicanos in the Southwest subsist on an annual income of $3,000 or less. In East Los Angeles, a special census showed that between 1960 and 1965 real income of

Chicanos actually dropped. Unemployment of Chicanos is frequently twice as high as that of Anglos; in one Chicano section of Denver, unemployment in the mid-1960s was about 20 percent. Moreover, as the United States Commission on Civil Rights pointed out in 1968, Chicanos are often *under*employed. According to the commission, almost four fifths of Chicanos who were employed in 1960 held semiskilled and unskilled jobs. Such underemployment seems no less persistent in the federal than in the private sector.

Perhaps the most discriminatory policies in the Southwest were directed against the use of the Spanish language. As a result, by 1900 most Chicanos attended segregated schools and were barred from voting. Today, lack of skills or facility with the English language are often an excuse for covert discrimination, while overt discrimination is widespread. As a group, Chicanos also attain far less schooling than either whites or other nonwhites. On the average, Chicanos have completed eight years of school while whites have completed twelve years and nonwhites ten years. In some predominantly Chicano high schools the dropout rate approximates 50 percent, and 35 percent among Chicanos is not uncommon. The educational handicaps of migrant youngsters are even more severe than the average, and few Chicanos have attended college. Between 1950 and 1960 there was only slight improvement in these statistics. In New Mexico, for example, about 1 percent more Chicano youngsters had completed the eighth grade in 1960 than in 1950, although high school and college enrollment had increased more significantly.

Contrasted with the urban Chicano population, the rural Chicano is even worse off. Chicanos represent a high percentage of farm labor in the Southwest, and wages frequently are low and employment seasonal. Since farm workers are specifically excluded from protection under the National Labor Relations Act, minimum wages and unemployment insurance are often nonexistent, while working conditions are poor. Initiated in 1942, the *bracero* program, by which Mexican nationals were employed for agriculture in the United States, made the position of the Chicano farm worker even more uncertain.

In addition to poor educational and job opportunities, Chicanos have frequently experienced infringements on their civil rights. The statements of Judge Gerald S. Chargin in the California Superior Court, County of Santa Clara, have become legend in the contemporary Chicano press and are a case in point. In addressing a Chicano youngster in court on September 2, 1969, the judge stated in part:

There is nothing we can do with you. You expect the County to take care of you. Maybe Hitler was right. The animals of our society probably ought to be destroyed because they have no right to live among human beings. If you refuse to act like a human being, then, you don't belong among the society of human beings.

Chicanos also cite police brutality, illegal arrest, and exclusion from juries. The United States Commission on Civil Rights in 1968 suggested that these allegations have considerable basis in fact, but there has not been a concerted effort to lessen the civil rights problems of Chicanos.

Chicanos in general have taken part in electoral politics with far less frequency than Anglos. The most notable exception is found in the history of New Mexico, both as a territory and a state. There ethnic voting was of critical importance in many statewide elections well into the twentieth century, and several members of the minority were elected to state offices and to Congress.

The reactions of Chicanos to inequities gained more public notice in the 1960s than previously, and the Chicano liberation movement is increasingly national in scope. The historical antecedents of the movement are more local in character, many of them involving labor disputes. As early as 1883 Juan Gómez organized a strike of *vaqueros* ("cowboys") in Texas. In the first three decades of the twentieth century, sugar beet workers in Ventura, California, workers on the Los Angeles street railway, and grape pickers in Fresno, California, initiated strikes against their employers. In Los Angeles, one issue was the hiring of Chicano conductors. In 1927 the first Chicano workers' union was formed in southern California. In the mid-1930s coal miners struck in Gallup, New Mexico, and there were strikes against copper mines in the Southwest in 1896, 1917, and 1946. The strikes of 1933 involving thousands of agricultural workers were the largest to that time. In addition to these largely rural strikes, there were in Los Angeles in June 1943 the "Zoot Suit" riots, provoked by soldiers, sailors, and marines without interference by the Los Angeles police. These riots were a prelude to riots involving Chicanos in other states. Thus, the activities of Cesar Chávez, "Corky" Gonzales, Reies Tijerina, and many others are part of a long struggle by Chicanos to achieve the full benefits of American citizenship.

While voicing specific grievances and organizing to be effective, Chicanos are also in the process of defining their own cultural heritage, which is often discussed unfavorably in Anglo literature and omitted from many school texts in the Southwest.

A major goal of the Chicano liberation movement is the education both of Chicanos and others about the unique cultural heritage of the minority. For Chicano youngsters, both bilingual and bicultural instruction are sought. Of particular note in this regard is the work of Sal Castro and Feliciano Rivera of Los Angeles, and Dr. Julian Nava, a member of the Los Angeles City Board of Education. Chicanos are thus contributing not only to their own advancement but also to a broader awareness of the cultural pluralism of the Southwest.

Carey McWilliams, *North from Mexico, The Spanish-Speaking People of the United States* (1948), is the seminal work on the history of the Chicano in the Southwest. Also valuable are John H. Burma, *Spanish-Speaking Groups in the United States* (1954), and a more recent series of essays edited by Julian Samora, in *La Raza* (1966). The most recent basic study is Matt S. Meier and Feliciano Rivera, *The Chicanos: A History of Mexican Americans* (1972). On a subject seriously lacking in statistical information, the United States Commission on Civil Rights, in *The Mexican American* (1968), has not only used available census data but also has reported the results of its hearings in the Southwest. Ernesto Galarza, *Merchants of Labor* (1964), is an important and highly factual account of the *bracero* program, 1942-60. Philip

D. Ortego, "Montezuma's Children," *Center Magazine* (November-December 1970) and *El Grito* (Spring 1970), provides an excellent analysis of Chicano youngsters' learning and language problems. Other issues of *El Grito* should be consulted for excellent articles by Chicanos discussing contemporary issues with various disciplinary approaches. See also issues of *Regenración*, which treats contemporary issues in the Chicano movement. *Atzlan*, a Center Publication of UCLA and *Con Safos* are important Chicano periodicals. *El Plan de Santa Barbara* (1969) discusses the Chicano and higher education.—J. R. V.

Chickasaw Indians. See FIVE CIVILIZED TRIBES.

Chief Joseph. Father and son, both Nez Percé leaders. The father, Tuekakas (1800?-1871), often called Old Chief Joseph, was a noted leader, fighter, and buffalo hunter of the Wallowa band. When a mission was established at Lapwai in 1836, he was one of the first converts. Henry Spalding baptized him, christened him Joseph, and in 1838 made him one of the two deacons of the Lapwai church. Joseph spent a part of each year at the mission until the local leaders quarreled with him, and he withdrew to the Wallowa area in northeastern Oregon in 1846.

As a tribal leader ranking in importance next to war chief Looking Glass, Joseph helped Governor Isaac Stevens in 1855 negotiate the treaty setting up the Nez Percé reservation. Then he went with Stevens and a number of influential leaders of the Columbia Basin tribes to a council at Cow Island on the Missouri River, where peace was made with the Blackfoot.

In 1863, angered by the new treaty that took the Wallowa area from his band, Joseph denounced the Americans, renounced his church membership, destroyed his New Testament and his American flag, and kept his band apart from the settlers as much as possible. He continued to hunt buffalo in Montana, where he was friendly with the settlers. He died near Lostine and was buried there, but in 1927 his bones were moved to the mouth of Wallowa Lake and a monument was erected over his grave.

Joseph's older son, Hin-mah-too-yah-lat-kekt ("Thunder Rolling Down From the Mountains," 1840-1904), and his younger son, Olikut (1845-1877), were born and raised in the Wallowa area. They hunted buffalo in Montana, where Olikut soon gained a reputation as a fighter. At the death of Old Chief Joseph in 1871, Hin-mah-too-yah-lat-kekt, although only thirty-one years old, was elected chief of the Wallowa band and was henceforth called Chief Joseph by the whites.

Through six troublesome years Chief Joseph stood firmly against the whites who sought to drive his band from their extensive grazing lands and settle them on the reservation in Idaho. Although he was a young chief and outranked in the tribal councils by several other chiefs, Chief Joseph was considered the most important Nez Percé leader by General Oliver Otis Howard, commander of the army units in the Northwest, and by John Monteith, the Indian agent at Lapwai, because Joseph's band owned large numbers of horses and cattle.

In the many meetings to argue the removal of the nontreaty bands, Chief Joseph held his own against a whole group of army officers and government officials. He was featured in several news stories and so became known to the general public.

Chief Joseph the Younger. (National Archives)

When the Sioux called a great council in 1874 in the Yellowstone valley to plan attacks against the whites, Chief Joseph attended but refused to join in the proposed war. Finally, in 1877, General Howard ordered him to bring all his people and livestock onto the reservation or he would be attacked by the cavalry. Joseph then led his band of about 55 fighting men and 300 others, mostly women and children, with about 3,000 horses and 1,500 cattle, away from the Wallowa, crossing the flood-filled Snake and Salmon rivers and losing many cattle in the turbid, raging waters. His band then went into camp with the other nontreaty bands to rest briefly. At that point about twenty young men from the Salmon River bands led a bloody raid along Whitebird Creek and the Salmon and started the NEZ PERCE WAR of 1877 (see also NEZ PERCE INDIANS).

Although Chief Joseph had little influence in the Nez Percé war councils and in time of battle had the important, if unglamorous, task of guarding the camp and the families, General Howard and the newspapers persisted in calling him the commander of the hostile faction and insisted that he plotted all the strategy and led the warriors in battle, when, actually, even the Wallowa warriors were led in battle by his brother, Olikut.

Chief Joseph opposed many of the plans adopted by the war councils. He did not want to go to Montana or to the Crow country but was overruled by his fellow chiefs. By chance, he was the only leader left alive to surrender the remnants of the Nez Percé bands to Colonel Nelson A. Miles at the Bear Paw battlefield in northern Montana on October 5, 1877.

Joseph was not considered a war leader by his own

people, although they recognized him as a brave fighter, a patriot, a skilled diplomat, and a statesman of first rank. His reputation, built up by the press and the army officers, spread through the country until the whites came to regard him as a superman, a military genius, a red Napoleon. White men who met Joseph, especially the army officers, were impressed by his personality. This regard was shown in Bismarck, North Dakota, where the local people gave a luncheon in honor of the captive chief. Joseph soon became a romantic figure in the eyes of the American people as the noble "red man," the unspoiled child of nature. His new friends and sympathizers helped him to secure better treatment for the war captives, who finally were allowed to return to the Northwest, about half of them to the Nez Percé reservation in Idaho and the rest, including Chief Joseph, to Nespelem on the Colville reservation in northern Washington. Worn out by trials and hardships, he died there and was buried in the Nespelem Cemetery.

See Francis Haines, *The Nez Percés* (1955); Mark Brown, *The Flight of the Nez Percé* (1967); and Lucullus Virgil McWhorter, *Yellow Wolf* (1940).—F. H.

Chihuahuan Desert. See VEGETATION: *deserts.*

Chihuahua Trail. See SANTA FE AND CHIHUAHUA TRAIL.

Chinatowns. In the early Chinese world in the West, Chinatowns provided an outlet for pent-up emotions and suppressed desires and furnished lonely sojourners drudging in a strange land with the illusion of home for a few fleeting hours. The excitement of the gambling table or the air of abundance pervading one of the great Chinese festivals added color to and brought relief from the monotony and discipline of an austere world of work. The headquarters of the district companies and tongs or the temples gave added significance to Chinatowns as the center of authority and power. Wherever a large number of Chinese worked in the West, in urban areas or distant mining camps, Chinatowns sprang into existence. In many places where they flourished before the end of free Chinese immigration in 1882, no traces of Chinese life have been preserved, but in some the remnants of a joss house or the skeleton of a gambling hall serves as a reminder. Those Chinese living in isolated camps focused their lives on a Chinese store or a restaurant until a traditional holiday lured them to the nearest Chinatown. The pageantry of celebrations centered around temples and extended to restaurants, theaters, gambling houses, opium dens, and brothels in the less ceremonious yet more popular pursuits of the holidays.

As occupations changed and the Chinese withdrew from the countryside, many of the small Chinatowns disappeared with the result that the size of Chinese quarters in the large cities swelled. In cities such as San Francisco, Oakland, Los Angeles, Sacramento, Portland, Seattle, Denver, Chicago, New York, Boston, and Philadelphia, the Chinatowns of popular fancy, if they ever existed at all, prospered between the 1880s and the 1920s. These sections were often considered the home of the Chinese. Actually, many Chinese lived outside Chinatown if their work demanded, but industry kept attracting a growing number to the teeming blocks of the quarters.

These populous Chinatowns became the focus of strife with Americans and magnified the bitter experience of the Chinese in the West. After repeated failures of reform drives, many westerners came to consider filth and immorality second nature to the Chinese and strongly resented many aspects of their world. On the other hand, this very concentration of human misery also stimulated humanitarian attempts and missionary work to alleviate the wretched conditions by bringing the Chinese into the realm of American culture. With the steady dispersal of Chinese through major metropolitan areas and their increasing integration into American society, Chinatowns lost their functions, while urban renewal projects diminished their size. The remnants of Chinatowns adjusted to the changes by consciously adapting to the needs of the tourist trade.

See Gunther Barth, *Bitter Strength: A History of the Chinese in the United States, 1850-1870* (1964); Rose Hum Lee, *Chinese in the United States* (1960); and Betty Lee Sung, *Mountain of Gold: The Story of the Chinese in America* (1967).—G. B.

China trade. The quest for a passage to India, a route through the West that could be used to tap the wealth of the Orient, is but an Americanized offshoot of Columbus' search for a westward path to the riches of the East and of the subsequent search for the Northwest Passage. The American dream of a route across the West to the Far East began even before the republic. In "The Rising Glory of America," a poetical oration delivered at the commencement exercises of the College of New Jersey (now Princeton University) in 1771, Philip Freneau and H. H. Brackenridge forecast a day when cities in the West would draw goods from Asia and dispatch them by caravan across the continent to the older population centers on the Atlantic seaboard. In various forms, this dream has survived to the present. The expectation of wealth through overland trade to the Orient has continued to beckon, even though the trade itself has never grown to the size expected and, indeed, its potential was always more myth than reality.

Americans first began trade with the Far East in February 1784 when the 300-ton ship *Empress of China* weighed anchor in New York harbor and stood out past Sandy Hook for Canton. In the years that followed, American participation in trade with China grew. This addition to the nation's commerce was most welcome, for after independence the traders of the young republic were more effectively shut out of the ports of the British Empire by the Navigation Acts than they had ever been shut in by them in colonial times, while high French tariffs and restrictive Spanish trade policies made it difficult to find markets in their domains.

But the routes to the East by sea were long and arduous, involving as they did rounding either the Cape of Good Hope or dangerous Cape Horn. A round-trip voyage consumed an entire year. The possibility of finding an easier, faster route overland to the western coast of North America and thence across the Pacific to Canton beckoned. John Ledyard and Thomas Hart Benton, as well as some historians, have argued that the desire for such a route prompted President Thomas Jefferson to dispatch the Lewis and Clark expedition. Similarly, John Jacob Astor may have been seeking an overland route to the Orient, as well as furs from the Pacific Northwest, when he laid plans for a trading post near the mouth of the Columbia River and, in 1811, sent

Wilson Price Hunt overland to help establish it. (See FUR TRADE: *in the United States.*)

Lewis and Clark's route was too tortuous to be useful, while Hunt's ill-starred expedition underscored the difficulties involved in overland travel. However, Astor and others already had successfully developed a trade in furs between the Pacific Northwest and China. Americans quickly came to dominate the trade, for they could engage in Far Eastern commerce while the North West and Hudson's Bay companies could not because of the monopoly on British trade in the Orient that the British crown had granted to the East India Company. The British firms had to dispatch their furs to less rewarding markets in eastern North America and London, sell the furs to Americans who would then transport them to China, or gain special dispensations from the East India Company to ship furs directly to Canton. The latter were granted only under conditions unsatisfactory to the fur companies. Yet for all the consternation American successes in the maritime fur trade caused officials of the British fur companies, the American trade was far from fulfilling hopes for a passageway to India. It was a westbound, transpacific trade only; transcontinental extension of the trade, easterly or westerly, remained undeveloped.

The discovery of South Pass in present-day Wyoming seemed to bring much closer the day when the prediction of Freneau and Brackenridge would be realized. By 1829 Caleb Atwater was confident that within fifty years this route would be the main channel of commerce between Occident and Orient. Not only would merchants prosper, but the trade would also serve as a catalyst speeding settlement of the then-empty lands that lay along the way. Benefits would redound to the entire country. Thomas Hart BENTON held similar views, as he made clear in 1818-19 in a series of editorials for the St. Louis *Enquirer* and in 1825 in a Senate speech advocating occupation of Oregon. In the 1840s Benton secured authorization for an expedition under John C. Frémont to survey the trail. Benton expected the expedition to bring a land route to Asia nearer to reality, as well as to hasten the settlement of the West. He predicted "a stream of Asiatic commerce pouring into the valley of the Mississippi through the channel of Oregon."

As the desire for acquisition of California and the Oregon country crested in the 1840s and as settlers moved in increasing numbers into these areas, the establishment of a viable overland passage to the Orient became a concern of a widening circle of Americans. The expansionists of the period included not only land-hungry settlers and nationalists who believed the United States had a special destiny to spread across the continent, but also men who saw western ports as valuable gateways to the trade of the East. In 1845 George Wilkes, promoter of a national transcontinental railroad, argued that Oregon ought to be acquired, for it would be of "incalculable" value as "a commercial avenue to the wealth of the Indies and the riches of the Pacific. . . ."

The territorial additions of the 1840s did nothing to quell the expansionism of aggressive nationalists. In 1852 Joseph Lane, delegate to Congress from Oregon Territory and a vocal enthusiast of manifest destiny, predicted that, even though the United States had reached the barrier of the Pacific shore, American institutions would spread "to the islands [of the Pacific], and ultimately, I trust, to the entire world." Rapidly developing American influence in the Hawaiian Islands and the surge of the country's commercial activity in the Pacific that accompanied the gold rush in California lent credence to the boast.

The growing number of Americans in the Far West included entrepreneurs as well as nationalists. Isolation from the rest of the nation prompted merchants on the Pacific Coast to look westward for markets for the products of the region. Nathaniel Crosby, Jr., a merchant sea captain from Portland, attempted to open a two-way trade between the Pacific Northwest and the Orient in the 1850s, and William D. Ralston, a leading banker-entrepreneur in California who had become convinced that San Francisco was the natural hub of Pacific trade, worked assiduously to develop a similar trade out of the bay area. Scores of others turned to the same markets, and a sizable commerce gradually developed, especially in lumber and agricultural products. Though of little importance to the nation as a whole, outlets in Asia and the Pacific were of real importance to the Far West because it had few others.

Spread-eagle nationalism and budding trade between the Far West and Far East helped pave the way for the expansionist schemes of Commodore Matthew C. Perry and Peter Parker, American commissioner to China in the mid-1850s. They pushed for American acquisition of the Bonin Islands, the Ryukyus, and Formosa, arguing that the islands lay along the natural trade routes between the West Coast and the Orient and therefore could be used to encourage and protect the growing transpacific commerce of the United States. As truly as Freneau and Brackenridge, Perry and Parker had caught the vision of a passage to India.

Despite the developments of the 1850s, overland trade with Asia still failed to materialize. High costs of transportation not only shut far westerners out of markets east of the Rockies, but also prevented the overland shipment of goods bound to or from the Orient. As Asa WHITNEY pointed out in the late 1840s, for commercial purposes the Oregon Trail was little better than the route of Lewis and Clark; only a railroad could make overland trade profitable. Whitney became a tireless crusader in the fight for a transcontinental railroad and found allies in Wilkes, Benton, William H. Seward, William Gilpin, and many others. The argument that railroads would stimulate overland trade with Asia was important in winning support for railroad construction, for it was apparent that the sparsely settled trans-Mississippi West could not then generate enough traffic internally to justify transcontinental rail lines. By the time the Union Pacific and Central Pacific met at Promontory Point in 1869, transcontinentals and trade with the Orient had become closely linked in the popular mind. Bret Harte gave voice to the idea. In a verse describing the occasion of the driving of the golden spike, Harte had an engine from the West snort triumphantly to its counterpart from the East:

> You brag of your East! *You* do?
> Why, I bring the East to *you!*
> All of the Orient, all Cathay,
> Find through me the shortest way. . . .

Leaders in the quest for a passage to India agitated for transpacific steamship lines as well as for transcontinental railroads. They argued that steam transport at sea linked to steam transport ashore would furnish the inexpensive means for the transit of goods that earlier modes of transportation had failed to supply. Californians justified their support of the Pacific Mail Steamship Company with arguments based on this expectation even though the line's freight rates were so high as to prevent shipment of bulky agricultural and forest products, which made up the largest portion of what far westerners had to sell in the Orient. Sailing vessels, which furnished less expensive tonnage, continued to dominate transpacific freight traffic long after they had all but disappeared on major sea lanes elsewhere.

In spite of Pacific Mail's failure to generate a major traffic in freight, entrepreneurs were quick to project similar lines connecting with the transcontinental railroads completed in the 1880s and 1890s. The Canadian Pacific and Northern Pacific had steamship lines operating to the Orient by the mid-1880s. Charles Francis Adams, Jr., head of the Union Pacific from 1878 to 1890, repeatedly spoke of the Union Pacific and its connecting lines to Portland as marvelously suited for handling Oriental traffic, but the UP system failed to follow its northwestern competitors in establishing connecting steamship service until 1895. Frank Upton, an American in Japan who had already accumulated a fortune in mining and commerce, moved more quickly. In 1891 he inaugurated his own line between Portland and the Far East. Then, in mid-decade, James J. Hill joined the competition. He first entered into an agreement with Nippon Yusen Kaisha, the leading Japanese steamship company, and then established his own steamship line to complement his Great Northern Railway. Anticipating that great quantities of goods would be carried by his company, Hill had two of the largest vessels then afloat, the *Dakota* and *Minnesota*, constructed for it.

Until the 1880s San Francisco dominated the American end of transpacific trade. The city's advantages as the financial center of the West Coast, its fine harbor, the Pacific Mail line, and Claus Spreckels' western sugar monopoly—which generated considerable trade between the bay area and Hawaii—all served to direct transpacific commerce to San Francisco. But in the 1880s ports in the Pacific Northwest became increasingly active competitors for Asian trade. In 1885 the British bark *Isabel* brought to Tacoma the first major shipment of Japanese tea to arrive at Puget Sound. The shipment filled ten trains that rushed the cargo to New York. Other trains were shunted to sidings to let the precious cargo pass, with the result that the record for a coast-to-coast rail run was reduced from seventeen to nine days. The Canadian Pacific, with both its rails and fleet subsidized, soon outstripped the Northern Pacific in the transcontinental shipment of tea, but the successes of the Canadian line served only to convince entrepreneurs on the American side of the forty-ninth parallel that the trade was practical and San Francisco's dominance could be permanently broken. The ports of the Pacific Northwest, they pointed out, were a thousand miles closer to Japan than was San Francisco.

For his steamship line to Portland, Frank Upton sought a traffic in rice similar to that emerging in tea.

For a brief period in the early 1890s he was successful in redirecting that grain to Portland and away from the established channels to San Francisco or via the Suez Canal to New York and New Orleans, thus adding to the conviction of many northwesterners that fulfillment of the dream of a great overland trade with the Orient was imminent. Soon, however, rival lines slashed their rates and forced Upton from the scene.

For all the enthusiasm of Harte, Benton, Wilkes, and the builders of rail and steamship lines, the fact was that by the time transcontinental railroads were opened the Far East was of declining importance to the American business community. Opportunities for investment seemed greater at home than abroad. Even men who had long been prominent in the China trade—including Franklin D. Roosevelt's grandfather, Warren Delano—had begun diverting profits earned in the Far East to domestic investments, with the result that their British rivals quickly outstripped them in the Orient. Other factors also contributed to the decline of American enterprise in East Asia. Unable to build sailing craft equal to American clippers, British builders, aided by government subsidies, early turned to steam-powered, metal-hulled vessels. Following the opening of the Suez Canal in 1869, British steamships quickly drove American clippers from trade between England and the Orient since contrary winds barred sailing craft from the new, shorter route. Americans continued to participate in Far Eastern enterprise, but they declined both in relative number and in stature during the late nineteenth century. In spite of the excitement occasioned by transcontinental trains laden with tea, rice, and silk, the glory days of the old China trade were past. With them vanished the possibility that an overland passage to the Orient would ever approximate the expectations of its early champions.

Yet in the United States, ironically enough, there was a surge of interest in Asian trade during the first decades of the twentieth century. The addition of the Hawaiian and Philippine islands to the country's domains and the publicity that attended John Hay's Open Door notes spurred interest in the Pacific area. So, too, did the increasing sale of American cotton textiles in China and the efforts of Robert Dollar, West Coast shipping and lumber magnate, who sought to persuade American businessmen of the great potential of transpacific trade. The success of Dollar's steamship company in Pacific commerce gave point to his arguments, and the number of Americans engaged in Far Eastern trade rose sharply. By 1921, only six years after its founding, the American Chamber of Commerce in Shanghai had three hundred members. In 1930 East Asia had the largest share of the maritime trade of the West Coast and was the area's largest market. Pacific Coast ports handled over sixty percent by volume of the Far Eastern trade of the United States (somewhat less by value).

As it had been earlier, this trade was of great importance to the West Coast, but it did not fulfill the old dream of an overland passage to the East. It was a two-way trade between the Far West and the Far East; only a small portion of the goods involved moved overland to or from the valley of the Mississippi or the Atlantic seaboard. For most areas east of the Rockies, the Panama Canal had become the main route to Asia.

Furnishing these areas with a less expensive means of transportation than rail lines to the West Coast, the canal virtually guaranteed that the predictions of Freneau, Brackenridge, and their successors would go unfulfilled.

Yet to this day echoes of the old chorus sound. Publicists for the Union Pacific Railroad speak of the line as the great commercial thoroughfare to a burgeoning Orient, while spokesmen for West Coast ports still describe them as gateways to the wealth of the Pacific and the East. At the same time, however, other westerners decry the importation of Asian manufactures into the United States at the expense of items produced domestically and the exportation of logs from the West Coast to Japan at the expense of American lumbermen and mill workers. They find sympathetic audiences in many quarters. Except among spokesmen for vested interests, Asian trade as a means of enriching the country would appear to have lost its appeal. Today the old dream of a flood of Asian goods entering the country through the West seems nearer than ever to being a reality, but for perhaps a majority of Americans the prospect now seems less a dream than a nightmare.

Material on the "passage to India" theme is scattered. Henry Nash Smith discusses its literary treatment in *Virgin Land* (1950). Norman Graebner analyzes mercantile interest in western ports in *Empire on the Pacific* (1955). Numerous books discuss the early days of trade with China. A good introduction is Foster Rhea Dulles, *The Old China Trade* (1930). There is no adequate overall treatment of American trade with China in more recent times; however, see Paul Varg, *The Making of a Myth: The United States and China, 1897-1912* (1968). Numerous specialized studies of individuals and firms connected with the "passage to India" theme and with Asian trade also exist. See especially Thomas L. Karnes, *William Gilpin, Western Nationalist* (1970).—T. R. C.

Chinese, riots against. The violence of the anti-Chinese movement erupted in a series of riots in the West culminating in the 1870s and 1880s. General economic unrest, racial antagonism, and specific grievances made the Chinese the object of official abuse and private harassment. The incorporation of the "Chinese Question" into national politics in the ELECTION OF 1876 seemed to sanctify open brutality, and the simplistic rhetoric "The Chinese Must Go" helped turn the continuing abuse and violence into riots. In the isolation of the countryside, Chinese were the prey of cruel whites and the targets of bands of vagabonds robbing them of their savings, while the legal restrictions barring Chinese testimony in court encouraged the brutish pranks of city hoodlums.

In 1871 a mob in Los Angeles killed eighteen or nineteen Chinese, ostensibly to avenge the shooting of a white man during a fight between warring district companies. The rationale of the rioters gathering on the empty sandlots in San Francisco in 1877, which made the Chinese *the* scapegoat for the difficulties besetting the workingmen, was readily accepted throughout the West. The Chinese were driven from the countryside into the towns and from the towns into the country, and a considerable number of the beleaguered laborers hastened their return to China. In October 1880 a Chinese was murdered in Denver during the height of the Garfield-Hancock political campaign, and the Chinese

quarter was gutted. On September 2, 1885, in Rock Springs, Wyoming, 150 whites killed 28 Chinese coal miners and laborers, wounded 15 others, and drove several hundred out of town. Bitterness against alleged mistreatment by the Union Pacific Coal Department and prejudice accentuated by the refusal of the Chinese to join in strikes were among the immediate causes of the riot. The survivors were allowed to come back to work, but they could get no restitution for their losses locally, although they were indemnified in 1887 after the United States government paid $147,748.74 to China. In the wake of the Rock Springs riot came the Pierce Chinese massacre in Idaho, where a gang of masked men lynched five Chinese who were being escorted to jail on suspicion of having murdered a white merchant. Also in September 1885, a group of white men shot into the tents of hop pickers at Squak valley in King County, Washington Territory, killing two Chinese. In November, Tacoma expelled its Chinese residents. In Seattle, six months of threats, burning, and violence culminated in riots in February 1886, which temporarily drove most Chinese from the city. With the restriction of Chinese immigration and the continuing return of Chinese to their homeland, public attention shifted to other racial and ethnic groups as scapegoats for the ills of American society.

See Gunther Barth, *Bitter Strength: A History of the Chinese in the United States, 1850-1870* (1964); Mary Roberts Coolidge, *Chinese Immigration* (1909); Paul Crane and Alfred Larson, "The Chinese Massacre," *Annals of Wyoming*, vol. 12 (1940); Jules Alexander Karlin, "The Anti-Chinese Outbreaks in Seattle, 1885-1886," *Pacific Northwest Quarterly*, vol. 39 (1948), and "The Anti-Chinese Outbreak in Tacoma, 1885," *Pacific Historical Review*, vol. 33 (1954); Stuart Creighton Miller, *The Unwelcome Immigrant* (1969); Elmer Clarence Sandmeyer, *The Anti-Chinese Movement in California* (1939); Alexander Saxton, *The Indispensable Enemy* (1971); and Roy T. Wortman, "Denver's Anti-Chinese Riot, 1880," *Colorado Magazine*, vol. 42 (1965).—G. B.

Chinese-Americans. The California gold rush first lured large numbers of Chinese to the United States. For the initial decades of their coming the mining region in the foothills of the Sierra Nevada designated the area of Chinese activities in the West. At the end of the period of free Chinese immigration to the United States in 1882, about one hundred thousand Chinese men and about five thousand women lived in the West, seventy-five percent of them in California. At first most of them planned to return to their families in China with their savings. But as ever-increasing numbers of these sojourners remained in the United States they could not easily send for their families, since the immigration laws complicated the coming of women. The resulting scarcity of females remained for many decades a characteristic of the Chinese population in the United States.

With the extension of the mining frontier into the Rocky Mountains and the increase in railroad construction in the West, new centers of Chinese life sprang up in other states and territories, notably Oregon, Nevada, Idaho, Washington, Montana, and Arizona. While growing numbers of Chinese found employment as fishermen, freighters, woodchoppers, washermen, gardeners, farmhands, cooks, and servants, the decline of mining and the completion of the major transcontinental lines shifted most Chinese into urban centers, where they sought work in the manufacture of cigars, clothing, and shoes. Driven from the countryside or discharged from factories and sweatshops as a result of the anti-Chinese movement, the Chinese often set up their own shops in these trades in addition to laundries and restaurants. In 1920, thirty percent of the Chinese employed were working in laundries, and for more than half a century the predominant occupation of the Chinese in the United States was the laundry business, with the operation of restaurants the next most frequent occupation. In later years, many Chinese went into the grocery business, but the professional class made the greatest gain, increasing between 1950 and 1960 from 7.2 to 17.9 percent of the employed Chinese-Americans.

The durable ties of social institutions kept the expanding Chinese world focused on San Francisco, which contained the headquarters of district companies, family associations, guilds, and secret societies. Based on loyalty to a native district, a family, a number of friends, or a political or religious creed, these organizations had long fulfilled functions intimately associated with the elevated Chinese view of personal relations. In the West, however, these institutions contributed not only to the traditional objectives of mutual aid and protection, but also in varying degree to the maintenance of an invisible Chinese world that controlled the indentured immigrants obligated to work for creditors who had paid for their passage. Under the management of the merchants who ruled through the Chinese Consolidated Benevolent Association ("Six Companies"), the overall organization of the district companies that emerged in the 1860s, the structure of the Chinese world in the West represented a change from the traditional Confucian value system, which relegated merchants to a lowly position in society. During the height of the anti-Chinese movement in the United States, the semiofficial functions of the Six Companies, acting as spokesman for all Chinese, enhanced their significance.

The major challenge to the rule of the district companies came from rebellious factions within the Chinese world. Untouched by any loyalty to family or district, these secret societies, anxious to manipulate and to coerce their countrymen for their own ends, disputed the authority of the Six Companies. These brotherhoods traced their origin to the Triad Society, which found its way from China to the United States like other institutions and customs. They came to be known in the United States as "tongs." The application of the term *highbinder*, which had originally characterized an Irish tough in New York City, to a professional killer for a tong—often also called a "hatchet man"—added to the distinctly American air that surrounded the brotherhoods. Behind the facade of social clubs and benevolent institutions, the secret societies linked together revolutionary groups, fraternities bent on righting imagined or real injustices suffered by their members, and gangs of criminals that controlled gambling, prostitution, and opium smuggling by means of extortion, physical coercion, kidnapping, and murder. The tong wars for the control of spheres of influence affected the imagination of the general public, which mixed fact and fancy indiscriminately to the detriment of all Chinese in the United States.

The dispersal of the Chinese through the West and their concentration in cities quickly brought them into all states, but primarily into the metropolitan centers. For several decades the effect of the multitude of local, state, and federal laws regulating Chinese immigration led to a steady reduction of the number of Chinese residents in the United States. By 1920 the population figure had declined from a high of 107,488 in 1890 to a low of 61,639. Although the size of the population increased to 74,954 in 1930 through natural gain and a more accurate enumeration, the great reversal of the trend came in the 1940s as a result of relaxed immigration laws and political developments in China. The changed regulations finally gave sojourners an opportunity to bring their wives and children permanently to the United States at the time when Communist conquest of China diminished the urge to return to the homeland. The establishment of the People's Republic of China also kept about five thousand students, scholars, businessmen, and officials in the United States. In the final analysis, the Communist success forced most Chinese-Americans to find a permanent place in American society. Their search for new directions intensified the dual nature of their struggle for identity, combining affection for the land of their ancestors with the willingness to take up those opportunities that American society offered. It explained also the rate of physical mobility among the Chinese-Americans during the 1950s, which was twice as high as the average for the United States. However, despite the population movement, the Chinese-Americans remained concentrated in the urban areas of a few states. In 1960, 237,293 Chinese lived in the United States, roughly three fourths of them in three states: California (40 percent), and New York and Hawaii (16 percent each). Illinois, Massachusetts, and Washington divided another 8 percent. Accentuating the concentration of Chinese-Americans, about 75 percent of them lived in just nine metropolitan areas: San Francisco (22.4 percent), Honolulu (15.5), New York (15.4), Los Angeles (8.2), Sacramento (2.7), Chicago (2.5), Boston (2.3), Seattle (1.9), Washington, D.C. (1.7), and Philadelphia (1.1).

Mary Roberts Coolidge, in *Chinese Immigration* (1909), wrote the general pioneering study, while Elmer Clarence Sandmeyer, in *The Anti-Chinese Movement in California* (1939), limited the perspective. The sociology of the immigrants' world is discussed by Rose Hum Lee in *Chinese in the United States* (1960). S. W. Kung outlines the general context in *Chinese in American Life* (1962). The complexity of the subject is examined by Kwang-Ching Liu in *Americans and Chinese: A Historical Essay and a Bibliography* (1963). Gunther Barth, in *Bitter Strength: A History of the Chinese in the United States, 1850-1870* (1964), focuses on the life of the people. Betty Lee Sung's compassionate observations on recent developments in the Chinese community gives significance to her *Mountain of Gold: The Story of the Chinese in America* (1967). See also Alexander Saxton's *The Indispensable Enemy* (1971).—G. B.

Chinese immigration. In the 1850s and 1860s a tidal wave of Chinese surged into California in pursuit of a dream: they would make money in the West to return to China with their savings for a life of ease, surrounded and honored by the families that their toil had sustained. The vast majority of arrivals from the Middle Kingdom were thus merely sojourners, and their name for their

native land as occupying the center of the world reflected their cultural pride. Their goal kept them apart
from other immigrants who came to the United States as
permanent residents, and as a result, the Chinese were
excluded from the privileges and obligations of immigrants. They became the docile subjects of bosses and
headmen, and thus were still directed in the West by the
dictates of the Chinese world. Strife and acculturation
left their daily life unchanged. Only when changes in
China and America modified their original goal were an
ever-increasing number transformed into Chinese
immigrants.

The newcomers came from the Pearl River Delta in
the province of Kwangtung in South China, where political and social unrest threatened their established way of
life and made it economically impossible to maintain a
large family. Deprived of their resources, the villagers
aimed at supporting their wives, children, and dependent parents by emigrating. They followed the example
of many South Chinese before them, who had supported their families by working in Chinese oversea
communities in Southeast Asia. When the social conditions of the Pearl River Delta compelled the Cantonese
to test the usefulness of the system of emigration as a
defense of their way of life, the rumors of easy riches in
California as a result of the discovery of gold gave their
emigration a new direction. The movement was stimulated in the 1860s and 1870s by labor contractors and
shipping companies who brought Chinese workers to
the United States for specific projects, such as railroad
construction.

The Cantonese sojourn in California took place within the framework of the traditional practices of the
Chinese oversea emigration. Poverty turned the mass of
sojourners into indentured emigrants, resembling those
who formed the backbone of the Chinese migration to
Southeast Asia. They obtained their passage under the
credit-ticket system from Chinese merchants, who were
reimbursed by relatives of the travelers or by their future employers. In return, the newcomers worked for
whoever extended credit until the debt was paid. In
other cases the merchant-creditors used the working
power of the migrants in any way that guaranteed a
profitable return on their investment. The system
camouflaged a world of debt bondage that turned indentured emigrants into slaves of their countrymen,
who ruled through influences unfamiliar to most
American observers.

Although Californians opposed the intrusion of debt
bondage into their state, Chinese merchants successfully
adjusted the pattern by extending the social structure of
the Chinese world of the Pearl River Delta into the West,
employing district companies and kinship organizations
as instruments of extralegal control. The sojourners'
loyalty to their families, left behind in the Pearl River
Delta, enforced the creditors' hold over the indentured
emigrants. Under merchant leadership the control system pervaded the entire West, spreading through isolated mining camps and crowded Chinese quarters. It
ensured the newcomers' work in gangs of miners and
railroad construction crews, where regimented labor
guaranteed the merchant-creditors a constant return on

Chinese laborers building the embankment for the Central Pacific's Secrettown Trestle in the Sierras in 1877. (Southern Pacific)

their investment in indentured emigrants. Laboring in the West furnished the mass of sojourners with compensation high enough to ensure their submission to the system and to perpetuate their dreams of success, yet small enough to secure their continuing dependence.

The extension of the mining frontier into the Rocky Mountains intensified the Chinese contact with the entire West, and the construction of the transcontinental railroad speeded their eastward movement. About 105,000 Chinese lived in the United States in 1880, two years before the Chinese Exclusion Act of 1882 brought an end to the free immigration of Chinese laborers. Of that number, 75,132 lived in California, 9,540 in Oregon, 5,416 in Nevada, 3,379 in Idaho, 3,186 in Washington, 1,765 in Montana, 1,630 in Arizona, 914 in Wyoming, 612 in Colorado, 501 in Utah, and 57 in New Mexico. The sugar plantations and the commercial enterprises of Hawaii had attracted 25,767 Chinese by the turn of the century, but with its annexation in 1898, the United States restriction measures were applied to Hawaii and the Chinese population remained almost static for four decades.

In time, the Chinese gained a new perspective on American life and began to feel more like immigrants than sojourners, but the initial experience of Americans with Chinese had left a lasting memory that long cast a shadow over the contact between Chinese and Americans as well as between other Oriental immigrants and Americans. Stereotypes and misconceptions faded slowly, and so did persecution and hostility. Customs and laws, already barring Chinese from citizenship and its legal and property rights, were often further construed to restrain sojourners and to curb the particular world of indentured emigrants, thus hindering their acceptance as Americans. Opponents of the Chinese readily absorbed the clichés into their arguments for exclusion. Such prejudice led to the abrogation of the clause in the Burlingame Treaty of 1868 recognizing the reciprocal right of citizens of China and of the United States to emigrate to either country at will. Their drive culminated in the Geary Act of 1892, extending for ten years the Exclusion Act of 1882. All Chinese workers in the United States were required to secure certificates of residence within one year, or be held liable to be deported. Enforcement of these regulations was tightened by other laws, among them the Immigration Act of 1924, and was continued until 1943, when Congress, mindful of the wartime alliance with China, repealed the Exclusion Act of 1882. In subsequent years new measures were designed to facilitate the immigration of Chinese, in part to ameliorate the hardships on families caused by the emergence of "two Chinas" as a result of the establishment of the Communist People's Republic of China and the Republic of China (Taiwan).

Mary Roberts Coolidge wrote the pioneering general study, *Chinese Immigration* (1909). Elmer Clarence Sandmeyer, in *The Anti-Chinese Movement in California* (1939), limited the perspective. The sociology of the immigrants' world is discussed by Rose Hum Lee in *Chinese in the United States* (1960). S. W. Kung outlines the general context in *Chinese in American Life* (1962). The complexity of the subject is examined in Kwang-Ching Liu, *Americans and Chinese: A Historical Essay and a Bibliography* (1963). Gunther Barth, in *Bitter Strength: A History of the Chinese in the United States, 1850-1870*

(1964), focuses on the life of the people. Betty Lee Sung's compassionate observations on recent developments in the Chinese community characterizes her *Mountain of Gold: The Story of the Chinese in America* (1967).—G. B.

Chinook Indians. See INDIANS OF THE NORTHWEST COAST.

Chinook Jargon. Chinook Jargon was a lingua franca developed before 1815 in Indian hamlets near and along the lower Columbia River, where dialects of the Chinook language were spoken. *Chinook* is the linguist's name for a small set of dialects that may be grouped into two principal dialects: coastal or Lower Chinook, and Columbia River or Upper Chinook. The name *Chinook* should be used only for these dialects, which comprise the natural Chinook language. Nonlinguists who have referred to "Chinook" in casual speech or in writing invariably have meant not the natural Chinook dialects, but the famous auxiliary language, Chinook Jargon, which was developed on the pattern of Chinook, but which was very much simplified in form and had a much smaller vocabulary. Unlike Chinook, the Jargon was not a natural language, but rather was a simplified communication system having no native speakers. The Jargon was used as a means of communication between people who could not understand each other's native languages.

In the short period from about 1810 to 1815, the Jargon spread south from the lower Columbia River to central-western Oregon, north almost a thousand miles to southern Alaska, and east for varying distances along coastal streams. Soon young speakers of from sixty to seventy Indian languages in this vast area used Chinook Jargon as a second language, but before 1880 only a few learned English as a third. Thousands of English- and French-speaking Caucasian pioneers also resorted to the Jargon to communicate with Indians. Rural preachers gave sermons in Jargon to Indian congregations. Beginning in the 1890s, however, immigration of English-speaking people, compulsory schooling, and the substitution of English for Indian languages in Indian households resulted in the progressive diminution of the number of people who knew Jargon. Almost no Caucasians born in the Pacific Northwest after 1880 learned it. By 1930 Jargon had become moribund. After 1930 only a few hundred older Indians and almost no Caucasians could speak the Jargon, and by 1970 it was virtually extinct.

Because of the lack of written records, it is impossible to determine the origin of Chinook Jargon precisely. Both before and after the arrival of white men in the Pacific Northwest, the Columbia River region was a great trading area. There are known to have been wide intertribal contacts among the Indians of the Northwest coast. The Chinook peoples served as middlemen in the active trade along the coast, and between the coast and the interior. The Chinook Jargon probably arose to facilitate communication between native residents of Chinook hamlets and their non-Chinook Indian visitors. It is known that the Jargon contained about four hundred of the commonest morphemes— meaningful parts of words, such as roots, prefixes, and suffixes—of natural Chinook as spoken sometime before 1815. By the 1820s or 1830s the Jargon had ingested some words from the French dialect of Quebec pioneers who had come to the lower Columbia districts, and it had also incorporated some English words. By the 1830s approximately ninety percent of the vocabulary of the Jargon was Chinook in origin, while five percent was English and five percent French. An additional word or two may early have entered Jargon from each of several coastal Washington and British Columbia languages unrelated to Chinook. But claims that Quileute, Nootka, and other Indian languages of the Pacific Northwest offered such contributions have not been proven. The speed of expansion of the Jargon over the Northwest has never been studied. The spread seems to have correlated with nineteenth-century advances in coastal wealth, trade, and communication principally north of the Columbia River.

Since Chinook Jargon had no native speakers, each person who used the Jargon spoke some other language as his native tongue: French or English, Chinook, or one of many non-Chinook Indian languages. Some linguists claim that Jargon was not entirely uniform in pronunciation or grammatical structure, but differed to some degree from one speaker to the next, depending on the native language of that speaker. Michael Silverstein claims, for example, that sentences of Jargon may be seen as grammatical simplifications both of English and of Chinook. Although there may have been variations in the grammar and pronunciation of Jargon from one speaker to another, these were evidently not severe enough to inhibit communication greatly.

With a much simplified grammatical structure and a vocabulary of only about five hundred words, all acquirable in one or two weeks of intensive practice, Jargon had a typical semantic manifestation of jargons everywhere: Many words had wide semantic breadth. For example, just one word served for *in*, *at*, *upon*, *beside*, or any location. The word for *female* also meant *woman*, *wife*, and *prostitute*. The word for *make* also meant *do*, *manufacture*, and *cause*. A principal feature of Jargon syntax was subject-verb-object word-order, as can be seen in the following Jargon text, obtained by Franz Boas from a Tsimshian Indian in 1888:

ikt man yɑ′kɑ ku·′li kopa la′motai yɑ′kɑ tiki łap
one man he   go   to mountain he   wish find

lə′muto.   tǝna′s le·′le yɑ′kɑ ku·′li pe   yɑ′kɑ
mountain sheep little long he   go   and   he

łap   ikta,   mɑs′ɔ′l. yɑ′kɑ ma·c bow pe
find something white bear he   throw bow and

yɑ′kɑ łap   mɑs′ɔ′l.
he   find white bear

(One man went to the mountain, wishing to find a mountain sheep. He went a little way and found something, a white bear. He shot a bow and he hit the white bear.)

The Jargon is only fragmentarily described. Melville Jacobs and Boas presented some Jargon texts. After 1960 anthropological linguists who were working on the many Salishan languages in the central part of the Northwest took notes from aged Indians who recalled some Jargon. Such spare data remain in manuscript. Many linguistically untutored Caucasians obtained word lists and idioms from the period of the 1840s through the 1920s, but these are often unreliable.

See Franz Boas, "Note on the Chinook Jargon," *Language*, vol. 9 (1933); Melville Jacobs, "Notes on the Structure of the Chinook Jargon," *Language*, vol. 8 (1932), and *Texts in Chinook Jargon*, University of Washington Publications in Anthropology, vol. 7, no. 1 (1936); Michael Silverstein, "Chinook Jargon, I," *Language*, vol. 48 (1972); and E. H. Thomas, *Chinook: A History and Dictionary of the Northwest Coast Trade Jargon* (1935).—T. G. D.

Chino Rancho (California). Chino Rancho, in southern California, was operated and owned by an Anglo, Isaac Williams. Created out of former Mission San Gabriel lands in 1841, the rancho was granted to Antonio Maria Lugo, who entrusted operations to Williams, his son-in-law. Through the decade Lugo gradually vested Williams with full title. The prosperous rancho became the scene for the so-called Battle of Chino in 1846, when Californios battling American occupation besieged several Anglo rancheros. Williams' equivocation and split loyalties on this occasion lost him the trust of both Anglos and Californios; only after befriending hundreds of emigrants on the southern routes to the gold mines in 1849-51 did he dispel Anglo suspicions of his loyalties. Williams died in 1856, leaving his estate to his daughters, who, over the years, sold the property until the rancho was decimated. The rancho is now the site of the city of Chino, California.

See George William Beattie and Helen Pruitt Beattie, *Heritage of the Valley: San Bernardino's First Century* (1939).—J. F.

Chippewa Indians. See OJIBWA INDIANS.

Chiricahua Indians. See APACHE INDIANS.

Chisholm, Jesse (1805-1868). Frontier trader. Born of a Scottish father and Cherokee mother in Tennessee, Chisholm drifted west during the 1820s and settled in a Cherokee community in northwestern Arkansas. Engaging in the frontier trade in the country west of Fort Smith, which became Indian Territory, he trafficked with the Osage, Wichita, Kiowa, and Comanche and operated several trading posts in the area, including one in Council Grove on the North Canadian River near the present site of Oklahoma City.

His wide acquaintance with the Indian tribes, their customs and languages (it is claimed that he could converse in fourteen different dialects), and his keen knowledge of the terrain made him useful to United States authorities at Fort Smith and Fort Gibson. He served as interpreter at several important councils attended by tribal leaders and federal officials, negotiated for the ransom of many captives held by the Kiowa and Comanche, and led several important expeditions into the Southwest, including the 1834 Dodge-Leavenworth expedition, an effort to contact certain Indian tribes (Kiowa and Comanche) and negotiate treaties providing for safe passage across their domain. During the Civil War he operated a trading post near present-day Wichita, Kansas. After the war he blazed a wagon trail south from the Kansas post to the Red River, and resumed trading with the wild tribes.

Chisholm died at Left Hand Spring near present-day Geary, Oklahoma. His trader's route across Indian Territory became the Chisholm Trail, a famous cattle highway connecting Texas ranches with markets on the railroad in Kansas (see CATTLE INDUSTRY).

See T. V. Taylor, *Jesse Chisholm* (1939).—A. M. G.

Chisum, John Simpson (1824-1884). Cattleman. Born in Madison County, Tennessee, Chisum moved with his family to Paris, Texas, in 1837. After working as a construction contractor for several years, the young man became engaged in the livestock business about 1854. Although he participated in several cattle drives, he was not associated with the famous Chisholm Trail, the name of which derived from a half-breed stockman, Jesse Chisholm.

During the Civil War, Chisum furnished cattle to the Confederacy. Later he became associated with pioneer rancher Charles Goodnight, who credited him with being "a good trail man." By 1873 Chisum had founded a vast ranch at South Spring on the Pecos River in New Mexico, being among the first Texas stockmen to begin operations in this area. The *Las Vegas Gazette* described his range as extending 150 miles along the river. He ran eighty thousand head of cattle in 1875 and employed one hundred cowboys. During the next five years he supplied fifty thousand beefs to the Kansas City market alone and became known as the Cow King of New Mexico. Rustlers, according to Chisum's own claim, relieved him of ten thousand head of stock, and it was this problem that involved him in the LINCOLN COUNTY WAR (1878-81), a conflict that pitted large ranchers against small cattlemen and merchants. His precise role in that affair is still in dispute. As a result of his participation in this skirmish and his continuing losses of cattle to Indian raiders, rustlers, and competition, he lost much of his wealth and power. Even so, when he died at Eureka Springs, Arkansas, he left an estate of $500,000. In 1884 J. J. Hagerman, with the help of several businessmen, bought the ranch, a part of which is still in operation as the South Spring Dairy Ranch.

A brief biography of Chisum appears in C. L. Douglas, *Cattle Kings of Texas* (1968). His life is detailed in Harwood P. Hinton, Jr., "John Simpson Chisum," *New Mexico Historical Review* vol. 32 (1956-57).—M. Si.

Chiswell's mines (Virginia). Chiswell's mines were developed at a large outcropping of lead ore located on the east bank of the New River, opposite the mouth of Cripple Creek at present Austinville, Virginia. Discovered early in the course of colonial exploration, the deposit was first worked in 1757 by Colonel John Chiswell, and the mines became an important backcountry center. In 1758 Fort Chiswell was established on the route of the Great Valley Road about ten miles north of the mines, and in 1772 the settlement that had grown up around the fort became the seat of the new Fincastle Country, which included all of western Virginia and Kentucky. The mines themselves were a pivotal point along the colonial Indian boundary established after the French and Indian War (1754-63). Tryon's Line (1767) and the Treaty of Hard Labor line (1768) used the mines as an anchor point.

During the American Revolution the mines were a principal supply of lead for the Continental Army and were taken over for that purpose by the state of Virginia in 1776. In 1779-80 loyalists in southwestern Virginia attempted to seize the mines, but they were crushed by a force led by mine superintendent Colonel John Lynch, and their leaders were summarily hanged. From the harsh reprisals of Colonel Lynch is supposedly derived the term "lynch law." After the Revolution the mines were acquired by Moses Austin. His failure to turn a profit in the business prompted him and his son Stephen to migrate first to Missouri and later to Spanish Texas, where their "colony" eventually led to American annexation.

The mines were an important source of lead for the Confederate Army during the Civil War, and they are still being worked in a small way today.

There is no concise history of the mines. The most concentrated information is found in various volumes of the *Virginia Magazine of History and Biography.* —P. R. M.

Chittenden, Hiram Martin (1858-1917). Engineer and historian. A graduate of the United States Military Academy in 1884, Chittenden was commissioned an officer in the Corps of Engineers. His duties in the corps took him to several western states. While residing in St. Louis in the service, he projected a history of the fur trade in the region west of the Mississippi River. *The American Fur Trade of the Far West* (1902) remains the definitive account of the topic. Clearly written and carefully researched in documents and in the field, the book deals with the years 1806 to 1843, emphasizing the institutional history of the trade against a background of the flora, fauna, and Indian cultures of the region. Chittenden attempted to be objective and scientific in his philosophy of history, but he did not hesitate at times to pass moral judgments, even though he sometimes overruled free will in favor of ethnic or racial determinism as the key ingredient in the historical process. Although a standard, the work has been criticized for omitting the trade of the Southwest beyond Santa Fe, for slighting the international context of the fur commerce, and for unsophisticated or incomplete economic analysis. Chittenden subsequently prepared two other works dealing in part with the fur trade. *History of Early Steamboat Navigation on the Missouri River* (1903) was woven around the thread of the career of a veteran river pilot, Joseph La Barge. With Alfred T. Richardson, Chittenden edited the *Life, Letters and Travels of Father Pierre-Jean De Smet, S.J., 1801-1873* (1905). The book on steamboat navigation has been superseded, and the De Smet book suffers from faulty translations and an incomplete collection of the letters. The brief biographical section does provide, however, a lucid outline of the missionary's career.

See Gordon B. Dodds, *Hiram Martin Chittenden: His Public Career* (1973), and Bruce Leroy, ed., *Western Epic* (1961).—G. B. D.

Chivington, John M. (1821-1894). Minister and soldier. Chivington, the "Fighting Parson," was born in Warren County, Ohio. He took up the ministry in 1844 and preached in Ohio, Illinois, Missouri, Kansas, and Nebraska before arriving in Denver, Colorado, in 1860 as presiding elder of the First Methodist Episcopal Church. Chivington spread the gospel to the surrounding mining camps and established the first Methodist Sunday school in Denver.

Following the outbreak of the Civil War, Governor William Gilpin offered Chivington a commission as chaplain of the First Regiment, but the parson refused and asked instead for a "fighting" commission rather than a "praying" one. During the summer of 1861 the First Regiment answered a call for help from the Union forces in New Mexico. The combined force of Coloradans and New Mexicans met the Confederate army at

La Glorieta Pass, located east of Santa Fe. Chivington led a force of men through the mountains south of the pass and attacked the enemy from the rear. This surprise attack began the campaign to drive the Confederate army from New Mexico and established Chivington as a military hero.

The remainder of Chivington's military career was spent fighting the Indians of the Colorado plains. In November 1864 he led a thousand territorial volunteers against a Cheyenne camp on Sand Creek (see SAND CREEK MASSACRE). The volunteers surrounded the camp where five hundred Indians slept, the Indians confident that they were under the protection of the federal government. At dawn on November 29 the militia attacked the camp, killing some 200 to 450 Indians, many of whom were women and children. Chivington was alternately cheered and condemned for his action. The official investigation by a government committee headed by Senator J. R. Doolittle in March 1865 resulted in a condemnation of Chivington for his acts and a rather lame attempt to court-martial him. Chivington, however, had resigned from the army in January 1865, thus putting himself beyond the pale of military justice. Nonetheless, he spent the remainder of his life trying to escape the stigma of Sand Creek.

See Reginald S. Craig, *The Fighting Parson* (1959); Stan Hoig, *The Sand Creek Massacre* (1961); Janet Le Compte, "Sand Creek," *Colorado Magazine* (1964); and Michael A. Sievers, "Sands of Sand Creek Historiography," *Colorado Magazine* (1972).—R. B. W.

Choctaw Indians. See FIVE CIVILIZED TRIBES.

Chorpenning, George (1820-1894). Pioneer stagecoach operator. Chorpenning was born in Somerset, Pennsylvania, and among other enterprises operated an inn in his youth. In 1849 he started for the California gold fields, walking with two companions as far as Pittsburgh and from there working their way on steamboats along the Ohio and Missouri rivers until they reached Independence, Missouri. There they purchased a wagon, drawn by two mules, in which they completed their journey.

In 1851 Chorpenning and his partner, Absalom Woodward, secured the first contract from the United States Post Office to carry the mail from Sacramento to Salt Lake City once a month for $14,000. Placing the mail on the back of a mule, they journeyed from California to Salt Lake in fifty-three days, having been delayed by snow in the Sierra Nevada. Woodward was killed by Indians in November 1851 on the Malad River in northern Utah. When Chorpenning's contract was canceled because of his failure to perform the required service during the winter of 1851-52, he went to Washington and succeeded in getting his mail contract reinstated with an increase in payment to $30,000 a year. He continued to be the successful bidder between 1854 and 1858, at which time the mail service was changed from a monthly to a weekly basis and the compensation raised to $130,000 a year. At this point Chorpenning purchased ten stagecoaches and operated a passenger service between Salt Lake City and California in conjunction with mail delivery. In May 1860 his contract was again canceled by the Post Office Department and transferred to the Central Overland California and Pike's Peak Express Company.

During the Civil War, Chorpenning raised two regiments of volunteers and became a major in one of them, the First Regiment of Maryland Volunteer Infantry. Congress at one time approved a claim for his losses in carrying the mails between 1851 and 1860 amounting to $443,010 and a Treasury warrant was issued to him, but payment was stopped and he received nothing. Chorpenning died in poverty.

See Raymond W. Settle and Mary L. Settle, *War Drums and Wagon Wheels* (1966).—W. T. J.

Chouteau, August Pierre (1786-1838). Frontier trader and Indian diplomat. Chouteau was born in Spanish Louisiana at St. Louis, the son of Jean Pierre Chouteau, a pioneer in western fur trade enterprises. Young Chouteau received an appointment to West Point, served for a time as aide to General James Wilkinson, and participated in western military and trading expeditions to the Mandan and Arikara on the upper Missouri River. In 1815 Chouteau undertook, with Jules De Mun, a trading venture to the central Rocky Mountain region. A Spanish force arrested him, confiscated his goods, valued at thirty thousand dollars, and detained him at Santa Fe. Chouteau subsequently concentrated his commercial activities in Indian Territory.

From a base trading post established by his father in 1802 among the Osage on Grand River at Salina, Kansas, Chouteau developed a bustling trading community at Three Forks, where the Verdigris, Grand, and Arkansas rivers converge, complete with shipyards for construction of boats for shipping furs to New Orleans. By the 1830s, Chouteau dominated the fur trade industry of Indian Territory with a chain of trading stations that extended from the mouth of Little River west to Chouteau Creek in central Indian Territory and southwest into the Wichita Mountains. It is said that Chouteau lived on his primeval estate at Salina like a feudal lord, surrounded by *engagés* and slaves. He built a racetrack for entertaining friends and bestowed lavish hospitality on visitors, including Washington Irving, Charles Latrobe, and Sam Houston.

Chouteau regularly rendered service to the United States government in opening the Southwestern wilderness, serving as adviser, providing guides and interpreters for councils with the tribes, and serving as government envoy to the Kiowa and Comanche tribes. His interest and influence augured success for the 1834 Dodge-Leavenworth expedition to the Wichita Mountains, and his influence with the Kiowa and Comanche led to the first great intertribal council at Camp Mason, situated on the Canadian River in Cleveland County, and, ultimately, to the first treaties between the United States government and the Kiowa and Comanche. Commissioner Montfort Stokes commented that Chouteau was "better acquainted with the situation of Indian tribes and Indian manners, habits and dispositions than any man west of the Mississippi River."

See Grant Foreman, *Pioneer Days in the Early Southwest* (1926).—A. M. G.

Chouteau family. Missouri fur traders. *René Auguste* (1749-1829), born in New Orleans, commanded at the age of fourteen a building party that started the city of St. Louis at a site chosen by his stepfather, Pierre LACLEDE. As early as the 1780s he and his half brother, Jean Pierre, were trading furs with the Osage Indians. From 1794 to 1802 the half brothers had by grant of the governor of Louisiana the monopoly of trade with this tribe. Until the close of the War of 1812 he shipped most of his furs to Montreal, the only St. Louis merchant with the requisite credit for so large-scale an enterprise. A man widely respected for his high character, René Auguste held local military and political offices and became the largest landholder and wealthiest citizen in St. Louis.

Jean Pierre (1758-1849) was born in St. Louis. During the monopoly years he was chief trader of the family firm with the Osage and commanding officer of its Fort Carondelet. When Manuel Lisa was given the Osage monopoly in 1802, Jean Pierre persuaded most of the tribe to move to the three forks of the Arkansas, which was outside of Lisa's monopoly. In 1806 he was appointed Indian agent for the Osage and in 1809 he became one of the ten partners of the St. Louis Missouri Fur Company and supplied the trading goods for the expedition of that year. When that company was reorganized in 1814, he thereafter operated several trading houses on the lower Missouri until 1820, when he went into semiretirement. Jean Pierre was the most prominent individual in St. Louis.

Pierre (1789-1865), a son of Jean Pierre, was born in St. Louis. He clerked in his father's store, worked for two years in the upper Mississippi lead mines, and in 1813 formed a partnership with Bartholomew Berthold in the Missouri Indian fur trade. He became a partner in Bernard Pratte and Company (later Pratte, Chouteau, and Company), which purchased the Western Department of John Jacob Astor's American Fur Company in 1834. The firm was renamed Pierre Chouteau, Jr., and Company in 1838 and as such came to dominate the still-valuable fur trade of the upper Missouri for more than twenty years. Pierre Chouteau became an investor in many enterprises, a patron of art and science, and a manifold millionaire who resided for many years in New York City (see CHOUTEAU, AUGUSTE PIERRE; and FRENCH HERITAGE).

See Hiram M. Chittenden, *The American Fur Trade of the Far West* (1902).—G. B. D.

Chu Pak (1797-1866). The "Venerable Old Man" of the Chinese in the West during the 1860s. Chu Pak came to California in 1850 at the age of fifty-three. One of the leading men from the Four Districts in the Pearl River Delta in the province of Kwangtung in South China, Chu Pak served for many years as a headman of the Sze Yap Wui Kun, one of the district companies. In the summer of 1862, when he was involved in a murder trial, the directors of all district companies came to his aid with an address to the public that helped to clear him in the American court.

See Gunther Barth, *Bitter Strength: A History of the Chinese in the United States, 1850-1870* (1964).—G. B.

Church, James E. (1869-1959). Developer of snow-surveying. Born in Holly, Michigan, Church received his A.B. degree from the University of Michigan in 1892 and his Ph.D. from the University of Munich in 1901. Although a scholar of the classics, his love for mountain climbing led him to the Sierra and to the discovery of a method for predicting from snow depth the amount of moisture in the spring runoff from the mountains. His system of snow-surveying was adopted throughout the United States and the world, bringing him renown as a scientist.

A large collection of Church's papers is at the University of Nevada, Getchell Library, Reno.—R. R. E.

churches, traveling. The traveling churches were one of the most important organizing influences in the early western frontier. These disgruntled Baptist congregations, which originated in Fauquier County, Virginia, were outgrowths of the Great Awakening of the middle of the eighteenth century. Between 1763 and 1781 the Baptists grew more resentful of discrimination against them by the government and established church, and so, in 1780 and 1781 two groups moved overland to Kentucky. The first congregation, describing themselves as the Ten Baptist Churches, settled in the Bluegrass. The second group, led by Lewis and Elijah Craig, John Waller, and others, settled in Kentucky from Gilbert's Creek near the Crab Orchard, to the Ohio River near Limestone (Maysville).

These moving congregations were influential in expanding the settlements of the early West, and in time some of their members were to make significant economic contributions in the new country.

See Thomas D. Clark, *Kentucky, Land of Contrast* (1968); George W. Ranck, *The Traveling Church* (1891); and John Taylor, *A History of Ten Baptist Churches* (1823).—T. D. C.

Church of Jesus Christ of Latter-day Saints. See LATTER-DAY SAINTS.

Cíbola. Legendary location of seven mythical cities in the Southwest. Cíbola is the most common spelling given to a group of pueblos along the Zuñi River of northwestern New Mexico. They comprised the reality of the mythical "Seven Cities," which attracted Francisco Vásquez de CORONADO.

The origin of the myth is obscure; but CABEZA DE VACA told of peoples possessing precious jewels, and Spanish conquistadores had heard of wealthy peoples to the north. Fray Marcos and Estevanito found the "fabulous" cities in 1539—Estevanito to die at one of them. Coronado followed, conquered the Zuñi pueblos, and went on to other explorations.

See Adolph F. Bandelier, *The Gilded Man* (1893, 1962), and several articles in the *New Mexico Historical Review*; and George P. Hammond, *Coronado's Seven Cities* (1940).—R. A. B.

cities, growth of. The rise of instant cities in the second half of the nineteenth century highlighted the emergence of urban society in the West. Thriving on mining booms, these cities telescoped into a generation the cycle of growth from wilderness to city and produced a sophistication of life symptomatic of full-grown and flourishing urban centers. San Francisco and Denver typified these communities. The discovery of gold and silver in nearby mountains attracted floods of newcomers and spurred the rapid development of commerce and finance, industry and technology, urban democracy and culture. The mining booms provided an instantaneous economic base for a population of varied origin, background, and position, who brought to the new cities some of the diverse patterns of urban life they had known before their migration. The process hastened the maturing of urban society, and the fullness of city life reflected the quickly emerging and complex social, economic, and cultural setting. This immediate flowering of urban life, coupled with a measure of social cohesion and cultural identity, set the instant cities apart from the score of other towns rising rapidly in the second half of the nineteenth century—frontier settlements like Kansas City, transportation links like Omaha, markets like Portland, or harbors like Seattle.

Citizens in the emergent urban societies of the Far West strove to inaugurate and to maintain a style and tone of life characteristic of great cities and to foster a quality of urban behavior symptomatic of large centers. In settings but a few steps removed from the wilderness, they would aspire to live a city life undeterred by the vast expanse of nature separating their new homes from their old ones in the East. The residents of the emerging cities and towns shared with the rest of the country the difficulties of adjusting to the strains of a maturing industrial society. They experienced the typical phenomena of expansion: problems of migration and immigration; racial and ethnic struggle; economic opportunities and limited social mobility; the adjustment of an agrarian democracy to the city; the rise of urban culture; and the incorporation of an intensified technology into the fabric of life. The process was aggravated in the West, since the vast open spaces still seemed to promise the virtues and rewards of Jeffersonianism while actually the city already dominated national development and affected its goals and mores.

On the eve of the rise of instant cities, four types of towns were prevalent: the economic town, epitomized by Santa Fe; the colonial outpost, for example, Monterey; the marketplace (Champoeg); and the temple city (Salt Lake City). They reflected in the West some of the variety of urban experience that characterized the growth of settlements in all America. These four towns were the products of the Spanish-Mexican world in the far Southwest and on the California littoral, the settlements in the Willamette valley of the Oregon country, and the Great Basin kingdom of the Mormons. They had come into existence in response to impulses dating back as far as 1598, when Don Juan de Oñate, in founding New Mexico, planted the roots for the settlements along the Rio Grande. As recently as 1844, the mob murdering of Prophet Joseph Smith in Illinois set into motion the events leading to the Mormon exodus and the establishment of the Zion in the Mountains by the Church of Jesus Christ of Latter-day Saints.

The oldest of the four towns, Santa Fe, founded in 1609, was transformed during the 1830s and 1840s by the commercial and military conquest of American traders and soldiers. Here resident merchants marketed their imports for sale to the local population in return for silver, blankets, buffalo skins, and mules, which were shipped to Missouri. Monterey, picked in 1775 by Carlos III as capital of the newest addition to his empire, remained the administrative center of settlements stretching from San Diego in the south to Sonoma in the north. American conquest destroyed the Californios' pattern of life, with work centered on socially and economically self-sufficient rancherías. For several years before the organization of the Oregon Provisional Government at Champoeg in 1843, the settlers of the Willamette valley—mostly Canadians formerly employed in the fur trade and Americans infected with the "Oregon fever"—had been trading their wheat at the river landing at Champoeg to an agent of the Hudson's Bay Company from Fort Vancouver. But the market-

place lost all significance after its fleeting moment of political importance, when the Great Migration of the 1840s to the Oregon country created a boom in town sites. While the economic town, the colonial outpost, and the marketplace represented familiar forms of urban life in the United States, an altogether different type of settlement, a temple city, appeared in the heart of the western mountains. In July 1847 Brigham Young and his followers laid out Salt Lake City according to the plat of the city of Zion. From the center of their Great Basin kingdom they would administer to the spiritual, ecclesiastical, and secular needs of a chosen people in the promised land.

These islands of urban civilization occupied only a small portion of the vast wilderness ocean in the West. Although most of the expanse remained wilderness, it was crossed and crisscrossed by lines of communication linking the urban islands to each other and to the mainlands of authority, commerce, culture, industry, and population. Red and white men had left their trails and river crossings, trading posts and military forts, rendezvous sites and burial grounds. Although few of the sites of the fur trade became the nuclei of towns, the economic and social philosophy of some of the mountain men prepared the West for the rapid transformation that accompanied the urban explosion and the rise of instant cities. As "Jacksonian men" of enterprise and expectant capitalists, the mountain men bypassed the civilizing influences of farms and homesteads in a region considered unsuited to agriculture. Finding the role of the roving entrepreneur more congenial to their temper than that of the farmer, their operations introduced elements of a mercantile and industrial society into the wilderness.

The coming RAILROADS intensified the urban explosion in the West in the second half of the nineteenth century, accelerating the development of San Francisco, Los Angeles, Portland, Seattle, Denver, Kansas City, and Omaha. In the early twentieth century the advent of the automobile presaged the disintegration as physical and social entities of those cities that had achieved a high measure of cultural distinctiveness. The spectacular rise of Los Angeles, paling in the shadow of San Francisco during the era of instant cities, epitomized the new trend initiated by the motor vehicle. The automobile enhanced the physical and social mobility of the residents of western towns, most of which were endowed with ample space for expansion, and made the pleasantness of cityfied living available in the sprawling rurban, neither rural nor urban, additions to the cities.

The established urban centers were submerged by waves of migrants surging west as a result of the relocation of industry during two world wars, the emergence of new industries (oil, entertainment, and aerospace), the Great Depression, and the intensified exploitation of natural resources with added emphasis on the marketing of climate and scenery. The influx made the conventional boundaries of cities and towns obsolete and brought into existence vast concentrations of people described as Standard Metropolitan Statistical Areas. Several of these large units of population exist in the West. In 1963, at least 1,000,000 people lived in San Diego, Los Angeles-Long Beach, San Francisco-Oakland, Seattle-Everett, and Kansas City; 500,000-1,000,000 in Anaheim-Santa Ana-Garden Grove, San

Bernardino-Riverside-Ontario, San Jose, Sacramento, Portland, Phoenix, Denver, and Oklahoma City; and 250,000-500,000 in Bakersfield, Fresno, Tacoma, Spokane, Salt Lake City, Tucson, Albuquerque, Tulsa, Wichita, and Omaha. These centers of population are struggling to achieve a measure of social cohesion and cultural identity, which the instant cities had gained when the motor vehicle overwhelmed and absorbed them into a nationalized urban scene created by the new technology of the automobile civilization.

See Leonard J. Arrington, *Great Basin Kingdom* (1958); Gunther Barth, "Metropolism and Urban Elites in the Far West," in F. C. Jaher, ed., *The Age of Industrialism in America* (1968); William H. Goetzmann, "The Mountain Man as Jacksonian Man," *American Quarterly*, vol. 15 (1963); W. Eugene Hollon, *The Southwest: Old and New* (1961); Earl S. Pomeroy, *The Pacific Slope* (1965); and Glenn Chesney Quiett, *They Built the West: An Epic of Rails and Cities* (1934).—G. B.

Civil War. The Civil War affected the lives of citizens living west of the Mississippi River in ways frequently different from those living in the North or South. Slavery was never a very controversial issue beyond the borders of Missouri, Kansas, Nebraska, Arkansas, and Texas, although many defenders of slavery lived in New Mexico and California. Most Americans in the West were unionists, and probably a majority of them favored Democratic presidential candidate Stephen A. Douglas at the outset of the war. In California, as in other states, the split in Democratic ranks pushed the state into the Republican column in the election of 1860. The Mormons in Utah, while actually neutral, were suspected of having southern proclivities. Only one far western region—the southern half of the New Mexico Territory—formally declared for the Confederacy. The Mexican portion of the population in New Mexico, generally indifferent to the North-South conflict, was nevertheless greatly influenced by anti-Texas sentiments, stemming back to the ill-fated Santa Fe expedition of 1841. Sectional feelings were undoubtedly strongest in the Mississippi valley states, where bitterness stemming from "Bleeding Kansas" continued throughout the war.

In the West, there were no major cities captured during the war, no great strategic prizes won. No major engagements occurred comparable to those taking place simultaneously to the East. In most western regions the Civil War was irretrievably connected with Indian relations and, ironically, the greatest impact of the war in terms of casualties was on the Indians, who had little or no interest in the issues dividing the North and South, except for the Five Civilized Tribes of Indian Territory, which individually signed treaties with the Confederacy and sent men into battle for the South. Some settlers always felt that the absence during the war of regular troops in strength prompted increased Indian hostility. There is little doubt, however, that continued pressure caused by advancing pioneers was the contributing factor to Indian-white agitation.

Lincoln's political tactics in the trans-Mississippi West were obvious and effective. He appointed pro-Union officials in the newly created territories of Dakota (1861), Colorado (1861), and Nevada (1861) and in the older territories of New Mexico, Utah, and Washington. Later he did the same when Idaho (1862), Arizona (1863), and Montana (1864) were organized by Congress. One of the significant accomplishments of the Lincoln administration during the war was to organize the entire West into viable political units each with a government loyal to the Union. Dr. William Jayne, Lincoln's friend and personal physician in Springfield, Illinois, became governor of the Dakota Territory, and a Unionist from Missouri, William Gilpin, was made governor of Colorado. Lincoln also appointed Stephen J. Field, a major California political figure, to the Supreme Court of the United States. In order to avoid dissension, moreover, he did not press the draft issue in the West.

The Lincoln administration maintained effective communication with the mining areas of the West and especially California in its desire to secure gold and silver with which to finance the war. The short-lived pony express raced messages between California and St. Joseph, Missouri, until October 1861, when the first transcontinental telegraph was completed. The old "oxbow" route of the Butterfield Stage Line, which ran through Texas and the Southwest to Yuma and then north to San Francisco, was abandoned in favor of a central route across the Great Plains, Utah, and the mining area of Nevada. Beginning in the spring of 1861, the Overland Mail Company delivered the mail to the West Coast. By the end of the war, Ben Holladay lines transported mail and passengers from the East to Salt Lake City, whence the Overland Mail carried them to California. Concern for effective communication inspired Congress on July 1, 1862, to pass a bill calling for the construction of a transcontinental railroad. Long demanded but postponed by the sectional controversy, the measure now received favorable action. Obtaining equipment and building materials was difficult and costly, since much had to be shipped around Cape Horn. In spite of the obstacles, by the end of the war the Central Pacific Railroad had managed to lay more than thirty miles of track.

The demand for soldiers on the eastern front was so great that few regular army units could be spared for duty in the West, so local volunteer or militia contingents replaced them. In the Dakotas, these troops battled the Sioux during the War of the Outbreak. Colorado volunteers supplemented regulars assigned to guard the overland trail and the road to Santa Fe and fought the Confederates when they threatened New Mexico in 1862. Washington and Oregon belatedly created volunteer units, but in California the response was overwhelming. Volunteers numbered nearly 17,000—more than the entire prewar United States Army. By 1865, upward of 20,000 troops were stationed at strategic locations in the West (see ARMY ON THE FRONTIER and ARMY TERRITORIAL COMMANDS). These garrisons were supposed to protect settlers and routes from real or fancied Indian troubles and from Confederate raiders. In the course of performing that mission, they provided a ready and often indispensable market for the produce of local settlers.

One of Lincoln's problems was Texas. Confederate sentiment was so strong there that its famed Unionist governor, Sam Houston, was forced from office when the state seceded in February 1861. General David E. Twiggs, commander of the United States Army's Department of Texas, soon after surrendered all federal property and supplies to the Confederates. The Texas coast became an entrepôt for military supplies, and its common border with Mexico afforded another source of supply for foreign goods. By 1863, however, the Union blockade of the Texas coast had become fairly effective; partial federal control of the Mississippi River after Admiral David G. Farragut's capture of New Orleans in April 1862 helped cut off Texas and the rest of the trans-Mississippi West from the eastern portion of the South (see LOUISIANA, STATE OF).

The greatest Texas threat to the Union was the invasion of the New Mexico Territory. Before the invasion Colonel W. W. Loring, who headed that army department, was actively seeking to win his officers over to the Confederacy. In July 1861 Colonel John R. BAYLOR moved north from Fort Bliss (El Paso) into the Mesilla valley, where he forced the evacuation of Fort Fillmore and received the surrender of Major Isaac Lynde's retreating command. Union forces also abandoned Fort Stanton in the face of his advance. Baylor's efforts coincided with a political effort by southern sympathizers in the Mesilla valley to create a separate Confederate territory out of the southern half of the New Mexico Territory, which then included present-day Arizona. Another group of southern adherents in Tucson, meanwhile, was also promoting a separatist movement. The Confederate Territory of Arizona was eventually organized and sent a delegate to the Confederate Congress (see ARIZONA: *Confederate Arizona*).

Baylor's actions were but the initial thrust. A greater effort by Texas and the Confederacy to capture the whole of New Mexico, to seize the Colorado mines, and perhaps even to take southern California, followed. During the winter of 1861-62, General Henry H. Sibley, commanding the Texas forces, moved up the Rio Grande valley toward Albuquerque and Santa Fe, his destination Fort Union, then the best-provisioned post in the Southwest. In the interim, Colonel E. R. S. Canby assumed command of the Union Department of New Mexico and concentrated his forces at Fort Union and at Fort Craig on the Rio Grande. Canby's Fort Craig troops met Sibley's Brigade at Valverde on February 16, 1862. The battle resulted in a Confederate victory. Sibley's mounted units then advanced rapidly up the Rio Grande valley, taking the capital at Santa Fe and forcing the pro-Union government of Governor Henry Connelly to retire to Las Vegas. Pushing eastward in hopes of seizing Fort Union, the Confederates unexpectedly met the Union command of Colonel John Slough in La Glorieta Pass, New Mexico. The ensuing battle, March 26-28, has been labeled "the Gettysburg of the West." Regulars, reinforced by Colorado volunteers dispatched to the scene by Governor Gilpin, engaged the Texas command under Lieutenant Colonel William R. Scurry. A flanking party led by the "Fighting Parson," Major John M. Chivington, happened upon the Confederate supply train parked in a side canyon. It destroyed the wagons and teams, thus precipitating the Texas retreat from New Mexico. Without support from the hostile New Mexican populace, with Canby's pursuit of the now disorganized invaders, and with the approach of the California Column, the Confederate dream of the conquest of the West went aglimmering.

California's major contribution to the Union cause was not so much men as money. Her gold proved indispensable in bolstering the North financially. Her citizens, moreover, inspired by the Unitarian minister Thomas Starr King, donated almost $1.25 million, or one fourth of all funds forthcoming in the nation, to the Sanitary Commission, the precursor of the Red Cross. An attempt by some Californians to form an independent Pacific Republic, which was also to include the Pacific Northwest, had a certain following but failed, as did a more concerted attempt by secessionists to turn southern California into a separate state with Confederate ties. Their efforts were quelled through legal and extralegal suppression of individuals and newspapers.

Meanwhile, Californians supporting the Union cause were encouraged to enlist in the so-called Army of the Pacific. Not counting the service of the "California Hundred" and a regiment that served with Massachusetts troops in the eastern theater of operations, the primary function of the California volunteers was to perform guard duty in the adjacent territories.

The California Column, General James H. CARLETON commanding, advanced into Arizona in the spring of 1862 to relieve the beleaguered forces in New Mexico. Forward elements of Carleton's command skirmished with a few Confederates at Picacho Peak on April 15 in the "westernmost battle of the Civil War," eventually forcing the retreat of the Confederate detachment that had taken post at Tucson. On July 15, a part of his brigade engaged Cochise at Apache Pass.

With General Canby's departure, General Carleton assumed command in New Mexico and proceeded to chastise the Navaho, whose raids upon New Mexican settlements had long distressed the inhabitants. A punitive expedition under Colonel Kit CARSON was sent against the Indians. The campaign of 1863-64 terminated when most of the Navaho were ousted from their haunts in the northwestern part of the territory and transplanted to the Bosque Redondo at Fort Sumner on the Pecos River. The forced migration and sojourn at the ill-suited reservation was extremely hard on the Navaho. Promising compliance with the white man's laws, the Navaho were finally permitted after the war to return to their former home. Carleton, in the meantime, kept close watch on the former secessionist strongholds of Mesilla and Tucson. When the Union Territory of Arizona was created in 1863 he persuaded federal officials to locate the capital at Prescott near the newly discovered gold mines rather than at Tucson. Throughout the war, Carleton exercised virtually unlimited power in New Mexico.

A thousand-man California contingent crossed into Nevada in the early days of the war and hastened to Salt Lake City, establishing Fort Douglas. Its task was to patrol the vital overland mail route between the Mormon capital and Sacramento. Except for a brief interval, the troops kept it open throughout the war. These units were commanded by Colonel Patrick Edward CONNOR, a Stockton businessman and veteran of the Mexican War, who feuded incessantly with the Mormon leaders while warring aggressively and unmercifully against the Shoshoni, Bannock, and Ute Indians. What success there was in handling civil and Indian problems in the extensive reaches west of the continental divide may be attributed in large measure to the skill of General George Wright, who commanded the Department of the Pacific for three years until replaced by General Irvin McDowell in July 1864.

East of the Rockies, the Cheyenne and Arapaho were perhaps the least offensive of the hostile Plains Indians, yet it was they who suffered the most grievous treatment at the hands of the whites during the war (see CHEYENNE-ARAPAHO WAR). Governor John Evans of Colorado Territory wanted to clear title to the Indian lands appropriated by miners and farmers who had moved into the region. The origin of the hostilities that broke out on the Plains in 1864 resulted from the mistaken belief that the Indians intended to fight.

Depredations occurred, engaged in by both sides. Political considerations and Colorado statehood ambitions came into play as the Indian became the scapegoat for the territory's many troubles, thus setting the stage for the SAND CREEK MASSACRE. John M. Chivington, now colonel commanding the Colorado District, led the Third Colorado Volunteer Cavalry, which had volunteered for a hundred days of service, into battle. Surprising Black Kettle's people, who were camped under a flag of truce near Fort Lyon on Sand Creek, the assaulting force decimated the Cheyenne village. The controversial event aroused ire among many easterners and, in 1865, gave rise to three investigations that condemned the perfidy and slaughter. Most frontiersmen, however, usually took an intolerant hard line regarding Indian affairs and felt the evidence justified the actions at Sand Creek. Sand Creek invited revenge, and soon raiding parties were ravaging the Platte River country through which the overland trail ran. Twice Julesburg, Colorado, was sacked, and at Fort Sedgwick more than a dozen soldiers were killed from ambush. These forays finally led to the abortive POWDER RIVER INDIAN EXPEDITION of 1865.

Farther north the Nez Percé acquiesced temporarily to the invasion of prospectors, signing a treaty in June 1863 that reduced their domains in Idaho considerably. Meanwhile, miners were also flocking to the mines of Montana. Throughout the war, migration, though on a reduced scale, went on continually all over the West.

The Indians who resented most intensely the intrusion of whites onto their lands were the Sioux of western MINNESOTA and eastern Dakota. They were mistreated by settlers and crooked agents and debauched by whiskey. The result was the so-called War of the Outbreak. It began with the unpremeditated killing of five farmers near Acton in August 1862. This precipitated depredations that brought about the Indians' attack on Fort Ridgely and New Ulm, resulting in the death of eight hundred settlers and the capture of several hundred others (see MINNESOTA UPRISING). General Henry Hastings Sibley, early-day fur trader and first governor of Minnesota, was assigned the task of relieving the distressed pioneers. His militia units, reinforced by a detachment of volunteers, met the hostiles in the Battle of Wooded Lake. Thirty-nine of the 303 Sioux warriors taken prisoner and convicted by a military commission of complicity in the uprising were hanged at Mankato in December.

The operations against the Sioux during 1863-64 conducted by Sibley and General Alfred SULLY were not successful in crushing them. Although defeated in combat at Big Mound, Dead Buffalo Lake, Stony Lake, Whitestone Hill, and Killdeer Mountain, the Sioux remained hostile. Marshaling between one thousand and three thousand warriors, they, in conjunction with the

Cheyenne and Arapaho, attacked Platte Bridge Station, 130 miles west of Fort Laramie, on July 26, 1865. They defeated the troops garrisoned there, killing in the process Lieutenant Caspar Collins, after whom the Wyoming community is named.

Indian-white troubles in the vast area from Minnesota to the Rockies had little to do with the Civil War, but many settlers and officers were convinced that the "Secesh" incited the Indians and saw it as a part of the North-South conflict. On the other hand, a noteworthy feature of the 1864-65 campaign against the Sioux was the use of "Galvanized Yankees" as support elements. These Confederate prisoners, recruited from the prisoner-of-war camp at Rock Island, Illinois, and led by Union officers, performed creditably in garrisoning posts and patrolling on the Great Plains. Other repatriated Confederates helped swell the mining camps of Montana.

The construction of two forts on the Missouri River indicated the stream's importance as an avenue to the newly organized Montana Territory, while the increasing use of the BOZEMAN TRAIL posed another threat to the northern tribes. The officer charged with administering and coordinating military affairs on the Great Plains was General John POPE. In 1862, following his defeat at Second Manassas, he was assigned command of the Department of the Northwest, where his attention was primarily devoted to the Sioux. After 1864, however, he was given control of the Division of the Missouri, which enlarged the scope of his authority to include the Southern Plains tribes and greatly extended his responsibility for maintaining peace on the prairie.

In the trans-Mississippi theater, action was centered in Louisiana, eastern Texas, Arkansas, Missouri, and Kansas. MISSOURI, for all the exertions of its governor Claiborne F. Jackson, did not secede. Two armed camps, however, quickly appeared in St. Louis. Street fighting ensued, with 28 deaths resulting. The Unionists, supported by the large German population in the state, followed the vigorous leadership of Francis P. BLAIR, Jr., and Captain Nathaniel Lyon. Southern sympathizers organized military forces that Governor Jackson placed under the direction of Sterling PRICE, a veteran of the Mexican War and a former governor of Missouri.

Conciliatory measures failing, engagements soon occurred in southern Missouri at Wilson's Creek, August 10, 1861, where General Lyon lost his life, and at Pea Ridge, March 6-8, 1862, where the secession forces were defeated (see ARKANSAS). Despite the fact that a shadow regime met at Neosho in November 1861, passed an ordinance of secession, and was recognized by the Confederate government, the victory at Pea Ridge clinched control of most of Missouri for the Union.

Fighting in Missouri degenerated into guerrilla warfare. This situation was not helped by the actions of General John C. FREMONT, who had been placed in charge of the Department of the West. Because of Frémont's unauthorized proclamations concerning confiscation of property and emancipation of the slaves and many other irregularities, he was removed from command by Lincoln in November 1861. In 1864 Sterling Price sought to wrench Missouri from the federals but during his invasion, which was partly for the purpose of recruiting men for the Confederacy, he lost more men by desertion than he gained as recruits.

Price's actions only worsened the internecine struggle in Kansas and Missouri. Missouri "bushwhackers" invaded Kansas to raid and kill, and Kansas "JAYHAWKERS" retaliated in kind. These border guerrillas, while claiming to represent one side or the other, more often than not were acting on their own. Most notorious of the practitioners was William C. Quantrill, a Confederate captain. His assault upon Lawrence, Kansas, in August 1863 resulted in the slaughter of 150 men and the injury of 30 (see QUANTRILL'S RAIDERS).

From 1862 to 1864 forts Larned and Riley were the bases from which efforts were made to stem bushwhacking tactics by Kansas jayhawkers. These posts were also points from which to counteract Confederate intrigue in the Indian Territory. Southern representatives to the Five Civilized Tribes negotiated treaties with the Creek, Choctaw, Chickasaw, Seminole, and, finally, the hesitant Cherokee. Owning many slaves themselves, most of the Indians readily sided with the Confederacy and contributed a brigade of troops that was utilized primarily in the Indian country and in Arkansas (see NEGROES ON THE FRONTIER). After the war, the tribes were penalized by the Union government when they were forced to make new concessions of land.

Confederate agents likewise endeavored to secure the Texas frontier from inroads by the Kiowa and Comanche; but neither the treaties drawn nor the occupation by Texas troops of Fort Arbuckle and other federally abandoned western posts stopped the incursions of these tribes and the Apache, all of whom continued to cause trouble for whites on both sides of the war. In November 1864 General Carleton ordered Kit Carson to punish the Comanche and Kiowa for raiding wagon trains on the Santa Fe Trail. After enveloping Chief Little Mountain's Kiowa village of 150 lodges in the Canadian valley, Carson's nine hundred soldiers suddenly came upon a combined Kiowa-Comanche force of more than one thousand warriors at Adobe Walls. Had it not been for the good service of the two howitzers attached to his command, the Indians probably would have overrun Carson's position. As it was, they severely harassed his retrograding column. Carson, although claiming victory after having destroyed the Kiowa encampment, acknowledged that he was lucky to get his troops out of their predicament. Despite Carleton's efforts, Apache raids throughout Arizona and New Mexico continued unceasingly during the war. And with the exception of the Mescalero, Apache warriors fought both Union and Confederate forces.

At sea, Galveston, Texas, was captured temporarily by a Union squadron in October, 1862. A regiment and battery of federal troops occupied the town in December, but it was almost immediately retaken by Confederates aboard river steamers converted into gunboats. The Gulf Squadron was unable to prevent blockade runners from making port at Galveston until it surrendered in June 1865. Northern naval vessels in the Gulf suffered another setback in January 1863 at Sabine Pass, Texas, where two ships, with a complement of 190 sailors and armed with eleven guns, were overpowered by Confederate riverboats. But these successes were canceled in 1863 when the Union finally gained control of the Mississippi River and cut off Texas from the South. Thereafter the mission of the Union forces west of the river was to prevent Confederate troops in Arkansas and Louisiana from crossing to reinforce their hard-pressed compatriots in the Cis-Mississippi region.

Throughout the war Lincoln encouraged southern Unionists to bring their states back into their "proper practical relations" with the rest of the Union. In pursuit of that goal, he issued a proclamation on December 8, 1863, by which Louisiana and Arkansas established "free state" governments upon renouncing their ordinances of secession, abolishing slavery, and holding new elections. These civil administrations proved unsatisfactory, since more than ninety percent of the population and area of Louisiana still remained loyal to the Confederacy. In Arkansas, military enclaves afforded the only security for northern forces. Furthermore, attempts by these "ten-percent" governments to function independently interfered immeasurably with military operations in the Mississippi valley.

President Lincoln also believed that acquisition of cotton was vital to the North. To obtain that commodity, trade was permitted with the South. This traffic was supposed to be regulated by licenses issued by the Treasury Department. A scandal soon developed, however, because unscrupulous speculators took advantage of the unprecedented opportunity to make money. General Nathaniel P. Banks's Red River expedition of March-May 1864 devolved into a cotton-raiding endeavor. This campaign, designed to take Shreveport and gain possession of East Texas, was a fiasco. The river terrain obviated the success of a joint army-navy venture. Kirby Smith's Confederate forces were not defeated; and the Confederates destroyed much of the cotton to keep it out of the hands of those aboard the troop-laden ships. Banks suffered two reverses at Sabine Cross Roads and Pleasant Hill, while the Union flotilla narrowly escaped being stranded high and dry by the falling river.

Kirby Smith's position in the Southwest remained firm; illicit commercial intercourse sustained his forces during the last year and a half of the war, supplying him with more war material than came into Texas via Matamoras, Mexico. General Canby, who replaced General Banks in May 1864 as commander in the entire Mississippi valley and adjacent states, complained bitterly to the president about the trade policy and the rump governments—to no avail. Finally, in New Orleans on May 26, 1865, Canby received the surrender of Smith's trans-Mississippi command, the last organized Confederate army in the field. With that capitulation the Civil War ended in the West and in the nation.

While the Civil War greatly affected the West and deeply embittered people in the tier of states to the west of the Mississippi River, it did not change patterns of settlement or result in any major political changes. It gave the Republican party a chance to gain a strong foothold in most of the western states and territories in the ELECTION OF 1864. While Texas and Arkansas suffered from the war, California boomed; and new mining areas opened up in Idaho, Montana, and Arizona. The Civil War in the West was actually a prelude to a lingering Indian war which lasted until 1890. In that intermittent conflict, many officers and troops were veterans of the Civil War, and some were ex-slaves who had joined the army.

There is no account of the Civil War in the West in print. The best general survey is in J. G. Randall and David Donald, *The Civil War and Reconstruction* (1961). Jay Monaghan, *Civil War on the Western Border, 1854-1865* (1955), is useful for the trans-Mississippi story. The Union efforts in the West are conveniently summarized in Robert M. Utley, *Frontiersmen in Blue: The United States Army and the Indian, 1848-1865* (1967). Ray B. Colton, *The Civil War in the Western Territories* (1959), covers the civilian and military history of the Southwest during the war years, as do Howard R. Lamar, *The Far Southwest* (1966), and Arthur A. Wright, *The Civil War in the Southwest* (1965). Ludwell H. Johnson, *The Red River Campaign: Politics and Cotton in the Civil War* (1958); Fletcher Pratt, *Civil War on Western Waters* (1956); and Stephen B. Oates, *Confederate Cavalry West of the River* (1961), cover aspects of Texas' role in the conflict. Joseph Ellison, *California and the Nation, 1850-1859* (1927); Aurora Hunt, *The Army of the Pacific* (1951); and Oscar Lewis, *The War in the Far West, 1861-65* (1961), focus on California. Many books treat the New Mexico campaign. Max L. Heyman, Jr., *Prudent Soldier: A Biography of Major General E. R. S. Canby, 1817-1873* (1959), provides a useful summary, as does Martin H. Hall, *Sibley's New Mexico Campaign* (1960). In addition to Utley's *Frontiersmen in Blue*, see C. M. Oehler, *The Great Sioux Uprising* (1959), for more information about the war on the Great Plains. Useful, too, is William E. Parrish, *Turbulent Partnership: Missouri and the Union, 1861-1865* (1963).—M. L. H.

Clagett, William Horace (1838-1901). Northwest lawyer and politician. Moving from his native Maryland to Iowa in 1850, Clagett studied law and was admitted to the bar in Keokuk, Iowa, at the age of twenty. Then he moved to Carson, Nevada, in 1861, where he joined Samuel L. Clemens (Mark Twain) in a prospecting trip to Unionville, which is described in detail in Twain's *Roughing It*. Clagett specialized in mining law thereafter and also served in the Nevada legislature before moving on to Montana Territory, where he was elected delegate to Congress in 1870, the only Republican to win before 1888. He had considerable success in Congress, where delegates often fared less well than Congressmen who could vote. There he got Yellowstone Park established, among other things. After four more years in Montana, he moved to Denver and then to Dakota's Black Hills, where he led a movement in April 1877 to get Congress to establish a new territory of Lincoln for the new Deadwood mines. When that effort failed, he returned to Montana. Next, he shifted to Portland shortly before settling in Idaho's new Coeur d'Alene lead-silver mining region. In Idaho he was president of the constitutional convention in 1889. In 1890 he was one of four senators elected by Idaho's first state legislature, but the Senate declined to seat so many, and he was one of the two left out.

As attorney for Idaho's largest lead-silver mining corporation, Bunker Hill and Sullivan, Clagett naturally joined almost everyone else in Idaho in upholding the silver standard. But he did so as a Populist rather than as a Silver Republican—much to the surprise of many of his political associates. He never did win the seat he wanted in the Senate, and eventually settled in Spokane, the headquarters of Idaho's Coeur d'Alene mining region.—M. W.

Claiborne, John Francis Hamtramck (1807-1884). Mississippi lawyer, journalist, politician, and historian. Born in Natchez, Mississippi, Claiborne was the grandson of the pioneer settler Colonel Anthony Hutchins, the son of General Ferdinand Leigh Claiborne, and the nephew of the territorial governor, William Charles Coles Claiborne. He practiced law, edited a Democratic newspaper, and served in the state legislature and briefly in the United States Congress. Because his health was always delicate, he retired from public life in 1838 but served as an editor of several papers in the 1840s. Opposed to secession, he held himself aloof from all official connection with the Confederacy.

Before the Civil War Claiborne published the *Life and Times of Sam Dale* (1860) and the *Life and Correspondence of John A. Quitman* (1860). He devoted his postwar energies to writing a history of Mississippi. The first volume, *Mississippi as a Province, Territory and State*, appeared in 1880 (reprinted in 1964), but the manuscript of the completed second volume was destroyed when Claiborne's home burned in 1884. Though biased, his works are very valuable sources on Mississippi history prior to the Civil War.—J. E. G.

Claiborne, William Charles Coles (1775-1817). Territorial politician. Claiborne was second governor of Mississippi Territory and only governor of Orleans Territory, as well as first governor of the state of Louisiana. He was noted for his ability to work with the federal administration and with territorial residents.

Born in Sussex County, Virginia, he was from an old Virginia family. He became a clerk to Congress at the age of fifteen, and later studied law. His law practice was first established in Sullivan County, Tennessee. Becoming involved in politics, he was a member of the constitutional convention for the new state of Tennessee. While serving on the state supreme court, he was elected to fill out Andrew Jackson's unfinished term in the United States House of Representatives. Despite his being under age, the people reelected him to the House in 1798.

In the House of Representatives he chaired the select committee to investigate charges of irregular conduct against Governor Winthrop SARGENT of Mississippi Territory and to consider the request from residents of the territory for second-stage government. The committee's report was accepted by Congress, and the territory was granted an elected legislature and congressional delegate. When the presidential election of 1800 was thrown into the House of Representatives, Claiborne voted for Thomas Jefferson. The reward for his party regularity and his interest in the frontier was appointment as governor of Mississippi Territory, to replace Sargent.

During his two years in Mississippi, Claiborne managed to avoid any serious political differences with the local politicians and supervised the first elections in the territory. With the acquisition of Louisiana, he and Major General James Wilkinson were appointed commissioners to receive the new land from Spanish authorities.

He became governor of the Territory of Orleans upon its creation in 1804, holding that post until 1812, when he was elected the first governor of the state of Louisiana. His first years in New Orleans were difficult ones. He knew no French, and the Louisianians were displeased with their small share in self-government, angered by imposition of the English language and common law, and unhappy with rigid enforcement of United States customs regulations after years of laxity under Spain. Claiborne's indecisiveness in the face of the arbitrary behavior of James WILKINSON during the confusion of the BURR CONSPIRACY also damaged his position. But he gradually won the respect and affection of his new compatriots as well as the federal administration. He married into a native Louisiana family, welcomed hostages from slave insurrection in the West Indies, and learned French. Unfortunately, his difficulties reemerged during Andrew Jackson's defense of New Orleans in 1814-15, when his old indecisiveness infuriated the impatient Tennessean. At the end of his gubernatorial term he was elected to the United States Senate in 1817, but death prevented his taking his seat.—J. T. B. and J. G. T.

claim association. The settlement of portions of the Middle West occurred prior to government surveys of the land. In order to settle disputes over land ownership in these areas, extralegal organizations called claim clubs, squatter clubs, squatter courts, or claim associations were formed. Often the club extended its jurisdiction to include the enforcement of general law and order if no law officers were in the newly settled region.

Each association registered and protected claims for an area about the size of a township. Settlers would hold a meeting, elect officers, and draw up a constitution. Members of the association registered their claims, usually for the nominal fee of one dollar, which was the requirement for joining. When a claim was disputed, the conflict was taken before a panel or jury composed of five members of the association elected to serve as arbiters. Appeals could be taken from the jury to the entire association membership.

When someone attempted to settle another man's claim, his punishment was meted out by the association's marshal. If the "jumper" did not heed verbal warnings, the marshal usually enlisted the aid of the membership to perform a "physical warning." Beatings and destruction of property were common inducements for the jumper to move on. Occasionally death was the result of an overzealous warning.

Claim associations differed from government land offices in several respects. According to federal law, claims in Nebraska and Kansas were not to exceed 160 acres, but associations commonly allowed members to register 320 acres. In addition, claim clubs allowed minors to register land. Finally, the books of these organizations were not always available to the general public. Claim clubs were common to the rapidly advancing frontier, but they seldom lasted more than three years. Their functions were taken over by government land offices.

See Everett Dick, *The Sod-House Frontier, 1854-1890* (1954).—D. J. T.

Clappe, Louise. See DAME SHIRLEY.

Clark, [Charles] Badger, Jr. (1883-1957). Cowboy poet. When Clark was three months old, his preacher father moved the family from Iowa to Dakota Territory (present-day South Dakota). After a year at Dakota Wesleyan University, Clark joined a group of colonists going to Cuba to try to farm. The expedition was prematurely interrupted for lack of funds, but Clark stayed on. While there he got involved in a feud between two Spanish families and spent a little time in jail. Charged with carrying a gun and stealing coconuts, he was finally brought to trial and acquitted. Returning to South Dakota, he became a news reporter for the *Lead Daily Call* but soon went to Arizona to arrest a minor tuberculosis attack. There he took a riding job on the Cross I Quarter Circle Ranch near Tombstone.

Clark became so enthusiastic about range life that he began writing letters in verse describing various aspects of cowboy life to his family. His stepmother sent one of these "letter poems" to the *Pacific Monthly* magazine. It was accepted and Clark was paid ten dollars. Later he explained to a group, "Boys, I knowed then I'd found my life's work—no boss, no regular hours and no responsibility—I was a poet." From then on Clark devoted his energies to his poetry: writing, lecturing, and reading before groups.

Clark's most famous poem, "The Cowboy's Prayer," has been reprinted in many collections and has received the approval of the severest critic of all, the old-time range man. His first book, *Sun and Saddle Leather*, (1915), a gathering of his early and best poems, was reprinted many times and is still in print. *Spike* (1925), his only novel, relates the story of Robert "Spike" Axtel, the foreman of the Cross I Quarter Circle Ranch.

Clark was poet laureate of South Dakota. His log-cabin bachelor home, "The Badger Hole," near Custer, is now a state shrine.—J. C. D.

Clark, [James Beau] Champ (1850-1921). Missouri politician. Born near Lawrenceburg, Kentucky, Clark was educated at the University of Kentucky and Bethany College, where he secured the usual classical education of that day and began developing the oratorical skills for which he would later be widely noted. Following a year as president of Marshall College in Huntington, West Virginia, he turned to the study of law at Cincinnati Law School.

In 1876 Clark settled in Pike County, Missouri, where he practiced law in the neighboring towns of Bowling Green and Louisiana and edited a country newspaper. After two terms as prosecuting attorney for Pike County (1885-89), he served a term in the state legislature before being elected to the United States Congress in 1892 as a Democrat. Here he took a stand for free trade, which he maintained throughout his career. Defeated for reelection two years later, he made a comeback in 1896 and remained in the House until his death.

In Congress Clark gained a reputation for sharp debate and hard work. He took care of more than one thousand pension claims for his constituents. He became the protege of Minority Leader John Sharp Williams and succeeded to the leadership of his party in 1907. In the sixty-first Congress he helped lead the fight that curtailed the powers of Speaker Joseph G. Cannon. Clark himself succeeded to that office in the following Congress, as the Democrats gained control of the House for the first time in sixteen years.

A leading contender for the Democratic nomination for president in 1912, Clark held a majority of the delegate votes through eight ballots but could not secure the two thirds requirement and ultimately gave way to Woodrow Wilson. He continued as speaker until 1919, when Democratic loss of the House made him once again minority leader. Defeated for reelection in 1920, he died two days before the expiration of his term.

Clark tells his own story in his two-volume *My Quarter Century of American Politics* (1920). The only biography of note is William L. Webb, *Champ Clark* (1912), written to support his bid for the presidency.—W. E. P.

Clark, Dan Elbert (1884-1956). Author and historian of the Middle West. Clark was born in Ogden, Iowa. Attending the State University of Iowa, he received his B.A. in 1907 and his Ph.D. in 1910. From 1910 to 1918, he remained at Iowa as a lecturer in political science. In 1918, he moved to Seattle and worked with the Red Cross and three years later joined the faculty of the University of Oregon. Until 1940, he devoted most of his time to the university extension division; thereafter he was chairman of the history department until he retired in 1951.

Clark was an active member of the Pacific Coast branch of the American Historical Association, serving as president in 1931. He was one of the founders of the *Pacific Historical Review* and served on the board of editors for nine years. He was also active in the Oregon Historical Society on whose board of directors he served from 1940 to 1956.

While still a student, Clark became an editor at the Iowa State Historical Society, publishing several short studies with the society's cooperation: *Border Defense in Iowa During the Civil War* (1918); *The Codification of Statute Law in Iowa* (1916); *Samuel Jordan Kirkwood* (1917); *The Spirit Lake Massacre* (1918); and *One Hundred Topics in Iowa History*, a compilation of texts.

Clark's major work was *The West in American History*, published in 1937 and reissued in a revised, condensed form in 1966 as *The Middle West in American History*. Clark focused on the frontier region that Frederick Jackson Turner felt was most important. Avoiding both romanticism and overly harsh realism, Clark stressed the evolution of various social, political, and economic practices. His book was the product of extensive reading in travel accounts, diaries, reminiscences, letters, and newspapers. "Few books about any region of the nation," Ray Allen Billington has written, "mirror such warm affection or convey such a sense of intimacy with a segment of the past."—P. L. N.

Clark, George Rogers (1752-1818). Soldier. Clark was born near Charlottesville, Virginia, and spent his early childhood on a farm adjoining that of Thomas Jefferson's father. It was in Caroline County, however, that he grew to young manhood. Like George Washington, Clark became interested in surveying and western lands. By 1772 he was in the western woods along the upper Ohio, where he was scouting the lands along the southern bank of the river in what is now West Virginia. In these early months he traveled as far down the Ohio as the mouth of the Kanawah. When Lord Dunmore's War occurred in 1774 Clark accompanied the governor in his march against the Indians and was present in the negotiation of the Treaty of Charlotte.

In June 1775 Clark appeared at Harrod's Town (later Harrodsburg), Kentucky, and quickly involved himself in the developing political affairs of that area. He led the fight to check Richard Henderson's scheme to establish the colony of Transylvania beyond Virginia territory. In the fall of that year he and John Gabriel Jones of Harrods Fort went back to Virginia to present a plea for the commonwealth's assumption of authority in the western country. This visit resulted in the creation of Kentucky County and the supplying of lead and powder for the support of the frontier posts. Clark's return to Kentucky was accompanied by several dramatic events, the most important of which was a running Indian attack in central Kentucky. He quickly saw that the outbreak of the American Revolution offered a severe obstacle to the survival of the new western settlements. During the spring and summer of 1777 he sent out two spies to gather information about British and Indian activities beyond the Ohio. With this information in hand, he returned to Virginia and persuaded Governor Patrick Henry and the general assembly to give sanction to a secret expedition against the northwestern British-Indian strongholds.

Clark was instructed secretly to raise a small army of 350 men to undertake his planned campaign. Floating down the Ohio from a rendezvous at Pittsburgh with militiamen and their families, Clark established his base of operations on Corn Island just above the Falls of the Ohio (present-day Louisville, Kentucky). On June 24, 1778, he left this place with between 170 and 180 men. His first major objective was to take Fort Massac in the Illinois country, just below and opposite the mouth of the Tennessee River. There he abandoned his boats and set out overland to Kaskaskia in an arduous passage over forest and swamp trails. On July 4 the tiny expeditionary force was before Kaskaskia, and that night the Virginians took the post by surprise.

Though victorious at Kaskaskia, Clark was left in a precarious situation. He no longer had the advantage of secrecy. Too, he had the diplomatic problem of dealing with the French, Spanish, and Indians. At Vincennes, Clark's emissary, Leonard Helm, was able to create a friendly attitude among the French population toward the Americans, but in October 1778 British Governor Henry Hamilton moved down from Detroit and established his headquarters at Vincennes, renaming Fort Patrick Henry as Fort Sackville. Hamilton's failure to keep his forces organized that winter gave Clark an opportunity to use once again the strategy of secrecy and surprise. With the trail guide Francis Vigo, Clark marched his tiny command of approximately seventy Americans and sixty French-Americans for eighteen days across the flooded swamp lands of southern Illinois in the dead of winter. Clark arrived before Fort Sackville at nightfall on February 23, 1779, and late the next day received the surrender of the post from Governor Hamilton.

Clark was severely disappointed in his Northwest campaign because of his inability to take his major objective, Detroit. The path was blocked, partly because of the abortive efforts of a poor frontier commander, John Bowman. Clark returned to the Falls of the Ohio and in the following years engaged in raiding the Indian villages above the Ohio. He also interested himself in land speculations in the region opposite the falls.

In later years Clark suffered tremendous anguish over the failure of Virginia and the Confederation to honor financial obligations incurred in the Northwest campaign. His service as Indian commissioner was discredited by the intrigues of turncoat General James WILKINSON, and Clark became involved in the Spanish and French attempts to found colonies in the Mississippi valley, even accepting a commission as French commander on the Ohio. Failure of these schemes added further to Clark's disappointment and even brought him under suspicion for lack of loyalty.

Between 1794 and February 13, 1815, General Clark lived for a time at Clarksville in the Northwest Territory, where he ran a mill, and then at Locust Grove in Jefferson County, Kentucky. He lived to see his younger brother succeed with Meriwether Lewis in the famous Lewis and Clark expedition to the far Northwest. In 1808 Clark's right leg had to be amputated under very crude surgical conditions, and this operation left the general partially paralyzed.

Clark demonstrated a high degree of leadership ability, and he had a broad vision of the defense problems of the Old West. Although his actual military ability under heavy fire went untested at both Kaskaskia and Vincennes, these two campaigns were well executed.

See John D. Barnhart, ed., *Henry Hamilton and George Rogers Clark in the American Revolution* (1951); Temple Bodley, *George Rogers Clark, His Life and Public Services* (1926); and James A. James, *The Life of George Rogers Clark* (1928).—T. D. C.

Clark, Thomas D. (1903-   ). Historian. Clark was born in Louisville, Mississippi, and educated at the University of Mississippi, the University of Kentucky, and Duke University. Most of his career as a historian was spent at the University of Kentucky, where he rose through the ranks from 1931 until his retirement in 1968. He then accepted an appointment as Distinguished Professor of American History at Indiana University, where he worked on a multivolume history of that institution.

Clark's interests in America's regions and sections led him to study the southward advance of the frontier in the Old West in the nineteenth century. Influenced by the views of Frederick Jackson Turner, Clark's own writings in western history are squarely within the Turnerian framework.

One of his first books was a *History of Kentucky* (1937). In the late thirties and early forties Clark began focusing on a relatively neglected aspect of western history, the development of business enterprise on the frontier. In 1945 he reported some of his findings in *Pills, Petticoats, and Plows*, an entertaining account of the country store on the nineteenth-century frontier. During the next decade Clark pulled together his ideas on western development and incorporated them into a textbook, *Frontier America* (1958). This well-written book, which had a decided Turnerian viewpoint, ended in 1890—coincidental with the closing of the frontier.

Clark's views on western history also gained wide currency because of his many-sided professional activities. He served as president of the Southern History Association in 1947 and editor of the *Journal of Southern History* from 1948 to 1952. He was also active in the Mississippi Valley Historical Association (later the Organization of American Historians), becoming its president in 1957; in 1970 he was appointed secretary of the organization.

Clark was the recipient of a number of honorary degrees from Lincoln Memorial University (1949), Washington and Lee University (1963), and Berea College (1966).—G. D. N.

Clark, Walter Van Tilburg (1909-1971). Novelist, short-story writer, and teacher. Clark was born in East Orland, Maine, and moved west with his family in 1917. The Clarks settled in Nevada, which was to become the fictional locale of almost all his later writing. He was graduated from the University of Nevada in 1931 and then devoted himself to teaching and writing.

In addition to numerous short stories, some of which have been collected in *The Watchful Gods and Other Stories* (1950), Clark has written three novels. *The City of Trembling Leaves* (1945), although set in Reno, can scarcely be called a western in any specific sense of the term, but *The Ox-Bow Incident* (1940) and *The Track of the Cat* (1949) are clearly recognizable adventure stories in the western idiom. The first is an ironic examination of frontier "justice," in which a posse on the trail of cattle rustlers mistakenly hangs three innocent men. The second is an examination of the nature of evil couched in the convention of the hunting story—in this case the pursuit of a panther that has been killing livestock on an isolated ranch.

Clark has the remarkable ability to transcend the apparent limitations of adventure stories. In his two western novels he transforms the clichés of blood-and-thunder writing into serious and thoughtful philosophical studies of the place of man in a world where he does not fully understand the dimensions of evil. *The Ox-Bow Incident* is, among other things, a study of fascism. A posse of ordinary citizens allows itself to be brought under the sway of a ruthless and power-hungry man who forces it to abandon good sense and humanity for an emotional, but perverse, ideal of justice. *The Track of the Cat* is at once more intriguing and less political in its implications. In this novel two of the four hunters of the marauding panther are killed because of their inability to understand it; the two successful hunters succeed in killing the panther because they come to comprehend what the panther—by extension, the evil principle in the world—represents. Both novels prove the remarkable adaptability of western writing, which when properly handled becomes a subtle and profound means for the examination of what are apparently nonwestern concerns.—J. K. F.

Clark, William (1770-1838). Explorer and politician. Clark was born on a plantation in Caroline County, Virginia. He was the youngest of six sons and the ninth of ten children of John and Ann (Rogers) Clark. He was the younger brother of George Rogers Clark, the hero of the American Revolution in the West.

Clark grew up on the frontier and as a young man was an Indian fighter. When he was fourteen years old, he moved with his parents to a new plantation, called Mulberry Hill, at the Falls of the Ohio in Louisville, Kentucky. Beginning probably in 1789, he participated as a militiaman in several campaigns against the Indians north of the Ohio River. In March 1792 he was commissioned a lieutenant in the army and two years later fought under General Anthony Wayne in the battle of Fallen Timbers. In 1796 he resigned his commission and returned home, where for the next seven years he managed the family plantation.

From 1803 to 1806, Clark was coleader of the LEWIS AND CLARK EXPEDITION. He was offered the position by his old friend, Meriwether Lewis, in July 1803, and quickly accepted it. During the winter of 1803-04 and the following spring, Clark played a major part in the expedition's final preparations at Camp Wood River,

Illinois. On the journey itself, he was the mapmaker and, of the two officers, the principal waterman and the more skillful Indian negotiator. His experience, talents, and disposition complemented superbly those of his partner.

Following the expedition's return from the Pacific, Clark spent the rest of his life mainly in the administration of Indian affairs for the federal government. In March 1807 President Jefferson appointed him principal Indian agent for the Louisiana Territory and brigadier general of its militia, posts which he held until 1813. In June of that year, he became governor of Missouri Territory, as Louisiana had been renamed the year before. In these positions Clark's chief concerns were to strengthen the defenses of the territory against attack by hostile Indians, for which reason he built FORT OSAGE, and to establish and maintain friendly relations with the tribes of the Missouri and upper Mississippi rivers.

When the government of the State of Missouri began to function in September 1820, Clark (who had lost his bid to become the state's first governor) ceased to be a territorial chief executive, but remained in charge of Indian affairs. In May 1822 he assumed the office (newly created by Congress) of superintendent of Indian affairs at St. Louis retaining the responsibility for the tribes of the Missouri and Upper Mississippi. Clark held this post until his death, although his jurisdiction was reduced by the act of 1834 that organized the department of Indian affairs and the act of 1836 that created Wisconsin Territory. As superintendent of Indian affairs, he was involved mainly with the removal of Indians living east of the Mississippi and in Missouri to lands assigned them in present-day eastern Kansas. From October 1824 to May 1825, Clark was also acting surveyor general of Illinois and Missouri and the Territory of Arkansas.

A big, good-natured redhead, Clark was an affectionate family man. His first wife was Julia Hancock, with whom he had five children. Following her death, he married Harriet Kennerly Radford, a widow, who bore him two sons. Four of his sons lived to manhood.

Although best known to history as an explorer, Clark was one of the nation's ablest and most successful Indian agents. By the standards of his own time, he treated the Indians with fairness, understanding, and compassion and, in return, enjoyed their respect and confidence.

The only biographical treatment of Clark worthy of note is John Bakeless, *Lewis and Clark, Partners in Discovery* (1947), and it deals only briefly with his activities after the expedition to the West.—J. L. L.

Clark, William Andrews (1839-1925). Montana mining magnate and politician. Born in Pennsylvania, Clark moved with his family to Iowa when he was seventeen. He taught school in Iowa and Missouri and studied law at Iowa Wesleyan University for two years. In 1861-62 he was at Central City, Colorado, and in 1863 he went to Bannack and Virginia City, Montana. After profitable ventures in freighting, contracting mail routes, and wholesale trading, he turned to banking in Deer Lodge and Butte. Pioneering in developing silver and copper mining in Butte, and always a perfectionist, he went for a year to Columbia University's School of Mines to learn mining procedures. He built the first smelter in Butte for silver and copper and, in part to assist with this

enterprise, he also built Butte's first water system and electric plant. His wide-ranging business interests included several railroads, the giant Mesa Verde Copper Company in Arizona, a wire works in New Jersey and a bronze works in New York, as well as a sugar plantation and refinery in California. Senator Robert La Follette designated him one of "the 100 men who rule America."

Clark served as president of the Montana constitutional convention in 1884 and again in 1889. Politically ambitious, he ran for territorial delegate to Congress in 1888 but was defeated, largely through the efforts of Marcus Daly, another of the three Butte copper kings." This election is reputed to have started the conflict with Daly and others known as the war of the copper kings (see MONTANA). He was chosen as United States senator in 1890 by the Democrats in the first state legislature in a contested election, but the Senate seated his Republican competitor. He was elected again in 1899, but when the Senate committee on elections made a report on Clark's campaign activities which seemed certain to lead to charges of bribery he resigned before taking his seat. He finally served in the Senate from 1901 to 1907.

Clark was an ardent patriot and was chosen state orator for the Philadelphia Centennial Exposition in 1876. He also led the civilian force aiding the injured in the battle of Big Hole River in 1877 when the retreating Nez Percé Indians rallied surprisingly from an early dawn attack and inflicted severe injuries upon United States troops. He gave the Columbia Gardens, an elaborate recreation park, to the city of Butte, in part to counter the political influence of Frederick Augustus Heinze, the third of the copper kings. His notable art collection was given to the Corcoran Gallery in Washington, D.C. The oldest of the warring copper kings, he outlived the other two by many years.

See C. B. Glasscock, *The War of the Copper Kings* (1935); William D. Mangam, *The Clarks, An American Phenomenon* (1941); and *Progressive Men of the State of Montana* (1901).—M. G. B.

Clay, Henry (1777-1851). Statesman. Clay was born in Hanover County, Virginia. His father was a Baptist preacher and a moderately well-to-do farmer who died when Clay was four. His mother quickly remarried, but the burdens of caring for the nine children of her first marriage and the seven of her second left little time or money for Clay's early education, which was brief and rudimentary. The boy's opportunity for more formal training came at the age of fifteen, when his parents migrated to the bluegrass country of Kentucky to open a tavern and left him behind in Richmond, Virginia, as a clerk. There Clay came under the tutelage of George Wythe, mentor of Thomas Jefferson, a signer of the Declaration of Independence, and first professor of law in Virginia. Clay began the study of the classics and the law under Wythe, as well as serving as his secretary, and concluded his preparation for the bar under the direction of Robert Brooke, a former governor of Virginia. Though attracted by the warm, gracious, cultivated society of Richmond, Clay found the city too confining for his temperament and ambition. In 1797 the young lawyer departed for the flourishing five-year-old state of Kentucky, where he arrived at the age of twenty.

Clay settled in Lexington, the state's thriving center of trade. He came penniless to the booming western town, but rapidly established himself as a crackerjack lawyer and enterprising land speculator. Fluent, deft at humor and sarcasm, and adept at reading the faces of frontier jurors, Clay became the foremost criminal attorney in the state. Success swelled his practice, and Clay prospered. Marriage in 1799 to Lucretia Hart, daughter of a prominent Lexington businessman, brought Clay into the circle of the developing bluegrass aristocracy of merchants, hemp manufacturers, and planters who dominated the life of the town.

Boldness and zeal marked Clay's first plunge into Kentucky politics. In 1798 he joined a campaign to democratize the state's constitution and to seek the gradual emancipation of slaves in Kentucky. Pitted for the moment against the ruling merchants and planters of the state, Clay denounced "aristocratic" control of state government. A new constitution passed, but without emancipation. Clay accepted Kentucky's verdict on slavery, never again to challenge the institution directly, and lost few friends by what most regarded as the excusable ardor of a twenty-one-year-old idealist. Wild acclaim followed Clay's debut in July 1798 as a stump speaker, a fiery denunciation of the recently passed Alien and Sedition Acts. The backwoodsmen and townsmen, massed to protest the oppressive measures, hoisted the defiant orator to their shoulders and paraded their champion through the streets of Lexington. An ardent supporter of Thomas Jefferson's rising Republican party, Clay stumped for the Virginian in 1800 and was elected to the Kentucky legislature in 1803. In 1806 Clay defended Aaron Burr, who was under grand jury investigation in Kentucky because of his designs in the Southwest. Though Clay won an acquittal for Burr—whom he and other Kentuckians believed the victim of a Federalist conspiracy—Clay repudiated Burr when later convinced of his client's guilt.

Shortly after his defense of Burr, the popular state legislator was appointed to fill an unexpired term in the Senate, where he took his seat at the age of twenty-nine. There he vigorously advocated the use of federal funds for roads, canals, and other internal improvements to promote western economic development. Clay regarded his short foray to Washington more as a tour of pleasure than a solemn mission. He established an enduring capital reputation as an all-night, high-stakes gambler.

Returning to Kentucky in 1807, Clay again was elected to the state legislature, where he was chosen Speaker of the House of Representatives. As a Republican and a nationalist, Clay defended President Jefferson and his foreign policy. He delighted his constituents when he introduced a bill to require members of the assembly to prove their patriotism by wearing homespun suits instead of British broadcloth. Accused of demagoguery by Kentucky's leading Federalist, Humphrey Marshall, Clay rushed to pummel the tall aristocrat on the floor of the house. A fistfight was avoided but a duel was not; and both men were slightly wounded in the exchange of shots.

The affray with the Federalist further enhanced Clay's popular standing, and in 1810 Kentucky again dispatched him to the Senate, where he commenced a career in the national capital that would span the next forty years of his life. In Washington, Clay's remarkable personal gifts, responsible in large part for his rapid rise in Kentucky politics, won the westerner immediate popularity and influence. Tall, warm-hearted, frank, easy of manner, he turned his charm and conviviality to account whether gambling or gathering votes. Ardent and impulsive, a man of generous impulse and instinctive courage, he inspired devotion among friends and the admiration of foes. Above all decisive, Clay came to the capital ready to command. When thwarted, his confidence could become arrogance, then men would complain of his colossal audacity and "disgusting vanity." But on his arrival in 1810 the young Kentucky senator was vibrant, optimistic, and sure, exuberantly ambitious for the West, the country, and himself. In the fluid society and politics of Washington, Clay's supreme sociability, his adroitness at managing men, and his power of passionate persuasion made him a natural leader.

In the Senate Clay was a zealous advocate of the needs of his constituents and the West. The infant industries and hemp interests of Lexington required protection from foreign competition; Clay supported a high tariff (see TARIFF POLICY). The West, anxious for the safety of the Mississippi River, worried over Spanish control of West Florida; Clay called for seizure of the territory from Spain by the federal government. Frontier speculators, Kentucky banking interests, and westerners fearful of the dangerous power of the Bank of the United States opposed its recharter; Clay helped defeat the recharter bill. Of greatest importance, Clay threw his support behind the growing movement to force a declaration of war against Great Britain. Westerners were convinced that the British in Canada were inciting the Indians to attack the American frontier. Clay demanded war with Britain to extinguish "the torch that lights up savage warfare."

When Clay's brief term in the Senate expired in 1811, his constituents elected him to the House of Representatives, and Clay gladly exchanged the "solemn stillness" of the upper chamber for the excitement and activity of the lower house of Congress. The new Twelfth Congress was dominated by young men impatient with their government's ineffectual response to British impressment of American seamen and arrogant disregard of American rights. Coveting Canada and determined to redeem American self-respect, Clay spoke for the West and the war hawks, when he declared that he preferred combat, "with all its calamities and desolation, to the tranquil and putrescent pool of ignominious peace." The young zealots for war agreed that they needed a leader of drive and dispatch to advance their aims and had no difficulty in selecting Clay—that "clever man . . . whom they call 'the Western Star' "—to champion their cause. In defiance of seniority, Congress chose the thirty-four-year-old Kentuckian as speaker of the house, and Clay, with bold disregard for age or party services, named committees dominated by the will to war. Clay and Congress steadily pushed President James Madison toward the War of 1812 and vigorously supported the war when it came.

Though Clay expected a war of "true glory," devoid of the "languor and imbecility" that had characterized the policy of peace, the military results of the conflict were disappointing. Little more could be salvaged by the five-man United States peace commission that traveled to Ghent in 1814, of which Clay was a member, than a treaty establishing the *status quo ante bellum*. Clay's major achievement in the negotiations was forcing Britain to abandon her right to navigate the Mississippi River, a privilege originally granted by the Treaty of Paris of 1783.

Clay left Ghent convinced that the peace commission had terminated an inept war with a meek treaty. But with the news of Andrew Jackson's stunning victory over the British at the Battle of New Orleans in January 1815, Clay revised his estimate of the war's results. The young country had fought the world's greatest power to a draw and had restored its self-respect. Above all, the war, and especially Jackson's triumph, had rekindled a spirit of patriotism in the land. But Clay, who had done much during the conflict to stir that patriotism with his call for a "new race of heroes," did not foresee that it would be the "Hero of New Orleans," and not himself, who would become the symbol of national pride and glory.

Clay returned home in 1815, and when Congress reconvened in December he was promptly reelected Speaker of the House. Acknowledged as the spokesman of Kentucky and a leading younger statesman of the land, he shared with the new leaders of his generation a determination to build a self-sufficient nation equal to any on the globe. To secure self-sufficiency in the years ahead Clay proceeded to develop what became known as the AMERICAN SYSTEM. A protective tariff would nurture the war-born industries of New England and the middle states, which in turn would provide a home market for the crops of western and southern farmers. An improved system of transportation at federal expense would bind the nation together by providing the West and South with reliable roads to eastern markets. A new national bank would give the nation the uniform currency and the regulated credit needed for the exchange of goods. And cooperation with South American patriots struggling for independence from Spain would establish United States hegemony in the hemisphere and open the trade of the Mississippi valley to the new Latin American republics. Clay recognized that there would be opposition to the bold agenda of the American System. But with his colleague in national consolidation, John C. Calhoun of South Carolina, Clay contended that the needs of the young country called for "enlarged views" and the abandonment of "selfish instincts." It was time, Calhoun argued, to subordinate the "interests of particular sections" to the "common good." It was a time, Clay exhorted, to elevate the nation to "that height to which God and nature had destined it."

Clay's program for western and national development met with partial success. Congress chartered the Second Bank of the United States and approved a protective tariff. But the executive branch and Clay's fellow congressmen rejected his demands for early recognition of South American independence, and presidents James Madison and James Monroe vetoed bills for internal improvements.

Most damaging to support for Clay's vision of federal economic stewardship were two crises that erupted in 1819. That year the country plunged into a deep depression. Bankers had overextended credit and when the financial bubble burst, the newly rechartered Second Bank of the United States sought to mitigate the calamity by clamping new restrictions on lending.

To westerners demanding relief from debts, the bank became the monster, as Andrew Jackson called it, that foreclosed mortgages and denied new loans. From small farmers and small capitalists of the West came the rising cry to "let us alone" in the pursuit of self-interest. In the harsh months of 1819, Clay sided with the bank and creditors against a hostile populace. Then and thereafter he underestimated the magnitude of western suspicion of power and finance that would eventually find a voice in Andrew Jackson and the rhetoric of *laissez-faire*.

A second crisis subverting Clay's program exploded in 1819 over the admission of Missouri to the Union as a slave state. Clay's own answer to the dilemma of slavery in the United States was the gradual colonization of slaves to Africa; meanwhile, he believed, Missourians should be free to enslave. Clay played a decisive role in achieving the MISSOURI COMPROMISE that resolved the dispute in 1820 and that earned him the title of "Great Pacificator." But after 1820 the South was rarely at peace with the Union again. Hereafter Calhoun and other southerners increasingly required that the "common good" be compatible with southern interests. To secure slavery against future attacks by the North, southerners looked to a political alliance with the West—but not with the West of Henry Clay. The costs of the internal improvements and high tariff that Clay favored, southerners saw as falling excessively on them. More ominously, the broad federal powers presumed in Clay's program might ultimately be used to tamper with slavery. Southerners sought instead to ally themselves with those westerners who wanted minimal government interference, minimal taxation, and maximum credit.

Not until the end of the decade would the centrifugal forces unleashed by the two crises of 1819 triumph. Until then Clay thought the American System would prevail—and with it his own ambition to become the first president from the West. Clay expected to ascend in the traditional manner: first to be appointed secretary of state and then to be named presidential nominee by the congressional caucus of the dominant Republican party. Bitterly disappointed in 1817 when President Monroe selected John Quincy Adams of Massachusetts for the premier cabinet post, the Kentuckian hoped to rally sufficient western and national support to overturn Adams when Monroe's second term expired in 1824. But in the presidential contest of that year Clay ran last among four candidates. Andrew Jackson of Tennessee won the suffrages of all but three western states and a plurality of votes in the nation. Since no candidate had a majority, the election was decided in the House of Representatives. Eliminated as a contestant and thus denied a chance to use his immense influence to advance himself, Clay as the speaker of the house made a fateful choice. Though he thought Adams a prig, he did not see how "killing two thousand five hundred Englishmen at New Orleans" fitted Jackson for the presidency. Defying the instructions of the Kentucky legislature, Clay threw his support to the New Englander, who won the contest. Adams promptly named Clay his secretary of state—and Jackson's followers promptly charged "bargain and sale!" No deal was made, but no honest mistake could have been more calamitous. Labeled "Judas of the West," Clay never entirely exonerated himself from the charge of intrigue. More fundamentally, his conduct undermined the moral basis of political stewardship and accelerated the demise of government by Washington insiders.

Clay's alliance with Adams was logical but costly. Adams proved a vigorous advocate of Clay's program of protection and internal improvements. In four years the Adams administration spent as much money on roads and canals as had been allocated in the previous twenty-four. Adams approved the high tariff in 1828, endorsed by the West but denominated the "Tariff of Abominations" by its enemies in the South. Following Clay's counsel to seek new markets for farmers and entrepreneurs of the Mississippi West, Adams made a strong effort to establish close relations with the new states of South America, though opposition in Congress thwarted his attempt to send delegates to the Pan-American Congress at Panama in 1826. But Clay's American System gained little popularity from Adams' blunt demand that it be enacted by congressmen "not palsied by the will of our constituents," and Clay's standing in the West suffered from his necessary affiliation with the tactless New Englander. The coalescing opposition charged that Clay and Adams had reincarnated eastern Federalism and claimed itself the true heir of Jeffersonian democracy. With "democracy" its battle cry and Jackson its candidate, the opposition triumphed in 1828 over Clay and Adams' National Republican party.

Clay retired to his estate in Lexington in 1829. There he anxiously waited for the expected mistakes of Jackson to dissolve the president's heterogeneous coalition. Jackson's use of patronage to elevate "unfit" men to office, his veto of bills for internal improvements in the West, and his continued ambivalence on the protective tariff did antagonize many Democrats, but few congressmen defected to the opposition. In 1831 Clay returned to the capital as senator from Kentucky and as the presidential nominee of the National Republicans, to lead the battle against Jackson.

Clay advanced a legislative program in 1832 that remained true to the goals of the American System but that proved out of touch with the wishes of the majority of westerners. To maintain federal support for INTERNAL IMPROVEMENTS, Clay advocated distribution of the revenue from the sales of public lands to *all* the states. Quite different plans found more favor in the newer states of the West, which were eager for cheap land and rapid settlement. But Clay doggedly opposed proposals to give the public lands to the western states in which they lay, to reduce gradually the price of land owned by the government, and to give the "squatter" the first option to buy (or preempt) land on which he had settled without legal title. Clay devised a new tariff in 1832. It found greatest support among manufacturers of the East, some support in the West, and none in the South.

Easily Clay's most critical choice of 1832, however, was his decision to persuade Nicholas Biddle, president of the Second Bank of the United States, to apply for a new federal charter that year (see BANKING AND CURRENCY). Clay anticipated Jackson's veto and expected the groups dependent on bank credit and the established congressional leaders anxious over growing executive power to muster a majority to the National Republican standard in the coming presidential election. What Clay did not envisage was that western enterprisers eager for easy money, small farmers and northern artisans suspicious

of the bank's great power, and politicians loathe to defy the popularity of Jackson, would rally instead to Jackson's call for the public to strike down the great financial "monster" that made the "rich richer and the potent more powerful." Underlying the volatile rhetoric of the veto message was Jackson's devastating argument that Clay's once-grand vision of guided national growth was now merely a guise for government aid to vested interests. The charge was both plausible and popular, and in 1832 Clay went down to calamitous defeat, winning the electoral vote of no western state but Kentucky.

Clay remained in the Senate and was the guiding spirit in the passage of the Compromise Tariff of 1833, which ended South Carolina's nullification of the tariffs of 1828 and 1832 and quieted Jackson's threat to use force against that state. Clay's role added to his reputation as the Great Compromiser of sectional disputes.

During the next eight years Clay led the motley Whig party in opposition to Jacksonian fiscal policies. They were years of frustration for the Kentuckian, now in his mid-fifties. Through 1836, the dazzling growth of western migration and land sales and the endless expansion of bank credit and state-sponsored improvements in transportation seemed to confirm Jackson's claim that no national guidance was needed to guarantee prosperity. Clay's continuing attacks on executive power and on Jackson's fiscal irresponsibility appeared remote from the actualities of western development. Prosperity bred Whig pessimism in the presidential contest of 1836, and the party chose to ignore Clay and to run instead three regional candidates in a futile attempt to defeat Jackson's hand-picked successor, Martin Van Buren.

No sooner was Van Buren inaugurated in 1837, however, than depression struck the country. The disaster renewed Clay's hope that the public might reconsider the need for government stewardship over the economy, and buoyed Whig prospects for victory in 1840. But sporadic signs of recovery in 1838 and 1840 undermined the first expectation and endangered the second. To guarantee victory, the emergent political brokers of the Whig party, led by master manipulator Thurlow Weed of New York, engineered Clay's defeat at the Whig presidential convention and secured the choice of General William Henry Harrison of Ohio. The Whigs presented Harrison to the country as the incarnation of simple frontier virtues, and the party—silent on its program—prescribed simple virtues as the cure for hard times. Though bitter at his loss, Clay guaranteed party unity by his generous endorsement of Harrison; though appalled at the ensuing Whig appeal to "the passions of our countrymen rather than to their reasons and judgments," Clay participated in the triumphant Log Cabin campaign.

Clay meant to command the new Whig administration and finally to win complete enactment of the program he had advanced for a quarter-century—a high tariff, a national bank, and federal support for internal improvements. Clay's program passed Congress, but the victory was Pyrrhic. Disappointment had jaded the joy of politics for the sixty-four-year-old Clay. Once the master of tact, he now brooked no opposition. Dictatorial tactics cowed his congressional colleagues, but his imperiousness antagonized President Harrison and mortally alienated John Tyler, who succeeded to the presidency upon Harrison's death in April 1841. Supreme tact might have reconciled the vain, thin-skinned Virginian, long opposed to a national bank and to federal encroachment on the rights of the states, to Clay's aggressive legislation. But Clay's unyielding demands brought Tyler's unyielding vetoes. Deadlocked irrevocably with Tyler, Clay and the Whigs expelled the president from the party in September 1841. Clay left the Senate in 1842, his supremacy in the Whig party assured, his program for the country a shambles.

Despite the party rupture, Clay by 1844 stood on the threshold of achieving at last his lifelong ambition of the presidency. He was the certain Whig candidate that year, and with the return of prosperity Whig chances for victory were excellent. But Tyler now avenged his expulsion from the Whig party by committing his administration to a cause fraught with hazard for Clay: the annexation of Texas. In Kentucky, the West, and the South, zeal for expansion had steadily mounted. But Texas was a slave republic and if annexed would become a slave state. Mexico still disputed Texas' claim to independence and threatened to fight if the United States annexed the territory. Clay saw nothing but "discord and distraction" in the issue, which threatened to divide his party and to embroil the nation in war. He sought to keep Texas out of the 1844 campaign by an ambivalent stand opposing "immediate annexation." But evasion appeared impossible to Clay after the Democratic convention rejected Martin Van Buren, also opposed to immediate annexation, and chose instead James K. Polk of Tennessee, an expansionist pledged to the prompt "re-annexation" of Texas. In a series of letters in the summer of 1844, Clay sought to mollify the West and South by insisting that he too favored acquisition of Texas if achieved "without dishonor, without war, with the common consent of the Union." Southerners were unappeased, and northern abolitionists damned Clay as "rotten as a stagnant fish pond, on the subject of Slavery." Perhaps, as Kentucky friends advised, the Whig candidate should have been "caged" throughout the campaign, then as president try to acquire Texas without war or domestic strife. Yet however impolitic was Clay's attempt to grapple with the Texas issue, his was a farsighted stand: events bore out his premonition of peril in pell-mell expansion; Clay's dilemma would soon be the country's. In the razor-close election of 1844, Clay won three western, two southern, and five northern states. But in the critical vote of New York, the defection of ten thousand Whigs to the abolitionist Liberty party gave a plurality to Polk—and cost Clay the presidency.

The defeated Kentuckian retired to his home in Lexington, where he watched with dismay as his forebodings of 1844 became fact. Congress annexed Texas in 1845, and the new president—his aim firmly fixed on expansion to the Pacific—maneuvered Mexico into war. Clay disapproved of the war, which in 1847 claimed the life of his son. He sought to pledge his party and the nation against acquisiton of new territory and against the extension of slavery into any new lands annexed. But the effort was vain. Vanquished, Mexico was compelled to surrender to the United States her vast southwestern territory from Texas to California, and the dispute Clay had sought to avert became unavoidable: would the nation permit slavery in the new lands? War hero Zachary Taylor, chosen over Clay as the Whig party's presidential candidate in 1848, straddled the slavery question, and his victory that year left the festering issue unresolved. Sectional rancor deepened. Northerners stood firm against slavery's extension and southerners retaliated with threats of secession. When Clay returned to the capital for the last time in 1849, as senator from Kentucky, the nation was convulsed in crisis.

In that crisis, the western nationalist again bent his efforts toward compromise between North and South. Clay gave his support to a comprehensive settlement that called for the admission of California as a free state, for the organization of the remaining territory acquired from Mexico without reference to slavery, and for a stringent fugitive slave law to guarantee southerners the return of their runaways. He enlisted the aid of Massachusetts Whig Daniel Webster for his compromise bill, and both argued that there was no need for Congress formally to bar slavery in the desert Southwest, where "nature itself" rendered slavery impractical. Clay's proposals set the stage for the COMPROMISE OF 1850, which was achieved through the parliamentary skill of Stephen A. Douglas of Illinois and by the decisive support of Democratic congressmen. Clay's compromise preserved the Union for another decade. In that time economic interest and improved communication cemented the alliance between West and East that Clay's programs had sought and gave the united North the strength to win the war that ultimately decided the fate of slavery. Clay did not witness the bloodbath he had dedicated his life to avoid; he died in Washington on June 29, 1852, at the age of seventy-five.

Clay's long and remarkable public career was dominated by a vision of a strong Union and an energetic national government. Sectional differences increasingly rendered the dual goals incompatible. Given the nation's highest trust, Clay might have demonstrated that public stewardship and the American System could advance the great interests of the West and the nation without bringing division. But the passing of personal politics, the revival of parties, and crucial errors of judgment combined to thwart Clay's ambition to become president. More fundamentally, Clay's concept of federal leadership stood at odds with the wishes of westerners and other citizens to decide their own destinies, without guidance or interference from any quarter. When parties later did adopt policies Clay had long advocated, it was in response to demands from below, not to visions from above. Yet if it was Clay's fate to fail at his ultimate ambitions and gradually to fall out of step with the aspirations of fellow westerners, it was his fortune and the nation's that he served four decades to keep the nation at peace. At times of sectional crises, the Kentuckian's fervent nationalism, his personal courage, and his parliamentary skill opened the way from impasse to compromise. Clay's lasting legacy was a Union preserved.

The best biographies of Clay are Clement Eaton, *Henry Clay and the Art of American Politics* (1957); Bernard Mayo, *Henry Clay, Spokesman of the New West* (1937); and Glyndon G. Van Deusen, *The Life of Henry Clay* (1937). Added insight into Clay's career is provided by Albert D. Kirwan, *John J. Crittenden: The Struggle for the Union* (1962); George Rawlings Poage, *Henry Clay and the Whig Party* (1936); and William Appleman Williams, *The Contours of American History* (1961). *The Papers of Henry*

Clay, edited by James F. Hopkins, is the comprehensive collection of Clay's speeches and correspondence. —S. N.

Clay, John (1851-1934). Cattleman. A native of Winfield, Berwickshire, Scotland, Clay was educated at Wellfield Academy, Smeaton's School near St. Andrews, and Edinburgh University. After several years of managing farms near his home, he visited the United States and Canada in 1874. As a result of this trip he became progressively more involved with the affairs of the Bow Park breeding farm near Brantford, Ontario. He assumed full-time responsibility for the farm in 1879 and the same year served as a subcommissioner on a royal commission to survey the American livestock industry.

In 1882 Clay moved to Chicago and began his career as an agent for Scottish companies with cattle investments in the West. During the next five years he represented such firms as the Scottish-American Investment Company, the Cattle Ranche and Land Company, and the Western Ranches Company. By 1886 he had opened his own commission office in Chicago. Canny and conservative, Clay built a reputation for sound judgment, and cattlemen committed stock to his firm because "they have done better by us than others."

From 1888 to 1896 Clay managed the financially troubled Swan Land and Cattle Company of Wyoming with only moderate success until his connection with the company was severed. He was president of the Wyoming Stock Growers Association from 1890 to 1896 and may have helped organize and finance the vigilante expedition against settlers in northern Wyoming that led to the Johnson County range war of 1892. He maintained his interest in the Wyoming economy during the last three decades of his life through ownership of such institutions as the Stock Growers National Bank of Cheyenne and remained active in western affairs generally through the John Clay Commission Company.

Clay was one of the most significant participants in the Anglo-American cattle boom of the mid-1880s, his special interest being the protection of British investors in the West. His autobiography, *My Life on the Range* (1924), is the most perceptive memoir about the financial side of the cattle business during its halcyon years. Clay demonstrated the intimate link between eastern and foreign investors and the economic growth of the American frontier in the late nineteenth century.

See Gene Gressley, *Bankers and Cattlemen* (1966); and W. T. Jackson, *The Enterprising Scot* (1968).—L. L. G.

Clayton, Powell (1833-1914). Arkansas politician. Clayton was born in Bethel County, Pennsylvania. A Union brigadier general, he served in Missouri and Arkansas. After the Civil War he was Reconstruction governor of Arkansas. He was elected to the United States Senate in 1871 and served until 1877, when Augustus Hill Garland, a Democrat, replaced him. Retiring to his home in Little Rock, he remained active as the leader of the state Republican party and, in 1882, moved to Eureka Springs, a resort town and watering place in north Arkansas, which he largely owned. From 1872 on, except for two years, he was a member of the Republican National Committee. President William McKinley appointed him ambassador to Mexico in 1897, and he served until 1905. In about 1912 he settled in Washington, D.C.—W. L. B.

Cleburne, Patrick Ronayne (1828-1864). Arkansas soldier. Cleburne was a native of Ireland and former British soldier who settled in Helena, Arkansas, in about 1850. A druggist and lawyer, he acquired considerable property. He became colonel of an Arkansas volunteer regiment at the onset of the Civil War and led it gallantly in the region immediately east of the Mississippi River. Rising to the rank of major general, he won fame as a combat leader on the fields of Shiloh, Perryville, Chattanooga, Missionary Ridge (where he beat William T. Sherman), and Ringgold Gap (where at his own personal risk he saved Braxton Bragg's artillery and wagon train). His elevation to higher command was doubtlessly prevented by his controversial proposal for freeing and arming the slaves as soldiers. He was killed at Franklin, Tennessee.—W. L. B.

Clemens, Samuel Langhorne. See Mark TWAIN.

clothing. See COWBOY CLOTHING.

Clum, John P. (1851-1932). Indian agent and Arizona pioneer. Clum was born near Claverack, New York. After a year at Rutgers College, he enlisted in the Signal Service and opened a weather station at Santa Fe in November 1871. In February 1874 he entered the Indian Service as an agent at San Carlos, the Apache reservation on the Gila River.

Clum had received his appointment under the PEACE POLICY, San Carlos being assigned to the Dutch Reformed church, which also supported Rutgers. In the East at the time of his appointment, Clum was briefed at the Indian Office on conditions at San Carlos and on the necessity of reestablishing civilian control over the reservation. To free himself from dependence on the military, Clum adapted to his needs the device of using Indian scouts, a tactic introduced into the area by General George H. Crook. He enlisted four Apache as policemen to help him control their 865 fellow tribesmen under his charge. Although Clum later claimed credit for originating the concept of Indian police, he was only one of several agents experimenting along these lines.

Clum's next step was to secure the grudging consent of the military to the removal of all troops from the vicinity of San Carlos. So impressed were his superiors at Clum's success in handling both the Indians and the army that Apache from Rio Verde were moved to San Carlos. Then, in April 1875, Camp Apache Agency was closed and its eighteen hundred resident Indians were moved to San Carlos. As the reservation population increased, Clum increased his police force.

In February 1876 Clum submitted his resignation. Meanwhile, in May he was ordered to relieve the agent of the Chiricahua Apache and move 325 more Indians to San Carlos. This accomplished, Clum set out in July for Washington with twenty Apache, planning to exhibit the Indians in the East. By October this venture had failed, and Clum had to apply to the government for funds to return the Indians to San Carlos. He also withdrew his resignation on the promise of a larger salary.

During the next few months Clum was engaged in a hot controversy in the columns of partisan Arizona newspapers. The issue was whether the Indians would be controlled by civilians or the military. His chief ally was Governor A. P. K. Safford, and his principal opponent was General August Kautz, Crook's successor. On

April 4, 1877, he resigned again and during the same month also carried out his most celebrated coup, the arrest of Geronimo. Ordered to relieve the agent at the Southern Apache Agency at Hot Springs, New Mexico, Clum took Geronimo prisoner and removed about 450 Apache from Hot Springs to San Carlos.

In a final show of bravado he offered to remain and supervise all the Apache in Arizona, dispensing with all regular troops in the territory, if his salary were increased and he was permitted two companies of Indian police. But his offer was rejected, and on July 1, 1877, Clum departed from San Carlos. An inspector for the Indian Service had described him as "the best agent for wild Indians that I know of in the service."

Clum next studied law in an attorney's office in Florence and then bought a Tucson newspaper, which he sold in 1880. For the next six years Clum published a new paper, *The Tombstone Epitaph*, and was active in the community affairs of Tombstone.

Leaving Arizona in 1886, Clum worked briefly for the San Francisco *Examiner* before joining the Post Office Department, serving until 1909 in west Texas, Alaska, and New York. Clum died in Los Angeles.

See Woodworth Clum, *Apache Agent: The Story of John P. Clum* (1936); and William T. Hagan, *Indian Police and Judges* (1966).—W. T. H.

Clyman, James (1792-1881). Fur trapper, explorer, soldier, and farmer. Clyman's eventful life spanned the entire period of American expansion to the Pacific. He was born in the Blue Ridge country of Virginia, the son of a tenant farmer living on lands owned by George Washington. In 1811 he moved with his parents to a frontier farm in Ohio. He served briefly as a scout on the lookout for raiding Indians during the War of 1812. Adept at hunting and farming and skilled in woodcraft and cabin-raising, Clyman migrated to Indiana in 1815 and started a farm. He soon moved on to Illinois, where he worked in a salt factory and later became a surveyor in the Sangamon River country.

On a visit to St. Louis, Missouri, in the spring of 1823, Clyman was attracted by the stories of William H. Ashley's daring fur-trade expedition up the Missouri to the Yellowstone River in 1822. He made himself known to Ashley, who promptly hired the tall, rawboned, thin-lipped Virginian to assemble a crew of boatmen for the 1823 trip. Clyman was appointed clerk in charge of one of the keelboats. The 1823 expedition proved to be disastrous. Ashley's men were attacked by Arikara; fifteen were killed and many goods and horses lost. Although Clyman nearly lost his life, he returned with Colonel Leavenworth's largely ineffective punitive expedition (see ARIKARA CAMPAIGN).

Ashley then mounted a second expedition, which included Jedediah Smith, Thomas Fitzpatrick, and Clyman, that went overland from Fort Kiowa through the Black Hills to the Powder River country.

This expedition, too, had its troubles, for on the trail Smith was badly mauled by a grizzly, who nearly tore off an ear. (Clyman was detailed to stitch it back on.) The group nearly froze to death during the winter of 1823-24. But their various explorations revealed two important pieces of information that were to affect the nature of the fur trade: first, that the upper Green River was rich with fur-bearing animals; and second, that the region could be reached more directly via the South Pass

(rediscovered by the Smith and Clyman party in 1824) and the Platte River route. Another Ashley party under Etienne Provost had discovered the true South Pass in 1824 while Smith and Clyman crossed to the south of the Pass, but the latter established the fact that the Sweetwater was a tributary to the Platte. In the course of his travels, Clyman became separated from his companions and walked seven hundred miles back to Fort Atkinson. He returned later in the year and spent the winter with Zacharias Ham trapping on the headwaters of the Green, where once again he nearly lost his life in an Indian ambush. He attended the first annual rendezvous at Henry's Fork on the Green in 1825 and sold his one hundred skins to Ashley.

During the next two years Clyman explored the Salt Lake area for furs with William Sublette and probably accompanied another party to the Yellowstone. By 1827 he was ready to leave the mountains; he piloted a returning party to St. Louis, sold his own catch, bought a farm near Danville, Illinois, and opened a store. Clyman's natural restlessness and his understandable dislike of Indians made it almost inevitable that he would volunteer to fight in the Black Hawk War of 1832. After two years of sporadic military duties he and Hiram J. Ross built a sawmill on the Menominee River west of present-day Milwaukee and dabbled in land speculation.

By 1844 Clyman's eyes had turned westward to Oregon. He joined a train led by Moses "Black" Harris, at Independence, Missouri, that spring; carved his name on Independence Rock; and once in Oregon was entertained by Dr. John McLoughlin, the Hudson's Bay factor at Fort Vancouver. After wintering in Oregon, he led a group of immigrants southward over the Umpqua trail to California before returning east with a party led by Caleb Greenwood, over the Sierra via the Hastings Cutoff. At Fort Laramie Clyman warned immigrant trains to avoid the dangerous and nearly impassable cutoff—advice that the Reed and Donner parties tragically failed to heed. While living in Wisconsin in 1848, he organized another party to California. As they were crossing Nevada, members of the returning Mormon Battalion told them of the gold discovery at Sutter's Mill.

Clyman married Hannah McCombs, who had been in his party, and the couple settled on a ranch in the Napa valley, California, where he lived for the rest of his life. Although Clyman's education was rudimentary, he kept a diary of his experiences and liked to try his hand at poetry. With the aid of his diaries he wrote reminiscences that contain valuable accounts of the earliest days of the Rocky Mountain fur trade and the best account of the 1844 trip to Oregon. His shrewd, wry observations, often ungrammatical and full of outrageous phonetic spellings, are a delight. Not every fur trapper could describe an Indian chief as "a tall lean wrinkld face Filthy looking man with a forehead indicating deceet Dissimulution and intriegue and more like a beggerly scape gallows than a Chief but nodoubt thse fine Qualities are highly prized in the Kaw nation. . . ."

Clyman was a true frontiersman and mountain man but with a difference. He never lost his Southern accent or his courteous manner, and he appears to have been a lifelong Whig. He was adventurous but never reckless and had, says his biographer, Charles L. Camp, "a feeling for history."

Clyman's writings are published in Charles L. Camp,

ed., *James Clyman, American Frontiersman, 1792-1881* (1928). A brief biographical sketch by Camp is in LeRoy R. Hafen, ed., *The Mountain Men and the Fur Trade of the Far West*, vol. I (1965).—G. B. D.

Coastal Plain. See GULF COASTAL PLAIN and PHYSIOGRAPHY OF THE UNITED STATES: *Atlantic and Gulf Coastal plains*.

Coburn, Walter (1889-1971). Writer and historian. Raised on the family's thirty-thousand-acre Circle C Ranch, located near the Little Rockies of Montana, Coburn learned the ways of range cows, horses, and cowboys, and, later, of sheep and shepherds. Although he had spent a year in prep school to prepare for Stanford University, one of his older half-brothers insisted that he go to the Butte College of Mines. Coburn refused and became, instead, a full-time hand on the Circle C. In 1916 the family sold the ranch, and he went to Arizona to work on a ranch owned by his half-brothers.

About 1922 Coburn began writing for the pulps and other magazines. He quickly established a reputation as a fine fiction writer whose stories realistically reflected western life as he knew it. Among his better-known novels are: *The Ringtailed Rannyhans* (1927), a tale of two fiddle-footed cowpokes who return to the Circle C in time to save it for the new tenderfoot owner; *Mavericks* (1929), a story of hanky-panky with water rights and brands; *Barb Wire* (1931), a description of the end of the open-range days and the activities of the Wild Bunch, the most notorious and best-known outlaw gang; and *Pardners of the Dim Trail* (1951), an exciting story of the Pony Express.

In recent years Coburn was best known as a cow-country historian. His *Stirrup High* (1957) is a delightful account of his first working summer on the Circle C. In a foreword to the book, Fred Gipson, author of *Old Yeller* (1956) and other tales, explains Coburn's success: "This shy little sawed-off ex-Montana cowhand knows which end of a cow gets up first—which end of a horse gets up first—and the color of burnt-hair smoke, curling up from under a hot branding iron—. His ability to re-live his first-hand experiences of cows and horses and men through his yarns is the quality that has made my friend Coburn one of the leading writers of the Old West. . . ." *Pioneer Cattleman in Montana* (1968), the story of the Circle C, completes the history he started in *Stirrup High* and includes additional material on the Wild Bunch.

See Walter Coburn, *Stirrup High* (1957), and *Pioneer Cattleman in Montana* (1968).—J. C. D.

Cochise (1824?-1874). Indian chief. Cochise is one of the most renowned figures in American Indian history. But in spite of the acclaim of a man who has become an American folk hero, surprisingly little is known of the facts of his life. A leader of the *chok'anen* (Central Chiricahua) band of APACHE INDIANS, he may have been born as early as the late 1790s, although the early 1820s is probably a better guess. An Anglo who knew him said he "was as fine a looking Indian as one ever saw. He was about six feet tall and straight as an arrow, built, from the ground up, as perfect as any man could be."

Cochise's wife was one of the daughters of MANGAS COLORADAS, and Mangas and Cochise were the staunchest of friends and allies until the former's death in 1863. Like other Chiricahua Apache living in the mid-nineteenth century, Cochise had as the objects of his enmity and raiding forays the hapless Mexican citizens living on both sides of the United States and Mexican border. It was not until 1861 that he became an enemy of Anglo-Americans as well.

The war between the United States and Cochise's band of Apache stemmed from an incident at an adobe ranch house along Sonoita Creek in southern Arizona. It was here that a rough-looking Irishman named John Ward and his Mexican common-law wife, Jesusa, were living with two of Jesusa's children by a former marriage and their own infant son. In October 1860, Apache attacked Ward's ranch, drove off some cattle, and kidnapped Felix Tellez, Ward's adopted son. Ward was away at the time of the raid, but on his return he complained to the commander of the nearby military post that Cochise had been the culprit and he asked the army to rescue Felix, who was about twelve years old. At the end of January 1861, Lieutenant George Bascom was dispatched to the northern end of the Chiricahua Mountains and the Overland Stage station in Apache Pass, next to which Cochise habitually camped in peace, to bring the Apache to account. In the events that followed, infamous in Arizona history as the "sixteen days in Apache Pass" or the "Bascom affair," the lieutenant, feigning friendship, had his men surround Cochise and other Chiricahua in a tent near the stage station, in which the Apache thought they were going to be entertained. Cochise told Bascom, truthfully, as it turned out, that he had neither kidnapped Ward's stepson nor raided Ward's ranch. Bascom refused to believe him, and he ordered Cochise held as a hostage to assure the return of the boy and the cattle. Cochise used his knife to cut himself out of the tent and escaped. Some of his fellow warriors, however, failed to get away.

Subsequently, Cochise's men killed one of the civilian employees of the stage station and took another as hostage. During the next several days people were killed on both sides, with the result that Cochise set off on a trail of plunder and pillage that was to terrorize the southern Arizona countryside and Mexican borderlands until 1872.

Within two months of the Bascom affair, more than 150 non-Indians were killed. Mangas Coloradas and Cochise pooled their efforts to attack settlers, miners, and small parties of soldiers. Settlements were abandoned in the wake of Apache destruction, which in time took more than four thousand lives and cost hundreds of thousands of dollars in ruined or stolen property. Cochise and Mangas even had the audacity to attack a contingent of General James H. Carleton's California Column in Apache Pass in 1862, although their ambush was unsuccessful.

Felix Tellez, the boy who had been kidnapped, reappeared in time as Mickey Free, an Apache-speaking scout for the United States Army in the 1880s. He had not, indeed, been captured by Cochise but by a band of Western Apache.

By 1872 it was apparent to official Washington that the success of President Grant's peace policy in the Southwest depended largely on the government's ability to secure a permanent armistice with Cochise. General Oliver O. HOWARD was dispatched to Arizona to undertake the job. Working through Thomas J. JEFFORDS, a close personal friend of Cochise, Howard was able to meet with the Apache chief in the Dragoon Mountains in southeastern Arizona and to promise the Apache a reservation of their own choosing. The result was the huge Chiricahua reservation, set aside by executive order in October 1872, which included most of the southeastern corner of the territory. Jeffords was made the reservation's special Indian agent.

Cochise died, possibly of stomach cancer, two years later. He was buried in secret in the Dragoon Mountains, leaving his name on modern maps of the area: Cochise's Stronghold. In 1876 the Chiricahua living on the reservation were transferred to San Carlos and the 1872 executive order was revoked.

Perhaps because of the unjust actions taken against him in 1862 and because of his peaceful capitulation in 1872, Cochise was destined to become a latter-day "noble savage," one enshrined by historians of the West, writers, and filmmakers as the symbol of the good Indian, an Apache whose hostility was understandable and even justified.

See R. A. Mulligan, "Apache Pass and Old Fort Bowie," *Smoke Signal*, no. 11 (1965); F. Stanley, *The Apaches of New Mexico, 1540-1940* (1962); and James H. Tevis, *Arizona in the '50's* (1954).—B. L. F.

Cody, [William Frederick] "Buffalo Bill" (1846-1917). Scout and showman. "Buffalo Bill" Cody typified the Wild West to more people in more parts of the world than any other person, yet he was actually a real part of the phases of the frontier he so successfully romanticized. He was born in LeClaire, Scott County, Iowa. He attended several sessions of country schools, most of them organized by his father, Isaac Cody, who dabbled in local politics. When Kansas Territory was opened to settlement in 1854, the family moved there and settled in Salt Creek Valley, near Fort Leavenworth. Isaac Cody was stabbed while speaking for the free-state cause. Although he survived to become a member of the unrecognized Topeka legislature, his family attributed his death in 1857 to his injury.

After his father's death young Cody was employed by Majors & Russell (later Russell, Majors & Waddell) as a mounted messenger. He later rode the Pony Express for the same company and is credited with the third longest (not *the* longest) emergency ride while working on the division headed by the notorious Joseph A. Slade.

In the early Civil War years Cody was associated with irregular militia companies, one of which he admits was a "jay-hawking enterprise," meaning horse thievery. In 1864 he enlisted as private, giving his occupation as teamster, in the veteran Seventh Kansas Volunteer Cavalry, with which he served in campaigns against Confederate generals Bedford Forrest and Sterling Price.

While stationed in St. Louis Cody met Louisa Frederici and married her in 1866. He tried his hand at hotelkeeping in his old Salt Creek Valley neighborhood with ill success and then went west and worked irregularly as a scout and guide. In 1867-68 he contracted to supply buffalo meat for construction workers on the Union Pacific, Eastern Division, later renamed the Kansas Pacific Railroad. He was first dubbed Buffalo Bill while on this job.

In carrying dispatches over a long route through hostile Indian country, Cody came to the attention of Lieutenant General Philip H. Sheridan, who employed him as chief of scouts for the Fifth United States Caval-

Pawnee Bill (Gordon W. Lillie) and Buffalo Bill (William F. Cody), the two best-known Wild West showmen, merged their companies in 1908. (Library of Congress)

ry. Cody's continuous employment as a scout for more than four years (1868-72) was exceptional, for scouts usually were hired by the month or for a specific expedition. Cody took part in sixteen Indian fights, including the defeat of the Cheyenne on July 11, 1869, at Summit Springs under Brevet Major General Eugene A. Carr. Carr noted his "extraordinarily good services as trailer and fighter . . . his marksmanship being very conspicuous" and asked for a special increase in pay for him from the War Department, saying, "I hope to be able to retain him as long as I am engaged in this duty."

Adding to Cody's fame as a scout was his *ex officio* services as a hunting guide for parties of notables, including the Grand Duke Alexis of Russia in 1872. Another minor celebrity was Edward Zane Carroll Judson, who signed himself Ned Buntline as a prolific writer of DIME NOVELS. In 1869 he made Buffalo Bill the hero of a sensational story that was later dramatized. In 1872 Buntline persuaded Cody to appear on the melodrama stage in Chicago. Cody broke with Buntline after a year but remained on the stage for eleven seasons, spending many of his summers scouting or guiding hunting parties. During the summer of 1876 Cody took part in Indian fighting during which he killed Yellow Hand (more correctly translated Yellow Hair), called "the first scalp for Custer."

The first and most authentic of several Buffalo Bill autobiographies was published in 1879. Cody also appeared as author of dime novels and was the hero of some one thousand seven hundred variant issues, written by Prentiss Ingraham and nineteen or so other authors.

In 1883, inspired by the success of a July 4 celebration in North Platte, Nebraska, Cody organized Buffalo Bill's Wild West, an outdoor exhibition that dramatized the contemporary western scene (see WILD WEST SHOW). Its showing in London in 1887 for Queen Victoria's Jubilee and other European tours made it an international success. The show's stars included Buck Taylor, "King of the Cowboys" and first cowboy hero; Annie OAKLEY, "Little Sure Shot"; Johnny Baker, "the Cow-boy Kid"; and, for one season, Sitting Bull. Its acts included a Pony Express relay race, the attack on the Deadwood stagecoach, the "Congress of Rough Riders of the World," spectacles such as Custer's Last Fight and the Battle of Summit Springs, and the roping, bucking broncos and "cowboy fun" that became the rodeo.

Buffalo Bill's Wild West scored its greatest success at home at the Chicago World's Columbian Exposition of 1893. After the death of his longtime partner, Nate Salsbury, in 1902, the show had financial difficulties but remained on the road for thirty years. In its last few seasons Pawnee Bill (Gordon William Lillie) was partner.

In the last Sioux outbreak of 1890-91 Cody volunteered his services to Major General Nelson A. Miles and made a vain effort to see Sitting Bull. Indians who had toured Europe with Cody's show were useful peacemakers, and some of the Indian prisoners of the final Sioux War were employed in the show for the following season. While Cody was sometimes denounced for exploiting Indian savagery, he employed many at a time when opportunities were few; and many for the first time saw a world beyond the confines of their villages. Cody's use of buffalo in his show had an effect on preserving the species from total extinction, although because he was Buffalo Bill he has seemed to the public to personify the buffalo killer. Actually he killed relatively few buffalo; it was the hide hunters, who came after his hunting days, who destroyed the huge herds.

Above all, Cody was able to see an aspect of life in his own time as romantic and historic even while deprecating his own part in it to the extent that he made no effort to authenticate his own actions, which were becoming legendary. On the contrary, his sense of humor often led him to add a touch of the incongruous with a tall story. His refusal to take himself seriously was unfortunately echoed by his partners, who looked upon him as a mere figurehead. Yet he went on with his show while they fell by the wayside. The staging of the Wild West show was done by Cody, and every event in its program, nearly all of them reflecting his personal experiences, retained its glamor. It was Buffalo Bill's Wild West that made the West of the cowboy and Indian appear to be forever romantic.

Don Russell, *The Lives and Legends of Buffalo Bill* (1969), is the most complete biography. Frank E. Bliss, *The Life of Hon. William F. Cody, Known as Buffalo Bill, the Famous Hunter, Scout and Guide: An Autobiography* (1879), was the basis for eight or more later publications with varied titles, most of which have added and garbled material. *An Autobiography of Buffalo Bill* (1920) is an independent work. Both books show evidence that Cody had a hand in their writing. There is an immense bibliography on Cody, some written by his associates and members of his family and much that was show publicity.—D. R.

Coe, William R. See COLLECTORS AND COLLECTIONS.

Coeur d'Alene or **Skitswish Indians**. The Coeur d'Alene are an interior Salishan tribe closely related to the Pend d'Oreille and Flathead. They formerly oc-

cupied the headwaters of the Spokane and Clearwater rivers in northern Idaho. Culturally they were of the eastern Plateau complex and, like neighboring tribes, also exhibited many characteristics of both the Northwest Coast and Plains cultures. They have no tradition of migration and evidently inhabited their homeland from early prehistoric times. The Coeur d'Alene were neither nomadic nor given to warfare. They generally lived in peace with surrounding tribes, though in the late eighteenth century they often joined the Flathead in sending war parties to the Plains against the expanding Blackfoot and Crow. During this time they became accustomed to hunting buffalo and as late as 1880 made annual trips east to lay in supplies of meat and hides.

First brought clearly to the attention of whites by the reports of Lewis and Clark, the Coeur d'Alene were generally friendly toward the fur-traders and early settlers. Their population was reduced from nearly four thousand to about eleven hundred by two onslaughts of smallpox, first in the general epidemic of the 1830s and again about 1850, but unlike many other tribes, the Coeur d'Alene did not blame it on evil white magicians. During the Cayuse War (1845-50) and the Yakima Wars (1855-56) they were neutral, but owing to dissatisfaction with treaty negotiations and the white influx to the Colville mines in Idaho they joined in the Spokane war of 1858. Coeur d'Alene warriors helped defeat Colonel Edward Steptoe at the battle of Steptoe's Butte (May 17, 1858) and participated in the battles of Four Lakes and Spokane Plains (September 1 and 5, 1858), where the army under Colonel George Wright decisively triumphed. The Coeur d'Alene submitted soon afterward and were placed on a reservation bordering Lake Coeur d'Alene in the heart of their traditional homeland, where the remnants of the tribe have remained to the present. Their population was reported at 523 in 1962 and has been close to that figure since the end of the nineteenth century.

See R. I. Burns, *The Jesuits in the Indian Wars of the Northwest* (1963); V. F. Ray, *Cultural Relations in the Plateau of Northwestern America* (1939); J. H. Teit, *The Salishan Tribes of the Western Plateaus*, Bureau of American Ethnology Forty-fifth Annual Report (1927-28); and U. S. Bureau of Indian Affairs, *Indian Population and Land* (1963).—P. R. M.

Colcord, Charles Francis (1859-1934). Kansas rancher and developer. Born in Kentucky of English stock, Colcord moved with his family to New Orleans after the Civil War. Suffering poor health, the thirteen-year-old was sent to a Texas ranch near Corpus Christi where he was a cowboy for three years; he liked it so much that when his father came for him, he ran away and roved for a year. His father then bought a place in Texas and went into the horse and mule business, and young Colcord came home. At age seventeen he trailed horse herds north across Indian Territory to Kansas and beyond. In 1877 he moved to a Kansas ranch where, with his father, he organized the Jug Cattle Company and went into the Comanche pool of ranchers running cattle on open range from the Cimarron River north to Flint Hills.

In 1884 Colcord went to Flagstaff to run the Arizona Land and Cattle Company for three years but came back to Wichita when the boom later ruined his father. He went to Oklahoma City when the area was opened to settlers in 1889 and traded his team, wagon, and gear for Lot 1, Block 1, on East Reno at the Santa Fe tracks. He was chief of police under three mayors in boomtown days, as well as a sheriff and United States deputy marshal.

He participated in the opening of the Cherokee strip in 1893 and got a corner lot in Perry. He bought a farm north of town for fifty dollars, built an eight-room house, planted the first orchard in the strip, farmed, ranched, speculated in real estate, and helped build the town. After several years he returned to Oklahoma City and, with profits from land and operations at Perry, went into real estate and insurance. He built Oklahoma City's first twelve-story skyscraper and later had a hand in the Biltmore Hotel construction. He was active in every phase of city and civic affairs.—C. H. F.

Colden, Cadwallader (1688-1776). Philosopher, scientist, historian, and New York politician. Colden was born in Ireland of Scottish parentage. After graduating from the University of Edinburgh in 1705, he studied medicine and practiced it after his emigration to Philadelphia in 1710. He moved to New York in 1718, where he was appointed surveyor-general of the province in 1720 and a member of the governor's council in 1721. He was lieutenant governor from 1761 until his death, serving on occasion as acting governor of the colony. In this capacity he strongly advocated submission to British authority and in 1765 was burned in effigy for his attempts to enforce the Stamp Act.

Colden's interests were far-ranging. He wrote treatises on moral philosophy, mathematics, botany, medicine, and physics, several of which were highly regarded by the intellectual community of his day. As a colonial official he was a leader in shaping New York policies toward the Iroquois. His *History of the Five Indian Nations* (1727) was intended partly as an anthropological work that explained Iroquois institutions and customs and defended them against the charge of barbarism. It had also a political purpose, to call attention to the economic value of the Iroquois fur trade and to the military value of retaining Iroquois support in the struggle against France for continental supremacy. The political impact of Colden's book in influencing opinion and policy at the time is hard to measure, but he remains a major figure in the history of both Indian relations and Indian scholarship.

See A. M. Keys, *Cadwallader Colden, A Representative Eighteenth Century Official* (1906).—A. W. T.

Cole, Phillip Gillett (1883-1940). Businessman and art collector. Born in Jacksonville, Illinois, Cole graduated from the Columbia University College of Physicians and Surgeons in 1910, and practiced medicine in Helena, Montana, until the outbreak of World War I. Returning to New York City from France in 1918, he did not resume his medical practice, but joined his father as a partner in an auto parts manufacturing firm in Brooklyn, becoming president of the company upon his father's death. In 1930 Cole retired from business to an estate near Tarrytown, New York, where he spent his remaining years in pursuit of various hobbies, the most extensive being his collection of western art and artifacts reminiscent of his earlier days in Montana.

Following Cole's death, his widow decided to sell the collection, and trustees for the estate contacted Tulsa oilman Thomas Gilcrease, who agreed to purchase Cole's entire inventory. Listed in the affidavit of appraisal at the time of purchase were sixty-two bronze sculptures and more than five hundred paintings, about half of which were the work of Olaf Seltzer, whom Cole had commissioned to paint a series of Montana historical subjects. Works by Frederic Remington, Charles M. Russell, Frank Tenney Johnson, Joseph Henry Sharp, and Charles Schreyvogel were also included, as well as numerous illustrated letters and a large number of books, manuscripts, and related reports of interest to western frontier history. The Gilcrease purchase of Cole's collection was regarded as one of the largest single transactions of its kind ever made. The entire Gilcrease collection was deeded to the city of Tulsa in 1958.

Cole's younger daughter, Katharine, became an amateur sculptor who exhibited widely in the United States and Europe.

See David C. Hunt, "The Old West Revisited," *American Scene*, vol. 8, no. 4 (1967); Paul Rossi and David C. Hunt, *The Art of the Old West* (1971); and Aline B. Saarinen, *The Proud Possessors* (1958).—D. C. H.

Coleman, William Tell (1824-1893). Merchant and San Francisco vigilante. Coleman was born in Kentucky, the son of Napoleon Bonaparte Coleman, a lawyer. He went to Sacramento in 1849 and the following year founded the merchandising firm of William T. Coleman & Company in San Francisco. In 1851 he replaced the erratic Sam Brannan as a leader on the city's Committee of Vigilance, formed to suppress crime, and in 1856 was the principal figure in the revival of the committee after the shootings of United States Marshal William H. Richardson and James King, editor of the San Francisco *Bulletin*. Though Coleman exerted a relatively moderating influence in the vigilante movement, he condoned many of the committee's gross violations of due process. In July 1877, after a series of destructive anti-Chinese riots, he organized a Committee of Public Safety against the rioters, and armed its supporters with pick handles. They were quasi-legal militia, whereas the vigilante armies had been clearly illegal although they operated with impunity.

In addition to his mercantile activities Coleman engaged in sugar refining and other enterprises, and in his later years launched an unsuccessful venture in borax production, which bankrupted him. He was a tall and handsome man of most impressive and commanding appearance. Robert Louis Stevenson characterized him as "the Lion of the Vigilantes," a phrase that provided the title for a highly laudatory biography by James A. B. Scherer (1939).—W. B.

Colfax County War. See MAXWELL LAND GRANT COMPANY.

collectors and collections of western Americana. Since the late 1920s western Americana has been one of the most popular fields for book and manuscript collectors. The activities of these collectors and the booksellers who served them have brought to light many formerly unknown pioneer narratives and saved from destruction of oblivion many important and rare sources for the history of the West.

As recently as the 1920s westerners were still too close to the frontier period of their own history to give much thought to the preservation of its sources, and eastern collectors met with little competition in the West. Today that picture has changed. State universities, state libraries, and state and local historical societies everywhere in the West have long since embarked on programs for the collection and preservation of the materials of their own history.

Perhaps the earliest major collector of western Americana was the historian Hubert Howe BANCROFT. Beginning in the late 1850s, he assiduously sought out the sources needed for his monumental history of the Pacific states. The collection eventually comprised more than sixty thousand books and pamphlets and an enormous group of manuscript materials, including original papers and letters, transcripts of archival materials, and stenographic interviews with pioneers. Its scope covered the whole Pacific Coast from Alaska to Mexico and the Southwest from Utah to Texas, ranging from the early history of the native races down to the third quarter of the nineteenth century.

The collection was eventually acquired by the University of California and established as the Bancroft Library on the Berkeley campus. Its growth has continued over the years and it remains the largest single collection in its field. A catalog of its manuscript holdings is in preparation, the first volume having been published in 1963.

If Bancroft was in a sense the grandfather of western Americana collecting, the father was undoubtedly Henry Raup Wagner (1862-1957). In the course of his long career Wagner pioneered many fields of western bookcollecting and opened them up to others with the bibliographies he compiled and published. His first collecting venture was the early history of Texas and the Mississippi valley. For some years he gathered both manuscripts and early printed books relating to this area. In 1916 this collection was acquired by Yale University, and Wagner turned to new fields.

In 1917, while working in Chile as a mining engineer, Wagner issued a tentative checklist of works relating to the part of the United States formerly included in New Spain. By 1924 he had amassed enough data so that the list could be published as a bibliography: *The Spanish Southwest, 1542-1794*. A revised edition appeared in 1937. His collection of books in this field had in the meantime been sold, principally to other collectors.

Wagner had also become interested in accounts of travel in the trans-Mississippi West. The first edition of *The Plains and the Rockies* appeared in 1920. A second edition, revised and enlarged by Charles L. Camp, appeared in 1937, and a third edition in 1953. For fifty years the bibliography has inspired and guided two generations of collectors. Wagner's own collection of books in this field is now in the Henry E. Huntington Library in San Marino, California.

Most collectors confine themselves to a single field and a single type of material—books, manuscripts, or maps—but Wagner's interests were diverse and far-ranging. Among his many contributions to historical and bibliographical scholarship, one more may perhaps be mentioned, his *Cartography of the Northwest Coast . . . to 1800* (1937). The collection of maps, voyages, and so forth that he assembled on this subject is now in the Honnold Library in Claremont, California.

Wagner was perhaps unrivaled in the range of his interests and abilities, but at least one of his contemporaries was his equal as a collector. Edward Everett Ayer (1841-1927) was himself a pioneer who made the overland journey in 1860, fought Apache Indians in the Southwest, and built up a highly profitable lumber business. In his later years he turned with enthusiasm to acquiring books about the West. The result was a collection that was truly extensive not only in number of volumes but also in the area covered, sweeping from the Mississippi to the Pacific Coast, from the Southwest to Alaska. It is now housed in the Newberry Library in Chicago.

The decades between 1920 and 1950 were the great age of western Americana collecting. Never before or since have so many major collectors all been active in the field at once. Perhaps the three greatest were William R. Coe (1869-1955), Everett D. Graff (1885-1963), and Thomas W. Streeter (1883-1965). Soon after acquiring a cattle ranch in Wyoming, Coe became interested in the early history of that area. As the years went by, his collecting interests widened until they included the whole Louisiana Purchase area, the Pacific Northwest, including Alaska, and the Canadian Northwest. In the forty-odd years of his activity he bought not only books but also maps, manuscripts, and pictures. In the late 1940s his collection was given to Yale University, where it forms the nucleus of the Yale Collection of Western Americana. A catalog of the manuscripts was published in 1952.

Everett D. Graff was as ardent a collector as Coe. Unlike the latter, he concentrated his efforts on books and other printed materials, but his range of interest was even wider and included the whole trans-Mississippi West. He was highly discriminating in his choice of books, insisting that only the truly significant ones be included in his collection, and whenever possible, choice copies. The Graff Collection is now in the Newberry Library, and a selective catalog has been published.

Thomas W. Streeter, who was perhaps the leading Americana collector of the twentieth century, covered an even wider field. His interests ranged from the discovery of America to the beginnings of American aviation, from the first settlements on the Atlantic Coast to the last frontier in Alaska. The recent sale of his collection, spread over a period of three years, was a landmark in American bookselling, both for the number and rarity of the books included and the prices realized. Though most of his books were dispersed at auction, one collection remained intact. In the 1920s Henry Wagner had suggested to him that a bibliography of the early history of Texas down to its entrance into the Union in 1845 would be a notable contribution to scholarship. Streeter embarked upon the project with enthusiasm. It was typical of him that he sought out not only titles but the books themselves. When the bibliography was finally published in five volumes, commencing in 1956, Streeter had acquired more than half of the sixteen hundred books, pamphlets, and broadsides included. The collection was then acquired by Yale, where it joined, appropriately enough, Wagner's earlier Texas collection.

If these three led the field, there were many others pressing at their heels. Most of their collections now grace various institutional libraries. Donald M. Frost (1877-1958) collected narratives of early western travels for thirty years and in 1948 presented them to the American Antiquarian Society in Worcester, Massachusetts, where they added to that library's already considerable strength. Philip Ashton ROLLINS, author of a well-received book on the cowboy, gave his western collection to Princeton University. The Robert Ellison collection is one of the treasures of the Lilly Library at Indiana University. Although part of W. J. Holliday's collection was sold at auction in 1954, much was given to the Arizona Pioneers' Historical Society at Tucson.

Some collections have achieved institutional status by themselves. Most notable, of course, is the Henry E. Huntington Library at San Marino, California. Though Huntington was only incidentally a western Americana collector, this is one of the great research libraries for western, and particularly southwestern, history. The Everette L. DeGolyer Library was established as a foundation in Dallas, and its collecting activity continued with new scope and emphasis by Everette L. DeGolyer, Jr. Thomas W. GILCREASE, himself of Indian blood, brought together a great collection of books, manuscripts, and pictures relating to the West and particularly to the Indians, which is now housed in its own building on the outskirts of Tulsa, Oklahoma.

One of the last of the great collectors was Frederick W. Beinecke (1887-1971). He came to collecting not only late in his own life but also as the other collectors were disappearing from the scene. In a decade and a half after 1950 he put together one of the major western collections, with particular emphasis on the Southwest and the Mexican War. Much of his collection was given to Yale University.

Almost all of these great collectors are now dead, and with them passed an era. Even with large financial resources, it would probably be impossible to duplicate their collections today. Too many of the key books exist only in a handful of copies, and those are now in institutional libraries. It is unlikely that they will reappear on the market. This does not mean the end of collecting western Americana, however. The next generation of collectors, instead of attempting to retrace their predecessors' footsteps, can seek out fields that have hitherto been ignored or only partially explored.

See Philip M. Hamer, *A Guide to Archives and Manuscripts in the United States* (1961).—A. H.

colleges and universities. West of the Mississippi, institutions of higher education were largely established through the agency of the state. Unlike the East and the Old Northwest, the trans-Mississippi lands did not inspire the denominational zeal of religious groups, which had dotted the older regions with a bevy of denominational colleges jealous of any state competition. Of course, there were exceptions—particularly in some of those states admitted to the Union before the Civil War. By 1860 the Methodists had founded Baker University (1858) in Kansas, the College of the Pacific (1851) in California, and Willamette University (1853) in Oregon. Presbyterian activity had launched the College of California (1855) at Berkeley and Pacific University (1854) in Oregon. In Iowa and Missouri a cluster of denominational colleges almost dominated higher education. But with the war the surge of denominational zeal waned, and the state moved to center stage. Symbolic of this shift, the University of Kansas (1863) received a $10,000 gift from Amos Lawrence, an abolitionist from Boston, because no denominational group was able to organize the Free-State College that

he had wished to endow in the 1850s after the travails of "Bleeding Kansas." And in 1868 the Presbyterian College of California offered its facilities as the liberal arts unit of a university created by the Morrill Act. Thus a private denominational college surrendered its autonomy to become the core of the University of California.

Still, most of the lands between the Mississippi River and the Pacific Coast were virgin territory for the state university. As the Rocky Mountains, the Southwest, and the Far West regions were organized first as territories and then as states, constitution drafters viewed a state university as one of a handful of institutions that must be immediately located. The companions of the university were the capitol, the penitentiary, the insane asylum, and sometimes a separate agricultural college. Often constitutions contained elaborate plans for the organization of a university long before the state possessed the resources or students to support such an institution. The 1864 Nevada constitution, for example, contains one of the most elaborate plans for a university ever proposed in any state, East or West.

For the most part, the university builders copied policies of support and control that had been developed in the state universities of the Old Northwest. They even duplicated the classical curriculum of eastern colleges.

Most western state universities owe their inspiration and initial support to a tradition of federal land grants originated in 1787.

Even before the Ohio Company of Associates began to settle the Old Northwest, its leader, Dr. Manasseh Cutler, insisted that the contract between the company and the federal government provide two townships of land (46,080 acres) for the endowment of a university. This grant clearly gave a force to the less specific proviso in the Northwest Ordinance, which stated that "schools and the means of education shall forever be encouraged." The Ohio Company endowment was used to found two universities in Ohio—Ohio University at Athens (1802) and Miami University at Oxford (1809).

The contract with the Ohio Company was not a piece of legislation and obviously did not require or guarantee future federal grants to states other than Ohio. But it became the practice of the federal government to grant two townships or seventy-two sections of land to most states for the endowment of a university. The enabling act for statehood usually provided this land grant. There was specific legislation, however, in the case of some of the territories to withdraw land from public sale during territorial days and to hold that land in trust until the states entered the Union. The Donation Act of 1850 provided land for Oregon, and the Land Act of 1881 authorized land to be selected and held inviolate for the territories of Dakota, Montana, Arizona, Idaho, and Wyoming. Although some of the territories (for example, Wyoming and Washington) organized universities before statehood, the federal endowment did not become available until the state entered the Union.

Every state, with the exceptions of Texas, Alaska, and Hawaii, received a "university grant." These lands were often managed irresponsibly, resulting in virtually no permanent income. However, in Wyoming wise management coupled with the fact that oil was discovered on the lands led to an endowment that provided almost one-third of the university's yearly budget. In Texas, where the state itself endowed the University of Texas in 1881 with two million acres, oil revenues have also generated a considerable income.

The two-township grants are different from the better known Land Grant Act of 1862, or Morrill Act. This legislation offered additional lands (30,000 acres for each senator and representative) for the endowment of colleges that offered instruction in agriculture and the mechanical arts. Such colleges would supposedly open opportunities to the "industrial" as opposed to the "professional" classes. The land endowments from the 1862 act naturally varied in size from state to state. Both to equalize the funds available to each college and to compensate for meager endowments, which again resulted from poor land management, Congress passed a second

Morrill Act in 1890 to provide annual cash allotments of up to $25,000 to the "land-grant" colleges.

The university grants and the land grants were in no way mutually exclusive. The A & M (Agricultural and Mechanical) college could also be a part of the state university. Or the state might sponsor two separate institutions. And in some of the western states admitted after the Civil War, such as Wyoming and North Dakota, the state found that it would receive lands both from the Morrill Act and from the two-township practice upon admission. Some states mixed the grants by combining them to form one university; others separated them.

The following lists give a breakdown of the state institutions supported from these grants:

(1) Universities combining the Morrill Act and the two-township grants:

University of Arizona	Tucson	1885
University of Arkansas	Fayetteville	1871
University of California	Berkely	1868
University of Idaho	Moscow	1889
Louisiana State University	Baton Rouge	1860
University of Minnesota	Minneapolis	1851
University of Missouri	Columbia	1839
University of Nebraska	Lincoln	1869
University of Nevada	Reno	1874
University of Wyoming	Laramie	1886

(2) Universities supported *only* by the two-township grant:

University of Colorado	Boulder	1861
State University of Iowa	Iowa City	1847
University of Kansas	Lawrence	1863
Montana State University	Missoula	1893
University of New Mexico	Albuquerque	1889
University of North Dakota	Grand Forks	1883
University of Oklahoma	Norman	1890
University of Oregon	Eugene	1872
State University of South Dakota	Vermillion	1862
University of Utah	Salt Lake City	1869
University of Washington	Seattle	1861

(3) Land-grant colleges supported *only* by the Morrill Act:

University of Alaska	College	1915
Colorado State University	Fort Collins	1870
University of Hawaii	Honolulu	1907
Iowa State College	Ames	1858
Kansas State University	Manhattan	1863
Montana State College	Bozeman	1893
New Mexico State University	University Park	1888
North Dakota Agricultural College	Fargo	1890
Oklahoma State University	Stillwater	1890
Oregon State College	Corvallis	1888
South Dakota State College	Brookings	1881
Texas Agricultural and Mechanical University	College Station	1862
Utah State University	Logan	1888
Washington State University	Pullman	1890

(4) Universities supported *only* by a state grant:

University of Texas	Austin	1881

In the West, preparation for higher education, where it was to be had, was usually limited to attendance at a one-room schoolhouse like this one in Kansas. (Kansas State Historical Society, Topeka)

It is interesting to note that in those states that established separate land-grant colleges, the state university was usually the most prestigious and favored institution. This held true even in such states as North Dakota, where agricultural and popular interests were strong. The prestige of the state university, and sometimes the anger directed against it by the farmers, stemmed from the fact that this institution was viewed as the avenue of upward mobility. This often meant that farm boys did not return to the farm. As North Dakotans asked, "How are you going to keep them down on the farm after they've seen Grand Forks?"

Before the Civil War, the older state universities in the Midwest, such as Wisconsin and Michigan, and trans-Mississippi institutions, such as Minnesota, were supported only by the income from university lands, small student fees, and an occasional state grant. It was not until 1867 that annual state appropriations or mill-tax levies became a dependable source of revenue. Under the influence of President Erastus O. Haven, the Michigan legislature first authorized a 1/20-mill-tax levy in that year for the university. Missouri also instituted a university mill tax for the first time in 1867. By the 1890s the mill-tax levy had become an accepted mark of many of the state universities in the West. Thus another principle established on the eastern side of the Mississippi became a legacy of those universities founded in the West. Even though some states preferred to make an annual or biennial appropriation rather than authorize a tax, it was still the Michigan tax that first established

the principle of annual rather than sporadic support. In most states the provision of free tuition was enacted with the mill-tax legislation.

Although state funds eventually supported the western universities, a number of institutions were rescued from financial bankruptcy in their early years by private citizens. Both the University of Washington and the University of Oregon were saved from financial collapse by gifts from the railroad magnate Henry Villard.

Along with the mill-tax levy, the state universities of the West adopted the form of government that had been accepted in the state universities of the East—a board of regents appointed by the governor, elected by the legislature, or elected directly by the people. Before the Civil War a few state universities in the Old Northwest, such as Indiana and Ohio, had allowed self-perpetuating boards of trustees to govern the institutions. By 1860 these trustees had been discarded in favor of state-elected or appointed bodies. Self-perpetuating boards generally proved unsatisfactory because a particular religious denomination would "seize" the board and turn it into a sectarian body.

Though a university might be the state university, many of these institutions had difficulty in establishing a reputation and in recruiting students throughout the entire state as opposed to one geographic region. For example, the University of North Dakota was known in its early days as Grand Forks University. There were a number of reasons for this. As mentioned earlier, the state university was usually located in a particular region as an act of patronage along with the capitol, the penitentiary, and the insane asylum. Legislators, criminals, and the insane were to some extent coerced to patronize the state institution erected for their benefit. This was not the case with the university. Students were not forced to attend the institution of their state. Gradually each university found a way to spread its influence throughout the state. In North Dakota fear of financial bankruptcy in the 1890s led friends of the university to campaign for a University Maintenance Fund of $25,000. The fund-raisers canvassed the state and raised the university out of its regional status. In 1909 the campus of the University of Washington was the site of the Alaska-Yukon-Pacific Exposition, thus bringing the university into the public light.

In those states in which the university was also the land-grant college, the institutions widened their sphere of influence through extension services that disseminated useful information to farms and towns. Again it was federal legislation that spurred this activity. The Hatch Act of 1887 provided annual cash allotments of $15,000 for the establishment of agricultural experiment stations that would make available to the public the latest findings on crop and animal research.

Finally, the state universities became identified with the state at large by accrediting high schools. Because the universities were anxious to develop reservoirs of students, they frequently sent teams to visit high schools and set certain standards of curriculum for a diploma. This high school certificate would then be a ticket of admission to the university. By standardizing the high schools and then depending upon them for students, the state universities could dispense with their own preparatory departments, which were often criticized as competitors to the schools. In some states the state university was declared by law to be the head of the public school system.

The western state university tended to copy the required classical curriculum of eastern colleges for the bachelor of arts degree even in the 1880s, when that curriculum was undergoing change in the East. Eventually news of the success, or at least the excitement, of Harvard's elective system and the "any man, any study" philosophy of Cornell caused westerners to demand that their institutions innovate on eastern models— particularly that of Cornell. Possibly the reason for this "innovation lag" can be explained by the fact that there was no native faculty in the West. The faculty members came from the East and often duplicated the education they had received a few decades before.

News of eastern innovations was often brought west by ambitious men who had not succeeded in achieving the fame of some of their friends, such as Charles Eliot, Andrew D. White, or Daniel C. Gilman. John W. Hoyt, who had labored for years to create a national university only to be defeated by Charles Eliot, left the East to accept the post of territorial governor of Wyoming in 1878. Nine years later he became the first president of the University of Wyoming. Homer B. Sprague, a Yale graduate, assumed the presidency of the University of North Dakota in 1887 because he thought he could lead that institution to the fame of Cornell or Johns Hopkins —and in as short a time as Gilman and White had developed those universities. Regrettably, these men left

the universities within a few years, realizing that their plans were too ambitious; some of the states were too underpopulated to achieve the prominence of the East, at least in the 1880s and 1890s. It was David Starr Jordan, president of the privately endowed Leland Stanford, Junior University, in California, who succeeded in building what he thought would be the ideal state university—the Cornell of the West.

See Wilson O. Clough, *A History of the University of Wyoming* (1937); Charles M. Gates, *The First Century at the University of Washington* (1961); Louis G. Geiger, *University of the Northern Plains: A History of the University of North Dakota* (1958); Allan Nevins, *The State University and Democracy* (1962); Earle D. Ross, *Democracy's College: The Land Grant Movement in the Formative Stage* (1942), and *A History of Iowa State College* (1942); Henry D. Sheldon, *History of the University of Oregon* (1940); Donald G. Tewksbury, *The Founding of Colleges in the United States Before the Civil War* (1932); and Louis B. Wright, *Culture on the Moving Frontier* (1955). —J. S. W.

Collier, John (1884-1968). Social reformer. Collier was born in Atlanta, Georgia, the son of a prominent banker active in civic affairs. Young Collier inherited from his father a commitment to the solution of social problems through what today would be called community development, and from his mother an equally strong interest in romantic literature and the out-of-doors.

After graduating from high school in 1901, Collier tramped through the forests of northern Georgia and western North Carolina, then left Atlanta for New York City. During 1902-04 he pursued non-credit course work at Columbia University, first in literature, then in biology. He also read intensively in the works of Nietzsche, sociologist Lester Frank Ward, and the Gestalt psychologists. In 1904 he embarked upon a utopian scheme to modify the conservative mentality of the South by bringing unemployed immigrants to that region. His plan was to draw upon his valuable family connections to convince southern railroads to supply the necessary transportation and local chambers of commerce to find employment for the immigrants. The project ended dismally after six months and Collier drifted into a position with the Associated Charities of Atlanta, where his efforts to replace the dole with work relief projects also failed. He next tried his hand at newspaper work. In 1906 he left for Europe to resume his academic training. During the next year and a half he attended lectures in abnormal psychology at the Collège de France, met and married Lucy Wood of Philadelphia, and studied at first hand the labor and cooperative movements of northern Europe under the informal guidance of a Harvard professor of social ethics.

Returning to the United States in 1907, Collier resolved to apply the lessons he had learned from the European cooperative movements to the problems of immigrants in New York City. He accepted the position of executive secretary at the People's Institute, the educational branch of Cooper Union, where nightly forums were conducted for the immigrant and working-class poor. He became deeply distressed by the physical and psychological strain that the Americanization process entailed for these people, and increasingly convinced that the cultural heritage they were rejecting was in many ways superior to the one they were being encouraged to accept. Like many other contemporaneous critics of American life, he denounced materialism and concluded that only through cooperative and collective action in pursuit of human values could the nation be saved from self-destruction.

After four years Collier decided that the charity and settlement house approaches to urban problems were unsatisfactory because they were essentially paternalistic. What was needed was some way for the people to begin solving their problems through their own community projects. With the approval of his superiors and the backing of a reform-minded city administration, he began an experiment utilizing the public school after hours as a center for neighborhood self-improvement. Initially the school-community centers were devoted only to adult education and recreational activities, but Collier gradually pushed for their development into centers of local self-government. When the reform administration was turned out of office in 1917, the city's support was withdrawn, but a modified community center program was continued with an emphasis on Americanization classes for immigrants, a popular cause after the United States entered World War I. The program was strengthened when President Wilson, through the Council of National Defense, pledged his support to the community center movement as a means of coordinating various local projects in support of the war effort. The signing of the armistice, however, ended federal support, and the People's Institute, under a new director, declined to continue financing Collier's efforts in this direction.

In 1919 Collier resigned his post with the People's Institute to accept a similar position with the California State Immigration and Housing Commission. For nine months he toured the state delivering lectures, conducting forums, and training teachers for work in the proposed community centers. But in the fall of 1920 his position was deleted from the budget when members of the legislature took offense at his discussion of cooperative enterprise, saying it smacked too much of Bolshevism.

At this time a combination of events propelled Collier into the field of Indian affairs. Mabel Dodge Luhan, Collier's friend from his New York days when her Fifth Avenue salon was a center of radical ideas, had moved to Taos, New Mexico, in 1918 and shortly thereafter she decided that Indian civilization needed to be rescued from harmful American influences. Learning that Collier had lost his job and convinced that he could organize the movement, she invited him to Taos in the winter of 1920. For the next nine months Collier lived among the Pueblo Indians. Gradually his disillusionment over his failures in New York and California were replaced by a determination to preserve the concept of community which "yet lived on in the embattled Red Indians." Financial support for this undertaking was provided by a group of wealthy women in southern California whom he had met and impressed in the course of his work for the Immigration and Housing Commission. In 1922 Secretary of the Interior Albert B. Fall unwittingly provided Collier with the issue that brought his program and philosophy to national attention. In that year Fall gave his support to a bill designed to end a long-standing

dispute between the Pueblo Indians and white settlers over land titles along the Rio Grande in New Mexico. The bill was worded in such a way that the white claimants were favored, and if it passed, the Indians would lose both land and water rights along the river. Marshaling his forces, Collier proceeded to Washington to testify against the bill and he succeeded in blocking its passage. In the process he organized the American Indian Defense Association, which, under his direction as executive secretary, became the most powerful voice for radical change of federal Indian policy during the 1920s.

From the beginning Collier's program had four main objectives: a halt to the division or allotment of Indian tribal lands into individually owned parcels, a practice that since 1887, when the DAWES SEVERALTY ACT was passed, had reduced Indian land holdings from 139 million acres to 47 million acres; the guarantee of "elementary civil rights" to Indians, including the right of limited self-government on their reservations, freedom of religion, and removal of arbitrary control over Indian lives by Indian Service personnel; the preservation and encouragement of Indian traditions and cultures; and access by Indian tribal groups to federal, state, and private sources of credit toward the end of economic self-sufficiency.

During the years 1922-32 the American Indian Defense Association successfully defended the Pueblo titles to the disputed land; organized, in defiance of government directives, the All-Pueblo Council to demonstrate the ability of Indians to govern themselves; secured congressional approval for the Indian claim to subsurface minerals on executive order reservations; forced modification of restrictions on the practice of Indian religious ceremonials; and exposed the hypocritical practice of financing highway and irrigation projects in the West through assessments against Indian tribal estates without Indian consent. However, the association was not successful in halting the policy of land alienation or in obtaining credit for tribal economic projects, but growing support for these goals was obtained as the result of investigations conducted by a Senate committee created in 1927 and of the publication in 1928 of the nonpartisan Rockefeller Foundation-sponsored Meriam Report. During the Hoover administration attempts were made to implement the reforms indicated by the Senate investigation and the Meriam Report, but except in the areas of education and health care they were not successful. The Democratic party sweep in the 1932 elections resulted in the appointment of Harold Ickes—a charter member of the American Indian Defense Association—as secretary of the interior, and to the appointment of Collier as commissioner of Indian affairs.

Collier's tenure as Indian commissioner lasted until 1945, making it the longest in the history of that office. By administrative action he abolished the remaining debts levied against tribal treasuries for highway and irrigation projects, forbade discrimination against Indian religious ceremonies, introduced instruction in Indian languages, arts, and crafts into the school curriculum, increased the proportion of Indian employees in the Indian service from thirty-three percent to sixty-five percent, and in conjunction with various New Deal relief agencies, funneled millions of dollars into projects to conserve and improve the Indian landed estate. The most important event of his administration, however, was the passage in June 1934 of the Indian Reorganization Act, or Wheeler-Howard Act.

Under the act as originally drawn by Collier and two of Felix Frankfurter's former students, Felix Cohen and Nathan Margold, Congress recognized the right of Indians to organize "for the purposes of local self-government and economic enterprise"; stated that future educational policy should be designed to "promote the study of Indian civilization, arts, crafts, skills, and traditions"; abolished the allotment policy and pledged the federal government to assist in "a constructive program of Indian land use and economic development," including annual appropriations for land purchases and a revolving credit fund for economic self-improvement; and created a special Court of Indian Affairs to remove Indians from the jurisdiction of state courts. During congressional debate, both the statement on educational policy, which promoted instruction in Indian culture and civilization, and the Indian court provision were deleted, as were various mandatory provisions relating to the restoration of allotted lands to the tribal estate. In addition, the Indians of Oklahoma were exempted from the act although remedial legislation passed in 1936 granted them access to funds for economic improvement and land purchases. The final bill was thus a compromise between Collier's goal of a new policy encouraging the growth of Indian society and culture and the traditional forces of assimilation.

Other legislation Collier successfully steered through the Congress were the Johnson-O'Malley Act in 1934, which enabled the federal government to contract with state governments for the provision of medical, educational, and agricultural services to Indians, and the Arts and Crafts Act of 1935, which created a federal board to encourage enlargement of the market for Indian goods and to protect Indian products from imitation through the use of government trademarks. His major defeat was the refusal of Congress to enact a bill creating a Court of Claims to settle Indian claims for past treaty violations. Following World War II, however, this legislation was secured.

Collier's effectiveness as commissioner declined after 1938 as the conservative coalition in Congress began to cripple New Deal programs through appropriation reductions. When the Indian Service was moved to Chicago in 1942 to make room in Washington for the expanding defense establishment, Collier was cut off from both administrative and legislative sources of power, and in February 1945 he resigned from office. With Saul Padover he formed the Institute for Ethnic Affairs which, until its demise in 1954, sought to establish civilian rather than military rule in the American-mandated islands of the Pacific and in Guam and American Samoa. In 1946-47 he served as an adviser on trusteeship matters to the American delegation to the United Nations General Assembly. In 1947 he was appointed professor of sociology and anthropology at the City College of New York, a position he held until retirement at the age of seventy in 1954. He then taught one year at Knox College as a John Hay Whitney Professor of Anthropology before retiring to Talpa, New Mexico, where he died.

Collier wrote two books that contain accounts of his career: *Indians of the Americas* (1947) and *From Every Zenith*, a memoir (1963). Collier's papers are in the Beinecke Rare Book and Manuscript Library, Yale University.—L. C. K.

Colman, Norman J. (1827-1911). Agriculturalist. Born near Richfield Springs, New York, Colman grew up in a farming area that was noted for the promotion of agricultural reforms and was the son of one of the leading activists. This influence later led Colman to promote similar programs of even greater magnitude in the Midwest.

After attending a local academy, Colman studied law at the University of Louisville. Following a successful law practice in New Albany, Indiana, with Michael H. Kerr, later a congressman and Speaker of the House, he moved in 1853 to St. Louis. Continuing the practice of law, Colman renewed his agricultural interests through the purchase of a country home and small farm on Creve Coeur Lake. He also purchased the *Valley Farmer*, an agricultural paper in which he was soon reporting the results of his experiments with different crops and varieties of fruit.

In 1856 Colman began lecturing on the need for agricultural improvement for Missouri's farmers and in 1858 helped organize the Missouri Fruit Growers Association. By the time of the Civil War he saw his influence spreading as numerous agricultural associations and fairs came into existence, and the circulation of the *Valley Farmer* grew.

The paper continued publication throughout the war, although the conflict hampered Colman's other agricultural activities. In 1865 he rechristened the paper *Colman's Rural World* and began to extend its influence beyond the Mississippi valley. Probably no man did more to popularize scientific agricultural improvement in the last half of the nineteenth century.

Meanwhile Colman was actively engaged in Missouri Democratic politics, serving in the legislature and as lieutenant governor (1874-76) and working hard to thwart the Grange effort to create a third party in the state. He was a strong supporter of the University of Missouri and played a major role in securing its agricultural college.

President Grover Cleveland appointed Colman commissioner of agriculture in 1885, and his subsequent work in enlarging the bureau led to its elevation to a separate executive department on February 11, 1889, with Colman as its first secretary. He also authored the Hatch Act, creating experiment stations with federal support in the states and territories. In March 1889 he resumed his varied agricultural pursuits from his St. Louis headquarters.

Colman received numerous honors for his work, including the decoration of *Officier du Merite Agricole*, presented to him by the president of France.

The standard biography is George F. Lemmer, *Norman J. Colman and Colman's Rural World* (1953). —W. E. P.

Coloma, California. Ghost town. Coloma is the site of the discovery of gold by James Marshall, who was erecting a sawmill on the south fork of the American River for John Sutter in January 1848. The discovery started the gold rush of 1849, and Coloma became a boom town almost overnight.

Today the discovery site is preserved as a state historical park, with appropriate historical markers and an extensive museum. A number of the original buildings have been preserved, including Marshall's home, the Coloma jail, four stores, and two churches: one Roman Catholic, the other Emmanuel Episcopal—the first Protestant church in the mining camps.

See Remi Nadeau, *Ghost Towns and Mining Camps of California* (1965); and Muriel S. Wolle, *The Bonanza Trail* (1953).—R. B. W.

colonial wars (1689-1763). Five nations colonized North America in the sixteenth and seventeenth centuries, competing for wealth, power, and prestige. Each was eliminated militarily by a stronger rival or, in the case of England and Spain, by the very colonies they had planted. Of these powers the Swedes on the Delaware and the Dutch along the Hudson were the weakest and first to go. Spain's feeble attempts to colonize north of Florida came to nought. And after the Dutch were expelled from New York for the second and last time in 1674 only England and France were left to contest for most of the Atlantic seaboard and the rich continental interior.

The first permanent French settlement was at Quebec in 1608. Montreal was founded in 1641 and other settlements were made in Acadia, or Nova Scotia, at the same time. French explorers, missionaries, and traders used the Great Lakes and Ottawa River as highways to penetrate the interior and trade with Indians as far west as Wisconsin and eventually the Dakotas. Permanent settlements in the West, however, came later and remained small and isolated. The English, in contrast, confined themselves to developing their seaboard colonies, the first of which was founded at Jamestown in 1607. England's colonies north of Maryland were limited to New England until they drove the Dutch from New York in 1664 and gained access to the Great Lakes by the Hudson-Mohawk route. Imperial rivalry for control of the interior did not fully develop until the two powers became definitely aligned against each other in Europe in 1689.

The origins of the first Anglo-French war in America (1628) lay in Europe. The English on this occasion actually captured Quebec, but the town was returned in the peace settlement. For a generation afterward the two nations were at peace. A similar war broke out in 1667, also from European causes, and with even fewer ramifications in America.

The Glorious Revolution of 1688 brought England into a coalition that William of Orange had created to contain the European expansionism of Louis XIV. The ensuing conflict, known in America as King William's War (1689-97), had separate roots in the New World in a growing intercolonial rivalry. The IROQUOIS CONFEDERACY of New York had allied themselves with the English in an effort to capture a major part of the western fur trade from the interior tribes who traded with Canada and were friendly with the French. By 1687 Governor Thomas Dongan of New York had begun to back the Iroquois against the French with armaments and promises of support in case of attack. As a result New York and New France were on the verge of a de facto war when war was formally declared in Europe. Moreover, border warfare had already broken out between the two nations and their Indian allies along the northern New England frontier, where control of the nearly uninhabited Maine coast was at stake. The chief French ally in this quarter was the powerful Abnaki tribe, which persistently raided the English settlements.

Although one of England's purposes in King William's War was to drive the French from Canada, other objectives at home prevented her from sending to America the necessary forces to fulfill this goal. The result was eight years of bloody but inconclusive border warfare involving primarily Indians and frontiersmen on both sides. In July 1689 the Iroquois staged the terrible Lachine Massacre near Montreal, and in the following winter Canada, under the governorship of Count Frontenac and with its Indian allies, retaliated with three raids on the English frontier, resulting in the destruction of Schenectady, New York; Salmon Falls, New Hampshire; and Falmouth and Portland, Maine. Massachusetts contributed the most significant efforts against Canada. With little outside help it organized a fleet under Sir William Phips, capturing Port Royal, Acadia, in May 1690, and then joined in an intercolonial plan for a joint invasion of Canada proper. The plan, calling for a seaborne attack on Quebec and a simultaneous overland attack from Albany on Montreal, failed because it lacked the active participation of England. The war dragged to a close in 1697, with the Peace of Ryswick changing no boundaries and settling nothing. The Iroquois, disillusioned by nonsupport from England, made a belated peace of their own with the French in 1701, adopting a policy of cautious neutrality.

Queen Anne's War (1702-13), as it was called in America, concerned the question of the Spanish succession. Even more than before, however, the respective colonies had a stake of their own in its outcome. France had used the interlude of peace to found a new colony in Louisiana in 1699 and to build a fort and trading post at Detroit in 1701, strengthening its position in the West and correspondingly alarming the Iroquois and British. So far as the northern frontier was concerned, however, most of the fighting in this conflict was limited to New England. The New England frontiersmen sustained repeated assaults, including the Deerfield Massacre of 1704, and often retaliated, but no serious effort was made to strike at Canada until 1709. This time the British were to provide the fleet to attack Quebec. But the British government changed its mind, and the fleet never appeared. In 1710 the British and colonials took Acadia. The following year the plan of 1709 was revived. Although the British fleet appeared, the attack was called off because of heavy fog, and the fleet returned to England, leaving in the lurch the colonial army which had assembled near Montreal. The Peace of Utrecht (1713) reflected Britain's limited successes, confirming its possession of Nova Scotia and the Hudson Bay country.

More than thirty years elapsed before the third intercolonial war broke out, but the formal peace was interrupted in the 1720s by an inconclusive war between Massachusetts and the French-inspired Abnaki in Maine. New York in 1727 made its strongest effort so far to tap the western fur trade directly by building a fortified post at Oswego, where the western Indians passed on their way to Montreal. But the French had already diminished its effect with an additional fort of their own at Niagara. In 1731 they built a fort at Crown Point on

Lake Champlain, designed to protect Montreal against further invasion attempts from Albany.

King George's War (1744-48), the third intercolonial war, resembled its predecessors in its European origin, its American ramifications, and its inconclusiveness. As before, border warfare predominated from New York to Maine, with the French and their Indian allies taking the initiative. The Iroquois, for the most part, adhered to their policy of neutrality, and the British did little to inspire hope of decisive action against Canada. The only significant accomplishment was Massachusetts' capture, with British naval assistance, of the major French fort at Louisbourg on Cape Breton Island in 1745. The fort was returned, however, in the peace settlement.

By 1748 the contest for North America had already been partially settled, not through the previous indecisive military operations, but by more than a century of intensive English colonization. Although the French still controlled the interior, 60,000 Canadians could never shake the hold that 1,250,000 British colonists had fastened on the Atlantic seaboard from Maine to Georgia. The last great intercolonial war, the French and Indian War, would decide whether the British could dislodge the French from North America.

In terms of men engaged, battles fought, and victories won, the French and Indian War dwarfed the earlier wars. Moreover, it broke out in America two years before its European counterpart (Seven Years' War) and constituted a major theater of action. The fall of Canada in 1759-61 was Britain's major victory, and with other French defeats around the world, Britain emerged as the dominant colonial power.

English and French expansion in America conflicted at many points, but the chief convergence came in the upper Ohio valley. Fur traders and land speculators from Pennsylvania and Virginia saw this area as their main source of future activity and profit, and had begun to move into it. The French felt bound to stop English penetration of the Appalachian barrier, lest control of the Ohio lead to control of the entire Mississippi valley. Thus, the French took the initiative.

In 1749 Céloron de Blainville was sent with a military force to the upper Ohio, where he formally laid claim to the region for France. In 1752 the French destroyed a British trading post on the Miami River. The following year they began a series of forts to connect Lake Erie with the forks of the Ohio, in response to which the British formulated the ALBANY PLAN OF UNION. When the Virginians tried to counter with a fort of their own at the latter point, the French forcibly expelled them and built a stronghold themselves, Fort Duquesne, in 1754. Virginia lost no time in sending a party of militia under the twenty-two-year-old Colonel George WASHINGTON to demand French evacuation, but he was defeated in July at nearby Fort Necessity in the battle of GREAT MEADOWS, the first battle of the war.

England responded to this challenge by sending General Edward Braddock in 1755 with two regiments of redcoats and orders to take Fort Duquesne. After elaborate preparations, Braddock carved his own road through the wilderness, only to suffer humiliating defeat—and to lose his life—in a French and Indian ambush less than ten miles from his destination (see BRADDOCK'S ROAD). Britain's position in the West was shaken, and for three long years it proceeded to worsen. The

New York Iroquois showed signs of defecting to the French despite the efforts of Sir William JOHNSON, superintendent of Indian Affairs for the northern colonies. In August 1756 the French captured the British post at Oswego on Lake Ontario and a year later took Fort William Henry on Lake George. Meanwhile the Delaware and Shawnee Indians took the warpath on the side of the French and lashed out unremittingly against the frontier settlements of Pennsylvania.

When the tide finally began to turn in 1758, it was owing in great measure to the organizing genius of William Pitt, the new English prime minister. Greater armies under better commanders were sent over. Also Johnson's diplomacy with the Iroquois took effect and they in turn commanded the Delaware Indians to lay down the hatchet in Pennsylvania. In July 1758 the British suffered their last significant defeat, when they failed to take the French fort at Ticonderoga. In the same month a British force under General Jeffrey Amherst captured Louisbourg on Cape Breton Island, guarding the ocean gateway to Canada. Soon afterward a colonial force captured Fort Frontenac at the juncture of the St. Lawrence and Lake Ontario, virtually cutting off Canada from the interior. A British army under General John Forbes pushed its way in November to Braddock's earlier destination, replacing Fort Duquesne with Fort Pitt at the forks of the Ohio (see FORBES' ROAD). In July 1759 an Anglo-Iroquois force under William Johnson captured Fort Niagara. At the same time the French evacuated Ticonderoga and Crown Point on Lake Champlain and withdrew northward to Montreal.

These earlier successes were soon overshadowed by Britain's supreme victory, the capture of Quebec. In this battle, the young British General James Wolfe was pitted against the Marquis de Montcalm, the French commander-in-chief in America and architect of earlier French victories. Wolfe led a fleet of 168 ships, with an army of more than nine thousand soldiers aboard, up the St. Lawrence to besiege and capture the city, situated almost impregnably atop a cliff high above the river. He discovered a narrow and unguarded path leading up from the riverbank and took his men onto the Plains of Abraham behind the city. In the ensuing battle both commanders lost their lives, but the British went on to rout the defenders, and Quebec surrendered on September 18, 1759. Cut off from outside help, Montreal fell before a three-pronged attack from east, west, and south a year later. Detroit and the other posts in the Great Lakes region were surrendered late in 1760 and the next year, bringing French control of Canada to a close.

In the peace negotiations that followed there was some talk in England of giving Canada back to France— Canada had never paid France for its upkeep—and of taking the sugar-rich West Indian island of Guadeloupe instead. But in the end, influenced by considerations of long-range imperial advantage rather than short-range profit, Britain retained Canada. The Treaty of Paris of 1763 (see PARIS, TREATY OF, 1763) also gave Britain that half of Louisiana lying east of the Mississippi, while the western half, with New Orleans, went to Spain. France had lost its American empire; but Britain soon found that the major external danger that had served to tie her own colonies to her had also been lost.

See H. Baker-Crothers, *Virginia and the French and*

Indian War (1928); H. Bird, *Battle for a Continent* (1965); D. H. Corkran, *The Cherokee Frontier* (1962); J. R. Cuneo, *Robert Rogers of the Rangers* (1959); L. H. Gibson, *The British Empire Before the American Revolution* (1942-54); C. E. Hamilton, ed., *Braddock's Defeat* (1959); W. R. Jacobs, *Diplomacy and Indian Gifts* (1950); Walter O'Meara, *Guns at the Forks* (1965); T. C. Pease, ed., *Anglo-French Boundary Disputes in the West, 1749-1763* (1936); Max Savelle, *The Diplomatic History of the Canadian Boundary, 1749-1763* (1940); and J. C. Webster, *The Forts of Chignecto* (1930).—A. W. T.

Colorado. When the Mexican War ended in 1848, the land that was to become Colorado was virtually void of white settlers. The Indian tribes of the region—the long-tenured Ute of Colorado's western slope and the more recently arrived Arapaho and Cheyenne on the eastern prairies, the Comanche, Kiowa, and Apache on the southern fringes, and the Sioux along the northern borders—had seen nomadic white men come and go for decades. Spanish explorers from New Mexico had searched for metals, blazed trails, and chased fugitives there since the seventeenth century; French traders from Illinois had wandered up the river courses en route to Santa Fe; Americans had followed Zebulon M. Pike and Stephen H. Long and John C. Frémont through the valleys and passes. Other men had pursued the beaver trails into and out of the region, some of them stopping long enough to establish temporary trading posts in the fur or buffalo-robe trade. None of these nomads had stayed.

Permanent white settlement in Colorado began in 1851 when New Mexican farmers moved north onto lands in the San Luis and (later) Arkansas River valleys originally granted by Mexico a decade earlier. In their small villages they established the Spanish-speaking Catholic culture that still survives in the southern counties of the state of Colorado.

English-speaking white men invaded the Colorado frontier in larger numbers a few years later. In July 1858 a remnant of a band of argonauts, prospecting for gold in the foothills of the Rocky Mountains near present-day DENVER, found "pay dirt" in their mining pans, precipitating the Pikes Peak gold rush (see GOLD AND SILVER RUSHES). An estimated fifty thousand men reached the new El Dorado in the spring of 1859, and perhaps half that many men remained long enough to engage in serious gold-seeking. In the beginning, simple "washing pan" placer mining prevailed. But rich lodes of gold ore were soon discovered, requiring more complex separation processes including smelting. As such metallurgists as Nathaniel Peter HILL developed more sophisticated techniques of mining and ore reduction, the lone prospectors and simple partnerships were replaced by corporations and such entrepreneurs as David Holliday MOFFAT, who were capable of securing requisite capital funds from eastern and midwestern investors.

Much of the mining was concentrated in what became Gilpin County, where CENTRAL CITY, Nevadaville, Black Hawk, and other towns long since turned ghost boomed into population centers. Denver retained its early lead as the principal supply town for the mining camps in the mountains. Like most frontiersmen, the Pikes Peakers soon sensed a need for "law and order." Too far removed from the seats of government of the organized territories encompassing the gold fields—in

Kansas and Nebraska—the miners and townsmen indigenously fashioned miners' courts and claim clubs to secure their property and lives. And they optimistically erected an extralegal government for what they called Jefferson Territory. It proved impotent for its purposes within a short time, but in February 1861, after Kansas became a state, Congress responded to local requests, creating Colorado Territory with the same boundaries as the present state.

William GILPIN, the first territorial governor, and his successor, John EVANS, found their principal duty in shoring up Colorado's defenses. They had reason to fear both invasion from without and a race war between whites and Indians within Colorado. The gold mines attracted Confederate attention to the area until March 1862, when a Union force, including a regiment of Coloradans, routed a Confederate column in the Rio Grande valley in New Mexico. The governors warily watched Arapaho and Cheyenne tribesmen, for their depredations on isolated settlers generated fears that they planned a general campaign against the whites (see CHEYENNE-ARAPAHO WAR).

As a defensive thrust, Colonel John CHIVINGTON, on November 29, 1864, attempted to exterminate a major part of those tribes on their reservation in southeastern Colorado (see CIVIL WAR and SAND CREEK MASSACRE). Far from ending the fears, however, the atrocities committed by Chivington's men led the Indians to seek revenge. Only the end of the Civil War, allowing the deployment of Union veterans on the smoldering frontier, brought peace to the region with the removal of the Arapaho and Cheyenne to reservations in present-day Oklahoma.

The end of the Civil War also brought answers to another territorial need: improved transportation. Although the route of the first transcontinental railroad ran north of the territory, in 1870 a branch line, the Denver Pacific, tied the territorial capital to the transcontinental by linking Denver with Cheynne, Wyoming. The Kansas Pacific linked Denver directly with Kansas City in 1870, and soon additional lines crossed the territory—the Colorado Central, the Denver and Rio Grande, and the Denver, South Park, and Pacific.

The railroads spurred the territory's population. Towns and mining camps, ranches and farms were more easily accessible, diminishing dramatically the isolated posture of the place. Farmers could not easily be convinced to take up lands east of the Rockies, however, for the legend of the Great American Desert (as Pike and other early explorers had described the region) permeated public thought. (On the problem of watering the western desert, see Moses HALLETT.) The railroads, with land subsidies to dispose of and interested in rapidly developing the area, advertised the virtues of the territory. Entrepreneurs attempted to "plant" colonies, particularly within the ARKANSAS RIVER valleys of the eastern slope, where waters were available for taming the desert through irrigation. Union Colony, settled in 1870 under the leadership of Nathan Meeker, aided by his friend Horace Greeley, was perhaps the best known of a series of adventures in Colorado colonization.

The issue of statehood permeated Colorado politics during the fifteen years of territorial status from 1861 to 1876. Local interests shifted between desire and distaste for statehood, and national political leaders also tended to vacillate in their opinions about the advantages and disadvantages of Colorado statehood. In 1864 national Republican leaders, seeking additional electoral votes, invited statehood, but the territorial voters spurned the offer. Then when statehood sentiment, promoted by such people as William Newton BYERS and Casimero BARELA, seemed improved in Colorado, federal officials were no longer interested. Local efforts in 1865, 1866, and 1868 were aborted by failure to win federal approval.

Not until 1876 did national Republican needs and local interests harmonize, and in this year Colorado was admitted to the Union. In preparation for their new status, the Colorado voters selected delegates to draft a constitution. Meeting from December 1875 until June 1876, the convention prepared a state charter. At the time observers commented on the failure to set clear directions on critical issues, including public regulation of corporations and woman suffrage. The delegates, however, were principally motivated by their desire to gain statehood and had purposefully skirted divisive issues. Given this goal, they succeeded admirably, for the electorate overwhelmingly voted approval on July 1—15,443 to 4,062. On August 1, 1876, President Grant issued the proclamation of statehood. (Now, decades since the charter's adoption, it has proved too detailed and inclusive.) Henry Moore TELLER and Jerome Bonaparte CHAFFEE were the first senators.

Colorado's early years as a state were marked with optimistic enterprise and rapid growth. While gold had lured the original Anglo population to the mountains, Colorado now entered its legendary silver era. Some silver had been mined earlier in the Georgetown area, such as at SILVER PLUME, and at Caribou, but Colorado's greatest silver camp—the "Cloud City" called LEADVILLE—was born in 1877, incorporated the next year, and by 1880 claimed itself the second largest city in the state. The Leadville story follows classic mining-lore contours, beginning when two prospectors (grubstaked by one of Colorado's favorite demi-heroes, Horace Austin Warner TABOR) almost accidentally discovered the Little Pittsburgh Mine. Then followed the rush of thousands to the camp to make their fortunes mining silver or mining miners. Demands for goods and services far outstripped supplies until the railroads, racing for the market, tied the place to Denver and other distribution centers. Leadville provided the high drama of fortunes made and lost overnight; those who were there claimed there never was another place like Leadville.

Of course there was; or, at least, there were other silver camps claiming mines as magic as Leadville's. ASPEN (even more remotely centered in the mountains), Gunnison, Silver Cliffe, and (later) Creede sought to duplicate the Leadville luck. And there were additional lodes of ore—silver and gold—in the farther reaches of the western slope. Eventually miners pushed onto lands reserved for the UTE INDIANS, and when the minerals there seemed promising they summoned methods to displace the Indians. New treaties could be arranged to clear temporarily the most promising terrain. Ultimately—or so almost every white man believed—"the Utes must go."

And go they did, much sooner than many expected, for in 1879 the Meeker Massacre proved excuse and occasion to force the issue. Nathan Meeker had won appointment as Indian agent to the northern Ute, but he proved less able in directing affairs at the White River Agency than he had in the town of Greeley. When he summoned federal troops to quiet troublesome tribesmen, he ignited an uprising among his charges. The Indians ambushed a military relief column and slaughtered Meeker and the male employees at the agency. They carried off the women and children as hostages; Chief Ouray and Otto MEARS were instrumental in gaining their release.

These events provided fuel enough to energize the total removal of the Ute. Forced negotiations brought cession of their reserved lands and resettlement in Utah and the extreme southwestern corner of Colorado. Now the western slope was cleared for white men's ways, and soon Grand Junction, Delta, Montrose, and Durango were advertising their merits as growing communities.

Silver strikes and Indian removals punctuated the history of central and western Colorado in the years from 1876 to 1890. The eastern slope created its own history in the rise and fall of the open-range cattle industry. Cattlemen trailed stock northward from the Texas ranges to unclaimed and unfenced lands for fattening and shipment to the Omaha, Kansas City, and Chicago slaughterhouses. The enterprise paralleled, in structure, the mining ventures. Cattle barons such as John Wesley ILIFF and John Wesley PROWERS dominated the early stages; corporations became active participants later. The cattle enterprises particularly attracted British investors, such as those involved in the Prairie Cattle Company. Ultimately the combined calamities of range overstocking, disease, weather, and hostile homesteaders and sheepherders collapsed the "boom." Then the cattle kingdoms along the watercourses of the Arkansas and South Platte valleys gradually converted to "ranch" operations.

Cattle, silver, colonies, and railroads all contributed to the growth of population during this era of optimistic enterprise. In the 1890 federal census Colorado registered a total of 413,249 people, more than twice the total of a decade earlier. As befitted a rapidly fading frontier, monuments to permanence in the form of opera houses, hotels, courthouses, and railroad stations attracted local enthusiasm. And cultural advancement could surely be observed in the new colleges opening their doors—the University of Denver, the University of Colorado at Boulder, the Agricultural College at Fort Collins, the School of Mines at Golden, and Colorado College at Colorado Springs.

These obvious achievements commanded respect from all newcomers, both those intending to settle in the state and the transient visitors—the tourists—who arrived in increasing numbers each year. Tourists had come to Colorado to see the mountains or hunt big game from its earliest days. Now an additional dimension was added. The high altitudes, with their thinner, sunlit air, promised relief from respiratory diseases, particularly tuberculosis. As the numbers of "lungers" increased, as well as the sanatoriums and "health hotels" to accommodate them (as those in COLORADO SPRINGS), a largely unchronicled but significant chapter of the state's history was created.

Colorado's age of optimism came to an abrupt and disappointing conclusion in the last decade of the nineteenth century. Depressed agricultural prices afflicted the farmers and ranchers on the eastern slope; decreasing silver prices alarmed the mine and smelter men of the mountains. The fragile nature of Colorado's economy was fully exposed. Not even the opening of the CRIPPLE CREEK gold mines, with their impressive production records, could reverse the deepening economic crisis which, in time, inflicted its wrath on the state's social and political structures.

In these circumstances, there was more than ordinary interest in the inflationary scheme of the free-silver advocates, who sponsored the idea of federal resumption of silver coinage on an unlimited basis. Free silver (see SILVER ISSUE) promised a panacea that would release Colorado from its economic distress. When neither the Republicans nor the Democrats seemed interested in sponsoring silver salvation, Colorado voters turned to the new Populist party, which had included free silver among its reform proposals. In 1892 the voters elected Populist Davis Hanson WAITE governor of the state.

Waite's term as governor was marked with turbulence, much of it generated by the country-wide Panic of 1893 and the depression that followed. Now Populist ideas and the silver issue in particular commanded greater attention. In 1896 the national Democratic party incorporated the concept into its platform and selected a silver spokesman, William Jennings Bryan, its presidential candidate. In Colorado, politician John Franklin SHAFROTH gathered support for Bryan.

Republican William McKinley and the gold standard triumphed in that contest. The legacy, for Colorado, was dislocated party allegiances in an era of continuing industrial warfare. The silver mines and smelters never recovered their former economic health; the dry-farming region on the eastern plains awaited another, later invasion of optimistic sod-busters. Labor conflicts added to the instability of the times. Working men organized unions for collective bargaining and met, head-on, determined resistance from the owners of mines, smelters, and factories.

The CRIPPLE CREEK STRIKES produced violent clashes between the mine owners and the Western Federation of Miners in 1894 and again in 1904. A decade later something of a climax in Colorado's labor warfare was reached in the southern coal fields at a place called Ludlow Station. The state militia destroyed a tent colony housing families of striking members of the United Mine Workers of America. Thirteen deaths resulted, bringing public demands for more rational methods of resolving industrial disputes. Those strikers indicted for murder were represented by Edward Prestiss COSTIGAN. Belatedly, the legislature responded by creating the Industrial Commission, adding in time such substantive reforms as workmen's compensation.

The outbreak of World War I in 1914 finally provided an impetus for economic revival as the extraordinary demands for products stimulated mines, ranches, and farms. Eastern wheat lands expanded as the war economy sent prices higher than two dollars a bushel. Colorado's newest irrigated crop—sugar beets—was in similar demand. In the mountains, Colorado's mining enterprises responded to the need for such rare metals as molybdenum, vanadium, and tungsten. These unusual demands proved short-lived, however, for with the end of the war markets collapsed. Wheat lands that

perhaps should never have been plowed and mines that could not compete with peacetime foreign producers declined and, in many cases, were deserted.

Thus the stage was set for what was to be Colorado's quietest era—the years between the world wars. During this time population grew less rapidly than at any other time in the state's history. From 1920 to 1940 the total population increased from 939,639 to 1,123,296—a rate of growth slightly less than 10 percent. That might be compared with earlier rates, such as 48 percent between 1900 and 1910, or later rates, such as 32.3 percent between 1950 and 1960 and 25.8 percent between 1960 and 1970. Between 1920 and 1930, for the first and only decade in its history, Colorado's proportional population growth was smaller than the national average. No new mining ventures appeared to duplicate the earlier gold and silver bonanzas. Agriculture, now more important economically than mining, and manufacturing advanced slowly. Even tourism declined, particularly after 1930, as the Great Depression limited the number of people who could afford railroad tickets or automobile excursions.

Oil production was an exception. In places such as Canon City, where the first well had pumped petroleum in 1862, oil had long been a neighborhood affair. But in 1925 petroleum took on new significance with the opening of the Wellington Dome near Fort Collins and the oil fields near Craig. Gas and oil could also be killers of dreams. A natural gas pipeline from Texas reached Denver in 1928. Colorado coal miners then found it more difficult to compete with the new fuels for the residential and industrial markets.

There was also excitement over another of nature's fuels—water-turning turbines for generation of electricity. A dramatic example of multipurpose reclamation planning, involving power production, captured much attention when Congress in 1937 authorized the construction of the Colorado-Big Thompson project. The scheme entailed a literal reversing of the flow of water through a tunnel under the Continental Divide to bring "artificial rainfall" from the better-watered but underpopulated western slope to the water-hungry farmers of the eastern slope. Irrigation waters, electrical power generation, recreational facilities, and forest conservation were all designed benefits from the project. World War II disrupted construction schedules and inflation drove the price tag upward, but by 1947 waters flowed under the divide through the Alva B. Adams Tunnel. Success indicated feasibility of additional dreams. During the 1960s the Blue Mesa, Rifle Gap, and Lemon dams of the Upper Colorado project and the Arkansas-Frying Pan transmontane systems were constructed.

Such federal reclamation projects are illustrative of the continuous and significant role the policies and programs of the national government play in Colorado's development. World War II provided additional demonstration of that role. Military needs again called for increased production from wheat and sugar-beet fields, factories, and some mines. But, in addition, the defense departments constructed training camps and bases and other major military installations that remained in operation (some in expanded circumstances) in the postwar years. Colorado Springs, for example, emerged from the war years with a complexion quite different from its resort- and college-town days. The city's wartime installations remained in active use; the North American Air Defense Command was headquartered at Ent Air Base; and the United States Air Force Academy was constructed just outside the city.

Other defense-oriented activities of the postwar era were concerned with uranium production and processing. Western slope Colorado, particularly the Grand Junction area, witnessed a genuine mining boom in the early atomic age. Processing plants, including the Dow Chemical facilities at Rocky Flats between Denver and Boulder, expanded the impact of uranium production upon the Colorado economy. In similar manner, the new missile enterprises brought a new dimension to the state's industrial character. Large-scale industrial operations within the state had always been relatively limited, hardly extending beyond the Colorado Fuel and Iron Company plants at Pueblo and the Shwayder Brothers (Samsonite luggage) and Gates Rubber operations at Denver. In 1956, however, the Martin-Marietta Company constructed the Titan missile plant near Littleton, a facility that at one time employed upward of fifteen thousand wage-earners. Electronic and space-oriented activities, especially research and development operations, clustered along the eastern foothills of the Rockies. Scientific institutions, such as the Federal Bureau of Standards and the National Center for Atmospheric Research at Boulder, expanded the state's scientific-industrial complex during the postwar years.

The effects of such development on population distribution within Colorado are not surprising: the state has become increasingly urban. In the 1960s almost three quarters of the Colorado people (in 1970 totaling 2,207,259) lived in urban centers, and ninety-five percent of the urban dwellers resided within a narrow strip about 30 miles wide and 150 miles long, stretching from Pueblo in the south to Fort Collins in the north along the eastern base of the Rocky Mountains. Former mining and agricultural regions have lost both absolute and relative population. Once-lively gold-, silver-, and coal-producing regions are now all but deserted; agricultural areas, responding to technological changes that have increased the size and reduced the number of operating units, have been drained of population. Today farm residents account for only about seven percent of the state's inhabitants.

As Colorado's population has become more urban, it has also become more native. During the latter nineteenth century, twenty percent of the state's population was foreign-born; today only two and a half percent are nonnative. The European immigrants who found employment in mines and smelters were gradually assimilated into the dominant Anglo culture. In contrast, Spanish-speaking residents have retained their own culture, both those within the southern counties, where their heritage extends to the earliest of Colorado's permanent white settlements, and the Mexican immigrants, mostly agricultural field workers, who have come to Colorado more recently. Negro population has always been small, representing now approximately 2.3 percent of the total population. Most Colorado blacks live in Denver or Colorado Springs.

Politically, contemporary Colorado lacks a dominant partisan party. For many years the two major parties divided the United States senatorial seats; Republicans and Democrats often have traded state offices, including the governorship. Although manifestations of extremist politics have appeared from time to time, the short-lived flirtation with the Ku Klux Klan in the 1920s marked the last deviation on the part of elected state officials from major party politics.

Throughout its history, from territorial creation to the present, Colorado's relationships with the federal government have been of greater significance than its internal partisan politics. From Indian removals to interstate water compacts, from railroad construction to uranium production, the state has remained, to some extent, a colony of the nation. More than one third of the land of Colorado is controlled by the federal government. Future exploitation of known resources, including enormous oil-shale deposits in western Colorado, depend on federal participation in development. Almost all residents of the state keep partial attention focused on Washington, D.C., for the future, no less than the past, seems inextricably related to federal policies.

Meanwhile, many Coloradans are aware of the unique opportunities their state's climate, scenery, and history affords to lure the tourist and his vacation dollars. Old mining towns have been revived to meet the challenge; Aspen, with its ski slopes and cultural enterprises in the summer, and Central City, with its summer opera, are but two examples. Cowboys and Indians, beaver trappers and gold prospectors—these and all the other tokens of the Old West provide a heritage enticing vacation-seekers of the lost frontier to the Centennial State.

The most detailed history of Colorado is LeRoy R. Hafen, ed., *Colorado and Its People: A Narrative and Topical History of the Centennial State*, 4 vols. (1948). Carl Ubbelohde, Maxine Benson, and Duane A. Smith, *A Colorado History* 3rd ed. (1972) is a briefer narrative. See also Frank Hall, *History of the State of Colorado*, 4 vols. (1889-95). Contemporary statistical data is conveniently gathered in the official *Colorado Yearbook*, published annually from 1918 to 1928 and biennially since then.
—C. U.

Colorado Plateau. See PHYSIOGRAPHY OF THE UNITED STATES: *Colorado Plateau*.

Colorado River. Named in the 1770s by the Spanish priest and explorer Garcés after the reddish color of its water, the Colorado River is the master stream of the Southwest and drains an area of 244,000 square miles, much of which lies in the desert and semidesert regions. The river is 1,440 miles long and carries the water draining off of seven states and a portion of Mexico. Its basin contains some of the most colorful and angular landscapes found in the United States created by the differential erosion of uplifted blocks of the earth's crust. Its source lies high on the western slopes of the Colorado Rockies in Grand Lake at an elevation of 8,369 feet. The upper river flowing across Colorado was long called the Grand, and the name is still used by some today. In this portion of its course the river flows through a mountainous region and at places has cut deeply into the rock. Its gradient is steep and the flow of water swift. At one point in Gore Canyon, eighty miles above Glenwood Springs, it tumbles precipitously through deep canyons, dropping 360 feet in five miles. The Gunnison is the principal tributary of this portion of the river, and the

The Colorado River as photographed by a Geological Survey member in 1871-72.

nature of the landscape begins to change below the point at which it joins the Colorado. Below Grand Junction the river crosses into Utah and is joined by the Dolores and Green rivers and later by the San Juan. This portion of the basin is an arid plateau into which the main river and its tributaries have cut deep trenches. Large portions of the area contribute little or no runoff to the river and many of the smaller tributaries contribute only sporadically to the flow of the Colorado. Shortly after entering Arizona from Lees Ferry until the river empties into Lake Mead, the river is entrenched into the southwestern margin of the Colorado Plateau. As the plateau rose during geologic time, the river eroded ever deeper, creating a series of canyons, the best known of which is GRAND CANYON. Tributaries of the river in this section are subject to flash floods and flow intermittently. Most are deeply incised in the plateau surface and have spectacular rapids and falls as they near the main stream. The largest of these secondary rivers is the Little Colorado, which drains much of northeastern Arizona. On the north side of the river, the Virgin River, Kanab Creek, and Muddy River flow into the Colorado. Below the Grand Wash Cliffs, which marks the lower end of the Grand Canyon, and the edge of the Colorado Plateau the river flows across the Virgin and Black mountain ranges, again cutting canyons along the way. Below Lake Mead the river flows in a broad flood plain until it reaches its delta area below the border with Mexico. Along the way it is joined by two tributaries draining much of the western part of New

Mexico and central Arizona, the Bill Williams and Gila river systems.

The higher portions of the basin are covered with forests of pine, fir, spruce, and silver-stemmed aspens, among which are grassy mountain meadows. Piñon and juniper forests and chaparral cover the intermediate slopes and more humid portions of the plateau country. At lower elevations clump grasses, desert shrubs, yucca, and cactus predominate; large areas are virtually devoid of vegetation. Because of the ruggedness of much of the country and its sparse human population, wild game abounds. Deer, elk, and antelope are found at higher elevations. Mountain lions, wildcats, lynx, and other predatory animals are still to be found in remote situations, while coyotes harass livestock and prey upon gophers, rabbits, and other small mammals. Birds are numerous.

Rain and snow fall in abundance on the upper basin of the river but much of the middle and lower portions of the basin are relatively dry. Most of the flow is derived from winter storms originating over the Pacific Ocean; summer rain comes from thunderstorms bearing water from the Gulf of Mexico or from the tropical Pacific Ocean off the west coast of Mexico. Most of the summer rain is lost by evaporation, but the larger storms create flash floods in the tributary streams and occasionally cause the Colorado itself to rise abruptly in its channel. It is estimated that over the basin as a whole only ten percent of the precipitation ends up as river flow. Thus, most of the flow is derived from the melting of the winter snowpack; after a wet winter, the Colorado becomes a raging torrent as the meltwater from the snow packs in the Rockies form rivulets and join forces in the tributaries and main stem of the river. Before the river was modified by man, the Colorado overflowed its banks below the canyon section and flooded vast areas of its floodplain, spilling occasionally into the Salton Basin to create temporary lakes and seas. In contrast, the flows during summers of seasons with low runoff became a trickle, fed only by the melting of snowbanks in the high mountains of the interior. The flow of the river also fluctuates greatly from year to year and is decreasing as man is diverting more and more water for agricultural use.

Man has occupied the basin for a long time, and some of the finest examples of pueblo dwellings are found in the drainage basin of the San Juan River and other tributaries of the Colorado in the Four Corners region of Utah, Colorado, Arizona, and New Mexico. Here primitive Americans diverted streams, grew their crops, and built their villages long before the first European arrived on the scene. Except for the Hopi, the Zuñi, and the Rio Grande pueblos, most of the Indians had abandoned these ancestral homes by the end of the thirteenth century, about the time that the nomadic tribes of Apache and Navaho entered the area. The seven "golden cities" of Cíbola, which drew the Spanish conquistadores into the region, turned out to be dusty adobe buildings housing relatively poor American Indians.

The first Spaniards to see the river were on board a ship under the command of Hernando de Alarcón, who explored the stream for a short distance upstream from its mouth in 1540. Two years later members of Coronado's expedition under Garcia López de Cárdenas discovered Grand Canyon but were unable to descend its steep walls to reach the river below. Permanent settlement by the Spaniards in the Colorado Basin was limited to its southern margins, where a few brave missionaries, soldiers, and settlers clustered around Tubac and Tucson in present-day Arizona. Here they utilized the waters of the Santa Cruz River to grow their crops in the shadow of the fort protecting them from marauding Apache warriors. During most of the period of Spanish and Mexican domination of the region the Colorado remained a barrier separating the northern frontier of New Spain from the California settlement. One abortive attempt to establish a foothold at the Yuma crossing failed when the Indians destroyed the missions established there, killing the missionaries sent there to convert them.

Fur trapping brought the first Americans to the region. Beginning in 1824 William H. Ashley brought a large band of trappers into the Green River country, and shortly thereafter some of the more famous mountain men made their appearance in various parts of the basin. James O. Pattie, R. W. Hardy, Jedediah Smith, Kit Carson, Ewing Young, and William Wolfskill all spent time in the area gathering pelts. In the early 1840s John C. Frémont led his exploring parties through much of the upper Colorado country. First exploration of the river from the north was by Major John Powell, who in 1869 led an expedition from Green River, Wyoming, to the mouth of the Virgin River in Nevada. Thus he became the first white man to see all of the Grand Canyon from the surface of the river.

Most of the basin was acquired from Mexico by the Treaty of Guadalupe Hidalgo (1848) and the Gadsden Purchase (1853) which added the land south of the Gila to the United States. After the discovery of gold in California thousands of Americans poured across the basin following the Gila Trail to the Colorado crossing at Yuma or at Needles farther north along the river. Earlier, Americans following the Oregon and California trails had crossed the headwaters of the Green River in their westward journeys.

With the establishment of Fort Yuma in 1851 and the use of steamboats to carry military personnel and supplies up the Colorado, American utilization of the Colorado River began in earnest (see TRANSPORTATION ON THE COLORADO RIVER). The first American settlements in the basin were military posts designed to protect Americans traveling across the region. However, shortly after the establishment of their settlements in the Salt Lake oasis, the Mormons began to penetrate the plateau country into the headwaters of streams tributary to the Colorado. In Arizona, the gold and silver discoveries led to the establishment of mining camps along the southern and western margins of the state. The need to supply feed for the army horses at the military posts led to the beginnings of agriculture in the Salt River valley in 1869, when Jack Swilling cleaned out and enlarged some of the prehistoric canals of the Hohokam Indians, who had developed a sophisticated system of irrigated agriculture some centuries earlier. In 1877 Thomas Blythe made the first filing on Colorado River water in California and diverted a portion of the river to water fields in the vicinity of the town that now bears his name. The discovery of rich mineral deposits in the upper Colorado resulted in the building of railroads and the evolution of mining and farming settlements in that region. Near the juncture of the Gunnison and Colorado rivers the Grand Valley Canal was constructed in 1883 to irrigate the lands of the Grand Valley in western Colorado. The potential for large-scale irrigation of portions of the lower basin and of the adjacent Salton Sink were observed early, and around the turn of the century the California Development Company began to divert Colorado River water into the Imperial Valley (see the IMPERIAL VALLEY AND THE SALTON SEA). Because of the faulty engineering works and an unusual spring flood, the canal leading into the Imperial Valley became enlarged, and soon all of the flow of the Colorado River was pouring into the valley, creating the Salton Sea. From 1905 to 1907 the Southern Pacific Railroad, whose transcontinental tracks ran through the area, attempted to divert the river back into its course. It finally succeeded. Because this disaster occurred just as the nation was embarking on a new course in the management of the water resources of the West, it sparked

Colorado River

the development of a number of attempts to control the flow of western rivers. The Yuma project on the Colorado and the Salt River project on the main tributary of the Gila were among the first of these to be completed. With the completion of Hoover Dam in 1936, the river was finally controlled.

A treaty with Mexico in 1946 guaranteed Mexico 1.5 million acre-feet of water with no mention of quality. Development of agriculture along the Colorado has brought increasing loads of salt into the river, and the water the Mexicans are getting is becoming saltier and saltier. They maintain that they are entitled to good-quality water for their farms on the Colorado delta. The United States government has agreed to install a desalinization plant near Yuma to take care of the problem.

See American Geographical Society, *Story of the Colorado River* (1970); Edwin Corle, *The Story of the Grand Canyon* (1951); Norris Hundley, Jr., *Dividing the Waters* (1966); Daniel B. Luten, "The Use and Misuse of a River," *The American West* (May 1967); National Research Council, Committee on Water, National Academy of Sciences, *Water and Choice in the Colorado Basin* (1968); Frank Waters, *The Colorado* (1946); and Arthur Woodward, *Feud on the Colorado* (1955). —R. W. D.

Colorado Springs, Colorado. Situated at the foot of the Rocky Mountains, sixty-eight miles south of Denver, Colorado Springs (population 103,000) is one of the most scenic cities in the West. The city's western horizon is dominated by Pikes Peak, which rises 14,110 feet above the floor of the Great Plains. Colorado Springs is blessed with a mild, invigorating climate that has attracted tourists for the last hundred years. In addition, the climate has made the city a virtual mecca for sufferers of respiratory diseases.

Among the chief attractions of the Colorado Springs area are the Garden of the Gods, the Will Rogers Shrine, and the Cheyenne Mountain Zoo. United States Department of Defense-supported activities, such as the Air Force Academy, Fort Carson, and the North American Air Defense Command, have been instrumental in the growth and prosperity of the city in recent years.

Colorado Springs was founded in 1871 by General William Jackson Palmer, an eccentric but imaginative railroad entrepreneur. Palmer called his city Fountain Colony and envisioned it as "the one spot in the West where nice people could gather together and live out their days in gentility and peace." Colorado Springs became a favorite spot for vacationing eastern brahmins. Today Colorado College and the stately Broadmoor and Antlers hotels stand as reminders of this eastern influence and the city's heyday as the "Newport of the Rockies."

See Robert Athearn, *Rebel of the Rockies* (1962); John Fisher, *Builder of the West* (1939); and Marshall Sprague, *Newport in the Rockies* (1961).—R. B. W.

Colter, John (c. 1774-1813). Member of the LEWIS AND CLARK EXPEDITION and discoverer of thermal phenomena in the northern Rockies. Colter was one of the nine young men enlisted for an expedition by Meriwether Lewis prior to Lewis' arrival at the Falls of the Ohio in 1803. Though having only the rank of private, Colter's abilities soon led Lewis and Clark to give him responsible and dangerous assignments. Near the Mandan villages on the return journey, he was released from the expedition to join two fur traders on their way up the Missouri.

Thus did Colter begin his four years as a mountain man in the northern Rockies, employed by fur trader Manuel Lisa and later by Pierre Menard and Andrew Henry. In these years he had two narrow escapes from the Blackfoot Indians and was a witness to some of the thermal phenomena in the region. He returned to Missouri in 1810, married, and conferred with William Clark in regard to a map of the northwest country. This map was included in the 1814 Biddle edition of the Lewis and Clark journals, and on it is a dotted line marked "Colter's Route"; not until 1835 did the term "Colter's Hell" appear in print (in Washington Irving's *The Rocky Mountains*, later changed to *The Adventures of Captain Bonneville*).

These references have given way to a great deal of conjecture. Where was Colter's Hell? Did Colter pass through the present Yellowstone National Park? What was his route? No one knows the answers, and most assumptions are all possibilities but are lacking in proof.

See Burton Harris, *John Colter: His Years in the Rockies* (1952); Merrill Mattes, "Behind the Legend of Colter's Hell: The Early Exploration of Yellowstone Park," *Mississippi Valley Historical Review* (September 1949); and Stallo Vinton, *John Colter* (1926).—R. A. B.

Colt revolver. See GUNS.

Columbia, California. Ghost town. Located in the foothills of the Sierra Nevada mountains, Columbia was one of the largest and most important mining towns in California. Gold was discovered in March 1850, and the area proved to be one of the richest placer-mining areas ever found. Because of its great wealth, it was called the "gem of the southern mines." Between 1850 and 1880 nearly $87 million in gold was extracted. The old business district of the town has been restored as a state park.

See Remi Nadeau, *Ghost Towns and Mining Camps of California* (1965); and Muriel S. Wolle, *The Bonanza Trail* (1953).—R. B. W.

Columbia Plateau. See PHYSIOGRAPHY OF THE UNITED STATES.

Columbia River. The Columbia, mightiest of the western rivers, originates in Columbia Lake in British Columbia at an elevation of 2,650 feet above sea level and flows to the northwest for over 200 miles before circling around the Selkirk Mountains to flow southward through Upper Arrow Lake and Lower Arrow Lake. Then it receives the flow of its principal Canadian tributary, the Kootenai (Kootenay), and the flow of the Clark Fork-Pend Oreille system, which drains almost all of western Montana but crosses into Canada just before entering the Columbia. From this point, 460 miles from its source, the Columbia enters the United States, flowing southward and receiving water from several small streams. Shortly below its confluence with the Spokane River, the Columbia makes its way westward and southward in a series of broad, sweeping curves across the dissected surface of the Columbia Plateau, flowing in a narrow valley incised in the layers of lava comprising the plateau. Its principal tributary, the Snake, joins it just northwest of Walla Walla, Washington, and just before it turns westward to form the boundary between Washington and Oregon. In cutting through the Cascades and the coast ranges the Columbia has created some of the finest scenery in the West—a route followed by the major transportation routes of the region. Finally, after a journey of almost 1,210 miles, the waters reach the ocean, meeting the ocean tides 145 miles from its mouth. In its lower reaches the river widens to a mile and a half after passing through the Cascade Range, reaches a maximum width of six miles near its mouth, and is discharged into the ocean between jetties that are two miles apart.

The mouth of the Columbia was apparently explored by sailors from a number of nations. The Spaniard Bruno Heceta is generally credited with the first recorded observation in August 1775. The Spanish called the river the San Roque. However, it was an American, Captain Robert Gray, in his little ship, the *Columbia Rediviria* of Boston, who first crossed the bar at the mouth of the Columbia and explored the lower reaches of the river. On May 11, 1792, he floated the Stars and Stripes on her waters and renamed the river the Columbia. Shortly thereafter Lieutenant William Broughton, a British naval officer on the H.M.S. *Chatham*, spent three weeks surveying the lower Columbia. Thus American and British claims to Oregon Territory were established.

Further conflict occurred as the first American and British exploring parties arrived overland. Fur traders from Canada apparently entered the Columbia Basin as early as 1800; the first Americans, the Lewis and Clark expedition, reached the mouth of the Columbia in October 1805, where they built Fort Clatsop on the Lewis and Clark River near Astoria, Oregon. Soon representatives of the two principal Canadian companies, the North West Company and Hudson's Bay Company, and a number of Americans began to establish fur-trading posts along the Columbia and its tributaries. Because of British strength to the north of the river, particularly at the post at present-day Vancouver, Washington, American settlement was diverted into the Willamette valley. The Columbia River, sometimes called the Oregon or the River of the West, remained the major magnet drawing Americans west until the discovery of gold on the American River in California in 1848. Oregon Territory, comprising most of the basin of the Columbia, became a part of the United States in 1846.

For centuries the Indian tribes of the Northwest lived on the incredible runs of salmon that ascended the river each year. Later the Americans exploited the salmon commercially and so thoroughly that a major source of Indian subsistence was depleted. Irrigated agriculture began early and formed the basis for the development of the livestock and fruit-growing industries of the many small valleys tributary to the Columbia. However, it was not until the 1930s that federal development of the Columbia Basin project began and not until 1952 that appreciable amounts of water were available to the farmers of the semiarid Columbia Plateau.

The Columbia and its tributaries are subject to wide variations in annual and seasonal flows, being chiefly dependent on precipitation from winter storms originating off the coast of Alaska. If the air masses in the storms are relatively cool, much of the precipitation falls as snow in the mountains, and the gradual melting of the snow in the spring brings peak flows in June. In some years, however, warm winter rains melt the snowpack, and peak flows may occur at any time from Oc-

tober to June. On the smaller tributaries, summer thunderstorms may cause flash floods and destruction of property located on the flood plains.

The large volume of water in the Columbia (180 million acre-feet at its mouth) is a tremendous asset for the people of the Pacific Northwest. It represents about half of the developable hydroelectric power in the United States and is more water than can be profitably used for agricultural development in the area. As is true with most natural resources, there are conflicting views as to the future utilization of the waters of the Columbia. Citizens of the arid Southwest would like to see some of the water diverted southward to supply their future needs. Conflicts with Canada over development of the river have apparently been taken care of by the Columbia River Treaty of 1964, which specifies the ways in which the water and power resources of the river will be allocated. Bitter conflicts over Indian fishing privileges erupted in the 1960s and continue to the present. In addition to the development of power and water resources, efforts have been made to improve navigation and prevent flooding. Most of these goals have been attained.

For map see SNAKE RIVER map.

See R. G. Bailey, *River of No Return* (1935); R. Cox, *The Columbia River* (1957); C. Dryden, *Columbia River Valley* (1950); S. H. Holbrook, *Columbia River* (1956); H. L. Keenleyside, "Columbia River Power Development," *Canadian Geographical Journal* (November 1965); J. V. Krutilla, *The Columbia River Treaty* (1973); W. D. Lyman, *Columbia River* (1963); D. W. Meinig, *The Great Columbia Plain* (1968); and D. Waterfield, *Continental Waterboy* (1967).—R. W. D.

Comanche Indians. The Comanche, of Uto-Aztecan stock, were the largest tribe of the Shoshonian language group. They came from the north, along the eastern flank of the Rocky Mountains, separating from the other Shoshoni in Montana. When the Comanche reached the foothill country in eastern Colorado, they stayed for many years, roaming around in a number of small hunting bands for the most part. Some of them lived in small farming villages on the upper Arkansas River. When the tribe finally moved onto the Great Plains, about a tenth of the tribe remained behind in the farming villages until they were attacked in 1717 by Spanish troops, who destroyed the villages and killed or enslaved the Indians.

The Comanche were a short people with powerful bodies mounted on stubby legs. Their short legs were a great hindrance to them on the Plains until they secured horses to ride. Because buffalo hunting was curtailed by their long-legged enemies, the Comanche were forced to live at a bare subsistence level until they obtained horses from the Spanish settlements in New Mexico toward the end of the seventeenth century.

The Comanche, so slow and awkward on foot, became graceful, skilled horsemen. Competent observers ranked them as equal to the Don Cossacks of southern Russia. By 1700 most of the tribe were mounted nomadic hunters who followed the buffalo year in and year out. In a short time their bands of mounted warriors became the scourge of the southern Plains from western Kansas to central Texas.

They combined a love of fighting with a strong desire to dominate vast areas of the Plains. Hence, they were in a continual struggle with most of the neighboring tribes as well as Texas colonists. They fought the Apache, Osage, Tonkawa, Pawnee, Ute, and in later years the Cheyenne and Arapaho. For their uncompromising hostility toward the Ute, a closely related Shoshoni people, that tribe gave them the name Comanche, "the people who fight us all the time."

The Comanche were considered cruel and relentless toward their enemies, even by Indian standards, and were mean even to one another in many petty ways. They brooked no restraint of any kind except on the occasion of a large communal buffalo hunt. Then one man was chosen as the hunt leader and was given the authority to line up the hunters and to give the signal to charge the herd. For all other regulation of their conduct, they relied on social pressure within the band.

After the Comanche became mounted nomadic hunters, they had ample supplies of food from the buffalo herds. They prospered and multiplied until they numbered several thousand. Many of the men became obese from overeating and lack of exercise, but they still strove to conquer more hunting grounds to provide for their large, increasing families. On foot these stubby, overweight men were slow and awkward, but mounted on their horses they were skillful, dangerous fighters, adept in the use of bow and arrows and lances.

As they moved south into Texas, driving the Apache out, they met the Spanish, who had put their first permanent colony in Texas at San Antonio in 1715. The fleeing Apache asked the Spanish for help and protection. The Spanish responded by building an Apache mission at San Saba, but it was wiped out by the Comanche in 1758. The Comanche also defeated the Spanish troops sent the next summer to punish them. The colonies in southern Texas continued to suffer from Comanche raids for the next hundred years.

After the remnants of the Apache bands had retreated into the mountains of New Mexico, they became much fiercer and more of a problem to the Spanish settlements. The officials of New Mexico decided to make a peace treaty with the Comanche and enlist them to fight against the Apache. The Comanche favored the treaty, for it gave them a place to trade for guns and ammunition as well as other goods. At the same time the tribe continued its hostility against the colonies in Texas and later began raiding south of the Rio Grande into northern Mexico, for to them the treaty applied only to New Mexico.

Mexico became an independent nation in 1821 and immediately relaxed many of the Spanish regulations hampering foreign trade. Traders from St. Louis then opened the Santa Fe Trail through the northern section of Comanche land. The tribe offered no opposition, welcoming the trading opportunities thus offered to increase their supply of guns and ammunition to use against their old enemies. They continued their enmity toward the Texans, who refused to offer them any attractive peace proposals. The Comanche and Texans both had excess horses to trade and both needed manufactured goods, and so, they had little to offer each other.

A detailed history of the Texas frontier is filled with accounts of many bloody raids by Comanche and Kiowa bands and retaliatory raids by the Texans.

For example, the Comanche believed that smallpox,

which wiped out hundreds of their people in 1837, had been introduced deliberately by a small Texas trading party, so the Indians killed all of them. Later that year when sixty-five of the Comanche leaders went to a peace parley at the invitation of the Texans, thirty-five were killed in a treacherous attack and the rest were captured and sold into slavery. Such events effectively prevented any lasting peace settlement on the Texas border.

As the enemy tribes to the north and northeast received more guns and ammunition, they organized large bands of allied warriors and drove the Comanche out of some of their hunting grounds. The Osage and Wichita took over part of Oklahoma, while in 1838 a combined force of Cheyenne and Arapaho moved down from the north, defeating the Comanche in a big fight and forcing them back across the Arkansas River. This disaster, and some prodding from the fur traders at Bent's Fort on the Arkansas, led the Comanche to agree to a peace treaty with the two tribes in 1840. A treaty in 1843 with the Osage opened up a brisk trade, the Comanche trading large herds of horses and mules captured from the Texans and Mexicans for guns, ammunition, and trade goods at exorbitant prices. In 1847 the Indian agent to the Osage reported that his charges had bought fifteen hundred mules from the Comanche that summer.

The Comanche lost more of their aggressiveness when a smallpox epidemic in 1848, followed by cholera in 1849, claimed about half the entire tribe. In their weakened state they were induced to make a treaty with federal officials at Fort Atkinson, Kansas, in 1853. The treaty gave the Comanche $18,000 in trade goods each year, thus freeing them from the Osage and their high prices. Within a few years the two tribes, no longer engaged in lucrative trade with each other, lapsed into sporadic fighting. The Comanche did not believe that their treaty with the United States officials obliged them to cease their raids on the Texans and Mexicans. The raids into northern Mexico over a period of many years usually came in August under a full moon, known as the Comanche moon, and spread a broad belt of destruction across the northern Mexican plateau, marked with piles of whitened bones of slaughtered men and animals. The plateau became known as the Desert of the Frontier.

An unprovoked attack by Colorado militia on a Northern Cheyenne village in southwestern South Dakota in 1864 aroused all the Plains tribes to the union. Some Cheyenne joined with Comanche and Kiowa in a force three thousand strong that camped in the Texas Panhandle along the Canadian River. Here Kit Carson with three hundred men from New Mexico took up a strong position at Adobe Walls, the ruins of William Bent's old trading post. By fighting desperately and by using well his two howitzers, Carson beat off the attacking force and retreated to the west after an indecisive fight.

In 1874 white buffalo hunters from Dodge City established a trading post at Adobe Walls. This was in the heart of Comanche buffalo country and near the remnants of the great southern buffalo herd, which was rapidly being slaughtered.

A force of seven hundred allied warriors, mostly Comanche, gathered to wipe out the few intruders with an overwhelming surprise attack at dawn on June 27. A ridgepole breaking in one of the cabins at 3 A.M. aroused the inmates. They had just finished their temporary repairs when the mounted Indians charged *en masse* across the open river bottom. In a fierce fight the besieged lost three men, but, although outnumbered twenty-five to one, they beat back the attackers with heavy Comanche losses. The Comanche never tried another mass attack against a well-entrenched foe.

During the 1870s the army was anxious to subdue all the nomadic Plains tribes. In 1874, during the winter storms, it resorted to surprise attacks against Indian villages, killing indiscriminately men, women, and children and destroying the lodges, supplies, and horse herds. The RED RIVER WAR was so effective against the Comanche that after one winter of fighting they gave up and surrendered at the reservations, although the young men still slipped away from time to time on raids into northern Mexico.

The Comanche in time realized that they could never roam the Plains again unless the buffalo herds were restored. For several years after 1875 they staged an elaborate SUN DANCE each summer. When the GHOST DANCE ritual reached the Kiowa in 1890, one group of the Comanche also adopted it, but most of the tribe, under the influence of QUANAH PARKER, had then turned to peyotism.

None of these religious movements could hold back the encroaching settlers. On three separate occasions federal officials reduced the size of the reservation, taking some of the land for homesteaders. In 1906, after each Comanche had been given his own allotment plot of 160 acres, the remainder of the tribal lands were taken and the reservation was ended.

The Comanche continued their peyote religion in the face of strong opposition from state and federal officials and missionaries. Finally, through the efforts of James Mooney of the American Bureau of Ethnology, Oklahoma passed a law recognizing the peyote religion as the Native American Church.

See H. D. Corwin, *Comanche and Kiowa Captives in Oklahoma and Texas* (1959); J. Harston, *Comanche Land* (1963); Rupert N. Richardson, *The Comanche Barrier to South Plains Settlement* (1933); and Ernest Wallace and E. Adamson Hoebel, *The Comanches: Lords of the South Plains* (1952).—F. H.

company towns. See MINING TOWNS.

Compromise of 1850. By the beginning of 1850 the nation faced a crisis over the disposal of the territories won from Mexico in 1848, following the Mexican War. Since 1846 every northern state legislature except Iowa's had endorsed the Wilmot Proviso, which prohibited slavery in all those territories. Southerners, led by John C. Calhoun, demanded equal rights in those areas and threatened to secede rather than submit to the proviso. To discuss such a course of action, they called a southern convention to meet in Nashville in June 1850. Suggested alternatives to secession included the extension of the 36°30' line to the Pacific with slavery legal below it, or the application of popular sovereignty to the areas. Another solution was offered by the new Whig president, Zachary Taylor, in 1849. He urged California and New Mexico to apply for statehood immediately and thereby avoid the explosive territorial phase that required congressional action. Since California would probably apply as a free state, this plan won the support of most northern Whigs, who were Free-Soilers. Exacer-

bating sectional difficulties were southern demands for a tougher fugitive slave law and increasing northern complaints about slavery and the slave trade in Washington, D.C.

An immediacy was added to the volatile situation in 1849. Texas claimed large parts of the New Mexico area, including Santa Fe; if Texas kept that area, it would be open to slavery. The United States denied this claim, and there was a genuine threat in 1849 and 1850 that the Texas militia might march against government troops in Santa Fe. The boundary dispute had to be settled. Furthermore, by the end of 1849 California desperately needed the organization of civil government to control the burgeoning population flocking to the gold fields, and it applied for statehood. Because its admission as a free state would upset the national balance of free and slave states, southerners opposed it. Such was the situation when Congress met in December 1849.

Traditionally, the compromise that evolved in Congress in 1850 is attributed to the Whig party and particularly to the conservative giants Henry Clay and Daniel Webster. Clay offered an omnibus bill in January that provided solutions to all the problems: California would be admitted to the Union as a free state, and Utah and New Mexico would be organized without the Wilmot Proviso. Webster supported it in a magnificent speech on March 7, a speech that cost him Whig support in the North. They argued that the Wilmot Proviso was unnecessary in Utah and New Mexico because nature would stop the spread of slavery there: the land was inhospitable to the development of the kind of agricultural economy that made slavery profitable.

This traditional interpretation, however, suffers from difficulties. President Taylor and most northern Whigs opposed the compromise, and only Taylor's death in July 1850 allowed it to pass. Secondly, the man most responsible for getting the compromise through both houses of Congress was not Clay or Webster but Democratic Senator Stephen A. Douglas, who did so by splitting up the omnibus and aligning different coalitions behind each bill. Thirdly, more Democrats than Whigs supported the compromise measures in both houses. Fourthly, outside interests such as a strong Texas bond lobby, which believed bondholders would benefit directly from the United States compensation to Texas, also influenced the passage of the bill. Finally, the ultimate compromise measures differed somewhat from Clay's proposals. California was admitted as a free state. Slave-trading was made unlawful in the District of Columbia. A much harsher fugitive slave law was enacted. The Texas-New Mexico boundary was adjusted with the United States paying Texas $10 million. Finally, the Utah and New Mexico territories were organized with popular sovereignty; their territorial legislatures were explicitly given power to decide on slavery in the territorial phase. Any such decision, however, was subject to a veto by the governor or to reversal by Congress.

In the end, the essential elements of the Compromise of 1850 were that the South admitted California as a free state and the North surrendered its demand for the Wilmot Proviso. The results were ironic, since California quickly sent pro-southern Democrats to the Senate and few slaves were ever taken to the new territories.

The best account of the Compromise of 1850,

stressing the importance of Douglas and the Democrats, is Holman Hamilton, *Prologue to Conflict: The Crisis and Compromise of 1850* (1964). For the traditional view, which lauds the conservative Whigs, see Allan Nevins, *Ordeal of the Union*, vol. I (1947).—M. F. H.

Comstock Lode. See GOLD AND SILVER RUSHES; MINING, METAL; NEVADA; and VIRGINIA CITY, NEVADA.

Conestoga wagon. Often called the "wagon of empire," the Conestoga wagon was developed in the Conestoga River valley in Lancaster County, Pennsylvania, early in the eighteenth century. Mention was made of a "Conestogoe" wagon as early as 1717. It was first used to haul furs from the fur-trade center of Lancaster some sixty miles to Philadelphia; later the wagons were used to haul farm produce to market and freight to the frontier. Conestogas served as the supply wagons for General Braddock in 1755 when he began his disastrous march toward Pittsburgh during the French and Indian War.

The Conestoga got its distinctive features when Pennsylvania Dutch craftsmen adapted earlier wagon designs to create a long, deep wagon bed, 42 inches wide and bowed downward in the middle somewhat like a boat. The rear and front panels were slanted, so that they resembled the rear of a frigate. The wagon box, or bed, was fitted with between eight and sixteen bows of bent wood over which was stretched canvas or Osnaburg cloth to keep out rain. Virtually all of the wagons featured a tool box on the left side, a feedbox chained to the rear, a lazy board on the left side, and an iron fixture to hold an axe.

The running gear, or frame and wheels, on which the wagon box rested was more complex than in most wagons. The back wheels were larger than the front. The wheels had wide tire irons for negotiating dirt roads. Depending upon the size of the wagon and the load, the Conestoga was pulled by four, five, or six horses, usually fat and docile bays or chestnuts, undoubtedly of Flemish or German origin, who came to be known as Conestoga horses.

The care with which the wagons were built, the attractive design of the ironware, and the graceful curving shape of the body made the Conestoga a work of art. The upper part of the wagon was often painted blue, the running gear red. The white-covered red and blue wagon pulled by matched teams who were decorated with harness bells and sometimes pompoms was a pleasing sight. Since the Conestoga was not designed as a passenger vehicle, the teamster or driver did not ride in the wagon but walked or sat on the left wheel horse.

When pioneer settlers began to push over the Appalachians to the Ohio River valley after 1763, Conestogas were used to haul household goods and freight. Conestogas were also used by settlers who pushed down the Shenandoah Valley and into the western Carolinas. A variation of the Conestoga was manufactured in Salem, North Carolina, by Moravian craftsmen.

Use of the original Conestoga wagons was at its peak between 1820 and 1850. The wagons were a common sight on the turnpikes leading West, but their use declined precipitately when the railroad crossed the Appalachians. Although the name Conestoga is commonly applied to all covered wagons, the wagons used by merchants on the Santa Fe Trail and by immigrants on the

Oregon and California trails differed in size, design, and purpose and so were not true Conestogas.

See also PRAIRIE SCHOONER.

See Seymour Dunbar, *History of Travel in America*, 4 vols. (1915); B. H. Meyer et al., *History of Transportation in the U.S. Before 1860* (1917); and George Shumway, Edward Durrell, and Howard C. Frey, *Conestoga Wagon, 1750-1850*.—H. R. L.

Congregationalists. The American Congregationalist denomination stems originally from an attempt in England late in the sixteenth century to give full scope to the Protestant principle, the priesthood of the believer. Robert Browne, a graduate of Cambridge, published in 1582 *A Booke which showeth the life and manners of all Christians*. In this work he described the church as a gathering of earnest believers bound together by a covenant entered into with God and with one another to abide by Christ's laws as ruling their conduct as individuals and as a collectivity. From the basic postulate of the covenant evolved ultimately the theory that God revealed his will with respect to the calling of a minister through the collective conscience of the congregation and the further affirmation that ministerial authority derived from the divine call made through the congregation.

English ecclesiastical repression of such a denial of royal and episcopal authority long prevented the open expression of the new radicalism. The congregation, which first gathered secretly at Scrooby in the early seventeenth century, finally established at Plymouth in New England in 1620 the pioneer Congregational church in America. When the persecutions of Archbishop William Laud led to the Great Migration of the Puritan party in the Church of England across the Atlantic between 1630 and 1640, the remoteness of the frontier and the hostility of the archbishop caused the congregations gathered both in Massachusetts and Connecticut to take on the character of the church in the Plymouth colony. Although the churches in New England became Congregational in government, they did not espouse, as did the pilgrims, a complete separatism of church and state. The Congregational churches in Massachusetts and Connecticut continued to hold a position of political privilege and influence well into the nineteenth century (see MASSACHUSETTS, SETTLEMENT OF).

New England Congregationalism took form in the first half of the seventeenth century, when in England the Newtonian reorientation of scientific thought brought the Renaissance to its climax. Before the middle of the seventeenth century New England Puritans, setting up a printing press and founding a college, achieved a sophisticated intellectual life. With the founding of Harvard and Yale, the Puritans initiated the independent liberal arts college. In Puritan discussions of the cosmos, of the deity, and of society, American thought finds its beginnings.

Puritan thinking concerned itself with three basic tenets, the depravity of man, the sovereignty of God, and the need to worship God and to order the church strictly in accordance with the prescriptions of the inspired Scriptures. Puritan thought came to focus on the individual person, an actor in a divinely ordained cosmic drama whose ultimate spiritual concern expressed itself in the experience of regeneration, the assurance of election, and the certainty that the covenant of grace was for him. "God has made a Couenant with you, and you are in couenant with him."

Beginning in the 1730s Jonathan Edwards gave new life to Puritanism, which had declined after the pioneers' zeal turned into a formalism of respectability in the second and third generations. The most important originator of the Great Awakening in New England, Edwards gave a thological setting to the emotional experience of conversion. He set forth a theology that affirmed the importance of the feelings and declared that salvation comes not as a reward for moral effort but only from the mind's illumination by the loveliness of divine holiness. His grandson, Timothy Dwight, who became president of Yale College in 1794, popularized Edwards and launched the New England Theology, which had a profound influence on REVIVALISM both east and west of the Appalachian Mountains.

Edwards sought to stop the drift of Congregationalism toward the cool rationalism of the French Enlightenment. When in the early years of the nineteenth century conservative Congregationalism, particularly in eastern Massachusetts, was moving toward Unitarianism, the Edwardians founded Andover Theological Seminary. This institution became the chief center for the training of an evangelical Congregational ministry to serve abroad and within the nation. The "Haystack Meeting" at Congregational Williams College in 1806 initiated a missionary crusade to convert the heathen, which received organization and direction with the founding in 1810 of the American Board of Commissioners for Foreign Missions. As the march of the pioneers across the continent was beginning, they also became concerned with the Indians beyond the Appalachians, with Asia, and with the Hawaiian Islands. As New Englanders moved into western New York State, into Ohio, and into the country beyond the Mississippi, Congregational leaders felt the loose association along state lines of their independent congregations to be ill adapted to the needs of the evolving and fluid communities of the frontier. They entered into a Plan of Union in 1801 with the Presbyterians, whose theology was quite similar to their own. By this agreement congregations formed west of the mountains could belong to both denominations. In the end most of them became Presbyterian. In the West Congregationalism made its impact not in the creation of a giant denomination but rather, along with the PRESBYTERIANS, in the founding of liberal arts colleges and universities.

See Sidney E. Ahlstrom, *A Religious History of the American People* (1972); Frederick L. Fagley and Gaius Glenn Atkins, *History of American Congregationalism* (1942); and W. W. Sweet, ed., *The Congregationalists, 1783-1850* (1939).—R. H. G.

Connecticut, settlement of. In 1634 the Dutch from the New Netherlands established a small trading post at Fort Hope (Hartford) in order to discourage New Englanders from encroaching upon the fur trade or upon Dutch land claims in the rich Connecticut valley. The men of the Plymouth Colony were not impressed, however, and within months after the Dutch arrival, they built a rival trading house nine miles farther up the river. The great flood of colonists that streamed into the region from Massachusetts Bay soon overshadowed these two commercial ventures. As early as 1634 the people of Newton (Cambridge, Massachusetts) announced "the strong bent of their spirits to remove thither," citing the need for more land as their chief motive. The ruling magistrates of the bay were not pleased by these requests to emigrate, but there was little that they could do. Groups of Puritans from Roxbury, Watertown, and Dorchester, Massachusetts, did not wait for official permission before moving, and in 1636 Thomas Hooker and John Haynes led a large body of Newtown settlers overland to a new home in Connecticut. By the end of the year more than eight hundred Puritans were living in the three "River Towns," Hartford, Wethersfield, and Windsor. Throughout the entire colonial period, the population of Connecticut remained remarkably homogeneous, a fact that helps to explain why the colony later acquired the description "the land of steady habits." It is important to note that the original Connecticut settlers did not leave Massachusetts because of religious differences. The majority of them were orthodox Puritans intent on finding prosperity in the New World.

The people of Connecticut believed that they had moved outside the jurisdiction of Massachusetts Bay, but unfortunately, they did not possess a royal charter giving them status as a separate colony. In 1637 the three River Towns set up a temporary government to deal with Indian problems and local matters. Two years later these communities adopted the Fundamental Orders of Connecticut, which stated that ". . . where a people are gathered together the word of god requires that to mayntayne the peace and Union of such a people there should be an Orderly and decent Goverment established." They placed supreme ruling power in an elected General Court, which had authority to make and repeal laws, to set taxes, to admit new freemen, and to distribute the colony's lands. Over the last century, there has been a good deal written about "democracy" in colonial Connecticut, and some historians have claimed that the Fundamental Orders was a crucial document in the development of American liberties. But more recent studies have revealed that democracy as it is understood today was not present in colonial Connecticut; for example, only men of "good religious carriage" were allowed to participate in civil affairs. For most of the colonial era, the political practices of Connecticut were vitually indistinguishable from those of Massachusetts.

When the Stuarts returned to power in 1660, the leaders of Connecticut decided to petition for a royal charter. The colony's most distinguished citizen, John Winthrop, Jr., was dispatched to London with instructions to see that the "liberties and privileges inserted in the Patent" should "not be inferior or short to what is granted to Massachusetts." Winthrop's able diplomacy, coupled with five hundred pounds in bribes, won for Connecticut in 1662 one of the most liberal charters issued during the Restoration period. The charter essentially sanctioned the political system that had already evolved within the province. Unlike other English colonies, Connecticut was not burdened with appointed royal officials, for her governor and the members of her General Court continued to be elected by the freemen. Moreover, the settlers did not have to pay quitrents on their land. The people of Connecticut were understandably protective of their semi-independent status, so much so, that in 1741 the Board of Trade complained that "they think themselves by their charters little dependent on the Crown, and seldom pay obedience to royal orders." The charter of 1662 also expanded Connecticut's boundaries by including all the NEW HAVEN COLONY and part of Rhode Island within its jurisdiction.

Connecticut was never as prosperous as her neighbors. The colonists raised livestock, flaxseed, and wheat, but they did not develop a staple crop, like cotton or indigo, that was suitable for export. Most of the lucrative overseas trade flowed to New York, Newport, and Boston, rather than to the ports of Connecticut. During the eighteenth century the western part of the colony was settled, but as early as 1760 it became apparent that Connecticut was suffering from overcrowding. Land prices rose, the size of individual farms decreased, and the quality of cultivated acreage deteriorated. The historian Charles Grant noted in his study of Kent that "Economic opportunity, bright in 1751, had turned dark by 1796." One anonymous writer captured the spirit of the colony when he explained, "our farms in general will not bear a further division; unless there be some new resource our most active, industrious, and enterprising young men . . . will emigrate to those parts of the continent where there is more vacant territory." After the American Revolution, Connecticut farmers did just that, moving in large numbers to Vermont, New York, and Ohio, where they attempted to reproduce the institutions that they had known in their home state.

On the founding, see Charles M. Andrews, *The Colonial Period of American History*, vol. II (1936), and Perry Miller, "Thomas Hooker and the Democracy of Connecticut," *The New England Quarterly* (1931). For the eighteenth century, see Charles S. Grant, *Democracy in the Connecticut Frontier Town of Kent* (1961), and Albert Laverne Olson, *Agricultural Economy and the Population in Eighteenth-Century Connecticut* (1935), number 40 in a series of pamphlets sponsored by the Tercentenary Commission of the State of Connecticut.—T. H. B.

Connor, Patrick Edward (1820-1891). Soldier and miner. An Irish immigrant, Connor entered the United States Army at the age of eighteen and served in the Seminole War in Florida. Leaving the service in 1844, he entered into various business activities in New York. In 1846 he moved his mercantile business to Texas, where hostilities soon broke out between the United States and Mexico. Connor was mustered into the army again, this time as a captain under Albert S. Johnston. Following the Mexican War, Connor migrated to California, where he engaged in business again. With the onset of the Civil War, he volunteered once more for military duty and, as a colonel, led the Third California Volunteers into the Great Salt Lake valley in 1862. His detail of 750 men had been ordered to Utah to protect the overland mail and transcontinental telegraph from Indian raids. Connor's instructions included orders to garrison Camp Floyd, forty miles south of Salt Lake City. Instead, he constructed Fort Douglas on Salt Lake City's east bench. Suspicious of the Mormons and their sympathies in the Civil War, Connor not only kept a cannon leveled on Brigham Young's home but demanded that persons supplying the camp must swear an oath of allegiance to the Union. In like manner, he started a weekly anti-Mormon paper, *The Union Vedette*, whose purpose was "the education of the Mormon people up to American views." Nevertheless, the Mormons prospered economically from the military's presence.

Connor's solution to "the Mormon problem" was to encourage his soldiers, most of whom were prospectors from the California and Nevada gold fields, to search the Utah mountains for metals. Through appropriate publicity he hoped to start a rush of miners that would overwhelm the Mormons. Although his men did find minerals, mining was not successful until after the completion of the transcontinental railroad in 1869.

Connor did establish a reputation as an Indian fighter, a reputation built primarily on a victory in 1863 over the Shoshoni at the battle of Bear River in Cache valley, southern Idaho. This won him the command of the District of the Plains in 1865, in which year he led the POWDER RIVER INDIAN EXPEDITION. Released from military duties in 1866, he returned to Utah to pursue his mining and business interests. He was the leading non-Mormon in the territory and his business endeavors were partly directed against the Latter-day Saint power structure. His hope for successful mining operations in Utah eventually was realized, as was the ebb of Mormon control of the political life of the territory.

See Fred B. Rogers, *Soldiers of the Overland* (1938). —L. J. A.

conservation, land. See CONSERVATION MOVEMENT and WILDERNESS.

conservation, water. See RECLAMATION AND IRRIGATION.

conservation, wildlife. See FISHERIES and WILDLIFE.

conservation movement. From his beginnings in the early Pleistocene until only yesterday, geologically speaking, man directed his energies to conquering, not conserving, the environment. Such behavior was entirely appropriate for a people whose very survival depended on breaking nature to their will. With the sabertooth only a jump behind, conservation was inconceivable. In the first place, natural resources seemed inexhaustible; the problem was too many rather than too few trees. Moreover, the Judeo-Christian tradition taught that as a result of a gift from God the natural world belonged to man for his exploitation. Genesis 1:28 commanded the first couple to "be fruitful, and multiply, and replenish the earth, and subdue it: and have dominion over the fish of the sea, and over the fowl of the air, and over every living thing that moveth upon the earth." The environment, it followed, existed solely for the satisfaction of man's immediate desires.

The first Americans stood squarely in this tradition. Their transatlantic migration to a wilderness stripped away centuries of the civilizing process, re-creating the fears and drives of primitive man. Later generations of frontiersmen continued the pattern. A massive assault was directed at the New World environment in the name of civilization and Christianity. Progress became synonymous with exploitation. Men slashed the earth in pursuit of raw materials. The long-term interest of society made little difference; considerations of immediate profit dictated relationships with the land. A scarcity of natural resources? Absurd! Over the next ridge was a cornucopia of wood, water, soil, and game. Up to the late nineteenth century, in short, Americans experienced a population density unconducive to the conservation idea. But as man gained control over nature and his needs pressed against the limits of the continent, conservation made sense.

The attitude toward natural resources subsequently labeled "conservation" received its first major statement in the writings of such men as Henry David THOREAU, George Perkins Marsh, and Frederick Law OLMSTED. They challenged the dominant conception of the land's purpose and exposed inexhaustibility as a myth. Just as the environment had to be conserved, free enterprise had to be controlled. The early conservationists thus challenged another citadel of American thought, that free enterprise should be exempt from government regulation. Head of the Department of the INTERIOR Carl SCHURZ and pioneer reclamationist John Wesley POWELL, among others, realized that land management was too comprehensive and too crucial a problem to be left to individual developers. Their ideas paved the way for the first major surge of the American conservation movement in the Progressive period of the early twentieth century.

Within the space of a few years the concept of conservation came to have wide public usage and was extended to subjects as diverse as the improvement of rural schools and the reform of the parcel post system. Even human health and the lengthening of the life span were regarded as "conservation" problems. In politics the conservation issue played a major role, contributing particularly to a schism in the Republican party in 1912 (see Gifford PINCHOT).

One way to understand the sudden emergence of Progressive conservation is in terms of its historical context. Americans in the early twentieth century were ready to be concerned about their environment as the growth of industrialization, urbanization, and population meant the ending of the frontier. The Census of 1890 simply announced this fact. Three years later Frederick Jackson TURNER wrote his famous essay, "The Significance of the Frontier in American History." Yet few were willing to confront the prospect of a frontierless America, and a vague uneasiness was widespread. The frontier had been almost synonymous with abundance, opportunity, and distinctiveness of the New World. For two and a half centuries its presence largely explained America's remarkable material growth as well as many characteristics of her people. Few, as a consequence, could regard its passing without regret.

One result was a general tendency to look favorably on conservation. It would "string out" the remaining abundance, deny the chilling implications of the census pronouncement, and assuage anxiety over population growth and industrial expansion. Conservation would be, in a sense, the new frontier, keeping the nation young, vigorous, prosperous, democratic, and wholesome. For a civilization that had begun to notice its first gray hairs, conservation was a welcome tonic for the land as well as for the minds of its inhabitants.

Several other factors figured in the growth and character of conservation before World War I. There was a technological capacity capable of at least entertaining the large-scale environmental engineering Progressive conservationists proposed. In addition, the national indignation, growing since the 1870s, over concentrated wealth conditioned some Americans to welcome a movement to check private exploitation with social responsibility. Progressive conservation would have taken a different and probably a less potent form had it not coincided with the widespread acceptance of the philosophy that the central government should be strong and willing to use its strength in the public interest. Along with the passing of the era of easy resources, such developments created a climate of opinion that was ripe for conservation.

Among the many individuals who contributed to the Progressive conservation movement, the names of Theodore ROOSEVELT and Gifford Pinchot stand out. As president and chief forester respectively, they popularized the concept of wise and efficient use of resources for purposes of sustained yield. Forests, for instance, came to be regarded as cropland; utilitarianism guided decisions respecting their management. John Muir, the founder of the Sierra Club, led those who took a different approach to the environment. This viewpoint stressed the need to preserve nature for aesthetic, spiritual, and recreational reasons.

The conservation philosophies of Pinchot and John MUIR clashed directly in the Hetch Hetchy controversy of 1908-13. San Francisco wanted Hetch Hetchy Valley in Yosemite National Park as a site for a municipal reservoir. Pinchot favored the idea. Muir, on the contrary, believed that national parks should be permanent wilderness preserves. Ultimately Hetch Hetchy went to San Francisco, but the preservationist wing of American conservation gained a notable victory in the creation of the NATIONAL PARK SERVICE in 1916 and went on to gain both numbers and political muscle.

In the final analysis progressive conservation produced considerably more smoke than fire. There were urgent calls to action, grandiose plans, and elaborate conferences, but relatively little help for the environment. Political in-fighting doomed the movement to an early death. Public opinion, however, was aroused, and after World War I the American conservation crusade resumed. Fortunately some of the shrillness disappeared. Conservationists spent more time acting; less time exhorting and scolding. There was less talk about "running out" of resources, and the people-versus-plutocrats approach gave way to an acceptance of the idea that the condition of the environment was a product of American civilization as a whole. Responsibility for land health fell on the entire nation, and it responded with resource programs even more comprehensive than those of the Progressive years.

After 1920 conservation benefited from several new approaches and circumstances. The conservationists' understanding of the interrelation of resource problems increased. The Pinchot school of forest management, for instance, scoffed at the "sentimentalists" and "romantics" who extolled the recreational values of the woods. But the next generation of foresters gradually recognized the importance of forests for both lumber and pleasure. The United States Forest Service began to adjust its policy to accommodate both demands. The utilitarian line even weakened enough to permit the reservation of some portions of the national forests as wilderness. In the same way the Bureau of Reclamation started to publicize the boating and fishing potential of its reservoirs.

The continued growth of federal power and responsibility, particularly under Franklin D. Roosevelt, had a profound effect on conservation between the wars. State and private efforts were not discouraged, but increasingly Americans recognized that managing the environment was a task requiring a degree of knowledge, power, and money that only the national government could command.

Representative of the main thrust of conservation in the 1930s was the Tennessee Valley Authority, launched in 1933 after a decade-long struggle. Based on the premise of multipurpose development of an entire watershed in the public interest (SEE RECLAMATION AND IRRIGATION), TVA became a byword for regional planning throughout the world. Also important for creative environmental management through the control of water was the Colorado River Storage Project, the keystone of which was Boulder (later Hoover) Dam and Lake Mead.

After World War II the driving force in the American conservation movement came increasingly from the quest for *quality* in the environment. At first, however, the familiar theme of providing for man's material needs was much in evidence. Books such as Fairfield Osborn's *Our Plundered Planet* (1948) and William Vogt's *Road to Survival* (1948) grimly raised the old Malthusian specter of population outreaching the world's productive ability. From this perspective conservation was the means of maintaining the physical bases of life. Indeed, this had been the movement's main rationale at the time of its inception. But the idea of protecting the environment for its *non*material values also had a long, if less potent, history in American thought. By the 1960s this concept challenged utilitarianism as the dominant purpose of conservation. Led by Secretary of the Interior Stewart L. Udall, many Americans were coming to realize that an environment conducive to survival—even to affluence—was not enough. The land, they insisted, had to do more than just support life. It had to offer beauty, solitude, challenge, and joy.

This "new conservation," as President Lyndon B. Johnson labeled it in 1965, emphasizes such things as recreational opportunities and the beautification of highways. The environment was to be groomed for man's happiness. But there were perplexing new problems. For one, what economists call benefit-cost analyses are extremely difficult to make in regard to nonmaterial, subjective values. The dollar-and-cent worth of a forest, for instance, is relatively easy to calculate compared to its importance an an element in a landscape or a place for a family picnic. Another problem results, ironically, from the growing appreciation of nature. This coupled with increasing leisure and mobility has created crisis conditions in outdoor recreation. It is not that existing parks and recreation areas cannot hold all who come, but after a certain saturation point the degree of satisfaction from wilderness decreases abruptly. Quotas and other limitations seem the only answer to maintaining the quality of the national park experience.

In the late 1960s conservation in the United States clothed itself in the magic words "ecology" and "environment" and enjoyed a dramatic rise in popularity. Indeed, if the Progressive and New Deal periods could be said to mark waves of growth in the conservation movement, then the current vogue constitutes a third wave. Measured by the amount of public concern and press coverage, it is the biggest wave of all. The hallmark of the current environment movement is not affluence or beautification, but survival. Man's capacity to pollute the planet has been called a real threat to its life-supporting abilities. The advocates of conservation today are not a handful of experts but a vast slice of citizenry united by a sense of outrage, mixed with fear, at the way man has treated his spaceship—the earth. They point out that man has overpopulated the world at the same time that he has rendered it less capable of supporting a burgeoning population. The key insight is that of the ecologist, with his awareness of the interrelationships and balances that sustain life. Today, concern for the environment is often linked closely to criticism of capitalism, consumption, and growth. Progress, the critics of the establishment contend, may lie in the direction of stabilizing population and the economy. Armed with the "land ethic" of Aldo Leopold, environmentalists believe man could live in harmony with his habitat. But beneath the cheery recycling efforts and the bicycle campaigns is the haunting fear that conservation today is merely a rearrangement of the deck chairs on the Titanic. (See the WILDERNESS.)

A useful source of the highlights in American conservation history and a comprehensive bibliography is Roderick Nash, ed., *The American Environment* (1968). The best general survey is Stewart Udall, *The Quiet Crisis* (1963).—R. N.

Continental Divide. See PHYSIOGRAPHY OF THE UNITED STATES: *Rocky Mountains.*

Conway, Elias Nelson (1812-1892). Arkansas politician. Born in Tennessee, Conway grew up and was educated in Missouri. He became a surveyor and in 1833 went to Arkansas Territory, where his brother James and his first cousin Ambrose Sevier were leaders of the pro-Jackson faction in territorial politics. Through them Conway became territorial auditor in 1835. After Arkansas achieved statehood in 1836, with James as governor and Sevier as senator, he continued as state auditor for fourteen years. He served two terms as governor, from 1852 to 1860, giving most of his attention to winding up the affairs of the defunct state banks, awarding federal land grants to competing railroad companies, and keeping peace within the ranks of his Democratic party. His term over, Conway took no further part in politics.—W. L. B.

Conway, James Sevier (1798-1855). Arkansas politician. Conway was born and educated in Tennessee. In 1820 he and his brother Henry went to Arkansas Territory to survey public land, remained there, and became prominent in territorial politics. Conway was Arkansas's first surveyor-general, and, after Arkansas entered the Union in 1836, its first governor. As governor, he supported the chartering of two state banks which went broke and involved the young state in a long controversy over its bonded indebtedness. Leaving office in 1840 he retired to his large Red River plantation in Lafayette County. Through his cousin Senator Ambrose Sevier, who married the sister of Robert Ward Johnson, Conway belonged to the Democratic Conway-Sevier-Johnson family clique that ruled Arkansas until 1860.—W. L. B.

Cook, James Henry (1857-1942). Cowboy, scout, and rancher. Cook was born at Kalamazoo, Michigan, the son of a Great Lakes ship's captain. When he was twelve years old he went to work in a machine shop. He followed that with some experience as a seaman on the lakes. He then worked as a cowhand in Kansas and Texas, where he was employed by several large ranches, including the Slaughter, Ellison, and Deweese companies. Cook was an excellent rifleman, and during this period he often fought Indians and rode with the Texas Rangers. He also made trail drives to northern points.

After a drive to Nebraska in 1876 Cook scouted for the Fourth and Fifth United States Cavalries, returning to Texas in 1877 to make another drive. He hunted buffalo in Kansas, serving as a scout against the Cheyenne, and in 1879 drove a herd from southern Nevada to Idaho. Cook served as a guide for American and English hunting parties for several years and for the scientific exploring parties of Hayden, Marsh, Cope, and King.

In 1882 Cook established and managed the WS Ranch in Socorro County, New Mexico, for Harold C. Wilson, an English sportsman whom he had befriended. In 1885 he joined in the campaign that resulted in the capture and imprisonment of the Apache warrior Geronimo. Although he did not care for Comanche and Apache, Cook greatly admired the Northern Cheyenne and the Oglala Sioux, particularly Chief Red Cloud. After he purchased the O-4 ranch on the Niobrara River in Sioux County, Nebraska, in 1887, later known as the Agate Springs Ranch, many Indians visited him there. His den at Agate ranch became so filled with Indian artifacts that it constituted a private museum honoring Red Cloud and his people. Cook also pioneered in importing purebred stock, helped organize stock growers' associations, and developed a model ranch.

Agate Springs Ranch became famous for its fossil beds, and Cook encouraged their excavation by a number of leading American universities. Conscious that the old western way of life was fading away, he sought unsuccessfully to have a replica of Fort Laramie built on his property, but it is his own autobiography, *Fifty Years on the Old Frontier* (1923), that serves as the most attractive, vivid, and enduring monument to the Old West. Now considered a classic, it recounts in a wry, humorous style his dangerous experiences as a cowboy on the open range, big-game hunter, military scout, and pioneer rancher. But perhaps most impressive is his attempt to defend the Indians and to explain their way of life. Unlike most westerners, Cook also appreciated the role of the scientist in developing and explaining the West, and his book ends with a plea to preserve the record of the past.—H. R. L.

Cooke, Philip St. George (1809-1895). Soldier and memoirist. Born in Leesburg, Virginia, Cooke graduated from West Point in 1827 and joined the Sixth Infantry on the Missouri frontier, where in 1833 he was transferred to the newly organized dragoon regiment. In 1843 Cooke, a tall, lanky officer who was well known for his "peppery language," captured a group of Texans led by Major Jacob Snively who were molesting caravans on the Santa Fe Trail. At the outbreak of the Mexican War in 1846, Cooke marched with General Stephen Watts Kearny's Army of the West to New Mexico and in October left Santa Fe with a battalion of Mormons and a small supply train to open a wagon road to California. Heading southwest, he passed through the vicinity of Guadalupe Pass into Sonora, Mexico. Turning north along the San Pedro River, his column was attacked by a herd of wild cattle, and the so-called Battle of the Bulls ensued. Cooke then veered west, entered Tucson in mid-December unopposed, moved north to the Gila, and west to the Colorado, arriving in San Diego on January 29, 1847. Cooke's wagon road later became a popular route for westbound emigrants and gold-seekers. That spring Cooke accompanied General Kearny from California to the East, and testified against Captain John C. Frémont in the latter's court-martial. Kearny and Frémont had struggled over the governorship of California, with Frémont refusing to obey Kearny, his superior officer. Joining the Second Dragoons in Mexico City, Cooke returned in July 1848 to the United States.

After the Mexican War Cooke was superintendent at Carlisle Barracks, commanded the Second Dragoons in Texas, fought the Sioux, and was on duty in Kansas during the civil unrest there. He commanded the cavalry in the Utah War of 1857, was sent abroad as a military observer, and served as a Union cavalry general during the Civil War. Brevetted a major general in 1865, Cooke at his retirement in 1873 had played a major role in developing the cavalry into one of the most important arms in the army. He died in Detroit.

In addition to his lively and interesting military career, Cooke was a diarist and author, whose publications include *Scenes and Adventures in the Army* (1857), *Cavalry Tactics* (1861), and the highly readable *Conquest of New Mexico and California* (1878).

See Otis E. Young, *The West of Philip St. George Cooke, 1809-1895* (1955).—H. P. H.

Cooper, Astley D. M. (1856-1924). Painter. Born in St. Louis, Missouri, the grandson of trader and Indian agent Benjamin O'Fallon and great-nephew of explorer William Clark, Cooper became interested in the art and history of the West at an early age. He was reputedly greatly impressed with the Indian portraits by George Catlin commissioned by his grandfather, who was the United States Indian agent for the Missouri River tribes. After attending Washington University in St. Louis, Cooper spent two years in Colorado, and before his twenty-first birthday is said to have attracted the attention of eastern art critics with his Indian portraits.

Cooper moved to San Jose, California, in 1883, established a studio, and contributed many illustrations to *Frank Leslie's Illustrated Newspaper*. Indians, wildlife, and western frontier history continued to be the subjects of his greatest interest and popularity, although he also produced numerous contemporary portraits. He produced a large volume of work of wide public appeal and was an early member of the San Francisco Art Association. He is represented in numerous collections, both public and private.

See Dorothy Harmsen, *Western Americana* (1971). —D. C. H.

Cooper, James Fenimore (1789-1851). Novelist. Cooper was born in Burlington, New Jersey, the son of William Cooper, who in 1785 had acquired a patent of thousands of acres at the headwaters of the Susquehanna River in New York State. There, on Lake Otsego, his father established Cooperstown—the Templeton of the Leatherstocking Tales—to which he brought his family in 1790. William Cooper was a man of property who ruled over his forty thousand acres of land in a manner befitting an English lord of the manor. Between 1796 and 1799 he built Otsego Hall in Cooperstown, an imposing edifice into which his son later moved and which is satirically described in *The Pioneers*.

After being dismissed for misbehavior in his third year at Yale, Cooper obtained a midshipman's commission in 1806. He found the life of a landowning squire more congenial than that of a naval officer, however, though the knowledge he gained during his five years at sea proved invaluable to him as a novelist. In 1811 he married Susan DeLancey, herself a member of the aristocratic landowning class. They settled first in Mamaroneck, New York, and in 1814 returned to Cooperstown.

Cooper came to a literary career more or less by accident. One day—so the story goes—when reading a novel aloud to his wife, Cooper remarked with characteristic quarrelsomeness that he could write a better book himself. Challenged to do so, he wrote *Precaution* (1820), a drawing-room novel derivative in both form and content from the then-popular novel of fashionable society. Though *Precaution* is not a particularly noteworthy novel, its success encouraged him to continue writing, and in quick succession he turned out *The Spy* (1821), *The Pioneers* (1823), and *The Pilot* (1823). These three novels, themselves among Cooper's best, are one of the firsts of their kind and indicate the range of most of his significant later writing. The first is a revolutionary war romance, the second marks the literary debut of the famous Leatherstocking, and the third is an adventure novel of the sea. They indicate as well the typical plot in most of his later writing. They are all stories of a man placed between two very different symbolic locations. Harvey Birch, the "spy," is a prototypical Cooper hero whose symbolic location in the novel, evocatively called "the neutral ground," is the no-man's-land between the British and American lines. Birch prefigures Leatherstocking, whose symbolic terrain is the neutral ground between the whites and the Indians.

Between 1826 and 1833 Cooper traveled in Europe, and in 1834 settled again in Cooperstown, which he was to make his home for the remainder of his life. While abroad he staunchly defended America and American ways, and inevitably sentimentalized life in the United States. The confrontation between his unconsciously romanticized picture of American life and its reality proved profoundly disillusioning. Cooper's immediate reaction was to strike out in various literary quarrels at what he considered the shortcomings of America. His *Letter to His Countrymen* (1834) and *The American Democrat* (1838) stirred up bitter hostility in the United States, as, more surprisingly, did his *History of the Navy of the United States of America* (1839). To silence his critics Cooper initiated a number of libel actions between 1837 and 1842, most of which he won. The victories proved to be Pyrrhic, however; the damages he was awarded were nominal, and the price of his litigiousness was, predictably enough, the still greater hostility of his critics. During these years Cooper completed the two remaining novels of the Leatherstocking Tales and later initiated a new series of three novels, now generally known as *The Littlepage Manuscripts*, dealing with the Anti-Rent War in New York State (1839-46). The first of these novels, *Satanstoe* (1845), is generally considered to be the best, although *The Chainbearer* (1845) and *The Redskins*

(1846) are well worth reading. In 1847 Cooper made a trip as far west as Detroit, but for most of his later years he lived quietly in Cooperstown.

Cooper is probably the most uniformly underpraised of major American writers. Although his influence has been widely recognized, he has been equally widely deplored. His fiction about the West has uniformly been interpreted as "romance," and then condemned as unrealistic, particularly by those who have expected from western literature that it be true to the facts of the American westward movement. In an 1827 review of *The Prairie* for the *Western Monthly Review*, Timothy Flint objected to Cooper's inexact descriptions of prairie geography; and Robert Montgomery Bird, a novelist contemporary with Cooper, in his introduction to his own novel *Nick of the Woods* (1837), deplored Cooper's sympathetic portrayal of Indians, which, in his opinion, owed more to François René de Chateaubriand's fanciful conception of the noble savage than to actual flesh and blood redskins. Mark Twain, in one of his least happy essays, "Fenimore Cooper's Literary Offenses" (1895), summed up this line of argument by gleefully recounting a list of Cooper's factual errors, which allegedly prove his absolute incompetence as a novelist and dismiss him as unworthy of consideration as a serious writer. Many later critics of Cooper have repeated, with greater or less ingenuity, these same charges.

The consistency of the various attacks on Cooper highlights a very real difference in critical expectations toward western literature. If on the one hand one wishes western literature to be a factual account of the events of western history, Cooper's writing can easily be dismissed as "romantic," and hence untrue. If, on the other hand, one views romance not as an escape from reality but as a fictional method of presenting a reality that is not primarily factual, Cooper's achievement becomes much more profound. Moreover, Cooper's overwhelming influence on later western literature may then be seen not as providing a convenient formula for literary escape, but rather a method of removing the trivia of anecdotal history and local-color fiction.

Though Cooper wrote a number of other novels that take place on the frontier, his influence on later western fiction is almost entirely traceable to the five novels of The Leatherstocking Tales: *The Pioneers* (1823), *The Last of the Mohicans* (1826), *The Prairie* (1827), *The Pathfinder* (1840), and *The Deerslayer* (1841). In this series Cooper wrote the definitive epic of the American West, and the magnitude of his achievement may justly be gauged by the host of imitators, both in America and abroad, whose stories have been conceived largely in terms of the structure he pioneered.

Cooper's most important legacy is the character of Natty Bumppo, the "Leatherstocking." Though Natty is based upon the figures of various historical pioneers, most notably Daniel Boone, his character has little in common with the character of actual frontiersmen, either then or later. Most crucial in Cooper's treatment is the fact that Natty is seen as a man between two societies. Unlike the historic Daniel Boone, he is not conceived as the first of the white settlers who will succeed him, nor, contrariwise, is he conceived as a renegade who has "gone native" and become an Indian. He is placed between the two societies in a kind of neutral ground over which they are both fighting, and is detached from both societies so that he may comment upon the strengths and weaknesses of each. Moreover, he is isolated from the rewards as well as the shortcomings of both white and Indian life, and as a result his opinions about the merits of either society are divorced from special pleading.

Significantly, Natty was first conceived as an old man, an ambiguous figure able to comment upon society from the perspective of age. In the subsequent Leatherstocking Tales Cooper's fascination with Natty as a detached and venerable figure broadens into a realization that the old pioneer can be a vehicle for the presentation of the conflict between the confused world of events and the detached perspective of history. He is involved both in the blood-and-thunder plots and divorced from them, a figure at once detached and active, simultaneously a causer of events and a commentator upon them. Thus, the exciting world of Indian peril, wilderness rescue, natural hazards—in short, all the staples of western adventure fiction—can be viewed both particularly and generally; the excitement of a tale of daring can be combined with philosophical concerns.

Western writers have copied Cooper because they have understood the larger implications and viability of telling exciting facts and at the same time commenting upon them, of setting up a neutral ground between two conflicting ideologies. In sum, the possibilities for ambiguity inherent in the paradoxes of Cooper's world have proved perpetually more intriguing to writers of fiction and their audience than straightforward factual accounts of western history.

Modern readers may best approach the Leatherstocking Tales by way of Allan Nevins' abridgment in *The Leatherstocking Saga* (1954), a volume that also contains a superb introductory essay. Biographical studies of Cooper have tended to concentrate upon his difficult personality and crotchety political opinions to the neglect of his fiction. Robert E. Spiller, *Fenimore Cooper: Critic of His Times* (1931), contains the best analysis of Cooper's social thought, to be supplemented by the biographical material in Thomas R. Lounsbury, *James Fenimore Cooper* (1883), and James Grossman, *James Fenimore Cooper* (1949). The essays by various hands in *James Fenimore Cooper: A Re-appraisal* (1954), edited by M. E. Cunningham, give differing new perspectives aimed toward a reevaluation of Cooper's place in American literature. The best short study of Cooper aimed primarily at literary rather than biographical criticism is Donald A. Ringe, *James Fenimore Cooper* (1962).—J. K. F.

Copper Kings, War of the. See MONTANA.

copper mining. A key metal in the industrialization process, copper has been far more important in the life of the modern United States than have silver and gold combined. With the electrification of industry and of homes after the 1870s, and with the advent of the automobile in the twentieth century, per capita consumption of copper increased tremendously. Production of that metal has expanded more than a hundredfold since the Civil War. Except for the years 1932 and 1934, the United States has been the leading copper producer since 1883. Its peak output of 1,429,000 tons in 1966 represented only about 26 percent of the total world yield, a percentage that had been steadily declining since

1916, when the United States produced nearly two thirds of the total.

Until the mid-nineteenth century, copper was not an important domestic commodity. In the 1840s, however, the exploitation of deposits in the small "mass veins" on Michigan's Keweenaw Peninsula began. Next and more important were the discoveries of the amygdaloidal lodes in the Keweenaw lava beds, and more important still were the great Calumet and Hecla conglomerate veins, also on Lake Superior, which concerns such as the Boston-capitalized Calumet and Hecla Mining Company—described as "a copper company with a Harvard accent"—tapped with great profit. From the dozen tons of copper produced in the Lake Superior area in 1845, its output jumped to 18,000 tons in 1875, and reached its peak of 135,000 tons in 1916. In all, about one in every three Lake Superior copper companies paid dividends, a remarkable record in a field where one success in ten is expected. Between 1871 and 1921, the Calumet and Hecla Mining Company paid dividends of $152,250,000 on an investment of $1,500,000.

Even before World War I, high-grade deposits at Butte, Montana, and in Arizona had overshadowed the Keweenaw conglomerates. Passing quickly through her days of gold and silver, Butte produced 5,000 tons of copper in 1882—the preliminaries to the development of "the Richest Hill on Earth." Entrepreneurs such as William A. CLARK on the one hand and Marcus DALY of the Anaconda interests and of new rail facilities to begin exploitation of the vast high-grade veins of copper sulphides that stood at steep angles and ran marvelously thick thousands of feet in length and depth. In 1887 Montana replaced Michigan as the leading copper region in the country and reached its peak production of 176,000 tons in 1916. Most of this was from the Butte area and was produced despite years of bitter litigation and intermittent underground violence, before Anaconda bought out its chief antagonist and consolidated its position as the leading corporation in the state.

Butte's rich veins were not equaled elsewhere, but in ARIZONA four large high-grade deposits were brought to full production near the end of the century, although all had been located much earlier, prior to settlement of the Indian and transportation problems. These were all copper sulphides, found in great "lenses" in limestone, and most were developed by large corporations. At Clifton-Morenci, a district in eastern Arizona, the Leszinsky brothers had mined on a limited scale before selling out to the Scottish Arizona Copper Company, Limited, in 1880. Under manager James Colquhoun, this firm built an advanced leaching plant and made the property a producer, ultimately selling its important mines to the Phelps Dodge Company in 1921. At Globe, deposits worked by the Lewisohns of New York in the 1890s also passed under the control of Phelps Dodge, whose brilliant engineer, Louis Ricketts, modernized the plant and brought success. Phelps Dodge also dominated at Bisbee, where James Douglas brought the Copper Queen mine into production in record time, but at Jerome, the fourth of the great Arizona high-grade districts, Douglas rejected the United Verde mine on behalf of Phelps Dodge in 1880. Eight years later William A. Clark of Montana acquired the property and ultimately took a profit of $60 million from it. Apart from lesser high-grade deposits found in Mexico and Alaska in this period, these were the major copper bodies of this type in the West.

The most revolutionary era of all began with the working of the low-grade porphyry, or disseminated ore, deposits on a new mass-production basis. The porphyries were primarily copper sulphides scattered to form a small percentage of a large mass, and their exploitation depended upon ability to handle bulk. It was a young engineer, Daniel C. Jackling, who made the technological breakthrough and in 1903 succeeded in forming the Utah Copper Company to work a huge deposit at Bingham on a scale unknown before that time. Jackling constructed a 2,000-ton-per-day concentrating plant at a time when a 500-ton plant was a large one; after the first few years, he used steam shovels to strip off the worthless overburden and scoop the ore into railroad cars on a nonselective basis. The success of Utah Copper was dazzling: in the sixty years prior to 1963, it took out more than 8 million tons of copper from "the richest hole on earth"—the largest man-made excavation in the world.

And its success sent engineers scurrying to find low-grade porphyry deposits the world over. Within the next few years they found a dozen important such bodies in the United States, among them deposits near Ely, Nevada, where Mark Requa paved the way and the Guggenheim's Kennecott Copper ultimately took over; at Ray, Arizona, and Santa Rita, New Mexico, where Kennecott also controlled the important fields; at Miami and at Inspiration, Arizona, the first independent, the second developed by the Anaconda group; at Ajo, where Louis Ricketts developed the New Cornelia mine, an exceptional addition to the Phelps Dodge Arizona holdings; and at Bisbee, where Phelps Dodge revitalized its mines, using low-grade techniques. From the early twentieth century, the low-grade porphyries have dominated American copper production, with Arizona ranking first since 1907, and Utah second since 1926.

Advancing technology was a vital factor in the low-grade mass-production revolution. Better methods projected on a larger scale meant cheaper per unit costs. Thus, because of high wartime prices during two global conflicts, and with the help of federal subsidies—especially in the 1950s—deposits once regarded as waste became profitable pay dirt. Where the Butte high-grade deposits often averaged 5 or 6 percent copper, Utah Copper in 1905 was working ore that ran 1.98 percent copper and the average dropped with time so that by 1962 the Bingham mines were working ore that was only 0.77 percent metal; by 1968, the average recoverable content of all copper ores in the United States was 0.60 percent.

Revolutionary in itself was the flotation process of concentration introduced in the 1912-25 era—an innovation which enhanced recovery as much as 50 percent as it gradually replaced gravity concentration except in a few important plants like those at Ajo or Inspiration where the oxide ores, as apart from the sulphides, were worked by leaching. But during the mid-1950s, many companies modernized their ore treatment, adopting either the "dual process" of combined leaching and flotation or Anaconda's example of the use of "LPF" (leaching-precipitation-flotation) units.

Underground block-caving techniques were employed at a number of porphyry mines, notably at Ray, Inspiration, and Miami, but by the end of the 1960s, 80 percent of the copper mined in the United States was by the open-cut method. Electric shovels replaced steam, and after World War II, except for Utah Copper, most open pit operations felt the impact of the heavy-duty, rubber-tired Diesel truck, which with other sophisticated earth-moving equipment either replaced or augmented railroad haulage and brought a whole new concept of flexibility to the industry.

Large-scale copper mining required huge concentrating works, electric generating plants, and vast armadas of expensive equipment. It has been estimated that to prepare an open-cut mine for production requires nearly four years, as opposed to half that time for an underground mine. Hence large amounts of capital were demanded, and even in Michigan and Montana, where vein mining predominated, the industry tended to concentrate in a relatively few major corporations. Today, some 360 mines produce copper in the United States, but the largest 25 account for nearly 96 percent of the nation's output. Together, the "Big Three"—Kennecott, Anaconda, and Phelps Dodge—mine about 75 percent of the total; with American Smelting & Refining Company, they refine more than 85 percent of the copper produced in the United States.

A general, but somewhat popularized, treatment of the subject is by Ira B. Joralemon, *Romantic Copper* (1936). Two excellent studies of the development of the low-grade deposits are by Arthur B. Parsons: *The Porphyry Coppers* (1933) and *The Porphyry Coppers in 1956* (1957).—C. C. S.

Cornish, Nellie Centennial (1876-1956). Sponsor of performing arts. Born in Greenwood, Nebraska, Nellie Centennial (so named because of her birth date) Cornish was educated in the public schools of Nebraska and by private music teachers. She taught piano in small towns of Oregon and Washington before moving to Seattle in 1900. There she founded in 1914 the Cornish School of Music and Art, with courses in painting, dance, theater, and music instruction. This was the first school of its type in the northwestern United States and one of the first in the nation. Countless well-known artists taught in her school, including Mark Tobey, Elena Miramova, Alexander Koiransky, and Moroni Olsen. Cornish withdrew from active direction of the school in 1939, but the school is still operating.

See Ellen V. Brown and Edward N. Beck, eds., *Miss Aunt Nellie: The Autobiography of Nellie C. Cornish* (1964); and Nancy Wilson Ross, "The Incredible Miss Nellie," *Seattle Magazine* (November 1964). —K. A. M.

Cornplanter. Also called **John O'Bail** or **Abeel** (c. 1732-1836). Seneca chief. Cornplanter was born between 1732 and 1740 at Conewaugus on the Genesee River in New York. His father was a white trader, and his mother was a full-blooded Seneca. Handsome Lake, the religious prophet, was his brother. As a young man Cornplanter earned a reputation as a warrior and orator. During the French and Indian War he joined the French and was present when General Edward Braddock was defeated near Fort Duquesne in 1755. During the American Revolution he joined Iroquois attacks against American settlements in New York and Pennsylvania. After the Revolution he emerged as an important

Seneca leader, playing major roles at the treaties of Fort Stanwix (1784) and Fort Harmar (1789). In 1791 he personally presented Seneca grievances to George Washington in Philadelphia. A Seneca faction, the Cornplanter Seneca, settled with him in Pennsylvania and followed his guidance.

Cornplanter advocated rapid assimilation of white ways and so sought to secure land to permit his followers to reorient their economy around white agricultural techniques. He undertook peace missions to hostile tribes for the federal government, but only in exchange for land. The land he chose was in an isolated area, away from white settlements and hopefully safe from encroachments.

A skilled politician, Cornplanter exercised his leadership to benefit himself as well as his followers. At numerous treaties in the 1780s and 1790s he made private agreements that brought him large amounts of land and money. By 1800 he owned 1,300 acres, 640 of which Governor Mifflin of Pennsylvania had granted him in 1796 "for his many valuable services to the whites." He also used his wealth to benefit his followers, thereby increasing his status and power in the Indian community.

Cornplanter remained an important Seneca leader through the 1820s. However, as he grew older he became convinced that the "Great Spirit" had told him to break all his ties with the whites. Thus he burned many presents given him by whites and rejected the idea of assimilation, which he had held earlier.

For further reference, see S. G. Drake, *The Book of the Indians of North America* (1845); F. W. Hodge, *Handbook of American Indians North of Mexico*, 2 vols. (1907-10); and A. F. C. Wallace, *The Death and Rebirth of the Seneca* (1970).—G. M.

corn production. Corn was a contribution of the western world to agriculture. Apparently originating in South America, it had long been known to the Indians of the Northeast along with the bean and the squash. Among the Iroquois it was a staple of their diet, being raised in considerable quantities and stored in their longhouses for winter consumption. The English learned that one of the most effective ways to weaken the Indians was to destroy their supplies of stored and growing corn. The Indians taught the early settlers how to plant corn, and by 1631 Virginia was producing enough that it became an item of export. Whites found corn equally important as a food item, making it their first staple. Wherever they settled, they placed heavy reliance on corn. In 1860 it was grown in every state and in practically every county. As the economy developed, wheat was more commonly used for human consumption and corn for livestock and poultry. Corn is less subject to the ravages of parasites and diseases than wheat—though the borer and viruses have taken their toll—and it is somewhat less vulnerable to the vagaries of weather. It is a questionable crop in the drier portions of the Great Plains, where sorghum grains are grown instead, and it often does not mature in regions having a short growing season. It is attacked by crows who unearth and eat the planted seed in the spring, blackbirds who unsheath the mature ear and rob it of its grain, and raccoons, squirrels, rats, and mice.

Maturing corn has been used in different ways by farmers. In the South, when other forage was exhausted leaves were pulled from the stalk and fed to cattle. The development of the wooden silo in the late nineteenth century made it possible for dairy farmers to cut the growing corn in the milk stage, shred the stalk, leaves, stem, and cob with the green grain, and elevate it into the silo for forage in the winter. In this way the entire plant except the roots was used. Silos became as characteristic of dairy farms as the milk house and the corncrib, and ensilage as important as hay, in the herd's forage. In the early frontier days of western Pennsylvania, Virginia, and Kentucky, liquor was distilled from boiling corn mash and was easily sold or consumed at home. Corn in the form of dried grain was fed to hogs and cattle who, when sufficiently fattened, were driven to market, a much easier way to utilize the grain than to haul it over the rough dirt roads of the early days. It took more capital than the farm maker ordinarily had when he began his operations to invest heavily in livestock. The production of grain absorbed his time and capital at first, and only when he was well established with sound credit could he begin to feed his corn to hogs and feeder cattle on an extensive scale. In the last half of the nineteenth century the feeder cattle business flourished, first in Ohio, then in Indiana and Illinois, and later in Iowa. Farmers were strongly urged to use their corn as feed rather than to sell it, for they would thus make two profits from it and would at the same time have the benefit of the manure to maintain their soil. Some farmers even began to purchase corn, so large were their feeding operations.

From maps prepared by the United States Department of Agriculture one can trace the development of the modern corn belt, which extends from Ohio to eastern Kansas and Nebraska. In 1839 the leading states were Tennessee, Kentucky, and Virginia, with Ohio ranking fourth and Indiana fifth. By 1859 Illinois was far in the lead, producing thirteen percent of the country's crop, followed by Ohio, Missouri, and Indiana. In 1919 Iowa led with sixteen percent of the crop; Illinois, Nebraska, Indiana, and Ohio ranked next. By 1880 the corn belt states were also leading hog producers with Iowa, Illinois, Missouri, Indiana, and Ohio well in the lead. Farmland in these states was too high in value to be used for raising beef cattle, but western steers were brought into them for fattening purposes, the leading feeder states being Iowa, Missouri, and Illinois.

Deep plowing, manuring of the land, and liming, if necessary, were urged by farm journals, though the frequency with which such admonitions appeared suggests that these practices were not commonly followed. Farmers in the prairies of Illinois and Iowa reasoned that their soil was inexhaustibly rich and needed no such attention. Furthermore, a relatively high proportion of the prairie lands, especially of Indiana and Illinois, was farmed by tenants who felt compelled to get as much from the soil as possible with the least expenditure of capital and labor. Unless checked by farm managers or owners they could and did do much damage to the land by such practices. There is a classic case of a landlord owning a number of thousand acres on the Illinois-Indiana line and who either gave no supervision to his tenants or was content to let them plant corn year after year without fertilizers or crop rotating. At his death the executors of his estate swore in an inheritance-tax pro-

Pueblo women grinding corn. (Library of Congress)

ceeding that a generation of neglect had so depleted the once-rich land as to justify an extremely low appraisal, and it was allowed.

Corn growing has gone through great changes from the early days, when corn was planted around stumps in clearings or in the turned-over sod of the prairies, to the modern highly mechanized operations. Early plantings for household consumption were small but were gradually expanded to provide for livestock. When matured, the stalks were cut and shocked in the field to dry. When needed the ears were shucked and shelled, all by hand, or the ears might be shucked and placed in cribs for drying and then thrown to the hogs without shelling. The old wooden, iron-tipped plow that did little more than scratch the surface was being replaced in the mid-nineteenth century by the chilled-steel plow. Then came the riding sulky plow to replace the walking plow, and with the tractor in the twentieth century came the gang-plow. Crude planting devices were being experimented with in the mid-nineteenth century, but the effective one-row seeder came later. Then came the two- and four-row planters, which speeded up the process of getting the corn in the ground between spring rains. Hand cutting of the stalks, an arduous and seemingly endless task on large fields, led to experiments with corn cutters. Only with the tractor in the twentieth century were effective one- and two-row corn-cutting devices perfected. Hand-operated corn shellers, in use before the Civil War, were distinct improvements over earlier primitive methods of shelling, but they were still too slow for large crops. Power shellers of a later day re-

lieved farmers of a part of their winter chores. With this array of machinery, farmers could take advantage of short breaks in weather to plant and harvest their grain and could plant larger acreages. Indeed, that larger acreage was needed to justify the heavy investment in machinery. In the years of most intensive mechanization, Illinois, for example, increased the average size of its farms from 124 acres in 1900 to 232 acres in 1960. The corn belt counties of Illinois had even larger farms, ranging from 232 acres on the average in McLean County to 262 acres in Vermilion County.

One of the outstanding scientific breakthroughs of the twentieth century has been the perfection of hybrid corn that yields from twenty-five to thirty percent more grain than the open-pollinated variety previously used. Hybrid vigor obtained from crossing or double crossing carefully selected inbred varieties was worked out in the laboratories in the 1920s. Commercial seedmen developed their own combinations and by the early 1930s were putting their high-yielding seed corn on the market, where in a short time it displaced open-pollinated seed. Since hybrid corn does not breed true, farmers have had to purchase their seed from the companies producing it in place of their earlier practice of selecting the best-looking ears for seed. The success of hybrid corn encouraged many experiments in crossbreeding and hybridizing other grains, notably wheat and rice, which blossomed into the "green revolution" of the 1960s that has produced vastly increased yields of grain in countries previously largely dependent on imports.

Other recent developments that have affected the growing of corn are the use of liquid weed killers, notably 2, 4-D, to eliminate or control weeds that otherwise would draw off the moisture and nutrients the corn needs, and the application of ammonium nitrate to give the growing corn an extra shot of liquid fertilizer.

In 1959 corn production averaged fifty-three bushels to the acre throughout the United States, as compared with twenty-six bushels in 1929. In the corn belt it was much higher. Weather, rainfall, the length of the growing season, and other natural factors may have contributed to this startling improvement, but most important was hybrid seed and technical improvements in soil management. Iowa was still the premium corn-producing state with Illinois, Nebraska, and Indiana next in line. Corn continued to be the most valuable of all crops, constituting twenty-three percent of the value of all crops harvested. It was followed by cotton and hay, the value of which was about half that of corn. Wheat, soybeans, and tobacco ranked next in order.

See United States Department of Agriculture, *Yearbook*, especially those for 1921 and 1922; see also Paul W. Gates, *The Farmer's Age: Agriculture, 1815-1860* (1960); and Fred A. Shannon, *The Farmer's Last Frontier, Agriculture, 1860-1897* (1945).—P. W. G.

Cornstalk (c. 1720?-1777). Shawnee chief. Cornstalk was probably born in Pennsylvania but was associated in his mature life with the Ohio country. The Shawnee had generally favored the French against the British before 1763, and Cornstalk spent most of his life opposing the remorseless advance of Anglo-Saxon settlement across the Appalachians. He led raids against the Virginia frontier in 1759 during the French and Indian War, and again in 1763 during Pontiac's Rebellion. Following this latter conflict he was briefly held hostage by a retaliatory British expedition. Cornstalk reluctantly went to war once more in 1774, vainly leading his warriors against Lord Dunmore's army of Virginians at Point Pleasant, on the Ohio River (see LORD DUNMORE'S WAR). In 1777 when he returned there on a diplomatic mission, he was again detained as a hostage and then murdered by lawless whites. This action helped confirm Shawnee hostility to the whites for years to come.—A. W. T.

Coronado, Francisco Vásquez de (1510-1554). Spanish explorer of the Southwest. As a result of the stories of cities of wealth and exotic peoples spread by Cabeza de Vaca and Fray Marcos, plus other rumors of the Seven Cities of Cíbola, which were alleged to be north of Mexico, the Spanish focused their attentions on that mysterious, unknown region. By land went three hundred ambitious Spaniards and eight hundred Indians. Their leader was Coronado, the thirty-year-old governor of New Galicia, a province in northwest Mexico.

In April 1540 the expedition was launched from the city of Compostela, five hundred miles northwest of Mexico City. Following ancient trails up the western corridor of Mexico, the expedition advanced northward into the region along the Arizona-New Mexico boundary, finding Cíbola (Zuñi), which is in northwest New Mexico. These towns were conquered with a minimum of bloodshed, but they brought forth no riches. Pedro de Tovar, one of Coronado's lieutenants, subjugated the Hopi villages to the north and west, and another lieutenant, García López de Cárdenas, explored west to the Colorado River, which he gazed down upon from the rim of the Grand Canyon. A marine branch of the expedition, led by Hernando de Alarcón, had meanwhile advanced some distance up the same river from its mouth, thus making Alarcón the first Spaniard to reach California.

Still another officer, Hernando de Alvarado, searched eastward and discovered the pueblo of Acoma, the "Sky City." He then worked north up the Rio Grande to Taos. Along the way he acquired two slaves of the local Indians, Ysopete and one the Spaniards dubbed "the Turk." Both of them told of their homes far to the northeast in a place called Quivira, and the Turk boasted of the fabulous riches there. Coronado wintered at Tiguex, between Albuquerque and Bernalillo, New Mexico, and then set off for Quivira in the spring of 1541.

He crossed the Pecos, worked northeast across the Texas and Oklahoma panhandles, discovered Tule and Palo Duro canyons, and saw buffalo and the nomadic Indians who hunted them. He continued northeast into KANSAS, reaching the Arkansas River at about the site of Ford, Kansas. Three days later he met the first Indians of Quivira, but they lived in huts and were anything but rich. From here Coronado made his way among the Wichita Indians along the Smoky Hill River, garroted the lying Turk, returned to Tiguex, and in April 1542 left for Mexico. No gold, silver, precious gems, or exotic cities had he found. His health affected by his journey, disappointed, and suffering from a painful injury, Coronado now had to submit to a lengthy official investigation.

The Coronado expedition, along with the explorations at almost the same time of Hernando de Soto in the Southeast and of Cabeza de Vaca before them, gave the Spanish a fairly accurate concept of the southern half of the present United States.

See Herbert E. Bolton, *Coronado, Knight of Pueblos and Plains* (1949), which is both exciting and scholarly; George P. Hammond and Agapito Rey, *Narratives of the Coronado Expedition of 1540-1542* (1940); and George Parker Winship, "The Coronado Expedition, 1540-1542," *Fourteenth Annual Report of the Bureau of Ethnology* (1896), Part 1.—R. A. B.

Cortez, Gregorio (1875-1916). Folk hero. "Then said Gregorio Cortez, with his pistol in his hand, 'Ah, so many mounted Rangers just to take one Mexican!' " Thus the "Corrido [Ballad] de Gregorio Cortez" tells the story of a man who came to symbolize the struggle between Mexicans and Anglo-Americans in Texas. He was born in northern Mexico, but his family moved to south Texas when he was twelve years old. He worked on various ranches as either a vaquero or a ranch hand until he and his brother finally settled down to farm. On June 12, 1901, the sheriff of Karnes County, Texas, attempted to arrest Cortez and his brother for horse-stealing. Cortez denied the charge and pointed out that he could not be arrested for nothing, whereupon the sheriff shot and wounded his brother. While trying to protect himself Cortez shot and killed the sheriff.

Knowing that in Texas there was one law for Anglos and another for Mexicans, Cortez fled and was pursued by Anglo posses of up to three hundred men. During the chase he eluded the law and fought off posse after posse, thus coming to represent to the Mexican people a man who fought for his rights and would not back down.

For ten days he remained at large, outwitting his pursuers. He rode more than 400 miles and walked at least 120 miles in a frantic effort to reach the Mexican border. Cortez was captured before he crossed the border but not until he had killed a second sheriff in a gunfight with a posse.

Cortez' crime was viewed as an act of defiance to Anglo injustice, and he was supported by his countrymen, who contributed money for his defense in a legal battle that lasted for almost four years. He was acquitted of killing the sheriff of Karnes County but was sentenced to life imprisonment for the killing of the second sheriff. In 1913 he was granted a pardon, but after only three years of freedom he died. In Texas the Mexicans still tell the "Corrido de Gregorio Cortez."

See Pedro Castillo and Alberto Camarillo, eds., *Furia y Muerte: Los Bandidos Chicanos* (1973); and Américo Paredes, *With His Pistol in His Hand: A Border Ballad And Its Hero* (1958).—P. C.

Cortina, Juan Nepomuceno (1824-1892). Rancher, general, governor, bandit, and revolutionary. "Cheno" Cortina was born in Camarago, a village on the Texas side of the Rio Grande. He was a member of a wealthy and prominent family who did not take advantage of their economic position. His heritage was not only one of wealth but also one of leadership within the Mexican community. With the coming of the Anglo this position of honor and responsibility was threatened.

During the Mexican War he joined the Mexican army and fought against the United States. After the war Cortina established a ranch on his mother's land near Brownsville in the lower Rio Grande valley. But he soon realized that the coming of the Anglo had pushed the Mexicans into a state of second-class citizenship. Mexicans had little protection from the law, since Anglos controlled the police and the courts and considered the killing of Mexicans no crime and the mistreating of them a pastime. Therefore, Cortina could never assume the role of leader, which he felt was his birthright.

On July 13, 1859, his career began in the classic social-bandit manner. As Cortina was riding home to his ranch one day, he saw a Mexican who had at one time worked on his ranch being beaten by the Brownsville marshal. Cortina demanded that the marshal stop, which he did not do; Cortina therefore shot him in the shoulder and fled with the Mexican servant. He became a hero immediately because he had taken matters into his own hands in order to defend the Mexican who had been mistreated. The local sheriff and later some Texas Rangers attempted to arrest Cortina, but they were unsuccessful.

On September 28, 1859, Cortina led some of his fellow Mexicans into Brownsville; meeting no resistance, he occupied the city and proclaimed the Republic of the Rio Grande. As Mexicans from the local area joined his gang, Cortina's men raised the Mexican flag and shouted, "Death to the gringos!" Cortina had the city at his mercy, but he did not pillage. He was far from being a simple bandit: he was a man resisting Anglo injustice and oppression. Cortina was able to defeat attempts by the local authorities and the Texas Rangers to subdue him. He continued his resistance in the area from Brownsville to Rio Grande City, attempting to regain the cattle and land that had been stolen from the Mexicans.

Faced with the combined force of the Texas Rangers, the United States Army, and the local authorities, Cortina had to dissolve his small army and flee to Mexico. There he was appointed a general in the army by President Benito Juárez and later became the military governor of the state of Tamaulipas. With the coming to power of Porfirio Díaz, Cortina was imprisoned in Mexico City in 1875 and was not released until 1890. He returned to the border and died in 1892. Cortina led an organized revolt and was a man fulfilling what he felt was his duty—both resisting the Anglos and standing up for the rights of his countrymen.

See José T. Canales, *Juan N. Cortina, Bandit or Patriot* (1951); and Pedro Castillo and Alberto Camarillo, eds., *Furia y Muerte: Los Bandidos Chicanos* (1973).—P. C.

Costigan, Edward Prentiss (1874-1939). Colorado lawyer and politician. Born in King William County, Virginia, Costigan moved with his family to Colorado while still a small boy. He entered Harvard in 1892, but an illness interrupted his studies. After reading law in Utah, he was admitted to the bar of that state in 1897, and only then did he return to Harvard, receiving his B.A. degree *cum laude* in 1899. After moving to Denver in 1900, he soon became involved in progressive reform movements, while continuing his law practice. He was an organizer and attorney for the Honest Election League and the Law Enforcement League and was a leader of the Colorado Direct Primary and Direct Legislation leagues. A spokesman for progressivism within the Republican party, he took the lead in founding the Progressive party of Colorado and was its unsuccessful candidate for governor in the elections of 1912 and 1914. Colorado's labor troubles were a primary issue in the 1914 campaign, and Costigan spoke forcefully for social, industrial, and political justice. During congressional investigations into the 1913-14 Colorado coal strike, which culminated in the notorious "Ludlow Massacre" (April 20, 1914), Costigan had been one of the principal attorneys for the United Mine Workers. After the strike he defended many of those indicted for murder, winning numerous acquittals. In 1917 he was appointed to the United States Tariff Commission, a position he held until 1928. Costigan affiliated with the Democratic party in 1930 and as a Democrat served one term in the United States Senate, from 1931 to 1937.

Costigan's career as a Colorado Progressive may be traced in Colin B. Goodykoontz, ed., *Papers of Edward P. Costigan Relating to the Progressive Movement in Colorado, 1902-1917* (1941).—M. B.

cotton culture. The growing of cotton became an impelling economic force in westward expansion and AGRICULTURAL EXPANSION after Eli Whitney's invention of the cotton gin in 1793. The cotton plant itself is one of the widely distributed plants of the world, although the specific origin of cotton as a commercial staple is somewhat blurred by lack of historical record. Perhaps it was first introduced to Europe and England from India. Columbus found it growing in the Bahamas, and it is known to have been cultivated by the Incas of Peru. Plants of the cotton family are indigenous to the United States, but they produce little, if any, fiber.

There are records of two varieties of cotton growing in Virginia and the Carolinas in the early eighteenth century: the long staple black-seeded, sea-island type, and the short staple green-seed plant of the highlands. The latter was developed in the expanding cotton belt after the opening of the nineteenth century. The mechanical gin made it possible to separate the lint from the small, tightly fibered green seed. By 1820 cotton planters had entered the Mississippi valley about Natchez and Vicksburg, and in the prairie lands up the Alabama and Black Warrior rivers. In the 1830s, with the opening of Indian lands around the Gulf coastal areas of the lower South, cotton-growing became a central agricultural activity.

In one respect cotton was a versatile crop. It was well suited to the needs of the small hillside yeoman farmer and at the same time to those of the slave-holding plantation owner. Too, it could be grown by the crudest sort of cultivation methods and could be harvested and housed without use of expensive equipment. People of almost all ages could be engaged in cultivating and harvesting cotton.

By 1860 the cotton belt had expanded from the southeastern counties of Virginia to central Texas, and as far north as the Purchase counties of western Kentucky known as the "Jackson Purchase" because of Andrew Jackson's role in the purchase of the area from the Chickasaw Indians in 1818) and those of southeastern Missouri. From the beginning of the nineteenth century it played a major role in the expansion of the southwestern frontier. Literally hundreds of thousands of people migrated to the cotton belt, where they developed a folkway and economic culture peculiar to the region.

By 1820 the slave-cotton system had already reached such a state of promise that the bitter sectional issue over the Missouri admission question and the expansion of slavery into the western territories was to have enormous political impact on the country.

Cotton culture itself was laborious, requiring long hours of work under a broiling sun both in the processes of cultivation and harvesting. The plant itself did not extract so many nutrients from the soil as to be exhaustive, but careless and wasteful methods of cultivation did destroy the soil. Erosion caused by primitive cultivation methods denuded hundreds of thousands of acres of land. This land abuse caused a constant movement of individuals within the cotton belt in search of fresh lands. Cotton planter and farmer alike were forced to depend upon foreign buyers to purchase the great bulk of the annual crop. Too, most areas of the cotton belt were dependent upon the steam boat and the rivers as means of transporting the annual harvest to market. Because of the latter conditions, southern economic views were severely limited by a belief that cotton culture was a central fact in world economics.

See Clement Eaton, *A History of the Old South* (1949); Matthew Brown Hammond, *The Cotton Industry* (1897); and Harold W. Woodman, *King Cotton and His Retainers* (1968).—T. D. C.

cotton production. Cotton, the chief item in American foreign trade until 1929, was regarded by southern leaders before the Civil War as so vital to the economic welfare of England that it was believed that that nation would throw its support to the Confederacy to get continued access to "King Cotton." Long-staple, sea-island cotton was a superior grade of fine cotton grown only in limited areas, but its price put it in the class of luxury commodities. Upland cotton, the better seed for which was imported from Mexico, likewise had a limited market because of the expense involved in separating the seed of this short staple cotton from the lint. Eli Whitney's perfection of the cotton gin in 1793, first operated by hand then by steam, so reduced the cost of labor in preparing the seed cotton for market as to create a demand for the fiber that sent production upward at a fantastic rate: 3,135 bales of 400 pounds in 1790, 73,145 in 1800, 177,638 in 1820, 731,452 in 1830, 1,345,292 in 1840, 2,133,851 in 1850, and 4,541,285 in 1859. Rarely has an invention so changed farm practices, manufacturing, and internal trade as the cotton gin.

Cotton in 1861 rivaled corn as the number one staple of the South, outranking tobacco, rice, and sugar. It was grown in practically every settled county from North Carolina to Texas both by small yeomen farmers and planters owning a few slaves, and by landowners possessing several plantations and hundreds of slaves. Cotton required year-round labor to prepare the soil and plant the seed, to thin out the growing plants and eliminate the weeds, to pick the fields a number of times, to gin and bale the cotton, and to haul it to steamboat landings where it could be taken to New Orleans or Charleston. In fact the final tasks on one crop were not completed before work on the next was begun.

The demand for cotton at home and abroad kept the average price at a profitable level most years and contributed to the rising value of slaves and the political movement for the reopening of the slave trade. Whereas in the earlier years there had been some slight support in the South for ending slavery, that section later would not tolerate any discussion of this question. The South demanded the removal of the Five Civilized Tribes of Indians from Georgia, Mississippi, and Alabama and the opening of their lands to settlement. Great excitement occurred at the public sales of some of the Creek, Chickasaw, and Choctaw lands when they were thrown open in the wildly inflationary years 1817-19 and 1834-37. With cotton bringing thirty-two cents a pound in 1818, planters and capitalists with credit rushed to buy Alabama and Mississippi land, some for development, others for speculation. Wild land that would take much capital and labor to bring into cultivation went for prices far beyond its worth at the time. Again in 1834-37 potential cotton land not previously offered for sale brought excited bidding at the auction sales in Mississippi and Alabama. A goodly portion of this land was purchased for speculation, although a large acreage was cleared and placed in cotton. It was only by segments that the Gulf Coast was acquired from France and Spain in 1803, 1810, 1813, and 1819, but so rapid was the rush of population into the region to take up land for cotton farming that Louisiana entered the Union in 1812, Mississippi and Alabama in 1817 and 1819, and Arkansas in 1836. The possibilities for expansion of cotton planting in the Mexican state of Texas attracted Americans there also. Finding Mexican authority too arbitrary, they declared their independence and asked for admission into the Union. This in turn contributed to the coming of the Mexican War and the acquisition of New Mexico and California. Even these additions did not satisfy the cotton-hungry expansionists among the proslavery elements; they conducted filibustering expeditions into Central America and induced President James Buchanan to attempt to purchase Cuba.

Because many planters in the cotton belt and in the sugar bowl of the Deep South were not raising sufficient corn, wheat, pork, and beef for their own needs and those of their slaves, that section was forced to depend upon states of the upper Mississippi valley for these items, thereby contributing to interregional trade by way of the Mississippi and to the growth of such states as Ohio, Indiana, Illinois, and Missouri.

Emancipation of the slaves and the destruction wrought by the marching armies together with the general disorganization of agriculture caused by the Civil War and the strife of the Reconstruction years, delayed the recovery of cotton production to its prewar level until 1879, though the average price in the intervening years was for the most part favorable. Failure of the government to bring about any redistribution of the land among the freedmen left them with no alternative but to become sharecroppers, for they had no capital to set themselves up as tenants or farm owners. The crop lien became the means by which they were tied to the land and virtually compelled to put their labor and the land assigned to them into producing cotton. They could not move from cotton to other crops when prices might seem to dictate such a change. This lack of flexibility was neither good for the land nor for the sharecroppers. It could well be questioned whether the average freedman on his small cotton patch was any better off than he had been in slavery.

By 1900 Texas had become the major producer of cotton, with Mississippi, Georgia, and Alabama following. In five years in the 1890s the output for the country was double what it had been on the eve of the Civil War, and the average price declined from 8.98 cents a pound in the 1880s to 6.93 cents in the 1890s. In 1894 the average was 4.59 cents, which, for many farmers, was less than the cost of production. Distressed southern farmers responded to rising production and diminishing returns by organizing the Farmers' Alliance and by taking an active part in the Populist revolt, but these movements of protest did them little good. Better prices returned in 1900 owing to improved demand abroad and the inflationary effect of the new supplies of gold that were flowing into circulation. Cotton was 10.5 cents a pound in 1903, 13.5 cents in 1909, 17 cents in 1916, and 35 cents in 1919. Such prices led to greatly increased production, which the market was able to absorb fairly well until 1930 and the following two years, when prices declined to 5.60 cents in 1931 and 6.52 cents in 1932.

Cotton farmers cried out for government assistance to reduce output and to raise prices. Congress responded with the crop-control program of the Agricultural Adjustment Administration, which has in one form or another provided a floor on prices for cotton ever since. Farmers learned to withdraw their lowest yielding acres and to use their most productive acres more intensively so that 17 million acres in 1956 yielded almost as much cotton as 43 million had yielded in 1929. The high price at which the controlled program has pegged cotton has led to its extensive planting in other parts of the world, stimulated the use of synthetic fibers, and reduced the foreign demand for American cotton. Whereas in 1925-30 the American production of cotton was fifty-seven percent of the world's output, in 1967 it was only twenty percent, and the number of bales exported has fallen from 11,299,000 in 1926 to 4,361,000 in 1967.

Meantime, great changes were occurring in cotton planting. With the substitution of tractor-drawn sulky plows, harrows and cultivators, and, most important, the cotton picker for the mule, crude shovel plow, hoe and handpickers which were used earlier, sharecroppers were becoming nonessential. They were being thrust off the land and their forty-acre tracts were being combined into large farms where the work was being done by machines. Cotton planting had moved into irrigated land in California, Arizona, and New Mexico where the product was of finer quality and the yield 1.7 bales to the acre compared with Texas' yield of .78 bales. Wherever it was produced, cotton was heavily subsidized by the government, but in California, Arizona, and New Mexico, where irrigation water was also heavily subsidized, the planter had an advantage over his competitors elsewhere. With diminishing demand abroad and competition from the doubly subsidized cotton produced on the irrigated acreage in the Southwest, the future of cotton in the traditional states of the Old South is in question. The statistics show what is occurring. Mississippi's average acreage in cotton in 1928-32 was 3,967,000 acres, whereas in 1967 it was 890,000 acres; South Carolina's acreage was down by five sixths; Georgia's by eleven twelfths; and Texas' by three fourths. California, however, has increased the area in cotton from 20,000 to 588,000 acres.

See Lewis C. Gray, *History of Agriculture in the Southern United States to 1860* (1933); and United States Department of Agriculture, *Yearbook* for 1921 and 1950-51.
—P. W. G.

Coues, Elliott (1842-1899). Ornithologist and editor. Born in Portsmouth, New Hampshire, Coues moved with his family in 1853 to Washington, D.C., where he attended Gonzaga Seminary and studied medicine at Columbian College (now George Washington University). (He returned to the college in 1877 as professor of anatomy, a post he held until 1886.)

In 1864 Coues was appointed assistant surgeon at Fort Whipple, Arizona, an assignment that provided him with an opportunity to explore much of the country. He served at Fort Randall, Dakota, in 1873 and was then appointed in the same year surgeon and naturalist to the United States Northern Boundary Commission. From 1876 to 1880 he was secretary and naturalist to the Geological and Geographic Survey of the Territories under F. V. Hayden. In 1880 Coues was again returned to Arizona, but finding that life as an army surgeon was interfering with his scientific work, he resigned his commission.

Coues' scientific career spanned four decades, beginning with *A Monograph of the Tringeae* (1861), a technical treatise. His most famous work, the *Key to North American Birds*, first published in 1872, grew, in large part, from his research in the West. Other notable scientific works include his *Birds of the Northwest* (1874), *Birds of the Colorado Valley* (1878), and *Fur Bearing Animals* (1877).

In the 1890s Coues turned his attention to a subject that had been in the back of his mind ever since he embarked on the Santa Fe Trail while stationed at Fort Whipple. In a flurry of editorial enterprise Coues turned out the *History of the Expedition of Lewis and Clark*

Cotton being picked in an Oklahoma field in the 1890s. (National Archives)

(1893), *Expeditions of Zebulon Montgomery Pike* (1895), *Journals of Alexander Henry and David Thompson* (1897), *Journal of Major Jacob Fowler* (1898), *Forty Years a Fur Trader on the Upper Missouri by Charles Larpenteur* (1898), and *Diary of Francisco Garces* (1900).

These works, totaling fifteen volumes, consisted entirely, except in the case of Lewis and Clark and Pike, of previously unpublished material. Coues annotated the volumes copiously, making special reference to the geography, ethnography, and general natural history of the regions. Coues himself retraced many of the explorers' routes, traveling thousands of miles in order to ensure geographical correctness. While on one of these arduous journeys in New Mexico and Arizona, his health deteriorated, and he was forced to return to the East, where he died after an extended illness.—R. B. W.

cougar. See MOUNTAIN LION.

Courtright, Jim [Timothy Isaiah] (1845?-1887). Lawman and detective. "Longhaired Jim" Courtright was born in Illinois. He was a scout during the Civil War and later moved to Texas to farm. Quickly abandoning the plow for the badge and the six-gun, he served in various capacities as a lawman and in 1876 was elected marshal of Fort Worth, Texas, where he was quite popular. Still, Courtright was a brooding man who drank too much and in 1878 he was fired. For a while he was marshal at Lake Valley, New Mexico, and in 1883 was hired by his old Civil War commander as foreman of a ranch in New Mexico. There he and Jim McIntyre killed two squatters. Courtright fled back to Fort Worth, where he was arrested and held for extradition. With the help of friends, he escaped to South America. In 1886 he returned to New Mexico to stand trial and was acquitted. He then returned to Fort Worth and opened a detective agency. When the business foundered, Courtright began to demand fees from local saloonkeepers in exchange for his protection. On February 8, 1887, he was

killed in a gunfight by Luke Short, a gambler who refused to pay.

See F. Stanley, *Jim Courtright, Two-Gun Marshal of Fort Worth* (1957).—G. L. R.

Couse, Eanger Irving (1866-1936). Painter. Born in Saginaw, Michigan, Couse began his formal art training at the Art Institute of Chicago at the age of seventeen. There followed a period of study at the Art Students League in New York City and approximately ten years abroad, where he was a frequent exhibitor at the Paris Salon. While studying in France, he met Virginia Walker, another American art student, whom he married in 1889. Returning to the United States, Couse and his wife visited her father's sheep ranch near Arlington, Oregon, and thereafter spent a number of seasons in Oregon between trips to New York and Paris. On one of his Paris trips, Couse met Joseph Henry Sharp, from whom he heard of the beauties of the country surrounding the little village of Taos, New Mexico. In 1902 Couse visited Taos and returned every summer for many years, retaining his New York studio, where he spent the winters producing pictures of the Southwest. His standing in New York circles enabled him to advance the cause of the Taos artists' colony, and when the Taos Society of Artists was formed in 1912 he was elected its president. One of the few artists permitted to observe the Indians' sacred ceremonial dances and other rituals, Couse painted many Pueblo Indian subjects.

Couse was elected to the National Academy of Design in 1911 and received numerous awards over the years. His paintings are at the Metropolitan Museum of Art in New York City; the National Gallery of Art in Washington, D.C.; the Brooklyn Museum, Brooklyn, New York; the Toledo Museum of Art, Toledo, Ohio; the St. Paul Art Center, St. Paul, Minnesota; the Fort Worth Art Center, Fort Worth, Texas, and in many private collections throughout the Southwest.

See Van Deren Coke, *Taos and Santa Fe: The Artist's Environment* (1963); and Mabel Dodge Luhan, *Taos and Its Artists* (1947).—D. C. H.

cowboy. Myth and reality have mingled in the popular image of the cowboy ever since he was introduced to the American public by the pulp fiction of the 1870s. The Fred Fearnots of the dime novels and their latter-day cinematic counterparts represent not an inversion of the truth but a distension of it: in them the very real courage of the cowboy becomes foolhardiness; his toughness, indestructibility; and the rootlessness of his life, romantic vagabondage. The cowboy myth notes and exaggerates the colorfulness of COWBOY CLOTHING but ignores its grim pragmatism: chaps protected legs from the thorns and nettles of range plant life; a bandanna absorbed sweat and, when worn over mouth and nose, kept dust from choking a man; the high heel of the cowboy boot was made to grip a stirrup and keep a rider from being thrown; and guns were used to kill predators. Thus armed against the occasional dangers that nature placed in his path, the cowboy yet had to cope with the insidious conditions of his everyday existence, all of which have been glossed over by the mythmakers: he was poorly fed, underpaid, overworked, deprived of sleep, and prone to boredom and loneliness. It is no wonder that most cowboys spent but about seven years on the range before seeking out a more human and settled existence in the towns of the West.

The motives that led men to become cowboys were seldom as romantic as those most often attributed to them. In the years following the Civil War—the peak years of the range CATTLE INDUSTRY—many young men of the Confederacy found themselves without family, property, or even work opportunities in the devastated South. For them the West was, if not the Promised Land, at least a land that promised a new beginning. A smaller number of Union veterans, especially those from New England, were likewise drawn to the range. The origin of many a cowboy in those early years was readily discernible in the scruffy remnants of a uniform that had now to serve him as work clothes.

Filling out the ranks of cowboys were Indians, Mexicans, blacks, and—most surprising of all—Englishmen and Scotsmen. The black cowboys were, for the most part, ex-slaves from Texas ranches; the rest had moved west to escape the constraints placed on blacks by local Southern governments in reaction to the North's Reconstruction policies. That one in seven cowboys was black does not mean that blacks were made welcome on the range. White cowboys were no more free of bias than their countrymen in the East, but given the fluid nature of western society and the absence of eastern institutions, which tended to foster discrimination, white cowboys would, if only grudgingly, acknowledge the skills of the blacks in their midst. A very few, fortunate blacks became trail bosses, but even they were subject to racial assaults. Two of the best-known black cowboys, Nat Love and Jessie Stahl, became celebrated rodeo performers, and Love's autobiography was widely read. Black cowboys were, of course, welcome—as long as they had money—in the saloons and brothels of the cattle towns. Mexicans—who, like blacks, formed about one-seventh of the cowboy population—and Indians fared little better, in part because in language and culture they were more foreign to the white cowboy than were blacks.

The British contingent included many of the "black sheep" of noble families, who, because they received remittances from home, were known as remittance men. The rigors of life in the American West seldom had the sobering effect on these dissolutes that their families had anticipated. A minority of transplanted Britons had the most romantic motivation of all the cowboys: a real desire for adventure and fortune.

If it was the American East and Europe that, to a large degree, provided the cowboys themselves, it was Spanish Mexico that provided the cowboys with the techniques and much of the jargon of their trade. The earliest Texas cowboys learned their trade from Mexican *vaqueros,* the heirs of Spaniards who had herded a type of Longhorn on the plains of Andalusia long before the conquest of the New World. The roundup, branding, the western saddle, roping, and cowboy clothing all originated with the vaqueros; indeed, the very idea of mounted herdsmen was almost uniquely Spanish, for in other European countries herdsmen usually moved about on foot. Words like *cincha* ("cinch"), *catallerango* ("wrangler"), *chaparejos* ("chaps"), *reata* ("lariat"), and *caballo* ("cayuse") permeated the colorful vocabulary of the cowboy and betrayed the origin of his trade.

The cowboy's work life centered on the roundup and the long drive to market. There were two roundups every year: the first occurred as soon as the grass turned green so that the cattle being gathered would be able to graze at the roundup site and not wander off again in search of food; the second took place in the fall. The drive to market generally followed the spring roundup in the Southwest and the fall roundup on the northern ranges.

The cowboy's first duty was to ride out over a given stretch of range and drive back scattered cattle to the roundup site. On the vast spreads of the arid southern ranges, wandering cattle gravitated to water holes and grassy patches and, consequently, were a little easier to find than they were on the northern ranges, whose long, unbroken stretches of grass lured the animals further and further from home. Northern cowboys therefore had a good deal more sorting-out to do than those in the south, especially since northern spreads tended to be smaller and closer together than southern spreads.

Traditionally the "first cut," or first selection of stock from the gathered cattle, fell to the foreman of the ranch on which the roundup was held or, if the roundup was on government land, to the foreman of the ranch that appeared to have the greatest number of cattle in the herd. The cowboy would chase a calf toward the branding fire, rope it to bring it down, and call for the appropriate branding iron. The iron to be used was determined by observing the brand of the calf's mother, who made herself known by bawling loudly when her calf was brought down.

Here, as always, roping presented the cowboy with dangers. A steer suddenly pulling a rope taut could easily topple both horse and rider. Fingers could, if misplaced on a saddle horn, be cut off by rope. And, of course, entanglement in the coils of his rope was a threat to the cowboy, especially the inexperienced. The rope tricks of show cowboys were merely a by-product of the real cowboy's efforts to counter these dangers by perfecting his technique.

Another of the cowboy's jobs was to castrate male

Roping a steer. (Library of Congress)

calfs, and this he could do while a calf was down for branding. Castration added weight to the animal and made it relatively docile, but the wound so created often became infected by the blowfly, whose eggs produced a worm that could cause the animal's death. This, too, was often dealt with around the branding fire, where the cowboy could easily daub various crude ointments on the wounds of animals castrated at some earlier time. Branding and other kinds of wounds were also vulnerable to this infection, and so, the cowboy always had to be on the watch for it, especially during the summer months, when blowflies were most numerous. Another year-round job most conveniently done at roundup was the dehorning of cattle whose horns had become so long and sharp as to be a potential danger to the other animals and the cowboys.

On the long drive—which could be as long as twelve hundred miles and take three or four months—the cowboy had to keep the line of cattle moving along the course set by the trail boss, who rode at its head. Cowboys flanked the herd at various points along the column, which might stretch out over two miles, with the animals five or six abreast. The cowboy had to drive strays back into line by maneuvering his horse and "quirting" the strays (i.e., striking them with the end of his rope). Rotating positions with the rest of the crew, the cowboy would eventually ride in the drag position, at the end of the column, where he would urge the cattle forward and keep an eye out for stragglers. One cowboy, the "wrangler," oversaw the "remuda," or "cavvy," a group of fresh saddle horses for the trail crew; on the trail a cowboy could easily wear out two horses in one day.

The relationship between cowboy and HORSE is one of the most highly romanticized elements of the cowboy myth, as one might guess from the function of the remuda: The cowboy needed a good cow horse—one that by training and instinct knew how to move among, and dominate, cattle—to do his job and would change horses with as little hesitation as any worker would in changing

tools of his trade. Most cowboys did not even own their own horses but rather were supplied them by their employers. In short, more sweat than sentiment passed between horse and rider. This is not to say that cowboys never felt affection for an animal—although cruelty to horses was not uncommon—but affection was likely to be reserved for some animal that was extraordinarily adept at performing a particular function; for example, there have been cowboys who would grow misty-eyed in recounting the wonders of some cutting horse they had long worked with (a cutting horse was one used to cut individual cattle from a herd). Such animals seemed to have a sixth sense: the mere gesture of a cowboy in the direction of a calf to be cut was enough for the horse to pursue and prod the calf for as long as was necessary. The legends that grew up around these horses inspired the creation of more than one of Hollywood's "wonder" horses.

The cowboy's working day on the trail lasted as much as fourteen hours, almost all of it spent riding under a blistering sun through clouds of dust kicked up by the herd. His sleep was limited to about six hours, because part of every night had to be spent keeping watch over cattle that might easily stampede. It was not uncommon for cattle to be "spooked" by lightning, noise, or sudden movement and to take off thunderously and blindly. Many luckless cowboys were killed or badly injured during such melees. At the very least, the fear of stampede made the cowboy's sleep uneasy when rain and insects did not. The cowboy's few hours of real relaxation were spent in the shadow of the chuck wagon, sitting around a campfire gossiping or spinning yarns that became grist for the myth mill.

A chuck wagon was more than a traveling kitchen because the cook had to be more than a cook: the chuck wagon was home, and to the cook fell any duty that smacked of domesticity. He was doctor, barber, seamstress, blacksmith, and keeper of the peace, and to his care were consigned all the provisions needed on the drive, from needles to bedrolls. His job was the most hectic on the trail, because he had to pack and unpack the chuck wagon twice a day, cook three meals, and stay one step ahead of the trail crew. Good cooks were difficult to find, but even the best was hard put to vary his menu; the conditions of the trail were such that only foods that would not spoil quickly could be stocked. Bacon, beans, sourdough bread, and coffee were the staples and were often supplemented by onions, potatoes, or dried fruit. Given the size of trail crews (only one man to every 250-300 cattle, or about ten men on the average drive), it was not practical to slaughter beeves on the trail, for most of the meat would spoil before it could be eaten; an occasional stray calf provided a tasty exception.

At the ends of the trails were the CATTLE TOWNS, and to a cowboy a cattle town meant letting off steam or simply luxuriating in the comforts he had so long done without. He was likely to squander the hundred or so dollars he made on a drive (the average cowboy made thirty to forty-five dollars per month) in the space of a few days, on clothes, liquor, and prostitutes. Innocent "hell-raising" by cowboys on a spree invariably met with the resistance of townspeople and earned the cowboy a not wholly deserved reputation for violence; indeed, many cowboys have testified that they never saw one man pull a gun on another. Charles GOODNIGHT, whose long career in the West embraced every aspect of cowboy life, claimed never to have heard of any real cowboy—as distinct from a professional "badman"—being tried for any crime in the Texas Panhandle and could recall only two fist fights in fifty years. Employers commonly prohibited gambling, drinking, or cursing among their hands, but almost as many men refrained from these of their own accord as found ways of circumventing such strictures.

Summer kept the cowboy busy on the home spread tending cattle, treating them for diseases, and dehorning them. As the years went by and fenced ranches replaced the open range, cowboys began to spend more and more time in the summer tending windmills, repairing fencing, and doing general farm chores. Always, though, summer brought with it one great danger— fire. Spontaneous fires on the sun-scorched ranges of the Southwest could spread rapidly and destroy grass and cattle over vast stretches of land. Thus, keeping fire watch and making firebreaks became essential duties of the cowboy, and fire fighting a common hazard. In the wake of fire or during periods of drought, the cowboy had to uproot himself again and move the cattle to new grazing lands, again giving up the minimal comforts of the bunkhouse, as he had to do when he went on long drives.

The bunkhouse, like the trail, offered a man little privacy. A bunk, and perhaps a shelf and a bit of wall space, served as the repository of the cowboy's few worldly goods. The bunkhouse itself was usually nothing more than a log cabin, often with a dirt floor; its walls were covered with newspapers to keep the wind from blowing through cracks. The single, not very large room was usually unkempt and had a thriving population of lice and bedbugs. Here the cowboy spent his evenings trying to alleviate the boredom of his existence with a little gambling, reading, or even taking potshots at pictures on the wall. Meals were usually taken in a nearby building that served as cookhouse and mess hall. Cookhouse food was better, and more varied, than chuck-wagon food, but bacon and beans remained staples. Slaughtered cattle furnished, in addition to fresh beef, the makings for one of the West's most characteristic dishes, "sonofabitch stew," a concoction of beef heart, liver, testicles, and other organ meats.

Fall saw the second roundup of the year and, on northern ranges, the drive to market. For most cowboys this meant the end of their work year; two-thirds of them would spend the winter working at what jobs they could find in the towns of the West or "grub-line riding." Grub-line riding consisted of nothing more than going from one ranch to another to get an odd job or free meal, an easy thing to do in a sparsely populated country, where a new face was usually welcome.

The cowboys who were kept on by their employers for the winter spent most of their time in the repair and maintenance of the ranch. Some took on the loneliest duty of all, line-riding. A line-rider, either alone or with one other man, had to patrol the boundaries of spreads too large to be overseen from the main house. The rider lived in a primitive hut and rode out every day to track down stray cattle, to kill predators (especially wolves, on which local governments often placed a bounty), and to do any other job necessary to protect the land and cattle.

The persistence of the cowboy myth in spite of attempts to portray range life accurately (see Andy ADAMS) has been attributed by some to the American taste for the simple and the homespun—itself a myth—epitomized for at least one generation in the cowboy-humorist Will ROGERS. In him—and in the cowboy—Americans perceived their self-image: a man with a hard-won knowledge of the world who had remained untainted by the world. But the cowboy myth, like any myth, survives because it embodies "rites of passage": the cowboy, who was often literally a boy (the average cowboy was only in his early twenties), wins his manhood by passing through trials of his strength and endurance. The appeal of the myth to American society, which provides no formal, institutionalized rites of passage, is so strong that it has obscured the fact that cowboys, although less numerous than they were, are still at work in the West, living a life not wholly unlike that of their predecessors.

See Andy Adams, *Log of a Cowboy* (1903); Lewis Atherton, *The Cattle Kings* (1961); Douglas Branch, *The Cowboy and His Interpreters* (1926); J. Frank Dobie, *Cow People*; Philip Durham and Everett L. Jones, *The Negro Cowboys* (1965); Joe B. Frantz and Julian E. Choate, Jr., *The American Cowboy: The Myth and the Reality* (1955); and I. Emerson Hough, *The Story of the Cowboy* (1924). —J. A. S.

cowboy clothing. Although cowboy clothing was distinctive, it was not intended to set the wearer apart but was designed as a practical work uniform especially adapted to the western climate and ranch work.

The most important items of western dress were hats and boots. The cowboy's hat had a flat brim, $3^1/2$ to $5^1/2$ inches wide, and a tall crown, 5 to 8 inches high, surrounded by a belt or band used as decoration and to regulate the fit. Thongs, or "bonnet-strings," were added to help secure the headgear during wind and storm. The height and crease of the crown and roll of the brim varied from place to place, and it was often possible to tell a man's home from the way he shaped his hat. Southwesterners favored the high crown and wide brim of the Mexican sombrero, while northern riders preferred a lower, flat crown and narrower brim. Outside the Southwest a cowboy who affected the Mexican style would be jeered at by his fellows and accused of "chucking the Rio" (an oblique reference to the Rio Grande).

At first cowboy hats came in many styles, were often homemade, and generally of poor quality. Then, in the 1860s, a young New Jersey hatmaker, John Batterson Stetson, went west for his health. Stetson quickly recognized the need for a practical, broad-brimmed hat especially designed for western and range wear. When Stetson returned east in 1865, he opened a one-man shop in Philadelphia and began designing and selling models for the western trade. Within a few years, "Stetson" and "John B." became synonymous with western headgear. By 1906 Stetson employed some thirty-five hundred workers and turned out two million hats a year. Of the many models produced by the Stetson company, the "Carlsbad" and the "Boss of the Plains" were the most popular and were widely imitated.

About the turn of the century western hats began to grow in popularity and size. During the 1920s the famous "ten gallon" (supposedly named for its approxi-

Cowboys at night awakening the relief watch. (Library of Congress)

mate liquid capacity, although the term may have derived from the Spanish *galleones*) with its high crown and wide, curled brim gained admirers among movie fans and drugstore cowboys, but these extreme styles were rarely worn by working hands. To the range rider, a hat was a tool of the trade. It protected him from sun and rain and served as a drinking cup for man and horse. It was used to fan the campfire, signal other riders, and slap a bronc when he was bucking. A Stetson was often the first thing a man put on in the morning and the last thing he took off at night.

The cowboy's footgear served as a badge of office to set the western horseman apart from others. Boots were made of top grade leather with a high arched vamp, a square or slightly rounded toe, and a heel that varied from a flat 1-inch rise to the more popular $1\frac{1}{2}$- to 2-inch tapered form. Soles were thin to give the rider a "feel of the stirrup," while the heel prevented the foot from slipping through the stirrup and served as a brace when roping on foot.

Since western boots had no laces, they were difficult to put on and remove. Leather straps, sewn inside the tops, helped in donning the footwear, while all kinds of gadgets were invented for their removal. Among the more popular bootjacks were iron "beetles" and "steers." Another variation of this design was the "Naughty Lady," evidently popular in bunkhouses and red-light districts, although this model may have existed more in imagination than in reality. Although short tops, or "peewees," were occasionally worn, most boot tops ranged from twelve to sixteen inches in height and were straight and plain in design. The first fancy tops had a wide red band and "Lone Star" motif, but in time modern inlaid or stitched and scalloped tops became popular. Until the 1890s most westerners stuffed their pants legs inside their boots, but about the time decorated tops began to gain favor men began wearing their pants over the outside of the boots to cover the new designs.

Plain or fancy, most cowboys preferred handmade boots to factory-manufactured items and would spend considerable sums on good footwear. Many had a favorite bootmaker. On the Southern Plains, Joe Justin of Texas was the choice of most riders, and "Justins" became *the* word for boots. Hats, varying in price from $10 to $20, and boots, ranging from $20 to $30, were the most expensive items in a working hand's wardrobe.

Spurs, also known as *espuelas* or "grappling irons," were a necessary accouterment. Each spur included a rowel, shank, heel plate, and spur button plus a leather strap or "spur leather" to hold the spur in place and protect the ankle from chafing. Two chains, passed under the instep, were sometimes added.

Spurs were used to control but never to punish the horse, and a man who used his spurs to cut a horse did not last long on most ranches. The first thing a cowboy did when he got a new pair of spurs was to blunt the points. Larger rowels were much favored because they did less damage than the smaller ones. Spurs came in all sizes, from the big Chihuahua and California models to the smaller five- or ten-point stars and the popular OK design. Shanks might be straight, raised, or dropped, depending on the individual's tastes or needs.

Spur wearing customs varied. In some places spurs were never removed from the boots and a man would sooner have gone without his pants than to be caught without his spurs. In other areas, particularly on the West Coast, spurs were worn only during working hours. Sometimes steel "danglers" or tiny bells were added to the head of the rowel to provide "saddle music," but with or without these added attractions, the jingle of the spurs was sweet music to any cowhand.

Other items of western dress were of plain but serviceable quality. Pants (never trousers or overalls) were designed for protection and comfort and also served as a handy place to strike a match. Just as westerners lacked a practical, well-designed hat before the advent of John B. Stetson, so they lacked good, durable work pants until 1850 when a young eastern merchant, Levi Strauss, landed in San Francisco with a load of merchandise he hoped to sell in the California mining camps. Unable to sell a large supply of canvas and finding a demand for work clothes, Strauss made his canvas into pants and became an overnight success. Within a few years these "wonderful pants of Levi's" were in demand throughout California. Strauss opened a factory at 98 Battery Street, San Francisco (where the company remains today), switched from canvas to heavyweight blue denim material, added copper rivets at the stress points, and made an impressive fortune. Not only did "Levi's" become standard western wear, but by the turn of the century people outside the ranch and mining company had discovered that these western pants were both comfortable and durable for travel, sports, and other outdoor activities. Although Strauss and his miners might be surprised at the recent popularity of his creation, both in the United States and Europe, Levi's remain a favorite for wearability and comfort.

But even Strauss's durable denim did not offer sufficient protection for a cowboy's legs, so Anglos added a device developed from the Mexican *armas*, large pieces of rawhide draped across the saddle horn and tucked over the legs like a lap robe. California vaqueros discarded the bulky armas for short leather panels called *armitas*, and from these came "chaps" (from the Spanish *chaparreras* or *chaparejos*—leather breeches). The first chaps, called "shotguns," were made with a closed or seamed leg fringed down the outer edge. Later open or wraparound legs became popular, with a number of variations, including the Texas or wing chap, the "Cheyenne" leg, and the wide, fancy batwings favored by rodeo performers. Although plain leather was used, most hands preferred Angora goat or similar material because it was more pliable and comfortable. Despite their protective qualities, chaps were hot and cumbersome, and few cowboys wore them outside of working chores or the rodeo arena.

In the Old West, shirts were always collarless, and a kerchief provided protection for the neck. In addition, this colorful neckpiece could be pulled over the nose and mouth when a man was "eating dust" or during a sand or ice storm. A neckerchief also served as a signal flag or as a handy rag or tie when nothing else was available.

When a jacket was worn, it was usually of denim, duck, or similar material and was cut short and loose to give the wearer freedom of movement. Except when needed for protection or warmth, most hands preferred not to wear a coat or jacket. Since coats were rarely worn and shirts were usually pocketless, most men wore a vest, which served as a container for small pieces of equipment, Bull Durham "fixins" (which included a small package of cigarette papers and the ubiquitous muslin tobacco sack with a round tag label proudly proclaiming that the contents were "Blackwell's Genuine Durham"), and some small talisman or pocket piece such as a gold nugget, arrowhead, or elk "tush."

For wet weather every rider carried a yellow slicker tied across the saddle cantle. These voluminous rubber coats had wide long skirts with slits and gores that formed a tent over man and saddle to protect them from the rain. Although they were hot in summer and cold in winter, they were standard equipment.

Gloves or guantlets were also used for warmth and to protect the cowboy's hands against rope and rein burns. Made with long, flaring cuffs and often beautifully decorated with beads, quillwork, or other materials, they added a touch of color to the cowboy's generally drab appearance.

Other pieces of equipment and finery such as a silver belt buckle or a gold or silver concho (a small shell-shaped or circular round disk) might have been added for "dress up," but westerners were generally conservative and tended to prefer plain styles and dark colors. Old-timers would undoubtedly be shocked by the elaborate design and bright colors of modern western wear.

Fashion and modesty forced women into less comfortable riding gear. Riding habits with cumbersome skirts and tight jackets were the order of the day until the turn of the century when ladies began to ride astride and adopted the divided riding skirt. By the 1930s they had begun to wear pants and shirts similar to those of men.

Despite the changing nature of ranch work, western wear remains popular. In addition to traditional range clothes, colorful costumes for rodeo performers, musicians, actors, and western buffs keep outfitters in business and emphasize the nostalgia attached to the Old West.

See Philip Rollins, *The Cowboy* (1922); Glenn Vernam, *Man on Horseback* (1964); and Fay Ward, *The Cowboy at Work* (1958), for extensive discussions of western styles. Ramon Adams, *Western Words* (1944) contains both history and vocabulary.—S. L. M.

cowboy songs. See MUSIC, WESTERN.

Cowles, Gardner, Sr. (1861-1946). Iowa newspaper publisher. Cowles was born in a Methodist parsonage in Oskaloosa, Iowa, and lived all his life in his native state. He graduated from Iowa Wesleyan College with a bachelor of arts degree in 1882 and took a master's degree from the same school in 1885.

Cowles's early professional interests were varied. His first job was superintendent of the Algona public schools. He acquired interests in several banks and became editor of the Algona newspaper, *Advance*. While residing there, Cowles served two terms in the Iowa House of Representatives.

In 1903 he launched a new venture when he purchased the ailing Des Moines *Register and Leader*. The weakest of several Des Moines papers, the publication was plagued with debts and low circulation. In 1908

Cowles expanded by purchasing the afternoon paper, the *Tribune*, and the paper's title became the *Register and Tribune*. Further consolidation was effected in 1924 through purchase of the Scripps-Howard afternoon paper, the *News*, followed a few years later by the purchase of the *Capital*. By 1927 the flourishing *Register and Tribune* was the only daily newspaper in Des Moines. By the time of his death Cowles had increased the paper's circulation from under fourteen thousand to a Sunday circulation of half a million. An indefatigable worker and a believer that a newspaper should be "entertaining and friendly," Cowles developed his newspaper into a nationally prominent publication.

Two of his sons, Gardner, Jr., and John, continued to expand the family's mass media holdings. In 1935 the company purchased the Minneapolis *Star*; it published the first issue of *Look* magazine in 1937. Investments were made in radio and television throughout the Middle West. Today the family's varied business interests are combined as Cowles Communications, Inc.

A brief sketch of Cowles's life is in *Gardner Cowles, 1861-1946* (1946), published by the board of directors of the Des Moines *Register and Tribune*. William Petersen, *The Story of Iowa*, vol. III (1952), also includes biographical information on Cowles.—D. S.

Cox, Ross (1793-1853). Adventurer and journalist. Cox was a youth of eighteen when he sailed from New York in 1811 for Fort Astoria as one of John Jacob Astor's clerks in the great enterprise of the Pacific Fur Company. Little is known of his early life except that he was born in Dublin and migrated to America shortly before his departure for the Pacific Northwest.

Cox spent six years in the Pacific Northwest fur trade, initially working for Astor, then, following Britain's takeover of Astoria, for the North West Company. He traveled up the Columbia River nine times and down it eight, had several encounters with Indians, and spent two weeks lost in the wilderness.

After returning to Ireland in 1818, he related his experiences in a narrative entitled *The Columbia River (Or scenes and adventures during a residence of six years on the western side of the Rocky Mountains among various tribes of Indians hitherto unknown, together with "A Journey Across the American Continent")*. It was published in 1831. The work was immensely popular on both sides of the Atlantic and reached a third edition in only a year.

Cox never returned to America. He was employed for many years as a clerk in the Dublin Police Office, and until 1837 he served as the Dublin correspondent for the *London Morning Herald*.

See Ross Cox, *The Columbia River* (1957).—R. B. W.

Coxey's Army. See INDUSTRIAL ARMY MOVEMENT.

Cramer, Zadok. See RIVERMEN.

Crater Lake National Park. Crater Lake National Park in Oregon contains one of the world's purest, deepest, and most beautiful lakes. The lake was discovered by John Wesley Hillman, a prospector, in 1853. It was rediscovered numerous times by other miners and cowboys, who named it Deep Blue Lake, Crater Lake, Lake Majesty, and Blue Lake. Crater Lake became its official name later in the nineteenth century. William Gladstone Steel visited the lake in 1885 and was so awed by its beauty that he launched a campaign to have it declared a national park and worked single-mindedly toward this objective for seventeen years. President Theodore Roosevelt approved legislation establishing the park on May 22, 1902.

The lake has an extraordinary deep blue color. It was formed when an ancient volcano, Mount Mazama, collapsed, leaving a caldera in which water gradually accumulated. The walls of the caldera rise five hundred to two thousand feet above the lake. At its deepest point, the water is about two thousand feet deep. The park, which forms a rectangular zone of 160,290 acres around the lake, is situated near national forests, ranch lands, and farms that are typical of south-central Oregon. It is about forty-five miles north of Klamath Falls, Oregon. The park may also be entered via Medford, Oregon, which is approximately seventy miles to the west. —D. C. S.

Crawford, Coe Isaac (1858-1944). South Dakota politician. From 1897 to 1903 Crawford served as general counsel for the Chicago and Northwestern Railroad. In 1904 he organized the Republican State Primary League and became a La Follette progressive, attacking railroads, insurance companies, and Standard Oil for unduly mixing in politics. He founded the Roosevelt League in 1905, and a year later he led progressive Republicans to victory over the state machine. After one term as governor, he was elected to the United States Senate in 1908. His main concern in politics was popular control of government by such means as the direct primary. In 1912 Crawford supported Theodore Roosevelt for the presidency. When his Senate term ended in 1915, he resumed his law practice.—D. J. T.

Crazy Horse (Tashunca-uitco) (1841 or 1842-1877). Military leader of the Oglala subdivision of the Teton Sioux. His name, perhaps better translated as "His Horse Is Crazy," was given him by his father, a holy man of the same name, after brave exploits against another tribe in battle. Crazy Horse took an active role in the campaigns of the Oglala chief Red Cloud against the forts and settlements of Wyoming in 1865-68. He participated in the Fetterman Massacre (1866), the Hayfield Fight (1867) and the Wagon-Box Fight (1867). His skill in battle and his bold spirit helped him become one of the leaders of that element of the Southern Sioux and Northern Cheyenne which refused to stay on the reservations and frequently raided whites or the rival Crow. Crazy Horse's first marriage, to a Cheyenne woman, brought him into closer alliance with that tribe.

After the Black Hills gold rush, he, like other "hostiles," did not follow the War Department order that all Indian bands return to their reservations by January 1, 1876. Instead, his village became the rallying point for most of the nontreaty bands. On June 17, his force of twelve hundred Oglala and Cheyenne were attacked on the upper Rosebud by the army of General George CROOK, thirteen hundred strong. Crazy Horse's tactics baffled Crook, and after a day's fighting, the general withdrew with severe losses. Crazy Horse then moved north and joined SITTING BULL and his large following in the valley of the LITTLE BIG HORN. In the famous battle of June 25, his mostly Cheyenne force attacked Custer from the north and west, while Chief GALL of the Hunkpapa Dakota, after routing Major Marcus A. Reno, charged Custer from the south and east.

Following the flight of Sitting Bull to Canada, Crazy Horse continued to war against army troops and carried on a brilliant campaign against General Nelson A. Miles. He surrendered on May 6, 1877, the last of the important chiefs except for Sitting Bull and Gall to do so. Crazy Horse had received favors from the military to induce him to surrender, which some other chiefs who had surrendered earlier resented. That summer on the reservation, he was asked to help gather Dakota as volunteer scouts for rounding up the Nez Percé, who were in flight or retreat from Oregon to Canada. Frank GROUARD is said to have mistranslated—perhaps deliberately—Crazy Horse's reply. By August, rumors had spread that Crazy Horse was planning another outbreak. Finally, on September 5, 1877, after having left the agency without authorization to take his sick senior wife, Black Shawl, to her parents, Crazy Horse was arrested at Fort Robinson. At first, he was calm; but when it was clear that he was being led to a guardhouse, he resisted. While his arms were held by a jealous rival warrior, he was killed by a bayonet thrust from a soldier.

See F. W. Hodge, ed., *Handbook of American Indians North of Mexico* (1910-11) and Mari Sandoz, *Crazy Horse* (1942). On the mistranslation, see *General George Crook, His Autobiography*, Martin F. Schmitt, ed. (1966). —E. I. S.

Credit Mobilier. A limited liability finance company organized to pay the construction costs of the UNION PACIFIC RAILROAD. Credit Mobilier was the solution to impossible financial restrictions put upon the Union Pacific by Congress. Under its congressional charter, Union Pacific was required to sell its stock for cash at the stock's par value of one hundred dollars per share. This the company could not do because of its uncertain future. Investors doubted whether a transcontinental rail line could be built, so they would not pay for company stock at par. But without the capital of investors, the road had no money to continue construction.

This dilemma was solved in 1864 when Thomas C. Durant purchased the charter of the Pennsylvania Fiscal Agency and renamed it the Credit Mobilier of America. Durant and other stockholders of Credit Mobilier were also the majority owners of the Union Pacific. As stockholders in Union Pacific, Durant, Oakes AMES, and the other men involved would give construction contracts for building the railroad to Credit Mobilier through dummy third parties. Credit Mobilier deliberately exaggerated construction costs, sometimes as much as doubling the actual mile-by-mile cost. Credit Mobilier was paid for its contracts by checks from the Union Pacific. It thereupon returned these checks to Union Pacific for Union Pacific stocks and bonds, thereby fulfilling the requirement that the company's stock be bought with "cash" and at par. Credit Mobilier, however, could sell the stocks and bonds any way it wanted to. The Union Pacific financial instruments were resold at prices considerably below par, but high enough to pay for construction. In addition, the stockholders in Credit Mobilier (i.e., the large stockholders of Union Pacific) made a profit on the resale. By doing so, they made a profit out of construction of the road at a time when they could make little money out of its actual operations.

The dealings of Credit Mobilier came to public attention in 1872, although there had never been a serious attempt to hide them. Union Pacific and its officers were criticized for their questionable practices, as well as for what appear to have been bribes to elected officials. A congressional committee investigating Credit Mobilier concluded that the company's stockholders, which included congressmen, had accumulated over $23 million in ill-gotten profits. More accurate estimates made recently put the profit figure at around $13 million to $16 million. Moreover, scholars now realize that the Union Pacific had had no other choice short of asking Congress for a new charter.

Credit Mobilier illustrates the way in which transcontinental rail lines could be built. The Southern Pacific Railroad, for example, used similar tactics in building east from California. It was spared an investigation only by a fire that just "happened" to destroy its financial records. Credit Mobilier was a system copied by other railroads, both large and small in all parts of the country. Investors unsure of a profit from the operation of a transcontinental road were induced to build one when they found a way to make a profit out of its construction.

For the public, Credit Mobilier dramatized two things. First, general incorporation or liability laws allowed separation of management from ownership. Union Pacific managers, having invested less than two percent of their own money in the railroad, nevertheless controlled a business owned by helpless stockholders. Second, the railroad corporations were powerful enough to influence the national government.

The best study of Credit Mobilier is Robert W. Fogel, *The Union Pacific Railroad: A Case in Premature Enterprise* (1960).—R. S.

Creek Indians. See FIVE CIVILIZED TRIBES.

Creek War. See HORSESHOE BEND, BATTLE OF.

Cremony, John C. (1815-1879). Soldier and writer. Cremony served as a second lieutenant in the First Massachusetts Infantry during the Mexican War and was interpreter to the United States Boundary Commission, which surveyed the Mexican-United States boundary in 1849-51. During the Civil War, Cremony served as a major in the Second California Cavalry, campaigning in Arizona and New Mexico under General James H. Carleton. After 1865 Cremony retired to San Francisco. In 1868 he published *Life Among the Apaches*, one of the most vivid and objective firsthand descriptions of the Indians in the Southwest.

There is no biographical study of Cremony. Except for information contained in his book, the details of his life are unknown.—P. R. M.

Cripple Creek, Colorado. Mining town. Cripple Creek was the last and the richest of Colorado's major mining towns. By 1890 most knowledgeable observers believed that the golden riches of Colorado had been tapped, but ironically, as historian Phyllis Dorset remarks, "only some twenty miles west of Pikes Peak, completely overlooked by the fifty-niners in their rush to find riches at the base of that famous landmark, there still lay waiting to be discovered a treasure box that would make the Clear Creek bonanzas and the placers of South Park look like hors d'oeuvres before a feast of gold."

This omission is not as surprising as it might seem, however, for the development of Cripple Creek's abundant resources hinged upon more advanced techniques in mining science and technology. Unlike the earlier large strikes in Colorado where the gold was relatively accessible, the veins of ore at Cripple Creek flowed between layers of igneous rock. Ambitious individual prospectors like "Crazy Bob" Womack, who alerted professional geologists to the possibilities of Cripple Creek in 1891, left the diggings frustrated at their inability to exploit their discovery. Soon, however, an alliance of geologists and large investors moved into the region and launched the kind of intensive, highly technological enterprise it would take to extract the vast wealth embedded in the volcanic rock. By 1892 five thousand people lived in Cripple Creek, and the nearby camps of Victor, Elkton, Goldfield, Independence, and Altman housed another five thousand.

From the beginning, the development of Cripple Creek was the pet project of the idle rich of the nearby "Newport of the Rockies," Colorado Springs. In particular, the fortunes of the town were linked up with the exploits of a group of ambitious young businessmen—Charles Tutt, Spencer Penrose, Horace Devereux, Charles MacNeill—who were styled the "Socialites." The contrast between these wealthy, Protestant, conservative capitalists and the poorly paid, Catholic, and (after the Western Federation of Miners had done its work) radicalized miners who toiled in the mines contributed to the violent strikes that hit the town in 1894 and 1904.

Gold production in Cripple Creek reached its peak in 1901, but advances in technology—extensive drainage tunnels and the cyanide process for reducing ore—kept the mines alive until after World War II, when rising production costs forced them to close. Today Cripple Creek is a popular tourist attraction.

See Phyllis Dorset, *The New Eldorado* (1970); Rodman Paul, *Mining Frontiers of the Far West* (1963); and Marshall Sprague, *Money Mountain* (1953).—R. B. W.

Cripple Creek strikes (1894-1904). Labor movement struggle. Three years after the discovery in 1890 of the rich gold field around Cripple Creek, Colorado, the United States was hit by a financial panic that ushered in four years of depression. This crisis struck particularly hard the silver mines of Colorado, many of which had to close down. As a result, the laborers from these mines, as well as thousands of other unemployed workers, flocked to the still-prosperous gold fields of Cripple Creek, setting the stage for a confrontation between capital and labor that would last intermittently for nearly ten years.

Fundamental to this confrontation was the stratification of Cripple Creek society into two layers. The mineral properties of the area were owned by shareholders in various companies that hired managers to undertake the actual development of the property. The owners and managers formed the upper stratum of the area's society, while the miners, who worked the claims for wages, formed the second layer. The tension between these two groups, of course, heightened by the influx of unemployed workingmen in 1893.

When the mineowners moved to extend the working day to ten hours with no increase in wages, the miners rebelled and demanded the restoration of their former wage-scale and recognition of their new union, the Western Federation of Miners. By February 1894 most of the mines and many of the smelters around Cripple Creek had been closed down. Soon the area became an armed camp, the union men facing the local police and the state militia called out by Governor "Bloody Bridles" Waite. Tempers cooled, however, and in June 1894 the strike was settled in the union's favor.

The ensuing nine years were relatively quiet, while both labor and management tried to build up their strength by further organization of their respective groups. Under the leadership of Charles H. Moyer and "Big Bill" Haywood, the Western Federation of Miners managed to enlist a majority of the miners in the Cripple Creek mines. The owners, on the other hand, had organized the Mine Owner's Association.

When these two factions did finally confront one another, it happened not in the mines but at the smelter in nearby Colorado City. In the summer of 1903 the Western Federation, hoping to increase its membership rolls among the mill-workers, called a sympathy strike to force union recognition in the mills. The effort snowballed, and by the end of October both the mill-workers and the gold-miners were on strike. The mine owners called in "scab" labor, Governor James Peabody called out the state militia, and the union workers barricaded the roads and railways leading to the gold fields.

On June 6, 1904, Harry Orchard, a professional terrorist in the union's employ, dynamited the railroad station at Independence, which resulted in the death of thirteen strikebreakers. Following this tragedy the mine-operators mobilized their forces. Workers were rounded up and confined in "bull pens"; many of them were driven from camp, including seventy-three men who were transported to the Kansas border and abandoned on the prairie.

This violence worked generally in the mine-operator's favor, for the public blamed the union for extremism and approved the institution of martial law in Cripple Creek. By midsummer 1904 the strike was over, and the mineowners reopened their mines with nonunion labor. The defeat was a crushing one for the Western Federation of Miners, for it never regained the power it had once held in the mining areas of Colorado.

See Stewart H. Holbrook, *Rocky Mountain Revolution* (1956); and Benjamin M. Rastall, *The Labor History of the Cripple Creek District* (1908).—R. B. W.

Crocker, Charles (1822-1888). Railroad builder and businessman. The son of an unsuccessful liquor merchant in Troy, New York, Crocker moved with the family to a farm on virgin land near Marshall, Iowa. He worked as a farmhand, sawmill operator, and owner of an iron forge. When gold was discovered in California he led a party, which included his two younger brothers, overland to the Pacific Coast. Two years of mining convinced Crocker that the real gold lay in retailing goods for the rapidly growing population of San Francisco; in a few years he was one of the richest men there.

When Crocker, in partnership with Collis P. Huntington, Leland Stanford, and Mark Hopkins, undertook to build the western segment of the transcontinental railroad (the CENTRAL PACIFIC) in 1863, he found his natural role as superintendent of construction. Men and nature conspired against him. Day laborers were virtually nonexistent on the Pacific Coast, and until the second Pacific Railroad Act was passed money was always short. Materials and equipment had to be shipped by water around Cape Horn, and high in the Sierra Nevada the project all but came to a standstill in subzero temperatures and deep snowdrifts. But the money came, and Crocker hit upon the use of Chinese laborers, generally cheerful people who worked like demons and had never heard the word "exploitation." Crocker's construction feats, which set records that stood for years, conquered the mountains. Having completed the Central Pacific seven years ahead of the government deadline, he turned his attention to construction of the SOUTHERN PACIFIC, and then to real estate, banking, and irrigation projects. Running ranches and building mansions, however, never absorbed his giant energies. Nor did he enjoy life in New York, where he bought a house in 1886, even though his daughter lived there. Seriously injured in a carriage accident, Crocker returned to San Francisco where, diabetic, overweight, and refusing to stick to his diet, he died.

Two old works provide details of Crocker's career: Stuart Daggett, *Chapters on the History of the Southern Pacific* (1922; repr. 1966); and Oscar Lewis, *The Big Four* (1938).—A. M.

Crockett, Davy [David] (1786-1836). Frontiersman, Tennessee politician, and soldier. The story of Crockett's life is so interwoven with the American frontier and literary legends that it is most difficult at times to determine where fact begins and fiction leaves off (see HUMOR). Crockett was born on the Nolichucky River in Greene County, Tennessee. He was the son of John and Rebecca Crockett, who had moved over the valley path of emigration from Virginia. Crockett was a somewhat willful boy who failed to profit at all from a meager exposure to schooling. Between his twelfth and sixteenth birthdays he labored as a hireling to cattle drovers and freight haulers and then as a farm laborer in East Tennessee. At none of these tasks did he make any money. On October 24, 1805, he made plans to marry Margaret Elder, even purchased a marriage license, but a rival cut him out on his wedding day, and the following August he married Polly Finley in a characteristic frontier wedding followed by a rollicking infare.

In September 1811 Crockett moved his family out to Middle Tennessee, where he settled first in Lincoln County and then in Franklin, near Winchester. When this country was aroused over news of the Indian troubles at Fort Mims, and Andrew Jackson was recruiting his volunteers, Crockett joined the local militia and took part in the general Creek campaign in Alabama. He was present in several of the preliminary skirmishes but was not in the famous battle of Horseshoe Bend. As a matter of fact, he had withdrawn from the militia by that time and was back at his home from December 24, 1813, to September 28, 1814. He then joined Major Russell's "Separate Battalion of Tennessee Mounted Gunmen" and marched off to southern Alabama and Florida, but this command arrived in Pensacola too late to help in the destruction of Fort Barancas. Again Davy Crockett missed a moment of fame by not going on to New Orleans with Jackson. After a bit of patrolling around Mobile, he returned to Tennessee.

After the death of his first wife, he married the widow Elizabeth Patton in 1816. After a fruitless land-hunting journey to Alabama, he went back to Tennessee a mere shadow of himself because of an acute attack of malaria. The next year he moved deeper into West Tennessee to Lawrence County, where he became a justice of the peace, then a court referee, and then an elected militia colonel. In 1820 he was elected to the Tennessee legislature, where he advocated easier land-granting terms. As the result of a practical joke sprung on him in a frontier tavern, Crockett was renominated a candidate for the

legislature in 1823 against three prominent rivals, and following a stormy campaign returned to Nashville to represent five newly formed western counties. In this term he incurred the wrath of the Jacksonians largely because he opposed their candidate for the United States Senate. Too, he favored the Bank of the United States.

In 1825 Crockett was defeated for election to the United States Congress, but in 1827 he was elected to that office, reelected in 1829, defeated in 1831, and reelected in 1833. While a member of Congress he toured the East from April 25 to May 14, 1834, for purposes, he said, of viewing the great eastern industries, but he no doubt was lured into this unsuccessful venture by scheming politicians who hoped to trump up charges against him back home because of his absence from duty.

Crockett ended his national political career in something less than a blaze of glory, even though he had been outspoken on many national issues. Defeated in 1835, he turned back to the frontier. On November 1 of that year, he and five companions set out to explore Texas. In February 1836 they arrived in San Antonio, and on March 6, Crockett lost his life when Santa Anna's Mexicans stormed the Alamo.

Memory of Crockett has thrived in a sizable body of folk literature, most of it in the strong vernacular of the backwoods. His tales were of the tall variety and his figures of speech rugged. He was the subject of a romanticized autobiography that he prepared in 1834 with Thomas Chilton, and an almanac bearing his name was issued.

See Edward S. Ellis, *The Life of Colonel David Crockett* (1884); and James Atkin Shackford, ed., *David Crockett: the Man and the Legend* (1956).—T. D. C.

Croghan, George (?-1782). Frontiersman and Indian diplomat. Croghan immigrated from Dublin, Ireland, to the United States, but his life prior to 1741 is not a matter of record. He was a Protestant Irishman and perhaps a native of Dublin. The first mention of his name in the western Pennsylvania Indian trade was in 1742, when he received goods of Edward Shippen in Philadelphia. He followed the road from this city westward through the German settlements to Lancaster, then to Harris' Ferry (present-day Harrisburg), and to the Condogwinet valley. In the years 1741-54 Croghan became a seasoned frontiersman and Indian trader. He formed friendships with the Indians, came to know the geography of the Ohio system of streams, and was a major source of information about Indian and French relations from 1754 to 1760. He likewise played a major diplomatic role in the closing years of the French and Indian War in bringing about British-Indian agreements.

As a trader Croghan experienced success and failure. The ravages of the French and Indian War cut deep into his activities, and following its end he played an active role in helping to establish British control in the West, as interpreter and as messenger to the distant outposts. He exercised sufficient influence over the Pennsylvania Indians to help them thwart some of the Quaker attempts to grab Indian lands. Croghan himself had a major interest in western land speculation, purchasing large tracts from the Indians by legal and illegal means. In May 1763 he sold to Daniel Clark and William Peters a huge block of western lands to which he did not have title; furthermore, he deliberately deceived the purchasers as to the ownership and quality of the land. Hardly had this sale taken place when the Indian uprising in western Pennsylvania (a part of Pontiac's Rebellion) virtually bankrupted Croghan by the heavy loss of property in that region.

Croghan accompanied Major Robert Rogers to Detroit and early in 1765 helped to negotiate a treaty with the Shawnee, Delaware, and Seneca at Fort Pitt. He also went on a diplomatic and trading expedition to the Wabash valley, where he was tomahawked by Kickapoo and Mascouten in a surprise attack. He managed to bring about peace among the Indians, however, and in July 1765 met with Pontiac and reached an agreement by which the English could take over the western posts.

Croghan was shrewd, courageous, a sharp trader, an Indian diplomat, a gambler, a cheat, a victim of circumstances that destroyed his trade, and in the end a bankrupt man. Nevertheless he enjoyed the backing of many important colonial officials. He lived through two major wars and died in obscurity in Passyunk, Pennsylvania, (near Philadelphia).

Before he died, Croghan had the satisfaction of seeing his name cleared in court on November 12, 1778, of a charge of treason. He was not, however, able to clear himself of a staggering debt that had been incurred in Indian trading and land speculation. His credit rating was practically nil, and events during the American Revolution injured further his hopes of making a profit from his lands. Croghan was a complex personality whose contributions to western frontier expansion were enormous on one hand, and perhaps a deterrent force on the other. Nevertheless, his name as much as that of any other person is indelibly associated with the formative period of the westward movement.

See A. T. Volwiler, *George Croghan and the Westward Movement, 1741-1782* (1926); and Nicholas B. Wainwright, *George Croghan, Wilderness Diplomat* (1959). —T. D. C.

Crook, George (1828-1890). Soldier. An Ohio farm boy, Crook was graduated from West Point in 1852, conspicuously near the bottom of his class. In the opinion of General William T. Sherman, he became the greatest Indian fighter and manager the army ever had. In an era when Indians were often regarded by military and civilian alike as so much wild game to be restricted to reserves or destroyed, Crook could probe the "little secrets of the inner Indian" and protected them from the worst excesses of the Interior Department and the army.

Crook's first assignment was to the Fourth Infantry, then stationed on the Pacific Coast, where the Indians were considered a threat to miners and settlers. For eight years he learned frontier lessons and formed habits that distinguished his later career. He learned to live off the country, to fight Indians, to understand frontier mentality, to sympathize with the plight of the Indians, and to mistrust the motives and abilities of volunteer militia. He also learned about the army and did not like what he found: drunkenness, laziness, inept leadership, and rank-consciousness. In the process, he served in the Rogue River War, the Yakima War, on escort duty, and as a builder of military posts.

The outbreak of the Civil War took Crook east, where

he was appointed colonel of the thirty-sixth Ohio Volunteer Infantry. He applied his frontier lessons by training recruits and fighting successful guerrilla actions against bushwhackers in West Virginia. His first major action was the second battle of Bull Run. In June 1863 he was placed in command of the Second Cavalry Division, which served at Chickamauga, and in patrol of the Tennessee River line. He served with distinction in the Shenandoah valley campaign of 1864.

Crook's own account of his Civil War experiences suggests that he was uncomfortable as part of a relatively amorphous military operation and little impressed with his fellow officers. "Stupidity" and "paltroonery" were his usual epithets.

After the Civil War Crook returned quickly, and gladly, to the western frontier, joining his regiment (Fourteenth Infantry) in the Pacific Northwest, where the Paiute Indians were actively hostile. After a few days in Boise, Idaho Territory, he set out to investigate an Indian raid, expecting to be gone a week. But he did not return to Boise again for more than two years. The rugged eastern Oregon desert country was ideal for Indian resistance and also for Crook's system of fighting. Within a year he had "pacified" the region.

When the Apache Indians of Arizona proved too much for the talents of Colonel George Stoneman, Crook, at the specific request of President Ulysses S. Grant, was placed in command of the Department of Arizona in 1871. Here, in an environment even less hospitable and among Indians more warlike and determined, Crook again applied his particular methods. He reorganized his command, employed Indian scouts, and put constant pressure on roving bands of Apache. By 1873 relative peace and calm reigned in the territory, and the Apache were on reservations—though not in locations approved of by Crook.

The Arizona experience made it plain to Crook's troops and to his superiors that when there was trouble the general would be found "in the skirmish line, not in the telegraph office." In 1875 he was placed in command of the Department of the Platte, where his first task was to clear the Black Hills of trespassing prospectors. In 1876 he led the Powder River and Yellowstone expeditions against the Sioux Indians, and on June 17 was defeated at the battle of the ROSEBUD. This battle prevented a junction of his command with that of General Alfred Terry, and may have contributed to the defeat of George Armstrong Custer at the Little Big Horn.

Crook's methods in the Department of the Platte were an adaptation of what he had practiced in Arizona and the Pacific Northwest. He used Indian scouts and allies, fought only when necessary, and engaged in diplomacy when possible. He believed he understood Indians and was certain that "Indian troubles" were the result of "tardy and broken faith on the part of the general government."

By 1881 the peace Crook had fashioned in Arizona had worn thin. Many of the Apache, particularly the Chiricahua, had fled the hot, dusty San Carlos Reservation into Mexico, a haven from which they raided into Arizona and terrorized the settlers. In 1882 Crook was called back, and after eight months of hard campaigning forced the return of the Indians to the reservation. The new peace, uneasy at best, was broken two years later. In March 1886, after a final campaign, and with the use of Indian scouts, Crook obtained the surrender of the Chiricahua, among them the well-known Geronimo. It was a short-lived surrender, for the Apache fled to the mountains once again before they could be returned to the reservation. Six months later, General Nelson A. Miles accepted the surrender of the remaining hostiles, who, together with the loyal scouts, were exiled to Florida. Crook, meanwhile, had been relieved of command.

For the next five years, first as commanding general of the Department of the Platte and after April 1888 as major general in command of the Division of the Missouri, Crook attempted to redress the injustice done to the loyal Apache scouts and arrange the return of the exiled Apache to their own land. He spoke before Indian rights organizations, corresponded widely, wrote pamphlets, and engaged in a bitter counterpropaganda operation against General Miles, who opposed any change in the status of the Apache prisoners. Crook also attempted to better the condition of the Sioux Indians by persuading them to accept a policy of land allotment, a policy he believed would "civilize" the Indians by making property owners of them.

General Crook's death in March 1890 ended his campaign for the relief of the Apache and saved him from witnessing both the failure of the allotment policy and the shame of the battle of Wounded Knee (1890), in which soldiers needlessly massacred Sioux Indians. His old adversary and friend, the Sioux Indian Red Cloud, summed up Crook's reputation: "He never lied to us. His words gave the people hope."

Major sources of information on Crook are John G. Bourke, *On the Border with Crook* (1891), and *General George Crook: His Autobiography* (1946).—M. S.

Crosby, Bob "Wild Horse." See RODEO.

Cross, Henry H. (1837-1918). Painter. Born in upstate New York, Cross early manifested an interest in the drawing of animals and at sixteen was sent to France for two years of study with Rosa Bonheur. Upon his return to the United States, he worked for a traveling circus. In 1862 he visited southwestern Minnesota at the time of the Sioux uprising, during which period he made sketches of many of the Indian participants in this conflict. Back in the East once again, he traveled for a time with P. T. Barnum's circus and menagerie as a wagon and poster painter and again turned his attention westward to the study of Indian and animal life.

While in the West, Cross spent a great deal of time among the various Plains tribes, became acquainted with "Buffalo Bill" Cody, and learned the Sioux tongue. Almost all of his Indian portraits reportedly were derived from living subjects, and his reputation rests largely upon the accurate likeness he achieved and the care with which he portrayed the details of Indian dress and equipment. Cross spent much of his time on private commissions in the decade preceding his death. One of the largest collections of his American Indian portraits is owned by the Thomas Gilcrease Institute of American History and Art in Tulsa, Oklahoma.—D. C. H.

Crow Indians. The Crow Indians, a wandering, buffalo-hunting, Siouan-related tribe with a population of about four thousand, inhabited the eastern Rockies along the tributaries of the Yellowstone River when whites first entered that region in the early nineteenth century. They originated from a village that had separated from the Hidatsa in late prehistoric times. After 1859 a majority of them, the Mountain Crow, usually lived in the mountains, while a minority, the River Crow, frequented the vicinity of the Missouri River. They were a proud, warlike people, openly disdainful toward white civilization and almost constantly in conflict with neighboring tribes. Yet they willingly traded with Americans, boasted of never killing a Caucasian, and furnished many scouts for the army's crucial expeditions against the Sioux and Nez Percé in the 1870s.

A variety of persistent problems, largely concerned with ratified and unratified treaties, dominated Crow-white relations after the Civil War. Having already recognized the government's authority, limited their territorial claims, and received annuities at designated agencies under earlier agreements, the Crow signed a treaty in 1868 that assigned them to a "permanent" reservation in south-central Montana. But repeated invasions by white hunters, ranchers, and miners, raids by hostile Indians, and prolonged absenteeism by the River Crow led to further negotiations on the size and location of their reservation, which failed to win Senatorial approval. These complications, plus nearby Indian wars, slowed Crow absorption into white culture. However, by 1890 a growing number of them were involved in freighting, ranching, and lumbering and were beginning to make social reforms.

Located southeast of Billings, Montana, the Crow Indian Reservation is now smaller than in 1890, but it is a major tourist attraction because it encompasses the famous Custer battlefield.

Robert H. Lowie, *The Crow Indians* (1935), is the only full-length study of the Crow currently available. This book is primarily concerned with matters of ethnographic interest. John C. Ewers' edition of Edwin T. Denig, *Five Indian Tribes of the Upper Missouri* (1961), includes a chapter featuring a perceptive eyewitness account of the condition of the Crow in the 1850s, supplemented by explanatory footnotes that expand upon background events. An important facet of Crow history is treated in A. Glen Humphreys, "The Crow Indian Treaties of 1868: An Example of Power Struggle and Confusion in United States Indian Policy," *Annals of Wyoming* (Spring 1971). The discussion of the Crow in Frederick W. Hodge, ed., *Handbook of American Indians North of Mexico* (1910-11), vol. II, also provides some helpful general information. Still, the annual reports of the commissioner of Indian affairs have to be consulted for most of the particulars of Crow-white relations and tribal developments since 1868.—H. G. W.

Croy, Homer (1883-1965). Humorist and writer. Born on a Missouri farm, Croy was the first student in the first school of journalism, at the University of Missouri. Getting his start with Theodore Dreiser, then an editor for women's magazines, Croy quickly moved into the young field of communications by writing magazine articles and stories, preparing radio scripts, and, supposedly, making the first trip around the world specifically to take motion pictures.

Croy's historical narratives, often about characters from his Missouri homeland and neighboring areas, covered an endless variety of western subjects. The new cinema industry was the subject of his *How Motion Pictures Are Made* (1918), *Headed for Hollywood* (1932), *Our*

Legendary Horse by Woodrow Crumbo. (Thomas Gilcrease Institute)

Will Rogers (1953), and *Star Maker* (1959), his last book, on D. W. Griffith. Outlaws figure in *Jesse James Was My Neighbor* (1949) and *Last of the Great Outlaws* (1956), while frontier justice has its due in *Trigger Marshal* (1958), the story of Chris Madsen, a famous United States marshal, and *He Hanged Them High* (1952), the biography of a frontier judge. The tragic epic tale of the ill-fated Donner party is retold in *Wheels West* (1955).

His novels, packed with his varied experiences and often spiked with his never-failing wit, such as in *Sixteen Hands* (1938), which features a Missouri mule, are just as wide-ranging as the historical pieces. One of the best known is *They Had to See Paris*, which was subsequently made into a motion picture starring Will Rogers (the two men later became close friends). Other well-known novels are *The Lady from Colorado* (1957), based on the true story of a washerwoman who became the first titled lady of Colorado, and *River Girl* (1931), a realistic romance of the high days of Mississippi steamboating. Croy himself preferred the novels that dealt with rural life and the small towns of his home state. Written with knowledge, sympathy, and humor, these include *West of the Water Tower* (1923), probably his best book and sold to Paramount Pictures; *R.F.D. No. 3* (1924), a novel of Missouri farm life; and *Boone Stop* (1918), a story of young love in a small town. In *Country Cured* (1943) Croy relates the story of his own life.—J. C. D.

Crumbo, Woodrow (1912-   ). Creek-Potawatomi artist, dancer, and musician. Crumbo was born in Lexington, Oklahoma. Educated in Indian schools, he early mastered the essentials of Indian art, which included the study of religion, dancing, music, history, and folklore. In 1934 he attended Wichita University in Kansas and studied painting from Clayton Staples. In 1936 and 1938 he taught at the University of Oklahoma in Norman and also studied under Dr. Oscar B. Jacobson, who is credited with having influenced the careers of a number of contemporary Indian artists. He toured the nation for eleven years with the Thurlow Laurance Symphony, organized and directed by the noted composer of Indian music.

From 1938 to 1943 Crumbo was art director of Bacone College in Muskogee, Oklahoma, where he designed the window for the memorial chapel. Moving to Tulsa to work at Douglas Aircraft as a designer during the latter half of World War II, he continued to pursue his artistic career, producing tempera and oil paintings, serigraphs, and etchings, at one point as artist-in-residence at the Thomas Gilcrease Institute of American History and Art in Tulsa under the sponsorship of its founder. When on the staff of the El Paso Museum of Art in El Paso, Texas, Crumbo divided his time between Taos, New Mexico, and his native Oklahoma.

Crumbo paints in the tradition of his people, rendering his subjects in a flat or two-dimensional, sometimes highly decorative style reminiscent of earlier pictographic productions. Many of his works exhibit a certain amount of modeling and perspective; others are highly abstract and symbolic. His paintings are on permanent exhibition at the American Museum of Natural History in New York City, the universities of Wichita and Oklahoma, the Corcoran Gallery of Art and the Department of the Interior in Washington, D.C., the San Francisco Museum of Art, and at the Philbrook Art Center and the Thomas Gilcrease Institute of American History and Art, Tulsa, Oklahoma.

See Edward Everett Dale and Morris L. Wardell, *His-*

tory of Oklahoma (1948); Angie Debo, *Oklahoma Footloose and Fancy Free* (1949); and Jeanne O. Snodgrass, *American Indian Painters: A Biographical Dictionary* (1968).—D. C. H.

Cumberland Compact. (1780). Contract made between settlers and a land company. On May 13, 1780, Richard Henderson, one of the partners of the Transylvania Company, and 263 settlers signed the Cumberland Compact, more fully entitled "Articles of Agreement, or Compact of Government Entered Into by Settlers on the Cumberland River." This document did two things. First, it explained the exact terms by which the settlers could purchase acreage from Henderson and his associates. The compact set a high price for land—more than twenty-six pounds for each hundred acres—but it promised that no payments would be demanded until Henderson received confirmation for his title from the government of North Carolina. Second, the contract established a temporary elective government to rule the eight small communities that had been founded in the area of the present-day city of Nashville, Tennessee. This democratic policy, conceived by Henderson himself, survived until 1783, when the region was incorporated into Davidson County, North Carolina.

See Archibald Henderson, "Richard Henderson: The Authorship of the Cumberland Compact and the Founding of Nashville," *Tennessee Historical Magazine*, vol. 2 (1916).—T. H. B.

Cumberland Gap. Cumberland Gap is one of the deepest passes through the great rock wall forming the spine of the Pine, or Cumberland, Mountain range, located at the point common to Virginia, Kentucky, and Tennessee. Thomas Walker visited this defile on April 13, 1750. He either knew it as Cave Gap or gave it that name. Subsequently, he gave the river and mountain the name Cumberland for the "bloody" duke of Cumberland. Walker, however, was not the first white man to see the gap, because he found there the sign of the cross and initials carved on trees.

After 1770 Cumberland Gap became the great gateway to the New West, via the WILDERNESS ROAD. Between 1775 and 1800 more than 300,000 immigrants crossed over it.

See Clarence W. Alvord and Lee Bidgood, *The First Explorations of the Trans-Allegheny Region by the Virginians, 1650-1674* (1912); W. E. Connelley and E. M. Coulter, *History of Kentucky*, 5 vols. (1922); and J. Stoddard Johnston, ed., *First Explorations of Kentucky* (1898).—T. D. C.

Cumberland Road (National Road). See NATIONAL ROADS.

Curry, John Steuart (1897-1946). Painter. Born on a farm near Dunavant, Kansas, Curry was a robust and athletic youth with a fascination for drawing pictures of his surroundings. His strong drive for a career in art led him to leave high school and enter the Chicago Art Institute, where he spent two years as a special student. After brief service in World War I he began serious independent work under Harvey Dunn, a well-known illustrator. During the early 1920s Curry made illustrations for popular magazines and for books published about the West. By 1925 editors desiring pictures as illustrative materials for magazine stories were complaining that Curry's illustrations were too much like paintings, and he lost most of his work in this line.

Through the help of friends Curry spent the next two years in Paris learning draftsmanship and a strict delineation of form. By 1928 his style had developed along impressionistic lines. During the next few years he had his first one-man show, and a few paintings—many based on Kansas themes—began to sell. He also traveled one season with Ringling Brothers Circus; taught in New York City at Cooper Union and the Art Students League; and obtained commissions to paint murals sponsored by the Federal Art Project. In 1936 he became artist in residence at the University of Wisconsin.

Two years later, through the influence of Kansas newspaperman William Allen White, Curry was commissioned to provide a series of murals for the Kansas State Capitol in Topeka. Unfortunately, after Curry had made all the preliminary studies and was painting the murals, controversy broke out over trivial details involving the content of his pictures and Curry refused to sign his name to his paintings. These murals are probably his best-known works. His remaining years were spent at the University of Wisconsin. Curry is generally classified with Grant Wood of Iowa and Thomas Hart Benton of Missouri in the American Regionalism school of art.

An extensive review of his work is Laurence E. Schmeckebier, *John Steuart Curry's Pageant of America* (1943). Two posthumous studies are Maynard Walker, "John Steuart Curry (1897-1946)," *Kansas Magazine* (1947); and "John Steuart Curry," *Kansas Quarterly* (Fall 1970).—H. E. S.

Curti, Merle Eugene (1897-   ). Historian. Born in Papillion, Nebraska, Curti was educated at Harvard University (B.A., 1920; Ph.D., 1927), where he was a student of Frederick Jackson Turner. He taught at Smith College (1925-37), Columbia Teachers College (1937-42), and the University of Wisconsin, where he became Frederick Jackson Turner Professor of History in 1947.

Curti's interests and publications ranged from pacifism to education and philanthropy. One of his best-known books, *The Growth of American Thought* (1943), received the Pulitzer Prize in history. This work of social and intellectual history, with its emphasis on conflict and change, is considered to be a progressive interpretation in the tradition of Turner and Charles Beard. It stands in contrast to Ralph Gabriel's conservative and consensus-stressing *The Course of Democratic Thought* (1940). Curti was noted for his treatment of the interaction of ideas in the context of social relationships and institutions. This theme was well developed in *Social Ideas of American Educators* (1935). His two-volume history *The University of Wisconsin, 1848-1925* (1949), written jointly with Vernon Carstensen, stands as one of the most thorough attempts by professional historians to write the history of an educational institution.

As a student of Turner and a historian of American society, Curti naturally held an interest in the continuing debates over the validity of the Turner thesis. With a desire also to ascertain the value of quantitative methods for the study of history, Curti and a team of researchers applied and examined the Turner thesis in a study of Trempealeau County, Wisconsin, during the period between 1850 and 1880. In *The Making of an American Community* (1959), Curti noted that the group had not been "testing" the Turner *thesis* "but rather our interpretation of Turner's theory that the ready accessibility of free or almost free land promoted economic equality and that this was followed by political equality." The team found that in Trempealeau County such equality did exist, and that it was stronger in the 1870s than earlier. Admitting that the development of political and economic equality was not limited to the frontier, Curti concluded, "In our county, however, that stimulus and that opportunity were largely provided, we believe, by frontier conditions."

Curti is also author of *Austria and the United States, 1848-52* (1926), *The American Peace Crusade* (1929), *Bryan and World Peace* (1931), *Peace or War* (1936), *The Learned Blacksmith—Elihu Burritt* (1937), *American Issues* (1941), *Introduction to America* (1944), *Roots of American Loyalty* (1946), *An American History* (1950), *American Scholarship in the Twentieth Century* (1953), *Prelude to Point Four* (1954), *Probing Our Past* (1955), *American Paradox* (1956), *Rise of the American Nation* (1960), *American Philanthropy Abroad* (1963), *Philanthropy in the Shaping of American Higher Education* (1965), and *Human Nature in American Thought* (1968). —J. S. W.

Curtis, Edward Sheriff (1868-1952). Photographer and ethnologist. Born near Whitewater, Wisconsin, Curtis moved with his family in 1887 to Seattle, Washington, where he made his first Indian photographs in 1896. Also an ardent outdoorsman, Curtis accompanied the E. H. Harriman expedition to Alaska in 1899 as an official photographer, traveling more than nine thousand miles by land and sea, and produced nearly five thousand photographs of mountains, glaciers, animals, and topography. Also with this expedition were naturalist John Muir, ornithologist John Burroughs, and George Bird Grinnell, editor of *Forest and Stream* magazine, who encouraged the young photographer's ambition to produce a lasting pictorial record of the culture and characteristics of North America's aboriginal peoples. For the next thirty years Curtis worked to complete what proved to be a monumental project in this field, visiting more than eighty tribes from Canada to Mexico, and taking more than forty thousand photographs of Indian subjects. Some two thousand of them finally appeared in Curtis' *The North American Indian*, issued between 1907 and 1930 in twenty quarto volumes of text, illustrated with 1,500 plates, and twenty larger folios of 722 unbound photogravure plates, each of the folios corresponding to a volume of the text. More than half the cost of this enormous effort was borne by millionaire J. Pierpont Morgan, to whom Curtis was introduced in 1906 by Theodore Roosevelt. Prepared under the editorial supervision of Frederick Webb Hodge of the Smithsonian Institution's Bureau of American Ethnology, the whole work was originally intended to be published in five hundred numbered copies. However, less than two hundred were actually subscribed and sold upon completion of the twentieth volume in 1930. Remaining copies of an undetermined number were subsequently purchased and resold, and a few unbound or "green" copies also survive, although, like many of the original bound sets, they have been broken up and distributed piecemeal.

Comparable both in volume and scope to the work of John James Audubon in the field of American ornithology, *The North American Indian* is acknowledged today as one of the largest photographic documentaries ever produced by a single photographic artist.

See *Portraits from North American Indian Life: Edward S. Curtis* with introductions by A. D. Coleman and T. C. McLuhan (1972).—D. C. H.

Cushing, Frank Hamilton (1857-1900). Ethnologist. Cushing was born in Erie County, Pennsylvania. In 1879 he joined the Bureau of American Ethnology and went to Zuni, New Mexico, with James and Matilda Coxe Stevenson. Within six months Cushing had made fast friends among the Zuñi, and for the next four and a half years Zuni was his home. Formally initiated into the tribe, he wore their clothing, resided with the Zuñi governor's family, spoke the language, participated in Zuñi ceremonies, and became a member of the tribal council. In 1881 he entered the Bow priesthood (an esoteric fraternity whose members are responsible for the leadership of war parties), becoming its assistant chief and, ultimately, head war chief. He earned his Zuñi name, Ténatsali, upon his initiation into the Macaw clan, one of the more than dozen clans among the Zuñi.

Cushing published more than twenty papers on the Zuñi and other southwestern groups before his death; his *Zuñi Breadstuff* (1884-85) continues to be a standard source. His voluminous notes, many of them written in Zuñi, are deposited in the Southwest Museum in Los Angeles (see ARCHAEOLOGY OF NORTH AMERICAN INDIANS).

See W. J. McGee, William H. Holmes, et al., "In Memoriam Frank Hamilton Cushing," *American Anthropologist*, vol. 22 (1900).—B. L. F.

Custer, George Armstrong (1839-1876). Soldier. Custer was born in New Rumley, Ohio, of Hessian ancestry. In 1857 he was appointed to the United States Military Academy by Congressman John W. Bingham. Never a good student, he distinguished himself by the number of demerits accumulated and graduated at the bottom of his class, under a disciplinary cloud.

Assigned to the Fifth Cavalry in the Army of the Potomac, Custer soon attracted the attention of generals Phil Kearny and George McClellan with his bold, reckless bravery and spectacular showmanship in several cavalry fights. Although his promotion in 1863 to brigadier general of volunteers was ascribed to the mistake of an overworked clerk and to politics, it was probably Custer's flair for the flamboyant and his success in whatever he undertook that was responsible. Several other similar promotions, all recommended by General Alfred Pleasanton, were made at the same time, in what might be termed a cavalry shake-up. Shortly afterward Custer participated in the cavalry fight on the right flank at Gettysburg, which turned back Jeb Stuart's encircling movement and is said to have constituted "the margin of victory" that enabled the North to win this decisive battle of the Civil War.

Early in 1864 Custer married Elizabeth Bacon. After his return to duty, he participated in most of the remaining battles of the war in the East and played a decisive role in the preliminaries that brought about the surrender of General Lee at Appomattox. By the end of the Civil War, Custer was the youngest major general in the army.

When peace returned Custer reverted to his regular army rank of captain. But with the enlargement of the

Gen. Custer (with rifle) posed with the visiting Grand Duke Alexis of Russia (c. 1872). (Library of Congress)

army to cope with the growing Indian menace on the Great Plains, he was appointed lieutenant colonel of the newly created Seventh Cavalry. In 1867 the regiment played a prominent part in the HANCOCK CAMPAIGN, but because of a number of indiscretions--such as cruel treatment of deserters and overmarching his troops— Custer was court-martialed, convicted, and suspended from rank and command for one year. Reinstated before expiration of his sentence, he led his regiment to victory at the WASHITA River, a battle that gave the Seventh Cavalry its reputation and also sowed seeds of dissension within it, for some of the officers did not trust Custer's judgment.

After a brief tour of duty in the Department of the South, the regiment was transferred to Dakota in 1873 and, under Custer's command, constituted a part of the Stanley expedition, which explored the Yellowstone River in that year. In 1874 the expedition to the Black Hills, an area that was guaranteed to the Sioux by treaty, and Custer's statement about there being "gold at the roots of the grass" led to a stampede of miners into the area. This brought the troubles with the Sioux to a climax. In 1876 a full-scale campaign against these Indians culminated in the battle of the LITTLE BIG HORN, in which Custer and his command lost their lives.

The news of the disaster created an uproar among the American people and led to a controversy that has not subsided to the present day. Custer had a reputation for victory; for him, attack and victory were synonymous. He was known as the "American Murat" and his regi-

ment as "the matchless Seventh." That the regiment had suffered defeat and its commander death led to the suspicion that there had been treachery somewhere. This was heightened by the actions of certain other figures in the tragedy, by somewhat contradictory official reports, and by dispatches of newspaper correspondents. Gradually, the blame came to center on Major Marcus A. Reno, the second in command. At Major Reno's request, a court of inquiry into his responsibility was ordered in February 1879. Although interested to put an end to the controversy, the testimony was so contradictory that the controversy was merely intensified.

Mrs. Custer also contributed her share to the confusion concerning Custer's career. Because her pension was inadequate and in order to protect her husband's memory against his detractors, she wrote several books about him. The first, *Boots and Saddles* (1885, reprinted 1961), deals with the period just prior to the battle of the Little Big Horn. This was followed by *Tenting on the Plains* (1887, reprinted 1969) and *Following the Guidon* (1890, reprinted 1966).

The literature on Custer and the battle of the Little Big Horn is voluminous. Frederick Whittaker, *Popular Life of General George A. Custer* (1876), is extremely pro-Custer, and his account has been generally followed by subsequent writers. In 1934 Frederic F. Van De Water published *Glory Hunter*, which is anti-Custer. Mari Sandoz, *Battle of the Little Big Horn* (1966), stresses the theory that Custer had political ambitions and that his reckless attack at that battle can be attributed to his hopes for a spectacular victory, which would assure him the Democratic nomination for the presidency. Two recent books are Jay Monaghan, *Custer* (1959); and Edgar I. Stewart, *Custer's Luck* (1955).—E. I. S.

Cutter, Donald C. (1922-   ). Historian. Cutter was born in Chico, California, and educated at the University of California at Berkeley, where his studies were briefly interrupted by naval service during World War II. Although Cutter was too young to study under Herbert Bolton, the well-known Berkeley historian of the Spanish borderlands, he was deeply influenced by Bolton's views on the significance of the Spanish era in western history.

After teaching one year at San Diego State College, Cutter moved to the University of Southern California in 1951. In 1962 he joined the faculty at the University of New Mexico, where in 1967 he directed the American Indian historical research project. Often invited to speak before professional organizations and at various universities, Cutter served as a Fulbright lecturer in Spain and at Guadalajara, Mexico.

Much of Cutter's research dealt with Spanish naval and colonizing activities on the Pacific Coast during the seventeenth and eighteenth centuries. In 1957 he edited *The Diary of Ensign Gabriel Moraga's Expedition of Discovery in the Sacramento Valley, 1808* and in 1960 produced a short monograph, *Malespina in California*, a detailed account of an earlier Spanish exploring party on the West Coast. In various articles Cutter investigated other aspects of Spanish exploration in the Pacific area.

Cutter placed a great deal of emphasis on the training of large numbers of graduate students in the Bolton tradition of Spanish borderlands history and by 1970 had trained more than two dozen students.

His contributions to western history have kept alive Bolton's concepts on the role of Spanish influence in the West and focused attention on little-known phases of Spanish exploration and discovery on the Pacific Coast in the years prior to American annexation.—G. D. N.

D

Dakota Indians. See Sioux Indians.

Dakota Territory. Largely because of the lobbying of promoters like John B. S. Todd, Congress passed a law in 1861 establishing the Dakota Territory. There was, however, no great rush of settlers to the territory. During its first years, the territorial capital, Yankton, remained the population center. The population in the northern part of the territory was centered around Pembina. The period 1878-87 brought the "Dakota Boom," during which more than twenty-four million acres of land were acquired through the public land office. The population of southwestern Dakota rose from 10,000 in 1870 to 81,781 in 1880. Railroads and territorial promotion by writer Moses K. Armstrong, among others, lured many people, primarily from Minnesota, Wisconsin, Iowa, and Illinois. Those who migrated directly from abroad came mostly from western and northern Europe. Between 1878 and 1890 the population of northern Dakota increased one thousand percent, from 16,000 to 191,000. The coming of the railroads also led to the growth of such towns as Sioux Falls, Huron, Aberdeen, Pierre, Fargo, and Grand Forks.

The overwhelming majority of Dakotans earned their livelihood from the soil. The summer that settlers broke ground little was raised except sod corn, potatoes, and vegetables. Although all grains were grown in Dakota, wheat became king. And because Dakota developed into an almost one-crop economy, when hard times struck, the times were indeed hard. The decline of the price of wheat in the 1880s and prolonged drought caused severe economic hardship on the farms of Dakota. The Farmers' Alliance prospered in Dakota, and when statehood was achieved for the Dakotas, the Populist party won the governorships in both states. But earning a living from Dakota's fertile land remained a difficult task with the hazards of nature and the abuses of man.

In addition to farming, mining and cattle ranching played significant roles in the Dakota economy. An estimated ten thousand people were drawn to the Black Hills between November 1875 and March 1876 by the lure of gold. The amount extracted in the vicinity of Deadwood has been estimated as worth from three to four million dollars. The backbone of the mining industry was the Homestake Mine in Lead, which between 1876 and 1935 removed $301 million worth of gold out of the total state yield of $358 million worth. The Black Hills agreement with the Teton Sioux in 1877 not only opened up the mining country but also rich grazing land, and by 1878 the range-cattle industry spilled over into Dakota. Increased population in the Black Hills brought demand for meat products. Andrew Voigt, Scotty Philip, and John D. Hale were some of the most successful ranchers, and soon many Texas outfits moved into the region; by 1880 cattlemen had occupied most of the range in Dakota.

Since territorial governors were presidential appointees, Republicans dominated the politics of the territory. William Jayne (1861-63), Andrew J. Faulk (1866-69), John A. Burbank (1869-73), John L. Pennington (1874-78), William A. Howard (1878-80), Nehemiah Ordway (1880-84), and Gilbert Pierce (1884-86) came directly to the territory as appointees to the governorship. Newton Edmunds (1863-66) came to Dakota in 1861 as chief clerk in the surveyor general's office, while Louis K.

Church (1887-89) was appointed to the court in 1885. Only Arthur C. Mellette (1889), who practiced law in Watertown, Dakota, was appointed directly from the territory.

Political pull or debt brought most of the appointments. Jayne was Lincoln's family physician and campaign manager in Illinois as well as the brother-in-law of Senator Lyman Trumbull of Illinois; Faulk was the father-in-law of delegate Walter A. BURLEIGH; and Burbank was the brother-in-law of Senator Oliver Perry Morton of Indiana. President Rutherford B. Hayes appointed Howard largely because the latter had been instrumental in switching the Michigan delegation's support to Hayes in the Republican convention of 1876. Ordway, Pennington, and Church were faithful party workers in their respective states of New Hampshire, North Carolina, and New York. Only Edmunds and Mellette, who were both in the territory prior to appointment, could not be regarded as carpetbaggers.

The governors of Dakota brought a variety of experience to the territory. Three were newspapermen: Faulk, editor of a small-town Pennsylvania paper; Pennington, associated with several papers in North Carolina; and Pierce, who worked with the Chicago *Inter-Ocean*. Of the newspapermen only Pennington seems to have dabbled in politics before coming to Dakota. Church and Mellette were practicing attorneys in New York City and Dakota Territory, respectively. Jayne was a physician, although he had been mayor of Springfield and a member of the Illinois state senate. Edmunds, of course, had been in Dakota with the surveyor general's office. Only Burbank, Howard, and Ordway could be classified as professional politicians. The governors were of different capabilities and motivations. Some were successful; some failed. Most were qualified; some were not. A review of two governors serves to illustrate this.

Edmunds serves as an example of the governor who took his charge seriously and who also paid a great deal of attention to his position as superintendent of Indian Affairs. In the latter capacity he initiated a movement for peace among the Sioux in the Missouri River valley. He believed that peaceful relations could be gained without the extensive military intervention that the army contemplated.

In contrast, Burbank was more interested in railroads than in governing. He came in with the Grant administration of 1869 and was reappointed in 1873, but within a year he was requested to resign by the secretary of the interior. He entered fully into the ambitious plans of railroad promoters and land speculators. When the secretary of state disapproved a Yankton County bond issue to support the Dakota Southern Railroad, promoted by a pro-Burbank group, Governor Burbank went to Washington and spent the entire winter and spring of 1871 lobbying for congressional approval of the county bond issue. He received an additional charter and a land grant for a "grand trunk" to connect Yankton to the Northern Pacific Railroad. As a reward for his efforts, he was made a director of the railroad.

The mid-1880s witnessed the development of a full-blown statehood movement. Complicated by the removal of the capital to BISMARCK and the corrupt governorship of Ordway, the movement resulted in the drafting and popular approval of two constitutions, in 1883 and 1885. Congress, however, because of political stale-mate between both Democrats and Republicans, failed to act until 1889, when NORTH DAKOTA and SOUTH DAKOTA were admitted to the Union.

See Howard R. Lamar, *Dakota Territory, 1861-1889* (1956).—D. J. T.

Dale, Edward Everett (1879-1972). Historian. To say that Dale's career as a historian is unique would be an understatement. He did not enter college until he was almost thirty years old, marry until he was forty, or receive his doctorate until he was forty-three. Even after passing "four score and ten," he continued to maintain a regular schedule of research and writing at his office at the University of Oklahoma. He has the additional distinction of being a native Oklahoman, even though he was born in Texas. The place of his birth was a small ranching community in Greer County, Texas, between the north and south forks of the Red River. After a Supreme Court decision in 1896 this area was transferred to Oklahoma and the local settlers were declared citizens of the Sooner State.

Greer County at the turn of the century offered few opportunities for an ambitious young man. "We were not exactly poor people," Dale later reflected, "we were just plain damn *pore*." After failing in a small ranching enterprise in partnership with his brother, the future historian entered college at an age when most men already had a sizable family. After he graduated from the University of Oklahoma in 1911, he taught in country schools for two years before enrolling in graduate work at Harvard University. He received his M.A. degree there in 1914 and went back to Oklahoma as an assistant professor. For the next eight years he continued intermittent work on his doctorate at Harvard during the summers and taught "every history course in the catalogue" in the history department at the University of Oklahoma during the regular terms.

Dale's dissertation, completed in 1922 under the direction of Frederick Jackson Turner, was eventually published under the title of *The Range Cattle Industry* (1930). By this time he already had published *Territorial Acquisitions of the United States* (1912); a small volume of poems entitled *Tales of the Teepee* (1919); and co-authored *A History of Oklahoma* (1924). His scholarly list exceeds twenty books, the best known of which is *The Indians of the Southwest* (1948).

Honors and administrative positions came late to Dale, but in large numbers. He was chairman of the history department at Oklahoma from 1924 to 1942, followed by ten years as research professor of history and twenty more years as emeritus research professor. Meanwhile, he was twice elected president of the Agricultural Historical Society (1925-27) and served one term as president of the Mississippi Valley Historical Association (1926-27). Among his other administrative positions was a short stint as dean of the Graduate College at Oklahoma (1929-30), member of the Indian Survey staff for the Brookings Institution (1929-30), and director of the Frank Phillips Collection of Western History at the University of Oklahoma (1926-52).

Dale was noted for his ability to relate personal experience to his writings about the southwestern frontier. He also enjoyed a successful reputation as a public lecturer, raconteur, and authority on modern Indians.—W. E. H.

Dallas, Texas. The second-largest city in Texas, Dallas began in 1841 when John N. Bryan located a farm and store on the banks of the Trinity River. The origin of the name, applied almost immediately to the community, is obscure, although generally it is thought to have been named in honor of George M. Dallas, vice-president of the United States from 1845 to 1849. Bryan, who planned the town, advertised it widely. By 1851 it had a population of 163 and was the county seat for Dallas County. A nearby European colony, La Réunion, disbanded in the late 1850s and many of its residents moved to Dallas, adding a cosmopolitan flavor that has endured.

A fire in 1860 destroyed much of the town, but it quickly was rebuilt and became a Confederate administrative center. After the war it was a banking and distributing center for farmers in much of North Texas. Then in 1872 the Houston and Texas Central Railroad arrived, as did the Texas and Pacific the following year, and immediately the town boomed; from 1,200 residents in 1872 it grew to 7,000 within months. In 1873 alone some 725 buildings were constructed. Apparently the Panic of 1873 did not slow this growth, for the town numbered 10,358 residents by 1880 and 42,638 at the turn of the century.

Flooding and water supply were problems plaguing the community in those early years. Water first was secured by drilling artesian wells, but eventually both flooding and water supply were controlled by erecting dams on the Trinity River. In 1900 Bachman's Lake was created on the Trinity, the first man-made lake of the many that would be constructed in the vicinity. And in 1912 the city fathers began construction of concrete-and-steel viaducts to channel the Trinity through the city, also providing an industrial park along the old waterway.

Dallas merchants continued in the twentieth century to dominate trade and wholesale distribution in North Texas, even expanding their trade area in recent years through the construction of the Dallas Market Center, the Trade Mart, the Home Furnishings Mart, the Apparel Mart, and the Market Hall. Moreover, its retail stores, such as Neiman-Marcus, have become world famous for the quality of their merchandise. Dallas also developed as a major fashion center specializing in the design and manufacture of wearing apparel. Today the city ranks third in the nation as a wholesale market.

Other sources of income include the marketing of cotton; in 1970 alone the Dallas Cotton Exchange exceeded $300 million in business. Some 450 oil companies have made their headquarters in Dallas, while banking and insurance have expanded until Dallas has become dominant as a financial center. World War II stimulated manufacturing on a wide scale, especially in the aircraft industry. After the war Chance-Vought began operations in Dallas, and later merged into Ling-Temco-Vought; this company, along with Texas Instruments and other such firms, have made Dallas a leader in the electronics and computer fields. Automobile assembly plants have located nearby, while Dallas has become a regional center for printing, publishing, and food processing. Tourism is a major source of income also; within the metropolitan area are major-league football and baseball teams, amusement parks, and convention centers.

Dallas—"Big D" its residents call it—emerged as a major metropolitan center because its leaders proved aggressive and farsighted. Today those same qualities are evident in the big air terminal recently opened near the city.

See James Howard, *Big D Is for Dallas* (1957); and J. W. Rogers, *The Lusty Texas of Dallas* (1951).—O. B. F.

Dalton gang. Outlaws. When Lewis Dalton, a rambler, saloonkeeper, and admirer of horseflesh, abandoned his wife, Adeline Younger Dalton, she was left on her own to instill moral principle into their fifteen children. It was an immense task to undertake on the Missouri-Kansas frontier in the troubled years of the Civil War and Reconstruction, when Kansas Jayhawkers and Missouri bushwhackers brought a particularly vicious and lawless warfare to the region. With men like Jesse James and Cole Younger for impressionable children to idolize it is perhaps surprising that so many of the Dalton brood (four boys and three girls) found satisfaction in mundane, but respectable, pursuits. The oldest boy, Ben, stayed with his parents through the years, and three more migrated to California, where they lived out their lives as farmers. Three other children died very young. Another, Franklin (?-1887), wore the badge of a lawman and died in the line of duty. The rest of the boys, however, left their mark on western history. Three, Grattan (1861-1892), Robert (1870-1892), and Emmett (1871-1937) became infamous as the heart of the Dalton gang. The other boy, William (1863-1894), embittered by political failure and the fate of his brothers, foolishly followed their example and died at the hands of the law in Oklahoma.

In the 1860s the Daltons settled in Montgomery County, Kansas, near the present site of Coffeyville. They soon moved to a farm in Missouri, and there their children grew up. In 1882, Lewis packed up his brood once again and moved into the Cherokee Nation in what is now Oklahoma. The boys still at home were soon working as cowboys and consorting with a rough crowd that included several men who would later become members of their gang.

In 1884 Frank became a federal deputy marshal serving under the jurisdiction of Fort Smith's "hanging judge," Isaac Parker. He proved to be an efficient officer who respected his badge, but he operated in a dangerous area and, in 1887, was killed by whiskey runners. Grat Dalton took his place and promptly chose Bob as a posseman; Emmett sometimes tagged along as an unofficial assistant. From the outset it was apparent that these Daltons lacked the respect for the law that had characterized Frank. In 1888 Bob was appointed chief of the Indian police in the Osage Nation. Emmett joined Bob as a posseman there. They were still wearing badges when they killed a man named Charlie Montgomery, who made the mistake of taking up with Bob's girl. That was the real beginning of their problems, although they managed to clothe the shooting with a charge of "resisting arrest."

The next year Oklahoma opened up to settlement, and the Daltons moved into a profitable horse-stealing operation, in spite of the badges they still wore. For a time after the Osage caught on to their activities, they carried on their clandestine operations as officers for the Cherokee. By 1890, however, they were discredited as lawmen and had turned to horse stealing as a full-time enterprise. They surrounded themselves with hardcases like Charley Bryant, Bill McElhanie, and George Newcomb. Grat left the territory to visit his brother Bill in California, and the rest of the boys drifted into Silver City, New Mexico, where they expanded their operations by robbing a gambling house. Emmett was badly wounded in the fight that followed and forced to go into hiding. The pressure from the law was so great that Bob followed Grat to California to visit Bill.

Bill Dalton's fortunes were on the rise when his brothers arrived. He was popular, prosperous, and politically promising, and the presence of his notorious brothers did him no good at all. Not long after their arrival a train was robbed, and the Daltons were blamed. Bob eluded capture, but Bill and Grat were arrested, although there never was any real evidence against them. Grat was convicted of train robbery, and although Bill was exonerated, his political future was ruined. From that point on his name was linked to that of his brothers. Grat was never sentenced in California. In September 1891 he escaped and headed home. He arrived in Oklahoma to find that Bob and Emmett and assorted cronies had gone into the train-robbing business for real.

For the next year, the Daltons indulged in robbery and murder while the forces of Oklahoma law pursued them. The Daltons had more crimes than loot to their credit, and the law was closing in on them by 1892. Then Bob and Grat made a fatal error. They decided to rob both banks in Coffeyville, Kansas, their old hometown. The decision split the gang, but the main problem was that Coffeyville was expecting them. On October 5, 1892, Bob, Grat, Emmett, Dick Broadwell, and Bill Powers rode into Coffeyville. They were recognized, and a wild gun battle followed in which the citizens killed all of the gang except Emmett, who was severely wounded. Four local citizens also died that day. Emmett was sent to prison for life, but he was paroled after fourteen years.

Bill Dalton had already returned to Oklahoma long before the Coffeyville raid. He could not get politics out of his system, but his efforts failed to overcome the Dalton name. So he also turned to outlawry. He disagreed with his brothers regarding the wisdom of the Coffeyville robbery and joined Bill Doolin's new gang instead of going to Kansas with his brothers. He rode with Doolin until 1894 and then formed his own gang. The new Dalton gang made one raid, a bank robbery in Longview, Texas, which was a fiasco. The gang was badly shot up, but Bill made it as far as Ardmore, Oklahoma. There on June 8, 1894, Bill Dalton was killed attempting to escape from law officers.

See Harold Preece, *The Dalton Gang* (1963); and Paul I. Wellman, *A Dynasty of Western Outlaws* (1961). —G. L. R.

Daly, Marcus (1841-1900). Montana mining magnate. Raised in a poor family in Ireland, Daly arrived in New York at the age of fifteen, but was soon engaged in mining in California, Nevada, and Utah. He went to Butte, Montana, in 1876, where he acquired the Anaconda and other mines rich in silver. When copper ore appeared, Daly was the first to recognize its value. An early friendship with his fellow copper magnate, William A. CLARK—Daly's wife's sister was married to Clark's brother—turned into a bitter personal, business, and political feud. When Clark obtained control of Butte's limited water supply, Daly built the town of

Anaconda and its huge smelter near a plentiful water supply. He also built the Butte, Anaconda & Pacific Railway to transport ore from Butte. When Clark blocked Daly's lumber enterprises near Missoula, Daly transferred his activities to Hamilton, where he also built a famous horse racing and training center and a palatial mansion.

When Clark defeated Daly's attempt to make Anaconda the capital city, Daly provided financial support to the investigation by the United States Senate into bribery of the Montana legislature, which caused Clark to resign before the committee report was acted upon. The feud between Daly, Clark, and Frederick Augustus Heinze, another of the battling copper kings, all of whom were Democrats, kept this party in turmoil for a full decade (see MONTANA). Daly had no personal desire for political office, but because of the loyalty of his workmen to him, his party and his political friends could expect substantial aid when it was needed.

Daly led in consolidating the vast mining enterprise he had assembled into the Anaconda Copper Mining Company in 1895 of which he was president until he died. With considerable reluctance he entered into the Amalgamated Copper Company in 1900, a holding company to enlarge still further the Anaconda company, because he feared its control would shift from the mining men in Butte and the West to the financiers in New York.

See Isaac F. Marcosson, *Anaconda* (1957); and *Progressive Men of the State of Montana* (1901).—M. G. B.

Dame Shirley. Pen name of **Louise [Amelia Knapp Smith] Clappe** (1819-1906). Writer. Dame Shirley is famous for her California gold-rush letters. However, she was not generally recognized as their author during her lifetime and little is known about her even today. Born in New Jersey, Louise Smith was orphaned early and raised in New England. There she attended Amherst Academy in 1839 and 1840, where she met Alexander Hill Everett, an author and diplomat. Everett introduced "Shirley" (as friends called her) to writing and coached her through an exchange of letters.

Shirley married Dr. Fayette Clappe, a man remembered only as her husband. In 1849 the couple moved to San Francisco. In June 1851, because of ill health, Dr. Clappe removed to the mining settlement of Rich Bar in the upper Feather River Canyon. His wife followed in September. From that area, Shirley wrote a series of twenty-three letters to her sister Molly in New England. The letters fall between September 1851 and November 1852. Copies of them were published in 1854 and 1855 in *The Pioneer: or California Monthly Magazine* under the pen name Dame Shirley.

These letters stand out as perhaps the best descriptions of the short-lived early gold-rush days. The language is picturesque and graphic, depicting the rough-hewn mining camps in full: "I am bound, Molly," wrote Shirley, "to give you a *true* picture (as much as in me lies), of mining life and its peculiar temptations, 'nothing extenuating nor setting down aught in malice.' " That task she amply accomplished. "I think I have never spoken to you of the mournful extent to which profanity prevails in California," she wrote in Letter Six. "You know that at home it is considered *vulgar* for a gentleman to swear; but I am told that here, it is absolutely the fashion, and that people who never uttered an oath in their lives while in the 'States,' now 'clothe themselves with curses as with a garment.' "

By the end of 1852 the diggings were giving out, forcing the Clappes to return to San Francisco. There Shirley became a teacher. Among her pupils were authors Charles Warren Stoddard and Mary Viola Tingley Lawrence. Shirley was divorced from her husband in 1857. In 1878, her health failing, she returned to New York. She lived there for some years, often giving lectures on literature. In 1897 she moved to a New Jersey home for the elderly run by a niece of Bret Harte, and there she died.

Many later authors, including Bret Harte, used the "Dame Shirley Letters" as the background for their own tales about the fabled gold-rush days in the mother lode.

See Carl I. Wheat, ed., *The Shirley Letters From the California Mines, 1851-1852* (1949).—R. S.

Dana, Richard Henry, Jr. (1815-1882). Writer. Dana was born in Massachusetts and entered Harvard College in 1831, but soon had to withdraw because of eye trouble resulting from measles. For reasons of health, he was sent off around Cape Horn to California in 1834 as a common sailor and in 1836 returned in vigorous health to Boston. He resumed his interrupted Harvard studies, graduated in 1837, studied law, and was admitted to the bar in 1840, the same year in which his account of his voyage to California, the famed *Two Years Before the Mast*, was published. As a lawyer Dana specialized in admiralty cases, and in later life he dabbled in politics. A founder of the Free-Soil party, his political ambitions were never fully realized, in part because of his distant personal manner and in part because of his aversion to machine politics. He died in Rome, Italy, while on a pleasure trip.

Dana's literary reputation rests entirely on *Two Years Before the Mast*, on one level a simple report of his experience as a sailor. The book's immediate popularity was in large measure the result of its concern with the hard and often brutal treatment given common sailors, a concern it shares with Melville's *White-Jacket* (1850) and, to a degree, *Moby Dick* (1851). Although this concern is presently only of antiquarian interest, the book ramains valuable for its descriptions of life at sea and for its superb eyewitness account of life in California before the American annexation of that territory.

See Robert L. Gale, *Richard Henry Dana* (1968); Charles Francis Adams, *Richard Henry Dana: A Biography*; and Henry Adams, *The Education of Henry Adams* (1907).—J. K. F.

Dancing Rabbit Creek, Treaty of (1830). The Dancing Rabbit Creek treaty, signed September 27, 1830, and ratified February 24, 1831, was an agreement made with the Choctaw Indians of Mississippi and eastern Alabama, by which the government schemed to carry out the Indian Removal Act of May 1830. The scene of the treaty ground was Dancing Rabbit Creek in southwestern Noxubee County, Mississippi, near the Noxubee River. Chief negotiators were General John H. Eaton and General John Coffee for the United States government and Greenwood Leflore, Mosholatubbee, and Nitakechi for the Choctaw.

When the white negotiators opened by stating that the Choctaw were required by a new law to immediately cede all their lands east of the Mississippi and remove to the West, the Indians were amazed. They refused outright and threatened death to any chief weak enough to consent. General Eaton then stated that they had no choice, because the president would in twenty days march an army against them if they refused. At this most of the Choctaw rose and left, but Eaton convinced a few, through bribery and threats, to sign an agreement. Under terms of the treaty the Choctaw ceded to the federal government about one fourth the area of Mississippi, from which sixteen counties were later formed. The Indians were paid $20,000 yearly for a period of twenty years, and the chiefs were each to receive $250 a year and four sections of land for their personal use. The tribe was promised a generous grant of land in the West.

The majority of the Choctaw were outraged by the treaty, but the government refused to recognize any objections, and intratribal dissension over blame for its signing prevented united resistance. Depressed and disorganized, the Choctaw had no choice but to submit. The Dancing Rabbit agreement was the first treaty executed under the Removal Act, and it set a pattern for the tactics used in the subsequent negotiations with the other southeastern tribes.

See Thelma V. Bounds, *Children of Nanih Waiya* (1964); A. W. Dillard, *The Treaty of Dancing Rabbit Creek* (1928); Dunbar Rowland, *Encyclopedia of Mississippi History*, 2 vols. (1907); and Charles C. Royce, "Indian Land Cessions in the United States," in Bureau of American Ethnology, *Eighteenth Annual Report, 1896-97* (1899). —T. D. C.

Darley, Felix Octavius Carr (1822-1888). Illustrator. Darley was born in Philadelphia, the son of John Darley, or Darly, English comedian. Although displaying a talent for art at an early age, he received no formal instruction but followed mercantile pursuits in his native city and executed woodcuts for a pictorial journal, *Scenes of Indian Life* (1843). He began his professional career as an illustrator after moving in 1848 to New York City, where he was engaged throughout the 1850s to produce illustrations for the novels of Washington Irving and James Fenimore Cooper. His work earned him the reputation of being a skilled and original draftsman, and he continued to furnish pictures for some of the finest editions of standard English and American authors for several years. He also produced a popular series of lithographs based upon American historical and frontier themes.

An exhibitor at the National Academy of Design in New York City, to which he was elected to membership in 1852, Darley also was a member of the Artists' Fund Society and the American Watercolor Society, although he worked almost exclusively in a black-and-white medium. His brother, E. H. Darley, and his sister-in-law, Jane Cooper, stepdaughter of artist Thomas Sully, also were artists.

See Robert Taft, *Artists and Illustrators of the Old West, 1850-1900* (1953).—D. C. H.

Davis, H[arold] L[enoir] (1896-1960). Short-story writer, poet, and novelist. Davis was born in Yoncalla, Oregon. He was educated rather informally in the Oregon public schools and began at an early age the series of miscellaneous jobs that became the staple of his later western fiction. His first job—at the age of nine—was as a typesetter on a country newspaper, followed by temporary employment in a varied succession of odd jobs as, among other things, sheep herder, cowboy, surveyor, editor, and deputy sheriff. His novel *Honey in the Horn* (1935) won both the Pulitzer Prize and the Harper Novel Prize, and he contributed short stories and poems to various magazines.

Davis might more truly be considered a regional than a purely western writer. Although the usual fictional locale of his tales is the Pacific Northwest, the time of his stories is approximately the time of his own youth. His tales are nostalgic, almost elegaic in tone, lamenting not so much the loss of the wild, free life of the frontier as the passing of the idyllic existence of a boy in the rural America of the turn of the century. They are humorous rather than melodramatic, and a good many of the staples of commonplace blood-and-thunder western fiction are absent from them. Although Davis is best remembered for his fiction, the fact that he considered himself to be primarily a poet explains much about his prose. He often writes a story as though it were an expanded poetic metaphor, and even his longer fiction is organized more in terms of the poetical techniques of metaphor and analogy than the more conventional fictional ones of plot and characterization.—J. K. F.

Davis, Jeff (1862-1913). Arkansas politician. Davis was a colorful native Arkansan whose agrarian appeal won him control of the state's Democratic party at the turn of the century. He served one term as Arkansas's attorney general (1899-1901), three terms as governor (1901-07), and had been elected to a second term in the United States Senate (1913) when he died at Little Rock. With the farmer-labor vote solidly behind him, he attacked the trusts, the railroads, the prison contractors, and secured much reform legislation. His platform style mixed humor, folksiness, and ridicule of his enemies. When the Baptist church withdrew fellowship from him for drinking, he declared that he was a "pint-a-day" Baptist booted out by "quart-a-day" deacons, and appealed to all those who had ever taken a drink to vote for him. They did.—W. L. B.

Davis, Jefferson (1808-1889). Soldier, politician, president of the Confederacy and writer. Born in Kentucky, Davis was the tenth child of a pioneer family. His father made a modest living as a tobacco planter and breeder of fine horses. During Davis' childhood, his father moved the family to Wilkinson County, Mississippi. Davis received most of his education at Transylvania University in Lexington, Kentucky, and at West Point, where he graduated in 1828. He then served in several frontier posts, but saw action only in the Black Hawk War (1832).

Davis left the army in 1835 to become a Mississippi cotton planter at his plantation home Brierfield, in Warren County. Having first married in 1835 the daughter of Zachary Taylor, Sarah Knox, who died after a few months, Davis took as his second wife in 1845 Varina Howell, the daughter of an aristocratic and wealthy Mississippi planter of Natchez. In the ten years of widowhood at Brierfield, Davis read widely in the fields of politics and history and engaged in endless discussions with his older brother, Joseph, who was a substitute father to him.

He entered politics in 1843 as the Democratic candidate for representative of Warren County and was defeated. In 1844 he canvassed the state as a presidential elector for the Democratic ticket. His first election to

public office, the United States House of Representatives, was in 1845. He resigned from the House in 1846, however, to serve as colonel of a volunteer regiment of Mississippi rifles in the Mexican War (1846-48). Distinguishing himself at Monterrey and Buena Vista, Davis returned to Mississippi to recuperate from his war wounds. But he soon reentered the political arena when Governor Albert Gallatin Brown appointed him to the Senate seat left vacant in 1847 by the death of Jessie D. Speight. Subsequently, Davis was elected in 1850 to a full six-year term.

As senator from Mississippi (1847-51), he tried hard to defeat the admission of California as a free state and opposed all the measures known collectively as the COMPROMISE OF 1850. In 1851 he was a candidate (for the first and only time in his career) for governor of Mississippi, but was defeated by his political and personal enemy and Senate colleague, Henry Stuart FOOTE, the candidate of the Union party. Davis' candidacy for the governor's office came about under unusual circumstances. In the midst of the campaign of 1851, Mississippians elected an overwhelming number of Union delegates to the proposed secession convention of 1851. The Union party in Mississippi was a coalition of Democrats and Whigs who believed that the Compromise of 1850 was the solution to sectional problems and who hoped to avoid secession in 1851. John Anthony Quitman, an avid secessionist and candidate for governor on the State Rights ticket, withdrew. Davis then resigned his seat in the Senate and campaigned against Foote. He lost the governorship by only 999 votes.

After his defeat in 1851, Davis retired once again to his plantation. Because of his efforts in behalf of the Democratic ticket in the presidential election of 1852, President Franklin Pierce selected him for the post of secretary of war in his cabinet. He held this post during the entire four-year administration of Pierce and became his close political and personal friend. Davis' West Point training and military experience were valuable assets to him in this post. As secretary of war he achieved some success in standardizing the army and bringing it up to date in equipment and organization. During his secretaryship, engineering surveys were undertaken to mark the routes that were to be used by four of the future great transcontinental railroads. Davis supported expanionist schemes in Cuba and Nicaragua and urged the building of a transcontinental railroad using the southern route.

Davis reentered the Senate immediately after the close of his term as secretary of war (1857), where he again became an ardent defender of the South. He interpreted the concept of POPULAR SOVEREIGNTY to mean that neither Congress nor a territorial legislature could exclude slavery and called for federal protection of slavery in the territories. He served in the Senate until his formal withdrawal on January 21, 1861, when he learned officially that Mississippi had seceded from the Union.

Davis became the first and only president of the Confederate States of America, serving in this capacity from his inauguration as provisional president on February 18, 1861, to his capture on May 10, 1865. Davis had believed in secession as a last resort and merely went along with Mississippi when she seceded. By 1860 he was considered to be a moderate, which is the principal reason why he was chosen to be president of the Confederacy. Those in the Confederacy who opposed Davis believed first in state sovereignty and then in the Confederacy. To Davis, a southern nationalist above all, the Confederacy came first. Yet almost from the time of his inauguration, Davis' critics both inside and outside the Confederate Congress began to increase their attacks on him. Favorite targets were Judah P. Benjamin in the cabinet for the tremendous influence he had in helping Davis make decisions, the conscription, impressment, and tax in kind acts, the presidential suspension of the writ of *habeas corpus*, and Davis' "interference" with generals and military affairs. One of the principal leaders of the opposition in the Confederate Congress was the same Foote, now a representative from Tennessee, who had defeated Davis for governor in 1851.

Davis lived until December 6, 1889. During this almost quarter-century of retirement at his home Beauvoir on the Mississippi Gulf Coast, Davis attended to his business affairs, read a great deal, did some writing, and enjoyed the company of many visitors. His *The Rise and Fall of the Confederate Government* (1881) and *A Short History of the Confederate States of America* (1890) were written at Beauvoir.

Davis is one of the most controversial figures in American history, not only because of his role during the Civil War but also because of his personality. In his childhood he seems to have been extremely sensitive and highly imaginative. As a young man he was fearless, generous, modest, self-confident, very loyal to his friends, but lacked humor. His years as a young military officer and a planter were important in the development of his character. A benevolent slave-owner, he developed a devotion to the South's social system and to the state-rights argument to maintain this system. He also had a deep-seated love of the military way of life and always thought of himself as a soldier. Except for the years as secretary of war, his health was poor. He suffered from neuralgia, nervous indigestion, and eye disease. As president of the Confederacy, most authorities agree that he was an astonishingly bad administrator, insensitive to public opinion and loyal to his friends even after they had lost the confidence of the public at large. He attempted to combine civilian and military leadership in his own person and was too short-tempered to get along with people. But he was honest, courageous, dignified, and looked the part of the leader. He was not very successful as war president, but it is doubtful that any other southern leader could have done a better job considering the difficulties faced by the Confederacy.

For a sympathetic appraisal of Davis, see Elizabeth Cutting, *Jefferson Davis, Political Soldier* (1930); Varina Howell Davis, *Jefferson Davis, Ex-President of the Confederate States of America: A Memoir by His Wife* (1890); Hudson Strode, *Jefferson Davis*, 3 vols. (1955-64); Allen Tate, *Jefferson Davis: His Rise and Fall* (1929); and Robert W. Winston, *High Stakes and Hair Trigger: The Life of Jefferson Davis* (1930). For a more critical appraisal, see Hamilton J. Eckenrode, *Jefferson Davis, President of the South* (1923); Robert McElroy, *Jefferson Davis, the Unreal and the Real* (1937); and Edward A. Pollard, *The Life of Jefferson Davis* (1869). See also *Jefferson Davis, Constitutionalist: His Letters, Papers and Speeches*, 10 vols. (1923), edited by Dunbar Rowland, and *The Papers of*

Jefferson Davis (1971-   ), edited by Haskell M. Monroe, Jr., and James T. McIntosh.—J. E. G.

Davis, Theodore Russell (1840-1894). Illustrator. Davis was born in Boston and moved to Brooklyn at the age of fifteen. Believed to have received some instruction in drawing from the engraver Henry W. Herrick, he exhibited at the American Institute in 1856. He joined the staff of *Harper's Weekly* in 1861 as a Civil War illustrator and correspondent and after the war traveled through the conquered South on assignments and later into the mining districts of the Far West. Best known today for his illustrations of western life, Davis continued to work for *Harper's* until about 1884, when he retired to Asbury Park, New Jersey, to do free-lance work.

See John C. Ewers, *Artists of the Old West* (1965); and Robert Taft, *Artists and Illustrators of the Old West, 1850-1900* (1953).—D. C. H.

Davis, William Watts Hart (1820-1910). Historian, attorney, and journalist. A native of Massachusetts, Davis was reared in the East, where he was trained in the law. Serving in the Mexican War as a first lieutenant, the swarthy Davis distinguished himself by his courageous conduct in several engagements. Appointed United States attorney for the Territory of New Mexico by President Franklin Pierce in 1853, Davis again went west, where he not only helped to administer the laws of the new territory but was also able to record in exhaustive detail his view of the Spanish-speaking Roman Catholic inhabitants of the former Mexican holding.

His *El Gringo, or New Mexico and Her People* (1857), while presenting an unfair and typically "Victorian-American" view of New Mexico's native population, has become a classic, because the author did capture certain aspects of life in the nineteenth-century territory that could have been lost to posterity. A detailed account of the noisy vaccination of babies at Taos Pueblo, for instance, or a careful description of a large and fashionable native wedding were the kind of activities that fascinated this curious, but prudish, man. He was a rigid moralist, condemning the habit of smoking on the part of the territory's "lovely and refined females," and somewhat of a bigot, bemoaning the darker skin of New Mexico's Hispanos and regretting the fact that no hope existed for their ever "improving in color." Nevertheless, if a student of southwestern history wanted to know what the people of Santa Fe wore or ate about a century ago, he would have to go to *El Gringo* for the best account.

Davis later became territorial secretary and was acting governor of New Mexico after David Meriwether's departure and before the arrival in 1857 of President James Buchanan's appointee, Abraham Rencher.

Davis returned to the East after his departure from New Mexico, settling in Doylestown, Pennsylvania, to edit the *Democrat*, a small politically partisan journal. During the Civil War he served as a field officer in command of the Pennsylvania State volunteers. Davis also maintained his interest in history, becoming a member of the Historical Society of Pennsylvania. In addition to *El Gringo*, Davis wrote *The Spanish Conquest of New Mexico* and the *History of the 104th Pennsylvania Regiment*. He died in Doylestown.

A brief biographical sketch of Davis can be found in Ralph Emerson Twitchell, *The Leading Facts of New Mex-*

ican History, vol II (1912). An insightful analysis of his character is provided by Harvey B. Fergusson in an introduction he wrote for a 1938 edition of *El Gringo*. —R. W. L.

Dawes, Henry Laurens (1816-1903). Politician and Indian reformer. A Republican from Massachusetts, Dawes equally divided his thirty-six-year congressional career (1857-93) between the House of Representatives and the Senate. His service during the Civil War on the "Committee of Five" (which investigated rumors that the South intended to capture Washington, D.C., before Lincoln's inauguration) and the War Contracts Committee early established his reputation among colleagues as a "working legislator." His chairmanship of the Committee on Elections obscured his name from public view, but from 1869 to 1875, when serving as chairman of the Committee on Appropriations and the Committee of Ways and Means, Dawes emerged as "father" and Republican leader of the House. Known for his parliamentary skills, he forced numerous policy decisions and quietly pressed for many administrative reforms so desperately needed to counteract shoddy procedures and to accommodate increased government activity after the Civil War. For instance, he stopped bills providing for unappropriated expenditures and the use of unexpended balances in government bureaus. More positively, he sponsored the bills establishing the weather bulletin, the Fish Commission, and Yellowstone National Park, and he consistently enlarged, for example, the appropriations for geological surveys of the West.

Dawes's interest in the Indian came to public attention in 1870, when his bill to discontinue the anomalous treaty-making system became the first definite step toward general allotment of land and eventual serious efforts to assimilate the Indian into American society (see INDIAN-WHITE RELATIONS: *United States Indian policy, 1860-present*). Ten years elapsed before Senator Dawes, with "Indian on the brain," took up the issue that remained the central concern both of his public acts and personal agony. In 1880, along with other Massachusetts "sickly sentimentalists," he took bitter exception to Secretary of Interior Carl Schurz's support of the forced removal of the Ponca. Then as the long-term Senate chairman of the Committee on Indian Affairs, he began the patient work that resulted in the DAWES SEVERALTY ACT of 1887. In conjunction with the Boston Indian Committee, the INDIAN RIGHTS ASSOCIATION, and the Lake Mohonk Conference of the Friends of the Indian, Dawes acted as the crucial "legislative medium" to bring justice to the Indian and "atone" for this country's sins against him. Put negatively, Dawes intended to de-Indianize the Indian, destroy his culture, and separate him from whatever previously gave him his identity. Put positively, Dawes wanted to provide the Indian with the economic base and education that would most expediently assimilate him into the American culture. In practice neither destruction of Indianness nor construction of Americanness clearly developed, yet Dawes persisted in his beliefs, and upon retiring from the Senate in 1893 he served as chairman of the Dawes Commission to place the Five Civilized Tribes in Oklahoma under the provisions of the Dawes Act.

The Henry L. Dawes manuscripts are in the Library of Congress, Washington, D.C.—F. N.

Dawes Severalty Act (1887). Indian land allotment policy. The Dawes Severalty Act, also known as the General Allotment Act, was intended both as a means of bringing security and "civilization" to the Indian and as a method of opening Indian reservations to white settlement. Drawn up by Senator Henry Laurens DAWES, it compromised between the Indian's need for some land and the encroaching white man's desire for most western land. Passed on February 8, 1887, after nearly a decade of intermittent debate, the Dawes Act gave the president discretionary power to survey Indian reservations and divide them in 160-acre plots for heads of families, eighty acres for single persons over eighteen years of age, and forty acres for minors. (There were no provisions for the unborn.) The Indians were supposed to farm their land, and the size of allotments doubled on grazing land. If an Indian failed to select his allotment within four years after the president directed allotment on any reservation, the Indian agent made the choice for him. Indians who did not live on reservations might choose to settle upon any unappropriated government land.

Each Indian allottee received a land patent allowing the United States to hold the untaxable land in trust for twenty-five years, during which time he could neither lease nor sell it. Despite this restriction, intended to protect the naïve Indian from the unscrupulous white man, each patented allottee, or any non-tribal Indian taking up the "habits of civilized life," became a citizen of the United States subject to the civil and criminal laws of his resident state or territory. After private land allotment, the government opened surplus reservation land for sale to whites. The United States Treasury held the money derived from such sales, and the three percent interest paid on it was subject to congressional appropriation for civilizing the Indian. Because of previous treaties, the act did not extend to the Five Civilized Tribes and five other tribes in Indian Territory or to the Seneca in New York State; it was this specific exclusion of the five civilized tribes that led to the creation of the Dawes Commission, which went to Oklahoma to arrange for the act's expansion to cover them.

In its conception, the Dawes Act embraced the most sincere humanitarian, though paternalistic and ultimately misguided, thinking of the time. While Indians generally opposed it because it broke up tribal ownership of land, basic to their culture, enthusiastic white supporters called it the Declaration of Independence and the Emancipation Proclamation for the Indian. Western congressmen generally approved it because it allowed their constituents to acquire Indian land. (Between 1887 and 1934 Indian land holdings declined from 138 million to 47 million acres.) Eastern congressmen followed the advice of religious and humanitarian "friends" of the Indian, who believed that the reservation system perpetuated barbaric tribalism and shut off the Indian from acquiring civilized qualities. The Commissioner of Indian Affairs, J. D. C. Atkins, cautioned that "The distance between barbarism and civilization is too long to be passed over speedily. Idleness, improvidence, ignorance, and superstition cannot by law be transformed into industry, thrift, intelligence, and Christianity. Thus the real work remains to be done."

In practice the disposal of surplus lands to whites encountered little difficulty, as was expected. Otherwise, everything from weakness in the law to racial prejudice to bureaucratic bungling frustrated the act's intended benefit to the Indian. Premature presidential allotments gave land to unprepared tribes. White squatters retained their land on reservations. Agents barred allotments on the best land to Indians. Small payments were made for surplus lands bought by white men. Meager congressional appropriations deprived Indians of essential money, while the prohibition against leasing allotted land caused further monetary loss. Exemption from taxation of allotted land, intended as a favor to the Indian, resulted in states refusing to construct needed Indian schools and roads, as well as Indian access to local courts. The prohibition against selling the land led to cases where multiple heirs possessed equal rights to small tracts of land. Subsequent legislation both strengthened and weakened (see the BURKE ACT) the Dawes Act until the Wheeler-Howard Act of 1934 (see John COLLIER and INDIAN-WHITE RELATIONS: *United States Indian policy, 1860-present*) repudiated it and attempted to retain the tribal relationship.

See Henry E. Fritz, *The Movement for Indian Assimilation, 1860-1890* (1963); D. S. Otis, "History of the Allotment Policy," Hearings Before the Committee on Indian Affairs, House of Representatives, 77 Congress, 2 Session, on H.R. 7902 (1934); and Loring B. Priest, *Uncle Sam's Stepchildren: The Reformation of United States Indian Policy, 1865-1887* (1942).—F. N.

Deadwood, South Dakota. Mining town. In its heyday Deadwood was one of the wildest towns in the West. It sprang up following the discovery of gold in Deadwood Creek in 1875. The history of the town is punctuated by violence: battles with the Sioux and spectacular murders like that of Wild Bill Hickok in 1876. The wildness of the town is in part attributable to its isolation. As historian Muriel S. Wolle observed: "Years after trains on the Georgetown Loop were hauling ore to smelters from Silver Plume, tucked in at the foot of the Colorado Rockies, even after the Northern Pacific railroad had celebrated its completion by driving a golden pike at Gold Creek, Montana, Deadwood and Lead were still without rail connections with the outside world." Not until 1890 did the rails of civilization find their way into town, calming the boistrous spirit of the northern Black Hills.

Deadwood remained a prosperous mining community until the early years of the twentieth century, despite the ravages of a major fire in 1879 and a disastrous flood in 1883. Today the town depends primarily on tourism to bolster its economy. The only mining income comes from the huge Homestake Mine in nearby Lead.

Many of the town's early buildings remain and have been maintained by a history-conscious population. Mount Moriah Cemetery is the final resting place of some of the West's mythic figures, including Wild Bill Hickok and Calamity Jane.

See Lambert Florin, *Ghost Town Trails* (1963); Albert M. Williams, *The Black Hills* (1952); and Muriel S. Wolle. *The Bonanza Trail* (1953).—R. B. W.

Deady, Matthew Paul (1824-1893). Oregon jurist and politician. Admitted to the Ohio bar in 1847, Deady got a job as a blacksmith with the United States Mounted Rifle Regiment en route to Oregon, and arrived in the territory in 1849 when most other westbound emigrants, and many Oregonians, were headed for San Francisco and gold.

Following a brief stint as a teacher, he was elected to the territorial house of representatives in 1850 from Yamhill, and in 1851 he was elected to the council. He prepared the first volume of territorial laws and twice codified all general state laws, in 1864 and in 1872. After seven years as an associate justice on the territorial supreme court (1853-59) Deady was made United States district judge for Oregon (1859) in which office he served for the rest of his life. An exemplary legislative draughtsman, he wrote a landmark law for corporations (1862) and Portland's charter (1864), which became a model for the incorporation of other cities. He was the only Democrat to run for delegate to the Constitutional Convention of 1857 on a proslavery platform, though he stayed loyal to the Asahel Bush wing of the Oregon Democrats when the pro-southern Joseph Lane forced an irreparable split in party ranks (1858-60). A paternalist, an anticapitalist, and a Tory before the Civil War, Deady became an advocate of laissez-faire Republicanism following it, his transformation reflecting changed times (see OREGON).

Ten volumes of Deady's diary and over three thousand letters are at the Oregon Historical Society, Portland. Deady's unpublished "History and Progress of Oregon" is in the Bancroft Library.—R. J. L.

Deas, Charles (1818-1867). Painter. Deas was born in Philadelphia and reared in the neighboring vicinity. Failing to win an appointment to West Point Military Academy, he decided on a career in art, studying first at the National Academy of Design in New York City. In 1838 he exhibited at the National Academy and was elected an associate member the following year. During this same period it is said that he chanced to view an exhibition of Indian paintings by George Catlin in Philadelphia and became interested in the places and people portrayed in the elder artist's works.

In 1840 Deas visited a brother stationed at Fort Crawford, Wisconsin, where he acquainted himself with Indian and frontier life. He also made trips to forts Winnebago and Snelling in 1841 and afterward established a studio in St. Louis, Missouri, where he spent several months each year. In 1844 he accompanied a military expedition from Fort Leavenworth to the Pawnee villages on the upper Platte. His paintings were shown with considerable success in the East, and Deas returned to New York City about 1847. A few years later he suffered a mental breakdown from which he never recovered. Of his works only a handful have survived to the present time. These present a general and romanticized view of the primitive West.

See Bernard DeVoto, *Across the Wide Missouri* (1947); and Perry T. Rathbone, *Mississippi Panorama* (1950). —D. C. H.

Death Valley. See PHYSIOGRAPHY OF THE UNITED STATES: *Basin and Range Province.*

deer. The deer family is represented in the West by four genera: elk (genus *Cervus*), moose (*Alces*), caribou (*Rangifer*, of practical importance only in Canada), and deer (*Odocoileus*) which comprise two species.

The white-tailed deer (*O. virginianus*) has a continent-wide distribution from southern Canada to Panama. West of the Mississippi River and north of Mexico, nine subspecies have been distinguished. They vary in size from the large northern form, in which the male may attain a shoulder height of 41 inches and a weight exceeding 300 pounds, to the small Coues or Arizona whitetail, of which males are less than 35 inches tall and rarely weigh more than 100 pounds.

The mule deer (*O. hemionus*) is more limited in range, occurring from western Minnesota and western Oklahoma to the Pacific Coast and from Great Slave Lake to north-central Mexico. Eight subspecies have been described in the United States and Canada. They are larger and vary less widely than the white-tailed forms; bucks have been taken in British Columbia and California that weighed about 475 pounds, while large males from the southern deserts scale 200 to 250 pounds.

Aside from size (an unreliable criterion), the two species can be distinguished by several characteristics. The spiked antlers of young males of the two species are quite similar, but the adult whitetail has simple, straight tines that rise in a series from the main beam, while at least some of the tines of the mule deer are branched or forked. In its summer coat the whitetail is decidedly reddish, but in winter this distinction is largely lost as the pelage changes to grayish, rather like the mule deer's coat. The tails of the two species are distinctive: that of the whitetail is long, broad at the base, and brown above, with a white fringe from base to tip; the mule deer's tail is much shorter and narrower with a completely black tip. (This gives rise to the often-used alternate name, "black-tailed deer.") In white-tailed deer, the metatarsal gland (on the inner side of each lower hind leg) is rarely more than 1 1/4 inches long and is fringed by white hairs; in the mule deer, the gland is more than 2 inches long and is surrounded with brown hair.

The mule deer was first recognized as distinct from the whitetail by William Clark, co-leader of the Lewis and Clark expedition, who wrote in his journal that on September 17, 1804, in Lyman County, South Dakota, John Colter (of later Yellowstone fame) had killed "a curious kind of Deer of a Dark Gray Colr. . . the ears large and long." From the latter attribute, the explorers settled on the appropriate name "mule deer."

Although both species may and often do occur in the same region, they live in different habitats. Throughout its range, the whitetail is an animal of forest margins and thickets. In the West it is found most often in canyon bottoms. Mule deer, on the other hand, usually feed in open parks and meadows.

Another important difference in the habits of the two species, at least in mountainous country, is in annual movement. The whitetail, living as it does in valleys where snowfall is minimal, usually stays in its home territory the year round. The mule deer, however, is generally forced by deep snow to migrate from the upper slopes to the lower range where it can still feed on shrubs and cured grasses. On this annual trek it is often ambushed and shot by hunters.

In outline, the life stories of the two species are similar. The fawns, generally twins but occasionally singles or triplets, are born in the months from May to July, after a gestation of seven months. They are nursed with rich milk (containing much more fat than that of the domestic cow) until autumn. Then the white-spotted birth coat is replaced by the plain pelage of the adults. Fall is also the mating season, when the polygamous

bucks compete for the does. They use their newly grown antlers to threaten, to win mates, to establish supremacy, and occasionally to scratch themselves. Most rutting battles are pushing contests, but sometimes a combatant is gored; very rarely the antlers become locked together and the duelists die of starvation or are devoured by predators.

When the rut is over, in late fall, the males shed both their antlers and their aggressive behavior, and live peacefully with small groups of does and their young. Winter food consists of hardwood browse; the summer diet includes many herbs as well as grasses.

By spring and the next fawning season, the yearlings are completely independent and the males begin to grow their "spike" antlers. (Only among the caribou, of New World members of the deer family, do both sexes have antlers.) The successive annual sets of these bony weapons are larger and more complex (branched) each year until old age sets in, at eight to ten years, and the antlers degenerate. The teeth also become worn. Most deer die or are killed by hunters or predators before the age of ten; in the wild very few live to be fifteen years old.

Excavations of prehistoric Indian mounds, middens, and caves have revealed more bones of deer than of any other animal. Folklore about deer developed over the ages and some clans of Indians had a special veneration for it. In the Omaha tribe, an early group called by anthropologists the Deer-Head Gens forbade the use of deer hide and oil, although they ate the flesh. Typical names of the clan members were "Deer Paws the Ground," "Deer in the Distance Shows Its Tail White Suddenly," "Dark Chin of a Deer," and "He Who Wags His Tail."

To all other Indians and white frontiersmen, the deer was a vital source of both food and clothing. Venison was the staple—a tasty and sustaining meat. Unlike the bison, which congregated in herds but moved with the seasons and irregularly according to the pasturage, deer were dependable; they were usually available and made only short, local, and predictable migrations.

All parts of the carcasses were utilized by the Indians, from the heart, liver, kidneys, and intestines to the brains and bone marrow. The hide was stretched, scraped, dried, worked with grease, soaked in water, and kneaded until pliable, then made into clothing (often elaborately trimmed with colored grasses, shells, and beading), utensils, tents, and many other articles. Bones were crafted into a wide variety of objects from sewing awls to fishhooks. Antlers became knife handles, forks, small tools, ritual ornaments, and decoys. Leg sinews made thread, bowstrings, and binding for weapons and tools.

Before manufactured goods became available, the whites adopted many of the Indian uses for deer and added some of their own. Deer tallow was melted into soap and candles; deer hair became stuffing for saddles and wagon seats, and deerskin—scraped as thin as possible—was sometimes substituted for window glass in primitive cabins. Many white explorers, trappers, missionaries, pony express riders, frontier farmers and cowmen dressed in buckskin clothing. Some of the whites became adept and even artistic at preparing the hides and sewing them into handsome garments ornamented with fringe and beading. Strips of deer hide were made into bullwhips fifteen and thirty feet long; smaller pieces spliced broken wires in the first western telegraph line. As civilization advanced, deer antlers were exhibited in white men's homes as umbrella stands, hat racks, and chandeliers.

Since venison was the staff of life, professional hunters shot deer and other big game for mining camps, cattle outfits, railroad construction crews, and boardinghouses. Deer provisioned the remarkable Lewis and Clark expedition across the continent from 1803 to 1806 and United States soldiers during the Indian wars. While washing stream gravels for gold in California in 1851, J. W. Audubon—John James Audubon's younger son, who painted many of the plates for his father's *Quadrupeds of North America*—and his little party generally consumed one or two deer every day. One miner turned to supplying deer meat and other game to his co-workers and in eighteen months made $5,000. (In those days a man could open up a bank and appoint himself president with that much capital.) As wildlife in the East became decimated, great quantities of venison were shipped from the West to restaurants and hotels in Boston, New York, Baltimore, and other cities.

Deer meat was sold for three cents a pound and up, depending on the place, the year, and the demand. Many agents and suppliers made tremendous profits on markups. At times, both deer hides and meat were used as barter; Indian tribes traded deer with other tribes for salmon, or occasionally with fur traders for cheap brandy. The General Assembly of the State of Franklin (in the 1780s most of present-day Tennessee) voted it lawful to pay taxes with pelts. The governor's annual salary was one thousand deer; the chief justice received five hundred. Perhaps fortunately for the local deer, the state was dissolved when the first three-year terms of office ended.

Next to bison, deer was the most valuable hoofed mammal in the western fur trade. Leather was much in demand and traffic in deerskins was brisk. In the accounts of the North West Company in 1784 and 1789, deer was second in value only to beaver. It was a close third in 1801, and second in the average of the three years 1803 to 1805. One agent estimated that the western fur trade handled 150,000 pounds of deerskins annually between 1815 and 1830. At thirty-three cents per pound, the total value of hides was nearly $750,000. (The individual hunter got only fifty cents to a dollar for each deer hide.)

Most of these deer undoubtedly were mule-blacktails, which were more easily obtained than the western whitetails. To the average hide hunter and trader, the leather of the two species was identical. The ratio in the accounts kept at Fort Nisqually, Washington, in 1835, where skins of the two deer were itemized separately, may be indicative: 220 blacktails as compared with 8 whitetails.

Indians usually sought deer by stalking; the lone hunter, armed with bow and arrows, crept silently through woods or thickets in the hope of approaching an animal unaware of danger. Some natives wore antlers on their heads as decoys. Other methods consisted of driving deer through a line of widely spaced archers or into water where the animals could be speared or clubbed, and of lying in ambush at water holes or at salt licks (natural, or if salt were available, man-made). Puget Sound Indians joined in long lines and with shouts and imitated wolf howls drove the animals into enclosures. In California, pits were dug in runways and concealed with a "basketwork" of branches and leaves; deer were then frightened into running onto the traps. Other tribes set snares or employed fire to stampede and then surround the animals. White men employed a number of these methods and devices; market hunters especially resorted to cooperative drives and to the use of dogs to chase deer into water or to an ambush on land. Firearms gave the hunters vastly greater advantage than did the bow and arrow, and they were adopted by the Indians as soon as possible.

The naturalist Ernest Thompson Seton estimated that there were fifty million deer on their primitive range in the entire United States. Certainly early travelers found them plentiful and it is on their reports that Seton based his calculations. Inevitably, unrestricted hunting for meat and for hides thinned the deer populations drastically. (Thousands of carcasses were abandoned where there was no commercial outlet for meat.) Because mule deer frequented more open habitat than did the whitetails, they bore the brunt of the onslaught. (However, the clearing of bottomlands for growing corn, hay, and other crops eliminated much whitetail territory.) While the slaughter continued, one man shot more than a hundred deer at a stand in Colorado; another killed thirty in six days in Idaho, and three hunters took a thousand deer during less than six weeks in Montana.

Finally, when the deer had been reduced to perhaps one percent of their original numbers, protective laws were enacted. Among the first of such conservation efforts in the West were those of Missouri and Wisconsin in 1851, California in 1854, Minnesota in 1858, Texas in 1860, and Idaho in 1864. Many years passed, however, before closed seasons and the "doe law" (protection of females) became effective. A spectacular recovery began in the decade from 1910 to 1920. Ultimately the prolific deer again became numerous, and even too abundant in some places for the winter food supply. Through excessive control of predators and prolonged application of the doe law, mule deer and, in places, western whitetails have done great damage to their winter ranges. Today the population (estimated very roughly at four million animals) is now stabilized at a level that affords sport for over one million hunters annually in the western states and provinces.

See Walter P. Taylor, ed., *The Deer of North America* (1956).—V. H. C.

Deitz, John F. See John F. DIETZ.

Delaware, settlement of. Interest in the region around the Delaware Bay developed slowly during the first half of the seventeenth century. In the 1620s the Dutch West India Company sent several small trading and whaling expeditions to the "South River," as the Delaware was then called, but those early commercial probings never yielded substantial profit. In 1634 Thomas Yong, an English sea captain, entered the bay hoping "to find a way that leadeth into the Mediterranean Sea." Despite Yong's enthusiastic description of the area, English colonists continued to flood into Virginia, Maryland, and Massachusetts. The Dutch held the land on the west side of the Delaware Bay almost by default, and as the historian John E. Pomfret has written, "No one bothered the Dutch on the Delaware River until the Swedes planted there in 1638, and the Dutch themselves . . . had manifested no great interest in the region."

In 1638 a small group of Swedish colonists under the leadership of Peter Minuit established New Sweden on the west side of the Delaware Bay. The settlement was originally sponsored by the New Sweden Company, but the resources of this corporation were never large enough to support the American venture properly. Governor Johan Printz, who ruled the Swedish colony from 1643 to 1653, tried to make the Delaware project prosperous. Despite his appeals for assistance, however, the directors of the company sent few new settlers to the New World, and between 1647 and 1654 no supply ship whatsoever reached New Sweden. Moreover, attempts to grow tobacco for the European market did not succeed. In 1654 the population of the colony, composed mostly of Swedes and Finns, attained its highest level— 368. The next year the Dutch, who had built Fort Casimir (later New Amstel and New Castle) in 1651, took over the Swedish settlements at Fort Trefaldighet and Fort Christina without bloodshed, and New Sweden ceased to exist.

The Dutch considered the territory that later became the colony of Delaware as part of the New Netherlands, and between 1658 and 1664 the autocratic Peter Stuyvesant governed the region from New Amsterdam. The Dutch province was weak, however, and in 1664 English troops had no trouble conquering the area for the duke of York, later James II. The duke's charter gave him proprietary rights only to the lands on the east side of the Delaware River, but both he and his governors assumed that the Dutch settlements on the west bank came under their jurisdiction by right of conquest. In 1676 Governor Andros of New York divided the region into three separate counties—New Castle, Kent, and Sussex. Lord Baltimore believed the west side of the bay belonged to Maryland, of which he was proprietor, but his claims were never upheld in England.

In 1682 William Penn realized that the land the crown had granted to him for Pennsylvania did not have an open access to the ocean. He therefore pursuaded his friend, the duke of York, to lease him the three lower counties on the Delaware. Unfortunately, the duke's own claims to the area had been questionable, and Penn was never certain of the legal status of Delaware. Several times he asked for a royal charter, but his efforts were always thwarted. In 1717 the earl of Sutherland unsuccessfully petitioned for the entire region on the grounds that the king had never granted Delaware to anyone.

Penn offered the people of the lower three counties equal representation with the settlers of Pennsylvania, but harmonious relations between the two areas were doomed probably from the start. The colonists on the Delaware realized that they had no opportunity for westward expansion, as the Pennsylvanians had. They were afraid that they would soon be outvoted in the rapidly expanding Quaker assembly that met in Philadelphia. Moreover, they were angry to see Quaker merchants taking trade away from New Castle, which before 1683 had been the major port on the Delaware. And lastly, the Swedes, the Finns, and the Dutch charged that the Quakers were unwilling to spend the money that was required to defend the bay settlements

from raids by French warships. Robert W. Johannsen has written, "The inhabitants of the lower counties throughout this period considered themselves subjects of the Crown, first, and recognized the authority of the Proprietor [Penn] as only secondary to this."

In 1701 Penn issued the Charter of Privileges, which gave the lower three counties the right to hold their own legislature. The area was still under the jurisdiction of the proprietor's governor in Pennsylvania, but for all practical purposes, Delaware became a separate colony in 1704 when its assembly met for the first time. Although the people of Delaware prided themselves on their independence, their colony was in fact economically dependent on the larger, more prosperous Pennsylvania. Throughout the colonial period, English administrators never recognized Delaware's separate status, and they continued to treat the region as if it were part of Penn's charter grant. In 1776 the three lower counties ratified a constitution, proclaiming themselves the state of Delaware.

The fullest account of the early period of Delaware is John E. Pomfret, *The Province of West New Jersey 1609-1702* (1956). Also helpful is Robert W. Johannsen, "The Conflict Between the Three Lower Counties on the Delaware and the Province of Pennsylvania, 1682-1794," *Delaware History*, vol. 5 (1952-53). There is no adequate study of the eighteenth century.—T. H. B.

Delaware Indians. The Delaware were a large Algonquian tribe occupying, when the white man arrived, all of New Jersey, northern Delaware, eastern Pennsylvania, Staten Island, and the western tip of Long Island. At that time they may have numbered eight thousand persons. The Delaware, who called themselves Lenni-Lenape ("real men"), had migrated from the West long before, and were probably the parent stock of a number of eastern Algonquian tribes. They were divided into a large number of independent village bands and had no tribal organization in historic times until the eighteenth century.

Due to their exposed seaboard location the Delaware were among the first Indians to be encountered and displaced by the Dutch, Swedish, and English colonists. The Delaware had little access to the interior peltry supply that the Europeans craved, they were not notably warlike, and their political disorganization made them comparatively easy to dislodge as settlement advanced. Delaware bands fought against the Dutch at New Amsterdam in the 1640s, and there was occasional friction along the Delaware River, but for the most part displacement was peaceful until the mid-eighteenth century. About 1720 they came under Iroquois domination, the latter symbolically designating them as women. The Delaware gradually moved westward through Pennsylvania as the Iroquois and whites together forced them off their lands, and by the 1750s most of them had located in eastern Ohio. But in Ohio they were influenced by western tribes and by the French, and with the outbreak of the French and Indian War in 1754, they joined the Shawnee and others in attacking frontier settlements in Pennsylvania. Hostilities continued sporadically until the defeat of these tribes by the Americans under General Anthony Wayne in 1795, by which time many of the Delaware had retreated into Indiana. Some of the Delaware moved into Ontario with the Iroquois after the American Revolution; others migrated by stages to Texas; but most were on a reservation in Kansas by 1835, whence the greater part went to Oklahoma in 1867. Like other eastern tribes, the Delaware have become widely scattered and their population decimated after three hundred years of warfare, disease, and displacement.

See F. W. Hodge, *Handbook of American Indians North of Mexico*, 2 vols. (1907-10); W. W. Newcomb, *The Culture and Acculturation of the Delaware Indians* (1956); and A. F. C. Wallace, *King of the Delawares: Teedyscung* (1949).—A. W. T.

Deloria, Vine, Jr. (1934-   ). Yankton Sioux writer, lawyer, and activist. Deloria is best known as author of *Custer Died for Your Sins* (1969), written while he was at the University of Colorado Law School; his second book, *We Talk, You Listen* (1970), is far more serious, although it has not enjoyed the popular success the first book has.

Deloria was born in Martin, South Dakota. Coming from a distinguished family of Indian churchmen and scholars, he considered a vocation in the ministry and entered Lutheran (Augustana) School of Theology, where he earned his bachelor of divinity degree. He took a job, however, with the National Congress of American Indians. He resigned his post as executive director to enter law school and, while in Denver, joined the staff of United Scholarship Service for American Indian and Spanish-American Students, where he developed a program to assist Indian students in private secondary schools. After passing the Colorado bar exam, Deloria accepted a position at Western Washington State College in the division of ethnic studies. He became very active in the fishing rights efforts of the tribes of the Northwest Coast and took their story to national television. During a trip to New York in September 1970, he visited the Fulton Fish Market at about 3:00 A.M. and, with the help of Jerry Kaplowitz, a New York cab driver who had been in the fish business, sold an unlimited quantity of Indian-caught salmon at a fair market price.

Deloria also wrote *God Is Red* (1973) and numerous articles for newspapers and magazines across the country and made many speeches and television and radio appearances. His most frequent topic was the need for Indians to have an economic base through land ownership. To help Indians regain and secure land, Deloria helped found an Indian legal services organization with headquarters in Washington, D.C. In September 1971 he began work at the American Civil Liberties Union in its Denver office.—C. C.

Democratic party, 1800-1860. The issues of most concern to the West between 1800 and 1860 were the easy accessibility of land for settlement, the acquisition of additional land, and federal aid to internal improvements. While the priority of these differed over the years, the policies of the Democratic party on them were generally more favorable than those of its opponents. On each issue, however, the Democratic position changed over the years as internal factionalism developed. One must note, moreover, that while general party policy can be delineated, throughout the period some Democrats in Congress followed local or sectional interest, not party policy.

As a whole, the Democratic party agreed with westerners that land should be used for settlement and not

revenue, and the party generally favored the rapid opening up and organizing of territories for settlement and the selling of public lands cheaply. Similarly, the Democrats pursued a policy of removing the Indians, first west of the Mississippi and then to the Great Plains. Thomas Jefferson and James Madison did so by negotiating treaties, and Andrew Jackson more forcefully after a Democratic Congress empowered him to with the Removal Act of 1830. Democrats also tried to lower the price of land throughout most of the period, despite opposition from New England Democrats. They passed the land laws of 1804 and 1820, which reduced the price per acre and the minimum number of acres a person had to buy. In the 1830s Democrats vigorously favored graduation of land prices—giving squatters the right to buy the land on which they had settled at minimum prices once those lands were open for purchase. Graduation could not be passed in this period, but preemption laws were passed in 1830, 1838, and 1841. By the 1850s, however, the southern and northern wings of the Democratic party were seriously divided over land policy. Southerners opposed organizing territories and making land cheaper because that policy would aid the growth of free states. Though a graduation act was passed in 1854 over southern opposition and though Kansas and Nebraska were opened to settlement, southern influence was strong enough to prevent passage of homestead acts in the 1850s and finally to cause Democratic President James Buchanan to veto such an act in 1860.

The Democratic party was always more favorable to territorial expansion than any of its opponents between 1800 and 1860. Democrats were primarily responsible for the Louisiana Purchase, the annexation of Texas (even though the states'-rights Whig John Tyler initiated the move), the Oregon Treaty, the Mexican War and subsequent cession, and the Gadsden Purchase. Democratic platforms persistently lauded expansion. Though their fervor for expansion was constant, it did change in these years. Jefferson and Madison wanted contiguous agricultural land, but they considered the Rocky Mountains a natural boundary. Jefferson thought independent republics should be created on the Pacific Coast. By the 1840s, however, the party was home for the advocates of manifest destiny; it now considered the Pacific the country's natural boundary, and some "Young America" Democrats such as Stephen A. Douglas wanted to acquire the entire North American continent.

The Democratic record on internal improvements was much weaker from the western point of view. Though Jefferson and Madison started the Cumberland Road and Jackson approved some interstate projects, throughout the period Democrats generally opposed federal internal improvements, althought they supported state action. Such negativism most hurt the Democrats in the West in the 1850s, when vetoes of rivers and harbors bills coupled with official opposition to homestead laws in part caused the shift of northwestern Democratic voters to the Republican party.

See ELECTIONS OF 1824-1896.

For excellent analyses of Democratic expansionism, see Harry V. Jaffa, *The Crisis of the House Divided: An Interpretation of the Issues in the Lincoln-Douglas Debates* (1959); and Frederick Merk, *Manifest Destiny and Mis-*

sion in American History: A Reinterpretation (1963). On Democratic land policy, see Glyndon G. Van Deusen, *The Jacksonian Era, 1828-1848* (1959). For the Democratic record in Congress and on internal improvements, see Thomas B. Alexander, *Sectional Stress and Party Strength* (1967); and Joel Silbey, *The Transformation of American Politics, 1840-1860* (1967).—M. F. H.

Denig, Edwin T. (1812-1858). Fur trader and ethnologist. Denig was born in Stroudsburg, Pennsylvania. His father, a successful physician, saw that Denig received a better-than-average education, though the details of his youth and schooling are unknown. In 1833 he went west to work for the American Fur Company and rose through its field ranks, becoming *bourgeois* in charge at the key Missouri River post of Fort Union in 1849. Through his work he became closely acquainted with the Indian tribes of the upper river and believed them to be as respectable as any other race. He took two Assiniboin wives and treated them always with love and consideration, sending their children to school in the East.

Denig's interest in the Indians and natural features of the upper Missouri led him to perform invaluable service in preserving knowledge of his era. In 1843 he assisted John James Audubon in gathering specimens and wrote for the naturalist what is still the most detailed description of Fort Union in existence. In 1850 he supplied the fledgling Smithsonian Institution with its first specimens of upper Missouri mammals. For Father Pierre de Smet, Denig wrote extensive accounts of Indian legends and usages, which were incorporated into the priest's book *Western Missions and Missionaries*. When during the 1850s Henry R. Schoolcraft was compiling his monumental study of American Indian tribes, Denig prepared such a detailed report for the ethnologist that it was eventually published separately by the Bureau of American Ethnology as *Indian Tribes of the Upper Missouri* (1928-29).

At the time of his death from appendicitis, Denig was writing a definitive summary of his knowledge of Indians. F. V. Hayden copied large portions of this unfinished manuscript verbatim in his *Contributions to the Ethnology and Philology* of 1862, but it was not until 1949, through the efforts of John C. Ewers, that Denig's authorship was established. During his lifetime and long afterward, Denig's writings were buried in the work of others, but it is now certain that he was the most prolific and knowledgeable student of the upper Missouri Indians in the nineteenth century.

See E. T. Denig, *Indian Tribes of the Upper Missouri*, Bureau of American Ethnology Forty-sixth Annual Report (1928-29) and *Five Indian Tribes of the Upper Missouri*, ed. John C. Ewers (1961); and L. O. Saum, *The Fur Trader and the Indians* (1965).—P. R. M.

Densmore, Frances (1867-1957). Ethnomusicologist. Densmore, who was born in Red Wing, Minnesota, contributed more to the scholarship and understanding of American Indian music than any person before or since. Trained in music in college, Densmore became interested in the music of Chippewa Indians living near her home. She cut wax cylinders of Chippewa songs in 1901 and sent them to the Bureau of American Ethnology, and thus began a lifelong association with this Smithsonian bureau. Her recordings and notes on more than twenty-four hundred American Indian songs today comprise the Smithsonian-Densmore Collection. Many of these have been reissued and sold as long-playing records through the Library of Congress.

Although her work was nationwide, most of her efforts were directed toward Indians of the West. The Papago, Cocopa, Yaqui, Isleta, Acoma, Zuñi, Quechan (Yuma), Teton Sioux, Northern Ute, Mandan, Hidatsa, Pawnee, Arapaho, Cheyenne, Nootka, and Quileute Indians are only some of the western tribes whose music she recorded and discussed in published monographs. As a chief of the folklore section of the Library of Congress noted, "The total collection is unique and constitutes one of the great recorded treasures of the American people."

See Nancy O. Lurie, "Women in Early American Anthropology," in June Helm, ed., *Pioneers of American Anthropology* (1966).—B. L. F.

Denver, Colorado. Since its incorporation in 1861, Denver, Colorado, has been transformed from a crude little town of tents and shacks into the largest city between the Pacific Coast and St. Louis. The natural advantages of the area made it likely that somewhere within it a city would develop. That it would be on the location where the Great Plains meet the Rocky Mountains at the juncture of the South Platte River and Cherry Creek was the result of luck and the talents of promoters.

The story of Denver began in 1858 when a prospector from California named William Green Russell pursued a hunch that gold existed in the creeks and streams on the eastern slopes of the Rocky Mountains. Russell and his party camped near the mouth of Cherry Creek and the South Platte River and there made a modest discovery of gold. Word of their find—grossly exaggerated—spread to the East and to California. By early 1859 thousands of prospectors, or "fifty-niners," descended upon the Kansas Territory between Pikes Peak and Longs Peak in present-day Colorado. Many of these prospectors stopped at Russell's settlement because it was already famous. Its location in the midst of a cottonwood grove with plenty of water made it a suitable point to camp and wait for the spring thaw. In haste, log and mud huts were constructed and tents were pitched on both sides of Cherry Creek on the site where Denver now stands.

In fewer numbers than the prospectors, but with just as much optimism and zeal, land speculators and town promoters moved into the region. The landscape between Pikes Peak and Longs Peak was soon dotted with towns—each, according to its founders, destined to become the commercial emporium of the Rocky Mountain West. Many of these visionary metropolises failed to materialize anywhere but on the maps on which they were plotted, but a few, such as Colorado City, Central City, Boulder, Golden, and Denver City, survived with some reasonable hopes for success. Denver City, astutely named for the territorial governor of Kansas, General James W. Denver, received his aid and became the county seat of Arapahoe County. In 1860 this little town merged with Auraria, its rival located on the left bank of Cherry Creek, because the promoters of both sites were growing fearful of the competing towns, especially Golden. Instrumental in the merger of Auraria and Denver were William Larimer, a promoter who had boosted towns in Pennsylvania and Nebraska, and William N.

Larimer Street in Denver, 1879. (Denver Public Library, Western History Department)

Byers, who had brought a printing press from Omaha to found the *Rocky Mountain News* in Denver in 1859.

When territorial status was accorded to Colorado in 1861, more people were drawn to the new Rocky Mountain towns. Nevertheless, uncertainties about the future caused by markedly fluctuating land values prompted Larimer to sell most of his town lots in Denver and move to Kansas on another town-promotional venture. Byers and a few others gambled on Denver's future and continued to promote the town. Through the pages of the *Rocky Mountain News*, Byers boosted the community and the entire region. Realizing that the natural advantages of gold were not great enough to support Denver in the long run, he joined the efforts of the territory's governor, William Gilpin, and inaugurated a campaign to change America's image of the "Great American Desert." The *News* circulated beyond Colorado and informed readers that the most profitable opportunities in the region were in farming, not gold digging. Byers argued that the land in eastern Colorado was more fertile than people believed and that it could provide thousands of new settlers with food, which they were forced to buy from farmers five or six hundred miles to the east at incredibly inflated prices.

The HOMESTEAD ACT, combined with local promotional efforts, attracted more settlers to Colorado. Throughout the 1860s a substantial portion of the raw materials and merchandise that supported Colorado's settlers came into Denver by wagon and were warehoused and distributed from that point. But everyone with vision recognized that ultimately the railroad would dictate which community would distribute the freight in the future. Denver's leaders hoped that the transcontinental railroad would go through their town and over the mountains as it made its way to the Pacific Coast. Their dreams seemed to shatter when the

Union Pacific took the less mountainous northern route through Cheyenne, Wyoming. Some speculators and businessmen moved out of Denver after the Union Pacific decision was made, but others felt they had too much invested to quit. A board of trade was formed to give new direction to the community. Through this vehicle and in the face of a scheme by Golden to construct a railroad to Cheyenne, Denver's power elite organized a local company and built the Denver Pacific line to Wyoming. In 1870 the 106-mile line was connected to the Union Pacific. Meanwhile, the Kansas Pacific finished its earlier projected line to Denver. Determined to keep their momentum, now that they controlled the approaches from the north and the east, Denver leaders next solicited Boston capital to construct a narrow-gauge line, the Denver and Rio Grande, to tap the Southwest. The line never reached the planned destination of Mexico City, but in 1872 it was opened to Pueblo and thereby provided Denver with access to that region's valuable coalfields (see DENVER AND RIO GRANDE WESTERN RAILROAD).

The effectiveness with which Denver businessmen had raised money and acquired land to build three railroads in little more than three years put the town firmly on the road to dominating the commerce and finance of the region. And soon, good fortune complemented the activities of the decisionmakers. Just as the discovery of silver came in the wake of dwindling gold mining to revitalize San Francisco a few years earlier, so the discovery of carbonate enlivened the mining industry of Colorado's mountains in the 1870s and 1880s. The already booming city now had new opportunities to haul mining equipment and other necessities to the new silver camps, which mushroomed as quickly as had gold camps earlier. Ambitious businessmen and investors now poured into Denver to build smelting works and various industries to serve Colorado's expanding and diverse needs. More merchandising houses, banks, hotels, and entertainment establishments moved into Denver and its environs to take advantage of the opportunities. By 1890 Colorado had over four thousand miles of railroad track, with most major lines passing through Denver.

In 1881 the citizens of Colorado voted Denver the state capital. This factor, plus concentrated campaigns to promote the city and state as a paradise for tourists and a haven for sufferers of respiratory ailments, brought still more people to the area. The state's population in 1890 was just over 400,000, with more than one fourth residing in Denver. During the second decade of the twentieth century, Denver's population increased from 213,000 to 256,000. This modest increase, though, was caused as much by annexations (the city expanded from seventeen to fifty-eight square miles) as by the attraction of newcomers. While Denver was in an impregnable position as the state's major city and the region's dominant metropolis, the boom was over.

The beginning of the cooling-off period coincided with the passage of a home-rule act in 1904, which gave the city fathers an opportunity to concentrate on some functional and aesthetic problems. Gas and water services were expanded and perfected, and an efficient sewer system was constructed. Gas and electric lighting adorned an impressive park and boulevard system. An excellent public school system was organized, and new libraries, museums, and theaters were built. Denver's wealthy citizens always maintained close ties with the East, entertained elegantly, and built handsome mansions. The tastes of the Hill, Evans, Moffat, Cheesman, and other prominent families were reflected in the construction of an imposing granite neoclassical capitol, which faces one of the most beautiful civic centers in the nation.

After the 1920s Denver continued to grow, but less spectacularly. The city became much more of a cosmopolitan community with modern buildings and tree-lined streets. It looked its new role of a financial, insurance, and mercantile center and struck visitors as more like an eastern city than the rough and tumble mining- and cattle-outfitting center it had been a generation earlier.

Between 1930 and 1970, Denver's population expanded from 287,000 to 514,000. By the 1970s that of the standard metropolitan area was nearly 1.25 million. The federal government in the 1930s selected Denver as a headquarters for the Bureau of Internal Revenue, the Veterans' Administration, the United States Forest Service, and Bureau of Reclamation. During and after World War II many more federal bureaus and agencies, especially those related to defense, were located in the Denver area. Vigorous lobbying helped the Colorado city acquire some of these plums, but the natural beauty and mild climate played no small role in the minds of Washington decisionmakers. After 1949, when the Soviet Union detonated its first atomic bomb but had nothing other than conventional airplanes with which to deliver it, leaders in Washington, D.C. gave serious thought to making Denver an alternate national capital. Federal officials believed that the Mile-High City, tucked against the mountains and located far from both coasts, was much less vulnerable to atomic attack than either Washington, D.C., or any West Coast city.

Numerous defense-related businesses, such as chemical and electronics corporations, also located in the Denver area. They gravitated to the region because they wanted to be close to the federal defense installations and because Colorado, a pleasant state, helps attract and retain the well-paid, but highly mobile, scientists and engineers who comprise the work force of these modern industries.

While Denver remains a stockyard center, gold and silver mining play almost no role in Denver's economy today. But the Rocky Mountains are still an important natural advantage. They are rich in uranium and molybdenum, which have in recent years grown increasingly important. Besides this, Americans, with more money and leisure than ever before, have made Colorado one of the busiest playgrounds in the United States. Skiing, camping, hunting, fishing, and backpacking draw throngs to Colorado twelve months out of the year. Using Denver as a point of rest and embarkation, tourists buy their sports clothes and equipment from the scores of factories that multiply yearly to meet their needs.

The prodigious growth of Denver has brought it serious problems as well as prosperity. The metropolitan area has grown rapidly—thanks in large part to the automobile—along the lines of the state highways and interstate systems. In 1974 newcomers were arriving in metropolitan Denver at the rate of twelve hundred per week, helping to clog the highway system and bring on a smog problem second only to that of Los Angeles. Today, rather than a city of clean air, mountain views, and clear streams, Denver is an increasingly crowded and dirty city that leads the nation in per capita automobiles. Denver is likewise plagued with racial and ethnic problems. The foreign-born population, never more than twenty-five percent of the total, has been well assimilated both economically and socially. But the Hispano and black members of the population (11 and 3.5 percent, respectively, in 1970) are still ghettoized and denied equality of opportunity. It is significant that bussing schoolchildren to achieve desegregation is the most talked about issue in the "Queen City of the Rockies" in the 1970s.

As natural resources attracted the first settlers to Denver in 1858, so they continue to do so in 1974. A local political leader said when discussing the city's social and ecological problems, "If Denver was located any place else other than 10 miles from the mountains, you couldn't pay people to live here." Nature has done her work; only talent and luck can improve the quality of life in Denver in the future.

Among the many schools whose campuses are in Denver are the University of Denver, Regis College, Loretto Heights College, the University of Colorado Medical School, the Iliff School of Theology (Methodist), and Westminster Law School. The city is the home of three museums: the Denver Art Museum, which owns a notable collection of Indian art; the Colorado State Historical Museum; and the Colorado Museum of Natural History.

No scholarly or reliable history of Denver exists. The most useful work for the city's early history is Jerome C. Smiley, *History of Denver* (1901). A brief but useful survey is in Constance McLaughlin Green, *American Cities in the Growth of the Nation* (1957). The most sophisticated framework in which Denver's history has been placed is by Carl Abbott, "Boom State and Boom City: Stages in Denver's Growth," *Colorado Magazine* (Summer 1973), pp. 207-230.—L. W. D.

Denver and Rio Grande Western Railroad. The Denver and Rio Grande Western Railroad, a strategic line connecting Denver, Colorado, with Salt Lake City, Utah, eventually placed those two cities on the main line of a transcontinental route. Incorporated in Colorado in 1870 and operated until 1887 as a narrow-gauge route, the Denver and Rio Grande's original promoter was General William Jackson PALMER. Impressed with the scenic grandeur of the country between Denver and Pueblo, Colorado, and with the economic value of a railroad that would connect the two thriving towns with El Paso, Texas, Palmer dreamed of "how fine it would be to have a little railroad a few hundred miles in length, all under one's own control, with one's friends."

Palmer's experience on the Denver and Rio Grande was anything but tranquil. After the railroad had reached Trinidad, Colorado, in 1876, Palmer discovered that the Santa Fe coveted the Royal Gorge route and was ready to fight for it. This route—a narrow ledge of rock alongside the Arkansas River that filled with water like a storm sewer during spring freshets—was the only access to the West from Pueblo. (There was no access to the West from Denver, inasmuch as the mountains that intervene on the "airline" between that city and Salt Lake City rise to an altitude of over eleven thousand feet.) The Denver and Rio Grande lost the gorge to the Santa Fe in a physical and legal fight, but finally won it back by a decision of the United States Supreme Court. Not so lucky in its second fight with the Santa Fe, over the Raton Pass in New Mexico, which the Santa Fe had to have for its main line, the Denver and Rio Grande agreed to end its plans to push south. Instead, having admitted Jay Gould and Russell Sage, two of the most prominent railroad speculators of the day, as important investors, Palmer's road advanced westward, reaching Salt Lake City and Ogden in 1883, where it made connection with the Union Pacific. Exhausted by these labors, the road was then rent with organizational strife and had to be reorganized in 1886 with David MOFFAT assuming the presidency in 1887.

In 1901 the Denver and Rio Grande and a rival line, the Rio Grande Western, which had made a gesture toward direct westward extension from Denver to Salt Lake City, seemed no closer than ever to becoming parts of a transcontinental line. In that year George Gould, heir to his father's far-flung but rather rickety railroad empire, gained control of both railroads and consolidated them in 1908 as one step in his grandiose plan to weld the first and only true transcontinental railroad. Since the Union Pacific and the Central Pacific, both now controlled by Edward H. Harriman, refused to exchange freight with the Denver and Rio Grande Western at Ogden (preferring to carry it on their own lines for the entire haul between Council Bluffs, Iowa, and San Francisco), Gould decided to build a new line from Salt Lake City to the coast. His WESTERN PACIFIC RAILROAD, incorporated in 1903, never developed enough traffic in Gould's time to pay its fixed charges; even so, he might have been able to carry it if he had not overstrained even his enormous resources in an effort to secure a route through intensely hostile Pennsylvania Railroad territory into Pittsburgh and on to tidewater. By 1911 Gould, widely called "the sick man of Wall Street," was out of the MISSOURI PACIFIC RAILROAD, and his railroad empire crumbled rapidly thereafter. The Denver and Rio Grande Western went into receivership and was reorganized in 1924, from which date it was closely identified with the Missouri Pacific.

Two events finally put Denver and Salt Lake City on a transcontinental route. In 1928 David Moffat's dream, a seven-mile-long tunnel under the mountains between the two cities, was completed under public financing. In 1934, under pressure from the Western Pacific and the Burlington route, the Rio Grande agreed to build the Dotsero cutoff, a 38-mile project which shortened the route by 175 miles. The introduction of diesel powered, streamlined trains in the 1930s made the Burlington/ Rio Grande/Western Pacific route of the California Zephyr one of the most popular in the United States before the widespread termination of rail passenger travel in 1970.

One of the best railroad histories is Robert G. Athearn, *Rebel of the Rockies, A History of the Denver and Rio Grande Western Railroad* (1962).—A. M.

deputy marshal. See MARSHAL, FEDERAL.

De Quille, Dan. Pen name of **William Wright** (1829-1898). Journalist. Born in Ohio, De Quille went to California in 1857 and to Nevada in 1861. He became a member of the staff of the *Territorial Enterprise* in 1862 and remained with that paper for thirty-one years. During the Comstock era he was considered the outstanding mining journalist of the region. He was one of the originators of the famous western "hoax" stories, which his friend Mark Twain developed and made even more popular. De Quille's major work on the Comstock, *History of the Big Bonanza*, was published in 1876. The book has become a standard reference and is indispensable for research on the history of the Comstock Lode. —R. R. E.

Derby, George Horatio (1823-1861). Topographical engineer and humorist. Born in Dedham, Massachusetts, and educated in New England schools, Derby was graduated from West Point and assigned to the army's topographical corps. He saw action in the Mexican War and was wounded in the battle of Cerro Gordo. After brief service in Minnesota, he was sent to the Far West in 1849 to participate in explorations of the Sacramento valley, the San Joaquin valley, the Colorado River, and parts of Oregon and Washington. His findings, published during 1850-56, were reissued in *The Topographical Reports of Lieutenant George H. Derby* (1933). In 1856, Derby was transferred to Mobile, Alabama, to direct the erection of lighthouse towers in Florida, Alabama, and Mississippi. His health slowly deteriorated after his California tour. Derby suffered a sunstroke in 1859 and died two years later.

Derby gained widespread popularity far less by writing official accounts than by publishing humorous pieces under such pseudonyms as Dr. Ellenbogen, John Pea Tarbox, H. Wadding Tallboy, Amos Butterfield, Squibob, and John Phoenix. Most of these, originally written for periodicals and California newspapers, were collected in two books, *Phoenixiana; or, Sketches and Burlesques* (1856), one of the most popular pre-Civil War works of American humor, and *The Squibob Papers* (1861).

Reared in the East and writing for and about the West, Derby was influenced by both. He demonstrated an easterner's finesse in playing with words and sentences, turning out with ease sophisticated burlesques and parodies of orations and *belles-lettres*, "lectures" on astronomy and other sciences; "reports" on geographical surveys; and "descriptions" of ingenious inventions, some of which foreshadowed cartoonist Rube Goldberg's complicated machines of a later period. But it was the western influence that prompted his irreverent attitudes, his imaginative tall tales, and his satires of overly romantic portrayals of western locales and activities.

In "Musical Review Extraordinary," which supposedly depicts scenes evoked by a musical composition, "The Plains," Derby describes a wagon train "consisting of seven families with forty-six wagons. . . . Each family consists of a man in butternut-colored clothing driving . . . a wife in butternut-colored clothing riding in the wagon, holding a butternut baby, and seventeen butternut children running promiscuously . . . ; all are barefooted, dusty, and smell unpleasantly." In one "official report," Dr. Ellenbogen, M.D., announces the capture by a surveying party in Oregon of two animals frequently celebrated in western tales, the gyascutus and the prock. The former was three feet tall, three feet long, and protected by a heavy shield like a turtle; the latter was identified as a beast commonly known as a "side-hill winder." Derby's solemn style and the playfully imaginative details he used in describing these and other mythical beasts delighted his western and eastern contemporaries.

A wit and prankster since childhood, Derby was the subject of many anecdotes. Stories traveling by word of mouth linked his name with General Winfield Scott, Secretary of State Jefferson Davis, and others. Long after his death, Californians continued to recall the time he stopped the Golden Eagle Bakery wagon to order "three golden eagles, baked crisp," and the time he brought his wife and his mother together after telling each that the other was hard of hearing. His most famous prank, related by Derby himself, was played when the San Diego *Herald* editor trusted him to edit the newspaper in the editor's absence: Derby blithely switched the paper's political alignment and enthusiastically backed a rival candidate for governor.

See John Kendrick Bangs, "John Phoenix and His Work," preface to the 1903 edition of *Phoenixiana*; and George R. Stewart, *John Phoenix, Esq., The Veritable Squibob* (1937).—W. Bl.

Dern, George Henry (1872-1936). Utah businessman and politician. Born in Dodge County, Nebraska, Dern received his education in his home state. In 1894 he moved to Utah, where he took a position as bookkeeper for the Mercur Gold Mining and Milling Company. Within a few years he became treasurer of the company and in 1900 became the company's general manager. From 1902 to 1913 Dern was named general manager of the Consolidated Mercur Gold Mine Company. His efficient superintendency was not unnoticed, and he was soon employed as general manager of the Tintic Milling Company (1915-19). He also invested in ranches, became a director of the Mutual Dairy Company, and was on the board of numerous companies and banks.

In 1914 Dern was elected as a Democrat to represent Salt Lake County in the state senate and served two four-year terms. During World War I he was a member of Utah's Commission of Defense, the chairman of the committee on war materials, and a member of the United States Fuel Administration for Utah. In 1924 and 1928 he was elected governor of Utah. He reformed the tax system, helped to secure development of the Colorado River, and improved the financial support of public schools. In 1929 and 1930 he was chairman of the Governor's Conference, where he met Franklin D. Roosevelt. When Roosevelt became president in 1932, he named Dern secretary of war. As such, he enlarged and motorized the army.

Deseret, state of (1849-51). Provisional state of the Mormons. As mapped by Brigham Young and the Council of Fifty, the geographical dimensions of Deseret included all of Utah, most of Nevada and Arizona, and parts of present-day Oregon, Idaho, Wyoming, Colorado, New Mexico, and California. It included seaports at San Diego and at the mouth of the Colorado River. Congress, embroiled in the Compromise of 1850 and suspicious of Mormon intentions, failed to approve statehood for Deseret and instead created the territory of Utah in 1851, with reduced boundaries but larger than present Utah. Hopeful of achieving statehood, a "ghost government" of the state of Deseret was main-

tained on a standby basis from 1862 to 1870.

deserts. See VEGETATION: *deserts*.

De Smet, Pierre Jean (1801-1873). Jesuit missionary. A Potawatomi missionary, this Belgian of great physical strength and charm founded the Pacific Northwest mission chain beginning in 1840. A publicist as much as a missionary, De Smet made sixteen trips back to Europe and published prolifically in six languages in his efforts to promote Indian missions. De Smet became the idol of the Plains tribes (especially Teton and Yankton Sioux and Blackfoot) and was a government peace agent in the Indian wars of the Great Plains and Northwest. He was also a friend of many eminent western and national figures. (See ROMAN CATHOLIC MISSIONARIES.)

See H. M. Chittenden and A. T. Richardson, *Life, Letters and Travels of Father Pierre Jean De Smet, S.J.,* 4 vols. (1905). See also Robert I. Burns, *The Jesuits and the Indian Wars of the Northwest* (1966). —R. I. B.

de Soto, Hernando (c. 1500-1542). Spanish explorer of Florida and the Southeast. De Soto, a captain under Francisco Pizarro, had earned a fortune in the conquest of Peru. When he heard stories of the "northern mystery," he organized an expedition to land in Florida and explore to the north. His flotilla of seven ships and six hundred men left Spain in April 1538, bound for Cuba and Florida.

Not until the last week of May 1539 were landings made somewhere in the Tampa Bay, Charlotte Harbor, or San Carlos Bay areas (the exact place of landing is in vigorous dispute). Then, following a policy of capturing the local *cacique* and by this means controlling and using the natives, the expedition started north.

After wintering at Apalachee (the region around Tallahassee), de Soto marched into present Georgia, then in a northeasterly direction into South Carolina. Here, two days' march from the sea, the expedition came upon the Indian capital of Cofitachequi. The Spaniards found many fresh-water pearls here, but hearing of a rumored land of wealth called Chisca, or Kuska, the conquistador directed his expedition up through western North Carolina, then over the mountains into Tennessee and down into Alabama. Here, in the heartland of the Creek, de Soto found cornfields and orchards and a hardy agricultural people. The expedition fought a pitched battle with the Indians and lost a number of men, then pushed westward into Mississippi. They came in contact with the Choctaw and Chickasaw, the latter of whom attacked them and left them nearly destitute. With ingenuity, however, the explorers replenished their supplies and pushed northwestward through Mississippi into southwest Tennessee. They crossed the Mississippi River about twenty-five miles below Memphis, and then advanced across Arkansas, into Oklahoma, then east again through bogs and canebrakes. On May 21, 1542, de Soto died, and was buried in the Mississippi.

His successor, Luis de Moscoso de Alvarado, explored southwestward into Texas, probably as far west as the Trinity River. Then he returned to the Mississippi River and constructed crude vessels on which the men floated down the river and along the Gulf until, in September 1543, they reached the Rio Pánuco in Mexico. Three hundred and eleven men—just about half the original

Father Pierre De Smet and some of the converts he made among the tribes of the Northwest. (Crosby Library, Gonzaga University)

number—survived this ordeal of four years and five months.

This expedition, which with Coronado's was the most ambitious Spanish intrusion into North America, explored all of the Southeast and discovered the Mississippi River. At one point de Soto's group was within two or three days' riding distance of Coronado's men, who were at that time in Kansas. Yet the expedition was considered a total failure, for the great riches that de Soto was seeking were never found.

See Edward G. Bourne, ed., *Narratives of the Career of Hernando de Soto* (1922); "Final Report of the U.S. de Soto Expedition Commission," House Doc. No. 71, 75th Cong., 1st Sess. (1939); Frederick W. Hodge and Theodore H. Lewis, eds., *Spanish Explorers in the United States, 1528-1543* (1907).—R. A. B.

Devol, Jonathan. See RIVERMEN.

De Voto, Bernard (1897-1955). Educator, novelist, and historian. De Voto was born in Ogden, Utah. He attended the University of Utah and later Harvard University, from which he was graduated Phi Beta Kappa in 1920. During World War I he served as a marksmanship instructor in the army. In 1922 he was appointed assistant professor of English at Northwestern University, but in 1927 left Illinois for Massachusetts, where he hoped to become a free-lance writer. From 1925 to 1936 he taught at Harvard and from 1936 to 1938 was editor of the *Saturday Review of Literature*. In 1948 he was awarded a Pulitzer Prize in history for *Across the Wide*

Missouri (1947), a history of the Rocky Mountain fur trade.

De Voto, true to the old saying, is something of a prophet without honor in his own country. His four novels of the West—*The Crooked Mile* (1924), *The Chariot of Fire* (1926), *The House of Sun-Goes-Down* (1928), and *Mountain Time* (1947)—have not received the critical notice they deserve quite simply because De Voto is often dismissed by literary critics as a "historian." At the same time his historical works—*The Year of Decision* (1943), *Across the Wide Missouri, The Course of Empire* (1952), and his edition of *The Journals of Lewis and Clark* (1953)—are summarily dismissed by many historians as popularizations of history written by a literary dilettante.

In fact, each assessment is unjust. Common to both his fictional and historical works is an attempt to interpret the significance of the West in the development of American culture. Coupled with this theme is his defense of the West as the most important positive force in the formation of the American character. This theme is best seen in De Voto's avowedly polemical works, notably *Mark Twain's America* (1932). This is an attack on Van Wyck Brook's *The Ordeal of Mark Twain* (1920), which puts forth the thesis that greatness eluded Twain because of the limitations of his western environment. De Voto's defense of western values as superior to eastern is also evident in *The Easy Chair* (1955), a collection of essays published in *Harper's Magazine* from 1935 to

1955, and in his one novel that is not set in the West, *We Accept with Pleasure* (1934).

Critics have often felt uneasy with De Voto because he did not sentimentalize the western experience, nor did he accept the easy clichés through which many Americans romanticize western history. An ardent conservationist in his later years, De Voto was uncompromising in his denunciation of the cattle interests, the vapid "good guys" of contemporary American mythology. Yet he was not rigidly doctrinaire. His *Easy Chair* essay on Eugene Manlove Rhodes is a sympathetic and kindly study of a cowboy author who stood for everything De Voto himself came to detest. In many ways his one extended attempt at literary criticism, *The World of Fiction* (1934), says more about De Voto than it does about its ostensible subject. It reveals, as do his other works, a complex and many-sided man, an individual firm in his principles and yet aware that all generalities falsify and that individuals of merit often affirmed positions of which he personally did not approve.

See Catherine Bowen, Edith Mirrielees, Arthur M. Schlesinger, Jr., and Wallace Stegner, *Four Portraits and One Subject: Bernard De Voto* (1963); Robert Edson Lee, *From West to East* (1966); Orlan Sawey, *Bernard De Voto* (1969); and Wallace Stegner, *The Uneasy Chair* (1974).—J. K. F.

dialects. See BLACK ENGLISH; CHINOOK JARGON; ENGLISH LANGUAGE AND THE WESTWARD MOVEMENT; FRENCH DIALECTS IN THE MISSISSIPPI VALLEY; HAWAIIAN PIDGIN ENGLISH; PENNSYLVANIA GERMAN; and SPANISH LANGUAGE IN THE SOUTHWEST.

Diamond Hoax. See GREAT DIAMOND HOAX.

Dick, Everett (1898-   ). Historian. Dick was born in Ozawkie, Kansas, and educated at Union College, an institution affiliated with the Seventh-Day Adventist church in Lincoln, Nebraska, and the University of Nebraska, where he worked with well-known historian John D. Hicks. At the suggestion of Hicks, he continued graduate work at the University of Wisconsin under Frederick L. Paxson until 1930. He then embarked on a teaching career at Union College that was to span the next forty years. In World War I, as in later years, he was active in counseling young men, who—as Seventh-Day Adventists—became conscientious objectors when subjected to the military draft.

Dick was one of the first frontier historians to place a special emphasis on the social life of western settlers. His books were among the earliest efforts to convey a realistic—rather than a romantic—account of the everyday life of average settlers on the nineteenth-century frontier.

His first important work on the subject was *The Sod House Frontier* (1937), a well-written narrative of pioneer life on the Great Plains in the later nineteenth century. This study was followed by a number of others, all using the same approach: *Vanguards of the Frontier* (1941), an account of early western travelers and explorers; *The Dixie Frontier* (1948), an account of the settlers' experiences on the southern frontier; and *Tales of the Frontier* (1963), a sprightly and attractive volume that recaptures the mood of many frontiersmen.

In 1970 he produced *Lure of the Land: A Social History of the Public Lands from the Articles of Confederation to the New Deal*, a rapid survey of the social aspects of public land policy since the later half of the eighteenth century.—G. D. N.

Diehl, Charles Sanford (1854-1946). Journalist. As correspondent for the Chicago *Times* from 1873 to 1883, Diehl accompanied reinforcements who joined Brigadier General Alfred Terry after the Custer defeat in 1876 and remained in the field from late August to early September. In 1877 he and Jerome B. Stillson of the New York *Herald* accompanied Terry's peace commission to Sitting Bull in Canada. En route, they received word of Chief Joseph's surrender and wrote the first news accounts, since no correspondents were present at the surrender; later, they interviewed Sitting Bull in Canada.

To cover Sitting Bull's anticipated surrender (which did not come about at that time), Diehl was living at Poplar River Agency, Montana. When Major Guido Ilges attacked the Sioux camp there on January 2, 1881, Diehl fought alongside troops, which was not unusual for Indian war correspondents, and was subsequently commended by Ilges in his report. Being "mentioned in the dispatches" was a coveted encomium for all war correspondents of the period.

From 1883 to 1911 Diehl was with the Associated Press, becoming assistant general manager, in which capacity he organized AP coverage of the Spanish-American War. From 1911 to 1924 he was co-owner of the *San Antonio Light*.

Diehl's service in the West is detailed in his autobiography, *The Staff Correspondent* (1931). An additional treatment is to be found in Oliver Knight, *Following the Indian Wars* (1960).—O. K.

Dietz (or **Deitz**), **John F.** (1861-1924). Wisconsin pioneer. Dietz was born in Winneconne, Wisconsin, and settled on a cutover farm on the Thornapple River in Sawyer County. When he discovered in 1904 that one end of a dam owned by the Chippewa Lumber and Boom Company was on his land, he began charging a fee for each log that went through his property on the way to the sawmill below. To do this, he defied law-enforcement officers and became known as the "defender of Cameron Dam." When a deputy, Oscar Harp, was killed on October 10, 1910, Dietz was charged with murder. He defended himself in court but was found guilty and sentenced to prison for life, although 10,000 people signed petitions asking for clemency. The sentence was finally reduced, and in 1921 he was pardoned.

Dietz's one-man fight against the big lumber companies evoked the sympathy of many who opposed big business. A play written by Harlow R. Hoyte of Wisconsin tells of his exploits, and several articles and books have contributed to the Dietz legend.

See Earl Chapin, "The Showdown at Cameron Dam," *The West* (May 1969).—W. D. W.

Diggs, Annie La Porte (1853-1916). Journalist and Populist leader. Diggs was a major female Populist leader who, unlike the tempestuous, erratic, and better-known Mary Elizabeth LEASE, remained influential in Populist councils throughout the 1890s. Lease and Diggs were both Kansas Populists, and no other woman in that state or elsewhere attained the prominence of these two. In fact, after Lease's disaffection, Diggs had no genuine competitor among the women who were active in the Populist movement.

Diggs, nee La Porte, was a Canadian by birth and a

New Jerseyite from early childhood to maturity. An attractive and adventurous woman, she pursued a journalistic career briefly in Washington, D.C., before taking a job in a Lawrence, Kansas, music store in 1873. Soon thereafter, marriage and children monopolized her energies. But in the early 1880s she became active in the Woman's Christian Temperance Union, the Unitarian church, and the Social Science Club of Kansas and western Missouri. She became a lecturer for these causes and also returned to journalism as the eastern (Boston) representative of several Kansas newspapers. Gradually she developed a broad interest in the issue of reform, and when the Farmers' Alliance grew in prominence in the late 1880s, she developed a popular Alliance column for a Lawrence newspaper. The column led to her appointment as associate editor and Washington correspondent for the Topeka *Advocate*, Kansas' major populist weekly. From 1890 to 1900, from the formation of the p arty in Kansas until it was thoroughly absorbed via the fusion route with the Democratic party, she waged a consistent and determined fight for progressive reforms.

Although she was inferior to Mary Lease in spectacular crowd-pleasing attributes, she held her own against Lease, and male politicos as well, when it came to intellectual abilities. Her charm was an antidote to the Populists' flamboyant and erratic element, which was often emphasized to discredit the movement. In an interview in 1907, she made an apt commentary on the Populist effort of the 1890s when she responded to a reporter's comment that Populism was apparently becoming respectable: "And don't you remember how the press denounced us as traitors and rebel sympathizers and Anarchists? How they twitted us . . . and declared that we wanted to confiscate everybody's property?" At the same time she stated that it was "worth all that to know now that we were right and that this good old world regards us in a different light as it comes to understand that many of the issues so crudely advocated were really safe and sane progressive measures."

See O. Gene Clanton, *Kansas Populism: Ideas and Men* (1969).—O.G.C.

Dillon, Sidney (1812-1892). Railroad builder and financier. Dillon was perhaps the most important independent railroad building contractor in the pre-Civil War history of American railroads. He was born in Northampton, New York, the son of a poor farmer. He began his railroad building career as water boy during construction of several of the lines that ultimately became the New York Central. Still in his twenties, he risked his slender capital to bid on a section of the Boston and Albany Railroad. From its completion in 1840 to the day on which he watched the golden spike driven on the first transcontinental railroad, his career as a railroad builder was highly successful.

A rich man by 1865, Dillon invested in the Credit Mobilier, then being promoted by Oakes Ames to marshal capital for construction of the UNION PACIFIC RAILROAD, and became chief contractor. From the time of the Union Pacific's organization in 1864 to his death Dillon was a member of the board of directors, and during two of its most critical phases, 1874-84 and 1890-92, also was its president. A close business associate of Jay Gould, he bore chief responsibility for management of the many enterprises in which Gould was involved. Dillon's for-

tune was the result of appreciation of common stock he had accepted, in lieu of cash, in payment for railroad construction. He therefore labored long and hard to build the Union Pacific into a strong carrier, despite the handicaps that government policy, adopted after the Credit Mobilier scandal laid upon it. He died on the eve of the 1890s depression, which brought a thoroughgoing reorganization of the corporate structure of American railroads. A decisive, impressive, technically and financially brilliant executive, Dillon might have altered the history of western railroads had he been ten years younger in 1892.

The importance of Sidney Dillon in the affairs of the Union Pacific has not been adequately appreciated. The best understanding of his role is in Robert G. Athearn, *Union Pacific Country* (1971).—A.M.

dime novels. The first of the notorious dime novels appeared on the literary scene in June 1860, when Erastus Beadle brought out the first of Beadle's Dime Novels, a series that was eventually to include more than three hundred titles and was to be followed by thousands of similar titles in more than thirty other distinct series for the next thirty years. Beadle, who had been a moderately successful publisher in Buffalo, New York, had moved to New York City in 1858 with the avowed intention of becoming a publisher of inexpensive books for a mass audience. When his earlier songbooks and handbooks—priced at ten cents apiece—proved successful, he launched his Dime Novel series as a speculative venture to exploit the undeveloped mass market that his earlier publications had unexpectedly turned up. These novels were short, rarely running over thirty thousand words, and were published regularly every week in a distinctive orange cover. They were patterned after an earlier series of miscellaneous adventure tales that Maturin M. Ballou and Frederick Gleason had been publishing in Boston since 1844, but Beadle's dime novel enterprise was more "businesslike" than that of the earlier series—and far more successful. Beadle's total sales between 1860 and 1865 were nearly five million copies, an amazing figure for the day. (The most successful of all dime novels—it sold more than four thousand copies—was Edward S. Ellis' *Seth Jones: or, The Captives of the Frontier* [1860].)

Beadle realized that in order to attract a mass audience one must offer a standardized product. With his able editor, Orville J. Victor, he managed to perfect a series of formulas for adventure fiction and to create a set of imaginative characters whose adventures readers would avidly follow. Many of Beadle's writers could grind out dime novels at the rate of one thousand words per hour for twelve hours at a stretch, or in other words, produce a complete novel in less than three days. Indeed, Prentiss Ingraham, one of his most prolific writers (he wrote more than six hundred novels in addition to short stories and plays), is said to have written a complete thirty-five-thousand-word story in one marathon session lasting a day and a night. Such facility is the result of fiction reduced to formula.

Some of Beadle's literary heroes are still remembered today, even though the dime novel has long been forgotten. Deadwood Dick, Hurricane Nell, and Calamity Jane were created by Edward L. Wheeler, one of Beadle's writers, in the late 1870s. Deadwood Dick goes through a number of permutations in, among other novels,

Deadwood Dick's Dream: or, The Rivals of the Road (1881); *Deadwood Dick's Protégée: or, Baby Bess, the Girl Gold Miner* (1887), and *Deadwood Dick, Jr., in Chicago: or, The Anarchist's Daughter* (1888).

Frederick Whittaker's *The Mustang-Hunters; or, The Beautiful Amazon of the Hidden Valley,* published in the late 1860s, apparently marks the first appearance of the western heroine in man's clothing, a promising character to be further developed in the figure of Wheeler's Hurricane Nell, who made her literary debut in *Bob Woolf, the Border Ruffian: or, The Girl Dead-Shot* (1878). Wheeler's Calamity Jane, the flower of this kind of characterization, is best met in *Deadwood Dick on Deck: or, Calamity Jane, the Heroine of Whoop-Up* (1885). Devotees may follow her adventures in *Blonde Bill: or, Deadwood Dick's Home Base* (1880) and elsewhere.

Literarily, dime novels descend from the adventure stories of James Fenimore COOPER, with a liberal admixture of "southwestern" HUMOR and, less predictably, Down East humor, which at the time was also a popular genre of burlesque writing. Cooper's influence is seen in the dime novel's plot of wilderness peril and rescue; in the ubiquitous, beneficent old hunter, who is a direct descendent of Cooper's Leatherstocking; in the love stories of courtship between two young, romantic lovers; and in the dependence upon disguise and mistaken identity, which is so pronounced a feature of nineteenth-century melodrama in general and of the Leatherstocking Tales in particular.

The importance of the dime novels, however, is commercial, despite the fact that they pioneered one form of subliterary writing in the western tradition. Most interesting, perhaps, is the pioneering effort of dime novel publishers in the tradition of press agentry; indeed, the transformation of "Buffalo Bill" CODY from a western scout for Major Frank North at Fort McPherson into an American myth hero is the first example of a character created by a mass medium to pander to a mass taste. Buffalo Bill was discovered accidentally in 1869 by Edward Z. C. Judson, a hack writer who, under the name of Ned Buntline, had been turning out a constant stream of blood-and-thunder stories since the late 1830s. Judson had sought out Major North at Fort McPherson with the avowed intention of turning him into a dime novel hero, but was referred by North to Cody. When Judson returned to New York he introduced a highly colored Cody to the readers of the New York *Weekly* in December 1869, in *Buffalo Bill, the King of Border Men.* This supposedly autobiographical account of Buffalo Bill is short on fact and long on sensationalism; it was, however, extremely successful—it was still being sold in 1928—and succeeded in turning the hunter into a temporary sensation. Judson managed to capitalize on this momentary notoriety during Cody's trip east in 1872 (which he may have in fact arranged) by bringing him to Chicago late in the same year, where he appeared in a play—the clear forerunner of the later WILD WEST SHOW—that Judson had written for him. After three years with Judson, Buffalo Bill and a friend, Texas Jack Omohundro, organized their own show with one John M. Burke as press agent and business manager. Burke continued the romanticization of Cody, as did Prentiss Ingraham, who became essentially a staff publicity writer for Buffalo Bill and who wrote more than two hundred ostensibly factual stories about him. Rather

pathetically, Cody himself became unable to tell the facts of his life from the myths created about him and in his old age used to repeat as sober truth the clichés manufactured by Burke and Ingraham.

Modern mass publishing has followed the lead of the dime novels in other ways. Like their nineteenth-century forerunners, modern magazine adventure tales are predictable standardized products, distinctively packaged. Nor is it farfetched to see in the modern television western the long shadow of Beadle, for, like his dime novels, these programs are repetitive adventures of characters who are nearly indistinguishable except for their names and for some superficial, but constantly emphasized, quality that, in lieu of characterization, serves to set them apart from their rivals.

An early, but still valuable, study of the dime novel is Edmund Pearson, *Dime Novels: or, Following an Old Trail in Popular Literature* (1929). The press agentry behind the Buffalo Bill legend has been exhaustively studied by Richard J. Walsh and Milton S. Salsbury in *The Making of Buffalo Bill: A Study in Heroics* (1928). The best general discussion of the dime novel is to be found in Henry Nash Smith, *Virgin Land: The American West as Symbol and Myth* (1950).—J. K. F.

Disciples of Christ. During the long colonial period immigrants from the British Isles and from the Continent brought to the New World many diverse expressions of Protestant Christianity. They ranged from the conservative Church of England, established in Virginia and the Carolinas, to the radical and democratic Baptists and Quakers. In government the Protestant churches fell into three categories: the episcopal polity of the Church of England, the presbyterian polity that had been brought originally from Scotland, and the congregational government as developed in Puritan New England and among the Baptists. The migrating Protestant groups brought to the colonies diametrically opposed attitudes toward the question as to whether the church should be part of the state or separated from it. The Great Awakening in the first half of the eighteenth century brought new divisions within the religious groups already emerging as American denominations.

Settlers streamed across the Apalachian barrier into Kentucky and Tennessee after the close of the American Revolution. After 1800 they began to fill up the Ohio valley and to move into the Old Southwest. The unchurched settlements west of the mountains presented a challenge to the denominations. Preachers from the different denominations set out to build churches to meet the religious needs of frontiersmen who were isolated from the centers of culture in the East. They used revivalism, of which the camp meeting was the most striking manifestation, as the means of recruiting new members. Inevitably rivalry developed between the denominations, and frontiersmen heard from the preachers the truth as set forth in diverse creeds. On occasion the preachers engaged in debates that provided a contribution to the limited intellectual life of the early western communities.

By 1805 one of the most successful frontier evangelists became disenchanted with creedal disputes and weary of denominational rivalries. He was young Barton W. Stone (1772-1844), a Presbyterian ordained in 1798. He participated in the Cane Ridge camp meeting in August 1801 in Kentucky, the most spectacular such meeting in the history of the frontier (see REVIVALISM). The intense emotionalism generated by Cane Ridge aggravated the creedal differences among Stone's Presbyterian colleagues. A theological liberal, Stone, with four others, withdrew two years after the camp meeting had ended from the Synod of Kentucky and formed the Springfield Presbytery. In the following year, 1804, Stone cemented the break by announcing in "The Last Will and Testament of the Springfield Presbytery" that he and his followers would accept no designation for their faith but "Christian" and no authority but that of the Bible. Stone went on to become one of the most successful evangelists of the frontier. He borrowed from the Baptists the practice of baptism by immersion. He founded a democratic church, which enjoyed a rapid growth in Kentucky, Tennessee, and Ohio. By 1830 it numbered around fifteen thousand members. Four years earlier Stone had established a paper called the *Christian Messenger.* Shortly before the first number of the *Messenger* appeared, Stone met and struck up a warm friendship with Alexander Campbell, whose followers were called Disciples of Christ. As a consequence of the similarity between the Christians and the Disciples, the Reverend John T. Johnson, a Disciple, became co-editor of the *Messenger* in 1832. The two bodies, however, never completely amalgamated.

Thomas Campbell (1763-1854), a Presbyterian minister in the north of Ireland, migrated in 1807 to western Pennsylvania in search of health. In the Old World he had disapproved of Presbyterian exclusiveness. The denominational divisiveness and particularism that he found on the American frontier shocked him. Campbell abandoned Presbyterianism and founded in 1809 the Christian Association of Washington (Pennsylvania). He wrote and the Washington Association endorsed a "Declaration and Address." It contained what became a much repeated maxim: "Where the Scriptures speak, we speak; where the Scriptures are silent, we are silent." For all practical purposes the New Testament comprised the Scriptures.

Alexander Campbell (1788-1866), on summons from his father, joined him in 1809. A year in Scotland, part of it at the University of Glasgow, had brought him under the influence of religious ideas quite similar to those of Stone and the elder Campbell. Within three years the younger Campbell had assumed the leadership of a movement that hoped to "restore the ancient order" of the early church as a step toward uniting all Christians. Accepting baptism by immersion in 1812, the Campbells achieved an uneasy fellowship with the Baptists, which continued until the early 1830s. Alexander Campbell founded in 1823 his first paper, the *Christian Baptist,* which continued under his editorship for seven years. Through this medium he presented his ideas with such persuasiveness as to draw to the Disciples of Christ large numbers of Baptists from western Pennsylvania, western Virginia, Kentucky, and Ohio. Along with his father, Alexander Campbell believed the Bible to be the sufficient guide, but he was no literalist. In an age in which biblical scholarship had barely begun, he practiced a scholar's approach to Scripture. His faith in the common man's ability was evidenced by his conviction that the common man could read the text of the Bible and gain a reasonably clear understanding of its meaning. Such faith helps to explain his leadership. For many years he edited the *Millennial Harbinger.* He achieved fame by extended debates with the Roman Catholic archbishop of Cincinnati, J. B. Purcell, and with the secularist Robert Owen, the founder of English socialism. Campbell was a member of the Virginia constitutional convention of 1829. He founded Bethany College in West Virginia, presiding over it as president until his death.

The Disciples' substitution of a simple gospel for elaborate creeds, their democratic church organization, and their emphasis on Christian unity made a strong appeal in communities emerging from primitive beginnings. Campbell's noncreedal, nonauthoritarian program for Christian unity permitted diversity of thought and belief among his followers. He saw baptism and the Lord's Supper as the most important sacraments of Christianity, binding through centuries of tradition the modern communicant to the early church. These commemorative and symbolic ceremonies provided, he taught, the core of institutional Christianity. Commitment and discipleship, rather than theological belief, comprised the essence of religion for the individual man or woman. So it was that the Disciples came to reflect the vigor and the diversity of Middle America. In their pulpits stood fiery backwoods exhorters and preachers of real social standing and sometimes of wealth. Some were unlettered and some possessed university degrees. Some never moved out of their native counties; some achieved recognition throughout the church. They gathered into the fold the poor and the rich, the country man and the city dweller over practically all of Middle America. The determination to "restore the ancient order" provided the bond of unity among them. The Disciples survived the tension over slavery and the tragedy of the Civil War without fracturing. But the dream of the two Campbells of a Christendom as united as the early church did not achieve reality. Ironically, in seeking to end denominational divisiveness, they succeeded only in adding another denomination to American Protestantism. The Christian Churches (Disciples of Christ) International Convention had a membership in the 1970s of something more than 1,875,000.

See Alexander Campbell, *The Memoir of Elder Thomas Campbell* (1861); David Edwin Harrel, Jr., *Quest for a Christian America* (1966); Robert Richardson, *Memoirs of Alexander Campbell* (1868-70); and Robert Frederick West, *Alexander Campbell and Natural Religion* (1948). —R. H. G.

diseases. The American pioneers who moved progressively westward from the 1790s onward experienced the same threats to their health that pioneers have always faced: new infections to which immunity had to be built up, injuries, malnutrition, poor sanitation, and similar hardships. There were some conditions, however, in these predominantly nineteenth-century migrations that were not present in previous times. Rapid settlement and technological developments in power, transportation, farming, and building had marked impact on disease conditions and medical practice as well as on other spheres of life.

The diseases faced by the western settlers were, in almost all respects, the same as they had encountered at home in the eastern United States or even in Europe. What made the western situation different was the amount of disease, its differing epidemic characteristics, and the conditions under which it had to be borne. The historical epidemiology of health and disease on the frontier varies according to the factors determining the incidence of any disease: time, season, climate, geographical location, crowding, sanitary conditions, and other similar physical and social factors. When speaking of disease in the West, then, one is limited in generalizations and conclusions by many things. There was no single disease, or group of diseases, that was entirely typical of the frontier or of pioneers. Some illnesses, such as malaria and scurvy, were widespread. Others, such as milk sickness, were more localized.

The frontiersmen, hardy as many of them were, nevertheless were subject to the usual accidents and injuries of an active life. Travel reports and diaries of the pioneers are full of accounts of major and minor accidents. Land clearing was not without its hazards. An improperly felled tree crushed more than one body or limb. The lack of surgeons, and, even if surgeons did treat an injury, the lack of good antiseptic technique, led to frequent amputation and to many postoperative infections. These latter could, themselves, be fatal at worst or very debilitating at best. Many of the health problems afflicting the pioneers were of a distinctly debilitating nature. Illness and prolonged convalescence are difficult in the best of modern circumstances. For the active frontiersman, whose daily hard physical work was essential for survival, this often meant failure.

Certain groups of pioneers were subjected to hazards peculiar to their mode of travel or their chosen work. The miners in California, for instance, suffered innumerable injuries in open-faced mining shafts, as well as from the violence rampant in some mining communities. The Indians were a constant threat, especially on the Great Plains and prairies. One of the earliest American medical journals carried a very serious article entitled "On the Management of a Scalped Head."

To provide sufficient daily food was a problem for most travelers and many already settled on the frontier. Dietary deficiency and the resistance to infection is still a topic being investigated by scientists. That severely deficient diets led to lowering of resistance, whatever that vague phrase may really mean, and to actual disease such as scurvy, there is no doubt. The more subtle factors involved in diet and health are not pertinent here. The pioneers believed that many of their woes were due to improper cooking and choice of foods.

John Woods, an English farmer who settled in the Illinois country around 1820, pointed out that although much sickness prevailed among the American settlers, the Europeans generally enjoyed good health. His reason was that the Americans ate but two meals a day and sometimes only one, while the Europeans ate regularly three times a day.

Sometimes a forced change of diet led to severe intestinal disturbances. Whether a bacterial infection in our modern terms would be implicated here is not clear. But the travelers' accounts leave no doubt as to their own cause-and-effect reasoning: "The sudden and entire change from flesh to fish affected us all more or less, with diarrhoea and pain in the abdomen. . . ." This note in the diary from the Oregon journey of John K. Townsend is typical. When the fish involved was salmon, the high fat and oil content was usually blamed for loosening the bowels.

While the ague was the most common disease on the frontier, diarrhea must have been the most common symptom. This debilitating condition, which in the large eastern cities killed scores of infants every summer under the name cholera infantum, was found on the mountain trails as well as on the Plains. In the East, the unsanitary streets and crowded tenements led to a wildfire spread of intestinal diseases. On the frontier, too, the sanitary conditions were often equally primitive and inadequate. Here at least there was usually no crowding of large masses of people into tenements. But the absence of wells in newly settled areas necessitated the use of water holes that were all too frequently contaminated and ready to spread their death-dealing germs.

One form of diarrheal disease was the most dreaded of all, the cholera, sweeping through the country in epidemics in 1832, 1849, and 1866. Also knows as Asiatic cholera or cholera morbus, this food-borne and waterborne bacterial disease caused great fear and panic because it was associated with the worst possible characteristics of any epidemic disease: it affected large numbers, struck extremely rapidly, caused many deaths, and the doctors really could do very little for the poor sufferers. Literature is replete with stories describing a healthy man in the morning who was in the throes of abdominal spasms, watery diarrhea leading to dehydration and prostration by evening. Soon thereafter he might be ready for burial. Even that final rite too often had to be in a ditch with dozens of his unfortunate fellow victims.

"Rain follows the plow" was a common belief on the Great Plains in the nineteenth century. But as rain followed the plow so did one of the most prevalent diseases the pioneers encountered, malaria, or the ague. The disease was so common that many travelers and physicians reported that many people didn't even consider it an illness. "He ain't sick," the saying went, "he's just got the ager." The term *malaria* (literally *mal aria,* or "bad air") relates to its supposed origin from air filled with miasms. Since the disease reached its greatest prevalence in the fall it was also known as "autumnal fever." The British term for malaria was *ague,* or *fever and ague,* the latter also commonly used by Americans. "Chills and fever" and "the shakes" were more descriptive and popular ways of referring to this widespread malady.

Malaria is an infectious disease with intermittent symptoms, hence its common name of intermittent fever. It is caused by parasitic protozoa that invade and multiply within the red blood cells. The disease more often debilitates than kills its victims. Patients with repeated attacks usually have anemia, weakness, depression, and enlargement of the spleen.

The economic and social consequences to those who had to perform hard physical work and to protect themselves from the elements or the Indians are obvious. Those who contracted the disease while traveling were equally unfortunate.

Among doctors and laymen of the nineteenth century, who before very late in the century knew nothing of the parasitic cause or the mosquito spread of the disease, the miasmatic doctrine of its origin was by far the most commonly held. According to this theory, the ague, and many other infectious diseases as well, was caused by decaying organic matter poisoning the air with a noxious effluvium. Watering the land was believed to increase the formation of miasms, a belief not without foundation as we now know, because mosquito larvae breed in collections of still water.

Many observers, such as Fortescue Cuming early in the nineteenth century, noted that the residents along the banks of the Mississippi, where overflow with resulting stagnant water was common, had annual attacks of ague leaving the sufferers weak and sallow in complexion. While Cuming's description, published in 1810, is not as clear and precise in its diagnostic labels as we might want today, it nevertheless graphically portrays the problem: "On the subsiding of the waters, the sickly season commences, and lasts with little variation from July to October, inclusive. This is more or less the case over the whole territory, particularly on the banks of the Mississippi, and in the neighborhood of swamps and stagnant ponds. The driest seasons are the most unhealthy. The prevailing malady is a fever of the intermittent species, sometimes accompanied by ague, and sometimes not. It is rarely fatal in itself, but its consequences are dreadful, as it frequently lasts five or six months in defiance of medicine, and leaves the patient in so relaxed and debilitated a state, that he never after regains the strength he had lost. It also frequently terminates in jaundice or dropsy, which sometimes prove fatal.

"All newcomers are subject to what is called seasoning, after which, though they may be annually attacked by this scourge of climate, it rarely confines them longer than a few days."

Paradoxically, malaria was probably an underreported disease despite its wide prevalence. For one thing it was so common as to escape any special notice. The disease strikes small children very frequently, though in the previous century there still existed the mistaken notion that only adults were afflicted. The many clinical and lay terms applied to malaria, such as intermittent, remittent, remittent bilious, congestive, tertian, quartan, and quotidian fevers, were bound to cause confusion. From the point of view of business and promotion of an area, there was also reason to play down any epidemic disease. The purported report from Wisconsin that the place was so healthy that a few men had to be killed in order to start a cemetery, describes this attitude very well. The truth is that throughout much of the Midwest malaria actually determined the daily habits of the people. The minister scheduled his preaching to avoid his shakes, and the courts avoided the sick days of the litigants or the justices.

While all travelers knew that the ague, or the fever as they called it, was the disease of the Mississippi River valley, it was also an important health factor in California. It was probably brought to the state by fur trappers who had become infected in an Oregon epidemic of 1829-30. The disease was well established in California before the forty-niners came in such large numbers, and it continued to be present and to flare up in local epidemics through the rest of the century. The secretary of the California state board of health reported, in 1875, that malarial fevers and consumption were the most prevalent forms of disease.

The American experience with malaria confirms the fact that a high incidence of malaria did not immediately follow settlement of a region. Only after a few years, or even decades, did the disease present a problem. Erwin Ackerknecht, the foremost historian of malaria in the

Midwest, has called this phenomenon an epidemiological latency period. One important judgment that the concept of latency period affords us is to be able to distinguish between a moving and a stationary frontier, using the evidence of sickness statistics.

Colonization of the American continent helped spread most diseases. Malaria was probably originally imported with Negro slaves, but white colonization spread it rapidly. For instance, the early housing of the western settlers, unbeknown to them, was ideally suited to the unwelcome but ever-present mosquito guests. Most of the malaria-transmitting types thrive in dark, moist, warm habitats, just the conditions provided by the log cabin. As housing improved, malaria decreased.

Malaria disappeared from the upper Mississippi River valley before any conscious antimalarial measures such as screening were instituted. Ackerknecht cites several factors, stressing that no one reason can be singled out. The coming of railroads was important because less reliance on water transportation resulted in a shift of settlements from the bottom lands of high mosquito density to the healthier uplands. As settlements progressed, livestock herds grew, and mosquitoes much prefer cows to men, thus reducing the chances for malaria passage.

Dr. John C. Gunn in his *Domestic Medicine* (see DOCTORS) clearly described for his readers the course of acute malaria. There are three stages to the attack, Gunn explained, cold, hot, and sweating. "In the first, there is much yawning and stretching, the feet and hands become cold, the skin looks shriveled, you seem to lose the use of your limbs by weakness, your pulse is small and frequent, you dislike to move, and finally take a chill succeeded by a cold shake. This shake continues about ten or fifteen minutes. . . . In the second stage, as the chill and shaking go off, a pain in the head and back comes on, succeeded by flushings of heat. . . . In the commencement of the third and last stage, the intense heat begins to subside, moisture begins to break out on the forehead, . . . fever abates. . . . You then feel considerably relieved as the sweat increases, which soon restores you to your usual feelings and sensations, except great weakness and extreme prostration of strength."

Obviously then, this very common malady took a terrific social, economic, and physical toll. The above description is of one attack. Depending on which of several malarial parasites caused the infection, the patient went through these paroxysms every twenty-four, forty-eight, or seventy-two hours. The quotidian variety, with chills and fever every twenty-four hours, was most common, the recurrences occurring over a period of weeks. Quinine, promoted in the 1820s by Dr. John SAPPINGTON, was able to abort the chills and fever.

There is evidence that around the middle of the last century typhoid fever gradually replaced malaria as the prevalent disease of the Midwest. Typhoid is a severe intestinal disease caused by a bacterium that is readily spread by flies, food, fingers, and water. It was an ever-present threat wherever sanitation was lax, that is to say, in most communities and settlements. Until proper sewage disposal was instituted and clean water made available, diarrheal complaints were routine. Some of these doubtless were typhoid, or continued fever, as it was often called.

Not until 1836 did Dr. William Gerhard, a Paris-trained physician of Philadelphia, clearly differentiate between the louse-borne disease typhus fever, also called ship fever or jail fever, and typhoid fever. The latter disease could be found in the gold-rush mining camps and along the trail, as well as in the large cities of the East or the new towns of the frontier.

Scurvy, ever the bane of travelers, was no less a problem in the great migration to the American West. Now known to be caused by vitamin C deficiency, the disease comes on slowly when the diet is deficient in natural sources of the vitamin, especially fresh fruits and vegetables. During much of the migratory period, travel was slow and food preservation not yet sufficiently advanced. Among the forty-niners the disease was especially prone to appear when they began doing hard physical work in the mines following the long water or overland journey.

Scurvy was often confused with rheumatism because muscle weakness and pain were common symptoms. Late manifestations, appearing after one hundred and fifty to two hundred days of vitamin deficiency, included skin lesions, swollen gums, swelling of the limbs, and anemia. The disease, as is apparent from the list of signs and symptoms, causes much lethargy and is, in itself, very serious. The emigrants usually made some provisions against scurvy on the trip west, but, too often, these were insufficient. The settlers knew which roots or fruits were good antiscorbutics. Service berries or June berries, for instance, were abundant in some areas. These are rich sources of vitamin C.

One apparently common health problem of women, rarely discussed in the travel journals and diaries, was prolapse of the uterus. Dr. William M. Wood of the United States Navy, writing in the *Maryland Medical Journal* in 1842 on diseases of the western states, told his colleagues that this condition ". . . among the women of the new states, presents itself to an extent so shocking as to indicate some sectional causes." Wood ascribed the frequency of uterine prolapse to the conduct of labor in childbirth and the subsequent medical management of the new mother. "It is a matter of religious vigilance," the outraged Dr. Wood continued, "during the progress of labor, to harass the patient by all manner of savage and violent aid . . . and by no manner or means permitting her to remain quiet in bed."

Where no physicians were available, as in isolated settlements or in the backwoods or on the trail, Wood blamed the barbarous practices on "old women" who managed the labor process. This harsh judgment, however, should certainly not be applied to all the many midwives who did creditable obstetric work throughout the frontier country.

As to psychological problems, the types and extent of these disorders among the pioneers are difficult to describe and to measure. The active habits of our countrymen, one observer wrote, made hypochondria much rarer than in Great Britain. One recent writer has drawn attention to the unimaginable solitude of the early West. The extent of its havoc is glimpsed in a few diaries, but the real toll is yet to be measured with any real precision.

One of the diseases encountered by the pioneers, the awesome and bewildering milk sickness, was truly a frontier disorder. Often called milk sick, or by even more descriptive names such as puking fever, swamp sickness, the tires, the slows, or the trembles, this affliction of man and cattle was widely prevalent in the states of the upper South and the Midwest. Reports from colonial times to the 1960s may be found in the medical literature. Many family tragedies resulted from this poorly understood disease.

We now know that milk sickness is due to poisoning by tremetol, the toxic ingredient of white snakeroot and rayless goldenrod. The disease occurs when man eats butter or drinks milk taken from cows poisoned by eating the leaves or stems of the white snakeroot plant. Exact figures are not obtainable, but the incidence of disease and death from this cause in eighteenth- and nineteenth-century America was great. It was especially prevalent in dry seasons, when the cattle strayed from their pastures into neighboring woods. The disease was more likely to occur in newly cleared areas without fenced pasturelands than in more settled regions with fences. Another important epidemiologic point is that the toxin in raw milk must reach fairly high concentrations to do its damage to human consumers. In rural areas, where heavy consumption of raw milk from single cows or a small herd was common, the disease was likely to hit entire families. In more populous areas, where milk from several sources was pooled, the toxin was diluted, hence less harmful.

The disease is directly related to the dose of toxin absorbed. Severe acid-base disturbances could lead to death within a few days. Nancy Hanks Lincoln died of milk sickness in 1818 when her son Abraham was a boy of nine. Mrs. Lincoln's great-aunt and uncle and two neighbors died shortly after her. Though Nancy Lincoln may have been the most prominent historical figure to die of milk sickness on the frontier, she was by no means the only one. Those lucky enough to recover after an illness, characterized by loss of appetite, weakness, muscle pain and stiffness, severe vomiting, and constipation, were often left to a slow recovery with much lethargy. This feature gave it the name sloes, or slows.

Finally, it should be said again that other diseases such as diphtheria, smallpox, tuberculosis, erysipelas, and various skin disorders, were as prevalent in the West as they were in the East. A significant number of emigrants came west in search of health, believing the lands beyond the Missouri to be rich as well as invigorating. It was true that an outdoor existence in the mountains of Colorado certainly proved beneficial for some consumptives, but they soon encountered numerous other threats to their health.

While preservation of good health was but one of many problems faced by the pioneers, it was an overriding one. Without health all else might be lost. Unfortunately, in most instances, nineteenth-century Americans had little direct control over disease and its prevention.

See Erwin H. Ackerknecht, *Malaria in the Upper Mississippi River Valley, 1760-1900* (1945); George W. Groh, *Gold Fever, Being a True Account, Both Horrifying and Hilarious, of the Art of Healing (So-called) During the California Gold Rush* (1966); Billy M. Jones, *Health Seekers in the Southwest, 1817-1900* (1967); and Madge E. Pickard and R. Carlyle Buley, *The Midwest Pioneer: His Ills, Cures and Doctors* (1945).—G. H. B.

Disney, Walt[er Elias] (1901-1966). Entertainment

entrepreneur. Born in Chicago, Illinois, but raised on a small farm near Marceline, Missouri, Disney was steeped in turn-of-the-century, small-town virtues. He was mostly self-educated and learned to be self-reliant—a proud, tough, and blunt man in the tradition of Edison and Ford. To the public he was an uncle figure, a kindly tinkerer and "dreamer," turning out bright, clean, uncontroversial amusements for the kids. Because of his location on the West Coast, his nature films, his historical films about western figures, and his "Frontierland," Disney became associated with the West in a special way.

Disney first ventured into animated films in Kansas City after completing army service in France. His early attempts proved unsuccessful, and in 1923, bankrupt, Disney moved to Los Angeles, joining Roy, his brother and financial mentor. There he achieved modest success with the nationally distributed series *Oswald the Rabbit* (1927). This was followed by the appearance of the spunky little rodent Mickey Mouse in *Steamship Willie* (1928), the first animated film to use sound. It gave Disney the competitive edge he needed.

Disney's good fortune continued in the 1930s: new popular characters were created; his staff expanded; the quality of animation rose; and new incomes from merchandising were created. Experimenting in other directions, Disney began the Silly Symphony series in 1929, blending classical music with animated film. The turning point was his first feature, *Snow White and the Seven Dwarfs* (1937). It cost so much that it almost broke the studio, but it grossed $8.5 million in its first release and continued the love affair between Disney and the intellectual critics, even Edmund Wilson. Many were convinced that Disney's cartoons kept alive the traditions of physical, nonverbal humor that had been America's greatest contribution to the silent screen. Neither *Pinocchio* (1939) nor *Bambi* (1942) was as financially successful as *Snow White,* however. And *Fantasia* (1940), a high-brow attempt to combine music by the world's greatest composers and complicated animation, appealed to few when it was first released.

In 1940 Disney opened a new studio. Unimpressed by his attempt to create a harmonious artistic community, his staff struck over their right to organize a noncompany union. The simultaneous failures of *Fantasia* and his paternal-communal studio plans embittered Disney. Thereafter his animation style remained fixed at a level of conventional realism, slick in execution and aiming at only the cute and sentimental. Although he still insisted on a certain informality with his staff—they continued to call him "Walt" and support the official line of easy accessibility—the old camaraderie ceased. Instead, Disney became remote and erratic, and finicky about details. Publicity was used as a smoke screen, hiding a shrewd, hard-driving go-getter behind an image. He began to diversify his film products and entire range of activities, producing a series of cheap but well-made historical adventures using real actors, a successful string of situation comedies, and nature films inexpensively obtained from naturalists.

Everything flowed together in the early 1950s. Disney's weekly television show became a way of plugging his new films without cost, and the networks, along with several of the sponsors, invested in his new venture, DISNEYLAND. Disney's personal worth, almost nothing prior to the park's opening, was in excess of $25 million

when he died. In 1965, the year *Mary Poppins* was released, Disney's empire grossed over $112 million. By the early 1970s it was surpassing $150 million annually. Five years after Disney's death, Disneyworld opened in Florida. The Disney machine hummed smoothly along: everything—the films, amusement parks, television show, merchandising and educational subdivisions—reinforced everything else in a time when other mass media firms were feeling a severe profit squeeze.

A believer in progress and the benign force of technology, Disney was always one of the first to take advantage of technological breakthroughs, such as color film and stereophonic sound. He was also in the promotional vanguard, committing his studio to regular television programming and diversifying by investing in non-movie entertainment. He managed to hold a virtual monopoly on the "family" audience.

Disney was convinced that what pleased him would please wholesome Americans. He wished to banish anxiety and ugliness from his carefully controlled world, smooth the rough edges off experience, and have others share with him a comforting, chucklesome, safe place. Many acknowledge that with all his talent and imagination Disney could have been a great American primitive, but that he chose to cut himself off from the anarchical exuberance of his earliest films and from that which was dark and interesting in his own background and sensibility in order to develop the skills of real-estate developer and merchant.—R. Sc.

Disneyland. A 185-acre amusement park founded by Walt DISNEY. Disneyland, located south of Los Angeles in Anaheim, California, consists of five different areas that reflect some of Disney's own basic interests. The entrance to the park is an idealized representation of a small town such as Disney knew when he was growing up. Once the visitor has passed through Main Street, he may visit four different "lands": Adventureland, offering a jungle boat ride and lifelike moving models of jungle animals; Frontierland, featuring a Mississippi River steamboat, Huck Finn's island, a mule train, and a pirate raid; Fantasyland, catering to younger children with its characters from Disney's animated films; and Tomorrowland, simulating space-age adventures.

Disney's idea for a clean, well-managed amusement park originated in the early 1930s, when he was looking, unsuccessfully, for places that were not too dirty or phony to take his own small daughters. When he was building a new studio in the San Fernando Valley, he considered adding a small amusement park, but it was during the Depression and money was unavailable. Meanwhile he and his technicians were trying to animate little three-dimensional dolls. Their experimentation became the basis for the complex system "audio-animatronics," which activates all the animal and human figures at the various Disneyland "adventures."

Disney commissioned the first plans for the park in 1952, using ten thousand dollars of studio money as well as the cash value of his own life-insurance policy. The American Broadcasting Company, the network that carried Disney's popular television show; Western Printing, long-time purveyors of Disney comic books and other publications; and various concessionaires, including some of the TV-show sponsors, joined Walt Disney Productions, Ltd., in providing $17 million for building the park in a former orange grove.

From its opening day in 1955, Disney's "Magic Kingdom" was an enormous success, grossing $195 million in its first decade. The average number of visitors rose to well over six million annually with yearly grosses of up to $50 million. The park has played host to no fewer than eleven kings and queens, twenty-four other heads of state, and twenty-seven princes and princesses.

In creating "the world's biggest toy for the world's biggest boy," as someone put it, Disney gave the public what it wanted—and what he wanted. He applied to a new form of entertainment the latest technology and set it in a pretty, clean, and orderly environment. The park has gently curving walks, sparkling water, plenty of shade, no long admission lines, an intensively trained platoon of youthful, cheerful, clean-cut guides and ride masters, and even carefully sanitized food concessions. All of which led city planner James Rouse to comment that "the greatest piece of urban design in the U.S. today is Disneyland. Think of its performance in relation to its purpose."—R. Sc.

Dobie, J[ames] Frank (1888-1964). Folklorist and writer. Born on a ranch in Live Oak County, Texas, the eldest of six children, Dobie attended ranch schools. He was educated at Southwestern University, Georgetown, Texas; Columbia University; and the University of Texas, where he finally gave up trying to get his Ph.D. During those early years he worked briefly as a reporter for the San Antonio *Express* and Galveston *Tribune,* a high school principal and teacher, and a college administrator. After World War I service in France, he returned to Texas to manage his uncle's ranch.

Deciding in 1921 to be a writer and teacher, Dobie joined the University of Texas faculty for two years. After briefly heading the English department of Oklahoma Agriculture and Mining College at Stillwater, he returned to the university in 1925. That same year he sold his first article, on cowboy songs, to the national magazine *Country Gentlemen.* At a time when the university's English department presumed that Texas had no literary tradition, and had even sent folk-song collector John Lomax packing to Harvard, Dobie insisted that Texas had a rich tradition that should be preserved orally and in writing and initiated a course in the life and literature of the Southwest.

World War II saw Dobie in Europe, teaching American history for a year at Emanuel College in England and lecturing to American servicemen in England, Germany, and Austria. Politically concerned, Dobie frequently challenged the status quo at the university and in state and national politics. His tiffs with the university's board of regents became legendary. The so-called Dobie rule limiting the number of successive leaves allowed a professor was instituted in 1947 to bring Dobie home or fire him; he refused to come home and was dropped from the faculty. Undaunted he continued to run a sort of sub-university at his home, administrators, faculty, and students crowding in for advice on academic problems, writing, and political procedures.

With the publication of his *A Vaquero of the Brush Country* and *Coronado's Children* in 1930, Dobie became a national literary figure. From 1939 until his death, he wrote a weekly column for Texas newspapers, eventually becoming the best-known academic and literary figure in the state; he also was held in highest regard as a collector and critic. A striking figure, with his white suit

setting off his bright blue eyes and unruly shock of snow-white hair, and a preeminent storyteller, Dobie enchanted audiences with his slow drawl, his slow way with a story that could not be hurried, and his knowledge of mustangs, coyotes, Longhorns, rattlesnakes, and cow people.

Dobie served as editor and secretary of the Texas Folklore Society from 1922 until 1942. He received an honorary degree from Cambridge in 1944, was named a member of the United States Commission, UNESCO, in 1945 and Consultant to the Library of Congress on American Cultural History in 1964, and awarded the Presidential Medal of Freedom four days prior to his death by his close friend President Lyndon B. Johnson.

Old quarrels long forgotten, Dobie directed his wife to place his working library, manuscripts, and several collections in the Dobie Room in the Academic Center of the University of Texas. His "Paisano" ranch, located fifteen miles southwest of Austin, was purchased by friends and given to the university as a writers' retreat, along with endowed fellowships.

See Winston Bode, *A Portrait of Pancho: The Life of a Great Texan, J. Frank Dobie* (1965).—J. B. F.

doctors. The story of the frontier doctors is similar to that of most nineteenth-century American physicians. While it is true that the American frontier physician was exposed to certain personal hazards and occasionally encountered diseases not seen by his eastern colleagues, in general, the medicine he practiced in Indiana in the 1830s or California in the 1850s was the same as that of his colleagues in New York, Philadelphia, or Boston.

On the early midwestern frontier, as well as in the West and Northwest, military surgeons were often the first doctors. They not only treated the members of their garrisons, but often rode out from the presidio or the fort to surrounding ranches or settlements. A number of these early physicians remained in the West to open their own practices. Many of the army's most famous physicians, such as William Gorgas, George Sternberg, and Walter Reed, served long tours on the frontier.

The early civilian medical men of the West more often than not turned to other work besides the practice of their profession. This, incidentally, was true of physicians throughout the country, with the exception of the populous cities where a man might support himself merely by his practice. In the West, medical men were involved in a large variety of business and scientific ventures. A number of the naturalists accompanying various exploratory parties, for instance, were doctors. In part this was necessary because only through the study of medicine was a man likely to receive training in biology, especially in early nineteenth-century America.

Some western physicians doubled as preachers. Others opened drugstores, which later became their main source of income. Claim buying, mining, newspaper work, and many other business enterprises found western doctors actively involved. Often they played a prominent role in local and state governments. In Kansas, for example, Doctors Charles Robinson and J. P. Root took active parts in the territorial council, and when Kansas achieved statehood, Dr. Robinson became its first governor and Dr. Root the first lieutenant governor. In North Dakota, California, Oregon, and elsewhere doctors played important civic and economic roles.

Dr. David Wall, who opened the first drugstore in Vancouver, Washington, is a typical example of a pioneer doctor whose shrewd business sense and ability to convince patients of his medical skills led to a successful career. Born in Ireland, Wall came to the United States as a young man. After serving in the army as a hospital steward in the Civil War, he came to the Northwest Territory, where he opened a drugstore in 1865 and proclaimed himself a physician. He practiced for forty years and eventually became vice president of a Vancouver bank.

Many doctors turned to nonmedical activities out of economic necessity. Where local medical societies were formed in the western states they usually published a fee bill stating the standard charges for house calls, bleeding, obstetrical care, and so on. Payment, unfortunately, often went uncollected. Many a nineteenth-century physician lamented that if only his patients would pay their outstanding bills, his economic worries would cease. Payment in fruit, vegetables, groceries, meat, or in services, such as painting or cutting wood, was also common. It is safe to conclude that the frontier doctor who relied solely on the income from his practice was not among the well-to-do. Only after he had established himself solidly and his patients themselves had become economically self-sufficient could the doctor expect to make a decent living from medicine.

Not all doctors were paid on a fee-for-service basis. In certain sections some form of contract by the year was fairly common. In the South, for example, plantation owners often paid the physician a lump sum to provide all the necessary medical care and hygienic advice. Mark Twain in his autobiography described the arrangements he knew as a boy. Frequent illness or accidents cost nothing extra, for the doctor worked by the year. He charged twenty-five dollars per year for the whole family, including the necessary medicines. But Twain also pointed out that "Doctors were not called in cases of ordinary illness; the family grandmother attended to those."

Many western areas suffered from a lack of physicians. From the 1830s on, some western medical schools were founded in order to increase the numbers of available doctors. Numerous reports, such as that of S. H. Long's expedition to Arkansas, related that, "Among recent settlers, the want of the most common comforts, of the advice and attendance of skilful physicians, and, above all, the want of cleanliness, and the destructive habits of intemperance, are causes operating powerfully to produce and aggravate . . . diseases."

One means by which doctors could spread their services more widely was by circuit-riding. Lawyers and preachers also carried out their duties in this fashion. These hard-working medical men were away from their homes for a week or two at a time, living with their patients en route. Gathering herbs along the trail and equipped with what medicines and appliances they could carry in the saddlebags, these were among the earliest pioneer doctors in the West. When roads improved and railroads were built consultation became easier. With the advent of the telephone, circuit-riding was no longer necessary at all.

Where doctors were unavailable their writings were not. The home medical adviser, usually a book written for the public in nontechnical language by a physician, was among the standard equipment of most pioneer wagons or pack trains. These guides began to be published in the seventeenth century with increasing frequency. John Wesley was as widely known for his *Primitive Physic* as he was for his particular brand of Christianity.

The titles of some of those do-it-yourself medical books plainly indicate their intentions. An early nineteenth-century example was Alexander Thomson's *The Family Physician; or, Domestic Medical Friend: Containing Plain and Practical Instructions for the Prevention and Cure of Diseases.* A similar book by an anonymous "physician and surgeon" was the 1818 *The House Surgeon and Physician; Designed to Assist Heads of Families, Travelers, and Sea Faring People.* An English book of the late eighteenth century that went through numerous editions and dozens of reprintings in the United States was William Buchan's *Domestic Medicine.* The later editions even included sections dealing with the care of livestock.

Which of these many domestic medical guides was the best or the most popular is hard to gauge. Certainly a prominent candidate would have to be *Gunn's Domestic Medicine, or Poor Man's Friend,* written by Dr. John C. Gunn of Virginia and Tennessee in 1830. A conservative estimate is that the early editions in the 1830s sold more than 100,000 copies. By the 1860s, it was much enlarged and still going strong, a best seller by any standard.

Dr. Gunn was convinced that medical knowledge need not be esoteric, that the time had come when all the technical language of medicine should be simplified for the people. He aimed his book, therefore, at the uneducated. They needed instruction to help them live healthier lives and to avoid the many schemes and medicines of the quacks that abounded. His rules for health were simple: exercise, temperance, and cleanliness.

In addition to the family grandmother and the handy home medical guide, in times of need the endurance, skill, and ingenuity of the pioneers themselves more often than not enabled them to give quite adequate medical care. A common experience was that of Captain Meriwether Lewis. In his journal he described a bout of intense abdominal cramps and dysentery incurred in June 1805 when he was approaching the Great Falls of the Missouri. Lewis was in such distress that he had to stop to make camp. "Having brought no medicine with me," he recorded, "I resolved to try an experiment with some simples; and the choke cherry which grew abundantly in the bottom first struck my attention. . . ." Lewis stripped the twigs, boiled them in water, and drank a pint of the bitter black "tea." He repeated the dose an hour later and by that evening reported that all symptoms had disappeared.

Much of the opinion about doctors found in the western travel literature has it that many men practiced many different brands of medicine or followed various doctrines regarding diseases and cures. Many practiced without proper medical training throughout the entire country. Licensing laws were repealed in most states by the mid-nineteenth century. Pretty much anyone who called himself a doctor could function as one. In the new settlements many men, with little less than good intention to go on, held life and limb in their hands.

Sometimes the title of doctor was thrust upon those

who, by virtue of good common sense and a bit more education than their fellows, sounded and looked like doctors. The experience of one pious New Englander, Estwick Evans, must have been very common. While traveling on the Ohio River in 1818, he wrote, the boatmen, who frequently became sick with fevers, applied to him for medical aid: ". . . and hence I acquired the title of Doctor. My prescriptions were always simple; and, strange to tell, I did not lose a single patient . . . I always told the sick, that in a few days, they would be perfectly well." Evans was a firm believer in nature's power to cure. In this he was in the best company, for by midcentury a movement toward a less heroic form of treating, without bleeding, purging, and blistering, was well under way.

How the pioneer physician actually practiced his profession and what modes of therapy he prescribed depended on his training, his allegiance to the so-called regular profession or to one of the numerous medical sects, and the availability of medical supplies. Some generalizations can be made. Since fevers were very common, some form of depletion therapy was usually used. Blood-letting was especially popular until the Civil War years. Several ounces to a pint or two might be let at one time by cutting into a vein or scarifying the skin. Leeches did the job more slowly. The theory was that a vascular fullness existed at the onset of an illness. This had to be reduced before any drug therapy could be effective.

In a similar way emetics and strong purges were used. All this therapy was based on the age-old humoral theory of disease. Blood, yellow bile, black bile, and phlegm were the four humors of Greek antiquity. These combined in hot, cold, moist, and dry combinations. If the humors were not in balance or in the wrong location within the body resulting in disease they might be favorably affected by release through the intestinal tract or via the blood vessels. By a theory of opposites, treatment was directed to cool those diseases deemed to be hot, dry those with excess of moisture, and the reverse.

The most commonly used purge was mercurous chloride, better known as calomel. Nineteenth-century doctors believed that, in addition to acting as a cathartic, calomel modified the secretion of the liver. That organ was believed to be sluggish in most fevers and in springtime.

To illustrate therapeutic concepts and their vagueness, witness what a physician writing the "Modus Operandi of Calomel" in the *Western Journal of Medical and Physical Sciences* in 1833 had to say: "When given in large doses, besides its primary action on the bowels, it produces its specific effects on the general system, called the mercurial impression; and thus whatever may be its nature, seems especially to affect the capillary vessels, and exerting the action of these parts, it has a tendency to equalize the general circulation, restore secretions, overcome local congestion, inflammations, etc."

We now know that there was some justification for thinking that calomel acts on a sluggish liver. Calomel causes a greenish stool, not because it stimulates an increased bile flow from the liver, but because mercury, acting as a mild antiseptic, interferes with the intestinal bacteria that are necessary to convert the stools to their normal color by acting on the bile pigments being excreted.

Calomel also causes salivation, and, when given for too long a period or in excess, causes bone damage and the teeth to loosen and actually drop out. The salivation was thought to assist in ridding the body of bad humors.

A typical picture of an early nineteenth-century American practitioner is one drawn by J. Fenimore Cooper. In his novel *The Pioneers,* Cooper portrays frontier life in the 1790s. Hence, the book is one of the first and most useful novels for our purpose. One of Cooper's characters is a young physician of formidable stature, Dr. Elnathan Todd. Elnathan, a sickly lad, took to doctoring because it was believed to be an easier calling than farming. After an apprenticeship with a local doctor and a very brief sojourn in the hospital at Boston, the young man was ready to minister to the ills of an upstate New York frontier village. Elnathan, Cooper tells us, ". . . had acquired a certain degree of knowledge in fevers and agues, and could talk with much judgement concerning intermittents, remittents, tertians, quotidians, etc. In certain cutaneous disorders very prevalent in new settlements he was considered to be infallible. . . ." Dr. Todd's surgical skills were perhaps questionable, but then what newly independent physician's were not?

As Cooper noted, Dr. Todd's ". . . reputation was hourly increasing, and, luckily for his patients, his information also." The description of his ministrations to the victim of a gunshot wound vividly pictured a scene that must have been reenacted countless times in the hundred years to follow. Dr. Todd carefully emptied the contents of his saddlebags and surgical case in preparation for dressing the wound. There were various vials filled with radiant colored fluids arranged on the table by the side of "murderous" saws, knives, and scissors, all with due effect of awe and respect from the audience. The doctor then successfully extracted a large shot from his patient's leg.

This scene and the actors in it were typical of nineteenth-century frontier medicine. Dr. Todd's training, or lack of it, and his empirical skills exemplify the large majority of the doctors of a century ago.

The average doctor on the frontier did what he could to ease the many health problems he encountered. (See DISEASES.) But there were a few men whose work won them recognition well beyond their frontier neighbors. Three men especially should be singled out: Ephraim McDowell, William Beaumont, and Daniel Drake. Their work won them worldwide fame because they made important contributions to the advance of medicine. That, in itself, was unusual for American doctors in the first half of the nineteenth century.

Ephraim McDowell (1771-1830) was born in Virginia and received his medical education as an apprentice and in Edinburgh. He set up practice in Danville, Kentucky, a small wilderness town. In 1809 Dr. McDowell was called in consultation to see Mrs. Jane Crawford in Green County, sixty miles from Danville. Her own doctors thought she had a complicated childbirth, but McDowell immediately diagnosed a large ovarian tumor. This diagnosis was virtually a death sentence, for no one had successfully removed such a growth surgically. Left alone, it was sure to cause death in a matter of weeks. Mrs. Crawford agreed to McDowell's proposal for surgical removal, fully aware that it had never been done, yet knowing too it was her only chance.

McDowell preferred to perform the historic operation at his own house with familiar assistance and equipment. The plucky patient was put on a horse supporting her huge abdomen on the horn of her saddle and rode the sixty miles through the Kentucky winter. She was warmly received by Mrs. McDowell and then on Christmas Day, 1809, with a hostile crowd outside the door ready to hang the doctor should he fail in his "experiment," McDowell was set to operate. He did so successfully. His patient was making her own bed five days after surgery and was perfectly well in twenty-five days.

This operation, performed nearly forty years prior to the introduction of anesthesia, was the first of several similar ones carried out by McDowell. He waited seven years to report the feat to the medical world. In 1816 and in 1819, McDowell published articles in a medical journal describing the operation. His surgical skill and his great courage and self-reliance were in the true pioneer spirit.

William Beaumont's pioneer work lay not in a miraculous cure but in a series of careful scientific experiments under crude frontier conditions. Beaumont (1785-1853) was a United States Army surgeon stationed at Mackinac Island, Michigan. In 1822 Alexis St. Martin, a young French-Canadian fur trapper, was shot in the left lower chest, sustaining a large open wound. Beaumont was called to treat him but despaired of saving the poor man's life. With careful dressing and cleansing of the wound, slow healing did take place. The only trace of the injury remaining two years later was an opening from St. Martin's stomach through the chest wall to the outside. In medical terms this is known as a fistula.

Through the fistula Beaumont could observe the lining of the stomach and food being digested. He thus began a long series of careful observations and experiments to study the process of digestion, then imperfectly understood. St. Martin, naturally enough, became impatient with science at times and had to be cajoled, bribed, and brought back after running off, all at great personal expense to Beaumont, who had made him a member of his household.

Finally, after seven years, St. Martin had had enough, and so Beaumont published the results of his experiments on digestion in 1833. The book was well received here and in Europe as an important contribution to medical science. Beaumont identified hydrochloric acid as one of the active chemicals in the digestive process, and he dispelled many misconceptions.

The third of the noteworthy pioneer physicians was Daniel DRAKE (1785-1852). Drake was a major force in the organization of several medical schools on the frontier in Ohio and Kentucky in the first decades of the nineteenth century. He not only lectured to scores of students but wrote for them as well. Drake founded and edited a widely read medical journal in Ohio and wrote several pamphlets and books on medical education, and on cholera and other diseases. Near the close of his illustrious career he traveled thirty thousand miles in the states of the Mississippi River valley, accumulating data for a massive two-volume study of geography and disease in that area. Students of western history are still indebted to Drake for his descriptions of living conditions, dietary habits, sanitation, topography, geology, climate, diseases, and medical practices.

It is difficult, then, to characterize frontier doctors. Some were obviously potential leaders of their profession; many were unschooled empirics who applied what balm they could. But all the men and the very few women who practiced on the western frontier must have been resourceful and hardy, as were their fellow pioneers.

See Richard Dunlop, *Doctors of the American Frontier* (1965); James T. Flexner, *Doctors on Horseback* (1937, reprinted in 1969); Robert F. Karolevitz, *Doctors of the Old West* (1967); and Madge E. Pickard and R. Carlyle Buley, *The Midwest Pioneer: His Ills, Cures, and Doctors.* (1945).—G. H. B.

Dodge, Grenville Mellen (1831-1916). Railroad builder, soldier, and Iowa politician. Dodge was born in Danvers, Massachusetts. After graduation from Norwich University in Vermont in 1851, he completed a survey course in civil and military engineering at Partridge's School in Norwich. Caught up in the excitement of western railroad building, Dodge moved to Illinois and then, in 1853, to Council Bluffs, Iowa, where he became a merchant and railroad construction contractor.

Commissioned a colonel of the Fourth Iowa Regiment after the outbreak of the Civil War, Dodge rose to the rank of major general of volunteers. Although he fought in many important engagements (he was severely wounded at Atlanta in 1864), his main contributions were bridge construction and the rebuilding of several southern railroads for use by the Union army.

In 1866 he became chief engineer for the UNION PACIFIC RAILROAD, the eastern segment of the nation's first transcontinental railroad. He supervised the building of the road until it was completed in 1870, set a construction record of 568 miles in one year, and was instrumental in the designation of Council Bluffs as a division point along the Union Pacific route. Often called a "railroad pathfinder," Dodge was chief engineer for the Texas and Pacific until its failure in the 1873 depression. In the next ten years he built some nine thousand miles of road for the Denver, Texas and Fort Worth and the Denver, Texas and Gulf railroads. Loath to retire, Dodge built railroads in Cuba from the end of the Spanish-American War to 1903. Over the years he had surveyed approximately sixty thousand miles of railroad line in the Midwest, the West, and Cuba.

Always active in the Republican party, Dodge served one term in Congress, in 1867-69; he reportedly refused other political offices or involvement, although his most recent biographer, Stanley P. Hirshson, does emphasize that he had an influential role in the "Des Moines Regency," controller of Iowa's Republican party for many years.

Later in life Dodge was in constant demand as a lecturer on the Civil War and western events and personalities. Dodge's Council Bluffs home, a three-story, fourteen-room mansion reminiscent of many sumptuous late nineteenth-century houses, is a national landmark.

The most recent biography of Dodge is Stanley P. Hirshson, *Grenville M. Dodge: Soldier, Politician, Railroad Pioneer* (1967). J. R. Perkins, *Trails, Rails and War—The Life of General G. M. Dodge* (1929), is the standard work. But Dodge's personality really comes through best in his own reminiscences, *How We Built the Union Pacific*

Railway (1910). The Dodge papers are at Iowa's State Department of History and Archives, Des Moines, and in the Council Bluffs Public Library.—A. M. and D. S.

Dodge, Henry (1782-1867). Wisconsin pioneer and politician. Dodge moved to Missouri with his parents in 1796, becoming a farmer, miner, and politician. He went down the Mississippi to join Aaron Burr's expedition, believed to be aimed at establishing an empire west of the Mississippi, but turned back when he heard that Burr had been arrested. When accused by a Missouri jury of being a participant in the Burr plot, he offered to fight each member singly until the indictment was quashed. He came to the Wisconsin lead region in 1827 and shipped the first pig-lead by flatboat to New Orleans. He led the miners against Red Bird and the Winnebago in 1827 and gained further prominence in the Black Hawk War when he served as colonel of the Iowa County militia. Between 1833 and 1836 he commanded several expeditions on the Plains.

When the Territory of Wisconsin was created in 1836, Dodge was appointed the first territorial governor by the Democratic president. After serving only one term in office, he was elected territorial delegate to Congress. When the Democrats returned to power, he was again appointed governor and was elected United States senator when Wisconsin became a state in 1848. He retired from public life in 1857, living in Burlington, Iowa.

See Louis Pelzer, *Henry Dodge* (1911).—W. D. W.

Dodge City, Kansas. See CATTLE TOWNS.

Dodge City War. See Luke L. SHORT.

Dog Soldiers. See TALL BULL.

Dolores, New Mexico. Ghost town. Dolores, located in the Cerrillos mining district, a few miles south of Santa Fe, became the site of the first gold strike in the present-day United States. In 1832 José Francisco Ortiz discovered the mother lode of the placer deposits and established the Ortiz Mine, one of the oldest lode mines in the country. The boom was short-lived, however, and the town's problems were accentuated by a shortage of water. Thomas Edison tried to solve this problem when he came to Dolores in 1900 and tried unsuccessfully to extract gold from the placer gravel using static electricity. Today little remains of the town, but ghostly relics will be found at the nearby towns of Madrid and Cerrillos.

See Ralph Looney, *Haunted Highways: The Ghost Towns of New Mexico* (1968); and Muriel S. Wolle, *The Bonanza Trail* (1953).—R. B. W.

Dolores Mission. See SAN FRANCISCO DE ASIS.

Donaldson, Thomas C. (1843-1898). Historian. The vade mecum of western historians is Donaldson's *The Public Domain: Its History, with Statistics*. Originally published in 1881, this work was revised and greatly extended for the 1884 edition. Notwithstanding the author's crotchets, Donaldson's experience equipped him admirably for preparing this great work, which is indispensable to students of the history of the West.

Donaldson was born in Columbus, Ohio, graduated from Capital University in his home town, served in the army during the Civil War, was admitted to the bar in 1867, and in 1869 was appointed by President Ulysses S. Grant register of the newly opened land office in Boise, Idaho Territory, where he served six years. There he familiarized himself with the land laws, the commission-

er's instructions, and the court decisions interpreting them, and he experienced pressures exerted by influential miners, stockmen, and lumbermen who expected the register to grant them special favors or to overlook their violations of the land laws.

Although a strongly partisan Radical Republican, Donaldson was close to President Rutherford B. Hayes, as his autobiographical sketch shows, and when Congress authorized the establishment of a Public Land Commission to codify the thirty-five hundred public land statutes, to prepare a land classification system, and to recommend improvements in surveying and ways to assure that the remaining public lands would be held for actual settlers, Donaldson was one of the three presidential appointees. Other members of the commission were J. A. Williamson, commissioner of the General Land Office; Clarence King, head of the United States Geological Survey; John W. Powell, like King an explorer and geologist; and Alexander T. Britton, head of the leading Washington law firm specializing in land law and widely employed by land-grant railroads and other large corporations interested in land cases. Only Donaldson, Williamson, and Britton were familiar with land legislation and the problems of settlers and corporations trying to gain ownership of public lands, and Britton was firmly committed to the "big business" interests he had served and continued to serve after the commission had completed its task.

Williamson, King, and Powell constituted the committee on classification. Because King and Powell were familiar only with the Intermountain West (between the Rockies and the Sierra-Cascade Mountains), the recommendations of the committee were applicable to conditions that existed in that region and not applicable to the higher portion of the Great Plains between the ninety-ninth meridian and the Rocky Mountains.

Britton was responsible for the codification of the land laws and accomplished the task with success.

Donaldson was assigned the task of making a detailed examination of the origins of the public domain, the cost of quieting Indian occupancy rights, and the methods of disposal. He investigated the background of the various land laws and the amount of land that had passed to private ownership under each, traced through the intricate and deeply involved question of private land claims and their adjudication, and presented this information in his great compendium. The first edition of *The Public Domain* was couched in the usual bland language of the government bureaucrat, factual, noncontroversial, and dull. Its comprehensive coverage and the quantity of statistics provided, drawn partly from the annual reports of the commissioner of the General Land Office and partly from compilations prepared especially for inclusion by the staff of the G.L.O, make it a most useful tool and the point of departure for any investigation of public-land policies. In its second edition (1884), *The Public Domain* was more than doubled in length by the inclusion of a vast body of regulations, instructions, forms, blanks and excerpts from reports of the commissioner, and lists of all officers, timber agents, clerks, messengers, and laborers and fifty pages of specimen field notes of surveyors. In this edition Donaldson was much less cautious and in a polemical tone denounced those acts of Congress he regarded as working badly. Donaldson's recommendations for legislation to safeguard the public lands for settlers were on the whole just and were embodied in the preliminary report of the commission, but the coloration he gave them in his expanded work was certain to win no support for them in Congress. For example, his xenophobic distrust of immigrants from southern Europe drove him to charge that they were given preference in the selection of public land.

The intense interest of Powell and King in the Intermountain West tended to concentrate the testimony presented to the commission on this area and the Pacific Coast states. But the region where the greater proportion of land entries was being made and where the abuses of the land laws were most common received little attention. This obvious neglect may be attributed to the desire to avoid the most controversial issues, though it is more likely that it was owing to the deeper interest of Powell, King, and also Donaldson in the mining and grazing areas rather than in the region suitable for farming. However that may be, the recommendations of the commission for the withholding of the remaining arable land for settlers under the Homestead Act, the repeal of the preemption law, the retention of the benefits of the Timber Culture Act solely for homesteaders, classification of the public lands, the elimination of receivers of the land offices who, the commission felt, were wholly unnecessary, the sale of irrigable and forest lands in unlimited amounts and of pasturage (grazing) lands in units of 2,560 acres at gradually reduced prices, the establishment of more safeguards in other laws, and numerous other minor suggestions were all neglected by Congress. Congress was not ready to make any fundamental changes in land policy, notwithstanding the fact that it had created the commission.

Donaldson left an imperishable record of public-land history, though much of it has to be used with care and discrimination. Also interested in Indian culture, Donaldson prepared a 939-page detailed description: *The George Catlin Gallery of the U.S. National Museum.* The memoir has been characterized as a "richly commented catalogue of the paintings, long excerpts and numerous line drawings from Catlin's books." Donaldson became an Expert Special Agent for the Eleventh Census, preparing and editing monographs on the Iroquois of New York, the eastern Cherokee of North Carolina, the Moqui Pueblo Indians of New Mexico, and the Five Civilized Tribes of Indian Territory.

A sketch of Donaldson by Paul W. Gates is in the 1970 printing of *The Public Domain.*—P. W. G.

Donelson's Line (1771). During the course of the negotiations leading to the Treaty of *Lochaber* (1770), the Cherokee Indians indicated a willingness to sell to Virginia all land lying between the Kentucky and Ohio rivers. Since such an extension of colonial territory was counter to the sense of the Proclamation of 1763, which prohibited settlement beyond the Appalachian crest, and to the specific treaty instructions of the British secretary of state, nothing came of it. Many colonial officials, however, felt that such a purchase would be very desirable and set about to persuade the British government to give approval. In the meantime, Colonel John Donelson of Virginia, head of the survey party to mark the Lochaber treaty line, took it upon himself to go ahead and negotiate the sale with the Cherokee representatives accompanying his party. The Cherokee

agreed to a price of £500, and instead of marking the line from Holston River directly to the mouth of the Kanawha River as prescribed in the treaty, Donelson's party turned northwestward across the Powell and Cumberland rivers to the Kentucky River and ran the line down its northern bank to the Ohio. Though Donelson's Line was disavowed by the British government and Virginia failed to pay the promised £500, the episode provided additional impetus for the speculators and settlers who were already pushing across the mountains in defiance of the law.

See J. R. Alden, *John Stuart and the Southern Colonial Frontier, 1754-1775* (1944).—P. R. M.

Doniphan, Alexander William (1808-1887). Lawyer and soldier. Born in Mason County, Kentucky, Doniphan graduated from Augusta College, and in 1830 moved to Missouri to practice law. As a brigadier general of militia he successfully negotiated with Joseph Smith for the disarming and removal of the Mormon colony from Missouri. Doniphan also served in the Missouri state legislature in 1836 and 1840, and again in 1854.

At the outbreak of the Mexican War in 1846, Doniphan, a colorful, redheaded giant of a man, was elected colonel of the First Missouri Mounted Volunteers and marched with General Saplen Watts Kearny's army into New Mexico. In Santa Fe, Doniphan and several others drew up the so-called Kearny Code, which became the basic law of New Mexico. In November he traveled west to Bear Spring, near the present Arizona line, and signed a peace treaty with fourteen Navaho chiefs. On December 14, Doniphan left Valverde on the Rio Grande with five hundred men and a large wagon train to join General John E. Wool in the conquest of Chihuahua. At Brazito, thirty miles north of El Paso, he defeated an army of one thousand two hundred Mexicans and two days later occupied the city. On February 8, 1847, Doniphan headed for the city of Chihuahua with about one thousand men, although he had heard that Wool had abandoned his attempt to invade Chihuahua. Moving south, the Missourians broke through a force of some four thousand Mexicans on the Sacramento River and entered Chihuahua City. The accomplishments of "Doniphan's Thousand," as his men were called, were all the more impressive since Doniphan himself was a casual officer who cared little for military discipline or order. His ragged, individualistic soldiers looked more like a battalion of tramps than a military unit.

Turning east to Saltillo and the coast, Doniphan and his men reached New Orleans in June and were discharged from service. Doniphan resumed his law practice in Missouri and was a delegate to the conference that met in Washington in February 1861 to find a way to avert the drift toward civil war. He served briefly as a Union major general in the Missouri State Guard and died in Richmond, Missouri.

See John T. Hughes, *Doniphan's Expedition* (1962). —H. P. H.

Donnelly, Ignatius (1831-1901). Minnesota third-party politician and writer. Donnelly was one of the most colorful political figures of the country. A native Philadelphian of Irish descent, well educated, ambitious, and a Democrat of the manifest destiny school, Donnelly decided to go west, like so many others, "to grow up with the country." In 1856, after appraising the area, the young lawyer was captivated by the scenic beauties of central Minnesota. He became an enthusiastic townsite promoter and was determined to make Nininger City, located a short distance south of St. Paul, the newest Athens of the West. When his dreams of riches were wiped out in the Panic of 1857, he turned to farming and aligned himself with the growing Republican party. The party's successes soon made the talented young leader lieutenant governor, and, with Governor Alexander Ramsey's sojourn in Washington, he became acting governor as Minnesota mobilized for the Civil War. He served three terms in Congress, from 1863 to 1869.

During this stormy and historically critical tenure he developed a reputation as Minnesota's most genuine Radical Republican. He was a staunch and consistent champion of Negro rights and congressional Reconstruction. He was never a mere agent for special-interest groups, but no less than other legislators in those corrupt times he used his office to obtain special favors and financial rewards for his businessmen constituents. It might be said that he was a minor yet skeptical guest at that "Great Barbecue" that passed for enlightened politics in the Civil War and postwar era, thereby acquiring, at first hand, insights that subsequently put him in the position of knowing exactly what he was agitating against.

In 1868, because of a split in the Minnesota Republican machine that he was unable to reconcile, Donnelly lost his congressional seat. Thereafter, he persuaded himself that the great battle of the future would be "between humanity and property, between men and money." He enlisted at once on the side of humanity and made his first independent fight against the protective tariff. When victory eluded him, he returned to the Republican camp in 1872 as a supporter of Liberal Republicanism under Horace Greeley. That also proved to be a losing cause, but political change was in the wind. On the eve of the great economic collapse of 1873, Donnelly became active in the Minnesota Grange, serving as state lecturer. He persuasively advocated a political course for the supposedly nonpartisan Grange and ulitmately was successful in aligning it with the Anti-Monopoly party, which elected him to the state senate. As a leader of the Anti-Monopoly legislators, Donnelly's successes, in the main, were in the important area of publicizing needed reforms.

The decline of Grangerism and the Anti-Monopoly forces, however, soon caused his return to private life, but not for long. The rise of the Greenback movement after 1875 brought him back into prominence. He dominated the party in Minnesota, was its temporary chairman at the 1876 national convention held in Indianapolis, and polled a large yet losing vote in his bid to return to Congress. In 1878, after a second and more productive term in the state legislature, Donnelly was again a congressional candidate. His Republican opponent won the election, but Donnelly claimed fraud had produced the result. He had a strong case, but the contest he entered prompted a long series of hearings that failed to gain him the seat.

Defeated, dejected, and financially drained, Donnelly retreated to his Nininger farm to write. In 1882 Harper and Brothers published *Atlantis,* his imaginative attempt to prove that Plato's lost continent had actually existed in the Atlantic. The book was an almost instant success and sales skyrocketed. The great popularity of *Atlantis* (Harper's offered a revised edition in 1949) encouraged Donnelly to set to work on another book, *Ragnarok* (1883). This commentary on the origins of the earth, while not as popular in the long run as *Atlantis,* surpassed it in early sales and went through numerous editions.

After his literary triumphs, Donnelly was even more in demand as a lecturer, and his political ambitions were reawakened. In 1884 he waged another unsuccessful campaign for Congress as a reform coalition candidate. But the ever resilient Donnelly would not be denied: by 1886, the Farmers' Alliance was a growing and influential movement in Minnesota and Donnelly was eager to take command. The alliance sent him to the legislature, where he fought his usual fight for reform. But the 1888 election was something of a setback to Donnelly's reform image; in a series of maneuvers, probably explained by his great and enduring ambition to become a United States senator, he accepted the Farmer Labor party's nomination for governor and withdrew only a few weeks before the election, throwing his support to the Republican candidate; to top it all off, he was also a Democratic candidate for the legislature.

Donnelly continued his writing in this period. In 1887 *The Great Cryptogram,* his effort to prove Francis Bacon's supposed authorship of Shakespeare's works, sparked some praise and much controversy. In 1889 he published *Caesar's Column,* his first novel, which provided an apocalyptic view of the future by extending to their logical conclusion what he saw as the current tendencies of his age—tendencies that culminated in a brutal anti-Utopian society in the year 1988. The novel also contained Donnelly's comprehensive assessment of the ills of late-nineteenth-century society and sounded an alarm that caught the ear of many of his contemporaries. Donnelly followed *Caesar's Column* with *Doctor Huguet* (1891) and *The Golden Bottle* (1892). Neither equaled the phenomenal success of *Caesar's Column,* but, historically, they were as important. *Doctor Huguet* stands as the most sympathetic and imaginative novel written in the period about the plight of Negro Americans. *The Golden Bottle* is a political tract "intended to explain and defend in the thin disguise of a story, some of the ideas put forth by the People's party."

By 1890 the combative, versatile, and magnetic Donnelly was more than ready to lead the Populist movement. He relished nothing more than a righteous cause. Having battled slavery as a Republican, the corporations as an Anti-Monopolist and an Independent, and the "money power" as a Greenbacker, he sensed in Populism the coming Armageddon. As president of the state Farmers' Alliance, legislator, candidate for governor, lecturer and propagandist, Donnelly contributed much color, talent, and drive to Populism. He applied the rhetoric of *Caesar's Column* to the preamble of the Omaha platform (see POPULISM), creating a stinging indictment of American society that became an inspiration to thousands of disenchanted citizens. Today, the image of Donnelly as a flamboyant and wildly speculative writer is stronger than that of Donnelly as a reform politician; in his own time, the picture struck a better balance. By 1901, the year of his death, his name had become "a synonym for reform," and rightly so, for in his political activities as in *Caesar's Column* he "had virtually taken off the skin and exposed the bare bones of what he felt to be the false American credo which placed its trust in progress through technology, laissez faire, and Social Darwinism."

Martin Ridge, *Ignatius Donnelly: The Portrait of a Politician* (1962), is the most authoritative work on Donnelly's life. Richard Hofstadter, *The Age of Reform* (1955), provides a critical interpretation, suggesting various illiberal strains in Donnelly's thought. For an antidote, see Norman Pollack, "Ignatius Donnelly on Human Rights: A Study of Two Novels," *Mid-America* (April 1965).
—O. G. C.

Donner Party. Ill-fated emigrant expedition. Of all the parties of California-bound settlers who braved the physical hardships of the westward trek, none was less fortunate than the Donner Party. In terms of sheer tragedy, few incidents in the history of the West surpass the story of this group of eighty-nine emigrants who headed their wagons westward in the summer of 1846.

The party was organized in Springfield, Illinois, and was led by two wealthy brothers, Jacob and George Donner. The Donners had read the *Emigrant's Guide to Oregon and California* by Lansford W. HASTINGS, and they decided to follow the author's advice and leave the regular California Trail at Fort Bridger, "thence bearing west southwest, to the Salt Lake; and thence continuing down to the Bay of St. Francisco." Hastings humbly named the new route "Hastings Cutoff," and he and his longtime partner James Hudspeth set up shop at Fort Bridger, offering to lead settlers along his self-proclaimed shortcut, later named the DONNER TRAIL.

The Donners were the third group of travelers to unwittingly place themselves under Hastings' guidance. When they arrived at Fort Bridger on August 3, 1846, the party learned that the author-adventurer was leading another party westward, but he had left word that he would mark the trail for them. Thus reassured, they headed southwest, following Hastings' trail to the head of Weber Canyon. Here they suffered the first of many fateful delays. Hastings had left a note on a forked stick at the head of the canyon, asking them to wait until he could show them a better route through the Wasatch Range. They waited for eight days and then decided to send a messenger to find Hastings. The messenger returned without Hastings but with instructions to follow another trail, which proved to be virtually impassable. After pushing their way past innumerable boulders, the party arrived in the valley south of the Great Salt Lake, having already wasted about eighteen valuable days.

It then took the Donner Party six days to cross the desert—a journey that Hastings had estimated would take two days. Most of the valuables that the settlers had brought from Illinois were left buried in the sand, along with four wagons and most of the livestock. Two men were sent ahead to bring back food from California, and the rest of the party struggled onward to the base of the Sierra. At this point the emigrants were exhausted both physically and emotionally. From the outset they had been plagued by quarreling and petty jealousies. John Reed, one of the leaders of the party, settled one argument by stabbing a man to death. Reed was banished on the desert, leaving his wife and five children to continue on alone.

On October 19 one of the men returned from Sutter's Fort with five mules laden with supplies and two Indian guides, and on October 23 the pioneers began the long climb over the mountains. Five days later they camped near a lake high in the mountains and looked forward to the final push through the pass and into the valley. That night, however, the first storm of the winter struck, a month early. By daylight the ground was covered with snow, the pass was blocked, and the Donner Party was snowbound in the high Sierra.

The panic-stricken emigrants hurriedly fashioned tents out of wagon canvas and huddled together to brave the winter cold. By the middle of December it was obvious that someone must go for help, or the whole party would perish from hunger. Fifteen of the strongest survivors (eight men, five women, and the two Indian guides) volunteered to attempt to reach civilization. They left on December 16 with six days' rations on what was to be a thirty-two-day ordeal by hunger.

On Christmas night the "Forlorn Hope," as the fifteen volunteers were called, was hit by a violent storm, and two days later four members of the band were dead. The survivors "stripped the flesh from their bones, roasted and ate it, averting their eyes from each other, and weeping." The remaining flesh was carefully packed and labeled so that no one would eat his kindred, and the band moved on. Two more men died, and the two Indians, who refused to touch human flesh, were shot and eaten. Finally, the seven survivors stumbled into an Indian village on January 10, 1847.

The first of several rescue parties reached the lake camp on February 19, and others followed until all the survivors were brought down the mountains. The main body of the pioneers had suffered as much as the Forlorn Hope. Many had died, and hunger had driven them to cannibalism as a last resort. Of the eighty-nine emigrants who set out from Fort Bridger, only forty-five survived the ordeals of the journey.

See Ray A. Billington, *The Far Western Frontier* (1956); and George R. Stewart, *Ordeal by Hunger* (1936).
—R. B. W.

Donner Trail. The Donner Trail is the name given the route to California taken by the DONNER PARTY in the fall and winter of 1846-47. The trail was the product of the fertile imagination of Lansford W. HASTINGS, a somewhat irresponsible author-adventurer who sought to direct the emigrant traffic away from Oregon and into the Sacramento valley by means of a shortcut he labeled "Hastings Cutoff." Hastings figured that his new route would reduce the traveling time to California to 120 days and the distance to 2,100 miles.

This trail differed from the older California Trail in one fundamental respect. Instead of looping northward over the Great Salt Lake toward Fort Hall and Oregon and then back southwest to the Humboldt River, the Donner Trail proceeded southwest from Fort Bridger, through the Wasatch Range and *south* of the Great Salt Lake until it reached the Humboldt River. From Humboldt Sink (a large lake in western Nevada that receives the waters of the Humboldt River) the trail followed the Truckee River to the foot of the Sierra and up the mountains through the narrow canyon of the Truckee. About two thousand feet from the summit of Donner Pass is Donner Lake, where the Donner Party was snowbound in October 1846. The trail then continued through the pass and down the mountains to Sutter's Fort in the Sacramento valley.

Though the Donner Trail appeared on paper to be just the shortcut that California emigrants were looking for, many pioneers discovered that Hastings had lightly discounted the hardships of "burning deserts and towering mountains" in his glowing account of the route. Legend has it that the blue haze that rests on the Utah foothills is the last remnant of the curses against Hastings that the emigrants scattered along the trail.

See Ray A. Billington, *The Far Western Frontier* (1956); and George R. Stewart, *Ordeal by Hunger* (1936). —R. B. W.

Dorsey, James Owen (1848-1895). Missionary and ethnologist. Dorsey was born in Baltimore, Maryland. He taught himself the Hebrew alphabet at the age of six and was literate in Hebrew four years later. After attending the Protestant Episcopal Theological Seminary in Alexandria, Virginia, he was ordained a deacon of the Episcopal Church in 1871.

Dorsey's first missionary assignment was among the Ponca Indians in Dakota Territory. In two years he learned to speak Ponca, but illness forced his return to Maryland. In 1878, under the direction of Major John W. Powell, he returned to the West, this time to the Omaha reservation in Nebraska. He gathered linguistic and ethnographic data there until 1880. He was hired as a permanent member of the Bureau of American Ethnology staff when Powell organized the bureau in 1879.

After 1880 Dorsey worked among various Siouan-speaking groups, expanding his efforts to include studies of Athapaskan languages as well. At the time of his death, he was one of America's leading linguists and the acknowledged authority on the Ponca, Osage, and Omaha tribes. His *Osage Traditions* (1888), *Siouan Sociology* (1897), and *Omaha Sociology* (1884) continue to be among the classic published works on these subjects.

See J. N. B. Hewitt, "James Owen Dorsey," *American Anthropologist*, vol. 8 (1895).—B. L. F.

Dorsey, Stephen Wallace (1842-1916). Arkansas politician. A resident of Ohio, Dorsey served as a captain in the Union army. He moved to Arkansas during Reconstruction as president of the Arkansas Central Railway Company. He joined the Republican party and went to the United States Senate in 1873, serving one term. He allegedly made fraudulent use of Arkansas railroad construction bonds, which the state later repudiated. He represented Arkansas in 1880 on the Republican National Committee and conducted James A. Garfield's presidential campaign, though he never returned to Arkansas after his Senate term ended. A speculator in the Star Route mail service, he and others were indicted in 1881 for conspiracy to defraud the federal government of a half million dollars. Acquitted, Dorsey thereafter ranched in New Mexico, invested in Colorado mining, and in about 1901 moved to California.—W. L. B.

Doty, James Duane (1799-1865). Politician. Doty came to Detroit from his home town of Salem, New York, in 1818. He was secretary to the exploratory expedition of Michigan led by Governor Lewis Cass in 1820 and judge of the region between Mackinac, Michigan, and the Mississippi River (1823-32). He next served in the Michigan territorial legislature (1833-35) and was a delegate to Congress from Wisconsin Territory (1838-

41). In 1829 he had laid out the townsite of Madison, Wisconsin, and by giving lots to members of the Wisconsin territorial legislature at the first meeting at Belmont, affected the decision to choose Madison as the capital. As a Whig, he was governor of Wisconsin (1841-44) and congressman (1849-53). President Lincoln appointed him superintendent of Indian affairs in Utah Territory in 1861, where he also was governor for a term and where he died.

See A. E. Smith, *James Duane Doty* (1954).—W. D. W.

Douglas, Stephen A[rnold] (1813-1861). Politician. Douglas, though born in Vermont, became congressman and then senator from Illinois and a presidential candidate in 1860. His career was intimately involved with the West and the events that preceded the Civil War. As chairman of first the House and then the Senate Committee on Territories, Douglas was a vigorous exponent of westward expansion and development. His efforts to deal with slavery in the West, however, had national consequences that transcended the interests of a single section.

Above all, Douglas was a fierce nationalist who loved the Union. His career was dedicated to preserving the Union from sectional conflict and to expanding its boundaries. Douglas believed that the American republic served the world as an experiment in democracy and had a mission to spread liberty in the world. The country would do that by increasing its physical size and applying to the new areas the institutions of American democracy. Among these, he considered the most essential to be the right of people in a specific locality or state to self-determination in choosing their institutions. Thus Douglas was an advocate of continental manifest destiny. Once areas were annexed to the United States, he favored the quick organization of territorial governments to promote their rapid settlement. Westward expansion would not only extend democracy but also divert attention in the older sections from the slavery question. Fearful of possible disunion, Douglas hoped development of the West would absorb the energies of both the North and the South, and the West, once settled, would balance those older sections and prevent disunion. Hand-in-hand with expansionism in Douglas' thinking went popular sovereignty—that is, local self-determination on the slavery question. Not only was a local decision essential to democracy, but it was also a compromise solution to the problem of slavery in the territories. Douglas regarded the sectional split over slavery expansion as the chief impediment to westward expansion, and popular sovereignty as a compromise seemed the best way to remove that obstacle. Equally important, by letting the people in the territories decide on slavery, it removed from Congress an explosive issue and thus strengthened the Union, a goal that was also a purpose of expansion itself.

These principles shaped much of Douglas' career. He favored all kinds of measures to speed up the organization and settlement of new areas, such as liberal immigration laws, easy terms for the purchase of lands, protection from the Indians, and federal aid to railroads. In 1844 Douglas spoke in the House in favor of the annexation of Texas, and in 1846 he demanded all of Oregon even though acquisition of the whole territory might produce war with England. In the Senate after 1846, Douglas backed President James K. Polk's Mexican War policy and opposed the Wilmot Proviso because it might have prevented the possibility of territorial cession from Mexico. In 1849, even before Henry Clay introduced his compromise plan for dealing with slavery expansion in the West, Douglas proposed admitting California as a free state and organizing the other territories with popular sovereignty. Douglas eventually backed Clay's plan, but it was his astute leadership in the Senate and behind the scenes in the House and his breaking up of the omnibus bill, not Whig rhetoric, that was primarily responsible for the passage of the Compromise of 1850. Douglas' concern for western development was also evident in his successful fight that year to secure federal land grants for the Illinois Central Railroad, which was to run from Chicago to the Gulf of Mexico. In the early 1850s Douglas sought land grants for a Pacific railroad with branches to St. Louis and Chicago, and he also advocated a homestead act.

Douglas' principles also help explain his introduction of the Kansas-Nebraska Act, the most controversial and divisive issue of the 1850s (see KANSAS-NEBRASKA ISSUE). His motives were complex, but, among other things, he was interested in removing Indians from the Platte region, encouraging "a continuous line of settlements to the Pacific Ocean," and building a railroad through the region to the Pacific. Recognizing the need for southern support to organize any such territory, which he fully expected to be free of slaves because of climate, Douglas included in his original Nebraska bill of January 4, 1854, a provision that states formed out of the territory could enter the Union "with or without slavery, as their constitution may prescribe at the time of admission." Douglas thought the Missouri Compromise ban on slavery in that area would apply in the territorial phase, but because of southern pressure and political maneuvers he was forced to amend his bill. In short, Douglas was not responsible for the final Kansas-Nebraska Act, which organized two territories, repealed the Missouri Compromise, and applied popular sovereignty to those territories, although it left vague at what time settlers could make the decision. Though not responsible for it, Douglas vigorously defended the act when it later came under attack.

His defense continued when events in Washington and Kansas threatened to make a shambles of the doctrine of popular sovereignty. When the Supreme Court ruled in the Dred Scott decision of 1857 that Congress could not prohibit slavery from a territory, Republicans argued that the decision meant no territorial legislature could do it either. In defense of local self-determination, Douglas replied that a legislature could prohibit slavery simply by refusing to pass a positive slave code protecting slavery in the territory, an argument that became the famous Freeport Doctrine in his debates with Lincoln the following year. Similarly, when President James Buchanan tried to make Congress approve Kansas' Lecompton constitution, even though a majority of settlers opposed it, Douglas broke with Buchanan and denounced the constitution as a denial of self-rule by a local majority. Douglas' interpretation of the impact of the Dred Scott decision on popular sovereignty and his opposition to Lecompton alienated southerners and ruined his chances of leading a united Democratic party in the presidential election of 1860. Nevertheless, he continued to struggle to preserve the Union. He was willing to sacrifice popular sovereignty in the 1860 platform to keep the party together. When that failed and he had the nomination of the northern half, he campaigned vigorously in the South in an effort to prevent secession if Abraham Lincoln won.

Douglas died in 1861 after touring the Northwest to rally Democrats there to the cause of the Union once the Civil War had actually started. The compromise he had advanced so energetically had failed to hold the country together.

Harry V. Jaffa, *The Crisis of the House Divided: An Interpretation of the Issues in the Lincoln-Douglas Debates* (1959), contains a superior analysis of Douglas' philosophy. Gerald M. Capers, *Stephen A. Douglas: Defender of the Union* (1959), is an able biography. Douglas' role in the Compromise of 1850 and in the Kansas-Nebraska Act is described in Holman Hamilton, *Prologue to Conflict: The Crisis and Compromise of 1850* (1964); and Roy Franklin Nichols, "The Kansas-Nebraska Act: A Century of Historiography," *Mississippi Valley Historical Review*, vol. 43 (1956). A recent major biography is Robert W. Johanssen, *Stephen A. Douglas* (1973).—M. F. H.

Douglas family. Arizona businessmen. *James* (1837-1918), a metallurgist, mining engineer, and industrialist, was born in Quebec, Canada, and attended Queens University in Ontario, the University of Edinburgh, and medical school at Laval University. While a chemistry professor at Morrin College, Douglas and Professor T. Sterry Hunt worked out a leaching process for treating low-grade ores, which Douglas later employed while superintendent of the Chemical Copper Company at Phoenixville, Pennsylvania. When a fire destroyed the plant there, Douglas became a mining consultant. He inspected the Jerome copper properties in Arizona for Philadelphia investors, and the Morenci and Bisbee mines for Phelps Dodge and Company, New York metal dealers. In 1885 Phelps Dodge organized the Copper Queen Consolidated Mining Company at Bisbee and made Douglas president; from 1908 to 1916, he served as president of Phelps Dodge. Still a Canadian citizen at his death, James Douglas was widely honored by the mining profession. As a student of Canadian history, he published *Old France in the New World* (1905) and several other books. Douglas, Arizona, was named for him.

James Stuart (1868-1948), son of James Douglas, was a mine owner and banker. "Rawhide Jimmy" Douglas was born at Copper Camp, Quebec Province. He was superintendent of the Commercial Mining Company, a Phelps Dodge subsidiary at Prescott, Arizona; became a naturalized citizen o; the United States in 1896; founded the town of Douglas; and organized banks in Bisbee and Douglas. He managed various mining and railroad interests in Sonora and by 1916 had opened the rich United Verde Extension Copper Mine near Jerome. Douglas served as an American Red Cross official during World War I. He retired in 1938 and resumed his Canadian citizenship.

Walter (1870-1946), a mining engineer and industrialist, and brother of James S. Douglas, was born in Quebec. He attended the Royal Military College in Kingston, Canada; was superintendent of the Commercial Mining Company at Prescott; and became general manager of the Copper Queen by 1900. In 1916 he succeeded his father, James Douglas, as president of the

Phelps Dodge Corporation and the following year played a principal role in the deportation of striking miners at Bisbee. Douglas became a naturalized citizen of the United States in 1913 and retired in 1930.

Lewis William (1894-1974), a politician, ambassador, and banker, and son of James S. Douglas, was born in Bisbee, Arizona, graduated from Amherst College, and during World War I served in France as an artillery lieutenant. Douglas then was a history instructor at Amherst, worked in his father's mines at Jerome, and beginning in 1922 was in the Arizona legislature for two terms. In 1926 he was elected Arizona's single congressman, held that position for several terms, and in1933 briefly was director of the budget under President Franklin D. Roosevelt. A government official during World War II, Douglas was ambassador to the Court of St. James's from 1947 to 1950. Lewis Douglas then settled in Tucson to become a bank executive.

See Douglas D. Martin, "The Douglas Family of Arizona," a typescript in Special Collections, University of Arizona Library, Tucson.—H. P. H.

Dousman, Hercules Louis (1800-1868). Wisconsin pioneer. Dousman was born in Mackinac Island, Michigan and became a clerk in John Jacob Astor's American Fur Company, serving at Prairie du Chien, Wisconsin (1824-34). He traded with the Chippewa and Winnebago, and then became a stockholder in the reorganized American Fur Company under Ramsey Crooks. In 1843 he transferred his trade to the Pierre Chouteau Company, became a partner, and in 1844 built Villa Louis, a large mansion at Prairie du Chien. In 1844 he married the widow of Joseph Rolette, an influential fur trader, and this increased his influence among the Indians. He owned extensive lands in the Chippewa valley and was the principal owner of the sawmill operated there by Jean Brunet. During the 1850s he was owner of five steamboats carrying immigrants to the upper Mississippi River ports and had interests in other lines. The first Wisconsin railroad to reach the Mississippi, which became the Milwaukee and Prairie du Chien, was promoted by Dousman. He spent his last years on his large estate at Villa Louis, now preserved by the State Historical Society of Wisconsin.

See A. Derleth, *House on the Mound* (1958); and P. L. Scanlan, *Prairie du Chien* (1967).—W. D. W.

Downieville, California. Ghost town. Located in the heart of the rugged Yuba River mining country, Downieville is one of the most picturesque of the old goldrush towns. The town sprang up in 1849 and flourished throughout the 1850s as the center for nearby camps. Although the town was twice destroyed by fire, many of the old buildings still remain. Of particular interest are the Sierra County Museum and the *Mountain Messenger*, a newspaper that has been published continuously since 1853.

See Remi Nadeau, *Ghost Towns and Mining Camps of California* (1965).—R. B. W.

Dozier, Edward P. (1916-1971). Anthropologist. A native-born speaker of Tewa from Santa Clara Pueblo, New Mexico, Dozier became to the Pueblo Indians what another native American, Francis La Flesche, had been to the Omaha and Osage: a sympathetic, sophisticated, and objective observer of his own people. Dozier was the son of a Tewa mother and French-American father. He grew up as an Indian, speaking only Tewa and Spanish until he was twelve. While attending the University of

New Mexico in the late 1930s, he met W. W. Hill, an anthropologist, and became Hill's interpreter at Santa Clara.

After serving with a Pacific bomber squadron during World War II, Dozier graduated from the University of New Mexico in 1947. In 1952 he became the first American Indian to receive a Ph.D. degree in anthropology. His dissertation at the University of California at Los Angeles was published in 1954 as *The Hopi-Tewa of Arizona*.

Although Dozier later worked with the Kalinga peoples in the Philippine Islands, his real lifework was in promoting understanding of native peoples of the Southwest, particularly the Pueblo Indians. Most of his more than eighty publications were on that subject. His *The Pueblo Indians of North America* (1970) was published shortly before he died, while he was teaching anthropology at the University of Arizona.

See Fred Eggan and Keith Basso, "Edward P. Dozier, 1916-1971," *American Anthropologist*, vol. 74 (1972).—B. L. F.

Dragging Canoe (Tsiyu-Gûnsíni) (1750-1792). Cherokee chief. Dragging Canoe was the son of the famous Cherokee chief Attakullakulla (called "Little Carpenter" by whites). He was a member of the Overhill Cherokee division, and was one of three major chiefs present when Richard Henderson and his partners negotiated the Treaty of Sycamore Shoals (1775). Because Dragging Canoe disapproved bitterly of the sale of Cherokee hunting lands and felt his people would not get sufficient pay for them, he threw the treaty council into an uproar, caused a delay in negotiations, and held out against agreeing to the treaty, informing Henderson that the Kentucky country would be a "dark and bloody ground." Dragging Canoe also played an active role in general Cherokee resistance to white invasion of the Tennessee valley, was especially active in the attacks in 1776 on the Watauga settlements, and led those Cherokee who espoused the side of the British during the American Revolution.

Dragging Canoe and his followers established a village on Chickamauga Creek near present Chattanooga, and became known as the Chickamauga Cherokee. From this base they carried out bitter raids on frontier outposts until their village was destroyed by Sevier and Campbell's attack in 1782. They then moved farther down the Tennessee River and established what were afterward known as the "Five Lower Towns." Aided by recruits from the Creek, Shawnee, and white Tories, they continued to attack American settlements. In 1784 these towns were also destroyed, and Dragging Canoe made a reluctant peace.

Dragging Canoe is mentioned in accounts of the Creek War (1813-14) as one of the Cherokee chiefs who allied with Andrew Jackson's campaign and participated in the climactic battle at Horseshoe Bend.

See John P. Brown, *Old Frontiers* (1938); Carl S. Driver, *John Sevier, Pioneer of the Old Southwest* (1932); F. W. Hodge, ed., *Handbook of American Indians North of Mexico*, 2 vols. (1907-10); William Stewart Lester, *The Transylvania Colony* (1935); and J. G. M. Ramsey, *The Annals of Tennessee* (1853).—T. D. C.

Drago, Harry Sinclair (1888-   ). Writer and historian. Drago began his professional writing career in Ohio as a cub reporter for the Toledo *Bee*. Two years later he moved to New York and became an all-around handyman in a small publishing house. Concluding that he could probably turn out better books than those submitted to his employer, he began to write. His first book, *Out of the Silent North* (1923), was an immediate hit. Within weeks, he had sold the magazine, book, and motion-picture rights.

During the next two decades, Drago became one of the most prolific fiction writers in America's history, rivaling Frederick Faust (Max Brand) and Zane Grey. Altogether, Drago wrote about one hundred novels under either his own name or various pen names, such as Bliss Lomax, Will Ermine, Stewart Cross, J. Wesley Putnam, Kirk Deming, and Grant Sinclair. Among these many novels were such early favorites as *Smoke of the 45* (1923), *Following the Grass* (1924), and *Rio Rita* (1929), as well as the thriller *Apache Crossing* (1950) and *Appointment on the Yellowstone* (1959). Despite this flow of fiction, Drago managed to spend five years in Hollywood as a film writer, and even found time to explore the West.

Encouraged by publisher Clarkson Potter, a fellow member of the New York Posse of the Westerners, an international organization of western-history buffs, Drago turned his attention to western history. His first historical piece, *Wild, Wooly and Wicked* (1960), won the Buffalo Award for best western book of the year. After 1960 he was a major contributor to America's written record of the West, writing such well-known books as *Red River Valley* (1962); *Great American Cattle Trails* (1966); *Lost Bonanzas* (1966), describing lost mines of the West; *Notorious Ladies of the Frontier* (1969); and *The Great Range Wars* (1970).—J. C. D.

Drake, Daniel (1785-1852). Doctor and educator. Drake was born of Scottish ancestry in Westfield, New Jersey. He was a precocious child who learned to do many things before he was five years of age. Before his third birthday his parents moved out to the Kentucky frontier. Traveling down the Ohio River with the Drake party were the families of the Reverend John Gano and Dr. William Goforth. The Drakes landed at Limestone, Kentucky, in June 1788 and moved south to lands near Mays Lick. Here they began life as pioneers on the raw frontier and with the meagerest sort of domestic equipment. Late in life, Drake was to describe this pioneer life for his children in a classic set of letters.

After twelve years of life in the frontier settlements at Mays Lick, fifteen-year-old Drake began the study of medicine under the tutelage of Dr. William Goforth in Cincinnati, Ohio. Seven years later he began an independent practice of medicine in that city. Dr. Drake became more than a physician, for like Dr. Goforth, he had broad cultural and scientific interests. He quickly became a leading figure in every movement for the improvement of Cincinnati. Sir William Osler said of him that he "founded nearly everything that is old and good in Cincinnati." This included the founding of a library, the beginning of schools, and museums.

In January 1817 Drake was elected to the medical faculty of the Transylvania Medical School in Lexington, Kentucky, and that fall he began teaching. There was bitter dissension in the Transylvania medical faculty, and Drake did not escape involvement in it. As a result he resigned his professorship in 1818, an act that stirred the wrath of crusty and selfish Dr. Benjamin W.

Dudley and resulted in a duel between Dudley and Dr. William Richardson.

Drake returned to Cincinnati, where he once again became active in public affairs, organizing a museum society, lecturing on mineralogy and conservation, and joining learned societies. A popular class in botany that he organized helped to begin the organization of both Cincinnati College and the Medical College of Ohio. The latter, however, was involved from the outset in a thoroughgoing western fight among the local doctors, in which Drake was a central figure. In 1820 Drake at last organized a faculty and began holding classes in November of that year. He was advanced in his thinking and planning for medical training, advocating among other things the use of a hospital as an adjunct to medical training.

In February 1823 Drake was again elected to the staff of the Transylvania Medical School and remained there for four years, during the golden age of Horace Holley's presidency. He resigned when Holley was forced out of the university. Between 1827 and 1839 Drake was back in Cincinnati. In the latter year he accepted a teaching position in the medical school in Louisville.

Despite the fact that Drake engaged in all sorts of public activities, which ranged from the founding of schools to the promotion of railroads, his most lasting contributions were his monumental *Principal Diseases of the Interior Valley of North America* (1850) and his twenty-two-year editorship of the *Western Journal of Medicine and Surgery*.

See Daniel Drake, *Pioneer Life in Kentucky,* ed. by E. F. Horine (1948); and Emmet Field Horine, *Daniel Drake, 1785-1852: Pioneer Physician of the Midwest* (1961). —T. D. C.

Draper, Lyman Copeland (1815-1891). Collector and writer. Draper was born in Erie County, New York, and attended Granville College in Ohio for two years. He became interested in the frontier and began to collect biographical material about the leaders of the westward advance into the Mississippi valley. Aided by Peter A. Remsen, husband of a cousin, he roamed the Allegheny region, Mississippi, and Alabama, interviewing old settlers and collecting their reminiscences and manuscripts. After moving to Madison, Wisconsin, in 1852, he became corresponding secretary of the State Historical Society (1854-86) and state superintendent of public instruction (1858-59).

Draper wrote *King's Mountain and Its Heroes* (1881), which recounted the role of frontiersmen in the American Revolution, and *The Helping Hand* (1870), a practical book on farming and household management. His chief contribution was bringing together his personal collection of 478 volumes of pioneer reminiscences and associated materials to form the nucleus of the frontier manuscripts of the State Historical Society of Wisconsin. This collection became one of the largest in the nation bearing on the trans-Appalachian and midwestern frontiers.

See W. B. Hesseltine, *Pioneer's Mission* (1954). —W. D. W.

Drexel, Katherine (1858-1955). Roman Catholic philanthropist and missionary. Born in Philadelphia, Drexel spent twelve million dollars of her family fortune for Indian missions and the betterment of Negroes, establishing Xavier University (for Negroes) in New Orleans in 1915. In all, she established fifty institutions. As a nun she founded the missionary Sisters of Blessed Sacrament.

See Katherine Burton, *The Golden Door: The Life of Katherine Drexel* (1957).—R. I. B.

dry farming. Dry farming originated in the late nineteenth century in the Great Plains, where men sought to farm a region that had little moisture. Dry farming involves the conservation of soil moisture during dry weather by special methods of tillage. It is important to note that dry farming is not farming *without* moisture, but rather the cultivation of certain crops where there is a minimum of moisture. Farming in regions that average eight to twenty inches of annual rainfall is necessarily dry farming. Dry farming is practiced in America west of the one hundredth meridian to the Pacific Coast, except in areas of greater moisture, on irrigated lands, and in the deserts.

Dry farming in the United States began when settlers found it necessary to push westward into the dry uplands of the Great Plains, away from streams and readily available water. A Californian, Professor E. W. Hilgard, did experiments on the fertility of arid soil and demonstrated the need for deep and frequent plowing in order to use this soil, a practice which is the basic principle of dry farming.

The first large-scale success with dry farming was in Utah. At first the Mormons irrigated the dry soil, but soon all the irrigable land was taken up and demands on the available water supply were increasing. Attempts were made to grow crops without irrigation on lands that had earlier been irrigated, but these failed because occasional irrigation ruined the soil for dry farming. Finally, when Bear River City was settled, the farmers, according to Walter Prescott Webb, simply "swung their plows into the hopeless sagebrush lands, planted their wheat, waited, watered, and prayed." Much to their surprise the plants sprouted and survived. The first victory for dry farming had been won.

Nebraska became the center of developments in dry farming in the Great Plains. It was here that the great evangelist of dry farming, Hardy W. Campbell, lived and did his work. To Nebraskans, Campbell was to farming what William Jennings Bryan, his contemporary, was to politics. Both were seen as men fighting to better the hard lot of the Great Plains pioneers.

The principles of dry farming are simple, although its practice varies in different sections of the country. Both the irrigator and the dry farmer attempt to store up water for use in time of drought. The difference is that the irrigator stores the water in reservoirs, while the dry farmer stores the water in the soil itself, just beneath the growing plants.

The dry farmer uses capillary water—water that surrounds the soil grains and supplies moisture to the growing plants. The amount of water in a given area depends in part on the texture of the soil; the finer the soil particles, the greater the capacity for holding water. Therefore the first essential of dry farming is to select soil of the right texture, preferably a sandy loam. This land is then plowed deeply so as to break up the soil particles and increase the capacity for capillary water. Thus a reservoir is formed in the deep soil bed.

Under the abuse of the hot sun and winds of the Plains this water would evaporate rapidly under normal conditions. To prevent this, the dry farmer packs the top layer of soil into a blanket called the dust mulch. This dust mulch acts much like a cork in a jug, preventing the moisture from passing out of the soil into the air.

In order to maintain the capacity of his subsoil reservoir, the dry farmer must cultivate his land after every rain, not only while the crops are growing, but also before they are planted. Cultivation keeps the soil loose so that as much water as possible is absorbed and stored. Stirring up the soil also prevents the moisture already in the soil from escaping and protects the land from the constant blowing of strong winds.

In dry-farming areas a rain is followed by a flurry of activity on the part of the farmer. The soil must be cultivated within twenty-four to forty-eight hours; a few days of neglect can result in untold damage as the soil becomes too hard to break up.

Successful dry farming requires big machines, strong horsepower, and rapid work. For this reason farming on the Great Plains is done on a much larger scale than elsewhere. Extensive acreage is necessary to compensate for losses from drought; this called for the development of improved machinery with increased power in order to accomplish a great deal of work rapidly. Without the industrial revolution, dry farming on a large scale would have been impossible.

Along with dry farming went the process of crop adaptation. It was necessary not only to find means of preserving water but also to find crops that needed relatively little water. Wheat is the leading dry-farm crop, especially in the northern section of the arid region. Russia probably has developed more dry-farm crops than any other country. In the southwestern United States the sorghums have proved the most successful, particularly as a forage crop.

When it was first introduced, dry farming was heralded as a panacea for all the ills of the arid Great Plains. Like many other phases of development in the West, it suffered from the overemphasis and misrepresentation of land speculators. Government agents warned farmers about the shortcomings of dry farming, but it was not until the 1890s that prairie farmers realized that this was not a cure-all but simply another possible alternative in their search for water.

See Gilbert C. Fite, *The Farmers' Frontier, 1865-1900* (1966); and Walter Prescott Webb, *The Great Plains* (1959).—R. B. W.

Dubois, Fred Thomas (1851-1930). Idaho politician. Dubois, the son of a prominent Illinois attorney general, graduated from Yale in 1872 and went to Idaho in 1880, settling in Blackfoot. As United States marshal (1882-86), he searched for Mormon polygamists with unparalleled diligence and revived the Independent Anti-Mormon party of Oneida County in 1884. His legislative followers succeeded in disfranchising all the Mormons, who voted in a bloc for Democrats, so that Dubois could be elected to Congress in 1886 as a Republican. By 1888 he managed to persuade Congress to reject a scheme to divide Idaho between Nevada and Washington and led the bipartisan effort to secure Idaho's admission as a state in 1890.

Dubois was elected United States senator in 1890 and became a national leader of the Silver Republican party in 1896. Although he could not assemble a combine of Silver Republicans, Democrats, and Populists to ensure reelection to the Senate in 1896, he nearly won anyway. During the Spanish-American War he emerged as a prominent anti-imperialist. In 1900 he managed to ally with the Democrats opposed to Democratic governor Frank Steunenberg, take over the Idaho Democratic party, and obtain another Senate term even though officially he still was a Silver Republican. At this point he became a Democrat but supported Republican president Theodore Roosevelt on progressive domestic issues, such as conservation. An ill-advised revival of anti-Mormonism from 1904 to 1908 (at a time when the Mormons could vote again) led to his 1906 defeat for reelection to the Senate and split Idaho's Democratic party once again.

Not embarrassed by his loss of control of the Idaho party organization, Dubois retained his national prominence, managing Champ Clark's national campaign for the Democratic presidential nomination in 1912. Clark had a majority of the convention delegates, but needed a two-thirds vote for nomination. Dubois once again showed his political flexibility by attempting to bring his old friend William Jennings Bryan into a combination with Tammany to get the necessary margin for Clark. After Woodrow Wilson was nominated and elected, Dubois was Wilson's campaign manager for the western states in 1916. In 1918 he persuaded Wilson quietly to endorse William E. Borah, a Republican, for reelection to the Senate in a combine that included Dubois's chief Democratic factional enemy, Senator John Nugent. As for Dubois himself, he wound up getting Calvin Coolidge to appoint him on July 15, 1924, to the International Joint Commission regulating boundary waters of the United States and Canada.

A political manipulator of rare skill, Dubois had his ups and downs. But in his earlier years, he had a steady influential position in the structure of Idaho politics.

See Fred T. Dubois, *The Making of a State* (1972). —M. W.

Dubourg, Louis (1776-1883). Roman Catholic bishop. Dubourg was the first Roman Catholic bishop of American New Orleans and the trans-Mississippi West. An *émigré* priest from revolutionary France, he was president of Georgetown College and founder of St. Mary's College in Washington, D. C. Dubourg administered the Louisiana country from 1812 and aided its defense in 1815 during the War of 1812. As bishop, he programmed western Indian missions, securing Jesuit help. He later became bishop of Montauban in France and then of Besançon.—R. I. B.

Dubuque, Julien (1762-1810). Iowa fur trader and miner. The first permanent white settler in Iowa, Dubuque was born in the village of St. Pierre les Brecquets in the Province of Quebec. As a young man, Dubuque headed west to seek his fortune and in 1785 located in Prairie du Chien, Wisconsin. Nearby he discovered lead deposits on land controlled by the Fox Indians. Dubuque quickly made friends with the Indians and in a short time received sole permission to work the mines on the Iowa side of the Mississippi River. He soon built a smelting furnace and opened new mines. Dubuque also opened a trading post and developed a thriving fur trade with the Indians; he made two trips yearly to St. Louis to exchange the furs for manufactured goods. He later renamed his holdings "the Mines of Spain" in anticipation of securing from the Spanish government legal title to his holdings, which was granted. When Dubuque died, the Indians buried the man they had named "Little Cloud" with the honors of a chief.

The major work on Dubuque is Richard Herrmann, *Julien Dubuque: His Life and Adventures* (1922). Dubuque's life is also covered in M. M. Hoffmann, *Antique Dubuque, 1673-1833* (1930).—D. S.

Duchesne, Rose Philippine (1769-1852). Roman Catholic saint and missionary. After a career as a nun in Napoleonic France, Duchesne opened the first free trans-Mississippi school. Among other such institutions, she founded the Potawatomi Indian girls' school (Kansas), becoming the tribe's nurse and oracle, at the age of seventy-two.

See Louise Callan, *Philippine Duchesne* (1957). —R. I. B.

Dull Knife (1820?-1883). A principal chief of the Northern Cheyenne. Also known as Morning Star, Dull Knife was most noted for his role in the so-called Dull Knife Outbreak of 1878 and its tragic sequel at Fort Robinson, Nebraska, in 1879. Earlier, although Dull Knife had usually counseled peace with the whites, his outrage at the Sand Creek Massacre led him to participate in the Cheyenne-Arapaho War of 1864-65. In 1876 many of Dull Knife's people, including one of his sons, fought the United States Army in the battles of the Rosebud and the Little Big Horn, but Dull Knife himself seems to have been directly involved in neither. Dull Knife's band went into winter camp in 1876 on the headwaters of the Powder River. There the village was found and destroyed in November by General Ranald Mackenzie's expeditionary force, with heavy loss to the Cheyenne. In the spring Dull Knife and his people surrendered to the army and were sent south to Indian Territory.

In September 1878, beset by hunger, homesickness, and the rapid spread of disease, Dull Knife's people joined those of Little Wolf to begin their epic march back to their homeland. Although they had announced that their intentions were peaceable, the Indians were regarded as renegades by the government, and they were forced to fight or evade soldiers sent against them from posts throughout the Plains. The Cheyenne party divided after crossing the Platte; Little Wolf led his band on to the north, while Dull Knife led his people to Fort Robinson to surrender in the belief that they would be permitted to remain in their old home. Instead, the Cheyenne were imprisoned until they would agree to return to Indian Territory. A desperate break for freedom in January 1879 cost the lives of more than a third of Dull Knife's band, including several members of his immediate family. Dull Knife himself escaped with part of his family, was concealed through the winter by white and Indian friends, and was eventually given a home by Red Cloud's Sioux, with whom he lived, broken in health and embittered, until his death; he was buried near the Rosebud River.

George Bird Grinnell relates much of Dull Knife's life in *The Fighting Cheyennes* (1915). Mari Sandoz, *Cheyenne Autumn* (1953), is a sympathetic account of the events of the fall and winter of 1878.—J. T. K.

Duluth [Du Lhut], Daniel Greysolon, Sieur. See EXPLORATION, FRENCH; GREAT LAKES, MEN OF THE; and MINNESOTA.

Duluth, Minnesota. At the western tip of Lake

Superior, on a great natural harbor, stands Duluth. The city was founded in the early 1850s; in 1880 its population was still only 3,000, but ten years later it had grown to 33,000 and by 1920 it had jumped to 98,917. This dramatic growth was the result of the development of the iron-mining resources in the wilderness north and west of Lake Superior. The presence of iron was known in the mid-nineteenth century, but no attempts were made to exploit the mineral wealth of the area until the 1870s. Then rich beds of ore were discovered near Lake Vermilion in the northeastern section of the state. In 1884 the first ore was shipped from the Vermilion Range by way of Two Harbors. Later Duluth developed into an important port for the shipment of ore from the great Mesabi Range, discovered by the Merritt brothers in 1890. With the opening of the smaller Cuyuna Range in 1911, Minnesota became a national center and Duluth the state center for iron mining.

Duluth, the third largest city in Minnesota, is today the commercial and industrial center in the northern part of the state. It is the western terminus of the Great Lakes-St. Lawrence Seaway.

See *Minnesota History* (September 1960), a special issue devoted to Duluth.—R. W. F.

Dundy, Elmer Scipio (1830-1896). Nebraska jurist. Dundy was born and reared on a farm in Trumbull County, Ohio, and as a young man taught school in Pennsylvania. He was admitted to the bar in 1854. In the summer of 1857 Dundy moved to Nebraska Territory and soon became active in politics. The following year he was elected to the territorial council and remained in the upper house of the legislature for four years, emerging as a leader of Nebraska's nascent Republican party. In 1863 Dundy was appointed a federal judge for Nebraska Territory. Five years later he was named United States district judge for Nebraska, a position he held until his death.

Judge Dundy's best-known decision was rendered in the case of *United States ex rel. Standing Bear* v. *Crook* (1879). In 1877 the government had removed the Ponca Indians from their homeland along the Niobrara River in Nebraska to a reservation in Indian Territory in Oklahoma. Early in 1879, Chief Standing Bear and some thirty of his tribesmen returned to Nebraska, whereupon the War Department directed General George Crook at Fort Omaha to arrest the Ponca and escort them back to Oklahoma. Through the efforts of Thomas H. Tibbles of the Omaha *Herald* and several local lawyers, a *habeas corpus* suit was brought before Judge Dundy's court in the hope of securing the release of the Ponca. General Crook, believing that the treatment of the Ponca had been inhumane, was most cooperative in the institution of this legal action. In his decision Dundy ruled that the government had no right to detain the Ponca and that an Indian was a person subject to the protection of the laws of the United States. Although this ruling did not sweep away all legal obstacles facing the Indian in his quest for fair treatment, it was a notable achievement in the realm of civil rights.

Dundy also rendered important decisions relating to railroads. Between 1871 and 1874, sitting in United States Circuit Court, he and Judge John F. Dillon of Iowa held in several cases that county governments could not tax federal lands granted to railroads until the railway companies had actually patented the lands in

question. During the Burlington Railroad strike of 1888, Dundy issued an injunction denying Union Pacific workers the right to boycott traffic from the former line. This decision was one of the first applications of the Interstate Commerce Act in the field of labor-management relations. In 1893 Dundy issued an injunction barring the application of Nebraska's Newberry Law, a statute establishing maximum railroad rates. This ruling was ultimately sustained by the United States Supreme Court.

See James T. King, " 'A Better Way': General George Crook and the Ponca Indians," *Nebraska History* (Fall 1969); and Donald L. McMurry, *The Great Burlington Strike of 1888: A Case History in Labor Relations* (1956). —H. A. D. and D. H. P.

Duniway, Abigail Scott. See WOMAN SUFFRAGE.

Dunmore's War. See LORD DUNMORE'S WAR.

Durant, Thomas Clark (1820-1885). Railroad builder. Durant is credited with convincing President Abraham Lincoln that the central route was the best for the first transcontinental railroad (see RAILROADS). He was born in Lee, Massachusetts. Although he was graduated from medical school, a taste for business led him first into grain and stock speculation in New York City and then into contracting to build sections of such major railroads as the Michigan Southern and the Rock Island. Later claiming to have supplied all of the initial capital for projecting what was to become the UNION PACIFIC RAILROAD, Durant pushed the Pacific Railway acts of 1862 and 1864 through Congress. When conventional sources of capital failed to produce the money required to build the road, he organized the CREDIT MOBILIER, which also became chief contractor. But it remained for Oakes Ames to get the project on a sound financial footing, and although Durant continued in charge of construction until 1868, pushing the line forward at record-breaking speed, he was frequently at odds with the Boston group. For a time thereafter Durant was associated with the Central Pacific, the western half of the transcontinental, but poor health forced his semiretirement to his lodge in the Adirondacks in New York. There he owned large acreages of land and was active in the area's early development.

Arthur M. Johnson and Barry E. Supple, *Boston Capitalists and Western Railroads* (1967), contains a good summary of Durant's participation in the building of western railroads.—A. M.

dust bowl. The term "dust bowl" was given to the region of the Oklahoma and Texas panhandles and the neighboring parts of Kansas, Colorado, and New Mexico by an Associated Press correspondent while visiting those drought-stricken counties in 1935 at the height of the dust storms. Billowing clouds of "black rollers" at that time spread far from the area of their origin. A native short-grass region, possessing an average yearly rainfall of twenty inches or less, much of the level-to-rolling land in the area had been planted to wheat during World War I and afterward. Abundant crops had been raised there but the region was plagued with a highly variable rainfall pattern. When rains failed to come in the early 1930s, the ground dried up, seed failed to germinate, and the dry, powdered soil began to blow, propelled by the usually strong spring winds. Local dust storms became massive regional storms when the scouring action of wind-driven dust laid bare fields wherever the plow had dug, or where grassland had been too heavily grazed. Drifts of blowing dust piled up along fence rows, on roads, and near buildings. Agriculture in this water-scarce Great Plains area (see GREAT AMERICAN DESERT) had to adapt or die, and many farmers became the migrants described in John Steinbeck's *Grapes of Wrath.*

With the return of heavier rainfall in the 1940s and high prices for farm products, the millions of acres of marginal wheat lands in the former dust bowl were again productive. Even drier years of the mid-1950s brought a new threat to the region. But the effects were far different from twenty years earlier. Farmers of the 1950s had the knowledge, technology, and the capital to keep their soil in place. Depression and drought had coincided in the 1930s. Twenty years later most farmers in the region had a prosperous base of operations and they understood the lesson learned from the previous drought. Moreover, the power of government could be employed more easily in soil-conserving practices.

Survival in drought-cursed years requires patience and special DRY FARMING techniques—among them maintaining stubble and other soil cover and not tilling. Implements that have a special adaptation for the area have been developed. Farming in the dust bowl area is "feast or famine," and local people have learned to work profitably in spite of the uncertainty caused by the climate.

Two views of the 1930s and the dust storms are Vance Johnson, *Heaven's Tableland: The Dust Bowl Story* (1947); and Lawrence Svobida, *An Empire of Dust* (1940). See also James C. Malin, "Dust Storms, 1850-1900," *Kansas Historical Quarterly* (1946); and Ira Wolfert, *An Epidemic of Genius* (1960).—H. E. S.

Dutch in America. In 1609 Henry Hudson, an Englishman hired by the Dutch East India Company, explored the river that now bears his name. As soon as the company heard that Hudson had not discovered a passage to the Orient, its interest in the region cooled. Over the next fifteen years Dutch traders stopped at Manhattan to gather furs, but no permanent settlement was attempted until 1624, when the newly formed Dutch West India Company sent thirty families to the New World. Some of these first settlers went to Fort Orange (Albany, New York), while others built homes along the Delaware River. It was not until 1626 that Manhates, renamed New Amsterdam, established itself as the largest and most important of the scattered Dutch communities, collectively known as New Netherland.

In certain respects the Dutch West India Company resembled the Virginia and Massachusetts Bay companies. Unlike the English ventures, however, the Dutch enterprise did not possess a charter for a specific area. During the mid-seventeenth century its holdings included Brazil, Surinam, and Curaçao. The company's leaders directed most of their resources toward these tropical colonies, letting New Netherland shift for itself. A body of nineteen delegates, called the Heeren XIX, controlled the West India Company. These men were elected by five local chambers. Regional jealousy, as well as private ambition, tended to undermine the company's effectiveness, and its vacillating policy in New Netherland was a manifestation of the internal division. The Dutch company differed from its English counterparts in another way. Its chief interest was trade, not

colonization, and the Heeren XIX showed little willingness to underwrite the cost of settlement.

One of the company's most powerful directors, Kiliaen Van Rensselaer, thought that New Netherland could never prosper by furs alone. He advocated the establishment of agricultural communities supported by private capital. His ideas were embodied in the Charter of Freedoms and Exemptions, ratified in 1629. This document promised a large American estate, called a patroonship, to any member of the company who sent fifty families to New Netherland at his own expense. The patroons held all the rights and powers of a feudal lord. Despite initial enthusiasm for the plan, only one successful patroonship, the Van Rensselaer manor, was ever established. Most of the great Hudson River estates were created long after the Dutch had lost control over the region.

By almost any standard, New Netherland was a failure. Its sparse population, which never exceeded eight thousand, was scattered over a wide area, and most of the tiny settlements were incapable of defending themselves from the Indians. The colonists themselves came from different countries, spoke different languages, and prayed in different churches. The Dutch colony might have developed a greater community spirit if it had possessed a representative government, but the Dutch West India Company never allowed the settlers a meaningful voice in civil affairs. Another divisive element was the unwillingness of local officials to tolerate non-Calvinist theology.

The colony's problems might have been eased if the company had chosen better administrators. Unfortunately, the director-generals were greedy, incompetent, and arbitrary men. One of them, Willem Kieft, caused an unnecessary Indian war (called KIEFT'S WAR, 1643) that nearly destroyed New Netherland. His successor, Peter Stuyvesant (1647-64), refused to listen to the advice of the settlers, whom he called "ignorant subjects." When English troops seized the Dutch colony in 1664, which marked the settlement of NEW YORK, few men were willing to come to the company's defense.

See Charles M. Andrews, *The Colonial Period of American History,* vol. III (1937); J. Franklin Jameson, ed., *Narratives of New Netherland* (1909); and Henry Kessler and Eugene Rachlis, *Peter Stuyvesant and His New York* (1959).—T. H. B.

DuVal, William Pope (1784-1854). Florida politician. Born at Mount Comfort near Richmond, Virginia, young DuVal left home at the age of fourteen and settled in Bardstown, Kentucky. There he studied law and was admitted to the bar at age nineteen. He was elected to one term in Congress in 1812 and was identified with the war hawks, who were encouraging war with England.

In 1822 DuVal was appointed district court judge of East Florida by President James Monroe, but his term was brief, for in April he was named territorial governor by the president to succeed provisional Governor Andrew Jackson. He served four three-year terms. During his first term he appointed commissioners to locate the site of a new capital city. On March 4, 1824, he proclaimed their choice, which was named Tallahassee. DuVal won the reputation of being the "veto governor" because of the large number of bills chartering banks that he turned back. DuVal was a quick-tempered but unassuming man. A contemporary politician, Robert

Raymond Reid, wrote of him, "He is, if I mistake not, a weak man and wants dignity, but his friends say he is a fine storyteller!" Much was made of his lack of "dignity" and his storytelling propensity. Washington Irving wrote of him as "Ralph Ringwood" and James K. Paulding as "Nimrod Wildfire." Noted by some as a man of courage, DuVal personally deposed Indian chief Neamathla in 1824 in a confrontation near Tallahassee when it appeared he would resist the Treaty of Moultrie Creek, which was to establish an Indian reservation. DuVal replaced him with John Hicks, who was then elected chief of all the Seminole.

In 1834 DuVal was not reappointed to the governorship and returned to Kentucky. In 1836, after an invitation from the Legislative Council, he returned to reside in Florida. During this period he associated with the political-economic-social group known as "the Nucleus," which later provided the core of the Whig party. He served in the Florida constitutional convention of 1838-39, losing the convention presidency by one vote to Robert Raymond Reid. In 1838 he was also elected to the first territorial Senate. In 1840 he was reelected as a Harrison Whig. Moving in 1843 to St. Augustine, a Democratic stronghold, he soon realigned with that party for the sake of expediency and presided over the East Florida Democratic convention in 1844. In 1848 he was named the Democratic candidate for Congress but was defeated by Whig incumbent Edward C. Cabell. He moved to Texas in the same year and lived there until his death.

See James Owen Knauss, "William Pope DuVal, Pioneer and State Builder," *Florida Historical Quarterly* (January 1933).—H. J. D.

Dye, Eva Emery (1855-1947). Historical novelist. Born in Prophetstown, Illinois, and growing up near the site of the Black Hawk War, Eva Emery acquired a taste for heroic tales. She began writing when she was fifteen, publishing verse in a local newspaper under the name Jennie Juniper. After graduation from Oberlin College, Ohio, in 1882, she married classmate Charles Henry Dye and moved with him to Iowa, where he studied law at the university. They returned to Oberlin in 1889, and the next year migrated to Oregon City, Oregon, where Mrs. Dye lived the rest of her life, studying local history, working to restore and preserve the home of Dr. John McLoughlin—chief factor of the Hudson's Bay Company, 1824-45—writing novels, and raising four children.

In 1900 she published a manuscript completed six years earlier, *McLoughlin and Old Oregon*. Meanwhile, she had begun *The Conquest* (1902), a novel about Lewis and Clark, in which she described the expedition members as "Homeric heroes who had wandered farther than Ulysses and slain more monsters than Hercules." This was followed by *McDonald of Oregon* (1907), a romantic fictionalization of the life of Ronald McDonald, Hudson's Bay Company trader and traveler to Japan in the 1840s. After a twenty-seven-year interval she returned to print with *The Soul of America* (1934), a rambling paean to the pioneer spirit.

Dye's writings were familiar to and widely read by several generations of Oregonians. For each novel she corresponded with dozens of pioneers or their descendants and searched archives and libraries for diaries and letters. Unfortunately, her resulting works were neither factually reliable nor effective fiction, for she wove a veil of romance so thick that it obscured and distorted the facts and had difficulty distinguishing between the significant and the trivial.

See Alfred Powers, *History of Oregon Literature* (1935).—E. R. B.

Dykes, Jefferson C. (1900-   ). Writer and book collector. A Dallas Texan, Dykes began collecting westerniana at an early age. Main features in his private library include an enormous assemblage on range livestock and producers, the largest assortment of privately owned ranger books, and a choice and inclusive collection of humorist and historian J. Frank Dobie's writings. In 1966 the late Earl Rudder, president of Texas A & M, Dykes's alma mater, assigned him to build the college range-livestock library into the best collection of its kind. In May 1971 Dykes presented the five-thousandth item in the range-livestock collection.

Dykes also wrote and reviewed books about the West. He was originator and president of The Old Bookeroos, a book-reviewing group including F. G. Renner, B. W. Allred, and R. E. Williams. They published about three thousand reviews of current western books over at least eighteen years. Dykes was a founder and sheriff of the Potomac Corral of Westerners in Washington, D.C., and an editor of "The Brand Book," a publication of the Chicago Corral of Westerners. Among his numerous books are *Billy the Kid* (1952) and *Flat Top Ranch* (1957), written with B. W. Allred. He was editor of and contributor to *Great Western Indian Fights* (1960) and author of a uniquely comprehensive series on the lives and works of fifty-five western artists and illustrators, published in the *American Book Collector*, May 1963 to May 1971.

After retiring in 1965 from the Soil Conservation Service of the United States Department of Agriculture, Dykes became a bookseller.—B. W. A.

E

Eads, James Buchanan (1820-1887). Engineer. Born in Lawrenceburg, Indiana, Eads spent his early years in Cincinnati, Louisville, and St. Louis, where he centered his career for the remainder of his life.

After holding a variety of jobs, Eads at eighteen became a purser on a Mississippi River steamboat. His observations here of the heavy losses in boats and traffic coupled with a boyhood interest in machinery induced him to produce a diving bell which he patented. With this, he formed a partnership for salvage operations on the river in 1842 that proved a highly successful venture. Except for a brief unsuccessful side trip into glass manufacturing, he pursued his salvaging career until he retired in 1857. During the 1850s Eads became interested in the river's flow, the problems of erosion and soil deposition, and the clearing of channels. His efforts to interest the United States Congress in a corrective program during the prewar era failed.

At the outset of the Civil War President Abraham Lincoln asked Eads to consult on the utilization of the western rivers in the war effort. Eads proposed and subsequently built a fleet of armor-plated, steam-propelled gunboats that performed remarkably well.

When Congress authorized the building of a bridge across the Mississippi at St. Louis in 1865, Eads undertook what many engineers considered an impossible task and saw it through to successful completion by 1874, in spite of numerous technical problems. The span subsequently came to bear his name.

Immediately upon completion of this work, Eads proposed to open one of the mouths of the Mississippi River into the Gulf and maintain its channel. Congress accepted after Eads agreed to assume sole risk of failure. Using a system of jetties that guided sediment deposition, he completed the task in four years. Thereafter he was sought as consultant by many governments and municipalities for a variety of projects.

The standard biography is Florence Dorsey, *Road to the Sea* (1947).—W. E. P.

Earp brothers. Peace officers, gamblers, saloonkeepers, and miners. The legend of Wyatt Earp and his brothers is of farily recent origin and may be attributed largely to the highly readable prose of two writers, Walter Noble Burns and Stuart N. Lake. Burns and Lake lifted the exploits of a clannish family of itinerant gamblers and sometime lawmen to the high plane of epic. They planted the seed of one of the most persistent controversies in western history, leaving it for others to sort out the truth. The response to the Earp legend produced a counterview of the Earps that is as tenacious as the first. In one view the Earps were lawmen of sterling quality who brought law and order to a wild frontier, as the very personification of all that is good and right in America's frontier heritage. In the other, the Earps were vicious, unprincipled thieves, killers, conmen, and frauds and were led by Wyatt Earp, whose boasting was ultimately responsible for a travesty on the truth. These opposing views have only increased the fascination of the Earps to students of western history.

The Earps were children of the Middle West, not unlike many other families with close ties and a father with wanderlust. There were five boys: James C. (1841-1926), Virgil W. (1843-1906), Wyatt B. S. (1848-1929), Morgan (1851-1882), and Warren B. (1855-1900). They had an older half-brother, Newton Jasper Earp (1837-1928), and a baby sister, Adelia. The Earp children spent most of their early lives in Illinois and Iowa.

When the Civil War came, the older boys, Newton, James, and Virgil, enlisted and marched away to fight for the Union. In 1863, James came home with serious wounds, the marks of which he bore for the rest of his long life. He reached home in time to join the family for a trek across the continent to California in 1864. The Earps settled at San Bernardino. In 1865, Virgil followed the family west. His trip carried him through Prescott, Arizona, a place he apparently liked, for he returned to it periodically all through his life. The next year Virgil and Wyatt took jobs as teamsters between Wilmington, California, and Prescott.

In 1868, Nicholas Earp, the patriarch of the clan, got the urge to move again, this time back to Monmouth, Illinois, and the old home place. Virgil and Wyatt left the family in Wyoming and went to work with a section crew on the Union Pacific Railroad. By the time they reached Monmouth they had become proficient gamblers. The family had already moved on again, to Lamar, Missouri, so Wyatt and Virgil visited relatives briefly, then headed to Lamar.

The Lamar experience is somewhat clouded, for documentation is sparse. Wyatt moved in with Newton, but in January 1870 Wyatt married. He also entered the race for constable against Newton and beat him at the polls in April 1870. Wyatt apparently did a good job as constable, although there is a hint of trouble between the Earp family and the Brummet brothers. Wyatt may also have had trouble with his wife's family. Then tragedy struck: Wyatt's wife died of typhoid. He soon departed Missouri, and shortly thereafter the rest of the family left Lamar.

Wyatt's life took a decided turn after Lamar. He drifted into Indian Territory, and within a matter of months he was arrested for stealing horses. He made his escape into Kansas and worked as a buffalo hunter in 1872. The next year found him in Hays City and

Ellsworth. In 1874 he arrived in Wichita, where James was a bartender and James's wife operated a brothel. Wyatt was hired as a policeman by Marshal Michael Meagher in April 1875 and again proved his mettle as a peace officer. The next year, however, Wyatt had a fist fight with Bill Smith, Meagher's opponent in the race for town marshal. Meagher was reelected, but Wyatt was dismissed at the end of the month.

Later that spring he joined the police force at Dodge City, a post he held until April 1, 1877, when he resigned to follow the gold rush to the Black Hills. He was back in Dodge that summer and was offered his old job back, but he did not accept it. After following the Texas gambling circuit, he again returned to Dodge in May 1878 and accepted the job of assistant marshal. Wyatt was an efficient lawman and well liked in Dodge. He made many of his most lasting friendships in Dodge, including those with Doc Holliday, Bat Masterson, and Luke Short. That year was a busy one in Dodge City, especially for the law, and Wyatt may have killed his first man there. It is really impossible to say that he did, since he was one of several officers who fired at a rowdy young cowboy named George Hoy. By 1879, however, Dodge had slowed down some, and in September, Wyatt left Dodge City for good, traveling to Las Vegas, New Mexico, with his second wife.

In the meantime the other Earps were also on the move. Morgan worked as a lawman in Dodge for a time while Wyatt was there and then went to Montana. Newton was living in Garden City, Kansas. Nicholas had packed his belongings and taken the rest of the family to California again. Virgil had wandered here and there before settling in Prescott with his wife. He operated a sawmill and dabbled in prospecting. He had been there for more than two years when Wyatt arrived and persuaded him to join the rest of the Earps, who were gathering in the new boomtown of Tombstone, Arizona.

The Tombstone years brought the Earp family together again and set the stage for the Earp legend. For a while Wyatt worked as a Wells Fargo guard, and Virgil arrived in Tombstone with a fresh commission as a deputy United States marshal. Wyatt soon resigned his job to become deputy sheriff of Pima County, and Morgan replaced him as shotgun messenger. James arrived and became a bartender in a local saloon, and young Warren soon joined his brothers. The Earps appear to have made a serious effort to establish themselves in Tombstone. They invested in real estate, secured mining properties, and courted local business leaders. They aligned themselves with local Republicans and cultivated the friendship of prominent citizens.

In October 1880 Virgil took over as town marshal following the death of Fred White. He served until a replacement could be found, and the Earps continued to promote their political position in the community. Their first real disappointment came when Wyatt failed to get the appointment as sheriff of Cochise County when it was formed, but Wyatt immediately set his eyes on the next election. He also acquired an interest in the gambling tables at the Oriental Saloon and imported gamblers like Bat Masterson and Luke Short to work for him. When the new town marshal disappeared mysteriously, Virgil was appointed to the position. Everything was going well.

They might have succeeded if they had not encountered opposition from small ranchers in the area, particularly from N. H. "Old Man" Clanton and his three sons, Ike, Phin, and Billy. The Clantons and their friends were mostly southerners, Democrats, and older residents of the region. They lived a simple existence that included cattle rustling, particularly in nearby Mexico. They were a rowdy, unsavory lot but were not regarded seriously by the Earps. The establishment of Tombstone crimped the cowboys' style, however. Practices that had been winked at in the past or had gone undetected because of the wild nature of the country were now regarded as criminal. The Clantons chafed under the Tombstone *Epitaph* editorials against their activities. Moreover, the wildest among them were involved in a large assortment of criminal activities.

From time to time the cowboys frequented Tombstone. One night in October 1880 Marshal Fred White was killed when he attempted to arrest Curly Bill Brocius for disorderly conduct. Wyatt, as deputy sheriff, disarmed Brocius and, with the help of Virgil and Morgan, rounded up his friends who were "hurrahing" the town. Marshal White said before he died that the shooting was accidental, but the episode sparked animosity between the Earps and the Clantons.

In the months that followed numerous small incidents contributed to the feud. Then in 1881 a series of events propelled the Earps toward a showdown with the Clantons. The real trouble began in March 1881 when the Kinnear and Company stage was attacked near Contention and two men were killed. Wyatt saw an opportunity to guarantee his election as sheriff. All he had to do was arrest the stage robbers. One man was arrested but escaped from the county jail under peculiar circumstances. Wyatt and his brothers made exhausting searches for the outlaws in the weeks that followed, but to no avail. Wyatt therefore sought out Ike Clanton and promised him the reward for telling him where the outlaws were hiding. All Wyatt wanted was the credit for capturing them. Ike agreed to betray his friends, but the deal fell apart when the three known outlaws were killed. Wyatt's negotiations with Ike now became a threat to both of them.

In June 1881 Wyatt's friend Doc Holliday was arrested as one of the suspects in the attempted robbery and murders. Although charges against Doc were dropped, the incident took its toll in the popularity of the Earps. More and more people suspected them of illegal activities, including stage robberies. Through the summer, conditions worsened. The Earps pointed to the illegal operations of the cowboys and accused the sheriff's office of being in league with outlaws. The other side promoted rumors that the Earps were themselves criminals. The confrontation raced toward a conclusion in the fall when a friend of Wyatt's accused Ike Clanton of selling out his friends who were implicated in the attempt to rob the stage near Contention. In a rage Ike accused Wyatt of revealing their secret negotiations.

On the night of October 25, 1881, Ike let it be known that the Earps would pay for their treachery. The next day he was still on the streets looking for a fight when Virgil arrested him and carried him into court. Outside the courtroom, Wyatt ran into Tom McLaury, a friend of Ike's, and after a heated exchange cracked him over the head with a pistol. With the town alive with rumors, Ike and Tom were joined by Frank McLaury and Billy Clanton. They apparently argued over whether or not they should leave town. In the meantime the Earps were repeatedly warned that the Clantons intended to kill them. In response to these warnings, Virgil, as town marshal, enlisted the aid of Wyatt, Morgan, and Doc Holliday to arrest them. They met the Clantons and McLaurys on a vacant lot on Fremont Street near the O. K. Corral. In a few bloody seconds, the McLaurys and Billy Clanton were fatally shot. Virgil and Morgan were wounded, Ike Clanton and Billy Claiborne had fled, and Wyatt was unhurt. Sheriff John Behan tried to arrest the Earps, but Wyatt refused to be taken. A hearing followed, and on December 1, 1881, a justice of the peace found that the Earps had been acting as officers of the law.

The verdict did not satisfy everyone, and the controversy still rages. Some hold that the judge was right, while others insist that the Earps shot down unresisting victims who had their hands in the air. The shootout on Fremont Street shattered the Earps' plans. Virgil Earp was dismissed as chief of police, and the popularity of the Earps began to wane.

Then followed a vendetta of assassinations and shootings. The first victim was Virgil, who was shot from ambush late in December 1881. He survived but never regained full use of his left arm. Then in March 1882 Morgan was killed by unknown assassins while shooting pool in Bob Hatch's saloon. Wyatt took command then. He sent Virgil and the Earp women to California with Morgan's body, and turned grimly to revenge. His first victim was Frank Stilwell, a deputy sheriff who was suspected of being involved in Morgan's murder. When Stilwell's body was found in the rail yard at Tucson, Wyatt and Doc Holliday were among those accused of the crime. Wyatt returned to Tombstone, hastily concluded his business affairs, refused to submit to arrest for the murder of Stilwell, and departed Tombstone with Doc Holliday, Warren Earp, and several friends. Outside of Tombstone, the Earp party killed a Mexican named Florentine, who was also suspected of being one of Morgan's killers. A few days later Wyatt shot and killed Curly Bill Brocius when the Earp party accidentally stumbled onto the outlaw's camp. Warrants were sworn out for Wyatt's arrest in the deaths of Stilwell and Florentine but were never served.

After hiding in Gunnison, Colorado, for a time, Wyatt moved on to Silverton, and then returned to Dodge City to help gambler Luke Short in 1883. He drifted from boom camp to boom camp after that, following his trade as a gambler. The next year he and James operated a saloon in Eagle City, Idaho, and got into trouble over mining claims. In 1885 he was in Cripple Creek, Colorado, where he met Virgil, and returned with him to Prescott, Arizona.

Virgil was also on the move. In 1887 he was elected marshal of Colton, California, and in 1889 he built a saloon there which was quite successful. He sold out in 1895 and joined Wyatt in Cripple Creek again. In 1889 and 1890 Wyatt operated gambling halls in San Diego and in the 1890s worked as a bodyguard for the editor of the San Franciso *Examiner.* He refereed the controversial Sharkey-Fitzsimmons fight in December 1896. After a brief stay in Yuma, Arizona, in 1897, Wyatt left for the gold fields of Alaska with his third wife and operated a saloon in Nome.

In 1900 Warren was killed in Wilcox, Arizona, in a saloon fight with a man named Johnny Boyett. The fight may have been related to the Tombstone troubles, for Virgil swore that he would kill the man responsible. He did not mean Boyett. Virgil was living in Prescott again, and people asked him to run for sheriff. He declined. In 1905 he moved again to Goldfield, Nevada. He left there only once and killed the man he blamed for Warren's death. Then, early in 1906, Virgil Earp died of pneumonia.

Wyatt returned from Alaska in time for the Nevada boom. He was at Tonapah and Goldfield. From 1906 until his death Wyatt lived in Los Angeles, but spent much time at Parker, Arizona. He dabbled in oil, gold and silver mines, and other business ventures, but he never really found success. By the 1920s Wyatt had to struggle. His money was gone, and he was an old man. He spent a lot of time on movie lots and befriended cowboy stars like William S. Hart and Tom Mix. But producers and directors exploited him rather shabbily by pumping him for information but not paying him for his services.

Wyatt had not found the success he had hoped for, but he had led an exciting life. For years he had hoped to write a book about his life and had in fact drafted a lengthy account, but he could not find a publisher. In 1928 he met Stuart N. Lake, a young journalist of considerable talent who was anxious to write his biography. Lake's controversial and fanciful biography of Earp did not appear until almost two years after Earp's death a few months later, on January 13, 1929.

The literature on the Earp brothers is vast. Walter Noble Burns, *Tombstone* (1927), and Stuart N. Lake, *Wyatt Earp: Frontier Marshal* (1931), made Wyatt Earp a hero. Frank Waters, *The Earp Brothers of Tombstone* (1960), and Ed Bartholomew, *Wyatt Earp: The Untold Story* (1963) and *Wyatt Earp: The Man and the Myth* (1964), take an opposite view. More useful than any of these are the writings of John D. Gilchriese, notably "The Odyssey of Virgil Earp," which appeared in the Tombstone *Epitaph* in 1968.—G. L. R.

East and West Florida question. Argument with Spain over the extent of the Louisiana Purchase. In the entire history of the American West, perhaps no issue is more difficult to hold in mind than the East and West Florida question, which was finally settled in the ADAMS-ONÍS TREATY of 1819. One writer has sought to drop it into the dustbin of history by describing the dispute over the Floridas as "tiresome reiteration," and it may have been that. Still, without comprehending the successive changes of the Florida boundaries, it is difficult to understand some of the present-day state lines in the Gulf area and also difficult to grasp the forces and factors that were moving the United States toward possession of all the lands between the Rio Grande and the forty-ninth parallel.

The question of the Floridas reached back a hundred years before the Adams-Onís Treaty to the year 1719 when after a petty local war France and Spain agreed that the line between French Louisiana and Spanish Florida would be the Perdido River (the western boundary of the present-day state of Florida). When Louisiana passed from France to Spain in 1763 and Spanish

Florida to Great Britain, the British also took the territory westward from the Perdido to the Mississippi River, except for the island of New Orleans. For administrative reasons the British named this strip West Florida and extended its jurisdiction eastward as far as the Apalachicola River (with Pensacola, just to the east of the Perdido, as its capital). Incidentally—and sometimes one of the confusing factors in the Florida question—it is necessary to remember that the Chattahoochee River becomes the Apalachicola River in Florida. In 1783 the Spanish acquired what by that time had become known as "the Floridas," including not merely their erstwhile Florida (renamed East Florida, most of the present-day state) but also the once French strip (1719-63) together with the territory between the Perdido and the Apalachicola, which was now West Florida. The Spanish placed West Florida within the jurisdiction of Louisiana, where it remained until 1803.

The Treaty of San Lorenzo of 1795 established the boundary between Spanish Florida and the United States at the thirty-first parallel, but this was only the opening American arrangement in regard to the Floridas, East and West, which, as mentioned, did not obtain settlement until 1819. No sooner had the United States government concluded the Louisiana Purchase than Minister Robert R. Livingston in Paris, and many individuals in the United States, began to argue that Napoleon had sold the Floridas as well as the Louisiana territory. It was a specious argument but had a certain cogency since at one time West Florida had been part of Louisiana under French rule. Actually, the Spanish (although unknown to the Americans) had reincorporated it for administrative purposes. The American claim to West Florida under the Louisiana Purchase treaty was better than the claim to East Florida, but undaunted by this fact the Americans proceeded to elaborate a claim to the latter area too, maintaining that the Spanish should give East Florida to the American government as an indemnity, because of the failure of Spain to restrain the Indians from raiding into American territory, as provided in the Treaty of San Lorenzo, the harboring of escaped slaves in the Floridas (see NEGROES ON THE FRONTIER), and the use of Florida ports by Spanish and French ships of war that preyed on American merchantmen. When the Spanish intendant in New Orleans in 1802 revoked the right of deposit, Americans charged the losses up to East Florida.

As a result of these injustices, real and imagined, and the rather thin American territorial claim to West Florida, the government of the United States undertook a piecemeal occupation of the Floridas, which progressed rather far prior to conclusion of the Adams-Onís Treaty. The Mobile Act of 1804 authorized organization of West Florida as a United States customs district. To pass an act of Congress was one thing and to take the territory something else: six years elapsed before the Americans seized West Florida up to the Pearl River. In April 1812 the seized section became a part of the new state of Louisiana. In May 1812 the section of West Florida between the Pearl and the Perdido (including Mobile) became a part of Mississippi Territory. The most notorious of the incursions into the Floridas was by General Andrew Jackson in 1818, in which the *Napoléon des bois* ("Napoleon of the woods," as the French minister in Washington dubbed him) captured West Florida's capi-

tal, Pensacola, and meted out a number of frontier hangings and shootings en route. Jackson's action, if not authorized, was at least condoned by the Monroe administration. (An argument raged ever afterward as to whether Monroe had authorized Jackson to move into the Floridas, the two principals taking opposite sides in the controversy.) But a year after the Jackson raid the Spanish gave in and signed the Adams-Onís Treaty, by which the Floridas became American territory.

Part of the controversy appears in Isaac J. Cox, *The West Florida Controversy, 1798-1813* (1918); see also Philip C. Brooks, *Diplomacy and the Borderlands: The Adams-Onís Treaty of 1819* (1939).—R. H. F.

Eastman, Seth (1809-1875). Soldier, surveyor, and painter. Born at Brunswick, Maine, Eastman graduated from West Point Military Academy in 1829. From 1831 to 1833 he was stationed at forts Crawford and Snelling, during which time he served as topographical draftsman for a number of western land surveys. From 1833 to 1840 he taught drawing at West Point. After participating in the Seminole War in Florida in 1840-41, he returned to Fort Snelling, where he remained until 1848.

Following a tour of duty in Texas in 1848-49, Eastman was given the task of producing illustrations for Henry R. Schoolcraft's *History and Statistical Information Respecting . . . the Indian Tribes of the United States,* a six-volume work published by the federal government between 1853 and 1856. After serving another period of time in Texas and in the office of the quartermaster general in Washington, D.C., Colonel Eastman was placed on the retirement list, brevetted brigadier general in 1866. From 1867 until shortly before his death, he was engaged in the painting of Indian scenes and views of western forts for the Capitol.

In addition to the Schoolcraft reports, Eastman's work appeared in *American Aboriginal Portfolio,* written by his wife, Mary, and published in 1853. Original works survive in the collections of the Corcoran Gallery of Art and the Capitol in Washington, D.C.; the Minneapolis Institute of Arts; and the Thomas Gilcrease Institute of American History and Art, Tulsa, Oklahoma.

See John Francis McDermott, *Seth Eastman, Pictorial Historian of the Indian* (1961); and Robert Taft, *Artists and Illustrators of the Old West, 1850-1900* (1953). —D. C. H.

East Texas missions. See SAN FRANCISCO DE LOS TEJAS.

Echohawk, Brummett (1922-   ). Pawnee artist. Echohawk's favorite subject matter was horses, and he raised them in addition to drawing and painting them. He began painting as a small child in Pawnee, Oklahoma, where he was born. His professional career began while on combat duty with the army, when he was chosen to be illustrator for the NEA newspaper syndicate and *Yank.* He painted some of the bloodiest battles in North Africa, Sicily, and Italy. Wounded in action twice, Echohawk went AWOL from the hospital to *return* to his unit to fight, in true Pawnee warrior tradition. The second time he was sent back to the United States, but by this time he had earned many military honors.

Echohawk began formal training at the Chicago Art Institute under the GI bill. His talents covered a wide range and included his own line of Christmas cards, a weekly comic strip ("Little Chief" in the Tulsa *Sunday World*), illustrations for magazines and newspapers, and, of course, his paintings. He used a variation of Van Gogh's palette knife technique in classic nineteenth-century tradition, though his Indian and horse themes are far removed from that era. He also sketched for animated films.

A history buff and something of an anthropologist, Echohawk recorded Pawnee songs and ceremonies and lectured and published widely, particularly on Pawnee tribal history and the Custer battle at the Little Big Horn. Along with Thomas Hart Benton, Echohawk was commissioned to do a mural for the Truman Library. His paintings have been exhibited nationally and internationally.—C. C.

ecological movement. See CONSERVATION MOVEMENT.

ecology. See FISHERIES; PHYSIOGRAPHY OF THE UNITED STATES; VEGETATION; and WILDLIFE.

Edmunds, Newton (1819-1908). Dakota Territory politician. In the autumn of 1863 President Abraham Lincoln appointed Newton Edmunds governor of Dakota Territory. A native of Michigan, Edmunds was serving as chief clerk in the surveyor general's office. As governor he also was the ex officio superintendent of Indian affairs for the territory and attempted to establish a humane policy toward the Sioux. He opposed the use of military force against the Indians and served as chairman of the Northwestern Indian Commission of 1865. He remained active in Indian affairs until his death, helping to lay the foundation for the federal Indian peace policy. After a political struggle with Walter A. Burleigh, agent to the Yankton Indians, Edmunds was removed from the governorship by President Andrew Johnson and replaced by Burleigh's father-in-law, Andrew J. Faulk.—D. J. T.

Edwardsen, Charles ("Ituk"), Jr. (1943-   ). Eskimo activist. Statehood and the discovery of oil in Alaska have, in the last decade, hurtled native peoples from a generally self-sustaining and materially adequate culture into chaos. Prior to this time, incursions by missionaries and government agents from Siberia, the United States, and elsewhere had been comparatively infrequent, and their effects were mitigated by the climate and the strength and harmony of the cultures. To be sure, infant mortality was high, but incidence of many common United States diseases—such as heart disease, ulcers, and venereal disease—was low. The federal government began to insist that teen-agers be "educated" in Bureau of Indian Affairs schools often as far away as Oklahoma and New Mexico. When these students returned to communities that had no jobs to fit their education, anomie, alcohol, and drugs began to take hold. Edwardsen, born in Point Barrow, grew up in this changing milieu and emerged against the background of a dispute involving tremendous amounts of money, land, and oil as a powerful spokesman of his land and peoples.

Edwardsen served as director of Friends of Alaskan Natives, Incorporated, a group based in Washington, D.C., founded to promote financial and political support by other Americans for the Alaskan Native Federation. Edwardsen's forceful congressional testimony during 1970-71, some of which was televised, along with a few articles in "liberal" magazines, marshaled the limited popular support the native movement enjoys in the shadow of massive publicity efforts by government and oil interests. The 55,000 native Alaskans belong to seven distinct cultural groups. Edwardsen and his group feel that each group should manage its own land and resources. The federal administration favors a single settlement and management of these vast lands and problems.

As executive director of the Arctic Slope Native Association, Edwardsen filed federal suit to evict the state and oil companies from the North Slope oil fields, where many Eskimos live. Under the 1958 statehood act, Alaska was allowed to select 103.5 million acres of federal domain, but land-claim disputes have complicated this process, and the state has clear title to only a fraction of this acreage, none of which is in the North Slope.

See Hugh G. Gallagher, *Etok: A Story of Eskimo Power* (1974).—C. C.

Eel River. The Eel, best known as the stream along which the giant redwoods of California grow, has the largest runoff of those streams whose watersheds are entirely within the Coast Range Province. It also has the dubious distinction of being the fastest eroding of the nation's larger river basins according to studies made by the United States Geological Survey. The average rate of erosion in the basin ranges from four to eight inches every one hundred years, a sediment load more than fifteen times that of the Mississippi.

The river was named by Dr. Josiah Gregg, an early American settler in California, when he saw a group of Indians carrying eels they had caught in the river. With a drainage basin that covers 3,565 square miles in northwestern California, the Eel transports almost half as much water on an annual basis as does the Colorado and dumps it into the Pacific Ocean about thirteen miles south of Eureka. Unlike most of the western rivers, the headwaters of the Eel lie in relatively low mountain areas, and most of its runoff comes from winter storms that drop rain instead of snow onto its basin. Its source receives some runoff from peaks that are almost seven thousand feet above the sea, but it drops quickly to lower elevations.

After flowing west for about fifty miles, the Eel turns toward the northwest and receives the flow of Middle Fork. It continues to the northwest through some of the most beautiful forests to be seen anywhere. The other two principal tributaries, South Fork and the Van Duzen, join the Eel as it reaches the coastal plain and shortly before it reaches the ocean.

Floods are a frequent occurrence along the stream, and damage from them has occurred with some regularity. But from July through October, the dry season of California, the Eel is a placid stream meandering around and over sand and gravel bars, which are dropped by the mighty torrents of water that follow winter storms.

Permanent settlement along the Eel proceeded slowly until the gold rush. Today tourism, lumbering, and some general farming constitute the area's main activities.

For map, see CALIFORNIA.

See S. T. Harding, *Water in California* (1960); and Lawrence R. McDonnell, ed., *Rivers of California* (1962).—R. W. D.

Ehrenberg, Arizona. See GILA CITY, ARIZONA.

election of 1824. The election of 1824 was the first in which there were prominent western candidates. The Republican caucus in Congress nominated William Henry Crawford of Georgia to succeed President James Monroe. But other candidates including John Quincy Adams with strong support in New England, Henry CLAY of Kentucky, and Andrew Jackson of Tennessee vied for the office, and the old Jeffersonian Republican party disintegrated.

The main issue in the campaign was opposition to Crawford and the right of a caucus, as opposed to conventions, to pick the nominee. Jackson's views on most issues, such as tariffs, internal improvements, and the national bank, were unknown. He was a national hero with support throughout the country, not just in the West; though Tennesseans first nominated him in 1822, it was Pennsylvania's nomination that made him a serious contender. Clay was the nationalist champion of the American system; Adams was also a nationalist. Only Crawford claimed to be a strict Jeffersonian states' righter who opposed an active role in the economy by the federal government.

In the election, Jackson won a plurality of the popular vote and the most electoral votes. He had strong popular support everywhere except New England, and carried Mississippi, Alabama, Tennessee, and Indiana in the West, also winning votes in Illinois and Louisiana. Clay, running fourth, carried Kentucky, Ohio, and Missouri, the newest state.

No candidate, however, had an electoral majority, and the election—among the top three contenders, Jackson, Adams, and Crawford—was thrown into the House. Speaker of the House Clay played kingmaker. Rather than supporting Jackson, his fellow westerner, he backed Adams because he considered Jackson inexperienced and a political threat. In the House, of the western states, Louisiana, Illinois, Ohio, Missouri, and Kentucky backed Adams and helped elect him.

See Samuel Flagg Bemis, *John Quincy Adams and the Union* (1956); George Dangerfield, *The Awakening of American Nationalism, 1815-1828* (1965); and Robert V. Remini, *The Election of Andrew Jackson* (1963). —M. F. H.

election of 1828. The election of 1828 marked the revival of formal competition between parties. The National Republicans backed the incumbent John Quincy Adams and his policy of a vigorous role for the national government in the economy. Opponents of the administration—a group including Martin Van Buren, Thomas Hart Benton of Missouri, and Vice President John C. Calhoun—rallied behind Andrew Jackson. These politicians had been carefully organizing the opposition since 1825, by starting newspapers and establishing local organizations. By 1828, though still a diverse anti-administration coalition, they were calling themselves the Democratic party.

In the background of the campaign were issues of importance to western voters. Westerners disliked Adams' demonstrated concern for the rights of Indians. Questions of land policy, internal improvements, banking, and debtor relief commanded western interest. Furthermore, Democrats had helped push the high tariff of 1828, the so-called Tarriff of Abominations, through Congress, and because it promised high rates on raw materials such as wool, it apparently won Jackson

support in Kentucky, Illinois, Indiana, Missouri, and Ohio.

During the campaign, however, these matters remained in the background. Both Jackson and his party newspapers were silent or vague on most issues; people simply did not know where he stood. Instead, the campaign revolved around personalities. Jacksonian propagandists skillfully made Adams a symbol of aristocracy, privilege, trickery, and the old order. Reiterating the charges of a corrupt bargain between Henry CLAY and Adams in 1825 was one of several ways in which they did this. Jackson, even though he belonged to the Tennessee gentry, seemed to represent honesty and opportunity and to personify the aspirations of the common man. By 1828 a new generation of Americans was rising, anxious to take economic and political power from older leaders whom they regarded as a privileged elite. Electing Jackson was a way to attack privilege. As the campaign progressed, it degenerated into savage mudslinging. Adams was accused of pimping for the czar while minister to Russia. Jackson was called an adulterer, and propaganda such as the Coffin Handbill portrayed him as a brutal murderer of his own militiamen.

In the end, Jackson's popularity and his party's organization overwhelmed Adams. Jackson carried every state west of the Alleghenies; Adams took only New England. Popular faith in Jackson as defender of the people's interests against a corrupt elite, more than any concrete issues, explains this victory. And while Jackson is often considered the representative of the New West or the frontier, his strength and appeal were national, not sectional.

The best account of the election of 1828 is Robert V. Remini, *The Election of Andrew Jackson* (1963). See also Richard P. McCormick, *The Second American Party System: Party Formation in the Jacksonian Era* (1966); and John William Ward, *Andrew Jackson: Symbol for an Age* (1953).—M. F. H.

election of 1832. The presidential campaign of 1832 was marked by several innovations. It was the first in which a major third party participated. The Anti-Masonic party, which was opposed to secret privileged societies and strong in the rural areas of New England and the Middle Atlantic states, nominated William Wirt. The second major innovation was the use by all parties of national nominating conventions rather than caucuses. The National Republicans nominated Henry CLAY, and their platform denounced Andrew Jackson's abuse of the veto power, endorsed the American system, and called for the rechartering of the Second Bank of the United States. The Democrats renominated Jackson and selected Martin Van Buren for vice president.

Jackson's record, especially his veto of the bill to recharter the Bank of the United States, was supposedly the major issue in the campaign. Nicholas Biddle, president of the bank, in alliance with Daniel Webster, Clay, and others, had pushed for recharter in 1832. In his veto message, Jackson denounced the bank as an unconstitutional and privileged monopoly. Democrats portrayed Clay and his party as the money power.

While the National Republicans tried to make the veto the central issue of the campaign and while Jackson took his overwhelming reelection (687,502 votes to a combined 566,297 for his opponents) as a popular mandate to destroy the bank, the real impact of the veto issue is questionable. For one thing, in the West, which Jackson carried except for Kentucky, many farmers and bankers favored the Bank of the United States. Moreover, Jackson's personality and his other policies, such as Indian removal and advocacy of graduation of land prices and preemption, made him a favorite in that section. Finally, while the total popular vote increased by ninety thousand since 1828, Jackson's majority fell by fourteen thousand. The bank veto actually cost Jackson votes. One of the closest students of the election concludes that Jackson won in spite of the veto because of a superior Democratic organization and a campaign that featured pole raisings, mass rallies, and barbecues, not issues, to draw out the vote.

See Robert V. Remini, *Andrew Jackson* (1966). For western support of the Bank of the United States, see Jean Alexander Wilburn, *Biddle's Bank: The Crucial Years* (1967).—M. F. H.

election of 1836. Between 1832 and 1836 the opponents of Andrew Jackson organized as the Whig party. It was a heterogeneous coalition of National Republicans, states' rights southerners, Anti-Masons, and probank Democrats with little in common except opposition to "King Andrew" and his successor, Martin Van Buren. As befit such a diverse coalition, the Whigs held no national convention in 1836 and nominated three candidates rather than a single standard-bearer. Daniel Webster was to have strength in New England, Hugh Lawson White of Jackson's own Tennessee was to appeal to the South, and General William Henry Harrison of Ohio, an old Indian fighter, was to appeal to the West. The last posed a real threat in that section to the Democrats, who nominated the New Yorker Van Buren without a platform and promised to continue Jackson's policies. Westerners were disillusioned with the Democrats because of Jackson's Specie Circular of July 1836, which required all payments for land to be made in specie. Since genuine settlers rarely possessed specie, the circular benefited eastern speculators and thus angered westerners. Even Jackson's plan for distributing the surplus revenue of the national government to the states and his endorsement of Van Buren could not appease them.

In November Van Buren won the election, but the Democrats' margin dropped to 25,688 in a total vote of 1,505,290. The newest states, Michigan and Arkansas, went for Van Buren, but Harrison carried Ohio and Indiana in the West, while White took Tennessee. Though Van Buren carried the other western states, the substitution of an eastern candidate for Jackson and unpopular policies obviously cut into Democratic strength in that section. .

The best account of the election of 1836 can be found in Glyndon G. Van Deusen, *The Jacksonian Era, 1828-1848* (1959). See also Richard P. McCormick, *The Second American Party System: Party Formation in the Jacksonian Era* (1966).—M. F. H.

election of 1840. The election of 1840 brought voters out in unprecedented numbers. It, and not the elections in which Andrew Jackson ran, saw a true outpouring of democracy. The total vote in 1840 was more than twice as large as that in 1828. In 1828 the national average of voter participation was 56.3 percent; in 1840 it was 78 percent. In Mississippi, Alabama, Tennessee, Arkansas,

Michigan, Illinois, and Indiana 85 percent or more of the voters went to the polls. Missouri's 74 percent turnout was the highest it had ever achieved.

The campaign of 1840 also marked the first victory of the Whig party in a presidential campaign. Of the western states, Ohio, Indiana, Michigan, Kentucky, Tennessee, Mississippi, and Louisiana were carried by William Henry Harrison and John Tyler, the Whig candidates; Arkansas, Missouri, and Illinois were won by Martin Van Buren, the Democratic standard-bearer.

Several factors explain the huge vote and the Whig strength in the West and in the nation. One was the Whig campaign that, by omitting a platform and stressing emotionalism and hoopla, aimed at increasing voter participation and drawing rural and western support to the party. Harrison, an old Indian fighter who lived in Ohio, had great appeal in the West when contrasted to the New Yorker Van Buren. The Whigs posed as the party of the common man and labeled Van Buren an aristocrat. They portrayed Harrison as the Log Cabin and Hard Cider candidate, and the campaign was filled with cabin raisings in various towns where free liquor was dispensed to thirsty voters. Barbecues, torchlight processions, and mass meetings entranced the public. Rather than discuss issues, Whigs sang songs and chanted slogans such as "Tippecanoe and Tyler, too." Ignoring some issues probably helped the Whigs in the West, especially the Democrats' record on land preemption and graduation to help settlers during Van Buren's administration. If the selection of a military hero and a boisterous campaign helped the Whigs, so too did the Panic of 1837 and the subsequent depression. Voters turned on the Democratic administration whose policies could facilely be blamed for the depression. Whigs promised to restore prosperity, while the strict constructionist Democrats wanted to limit the role of the federal government in the economy still further. A final reason for the increased voter participation is that by 1840 the two opposing parties were well organized and closely balanced in almost every state. The very closeness of competition increased the interest of hitherto apathetic citizens, and the improved organizations brought out their votes.

R. G. Gunderson, *The Log Cabin Campaign* (1957), is a lively account of the 1840 election. A briefer, yet more balanced, account can be found in Glyndon G. Van Deusen, *The Jacksonian Era 1828-1848* (1959). Richard P. McCormick, "New Perspectives on Jacksonian Politics," *American Historical Review*, vol. 65 (1960), provides statistical evidence to show that if any democratic revolution occurred in presidential elections, it occurred in 1840.—M. F. H.

election of 1844. Westward expansion was a central issue of the campaign of 1844. After 1842 John Tyler, who succeeded to the presidency upon the death of William Henry Harrison, made the annexation of the Republic of Texas a major goal of his administration in order to build a new third party. In 1844 Texas annexation was explicitly linked to the protection of southern slavery by Tyler's third secretary of state, John C. Calhoun. These sectional overtones in large part account for the fate in the Senate of the treaty of annexation that Tyler negotiated. Several northern Democrats combined with almost all the Whigs to defeat the treaty.

Initially, the front-runners of both parties—Henry

CLAY and Martin Van Buren—tried to avoid the slavery issue by opposing immediate annexation in public letters. The Whigs followed Clay's lead by nominating him and omitting any reference to expansionism in their platform. In sharp contrast, the Democrats shoved aside Van Buren, who was unpopular in the South, and nominated James K. Polk of Tennessee, the first dark-horse candidate. To combine the expansionist desires of both the South and Northwest, the platform demanded "the reoccupation of Oregon and the reannexation of Texas at the earliest practicable period," although it seems that Oregon was tacked onto the platform without any unusual popular demand beforehand. While a few northern Democrats opposed Texas annexation and some southern Whigs favored it, and although Clay frantically shifted positions on the issue, expansionism became essentially a party issue with most Democrats everywhere favoring it and Whigs opposing it. The abolitionist Liberty party, staunchly against Texas annexation, ran James Birney of Michigan as its candidate.

The actual impact of the expansion issue on voting is difficult to determine. The election was remarkably close: Polk won 1,337,243 votes to Clay's 1,299,062 to Birney's 61,999. Every state west of the Alleghenies except Ohio, Kentucky, and Tennessee went for Polk. Nevertheless, the closest student of the election argues that while Texas weakened the Whigs in the South, it helped the Democrats carry only Indiana and Georgia of states they could not expect to carry for other reasons, and that it probably helped the antislavery Whigs carry Ohio. New York was the crucial state, since Birney drew off enough votes from Clay to throw the election to Polk, but the closest student of the election in that state denies that Texas caused the result. The strength of party loyalty and other issues such as the tariff and nativism probably had more influence on the results than Texas.

The best account of the 1844 election, which minimizes the importance of Texas on voting, is Charles G. Sellers, *James K. Polk: Continentalist, 1843-1846* (1966). A more traditional account, stressing Texas, can be found in Glyndon G. Van Deusen, *The Jacksonian Era, 1828-1848* (1959). Lee Benson, *The Concept of Jacksonian Democracy: New York as a Test Case* (1961), questions the importance of the Texas issue in New York in 1844.—M. F. H.

election of 1848. The disposition of slavery in the territories won from Mexico was the crucial issue behind the election of 1848. Both national parties had split sharply over that issue since 1844. Northern Democrats and Whigs, at the urging of their state legislatures, supported the WILMOT PROVISO, which would prohibit slavery in those territories. Southern Whigs and Democrats firmly opposed the proviso as an assault on southern rights. Indeed, extreme southern rights men, led by John C. Calhoun, argued that slavery should be allowed in all national territories.

Both parties, then, faced the problem of patching up internal differences in the 1848 campaign. Both solved it by avoiding any open position on the Wilmot Proviso. Ignoring Henry Clay and other established party leaders, the Whigs nominated Zachary Taylor, a Mexican War hero whose stance on important issues was unknown. To further obfuscate the situation, they adopted no national platform. Northern Whigs claimed Taylor supported the proviso, while southerners emphasized his background as a Louisiana slaveholder. The Democrats did almost as well. As a presidential candidate they selected Lewis Cass of Michigan, who along with other northwestern Democrats was a proponent of popular sovereignty as a compromise solution to the problem of slavery in the territories, and nominated William O. Butler of Kentucky for vice president. Cass, who had great strength in the Northwest, was also a firm expansionist and outspoken opponent of the proviso. The platform, however, while praising Polk's policy in the Mexican War and his territorial acquisition, was purposefully vague on the question of slavery in the territories. In the campaign Democrats stressed popular sovereignty. Antislavery men of both parties as well as Liberty party men, outraged at this attempt to dodge the issue, formed the FREE-SOIL PARTY, pledged to congressional prohibition of slavery in the territories. They nominated Martin Van Buren.

By carrying half the states Taylor won with a total vote of 1,360,099. Cass garnered 1,220,544, while Van Buren won 291,263, mainly in New York, Massachusetts, and Ohio. All of the western states admitted since 1844—Texas, Iowa, and Wisconsin—went for Cass, as did Arkansas, Missouri, Ohio, Indiana, Illinois, and Michigan. Taylor's strength in the Middle Atlantic states may have resulted from the tariff, not the slavery-extension, issue.

The best account of the 1848 election is Chaplain W. Morrison, *Democratic Politics and Sectionalism: The Wilmot Proviso Controversy* (1967). See also Allan Nevins, *Ordeal of the Union*, vol. I (1947).—M. F. H.

election of 1852. The campaign for the presidency in 1852 involved no issue of particular importance to the West. While the Democratic platform exulted in the territorial acquisitions from Mexico and opposed distribution of the proceeds of the sale of public lands to the states, the central issue was the COMPROMISE OF 1850, especially the explosive and hated Fugitive Slave Act. The Democrats, who had split in 1848, pledged to enforce the Compromise of 1850 in all its provisions and to resist new agitation of the slavery issue. Their candidate was dark-horse Franklin Pierce of New Hampshire, a Mexican War general. By 1852 they had managed to pull back into the party many of the antislavery Barnburners who had supported the Free-Soil party in 1848.

The Whigs were seriously divided between supporters of the Compromise of 1850 and incumbent Millard Fillmore and antislavery Conscience Whigs who abhorred the Fugitive Slave Act and refused to accept it as a finality. At their convention the Whigs rejected Fillmore and Daniel Webster, another conservative, and nominated Winfield Scott, a military hero and the choice of the Free-Soil wing of the party. But the conservatives and southerners controlled the platform, which lukewarmly accepted the compromise, including the Fugitive Slave Act, and contained a moderate tariff plank. The Free-Soil party, asserting that southerners dominated both major parties, denounced the compromise and nominated John P. Hale of New Hampshire.

The election dealt a mortal blow to the Whigs, who carried only four states even though the popular vote was reasonably close. Southerners feared Scott, and the

Whig vote dropped in almost every slave state including Kentucky and Tennessee, which Scott carried. Every western state, including the newest, California, went for Pierce. Support for the Compromise of 1850 may have helped the Democrats in the North, but much of their increased support probably came from the growing immigrant vote. The Free-Soil vote dropped, but the party remained strong in Ohio.

Able accounts of the 1852 election can be found in Allan Nevins, *Ordeal of the Union,* vol. II (1947), and Robert J. Rayback, *Millard Fillmore: Biography of a President* (1959).—M. F. H.

election of 1856. The problem of slavery in the territories and the actual situation in Kansas played a major role in the election of 1856. Since 1854 opponents of the Kansas-Nebraska Act (see KANSAS-NEBRASKA ISSUE) had been coalescing into anti-Nebraska coalitions, and in February 1856 they formed the national Republican party. With the addition of most northerners of the KNOW-NOTHING PARTY in June 1856, the Republicans managed to unite most opponents of slavery expansion, including the old Free-Soilers. The incipient party nominated for president John C. Frémont, famous for his explorations of the West and known as the Pathfinder. The Republican platform, obviously concerned with the Mormons in Utah, announced "the right and duty of Congress to prohibit in the territories those twin relics of barbarism, polygamy and slavery," denounced the aggressions on the rights of northern settlers in Kansas, and demanded the immediate admission of Kansas as a free state. It also called for a railroad to the Pacific and river and harbor improvements. Throughout the campaign Republican orators exaggerated the violence in "Bleeding Kansas" and called on northerners to unite against the South.

Democrats, on the other hand, while also calling for a Pacific railroad, endorsed the Kansas-Nebraska Act and asserted in their platform that popular sovereignty, "non-interference by Congress with Slavery in States and Territories," was the proper solution to the problem of slavery in the territories. They rejected, however, the champion of that doctrine, Stephen A. Douglas of Illinois, and nominated James Buchanan of Pennsylvania, primarily because he was in England in 1854 and therefore unconnected with the unpopular Kansas-Nebraska Act. The remnant of the Know-Nothing or American party, primarily southerners and conservative northerners, ran Millard Fillmore as a conservative pro-Union candidate.

The Republicans carried every free state except Indiana, Illinois, California, Pennsylvania, and New Jersey; Buchanan took the rest of the states except Maryland, which Fillmore carried. Free-Soil and antisouthern sentiment undoubtedly contributed to Republican strength in northwestern states, just as racist sentiments helped Democrats there. But nativism, antiCatholicism, temperance, and ethnic allegiance also influenced voting in the election.

See Eugene H. Berwanger, *The Frontier Against Slavery: Western Anti-Negro Prejudice and the Slavery Extension Controversy* (1967); Allan Nevins, *Ordeal of the Union,* vol. II (1947); and Joel Silbey, *The Transformation of American Politics, 1840-1860* (1967).—M. F. H.

election of 1860. Western issues and considerations were important, perhaps crucial, factors in the campaign of 1860. Disposition of western lands, the availability of candidates in important states, and formulas for slavery in the territories concerned both major parties.

When the Democrats convened in Charleston in May 1860, Stephen A. Douglas of Illinois, champion of popular sovereignty in the territories—that is, local self-determination on slavery—was the front-runner for the nomination. Southern Democrats, however, disliked him because of his opposition to the Lecompton constitution (see KANSAS-NEBRASKA ISSUE) and his insistence, after the Dred Scott decision, that territorial legislatures could prohibit slavery by refusing to pass slave codes protecting it. Followers of President James Buchanan were also determined to deny Douglas the nomination. Most important, a group of southern Democrats led by William Lowndes Yancey and the Alabama delegation were pledged to walk out of the convention if it did not adopt a platform calling for a federal slave code in the territories—that is, positive protection of slavery by the federal government in all territories. Douglas' followers realized this platform would be suicide in the North, and they insisted on readoption of the 1856 platform, which called for nonintervention by Congress in the territories—that is, self-government there. When southerners lost the platform fight, most of the delegates from the lower South bolted the convention. Eventually the Democrats nominated two tickets—one headed by Douglas for president and Herschel V. Johnson of Alabama for vice president, favoring nonintervention; and a southern ticket with John C. Breckinridge for president and Joseph Lane of Oregon for vice president, supporting a federal slave code. Support for either ticket was not exclusively sectional, but the split severely weakened the Democrats.

Meanwhile, the confident Republicans met at Chicago. They wanted a candidate with availability in Illinois, Indiana, and Pennsylvania, a man who did not seem too radical on the slavery issue and who would not alienate Know-Nothings in those states. For these reasons, they nominated Abraham Lincoln, the Illinois rail-splitter who would have great appeal in the northwestern states. To augment that appeal, the Republicans denounced the Lecompton constitution and denied the authority of Congress to legalize slavery in any territory. Equally important so far as western states were concerned, the platform called for rivers and harbors improvements, a Pacific railroad, and a homestead act granting free land to actual settlers. The latter plank evoked acute interest in the West because Democratic President James Buchanan had recently vetoed such a law. During the campaign Republican orators stressed the homestead issue in places such as Michigan, Iowa, and Minnesota, and it was very influential there.

A fourth party, of conservatives fearful for the Union if Republicans won, entered the race. Named the Constitutional Union party, it nominated John Bell of Tennessee and Edward Everett of Massachusetts and ran on a platform of the Constitution and the Union.

While Lincoln won the election with a clear majority in the electoral college, he had only a minority of the popular votes. Douglas, the old advocate of expansion and territorial self-determination, carried only Missouri and part of New Jersey. Bell carried Tennessee, Kentucky, and Virginia and ran well in Missouri and Arkansas. Breckinridge carried all the other slave states including Texas, while Lincoln took the remaining free states including California, Oregon, and Minnesota, the newest states. A combination of factors—the Democratic division, free-soil sentiment, hostility to the South for obstructing economic measures, and ethnic and religious issues and allegiances—explains this result.

For the Democratic campaign, see Roy F. Nichols, *The Disruption of American Democracy* (1948); and Allan Nevins, *The Emergence of Lincoln,* vol. II (1950). For the Republicans, see Don E. Fehrenbacher, *Prelude to Greatness: Lincoln in the 1850's* (1962). Reinhard Luthin, *The First Lincoln Campaign* (1944), stresses the importance of economic issues in the Republican victory, while Joel Silbey, *The Transformation of American Politics, 1840-1860* (1967), argues that a combination of economic, moral, and sociocultural issues determined voting behavior.—M. F. H.

election of 1864. The election of 1864, not surprisingly, reflected the tensions that had been generated by three years of civil war. The Lincoln administration's lackluster management of the Civil War and its suppression of civil liberties on the home front troubled many politicians, both Democrat and "Unionist" (the name taken by the Republicans upon the outbreak of the war). The president had angered Missouri radicals when he discharged General John C. Frémont, and many moderates were disturbed by his Emancipation Proclamation and his suspensions of habeas corpus.

Lincoln's reelection, in short, was far from certain, and the president himself realized that it was highly "probable that this Administration will not be reelected." The uncertainty of the situation can be seen in the Republicans' unsuccessful last-minute effort to admit the territories of Nebraska and Colorado to the Union in time for the election. It was hoped that these states would cast the necessary votes to return the party to power.

Each of the major parties was split into radical and moderate factions over the issue of the war, with the fundamental difference being that radical Democrats were advocates of peace while radical Republicans urged a more vigorous prosecution of the war. The Peace Democrats, called Copperheads by their detractors, were centered in the Old Northwest, particularly in Ohio. Despite the eventual prosperity which wartime prices brought to the western farmer, many of the residents of the Ohio and Mississippi valleys were upset at the loss of their southern markets, for they were still accustomed to thinking of the flow of goods in terms of river transportation. In addition, many of the Peace Democrats were former southerners, and they dreaded the influx of blacks across the border they feared would result from emancipation.

The radical Republicans, on the other hand, found Lincoln's policies too soft. In May 1864 a group of radicals, primarily German-Americans from the Old Northwest and Missouri, gathered in Cleveland prior to the regular Union party convention and nominated Frémont for president. Most of the radicals, however, grudgingly stuck with Lincoln, and "Honest Abe" was the unanimous choice of the party's Baltimore convention. Lincoln dropped Vice President Hannibal Hamlin in favor of Tennessean Andrew Johnson, and the party platform called for unity in the prosecution of the war,

declared slavery to be the cause of the war and demanded its elimination, and advocated a Pacific railroad.

The Democrats, seeking to capitalize on both the disaffection with war losses and the strength of the peace movement, nominated General George B. McClellan to please the war faction while at the same time inserting a peace plank in their platform. It described the war as a failure and called for an armistice and peace negotiations based on a restored Union.

In August 1864 the war took a favorable turn for the North and for Unionist election hopes. Admiral David Farragut captured Mobile, General Philip Sheridan secured the Shenandoah valley, and General William Sherman took Atlanta. Frémont now found himself without an issue and withdrew from the race, and the Radical Republicans closed ranks behind Lincoln. The Democrats and Copperheads saw their hopes for a victory at the polls shattered by victory on the battlefield. The president won the election handily, polling 55 percent of the popular vote and winning the electoral vote by a decisive margin of 212 to 21. Lincoln carried every state except Kentucky, Delaware, and New Jersey.

The Republicans ran very strong in the Midwest and Far West. Except for the border state of Kentucky, where emancipation and internal security policies aroused severe resentment, every state in the heartland went to the Republicans with large majorities. This was, in part, a response to Republican support for homestead legislation and military aid against Confederate armies and pro-Confederate guerrillas. The Republicans captured the new state of Nevada and the Pacific Coast states, overcoming the former Democratic edge in the West. Of great importance to this realignment was the policy of the Lincoln administration on behalf of a transcontinental railroad.

See Harold M. Hyman, "The Election of 1864," in Arthur M. Schlesinger, Jr., ed., *History of American Presidential Elections,* 4 vols. (1971); F. L. Klement, *The Copperheads in the Middle West* (1971); Eugene H. Roseboom, *A History of Presidential Elections* (1970); and William F. Zornow, *Lincoln and the Party Divided* (1954).—R. B. W.

election of 1868. The election of 1868 was in large part a test vote on the policies of radical Republican Reconstruction. Few Republicans seriously considered the renomination of Andrew Johnson, and the Democrats, as well, showed little interest in a president who had barely survived an impeachment trial. The Republican party was firmly in the hands of the radicals, who were determined to guarantee that the South would be reconstructed from Capitol Hill with little interference from the White House.

The radical Republicans were aware that the election would be won or lost in the North, and northern uneasiness over the question of Negro suffrage cast doubt on their prospects in the presidential election. Three northern states had voted down Negro suffrage, and only two northern states outside New England allowed the black man the right to vote in 1868. In order to protect themselves from this anti-Negro prejudice, the Republicans chose as their presidential candidate the most popular man in the North, Ulysses S. Grant. Grant had shown an interest in the radicals' point of view, and his political inexperience made him an ideal figurehead for the policies of the radical congressmen. The Republicans provided themselves with additional insurance by inserting ambiguous planks in their platform concerning Negro suffrage and monetary policy.

It was the money issue that most interested western voters. During the war the government had issued some $450 million in greenbacks without gold backing. The value of the greenbacks had fluctuated but was always below the value of coins or gold-backed currency. Between 1866 and 1868 some $100 million of these greenbacks had been retired from circulation, but pressure by western farmers had stopped the deflation in 1868. The farmers further demanded that greenbacks be reissued to redeem those outstanding war bonds that did not explicitly require redemption in gold. The farmers maintained that more greenbacks in circulation would strengthen farm prices and expand credit.

The Democrats, hoping to compensate for Grant's popularity and the stigma of disloyalty, armed their candidate, Horatio Seymour, with a platform a great deal more explicit than that of the Republicans. They denounced Republican Reconstruction and defined the issue of Negro suffrage as properly belonging to the states for settlement. They hoped to appeal to western agricultural interests by incorporating into the platform the "Ohio Idea" of Peace Democrat George H. Pendleton. Pendleton, who was for a time the leading contender for the Democratic nomination, advocated the use of greenbacks to pay off outstanding war bonds and to replace national bank notes, which were highly unpopular in the West. This "idea," he insisted, guarded against both contraction *and* inflation, for the bonds, argued Pendleton, could be retired without new issues of greenbacks. Seymour, a "hard-money" man, did everything he could short of outright repudiation to avoid this plank of the platform, a stance that contributed to his failure to arouse much enthusiasm for his candidacy in the West.

The campaign was marked more by an appeal to the hatred and divisiveness engendered by the Civil War than by a discussion of the issues of money and suffrage. The Republicans charged the Democrats with disloyalty and "waved the bloody shirt," and western voters like those in the North generally reacted more to the passions of the war than to anything else. The emotional issues of the campaign and the GOP's liberal land and resource policies were more than able to overcome any concern western interests had over the party's conservative stand on the currency issue.

Nevertheless, the Democrats did surprisingly well in the West. Seymour captured Oregon and lost Nevada by only 1,200 votes and California by only 500 votes. Nebraskans, voting for the first time in a presidential election, provided Grant with three electoral votes. Overall, Grant garnered 52.7 percent of the popular vote and 214 of 294 electoral votes. The radicals could claim a victory, but not a decisive one. Without the "bloody shirt" and the votes of the six southern states manipulated by the radicals, the Republicans would have been hard pressed to bring in a winner.

See Charles H. Coleman, *The Election of 1868* (1933); John Hope Franklin, "The Election of 1868," in Arthur M. Schlesinger, Jr., ed., *History of American Presidential Elections*, 4 vols. (1971); Eugene H. Roseboom, *A History of Presidential Elections* (1970); Robert P. Sharkey,

Money, Class, and Party (1959); and Irwin Unger, *The Greenback Era* (1964).—R. B. W.

election of 1872. The election of 1872 signified the extent to which American politics was scraping rock bottom in the age of what Vernon L. Parrington called the "Great Barbecue." The Democratic party, still hampered by the Copperhead legacy, was forced to seek a coalition with a disaffected liberal Republican faction led by Horace Greeley, a man who had made his name by attacking the Democrats. The Republicans, on the other hand, stuck with Ulysses S. Grant, who had proved amenable to the control of both Congress and greedy office-seekers.

The Liberal Republican party grew out of a sincere desire to quell the runaway corruption of Grant's administration. The movement originated in Missouri, where a group of reformers led by Carl Schurz captured the state's gubernatorial election in 1870. The Liberals stood for civil-service reform, downward revision of the tariff, and more lenient treatment of the South. At the party's convention, however, the reformers were faced with a wide spectrum of delegates who had in common only their discontent with Grantism. Such an odd collection of politicians could have picked a scarcely less odd candidate than Horace Greeley, a strong advocate of high tariffs and lifelong enemy of the party of Jackson. The Democrats, however, realizing that their chances were nil without a coalition, temporarily buried their enmity and nominated the intrepid editor as their candidate also.

Historian Eugene Roseboom has characterized the campaign as a contest that pitted "the man of no ideas . . . against the man of too many." The outcome was never really in doubt. Grant was still the honest hero to many voters, and the "bloody shirt" was still a persuasive symbol. Grant polled 55.8 percent of the popular vote and secured an electoral college majority of 286 to 63.

The Republicans did well in the Far West, capturing California and Nevada by substantial margins. Texas, voting for the first time since the Civil War, gave Greeley a twenty thousand-vote plurality. The Democrats also made a strong showing in the border states, particularly Missouri, birthplace of the Liberal Republican movement. Here Greeley outpolled Grant 151,434 to 119,196. For Greeley, Grant's overwhelming victory was a mandate for corruption. The victory broke his heart and, coupled with the death of his wife and the loss of his newspaper, led to his death a few weeks after the election.

Although the West and western issues played a relatively minor role in this election, beneath the overt concerns of the campaign lay the beginnings of the discontent that was to subsequently influence the course of national politics. Western farmers were beginning to suspect that their interests were less than secure in a Republican party that looked first to the needs of eastern bankers, railroad promoters, and manufacturers and was beginning to coalesce around a firm high-tariff, sound-money platform. Some of the concerns that were to activate western agrarians for the next quarter century can be found in the third-party platform of the Labor Reform party in 1872. This platform called for monetary inflation, the taxation of government bonds, reservation of public lands for actual settlers only, the prohibition of the importation of Chinese labor, and government regulation of railroad and telegraph corporations. Western tillers of the soil, observes historian Roseboom, "harassed by debts, high taxes, and falling farm prices, and disillusioned over the benefits of railroads were developing heretical views on economic problems." The Panic of 1873 would bring these views to bear on national politics.

See William Gillette. "The Election of 1872," in Arthur M. Schlesinger, Jr., ed., *History of American Presidential Elections,* 4 vols. (1971); E. D. Rose, *The Liberal Republican Movement* (1919); Eugene H. Roseboom, *A History of Presidential Elections* (1970); and G. G. Van Deusen, *Horace Greeley: Nineteenth-Century Crusader* (1953).—R. B. W.

election of 1876. By 1876 the corruption and ineptitude of the Grant administrations had almost completely destroyed public faith in the national government and had brought the Republican party to the brink of disaster. Nothing damaged the party's prestige in the West more than the Panic of 1873 and the economic collapse that followed in its wake. Westerners were particularly disillusioned by the financial collapse of the railroads and the depressed agricultural prices that persisted through four years of economic stagnation. The Republicans averted disaster at the polls by "stealing" the presidency from the Democrats in the dramatic disputed election of 1876. This election was marred by widespread electoral corruption on the part of both parties and did little to restore public confidence in the electoral process. Nevertheless, the closeness of this contest was significant, for it marked the resurgence of the Democrats and the full-scale reentry of the South into the politics of the Union.

Once Grant had been disabused of any notion of running for a third term, the leading Republican candidate for the nomination was James G. Blaine of Maine, a bitter enemy of both the reform wing of the party and Roscoe Conkling's New York machine. In the face of a Blaine stampede the reformers and reactionaries pooled their delegate strength in an unlikely alliance and nominated Governor Rutherford B. Hayes of Ohio on the sixth ballot. The platform was the model of vagueness. It eulogized the party for its work during the Civil War and Reconstruction and, out of deference to western inflationists, did not refer specifically to the controversial Resumption Act of 1875, which had provided for the redemption of greenbacks in coin after January 1, 1879. Instead the platform urged "a continuous and steady progress to specie payment," an ambiguous statement that satisfied few westerners interested in an inflationary monetary policy, particularly since Hayes had made his political reputation as a foe of Ohio greenbackism (see SILVER ISSUE).

Governor Samuel J. Tilden, a wealthy corporation lawyer in New York and leading aspirant for the Democratic nomination, was a first-ballot victor in that party's convention in St. Louis. In order to compensate for Tilden's eastern, hard-money leanings, Thomas A. Hendricks of Indiana, a leading soft-money man, was given second place on the ticket. This move appeased the western wing of the party but alarmed eastern conservatives who worried over Tilden's chronic poor health and the possibility of inadvertently putting a greenbacker in the White House.

Reform was the keynote of the Democratic platform. The scandals of the Grant administration were denounced in unsparing terms, and reform was promised in government administration, banking and currency, the tariff, taxation, public expenditures, the public-land system, immigration policy, and the civil service. The currency and immigration reforms were aimed particularly at westerners, who were seeking an inflationist monetary policy and exclusion of Oriental immigrants. This latter issue, which inflamed passions and influenced West Coast politics throughout the 1870s and 1880s, can most logically be traced to the interests of western labor, but this is to ignore the larger ethnic animus that extended beyond such straightforward economic motivations. As one San Franciscan explained the Chinese problem: "The burden of our accusation against them is that they came in conflict with our labor interests; that they can never assimilate with us . . . that their civilization is demoralizing and degrading to our people . . . and that an alien, degraded labor class, without desire of citizenship, without education, and without interest in the country it inhabits, is an element both demoralizing and dangerous to the community within which it exists." The Republicans, ever alert to the needs of capitalists, answered this sentiment with the mere promise to "investigate the effects" of Chinese immigration, while the reform-minded Democrats promised to press for legislation to "prevent further importation or immigration of the Mongolian race."

The stand of neither party on currency issues satisfied extreme inflationists, and in May 1876 this element met as the GREENBACK PARTY in Indianapolis and nominated Peter Cooper of New York for president and Senator Newton Booth of California for vice president. (Samuel F. Cary of Ohio later replaced Booth.) The party's platform called for the repeal of the Resumption Act of 1875 and issuance of legal tender notes convertible into government bonds with an interest rate not to exceed one cent a day per hundred dollars. This party's campaign, a forerunner of the agrarian politics of the 1890s, managed to win 81,737 votes, most of these from Indiana, Iowa, Illinois, and Michigan. More importantly, the party's vote not only influenced the outcome in the key state of Indiana but also revealed the political appeal that the money issue had in a national campaign.

During the campaign, the Democrats dwelt heavily on the corruption of the previous Republican administrations and emphasized the need for thoroughgoing reform. The Republicans once again waved the "bloody shirt" and banked heavily on Hayes's spotless military and political record. Joseph Pulitzer, recognizing the narrowness of this approach, remarked, "Hayes has never stolen. Good God, has it come to this?" The campaign in the South was marked by violence and bloodshed as both parties tried to influence the Negro vote.

Although the election gave Tilden a margin of 250,000 popular votes, the electoral vote in some southern states and in Oregon was disputed, leaving Tilden one vote short of the needed 185 electoral votes. Ultimately, the power to decide the result of the election was vested in a fifteen-man electoral commission. It ruled in every case in favor of Hayes by an identical eight to seven margin. Hayes won the election by a single electoral vote, 185 to 184. The danger of another civil war was averted when southern Democrats agreed to acquiesce in Hayes's election in return for the withdrawal of federal troops from the South and aid for southern internal improvements.

Once again the western states were securely in the Republican column, although the closeness of the vote in California, Oregon, and Nevada reflected that of the nation as a whole. Texas, voting still as a southern state, gave Tilden an overwhelming two thirds of its popular vote. The Democrats were disappointed to discover that Colorado, a state they had voted to admit to the Union upon the expectation that it would be safely Democratic, voted overwhelmingly Republican. The reform emphasis of the Democrats was not sufficient to overcome the long-standing loyalty of the important interests of the West—grain, cattle, sheep, and mining—to the party of nationalism, the transcontinental railroad, and a liberal land policy.

See Harry Barnard, *Rutherford B. Hayes and His America* (1954); Alexander C. Flick, *Samuel J. Tilden: A Study in Political Sagacity* (1939); Sidney I. Pomerantz, "The Election of 1876," in Arthur M. Schlesinger, Jr., ed., *History of American Presidential Elections,* vol. II (1971); Eugene H. Roseboom, *A History of Presidential Elections* (1970); Irwin Unger, *The Greenback Era* (1964); and C. Vann Woodward, *Reunion and Reaction* (2nd ed., 1966).—R. B. W.

election of 1880. The election of 1880 was largely one of personalities, with neither of the major-party candidates taking a strong position on the problems of the day. As historian Leonard Dinnerstein has noted, "The election of 1880 highlighted the worst features of the electoral process: vicious squabbles among intransigent party bosses; competitors for the major nominations who differed only in name, place of origin, and zeal in pursuing the party's highest honor; purchased votes, forgery, calumny, and vindictive politics."

The Republicans overcame a divisive intraparty struggle between factions headed by New York's Roscoe Conkling and Maine's James G. Blaine by nominating James A. Garfield of Ohio, a virtually unknown dark horse, over former President Ulysses S. Grant, who had just returned from a triumphant world tour with his eyes on a third term in the White House. In order to placate the Conkling faction, which had supported Grant, second place on the ticket was given to Conkling's lieutenant, Chester A. Arthur. The Democrats displayed a similar instinct for the innocuous by nominating a little-known Civil War general, Winfield Scott Hancock of Pennsylvania, for the presidency.

The Greenback party tried once again to rouse national interest in a program of reform, but the results were disappointing. The party failed to do well because its platform appealed only to debtors struggling to pay off debts. Farmers were enjoying boom conditions and were busy acquiring new debts rather than thinking about how to pay off old ones. The party's candidate, General James B. Weaver of Iowa, polled only 307,000 votes. However, the Greenback party did manage to influence the outcome of the vote in the key states of California, Indiana, and New Jersey, where the major candidates were involved in close contests.

The election resulted in a narrow victory for the Republicans. Garfield held a 10,000-vote plurality in the popular vote and a margin in the electoral college of 214 to 155. Garfield carried the entire Midwest and West with the exception of Missouri, Texas, Nevada, and California, which Hancock won by a margin of 78 votes.

See Herbert J. Clancy, *The Presidential Election of 1880* (1958); Leonard Dinnerstein, "The Election of 1880," in Arthur M. Schlesinger, Jr., ed., *History of American Presidential Elections,* vol. II (1971); H. Wayne Morgan, *From Hayes to McKinley: National Party Politics, 1877-1896* (1969); and Eugene H. Roseboom, *A History of Presidential Elections* (197|).—R. B. W.

election of 1884. The election of 1884 was marked by one of the most vituperative campaigns in the history of American politics. There was little division on major issues between the two major parties or their presidential candidates, James G. Blaine and Grover Cleveland; the campaign centered on the public failings of Blaine and the private indiscretions of Cleveland.

After twenty years of dedication to partisan politics Blaine was finally nominated by his party for the presidency at the Republican convention in Chicago. His nomination was popular among the great majority of Republicans, but the reform wing found him totally unacceptable and seceded from the Republicans to form the Cleveland Democrats, or Mugwumps. The Democratic convention, meeting also in Chicago, was a generally harmonious affair. The party, eager for its first victory since the Civil War, united behind Governor Grover Cleveland of New York, who was nominated on the second ballot despite the opposition of Tammany Hall.

The year 1884 marked the demise of the Greenback party. It united with the upstart Anti-Monopoly party behind General Benjamin Butler of Massachusetts and Greenbacker Alanson M. West of Mississippi and reiterated its reform proposals of 1880. Butler, however, received only 175,370 votes; the poor showing marked the end of national politics for the Greenbackers. However, the death of the Greenback party did not mean the end of the inflationist sentiment, which was the bread and butter issue of the party and its western agrarian constituency. This sentiment merely changed colors, from green to silver. Both major parties assiduously avoided the monetary issue in 1884 and the supporters of free silver had yet to find a political vehicle with which to express their discontent.

In the major campaign, reformers of all political persuasions led the attack on Blaine; he was characterized as a spoilsman, a tool of big business, and a sentimental Don Quixote whose baiting of the South was little more than a jousting match with "rebel windmills." More specifically, Blaine was indicted for the use of his official position to promote railroad transactions for personal profit. The Republicans counterattacked by uncovering evidence showing that Cleveland had fathered an illegitimate child in Buffalo ten years prior to his nomination. This mudslinging prompted one reformer to wryly propose that Blaine, whose private life was blameless, be remanded to private life, and let Cleveland, whose public life was a model of integrity, be kept in public life.

The campaign of 1884 was more notable for the issues that were not confronted than for those "moral" issues that were. Neither party came to terms with such important issues as labor unrest, farmer discontent, public-land policies, railway regulation, monopolies, or even tariff reform. This can be partially explained by the fact that the parties were very close to agreement on these issues; the Democratic party was no longer the party of Jeffersonian agrarianism but was drifting toward a concern with industry, commerce, sound money, and nationalism. The party platforms left the voter with little choice, particularly if he opposed this drift toward consensus. This was not lost upon western and southern farmers, who recognized that Bourbon Democracy was no more sympathetic to their demands than was the GOP.

The race was an extremely close one, and was ultimately decided by the vote of New York State, which went to Cleveland by a narrow margin. Cleveland polled a popular vote of 4,874,986 against Blaine's 4,851,981 and won the electoral vote by a margin of 219 to 182. The West played no role in electing the first Democratic president since Buchanan. The Republicans captured the vote of all the western states, regaining the electoral votes of California and Nevada they had lost in 1880.

See Mark D. Hirsch, "The Election of 1884," in Arthur M. Schlesinger, Jr., ed., *History of American Presidential Elections*, 4 vols. (1971); H. Wayne Morgan, *From Hayes to McKinley: National Party Politics, 1877-1896* (1969); David S. Muzzey, *James G. Blaine: A Political Idol of Other Days* (1936); Allan Nevins, *Grover Cleveland: A Study in Courage* (1932); and Eugene H. Roseboom, *A History of Presidential Elections* (1970).—R. B. W.

election of 1888. The central issue shaping the election of 1888 was tariff reform. It was, in fact, virtually the only issue the Republican party had, for Grover Cleveland had proven to be an able and widely popular president. However, it was Cleveland himself who gave new life to Republican hopes for victory when he devoted the entirety of his annual message of 1887 to a vigorous argument for a downward revision of the tariff. The Republicans were jubilant over Cleveland's strong statement, for it provided them with a ready-made coalition of manufacturers, businessmen, workers, and Anglophobes.

The Democratic party convention in St. Louis was a perfunctory affair; Cleveland was nominated by acclamation and the leading issue, tariff reform, had already been settled in advance. After James G. Blaine pulled himself out of the race for personal considerations and leading contenders John Sherman of Ohio and Walter Q. Gresham of Indiana failed to galvanize the necessary support, the Republican bosses turned to Senator Benjamin Harrison of Indiana. The platforms of the two parties reflected the central importance of the tariff issue. The Democrats denounced the evils of the existing protective system and called for downward revision, while the Republicans dragged out the spectre of free trade and spoke "uncompromisingly in favor of the American system of protection." Both parties pledged themselves to facilitate the entrance of the western territories (except Utah) into the Union, and the Republicans denounced the pernicious political power of the Mormon Church in the territories.

The Republicans waged a vigorous and flamboyant campaign, relying heavily on the rhetorical flourishes of both Harrison and the old master, Blaine. They attacked the Democrats as free-traders with the interests of Europe, particularly Great Britain, more at heart

than those of the United States. Much of this campaign was aimed at western farmers whose loyalty was considered essential to Republican success but whose interests in high tariffs were more theoretical than real. Tariff tracts flooded the midwestern states, raising the spectre of competition with European agriculture and extolling the virtues of the shield offered by the protective system. While some grumblings were heard from western agrarians, particularly in Minnesota, who resented the disproportionate benefits protectionism offered manufacturing and labor over agriculture, the Republican's propaganda campaign was successful in holding the votes of the heartland. The Democratic campaign never got off the ground. Cleveland thought it improper for him to campaign actively, and his campaign managers, William H. Barnum and Calvin S. Brice, were wealthy businessmen with a marked aversion to tariff reform.

Inflationist sentiment found its outlet in 1888 under the aegis of the Union Labor party, which held its convention in May in Cincinnati. The party nominated for president Alson J. Streeter, a former president of the Northwestern Farmers' Alliance. The platform showed the party's debt to Greenbackism and foreshadowed the agrarian demands of the 1890s. It opposed land monopoly and advocated the nationalization of transportation and communication facilities, a legal tender currency issued directly to the people, and the free coinage of silver. Indeed, the party's name belied its true interests, for its concerns were more agrarian than labor.

The election was close, but Harrison carried the key states of Indiana and New York, giving him an electoral vote margin of 233 to 163, despite the fact that Cleveland outpolled him in the popular vote 5,540,329 to 5,439,853. The Republicans again captured the whole of the western electoral vote, but the race was closer in this region than it had been in 1884. The issues that were to become so prominent in the next decade—depressed agricultural prices, grievances against railroads, and antimonopoly sentiment—threatened Republican hegemony in Minnesota, Iowa, Nebraska, and Kansas. Although the immediate impact of these issues was minor, the grumblings of 1888 portended the upheaval that rocked the GOP and then wrecked the Democrats.

See Robert Marcus, *Grand Old Party* (1971); H. Wayne Morgan, *From Hayes to McKinley: National Party Politics, 1877-1896* (1969); Allan Nevins, *Grover Cleveland: A Study in Courage* (1932); Eugene H. Roseboom, *A History of Presidential Elections* (1970); Harry J. Sievers, *Benjamin Harrison* (1959); Tom E. Terrill, *The Tariff, Politics, and American Foreign Policy* (1973); Robert F. Wesser, "The Election of 1888," in Arthur M. Schlesinger, Jr., ed., *History of American Presidential Elections*, vol. II (1971); and R. Hal Williams, " 'Dry Bones and Dead Language': The Democratic Party," in H. Wayne Morgan, ed., *The Gilded Age* (2nd ed., 1970).—R. B. W.

election of 1892. The election of 1892 was a rematch of the election of 1888 with "honest bearded Benjamin Harrison confronting honest mustached Grover Cleveland in a tariff debate." The dullness of this confrontation was mitigated somewhat by the appearance of POPULISM, as the storm of agrarian discontent began to manifest itself on the national level. A key feature of this election was the unusual voting pattern of the western states, where the message of the People's party met with the greatest sympathy.

Republicans were not entirely happy with the presidency of Harrison, despite the fact that this administration had managed to fulfill nearly all of its campaign promises in one of the most active periods of legislation in the country's history. Harrison, however, was not an endearing personality, and his cold aloofness contrasted sharply with the dynamism of his chief rival for control of the party, the "Plumed Knight," James G. Blaine. Harrison, nevertheless, overcame the Blaine challenge at the Minneapolis convention and captured the Republican nomination.

At the Democratic convention the only challenge to former President Cleveland was mounted on behalf of New York governor David B. Hill, who avoided any concrete statement on the issues by asserting enigmatically: "I am a Democrat." Cleveland gained the nomination on the first ballot and chose as his running mate Adlai E. Stevenson of Illinois.

The campaign between the major parties once again centered on the tariff issue, with the Democrats denouncing the existing protectionist system and the Republicans defending it (see BANKING AND CURRENCY and SILVER ISSUE). The two parties were equally vague on the issue of monetary policy, but both Cleveland and Harrison stood firmly on the side of the conservative East with regard to this issue. Both parties spoke out in favor of the earliest possible admission of Arizona and New Mexico to the Union, but otherwise slanted their campaign toward the key eastern states, particularly New York.

The narrowness of the major-party campaign was not lost on the discontented farmers of the South and West, and in July 1892 various spokesmen involved in the AGRARIAN MOVEMENTS came together in Omaha and formed the People's, or Populist, party in an atmosphere of bitterness and frustration. The Populists denounced the American economic system and condemned the major parties for "a sham battle over the tariff, so that capitalists, corporations, national banks, rings, trusts, watered stock, the demonetization of silver, and the oppressions of usurers may all be lost sight of." The party's platform, largely written by Ignatius DONNELLY, demanded a national currency issued by the government without the use of banks, the free and unlimited coinage of silver and gold at the ratio of sixteen to one, a circulating medium of fifty dollars per capita, a graduated income tax, a system of postal savings banks, government ownership and operation of railroad, telegraph, and telephone systems, and measures to end land monopoly by railroads and corporations. James WEAVER of Iowa, the old Greenbacker, was nominated for president and James G. Field of Virginia, a former Confederate general, was named for vice president.

The election produced a near landslide for the Democrats and a surprising show of strength by the Populists, especially in the West. Cleveland netted 5,556,543 popular votes; Harrison, 5,175,582; and Weaver, 1,040,886. The electoral vote was won by Cleveland by a 277 to 145 margin. Weaver gained 22 electoral votes, these coming from Colorado, Idaho, Kansas, Nevada, North Dakota, and Oregon. Cleveland regained California for the Democrats (except one elector) and managed to gain one of North Dakota's electors. Mon-

tana, Nebraska, Oregon, South Dakota, Washington, and Wyoming gave all or most of their electoral votes to Harrison. This was the first election for the Omnibus States (Idaho, Montana, the Dakotas, Washington, and Wyoming) admitted in 1889 and 1890, and the diverse nature of their balloting added to the interest of the election.

See D. M. Dozer, "Harrison and the Campaign of 1892," *American Historical Revue*, vol. 54 (1948); John D. Hicks, *The Populist Revolt* (1931); G. H. Knoles, *The Presidential Campaign and Election of 1892* (1942); Horace S. Merrill, *Bourbon Leader: Grover Cleveland and the Democratic Party* (1957); H. Wayne Morgan, *From Hayes to McKinley: National Party Politics, 1877-1896* (1969), and "The Election of 1892," in Arthur M. Schlesinger, Jr., ed., *History of American Presidential Elections,* 4 vols. (1971); Allan Nevins, *Grover Cleveland: A Study in Courage* (1932); Eugene H. Roseboom, *A History of Presidential Elections* (1970); and Harry J. Sievers, *Benjamin Harrison* (1959).—R. B. W.

election of 1896. The presidential election of 1896 climaxed four years of economic upheaval, political turmoil, and vigorous protest from the discontented South and West. The result of the contest between Democrat-Populist William Jennings BRYAN and victorious Republican William McKinley was that the American people rejected the aspirations of POPULISM, condemned the Democrats to minority status for a generation, and made the Republicans the majority party. After two decades of partisan stalemate, a national two-party system replaced the divided and discordant organizations of the 1870s and 1880s. The GOP was in clear control of the country's political destiny.

The Panic of 1893 did the most to produce these results. The depression drove voters away from the Democrats among crucial ethnic groups in the Middle West and Plains states and eroded party strength in the major cities. Americans were forced to choose between the protest doctrines of Populism—most notably the demand for a silver standard of currency and unlimited purchase of silver by the federal government—and such nationalizing policies of the Republicans as the protective tariff. In 1894 and 1896 voters overwhelmingly opted for the GOP.

President Grover Cleveland's disastrous leadership shattered the Democratic party between 1893 and 1895. Forcing a split on the money question over repeal of the Sherman Silver Purchase Act (see SILVER ISSUE) in 1893, he further ruptured the party with inept handling of the Wilson-Gorman tariff in 1894, patronage in states such as Nebraska, Colorado, and California, and manifestations of popular unrest, such as Coxey's Army (see INDUSTRIAL ARMY MOVEMENT) and the Pullman strike. Catastrophic Democratic reverses in the congressional elections of 1894 left little chance for victory unless the party repudiated Cleveland's abysmal record of failure.

For the young People's party, the election represented an opportunity and a challenge. Organized to express the grievances of southern and western farmers at their subordinate economic place in society, the party did well in the 1890 and 1892 elections. But its performance in 1894 was disappointing, and it needed a good showing in 1896 to maintain any hope of attaining major party status. The Populists had laid aside most of their earlier programs of railroad regulation, subsidies to agriculture, and political reform and were concentrating on the panacea of unlimited coinage by the government, so dear to western silver miners and southern agrarians. Confident that both the GOP and the Democrats would select candidates unfriendly to silver, the Populist leaders expected to have the only candidate in the field acceptable to discontented rural Americans.

After 1894, however, silver sentiment within the Democratic party grew rapidly,. When the national convention met, the supporters of the white metal were in secure control, and the platform endorsed silver. In addition, the Democratic party found a candidate who could express the frustrations of the agricultural regions. William Jennings Bryan capitalized on months of patient wooing of delegates, delivered the "Cross of Gold" speech that established him as silver's champion, and was nominated on the fifth ballot. The People's party could only second Bryan's selection and choose him as their candidate too. Divided over the vice-presidential nominee and mutually suspicious, the fused forces of the Democrats and the Populists moved to do battle with the Republicans. This marriage of convenience ended the People's party as a serious national force.

Their overwhelming triumph of 1894 had made the Republicans almost certain of success in 1896. The nomination of William McKinley further enhanced their prospects. He was the most popular figure in the party, an attractive blend of protectionism and moderate views on the monetary issue. His brilliant campaign for the nomination brought the GOP together, and McKinley's advisers fully anticipated that he could beat any potential Democratic challenger with a tariff-oriented canvas.

Bryan's candidacy temporarily disrupted this plan of action during the summer and early fall. The evangelistic Democrat roused the South and West with his silver crusade. Harried Republicans reported rampant enthusiasm for the Democrats in usually safe areas. Bryan put new life into his party's cause and went out on the stump in a dynamic, personal effort. Hysterical eastern orators, such as Theodore Roosevelt, associated the Democratic standard-bearer with fancied western radicalism and compared him to the leaders of the French Revolution. But the Bryan surge was evanescent, and his one-issue campaign faltered in the face of money shortages, defections within his own party, and an electorate receptive to Republican counterappeals.

The superior financial resources, strategy, and political arguments of the Republicans turned the tide. The party made adept use of newspapers and orators. It stressed the virtues of the tariff to middle western farmers and western advocates of silver. To industrial workers in the cities it exposed the inflationary drawbacks of unlimited silver coinage. McKinley, modest and dignified on his front porch in Canton, Ohio, made incisive speeches to throngs of visitors, and always sounded the theme of protection and prosperity. Bryan's narrowly focused campaign wilted in September and October under this merciless professional pounding.

The Republicans won a decisive victory. McKinley garnered 271 electoral votes to Bryan's 176, and his nearly 600,000-vote margin was the largest since 1872. Bryan detached some normally Republican adherents with his moralistic rhetoric and did better than any other

Democrat could have done, but he could not overcome the GOP's secure hold on the nation's voters. McKinley ran well among urban residents, previously Democratic ethnic groups, and prosperous farmers. He consolidated a solid Republican base in the Northeast and the industrialized Middle West. For more than a generation these centers would be the core of party dominance of American politics.

The election of 1896 has been variously depicted as a contest between western good and eastern evil, a confrontation of an older and newer America, and a struggle of a virtuous Democratic hopeful against a weak Republican rival. It was none of these things. The election was the culmination of a quarter of a century of party combat to decide whether the nation would have a functioning two-party system, and which party would be the preeminent force. The Democrats under Cleveland convinced the people that their party was unfit to govern, and Bryan's candidacy never surmounted this obstacle. The Republicans contended that the tariff and the economic nationalism that it represented would counteract the depression and restore prosperity. In 1896 the Americans agreed and chose the embodiment of Republican party doctrine in McKinley.

See Richard J. Jensen, *The Winning of the Midwest* (1971); Stanley L. Jones, *The Presidential Election of 1896* (1964); and H. Wayne Morgan, *From Hayes to McKinley* (1969).—L. L. G.

Eliot, John (1604-1690). New England's "apostle to the Indians." Eliot was born in Widford, England, and studied at Jesus College, Cambridge. In 1631 he migrated to the Massachusetts Bay Colony and the next year became pastor of the Roxbury church, keeping that post until his death. Encouraged and supported by his congregation and fellow ministers, he began a mission to the Indians in 1646. Financial aid was provided by regular small grants from the General Court of Massachusetts and by larger sums from England, where Eliot's efforts inspired the founding in 1649 of the Company for Propagating the Gospel in New England and Parts Adjacent in North America.

Eliot began preaching to the Indians at Newton after intensive study of their language and religious customs. A town of "praying Indians" gathered there and moved to the less-populated location of Natick in 1651. Eliot believed his work would glorify God and honor Christ by revealing the compassion of civilization for the physically and spiritually destitute heathen. He felt that only through evangelization could the Indians reach a civilized state. Accordingly, Indian converts won in public preaching were gathered into Christian towns governed by a biblical code and were gradually introduced to English manners and customs. Each village had a school that instructed in elementary subjects and doctrine, taught the English language, and trained the Indians in handicrafts by which they could become self-supporting. Native teachers and evangelists were trained and employed. After severe testing, believers were covenanted into the Puritan church commonwealth. The literature in the Massachusetts Algonquian language necessary to this enterprise was produced by Eliot himself, beginning in 1653 with the *Catechism*. In 1661 he completed a translation of the New Testament and two years later of the Old Testament. This Bible was the first in any language to be printed in America.

By 1674 there were fourteen villages containing more than four thousand converts scattered across Massachusetts, but during King Philip's War of 1675-76 they were nearly all destroyed. The warring Narragansett Indians viewed their Christianized brothers as traitors and apostates and attacked them at every opportunity. At the same time frustrated and embittered colonists, despite Eliot's desperate efforts, found it far easier to burn and slaughter the unresisting and easily approachable convert towns than to hunt down King Philip and his warriors in the New England swamps. While the original villages never completely recovered from these massacres, the Indian mission as a whole expanded throughout New England. Even after the Massachusetts Indian towns were extinct, Eliot's influence grew as his example inspired the rising missionary movement and his methods became their pattern for two centuries to come.

See Douglas Leach, *Flintlock and Tomahawk: New England in King Philip's War* (1958); Alden Vaughan, *New England Frontier: Puritans and Indians, 1620-1675* (1965); Williston Walker, *Ten New England Leaders* (1901); George P. Winship, *The Cambridge Press, 1638-1692* (1945); and Ola Winslow, *John Eliot: Apostle to the Indians* (1968).—P. R. M.

Elizabethtown, New Mexico. Ghost town. Located in the Sangre de Cristo Mountains near the state's northern border, Elizabethtown was a mining town with a roller-coaster history. Gold was discovered in the area in 1866 and the town soon grew to a population of seven thousand. Elizabethtown was the first incorporated town in New Mexico Territory, and over $5 million in gold was produced in the town's early years. By 1875, however, the placers were wearing thin and the town, often called "E-town," was virtually abandoned. In 1901 H. J. Reiling took his gold dredge to the Moreno valley, and Elizabethtown again began to prosper. Reiling's company went bankrupt in 1905, and with the demise of the dredge, the fortunes of Elizabethtown dropped once more. A disastrous fire delivered the final blow, and today the ghostly remains of the town stand out starkly against the background of Baldy Peak.

See Ralph Looney, *Haunted Highways: The Ghost Towns of New Mexico* (1968); and Muriel S. Wolle, *The Bonanza Trail* (1953).—R. B. W.

elk, American. Described in prose as majestic and noble, a monarch, and the king of the mountains, the American elk, or wapiti, commands emotional appeal unmatched by other animals of the West. The name *elk* is somewhat a misnomer that has persisted in common usage since presettlement days. *Wapiti*, as the animal was known among the Shawnee Indians, is considered more proper and applied in scientific writing to differentiate the American *Cervus* from the European moose, *Alces*, which is commonly known as the elk in the Old World. American elk are closely related to the red deer of Europe and Asia, and some authorities consider them a single species.

The elk is the second largest member of the deer family (Cervidae) in North America, the moose being the largest. Adult males, or bulls, average more than five feet in shoulder height and more than 600 pounds in weight; the largest may stand nearly six feet and weigh 1,000 pounds. Females, or cows, are smaller and average about four and one-half feet in height at the shoulder and 400 pounds in weight. A very large cow may stand over five feet and weigh 650 pounds. In addition to size, the elk is distinguished by its coloration. The body is gray to brown grading to dark chestnut brown in the long, heavy mane, the head, and the legs. A conspicuous buffy-white or tawny rump patch surrounds a short white tail. Males may also be distinguished by the large, widely branching antlers that consist of a main beam and five to seven points on each side in mature animals. Females are antlerless.

When white men first came to America, elk were common in much of the woodland, prairie, and mountainous country north of Mexico and south of the broad coniferous forest that extends from the northeastern United States across Canada to Alaska. Absent only from parts of the deep South and the Great Basin, elk were the most widely distributed American deer. The eastern, prairie, and woodland elk disappeared early in the period of settlement, as did the Merriam elk of isolated mountain areas of Arizona and New Mexico; and elk in other areas generally became more restricted and reduced in numbers. The present distribution is restricted mainly to the mountainous western United States and Canada. Historical records and archaeological surveys refute a popular misconception that elk were originally only found on the prairies and were driven into the mountains by settlement and exploitation.

Although the hide and flesh were used extensively by the American Indian and later provided food and clothing for early explorers, trappers, and settlers, this probably had little or only local impact on elk populations. The disappearance and reduction of herds was more likely the result of widespread elimination and alteration of habitat by logging, farming, ranching, and other human activities and developments. Commercial hunting may have been important in some areas, such as mining camps. Given protection and relatively stable habitats, elk populations have generally increased and spread under careful management to fully occupy suitable range and forest land throughout the western mountains.

Four races of elk persist in the West. The Rocky Mountain elk *(C. canadensis nelsoni)* is most common and abundant and is widely distributed through the Rocky Mountain region of the United States and Canada. The Roosevelt elk *(C. c. roosevelti),* slightly darker in color and larger than the Rocky Mountain elk, occurs in the rain forests of the Pacific Coast intermittently from northern California to Vancouver Island and on the Afognak and Kodiak islands of Alaska. The Manitoba elk *(C.c. manitobensis)* is found locally in the provinces of Manitoba and Saskatchewan, while the Tule elk *(C. nannodes)* persists only in remnant herds totaling less than five hundred animals in three areas of interior California.

Elk are extremely adaptable and tolerant of diverse environments, as shown by their wide distribution and the varied habitats they occupy. Ecologically, they appear to bridge successional stages from pioneer to near climax grassland and forest vegetation. In much of the intermountain West larger and more productive populations are associated with extensive areas of open forest at moderate to high elevations and open grass or grass-shrub vegetation at lower elevations. In more heavily forested areas they are associated with extensive areas of early forest regrowth following fires. Elk are migratory over most of their range, spending the summer months at higher elevations where they frequent mountain meadows and open forest. With the arrival of severe weather in the fall they move to lower elevations to winter on open foothills or brushy mountain slopes. Migration is not universal and some animals may spend the entire year on the same area.

The foods and feeding habits of elk are also diverse, depending upon the area, season of the year, and availability of different kinds of plants. They are primarily grazing animals, utilizing a wide variety of grasses and weeds, but readily browse when shrubs are available. During late spring and summer, the diet usually consists of succulent forbs, or weeds, though the leaves of some shrubs as well as green grasses and sedges are also eaten. From fall through early spring elk eat dry bunchgrasses, if available, and browse on shrub ranges when grasses are covered by deep or crusted snow. The feeding habits of elk and cattle are similar, and competition for forage frequently occurs when both animals graze the same area. Because of this and their highly gregarious nature, elk are considered a problem on private rangelands. Cattle grazing on important elk winter ranges is also a problem in many areas because the size and productivity of elk herds is most often limited by the amount of forage consistently available during the winter.

The elk breeding season, or rut, generally occurs during September and October. The rut is characterized by the musical bugling of bulls, which often provides a thrilling experience for the elk-country visitor, and by the collection of cows into harems by dominant bulls. Younger bulls, including animals one and one-half years old are capable of breeding but rarely do in the presence of aggressive older bulls. The cow is also capable of breeding as a yearling, but most do not breed until they are two and one-half years old. Mature cows usually produce one calf each year; twins are extremely rare. Most calves are born in late May or early June, after a gestation period of about 235 days. They are born spotted and weigh about thirty-five pounds. Growth is rapid and by late fall the calves may weigh 250 pounds or more.

Intensive elk management programs are conducted by all states and Canadian provinces in which the species occurs, as well as by federal agencies in some areas. Most management effort is directed toward careful regulation of populations and maintaining or improving elk habitat.

See Olaus J. Murie, *The Elk of North America* (1951), or the more than 1,200 miscellaneous publications listed in J. B. Kirsch and K. R. Greer, *Wapiti—American Elk and European Red Deer . . . Bibliography,* Montana Fish and Game Department (1968).—R. J. M.

Elkins, Stephen Benton (1841-1911). Industrialist and New Mexico and West Virginia politician. Elkins used frontier politics as a stepping-stone to success in national business and politics. He got his start in New Mexico, to which he came in 1864 as a young lawyer from Missouri, where he had also been a teacher (see YOUNGER BROTHERS). With another Missourian, Thomas B. Catron, he established a lucrative practice specializing in the disposition of New Mexico's Spanish land grants and rose swiftly in territorial politics (see MAXWELL LAND GRANT COMPANY). As a member of the "Santa Fe Ring" of officials and land speculators, he served successively as territorial attorney, attorney-general, federal attorney, and delegate to Congress. After two terms as delegate (1873-77) he remained in the East as a lobbyist in Washington and a stock speculator in New York, although New Mexico remained his political residence until 1888.

Meanwhile Elkins acquired two patrons who aided in his movement into the eastern business wing of the Republican party. One was Speaker James G. Blaine, who made Elkins his confidant and manager in the 1880 and 1884 presidential campaigns; the other was Senator Henry G. Davis, a West Virginia Democrat, whose daughter Elkins married in 1875. Blaine supported statehood for New Mexico in hopes of making Elkins a United States senator and, failing that, a member of Garfield's cabinet. But with New Mexico still a territory and Blaine's career in suspense after 1884, Elkins turned to Davis and to Benjamin Harrison, a long-time acquaintance of the Davis family whose nomination and election as president Elkins helped to secure in 1888. His reward was a place in Harrison's cabinet as secretary of war (1891-93) and undisputed control of federal patronage in West Virginia, which enabled him to place himself at the head of a resurgent Republican party there. Elkins' election to the Senate from West Virginia followed in 1895. Here he became a charter member of the Senate's conservative "Old Guard," although not of its inner circle. As chairman of the Committee on Interstate Commerce (1901-11), he stood guard over the protective tariff and helped to frame a series of measures designed to meet public demands for railroad regulation while accommodating the trend to consolidation among the carriers. The Elkins Anti-Rebate Act (1903) and Mann-Elkins Act (1910) bear his name.

As a lobbyist, speculator, and business manager, Elkins developed a broad range of business interests, the most important of which were western agricultural and mineral lands and coal mines and railroads in West Virginia and Maryland. His other business associations included one involving mail contractors implicated in the Star Route mail frauds exposed in 1881 and another involving the exploitation of the government-owned Alaska fur seal fishery, both notable for their political complications. Altogether Elkins' business career brought him a handsome personal fortune and a deserved reputation as "a classic example of a man who rose by exploiting political office for private gain."

Oscar D. Lambert, *Stephen Benton Elkins: American Foursquare* (1955), must be supplemented by his private papers and those of Davis, John W. Mason, A. B. White, and other political leaders housed in the West Virginia Collection, West Virginia University Library, Morgantown. Howard R. Lamar, *The Far Southwest, 1846-1912: A Territorial History* (1966), and Jim Berry Pearson, *The Maxwell Land Grant* (1961), develop the context of Elkins' New Mexico career. His trail in national business and politics must be followed through a variety of published and unpublished sources. Two useful scholarly treatments are Gabriel Kolko, *Railroads and Regulation, 1877-1916* (1965) and Harry J. Sievers, *Benjamin Harrison, Hoosier Statesman, from the Civil War to the White House, 1865-1888* (1959).—J. A. W.

Ellet, Charles R. See RIVERMEN.

Ellsworth, Kansas. See CATTLE TOWNS.

El Paso, Texas. The city of El Paso is situated at the far western tip of Texas, near a point where New Mexico and the Mexican state of Chihuahua meet. Indeed, one may easily view the three states from the slopes of Mount Franklin, about which the city has been built. El Paso has a population of about 375,000, fifty-five percent of whom are Spanish-speaking. To the south across the Rio Grande is El Paso's twin city, Ciudad Juárez, with a population of about 600,000, the largest city on the Mexican border. El Paso is the product of the Spanish-Mexican northern frontier and the Anglo-American West, and the blending of the two cultures gives the community a personality and charm that are fascinating and unique.

In the sixteenth century, Spaniards coming northward from Santa Bárbara in Chihuahua viewed, as they approached the Rio Grande, two mountain ranges rising out of the desert, between which ran a deep chasm that is thought to be the lowest pass through the Continental Divide between the Arctic Sea and the Isthmus of Tehuantepec. On the left was the Sierra de Juárez, while slightly to the right and set back were the Franklin Mountains; in the deep gorge, slicing its way between in a southeasterly direction, was the Rio Grande. This site they named El Paso del Norte. It would be the future location of Ciudad Juárez, on the south or right bank of the Rio Grande, and El Paso, Texas, on the opposite side of the river. Since the sixteenth century, the El Paso area has been a continental crossroads and was a major link between north and south during the Spanish and Mexican periods and between east and west in the years following the Mexican War.

The El Paso area was inhabited for centuries by various Indian groups prior to the coming of the Spaniards. In all probability, Alvar Núñez CABEZA DE VACA was the first European to enter the El Paso area; most authorities agree that his reference to "the river which ran between some ridges," written in 1535, was most likely to the Rio Grande at a site approximating that of El Paso del Norte.

More reliable documentation is offered in support of the expedition of the Franciscan Fray Agustín de Rodríguez, who left the little mining community of Santa Bárbara in 1581 and moved northward along the Conchos and Rio Grande to study the possibilities for missionary work in New Mexico. In the following year the expedition of Antonio de Espejo followed the trail taken by Fray Rodríguez to a point where it could view "a mountain chain on each side of the river, both of which were without timber throughout the entire distance."

The Rodríguez and Espejo expeditions aroused such interest in New Mexico that it occasioned the 1598 colonizing enterprise of Juan de OÑATE. His expedition took the more direct northerly route through the sand dunes of Chihuahua, camped on the banks of the Rio Grande below the present site of Ciudad Juárez, took formal possession of New Mexico in the name of the king of Spain, and laid the foundations of Spanish administration and institutions in that frontier province. The Oñate party then crossed the river, which it called the Río del Norte, the name still used by Mexicans.

A caravan service through the pass was soon organized to supply New Mexico, and in 1630 Fray Alonso de Benavides recommended the establishment of a mission to minister to the Manso Indians and serve as a way station on the caravan route, soon to be known as the Camino Real (see SANTA FE AND CHIHUAHUA TRAIL). Benavides' suggestion was at length honored when in 1659 Fray García de San Francisco y Zúñiga founded the mission of Nuestra Señora de Guadalupe on the south bank of the Rio Grande, "the flower of all the New Mexican missions" and the real beginning of El Paso (see NEW MEXICO MISSIONS).

The Pueblo Indian revolt of 1680 sent Spanish colonists of New Mexico fleeing southward to take refuge at the pass, transplanting the names of the New Mexico river pueblos—Isleta, Senecú, and Socorro—to the area, where they were reestablished in a chain along the south bank of the Rio Grande (see PUEBLO INDIANS). Shortly afterward the presidio of El Paso del Norte and five missions to serve the presidio and the pueblos were established. With the Spanish reconquest of New Mexico in 1696 and the founding of Chihuahua in 1709, the role of the El Paso settlements as a way station on the Camino Real took on added significance. Here was a true oasis in the desert, bounded by the Jornada del Muerto on the north and the sand dunes of Samalayuca on the south.

By the middle of the eighteenth century about four thousand people lived in the El Paso area—Spaniards, mestizos, and Indians, most of whom belonged to the Piro, Suma, and Tiwa tribes. The settlements were administered by the governor of New Mexico; but their ecclesiastical administration became a source of jurisdictional controversy between the regulars and seculars, involving the Franciscans and the bishop of Durango. Contemporary reports affirm that the pueblos flourished and produced wheat, corn, and beans in great quantity. A large dam and series of canals provided an ample supply of water for the fertile soil. The large number of vineyards produced grapes in abundance, and the quality of the wine and brandy was said to have ranked with the best in the realm. The celebrated Prussian scientist Alexander von Humboldt found the environs of the pass to be "delicious," resembling the finest parts of Andalusia, and the wine to be preferable to that of Parras in Nueva Vizcaya. During the 1830s American traders in Santa Fe came to like "Pass" wine and brandy.

The Apache problem in the second half of the eighteenth century demanded a comprehensive reorganization of Spain's northern frontier defenses. In accordance with the Reglamento of 1772 a cordon of fifteen presidios roughly one hundred miles apart, extending from the Gulf of Mexico to the Gulf of California, was established in a line approximating the boundary between the United States and Mexico fixed some seventy-five years later. The pueblo of El Paso del Norte was considered to be of sufficient population to organize a militia for its own protection, and a recommendation to establish a new presidio north of the pueblo to protect the Camino Real was never implemented. A vast military-administrative jurisdiction called the Provincias Internas, or Interior Provinces, was established in 1776 under a commandant-general with headquarters in Chihuahua, and the presidio of San Elizario was transferred to its present location, about twenty miles down river from El Paso del Norte, to aid in its defense. Yet the

El Paso in 1875. (National Archives)

Apache remained a problem that Spanish officials could never completely solve, and the frontier settlements, including El Paso del Norte, were ravaged repeatedly.

During the war for Mexican independence the El Paso area chose the path of constitutional government in preference to insurgency. While King Ferdinand VII of Spain was a prisoner of the French, a representative assembly known as the Cortes drafted the constitution of 1812, which transformed Spain into a limited parliamentary monarchy and created a representative system for Spain and its overseas dominions. El Paso del Norte was authorized to establish its own *ayuntamiento,* or municipal council; and a provincial *junta,* or assembly, of deputies elected from the towns of New Mexico and Chihuahua met in El Paso del Norte in 1814 to select a deputy to the Spanish Cortes. Although this action was nullified with the return of Ferdinand VII and his suspension of the constitution, representative government was restored in Spain in 1820, and a second provincial *junta* meeting in El Paso del Norte in 1821 was actively engaged in the selection of a deputy to the Spanish Cortes when news was received that Agustín de Iturbide had liberated Mexico from Spanish rule.

Meanwhile, the first Anglo-Americans had entered the El Paso area. Zebulon Pike, captured by Spanish officials above Santa Fe in 1807, was brought to Chihuahua for questioning. Pike found El Paso del Norte to be a friendly and flourishing community, and the hospitality of San Elizario, he said, was unmatched. His arrival in El Paso marked the beginning of the Anglo-American advance into the area.

With the establishment of Mexican independence

from Spain in 1821 and the subsequent adoption of the constitution of 1824, which created a federal republic, the El Paso area was incorporated into the state of Chihuahua and, once again, El Paso del Norte was accorded its own ayuntamiento. In 1827 this body granted two tracts of land across the river to Juan Ponce de León, an influential citizen of El Paso del Norte. It was the first attempt to settle the north bank of the river on what would become the future site of El Paso, Texas.

Although the El Paso settlements seemed to have been little affected by the Texas revolution of 1835-36 and the establishment of the Republic of Texas, a number of significant developments in the late 1840s had profound implications for El Paso history: the outbreak of the MEXICAN WAR in 1846; the invasion of Chihuahua by an American force under Colonel Alexander DONIPHAN; the signing of the Treaty of GUADALUPE HIDALGO in February 1848, which fixed the boundary at the Rio Grande as far north as the thirty-second parallel and gave the United States the vast area from Texas to the Pacific as far north as Oregon; the arrival of the forty-niners en route to California; the establishment of a military post on the Texas side of the river (the future Fort Bliss); the authorization of a post office for El Paso, Texas; and the periodic shifting of the Rio Grande, which placed Ysleta, Senecú, Socorro, and San Elizario first on an island and then on the Texas side.

Four settlements along the north bank form the nucleus of modern El Paso, Texas. Following the Mexican War, Franklin Coons bought the Ponce de León property, located in the present downtown area, and thus, the settlement frequently was called Franklin during the

1850s and 1860s. A second settlement was located down the river from Franklin on property that had been granted to Juan and Jacinto Ascárate in 1836 and developed by Hugh Stephenson, Juan's son-in-law. Between the Ponce de León and Ascárate grants, James Wiley MAGOFFIN established Magoffinsville in 1850, and a fourth settlement developed around Simeon Hart's mill to the west near the river. Visitors entering the area around the middle of the nineteenth century found a population of some six thousand on the south bank and about three hundred on the Texas side. All were impressed with the fertility of the soil, the delightful climate, the vineyards and the wine, and the possibilities for ranching and agriculture. With proper cultivation, observed one, the area could support a million inhabitants.

During the Civil War most of the Anglo-American population in El Paso supported the Confederacy and voted for secession. Confederate troops occupied Fort Bliss briefly, but in August 1862 a force of California volunteers called the California Column took Fort Bliss, and El Paso remained in Union hands for the remainder of the war. Some Confederate sympathizers fled to El Paso del Norte, an interesting example in miniature of the Confederate exodus to Mexico at the close of the war. Moreover, about this time the itinerant republican government of Benito Juárez took refuge in El Paso del Norte from the French forces of Napoleon III in 1865 and 1866, and in 1888 the town was named Ciudad Juárez in honor of this great Mexican patriot.

In 1881, a memorable date in El Paso history, the railroads arrived, and the future of a western town, already bilingual, binational, and bicultural, was assured. For two decades or more, the gunfighters, gamblers, and girls prevailed, but ultimately, the regular processes of civilized society gradually became the pattern.

Three major trends are discernible in the history of El Paso in the twentieth century. One is the city's population growth and economic development. From a community of some 16,000 people at the turn of the century and an economy largely geared to copper, cotton, and cattle, it has grown to a metropolis of nearly 375,000, with a diversified economy based on natural gas, electric power, oil refining, textiles, banking and finance, building materials, international trade, agriculture and ranching, governmental and military establishments, and tourism.

A second trend is the growth in size and influence of the military establishments, particularly Fort Bliss, all of which was augmented greatly by the nation's involvement in four major conflicts in this century and by advances in missile warfare. At the beginning of the Mexican Revolution, Fort Bliss became a major cavalry post, and General John J. Pershing, who took command in 1916, led the expedition into Mexico in pursuit of the revolutionary chieftain Pancho Villa. Military aircraft were used for the first time in the search. During World War II, Fort Bliss became an antiaircraft-artillery post, and today it is the Army Air Defense Center, where training is conducted in the latest advances in missile systems and antiballistic warfare.

Third, there is the special relationship with Mexico in general and Ciudad Juárez in particular. The historic Taft-Díaz meeting in 1909 took place in Juárez, and for a brief time, Ricardo Flóres Magón, best known of the precursors of the Mexican Revolution, made El Paso his headquarters. Francisco Madero, whose revolt eventually overthrew Porfirio Díaz, came to El Paso in 1910, and in the subsequent battle for Ciudad Juárez, El Pasoans by the thousands stood on hills and rooftops to watch the revolutionary forces take the city. Pancho Villa visited El Paso on numerous occasions to purchase arms and supplies and was frequently entertained by national and local dignitaries. But with the United States recognition of Villa's enemy, Venustiano Carranza, came the retaliatory Villista attack on Columbus, New Mexico, followed by Pershing's punitive expedition of 1916, and so, the friendly relations between Pancho Villa and the El Pasoans deteriorated. A dreaded Villista attack on El Paso never materialized, however, and eventually the border returned to normal.

Mexican families of property during and after the Mexican Revolution fled Chihuahua by the thousands; many of them, like the wealthiest of them all, Don Luís Terrazas, took up residence in El Paso, thus intensifying the city's basic bilingual, binational, and bicultural character. Moreover, bootlegging activities during the Prohibition Era and the growing economic interdependence of the two cities within recent decades also fostered a unique relationship between El Paso and Ciudad Juárez, which, however, was strained by the Chamizal dispute. The Chamizal, a 630-acre area on the south side of El Paso, belonged to Mexico until the 1850s, when a shift in the course of the Rio Grande put the property north of the river. By an agreement made between the two nations in 1963, and formalized in 1967, 437 acres of the Chamizal were returned to Mexico. The Chamizal National Memorial, constructed on the new border, stands as a symbol of cooperation between the two cities and two nations.

See Hubert Howe Bancroft, *History of Arizona and New Mexico* (1962); William Weber Johnson, *Heroic Mexico* (1968); Florence C. Lister and Robert H. Lister, *Chihuahua, Storehouse of Storms* (1966); Frank Mangan, *Bordertown Revisited* (1973); John J. Middagh, *Frontier Newspaper: The El Paso "Times"* (1958); C. L. Sonnichsen, *Pass of the North* (1968); and Owen White, *Out of the Desert: The Historical Romance of El Paso* (1923). —W. H. T.

emigrants' guidebooks. Travel accounts of the cross-continental journey to the Pacific Coast, used primarily to assist in the practical matters of migration. Until the 1840s westward trails were known only to a few fur traders and scouts. But with the beginning of popular interest, the guidebooks filled this information gap and stimulated further interest by acquainting potential emigrants with the route of travel, time schedules, needed supplies, crude maps, and the dangers and scenic wonders of the trip. Travelers were warned that they could not expect to cover more than twenty miles a day and were advised to pack ammunition, watertight containers for flour and grains, and preserved foodstuffs such as jerky and salt meat.

Several books appeared in the early 1840s. Like the account by John BIDWELL of his pioneering trip of 1841, *A Journey to California* (1842), they described the cross-continental trip and sparked considerable interest but provided little practical detail. Somewhat more helpful, but still noted mainly for its effect in stirring up en-

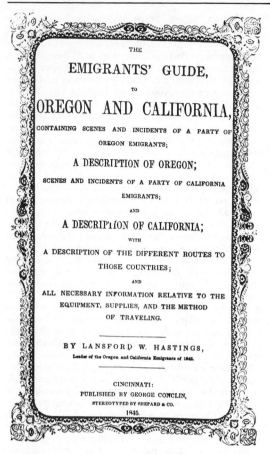

THE

EMIGRANTS' GUIDE,

TO

OREGON AND CALIFORNIA,

CONTAINING SCENES AND INCIDENTS OF A PARTY OF
OREGON EMIGRANTS;

A DESCRIPTION OF OREGON;

SCENES AND INCIDENTS OF A PARTY OF CALIFORNIA
EMIGRANTS;

AND

A DESCRIPTION OF CALIFORNIA;

WITH

A DESCRIPTION OF THE DIFFERENT ROUTES TO
THOSE COUNTRIES;

AND

ALL NECESSARY INFORMATION RELATIVE TO THE
EQUIPMENT, SUPPLIES, AND THE METHOD
OF TRAVELING.

BY LANSFORD W. HASTINGS,
Leader of the Oregon and California Emigrants of 1842.

CINCINNATI:
PUBLISHED BY GEORGE CONCLIN,
STEREOTYPED BY SHEPARD & CO.
1845.

Title page of an emigrants' guidebook. (Library of Congress)

thusiasm, was the *Report of the Exploring Expedition to the Rocky Mountains in the Year 1842, and to Oregon and North California in the Years 1833-'44* (1845), by John Charles FREMONT. The first real guidebook appeared the same year, *The Emigrants' Guide to Oregon and California* (1845) by Lansford HASTINGS. It gave detailed, helpful advice of the Oregon Trail but, despite the title, said little of the California trip. The next year Joel Palmer added his detailed guide to the Oregon Trail in his *Journal of Travels . . . to the Mouth of the Columbia River* (1846). Palmer planned his book to take advantage of the favorable climate for migration in the wake of the United States-English compromise on the Oregon question. Edwin Bryant's *What I Saw in California* (1848) provided the first detailed guide to the California Trail. After 1848 overland travelers frequently utilized the "Mormon Guide," William Clayton's *The Latter Day Saints' Emigrants' Guide* (1848), an excellent aid except that it covered only the Council Bluffs route and only as far as Salt Lake City. The most popular and helpful guide was Joseph E. Ware's *The Emigrants' Guide to California* (1849), prepared to capitalize on gold fever. Although Ware, unlike other authorities, had never been to the coast, he specifically designed his work as a no-nonsense, instructive guidebook for the routine of

day-to-day travel. He told his readers how much food to bring and how to best picket the animals at night.

All the books were filled with inaccuracies—most minor, some serious. Hastings' book, for example, was partly responsible for the DONNER PARTY tragedy. Few emigrants were foolish enough to rely solely on the books; conversely, few failed to consult them seriously before beginning the journey, and there was nearly always a guidebook in each train. For the realities of day-to-day travel, the guidebooks were relatively useless. They were, however, essential items in evoking a public discussion of the trails and in creating a public confidence in the ability of ordinary people to make a perilous, lengthy journey that only a few years before had been reserved for mountain men and missionaries.

See David M. Potter, *Trail to California: The Overland Journal of Vincent Geiger and Wakeman Bryarly* (1962); and George R. Stewart, *The California Trail* (1962). —J. F.

Emma Mine. The Emma Mine was the most notorious, or infamous, mining property in the United States promoted by an Anglo-American company. Located in Little Cottonwood Canyon, near Alta, Utah, this silver deposit was discovered in 1868 by two prospectors who, for lack of capital to work their claim, were forced to transfer a one-third interest to James E. Lyon of New York for funds advanced. In 1871 the partners also gave a San Francisco mine promoter an option to purchase the property for $1.5 million, subject to the settlement of Lyon's interest. In turn, the San Franciscan succeeded in interesting Trenor W. Park of Vermont and General H. Henry Baxter of New York in buying a half interest in the mine for $375,000. The Emma Silver Mining Company of New York was organized and the promoters resolved to take the mine to England for sale. Lyon engaged Senator William M. Stewart of Nevada to represent his interest, and an agreement was negotiated whereby Lyon would profit from the sale abroad but not in excess of $500,000 for his one-third interest.

The Emma Mine had been described as "one of the most remarkable deposits of argentiferous ore ever opened" by mining experts in the employ of the United States government. The mine was well known in England because some of the ore was rich enough to justify its shipment by rail and sea to Liverpool for refining and sale as bullion. The promoters secretly obtained the services of Baron Albert Grant, a London financier of dubious reputation but a masterful promoter. The Emma Silver Mining Company, Ltd., was registered with a nominal capital of £1 million with half the shares, worth $2.5 million, being given to the vendors as paid up on the books. Professor Benjamin Silliman, Jr., of Yale was engaged to make a favorable report on the mine for a fee of $25,000. Grant and his associates prevailed upon a distinguished group of men to serve on the board of directors, including the United States minister to the Court of St. James's, three members of Parliament, a former president of the New York Central Railroad, Senator Stewart, and Park. Within twenty days the £20 shares were selling for a £4 premium. The public contributed between £500,000 and £600,000 to the enterprise. This was twice the sum the American vendors had paid for the property. Baron Albert Grant received £170,000 for his contribution in floating the company. Stewart succeeded in eliminating Lyon for a mere

£50,000, half the amount he had expected. Emma shares went as high as £50. Then the bubble burst. A rival neighbor, the Illinois Tunnel Company, asserted that the Emma claim had been incorrectly recorded and that the English company was working its property to obtain silver for initial dividends. There also had been a cave-in at the mine. By the end of 1872 the directors admitted the available ore was exhausted. Evidence piled up to prove that a gigantic fraud had been perpetrated on the investors.

Public reaction forced an investigation of the United States minister's conduct by the Committee on Foreign Relations of the House of Representatives. His resignation was promptly accepted. When Trenor W. Park was found to be the owner of the Illinois Tunnel Company as well as a shareholder in the Emma Mine, extensive litigation followed. The suit of the English company against the vendors of the Emma resulted, after a long and exhaustive trial, in a verdict for the defendants in May 1877. The London shareholders were then forced to sell the silver mine to Park for less than $150,000, five percent of their investment. The Emma was operated by an American company until 1882, when the first of a series of "New" Emma Silver Mining Companies was organized under Britain's limited liability laws. The dismal end came with the collapse of the price of silver in 1893.

The history of the Emma Mine is often cited to illustrate the perils of foreign investment in United States mines: the hapless discoverers, the unscrupulous American vendors, the unreliable geologists, the scheming British promoters, the gullible boards of directors, the duped investing public, and the problems of long-distance management. Utah historians have criticized the pioneer generation for a lack of interest in mining development, which opened the door for outside, exploitative capitalists, domestic and foreign. The record of Utah's silver mines was so disastrous in the 1870s that the territory was shunned by legitimate mining investors for almost a generation.

See W. Turrentine Jackson, "The Infamous Emma Mine: A British Investment in the Little Cottonwood District, Utah Territory," *Utah Historical Quarterly* (October 1955), and Clark C. Spence, "The Emma Silver Mining Company, Limited: A Case Study," in *British Investments and the American Mining Frontier, 1860-1901* (1958).—W. T. J.

Emory, William Hemsley (1811-1887). Career soldier, topographical engineer, explorer, and cavalry officer. Major Emory, scion of an aristocratic Maryland family, was graduated from West Point in 1831, fourteenth in his class, and breveted second lieutenant in the Fourth Artillery. He resigned in 1836 but was reappointed as first lieutenant in the Corps of Topographical Engineers on July 7, 1838. His contribution to western American history began with his service on General Stephen Watts Kearny's expedition to California, 1846-47. Emory was breveted captain and a few weeks later major for "gallant and meritorious conduct" in the small but important battles Kearny fought in southern California.

After the Mexican War Emory was assigned to the United States-Mexican Boundary Commission, in which he served as astronomer under the difficulties of a civilian-controlled, politically conscious, sectionally oriented organization. This commission had hardly ended its tasks when the Gadsden Purchase of 1853 necessitated the running of a new boundary line. Emory was appointed commissioner and astronomer for this survey, and between 1854 and 1857, when his report was issued, he fulfilled his task in admirable fashion. He was also involved in the planning for the Pacific railroad surveys.

He left the Topographical Engineers and was attached to the First Cavalry with the rank of major (May 1855). In this capacity, but following his survey work, he was on duty at Fort Riley, Kansas, and participated in the Utah Expedition (or Utah War) of 1858. At the beginning of the Civil War he commanded troops at Forts Cobb, Smith, Washita, and Arbuckle in the Southwest. His later Civil War career included a wide range of assignments, and he was retired with the rank of brigadier general in 1876. Emory was a capable, even brilliant officer whose varied and worthy career has so far escaped the attention of biographers.

See George W. Cullom, *Biographical Register . . .*, vol. I (1868); William H. Goetzmann, *Army Explorations in the American West* (1959); and Edward S. Wallace, *The Great Reconnaissance* (1955).—R. A. B.

empresario system. Under a system used by the Mexican government in the 1820s to encourage colonization of its northern frontier, especially Texas, an empresario was an independent land agent who contracted to settle at least one hundred families in a predetermined location within a six-year period. Upon fulfillment of his contract with the government, the empresario, in return for his services, was given personal title to a generous portion of land (67,000 acres for every two hundred families settled).

Because individual acquisition of land title from the Mexican government was often a long and costly undertaking, new colonists usually preferred to deal with an empresario, paying him a fee to act as intermediary with the Mexican government. Another reason for dealing with an empresario was the desire of the new colonist to enjoy the security and benefits of an established community.

Each new colonist was allotted a portion of land (4,428 acres was a typical allotment for a family engaged both in soil cultivation and cattle raising) on which to settle and begin improvements. Over the period of the next six years the colonist could then purchase the land from the Mexican government for a nominal amount that could be paid in several installments. When payment was complete, the colonist was issued his land title by the empresario.

The outstanding empresario in Texas was Stephen F. Austin. Under authority of a grant made to his father, Moses Austin, immediately before his death in 1821, Austin established several thriving colonies. Austin enjoyed the respect not only of his fellow Texans but of many Mexican officials as well.

Other notable empresarios were Green C. DeWitt, Haden Edwards, James Hewetson, Martin de Leon, James McGloin, John McMullen, James Power, Sterling C. Robertson, Arthur G. Wavell, and Samuel May Williams.

See Eugene C. Barker, *Life of Stephen F. Austin* (1925).—J. B. F.

English language and the westward movement. English vocabulary change and the westward movement are in some cases directly related to each other and sometimes not related at all. *Mesa* entered western American English because English-speaking settlers needed a word for this new geographic feature and adopted it from the Spanish. But when *howdy podnuh* was created, *hello* was already at hand. Historical circumstances leading to *mesa* and *howdy podnuh* were different. The first was borrowed directly from New World Spanish. The second came from a slow reduction of British English *how do ye do* to *howdy* and of *partner* to *podnuh*, changes that began while the American colonies were being settled. Thus, to understand some changes that occurred as English-Americans moved westward, one should start with the British English of the seventeenth and eighteenth centuries.

British English. By 1600 printed English had developed a uniform spelling as a convenience for printers. Such uniformity encouraged readers at home and overseas to learn about new things in science, religion, politics, and social belief. Famous writers demonstrated that the national language was no longer barbarous and that it would serve for great literature. As early as 1700, however, Jonathan Swift, Joseph Addison, and others had begun to find it a "decaying language." Their remedy was to urge the rising middle class to avoid using foreign words such as the French *ballet,* or current slang such as *mob,* or the Latinate *agricultural implement* when the Saxon *spade* would do.

Spoken English had distinctive social and regional dialects. At the top was the social dialect that nobles spoke in London at the court; lower was that of merchants and other middle-class persons; at the bottom was that of thieves and vagabonds—except when slumming aristocrats took this speech back to the court and made it fashionable. In any direction twenty miles or so beyond London were regional dialects with their own special social usages.

Conflicts could arise when someone used socially improper forms: consider what happened to a young county gentleman who became a Quaker. This sect, following biblical precepts, used plain speech as a sign of their faith; its plainness was influenced by the northern weavers' dialect of its founder, George Fox. Among other characteristics was its use of *thou* and *thee* to all persons regardless of their rank. Thus, when the young gentleman convert spoke to his father with *thee,* his father's response to this rudeness was, "Sirrah, if ever I hear you say *Thou* or *Thee* to me again, I'll strike your Teeth down your Throat."

colonial American English. Early American English was formed by persons speaking middle-class county dialects of British English: the rich and the poor, felons who for stealing a handkerchief had a choice of hanging or of being sent to the colonies, and indentured servants who sold themselves in payment for passage to America. With them they brought the prevalent ideas about language as a sign of social position.

Three colonial settlements illustrate the first placing of British dialects in the New World and some attitudes that caused colonists to look to themselves or to England for further instruction. Middle-class Massachusetts was settled by persons speaking a dialect from southeastern England. According to enemies, they affected a whining talk in order to show piety. Middle-class Pennsylvania

was settled by Quakers whom New Englanders denounced as "Ranters . . . , Divils, and Jesuits." Their speech was colored by humble dialects of northern and northwestern England. Both colonies were peopled by dissenters who thus would have little reason to send their sons back to England for training in universities, which were Anglican. But the settlers of Virginia were cavaliers in that many had served in King Charles's cavalry, where they were addressed as "Tom" or "Dick" and not as "milord" or "Sir Richard." Their dialect was mainly southern British, their allegiance Royalist, and their faith Anglican. When they became wealthy enough, it was natural to consider sending their sons to Oxford or Cambridge University.

Some colonists used fashionably upper-class pronunciations: *jine, gwine,* and *pizen* rather than *join, going,* and *poison;* or *varmint, starling, (uni)varsity* rather than *vermin, sterling, university.* Other pronunciations are not easily placed on a social scale. *Aint* might have been the fashionable shortening of *am not* and *are not* or the rustic shortening of *haenot* and *haint,* a northern dialectal form of *have not.* Similarly, *dived* and *dove, helped* and *holp,* and *had et* and *had eaten* reflect social differences unclearly. Among pronouns, *hit* and *his* were old neuters that competed with the new *it* and *its* (Shakespeare, for instance, wrote "yond candle throws *his* beam"). *You* had begun replacing *thee, thou,* and *ye,* as in *you was* from *thou wast.* The decision to use *you were* in writing for both singular and plural was not accepted until the end of the eighteenth century. *You was* lasted much longer in the speech of the uncultivated. In spite of laws, swearing was fashionable. One could judge the wealth of a family by the frequency with which its women imitated the swearing among British noble ladies; in a Boston first family, the mildest female oath was *good God.* Furthermore, people of all classes talked with a coarseness that will not be illustrated here.

In the New World many place names came from the English. English words were combined for *Goose Creek, Shallow Ford Road, Wall Street.* Royal and noble persons were remembered in *Carolina* (after the Latin *Carolus,* "Charles"), *Charles Town, King* or *Duke of Gloucester* streets, and *Fincastle* for George Lord Fincastle. Anglicized Hebrew, Latin, or Greek provided others: *Bethlehem, Philadelphia, Athens,* and *Rome. Pennsylvania* was a hybrid from English *Penn* and Latin *sylvania,* "woods."

American Indians exerted a special influence. *Indian,* probably pronounced *injun,* had become English by 1600; thus any colonist could have brought the word with him to North America. There he used it with existing English to form new words: *Indian Orchard,* a place, and *Indian paintbrush,* a plant. He gave English names to Indian practices: *warpath, peace pipe, scalp* (pronounced *skelp* if one can judge from local spellings). He also used French words, as in "to count *coup.*" But for things "for which the *English* tongue hath no name" he turned to the tribal languages. The gap between English and Indian words is suggested by a spelling in Captain John Smith's description of his meeting with Powhatan: the seated chief was covered with a robe of "Rarocun skinnes." The Indian word would be later spelled *raccoon* and *coon.* For the tribal words behind *Massachusetts, moose, woodchuck, skunk,* and *squash,* one should consult a dictionary. Of these, *skunk* became a regional usage with a later competitor—the European *pole cat,* the name of a very different animal in Europe.

The backwoods were settled by dissenters—Baptists, Presbyterians, and Methodists—whom English aristocrats described as having "impertinence and disrespect toward their superiors." Class distinctions were reflected in styles of religious service as is shown by an Anglican clergyman who preached in the Old West, meaning the hill country of South Carolina. There he observed a "gang" of ignorant Methodist and Baptist preachers, "yet the lower Class chuse to resort to them rather than to hear a Well connected Discourse."

Settling western Virginia and North Carolina after 1740 were Scotch-Irish Presbyterians who kept ties with Scotland by sending their ministers there for religious training. The Scots' northern dialect included *gin* for *if, wha* for *who,* and *hae* for *have.* Their ballads, such as "Lord Randall," and the ballads of other English settlers furnished models for this form of storytelling in the next century. If today some listeners think that this mountain speech is "pure Elizabethan," they forget that Elizabeth I died one hundred and fifty years before the first Scotch-Irish migrated to America.

In coastal colonial settlements, wealth and distinction came from the sale of cod, African slaves, rum, gunpowder, tobacco, rice, and sea island cotton. In the back country it came from raising cattle and driving them to market towns on the *fall line* and at the ports. Contact between the coast and the backwoods, however, was not always direct. While Virginia claimed political control over persons living in the Great Valley within its western borders, mountains and *pine barrens* formed a barrier between eastern and western Virginians. From the valley it was easier to follow the Great Philadelphia Wagon Road to Philadelphia itself than to cross the mountains to Williamsburg.

Under most circumstances a twenty-five-mile journey was a major undertaking. Difficulties of travel made it logical for German settlers in the Shenandoah valley to say, "We have no need of English if we hold fast to our language and religion . . . and support ministers and schoolmasters out of our scanty means."

In British eyes the development of North American English was colonial. Its crudities are suggested in Francis Moore's *A Voyage to Georgia* (1744), where he notes that Savannah was situated on a steep riverbank "which they in barbarous English call a *bluff.*"

agrarian American English. After the new nation was founded, its people pushed west into new cotton and corn lands, the Old Northwest and the Old Southwest, and then into cattle country, the wild West of the second half of the nineteenth century.

Letters, diaries, account books, church records, and other ordinary documents give evidence of some speech changes. Once-aristocratic pronunciations like *varmint* and *pizen* appeared everywhere. *Passel,* a form of *parcel,* was reported in New England as early as 1650. The expansion in Virginia and the Carolinas of *fouth* and *couse* for *fourth* and *course* was paralleled by a more general spread of *widder* for *widdow, winder* for *window,* and *piller* for *pillow*—all instances of variation in the *r* sound. Both vowel and *r* are shown in Daniel Boone's 1760 spelling of *bar* for *bear.* One cannot always know the social position of the writer; yet, it is certain that in the nineteenth century no gentleman pronounced the *l*

in *calm* and *psalm;* polite pronunciation rhymed with *cam* and *sam.*

The self-sufficient frontier is symbolized by *log cabins* (1770) built near *bottom land* held by purchase or granted as reward for military service, or by *homesteaders'* or *squatters' rights.* When a second, larger cabin was adjoined, the open space between was roofed and called a *dog trot;* the larger cabin, the *big house,* later became synonymous with regional variations such as *parlor, living room,* or *best room.* Shingles were split with a dull wedge called a *froe* or *frow,* hence the comparison "dull as a froe." Settlers sawed *firewood,* steadying it in a *buck, horse, rack, jack,* or *trestle.* The largest log was a *back stick, back chunk,* or *back log* if put in a fireplace, and the smaller pieces were *kindling, pine knots,* or *fat pine.* Supports in the fireplace were *andirons, hand irons, fire dogs,* or *fire irons;* the shelf above was a *fireboard* or *mantel.*

Surrounding the cabin were dying *girdled* trees, a *deadening.* Here settlers planted crops, protecting them from animals by *zigzag, rail, snake,* or *worm fences* made from split logs, or by *rock* or *stone walls* (nineteenth-century prudery rejected *stone* as indecent; the uncastrated horse was known as a "stone horse"). Slovenly farmers did not remove stumps from their fields; hence *stump farmers* was a term of contempt. Cattle roamed in the *cow woods* after owners had cut identifying notches into their ears, *earmarks.* Identifying them by *branding* was reported in Georgia in 1740. When cattle were driven to market, they were herded into *cowpens*— probably pronounced *cuppins.*

When the frontier reached the Plains some colonial words became relatively useless; others provided models for new words. The first persons to build a *sod house* (not in print until 1872) had little use for "dull as a froe." On the other hand, *rock fence* lay behind *sod fence* (1839).

Corn was an old word that took on a new American meaning. For the British, *corn* meant "small grain" like wheat. Doubtless this meaning was in Captain John Smith's mind when he wrote (1608), "It pleased God- . . . to moue the Indians to bring vs Corne, ere it was half ripe." Then colonial usage began to change so that speakers began to distinguish between *corn bread* and *wheat bread.* This distinction lies behind *corncob pipe* and the simile *rough as a cob.* Corn for fodder was *field corn;* that for human use was given regional names—*sweet corn, sugar corn, mutton corn, green corn,* and *roasting ears.* Of these *mutton corn* became obsolescent; in the twentieth century it was reported only from a few counties in Florida and Georgia. As for the covering of ears of corn, two regional names appeared: *husks* and *shucks.*

Terms for food and drink from corn range from *corn meal, corn soup, corn bread, corn pone, hominy grits, hasty pudding, samp, batter bread, spoon bread, ash cake, ash pone, hoe cake, johnny cake, pone bread, poor do, hush puppies, corn whiskey,* and *corn squeezings* to *moonshine.* Except for *pone, hominy,* and *samp,* which originally were Indian words, the names are formed from English. Dictionaries list several hundred combinations with *corn,* by no means all of them names for food.

Regional vocabularies and pronunciations were not so clearly established in 1800 as they were a century later. Even so, it is possible to trace the westward path of selected local words. From New York and New England, pioneers settled along the Great Lakes taking with them *darning needle,* the name of a four-winged insect. Other pioneer planters advanced south from Maryland, Virginia, and the Carolinas and, skirting mountain barriers, settled the Gulf Coastal Plain as far west as Texas; their name for the same insect was *mosquito hawk.* Between these streams of westward settlement were Pennsylvanians and Scotch-Irish mountain people; the first used *snake feeder,* the second *snake doctor;* both regional words intermingled as groups from these localities moved south, north, and west along rivers into the interior. Maps now enable us to trace *snake feeder* from the Atlantic states to Oregon and Washington, and *mosquito hawk* into New Mexico. (The book word *dragon fly* may replace all of them.) From northern states one can find similar patterns of distribution for *skunk, outhouse, angleworm,* and *stoop* (a porch); from Pennsylvania, *green beans* and *hotcakes;* and from coastal southern states *snap beans* and *hand irons* (andirons). Once settlers reached the Rockies, the regional vocabularies spread north or south with the deflected course of migration.

The Mississippi valley became an avenue for the spread of some regional words north and south. Dutch provides instances. The point of origin was New York, where, in 1732, according to the historian William Smith, "English is the most prevailing language among us, but not a little corrupted by the Dutch dialect." Among the corruptions was *Yankee,* which English speakers pluralized as *Yankees.* The Dutch was *Jan Kees,* "John Cheese," a sneering word that New Englanders applied to the Dutch. How it became a favorable term for Americans is not clear. Other Dutch words were *Santa Claus, cookie, stoop* (a small porch), *sleigh,* and *cole slaw,* which some people mistakenly believe is *cold slaw.* From New York these words crossed Pennsylvania to the headwaters of rivers that flowed into the Mississippi, or they went generally westward at many points.

Along the Mississippi, English-speaking pioneers found French again. The first introduction of French, such as *prairie,* had occurred in the 1700s; now the settlers met or remet *levee* and *bayou,* a word that had gone into Mississippi French from the Choctaw *bayuk.* By the 1840s Americans "rather loosely applied [bayou] in the topography of Texas and the West," according to William Kennedy, a mid-nineteenth-century writer on Texas. These and place names are indications of the north and south pattern of language change found in the midcontinent.

Spanish can be conveniently noted at this point. New World Spanish had entered British English before 1600 in such words as *alligator* from *el lagarto,* "the lizard." But western Spanish came into English along with a new cattle industry. *Mesa, stampede, mesquite, pinto, lariat,* and *corral* are instances. *Ranch* (from *rancho*) combined with English as in *ranching* and *ranch hand.* For other matters on the range, English was often sufficient: *sod-buster, cattle drive.*

Colonial religious language went everywhere. One's best clothes were *Sunday-go-to-meeting clothes,* a recollection of Quaker plain speech that chose *meeting* and *meeting house* instead of *church.* Religious services were often held in a *brush arbor.* A revivalist would hold an *all-day camp meeting with a picnic on the ground.* There he preached *hell fire and damnation* and the congregation

sang about *the good old-time religion* or about being *a wayfaring stranger in this land of woe.* The style of public spontaneous prayer required *thou wast* and *ye are,* the language of the King James Bible or its American revisions. An admired *preacher man* was *the reverend;* one not admired, a *bible banger, chair backer,* or *jackleg preacher.* At home children were warned that Satan might take them, though speakers usually chose a less dangerous term—*Old Harry, Old Scratch, raw head and bloody bones, plat eye,* or *booger man.*

the industrialized Union. The industrializing nation reshaped the emerging regional dialects. One of the signs of national unity and independence is a national language. An important question was how it should be shaped. To this end, and influenced by Addison's ideas about purifying English, Benjamin Franklin urged that Americanisms such as *to advocate* and *to legislate* should not appear in a national dictionary. Noah Webster, however, included Americanisms such as to *girdle* trees and to *gin* cotton in his *American Dictionary of the English Language.*

Although he needed their printing presses, Webster was hostile to city people. "City coxcombs," he said, "have a large share in directing the *polite part* of pronunciation, which of course is as vicious as that of any class of people." Farmer at heart, he said that "it is always better to be *vulgarly* right than *politely* wrong." On those grounds he defended his use of *them horses* and his pronunciation of *deaf* to rhyme with *leaf.* Yet he proposed his dictionary as "the fairest opportunity of establishing a national language, and giving it uniformity and perspicuity in North America." Perhaps his *Blue-Backed Speller* did lead to pronunciation according to letters, to the favoring of *join* over *jine* for instance.

When schools were established, children learned and recited famous speeches such as Patrick Henry's. His "Gentlemen may cry, peace, peace—but there is no peace" is from classical oratory. The style that students did not learn in school was that which Henry used for backwoods constituents: He talked "in their own vicious and depraved pronunciation," saying, *"Naiteral parts is* better than all the *larnin* upon *yearth."* As children grew older and *stumped* for offices of *selectman, trustee, supervisor, reeve,* or *councilman,* they must have also observed that political styles were necessary—one for country people and the other for city coxcombs.

The naming of cities, states, rivers, and so on followed colonial practices: Washington, Jefferson, Hamilton, and Madison became the persons for whom places were named. Indian names served also—*Tuscaloosa,* the *Ohio, Illinois;* so did French names in *Sainte(e)* and in other forms such as *Detroit.* Spanish contributed *Florida, California,* and towns with *San.* Finally there were English combinations like *Mule Shoe.*

One new product introduced by the mid-nineteenth-century oil industry illustrates how rapidly words could rise or fall in social standing. The product was named regionally *lamp oil, coal oil,* or *kerosene* (the latter pulled out of a Greek dictionary in which *keros* meant "wax"). By 1900 the distribution of this product in the Mississippi valley had brought the names *kerosene* and *coal oil* together along with a social judgment that common people said *coal oil* while persons pretending to background and breeding chose *kerosene.*

Commerce from the cities influenced vocabulary

everywhere. Manufactured products such as *store-bought bread* began to replace the homemade kind, although, in this instance, the bread was considered to be poor and tasteless. Magazines and catalogs, arriving by *rural free delivery*, led people in the country to contrast their homemade clothes with what seemed to be the latest city fashions. And from catalogs farmers learned that the city names for certain familiar things were *gutters, mantel, frying pan, counterpane*, and *faucet;* what they did not know was that the catalog words were also regional and thus were no more appropriate or elegant than their own local *eaves troughs, fireboards, creepers, coverlids*, and *spigots*.

The cotton *gin* was an important contributor to the change in regional patterns. It led northerners and southerners—with and without slaves—to new agricultural wealth from cotton and corn, and to a desire by the newly rich to imitate the manners of first families on the Atlantic seaboard. Along with *who are his kin* the new rich had to know *what is he worth* and, particularly of politicians, *what is his price*. Their poor neighbors were *trash, poor whites, hooziers, red necks, country jakes,* and *share croppers*. With the introduction of railroads, the poor were *born on the wrong side of the tracks*. Finally, as an outcome of the Civil War, a host of new emotions and meanings attached themselves to *Yankee, Rebel,* and so on.

After 1850 increasing numbers of people moved from farms into industrial cities. Forming communities within the city, they preserved their local usages. Their children, fourth- or fifth-generation speakers of American English, were taught by first-generation urban-English speakers. All were influenced by print and, later, by radio and television. If these forces of instruction led to national uniformities, they also showed how quickly English could change. Illustrative words from sports reporting will serve: *football*, a British name with a new American meaning; *varsity*, an eighteenth-century pronunciation and a changed meaning; *scrimmage*, re-pronunciation of *skirmish; Gator*, a team name from Spanish; *skunked*, an Indian name changed to a verb with new meaning. From the field these words spread to business and government, where one is a *team player* who has a *game plan* and *keeps his eye on the ball*.

The city regularly revisits the country. Refined women who find *tote* vulgar usage nevertheless carry things in *tote bags*. Editors may order their authors to change *to quickly answer* to the genteel *to answer quickly*, while at the same time publishing advertisements containing *This here Stormalong, he was*, etc. Some dictionaries will list Bostonian pronunciations first; others will give midwestern ones. An uninformed reader can learn from a dictionary panel "just how and to what extent his presumed betters agree on what he ought to say or write," as Morris Bishop points out in *The American Heritage Dictionary of the English Language*, but he cannot discover whether any member of the panel is a genuine aristocrat. At the same time, candidates for national office go "stumping in a fire and brimstone style." And entertainment regularly depicts the myth of the cowboy West, which began with Owen Wister's *The Virginian* (1902); Wister himself was a city-bred easterner who, having visited Wyoming, returned east to sympathize with cattlemen against sod-busters.

This account has not examined what happened in the United States when other languages became Anglicized or resisted the process. Such a study would include the reactions of European and Asian speakers, including Cajun French and Pennsylvania Dutch, of American Indians, Eskimos, and Hawaiians, and of those blacks who have retained traces of African usage—these are important matters which must be sought elsewhere.

See BLACK ENGLISH; CHINOOK JARGON; FRENCH DIALECTS IN THE MISSISSIPPI VALLEY; HAWAIIAN PIDGIN ENGLISH; PENNSYLVANIA GERMAN; and SPANISH LANGUAGE IN THE SOUTHWEST.

For words and senses see W. A. Craigie and J. R. Hulbert, eds., *A Dictionary of American English on Historical Principles*, 4 vols. (1938-43); and M. M. Mathews, ed., *A Dictionary of Americanisms on Historical Principles*, 2 vols. (1951). A convenient bibliography is Harold B. Allen, ed., *Linguistics and English Linguists* (1966), esp. "British and American English" and "Dialect Geography." A brief survey of regional variations is in Carroll E. Reed, *Dialects of American English* (1967). Numerous word maps for the thirteen original states and for parts of the South and Southwest are in E. Bagby Atwood, *The Regional Vocabulary of Texas* (1953); and Hans Kurath, *A Word Geography of the Eastern United States* (1949); and Gordon R. Wood, *Vocabulary Change . . . in Eight of the Southern States* (1971).—G. R. W.

engraving. See PRINTS.

Erie Canal. See CANAL ERA.

Eskiminzin (?-1896). Indian chief. Eskiminzin was one of the leaders of the Arivaipa band of Western Apache, a division of the San Carlos group. He had married into the band, having been born in the Pinal band. The name by which he was best known to Apaches was Hackibanzin, or "Angry—men stand in line for him." He was squat and stout and stuttered. In spite of his stutter, however, he was reputed to be eloquent in speech and his words commanded respect.

Eskiminzin was at Camp Grant, Arizona, on the San Pedro River in April 1871, when about a hundred—estimates range from 25 to 144—of his people were murdered by a mob of Papago and non-Indians from Tucson (see CAMP GRANT MASSACRE). Seven of the eight members of his immediate family were killed in this debacle.

He survived the massacre and in 1873 was taken back to Camp Grant as a prisoner. He was transferred to San Carlos in 1874, and Indian agent John CLUM restored Eskiminzin as head chief of the many Arivaipa Apache assembled there by the United States Army. Said Clum, "[He] ever thereafter proved himself a worthy and faithful friend to me, to his people, and to peace. His conduct was most exemplary, and he was foremost among those making strenuous efforts toward self-support and civilization."

By 1876 Eskiminzin had become something of a celebrity, and with Clum and several Apache he made a trip to Washington, D.C., stopping off in St. Louis long enough to take part in a theatrical production. When Clum left the reservation in 1877, Eskiminzin returned to his former lands on the San Pedro River, where he farmed peacefully for the next ten years, becoming wholly self-sufficient. In 1888, however, he was arrested for allegedly having communicated with an outlaw known as the Apache Kid. Eskiminzin had rescued a girl named Chita—Clum says she was his daughter—during the Camp Grant massacre, and Chita had later become the wife of the Apache Kid. For his indiscretion, Eskiminzin was deported first to Florida, where he was imprisoned with Chiricahua Apache, and subsequently to Mount Vernon Barracks, Alabama, where he became head gardener. Clum succeeded in effecting his release in 1894, and Eskiminzin was secretly returned to San Carlos, where he died of "chronic stomach trouble" in 1896.

See John P. Clum, "Es-kim-in-zin," *New Mexico Historical Review* vol. 3, no. 4 (1928) and vol. 4, no. 1 (1929); and Don Schellie, *Vast Domain of Blood* (1968).—B. L. F.

Eskimo-Aleut language. See INDIAN LANGUAGES: *Eskimo-Aleut.*

Evans, John (1814-1897). Colorado businessman and politician. Born near Waynesville, Ohio, Evans was educated in Quaker schools and received a medical degree from Cincinnati College in 1838. He practiced in Ohio, Illinois, and Indiana, where he was a founder and first superintendent of the Indiana Hospital for the Insane. Moving to Chicago, he taught at Rush Medical College (1845-57), becoming editor and subsequently owner of the *North-Western Medical and Surgical Journal*. While in Chicago he began investing in real estate, later regarding these ventures as the basis of his large fortune, and seved on the city council. Although born a Quaker, Evans later became a Methodist and was instrumental in founding Garrett Biblical Institute and Northwestern University in Evanston, Illinois (named for him), both Methodist institutions.

Entering politics, Evans was defeated in his bid for nomination for a congressional seat in 1854. In 1862, when Abraham Lincoln appointed him the second governor of Colorado Territory, he moved to Denver, where he spent the rest of his life. He also served simultaneously as *ex officio* superintendent of Indian affairs, and his role in the events that culminated in the SAND CREEK MASSACRE, November 29, 1864, in which Indians were brutally massacred while under a flag of truce, is still a matter of debate. Whatever Governor Evans' motives and actions, his political enemies were successful in using the Sand Creek episode to discredit him, and he was asked to resign in 1865.

Evans continued to reside in Denver, where he became a prominent figure in business and educational circles. When word arrived in Denver that the transcontinental railroad would bypass the city, Evans and other businessmen organized the Denver Pacific Railroad to connect Denver with the UNION PACIFIC line at Cheyenne. Built with Kansas Pacific aid, the Denver Pacific brought the first trains to Denver in 1870. Evans' other railroad enterprises included the Denver, South Park and Pacific, and the Denver and New Orleans. Continuing his interest in education, he was a founder in 1864 of Colorado Seminary, which later became the University of Denver.

See Harry E. Kelsey, Jr., *Frontier Capitalist: The Life of John Evans* (1969); and Edgar C. McMechen, *Life of Governor Evans* (1924).—M. B.

Ewers, John Canfield (1909-   ). Ethnohistorian. Ewers was born in Cleveland, Ohio. After graduation from Dartmouth College, he studied at the Art Students League in New York before entering Yale University graduate school. There his interest in Plains Indian studies was stimulated by anthropologist Clark Wissler.

Ewers' first book, *Plains Indian Painting* (1939), was based largely upon his graduate thesis.

Throughout his career Ewers was concerned with the interpretation of history, ethnology, and art through museum exhibits as well as writings. He was field curator for the National Park Service (1935-40) and the Museum of the Plains Indian on the Blackfoot reservation, Montana (1941-44). In 1946 he joined the Smithsonian Institution, where he planned, developed, and administered the Smithsonian's new Museum of History and Technology for nine years and was its director during its first year (1964-65). In 1965 he became the senior ethnologist in the anthropology department.

Ewers' museum background is reflected in his writings, which are based upon studies of artifacts and pictures, extensive fieldwork among Indians of several tribes, and documentary history. Among his books are *Blackfeet Crafts* (1945); *The Horse in Blackfoot Indian Culture* (1955); *The Blackfeet, Raiders on the Northwestern Plains* (1958); *Crow Indian Beadwork* (with William Wildschut, 1959); *Artists of the Old West* (1965); and *Indian Life on the Upper Missouri* (1969). His 1958 study of the Blackfoot continues to be the standard published work on that group and is considered to be among the best ethnographies ever written concerning any American Indian tribe. He edited works by nineteenth-century observers of the Plains Indians, including George Catlin's *O-kee-pa, a Religious Ceremony and Other Customs of the Mandans* (1967); Edwin T. Denig's *Five Indian Tribes of the Upper Missouri* (1961); and Jean Louis Berlandier's *The Indians of Texas in 1830* (1969). Ewers contributed chapters to a score of books and more than one hundred articles to journals of history, anthropology, and art. He also conducted numerous studies of Indian painting and sculpture, based on research in museums and libraries throughout the world.

Ewers was the recipient of the Smithsonian Institution's first Exceptional Service Award in 1965, an honorary doctor of law degree from the University of Montana in 1966, and a doctor of science degree from Dartmouth College in 1968.—B. L. F.

"Exodusters." See NEGROES ON THE FRONTIER.

exploration, English. Most English exploration was of the Canadian West rather than of the land south of the forty-ninth parallel. John Cabot, a Genoese in the employ of Henry VII, established England's claim to North America by his landfall, probably on the south shore of Newfoundland, in June 1497. For nearly eight decades thereafter the English manifested little interest in North America, and not until the 1570s in the age of the Elizabethan "sea dogs" did they begin exploring again. In 1578 Sir Francis Drake sailed his *Golden Hind* up the California coast, anchoring probably in the present Drake's Bay. In 1583 Sir Humphrey Gilbert tried to establish a colony in Newfoundland, and in 1607 Jamestown was established. As the decades passed and thirteen English colonies came to occupy the eastern seaboard, there was exploration as far west as the Mississippi. This was a by-product of land speculation schemes or of the fur trade.

Meanwhile, the British received Hudson's Bay by the Treaty of Utrecht (1713). One Henry Kelsey, working southwest from York Factory on Hudson's Bay, had already seen the vast Canadian plains in 1691. In 1717

Captain James Knight founded a fort at Churchill. In 1754-55 Anthony Henday reached Blackfoot country along the foothills of the northern Rockies. In 1769 Samuel Hearne explored in the vast area northwest of Hudson's Bay and helped destroy the legend of a short Northwest Passage or a Strait of Anian connecting East and West. In 1787 a young Scotsman, Alexander Mackenzie, who was stationed near Lake Athabaska, was inspired by a belief of Peter POND that there was a feasible route across the vast northland to the Pacific. In 1789 Mackenzie discovered the river that now bears his name, but he christened it "River Disappointment" because, although it flowed west out of Great Slave Lake, it veered to the north and discharged into the Arctic. In 1793 he made his second and more famous exploration. On July 19 after discovering the Fraser River (which he thought was the Columbia), he saw "a narrow arm of the Sea": he had reached the Pacific. By August 24 Mackenzie was back at the Peace River Fort, from which he had launched his enterprise. In 1808 Simon Fraser traversed the river and gave it his own name.

Meanwhile English navigators had coasted the northeastern shores of the Pacific. In 1778 Captain James Cook cruised from the forty-fourth parallel to northern ALASKA, and in 1792 Captain George Vancouver mapped the coast from San Diego to Alaska. Furs were the attractions, and first the NORTH WEST COMPANY, and after its merger in 1821, the HUDSON'S BAY COMPANY, manifested interest in the Pacific Northwest. FORT VANCOUVER became the center of exploration activities, some as far to the southeast as the Great Salt Lake, by such adventurers as Peter Skene OGDEN and Alexander ROSS.

See Lawrence J. Burpee, *The Search for the Western Sea,* 2 vols. (1907; rev. ed. 1935); Frederick Merk, *Fur Trade and Empire: George Simpson's Journal* (1931; rev. ed. 1968); and publications o; the Champlain Society and the Hudson's Bay Record Society.—R. A. B.

exploration, French. In the nearly two and a half centuries in which France was in possession of much of North America, her explorers, fur traders, and Catholic missionaries gained knowledge of the Great Lakes and the watersheds serving them, of Hudson's Bay, of the Mississippi valley, of the vast prairies west of the Lakes (see MINNESOTA and KANSAS), and even some knowledge of the Rocky Mountains and of the Great Salt Lake. They discovered the mouth of the Mississippi and even attempted to establish a trading post on the coast of Texas. The loss to France of her North American empire is massive when equated with the energies expended in its acquisition.

French fishermen may have been drying their fish on islands of the St. Lawrence estuary for many years prior to the first official probing of that area by mariners in the pay of the French king. Such official exploration was first accomplished by the Italian Verrazano, who in 1524 coasted from the Delaware to Cape Breton and established France's initial claim to North America. In 1535 Jacques Cartier discovered the St. Lawrence estuary, and for a little more than a decade efforts were made at colonization, but they failed. Then France entered the troubled times of religious wars, and not until the ascension of the Bourbon King Henry IV was there a renewal of activity.

Samuel de Champlain sailed in 1608 for New France as an agent for the monopolistic French company that controlled the trade there. For the next twenty-eight years this man was to dominate New France and encourage exploration (see TRANSPORTATION ON THE GREAT LAKES). In the course of his activities he explored up the Richelieu River to Lake Champlain, up the Ottawa, and west to Lake Ontario.

In 1634 Champlain sent Jean NICOLET, one of his "young men" (Frenchmen whom he had trained for service in New France), westward to investigate tales about a distant sea. This adventurer reached Green Bay and explored Lake Winnebago and the Fox River. Meanwhile Champlain died in 1635, and there was a lull in exploring activity until the 1650s, when the fur country west of the Great Lakes began to figure in the economy of New France. Deeply involved in this area were two adventurers, Pierre Esprit Radisson and Médart Chouart Groseilliers. They probably saw much of present Minnesota and the upper Mississippi, but their controversies with the French led them to deal with the British at Albany, and the final outcome was the creation of the HUDSON'S BAY COMPANY.

ROMAN CATHOLIC MISSIONARIES were also active. Recollects, affiliated with the Franciscans, came first, to be followed by the Jesuits in 1625 and finally by the Sulpicians a generation later. These valiant men lived in the wilderness with the Indians, especially with the Huron, and risked their lives as the hated Iroquois pushed warfare into the heart of Huronia. By 1670 Father Jacques MARQUETTE was at Michilimackinac. In the summer of 1671 France officially took possession of "the West" in a formal ceremony at Sault Sainte Marie. One reason for this expansion westward was the diaspora of the Huron and neighboring Algonquian tribes in the face of Iroquois raids.

In 1673 the French began their exploration of the vast Mississippi valley. In that year Louis JOLLIET and Father Marquette paddled their canoes down the Wisconsin River to the Mississippi and thence downstream to the mouth of the Arkansas. Indians were unfriendly, however, and the Frenchmen concluded that the Mississippi flowed into the Gulf without actually sailing down to the mouth of the river. With this much information they returned to New France.

In the next two decades such explorers as Henri de TONTI; Daniel Greysolon, Sieur Duluth; Father Louis Hennepin and Louis-Armand de LAHONTAN (of questionable veracity); and René Robert Cavelier, Sieur de LA SALLE were all busy in the Mississippi valley. On April 7, 1682, La Salle, a seigneur (landowner) of New France, reached the Gulf of Mexico. Two days later he claimed the entire Mississippi valley in the name of France and christened it Louisiana in honor of his king. In 1687, somewhere in Texas, the explorer was murdered by his men as he tried to make his way back to New France from a colony he had founded on the Texas coast. Meanwhile, French fur trading posts were springing up along the tributaries of the Mississippi and at strategic points along the Great Lakes. French traders even reached Santa Fe, in Spanish territory.

In the late seventeenth and early eighteenth centuries there was again an advance westward. Daniel Greysolon, Sieur Duluth, in 1679 pushed into Sioux country west of

Lake Superior. Three of his men accompanied a war party to Dakota and heard of a salty sea some twenty days' ride to the west. Yet from the 1680s on the Sioux proved treacherous, and the French advanced westward by staying north of the Sioux country. In the 1730s Pierre de LA VERENDRYE and his sons pushed westward to the Lake of the Woods and Lake Winnipeg, searching for the western sea and trading for furs. Hearing of the Mandan, they sought their domain and arrived at one of their villages in 1738. From there, some three years later (April 1742), two of La Vérendrye's sons headed southwest, hoping to make contact with some "horse Indians." The Frenchmen appear to have reached the Black Hills of South Dakota, and possibly they saw the Big Horn Mountains in Wyoming.

These explorations laid the foundations both for France's claim to a vast portion of North America and for a lucrative fur trade, which was the envy of other nations. By 1763 the French knew the interior of North America from Hudson's Bay to the mouth of the Mississippi, westward beyond the Missouri, southwest to Santa Fe, and south to FLORIDA, though they fared less well there. It is doubtful that they ever actually reached the front range of the Rocky Mountains. However, the French-Canadian half bloods, the *coureurs de bois*, carried on as laborers in the fur trade to all parts of the West until the trade ended in the nineteenth century.

See John Bartlett Brebner, *The Explorers of North America* (1933); Nellis M. Crouse, *In Quest of the Western Ocean* (1928); John Francis McDermott, ed.; *The French in the Mississippi Valley* (1965); Frances Parkman, *A Half-Century of Conflict* (1892), *The Old Regime in Canada* (1874), and *La Salle and the Discovery of the Great West* (1879).—R. A. B.

exploration, Russian. In 1725 Peter the Great sent a Dane, Vitus Bering, to determine the whereabouts of North America in relation to Siberia. Bering finally saw the American coastline on July 16, 1632. In December he died, but a subordinate named Chirikov returned with magnificent peltry. The lust for furs was the cynosure that drew Russians to the northwest coast of America.

These fur trappers began their conquest by island-hopping the Aleutians. Subsequently, a merchant named Shelikov established a trading colony on Kodiak Island, and from this beginning, with the involvement of explorers Nikolai Petrovich Rezanov and Aleksandr A. BARANOV, there came into being in 1799 the monopolistic Russian-American Company.

By this time Baranov had explored the coast of southeastern ALASKA, and in 1800 a Russian settlement was established at Sitka. It was to become the American headquarters of the Russian-American Company, which maintained small hunting and trading settlements up and down the coast and among the hundreds of islands between Alaska and Siberia. Scurvy was a danger, and the search for fruits and vegetables led Rezanov to sail to San Francisco in 1806. In the next few years Baranov commissioned crews of Aleuts to poach along the California coast, and in 1812 employees built FORT ROSS at Bodega Bay, about fifty miles north of San Francisco. By 1819, when the first charter of the Russian-American Company expired, that organization had posts from the Bering Sea to California.

From about 1817 until the Alaska purchase in 1867, the Russians, anxious for new sources of furs, pushed their explorations into the interior of the West Coast. By the end of their era, the mountains and river systems of that vast land were sketchily known.

See Hector Chevigny, *Russian America: The Great Alaskan Adventure, 1741-1867* (1965), and Clarence C. Hulley, *Alaska, Past and Present* (1958).—R. A. B.

exploration, Spanish. The successful Spanish conquest of Mexico and of Central and much of South America is a testament to the Spaniards' aggressiveness, be they soldiers or friars. The story of the lands north of Cuba and Mexico—of North America and especially the part that became the United States—is, in contrast, one of failure. There lay the "northern mystery." If Mexico had revealed such great riches, then what prevented the existence of other exotic and fabulously wealthy heathen civilizations in the land mass that extended in a wide arc from northeast to northwest? Indians related stories of such places as the Seven Cities of CIBOLA, of a fountain of youth, of a land governed by amazons.

The "northern mystery" embraced the secrets of a continent three thousand miles wide, and the Spanish succeeded in exploring a substantial part of it. They were disappointed in what they discovered, but even in disappointment their expeditions added greatly to geographical knowledge. So extensive was the land and so widespread their perambulations that, in order to retain a semblance of clarity, the continent will be divided into a southeast and a southwest, with a chronological break in the year 1542.

By 1507 the Spanish were well established in the Caribbean. The trails to gold and jewels seemed to lie in all directions, and adventurers pursued the rumors with unquenched energy. This spirit, which carried Hernán Cortés to Mexico in 1519 and Francisco Pizarro to Peru in 1532, likewise stimulated the search into the north. In 1513 Juan PONCE DE LEON dropped anchor near the mouth of the St. Johns River and named the land Pascua Florida (see FLORIDA). He then sailed southward, around the Florida Keys and the Tortugas and up the Gulf Coast to above Charlotte Harbor. In 1521 he returned to the latter place, landed, engaged in a skirmish with the Indians, and returned to Cuba, where he died of his wounds.

In 1519 Alonso de Pineda sailed along the Gulf Coast and discovered either Mobile Bay or the mouth of the Mississippi. In 1520 or 1521 Francisco Gordillo took Indian slaves in the vicinity of Cape Fear in North Carolina. His superior, Lucas Vásquez de Ayllón, followed in 1526 with an unsuccessful attempt to establish a colony at the mouth of the Cape Fear River. He did determine, however, that Florida was a peninsula, and not an island. In fact, it appears that in 1524 or 1525 one Stephen Gomez actually coasted the Atlantic from Nova Scotia southward.

Then in 1528 the incompetent Pánfilo de NARVAEZ landed at Tampa Bay and began a march through the interior of Florida. Failing to discover any wealth, the men embarked in crude boats from near St. Marks, hoping to find their way to Pánuco, on the Mexican coast. A shipwreck, on either Galveston Island or nearby San Luis Island, ended this expedition, and eventually all but four died. The four survivors expanded Spanish knowledge of North America by traversing several thousand miles from where they were shipwrecked to the province of Sinaloa, in northwest Mexico, where they were rescued in 1536. These men were Alonso del Castillo Maldonado, usually called simply Castillo, Andrés Dorantes de Carranca, usually called Dorantes, Alvar Núñez CABEZA DE VACA, and the Arab slave Estevanito.

Cabeza de Vaca related his experiences to receptive and gullible audiences both in Mexico and Spain. Rumors of a wealthy Seven Cities of Cíbola to the north and of a strait through which ships could pass from the Atlantic to the Pacific were intriguing the Spanish even before Cabeza de Vaca's timely rescue. His stories served as a catalyst to action. Between 1538 and 1542 a whole wave of explorations took place.

To the east in Florida the conquistador Hernando DE SOTO landed in May 1539 with six hundred men, horses, and a few swine. Following a policy of merciless cruelty toward all the natives they met, the expedition wintered in Apalachee, in the vicinity of present Tallahassee. In the spring of Soto's men advanced northeastward to South Carolina, turned northwest over the mountains into Tennessee and then south into Alabama, west into Mississippi and north into southwest Tennessee, where, somewhere below Memphis, they crossed the Mississippi. Then they advanced through Arkansas into Oklahoma and returned to the Mississippi, where de Soto died. His successor explored into East Texas, then returned to the Mississippi, ordered boats constructed, and led the survivors down the Mississippi. Following the southwestern curvature of the Gulf, some 311 men—about half of de Soto's original force—reached the Rio Pánuco in Mexico in September 1543. The only gain for the Spanish was knowledge.

Meanwhile, the conquistadores in the West had been busy also. Fray Marcos de Niza and the slave Estevanito had discovered some pueblos far to the north. Estevanito was killed there, but Fray Marcos returned to Mexico with the news that he had viewed the fabled Cíbola from a far distance. Cortés sent Francisco de Ulloa up the West Coast in search of the Seven Cities of Cíbola. Ulloa discovered the mouth of the Colorado and in the same year (1540) Hernando de Alarcón, a lieutenant of Francisco Vásquez de CORONADO, likewise found the Colorado River and actually sailed up it some distance. In 1542 Juan Rodríquez CABRILLO sailed as far north along the California coast as Drake's Bay, and after his death his successor, Bartolomé Ferrelo, explored northward to just above the California-Oregon boundary.

The chief land expedition, from 1540 to 1542, was Coronado's exploration in search of wealth and/or a strait linking the Atlantic with the Pacific. Coronado advanced up the western corridor of Mexico, northward across eastern Arizona, and took Cíbola, in reality the Zuñi pueblos of northwestern New Mexico. Coronado's lieutenants explored west to the Colorado River, which they observed from the crest of the Grand Canyon, and then northward, capturing the Hopi pueblos. They then explored first eastward, discovering Acoma (the "Sky City") and the Rio Grande, and then northward up that stream at least to the Taos pueblo. Coronado wintered at Tiguex, near Bernalillo, New Mexico, and in 1541 headed northeast toward a rumored land of wealth called Quivira, in KANSAS. This brought him as far as the land of the Wichita Indians, along the Smoky Hill River

of Kansas. Finding no wealth, he returned to Mexico in 1542. Thus ended the explorations of the conquistadores in North America.

Yet Spanish exploration continued, albeit within a great geographical frame of knowledge. It was usually a by-product of colonization schemes or of the extension of borders for purposes of defense against the French, English, or Russians, or it was a result of missionary work, first of the Jesuits and then of the Franciscans. Whatever the prime motive, the net effect was a more detailed knowledge of the vast southern half of the United States-to-be. See ARIZONA: *Spanish and Mexican Arizona (to 1846),* and TEXAS.

The settlement of Florida at St. Augustine in 1565 by Pedro Menéndez de Avilés is significant, for this was the base from which a chain of missions was extended westward across the peninsula. Fear of the French also prompted the exploration of Texas, with Martin de Alarcón founding San Antonio in 1718. This, after earlier attempts south and east had failed, was to prove a permanent base of military operations in that vast land. The settlement of New Mexico in 1598 by Don Juan de ONATE and the establishment of Santa Fe in 1609 also contributed significantly to the body of Spanish knowledge.

Similarly, CALIFORNIA was occupied as a defense measure. In 1602 Sebastián Vizcaíno explored the coast and recommended that Monterey be made a defensive post, although no action was taken. Nearly a century later the Jesuit Father Eusebio KINO trod a path across the desert wastes into California, establishing missions along the way (see also ROMAN CATHOLIC MISSIONARIES). Nearly seven decades elapsed before threats of a Russian advance down the Pacific Coast renewed Spanish activity in the forging of trails into California. In 1769 a joint land and sea expedition led by Father Junípero SERRA and Gaspar de Portolá resulted in the settlement of San Diego. From there, settlement and missions spread northward as far as Monterey. During the 1770s a search was under way for an overland route from New Mexico to California. The Franciscan Father Garcés explored into southern California, while Fathers Dominguez and Escalante ventured northwest from Santa Fe through the Rockies and into much of eastern Utah, thus exploring a part of the Great Basin. In 1776 Juan Bautista de ANZA established the presidio at San Francisco. This constitutes in many ways the high-water mark of Spanish colonization in North America, for after the 1770s both internal difficulties and the coming of the French Revolution and the Napoleonic wars weakened Spain's control and taxed her energies.

In sum, Spain's conquistadores, missionaries, and colonizers were the first Europeans to tread an enormous portion of North America. For a fleeting moment in time a Spanish Jesuit mission was established on the Chesapeake, within thirty miles of Washington, D.C. Spaniards advanced as far north as St. Joseph, Michigan, and the Spanish flag once waved over the Mandan villages in North Dakota. Her vessels coasted southward from Nova Scotia and off the West Coast contested British ownership of Nootka Sound on Vancouver Island. Pedro VIAL trod the lands of the Santa Fe Trail to St. Louis, and many other explorers, pathfinders, and trail breakers wove a web of geographical knowledge across the continent. In reality, Spain once possessed a frontier extending from St. Augustine to San Francisco, with missions and presidios at strategic points all the way. As with most frontiers, all parts of it were never at one time under her uncontested control, but the dream was there.

Spain's failure was due in part to her inability to adjust her colonization techniques, so successful in Mexico and Peru, to a sparsely settled, temperate-zone land in which the peoples were nomadic and warlike. Then, too, the incentive of fabulous treasure was missing, as was the challenge of civilized peoples to be converted to the "true faith." The American pioneers working west from the Atlantic were more numerous and more interested in permanent settlement. Finally, the complexities of European politics as well as the internal difficulties of Spain in the period after 1776 contributed to her failure in North America.

The outstanding historian of the Spanish in North America is Herbert Eugene Bolton. A brief survey is his *The Spanish Borderlands* (1921), and of special merit is his *Coronado, Knight of Pueblos and Plains* (1949). A good survey of Bolton's work is John Francis Bannon, ed., *Bolton and the Spanish Borderlands* (1967). A general view of the exploration of North America, including the Spanish, is John Bartlett Brebner, *The Explorers of North America* (1933). See also Gloria Griffin Cline, *Exploring the Great Basin* (1962); Warren L. Cook, *Flood Tide of Empire: Spain and the Pacific Northwest, 1543-1819* (1973); and Noel M. Loomis and Abraham P. Nasatir, *Pedro Vial and the Roads to Santa Fe* (1967).—R. A. B.

exploration, United States. The energetic push westward of the American people from 1789 to 1890 was so rapid that official explorations usually lagged behind the discoveries of the curious, profit-seeking private citizen. The California and Oregon coasts were known to Yankee traders who were anchoring in the bays and inlets of that vast and beautiful seascape before there was a single state west of the Appalachians. John Ledyard, a Connecticut Yankee, was encouraged in 1786 by Thomas Jefferson to walk across Siberia, then cross to the northwest coast and walk eastward to St. Louis. (He never got beyond Irkutsk in Siberia.) Captains Robert Gray and John Kendrick headed for the northwest coast of the Pacific in 1787; on a second voyage in 1792 in his ship, the *Columbia*, Gray passed over the sandbar and set his anchor in the Columbia River estuary. Prior to 1800 Yankee traders were killing off the sea otter along the California coast. When the seals were nearly exterminated, the Americans began trading with the Californians for hides and tallow, and agents of these trading concerns traveled from ranch to ranch, learning much of the lay of the land.

Inland, prior to 1800, the peripatetic American was nearly always ahead of official explorations and international diplomacy. Americans out of Natchez and New Orleans were trading deep into the Southwest, and Jefferson encouraged one Philip Nolan to investigate Texas. Traders were to be found throughout the Great Lakes region, and by the beginning of the nineteenth century they were even probing up the Missouri River.

Trade was the great magnet that drew men westward, although curiosity and the possibility of adventure added to their incentives. When Meriwether Lewis and William Clark moved up the Missouri in 1804 they met a number of fur traders floating down the river with cargoes of peltry. At about the time Stephen H. Long was returning from his expedition to the front range of the Rockies in the early 1820s, William Becknell was planning a journey far to the southwest, to Santa Fe.

The fur trade west of the Mississippi, and especially that part of it centering west of the Missouri from the mouth of the Platte into the vastnesses of the Rockies beyond the three forks, soon became of great importance. John Colter, who had left Lewis and Clark and had returned upstream with some trappers, was the first witness of the thermal phenomena of the Yellowstone region. John Jacob Astor established Astoria on the Oregon coast and sent Wilson Price Hunt overland to the fort. Hunt traveled through new country south of Lewis and Clark's route in order to avoid the bloodthirsty Blackfoot. When the Robert Stuart party of returning Astorians came east, they crossed the Continental Divide just south of the Wind River Range—the general area of the South Pass of the Oregonians and the forty-niners.

The great decades of the mountain men were from about 1820 until 1840. These freedom-loving individuals traversed the entire West in search of peltry, so that by the 1840s there was scarcely a prominent pass or geographical landmark they did not know. Major Andrew Henry and William Henry Ashley provided the impetus that started a number of these men on their way to fame. Jedediah Smith crossed the Black Hills of present South Dakota, trapped in the Big Horn Mountains, and in 1826 forged from Salt Lake through the desert wastes of the Southwest to the San Gabriel Mission. He then advanced up the San Joaquin valley, turned northeast, crested the Sierra, and continued northeasterly until he arrived back at Great Salt Lake, in June 1827.

By 1827, James Ohio Pattie and his father, Sylvester Pattie, had made their way from Santa Fe west to southern California, and in 1829 Ewing Young and William Wolfskill began forging the Old Spanish Trail from Santa Fe to Los Angeles. In 1833 Joseph Reddeford Walker trekked to California over the Sierra, working from east to west. Other mountain men—Jim Bridger, Thomas Fitzpatrick, William S. Williams, Milton Sublette (see Sublette brothers), Osborne Russell, to name a few—made discoveries some of which, because they were not recorded, had to be rediscovered at a later date. Frontiersmen or wayfarers such as Kit Carson, Benjamin L. E. Bonneville, Hall J. Kelley, and Nathaniel Wyeth also added to the easterner's knowledge of the West.

So too did missionaries make a contribution. If they were not native-born, most of them became United States citizens. Father Pierre De Smet and a number of his brethren of the Jesuit order advanced into the Northwest, as did the Protestants Jason Lee, Elijah White, and Marcus Whitman. Totally different, but still discovering and adding to the knowledge of the West, were the Argonauts of 1849 (see trails of the Forty-niners). In the following decades the lonely prospector with his loyal pack jack was to be encountered all over the transmontane region, searching for "color" but also discovering other secrets of the land.

The government was not far behind these people, and in the final anaylsis, American official exploration of the West was vigorous and thorough. Jefferson, once he was president, lost little time in implementing his plans. Meriwether Lewis and William Clark explored to the Pacific Northwest, William Dunbar and John Hunter explored the Ouchita River, Thomas Freeman the Red River, and Zebulon PIKE to Leech Lake in the north woods and on a later expedition west to the upper Rio Grande, where he was captured by the Spanish. During Monroe's administration, Stephen H. Long explored to the north woods and to the front range of the Rockies in the present Colorado. In the period from 1838 to 1842 Charles Wilkes led the WILKES EXPEDITION to Antarctica, the South Seas, Hawaii, and the coast of Oregon.

After the Corps of TOPOGRAPHICAL ENGINEERS was established as a separate unit in 1838, American exploration was concentrated in that office. These engineers explored much of the Southwest during and following the Mexican War. John C. FREMONT made three official expeditions west, and his reports were widely read by a public eager to acquire lands in Oregon and California. The TRANSCONTINENTAL RAILROAD SURVEYS of 1853-55 likewise contributed greatly to American knowledge of the West. These surveys were also characterized by a substantial amount of purely scientific work.

After the Civil War, exploration became a matter of scientific investigation and mapping. The surveys made by Ferdinand V. HAYDEN, Clarence KING, John Wesley POWELL, George M. WHEELER, and Walter P. Jenney—the latter of the Black Hills—figure most significantly until the creation of the United States GEOLOGICAL SURVEY in 1879. Coexisting through these years, and in some cases antedating them, were several state-sponsored geological surveys, such as the California Geological Survey. In the 1880s Henry T. ALLEN and other soldiers explored ALASKA. Thus by 1890, when the nation was just barely more than a century old, American energy, curiosity, desire for profit, and scientific endeavor had unlocked the secrets of the greatest and most diverse area on earth.

The material on American exploration is voluminous. A good beginning would be the pertinent chapters in the principal college texts on the American frontier, such as Ray Allen Billington, *Westward Expansion* (various editions); Thomas D. Clark, *Frontier America,* 2nd ed. (1969); and Robert E. Riegel and Robert G. Athearn, *America Moves West,* 4th ed. (1964). The American Exploration and Travel series and the numerous publications of the Arthur C. Clark Company embrace an unusually large percentage of the scholarly works on American exploration. See also Bernard De Voto, *Across the Wide Missouri* (1947) and *The Course of Empire* (1952); and William G. Goetzmann, *Exploration and Empire* (1966).—R. A. B.

F

factory system. See FUR TRADE: *in the United States.*

Fair, James Graham (1831-1894). Miner and financier. Born in Ireland, brought to Illinois at the age of twelve. At eighteen he joined the gold rush to California, and at thirty was the owner of a quartz mill on the Washoe River in Nevada. He was soon in association with three other sons of poor Irish immigrants—John W. Mackay, James C. Flood, and William S. O'Brien—and the "Irish four" became the wealthiest of the kings of the Comstock Lode. Fair and Mackay began as mine superintendents. Flood and O'Brien were originally partners in a San Francisco saloon catering to the city's leading stockholders, from whom they gleaned much inside information that was of great value when they opened a stock brokerage firm of their own. The combination of expert knowledge about the mines and about the San Francisco stock market was tremendously effective, and the four associates were able to establish the Bank of Nevada in successful competition with the Bank of California. In 1873 Fair discovered the "big bonanza," a vast deposit of silver and gold directly under his Consolidated Virginia Mine. This was the largest single ore pocket ever found, and it yielded more than one hundred million dollars in the next six years. Fair purchased a seat in the United States Senate from the Nevada legislature in 1881, though he took little part in Senate debates. His relations with his wife, three daughters, and two sons were tragically unhappy, and his attempt to tie up his estate in a trust resulted in many years of famous and frequently scandalous litigation after his death.

William Wright (Dan DeQuille) published a classic account, *The Big Bonanza,* in 1876. Oscar Lewis, *Silver King* (1947), includes a biography of Fair emphasizing his personal life.—W. B.

Fall, Albert Bacon (1861-1944). New Mexican businessman and politician. The name of Fall will always remain inextricably associated with the Teapot Dome scandal of the 1920s, an event which terminated the political career of this bluff and competent westerner. He was born in Frankfort, Kentucky. Ill health as a youth drove him to the salubrious climate of the West, where he taught school briefly in Indian Territory, became a cowhand on a Texas cattle drive, and engaged in several mining ventures in Mexico. In 1885 he began prospecting in southwestern New Mexico around Kingston and there became acquainted with Edward L. Doheny. With his family, Fall settled in Las Cruces in 1887, where he was shortly admitted to the bar, and by 1905 had begun the development of his huge ranch at Three Rivers, New Mexico.

During these years he became increasingly active in

politics, filling various positions in the territorial government. With statehood in 1912, he was elected on the Republican ticket to serve as one of New Mexico's first senators. Nine years later his friend President Warren G. Harding made him secretary of the interior, the highest post thus far attained by a New Mexican. While in this office he leased government oil lands at Teapot Dome, Wyoming, and Elk Hills, California, to associates Harry F. Sinclair and Doheny. The storm that arose forced his resignation, and when subsequent investigation disclosed he had accepted a $100,000 bribe from Doheny, he was sent to prison in 1931. Fall thus became a convenient scapegoat for all the misdeeds of the Harding administration. Fall died in poverty in El Paso, his reputation permanently blackened.

Fall's early life is treated in David H. Stratton, ed., *The Memoirs of Albert B. Fall,* Southwestern Studies, No. 15 (1966). A full biographical sketch appears in William A. Keleher, *The Fabulous Frontier, Twelve New Mexico Items* (rev. ed., 1962).—M. Si.

Fallen Timbers, battle of (1794). The battle of Fallen Timbers grew out of Indian resistence to American settlement north of the Ohio River, and England's attempts to create an Indian buffer state in the Old Northwest. Indian victories against General Josiah Harmar near the Maumee River in 1790 and against General Arthur St. Clair on the Wabash River in 1791 gave the British an advantage in their diplomatic offensive. President Washington therefore appointed a new military commander in the West, General Anthony Wayne, and ordered him to make a major offensive campaign.

Wayne began the long preparation for his drive against the Indians and British of the upper Miami River in May 1793, when he moved his forces down the Ohio River to Fort Washington. The British were in posts they had occupied since the French and Indian War. In the winter of 1793-94 he again moved his troops northward and established Fort Greenville, where he drilled his men for battle. He had with him as commanders Charles Scott, James Wilkinson, and William Clark. Historians' estimates of the number of troops range from 4,700 down to 3,000, and estimates of the Indians who were to oppose him vary from Wayne's guess of 2,000 down to 900.

The Indian resistance at Fallen Timbers did not come as a surprise to Wayne, for on the way north a part of his command had been attacked while constructing Fort Recovery at the site of St. Clair's defeat. Wayne's troops withstood the Indians and shattered their hopes for repeating their successes against Harmar and St. Clair. General Wayne was methodical and organized in his troop advance to the Auglaize and Maumee rivers, leaving little if any opportunity for surprises. At the confluence of the Auglaize and Maumee Wayne was successful in scaring the Indians away from their crops and villages. There he established Fort Defiance almost in the face of the British Fort Miamis. Wayne wanted to treat with the Indians without attacking (despite the fact that he was ready for battle), but their dilatoriness made this plan impossible. On August 20, 1794, he was engaged in battle with the Northwest Indians, some French, British, and even renegade Americans.

The battle of Fallen Timbers was fought in the path of an earlier cyclone in which timber had been tossed about in confusion. This was difficult ground on which to fight, but Wayne so deployed his troops as to keep the enemy surrounded and in a position where he could press against them with advantage. In less than an hour the Indians were thrown into confusion and retreated toward the British fort, but the British closed the gates to them. The Americans lost thirty-three men killed and about one hundred wounded. Indian losses were rather heavy.

Wayne no doubt could have pursued the Indians and all but annihilated them. At the same time he might have become involved in a fight with the British garrison, and, in fact, there was a sharp exchange of notes between Wayne and the British major William Campbell in which the American commander asked Campbell to abandon his post, which he later did. Wayne destroyed the Indian villages on the Maumee and Auglaize, then went on to the confluence of the St. Marys and St. Joseph rivers, where he built Fort Wayne. He then moved back to Fort Greenville to spend the winter and prepare for treaty-making the following spring and summer with the Indians. The battle of Fallen Timbers went far toward reducing Indian influence in the area and led directly to the Indians' cession of southern Ohio in the Treaty of GREENVILLE and to JAY'S TREATY.

See W. E. Connelly and E. M. Coulter, *History of Kentucky* (1922); and John Hyde Preston, *A Gentleman Rebel* (1930).—T. D. C.

Fargo, William George (1818-81). Businessman. Fargo was born in Pompey, Onondaga County, New York. At thirteen he became a mail carrier riding on horseback over a thirty-mile route twice each week. In 1835 he worked as a grocer's clerk in Syracuse; later he and his younger brother ran their own store, which was to prove a financial failure. In January 1840 Fargo married Anna H. Williams of Pompey. At that time he became the freight agent in Auburn for the Auburn & Syracuse Railroad. Soon he turned his attention to the express business, first as a messenger for Livingston, Wells, and Pomeroy between Albany and Buffalo and later as their agent in Buffalo. In 1844 he became one of three partners, with Henry Wells and Daniel Dunning, in Wells & Company, the first express firm operating west of Buffalo, and served as a messenger. In 1850 three competing companies were combined to form the American Express Company, with Wells as president and Fargo as secretary. Mail and packages were delivered from New York to Buffalo and on west to Chicago, Milwaukee, St. Louis, Galena, Illinois, and Dubuque, Iowa.

With the advent of the gold rush to California, the need for improved communication and transportation service from the East Coast to the Pacific Slope as well as within California became obvious. In response to this need, WELLS, FARGO & CO. was organized in 1852 and soon gained a dominant position in the express business and in time a monopoly in California. The company collected gold dust and transported mail, packages, and passengers; it also successfully engaged in banking. Wells and Fargo were highly successful as a team, with the former concentrating on the financial aspects of the business and the latter serving as supervisor of field operations. In 1868 Fargo became president of the American Merchants Union Express Company, known by the shorter title of American Express Company after

1873, and held that position until his death. He was also president of Wells, Fargo & Co. from 1870 to 1872.

Throughout his life, Fargo was identified with the economic development and political activity of Buffalo, New York. He was the Democratic mayor for two terms, 1862-66, but was an unsuccessful candidate for the state senate in 1871. His family ties were strong, and two of his brothers, James C. and Charles, were associated with him in the express business for many years. While his partner, Henry Wells, apparently was shy, retiring, and sensitive by nature, Fargo had a dynamic personality, a commanding presence, and was gregarious and popular.

See Alvin F. Harlow, *Old Waybills* (1934); Edward Hungerford, *Wells Fargo: Advancing the American Frontier* (1949); and A. L. Stimson, *History of the Express Business* (1881).—W. T. J.

Fargo, North Dakota. Settlement in the area around present-day Fargo began in 1871. The Northern Pacific Railroad had built its main line to the Red River of the North at Moorhead, Minnesota. The site for the future town was just across the river. In 1872 the town's name was changed from Centralia to Fargo. Like other towns along the main line of the Northern Pacific, it was named by the railroad—in this case by William G. Fargo, on the board of directors of the Northern Pacific and a founder of Wells, Fargo & Co.

As other railroads extended into the Red River valley, land offices and settlers followed. In 1885 Fargo boasted a population of 7,394. After the land boom subsided, Fargo lost approximately 2,000 people. In 1890, a year after North Dakota entered the Union, Fargo's population was 5,664. By 1920, however, Fargo was the largest town in the state, with a population of 21,961. This distinction has been retained to the present day; the 1970 census showed the population to be 53,365. —D. J. T.

farm movements. See AGRARIAN MOVEMENTS.

Farnham, Thomas Jefferson (1804-1848), and **Eliza Woodson** (1815-1864). Diarists and historians. The early life of Thomas is obscure. He was probably born in Vermont, but first definite biographical data places him in Peoria, Illinois, where he practiced law. In 1836 he married Eliza Woodson Burhans. Farnham was chosen captain of a group of nineteen who, inspired by a lecture about Oregon given by the Reverend Jason Lee, decided to make a trip across the continent. They outfitted at Independence, Missouri, and in May 1839 set off on the Santa Fe Trail. The party split up and only five members, including Farnham, reached the Pacific. From there Farnham sailed to Hawaii and returned via California and Mexico, crossing the isthmus and ascending the Mississippi River to Peoria in the summer of 1840. In 1841 the Farnhams moved to New York. In 1846 or 1847 Farnham moved to San Francisco, where he practiced law until his death.

From 1844 to 1848 Eliza Farnham was matron of the female department of the state prison at Sing Sing. After her husband's death she went to California but returned in 1856 to New York, where she died.

Both Farnhams are remembered as reporters of western life. Thomas published the account of his 1839-40 journey as *Travels in the Great Western Prairies* (1841) and supplemented it with *Life and Adventures in California* (1846). Since the *Travels* covered a partially new route to the West, the descriptions are of value, but both books are marred by erratic and irresponsible personal observations.

Eliza's account of western life, *Life in Prairie Land* (1846), and two semiautobiographical novels are primarily of antiquarian interest.—J. K. F.

Farny, Henry F. (1847-1916). Painter. Farny was born in Alsace, France, and brought to the United States by his parents in 1853, the family living in western Pennsylvania and then Cincinnati, Ohio. In Cincinnati Farny served an apprenticeship as a lithographer in one of the city's numerous publishing firms that produced prints of Civil War battle scenes, theatrical portraits, and the like. After studying abroad from 1866 to 1870, he decided in 1881 to make a study of the American Indian and until about 1900 made frequent journeys into the West in search of appropriate material. He was a frequent contributor of illustrations to *Harper's Weekly* during this period and produced some pictures for an edition of a McGuffey Reader. He also illustrated the memoirs of New Mexico ethnologist Frank Hamilton Cushing, published in *Century* magazine in serial form in 1882-83.

About 1890 Farny seems to have abandoned commercial illustration to devote himself entirely to painting, and his present fame rests largely upon the pictures produced during this time and afterward. Overlooked by most modern art historians, his work nevertheless is of historic value because of his efforts to secure authentic material for his pictures and to certify through observation and study that they represented not only the facts but the spirit of his time. Presidents Ulysses S. Grant and Theodore Roosevelt praised his portrayals of Indian and latter-day frontier life, delighting in his realistic, sympathetic approach to his subject. It is difficult to know how many western paintings Farny produced during the last phase of his career, but he is represented widely in collections in the United States, and the Cincinnati Art Museum owns a great many of his works.

See E. M. Clark, *Ohio Art and Artists* (1932); and Robert Taft, *Artists and Illustrators of the Old West, 1850-1900* (1953).—D. C. H.

Faulk, Odie (1933-   ). Historian. Faulk was born in Winnsboro, Texas. After serving in the marine corps from 1950 to 1955, he attended Texas Technological University. He taught for a year at Texas A. and M. University, served as assistant editor of *Arizona and the West* from 1963 until 1967, then returned to teaching, first at Arizona Western College in Yuma, Arizona, then at Oklahoma State University.

Faulk quickly became a prolific writer on the history of the Southwest, especially Arizona and Texas, and more than a dozen pamphlets and books came from his pen during the first decade of his career. Most of these were well-written narratives or works of synthesis rather than products of original research. Among his books were several short histories of Texas and a short general survey of the Southwest, from early origins to the twentieth century, *Land of Many Frontiers* (1968). Faulk also wrote a brief *History of Arizona* (1970), designed for general readers rather than historians. In 1971, with Seymour V. Connor, he published *North America Divided: The Mexican War, 1846-1848*.—G. D. N.

Faust, Frederick Schiller. See Max BRAND.

Fayetteville, Arkansas. Fayetteville, located in northwest Arkansas, is the seat of Washington County and is situated in the picturesque Springfield Plateau of the Ozark Mountains. The settlement began in 1828, was named Fayetteville in 1829 after Fayetteville, Tennessee, was incorporated as a town in 1836, and received a city charter in 1859. The city charter was revoked in 1867; it was incorporated as a town in 1869 and again as a city in 1906. Fayetteville was an educational center from its earliest days, Arkansas College, founded in 1852, being its best-known early institution. The college was burned down during the Civil War, but College Avenue, Fayetteville's principal street, still bears its name. Fayetteville suffered severely during the Civil War, as contending armies marched and countermarched through it, and it was the target of a Confederate attack in 1863 after it had fallen into Union hands. The city was a stop on the Butterfield Overland Mail Stage Line in 1858; a telegraph line reached it in 1860. Since 1871 it has been the site of the University of Arkansas. Lying in the center of northwest Arkansas's poultry-raising country, the city has several industries related to that pursuit. Lakes, streams, and mountains attract tourists and residents in search of recreational facilities. Its population in 1970 was 30,729. —W. L. B.

Feather River. The Feather River country contains some of the most spectacular mountain scenery found in the West. The river was given the name El Rio de las Plumas ("The River of the Feathers") by the Spaniard Luis Arguello, who had led an exploring group up the river. The three great forks of the river meet near Oroville, California. Each of them rises in snow-fed rivulets high on the sides of peaks in the Cascade and Sierra Nevada ranges.

The north fork of the Feather has its source on the slopes of Lassen Peak. Its upper watershed consists of a broad plateaulike basin extending to the southeast of Lassen Peak. The surface is mostly volcanic in origin and is densely timbered except for several large meadows. Big Meadows, the largest of these, has been converted into a reservoir, now called Lake Almanor. Below the lake the river has cut through a deep lava flow and plunges into a rugged canyon in which it flows until it reaches Lake Oroville, the new reservoir built to store the water of the Feather.

The middle fork rises in Sierra valley, an old lake bed lying at about 5,000 feet elevation. After a short distance, it, too, plunges into a deep canyon and falls more than 3,000 feet before its junction with the north fork. This part of the Feather is relatively undeveloped and free-flowing.

The south fork has the smallest basin, and although the stream has a steep gradient, the topography is less rugged than that of the two other branches of the river. Below Oroville Reservoir, the Feather is joined by the Yuba River and the Bear River before emptying into the Sacramento River at Verona. In all, the basin occupies 5,980 square miles, much of it in the forested Cascade Mountain region.

That portion of the river valley that lies in the Central Valley was settled by Americans who had come across the Overland Trail in the early 1840s. They had procured land grants from the Mexican government and were grazing their cattle and raising their crops in relative seclusion until the discovery of gold at Bidwell Bar

on July 4, 1848. Soon mining camps covered the sides of the river and men and equipment began to tear into the placer deposits along the banks. One party to arrive in 1851 was led by James P. Beckwourth, who brought the group through the pass that bears his name and down the river canyon to Marysville. This became the famous Feather River route, now a much traveled highway and the route of the Western Pacific Railroad.

The waters of the Feather have long been used for the generation of electric power and now contribute to the flow of water pulsing through the California aqueduct to southern California. The creation of Oroville Lake has given Californians another large body of water for recreational use. The Feather River country is a well-known recreational paradise with almost a thousand miles of trout streams and salmon, bass, steelhead, and shad available at lower elevations. Hunters find deer, bear, and an occasional mountain lion. There are extensive acreages of woodlands, mountain peaks, streams, lakes, and meadows. In the valley below, rich alluvial soils support bountiful crops during most of the year.

For map, see CALIFORNIA.

See California Department of Water Resources, *The California Water Plan* (1957); S. T. Harding, *Water in California* (1960); and Lawrence R. McDonnell, ed., *Rivers of California* (1962).—R. W. D.

Feikema, Feike. See Frederick MANFRED.

Ferber, Edna (1887-1968). Novelist. Ferber was born in Kalamazoo, Michigan, but spent most of her childhood in Appleton, Wisconsin, where her family moved when she was two years old. Upon graduation from high school she became a journalist. As a reporter Ferber developed her distinctive literary style, and her different assignments suggested the subject matter of many of her later books. Her novel *So Big* (1924) received the Pulitzer Prize and, among other honors, she was made a member of the National Institute of Arts and Letters.

Ferber was one of the relatively few contemporary authors who wrote in the satirical western tradition. Indeed, some of her novels about the West—notably *So Big, Cimarron* (1929), and *Giant* (1952)—were widely read at the time of their publication as polemical attacks upon the crudity and boorishness of life in the Southwest. Typically her novels follow the classic story of the dude who goes west and is appalled by the crudity and lack of refinement he discovers. Actually, Ferber's fictional achievement is much more subtle, for she attacked not only the vagaries of southwestern life but the pretentious and often effete criticism of western ways by those who are supposedly more cultivated. The superficiality and the often bogus gentility of much of the dude's criticism is satirized when seen in the light of those very western values he finds so contemptible. At her best Ferber manages to transform what seems fairly straightforward social criticism into a probing analysis not only of the shortcomings of society but of the imperceptiveness of various social critics.—J. K. F.

Ferguson, James Edward (1871-1944). Texas politician. The son of a Methodist minister, Ferguson was born in Bell County in central Texas. He was expelled from Salado College at sixteen over a prank and spent two years in the West as an itinerant laborer. Returning to Texas, he acquired a law degree, married the daughter of a prosperous farmer, and became a banker in

nearby Temple. By the age of forty-two he was successful, restless, and politically ambitious.

In November 1913 Ferguson announced his candidacy for governor. Opposing prohibition, a leading issue
in Texan politics, he promised to strike all temperance
legislation "where the chicken got the ax." He appealed
to the growing number of tenant farmers with a program to limit the rents they had to pay. In a campaign
that combined persistence, a vicious assault on the weaknesses of a prohibitionist opponent, and brilliant stump-
speaking, Ferguson won the Democratic primary in July
1914.

Ferguson's interest in tenancy soon disappeared, but
he did secure laws to compel school attendance and
larger appropriations for public education. These
achievements brought reelection in 1916. A bitter controversy with the University of Texas then erupted.
Skeptical of the conduct of the institution and the value
of higher education generally, the governor quarreled
with the university and vetoed its appropriation in June
1917. Partisans of learning fought back and charged
him with mismanagement of state funds, and a refusal
to disclose the source of a $156,500 personal loan sealed
his fate. In August 1917 Ferguson was impeached. A
month later the state senate found him guilty and
sought to bar him from holding office again.

To win vindication, Ferguson defiantly ran for governor in 1918, president in 1920 and senator in 1922.
Despite support from anti-prohibitionists ("wets"), and
some urban workers, he could not overcome the dominant prohibitionist wing of the Democratic party. In
1924 he put his wife forward as a gubernatorial hopeful,
promising "two governors for the price of one." Miriam
Amanda "Ma" Ferguson defeated an opponent endorsed by the Ku Klux Klan, and the husband-wife team
took office. After one scandal-ridden term, in which
Ferguson was governor in all but name, his wife was
defeated for reelection. Candidates again in 1930, they
lost another race, but the depression helped them eke
out a close victory in 1932. During a last term, they
provided honest government but had little success in
coping with the troubled economy. Weary from two
decades of politics, the Fergusons retired in 1934. Six
years later "Ma" again ran for governor but finished a
poor fourth.

Ferguson's stand on tenancy and his opposition to the
Klan and prohibition have given him a place among
Texas liberals. This judgment, however, ignores his
consistent opportunism, an inability to distinguish personal desires and the public interest, and the lack of
constructive results from his public career. His impact
on higher education was disastrous. More than a demagogue but less than a statesman, Ferguson illustrates
how charismatic personalities have exploited the fluid
nature of one-party politics in southwestern states.

See Lewis L. Gould, *Progressives and Prohibitionists:
Texas Democrats in the Wilson Era* (1973); S. S. McKay,
Texas Politics, 1906-1944 (1952); and Ouida Ferguson
Nalle, *The Fergusons of Texas* (1946).—L. L. G.

Fergusson, Harvey (1890-1971). Novelist. Fergusson
was born in Albuquerque, New Mexico, where he spent
most of his boyhood. In 1911 he was graduated from
Washington and Lee College in Lexington, Virginia,
after which he made his home primarily in the East.
Until 1923 he worked as a newspaperman in Washing-

ton; then he moved to New York, where he became a
free-lance writer. In 1932 he moved to California,
where he continued to write fiction and also for most of
the major motion-picture companies.

Though Fergusson left his native Southwest to live
elsewhere, he did not abandon it in his fiction. In general his historical novels—notably *Wolf Song* (1927), *Grant
of Kingdom* (1950), and *The Conquest of Don Pedro*
(1954)—are more interesting than his studies of contemporary southwestern life. Two of his books about the
modern Southwest, however, will repay reading. *Footloose McGarnigal* (1930) is a richly comic novel about the
adventures of a young man seeking a life of romance
and adventure in the Wild West, and *Home in the West*
(1944) is an autobiographical memoir of his early life in
New Mexico.

In his Introduction to the trilogy *Followers of the Sun*
(1936), Fergusson tells how his own attitude toward life
had changed from a passionate longing to relive the past
into acceptance of "the prickly stuff of the inescapable
present." This change of attitude is reflected in his
southwestern fiction, which is noteworthy for its lack of
sentimentality. Its values are uncompromisingly
oriented toward the future rather than the past, welcoming change rather than deploring it. As a result
Fergusson's writing is something of an anomaly in western fiction, which tends to be nostalgic and retrospective, looking—in his phrase—"backward with longing"
rather than "forward with hope."—J. K. F.

Ferris, Warren Angus (1810-1873). Civil engineer,
fur trapper, and surveyor. Ferris recorded his six adventurous years as a mountain man (1829-35) in his
valuable journal, *Life in the Rocky Mountains* (1842). He
liked a good chase while hunting on the Plains, enjoyed
the fare of buffalo and venison, and vividly depicted the
dangers and hardships of trapping. Trained as a civil
engineer, Ferris prepared one of the best early accounts
of the Yellowstone region and drew an excellent and
influential "Map of the Northwest Fur Country" in 1836
describing the region between the thirty-ninth and forty-eighth parallels and from the one hundred and ninth
meridian on the east to the one hundred and sixteenth
meridian on the west. Both the map and his journal
locate and preserve many of the original place names
used by mountain men.

Just why the son of a Glens Falls, New York, Quaker
family would seek a career in the Rockies is hard to
determine. During his youth his family did live on the
frontier, first in Erie, Pennsylvania, and later in Buffalo,
New York. Tradition has it that he left for the West after
a quarrel with his mother over smoking. Ferris appeared in St. Louis, Missouri, in 1829 as a trapper and a
year later joined an American Fur Company party led
by Andrew Drips and Joseph Robidoux. While Ferris
did not make any notable explorations, he was associated with some of the most famous men in the trade,
and his descriptions of Lucien Fontenelle, William H.
Vanderburgh, James Bridger, Robert Newell, James
Fitzpatrick, Joseph R. Walker, and others are
invaluable.

Soon after Ferris left the mountains, he and his
brother Charles participated in the Texas Revolution of
1836. The Lone Star State apparently attracted him, for
he became the county surveyor at Nacogdoches from
1837 until 1840 and then surveyed and settled in the

region of the present city of Dallas. After his first wife and all their children died of illness, Ferris settled in Reinhardt, Texas, where he raised a second family. Some of his children were still alive in 1940.

See Lyman C. Pedersen, Jr., "Warren Angus Ferris," in LeRoy R. Hafen, ed., *The Mountain Men and the Fur Trade of the Far West,* vol. II (1965); and Paul C. Phillips, ed., *W. A. Ferris: Life in the Rocky Mountains* (1940). — G. B. D.

Fetterman Massacre (December 21, 1866). The Fetterman Massacre was fought near Fort Phil Kearny, Wyoming, between Sioux, Cheyenne, and Arapaho warriors and eighty men under command of Brevet Lieutenant Colonel William J. Fetterman. Fetterman's detachment was annihilated.

Resentful of the intrusion of white soldiers into unceded Indian lands, the Plains tribes constantly harassed Fort Phil Kearny's undermanned and poorly equipped garrison and raided its wood and supply parties. During such an attack on the wood train, post commandant Colonel Henry B. Carrington ordered Fetterman's command to its relief. The Indians had carefully planned an ambush, and although the wood train escaped to the fort, Fetterman's troops perished to a man. In the furor that followed the incident, Carrington was relieved of his command and his military career was virtually ended.

Historians have tended to accept Carrington's assertion that Fetterman had disobeyed orders and therefore was to blame for the catastrophe; that viewpoint is well presented in Dee Brown, *Fort Phil Kearny: An American Saga* (1962). J. W. Vaughn, however, has argued in his *Indian Fights: New Facts on Seven Encounters* (1966) that Fetterman instead was probably following an order by Carrington to make an offensive movement against the small group of Sioux that had ridden out to decoy the soldiers into a trap, and that Carrington's story was an attempt to shift the blame from himself. Since there is much conflicting testimony, which is difficult to resolve, the full truth of the episode probably will never be known. The Indians' version of the battle is related in George Bird Grinnell, *The Fighting Cheyennes* (1915). —J. T. K.

Fewkes, Jesse Walter (1850-1930). Naturalist and anthropologist. When a group of Tiwa Indians were "rediscovered" living on the outskirts of El Paso, Texas, in the mid-1960s, it turned out they already had been described in an article by Fewkes in the *American Anthropologist* in 1902.

Born in Newton, Massachusetts, Fewkes was trained at Harvard in natural history with specialization in marine zoology. This remained his field of interest until 1888, when a trip to California turned his interest toward ethnology. In 1889 he took over leadership at the Hemenway Southwestern Archaeological Expedition from Frank CUSHING. In this post he became the first to record Zuñi songs with a phonograph.

Fewkes next directed his attention toward the Hopi Indians, which deeply involved him in questions of prehistory and in archaeology. For the next several years he also worked at Casa Grande ruins in southern Arizona and Mesa Verde in Colorado. He also found time for researches in Cuba, Puerto Rico, Trinidad, and Grand Cayman.

While Fewkes was working in the Hopi country, a Hopi-Tewa potter, Nampeyo, visited the site of his excavations and copied prehistoric pottery designs on her own wares. Thus began a revival of decorated Hopi pottery on First Mesa that has continued down to the present.

Among his many publications about the Southwest were *A Few Summer Ceremonials àt the Tusayan Pueblos* (1892); *Archeological Expedition to Arizona in 1895* (1898); *Hopi Katcinas Drawn by Native Artists* (1903); *Casa Grande, Arizona* (1912); *Archeology of the Lower Mimbres Valley, New Mexico* (1914); and *Designs on Prehistoric Hopi Pottery* (1919).

See Walter Hough, "Jesse Walter Fewkes," *American Anthropologist,* vol. 33 (1931).—B. L. F.

Ficklin, Benjamin F.. (fl. mid-nineteenth century). Road builder and transportation manager. Ficklin was associated with William M. F. McGraw in the improvement of the Fort Kearny, South Pass, and Honey Lake Road in 1857 as a part of the Pacific Wagon Road program of the United States. McGraw's party was responsible for the route only as far as the South Pass. When the work was abandoned, Ficklin served as deputy United States marshal in Utah Territory, and shortly thereafter became an express rider for Albert S. Johnston, in command of the army of Utah. Among other services, Ficklin made one trip to the Flathead country to secure cattle and mules for the army and to deliver dispatches to Fort Leavenworth, Kansas. He was employed by the Overland Mail Company to supervise the construction of way stations and the stocking of the route from San Francisco to El Paso. In 1859 he was employed by the Leavenworth and Pike's Peak Express Company, and when this firm expanded into the Central Overland California and Pike's Peak Express Company, he became a road superintendent. He assisted in the organization of the Pony Express. Upon his dismissal from this enterprise, Ficklin worked for the Pacific Telegraph Company. When the Civil War broke out, he went to Virginia and joined the Confederate army, being commissioned a major in the Transportation Department. After the war was over, he returned to the Southwest, where he engaged in the stagecoach business. He was in Washington, D.C., at the time of his death.

See Raymond W. Settle and Mary L. Settle, *Saddles and Spurs: The Pony Express Saga* (1955).—W. T. J.

fiddle. See MUSIC, WESTERN.

Field, Stephen Johnson (1816-1899). California lawyer and Supreme Court justice. Field was born in Haddam, Connecticut. When Stephen was two years old, his father, a distinguished clergyman, was called to the First Congregationalist Church of Stockbridge, Massachusetts. There nine Field children grew up imbued with the Puritans' typical high valuation of hard work. Stephen first traveled abroad when he was thirteen, to visit a sister whose husband was a missionary in Turkey. Almost three years later he returned to New England and soon thereafter entered Williams College, from which he graduated at the head of his class in 1837.

Field then read law in the New York office of his eldest brother, David Dudley, by then a noted lawyer deeply involved in the codification of the state's laws. Upon admission to the bar in 1841, Stephen entered an uneasy partnership with his strong-willed brother that lasted until 1848. Stephen's own aggressiveness asserted itself when, after a brief sojourn in Europe, he embarked from New York for the gold fields of California.

Field headed to the mining country on the Feather River. He never got around to mining for gold, for he found his training in law to be a more ready means for making his fortune in a country short on law and order, where land and mining rights were constantly and vigorously contested. Arriving in a newly formed town called Yubaville, shortly afterward renamed Marysville, Field immediately became involved in real estate speculation and in the formation of a local government. Within three days of his arrival he was elected alcalde of the town. Administering justice enthusiastically and with a free hand, superintending the grading of town landings, and attending to his private legal and real estate interests, Field led a busy and profitable life. He later boasted that under his administration Marysville "was the model town for the whole country for peacefulness and respect for law."

Under the 1849 constitution of California, Field's office was abolished and a new district judge, William R. Turner, took the bench. Field and Turner soon entered into a conflict over a minor point of court etiquette that was to dominate Field's life for a decade and do lasting damage to his reputation. Turner disbarred Field and attempted unsuccessfully to block his election in 1850 to the state legislature; Field in turn successfully urged a redistricting of the state circuits so that Turner would be banished to the wilderness of northern California. Threats against Field's life drove him to wearing pistols, and Turner's vilification of him made Field greedy for the last word in the many controversies that attended his career.

As a state legislator Field made several important contributions to the new California government. As the dominant member of the judiciary committee, he adapted the codes of civil and criminal procedure developed by his brother David Dudley for New York to the needs of California, recasting hundreds of sections to fit the new state's particular needs. The liberal tendency of many of Field's efforts at this time are noteworthy; for example, he inserted into the Civil Practice Act provisions that were distinctly liberal to debtors, exempting work tools and animals and homesteads up to five thousand dollars from bankruptcy proceedings.

During his term in the legislature, for reasons never made completely clear, Field lost the money he had made in Marysville real estate. Heavily in debt, he returned to Marysville determined to repay his obligations. In this financially austere period, Field established a reputation that assured his election in 1857 to the state supreme court.

Among the pressing needs of California, in these formative years, was a law to govern mining rights and claims. Three legal problems of crucial significance were mineral rights and what precedents should govern them; property titles in San Francisco, which were hopelessly confused by the uncertain actions of the city council; and the pueblo lands, four leagues of land given to each organized town (or pueblo) by Spanish-Mexican practice. The United States was pledged to honor valid grants made by the Mexican government, but some of the pueblo grants were of doubtful validity. The decisions rendered in these cases did much to bring legal order out of the chaos deriving from the Mexican cession. Many of the great Mexican land grants, especially those of John C. Frémont and John A. Sutter, had never been properly surveyed, and the ill-defined boundaries of these lands became an invitation for miners to enter and take up claims in the areas near the boundary lines, upon the rationale that these were really public lands belonging to the United States, and therefore available for claim. When farmers also came in numbers and began improvements, the conflicts became more constant, and more serious infringements of property rights were involved.

In general, Field tended to support the claims of those with paper titles to the land, even if these were not in all respects clear, and he determined that settlers could not of their own will decide whether the United States owned land within the great private tracts, nor could they appropriate the same to their own use. Only the federal government could do that.

The general tendencies in Field's decisions in disputes over mineral rights were to give private owners control over their property and to limit the free-wheeling enterprises of the miners. In *Biddle Boggs* v. *Merced Mining Co.* (1859), Field ruled that neither California nor the United States could authorize entry of private property for the purpose of mining. He ruled subsequently, in *Moore* v. *Smaw* (1861), that minerals in the earth belonged to the owner of the land itself, and not to the state or federal government. Field antagonized the miners by these decisions and antagonized many of the settlers by his decisions concerning land ownership.

Field's approach to these problems was essentially pragmatic, and the general tendency of his work was to supplant older and inapplicable precedents with newer doctrines that met the problems of California in a practical spirit of justice. Although a vast respect for property rights is discernible and although Field was himself enough the "rugged individualist" to favor the trait in others, he did not at this time believe in laissez-faire doctrine so strongly as to deny the power of the state to interfere with the rights of individuals when they came into conflict with the general welfare of the citizenry at large.

These later extensions of individualism in the interpretation of the law were only manifest after Field became a justice of the Supreme Court of the United States. Although a Democrat, Field owed his appointment to the highest court to Abraham Lincoln, who had two reasons for choosing Field. The land disputes originating in California required some member of the bench who understood Mexican land law, and Field's experience in California made him a logical choice. The other reason lay in the support that David Dudley Field had given to Lincoln in 1860, when the Republicans nominated him for the presidency. In March 1863 Field's appointment was confirmed. He served on the Supreme Court from 1863 until 1896, longer than any other justice had done.

Because as Supreme Court justice Field was required to spend part of every year in California as chief justice of the tenth circuit court of the United States, his direct associations with his adopted state continued. Loyal as he was to California, California never showed a marked preference for Justice Field. This was in part a result of Field's previous decisions in the pueblo lands cases, his past history of conflict with men like Judge Turner, and his haughty mien, which did him no good among the poorer and more populistic elements. More harmful to him, however, were his personal friendships with the great railroad builders of the West Coast and his unpopular judicial decisions while on the United States Supreme Court.

With the rapid development of California many Orientals had immigrated, bringing with them social values and customs so different from those of their neighbors as to incur much hostility and discriminatory legislation. Because many poor Chinese preferred being jailed to being fined, San Francisco began an effort to make jail unattractive by cutting the hair of the prisoners within an inch of the scalp. This not only humiliated the Chinese, who still wore queues, but also quashed their hope for a good reception beyond the grave. Field struck down this law in the case of *Ho Ah Kow* v. *Nunan* (1879). He also was against laws that made it difficult for Chinese laundrymen to ply their trade. Although Field doubted the advisability of continued mass immigration from the Orient, he maintained that once here the Chinese were subject to the same laws to which others were subject. Field's decisions were obnoxious to citizens who dreaded competition from laborers who could, and were willing to, live on small wages.

In his decisions concerning the role of the state in the taxation of railroads, Field earned a few powerful friends among the railroad magnates but hurt himself badly with the general population, especially the followers of Dennis Kearney and his workingmen's organization, the "Sand-lotters," who could see that the railroads, under Field's interpretation of the rights of corporations, were escaping taxation almost entirely. Field, who was among the first to apply the due process clause of the Fourteenth Amendment to corporations, in case after case reached decisions favorable to the railroads, on the assumption that corporations are "persons" for the purposes of business enterprise in exactly the same sense that individuals are, and are therefore guaranteed equal protection under the Constitution. This interpretation was used successfully to strike down efforts of popular movements to gain control over rates as well as to provide immunity from special taxation through state legislation.

Field's unpopularity in California frustrated his desire—which was real enough, although never publicly stated—to become the Democratic nominee for president in 1880 and 1884. In 1884 the state Democratic convention specifically repudiated Field and pledged to vote only for delegates who would work to defeat Field.

The climax of Field's troubles in California developed out of the litigation of the will of United States Senator William Sharon of Nevada. Field came into the case after conflicting opinions had been given in the state and federal courts and after Althea Hill, who claimed to be Sharon's widow, had captured the sympathies of many common folk in California and, not incidentally, the hand and heart of her lawyer, a former state supreme court justice named David Terry. Both Terry and his wife were boisterous, passionate personalities, and Field's efforts to keep order in his court on the day he rendered a decision adverse to their claims led to a broil that involved fisticuffs and a display of knife and

gun and culminated in the arrest and incarceration of the Terrys. In response to Terry's numerous threats upon his life, Field was accompanied by a bodyguard, David NEAGLE, when he took a train to go back to San Francisco from Los Angeles, where he went in the spring of 1889 to hold court. At a train stop in Lathrop on August 14, when Field was having breakfast, he encountered the Terrys. Neagle shot Terry, claiming that Terry had been in the act of drawing a knife on Field. Terry died upon the floor, and a turmoil ensued that resulted in the arrest of both Neagle and Field. Both were cleared of blame, but in the meantime all the old grudges of rank-and-file Californians against Field were aired again, and the case threw into relief Field's least attractive characteristic: his unwillingness to forgive or forget any person who had ever sided against him in a controversy.

Known as the strongest pillar of rugged individualism on the Supreme Court during the heyday of laissez-faire, Justice Field is less well recognized for his courageous decisions in the area of civil liberties and in his role as a pioneer Californian.

See Robert G. McCloskey, *American Convervatism in the Age of Enterprise: A Study of William Graham Sumner, Stephen J. Field, and Andrew Carnegie* (1951); Wallace Mendelson, *Capitalism, Democracy, and the Supreme Court* (1960); George A. Shipman, *The Constitutional Doctrines of Stephen J. Field* (1931); and Carl Brent Swisher, *Stephen J. Field: Craftsman of the Law* (1930).—W. L. R.

films, western. The first "western" was Edwin S. Porter's ten-minute *The Great Train Robbery* of 1903. Since that time the genre has become the most enduring, popular, and flexible of all those created by the American cinema. In the hands of some of the country's greatest directors, the western has become the vehicle for communicating complex interpretations of history and morality. At least a dozen westerns are ranked among the finest works of art the United States has produced. Dramatic, epic, poetic, pastoral, ironic, and satirical modes have proven adaptable to the western story, whose popularity has persisted unabated through four generations and across all national boundaries. In Western Europe, the Middle East, India, and Japan the western continues to draw crowds and to be identified with the American film itself.

The western is difficult to define. At one time, a working definition might have identified a western as a story taking place between 1865 and 1890 somewhere along the American frontier and involving at least one violent confrontation with outlaws or Indians. But such a definition has been difficult to sustain. A western is any film that has the "feel" of one. Howard Hawks's *The Big Sky* (1951), about fur-trading along the Missouri River, and John Wayne's *The Alamo* (1960) both occur during the mid-1830s; the first is not considered a western, while the second is. A Civil War story involving the cavalry and concerned with the fighting in Louisiana and Mississippi, such as John Ford's *The Horse Soldiers* (1959), can be a western. Even a modern-day story such as David Miller's *Lonely Are the Brave* (1962) comes to be termed a "modern western" because its protagonist is a traditional cowboy. At one time the very appearance of an automobile in a film meant that it could by no means be considered a western. Yet in recent years the most popular period of interest for makers of westerns has been that time between the turn of the century and the beginning of World War I.

Indeed, such movies as *The Professionals* (1966), *Ride the High Country* (1962), *The Wild Bunch* (1969), *Butch Cassidy and the Sundance Kid* (1969), *The Ballad of Cable Hogue* (1970), *Tell Them Willie Boy Is Here* (1969), *McCabe and Mrs. Miller* (1971), *The Life and Times of Judge Roy Bean* (1973), and *Kid Blue* (1973) have such themes as the decline of the frontier, the displacement of gunfighters following the great cattle depression of 1886-87, the "obsolescence" of the western hero confronted with modern technology, and the passing of the western saga into legend and myth. In recent years the master disseminator of these themes has been Sam Peckinpah, but many directors' films suggest that the western has reached a "decadent" stage; its subject, perhaps heralded by George Stevens' *Shane* (1952), has become the western itself.

What is that subject, and what accounts for its popularity and artistic achievement? That western movies, taken individually or as a group, are immeasurably superior to dime and popular novels, on which they are sometimes based, has presented a challenge to students of American studies. Credit is normally given to certain visual elements, which lend themselves to epic and dramatic presentation: landscape, action, the virile personalities of a group of male stars (from William S. Hart to John Wayne), and the development of an "iconography" of symbols, including costumes, animals, and weapons. The western's immense popularity has been seen as confirmation of Frederick Jackson Turner's thesis that the winning of the frontier was the central American experience. Some see the stark confrontations between good and evil that characterize the western as indicative of the Puritan morality, which, according to such social historians as Perry Miller, has governed America. Moreover, the western provides a means for expressing key oppositions crucial to American history: civilization versus savagery, nature versus law, individualism versus conformity, and the desert versus the garden.

One- and two-reel western stories continued to be made following *The Great Train Robbery*, but the primitive history of the western proper rightly begins in 1908 with the emergence of G. M. "Broncho Billy" Anderson, who wrote, starred in, and directed some 375 short films between then and 1914, and became the first important western actor. Never a very slim or dashing figure, Anderson portrayed a virtuous, self-sacrificing man in a series of stories that rarely rose above dime-novel level. His kind of film-making was outdated by the time Cecil B. De Mille made two moralistic but financially successful feature-length westerns, *The Squaw Man* (1914) and *The Virginian* (1915), the latter based on the classic and controversial novel by Owen Wister, which justified lynching. De Mille's successes spurred and coincided with the emergence of William S. Hart, star-writer-director of a series of feature westerns until 1925. The taciturn Hart created many of the traditions now common to westerns and was the first to emphasize "realistic" settings and action in his stories, which more often than not were about reformed badmen. The most famous of his films is one of the earliest, *Hell's Hinges* (1915). Hart's only important rival as a western star during the silent era was Tom Mix, a veteran of the

WILD WEST SHOW whose popular short films (few longer than three reels) marked a return to the simplicity rejected by Hart: Mix was clean-living and virtuous and had encounters with evil outlaws.

The western might have remained a secondary genre were it not for the surprise success in 1924 of James Cruze's *The Covered Wagon,* the first of the big-budget epics, which detailed the hazards faced by an early group of pioneers. The following year it was surpassed artistically by John Ford's *The Iron Horse,* which delineated the building of the first transcontinental railway. Though these films established once and for all the aesthetic respectability of the western, their emphasis on a schoolboy sense of history has provided but a minor influence on subsequent production. This merger of the historical epic with the western mode reached an artistic peak in 1950 with Ford's *Wagonmaster,* which concerned a Mormon wagon train, and a commercial peak in 1962 with *How the West Was Won,* an episodic Cinerama production co-directed by Ford, Henry Hathaway, and George Marshall. Present-day attitudes perhaps best can be gauged by the sardonic and bitter tone achieved in Arthur Penn's *Little Big Man* (1970), a mock epic that questions traditional assumptions about the winning of the West.

Still, the epic stance was viable enough during the early years of the talkies for it to be a crucial factor in the group of western spectaculars that appeared in the years 1928-32. Two by Raoul Walsh—*In Old Arizona* (1929), for which Warner Baxter won an Oscar as the Cisco Kid, and *The Big Trail* (1930), which gave John Wayne his first big role—began for that director a long and distinguished career as a maker of westerns, most of which featured a spunky and simple-minded adventurer as hero. The best of these include *They Died with Their Boots On* (1941), *Pursued* (1947), *The Tall Men* (1955), and the underrated *A Distant Trumpet* (1964). Other important westerns of the early 1930s are King Vidor's *Billy the Kid* (1930), Wesley Ruggles' *Cimarron* (1931), and Edward Cahn's *Law and Order* (1932).

Until the end of the decade, the "A" western was in eclipse. This was the great era of the "B" western, cheap serials, and short, simple stories featuring such stars as Bill Boyd, Johnny Mack Brown, and Ken Maynard. The singing western also emerged during this depression era, with Gene Autry and his horse Champion rivaling Roy Rogers and his horse Trigger (see MUSIC, WESTERN). Years later the most popular serials—*Hopalong Cassidy* and *The Lone Ranger*—were revived and continued on television.

Then, in 1939-40, the larger-budgeted western made a triumphant return with such movies as John Ford's *Stagecoach,* Henry King's *Jesse James,* William Wyler's *The Westerner,* and—the first important comedy western—George Marshall's *Destry Rides Again.* These and other films represent the height of the western's "classical period"; their purity and simplicity in dealing with codes of the Old West have never been equaled. Still, most critics today understand the decisive turn the genre took during and immediately after World War II as being crucial to its sustained vitality. Beginning in 1943, with William Wellman's liberal anti-lynching tract, *The Ox-Bow Incident,* the western became a vehicle of astonishing richness and variety, a means of intense personal expression. With Ford's *My Darling Clementine*

(1946) and Hawks's *Red River* (1948) the western became the main genre with which to explore relationships between two men—a pattern that continues to this day. Erotic elements entered with Howard Hughes's controversial *The Outlaw* (1943) and King Vidor's *Duel in the Sun* (1946). Walsh's *Pursued* is generally considered the first "psychological" western. Ford's *Fort Apache* (1948) is perhaps the initial anti-western—the first to attack prevailing American myths about the building of the West. Its upholding of the Indian cause influenced Delmer Daves' *Broken Arrow* (1950) and subsequent films defending the red men, the most complex of which are probably Samuel Fuller's *Run of the Arrow* (1956) and Robert Aldrich's *Ulzana's Raid* (1972). The theme of the aging gunfighter forced to embark on "one last moral mission," which has so influenced postwar westerns, was first enunciated in Henry King's *The Gunfighter* (1950); this idea, plus a strong political message attacking apathy, conjoined in Fred Zinnemann's *High Noon* (1952).

Ford's series of postwar westerns constitutes a singular achievement in examining the meaning of American history. An optimistic believer in values of gallantry and civilization in such films as *She Wore a Yellow Ribbon* (1949) and *Rio Grande* (1950)—along with *Fort Apache* they form what is known as the Cavalry Trilogy—Ford first questioned these values in his masterpiece, *The Searchers* (1956). Its theme is the relativity of environment—white and Indian. By the time of *The Man Who Shot Liberty Valance* (1962), Ford deplored the decline of anarchy and frontier justice. In *Cheyenne Autumn* (1964) Ford, deeply inbued with pessimism, called for the return of the savage wilderness that existed before the arrival of the white man. As opposed to Ford's approach, Hawks's westerns are based on stories that could be transferred to other times and places without losing impact, explorations of timeless professionalism and camaraderie among groups of men who do not expect help from outsiders. *Rio Bravo* (1959), *El Dorado* (1968), and *Rio Lobo* (1970), for all their excellence, utilize the genre's conventions more than they are "about" the West.

Two series of westerns during the 1950s are especially notable. Beginning with *Winchester '73* (1950), director Anthony Mann made a group of revenge stories, all featuring a hero driven by an emotion that subsumes reason and humanity. The best were *The Naked Spur* (1952) and *Man of the West* (1958). A related if different sort of existential agony motivated the heroes, all played by Randolph Scott, in seven movies made by Budd Boetticher between 1956 and 1960. Morality plays pitched between tragedy and comedy, the best-known being *Seven Men from Now* (1956) and *Buchanan Rides Alone* (1958).

Foreign-made westerns have become increasingly popular in the past few years. This trend began in 1962 with the German *Der Schatz im Silbersee (The Treasure of Silver Lake),* which was quickly eclipsed by Italian westerns ("spaghetti westerns"), beginning in 1964 with Sergio Leone's astonishingly successful *Per un pugno di dollari (A Fistful of Dollars).* More than two hundred westerns have now been made in Europe (mostly in Yugoslavia and Spain, although in large part bearing an Italian imprint). Amoral heroes provide an important element, along with generous helpings of parody, Catholicism, and violence. A number of recent American-made westerns, too, have been considered "explorations of violence."

The most frequently utilized historical event featured in westerns is probably the gunfight in Tombstone, Arizona, in 1881, which pitted Wyatt Earp and Doc Holliday, on the side of the law, against Ike and Billy Clanton. *Law and Order, My Darling Clementine,* Jacques Tourner's *Wichita* (1955), John Sturges' *Gunfight at the O.K. Corral* (1957), and Frank Perry's *Doc* (1971) all relate this story. Another often repeated theme is the defeat of General Custer at the Little Big Horn, recreated in *They Died with Their Boots on, Fort Apache,* Robert Siodmak's *Custer of the West* (1967), and *Little Big Man.* The career of the outlaw William Bonney has been traced from diverse angles in *Billy the Kid, The Outlaw,* and Arthur Penn's fine *The Left-Handed Gun* (1958), Stan Dragoti's *Dirty Little Billy* (1972), and Peckinpah's *Pat Garrett and Billy the Kid* (1973). After providing the material for *The Great Train Robbery* in 1903, the exploits of the Hole-in-the-Wall Gang have been reprised in Elliot Silverstein's *Cat Ballou* (1965), Peckinpah's *The Wild Bunch,* and George Roy Hill's *Butch Cassidy and the Sundance Kid.*

Since World War II, John Wayne has been the chief star of westerns for Ford, Hawks, and other directors, along with actors Joel McCrea, Scott, Gary Cooper, James Stewart, and Clint Eastwood. Key script writers include Leigh Brackett and Jules Furthman (for Hawks), Frank Nugent and James Warner Bellah (for Ford), Burt Kennedy (for Boetticher), Borden Chase (for Mann), and Peckinpah (for his own films). Such directors of photography as Lucien Ballard, William Clothier, and William Daniels have expertly caught the vistas and landscapes of the West. And such composers as Max Steiner, Richard Hageman, Dimitri Tiomkin, Jerome Moross, Elmer Bernstein, and Jerry Goldsmith have made important atmospheric contributions.

The first book-length study of the western in English, George N. Fenin and William K. Everson's *The Westerns: From Silents to Cinerama* (1973), contains a mass of historical and anecdotal detail, but critical attitudes have made its nostalgia for the "pure" western of the prewar period appear dated in retrospect. Allen Eyles's *The Western: An Illustrated Guide* (1968) contains, in dictionary format, entries for cameramen, script writers, and characters, as well as the actors and directors who form the bulk of the entries. Jim Kitses' *Horizons West: Studies of Authorship Within the Western* (1970) is the most formidable study to date, concerning itself with the mythical and dramatic realities explored by the genre. Frank Machel's *Cameras West* (1971) is an excellent introduction to the subject for readers from age twelve to sixteen.—S. B.

Findley, John. See John FINLEY.

Finerty, John Frederick (1846-1908). Journalist. As correspondent for the Chicago *Times,* Finerty covered more Indian war campaigns than any other reporter: George Crook's campaign of 1876 against the Sioux; Colonel Nelson Miles's operations against the Sioux in 1881, during which Finerty visited Sitting Bull's camp in Canada; the Ute campaign of 1879; and an Apache uprising in 1881. He recounted his war experiences in *War-Path and Bivouac* (1890, 1961), which closely follows his dispatches. Colleagues on the *Times* remem-

369 Fisher, John King

bered him as outstanding in an outstanding staff, and an officer with Crook rated him as the "gem of the lot" among the correspondents.

Finerty also served one term in Congress (1883-85) and, having been born in Ireland, served three terms as president of the United Irish League of America.

Oliver Knight, *Following the Indian Wars* (1960), contains a brief biography.—O. K.

Fink, Mike (1770 or 1780?-1823). Mississippi valley keelboatman and folk hero. The documented details of Fink's life are few, but the pattern is clear. Born in the Pittsburgh vicinity, Fink came to young manhood in the great age of the Ohio-Mississippi keelboat. The long, narrow keelboats were propelled upstream by the muscle of their crews, whose brawling members were dominant on the river. Fink soon became captain of his own keelboat and before long was a living legend in the river network bounded by Pittsburgh, St. Louis, and New Orleans. In this far-flung expanse he became well known for fighting Indians, for deadeye marksmanship (in St. Louis he once shot off a Negro's heel to enable him, as he said, to "wear a genteel boot"), for heroic feats of fighting and drinking, for practical jokes, and for his tall tales. In his own time the name of Mike Fink became synonymous with the ultra-exaggerated braggadocio of the Mississippi valley frontiersmen. Perhaps because of the eclipse of the keelboat by the new steamboats or perhaps because of the lure of a new frontier, Fink joined General William H. Ashley's first fur-trapping and trading expedition to the upper Missouri River country, 1822-23. Some time during the winter of 1823, at Ashley's trading post where the Yellowstone River flows into the Missouri, Fink was killed by a member of the expedition after he himself had slain a companion, accidentally or not, while trying to shoot a tin cup from his head.

More significant than the historical Fink is the mythic persona. As late as 1847 a rich oral tradition of Mike Fink stories flourished along the length and breadth of the Ohio-Mississippi River system. Aside from a brief death notice in the St. Louis *Republican,* July 16, 1823, the first of many printed accounts of Fink was Morgan Neville's "The Last of the Boatmen" in the *Western Souvenir* (1829). Especially influential in perpetuating the legend were two mid-nineteenth-century books, *Mike Fink: The Last of the Boatmen* (1847) by J. M. Field and *Mike Fink: A Legend of the Ohio* (1848) by Emerson Bennett. The great frontiers of American history have usually produced their real or mythical heroes in the style of Daniel Boone as forest pioneer, Paul Bunyan of the loggers, and Pecos Bill of the Southwestern cowboys. Representing the keelboat era is the legendary Mike Fink.

See Walter Blair and Franklin J. Meine, *Mike Fink: King of Mississippi Keelboatmen* (1933); and Leland D. Baldwin, *The Keelboat Age on Western Waters* (1941).—R. M. B.

Finley (or **Findley**), **John** (1722-?1769). Frontiersman. Finley was born in northern Ireland and immigrated with his parents in the early 1740s to Pennsylvania. In 1744 he was licensed by Pennsylvania as an Indian trader, and this license was renewed subsequently until 1748. He traded afar in the Ohio country, including in the Pickawillany Plains and Eskippakithiki in present-day Kentucky. In 1755 he, with Daniel Boone,

was a wagoner on Braddock's march against the French and Indians at the head of the Ohio River. Between that date and 1769, when he appeared at Boone's cabin on the upper Yadkin River, he was a fur trader, peddler, and resident of Fort Pitt. Finley was with Boone in Kentucky during the summer of 1769 and then returned to the great wilderness, where he met his death under unknown circumstances. Finley has been almost forgotten by historians of the early frontier.

See Lucian Beckner, "John Findley: The First Pathfinder of Kentucky," *Filson Club History Quarterly* (April 1927); and Richard H. Collins, *History of Kentucky,* 2 vols. (1874).—T. D. C.

Finney, Charles G. See REVIVALISM.

Fisher, John King (1854-1884). Rancher, outlaw, and lawman. Fisher was one of many born to the chaos of Civil War and Reconstruction. He was raised in south Texas by simple, hard-working parents. In 1869 he was accused of stealing a horse after he borrowed it without telling the owner. He was arrested but escaped. Shortly thereafter he was arrested for housebreaking at Goliad and sent to prison. Only four months later he was pardoned, but his brief incarceration merely hardened him. Within a short time Fisher showed up in Dimmit County near the Rio Grande in the area known as the Nueces Strip. It was a lawless area, filled with desperate men, harassed by Mexican bandits, including the notorious Juan Nepomuceno Cortina, and raided by hostile Indians. Rustling was a major industry, and the law was enforced in only the most limited way.

Young Fisher was soon a popular hero in the area with a growing reputation as a bad man to tangle with, in spite of his mere seventeen years. He set up a ranch on Pendencia Creek that became a haven for a collection of criminals, drifters, and shady characters who repaid him with loyalty. He soon controlled the area to a large degree. Operating out of Eagle Pass and the Pendencia ranch, Fisher's escapades and reputation grew. He was one of those frontier characters, like Clay Allison, who became the law unto themselves and won as many admirers as detractors in the process. His notoriety was attested to by a crude sign nailed to a tree near his ranch. "This is King Fisher's road," it said. "Take the other."

But his supremacy in the chapparal of the Nueces Strip did not last. By 1875 the Texas Rangers, under the leadership of Captain Leander H. McNelly, were prepared to bring law and order to the Strip. Fisher was one of their prime targets. So far he had avoided conviction on any charge. In April 1876 King was married and the next month was arrested by Rangers at his ranch. He was almost immediately released, but Ranger harassment was only beginning. McNelly sternly warned him to change his ways. For the moment, however, Fisher had won, and he enjoyed the acclaim. The "King of the Strip" was indeed imposing. He was described as tall and handsome with black, wavy hair and a handlebar mustache. One of the Rangers who saw him then recorded that he was decked out in a beaver hat with a solid gold hat band in the shape of a rattlesnake, a silk shirt with a bandana about his throat, a pair of chaps made from the skin of a tiger he allegedly killed at a circus, and a brace of silver-plated, ivory-handled six-guns.

The Rangers were persistent. Lee Hall replaced the consumptive McNelly, and Hall went after Fisher with a vengeance, armed with warrants charging him with murder and horse stealing on numerous counts. In the fall of 1877 Fisher was again arrested by Rangers and carried to San Antonio, outside his sphere of influence. It was the beginnning of a whole train of trials and legal proceedings, and although he managed to avoid conviction on more than a score of indictments, the legal ordeal took its toll.

Fisher was older now, with a wife and children. He bought a ranch near Eagle Pass, got interested in religion, and settled down considerably. In 1881 he was appointed deputy sheriff of Uvalde County and began making plans to run for sheriff. He was an efficient officer and extremely popular. He became acting sheriff in 1883 after the sheriff was indicted, and it appeared a certainty that he would be elected to the office in 1884. Then, early in March 1884, he went to Austin on official business. He never returned.

In Austin he ran into Ben Thompson, a noted gunman and an old acquaintance. The two talked, and when Fisher boarded the train west, Thompson, who was drinking heavily, accompanied him. At San Antonio, Thompson and Fisher made the rounds of the local saloons and ended up at the Vaudeville Variety Theatre, apparently at Fisher's suggestion. Thompson was embroiled in a feud with the owners of the theater, and one man had already met death at his hands. The owners, Joe Foster and Billy Simms, had been warned that the two gunmen were in town. There is evidence that Fisher was trying to settle the feud, since he was on good terms with both sides. It is also possible that he was merely the victim of circumstance. At any rate, a quarrel ensued between Thompson and Foster. A fusillade was fired by several parties, and Fisher was killed in the melee along with Thompson. But for the chance meeting with Thompson, Fisher might well have lived out his life as a respected rancher and lawman.

See O. C. Fisher and Jeff C. Dykes, *King Fisher: His Life and Times* (1966).—G. L. R.

Fisher, Vardis [Alvero] (1895-1968). Novelist and teacher. Fisher, born in Annis, Idaho, was educated at the University of Utah, and the University of Chicago, from which he received his Ph.D. in 1925. He taught English at various institutions but regarded himself primarily a writer.

Fisher's basic literary theme, in evidence since his first novel, *Toilers of the Hills* (1928), may be stated as the bondage in which unreal ideals hold mankind. The attempt on the part of the hero of this novel, Dock Hunter, to dry-farm the high lands of Idaho is frustrated simply because this high country is not amenable to farming, however much the unreal ideals of the agrarian myth may affirm that it is. Rather than bow to the facts of life, Dock cleaves more and more firmly to the agrarian myth as it becomes less and less applicable to the facts of the life in which he finds himself.

A basically similar concern informs Fisher's novel about the Mormons, *Children of God* (1939), for which he received the Harper Novel Prize. Though this novel received a certain notoriety when it was published as an exposé of the Mormons, Fisher was less concerned with revealing the depth of Mormon bigotry than with showing the evils that are inherent in the single-minded acceptance of any ideal. In Fisher's other novels as well, his heroes face Hobson's choice: they may see things as they

are only when they sacrifice cherished wishes for the way things ought to be.—J. K. F.

fisheries: *the West*. The native fishes of the Pacific Coast drainages are similar in many respects. Several fish species of the Columbia River also live in the Sacramento-San Joaquin, but in both rivers live species that exist nowhere else. For example, the Sacramento-San Joaquin system has thirty-eight native fish species (83 percent endemic), the Columbia River has fifty-seven (58 percent endemic).

The best known and most heavily used native species have been the salmonids (salmon and trout), whitefish, and sturgeon, although local fisheries often developed for suckers, squawfish, and the Pacific lamprey.

East of the Continental Divide, paddlefish, bowfin, garpike, darters, and pickerel were probably used locally by Indians. The abundance of buffalo and other large animals east of the Divide minimized the need for intensive Indian fisheries. But the salmon was the buffalo of major Pacific Coast streams. It provided a staple in the Indian diet.

The largest native minnow in North America, the squawfish, and the largest anadromous (migrating to the sea and returning to fresh water to spawn) fish, the white sturgeon, are both found in Pacific coastal drainages.

The Great Basin is a land of relicts. Between the Wasatch and Sierra Nevada ranges are remnants of animals that indicate a moist land of many lakes and streams. The moist period probably occurred in the late Pleistocene, when glaciation occurred in mountains and across much of the northerly parts of the North American continent. In that period Lake Bonneville, in the northern Great Basin, overflowed to the north, into the upper Snake River. About twelve fish species moved one or both ways throughout the connection.

Native fishes of the Great Basin occur in habitat that was reached, either actively or passively, through long-desiccated surface connections. At one time Lake Bonneville covered most of western Utah to depths up to one thousand feet and an area of twenty thousand square miles. Ichthyologists have noted that the presence in the Great Basin of a fossilized stickleback and killifish, both coastal fishes, tells us that the Lahontan basin must once have connected to the Pacific Ocean, probably via the Southwest when Nevada was a coastal lowland. Hundreds of lakes have come and gone in arid areas of the western United States. The interior drainage of the Great Basin is surrounded by stream systems that contain the main freshwater fishes of the West.

The Colorado River Basin, a region of rugged, dissected mesas and mountains, drains much of the interior, more southerly parts of the West. It once contained native Utah cutthroat, now extinct, and Colorado cutthroat, as well as mountain whitefish, Colorado chub, Colorado squawfish, and various suckers and minnows. The theory of animal distributions and geological history, mentioned earlier, that a very large area in the Southwest and including much of the Great Basin was connected to the sea by streams elevated in the Pleistocene would help explain not only ranges of certain fossilized and relict forms, but also the rapid erosion of Colorado River canyons.

Important native fishes in Montana included cutthroat trout, grayling, mountain whitefish, and the

Dolly Varden, a char. The pygmy whitefish is also native to western Montana. Native suckers, dace, chub, and sculpins also lived in Montana streams.

Pacific salmon and steelhead trout were native to all major streams and most small ones along the Pacific Coast and British Columbia. They form an important part of anthropological history in the approximately ten thousand years of known human residence in the West. These fishes also played an important role in the economic exploitation and settlement of Pacific drainages by white men.

Native oceanic fishes important to humans include the halibut, herring, tuna, several species of cod, rockfish, sole, clams, crabs, and oysters. These were often used by Indians and later formed important commercial fisheries.

In "The Coming of the Pond Fishes," Ben Hur Lampman chronicles the introduction of dozens of fishes exotic to the western United States. For many reasons, perhaps including homesickness, white men introduced carp, green sunfish, largemouth bass, black, brown, and yellow bullhead, channel catfish, smallmouth bass, tench, black and white crappie, and yellow perch. Salmonoid introductions from eastern waters include eastern brook trout, Atlantic salmon, brown trout, and lake trout. Striped bass, shad, eastern soft-shell clams, and several exotic oysters have flourished largely in estuarine waters. In fact, the explosive growth of striped bass and shad populations on the Pacific Coast after introduction in the late 1800s has been nothing short of spectacular, and furnishes two examples of successful and desirable exotic introductions.

In addition to the exotics brought in from eastern waters or from other continents, hundreds, perhaps thousands, of transfers of fishes were made and are still made, legally by conservation agencies and illegally by laymen. Fish transfers have stirred the kinds of fish in many areas into a veritable muddle no longer reflective of the population structures that existed before about 1825. Fishes exotic to a body of water are initially not integrated in the ecological system. Since predators and competitors are not yet adapted to the exotic presence, explosive population increases frequently occur after introductions.

In many waters introductions and transfers have increased species diversity to the detriment of the production of species presently desired by man. In waters formerly barren of fish, introductions have added recreational opportunities and food for man. A few species, such as striped bass and shad, have offered striking success and occupancy by a new fish of a niche apparently used before by less desirable species. Introductions and transfers reflect, in part, man as the inveterate tamperer and nature tamer.

Fisheries of the Pacific Ocean and estuaries were pursued to a limited extent by Indians. Halibut, cod, herring, and miscellaneous other species were harvested. The Indians of the British Columbia coast fished for halibut with wooden hooks made of a forked branch, or with two pieces of wood locked together to form an acute angle. The line was made of crushed and braided cedar bark or of seaweeds and tied to one branch of the fork. A bone or sharpened stone barb was lashed to the other branch of the fork. The duped fish often drowned because the hook prevented it from closing its mouth and from ventilating its gills. Halibut meat was dried in thin slices and used for barter and food.

Indians harvested herring with dip nets made of woven baskets, with herring rakes made of thin laths into which sharp bone spokes were set, or with dragnets. Salmon dip nets made of nettle or kelp fibers or Indian hemp were also used. Dip nets and rakes also were used to harvest eulachon, one of the smelts.

Much information on Indian fishing can be found in the journals of early explorers. In 1793 Alexander MacKenzie, the first Caucasian to cross the North American continent north of the Spaniards' exploration, secured salmon from Indians on the Bella Coola River, where he saw a "great weir" on the stream. Lewis and Clark in 1805-06 reported that Clatsop and Chinook Indians used gigs, bone hooks, and lines to capture salmon. The natives also used straight nets, dip nets, and weirs. Salmon, fresh or dried, was the chief staple item in the diet of the Indians of coastal British Columbia, the Columbia Basin, and the coastal rivers to the south of the Columbia River. Lewis noted that the Indians opened up the captured fishes and exposed the carcasses to the sun on a scaffold to dry the meat. When the meat had dried, the Indians pulverized it by pounding it between two rocks, then placed it in a basket of grass and rushes lined with a skin of a salmon stretched and dried for the purpose. The fish powder was pressed down, covered with skins, and the baskets were bound together. Fish thus preserved as pemmican remained sound and sweet for up to several years. Dried fish was often buried in holes lined with straw and skins and covered with dirt. Smoking was also used to dry and preserve salmon flesh.

Perhaps the most spectacular fishing method used by Indians on the rivers of the Pacific Coast was dipnetting at falls or rapids. The nets were hoops up to five feet in diameter on which a bag of mesh webbing was hung. The Indians fished the nets from rocks or platforms suspended over the current. This fishing technique at Celilo Falls ended after the Dalles Dam flooded the rapids. That the fishing technique was effective is evidenced by the sharp rise in escapement of anadromous fishes to tributaries above the falls after the fishery ended in 1957.

Seine nets were used where salmon congregated over a smooth bottom. The nets, constructed of fibers of a wild hemp or silk grass that grew east of the Cascades, were as large as eight feet deep and three hundred feet long. Such nets were used in the main Columbia and Snake rivers.

Indians in British Columbia trolled with a handline, speared fish, seined, and even gillnetted with stationary nets. Dip nets were used in fast water. Weirs served well to capture fish in the upper tributaries of Pacific Coast streams. They were placed near the edge of or across large streams. Stakes were driven into the stream bed and a willow barricade was woven among the stakes. Other weirs contained basket structures into which the fishes moved. Juvenile fishes were considered a delicacy, either fresh or dried. Steelhead and cutthroat trout were probably taken with traps, dip nets, and spears.

From all available accounts, one can conclude that Indians settled heavily along streams on the Pacific Coast. One estimate of Indian density in the Oregon country (Columbia River area) places the population at fifty thousand at the beginning of the 1800s, although some historians believe the population was much smaller.

One author estimates that the annual catch by Indians was about eighteen million pounds per year. (In 1933 the total commercial catch of salmon and steelhead in the Columbia River was about twenty-six million pounds.)

The first exploratory groups, settlers, and traders obtained fishes from Indians in barter or by fishing themselves. They used handlines, nets, and sometimes spears to capture fishes, and apparently did not hesitate to adopt methods used by local Indians. By 1830 a standard of barter on the Columbia River was reached and salmon were purchased from Indians, salted, and used locally and for a small amount of trade. In 1829 Indians traded each salmon for three leaves from a twist of tobacco. In the same year on the Fraser River each salmon was traded for goods worth less than one cent. By the mid-1850s, salmon was British Columbia's second export item (after furs). In many drainages along the Pacific Coast salmon contributed markedly to development of the region. Whole carcasses and offal were used for fertilizer, and fish grease lubricated wheels, hinges, harnesses, and guns.

Early settlers usually prepared fresh fishes for the table by boiling and frying. Fresh salmon eggs were occasionally consumed. One report indicates that fresh salmon were combined with pork cracklings and boiled in a stew with potatoes, and that leftover fresh salmon were salted or smoked. Smelt were often smoked whole and put away for winter. Sturgeon flesh and roe were fried or smoked for consumption by residents along the Snake and Columbia rivers. Early trading, although quite limited in scope, established Pacific salmon in the markets of the world. By 1861 in Oregon and in the 1860s in Canada, salmon fishing and processing began to take on the trappings of an industry. Gillnets, seines, and traps were being used to harvest fish, and canneries were developing apace and going broke at nearly the same rate.

Halibut, shellfish, herring, and eulachon were also caught or bartered for by early settlers and traders. Significant commercial fisheries for halibut did not commence until about 1880, although the species was earlier sold for local consumption in Pacific coastal ports. By 1900 halibut were sold frozen as well as fresh. Sturgeons were harvested on the Columbia River commercially beginning in 1880, and marketed fresh, pickled, salted, and smoked. A systematic commercial fishery developed on the Fraser about 1892.

Other food fishes of coastal waters and Pacific coastal streams were used for subsistence and limited trade until late in the 1800s, when systematic fisheries developed.

Freshwater fishes, such as trout, suckers, and native minnows, were used for subsistence and limited local barter, and for some sport. Fishes frequently supplemented the diet of settlers in the interior. Later, after spiny-rayed fishes such as perch, sunfish, and bass were introduced, warmwater fishes were used both for sport and food.

At present one need only read national sporting magazines or visit the local supermarket to learn the importance of sport and food fish resources. In spite of widespread abundance of introduced spiny-rayed fishes, such as bass and crappie, the most-sought sport fishes of the West are Pacific salmon and several kinds of trout. Chinook and coho salmon, steelhead trout, rainbow and cutthroat trout, and introduced brown trout form the backbone of western sport fisheries. The most significant commercial harvests are salmon, halibut, tuna, herring, shellfish, and several species of bottom fishes. Freshwater species are pursued most intensely near human population centers, of course, but the automobile and affluence have put quality western sport fisheries in reach of masses of people. To many of these anglers, distance is of little concern. Thus, Idaho residents often travel in summer to the Washington coast to fish for salmon on charter boats and Californians visit Montana in trailers and pickup campers to pursue brown trout. And affluent easterners can leave New York after breakfast and find themselves casting to western trout or salmon before suppertime the same day. To many westerners, high quality recreation, a few minutes from home, is a benefit that amounts to real income.

Regulatory measures developed in the West as fish populations declined and intensity of exploitation increased. Beginning in the last quarter of the nineteenth century, regulations everywhere in the West for food fishes and later for sport fishes have usually had one feature in common: they promoted inefficiency. Whether the reason for regulation of harvest was to protect particular spawning stocks, provide for adequate escapement of mature fish, or spread a limited amount of fish among all fishery participants, most regulatory measures have led to excessive capital outlay and operating costs and to less than maximal net return to commercial and sport fisheries. Why has this been so?

Ecologically healthy fish stocks can sustain a harvest by man as long as the habitat of the stock does not deteriorate. The phenomenon permitting stocks to absorb mortalities is called compensation. Losses at one life history stage or in one population component can be compensated for by reduced mortalities or greater growth of population members. Every stock has some average annual yield of fish flesh that it can sustain at various levels of fishing. And all stocks have some average maximum sustainable yield of fish flesh. For example, if adult salmon numbers are reduced, survival to adulthood of embryos deposited in the spawning beds improves, *compensating* for the adult mortality. As long as the habitat of the animal remains undamaged, the stock can absorb rather heavy mortalities, perhaps as great as eighty to ninety percent of the adult stock.

This maximum yield can be harvested by many people fishing inefficiently or by fewer people fishing very efficiently. Monopoly would be an undesirable extreme in promoting efficiency. On the other hand, fisheries are considered common-property resources; they are owned by all or by no one. Such resources are open to exploitation by anyone who wishes to enter the harvest and has paid some minimal license fee.

As long as some profit can be made, fishermen will enter the fishery with the result that potential profits are dissipated among many fishermen. So one of the major issues facing lawmakers and conservation agencies is the social problem of legal restraints on unlimited entry in common-property resources. An example is the offshore troll fishery for Pacific salmon. A decreasing

Drying squid at a fishery in Monterey, California, in the 1880s. (Library of Congress)

total yield has been shared by an increasing number of vessels since World War II. Catches are spread over so many vessels that little profit, on the average, is made on dollars invested. Net economic return would be increased if entry were controlled in at least the salmon fisheries and probably in halibut and some shellfish fisheries. Another major problem in marine fisheries is fishing by other nations on stocks coveted by American commercial fishermen of the Pacific Coast. Conservation of fish stocks and the partitioning of catches among nations offer one of the thorniest problems in fishery management.

Western fishery management also faces great challenges in attempting to maintain aquatic habitat for desirable fish species in the face of increased conflicting demands for the same water. Seen from an ecological point of view, Indian activities in the West before the arrival of the invading white men were integrated with nonhuman life. But the settlers who invaded and dominated the Indians did not integrate with the ecological system. Rather, they altered it drastically. The history of human activity from the 1800s to the present is a record of domination of nature. From the viewpoint of aquatic ecology, water development for irrigation, hydropower, navigation, flood control, and pollution dilution have drastically reduced the productive capacity of the major stream drainages of many lakes.

Fortunately, there has been a shift in recent years toward a social ethic in which the environment has assumed greater importance. Society now more frequently opts for controlled technological development and preservation of natural systems. With this shift, western fishery managers have noted somewhat increased public sympathy for fish habitat maintenance and improvement.

Fishery management does not operate in a vacuum. In much of the West, the United States Forest Service, Bureau of Land Management, and private parties (to a lesser extent) control the habitat in which fish live and limit the number of fishermen who have access to that habitat. The major problem now is for fishery management to be integrated with other land uses so that the combined benefits will be realized.

See Joseph A. Craig and Robert L. Hacker, *The History and Development of the Fisheries of the Columbia River,* (1940); Carl L. Hubbs and Robert R. Miller, *The Zoological Evidence: Correlation Between Fish Distribution and Hydrographic History in the Desert Basins of the Western United States,* University of Utah Bulletin No. 38 (1948); and Cicely Lyons, *Salmon and Our Heritage* (1969). —D. W. C.

Alaska. Alaska is bounded on three sides by rich seas and vast continental shelves. It has a shoreline of thirty-four thousand miles, and the land is richly endowed with freshwater lakes and streams from which have arisen five species of Pacific salmon that have been worth more than any other single natural resource of the fiftieth state.

Great Alaskan glaciers pulverize rocks and soil, and streams carry the nutrients released by this action swiftly to the sea, enriching the waters to the benefit of the myriad plankton, upon which all fishes utilized by man depend.

In the Bering Sea during the summer, when the water of the polar seas divests itself of its ice and meets the warm water from the south, there are virtually twenty-four hours of daylight, and there is a sudden and tremendous development—almost an explosion—of marine life. Planktonic life blooms in such profusion that the sea often assumes a greenish-brown color.

When the Europeans arrived, Alaska's waters teemed with salmon, halibut, herring, cod, trout, whitefish, flounder, several kinds of crab, shrimp, and clams. But these renewable resources are not endless, and heavy exploitation has proven this time and again.

It is to these rich northern waters that herds of great whales have annually migrated, and, although the whale is not a fish but a mammal, the pursuit of whales has always been considered part of the fishing industry.

Toward the end of the eighteenth century the pursuit of whales was extended to the Pacific from the Atlantic, and there it greatly expanded. By 1839 there were 555 American whalers, most of them involved in Pacific sperm whale (*Physeter catodon*) fishing.

The whale fisheries of the Pacific-Alaskan coast were first visited in about 1835, and the hunt was soon extended into the Bering Sea. In 1848 the whaler *Superior* ventured into the Alaskan Arctic and made an enormous catch. Soon others followed, and by 1852, 278 American vessels were whaling along Alaska's coast, and in 1855, 154 American whalers passed through the Bering Strait seeking their prey.

Russia, which owned Alaska, organized a whaling company, but the Russians were not a seafaring people and the venture soon died.

In June 1865, the Confederate privateer *Shenandoah* destroyed thirty-eight Northern whalers in the Bering Sea. Finally she captured a ship on which there were newspapers telling of the ending of the Civil War in April and she fled.

Whales, including the blue whale (*Balaenoptera musculus musculus*), the North Pacific right whale (*Eubalaena sieboldi*), the gray whale (*Eschrichtius gibbosus glaucus*), and the sperm whale, were depleted during the first three quarters of the nineteenth century. However, with the introduction of petroleum for illumination and other purposes formerly supplied by whale oil, plus the loss of the baleen market for corset stays, the industry rapidly declined. In 1902 there were but eight vessels left in the Alaskan whaling industry.

The exploitation of whales—with little thought of conservation, an abrupt plunging of investors into the industry, great expansion of the fleet, fortunes being made and lost almost overnight—has been characteristic of most of Alaska's fisheries since the United States purchased the territory from Russia in 1867.

In turn, halibut, salmon, cod, and king crab—the major fisheries of Alaska—have all been exploited without reasonable controls, to the ultimate detriment of the resource and the various industries. Only when it has become obvious that a resource was depleted have measures been taken to attempt to rebuild it.

The best known, the most valuable over the years, and the most heavily exploited fishery of Alaska has been that of salmon. The five species in Alaska include the king salmon (*Oncorhynchus tschawtscha*), the coho salmon (*O. kisutch*), the chum salmon (*O. keta*), the pink salmon (*O. gorbuscha*), and the red salmon (*O. nerka*). An anadromous animal, the Pacific salmon hatches and spends varying times in freshwater, then travels to the sea, where it grows rapidly, reaching maturity in from scarcely a year to as much as five or six years, depending upon the species.

While at sea Alaska's salmon penetrate deeply into the Pacific, some traveling nearly as far south as the Hawaiian Islands. When sexual maturity nears, they return to the streams of their birth, where they spawn by burying fertile eggs in the gravel of stream and river beds, and then they invariably die. With the new births the cycle then starts again.

Before the Russians arrived, an estimated seventy-six thousand natives lived within the salmon-producing areas of Alaska, and anthropologists believe they consumed about 33.5 million pounds of salmon each year. When the Russians came to Alaska they sought first the rich furs of the seat otter and fur seal. They forced the natives to hunt furs for them, pillaging, raping, and mercilessly uprooting villages and moving them great distances. They also inflicted European diseases and alcoholic drink upon them. As a result, the natives of Alaska declined greatly in number and many turned to types of food introduced by Europeans, thus materially reducing the use of salmon. This may help to explain the high productivity experienced on nearly every Alaskan salmon stream at the beginning of the commercial era, which commenced in 1878 with the establishment of two salmon canneries in southeast Alaska. Prior to that, the Russians, who seldom looked to the sea for food, had traded some dried salmon in California, and as early as 1830, they had shipped some choice salted Yukon River king salmon to Russia as a special delicacy.

Salmon is highly perishable, and Alaska was isolated from the main food-consuming parts of the world. Drying and salting as means of preservation, while fine for local use, have commercial limitations. Both processes are slow and time-consuming, and the final product is subject to deterioration. When a method for preserving salmon in tinned cans was developed in the 1860s, the potential of the Alaska salmon industry could be developed. Today, nearly a hundred years after the first canneries were established, the bulk of Alaska's salmon is canned essentially as it was in 1878. Even through the 1950s and 1960s about 90 percent of the total Alaskan salmon catch went into cans.

The patterns of early development have influenced today's industry. Because of the remoteness of various fishing grounds from each other, and Alaska's huge coastline, salmon canneries were often constructed in areas isolated from cities or villages. Many such canneries continue to exist; during the winter they are ghost towns with only a watchman on hand, while during the relatively brief harvest time of June, July, and August, they are bustling centers of life.

In the early years the remote location of many of the fishing areas and the lack of local labor in Alaska required the yearly importation of fishermen, cannery laborers, and supplies, mostly from Seattle and San Francisco. In the early years much of the labor of fish handling and canning was done by Chinese-Americans, but in recent years Filipino-Americans have largely taken their place. Workers and fishermen were transported to Alaska aboard large tender-type vessels. They were housed at the cannery, which was often a virtual small city, and at the end of the season they were transported back to the place of hire, where they were paid for the season of work. Nowadays the companies charter large airliners to accomplish the transport of fishermen and workers.

Seattle and San Francisco were the early financial

centers for Alaska's canned salmon industry, and they were the storage and marketing centers from which canned salmon was shipped to other markets. Seattle is still the major financial center and shipping and storage depot for Alaska's salmon.

This pattern of economic absenteeism in the face of a growing and stable Alaskan population has created numerous problems, conflicts, and disagreements. For at least fifty years there has been resentment within Alaska of the domination of the salmon industry by non-Alaskan investors, fishermen, and laborers.

Consolidation of companies involved in Alaska's salmon catching, processing, and marketing became commonplace. In 1919 five canning companies controlled more than 53 percent of the total Alaska salmon pack. In 1939, of 111 companies operating in Alaska, the nine largest canned 58.3 percent of the total American (not Alaskan) production of salmon. As late as 1959 six of the largest concerns owned more than 40 percent of the canneries and produced 53 percent of the total Alaskan output.

Often Alaskan fishermen, independent because they own their boats, find themselves unable to sell the salmon they catch because the canneries are obligated to take salmon from their own boats, usually operated by non-Alaskan fishermen.

The first thirty years of the salmon industry were particularly crude; streams were blocked so as to catch all salmon ascending them. Traps were placed at river mouths, and no concern whatever was given to future runs.

In 1924 the so-called White Act gave the federal government responsibility for controlling the type and placing of gear, and for setting the fishing seasons. It made clear that escapement of breeding stock into spawning streams was to be accomplished by the fisheries people in charge.

From 1915 until 1958, traps, both the floating type and the pile-driven or hand-pole-driven—caught more than 40 percent of Alaska's salmon. During those years from 75 to 90 percent of the traps were owned and operated by canning companies that were based outside of Alaska.

When Alaska became a state in 1959, one of its first moves was to abolish, by state law, the use of salmon traps.

After a slow growth from 1878 to 1900, the salmon pack had skyrocketed, reaching a high in 1918 of more than 6.5 million cases (one case equals 48 one-pound cans). After a drop to 2.3 million cases in 1921, the pack increased again. The all-time peak occurred in 1936, when a total of 8.5 million cases were packed. In 1959 the total pack amounted to only 1.6 million cases, the lowest since 1900.

While the Alaska pack declined in the 1920s, the pack of adjacent British Columbia remained stabilized at around 1.5 million cases, which tends to discount the likelihood of any widespread natural phenomena causing the Alaska salmon decline. There is little doubt that Alaska's salmon declined because of abusive over-exploitation.

The state of Alaska assumed management of its fish and game on January 1, 1960. During the first eleven years of state control the salmon pack averaged 2 million cases—the exact average for the last eleven years of

federal control. However, indications are that the federal average was based on a declining fishery, and the state average shows indications of trending upward. State management is more flexible than that of the federal government.

Alaska, however, has been reluctant to invest heavily in rehabilitating its depleted salmon, and, in fact, it has so far managed and protected the remnants of this great resource with only a skeleton force of biologists and protection personnel.

Since the 1930s Japanese fishermen have caught giant king crab *(Paralithodes camtschatica)* in the Bering Sea and canned them for domestic consumption and for the world market. Unusually large specimens of this northern crab may weigh more than twenty pounds and have a span of nearly six feet.

In 1947, Wakefield Fisheries, a pioneer Alaskan firm, fitted out a catching and processing vessel to fish the Bering Sea for king crab; the fishery started to build from this. In 1953 Alaska produced 4.6 million pounds of this species, and from that time until the peak of the catch was reached in 1966, king crab production skyrocketed. Once again it was the story of intense exploitation, with fortunes being made by investors, processors, and fishermen but little thought given to the future of the resource.

At the start of the Alaskan king crab fishery the huge crustaceans were caught by both pots (traps) and by otter trawls. Pots work in a manner similar to lobster traps, with a one-way funnel through which the crab passes, seeking the bait placed inside by the fishermen. In the early 1960s otter trawls were prohibited for taking of king crab because of damage caused to female and undersized crab—they were often crushed. Large males only may be taken. All females and undersized males are returned to the water. Early pots measured about four feet square and weighed less than one hundred pounds. By the late 1960s the most efficient pots were found to be those that measured about seven feet on a side, made of a heavy steel frame, with webbing used to close it in. Such pots weigh four hundred to five hundred pounds, and they are not easily moved by the swift tides of Alaska's waters.

When the production of king crab peaked in 1966, landings totaled 159.2 million pounds for the state. But production has since declined. In 1970 the catch was 51.9 million pounds, the lowest since 1961, when the fishery was still growing.

The tanner crab *(Chionoecetes bairdi* and *C. opilio),* which was marketed for the first time in quantity during the 1960s under various names such as "snow crab" and "queen crab," has long presented a problem to processors in Alaska because its narrow, spidery legs make it difficult to extract the meat. Only in the last half of the 1960s has a practical method been found of accomplishing this.

In the early 1960s production of tanner crab amounted to a few thousand pounds. In 1967 42,000 pounds were landed. However, as king crab production declined interest in tanner crab grew, and by 1969 11.2 million pounds of tanner crab were landed, while total landings for 1970 came to 14.5 million pounds.

It is apparent that this species has started to fill the void left by the over-exploited king crab, for the same vessels and same processing plants catch and prepare it for market. Fisheries biologists believe that the total poundage of tanner crab in Alaskan waters exceeds that of the highly prized king crab.

Production of significant poundage of Dungeness crab *(Cancer magister)* commenced in southeast Alaska, and in Prince William Sound in the 1920s; it has fluctuated with the condition of Alaskan stocks and in response to West Coast demands since that time.

Never a high volume product, in 1968 Dungeness Crab reached a maximum production since 1950: West Coast demands for Dungeness were great and in that year 13.2 million pounds were taken. The low of 500,000 pounds was hit in 1957. The advent of modern air transport has been responsible for an annual production exceeding 10 million pounds since 1967.

Alaska has several species of commercially marketable shrimp, including the ocean pink *(Pandalus borealis),* the sidestripe *(Pandalopsis dispar),* the humpback *(Pandalus goniurus),* and the coonstripe *(Pandalus hypsinotus).* The ocean pink is the major volume species, and a boom-type fishery for this shrimp developed in the mid-1960s. Prior to that, Alaska produced 2 or 3 million pounds of shrimp annually.

Until development of the efficient automatic peeler in the 1950s, all Alaskan shrimp was hand-peeled, with a minor amount of the product being marketed unpeeled. Since the pink shrimp is too small to peel efficiently by hand, early production was limited largely to sidestripe, humpback, and coonstripe shrimp.

From an average of below 10 million pounds a year in the 1950s, shrimp production climbed to an average of nearly 24 million pounds in the 1960s. Peak production at this writing was 74.3 million pounds in 1970. The bulk of this (62 million pounds) was taken in waters surrounding Kodiak Island and landed at the port of Kodiak.

In the late 1960s, after exploration by the state and federal governments indicated the presence of weather-vane scallops *(Patinopecten caurinus)* in Alaskan waters, a fleet of East Coast scallop vessels traveled to Alaska and immediately engaged in a fishery.

In 1968, these boats, along with some Alaskan vessels that were rigged for scallop fishing, landed 1.5 million pounds of shucked scallop meats. In 1969, 1.9 million pounds of Alaskan scallop meats were landed. In 1970, with about six vessels involved, landings of scallop meats totaled 1.4 million pounds.

Largest of the Alaskan food fishes, halibut *(Hyppoglossus stenolepis)* can weigh 300 to 400 pounds, occasionally more. Halibut fishing started in a large way on the Pacific coast about 1890, centering in waters off Oregon and Washington. Halibut schooners began to visit Alaskan waters as early as 1895, and by 1899 an icing plant was established at Petersburg in southeast Alaska. Within thirty years the center of the industry had moved northward to southeast Alaska, and a striking depletion of Alaskan halibut was evident by the 1920s.

In 1924 the United States and Great Britain signed an agreement for the control of Pacific coast halibut; this agreement is still in force. This is one of the best examples of a properly regulated fishery in the world. A commission was established that set catch quotas for various districts along the Pacific coast. Seasons were set, and for a time some waters were closed for brood purposes. Methods of fishing are rigidly controlled. As a result, the badly depleted fishery rebuilt within about three decades.

Today both United States and Canadian fleets harvest halibut in territorial waters and on the high seas. Landings of the fleet's production are made in either nation's ports by both fleets. Canadian vessels caught more of the 54 million pounds of Pacific halibut in 1970 than did United States vessels. Landings of halibut in Alaska in 1970 totaled nearly 26 million pounds, while the 28-million-pound balance of the Pacific catch was landed in Canada and the Pacific states.

In about 1865 cod *(Gadus macrocephalus)* was the first fish to attract American fishermen to Alaskan waters. Early fishing was by vessels that sailed from Pacific ports, usually San Francisco. When a vessel caught and salted its catch, it returned to its home port.

During the 1920s, peak years of production were reached and catches approximated 15 million pounds annually. Prices obtained for Alaskan cod never equaled those paid for East Coast cod. The fishery gradually diminished, until today the catch is from 1 to 2 million pounds annually, taken almost entirely in southeast Alaska.

Herring *(clupea* sp.) is probably the most abundant and widely distributed food fish of Alaska. While during the 1920s a certain volume of Scotch-cured herring was put on the export market for human consumption, most of Alaska's herring is used for the manufacture of fertilizer and for bait to catch crab, halibut, and cod. By the late 1960s the plants using herring to make fertilizer had shut down.

In the mid-1960s a new use was found for herring—the Japanese market paid high prices for herring roe, which is cut from the females in a whole skein, and as much as 500,000 pounds of roe are now processed and exported to Japan. Carcasses of the males and of the eviscerated females are generally discarded as waste.

Other fishery products from Alaska include several species of clams, freshwater whitefish, lake and Dolly Varden trout, sheefish, flounder, abalone, oysters, and herring roe on kelp, a specialty product prized by the Japanese and by some Alaskans.

See Alfred Hulse Brooks, *Blazing Alaska's Trails* (1953); Richard A. Cooley, *Politics and Conservation* (1963); and Ernest Gruening, *The State of Alaska* (1954).—J. R.

Fitzpatrick, Thomas (1799-1854). Fur trader, mountain man, guide, and Indian agent. Fitzpatrick was born in County Cavan, Ireland, but came to America while still a young man. He joined Ashley's fur-trapping expedition of 1823 and aided him in the campaign mounted against the Arikara after the latter had attacked Ashley and his party. When Ashley sent Jedediah SMITH on a new overland route to the mountains in the late summer of 1823, Fitzpatrick accompanied him. A highly intelligent, serious man, Fitzpatrick soon became one of Ashley's brigade leaders and was present at the first fur-trading rendezvous in 1825. Earlier that year he and Ashley had pioneered the Platte River route to the mountains, but Fitzpatrick, traveling on his own, was attacked and pursued by Indians and arrived at the rendezvous emaciated and starving. Contemporaries assert that the ordeal turned Fitzpatrick's hair white almost overnight and led Indians to address him as White Hair, although he was also called Broken Hand or Bad

Hand, a reference to the fact that one of Fitzpatrick's hands had been permanently injured by the bursting of a gun barrel.

After Ashley sold out in 1826 Fitzpatrick was employed by Jedediah Smith, David Jackson, and William Sublette's company until 1830, when he, James Bridger, Milton Sublette, Henry Fraeb, and Jean Baptiste Gervais bought out the firm and formed the ROCKY MOUNTAIN FUR COMPANY. Fitzpatrick was, in the words of Dale L. Morgan, the "brains" of the firm.

The following year Fitzpatrick went to St. Louis seeking supplies from Smith and Sublette and decided to join their caravan to Santa Fe, buy his goods there, and return to the mountains from New Mexico, a roundabout trip that he undoubtedly took in order to assess the prospects for the beaver-fur trade in the Southwest. Fitzpatrick also recruited forty men in Taos for the mountains, one of whom was young Kit Carson. In the next seven years Fitzpatrick, often accompanied by Jim Bridger, ranged over a vast region of the West, trapping in eastern Oregon, in Blackfoot country, and in the Great Basin. David Lavender has aptly called him one of the "openers of the West." The Rocky Mountain Fur Company was broken up in 1834, but a new firm, Fontenelle, Fitzpatrick, and Company, was created and lasted until 1837. Despite its independent name, the partners appear to have been employed by the American Fur Company during this time.

When profits from the fur trade began to decline, Fitzpatrick went to work as a guide. Marcus Whitman traveled for a time in his train in 1836, and in 1841 Fitzpatrick guided the Bartleson-Bidwell party, which included Father Pierre De Smet, and the Oregon caravan of 1842, which included Elijah White. He is credited with saving the life of a missionary, A. L. Lovejoy, at Independence Rock when the latter fell into the hands of an Indian party. He accompanied Frémont on his second expedition (1843-44); guided Stephen W. Kearny on his military patrol of the West in 1845; and assisted Lieutenant James W. Abert's expedition to explore the Canadian and Arkansas rivers. He served as one of Kearny's guides in the Mexican War and intended to accompany the general to California but was sent east from New Mexico with important messages for the government.

During 1845 Fitzpatrick was appointed Indian agent to the tribes of the upper Platte and Arkansas rivers, with headquarters at Bent's New Fort. Fitzpatrick took his new job seriously and labored to bring peace between the warring Plains tribes by convening the famous Indian conferences at Fort Laramie in 1851 for the purpose of marking tribal boundaries. He also secured treaties with key tribes living north of the Arkansas River. Two years later he held a second Indian conference near present-day Dodge City, Kansas, to make treaties with the Southern Plains tribes. During the winter of 1853-54 he went to Washington to see that the treaties would be approved, but while there he became ill and died of pneumonia.

Historians are in general agreement that Fitzpatrick was an outstanding figure in the Rocky Mountain fur trade, a shrewd businessman, an excellent guide, and a fair-minded, sensitive Indian agent. The keen-eyed, gaunt-framed, taciturn Irishman, often portrayed in rough costume with rifle in hand, also seemed the epitome of the mountain man; yet he was well educated and intelligent, and his surviving letters suggest that he was one of the most perceptive minds in the fur trade. Fitzpatrick's arduous life in the mountains and Plains kept him from marrying until 1850, when he took as his wife the half-breed daughter of John Poisal, an Indian trader.

See LeRoy R. Hafen and William J. Ghent, *Broken Hand: The Life Story of Thomas Fitzpatrick* (1931); David Lavender, *Bent's Fort* (1954); and Dale L. Morgan and Eleanor T. Harris, eds., *The Rocky Mountain Journals of William Marshall Anderson* (1967).—G. B. D.

Five Civilized Tribes. Indian confederacy. The Five Civilized Tribes, created in 1843, were composed of Cherokee, Creek, Choctaw, Chickasaw, and Seminole. In the seventeenth century the Cherokee, an Iroquoian tribe, lived in and about the southern Appalachians in northwest Georgia and northern Alabama. The Creek Confederacy, made up of Northern Towns and Southern Towns, had a territory extending from the Savannah River westward to the Alabama River. West of the Creek, the Choctaw occupied western Alabama and Mississippi. North of them lived the Chickasaw, in northern Mississippi and western Tennessee. The Creek, Choctaw, and Chickasaw were of the Muskogean family. In the seventeenth century English agents, in an attempt to combat Spanish influence in Florida, incited the Creek to destroy the Indians in the northern part of the peninsula who had been Christianized by Jesuit missionaries. After this adventure some Creek moved into Florida, their numbers augmented by runaway slaves (see NEGROES ON THE FRONTIER). They came to be called Seminole.

From the beginning of English settlement to 1783, white traders penetrated all the tribes. Many married Indian women and founded mixed-blood families, which were to play an important part in the history of the tribes. As the eighteenth century progressed the commodities provided by the traders enabled the Indians to move out of the stone age. Guns diminished at the same time that plows made agriculture possible. From the whites the tribes obtained horses, cattle, sheep—and liquor, which introduced drunkenness. Smallpox had reduced the Cherokee to about seventeen thousand by 1783. The sprawling and loosely united Creek Confederacy enjoyed a period of prosperity in the eighteenth century as they began to improve their economy with the animals and implements made available by the white man. Increasing their population by incorporating defeated tribes or those who became refugees as a result of the advance of the white frontier, they stood out as the most powerful nation in the Old Southwest.

The Creek, Choctaw, Chickasaw, and Cherokee all became involved in the imperial struggles of Spain, France, and Great Britain for North America. From the beginning of French power in Louisiana the Choctaw, occupying a strategic position, found themselves objects of attention by French governors. The French managed to bring the Choctaw into a war with the Natchez, in which that culturally advanced but small tribe was virtually exterminated in 1730. Louisiana's Governor Philippe de Rigaud, Marquis de Vaudreuil, hoped also to liquidate the Chickasaw, who were under the influence of British traders, and to make the Choctaw a French protectorate. He only succeeded in dividing the Choctaw into pro-British and pro-French parties and in starting a bloody fight between them. The episode ended with the graduation of the Choctaw from the school of white diplomacy, in which art in later years a reunited nation proved adept.

The colony of South Carolina controlled British relations with the powerful and, by the middle of the eighteenth century, prosperous Creek. The Creek Confederacy favored the British side as against Spain in Florida. Under British urging it wiped out the Yamasee Indians on the south, who were allies of the Spaniards. But the Creek maintained their independence. Their ability to muster a large force of warriors caused them to be respected and even feared by the representatives of all the powers. As for the Cherokee, whose towns were closer than those of the Creek to the English settlements of South Carolina, British influence early nullified French efforts at penetration, despite the CHEROKEE WAR and other signs of latent hostility. The English established an ascendency that continued throughout the colonial period and were able to conclude several treaties that advanced the cause of white settlement (see the treaties of AUGUSTA, HARD LABOR, LOCHABER, and SYCAMORE SHOALS).

During the American Revolution the Cherokee under DRAGGING CANOE allied themselves with the British, having learned that it was the American frontiersman who wanted their land. Invading American troops from the southern states punished them severely and also brought a second epidemic of smallpox. The Creek also sided with the British. They attacked frontier settlements, whose men were away at the battle of Kings Mountain (1780). A party of Creek warriors attempted unsuccessfully to end Anthony Wayne's blockade of Savannah in 1781. On the other hand, Choctaw, whose friendship the British had never won, provided scouts who served under George Washington, Daniel Morgan, Anthony Wayne, and John Sullivan.

After the American Revolution Spain continued intrigues with the Creek until issues with the United States were settled in the Treaty of San Lorenzo in 1795. During Washington's administration the United States made the Creek Confederation a protectorate by establishing an Indian agent among them. From time to time the United States pressed for land cessions. In negotiating treaties, federal officials commonly plied the Indians with liquor and encouraged the chiefs with bribes. Sometimes they entered into fraudulent treaties by negotiating with subservient individuals who had no authority from the tribe. At the same time in Georgia, the Creek faced a state determined to drive all Indians from its territory by any means that might prove effective.

For a time after the Revolution the Creek had a centralized government and a unified foreign policy under an educated and brilliant mixed-blood, Alexander McGILLIVRAY, whose devious diplomacy in the Treaty of NEW YORK (1790) matched that of the United States. But the old decentralization of a loose confederacy appeared after his death in 1793. In the early years of the nineteenth century the United States agent to the Creek, Benjamin Hawkins, attempted with some success to change and develop the economy of the tribe. He brought in blacksmiths and encouraged stock-raising

and the weaving of cloth from cotton raised by the Indians. The growing number of mixed-bloods took more readily than did the full-bloods to the white man's way of life. Some amassed wealth in livestock and slaves.

In 1811 Tecumseh's appeal to the Creek to join his confederacy of tribes in the Ohio valley to oppose the white advance split the Creek, but one group called the Red Sticks did go on the warpath. In 1813 General Andrew Jackson, with the aid of a considerable force of Choctaw led by PUSHMATAHA, killed more than five hundred Red Stick warriors at HORSESHOE BEND. The defeat broke the power of the Creek nation, and the United States exacted a large amount of land as an indemnity.

After the Revolution the leading men of the Cherokee concluded that the safety of the tribe could only be insured by taking over the white man's civilization. In the early 1820s the chiefs accepted the syllabary of SEQUOYAH, and in a short time the Cherokee became literate. Congregational missionaries established schools. One, Samuel A. Worcester, with the aid of Elias BOUDINOT, an educated full-blood, began translating the New Testament into Cherokee. In 1828 Boudinot became editor of the *Cherokee Phoenix,* a weekly paper published in English and Cherokee. The year before John Ross had taken the lead in drawing up a constitution modeled somewhat on that of the United States, which was adopted by the tribe. Ross, almost wholly white and married to a Cherokee wife, became principal chief. The Cherokee made great progress in achieving an agricultural economy. Their advance stiffened the determination of Georgia to rid the state of the tribe.

The Choctaw in the early nineteenth century also made rapid advance in developing an agricultural economy. They welcomed missionaries and the schools they maintained and created a code of laws appropriate to their civilized state. Roads across their country helped to increase the pressure of white settlers on their borders. Mississippi became anxious to move them out.

At the time of the purchase of Louisiana, President Thomas Jefferson suggested that the tribes of the Old Southwest be removed across the Mississippi River. A company of Cherokee moved west early in the century. The Chickasaw, under pressure, began moving in the 1820s. The Jackson administration began with the declared policy of completing the removal of all the Indians, a policy expressed in the Removal Act of 1830. In 1830 the Choctaw were forced to accept the Treaty of DANCING RABBIT CREEK, and their change of location, which was complete by 1833, was characterized by great suffering. The Creek, forced to give up their old homeland, suffered heavy loss of life during their migration in the winter of 1834-35 (see OKLAHOMA).

The Cherokee contended with both Georgia and the United States. In December 1828, after the election of Jackson, Georgia extended its jurisdiction and laws over Cherokee territory within the state. The Cherokee sued to restrain Georgia. The Supreme Court ruled in 1831 in CHEROKEE NATION v. STATE OF GEORGIA that the Indians could not sue, Indian tribes being only "domestic dependent nations." In an attempt to blunt the influence of missionaries who encouraged Cherokee aspirations for a better life in their old homeland, Georgia had required that all white men living in Indian country take an oath of allegiance to the state. Worcester refused and was jailed. In WORCESTER V. STATE OF GEORGIA the Supreme Court declared in 1832 that the state's extension of its jurisdiction to Cherokee country was unconstitutional on the ground that the Cherokee Nation was a distinct community occupying its own territory. President Jackson took no action to enforce the decision, however, and Worcester remained in jail. Georgia then began surveying Cherokee lands, dividing them into parcels, which were then distributed by lot to white settlers. Principal chief Ross refused to negotiate a treaty of removal or to permit a discussion of the desperate situation in the Phoenix. But Boudinot and John Ridge, in the hope of saving their people from utter demoralization signed a treaty of removal in 1852, and the Treaty of NEW ECHOTA in 1835. Ross and the majority offered passive resistance to the United States. A federal military force rounded them up in 1838. In 1839 United States soldiers marched them west with heavy loss of life along the "trail of tears." At the time of the roundup some Cherokee hid in the mountains. They became the eastern band of Cherokee now dwelling in North Carolina. Meanwhile, the Seminole, under the leadership of OSCEOLA, moved only after the longest and costliest war fought by the United States against Indians (see SEMINOLE WAR and FLORIDA).

Desire to rid the Old Southwest of Indians caused the United States to make large grants of land (thought to be of little value) to the migrating tribes in what became Indian Territory. The migrating nations reestablished their governments. The Cherokee who had been moved united with the western band that had long been in the area. The newcomers brought agriculture to the Great Plains, and with them came a considerable number of slaves and free Negroes. But the Plains Indians, such as the Kaw and the Cheyenne, caused anxiety. A compact entered into at Talequah (in what is now Oklahoma) in 1843 and strengthened in 1859 created the Five Civilized Tribes with an intertribal code of law and a common front against the "wild tribes" of the buffalo country.

The Five Civilized Tribes faced the necessity of decision in 1861 with the coming of the Civil War. Negro slavery existed in all the tribes, the largest slave owners being the mixed-bloods. The Chickasaw, Choctaw, and Seminole sided promptly with the Confederacy. The Cherokee at first tried to remain neutral but soon entered into a treaty with the Confederate government. The Creek divided into a Confederate and a Union party. Military action between Union and Confederate forces involving campaigns in Indian country brought suffering, especially to the Cherokee and the Creek. At the end of the war the United States exacted large cessions of land but the tribal governments remained intact.

In 1903 an act of Congress authorized the president to appoint a commission of three (later increased to five) to negotiate with the Five Civilized Tribes. The act instructed the commissioners to effect the extinction of the land titles of the nations either by cession to the United States, allotment of parcels of land to individual members of the tribe, or any other method. The declared purpose of the act was the creation of a state or states in the Union out of an area occupied by the Five Civilized Tribes. Henry L. Dawes became head of what came to be called the Dawes Commission.

Understandably, negotiations with the reluctant tribes were long, difficult, and of varying outcomes in detail. But the end of the tribes as separate and independent political entities had come. In 1901 Congress had prepared the way by granting citizenship to every Indian in Indian Territory. In 1905 delegates not only from the Five Civilized Tribes but from all parts of Indian Territory met in the so-called Sequoyah Convention in Muskogee. The Indian convention drafted a constitution that the framers hoped Congress would accept as the basic law of a separate state. But Congress rejected the idea of what, in effect, would have been an Indian state. Instead, it passed in 1906 an enabling act that joined Indian Territory with Oklahoma. The new state was admitted to the Union in 1907. With that event, the history of the peoples of the Five Civilized Tribes became fused with the larger history of the state of Oklahoma.

See Angie Debo, *The Road to Disappearance* (1941); Grant Foreman, *The Five Civilized Tribes* (1934); and M. H. Wright, *A Guide to the Indian Tribes of Oklahoma* (1951).—R. H. G.

Flaget, Benedict (1763-1850). Roman Catholic missionary. A Sulpician priest from France, Flaget taught at Georgetown and Baltimore colleges from 1792 to 1808. He then worked in frontier Vincennes, Indiana, and, as Kentucky's first bishop, for forty years among Indians and settlers over seven states.

See J. Schauinger, *Cathedrals in the Wilderness* (1952).—R. I. B.

Flagler, Henry Morrison (1830-1913). Florida developer. Born in Hopewell, New York, into a Presbyterian minister's family, Flagler attended public school until he was eighteen. Deciding to enter the business world, he got work in mercantile establishments in Republic, Fostoria, and Bellevue, Ohio. He entered the grain-commission business in Bellevue and in 1852 joined a flourishing firm of grain shippers and distillers. Cleveland was the focal point for this business and John D. Rockefeller the principal commission merchant there. Flagler's dealings with him developed into friendship. After an abortive venture in the salt manufacturing business in Michigan, Flagler moved to Cleveland and became associated with Rockefeller in the oil industry. The firm of Rockefeller, Andrews, and Flagler appeared in 1867, being supplanted by the Standard Oil Company in 1870. The relationship between Flagler and Rockefeller in this enterprise was personal and close. Ida M. Tarbell, the *McClure's Magazine* editor, in her muckraking *History of the Standard Oil Company* (1904) judged Flagler to be Rockefeller's strongest colleague. Throughout its turbulent early years, Flagler was active in the direction of the giant concern, remaining on the board of directors until two years before his death.

Visiting Florida on a honeymoon in 1883-84, Flagler became interested in the undeveloped possibilities of that frontier region. In 1885 he decided to construct a luxury hotel in old St. Augustine, the magnificent Ponce de Leon, which opened January 10, 1888. This was his first Florida enterprise. In 1887 Flagler started construction on the Alcazar across the street, for guests of lesser means, completing it in 1889. A third hotel, the Cordova, was bought in 1889. Soon after the Ponce de Leon was begun, Flagler bought the Jacksonville to St.

Augustine railroad, rebuilding it to suit the demands being placed on transportation by his construction projects. By 1888 he had bought short lines reaching as far south as Daytona. By 1890 he had standardized his railroads, bridged the St. Johns River at both Palatka and Jacksonville, and provided a convenient means of access to his hotels for northern tourists.

Flagler's interest then turned to further development of the east coast of Florida and in 1892 his Florida East Coast Railway began to push south from Daytona, reaching West Palm Beach in 1894 and the village of Miami in 1896. Palatial hotels were built at Ormond, Palm Beach, and Miami. Along the railroad line, agricultural improvements were stimulated, settlers were attracted, and business and commerce were fostered. Having pushed back the frontier to the southern tip of Florida, Flagler became determined to conquer the watery wilderness of the Keys. In 1905 the work was begun. Almost overwhelming difficulties were presented by this project and they were overcome only with great expenditures of both money and life. The sum of $20 million was spent on the overseas extension; all Flagler's other Florida projects to that point had taken but $30 million. In 1912 this immense task was completed and Flagler rode into Key West in his own railroad car at eighty-two years of age. He died in his home Whitehall in Palm Beach and was buried in St. Augustine.

See Sidney Walter Martin, *Florida's Flagler* (1949). —H. J. D.

Flake, William (1839-1932). Arizona cattleman and developer. Born in North Carolina, Flake moved by wagon train to Utah with his Mormon parents in 1849. A year later his father was killed while examining a colony site in California; undaunted, his mother went on with the family to the new settlement near San Bernardino. The family returned to Utah in 1857. In 1858 Flake was married, and a year later he started a cattle ranch at Beaver, Utah.

In 1877 Flake and other Mormon colonizers took a wagon train and their cattle herds to the Little Colorado region of Arizona, arriving in January 1878. They lived in their wagons through the rough winter and were forced to cut up sacks and canvas for clothing. In the spring Flake exchanged cattle for James Stinson's ranch, then under irrigation and growing crops of corn and wheat. That summer Flake and his family lived mostly on beef and corn but by autumn had provisions for winter. In the fall of 1878 Erastus Snow, an apostle of the church, visited there. Deciding that Flake's ranch was a promising place for a settlement, he joined Flake in creating the town of Snowflake, named for the two men.

When Apache County was created, Snowflake was county seat for a time, and the first court was held in Flake's home. Noted for generosity throughout his life, Flake gave many a helping hand to settlers; his practice of giving wood and food to the needy at Thanksgiving still is followed in that area.

Flake rode the range until just before his death. He was known and respected as a cattleman and humanitarian.—C. H. F.

Flathead Indians. The Flatheads proper, or Salish, were one of a group of small Salishan tribes loosely identified as "flatheads," although they did not artificially deform their infants' foreheads, as was the custom in certain other tribes of the Pacific Northwest. The presence among the Salish of slaves from those other tribes was responsible for the adoption of the misnomer. By 1855, when the government first attempted to confine them to a reservation in northwestern Montana, they claimed the Bitterroot valley as their home and hunted, fished, and foraged throughout the region between the headwaters of the Columbia and Missouri rivers. Meanwhile, their relations with the whites who followed Lewis and Clark into their country were remarkably peaceful and friendly. Although belligerent toward Indian rivals, they took no part in their neighbors' sporadic hostilities against settlers and troops in the period 1847-77. Moreover, the Flatheads eagerly engaged in commerce, and to the disappointment of Protestant missionaries, who responded to their alleged appeals for Bibles and preachers, many became devout Catholics.

After 1855 the United States's major difficulty with the Flatheads was their reluctance to join the Pend d'Oreille and Kutenai on Jocko Reservation. Taking advantage of ambiguities in their 1855 treaty and later directives, a large segment of the 500-plus Flatheads— "Charlos' Band"—spurned government aid and fended for themselves south of Jocko until the late 1880s. But then the disappearance of game, bad crops, increasing white settlement, and political pressures forced the self-reliant Flatheads to begin reservation life.

A detailed history of the Flathead Indians has not yet been published. Some revealing, episodic comments on their condition and relations with the government in the nineteenth century appear in the brief *Historical Sketch of the Flathead Nation* (1890) by Peter Ronan, who served as the Flatheads' Indian agent throughout the 1880s. A general survey of the life and environment of the Flatheads is included in Olga W. Johnson, *Flathead and Kootenay: The Rivers, the Tribes, and the Region's Traders* (1969). Neither James A. Teit, "The Salishan Tribes of the Western Plateau: The Flathead Group" (1930), nor Harry H. Turney-High, *The Flathead Indians of Montana* (1937), is primarily concerned with historical events, but both shed some light on the Flatheads' traditions and early activities. Also helpful are the brief commentaries presented in Frederick W. Hodge, ed., *The Handbook of American Indians North of Mexico*, 2 vols. (1907-10). The basic source of information on Flathead-white relations, though, is the annual reports of the commissioner of Indian affairs, published by the federal government. —H. G. W.

Flint, Timothy (1780-1840). Minister, social historian, editor, and novelist. Flint was one of the most influential western men of letters of the first half of the nineteenth century. He was born near North Reading, Massachusetts, and was graduated in 1800 from Harvard. After an abortive attempt at a career as a Congregationalist minister in New England (1802-14), Flint and his family moved west to Cincinnati, Ohio, and later to Alexandria, Louisiana. The vicissitudes of the trip form the basis of much of the narrative of the semiautobiographical *Recollections of the Last Ten Years* (1826), his first book, written when he was forty-five years old. Flint eventually took up the editorship of the *Western Monthly Review* (1827-30), which he turned into the first successful literary periodical to be printed west of the Allegheny Mountains. Finding a literary career more to his taste than an ecclesiastical one, he devoted the rest of his life to writing.

To his contemporaries, Flint was probably best known as the author of the extremely popular *Biographical Memoir of Daniel Boone* (1833). Though the *Memoir*, together with its companion, *Indian Wars of the West* (1833), is almost forgotten today, the modern reader will be most struck by Flint's treatment of Boone and the other pioneers, who are presented not as outcasts or exiles from society but as willing servants of the process of civilization. Boone's "heart swelled with joy, and warmed with a transport which was natural to a mind so unsophisticated and disinterested as his," Flint tells us, when he contemplated those who would succeed him and civilize the wilderness. Most readers today would expect, and probably prefer, his enthusiasm to be more qualified and his transports of joy to be more self-contained at the prospect of the destruction of his wild, free way of life.

Flint is also noteworthy as the writer of the first "western," *Francis Berrian, or, The Mexican Patriot* (1826), which in thematic concern as well as subject matter clearly prefigures many later novels of the American West. Ostensibly the story of the Mexican revolution of 1823, the novel, in two volumes, is the first clear articulation of the ubiquitous later theme of the rivalry between the clean-living American and the corrupt Mexican for the hand of the exotic Spanish maiden. A later novel, also in two volumes, *The Shoshonee Valley* (1830), is an effective descant on the perennial frontier theme of Indian captivity. It tells of a group of whites who, while living among the Shoshoni Indians, discover that life in a state of nature is not—Rousseau to the contrary—an ideal state. As in the *Biographical Memoir*, Flint favors a state of social order to a state of anarchic primitive life. Flint also edited *The Personal Narrative of James O. Pattie, of Kentucky* (1831), for which he is probably most widely remembered today. Though the *Narrative* masquerades as sober history, it is really semifictional; whether its unreality of the story is primarily due to Pattie's vivid imagination or to Flint's fictional gifts is uncertain.

Flint's other fiction includes a number of short stories and three other novels. *George Mason, the Young Backwoodsman* (1829) is a novel of life in the Mississippi valley; *The Life and Adventures of Arthur Clenning* (1828) is another study of life in a state of nature, and owes much to Daniel Defoe's *Robinson Crusoe;* and *The Lost Child* (1830) is a banal anecdote of Mississippi valley history written for a juvenile audience. Flint's nonfictional studies of western life, *A Condensed Geography and History of the Western States* (1828) and *The History and Geography of the Mississippi Valley* (1832), still repay perusal by the social historian, though neither achieves the quality of his earlier *Recollections.*

However dated much of his writing may seem today, Flint is an important literary pioneer and social historian. He was one of the first writers to articulate the possibilities of western life as a subject for serious fiction.

See James K. Folsom, *Timothy Flint* (1955); John Ervine Kirkpatrick, *Timothy Flint* (1911); and William H. Venable, *Beginnings of Literary Culture in the Ohio Valley* (1891).—J. K. F.

Florida. Although credit for the discovery of Florida usually goes to Juan PONCE DE LEON because his voyage was officially authorized by the Spanish monarchy, there is evidence that Juan and Sebastian Cabot and perhaps Amerigo Vespucci were earlier visitors to the shores of Florida. Three maps published before Ponce de León's voyage represent Florida, the earliest being the Alberto Cantino map of 1502. In 1513 Ponce departed Puerto Rico under a royal patent to explore and govern the island of Bimini and such other lands as he might discover. On April 2 he reached the Florida coast a few miles south of the St. Johns River. Naming the land Florida for Pascua Florida, the feast of the flowers associated with the Easter season, Ponce took possession for Spain. After exploring the east and west coasts, he went back to Puerto Rico. Before Ponce could return to govern and exploit the land he had discovered he was delayed by a mission to the Lower Antilles. Ponce de León met disaster on his second voyage in 1521. His expedition of colonists reached the Florida west coast, perhaps in the Charlotte Harbor area, where they were attacked by Indians and Ponce was wounded. The survivors sailed to Cuba, where their wounded leader died.

Meanwhile, in 1519, Francisco de Garay mapped the Gulf Coast, and Lucas Vásquez de Ayllón sent an exploratory expedition to the Atlantic Coast in 1521. These probes showed that Florida was not an island but part of a vast continent, which became known as Florida to sixteenth-century Spaniards.

The next important exploration was led by Pánfilo de NARVAEZ in 1528. With four hundred men he sailed into Tampa Bay in April. Lured on by Indian tales of gold he fixed a rendezvous with his ships and marched off toward the north. More than two months later he reached the region of present-day Tallahassee. Finding no riches, he turned southward to the coast but found no ships. Constructing five crude boats, his group set sail for Mexico but was shipwrecked off Texas, losing two thirds of its members, including Narváez. Eight years later four survivors, headed by Alvar Núñez CABEZA DE VACA, reached Mexico City.

Hernando DE SOTO, a former associate of Pizarro in Peru, departed Europe in 1538 with an elegantly equipped expedition of notables. At the end of May 1839 they landed in Tampa Bay. In August, de Soto's force of five hundred armed men, two hundred horses, and some priests set out for Apalachee (the Tallahassee region), arriving there in October. Wintering in the area, de Soto sent out an exploring party that discovered Pensacola Bay. Sending to Cuba for more supplies to meet him in Pensacola late in 1540, de Soto then moved northward, traversing parts of Georgia, North Carolina, Tennessee, Alabama, and Mississippi. Deciding not to rendezvous with his supply ships at Pensacola, de Soto moved across the Mississippi River into Arkansas, Missouri, and Oklahoma. In the spring of 1541 he died near the mouth of the Arkansas River and was buried there. Luis de Moscoso, who succeeded de Soto, constructed vessels for departure to Cuba and returned with three hundred and ten Spaniards and Indian slaves. After this expedition, interest in Florida lagged noticeably.

In 1559 a major colonizing expedition set out from Mexico to the Pensacola Bay area under Tristán de Luna y Arellano. In the summer of 1559 the party reached its destination after suffering significant losses in storms at sea. Achieving no successes, de Luna was relieved in 1561 by Angel de Villafañe, but he failed to found a permanent settlement and shortly thereafter abandoned Pensacola Bay.

At this point, to many Spaniards, Florida appeared to be impossible of colonization, but a challenge to try again was shortly to come from the threat of interlopers. In 1562 Jean RIBAULT landed at the mouth of the St. Johns River with a colony of one hundred fifty French Huguenots. The rise of nationalistic and Protestant-Catholic rivalries in Europe sparked the first challenge to Spain's imperial power. Naming the St. Johns the River of May, Ribault planted a stone column, claimed the land for France, and sailed northward to Port Royal, South Carolina, where he planted a small colony before returning to France. Changes in the French government delayed Ribault's early return to Florida. Meanwhile, in 1564, a second French expedition under René de Laudonnière planted a colony in Florida on the St. Johns River and there constructed Fort Caroline. Though the local Timucua Indians, under chief Saturiba, were friendly and helpful, the colony did not prosper, and by mid-1565 they had decided to go back to France. In their preparations they were discovered by the Englishman Sir John Hawkins, who traded them an additional ship for guns, ammunition, and fresh water. Shortly after, Ribault unexpectedly arrived with reinforcements, relieved Laudonnière, and began to strengthen Fort Caroline. Spanish officials, learning of the French incursions, had hoped to destroy the settlement before Ribault's arrival.

About the time of Ribault's return, a Spanish force under Pedro Menéndez de Avilés arrived in the region of what is now Cape Kennedy and then sailed north to the area of present-day St. Augustine. Menéndez' orders were to eradicate the French, establish Spanish settlements, and promote Christianity. On September 8, 1565, he founded the settlement of St. Augustine and sent to Havana for reinforcements. A few days later Ribault sailed for St. Augustine, but his expedition was driven south by a storm and wrecked. Menéndez then marched overland to Fort Caroline and destroyed its undermanned garrision except for some fifty-six prisoners and sixty escapees. He garrisoned the fort and returned to St. Augustine, where word was received of the Frenchmen stranded south of the colony. Menéndez took fifty men south to Matanzas Inlet, finding there some two hundred of Ribault's men. They surrendered and most were executed. Two weeks later Ribault and one hundred fifty men surrendered at Matanzas and all but sixteen were executed. The massacre of the French gave the name Matanzas ("Place of Killing") to the location. About one hundred seventy others, refusing to surrender, fled southward. Menéndez located them near Cape Kennedy, induced all but twenty to surrender, and kept his promise to send them to Europe.

Although Menéndez established several settlements on the Florida coasts, none survived except St. Augustine. By 1585 St. Augustine had a population of about three hundred, a government house, church, and several other buildings The next year Sir Francis Drake attacked and destroyed the town, but it was later rebuilt and strengthened. The continuing vulnerability of the town, however, led to the consideration of its abandonment in 1602. Conceding that Florida could probably not be a self-supporting colony, a decision to sustain it was made nonetheless and a new direction was given to

administrative policy. A chain of Franciscan missions was created in the seventeenth century to teach the Indians Christianity and loyalty to Spain. They made much headway toward that end despite the failure of Jesuit attempts in the previous century. During the 1670s the Franciscans achieved their most widespread influence, extending their mission stations from San Diego de Salamototo, on the St. Johns River west of St. Augustine, westward to the Apalachicola River. The heaviest concentration was in the Apalachee area. Northward from St. Augustine missions extended along the coast into the upper sea islands of Georgia.

The earliest Indian inhabitants of Florida appeared, by many accounts, as long as twenty thousand years ago and are believed to have been part of a great migration from northeastern Asia, which crossed the land bridge from Siberia to Alaska during the Ice Age. The earliest inhabitants were almost exclusively hunters of large, now-extinct animals. Archaeologists have discovered many evidences of the tools and weapons they used and the animals that fell prey to their skill. About 5000 B.C. villages began to appear housing people more dependent upon shellfish, snails, mollusks, nuts, and roots. Significant evidence of fairly early and extensive trading is present. Manufacture of pottery appeared in Florida and Georgia about 2000 B.C., some eight hundred years earlier than the rest of the continental United States. Cultural diffusion resulted in the development of an agricultural economy among the Florida Indians around 1000 B.C. Burial mounds began to appear in Florida around the beginning of the Christian era, followed by the appearance along the Gulf Coast about A.D. 500 of a considerable cultural homogeneity, which many authorities believe to have been rooted in a common religion. This culture spread in Florida but had little impact upon the extreme southern Indians. In the Lake Okeechobee area about this time, however, appeared a complex of large ceremonial centers that showed Gulf Coast influences. Mounds with temples atop began to appear near the Gulf Coast in the fourteenth century. Archaeologists see in this evidences of changed ceremonial life and more emphasis upon agriculture.

By the sixteenth century Florida Indians numbered about 25,000 and had developed relatively complex cultures. There were five major groups: the Timucua (14,000), occupying the interior of the peninsula from Cape Kennedy to Georgia; the Apalachee (7,000) in the "panhandle" from the Aucilla River to the Ocklockonee; the Ais (900) on the east coast south of Cape Kennedy; the Tequesta (800) on the lower east coast; and the Calusa (2,500) on the west coast south of Tampa Bay. Of these, almost none remained at the end of the eighteenth century.

The founding of English Charleston in 1670 promised trouble for Spain, her Franciscan missions, and the Florida Indians. British influence was soon exerted upon the Guale Indians of Georgia and they were won over with goods, guns, and money. Scattered attacks upon the northernmost missions followed. In 1702 and 1704 Governor James Moore of South Carolina invaded Florida with Indian allies and laid waste the coastal missions first and later the Apalachee missions. Other raids in 1706 and 1708 destroyed the Timucua villages. The Spanish estimated that some ten thousand to twelve thousand Indians were killed or carried into slavery. After 1708 no Spanish missions remained except those around St. Augustine. With the missions destroyed and most of the aboriginal Indians gone, Indians from Alabama and Georgia began to move into depopulated north Florida in the 1700s. Lower Creek Indians moving into Apalachee were the first to come, probably at Spanish invitation. By 1750, the Lower Creek of the Oconee band were settled in the Alachua area, and more came into Florida during the British period. In the same period the first Upper Creek came, settling near Tampa Bay. The last major movement came after Andrew Jackson's defeat of the Creek in Alabama in 1814. The "Red Stick" faction of Upper Creek, bitter in defeat, moved to Florida. During the British era all the fragmented bands of Creek had begun to be called Seminole, a name identifying them as detached from the Creek Federation north of Florida.

The eighteenth-century British incursions had done permanent damage to Spanish Florida. Though they never were able to take the powerful Castillo de San Marcos (construction of which was begun in 1672) in St. Augustine, they did destroy virtually everything outside its walls. Despite the building of the small Fort San Marcos in Apalachee country in 1718, Spanish authority in Florida was rarely to be effective again beyond gunshot of the walls of her fortresses, and English traders and adventurers pushed British influence deep into the province.

Meanwhile, another threat had appeared with the spread of French influence down the Mississippi valley. The disturbed Spaniards made investigations, decided to place an outpost on Pensacola Bay, and began construction in November 1698. Three months later a French expedition arrived and, upon being turned away, settled at Biloxi, later moving to Mobile. The Pensacola settlement lived even more precariously than that at St. Augustine and was never self-supporting. In 1719 a French fleet seized Pensacola and retained it until 1723. In the mid-decades of the eighteenth century international rivalries led to recurrent clashes between the English stronghold at Charleston and that of the Spanish at St. Augustine. In 1740 Governor James Oglethorpe of Georgia attacked St. Augustine and besieged the fortress, withdrawing only upon the appearance of Spanish warships. A second attack was made in 1742, but again Oglethorpe had to withdraw without conquest. For twenty years thereafter St. Augustine was peaceful and almost prosperous. The population grew, durable houses were constructed, and life seemed more normal. At the close of the Seven Years' War (in 1763), however, Spain ceded Florida to England in exchange for Cuba, which Britain had taken during the hostilities, and almost all the Spanish inhabitants left the peninsula. In addition, some two hundred of the surviving aboriginal Indians near St. Augustine went with them. Before evacuation, the 1763 population of St. Augustine had been 3,046; that of Pensacola was less than 800.

By proclamation of October 7, 1763, the British reorganized the administration of Florida and altered its boundaries. All present-day Florida east of the Apalachicola River was constituted as East Florida. West Florida was bounded on the west by the Mississippi River and on the north by the 31 degrees latitude from the Mississippi River due east to the Chattahoochee River, thence southward down the Chattahoochee and Apalachicola rivers to the Gulf. St. Augustine and Pensacola were the respective capitals. In 1764 the northern boundary of West Florida was pushed up to 32°28'—a line running eastward from the mouth of the Yazoo River to the Chattahoochee. Under Governor James Grant, East Florida soon became a bustling area; wealthy settlers entered, and amicable Indian relations were established. More than one hundred estates were established on the northeast coast and in the St. Johns valley, but the most remarkable colony was that founded at New Smyrna by Dr. Andrew Turnbull. More than one thousand persons were brought there from the Mediterranean area, the largest number coming from the island of Minorca (located off the east coast of Spain). By 1769 the colony was growing corn, cotton, sugarcane, rice, and indigo. Conflicts between the culturally diverse settlers and political controversies in which Turnbull became involved, related to demands for an elective assembly, led to the disruption of the colony after a few years, and most settlers moved to St. Augustine.

West Florida was less fortunate. It was more inaccessible than East Florida and its capital, Pensacola, was isolated from its richest lands, which were along the Mississippi. George Johnstone, who took office as the first governor in 1764, was contentious and unable to lead his people or conciliate the Indians. After he was removed in 1767, the brief terms of his three successors were little better. In 1770 Peter Chester arrived to rule until the end of the British period. In the west, the hide and fur trades seem to have been more important than agriculture. Neither province was self-sufficient, and no other colony save Georgia got the kind of support from London that the Floridas did.

During the American Revolution, the Floridas were havens for loyalist refugees; the provinces were too dependent on London to be moved to revolt. West Florida, however, faced the threat of Spain's desire to profit from England's involvement. Bernardo de Gálvez, governor of Spanish Louisiana, moved against the region, seizing Natchez in 1779, Mobile in 1780, and Pensacola in 1781. No serious fighting took place in East Florida. The Treaty of Paris of 1783 returned the Floridas to Spain to the disappointment of the thousands of refugee British loyalists. Of the British inhabitants, only the Minorcans remained in any numbers.

Disorders, banditry, and incursions by the Americans from the north were characteristic of Spain's weak rule throughout the second occupation. The possession of both Louisiana and the Floridas after 1783 gave Spain more territory in North America than ever before, but she was unable to govern it. In order to maintain good Indian relations in the Floridas, the Spanish allowed Panton, Leslie and Company, which had handled Indian trade for the British, to continue lest the Americans move into the field. Panton, Leslie and Company was a big business operating fifteen oceangoing vessels and employing fifteen clerks in its Pensacola headquarters. After the death of William Panton, however, prospects for the firm declined. Indian indebtedness grew and the Treaty of San Lorenzo (1795), which settled the disputed northern boundary of West Florida at 31 degrees north latitude, cut off access to Indians north of the line. John Forbes, who inherited control of the company, induced the Indians to cede 1.2 million acres of land on the Apalachicola River to settle their debts. The Spanish approved as did, ultimately, the United States Supreme Court.

In 1803 Louisiana, which Spain had returned to France in 1800, was sold to the United States with the implication that she should make the most of the territory's vague boundaries (see EAST AND WEST FLORIDA QUESTION). In 1810 President James Madison claimed Florida from the Mississippi to the Perdido River as part of that purchase, and in 1813 the United States seized the Mobile Bay area, thus reducing the Spanish Floridas to the boundaries of present-day Florida. On the eve of the War of 1812 efforts were made by United States agents to foment a revolution among the growing American population in northeast Florida in the expectation that they would then deliver the province to the United States. The revolt occurred and the "Republic of Florida" was set up, but in the face of war with England and declining enthusiasm in Congress, the expected American military support was withdrawn. When war with England commenced the whole project was abandoned, leaving northeast Florida in virtual anarchy.

In 1814 the British occupied Amelia Island, which was used briefly as a base for raids against southern Georgia. A few months later, with Spanish consent, a strong force of British marines landed in Pensacola as part of the British move against the southern United States. Major General Andrew JACKSON, in command in the southwest, drove the English out on November 6, 1814, and then turned west to fight the famous battle of New Orleans. After the war Amelia Island became a refuge for pirates, adventurers, revolutionaries, and smugglers until seized by the United States in December 1817. Elsewhere on the Florida border Indian troubles marked the postwar years, leading in 1818 to orders to General Jackson to undertake punitive action in what became the long SEMINOLE WAR. He was told to avoid all Spanish posts. After asking permission to seize all Florida, Jackson proceeded into the territory in the belief that he had received approval, though the Monroe administration repudiated him. With about two thousand men he seized St. Marks, searched for Indians as far east as the Suwannee River, and then turned toward Pensacola, which he took in May 1818. There he expelled the Spanish and established a provisional government. Negotiations were already under way for the cession of Florida. Jackson's actions had demonstrated Spanish weaknesses. On February 22, 1819, the ADAMS-ONÍS TREATY was signed, ceding Florida to the United States and obligating the United States to pay debts up to the amount of $5 million which Spain owed American citizens. Perhaps more importantly, this treaty delineated the western boundary of the United States from the Sabine River on the Gulf to the Oregon boundary on the Pacific.

Because of a delay in exchanging ratifications, the transfer did not occur until 1821, when, on July 17, provisional Governor Andrew Jackson received West Florida "with the tune of 'long may it wave, o'er the land of the free and the home of the brave.' " On July 10, East Florida had been received by Colonel Robert Butler. Jackson lingered in Florida only about twelve more weeks, long enough to organize the local government. In March 1822, Congress enacted a territorial government and President Monroe appointed William P. DU-VAL (of Kentucky) governor. During his twelve-year term DuVal saw the rapid growth of this frontier territory. A new capital site, Tallahassee, chosen midway between the populated extremities, was occupied in 1824. The richness of the lands around the capital (the old Apalachee mission region) attracted settlers rapidly and it soon rivaled the older areas as an economic, political, and population center.

Problems with Indian tribes comprising the FIVE CIVILIZED TRIBES beset the new government as they had preceding ones. The removal of Indians from fast-growing northern Florida was accomplished in consequence of the Treaty of Moultrie Creek of 1823, which set aside a large interior region south of Ocala and north of Charlotte Harbor for the Indians. Before a decade had passed, however, Florida frontiersmen were pressing hard upon Indian lands and demands were made that the Indians go to the trans-Mississippi West. With objections and misgivings, a number of chiefs agreed in 1832 to move if they could inspect the proposed western lands. After visiting the region they signed a treaty in 1833 agreeing to the move, but upon their return some repudiated their actions and a number of Indians denied that they could be bound by the signers. Ignoring the protests, the government set January 1, 1836, as the deadline for removal. Young Seminole braves led by the fiery OSCEOLA repudiated the leadership of the older chiefs and vowed resistance. Attacks upon Indians who had agreed to move and raids on white settlements in 1835 presaged the war, which erupted on a large scale in December. Though General Duncan L. Clinch was initially in command, President Jackson put General Winfield SCOTT in charge in January 1836. Regular troops were committed and a naval blockade of Seminole coasts established. In May Governor Richard K. CALL was put in charge of all the forces and conducted a brief, unsuccessful offensive. General Thomas S. JESUP took command at the end of 1836 and conducted an unsuccessful conciliatory policy aimed at protecting Indians who would move. In the fall of 1837 Seminole leaders King Philip, Coacoochee, and Osceola indicated to militia General Joseph M. Hernandez their desire for a conference near St. Augustine. There, on the orders of Jesup, they were taken prisoner under a flag of truce and imprisoned in Castillo de San Marcos. Coacoochee and nineteen other escaped and Coacoochee assumed leadership of the resistance. Osceola was moved to Charleston, South Carolina, where he died in Fort Moultrie on January 31, 1838. Jesup's plan thereafter was to drive the Seminoles to the south and away from the areas inhabited by whites. The last pitched battle was on December 25, 1837, northeast of Lake Okeechobee, where American forces fighting under Colonel Zachary TAYLOR were victorious.

Jesup was not able to conclude the war, but he did severely weaken the Indians by fighting, capturing important chiefs, and persuading many to leave. In November 1841, Coacoochee and his followers finally surrendered. In August 1842, Colonel William J. Worth declared the war finished and gave the remaining Seminole permission to stay in the Everglades. The war had cost $20 million, approximately fifteen hundred

American lives, and much destruction of property. About three thousand eight hundred Indians were removed. Only a few hundred remained and these were involved in recurrent acts of violence for almost two more decades. In the course of the hostilities the army explored and mapped hundreds of square miles of unknown territory and built a network of roads and many new settlements, thereby opening up more of the region.

During the first governorship of Richard Keith Call (1836-39), a constitutional convention led by Robert Raymond REED had been held to prepare for statehood. The Indian wars and the long depression that began in 1837 delayed Florida's admission to the Union, however, until 1845. One of the results of the convention, in addition to a constitution, was a political division that eventually led to the founding of the Democratic party in 1839 under the leadership of James D. Westcott and David L. YULEE. The opposition took the Whig name and was led by Call, Thomas Brown, and Edward C. Cabell. The territorial economy was almost completely agricultural and extractive—cotton, tobacco, rice, and lumber being the cash crops. A number of banks operated, only one railroad of any consequence existed (from Tallahassee to St. Marks), some shipbuilding was carried on, and canals were projected, but such business activity was largely supportive of agriculture.

When Florida finally entered the Union, the Democrats organized the new state government under Governor William D. Moseley. Until after the Civil War they managed the affairs of the state except for the period 1849-53, when Whig Thomas Brown was governor. The population, seventy thousand in 1845, doubled in the next fifteen years. Antebellum settlers in frontier Florida were overwhelmingly from the South, mostly from Georgia and South Carolina. Through the period slaves comprised forty percent of the population. There were only 932 free Negroes in 1860. In this period the region surrounding Tallahassee became Florida's "black belt"—the center of cotton planting, population, wealth, and slaves. In 1845 only the twenty-mile Tallahassee Railroad had been in operation. By 1860 Senator David L. Yulee was heading the corporation constructing the Florida Railroad from Fernandina to Cedar Key. Another line connecting Jacksonville and Tallahassee was complete. The first state-chartered bank was approved in 1855 and four others were in business by 1860. One successful textile mill was operating by 1860 and some two dozen sawmills. South and east of Tampa Bay an open range cattle industry that had begun after the Seminole War was to be an important source of supply for Confederate forces after 1861. Antebellum public education was almost nonexistent except for the Ocala East Florida Seminary, established in 1853, and the Tallahassee West Florida Seminary, begun in 1856.

On January 10, 1861, Florida left the Union to join the Confederate States of America. The state's role in the Civil War was relatively insignificant because of the smallness of its population, the paucity of its developed resources, and its relative isolation from the Confederacy once the federal blockade was established. Throughout the war Key West and the main forts at Pensacola remained in federal hands, and during much of the war the other port cities were under federal occupation.

Some salt and a considerable amount of beef and pork were produced for the Confederacy, all of which was shipped out by wagon. The most important battle in Florida was caused in part by an attempt to cut this supply route. On February 7, 1864, federal troops moved west out of Jacksonville along the railroad to Tallahassee. On February 20 they met the Confederates near the village of Olustee. About five thousand men were arrayed on each side. Losses were heavy and the federals withdrew, but the Confederates were unable to pursue. A month before the end of the war a federal force of one thousand was landed at St. Marks to seize Tallahassee but was turned back at the battle of Natural Bridge by a force of militia and seminary cadets.

The close of the conflict saw economic ruin in Florida. Many of the major ports had been destroyed, the railroads were in shambles, both the Gulf and Atlantic terminals of the Florida Railroad had been destroyed, banking and credit facilities had been shattered, the slaves were free, and the value of farm property had drastically declined. The percentage decline in property value was greater than in Virginia—the main seat of war. The promise that postwar Florida held, however, lay in the fact that it was still largely an undeveloped frontier offering many opportunities to those capable of developing them. The Freedmen's Bureau was effective in helping new black citizens to adjust, the sharecropping system haltingly restored agricultural production, and the possibilities of the tourist trade were beginning to be seen. During Reconstruction Florida's promise was not fully realized. Timber and land resources and the transportation system were manipulated for corrupt ends. Bankrupt railroads were sold for a fraction of their cost, frequently to those who exploited rather than improved them. Politicians attempted to dispose of large tracts of state lands at pitiful prices, but were thwarted by federal injunctions favoring railroad bondholders whose bonds were backed by prewar pledges of state lands. On the whole, economic recovery was slow in the fifteen years after the war.

The year 1876 was a turning point on the road to recovery and the beginning of the end of Florida as a frontier state. In that year the Democrats elected George F. Drew, an ex-Whig, to the governorship and the era of the developers was about to begin. Drew initiated an austerity regime in government and drastically reduced taxes. His successor, William D. Bloxham, turned to positive growth and prosperity policies and began freeing the public lands from federal receivership. He induced Philadelphia millionaire Hamilton Disston to buy four million acres of state land for $1 million, thus providing the funds to pay off the railroad bondholders and clearing the title to state lands. Though an unpopular sale, Bloxham's act opened up a boom decade of railroad building. Disston was also persuaded to embark on a vast canal-building and river-clearing program, which opened up rich lands to settlers and furthered water transportation.

Through the remainder of the nineteenth century, railroads probed into almost every unfamiliar corner of the state, eliminating the last frontiers. West of the Apalachicola River, W. D. Chipley and the Louisville and Nashville Company developed a network tying Pensacola to Alabama, Georgia, and east Florida. Another developer, Henry B. PLANT, tied a number of short lines in South Carolina, Georgia, and Florida into the Plant System. Pushing down to the Tampa Bay area, his system operated more than six hundred miles of track in Florida alone when it merged into the Atlantic Coast Line in 1902. A system of similar size had been developed by John Shelton Williams, who tied together lines from Richmond and Columbia with the old Yulee system and other short lines in Florida. In 1903 it was merged with the Seaboard Air Line. Closer to the hearts of Floridians is the role of Henry M. FLAGLER and his Florida East Coast Railroad in developing the east "Gold Coast" and banishing the watery frontier of the Florida Keys. Having built a fortune in the Standard Oil Company, Flagler first came as a tourist in 1878. Initially interested in building luxury hotels in St. Augustine, which expanded into a chain of hostelries down the coast, Flagler got involved with railroads as a means of transporting building materials and later tourists to his hotels. From Jacksonville to Daytona he put together three short lines, but thereafter constructed his own lines, receiving land grants of eight thousand acres per mile. At the end of 1894 he had reached West Palm Beach and in 1896 his first trains reached Miami. Flagler's last great venture was the expensive but monumental overseas branch that reached Key West in 1912.

The last two decades of the nineteenth century were a turning point in Florida's history: the real beginnings of the modern public school system, under the direction of Jonathan GIBBS, were made; effective state railroad regulation was instituted; national banks appeared in the growing cities; the tourist industry was firmly established; the Democratic white primary was introduced in politics; naval stores, timber, and phosphate industries flourished; citrus-growing gained importance and spread ever farther south; and the population rose from 270,000 in 1880 to 529,000 in 1900. Though Florida's population was predominantly rural until after 1920, by 1900 the rural Floridian was no longer a frontiersman in the primitive rugged sense of even 1870.

The best general history is Charlton W. Tebeau, *A History of Florida* (1971). An indispensable source for articles and book reviews on all phases of Florida history is the *Florida Historical Quarterly*. The most readable short history is Rembert W. Patrick and Allen Morris, *Florida Under Five Flags* (1967). See also Michael V. Gannon, *The Cross in the Sand: The Early Catholic Church in Florida, 1513-1870* (1965); John E. Johns, *Florida During the Civil War* (1963); John K. Mahon, *History of the Second Seminole War* (1968); Charles L. Mowatt, *East Florida as a British Province* (1943); and John J. TePaske, *The Governorship of Spanish Florida, 1700-1763* (1964). —H. J. D.

Folwell, William W. (1833-1929). Minnesota educator and historian. Born on a farm in New York, Folwell was the first president (1869-84) of the University of Minnesota and laid out a farseeing plan for a state university—a federation of schools. He stressed both science and the humanities, calling for a museum, a department of public health, a state geological survey, a program for training experts in legislation, a great library, an observatory, and a faculty research program to be incorporated into the university. He also urged the state to establish junior colleges, an idea that proved to be a half-century ahead of its time. None of Folwell's ideas came to fruition during his tenure as president, but most of them did emerge later.

Folwell wrote the outstanding four-volume *History of Minnesota* (1921-30).—R. W. F.

Fontainebleau, Treaty of. See NEW ORLEANS.

Fontenelle, Lucien (1800-?1840). Fur trapper. One of the most shadowy and romantic figures in the history of American fur trade, Fontenelle was born on his family's plantation, located south of New Orleans. After the death of his parents, who were killed in a hurricane, young Fontenelle was sent to live with his aunt. Incensed at her harsh discipline, he ran away from home and went to St. Louis, where he began his career as a fur trader.

According to historian H. M. Chittenden, Fontenelle was one of the best examples of the Rocky Mountain "partisan," the leader of a "brigade," or itinerant party of hunters and trappers. After trapping briefly for the Missouri Fur Company, Fontenelle formed a partnership with Andrew Drips, and the two built a post at Bellevue, near the present city of Omaha. In 1830 Fontenelle signed on with the American Fur Company and spent the rest of his career leading the company's mountain expeditions.

As the cutthroat competition of the fur-trapping business intensified, the need for consolidation became apparent. In 1835 Fontenelle negotiated a new partnership with Thomas Fitzpatrick, Jim Bridger, and Milton Sublette, the giants of the recently dissolved Rocky Mountain Fur Company, and formed Fontenelle, Fitzpatrick & Co. This partnership thus consolidated the control of the American Fur Company and brought a temporary reprieve for the entire fur trade. The new partnership purchased Fort Laramie, thereafter referred to occasionally as Fort Lucien.

Fontenelle married the daughter of an Omaha chief, La Cerf, and fathered four children. Fontenelle's death in 1839 or 1840 is one of the most mysterious aspects of his career. Some say he committed suicide at Fort Laramie "in a fit of *mania a potu*" (drunken madness), but the weight of the evidence indicates that he died a natural death.

See H. M. Chittenden, *The American Fur Trade of the Far West*, vol. I (1902); Dale L. Morgan and Eleanor T. Harris, eds., *The Rocky Mountain Journals of William Marshall Anderson* (1967); and Alan C. Troutman, "Lucien Fontenelle," in LeRoy Hafen, ed., *The Mountain Men and the Fur Trade of the Far West*, vol. V (1968). —R. B. W.

Foote, Henry Stuart (1804-1880). Southern lawyer, politician, and writer. Foote spent the early years of his life in Virginia. In 1825 he moved to Alabama and five years later settled in Mississippi, where he remained until 1854. His elective offices in Mississippi include state representative (1839), United States senator (1847-52), and governor (1852-54).

Foote was small in stature, being five feet five and weighing 145 pounds, and was almost completely bald at an early age. Yet this physically unimposing man was pugnacious throughout his life; indeed, he fought four duels, though he was a notoriously poor shot. He excelled as a stump speaker, and many Mississippians considered him to be one of the outstanding public speakers in the country. As a writer Foote gained recognition for his journalism and for his four published works. His memoirs, published in 1874 under the title *Casket of Reminiscences*, is an important source for information on people and events in the United States from 1830 to 1870. As a lawyer he had a thriving practice and achieved some measure of fame in the Old Southwest for his handling of criminal cases.

While a Mississippian, Foote fought valiantly for temperance, authoring in 1839 "An Act for the Suppression of Tippling-Houses, and to Discourage and Prevent the Odious Vice of Drunkenness," which prohibited the sale of liquor in quantities of less than a gallon. This "gallon law" was not a popular measure and was repealed by the legislature in 1842. He also favored an elective judiciary, the maintenance of the Union in the secession crisis of 1850-51 (see COMPROMISE OF 1850, which he helped formulate), and the annexation of Texas.

A Unionist, Foote was unsuccessful in Mississippi politics. His amicable relationship with Jefferson Davis did not continue after 1847, when both men were in the Senate. Their views of the Compromise of 1850 were especially conflicting, for Foote favored the Union and Davis held secessionist beliefs. There were personality differences too. Foote wrote that "Serious incompatibilities, both of taste and temper, as well as exceedingly conflicting views of men and measure" developed between them. The rupture became complete when they exchanged blows for some unknown reason at a Mrs. Owner's on Christmas morning, 1847. The break never healed, and they remained estranged the rest of their lives.

Foote's gubernatorial administration was a failure, and by the end of 1853, after failing in his bid to return to the Senate, Foote decided to retire from politics. Had Foote been able to unite behind his banner all the people who voted for him in November 1851, the record of his administration would have been different. But Foote did not possess this needed creative ability. He was more adept at attacking those entrenched in power than at consolidating gains. Foote blamed his defeat primarily on Davis, who, he claimed, as President Franklin Pierce's secretary of war, wielded the powerful weapon of executive patronage against him.

In 1854 Foote moved to California. Returning to the East three years later, he settled and became politically active in Tennessee. The remainder of his career is a part of the history of that state.

See John Edmond Gonzales, "Henry Stuart Foote: A Republican Appointee in Louisiana," *Louisiana History* (1960); "Reminiscences of a Mississippian [Foote]," *Journal of Mississippi History* (1960); "Henry Stuart Foote: A Forgotten Unionist of the Fifties," *Southern Quarterly* (1963); and "Henry Stuart Foote: Confederate Congressman and Exile," *Civil War History* (December 1965). See also Holman Hamilton, *Prologue to Conflict* (1964).—J. E. G.

Foote, Mary Hallock (1847-1938). Novelist and illustrator. Born in Milton, New York, Foote received her early art training at Cooper Union in New York City and began a professional career as an illustrator for *Harper's Weekly* at the close of the Civil War. Following her marriage to a mining engineer, she spent a number of years in the West in a succession of frontier towns in California, Colorado, Idaho, and Mexico. Her first western experiences were published in *Scribner's Monthly*. While residing in Leadville, Colorado, she produced three novels, the first of which featured her own illustrations. All three novels were issued in serial form by *Century* magazine and featured the mining country of central Colorado as the setting. Between 1883 and 1893 Foote was in Idaho, where she produced more novels as well as her most notable series of western illustrations, published by *Century* magazine in 1888-89 under the title "Pictures of the Far West," each accompanied by a brief commentary by the artist. Few of her original drawings survive, many having been executed directly upon the engraving block and the later ones, reproduced by photogravure, never returned to her by her publishers. She spent the latter years of her life in Grass Valley, California, before moving to Boston to live with a daughter.

See Robert Taft, *Artists and Illustrators of the Old West, 1850-1900* (1953).—D. C. H.

Forbes, John Murray (1813-1898). Financier and railroad executive. Forbes, the leading figure in the early financing of major midwestern and western railroad lines, was born in Boston, Massachusetts. At fourteen he entered the shipping business of his maternal uncles, the Perkinses, and at seventeen went to Canton, China, to manage their far eastern shipping interests. Seven years later he returned to Boston with sizable capital; in another nine years he was a rich man. In the 1840s Forbes and a group of associates invested in the floundering railroads of the Midwest. Buying the Michigan Central from the state of Michigan, the group rebuilt it, completed it to Chicago, and eventually sold it for a handsome profit.

Forbes's major involvement with railroads then began with an interest in what eventually became the Chicago, Burlington and Quincy Railroad. By construction and judicious acquisition of existing lines, Forbes built what was later called the BURLINGTON NORTHERN RAILROAD into the most important railroad between the transcontinentals to the West and the trunk lines to the East—a railroad destined to become the "main street" of the most productive agricultural area in the world. Forbes and his kinsman and close associate, Charles E. Perkins, extended the Burlington as far north as Minneapolis, as far west as the Rockies, and as far south as Texas and the Gulf of Mexico.

The paragon of the self-made man, Forbes was witty, urbane, and cultivated. "He is not likely, in any company, to meet a man superior to himself," was Ralph Waldo Emerson's tribute to him. A prodigious worker and shrewd judge of men, Forbes was one of the very first to manage a large, far-flung enterprise. The managerial practices he innovated are among the earliest examples of "big business" techniques.

A tradition of historical writing that ignores the fact that there were great men of business before the "robber baron" era is responsible for the lack of a definitive biography. Of some help is Henry G. Pearson, *An American Railroad Builder, John Murray Forbes* (1911). For Forbes's role in the development of the Burlington lines, see Richard C. Overton, *Burlington Route: A History of the Burlington Lines* (1965).—A. M.

Forbes' Road. Forged in Pennsylvania during French and Indian War. By 1758 the tide was turning in favor of the British in the French and Indian War. In late July, British forces captured Lewisburg, Pennsylvania, and a campaign against French-occupied Fort Duquesne was planned for autumn. Led by Brigadier General John Forbes, with Lieutenant Colonel Henry Bouquet second in command, the troops were to build a chain of supply depots and fortified posts across western Pennsylvania as they moved slowly on the fortress. Although George Washington attacked the plan and others questioned it, Forbes and Bouquet persisted. From Raystown (present-day Bedford), his supply base, Forbes and his men set out in July. By late August they were across the Alleghenies and within forty miles of Fort Duquesne. At this juncture they built Fort Ligonier.

In October, Forbes held a conference with some of the tribes of the Ohio country at Easton, which helped undermine Indian support of the French. Meanwhile, a French and Indian assault on Fort Ligonier on October 12 was successfully repelled. In November, Forbes approached Fort Duquesne, but before he could assault it, the men inside decided to evacuate and destroy the fort.

In addition to leading the way to a military triumph, Forbes' Road later served as an important migratory route westward for Pennsylvanians and others entering the Ohio country.

An exhaustive discussion of Forbes' Road is in Lawrence H. Gipson, *The British Empire Before the American Revolution*, vol. VII (1949).—E. W. K.

Ford, John. See FILMS, WESTERN.

forests. See VEGETATION.

Forsyth, George Alexander (1837-1915). Soldier. Forsyth entered service as a private during the Civil War and rose to the rank of brevet brigadier general, taking part in eighty-eight engagements. Detached from the personal staff of Major General Philip Sheridan, he organized in the summer of 1868 a detachment of fifty frontiersmen to search out Cheyenne who were raiding Kansas. In one of the classic encounters with Indians, a force of about 750 Cheyenne and Sioux attacked and besieged his force for six days (September 17-23, 1868) on BEECHER'S ISLAND in the Arickaree Fork of the Republican River, near present-day Beecher's Island, Colorado. Couriers, who slipped out by night, brought a relief column on September 25.

Although he also participated in Apache campaigns in New Mexico from 1881 to 1883, it is in the Beecher's Island fight that Forsyth gained prominence.

See G. A. Forsyth, *The Story of the Soldier* (1900) and *Thrilling Days in Army Life* (190); see also Dee Brown, *Bury My Heart at Wounded Knee* (1971); and L. J. White, "The Battle of Beecher Island: The Scouts Held Fast on the Arickaree," *Journal of the West*, vol. 5 (1966).—O. K.

Fort Beauharnois and Fort St. Charles (Minnesota). Forts Beauharnois and St. Charles were the two most significant centers of French occupation in Minnesota. They were both military outposts and fur-trading centers. Fort Beauharnois, established in 1727 on Lake Pepin by an expedition led by Sieur de la Perrière, was also the site of the first Christian mission on Minnesota soil. Fort St. Charles, situated on what is now the Northwest Angle on Lake of the Woods, was built by Sieur de La Vérendrye in 1732 and remained the hub of French exploration over a vast area for a decade. Both posts were intended to control the surrounding Indian tribes and to serve as jumping-off places to search for the Western Sea, the all-water route to the Orient. —R. W. F.

Fort Belknap (Texas). Established in 1851 to protect the road from Fort Smith to Santa Fe and to provide protection from marauding Kiowa and Comanche, Fort Belknap on the Salt Fork of the Brazos River was part of the new defense system in Texas in the 1850s. It was a base for Captain Randolph Marcy's exploration of the Red River in 1852. In 1855 the abortive Comanche reservation was established near the post, and when the army took the offensive against the Comanche in 1858, Fort Belknap was a base for Captain Earl Van Dorn's campaign, which resulted in a victory over the Comanche at Rush Springs. Texas troops occupied the post during the Civil War and used it to operate against the Kiowa and Comanche. After a brief reoccupation by United States troops in 1867, Fort Belknap was abandoned because of an inadequate water supply and was replaced by Fort Griffin and Fort Richardson.—R. N. E.

Fort Bonneville (Wyoming). The fort was built by fur trader Benjamin L. E. Bonneville five miles north of Horse Creek on the Green River (near present-day Daniel, Wyoming) in August 1832. Derided by the trappers as "Fort Nonsense" or "Bonneville's Folly" because of the extreme coldness of the area, it actually was strategically located in a military sense and helps confirm the theory that Bonneville was an agent of the United States government.

See William H. Goetzmann, *Exploration and Empire* (1966).—G. B. D.

Fort Bowie (Arizona). Fort Bowie was established on the east side of Apache Pass by the California Volunteers under General James Henry Carleton in 1862. The strategic pass, with an important spring, was on the Mesilla-Tucson road and Butterfield Trail. It had been the site of the BASCOM AFFAIR in 1861, when Lieutenant Bascom had tried to hold Cochise hostage, and a battle between advance units of the California Column and Apache under Cochise and Mangas Coloradas in 1862. The post, built on a new site in 1868, was of major importance in the Apache campaigns. It watched over the Chiricahua Apache, who were located on a reservation selected by General Oliver Otis Howard and Cochise in 1872. Fort Bowie was a base of operations for General George Crook and General Nelson A. Miles, and Geronimo's band was sent there before entraining for Florida in 1886.—R. N. E.

Fort Bridger (Wyoming). The fort was established on Black Fork of the Green River (present-day western Wyoming) by James Bridger and Louis Vasquez in 1843. The post was important, for its purpose was to sustain the migrants on the Oregon Trail rather than to collect furs. It thus helps mark the conclusion of the mountain trapping era. After conflicts with the Mormon authorities Bridger was forced from the fort in 1853 and Vasquez sold it to the Mormons in 1855. In 1858 the fort became an army post.

See J. Cecil Alter, *James Bridger* (1925).—G. B. D.

Fort Brooke (Florida). Fort Brooke was established at the mouth of the Hillsborough River on Tampa Bay in 1824 after the Treaty of Camp Moultrie had established a reservation for the Seminole in south-central Florida in 1823. A key post during the second Seminole War, Fort Brooke was a gathering place for friendly Indians and the point from which the Seminole were removed to the West. Major Francis Dade and more than one hundred men marched to their death from Fort Brooke in December 1835. General Edmund Gaines also operated from Fort Brooke in 1836, and as late as 1841 the garrison totaled 680 officers and men. Used as a seasonal camp after the Civil War, Fort Brooke was abandoned in 1882.—R. N. E.

Fort Craig (New Mexico). Located on the west bank of the Rio Grande at the northern end of the Jornada del Muerto, Fort Craig was established in 1854 to replace Fort Conrad, nine miles to the north. It was built on private land by mistake and had to be leased by the government. The post was strengthened by General E. R. S. Canby following the Confederate invasion of New Mexico, and although the Confederates won the battle of Valverde at a fort just north of the post, they did not attack Fort Craig itself. After the Confederate retreat it was a base of operations for campaigns against the Apache. The post was abandoned in 1885.—R. N. E.

Fort Crawford (Wisconsin). During the War of 1812, William Clark occupied Prairie du Chien, one of the great crossroads of the frontier, and built Fort Shelby there in 1814. In July the post was surrendered to the British, who renamed it Fort McKay and burned it when they evacuated the area at the end of the war. Fort Crawford was established in 1816 to check the influence of the British in the Northwest and to watch over the Winnebago, Sauk and Fox, Ojibwa, and Sioux, and was an important fort in the western defense system developed after the War of 1812. A series of floods caused its abandonment in 1826, but the Winnebago outbreak in 1827 caused a temporary reoccupation and the construction of a new fort. It was a major treaty ground, the location of a government-operated trading post, and important in the Black Hawk War and in the removal of the Winnebago in 1840. Abandoned in 1849, Fort Crawford was briefly reoccupied in 1855-56 and 1864-65. —R. N. E.

Fort Davis (Texas). The need to protect travel on the San Antonio-El Paso road caused the construction of Fort Davis in 1854 at a site chosen by General Persifor Smith. The post was on a federal mail route and was involved in the army's experimental use of camels. It was abandoned in 1861 by United States troops and was occupied by the Confederates until California troops briefly visited the area in 1862. In 1867 Lieutenant Wesley Merritt built a new stone fort, which grew to more than sixty buildings by 1890. Black soldiers of the Ninth and Tenth Cavalry and Twenty-fourth and Twenty-fifth Infantry who garrisoned the post between 1867 and 1885 campaigned against the Kiowa, Comanche, and Apache and scouted the Llano Estacado, Guadalupe Mountains, and Big Bend country. During 1878 troops from Fort Davis and its subposts had a scouting mileage of 6,724 miles. The Tenth Cavalry from Fort Davis helped disarm Mescalero Apache in 1880 and played a major role in the Victorio campaign by forcing Victorio back into Mexico, where he was killed in 1880. Peace with the Indians caused the abandonment of Fort Davis in 1891. It is now a national monument.—R. N. E.

Fort Defiance (Arizona). The first United States post in Arizona, Fort Defiance was constructed in 1851 to control the Navaho. A by-product of Colonel Edwin Vose Sumner's expedition into Canyon de Chelly, the fort was part of Sumner's defense plan for New Mexico Territory. Several skirmishes were fought in the vicinity during the 1850s, and on April 30, 1860, the post was unsuccessfully attacked by an estimated one thousand Navaho. Abandoned in 1861 because of the Civil War, Fort Defiance became the site of the Navaho Agency in 1868.—R.N.E.

Fort Douglas (Utah). Established in 1862 on a bench overlooking Salt Lake City, Fort Douglas was designed to house United States Army troops assigned to suppress the Indians and discourage the Mormons from possible rebellion against the Union. The camp's first commander, Colonel Patrick E. Connor, sought to subvert the Mormons by encouraging a stampede of miners to Utah Territory. The camp was rebuilt with permanent facilities during the 1870s and 1880s.

Fort Douglas was a key induction and training center during the Spanish-American War and World War I, but its real potential was not realized until the Japanese attack on Pearl Harbor in 1941. At that time, the West Coast's military headquarters moved to the site. After 1945 the facility was used for both military and governmental offices. By 1967, the fort's role in the federal military complex had drastically changed, and its facilities were divided up between the Department of Agriculture, the National Guard, the Veterans Administration, and the University of Utah. In 1972 it was announced that the Fort Douglas property would revert to the University of Utah.

Fort Garland (Colorado). Established in 1858 to replace Fort Massachusetts six miles to the north, Fort Garland protected settlers in the San Luis valley, guarded Sangre de Cristo (La Veta) Pass, and provided protection for travelers on the road to Taos, New Mexico. The two-company post, made of adobe, watched over the Ute and Jicarilla Apache and was the only military installation in southwestern Colorado until the establishment of Fort Lewis at Pagosa Springs in 1878 (moved to the La Plata in 1879). Some fifteen hundred troops were concentrated at Fort Garland following the Meeker Massacre in 1879 and marched to the Los Pinos Agency in 1880, where Fort Crawford was established. The establishments of Fort Crawford and Fort Lewis eliminated the need for Fort Garland, and it was abandoned in 1883.—R.N.E.

Fort Hall (Idaho). The fort was established by Nathaniel Wyeth in 1834 on his second fur-trapping expedition, after the Rocky Mountain Fur Company refused to purchase his goods. It was the first permanent United States post west of the Continental Divide. Located on the Snake River above the mouth of the Portneuf, the post could not sustain the competition of the Hudson's Bay Company and was sold to that corporation in 1837, which in turn abandoned the fort in the winter of 1855-56. The post was later an important way station for migrants to California and Oregon.

See William H. Goetzmann, *Exploration and Empire* (1966).—G.B.D.

Fort Kearny (Nebraska). One of the most important posts on the Oregon Trail, Fort Kearny was established on the south bank of the Platte River in 1848. The trails from the Missouri River towns converged here, and some thirty thousand emigrants passed the post in 1849. It provided protection and assistance to travelers and was the organizational point for Colonel William Harney's 1855 expedition against the Sioux. The gateway to the Plains for some twenty years, Fort Kearny was made obsolete by the Union Pacific Railroad and was abandoned in 1871.—R.N.E.

Fort Laramie (Wyoming). Originally called Fort William, Fort Laramie was built in 1834 by fur traders William Sublette and Robert Campbell at the junction of the Laramie and North Platte rivers. In 1835 it was sold to Fontenelle, Fitzpatrick & Company (which was absorbed by the American Fur Company in 1836) and became increasingly important after the abandonment of the fur-trading rendezvous in 1840. It was also an oasis for those traveling the Oregon Trail. In 1849 Fort Laramie was sold to the United States government for a military post.

See LeRoy R. Hafen and Francis M. Young, *Fort Laramie* (1938).—G.B.D.

Once acquired by the government, Fort Laramie was used to protect travel on the Oregon Trail during the gold rush. It became a shakedown point for countless emigrants before they began the long upgrade haul to the mountains.

The close relationship of the fort with Sioux affairs on the northern Plains began with the Treaty of Fort Laramie in 1851. In 1854 inexperienced Lieutenant John Grattan made an issue of a missing cow or ox (supposedly stolen by Sioux) and led thirty men to their death, causing Colonel William Harney's retaliatory expedition against the Indians the following year. In 1865 Colonel Thomas Moonlight executed two Sioux chiefs. An attempt to remove the friendly Laramie Sioux led to conflict, and the post was a main base for the unsuccessful Powder River expedition against the Sioux and Cheyenne. The site of negotiations with the Sioux in 1866 and 1868, it remained an important post on the northern Plains. Fort Laramie was abandoned in 1890 and is now a national monument.—R.N.E.

Fort Laramie, Treaty of (1851). The Treaty of Fort Laramie was negotiated by United States commissioners Thomas Fitzpatrick and D. D. Mitchell with representatives of the Sioux, Cheyenne, Arapaho, Crow, Arikara, Assiniboin, Mandan, and Gros Ventre. Sometimes called Fitzpatrick's Treaty, or the Treaty of Horse Creek, it divided the Great Plains into specific tracts for each of the signatory tribes, although the concept of the Plains as "one big reservation" for all Indians was retained until the 1860s. Other provisions of the treaty bound the Indians to abstain from warring among themselves, to recognize "the right of the United States Government to establish roads, military and other posts" within the Indian territories, and to make restitution for any future depredations upon other Indians or upon whites.

The United States government promised, in return, that the Indians' lands would be theirs forever, that they would be protected against white depredations, and that the government would distribute among the tribes fifty thousand dollars in supplies and provisions during each of the next fifty years. Before ratifying the treaty, the Senate reduced the annuity period to fifteen years but increased the amount of goods to seventy thousand dollars, a provision that was never ratified by the Indians.

It was hoped that the treaty would protect the increasing traffic on the emigrant road and maintain peace on the Plains, but even if the chiefs had understood the treaty provisions and intended to abide by them, it nevertheless would have been impossible for the signatory individuals to impose their will on other tribesmen. Consequently, the treaty did not end either conflicts among the Indians or incidents between the Indians and emigrant whites, and the "peace" lasted little longer than the treaty conference. Even had the Indians obeyed the treaty strictly, its effect would have been brief, for the discovery of gold in Colorado in 1859 brought in a population of miners, farmers, and speculators with little regard for Indian rights.

The treaty council is described in LeRoy R. Hafen and Francis M. Young, *Fort Laramie and the Pageant of the West* (1938); and Hafen and W. J. Ghent, *Broken Hand, The Life Story of Thomas Fitzpatrick, Chief of the Mountain Men* (1931). For a discussion of the implications of the Senate's revision of the treaty, see Harry Anderson, "The Controversial Sioux Amendment to the Fort Laramie Treaty of 1851," *Nebraska History* (September 1956).—J.T.K.

Fort Larned (Kansas). Designed to protect travel on the Santa Fe Trail, Fort Larned was established in 1859 and immediately became an important way station on the trail. Moved three miles in 1860 and reconstructed of stone during the Indian troubles of the mid-1860s, Fort Larned served as a base for the Cheyenne campaigns of 1864 and the abortive campaigns of 1865 against the Kiowa and Comanche. General Winfield S. Hancock used it as a base in 1867, and it was important in the 1868-69 campaigns on the southern Plains. It was also an Indian agency and a distribution site for annuities and later helped protect construction crews for the Santa Fe Railroad. The completion of the railroad made it obsolete, and Fort Larned was abandoned in 1878.—R.N.E.

Fort Leavenworth (Kansas). Established in 1827 to protect travel on the Santa Fe Trail, Fort Leavenworth was at the head of the Santa Fe, Smoky Hill, and Oregon trails and was an important part of the western defense system. It was a base for western expeditions under Colonel Henry Dodge in 1835 and Colonel Stephen Watts Kearny in 1839 and 1845, and was the point of origin for Kearny's march to New Mexico and California during the Mexican War (1846-48). It was an important supply depot during the Civil War and continued to fulfill that function for several decades as well as being headquarters for the Department of the Missouri. In 1881 a school for infantry and cavalry officers was begun. It became the General Service and Staff School and later the General Staff College, which is still in operation at the fort—R.N.E.

Fort Manuel. See FORT RAYMOND.

Fort Osage. Reaching a narrow portion of the Missouri River near present-day Kansas City on June 23, 1804, Lewis and Clark observed a seventy-foot-high bank that commanded a great eddy. Clark noted that it would "be a good site for a fort and trading house with the Indians" and four years later, when he had become brigadier general of militia in Upper Louisiana, led the St. Charles dragoons west to accomplish the task. Guided by Nathan Boone, they set out on August 25, 1808. Clark's journal of their trip gives the first detailed description of the land route across what became Missouri, following the approximate location of Interstate 70. Eighteen days earlier six keelboats had left Fort Bellefontaine, carrying the commissary and goods of

George C Sibley, the federal Indian factor, and other goods for the Indian trade and maintenance of the fort.

Clark's men erected a square defended by four block-houses with an outwork defended by a single block-house on the point. While the fort was being built, Clark sent word to the Osage to take up residence near the fort if they wished the protection of the United States government. The Indians came gladly, for Governor Meriwether Lewis had declared them and the Kansas Indians beyond protection, thereby inviting other tribes to make war on them. Clark quickly made a treaty in September with the Osage that transferred to the United States government all Osage claims to land east of a line drawn south from Fort Osage to the Arkansas River—virtually half of Missouri and a good part of Arkansas. In return the Indians received annuities, the benefits of the blacksmith shop and smith, a mill, some plows, a house for each of the two great chiefs, use of the government trading house, and cancellation of certain debts. Although the Clark treaty was never ratified, a similar one negotiated by trader Pierre Chouteau two months later was.

The history of Fort Osage falls into two principal periods. The first lasted from 1808 until June 1812, when the need for shortening the defense lines of the Mississippi-Missouri River frontier necessitated its evacuation. During that time it served as the jumping-off place for western trappers and others venturing into the wilderness. Internally it was torn by continuous enmity between the government traders and those private entrepreneurs like the Chouteaus, whom they were underselling and outbidding. There was also friction between the government trading house and the military garrison as Indian warfare increased as a result of the removal of the eastern tribes. During the evacuation, Sibley and John W. Johnson opened trading houses outside the lines: one for the Osage at Arrow Rock, another for friendly Sauk, who had been moved to the Little Moniteau River near present-day Jefferson City.

Sibley returned to Fort Osage in the spring of 1816 to open the second period, which was marked by increasing friction between the Osage and the Cherokee and the consequent decline of the Indian trade. Sibley and the Chouteaus vied increasingly for what remained. With the establishment of military posts farther up the Missouri, the need for a garrison at Fort Osage lessened; it was removed in 1819. The trading house continued for another three years until the private operators secured the passage in March 1822 of a law abolishing the system of federal factors. Sibley closed out his operations in August. The Osage signed away the benefits they had enjoyed under the treaty of 1808. In 1827 the site passed into private hands.

A more thorough account may be found in Kate L. Gregg, "The History of Fort Osage," *Missouri Historical Review* (July 1940). A good study of the man most closely associated with Fort Osage is Charles T. Jones, Jr., *George Champlin Sibley: The Prairie Puritan* (1970).—W.E.P.

Fort Phil Kearny (Wyoming). Designed and constructed by Colonel Henry Carrington in 1866, Fort Phil Kearny was the largest and most important of the forts established to protect travel on the Bozeman Trail to the Montana mines. The large, stockaded post had a brief but eventful history. Red Cloud's Sioux were opposed to use of the Bozeman Trail and constantly harassed Fort Reno and Fort C. F. Smith while concentrating their efforts on Fort Phil Kearny. The Fetterman Massacre of December 21, 1866, and the Wagon-Box Fight of August 2, 1867, occurred near the post. In 1868 the Peace Commission agreed to abandon all three forts because of Sioux intransigence and because the Union Pacific Railroad made the Bozeman Trail unimportant. —R.N.E.

Fort Raymond (Montana). The fort was built by Manuel Lisa at the confluence of the Bighorn and Yellowstone rivers in November 1807 for fur trading. It was in the winter ground of the Crow nation and in an excellent region for game. From this post Lisa sent out his trading expeditions to the Crow tribe. The fort was also known as Fort Manuel and Manuel's Fort.

See Richard E. Oglesby, *Manuel Lisa and the Opening of the Missouri Fur Trade* (1963).—G.B.D.

Fort Rice (North Dakota). Forts Randall and Sully were the only military posts on the upper Missouri when Fort Rice was built in 1864 as one of a series of new forts established on the northern Plains between 1863 and 1866. Intended to protect travel on land and river and to control the Sioux, it was built while General Alfred Sully marched against the Sioux west of the Missouri River. The garrison of United States Volunteers (Galvanized Yankees) at the fort suffered from scurvy and other diseases, and eighty-one men died between October 1864 and May 1865. Fort Rice was the base for Sully's 1865 expedition to Devil's Lake and was the site of councils with the Sioux throughout the later 1860s. In 1871, 1872, and 1873 it was the base of expeditions to the Yellowstone River under Major Joseph Whistler and Colonel D. S. Stanley. The post was abandoned in 1877 after the establishment of Fort Yates.—R.N.E.

Fort Robinson (Nebraska). Constant dangers at the Red Cloud Agency and the murder by Indians of the acting agent led to the permanent establishment of Fort Robinson in 1874, about a mile from the agency. Troops from the post tried unsuccessfully to halt the movement of miners into the Black Hills in 1874, and the post was important during the 1876 Sioux campaign. General George Crook disarmed the Sioux and sent Colonel Ranald Mackenzie on a successful expedition against the Northern Cheyenne under Dull Knife. In 1877 Crazy Horse was bayoneted and killed at the fort as soldiers were attempting to arrest him, and in 1879 some sixty-four Northern Cheyennes who had fled from Indian Territory and been confined at Fort Robinson were killed while attempting to escape. Troops from Fort Robinson were the first to arrive at Pine Ridge (the Red Cloud Agency had been moved about fifty miles north in 1878) during the Ghost Dance uprisings of 1890. During World War I it became a quartermaster remount depot, and during World War II it was a training center for war dogs and a P.O.W. camp. Fort Robinson was abandoned in 1948 and is now a state park. —R.N.E.

Fort Ross (California). Russian settlement. The Ross (short for Russia) settlement in California, on the coast north of San Francisco, was founded in 1812 by a large party of Russians and Aleuts commanded by I. A. Kuskov, an official of the Russian-American Company. The California coast had already supplied the Russians with sea otter pelts, taken by Aleut hunters working off

American ships under contract to the company, and Kuskov had in 1809 and 1811 constructed shelters from Bodega Bay northward. Even earlier, Nikolai Rezanov, after a visit to the presidio of San Francisco, had recommended Russian expansion to California, in part to develop a source of foodstuffs for the Alaskan colonies. Neither function of the new settlement was permanently realized. By the 1820s the sea otters were scarce; the fur seal population declined sharply in the next decade. Both private and company agricultural experiments with grain, fruits, and livestock were disappointing in the foggy summers of the coastal slopes. Potatoes did thrive, but they could be grown in Alaska too. In the 1830s the company manager, Ferdinand Wrangell, failed to strengthen the Russian title to Fort Ross and to extend the company's holdings to more suitable locations inland.

The reduction in peltry, the marginal agricultural activities, and increasing friction with American squatters and Mexican officialdom combined to persuade the Russians to abandon Ross. Attempts to sell the property to the Hudson's Bay Company and to General Mariano Vallejo preceded an agreement with John A. Sutter of Sacramento. Sutter bought Ross for $30,000 in 1841. The property changed hands several times thereafter, eventually going to G. W. Call in 1874, in whose hands it remained until 1903. In 1906 the site was presented to the state of California, which has, with extensive restoration, made it a state historical monument. Fort Ross is now a favorite tourist stop on the beautiful Sonoma coast.

See H. H. Bancroft, *History of Alaska* (1886); and *Quarterly of the California Historical Society* (September 1933).—M.B.S.

forts. The regular army of the United States moved westward across the continent with the expansion of the nation. American sovereignty had to be exerted over new territorial acquisitions, and settlers moving west called for protection against the Indians. The military presence in the West came largely in the form of small installations (variously called posts, forts, camps, cantonments, or barracks), which were built at strategic sites along the lines of communication or in areas of Indian disturbances. They were frequently no more than log palisades with blockhouses at the corners, similar to the defenses thrown up by frontiersmen themselves, but a few of the more permanent posts became imposing structures of brick or stone. In the trans-Mississippi West the forts usually lacked defenseworks altogether and were no more than garrisons to house the troops. The forts, in fact, were seldom attacked. Their importance lay in the presence of the troops, who were a symbol of American authority in the region, and the posts served as bases of operation when campaigns against the Indians became necessary. The history of the western military frontier is primarily the history of the establishment of successive lines of forts as the frontier advanced.

the Revolution to the War of 1812. Having disbanded the army that fought the Revolution, Congress in 1784 began anew to build up a defense organization, for the frontier situation demanded protection and assertion of American authority. With a mere handful of troops, Colonel Josiah Harmar, the first commander, began the construction of a series of small forts along the Ohio, in order to protect the surveyors who were laying out the Seven Ranges and the settlers who were moving down the Ohio in ever larger numbers. Fort Pitt at the confluence of the Monongahela and Allegheny rivers and Fort McIntosh, thirty miles down the Ohio, which had served as forts during the war, were reoccupied in 1784. In September 1785 Fort Harmar was built at the mouth of the Muskingum (present-day Marietta, Ohio), and a temporary post at the mouth of the Miami (Fort Finney) was set up in 1785 for a special treaty with the Indians. Treaties, however, did not pacify the Indians, who continued to object to white settlement north of the Ohio River.

In 1789 the army built Fort Washington at the site of Cincinnati. The fort was the chief outpost in the Northwest for a decade or more and the center from which the attacks of Generals Harmar, Arthur St. Clair, and Anthony Wayne moved against hostile Indians. A series of smaller forts, strung between Fort Washington and the Indian concentrations on the Wabash and the Maumee, furnished depots and refuges for the campaigns. After Wayne's defeat of the Indians at the battle of Fallen Timbers in 1794 and the Treaty of Greenville (1795), in which the Indians ceded much of Ohio, these small posts were abandoned. FORT WAYNE, which had been built at the headwaters of the Wabash in the heart of the Indian country in 1794, remained as a key post in the defense of the Northwest.

The limited number of regular troops allowed by Congress fought against the Indians north of the Ohio; few were available for protection of the settlers in the South, where the Creek, Chickasaw, Choctaw, and Cherokee objected to white encroachment on their lands. These tribes signed peace treaties with the United States after the Revolution, but the aggressive advance of the whites onto lands guaranteed to the Indians by treaty created almost continual tension. Militia troops in the Southwest Territory and in Georgia furnished protection for the settlers and restrained the hostile tribes, but these citizen soldiers were much too agressive against the Indians to be relied upon for the development of a permanent peace. When the Indians of the Northwest were pacified in 1794, a few regular troops were sent to eastern Tennessee (Tellico Blockhouse and Southwest Point) and to Georgia (Fort Wilkinson, near present-day Milledgeville).

The military frontier in the West expanded greatly as the result of diplomatic settlements with Great Britain and Spain. Jay's Treaty in 1794 with Great Britain provided for the transfer of the British posts still maintained on American soil, and in 1796 United States troops received the posts at Niagara and Detroit and Fort Mackinac on Mackinac Island. Pinckney's Treaty with Spain in 1795, which recognized American claims east of the Mississippi south to the thirty-first parallel, made it possible for the army in 1797-98 to garrison posts on the Mississippi evacuated by the Spanish. The troops also built a new post, Fort Adams, on the east bank of the Mississippi in the southeasternmost corner of the United States in 1798, and in 1799 erected Fort Stoddert on the Tombigbee River above Mobile to replace the abandoned Spanish fort in the region.

Fears of foreign intrigue in the Mississippi valley brought emergency plans in 1798 for an augmented army, but the fears proved groundless, and in 1803 dangers from foreign powers in the trans-Mississippi region were removed by the Louisiana Purchase. The new territory, however, expanded American defense lines. In 1804 the army occupied the post at New Orleans and the outlying forts held by the Spanish on the Red and Arkansas rivers. At the same time troops moved into St. Louis, but in 1805 Fort Bellefontaine (on the Missouri just above the confluence with the Mississippi) became the center of army activity on the upper Mississippi. Meanwhile, to overawe the Indians and to protect the government trading house, Fort Dearborn was built in 1803 on the site of the future city of Chicago. To counteract the growing British influence among the northwest tribes, new government trading factories with accompanying military posts were established in 1808 on the Missouri (FORT OSAGE) and on the upper Mississippi (Fort Madison).

By the beginning of the War of 1812 the small American army, with an authorized strength of fewer than ten thousand men, was drawn in a thin line around the periphery of the nation. The posts along the Canadian border were weak, and those along the Mississippi were hardly more impressive. The war itself erased many of the marks of American control in the West. Indians massacred the troops at Fort Dearborn as they evacuated the post in 1812. The troops at Fort Madison abandoned the post, which they considered indefensible, and Fort Mackinac fell to the British and their Indian allies. General William Hull's surrender of Detroit in 1812 meant that the Americans would have to begin anew to gain dominion over the Northwest. The attempt of the Americans to move up the Mississippi in 1814 in order to establish a post at Prairie du Chien (Fort Shelby; see FORT CRAWFORD) was abortive, for the British and the Indians easily forced the garrison to surrender. The defeat of the British and the Indians at the battle of the Thames (October 5, 1813), however, meant that American control of the Northwest was again possible.

In the South hostile Creek were defeated by Tennessee volunteers and regulars under Andrew Jackson in the battle of Horseshoe Bend (March 27, 1814). At Fort Jackson in central Alabama the Creek signed a treaty by which they ceded large tracts of land in Alabama and Georgia.

the War of 1812 to the Mexican War. Although the Treaty of Ghent upheld American claims to the Northwest, the Indians of the area had largely supported the British in the war, and the United States needed to reassert its authority with a show of military strength. The War Department began to block the channels through which the British traders moved into American territory from Canada. The army reoccupied Fort Mackinac in 1815 and in 1816 reestablished Fort Dearborn and built a new post at the mouth of the Fox River (Fort Howard). At the same time troops moved up the Mississippi to build Fort Armstrong on Rock Island and Fort Crawford at Prairie du Chien.

Not satisfied with the line of posts from Green Bay to Prairie du Chien and Rock Island, the War Department soon began a dramatic extension of the military frontier up the Missouri and up the Mississippi to counteract the influence of British traders upon Indians within the United States. The first of these movements was the so-called Yellowstone expedition, which aimed original-

ly to build a post on the Missouri at the mouth of the Yellowstone River or at least as far up the river as the Mandan villages (near present-day Bismarck). This grand scheme was not fulfilled, for transportation difficulties and opposition to the high costs cut short the expedition. Fort Atkinson was built at the Council Bluffs (above present-day Omaha) in 1820, however, and for almost a decade it was the westernmost outpost and one of the largest garrisons in the nation. On the upper Mississippi a key post (eventually named FORT SNELLING) was established in 1819 at the confluence of the Minnesota and Mississippi rivers. Fort Brady, built in 1822 at Sault Ste. Marie, completed the cordon in the Northwest.

A similar advance took place in the Southwest, where white settlement as well as emigrating southern Indians entering Arkansas and the region to the west demanded protection. In 1817 FORT SMITH was established on the Arkansas River at what is now the western border of Arkansas, and in 1822 Fort Jesup was built in western Louisiana, midway between the Red and Sabine rivers, to keep a watchful eye on the Spanish border. As more of the eastern Indians migrated to the West, the army in 1824 built Fort Gibson on the Neosho River near its confluence with the Arkansas and Fort Towson near the Red River to protect the immigrant Indians from the hostile Indians of the Plains. As the new western forts appeared, older posts in the more settled parts of the nation were abandoned.

The army opened two posts of lasting importance in 1826 and 1827. The first was JEFFERSON BARRACKS, on the Mississippi just south of St. Louis, which replaced Fort Bellefontaine and became the most important military post and depot on the upper Mississippi. The other was FORT LEAVENWORTH, on the Missouri River just west of the border of Missouri; it replaced Fort Atkinson, which was considered too far in advance of the frontier. These were administrative moves, determined by a consideration of the overall needs of defense in the West, rather than by needs for protection in a given region. But specific Indian dangers, too, caused the erection of new posts. An incipient uprising of Winnebago Indians in southwestern Wisconsin in 1827 called for more troops to be sent to that area. Fort Crawford at Prairie du Chien, which had been abandoned the year before, was reestablished on higher ground, and Fort Winnebago was built in 1828 at the portage between the Fox and Wisconsin rivers.

In the 1830s the eastern Indians were removed to the trans-Mississippi West. Indians in the North migrated with little disturbance to reservations in Iowa and in the region west of Missouri. Only the Black Hawk War of 1832 marred the generally peaceful movements. In the South the Choctaw, Chickasaw, Creek, and Cherokee created greater problems. They were powerful nations, politically and economically advanced, and with strong attachment to their ancestral lands. Treaties of removal with the Creek and the Cherokee took military force to carry out, but the Indians were eventually transported to lands allotted to them in what is now Oklahoma. The Seminole in Florida were even more adamant in their refusal to migrate. Under the leadership of astute chieftains, they engaged the United States Army in a long and costly war from 1835 to 1842, until at last all but a few of the Seminole were killed or rounded up at FORT BROOKE for removal to the West.

The movement of these thousands of eastern Indians to the West and the advance of white settlement into the valleys of the Mississippi and the Missouri led to extensive planning by the War Department for the defense of the western frontier. Secretary of War Lewis Cass in 1836 drew up a detailed plan for western defense, which consisted fundamentally of a military road running along the frontier and joining an exterior line of military posts. The road was to begin on the Red River near Fort Towson, pass west of Arkansas and Missouri, and join the Mississippi somewhere between the Des Moines and Minnesota rivers. Cass's successor, Joel R. Poinsett, objected to this plan and insisted instead that the lines of communication should run from interior sources of supplies and manpower as radiating spokes to the military posts on the frontier line. General Edmund P. Gaines in 1838 proposed an elaborate plan of his own, which rested upon railroads built by the soldiers to tie the defenseworks together. A board of officers that convened in 1840 offered still another proposal. All the plans, however, were similar in the locations for military posts in the West—a cordon running from Fort Brady or Fort Snelling in the North, down through Fort Leavenworth and Fort Gibson, to Fort Towson or Fort Jesup in the South. Jefferson Barracks was considered a reserve post, where a large disposable force should be maintained, capable of rushing to any part of the frontier when trouble threatened.

The defense of the prairies and the Great Plains, where Indians on horseback could easily escape infantry troops sent to dispell or punish them, called for the reinstitution of mounted troops, which had been discontinued after the War of 1812. For one year (1831) a special battalion of mounted volunteers, called Rangers, was tried, but in the following year Congress authorized a regiment of dragoons. These mounted troops, considered an elite corps, performed valuable service in escorting traders on the Santa Fe Trail and marching on reconnaissance expeditions into the Great Plains, where they impressed the Indians with their military power and rapidity of movement. From new posts built in Iowa (Fort Des Moines, 1835, and Fort Atkinson, 1840) the dragoons explored the prairies of Iowa and Minnesota and made an excursion into Dakota to investigate the activities of Canadian half-breeds, who came into the United States yearly for buffalo hunts. The dragoons, crisscrossing the prairies and the plains, cast a web of American authority over the West that the Indians could not escape.

The nation also faced two threats along her borders that came from foreign disturbances, not Indian dangers. The Texas Revolution (1835-36) upset the peace in the Southwest, and army troops rushed to the Sabine boundary between Louisiana and Texas in 1836, lest the troubles in Texas be the occasion for Indian uprisings and lest the Texas patriots or the Mexican forces violate American soil. Along the northern border the Canadian Rebellion of 1837 and the resulting agitation of "Patriots" on both sides of the line brought imminent danger of war in 1838. But the concentration of troops along the border, the peaceful policy of the United States government, and the prudent action of military commanders eased the tension.

The Canadian border troubles, the Seminole War, and the increasing demands for troops on the western frontier forced a reluctant Congress in 1838 to increase the authorized strength of the regular army from a meager six thousand men, to which the army had been cut in 1821, to ten thousand troops and a proportionate corps of officers.

the Mexican War to the Civil War. The Mexican War (1846-48) seriously disrupted frontier defense plans. Even before the beginning of the war large numbers of troops moved to Texas, leaving the regular posts with skeletal garrisons or with no soldiers at all. Forts Crawford, Winnebago, and Howard in Wisconsin were evacuated, and at other posts handfuls of regulars or temporary volunteers maintained the defenses.

The cession of New Mexico and California to the United States in 1848 was a great turning point in the western military frontier, for vast new regions were opened up to American settlement and exploitation. The mass movement to the Pacific Coast that came after the acquisition of California called for increased military protection, not only in the new regions but also in the Great Plains and the mountains, where Indians resisted the opening of their country that the transcontinental migration effected. The problems of establishing and maintaining new posts were greatly multiplied, for the frontier no longer was along the edge of the settled areas, easily reached by river or road. Scattered now at great distances from the sources of supply and frequently in remote regions that were hard to reach, the posts seriously drained the resources of the War Department.

In Texas alone, between the signing of the Treaty of Guadalupe Hidalgo on February 2, 1848, and the end of 1849, a dozen new military posts were established to ward off Indian incursions and to protect the trails that crossed Texas toward the Far West. The posts stretched along the Rio Grande from Fort Brown near the mouth to El Paso, and another string through central Texas protected the frontier from the Trinity to the Nueces. Army authority in New Mexico was located at Santa Fe (Fort Marcy), Taos, Albuquerque, and Las Vegas, while other troops occupied the Spanish presidios at Monterey and San Francisco on the Pacific.

The Mexican cession was balanced at the north by the acquisition of clear title to the Oregon country south of the forty-ninth parallel. To protect the citizens moving in ever-increasing numbers across the continent to the Pacific Northwest, the War Department established forts not only at Fort Vancouver and Fort Dalles on the Columbia, but also at FORT KEARNY and FORT LARAMIE on the Platte along the path of the emigrants. By 1850, only five years after the onset of the Mexican War, the defense system of the nation had jumped across half a continent, with the military installations in Texas, a string of small posts along the upper Rio Grande in New Mexico, and a scattering of strategically placed posts in California and the Pacific Northwest. It was merely a beginning.

The decade of the 1850s brought a multiplication of military posts, as continual Indian troubles forced expansion of defenses. In Texas a supplementary chain of posts was added, such as FORT DAVIS in 1854 and FORT BELKNAP in 1851, and additional forts appeared along the upper Rio Grande. In 1851 FORT DEFIANCE was built in the heart of the Navaho country, and in the same year FORT UNION was built as a central supply depot in northeastern New Mexico. Also built in New Mexico was FORT CRAIG in 1854. In 1858 FORT GARLAND was established to protect Colorado settlers, and the next year FORT LARNED was established to protect travel on the Santa Fe Trail. In California the native Indians were overrun by the influx of miners that followed the discovery of gold. The Indians were no match for the aggressive wealth-seekers, but their sporadic resistance to the invaders forced the building of scattered forts to protect the settlements on the coast, the mining areas, and the routes of communication to and from the mines. The line of forts extended up into the present state of Oregon, where Indian threats and outbreaks terrified the white inhabitants.

The mid-1850s witnessed serious troubles in present-day Washington. A general outbreak in 1855, known as the Yakima War, brought a new influx of regular troops, who established FORT WALLA WALLA in the southeastern corner of the territory and Fort Simcoe in the Simcoe valley. The same decade brought a heavy concentration of troops in Utah as a result of the Mormon War. The trading post of Fort Bridger in what is now southwestern Wyoming became a United States Army post in 1858, and Camp Floyd (later called Fort Crittenden) was established between Salt Lake City and Provo as a center of American authority until the tensions between the Mormons and their hostile neighbors ended. Fort Ridgely on the Minnesota River (1853), Fort Riley on the Kansas River (1853), and Fort Randall on the upper Missouri (1856) all reflected the movement of white settlers into regions threatened by Indian resistance.

This rapid expansion of military installations caused concern for the War Department. Secretary of War John B. Floyd in 1857 spoke of the need to garrison "68 forts of a large and permanent character, so far, at least, as it is possible to supply men for the purpose; and to occupy 70 posts less permanently established, where the presence of a force is absolutely required." And two years later he scoffed at the use of the term "peace establishment" to describe the army scattered over an area of three million square miles. On the eve of the Civil War the American army was distinctly a western frontier army. The artillery posts along the East Coast had all but lost their garrisons, as imminent dangers in the West called for more and more troops.

the Civil War and after. The Civil War became the center of attention for the army and the nation, but Indian dangers did not disappear nor the need for army garrisons on the frontier. While the fighting was going on in the South, the posts in the West (often with volunteer troops in place of regulars) maintained a patrol in the Indian country.

The secession of the southern states created critical problems for the posts within their borders. General David E. Twiggs, commanding in Texas, surrendered all the federal property under his command to the Confederates, and the regular troops marched out of the posts in April and May 1861, leaving the forts unmanned or turning them over to southern soldiers. The troops in Indian Territory abandoned their posts and marched to Fort Leavenworth. The Confederate invasion of the Territory of New Mexico brought the abandonment or surrender of the military posts there, and Santa Fe and the other principal towns of the territory fell to Confederate control. The victory was short-lived, however, for the aggressive action of Colorado volunteers and then of California volunteers forced the Confederate troops out.

The mining activities in the West did not cease because of the sectional conflict. More military posts in California were established in the 1860s to protect the miners as they moved into new areas, and coastal fortifications, too, were added. In New Mexico and Arizona Indian depredations kept the troops occupied after the retreat of the Confederate forces, and new military posts were set up in strategic positions to control the tribes. In 1862 a fort was built at Tucson, and FORT BOWIE was established at Apache Pass to guard the road to Tucson. In the same year the army built Fort Wingate in the Navaho country and Fort Sumner at the Bosque Redondo on the left bank of the Pecos River to guard Apache and Navaho prisoners. Fort Bascom (1863) on the Canadian River kept the Comanche and Kiowa under control. New posts in the following years appeared at Prescott and at other points in Arizona.

While the attention of the army was turned to the South, the Sioux Indians in 1862 rose up against the whites in the Minnesota River valley. The whites quickly struck back and an Indian war of considerable dimensions resulted. As campaigns were set afoot up the Missouri River into Dakota, Fort Sully and FORT RICE were built and the fur posts of Fort Union and Fort Berthold far up the river became military installations. Fort Totten, Fort Sisseton, and Fort Ransom controlled the Sioux in eastern Dakota and helped to keep open the routes of travel to the mining areas of Montana. Another significant extension of the military frontier was along the Bozeman Trail, which approached the Montana mines from Fort Laramie through the Powder River country of Wyoming. A series of small forts was built to protect the miners on the trail (Fort Reno, FORT PHIL KEARNY, and Fort C. F. Smith). FORT DOUGLAS was built to control Mormons as well as Indians.

Everywhere in the West after the Civil War, as miners and farmers probed into lands claimed by the Indians, military posts sprang up like mushrooms until the whole trans-Mississippi West was dotted with garrisons. Posts along the upper Missouri River in Montana extended the line of forts running through Dakota. In Kansas and eastern Colorado new forts provided bases of operation against the hostile Kiowa and Comanche of the Southern Plains and protected the newly developed routes of emigrants to Colorado. When the mining frontier moved into Nevada, Oregon, and Idaho, the call for military protection was answered by a group of one-company posts, most of which had a very short existence.

Another function of the military in the West was the protection of Indian reservations, as the government pursued its policy of concentrating Indians at spots where they could be watched and provided for. In 1870 the army established garrisons at the Indian agencies along the upper Missouri, three of which were turned into regular military posts—Fort Hale at Lower Brulé Agency, Fort Bennett at Cheyenne River Agency, and Fort Yates at Standing Rock. But there was a widening of the military frontier in other areas as well. Fort Sup-

ply and FORT SILL in Indian Territory were opened in
1868 and 1869 to serve against the Kiowa, Comanche,
and other hostiles of the Great Plains, while in Arizona a
sprinkling of new forts appeared, including Fort
Apache (1870) on the White Mountain River. In 1874
FORT ROBINSON was established because of constant Indian threat at the Red Cloud Agency.

The transcontinental railroads, which the Indians
knew would open channels for white penetration of
their lands, needed extensive military protection, and
new posts were established to protect the crews who laid
the rails. Fort D. A. Russell at Cheyenne and Fort Fred
Steele at Rawlins guarded the Union Pacific as it moved
west across Wyoming. In 1872 Fort Seward, at the
Northern Pacific crossing of the James River, and Fort
Abraham Lincoln, on the Missouri near present-day
Bismarck, were built to protect the construction crews.

The 1870s were a time of wars on the Plains. The
government declared that agency Indians who were not
on their reservations by January 31, 1876, were to be
considered hostiles, and when the ultimatum was not
met, the army prepared for action. Soon the army found
most of the Sioux and Cheyenne warriors arrayed
against it, and steps were taken to begin their subjugation. Three columns of troops began to move against the
Indians in Montana, and it was in this campaign that the
"massacre" of General George A. Custer's troops at the
Little Big Horn occurred.

This victory did the Indians little good, however, for
reinforcements were rushed into Indian country, and
the Sioux chiefs were relentlessly pursued until they
were captured or driven into Canada. Defenses in the
West were strengthened by the erection of new, permanent fortifications in the region where Indian troubles
were centered. In 1876 Congress appropriated money
for two new posts on or near the Yellowstone—Fort
Keogh, built at the mouth of the Tongue River, and Fort
Custer, erected at the junction of the Big Horn and the
Little Big Horn rivers. At the same time the army established Fort Missoula in Flathead country and Fort
Meade in the Black Hills.

Along the Oklahoma-Texas border the Red River
War of 1874-75 was the last major struggle, and additional posts in the area served the troops engaged in the
operations. In 1874 Fort Reno was located on the north
fork of the Canadian River, near the Cheyenne and
Arapaho Indian Agency, and the next year another
cantonment was built farther up the river. To aid in the
opening of a cattle route that would avoid the settlements in Indian Territory and Kansas, Fort Elliott was
established in the Texas panhandle in 1875.

The victories over the Indians on the Northern and
Southern Plains marked the high point of post-Civil
War military action against the western Indians. In the
1880s the general movement was toward retrenchment
rather than expansion of the military frontier. The
tribes were placed on reservations where they became
dependent upon government supplies for their existence. At the same time the extension of the railroad
network made it possible to transport troops quickly to
areas where they were needed. With settlers swarming
into the region, the posts along the Missouri River no
longer served a useful purpose, and one by one they
passed out of existence. What was true along the upper
Missouri was true in other parts of the West as well.

Everywhere there was consolidation of troops and abandonment of the smaller posts. The secretaries of war
rejoiced at the economy and improved conditions for
discipline and instruction of the troops that this concentration afforded.

The year 1886 was a busy one for the troops in the
Southwest, who pursued and finally captured
Geronimo and his band. But consolidation was going on
apace, and if new posts appeared in the West, Indians
were not the reason for their establishment. Camps
Medicine Butte and Pilot Butte in western Wyoming
were set up in 1885 to control anti-Chinese rioting along
the construction route of the Union Pacific, and Fort
Logan, built at Denver in 1887, resulted from pressure
of civic-minded citizens, who thought that a military
post would be good for the business of the region.

In 1891 the secretary of war declared that a quarter of
the posts that had been occupied in 1889 had since been
given up, and ten or twelve more were set for abandonment as soon as suitable shelter for the troops could be
found at other garrisons. By 1892 the War Department
believed that the Indian wars were at an end. "In the
march of population and civilization westward," the department's annual report asserted, "that which was so
long known as the frontier has disappeared." In that
year ninety-six posts were reported, thirty-three of them
located east of the Mississippi. At the end of 1894 the
number of posts had been reduced to eighty, and the
next year saw another small reduction. It was then simply a matter of housing the troops of the peacetime
army, and all sections of the country wanted to be considered. By 1895, although some small forts in the Indian areas were retained, especially to guard reservations, the troops were spread more or less equally over
the whole United States. The defense of the western
frontier was over.

(See also ARMY ON THE FRONTIER; and ARMY TERRITO-
RIAL COMMANDS.)

A brief account of frontier defense, together with a
catalog of regular army posts and detailed maps showing their location is Francis Paul Prucha, *A Guide to the
Military Posts of the United States, 1789-1895* (1964). Essential information about forts west of the Mississippi is
given, state by state, in Robert W. Frazer, *Forts of the
West: Military Forts and Presidios and Posts Commonly
Called Forts West of the Mississippi River to 1898* (1965).
For excellent illustrations of western forts, see the four
volumes in the Western Forts Series, by Herbert M. Hart
(1963-67). A full story of frontier defense appears in
Francis Paul Prucha, *The Sword of the Republic: The United States Army on the Frontier, 1783-1846* (1969), and
Robert M. Utley, *Frontiersmen in Blue: The United States
Army and the Indian, 1848-1865* (1967) and *Frontier Regulars: The United States Army and the Indian, 1866-1891*
(1974).—F.P.P.

Fort St. Charles. See FORT BEAUHARNOIS AND FORT
ST. CHARLES.

Fort Sill (Oklahoma). General Philip Sheridan's 1868-
69 campaign against the tribes of the southern Plains
indicated the need for a post in the heart of the Indian
country. Established in 1869 by the Tenth Cavalry on a
site selected by General Benjamin Grierson, Fort Sill was
also the location of the Kiowa-Comanche Agency.
Atrocities on the reservation and raids into Texas
caused the arrest of three Kiowa leaders on the front

porch of Grierson's headquarters in 1871. Fort Sill was a major base of operations in the Red River War of 1874-75 and in 1894 it became the new home for Geronimo and the Chiricahua Apache who had been imprisoned in Florida. In 1911 the Field Artillery School was located at Fort Sill, which continues to be an important army post.—R.N.E.

Fort Smith (Arkansas). The city of Fort Smith is at the western border of the state. It lies on the south bank of the Arkansas River at the mouth of the Poteau River, and is the seat of Sebastian County. First known as Belle Point, a United States Army post was established there in 1817 and named Fort Smith for General Thomas A. Smith. Adjacent to the post a settlement grew up, which was also called Fort Smith and which in 1829 received a post office by that name. In 1834 the army fort was abandoned, but in 1838 a new post was built and garrisoned. The same year, Captain John Rogers, a retired army officer who owned the land adjacent to the new post, plotted and sold lots at public auction in his "town of Fort Smith." Four years later, in 1842, Fort Smith was incorporated as a town; it was chartered as a city with the mayor-council form of government in 1851. The town and city flourished as the site of Fort Smith Post, as the supply base for the Indian Service, and as a shipping and commercial center at the head of navigation on the Arkansas. It was the jumping-off place in 1849-50 for several California-bound wagon trains, the outfitting of which brought good profits to its merchants. The city, in 1858, became an important station on John Butterfield's Overland Stage Line, being at the juncture of the St. Louis-Fort Smith and Memphis-Fort Smith branches of the line.

The Civil War brought five years of struggle and economic stagnation, but the city regained its prosperity with peace. The post continued as a garrison until 1871, and since 1872 the city has been the seat of the United States District Court for the Western District of Arkansas. There Judge Isaac PARKER held court from 1875 to 1896. In the twentieth century Fort Smith developed as an industrial city with factories turning out wood, metal, paper, glass, fabric, and electronic products. A large natural gas field surrounds the area, as well as the valuable Arkansas-Oklahoma coalfield. It is also a center for cattle raising, truck farming, and of the poultry industry. World War II saw the establishment of Fort Chaffee, a huge installation for training armored forces, which was abandoned after the Korean War but is still used as a training area for the United States Army Reserve and National Guard. The completion, in 1970, of the Arkansas River Navigation Channel, which allows the largest river barges to reach the city, promises to be an economic boon to the city. Its population in 1970 was 62,802.—W.L.B.

Fort Snelling (Minnesota). In 1820 Colonel Josiah Snelling laid the cornerstone of the fortress that became Fort Snelling. It was the only United States military post in the Northwest north of a line from Prairie du Chien, Wisconsin, to the Pacific. Strategically located on the crest of the bluff above the junction of the Minnesota and Mississippi rivers, the fort was the only tangible evidence of United States sovereignty in a vast unsettled wilderness. Its Indian agent, Lawrence TALIAFERRO, kept an uneasy peace between the Sioux and Ojibwa Indians.

Within its walls, the first school in Minnesota opened its doors in 1823 and the first hospital and circulating library came into being. The fort's brass band and its amateur theater were the first such entertainments on the Minnesota frontier, and the first Protestant church in the area was organized there in 1835. The post's commandant directed the first development of the region's natural resources, harnessing the water power of the Falls of St. Anthony to run Minnesota's first sawmill and gristmill. Near its walls gathered the pioneers who founded the Twin Cities of St. Paul and Minneapolis.

Fort Snelling continued to be the cradle of settlement in the Northwest until Minnesota entered the Union as a territory in 1849. In the 1860s it served as a rendezvous point for all the Minnesota troops mustered into the Union army during the Civil War, and its military functions continued through all of the nation's wars until 1946, when the fort's 126-year career as an army post came to an end.

See Marcus Hansen, *Old Fort Snelling* (1958); and Marilyn Ziebarth and Alan Ominsky, *Fort Snelling: Anchor Post of the Northwest* (1970).—R.W.F.

Fort Stanwix, Treaty of (1768). Indian treaty. During the years immediately following the Proclamation of 1763 it became apparent to British policy-makers, both in England and the colonies, that the Proclamation Line would not contain colonial expansion and that settlers were in fact already established beyond the Appalachian crest. Fearing that a general frontier Indian war might erupt, the Lords of Trade and the Privy Council in 1767 authorized the Indian superintendents in America to negotiate a new boundary with the Indians, to be west of the Proclamation Line. Northern district Indian superintendent Sir William Johnson accordingly summoned the Six Nations (Iroquois) and their allies and dependents to meet with him in September 1768 at Fort Stanwix, on the upper Mohawk River in New York.

Indian and white agents began to gather on September 19. Colonial officials present during the conference in addition to Johnson included Thomas Penn, lieutenant governor of Pennsylvania; Richard Peters and James Tillman, members of the Pennsylvania Council; William Franklin, governor of New Jersey; Frederick Smith, chief justice of New Jersey; Thomas Walker, official commissioner from Virginia; and George Croghan, deputy Indian superintendent; as well as numerous individual traders and speculators pursuing private interests. Iroquois representatives were slow in arriving, and the conference did not officially open until October 24, by which time there were 2,200 Indians present, including all the leading sachems of the Six Nations, Delaware, and eastern Shawnee. If the legitimacy of an Indian treaty is determined by the authority and position of the negotiators, then this treaty was the most important of the colonial era.

Johnson's long and intimate association with the Iroquois had gained him much practical insight into the Indians' character, and he wasted little time in preliminaries. Displaying twenty boatloads of trade goods to the assemblage, he offered an immediate exchange for a grant of land to the king. Supplementing this general bounty with large private gifts to influential Iroquois leaders, Johnson gained a quick acquiescence from the Indians, who were themselves desirous of establishing a definite boundary, particularly between the

Mohawk and upper Susquehanna river valleys, where white settlement was encroaching on the heart of the Iroquois homeland. After a period of discussion on the exact terms of the cession, a treaty was signed on November 5.

In return for goods valued at £10,460, seven shillings, and threepence sterling, the Indians ceded to the crown all lands lying east and south of a line beginning at the mouth of the Tennessee (Cherokee) River on the Ohio, running up the south bank of the Ohio and Allegheny rivers to Kittaning village above Fort Pitt, thence directly to the west branch of the Susquehanna River and down it to the mouth of Tiadaughton Creek, up that creek and along the north side of Burnett's Hills to upper Awandee Creek, down Awandee Creek to the east branch of the Susquehanna River, up that river's east bank to Oswego village, thence due east to the Delaware River and up its west branch to a point due south of where Tianaderha Creek empties into the Susquehanna, across to that creek and up to its head, and thence directly to the mouth of Canada Creek on Wood Creek at the west end of the portage from Fort Stanwix to Lake Oneida.

The original intent of Johnson and the British government had been to establish a line only as far west as the mouth of the Great Kanawha River on the Ohio, where the line being negotiated by southern district superintendent John Stuart was expected to terminate. The extension of the Fort Stanwix line three hundred miles farther west was apparently the result of machinations by land speculators, who wished to obtain lands in the Kentucky country. The Six Nations were quite amenable to this extension, and in fact insisted on it, since their claim to those lands were tenuous; they saw British acceptance of their cession as proof that they, not the Cherokee, had really ruled that region. Whether or not the British government, as distinct from their colonial agents, intended the new Indian boundary to authorize settlement west of the 1763 Proclamation Line, is still a matter of debate. In reality, settlers continued to push into the country between the two lines, and beyond, with little regard for proclamations, treaties, governors, or Indians; and the speed of that advance was probably affected not at all by the government's efforts at Indian diplomacy.

See C. W. Alvord, *The Mississippi Valley in British Politics* (1917); and Max Farrand, "The Indian Boundary Line," *American Historical Review*, vol. 10 (July 1905). The minutes of the treaty council, treaty text, and official map of the line and Johnson's report to his superiors are printed in E. B. O'Callaghan, ed., *Documents Relative to the Colonial History of New York*, vol. 8 (1857).—P.R.M.

Fort Stanwix, Treaty of (1784). Indian treaty. This was the first Indian treaty negotiated by the United States government after the American Revolution and involved not only Indian-white relations, but also the controversy over the powers of the national government under the Articles of Confederation versus the powers of the individual states. During the war, the campaigns of Sullivan and Brodhead into the country of the Six Nations (Iroquois) in New York and Pennsylvania had greatly reduced the Iroquois' strength. Sporadic Indian raids continued, however, and after the British surrender the Continental Congress and the governments of

New York and Pennsylvania determined to conclude a quick peace with the Six Nations. New York and Pennsylvania wished also to take advantage of the Indians' weakened condition to exact land cessions. Accordingly, all three governments began in the fall of 1783 to prepare for individual councils with the Iroquois. Governor Clinton of New York arranged to meet the Indians at Fort Stanwix in the summer of 1784, and suspicions of his intentions by Pennsylvania and the Congress led the commissioners of these governments to arrive at the same time and place.

In a series of conferences between August 31 and October 23, the white representatives clashed bitterly over the question of which government had the right to deal with the Indians for land. In the process they concluded two separate treaties, neither of which resolved the problem. Governor Clinton decided a better day would come to settle the matter of land cessions within New York and went home in early September without accomplishing anything but stirring up ill will between his state and the Congress. The congressional commissioners, backed by several hundred soldiers, dictated on October 23 a treaty of peace between the Iroquois and the United States. By its terms the western boundary of the Six Nations was established, running from Niagara roughly parallel to the western borders of present New York and Pennsylvania south to the Ohio River; and the Indians handed over six chiefs as hostages for the safe return of white prisoners—which occurred soon after. In separate negotiations on the same day, Pennsylvania secured a cession of all Iroquois lands lying within its borders that had not already been ceded in the 1768 Treaty of Fort Stanwix—amounting to a quarter of the state's present area.

The treaties' effects were more than immediate. Future Presidents Monroe and Madison were both present at the conference and took away definite ideas about Indian diplomacy and the relation of state to national jurisdiction. The easy acquiescence of the Seneca leader Cornplanter led to his decline and the emergence of the famous Red Jacket as the Iroquois' champion. And the specific failure to determine the precise jurisdiction of state or nation over the Iroquois' affairs led to administrative difficulties that adversely affected these Indians well into the twentieth century.

See H. S. Manley, *The Treaty of Fort Stanwix: 1784* (1932).—P. R. M.

Fort Union (Montana). The fur-trading fort was built by Kenneth Mackenzie of the Upper Missouri Outfit of the American Fur Company on the north bank of the Missouri River five miles above the mouth of the Yellowstone. Construction began in 1829 and the fort was placed in full operation in 1833. The steamboat *Yellowstone* reached the fort in 1832. The fort was designed to tap the trade of the Blackfoot country. It was purchased by the United States government and torn down in 1866.

See Herbert M. Hart, *Old Forts of the Northwest* (1963).—G. B. D.

Fort Union (New Mexico). Lieutenant Colonel Edwin Vose Sumner was sent to command the Ninth Military Department (New Mexico Territory) in 1851 and immediately began to revise the system of defense. On July 26 he established Fort Union and moved his headquarters from Santa Fe ("that sink of vice and extravagance") to the new post. Strategically located near the junction of the Mountain and Cimarron branches of the Santa Fe Trail, the post provided protection for travel and acted as a deterrent to nearby Ute and Jicarilla Apache. It was a base of operations during the Jicarilla War of 1854 and the Ute War of 1855, and troops from Fort Union participated in a campaign against the Kiowa and Comanche in 1860-61, destroying a village of 175 lodges on the Cimarron River. During the Civil War a large earthen star-shaped fort was constructed, which served as a staging ground for the Colorado Volunteers before their victory over the Confederates at Glorieta Pass. A new fort of adobe and brick was begun in 1863 by General James Henry Carleton and served as military post, quartermaster depot, and ordnance depot. The arrival of the railroad in 1879 ended its utility, and Fort Union was abandoned in 1891. It is now a national monument.

See Chris Emmett, *Fort Union and the Winning of the Southwest* (1965).—R. N. E.

Fort Vancouver (Washington). The fort was founded by the Hudson's Bay Company in 1824-25 as the headquarters of its Columbia Department. It was located on the north bank of the Columbia River six miles above its junction with the Willamette River and about one hundred miles from its mouth. A fur-trading post and supply depot, it was the chief settlement in the Pacific Northwest. In 1845 the supply depot of the Columbia Department was moved to Fort Victoria on Vancouver Island, and in 1849 the departmental headquarters followed. In 1860 the company abandoned the post. The Department of War used the fort as a military post after the Mexican cession in 1848.

See John A. Hussey, *Fort Vancouver* (1957).—G. B. D.

Fort Walla Walla (Washington). The Yakima War and continued Indian trouble in the Northwest caused the establishment of Fort Walla Walla in 1856 to control the Yakima Indians and to enforce General John Wool's determination to prevent white settlement east of the Cascades. In 1858 Lieutenant Colonel Edward Steptoe led an expedition from Fort Walla Walla against hostile factions of Spokane, Coeur d'Alene, Yakima, and Palouse that nearly ended in disaster, and Colonel George Wright used it as a base for his expedition of the same year, which crushed the resistance of the Spokane tribe. Troops stationed there also participated in the Nez Percé War in 1877 and the Bannock War of 1878. It was abandoned in 1911.—R. N. E.

Fort Wayne (Indiana). Fort Wayne was established by General Anthony Wayne in 1794 at the strategic location that controlled the portage between the Maumee and Wabash rivers. It had been the site of a French and later British post, which fell to the Indians during Pontiac's Rebellion. General Josiah Harmar was defeated in the vicinity in 1790.

Fort Wayne was also the site of an Indian agency, a government-operated trading post, and several councils and treaties with the Indians, including the Treaty of Fort Wayne in 1809, which was rejected by Tecumseh. During 1812 it was besieged by the Indians. The fort was abandoned in 1819.—R. N. E.

Fort William. See BENT'S FORT.

Fort Worth, Texas. On June 6, 1849, Major Ripley A. Arnold established a military post on the Clear Fork branch of the Trinity River. He named it Fort Worth in honor of General William J. Worth, who had died a month earlier. A few merchants gathered nearby to open stores, and they chose to retain the name of Fort Worth for their settlement when the army closed the fort in 1853. Seven years later, after the state legislature created Tarrant County, the voters chose Fort Worth as the county seat and thereby ensured its survival. However, growth was slowed by the Civil War, and not until 1873 was the city incorporated, at which time it had a population of only five hundred.

During the hard years of Reconstruction in Texas, merchants in Fort Worth prospered by selling supplies to cowboys and cattlemen pushing their herds north along the Chisholm Trail. Then on July 19, 1876, the Texas and Pacific Railroad pushed its tracks into the city, and stock pens hastily were built in anticipation of Fort Worth becoming a major shipping point. Merchants in the city specialized in supplying ranchers to the west as far as the Panhandle, making their town a supply and distributing point. In addition, farmers in the vicinity of Fort Worth began raising wheat, and in 1878 the first elevator was constructed. Cattle and milling therefore produced the income for residents of the city, especially after 1890 when the first major packing plant opened there. Gradually Fort Worth had made itself the southwestern center for the processing of beef and flour.

Early in the twentieth century came two major advances: the erection of a dam on the west fork of the Brazos River, at once controlling flooding and creating Lake Worth as a permanent water supply; and the discovery of oil in Wichita County in 1911 and in other nearby counties shortly thereafter, making Fort Worth a major center for oil-well supplies as well as the headquarters for several oil companies.

At the outbreak of World War I in 1914, the Canadian government established three air training fields near Fort Worth. When the United States entered that conflict in 1917, these bases were taken over for the training of American flyers, while Camp Bowie was opened to train soldiers. These posts were later closed, but aviation became a permanent part of the city's future. During World War II, Tarrant Field was established there (to become Carswell Air Force Base in 1948), and Consolidated Aircraft Corporation began manufacturing airplanes in the city. Since the end of that conflict, aviation has joined beef, flour, and oil as a base of the economy of the city. Moreover, city fathers made a concerted effort to diversify the economy; items now manufactured in Fort Worth include containers, machinery, and automobiles, while breweries and food processors have contributed to the economy.

Fort Worth, in addition to being a distributing point for much of West Texas, also has been an educational center. It is the site of Texas Christian University, Texas Wesleyan University, the Southwestern Baptist Theological Seminary, and several junior colleges. The AMON CARTER MUSEUM OF WESTERN ART is nationally famous. It is endowed by Amon G. Carter (1879-1955), who for many years was editor and publisher of the Fort Worth *Star-Telegram*. The population of the city, which reached 26,668 in 1900, grew to 393,476 in 1970, but the residents never turned their backs on their regional heritage. They have advertised their city as "Out Where the West Begins," and they refer affectionately to it as

"Cowtown." Both are true, although with a modern flavor.

See Oliver Knight, *Fort Worth: Outpost on the Trinity* (1960), and R. H. Talbert, *Cowtown-Metropolis* (1956). —O. B. F.

forty-niners. See GOLD AND SILVER RUSHES; PROSPECTOR.

forty-niners, trails of the. With the discovery of gold in California in 1848, the gold-seeking forty-niners, or Argonauts, came to the Pacific Slope by both sea and land. The sea routes drew the heaviest traffic during the winter and early spring of 1849, before it was convenient and safe to travel across the Great Plains and through the passes of the Rockies and the Sierra. The most reliable and comfortable water route was around the tip of South America at Cape Horn, but the journey was long, eighteen thousand nautical miles, and took anywhere from five to eight months. The sea route could be shortened by a land crossing through Panama, Nicaragua, or Mexico. The United States Congress had granted subsidies to two steamship companies prior to the discovery of gold: the UNITED STATES MAIL STEAMSHIP COMPANY, operating between New York and Chagres on the Atlantic side of the Isthmus of Panama; and the Pacific Mail Steamship Company from Panama, on the Pacific, to California and Oregon. Travel across the Isthmus on foot or with a pack animal was difficult, costly, and unhealthy, because cholera, dysentery, and yellow fever were rampant. The pressure of the crowds was so great that obtaining passage on the steamer coming up the Pacific Coast was uncertain. Some travelers chose the longer crossing by way of Nicaragua because of the overcrowding in Panama. Still others crossed Mexico, and if water transportation proved unavailable on the Pacific shore, many elected to make their way to California by land.

At least twice as many gold-seekers traveled to California by land as by sea. Every known route along the valleys of the rivers tributary to the Missouri were traversed in 1849. The most popular route was the CALIFORNIA TRAIL by way of the Platte River, the South Pass, and the Humboldt River. The migration in 1849 differed from that of earlier seasons; because of the numbers on the trail, there no longer was any danger of getting lost or the threat of an Indian attack. However, so many traversed the favored routes that the grass supply was exhausted, and some parties had to make detours to find food for their animals. The water holes became infected with the dread Asiatic cholera and many perished along the road. The desert crossing between the sink of the Humboldt River and that of the Carson River, a distance of forty miles without water, proved an ordeal. Wagons and property were many times abandoned along this stretch of the trail, as the Argonauts struggled for survival. On reaching the Sierra, slightly more than half chose the direct route westward by way of the Truckee River, though many, frightened by the reputation of the DONNER TRAIL, elected to use Carson Pass about twenty miles south of Lake Tahoe.

Many travelers starting out along the PLATTE RIVER chose alternate routes to California. A number of forty-niners branched off the main California Trail at Fort Bridger in Wyoming, traveling to Salt Lake City and southwestward through Utah to the Colorado River,

thence westward across the Mojave Desert and into southern California. Some parties eager to reach the gold fields without going so far south struck out westward from the Colorado River and experienced death and disaster in an attempt to cross the area now known as Death Valley. Others turned off the California Trail at the bend of the Humboldt in north central Nevada and started through the Black Rock Desert, expecting to swing north of the Sierra and into the upper end of the Sacramento valley. This roundabout way was known as Peter Lassen's Cutoff. The comparative popularity of the various alternate routes is indicated by extant diaries. Of the 132 diarists on the overland trails in 1849, 110 went west along the California Trail. A surprising number of 41 out of the 110 chose the Lassen Cutoff. Of the remaining 69 who continued down the Humboldt to its sink, 37 took the Truckee route across the Sierra, and 32 chose the Carson route. In the early 1850s the majority of wagon trains elected the Carson route, largely because Mormon way stations had been established on the trail, where supplies could be replenished. Those insisting on crossing the Sierra farther north had three passes to chose from: Donner, Henness, or Beckwourth.

Southern routes to the gold fields were also popular, with the routes across Texas converging at El Paso and continuing west by way of the Gila River. Santa Fe became a rendezvous for those using the old SANTA FE AND CHIHUAHUA TRAIL along the Arkansas River or those ascending the Canadian River. Here some turned south along the Rio Grande to pick up the Gila route, and others turned northwesterly across the Grand and Green rivers by way of the OLD SPANISH TRAIL to the Colorado River. Crossing the desert west of Yuma proved as difficult for many as was the section between the Humboldt and Carson sinks on the California Trail. Tens of thousands were on the various overland trails in 1849, participating in one of the largest folk movements in modern history.

John H. Kemble, *The Panama Route, 1848-1869* (1943), is a standard, scholarly account of the Panama steamer lines. Oscar Lewis, *Sea Routes to the Gold Fields* (1949), describes in a popular style all aspects of travel by ocean. An early account of the various land journeys is Owen Coy's *The Great Trek* (1931). Ralph P. Bieber, *Southern Trails to California in 1849* (1937), is authoritative and concentrates on original sources. Two distinguished scholars, Dale Morgan in *The Overland Diary of James Avery Pritchard, 1849* (1959) and David M. Potter in *Trail to California: The Overland Journey of Vincent Geiger and Wakeman Bryarly* (1945), incorporate the latest statistical analysis and interpretation of the rush of 1849 in their introductions—W. T. J.

Fraeb, Henry (?-1841). Fur trader. Little is known of the early life of Fraeb, known to his fellow mountain men as "Old Frapp." Contemporaries reported that he was a German from St. Louis, who spoke with a heavy "Dutch" accent. Still less is known of Fraeb's entrance into the fur trade; initial reports in 1829 reveal that he was enough of a veteran at that time to be a leader of trappers. He emerged from the shadows in 1830, when he joined Thomas Fitzpatrick, Milton Sublette, James Bridger, and Jean B. Gervais as a founder and proprietor of the ROCKY MOUNTAIN FUR COMPANY.

Fraeb spent the next four years leading a variety of expeditions for the Rocky Mountain Fur Company that carried him as far afield as northwestern Idaho and northern Arizona. At the 1834 rendezvous on Ham's Fork on the Green River Fraeb was the first partner to sell out. Sublette's brother, William, bought his share for "Forty head of horse beast, forty beaver traps, eight guns, and one thousand dollars worth of merchandise." In the summer of 1837 Fraeb formed a partnership, backed by Pratte, Chouteau & Co. of St. Louis, with Peter Sarpy and began working the South Platte region. The partners built Fort Jackson as the base for their operations and sent out trading expeditions to the north and south. Competition in the area proved to be too intense, however, and in 1838 Sarpy and Fraeb sold out to Bent & St. Vrain.

In 1840 Fraeb formed yet another partnership, this time with Jim Bridger. In the summer of 1841 the partners began building the first Fort Bridger, on the west band of the Green River. While on a hunting expedition southeast of the fort, a party of trappers led by Fraeb encountered a band of Cheyenne, Arapaho, and Sioux. In the ensuing battle "Old Frapp" was killed.

See LeRoy R. Hafen, "Henry Fraeb," in Hafen, ed., *The Mountain Men and the Fur Trade of the Far West*, vol. III (1966), and "Fraeb's Last Fight and How Battle Creek Got Its Name," *Colorado Magazine* (May 1930); and Dale L. Morgan and Eleanor T. Harris, eds., *The Rocky Mountain Journals of William Marshall Anderson* (1967).—R. B. W.

Franchère, Gabriel (1786-1863). Fur trader. Of the several written accounts describing the Astorian phase of American fur trade, none is better than that of Franchère, one of John Jacob Astor's young clerks. Franchère was born in Montreal, Canada, and worked in his father's mercantile business. In 1810 he signed on with Astor's enterprise and departed from New York aboard the *Tonquin*.

Franchère kept notes in his journal of the voyage, the founding of Astoria, the sale of the post to the North West Company, and most of the incidents in the Oregon country until 1814, when he returned to Montreal. The journal was first published in 1820 in a French edition and translated into English a generation later. Shortly after his return, Franchère was made Montreal agent of the American Fur Company, a post he held for twenty years. He then served as the company's agent at Sault Ste. Marie until 1842, when the American Fur Company went into bankruptcy—a collapse that appears to have inflicted heavy personal financial losses on Franchère as well.

In spite of these reverses, Franchère remained in the fur business; in 1842 he became New York agent for Pierre Chouteau, Jr. & Company and in 1857 with his son-in-law took over the business from Chouteau. He remained actively engaged in this partnership until his death.

See Gabriel Franchère, *Journal of a Voyage on the North West Coast of North America during the Years 1811, 1812, 1813 and 1814*, edited by W. Kaye Lamb (1969). —R. B. W.

Franciscan missions. See NEW MEXICO MISSIONS; RoMAN CATHOLIC MISSIONARIES; and entries on individual missions.

Frank, Michael (1804-1894), Wisconsin reformer and politician. Frank was born in Virgil, New York, and came to Southport (Kenosha), Wisconsin, in 1839, where he and Christopher L. Sholes founded the first newspaper in Kenosha County. While in the territorial legislature (1843-46), he won support for establishing the first free school in Kenosha, Wisconsin (1845), and with others got public education written into the constitution of 1848, earning him the title of "father of Wisconsin's free school system." He then became state assemblyman (1861), university regent (1861-66), Kenosha postmaster (1861-66), and co-editor of the Beloit *Journal* (1869-70). Throughout his career, Frank supported abolition, free schools, temperance, and other reforms.

See L. P. Jorgenson, *The Founding of Public Education in Wisconsin* (1956).—W. D. W.

Franklin, Benjamin (1706-1790). Philosopher, statesman, inventor, and man of letters. Although Franklin was as great a devotee of urban living as America ever produced, he was deeply involved in western matters. He once held a mortgage on the Daniel Boone family farm; as "General" Franklin, he fought Indians in northeastern Pennsylvania; transport that he had collected rolled General Edward Braddock to defeat before Fort Duquesne; his advice shaped the policy toward the American West of a British secretary of state (Lord Shelburne, 1766-68); and he helped win the West from the British at the Paris Peace Conference of 1782. But the primary reason why Franklin should be discussed in the context of the West is that, with the possible exception of Frederick Jackson Turner, no man ever wrote on its role in shaping the character of American life with as much influence and conviction.

Like Turner, Franklin believed that the West or frontier (he used the terms interchangeably and generally equated them with free land) was the decisive factor in creating what he considered to be the distinctive aspects of American society of his day—its phenomenal population growth and its peculiar economic profile. Like Turner, Franklin commanded a felicitous pen that insured wide currency for his opinions. Unlike Turner, however, Franklin produced ideas that had a demonstrable impact on the public events of his time and can even be said to have contributed to the coming of the American Revolution.

Franklin first presented his notions about the influence of the West on his country's character in his *Observations Concerning the Increase of Mankind* (1751), but his most polished exposition is in *The Interest of Great Britain Considered* (1760). His ideas were based on the knowledge that the West (by which he meant the Old Northwest) was a farmer's paradise, one of the finest pieces of real estate in the world "for the extreme richness and fertility of the land," for the salubriousness of the climate, and for its network of navigable waterways. Having never crossed the Alleghenies (he was never west of Winchester, Virginia), he obtained his information from fur traders, such as George Croghan, William Trent, and Conrad Weiser. For this class of men to be conduits of knowledge about the interior was a common phenomenon, and one should not be surprised that the intelligence they imparted encouraged more than one kind of speculation: the theorizing of reflective men like Franklin and the land jobbing of acquisitive men, in which category Franklin also fits. But who would have suspected that their information would have set the Doctor to meditating about marriage?

Franklin considered it axiomatic that the number of

marriages in any society was determined by the economic opportunities it afforded. He observed that in old, settled countries such as those of Europe "all trades, farms, and offices and employments are full and many people refrain from marrying till they see an opening, in which they can settle themselves, with a reasonable prospect of maintaining a family." Often such openings never came or else came so late that marriages produced few, if any, children. Things were different in America, Franklin declared, because of the limitless supply of good, cheap land in the West. There any able-bodied man could get a homestead that would repay moderate labor with "subsistence and something to spare." Thus, there was no hesitation about marriage; people took their vows early and produced flocks of children whose futures, with the broad expanses of western lands beckoning, looked as bright as their own. Franklin estimated that in a given period of time there would be twice as many marriages in America as in Europe and that these unions would produce twice as many offspring; hence his famous dictum that the population of America would double every twenty-five years and would continue to do so in the foreseeable future. The frontier's ardent champions have credited it with producing everything vital to America except fecundity; for Franklin this was its principal function.

He also believed that the West accounted for the middle-class agrarian character of America and for its "happy mediocrity," by which he meant a society in which the predominant producing units were self-sufficient family farms, all of about the same size, all generating comfort, but not affluence, for their proprietors. (This characterization applied to New England and Pennsylvania, where Franklin grew up and lived, but not, of course, to the South.) In his view the West created this kind of society by discouraging manufacturing, which he believed was a product of poverty. Only if there were a labor pool forced to work for the same starvation wages as European workers received could American entrepreneurs compete with their Old World counterparts, he averred. But he was convinced that there would be no supply of cheap American labor as long as men could make decent livings farming the West. And how long would that be? So vast did the trans-Allegheny region seem to him that he thought it would take his countrymen "centuries," "ages," to settle it. Just so long, then, would good land be available there and just so long would the business of America be agriculture, not manufacturing.

One of the elements of Franklin's genius in both science and statecraft was his facility in making specific applications of general principles and observations. Never did he employ this talent to better effect than at the end of the Seven Years' War, when he argued that Britain should not restore Canada to France. No hostile power should be allowed to impede the westward thrust of the American people, he declared, because if they were allowed to develop and double as they had previously done, a future America settled all the way to the Mississippi with as many as 100 million prosperous farmers was a certainty. And what a market this agrarian host would provide for British manufactures! The British industrial plant would have to expand enormously to meet the demand, and the population and wealth of the metropolis would expand with it, he predicted. British

shipping carrying the goods to America would increase proportionally and, as the nation's merchant marine increased, so would its naval power until it would awe not only Europe, but the world, making Britain the greatest power on the planet.

Franklin demonstrated no originality in connecting American consumption to British shipping, naval power, and national strength; in a mercantilist age most Americans thought in these terms. Where he broke new ground was by adding the West to the equation and showing that, owing to its matchless market potential, the American colonies would be not merely a factor in the European balance of power, but the decisive factor.

Americans absorbed this idea eagerly, and it became, in fact, one of that congeries of notions that helped bring about the Revolution; it gave the colonists confidence that other countries would be willing, even anxious, to help them defeat the mother country in order to gain access to their markets, and thereby increase their own power at Britain's expense and alter the balance of power against that "arrogant" nation. These were the calculations on which the United States offered to treat with France, the correctness of which the French Alliance of 1778 confirmed.

Franklin's frontier-inspired formula that the population of America doubled every twenty-five years also contributed to the coming of the Revolution. As widely accepted by the world as his theory about the relationship between lightning and electricity, it was an article of faith with all American patriots and served as their principal morale-builder, convincing them that success against Britain was possible because the British could not kill their countrymen fast enough to defeat them. Franklin himself stated this argument best when he wrote English clergyman and chemist Joseph Priestley in the fall of 1775 that "Britain, at the expense of three million, has killed one hundred and fifty Yankees this campaign, which is twenty thousand pounds a head. . . . During the same time sixty thousand children have been born in America. From these data his [Richard Price's] mathematical head will easily calculate the time and expense necessary to kill us all, and conquer our whole territory."

Franklin's convictions about the importance of the West led him to labor for years to put his country—first Great Britain and then the United States—in possession of it. Indeed, so assiduous were his efforts that a recent writer believes that he, rather than Jefferson, deserves the designation of "America's first great expansionist." As a subject of George II and George III, he favored British expansion into the Old West for strategic reasons, finding it unthinkable that Catholic, authoritarian France should gain control of the region and tilt the balance of power against Britain in her own favor. Considerations of security also weighed heavily with him. The prospect of sharing a common western border with France and, after American independence, with Britain appalled him because of what he considered to be the licentiousness of frontiersmen of all nationalities. These men, whom he always distinguished from the industrious farmers who followed in their wake, he branded "the refuse of both nations, often of the worst morals and least discretion," "bold in committing Offences against Neighbours, and for ever occasioning Complaints and furnishing Matters for fresh Differences between the States." The proximity of American and foreign frontiersmen would, Franklin feared, precipitate constant warfare in which the United States (or earlier Britain) would be compelled to pour endless amounts of men and money. To secure his country against such a calamity, he favored supplanting foreign nations on the frontier, using the arts of diplomacy to persuade them to leave or, if necessary, buying them out. In this connection his strategy, advanced in 1776 and again in 1782, of buying Canada from Britain has been hailed as a model for the Louisiana Purchase.

Franklin also believed that westward expansion was vital to the preservation of the quality of American life. If his countrymen could not move westward, he foresaw them being forced to huddle in cities and work for pittances in manufacturing, a prospect fatal to his vision of America as a land of "happy mediocrity." He feared, moreover, that a large urban proletariat would be fatal to American democracy itself. It was one of the tenets of the time, which Franklin considered confirmed by personal experience and observation, that the urban poor were inordinately susceptible to vice and could not, in fact, resist it. Another article of his and his contemporaries' credo was that widespread virtue was essential for the survival of democratic government. Hence, Franklin believed that because the free lands of the West kept the population from concentrating in urban industrial centers, it discouraged the vice that they bred and created, instead, an environment in which free government could flourish. Westward expansion, then, became for him a process that promoted democracy and that was desirable because it did. Here he anticipated one of Turner's most celebrated claims on behalf of the frontier, although the two men came to their conclusions from very different directions and premises.

A final reason for Franklin's enthusiasm for westward expansion anticipated the attitude of nineteenth-century Americans. The West, he felt, was just over the horizon, vacant, rich, and alluring. Poised to settle it was a British Protestant population, infinitely superior, he thought, to any of its actual or potential inhabitants, red Indians or French or Spanish Papists. Therefore, it seemed to him to be "natural," to be the design of providence, that Americans should have it. As early as 1751 he articulated these sentiments in such a way as to persuade a perceptive writer that he had produced "the first conscious and comprehensive formulation of 'Manifest Destiny'" in American history.

Franklin knew the Indians well. He saw them constantly in Philadelphia, where they came to confer with the proprietary governors and trade with the local merchants. For years he printed, and in the process studied, the minutes of their conferences with provincial officials. After becoming a member of the Pennsylvania Assembly in 1751, he personally participated in these palavers, going so far on one occasion as to write the governor's speeches to the assembled savages (Easton, 1756). Finally, his scientific curiosity was aroused by the Indians, and he interrogated traders and travelers to glean scraps of information about them that he could not acquire in other ways.

His views about the Indians varied according to where and when he expressed them. Late in life, in the salons of Paris, he was apt to wax philosophical about them and flatter them with genial productions such as the famous

Remarks Concerning the Savages of North America (1784). For most of his life, however, he viewed the Indians with contempt, his opinions being colored by such firsthand experiences as their drinking bouts at the Carlisle treaty of 1753. Although Franklin realized that all Indians were not drunken brutes, their wandering, catch-as-catch-can style of life was the very antithesis of his ideals for man in society—industry, frugality, and steadfastness. Therefore, he believed that the Indian did not deserve to stand in the way of the Englishman, and he looked upon his disappearance from the American continent with equanimity.

But he did not favor exterminating him summarily, as some of his Pennsylvania contemporaries did. He laid it down as a kind of demographic rule that whenever the red man and the white man lived in proximity, the former steadily decreased, principally because of the baleful effects of liquor and disease, until he disappeared. Therefore, he was convinced that as the Americans steadily pushed their settlements westward, the Indians would be gradually and peacefully extinguished. This belief helped to account for the relatively humane Indian policy that he espoused as a public man. He demanded that the Indians be treated honestly and that their lands be purchased whenever settlement was intended. And he consistently advocated putting the Indian trade under government regulation to protect the natives from unscrupulous traders. He supported these policies not only because he was a just man, but because he thought it would be pointless to provoke the Indians to warfare. Why goad people whose days were numbered into killing others who owned the future? This reasoning accounted for his indignation at the Paxton Boys' annihilation of the remnants of the Conestoga Indian nation in 1763. Besides being horrified at the slaughter of these defenseless people, he was enraged by the gratuitousness of the deed, for in a few years the Indians would have disappeared under their own power, without obliging the frontiersmen to dishonor themselves by dispatching them.

Finally, Franklin exerted great political and diplomatic pressure to win the West for the Hanoverian kings of Great Britain and later for the United States. His first major effort to secure the West resulted in the ALBANY PLAN OF UNION of 1754, in which he proposed that the colonies unite to command the strength to establish two strong colonies in the Ohio country in order to deny it to the French and to deal more effectively with the Indians, who were being wooed away from the British by Gallic blandishments. The next year witnessed his famous exploit of procuring transportation for General Edward Braddock's expedition against French-held Fort Duquesne during the French and Indian War. In the wake of Braddock's defeat, Pennsylvania was exposed to the fury of Indian warfare for the first time in its history, and until 1757, when he was sent to England by the Assembly, Franklin was a tower of strength in opposing the enemy. He led efforts to force the Quakers in the Assembly to vote military appropriations and to enact a militia law; he himself took the field at the head of Pennsylvania troops to build a fort in the northeastern part of the province; and he was a confidant and adviser of British military men in the middle provinces. His aim was consistent and single-minded—to defeat the French and clear them from the West.

The TREATY OF PARIS of 1763, which confirmed the demise of French power in North America and awarded the West to Great Britain, galvanized colonial land speculators, among whom none were more ardent than Franklin. At first he pinned his hopes for acquiring western lands on his and his British friends' influence in obtaining royal confirmation of the claim of the descendants of Dr. Daniel Coxe to the ancient and enormous grant of "Carolana" (not Carolina). Hopes for this scheme receded about the time he returned to England in 1764. Then he devoted himself to obtaining royal confirmation for a plan, conceived by his son and his Pennsylvania political associates, to form a colony in the Illinois country. With the arrival of land speculator Samuel Wharton in London in 1769, his and his friends' energies were diverted from the Illinois scheme to a series of grandiose speculative ventures. The history of the metamorphosis of the Illinois adventurers into the Walpole Associates into the Grand Ohio Company into the Vandalia project, superintended at each phase by Wharton, is a familiar, though complicated, chapter in the story of American westward expansion. (See BRITISH ADMINISTRATIVE POLICY.) Suffice it to say that Wharton's projects failed because of the eruption of troubles between England and America in 1773-74. His failure was also Franklin's, and when Franklin left England in 1775 to begin a new career as a revolutionary statesman, he carried with him the knowledge that eleven years of lobbying for various land speculating ventures had netted him nothing (except some blustery acres in Nova Scotia, the titles of which had already lapsed).

The next episode in Franklin's association with the West is perhaps the most important of all, his role in the peace negotiations with the British in 1782-83. It was Franklin who first demanded from the British negotiators, as an indispensable condition for peace, that George III grant America possession of the trans-Allegheny West, bounded on the north by the Great Lakes and on the west by the Mississippi River. Owing to his and his colleagues' magnificent intransigence, this area was won.

Franklin returned to Philadelphia from France in 1785. Sometime during the last five years of his life, his son-in-law, Richard Bache, purchased for him at public auction eleven lots in the wilderness north of Pittsburgh. The only western lands he ever owned, they seem a poor payment for his years of promoting westward expansion. But Franklin did not resent his failure to profit materially from the West. He considered himself amply rewarded by the knowledge that his efforts to win the West would assure the happiness and prosperity of thousands of his countrymen in future years.

Among the selected editions of Franklin's writings, the most reliable is Albert H. Smyth, ed., *The Writings of Benjamin Franklin*, 10 vols. (1905-07). It will eventually be superseded by the definitive *The Papers of Benjamin Franklin*, Leonard W. Labaree et al., eds., of which twelve volumes, covering Franklin's life through 1765, have so far been published. Numerous books describe Franklin's interests—speculative, contemplative, and otherwise—in the trans-Allegheny West. Clarence W. Alvord, *The Mississippi Valley in British Politics*, 2 vols. (1917), is still valuable, although it should be supplemented by two fine recent monographs, Jack M. Sosin, *Whitehall and the Wilderness* (1961), and Michael

G. Kammen, *A Rope of Sand: The Colonial Agents, British Politics, and the American Revolution* (1968), and by two articles, Alfred P. James, "Benjamin Franklin's Ohio Valley Lands," American Philosophical Society, *Proceedings*, (August 1954), and Peter Marshall, "Lord Hillsborough, Samuel Wharton and the Ohio Grant, 1769-1775," *English Historical Review* (October 1965). A superb work on Franklin's diplomacy, including his efforts to win the West, is Gerard Stourzh, *Benjamin Franklin and American Foreign Policy* (1954). A stimulating recent work on Franklin's ideas on various subjects, among them the West, is Paul W. Connor, *Poor Richard's Politicks: Benjamin Franklin and His New American Order* (1965).—J. H. H.

Franklin, state of. In June 1784 the North Carolina legislature ceded to the United States its western lands and proposed to close its western land office, since the western counties had become burdensome to the mother state. This cession included the region of the Watauga settlements in present Tennessee and the vast area of unclaimed lands to the west. In back of this action were not only the troubled economic issues arising out of the American Revolution but also a tremendous pressure on legislators to cede the western lands so as to open them to land speculators and traders. In the latter group was the Caswell-Blount-Martin combine, which had a large stake in the control of the western territory.

Without jurisdiction from North Carolina, the western counties now found themselves in a precarious situation, for they needed political and militia protection from constant threats of Indian attacks. It was proposed that each militia captain's company send two representatives to a general meeting to discuss the affairs of the western counties and to adopt such measures as seemed advisable. These were the initial steps toward the organization of the state of Franklin. In August 1784 the assembly of the western counties met in Jonesboro and voted unanimously for the creation of a new state. A call went out for an assembly to meet in December to draft a constitution. The document that was formulated followed closely the terms of cession drafted by the North Carolina legislature.

By this time the speculators were troubled over the location of the new state's boundaries. They feared that it would incorporate the great bend of the Tennessee, the plum of the speculators' eyes. They thus opposed ratification of the original constitution in November 1785 and an entirely new document was submitted. The new instrument, said to have been the handiwork of ministers, caused controversy from the outset because of its pretended sectarian nature. John Sevier, a leader of the WATAUGA ASSOCIATION, successfully proposed adoption of the North Carolina Constitution with modifications.

From 1785 to 1790 the state of Franklin functioned until it collapsed under the weight of other circumstances, such as personal rivalries and friction between pro-North Carolinians and the independents. The new state opened a land office in 1787 to sell lands acquired in a treaty made by Sevier with the Cherokee, in which they ceded lands between the French Broad and Little Tennessee rivers. The creation of the SOUTHWEST TERRITORY in 1790 set political administration and organization on a new tack in the Tennessee country. It helped open the way for unification of the two parts of Tennessee.

See Thomas Perkins Abernethy, *From Frontier to Plantation in Tennessee* (1932); and Samuel Cole Williams, *History of the Lost State of Franklin*, rev. ed. (1933). —T. D. C.

Frantz, Joe Bertram (1917-   ). Author and historian of the West and American business. Frantz was born in Dallas, Texas. A student at the University of Texas, he received his B.A. degree in journalism in 1938 and his M.A. and Ph.D. in history in 1940 and 1948, respectively. He began teaching as an assistant professor at the university in 1949; he was a full professor and chairman of the department from 1959 to 1965, succeeding his mentor Walter Prescott Webb.

Frantz was unusually active in both professional and federal organizations and commissions. In 1942-43 he was archivist and acting director of the San Jacinto Museum of History. He served in the United States Navy Reserve in 1943-46. He was a member of the National Parks Board (1964-70, the National Historical Publications Commission (1964-69), the Committee on the International Exchange of Persons (1969-72), and the Business History Foundation. In 1967 he was named a consultant to the NASA Historical Advisory Commission and, in 1968, a consultant to the White House. He held office in many professional organizations: president of the Texas Institute of Letters (1967-69); a member of the executive councils of the Mississippi Valley Historical Organization (1962-64), the Western Historical Association (1965-68), and the Southern Historical Association (1961-63); president of the Southwest Social Science Association (1963-64); and national councillor (1956-58) and president (1962-64) of Phi Alpha Theta, the international honor society in history.

Frantz was a Social Research Council Fellow, a Ford Foundation Fellow in 1953-54, and an E. D. Farmer Fellow in 1959. He served as visiting professor at Northwestern University and the universities of Chicago, Colorado, Chile, and San Marcos (Peru).

Frantz's first book, *Gail Borden, Dairyman to a Nation* (1951), revealed his interest in the cattle and dairy business, as did *The American Cowboy: The Myth and the Reality* (1955, with T. G. Choate) and *Six Thousand Miles of Fence: Life on the XIT Ranch of Texas* (1961, with Cordia Duke). Frantz edited or contributed to *Readings in American History* (1964), *Turner, Bolton and Webb* (1965, with John Caughey and Wilbur Jacobs), and *Violence in America* (1969).

Frantz was instrumental in the establishment of the Lyndon Baines Johnson Library. He became director of the Texas State Historical Association in 1966 and director of the University of Texas Oral History Project in 1968.—P. L. N.

Fraser, James Earle (1876-1953). Sculptor. Born in Winona, Minnesota, Fraser had at the age of eight years already begun to carve small sculptures in chalkstone, and began his study in art at the Art Institute of Chicago while in his teens. Traveling to Paris in 1895 for further study, he came to the attention of the noted sculptor Augustus Saint-Gaudens, with whom young Fraser soon after began to study and work. This association continued in Paris and later in Windsor, Vermont, until Saint-Gaudens' death in 1907. Fraser afterward maintained a studio in Cornish, New Hampshire.

A prolific sculptor, Fraser's commissions over the years ranged in size and scope from the familiar Indian-head nickel issued by the Treasury Department (1919) to the heroic equestrian groups on the Arlington Memorial Bridge Plaza in Washington, D.C. He also produced a bronze of Alexander Hamilton for the front of the nation's Treasury Building, a statue of Benjamin Franklin for the Franklin Institute in Philadelphia, and a famous bust of Theodore Roosevelt. His architectural sculptures include the pediment for the Constitution Avenue side of the National Archives Building in Washington, one of the largest of its kind in the world. Many honors were bestowed upon Fraser during his lifetime, and his work is represented widely in collections throughout the United States. The monumental plaster model for his now famous *End of the Trail*, which was featured in the Panama-Pacific Exposition of 1915, is permanently installed at the National Cowboy Hall of Fame in Oklahoma City, Oklahoma.

See Lorado Taft, *History of American Sculpture* (1924); and Albert E. Wier, *Thesarus of the Arts* (1943).—D. C. H.

Frazier, Lynn Joseph (1875-1947). North Dakota politician. Frazier was born in Minnesota. After his graduation in 1901 from the University of North Dakota he was a rural schoolteacher and then made an unsuccessful attempt at farming near Hoople, North Dakota.

Frazier became involved in politics with a university friend, William Lemke. The Nonpartisan League, an organization that advocated reform through socialistic legislation, nominated Frazier as its candidate for governor of North Dakota in 1916. Because the league was not a political party at this time, Frazier ran on the Republican ticket. He won the election and was reelected in 1918, despite attempts by the opposition to cast doubts on his loyalty during the war.

As the league elected more of its candidates to state offices and the legislature, it began to put its program of reform into operation. Charges of socialism, communism, and corruption were thrown at the league during the 1920 election. The opposition, the Independent Voters' Association, did not succeed in defeating Frazier in 1920, but they did successfully launch a recall drive and election in 1921. Frazier and two other state officers became the first state officials ever to be recalled in American history.

The voters who recalled him in 1921 then elected him to the United States Senate in 1922. Porter J. McCumber had held that Senate seat for several years, but he was not supported by the Independent Voters' Association, because he had never actively opposed the league. Frazier was able to take advantage of the split in the Republican party and emerge victorious: he was reelected in 1928 and 1934. In 1940 he lost the endorsement of the Republican party because of his isolationism and hostility toward banks and insurance companies. —D. J. T.

Fredonian Rebellion (December 1826-January 1827). The Fredonian Rebellion began in East Texas on December 16, 1826, after a dispute between empresario Haden Edwards and his brother Benjamin and authorities of the Mexican government in Texas. Haden Edwards himself was in the United States seeking financial support for his Texas colony when his brother and a force of about thirty men seized a stone fort in Nacogdoches and proclaimed the Republic of Fredonia under the motto "Independence, Liberty, and Justice." Benjamin Edwards then made an agreement with the Cherokee, offering to divide Texas betwec. 'iis republic and the Indians in return for mutual defense. Local inhabitants at Nacogdoches refused to support the revolt, and when the Mexican militia, including some members of the Stephen F. Austin colony, approached Nacogdoches on January 31, the revolutionists fled across the Sabine River into sanctuary in the United States. The revolt was an adumbration of more serious difficulties between dissident Texans and their Mexican sovereigns.

See Eugene C. Barker, *Mexico and Texas, 1821-1835* (1928); and William C. Binkley, *The Texas Revolution* (1952).—J. B. F.

free silver. See SILVER ISSUE.

Free-Soil party. The Free-Soil party was the first major effort to unite politically northern opposition to slavery expansion into western territories. That opposition had crystalized in the popular reaction to the Wilmot Proviso of 1846, which prohibited slavery in any territory to be ceded to the United States by Mexico. When both the Whig and Democratic parties avoided any national commitment against slavery expansion in 1848, a coalition of Barnburner Democrats, Conscience Whigs, and erstwhile Liberty party men formed the Free-Soil party in Buffalo, New York, in August 1848. That convention nominated Martin Van Buren for president and Charles Francis Adams, a Massachusetts Conscience Whig, for vice president. The platform called for "free soil, free speech, free labor, and free men" and demanded "no more slave states and no more slave territories." Growing also out of the LAND REFORM MOVEMENT, the platform advocated free homesteads for actual settlers.

While most leaders of the Free-Soil party were idealistic and while the party was staunchly sectional in principles, it was not a simple extension of the abolitionist Liberty party. Prohibition of slavery expansion could attract wider but less humanitarian support than abolitionism; it could even attract racists. Just like many who supported the Wilmot Proviso, some Free-Soilers were anxious simply to keep all Negroes out of western territories or to limit the political base of the slave power. The party also attracted land reformers who wanted homesteads and advocates of cheap postage. Because of this broader support, the party won about ten percent of the popular vote in 1848, primarily in New York from Van Burenites, Massachusetts, and the Western Reserve of Ohio. It also managed, usually through coalitions with other parties, to elect several influential congressmen and senators, such as Salmon P. Chase, John P. Hale, and Charles Sumner. In 1852, with Hale as its presidential candidate, the party's vote fell by almost half, and in 1854 the remnants of the party were among the first to join anti-Nebraska coalitions and to start the Republican party.

For information on the Free-Soil party, see Martin Duberman, *Charles Francis Adams, 1807-1886* (1961); Louis Filler, *The Crusade Against Slavery, 1830-1860* (1960); Allan Nevins, *Ordeal of the Union*, 2 vols. (1947); and Theodore C. Smith, *The Liberty and Free Soil Parties in the Northwest* (1897). The racist basis of western Free-Soil sentiment is described in Eugene H. Berwanger,

The Frontier Against Slavery: Western Anti-Negro Prejudice and the Slavery Extension Controversy (1967).—M. F. H.

Frémont, Jessie [Anne] Benton (1824-1902). Writer. Passing her girlhood in St. Louis and Washington, Jessie Benton received most of her education from her father, Senator Thomas Hart Benton. She also had many of his characteristics: a bold intellect, a strong will, a militant pride, and on occasion the power of invective.

Her pen was used first to help her father, and as his secretary and confidant she became fully educated in Washington politics and was made aware of the importance of the West. After her marriage to John C. FRÉMONT, she used her talent in the interests of her husband, helping him compose the official reports of his western expeditions, writing many of his letters—even signing his name to many of them and virtually completing his memoirs in 1886. She sometimes wrote, often with embellishments, in defense of his controversial decisions and questionable behavior. In the 1870s and 1880s, when the Frémonts were reduced to poverty, her facile pen brought in an income. To Robert Bonner of the New York *Ledger* and to the editors of *Harper's* and *Wide Awake* she sold stories about prominent Americans, of her experiences in Washington and Paris, of her travel across the Isthmus of Panama in 1849, and of her life on their Mariposas estate in California. Many of these were later republished in book form under the titles *A Year of American Travel* (1878), *Souvenirs of My Time* (1887), and *Far West Sketches* (1890).

Mrs. Frémont was not blind to her husband's faults, but she had an unswerving loyalty to him—a loyalty that prompted an unsuccessful intervention in his behalf with presidents Polk and Lincoln, the breaking of the long and close friendship with the Blair family, and a recognition that her adored father had given Frémont "a sort of Brutus stab" in the campaign of 1856. But a few months after her dream of being a "presidentess" was crushed at the ballot box, she could write F. P. Blair, "I find myself thinking it was the 'world well lost,'" since family harmony and peace for my Father's old age has come out of defeat." Ambitious for power and prestige, she adjusted well to the various circumstances into which she was plummeted by the fluctuations of her husband's career. Although her poverty of later years was somewhat lightened by the widow's pension of a retired major general and by the gift of a home from the ladies of Los Angeles, she bore it nobly as she had the death of two of her five children. When her own death came in Los Angeles, her ashes were taken to Piermont on the Hudson and buried beside Frémont, not far from their old home, Pocaho.

The best biography, although uncritical, is Catherine C. Phillips, *Jessie Benton Frémont, A Woman Who Made History* (1935).—M. L. S.

Frémont, John Charles (1813-1890). Explorer, politician, and soldier. Frémont was born in Savannah, Georgia, the son of Charles Fremon, a French émigré, and of Ann Beverly Whiting, who had scandalized Richmond, Virginia, by leaving her elderly husband, John Pryor, to run away with her lover. The Frémonts (it is not clear when the *t* was added to the name, but young Frémont began using the accented form when he became associated with Joseph N. NICOLLET in 1838) were nomadic, their finances unstable, and soon after the death of the father in 1818, the mother took the family, which now included a second son and a daughter, to live in Charleston, South Carolina. Young Frémont enrolled as a junior in the Scientific Department in the College of Charleston in 1829; although he did well at first and showed promise, he was dismissed in 1831, three months short of graduation, for "incorrigible negligence." Five years later, however, he applied successfully to the trustees for a B.A. degree.

In 1833, through the influence of Joel Poinsett, Frémont obtained a civilian post as teacher of mathematics to the midshipmen on board the U.S.S. *Natchez*. In 1836-37 he assisted in surveys of the projected Charleston and Cincinnati Railroad and the Cherokee country, and it was this assignment that determined his career. The great opportunity came in 1838, when, again due to Poinsett's influence, he was commissioned a second lieutenant in the United States Corps of Topographical Engineers and assigned to accompany the distinguished French scientist Nicollet on a reconnaissance of the northern territory lying between the upper Mississippi and Missouri rivers.

Frémont made two expeditions with Nicollet into the Minnesota country and received invaluable training in cartography, not only in the field but in Washington where the young man and the ailing scientist refined their sketches and calculations and drew the all-important Nicollet map. It was in Washington on October 19, 1841, that Frémont, after conducting a survey of the lower course of the Des Moines River, eloped with seventeen-year-old Jessie, the vivacious daughter of influential Senator Thomas Hart Benton of Missouri (see Jessie Benton FRÉMONT).

The following spring Frémont received orders from the chief of the Topographical Bureau to survey the Platte River "up to the head of the Sweetwater" and, if the season were favorable, to make a similar survey of the Kansas River. Taking along twenty-one voyageurs, the skilled German topographer Charles PREUSS, Lucian B. Maxwell as hunter, and Kit Carson as guide, and such interesting items as a daguerreotype camera and an india rubber boat, Frémont reached South Pass and then struck northwest to reconnoiter the Wind River Mountains and to scale Woodrow Wilson, one of the high peaks in the chain. The report of his expedition and its accompanying map were ordered printed by Congress, and shortly after it reached the public Frémont was on his way West again.

In applying for a mountain howitzer at St. Louis (which he abandoned later, probably on Mill Creek in Nevada), Frémont wrote Stephen Watts Kearny, "I have been ordered to make an exploration, military and geographical, principally to connect, on the line of communication usually travelled, the frontiers of Missouri with the mouth of the Columbia." But he did more than connect his South Pass reconnaissance of the previous year with the surveys Commander Charles Wilkes had made on the Pacific Coast. When Frémont returned to St. Louis some fourteen months later, he had made a virtual circuit of the entire West. Not only had he examined the northeastern extremity of Great Salt Lake and penetrated Oregon, but he had also effected a rash midwinter crossing of the Sierra Nevada at a still unidentified and unnamed pass lying south of Carson Pass, "1,000 miles by our traveled road from the Dalles of the Columbia," he wrote in his journal. His starving men recouped and refitted at Sutter's Fort on the Sacramento, and then traveling south through California with the Sierra on their left, they went through Oak Creek Pass, picked up the Old Spanish Trail and kept to it until the desire to make a cursory examination of Utah Lake forced a departure. After penetrating the Wasatch and Uinta Mountains, Frémont headed for Bent's Fort on the Arkansas, traversing the Three Parks of the Rockies en route.

He wrote another official report and with the assistance of his traveling companion, Preuss, drew a map, which according to Carl I. Wheat "changed the entire picture of the West, and made a lasting contribution to cartography." True, it had errors, but more important it depicted Frémont's "Great Basin" (see GREAT AMERICAN DESERT), a term he applied to the vast intermediate region between the Wasatch and the Sierra Nevada with its own systems of lakes, rivers, and creeks, and having no exterior drainage. Again the Congress ordered the map and the report (in combination with the one of 1842) printed. A number of editions were issued by commercial publishers in the United States and in Europe. Frémont, who had already departed on his third expedition, became a national hero. In the summer of 1847, as he was marched east from California by Kearny and was feeling that general's "unjust and aggravating conduct," he had the satisfaction, he wrote Pierson B. Reading, "to meet in all the great emigration many strong and warm friends. They were using my maps on the road, travelling by them, and you may judge how gratified I was to find that they found them perfectly correct & could do so."

The instructions from the Bureau of Topographical Engineers under which Frémont mounted his third expedition contemplated a survey of the Arkansas and Red rivers, of localities within reasonable distances of Bent's Fort, and of the streams that ran east from the Rocky Mountains. The *Western Expositor*, however, announced that Frémont would complete the survey of the Great Salt Lake and enter California, and this is exactly what Frémont did—and under official instructions, he wrote in his memoirs many years later. He was in California before Christmas but soon became involved in a conflict with the Mexican authorities, and after audaciously defying them he led his party north into Oregon. He was overtaken by Lieutenant Archibald Gillespie who brought not only a letter of introduction from Secretary of State James Buchanan and letters from the Benton family, but also news that war with Mexico was imminent and that the American consul in California had been appointed a confidential agent of the United States government. For decades historians have pondered the question, Did Gillespie deliver secret instructions to Frémont? Most concluded that he did not.

But Frémont returned to California with Gillespie, and shortly before the United States flag was hoisted joined the Americans in their BEAR FLAG REBELLION against Mexico. His battalion of volunteers, composed of voyageurs from his topographical party and American settlers in California, became known as the California Battalion and served under the command of Robert F. STOCKTON, who became chief of naval and land operations on the Pacific Coast. The Frémont and Stockton forces occupied Los Angeles in August 1846, and ostensibly the conquest of California was completed. Stockton promised Frémont the governorship. A revolt by the native Californians, however, made necessary new war measures and it was not until January 1847 that victory was finally won, aided by Brigadier General Stephen Watts KEARNY and his Dragoons, who had entered California from the southeast. In the controversy that ensued between Stockton and Kearny as to the chief command, Frémont refused at first to obey the orders of Kearny, a refusal that caused him to be court-martialed in Washington on charges of mutiny, disobedience, and conduct prejudicial to military discipline. Frémont's defense counsel was his brother-in-law William Carey Jones and Benton, who was ragingly indignant at his son-in-law's treatment. The verdict was guilty on all three counts, but since the court recommended leniency, President James K. Polk ordered him to duty again. An embittered Frémont, however, resigned from the army.

He hurriedly completed a "geographical memoir" to accompany the map of Oregon and Upper California that Preuss was drawing, and with contributions from private sources, launched another expedition to California in the hope of finding passes for a Pacific railroad along the thirty-eighth parallel. This winter expedition of 1848-49 ended in disaster in the San Juan Mountains, but Frémont got out with some of his men. (See KERN brothers.) He continued on to California to his Mariposa estate, which had been purchased for him by Thomas O. Larkin in February 1847 and which proved to have rich gold-bearing veins. For the next few years he was occupied with raising capital, some of it European, for the development of the gold mines, and with litigation over title to the estate which he finally received in February 1856. But the mercurial explorer had little business acumen and in 1864 he lost control of the seventy-square-mile property. In 1850-51 he served California as a United States senator, and in 1853-54, half-ill but seeking new laurels and a railroad pass, he made his fifth and last expedition into the West.

In 1856 Frémont was the presidential nominee of the newly formed Republican party, and thousands marched to the slogan, "Free Soil, Free Men, Frémont and Victory." The Democrats, however, heaping personal invective on the explorer and capitalizing on Whig fear of the consequences of the election of a sectional candidate by a sectional party, were able to win the election for James Buchanan. The electoral vote was 174 to 114.

When the Civil War began, Frémont was in Europe. He hurried home, was made a major general, and was put in command of the western department with headquarters at St. Louis. In this command he lasted approximately one hundred days. Missouri was divided in its loyalty; arms and supplies were insufficient; unscrupulous speculators—some his own California friends—surrounded him; and criticisms and military defeats cost him President Lincoln's confidence. When he foolishly issued a proclamation declaring the property of Missouri rebels confiscated and their slaves emancipated, the president removed him from the command, but the next spring—1862—put him in charge of the mountain department in western Virginia. When Frémont was outgeneraled by Stonewall Jackson, Lincoln placed him under John Pope, whom Frémont detested. He re-

quested to be relieved of his command, a request which the president accepted with alacrity.

Frémont was nominated again for the presidency in 1864 by the radical wing of the Republican party, but withdrew before the election and retired from public life to make money. He became involved in railroad promotion, particularly that of the Memphis and El Paso, which he dreamed would ultimately extend from the East Coast to San Diego. Its bankruptcy in 1870 blemished his reputation further and left him virtually penniless. Mrs. Frémont's writing brought some income, and her husband sought appointment as territorial governor of Arizona. Frémont reminded the leaders of the Republican party that it had been his withdrawal in 1864 which had been of "deciding importance" in the reelection of Lincoln. His appointment as governor in 1878 brought with it a salary of $2,600 and an opportunity to recoup his finances in mine promotion and speculation and various land and railroad schemes, some even across the Mexican border. Frémont averted criticism of a conflict of interests by remaining a silent partner in many of the sales and purchases, but long absences from the territory did bring criticism and a request for his resignation, which he submitted on October 11, 1881.

A second grand fortune was never made. Even his *Memoirs*, published in 1887, did not bring the expected royalty. A few months before his death in New York, Congress authorized the president to appoint him a major general in the army and to place him on the retired list for pension purposes.

Frémont's proudest achievements came before he was forty—exploring the West and making it known through his narratives to an eager public. He was not a "pathfinder," but his first two expeditions followed the very early westward-moving emigrant trains. Allan Nevins, whose biography of Frémont (3rd ed., 1955) remains the most authoritative, has correctly defined his role as a "pathmarker." By 1973 a map portfolio and two volumes of a three-volume series, *The Expeditions of John Charles Frémont*, were published. Bert Fireman's article in *American West* (Winter 1964) sheds new light on his Arizona career.—M. L. S.

French, Peter (1849-1897). Oregon rancher. Born in Callaway County, Missouri, French was christened John William but later adopted the name Peter. In 1850 his parents moved to California, where they engaged in sheep raising in Tehama County. Although French had only a limited education, his ability and energy brought him to the attention of Dr. Hugh James Glenn, a prominent California rancher and one of the largest wheat growers in the United States. Glenn hired the dark and wiry little man to work on his ranch at Jacinto, California, a holding of 55,000 acres adjacent to the Sacramento River. The coming of agricultural settlers to Colusa County and their opposition to open-range ranching persuaded Glenn to move his cattle elsewhere. French was taken on as a younger partner and ordered to establish a ranch in Harney County, Oregon. In June 1872 he drove some twelve hundred cattle and other livestock to the valley of the upper Blitzen River west of the Steens Mountain, where he established the P Ranch. Although other pioneer ranchers had preceded French into Harney County, French was the first to locate on the Blitzen.

Once in Oregon, French improved the herd by importing purebred Shorthorns from the East. He also cut and dried the lush Blitzen meadow grasses for hay during the summer months, while the cattle grazed on bunch grass on the mountain slopes. He irrigated dry lands for pasturage and drained swampy areas to make the operation more efficient. Eventually the French-Glenn Livestock Company ran some 30,000 cattle and 3,000 horses and mules on its 132,000-acre holdings. Isolated in the sparsely settled region of southeastern Oregon, French and his men experienced an Indian attack during the Paiute-Bannock outbreak of 1878. He had to drive his cattle two hundred miles to Winnemucca, Nevada, before they could be shipped to market.

In 1883 French married Glenn's daughter Ella, but the marriage ended in divorce after a few years. French, however, had already assumed the management of the French-Glenn company only a few weeks after his marriage, when his father-in-law was murdered by an ex-employee.

A tough, aggressive man who was always anxious to enlarge his holdings, French engaged in arguments over ownership of the range lands with the federal government and with settlers who began to come into Harney County during the 1890s. His feud with a settler, Ed Oliver, came to a climax early in 1897 when Oliver killed French. In 1935 the area of the original P Ranch was incorporated as part of the Malheur National Wildlife Refuge.

See George F. Brimlow, *Harney County, Oregon, and Its Range Land* (1951); Robert G. Ferris, ed., *Prospector, Cowhand, and Sodbuster*, vol. XI in the National Survey of Historic Sites and Buildings (1967); and Giles French, *Cattle Country of Peter French* (1964).—H. R. L.

French and Indian War. See COLONIAL WARS.

French dialects in the Mississippi valley. Most linguists distinguish three varieties of French in the southern part of the Mississippi valley: Louisiana Standard French; Acadian French, more colloquially known as Cajun; and Louisiana Creole. There also existed until recently vestiges of a French dialect that used to be spoken in some regions of Missouri and Illinois.

Louisiana Standard French remained for a long time the language of the white French settlers of the colony of Louisiana. Most of them lived in New Orleans, and the rest, in the plantations facing the Mississippi, going north beyond Donaldsonville. They were descendants of the French aristocracy and came from the region called Ile-de-France, where the variety of French spoken is still supposed to be the purest. Usually, colonial children received their early education from French teachers and were later sent to France to complete their schooling. This tradition was not discontinued during the Spanish rule from 1763 to 1800, nor was it disturbed after the American purchase of Louisiana. The position of French culture and language in Louisiana was reinforced well into the nineteenth century by an influx of French journalists and political refugees who had gone into exile after the failure of various plots against the French monarchy and the Second Empire. They became the intellectual nucleus of the territory, founding schools and newspapers and encouraging the development of a local French literature that displayed their talents.

The first great threat to French hegemony in the lower Mississippi valley was the Civil War. The defeat of Confederate Louisiana impoverished and scattered the French settlers as well as native southerners. They could no longer afford to import French teachers or send students to France. Some young ladies of French descent even found that teaching the French language had become a useless pursuit. For a time, French was only tolerated at some bilingual schools; it was finally abandoned and replaced by English everywhere. While many children of French stock continued to speak French at home, they were reluctant to use it at school among themselves for fear of being called "Kis-kee-dees," a scornful parody of "Qu'est-ce-qu'il dit?" ("What does he say?"), which Creoles asked anyone addressing them in English. Because of the influx of immigrants from the northern states and various economic and political forces, the use of French declined. The founding in 1876 of the Athénée Louisianais, an academy devoted to French culture directed by Alfred Mercier, a humanist, physician, and writer, represents just one desperate effort to revive a dying tradition.

By the beginning of the twentieth century most French newspapers and periodicals had ceased publication. The last to vanish was the century-old *Abeille*, discontinued in 1919, three years after passage of a law declaring that French transcription of judicial notices was no longer mandatory. The fact remains that as late as 1930 the Bureau of the Census reported that French was still spoken in many families in several localities throughout Louisiana. In an article on Louisiana French (*Language*, December 1934), George Lane described the situation of Standard French in the town of St. Martinville, some 110 miles west of New Orleans. He found that Standard French was still spoken by seventy-five percent of the white people who were over forty years old and used by those between twenty-five and forty only when among associates or older people; it was not used at all by those under twenty-five, although some could understand it and others were able to speak it. Apart from a few peculiarities, mostly related to archaisms, localisms, and semantic changes, it was observed that there were no significant differences between Standard French spoken by the older generation of St. Martinville and by Frenchmen but that many anglicisms had contaminated the variety spoken by the younger generation. The contamination has since spread and completely corrupted French almost everywhere in Louisiana. Until recently, French could still be heard in the cultured circles of a few cities, such as New Orleans, Baton Rouge, and Lafayette; in a few old Creole families; and in some churches. In 1968 the state senate of Louisiana decided to reintroduce French in the schools with the assistance of teachers imported from France. An organization called Committee of Defense of French Language in Louisiana (CODOFIL) is now encouraging bilingualism in Louisiana and is also publishing the *Louisiana Review* in French and English. Should their efforts succeed, Standard French will no longer be solely the property of a privileged class or culture.

Acadian French was spoken mostly by the descendants of the French who had been expelled by the English from Acadie (the French name for Nova Scotia) in 1755 and managed to reach Louisiana a few years later. They settled along Bayou Teche, Bayou Terre aux

Boeufs, and Bayou Lafourche; in some parts of the Attakapas and Opelousas districts of southwestern Louisiana; on the banks of the Mississippi in Pointe Coupée Parish and at Baton Rouge and New Orleans. Most of them were descendants of peasants from the French provinces of Normandy, Brittany, Picardy, and Perche, whose patois they could speak. Community life and intermarriage had produced a degree of linguistic unity among Acadians before they moved to the Mississippi valley. This did not preclude, however, the emergence of local peculiarities, sometimes within a parish.

Generally, there are phonetic peculiarities and certain words and expressions typical to certain districts. Despite these differences, some general remarks can be made concerning the Acadian language. Unlike Standard French, Acadian French contains a great number of archaisms and provincialisms. Since it was spoken mostly by illiterate people, no attention was paid to the correctness of its phonetics, semantics, or grammar. Many closed vowels in Standard French have become open and vice versa. There are also a certain number of vocalic substitutions. For example, *a* becomes *e*, as in *alle* for *elle* ("she"). Metathesis is a frequent phenomenon, as in *cocodrile* for *crocodile*. Excrescent consonants and syllables (e.g., *croquecignole* for *croquignole*, a fried cake resembling a doughnut in taste) and assimilations (e.g., *gigier* for *gésier*, "gizzard") may occur. Levelings (*j'avions* for *j'avais*, that is, use of first-person singular pronoun with first-person plural verb) and agglutinations of articles (*lendroit* for *l'endroit*, "the place" or "the right side") become the rule. Not only does the pronunciation appear distorted and the grammar broken, compared to Standard French, but there are also many semantic discrepancies: *colline* ("hill") for *vallée* ("valley"), *consommer* ("to consummate" or "to use up") for *consumer* ("to burn" or "to consume"), *corrompre* ("to corrupt") for *convaincre* ("to convince"), *incredule* ("incredulous") for *indocile* ("indocile"), *intrigant* ("intriguing") for *intelligent*, *sortir* ("to go out") sometimes for *venir* ("to come").

Many scientific words are so completely corrupted as to become malapropisms: *certifie* ("certify") for *salsifis* ("salsify"), *l'eau d'anon* ("donkey water") for *laudanum,* *ordure de fer* ("iron trash") for *iodure de fer* ("iron iodite"), and even *téléformer* for *téléphoner* ("to telephone").

It is easy to see that in many cases these changes were originally caused by illiteracy or ignorance. In the past, Standard French has been an influential force in bringing about the disappearance of these anomalies.

It is also interesting to note that Cajun makes use of a great deal of nautical terms, such as *amarrer* ("fasten"); *au large* ("in the open"); *virer de bord* ("to turn around"); and *haler* ("to pull").

Acadian French has also been exposed to foreign influences, among which English has been the most important; this is shown not only phonetically, as in the palatalization of dental *di* and *ti* before vowels (to *dji* and *tchi*) and the vocalization of final *r* (*faire* is pronounced as English *fair*), but also lexically and even syntactically, since there are many borrowings of words and syntagms from English, such as *raide rôle* from "railroad," *estimbote* from "steamboat," and *passer des remarques* from "to pass remarks." Contacts with Indians also enriched the vocabulary with words like *picouette* ("thin, ill-tempered child") and *sacacoua* or *sasacoua* ("uproar," "shouts"). African words such as *gombo* ("ok-

ra") and *gris-gris* ("charm") were taken over from African-born slaves. Similarly, a great many Creole expressions were borrowed from them (e.g., *mon gardemanger*, "the stomach"; *mon tendé*, "the ear"; *mon senti*, "the nose"; *mon oi clair*, "the eye").

One may finally add to this linguistic cocktail a certain number of words taken from Canary Islanders (the "Islingues"), who were established near the Acadian settlements during the administration of Governor Bernardo de Galves (1777-85); an example is *pobon* ("earthen jar").

Isolated in remote villages, Acadians managed for a time to preserve their culture, but ultimately they could not insulate their language from outside influences. As a result, their linguistic heritage gradually decayed with each generation, and those who can still speak Cajun are a few aged people who, more often than not, are incapable of discriminating what is pure Acadian from what is not.

Louisiana Creole used to be called Negro-French or Gombo. It is generally agreed that this was the language that originated from the working communication between the white French Creoles and their African slaves. Having been systematically severed from their own linguistic groups and joined with other people from various tribes, the slaves did not have any choice but to learn the language of their masters. Without necessarily using "broken" French or baby talk, slaveholders reduced and simplified Standard French to facilitate understanding between themselves and their slaves. The learners would in turn catch by ear these more or less indistinct utterances and reproduce them in their own way, with still more simplification, if not distortion, of pronunciation and grammar. This process was not peculiar to Louisiana: it was repeated in other areas where European languages were imposed on non-Europeans, especially on the slaves in the Caribbean. More often than not, any variety of a given Creole is intelligible to anyone who speaks any other variety of that Creole. For example, there are close resemblances between Louisiana Creole and Haitian Creole. These affinities may be the result of the influence of the great many slaves who emigrated with their masters from Santo Domingo to Louisiana at the outbreak of the island's Negro insurrection in 1791.

Interestingly enough, the use of Creole spread in Louisiana at the expense of Standard French and Cajun. This is easily understandable if one bears in mind that for some time the slaves outnumbered not only their masters but also the Acadians. Moreover, most of the younger children of the white settlers were entrusted to the care of their Negro nurses, who would teach them Creole before they could learn Standard French at school. They would in turn speak this language to both the whites and Negroes of the urban or plantation population, thus acquiring and propagating Creole habits. As a result, not only did all Negroes speak Creole, but many whites spoke it as well. Needless to say, it was regarded as a disreputable patois and its use was discouraged among the children of the privileged class. This did not handicap the vitality or the growth of Creole, however. In spite of the scorn and contempt of the elite, it took hold because it managed to build up its own folklore and literature. Some folk songs in Creole became popular, the best known being "Le Chanson du vié Boscoyo," also called "La Calinda" after a dance imported by Negroes of Santo Domingo. Its syncopated rhythm and its tune were subsequently used in musical lampoons against politicians. Negroes improvised many other songs and verses that were repeated by Creoles. Very popular also were animal fables, of which Lapin, the clever rabbit, with which the audience liked to identify itself, was the most famous hero and the inspiration for Joel Chandler Harris' Br'er Rabbit. Another well-known character was Compair Bouki, or Friend Goat, who also belongs to Haitian folklore. Louisiana tales would usually begin with "Bonne foi! Bonne foi!" ("Good faith!"), to which the audience would answer "Lapin, Lapin." The Creole repertory also contains a great number of proverbs that reveal a certain philosophy derisive of the foibles of human beings whether black or white. There is also a good deal of wisdom in the so-called *ditons* ("sayings"), in which images of animals are used to comment on human behavior: "Coupé zoreil à milet, ça pas fai choual" ("Cutting a mule's ears can't make him a horse").

So attractive did Creole become for its humor, wit, and understatement that many Louisiana French periodicals such as *Le Carillon*, a New Orleans weekly, used it regularly in their columns. During the period of Reconstruction expecially, it published hundreds of lampoon poems in Creole; among them was the well-known "Ti Macaque vini grand" ("Little Monkey Became Big"), which satirized a poor parish barber named Caïus César Antoine, who had risen to the post of lieutenant-governor.

The written expression of Creole was to suffer from the failure of French publications in Louisiana. This does not mean, however, that Creole experienced the same decline as Standard French; indeed, it resisted social change far more effectively, and despite the inevitable impact of English, it is still spoken even by some people of the younger generation in many parts of southern Louisiana. This is particularly true in some parts of New Orleans, Baton Rouge, Lafayette, St. Martinville, and Broussard. It may, however, suffer from the teaching of Standard French in force in Louisiana schools today.

The structure of Louisiana Creole has been studied extensively by amateur linguists and scholars, whose findings have been printed in folklore periodicals and specialized journals. Many theses and dissertations have been devoted to the subject. It is therefore impossible in this brief presentation to give an accurate description of this language, for any simplification may appear to be mere caricature. All that can be ventured here are a few remarks based on some comparisons with Standard French.

Most rounded vowels of Standard French become unrounded in Creole. The *u* in *plume* ("pen") becomes *i*, giving *plim*; *e* (schwa) may become a mid-frontal *e*, as in *dèmain* for *demain* ("tomorrow"), or an *i* as in *vini* for *venir* ("to come") or in *piti* for *petit* (by assimilation). The Standard French *eu* is reduced to *e* as in *de* for *deux* ("two") or *è* as in *pè* for *peur* ("fear"). Another unrounded case is that of the indefinite article *un*, which is pronounced *ein*.

Nasalizations occur after nasal consonants, as in *moin* for *moi*, whereas vowels are denasalized after *d* and *b*. Similarly, *ja*, *jou*, and *ge* are often depalatalized to slip

into flat sibilant *z* as in *touzou* for *toujours* and *manze* for *manger*, but there is palatalization after dentals followed by vowels *i* and *u* as in *tiens*, *tuer*, and *diable*, which become *tchen*, *tchwer*, and *djab*. The Standard French *r* disappears in Creole, as in *apè* for *après* or *di* for *dire*. Finally, *v* is converted into *w*, as in *wa* for *voir* ("to see").

There are also many morphological features, some of them based on leveling of the original French forms. Grammatical genders are abandoned (e.g., *nom-la*, "the man"; *fem-la*, "the woman." The phenomenon of agglutination where definite and partitive articles are attached to nouns and pronouns to verbs is frequent in Louisiana Creole. For example, *la soupe* becomes *lasoup*, *du vin* becomes *divin*, and *vous étiez* becomes *voute*. Plurals are usually made by adding the suffix *-je* to nouns (e.g., *nom-je*, "the men," although the irregular plurals are leveled, as in *chwal* for both *cheval* and *chevaux* ["horse" and "horses"]). Adjectives are invariable. The possessive adjective is generally expressed by the dative, which is believed to be imported from Santo Domingo (e.g., *ziés à moin* for *mes yeux*, "my eyes"). Reduced to a single form for each person, the pronoun is generally the only marker for the person of the verb. The tenses—mostly reduced to present, past, and future—are indicated by added particles. The copula *être* ("to be") is omitted in the present, except in the interrogative with pronoun subjects and the progressive form, which occurs very frequently in Creole. The relative pronoun as object of a verb is generally omitted. In negative sentences, the *ne* of the French *ne . . . pas* is suppressed and *pas* often elides in front of vowels.

As far as vocabulary is concerned, it is based on the French with a few exceptions. It is interesting to note that aphaeresis in words of two or more syllables is a favorite process of Louisiana Creole (e.g., *garder* for *regarder*, *réter* for *arrêter*, *mander* for *demander*, *mener* for *amener*); however, the first syllable of *revenir* ("to come back") is preserved to avoid ambiguity with *venir:vini* ("to come").

Another lexical peculiarity of Louisiana Creole is its remarkable polysemy: words like *capab* and *gain*, for example, are rich in nuances not possessed by their Standard French counterparts, *capable* and *gagner*. This is indeed part and parcel of the basic principles of Louisiana Creole—namely, economy and concision.

Concurrent with the usage of the lower Mississippi valley dialects, another variety of French was spoken in Missouri and Illinois. Being first an amalgam of various patois of northwestern and central France, it had been introduced as early as 1700 in such localities as Cahokia, Kaskaskia, St. Louis, and Ste. Genevieve, mostly by Canadian French who happened to be adventurers, explorers, seekers of metals, trappers, or farmers. The complete isolation of this French-speaking community effected a French dialect with features of its own. Yet, a few terms related to animals, plants, foods, and geographical data seem to have been borrowed from lower Louisiana French. Some examples are *aile-rouge* ("redwing blackbird"), *moqueur* ("mocking bird"), *bois d'arc* ("osage orange"), *taffia* ("rum"), and *bayou*. The pronunciation also shows some metatheses as in *mequerdi* for *mercredi* ("Wednesday"), *gernouille* for *grenouille* ("frog"), or *garlie* for *galerie* ("porch" or "veranda"); these pronunciations are shared with Cajun. There are possible influences of Creole, such as the change of nasal *on* to *o*, the depalatalization of *je* or *ge* into alveolar sibilant *z*, some unroundings of *u* into *i*, and the abbreviation of a few polysyllabic words like *demander* ("to ask") and *appeler* ("to call"), into *'mander* and *'peler*. Elements of folklore, particularly those related to animal fables like the stories of Lapin and Bouki, are borrowed from Louisiana Creole.

Such common features among Louisiana dialects resulted, on the one hand, from subsequent occasional relations in government or trade and, on the other hand, from the import of slaves purchased downriver. It is important to emphasize at this point that, whatever influence Creole may have exercised on Missouri French, Creole cannot be technically assimilated to this dialect. Regardless of influences and evolution, its basic structure remains akin to the Canadian French of the early eighteenth century. To the few alterations mentioned above may be added some slight changes in pronunciation, as when Canadian *beigne* ("pancake") becomes *bagne* in Missouri; a number of semantic shifts, so that *barbote*, meaning "catfish" in Canada, came to mean "tadpole" in Missouri. Certain meanings may have been sheer inventions of the Missouri settlers, while others were current during the French colonial period.

Under the impact of Anglo-American settlers, who rushed in after the Louisiana Purchase of 1803, Missouri French began to decline, although sermons were preached in French in St. Louis until 1842 and an unlettered French dialect was spoken in counties around Ste. Genevieve until 1930.

Since Frenchmen played a major role in the early American fur trade, the early American fur companies not only depended on French *voyageurs* and *engagés* ("canoemen" and "workers") but borrowed the structure of French company organization. The chief clerk or trader on an expedition was the *bourgeois* (which Americans pronounced "booshway"); he was accompanied by his *commis* ("clerks"). Americans called newcomers or lowly hirelings in the trade *mangeurs de lard* ("grease eaters"). Many French words and phrases were used by Anglo-American frontiersmen between 1803 and 1850.

The presence of Frenchmen and the French language in the Mississippi valley and throughout the American West revealed both the persistence of a second European culture there and the process by which American frontier conditions affected language itself.

See James F. Broussard, *Louisiana Creole Dialect* (1942); Alcée Fortier, "The French Language in Louisiana and the Negro-French Dialect," *Transactions of the MLA*, vols. 1-2; Morris F. Goodman, *A Comparative Study of Creole French Dialects* (1964); Raleigh Morgan, Jr., "Structural Sketch of Saint-Martin Creole," *Anthropological Linguistics*, vol. 1, no. 8; and Daniel L. Racine, "Le Créole de la Guadeloupe," *N.A. French Lang. Lit. Bull.* (French VIII, MLA), no. 12.—D. L. R.

French heritage. French settlers in the Mississippi valley bequeathed a rich heritage of urban settlement, customs, and language to the new American nation. Not only did they have a cultural impact right up to the 1850s, but French Creole merchants, traders, and mountain men were in the vanguard of American frontiersmen (see MISSISSIPPI VALLEY: FRENCH AND SPANISH PERIODS).

By 1763 French settlements had already crystallized into three distinct sections: Canada, Upper Louisiana, and Lower Louisiana (see LOUISIANA TERRITORY). The main settlements of Canada—Quebec (founded 1608), Trois-Rivières (1634), and Montreal (1642)—were well established, and each had a consciously independent population. The Illinois country of Upper Louisiana was politically and economically tied more closely to Louisiana than to Canada, although many of its settlers came from the north. Once in the Ohio and Mississippi valleys, Frenchmen had absorbed various Indian villages and established trade relations, and by 1700 their settlements had taken on a veneer of European culture. Parish records for St. Francis Xavier's Church at Vincennes, Indiana, start in 1704, as do those of Ste. Anne's of Detroit. Cahokia (1699) and Kaskaskia (1703) in present-day Illinois were thriving French villages up until British occupation in 1765, which date marks the beginning of French emigration to the western side of the Mississippi (see EXPLORATION, FRENCH). The first settlement on the Missouri side, Ste. Genevieve, can be dated as far back as 1732, although Philippe François Renault was operating a lead mine in the area in 1723. Between the upper Mississippi valley region and Canada, Detroit (1685) stood as something of a way station. To the south, Arkansas Post occupied a similar position between the towns of Upper Louisiana and those of Lower Louisiana—Biloxi (1699), Mobile (1702), and New Orleans (1718). Up until the Louisiana Purchase—that is, for a period of forty years after the Treaty of PARIS of 1763—Frenchmen retained their hegemony in the Mississippi valley despite conflicts with the English and the Americans in Illinois and Spanish rule in Louisiana itself.

That the domination by citizens of French blood did not end when France ceded Louisiana to Spain in 1763 is crucial to an understanding of the Mississippi valley frontier between that date and 1804. In this period New Orleans, after a shaky start, grew rapidly in importance. Having reached some accommodation with the Spanish administration, French merchants directed their city to a new age. New Orleans became an energetic depot for goods flowing in and out of the heartland and was a vital link in the trade nexus of the Atlantic seaboard. The French population of Lower Louisiana was actually reinforced in 1755 when the Acadians, driven from Nova Scotia by the British, came to the delta region.

Stimulated by New Orleans' new connections and unencumbered by colonial mercantilism or patriotic visions, two Frenchmen, Pierre LACLEDE and Auguste CHOUTEAU, founded St. Louis in 1764, a town that would become the urban focus for the upper Mississippi valley region and a commercial jumping-off place for the entire American West. Rarely has the vision of a city's future importance been so clearly seen by its founders. French settlers quickly built up their contacts with Indian nations to the west and established themselves as an urban population to be reckoned with. The merchant companies that some of them established, though slightly archaic in structure, represent the first native American business interests in the vast area. Chouteau emerged as the patriarch of a family commercial dynasty whose intricacy and scope could be compared to those of medieval Italy. Though still small in 1804 when Captain Amos Stoddard arrived to take over Missouri for the United States, St. Louis had already established the patterns and directions, both social and economic, that would take its citizens all over the West in the next forty years.

Historians have so neglected the social and economic role of the French on the American frontier that it is difficult to place the French and their activities in perspective. They spoke French and maintained their cultural associations with France just as the Americans had done with England during the American Revolution. Yet their ancestors had been on the American continent for a hundred years by the time St. Louis was founded, and they clearly saw themselves as distinctly native in many ways. They referred to themselves as Creoles or simply as French and regarded the Americans as intruders.

The Creoles were able to maintain their Frenchness and their relative independence in part because of their insistence on an urban culture even on the frontier. Towns and cities demand a political allegiance all their own; yet, as cultural centers, they are open-ended. Their citizens are often international in outlook, so that one is hard put to see the frontier thesis embodied in the French frontier. The Chouteaus were not foot-weary pioneers in raccoon hats but eager merchants and cultured gentlemen who took time to read Voltaire and Rousseau as fast as their works could be imported. Even the mountain men of French extraction always carried with them this urban impulse, for many of them came from Canadian villages or from St. Louis and its suburbs, and most of them either returned to their towns or became citizens of new towns.

St. Louis was the capital of the region. As the operations of its merchants began to expand, suburbs grew up. Carondelet was founded in 1767. In 1769 the village of St. Charles began its existence. Before the turn of the century, new villages began all over Missouri: Florissant (1786), New Madrid (1783), New Bourbon (1793), Cape Girardeau (1793), and Portage des Sioux (1799). Some were agricultural hamlets producing foodstuffs for the growing city; others were garden suburbs containing the country homes of rich merchants, such as Chouteau's farm at Florissant; still others were military and trading posts bringing Indian groups within the sphere of influence of St. Louis.

The leaders of the region and of St. Louis were the successful merchants. To them the rest of the inhabitants looked for guidance. Politics before the advent of the Americans was quite a straightforward affair. Not unlike the preindustrial Puritan communities of New England, each village had an established elite or a single paternalistic *bon papa* whose role sometimes resembled that of the New England village squire. The communities were small, and class distinctions were a well-kept tradition. Prominent men like François Vallé of Ste. Genevieve naturally assumed the position of justice of the peace, commandant of the local militia, or sometimes both. Sole civil authority rested with these men. If a matter of importance arose, they presided over an election of syndics from the community whose decisions would be irrevocable. Such elections were decided by voice vote. Criminal cases, which were exceedingly rare, also came under the jurisdiction of the town father. If a criminal or civil case proved particularly difficult, appeals were made to the Superior Council, on which the governor himself sat. The community usually felt well represented by the town father, and if they did not, they said so. While such arrangements were not exactly democratic, they formed a heritage of self-government somewhat similar to that of the English colonies. Far removed from the absolute monarchy of France, these Creoles probably gave that institution little ideological credence. Moreover, there was probably greater separation of spiritual and civil matters in Upper Louisiana than in New England. Priests, when they could be found, were looked to for confession and education, and little else.

When the American political tradition was introduced in 1804, the Creoles reacted with caution and some alarm. They had listened carefully to all the talk about liberty and independence that accompanied the American Revolution, and they knew of the ideals of liberty, equality, and fraternity voiced in the French Revolution. The leaders of St. Louis and New Orleans sought somehow to preserve their power and the sovereignty of their communities with the status of statehood within the Union. When Lower Louisiana became Orleans Territory in 1804, its citizens resented territorial status and absentee governors and by 1812 had joined with American settlers to secure statehood for Louisiana. St. Louis also resented inferior status, and an American law that first attached Upper Louisiana to Indiana Territory struck the St. Louisans particularly hard. A committee of five—Auguste Chouteau, Charles Gratiot, Bernard Pratte, Louis Labeaume, and Pierre Provenchere—called a town meeting and denounced dictates of a "foreign government" that threatened some of the "dearest rights enjoyed by freemen!" Holding American politics in little esteem, the St. Louis Creoles pushed for territorial status of their own. In 1805 they came under the jurisdiction of Louisiana Territory. Finally, in 1812, Missouri Territory was organized. Unlike Louisiana, it sought to avoid statehood as long as possible.

The Creoles saw Americans as rootless, drifting individuals, entering their region without social ties and without true public instincts. François Vallé described Americans as a "peuple sans loix ni discipline," to be feared more than Indians. The furor died with time, however, and the English common law replaced the *coûtume de Paris*. Prominent Creoles held various offices, usually judgeships, preferring to leave the more "abstract" executive positions to ambitious young American lawyers. Busily engaged in building a city and expanding their businesses, the Creole elite, unlike their counterparts in New Orleans, allowed the old civil code to disappear.

While the French Creoles were not as politically aggressive as they might have been, they continued to be active in the Indian and fur trade. The merchants of St. Louis formed extended-family companies. More complex than simple partnerships and less abstract and safer than corporations, these companies enabled the Creoles to pool their credit resources, keep the profits and the opportunities in the region, and minimize risks by working with trusted relatives. The complexities of family-commercial relations defy any historian. One example will suffice: In 1813, at the age of twenty-four, the younger Pierre Chouteau opened a store in St. Louis with Bartholomew Berthold. They sold crockery and hardware in the city's first brick building. As the son of the elder Pierre and the nephew of Auguste, the first citizen of the city, Chouteau's first business experience came from managing his uncle's lead mines in Dubuque, Iowa. Berthold was married to Chouteau's sister Pelagie in 1811. In 1813 young Pierre married Emilie Anne Gratiot, his first cousin, daughter of Charles Gratiot and Victoire Chouteau. One sister-in-law, Julie, married Jean Pierre Cabanné, who was to be a business partner for many years. Another, Isabelle, was the wife of his brother's business partner, Jules De Mun. A later senior partner was Bernard Pratte, grandson of Chouteau's aunt. Two other junior partners, John B. Sarpy and Pierre Melicourt Papin, were also cousins.

Within companies the partners played different roles. Chouteau served as overall superintendent of his firm's affairs. Pratte kept in close contact with other companies and merchants in New Orleans and New York. General Charles Gratiot, Chouteau's brother and therefore his first cousin, had connections in Washington. Other partners, such as Papin, Berthold, and Cabanné, often took to the road and managed the trade at distant outposts. Sarpy stayed in St. Louis and acted as treasurer of the company. The merchant who did not leave St. Louis frequently on trading expeditions to the West was the exception.

Partners often acted as agents at frontier trading posts, where other French Creoles, ranging in status from simple laborer to salaried middleman with the right to trap for himself to some extent, could be found. The enterprising trapper, depending upon his ability and intelligence, could aspire to independent merchant status. To the southwest, Santa Fe and Taos offered many of these young entrepreneurs the chance to marry into important New Mexican families and set themselves up as community leaders. One is not surprised to find Frenchmen such as Ceran St. Vrain, Antoine Leroux, and Charles Beaubien among the elite of New Mexico before and after American occupation.

The lifeblood of the economy of St. Louis was the FUR TRADE. Through the fur trade, St. Louis merchants established markets with most of the Indian tribes of the West, and equally important, with New Mexico. From Santa Fe hard money flowed into the Mississippi valley. Accumulating a capital reserve, many of the Creoles sought to diversify the economy of the region. Some entered the lead-mining operations in Missouri and present-day Iowa. The Chouteaus eventually invested some of their wealth in railroads, and when the younger Chouteau died his estate included $400,000 in railroad bonds.

Other merchant-mountain men became founders of new towns: Joseph Robidoux II laid out St. Joseph, Missouri, in 1843; his brother Louis established himself south of Los Angeles on the Jurupa Rancho. Antoine and Nick Janis founded Laporte, Colorado, in 1859. Others, having taken Indian wives, took their métis families up to Oregon upon retirement from company service. The French, then, contributed an urban experience, a commercial drive, and a feel for the social graces to the western experience.

As a commercial people, the Creoles were quick to learn the customs and languages of others. Many of them were bilingual, often multilingual; yet the French language remained their mother tongue for three generations and only gradually faded away by the 1850s. In

the West, French remained throughout this period one of three important languages. Indian agents were often required to have some ability in it, and many Indian villages employed it as a lingua franca. Certain isolated villages in Missouri spoke French as late as the 1930s.

Most educational institutions in the region were established by churchmen. Bishop Louis Debourg, who administered the area from 1812, started a Jesuit seminary (Saint Mary's in the Barrens) and a boys academy in St. Louis. Meanwhile, Mother Duchesne began a girls school at nearby Florissant. Even though a deist outlook was held by much of the population, Roman Catholicism certainly struck deep roots in the region. Even today one may notice the persistence of Roman Catholic institutions in Dubuque, St. Paul, and St. Louis and in scattered places throughout the Creole's sphere of influence in the West (see ROMAN CATHOLIC CHURCH).

Many Creoles were slaveholders, although plantation life did not catch on in Missouri as it did in Louisiana. François Vallé of Ste. Genevieve was said to have owned a hundred slaves at the time of his death in 1804. Auguste Chouteau owned at least fifty. Sympathy among the Creole population during the Civil War, to the extent that it can be gauged, seems to have been with the Confederacy.

Other aspects of the French heritage—customs, ideas, words, and foods—are less measurable but certainly present in American life. Architectural styles ranging from the formal designs of the Ursuline convent in New Orleans (the work of French engineer Ignace François Broutin) to the shady gallery or veranda of French-Canadian houses, which became a major feature of Mississippi valley planation houses, all left their mark. French music performed on feast days or at parades and balls played some role in the development of jazz, while composer Louis Moreau Gottschalk borrowed much from French Creole songs. The willingness of Creoles on the frontier to intermarry with Indians produced hundreds of half-breed families and scores of part-French Indian leaders in the West over many generations.

See N. M. Belting, *Kaskaskia Under the French Regime* (1948); W. A. Dorrance, *The Survival of French in the Old District of Ste. Genevieve* (1935); W. J. Eccles, *The Canadian Frontier* (1969); W. E. Foley, *A History of Missouri*, vol. I: 1673 to 1820 (1971); L. R. Hafen, ed., *The Mountain Men and the Fur Trade of the Far West*, 10 vols. (1965-72); and J. F. McDermott, ed., *The French in the Mississippi Valley* (1965), *Frenchmen and French Ways in the Mississippi Valley* (1969), *The Frontier Re-examined* (1967), *A Glossary of Mississippi Valley French, 1673-1850* (1941), and *Private Libraries in Creole St. Louis* (1938).
—J. Gɪ.

French rule in the Mississippi valley. See MISSISSIPPI VALLEY: FRENCH AND SPANISH PERIODS.

Frenzeny, Paul. See Jules TAVERNIER.

frontier, Australia. The FRONTIER THEORY associated with Frederick Jackson Turner's analysis of the American experience has on occasion been applied to Australia. It, along with Canada and South Africa, has shared certain aspects of the Turnerian model, especially as recounted by the Australian historian Russel Ward. For the most part, however, the Australian frontiers have so differed from that in the United States as to lend added weight to the Turnerian assumption of uniqueness.

There have been four clearly distinguishable Australian frontiers. Further, Australia (together with New Zealand) was itself viewed as a frontier of European civilization from the end of the eighteenth until the latter decades of the nineteenth centuries. Fundamental to the development of Australia and its frontiers is the fact that the Australian population has always been ninety-five percent or more British in stock. Unlike the United States frontier, where diverse European peoples came together to rub customs off on one another, Australia represented a transplantation of British working-class culture: Australia therefore was a *British* frontier, a land of beginning again for a variety of peoples who had been unsuccessful, or unhappy, in Britain: convicts, remittance men, Chartists, Irish who opposed the church and the rule of the United Kingdom, and dissident religious groups, Methodist foremost. To Australia were transplanted the religious and class quarrels of nineteenth-century Britain, with little notion that such quarrels could be left behind for long.

Internally, the four frontiers were relatively distinct. The first lay around Sydney Cove, where in January 1788 the First Fleet under the command of Arthur Phillip disgorged their contents together with over a thousand convicts and jailers. About them lay the Bush, and within the Bush lay aborigines who were ill-prepared to deal with newcomers from within their Stone Age culture. Convicts were sent to New South Wales until 1840 and to Tasmania until 1852; in all some 160,000 arrived, primarily after 1815. (Western Australia also received convicts from 1850 to 1868.) Convict settlements were the antithesis of those in North America: The men were tied to a system, itself ill-organized and inefficient, which precluded free land, social innovation, and the breaking of class barriers through individual performance. In time the majority of convicts were assigned to free settlers, providing a labor force, intensifying class awareness, rooting settlement near the ports of entry, and retarding the growth of forms of agriculture not amenable to a gang labor system. If there was a frontier at this time, it lay in the Bush, which, precisely because it was at the outer edge of imprisonment, became increasingly attractive, romantic, and remote.

The Bush was not, in fact, attractive at all, but exceptionally inhospitable to settlement. Australian ground cover was prickly, poor, and weakly rooted; the land was arid, water evaporated quickly, and the timber cover was sparse except in relatively limited areas, such as the Blue Mountains. Compact settlements were difficult to establish, even as the convict period ended, for lack of water and the poverty of transport kept most Australians rooted to the seacoast, as they remain to this day. The obvious solution to the near interior was a pastoral economy, and the second frontier emerged based on sheep.

The second frontier was founded by the squatters. Climate and soil did not favor small settlers, and the grants made to "emancipists" and garrison men were too small to permit wheat farming. Small settlers lacked capital for expansion, limiting most free settlers to market gardening near the towns. The economy that arose was not a democratic one, resting as it did upon men of capital. From 1821, the first year for commercial export of wool, to 1850, Australian wool-growers moved from

being experimenters upon the fringes of an empire to being the proven producers of wool; in 1850 they sold more wool to England than did Germany and Spain together. Middle-class immigrants were now attracted to Australia; many had been comfortable in Britain but faced the prospect of an economic decline. They took with them sufficient capital to establish a squattocracy upon the land, a local equivalent of the gentry-bred squireocracy of England. Because of the sheepman's frontier, the Australian squattocracy has at times been compared to the cattleman's position in the American West. However, the frontier of the squatter bore more resemblance to that of the trekboer in South Africa.

The Australian frontier clearly did not lay in a westerning process. Initial movement was along the coastal lowlands. In 1813 the Blue Mountains were penetrated deeply enough to reveal open woodland to the west, and the first inland town, Bathurst, was founded two years later. In 1837 Sir Thomas Mitchell, the surveyor-general, traveled from Sydney to Portland Bay (in western Victoria), opening a rich pastoral area that he named Australia Felix. Most important, Charles Sturt sought to find some Australian equivalent of the North American Great Lakes by following the westward-draining rivers from the eastern highlands, only to prove that nothing lay in the interior save more saltpans. Farther to the north a German, Ludwig Leichardt, crossed to a point north of Darwin, in the present-day Northern Territory, discovering that the North was as arid as the South once away from the tropical lowlands. In 1848 Leichardt disappeared while attempting a transcontinental journey, and he above all became the symbol of the unpromising, omnivorous Outback, the land not of "beginning again" or of "the eternal return" but of "never return." Upon Leichardt were built many of the legends of the Australian "frontier," including the finest work of the continent's finest author, Patrick White, in *Voss*.

In truth, there was no Turnerian frontier, and certainly no westward movement in Australia. Exploration, settlement, and interior development (to the degree that such took place) proceeded from all directions. Emphasis was placed on the eastern and southeastern coasts, however, leaving the Far West isolated by the great distances of the interior. Communication continued to be by sea, and Australians continued to cluster in seaport villages. Railways were built by the state governments, since private enterprise could not expect profit from intermediate communities of settlers, and the Australian grain-farmer, in particular, demanded cheaper transportation to the ports. Victoria had more capital and began the railway boom of the late 1850s, but its railways did not reach the South Australian border until 1885—less than halfway across the continent—in the same year that the first trans-Canadian railway was completed. Western Australia, therefore, was left isolated to develop its own frontier.

This third frontier lay to the east of Perth, and it rested on sheep, minerals, and timber. In 1883 one of the richest silver-lead-zinc fields in the world was found at Broken Hill, in New South Wales. From it, from Tasmania, and from Western Australia came much of the capital that made the latter part of the nineteenth and early part of the twentieth centuries boom years for Australia. "Westralia" remained an appendage of the

East, however, just as Queensland—where sugar cane began to be grown commercially in the 1850s—did to the Southeast, and the dryland farmers of South Australia to Victoria and New South Wales. Rather than creating new centers of settlement, as the gold rushes and mining booms of the United States had done in California and the Rocky Mountains, mining in Australia sharpened the focus of the continent on its two rapidly growing cities, Melbourne and Sydney.

The fourth frontier showed more superficial similarities to that of the United States, although it lay not within the continent but outside: to the far north, in New Guinea. Populated with Stone Age cultures that European imperialism had passed by until the 1870s, New Guinea was at first of interest to Britain only because it attracted Germany and because it could provide some black labor for the Queensland cane fields. Australia's Africa, it was regarded as too tropical for white settlement. Britain transferred Papua to Australia in 1902, and in 1914 Australian troops took over the German portion of the island. This land was confirmed to the Commonwealth of Australia—itself born in 1901—by the League of Nations in 1919. There was no immediate rush of settlers.

The rush came later, and briefly New Guinea passed through in miniature the phases associated with a Turnerian frontier. New Guinea was a belt of relatively free land that had attracted some Europeans from the 1870s and 1880s. In the 1930s the discovery of the central highland valley system directed attention to the interior, and miners and missionaries sought out the El Dorado so long denied the Australian dream. Planters began to expand after 1951. Encounters between settlers and the aboriginal population were bloody, the land was dangerous, and the sense of being under siege was acute. The last was self-romanticizing, for, in fact, the native societies of New Guinea did not reach out to attack white settlers, being content to defend themselves from within the interior against unwanted incursions. No new European society emerged, for the New Guinea frontier was closely controlled by the Australian government, aware of its responsibilities to the League of Nations and its successor, the United Nations. The white settlements replicated those of northern Queensland, neither notably democratic nor notably innovative.

Much of Australia remains unsettled today; in this sense it is frequently referred to as one of the world's last frontiers. But if by "frontier" is meant something more subtle than the mere absence of people, Australia is not and never was a true frontier. In particular, very little of the classic formulation of a frontier, as given by Turner, applies to the Australian story.

Australia was settled from all sides, its interior proved to be desert, and those moving onto the land were overwhelmingly of British stock. Australia did not initially offer a range of entrepreneurial opportunities and so encouraged concentration of land and monopolistic trading practices rather than free enterprise on the United States model. Australia was an urban society, and Australian democracy sprang less from its frontier than from its asphalted cities. "Mateship," the Australian term for comradeship, reflected a fear of the Outback, not romantic involvement with it. Still, Australians did embrace the myth of the frontier just as Americans and Canadians embraced similar myths. Australian lit-

erature is filled with the balladry, the poetry, and the plain voices of the harsh and empty land. Ned Kelly and other bushrangers became the plain man's cultural hero for opposing a system that was urban, capitalistic, and imperially oriented. Australia's most famous painter, Sidney Nolan, caught exactly the Australian frontier and its uniqueness: alone and alienated, yet fascinated with a mechanical civilization. However far across the horizon train tracks might run, they inevitably ended at a port beyond which stood the world upon which Australia depended.

Two historians have compared the Australian and American frontiers: Frederick Alexander, in *Moving Frontiers: An American Theme and Its Application to Australian History* (1947), and H. C. Allen, in *Bush & Backwoods* (1959). The best examination of the impact of the frontier myth on Australia is Russel Ward, *The Australian Legend* (1958). A fresh new look is taken by Geoffrey Blainey in *The Tyranny of Distance* (1966). For revealing case studies, see D. W. Meinig, *On the Margins of the Good Earth: The South Australian Wheat Frontier, 1869-1884* (1962); T. M. Perry, *Australia's First Frontier: The Spread of Settlement in New South Wales, 1788-1829* (1963); and C. D. Rowley, *Australians in New Guinea* (1958). Norman Harper, "The Rural and Urban Frontiers," *Historical Studies, Australia and New Zealand* (May 1963), is a thoughtful bibliographical essay.—R. W. W.

frontier, Canada. There have been four distinct frontiers in Canada. There was a French frontier in the New World that lasted approximately from 1534, when Jacques Cartier sailed into the St. Lawrence River, until 1760, when the British occupied French Canada. There was an English and Scots frontier of settlement associated primarily with Upper Canada (later to be called Canada West and later yet Ontario) concentrated in the years between 1783 and 1837. There was a western frontier of open spaces, essentially unwooded, explored and developed between the 1840s and 1920. And then there was a frontier of the Far North, known from the earliest days of European contact when Martin Frobisher first sought a Northwest Passage, and not fully exploited to this day. Physically and chronologically these frontiers roughly paralleled those of the United States.

Because of certain superficial similarities, until the late 1930s much of Canadian history was interpreted in the light of the FRONTIER THEORY associated with the United States historian Frederick Jackson Turner. Today, most scholars would agree that, while there were a series of frontiers both in Canada and the United States, the total meaning of the frontier experience for Canada was quite different from that of the United States. This reinterpretation has come about partly as a result of the rise of the Laurentian School of Canadian historians, who emphasize east-west trading routes and the influence of the St. Lawrence River, partly because of the general decline in Turner's influence, partly because of the rising sophistication in comparative history and sociology, and partly because of nationalism. For some in Canada, Turner was a continentalist: one who saw the entire North American continent as a geographical unit that led to cultural similarities. Although this view ignored Turner's work on sectionalism and multiple causation, Canadian nationalists distrusted Turnerian models. They were right to do so.

The French frontier in Canada was at the outer limit of continental European culture. The initial thrust was an almost entirely mercantile concern for furs and fish. Control was vested solely in Paris, a distant, politically conservative capital. There was little opportunity or need for religious, political, or commercial innovation on the New French frontier. Historian Walter Prescott Webb has argued that through exploiting the New World, the stable European population was presented with a surplus of land and capital which launched four hundred years of boom. Yet for the most part the closed mercantilistic world of New France did not significantly alter the land-people-capital ratio, and the French frontier in Canada was neither a primary source of food for France nor itself a land of opportunity. As French mercantilism differed from British, so did the French frontier differ from the British frontier.

New France experienced four types of frontier: commercial, religious, military, and settlement. They were not geographical frontiers moving west in successive waves, as Turner described the United States frontier. Rather, they were simultaneous, coterminous, and static, all aspects of a single, obsessive concern for profit. Few settlers came to New France with the intention of remaining permanently. Little economic opportunity was open to the residents, dependent on the fur trade and the success of the *coureurs de bois*. The efforts of Samuel de Champlain, Sieur de La Salle, Jean Talon, and other leaders of New France were made in behalf of the mercantile interests of the crown and not to advance settlement or create a new society.

The second, or British, frontier was essentially in Upper Canada, but it was found in all areas of new settlement (especially after 1783)—in the Maritime colonies of Nova Scotia and New Brunswick and in the Eastern Townships of Lower Canada (later Quebec). Upper Canada received a steady influx of settlers after 1793. Loyalists (settlers from English colonies farther south who remained loyal to the British crown during and after the American Revolution), Quakers, Mennonites, Dunkers, Irish, Negroes, land speculators, foresters— all mixed in the Eastern Townships and from the Bay of Quinté to the Niagara River. Here the Canadian frontier was, for the first and also for the last time, truly similar to the American frontier. Upper Canadian farmers, in a wooded temperate zone, grew wheat, oats, and barley, produced whiskey, sought improved transportation through canals and railroads, and were dependent on faraway markets. In common with most frontiers, Upper Canada lacked capital, and a few merchants took leading positions in shaping society. The settlers showed the usual concern for education, for temperance societies, and for a rude equality in speech, manners, and dress. But there were differences between the Canadian and American frontiers as early as the 1830s.

Some of these differences were obvious at the time. Except for Spanish-speaking frontiersmen and the Indians, the United States frontier was ethnically one. There were minorities, to be sure, and many languages were heard on the American frontier, especially in river towns such as St. Louis. But in Canada one third of the population was French-speaking—too large a minority to ignore, to isolate, or to dominate. However, French-Canadians initially remained within their province of Lower Canada, leaving the exploitation of the cheap lands of Upper Canada to the new arrivals.

The majority of the new arrivals were Americans, and many were loud in their desire for annexation of this frontier, which was physically so similar to Ohio or Indiana. On the American frontier, each new arrival strengthened the settlement against a primary source of fear, Indian attacks, so that growth meant greater national security. On the Upper Canadian frontier, the Indian posed little threat while the potentially subversive American did. In short, in the United States more meant safer; in Canada more meant weaker. Finally, once Upper Canada had been developed, once the Rebellion of 1837 had been suppressed by the British crown, and once Montreal's Annexation Manifesto of 1849 had been proven hollow bombast, Canadians who chose to move westward often did so by moving into the United States. The great Canadian Shield, on which agriculture was most difficult, swept down to touch Lake Superior at Thunder Bay, severing any possibility of a continuous line of agricultural settlements and diverting the Canadian westward movement to south of the Great Lakes.

It is at this point—the development of the western frontier—that the Canadian experience began to diverge most strikingly from the Turnerian model. For example, Canada remained a monarchy. This is of fundamental importance if one accepts the concept that frontiers create a selecting, or at least a filtering, process. Encounters with new environments in North America forced Europeans to reconsider the cultural baggage they had brought with them, ultimately to create new responses to new demands. In Canada different selectors were at work, and different cultural baggage was involved from the outset.

After the American Revolution the Loyalists were innovative with tools and other physical artifacts but remained conservative in political and social expression. To this day comparative sociologists would agree that Canadian customs are more conservative than those of the United States, at least marginally closer to European norms. While French-speaking Canadians had no reason to love the British crown, they feared it less than they feared the United States, because the crown had confirmed their religion, language, and law.

Despite vast empty tracts of land stretching back from the St. Lawrence, most French Canadians lived in towns from the outset, and their culture, while often rural, seldom partook of the distances and the dangers of a genuine frontier. The British settlers, many of them demobilized soldiers given grants of land or colonists sent from Scotland as a group, moved onto the soil far more slowly than American settlers did. Moreover, they were from the outset under the control of the common law. This difference is especially telling. Americans felt that they could shape their own laws to fit their new experiences. The riparian codes or mining laws of the new western territories were in part copied from the eastern states. Settlers often established themselves before Congress provided territorial government, so that in many local ways the settlers along the pushing edge of the American frontier were shaping their own laws. This was not so in Canada. Long before Canadian settlers pressed into the western lands, both the common law and the specific regulations of a powerful, semifeudal, chartered enterprise—the Hudson's Bay Company—had been placed upon the land. Settlers could conform or leave. With the important exception of settlers in Vancouver Island and British Columbia before 1871, they were not free to shape laws in accordance with their own perceptions of their immediate environment. Thus Canadians showed different attitudes toward the law itself, toward education, toward the function of the state, and toward governance. While these differences with Americans were of degree rather than of kind, the degree was significant.

Turner suggested that the American frontier was partially responsible for the American economy of abundance, an insight later refined by David M. Potter. In Canada transportation developed less rapidly—a trans-Canadian railroad not being completed until 1885 and a paved trans-Canadian highway not until the 1960s—and movement westward beyond the fertile agricultural lands of Ontario was slow. When that movement took place, it often was through the United States, where many settlers stopped without going farther. Between 1910 and 1930, when the Canadian West received its greatest proportionate population increase, land was cheap, but at the end of this period the crops best grown on that land were no longer in high demand. The economic role of Canada was played primarily within the British Empire, and after 1931, the British Commonwealth. The American economic role was worldwide. Canadian staples themselves, while abundant, often were brought into the world market just when there was less demand for them. Thus Canada showed many of the characteristics of a staple-dependent economy, such as Cuba has been, while the products of the American frontier were far more varied, moved into world markets at an earlier time, and could tap a substantial domestic market.

As Turner and, more recently, C. Vann Woodward have pointed out, the American West provided the United States with distance—with space—as a protection against potential enemies. The Canadian West led not to security but to a constant fear of annexation. The farther west settlement moved from its essentially transatlantic political, social, and economic ties, the more exposed Canada was. The Canadian West did not, therefore, become a symbol of the Canadian future. The only exception was during a short period preceding World War I, when the minister of immigration asked for strong-armed yeomen in sheepskin jackets to people the Plains. Many of these men came from the adjacent American states, however, increasing the dangers of an American cultural, if not political, annexation. The cry for more men meant to many Canadians an increased danger of losing a precarious identity rather than, as in the American West, a reinforcement of a unique identity.

Another difference of importance between the far western frontiers arises from the fact that they were not settled at the same time. Advances in technology meant that Canadian settlement, when it occurred, moved more rapidly. To the extent that they existed at all, the various frontier "stages" were telescoped. Canadians could benefit from American mistakes, not only in adaptation to sod huts and barbed wire, but in land ordinances, administration of Indian reservations, and power projects.

That the uniquely Canadian frontier lay primarily to the north of a thin line of towns meant that the frontier was essentially a story of exploitative movement northward rather than westward. Environmental similarity marked the northern lands, and this similarity included the impracticality of large-scale settlement on semibarren tundra and the inability to create chains of villages to sustain railroads built by private enterprise (hence the growth of a mixed-enterprise economy). The northern frontier did produce a mining economy, but the riches flowed into Bay Street or other financial centers in Montreal and Toronto. They did not create local metropolitan centers and locally oriented sub-economies, as settlement did in such climatically diverse environments as the Dakotas, New Mexico, and Florida.

The fourth Canadian frontier, that of the Far North, had no parallel in the United States outside Alaska. Beginning about 1870, carried into the Yukon region by the Klondike gold rush of 1896-98, and with an Arctic thrust after 1914, this frontier provided the mystique for a unique Canadian romanticism that, in the United States, was best supplied by the cattleman's frontier. This frontier of the North remains relatively unexploited to the present time, although development has been much intensified since World War II.

Canadians showed an affinity for group or collective heroes rather than individuals, since their environment was mastered more by organization men: the Hudson's Bay Company trapper, factor, or trader; the Royal Canadian Mounted Policeman; the Saskatchewan grain-growers' association; or earlier, the servants of New France. Neither the British government nor the Canadian settlers turned to sustained genocidal practices to clear the aboriginal population from the land. Since there was no cattle kingdom, no trail drives, and little vigilante justice, the most colorful episodes associated with the American West could not be transplanted to Canadian locales. Nor did the Canadian West experience Turner's successive waves of newcomers in the order he suggested. Since the Canadian frontier was not turbulent, direct governmental intervention was required only twice: in the two rebellions of 1869 and 1884 by the *métis* (persons of mixed Indian and European descent), both led by Louis RIEL. Thus the horse, the gun, and the "shootout at the O.K. Corral" did not become part of the glamour of the Canadian frontier as they were of the American frontier.

This being so, the Canadian frontier did not take root in the national literature in the way it did in American literature. To be sure, Canadian literature is marked by an awareness of environment, landscape, waterscape, and cloud; yet this awareness springs from the romanticism of William Wordsworth and the Lake Poets as much as from the frontier. The Canadian West did produce a literature of agrarian defeat. It also produced a literature of spiritual uplift, which suggested that frontiersmen and those close to the soil were closer to God—especially in the work of Ralph Connor, pseudonym for Charles W. Gordon.

The United States became independent by revolution. The revolution itself was, in numerous ways, a product of the American frontier. Canada became independent by evolution. That evolution provided a different ethos; it also gave Canada a continuing role within the British Empire and thus meant that until the twentieth century Canada continued to look eastward rather than westward. In the United States, the visible symbols of the past—the living evidence of what a people most wishes to believe of itself—are best represented by the choices made under the National Registered Historic Landmarks Act. Three types of historic sites outnumber all other kinds: those relating to the settlement of the eastern seaboard, those relating to the Civil War, and those relating to prospector and sod-buster, Indian and cavalryman. The scenes memorialized by the National Historic Sites Board of Canada were, numerically, dominated by Loyalist sites, by east-coast and fur-trade settlements and factories, and by constitutional and legislative precedents. Relatively few sites from the Canadian West were honored, for the western and frontier experiences had bitten less deeply into the Canadian consciousness.

See Gerald M. Craig, *Upper Canada: The Formative Years, 1784-1841* (1963); Michael S. Cross, ed., *The Frontier Thesis and the Canadas* (1970); William J. Eccles, *The Canadian Frontier, 1534-1760* (1969); H. A. Innis, *The Fur Trade in Canada* (rev. ed., 1956); A. R. M. Lower, *Canadians in the Making* (1958); Frederick Merk, "The Strategy of Monopoly," in *Fur Trade and Empire: George Simpson's Journal* (rev. ed., 1968); Arthur S. Morton, *A History of the Canadian West to 1870-71* (1939); E. E. Rich, *The Fur Trade and the Northwest to 1857* (1967); Paul F. Sharp. *Whoop-Up Country: The Canadian-American West, 1865-1885* (1955); G. F. G. Stanley, *The Birth of Western Canada* (2nd ed., 1960); Robin W. Winks, *The Myth of the American Frontier* (1971); and Morris Zaslow, *The Opening of the Canadian North, 1870-1914* (1971).—R. W. W.

frontier life, 1750-1850. By the end of the eighteenth century there were nearly 900,000 people on the American frontier, and the number was increasing annually. Most of the individuals who emigrated westward during this period had already undergone a seasoning experience that had prepared them to meet the challenges of nature, the land, and Indian resistance. This process of conditioning had begun before the middle of the eighteenth century. Virginians moving up to the falls of the James and beyond, Marylanders migrating toward the headwaters of the Potomac, Pennsylvanians moving up the Susquehanna, New Yorkers up the Hudson and Mohawk, and Carolinians moving into the Yadkin and Catawba valleys created a wide realm of backwoods settlements. As new immigrants reached North America from the British Isles and Europe, they pushed into the backcountry.

Thus by the middle of the eighteenth century the major westward movement had begun. Joist Hite, for instance, had made a settlement at the head of the Shenandoah Valley in 1731, and soon after that new settlements were being formed all across the eastern valley frontier. People moving into these great land troughs were the first to be almost completely isolated from both Old World and established eastern seaboard economic and social communications.

Once out of immediate reach of established associations with the older centers, the American pioneer was forced to depend largely upon the immediate resources of the land. He gathered his food from the woods, from the tiny clearings he chopped out of the virgin forest, and from the streams. His cabin, furniture, implements, and vehicles of travel were hewn and fashioned from materials readily at hand. His clothing was homemade from native fibers and skins, and his medicines came from native herbs. For the early American pioneer of the Old West the woods offered both succor and death. In most areas the frontiersman could never be certain when death and injury would pitch out of the woods in the form of a surprise Indian attack, a storm, or an accident. This condition tested the pioneer's inner courage and self-reliance.

The forms of economic and social life were elementary. Even though towns with merchants sprang up around the forts and stations, stocks of goods were severely limited, and in the earliest years exchange of goods and products was carried on by a crude form of barter. Life in towns and villages was generally no more refined than that of the isolated backcountry farm. People lived in severely limited cabin space, where they cooked, ate, slept, entertained and carried on several types of fireside industries, such as spinning, weaving, knitting, shoe-making, and woodwork—all in a single room. Modesty between sexes was both impossible and, in many cases, unknown. Family, relatives, and wayfaring strangers undressed and dressed before the fire and slept wherever there was floor space to lay a body. Sometimes cabins became smelly and nearly always bug-ridden. There were no insecticides, except for a form of crude wood lye soap, and no knowledge of the importance of personal hygiene.

DISEASES took a relatively heavy toll of life and human energy. Among the most virulent were malaria, typhoid and yellow fevers, the endemic diseases and smallpox, and, after 1833, Asiatic cholera. There were almost no DOCTORS of dependable training and capability in most areas of the frontier. Because of this lack, frontiersmen had to depend almost completely on folk remedies, mineral curatives, and superstitions. Children were delivered by often clumsy fathers or by neighboring "granny women." Cuts and wounds were treated with materials and methods that were often more infectious than the original injuries. Indian lore was the basic *materia medica* of the frontiersman, and the earth and the forest the source of supply. Life on the frontier was hard for women, and many of them died at an early age.

Socially the American frontiersman was hospitable. He was not only ready to take the benighted stranger into an already overcrowded cabin for humane reasons, but he craved company and news. Many a frontiersman wore his foreign guest out before bedtime by asking him unending questions. The backwoodsman had curiosity about everything from the place of origin of the stranger to what he had paid for his coat and hat. It never occurred to him that he was being rude or personal. The last thing he intended was to offer offense to a guest.

Not only was the backwoodsman tireless in asking questions, he was proud of his own accomplishments. He bragged of his physical strength, his marksmanship, his horse, wife, dog, land, and even of the brightness of the sun and moon over his head. In time he became exceedingly sensitive about his place and influence in the territorial, state, and national political systems. Bragging was often a way of renewing courage for the frontiersman. He early became an incurable promoter, whether or not he had a philosophical conviction about the Eden-like qualities of his country. He often proclaimed his community the center of the "garden" and his neighbors the hardy souls who were the chosen ones. He did this knowing full well that the backwoods garden was full of thorn trees.

Isolation was a leading environmental fact in the shaping of the frontier way of life. It limited the pioneer in many areas of activity, stunted his intellectual growth, and coarsened his manners, folk mores, and mode of speech. As to speech, the backwoodsman contributed significantly to making the English language highly functional. His nomenclature, colloquialisms, adoptions of Indian words, the challenges of a highly variable fauna and environmental conditions, all had their influences. Added to this, great pockets of western settlers clung to the idiom and speech forms of seventeenth-century Britain (see ENGLISH LANGUAGE AND THE WESTWARD MOVEMENT).

The American frontiersman practiced a religion that matched his environment and condition of life. Most of his ministers were laymen, and his scriptural interpretations were literal. At the turn of the nineteenth century a series of highly emotional revivals in Kentucky set a pattern for future religious responses. The Methodist church especially had a wide impact on the frontier. Circuit riders followed the settler to his westernmost points of penetration, and the annual revival meeting was of as much social as religious importance. The names of Francis Asbury, Peter CARTWRIGHT, David Rice, William Magee, James B. Findley, and Charles G. Finney (see REVIVALISM) were almost as well known as those of the old trailbreakers.

In politics the frontiersman supported the local heroes for county and state offices and the victors of frontier wars for national offices. He was particularly sensitive about issues that tended to slight his region and its needs, especially the proposed Jay's Treaty of 1785, the excise taxes on distilled spirits, and the Alien and Sedition Acts. He helped to create the western folk type of political hero that sent Andrew Jackson, William Henry Harrison, James Knox Polk, and Abraham Lincoln to the White House. He was sensitive on issues of banking, internal improvements, taxation, and Indian policies.

Elections, militia musters, stump speakings, and political debates were always attractive to the backwoodsman. Whether or not he understood what an orator had to say, he liked to hear him say it. The more grandiloquent the phraseology and the flights of oratory the better he liked it. Joseph Hamilton Daviess, Jonathan Jennings, Henry Clay, Felix Grundy, Thomas Hart Benton, and scores of others were able to satisfy even the most demanding audiences with their golden phrases.

There was little place on the frontier settlement for the rugged individualist. Settling the backwoods was a highly cooperative affair. Neighbors helped the newcomer to raise a cabin, clear his ground, roll his logs, and harvest his crops. Log rollings, cabin raisings, corn shuckings, quiltings, bean-stringings, and housewarmings were as much a part of frontier life as the passing of the seasons. This is the way the backwoodsmen got their heavy tasks performed. Even the various forms of entertainment, from barn dances, to preparing a new cabin for occupancy, to party games, helped to break the monotony of life, and to break the ice in courting.

The backwoods way of life went far toward shaping the American personality. Accomplishments of common backwoodsmen in clearing the land, building flatboats and steamboats, opening the roads, building the towns and industries, and establishing schools and churches became their proud boasts. Their adaptability was the magic quality that made life on the frontier possible. It is indeed doubtful that after 1830 any really new and innovative changes were made in the art of American pioneering.

See R. C. Buley, *The Old Northwest: Pioneer Period, 1815-1840* (1950); Mann Butler, *A History of the Commonwealth of Kentucky* (1834); Thomas D. Clark, *The Rampaging Frontier* (1939); Everett Dick, *The Dixie Frontier* (1948); Timothy Flint, *Recollections of the Last Ten Years* (1826); and Baynard Rush Hall [Robert Carlton], *The New Purchase* (1916).—T. D. C.

frontier theory. The frontier theory of American history, developed by historian Frederick Jackson TURNER, is that the westward-moving American frontier was a unique historical phenomenon which gave a special tincture to the development of American society. The theory provided a key to understanding the origins of American democracy, the American character, and the evolution of the American society. The theory provided a key to understanding the origins of American democracy, the American character, and the evolution of the American political system. In varied and subtle forms the theory continues to be a main thread of interpretation in textbooks and monographs, not only of United States history but of the history of other nations such as Australia, Russia, and Brazil.

The theory was presented in Turner's paper "The Significance of the Frontier in American History," read at the Chicago meeting of the American Historical Association in 1893 and published in the *Proceedings* of the State Historical Society of Wisconsin in December 1893. Turner unhesitatingly called for a revision of United States history and said that the waves of frontier advances by Indian traders, miners, cattle-raisers, and farmers provided a "record of social evolution." "The result is," Turner wrote, "that to the frontier the American intellect owes its striking characteristics. That coarseness and strength combined with acuteness and inquisitiveness; that practical, inventive turn of mind, quick to find expedients; that masterful grasp of material things, lacking in the artistic but powerful to effect great ends; that restless, nervous energy." The frontier promoted "the composite nationality" of the American people. Indeed, Turner went so far as to argue that "the frontier individualism from the beginning has promoted democracy."

In his later writings and teachings Turner softened his argument, but never abandoned the theory as a basic tenet in all his research and writing. He portrayed the frontier areas as regions that witnessed generations of historic change with gradually emerging sectional characteristics. This transformation Turner called "the frontier process," involving a complex of interrelated social, economic, political, and geographical forces. The distinct physiographic "provinces," or sections, that emerged in the wake of the advancing frontier were readily identified after 1890 when the census demonstrated that the westward advance had at last come to a halt.

In his essay "Sections and the Nation," published in the *Yale Review* in October 1922, Turner set forth the concept of multiple hypothesis in historical causation by pinpointing the multiple factors such as soil, climate, economic interests, and inherited ideals that comprised the background of sectional loyalties and rivalries. Yet it was actually the federation of sections that gave nourishment to the American spirit, what Turner called "Uncle Sam's psychology." The frontier theory, then, actually set forth a frontier-sectional theory to explain the whole development of American society. Turner hoped to provide a theoretical scaffolding that would provide a better understanding of the origins of the American character and the American system of government.

In several essays Turner, developing the SAFETY VALVE THEORY of George Henry Evans, suggested that the frontier had been a safety valve for Americans seeking a better way of life. The closing of the frontier introduced a period of dwindling resources, making governmental planning more necessary than it had been in the past. These concepts were later altered by Turner's followers to include an explanation for business cycles and unemployment patterns which came under attack by historians of American economic history. However, Turner's general view of the frontier as a safety valve for those who wanted a new start in life is generally accepted.

Turner's work has been the subject of much criticism. A decade of controversy in the 1930s was followed by searching criticism and reexamination in the years from 1950 to 1970. Turner's more extreme claims of the frontier's determinative influences have been rejected, but the broad implications of his environmentalist view of the origins of the American nation are still generally accepted. Certainly his interpretations give scant attention to nonwhite people, especially Negroes and Indians, and he tended to neglect the influences of the city, the clash of labor and capital, and the frontiersman's exploitation of rich national resources. But it is also true that his writings and teachings have encouraged a persistent debate about the nature of historical change. And in that debate, the frontier-sectional theory remains one of the most important contributions to historical thought made by an American writer.

See Ray A. Billington, *America's Frontier Heritage* (1969) and *The Genesis of the Frontier Thesis* (1971); and Wilbur R. Jacobs, *The Historical World of Frederick Jackson Turner* (1968); "Turner's Methodology: Multiple Working Hypothesis or Ruling Theory?" *Journal of American History*, vol. 55 (1968); "Colonial Origins of the United States: The Turnerean View," *Pacific Historical Review*, vol. 40 (1971); and (ed.) *America's Great Frontiers and Sections* (1969).—W. R. J.

Fung Ching (1863-1897). Chinese merchant and shoe manufacturer. Fung Ching was known as "Little Pete" from the brand name of his shoes, F. C. Peters & Company. He came to San Francisco as a teen-ager in the 1870s. A brilliant organizer and a thoroughly unscrupulous man, he rose rapidly to power within Chinatown and to a position of influence in the community at large. His contacts spanned almost the entire range, from political bosses to racetrack jobbers. In 1887 he was convicted of attempting to corrupt officials investigating a murder. He spent five years in prison but continued to wield influence after his release. Fung Ching was assassinated by "hatchetmen" at the age of thirty-four in January 1897.—G. B.

Furnas, Robert Wilkinson (1824-1905). Nebraska editor, soldier, politician, and agriculturalist. Furnas was born near Troy, Ohio, and as a young man with little formal education served a printer's apprenticeship in Covington, Kentucky. He then conducted a printing business in Cincinnati and later became editor and publisher of a newspaper in his home town of Troy. In 1856 Furnas settled in Brownville, Nebraska, and established the *Nebraska Advertiser*, which soon became one of the most important papers in the territory. Through the *Advertiser*, which he operated until 1861, he vigorously promoted the settlement of Nebraska, placing particular emphasis upon the agricultural potential of the area. As a member of the territorial legislature from 1856 to 1860 Furnas was largely responsible for the adoption of a public school law and the creation of a board of agriculture. In 1860 he joined Nebraska's recently established Republican party.

When the Civil War began, Furnas was commissioned a colonel in the Nebraska militia. In 1862 he received a commission as a colonel in the regular army and was sent to southern Kansas, where he organized three Indian regiments for Union service in the Indian Territory (Oklahoma) and along the Kansas-Missouri border. He later commanded the Second Nebraska Cavalry, which, as part of a larger force under Brigadier General Alfred Sully, shared in a significant victory over the Sioux on September 3, 1863, at White Stone Hills, Dakota Territory.

In 1864 President Abraham Lincoln appointed Furnas agent for the Omaha Indians. When the Winnebago, who were akin to the Omaha, faced hardship on their reservation in Dakota, they moved down the Missouri River to reside on the Omaha reservation in northeastern Nebraska. Furnas assisted in the relief of the newcomers. In 1865 he was instrumental in arranging the cession of a portion of the Omaha lands to the Winnebago people. He remained Omaha agent until President Andrew Johnson removed him from that position in 1866 for political reasons.

Returning to Brownville, Furnas began farming and developed a nursery business. As president of the State Board of Agriculture and secretary of the State Horticultural Society, he achieved prominence as an advocate of tree-planting, fruit-raising, and improved methods of farming.

As a leading Nebraska Republican, Furnas was elected governor in 1872. When the state was beset with a devastating grasshopper plague in 1874, Governor Furnas formed the Nebraska Relief and Aid Society, which solicited and secured a great deal of material assistance for the victims of the natural disaster.

Tiring of the governorship, Furnas did not seek reelection in 1874, but he did devote the rest of his life to public enterprises, particularly in agriculture.

See Robert C. Farb, "The Military Career of Robert W. Furnas," *Nebraska History* (March 1951); and "Robert W. Furnas as Omaha Indian Agent, 1864-1866," *Ibid.* (September-December 1951); Robert N. Manley, "In the Wake of the Grasshoppers: Public Relief in Nebraska, 1874-1875," *Ibid.* (December 1963);

and James C. Olson, *History of Nebraska*, 2nd ed. (1966).—H. A. D.

fur trade: *in the colonies.* Fur trading, perhaps more than any other single activity, provided the impetus for exploring and colonizing North America. This trade remained an economic mainstay for generations among the French of Canada and the Dutch and English of New York because these two areas enjoyed easy access to the great interior fur supply of the Great Lakes and beyond, via the St. Lawrence and Hudson-Mohawk routes, respectively. Elsewhere the trade declined in importance as the limited seaboard supply of fur-bearing animals became exhausted. In the Southeast, Charleston, South Carolina, became a major center for the deerskin trade, and well into the eighteenth century some fifty thousand deerskins a year found their way through that port to the London market.

As early as 1600 Henry IV agreed to send an expedition to America, hoping that the group would return to France with enough beaver hides to replenish his dwindling treasury. By the beginning of the eighteenth century French, Dutch, and English traders were pushing into North America's interior in pursuit of this creature, whose fur was used in elegant felt hats and fur coats. By 1750 they had penetrated the entire Mississippi valley and had explored as far west as the Big Horn Mountains of Montana and Wyoming.

During the seventeenth and eighteenth centuries nearly all the hunting was done by Indians, who sold the pelts to traders for a variety of European goods, including woolen cloth, iron tools and cooking implements, liquor, guns, and ammunition. Taken collectively these items, and the activity required to secure them, transformed Indian life. The most favored tribes were those who lived in the interior or had access to it; coastal Indians soon lost their economic value to the whites and came to be regarded primarily as obstacles to the expansion of settlement and progress.

Fur trading was the only significant economic activity that demanded close cooperation between the races. Wherever it dominated Indian-white relations, they were apt to be friendly, for the trade was mutually beneficial and made the races interdependent. It encouraged commercial, political, and military alliances between tribes and colonies whose interests were complementary. It also created rivalry (often culminating in warfare) between those who found themselves competitors. In time trade rivalry tended to become almost imperceptibly a competition for empire itself, with trade serving more as a means than an end. Such was the case by the 1680s, when colonial competition had narrowed down to England and France.

In general, the French enjoyed happier Indian relations than did the Dutch and English, owing partly to their far-flung trading activity and partly to the small volume of French migration to North America, which never seriously threatened Indians with displacement and loss of lands. Over the years the French built up a trade and alliance system with widely scattered tribes: the Abnaki of Maine; the Huron around Georgian Bay; the Ottawa near the Straits of Mackinac; the Miami of Ohio and Indiana; and the Illinois. The IROQUOIS CONFEDERACY was the only Indian group to whom the French were hostile. Trade was carried on in two ways: either the Indians brought their peltry to Montreal or other French settlements by canoe or French traders (*coureurs de bois*) ventured into the interior, often remaining for months in remote Indian villages, where they acquired wives and sired children. Whether the trade occurred at Montreal or deep in the interior, it was usually conducted directly with the tribes that hunted the animals; but the Huron and Ottawa in particular seem to have developed a middleman position between the French and more distant tribes that seldom if ever reached Montreal.

French interest in the Indians was never entirely commercial. The fur trade was a means of extending French influence and power across the continent. Military posts were gradually established in the interior both to protect the trade against interlopers and to confirm French control. Jesuit and other missionaries also ventured into the Indian villages, primarily to convert the heathen to Christianity but also to France. More permanent missions were founded near Montreal, and the Indians who were induced to settle there became a buffer for Canada and useful auxiliaries against the Iroquois and English of New York.

The HUDSON'S BAY COMPANY, chartered by the British government in 1670, began establishing trading posts in the Hudson's Bay country, far to the north, which tapped the rich northern peltry supply. (Great Britain formally acquired the Hudson's Bay region from France when the Treaty of Utrecht was signed in 1713.) Private individuals and company employees were used as trappers. In 1727 New York built a fortified post at Oswego on Lake Ontario that intercepted some of the western Indians carrying furs to Montreal. By the 1730s Pennsylvania traders were penetrating the upper Ohio valley. The French responded by building more forts. The most potentially dangerous French outposts were those constructed between 1749 and 1754 connecting Lake Erie with the forks of the Ohio at present-day Pittsburgh. They blocked English westward expansion. A direct confrontation at the forks of the Ohio in 1754 precipitated the last and greatest of the Anglo-French conflicts, the French and Indian War, which resulted in France's final defeat and expulsion from North America in 1763.

New York and the Iroquois profited little more than the French from England's victory. Once Canada was in English hands most of the northern trade gravitated to Montreal, bypassing the Iroquois altogether. Some of the western tribes revolted against British domination in Pontiac's Rebellion in 1763. Although the rebellion failed, it helped bring greater uniformity and central control of Indian policy.

See INDIAN-WHITE RELATIONS: *British Indian policy, 1763-1775*; and BRITISH ADMINISTRATIVE POLICY.

See Paul C. Phillips, *The Fur Trade*, vol. I (1961); W. J. Eccles, *The Canadian Frontier, 1500-1760* (1967); Allen W. Trelease, *Indian Affairs in Colonial New York: The Seventeenth Century* (1960), and "The Iroquois and the Western Fur Trade: A Problem in Interpretation," *Mississippi Valley Historical Review*, vol. 54 (1962); and J. T. Flexner, *Mohawk Baronet: Sir William Johnson of New York* (1959).—A. W. T.

in the United States. Even after the Treaty of Paris of 1783 secured United States independence, an essentially colonial, European-oriented fur commerce continued, with most American furs being exported. The

Hudson's Bay Company and various Montreal businessmen used the capital outflows generated by the industrial revolution to dominate not only the trade of Canada and Rupert's Land but also the Old Northwest of the United States. This was done in violation of the peace treaty until Jay's Treaty (effective in 1796). Only after the War of 1812 did the British finally yield all hopes of creating an Indian buffer zone in the Old Northwest, but the fur trade itself continued to be controlled by the British. Spanish traders also, operating out of Florida and New Orleans and using especially the Florida-based Scottish firm of Panton, Leslie, and Company, challenged the United States for the deerskin trade within its own borders in the Southeast until the Treaty of San Lorenzo (1795). By a decade later, however, the advance of the agricultural frontier had ended the trade in this region.

The only fruitful outlet for American fur traders in the eighteenth century was the maritime trade, starting with the Pacific voyages involving the sea otter and seals obtained in the Pacific Northwest, the sandalwood of the Sandwich Islands (Hawaii), the spices of China, and the ginseng roots and manufactured goods of New England.

Only in the closing years of the eighteenth century did the United States enter, timidly, into the race for beaver—the most valuable trade good on the frontier, providing peltry not only for fancy continental hats and coats but for muffs, collars, and linings as well. For the next fifty years the fur trade went hand in hand with the westward push of the American frontier. Only with the decline in the beaver population during the 1840s did fur trading cease to provide an incentive for exploration and settlement.

In the 1790s goods from Montreal, Hudson's Bay, and St. Louis (the three main terminals) were moved largely on water. Manning the boats was the *voyageur*, typically the halfbreed son of a French father and Indian mother first employed by the British NORTH WEST COMPANY in Canada. His work was generally the same whether he worked in the far north near Hudson's Bay or on the lower Mississippi: get the boat through the rapids, shallows, or floods for the TRAPPERS or traders.

The transport of the furs back to the centers was also mainly by water during these early years. Normally the pelts were bound in one-hundred-pound packs, which the voyageur carried in slings on his back over the frequent and sometimes long portages. The fur brigade usually got started before daylight, worked a few hours, rested at breakfast, then worked throughout the day, quitting only for the large evening meal. (Food was usually easy to procure, for game was plentiful. Goose was popular in the Hudson's Bay region, large white fish on the large rivers, buffalo on the Plains, and rabbit and salmon west of the Rockies, where game might be scarce.) Dinner finished, the voyageur lighted his pipe, a small clay one if he came from the east. If he had grown up in an Indian village, he generally carried a long fire bag, fringed or beaded, that contained his fire tools: flint and steel, a pipe, and some tobacco. The men slept under their upturned canoes.

Early each spring, when the ice was beginning to melt, the voyageurs began the long trips in frail birchbark canoes. Over the years the canoes grew in size and weight; large ones, called *canotes de maître*, required four

men to carry them when empty and fourteen men to paddle them well. On the Missouri, goods were usually carried in pirogues, hollowed-out cottonwood logs, which were stronger than the birchbark canoes and which sometimes reached seventy feet in length and four feet in width. If the pirogues could not be paddled for one reason or another, ropes, or cordelles, were tied to the bows and the voyageurs dragged the boats along the banks on cordelle paths. Two pirogues when lashed together and boarded across could carry ten to fifteen tons of cargo. Where streams were broad and shallow, as on the Yellowstone, Athabasca, and Missouri (during the summer), keelboats were used. The ones on the Missouri, about sixty feet long and eighteen feet across, were capable of carrying ten to twenty tons of goods. When the water was calm, the men poled the boat along. They positioned themselves along both sides of the boat, facing toward the stern. On a given signal, they leaned into their poles and walked the boat forward under their feet. Reaching the stern, they ran back to the bow and began again. If the water was deep or the bottom soft, they attached a cordelle to the mast and pulled the keelboat along the shore. Oars were used to supplement poling and cordelling. Although sails were available, they were rarely used.

It was not until after the Louisiana Purchase (1803) and the Lewis and Clark expedition (1804-06) that the United States fur trade began a serious invasion of the trans-Mississippi region, penetrating the upper Missouri area by 1806. The Lewis and Clark expedition was designed in part to detach the fur resources held by the Indians of the Plains and mountains from the British and to add them to the United States. The expedition, having moved through some of the richest beaver country in the nation, proved that furs could be transported overland by horse to the Columbia River and shipped to the Orient more cheaply than the British could ship them via water through Montreal or Hudson's Bay. Encouraged by reports circulating even before the expedition was completed, men began moving westward.

Manuel LISA, one of the expedition's suppliers, was among the pioneers in the upper Missouri trade. In 1807 he opened dealings with several tribes along the river and established the first trading post, Fort Raymond, in present-day Montana. In 1809 Lisa, William Clark, (Jean) Pierre Chouteau, Auguste Pierre CHOUTEAU, Pierre MENARD, and others founded the St. Louis-based MISSOURI FUR COMPANY. (The CHOUTEAU FAMILY had been operating in the area since the 1780s.) In the Southwest Zebulon Pike's expedition of 1806-07 stirred the first serious interest there, and in 1814-15 American traders were looking for beaver on the upper Arkansas River.

Meanwhile, John Jacob ASTOR began a duel with the British-Canadians in the Old Northwest, organizing the AMERICAN FUR COMPANY in 1808 and the Pacific Fur Company in 1810. The American Fur Company, which became the most powerful American company, freed Astor from having to depend on the British for supplies and allowed him to build up trade with the East Coast, the Pacific Northwest, and China (see CHINA TRADE). (Although the Chinese had not taken a fancy to the popular beaver hats of Europe, they did make use of the fur in other types of garments.)

With the organization of the Pacific Fur Company, Astor hoped to tap the fur resources of the Pacific Northwest and blend them into world commerce (see OREGON and WASHINGTON). Following the dispatch of a maritime expedition in 1810 and an overland party led by Wilson Price HUNT in 1811, which were to meet at the mouth of the Columbia River, Astoria was founded in March 1811. American ownership of the post was short-lived; in October 1813 Astor's partners, most of whom were Canadians, sold the post to the British North West Company—much to the regret of certain Britishers, for shortly thereafter the post was formally captured by a British warship during the War of 1812. With the sale and subsequent capture of the post, Astor abandoned the Pacific Fur Company. (One of his company clerks, Gabriel FRANCHERE, wrote an account of this period beginning with the 1810 voyage.) In 1821 Astoria was absorbed into the Hudson's Bay Company.

In 1817 Astor was able to gain control of the South West Company and to found a northern department with a key post at Michilimackinac. His financial and political power enabled him to destroy the United States government factory system in 1822 and to defy other regulations and laws inimicable to his interests. His companies became the monopolists of the fur trade in the Old Northwest.

The factory system, originally conceived in a plan presented to the Continental Congress in 1776, had been unstable since its adoption in 1796. (Congress had passed the plan at President George Washington's urging after an experimental trial of the system with the Creek and Cherokee Indians in the preceding year.) The plan was designed to establish posts, or "factories," where the government would exchange goods, excluding liquor, with Indians for fur. In addition to luring the Indians away from the British, the purpose of the system was to let the Indians do the hunting and trapping in their own areas, without being hampered and degraded by whites and liquor. The Indians were to function independently, getting furs to trade for reasonably priced goods. The system operated well until after the War of 1812, when British traders left the Northwest and American private enterprise began to grow.

The factory system had a number of problems. Trappers, white or Indian, were accustomed to one-year credit allowances. The factors, who were in charge of the posts, were prohibited from extending any credit. Consequently the tribes went to whoever would agree to give them traps, ammunition, and supplies on credit. Moreover, the government was handicapped by another regulation that compelled the factories to utilize home industries, not yet producing quality goods. The Indians preferred to get the best quality they could from whoever could give it to them. Finally, private traders mixed with and knew the language and social patterns of the Indians; they always knew what kind of gift which chief would prefer. The factor, a salaried government employee, was often ignorant about such matters. So, despite the low prices and honest trade ratings, the Indians continued to go to the private trader. In 1822 Congress gave in to the opposition, the American Fur Company and the St. Louis fur firms and their spokesman, Missouri senator Thomas Hart BENTON, and finally killed the program. If the system had been placed on a

firmer base, it might have helped ease trade relations between the Indians and white men.

By 1810 it no longer took only a day, week, or month of portage between the market and the fur country. Now there were months of work on the Missouri and large overland areas to cross (buffalo country, widely separated streams, plains, and mountains). The Americans moving into the new fields from the South were almost running into the Hudson's Bay group and the North West Company penetrating from the North. Competition got steadily keener. More and more the traders had to match wits against one another. Trapping during the period 1810-20 was no easy matter either. Not only was access to the rich beaver areas becoming increasingly difficult because of distance, it also was becoming dangerous. Accounts of this period often refer to the Blackfoot "wall," which made trading and trapping difficult and sometimes impossible in the Missouri region. (That wall was one of the factors contributing to the demise of the Missouri Fur Company in 1830.) Finally, the fur market itself was experiencing problems: the Napoleonic wars had impoverished many Europeans, particularly those who had been the most important fur consumers; thought was being given to using nutria (the fur of the coypu, a rodent native to South America) as a cheaper substitute in the felting markets; and English wool was competing against fur wearing apparel.

After the 1819 depression many entrepreneurs sought to recover their losses by entering the fur business. Foremost among these businessmen was William H. ASHLEY, who with Andrew HENRY sent his first expedition up the Missouri in 1822. In the next year, following an attack upon his party by the Arikara Indians and the failure of the subsequent military expedition (see ARIKARA CAMPAIGN) under Colonel Henry Leavenworth and Joshua PILCHER to redress this injustice, Ashley was determined to reach the Rockies overland. The classic era of discovery followed, personified by the work of Ashley men; Jedediah SMITH, James CLYMAN, John WEBER, Etienne PROVOST, and James BRIDGER discovered or rediscovered, among other sites, the South Pass, the Great Salt Lake, and overland routes to California and Oregon.

Ashley was also responsible for popularizing the brigade-rendezvous system as a replacement for the trading post in the central Rockies. Under the old system, used by the North West Company and Hudson's Bay Company as well as the Missouri River traders, men were hired as *engagés*, signing a contract to work for a specified period of time as either a boatman or a hunter for a regular salary. "Free trappers," individuals who had not bound themselves to serve one particular company, were the exception rather than the rule. Historically the British had considered the animals in a given tribal area to belong to that tribe and left the hunting to the Indians. The pelts were exchanged for goods at the trading post. (Americans, on the other hand, had often invaded Indian areas and obtained the furs on their own. Although the government had banned such activities—through such devices as the factory system—violations continued.) The old British system worked poorly in the Rockies, where the mountain Indians remained indifferent to trapping, preferring to spend their time in the traditional pursuit of food and clothing.

An 1868 Harper's Weekly *wood engraving, after a sketch by W. M. Cary, showing fur traders on the Missouri being attacked by Indians. (Library of Congress)*

By 1818 trade had begun to decline. Then Donald MAC-KENZIE of the North West Company revitalized the system. He took into the mountains teams, or "brigades," of experienced trappers, former engagés whose contracts had run out and who had preferred to remain in the mountains, and supplied them with long strings of pack horses rather than the traditional canoes and barges. The system worked well as long as Mackenzie was in charge; soon everyone in the area had heard of his brigades, rendezvous, and Snake country expeditions. After the absorption of the North West Company by the Hudson's Bay Company in 1821, however, Mackenzie quit, and the "new" method seemed doomed. (None of Mackenzie's successors were able to hold together and control the bands of "mountain men.")

Ashley decided to give Mackenzie's experiment a try, holding the first American rendezvous at Henry's Fork on the Green River in 1825. To the rendezvous came company trappers, free trappers, and Indians in a colorful medley classically described by Washington Irving in *The Adventures of Captain Bonneville* (1837), based on the journals of trader Benjamin BONNEVILLE. For the next fifteen years, until 1840, each summer the trappers left their camps to trade at the annual rendezvous. After the isolation of winters spent setting up new camps and falls and springs setting traps and following the beaver, the men were delighted to tear loose and spend money on goods brought by pack trains from St. Louis. At the carnival-like rendezvous they picked up letters from home, newspapers, and news from the men of the

freight caravans. The first year Ashley had neglected to bring liquor; the next he remembered to carry it in.

In his *Adventures in Mexico and the Rocky Mountains* (1849) George Frederick Ruxton described the rendezvous:

> The trappers drop in singly and in small bands, bringing their packs of beaver to this mountain market, not unfrequently to the value of a thousand dollars each, the produce of one hunt. The dissipation of the "rendezvous," however, soon turns the trapper's pockets inside out. The goods brought by the traders, although of the most inferior quality, are sold at enormous prices. . . .
>
> The rendezvous is one continued scene of drunkenness, gambling, and brawling and fighting, as long as the money and the credit of the trappers last. Seated, Indian fashion, round the fires, with a blanket spread before them, groups are seen with their "decks" of cards, playing at "euker," "poker," and "seven-up," the regular mountain games. The stakes are "beaver," which here is current coin; and when the fur is gone, their horses, mules, rifles, and shirts, hunting-packs, and *breeches*, are staked. Daring gamblers make the rounds of the camp, challenging each other to play for the trapper's highest stake,—his horse, his squaw (if he has one), and, as once happened, his scalp. There goes "hos and beaver!" is the mountain expression when any great loss is sustained;

and, sooner or later, "hos and beaver" invariably find their way into the insatiable pockets of the traders.

After the riotous debauch, which also included horse racing, wrestling, shooting matches, duels, buffalo chases, and fighting, to name just a few of the activities, the trappers withdrew for another laborious season in the mountains.

Ashley sold out in 1826 for $16,000 to Jedediah Smith, David E. Jackson, and William L. Sublette (see SUBLETTE BROTHERS.) This partnership opened up great areas of the West to the fur trade, principally through Smith's explorations. Although the Smith, Jackson and Sublette company made a substantial profit, it was sold in 1830 to the ROCKY MOUNTAIN FUR COMPANY, run by Thomas FITZPATRICK, Milton Sublette, Henry FRAEB, and Jean Baptiste Gervais—all experienced mountain traders. Competition from the American Fur Company had proved too stiff, as it would also be for the Rocky Mountain company. Among Smith, Jackson, and Sublette's accomplishments were to open up the Blackfoot country in 1829 and to introduce the first wheeled vehicles except for the cannon—ten wagons and two carriages—into the Rocky Mountains in 1830.

Trade was not limited to the upper West during this period. With Mexican independence, William BECKNELL opened up the Santa Fe trade in 1821 and was joined later by the BENT BROTHERS and Ceran ST. VRAIN. Over the Santa Fe Trail flowed a commerce that enhanced the fur trading and mercantile wealth of St. Louis and Missouri and gave rise to a huge business, BENT, ST. VRAIN AND COMPANY. Bent's Fort on the Arkansas River, the firm's adobe headquarters, vies with Fort Laramie as one of the most colorful frontier outposts in American history. Into the Southwest to Taos and Santa Fe also came a "reckless breed" of trappers who scoured the southern Rockies and the Great Basin region for furs. Of these Antoine Robidoux (see ROBIDOUX BROTHERS) was considered the chief operator in the Green River region for twenty years. Young Kit CARSON got his start as a trapper in the region in the company of such men as William S. WILLIAMS, Ewing YOUNG, and others. In the Southwest the geographical discoveries of such men as Joseph R. WALKER and Sylvester and James Ohio PATTIE also had a political function in that they pointed the way to California and thus helped initiate a string of events leading to the eventual acquisition of the far Southwest and California.

In the Pacific Northwest, Americans such as Nathaniel WYETH followed up the maritime trade with Astor's Pacific Fur Company enterprise, which, though it failed economically, did add to geographic knowledge and later facilitated American diplomatic claims to the Oregon country. Originally trappers, Joseph L. MEEK, Robert NEWELL, and Osborne RUSSELL became prominent Oregon figures. In spite of American expeditions, however, the Northwest's fur trade remained in British hands after the merger of the North West Company and the Hudson's Bay Company in 1821. During the 1820s Peter Skene OGDEN and Alexander Ross led the expeditions for the latter company into the interior all the way to the western slope of the Rockies. They, and John WORK in the 1830s, practiced a "scorched earth" policy, trapping all the fur animals so that Americans would be

kept out of the Columbia River, Great Basin, and Snake country areas.

During the 1830s, the beginning of the beaver decline, the Rockies were dominated by the American Fur Company moving westward (their only "thorn" was the Robert CAMPBELL-William Sublette partnership in 1833-34) and the Hudson's Bay Company, under John McLOUGHLIN, moving eastward. They, in turn, were increasingly threatened by the growing numbers of free trappers, who, moving singly or in small groups, were penetrating remote mountain regions in the West to find fertile beaver peltries. R. L. WOOTTON and his party, for example, roamed for two years all over the West, going as far as Los Angeles. The area became crowded, the beaver were fewer; the trappers had to follow obscure little trails and streams, usually on the heels of one another. Too, by the late 1830s the beaver hat market in Europe had been ruined by the introduction of the tall silk hat. Indians were increasingly hostile, and more fortified fur-trading forts were being built. The days of the rendezvous were rapidly drawing to a close. The last rendezvous took place in 1840.

In its later days the continental trade shifted from beaver to buffalo (1870-83) and raccoon, from the rendezvous to the fort, and from the Rockies to the Great Plains. The raccoon was succeeded by the fur seal from the 1870s to the end of the century.

The significance of the fur trade in American history was momentous. Through their journeys, the trappers and traders added geographical and scientific knowledge that became useful for commerce, settlement, and pioneer routes. The fur trade ultimately led to the expansion of America's domain and served as the advance agent for destroying Indian culture. The trade created a popular and literary myth of the independent mountain man, which became a symbol of great power.

In the economic realm the fur trade was far less significant. From 1790 to 1890 the bulk of American furs were sent abroad (principally to England); even so fur still averaged only about one percent of America's annual exports. Even though the fur trade was of minimal importance in terms of profit to the United States and the frontier regions, it was economically significant in that it was one of the earliest industries to organize large companies with monopolistic practices.

See Ray A. Billington, *Far Western Frontier* (1956); Hiram M. Chittenden, *The American Fur Trade of the Far West* (1902); William H. Goetzmann, *Exploration and Empire* (1966); and Paul C. Phillips, *Fur Trade* (1961). —G. B. D.

fur-trading forts. Fortified places of exchange between Indians and whites. The forts were ideally located in Indian country adjacent to the haunts of fur-bearing animals, on easily defensible ground, and with convenient means of transportation. Such posts were characteristic of the United States fur trade, except during the era of the rendezvous system in the Rocky Mountains. Some of the most famous of the fortified trading posts were BENT'S FORT, FORT BONNEVILLE, FORT BRIDGER, FORT HALL, FORT LARAMIE, FORT RAYMOND, FORT UNION, and FORT VANCOUVER. Trade was carried on with every safety precaution, for there was always danger that Indians would attack the posts to steal the goods, especially liquor. Besides being trading centers, the posts were social centers, and the larger ones also sustained farming and boat-building enterprises.

See Hiram M. Chittenden, *The American Fur Trade of* the Far West (1902); and Paul C. Phillips, *Fur Trade* (1961).—G. B. D.

G

Gadsden Purchase (1853). Wedge of territory between Texas and California purchased from Mexico. The Gadsden Purchase was the last continental territorial addition to the United States, except for the purchase of Alaska in 1867. This purchase of 29,142,400 acres of land within the present states of New Mexico and Arizona, by the American minister to Mexico, James Gadsden, was largely to obtain a railroad route along a southern line from the Mississippi to the Pacific Coast. Gadsden's commission also came out of the spirit of "young America" that flourished in the 1850s, from the discovery of gold in California in 1848, from the active foreign policy of the administration of President Franklin Pierce during that administration's first two years, and for the purpose of establishing a natural boundary between the United States and Mexico.

Pierce's secretary of war, Jefferson Davis, reportedly had a large influence upon the president and seems to have been instrumental in obtaining the appointment of Gadsden. The negotiation in Mexico turned out not to be difficult, for in the years after the Mexican War (1846-48) the governments in Mexico City were in desperate financial straits. For example, there were sixteen different Mexican finance ministers between June 1848 and January 1851. When Gadsden arrived in the Mexican capital, the arch-adventurer Santa Anna was again in power and was in grave danger of losing office unless he secured immediate funds. The result was a treaty that gave Mexico $10 million in exchange for land. Signed in Mexico City on December 30, 1853, the treaty encountered the intense partisan strife in the American capital incident to passage of the Kansas-Nebraska Act and to the larger issue of slavery expansion into new territories. But the treaty eventually received the consent of the Senate, and President Pierce ratified it on June 29, 1854. Santa Anna promptly squandered the money. Because of the approaching Civil War in the United States, the railroad project never materialized.

See Paul N. Garber, *The Gadsden Treaty* (1923). —R. H. F.

Gall (Pizi) (c. 1840-1894). A chief of the Hunkpapa Sioux. Gall was considered by Indian Agent James McLaughlin to be one of the greatest men of his nation, the peer of Red Cloud and Spotted Tail. He was born on the Moreau River in South Dakota. Two stories are told to explain his unusual name. One relates his attempt as a famished orphan to eat the gall of an animal killed by a neighbor. The other holds that his name signifies a mean, bitter nature. After the treaty of 1868 that created a reservation for certain Sioux tribes in the Black Hills and Montana, as a warrior of note, he allied himself with the hostile element that refused to remain on the reservation. At the assumption by Sitting Bull of the position of holy man and political leader, Gall became his military chief. Gall's true importance is difficult to evaluate because of Sitting Bull's prominence. Gall fought in battles against army troops on the Yellowstone River in 1872 and 1873 and was one of the principal chiefs at the battle of the LITTLE BIG HORN, although his exact role is a matter of controversy. He did lead forces that routed Major Marcus Reno and then cooperated with Crazy Horse in surrounding and annihilating Custer.

Gall followed Sitting Bull into exile in Canada. In the fall of 1880, he returned to the United States after a quarrel with his leader. At first, his band was belligerent,

Gall, chief of the Hunkpapa Sioux, in 1881. (National Archives)

but on January 3, 1881, he surrendered with three hundred followers at the Poplar River Agency in Montana. He settled on Standing Rock reservation, where he became friends with McLaughlin. As a person of some importance, Gall supported the federal government's plan to educate Indian children. In 1889, he became a judge of the Court of Indian Offenses at the agency. That same year, he accompanied McLaughlin to Washington on a mission in behalf of the Sioux. Gall opposed the policies of Sitting Bull and toward the end, fearing assassination, asked to be armed. He strongly disapproved of the GHOST DANCE religion but did not openly oppose it. He died at his home on Oak Creek in South Dakota from a supposed overdose of medicine.

See F. W. Hodge, ed., *Handbook of American Indians North of Mexico* (1910-11); Mari Sandoz, *The Battle of the Little Big Horn* (1966); and Stanley Vestal, *Sitting Bull: Champion of the Sioux* (rev. ed., 1951).—E. I. S.

Gallegos, José Manuel (1815-1875). New Mexican politician. Born in what is now Rio Arriba County, New Mexico, Gallegos was educated in parochial schools and later at the College of Durango in Mexico, where he studied theology and was graduated in 1840. He sought the restoration of the Catholic church in what was then the Department of New Mexico, Republic of Mexico. Between 1843 and 1846 he served in the department's legislative assembly, and, after the Treaty of Guadalupe Hidalgo (1848), became in 1851 a member of New Mexico's first Territorial Council.

A powerful priest in Albuquerque, Gallegos was one of five Spanish-speaking clergymen excommunicated by reform-minded Bishop Jean Lamy, ostensibly for concubinage. Shortly thereafter he married and entered politics. In 1853 Gallegos was elected territorial delegate in a bitterly contested election, in which he was supported by the powerful Penitentes and was recognized as "anti-Lamy." He thus had the support of many of the Spanish-speaking clergy in New Mexico. Two years later, running for delegate, Gallegos was defeated by the elder Miguel A. Otero, who had the support of Bishop Lamy. Gallegos had first been declared the winner, but the election was contested by Otero. Gallegos served in Congress from March 4, 1855, to July 23, 1856, when Otero succeeded him after the contest. During his tenure in Congress, Gallegos' effectiveness was seriously hampered by his inability to speak English and by the refusal of the House to suspend its rules to allow Gallegos an interpreter.

Gallegos served in the territorial legislature from 1860 to 1862, during which time he was chosen speaker. In 1860, at a convention in Santa Fe considering defense against the Indians, Gallegos was an advocate of "home rule," an issue that also was part of his campaign platform in 1853. He ran unsuccessfully for delegate in 1862 and later that year was taken a prisoner of war by the Texas Confederate troops in New Mexico. He was treasurer of the territory in 1865 and 1866 and Superintendent of Indian Affairs in New Mexico in 1868.

A Democrat, Gallegos was returned to the Forty-second Congress, unseating incumbent José Francisco Chaves in a heated campaign which included a riot at Mesilla where several were killed. He was an unsuccessful candidate for reelection in 1872 and died shortly thereafter in Santa Fe.

For a discussion of Gallegos' political stance in the context of territorial politics, see Howard R. Lamar, *The Far Southwest, 1846-1912* (1966).—J. R. V.

Galvez, Bernardo de (1746?-1786). Governor of Spanish Louisiana. Born in Malaga, Galvez was the son of Matías de Galvez, viceroy of New Spain (1783-84), and nephew of José de Galvez, minister general of the Indies and guiding force in the Council of the Indies. After a brilliant military career in Portugal, New Spain, and North Africa, Galvez came to Louisiana in 1776 as commander of the Louisiana Regiment, succeeding to the governorship in January 1777. Marriage to a native Louisianian put him in the good graces of the colonials, a position he strengthened by allowing Oliver Pollock to establish in New Orleans a base from which to supply the American colonists in their rebellion against the mutually hated British. He also encouraged settlement of groups of Canary Islanders in Louisiana, where they became known as *Islenos*, and gave refuge to early bands of Acadians along the Mississippi and the bayous southwest of New Orleans. When Spain declared war against Britain in 1779, Galvez launched highly successful attacks into West Florida, capturing Baton Rouge and Natchez in 1779, Mobile in 1780, and Pensacola in 1781. His campaigns were largely responsible for Spanish acquisition of East and West Florida in the Treaty of Paris of 1783, and won him title as the count of Galvez, rank as lieutenant-general, captain-general of Louisiana, the Floridas and Cuba, and eventual appointment to succeed his father as viceroy of New Spain in 1785. His brilliant career was cut short by death from fever in Mexico.

See John W. Caughey, *Bernardo de Galvez in Louisiana, 1776-1783* (1934).—J. G. T.

gambling. In the early nineteenth century gambling became the great American pastime, which it has ever since remained. New Orleans was the font, with play spreading up the Mississippi valley and then on to the West.

Frontier gambling took two major forms: games of chance and confidence games. The confidence games were mainly variations of the "bunco" or "old shell" game—under which of the three shells is the pea? The varieties included three-card monte—which of the three face-down cards is the queen?—soap, and thimblerig. The confidence "games" weren't games at all, for the pea, in the hands of a skilled manipulator, was under *none* of the three shells when the gambler made his choice. Secreted between the dealer's fingers, the pea was replaced under the shell the gambler had not chosen in time to show the sucker that he had lost. The gullible contestant had virtually no chance of winning when he played against seasoned operators such as the "King of the Thimbleriggers" Jefferson Randolph ("Soapy") Smith, who won a fortune before being killed by a vigilante in Skagway, Alaska, in 1898.

The more legitimate games of chance were mainly faro, poker—usually five-card draw—twenty-one (blackjack), and roulette. In faro, a game that has virtually disappeared, the dealer alone handles the deck and the players bet against the dealer on the order in which certain cards will show up. Poker was played with no cards wild. The house percentage (varying from $1\frac{3}{4}$ percent to 6 percent) was against the player but not so strongly as to discourage him. Poker (the most popular short card game in American history) and faro (attrac-

Gambling was a favorite pastime in mining-town saloons, such as this one in Telluride, Colorado. (Library of Congress)

tive because its house percentage of 1¾ percent was the lowest) were the favorite frontier games. Policy, a lottery-type game played by the smallest bettors, was common in the West from the 1870s to the 1890s.

Mississippi gambling flourished from 1800 to the Civil War. Some of the famous gambling centers were the Swamp in New Orleans, the Landing at Vicksburg, the Pinch Gut at Memphis, and infamous NATCHEZ-UNDER-THE-HILL. More colorful were the 1,000 to 1,500 steamboat gamblers, who by the early 1830s were plying the rivers from New Orleans to St. Louis and Cincinnati. Notable among these stylishly dressed gents were Kentuckian Elijah Skaggs, whose command of faro teams throughout the region made him a wealthy man in the 1839-59 period; Bill Jones, the top monte dealer in the Mississippi valley; George Devol, who went West after the Civil War; James Ashby; Charles Starr; and many others.

So well organized and predatory were the operations of the Mississippi valley gamblers that they induced the first major antigambling crusade in American history: In 1835 five professional gamblers were lynched in Vicksburg, Mississippi, in the initiation of a campaign that spread to other cities such as Natchez, Mobile, and Cincinnati. The antigambling movement entered a new phase eight years later with the launching of a series of exposés by the reformed Mississippi valley gambler

Jonathan F. Green. Green's most famous book, *An Exposure of the Acts and Miseries of Gambling* (1843), was followed by *The Gambler's Mirror* and *Gambling Unmasked*. But crusades and exposés could only temporarily reduce the mania for gambling in the great river valley. Vain and naïve slave-owning planters, flushed with the profits of the pre-Civil War cotton boom, were easy, even eager, prey for the adroit professional gamblers. The catastrophic Civil War terminated the golden age of Mississippi valley gambling.

The combination of Civil War decline and the lure of California gold and other bonanzas caused many erstwhile Mississippi valley gamblers to migrate to the West. San Francisco became a rousing gambling center in the gold-rush era, with activity concentrated in Portsmouth Square. Houses like the El Dorado had a daily turnover of $100,000 to $200,000. Here the largest single faro bet ever made in America, $60,000, was made (and lost) by Ed Moses in a heroic eight-hour session that found him out $200,000. Although professional gamblers such as J. J. Bryant (originally from Vicksburg), Bill Briggs of the gold-rush time, and Charles Felton highlighted the gaming history of nineteenth-century San Francisco, not all the players were full-time operators. Two of the most notable San Francisco gamblers were nabobs in finance and politics: the leading San Francisco banker, William C. Ralston, was an indefatigable player for high stakes, and United States Senator William Sharon of Nevada, in the course of frequent visits to the Golden Gate metropolis, is said to have won more than a million dollars at the Pacific Club over a fifteen-year period.

While none could equal San Francisco's big games and continuous betting, gambling centers were legion in the West from the Missouri to the Pacific. Kansas City gamblers led by Albert Showers and Bob Potee steadily fleeced free-spending cowboys and cattle kings during the 1870s until a Missouri antigambling law shut them down. Unlike the case of Kansas City, antigambling state provisos were usually honored in the breach as betting boomed throughout the West from the 1870s to the 1920s. Typical of the smaller, more transitory boomtowns was the mining camp of Tombstone, Arizona, where Doc HOLLIDAY and John Dougherty made gambling reputations. Among the main centers, Denver had two hundred gaming houses in 1885, and the mile-high city's king of chance, Ed Chase, died in 1921 worth $650,000. Widely known among the roving professional gamblers of the West was the exotic "Madame Moustache," who operated casinos and brothels from 1854 to her death in 1879.

A new phase began with the legalizing of gambling in Nevada in 1931 (see GAMBLING, NEVADA). With its world-famous Harolds Club ("the poor man's Monte Carlo"), Reno was the mecca for legal gambling in Nevada until the rise of the luxury hotel-casinos along the Strip in Las Vegas after World War II. Allegedly dominated by organized crime, Las Vegas' gambling industry by 1962 was annually attracting twelve million tourists who bet three billion dollars.

Postwar affluence among a pleasure-loving people accounts for the lure of modern Las Vegas, but what was the appeal of old-time frontier gambling? In part it was for amusement, but, more basically, the gaming table was an extension of frontier life in general, in that men had to stake their lives and labor on speculative ventures in Mississippi valley cotton or western mining, cattle, or wheat. Finally, the windfall riches of the mining frontier in the Mississippi valley and later in the West created a reservoir of wealth that the professional gamblers gladly tapped.

See Herbert Asbury, *Sucker's Progress: An Informal History of Gambling in America from the Colonies to Canfield* (1938); Henry Chafetz, *Play the Devil: A History of Gambling in the United States from 1492 to 1955* (1960); Philip D. Jordan, *Frontier Law and Order: Ten Essays* (1970); Oscar Lewis, *Sagebrush Casinos: The Story of Legal Gambling in Nevada* (1953); and Ed Reid and Ovid Demaris, *The Green Felt Jungle* (1963).—R. M. B.

gambling, Nevada. On March 19, 1931, Governor Fred B. Balzar signed into law a bill legalizing gambling in Nevada. Gambling had been legal in Nevada from 1869 until 1910, when a reform movement throughout the state resulted in a law banning it. The origin of the 1931 law is still somewhat of a mystery, but it probably seemed advisable in part because gambling was being carried on illegally in many parts of the state and efforts to stop it were ineffective. Gambling grew slowly in Nevada during the 1930s but it became a major revenue producer during and after World War II. The state did not attempt to control the industry until 1945 when gambling was placed under the Nevada Tax Commission and a one percent tax was levied on gross revenue.

By that time it was evident that the loose control permitted under the 1931 act had attracted a number of underworld figures to Nevada gambling. The unsolved murder of mobster Benjamin "Bugsy" Siegel in 1947, the Kefauver Crime Committee hearings at Las Vegas in 1951, and a series of exposés in the Las Vegas *Sun* in 1954 all emphasized that additional state control was necessary. In January 1955 Governor Charles Russell recommended to the legislature that a gambling division be established under the Nevada Tax Commission. Thus there came into existence the Gaming Control Board to act as the enforcement and investigating unit for gambling. Continued suspicions of underworld infiltration led the next governor, Grant Sawyer, to ask the legislature in 1959 for a separate commission for gambling. The legislature then passed a new gambling control law, which established a five-man Nevada Gaming Commission, independent of the Tax Commission. The three-man Gaming Control Board was moved from the Tax Commission to the new Gaming Commission. The procedure for gaming control established with the Sawyer administration remains basically in effect today. However, Governor Paul Laxalt, who followed Sawyer, made use of a third body, which had been authorized earlier but not used by Sawyer, known as the Gaming Policy Board, made up of the combined membership of the two other boards plus the governor as chairman.

The most important recent legislation concerning gambling is the Corporate Gaming legislation, first passed in 1967 and made more effective in 1969. The new law opens Nevada gaming to publicly traded corporations without the necessity of licensing, and thus investigating, all stockholders. Thus the support for gaming is widened but many think that control is made more difficult, especially of such a large empire as that owned by Howard HUGHES. And the problem of gambling control is a basic one for Nevada, since gambling has become the number one revenue producer for the state.

There is no scholarly history of gambling available at the present time although there are a number of romanticized works. The Annual Reports of the Nevada Gaming Commission are useful.—R. R. E.

games. See GAMBLING; RODEO; SPORTS AND PASTIMES.

Garcia, Hector Perez (1914-   ). Mexican-American leader. The son of José and Faustina (Perez) Garcia, Garcia was born in Mexico. He received his B.A. and M.D. degrees from the University of Texas in 1936 and 1940, respectively. Between 1942 and 1946, Garcia served as a major in the Medical Corps, after which he entered private medical practice.

In 1950 Garcia founded and became chairman of the board of the moderate American G.I. Forum, which eventually was organized in about half of the states. He was active in other organizations and political groups concerned with Americans of Mexican and Spanish descent. In 1953 he was vice president of the Catholic Council for Spanish-Speaking People in the Southwest. In 1952 he was a member of the Texas State Democratic Committee and two years later a member of the advisory council of the Democratic National Committee. In 1960 he was both chairman of the Mexican-Spanish section of the Nationalities division of the Democratic National Committee and co-chairman of the Latin American division of the Texas Democratic campaign.

In 1955 Garcia received the Outstanding Democracy

Forward award from the Texas Conference of Negro Organizations and was chosen the outstanding Latin American citizen by the University of Texas Alba Club in 1949. He was a member of the council of LULAC, the League of United Latin American Citizens.—J. R. V.

Gard, [Sanford] Wayne (1899-   ). Teacher, journalist, and historian. Gard spent his childhood years in Illinois, Kansas, and Missouri. His studies at Illinois College were interrupted by army service in World War I. Returning to college, he began his early apprenticeship in journalism, writing for the student magazine, editing the college yearbook, and working during one summer as a news reporter. In 1921, he went to Burma, where for three years he taught high school English and history and served as a part-time correspondent for the Associated Press. Deciding that he wanted to make writing his career, Gard applied for and was awarded a fellowship to study at the Medill School of Journalism, Northwestern University.

From 1925 until 1930, only Gard's summers were devoted to news reporting; the rest of the time was spent teaching journalism at Grinnell College in Iowa. While at Grinnell he published his first book, *Book Reviewing* (1927). He then did brief stints with the *Register* and the *Tribune* in Des Moines, Iowa, and *Vanity Fair* magazine in New York. In 1933 he joined the *Dallas Morning News*, moving quickly from copy editing to editorial writing, a post he held for thirty-one years. Gard soon became well known for his many signed feature articles and numerous book reviews.

Through the years, Gard became increasingly intrigued with the history of Texas and the Southwest and delved deeply into available source material for the various magazine and newspaper articles and books he was writing. In 1936, he produced an excellent biography of a Texas outlaw, *Sam Bass*. This was followed by the *Chisholm Trail* (1954), probably his best book; *Frontier Justice* (1954); *The Great Buffalo Hunt* (1959); *Reminiscences of Range Life* (1970); an excellent guide to first-person range books; and many others. Gard's years of experience as a news writer taught him to spot the significant. As a result, he was always economical in his use of words, and his writings reflect strength and vitality.

See Ramon F. Adams, *Wayne Gard, Historian of the West* (1970), Southwest Writers Series No. 31.—J. C. D.

Garland, Augustus Hill (1832-1899). Arkansas politician and attorney. In 1867 Garland was the central figure in an important case decided by the Supreme Court, *Ex Parte Garland*. In 1865 Congress had passed a law prohibiting anyone who had borne arms against the United States or had held office in a government hostile to the United States from practicing law before the federal courts. Garland, who had served Arkansas in the Congress of the Confederate States during the Civil War, argued that the law was in effect a bill of attainder and was also an ex post facto law, both of which are prohibited by the Constitution. The Court found the law unconstitutional and Garland's right to practice his profession in the federal courts was upheld.

He led the Democratic party in postwar Arkansas, served as governor (1874-77) after the "carpetbag" administration had been overthrown, and was elected to the United States Senate in 1877. In 1885 he resigned to accept appointment as attorney general in President

Grover Cleveland's administration. Retiring from the cabinet in 1889, he practiced law in Washington, D.C., until his death—W. L. B.

Garland, Hamlin (1860-1940). Novelist and short-story writer. Garland was born near West Salem, Wisconsin, where his father farmed unsuccessfully. The family later moved by covered wagon to another farm near Osage, Iowa, and, in 1881, to Brown County in the Dakota Territory. Garland's formal schooling consisted only of brief attendance at the seminary in Osage, but this, combined with a brief trip to the East when he was twenty-one, strengthened his determination to quit the hard life of pioneering. In the winter of 1882-83 he taught school briefly in Illinois, and in 1884 mortgaged his claim in the Dakota Territory and went to Boston. There he eked out a bare living by teaching school and placing an occasional book review. He read voraciously, particularly the works of the American economist Henry George and the English philosopher Herbert Spencer, both of whom were to have a lasting effect upon him. After a brief trip to Iowa and Dakota in 1887 Garland returned to Boston determined to write a truthful explanation of the hard facts of life in the West he knew. Some of his stories were published in *Harper's Weekly* and others, from 1890 on, in B. O. Flower's *Arena*. Flower collected the *Arena* stories in *Main-Travelled Roads* (1891), Garland's first and probably best book. Another collection of short stories, *Prairie Folks*, followed in 1893, together with a number of novels of political reform, *A Member of the Third House* (1892), *Jason Edwards* (1892), *A Spoil of Office* (1892), and *Rose of Dutcher's Coolly* (1895).

After 1895 Garland turned from reform novels to western romances, the best known being *The Captain of the Gray-Horse Troop* (1902), and, later, to autobiographical reminiscences. The best of these, *A Son of the Middle Border* (1917), was followed by *A Daughter of the Middle Border* (1921), *Trail-Makers of the Middle Border* (1926), and *Back-Trailers from the Middle Border* (1928). In 1916 Garland moved to New York, and in 1929 to Los Angeles, where he died.

Garland's work as a whole has a curious duality that critics have been hard pressed to explain. The cause of what many have called the complacency and romanticizing of novels like *The Captain of the Gray-Horse Troop* may ultimately remain mysterious, but the fact is that Garland's worst work is so vastly inferior to his best writing that it scarcely seems to be by the same hand. With one exception, *The Book of the American Indian* (1923), Garland's work concerns itself with the hardships faced by farmers on the Great Plains. His first book, *Main-Travelled Roads*, consists of six stories of Mississippi valley life, of which two—"Up the Coulé" and "Under the Lion's Paw"—are among the best of American short stories. Though the second of these is a fairly straightforward sermon on the virtues of Henry George's single tax and the evils of unearned increment, the first is a much more somber tale of the hardships inherent in farming life.

Garland's view of the deprivations of rural life gains much of its bite from a deep feeling of betrayal. At times this betrayal is personal, as in "Under the Lion's Paw," in which the hero is swindled by a legal unfairness that ironically penalizes him for being a good farmer. Garland's real animus, however, is directed against the agrarian myth that conceives of farmers as nature's noblemen living a life of idyllic happiness surrounded by the beneficent influences of a kindly and bountiful natural world. Against this romanticized picture (a myth that descends through Thomas Jefferson from eighteenth-century primitivism), Garland pits the more somber facts of the farming life he had known as a boy living in the MIDDLE BORDERS. For example, the concluding metaphorical statement of *A Spoil of Office* takes place at the theater, when two people with firsthand experience of rural life are treated to a romanticized account of it. The effectiveness of "Up the Coulé" depends almost entirely on the skill with which Garland probes the ironies of the confrontation of the hero's mental pictures of an almost Edenic rural life with the facts of the squalid existence he actually finds. In *The Moccasin Ranch* (1909) the true nature of the Dakota prairie, which when first seen is covered with beautiful wild flowers, is finally revealed in the horrors of a prairie blizzard. "The Story of Howling Wolf," the best of the stories of *The Book of the American Indian*, relates how the Indian Howling Wolf accepts at face value the myth told him by the whites, that if he adopts white ways he will be freely accepted into their society. In fact, he is beaten almost to death by a group of cowboys.

At his best Garland is a superb, albeit perhaps unconscious, ironist; at his worst he is unable to see the realities of life for the glittering surface of cliché that covers them.

Thomas A. Bledsoe's introduction to his edition of *Main-Travelled Roads* (1954) is the most useful and perceptive single short study of Garland; see also Jean Holloway, *Hamlin Garland: A Biography* (1960), and Donald Pizer, *Hamlin Garland's Early Work and Career* (1960). —J. K. F.

Garrard, Hector Lewis (1829-1887). Diarist. Garrard, who for reasons best known to himself reversed his two first names for a *nom de plume*, was born in Cincinnati and lived there most of his early life. He persuaded his parents to let him go west and follow in the footsteps of John C. Frémont, whose accounts of western travel he had read. In July 1846 he left Cincinnati, descended the Santa Fe Trail to Bent's Fort on the Arkansas, wandered south to New Mexico, and returned to Cincinnati in 1847. He later practiced medicine, first in Cincinnati and after 1859 in Frontenac, Michigan, where he lived most of the remainder of his life.

Garrard's *Wah-to-Yah and the Taos Trail* (1850) would be little more than another traveler's journal were it not for an accident of history. For his descent of the Santa Fe Trail came at the time of the Taos revolt against the American occupation of New Mexico, in January 1847. His account in *Wah-to-Yah* of the events of the winter of 1846-47 is the best nonmilitary firsthand report in English.—J. K. F.

Garrett, Pat[rick Floyd] (1850-1908). Lawman. Garrett killed Billy the Kid, and that single act dominated his life and what history remembers of him. He was born in Alabama and reared in Louisiana, where his family was prominent. In 1869 he abandoned the piney woods for Texas and the life of a cowboy, and in 1874 he joined the hide hunters in the great buffalo slaughter. He arrived too late to make much money, however, and in 1877 he moved west again, drifting into Tascosa, Texas, and more of the cowboy's life. In 1879 he moved to Lincoln County, New Mexico. where he became sheriff

the next year. In the months that followed Garrett pursued Billy the Kid and his cronies until that fateful July night in 1881 at Pete Maxwell's ranch, when Garrett ended the life of the Kid with a bullet in the heart.

Life was pretty tame after that. In 1882 a book entitled *The Authentic Life of Billy the Kid* appeared under Garrett's name, although it was actually written by his friend Ash Upson. Garrett turned again to ranching, except for a brief interlude with the Texas Rangers. He also pursued unsuccessful irrigation schemes for southeastern New Mexico. In 1897 he became the sheriff of Dona Ana County, mainly to solve the murder of Judge Albert J. Fountain and his son. Although frustrated in this effort, he was reelected sheriff in 1898. In 1901 he was appointed customs collector at El Paso, Texas, by Theodore Roosevelt and in 1905 returned to New Mexico.

When Garrett returned to New Mexico he purchased a horse ranch that proved to be a bad investment. By 1908 he was in severe financial straits. He had already leased his ranch to Wayne Brazel when he was offered a better deal by Carl Adamson, a man of questionable character. Garrett tried to break his arrangement with Brazel. On February 29, 1908, Garrett and Adamson were en route to Las Cruces, the deal apparently made, when they were joined by Brazel. Brazel and Garrett argued violently. Then Adamson stopped the buggy in which he and Garrett were riding to relieve himself. Moments later Pat Garrett was shot dead. Adamson and Brazel later claimed that Garrett angrily told Brazel that he would get him off his property one way or another and that Garrett started toward Brazel with a shotgun, whereupon Brazel shot him in self-defense. Evidence at the scene contradicted the Adamson-Brazel story and strongly suggested that Garrett was shot in the back of the head while relieving himself. Moreover, circumstantial evidence suggested that he was actually murdered by Jim Miller, a professional killer and a cousin of Adamson. Nevertheless, Brazel immediately confessed to the shooting, and Adamson corroborated it.

The lengthy investigation that followed revealed many contradictions in the Brazel-Adamson version. By the time Brazel came to trial more than a year later, however, Adamson had been jailed for smuggling Chinese into the United States, and with no eyewitnesses to directly contradict Brazel's story and an inept prosecution, Brazel's tale of self-defense stood unchallenged. He was acquitted. The verdict satisfied few people. Ironically, the same day that Brazel was acquitted, April 19, 1909, Jim Miller was lynched at Ada, Oklahoma, for another murder.

Controversy still rages over Garrett's death. Some speculate that Adamson fired the fatal shots. Others, on the basis of the strongest evidence, point to Jim Miller, and a few maintain that Brazel did indeed kill Garrett. In any event, there is strong evidence that Garrett was the victim of a conspiracy to murder him. Brazel's story of self-defense fails to hold up under even cursory examination of the evidence. Many New Mexicans were convinced that Garrett died because he got too close to solving the murder of Judge Fountain and his son. The truth may never be known.

Leon C. Metz, *Pat Garrett* (1974), is the best biography; Richard O'Connor, *Pat Garrett* (1960), leaves much to be desired. See also Jeff C. Dykes, *Law on a Wild*

Frontier (1969); Robert N. Mullin, *The Strange Story of Wayne Brazel* (1969); and Colin W. Rickards, *How Pat Garrett Died* (1970).—G. L. R.

Garry, Joseph R. (1910-   ). Coeur d'Alene political leader. Garry was born in a tepee on the Coeur d'Alene reservation in Idaho and did not learn English until he was ten years old. He attended Haskell Indian School and several universities and served in the army during World War II and the Korean war.

He was probably the only Indian ever to hold tribal, state, regional, and national offices at the same time, and is perhaps best known nationally for his five distinguished terms as president of the National Congress o, American Indians (1953-59) During his tenure at NCAI, Garry completed extensive research regarding federal claims on behalf of the Oto-Missouri tribe. Garry was elected a representative to the Idaho legislature in 1956 and then became a state senator. He was chairman of the Coeur d'Alene Tribal Council and president of the Affiliated Tribes of Northwest Indians. Garry's most important achievement was bringing the Eisenhower administration's disastrous tribal "termination" policy to a congressional stalemate. His ability to mobilize quickly northwestern tribes into a strong coalition loud enough to be heard in Washington (which encouraged other tribes to lobby) prevented nothing less than wholesale destruction of Indian tribes and their lands throughout the country. Only one major tribe, the Menomini (Wisconsin), was terminated, and the record of social and economic depression and disintegration of a tribe that had to be self-supporting is appalling.

Unquestionably, many supporters of termination proposals sincerely believed that the policy would "raise" Indians to mainstream status, while others seemed to have been motivated by other kinds of reasons. But the plan obviated self-determination. It was frequently attached as a rider to a federal bill awarding money to tribes in claims cases, usually involving "taken" lands; the tribes could get the money, usually in per capita payments, if they agreed to legally end their existence as a tribe, an implicit and total abnegation of Indian cultural values. Garry hoped that plans for termination or changes in any of the many kinds of federal-Indian relationships would originate in the individual tribes, and his efforts while in office accomplished that end, at least for a time.—C. C.

Gates, Paul Wallace (1901-   ). Historian. Gates was born in Nashua, New Hampshire. He was educated at Colby College in Waterville, Maine, Clark University in Worcester, Massachusetts, and Harvard University, where he worked under Frederick Merk, Frederick Jackson Turner's successor. In 1930 he began teaching at Bucknell University in Lewisburg, Pennsylvania, and in 1936 moved to Cornell University, New York, where he taught for thirty-five years, after 1956 as Carl Stambaugh Professor of American History.

In a succession of books and articles Gates quickly established himself as one of the most profound students of federal and state land policies in the United States. His path-breaking monograph, *The Illinois Central Railroad and Its Colonization Work* (1934), set new standards in the field. By painstaking analysis of railroad and county records, as well as the United States census returns, Gates traced the impact of land disposal policies of the railroad. Prior to Gates, most western historians had concerned themselves with the legislative origins of land policies; Gates shifted perspectives to the actual administration of land disposal, perhaps a more important, and certainly a more difficult field for investigation.

In succeeding years Gates continued his meticulous examination of American land policies. A major theme that ran through his writings was his deep disappointment over the failure of land policies to achieve the Jeffersonian dream of family-size farms as a characteristic of twentieth-century American agriculture. Some of his major books include *The Wisconsin Pine Lands of Cornell University* (1965), *Fifty Million Acres: Conflicts over Kansas Land Policies* (1954), and in preparation for a comprehensive history of federal land policy in California, *California Ranchos and Farms* (1967). Meanwhile, Gates also wrote about the history of American agriculture, and his *Agriculture, 1815-1860* (1960), part of the Rinehart Economic History of the United States series, is perhaps the best available synthesis of the subject. Similarly, his *Agriculture and the Civil War* (1965) is a distinguished work. Gates amplified these various books in scores of articles in professional historical journals.

Gates was also active in a variety of consulting responsibilities. During 1934-35 he served as an agricultural economist in the land policy section of the Agricultural Adjustment Administration. After 1949 he was consultant to the United States Department of Justice on Indian Claims and advised the second Commission on Government Reorganization (Hoover Commission). One of his most important assignments was with the United States Land Law Review Commission between 1966 and 1968, when with R. W. Swenson, he wrote a massive study, *History of Public Land Law Development* (1968), a work in which he took special pride.

In 1969 Gates's students presented him with a *festschrift—The Frontier in American Development: Essays in Honor of Paul Wallace Gates*, edited by David M. Ellis.

Gates was also active in many professional organizations. In 1961-62 he was president of the Mississippi Valley Historical Association.—G. D. N.

Gates, Susa Young (1856-1933). Writer and educator. The second daughter of Brigham Young and Lucy Bigelow, and the first child born in the famed Lion House in Salt Lake City, Gates was educated in her father's private school. By the age of fourteen she had also received a practical education and was considered capable as a stenographer and as a telegrapher. While attending the University of Deseret in Salt Lake City (now the University of Utah), she launched the first college literary journal in the West. She was the first Mormon to write a novel of Mormon life and published other novels, biographies, manuals, and hundreds of articles for national and local magazines. She also founded and edited the *Young Women's Journal* (Salt Lake City) from 1889 to 1929.

In 1878 Gates went to Brigham Young Academy (later Brigham Young University) to teach and organized the music department there. After her marriage in 1880 to Jacob F. Gates, she served a proselyting mission with him in Hawaii, the first woman to accompany her husband on such a mission. Returning to the Brigham Young Academy, she organized the domestic science department in 1897. Besides teaching theology, music, and domestic science, she bore thirteen children, some of whom achieved distinction. An active suffragette, she was an officer and delegate to the National and International Council of Women. She was also a long-time officer of the Young Women's Mutual Improvement Association and the Relief Society of the Mormon church, editing the *Relief Society Magazine* (1914-33). —L. J. A.

General Allotment Act. See DAWES SEVERALTY ACT.

Genoa, Nevada. Genoa, formerly Mormon Station, was the site of Nevada's first trading post and of its first settlement, the former established in 1850 by a party under Captain Joseph DeMont and Hampton S. Beatie and the latter by a group under John Reese in 1851. The site was surveyed and renamed Genoa by Orson Hyde in 1856. Genoa was the county seat of Carson County, Utah Territory, until January 18, 1861, when the seat was moved to Carson City. Genoa became the county seat of Douglas County, Nevada Territory, in November 1861. It lost its county seat status to Minden in 1915.

See Russell R. Elliott, "Nevada's First Trading Post: A Study in Historiography," *Nevada Historical Society Quarterly* (Winter 1970).—R. R. E.

Geological Survey, United States. A bureau devoted to the geologic exploration of the United States and its territories. The United States Geological Survey was created by act of Congress in 1879 to classify the public lands and examine the geologic structure, mineral re-sources, and products of the national domain. From its beginning it has been under the administration of the Department of the Interior.

There is much misunderstanding as to the origin of the Geological Survey. When it was created a number of other geological groups, all under the aegis of the government, were abolished. These included the groups headed by Ferdinand V. HAYDEN, John Wesley POWELL, Clarence KING and Lieutenant George M. WHEELER. At times, one or all of these earlier surveys had been loosely called "the U.S. Geological Survey."

Clarence King was the first director of the Geological Survey. He framed the administrative structure and directed the survey toward practical geology, sending George Becker to the Comstock Lode and Samuel Franklin Emmons into the silver district of Leadville, Colorado. John Wesley Powell, who succeeded King in 1881 and remained director until 1894, extended the work of the survey into paleontology, nationwide geologic research, and a projected national topographic map. He also turned to problems of land use and irrigation.

In the twentieth century the Geological Survey has continued to concentrate on economic geology. It has always cooperated with other departments, such as Defense, in aiding in land use or strategic metal surveys, and is still aiming at the completion of a national topographic map. Under the leadership of such men as

A U.S. Geological Survey pack train on the trail in the Yellowstone region in 1871. (Library of Congress)

Charles D. Walcott and George Otis Smith, the Geological Survey has expanded its scope of operations. It has investigated water resources, evaluated hydroelectric power sites, and provided maps for the T.V.A. and other depression-spawned projects. Besides pioneering in military geology and lunar geology, it is at present developing new techniques of geologic research using photographs and statistics compiled from instruments in manned and unmanned spacecraft. Photomapping, ecology, and research under the sea are also matters of concern to the present Geological Survey.

See A. Hunter Dupree, *Science in the Federal Government* (1957); Thomas G. Manning, *Government in Science: The U.S. Geological Survey, 1867-1894* (1967); and J. S. Rabbit and M. C. Rabbit, "The U.S. Geological Survey: 75 Years of Service to the Nation, 1879-1954," *Science* (May 28, 1954).—R. A. B.

Georgia, settlement of. During the 1730s the founders of Georgia argued that their colony would serve three quite different ends. Georgia's most energetic promoter, James Oglethorpe (1696-1785), stressed the philanthropic character of the proposed settlement, explaining that the colony would become a refuge for the poor of England as well as for the persecuted Protestants of Europe. But at the same time, Oglethorpe and his associates were aware of Georgia's strategic value as a military buffer between South Carolina and Spanish Florida. They recognized that a successful colony in this area would frustrate Spain's claim to all lands south of Charleston. The founder's third argument was economic, and during the first years of colonization, they predicted that Georgia would "increase the trade, navigation, and wealth of these our realms."

Oglethorpe's reasoning was apparently persuasive, for in 1732 the crown granted twenty-one Georgia "trustees" the land between the Savannah and Altamaha rivers. These men, many of whom were members of Parliament, were to hold this territory "in trust" for twenty-one years, during which time they were not allowed to own land or to profit from the colony in any way. Although the trustees knew little about the region, they drew up an elaborate blueprint for its settlement. Their plans called for compact, easily defensible villages. Small farms were to be located on the edges of these communities, and no one could possess more than five hundred acres. In order to maintain their tight control over the character of Georgia, the trustees prohibited the settlers from selling, renting, or alienating any land within the colony. Only males could inherit land, and the acreage of a man without sons reverted to the trustees upon his death. It was declared illegal to import Negro slaves or liquor into the colony. No provision was made for a representative assembly. The trustees seemed unaware that the colonists might regard these policies as paternalistic or oppressive, and in 1735 the directors piously announced, "The Board will always do what is right and the people should have confidence in us." The historian Daniel Boorstin was probably correct when he declared that had the trustees' blueprint succeeded, Georgia "would have been a neat, antiseptic, efficient, and thoroughly dull community."

The Georgia trustees had originally hoped to finance their colony through private subscriptions, but it soon became evident that this source was inadequate. During the period of trustee rule, from 1732 to 1752, the British government paid approximately ninety percent of Georgia's expenses. Although many trustees were members of Parliament, they seldom voted or acted as a cohesive lobby, and their success in winning Parliamentary grants depended more upon public enthusiasm for the colony than upon their own political skill. When popular interest in Georgia waned in the 1740s, British ministers became less inclined to support requests for additional money, and by the end of the decade, it was clear that the trustees lacked both the revenue and the energy necessary to put their plans into effect.

Despite the efforts of Oglethorpe and his associates, Georgia did not prosper. Before 1750 only a few thousand people had settled there, and many of those, like the Moravians, moved north to other American colonies. The men who remained in Georgia did indeed complain of the trustees' paternalism and pointed to the plantation system of South Carolina as a model that Georgia should have been following. Discontent within the colony forced the trustees to retreat on almost every one of their original points. In 1738 they raised the maximum size of estates to two thousand acres. The restrictions on the sale and the inheritance of land were lifted. An assembly was created to hear the settlers' grievances, and in 1750 Negro slaves were allowed into the colony for the first time. In 1752, a year before their charter ran out, the discouraged trustees surrendered their rights over the colony. The founders of Georgia had made the same mistake that the Virginia Company had made more than a century earlier: They had formulated plans for settlement without considering either the American environment or the weaknesses of human nature.

When the first royal governor arrived in Georgia in 1755, he found the colonists occupying only a narrow strip of territory along the Atlantic coast. The Indians claimed that they had ceded land only as far as the "Flowing of the Tides," and they made it clear that they would tolerate no violation of this agreement. Georgia's defenses were almost nonexistent, and she had no staple crop suitable for export. Over the next twenty years, however, this bleak picture changed, and the colony prospered under royal government. The introduction of rice and indigo, coupled with the establishment of the plantation system, led to an economic boom. By 1760 Georgia was controlled by a planter-aristocracy similar to that which dominated the other southern colonies. The removal of the Spanish threat in 1763 and a treaty with the Creek Indians opened the western part of Georgia to expansion. Despite protests from British officials who wanted to discourage westward migration, Governor James Wright (1760-76) supported plans for inland settlement.

The most important feature of Georgia politics before the American Revolution was the dominance of the royal governor. He was assisted by an appointed council, composed chiefly of crown officials, who served also as members of the colony's legislative upper house. The elected lower house, called the Commons House of Assembly, was generally controlled by the wealthiest planters. There was almost no internal political conflict within Georgia, and the colonists seemed almost reluctant to follow the rest of America on the road toward independence. The scholar W. W. Abbot has understandably claimed that if the Savannah River had been fifty miles wide Georgia might have remained part of the British empire. The pressure from the other colonies was too great to resist, however, and Georgia severed ties with the mother country despite the success of her royal governors.

See W. W. Abbot, *The Royal Governors of Georgia 1754-1775* (1959); Daniel Boorstin, *The Americans: The Colonial Experience* (1958); Richard Dunn, "The Trustees of Georgia and the House of Commons, 1732-1752," *The William and Mary Quarterly*, vol. 11 (1954); and David M. Potter, Jr., "The Rise of the Plantation System in Georgia," *Georgia Historical Quarterly*, vol. 16 (1932). — T. H. B.

German Russian immigration. At the invitation of the German-born empress of Russia Catherine II in 1762 and later of Alexander I, German peasants migrated to Russia to establish colonies as frontier buffers against Mongols and Turks. Catherine promised them freedom of religion, exemption from military service, free land, and monetary subsidies. Their homes and lands devastated by war, Germans from Württemberg and other Rhenish provinces settled along the Volga River from 1763 to 1768, establishing 104 colonies, with 23,184 inhabitants. From 1789 to 1824 Germans with the same special privileges formed 214 colonies in the region north of the Black Sea. Later, others settled elsewhere in the Ukraine and the Caucasus. The Germans lived in farming villages isolated from the Russians, prospered, bought more land, set up more colonies, and remained German.

In 1871 Czar Alexander II withdrew their special privileges. From 1873 to 1914 some 115,000 German Russians emigrated to the United States; some 150,000 (almost half of them Mennonites), to western Canada; and an unknown number, to South America. By 1920 there were 303,532 first- and second-generation German Russians living in the United States: 65 percent were Evangelicals; 23 percent, Catholics, and 12 percent, Mennonites. North Dakota had the largest number (69,985), followed by Kansas (31,512), South Dakota (30,937), Nebraska (22,421), Colorado (21,067), and ten other states with 5,000 or more. On the Great Plains, as in Russia, the German Russians became grain farmers. They worked hard, lived frugally, and clung to the German language. With few exceptions their communities were of one faith and from one region in Russia. They married early and raised large, patriarchal families. Men, women, and children worked together in the fields. After their experience on the steppes of Russia, they quickly adapted to the Great Plains of America, taking pride in their conquest of the land. Even today the German Russians remain generally isolated throughout North Dakota, South Dakota, and Kansas.

See Elwyn B. Robinson, *History of North Dakota* (1966).—D. J. T.

Geronimo (1829?-1909). Indian leader. This famous medicine man and leader of the southernmost band of Chiricahua Apache, the *Nde'indai* ("enemy people"), made his mark in American history by being the last American Indian to surrender formally to the United States. Ironically, most of his native homeland was actually a large area in the northern parts of the Mexican states of Chihuahua and Sonora. It was in Mexico, in 1886, that he and his heroic band were finally brought to heel.

Called Goyakla, or "One Who Yawns," by the Apache, Geronimo (the Spanish for Jerome) is the name by which this Indian warrior came to be known to the world at large. He was born and grew up somewhere in the country around the headwaters of the Gila River. His youth was a time of increasing hostilities between his people and non-Indians, both Mexicans and Anglos, on both sides of what became the International Boundary in 1848 and 1854. In 1858 Geronimo and other Apache were near the "friendly" town of Janos, Chihuahua, drinking and having a good time when Mexican soldiers attacked the Apache camp and killed Geronimo's mother, wife, and children. His animosity toward Mexicans was thereby assured. He later acquired another wife and had more children, but the loss of his first family became a cross he was always to bear.

During the ensuing years, Geronimo's fame as a warrior grew, especially in Mexico. In April 1877, at Ojo Caliente, New Mexico, he was arrested by Indian agent John Clum and taken to San Carlos, Arizona, with 110 of his band. From then until his final capture in 1886, Geronimo enjoyed an amazing career, alternating between the roles of "ruthless renegade" and privileged prisoner of war. He remained inconspicuous on the reservation until 1881, when he and many other Apache broke out, proceeding to terrorize the southwestern countryside. Geronimo operated chiefly in the Sierra Madre of Mexico and in southeastern Arizona and southwestern New Mexico. In 1883 he was persuaded by General George Crook to surrender, although he did not actually give himself up until February 1884—and pretty much on his own terms. He again broke out from the reservation in May 1885: and in March 1886, Crook again effected a conditional surrender. En route to Fort Bowie, Arizona, the agreed-upon place of surrender, Geronimo encountered an Anglo whiskey peddler, got drunk, and fled to the mountains once more. At last, on September 3, 1886, General Nelson Miles presided at the final and unconditional surrender of Geronimo, although the warrior had not understood the "unconditional" part of the terms. He and the other Apache of his band were sent to exile and prison in Florida. Here and at Fort Sill, Oklahoma, five years later Geronimo earned money by selling pictures of himself and small bows and arrows with his name on them. He came to be regarded as a "most valuable asset as an attraction at prominent public affairs," such as the 1898 Trans-Mississippi and International Exposition at Omaha; the Pan-American Exposition at Buffalo in 1901; and the St. Louis World's Fair in 1904. He died at Fort Sill on the federal payroll as an army scout.

The greatest tribute paid Geronimo for his 1885-86 exploits can be found in the words of the federal judge who presided in the case of *Scott* v. *United States and Apache Indians* (33 Ct. Cl. 486), in which Scott was trying to collect money for Apache depredations:

The military forces engaged at the time of the surrender consisted, on the part of the United States, of 42 companies of cavalry and infantry; on the part of our ally, the Republic of Mexico, of 4,000 men; and on the part of the common enemy, the Apaches, of not more than 50 men and a few women. . . .

But the costly record of Geronimo is one which can never be questioned. His campaign taxed the powers of two great civilized governments; it involved a treaty which allowed the forces of the one to cross the frontier of the other; it received the energy and experience and ability of our two greatest masters of Indian warfare, General Crook and General Miles. The war was waged, on the part of the United States at least, with the best military apparatus of modern warfare, including steam, electricity, and the heliostat; and more valuable than any other element in the military case, it was an instance of Apache against Apache, for our troops were led by Apache scouts who faithfully and heroically served the Government. Yet Geronimo armed his band with the best of modern breechloaders and ammunition, and even equipped them with field glasses taken from us, and drew his supplies from wherever he would, and inflicted incalculable damage on the country of both of his enemies, and carried on his last campaign successfully for five months. There is not, probably, in the history or traditions or myths or the human race another instance of such prolonged resistance against such tremendous odds.

Moreover, the Indian soldier was successful even in the ending of his campaign, for the surrender of this paltry band involved more prolonged negotiation than the army of Burgoyne at Saratoga or of Lee at Appomattox, and concluded by the granting of terms that the surrender be "as prisoners of war to an army in the field"—terms which effectually removed the sagacious savage and his followers beyond the jurisdiction of the civil authorities (pp. 487-488).

See Angie Debo, *Geronimo* (1977.)—B. L. F.

Ghent, Treaty of (1814). Termination of the War of 1812. The War of 1812 had no sooner begun than President James Madison desired to end it. In the spring of 1813 he seized upon an offer of mediation extended by the czar of Russia to the United States and Great Britain to appoint peace commissions even before he knew that the British government would go along with the czar's proposal. The American commissioners—John Quincy Adams, Albert Gallatin, and James A. Bayard—soon were together in St. Petersburg (as the American minister to Russia, Adams was already there) in July 1813, awaiting the czar's pleasure. Nothing happened for quite some time, and it began to appear that the commissioners might have to return home with nothing accomplished.

At last, in 1814, the fortunes of war smiled upon the fourth coalition—it had taken four coalitions to defeat the French—as the British army occupied Paris and Napoleon exited to Elba in the Mediterranean. At the outset, the ending of the Napoleonic wars promised nothing of peace for the Americans, for the victory of the coalition gave the British the opportunity to send troops to the New World to chastise the Americans properly for their entrance into the war. But then the coalition began to disintegrate and rumors of a possible return of Napoleon from Elba spread in Paris. In this disquieting situation the British decided to end the war with America. England arranged for negotiations in the Flemish city of Ghent, which she controlled and which was close to the Channel and made for easy communication with London. There the American commissioners, with the addition of Henry Clay and Jonathan Russell, after a considerable parley, signed a treaty on Christmas Eve, 1814. There was, incidentally, no decision on impressment, one of the major issues over which the Americans had gone to war. The British delegates sought the creation of a great Indian barrier state in the Old Northwest, and this the Americans refused. The British then asked for the military situation of the moment, *uti possidetis*, meaning that they would have kept part of Maine along with other portions of American territory. The Americans held out and obtained the *status quo ante bellum*.

The first copy of the treaty of peace reached Washington on February 14, 1815, and three days later the Senate unanimously advised and consented to its ratification. At eleven o'clock that night, Secretary of State James Monroe exchanged final ratifications with the British minister. Next morning, February 18, the president proclaimed the treaty. It is possible—but, of course, who knows?—that if General Andrew Jackson had not won the battle of New Orleans on January 8, 1815, the British government might have tried to revise in its favor the treaty as concluded at Ghent. Fortunately history did not happen that way. The swirl of events in Europe was so fast, anyway, that afterthoughts probably would have been impossible. Napoleon landed on the coast of southern France on March 1, 1815, and thereafter the British and their allies had their hands full.

See John Quincy Adams, *Memoirs*, 12 vols. (1874-77); George Dangerfield, *The Era of Good Feelings* (1952); and Fred L. Engelman, *The Peace of Christmas Eve* (1962).—R. H. F.

Ghost Dance. Indian religious movement. The Ghost Dance was a messianic movement among Indians that spread widely throughout the West in two waves during the latter third of the nineteenth century. In 1869 or 1870 Tävibo, a Northern Paiute (or Paviotso) from Mason Valley, south of Virginia City, Nevada, began to preach a doctrine proclaiming that all white people would fall into holes in the ground and be swallowed up, while dead Indians would return to enjoy the earth and all the things left by the whites. He claimed to communicate with the dead during trances and instructed his followers to dance the traditional circle dance of the Great Basin and sing songs divinely revealed to him. The doctrine was called the Ghost Dance because it held to belief in the return of the dead. The Ghost Dance of 1870 spread only to California, Oregon, and other parts of Nevada; in some of these areas, local prophets and cults arose. The movement subsided within a few years when the prophecies did not come to pass.

A great resurgence was led by another Paiute messiah, Wovoka (c.1856-1932). Having lived for a time with a family named Wilson, near Yerington, Nevada, Wovoka was known to white men as Jack Wilson. He was said to be the son of Tävibo, but some contemporary scholars doubt the relationship. In any case, he lived in the same area and learned the doctrines of Tävibo as a boy, since he was about fifteen when Tävibo died shortly after 1870.

In 1889 a major eclipse of the sun occurred while Wovoka was stricken with a severe fever. In the words of his own language, he reported being taken to the afterworld to see the Supreme Being. All the people who had died long ago lived there, youthful and happily engaged in old-time occupations and sports. The Supreme Being told him to return to earth and tell his people to love one another, live in peace with the whites, and devote themselves to work. If they followed these instructions and danced a ceremony that the Supreme Being taught him, they would be reunited with the dead, death would be no more, and the whites would disappear forever. The Supreme Being also gave him songs to control the elements.

The California Indians, disillusioned by the earlier movement, were unimpressed by the Ghost Dance of 1890; but it spread rapidly through the Rocky Mountains and widely across the Great Plains, where it was eagerly embraced by the Sioux, Cheyenne, Comanche, Arapaho, Assiniboin, Shoshoni, and others. In the Southwest the Navaho, fearing ghosts, were unreceptive to the doctrine.

Among all these groups the basic ceremony involved men, women, and children dancing in a circle to the accompaniment of songs. For some, the dancing and chanting led to a state of trance, with visions of meetings with dead friends and relatives returned from the afterworld. Many new songs were composed to recount these visions. To these elements the Sioux added "ghost shirts," made of white muslin and painted with the sun, moon, stars, and eagles or sage-hens. The shirts were thought to give protection against danger, including bullets.

The Plains Indians had recently suffered defeat in warfare, the destruction of the bison, the advent of new and often fatal diseases, and confinement on reservations. The Ghost Dance promised a new world, with the return of the dead and of the great bison herds. The movement had the greatest impact on the Teton Dakota, the western division of the large linguistic group also known as the Sioux. For them it became a focus of resistance to further encroachment of the whites. After hearing about Wovoka in 1889, the Teton chiefs sent a delegation west to learn more about his doctrine. Upon their return in the spring of 1890, the Ghost Dance was inaugurated; the excitement it created reached a peak in the summer.

Indian resentment over the decline of their culture and the failure of the government to keep its promises, combined with white fears of Indian outbreaks, led to a series of conflicts on the Pine Ridge reservation, which reached a tragic climax at the WOUNDED KNEE MASSACRE (1890), in which almost three hundred men, women, and children were massacred.

The Ghost Dance subsided quickly at Pine Ridge and died out more gradually over the next few years among other tribes.

Anthony Wallace interprets the Ghost Dance as a "revitalization movement" that aimed to restore the vitality of a culture under attack. Weston LaBarre prefers the term "crisis cult," and he sees in the Ghost Dance a model for understanding religion as an adaptive response to misery and despair. Most scholars, regardless of their theoretical predilections, agree that the rapid spread of the Ghost Dance of 1890 was a reaction to the severe deprivation that the Plains Indians had suffered at the hands of the encroaching whites.

See Cora DuBois, "The 1870 Ghost Dance," *Anthropological Records*, vol. 3, no. 1 (1939); Weston La-Barre, *The Ghost Dance: Origins of Religion* (1970); James Mooney, *The Ghost Dance Religion and the Sioux Outbreak of 1890*, Bureau of American Ethnology Fourteenth Annual Report, Part 2 (1896); and Anthony F. C. Wallace, "Revitalization Movements," *American Anthropologist*, vol. 58 (1956), and the introduction to an abridged edition of Mooney's report (1965). For information on Wovoka, see Paul Bailey, *Wovoka, the Indian Messiah* (1957).—F. C. M.

"Ghost of Sonora." See Joaquin MURIETA.

ghost towns. For ghost towns in Arizona, see GILA CITY, SILVER KING, TOMBSTONE, and WHITE HILLS; in California, GOLD-RUSH TOWNS OF CALIFORNIA, AUBURN, BODIE, CALICO, COLOMA, COLUMBIA, DOWNIEVILLE, OLD SHASTA, PANAMINT CITY, RANDSBURG, WEAVERVILLE, and YREKA; in Colorado, CENTRAL CITY and SILVER PLUME; in Montana, BANNACK and VIRGINIA CITY; in Nevada, AURORA, GOLDFIELD, RHYOLITE, and VIRGINIA CITY; in New Mexico, DOLORES, ELIZABETHTOWN, GOLDEN, HILLSBORO, KELLY, MOGOLLON, and WHITE OAKS; in Utah, OPHIR and SILVER REEF. See also BOOM TOWNS and MINING TOWNS.

Giannini, Amadeo Peter (1870-1949). California banker and financier. The founder of the Bank of America and the "greatest innovator in modern banking," Giannini was born in San Jose, California. Shortly after his birth, his parents, Italian immigrants, purchased a farm in nearby Alviso. Two more sons were born before the father's premature death in 1877. The young widow married Lorenzo Scatena, a drayman, who moved the family to San Francisco in 1881. Scatena became a salesman for a produce commission house prior to establishing his own firm in 1883. Eventually L. Scatena & Co. became one of the largest commission houses in the state.

Giannini joined his stepfather in the business; and the success of the firm was due partly to the young man's business acumen as he traveled to the farming areas throughout the state soliciting customers. His ability soon gained for him the patronage of many farmers as well as the reputation of being a shrewd judge of men and commodities. By 1901 the company was well established and Giannini, now married and half-owner of the business, decided to retire. Financially secure, he had already developed his life-long policy against accumulating a large personal fortune. "Too much money spoils people," he believed.

The death of his father-in-law in 1902 determined the career to which Giannini devoted the remainder of his life. Appointed by the family to manage the estate, he was given the additional task of filling his father-in-law's seat on the board of directors of the Columbus Savings & Loan Society. However, he soon clashed with the other directors. He opposed the conservative, tight-fisted policies of the "Banca Colombo," which stressed the self-enrichment of the directors. When the "Banca Colombo" refused to change its policies, Giannini resigned his directorship and proceeded to organize his own bank, the Bank of Italy.

Located in San Francisco's Italian quarter, the "Banca d'Italia" opened for business in October 1904. As a matter of policy, stock ownership in the bank was broad so that many people would have an interest in its success and no one would have a controlling interest. The bank's loan policy was designed for the "little fellow"— the man of modest means in need of a bank. If he needed a small sum, the bank made it available to him at reasonable rates. This liberal policy enabled many borrowers to reconstruct their homes and businesses after the earthquake and fire of 1906.

A maverick in its loan policy, the Bank of Italy was equally unconventional in advertising. Giannini advocated the unheard-of practices of soliciting new accounts on a door-to-door basis and placing eye-catching advertisements in newspapers.

Giannini's greatest contribution to modern banking was the practice of branch banking. Branch banking was not a new idea, but it was Giannini who made it flourish. He was convinced that a system of branch banks was better suited to meet the diversified needs of California's industry and agriculture than unitary banks because it possessed greater resources and the ability to funnel money from area to area as needed. For example, when hard times hit the state's bean growers in 1919, the Bank of Italy's branches in the depressed areas were able to make loans at lower rates of interest than competing unitary banks because they could tap the resources of the entire Bank of Italy system. The strength of this system enabled the bank to become a major source of loans to the suffering raisin and cotton industries in the 1920s. Indeed, California was the only state able to finance its cotton crop through its own banks in that period.

Beginning with its first out-of-town branch in San Jose in 1909, the Bank of Italy gradually expanded throughout the state. By 1921 it had evolved from a small, sectional institution into a potent force in the national banking arena. Throughout these years of expansion, Giannini's restless and fertile mind directed the bank into new fields of endeavor. It purchased bonds for highway construction, financed the nascent movie industry, and established school bank accounts for children.

In the mid-1920s, the empire-building Giannini began a long struggle to establish nationwide branch banking, but state and federal regulations prevented him from accomplishing his goal. Despite this setback, he did continue expanding the bank throughout the state, and by 1927 the Bank of Italy was the third largest bank in America. In 1930, with 280 branches, it was renamed the Bank of America, National Trust & Savings Association.

During the Great Depression, the Bank of America was actively involved in the movement to revitalize California's economy. It bolstered the job market through the purchase of construction bonds of every kind, including that which financed the Golden Gate Bridge. To meet the monetary needs of California's increasing population—a growth due in part to the "dust bowl" migration—the bank initiated its "timeplan" loan, whereby money could be borrowed with the only collateral required being a good reputation and sound plans. Meanwhile the bank continued to assist new businesses, such as the state's clothing industry. It expanded this role during World War II when it became a major financier of wartime industries in California.

In 1945, four years before Giannini's death, the Bank of America became the largest commercial and savings institution in the world. Born in the West and designed to serve western needs, the bank symbolized the economic coming of age of the West.

See Joseph Giovinco, "Democracy in Banking: The Bank of Italy and California's Italians," *California Historical Society Quarterly* (September 1968); and Marquis James and Bessie R. James, *Biography of a Bank* (1954).—J. G.

Gibbs, Jonathan (1826?-1874). Minister, educator, and Florida politician. Born in Philadelphia of free, black parents, Gibbs was a carpenter's apprentice until twenty-one years of age. At that time he entered Dartmouth College, assisted by the Presbyterian Assembly. After graduating from Dartmouth he studied two years at the Princeton Theological Seminary and thereafter was pastor of a Presbyterian church in Philadelphia. Sent to North Carolina after the Civil War as a missionary to the freedmen, he opened a private school for them. Late in 1867 he moved to Florida to continue this work. There he came to the conclusion that the newly enfranchised blacks needed able leadership in secular as well as religious affairs.

He was elected to the state constitutional convention in 1868 and served with distinction, being recognized by parties on all sides as the most cultured member of the convention. He followed an independent course, working for a constitution that would protect the rights of blacks and of property. Late in 1868 Governor Harrison Reed appointed Gibbs secretary of state, a move that strengthened the governor's standing with the freedmen. He was a close, trusted collaborator of Reed's and won wide respect for his evenhanded fairness. His ability and impartiality, however, did not shield him from the hatred of the Ku Klux Klan.

In 1873 Reed was succeeded as governor by Ossian B. Hart, who appointed Gibbs superintendent of public instruction. Having an abiding interest in developing public schools, Gibbs supervised county superintendents closely and insisted on regular, accurate reports. He made some headway in establishing a uniform textbook system. Though he professed to be unsatisfied with his accomplishments, public education grew rapidly under his leadership. In 1873 he addressed the National Education Association in Elmira, New York, the first Florida educator to be so honored. He spoke eloquently of the development Florida education had made since the war.

On August 14, 1874, in apparent good health, Gibbs delivered a ringing oration at a Republican party meeting in Tallahassee. Later that night he suddenly died. Although his brother reported that his death was due to apoplexy, it was widely believed that he had been poisoned. The Jacksonville *Tri-Weekly Florida Union* eulogized, "in all the elements that go to make up what is termed a good citizen and a capable and honest public servant, he leaves few superiors."

See William Watson Davis, *The Civil War and Reconstruction in Florida* (1913); and Joe M. Richardson, *The Negro in the Reconstruction of Florida, 1865-1877* (1965).—H. J. D.

Gibson, Arrell M. (1921-   ). Historian. Born in Pleasanton, Kansas, Gibson was educated at the University of Oklahoma. In 1949 he began teaching at Phillips

University in Oklahoma and remained there until 1957, when he joined the history department at the University of Oklahoma. In addition to his teaching duties, in 1966 he was also appointed curator of history in the Stovall Museum of Science and History and in the following year became curator of the university's Western History Collections. During 1967-69 he also directed the university's American Indian history research project. Meanwhile, he succeeded John Porter Bloom as secretary-treasurer of the Western History Association in 1967, remaining in this post for the next three years.

Gibson dealt mainly with various aspects of Indian history. His first study, *The Kickapoos: Lords of the Middle Border* (1963), won a favorable reception from reviewers. Two years later his study of an Indian fighter, *The Life and Death of Colonel Albert J. Fountain* (1965), provided new data about Indian warfare on the Plains frontier. He was also the author of a text on Oklahoma history, *Oklahoma: a History of Five Centuries* (1965), in which the Indian experience was prominent. In 1971 appeared *The Chickasaws*, in which Gibson continued his detailed examination of particular Indian tribes.
— G. D. N.

Gibson, Paris (1830-1920). Montana businessman and politician. Born in Maine, Gibson was graduated from Bowdoin College in 1851 and served in the state legislature in 1854. In 1858 he went to the infant city of Minneapolis, where he built its first flour mill and first woolen mill. Active in community affairs, he was a founder of the Minneapolis Public Library and served on the University of Minnesota Board of Regents from 1871 to 1879. He went to Fort Benton, Montana, in 1879 and began to raise blooded sheep on a large scale. In 1883 Gibson helped to found the Montana Woolgrowers Association, which he served as president until 1906. In 1884 with railroad builder James J. HILL he developed the townsite of Great Falls, which prospered after 1887 when the Great Northern Railway reached the city. He was a member of the constitutional convention of 1889, and a Democratic senator in the second and third state legislatures, 1891 and 1893. His urgent plea for a single university to be located in Great Falls was a major issue of the 1893 legislative session. He was elected to the United States Senate in 1901 and worked effectively in Indian affairs, reclamation, and related interests of the West. The progress of Great Falls was always his chief concern but he was also active in promoting agricultural growth, particularly in connection with sheep, dry land wheat culture, and increased irrigation through the use of water storage projects on the Milk and Sun rivers.

See *Progressive Men of the State of Montana* (1901).
—M. G. B.

Gila City, Arizona. Ghost town. Gila City is on the banks of the Gila River just east of its junction with the Colorado. It was the site of the first placer gold rush in Arizona in 1858. In 1864 the placers at Gila City became washed out, and the town's twelve hundred citizens moved upstream to La Paz, where gold had been discovered in 1862. La Paz and its successor, Ehrenberg, were important river ports and commercial centers until the completion of the Southern Pacific Railroad in 1878. Today Gila City, La Paz, and Ehrenberg are little more than windblown adobe ruins.

See Nell Murbarger, *Ghosts of the Adobe Walls* (1964);

and Muriel S. Wolle, *The Bonanza Trail* (1953).
—R. B. W.

Gila River. The Gila, master stream of central Arizona, rises in the mountains of western New Mexico, is joined by several minor tributaries from the south, including the San Pedro and Santa Cruz, and joins with the Salt River at a point just southwest of metropolitan Phoenix. From here it flows in a generally southwesterly direction to reach the Colorado River near Yuma. It used to be a permanent stream, navigable in wetter seasons by flatboat as far upstream as the Pima villages above Gila Bend. At that time it probably contributed well over a million acre-feet of water to the Colorado. Today the Gila is generally a dry riverbed except where drainage from irrigated fields escapes into its bottoms. An exception to this occurred in 1973, when for the first time in many years water ran along the whole course of the river as a result of unusually heavy winter precipitation in the mountains of Arizona and New Mexico.

During historical times the channel has widened and become a sandy waste into which salt cedar and mesquite thickets have become well established, much to the delight of hunters and to the regret of people living along the banks of the stream. The thickets provide excellent cover for game birds and animals but cause the river to overflow when in flood.

The flow of the Salt, the principal tributary of the Gila from the north, exceeds a million acre-feet annually, but little of its water enters the Gila because the Salt and its tributary, the Verde, are controlled by a series of dams that date back to 1911, when the major structure on the Salt, Roosevelt Dam, was completed. The seasonal flow of the whole system is highly irregular, but the major portion of the flow is derived from the melting of the winter snows along the Rim country of the Colorado Plateau and the White Mountains of eastern Arizona. Thus, the rivers are generally highest in the spring.

The rivers flow from alpine tundra zones through verdant forests of spruce and pine, down to the piñon and juniper forests and the chaparral zone, and into the grass and desert shrubs of the Sonoran Desert. Much of the water comes from slopes above seven thousand feet. Most of the runoff is derived from the snows that fall from cyclonic storms that generally pass across the plateau country to the north. Most of the summer precipitation comes from thunderstorms that occur in the moist air sweeping up from the Gulf of Mexico or the Pacific Ocean off the coast of Mexico. An occasional hurricane across Mexico may recurve northward and cause extensive flooding in late August or September.

At the time of the first Spanish incursion, the basin of the Gila was occupied by a number of Indian tribes. Some had dwelled there for thousands of years and some, like the Apache, had arrived only shortly before the Spaniards. The Apache proved too much for the Spaniards, who were able to establish only tenuous holds at Tubac and Tucson in the upper Santa Cruz valley, leaving most of present-day Arizona to various native groups.

The first Americans to reach the Gila were mountain men searching for beaver. The Patties may have reached the river in 1824, and by the 1840s most parts of the river were known to the mountain men who traveled between the Rio Grande and the Pacific Coast. One of them, Kit Carson, guided General Kearny and the Army of the West to California when war with Mexico broke out in 1846. The Treaty of Guadalupe Hidalgo in 1848 transferred all of the basin north of the Gila to the United States, but because the best route westward lay south of the river the Gadsden Purchase was completed to add most of the Gila drainage to the United States.

Discovery of silver and lead near Tubac and gold along the lower Gila and the Colorado brought a return flow of settlers to Arizona. Military posts established to control the Navaho and Apache needed supplies, and in 1869 irrigation of fields along the Salt began using canals built centuries earlier by the Hohokam Indians to water their fields.

Eventually, it was seen that dams were needed in the mountain headwaters of the Salt and Gila rivers to control the floods and store water for irrigation. The creation of the Bureau of Reclamation in 1902 made this possible, and the Salt River project became the first reclamation project to be funded. It, plus the water now being pumped from the ground, continues to supply the metropolitan area of Phoenix with water and power and helps to maintain the surrounding cotton, citrus, and alfalfa fields. San Carlos Dam on the Gila stores water for the land along the Gila south and east of Phoenix. However, in central Arizona, the ground water levels continue to decline as water is pumped to water the farms. The Central Arizona project, begun in 1972, is designed to bring water from the Colorado River to alleviate current water shortages.

For map, see COLORADO RIVER.—R. W. D.

Gilcrease, [William] Thomas (1890-1962). Oilman and art collector. Born in Robeline, Louisiana, of Creek Indian ancestry, Gilcrease moved with his parents in 1899 to Indian Territory, where each member of the family received 160 acres of land in the Creek Nation. Gilcrease's tract lay in what became Oklahoma's first major petroleum field in 1905, and on initial earnings from this source he attended Bacone Indian College near Muskogee, later enrolling at the state school in Emporia, Kansas. In 1922 he organized the Gilcrease Oil Company, which later was moved to San Antonio, Texas, and in 1925 he made the first of many trips to Europe to further educate himself in art and history, pursuing what proved to be a lifelong preoccupation with the collection of historical Americana.

In 1942 he established the Thomas Gilcrease Foundation "to maintain an art gallery, museum, and library devoted to the preservation for public use and enjoyment of the artistic, cultural, and historical records of the American Indian. . . ." A museum built on the grounds of the Gilcrease estate in Tulsa, Oklahoma, was opened to the public in 1949. In 1958 Gilcrease deeded the museum collection, building, and grounds to Tulsa. Today the Thomas Gilcrease Institute of American History and Art is acknowledged as one of the largest repositories of its type in the world. Displayed in its galleries are paintings and sculptures by a host of western artists, including Frederic Remington, Charles M. Russell, Olaf Seltzer, and William R. Leigh. Also represented are extensive catalogs of works by Albert Bierstadt, William Cary, George Catlin, Henry H. Cross, Alfred Jacob Miller, Thomas Moran, Joseph Henry Sharp, and many others. Large collections of historic plains and woodlands Indian artifacts, and assorted materials excavated by Gilcrease from prehistoric sites

in New Mexico, Arkansas, Illinois, and Oklahoma, form an important part of the museum's assets. The extensive manuscript holdings of the Gilcrease Institute are listed in the *National Union Catalog*, published by the Library of Congress.

See David Milsten, *Thomas Gilcrease* (1970); Paul Rossi and David C. Hunt, *The Art of the Old West* (1971); and Aline B. Saarinen, *The Proud Possessors* (1958). —D. C. H.

Gillette, John Morris (1866-1949). Rural sociologist. A graduate of the University of Chicago and Princeton, John M. Gillette studied sociology after a brief tenure as a Presbyterian minister in Dodge City, Kansas, and became the founder of the rural sociology movement in the United States. He taught for his entire career after 1907 at the University of North Dakota. His *Constructive Rural Sociology* (1913) was the first textbook in the field of rural sociology. He published seven books and many articles.

Gillette was a progressive reformer who worked for improved jails, abolition of child labor, woman suffrage, and welfare legislation. In 1928 he was elected president of the American Sociological Society.

The John M. Gillette papers are in the Orin G. Libby Manuscript Collection at the University of North Dakota.—D. J. T.

Gilpin, William (1815-1894). Politician, soldier, and entrepreneur. The son of wealthy Quaker parents, Gilpin was born at the family estate, Kentmere, on the Brandywine River, north of Wilmington, Delaware. Tutored at home in an atmosphere of affluence and refinement, and then schooled in England for two years, Gilpin graduated from the University of Pennsylvania in 1833. Thereafter, he received an appointment to West Point, but resigned within eight months, despite his later statement of having remained through graduation.

After a brief period studying law in Philadelphia, Gilpin was appointed a second lieutenant during the Seminole War. This marked a turning point in Gilpin's life, for he was assigned primarily to recruitment duty in Missouri. While there he came to believe in the importance of the settlement and development of the Mississippi valley. Resigning from the army in 1838, he settled in St. Louis and the following year began to practice law. He developed an active interest in Missouri politics and, as a Democrat, supported the policies of Senator Thomas Hart Benton. This support was particularly evident in occasionally vigorous, if not vehement, editorials Gilpin wrote for the *Missouri Argus* in 1839-40.

A move to Independence in 1841 placed Gilpin in a more advantageous position for contact with the increasing migration of settlers to Oregon. It also offered him an opportunity to visit the Columbia River region in company with Captain John Charles Frémont's 1843 western expedition. Gilpin left Frémont's party in Oregon. He aided the Willamette settlers in forming a government and drafting a petition requesting congressional support. This petition Gilpin carried with him when he began his return journey east in April 1844. He followed a route that took him to Bent's Fort on the Arkansas, and there he became familiar with the very large Mexican land grants of northern New Mexico, one of which, the Sangre de Cristo grant, he later purchased.

In Missouri, Gilpin was detained for a period, in part

because he was elected clerk of the legislature—the second time he held that position. Meanwhile, he publicized the Northwest through articles in the local press, thus contributing to the "Oregon fever." In the spring of 1845, he resumed his trip east, delivered the Willamette petition in Washington, and responded to congressional requests for information by preparing a report. His report emphasized the need for western settlement and improved overland communication facilities. It also stressed the potential for trade between prospective Pacific Coast ports and the newly opened Chinese empire and other Asian countries. Published as a congressional document in March 1846, Gilpin's writing was widely circulated and discussed.

When the Mexican War broke out in May 1846, Gilpin returned to Missouri and was elected a major in Colonel A. W. Doniphan's regiment of Mounted Volunteers. He led his battalion over the Santa Fe Trail to take part in the bloodless conquest of New Mexico. His next assignment involved treaty-making with the Ute and Navaho. Doniphan then led his army deep into Mexico on a march that has been compared favorably with Xenophon's famous exploit. At Brazito, north of El Paso, on December 25, 1846, Gilpin's troops fought bravely and skillfully, defeating a determined Mexican force. At the next battle two months later, along the Sacramento River near Chihuahua, Gilpin provided especially courageous leadership, thus contributing to another victory.

The invading army then rested in Chihuahua, uncertain of its next objective. Gilpin urged a march on Mexico City but orders reached the commander in April 1847 to move southeastward to Saltillo. Gilpin's unit was assigned the lead, and after reaching its destination it was ordered to return to Missouri. Gilpin was discharged from the army in New Orleans.

The next dozen years of Gilpin's life centered in Independence. He resumed his law practice and interest in politics, although he was unsuccessful as a candidate for governor and then congressman. Stimulated by the writings of Alexander von Humboldt, Gilpin developed his theories of geopolitics, with an emphasis on an isothermal line along the fortieth parallel north, which he believed marked the region where major world civilizations had flowered. His theories fitted in with prospects for the growth of Missouri, so he could readily support, through his addresses and writings, the local demand for the construction of a transcontinental railroad line through the state. As a side issue, he endeavored to promote, rather unsuccessfully, his projected city of Gilpinton, near Independence.

The discovery of gold along the South Platte River bore out Gilpin's belief in the abundance of such treasures in the Rocky Mountains. His address in 1858, "Pike's Peak and the San Juan," was published as part of an 1859 Colorado guidebook. A year later, he issued his own book, a visionary study entitled *The Central Gold Region*, in which he described the Mississippi valley as the future center of civilization, with Denver, a tiny settlement just two years old, as its capital city.

Meanwhile, the Kansas question had taken the forefront in public debate and forced political realignments. Gilpin joined the Republican party and was in the minority in his region when he gave strong support to Abraham Lincoln in the election of 1860. Thereafter, he was called to Washington. Because of his prominence as a westerner, he was rewarded with appointment as the first governor of the newly created Territory of Colorado. He was given primarily oral instructions for his administrative duties in that critical time, and reached Denver on May 27, 1861.

He toured the mining camps, directed that a census of the territory be taken, studied the distinctive characteristics of the former unofficial Territory of Jefferson, and presented the first meeting of the legislature with a full set of gubernatorial recommendations. His greatest responsibility was to hold the territory for the Union in the face of much sympathy among the residents for the Confederacy. At the same time, he had to raise a military force for the federal government. He early endeavored to forestall Confederate sympathizers from buying up arms locally, organized a military staff, and began to recruit two companies of militia. By August, he had been authorized to increase the number of military to a thousand. Despite the fact that he lacked clear-cut sanctions for doing so, he issued drafts on the federal treasury, amounting to a total of $375,000, to meet these expenses.

As a result, Colorado had troops available when, early in 1862, a threatened Confederate invasion of New Mexico led to an urgent call from the Union commander for aid from Governor Gilpin. He promptly dispatched the First Colorado Volunteer Regiment to the vital post of Fort Union in New Mexico. From there, the troops were ordered to Santa Fe; en route they encountered the Confederates at Glorieta Pass. In the battle which ensued on March 27, the Colorado Volunteers played a decisive role in helping turn back the invaders.

The drafts Gilpin had issued were not honored by the treasury, and the ensuing dispute led to Gilpin's removal as governor in March 1862. (In later years the federal government did pay the drafts). Gilpin's pride was deeply wounded; he sought justification by seeking election as the territorial delegate to Congress, but failed.

Gilpin seemed to lose his enthusiasm for political office as he became involved in the purchase of Mexican land grants. Apparently as early as March 1862, he acquired an option to buy title to one hundred thousand acres of land—the Baca Grant Float No. 4, and during the following summer he located the grant in the upper San Luis valley. He did not purchase the grant for himself until 1870, and seven years later he sold it at a profit of seven thousand dollars.

A more important speculative enterprise concerned the Sangre de Cristo grant, embracing one million acres located in the southern part of the same valley. Gilpin borrowed money in New York to purchase the grant from the heirs of Charles Beaubien in 1864, and soon sold shares in it to eastern investors. He worked diligently to prove its mineral worth; lobbied in its behalf in Congress; visited England to promote its sale; and became local manager of the grant on which thousands of settlers of Mexican descent already resided. He gained a considerable financial return from this venture, but his role in handling it was not entirely to his credit.

Gilpin also displayed an interest in the West's Granger organization, railroad enterprises, and the cattle industry. He continued to respond to demands for public addresses and in 1873 published a revised edition of his previous book under the title *Mission of the North American People*. Later, in connection with H. H. Bancroft, he wrote *The Cosmopolitan Railway* (1890). In this book, Gilpin again foresaw a glorious future for America. He suggested that the world could be united under the leadership of the United States through a network of railroads, including one that would connect Asia and North America at the Bering Strait.

Gilpin was an impressive-looking man, bearded, just over six feet tall, and slim and athletic in build. He was known as an intellectual with a storehouse of information on many subjects. His acquaintances considered him visionary and somewhat impractical—even eccentric. He was an entertaining companion, especially on outdoor trips, and was an excellent monologist. His death was the result of a carriage accident.

See H. H. Bancroft, *History of the Life of William Gilpin* (1889); and T. L. Karnes, *William Gilpin: Western Nationalist* (1970).—H. H. D.

Gipson, Fred (1908-1973). Novelist. Gipson was born in Mason, Texas, the son of a German-Irish farmer. After studying journalism for three years at the University of Texas, he worked as a news reporter and feature writer for the Corpus Christi *Caller Times* and the San Angelo *Standard Times*. In 1946 his first book, *Fabulous Empire: Colonel Zach Miller's Story*, was published. From then on books and articles, both fiction and nonfiction, appeared frequently: *Hound Dog Man* (1949), *The Home Place* (1950), *Big Bend: A Homesteader's Story* (1952), *The Trail Driving Rooster* (1955), *Recollection Creek* (1955), *Old Yeller* (1956), and *Savage Sam* (1962). Movies were made from several of Gipson's novels, the most successful of which were *Old Yeller*, a Disney film that has become something of a young people's classic, and *Savage Sam*. *Old Yeller* describes a frontier family, the young son's expanding awareness, and the part a dog plays in the boy's maturing. The novel won several awards. It presents Gipson at his best, a skillful storyteller who knows teen-age farm boys in the early years of the twentieth century.

Gipson was also an editorial consultant for *True West* and *Frontier Times*, magazines that attempt to present authentic popular accounts of the West, and president of the Texas Institute of Letters.—J. B. F.

Girty, Simon (1741-1818). Soldier. Simon Girty was born near Harrisburg, Pennsylvania. When he was fifteen, Indians captured him and his three brothers and divided them among separate tribal families. Girty ended up with the Senecas and quickly adopted their customs and language. Three years later the Senecas released him and other prisoners to the British near Pittsburgh, and the young man seems to have remained in the general area as a military scout until the outbreak of the American Revolution. In 1776 the Continental Congress employed Girty as an interpreter, only to dismiss him because of his "ill behavior." Shortly thereafter he deserted the American cause and fled to Pittsburgh, where he later joined the British as an interpreter and agent among the Indians of the Old Northwest; thus he earned the sobriquet "The Great Renegade."

His previous life with the Indians undoubtedly shaped his character to the extent that he delighted in employing their torture techniques on his enemies. On several occasions he led bands of warriors against American settlements in western Pennsylvania and was sadistic in his treatment of white captives. After taking Colonel William Crawford as a prisoner of war in June 1782, he ordered him burned at the stake. Following the Treaty of Paris in 1783, the Great Renegade settled near the site of present-day Detroit, married Catherine Mallet, and continued his work as an agent among the Indians in the Ohio country in an effort to keep out American settlers. He bitterly opposed participation by the various Northwest tribes in the Treaty of Greenville, a few months after the battle of Fallen Timbers near the site of Toledo. When the British turned Detroit over to the United States the next year (1796), Girty fled to Canada and settled on land granted to him by the British. He was almost captured in 1813 when William Henry Harrison invaded Canada and won a decisive victory at the battle of the Thames.

By this time the once strong and agile renegade was an old man, totally blind and in extremely poor health. Although his wife had long since left him, because of his drunkenness and brutality, she returned to look after him until his death at the age of seventy-seven.

See Thomas Boyd, *Simon Girty, The White Savage* (1928).—W. E. H.

Gist, Christopher (c.1705-1759). Frontiersman. Gist was born sometime between 1705 and 1708 in Baltimore County, Maryland. He grew up in this vicinity, though there is no record of his boyhood. In 1728 he married and settled down on a farm, where he became the father of five children, and in 1745 he moved to the Yadkin valley in North Carolina. Gist became a frontier scout, land surveyor, and trader. He enjoyed the confidence of many people, including General Edward Braddock, George Washington, and officers of the Ohio Land Company. Gist's journal of his journey above the Ohio River and back across Kentucky in 1751 for the Ohio Company is one of the truly fascinating pieces of early frontier literature. This adventure was followed by a journey with Washington to Logstown village in Pennsylvania, and then up the Allegheny River to the French posts. During the stirring years of the French and Indian War, Gist was active in the affairs of the frontier as trader, Indian diplomat, and frontier scout.

See Kenneth P. Bailey, *The Ohio Company of Virginia and the Westward Movement, 1748-1792* (1939); Douglas Southall Freeman, *George Washington: A Biography*, vol. I (1948); Christopher Gist, *Journals*, ed. by William M. Darlington (1893); and J. Stoddard Johnston, ed., *First Explorations of Kentucky* (1898).—T. D. C.

Glacier National Park. Glacier National Park lies along the Canadian border in northwestern Montana. This stretch of the Rocky Mountains is unrivaled for its rugged, bold landscape. Jagged mountain peaks, glaciers, lakes, ice-carved valleys, and extraordinary alpine meadows combine in a continuous scenic panorama. The Blackfoot Indians used the area as fishing and hunting grounds for centuries before the white man discovered it. Their reservation borders the park on the east. Representatives of the Hudson's Bay Company were probably the first Europeans to visit the region. The Lewis and Clark party bypassed it to the south, though noting some of its mountains from a distance. The first serious exploration of this part of the Rocky Mountain range took place in 1853, when A. W. Tinkham trekked through Pitamakin Pass, and in 1854, when James Doty explored Glacier National Park's eastern slope. The United States-Canadian boundary was surveyed by a government expedition in the 1860s. The search for a suitable rail line over the northern Rockies brought a number of engineers to the region in the 1880s. In 1889 John F. Stevens surveyed a route through Marias Pass for the Great Northern Railroad. The rail company laid its main track there in 1891, and its trains still pass along the southern boundary of the park.

In 1901, George Bird Grinnell, an early conservationist, published an article in *The Century* about the remarkable scenery of this mountainous region, suggesting that it be preserved for the enjoyment of future generations of Americans. A campaign for the creation of Glacier National Park began soon after that. Lobbyists for the Great Northern Railroad assisted in the campaign, for the company was sure the park would become a tourist attraction of major proportions to which people would come by rail. Legislation establishing the park was approved on May 11, 1910.

A large part of the park is maintained as a wilderness area. The Waterton Lakes National Park of Canada adjoins Glacier on the north and combines with it to become the Waterton-Glacier International Peace Park, established by joint agreement between Canada and the United States in 1932. The fifty-mile Going-to-the-Sun Highway, which passes through the park from east to west, is one of America's most scenic mountain roads. The park of 1,013,129 acres may be entered from Kalispell, Montana, which is about thirty-five miles to the southwest.—D. C. S.

Glass, Hugh (?–?1833). Mountain man. Little is known of Glass until he joined William H. Ashley's fur-trading expedition of 1823 as a trapper. A fellow mountain man, George C. Yount, stated that Glass once served as a pirate under Jean Laffite and later lived with the Pawnee Indians before entering the fur trade, but the evidence for Yount's assertions is fragmentary. Nevertheless, it does appear that Glass was older than most men who entered the arduous Rocky Mountain fur trade.

Glass was wounded in the leg during the famous encounter between Ashley's party and the Arikara Indians in 1823, but he recovered sufficiently to join Major Andrew Henry's party that set out overland for the Yellowstone River after the fight with the Arikara. While on their way Glass was bitten and severely mauled by a grizzly bear at Grand River, South Dakota, in August and left with two companions, John Fitzgerald and James Bridger, to guard his final hours. Heartlessly they abandoned him to die, took his rifle, and reported that he was indeed dead. Glass, however, according to his own unsupported testimony, crawled many miles down the Grand River where he joined another party headed up the Missouri. On his painful journey Glass had survived on berries and on the carcasses of buffalo calves brought down by wolves. In his second effort to go up the Missouri, Glass was attacked by Indians and narrowly escaped with his life. He reached Fort Henry on the Yellowstone only to discover that it had been abandoned, but after seeking out Henry's new fort on the Bighorn, he traveled to safety at Fort Atkinson, where it is said he confronted Fitzgerald and recovered his rifle.

Later Glass journeyed over the Santa Fe Trail, but by 1828 he was back in the mountains. At the request of independent fur trappers who were discontented with the prices they had to pay for supplies brought to the mountains by St. Louis merchants, Glass asked Kenneth McKenzie, the powerful chief factor at the American Fur Company post of Fort Union, to send supplies to the 1829 fur-trading rendezvous. According to Dale Morgan, Glass was wounded in an Indian attack at Bear Lake in 1828. Thereafter he lived in and around Fort Union. Sometime during the winter of 1832-33, he, Edward Rose, and a trapper named Menard were killed by the Arikara on the frozen Yellowstone River. A few weeks later, Johnson Gardner and a party of trappers recognized Glass's murderers and killed them.

Glass's incredible crawl over scores of miles has inspired writers to dramatize both his grueling trip and the moment when he appeared like a specter from the grave to berate Bridger and Fitzgerald for abandoning him to die. In 1915 John G. Neihardt wrote an epic poem entitled *The Song of Hugh Glass*, and in 1954 Frederick Manfred published *Lord Grizzly*, a powerful novel that fictionalized Glass's traumatic experience.

The older account of Glass in Hiram M. Chittenden, *The History of the American Fur Trade in the Far West* (1902) has been corrected by Dale L. Morgan, *Jedediah Smith and the Opening of the West*. See also Charles L. Camp, ed., "The Chronicle of George C. Yount," *California Historical Quarterly*, vol. 2 (April 1923), and Leroy R. Hafen, ed., *The Mountain Men and the Fur Trade of the Far West*, vol. VI (1968).—G. B. D.

Glenn, Hugh James (1824-1883). California rancher. Glenn was born near Staunton, Virginia. After earning a medical degree he served as a doctor in the Mexican War. When the gold rush began in 1849 Glenn drove a herd of livestock to California to sell. So profitable was his venture that he returned east several times to buy horses, cattle, and sheep for the California market. In 1867 Glenn purchased a part of the Mexican Jacinto grant on the Sacramento River in Colusa County, where he first raised cattle and then turned to wheat. Enlarging his land holdings to 55,000 acres, in 1879 he produced a million bushels of wheat on 45,000 acres. Understandably he was called the "wheat king" of America. Part of his success was undoubtedly due to the fact that he used cheap Mexican and Chinese labor in his farming operation.

Glenn's way of life fully reflected his financial success. He built a twenty-three-room house at Jacinto and later built an ornate mansion in Oakland. His properties were dotted with imposing barns, and he ran his business from a large brick warehouse at Jacinto, which also served as a store. His prominence and wealth led a dissident group in California's Democratic party to nominate Glenn for the governorship in 1879. He was the runner-up, with 47,562 votes.

Glenn is best remembered, however, as the senior partner of a famous ranching partnership, the French-Glenn Livestock Company. When farmers began to settle in Colusa County, Glenn encountered increasing opposition to his open-range cattle operations. In 1872 he and Peter FRENCH, one of his foremen, agreed to establish a ranch in southeastern Oregon in Harney County with French in charge. Under the latter's management the famous "P" Ranch, located on the Blitzen

River, prospered; at one time 30,000 cattle and 3,000 horses and mules grazed on its 132,000 acres. In 1883 French married Glenn's daughter Ella (one of nine children), and when Glenn was killed a few weeks later by a bookkeeper he had recently fired, French managed the French-Glenn Livestock Company until his own death by a settler's bullet in 1897.

The vast Jacinto estate was eventually divided into small farms, but the old mansion has remained. Glenn also purchased a ranch in Paradise valley, Nevada, where his nephew E. W. Crutchers superintended 15,000 head of cattle and a herd of 1,000 horses.

See Giles French, *Cattle Country of Peter French* (1964).—H. R. L.

Glenn-Fowler expedition. (1821-1822) The Glenn-Fowler expedition was one of several groups to discover quite independently of each other the reopening of the New Mexico trade with America, a development that came as a result of the establishment of Mexican independence. Its leader was Hugh Glenn of Cincinnati, Ohio, who only a year or two earlier had established himself on the Verdigris River near the later site of Fort Gibson in northeastern Oklahoma. Glenn had been involved in a variety of trading enterprises since the War of 1812, primarily as a supplier to military posts in the Old Northwest and the Mississippi valley. At various times he had been joined in these operations by Jacob Fowler of Covington, Kentucky.

In September 1821 Glenn set out, with Fowler acting as guide, with a party of twenty men on a hunting and trapping expedition into the Rocky Mountain area. He had rejected an offer from St. Louis merchant Thomas James, who had come by his outpost with a trading expedition, that they join forces. The two would next meet in Santa Fe the following spring.

While James continued west through present-day Oklahoma and into the Texas Panhandle, encountering numerous difficulties, the Glenn-Fowler party proceeded up the Verdigris into present-day Kansas. They reached the Arkansas somewhere around the later site of Wichita and followed the river west to the vicinity of present-day Pueblo, Colorado, where they wintered among the friendly Kiowa and Arapaho. The only untoward incident was the fatal clawing of one of the party by an unfriendly bear.

On December 30 they encountered a party of some sixty Spaniards, who assured them of a welcome at Taos beyond the Sangre de Cristo Mountains. Glenn subsequently took four men and returned with the Spaniards to the outpost. A month later he sent word to the others that he had arranged with the New Mexican authorities "to Hunt and trap and trade in the Spanish provinces," and that they should join him.

Fowler, who had remained behind, now led his companions over the windswept crest of the Sangre de Cristos, and for the rest of the winter they trapped and hunted in the mountains north of Taos. Glenn went on to Santa Fe late in April, apparently by himself. By June 1822 the entire party was headed back to the United States, accompanied by what was left of the James group. They had pioneered the "old Taos trail," as Fowler called it, into New Mexico, but it would not become a generally followed route for another two decades.

Elliott Coues edited *The Journal of Jacob Fowler* (1898),

retaining Fowler's semiliterate prose and spelling. A good secondary account is R. L. Duffus, *The Santa Fe Trail* (1930). Thomas James told his story in *Three Years Among the Indians and Mexicans* (1926), edited by Walter B. Douglas.—W. E. P.

Godbe, William (1833-1902). Mormon schismatic. Born in London, England, Godbe was a sailor prior to his conversion to Mormonism. After his arrival at Salt Lake City in 1851, he became a merchant and member of the city council. Foreseeing that transcontinental railroads, bringing with them a flood of cheaper goods, would threaten the self-sufficient Mormon economy, Godbe advocated policies to bring Utah's economy into line with the capitalistic economy of the nation. He and other intellectuals, known as the Godbeites, contended that the Mormon church's isolationist economic policy should be replaced by a policy of specialization and trade, and that the Mormons should cooperate with non-Mormons in the development of Utah's mineral resources. Brigham Young and his associates, however, opted for preservation of the distinctively Mormon "Great Basin Kingdom." Godbe and several of his associates, after their excommunication in 1869, organized the Liberal party in 1870 and conducted political campaigns against the Mormon theocracy. —L. J. A.

Goetzmann, William Harry (1930-   ). Historian. Goetzmann, a native of Washington, D.C., was educated at Yale University (B.A., 1952; Ph.D., 1957), where he was a student of David Potter and Norman H. Pearson. After teaching at Yale he joined the faculty of the University of Texas in 1964, where he became Stiles Professor and director of the American studies program. In 1967-68 he was Fulbright Professor of American History at Cambridge University, England.

Goetzmann's scholarly interests concerned the exploration of the West with emphasis on the role of scientifically trained men and the direction given the explorations by eastern ideas and preconceptions. *Army Exploration in the American West, 1803-1866* (1959) examines the activities of the Corps of Topographical Engineers. *Exploration and Empire: The Explorer and the Scientist in the Winning of the West* (1966), which received the Pulitzer Prize in history, views the West as a case study in exploration. This work divides western exploration into three periods: "Exploration and Imperialism," or the period between the Lewis and Clark expedition (1804-06) and 1845; "The Great Reconnaissance and Manifest Destiny," 1845-60; and "Exploration and the Great Surveys," 1860-1900. In each period Goetzmann examined the training and background of the explorers as a key to what each discovered. The author also traced the role of the federal government in devising a public policy for the West as a part of the nation. In contrast to Frederick Jackson Turner's view of the West as a distinctive region, Goetzmann argued that the area "has offered a theater in which American patterns could be endlessly mirrored."

Goetzmann also wrote *When the Eagle Screamed: The Romantic Horizon in American Diplomacy, 1800-60* (1966), and *The Colonial Horizon: America in the Sixteenth and Seventeenth Centuries* (1969).—J. S. W.

gold and silver rushes. Gold and silver rushes were paradoxical in nature and effect. If measured by criteria that stress logic, efficiency, and results, they seem to be "full of sound and fury, signifying nothing." Here was a series of dramatic episodes in which thousands of persons braved hardships, danger, and exorbitant prices in order to hurry to some distant place about which they knew little save that it was alleged to have fabulous deposits of gold or silver. Often the rumors proved to be exaggerated, and often the returns to the average participant were less than the effort and money expended and risks run. Yet for half a century, from California in 1848-49 to Alaska in 1896-97, the siren call of gold or silver successfully lured its victims.

Did they regard themselves as victims? Not necessarily. Immediately after the collapse of a boom the diary of a returning gold-seeker was apt to be heavy with disillusionment, but some years later that same fortune hunter was likely to look back upon the affair with something close to anecdotal affection. Perhaps each generation has, especially among its younger people, a quota of restless individuals who find it appealing not only to take a gambling chance for sudden wealth, but also to break away from society's normal restraints. If so, then for fifty years the Far West's mineral regions afforded ample opportunity.

But the gold and silver rushes were much more than just a social outlet. They were a great elemental force that swept tens of thousands into a wild and forbidding country that, but for the abnormal call of gold or silver, would long have been left to the Indians and to a scattering of hard-scrabble pioneers. Much of the land west of the Great Plains is dry, elevated, remote. Some of it is ruggedly mountainous, some is virtually desert, some is semiarid plain. For a nation of farmers and small-scale stock raisers, which is what most Americans were in the 1840s, the few good places were precisely the most distant, such as the Willamette valley of Oregon or the valleys of central California; the journey to them was a severe test of a pioneer's endurance and a drain on his material resources. Short of the Pacific Coast there were occasional favored places, as the Mormons' unusually well-disciplined group effort was demonstrating at Great Salt Lake. But taken as a whole, the huge and incompletely known land beyond the Great Plains was very distant in 1848, decidedly strange, of uncertain value, and in the hands of Indians, Mexicans, and a dwindling number of fur trappers and traders. The region had the inherent difficulty of being remote from large markets. The Spanish-speaking ranchers of New Mexico and California and the American settlers of Oregon, Utah, and California all found it necessary to reach across great distances of land or water to find outlets for the simple products they raised.

If viewed against these basic conditions of the 1840s, the importance of the gold and silver rushes almost leaps into sight. However irrational the thinking of some of the participants, here nevertheless was a stimulus that caused several hundred thousand Americans, Europeans, Latin Americans, and Chinese to abandon their customary occupations and hurry themselves, their skills, and their capital to far western North America. Once there, the majority went scrambling off in search of rich diggings, and their efforts, however unskilled, proved to be the essential prelude to the real mining that presently developed in the West, for it was through the unplanned, uncoordinated searching of many individuals during a rush that thousands of "claims" were dis-covered, recorded, and made available for purchase or use. If a high percentage were of little value, from a few of the claims gold or silver did indeed pour forth in the profusion hoped for, and from many there was at least a significant return.

Nor was the impact of the gold and silver rushes limited to the creation of the major new industry of precious-metal mining. Wherever they went, the gold-rush crowds attracted merchants in great numbers; freighting, stagecoach, and express companies; skilled craftsmen, especially of the metals trades; lawyers; newspaper publishers; politicians eager to create offices that they themselves might fill; and the saloonkeepers, gamblers, "madams," and "bad men" that dominate fictional portrayals. Many of these business and professional people were no more permanent than the rushes they served, but when the boom passed, some of them remained to become lasting influences in their communities (see BOOM TOWNS and MINING TOWNS). A few great cities, of which SAN FRANCISCO and DENVER are the clearest examples, began primarily as a response to the demands of a gold-rush crowd, while cities that had other origins, such as SALT LAKE CITY; Portland, Oregon; and SEATTLE, Washington, were sharply changed in character when the opportunity came to serve a gold-rush population. Similarly, the sudden appearance of a market for food stimulated the rise of a local agriculture and ranching that would otherwise have been long postponed.

Beyond all that, the influence of the rushes had a cumulative effect. Out of them grew the western LABOR MOVEMENT, specifically the WESTERN FEDERATION OF MINERS and with the appearance of clusters of population west of the 100th meridian, the construction of railroads was encouraged—sometimes, to be sure, before there was enough business to justify it—and the availability of railroads, in turn, presently hastened the settlement of both the Pacific Coast and the lands between that region and the Missouri frontier.

Gold and silver rushes, then, played an essential role in opening the land beyond the Great Plains; yet the value of their contribution would have been far greater if by their very nature they had not been so transitory and wasteful. In any one locality a rush lasted only so long as optimism persisted, and during that relatively brief period boom conditions led to an extraordinary carelessness with human lives and natural resources. Men, minerals, the soil, trees, and the rivers and creeks were all spent in profligate fashion, with no regard for efficient utilization or the future. Much of the capital brought in from outside or generated locally was lost in ventures that failed to "pan out," or in towns that were abandoned as hastily as they had been built. A federal report for 1868 cited the unhappy example of Star City, Humboldt County, Nevada, in a district that had been organized in 1861 and had attracted large amounts of capital for opening mines and erecting buildings of adobe, stone, and wood. Star City had become a "flourishing town, with two hotels, post office, and daily United States mail, a Wells-Fargo express office, a telegraph office, connected by a special line with Virginia City, and a population of more than one thousand souls. So sudden has been its decline that the daily mail, the express office, and the telegraph office are all in operation yet, though the entire population consists of a single family."

The net useful residuum of the rushes was therefore much less than the total amount of energy expended.

The far-reaching cycle associated with these stampedes started with the discovery of gold on land owned by John A. SUTTER in California in January 1848, in the period between the end of the Mexican War and the ratification of the peace treaty (see GOLD-RUSH TOWNS OF CALIFORNIA). Very probably the resulting "excitement" was the greatest of all the nineteenth-century rushes. It stands up impressively whether measured by the number and variety of men engaged, quantity of treasure extracted, capital committed, or extent of influence. Certainly it was the one that set the pattern for all the rushes that followed.

How it could have become so big so quickly has always been something of a puzzle. Improved means of communication through widely circulated newspapers and a better mail service, and faster transportation by sea as ocean-going steamers and clipper ships became available, do something to explain the rapid spread of the "California fever." The genuineness of the large yields reported by the first-comers and the extraordinary overall richness that was so soon revealed not only help to explain the intensity of contemporary reactions but almost serve to justify it. It is clear also that many a veteran of the Mexican War, not yet ready to settle down, proved especially susceptible to the "California fever."

There had been a few small-scale forerunners on United States soil, notably in Georgia, starting in 1828-30, when gold discoveries attracted a surprisingly large and cosmopolitan crowd, but California quickly dwarfed its southern predecessor. At least a quarter of a million men came to California during the five years that constituted the gold rush proper, and while all mineral statistics should be viewed with caution, it appears that these men dug more than $200 million in gold. Nothing in any way so rich had ever before been encountered in any part of the world.

Although the majority of those who came to "El Dorado" were Americans, gold-seekers from every part of the world were attracted. Countries with which the United States had only limited relations, such as nearby Latin America and distant China, sent literally thousands. For example, customhouse figures assert that twenty-five thousand Chinese passed through the port of San Francisco in 1852 alone.

Some of the foreign-born played an essential role as teachers, because most of the gold-rush crowd were totally unfamiliar with mining. Veteran miners from Mexico, South America, Cornwall, Wales, and Germany joined with Americans from Georgia in showing the tenderfoot majority how to go about this novel business and how to establish boundaries between adjacent claims.

What made success possible for so inexperienced and badly equipped a crew as the early gold-rush crowd was the fact that all but a tiny fraction of the gold recovered during the first five years came from placers rather than veins. The difference was essential. All gold is derived originally from veins that are encased in rock. Extraction directly from the rock is a difficult and costly business, almost impossible for the untutored. But if veins and their surrounding rock have been exposed to ero-

sion and weathering over a very long period of time, the rock breaks down and its hold upon the gold is loosened, so that the latter can be transported away by streams and the runoff from seasonal rains. While being transported, the fragments of gold are abraded and reduced in size, so that ultimately pieces of placer gold may be found in any size from substantial chunks (nuggets) to thin flakes or fine dust. The gold-seeker's task is thus simplified. He must find a deposit, usually of dust or tiny fragments, and must use some means of separating the gold from the debris into which it has happened to be dropped by water and gravity, but the onerous work of freeing the treasure from solid rock has been done for him by nature.

The California gold rush, like most of those to the Rocky Mountains in the 1860s and to regions as far afield in place and time as the Yukon, Klondike, and Nome at the turn of the century, was primarily a placer rush and as such was well suited to the limited skills, equipment, capital, and patience of the great majority of the gold-rush crowd. It is true that vein (or "quartz" or "rock" mining) began in California during the gold rush, but real success in that difficult branch of mining began to come only late in the decade of the 1850s, by which time the gold rush itself was over. Indeed, an important means of determining the end of any gold rush was the advent of types of mining that made higher demands upon the participants, such as requiring considerable previous training or experience, expensive and sometimes complex machinery, heavier capital investment, and employment of hired labor or labor organized in accordance with a definite plan of cooperation.

Placer mining, then, was the ideal foundation for a rush. But not all rushes were based on placer deposits. In some regions, such as Colorado, vein gold was important from almost the beginning, while silver is not ordinarily found in placer deposits at all. In contrast to gold, which is chemically inert and thus preserves its original form while being eroded, transported, and deposited, silver combines readily with most acids, forms soluble compounds, and is carried off during erosion, thus failing to form placer deposits. Therefore rushes like those to Colorado in 1859-79 and to the Comstock Lode and other parts of Nevada in 1859 and later years were based on the presence of veins, but in such instances the man of little capital or training found his opportunity by speculating in "claims" or shares in claims, while making a minimum effort actually to extract ore.

Rushes could be defined as the relatively brief period —usually from a few months to a few years—during which a remarkably varied crowd poured into an area in which rich deposits were alleged to have been discovered. (The reports of discoveries did not even need to be true to precipitate a rush; a rumor would suffice.) Usually but not always the area was a new one, which was precisely why the find had not been made at an earlier date. But there were exceptions to that, too. The silver-lead carbonates of Leadville, Colorado, were recognized in the mid-1870s on the site of a decaying gold camp that had been worked over more than a dozen years earlier, while the telluride gold deposits of Cripple Creek, Colorado, were identified only in 1890-91 on a cow ranch that was near the Pikes Peak whose name was mistakenly given to the original Colorado rush.

The bulk of a gold-rush or silver-rush crowd usually confined itself to the less complex types of mining, or to speculation, or to serving or "fleecing" the rest of the crowd, or to wandering or loafing about. Contemporary descriptions frequently expressed astonishment at the high percentage of the population that was engaged in everything except mining. It seems clear that the excitement—some called it hysteria—aroused by rumors of rich findings usually swept into a stampede a great many men who knew little about actual mining and never took the time to learn. Any major rush offered many opportunities to profit suddenly and dramatically from the greed, necessities, or gullibility of the crowd, or from the ill-justified expectations of distant speculative investors who could be persuaded to risk their money *in absentia*.

For many, participation in a gold or silver rush brought hardship, danger, and net financial loss. Yet as Senator William M. Stewart of Nevada remarked, the occasional rich rewards to the lucky few so emboldened the majority that they kept on seeking. An atmosphere of excited anticipation, of bold chance-taking was characteristic. It lasted as long as the deposits yielded a high daily return to the self-employed miner, or a high daily wage to the hired hand. When the daily yield began to decline sharply and the speculative opportunities to dwindle, then suddenly the unstable crowd would become conscious of the poor chances before them; of the very high prices for food, lodging, and everything they bought; of their present discomforts; and of the wonderful possibility that perhaps rich diggings had in fact been discovered in some new, unknown, and distant place that had just begun to trumpet its new-found treasure. Gold and silver rushes lived as much on hopes as on realities.

There was quite enough of the bizarre and dramatic about gold rushes to justify the novels, plays, and movies that have been written about them. The social elements were highly unusual. The average rush was composed primarily of men; thus the rise of the PROSTITUTION industry. The men came from all kinds of backgrounds; some were in fact fugitives from justice or unhappiness, as the fiction writers so often allege; and all led a highly abnormal existence in a society that asked few questions, imposed few restraints, and offered much of a rough, thoroughly masculine kind of companionship. Over the whole disorderly scene presided a rapidly changing fortune that did indeed warrant the omnipresent contemporary stereotype of "fickle goddess." While hard work, endurance, good judgment, and skill had much to do with how well one succeeded, so did the sheer chance of making a "lucky strike," of being the discoverer or exploiter of an outstandingly rich claim. The point at which fiction and movies become misleading is when they present the dramatic and bizarre as constituting the whole scene. Little is said, in most cases, of the hard work, suffering, failure, and sheer discomfort of life in a gold or silver rush.

As the first of the mining "excitements," the rush to California had an especial importance because it was there that Americans learned a way of life that thereafter they sought to reproduce on each subsequent mining frontier. In California nature had provided remarkably extensive and rich placers, located primarily along the western slopes of the Sierra Nevada. The rush to the mountains began during the spring and summer of 1848, at a time when California's total population must have been not more than 14,000, other than Indians. The rewards to the first few thousand to reach the diggings were extraordinary and were well advertised. Placer gold in that halcyon period was literally to be had for the gathering. Word spread rapidly to all parts of the Pacific world, of which California, in its remoteness from eastern America and Europe, was then a part. Before 1848 was over, the Hawaiian Islands, Oregon, Mexico, Peru, and Chile were exporting restless contingents. In 1849 Americans from east of the Great Plains began arriving, then men from all parts of the British Isles and all the countries of continental Europe, from Australia, China, and a scattering of other exotic places. Probably there were more than 100,000 people in California by the end of 1849 and 250,000 by the end of 1852, which was close to being the end of the gold rush, though neither the influx of people nor the pattern of characteristic conditions ceased abruptly.

Despite the limited knowledge and equipment of the majority, the daily income of the working miner may have been as high as twenty dollars in 1848 and sixteen dollars in 1849. It sank gradually to about five dollars in 1853, and there remained until the later 1850s, at which time a level of three dollars became common. Just how much this meant in terms of annual income is hard to calculate, because of the wide variation in number of working days lost because of illness, traveling about, waiting for water in summer, or being flooded by too much of it in winter. Very high costs for food, tools, recreation, and transportation reduced the net value of whatever the miner earned.

California mining started with the simplest possible equipment: the pick and shovel, with which to dig out auriferous gravel, and a pan or bowl in which to "wash" it, so as to separate the heavy bits of gold from the lighter worthless material. Very quickly, in 1848, miners added the rocker or cradle as a much faster way of washing "dirt" than the pan. In 1849 they began to improve their efficiency—that is, to increase the percentage of gold that was saved rather than washed away by mistake—by using mercury to amalgamate with the gold. Presently they introduced the "long tom," which was an improvement over the rocker, and this, in turn, led to the sluice, which was a series of long wooden boxes through which auriferous gravel could be washed, in the hope that the heavy bits of gold would be caught behind the numerous "riffle" bars that were placed crosswise in the bottom.

Most or all of these relatively simple implements had long been known to miners of earlier regions, such as those of Europe, Latin America, and Georgia. Since they could be made by local blacksmiths, carpenters, and handymen, they were readily available. Passing into universal use during 1848, 1849, and the early 1850s, they became the standard tools of each gold rush that followed California. Add to them the simplest types of machinery for crushing quartz rock, namely, the Mexican arrastra and a small version of the stamp mill, and one has the whole assortment of equipment accessible to the rank and file of the gold rushes.

At some early and indeterminable date, the men in gold-rush California who called themselves miners began gradually to separate into two categories: the PROSPECTOR, that true pioneer who wandered off far beyond all known diggings to hunt for promising "indications"; and the miner, who hastened to follow the prospectors whenever the latter claimed to have found something. While there was enough overlapping between the two groups to prevent them from being mutually exclusive, nevertheless an identifiable class of prospectors emerged who served as the first comers, or the precipitating element in all later rushes.

If California was the pioneer in introducing most Americans and Europeans to prospecting and mining, so was it the theater in which Americans learned how to supply and serve a newly populated wild region and how to provide that minimum of property law and criminal justice needed to prevent total disintegration. The first was much the easier of the two. The private-profit motive operated sufficiently well so that many kinds of goods and services, including both essentials and luxuries such as champagne and oysters, were provided in the most remote places. The enterprising resourcefulness of the frontier storekeeper and saloonkeeper (sometimes the same, sometimes separate) became proverbial. Always there was a severe shortage at the beginning of any boom, and cyclically thereafter supplies gave out when bad weather closed the trails and wagon roads, but communications were opened or reopened with surprising quickness.

Property law and justice in criminal cases were something else again. Extralegal systems of law and law-enforcement were a familiar story on American frontiers. When legitimately established codes of law, courts, and police were slow in arriving on a frontier or were deemed inadequate or corrupt, the people "took the law into their own hands" or resorted to "popular justice," to quote two current phrases.

Faced by a new problem in property law—mining claims—and receiving no guidance from the federal government, which owned the mineral lands, the Californians borrowed from the old, well-proven mining codes of New Spain, Europe, and Britain, finding there regulations for determining the nature, size, and ownership of mining claims (see MINING LAW and Stephen J. FIELD). Each camp enforced its own rules and tried disputes, sometimes before the whole camp, sometimes before a committee or judge chosen by popular vote. In similar fashion criminal cases were often handled by locally chosen and locally imposed arrangements for "justice." The difficulty was that popular emotions at times of great stress, such as in the aftermath of a particularly disturbing murder, were apt to turn the extralegal "trial" into vigilantism or lynching. With little else available, and given the perennial weakness of federal and state provision for new areas, it is not easy to suggest what alternatives were available. Reckless drifters, outcasts, and criminals were a small minority but an unavoidable problem on each mining frontier.

Presently the contagion of rushes spread from California throughout the mountainous parts of western America. Nearly always, if we are to believe contemporary accounts, there could be found among the early participants in any given rush a few veterans of California, who brought their mining technology and its attendant skills, and their habits and attitudes, including their mining codes and their partiality to popular handling of mining disputes and criminal cases.

The former Californians were thus the conductors who transmitted to later rushes whatever had been learned for good or ill. Their presence gave a limited degree of unity to what were otherwise totally unplanned and uncoordinated movements of large numbers of individuals and small groups, who roved over difficult regions of immense size and considerable geographical and geological diversity. If nothing else, the participant in a gold or silver rush was a thoroughly free man who could make what he would of the opportunities before him.

First in time after California was the rush to Fraser River, British Columbia, in 1858. Although soon revealed as being based on exaggerated reports, the "Fraser River fever" nevertheless temporarily drew at least twenty-five thousand men into that unknown northern wilderness. As with California of a decade earlier, one marvels at the speed with which so many people managed to make up their minds, liquidate their affairs, and find transportation.

Far more important in ultimate significance were the two rushes of 1859, those to the Comstock Lode in NEVADA and to COLORADO. The two were in some respects quite different. A high percentage of the early participants in the Comstock boom were escaping from the decaying placer camps of California and from an industry and a state that were then undergoing basic changes that gave less opportunity to the man of modest capital. In short, the Comstock rush was started as an eastward movement out of California. It soon attracted recruits from east of the Great Plains, but Californians were dominant from the beginning and so continued after the first rush had ended and attention had to be focused on actual mining. Supplies and equipment were ordered primarily from California and were delivered speedily despite the barrier of the Sierra Nevada.

Colorado had a different experience. Being only 600 to 700 miles from the Missouri River, it drew most of its gold-rush enthusiasts from the east. Although former Californians played a significant role in early prospecting and mining, their contribution soon became much less important than that of the new arrivals from east of the Great Plains. Supplies, of course, came from that same direction.

In terms of numbers of participants, the Colorado rush was probably much larger than that to Washoe, as the Comstock region was called. Indeed, in size the mistakenly labeled "Pikes Peak" rush of 1859 may have been second only to the California "excitement" of 1849. Estimates suggest that more than fifty thousand took part, and some prefer a higher figure. Having been hard hit by the depression of 1857, the Mississippi valley was filled with restless people who were ready for a speculative chance farther west.

The Pikes Peak rush of 1859 was still on when disillusioned gold-seekers began trudging back across the plains to the Missouri frontier, convinced that they had been fooled by exaggerated reports. Yet newcomers continued to arrive and new placer and lode diggings were opened, until the boom collapsed decisively in the middle 1860s. There is a question of nomenclature here. At what point did a rush cease to be a rush? In the case of Fraser River, the answer was clear, for the enthusiasm diminished suddenly and dramatically and the majority of the would-be millionaires were back home within six months of their original departure. In Colorado, the first enthusiasm diminished but prosperity and speculation continued until the major collapse in the middle 1860s. On the Comstock Lode, after the rush of 1859-60 "the flush times held bravely on" until the middle 1860s. There was nothing very precise about the termination of rushes.

An important factor in both the Comstock and Colorado rushes was that from the beginning the former was based on vein mining for silver, while with the latter vein mining for gold was very important. In both instances, technical difficulties and the need for capital expenditures presently checked the kind of unbounded enthusiasm so essential to maintaining a boom.

A better chance for men of limited means was offered by IDAHO, where prospectors discovered a whole series of very rich placer diggings in 1860-62, and Montana, where rich placers were found in 1862-64. Discontented men from the mining regions of California, Nevada, and Colorado quickly opened both states and were joined by recruits from Oregon to the west and the Missouri frontier to the east. The inaccessibility of both Idaho and Montana and the relative severity of their climates tended to hold down the size of the rush to both places, but in the richness of their deposits and the fact that so many were placers, they offered the best chance since California of the early 1850s.

These were the biggest and most important rushes of the 1850s and 1860s. Save for the Comstock, each of them involved a sudden advance into a wide sweep of new territory. Indirectly the Comstock rush, too, led to extensive pioneering, for once Nevada's richness in silver had been demonstrated, prospectors swarmed over the state's forbidding mountains and valleys in pursuit of new districts.

Contemporaries, though, were impressed also by the smaller rushes, the ones that involved a single locality. White Pine, in eastern Nevada, was an example. The boom there began in 1868, when rumor began to circulate that rich superficial deposits of horn silver (silver chloride) had been discovered on a bleak hill, more than a hundred miles from a railroad or supply center. Despite snow, zero temperatures, smallpox, and an acute shortage of housing and supplies, this desolate place attracted so large a rush of fortune seekers in the winter of 1868-69 that a veteran observer termed it "one of the most violent of these extraordinary epidemics ever experienced on the Pacific Coast." Doubtless the claim that 10,000 to 12,000 reached White Pine that first winter was an exaggeration, for a year later the census of 1870 recorded only 6,765 in the three towns that had sprung up.

An obvious reason for the size of the White Pine "epidemic" was the uneasy realization that the major mineral regions within the United States mainland had been discovered, and that henceforth prospectors and men of little wealth would find themselves confined to the relatively few districts that for some reason had been overlooked hitherto. The towns of DEADWOOD and LEAD in the Black Hills of DAKOTA TERRITORY were an example. An isolated block of mountains east of the Rockies, and located in an area reserved for the Indians by solemn treaty, prospectors only began to penetrate past the Indians and their army guards in 1874-75, and a real rush developed only in 1875-76. When it came, the Black Hills "excitement," based on placers and gold

veins, quickly mushroomed into the sort of frenzied rush that was more characteristic of the 1850s and 1860s than of this much later date. Veterans of earlier "excitements" came from all parts of the mining West to join greenhorns from the Midwest. Contemporaries said that the scenes were precisely like those of Idaho and Montana a dozen years earlier.

Comparable rushes to hitherto neglected districts took place at LEADVILLE, COLORADO, in 1877, when an almost abandoned gold camp at 10,000-feet altitude was found to be rich in silver-lead ores, and at TOMBSTONE in ARIZONA, in the same year, when Ed Schieffelin's discovery of silver in a desolate, Apache-controlled corner of Arizona inspired intense activity. Although its history was sufficiently rounded to deserve better treatment, Tombstone seems fated to be known only for the famous shootings between the Earp brothers and the Clantons and their friends. A less dramatic but very real rush to another neglected area began in 1883, when news leaked out of gold discovered in the Coeur d'Alene region of mountainous, remote northern Idaho. Eager to build up traffic to points along its new line, the Northern Pacific Railroad enthusiastically publicized the great news and helped to attract a crowd into a wilderness where in fact difficult silver-lead ores proved to be more important than gold.

Prospectors had long been pushing deep into British Columbia and into ALASKA to the north of it. Ed Schieffelin of Tombstone fame was one of these pioneer searchers. But the remoteness and inaccessibility of the region and the severity of the climate discouraged any substantial invasion until gold was discovered in the summer of 1896 on Bonanza Creek, a tributary of the Klondike River, in Canadian territory. This led to numerous expeditions in the spring of the following year, with the result that substantial amounts of gold were brought to San Francisco and Seattle in midsummer of 1897. There being no other big news at just that time, the mass-circulation newspapers quickly inflated the reports into a nationwide sensation, which the steamship companies and outfitting concerns eagerly encouraged, for obvious reasons.

From this news-making discovery further exploration during the next several years revealed the richness of the vast Yukon valley on United States soil, of the Tanana River at Fairbanks, and the seacoast at Nome. It has been asserted that one hundred thousand people started for Alaska but that less than half that number reached the diggings. Losses from sickness, starvation, and cold were unusually heavy, in part because of the high percentage of inexperienced people. The supply of men who were hardened veterans of the many western rushes was no longer as large as it once had been. The day of the old-fashioned gold or silver rush to virgin territory was very nearly over. One hears of "old Californians" in Alaska at the end of the century, but if the phrase meant literally men who had learned their trade during the earliest of all the gold rushes, then they must have been very old indeed. (See also MINING, METAL.)

See Rodman W. Paul, *Mining Frontiers of the Far West, 1848-1880* (1963) and *California Gold: The Beginning of Mining in the Far West* (1947, repr. 1965). See also William S. Greever, *Bonanza West: The Story of Western Mining Rushes* (1963); W. P. Morrell, *The Gold Rushes* (1941,

Gold seekers set out for the Klondike through Alaska's Chilkoot Pass in 1898. (Library of Congress)

repr. 1968); and William J. Trimble, *Mining Advance into the Inland Empire* (1914, repr. 1972).—R. W. P.

Golden, New Mexico. Ghost town. In Santa Fe County, Golden was a mining town with a long and colorful past, stretching back to the early 1830s when gold was discovered in the nearby Cerrillos hills. New gold discoveries came in 1879. The town remained prosperous throughout the nineteenth century, for silver, copper, turquoise, coal, and zinc were also found there, but the town was continually plagued by a shortage of water, which ultimately led to its decline. Today the town is virtually a ghost, but several of the buildings from its early days remain, most notably the little mission church dating from the late 1830s. It is extremely well preserved.

Just over the hill from Golden is the sister town of San Pedro, which is in a much more advanced state of ruination. San Pedro was largely a copper mining town, and

it, like Golden, suffered severely from a shortage of water.

See Ralph Looney, *Haunted Highways: The Ghost Towns of New Mexico* (1968); and Muriel S. Wolle, *The Bonanza Trail* (1953).—R. B. W.

Goldfield, Nevada. Ghost town. Goldfield was the site of a highly prosperous mining operation in the early 1900s. The mines around the city yielded an estimated $150 million and the area achieved a population of thirty thousand. By 1918, however, the mines had played out and Goldfield began its slow demise. Today the city is trying to revive its mining operations, but it still lingers on the thin edge between life and death. Many of the original stone buildings still stand despite the effects of fire and wind.

See Nell Murbarger, *Ghosts of the Glory Trail* (1956); and Muriel S. Wolle, *The Bonanza Trail* (1953). —R. B. W.

gold-rush towns of California (1849-1859). Preconquest California was dominantly pastoral. With the discovery of gold in early 1848 at COLOMA, fortune-hunting emigrants from the United States, Mexico, Latin America, and China began to flood the state, and new settlements began to spring up, especially in the valleys and hills of the mother lode. This random settlement soon assumed an order and interrelationship dictated by the mining economy. SAN FRANCISCO became entrepôt for the state. New cities like SACRAMENTO, Stockton, and Marysville were forged as distribution centers for the vast inland valleys and the mountain mines, the metropoli of the mining hinterland. In the mining sections themselves, smaller temporary camps met the immediate social and economic needs of the miner himself. Most miners lived in the camps, but the character of these communities was temporary and single-purpose. Some of them became towns, however, when local trade routes and the commercial needs of a district found a logical center in a particular mining camp, or when large numbers of miners were attracted to an unusually rich strike.

To a significant degree mining life was semiurban. Camps were generally within a few hours of the town, to which miners made at least weekly excursions, often on Sundays. The towns offered gambling casinos, saloons, and brothels. But there was also legitimate theater. The Nevada Theater in Nevada City offered, in one season, *Hamlet, Richard III,* and *Camille* among other plays, ballets, and dramatic readings. Among night schools, one in Grass Valley offered classes in arithmetic, mechanics, surveying, Latin, and Greek. For the pious, there were a few churches. The service personnel in the towns constituted a significant proportion of the population; by one estimate, nearly half of the mother lode population lived and worked in the towns.

Historians have frequently divided the mother lode into the southern and northern mines. In the southern districts SONORA was one of the largest and most important towns. Mexican miners located the town just south of the Stanislaus River, an important trade route, in 1848, but Anglos literally drove the Mexicans from the area in 1850. While the town was able to develop three lending libraries by 1855, it was best known for its raucous character: "Greenwich Fair might be spoken of as a sober picture of domestic life," one traveler wrote, "compared to the din and clamor that resounded through the main street of Sonora." Directly north lay two other important towns: COLUMBIA, which, at its peak in the mid-1850s included within its boundaries more than 30,000 people; and Angels Camp, where the techniques of hydraulic mining were first utilized in California. Some forty miles to the south was Hornitos, whose predominately Mexican population remained firmly in control despite periodic attempts by Anglos to invade the district. In the mid-1850s these 15,000 Mexicans built a fine adobe civic center with a quiet marketplace and plaza. Mexicans were frequently excluded from the mining towns, and many formed their own communities similar to Hornitos. The Chinese, on the other hand, were allowed to stay, and nearly every mining town had a large and vital Chinese section.

Among the northern towns, PLACERVILLE, better known as Hangtown, was perhaps the most famous. Because of its location on important trade routes, in-cluding one fork of the Overland Trail, many emigrants were introduced to the mining life there. Upstate, between the Bear and the Yuba rivers, lay GRASS VALLEY, where substantial gold-bearing quartz attracted more than ten thousand miners by 1855, and DOWNIEVILLE. A few miles north, NEVADA CITY, named ten years before the state, outshown its larger valley neighbor, Marysville, in the area of cultural life. And at the northern end of the mother lode was Rich Bar, where Louise Clappe (better known as DAME SHIRLEY) wrote her famous descriptions of mining life. In 1851 this town was large enough to support some twenty-nine physicians. Outside the mother lode country, in the gold district of Trinity County, in the shadow of Mount Shasta, was WEAVERVILLE, whose society boasted two legitimate theaters, three newspapers, a lending library, and even a lyceum in the 1850s.

The early and mid-1850s were the golden years for these mining towns. But by the end of the decade many of the mines had begun to play out. The Frazer River rush to Canada in 1858 and the Comstock discovery in Nevada a year later evacuated many of the miners from the mother lode, and with their departure camps quickly died, while towns went into decline. Some communities took it gracefully: many of Hornitos' residents returned to Mexico, and the adobe gradually began to return to the earth. In Columbia, on the other hand, miners, frustrated by the exhausted diggings, tore down the town building by building, sifting every inch of the exposed topsoil for gold dust; Columbia finally stabilized at a population of two hundred. Other towns disappeared entirely: Rich Bar vanished in the 1860s, leaving only traces of its foundations. But other towns lingered on. Angels Camp, Grass Valley, and Nevada City continued as important gold-producing districts, although the shift from individual to corporate mining drastically changed their character. Sonora, Placerville, and Weaverville, thanks to their strategic location on trade routes, maintained some status as depots and commercial centers. For at least one gold town in each of the counties, the administrative functions of the county seat was enough to sustain a small population. After the 1850s, however, the gold-rush towns left little evidence of the important role they had played in the development of California society.

See also AUBURN; BODIE; OLD SHASTA; and YREKA.

See Joseph Henry Jackson, *Anybody's Gold* (1941); and Rodman W. Paul, *California Gold* (1964).—J. F.

Goldwater family. Arizona businessmen and politicians. *Michael* Goldwater (1821-1903), a merchant and freighter, was born Michel Goldwasser in Konin, Russian Poland. He emigrated first to England and then in 1852 to California. He ran a store in the mining town of Sonora and in Los Angeles and obtained American citizenship. By early 1863, Goldwater and his brother Joseph joined Bernard Cohn in operating a store in the boom town of La Paz, on the Colorado River north of Yuma. In 1867, the brothers bought the store, established the firm of J. Goldwater and Brother, and moved their business six miles downriver to the new town of Ehrenberg. Here they built a large warehouse, obtained government contracts, and began freighting into the interior of Arizona. In 1872 Michael opened a store in Phoenix, but four years later closed out and moved to Prescott. Joseph sold his interest in the business to his brother in 1880, ran a store in Bisbee for a few years, and then left for California. Michael served as mayor of Prescott in 1885 and died in California.

Morris (1852-1939), a merchant, politician, and civic leader and son of Michael Goldwater, was born in England. He was running the Goldwater enterprises by the mid-1870s. As mayor of Prescott on numerous occasions between 1879 and 1927, he promoted local civic organizations, a militia unit, a modern waterworks, and railroads. In the early 1880s he helped organize a nationally oriented Democratic party in Arizona and was chairman of the Central Territorial Committee. Elected to the territorial council in 1885, Goldwater was vice president of the state constitutional convention in 1910 and served as state senator, 1915-16. He also founded the Prescott National Bank.

Baron M. (1867-1929), Morris' brother, opened a store in Phoenix, was a ranking stockholder and director of the Valley Bank, and helped build the Arizona Biltmore Hotel.

Barry Morris (1909-   ), a businessman and politician and a son of Baron Goldwater, was born in Phoenix and graduated from Staunton Military Academy. He became a well-known photographer and sportsman, assumed direction of the Goldwater enterprises in 1929, and was company president from 1937 to 1953. In 1949 he was elected to the Phoenix City Council for two terms and beginning in 1952 served two terms in the United States Senate. In 1964 Goldwater was the Republican nominee for president; he was defeated by President Lyndon Johnson. After four years out of office, Goldwater was reelected to the Senate in 1968 and again in 1974.

See Richard Carlson, "Goldwaters, Merchants Since 1862," *Arizona Highways* (May 1939); William M. Kramer and Norton B. Stern, "Early California Associations of Michael Goldwater and His Family," *Western States Jewish Historical Quarterly* (July 1972); and Edwin McDowell, *Barry Goldwater, Portrait of an Arizonian* (1964).—H. P. H.

Goliad, battle of (1836). To counter the attempt of General Antonio López de Santa Anna and his army of Mexican regulars to overrun Texas in 1836, leaders of the Texas Revolution placed such volunteer armies as they could raise at strategic points in the path of the advancing Mexicans. Colonel James W. Fannin, commander of one of these units, chose to defend Goliad, a position that commanded Gulf Coast supply routes from Matagorda Bay. Mexican victories in several skirmishes prior to the main confrontation, coupled with loss of vital supplies to shipwreck and capture by the enemy, weakened the Texas position at Goliad. Unfortunately, Fannin, who had orders "not to make a retrograde movement," did not seriously consider retreat until it was impractical.

When Fannin finally ordered a withdrawal, the maneuver was slow and disorganized. Overtaken on an open prairie, the three hundred Texans were surrounded by some one thousand Mexicans under command of General José Urrea. Lacking food and water and helpless under the superior range of the Mexican artillery, Fannin surrendered on the second day of the fighting.

By terms of the surrender with Urrea, Fannin was led to believe that the lives of the Texans would be spared.

Urrea's recommendation of clemency for his prisoners was ignored by General Santa Anna, however, who ordered the immediate execution of the Goliad prisoners. On Palm Sunday, March 27, 1836, in an act known as the Goliad Massacre, Fannin and his men were lined up in a field and shot to death without warning. Thereafter "Remember Goliad!" ranked with "Remember the Alamo!" as a challenge to the Texas troops.

See William C. Binkley, *The Texas Revolution* (1952); and Wilfred H. Calcott, *Santa Anna* (1936).—J. B. F.

Gonzales, [Rodolfo] "Corky" (1928-   ). Chicano leader. Born in Denver, Colorado, Gonzales was the son of a migrant worker. He was a professional boxer and Golden Gloves champion, a packinghouse worker, lumberjack, businessman, farm worker, bail bondsman, and director of the Denver Neighborhood Youth Corps program. In 1965 he was instrumental in forming the Crusade for Justice, a militant Chicano organization in Denver, which he headed as president and director. The Crusade emphasizes Mexican and Chicano cultural heritage and conducts both adult and youth educational programs. The Crusade grew out of Los Voluntarios, the Mexican-American political arm of the Democratic party in Denver. Gonzales described the Crusade as "grass roots" and claimed three thousand members in Denver in 1969. On March 27-31, 1969, the Crusade sponsored a national conference on Chicano liberation, where participants learned firsthand about sit-in and demonstration techniques. One of the early publicized activities of the Crusade was a 160-mile protest march from Walsenburg to Denver, which Gonzales headed.

In 1967 Gonzales led a contingent of Crusade workers to New Mexico to investigate the Tierra Amarilla raid, allegedly led by Reies TIJERINA. On June 9 he sent a telegram to President Lyndon Johnson and others in defense of the Alianza, seeking a federal inquiry and legislation for partial reparations to land grant descendants. He later assisted with the Tijerina Defense Fund in Albuquerque and spoke at the fifth annual convention of the Alianza in New Mexico in the fall of 1967.

In 1970 Gonzales was editor of the Crusade's paper, *El Gallo*. His plays include *The Revolutionist* and *A Cross for Maclovio*, and he has written an "epic poem" about the Chicano entitled "I Am Joaquin" (1967).

Peter Nabokov, *Tijerina and the Courthouse Raid* (1969), recounts Gonzales' support for Tijerina in 1967.—J. R. V.

Gooding, Frank Robert (1859-1928). Idaho politician. Born in Tiverton, England, Gooding came to Michigan in 1867 and moved to California ten years later. A farmer and miner for four years around Shasta, California, he became interested in Idaho's Wood River mines and moved to Ketchum, Idaho, in 1881. There he carried mail for a while and contracted to provide charcoal to a smelter. When the smelter had to shut down in 1888, Gooding moved out into the plains of the Snake River, starting a ranch near the later city of Gooding. There he went into politics: he was elected to the Idaho state senate in 1900 and 1902 and was governor of Idaho, 1905-1908. He based his reelection campaign upon a promise to prosecute William D. Haywood and other officials of the Western Federation of Miners for conspiracy in the assassination in 1905 of former governor Frank Steunenberg. He carried out his pledge, but Haywood was found not guilty. Gooding then sought a seat in the United States Senate in 1913 and 1918 before winning in 1920 and again in 1926. An active member of the Senate farm bloc in 1921 and an internationalist who favored the League of Nations, he led the party organization Republicans who so often were at variance with the more independent-minded senator, William E. Borah.—M. W.

Goodnight, Charles (1836-1929). Cattleman. Born in Macoupin County, Illinois, Goodnight was brought to Texas in 1846 by his mother and stepfather. In 1857 he became a ranger and Indian scout, thus preparing him for his Civil War service as a scout and guide for a frontier regiment.

By 1865 Goodnight had a herd of cattle in Palo Pinto County, Texas. Seeking a better market for the herd than was offered in Texas during Reconstruction, he and Oliver Loving decided to sell their cattle in New Mexico. The route they followed in 1866 from Fort Belknap, Texas, to Fort Sumner, New Mexico, became known as the Goodnight-Loving Trail, later one of the most heavily used cattle trails in the Southwest. On their third trip west Loving was killed by Indians, but Goodnight continued to drive cattle to New Mexico for the next three years, working with John Chisum in 1871 to clear a profit of seventeen thousand dollars.

In 1875 Goodnight marked out the Goodnight Trail from Alamogordo Creek, New Mexico, to Granada, Colorado. His Colorado ranching venture was not successful, and in 1876 he moved his eighteen hundred head of Durham cattle from Colorado to Palo Duro Canyon in the Texas Panhandle. In 1877 he went into partnership with John G. Adair in the JA Ranch. In time they ran one hundred thousand cattle on one million acres of land. An early believer in herd improvement, Goodnight developed one of the nation's best blooded herds through the introduction of Hereford bulls. He also developed "cattalo" by breeding buffalo to Polled Angus cattle.

Goodnight was one of the founders of the Panhandle Stockmen's Association (1880), which was instrumental both in improving breeding methods and in ridding northern Texas of outlaws and cattle thieves. In 1887 the JA Ranch was divided between Goodnight and Adair's widow, Cornelia Adair, and in 1890 Goodnight sold his portion, the Quitaque division. In his last years he invested in a Mexican mining venture and operated his small ranch at Goodnight, the Panhandle town named for him.—C. H. F.

Goodwin, Cardinal B. (1880-1944). Historian. Born in Pine Bluff, Arkansas, Goodwin was educated in the Northeast and attended Brown University, where he supported himself by teaching in preparatory and high schools.

In 1910 he was drawn westward to the University of California, where Herbert Bolton was soon to develop his ideas about the common history of the Americas and Spanish influence on the American frontier. Goodwin continued his graduate studies under Bolton, again supporting himself by teaching in various high schools.

In 1918 Goodwin accepted an appointment at Mills College in Oakland, California, where he remained until his death. He was a frequent visiting lecturer at other universities in the West.

Goodwin was a prominent member of the "Bolton school" of southwestern history. After his first book, *The*

Establishment of State Government in California (1914), a competent narrative about the early American period of California history, he broadened his vistas to include the trans-Mississippi West. In 1918 he produced *A Larger View of the Yellowstone Expedition*, a monograph, and four years later a general survey volume, *The Trans-Mississippi West from 1803 to 1853: A Brief History of Its Acquisition and Settlement*.

Goodwin's role in popularizing the history of the Spanish borderlands won recognition in 1927, when he was elected president of the Pacific Coast branch of the American Historical Association. His reputation was further strengthened by his short study *John C. Frémont, an Explanation of his Career* (1930) and his editing of a collection of documents in honor of Bolton, *New Spain and the Anglo-American West* (1932).

Goodwin's major contributions to western history were to undertake a deeper exploration of nineteenth-century California history and to popularize Bolton's ideas in books, articles, and lectures.—G. D. N.

Goodykoontz, Colin B. (1885-1958). Historian. Born in Atlanta, Indiana, Goodykoontz was educated at the University of Colorado, the University of California, and Harvard University, where the seminars in western history led by Frederick Jackson Turner provided a major attraction. While working under Turner at Harvard, Goodykoontz taught for a year each at Bowdoin College and Yale University.

In 1921 he joined the history department at the University of Colorado, where he remained until his retirement in 1954. Goodykoontz's dissertation, *Home Missions on the Frontier*, was eventually published as a book in 1939. In accord with the typical Turnerian approach, it dealt with the impact of the frontier on American religious organizations.

Meanwhile, Goodykoontz expanded his interest to the history of Colorado and, with James F. Willard, edited *Experiments in Colorado Colonization, 1869-1872* (1926) and contributed an essay to *Colorado: Short Studies of its Past and Present* (1927). In later years Goodykoontz investigated the career of Edward P. Costigan, a leading Colorado progressive politician and United States senator, and edited the *Papers of Edward P. Costigan Relating to the Progressive Movement in Colorado, 1902-1917* (1941).

Goodykoontz was also active in professional organizations and sought to further interest in western history by arranging conferences of frontier historians, one of which resulted in a book he edited, *The Trans-Mississippi West: Papers Read at a Conference held at the University of Colorado, June 18-June 21, 1929* (1930). A popular teacher, Goodykoontz trained a competent group of graduate students in frontier history. But his main contributions to western history were to stimulate interest in the trans-Mississippi West and to encourage the further exploration of Colorado's history.—G. D. N.

Gore, Thomas P. (1870-1949). Oklahoma politician. Gore was born in Webster County, Mississippi. Although he lost the sight of both eyes in a series of childhood accidents, he refused to permit this physical disability to interrupt his education. He graduated from the Walthall Normal School in Mississippi in 1890 and, after teaching school for two years, entered Cumberland University Law School at Lebanon, Tennessee. Gore practiced law in Mississippi and Texas before settling down in Lawton, Oklahoma Territory, in 1901 and establishing a law office there.

Gore entered politics and during the 1890s was a leader in the Populist party of Texas, serving as a delegate to national conventions and seeking election as congressman. In Oklahoma Territory he joined the Democratic party and won election to the Oklahoma territorial legislature. On the eve of Oklahoma statehood Gore campaigned in both Oklahoma Territory and Indian Territory for the adoption of the Oklahoma constitution and for the election of the slate of nominees for state office put forth by the Democratic party. His sparkling and entertaining oratory made him a popular public figure. When Oklahoma was admitted to the Union in 1907, he ran on the Democratic ticket as a candidate for the United States Senate. He won his seat but drew the short term and had to run for reelection in 1908. He was victorious and continued his tenure until 1920, when he lost his bid for the Democratic nomination in the Oklahoma primary. Gore returned as a candidate in 1930 to serve one more term.

As a senator Gore was conspicuously attentive to Oklahoma and southwestern interests in oil, agriculture, and transportation. His early Populist affiliation influenced his political action as a Democratic senator. During World War I he was consistently in opposition to the military and diplomatic policies of President Woodrow Wilson. And as a senator during the early days of the New Deal he opposed President Franklin D. Roosevelt's programs for national economic rehabilitation.

See Monroe Lee Billington, *Thomas P. Gore: The Blind Senator from Oklahoma* (1967).—A. M. G.

Gould, Jay (1836-1892). Financier. Gould, the leading exemplar of the "robber baron" legend, was a descendant of Nathan Gold, an Englishman who settled in Milford, Connecticut, in 1647. From the beginning he had a talent for making money, saving five thousand dollars from surveying work in upstate New York, Ohio, and Michigan. The nest egg, invested in a tannery, grew to an amount sufficient to establish Gould in New York City in 1859, while his treatment of his partners, according to legend, drove one to suicide.

"Undersized, keen-witted, and unscrupulous," in the words of historian Allan Nevins, Gould was soon speculating in railroad bonds. His roughshod tactics in a quick succession of spectacular operations, such as the fight with Commodore Cornelius Vanderbilt for the Erie Railroad and his attempt, with James Fisk, to corner the market for gold, brought him permanent obloquy, and a large fortune. Gould then seized control of the Union Pacific and Kansas Pacific railroads. When he merged them at great profit to himself, the public outcry was bitter. Control of the Denver Pacific followed, and with acquisition of the Missouri Pacific, the St. Louis, Iron Mountain and Pacific, and the Texas and Pacific, the "Gould system" of southwestern railroads, constituting about the only competition with the Santa Fe system, was formed. Meanwhile, Gould had acquired the Western Union Telegraph Company, newspapers, and the New York elevated rapid transit system. Badly overextended when the short but sharp Panic of 1884 came, he had to abandon his efforts to invade the trunk-line territory of the northeast, for which he had acquired the Wabash Railroad, and thereby an ambition, which he shared with other railroad financiers of his day, to control a single coast-to-coast system.

Interested in little beyond business except gardening and books (he left a valuable library), Gould lost a long struggle with tuberculosis on the eve of the depression of the 1890s.

Gould's name is perhaps permanently welded to the image of the heartless, destructive monopolist and Wall Street manipulator, which was expanded to cover all men of big business in the Populist-Progressive era. The growth of sophisticated scholarship in business history, however, is leading to the conclusion that many of Gould's operations were highly constructive and frequently dictated by factors outside his control. The Union Pacific-Kansas Pacific merger, for example, is now realized to have been necessitated by unwise restrictions placed on the Union Pacific by its charter, which threatened its ability to compete after later transcontinental lines were built.

Jay Gould's lofty seat in the robber-baron pantheon was firmly established in Gustavus Myers, *History of Great American Fortunes*, 3 vols. (1910), a bitter, naïve work to which Matthew Josephson, *Robber Barons: The Great American Capitalists, 1861-1901* (1934), added little scholarship or sophistication. Gould will probably never be "rehabilitated" to the extent implied in Julius Grodinsky, *Jay Gould: His Business Career, 1867-1892* (1957), but perpetuators of the robber-baron legend will ignore this monumental work at their peril.—A. M.

Graff, Everett D. See COLLECTORS AND COLLECTIONS OF WESTERN AMERICANA.

Graham, Charles (1852-1911). Scenic designer, illustrator, and draftsman. Graham was born in Rock Island, Illinois. With no formal art training, he gained experience in the West as a topographer with a surveying party for the Northern Pacific Railroad in 1873. His professional career began as a scenic artist for a Chicago theater, followed by several years in this same capacity in New York City. About 1877 he joined the staff of *Harper's Weekly*. Nearly every issue of *Harper's Weekly* between 1880 and 1893 featured a full page or double spread by Graham. In addition to his first trip with the railroad survey, he made subsequent western tours to record views of frontier life that later served as material for his published illustrations. His emphasis on town and city views is considered important today in showing how the West grew out of its primitive frontier state. After 1892, Graham became a free-lance illustrator for a number of New York newspaper and magazine publishers, contributing some work to the American Lithography Company. He took up oil painting very late in life.

See Robert Taft, *Artists and Illustrators of the Old West, 1850-1900* (1953).—D. C. H.

Graham-Tewksbury feud (1886-1892). Feud in Arizona. The Graham-Tewksbury feud stands in the history of the American West as a reminder that western violence was often directed at basically honest men by other basically honest men. The bloody events of that affair also reflect the somber truth that jealousy, hatred, and blind passion between neighbors is often exploited by economic interests, law enforcement authorities, and well-intentioned friends. Although the feud is often described as a conflict between cattlemen and sheepmen, that aspect of the affair seems almost incidental in a broader context. Certainly it did little more than trigger the violence. Prejudice and irrational hatred were the factors that kept the war alive and took the lives of more than twenty men before it ended. Consequently, the origins of Arizona's most infamous feud are difficult to unravel because the bitterness of family hatreds has colored the record with partisanship and because the root causes were never explained by the principals if indeed they understood them. Most of the leading figures in the drama died in the feud, and the things that historians would most like to know lie precisely in those areas least likely to be documented.

Pleasant Valley in the Tonto Basin seemed a safe enough place in the 1880s. It was remote to be sure, and there were problems, but it was attractive enough to draw the families of John D. Tewksbury, an old man with three half-breed sons, and of two brothers, Thomas H. and John Graham. Both families had modest means but were respected by their neighbors. The Tewksbury boys and the Grahams rode as cowhands for neighboring ranchers and were apparently friends until 1884, when they quarreled over cattle. The nature of the dispute is not clear. Some sources claim that the Grahams and Tewksburys stole strays from ranchers in the area. Others suggest that they simply gathered unbranded and unclaimed calves and applied their own brand to them. The partnership proved so profitable that one of the Grahams succumbed to temptation and registered the new brand in his own name, refusing to acknowledge any partnership with the Tewksburys. Whatever the truth, two things are clear: members of both families were arrested on charges of cattle rustling and released for lack of evidence, and the families soon became fierce enemies. The Grahams found allies in the five sons of Mark Blevans, and the stage was set for tragedy.

The feud might never have developed beyond a family quarrel if outside interests had not interfered. The Grahams, by reason of their newly acquired cattle interests, moved into a closer relationship with the area's larger ranchers, while the Tewksburys, denied the rewards of their labors, were increasingly excluded from Pleasant Valley affairs. They grew bitter and touchy, and in 1886, when the foreman of a prominent local rancher accused Ed Tewksbury of stealing horses, Tewksbury shot him. But the real trouble began when the Tewksburys violated the valley's strongest prohibition. The Tonto Basin was cattle country, and the ranchers had specifically forbidden sheep to enter the valley pastures. In the fall of 1886 the Tewksburys, who were still looking for a way to get even with the Grahams, made a deal with prominent sheepmen from Flagstaff to graze sheep in Pleasant Valley. When woolies by the thousands began to pour into the valley, the feud exploded with violent fury as the cattlemen moved to crush the sheepherders and the Tewksburys. At first they killed only sheep, largely because of the restraining hand of Tom Graham, who argued against bloodshed; but in February 1887 a Navaho shepherd was brutally murdered. The Grahams and Tewksburys had sparked something bigger than a family feud and were dragged along by events.

When summer arrived, the sheep were gone. The cattlemen had won, and there was reason to hope that the trouble was over. But the animosities remained. In July 1887 Mark Blevans, who had avoided the feud so far, disappeared. On August 10, 1887, Hampton Blevans and five other men, including riders from the powerful Aztec Land and Cattle Company (the Hash Knife brand), stopped to exchange a few polite and apparently innocent words with Jim Tewksbury. As they turned to go, Tewksbury fired on them from the doorway. The cowboys said the shooting was unprovoked, but the Tewksburys claimed that Blevans and John Paine, a hired gun for the Hash Knife, drew their revolvers as they turned away. In any case, Hamp Blevans and John Paine were killed.

Even then Tom Graham tried to avoid further violence, but other cattlemen pushed the issue and more killing resulted. A Graham partisan tracking Jim Tewksbury became the third victim of his marksmanship. The law now moved into the controversy but failed miserably to restore order. Instead, Bill Graham, the youngest of the Graham boys, was murdered by a deputy sheriff in sympathy with the Tewksburys. Overcome with grief, Tom Graham abandoned his opposition to violence and personally led a raid on the Tewksbury ranch on September 2, 1887. John Tewksbury and William Jacobs were caught in the frontyard and died in the first fire. For hours the Grahams and their friends kept up a murderous barrage. Then suddenly the cabin door opened, and John Tewksbury's wife stepped outside. The shooting stopped as the woman drove off hogs that were rooting at the bodies of her husband and his friend and buried the two dead men. When she returned to the safety of the cabin, the shooting began again until a posse arrived and dispersed the attackers.

Two days later Commodore Perry Owens, the new sheriff of Apache County, attempted to arrest Andy Blevans at Holbrook on charges that had nothing to do with the feud. In the fight that followed, Owens killed three of the Blevans boys and their brother-in-law. In spite of the steady attrition, the feud dragged on. In September, William Mulvenson, the sheriff of Yavapai County, determined to end the feud by arresting the leaders of both factions. The Grahams were his first quarry, and John Graham and Charles Blevans died when they resisted arrest. Mulvenson then turned his attention to the Tewksburys. At the Tewksbury ranch seven men, including the two remaining Tewksburys, surrendered without a fight. They went to jail and were indicted for murder. This seemed to herald the end of the feud. The cost had been high: only one of the Blevans boys was still alive, and Tom Graham was the only surviving Graham.

In October the shooting started again when a friend of Tom Graham's was ambushed. The law again proved ineffectual in dealing with the grudge war, and the killing continued. The atmosphere of hate and fear was so pervasive that when the Tewksburys were brought to trial in June 1888 for the murder of Hamp Blevans no one would testify against them, and they were therefore released. Fear controlled community conscience, and human life had become so cheap in the basin that three men who had not participated in the feud were lynched by Tewksbury partisans.

In December 1888 Jim Tewksbury died of tuberculosis, leaving Ed Tewksbury and Tom Graham as the only survivors of their respective families. They seemed willing to let the feud die. Graham even moved out of the valley to avoid further trouble. But the animosities had grown larger than two families by then, and Pleasant Valley had not heard the last of gunfire. A friend of the Tewksburys' disappeared in September 1891 and was never heard from again. Evidence suggested foul play.

In June 1892 Tom Graham returned to Tonto Basin to settle business affairs. He moved his cattle to a new location near Tempe and even made peace with some of his former enemies. The following August, however, Graham was ambushed near Tempe by two assassins. Witnesses identified them as Ed Tewksbury and John Rhodes. Rhodes was released for no good reason, but Tewksbury finally stood trial for the murder in December 1893 and was convicted. The case was appealed, and a new trial was granted on a technicality. The second trial ended in a hung jury. The charges were finally dropped in 1896. Oddly, Tewksbury later became a lawman at Globe, Arizona, and died in 1904 of tuberculosis.

The war has been celebrated in many forms, including Zane Grey's novel *To the Last Man*, but beyond the personal vendetta and the cattle-sheep conflict, the Tonto Basin feud loosed passions and feelings that make it virtually impossible to define its causes clearly. The inefficiency of law enforcement in a wild country certainly contributed to the longevity of the feud, and that inefficiency was exploited and promoted by economic forces at work in the dispute. Not only was law enforcement hampered if not hamstrung, but the judicial system was virtually paralyzed by fear. Hatred and fear so thoroughly permeated the valley's populace that violence became the only means of solving disputes upon which all parties could agree. The Grahams and Tewksburys were impelled deeper and deeper into the bloody business, almost reluctantly, by associates who stood to gain more than either of them. And when it was over, the only thing the basin had to show for it all were scattered tombstones, a legacy of hate and suspicion, and a reputation as Arizona's "dark and bloody ground."

See Earle R. Forrest, *Arizona's Dark and Bloody Ground* (1936); and Wayne Gard, *Frontier Justice* (1949). —G. L. R.

Grand Canyon. national park. The Grand Canyon is surely one of the most awesome natural spectacles in the world. A gigantic chasm, it extends for 217 miles through northern Arizona. Approximately 105 miles of it are protected in the national park. It is more than five thousand feet deep, and it exposes strata of sandstone, limestone, shale, and, in the inner canyon, Archean rocks more than two billion years old. The silt-laden Colorado River, gouging at the rocks for millions of years, cut through a great flatland, leaving the Kaibab Plateau on the north rim and the Coconino Plateau along the south rim. (See PHYSIOGRAPHY OF THE UNITED STATES.) Prehistoric Indians lived in the canyon for centuries. About five hundred ancient pueblo sites have been identified in the rocky walls and along the rim. The Havasupai Indians still live in the canyon on a small reservation. The Navaho also frequented the area. The Hopi, Walapai, and Paiute tribes lived in the vicinity.

Grand Canyon National Park was authorized by Congress on February 26, 1919, culminating a long crusade by conservationists and preservationists to bring the canyon into the national park system. Mining claims in the canyon impeded National Park Service administration of the area for a few years, but during the 1920s, a series of court cases invalidated these claims. The park contains 673,575 acres. The adjoining Grand Canyon National Monument, proclaimed by President Herbert Hoover in 1932, contains 198,000 acres, including Toroweap Point, one of the most scenic viewpoints along either rim. Efforts are under way to enlarge the park to the east. Flagstaff, Arizona, is the city through which most visitors enter the park.—D. C. S.

history. In 1540, Don García López de Cárdenas, one of Coronado's soldiers, became the first European to look upon the gash cut by the Colorado River through the high plateau country of northern Arizona. More than two centuries elapsed between the visit of Coronado's men and that of the next white visitors. In 1776 the priest-explorer Francisco Garcés found himself on the south rim of the Grand Canyon. Accepting the invitation of the Havasupai Indians, Garcés descended into the canyon and spent several days at their village. "I am astonished," he wrote in his journal, "at the roughness of this country, and at the barrier which nature has fixed therein." Another half-century slipped by before the next visitor confronted the canyon. This time it was the quest for furs, not souls, that led James Ohio Pattie along the south rim in the 1820s.

Essentially, however, the Grand Canyon was *terra incognita* until 1869, when John Wesley Powell and nine companions embarked on one of history's greatest explorations. They proposed to run the Green and Colorado rivers in small wooden boats from Wyoming through the upper canyons and finally through the Grand Canyon itself. August found them at the entrance to the Grand Canyon. "We are now ready to start," Powell wrote, "on our way down the Great Unknown. . . . We have an unknown distance yet to run; an unknown river to explore. What falls there are, we know not; what rocks beset the channel, we know not; what walls rise over the river, we know not. Ah, well! we may conjecture many things. The men talk as cheerfully as ever; jests are bandied about freely this morning; but to me the cheer is somber and the jests are ghastly." During the next month, Powell's party overcame rapids, whirlpools, rocks, and their own fears, arriving at Grand Wash, the end of the canyon, on August 29. There were no casualties on the river, but three men who chose to desert Powell and walk out of the canyon to the north rim were killed by Indians.

Powell returned to the Grand Canyon with a more elaborate expedition in 1871-72, and others followed his lead, but before 1900 those who knew this vast wilderness even casually could have been seated in a small room. Among them Robert B. Stanton stands out for the boldness of his imagination if not for his practicality. In 1889 Stanton, an engineer, organized an expedition for the Denver, Colorado Canyon, and Pacific Railroad along the Colorado River. Its purpose was to survey a water-level railroad route to the West Coast *through* the Grand Canyon. Nothing came of Stanton's plans, however, nor did a series of early mining ventures bear much fruit. Tourism and recreation, it appeared, would be the main canyon industry.

Attempts to capitalize on the Grand Canyon as scenery began in the 1890s with the construction of several rickety "hotels" on the south rim. But the canyon was still a two-day stagecoach ride from Flagstaff, Arizona, itself an isolated hamlet, and the number of visitors remained small. The situation changed radically, however, when the Santa Fe Railroad built a spur line to the Grand Canyon. In 1904 the Fred Harvey Company opened the El Tovar Hotel at the terminus of the railroad. Soon the Grand Canyon was on the "must see" list of every western tourist.

One of the first was President Theodore Roosevelt. Standing on the south rim in 1903, he admonished his countrymen to leave the canyon as it is. "You cannot improve on it," Roosevelt declared. "The ages have been at work on it, and man can only mar it." As good as his word, Roosevelt in 1908 created the Grand Canyon National Monument. Eleven years later Congress changed the designation to "national park," and in 1932 a new national monument was carved out downstream from the park.

By this time plans to harness the Colorado River with dams were well under way. The isolation of potential dam sites in the Grand Canyon provided temporary immunity, but the two-thousand-foot drop of the Colorado as it passed through the gorge made engineers' mouths water. In 1963 the United States Bureau of Reclamation unveiled its Pacific Southwest Water Plan. Part of it called for two hydropower dams in the Grand Canyon. One dam would have flooded fifty miles of the upper canyon; the other more than one hundred miles in its heart. Friends of wilderness and national parks objected strenuously, and David Brower led the Sierra Club in an all-out, no-compromise fight that commanded public attention as no other controversy in American conservation history. If we can't protect the Grand Canyon, preservationists asked, what *can* we save from development? The nation is not so poor, they continued, that it must turn the Grand Canyon into a "cash register." Ultimately this view prevailed, and in 1968 plans for the dams were dropped.

In the aftermath of the dam controversy, President Lyndon B. Johnson protected the upper Grand Canyon with the Marble Gorge National Monument (1969). Congress also began consideration of a proposal to create an enlarged national park encompassing the entire Grand Canyon. As it currently stands, only seventy-three out of almost three hundred river miles are within a national park.

In the recent past lovers of the Grand Canyon have had to face the ironical fact they may be its worst enemies. Crowds on the rims are already at crisis levels during the peak vacation months. When double parking is necessary for a glimpse of the canyon, and when boats are bumper-to-bumper on the Colorado River, something of the canyon's beauty is lost. Wilderness is a fragile commodity. An important new problem of conservation is maintaining a quality wilderness experience in the face of its growing popularity.

A convenient and beautiful source of information about the Grand Canyon is T. H. Watkins, ed., *The Grand Colorado* (1969). The Sierra Club has had a hand in two volumes: François Leydet, *Time and the River Flowing: Grand Canyon* (1964); and Roderick Nash, ed., *Grand Canyon of the Living Colorado* (1970). John Wesley Powell's journals are found in numerous paperback editions, among them *The Exploration of the Colorado River and Its Canyons* (1961).—R. N.

Grand Forks, North Dakota. French-Canadian explorers, traders, and trappers for Hudson's Bay Company named Grand Forks, located at the confluence of the Red River of the North and Red Lake River, nearly one hundred years before the first white settlers came to the area. In French it was known as Grandes Fourches or, more commonly, as La Grande Fourche.

In 1870 the English version became the official post office name. Grand Forks was the second permanent settlement by white families in what was to become North Dakota. The first was Pembina. Initially the town thrived because of steamboat traffic on the Red River of the North. In 1872 it had a boardinghouse, a hotel, a steamboat warehouse, three saloons, a stage station, a sawmill, and seven residences. A branch line of the Northern Pacific Railroad was built through Grand Forks in 1880, which further stimulated the town's growth. The 1889 state constitution established Grand Forks as the site for the University of North Dakota.

In the first census taken after statehood, Grand Forks had a population of 4,979. By 1920 it had grown to 12,478. According to the 1970 census, the Grand Forks population was 39,008.—D. J. T.

Grand Portage National Monument. Grand Portage National Monument, so designated in 1958, is located at the northeastern tip of Minnesota on Lake Superior. It includes the sites of the British North West Company's posts on Grand Portage Bay and at Fort Charlotte as well as the nine-mile "carrying place" over a trail that bypasses the falls of the lower Pigeon River. It was the inland center of the British fur trade in North America at the time of the American Revolution. Each summer a rendezvous of as many as one thousand men was held at Grand Portage, the emporium for an international trade based on capital and credit. Three or more years elapsed between the placing of orders for goods in London by Montreal merchants and the return of profits from the sale of furs in the markets of England. Such lengthy and involved procedures led to combinations and then to a kind of organized monopoly, fashioned by businessmen rather than created by the government, as it had been under the French.

The trade at Grand Portage in 1778 was measured at £40,000, and five hundred persons took part in it. There were a number of buildings at the post enclosed by a stout stockade. A small military fort held a dozen British soldiers in 1778—the only military force to operate on Minnesota soil during the Revolution.

The significance of Grand Portage faded after 1803, when the North West Company, fearful that American authority might be extended over the region and wishing to be sure that its traders were operating on British soil, removed its headquarters to Fort William at the mouth of the Kaministikwia River. The company's uneasiness was justified, for in 1803 the United States bought the Louisiana Territory from Napoleon.

See Solon J. Buck, "The Story of Grand Portage," in Rhoda R. Gilman and June D. Holmquist, eds., *Selections from "Minnesota History": A Fiftieth Anniversary Anthology* (1965).—R. W. F.

Grand Teton National Park. Grand Teton National Park, which lies a few miles south of Yellowstone National Park in Wyoming, is a territory rich in the lore of the old West. John Colter, who departed from the Lewis and Clark expedition on its return trip from the Pacific in 1807, was probably the first man of European descent to see the Grand Tetons and the adjoining valley known as Jackson Hole. Indians, trappers, adventurers, traders, and outlaws all roamed this remote region. It was not until 1887 that the first permanent settlers came to the Jackson Hole country. They set up cattle ranches, and later, as the beauty of the Tetons became known to easterners, dude ranches were established.

For many years the National Park Service hoped to add the Teton range and the Jackson Hole region to Yellowstone National Park. Stephen T. Mather and Horace M. Albright, of the National Park Service, made tentative efforts in this direction as early as 1916. But these early plans came to nothing. In the next thirty years, Albright was to become the central figure in the long battle to establish Grand Teton National Park. He worked persistently to bring this scenic territory into the national park system, first as superintendent of Yellowstone, then as director of the National Park Service, and finally as a private citizen.

As soon as the planned extension of Yellowstone was publicly disclosed in 1919, strong opposition developed from the livestock men, dude ranchers, and sportsmen of Jackson Hole who did not want federal ownership of this region. The Forest Service, out of whose Teton National Forest the proposed park would largely be carved, also opposed it. The political battle was intense. On January 26, 1929, Congress passed a compromise bill sponsored by Senator John B. Kendrick of Wyoming to set aside part of the Grand Teton Mountains and a narrow strip at their base as Grand Teton National Park, a scenic preserve separate from Yellowstone park. Jackson Hole, the natural foreground of the Teton range, was excluded from the compromise bill because of the opposition of local residents.

Meanwhile, Albright had introduced John D. Rockefeller, Jr., to the Jackson Hole country and had persuaded him to begin purchasing land there for eventual inclusion in Grand Teton park. Rockefeller's plan was to give the land to the federal government as soon as he could be assured it would be administered by the National Park Service. By 1933 he had purchased more than 33,000 acres in the northern part of Jackson Hole. As his Snake River Land Company acquired property, local opposition to its inclusion in Grand Teton park increased. Cattlemen, invoking the traditions of the old West, raised the issue of local control, accusing the "eastern money interests" of trying to "lock up" natural resources and of dictating the economic development of the West. In the 1930s, the fight over Jackson Hole became the central issue in Wyoming politics. In 1943, in spite of strong political opposition, President Franklin D. Roosevelt created the Jackson Hole National Monument in an effort to bring the Rockefeller lands into the national park system. Attempts were made to overturn this action both in Congress and the courts, but to no avail. By 1948 opposition in Wyoming had begun to diminish, largely because of the economic benefits of tourism to the state. Rockefeller gave the federal government title to his Jackson Hole holdings in December 1949. An act of Congress authorizing the consolidation of Jackson Hole National Monument and Grand Teton National Park was approved in September 1950.

The Grand Teton range rises abruptly from the flatlands of Jackson Hole, providing one of the best examples in North America of the geological phenomenon known as block faulting. Glaciers have gouged and carved the peaks. Lakes have formed in the moraines left by the glaciers. For alpine beauty, the scenery is unsurpassed in the national park system. Elk are plentiful in the region, and moose are frequently seen feeding in the marshes along the Snake River. Beaver ponds are common. The park, which now contains 310,350 acres, may be entered from Yellowstone park to the north or via Jackson, Wyoming, to the south.—D. C. S.

Granger laws. In the depression years between the Panic of 1873 and the restoration of the gold standard on January 1, 1879, western farmers suffered seriously from low prices for grain while their costs, such as railroad rates (especially between noncompetitive points), warehouse charges, and purchases of tariff-protected goods, remained uniformly high. High freight rates on grain were the farmers' greatest grievance, while discrimination in favor of large shippers by railroads and grain elevators, and the uncertainty of their charges, convinced farmers that only by government regulation could they gain lower rates and the elimination of what they regarded as unfair practices. The need for government intervention to compel the railroads to pursue a fairer policy became apparent coincidentally with the growth of the National Grange or the Patrons of Husbandry in the years following its founding in 1867 by Oliver H. KELLEY. Organized for social, cultural, and educational purposes, the Granges provided meeting places where farmers came together to discuss common interests and problems, and of these problems the chief was railroad "extortions." These meetings so focused attention upon economic issues that in a short time the Granger movement was sweeping the upper Mississippi valley, where state legislation was enacted to deal with farmers' grievances.

Illinois, Minnesota, Iowa, Wisconsin, and Missouri led in the adoption of acts to establish maximum freight and passenger rates; outlaw discriminatory rates; prohibit consolidation of competing or parallel lines; forbid the issuance of passes to legislators, judges, and public officials; and create railroad and warehouse commissions to enforce these provisions. To this type of legislation the term *Granger laws* has come to be applied.

From the outset the railroads and warehouses denied the power of the legislatures to enact such laws. They contended that the measures were in contravention of the rights granted them in their charters as protected by the Supreme Court in the Dartmouth College case in 1819, that they violated the due process clause of the Fourteenth Amendment, and were an infringement of the federal government's power to control interstate commerce. They sought injunctions to prevent the enforcement of the laws, and when the state courts upheld the acts they took them on appeal to the Supreme Court of the United States. There Chief Justice Morrison R. Waite in a series of landmark decisions in 1876, the most notable being *Munn* v. *Illinois*, declared that the warehouses and railroads were "clothed with a public interest," and by interpreting the Fourteenth Amendment narrowly and the powers of the states generously he upheld the constitutionality of the measures, over the vehement opposition of the two rigid conservatives on the Court, Stephen J. Field and William Strong.

Failing in the Supreme Court, the railroads adopted the maximum—not the minimum—rates allowed by the Granger laws, and began a massive publicity campaign to secure their repeal. Improving economic conditions and increasing commodity prices, combined with a renewal of the flow of capital into western railroads—especially branch lines, which all communities wanted—and the somewhat more benevolent attitude toward farmer problems, which company officials now showed, produced a reversal of attitude toward the railroads. In this atmosphere, developing even before the Supreme Court rendered its decisions, the Granger laws, which had not proved workable and had perhaps harmed farmers as much as they had benefited them, were repealed. Repeal did not end the agitation in behalf of federal government regulation, however, for within a few years the demand for regulation of railroads was renewed and led to the adoption of the federal Interstate Commerce Act of 1887.

See Lee Benson, *Merchants, Farmers, and Railroads: Railroad Regulation and New York Politics, 1850-1887* (1955); and Solon J. Buck, *The Granger Movement* (1913).—P. W. G.

Grant, Heber Jeddy (1856-1945). Mormon leader. Born in Salt Lake City, Utah, Grant was the son of the renowned Mormon speaker and leader Jedediah M. Grant, who died when Heber was nine days old. In 1875, at age eighteen, he became a counselor in the first Young Men's Mutual Improvement Association. When only twenty-four years old he was called to be president of the Tooele Stake, a position equivalent to that of archbishop in the Roman Catholic faith. Two years later (1882) he was ordained a member of the Quorum of the Twelve Apostles. Called upon many times to serve financial missions for the church, he was also president of the Japanese mission (1901-04) and of the European mission (1904-07). He became president of the Quorum of the Twelve Apostles in 1916.

In 1918 Grant became the seventh president of the Church of Jesus Christ of Latter-day Saints, the first native Utahan to hold that position. He served as president until 1945, a period characterized by increasing prominence and acceptance of the Mormon Church in the United States. During these years the church doubled its membership and constructed four hundred new chapels and four new temples. In addition, during his presidency over the church, Grant vigorously suppressed the unauthorized practice of polygamy by Latter-day Saint members and also emphasized observance of the Word of Wisdom (abstinence from alcoholic beverages, tobacco, tea, and coffee).

Besides private banking and insurance holdings, Grant was the president or director of numerous companies, including the Union Pacific Railroad, State Bank of Utah, Salt Lake *Herald*, Provo Woolen Mills, and Zion's Co-operative Mercantile Institution.

See Bryant S. Hinckley, *Heber J. Grant: Highlights of the Life of a Great Leader* (1951); and Andrew Jenson, *Latter-day Saint Biographical Encyclopedia* (1901). —L. J. A.

grasses. See VEGETATION: *prairies.*

Grass Valley, California. Mining town. Grass Valley, in Nevada County, is one of the least ghostly of the mining towns of the California gold boom. The large quartz gold mines surrounding the town, most notably the Empire and Idaho-Maryland mines, were productive for more than a century, beginning in 1850. The Empire, with nearly two hundred miles of tunnels, is still in operation. The town still prospers, although gold-mining no longer dominates its economy. Grass Valley contains many fine buildings that date back to 1855, including the home of Lola Montez, notorious dancer, actress, and adventuress who retired in Grass Valley. The Nevada County mining exhibit features a full-size reconstruction of mine shafts with original equipment.

See Remi Nadeau, *Ghost Towns and Mining Camps of California* (1965); and Muriel S. Wolle, *The Bonanza Trail* (1953).—R. B. W.

Grattan Massacre (1854). Indian-white conflict. The Grattan Massacre was the first armed clash between the United States Army and the Teton-Sioux to involve major casualties on either side. During late July and August 1854, more than four thousand Indians, mainly from the Brulé and Oglala divisions of the Teton-Sioux, gathered in the valley of the North Platte River near Fort Laramie, Wyoming, to receive the annual distribution of annuity goods guaranteed them by the Horse Creek treaty of 1851. While awaiting the arrival of the Indian agent who would supervise the distribution, tensions mounted between the Indians, the army garrison at Fort Laramie, and the stream of westward-bound immigrants moving up the valley on the Oregon-California Trail. Late on the afternoon of August 17, while a Mormon caravan was passing the Indian camps, a footsore cow fell behind the wagons and strayed toward the Brulé lodge circles, where it was killed by a Miniconjou Sioux visiting Brulé relatives. The cow's owner reported the incident to the commander at the fort, Second Lieutenant Hugh B. Fleming, and demanded the arrest and punishment of the Indian. Although hesitant to act in the absence of the Indian agent, Fleming decided on the morning of August 19 to send Brevet Second Lieutenant John L. Grattan to make the arrest.

Grattan was only a year out of West Point, not yet commissioned in the regular army, and itching to prove his mettle. He had often stated his desire to "crack it to the Sioux" and regarded the fort's meager complement of seventy-five infantry as fully adequate for the task. With twenty-nine volunteers, an interpreter, and two cannon, Grattan set out for the Brulé camp. Along the way the interpreter, who was drunk, called to the Sioux that the army was coming to kill them all and that he would eat their hearts raw. Forming a battle line in the open center of the Brulé camp, Grattan demanded that their head chief, Conquering Bear, deliver the offender for arrest. The chief, who had already offered many horses in payment for the cow, tried to calm the lieutenant and the Miniconjou, who was standing before his lodge dressed in war clothes. But the drunken antagonism of the interpreter garbled his words. Grattan, apparently oblivious to the large number of Indians gathering from other camps, lost his patience and gave an order. His men leveled their guns and shots were fired. Witnesses were unable to tell whether the soldiers or the Miniconjou fired first. Conquering Bear called for his people not to shoot, but the soldiers fired a second volley and discharged the cannon. The chief fell dying, and the Sioux swarmed over Grattan's command. Within minutes all the whites were killed. The Miniconjou survived unscathed.

Older chiefs restrained the young warriors from destroying the fort and the forty-two soldiers remaining there. After emptying the annuity warehouse, the Sioux broke camp and moved off in small bands. The commissioner of Indian Affairs said soon afterward that "no officer of the military department was authorized to arrest or try the Indian for the offence charged against him." Nevertheless, the government responded to the Grattan incident the following year by sending General William S. HARNEY to mount a ruthless punitive expedition against the Sioux.

See L. R. Hafen and F. M. Young, *Fort Laramie and the Pageant of the West, 1834-1890* (1928); George Hyde, *Red Cloud's Folk* (1937); and L. E. McCann, "The Grattan Massacre," *Nebraska History Magazine*, vol. 37 (1956). —P. R. M.

Gray, Robert (1775-1806). Discoverer of the Columbia River. Since the 1760s rumors had been rife of a great river in the West, in "Oregon," that flowed into the western sea. When the American Revolution was over and merchants were seeking new avenues of trade, John Ledyard published his book narrating the voyage of Captain Cook and suggesting profits in a fur trade between the Pacific Northwest and China. In 1787 Captain John Kendrick set out in the *Columbia*, accompanied by Captain Robert Gray in the *Lady Washington*, to engage in this trade. In 1789 Kendrick placed Gray in command of the *Columbia* with orders to trade the furs they had obtained for tea in China, and then to sail on around the world to Boston. He arrived there in August 1790.

The next month Gray set sail again and arrived in Oregon in June 1791. During a coastal trading expedition the following spring he ran the sandbar and entered the Columbia River estuary (May 1792). He had found the great river of the West, but Gray never published the fact. The world learned of his discovery from Captain George Vancouver's published journals. Yet Gray's discovery constitutes the American claim to Oregon.

See Hubert Howe Bancroft, *History of the Northwest Coast, 1543-1800* (1884); Frederick W. Howay, ed., "Voyages of the *Columbia* to the Northwest Coast, 1787-1790 and 1790-1793," in Massachusetts Historical Society, *Collections*, No. 79 (1941).—R. A. B.

Gray, William H. (1810-1889). Oregon missionary and politician. Born in New York, Gray first went to Oregon with Marcus Whitman and Henry Spalding in 1836 as a member of the first missionary group sent out by the American Board of Commissioners for Foreign Mi,sions. Hoping to get a mission of his own, Gray returned east in 1837. Against the advice of trappers at Green River, Gray decided to travel through dangerous Indian country with only a small party of Nez Percé and French-Canadians. On the Platte River a Sioux war party offered Gray his life for the lives of his Indian companions, and Gray obliged. He earned the lasting enmity of the mountain men and others for his decision, and on his way back to Oregon the following year, barely escaped from a group of mountaineers bent on vengeance. The group making the second trip included Gray's new wife, Mary Augusta Dix of Ithaca, New York, whom he had met and married within seven days;

missioners Cushing Eells, Elkanah Walker, Asa Smith and their wives; and bachelor Cornelius Rogers. This trip was marked by even greater disagreements among the party than those on the first trip to Oregon. Finally, in 1842 Gray left the board and went to work for the Methodists in the Willamette valley, where he farmed and engaged in various other activities, including mining and milling.

A man remarkable for his petulance and quarrelsome spirit, Gray was capable of complete and consuming antipathies, especially for the British, the Hudson's Bay Company, and Catholics. In early Oregon, where many held similar prejudices but held them with less tenacity, the articulate and energetic Gray rose to positions of prominence. His influence in the formation of the provisional government in 1843 was considerable. As a member of the legislative committee he assisted in drafting the organic law. Though only once elected to the provisional legislature, in 1845, Gray maintained his initial prominence in some degree by writing the extensive *History of Oregon, 1792-1849* (1870).

A collection of Gray's letters is in the Beinecke Library, Yale University. See Clifford M. Drury, *Henry Harmon Spalding* (1936) and *Marcus Whitman, M.D., Pioneer and Martyr* (1937); and *The Diaries and Letters of Henry Spalding and Asa Bowen Smith* (1958).—R. J. L.

Great American Desert. The semiarid region lying between the 100th meridian and the Rocky Mountains of North America. The name was given to it by explorers of the area after 1800, among them Zebulon Montgomery Pike and Stephen H. Long. Both considered it a barrier to western expansion but at the same time well suited as a future home for the so-called uncivilized Indians. Lieutenant Pike referred to the vast expanse of open land as the Great Sandy Desert and compared it to the Sahara. Fourteen years later (1820) Major Long preferred the appellation Great American Desert, a term that remained fixed on maps and in the American mind until the post-Civil War period. Today the area is more often called the Great Plains.

To travelers and settlers familiar with an environment where the annual rainfall approximated forty inches, an area with less than half that amount was a desert—in fact as well as in name. The apparent sterility of the soil, absence of trees, sparseness of vegetation, and long, hot summers reinforced the belief. Moreover, it did not seem possible that traditional agriculture could be practiced under such conditions.

The first official explorer to challenge the concept of a desert in the heartland of North America was the flamboyant John Charles Frémont. He traversed the Plains in 1838 and again in 1843-44, years of abnormally high rainfall. Frémont discovered that livestock could subsist on the native grasses, and he saw no reasons why settlers could not practice subsistence agriculture there. At the same time he pointed out that the region farther west, between the Rockies and the Sierra Nevada Mountains, was a true desert and he subsequently labeled it the Great Basin, a term that remains unchanged.

Throughout the pre-Civil War years travelers continued to view the Great Plains as unfit for white settlement and as a wasteland to be crossed before reaching California or Oregon. Railroad builders and land speculators, anxious to erase the desert image of the Plains, found support by the late 1860s in Frémont's earlier observations. Soon the Plains were dotted with ranchers and farmers taking advantage of the Homestead Act of 1862. The boosters hired journalists and pseudoscientists and launched a massive campaign to abolish the desert. They put their faith in the slogan "rains follow the plow" and in the theory that the planting of trees would increase moisture and alter the climate. The TIMBER CULTURE ACT of 1873 gave statutory support to the latter idea, but the results proved negligible.

Because of above average rainfall during the late 1870s and early 1880s, the area prospered. A series of such years led to the general acceptance of what Henry Nash Smith in *Virgin Land* calls "the myth of the garden." There were many, however, who doubted the ability of the Great Plains to sustain agriculture indefinitely. Cattlemen knew from experience that dry years inevitably follow wet ones and they bitterly opposed the intrusion of "nests" of farmers. In his famous essay of 1878, "Report of the Lands in the Arid West," John Wesley Powell argued that the 160-acre homestead was too small and that in the end agriculture would prove destructive to the semiarid lands. His warning went unheeded until the disastrous drought, dust storms, blizzards, and grasshopper plagues of the late 1880s. Many settlers were suddenly reminded that it was easier to abolish the "myth of the desert" than the reality of nature.

Near the end of the nineteenth century science and technology came to the aid of the settlers on the Plains, along with the return of another wet cycle. In time the application of DRY FARMING techniques, the invention of radically new farm machines, widespread use of BARBED WIRE and windmills, development of drought-resistant plants, and the extension of irrigation facilities greatly assisted the integration of the arid West into the national economy. The dust storms of the 1930s (see DUST BOWL) and the prolonged drought of the 1950s brought temporary setbacks. Finally the rains returned, and legislation such as the Soil Conservation Act and the Taylor Grazing Act and new farming practices made the desert once again "blossom like the rose." (See also AGRICULTURAL EXPANSION; WHEAT PRODUCTION.)

Today the Great Plains region is thinly settled compared to the lands east of the Mississippi River. At the same time it is the largest producer of beef and wheat of any comparable area of the world. The network of interstate highways, airlines, and railroads has made possible widely separated cities and industrial plants, while air-conditioning, expansion of irrigation projects, and the revolution in agriculture have all but erased the once-forbidding image of the Great American Desert.

See W. Eugene Hollon, *The Great American Desert: Then and Now* (1966); Henry Nash Smith, *Virgin Land: The American West as Symbol and Myth* (1950); Wallace Stegner, *Beyond the Hundredth Meridian: John Wesley Powell and the Second Opening of the West* (1953); and Walter Prescott Webb, *The Great Plains* (1931). —W. E. H.

Great Basin Desert. See PHYSIOGRAPHY OF THE UNITED STATES: *Basin and Range Province*; and VEGETATION: *deserts*.

Great Basin Indians. See INDIANS OF THE GREAT BASIN.

Great Basin streams. The Great Basin is the only part of the United States without drainage to the sea. It is arid, and the amounts of runoff from the mountain peaks within and surrounding it are meager. On the west small turbulent streams such as the Owens, the Carson, the Truckee, and the Walker quickly waste their waters in desert lakes or sinks. On the east the many small streams issuing forth from the Wasatch front become lost in Utah Lake or Salt Lake.

The Humboldt River is the only stream that flows for any distance across this arid land. It is a small stream with a total watershed of about 17,000 square miles in north-central Nevada. It rises among lofty peaks that reach almost 12,000 feet and flows westerly to empty into the Humboldt Sink at an elevation of 3,900 feet. The total runoff in its basin is less than 900,000 acre-feet per year—puny when compared to such coastal streams as the Willamette and Klamath rivers. Its flow at any one point in any one year is, of course, much less than that. Floods along its course may occur at almost any time during the year. In winter, rain falling on frozen ground may run off quickly. In spring, sudden melting of snow in the mountains is quickly translated into a flood at lower levels. In summer a thunderstorm located over the stream can transform it into a raging torrent. In dry years many parts of its channel are devoid of water.

The significance of the Humboldt is obviously not derived from its length or the magnitude of its flow. Nor does the fact that it is the only stream of any size in an otherwise arid land completely account for its fame. Rather, it was the accident of location astride the CALIFORNIA TRAIL, which ran from the frontier settlements along the Missouri to the gold fields of California, that accounted for the fact that the Humboldt became known as the "highway of the West." Mark Twain added to its notoriety when he said that if a man was bored and wanted to entertain himself, he could jump back and forth across the river until exhausted and thirsty and then drink it dry.

The Humboldt is also notable for being the last stream of any significance to be found by western explorers. For years maps of the West had indicated a major stream, the Buenaventura, flowing from the Rockies to San Francisco Bay, and many men had sought it. Peter Ogden of Hudson's Bay Company finally found it in 1828, trapped along it, and reached its mouth in Humboldt Sink. Beaver abounded along it, and other mountain men followed. Called the Unknown River by Ogden and then Mary's or Ogden's River, it was renamed by John C. Frémont in honor of the great German naturalist and geographer Alexander von Humboldt. By the time that Frémont first saw it, the river had already become known as the California Trail's best and safest route between the Great Salt Lake and the foothills of the Sierra below Lake Tahoe. It had been used by immigrant trains as early as 1841 and was a continuation of the Overland Trail, which led up the Platte River in Nebraska. It carried the burden of the many thousands of travelers bound for the California mines.

The first settlements along the river were built by Mormons moving west from their Salt Lake oasis. They built villages near present-day Carson City, Nevada, and at other strategic places as early as 1851. The Mormons' wagon road was later paralleled by the tracks of the Central Pacific built eastward out of Sacramento in the 1860s, and railroad towns added population to the area.

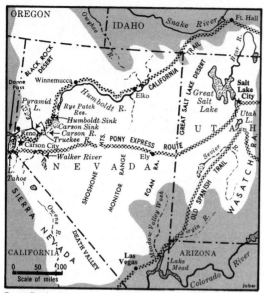

Great Basin Streams

Livestock ranching came to dominate the area, and the railroad towns served as collecting points and supply centers for the ranches. Highway 40, built in the 1920s, continued the route function of the valley of the Humboldt—a function continued by the interstate highway system today.—R. W. D.

Great Diamond Hoax. Two Kentucky cousins, Philip Arnold and John Slack, prospectors and mining speculators, turned up in San Francisco early in 1872 and attempted to deposit a bag of uncut diamonds in the Bank of California. They disappeared but were quickly located when their actions came to the attention of William C. Ralston, a bank director, and other men prominent in California financial circles. The financiers, assuming that they were dealing with unsophisticated miners, resolved to get control of the diamond field where the samples had been gathered. An agreement was reached whereby the prospectors were persuaded to escort a representative of the tycoons to the site with the stipulation that he would travel blindfolded. Leaving the Union Pacific at Black Buttes, Wyoming, the inspection party traveled four days on horseback to their destination on a mesa in the northwestern corner of Colorado. The presence of precious stones, both diamonds and rubies, was confirmed. Convinced about the quantity, the businessmen sought the opinion of jewelers concerning the quality. Sloan of San Francisco and Tiffany of New York certified to the genuineness of the diamonds, the latter suggesting that in quantity they would be worth "a rajah's ransom."

The investing syndicate next organized the San Francisco and New York Mining and Commercial Company, capitalized at $10 million, with grandiose plans for moving the diamond-cutting industry from Amsterdam to San Francisco. Arnold and Slack were paid approximately $600,000, only a fraction of the worth of the diamonds in hand according to Tiffany's estimates. Still exercising caution, the syndicate employed the presti-

gious engineer Henry Janin to make another inspection, and he returned dazzled by what he saw and publicly announced his intention of investing personally. Secrecy concerning the site was most difficult to maintain; the wildest rumors circulated. Prospecting expeditions fanned out all over the West, some led by guides employed by the syndicate to deceive the curious. Twenty-five known companies were incorporated with an authorized capital of more than $200 million to seek out and develop diamond fields in the American West.

In the end, Clarence King and his associates, who had just concluded the fortieth-parallel survey, which encompassed the rumored diamond site, determined its exact location by shrewd detective work, found it, and proved that the precious stones had been "salted." King convinced his friend Janin of his error and forced the syndicate to admit being duped and make restitution. Some of the stones found had lapidary marks on them. News also came from London that interested investors had learned that Arnold and Slack had purchased $35,000 worth of inferior South African diamonds there the previous year.

Arnold returned to Elizabethtown, Kentucky, lived lavishly on his ill-gotten gains, and made a settlement of $150,000 with his victims to quash further legal action. He was gravely wounded in a street duel in 1878 but survived, only to succumb to pneumonia a few months later. His partner, Slack, spent his last days as a coffin-maker in White Oaks, New Mexico.

Conditions were ideal for such a hoax in 1872, because the great gold rushes were over, a depression was in the offing, and the South African diamond discoveries had fired the imagination of the restless and venturesome. The potential impact of this episode on the world's diamond supply and market gives significance to the sequence of events. Although Ralston and his partners in the syndicate magnanimously repaid all the stockholders' losses, it is Arnold and Slack who have been admired, even lionized, for having victimized the sophisticated tycoons of the Pacific Slope.

A selection of documentary evidence concerning this incident was compiled in James H. Wilkins, ed., *The Great Diamond Hoax and Other Stirring Incidents in the Life of Asbury Harpending* (1915), thereby stimulating the continuing interest in the fraud. Bruce A. Woodward, *Diamonds in the Salt* (1967), provides additional material and the most recent interpretation. —W.T.J.

Great Lakes. See GREAT LAKES, MEN OF THE; PHYSIOGRAPHY OF THE UNITED STATES: *Central Lowland*; and TRANSPORTATION ON THE GREAT LAKES.

Great Lakes, men of the. Many men developed the extensive system of TRANSPORTATION ON THE GREAT LAKES:

Anderson, John (1837-1909). Harbor master. After working on Norwegian square-riggers as a youth, Anderson came to America in 1857. On the Great Lakes he commanded brigs and schooners of his own until 1870, when he was appointed harbor master of Chicago.

Bayfield, Henry W. (1795-1885). Admiralty surveyor. Bayfield came to Canada by way of the British Navy and spent nine years on surveys of Lakes Erie, Huron, and Superior. His charts, dating from the 1820s, were the first comprehensive navigation aids for Great Lakes mariners.

Bradley, Alva (1814-1885). Vessel operator. After

twenty years as a schooner captain, Bradley began building vessels on Lake Erie. In 1868 he developed shipyards in Cleveland, where he launched some twenty schooners and steamships. At his death he was a leading vessel operator on the Lakes.

Duluth (Du Lhut), Daniel Greysolon, Sieur (1649-?1709). Explorer. In 1669 Duluth made his first trip to the head of Lake Superior, the site of present Duluth. At an Indian council there he tried to make peace between the warring Chippewa and Sioux, so that French traders could work that region. (See EXPLORATION, FRENCH; and MINNESOTA.)

Hanna, Marcus A. (1837-1904). Merchant, politician, and shipping executive. In 1867 Hanna entered the coal and iron trade in Cleveland. With his brother, Howard M. Hanna, he organized the Cleveland Transportation Company in 1876. They ran a fleet of ten steam freighters that could carry 100,000 tons of cargo.

La Salle, René Robert Cavelier, Sieur de (1643-1687). Explorer. The son of a rich merchant in France, La Salle came to Canada in 1666. On the Niagara River, he built in 1678-79 the two-masted *Griffin*, the first decked vessel on the Great Lakes. It was wrecked in upper Lake Michigan on its first voyage. (See entry on LA SALLE.)

Mather, Samuel Livingstone (1817-1890). Industrialist. Attracted to upper Michigan by the discovery of iron ore, Mather organized in 1850 the Cleveland Mining Company, which began development of the Marquette Range. His company sent the first cargo of iron ore through the Soo Canal in 1855. His sons, Samuel Mather of Pickands Mather & Co. and William G. Mather of the Cleveland-Cliffs Iron Company, carried on his mining and shipping interests in the twentieth century.

McDougall, Alexander (1845-1923). Ship captain and shipbuilder. A Great Lakes deckhand at sixteen, a mate at eighteen, and a captain at twenty-one, McDougall gave up navigation for shipbuilding in the 1880s. The "whaleback" freighter was his invention. During the 1890s his shipyards in Duluth, Minnesota, and Superior, Wisconsin, launched forty-seven whaleback vessels.

Michelson, Halvor (1838-1923). Shipbuilder. Michelson came to America from Norway in 1854, settled in Chicago, and took up sailmaking. After his sail loft was destroyed in the great fire of 1871, he built a fleet of schooners for the grain and lumber trade. He was an early president of the Lake Carriers Association.

Newberry, Oliver (1789-1860). Vessel operator. As a young Chicago merchant, Newberry saw the future of the Great Lakes trade and by 1832 had acquired eight sailing vessels. In 1833 he built the steamer *Michigan*, largest of her time, and in 1835 established regular service between Chicago and Detroit. In the mid-nineteenth century he was known as the Admiral of the Lakes.

Nicolet, Jean (1598-1642). Explorer. Coming from France to Quebec in 1618, Nicolet was sent into the wilderness to learn Indian languages and lore. On an exploring expedition in 1634 he became the first white man to see Lake Michigan, Green Bay, and Wisconsin. (See entry on NICOLET.)

Perry, Oliver Hazard (1785-1819). Naval hero. During the War of 1812 Perry commanded United States naval forces on Lake Erie. Constructing ten vessels at present Erie, Pennsylvania, he sailed to Put-in-Bay in the Bass Islands. From there he engaged the British fleet in a decisive battle on September 10, 1813. His victory gave America control of the Great Lakes.

Poe, Orlando M. (1832-1895). Engineer. As a young army officer Poe surveyed the northern lakes during the years 1856-61. After the Civil War he became superintendent of river and harbor work on the Great Lakes. He built the Spectacle Reef Lighthouse in tossing waters near the head of Lake Huron and designed the Soo lock (replaced in 1969 by a greatly enlarged lock) that bears his name.

Simpson, Jerry (1842-1905). Vessel captain and congressman. At the age of fourteen Simpson signed as cook on a Great Lakes schooner. After Civil War soldiering he returned to the lakes and became a captain, commanding some of the biggest vessels of the 1870s. About 1880 he left the Great Lakes for a cattle ranch in Kansas. From there, as "Sockless Jerry," he was elected to Congress on the Populist ticket. (See entry on SIMPSON.)

Sorenson, Elias (1825-1911). Shipbuilder. As a young man Sorenson established a shipyard at Manitowoc on Lake Michigan. With his three brothers, all Great Lakes captains, he built more than one hundred schooners, steamers, barges, scows, and tugs. One of their vessels was the topmast schooner *Four Brothers*.

Tomlinson, George A. (1869-1942). Shipping executive. Tomlinson grew up in Michigan, spent two years as a cowboy in Wyoming, and was a bronco rider in Buffalo Bill's Wild West Show. Back in Michigan, he wrote for a Detroit newspaper and married the daughter of Captain James Davidson, the leading vessel builder of Saginaw. In 1893 he went into the ore shipping business, operating from Duluth and Cleveland. Eventually he acquired seventeen steam freighters, the last and largest one-man fleet on the lakes.

Ward, Eber Brock (1811-1875). Shipbuilder. In partnership with his uncle, Captain Sam Ward, Ward was a leading shipowner in the mid-nineteenth century. Anticipating the growth of commerce on Lake Superior, the two Wards had built fifteen steamships by 1855, when Soo Canal was opened. With an eventual total of thirty steamers, they were the largest shipowners on the Great Lakes.

Weitzel, Godfrey (1835-1884). Canal builder. As an officer in the United States Army Corps of Engineers, Weitzel enlarged the St. Marys Falls Ship Canal and built the 101-foot light tower on wave-swept Stannard Rock in Lake Superior. When completed in 1873, the Weitzel Lock at the Soo, 515 by 80 feet, was the largest canal lock in the world.

White, Peter (1831-1908). Pioneer iron magnate. Shipping as a deckhand on a Detroit schooner in 1846, White arrived in Marquette at the beginning of iron mining there. For half a century he was a leader in the development of mining and shipping enterprise in upper Michigan.

Wilkeson, Samuel (1781-1848). Harbor builder. As a trader and vessel operator, Wilkeson became a leading citizen of frontier Buffalo, New York. Though without engineering training, he took charge in 1820 of construction of a harbor at the mouth of Buffalo Creek, the western terminus of the Erie Canal.—W. H.

Great Meadows, battle of (1754). On April 2, 1754,

Lieutenant Colonel George Washington began a march with his troops from Winchester, Virginia, toward the forks of the Ohio by way of the Nemacolin Trail. He had been ordered by Governor Dinwiddie to reinforce the forks and prevent the French from locating there. Along the way Washington was informed that the French had already established Fort Duquesne on the site of present-day Pittsburgh. Washington's troops were poorly equipped and even more poorly supplied with transportation. The trail grew more impassable to wagons as they advanced. By May 24 the command was at Great Meadows, and four days later it engaged a French party in a skirmish near Fort Duquesne in which Coulon de Jumonville was killed; murdered, said the French. This was the letting of the first blood in the French and Indian War.

Despite his victory at the Jumonville camp, Washington found himself in a precarious situation. Messengers reported a rather large French and Indian force advancing from Duquesne, and he lacked men and supplies to combat such a force. On top of this, his aide Colonel Joshua Fry had fallen from his horse and died from injuries. Washington's command responsibilities were complicated by the arrival of colonial British troops under the command of the Scotsman James Mac-Kay, who was less than cooperative and uninformed as to the situation of the colonial troops. Washington dropped back to the inadequately built Fort Necessity at Great Meadows, where he was hemmed in by French and Indians, and was seriously handicapped by a heavy downpour of rain that practically drowned out his guns. Too, he lost his Indian support. On July 3 and 4 he was forced to surrender and evacuate Fort Necessity. With his badly depleted and mauled troops, he moved back to Virginia. The odds of support, the elements, and lack of experience were against the colonials. Washington's ranks had suffered heavy losses, but he was lucky to escape complete annihilation by the Indians.

See Douglas Southall Freeman, *George Washington, A Biography*, vol. I (1948); and Lawrence H. Gipson, *The British Empire Before the Revolution*, vol. VI (1956). —T. D. C.

Great Northern Railroad. See BURLINGTON NORTHERN RAILROAD.

Great Plains. See GREAT AMERICAN DESERT; and PHYSIOGRAPHY OF THE UNITED STATES.

Great Renegade. See Simon GIRTY.

Great Road of the Valley. This road had its historical beginnings in the game paths that followed the course of the Shenandoah Valley streams. The road was gradually opened and extended from Wadkin's Ferry, near Harpers Ferry, southward across the headwaters of the James and Roanoke rivers to Fort Loudoun at the forks of the Tellico and Little Tennessee rivers in present-day eastern Tennessee. The middle part of this road was opened in 1760 by Colonel William Byrd III. He located along its route the famous Fort Chiswell, which was near lead mines that were important during the American Revolution.

The Great Road of the Valley was a main passage of immigrants and traders going back and forth between the HOLSTON RIVER SETTLEMENTS and the New River country, and the Shenandoah Valley. In the great migration westward in the last quarter of the eighteenth century, it became a main artery of travel.

See Robert L. Kincaid, *The Wilderness Road* (1947); and Lewis P. Summers, *History of Southwest Virginia, 1746-1786* (1903).—T. D. C.

Great Warrior's Path. The Great Warrior's Path had its beginnings long prior to the era of historical notation. It no doubt originated as a combination game and Indian trail and led from Cumberland Gap northwestward to the mouth of the Scioto River at present-day Portsmouth, Ohio, and thence to the Shawnee village of Sonioto. A second branch of the trail led from central eastern Kentucky to the Limestone Crossing of the Ohio, near present Maysville, Kentucky, and northward to the Mingo village in southern Ohio. Actually, this path was the continuation of several Indian trails that came up from the East and South.

In 1750 Dr. Thomas Walker, scout and surveyor for the Loyal Land Company, came upon this trail and traveled along it intermittently as far north as the mouth of Station Camp Creek in present-day Estill County, Kentucky. In time, other pioneer travelers came this way. Daniel Boone and John Finley traveled it for a distance on their famous journey in 1769, but because the path traversed rough mountain and knob country it was never opened as a thoroughfare by subsequent settlers coming to Kentucky. Before the arrival of the settlers, however, both northern and southern Indians used it as a main line of travel between Cumberland Gap and the Ohio River.

See J. Stoddard Johnston, ed., *First Explorations of Kentucky* (1898); Robert L. Kincaid, *The Wilderness Road* (1947); William E. Meyer, "Indian Trails of the Southeast," in Bureau of American Ethnology, *Forty-second Annual Report, 1924-25* (1928); and Thomas Speed, *The Wilderness Road* (1886).—T. D. C.

Greeley, Horace. See LAND REFORM MOVEMENT.

Green, Joshua (1869-). Washington banker. Born in Jackson, Mississippi, Green withdrew from school at the age of fourteen to become a post office employee. In 1886 he moved with his parents to Washington Territory, where he soon became a prominent businessman. Before he was twenty-five he was purser of a small steamer and then part owner and a ship's officer on three trading vessels. With his partners, he founded and became president in 1901 of the Puget Sound Navigation Company, with a fleet of fifteen passenger and freight steamers. He is best known as part owner, president, and chairman of the board of the fifty-two-branch Peoples National Bank of Washington (1926-62). A member of the board of directors of six corporations, including the Chbicago, Milwaukee, St. Paul and Pacific Railroad and the Puget Sound Power and Light Company, he has also been a director of hospital boards, pioneer and historical societies, chambers of commerce, and of many Seattle private and social clubs.

See "The Hundred Years of Joshua Green," *Seattle Magazine* (October 1969); and Gordon Newell, *The Green Years* (1969).—K. A. M.

Greenback party. Known also as the National Greenback party, the Greenback party was formed in the 1870s with the purpose of easing the tight currency situation of the period. During the Civil War, the government had issued $432 million worth of paper money called greenbacks with which to help finance the war. They fluctuated widely in value and were held beneath the value of gold and so were popular with farmers and other debtors. Of course, creditors and businessmen desired a "tight" or "hard" money policy—specie and a stable paper currency. In 1866 a law was passed providing for the gradual retirement of some of the greenbacks, and in the next two years almost $100 million worth of the paper was taken out of circulation.

This policy was hard on long-term debtors, the worst hit being the farmers of the Midwest and West who had gone deeply into debt during the war expanding their production to meet the foreign and domestic wartime demands for food. Further, agricultural prices fell after the war and farmers' costs increased greatly. In 1873, there was a severe economic depression. Between 1865 and 1875, circulating money per capita declined from $31.18 to less than $19.00.

The Greenback party was an outgrowth in part of the Grange movement (see GRANGER LAWS), and was formed in 1874 to stem the governmental policy of monetary contraction. In November 1874 the Indiana Granger party held a conference in Indianapolis; out of this meeting emerged a national party in 1876. The Resumption of Specie Payment Act in 1875, which required the government to resume withdrawing greenbacks from circulation until the amount in use was stabilized at $300 million, and to start paying specie on demand for all its paper currency, including greenbacks, after 1878, put the greenbacks on a par with gold-backed paper. For the "hard" money interests, this was a victory, but for the farmers and other debtors and the small businessmen, this made their situation more acute. The Resumption Act contributed significantly to the Greenback party's political appeal.

The old philanthropist Peter Cooper, known as the New Yorker who built the nation's first locomotive, polled fewer than one hundred thousand votes as the party's first presidential candidate in the ELECTION OF 1876, but the party continued to grow at a remarkable rate between 1876 and 1878. Reorganized in the latter year as the Greenback-Labor party, its vote increased from eighty-three thousand to over one million. The vote was no western and southern aberration either. The largest vote came in Iowa, followed in order by Massachusetts, Pennsylvania, and New York. Fusion with the Democratic party and Independents on the state level resulted in the election of fourteen congressmen. Undoubtedly, discontent that made these successes possible had something to do with the passage of the Bland-Allison Act in 1878, as well as another measure in 1879 preventing the planned continuing retirement of a portion of the greenbacks. Both of these measures were viewed as ineffective sops by Greenbackers, who favored a more fundamental reform of the monetary system.

In the ELECTION OF 1880, the party ran James B. WEAVER of Iowa as its presidential candidate; he polled slightly over three hundred thousand votes with a stronger western support. By 1884, when the party was clearly on the way out, it joined with the Anti-Monopoly party in nominating Benjamin F. Butler, the old Radical Republican-turned-Democrat-then-Greenbacker, for president.

The vote-getting appeal of the party does not reflect its full impact. The movement was extremely important in opening the debate on the many problems confronting a rapidly industrializing America. As a matter of fact, the pattern of reform demands to dominate American politics for the remainder of the century was first enunciated during the Greenback era, and the party's spokesmen played a key role in its formulation. Its orientation was by no means exclusively rural and agricultural. In addition to publicizing the inadequacies of an inflexible and contractive monetary system, Greenbackers introduced the proposal for the graduated income tax and highlighted such demands as a postal-savings system, a federal labor bureau, equal pay for equal work of men and women, reduced hours of labor, abolition of convict-labor contracts, restriction of immigrant labor, an end to employment of children under fourteen years of age, an interstate commerce law, opposition to railroad land grants, payment of wages in cash, and woman suffrage. Practically all their proposals were eventually enacted into law by the two major or third parties that succeeded them, and former Greenbackers were prominent in these later parties.

See F. E. Haynes, *Third Party Movements Since the Civil War* (1916); Robert P. Sharkey, *Money, Class, and Party: An Economic Study of Civil War and Reconstruction* (1959); and Irwin Unger, *The Greenback Era: A Social and Political History of American Finance, 1865-1879* (1964). —O. G. C.

Greenville, Treaty of (1795). In 1794, after General Anthony Wayne defeated the allied Indians of the Northwest at the battle of Fallen Timbers, he established Fort Defiance and Fort Wayne and continued to move his army about the vicinity, menacing the demoralized tribes and razing their villages. The British at nearby Fort Miami refused to aid them, and the Indians were probably relieved when in spring 1795 Wayne called them to a great peace council at Fort Greenville, Ohio. Their power broken, deserted by their British supporters, and harassed by Kentuckians raiding across the Ohio River, the Indians were in no position to resist any demand Wayne might make.

From June 16 to August 10, 1795, representatives of the Wyandot, Shawnee, Delaware, Ottawa, Chippewa, Potawatomi, Kickapoo, Miami, and other smaller tribes counciled with Wayne at Greenville. On August 3 a treaty was signed in which the Indians gave up twenty-five thousand square miles of territory north of the Ohio. The general boundary began opposite the mouth of the Kentucky River on the north shore of the Ohio and ran to Fort Recovery, to Loramie's Creek, to Fort Laurens on the Tuscarawas branch of the Muskingum River, across the portage to the Cuyahoga River and along it to Lake Erie.

The result of the Treaty of Greenville was phenomenal. Peace was restored in the Northwest. With the extension of active United States jurisdiction into the area, the British were impelled to abandon the posts south of the Great Lakes that they had been occupying in defiance of the Treaty of Paris of 1783, although they continued to trade with the Indians as was permitted by Jay's Treaty of 1795. American settlers flocked in droves into the Ohio country, the population reaching forty-five thousand before 1800. But although the treaty bore the names of nearly all the Indian leaders, many of their warriors, including the young Tecumseh, refused to recognize its legitimacy and in coming years violently resisted further encroachment on Indian lands.

See Richard C. Knopf, *Anthony Wayne, A Name in*

Arms: Soldier, Diplomat, Defender of Expansion Westward of a Nation (1960); and Charles C. Royce, "Indian Land Cessions in the United States," in Bureau of American Ethnology, *Eighteenth Annual Report, 1896-97* (1899). —T. D. C.

Greenway, John Campbell (1872-1926). Mining engineer. Born in Huntsville, Alabama, Greenway graduated from Yale University with a mining degree and the laurels of a star athlete, worked for Carnegie Steel, and served with the Rough Riders in the Spanish-American War, attaining the rank of brevet captain. Returning to the business world, he was a mining superintendent for the United States Steel Corporation first in Michigan and later in Minnesota, where he built company towns and developed the mines in the Mesabi Range. In 1910 Greenway, a tall, amiable man with an engaging personality, came to Bisbee, Arizona, as general manager of the Calumet and Arizona Copper Company. He promoted the Warren (Development) Company, erected a smelter at Douglas, and invented and patented a furnace for melting metal and a new concentrator process (turbo log washer) for extracting copper from low-grade ores. Becoming interested in the Ajo copper mines west of Tucson, Greenway formed the New Cornelia Copper Company, sank deep wells to underground water, experimented with a pilot mill, and built the model town of Ajo. Although completely devoted to his profession, he also found time to engage in political activity. In 1912 Greenway helped promote the Republican Bull Moose movement in Arizona but by the 1920s was a prominent figure in the Democratic party, being a nominee for the vice presidency in 1924. An officer during World War I, he later attained the rank of brigadier general in the reserves. Greenway was buried at Ajo, and in 1930 Arizona placed a bronze statue of him in Statuary Hall in Washington.

See "Acceptance and Unveiling of the Statue of Gen. John Campbell Greenway," in *Senate Document 167,* 71 Congress, 2 Session, Serial 9213.—H. P. H.

Greenwood, Caleb (1763-1850). Mountain man. "Old" Greenwood was one of the iron men of the West whose greatest adventures came at an age when most retire. While he neither read nor wrote, his singular exploits were described in the diaries and reports of several people who knew him during different periods of his life.

Starting as a hunter for both the John Jacob Astor (1810-11) and Manuel Lisa (1812) fur-trapping expeditions, he later trapped beaver for the Missouri Fur Company. Afterward he became a member of W. H. Ashley's mountain men and attended the first fur rendezvous in 1825 at Henry's Fork of the Green River on the Wyoming-Utah border. Records show that he also attended subsequent gatherings at the head of the same stream.

Celibate until age sixty-three, Greenwood married the half-breed daughter of a French fur trader. They had five children. At age eighty-one, in 1844, Greenwood guided the first wagon train across the Sierra. When eighty-four years old, the hardy old man and his son led the second group of volunteers who helped rescue the last of the snowbound Donner Party who were still able to travel.

Catching gold fever in 1849, he and his sons panned for gold in California. Greenwood also sold advice to green easterners he conned into believing he could direct to dazzling bonanzas. His neighbors believed he died with his boots on in 1850, but no record remains of where he was buried.

See Alexander L. Crosby, *Old Greenwood, Pathfinder of the West* (1967); and Charles Kelly and Dale Morgan, *The Story of Caleb Greenwood—Trapper, Pathfinder, and Early Pioneer* (1965).—B. W. A.

Gregg, Josiah (1806-1850). Trader and historian. The foundation stone for all studies of the Santa Fe Trail must forever remain Gregg's *Commerce of the Prairies* (see SANTA FE AND CHIHUAHUA TRAIL). Universally regarded as the classic account of the early merchant-traders in New Mexico, this book was the fruit of Gregg's firsthand experience, acute powers of observation, and his meticulous note-taking. While presenting the most authentic and complete story of the Santa Fe trade, the author reached beyond his subject to include a treasury of frontier lore and natural history.

Gregg was born and raised on a Missouri farm. Formal schooling was rude, but he indulged his early bent for the intellectual life by reading in a wide variety of fields, including mathematics, surveying, medicine, and law. In his mid-twenties a debilitated constitution prompted him to join a merchant train bound for Santa Fe, and to his good fortune the open-air life of the trail quickly restored him to proper health. From 1831 to 1840 he was active in the New Mexico trade, at the same time collecting the material that was to furnish the basis for his *Commerce of the Prairies*. It appeared in two volumes in 1844 and went into several editions.

At the time of the Mexican War, Gregg joined the Arkansas Volunteers and saw brief service in the northern provinces. In 1847-48 he practiced medicine in Saltillo, Mexico, then joined a botanical expedition to western Mexico and California. He died shortly after discovering Humboldt Bay in 1850. Of Gregg, writer Paul Horgan has pointed out that the fatal flaw in his character was his lack of a sense of humor: "Nowhere was there a healing gust of laughter."

An authoritative edition of *Commerce of the Prairies,* together with a biographical sketch of Gregg by Max L. Moorhead, was published in 1954. A sequel to this work is Maurice Garland Fulton, ed., *Diary and Letters of Josiah Gregg,* 2 vols. (1944)—M. Si.

Grey, Zane (1875-1939). Novelist. Grey, born in Zanesville, Ohio, led an almost abnormally typical boyhood, punctuated by occasional fights with local youths who took exception to his Christian name of "Pearl," which he was later to abandon for his mother's family name of Zane. As a boy he read DIME NOVELS voraciously and excelled in sports, though he showed little interest in studies. He was particularly proficient at baseball, and while playing for the Baltimore, Ohio, team was spotted by a scout for the University of Pennsylvania, who persuaded him to matriculate at that institution. In 1896 he received a degree in dentistry, his father's profession, and settled down to a halfhearted practice in New York.

In New York Grey turned his hand to writing, first attempting a historical romance about an ancestress. In 1908 he met Colonel C. J. ("Buffalo") Jones, who persuaded him to be his biographer and, more important, took him out west on a trip to gather material. On this excursion Grey discovered the trappers, hunters, miners, and cowboys who were to become the heroes of most of his later fiction.

The biography of Buffalo Jones was published in 1908 as *The Last of the Plainsmen*. Grey's work on it had already led to a meeting with Ripley Hitchcock of Harper & Brothers, which published *The Heritage of the Desert* (1910) and the enormously successful *Riders of the Purple Sage* (1912), which sold more than a million copies. The popularity Grey achieved in *Riders of the Purple Sage* never left him, despite his immense literary output. In his lifetime he wrote seventy-eight books, seventeen of which were published posthumously. Most of these were westerns, some were boys' books, and others miscellaneous tales of outdoor adventure, which Grey could turn out at an average of two a year. By 1955 his books had sold more than twenty-seven million copies in the United States and four million abroad. His western writings include *The Border Legion* (1916), *The U. P. Trail* (1918), *To the Last Man* (1922), *The Wanderer of the Wasteland* (1923), *The Thundering Herd* (1925), *The Vanishing American* (1926), *Raiders of Spanish Peaks* (1938), and *Western Union* (1939).

Though Grey began as a historical novelist, and though his westerns often have a certain historical content, he considered his novels to be "romances," true to the western spirit rather then to the particular facts of western history. As a result, the historical content in his books tends to be generalized rather than specific, even in those novels that, like *The U. P. Trail* and *Western Union*, are ostensibly concerned with particular events of western history. He is remembered today primarily as the author who, almost single-handedly, succeeded in convincing the average reader that absolutely no merit can possibly be discovered in any western writing whatever. His books are now little read, though their notoriety lingers on. At worst Grey wrote sentimentalized escape literature of the most banal kind, marred by pompous moralizing against various kinds of simplistically conceived sin, and by an unthinking racism, presented in pretentious and awkward style; at best he wrote little differently.

See Frank Gruber, *Zane Grey: A Biography* (1970); and Carlton Jackson, *Zane Grey* (1972).—J. K. F.

Grierson, Benjamin Henry (1826-1911). Soldier. Born in Pittsburgh, Grierson was a small-town music teacher in Ohio and Illinois who did not like horses, having been kicked in the face as a boy. When he enlisted during the Civil War, however, he was put in the cavalry and rose rapidly in rank, being mustered out of the volunteer service as a major general in 1866. He served in Mississippi and Tennessee during the war and became famous for his raid from La Grange, Tennessee, to Baton Rouge, Louisiana, in April 1863, which contributed to the Union victory at Vicksburg.

In 1866 Grierson became colonel of the Negro Tenth Cavalry, which he formed and trained. Grierson complained about the "old fogies" in the army who were opposed to Negro troops, and under his command, the Tenth compiled an excellent record as a frontier regiment. Grierson built Fort Sill in Oklahoma. He supported the peace policy of the Grant administration and demonstrated an unusual ability to cooperate with the Kiowa and Comanche agents at Fort Sill. He also carried out the dramatic arrest of Indian chiefs Satanta, Satank, and Big Tree in 1871. From 1875 until 1885 he cam-

paigned against Comanche, Apache, and Kickapoo in West Texas and played an important role in the campaign to capture Victorio, an Apache leader, by driving him back into Mexico. In 1885 he was sent to the Department of Arizona.

Retiring as a brigadier general in 1890, Grierson was an able frontier officer who combined a knowledge of Indian tactics with a humane interest in the well-being of the Indians. He commanded a Negro regiment and defended his men at a time when other officers refused to serve with black soldiers.

The Benjamin Grierson papers are in the Illinois Historical Society. See also Dee Brown, *Grierson's Raid* (1954).—R. N. E.

Grinnell, George Bird (1849-1938). Anthropologist, historian, and zoologist. Born in Brooklyn, New York, Grinnell was trained as a zoologist at Yale University (A.B., 1870; Ph.D., 1880) and was active throughout his life as a businessman and publisher. However, he is best known for his work on the ethnology and history of the West. He had his first contact with the frontier in 1870, on a paleontological expedition headed by Yale professor O. C. Marsh. Grinnell's interests soon broadened to include the anthropology, history, and geography of the trans-Mississippi region. He was a member of the Peabody Museum staff at Yale from 1874 to 1880, while studying for his doctorate, but his trips to the West became almost annual until shortly before his death. In the summer of 1872 he participated in the last great hunt of the Pawnee; he served as naturalist with General George A. Custer's expedition to the Black Hills in 1874 and with Colonel William Ludlow's reconnaissance from Carroll, Montana, through Yellowstone National Park in 1875, and was one of the naturalists invited to participate in E. H. Harriman's Alaska tour in 1899.

Long associated with *Forest and Stream*, Grinnell also published numerous articles in *Scribner's, Atlantic Monthly, Harper's, Century*, and other magazines. His popular works include, in addition, a western fiction series for children and several books intended to prompt reform in the treatment of Indians. His most highly regarded work is the comprehensive two-volume study *The Cheyenne Indians* (1923), based on his thirty years of close contact with that tribe. The Cheyenne wars and legends are ably related in his *The Fighting Cheyennes* (1915) and *By Cheyenne Campfires* (1926), respectively. The legends of other tribes receive sympathetic and careful presentation in *Pawnee Hero Stories and Folk Tales* (1889) and *Blackfoot Lodge Tales* (1892). His treatment of Frank and Luther North in *Two Great Scouts and Their Pawnee Battalion* (1928) unfortunately rests heavily on his friend Luther North's often inaccurate recollections. Grinnell's long relationship with the Indians, he himself felt, made it impossible for him to treat them as "mere objects for study"; his regard for them as "acquaintances, comrades and friends" is clear in the warmth and sympathy of his work.—J. T. K.

grizzly bear. The grizzly bear (*Ursus arctos horribilis*) is an intelligent, extremely efficient omnivore and a relatively inefficient carnivore. Within recent geological time, this animal competed with the North American Indian for a wide variety of foods. Wherever the species existed, it was either the dominant mammal or a coequal with man.

In pre-Columbian times the range of grizzly bears

extended from the Pacific Ocean to the Mississippi River, south into Mexico, and north to the Arctic Circle. At the beginning of the white era, they frequented the brushlands, foothills, and river valleys of the Rocky Mountain region, where large bison herds and rodents furnished an abundant source of food. With the settlement of the West, the grizzly disappeared from much of its former range. It was estimated by T. I. Storer and L. P. Tevis in *The California Grizzly* (1955) that California once supported 10,000 grizzly bears. By 1924 they were extinct. Grizzlies have also disappeared from Texas, Nebraska, Oklahoma, Kansas, Arizona, New Mexico, Oregon, Utah, and the Dakotas and probably Colorado and Washington. They are now generally found only in the high mountain country and wilderness areas of large national parks and forests, and only in Alaska and western Canada are they still relatively abundant. In the continental United States (with the exception of Alaska) probably fewer than 800 grizzlies now exist. In Mexico only a remnant population of a dozen bears or less still persists in the upper Yaqui Basin of Sonora. In Glacier and Yellowstone national parks and the adjoining national forests there are from 350 to possibly 400 grizzlies.

In 1966 the Committee on Rare and Endangered Wildlife Species of the Bureau of Sport Fisheries and Wildlife officially listed the grizzly as "endangered," meaning that its prospects of survival and reproduction are in immediate jeopardy and that, without help, extinction will probably follow.

To many Indian tribes in North America the grizzly was a sacred animal, but it was also hunted as a test of strength and for its claws, which symbolized the high status of the hunter. Eating raw bear heart was thought to give the hunter the physical powers of the bear and also its supposed courage and cunning.

Because of its size, aggressiveness, and habit of congregating where food was abundant, the grizzly was especially noted by the early explorers. Coronado was probably the first among the early explorers to see and record the grizzly in 1540 in west-central New Mexico. Sebastián Vizcaíno in 1602 described seeing a number of grizzlies feeding on a whole carcass near Monterey, California. Samuel Hearne was perhaps the first white man to describe grizzlies in the Canadian Arctic. His account was based on hides he had seen in 1771. William B. Grinnell reported them still common along the Missouri River in 1875. From the time of these early records, however, the number of grizzlies steadily declined as they were shot, trapped, and poisoned by explorers, homesteaders, ranchers, and hunters.

The grizzly was first scientifically described and named by George Ord in 1815 upon observing an animal collected by the Lewis and Clark expedition in 1805 along the Missouri River in Montana. It was not until the early 1900s, however, that scientists began to take an active interest in the grizzly. In 1918 C. Hart Merriam described eighty-six forms, designating most of them as species. In 1928 Harold E. Anthony reduced this to eleven species. In 1953 Robert Rausch concluded that all North American grizzlies and brown bears belong in one highly variable species, *U. arctos*. Thus the European brown bear (*U. arctos arctos*), its North American relative, the grizzly (*U. arctos horribilis*), the Alaskan brown, or Kodiak, bear (*U. arctos middendorffi*), and the

peninsula brown bear (*U. arctos gyas*) are believed to be subspecies. In addition there are two other North American bears belonging to the same genus, the American black bear (*U. americanus*) and the polar bear (*U. maritimus*), but they are different species.

Grizzly bears eat the bulbs of blue camas, the tubers of yampa, the biscuit-root and other starchy roots; berries; pine nuts; acorns; fish; and large herbivores, especially those weakened by severe winters. In early spring, when they emerge from their winter dens, grizzlies eat the carcasses of elk, deer, bison, and other large herbivores that have died during the winter. After feeding on carrion or a fresh kill, a grizzly will generally cover the remaining portion of the carcass with soil and debris and return to it to feed for several days or a week. Normally it does not vigorously defend its food against other grizzlies, but will defend it against black bears, coyotes, and wolves. When man approaches too closely or unexpectedly he also may be attacked. Grizzly bears are not efficient predators on large game and their depredations do not control population levels of game animals. Their role as a carnivore is first as a scavenger, second as a predator on small prey species, and last as a killer of large prey animals.

During the summer months the bears may congregate in meadows and river bottoms to dig roots and tubers and graze on sedges, clover, and grasses. They also eat berries, feeding almost exclusively on them when they are abundant. In the fall they feed mainly on mice, other small rodents, and on pine nuts. Before going to the winter den, they may eat carrion or kill and feed on elk or deer.

The grizzly has poor vision and appears unable to identify man beyond 100 or 200 yards away, but it can detect motion beyond 200 yards and, if upwind, the animal frequently will investigate by circling the intruder to get a scent. If human scent is detected, the grizzly normally retreats, but its behavior is determined by the distance between bear and man at the moment of discovery. There is a critical attack distance within which the bear apparently feels sufficiently threatened to attack, by automatic response, rather than retreat. The attack distance varies according to sex, age, and the specific situation, but generally it is less than 100 yards in open country.

The temperament of individual grizzlies varies greatly and may change with their physical and psychological condition. A hungry, malnourished, or injured grizzly may become aggressive. When weaning their offspring, females (sows) become very irritable. The weaned offspring, whether yearlings or two-year-olds, are normally not aggressive. A female with cubs is noticeably nervous and alert and becomes anxious easily. Her critical attack distance is less than for other animals in the population and less than when she has yearlings or is without offspring.

Attacks occur when grizzlies are startled, cornered, or injured, and at times without discernible provocation. The victim is generally knocked down by blows from the forepaws or by the sheer weight and momentum of the bear. The bear inflicts injury primarily by multiple bites, often on the head. The grizzly may retreat soon after the attack, but resistance during the attack may prolong it, and movements or an attempt to flee may initiate additional attacks. The behavior of the female appears to be largely a defense reaction. Often one or more females with cubs will attack large boars (male bears) when they approach too closely or exhibit aggressive behavior. A female with cubs at initial confrontation, whether with a boar or with a human, reacts suddenly. The cubs are alerted by their mother and often flee in different directions. The female is thus unable to retreat with her litter in an orderly fashion. She appears confused. With head and neck extended and ears laid back, she rotates, stepping first in one direction, then in another. Suddenly she wheels and attacks. If her victim is another bear, her attack may last only seconds followed by a quick retreat in search of her cubs.

Grizzly bear attacks on man are rare, but during the time of the western fur trade they were the subject of conversation at the traders' rendezvous. Perhaps the most authentic anecdote that has been passed down to us is Hugh Glass's encounter with a grizzly and his miraculous escape. In the 1820s Hugh Glass was on a trapping expedition in Montana under the direction of Major Andrew Henry. Scouting ahead for game, Glass jumped a female grizzly with two offspring. The sow attacked and severely mauled him before the rest of the party arrived and killed the bear. Glass was in great pain and unable to stand. The expedition was in hostile Indian country and to delay until he had recovered would have endangered the whole party. Major Henry offered a reward to anyone who would stay with Glass until he died or recovered. Two volunteers remained with him for five days, but seeing no hope of recovery, they abandoned Glass and took his rifle and supplies. This enraged Glass and gave him renewed determination to live and seek revenge. He survived on wild cherries and buffalo berries until he gained enough strength to travel toward Fort Kiowa, a hundred miles away. His injuries prevented him from walking, so he started the long trek on hands and knees with no provisions or means of securing any. He encountered a buffalo calf killed by wolves, ate the meat raw, took what remaining food he could with him, and finally reached Fort Kiowa.

In recent times grizzly bear attacks have provided exciting news copy and have generated apprehensive public response. On the evening of August 13, 1967, at two widely separated locations in Glacier National Park, grizzly attacks resulted in the deaths of two nineteen-year-old employees of the park and serious injury to an eighteen-year-old boy. Both attacks were linked to food handouts. Attacks are rare, however, and even in Yellowstone National Park, where the grizzly population is relatively high and the number of visitors increases each year, the probability of being injured or killed by a grizzly is very small. From 1900 to 1970 there have been two fatalities in Yellowstone caused by grizzlies, both occurring in the early 1900s. From 1931 to 1970, Yellowstone records show sixty-three injuries and no fatalities. During these thirty-nine years, an average of a million people visited Yellowstone each year. Thus, the injury rate from grizzlies has been one person per 600,000 visitors.

Color variations in the grizzly range from dark brown to straw-colored blond. Often the hair is lighter (almost white) on the distal ends, giving the animal a silver or frosted sheen. From this appearance the name "silver tip" evolved. Collars of light-colored hair are common, especially among the young.

The grizzly is characterized by a noticeable shoulder hump and a concave profile. The claws on the forefeet, which may be three or four inches long or longer, immediately distinguish the grizzly and brown bears from other bears. Generally the dorsal curvature of the claws becomes white with age.

A large adult female may weigh 350 to 450 pounds, whereas a large male may be 800 to 1,000 pounds. This difference in weight is evident in cubs but becomes more apparent in adult animals.

Adult females without offspring come into estrus about the first of June and conceive between June and mid-July. During the breeding season the large males contend for the females in estrus. Fur flies and deep wounds may be inflicted; it is not uncommon for a male's ear to be severed, a lip torn (permanently exposing the large canines), or a jaw fractured.

The females first breed successfully at four and a half years, though many may not produce cubs until they are eight or nine years old. Only one third of the adult females breed each year, and females may breed in alternate years or with a two-year interval. One third of the cubs born do not survive the first year and a half of life. Among cubs, males outnumber females two to one, but because of a differential mortality rate among males, females become equally numerous in the population at the age of three to four years. Among adults, females are more numerous than males.

Unlike the reproductive process in most mammals, the blastocysts (or early embryos) formed by the union of sperm and egg do not immediately implant, but remain free in the uterus. This period of embryonic arrest, or delayed implantation, lasts five to six months, usually June to December. Then, at about the time that the female grizzly digs and enters her den, the microscopic blastocysts implant and one to four cubs begin to grow. The true gestation period is only six to eight weeks; birth occurs about February 1.

At birth the cubs weigh twelve to sixteen ounces and are blind and naked. They remain in the den for two and a half to three months, and about mid-April or early May the female and cubs leave the den and move to spring feeding areas, usually many miles from the winter den. At this time the cubs weigh ten to twelve pounds.

The female cares for her offspring during the spring and summer months. At about six months the cubs start feeding on vegetation and meat. In September and October, when the cubs weigh about 125 pounds apiece, they accompany their mother to an area where a new winter den is dug. Seldom is a den reused. About the middle of November, following a heavy snowfall, the family enters the 5 x 4 x 8-foot den lined with evergreen boughs. Often the dens are dug under trees with northern exposures, where the insulating snow will pile deep.

The grizzly does not truly hibernate but goes into a state of shallow hypothermia in which the body temperature drops about 5 degrees F. Because the body temperature is still relatively high, 96 degrees, and the metabolic rate is correspondingly high, grizzlies can be easily roused and can, if disturbed, come charging out of the den. In contrast, the true hibernators, such as the ground squirrel, maintain a body temperature that closely approaches the environmental temperature.

The following spring the female may wean her now

one-year-old cubs or may suckle them through another season, den with them, and wean them as two-year-olds. Weaning takes place just prior to the breeding season, and until she has weaned her offspring, the female will not accept a mate. Grizzlies are polygamous and a female may accept as many as four or more different males.

The male has no role in the family life; in fact, adult males are avoided or even attacked by females with cubs because it is not uncommon for them to kill the helpless young. This may be a natural mechanism to regulate grizzly bear numbers when these animals overpopulate an area.

In 1959 Drs. John and Frank Craighead and their students and colleagues began an intensive twelve-year study of the grizzly bear in Yellowstone National Park. Because the species was endangered it was not possible to kill animals for study, so a technique was developed for immobilizing the bears with muscle-relaxing drugs. This enabled the research teams to gather physical and physiological measurements and to individually color-mark the bears for identification after they were released back into the population.

Since 1959 the Craigheads have captured, examined, and released more than 550 grizzlies, immobilized and individually color-marked 256, and logged more than 40,000 man-hours observing and recording their activities and behavior. In addition, 24 grizzlies have been fitted with radios and radio-monitored for approximately 30,000 hours in order to obtain data on movements, home ranges, food habits, social and denning behavior, and an understanding of relationships between bears and men.

From population data, the researchers have calculated a minumum of 175 grizzly bears in the Yellowstone area. This population annually produces an average of 33 cubs, a 19 percent annual increment in the population. The increase rate slightly exceeds the mortality rate; thus, the population grew at an average annual rate of approximately six grizzlies per year from 1959 through 1966. An increase in the death rate, especially of adult females, could jeopardize the population.

During this same period, 34 percent of all the deaths recorded for grizzlies were caused by control measures within Yellowstone National Park, 34 percent by hunting outside the park, and 23 percent by all other factors.

Grizzly bears are not territorial but do have home ranges. The ranges of some females are only 20 to 30 square miles, while some males may encompass 1,000 square miles. Once a female weans her young she establishes her home range. Home ranges of grizzlies overlap but are not defended.

It was also found that a dominance hierarchy develops where the bears congregate at food sources. In Yellowstone these sites are most often garbage dumps, and consequently a relatively stable hierarchy is established because the same bears tend to frequent the same dump areas. Fighting occurs in the spring during the breeding season, and a large male usually becomes the ruling monarch. Smaller or less aggressive males, lower on the social scale, defer to him in matters of food and females. Females with offspring may be high in the hierarchy. When necessary they will vigorously defend their young against the males; a 300-pound female with three 200-pound two-year-olds makes a formidable team! Orphaned cubs and weaned yearlings and two-year-olds are lowest in the hierarchy.

A hierarchy is a substitute for territorial defense. It tends to reduce conflict because subdominant animals display certain submissive signs and postures to dominant animals. Submissive behavior can also terminate a fight before lethal wounds are inflicted. The most common submissive posture is lowering and turning the head to the side while slowly retreating. The hierarchy is a dynamic structure that changes as bears challenge and defeat dominant animals or as bears move in and out of the population.

Only bears captured and marked as cubs or yearlings could be positively aged in the field by the research teams. Therefore, in order to age adult animals, the bears' lower fourth premolar was pulled after they were captured and immobilized. The extracted tooth was sectioned and stained. One layer of cementum is deposited on the root of the bear's tooth each year. By counting these annuli in the stained-root section it was possible to accurately age grizzlies from one to twenty-five years old.

Information obtained in the study has been valuable in understanding the ecology of the grizzly bear and can be used to implement a scientific bear management program in Yellowstone National Park. Knowing the rate of reproduction, the size of a population, and the percent of natural mortality, as well as the number of those killed for control purposes and by hunters, will insure the grizzlies' survival as a species and help to reduce conflicts between them and men.

See H. M. Chittenden, *The American Fur Trade of the Far West* (1935); F. C. Craighead, Jr., and J. J. Craighead, "Knocking Out Grizzlies for Their Own Good," *National Geographic* (August 1960); "Tracking Grizzly Bears," *BioScience*, vol. 15 (1965); and "Trailing Yellowstone's Grizzlies by Radio," *National Geographic* (August 1966); J. J. Craighead, M. Hornocker, W. Woodgerd, and F. C. Craighead, Jr., "Trapping, Immobilizing and Color-Marking Grizzly Bears," North American Wildlife Conference, *Transactions*, vol. 25 (1960); W. P. Hubbard and S. Harris, *Notorious Grizzly Bears* (1960); A. S. Leopold, "Weaning Grizzly Bears," *Natural History* (January 1970); G. B. Moment, "Bears: The Need for a New Sanity in Wildlife Conservation," *BioScience,* vol. 18 (1968); J. Olsen, *Night of the Grizzlies* (1969); and annual reports of the superintendents of Yellowstone National Park.—J. J. C.

Gros Ventre of the Missouri. See HIDATSA INDIANS.

Gros Ventre of the Prairie. The Gros Ventre of the Prairie is the more common name given the Atsina Indians, an Algonkian-speaking tribe whose language closely resembled Arapaho. This resemblance indicates a union of these tribes that ended before 1700. The Gros Ventre of the Prairie were an entirely separate people from the Gros Ventre of the Missouri (Hidatsa), although both tribes were given the same name ("big bellies") by early French traders. By the time of their first contact with the Hudson's Bay Company in the 1770s, the Gros Ventre of the Prairie were buffalo-hunting "equestrian natives" of the area between the branches of the Saskatchewan River. Both the Hudson's Bay Company and the Northwest Company established trading posts accessible to the Gros Ventre and their allies, the Blackfoot, before 1800. Both tribes traded primarily in wolf and buffalo pelts instead of the preferred beaver, which the Cree and Assiniboin trapped. The Gros Ventre bitterly resented the more-favored treatment accorded the Cree and Assiniboin by the traders. They were slowly pushed south and east by these allied tribes, who were better armed and took advantage of the Gros Ventre's reduced numbers after the smallpox epidemic of 1780.

By 1808, the Gros Ventre had settled between the South Branch and the Missouri, thus no longer serving as a buffer between the Blackfoot and the Cree-Assiniboin to the north. The Gros Ventre, like the Blackfoot, carried on friendly trade with the British and did not like American penetration of their territory. Moreover, the American reliance on white, instead of red, trappers to bring back the beaver led to bloodshed. In 1810, a white party from Illinois was murdered and its marked skins stolen. Hostilities continued, with the Gros Ventre often being confused with the Blackfoot by the mountain men. In 1826, the threat of a Crow-American offensive against the Gros Ventre led to a desperate pillaging of the Hudson's Bay Company's Chesterfield House in order to obtain guns and ammunition. After this raid, as many as six of the tribe's twelve bands fled south to join their Arapaho kinsmen. For five years, the Arapaho and Gros Ventre hunted together and traded with Mexicans in the Cimarron area. A devastating attack of smallpox in 1829 reduced the southern Gros Ventre group by half. In 1832, the remnant returned north. They lost nine warriors in the famous battle against the mountain men at the Pierre's Hole rendezvous in July, and later sixty-siven were killed in an ambush by the Crow. The reunited tribe lost 400 after an attack on their village in 1834 by the Cree-Assiniboin.

By the mid-1830s, the value of buffalo robes in trade had increased and the interest in beaver declined. The Gros Ventre profited by this change. As a result of improved trade relations with whites, guns were more readily available, as was liquor. In addition, the Gros Ventre, possibly because of their previous exposure to smallpox, suffered relatively few losses (two hundred out of some three thousand) in the great epidemic of 1837-38. The Blackfoot and Assiniboin were decimated, costing the Gros Ventre a powerful ally but also leaving only the Crow as a strong enemy and thus generally improving the Gros Ventre's position among the Indians of the northern prairie. Peaceful relations with whites continued into the 1850s, with the Gros Ventre gaining a reputation among French-Canadian traders as "demanders," or shameless beggars who were nonetheless not offended if refused.

In 1855, the treaty at Judith River established a common hunting ground for the Gros Ventre and Blackfoot with the United States government promising ten years of provisions as well as agricultural instruction. Hunting and raiding other tribes went on much as before except in 1866-70, when the Blackfoot turned against both the Gros Ventre and the whites. In 1873, the Fort Belknap Reservation for the Blackfoot and Gros Ventre was established. The buffalo hunt continued, however, until 1884, when the northern herd became extinct. From an estimated total of 2,520 in 1853, the Gros Ventre were reduced to 970 in 1883 and to 596 by 1895.

See J. M. Cooper and R. Flannery, *The Gros Ventre of Montana*, 2 vols. (1953-56); F. W. Hodge, ed., *Handbook of American Indians North of Mexico* (1901-10); A. L. Kroeber, *Ethnology of the Gros Ventre* (1901); and J. R. Swanton, *Indian Tribes of North America* (1953). —C. A. M.

Grouard, Frank (1850-1905). Army scout. Grouard claimed to be the son of a Mormon missionary and a Polynesian woman, but others said he was the son of a Negro steamboat cook and one of his several Indian wives. In any event, he was in the Helena, Montana, area in 1870, and while serving as a mail-carrier Grouard was captured by the Sioux and adopted by Sitting Bull. In 1873 he fought with the Sioux against army troops on the Yellowstone River. Shortly after, he quarreled with Sitting Bull and joined the camp of CRAZY HORSE, where he was known as "The Grabber." He soon deserted the Sioux entirely, probably because of in-law trouble, and went to Fort Robinson, dressed, it is said, only in a breechclout and moccasins. Later he met and was employed by General George Crook as a scout. His familiarity with Indian ways, especially his knowledge of where the Sioux winter camps would probably be found, made his services of the greatest value. Crook had a very high opinion of him and said he would rather lose half his command than Grouard; others, however, were not so kind in their evaluation. When Crazy Horse surrendered at Camp Robinson in 1877, Grouard is said to have disappeared because of his fear of this Indian who knew so much about his past; later, he returned to the fort. It was said that his mistranslation of Crazy Horse's reply to a question led to the killing of the Indian leader.

Because of his knowledge of the terrain, Grouard reported the progress of the Ghost Dance religion (1890-91) among the Sioux. Later he was of great assistance to the peace officers in clearing the region of horse thieves and other desperadoes.

The only book about Frank Grouard is Joe DeBarthe, *Life and Adventures of Frank Grouard*, edited by Edgar I. Stewart (repr. 1958).—E. I. S.

Gruening, Ernest (1887-1974). Journalist and Alaskan politician. Gruening was born in New York City. Determined to follow in the footsteps of his father, a prominent eye-and-ear surgeon, he entered Harvard Medical School. But even before Gruening received his M.D. in 1912, he had become interested in journalism and public affairs. He first worked for Boston newspapers. After service in World War I he was managing editor of the New York *Tribune* (1918-19); general manager of *La Prensa* (1919-20), in which capacity he bacame an expert on Latin American affairs; and on the staff of *The Nation* (1920-23). In 1927 Gruening founded the Portland (Maine) *Evening News*. Its columns became famous for their courageous assaults on the power trust then blocking public power in New England, a concern that led to *The Public Pays* (1931), an analysis of public utilities. He stepped down as editor in 1932 and the next year became an editor of *The Nation* for a year.

As a journalist Gruening frequently expressed his abhorrence of war and Latin American military chieftains who fattened on it. He repeatedly denounced the United States's involvements in the Caribbean. In *Mexico and Its Heritage* (1928) he described a land still bleeding from its earlier revolutionary holocaust.

Predictably, the New Deal wave washed Gruening into the mainstream of political life. In 1924 he had been national publicity director for Robert La Follette, a Progressive, during his presidential campaign. In 1934 President Franklin D. Roosevelt appointed him director of the newly created Division of Territories and Island Possessions. As such, he had jurisdiction over Alaska, among other lands, and played an important part in preparing Rear Admiral Richard E. Byrd's South Pole expedition.

When Secretary of the Interior Harold Ickes first offered Gruening the governorship of Alaska Territory in August 1939, he rejected it. Gruening was acutely aware of the northlanders' aversion to carpetbaggers and urged that the post go to an Alaskan. After he heard over the radio that Roosevelt had appointed him, he reluctantly accepted.

Extensive travels in the Pacific in his previous office had supplied Gruening with a deep appreciation for the attitudes of America's insular citizens. Alaskans viewed themselves as rugged individualists—justified by their rigorous climate, embryonic communities, and very real isolation—yet they were precariously dependent on large federal aid. Gruening recognized the latter, but criticized congressional and Interior Department paternalism with as much ardor as he did the irresponsibility of those Alaskans who were interested only in exploiting the Great Land.

Greeted by an initially hostile legislature, Gruening soon began to win support for his policies. His victory against Seattle labor monopolists and their standpat allies in the military produced jobs for Alaskans, while the outbreak of World War II in Europe compelled Congress to enlarge defense expenditures in the North. In Alaskan eyes steamship companies had the same public image as the western railroads. Gruening challenged the shipping companies by introducing tax measures that sought to block some of the wealth made in Alaska from draining away to the south. Into a territory so preoccupied with fishing, mining, and physical transformation, the governor and his wife brought distinguished artists. Gruening struggled to protect the easily manipulated Indian population, while his campaign to protect animal life gained the expected denunciations from domestic hunters.

Despite Governor Gruening's best efforts, Alaska was ill-prepared to defend itself after the Japanese attack on Pearl Harbor. As commander-in-chief of the Alaskan Territorial Guard, he was appalled at how little attention was accorded Alaska's defense needs even after the Aleutian islands of Attu and Kiska were occupied by the Japanese, but this seizure of American soil by a wartime enemy did draw public attention northward. Alaska got airfields, docks, and military facilities of every description. With the peace, a variety of them remained as viable parts of the territory's economy. Most famous was the "Alcan" highway connecting Alaska to the United States via Canada, of which Gruening had been an early and ardent advocate.

How ironic that yet another war, the cold war with Russia, eventually would bring to a man so dedicated to peace the honor of winning Alaska its statehood. Once again enormous sums of federal construction money poured into the territory. The Republican party's return to power in 1953 terminated Gruening's governorship, but not his campaign for Alaskan statehood.

The following year his *The State of Alaska* appeared. Purportedly an historical study, it skillfully summarized his arguments for statehood, based on much of the same logic used by Alaska's great nineteenth-century advocate, Sheldon Jackson. Its essence: The Great Land, a region of fabulous wealth, had been misunderstood, mistakenly handled, and treated as a virtual colony by the United States.

Throughout the 1950s Gruening crisscrossed Alaska galvanizing support for statehood, a struggle recounted in *The Battle for Alaska Statehood* (1967). At the nation's capital, he proved a tireless lobbyist. Finally, in 1959, Alaska became the forty-ninth state. Its citizens rewarded Gruening with a seat in the United States Senate and reelection in 1962. His Alaskan projects were a vastly expanded highway system and the ecologically controversial Rampart Dam proposal, subsequently defeated. As a senator he continued to confront the threat of unleashed militarism, being one of two senators who voted against the critical Tonkin Gulf resolution, which approved what soon became the American war in Southeast Asia.

In 1968 Gruening had the dubious distinction of being the oldest senator seeking reelection. Defeated by his Republican challenger, Michael Gravel, he returned to his home in Juneau, Alaska.—T. C. H.

Guadalupe Hidalgo, Treaty of (1848). Termination of the Mexican War. The treaty ending the war with Mexico rounded out the present-day continental limits of the United States, with the exceptions of the Gadsden Purchase of 1853 and the Alaska Purchase of 1867. Together with the Louisiana Purchase, the Treaty of Guadalupe Hidalgo of February 2, 1848, constituted one of the two most important territorial additions in the entire history of the United States.

Its negotiation was nothing if not complicated and, for President James K. Polk, painful and embarrassing, if nonetheless acceptable. The president had dispatched to General Winfield Scott's army the chief clerk of the State Department, Nicholas P. Trist, with a commission to make a suitable peace. The fact that Trist, an impeccable Democrat, soon made friends with Scott, a (to Polk) horrible Whig, led President Polk to believe that Trist and Scott were plotting to embarrass him and the administration and perhaps to subvert the entire arrangement of the war. Trist instead showed his good judgment by drawing up, admittedly with Scott's assistance, the Treaty of Guadalupe Hidalgo, which obtained for the United States—and, if Polk wished to put it that way, the Democratic party—everything that the president could have desired. That, to be sure, was a good part of the presidential embarrassment—that Trist, the "enemy" to Polk's mind, had done such a successful job.

Trist arranged for the transfer to the United States of New Mexico and California and Mexican acceptance of the Texan boundary at the Rio Grande. The United States was to pay $15 million and assume the adjusted claims of its citizens against the Mexican government. These terms, Polk realized, were virtually the maximum that James Slidell, his previous envoy before outbreak of the war, had been empowered to negotiate in an abortive mission of 1846, and despite Polk's intense suspicion of Trist, whose commission meanwhile he had revoked, he sent the treaty to the Senate, which gave its advice and consent on March 10, 1848.

By the treaty the United States added altogether (including Texas) 1.2 million square miles to its domain, an increase of more than sixty-six percent. Despite ratification of the treaty, desire for the Mexican territory later comprised in the Gadsden Purchase, and thereafter a long series of border incidents, continued to strain relations between the United States and Mexico.

There is no monograph on the Treaty of Guadalupe Hidalgo. The best resort is the more general account of the fighting, together with the peace, in Justin H. Smith, *The War with Mexico*, 2 vols. (1919); Otis A. Singletary, *The Mexican War* (1960); and especially Milo M. Quaife, ed., *The Diary of James K. Polk: During His Presidency, 1845 to 1849*, 4 vols. (1910), and abridged by Allan Nevins, ed., *Polk, The Diary of a President: 1845-1849* (1929).—R. H. F.

Gue, Benjamin F. (1828-1904). Iowa politician and journalist. Born in Greene County, New York, Gue attended academies at Canandaigua and West Bloomfield in New York and taught school in that state for one year before moving to Iowa in 1852. He settled on a farm in Scott County.

Reared in a Quaker home, Gue's strong abolitionist views prompted his involvement in politics. In 1856 he helped to organize the Republican party in Iowa. He served several terms in both houses of the Iowa legislature. While a member of that body, Gue played a leading role in the establishment of the Iowa State Agricultural College (now Iowa State University); he first authored a bill to establish the institution and then successfully fought for its passage. Gue served on the college's board of trustees and successfully worked for admission of women on an equal basis with men.

In 1864 Gue embarked on a new career when he purchased the Fort Dodge *Republican*. Changing the name to *Iowa North West*, Gue, as editor and publisher, expressed his views on behalf of temperance, woman suffrage, and mass education. He was nominated and elected as the Republican lieutenant governor in 1865, serving one term. He later earned the title "founder of Iowa's first successful farm journal" by editing the *Iowa Homestead*.

In his later years Gue turned to historical writing and published the four-volume *History of Iowa from the Earliest Times to the Beginning of the Twentieth Century* (1903). He was the first assistant curator and secretary of the State Historical Department in Des Moines.

Gue's life and achievements are treated in E. H. Stiles, *Recollections and Sketches of Notable Lawyers and Public Men of Iowa* (1916); and Johnson Brigham, *Iowa: Its History and Its Foremost Citizens*, vol. I (1916).—D.S.

Guevavi. Spanish mission. Guevavi, the first Spanish mission in what is now Arizona, was founded in January 1691 by Father Eusebio KINO, the remarkable Jesuit "Apostle to the Pimas," who also founded SAN XAVIER DEL BAC and TUMACÁCORI. All were located on the northward-flowing Santa Cruz River in southern Arizona. Guevavi (or Guebavi, as Kino and others have spelled it), the southernmost of the missions, was situated in an Indian town of the same name. It lay just north and east of the modern border town of Nogales, Arizona. At various times the mission carried the names of various archangels; it was best known as San Gabriel de Guevavi, but was also referred to as Los Angeles de Guevavi.

Kino had come to New Spain's northern frontier province of Sonora in 1686, after a futile attempt to convert the natives of Baja California. A year after his arrival in Sonora he was ordered to use Mission Nuestra Señora de Los Dolores on the San Miguel as a base from which to missionize Pimería Alta (or land of the Upper Pima), an area embracing northern Sonora and present-day southern Arizona. After exploring the region with Father Juan María Salvatierra, Kino located the missions in the Santa Cruz valley, for the Sobaipuri, PIMA, and PAPAGO Indians were concentrated there in small rancherías or villages, where they practiced irrigation farming to raise corn, beans, melons, wheat, and cotton. Of these rancherías Guevavi was one of the largest.

Kino baptized a number of the local population in 1691 and introduced the Indians to sheep, goats, cattle, and horses. But Guevavi continued to be little more than a set of brush shelters erected to house church services and visiting priests until 1701, when Father Juan de San Martin became the first resident priest and a church and adobe house were built. By 1697 Tumacácori had been made a *visita*, or town under the jurisdiction, of Guevavi. Guevavi endured rather than thrived during the years the mission was run by the Jesuit order. After Kino's death in 1711 the mission declined and probably was abandoned until new priests came during the 1730s and a permanent church was built. Yet while the Indians benefited from Spanish herds, fruit trees, new foods, and better farming methods, the very presence of cattle and horses attracted Apache raiders, who harassed the mission and their enemies, the Pima, continually. The Apache threat was so great that the priests sometimes feared to travel to the mission's three or four *visitas*. Meanwhile, European diseases caused so many native deaths that the missionaries had to travel to even more distant villages to seek new converts for the mission.

At its height Guevavi probably never had more than two or three hundred families living there. Unlike the California mission Indians, the Pima neophytes retained much of their independence, moved with the seasons to hunt and gather food, and went on forays against the Apache. They retained many of their own religious customs and shocked the fathers by holding their riotous cactus wine festival on the feast day of St. Francis of Assisi. Priests, many of them Swiss and German after 1732, came and went. Often the fathers were so shorthanded that they had to take on duties at Tumacácori or Bac as well. The records suggest periods of confusion and despair and hint that some of the less popular priests were poisoned by the Indians. On the other side the missionaries demanded hard labor from the Indians and sometimes abused them so that even Juan Bautista de ANZA, the famous commander of TUBAC presidio, felt that the mission system had accomplished little in Arizona. Mistreatment of the Indians and the silver discoveries at Arizonac, less than fifty miles southwest of Guevavi, which brought thousands of rough and ready treasure seekers into Pimería Alta in 1733, helped provoke the Pima rebellion of 1751. That year the Indians nearly wiped out the Arizona missions. The fathers fled or were murdered, and the missions were looted. But the establishment of a presidio at Tubac in 1752, a few miles down the river, allowed the fathers to reoccupy the missions. By the 1760s Father

Ignatius Pfefferkorn noted that 111 Indians lived at Guevavi.

Guevavi's fate was sealed in 1767, when Charles III of Spain, swayed by the secular ideals of the Enlightenment, expelled the Jesuits from the New World missions; a year later Franciscan friars took over the Arizona posts. Although the Franciscans worked energetically to foster existing missions and tried to build new ones to the north and west along the Gila River, government officials wanted to free the Indians from the economic control of the missions and turn the neophytes into farmers and ranchers who could pay taxes. Then the Franciscans decided to make Tumacácori the head mission, for it was located less than five miles from the presidio of Tubac. Guevavi was reduced to the status of a *visita* and its inhabitants began to drift to Tubac and Tumacácori as Apache raids increased. In 1773 Father Bartholomé Ximeno wrote despairingly that with only nine families remaining, Guevavi "has no strength to defend itself."

It is clear that unrelenting Apache raids during the Franciscan period (1768-1828) were the real cause of the mission's decline, but its fortunes were also affected by Spain's new interest in an overland trail to California, which de Anza and Father Garcés, the energetic priest at Bac, opened during the 1770s. In essence the frontier had moved northward to Tucson and west along the Gila to the Colorado. In 1775 the soldiers at Tubac were moved to the new presidio of San Agustín de Tucson, and Father Garcés himself tried to found a mission and colony at Yuma. Though it was designated as a mission until 1828, Guevavi quickly fell into ruins. A modern cattle ranch now occupies the area where Jesuits, Franciscans, and Indians once labored; the actual site of the mission has been fenced in, but only traces of the buildings remain.

The fortunes of Guevavi have been carefully recounted in Will C. Barnes, *Arizona Place Names* (rev. ed., 1960); Herbert E. Bolton, *Rim of Christendom: A Biography of Eusebio Kino, Pacific Coast Pioneer* (1939); and John L. Kessell, *Mission of Sorrows: Jesuit Guevavi and the Pimas, 1691-1767* (1970).—H. R. L.

Gulf Coastal Plain. The Gulf Coastal Plain extends from Florida to Mexico along the Gulf of Mexico. It was one of the first parts of the North American continent to be explored by Europeans (see PHYSIOGRAPHY OF THE UNITED STATES: *Atlantic and Gulf Coastal plains*). In 1519 the Spaniard Alonso de Piñeda sailed along the southern coast in his journey from Jamaica to Tampico. Nine years later Pánfilo de NARVAEZ reached the Florida coast, where his party suffered intensely. Alvar Núñez CABEZA DE VACA and a small party from this venture finally reached Texas and underwent further hardships before they reached Mexico City and relief. The major penetration of the Gulf coastal area was by Hernando DE SOTO. He gained permission from Charles V on April 10, 1537, to exploit Florida, and on May 18, 1539, he landed on the Gulf coastal shore. (See EXPLORATION, SPANISH and FLORIDA.)

Despite Indian hostility, the Spanish invasion of the Gulf Coast had begun and was continued for the next two centuries. A rivalry developed between the French and Spanish when Pedro Menéndez de Avilés undertook to drive the French Huguenots away from Fort Caroline in 1565. This rivalry eventually resulted in the establishment of Pensacola in 1698 as a fortified barrier against French expansion into the Gulf coastal territory.

A second approach into the Gulf area was made during the seventeenth century by both Jesuit and Franciscan missionaries. In time small missions were located in several places in the territory of Florida as far north as the English Carolina border. The major European expansion was westward around the coast toward the Mississippi River in the eighteenth century. In 1702 the Frenchman Jean Baptiste Le Moyne, Sieur de BIENVILLE moved into Mobile Bay and established the French stronghold of Mobile. A decade and a half later Bienville pushed up the Mississippi approximately a hundred miles to establish on the eastern side of the wide sweeping bend the city of NEW ORLEANS. The precise date of the founding of this city is not definitely known, but various dates are given from 1715 to 1718. Elsewhere along the Gulf Coast both French and Spanish established toeholds—the French along the Mississippi coast, and the Spanish along the Texan coast.

Most of the Gulf coastal areas east of the Mississippi fell into the hands of the British after the end of the French and Indian War in 1763. In 1783 the coastal claims were ceded back to Spain. In this latter cession the British created an aggravating diplomatic situation for the Americans by the variable boundaries prescribed in the cession (see EAST AND WEST FLORIDA QUESTION). In fact, the British cession set the stage for a quarter-century of rivalry between the young American nation and Spain. The dispute involved areas extending from the coastal area up the Mississippi.

Pressures from American Indian traders, land speculators, and, after 1785, frontier American farmers created a continuously troubled situation. The so-called SPANISH CONSPIRACY centering about the ambitions of Spanish colonial officials and James WILKINSON reached far up the river and had an influence on Kentucky and Tennessee politics. By the opening of the decade of 1790 the tight policies of the Spanish relating to the free use of the harbor at New Orleans by American backwoodsmen promised to have serious international consequences. Spain after 1790 also attempted to organize a captaincy-general, which would form a strong barrier against American expansion. Actually, Spain feared the wild, uncontrolled backwoodsmen more than the forces of the young republic itself. The activities of the various Yazoo land companies offered a serious threat to Spanish welfare along the Gulf in both the Floridas and Louisiana. Too, there was grave danger that a strict trading policy at New Orleans and along the Gulf Coastal Indian frontier would only stimulate a forceful invasion of Americans.

The signing of the Treaty of SAN LORENZO on October 27, 1795, opened the Mississippi to American trade in an uneasy truce. The treaty, however, by no means ended Spain's attempt to defend the Mississippi, nor did it end American pressures on the Gulf coastal region. West Florida was reserved in Spanish hands. In 1804 the so-called Kemper Revolution at Baton Rouge sought to establish a filibustering foothold there. This was followed by continued invasion and friction in West Florida until the United States acquired the territory in 1810 and 1811. It was not until the conclusion of the LOUISIANA PURCHASE in 1803 that the river was in American hands.

The WAR OF 1812 and Andrew Jackson's campaign against the Creek Indians at HORSESHOE BEND took American forces into both East and West Florida. Following the end of that war forays against the Creek and Seminole and against Indian traders resulted in a series of political incidents that led to the conclusion of the ADAMS-ONIS TREATY of February 22, 1819. This filled out the southeastern territory of the United States and opened the Gulf Coast to free access for Americans. The cities of Pensacola, Mobile, Gulfport, and Biloxi were developed, and free access was established to the Pearl, Alabama, and Chattahoochee river systems. These streams became inland paths for settlers moving to the Old Southwest and its cotton lands during the 1830s and 1840s.

Samuel Flagg Bemis, *The Latin American Policy of the United States* (1943), gives the background of the Floridas. Thomas A. Bailey, *A Diplomatic History of the American People* (1969), explores the major incidents of Gulf coastal diplomacy. Thomas D. Clark, *Frontier America* (1959), deals with both the Spanish and American occupation. Arthur P. Whitaker, *The Spanish-American Frontier, 1783-1795* (1927) and *The Mississippi Question, 1795-1803* (1934), discuss late Spanish occupation of the region. Hubert Bruce Fuller, *The Purchase of Florida, Its History and Diplomacy* (1906), is a full discussion of the complex political and diplomatic history of the Spanish Florida territory.—T. D. C.

guns. Rifles were introduced into the American colonies from central Europe—particularly southern Germany, Austria, and Switzerland—in the latter part of the seventeenth century, and by the early eighteenth century they were well established on this continent. The settlers in the central and southern colonies, particularly Pennsylvania, were of Germanic origin, and many had served as foresters on the game reserves of the nobility in their native land. These men knew that rifles were more accurate than smoothbores and were quick to see the usefulness of employing such arms in the wilderness of America. For although game was plentiful, shots often had to be made from the comparatively long range of 100 to 150 yards, and the accuracy of a rifle was of great advantage. It soon became evident, however, that the European rifle was not well suited for use in the wilderness of America, for it was heavy, of large caliber, and quite poorly balanced. Consequently, it was tiring to carry on long trips through the forest and consumed a large amount of powder and lead in proportion to the results that could be obtained with it. There then appeared in the central colonies, a lighter and more slender rifle, bored to a smaller caliber, known as the KENTUCKY RIFLE. This rifle was the first truly American firearm, having been designed to meet the requirements of the frontier.

In about 1840 the Plains rifle appeared. It was made along the same general lines as the Kentucky, except that the stock was made to go only halfway up the barrel, rather than to the muzzle. The barrel on this rifle was heavier, supposedly for better accuracy at longer ranges in the more open Plains country. This type gradually superseded the true Kentucky.

In 1836 Samuel Colt patented a revolving type of handgun. His first venture into the firearms field was short-lived, lasting from 1836 to 1842. Because of the rather weak construction of his first revolvers, they were

The .44-caliber Colt Army Model (1860).

not enthusiastically received by the public. Financial difficulties also plagued Colt, forcing him to close his firm in Paterson, New Jersey. In 1847 a new model with improvements was introduced by Captain Samuel Walker of the Texas Rangers. Colt had no factory at this time, and so he contracted with the Whitney Armory at Whitneyville, Connecticut, to manufacture Walker's type of revolver. About 1,100 were produced in 1847, and the profit made from them started Colt in business in Hartford, Connecticut. New models were brought out and almost immediately became popular, for with many men going west as the result of the discovery of gold in California in 1849, there was a ready market for revolvers. During the 1850s the use of the Colt became widespread. In the Civil War thousands of Colt revolvers were purchased by the government. The Model 1851 Navy in .36 caliber and the Model 1860 Army in .44 caliber were the most prominent. Many of these revolvers were also used in the West by civilians during the latter part of the nineteenth century.

Although the earlier Colt models were six-shooters, they were still fired by percussion caps, with the ammunition in the form of loose powder and ball or cartridges made of paper or linen. In 1873 a new model was brought out that fired a metallic cartridge. This cartridge contained its own primer, and the powder was contained in a copper or brass case with the bullet seated at the open end. With slight variations this Colt, known variously as the Single Action Army, the Frontier, and the Peacemaker, became the most famous six-shooter of the West. Other makes of revolvers used in the West were the Remington, Savage, Smith & Wesson, and Merwin & Hulbert, but the Colt was predominant.

Contemporary with the early Colt was a single-shot breechloading rifle, patented in 1848 by Christian Sharps. Known as a falling breechblock, it was operated by a finger-lever trigger guard. During the 1850s a large number of Sharps rifles and carbines were used. At the time of the Civil War more than 80,000 Sharps carbines and more than 9,000 Sharps rifles were bought by the government. They were fired by percussion caps and used paper or linen cartridges of .52 caliber. Like the Colt, many Sharps were used in the West after the war.

Although the Sharps had the advantage of being a breechloader, it leaked burning powder gas at the breech when it was fired. It was not until a satisfactory metallic cartridge had been developed that breechloading arms became really practical. In 1860 B. Tyler Henry patented a breechloading repeating rifle that fired a metallic cartridge. The Henry rifle was manufactured by the New Haven Arms Company, of which Oliver

Winchester was president. The Henry rifle was a lever-action repeater with a tube magazine below the barrel. It was made to hold fifteen .44 caliber rim-fire cartridges; one cartridge in the chamber made it a sixteen-shot repeater. During the Civil War the company sold some 1,700 Henry rifles to the government and several thousand to state troops. By 1866 about 13,500 had been manufactured. Some were sold in western states and territories and others were taken west after the war.

Another repeating rifle, contemporary with the Henry, was the Spencer rifle. It was manufactured in Boston and Providence. Some 87,000 had been purchased by the Ordnance Department by the end of 1865. Many more were purchased to equip state militia units. The Spencer was a lever-action repeater with a tube magazine in the buttstock made to hold seven .50 or .52 caliber rim-fire cartridges. Like the Sharps and the Henry, many Spencer guns were sold after the Civil War as government surplus.

A sixteen-shot repeater, the Henry rifle had far more fire power than any other firearm of the time. But because the magazine was of frail construction and had to be filled from near the muzzle end, it was never widely used. In 1866 a patent for a loading port in the side of the receiver, so that the magazine could be filled from the breech, was granted to Nelson King. On the strength of this patent, the New Haven Arms Company was reorganized and expanded and called the Winchester Repeating Arms Company. King's patent was assigned to the new company, and the first Winchester, the Model 1866, was born. At first this model was known as the Improved Henry. It retained the lever action and the position of the magazine tube below the barrel.

In the early days of the Winchester Company, testimonial letters from users of its guns appeared in its catalogs. The following letter appeared in the 1869 catalog.

Omaha, Nebraska Territory
February 28, 1867
Winchester Repeating Arms Co.

Having been requested by Gen. L. P. Bradley, now stopping in this city, to make a statement in regard to the qualities of the Henry Rifle, I take the greatest pleasure in testifying to the many excellent qualities of the rifle.

I have used one for the past eight months on the new route to Montana, in all kinds of weather, on foot and horseback, in several Indian fights, where rapidity of firing was an essential quality, and never had the slightest trouble with it, nor never knew it to fail. I have fired the whole sixteen shots nearly as fast as I could count, without heating the barrel, or failing to

The .36-caliber Colt Navy Model (1851).

The .45-caliber Colt Peacemaker (1873).

throw out the old shell of the cartridge, (a fault no other gun has obviated in rapid firing.)

I have tried the range and accuracy, and had it tried by some of the best shots in that country, from one hundred to nine hundred yards, and found it the most accurate rifle I ever saw, either muzzle or breech-loading. The Henry Rifle is now considered by the miners and hunters in this country the best arm in use, and will pay more for it than any other.

From the description given me by General Bradley of the new improvement, in loading at the breech without unloading the magazine under the barrel, I am convinced it must greatly improve the efficiency of the arm, as the magazine can then be kept full on emergency. If my testimony to the value of this splendid rifle can aid in influencing any, it is here fully and cheerfully given, the more so because in two Indian fights I owe to this rifle, and its splendid execution, my own life, and, perhaps, the lives of others,

Very truly,
A. H. Ward,
Lieut. 36th U.S. Inf.

To Gen. L. P. Bradley,
Lieut. Col. 27th U.S. Infantry

The Model 1866 Winchester used the same .44 caliber rim-fire cartridge as did the earlier Henry rifle. At first the Model '66 was made in sporting rifle and carbine style. In 1869 a military type, the musket style, was added.

In 1873 Winchester brought out a new model, chambered for a .44 caliber center-fire cartridge. It was more powerful than the Model '66 and was used more extensively than any other make of shoulder arm in the West. It has often been called "the gun that won the West." In numerous western novels it is said that many a western baby cut his first teeth on the sling (saddle) ring of a Winchester Model 1873. Dime novels of the late 1800s and early 1900s said, "crack-crack-crack went the Winchester and fifteen Indians bit the dust."

An interesting testimonial letter from a famous user of the Model '73 appeared in an 1875 Winchester catalog:

Fort McPherson, Neb.
I have been using and have thoroughly tested your latest improved rifle. Allow me to say that I have tried and used nearly every kind of gun made in the United States, and for general hunting, or Indian fighting, I pronounce your improved Winchester the boss.

An Indian will give more for one of your guns than any other gun he can get.

While in the Black Hills this last summer I crippled a bear, and Mr. Bear made for me, and I am certain had I not been armed with one of your repeating rifles I would now be in the happy hunting grounds. The bear was not thirty feet from me when he charged, but before he could reach me I had eleven bullets in him, which was a little more lead than he could comfortably digest.

Believe me, that you have the most complete rifle now made.

W. F. Cody,
"Buffalo Bill"

The use of the '73 Winchester had become so widespread by 1878 that Colt announced its Single Action Army Revolver, chambered for the same .44 WCF caliber as the Winchester Model '73. This enabled a man to have both his shoulder arm and side arm chambered for the same cartridges.

In addition to the repeating rifles, several makes of single shots were used. The two best known were the Remington and the Sharps. Some were made to fire the most powerful cartridges of the day and were widely used in the open plains country for shooting big game. The Sharps in particular became famous as a "buffalo rifle." It had a heavy octagon barrel and fired some of the longest .40 to .50 caliber cartridges, which were very effective at long range. In 1873 the army adopted a single-shot rifle in caliber .45-.70, known as the Trap Door Springfield. (The breech-block was made to lift up like a trap door, and the place of manufacture was the United States Armory at Springfield, Massachusetts.) These were much used in the West by both federal and state militia troops. Because of the very long firing pins used in these guns, they were often referred to as needle guns.

In 1876 Winchester brought out a new model repeating rifle. In announcing the model the following statement was made:

The success attending the sale and use of Model 1873 and the constant calls from many sources, and particularly from the regions in which the grizzly bear and other large game are found, as well as from the plains where the absence of cover and the shyness of the game require the hunter to make his shots at long range, made it desirable for the Company to build a still more powerful gun. Retaining all the essential mechanical elements of the former model, and adding such improvements as seemed possible, the result has been a gun carrying a central fire cartridge capable of reloading, caliber 45/100 with 75 grains of powder and 350 grains of lead, being nearly double the charge used in Model 1873, and about the same as that adopted by the U.S. Government. The materials used in the construction of the gun are the same in kind and quality as in the Model 1873.

Although not mentioned in the above announcement, it is believed that this heavier model was brought out to make a repeating rifle available for buffalo hunting, but by the late 1870s the herds had been so greatly reduced that the model never reached great popularity.

Other makes of guns used to a limited extent were the Adirondack, Whitney, Marlin, Stevens, Wesson, and Ballard. In fact, guns of every make and type were used. Handguns ranged from tiny pocket pistols and revolvers of derringer type and size to large and heavy military pistols and revolvers. Shotguns, both single and double barrel, were used for hunting birds and small game. Except when stagecoach or bank guards carried it, the shotgun never found a niche in the West as did the rifle, carbine, and revolver.

People bought their guns from jobbers and dealers rather than directly from the manufacturers. Some of the smaller gun makers, such as John P. Gemmer of St. Louis, C. Freund of Cheyenne, and John Krider of Philadelphia, did sell directly to the customer. Two of the more prominent outfits that sold guns and supplies to people heading west were the Edward K. Tryon Company of Philadelphia and the Great Western Gun Works of Pittsburgh.

For later developments in firearms, see John Moses BROWNING.

See Charles Edward Chapel, *Guns of the Old West* (1961); Henry J. Kauffman, *The Pennsylvania-Kentucky Rifle* (1960); John E. Parsons, *The First Winchester* (1955); Carl P. Russell, *Guns on the Early Frontier* (1957); and James E. Serven, *Colt Firearms from 1836* (1954) and *The Collecting of Guns* (1964).—T. L. H.

Guthrie, A[lfred] B[ertram], [Jr.] (1901-   ). Short-story writer and novelist. Guthrie was born in Bedford, Indiana, but went west for his education. After his graduation in 1923 from the University of Montana he returned east, settling this time in Lexington, Kentucky. There, from 1926 until 1947 he served in various positions on the staff of the Lexington *Leader,* writing in his spare time and contributing short stories to various magazines. From 1947 to 1952 he taught creative writing at the University of Kentucky. He then followed the example of his fictional characters and moved west again, this time to Montana. In 1950 Guthrie received a Pulitzer Prize.

Although Guthrie has written many short stories, a number of which have been collected in *The Big It and Other Stories* (1960), his reputation as a novelist depends primarily upon his historical trilogy, *The Big Sky* (1947), *The Way West* (1949), and *These Thousand Hills* (1956). These three novels are a loose sequence, each one dealing with a different aspect of the settlement of the West. The first tells the story of the mountain men living "across the wide Missouri"; the second is a fictionalized history of a wagon train traveling the Oregon Trail from Missouri to the Pacific; and the final novel chronicles the later settlement of Montana. The interest of all three novels is very largely due to Guthrie's ability to re-create past historical periods believably. The trilogy is fascinating reading as fictional history, true to the spirit of the pioneers as well as to the facts of the westward movement.

Guthrie's fictional West is primarily a place where settled, conventional values are challenged by the unexpected and often unconventional demands of a new environment. His characters succeed or fail on the basis of their resilience and their willingness to accept the demands of their new surroundings without trying to fit them into preconceived expectations.—J. K. F.

Guthrie, [Woodrow Wilson] Woody (1912-1967). Folk singer and composer. Born near Okemah, Oklahoma, the son of a successful politician and businessman, Guthrie had a relatively comfortable childhood. But during his early teens a number of tragedies, including the illness of his mother and the death of his older sister, split up the family. During the separation Guthrie spent winters in school in Okemah and summers working as a migrant agricultural laborer. In 1929 he was reunited with his family in Pampa, Texas, and spent the next several years living with the fury of the Dust Bowl.

In 1937 he traveled to Los Angeles, California, with the hope of becoming a successful western singer. For the next couple of years he appeared on various radio stations and sang both folk songs and his own songs, including "Oklahoma Hills" and "So Long, It's Been Good to Know You." "This Land Is Your Land" and "Philadelphia Lawyer," two other well-known Guthrie songs, were written in the 1940s after he left California.

While in California he came into contact with the Communist party and, finding that he was in sympathy with many of its causes, began writing for some leftist newspapers, including the *Daily Worker*. This was later to become a source of much right-wing criticism against him.

In 1940 Guthrie traveled with the actor Will Geer to New York City. That same year folk-song collector Alan Lomax decided to record Guthrie's Dust Bowl ballads for the Library of Congress Folk Song Archives. With the release of an album, *Dust Bowl Ballads*, by RCA Victor, Guthrie gained national attention. During the 1940s and early 1950s he worked with a number of performers, including the Almanac Singers, Burl Ives, Josh White, Leadbelly (another Lomax "discovery"), Cisco Houston, and Pete Seeger. Guthrie's burgeoning career was cut short in 1954, when he was hospitalized with Huntington's disease, the same illness that had struck down his mother. His remaining years were spent in fighting the effects of the disease.

In all, Guthrie wrote over one thousand folk songs and children's songs, most of which were issued by Folkways Records and Stinson Records. His songs expressed a deep love for his native Oklahoma and his country and were characterized by humor and optimism. Even when he was unable to cope with increasingly poor health, he continued to feel that music should "make you feel good." His material was drawn primarily from his early years: as a youth in Okemah, an oil boomtown, where he came into contact with black and Indian culture; his early travels as a migrant agricultural worker; and the desperate Depression years spent in Dust Bowl country. Guthrie never composed his music, but rather simply took his verses and combined them with old tunes and traditional folk-song melodies. Later, when he discovered a "writing style" in New York, he lost some of the natural spark of folk-art quality that had characterized his earlier pieces. Increasingly he became a professional Okie—often to the point of overworking the misspelled word and poor grammar. Since he was an admirer of Will Rogers, it is probable that he patterned much of his "illiterate" style after that of Rogers. In fact, both men were educated and well read.

Guthrie was the inspiration of the folk-music revival of the late 1950s led by Pete Seeger and the Weavers and of the folk-rock development of the 1960s led by Bob Dylan, who early in his career copied Guthrie's style.

He occasionally wrote of his own experiences, and his autobiographical novel, *Bound for Glory* (1943), drew praise from Clifton Fadiman, who enthusiastically compared him to Walt Whitman.

In 1966 Secretary of the Interior Stewart Udall presented Guthrie with a Conservation Service award for making "our people aware of their heritage and the land."

See Woody Guthrie, *American Folksong* (1947), and *Born to Win* (1965); Millard Lampell and others, *A Tribute to Woody Guthrie* (1972), with two records, Part I issued by Columbia and Part II issued by Warner Brothers; Richard Reuss, *A Woody Guthrie Bibliography, 1912-1967* (1968); and Henrietta Yurchenco, *Hard Traveling: The Life of Woody Guthrie* (1970).—G. L.

Gwin, William McKendree (1805-1885). California politician. Trained as a physician, Gwin entered politics during the Jacksonian era as a congressman from his native Tennessee. Moving to California in 1849, he participated in the state constitutional convention of 1849 as a chief spokesman for Anglo settlers. After election to one of California's first senatorial seats, he introduced the bill establishing the land commission that decided the land claims of Mexican Californians. He also successfully led the fight against the ratification of the California Indian treaties of 1851. Through his control of federal patronage, he dominated the state Democratic party in the 1850s, bringing him into conflict with his Senate colleague David C. BRODERICK. As a result of his battle with Broderick, Gwin's pro-Southern sympathies became an issue in California politics. During the Civil War he was twice arrested as a Confederate supporter and spent some months in federal prison. With the ascendency of the California Republican party during the war, Gwin fell from power and lived out his last years in obscurity.

See William H. Ellison, ed., "Memoirs of Hon. William M. Gwin," *California Historical Society Quarterly*, vol. 21 (1940); Earl Pomeroy, "California, 1849-1860: Politics of a Representative Frontier State," *California Historical Society Quarterly*, vol. 32 (1953); and Lately Thomas, *Between Two Empires: The Life Story of California's First Senator, William McKendree Gwin* (1969). —J. F.

H

Hafen, LeRoy R[euben] (1893-   ). Historian. Hafen was born in Bunkerville, Nevada, grew up in Utah, graduated with a bachelor's degree from Brigham Young University in 1916, and in 1924 was awarded the doctorate from the University of California at Berkeley, where he studied under Herbert E. Bolton. Shortly afterward Hafen assumed the post of Colorado state historian at the State Historical Society of Colorado, which he held for thirty years. During this period he edited *Colorado Magazine* and directed the activities of the Colorado State Museum. Author of numerous books and articles on Colorado and western history, he collaborated with his wife, Ann Woodbury Hafen, in many enterprises, including the editing of The Far West and the Rockies series. He was visiting professor at the University of Glasgow, Scotland, in 1947-48, and during 1950-51 did research at the Henry E. Huntington Library as a recipient of a Rockefeller fellowship. Upon his retirement from the State Historical Society of Colorado in 1954, Dr. Hafen joined the faculty of Brigham Young University.

See LeRoy R. Hafen, *The Joyous Journey of LeRoy R. and Ann W. Hafen: An Autobiography* (1943); and *LeRoy R. and Ann W. Hafen: Their Writings and Their Notable Collection of Americana Given to Brigham Young University Library* (1962).—M. B.

Haida Indians. See INDIANS OF THE NORTHWEST COAST.

Hailey, John (1835-1921). Idaho politician. Hailey grew up in his native Tennessee and Missouri and crossed the Plains to Oregon at the age of eighteen. Two years later he was an officer in the Rogue River Indian war. In 1862 he joined the gold rush to the Idaho mines, where he decided to become a packer and stage driver. After building up a substantial stage line, he went into stock raising. One of the most popular men in Idaho Territory, Hailey was persuaded in 1872 to serve a term in Congress as a Democrat but in 1874 decided he didn't want another term, although he easily could have been reelected. He was willing in 1880 to try for the territorial legislature, where he served as president of the council. After the Republicans unexpectedly took control of Idaho in the election of 1882, he was thought to be the only Democratic candidate who had a chance to win a seat in Congress. He was again persuaded to run and was elected to a second congressional term in 1884. In this year the anti-Mormons took over the Idaho legislature and disfranchised every Mormon in the territory; in 1886, therefore, Hailey (who was not a Mormon) no longer could rely upon the solid Mormon-Democratic vote and had to straddle the Mormon issue in his reelection campaign for Congress so as not to lose too many Democratic votes. He still ran strong, and his North Idaho supporters concluded that he was defeated only by fraud in their part of the territory.

After his first and only defeat, Hailey retired from politics but accepted a position as warden of the state penitentiary in 1899. In 1907 he took over the management of the Idaho State Historical Society when that agency became a state-supported government corporation and continued in charge for the rest of his life. In 1910 Hailey published his *History of Idaho*, a useful compilation of information relating to pioneer days in Idaho.—M. W.

Hale, John D. (1847-1929). Freighter and cattleman. Born in Old Town, Grayson County, Virginia, the fourth child of a family of eleven children, Hale was the son of a farmer and stockman. When he was twenty years old, he went west to Omaha, Nebraska, where he lived with a distant relative, the first postmaster of Omaha. From Omaha he moved to Cheyenne, Wyoming; then to Montana, where he mined; and finally to Salt Lake City, Utah. When the Black Hills gold rush began in 1876, Hale and a younger brother organized a freight outfit consisting of seven 8-yoke teams of oxen. Each team could handle two or three wagons. The Hales loaded their wagons with merchandise and food, and after acquiring nearly five hundred hogs, eighty-four cows, and eighteen horses, set out from Norfolk, Nebraska, for the Black Hills. They made camp near Deadwood and quickly sold all the merchandise and livestock.

In 1877 Hale helped move the Sioux Indians, under Chief Spotted Horse, from Camp Sheridan to the Ponca agency on the Niobrara River in Nebraska. Knowing that Spotted Horse and his people were not satisfied with their new home and would ask the Indian Bureau to move them back again, Hale secured two jobs: moving them back and supplying them both on the journey and after they had settled at the Rosebud agency. Hale then set out for Deadwood in the spring of 1879 with more supplies and livestock. Next Hale turned to ranching near Tilford, South Dakota, stocking the ranch with forty-five hundred sheep bought in Denver. Despite a severe setback when the harsh winter of 1880-81 killed over two thousand of his sheep, he eventually enlarged his ranching operations in both South Dakota and Crook County, Wyoming, where he raised cattle and horses. Always willing to take a chance, in 1893 Hale decided to enter an endurance horse race in which the first rider to cover the distance from Chadron, Nebraska, to Chicago would win a total of fifteen hundred dollars. The two horses Hale selected for his rider, John Berry, won the 1,050-mile race in thirteen days and sixteen hours.

In 1905 Hale and others from South Dakota were invited by President Theodore Roosevelt to ride in the inaugural parade up Pennsylvania Avenue and to attend the banquet at the White House. At the banquet Hale was introduced as a dyed-in-the-wool Democrat. A shrewd man and a colorful figure, Hale epitomized the western ranching life that Roosevelt admired.—H. R. L.

Haley, James Evetts (1901-). Cattleman and historian. Born near Belton, Texas, and raised on the family ranch near the town of Midland, Texas, Haley became a cowhand at the age of fifteen, a broncbuster as sixteen, and an accomplished rider at nineteen. His writing experience began while he was attending West Texas State University at Canyon, where he worked for the school's newspaper and annual. His first published article, "Cowboys' Part in Plains History Was Vital," appeared in *The Cattleman* (December 1925). While doing graduate work at the University of Texas, he continued submitting historical pieces to *The Cattleman*, as well as to other publications. He became the first secretary and editor for the Panhandle-Plains Historical Society and was instrumental in establishing the well-known museum at Canyon (regarded in museum circles as the best in regional classification and containing perhaps the largest collection of cattle-range materials to be found in the world).

In 1929 Haley joined the University of Texas' history department, where his primary duties were to locate and acquire historical items for the university library. For seven years he toured throughout Texas, persuading owners of historical documents to make donations. In 1931 he was named historian of the Texas and Southwestern Cattle Raisers' Association.

Haley left the university in 1936 and, with the exception of a three-year period during which he was the director of the Institute of Americanism, devoted his life to cattle ranching and writing.

He first managed the Zeebar Cattle Company, south of Navaho, Arizona, with holdings of three hundred thousand acres of range in Arizona, New Mexico, and Texas, and later became general range manager for the J. M. West Ranch, one of the major independent cattle operations in Texas. In 1941 Haley himself acquired ranches on the Pecos and Canadian rivers in Texas and, in partnership with his son Evetts, Jr., on the Arkansas River in Oklahoma.

Haley's own experiences as a rancher, his straightforward narrative style, and his inquiring mind all contributed to his reputation as an outstanding cow-country historian. His first book, *The XIT Ranch of Texas and the Early Days of Llano Estacado* (1929), elicited the comment from cow-country historian J. Frank Dobie that though many "ranches have afforded bases for various range country histories. . . . this is tops." *Charles Goodnight: Cowman and Plainsman* (1936) is thought to be the best biography ever written about a cowman. These books were followed by a number of other successes, such as *George W. Littlefield, Texan* (1943) and *Charles Schreiner, General Merchandise* (1944), both fine cow-country sagas, *Story of the Shamrock* (1954), and *A Texan Looks at Lyndon* (1964). Haley also edited a number of range-life memoirs, including Bill Arp Oden's *Early Days on the Texas-New Mexico Plains* (1963).

In 1956 Haley sought but failed to obtain the Democratic nomination for governor of Texas.

See Chandler A. Robinson, *J. Evetts Haley, Cowman-Historian* (1967).—J. C. D.

Hall, Frank (1836-1917). Colorado newspaperman. Hall was born in Poughkeepsie, New York. In 1859 he went to St. Louis, where he managed a harness and saddlery house before moving to Colorado in spring 1860 to prospect for gold. While in Black Hawk, Colorado, he became associated with Ovando J. Hollister in the publication of the *Mining Journal*, later buying an interest in the Central City *Miners' Register*. Since he had received thorough military training in New York, he organized a volunteer militia at Black Hawk known as the Elbert Guards. He was elected to the house of the Colorado territorial legislature in 1865 and in 1866 was appointed territorial secretary, a post he held until 1874, often serving as acting governor in the absence of the chief executive. From 1878 to 1880 he served as adjutant general of the state. Moving to Denver in 1877, he subsequently became editor of the *Daily Evening Times*. During the years 1889-95 his four-volume *History of the State of Colorado* was published, for which he is best remembered today. In 1895 Hall became mining editor of the Denver *Post*, a position he held until his death.—M. B.

Hall, James (1793-1868). Historian and novelist. Hall, born in Philadelphia, Pennsylvania, received an excellent, though informal, education, primarily under the direction of his mother. When he was twelve he was sent to an academy, but disliked it so intensely that he was allowed to continue his studies at home. During the War of 1812 he joined the Washington Guards, the first regiment of volunteers from Philadelphia. After the end of hostilities he was a member of Stephen Decatur's expedition against the Algerian pirates, but his ship arrived too late for him to see action in this campaign. He was subsequently stationed at Newport, Rhode Island, and in 1817 was posted to Pittsburgh. While in the army Hall continued his study of law, which he had briefly undertaken before the War of 1812, and when in 1818 he was admitted to the bar he resigned his commission. In 1820 he moved to Illinois, where in quick succession he was made prosecuting attorney and elected circuit judge. In 1828 Hall became state treasurer, a position he held until 1833. In that year he moved to Cincinnati and resided in Ohio until his death.

Hall had an enormous capacity for work. In addition to a strenuous legal and political career he found time to serve as trustee of the infant Illinois College in Jacksonville (founded 1835), to edit (1833-35) the *Western Monthly Magazine*, and to write a number of historical and geographical texts in addition to a considerable body of fiction. His nonfictional works include two semiautobiographical accounts of western life, *Letters from the West* (1828) and *Sketches of History, Life, and Manners in the West* (1834-35), his once-famous *History of the Indian Tribes of North America* (coauthored with Thomas L. McKenney; 1836-44), and his enormously popular *Notes on the Western States* (first published in 1836 as *Statistics of the West*). Though these books are of necessity limited in their interest to the present-day reader, they are still valuable to the social historian and to the curious antiquarian.

Hall said that the sole intention of all his writing was to convey accurate information about the scenery and population of the western country. As a result, his fiction is not greatly different from his nonfiction. Both the strengths and weaknesses of his novels may equally be traced to his overwhelming desire to impart true information about the West in order to counteract the erroneous impressions current at the time. His writing tends to be anecdotal, and often—as in his short novel *The Harpe's Head* (1833)—combines an account of an actual event with a plot very clearly, if often ineptly, designed to hold the attention of readers who, he felt, would be put off by a straightforward historical chronicle. His style is vigorous, colloquial without being crude, cultivated, but certainly not bookish. It is dated more by its reliance on romantic cliché than anything else; he is, for instance, excessively fond of beginning a story or a chapter of a novel with the figure of a solitary horseman etched against the sky, an image which has long lost whatever evocative power it once presumably possessed. His great failure as a writer of fiction lies in his inability to transform the raw material of history into successful imaginative expression. As a result, the stories he tells in *Legends of the West* (1832), *The Soldier's Bride and Other Tales* (1833), and *The Romance of Western History* (1857) are read today primarily by those with antiquarian inclinations.

See John T. Flanagan, *James Hall, Literary Pioneer of the Ohio Valley* (1941); Randolph C. Randall, *James Hall, Spokesman of the New West* (1964); and William H. Venable, *Beginnings of Literary Culture in the Ohio Valley* (1891).—J. K. F.

Hallett, Moses (1834-1913). Colorado judge. Hallett was born in Galena, Illinois, attended Rock River Seminary and Beloit College, and commenced the study of law in Chicago at the age of twenty. He was admitted to the bar in 1857 and practiced in Chicago for three years before going to Colorado in 1860 upon hearing reports of the gold discoveries. Although he engaged in mining for a short time, he soon resumed the practice of law in Denver. A member of the council of the territorial legislative assembly in 1864 and 1865, he was appointed chief justice of the Colorado territorial supreme court in 1866, remaining in this position until statehood was achieved in 1876. The next year he was appointed judge of the United States district court and served in this capacity until his retirement in 1906. In 1892 he became the first dean of the University of Colorado law school in Boulder.

During his tenure as territorial chief justice, Hallett handed down numerous landmark decisions, particularly in the areas of mining and irrigation. In legalizing miners' union organizing, he stated, for example, that claims must comply with the laws of the mining districts in which they were located. Hallett diverged from the English common law doctrine of riparian rights when he stated: "In a dry and thirsty land it is necessary to divert the waters of streams from their natural channels, in order to obtain fruits of the soil, and this necessity is so universal and imperious that it claims recognition of the law." Hallett's opinion and the subsequent codification of this "doctrine of prior appropriation," which permitted diversion of water from rivers and streams without regard to ownership of the land along the stream banks, led to its being termed the "Colorado system."

Hallett's career is treated in John D. W. Guice, "Moses Hallett, Chief Justice," *Colorado Magazine* (Spring 1970). A biographical sketch is in *Portrait and Biographi-*

cal Record of Denver and Vicinity, Colorado (1898).—M. B.

Hamilton, William T. (1822-1908). Mountain man, fur trapper, merchant, and guide. Hamilton was born in England, but his parents migrated to the United States in 1824. Hamilton grew up in St. Louis and was undoubtedly affected by the color and excitement of the fur trade in its heyday. As a youth Hamilton suffered from ill health, and so, when his father arranged for William S. (Bill) Williams to take young Hamilton to the mountains in order to recover, Hamilton accepted the opportunity to go west with alacrity. He was gone three years, trapping with Williams and others along the North Platte and in the Green River valley.

Hamilton joined the California gold rush in 1849 but was soon engaged in chasing and killing California Indians whose situation had been made desperate by the white invasion of their lands. Hamilton, who soon earned the nickname "Wildcat Bill," appeared as an Indian fighter in the Rogue River War of 1855 and in the Modoc War a year later. He proved an excellent scout and was unusually adept at sign language. Later he served as a spy for Colonel George Wright, to whom he reported the activities of the Blackfoot, the Nez Percé, and the Crow during the late 1850s.

In 1858 Hamilton set up a trading post on the site of present-day Missoula, Montana, and in 1864 he began trading at Fort Benton, Montana, and serving as sheriff of Chouteau County. He was an Indian agent to the Blackfoot, with special orders to intercept the whiskey trade, in 1873; three years later he served as a scout to General George Crook in the Sioux campaign and fought in the battle of the Rosebud. Hamilton eventually settled on the Stillwater River at Columbia, Montana, and from that base acted as a guide to hunting and scientific parties. Shortly before his death he moved to Billings, Montana.

Hamilton's reminiscences, which appeared as *My Sixty Years on the Plains, Trapping, Trading, and Indian Fighting* (1905), actually details only the years 1842-60, but it is a valuable source for a history of the declining years of the fur trade. Hamilton's account is sometimes inaccurate and his cruel treatment of Indians seems indefensible, but it remains an honest and arresting story.

A new edition of *My Sixty Years* (1960) contains a useful biographical introduction by Donald J. Berthrong. See also L. Custer Kern, "William T. Hamilton," in LeRoy R. Hafen, ed., *The Mountain Men and the Fur Trade of the Far West*, vol. IX (1972).—G. B. D.

Hancock campaign (1867). On the basis of rumors that the Cheyenne planned to attack Kansas settlements and transportation routes, Major General Winfield Scott Hancock led about one thousand four hundred men onto the Kansas plains in April 1867. On April 12, he conferred with Cheyenne chiefs at Fort Larned, telling them that the soldiers would fight if the Cheyenne wanted war; if not, the Cheyenne were to abide by the terms of the treaty of 1865, which assigned them to lands south of the Arkansas River. Hancock then moved his command to the vicinity of a Cheyenne camp on the Pawnee Fork of the Arkansas River. Discovering that the Indians had abandoned the camp, Hancock sent Lieutenant Colonel George Armstrong Custer with part of the Seventh Cavalry in pursuit. The Indians gave Custer the slip, but he learned that they had burned a stage station on the Smoky Hill route. When Hancock received that report, he burned the village and marched to Fort Larned, where the campaign came to an end in May.

Meantime, Custer's cavalry had been immobilized when it reached Fort Hays, Kansas, because forage—which was to have been stored there for him—had not arrived. During that time, the Indians began attacking throughout the area. Ultimately, Custer took the field under orders from Lieutenant General William Tecumseh Sherman and ranged through Kansas and Nebraska, engaging Indians several times. His part of the campaign came to an end in July, when he went to Fort Riley, Kansas, to see his wife and obtain supplies. He was court-martialed for absenting himself from his command without leave and for abusing men and animals, and sentenced to suspension from rank and pay for one year.

An Indian agent with Hancock, E. W. Wynkoop, severely criticized Hancock's management of the campaign. Others blamed Hancock and Custer for the Indian depredations that spread along the Kansas frontier that summer.

The controversial Hancock campaign remains controversial in the literature. Having come under severe criticism, Hancock defended himself in a pamphlet, *Reports of Major General W. S. Hancock upon Indian Affairs with Accompanying Exhibits* (c.1867), which at least has the merit of centralizing documents without which the episode would not be clear. Another contemporary account is George Armstrong Custer, *My Life on the Plains* (1952), in which Custer as usual makes a hero of himself. More recent appraisals are to be found in Donald J. Berthrong, *The Southern Cheyennes* (1963); and William H. Leckie, *Military Conquest of the Southern Plains* (1963).—O. K.

handcart companies (1865-1860). Mormon system of overland transportation. Since money was scarce following the harsh winter of 1855-56, the Mormon leadership in Utah needed to devise new methods by which to transport poor emigrants from the Missouri valley to Salt Lake City. Brigham Young conceived the idea that incoming converts, mostly British and Scandinavian immigrants, could walk across the Great Plains, thus avoiding the cumbersome and costly plan of outfitting wagon trains; the pioneers traveling in wagon trains had generally walked across the Plains anyway. Young reasoned that the people could pull enough food by handcart across the Plains to survive the three-month journey. The jumping-off point was Iowa City, Iowa, and in 1856 the first of five companies departed. In 1859 the point of departure was changed to Florence, Nebraska. The first three were successful, but the last two, Martin's in July and Willie's in August, were caught in a blizzard on the Wyoming plains. About two hundred died before relief arrived. Over the next four years, a few handcart companies made their way to Salt Lake City, but the practice was ended in 1860.

During the years of its operation, about three thousand people walked across the Plains in this manner.

See LeRoy R. Hafen and Ann W. Hafen, *Handcarts to Zion* (1960).—L. J. A.

Hanna, Marcus A. See GREAT LAKES, MEN OF THE.

Hannibal and St. Joseph Railroad. See BURLINGTON NORTHERN RAILROAD.

Hansen, Marcus Lee (1892-1938). Historian. Born in Neenah, Wisconsin, Hansen was educated at Central College, Iowa, the State University of Iowa, and Harvard University. His studies were interrupted for a year's army service during World War I. Hansen then returned to Harvard, where Frederick Jackson Turner had first aroused his interest in immigration and westward population movements. Hansen was also greatly influenced by Arthur M. Schlesinger, Sr., who was then one of the early pioneers in American social history. Schlesinger, like Turner, believed immigration to be one of the most significant and neglected topics in American history, as he was wont to point out in his seminars and in his *New Viewpoints in American History* (1922). Hansen became his most profound student. Meanwhile, he had begun to teach at Smith College, where he remained until 1928, when he joined the history department of the University of Illinois.

Hansen's publications were varied. His first monograph, *Old Fort Snelling, 1819-1858* (1918), was followed in 1920 by *Welfare Campaigns of Iowa*, part of a Chronicles of World War I series edited by Benjamin F. Shambaugh. His interest in immigration was first reflected in *German Schemes of Colonization before 1860* (1924), a short monograph stemming from his graduate studies.

Then Hansen planned an ambitious three-volume study on the history of immigration to America, primarily from Central Europe. To prepare himself for this ambitious and path-breaking work, Hansen perfected his mastery of at least eight foreign languages and conducted an extensive search of European archives, diaries, and newspapers between 1922 and 1927. At that time he estimated that it would take him at least twenty years to complete his work, for he was not merely interested in personalities of leaders, but in the masses. For more than a decade after 1927 Hansen worked on his project, which was left unfinished at the time of his early death. In 1935 he did summarize his findings in a series of eight lectures at the University of London on "The Influence of Nineteenth-Century Immigration upon American History."

After his death, former friends of Hansen began to edit some of his unfinished works. Arthur M. Schlesinger, Sr., helped to bring out what had been planned as the first volume in the trilogy, *The Atlantic Migration: A History of the Continuing Settlement of the United States* (1940), which deals with the period between 1492 and 1860. This work won the Pulitzer Prize in history for 1940. In this same year John Bartlett Brebner edited *The Mingling of Canadian and American Peoples* (1940). In 1941 Schlesinger edited Hansen's University of London lectures of 1936, which appeared as *The Immigrant in American History* (1941). Another study on which Hansen had been a principal investigator appeared in 1943: the *Linguistic Atlas of New England*, a demographic study of the type that Turner had urged upon frontier historians.

See Oscar Handlin's introduction to *The Atlantic Migration: A History of the Continuing Settlement of the United States* (1961).—G. D. N.

Hardin, John Wesley (1853-1895). Gunman. Although not as famous in the annals of western gunplay as Billy the Kid, Jesse James, or Wild Bill Hickok, Wes Hardin was the greatest killer of them all. In a relatively short time span, from 1868, when he was only fifteen, to 1878, Hardin killed well over twenty men.

Hardin entered his teen years in central Texas during the early Reconstruction period, a locale and time among the most violent in American history. Born at Bonham, Texas, of a highly respectable family (his father was a Methodist circuit rider, and a great-uncle signed the Texas Declaration of Independence), young Hardin was traumatized—according to family tradition—by a tragedy typical of this brutal age. Shortly after the war the wife, son, and daughter of a maternal uncle were massacred by Unionist miscreants; the women were also raped and the house burned. Although the massacre party did not include Negroes, highly partisan southern sympathies and raging anti-Negro prejudice set Hardin on his murderous career. In 1868 he killed his first man, an ex-slave, with his own .44 caliber pistol, which he first carried as an eight-year- old. This was not his first violent action, however; he had already stabbed, nonfatally, a boy in a schoolyard quarrel over a girl.

Hardin's murderous career must be understood in terms of the turmoil of Texas politics and life during the Reconstruction era that came to a climax during the turbulent administration of Governor E. J. Davis (1870-74). Adhering to Davis's Reconstruction regime was a faction of white Unionists and Radical Republicans allied with former slaves and bolstered by the strong arm of state police force composed of both whites and blacks. The biracial Davis coalition aroused the strong opposition of those white Texans (including Hardin) who were Confederate-minded, Democratic in politics, and hotly prejudiced against blacks; many of the members of this Old South faction had suffered abusive treatment by the racially mixed state police force. Hardin's background made him an enthusiastic and fearless enlistee in the anti-Reconstruction bloc, and many of his killings stemmed from the complex of political and racial hatreds generated by these postwar troubles. The large anti-Reconstruction, white racist element of the Texas population elevated Hardin to heroic status. His killings were excused as being either in the interest of a good cause (hostility to Reconstruction and to blacks) or in self-defense. While charges of psychopathy have been leveled against such notable frontier killers as the Earp brothers and Billy the Kid, no such accusations have been made against Hardin. By the standards of strife-ridden Texas of the 1860s and 1870s Hardin was entirely sane, and to his thousands of sympathizers his killings were honorable.

At the peak of his gun-slinging career in 1871 Hardin was lithe and athletic with a hair-trigger temper (ready to deal fatally with foolhardy attempts to challenge his increasingly famous prowess as a gunman), a gift for horsemanship, and a penchant for gambling, drinking, and good times. Proud of his own reputation, Hardin cared little for the fame of others. Thus, he was unawed by Wild Bill Hickok, whom he encountered in Abilene, Kansas, in 1871. Hardin brashly ignored the local regulation (enforced by Wild Bill as town marshal) against carrying guns in town. When Hickok attempted to disarm him Hardin faced down Wild Bill in a tense confrontation (so Hardin claimed; Hickok partisans have disputed this).

Hardin's victims lacked the good sense to back down before the youthful killer. The most notable of Hardin's typically indiscreet opponents were Jack Helm and Charles Webb. Helm, a famous bravo, was a former captain in the hated state police force who had taken a prominent part on the Sutton side in the frightful Sutton-Taylor feud of central Texas (1867-77). In the Sutton-Taylor feud the Sutton faction was generally pro-Reconstruction, while the large Taylor group (which Hardin joined) was anti-Reconstruction. Helm had harried the Taylor connection for some years, and Hardin, among others, was thirsting for revenge. The end came for Helm in front of a blacksmith shop in the little town of Albuquerque, Texas, on May 17, 1873, when Hardin blasted Helm with a shotgun as the latter advanced on Hardin's friend and fellow feudist, Jim Taylor. All of this happened in the midst of a crowd of Helm's supporters, none of whom dared retaliate against Hardin. As Hardin later wrote, "The news soon spread that I had killed Jack Helms [sic] and I recieved many letters of thanks from the widows of the men whom he had cruelly put to death. Many of the best citizens of Gonzales and DeWitt counties patted me on the back and told me that was the best act of my life."

Even more dramatic was Hardin's slaying of deputy sheriff Charles Webb in the wild town of Comanche, Texas, on May 26, 1874. Encouraged by Comanche's anti-Hardin citizenry (who had been angered by the land-fraud activities of John Wesley's brother, Joe, a county resident), Webb maneuvered to get the drop on Hardin at sundown (after a festive day of horse races in which Hardin had been a big winner) as the two walked the dusty street toward a saloon while Webb falsely denied to Hardin any hostile intent. The arrogant, overconfident Webb miscalculated. Webb drew his pistol first when Hardin turned for an instant, but in one lightning-fast action Hardin jumped aside, drew, and put a fatal shot in Webb's head before Webb could get off his late shot, which only wounded Hardin.

The killing of Webb catapulted Hardin (who by then had a wife and growing family) into a refugee life in Florida and Alabama. Captured in the latter state, he was tried, convicted, and in 1878 put in the Texas state prison. Up to then Hardin had enjoyed his wild life, but entry into prison began a tragic period that was to end in ignominious death years later in El Paso. While Hardin was in prison his beloved wife died. After his release in 1892 he resumed life, nonviolently, with his three children. He had taught himself law in prison, but his entry into politics in Gonzales, Texas, came to nothing.

A marriage to young Callie Lewis on January 8, 1895, ended mysteriously in separation after only a few hours spent together after the wedding. Whatever the cause of the rupture, the bride's family did not blame Hardin and unsuccessfully urged Callie to rejoin her husband. A failure in spite of his best efforts, Hardin drifted on, without his children, to violent El Paso, where he led a life of dissipation, took up with Beulah Morose—a bosomy blonde of low reputation—and for the only time in his life used his gun to rob for money. While standing at the Acme bar on the night of August 19, 1895, Hardin was fatally shot in the back by John Selman, an El Paso policeman and old-time professional Texas gunman, who apparently shot down Hardin to enhance his own fame as a gunfighter. In his last months in El Paso, Hardin had spent his leisure hours (which were many, for few calls came for his legal services) in the composition of his autobiography. It was published posthumously and, by virtue of its well-written, graphic account of Hardin's exploits and the violent spirit of the time, is now recognized as a classic in western Americana. Had he grown to manhood in a quieter time and place, Hardin might have had a respectable career as a lawyer or politician, for he had the intellectual gifts for both.

See John Wesley Hardin, *The Life of John Wesley Hardin as Written by Himself* (1896, repr. 1961); Lewis Nordyke, *John Wesley Hardin: Texas Gunman* (1957); and C. L. Sonnichsen, *Pass of the North: Four Centuries on the Rio Grande* (1968).—R. M. B.

Hard Labor, Treaty of (1768). British southern district Indian superintendent John Stuart assembled representatives of the Cherokee tribe at Hard Labor Creek in South Carolina, October 13-17, 1768, to discuss with them the boundary between their hunting lands and Virginia, which had been left indefinite by the Treaty of Augusta of 1763. At the conference the North and South Carolina Indian boundaries of 1766-67 were ratified, and a Virginia boundary agreed to. The new Virginia line was to be run from the point where the North Carolina boundary survey had ended at Chiswell Lead Mine, straight northwestward to the mouth of the Kanawha River. Because this agreement was not made until late in October, it was agreed that the actual survey of the line across the rugged mountain country would not be undertaken until May 10, 1769.

Before the Hard Labor line could be established, however, there arose a dispute between Virginia and John Stuart and between Stuart and the private land speculators. Stuart had the backing of Lord Hillsborough and the English Board of Trade. The problem was that the Hard Labor line cut off Virginia settlers who had overstepped the Proclamation Line of 1763 and settled west of the Kanawha River. Virginia was anxious to push the negotiated Indian line south and west in order to take in a large slice of territory and to govern the outlying settlers. The Hard Labor line was subsequently revised as a result of this complication by the terms of the Treaty of LOCHABER, made in South Carolina, October 21-22, 1770, where a new line was agreed upon enclosing the white settlements west of the Kanawha.

See John R. Alden, *John Stuart and the Southern Colonial Frontier, 1754-75* (1944); and Louis De Vorsey, Jr., *The Indian Boundary in the Southern Colonies, 1763-1775* (1966).—T. D. C.

Harmar, Josiah (1753-1813). Soldier. Born in Philadelphia, Harmar began his military career with the Third Pennsylvania Regiment in 1776. By the end of the American Revolution, in which he served under both generals George Washington and Henry Lee, he had attained the rank of colonel. Harmar was made commander of the army on August 12, 1784, and following the approval of the peace treaty by Congress, he carried the ratification to France.

Returning home as the commander of the force stationed on the Ohio frontier, Harmar encountered difficulties with both white and Indian residents of the area. In 1785, in accordance with the treaties of Fort Stanwix and Fort McIntosh, he was ordered by Congress to expel the frontiersmen swarming across the Ohio into lands claimed by the Indians. Harmar was only partially successful in his attempt to remove these

"banditti whose actions are a disgrace to human nature." As was often the case in such frontier conflicts of interest, the army abandoned its attempts to control white settlement and instead turned its guns on the Indians, who opposed the encroachment on their lands and repudiated the obviously worthless treaties.

Rather than allow the frontier adventurers to carry on private guerrilla warfare with the Indians, Congress instructed Harmar to lead a formal expedition against the rebellious red men. The expedition was a dismal failure. In the autumn of 1790 Harmar marched northward from Fort Washington, but he moved so slowly that the Indians were able to retreat into the forests surrounding the Maumee River. Failing to find any Indians, Harmar began to march southward, but then waited while a detachment of 400 men slipped back toward the Maumee in the hope of surprising the Indians; instead, they were ambushed and lost 183 men. The Indians followed upon Harmar's retreat, raiding the struggling Ohio settlements at will. Harmar's failure was duplicated by another expedition led by Arthur St. Clair, and not until 1794 were the Indians subdued by a force led by General Anthony Wayne.

In 1791 Harmar was redeemed by a court of inquiry into the failure of his expedition. He continued to command the army until March 1791. Harmar resigned from the service in 1792 and spent his last years of official life as adjutant general of Pennsylvania.

See Ray A. Billington, *Westward Expansion* (1967). —R. B. W.

Harney, William Selby (1800-1889). Soldier. General Harney was labeled the "military Humboldt" of America by his biographer, and even those most critical of this officer's escapades must admit that he was well-traveled. Harney's career as a front-line soldier provided him with the opportunity to do battle on virtually every frontier his nation had to offer—from the Florida Everglades to the Oregon forests.

Born and raised near Nashville, Tennessee, Harney was groomed for a naval career by his mother but went against her wishes and joined the First Infantry in 1818. He distinguished himself in numerous expeditions against the Indians of Florida, and by the end of the Seminole campaign in 1840 had attained the rank of brevet colonel. Shortly before the outbreak of the Mexican War in 1846, Harney was promoted to colonel of the Second Dragoons, a position that made him ranking cavalry officer under General Winfield Scott. Harney and Scott clashed almost immediately, Harney believing Scott too weak-willed to capitalize on Mexican military incompetence. Scott did not trust his impetuous subordinate and attempted to replace him. Harney refused to step down, and a pointless battle of words ended with the restoration of Harney's command. He justified his reinstatement by performing brilliantly in the Mexican War, and thereby earning the rank of brevet brigadier general.

In August 1854, a foolish young lieutenant at Fort Laramie got himself and thirty other soldiers killed while trying to arrest an Indian in the midst of a large Sioux encampment (see the GRATTAN MASSACRE). Although the arrest was illegal and Lieutenant Grattan entirely to blame for his own fate, public opinion demanded revenge, and the army recalled Harney from a European vacation to lead a punitive expedition against the Sioux. In August 1855 he led a combined force of seven hundred infantry, cavalry, and artillery out of Fort Leavenworth, Kansas, and on September 2 came across the Brulé Sioux village of Little Thunder near Ash Hollow, Nebraska. Surrounding the village by day-break of September 3, Harney refused Little Thunder's attempt to surrender and attacked, destroying the village and killing more than a hundred men, women, and children.

Harney then moved on up the Oregon-California Trail to Fort Laramie, where he counciled with the several Sioux bands that had gathered there at the behest of Indian agent Thomas Twiss. Harney's message was simple: Stay away from the white man's road or suffer the consequences, and surrender those responsible for robberies or murders along the trail. The Sioux were in no position to resist, and several warriors, including the noted Brulé chief Spotted Tail, gave themselves up and were taken to imprisonment at Fort Leavenworth.

At the end of September, Harney left Fort Laramie and marched northeast across the heart of the Sioux hunting grounds to Fort Pierre, arriving there on October 19. This thrust into their previously inviolate country greatly disturbed the Indians, and in November Harney was visited by several large Sioux delegations who pleaded for peace. Convinced by then of the Indians' sincerity, and finally aware of where true responsibility lay for the Grattan affair, Harney called for representatives of all the Sioux tribes to meet at a peace conference in March 1856. At this council the Sioux reaffirmed the Fort Laramie treaty of 1851 and agreed to surrender those warriors still wanted in connection with the Grattan incident. Harney, though stern, demonstrated the benevolent posture of the government by freeing those warriors as soon as they gave themselves up, and by ordering the release of all other hostages. For all its harshness, the Harney campaign was the most effective ever undertaken by the army against the Plains Indians.

Harney's next assignment was to restore order in Kansas and Utah. Kansas was at that time nearly in a state of civil war over the slavery issue; and in Utah the Mormon hierarchy had been flagrantly ignoring federal authority. He proved to be as harsh with the pioneers as he was with the Indians. However, before he could carry out his plan to settle the Mormon question by hanging Brigham Young and his apostles, Harney was sent to Oregon. Never one to avoid a fight, he aroused British animosity by seizing the island of San Juan in 1859. This bit of adventurism caused Harney's recall to St. Louis, where he served as commander of the Department of the West until 1861.

With the outbreak of the Civil War Harney came under suspicion as a southern sympathizer. He was given no active command and was retired in 1863. Harney's retirement years were the only restful, uneventful period of his life, and he died in Florida, where his exploits began.

See L. U. Reavis, *The Life and Military Services of Gen. William Selby Harney* (1878).—R. B. W. and P. R. M.

Harriman, Edward Henry (1848-1909). Financier and railroad executive. Harriman is the chief figure in the railroad consolidation movement at the turn of the century. He was born in Hempstead, Long Island, New York, the son of an Episcopal minister. Disliking school, he became a "broker's boy" at the age of fourteen. He rose swiftly, as a result of a superb talent for stock trading, to a seat on the New York Stock Exchange at twenty-one.

Harriman's interest in railroads began as a result of his highly successful physical and financial rehabilitation of properties owned by his wife's relatives. In 1883 he bought into the Illinois Central Railroad and in close cooperation with its president, Stuyvesant Fish, made it into one of the leading carriers in the country. When Jacob Schiff set out to refinance the bankrupt UNION PACIFIC RAILROAD in 1897, he discovered that Harriman, then still almost entirely unknown outside Wall Street, had inserted himself firmly in the picture. Thus began a close relationship between Harriman and the dilapidated transcontinental line; ten years of prodigious labor by the financier made the Union Pacific one of the best-built and -operated railroads in the country—a foundation of excellence upon which subsequent managements have continued to build. Harriman also restored the Union Pacific's connections in the Pacific Northwest and, desiring to extend the line to the Pacific, tried to buy the old Central Pacific from the SOUTHERN PACIFIC, but it was not for sale. Upon the death of Collis P. Huntington, however, the controlling interest in the entire Southern Pacific became available, and Harriman and his syndicate bought it.

By 1906 it was clear that Harriman aimed at a "community of interests" in the central western and southwestern United States, which would have left only the Hill lines (the Great Northern, the Northern Pacific, and the Burlington lines) in the North and the sickly southwestern lines of George Gould under separate management. Such a sweeping consolidation of railroad interests was more than public opinion would tolerate. When Harriman and James J. HILL, both seeking to control the Burlington route as an entry into Chicago, precipitated the "Northern Pacific corner" panic of 1901 and followed it with plans to pool their holdings in the Northern Pacific and the Burlington in a gigantic holding company to be known as the Northern Securities Company, President Theodore Roosevelt attacked the combine as a violation of the Sherman Anti-Trust Act (see BURLINGTON NORTHERN RAILROAD). In 1904 the Supreme Court ordered the holding company dissolved in a split decision, of which the most illuminating part is Justice Oliver Wendell Holmes's spirited dissent. By then the Union Pacific-Southern Pacific tie was also under fire and was ordered dissolved four years after Harriman's death.

The techniques Harriman used to reorganize railroad properties were so dazzling and so little understood by historians and economists of the Progressive era that it was inevitable that he should have been condemned as a "broker's boy," a mere "money man" who sought illicit, if not illegal, profits to the detriment of the properties and the public they served. That he was one of the leading experts on the physical rehabilitation of railroads has been ignored, despite his brilliant transformations of the Union Pacific and the Alton Railroad. The Alton reorganization was beyond the comprehension even of such a transportation expert as Frank H. Dixon, who could write as late as the 1930s that the Alton affair "was an illuminating example of the manner in which a road may be drained of its resources for the benefit of insiders," thus begging the question of why no legal proceedings were ever brought against Harriman in this case. Forgotten today are Harriman's services to the city of San Francisco following the earthquake of 1906 and his triumphant and expensive fight to save California's Imperial Valley from the incursions of the Colorado River.

Slight of stature, bespectacled, and with a droopy walrus mustache, Harriman was frank to the point of bluntness on the witness stand during the frequent government investigations of his activities, but otherwise refused cavalierly to accede to demands that he justify his policies. It was perhaps Harriman's contempt for public opinion that assured that the "robber baron" myth would be carried over into the twentieth century.

George H. Kennan, *Edward Henry Harriman: A Biography*, 2 vols. (1922), is a touching effort by a close friend to correct the false judgments that Harriman himself ignored. A definitive biography is badly needed.—A. M.

Harris, Daniel Smith. See RIVERMEN.

Harris, La Donna (1931-   ). Comanche civic leader. Harris was born in Cotton County, Oklahoma, and was reared in the home of her grandparents, where the primary language was Comanche. While working to put her husband, who later became a United States senator, through college, she became interested in Indian rights and founded Americans for Indian Opportunity (AIO). Located in Washington, D. C., AIO serves as an Indian information resource center to recommend books and films and to provide teaching materials and statistical data. It has a legal program modeled on the NAACP Legal Defense Fund. Harris was also honorary president and a founder of Oklahomans for Indian Opportunity, a success in many areas of Indian self-help.

Harris was appointed by President Johnson to the National Indian Opportunity Council and was chairman of its committee on urban and off-reservation Indians. On behalf of all minorities, she was a member of the National Rural Housing Conference, the Joint Commission on the Mental Health of Children, the National Steering Committee of the Urban Coalition, and many other organizations.—C. C.

Harrison, William Henry (1773-1841). Soldier and politician. No figure in the history of the American frontier was more a part of the events that resulted in the opening of the early West than Harrison. Born on Berkeley Plantation along the James River in Virginia, this young son of a fairly well-to-do family received part of his education in the Presbyterian college of Hampden-Sydney at Farmville, Virginia. He had an ambition to study medicine after a brief introduction to the subject in Richmond and then went to Philadelphia in 1791 to study in the major center of the science. His interest in medicine quickly faded, however, and he joined the army instead, just after the disastrous defeats of Josiah Harmar and Arthur St. Clair in the Miami country of Ohio.

Harrison was sent west immediately, and in the winter of 1791-92, he experienced some of the rigors of frontier military life. During these months he helped with the construction of Fort Washington on the Ohio River. Later he was sent back to Pittsburgh to help recruit and condition a part of Anthony Wayne's western forces. While there, Captain Ballinger Smith became involved

in a row with a sergeant over the latter's wife, and Harrison was placed in command of the first sublegion commanded by Smith.

In the Miami-Fort Wayne campaign, Harrison went through all the experiences of Wayne's army on the move. In 1794 he was at Fort Greenville and was present at the defeat of the Indians in the battle of Fallen Timbers.

Following his marriage to Anna Symmes, Harrison was advanced to the rank of captain in 1797 and placed in command of Fort Washington. The next year he resigned his commission to enter politics. He was appointed secretary of the Northwest Territory under the governorship of Arthur St. Clair. The story of the relationship of the two is colored with disagreement and rivalry, since Harrison and St. Clair hardly spoke the same political language.

Opposing General St. Clair's son, Arthur St. Clair, Jr., for election as delegate to Congress from the Northwest Territory in 1799, Harrison won by a single vote. In Congress Harrison was in a position to relieve some of the frontiersmen's complaints about the administration of the land laws under the terms of the Northwest Land Ordinance and the revisionary law of 1796. He presented a report that resulted in the formulation of the Harrison Land Law of May 10, 1800, which provided for the sale of lands west of the Muskingum River in Ohio in blocks of 320 acres, while sale of 640-acre sections continued as standard practice east of the river. A minimum price of two dollars per acre was set and the terms of credit liberalized. Four new land districts were established, to be located in Cincinnati, Chillicothe, Steubenville, and Marietta.

Harrison was active in the passage of the division act that separated the Ohio and Indiana territories and placed the location of the territorial capital of Ohio at Chillicothe. In 1800 he was appointed governor of Indiana Territory (see INDIANA, SETTLEMENT OF). In this office he was confronted with the problems of dealing with complex Indian affairs. In the western and northern parts of the territory were located Potawatomi, Wea, Sauk, Foxes, Piankashaw, and Shawnee, all of them in the path of western advance. During Harrison's Indian administration, a series of treaties were made that resulted in the cession of large blocks of lands to settlers. In the Treaty of Fort Wayne (1803), for instance, the Indians surrendered 1,152,000 acres. Obviously, none of these treaties made the Indians happy.

Harrison established the territorial capital in Vincennes. At his estate, Grouseland, he carried on many other activities, some of them self-interested, besides his administrative duties. He was at one time or another miller, farmer, and trader. He was always active in matters pertaining to lands and opened land offices for potential white settlers in Vincennes and Kaskaskia. Twelve years as governor of Indiana Territory turned Harrison into a conservative, partly from age and partly from the struggle to control the territory. From approximately 1810 on he found himself at odds with the rising political leadership of the territory, especially with Jonathan Jennings, who was to play a key role in the organization of the state of Indiana.

Perhaps it was Harrison's good fortune as far as his political future was concerned that the War of 1812 threatened. When the Shawnee under the leadership of TECUMSEH and TENSKWATAWA threatened the peace of the upper Wabash valley, Harrison organized militia forces and began a drive against these Indians. On November 7, 1811, his forces were caught by surprise in the early morning attack at TIPPECANOE. The whites, although not overwhelmingly victorious, were left in control of the field. Tippecanoe was to be associated with Harrison the rest of his life. In 1812 he was elevated to the rank of brevet major general and almost immediately to the rank of brigadier general in the regular army. During the WAR OF 1812 Harrison was the chief western officer in the march toward Detroit following General William Hull's surrender of the fort to the Canadians. In subsequent campaigning Harrison was to become an even greater western hero as a result of his victory over the British and Indians at the battle of the THAMES, October 5, 1813.

In spite of the glorious esteem with which westerners held General Harrison, he had opposition from several sources in Congress. In fact, the United States Senate refused to vote him a gold medal for his military victories until 1818. This became a celebrated cause with some westerners and revealed pettiness on the part of some senators. Following the end of the War of 1812 Harrison retired to his farm at North Bend, Ohio, just below Cincinnati and overlooking the Ohio. He participated in the making of the Spring Wells, or Miami Rapids, treaty with the Northwestern Indians in August 1815 and began anew his political career by being elected to Congress in November 1816. Ultimately his popularity and hero's reputation in the West gained him the presidency in 1840, but he died only six weeks after taking office.

See Freeman Cleaves, *Old Tippecanoe* (1939); Dorothy Burne Goebel, *William Henry Harrison: A Political Biography* (1926); and Bennett H. Young, *The Battle of the Thames* (1903).—T. D. C.

Harrod, James (1742?-1793). Land speculator. There is no definite information about Harrod's birth, except that he was born in Bedford County, Pennsylvania. In 1754 his father died and left his mother, Sarah Moore Harrod, a widow with six sons. The Harrods then moved to Virginia, but they were caught in the path of the Indian attacks in the French and Indian War and moved back to Pennsylvania. In these years Harrod was schooled in the ways of the frontier. He served as a private soldier in Forbes's army in the closing phases of the French and Indian War, and between 1760 and 1774 was engaged in farming with his family, in long hunting, and in trade ventures in the western woods. Harrod became excited over the prospects of acquiring a large block of western lands in 1773 on a trip to the Falls of the Ohio, and in the spring of 1774, with a party of forty-one men, he entered the Kentucky country by way of the Kentucky River. Early in June, Harrod's party began building cabins on the site of what was to be called Harrod's Town (later Harrodsburg). This was the first settlement to be established in Kentucky. The establishment of this station was interrupted by Lord Dunmore's War (1774), but it was resumed in 1775.

Harrod was a quiet man who demonstrated genuine leadership ability. His courage was put to severe tests in the troubled years of the American Revolution, when his fort was threatened several times with destruction. After the war he was engaged in combatting Indian raiders beyond the Ohio, in politics, land-claiming, and

farming. In July 1793 Harrod went into the woods, perhaps in search of the legendary Swift Silver Mine, and never returned. His wife, Ann, told Dr. Christopher Columbus Graham that she suspected her husband had been murdered by a man named Bridges, with whom he had a law suit over some property.

See Richard H. Collins, *History of Kentucky*, 2 vols. (1874); Kathryn Harrod Mason, *James Harrod of Kentucky* (1951); and Charles Talbert, *Benjamin Logan, Kentucky Frontiersman* (1962).—T. D. C.

Harte, [Francis] Bret[t] (1836-1902). Short-story writer. Harte was born in Albany, New York, the son of an intellectual but impoverished schoolteacher who, at the time of his son's birth, was unsuccessfully attempting to conduct a private boarding academy. The Harte family was forced to move several times because of straitened financial circumstances. When in 1845 Harte's father died, the family settled in Brooklyn, New York, until 1853. Harte's family was intellectually interested and his father possessed a good library, in which Bret soon became an avid, if solitary, reader. Though his formal schooling ceased when he was thirteen the habit of reading never left him; indeed Charles Dickens, his favorite childhood author, left an indelible stamp on Harte's own later fiction.

In 1853 his mother moved to California. In 1854 Harte followed her by the Nicaragua route. Not much is known of his life in California from 1854 to 1860. He had a number of odd jobs and wrote desultorily, and at some time during this period picked up whatever knowledge of mining and the frontier gold camps he later possessed. Harte's firsthand experience of mining life has consistently been overemphasized because his stories seem to ask to be read autobiographically; indeed, if one may trust the internal evidence of his stories, Harte's knowledge of mining was sketchy, and his "typical" frontier characters owe more to Dickens' literary treatment of English character types than to his own personal acquaintance.

In 1860 Harte moved to San Francisco, where he became a typesetter for, and occasional contributor to, *The Golden Era*. He soon left this job for more lucrative positions with the government, first, in 1861, with the surveyor-general's office and in 1863 with the mint. He married in 1862. When his first book—a collection of California poems called *Outcroppings*—appeared in 1865, Harte was already well known on the San Francisco literary scene. *Outcroppings* was followed by another book of poems, *The Lost Galleon and Other Tales* (1867), and by *Condensed Novels and Other Papers* (1867), a good-humored collection of parodies, notably "Muck-a-Muck," a burlesque of the *Leatherstocking Tales* by James Fenimore COOPER.

Harte's serious literary career began in 1868, however, when he became editor of *Overland Monthly*. "The Luck of Roaring Camp," the first story he contributed to that periodical, became famous immediately not only in California but in the East. This tale and other equally successful stories were published in book form as *The Luck of Roaring Camp and Other Stories* (1870). On the strength of the literary notoriety of this collection Harte went east in 1871 and signed a one-year, $10,000 contract with *Atlantic Monthly* for his subsequent literary work. But the quality of Harte's later stories proved disappointing to *Atlantic*, and the contract was not renewed. Indeed, the decline of Harte's literary reputation after 1870 was almost as sudden as its meteoric rise. Personally as well, Harte was something of a disappointment in the East, which had expected to find in him a colorful rough-and-ready personage like one of his characters, but found instead a dapper, almost foppish, young man with stylish clothes and a well-trimmed beard.

Another collection of California stories, *Tales of the Argonauts* (1875), was followed by a novel, *Gabriel Conroy* (1876), and two dramas, *Two Men of Sandy Bar* (1876) and *Ah Sin* (1877), the latter a collaboration with Mark Twain, whom he had met in California in 1864. Though Harte earned a good income from these books, he was constantly in financial embarrassment, partly because of his wife's extravagance and partly because of his own inability to manage money. In 1878 Harte accepted the position of consul in Rhenish Prussia, and in June of that year sailed without his family for Europe. He never returned to the United States. In 1880 he was appointed to the more remunerative position of consul at Glasgow, but in 1885 a change of administration caused the loss of his appointment. Until his death from cancer, Harte lived in London, devoting himself to writing and hoping to find once again the financial success he had enjoyed in 1870. Though this eluded him, his literary reputation in England as a chronicler of the American West remained high.

Harte's reputation today depends almost entirely upon his stories of the California gold rush. Though he wrote one novel and throughout his life attempted unsuccessfully to break into the lucrative literary market for drama, he is remembered only for his short stories of life in the mining camps of the forty-niners. These stories have guaranteed in western folklore a place to the picturesque miners, cowboys, prostitutes, and gamblers of this memorable chapter in American history. The bulk of his stories is generally forgotten today, but a few—"Miggles," "Tennessee's Partner," "The Luck of Roaring Camp," "The Iliad of Sandy Bar," and "The Outcasts of Poker Flat"—have earned themselves a permanent place in American letters. His stories, anecdotal and sentimental, concern themselves with social pariahs possessed of too predictable hearts of gold, gamblers (such as Mr. John Oakhurst of "The Outcasts of Poker Flat"), and prostitutes (such as "Miggles") who comment on the hypocrisy of society. Much of Harte's particular social comment has lost its sting—it is difficult to believe, for example, that he had considerable difficulty in getting so innocuous a story as "Miggles" accepted for publication—and a later generation finds his characters too close to romantic and sentimental clichés to take seriously. At his best, however, Harte was a master of plotting and wrote superb scenes of action. He had as well a real comic gift, and some of his humorous scenes are among the best of the often overrated western "folk humor" tradition.

See A. F. Harlow, *Bret Harte of the Old West* (1943); and G. R. Stewart, *Bret Harte, Argonaut and Exile* (1931) and *A Bibliography of the Writings of Bret Harte in the Magazines and Newspapers of California, 1857-1871* (1933).—J. K. F.

Harvey, Ford Ferguson (1866-1928). Restaurant and hotel operator. Born in Leavenworth, Kansas, Harvey left college to work in the family restaurant, one of several that his father had opened along the route of the Atchison, Topeka and Santa Fe Railroad, beginning with an eating house in Topeka, Kansas. Harvey took over the business when his father died in 1901 and expanded it into a chain of hotels and dining rooms on the Santa Fe route, for which he also operated the dining-car service. In 1906 he named the business "Fred Harvey's" after his father.

Headquartered in Kansas City, Missouri, the chain operated the Grand Canyon National Park concessions and such famous hotels as the Bisonte, in Hutchinson, Kansas; the La Fonda, in Santa Fe, New Mexico; the Alvarado, in Albuquerque, New Mexico; and the El Tovar, in Grand Canyon National Park. Western tourism grew rapidly after the depression of the 1890s, and in these cities and in the Union Stations in Chicago, St. Louis, and Kansas City, the name "Fred Harvey" greeted millions of travelers each year until the automobile and the jet airplane all but destroyed the passenger train.

There is no biography of the man who was "Fred Harvey." His life is bound up with the history of the Santa Fe Railroad and the cities along its route.—A. M.

Hastings, Lansford Warren (1818?-?1868). Writer, lawyer, and emigrant guide. Although Hastings' name is forever linked to the DONNER PARTY tragedy, he was, in a broader context, a key participant in several 1840s events that aided the Americanization of the Pacific Coast. Born in Ohio, he made his initial appearance historically in 1842, when he and Elijah White led the first planned overland wagon migration to Oregon. That winter Hastings served as land claims lawyer and surveyed the town of Oregon City for John McLoughlin of the Hudson's Bay Company. He moved on to California that spring. In 1845 he wrote one of the early and more controversial overland guidebooks, *The Emigrants' Guide to Oregon and California*, used by the Donner Party. In 1846 Hastings led the first California emigrants west of Fort Bridger across the Salt Desert cutoff that now bears his name. Upon arrival he enlisted in John C. Frémont's California Battalion, where he served as captain of Company F. In the fall of 1849 he was elec ed a delegate to the state constitutional convention in Monterey. Following that he settled down during the gold-rush years to practice law in northern California. In the late 1850s he moved to Arizona City (present-day Yuma) for reasons of health.

After the outbreak of the Civil War, Hastings devised an elaborate but financially unfeasible plan to capture southern California, Arizona, and New Mexico for the Confederacy. The defeat of the South sent him off to Brazil, where he secured permission to colonize Americans on the Amazon River. In 1867 he was in Alabama, publishing a guidebook to the Amazon region. The next year, after planting a colony of unreconstructed rebels near present-day Santarém, Brazil, he died on the return voyage to Alabama for additional emigrants.

See Dale L. Morgan, ed., *Overland in 1846*, 2 vols. (1963).—T. F. A.

Hauser, Samuel Thomas (1833-1914). Montana businessman and territorial governor. Hauser was born in Kentucky and moved to Missouri in 1854, where he engaged in railroad construction. He went to Montana in 1862 and in 1863 participated in James Stuart's Yellowstone prospecting expedition. In 1864 he built the first Montana silver mill at Argenta, and he later built another at Philipsburg. The first territorial legislature gave him a franchise to operate a toll road from the mouth of the Yellowstone River to Virginia City, and a telegraph line from Virginia City to Salt Lake City. Hauser's varied operations included short-line railroads, electric power transmission, irrigation projects, and partnership in the D-H-S cattle ranch. His First National Bank in Helena and others in Missoula, Virginia City, and Butte financed much of Montana's growth. He participated in the Washburn-Langford-Doane 1870 upper Yellowstone expedition and helped promote the area as the first of the national parks in 1872. In 1885 he was appointed governor of the territory but resigned two years later. A Democrat in politics, he was one of the "Big Four"—with Charles A. Broadwater, William A. Clark, and Marcus Daly—all of whom strongly influenced Montana's business and politics.

See *Progressive Men of the State of Montana* (1901). —M. G. B.

Hawaii. Admitted to the Union in 1959 as the fiftieth state, Hawaii consists of a group islands in the eastern area of the North Pacific, about 2,400 miles from California and about 3,800 miles from Japan. Because of its strategic location as a link between the western hemisphere and Asia, Hawaii has long been called the crossroads of the Pacific and a meeting place of East and West. The islands in the state of Hawaii encompass an area of about 6,400 square miles, about the same as that of Connecticut and Rhode Island combined. The seven main islands, which extend in an arc some 350 miles long in a southeast to northwest direction, are, in order of size, Hawaii (the Big Island), Maui, Oahu (the site of Honolulu and Pearl Harbor), Kauai, Molokai, Lanai, and Niihau (privately owned and a refuge for full-blooded Hawaiians). Of volcanic origin, supplemented by coral deposits, the islands are in fact the peaks of immense mountains, resting on ocean bottom 15,000 feet deep. Hawaii's highest point is Mauna Kea (White Mountain, often topped with snow), 13,784 feet above sea level, on the island on Hawaii. The volcano there is still active, as is another on the island of Hawaii, Mauna Loa (Long Mountain). The Hawaiian Islands have many other mountains (such as Diamond Head, an extinct volcano on Oahu overlooking Waikiki Beach), steep foothills, and deep valleys, fertile with volcanic soil. There are excellent harbors and unsurpassed broad beaches. Fish thrive in the surrounding ocean. The climate is mild. The year-round temperature at sea level is about seventy-five degrees and changes only slightly from month to month. Warm rainfall nourishes Hawaii's luxuriant vegetation, much of it imported at one time or another by traders, missionaries, and other settlers. The rainfall varies considerably from place to place, for Hawaii has much desert land similar to that of Arizona. The rainfall also varies somewhat throughout the year, with storms in the early spring brought by southerly (*kona*) winds. But even in *kona* weather the sun shines for a part of each day. Unlike many other subtropical regions, Hawaii has no snakes. For this and many other reasons, it has become traditional to call Hawaii "the Paradise of the Pacific."

The origins of ancient Hawaii are fairly well known. Polynesians, ancestors of Hawaiians, came from In-

donesia and migrated eastward in the South Pacific mainly in the first millennium B.C. About A.D. 900, many Polynesians in Tahiti moved northward to Hawaii in sturdy double canoes across about 2,700 miles of mostly open water, an odyssey that has few equals in human annals. Both ancient traditions, in oral Hawaiian genealogies later recorded, and modern linguistic and archaeological research support this account. The society of ancient Hawaii was primitive and, on occasion, oppressive. Chiefs ruled in often despotic fashion, with a complex system of taboos, called *kapus* in Hawaii. A vigilant priesthood, which demanded worship of many gods, supported the chiefs. The common people caught fish, raised pigs, and cultivated the starchy root taro to make the nutritious paste called poi. Like their overlords, the people lived in grass houses.

On January 18, 1778, Captain James Cook of the British navy discovered Hawaii by accident during a voyage from Tahiti to the Pacific Northwest. Hawaiians welcomed him warmly, but later murdered him in a brawl on February 19, 1779, on the southern coast of the island of Hawaii. Nonetheless, Cook's discovery encouraged both Westerners and Orientals to come to the islands. Their coming put an end to the epoch of ancient Hawaii.

Up to this point Hawaiian history has no connection with the American frontier; but just as the coming of white Europeans put an end to the old Indian way of life on the North American mainland, the Americans who came to Hawaii engaged in trade with the natives and used the islands as a port of call in the whaling and sealing business. This was followed by a "mission period" in which American missionaries tried to Christianize and educate the natives and even introduced the homestead concept of land in severalty to replace the feudal land system practiced by the Hawaiian monarchy. Later, settlers gradually seized the best native lands for large commercial farms, which then experienced bonanza profits from sugar and pineapple production. Toward the end of the century Americans seized political power and established a republic. Then with the annexation of Hawaii in 1898, American territorial government was introduced, under which many American states had experienced political tutelage. While no native-white wars occurred, many stages of the American takeover bore a remarkable resemblance to certain stages of western history, even to the point of establishing a reservation for full-blooded Hawaiians.

With the help of foreigners, King Kamehameha I (c. 1758-1819) unified the Hawaiian Kingdom by conquest. Meanwhile foreigners made a major and tragic impact on Hawaii. Although they introduced valuable livestock, such as horses, cattle, and goats, and valuable trees and fruits, such as eucalyptus and guava, they also brought measles and smallpox, to which the Hawaiians, long isolated, had slight immunity. Consequently Hawaii's population, estimated at 300,000 in 1778, fell to about 135,000 in 1819. Kamehameha II, who became king in 1819, abolished the *kapu* system, which had provided moral values and, therefore, stability in ancient Hawaii. The abolition of *kapus* brought psychological tensions that accelerated the decline of the Hawaiian people.

In 1820 Protestant missionaries from the United States reached Hawaii and dominated the kingdom for a generation or more. These missionaries, in the new spirit of secular (reformist) Calvinism, not only preached the gospel but also founded schools and promoted agriculture. The Reverend Hiram Bingham became, in effect, dictator of Hawaii until he returned to America in 1840. His successor, the missionary-physician Gerrit P. Judd, who served as prime minister of Hawaii from 1842 to 1853, successfully defended Hawaii from British and French imperialist threats. During this period whaling and ranching were Hawaii's main sources of wealth. Young Hawaiians (Kanakas) often formed part of the crew of sailing ships, and by the 1850s Kanakas were to be found in San Francisco and San Diego. Hawaiian growth necessitated the importation of salmon and timber from Oregon.

After 1854, however, Hawaii's economy shifted toward plantation agriculture, and American missionary political influence declined. The successors of Kamehameha III in the last forty years of the Hawaiian monarchy were unsympathetic to the American mission. Hawaiian politics fell into considerable corruption, abetted by adventurers. This was especially true in the reign of Kalakaua (1874-91), Hawaii's last king, and of his sister, the reactionary and strong-willed Queen Liliuokalani (1891-93), Hawaii's last monarch, who composed the haunting song "Aloha Oe." Nonetheless, the influence of American settlers in Hawaii persisted, particularly after the American development of sugar plantations, which had an ample market in America following the Reciprocity (reciprocal trade) Treaty of 1875. Sugar quickly became Hawaii's biggest source of income. Since the Hawaiian population continued to decline (to about 40,000 in 1890), and the remaining Hawaiians disliked the hard labor on the sugar plantations, enterprising planters brought in many foreign workers, primarily from China, Japan, and Portugal. In so doing, the planters created Hawaii's unique racially mixed population, a pluralism that is echoed in the Southwest and California. At the same time, imaginative descendants of American missionaries and others, in sugar and in enterprises such as shipping, banking, and wholesaling, overthrew the autocratic regime of Queen Liliuokalani and formed a provisional government, which became, in 1894, the Republic of Hawaii under the presidency of the controversial Judge Sanford Ballard DOLE.

After halting complex negotiations, the United States annexed the Republic of Hawaii in 1898, thus continuing American territorial expansion started in the Spanish-American War. Understandably, American residents of Hawaii were delighted. On June 14, 1900, American legislation to make Hawaii a territory of the United States went into effect. The newly formed territory of Hawaii had three basic problems: the establishment and maintenance of stable government; the promotion of an expanding economy; and the Americanization of the diverse racial and ethnic groups in the islands. The new government had difficulties, for like other territories, such as Alaska, it had limited self-rule. Although Hawaiian voters elected the two-house legislature, the president of the United States appointed Hawaii's governor, secretary (lieutenant governor), and high-ranking judges, and the United States Congress had the power to review Hawaii's legislation. The territory of Hawaii, although officially an "integral part" of the United States, had what amounted to colonial status.

Conflicts of interests occurred, with Hawaii's positions on many issues, such as duties on sugar and federal funds for roads, primarily presented by Hawaii's nonvoting delegate to the United States Congress.

While Hawaii's political leaders battled for their rights, Hawaii's business leaders labored to promote the economy, particularly in the monopolistic "Big Five" firms (American Factors, Brewer & Co., Alexander & Baldwin, Castle & Cooke, and The Davis & Co., Ltd.). Sugar, produced with increasingly improved techniques, remained Hawaii's prime crop. Profitable cultivation of pineapples began in 1903 on the plantation of James Drummond DOLE (a cousin of President Dole). By the 1930s pineapples, canned for export, were well established as Hawaii's second most valuable crop. Diversified agriculture, such as truck farming, was less successful mainly because of inexperience. The tourist trade, carried on almost entirely by steamship, had slow beginnings. In 1941 only 32,000 tourists came to the islands. As Hawaii's economy gradually matured, the expanding school system in the islands, supplemented by the Boy and Girl Scouts and similar organizations, brought the American way of life and thought to Hawaii's polyglot population.

Hawaii's gravest crisis came just before 8:00 A.M. (local time) on December 7, 1941. Without a declaration of war Japanese carrier aircraft bombed Pearl Harbor. The Japanese sank or severely damaged twenty-two United States naval vessels. More than twenty-four hundred Americans were killed. The Japanese lost probably fewer than one hundred men. The surprise attack on Pearl Harbor thrust the United States into World War II and gave Hawaii unprecedented importance in world affairs. On Oahu, as on other islands, the first reaction was a combination of shock and fury. In response to appeals by radio, hundreds of residents donated blood for wounded servicemen. Rumors multiplied, particularly those asserting that Americans of Japanese descent had committed numerous acts of sabotage. Later investigation, however, proved that no Hawaiian resident, of whatever racial or ethnic origin, was involved in sabotage. Nonetheless, American military authorities, poorly informed about Hawaii, imposed on the islands severe martial laws, some of which were unconstitutional. Americans of Japanese ancestry were dismissed from Hawaii's National Guard. But they persevered in loyalty to the United States. After long entreaty they were allowed to enter the American army and fought with unsurpassed distinction in Italy and France. World War II made possible Hawaii's later statehood.

Over a million United States troops passed through Hawaii to war zones in the western Pacific, and thousands of Americans came to Hawaii as war workers. After the war many settled in the islands. This situation transformed Hawaii from a dimly known overseas outpost of the American western frontier into an area well known to residents of the American mainland. At last a substantial proportion of mainland Americans came to realize that the territory of Hawaii was really an "integral part" of the United States.

Meanwhile Hawaii faced difficult problems in the postwar years 1945-59. The substantial influx of war workers created a severe housing shortage, especially as wartime needs restricted the allocation of labor and materials necessary to build new dwellings. In addition, the labor union movement, stimulated by the entry of about twenty-five thousand unionized workers during the war, grew increasingly strong, particularly in the International Longshoremen's and Warehousemen's Union. Conservative business leaders (especially in the Big Five firms) fought the unions but lost. Crippling strikes occurred in 1947, 1949, and 1958. In the end, the unions raised wages and brought other benefits to Hawaii's laborers. While these adjustments were taking place, Hawaii's leaders increasingly agitated for statehood, in order to gain a greater degree of self-government and some authority in the affairs of the federal government (such as elected representatives to the United States Congress). The issues and arguments were complex and heated, but Hawaii won the long battle. Congress finally approved statehood in March 1959 and on August 21 President Eisenhower proclaimed Hawaii the fiftieth state of the United States. Hawaii's first elections to Congress reflected the diverse racial composition of its population. The first United States senators were former governor Oren E. Long (Caucasian) and Hiram L. Fong (Chinese), America's first senator of Oriental ancestry. Hawaii's first member of the House of Representatives was Daniel K. Inouye (Japanese), a veteran of World War II who had lost an arm in the Italian campaign.

During the postwar years Hawaii made, on the whole, unprecedented economic progress. In the years 1950-70 the population increased by fifty percent, from 511,000 to just over 750,000. In the same period the gross state product increased almost fivefold, from $830 million to about $4 billion, and per capita income rose from about $1,350 to about $3,900. The most spectacular increase took place in the tourist trade (politely called in Hawaii "visitor industry"). The number of tourists soared from about 46,000 in 1950 to about 1.4 million in 1970. Estimated annual tourist expenditures in Hawaii rose from $18 million to $575 million over these two decades. The increasing influx of tourists created a boom in the construction industry (from $60 million in 1950 to $625 million in 1970), evidenced by the many high-rise hotels and apartments in the crowded Waikiki Beach area and by numerous new resorts on the outlying islands. Real-estate values reached unprecedented heights, with some land in Waikiki selling for well over $100 per square foot.

At the same time Hawaii's economy flourished in many other enterprises, prompting business leaders in the islands to express cautious optimism concerning economic stability. The two great cash crops of the past persisted: sugar (about $300 million in 1970) and pineapples (about $160 million in the same year). Hawaii's many industries, including an oil refinery, cement plants, a brewery, and factories making such items as clothing, chemicals, and furniture, rose in production from about $65 million in 1950 to about $400 million twenty years later. Diversified farming (in order of importance: beef, dairy products, vegetables, eggs, coffee, fruit, poultry, and flowers) rose from about $27 million in 1950 to $58 million in 1970. In addition, in 1970 the United States government spent almost $1 billion in Hawaii, about two thirds of which was allocated to the extensive American military establishment in the islands. Such prosperity transformed Hawaii's economy,

and the accompanying building boom changed somewhat Hawaii's physical appearance.

But away from the tourist resorts, the "old" Hawaii is as beautiful and easygoing as before, with water buffalo cultivating rice paddies less than an hour's drive from Waikiki. Hawaii's mixed population continues to grow. In 1970 about one third of the people were Caucasians, and about the same fraction were of Japanese origin. About one sixth were Hawaiians or part-Hawaiians. The remainder were Chinese, Filipinos, and people from other racial and ethnic groups. Interracial marriage persists and is apparently increasing. Members of Hawaii's mixed population have learned to live in peace, with mutual toleration and respect. (See HAWAIIAN PIDGIN ENGLISH.)

See Gavan Daws, *Shoal of Time: A History of the Hawaiian Islands* (1968); Gerrit P. Judd, *Hawaii: An Informal History* (1961); and Ralph S. Kuykendall, *The Hawaiian Kingdom*, 3 vols. (1938-67).—G. P. J.

Hawaiian pidgin English. Beginning in 1785 Hawaii was frequented by ships from the Western world, predominantly American and British. This soon resulted on the one hand in a small resident foreign population, and on the other in Hawaiians shipping out as seamen. Intercourse was increased by the whaling trade, which was at its height during the period 1840-60. An average of four hundred ships arrived each year; in 1846 about three thousand Hawaiians were serving on foreign vessels—and carrying Hawaiian words into whalers' jargons—and by 1860 foreigners numbered 2,816 as contrasted with 66,984 natives.

In the ports, natives and foreigners learned something of each other's language, with the Hawaiians usually doing most of the learning. In the back districts, as late as the 1870s, only Hawaiian was spoken. A folktale from about 1800 tells how a mischievous Hawaiian coached some rustics in the proper greeting for foreign traders: "Go to hell, you bugger"—with the result that the rustics were promptly kicked out the door. Probably both pidginized Hawaiian and pidginized English (the latter sometimes called *hapa haole*—"half white") were spoken, but neither pidgin became standardized. A traveler in 1873, Isabella Bird Bishop, recorded examples of *hapa haole* on two levels of adequacy and exactness:

Too much chief eat up people! You good Queen, you Bible long time, you good! [Having too many chiefs impoverishes the people. You have a good Queen, you have had the Bible for a long time, your life is good.] But can't go back, we no stay here, water higher all minutes, spur horse, think we come through.

The first missionaries, who arrived in 1820, adopted an alphabet and by January 1822 were printing in Hawaiian. Adult literacy spread rapidly and in the 1830s a primary school system was begun. A small minority of half-white and upper-class Hawaiians became literate in English, and there was continual pressure for the schools to change from Hawaiian to English as the language of instruction. This process was speeded by the importation of Portuguese labor, beginning in 1878, whose children were guaranteed free public schooling. From 1 percent of the school enrollment receiving instruction in English in 1848, the proportion rose to 12 percent in 1860, 25 percent in 1870, 43 percent in 1880, 92 percent in 1890, and 100 percent in 1902.

Without the influx of foreign labor, Hawaii might have become a bilingual country somewhat like Samoa. But shortage of plantation hands led to the importation of thousands of Chinese, Portuguese, Japanese, and Filipinos, and smaller numbers of Micronesians, Puerto Ricans, Koreans, and Spaniards and other Europeans, mostly between 1877 and 1930. Most of these nationalities still are distinct ethnic groups retaining more or less of their languages, but their languages and what is left of Hawaiian are usually spoken with marked impoverishment of vocabulary, some disregard of grammatical and stylistic niceties, and much intermixture of English, to the point where an individual switches from one language to another in the same sentence.

By about 1885 the Hawaiians were outnumbered in their own land and the predominance of English was assured among a polyglot population. It is probable, though not certain, that pidgin English arose on the plantations in the late 1870s, building on the already common *hapa haole* broken English. While each nationality spoke pidgin with its own "accent" and grammatical peculiarities, the various forms of pidgin were enough alike to be generally intelligible. The following is an example of plantation pidgin from the 1910s, an American telling a Chinese gang how to cut sugar cane:

Luna, big boss speak, all men down-below cutch; suppose too much *mauka* cutch, too much sugar *poho—keiki* no-use. Savvy? All men *opala* cutch, one side t'row—byenbye mule men come, *lepo* too much guru. Savvy? [Foreman, the big boss, says for everybody to cut the cane low; if they cut too high, too much sugar is lost and the shoots are worth less. Understand? All men are to cut the trash (leaves) and throw them to one side; when the plowmen come, the soil will be very good. Understand?]

True pidgin, the makeshift second language mainly of immigrants, is approaching extinction. The term *pidgin English* has long been applied in Hawaii to a continuum ranging from actual pidgin to minor deviations from socially acceptable English. Sometimes—as in parts of the West Indies—a pidgin develops into a creole, the native tongue of most of the people—relatively stable—differing substantially in structure from the language on which its lexicon is based. Is any part of the pidgin English continuum a creole? Some scholars, among them Carl and Florence Voegelin, hold that the pidgin passed directly into a substandard dialect, skipping the creole stage. Others believe that parts of the continuum can be identified as pidgin, creole, and dialect respectively, as Stanley M. Tsuzaki wrote in 1966. The answer to the question turns on the extent to which the hard core of pidgin English differs from Standard English.

As the children of immigrants and Hawaiians entered the schools during the period of rapid transition to instruction in English, on the one hand they spoke the broken English of their elders and on the other they learned school English. The intermediate type of speech they arrived at was passed from one generation of children to the next, always getting closer to Standard En-

glish but not losing its identity. Children still speak the most distinctive pidgin; next are working-class young men who value it as a mark of masculinity and distinctiveness as "local boys." For many years pidgin was scorned by the educated. Now it is becoming accepted to some extent as a part of local culture. Some recall with pride its use by island soldiers to confuse German intelligence during World War II. At the same time, heavy immigration from the mainland and increasing familiarity with mainland speech increase the pressure toward the use of Standard English.

When "talking fas[t]" among themselves, islanders are almost unintelligible to the newcomer. The rhythm and intonation of pidgin are distinctive, there are some differences from other American dialects in pronunciation and a few in the use of words, and there are some basic differences in grammar. Completed action is usually marked by *went* or *went go* (formerly by *been*) with regular verbs, and past negative by *never*: "Ronnie wen[t] go jus[t] rap 'm [hit him]. [But] da guy ne[ver] fall down." *Stay* formerly indicated continuing action, as in *He stay eat* (or *eating*), but now its use is less standardized: "You been stay go or what?" ("Did you go or not?") *Get* equals "there is/are": "Get God?" ("Is there a God?") *Had* equals "there was/were": "An'[th]en had dis guy Teapot was comin' up da road in one cah." Proposed action is unmarked: "Us we go." ("Let's go.") But anticipated action is marked by *go'n*: "Us we go'n go." ("We shall go.") The passive is little used: "Da keys lose." ("The keys are/were lost.") Questions do not take inverted word order: "What you did?" ("What did you do?")

Suffixes and words not absolutely necessary to the sense are often dropped, resulting in a concise but sometimes ambiguous style. "Poho ink, no?" ("It's a waste of ink, isn't it?") "Easy for catch; I little mo[re] catch one." ("They're easy to catch; I nearly caught one.") "I [or Me I] no like go; was[te] time [th]asswhy." ("I don't care to go, because it bores me.")

Contrary to popular belief, pidgin English is not a "mixed" language. Almost none of its grammar can be attributed to other languages, although there are a few loan-translations such as *cut the neck* ("behead") from Japanese. Local English has borrowed possibly one thousand Hawaiian words, including names of flora and fauna, and one hundred words from immigrant languages, mainly Japanese and Chinese. These with few exceptions are as common in Standard English as in pidgin. Some, including *aloha, hula, lei, ukulele, luau, poi, muumuu*, and *zori* (a Japanese slipper), have attained national or international use.

See Elizabeth B. Carr, *Da Kine Talk: From Pidgin to Standard English in Hawaii* (1972); John E. Reinecke, *Language and Dialect in Hawaii: A Sociolinguistic History to 1935*, Stanley M. Tsuzaki, ed. (1969); Reinecke and Aiko Tokimasa, "The English Dialect of Hawaii," *American Speech*, vol. 9 (1934); Stanley M. Tsuzaki, "Hawaiian-English: Pidgin, Creole, or Dialect?" *Pacific Speech*, vol. 1 (1966); Tsuzaki and Reinecke, *English in Hawaii: An Annotated Bibliography*, Oceanic Linguistics Special Publication No. 1 (1966); and Carl F. Voegelin and Florence M. Voegelin, "Hawaiian Pidgin and Mother Tongue," *Anthropological Linguistics*, vol. 6 (1964). —J. E. R.

Hawley, James Henry (1847-1929). Idaho lawyer and politician. Leaving his original home in Dubuque,

Iowa, a year after he graduated from high school, Hawley came to Boise Basin, Idaho, in 1862. Active as a miner in that region, he left Placerville, Idaho, for San Francisco to study law in October 1864. He returned to Idaho to resume his mining career in 1868 and was elected to the legislature in 1870. He was admitted to the bar at the end of that legislative session, and it is law rather than politics in which Hawley became most prominent.

During the 1870s he held several political posts and almost became the Democratic congressional candidate in 1884, but with Grover Cleveland's presidential victory that year, he served a four-year term as United States attorney instead. Four years later he did capture the Democratic congressional nomination, but could not overcome the Republican anti-Mormon ticket. Following his election in 1902 to a term as mayor of Boise, Hawley was elected governor of Idaho in 1910. Missing reelection by a narrow margin in 1912, he ran for senator in 1914 and tried for another nomination in 1918, unsuccessfully both times.

As a lawyer Hawley first took the side of the growing labor movement in Idaho. After the Coeur d'Alene mine labor conflict in 1892, he acted as attorney for the miners' union at the time his clients organized the Western Federation of Miners. In 1899, though, he served as special prosecutor for the state against the union in the case of the dynamiting of the Bunker Hill and Sullivan concentrator at Wardner. He continued to prosecute labor officials during the conspiracy trials following the assassination of·former governor Frank Steunenberg in 1905. Hawley was one of the outstanding criminal lawyers of the West. His most notable success was the freeing of Diamondfield Jack Davis, who was convicted by mistake of shooting some sheepmen in a sheep and cattle war of 1896-1902. He also specialized in irrigation law, dealing in water litigation over a forty-year period.

John F. MacLane, *A Sagebrush Lawyer* (1953), is a biography by an attorney. Melvyn Dubofsky, "James H. Hawley and the Origins of the Haywood Case," *Pacific Northwest Quarterly* (January 1967), and two books by David H. Grover, *Debaters and Dynamiters* (1964) and *Diamondfield Jack* (1968), treat important aspects of Hawley's career.—M. W.

Haycox, Ernest (1899-1950). Writer. Haycox was born in Portland, Oregon. His early years were restless and uncertain: His father was in turn farmer, logger, shingleweaver, and steamboatman, and the Haycoxes divorced before Ernest was eleven. Joining the Oregon National Guard at age sixteen, Haycox participated in the American expedition to Mexico in pursuit of Pancho Villa. Back in Portland in the fall of 1916, he began writing in his senior year of high school. During World War I he served for fourteen months in France. Returning to Portland to study journalism, he attended Reed College and the University of Oregon, where he served in various editorial roles on university publications and worked under writer W. F. G. Thacher.

During the fall and winter of 1923 as a police reporter on the Portland *Oregonian* Haycox papered one wall of the editorial office with rejection slips. Finally, making as much money from his fiction as he was earning as a reporter, he left the paper and made his way to New York, where he was "nearly starved out." Before he returned to Oregon, temporarily defeated, a friendly

editor of pulps urged Haycox to master the technique of the western. It was good advice. After a second trip to New York in 1925, he returned to Portland in 1926 and remained there for the rest of his life.

For the next quarter of a century Haycox wrote for a living, mastering the formula western and influencing a generation of popular writers. Bernard De Voto, writing in *Harper's* in 1954, described Haycox as "the old pro of horse opera" and insisted that Haycox came closer than anyone else to making effective novels of the western. Luke Short (Frederick Glidden), a self-confessed inheritor of the Haycox western, discovered Haycox in *Collier's* and sensed at once that Haycox's hero was much more complex and sophisticated than the traditional "gun dummy" of many early westerns. Short was drawn to the new Hamlet-like hero that Haycox had created. Frank Gruber, another successful writer of westerns, testified that he had "read all the books of Ernest Haycox" as a kind of informal course in the art of writing westerns.

Haycox produced more than twenty novels and hundreds of short stories, progressing from the pulps to *Collier's* and the *Saturday Evening Post*, and from action-dominated yarns, such as *Bugles in the Afternoon* (1944), the Custer story, to books dealing with the historical West, such as *The Earthbreakers* (1952), his most ambitious work. In this last novel he used universal themes convincingly, treated the settlers' experience realistically, and developed protagonists that were complex human beings rather than stereotypes. Although he never attained the rank of Conrad Richter or Walter van Tilburg Clark, he did succeed with *The Earthbreakers* in producing not just another western but rather a novel of the West.

Films made from Haycox's stories include: *Union Pacific*, adapted from *Trouble Shooter*, serialized in *Collier's* (Summer 1936); *Stage Coach*, taken from *The Stage to Lordsburg*, in *Collier's* (April 1937); and *Canyon Passage* (1943).

See Jill Haycox and John Chord, "Checklist of Haycox Fiction," *The Call Number* (Fall 1963, Spring 1964). —E. R. B.

Hayden, Ferdinand Vandeveer (1829-1887). Geologist. Hayden was a pioneer geologist of the West and head of the United States Geographical and Geological Survey of the Territories. He was a nineteenth-century self-made man, being reared by an uncle near Rochester, New York, teaching school at sixteen, and entering Oberlin College two years later. After graduation he entered Albany Medical School and became acquainted with the geologist Dr. John S. Newberry and the paleontologist James Hall. Upon receiving his M.D. in 1853, Hayden chose to make a fossil-collecting trip to the White River Bad Lands of Dakota, accompanied by the invertebrate paleontologist Fielding Bradford Meek.

Thus was launched Hayden's career as geologist. Until the Civil War he was engrossed in exploration in Kansas, Nebraska, and Dakota. He was with Lieutenant Gouverneur K. Warren in 1856-57, and in 1859-60 he accompanied Captain William F. Raynolds on an unsuccessful attempt to break through the snowy mountain barriers into the mysterious upper Yellowstone country. All the while Hayden was publishing the results of his work in numerous scientific publications.

Hayden made use of his medical training as a surgeon

during the Civil War, and he then accepted a professorship at the University of Pennsylvania, which he held until 1872. But when, in 1867, he was appointed geologist in charge of the geological survey of Nebraska, he was launched on his life's career. From its modest beginnings in that year he changed its name and expanded his survey into the most ambitious scientific undertaking in the American West. In 1871 and 1872 he led the first scientific parties into the Yellowstone, and the subsequent publicity, along with distribution of the photographs taken by his photographer, William Henry Jackson, aided in the passage through Congress of the bill creating the Yellowstone National Park.

From 1873 through 1876 the survey concentrated on Colorado, making an excellent atlas of that state and discovering the Mount of the Holy Cross and the cliff dwellings of the Southwest. Until its merger in 1879 with the United States Geological Survey, the Hayden survey continued to function throughout much of the Rocky Mountain West. Hayden continued his work until he retired, December 31, 1886; he died December 22, 1887.

Hayden has not been honored with a good biography and has fared poorly at the hands of the biographers of his competitors. Certainly his accomplishments were substantial. The publications of his survey were multifarious: see Laurence F. Schmeckebier, *Catalogue and Index of the Hayden, King, Powell, and Wheeler Surveys*, U. S. Geological Bulletin 222 (1904). See also Richard A. Bartlett, *Great Surveys of the American West* (1962).
—R. A. B.

Hayden family. Arizona businessmen. *Charles Trumbull* (1825-1900), a freighter, merchant, and town builder, was born at Haydens, Connecticut, taught school in New Jersey, and studied law in New York City. Contracting "lung fever," he moved west and settled in Independence, Missouri, entering the employ of a cousin who operated a mercantile business. When in his twenties he purchased the firm, began freighting to Santa Fe, and established a store there. In the late 1850s Hayden opened a store near Tubac and by the next decade was in business in Tucson, with property valued at $20,000. A Union sympathizer, he left Tucson during the Confederate occupation but two years later was back and was appointed probate judge. In 1866, while on a business trip, he reached the Salt River and saw trade opportunities there; four years later he organized with several others the Hayden Milling and Farming Ditch Company. Granted ditch privileges by the neighboring Tempe Canal Company, Hayden moved to the Salt in 1871, opened a store, started a ferry, and built a gristmill. By the late 1870s the vicinity of Hayden's Ferry was called Tempe. Hayden served on the board of supervisors of Maricopa County and promoted the establishment of the Tempe Normal School, which became Arizona State University.

Carl Trumbull (1877-1972), a businessman and politician, and son of Charles T. Hayden, was born at Hayden's Ferry (Tempe), Arizona. He attended Tempe Normal School and Stanford University, and at his father's death assumed the direction of the C. T. Hayden Company. In 1902 he was elected a member of the Tempe town council, joined the Arizona National Guard, and was treasurer and then sheriff of Maricopa County. From 1912 to 1926 Hayden was the congressman from Arizona, then won a seat in the United States Senate. He promoted highway building, irrigation, and mining legislation beneficial to Arizona. At his retirement in 1969, Hayden had served under ten presidents and was president pro tempore of the Senate. He died in Tempe.

See Bert M. Fireman, "Charles Trumbull Hayden," *Smoke Signal No. 19*, Tucson Westerners (Spring 1969); Carl Trumbull Hayden, *Charles Trumbull Hayden: Pioneer* (1972); and Charles F. Parker, "Senator Carl Hayden," *Arizona Highways* (February-March 1962).
—H. P. H.

Hayes, Ira (1923-1955). Pima war hero. Born on the Pima reservation in Arizona, Hayes is one of the soldiers immortalized in the famous statue of the World War II flag-raising at Iwo Jima. Probably because he was an Indian, he was singled out and hailed a super-hero, perhaps out of proportion to his act of courage (after all, many had *died* making the way safe for that flag), and was toured across the United States selling war bonds. But suddenly, it was all over; he was a drunken Indian, and dead.

Schoolchildren's history books always tell the beginning of the story, and in a college book one may even find the end. Stan Steiner, in *The New Indians* (1969), sees in Hayes's life and death the story of an Indian who lost his identity to the values of white men. Hayes was an exemplary soldier not only for his courage but for the fact that he was a "good Christian," a "good Indian," Steiner says. After being wined, dined, and decorated with medals, he was promptly forgotten. With no "Indianness" to sustain him, he was left defenseless in a cultural no-man's-land. When he wandered home to the Pima reservation he was without money, job, or future. He was found in a drainage ditch, in two inches of water.

Hayes's life as immortalized in songs, books, and films was a myth, while the meaning of his death and the lessons that might have been learned about the disastrous effect of cultural annihilation were not understood by those *in charge* of federal Indian policy, notably those in the education programs and in the relocation programs of the Bureau of Indian Affairs. Continuing high rates of Indian suicide and alcoholism are testament to the fact that Hayes's death is still not understood.—C. C.

Hays, William Jacob (1830-1875). Painter. Born in Catskill, New York, Hays spent most of his life in New York City, where he studied art at the National Academy of Design. Known chiefly as a painter of animal life, he owes his continuing reputation as a western artist to material gathered on a steamboat trip up the Missouri River to Fort Union in the summer of 1860, during which time he made drawings of the various trading posts visited along the way and scenes of Indian and animal life. He seems to have been impressed particularly by the immense herds of buffalo and abundance of other animals on the Great Plains at this time. Following his western excursion Hays produced many pictures illustrative of this aspect of nature, which were exhibited in New York City and later in London. His *Buffalo Hunt* and *The Bull at Bay* presently are owned by the American Museum of Natural History, New York City. Another of his large pictures, *Herd on the Move*, was reproduced as a colored lithograph in 1863 and exhibited in 1865 in London, where it remained in relative obscurity until after World War II. It is now included in the collection of the Thomas Gilcrease Institute of American History and Art, Tulsa, Oklahoma. Hays also produced many paintings representative of eastern game animals.

See Robert Taft, *Artists and Illustrators of the Old West, 1850-1900* (1953).—D. C. H.

Haywood, William Dudley (1869-1928). Labor leader. "Big Bill" Haywood was born in Salt Lake City, Utah. At the age of nine he lost an eye. Haywood had a knockabout youth as a hard-rock miner, cowboy, and homesteader in Utah, Nevada, and Idaho. In 1896, in Silver City, Idaho, he joined the fledgling Western Federation of Miners (WFM) and found his métier as a militant labor unionist, quickly rising to the highest strata of WFM leadership. It was as a WFM official that he was tried for plotting the assassination by Harry Orchard of former governor Frank Steunenberg of Idaho in late 1905. With the famous lawyer Clarence Darrow defending him and future senator William E. Borah prosecuting him, the trial in 1906-07 was a national sensation. In effect, it pitted the surging radical labor movement against the embattled capitalists of the West, for the charge was that Steunenberg was killed in retaliation for pro-management actions during his gubernatorial term in regard to the bitter labor conflict in the Coeur d'Alene mining region of northern Idaho. With Darrow and Borah—two of the notable public figures of the twentieth century's first half—engaged in an epic courtroom struggle, the public reacted with fascination to this legal test of strength between the forces of capital and labor. Haywood's acquittal was hailed as a striking victory for Darrow, Haywood, and the radical union forces of the West.

Whether guilty or not of planning the Steunenberg assassination (although historians disagree on this, the weight of opinion favors Haywood's claim of innocence), Haywood emerged from the *cause célèbre* as the personification of the revolutionary-minded labor movement in America. Basic to the way people reacted to Haywood was his appearance and personality. To the capitalist this big, one-eyed, very "physical" man was a menacing portent of the feared uprising of the proletariat. To workers, their wives, and their children, however, this friendly, direct, forceful "tall Cyclops" was cut in heroic proportions. Such was Haywood's charisma that through many a vicissitude from 1905 to 1917 he never lacked an enthusiastic following.

Internal broils ultimately caused Haywood's virtual expulsion from the WFM in 1908. Thereafter he devoted his ebullient energies to the Socialist party (until ousted once again as a result of sectarian differences) and, even more crucially, to the Industrial Workers of the World (IWW). Haywood had been an IWW founding father at Chicago in 1905, and after his break with the WFM he was increasingly identified in the public mind with the IWW. In 1918, during a national mood of wartime hysteria, Haywood and other IWW leaders were tried and convicted for sedition by the federal government in a proceeding that has been termed "a shabby affair at best and an indelible blot on American civil liberties at worst."

In a life that oscillated between the pursuit of practical unionism and a romantic vision of revolution, Haywood's last phase was an escape, while free on bail from the sedition sentence, to Soviet Russia in 1921. Viewing the Russian revolution as the "dawn of freedom and industrial democracy," Haywood wished to participate in that historic event. He was probably also motivated, to a lesser extent, by the fear that his American prison term was in reality a death sentence, given the poor state of his health. His stay in the Soviet Union began in exhilaration as, for a short time, he took a leading part in the construction of the huge coal-mine complex at Kemerovo in the Kuznetsk Basin. But continuing ill health forced him to settle down in Moscow, where, lonely and sick, he died.

One of the best-known Americans of his day, Big Bill Haywood nevertheless departed life, at first glance, with little accomplished in a full, active existence. His undertakings—with the WFM, IWW, Socialist party, and communism—invariably ended in disappointment. Yet he was far from a failure when considered from the long-range perspective of the American radical and labor movements. Although often defeated, he spearheaded many a significant struggle against the uncompromising, brutal capitalists of his time and in this sense contributed vitally to the ultimate success of the labor movement in America. As a symbol of dauntless resistance to the established capitalist structure, Haywood has earned the unflagging admiration of American radicals. Not the least of Haywood's legacies is his posthumously published autobiography, *Bill Haywood's Book* (1929), a colorful account of his lifelong battle for the underprivileged. It remains to the present a classic product of the turbulent era of American labor history.

See Joseph R. Conlin, *Big Bill Haywood and the Radical Union Movement* (1969); and *Bill Haywood's Book: The Autobiography of William D. Haywood* (1929).—R. M. B.

headright system. A grant of land given by colonial governments to any man who paid the transportation costs to America either of himself or some other person. During the seventeenth century most of the colonies used headrights as an inducement to draw settlers to the New World, but the system was most fully developed in Virginia, Maryland, Carolina, and Georgia.

In 1618 the reorganized Virginia Company attempted to enlarge its labor force by offering a headright of fifty acres. The company hoped that its proposal would encourage wealthy Englishmen to transport to America as many people as they could afford, since each additional person represented another headright and, thus, a more extensive plantation. The headright system quickly became the basis of Virginia's land policy, and even though the Virginia Company went bankrupt, the colony's government continued granting headrights to planters who brought in indentured servants and Negro slaves. In the 1630s Maryland's proprietor tried to divert the stream of settlers going to Virginia by offering a more liberal headright. In 1633 Lord Baltimore promised "first adventurers" two thousand acres for every five men they sent to his colony. By 1658, however, the Maryland headright had been reduced to fifty acres. The headright system in other colonies was basically the same as that of Virginia and Maryland, although the size of the land grant varied from place to place.

By the middle of the seventeenth century, the original purpose of the headright system in Virginia and Maryland had been undermined by fraud. Instead of serving as an inducement for immigration, the system became a means by which men were able to engross thousands of acres. A person could get around the letter of the head-right laws in several ways. Some planters who crossed the Atlantic several times claimed a new headright whenever they returned to the colonies. Sea captains frequently demanded a grant of land for every member of their crews, and when a slave or indentured servant was brought to America, the captain, the merchant, and the planter, each in his turn, would ask for a headright for the same individual. Colonial officials were aware of these corrupt practices, but they seldom did anything to discourage their spread. By the end of the century any Virginian who had five shillings could purchase a head-right from the government, no questions being asked about the Atlantic crossing.

During the eighteenth century the headright system lost its earlier significance, and in several colonies it disappeared altogether. Lord Baltimore, angry about the corruption, abandoned headrights in favor of the direct sale of land. In Virginia headrights were superse-ded by "treasury rights." After 1699 a planter could buy a treasury right of fifty acres for a stated price from the Commonwealth of Virginia. As the historian Lewis C. Gray pointed out, "Since the authorities for some time had been selling headrights for uniform fees, the treas-ury right provided legality for a practice already in vogue." On the whole, headrights appear to have en-couraged the development of the plantation economy and a system of involuntary labor in America.

See Lewis C. Gray, *History of Agriculture in the Southern United States to 1860*, 2 vols. (1941); and Marshall Harris, *Origin of the Land Tenure System in the United States* (1953).—T. H. B.

health. See DISEASES.

Hearst, William Randolph (1863-1951). Newspaper publisher. Born in San Francisco, Hearst was the only child of George Hearst, United States senator from California from 1886 until his death in 1891. The elder Hearst made his fortune by buying proven mining properties in Missouri, California, Nevada, Utah, South Dakota, Montana, and Mexico. While attending Har-vard College (1882-85) young Hearst came to admire the methods of Joseph Pulitzer, owner-publisher of the New York *World*, and after he was expelled from Har-vard he worked briefly for the *World* as a reporter. He then persuaded his father to give him charge (1887) of the San Francisco *Examiner*, which George Hearst had bought in 1880 to advance himself in Democratic party politics.

Although Hearst spent lavishly on eastern personnel and techniques, yellow journalism as he developed it on the *Examiner* followed the San Francisco traditions of sensationalism and invective. He used similar methods at the New York *Morning Journal*, which he bought in 1895, appealing particularly to immigrant working-class readers; in California, despite frequent complaints about his taste, all classes read his papers.

While establishing and acquiring newspapers in all parts of the country after 1900, when he founded the Chicago *Evening American*, Hearst made New York City his base both for editing and publishing and for politics from 1895 until the mid-1920s. He won election twice (1902 and 1904) to the House of Representatives as a Democrat, ran unsuccessfully for mayor as an indepen-dent in 1905 and 1909, and ran as the Democratic

nominee for governor in 1906 but lost to Charles Evans Hughes. In 1908, hoping to prepare for his own nomi-nation in 1912, he organized a presidential ticket for his Independence party. In *The Industrial Repub-lic . . .* (1907), Upton Sinclair compared Hearst with Abraham Lincoln and described him as the country's best hope for the presidency in 1912.

Hearst maintained western loyalties after moving east, in 1896 conducting a campaign against the South-ern Pacific Railroad, for which he brought Ambrose Bierce to Washington. He drew western insurgent votes for the Democratic presidential nomination in 1904. After the early 1920s, when he failed to get the Demo-cratic nomination in New York for either governor or senator, he became more interested in California as a residence and as a field for political influence. Upon his mother's death in 1919 he inherited the ranch at San Simeon where he had vacationed as a boy. He began building the castle on Camp Hill, or La Cuesta Encanta-da, which was ready for occupancy in 1925, and in-creased the size of the original ranch from 60,000 to 230,000 acres. In 1924 he shifted his motion picture company, Cosmopolitan Productions, to Los Angeles; in 1925 he took charge of the Los Angeles *Examiner* (founded 1903), and his California papers became the bellwethers of his chain. As publisher and producer thereafter and until World War II he commuted be-tween San Simeon, Malibu, and Beverly Hills, adminis-tering his empire by telephone and telegraph. His west-ern papers included the San Francisco *Call* (purchased in 1913, named the *Call-Bulletin* from 1929 to 1959, when it became the *News-Call-Bulletin*), the Oakland *Post-Inquirer* (formed in 1922 from the *Post*, established in 1917), the Seattle *Post-Intelligencer* (purchased 1921), the Los Angeles *Herald* (1922, combined with the *Eve-ning Express* in 1931 as the *Herald-Express*, combined with the *Examiner* in 1962 as the *Herald-Examiner*), the Fort Worth *Record* (1923), and the San Antonio *Evening Light* (1924). He supported Senator Hiram Johnson (Republican, California, 1917-45) for reelection, and first John Nance Garner and then Franklin D. Roosevelt for the presidency in 1932. By 1935, however, when he announced that he would leave California because of the state income tax, he was supporting right-wing vigilante groups; later he tried to control the state Re-publican party.

During the depression of the 1930s Hearst liquidated and consolidated part of his publishing empire; by the time of his death appreciation of his vast real-estate holdings may have made them the most valuable part of his estate. The Hearst Corporation gave the castle at San Simeon to the state of California in 1957. The Los Angeles *Examiner* ceased publication in 1962; the San Francisco *Examiner* published a joint Sunday edition with the San Francisco *Chronicle*, its old rival, after 1965, used the same printing plant, and became an afternoon paper, replacing the *News-Call-Bulletin*; the New York *Journal-American* merged in 1966 with the *Herald Tribune* and *World Telegram and Sun* into a composite operation but ceased publication the same year.

While Hearst lived in New York over nearly half of his journalistic career and held and sought public office only as a New Yorker, the history of the western press, of California politics, and even of the motion-picture in-dustry is incomplete without an account of him.

The most substantial biographies are W. A. Swanberg, *Citizen Hearst* (1961); John Tebbel, *The Life and Good Times of William Randolph Hearst* (1952); and John K. Winkler, *William Randolph Hearst* (1955). Papers of William Randolph Hearst and of his mother, Phoebe Apperson Hearst, are at the Bancroft Library, University of California at Berkeley.—E. P.

Hebard, Grace Raymond (1861-1936). Feminist writer and educator. An Iowa-born daughter of a pioneer Congregational missionary, Hebard obtained a job in 1882 as a draftsman in the Wyoming Territorial Surveyor General's office. From 1891 until her retirement in 1931 she served the University of Wyoming at Laramie variously as secretary of the board of trustees, librarian, and professor of political economy. As the university's librarian she gathered and organized an important collection of manuscripts and books related to western history.

Hebard wrote widely read books: *The History and Government of Wyoming* (eleven editions beginning in 1904); *Pathbreakers from River to Ocean* (six editions beginning in 1911); *The Bozeman Trail* (with E. A. Brininstool, 1922); *Washakie* (1930); and *Sacajawea, Guide and Interpreter of the Lewis and Clark Expedition* (1932).

As a historian, Hebard was essentially self-taught. Her B.S. degree (1882) from the University of Iowa was in civil engineering. Her M.A. in English from the University of Iowa and her Ph.D. in political science from Illinois Wesleyan were obtained through correspondence study with little if any resident instruction. All too often her practice in historical writing was to set out to prove her preconceptions, quickly rejecting contrary evidence. She gave high priority to glorifying the pioneer. In her efforts to offset the neglect of women in the history of the West she sometimes overcompensated.

She regarded Sacajawea (Sacagawea) as the indispensable guide of the Lewis and Clark expedition. Similarly, Hebard acclaimed Esther Morris as the founder of woman suffrage, giving her credit for bringing woman suffrage to Wyoming in 1869, although the evidence unmistakably points to several men as the responsible parties.

A poised, forceful public speaker, Hebard took the lead in marking points of interest and in commemorating historical events. She championed the cause of woman's rights, worked for child welfare, and endowed scholarships. Her enthusiasm for the splendid achievements of the pioneers was imparted to many who heard her or who read her books.

See W. O. Clough, *A History of the University of Wyoming, 1887-1937* (1937); and University of Wyoming faculty, *In Memoriam: Grace Raymond Hebard, 1861-1936* (1937).—T. A. L.

Heinze, Frederick Augustus (1869-1914). Montana mining engineer and financier. Heinze was born in Brooklyn, New York, and educated at the Brooklyn Polytechnic Institute, Columbia University School of Mines, and in Germany. He went to Butte, Montana, in 1889 as a mining engineer at the age of twenty. He evaluated mines shrewdly, actually worked in them, and soon owned some of the richest mines in Butte and in Trail, British Columbia. His competitors tried unsuccessfully to search out the source of his financial assistance in order to cut it off. It was later traced to his brother who secured almost unlimited loans from German financiers. Heinze was marked as a "public enemy" by other mining operators, particularly one of the copper kings, Marcus Daly, when he formulated his "apex" theory, whereby whoever owned the location where a mineral vein "apexed," or came to the surface, could follow this vein and mine its wealth, even if it led into the richest ore bodies of the neighboring mines. Heinze secured the election of notoriously corrupt judges who supported his claims. In 1903 the mining interests opposing Heinze demanded the convening of a special session of the state legislature which passed a bill allowing a change of venue in court proceedings when the request appeared to the state supreme court to be reasonable.

Heinze was politically conscious and genuinely interested in his employees. He introduced the eight-hour day for underground mining about 1900, well ahead of the other mining operators in the nation, and his pay scale was progressive. This action, together with his powerful oratory and attractive personality, enabled him to exercise formidable political power. This quality worried William A. Clark, the third warring copper king, although Clark usually worked with Heinze and against Daly. In 1906 Heinze sold his Butte interests to the Anaconda company for a reported $12 million and returned to New York. He annoyed the brokers on the stock exchange by his frenetic operations to the extent that an important part of the 1907 financial panic was a planned slump by his fellow operators to force the sale of many of Heinze's holdings at severe losses. He still retained large mining properties, however, which he operated until his sudden death at the age of forty-five from cirrhosis of the liver resulting from the stress of his business life and extravagant social living.

See C. B. Glasscock, *The War of the Copper Kings* (1935); Sarah McNelis, *Copper King at War* (1968); and *Progressive Men of the State of Montana* (1901).—M. G. B.

Henderson, Richard (1735-1785). Land speculator. Henderson was born in Hanover County, Virginia, but in 1742 the family moved southward to Granville County, North Carolina. Educated by private tutors, Henderson received a license to practice law and quickly developed a numerous western clientele. This ambitious young lawyer followed the court circuit into the Piedmont towns of North Carolina, where he met men who had ventured out onto the frontier either as long hunters or Indian traders. Among them were the elder Squire and Daniel Boone. Their stories of the western country were enticing.

Between 1763 and 1771 there was marked excitement over the extension of the settlement line into the Tennessee valley country. With the negotiations of the treaties of Fort Stanwix, Hard Labor, and Lochaber, by which the Indians lost much of their land, land fever became more virulent. Between 1769 and 1771 Daniel Boone wandered over the central Kentucky country. Although the evidence is not thoroughly conclusive, he perhaps was partially in the employ of Richard Henderson and Company. This organization was composed of a group of North Carolinians and Virginians, including Thomas and Nathaniel Hart.

The "War of the Alamance" (1771) brought an abrupt change in Judge Henderson's career. With the opening of the Watauga settlements in eastern Tennessee, the

North Carolina judge's attention was turned in this direction. Following the advice of Boone, Henderson reorganized his company at Hillsboro, North Carolina, on August 27, 1774, as the Louisa Company (later Transylvania Company). The partnership was expanded, and immediate plans were made to move into the scene of western activity. Trade goods were purchased in Fayetteville, and communication was opened with the Cherokee chiefs. In the winter of 1774-75, the company negotiated the Treaty of SYCAMORE SHOALS by which the Cherokee Indians surrendered their claims beyond Cumberland Gap.

In April Henderson and his company followed Boone to the south bank of the Kentucky River and Boonesboro. He quickly called into session a general assembly of representatives from the newly formed settlements and laid the groundwork for the organization of Transylvania Colony. Henderson's ambitious plans were thwarted by Virginia. The arrival of George Rogers Clark at Harrod's Town in 1775 created an organization of Virginia interest in the region. Late in 1776 the Virginia assembly created Kentucky County, and attempted to conciliate Henderson by recognizing his personal title to two hundred thousand acres of land on the Ohio. Henderson still held his land claims in the bend of the Cumberland, however, and in 1780 drew up the CUMBERLAND COMPACT with settlers in the area. Failure of the Transylvania Colony project was in good measure due to the fact that its promoters never could secure congressional recognition over the staunch opposition of Virginia in the Continental Congress. Following the failure of his western venture, Henderson returned to North Carolina, where he died.

See John Bakeless, *Daniel Boone, Master of the Wilderness* (1939); Archibald Henderson, "Richard Henderson and the Occupation of Kentucky, 1775," *Mississippi Valley Historical Review* vol. I (1914)), and *The Conquest of the Old Southwest* (1920); James A. James, *The Life of George Rogers Clark* (1928); and William Stewart Lester, *The Transylvania Colony* (1935).—T. D. C.

Henry, Andrew (1775?-1833). Lead miner and mountain man. Henry was born in York County, Pennsylvania. After living in Nashville, Tennessee, for a time, he moved to Ste. Genevieve, Missouri, where he became a lead miner in 1808 or 1809. He became a partner of the St. Louis Missouri Fur Company in 1809 and was on its first expedition (1809-10), which opened up the little-known Three Forks of the Missouri to organized trapping. In the winter of 1810-11 his party was the first of United States trappers to trap along, and build a post on, the Continental Divide (on Henry's Fork of the Snake River). Henry returned to the lead-mining business in 1811, however, and at the outbreak of the War of 1812 worked out a profitable business relationahip with William H. Ashley, whereby Henry produced needed lead while Ashley produced saltpeter for the American armed forces. Both Ashley and Henry joined Missouri volunteer forces (Henry's success as a major led to his being addressed as "Major Henry" for the rest of his life).

In 1822, he and Ashley became partners in the fur trade, and once again Henry ascended the Missouri, this time to establish a post, Fort Henry, near the mouth of the Yellowstone. Although he was skilled in wilderness craft and was greatly liked and respected by his men, Henry's luck had begun to run out. When he tried to trap in hostile Blackfoot country, he and his men were driven out. When Ashley's 1823 expedition was ambushed by the Arikara, Henry rushed downriver to assist him. On his return upriver Henry lost two more men on the arduous land trip through Nebraska and the Dakotas, and when he arrived at Fort Henry, he discovered that the Indians had stolen his horses and showed little interest in bringing in furs to his post. Desperately Henry moved his fort up the Yellowstone to the Bighorn River. Later, after another group of Ashley's men, led by Jedediah Smith, had rediscovered the South Pass, Henry led his own trappers across that historic pathway to the Green River trapping grounds, but during 1823 he lost more men to Indian attacks. Undoubtedly disheartened by setbacks and heavy debts, Henry left the fur trade in 1825, and Jedediah Smith replaced him as Ashley's partner. Capable, fearless, and honest, Henry appears to have been a hero to the men with whom he worked, but his own career was eclipsed by that of his more flamboyant and successful partner, Ashley.

See Hiram M. Chittenden, *The History of the American Fur Trade in the Far West* (1902); William H. Goetzmann, *Exploration and Empire* (1966); Thomas James, *Three Years Among the Indians and the Mexicans* (1916); Dale L. Morgan, *Jedediah Smith and the Opening of the West* (1953); Dale L. Morgan, ed., *The West of William H. Ashley* (1964).—G. B. D.

Henry, Patrick (1736-1799). Orator. Henry was born in Hanover County, Virginia, the son of a moderately successful but well-educated planter. As a young man, Henry failed both in business and farming, but after he turned to the law, he quickly became one of the most celebrated lawyers in the colony. Jefferson once described him as "the greatest orator that ever lived."

In 1763 Henry gained notoriety by taking a leading part in the so-called Parson's Cause. When the local Anglican clergy asked the king to annul a Virginia act favoring debtors, Henry argued passionately that laws should be framed for the good of the people, not a narrow clique, and that the king had no business disallowing popular colonial legislation. A few years later, he was the most vigorous opponent of the Stamp Act within the Virginia House of Burgesses. Henry was an outspoken nationalist before the American Revolution. He told his fellow delegates to the first Continental Congress, "I am not a Virginian, but an American." Between 1776 and 1779, he served Virginia as governor. During the last twenty years of his life, Henry held a number of important political positions and strongly opposed the passage of the Constitution in the belief that it gave too much power to the federal government. His contemporaries often criticized Henry's vacillating policies, but all agreed that he was the most popular leader in Virginia.

As early as 1767, Henry became interested in the Ohio valley and apparently was a leading figure in several pre-Revolutionary land companies. While serving as governor of Virginia during the American Revolution, Henry dispatched Colonel George Rogers Clark to the Illinois country. Clark's military successes over the British reestablished Virginia's long-standing claim to the region. Henry was convinced that the Mississippi River was the crucial factor in western settlement, and in 1779 he warned George Washington that English forces in the Southwest endangered ". . . our trade on the Mississippi, on which river the Spaniards wish to open a very interesting commerce with us." In 1786 Henry again came to the defense of the western interests. He condemned John Jay's proposed Spanish alliance (the Jay-Gardoqui Negotiations), which would have surrendered navigation rights on the Mississippi River for a number of years in exchange for commercial reciprocity between the United States and peninsular Spain. Henry was probably behind a Virginia resolution passed in 1786 that declared, "The common right of navigating the river Mississippi . . . ought to be considered as the bountiful gift of nature to the United States." Henry was most angry at the states north of Maryland, which he believed had been willing to sacrifice the West in order to expand their own trade.

Henry was obviously concerned about the economic development of the Ohio valley, but he was no backwoodsman as some scholars have incorrectly claimed. In fact, after examining Henry's legislative behavior, historian Charles S. Sydnor concluded, "Here was no case of a demagogue leading the poor people of the upcountry to victory over the periwigged gentry of the East."

See Thomas Perkins Abernethy, *Western Lands and the American Revolution* (1937); Bernard Mayo, *Myths and Men: Patrick Henry, George Washington, Thomas Jefferson* (1959); and Charles S. Sydnor, *American Revolutionaries in the Making: Political Practices in Washington's Virginia* (1952).—T. H. B.

Heyburn, Weldon Brinton (1852-1912). Idaho politician. Prominent as a mining attorney, Heyburn practiced law in his native Pennsylvania from 1876 to 1878, moved to Leadville, Colorado, and then joined Idaho's Coeur d'Alene gold rush in 1883. With two partners, he located an important lead-silver property, the Polaris, in 1884, and settled down to a law practice in Wallace, Idaho, He held a local Republican party office and then served in Idaho's constitutional convention in 1889. Although he opposed the Republican party's advocacy of the gold standard, Heyburn declined to become a Silver Republican in 1896, and this cost him votes in an area where the silver cause was extremely popular. He thus had to wait until 1903, when the two Republican parties had reunited, to get elected to the United States Senate. As a senator he fought President Theodore Roosevelt's conservation and forest reserve programs, as did most westerners; his campaign against forest-fire protection succeeded almost completely until the disastrous North Idaho fire of 1910 burned all the way into his home town of Wallace. He sponsored the Pure Food and Drug Act, but that marked the limit of his progressive efforts. Heyburn had a lot of western support, though, for his stand against conservation and for his representation of Idaho's mining interests.—M. W.

Heye Foundation, Museum of the American Indian. The purpose of the Heye Foundation, Museum of the American Indian, located in New York City, is the preservation, exhibition, and study of the material culture of the Indians of all of the Americas, from prehistory to today.

While a young engineer engaged in a late nineteenth-century survey of Arizona, George G. Heye became intrigued with Indian arts and crafts. He amassed his first large collection of New Mexico's Indian pottery in 1903, and the next year added a large collection from Arizona. Gradually Heye's acquisitions included pottery, textiles, and a vast variety of Indian artifacts from most of the United States, South America, Mexico, and the West Indies. Heye founded the Museum of the American Indian in 1916, endowed it, and deeded the entire collection to a board of trustees. Through the trustees and interested friends, sufficient funds were obtained to erect the museum building.

The major exhibits include items used by the League of the Iroquois, Indians of the Southeast, and various tribes of the Plains. The League of the Iroquois display includes intricately quilled and beaded garments, finger-woven sashes, headdresses, rhythm instruments, utensils, games, and weapons. In a special case are two wampum belts given to William Penn in 1683 at the signing of the Treaty of Shakamaxon. Another special case features the masks of the False Face Society and another defines the role of Iroquois women.

The Indians of the Southeast collections show the culture of the Creek, Chickasaw, Cherokee, Choctaw, Seminole, Alibamu, Koasati, and Houma. Here can be seen rare beadwork, colorfully dyed river-cane baskets, and an ornate beaded pouch presented to General Andrew Jackson by Sam Houston. The Plains Indian display has, among other things, splendid examples of the attire, headdresses, weapons, jewelry, and games of such Great Plains tribes as the Sioux, Crow, Cheyenne, Blackfoot, Kiowa, and Comanche. Even a small hand mirror is to be seen here.

The museum also houses Indian paintings, prehistoric artifacts, and examples of contemporary southwestern Indian art, such as pottery, kachina dolls, and silverwork. A grand display of the art forms of the pre-Columbian cultures from northern Mexico to southern Panama exhibits sculpture from Oaxaca and Colima, pottery from Guatemala and Honduras, and gold-, bronze-, and silverwork from Colombia, Ecuador, and Peru.—B. P. D. and M. L.

Hiawatha legend. An Iroquois myth that explains the creation of the IROQUOIS CONFEDERACY. Like most stories of its kind, the Hiawatha legend is probably a mixture of fact and fancy in proportions no longer ascertainable. It begins with Deganawidah, a Huron Indian from north of Lake Ontario, who was a son of the Great Spirit and born of a virgin. On reaching manhood Deganawidah crossed Lake Ontario to bring a divinely inspired message of peace and unity to the warring Iroquois tribes. After winning over Hiawatha, an Onondaga chief (who bears no other relation than his name to Longfellow's hero), Deganawidah moved on to convert the Mohawk tribe. With Hiawatha's aid he successively converted the Oneida, Cayuga, and Seneca. The main obstacle to peace and unity was the Onondaga sachem Atotarho, a demonic figure with crooked mind and body and with snakes in his hair. Hiawatha combed the snakes from Atotarho's hair, straightened his mind and body, and won him over to the idea of an Iroquois confederacy. This done, Deganawidah planted the Tree of Peace and gave the people their Great Law, or Constitution of the Five Nations.

Whatever the factual basis of this story, the Iroquois confederacy was real enough, consisting of five—and later, six—Indian tribes. In the absence of written records, precise dating of its origin is impossible, and authorities have assigned a variety of probable dates, ranging from A.D. 1390 to 1630.

See F. W. Hodge, ed., *Handbook of American Indians North of Mexico*, 2 vols. (1907-10); A. M. Josephy, Jr., *The Indian Heritage of America* (1968); and L. H. Morgan, *League of the Ho-dé-no-sau-nee, or Iroquois*, 2 vols. (1851). —A. W. T.

Hickok, [James Butler] "Wild Bill" (1837-1876). Soldier, scout, and lawman. Born on a farm in Illinois, Hickok left home for the Kansas frontier in 1855. Footloose and unattached, he worked at various jobs, supported Kansas politician Jim Lane and his free-state army, and spent two years driving wagons and stagecoaches. Badly mauled by a bear on a trip over the old Santa Fe Trail in 1861, he was put on light duty at Rock Creek Stage Station, Nebraska, where the "Wild Bill" legend began. There he quarreled with David McCanles, killing him and two accomplices. This fight was later exaggerated in dime novels and his three victims were increased to ten and sometimes to as many as thirty.

Hickok's Civil War services in the Union army are shrouded in mystery, but his wartime activity and a gun duel on the main street of Springfield, Missouri, added to his "gunman" image. After the war he was briefly a United States deputy marshal. His handsome appearance, his long flowing hair and buckskin clothes, his accuracy with a pistol, his gambling avocation, and his role as General Philip H. Sheridan's scout enhanced his reputation. Hickok also was a guide for a hunting party organized by a Massachusetts senator and marshal of Hays City, Kansas. In 1870, according to some accounts, he secretly married CALAMITY JANE. Bored with inactivity—his "dexterity with cards was inferior to his dexterity with pistols"—he was considering army scouting duty when he was offered the position as marshal at Abilene, Kansas, on April 15, 1871. There, at the end of the Chisholm Trail, he served during Abilene's last season as a cattle town. Those eight months were the climax of Wild Bill's career, and his legend was spread down the trail to Texas.

During his last five years he roamed the West. His reputation as a gunfighter grew with each retelling. He spent some time in Buffalo Bill's Wild West show, and in 1876 he married Mrs. Agnes Lake Thatcher, owner of another circus. Two weeks later he set out for the Black Hills. There at Deadwood in Dakota Territory on August 2, 1876, he was assassinated in a saloon. His killer was tried, convicted, and hanged.

The most recent biography is Joseph Ross, *They Called Him Wild Bill: The Life and Adventures of James Butler Hickok* (1964). See also the account in Nyle H. Miller and Joseph W. Snell, *Why the West Was Wild* (1963). —H. E. S.

Hicks, John D. (1890-1972). Historian. Hicks was born in Pickering, Missouri. Before entering Northwestern University in 1909, he spent a year as a schoolteacher in rural Wyoming. He then continued his graduate studies at the University of Wisconsin, where he worked with Frederick L. Paxson, already a well-known frontier historian. In 1916 Hicks joined the history department at Hamlin University in Minnesota, in 1922 spent a year at the North Carolina College for Women in Greensboro, and in 1923 moved to the University of Nebraska in Lincoln, where he was dean of arts and sciences between 1929 and 1932. In 1932 he joined the University of Wisconsin and a decade later succeeded Paxson at the University of California at Berkeley, where he remained until his retirement in 1957.

Hicks early became interested in the frontier experience of the nineteenth-century Midwest. His first published book, *The Constitutions of the Northwest States* (1923), a study of political structure, applied Frederick Jackson Turner's frontier theories in studying the growth of political democracy. Meanwhile, he became involved with investigating the frontier in the late nineteenth and early twentieth centuries, and after more than a decade of research he presented the fruits of his labors in *The Populist Revolt* (1931). Appearing in the midst of another great depression, this work was as relevant as it was impressive and won immediate acclaim as a definitive study. A convinced Turnerian, Hicks also did much to popularize the frontier theories of Turner through his widely read United States history textbooks, *The Federal Union* and *The American Nation*, which began to appear in 1937. Hicks joined with Theodore Saloutos, one of his former students, to collaborate on a monographic study, *Agricultural Discontent in the Middle West, 1900-1939* (1951), bringing his earlier account of Populism into the twentieth century.

After he moved to California, Hicks shifted his interests primarily to the twentieth century. In 1968 Hicks published his reminiscences, *My Life with History*, a charming account that tells much about himself and the historical profession during his active years.

Hicks was one of the youngest men ever elected to the presidency of the Mississippi Valley Historical Association (1932). He was also president of the Agricultural History Society in 1948 and the Pacific Coast branch of the American Historical Association in 1955, a frequent guest lecturer at scores of universities, and Pitt Professor of American History at Cambridge University in England (1950-51). Various institutions bestowed honorary degrees upon him, including Northwestern University, the University of San Francisco, the University of California, and the University of Nebraska.—G. D. N.

Hidatsa Indians. The Hidatsa are also called Gros Ventre of the Missouri or the Minitari. The Hidatsa Indians were a sedentary agricultural Siouan tribe, which in historic times occupied the Missouri River valley of North and South Dakota and was closely connected with the Mandan and Arikara. The ancestral Hidatsa people migrated into the northern Plains region from the Southeast, either in advance of or connected with the early Sioux (Dakota). For a time they inhabited the country centering around Devil's Lake in North Dakota as seminomadic hunters, but for undetermined reasons moved to the Missouri valley during the seventeenth century, where they met the linguistically related Mandan and from them learned—or relearned —field agriculture. By the 1760s the Hidatsa, Mandan, and Arikara (who were a Pawnee offshoot from the Southwest) were established in several large villages of earth lodges in the vicinity of the Heart River. They were a powerful though generally nonaggressive combination, and posed an impenetrable barrier to expansion by surrounding nomadic tribes. The Hidatsa population at that time was approximately four thousand.

Culturally the Hidatsa were nearly identical to the Mandan. It has not been established whether this similarity was acquired by merging their respective patterns or if it had existed before they came in contact. Probably both factors operated, since both tribes were of Siouan stock. Hidatsa social organization was based on seven exogamous clans, which were evidently originally associated with separate villages, which in turn had been formed from the independent bands of the earlier nomadic phase. There was also a system of age-graded societies through which both men and women passed from youth to old age. Each village was politically independent, although close kinship ties usually resulted in concerted action on matters of tribal importance. Performance of most religious rituals was the right of whichever clan owned the associated symbolic objects, and participation privileges had to be purchased from the clan. Their one unitribal ceremony was a form of the Plains sun dance, which was noted for the severity of its self-torture aspect. Besides agriculture, Hidatsa subsistence depended on annual spring buffalo hunts, which became more important to their economy with the acquisition of horses after 1750 and the advent of white fur traders. Following a dispute traditionally associated with one such hunt, one of the village-bands in the late eighteenth century separated from the rest of the Hidatsa and became entirely nomadic. This group was subsequently known to whites as the Crow Indians.

During the 1770s an epidemic of smallpox drastically reduced the Hidatsa, Mandan, and Arikara populations. Subsequent raids by the expanding Teton-Sioux forced the survivors to move north and resettle near the mouth of the Knife River, where the Hidatsa established three new villages containing about 2,100 people. At this location the Hidatsa were visited by the explorers and traders who began traveling the Missouri after 1790. The tribe was friendly to the whites and welcomed the establishment of trading posts near their villages. In 1837 another smallpox epidemic swept the Missouri valley, and the Hidatsa population was so reduced that they consolidated into one village. By 1845 predatory raids from the Sioux had again become so severe that the remaining Hidatsa and Mandan moved to near Fort Berthold, where they established a combined village and were joined in 1862 by the Arikara survivors. In 1880 the Fort Berthold Reservation in North Dakota was created for the three tribes, where their descendents merged into one group that today can claim no specific tribal identity.

See E. M. Bruner, "Assimilation Among the Fort Berthold Indians," *American Indian*, vol. 6 (1953); F. W. Hodge, ed., *Handbook of American Indians North of Mexico*, 2 vols. (1907-10); R. H. Lowrie, "Social Life of the Hidatsa," American Museum of Natural History *Anthropological Papers*, vol. 21 (1917), and "Some Problems in the Ethnography of the Crow and Village Indians," *American Anthropologist*, vol. 14 (1912); and W. Mathews, *Ethnography and Philology of the Hidatsa Indians* (1877).—P. R. M.

Higgins, Victor (1884-1949). Painter. Born in Shelbyville, Indiana, Higgins studied at the Chicago Art Institute and the Academy of Fine Arts in New York City, as well as in Paris and Munich, before returning to Chicago to teach at the Academy of Fine Arts. He gained fame following a move to Taos, New Mexico, in 1914, when he was promptly invited into the exclusive membership of the Taos Society of Artists along with Walter Ufer, who arrived in Taos at about the same time. Influenced toward impressionism by Andrew Dasburg, also of the Taos art community, Higgins began to experiment in this direction and with E. L. Blumenschein and O. E. Berninghaus was one of the few pioneer artists of Taos to risk popular and commercial success to develop new styles and approaches in his work. He won the first Altman Prize of the National Academy of Design and the French Memorial Gold Medal from the Art Institute of Chicago in 1932. The following year his work was first represented in a showing at the Museum of Modern Art in New York City. He lived in Taos for the remainder of his life and produced many pictures of New Mexican Indian life and landscape, which are in a number of collections throughout the United States. An important collection of Higgins' work is owned by the Stark Foundation in Orange, Texas.

See Van Deren Coke, *Taos and Santa Fe, the Artist's Environment* (1957); Dorothy Harmsen, *Western Americana* (1971); and Mabel Dodge Luhan, *Taos and Its Artists* (1947).—D. C. H.

highways. See NATIONAL ROADS; and ROADS AND HIGHWAYS.

Hill, James Jerome (1838-1916). Railroad builder. Hill was born near Rockwood, Ontario, of Scottish and northern Irish parentage. He was blinded in his right eye as a result of a boyhood accident with a bow and arrow. At his father's death in 1852 Hill, who had thought of becoming a doctor, ended his formal education but continued to read widely while clerking in stores in Rockwood and nearby Guelph. Although fascinated with the prospect of a trip to the Orient, Hill had heard much about the Minnesota Territory and "took a notion to go and see St. Paul." Finding work on the levee and on Mississippi River steamboats, he was soon permanently established in the fast-growing city. By 1865 he was freight agent for the Northwest Packet Company and the St. Paul and Pacific Railroad, and continued to add to his capital from earnings as a general merchant. He began to promote coal as a substitute for fast-dwindling wood supplies and by 1877 was a major coal dealer. In partnership with Norman W. Kittson, an early trader between St. Paul and the Hudson's Bay Company to the north, Hill operated a lucrative steamboat service down the Red River to Winnipeg. The chief fruit of these ventures was his conviction that the time was ripe to complete the bankrupt St. Paul and Pacific Railroad between St. Paul, the Red River valley, and Winnipeg.

In association with Kittson, Donald A. Smith of the Hudson's Bay Company, and George Stephen, president of the Bank of Montreal, Hill risked his entire capital to buy up the railroad's bonds from the disheartened committee of Dutch bondholders who held most of them. By the spring of 1879 the associates had completed the takeover and Hill had supervised the completion of construction to the international boundary. The Great Northern Railway, as it was renamed in 1890 (see BURLINGTON NORTHERN RAILROAD), progressed westward prudently but steadily and without the aid of a single grant of land or other form of government aid, reaching Puget Sound in 1893. With its more favorable grades and lower operating costs, the Great Northern, along with Huntington's Southern Pacific, was the only transcontinental to avoid bankruptcy during the 1890s depression. These years brought Hill the opportunity to end cutthroat competition with the Northern Pacific by acquiring it, and to give both roads a controlled entry into Chicago by joint acquisition of the Burlington. But Edward H. HARRIMAN, by then head of the Union Pacific, also wanted the Burlington, which set the stage for the "Northern Pacific corner" of 1901 and the gigantic holding company that was dissolved in 1904 by the Supreme Court's Northern Securities decision. Although these events began the "trust-busting" phase of the Progressive era, the Northern Securities decision had no practical effect on the "community of interests" Hill had long since put together between the Great Northern, the Northern Pacific, and the Burlington lines, which were finally permitted to merge as the Burlington Northern in 1970.

Hill was a member of the syndicate formed in 1881 to build the Canadian Pacific Railroad, but his opposition to the uneconomic segment north of Lake Superior led to his withdrawal. A major project in the development of the Northwest was his acquisition, on behalf of the Great Northern stockholders, of the Mesabi iron range, chief source of iron ore for the American steel industry until after World War II, an enterprise originally conceived of by two of his sons, James N. and Louis W. Hill.

In his last years Hill spoke and wrote in fervent support of the agricultural diversification of the grain-conscious Northwest, and of the constructive role of big business. "A barn-raising is a combination," he noted. Convinced that the railroads, during the prosperous first two decades of the twentieth century, when the traffic burden doubled and redoubled, were "trying to bore a one-inch hole with a half-inch auger," he urgently called for further development of the national system. He was therefore greatly discouraged at the repression of capital formation in the railroad industry, as a result of the Interstate Commerce Commission's repeated refusal to grant rate increases in an inflationary era. "It does seem hard," he declared, thinking of what he and his fellow railroad leaders had accomplished since the Civil War, to find themselves being ruled by politicians "who have never done a thing but pose and draw a salary."

J. G. Pyle's authorized biography of Hill, *The Life of James J. Hill*, 2 vols. (1917), contains most of the essential facts. B. H. Meyer, *A History of the Northern Securities Case* (1906), is heavy going, but a revelation to devotees of the robber-baron legend. A definitive biography of Hill is badly needed.—A. M.

Hill, Joe. See INDUSTRIAL WORKERS OF THE WORLD.

Hill, Nathaniel Peter (1832-1900). Colorado metallurgist and politician. Hill was born in Montgomery, New York. He was graduated from Brown University in Providence, Rhode Island, in 1856 and subsequently became a professor of chemistry. In 1864 he was employed by a group of eastern capitalists to travel to Colorado to examine the geological formation and mineral character of land in Gilpin County, which they were considering purchasing. He made two additional trips in 1865, during which time he observed the difficulty of reducing Colorado's "refractory" ores with the processes then in use. To solve this problem of ore reduction, he had a quantity of the ore hauled to the Missouri River and then shipped to Swansea, Wales, for analysis. After returning from Wales to the United States, Hill or-

ganized the Boston and Colorado Smelting Company in Boston in the spring of 1867. A few months later he began construction of the company's smelter in Black Hawk, Colorado, which commenced operations in January 1868. The company was most instrumental in stimulating Colorado's declining mining economy. In 1878 a larger facility was built just north of Denver at Argo.

Turning to community affairs and politics, Hill was elected mayor of Black Hawk in 1871 and was a member of the council of the territorial legislature in 1872. During the years 1879-85 he served as a United States senator from Colorado, speaking for the continued coinage of silver. After his Senate term he became proprietor of the Denver *Republican* while continuing as manager of the smelting company. Hill was also president of the United Oil Company, which operated in Florence, Colorado, and invested in real estate.—M. B.

Hill, Thomas (1829-1908). Painter. Born in Birmingham, England, Hill came to the United States in 1840 and settled in Taunton, Massachusetts. He later studied art at the Pennsylvania Academy of the Fine Arts in Philadelphia and established a reputation as a portrait and historical painter. In 1853 he was awarded a first medal at the Maryland Institute in Baltimore. In 1861 he moved to San Francisco, where he began painting the landscapes for which he later became famous. In 1866-67 he studied under Paul Meyerheim in Paris. After returning to America, he traveled throughout the West. Particularly noted for his mountain landscapes, Hill painted many scenes of Yellowstone National Park, the Grand Canyon, Donner Lake, and the Sierra Nevada. His canvas *The Last Spike*, measuring 8 by 11 feet, was painted to commemorate the completion of the first transcontinental railroad at Promontory Point, Utah, May 10, 1869, and now hangs in the California state capitol at Sacramento.—D. C. H.

Hillsboro, New Mexico. Ghost town. Hillsboro, in Sierra County, was a prosperous mining and cattle town throughout the 1880s and 1890s. During this time the mines in the area produced over $6 million in gold and silver despite Apache raids. Today the town is virtually a ghost, although many of the old stone and adobe buildings still remain.

Also of interest is the nearby silver town of Kingston, which thrived alongside Hillsboro in the latter part of the nineteenth century. Today Kingston is even more ghostly than its neighbor, but a few recognizable ruins still remain of the elegant hotels and twenty-two saloons that once existed there.

See Ralph Looney, *Haunted Highways: The Ghost Towns of New Mexico* (1968); and Muriel S. Wolle, *The Bonanza Trail* (1953).—R. B. W.

Hindman, Thomas Carmichael (1828-1868). Arkansas politician and soldier. A Mississippian by birth and a Mexican War lieutenant, Hindman settled in Helena, Arkansas, in 1856 and practiced law. He was elected to Congress as a Democrat in 1858 and 1860. He helped overthrow the Conway-Johnson family clique and strongly supported the successful campaign by Henry Rector for the governorship in 1860. A secessionist, Hindman raised a regiment of Arkansas troops during the Civil War and rose to the rank of major general in the Confederate army east of the Mississippi. His harsh methods and rash military action as commander in Arkansas in 1862-63 resulted in his transfer back to the East, where he served creditably as a subordinate field commander until disabled by battle wounds.—W. L. B.

Hine, Robert V. (1921-   ). Historian. Born in Los Angeles, California, Hine attended Pomona College and Yale University. He began teaching at the University of California at Riverside in 1954.

Through his research and writings Hine made many contributions to the history of social and cultural development of the West. His first book, *California's Utopian Colonies* (1953), skillfully analyzed a significant phase of western reform. Hine then turned to the career of Edward Kern, an important nineteenth-century scientist, and wrote a pioneering work, *Edward Kern and American Expansion* (1962). A few years later Hine's study of a nineteenth-century cartographer in the West appeared, *Bartlett's West: Drawing the Mexican Boundary* (1968). Meanwhile, in 1963, Hine collaborated with Edwin Bingham in editing an anthology for college courses in western history, *The Frontier Experience: Readings in the Trans-Mississippi West* (1963). He is also the author of various articles dealing with aspects of the history of frontier cultural life.—G. D. N.

Hitchcock, Gilbert Monell (1859-1934). Nebraska newspaper publisher and politician. Born in Omaha, Nebraska, Hitchcock studied in Germany in 1881. He established the Omaha *Evening Herald* in 1885 and in 1889 purchased the Omaha *Morning Herald*. Hitchcock amalgamated these two publications into the *World-Herald*, Nebraska's largest newspaper. Unlike his father, Phineas Warren HITCHCOCK, he was a Democrat and was elected to three terms in Congress (1903-05, 1907-11) and two terms in the Senate (1911-23). From 1914 to 1916 he worked unsuccessfully to secure the enactment of a statute barring the sale of arms and munitions to the belligerents in World War I. As Senate minority leader in 1919-20, he struggled in vain to secure the ratification of the Treaty of Versailles.

See Robert Foster Patterson, "Gilbert M. Hitchcock: A Study of Two Careers," *University of Colorado Studies* (November 1940).—H. A. D.

Hitchcock, Phineas Warren (1831-1881). Nebraska politician. Hitchcock was born in New Lebanon, New York, and graduated from Williams College. In 1857 he established a law practice in Omaha and became an early leader in Nebraska's Republican party. He was United States marshal for the territory (1861-64), delegate to Congress (1865-67), surveyor-general of Nebraska and Iowa (1867-69), and United States senator from Nebraska (1871-77).

As chairman of the Senate Committee on Territories, Hitchcock did much to bring about the admission of Colorado to the Union in 1876. He was also the author of the TIMBER CULTURE ACT of 1873, which provided that persons planting trees on forty acres of public land and maintaining such groves for ten years would receive title to the quarter section upon which this activity was undertaken. Although the required acreage of trees was soon reduced to ten and the time of cultivation to eight years, the statute was no panacea either in foresting the western plains or in assisting a majority of homesteaders. The act was repealed in 1891.

See Roy M. Robbins, *Our Landed Heritage: The Public Domain, 1776-1936* (1942).—H. A. D.

Hittell, John Shertzer (1825-1901). California jour-

nalist. Hittell emigrated to California looking for gold and excitement in 1849, but turned to journalism. He established his reputation as an important California intellectual as correspondent and editor for the *Alta California* and by writing a series of nationally circulated books on the resources and economic potential of California. Like his California contemporaries H. H. Bancroft and Theodore H. Hittell (his brother), Hittell very much reflected his times, dabbling in utopian socialism and phrenology in his youth and developing into a spokesman and apologist for industrial capitalism in his mature and productive years. His work remains a valuable source for the economic history of California.

See Claude Rowland Petty, "John S. Hittell and the Gospel of California," *Pacific Historical Review* (February 1955).—J. F.

Hodge, Frederick Webb (1864-1956). Anthropologist and historian. Born at Plymouth, England, Hodge came to America with his parents when he was a small boy. He went to public schools in Washington, D. C., and attended Columbian University (present-day George Washington University). After a brief stint in a law office, he became secretary of the United States Geological Survey and Bureau of American Ethnology. From 1886 to 1889 he was secretary of the Hemenway Southwestern Archaeological Expedition.

During the early twentieth century Hodge moved back and forth between the Smithsonian Institution and New Mexico and Arizona, completing the monumental two-volume *Handbook of American Indians* (1907-10) and excavations of the prehistoric and early historic ruins of Hawikuh along the way. (Hawikuh was the Zuñi Indian site stormed by Coronado and his men in 1540.)

Hodge, one of the founders of the American Anthropological Association, edited the association's journal, *American Anthropologist*, from 1902 to 1914. He was also editor of the classic twenty-volume set of Edward Curtis' photographic depiction of North American Indians.

In 1932 Hodge became director of the Southwest Museum in Los Angeles, a position he held until his retirement in 1956. Afterward he and his wife moved to Santa Fe, New Mexico, where he continued to work almost to the day of his death.

Known to his intimate friends by his Zuñi name, Teluli ("Mouse Who Digs Holes"), Hodge left behind him a legacy of more than three hundred and fifty published works, most of them concerned with Indians and western history, in addition to journals he started and helped to start. His many boxes of private papers and correspondence were placed by his wife in the Southwest Museum, which continues a publication series in his name. Not too long before he died, Hodge commented that he would have to live for another two hundred and fifty years to finish the many research and writing projects in which he was involved.

See Fay-Cooper Cole, "Frederick Webb Hodge, 1864-1956," *American Anthropologist*, vol. 59 (1957).—B. L. F.

Hoecken, Adrian (1815-1897). Roman Catholic missionary. A Dutch Jesuit, Hoecken was a peacemaker with the Kalispel and Flathead tribes from 1844 to 1861. His brother, Christian, was a peacemaker with the Potawatomi and Osage.

See Robert I. Burns, *The Jesuits and the Indian Wars of the Northwest* (1966).—R. I. B.

Hogg, James Stephen (1851-1906). Businessman and Texas politician. Hogg was born near Rusk in east Texas in comfortable circumstances. The deaths of his father, a Confederate general, in 1862, and his mother a year later forced twelve-year-old Hogg to seek a living. Later he went to journalism school and taught himself law. Heritage and temperament made him a Democrat, and he never wavered from the party's commitment to states rights, localism, and segregation. This partisan allegiance and his striking oratorical ability brought election as a county and district attorney in east Texas in the decade after 1878. The reputation he acquired as a prosecutor, as well as connection with the influential politicians of his section, won him the Democratic nomination for attorney general in 1886.

Over the next four years, Hogg prosecuted the railroads and other corporations whose policies had irritated Texas farmers, processors, and shippers. He became an advocate of a state railroad commission under the tutelage of United States Senator John H. Reagan. The two men believed that a commission could bring offending lines to heel, shape a rate structure more favorable to local economic interests, and preserve the agrarian character of Texas society. Hogg's endorsement of this program, his record in office, and the support of the Farmers Alliance led to the Democratic party's gubernatorial nomination in 1890. With it went certain victory.

As governor, Hogg secured passage of a railroad commission law in 1891. This victory aroused the enmity of the railroads and their corporate allies. Refusal to appoint a farmer to the commission alienated his rural constituency. But the wily Hogg had a firm hold on the middle ground of state politics. Simultaneous denunciations of outside economic forces and the federal courts played skillfully on grievances against the railroads and the chronic distrust of governmental power among his fellow Democrats. Promising that Texas "will regulate the railroads and not be regulated by them," the portly chief executive overcame opposition from conservative and Populist candidates in the frenetic election of 1892.

His last two years in office were less eventful, though he did obtain laws to regulate corporate securities and to limit alien landholding. Although he never lost his taste for politics, he did turn to the oil business upon retirement. Before his death he made a fortune. Like so many erstwhile progressives, Hogg was no enemy of capitalism as such; he wanted to redistribute the benefits of the system, not exterminate them.

Hogg left a mixed legacy. His adherents called him a reformer, a liberal, and a champion of the people. Texans remember him as one of the state's few progressive governors. But he was also a segregationist, a naïve economic thinker, and a ruthless foe of Populism. His career indicates the danger of turning the movement for reform in the Southwest in the Gilded Age into a simple struggle of good and evil. In Hogg's case the impulse for change, and what he defined as "good," was limited to the state context, designed to benefit local interests at the expense of the national economy, and was rigidly confined to the white middle-class members of the ruling Democratic party.

See the James Stephen Hogg papers, University of Texas Archives; and Robert C. Cotner, *James Stephen Hogg* (1959).—L. L. G.

Holbrook, Stewart Hall (1893-1964). Writer and historian. Born in Newport, Vermont, Holbrook went to a rural school in Vermont and to Colebrook Academy in New Hampshire. In 1911 he went to Canada and found a job on the Winnipeg, Manitoba, *Telegram* and, after a time, toured the western provinces in "one of the worst repertoire companies ever seen." A job as scaler in a Vermont logging camp was interrupted by service with the field artillery in France during World War I, after which he returned to drive logs on the Connecticut River.

Early in 1920 Holbrook went to Boston and bought a derby and a round-trip ticket to Victoria, British Columbia. He sold the return half of his ticket and went logging on the Fraser River. He began writing in camp and was encouraged when some of his work was accepted by Harold Ross and H. L. Mencken. In 1923 Holbrook moved to Portland, Oregon, to be associate editor (later editor) of the *Four L Lumber News*, the organ of the conservative Loyal Legion of Loggers and Lumbermen. In 1934 he turned to free-lance writing.

Holbrook has been described as "a deep well of nostalgia." Over a long career he wrote more than twenty books and countless essays and articles dealing with a wide variety of Americana: logging; iron-making; folklore; railroads; tycoons; forgotten figures of American history; forest fires; and the Columbia River. Because Holbrook's essential conservatism and romanticism made him shun analysis and social or economic criticism, his histories were straightforward descriptions and narratives and fraught with many an anecdote. As he once put it: "My only ambition as a writer is to put into books the figures and portions of American history that I think have been largely ignored or badly treated." Although Holbrook took all of America's past for his province, his long residence in Portland, his role as columnist for the Portland *Oregonian*, and the number of his books that focus on the region link him to the Pacific Northwest.

Holbrook's best-known books include: *Holy Old Mackinaw* (1938, reprinted in 1962 as *The American Lumberjack*), an informal history of logging from Maine to Seattle; *Burning an Empire: America's Greatest Forest Fires* (1943); *Little Annie Oakley and Other Rugged People* (1948), a collection of short pieces on heroic or sensational figures out of our past such as Calamity Jane, the James and Younger brothers, Kit Carson, and Buffalo Bill; *Far Corner* (1952), Holbrook's personal view of the Pacific Northwest as expressed through vignettes on such topics as the Heppner flood, the myth of Marcus Whitman's "saving Oregon" in 1843, and the society of anarchists at Home, Washington; and *The Columbia* (1956), a book in the American Rivers series, in which Holbrook develops the history of the Pacific Northwest around the Columbia River system and the vast area that system drains.—E. R. B.

Holladay, Ben (1819-1887). Transportation entrepreneur. Holladay was born in Carlisle County, Kentucky, but in his early boyhood he moved to western Missouri, some accounts suggesting that he went with his family, others that he ran away from home. He had a minimal education. At Weston, Missouri, he met Notley Ann Calvert, with whom he eloped and was married without the consent of her parents. The couple had seven children. Shrewd and energetic, he tried many occupations: soloonkeeper, postmaster, and general-store and hotel keeper in Weston. During these years he became known as a boisterous, coarse, and crude man, fond of whiskey and gambling. He also had successfully engaged in trade with Indians in Kansas.

When the Mexican War broke out in 1846, Holladay furnished and freighted supplies for Stephen W. Kearny's Army of the West. At the end of the war he purchased wagons and oxen from the government at bargain prices and in partnership with Theodore F. Warner, of Weston, took fifty wagonloads of goods to Salt Lake City in 1849. To insure success in marketing his goods profitably, Holladay took along a letter to Brigham Young from Colonel A. W. Doniphan, who had befriended the Mormons during their difficulties in Missouri and who also knew Holladay as a reliable trader and freighter during the Mexican War. In 1850 Holladay and his partner bought a herd of oxen and drove them to California, making a handsome profit.

Success seemed to characterize all Holladay's promotions. In 1858 he became associated with Russell, Majors and Waddell when he bought large quantities of livestock for them in connection with their freighting operations. He also joined William H. Russell in undertaking a contract to deliver flour between Camp Scott and Camp Floyd in Utah. In 1860 he advanced money and cashed drafts to assist the Central Overland California and Pike's Peak Express Company, owned by Russell, Majors and Waddell, in establishing the Pony Express. In time, he had to assume a mortgage on the holdings of that partnership and took over its properties at a foreclosure auction in March 1862 for $100,000. At this juncture he organized the Overland Stage Line, which, taking over the responsibilities of Russell, Majors and Waddell's firm, operated the eastern section of the trans-Missouri stage mail until 1864 under subcontract to the Overland Mail Company, with whose stages Holladay's line connected at Salt Lake City. He also operated branch lines in Nebraska and Colorado at this time, on which he had government mail contracts. In 1864 Holladay was awarded a four-year contract from the government for the mail eastward of Salt Lake City and on extensive new branch and feeder lines he had established in Idaho, Montana, Oregon, and Washington. Suffering financial reverses as a result of Indian attacks upon his stagecoaches, way stations, and stock in 1865, Holladay sold out the following year to Wells, Fargo & Co. Immediately, he invested his capital in the Northern Pacific Transportation Company, operating vessels from Alaska to Mexico. He had been interested in the steamship business since 1863, when he organized the California, Oregon and Mexican Steamship Company. In 1868 he became the chief owner of the Oregon Central Railroad Company and sold his steamship interests to construct 240 miles of track. In the Panic of 1873 he suffered tremendous financial reverses. German bondholders who had invested in his railroad promotion took control of the company in 1876, eliminated Holladay's influence, and he retired from business.

A self-made man who trusted no one, his business and political morals were deplorable: he lied to investors; he juggled his books; he bought influence. One of his favorite tactics was to wage a price war with a competing stage line and then, when the competition had been driven out of business, raise his prices to unheard-of levels. He was even reputed to have staged "Indian" attacks on rival lines. The personification of the expression "Easy come, easy go," he championed the underdog, grubstaked many a prospector, and generously contributed to charities. He built a pretentious mansion known as Ophir near White Plains, New York, for his family to which he was devoted, but he spent most of his time in an elaborate home in Washington, D.C., where he lavishly, and somewhat vulgarly, entertained politicians and men of influence when Congress was in session. He traveled in a private coach, drawn by blooded horses, which was trimmed with silver and outfitted with a food locker and silver decanters. His two daughters by his first wife married titled Europeans. Left a widower in 1873, he married Esther Campbell and had two additional children. Holladay died in Portland, Oregon.

See J. V. Frederick, *Ben Holladay, the Stagecoach King* (1940); Ellis Lucia, *The Saga of Ben Holladay* (1959); and Raymond W. Settle and Mary L. Settle, *War Drums and Wagon Wheels* (1966).—W. T. J.

Holladay's stagecoach lines. Ben HOLLADAY entered the field of western transportation as a freighter during the Mexican War (1846-48). After accumulating a small fortune in freighting, he transferred his interest to stagecoach lines. His business affairs were closely intertwined with the Russell, Majors and Waddell company, to which he made financial advances for the purchase of equipment and supplies. This freighting firm had also entered the stagecoach business and in time organized the Central Overland California and Pike's Peak Express Company. When the Overland Mail Company obtained the government contract for a daily mail service after March 1861 on the central route, the decision was made to subcontract the line east of Salt Lake to the C.O.C. and P.P. Express Co. When Russell, Majors and Waddell became insolvent in 1862, Holladay obtained control of its defunct staging operations at a bankruptcy auction. He also took over its unexpired mail contract and the Kansas charter under which it had operated. The contract for the daily overland mail was up for bids again in 1864. At this time the bifurcation of the route was officially recognized when Holladay was issued a contract for the area east of Salt Lake and the Overland Mail received the contract to the west. Between 1862 and 1866 Holladay successfully obtained eight mail contracts.

These mail contracts were used to subsidize his passenger service by stagecoach. Holladay organized the Overland Stage Line to book passengers traveling from Kansas to California, and he actually operated daily stagecoach service west of Atchison, Kansas, to Salt Lake City. The Colorado legislature also passed an act permitting him to run a branch line into Denver. In the uprising following the Sand Creek massacre Indians along his routes burned way stations, drove off cattle and horses, and stole supplies. He demanded, and succeeded in getting, military protection. Mining developments in Idaho and Montana necessitated improved communication into the Northwest, and Holladay ran triweekly stages from Salt Lake to Boise, Idaho, and Walla Walla, Washington, also delivering the mail. A tremendous network of stage lines was built radiating not only out of Salt Lake but from Denver into Central City and Black Hawk, Colorado, and between Nebraska City and Kearney City, Nebraska. By the middle of the 1860s Holladay

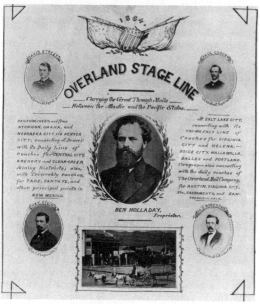

A poster for Holladay's Overland Stage Line. (Wells Fargo Bank)

was operating five thousand miles of stagecoach lines and was known as the Napoleon of the Plains.

Competition developed on the overland mail line when D. A. Butterfield organized the Overland Despatch Company to transport freight, express, and passengers along an alternative route between Missouri and the central Rocky Mountains. The eastern express companies had encouraged Butterfield in his venture, particularly Wells, Fargo & Co., which now had control over the Overland Mail Company operating west of Salt Lake City. Having made an arrangement to cooperate with Butterfield into Denver, the express companies threatened to stock the route between Denver and Salt Lake, and thereby have a through route. Holladay anticipated their move, purchased Butterfield's Overland Despatch Company, and thwarted the plans of the express companies. The upshot of this situation was the "Grand Consolidation" of the Holladay stagecoach, express, and mail interests with the American, United States, and Wells, Fargo & Co. express business, operating under the latter name and under a liberal charter that Holladay had obtained from the Colorado legislature a few months previously. Wells, Fargo & Co. was capitalized at $10 million and controlled all the large express and stage lines between the Missouri River and the Pacific Coast. Holladay was issued stock in the new company. He held the stock for a short time, then sold it for cash, and withdrew from the transportation business.

Holladay's financial success was largely based upon his organizational ability and his skill in the selection of reliable personnel. The supervision of each section of his main line was entrusted to a superintendent, and a company representative, known as a conductor, periodically rode on the stage to inspect the service. Stations were maintained at intervals of ten to fifty miles along the route. Some were known as "swing stations," where only corrals were maintained to provide a change of horses, and "home stations," where passengers could obtain meals and lodging. The best of these were crude, made of logs or adobe and often without flooring. Holladay had hundreds of employees engaged as drivers, station keepers, blacksmiths, and stock tenders.

See J. V. Frederick, *Ben Holladay, the Stagecoach King* (1940).—W. T. J.

Holliday, Doc [John Henry] (1851-1887). Dentist, gambler, and gunman. Holliday was born in Griffin, Georgia, to a moderately successful family and reared in the genteel tradition of the South. When Major Henry Holliday, John's father, came home from the Civil War in 1862, the family moved to the little village of Valdosta in southern Georgia. Those years are clouded, but it seems clear that Holliday and his father had difficulties, particularly after his mother died and the major remarried. Following the war, Valdosta was occupied by federal troops, and feeling against them ran high. Young Holliday may have been involved in an effort to blow up the county courthouse (which housed the Freedman's Bureau office) in 1867 or 1868. At any rate, he left home at about this time. He was back home when the census taker came in 1870 and listed his occupation as "student." He returned to his studies after that and graduated from the Pennsylvania College of Dental Surgery in 1872. In July 1872 he practiced dentistry briefly in Atlanta in the office of Dr. Arthur C. Ford. Later he opened an office in Griffin, but he had developed a bad cough. Doctors told him he had contracted chronic pulmonary tuberculosis and advised a drier climate. Doc visited Valdosta then and later stayed briefly with relatives at Jonesboro. Sometime late in 1872 or early in 1873, Doc headed west. It was his only hope for survival.

The Georgia years of Doc Holliday are still clouded, and family tradition insists that he was involved in a shooting incident on the Withlacoochee River. The family version reports that he fired several shots over the heads of Negroes who were swimming on family property. Other accounts claim that he killed one or more of them. No contemporary record has been found of the incident, and efforts to pin down the date have generally failed. It could have happened just prior to any of the times he is known to have left Valdosta, in 1868, 1870, or 1872.

In Dallas, Texas, Holliday practiced dentistry with Dr. John Seegar. The practice was apparently successful, but Doc was soon drawn into the life of the frontier gambler. He was adept at poker and faro and gradually built a reputation as a successful gambler. In 1875 he was involved in a shooting scrape and was arrested for the first time. Later that year he abandoned Dallas for Fort Griffin. He was a drifter in trouble after that—in Jacksboro, Pueblo, Denver, Cheyenne, Deadwood, Denver again, and finally in Dodge City—gambling, drinking, and coughing all the way. Rumors of dead men on the trail are numerous but difficult to confirm. He met Mary Katherine Michael, known in the West as Kate Elder, at some point in his wanderings and married her. In Dodge City he became a friend of Wyatt Earp and even practiced dentistry again, if only briefly. But mostly he gambled and kept out of trouble. Wyatt Earp insisted that Doc had saved his life in Dodge by coming to his rescue when he was surrounded by rowdy cowhands. Doc reportedly disarmed a cowboy who drew his gun on Wyatt from behind. Just when the episode took place is not clear, but it seems to have cemented the friendship of Earp and Holliday and linked their futures.

In 1879 Holliday moved to Trinidad and then to Leadville, Colorado, before finding his way to Las Vegas, New Mexico. He opened a saloon in Las Vegas in partnership with another man, but the enterprise did not last long. He killed one Mike Gordon, who tried to wreck Doc's establishment, and wounded bartender Charley White in a personal quarrel. In 1880 Doc followed Wyatt Earp to Tombstone, Arizona. His presence proved to be an embarrassment to Earp, who had become a deputy sheriff and was trying to build a political future there. In October 1880, Earp had to arrest Holliday for a run-in with gambler Johnny Tyler and saloonkeeper Milt Joyce. Thereafter, Holliday's quarrelsome nature, his drinking, his reputation as a shady character and killer, and, later, suspicions that he was involved in an attempted stage robbery proved liabilities to Earp. The stage robbery occurred in March 1881. Two men were killed in the attempt, and Earp saw a chance to enhance his political stature by capturing the outlaws responsible. Then Earp discovered that Holliday was suspected of being involved. In May 1881 Doc was arrested for murder and attempted robbery. The principal witness against Doc was Kate Holliday. Although the charges were later dropped, the suspicions remained and took their toll in Earp's popularity.

Few of Earp's friends liked Holliday, but they tolerated him because of Earp's friendship for him. And when the Earps needed a friend, he was there. He was at the O. K. Corral fight and stood at Wyatt Earp's side in the ensuing vendetta against the EARP BROTHERS. He was on hand when the Earp party killed Frank Stilwell and a Mexican named Florentine, both suspected of having a hand in the murder of Morgan Earp. Doc fled Arizona with Wyatt Earp in 1882.

He was arrested at Denver on trumped-up charges designed to keep him in custody until extradition papers could be drawn up to return him to Arizona for the murders of Stilwell and Florentine. Holliday would surely have been extradited if not for the behind-the-scenes manipulations of friends of Wyatt Earp. The most visible instrument of that effort was Bat Masterson, who intervened on Doc's behalf with the governor of Colorado.

From that point on, Holliday was a drifter, a celebrated gambler with a shady past and worsening tuberculosis. Contemporary newspapers place him in Dodge City during the Dodge City War in 1883. In 1884 he shot gambler Billy Allen in Leadville and renewed his quarrel with Johnny Tyler, a gambler from Holliday's Tombstone days. But time was running out for Doc. His tuberculosis reached its final stages, and in 1887 he had to go to Glenwood Springs, Colorado, for treatment. He died there in November at the age of thirty-six. Kate Holliday remarried and found a better life for herself as proprietress of a boarding house in Globe, Arizona, and lived to write her personal account of life with Doc Holliday.

There are two biographies: Pat Jahns, *The Frontier World of Doc Holliday* (1957), and John Myers Myers,

Doc Holliday (1955). The Georgia years are dealt with in Albert S. Pendleton, Jr., and Susan McKey Thomas, *In Search of the Hollidays* (1973).—G. L. R.

Hollister, William Welles (1818-1886). California rancher and developer. Born in Ohio, Hollister studied at Kenyon College but withdrew because of faulty vision. For fifteen years he managed farms for his merchant father until he had a stake to start on his own. He bought two hundred head of cattle and in 1851 drove them from Ohio to California. The venture was so successful that he returned to Ohio and with financial help from a sister organized a party to take on a larger venture.

With fifty herdsmen and drovers he took nine thousand sheep, four hundred head of cattle, and some horses west, across rivers, mountains, and desert. They were eighteen months on the road, hitting the coast near present-day Los Angeles and then going north. With the profits from his venture, Hollister settled in Monterey County (present-day San Benito) on the old San Justo grant of sixty thousand acres. Here he was a stockman from 1854 to 1869 and one of the state's largest sheep raisers. Hollister sold most of his land to settlers, whose payments and interest Hollister reduced when hard times hit; in gratitude the town of Hollister was named for him. In 1869 Hollister formed a partnership at Santa Barbara with Thomas and Albert Dibblee. They acquired four large ranches: Ranchos Nuestra Señora del Refugio, Las Cruces, Salsipuedes, and Las Armitas. Included were 150,000 acres of the original Rancho Lompoc, part of which was sold to an immigrant company in 1874. In 1881 the partnership was dissolved.

Hollister helped develop both northern and southern California. He helped found Santa Barbara College and engaged in many civic enterprises.—C. H. F.

Hollon, W. Eugene (1913-   ). Historian. Hollon was born in Commerce, Texas, and received his undergraduate education at East Texas State University in Commerce. Attracted by Walter Prescott Webb, a prominent western historian at the University of Texas, Hollon went there to pursue graduate studies in history.

He began teaching at Schreiner Institute in 1942. In 1945 he joined the University of Oklahoma, where he stayed until 1967. He was also curator of history for the university's Stovall Museum of Science and History. In 1967 he accepted a Regents professorship at the University of Toledo.

Hollon early revealed a penchant for broad general narrative histories about various aspects related to the development of the trans-Mississippi West. His first book, *Lost Pathfinder: Zebulon Pike* (1949), both competently summarized much that was then known about that explorer and added new data. Hollon also contributed other works on the history of exploration in the trans-Mississippi West, including *Beyond the Cross Timber: The Travels of Randolph B. Marcy* (1955), one of the finest accounts of the Great Plains prior to the arrival of the railroads, and, as collaborator, *William Bollert's Texas* (1956), one of the best descriptions of social life in Texas on the eve of annexation. In the succeeding decade Hollon extended the breadth of his writings. In 1961 appeared his *The Southwest, Old and New*, designed as a comprehensive general work that surveyed and synthesized the development of the region from its earliest beginnings until the middle of the twentieth century. In addition, Hollon attempted to extend some of Walter Prescott Webb's concepts about desert areas in the West in *The Great American Desert* (1966), an effort to sketch general outlines of historical development in the arid portions of the trans-Mississippi region. In 1968 Hollon aided in the revision of a well-known textbook in western history, LeRoy Hafen and Carl Coke Rister's *Western America*.

During 1958 Hollon served as a visiting professor at Peruvian universities, and in 1966-67 as a Fulbright lecturer at the University of Madrid in Spain. Active in professional organizations, Hollon was selected as president of the Western History Association in 1966-67. In 1971 his alma mater awarded him its Distinguished Alumnus Citation.—G. D. N.

Holmes, David (1769-1832). Mississippi politician. Holmes was born in Virginia, practiced law there, and served as United States representative from Virginia. He came to Mississippi as an appointed territorial governor in 1809 and served during the remainder of the territorial period. He was president of the Mississippi constitutional convention of 1817, first governor of the state of Mississippi, and one of the first United States senators from Mississippi. He returned to Virginia in 1826 because of ill health and spent the remaining years of his life there.

Holmes was one of the last presidential appointees of Thomas Jefferson and was a staunch and loyal Republican throughout his life. As territorial governor his attention centered on the problem of defining the boundaries of the territory as it prepared for statehood, public lands, Indian affairs, and the territory's role in the War of 1812 and the Creek War (1813-14). It was Governor Holmes's task to supervise the sale of public lands in the territory and to see that only proper claimants were sold lands. In his role as superintendent of Indian affairs he had to deal with the problem of liquor sales to Indians and the demands of white settlers for additional Indian lands. A quiet and effective worker, he was unopposed for election as the first state governor and put into operation the machinery of the state government with a minimum of difficulty.—J. E. G.

Holston River settlements. The settlements along the Holston River were only part of a much wider pattern of settlement west of the Appalachian Mountains. There was no one place that can be called the Holston settlements since stations appeared along the Holston, and nearby Clinch, Powell, French Broad, Nolichucky, and Watauga rivers. These settlements grew out of the restless expansion of Virginians and North Carolinians into the Tennessee country.

There is no doubt that the War of Alamance (1771) and its aftereffects stimulated the North Carolina migration. Also negotiation of the Treaty of HARD LABOR in 1768 and its revision in 1770 in the Treaty of LOCHABER made available generous slices of Cherokee lands for Anglo-American settlement. From 1763 on, the headstreams of the Tennessee River were visited by numerous hunters and land scouts. It was here that the famous long hunters first appeared in the western country, and behind them came cabin settlers under the leadership of various men, most important of whom were John SEVIER, James ROBERTSON, John Carter, and William Bean.

The so-called Holston, or Watauga, settlements were of the utmost importance in the opening of the broader trans-Appalachian frontier beyond Cumberland Gap. People learned to live separated from the oldest centers of population, to use the basic resources of the country in building their houses and supplying themselves with food and clothing, and to live with a constant threat of Indian hostility. The Holston region was the schooling ground for future pioneering, and its settlements became a base of operation in opening and defending the frontier (see WATAUGA ASSOCIATION). Especially important was the fact that the settlements became strong enough by the middle of the revolutionary war to form a very real block to British and Indian attacks from the rear. Holston settlers in time fought against both Cherokee and British, east and west of the mountains.

See John P. Brown, *Old Frontiers* (1938); Carl S. Driver, *John Sevier, Pioneer of the Old Southwest* (1932); Philip M. Hamer, ed., *Tennessee: A History, 1673-1932*, 4 vols. (1933); J. G. M. Ramsey, *The Annals of Tennessee* (1853); and Samuel Cole Williams, *Tennessee During the Revolutionary War* (1944).—T. D. C.

Homestake Mine. See LEAD, SOUTH DAKOTA.

Homestead Act (1862). The western pioneers in the first half of the nineteenth century who created farms on the public lands regarded themselves as making America with their capital and labor. They felt that the heavy cost of clearing, breaking, fencing (see BARBED WIRE), and erecting homes, while paying taxes, building roads, and supporting schools and churches, was enough of a drain on their resources and that for the government to exact payment for the land they were improving was to place another serious hurdle in the way of their success. They thought that they should not be penalized by having to pay $1.25 an acre for land that was worthless before the improvements of society gave it value, particularly when that money was needed to buy livestock, farm implements, tools, household goods, and food for a year or more until they could raise enough for their own needs. By selling them land the government was forcing them into debt, perhaps even additional debt to that which they already had. Eastern workingmen began the movement for free land. It was taken up by Horace Greeley through his powerful New York *Tribune* and received the support of western Democrats and Republicans. An emasculated homestead bill was passed by Congress in 1860 but vetoed by President James Buchanan because he was under heavy obligation to the proslavery southerners who wanted to slow the growth of the West. The veto, plus Buchanan's subserviency to the slave interests on the Kansas question, divided the Democratic party and made possible the election in 1860 of Abraham Lincoln, candidate of the Republican party, which was pledged to enact a homestead measure.

By withdrawing from the Union in 1860 and 1861 the South enabled Congress to adopt a truly free land measure, which President Lincoln signed on May 27, 1862. The Homestead Act authorized any citizen or intended citizen to select any surveyed but unclaimed tract of public land up to 160 acres and to gain title to it after five years' residence, making prescribed improvements, and paying a modest fee for the service of the register and receiver. If the homesteader wished to gain title at the end of six months' residence on the land in order to borrow on it for additional improvements, he could

A homesteader and his family. (National Archives)

commute his homestead entry to a preemption entry, pay $1.25 an acre, and receive title to it. Later amendments permitted Civil War veterans to count their years of service toward the five years of residence the law required.

Although much of the government land in the humid sections of the Middle West had already been sold or granted to railroads (see RAILROAD LAND GRANTS) or states and was not subject to homesteading, there still remained millions of acres in the upper Mississippi and Missouri valleys capable of being made into farms. Unfortunately, Congress did not reserve the remaining public lands for actual settlers, as Greeley had urged, and after 1862 much of that land was either bought by speculators or granted to railroads, thus frustrating the purpose of the Homestead law to some extent.

As settlers pressed into the drier portion of the Great Plains the quarter-section unit was found to be too small for the extensive type of farming required there. By making use of the Preemption Act, which was retained until 1891, and the TIMBER CULTURE ACT of 1873, homesteaders could acquire 480 acres of public land. In 1904, 640-acre homesteads were permitted in the Sandhills of western Nebraska and in 1916 full-section homesteads were permitted elsewhere on land suitable for grazing. Laxness in administering these laws enabled cattle and mining companies and speculators to use dummy entrymen to acquire large areas of the public domain (see LAND POLICY: *1780-1896*). After 1890 the rate of failure on the dry lands was high, at least one half of the original homesteaders failing to complete their

entries. In the mountain states for every farm or ranch successfully established there were four original homestead entries and two final entries. Yet the 1,623,691 homestead applications that were carried to patent were the chief means by which settlers west of the Missouri were successful in establishing ownership of farms. The Homestead Act aided materially in reversing the trend toward tenancy that was so characteristic of the older public land states where speculators had anticipated settlers by acquiring millions of acres for resale at high prices or to rent to tenants.

See Paul W. Gates, *History of Public Land Law Development* (1968).—P. W. G.

hoof-and-mouth disease. Hoof-and-mouth disease is a highly infectious disease of cattle and other clovenfooted animals. It is caused by a filterable virus that is only one millionth of an inch in diameter and is believed to be the smallest of the viruses affecting men or animals. Cattle and swine are most susceptible to the disease, but sheep, goats, buffalo, camels, deer, llama, and antelope may also be infected. Even man is susceptible to a mild form of the disease.

The disease has reached the epidemic stage periodically throughout the cattle-raising areas of the world, including the American West. The worst outbreak of the disease in the United States occurred in 1914, at which time the infection struck livestock in twenty-two states. The only solution to the problem was eradication of the diseased animals and the quarantine of affected areas, procedures that cost cattlemen untold thousands of dollars. Mild outbreaks continued to occur throughout the rest of the century, and the disease is still a threat despite the development of an effective vaccination program in the 1950s. The last epidemic was in England in 1967. During a five-week period the disease took a toll of 422,500 animals, and eradication cost cattlemen 240 million dollars.

See Edward E. Dale, *The Range Cattle Industry* (1960); and John T. Schlebecker, *Cattle Raising on the Plains, 1900-1961* (1963).—R. B. W.

Hooker, Henry Clay (1828-1907). Arizona cattleman. Hooker was born in Hinsdale, New Hampshire, left home at an early age, worked briefly in Kansas City, and in 1853 settled at Placerville, California, where he ran a hardware business. In 1866 Hooker became a cattle buyer for Hugh L. Hinds, who held the beef contracts for the Arizona forts and reservations; in 1871 he entered the employ of William B. Hooper and James M. Barney, merchant-freighters at Yuma, when they secured the Arizona contracts. The following year Hooker filed on a 160-acre homestead in the Sulphur Springs valley in Arizona and started the Sierra Bonita Ranch. Local markets soon developed at the neighboring San Carlos Apache reservation and forts Grant and Thomas. By the late 1880s Hooker expanded his holdings by location, purchase, and prior occupation to cover more than eight hundred square miles of rangeland, on which more than ten thousand head of blooded cattle wore his Crooked H brand. He also maintained a dairy herd, raised Poland China hogs, and engaged in experimental farming.

A quiet little man who dressed neatly, Hooker loved fast horses and maintained a large herd of fine brood mares and blooded stallions. Catering to health-seekers, he developed Hooker's Hot Springs in the neighboring Galiuro Mountains. Famous dignitaries were frequent guests at the Sierra Bonita, where Hooker entertained lavishly at his fortlike hacienda; life on the ranch was even depicted in a Broadway play, *Arizona: A Drama in Four Acts* (1889), by Augustus Thomas. By the 1890s Hooker had reduced his herd and shifted to closed-range operations. He built a townhouse in Los Angeles, where he made his residence until his death.

See Earl R. Forrest, "The Fabulous Sierra Bonita," *Journal of Arizona History* (Autumn 1965); and Frank Lockwood, *Pioneer Portraits* (1968).—H. P. H.

Hooper, William Henry (1813-1882). Utah politician and Mormon businessman. Hooper was born in Dorchester County, Maryland. He was a senator in the provisional State of Deseret, and when Utah became a territory in 1851, he served as its secretary (1857-58). He was Utah Territory's second delegate to Congress (1859-69), serving five separate terms. Though a monogamist, Hooper strongly defended the constitutionality of polygamy and religious liberty.

Hooper became a vice president of Zion's Cooperative Mercantile Institution in 1868 and in 1873 was named superintendent. He and others organized the Bank of Deseret in 1870, now a key element in the First Security Bank of Utah, National Association.

See Andrew Jenson, *Latter-day Saint Biographical Encyclopedia* (1901).—L. J. A.

Hopi Indians. Situated in the plateau country of northern Arizona, wholly surrounded by the Navaho Indian reservation (see NAVAHO INDIANS), are ten traditional Hopi Indian settlements, most of which have been

in or near their present locations since at least the early sixteenth century. One of them, ORAIBI, is very probably the oldest continuously inhabited town in the United States, having in all likelihood been occupied since the middle of the thirteenth century.

The Hopi's initial contact with non-Indians took place in 1540 when Pedro de Tovar, a captain among the soldiers of Francisco Vásquez de Coronado, set out to visit them from the Zuñi villages. While he was there he heard of a great river, and in late August 1540 Captain García López de Cárdenas set out under Coronado's orders and returned to the Hopi pueblos. The Hopi furnished him with guides, and Cárdenas became the first European ever to see the Grand Canyon.

From time to time throughout the entire period of Spanish and Mexican occupation of New Mexico and Arizona there were attempts made by Franciscan missionaries to bring the Hopi into the fold of Christianity. The friars dedicated a church at the Hopi village of Awatovi in 1629. By 1680 there were two additional *visitas*, or mission visiting stations, among the Hopi, and there were churches at Oraibi, Mishongnovi, and possibly Walpi. The rebellion of the PUEBLO INDIANS in New Mexico in 1680 brought missionizing attempts to a temporary halt, and the Hopi—remote as they were from the Rio Grande valley of New Mexico and the heartland of the revolt—took in Pueblo Indian refugees in the wake of the turmoil. The Hopi-Tewa village of Hano was one result.

After the reconquest of New Mexico by the Spaniards in 1692, the church at Awatovi was rebuilt, but other Hopi attacked the pueblo in 1700 and destroyed it. Between 1700 and the end of the Spanish and Mexican periods there were several attempts made to convert the Hopi, but all of them ended in failure. There are missionaries working among the Hopi today, but their influence appears to be minimal.

The coming of Anglo-Americans to the Southwest had no immediate effect on the Hopi, and until the 1880s the Hopi remained largely in splendid isolation in their mesa-top settlements, unmolested by Indian agents—they saw their first one in 1869—and taking no part in warfare against non-Indians. Their military troubles were chiefly with neighboring Navaho.

On December 16, 1882, the United States government, by executive order, set aside the Hopi Indian reservation of 2,472,320 acres. A government school was built at the Indian agency at Keams Canyon in 1887.

In addition to residing in their ten traditional villages, Hopi also live at Lower Moenkopi and Upper Moenkopi (which are Hopi-owned but beyond the limits of the 1882 reservation); at Keams Canyon, the federal administrative center for the Hopi agency of the Bureau of Indian Affairs (see INDIAN AFFAIRS, BUREAU OF) and for the United States Public Health Service; and at Polacca, a modern settlement below the villages of Walpi and Sichomovi and the Hopi-Tewa town of Hano.

There are slightly more than six thousand Hopi people, most of whom are involved in farming, cattle-raising, or off-reservation wage labor. There is also a high percentage of college graduates among the Hopi, and many of them are engaged in various professional occupations both on and off the reservation.

When the Hopi reservation was created in 1882 it was

Masked katcina dancers of the Hopi village of Shongopovi in Arizona. (Library of Congress)

bounded on the east by the Navaho reservation. Subsequent additions to the latter in 1884, 1900, 1901, 1907, and 1934 succeeded in engulfing Hopi lands entirely. The Hopi, traditionally sedentary farmers, hunters, gatherers, and small-scale pastoralists who speak an Uto-Aztecan language, had long been at odds with their more nomadic, expansionist, Athapaskan-speaking Navaho neighbors. The Navaho moved into most of the 1882 reservation, and in 1962 a special federal court gave the Hopi exclusive use of only 631,194 acres of their original reserve, decreeing they should use the remaining 1,822,080 acres jointly with the Navaho. In 1975 congressional legislation provided for the division of the joint-use area into two mutually exclusive areas, a move that eventually might entail the forced removal of some eight thousand Navaho from Hopi lands. The situation is one that fosters continued acrimony between the two groups.

Hopi religion, social organization, and political structure remain the mainstay of Hopi life. The basic unit of social orgainzation is the extended family. When a Hopi man marries, he moves into the household of his wife's family. The Hopi are monogamous, but divorce is not at all uncommon. In addition to the households there are twenty-one matrilineal clans, each clan consisting of all people presumed to be descendants of a common ancestor. Clans "own" the control of agricultural lands as well as the major ceremonies, which are performed by members of secret religious societies within the clan.

Hopi architecture, like that of other pueblos, is typified by the Hopi's traditional multi-storied stone homes—apartmentlike complexes perched on the tops of three mesas on the Hopi reservation.

The Hopi people are world-renowned for their religious dance dramas and their religious paraphernalia, including dolls made in the likeness of *katcinas*, the spirits of Hopi religion. Given by the Hopi to their children to enable them to learn the names and attributes of katcinas, these dolls are also sold widely on the non-Indian market. Hopi weaving, coiled and wicker basketry, and pottery—most of the latter actually made by Hopi-Tewa Indians of Hano village—are widely sought after. Hopi silversmiths and jewelers are among the finest in the world (see POTTERY, SOUTHWESTERN

INDIAN; SILVERWORK, SOUTHWESTERN INDIAN; and SANDPAINTINGS).

What is most remarkable about the Hopi people has been their ability to accommodate to the non-Indian world while retaining the most essential features of their native culture—their religion and their world view.

See Robert C. Euler and Henry F. Dobyns, *The Hopi People* (1971); and Ruth D. Simpson, *The Hopi Indians* (1953).—B. L. F.

Hopkins, Mark (1813-1878). Merchant and railroad builder. The oldest, by eight years, of the "Big Four" who built the CENTRAL PACIFIC and SOUTHERN PACIFIC railroads, Hopkins was less important in those enterprises than Collis P. Huntington, Leland Stanford, and Charles Crocker. He was thirty-five—already middle-aged for a forty-niner—when he left his native town of Henderson, New York, and moved to California in 1849. Tall, thin, and gangling, and with a bookkeeper's stoop, Hopkins never intended to pan for gold, but set up a store to supply the miners' needs. The business flourished, and in 1856 he became Huntington's partner in an even more successful store in Sacramento. Known by then as "Uncle Mark," Hopkins was conservative in outlook but had a talent for recognizing the true enterprising bent in others. Once he was in the transcontinental railroad venture, his expertness at paperwork made him the day-to-day administrative chief of the project. A modest vegetarian, Hopkins nevertheless proved to be "hell on wheels," as Crocker said, in matters of efficiency and economy and "the stubbornest man alive" in matters of fact, because, as Huntington admitted, Hopkins was usually right. The only exception to his simple life-style was the mansion with which he made Nob Hill famous, built primarily to please his wife. Hopkins' efficient administration was probably indispensable to the Central Pacific-Southern Pacific's successful efforts to weather the 1870s depression. Unlike Huntington, he was not to live to see the railroad freed of its enormous debt to the government and established as a fully independent railroad at the end of the century.

Biographers have generally ignored Mark Hopkins or confused him with the prominent educator of the same name. Oscar Lewis, *The Big Four* (1938), includes a short chapter on Hopkins.—A. M.

Horgan, Paul (1903-   ). Novelist and historian. Horgan was born in Buffalo, New York. His studies at the New Mexico Military Institute from 1920 to 1923 fed his interest in the Southwest and in military affairs. He returned to the institute from 1926 to 1942 as librarian and again from 1947 to 1949 as assistant to the president. For his scholarly and literary achievements he received twelve honorary degrees from such schools as the University of New Mexico, Notre Dame, and Wesleyan University. Twice a Guggenheim fellow, he was affiliated with the University of Iowa, Yale, and, since 1959, the Center for Advanced Studies at Wesleyan, where he has served as a senior fellow and director.

Literary recognition came in 1933 when he was awarded the Harper Novel Prize for *The Fault of Angels*. In 1954 Horgan received a Pulitzer Prize and the Bancroft Prize for *Great River: The Rio Grande in North American History*, written in 1954, a wide-ranging, inclusive biography of the river and its users. The Campion Award of the Catholic Book Club followed in 1957.

From 1942 to 1946 he served in the United States Army, achieving the rank of lieutenant colonel. He is a member of the National Council of the Humanities; the National Institute of Arts and Letters; the American Catholic Historical Association, of which he was elected president in 1960; and the board of the Santa Fe Opera. His published works include ten novels, eight collections of stories, two children's books, and ten histories. Outstanding among his other books are *Three Centuries of Santa Fe* (1956) and *A Distant Trumpet* (1960), a novel following individual careers that converge at Fort Delivery in the final Apache defeats and dramatizing Indian-policy issues by focusing on the conscience and idealism of a young lieutenant. His latest work, the culmination of a life-long interest, is *Lamy of Santa Fe* (1975), a biography of the remarkable first bishop of the Desert Diocese, who arrived in Santa Fe in 1851.—P. L. N.

Horn, Tom (1860-1903). Hired killer and scout. Horn was at various times a cowboy, miner, army scout, deputy sheriff, packer for the Rough Riders in Cuba, and livestock detective, but he gained notoriety as the killer of a Wyoming youth, Willie Nickell.

Horn was born in Memphis, Missouri. As a boy he became an expert hunter and dead shot. Striking west to make his fortune, he first ran amok with misfortune, hunger, and bankruptcy. Once in Prescott, Arizona, in 1875 his luck improved and he became in turn a stage-driver, nightherder of work oxen, and Mexican interpreter and straw boss for Al Sieber, chief army scout at the San Carlos Indian Reservation. Learning to speak fluent Apache, he became a useful aide to Sieber and worked for him on and off from 1875 to 1886. They trailed Geronimo and other "reservation jumpers" into Mexico and brought some of them back to the reservation. Horn claimed to have arranged Geronimo's final surrender in 1886 to General Nelson A. Miles in Skeleton Canyon in the United States. Several army officers who were contemporaries of Horn discount some of his statements about his military actions with the Apache, yet their probable envy might account for their doubting Horn's veracity.

Need for scouts dried up after Geronimo's surrender. In 1888 Horn worked as deputy sheriff under Arizona's favorite adopted son, sheriff "Bucky" O'Neill, and for sheriff Glenn Reynolds, later murdered by the Apache Kid. An expert rodeo cowboy, Horn won the steer-roping contest in Phoenix in 1891. He snared and tied his steer in 45.5 seconds, excellent speed on a three-year-old "critter." He also served with distinction as a mule-pack-train operator with the Rough Riders in Cuba, in the Spanish-American War.

During 1890-94 the Pinkerton Detective Agency hired Horn to run down outlaws who raided banks, railroads, and mine payrolls. The job being too tame, he resigned and in 1894 hired himself out to members of the Wyoming Cattlemen's Association to clean out rustlers. Horn was employed to hunt and kill livestock thieves, an occupation for which his training under Sieber and Pinkerton had prepared him. He effectively reduced rustlers so much that word of his presence in an area was sufficient to scare off many cattle and horse thieves.

Horn's career ended when he was hanged for bushwhacking Willie Nickell, fourteen-year-old son of a southern Wyoming sheepman, Kels Nickell. A jury voted him guilty based on his so-called confession, allegedly obtained by detective Joe LeFors and Charlie Ohnhouse when Horn was drunk. Dean Krakel, Horn's major trial biographer, considers the confession a frameup. He believes modern jurists would have thrown out LeFors' testimony as an inadmissible ruse. The court gave little consideration to depositions by such credible witnesses as Sieber; General Nelson A. Miles; John C. Coble, a Wyoming rancher; and Horn's part-time girl friend, Glendolene Kimmel. While Krakel believes that Horn was a hired killer, he considers him innocent of the Nickell shooting.

Horn wrote a coherent story of his youth and life as a scout with Sieber, *The Life of Tom Horn* (1904; repr. 1964, with an excellent introduction by Dean Krakel); he tells nothing about his service in the Spanish-American War and obviously omits his experiences while exterminating rustlers in Wyoming. See also A. McKinney Griffith, *Mickey Free: Manhunter* (1969); Charles Kelly, *The Outlaw Trail: The Story of Butch Cassidy* (1959); Dean Krakel, *The Saga of Tom Horn* (1954); Joe LeFors, *Wyoming Peace Officer* (1953); and Lauran Paine, *Tom Horn, Man of the West* (1963).—B. W. A.

horse. The wild horse (see HORSE, WILD) was indigenous to North America. Fossil remains indicate the wild horse was widely spread in large numbers over much of the continent until about fifteen thousand years ago, when, for some unknown reason, the wild herds disappeared entirely over a period of about seven thousand years. Indian hunters had killed horses for food for perhaps forty thousand years before the last of the herds vanished.

Domesticated horses were brought to the New World by the Spanish, first to the West Indies by Christopher Columbus in 1493, then to Mexico by Hernán Cortés in 1519. A series of Spanish exploring expeditions from 1520 to 1542 brought horses into the area between Florida and Arizona. None of the horses from these early expeditions survived to produce progeny, although there is a colorful legend concerning the strays from de Soto's herd meeting strays from Coronado's somewhere in the heart of Texas.

When the Spanish colonists occupied the large plateaus of northern Mexico, they developed a new method of pasturing cattle and horses. Instead of herdsmen on foot being in charge of small bands, the stock was turned loose on the open range to be supervised by riders who visited each range band every few weeks. Twice each year all the cattle and horses were rounded up separately. At the spring roundup the new calf and colt crop was branded, and the four- and five-year-old unbroken horses were taken to be trained. In the fall the mature animals were cut from the herds to be taken to market. This pattern of handling stock on the open range is of special interest, for it spread all over the western United States and is used in modified form even today. It required a fairly large horse herd on each ranch to furnish the necessary mounts.

Spanish stockman colonized along the Rio Grande in New Mexico in the early seventeenth century and soon had large herds of range cattle and horses, which they handled with the help of many Pueblo Indians. Some of these Indian servants became dissatisfied with their lot and ran off to join the wild tribes of buffalo hunters on the Great Plains. They usually took along a few tame,

well-broken horses; and with their skill in breaking, handling, and using horses, they soon taught their hunter friends how to use the animal. In a few years these Indians, in turn, gave one or two of their older, gentle horses to their neighbors to the north and instructed them in their use and care. In this manner Spanish horses and horse culture spread rapidly through the sparsely peopled Plains, reaching all of the tribes between 1650 and 1770.

West of the Rocky Mountains horses moved northward to the Navaho, Ute, and Shoshoni tribes, reaching the upper Snake River country and southwestern Montana about 1690. Shoshoni herds supplied horses to the Crow Indians on the upper Yellowstone River and to the tribes of the Columbia Basin, where the Nez Percé soon became noted for their fine horses. Thus, when the Americans moved westward, they found the entire country well endowed with horses from Spanish stock, which has remained by far the most numerous group throughout the West to the present time.

Wild horses had developed into two types. One, with small bones and a trim shape, was called the light, or riding, horse. The other, with heavy bones and a stockier build, was called the heavy, or draft, horse. A subdivision of the light horse type, the rather sturdy, close coupled light horses also are known commonly as belonging to the stock horse type. Western horses vary from fourteen hands high at the withers (one hand equals four inches) to fifteen hands two inches. Full-grown animals weigh from 800 to 1,050 pounds. Animals smaller then fourteen hands are called ponies, and many horses raised on the Plains by the Indian tribes fell into this category, their growth being stunted by scanty feed.

The horse had an immediate, profound influence on all the buffalo-hunting tribes, giving them the necessary help to kill an abundance of meat and to secure many hides for robes (see BUFFALO). This new method of killing buffalo also allowed the hunters to have a great deal of leisure time, which they used to develop the complex, colorful Plains culture that came to full flower in the early nineteenth century. The war games and spectacular religious rites belong to this period.

When explorers and fur traders moved west after the Louisiana Purchase in 1803 they found a plentiful supply of Indian horses at moderate prices to use on their ventures. Meriwether Lewis and William Clark, on their way to the Pacific coast, traveled from St. Louis to the headwaters of the Missouri by water, but when they reached the Continental Divide in southwestern Montana they were able to cross the mountains only with the help of a string of pack animals purchased from Sacagawea's people, the Lemhi Shoshoni. Zebulon M. Pike, exploring westward from the Missouri River to the Colorado Rockies, depended on the Indian horse herds to furnish his pack animals in 1806.

Fur traders in the West bought hundreds of Indian horses each year to ride and to load with supplies and furs. One of the first traders was Wilson Price Hunt, who led a party of fur men from St. Louis to the mouth of the Columbia River, starting in 1811. He left his boats at the Arikara villages in South Dakota and proceeded westward across the mountains to the Snake River with Indian horses.

Adventurous horse traders from the Mississippi valley were buying animals from the Indian tribes in northern Texas as early as 1793 and driving them to market at New Orleans or Natchez for use on the plantations. From Natchez a steady stream of horses moved into Tenessee, Kentucky, and Ohio. Other traders took horses north to the market at St. Louis.

In 1821 traders from St. Louis opened up the Santa Fe Trail to the markets of New Mexico, furnishing cloth and hardware in return for silver, horses, and mules. In a few years the demand for horses at Santa Fe had increased to the point that large herds were driven across the desert from California to supply the trade. Some of these horses were legally purchased, but many more were stolen by Ute Indians and their ally, Peg-leg Smith, a mountain man. During the period 1800-60, Comanche raiders stole large herds of horses from Mexico and Texas for the northern market. For sheer numbers stolen, this was the greatest period of horse rustling the West has ever known.

In 1843 trains of covered wagons started rolling westward along the Oregon Trail. The Rocky Mountains and the desert of southern Idaho took a heavy toll of the teams. The animals lost were often replaced by horses bought from the Nez Percé and Cayuse tribes to haul the wagons across the Blue Mountains in northeastern Oregon and down the Columbia River. This trade led in time to all western horses being called cayuses.

The gold rushes that began in the Columbia Basin in 1861 and spread over into Montana demanded a large number of pack animals to transport food and supplies to the new boomtowns and many teams to haul stagecoaches to the new camps. From the first these horses came largely from the Nez Percé and Yakima herds. As the prospectors flooded the Indian country, some were killed for trespassing. When the army chased the mounted Indians to punish them, it was often frustrated by the ease with which the well-mounted Indians evaded such pursuit. As a drastic form of punishment, Colonel George Wright in 1858 slaughtered an entire band of 850 horses captured near Spokane Falls. Ten years later on the Plains, Colonel George A. Custer killed about 800 horses captured from a Cheyenne village on the Washita River. However, the captured horses were driven back to the army posts when this was practicable and were then sold to eastern buyers. Colonel Nelson A. Miles thus took about 1,100 horses captured at the Bear Paw battlefield from the Nez Percé in 1877 back to Fort Keogh on the Yellowstone.

At the end of the Civil War, Texas had a shortage of ready cash, and cattle ranges were overstocked with Longhorns that could be bought for $2 or $3 a head, while in the Kansas markets eastern buyers were paying $30 or more for such steers. As a result, a large number of young veterans rounded up the cattle and drove them north to market at the rate of several hundred thousand a year. The average trail herd of fifteen hundred steers was handled by a crew of about ten cowboys, each of them using about ten horses on the drive north, but needing only one or two for the return trip. Thus there were about a hundred well-broken horses from Texas on the Kansas market for each herd of cattle brought north.

Once the buffalo had been killed, Texas cattle stocked the Plains. Many cattle ranches were established with the stock, both cattle and horses, handled in the pattern developed by the Spanish stockmen in Mexico and used extensively in New Mexico and California. Each cowboy needed a saddle string of about ten mounts for the entire working season, from April until the end of the fall roundup. He usually had two specially trained for cutting cattle from the herd and for roping stock. The rest of the string were "green broke" young animals just off the range in the spring, four- and five-year-old geldings that had been ridden three times each by the ranch broncobuster before being turned over to the cowboys. In the fall all of the aged riding horses and the ordinary young animals, together with the excess mares, were sold off. Only the best of the cutting and roping horses were kept through the winter.

Throughout the West, horses were as necessary to the rest of the people as they were to the stockmen. All mail, express, and passenger service away from the few railroads was handled by a network of stage lines with several hundred stages running each day, each coach drawn by four or six horses with a change of teams needed for each fifteen miles of travel. In the settled areas horses furnished all the local transportation, carrying riders and packs, pulling buggies, carts, buckboards, light and heavy wagons, delivering milk, meat, groceries, and other supplies to the homes, bringing the poles, logs, lumber, and firewood down from the forests, hauling supplies out to the mines and ore back to the smelters. The livery stable was the center of much of the activity of the smaller towns.

The West raised enough horses for all its needs and each year shipped many thousands to eastern markets. Until barbed wire supplied practical fences for the western grasslands and the federal government insisted on collecting grazing fees for all animals pastured on public lands, horses could be raised on the open range at a cost of $5 or less per head. The unbroken geldings were usually rounded up and sold when four years old, while the mares were kept until about ten years of age to raise colts. These range mares, when shipped to stock farms and bred to draft stallions such as the Percheron, produced a good-grade draft animal weighing 1,200 to 1,400 pounds. They were in demand for farm work and for much of the hauling of freight in the cities. Range horses gentled and broken to ride or drive before being marketed brought much better prices than those just off the range. On many of the ranches and farms, breaking these horses filled in the slack periods from late fall until early spring.

When times were hard in the East, the market for western horses suffered. The Panic of 1893 and the resulting depression were especially severe. Horses on the western ranges could not be sold for enough to pay the freight to market. But then Great Britain needed many horses for the Boer War in South Africa, and British buying agents came to western shipping points, the most important being Miles City, Montana, Sheridan, Wyoming, and Denver, Colorado. There they purchased range horses by the thousands, and the large amount of British cash paid out greatly stimulated the business of these towns and brought immediate prosperity to the western stock country. By the time the Boer War ended, eastern markets were again buying all the yearly crop of range horses.

Although barbed wire fences greatly modified the general pattern of feeding range cattle, range horses were still common throughout the western mountains and the Great Basin until the 1920s.

Meanwhile homesteaders had filled the eastern part of the Plains and had occupied many valleys to the west as soon as the land had been freed of buffalo and Indians. They depended largely on wheat as a cash crop and learned that each man must farm a large acreage to be successful. Weather and climate strictly limited the time that could be spent on each operation. Plowing, seeding, and harvesting had to be done rapidly, with one man in charge of many horses hitched to a number of machines. For plowing and seeding, usually done as one operation, the teams varied in size from six to thirty-six horses drawing a number of disc harrows with seeders hitched on behind, all operated by one driver. The harvesting combines used from eighteen to forty-two horses, and required a team of several men on each combine. Other teams were needed at harvest time to haul the threshed grain to the storage bins or the railroad shipping point. For these operations the farmers considered the western range horses too small. They preferred the grade draft animals produced by breeding range mares to draft stallions, and these they usually bought from regular horse breeders.

World War I brought drastic changes to the users of draft animals. Even before the war, vans, drays, buses, and taxicabs were taking over the hauling in the large cities. Then, under the stimulus of rich military contracts, makers of gasoline motors and motor vehicles rapidly improved their products and greatly expanded their field of usefulness. An important factor in speeding the change from horse-drawn to motor-propelled vehicles was the great saving in food grains so greatly needed to feed the hungry peoples of war-torn Europe, and the releasing of hay meadows for food crops. By the mid-1920s, horses had almost entirely disappeared from city streets. On the farms the replacement of horses by trucks and tractors was slower but just as decisive. The aged horses from the farms, and most of the range bands, some of them truly wild from neglect, were shipped to the canneries to be turned into dog and fox food.

Although draft horses almost vanished after 1920, many saddle horses were still used on western stock ranches and in the mountains. Pleasure riding increased all over the country until the ownership of a good saddle horse or two gave a family definite social prestige. Teenage girls especially turned to pleasure riding as their chief pastime.

The cowboys of the 1880s, glamorized by the Wild West shows, western fiction, and western movies, became romantic figures in America's past. Dude ranches throughout the West featured saddle horses and range riding, and many western towns staged frontier-day celebrations to lure the tourists. As a result of these factors, when a teen-ager wanted a horse, it had to be a western stock horse type with western equipment. Soon the young people and their parents were demanding registered horses eligible to compete in stock shows and fairs.

While there are several breeds of fine riding horses, only two of these breeds are closely associated in the minds of the general public with the romantic period of western range history. The first is the quarter horse, developed as a sprint racer in the American colonies and later raised in large numbers in Texas, where the breed registry was established. These horses are good both for handling stock and for pleasure riding. The quarter horse people claim the largest breed registry in the world, with more than 600,000 animals on their books. The quarter horse registry is unusual in that it will register sprint horses registered in some of the other breeds, particularly the Thoroughbreds.

The second breed closely associated with western history is the Appaloosa, used by the Nez Percé tribe since about 1750. This horse has a long and varied history, having been known in ancient Egypt, Persia, and China. Later it was common throughout Europe before its introduction into Mexico about 1621. This long historical background lends a special appeal to the Appaloosa that is heightened by the horse's colorful and unusual coat patterns. The Appaloosa is valued both as a stock horse and for pleasure riding.

Both the Arabian and the Morgan horse are excellent for pleasure riding and for handling stock. Their numbers are increasing rapidly in the West, but neither of them is associated in the public mind with the exciting phases of western development.

See J. Frank Dobie, *The Mustangs* (1952); Francis Haines, *The Horse in American History* (1971); and Frank Gilbert Roe, *The Indian and the Horse* (1955).—F. H.

horse, wild. *Wild horse* is a term some horse ranchers used for a feral or undomesticated horse. The term *mustang* was reserved for Spanish-blooded horses. However, the description of what constituted "Spanish" varied with each individual or area. It is now obvious that the wild horses of today are the result of many introductions of domestic stock, beginning with the Spanish breed. The so-called Spanish breed was a mix of other breeds itself and there probably were not "pure Spanish" herds at any time. It is interesting that even where a non-Spanish bloodline of past releases is known, if the horses are undisturbed for many generations, the resulting horses are often Spanish in coloration, are short coupled (one less vertebra), and have Roman noses. A more acceptable modern definition would use *wild horse* and *mustang* interchangeably and would mean any wild, free-roaming, and unclaimed horse.

The history of the wild horse (as distinct from the domesticated HORSE) since the West was settled by white men has been one of removal as a pest or exploitation as a cheap, unwanted commodity. The wild horse has been blamed for abuse of the range by overgrazing, and even today many range users are opposed to wild horses as representing a nonproductive part of the public domain. These users feel that if wild horses are protected, the policy will set a dangerous precedent.

The numbers of wild horses fell from estimated millions in the nineteenth century to about seventeen thousand in the eleven western states at the present time. The use of wild horses by the pet-food industry has virtually guaranteed their extinction unless they are protected. Because inhumane methods were used to capture wild horses, and because there was the danger of possible extinction, a well-organized campaign has led to legislation that has placed these animals under federal jurisdiction and recognized them as representatives of the American heritage. These free-roaming animals are now seen as symbols of ruggedness and stamina, traits that American pioneers themselves needed to enable them to tame and settle the harsh western environment. The wild horse is also aesthetically important as a symbol of unbridled freedom while being an integral part of the wilderness scene.

Much of the credit for the immense public interest today is due to a one-woman fight by Mrs. Velma Johnston (known as Wild Horse Annie) of Reno, Nevada. She is responsible for the "Wild Horse Annie Act" (Public Law 86-234), which prohibits the use of airborne and mechanized vehicles in rounding up wild horses. She was at the forefront of the effort for broader federal legislation (Public Law 92-195), passed in December 1971.

To date, two areas have been set aside for wild horses by the federal government. One is a refuge in Nevada, presently unavailable to the public since it is in the Nellis Air Force Base bombing range, and the other is the Pryor Mountain Wild Horse Range along the Montana-Wyoming border.

Virtually nothing was known about the natural history of the wild horse or its role as a component in the ecology of the range. However, some recent ecological and behavioral studies are shedding light on the many controversies based on bias rather than fact. When there is enough scientific information, a sound management program for wild horses will be possible.

See Marguerite Henry, *Mustang, Wild Spirit of the West* (1966); and Walker D. Wyman, *The Wild Horse of the West* (1945).—M. J. P.

Horseshoe Bend, battle of (1814). The battle of Horseshoe Bend was the climactic confrontation of the Creek War (1813-14). On his visit to the southern Indians in 1811, Tecumseh had stimulated the younger Creek to stronger resistance to white encroachments on their lands. American occupation of the West Florida strip to the Pearl River, and subsequently to the Perdido River, further stimulated anxiety on the part of the Creek Confederacy. Relations between the Upper Creek on the Tallapoosa and Coosa rivers in Alabama, who were generally antiwhite, and the Lower Creek of Georgia, who had come under the influence of United States Indian agent Benjamin Hawkins, deteriorated into open civil war. By mid-1813 the war faction had gained control of the tribe. In July 1813 a party of young warriors went to Pensacola, the historic source of Creek supplies, to secure arms and materials from the Spanish. This journey excited the settlers on the Tombigbee River, and they made an assault on the returning party of Indians. Although the settlers were partially victorious in their attack on the Creek, the Indians retaliated, with disastrous consequences. The white settlers gathered for protection inside the flimsy stockade of Fort Mims, but the militia failed to take adequate defensive measures. An attack by the Creek on August 30 wiped out this fort, killing most of the occupants, more than five hundred men, women, and children.

The Fort Mims massacre resulted in a wave of excitement all across the frontier bordering on Creek country. Andrew Jackson in October 1813 led an army of two thousand Tennessee Volunteers down by way of Huntsville to Fort Deposit, Alabama, and into the Creek country along the Coosa River, where he established Fort Strother. Supported by General John Coffee's volunteer cavalry, Jackson destroyed the Creek villages of Tallushatchee and Talladega in November. On January 22, 1814, he gained a victory in a heated battle at Emuckfaro Creek, but two days later was driven back into Fort Strother after being ambushed while his force was crossing Enitachopco Creek. Reinforced by two thousand more volunteers and a regiment of United States infantry, Jackson and Coffee determined to advance on the Creek's principal stronghold of Tohopeka, which was situated on the hundred-acre peninsula of Horseshoe Bend in the Tallapoosa River, near present-day Dadeville, Alabama. Over a thousand warriors and about three hundred women and children had gathered there under the war leader Menewa and the leading Creek prophet, Monahee. In the predawn hours of March 27, the army quietly surrounded the village and then began a cannonade. Coffee's Cherokee scouts crossed the river and attacked the Creek from the rear, while Jackson mounted a frontal assault on the log wall the Creek had constructed across the neck of the peninsula. Caught in a crossfire, the Creek were nearly annihilated; more than eight hundred were killed. Jackson's army lost only forty-nine men. The power of the Creek Confederacy was broken, and in the subsequent parley with Andrew Jackson at Fort Jackson on August 9, surviving second-level chiefs were forced to cede twenty million acres, over half their hunting grounds. Jackson was rewarded with a commission as major general in the regular United States Army and command of the Seventh Military District, which led him to the battle of New Orleans and later the White House.

See Thomas Perkins Abernethy, *The Formative Period in Alabama, 1815-1828* (1965); Marquis James, *Andrew Jackson, the Border Captain* (1933); and Albert J. Pickett, *History of Alabama* (1900).—T. D. C.

hotels. See TAVERNS AND HOTELS; TOURIST TRAVEL.

Hot Springs National Park. Hot Springs National Park is a city, a spa, and the seat of Garland County, Arkansas. Located at the eastern edge of the Ouachita Mountains, it is a popular resort. The springs, supposedly visited by Hernando de Soto in 1541, were widely known by the time the United States acquired them as part of the Louisiana Purchase in 1803. The next year President Thomas Jefferson had them explored, mapped, and analyzed. The first permanent settlers arrived about 1807, but the forty-seven thermal springs were set aside as a United States reservation in 1832 and not put up for public sale. Thus began a forty-year legal dispute over the title, which was settled in favor of the federal government. A town was incorporated in 1876, and in 1921 the name was changed to Hot Springs National Park. The city operates, however, under its own state charter and municipal ordinances and is independent of the federal government. There are twenty bathhouses and a physical medicine center under federal regulation that offers physiotherapy and hydrotherapy. Resort hotels, horse racing, fine golf courses, good fishing lakes, and mountain scenery also attract tourists to the city. Its population in 1970 was 35,631.—W. L. B.

Houck, Louis (1840-1925). Entrepreneur and historian. Houck was born in Belleville, Illinois. His father was associated with several German-language newspapers in the St. Louis area and taught young Houck the craft. After attending the University of Wisconsin and then studying law, Houck was appointed assistant United States attorney at St. Louis in 1868. He resigned the following year to locate in Cape Girardeau, his home for the remainder of his life. He practiced law and engaged in a variety of economic enterprises.

Houck was largely responsible for the completion of more than five hundred miles of railroad in southeast Missouri in the late nineteenth century. He also helped secure Southeast Missouri State College for his adopted city in 1873 and served on its board of regents until his death.

Houck's fame, however, rests on his authorship of a three-volume history of Missouri, *A History of Missouri from the Earliest Discoveries and Explorations Until Its Admission to the Union* (1908), regarded as the most thorough and authoritative work on the colonial and territorial periods. In 1909 he edited an important two-volume documentary set in translation, *The Spanish Regime in Missouri*, based on the archives of the Indies at Seville.

The standard biography is William T. Doherty, Jr., *Louis Houck: Missouri Historian and Entrepreneur* (1960).—W. E. P.

Hough, Emerson (1857-1923). Novelist. Hough was born in Newton, Iowa, and attended the State University of Iowa, from which he was graduated with a B.A. degree in 1880. He then traveled extensively in the wildest parts of the American West. In the winter of 1895 he explored Yellowstone National Park on skis, and as a result of this expedition became involved in various conservation activities aimed at protecting vanishing American wildlife. He was responsible for, among other things, the act of Congress protecting the Yellowstone Park buffalo from indiscriminate hunting. In addition to his western fiction Hough wrote stories for children and a number of popular historical studies of the Old West, including *The Story of the Cowboy* (1897) and *The Story of the Outlaw* (1906).

Hough's primary importance to western literature is that he pioneered in the method of wedding the sentimental romance to the western novel. It is no accident that *The Covered Wagon* (1922), a fictionalized history of a migrant wagon train on the Oregon Trail, was made in 1923 into one of the earliest western motion-picture spectaculars. The plot details what has now become a total commonplace in this kind of film: a misunderstood hero and a plausible but evil villain vie for the hand of the beautiful heroine while the wagon train plods westward, overcoming en route various and sundry perils. Though the novel is allegedly factual, its real concerns are sentimentally romantic. The same thing is true of Hough's other most famous western story, *North of 36* (1923), a fictional history of a trail drive from Texas to Abilene, Kansas.

Though Hough cannot be credited with originating the combination of love interest with he-man adventure, which is the hallmark of his fiction, he certainly was one of the most successful practitioners of this kind of western writing, in which the West, dotted with picturesque Indians, shaggy buffalo, and Longhorn cattle, serves as a panoramic backdrop to a sentimental tale.—J. K. F.

Houston, Sam[uel] (1793-1863). Soldier and politician. Houston was born in Rockbridge County, Virginia. After the death in 1807 of his father, a revolutionary-war veteran, Houston's mother moved with her nine children to Maryville, Tennessee. There young Hous-

ton worked at the village store and spent time with nearby Cherokee Indians, whose language and customs he learned. Joining the army in 1813, he established a distinguished record and became friendly with Andrew Jackson, his commanding general. In 1818 he completed an eighteen-month law course in six months and became a district attorney of the Nashville district.

In 1823 Tennessee sent Houston to Congress, where he served two terms and helped to build the Democratic party that later sent Andrew Jackson to the White House. Houston was twice elected governor of Tennessee. In 1829 his wife left him, and he resigned his post and went to live with the Cherokee Indians in Arkansas. He became a spokesman for the Indians and periodically traveled to Washington to negotiate in their behalf.

After several trips to TEXAS on Indian affairs, Houston decided to remain in Nacogdoches. Becoming involved in the imminent revolution against Mexico, Houston was elected delegate to the San Felipe Convention in 1833 and to the Consultation in 1835, signed the Texas declaration of independence in March 1836, and was chosen as commander-in-chief of the Texas army. His initial military tactics were criticized, but the battle of SAN JACINTO proved a brilliant victory over Santa Anna's superior forces, with negligible casualties for the Texans.

A military hero, Houston was elected first president of the Republic of Texas in 1836, whereupon he obtained United States recognition of Texas and returned Santa Anna safely to Mexico. In 1841 he again served as president, stabilizing the republic's finances and improving the Indian situation. After Texas became a state in 1846, Houston served as United States senator for fourteen years, during which time he spoke out eloquently on Indian matters and in support of the Union. He became separated from the Southern ideology, voting for antislavery provisions in the organization of Oregon, for all the items in the Compromise of 1850, and against repeal of the Missouri Compromise. Houston's antisecessionist views were unpopular with the Texas legislature, which voted for his successor two years before his term expired.

Surprisingly, in 1859 Houston was elected governor of Texas, where he continued to oppose secession. After the secession convention in 1861 and a plebiscite favoring separation from the Union, Houston considered Texas again a republic and refused to swear allegiance to the Confederacy. His office was declared vacant, Lieutenant Governor Edward Clark was chosen to fill it, and Houston returned to his farm near Huntsville, where he died.

Houston was a large man of giant appetites and talents, equally hailed and accepted at Indian tribal councils, in roistering bars and barracks, and in the halls of the politically great.

The Autobiography of Sam Houston has been edited by Donald Day and Harry H. Ullom (1954), but more useful are two superior biographical studies: Marquis James, *The Raven: A Biography of Sam Houston* (1929), and Llerena Friend, *Sam Houston: The Great Designer* (1954).—J. B. F.

Houston, Texas. Houston, the largest city in Texas and sixth largest in the nation, had its beginnings in August 1836, just four months after the battle of San Jacinto. John K. and Augustus C. Allen, two brothers, bought 6,642 acres and planned a town they named in honor of Sam Houston. In November that year their city was named capital of the Republic of Texas, and by the end of the year the population numbered 1,500, some of them government officials but many of them newly arrived immigrants.

The capital moved to Austin in 1839, but by then Houston was beginning a period of phenomenal growth. A chamber of commerce had already been established, and the following year, development began on a ship channel from Houston to the Gulf of Mexico by way of Buffalo Bayou, and planning was undertaken for a railroad (completed in 1853 as the Buffalo Bayou, Brazos, and Colorado line). Periodic fires and floods, along with occasional outbreaks of cholera and yellow fever, failed to slow growth, and by 1885 the city had 23,000 residents.

Houston's economy was based on the availability of transportation, and city fathers continued to fight for advances. In 1873 they secured out-of-state rail connections when the Houston and Texas Central made connections at Denton, Texas, with the Missouri, Kansas, and Texas line; and in 1882 the Southern Pacific was completed, allowing connections with New Orleans and San Francisco. Moreover, in 1899 Congress approved dredging a ship channel to Galveston Bay, and by 1914 the Houston Ship Channel had a uniform depth of twenty-five feet. In 1934 came the opening of the Intercoastal Waterway, which gave Houston shippers access to traffic on the Mississippi River. Today Houston is the third largest port in the nation.

The discovery of oil near Houston early in the twentieth century allowed diversification of the economy. The city soon became a major site for refineries (30 percent of the nation's capacity now is in the vicinity), for pipeline companies, and for petrochemical operations, while the forty-mile ship channel is one vast industrial complex. Other industries include cement, breweries, grain elevators, food processing (especially rice), and the manufacturing of oil-field equipment and light industrial goods. An electronics industry presently has developed to supply the National Aeronautics and Space Administration (NASA), which is headquartered just outside the city.

Houston's early leaders made their city grow by reinvesting their profits in their businesses rather than ostentatious living, a pattern that has continued to the present; Houston therefore has been less showy than Dallas, less "charming than San Antonio, less openly gilded than Galveston." Always the goal was to make the city not only dominant in the vicinity but in the South and Southwest as well. As a result the city today is a banking center, a gateway to Latin America through the Houston International Airport, an import-export center through the World Trade Center, and an internationally known medical center. Located in Houston are the Baylor University School of Medicine and the University of Texas School of Dentistry, as well as Rice University and the University of Houston.

The city chamber of commerce likes to advertise Houston as "the largest city in the South," which is true. From 44,633 residents in 1900, it has grown to 1,232,802 in 1970, with a metropolitan population of 1,985,031. Yet Houston today is neither southern nor southwestern. High-rise buildings produce a skyline not unlike that of eastern cities, while the Astrodome, a roofed sports stadium capable of seating fifty thousand in air-conditioned comfort, defies a regional label. Houston also boasts major-league athletic teams in all sports and has a nationally famous symphony orchestra, an opera association, museums, and art galleries, and thereby benefits heavily from tourism. Although plagued with problems of pollution and racial conflict, Houston shows potential of continuing to grow and dominate the South and Southwest.

See David G. McComb, *Houston: The Bayou City* (1969); and M. M. Sibley, *The Port of Houston: A History* (1968).—O. B. F.

Howard, James. See RIVERMEN.

Howard, Joseph Kinsey (1906-1951). Journalist and historian. Born in Iowa, Howard moved to Canada with his family and then went to Great Falls, Montana, in 1919. After his graduation from high school in 1923 he joined the staff of the Great Falls *Leader*, where he remained for twenty years. His first book, *Montana, High, Wide and Handsome* (1943), reflected his bitterness at what he considered the political and economic exploitation of Montana. It is regarded as one of the nation's best regional histories. He worked with the Montana Study (1943-45), which attempted to evaluate the social and cultural resources of the state and to stimulate the growth of its small communities. Here he collected some of the best writing which had been done in the state and published the anthology *Montana Margins* (1946). His third book, *Strange Empire* (1952), the story of the western Canadian rebel Louis Riel, is an account of regional unrest and racial maladjustment.

As correspondent for *Time, Life*, and the St. Louis *Post-Dispatch* and book reviewer for *The New York Times* and for the New York *Herald Tribune*, Howard was the voice of the state. He was a long-time lecturer at the annual national writers' conference at Bread Loaf, Middlebury, Vermont, and was the first director of the Northern Rocky Mountain Writers' Conference at the University of Montana. He was a founding member of the Montana Institute of the Arts, and a member of the board of trustees of the Montana Historical Society.

Bernard DeVoto characterized Howard as one of the West's "few writers of first rank and one of its most valuable citizens." With an incisive mind and facile pen, he led a turbulent but effective campaign against political and economic evils in the state and region and assisted immeasurably in creating an atmosphere in the state in which cultural progress could be made.

See biographical sketch of Howard by Bernard De Voto in *Strange Empire* (1952), and see Norman Fox, "Joseph Kinsey Howard: Writer," *Montana Magazine of History* vol. 2 (1952).—M. G. B.

Howard, Oliver Otis (1830-1909). Soldier. Known as the "Christian general" (often, in the Bible-thumping sense), Howard became known as a humanitarian while directing the Freedmen's Bureau (while still a regular army officer) and through publicly prominent church work. He also maintained influential connections with national Republican leaders. Thus, he was enlisted in furtherance of President Ulysses S. Grant's PEACE POLICY. However, Howard figured in only three episodes, leaving but a faint impress on Indian affairs.

Howard gained his first experience in the West when Secretary of the Interior Columbus Delano asked him to go to the Southwest as a peace commissioner in 1872. In addition to some minor accords with various tribes, he reached an agreement with COCHISE, whose Chiricahua Apache had been at war with white men since 1861. Howard made contact with the Indian chief through Thomas J. JEFFORDS, a frontier figure who was the only white man Cochise would trust. In an act of unquestioned courage, Howard went to Cochise's stronghold in the Dragoon Mountains in October 1872, accompanied by only two white men—his aide, Captain Joseph A. Sladen, and Jeffords. After eleven days of conferences he reached a peace agreement with Cochise, who insisted that his people remain in their homeland in southeastern Arizona and that Jeffords be their agent. Howard's work was justly criticized on the grounds that it was a verbal agreement and hence open to misinterpretation, that it gave the Chiricahua a reservation bordering Mexico, where the Apache continued to raid freely, and that the reservation was exempt from the close supervision by which the army was regularizing the reservations of other recently hostile Apache. Colonel George Crook, commanding the Department of Arizona, called the agreement "a fraud." Perhaps indicative of a characteristic self-puffery, Howard said in his autobiography that he and Cochise "concluded a lasting peace." Actually, the peace lasted only four years, for a majority of the Chiricahua resumed their depredations when the government insisted that they move to the San Carlos Reservation in 1876, two years after Cochise's death.

Commanding the Department of the Columbia, Howard intensified the attrition that eventuated in the Nez Percé War of 1877. During this war he fought the nontreaty Nez Percé in the battle of Clearwater, the only Indian battle in which he participated. It was primarily his inept pursuit of the Nez Percé toward Montana that made the army appear incompetent in that war. In 1878 he planned and commanded army operations in the minor Bannock War, but did not participate in any of the engagements.

The quality of Howard's dealings with the Indians is open to dispute. One historian says that he treated Indians with understanding, justice, and resolution; that he believed in equal justice for both white and Indian; that he was in favor of the peace policy while yet an army officer (which is hard to reconcile with his behavior toward the Nez Percé); that he nonetheless did not go to the extreme of a sentimentalist view of the Indian; that he opposed the reservation system; and that he believed in assimilation and education of the Indian along with division of land in severalty. The record indicates, however, that the self-righteous Howard lacked the temperament, empathy, and knowledge to deal with Indians effectively, in council or in the field. For instance, he once approached a council of Apache leaders, suddenly dropped to his knees, and started praying out loud, without previous explanation. The Indians fled, furious that such a man had been brought among them to make "bad medicine" against them. Certainly, Howard's energetic efforts to alleviate the plight of the Negro did not extend to the plight of the Indian.

Howard was his own best public relations man through frequent lecture appearances and his *Autobiography*, 2 vols. (1907), and *My Life and Experiences Among Our Hostile Indians* (1907). His biographer—John A.

Carpenter, *Sword and Olive Branch* (1964)—does not handle Howard's western service as well as one might wish. Howard's Indian service is treated in Alvin Josephy, *The Nez Percé Indians and the Opening of the Northwest* (1965); Frank C. Lockwood, *The Apache Indians* (1938); and Dan L. Thrapp, *Conquest of Apacheria* (1967).—O. K.

Hudson's Bay Company. British colonizing and trading company. Chartered by King Charles II on May 2, 1670, the Hudson's Bay Company was a proprietary grant in lands and trading rights to eighteen "adventurers" or stockholders and to their successors. As such, it did not differ in kind or purpose from other chartered colonizing companies. The proprietary grants, such as those to the Virginia Company (1606), the South Virginia Company (Carolina, 1663), and the proprietors of New York and New Jersey (1664), all shared the common goal of appropriating for England's use the resources of the New World. Britain's trading companies in America all played vital roles in America's development, and the Hudson's Bay Company was no exception. In addition to a common goal and similar histories, the chartered companies shared among themselves some of the most important and colorful men of London. For example, the first earl of Shaftesbury, London's leading Whig, was a member of both the Hudson's Bay Company and the Carolina company. Members of the Colleton and Carteret families were represented on the governing boards of several companies.

As European rivalries between England, France, Spain, and the Netherlands were extended into the New World in the sixteenth and seventeenth centuries, so cis-Atlantic affairs were inevitably made a part of Old World politics. Commercial and imperial considerations underlay the creation of the Hudson's Bay Company and figured prominently in the company's history. Lord Shaftesbury and others were first stirred by reports from Sieur de Groseilliers and Pierre Esprit Radisson, French-Canadian trappers, that New Wales (Hudson's Bay), and not the St. Lawrence, where the French held sway, was the natural outlet for North American furs. Moreover, furs could be put to valuable commercial use by England. Injected into the European market at the Baltic, they could be sold direct to suppliers of naval stores. This would preclude relying on the Dutch to supply them.

With the return of the *Nonsuch* (1668) from Hudson's Bay, vindicating the geographical views of Groseilliers and Radisson, the company was formed. Factors incident to the trading of furs led to an early decision in favor of the joint-stock mode of ownership, and to the conviction that trade, not colonization, would best serve company interests. Directed by a governor, a deputy, and a committee of seven—all subject to the stockholders who were to meet periodically in general court—the company's domain covered about 1.4 million square miles of North America, or all the lands draining into Hudson's Bay, more than one third of present Canada. This region was called Rupert's Land in honor of Charles's cousin Prince Rupert, the first governor of the company.

From 1821 until 1859 it represented British interests from the Rocky Mountains to the Pacific Ocean while operating under a specially granted license, in addition to its grant of monopoly conferred in 1670, to trade in that area. (Although the license was not renewed in 1859, no British administration was sent to present British Columbia, making the company de facto conservator of England's sovereignty.) These first two centuries of company history fall into four periods marked by challenges to the company charter and by competitors in the field.

The first and formative period included the years from 1670 to 1713, when the Treaty of Utrecht transferred possession of Hudson's Bay from France to England, thus legally—though not in fact—eliminating French competition in that area. The second period, from 1713 until 1763, when the Treaty of Paris transferred all of Canada from France to England, witnessed the expansion of company operations from Winnipeg to the Rockies and into present west-central Canada, later organized as the district of Athabasca. The third period, from 1763 to 1821, was the company's most difficult. While Napoleon upset Europe's markets, the NORTH WEST COMPANY, organized in 1784 with headquarters in Montreal, provided the most severe competition the company was ever to face. But though the "Nor'westers" outtraded and outfought the men of Hudson's Bay, they could not outlast then, and in 1821, prodded by government, the North West Company was merged with the Hudson's Bay Company. At the center of the conflict had been the doughty fifth earl of Selkirk. Granted some lands from the Hudson's Bay Company for the purpose of colonizing Scots farmers, the earl and his friends gained controlling shares of that company's stock. His settlement along the Red and Assiniboine rivers was at the core of the North West Company's transportation system, and Selkirk waged a ten-year struggle with that company until his death. The merger ended the warfare. His Red River colony left a half-breed population of free traders who were continually pulled in the direction of other free traders on the American side of the border (which had been drawn in 1818), while Americans, traders and farmers, began looking north into unguarded company lands.

From 1821 to 1870 the company was faced with Americans along the international border and in the Oregon country, where no border was drawn until 1846. During this period the company was under the direction of highly able men, among them the resident governor in North America, George Simpson, John McLOUGHLIN, Peter Skene OGDEN, and John WORK. Simpson's imagination together with the company's resources in talented men and capital reserves provided shareholders with dividends at a time when neither the British government nor British opinion was inclined to support the monopoly. The company was not equipped to handle agricultural settlements and the fur trade and to administer government at the same time, any more than other trading and colonizing companies had been. And yet Englishmen were increasingly demanding that the fur monopoly justify its existence by accommodating settlers, although the British government consistently chose not to assume the duties of colonial administration.

In Oregon the company learned that it could count on British pride to protect company property, but could not expect Englishmen to recognize the imperial value of the Oregon country itself. This was as unfortunate for Britain as it was frustrating and ironic from a company point of view, since the Oregon country was always of greater value politically to Britain than was the fur trade of the disputed territory to the company. At the Red River during the 1850s and 1860s, when Americans from Minnesota were ready to migrate and annex prairie lands to the north, and during the long period from 1846 to 1871 when the company tried to collect the money owed to it under the Treaty of 1846, which promised payment for the company's "possessory" rights—that is, for previously owned lands now in American territory—the British government displayed the same unrelenting backwardness. Interestingly, it was the threat of American expansionists in Oregon and at the Red River that finally aroused Englishmen to defend the company in 1846.

Simpson did the best he could to make virtues of necessities. With the growth of Red River and the company's charter rights ignored and unenforceable, he tried various experiments. The "general trade" store at Fort Garry—now Winnipeg—was made to turn a fair profit by 1860, by which time railroad access from St. Paul had largely replaced Hudson's Bay as the natural outlet that had provided incentive for the company's beginnings in 1670. In 1863, already in administrative decline, the governing body of the company, the governor and committee, resigned en bloc and sold its interests to the International Financial Society, a holding company.

After some abortive efforts to sell its assets for as much as £5 million, the company surrendered its territorial rights under a provision of Parliament (Rupert's Land Act of 1868), and the new British dominion of Canada agreed the following year to buy those territories for £300,000. The company continued to operate as a fur trading enterprise and as a retailer and wholesaler of department-store goods throughout western Canada. Sales of land retained in 1869 provided revenue into the twentieth century. The Hudson's Bay Company continues its commercial contacts with the United States by selling various commodities, particularly in Alaska. No longer an "imperial factor" after 1870, the company is now not even an English factor, having moved its corporate offices from London to Winnipeg in 1970.

See E. E. Rich, *Hudson's Bay Company 1670-1870*, 3 vols. (1960). The archives of the Hudson's Bay Company are in Winnipeg and London. The Champlain Society has published many volumes of company documents.—R. J. L.

Hughes, Howard [Robard] (1905-1976). Nevada businessman. Hughes was born in Houston, Texas. His father's death in 1923 left him with a fortune estimated at less than a million dollars. More importantly, he inherited control of the Hughes Tool Company, which held rights to a revolutionary oil drill. Through expansion of that company and investments in West Coast motion-picture and aviation industries; in California, Arizona, and Nevada real estate; and in Nevada gambling, Hughes became one of the world's richest men with a fortune estimated at well over one billion dollars. Although shy as a youth and a veritable recluse after the 1940s, his name and activities were seldom out of the news.

Between the late 1920s and the early 1940s he produced a number of films, the best known being *The*

Outlaw. From movie production he shifted to aircraft manufacturing, design, and speed flying, which brought him three major speed records, a short experience as a national hero, a number of aviation honors, and the Congressional Medal in 1941. His activities as a speed and test pilot ended with the near-fatal crash of an experimental FX-11 plane in 1946. His reputation as an aircraft designer and builder suffered badly as the result of a Senate committee's investigation of the world's largest plane, the "Spruce Goose," which he designed and built under army contract during World War II. The plane flew just once, November 2, 1947, and has been stored at Long Beach, California, since. These two events combined to focus Hughes's aviation interests more directly on production and transportation and to drive him into hiding from public view.

His activities in air transportation were highlighted in the 1950s with his purchase of TWA. Although accused of mismanagement, Hughes was able to sell his stock in TWA in 1966 for $546.5 million, thereby making a profit of many millions of dollars. It was the possibilities of quick investment of the TWA profits that led him to Nevada in the fall of 1966. He began his Nevada investments in 1967 with the purchase of the Desert Inn Hotel on the Las Vegas Strip for a reputed $13 million. In the next few years he added the Frontier, the Sands, the Castaways, and the Silver Slipper. However, when he attempted to purchase the Stardust Hotel in 1968, he was blocked by the Justice Department. Later the Justice Department gave its blessing to the purchase of the Landmark Towers Hotel, a turnabout that interested the Senate Watergate Committee when it found in 1973 that Hughes had contributed heavily to the 1968 and 1972 Republican campaigns. Hughes completed his gambling chain in Nevada with the purchase of Harolds Club in Reno in 1970. He was welcomed to Nevada gambling by Nevada officials who saw in Hughes a perfect antidote to the persistent rumors of Mafia operations, particularly in the Las Vegas area. Nevada gaming officials even went so far as to waive a number of licensing requirements, including a personal appearance, a recent photo, a recent set of fingerprints, and a complete personal history. Besides his gambling investments, Hughes purchased a number of ranches, some 2,700 mining claims, a television station in Las Vegas, Alamo Airlines, Air West Airlines, and additional real estate in Las Vegas. These purchases totaled about $300 million and made Hughes the state's largest employer, with some eight thousand employees, and the largest single landowner and gambling figure. His Nevada activities were further publicized by his agreement to give the University of Nevada Medical School a grant of $4 million spread over twenty years and by a continuing quarrel with the Atomic Energy Commission over the question of nuclear testing in the southern Nevada desert.

The wall of secrecy surrounding Hughes and his corporate empire began to crumble somewhat when he left Nevada for the Bahamas on Thanksgiving eve, 1970. His departure, kept secret for a time, added credibility to the rumor that he was losing millions of dollars from his gambling investments and that a reorganization of the Nevada operations was taking place. The internal shake-up was confirmed by a telephone call from Hughes to Governor Paul Laxalt and by a memo from

Hughes to one of his aides, Chester Davis, which terminated Robert Maheu as chief of the Hughes Nevada operations. Maheu refused to give up his position until a Las Vegas court upheld the validity of the Hughes memo. He then brought suit against Hughes for some $52 million for events surrounding his dismissal. One of the fascinating results of these events was the admission that neither Maheu nor Davis, two of Hughes's most trusted employees, had ever seen him.

After his departure from Nevada and the Maheu difficulty, Hughes was beset by an almost unbelievable series of events. The new administration under Governor Mike O'Callaghan refused at first to license Maheu's successor, Chester Davis. This issue was not resolved until O'Callaghan and Phil Hannifin, the Gaming Control Board chairman, held a face-to-face meeting with Hughes in London in 1973. Additional publicity was directed to the "bashful billionaire" when his wife of fourteen years, Jean Peters, divorced him in June 1971. Then in late 1971 and early 1972 came the famous "hoax." This involved a supposed autobiography of Hughes, obtained through the obscure novelist Clifford Irving, and announced to be published in March 1972 by the McGraw-Hill Book Company. The extent of the hoax was apparent by the end of January and ended on March 14, 1972, when Irving, his wife, and an aide, Richard Suskind, pleaded guilty to the charge of conspiracy.

Bad publicity plagued Hughes throughout 1973. The Watergate investigation first brought his name into that picture in May 1973, and a great deal of publicity followed concerning a $100,000 contribution to "Bebe" Rebozo, a close friend of President Richard Nixon. On December 27, 1973, Hughes and four associates were indicted in Las Vegas for conspiring to manipulate stock in Air West so that Hughes could buy at a lower price. Although the indictment was dismissed, Hughes's legal difficulties involving his Nevada transactions continued until his death two years later.

See Stephen Fay, *Hoax* (1972); Albert B. Gerber, *Bashful Billionaire* (1967); and John Keats, *Howard Hughes* (1966).—R. R. E.

Humboldt River. See GREAT BASIN STREAMS.

humor. Three environmental forces shaped the humor of life on the frontier and in the West: the physical world, the political dialog, and the heterogeneous society. From early times, settlers and natives had fun giving newcomers inaccurate information about the geography, the flora, and the fauna of the New World. Soon after British John Josselyn sailed to New England in 1638, "neighboring Gentlemen" gravely told him yarns about a baby-sized frog, a Cape Ann sea serpent, and a Casco Bay merman. Two hundred years later, natives told the author of a very famous travel book, Mrs. Trollope, tales about man-eating Mississippi River "crocodiles" and a bear that hijacked a canoe and sailed into New Orleans, where it was mistaken for "an Englishman of fashion, dressed in a driving coat." Through the years, to while away long hours of travel or evenings by fires, men hoaxed strangers or entertained one another with tall tales—high-handed amalgamations of facts and audacious imaginings.

Journeying westward, credulous or mendacious storytellers recorded a parade of remarkable animals. In eighteenth-century New England, Cotton Mather heard about a rattlesnake that changed the color of an ax-head by sinking fangs into it. Soon after, in the same area, a somewhat less pious but equally credible historian encountered a dog that, split in two, was so hastily reassembled that it ran around with two legs up and two down. After John Darling of Sullivan County, New York, helped a sow with a broken back get around by lugging her hindquarters on a two-wheeled truck, she birthed a litter in which each piglet had "a nice little two-wheeled truck under its hind-quarters." In Surry County, North Carolina, gunsmith Davy Lane watched hoop-snakes chase their prey by tucking their tails in their mouths and rolling after it at an astonishing speed—and later settlers farther west saw descendants of the same reptiles carry on in the same way. In frontier Arkansas, a canny settler crossed bees with lightning bugs, got a crossbreed that worked day and night, and doubled honey production. In Texas, Bigfoot Wallace regrettably was compelled to chaw tobacco and swig whiskey because he found that was the only way to fend off the Sante Fe, a critter with " a hundred legs and a sting on every one of them, besides two large stings in its forked tail, and fangs as big as a rattle-snake's."

Travelers westward (it was claimed) discovered countrysides and climates that just naturally produced such creatures. The soil was fertile down to the center of the earth and the air made those breathing it snort like a horse. Or the soil was sterile and scant and the climate dry or wet or hot or cold (or all these combined) enough to make survival most unlikely. Grass, trees, vegetables, fruit, varmints, and men all had a terrible time of it.

And since this was a nation in which newspapers, magazines, almanacs, and books, as well as storytellers, flourished, accounts of these wonders were broadcast not only by voice but also by print. Old World concepts of folk humor became quaint and outmoded as journalists and raconteurs collaborated to create semioral, semiliterary celebrations of the vast countryside, its beasts, and the men who outmatched both them and one another. And though the men had lives and performed feats somewhat like those of Old World demigods, because Americans celebrating them were not credulous, solemn, and reverent as a rule but were sceptical, jocose, and irreverent, many heroes became comic figures.

The generic frontiersman initially was called "a Kentuckian" or "a backwoodsman" and stereotyped in hosts of stories as lawless, ignorant, uncouth, hard-drinking, and hard-fighting. When Ohio and Mississippi River traffic offered particularly rough adventures and tests of manhood, "the boatman" became famous as a super-Kentuckian, all virtues and faults magnified. Archetype of the boatmen was one Mike Fink (1770?-1823), who began as a meat hunter, scout, and Indian fighter around Pittsburgh, later became a champion keelboatman, and ended his days as a Rocky Mountain trapper with Andrew Henry and William Ashley. Stories told about him along the rivers and in the Far West portrayed a "helliferocious fellow" and a prankster who talked tall, fought fiercely, shot straight, and doted on killdevil whiskey and wild women.

Slightly later, Davy Crockett joined him as a hero-clown. There was, of course, a real Davy (1786-1836), as there was a real Mike, but Davy's story too was enlarged and embroidered in fireside tales, almanacs, newspa-

pers, and books. "Everything here is Davy Crockett," wrote a British visitor to Kentucky in the 1840s. "His voice was so loud it could not be described—it was obliged to be drawn as a picture. He took hailstones for 'Life Pills' . . . picked his teeth with a pitchfork . . . fanned himself with a hurricane . . . could drink the Mississippi dry—shoot six cords of bears in one day." Crockett almanacs (1835-56) and books, purportedly telling about Crockett's feats in his own words, playfully added outrageous details, as did plays and books by inventive biographers.

A series of heroes with comic qualities plied their trades and had strange adventures on successive frontiers. Johnny Appleseed, a mite touched in the head and a fanatic who was smug about being a saint, planted orchards. Pecos Bill invented the cowboy business and made improvements. Paul BUNYAN, a giant aided by a huge blue ox, was a prodigious lumberman and eventually a great oil man in Texas. This second stage in Paul's career came after the booming Far West's mining frontier and achievements of engineers had helped popularize science. Jim Bridger won laughs with fabrications about natural wonders such as geysers and the petrified forest, and Febold Feboldson, in stories, used science to cope with Nebraska's cantankerous weather. In California, George Horatio DERBY parodied scientific lectures and reports to recount "discoveries" about mythical animals; in Nevada Dan DEQUILLE told about solar armor that conquered Death Valley heat. Working the same vein, the young Mark TWAIN pleased West Coast readers with his story about the finding of a petrified man, a "hardened creature" who had turned to stone while thumbing his nose.

Political battles, like the physical world, stimulated humor. In his account of a visit to frontier North Carolina in 1728, aristocratic William Byrd satirized the way "every one does just what seems good in his own Eyes" instead of depending upon well-educated gentlemanly governors to decide what he should do. The subsequent debate that pitted uneducated against educated candidates was a rich source for humor. Partly this was because many Americans believed that, as Jefferson put it in 1787, a ploughman might decide "a moral case" better than a professor "because he has not been led astray by artificial rules." And partly it was because there was a feeling, just as widespread, that this phenomenon was an endless source of comedy.

Many newspapers printed comic speeches by generic frontier politicians who made a virtue of their lack of book learning and played up their ability to do things. One "Candidate Earth" in a comic sketch urged voters to elect him sheriff because: " . . . if Bob Black has floated farther on a log, killed more Injuns, or stayed under water longer than I have, elect him; if not, I say what has he ever done to qualify him for the office of sheriff?" A visitor to Texas told about the rebuke of a newly elected justice of the peace to attorneys who brought him law books: "Do you expect to read them through to me? If you do, I shall tell you once and for all that I am appointed, not to judge the nice points of law, but to give my decisions according to the simple dictates of justice and common sense."

Crockett became the most famous comic frontier politician of the pre-Civil War period as a result of claims about him made in some instances by storytellers, in other instances by himself or by journalists using his name. A tale had him tell an audience in a Raleigh tavern: "I'm that same David Crockett, fresh from the backwoods . . . can wade the Mississippi, leap the Ohio, ride upon a streak of lightning, and slip without a scratch down a honey locust—can whip my weight in wildcats . . . and whip any man opposed to Jackson." His *Autobiography* explains how he succeeded when he had the office of a squire in the canebrakes: "My judgments were never appealed from, and if they had been they would have stuck like wax, as I gave my decisions on the principles of common justice and honesty between man and man, and relied on natural born sense, and not on law learning to guide me; for I had never read a law book in all my life." When Crockett was elected to Congress and made a stir in Washington, the Democratic party made use of him as a popular spokesman. Later, when he turned against Jackson and joined the opposition, the Whigs took advantage of his popularity to stress their claim that they too loved common men.

A political strategy in the old Southwest and elsewhere in antebellum days was to play up the good or bad qualities of an uneducated political figure. So Johnson J. Hooper of Alabama in *Adventures of Captain Simon Suggs* (1845) satirized adulatory campaign biographies with a parody of one that praised, tongue in cheek, an illiterate confidence man and office-seeker whose motto was "It is good to be shifty in a new country." Simon expressed a typical belief of an ignoramus such as he was: "Booklarnin spoils a man if he's got mother-wit, and if he ain't got that, it don't do him no good. . . ." Just such "mother-wit" qualified a contemporary uneducated political commentator, Major Joseph Jones, to serve as a voice for his sympathetic creator, William Tappan Thompson, particularly in *Major Jones's Sketches of Travel* (1847). The major's letters, written for a Madison, Georgia, newspaper, were effective and popular among local country readers and others.

At an auction in Pappville, Illinois, in 1832, young Abe Lincoln helped a friend who was having a fist fight, climbed atop a box, and made a speech: "Gentlemen and fellow citizens, I presume you all know who I am. I am humble Abraham Lincoln . . . candidate for the legislature. My politics are short and sweet, like the old woman's dance. I am in favor of a national bank . . . of the internal improvements system and a high protective tariff. These are my sentiments and political principles. If elected, I shall be thankful; if not, it will be all the same." Kinship with Crockett and his ilk is indicated by the straightforward tone, the comic simile, the wry self-characterization. This was the early Lincoln of the stump and the debates with Douglas—the rail-splitter who stressed in an 1859 autobiography that "when I came of age, I did not know much [and] I have not been to school since." Though his mature speeches were, of course, much more dignified, his use of common-sense arguments and of droll, homespun anecdotes to illustrate points related him to the tradition throughout the rest of his life.

Horse-sense approaches to issues, horse play, and horse laughs continued to loom large in politics in the Nevada of the 1860s, where Mark Twain reported on the territorial legislature for the Virginia City *Enterprise*. His articles, laced with satire, initiated activity as a political commentator that continued until 1910. In 1866,

about the time when Twain left the West Coast, Ambrose BIERCE arrived in San Francisco. There as a journalist this ex-soldier became "Bitter Bierce," whose witty comments, definitions, fables, and essays often commented sardonically on American politics until 1913, when he disappeared in war-wracked Mexico.

Like Bierce, Edgar Wilson NYE was not born in the West but became famous there. Better known as Bill Nye, he was born in Maine and reared in Wisconsin. In 1876 he moved to Wyoming Territory, where he dabbled in law and politics and edited a thoroughly western newspaper, the Laramie *Boomerang*. Thanks to wide reprintings in other newspapers, Nye's comic writings became internationally known, well enough known to trigger his removal to the East and his employment there by the New York *World*. His syndicated columns and books, beginning with *Bill Nye and Boomerang* (1881) and continuing through *Bill Nye's History of the United States* (1894), had huge sales. When he chose to write on politics, he scored very palpable hits. Deservedly admired were his bland letters of acceptance of the Laramie postmastership and his subsequent resignation, exposing the ridiculous aspects of political patronage and the grandiloquence of politics. His story of a visit to the Brooklyn Navy Yard, where he found "as pleasant a navy as one could see in a day's journey," neatly pilloried shortcomings. His characterization of a famous amendment was a high point in his comic history: "The Fourteenth Amendment, a bright little *bon mot*, became a law June 28, 1868, and was written in the minutes of Congress, so that people could go there and refresh their memories of it."

In addition to the landscape and the political scene, a wonderfully varied society on the frontier and in the West provided rich stuff for humor. When folk of many ethnic backgrounds mingled—English, Scots, Irish, Germans, Dutch, French, Spaniards, Indians, Afro-Americans, and mixtures thereof ad infinitum—hilarious contrasts and confrontations were assured. Juxtaposed religionists ranging from Catholics to Holy Rollers, social groups ranging from the quality to the "trash," and workers in every conceivable field provided additional incongruities. Humorous writers often remarked on the heterogeneity of the society and vowed that they would portray a wide range of its elements. Augustus Baldwin Longstreet, whose pioneer collection of sketches and stories, *Georgia Scenes* (1835), set forth that "the aim of the author was to supply a chasm in history which has always been overlooked—the manners, customs, amusements, wit, dialect, as they appear in all grades of society to an ear witness to them." Another author, whose book was subtitled "A Series of Humorous Sketches Descriptive of Incident and Character in the Wild West," noticed in 1846 that "the west abounds with incident and humor," and asserted that he would offer proof.

William T. Porter, whose magazine *The Spirit of the Times* (1831-61) did more than any other to search out and popularize frontier humorists, prefaced a famous anthology by them with a claim that contributors "furnished most valuable . . . reminiscences of the pioneers of the far West—sketches of thrilling incidents and adventures in that then comparatively unknown region, and the extraordinary characters occasionally met with—their strange language and habitudes, and the peculiar characteristics of . . . early settlers." Porter claimed that the humorists opened "a new vein of literature, as orginal as it is inexhaustible in its source."

The unusually varied backgrounds and experiences of these ebullient humorists gave some of our best humor panoramic variety. Sol Smith (1801-69), actor and theatrical manager, wrote about his traveling company's strenuous experiences when it appeared in towns along the Ohio and Mississippi rivers and in the old Southwest in *Theatrical Apprenticeship* (1845) and *Theatrical Journey Work* (1854). Governor Alexander McNutt (1802-48) of Mississippi wrote for *The Spirit of the Times* ebullient sketches about two rough and ready hunters and storytellers, Jim and Chunkey. Joseph M. Fields (1810-56), St. Louis actor and journalist, recorded many aspects of frontier life in *The Drama in Pokerville; or the Bench and Bar of Jurytown, and Other Stories* (1847). William Tappan Thompson (1812-82), Georgia soldier, printer, law student, and journalist, acted as amanuensis not only for Major Joseph Jones of the militia but also for some superb rustic yarnspinners. George Washington Harris (1814-69) of Tennessee, jeweler's apprentice, steamboat captain, silversmith, officeholder, inventor, and journalist, invented the trick-playing, hell-raising mountaineer in *Sut Lovingood: Yarns Spun by a "Nat'ral Born Durn'd Fool"* (1867). Thomas Bangs THORPE of Louisiana, painter, war correspondent, politician, and journalist, wrote authoritatively on the arts of hunting and dwelling in the backwoods in such stories as "The Big Bear of Arkansas." Johnson J. Hooper (1815-63) of Alabama, lawyer, legislator, and newspaper editor, wrote about the peerless confidence man Simon Suggs and those whom he encountered—and usually defrauded. Joseph Glover Baldwin (1815-64), lawyer and legislator, recorded his picturesque career and memorialized his rambunctious acquaintances in *The Flush Times of Alabama and Mississippi* (1853) and "California Flush Times" (1853). Henry Clay Lewis (1825-50), pseudonym Madison Tensas, physician in northeastern Louisiana, described his harassing experiences—equaled only by those of his associates and patients—in *Odd Leaves from the Life of a Louisiana Swamp Doctor* (1850).

From the writings of these men, as historian Bernard DeVoto has said, "No aspect of the life in the simpler America is missing." Hence, in addition to being amusing, these works offer a superb historical survey of southwestern frontier life in the antebellum decades. Historians of literature find them important for another reason: in a period when romantic fiction was being produced by the most admired authors, these humbler and more playful writers sneaked in a realistic mode of portrayal not destined to become respectable until much later.

Though other frontiers of the antebellum period produced fewer humorous writers, they inspired some fine books. Caroline Kirkland (1801-64) ruefully contrasted the actual frontier with that of romantic picturings in her *A New Home—Who'll Follow?* (1839), based upon her experiences as an early settler in Pinckney, Michigan. Her wide spectrum included upper-class British settlers, an overromantic girl, a gossipy spinster, and an embezzler, in addition to log-cabin democrats. Alonzo Delano (1802?-74), pseudonym Old Block, employed similarly wry wit in *Pen-Knife Sketches* (1853) and *Old Block's Sketch*

Book (1856) to tell the story of California gold-seekers and settlers who did not strike it rich. Like Mrs. Kirkland, he was panoramic: his range included prospectors, greenhorns, traders, gamblers, and other assorted California types.

Humorists of the old Southwest often claimed that, thank the Lord, the uncouth ways of living they pictured were things of the past. Their writings, nevertheless, had a feel of contemporaneity about them. Most post-Civil War humorists, by contrast, looked back nostalgically, dealing with specified antebellum periods or so playing up sentimental and genial aspects of life in their areas as to give their picturings a remote semiromantic quality.

A powerful impetus was Bret HARTE, whose local color writings about California gold-rush days were shaped by impressions he got as a visitor to the scene at a later date. Strongly influenced by Dickens and (as he himself acknowledged) by American humorists, Harte, in *The Luck of Roaring Camp and Other Stories* (1870) and in fiction that followed, stressed rosier and more amusing features of life in the mother lode country. Many contemporaries understandably classified these not as fiction but as humor. Except for black-hatted villains—missing from his pages—Harte "discovered" most stereotypes constantly used by writers of westerns who followed him—gamblers, miners, drunkards, pretty schoolmarms, and whores—and endowed the lot of them with hearts of gold.

Mark Twain was another powerful influence—not so much in *Roughing It*, which told of his years in the Far West, as in the books that revisited the Missouri of his boyhood and the Mississippi River of his pilot days. The best of these, of course, was *The Adventures of Huckleberry Finn* (1884). From 1908 on it begat numerous books with strong family likenesses. Their earmarks were naive but sensible narrators whose speech was illiterate, salty, and amusing, picaresque plots, and a generally comic tone. Those with western backgrounds include, notably: the stories told by a modern Simon Suggs, Jeff Peters, in O. Henry's *The Gentle Grafter* (1908); Robert Lewis Taylor's best-sellers in the Huck Finn manner, the best of which is *Travels of Jaimie McPheeters* (1959 Pulitzer Prize); the superb Pulitzer Prize-winning novel by H. L. DAVIS about pioneer Oregon, *Honey in the Horn* (1936); and three fine books of very recent years—Thomas Berger's *Little Big Man* (1967), Charles Portis' *True Grit* (1968), and David Wagoner's *Where Is My Wandering Boy Tonight?* (1970).

Among the shelves of books about cowboys, few that were predominantly humorous were outstanding. This was true despite the fact that Owen WISTER revealed many potentialities of the genre in 1902 in *The Virginian*, when he recounted at length in climactic chapters a tall-tale-telling contest involving the hero and the villainous Trampas. Two authors proved exceptions. Even before Wister's book appeared, Alfred Henry Lewis had begun to publish "Old Cattleman's" Wolfville stories (most of them comic, though a few were bathetic), based upon Lewis' youthful years as a wandering cowboy and miner in the Southwest. Between 1897 and 1913, Lewis published six volumes which were much admired. Often more amusing, better written, and, in the opinion of Texans who know, more authentic, are the campfire tales by another ex-cowboy and ex-miner, Andy ADAMS, in *The Log of a Cowboy* (1903) and *Cattle-Brands* (1906).

Walter Blair, in *Native American Humor* (1937; rev. 1960), *Horse Sense in American Humor* (1942), and *Tall Tale America* (1944), discusses humor at great length and in a broad context. Mody C. Boatright, *Folk Laughter on the American Frontier* (1949), and Norris W. Yates, *William T. Porter and the Spirit of the Times* (1957), are both readable and authoritative.—W. BL.

Hunt, George W[iley] P[aul] (1859-1934). Arizona pioneer and politician. Born in Huntsville, Missouri, Hunt left home in 1877, prospected in Colorado, followed the railroad into southern New Mexico, and in 1881 arrived in the copper camp of Globe, Arizona. He entered the employ of the Old Dominion Commercial Company and by 1900 had become president of the company, which owned a mercantile establishment, a bank, and other properties. Elected to the territorial legislature as a Democrat in 1892, Hunt served two terms in the lower house, where he was chosen speaker, and two terms in the Senate, where he was president. A large, bald-headed man with a handlebar mustache, he became known as the "Old Roman." Hunt was a master politician, skillfully drawing support from both business and labor, while at the same time appealing to the common people by his unpretentious personal habits and speech. He was chairman of the Constitutional Convention in 1910; two years later he ran on a Democratic ticket, portraying himself as a progressive, and was elected the first state governor of Arizona. He won reelection in 1914 but in 1916 lost to Thomas G. Campbell, a Republican—only to be awarded the office in December 1917 after a recount of the votes. During 1917 he was a federal strike mediator in Arizona. He lost in the state election of 1918, was appointed the minister to Siam in 1920, and regained the governorship in 1922. As governor he promoted railroad regulation, a state highway system, and prison reform, but opposed the development of federal power dams on the Colorado River, regarding it as a violation of states' rights. Defeated in 1928, Hunt won his seventh and last gubernatorial race in 1932. He died in Phoenix.

See Frank Lockwood, *Pioneer Portraits* (1968). —H. P. H.

Hunt, H[aroldson] L[afayette] (1889-1974). Industrialist. One of eight children, Hunt was born on a farm near Vandalia, Illinois. He left home at the age of sixteen and traveled across the western United States, working as a farmhand, cowboy, lumberjack, and muleskinner. When his father died Hunt inherited $6,000, which he invested in cotton land in Arkansas and Louisiana. The collapse of cotton prices in 1920 nearly wiped him out, but he managed to scrape together enough money to follow up on rumors of oil strikes in southern Arkansas. Here he began to accumulate the oil leases that were to bring him his fortune. By 1930 he had one hundred wells working throughout the South and Southwest. That same year he acquired the rights to the oil strike of C. M. (Dad) Joiner in eastern Texas; the site proved to be the greatest oil discovery in the world at the time and the first major field in oil-rich east Texas.

Reputed to be the richest man in the world, Hunt became increasingly concerned with the preservation of his fortune in the face of those he labeled the "mistaken"—the combined forces of communism, socialism, and liberalism. He backed the political campaigns of both General Douglas MacArthur (1952) and Senator Barry Goldwater (1964), hoping for a return to the "enlightened" policies of Calvin Coolidge, who, Hunt felt, had "turned in the last successful Administration in Washington." In order to guarantee a larger audience for his "constructivist" point of view, Hunt started "Life Line," a daily fifteen-minute commentary on public affairs that was distributed to more than three hundred radio stations.

Hunt made his home—an outsized replica of George Washington's Mount Vernon—outside of Dallas, the hub of his vast empire.

For an interesting look at Utopia, according to Hunt, see his *Alpaca* (1960). The best glimpse of Hunt's politics can be found in his interview with *Playboy* (August 1966).—R. B. W.

Hunt, Wilson Price (1783-1842). Fur trader. Hunt was one of the first businessmen to attempt to exploit the rich potential of the fur trade. Despite the fact that Hunt more or less ranks as the hero of Washington Irving's *Astoria* (1836), he was, in fact, no mountain man, but rather a hard-headed merchant who found himself in the incongruous position of leader of an exciting and harrowing expedition to the Pacific Coast.

Born in Asbury, New Jersey, where he was "bred to mercantile pursuits," Hunt in 1804 went west to St. Louis, where he established a store with a partner, John Hankinson. He soon came to the attention of John Jacob Astor, who was in need of young American merchants to help launch his Astoria enterprise. Astor planned to send two expeditions to the mouth of the Columbia River, one by sea and the other by land. Despite his inexperience, Hunt was put in charge of the overland expedition, and on October 21, 1810, the expedition left St. Louis.

Although the expedition was labeled inefficient and Hunt charged with mismanagement by such historians as Hiram Chittenden and Hubert Bancroft, Washington Irving and others praised Hunt for his coolness under fire and his administrative skill. It is true that Hunt made a number of blunders—most notably that of losing the horses in an attempt to navigate the wild and unpredictable Snake River. On the other hand, before Hunt and his party stumbled into Astoria in 1812, they had managed to trace the route between the Snake and Columbia rivers that was to become an important part of the western Oregon Trail.

After the sale of Astoria to the British in April 1814, Hunt returned to St. Louis, where he prospered as a landowner and provincial merchant. In 1822 he was appointed postmaster of St. Louis, a relatively important political position he held for eighteen years. The last half of Hunt's life was marked by none of the excitement which attended his one great adventure, and he appears to have preferred it that way.

See William Brandon, "Wilson Price Hunt," in LeRoy Hafen, ed., *The Mountain Men and the Fur Trade of the Far West*, vol. VI (1968); and T. C. Elliott, "Wilson Price Hunt, 1783-1842," *Oregon Historical Quarterly*, vol. 32 (1931).—R. B. W.

Hunter, Walter L. See RIVERMEN.

Huntington, Collis Potter (1821-1900). Railroad builder. Huntington was the most important of the "Big Four" (others included Charles Crocker, Mark Hopkins, and Leland Stanford) who built the CENTRAL

PACIFIC and SOUTHERN PACIFIC railroads. The fifth of nine children of a Harwinton, Connecticut, tinker, he left school at fourteen and the next year went to New York City. After six years of peddling watches and parts in the South, Huntington earned enough capital to start a store in Oneonta, New York. Attracted to California in 1849, ostensibly by thoughts of gold mining but with a stock of trading goods in his baggage, he took the quickest route, across the Isthmus of Panama. After trying just one day of mining, he set up a miners' supply store in Sacramento in partnership with Mark Hopkins.

A shrewd merchandiser, Huntington was relatively content with ocean transportation, but he saw the profits to be made in an overland route and contributed part of the cost of a survey over the Sierras for the Theodore D. JUDAH transcontinental project. He was Judah's apt pupil in lobbying for government assistance in Washington and a major influence in enactment of the second, and more generous, Pacific Railroad Act of 1864, after Judah's death. Thenceforth Huntington served as eastern agent for the Central Pacific and later the Southern Pacific, shouldering the burden of procurement of materials and equipment and, during the 1870s depression, of keeping the road solvent.

To protect the western end of their railroad, Huntington and associates built and acquired lines from Sacramento to San Francisco and then built ambitiously south to Los Angeles and San Diego and west to El Paso, Texas, incorporating this enterprise separately as the Southern Pacific. Thomas A. Scott of the Pennsylvania Railroad was then pushing the Texas and Pacific as part of his scheme for an Atlantic-to-Pacific railroad, but Huntington, aided by adverse publicity of the Credit Mobilier affair, frustrated Scott's efforts to get a federal land grant. The Texas and Pacific stopped at the main line of the Southern Pacific a few miles east of El Paso, while the Southern Pacific eventually pushed farther east to New Orleans. This southern route, over which the Big Four could route transcontinental freight and passengers to the complete exclusion of the Union Pacific, assured that the Union Pacific would share through revenues generously with the Central Pacific, upon which it depended west of Ogden, Utah.

The profits that the Big Four made on their construction of the Central Pacific were huge when compared to their direct cash investments, but not in view of the extremely high interest rates money commanded on the Pacific Coast in the 1860s and the risks involved. Since outside capital was unavailable at any price, payment for construction had to be taken in government subsidy bonds, which could be sold to raise cash only at heavy discounts. Net profits to the promoters were slight, therefore, until the common stock in which they were embodied gained a substantial market value.

Childless and grumbling at the heavy burden he carried, Huntington tried to sell out in 1884, but there were no takers, mainly because the Thurman Act of 1878 had tied up much of the profits in an untraconservative sinking fund to assure payment of the government bonds when due. The eventual value of the Central Pacific-Southern Pacific owed as much to Huntington's managerial skill in the 1880s and 1890s as anything else, although he did not take over the office of president until 1890.

Thrifty to the point of parsimony, openly contemptuous of venal public officials, "a hard and cheery old man, with no more soul than a shark," Huntington spent long days at his desk in the Mills Building in New York's financial district, looking after the western roads and other projects such as the Chesapeake and Ohio Railway. His philanthropies were negligible, his generosities confined to a niece and nephew. His true legacies were the debt-free Central Pacific and the independent Southern Pacific, which controlled the Central Pacific absolutely. (At the critical moment he had thrown the entire credit of the Southern Pacific behind the financial settlement with the government in 1899.) His life work completed, Huntington retired to his Adirondack mountain lodge in New York.

David Lavender, *The Great Persuader* (1970), is the most perceptive biography, although Cerinda W. Evans, *Collis Potter Huntington*, 2 vols. (1954), contains much additional detail. Stuart Daggett, *Chapters on the History of the Southern Pacific* (1922; repr. 1966), is still indispensable.—A. M.

Huron, South Dakota. In 1880 the townsite for Huron was platted as the Chicago and Northwestern Railroad progressed across Dakota Territory. The town served as a construction camp for rail workers, and the tracks came to the settlement in the summer of 1880. Many other rail lines went through Huron; by 1882 it was said that as many as eighteen trains might arrive daily on the several tracks.

Dakota land booms also centered around Huron, and its land office was the busiest of any land office in Dakota Territory on its opening day in 1882. Prior to the slump after the booms subsided, Huron boasted a newspaper, four churches of different denominations, an Odd Fellows Lodge, a Freemasons Lodge, three hotels, and even a town brass band.

Huron was considered as a site for the territorial capital but lost to Bismarck when the capital was moved from Yankton. Huron's 1898 population was 3,038, while its 1970 total was 14,299.—D. J. T.

Huron (Wyandot) Indians. The Huron Indians were in the early seventeenth century one of the strongest and most populous of the Iroquoian peoples. Called "Hurons" (ruffians) by the French, their own name for themselves was *Wendat*, meaning "peninsula dwellers." When contacted by the French in 1615, they were a confederation of four highly organized agricultural tribes and dependent communities, numbering about twenty thousand people and inhabiting fortified villages in a relatively small region between Georgian Bay and Lake Simcoe in southeastern Ontario. This unusual concentration of population was apparently due to the easily tillable soil of the area and to its geographic advantages for trade with the northern Great Lakes Algonquian peoples, which was an important aspect of the prehistoric Huron economy.

Huron social organization was based on a system of exogamous matrilineal clans, whose matrons determined the choice of hereditary lineage chiefs. These chiefs together formed the tribal and larger confederation councils. Their function was to coordinate intertribal activities and to act as conciliators in internal conflicts. Chiefs had little, if any, coercive powers, and acts such as murder and theft were redressed by compensatory payments between families of the parties involved. Huron religion was basically the general American Indian form of pantheistic animism, but they were noteworthy in their large amount of concern for matters of death; their primary communal ceremony was a periodic reburial ritual known as the "feast of the dead." Huron subsistence was primarily horticultural; the women tended fields that the men had cleared. Fishing was of greater importance than hunting, and a large percentage of the animal skins used in clothing were obtained by trade with other tribes.

Because of their geographic location and traders' traditions, the Huron became important middlemen for the French fur trade, and Jesuit missionaries were sent to convert them and ensure their loyalties. Along with Christianity the French brought smallpox, which ravaged the Huron in 1636. At the same time, the depletion of beaver in the New York region led the Iroquois Confederacy, which traded with the Dutch, to compete strongly for the Huron's northern fur sources. The traditional feud between the two peoples became a bloody war, which the Iroquois won. In a series of devastating raids in 1648-49 the Iroquois destroyed the Huron Confederacy and expelled the people from their homeland. Scattering in fragmentary bands, most of the survivors were captured and absorbed by the Iroquois. Others found temporary refuge with smaller tribes that the Iroquois destroyed in turn.

One sizable Huron group escaped west across lakes Huron and Michigan. After half a century of wandering, they settled on the south shore of Lake Erie, where they were known to the British and Americans as the Wyandot (a corruption of *Wendat*) and became an important tribe in northern Ohio during the eighteenth century. It was only through their permission that the Shawnee and Delaware were resettled in that region, and while few in numbers (1,500 in 1794-95) they joined all the antiwhite Indian movements in the Ohio valley and Lake region. Although they supported the British during the War of 1812, the Wyandot were confirmed a large tract in Ohio and Michigan after the peace of 1815. Most of this land was ceded in 1819. In the 1830s Wyandot chief William WALKER recommended against removal, but by 1842 the entire tribe had been removed to Wyandotte County, Kansas. In 1855 they were made citizens and granted land in severalty, but by 1867 increasing white settlement in Kansas resulted in their tribal organization being restored, and they were placed on a small reservation in northeas Oklahoma. Federal trusteeship of their affairs was terminated in August 1959, at which time the Wyandot population was given as 423.

See V. W. Kinietz, *The Indians of the Western Great Lakes, 1615-1760* (1940); J. R. Swanton, *The Indian Tribes of North America* (1952); Elizabeth Tooker, *An Ethnography of the Huron Indians, 1615-1649* (1964); and B. G. Trigger, *The Huron: Farmers of the North* (1969). —P. R. M.

Hutchinson, William Henry (1911-   ). Historian. When Hutchinson was only six weeks old, his family moved from Colorado to Goldfield, Nevada. Then, while his father served with the army in World War I, he lived with his grandmother in Oxford, Mississippi, and joined a boy scout troop led by William Faulkner. Reunited with his father, he lived for varying periods of time in Texas, Arizona, California, and Nevada, working in Arizona on a ranch as "an incompetent horse wrangler and inept rough string rider," as he described himself, and in Nevada as a harvest hand. In 1933 he joined the Matson Navigation Company, which operated primarily between America and Australia, and spent the next twelve years at sea. In 1940 he helped evacuate American women and children from Shanghai and during World War II served on convoy duty. He spent his last year with Matson as a labor negotiator.

In 1946 Hutchinson decided to try his hand at writing and moved to Chico, California. His first venture could best be termed a labor of love. Like his father, he had been a great fan of Eugene Manlove Rhodes, a western novelist. After Rhodes's death he collected a number of the author's short stories that were tied together by a central character, persuaded cow-country historian J. Frank Dobie to do the introduction and Harold Bugbee the drawings, and marketed a thousand copies of the book, *The Little World Waddies* (1946). He then turned over the book's entire proceeds to Rhodes's widow. Later he wrote *A Bar Cross Man* (1956), the life and personal writings of Rhodes, selected the stories for *The Rhodes Reader* (1957), compiled *A Bar Cross Liar* (1959), a bibliography of Rhodes's writings, and wrote introductions to reprints of five of Rhodes's novels. Hutchinson undoubtedly did more than any other person to assure Rhodes a permanent niche in America's literature of the West.

Hutchinson's literary pursuits were by no means limited to Rhodes. Over the years he produced a number of books dealing with the West, such as *A Notebook of the Old West* (1947); *California Heritage* (1958); *Oil, Land, and Politics* (1965), which covers the California political life of Thomas Robert Bard and was nominated for the Pulitzer Prize in biography; and *California* (1969), which emphasizes the cultural and commercial development of the Golden State. In addition, he wrote well over two hundred articles and stories for magazines and scholarly journals and reviewed more then three hundred books for the San Francisco *Chronicle*.

Hutchinson became a history professor at Chico State College in 1964, joined the Western History Association and the Western American Literature Association, and was invited to be a contributing editor for *The American West*. In the mid-1960s he began a weekly radio program and soon thereafter a highly successful television show.—J. C. D.

I

Iberville, Pierre Le Moyne, Sieur d' (1661-1706). Founder of the French colony of Louisiana. Born in Ville-Marie, Montreal, Iberville was the older brother of Jean Baptiste Le Moyne, Sieur de Bienville. As a young naval officer during the War of the English Succession, he distinguished himself against the British in Hudson's Bay in 1797. His heroism brought him to the attention of the Count de Pontchartrain, Louis XIV's minister of marine, who was anxious at the war's end to reestablish French title to the regions claimed by La Salle in 1682 as the "country of Louisiana."

Commanding the *Badine* and the *Marin* and two smaller vessels, Iberville departed upon this mission from Brest in 1698. After a brief stop at Santo Domingo, he put into Pensacola Bay in January 1699, then pushed westward to Mobile Bay and the island at its mouth, which his men christened Ile Massacre. From here he moved on to two small islands off the coast of the present state of Mississippi, which he named Ship Island and Cat Island. There he left his larger vessels in safe shelter while he, the Sieur de Bienville, and some 50 members of the crew made their way westward along the coast in search of the great river whose mouth had eluded La Salle in his tragic voyage of 1684. On March 3, 1699, he entered the Mississippi through North Pass and made camp on the east bank at a spot he called "Mardi Gras Bayou," thus fixing the first place-name in the present state of Louisiana. After exploring the mighty river, Iberville returned via Bayou Manchac, Lake Maurepas, and Lake Pontchartrain to the Mississippi Sound and Ship Island, from which he proceeded to shore to plant the first permanent settlement in French Louisiana, Fort Maurepas or Biloxi, at the present site of Ocean Springs, Mississippi. On two later voyages, 1700 and 1701, he established a post on the lower Mississippi, Fort de Mississippi or de la Boulaye, placed a settlement on Ile Massacre, which he rechristened Ile Dauphine, and built Fort Louis, now Mobile, on the western shore of Mobile Bay.

The War of the Spanish Succession called Iberville from these pacific duties, and he left the colony of Louisiana in 1702, never to return. He ousted the British from Nevis and St. Christopher in 1706, but as he planned to strike at New York and Boston he succumbed to yellow fever and died in Havana.

See Nellis Crouse, *Le Moyne d'Iberville: Soldier of New France* (1954).—J. G. T.

Idaho. Highly skilled Indians have lived in the area that is now Idaho for at least the past twelve or fifteen thousand years. Some of them—ten thousand or more, in fact—still were around in 1800, just before white men entered the area. North Idaho included bands of Kutenai, Coeur D'Alene, and Nez Percé. Northern Shoshoni, Northern Paiute, and Bannock lived to the south. Remote from Spanish, French, and British bases for exploration, Idaho turned out to be the last of the fifty states to be seen by white men.

Searching for a good route from the Great Plains across the Rockies to the Columbia River, Lewis and Clark introduced the Indians of Idaho to the white man's way of life in 1805-06. British fur hunters followed in 1808-09, and from 1824 to 1840 Idaho was a disputed borderland between rival British and American trappers. The mountain men of the fur trade, such as Donald MACKENZIE, traveled over the country and lived pretty much the way the Indians did. But they were joined by missionaries who began to settle some of the Indians down to a life similar to the white man's. Some of the Nez Percé and Coeur d'Alene became farmers, with flour mills, sawmills, and even a mission printing press. A great wave of white emigrants followed the missionaries through Idaho over the Oregon Trail after 1840, and in 1846 this migration led to an Oregon boundary settlement between Great Britain and the United States. Present-day Idaho became part of the United States, but the land still belonged to the Indians. Yet the founding of Mormon settlements to the south, followed by the California gold rush across Idaho in 1849, foreshadowed a new day of white settlement. In the spring of 1860 Mormon colonists advanced northward into land that soon became Idaho.

Gold discoveries in the Clearwater country on September 30, 1860, laid the foundations for a new mining commonwealth of Idaho. After the original success of Elias Davidson PIERCE, prospectors radiated out over the vast mountain ranges, and miners such as J. Marion MORE followed up on the more promising leads. Literally thousands more miners and settlers flocked to the fabulous gold discoveries at he Clearwater country and Salmon River mines and founded a new mineral empire that expanded southward in 1862 to Boise Basin and eastward to the upper Missouri River.

Like Nevada a year or two before, Idaho was settled originally by an eastward movement from the Pacific Coast—mainly from California. By 1862 the Idaho mines overshadowed Washington Territory's original settlements west of the Cascades. As soon as the mining counties could gain control of the Washington legislature, Olympia faced the dismal prospect of losing its status as territorial capital of Washington to the new community of Walla Walla, nearer the mines. But in the 1862 legislative elections the mining counties went along with Walla Walla's plan to keep Washington Territory intact so that Walla Walla could be capital of, hopefully, the mining state of Washington.

By 1862 a westward movement to the Idaho mines reinforced the initial wave of settlers, but many who came from Colorado could not get through the mountains to Florence and the Salmon River mines. Diverted to new gold discoveries at East Bannock (then in Dakota Territory), they quickly surpassed in numbers the Dakota farming settlers around the capital at Yankton, some eight hundred miles to the east. This development, along with the still greater Boise Basin gold rush, required that Dakota as well as Washington Territory had to be split up. Taking advantage of the situation, Olympia made certain that *all* Washington's mining region went to the new territory of Idaho, created March 4, 1863. Dakota's mines were thrown in for good measure, so that Idaho Territory's boundaries included all later Montana and just about all later Wyoming as well. Substantially larger than Texas in area, Idaho proved to be the last of the huge western territories.

In choosing a boundary for the new territory of Idaho, Olympia's partisans went just as far beyond the Cascades as they dared: their line separated most of the farmlands of the Palouse country from the mountainous mining area beyond. As a result, Washington never developed very many mines of consequence, and most of Idaho's farms have had to be irrigated, since Washington kept almost all the farmland that did not require supplementary water.

Even at the time, the Washington-Idaho boundary had little or no merit aside from preserving Olympia's political interest of remaining the capital of Washington Territory. Inclusion of all the mining region in the new territory of Idaho was a mistake because the mines were too scattered in a mountainous region, much of which still has no roads. The Olympia people wanted to have two mining territories but were denied more than one. Thus they lumped all the mines together, regardless of natural barriers. The Washington-North Idaho boundary was a particularly unfortunate choice, because it ran through one of the few naturally connected sections that ought not to have been divided. The basis for these mistakes was the original Washington-Oregon boundary of 1853, followed by an unfortunate eastern Oregon state boundary in 1859.

Lewiston, a service community for the northern Idaho mines, had been anxious to occupy a central location that would make it capital of a new territory. This would have required a boundary farther west. Instead, Lewiston wound up on the western boundary of an immense territory that included all the northern Rockies along with vast unsettled tracts of the northern Great Plains. The mountainous western portion, where the miners lived, had three sections separated by nearly insurmountable natural barriers. These were the Clearwater and Salmon River mines near Lewiston, the Boise region to the south, and the upper Missouri mines east of the Continental Divide. When Idaho Territory was organized in Lewiston, on July 10, 1863, the original Idaho mines around Pierce City, Elk City, Florence, and Lewiston had already declined dramatically. Idaho's population exceeded forty thousand during that initial summer, with more than half in the Boise region. But by the time an official census was taken in September, many of the miners had left. The Boise area had more

than sixteen thousand people; Virginia City and East Bannock (later Montana) approached twelve thousand; and only four thousand or so remained in the Clearwater and Salmon River region, where well over ten thousand had rushed in the summer of 1862.

Meeting in Lewiston during the winter of 1863-64, the Idaho legislature agreed unanimously that Idaho Territory should be divided but did not choose a site for a territorial capital prior to adjournment on February 4, 1864. More than any other group, the delegation from east of the Continental Divide, where new mines at Virginia City were attracting special attention, knew that something had to be done about Idaho's unsatisfactory boundaries. To return home to Virginia City, the members had to go down the Columbia River to Portland, head south to San Francisco, turn east to Salt Lake, and finally proceed north back to Idaho. This hard, circuitous trip from Lewiston to Virginia City was enough to convince just about anyone that another territory was needed, and Congress responded by creating Montana Territory on May 26, 1864. At the same time, most of later Wyoming was returned to Dakota. Idaho thus emerged with something close to its final boundaries, but with an isolated North Idaho projecting between Washington and Montana.

That solution again proved entirely unsatisfactory for Lewiston and North Idaho. The Salmon River Mountains effectively separated North Idaho from the rest of the territory. A second session of the legislature assembled in Lewiston, but the members decided to locate the territorial capital in Boise, effective December 24, 1864. With more than ninety percent of Idaho's population in the Boise region, Lewiston had no chance. Efforts to delay the matter by getting the local probate judge to declare the legislative session illegal (because no one could be sure what day it was supposed to convene) only made the situation worse. Alonzo LELAND and other leaders from Lewiston and North Idaho, embittered by the capital controversy, spent the next quarter-century trying to get something done about the North Idaho boundary. For a time, Boise concurred in asking Congress to set up a new interior Columbia territory for Lewiston, Walla Walla, and Missoula. Montana objected, and Congress failed to respond to the Idaho legislature's revised request to form a new Columbia territory out of northern Idaho and eastern Washington, with western Montana left out.

Even without the boundary arguments, few territories had anything like the sad experience that afflicted Idaho while setting up a territorial government. William Henson Wallace, the governor who organized the territory, immediately got himself elected to Congress as Idaho's delegate. His successor, Caleb Lyon, a political oddity from upstate New York, moved from one catastrophe to another. During the 1864 capital dispute, Lyon attempted to solve the problem by delivering five speeches on his experiences in the Holy Land. He also escaped clandestinely from Lewiston under the pretence of hunting ducks. "Fleeing from the mandate of a probate judge," he left Idaho with no executive department at all; finally his private secretary decided to take over until a legal official might show up. After three months a new territorial secretary, C. DeWitt Smith, reached Lewiston. With military support, he took the territorial seal and archives away from a vigilant armed guard provided by Lewiston's alert citizens, who were resisting permanent location of the capital in Boise. Smith did not last long in Boise. At the end of a strenuous chess game in Rocky Bar, August 19, 1865, he suddenly expired from the effects of a "dismal and melancholy disease." That left Idaho once again with no government. No one knew for sure where the capital was, and the supreme court had not yet succeeded in organizing itself into existence. Meanwhile, in Washington, D.C., Caleb Lyon beat W. H. Wallace in a hardfought contest for the dubious honor of returning to Idaho as governor.

While Lyon was on the way to Boise, Horace C. Gilson took over the government and soon got himself appointed secretary. An ill-chosen associate of C. DeWitt Smith (who had found him in a San Francisco saloon), Gilson came poorly recommended because of his doubtful "moral antecedents." Gilson and Lyon made an interesting pair. They managed to dodge serious conflict with a bitterly hostile Democratic legislature, but in the spring of 1866 they quietly left town. Gilson took along the entire territorial treasury of $41,062 in federal funds, and Lyon escaped with the entire Nez Percé Indian treasury of $46,418.40, to have been used for treaty payments. Lyon had been dismissed because of his policy of treating the Indians decently. Refusing to go along with local sentiment, he blocked a campaign to exterminate the local Shoshoni. But he learned his lesson quickly, and when he got through, no one could doubt that he had made up for his mistake in trying to help the Indians. No recovery ever was made from either Lyon or Gilson in this defalcation.

With Lyon's departure in April 1866, Idaho ended up with no government again. Location of the capital was still in litigation, but at last the supreme court got organized in time to dismiss the Lewiston complaints and injunctions on June 14. Just then David W. Ballard turned up as governor, and from then on, Idaho at least had a functioning territorial administration. It was about time. A few loose ends from the period of original chaos still had to be cleared up. The supreme court, for example, noticed at last that congressional delinquency in drafting the Idaho organic act had forced the territory to operate without criminal law until early in 1864, when the legislature corrected the oversight. Straightening out territorial finances posed more of a problem and took until 1869.

During the ensuing fourth session of the legislature, disagreements on the application of the Civil War test oath to the secessionist Idaho legislature, exacerbated by Gilson's theft of the treasury, led to a dangerous eruption at the close of the session. An influx of Confederate refugees from Missouri made Idaho an overwhelmingly southern Democratic territory after 1864. A mildmannered Radical Republican, Ballard called out troops from Fort Boise to protect himself from a hostile legislature excited over the question of whether it could or would be paid, and for the next two years a relentless campaign was waged for his removal from office. Protected by Oregon's United States senators, Ballard survived the onslaught. But Idaho's territorial administration suffered severely from the fight, and from that time on Idaho rarely had political harmony between the governor and territorial legislature. (This was a result of a defect in the territorial system in which the governor

was appointed nationally and the legislature elected locally.)

As late as the gold rush to Loon Creek in 1869, placermining excitement continued to support Idaho's economy. By 1870, though, the typical Idaho miner was Chinese, and the population (exclusive of Indians) had declined to 17,804. Lode mining, which had gotten off to an optimistic start in 1864, held great promise for the future. But lack of rail transportation, shortage of capital and of trained labor, and difficulties of operating in a wilderness, coupled with technological failures, retarded the development of this more stable kind of mining. Yet lode-mining attempts (even when they flopped) supported a number of service and farming communities that otherwise would have lacked markets. Stock raising expanded rapidly after 1870, no longer depending mainly upon local mining markets. With the Panic of 1873 and Indian wars against the Nez Percé in 1877 and the Bannock in 1878, Idaho did not really begin to emerge from the frontier until after 1880.

Factional disputes and local issues gradually replaced the hard feelings engendered by national issues associated with Radical Reconstruction after the Civil War. President Grant sent out several carpetbag appointees in 1869 who got into a lot of party trouble, and for the next two years he had to try six candidates for governor before he could get one to accept and stay in office. Then the Utah boundary survey awarded Idaho the Bear Lake Mormon settlements founded by Charles Coulson RICH. The Mormons decided in 1872 to vote unanimously Democratic, and a local anti-Mormon campaign kept most of that section under the control of the Independent Anti-Mormon party of Oneida County from 1874 through 1880. North Idaho renewed its demand for boundary revision, settling in 1873-74 upon annexation to Washington as an initial step. Southwestern Idaho was entertained by Governor Mason Brayman's crusade against the Boise ring, particularly from 1878 to 1880. Milton KELLY and the other politicians and civic leaders of the Boise ring really were not the corrupt gang of swindlers that the governor alleged, but they objected to Brayman's "garrulous vaporings of senile vanity." Brayman's successor proved to be a vigorous anti-Mormon from Salt Lake. From 1880 on, this religious issue was involved in continual factional battles that plagued Idaho through the rest of the territorial period.

In spite of hard times, Idaho's population grew to 32,610 by 1880. That was only the beginning of rapid expansion associated with railway construction and major new mining developments. Completion of the Utah and Northern Railway across southeastern Idaho to Montana in 1880 opened the way for Mormon expansion in the upper Snake River valley. Lines throughout the rest of the territory followed immediately, and mining rushes to Wood River in 1880 and to the Coeur d'Alene region early in 1884 brought large-scale leadsilver mining development. (Coeur d'Alene proved to be one of the major mining areas of the world. There, a single silver mine—not the largest one, at that— outproduced Nevada's entire Comstock lode.) Anti-Mormonism had great strength in the Wood River mines, and a Republican carpetbagger changed the political complexion of the territory in 1882 by running for Congress as an anti-Mormon. Continued anti-

Mormon success in 1884 led to legislation under which no Mormon was allowed to vote, to hold office, or to serve on a jury. Ostensibly related to Mormon practice of plural marriage, this discrimination against the Saints was directed primarily against Mormon participation in politics as a powerful Democratic voting bloc. Church economic cooperatives also were a target of the anti-Mormons.

Deprived of their solid Mormon vote, Idaho's Democrats relinquished political control to a Republican-anti-Mormon combine in 1886. This shift, which traced back to the anti-Mormon tidal wave in the congressional election in 1882, came in time to enable Idaho to secure admission as a Republican state four years later. During that same time, Alonzo Leland's Lewiston project to place the northern counties back in Washington fell into discard. North Idaho solidly favored the transfer until 1886, when Coeur d'Alene mining interests objected to Washington and disrupted northern unanimity on the issue. Congress adopted legislation to accomplish the change in 1886-87, but President Grover Cleveland, responding to a timely plea from Governor Edward Augustus STEVENSON, declined to approve the measure. Then, when the Republicans elected Benjamin Harrison as president and regained control of Congress by a very narrow margin in 1888, Idaho suddenly came under strong national Republican pressure to become a state. The Republicans foresaw the need for more representatives in order to gain a working majority in the new House of Representatives. Thus six Republican northwestern states were scheduled for early admission in order to provide the necessary congressmen.

Leaders of both Idaho parties entered into a bipartisan drive for statehood. Former Democratic congressional delegate John HAILEY joined his Republican successor, Fred T. DUBOIS, who had a number of influential allies (including a former Montana congressional delegate, William H. CLAGETT, who was to serve as president of the Idaho constitutional convention) to strengthen the movement. Democratic Governor E. A. Stevenson summoned a constitutional convention, and his Republican successor, George Laird SHOUP, went ahead to perfect the arrangements by which a strongly anti-Mormon document was adopted and ratified in 1889. William BUDGE, leader of the disfranchised Mormons, had no chance whatever to induce Congress to reject the offending constitution, and Idaho became a state, July 3, 1890.

Responding to declining silver prices and to excitement over the silver coinage issue, Idaho rewarded Grover Cleveland (who was returned to the White House, where he fought silver coinage) in 1892 with only two popular votes (out of more than nineteen thousand) for having saved the territory from division between Washington and Nevada. Plagued with a bitter Coeur d'Alene mine labor war that grew out of the silver price collapse in 1892, Idaho supported a Populist candidate for president. A decade of industrial strife ensued. The 1892 clash led directly to organization of the WESTERN FEDERATION OF MINERS, and in 1899 the struggle over wages, mine conditions, and union recognition erupted again with the dynamiting of the Bunker Hill and Sullivan concentrator at Wardner. Governor Frank STEUNENBERG proclaimed martial law in 1899 and finally was assassinated in 1905 by Harry Orchard, a disaf-

fected Coeur d'Alene miner. In 1906 Governor Frank R. GOODING gained reelection upon a pledge to prosecute William D. HAYWOOD of the Western Federation of Miners for conspiracy in the Steunenberg murder. Haywood's trial gained international attention, pitting capital against labor over the nation. Lack of evidence essential for conviction defeated the efforts of James H. HAWLEY and William E. BORAH, who served as attorneys for the state, and the jury found Haywood not guilty. Borah emerged from his legal duel with Clarence Darrow with a national reputation and won election six times (the last over popular Democratic Governor Charles Benjamin ROSS in 1936) to the United States Senate.

Development of major reclamation projects, mostly after 1900, and the simultaneous rise of a commercial lumber industry left Idaho less dependent upon mining after 1890. Besides forest products, the state today produces wheat, corn, barley, apples, and the famous Idaho potato. Antagonism against the Mormons diminished, and better transportation facilities reduced the geographic separation that had plagued Idaho Territory. Unlike Oregon and Washington, Idaho's regions were not diverse economically, and as improved communications gradually overcame the central Idaho mountain barrier, sectionalism diminished. North Idaho still has Spokane for a commercial and cultural center, and southeastern Idaho still looks to Salt Lake. But Idaho continues to demonstrate that a state can survive even the most awkward boundary arrangements and can profit from geographic diversity that resulted from unfortunate territorial decisions that Congress made more than a century ago.

Because of its great potential for hydroelectric power —due to the extensive Snake River drainage system— Idaho is becoming increasingly industrialized while enjoying a large influx of tourists attracted by Idaho's spectacular mountain scenery and unspoiled rivers. Some of the great wilderness areas left in the United States may be found in the mountain ranges of the Cabinet, Coeur d'Alene, Bitterroot, and Clearwater as well as in the Sawtooth, Salmon River, and Lost River mountains. The deep canyons of Snake River, the volcanic formations of the Craters of the Moon National Monument, the famous SUN VALLEY resort built by the Harrimans, and Bear Lake also attract sportsmen and campers in large numbers.

Several pioneers have left accounts of the early years of Idaho: Thomas Donaldson, *Idaho of Yesterday* (1941); W. A. Goulder, *Reminiscences: Incidents in the Life of a Pioneer of Oregon and Idaho* (1909); John Hailey, *History of Idaho* (1910); and W. J. McConnell, *Early History of Idaho* (1913). H. H. Bancroft, *History of the Pacific States of North America*, vol. XXVI: *Washington, Idaho and Montana* (1890), provides an early general survey. Special studies include Leonard Arrington, *Beet Sugar in the West: A History of the Utah-Idaho Sugar Company* (1966); Merrill David Beal, *Intermountain Railroads* (1962); D. E. Livingston Little, *An Economic History of North Idaho* (1965); Boyd Martin, *The Direct Primary in Idaho* (1947); D. W. Meinig, *The Great Columbia Plain* (1968); and W. J. Trimble, *The Mining Advance into the Inland Empire* (1914).—M. W.

Iliff, John Wesley (1831-1878). Colorado cattleman. Iliff, named after the well-known Methodist minister, was born in McLuney, Ohio, and attended Ohio Wesleyan University. Convinced that opportunity and adventure lay in the West, he declined his father's offer of $7,500, so the story goes, to purchase an Ohio farm, saying, "No! Give me the $500 and let me go West." From Ohio he journeyed first to Kansas, where he helped organize the Ohio City Town Company and was active in merchandising and farming. In 1859 he traveled farther west to the Cherry Creek settlements in Colorado, where he engaged in business for a short time. He sold out in 1861 and invested in a small herd of cattle, beginning a successful career as a cattleman. Often called the "cattle king of the Plains," at his death he dominated a range of 150 miles along the South Platte River through the judicious purchase of water sites that allowed him to control many times more land than he actually owned. At one time he reportedly had more than 50,0⟨0⟩ head of cattle grazing the Plains, and it was said that he could travel from Colorado towns Greeley to Julesburg and always stay at one of his own ranches. "He was the squarest man that ever rode over these Plains," said Wyoming cattleman Alexander Swan after Iliff's death, echoing the respect and esteem he enjoyed among his peers. The Methodist Iliff School of Theology, on the campus of the University of Denver, memorializes his contributions to Colorado and the nation.

See Edward W. Milligan, "John Wesley Iliff," Denver Westerners *Brand Book*, vol. 6 (1950); and Agnes Wright Spring, " 'A Genius for Handling Cattle': John Wesley Iliff," *When Grass Was King* (1956).—M. B.

Illinois, settlement of. Long before Illinois was "land of Lincoln" it was the land of prairies. Stretching unbroken to the horizon over half the state, they inspired De Liette, nephew of La Salle's good friend and partner, Henri de Tonti, to comment that the country was "undeniably the most beautiful that is known anywhere between the mouth of the St. Lawrence river and that of the Mississippi." The prairie could be flat or rolling, dry or wet, bottomland or hilltop. The marvel of it was its prairie vegetation—not forest, not grass, but a whole luxuriant vegetation of grasses, herbs, flowers, reeds, and roots from early spring until fire or frost. The prairie brought German noblemen and European tourists to the new state after 1818 and gained the admiration of the English radical William Cobbett, although he scoffed at the idea that prairies would make suitable homes for Englishmen. ". . . the first view of an Illinois Prairie is Sublime," wrote Morris Sleight, a New York sea captain, in 1834. "I may almost say awfully grand, as a person needs a compass to keep his course—but the more I travel over them the better I like them."

The prairie was unique to northern and central Illinois. Only a thin arm of it reached into northern Indiana and touched the tip of northwest Ohio. Only a few tendrils of it curved narrowly across the Mississippi into Iowa and Missouri. The sweeping Illinois prairie seemed eternal in its solitary beauty. But its days were numbered when, in the eighteenth century, it became a region in which two imperial powers collided. Conflict over the land was inevitable from the day when Jamestown was established in 1607 and Quebec in 1608. While the first Stuarts were granting Englishmen sea-to-sea charters and Virginians were already considering the land beyond the Alleghenies theirs, Champlain was dreaming of a French empire in the heart of the continent that would extend from the Arctic to the Gulf of Mexico. Thirty or so years later Frontenac, governor of New France, foresaw that coming conflict and set about building an arch of empire, at once a support and a defense, with settlements from the mouth of the St. Lawrence upriver, around the Great Lakes, and south following the river that Jolliet and Marquette had explored at his behest. La Salle, newly come to Canada, fell in with the governor's view. With a royal grant in Illinois in hand, he set out in 1679 to build a political empire for France and a business empire for himself as a feudal lord.

In the seventeenth century, the Illinois country was the land of the Illinois Indians. A nation numbering close to 10,500 persons, it was the largest Indian nation north of the Ohio and east of the Mississippi. Handsome—the men were better looking than Frenchmen, Frenchmen acknowledged—and already acquainted with the Christian faith through the Jesuit mission on Lake Superior, the Illinois were easily won as allies and kept as friends until New France was lost and they themselves were reduced to a few hundred persons.

As for the land itself, the French described it as an earthly paradise, a land of treasures. More importantly, as exploration soon showed, it cut athwart the principal routes by which the English might try to penetrate west beyond the mountains to make good their claims under their colonial charters.

The dream of western empire survived La Salle's bankruptcy and murder. From 1681-82, when he built Fort St. Louis as his headquarters on the Illinois River near the great Indian village at Starved Rock, past the time of the French and Indian War and the British conquest, to the days of the American Revolution, Illinois was the keystone in the arch of empire. The alliance of its Indians was of strategic importance, and its settlements were so located that control of them meant ultimately control of the Ohio valley.

Illinois, with about the same boundaries in the eighteenth century as now, was, for several administrative purposes, considered to be part of the province of Quebec; for other purposes, part of the province of Louisiana. Confusion as to the source of authority, compounded by the fact that Illinois was at least three arduous months distant upstream from the capital of Louisiana, New Orleans, and a like dangerous distance overland from Quebec, mocked the strictly regulated empire Louis and his ministers described in official documents. The *habitants* were as free in fact as any English colonial. They did as they pleased, to the extent of refusing the use of their horses when the commandant of Fort de Chartres needed them to hunt deserters, and digging under the jail of the fort to release the town's leading men when the commandant arrested them. When the parishioners of Ste. Anne of Fort de Chartres refused to pay their Easter tithe, the priest refused for months to display the Host on the altar. He seems to have had no more success asserting his authority than did the commandant.

There were six villages built on the rich alluvial bottomland bordering the east side of the Mississippi for some seventy to eighty miles south from the mouth of the Missouri. Their total population was never more than a few thousand, yet from about 1720 to 1752 they were the *entrepôt* of the French fur trade in the West. Kaskaskia (1703), Ste. Geneviève (c. 1735)—on the west bank of the Mississippi opposite Kaskaskia but regarded as part of Illinois— Fort de Chartres (1721), St. Philippe (c. 1722), and Prairie du Rocher (c. 1735) were alike in all save location. Cahokia, founded in 1698 by the priests of the foreign missions, was during the French period a mission to the Tamaroa and Cahokia Indians. Less than half a dozen French families lived there.

The settlements bore little resemblance to contemporary American villages. Indeed, the largest, Kaskaskia, was remembered into territorial and early state days as having been the "Versailles of the West." While no village was a Versailles, the Illinois settlements were like no others, even in New France. Houses were built of logs set upright in the ground or upon wood or stone foundations; many were built of blocks of native limestone. All were in an architectural style unique to the Illinois country. The style originated when the early French, coming down from Canada, added to their steep-hipped Norman roofs a second roof. This roof flared out below the line of dormers to cover a seven- or eight-foot *galerie*, which circled the house after the fashion of the French houses in the Caribbean islands. Most houses were a story and a half, but some were two or three. Close by the house were stable, barn, garden, and orchard, the whole palisaded, by Louisiana law, against enemies that never came. Thus each Illinois village counted as many "forts" as homes.

The French villages flourished in Illinois until it began to be apparent after 1752 that British conquest was inevitable, even though the king was building at Fort de Chartres the largest stone fort in the interior of North America. More and more Illinois French moved to New Orleans. The most wealthy fur traders, preferring to stay in the neighborhood, moved to Ste. Geneviève. In 1764, with Pierre LACLEDE, they built a new town near the mouth of the Missouri, dedicated it to St. Louis, and made it the trading center of the Missouri valley. When the British detachment of the Black Watch was finally able to outflank the hostile Indians and ascend the Mississippi to accept the surrender of Fort de Chartres in 1765, there was only a sad remnant of a few hundred French farmers and even fewer Illinois Indians left from a remarkable past.

The following period of British administration was chaotic. British commanders without sufficient authority tried to govern. Commandant followed commandant as new garrisons came in to replace old. Lieutenant Colonel John Wilkins, reaching Illinois in 1771, established a civil court composed of his friends, who then tried to collect money from French merchants. This illegal and dishonest proceeding, in cahoots with the interests of American businessman Samuel Wharton, forced the unhappy French to protest to the British commander-in-chief, General Thomas Gage. To no avail they begged to be given their own colony, like their American compatriots on the seaboard. Nothing was done. Even the fur trade fared badly as St. Louis stole commerce to the western bank of the Mississippi. The Illinois French welcomed the American Revolution as a chance to get rid of British mismanagement.

But if the inept years of British rule had been despairing, the first American ones were worse. On December 9, 1778, hearing of George Rogers Clark's victory at Kaskaskia the preceding July, the state of Virginia established the county of Illinois "for the more effectual protection and defence thereof." The plantation legislators could neither protect nor defend the area, however, and finally gave the whole affair up as a bad job in 1782. Illinois then suffered total anarchy. A few local courts tried vainly to preserve order, and some French settlers moved west of the Mississippi. To make matters worse, the Spanish possessors of Louisiana encouraged Indian raids to attract settlers to the relatively peaceful Spanish side of the Mississippi. The outlook in Illinois was bleak until Governor Arthur St. Clair arrived on March 5, 1790, to pick up the reigns of law and order under the Northwest Ordinance.

One of St. Clair's first acts of office was to form a county for the populated southwestern portion of Illinois, from the Mississippi and Illinois rivers in the west to a line drawn between the mouth of Mackinaw River and Fort Massac on the east. The new county was named after one of the Northwest Territory's most eminent citizens (or so the governor must have thought)—St. Clair himself. The county's boundaries took in all the major settlements west of Vincennes (Indiana). Even though the French continued to leave and the population to decrease, Governor St. Clair created another county, Randolph County, out of the southern part of St. Clair County in 1775. These two counties, still existent today, were the first permanent institutions of government to be established in Illinois by its new American possessors.

In May 1800 the Northwest Territory was divided. Illinois became a part of Indiana Territory, governed by William Henry Harrison. The nine years in which Illinois was joined to Indiana were not happy ones for the steadily increasing Illinois population (See INDIANA, SETTLEMENT OF). The territorial capital, Vincennes on the Wabash River, was too far from Mississippi riverside settlements, such as Cahokia, Kaskaskia, or Prairie du Rocher. Nor was the trip to Vincennes easy. The route led "through a dreary and inhospitable wilderness . . . [in which] the traveler is not only subjected to the greatest difficulties but his life placed in the most imminent danger," as an 1805 petition to Congress from Illinois complained. In addition, the issue of slavery became increasingly controversial. Settlers in Illinois asked for a modification of the Northwest Ordinance to permit slavery, while increasingly abolition-minded Hoosiers of eastern Indiana counties wanted no such thing. A compromise satisfactory to both sides was reached when they united in the 1808 session of the Indiana territorial legislature to petition Congress for the erection of a separate territory for Illinois. Following this request, Congress created Illinois Territory on February 9, 1809.

At this time most of Illinois' population was in the south. There the grassland was interspersed with trees along the rivers and barren uplands. With few bushes and trees, the uplands seemed hospitable to settlers accustomed to clearing forests. While the new territory grew rapidly after the War of 1812, few men were willing to try farming the vast prairie of northern Illinois. Illinois was admitted to the Union as a state on December 3, 1818 (see OLD NORTHWEST), but its frontier days were far from over.

If land did not attract men to the upper country, LEAD

MINING did. Almost as unique as the prairies, these mines, which Illinois shared with neighboring Wisconsin, Iowa, and Missouri, produced the enormous amounts of lead needed in the days before the development of the steel industry. Galena, Illinois, the principal lead port on the Mississippi, lay within the four million acres ceded by the Potawatomi and associated tribes in the 1829 Treaty of Prairie du Chien. But before the Indian title had been extinguished, even two years before Illinois became a separate territory, Congress in 1807 reserved for the federal government all lead mines in Indiana Territory and approved a leasing system.

The rush to the lead mines began in the 1820s. In 1825 Lieutenant Martin Thomas, superintendent of the United States Lead Mines, initiated a strictly controlled leasing system. (A miner could not fell even one tree without permission and was required to sell all his lead to certain smelters who held federal leases.) Nevertheless, two to three thousand men crowded the roads and rivers up from southern Illinois each spring like suckers to their spawning grounds, returning home late in the fall. Some, though, came to stay.

Lead production brought prosperity to the mineral region in northern Illinois. Seven million pounds were freighted in 1827 from Galena to St. Louis. Twelve steamships made regular runs between the two cities, carrying lead downstream and food and provisions upstream. Two years later a depression set in in the lead market and recovery came only after 1833. By then, however, the number of persons engaged in lead mining was down from ninety percent to little more than thirty percent. The population of the prairie area kept mounting. Yankee farmers were beginning to make their homes in the region, coming by canal and lake and trail from Chicago. The settlement of the rolling open prairies was beginning.

The prairies were still frontier in 1830. Scarcely anywhere did the population exceed two persons per square mile, and often there was no population at all. When Illinois became a state in 1818, it had only about 35,000 persons all told, considerably under the figure required by law. In 1830 157,000 residents were counted, but they still lived largely along the banks of the Wabash in the vicinity of Shawneetown and in the American Bottoms, that extraordinarily fertile strip of land bordering the Mississippi River for seventy-odd miles from Kaskaskia to Cahokia, opposite St. Louis.

The census of 1840 reported a population of 475,000. Most of the newcomers had settled in the prairie counties, but usually on the fringe of the prairies, close by timber and a stream. Two thirds of the Military Tract between the Illinois River and the Mississippi, originally designed as bounty-lands to encourage men to enlist in the army during the War of 1812, was prairie. As soon as the surveying of it was completed in 1822, settlers, many of them squatters, from southern Illinois began moving into it, they followed the Illinois River, spreading out into central Illinois along its tributaries. The opening of the Quincy land office in 1831 speeded the process of land entries. Out-of-state settlers came along the old trails and river routes from Kentucky, Georgia, and the Carolinas into the prairie counties of east-central Illinois.

New Englanders and New Yorkers for the first time began to come in considerable numbers as traffic by way of the Erie Canal and the Great Lakes developed after 1825. Chicago in the 1830s became the terminus of roads leading to the prairies, to the Illinois River valley, and to the booming lead-mine region around Galena. In the East promoters successfully sold the idea that the difficulties of prairie farming could be overcome by the cooperative action of large groups, and in 1836 the Providence Company of Rhode Island bought seventeen thousand acres of prairie in Bureau County, in the Military Tract. A New York Presbyterian congregation purchased sixteen sections of land in Knox County, built the town of Galesburg (named for their minister), and established Knox College. Other New England colonists built the towns of Wethersfield, La Grange, and Geneseo.

By 1840 the population distribution in Illinois had shifted dramatically from south to north. Now it was the northern counties in which farm abutted farm. Chicago's bustling citizens were rapidly dominating the region's commerce. St. Clair County, across from St. Louis and venerable with its memories of the French and early territorial days, saw the number of its inhabitants reduced to less than two per square mile, while the four grand prairie counties (last to be settled) had more than eighteen persons per square mile. Illinois was entering a new period of internal improvement and national politics. For better or for worse, none of the isolated prairie frontier remained. Illinois was no longer the West.

The single best account of frontier Illinois is Theodore C. Pease, *The Frontier State, 1818-1848*, vol. II of Centennial History series (1922). For the British period and territorial days see Pease, *The Story of Illinois* (1965). Printed source material on the French period is scarce. A single study on the French villages of the Illinois country is Natalia M. Belting, *Kaskaskia Under the French Regime* (1948). For a general survey of the period, see C. W. Alvord, *The Illinois Country*, vol. I of Centennial History series (1920).—N. M. B.

immigration. Until recently, the standard image of the West has been that it was and is Anglo-American with only a few isolated exceptions. Historians have focused attention upon the immigrant's trip across the ocean or his settlement along the eastern seaboard rather than in the interior. Yet there is evidence that many ranches, mining towns, and lumber camps throughout the West teemed with Chinese, French, German, and Mexican immigrants. In 1870 nearly three out of ten westerners were foreign-born. In that year sixty percent of Arizona's population was born abroad, while more than half of the men aged twenty-one and over in Utah, Nevada, Arizona, Idaho, and California were foreign-born. In 1870 also, California's Irish constituted one in four of that state's residents.

After 1880, however, neither the West nor the South was a favorite destination for new immigrants; both areas together attracted only half as many foreigners as did New York City alone. In the Far West the number of immigrants eventually reached only 5.6 percent of the total white population, although in San Francisco, Denver, and Kansas City the percentages were much higher.

To move westward was a chancy endeavor. But restless immigrants, of the sort that could never be content in a crowded urban invironment, took the gamble. To

A trainload of European immigrants bound for the Far West poses with the train's crew in Mill City, Nevada, in 1886. (Southern Pacific)

pass beyond the squalor of the eastern cities toward the grandeur of the West's prairies and mountains was finally to separate oneself from memories of Europe. To a degree, such thinking may have been escapism. Critics of immigration in the homeland thought abandoning one's native soil was an illusionistic opiate. But the call of virgin lands acted like a magnet. Furthermore, many of the immigrants had farm backgrounds. From 1860 to 1900, when immigrants swelled the growth of America's cities by almost 36 million persons, agricultural workers helped increase the farm population by about 9 million. In 1901 an observer noted the character of this immigration: "Our immigrants as a whole are a peasant population, used to the open, with the simple habits of life. . . . Practically all the immigration from Austria-Hungary . . . is from the country, as is also the immigration from Italy."

The move beyond the confining steel and concrete skyline of the eastern city was complicated, requiring money, which the newly arrived immigrant did not have, and involving great distances of travel in a totally unfamiliar land. Out West they became acculturated usually more easily than did the immigrant in an eastern city or in Chicago or Kansas City. As viticulturists, cotton raisers, hostelers, miners, or restaurateurs, to name only a few occupations, immigrants were accepted quite readily as members of the society in which they lived. Because foreigners have been assimilated so rapidly west of the Mississippi River, loss of national identification has been the rule rather than the exception. Indeed, acculturation proceeded so rapidly that the story of western immigrants can be constructed only with difficulty.

In San Francisco during 1880, out of a population of 233,959 persons, 104,244 had been born abroad. By 1900, with a foreign-born population of close to forty

percent, San Francisco (along with New York, Chicago, Los Angeles, and Denver) was a major cosmopolitan center. It was peopled by more Italians than by any other foreign group, and it bore the name of their fellow countryman Francis of Assisi. Not only was there a large European resident population, but sizable Chinese and Japanese representation. The city's "Chinatown," "Japantown," and "Little Italy" on North Beach retain this individuality. After the end of the California gold rush, thousands of Oriental males poured into the state to work on the railroads. Their strange ways and a willingness to labor for low wages led "Anglos" to discriminate against them. Eventually, however, fine Cantonese cooking helped to make San Francisco's Grant Street ghetto a mecca for tourists in the same way that the city's Columbus Avenue attracted lovers of Italian food.

Outside the cities as well, the immigrant pattern was readily discernible. In the Plains states lived a sprinkling of Scandinavians, Germans, and other nationalities among the ranches and towns. One can hardly think of Wisconsin without its Danish dairymen, St. Louis devoid of its German brewers, or Minnesota's mining camps bereft of Norwegians and Swedes. Willa Cather has described charmingly Nebraska's "French farm country" in her *O Pioneers!* (1913), and Mari Sandoz wrote a graphic account of her crusty immigrant father and of his life in Nebraska in *Old Jules* (1935). In the midst of Montana a sizable number of Italian priests were settled as missionaries among the Bitteroot Indians and other tribes in the 1840s by the Belgian Jesuit Pierre de Smet.

Both the Italians and the French, however, flourished best in a more Mediterranean environment, such as the wine-growing regions of California's Napa and Sonoma valleys. Armenian fig and date growers were attracted to the state's warmer Imperial and great Central valleys.

Millions of Mexican-Americans settled in that state and throughout the southwestern states of New Mexico, Arizona, and Texas. Los Angeles still has the largest Mexican population outside Mexico City. In Utah the Mormon religious experiment attracted persons of all nationalities, with heavy recruiting of northern Europeans by missionaries sent abroad in search of immigrants. Nevada, long passed over by Anglo pioneers, had the largest percentage of foreign-born for two decades after the Civil War and before the mass immigration of the late nineteenth century. From the 1880s onward the westward push of the transcontinental railroads encouraged migration into the rich farm valleys of the Pacific Northwest. The Oregon and Washington coast attracted numerous Norwegian and Swedish seamen as well as Portuguese and Sicilian fishermen, while the lumber industry utilized immigrants of every nationality in its camps. Frequently railroad construction workers would settle in a lumber or mining camp at track's end. The foreign-born residents of cities like Omaha, Denver, Reno, and Sacramento reached their destinations under the aegis of the railroads, where they (like the Mormons) promoted foreign immigration.

Without adhering to Frederick Jackson Turner's concept that the western environment was the major determinant in shaping pioneer life, one must conclude that immigrants fared better in the West than elsewhere. With certain notable exceptions (the Chinese in gold-rush California, the Japanese there during World War II, as well as the Chicanos in the Southwest), the immigrant record was successful. Although they also encountered prejudice and discrimination, Caucasian immigrants often re-found themselves in a tradition-free setting. In short, the immigrant on the western land was as upraised as he was uprooted.

See CHICANO LIBERATION MOVEMENT; CHINESE IMMIGRATION; GERMAN RUSSIAN IMMIGRATION; IOWA; IRISH IMMIGRATION; ITALIAN IMMIGRATION; JAPANESE IMMIGRATION; JEWISH IMMIGRATION; MEXICAN-AMERICANS; MINNESOTA; and ROMAN CATHOLIC CHURCH.

See Gunther Barth, *Bitter Strength: A History of the Chinese in the United States, 1850-1870* (1964); Kenneth O. Bjork, *West of the Great Divide: Norwegian Migration to the Pacific Coast, 1847-1893* (1958); Roger Daniels, *The Politics of Prejudice: The Anti-Japanese Movement in California* (1962); William Mulder, *Homeward to Zion: The Mormon Migration from Scandinavia* (1957); Moses Rischin, "Beyond the Great Divide: Immigration and the Last Frontier," *Journal of American History* (June 1968); Andrew Rolle, *The Immigrant Upraised: Italian Adventurers and Colonists in an Expanding America* (1968); and Wilbur S. Shepperson, *Restless Strangers: Nevada's Immigrants and Their Interpreters* (1970).—A. R.

Imperial Valley and the Salton Sea (California). Imperial Valley is one of the largest, most prosperous reclaimed agricultural areas in the United States. Once known as the Colorado Desert or the Salton Sink, it formed a natural depository for overflow from the Colorado, which normally flows into the Gulf of California. The possibilities for irrigating this area for agricultural use were first proposed in the 1850s, but it was not until 1896 that the privately financed California Development Company, a consortium of eastern capital, began to lay definite plans for reclamation. Beginning in 1900, water was diverted from the Colorado by means of a

canal system running north through Mexico to Salton Sink, rechristened, in good real estate fashion, the Imperial Valley. By 1905 the formerly uninhabited desert boasted more than 120,000 acres under cultivation and a settled agricultural population of 12,000. The hothouse characteristics of the irrigated desert contributed to an unusually high agricultural yield.

Extremely high flood waters on the Colorado in 1905-07 threatened to destroy this progress by inundating the valley. Before engineers had successfully dammed the river, allowing only enough water for agricultural purposes, a massive inland sea had been formed at the valley's basin. The Salton Sea, which is now fed only by the run-off of the valley's irrigation system, has become a highly popular recreational district in the agricultural desert.

See John S. Brown, *The Salton Sea Region, California*, in United States Geological Survey, *Water-Supply Paper 497* (1923); and George Kennan, *The Salton Sea* (1917).— J. F.

Independence, Missouri. Independence was established in 1827 near a site that had been used for some time as a rendezvous point for traders going west from the Missouri border. With the Santa Fe trade well under way, Independence soon became a bustling center and outfitting place, replacing Franklin (some hundred miles farther down river in central Missouri) as the jumping-off place to the West. An early settler, John C. McCoy, remembers that "it was well worth while to witness the arrival of some of the pack-trains. Before entering they gave notice of their arrival by the shooting of guns, so that when they reached Owen's and Aull's store a goodly number of people were there to welcome them. A greasy, dirty set of men they were."

Independence continued to hold its dominant position until the 1840s when it gradually yielded to Westport, a few miles farther up the river. This decline set in after the great push to Oregon had taken place, during which time Independence remained the key starting point for settlers going out on the trail.

In July 1831 Joseph Smith arrived to announce that he had chosen Independence as the "New Zion" for his recently established Church of Jesus Christ of Latter-day Saints. Within a year some three hundred Mormons had settled in the vicinity. They established the area's first newspaper, *The Evening and Morning Star*; but their doctrines, as proclaimed therein and elsewhere, soon led to difficulties with their neighbors. In the winter of 1833-34 mob action drove them from Jackson County to the areas north of the Missouri River and there began a series of difficulties which would take them ultimately to Salt Lake City by way of Nauvoo, Illinois. One branch of Smith's followers, the Reorganized Church of Jesus Christ of Latter-day Saints, would find its way back to Independence in the late nineteenth century, eventually establishing its headquarters there in 1922.

Later in the twentieth century, Independence regained a measure of fame as the home of President Harry S. Truman and the site of the Truman Museum and Library.

Good descriptions of Independence's several roles may be found in David D. March, *The History of Missouri*, 4 vols. (1967).—W. E. P.

Indiana, settlement of. The Hoosier State, Indiana, is best known today for its corn, hogs, and automobile races. The southern part is extensively urban while farms abound on the northern prairies. Yet the state's name is a reminder that the region was once a wilderness whose only inhabitants were Indians.

When the pioneers first crossed the Indiana countryside, its principal inhabitants were the Delaware, Miami, Piankashaw, Potawatomi, and Shawnee tribes. The area was inhabited by Indians from the early Paleo-Indian cultural period, and it still had a relatively small number of hunters and a few semipermanent settlements when Europeans arrived there.

The first explorers to greet the Indian tribes were the fur trappers and priests from Canada. René Robert Cavelier, Sieur de La Salle, originally crossed the northwest corner of the state in 1679 while trying to find a portage connecting Lake Michigan with the Mississippi River. His successors gathered furs in the area for shipment from Quebec to Europe. Eventually posts were established on Indiana soil to facilitate operations. The first of these was Ouiatanon, near present-day Lafayette, settled in 1717. The most important post was Vincennes on the Wabash River. Established in 1731, it grew to be a prosperous town whose inhabitants had a happy and peaceful life for some fifty years. Their period of stable tranquility ended when the French government went to war with the British.

Within a short space of time, from 1763 to 1783, the region changed hands twice. The English won it from the French in the French and Indian War. Then the Americans won it from the English in the American Revolution. The battles that effected these territorial transfers were generally remote from Indiana, but the days of wilderness and a fur-trapping economy were numbered when the land came into possession of the expansion-minded American government.

During the years between the Treaty of Paris of 1783 and the Division Act of 1800, which established Indiana Territory, the region was an undifferentiated part of the Northwest Territory. During this time the first American settlements pressured the Indians. The Indians were led to retaliate with prodding from the British. The skirmishes culminated in the battle of FALLEN TIMBERS (1794), which pitted General Anthony Wayne against Little Turtle, a Miami war chief. Decisive defeat of the Indians opened most of Ohio and an eastern strip of Indiana to peaceful settlement by the Americans. Fallen Timbers had another direct effect upon Indiana. Among General Wayne's officers was a lieutenant whose distinguished fighting earned him a special commendation. This same man was promoted to secretary of the Northwest Territory three years later. And when Indiana Territory was created in 1800, he was appointed its first governor. His name was William Henry HARRISON.

The original Indiana Territory (which included all of present Indiana, Illinois, and Wisconsin and parts of Michigan and Minnesota) was established July 22, 1800. Harrison arrived at its capital, Vincennes, on January 10, 1801. In the beginning his most important function was as a land agent. Harrison worked diligently to widen the boundaries of Indiana land open to white settlement. He began by resolving grants in the Vincennes area and continued by making treaties with Indian tribes elsewhere (not being too scrupulous in his dealings with the Indians). By 1806 he had federal title over all of southern Indiana and by 1809 the Indians had ceded approximately three million acres to the government. While acting for the nation Harrison engaged in private land speculation, giving rise to complaints that all the best land went to him and his friends. His vigorous policy also alarmed the Indians. TECUMSEH, the great Shawnee leader, recognized the dangers of American migration and tried to organize the Indians of the region into a force that could counter the settlers. To prevent such a union, which could have decimated the territory's white population, Harrison broke a truce with Tecumseh and while Tecumseh was away attacked the Indians at Prophetstown. The resulting battle of TIPPECANOE on November 7, 1811, was indecisive, but it broke the Indian confederation and forced Tecumseh to flee to the British. By the time the leader died in 1813, the Indians in Indiana were a fully subjugated people.

Another problem in territorial Indiana was that of slavery. Many of the early immigrants came from the South. The slaveholders among them, mostly centered in what was later to be Illinois, tried to make slavery legal. Those opposed to slavery in the territory pointed to an antislavery clause in the Northwest Ordinance. The slavery forces convinced Harrison to adopt a part of the Virginia Code that required all slaves in the territory to remain as slaves. When the territory was elevated to a second-grade government in 1805, the proslavery party enacted various slave laws and asked Congress to repeal the antislavery clause of the Northwest Ordinance. As opposition to slavery in Indiana Territory mounted, the slavery forces of Illinois agitated for a separate government. For this and other reasons, Illinois Territory was established in 1809. Indiana was now left with a predominantly antislavery population. In November 1810 its legislature repealed any previous laws allowing slaves to be brought into the territory. Slavery as an issue was finally settled in 1816 when the Indiana constitution adopted an antislavery clause.

The final problem for Indiana Territory was that of self-government. In the early years of Indiana's existence, Harrison ruled the territory almost by himself, but opposition to Harrison grew until Indiana received its territorial legislature in 1805. In the same year Michigan Territory was formed out of Indiana. From that time, the political forces in the state were split into pro-Harrison and anti-Harrison camps, the opposition rallying around Jonathan Jennings. Jennings was a populist and against slavery; Harrison, aristocratic and for slavery. The two sides started off reasonably well-balanced, with the proslavery side in a slightly superior position. But by 1809, when the Harrison forces were reduced by the creation of Illinois Territory, the political complexion of the land had begun to change. Jesse B. Thomas, a well-known foe of the governor, was voted as the territory's first congressional delegate. In 1811 Jennings was elected to the same office after a bitterly fought contest with Thomas Randolph of the Harrison party. Jennings won by only 26 votes out of 911 cast. Small as his margin was, it was increasingly clear that Indiana was dissatisfied with Harrison. Had he not quit as governor to fight in the War of 1812, he might have been forced out of office.

After the War of 1812, Indiana moved rapidly toward statehood. Its population in 1800 was estimated at 5,600. In the spring of 1812 Congress agreed to admit

Indiana as a state when the population reached 35,000. Due to the war the census was not completed until 1815, but when finished, it indicated a population of more than 60,000. Most of the new citizens had migrated within the years 1810-15. On April 19, 1816, Congress passed an enabling act, and on June 10 of that year a constitutional convention convened at Corydon (the capital since 1813) to establish a state government. The constitution the delegates wrote was taken almost entirely from the Kentucky and Ohio constitutions. Its one innovation was Article IX, which stated the government's responsibility for education (a principle honored in the breach for some years). On November 7 Jennings became the state's first elected governor.

Just as speedy as the statehood movement was Indiana's growth. In 1820 a new census listed the population at 147,000. The immigrants came predominantly from the South, although there were substantial numbers from the East. By 1850 the population was approaching one million. Figures from that time indicate that Indiana was settled chiefly from Virginia, North Carolina, Kentucky, Pennsylvania, and Ohio. Most of the early settlements were in the southern and eastern portions of the state. However, as the Indians ceased to be formidable the settlers moved north onto the flat Indiana prairies. By 1840 the entire state was settled and the last Indians forced out. The geographic shift of the population had caused the capital to be moved to a central location, Indianapolis, in 1825.

Economic development moved apace with the population. As more and more farms were brought under cultivation, so roads and canals tied Indiana into the bustling national economy. Plans for internal improvements reached their climax in 1836, when Indiana passed the "Mammoth Bill." The $10 million it allocated for internal improvements was much too large to handle and the state promptly went bankrupt in 1839. But otherwise Indiana had a typical development. In its early years its principal commodity was pork. Hogs were raised chiefly in the southern portions of the state and exported to the South via rivers. As the northern prairies came under cultivation, wheat began to be exported to the East. Transportation was facilitated when the National Road was completed in 1832 and when the Jeffersonville Turnpike and Michigan Road connected the state along its north-south axis. By the time railroads reached Indiana in the 1840s, it had passed from the wild forests of the frontier to the well-laid fields of a developed agricultural community. But just as states to the east of it had done before, Indiana contributed portions of its own population to the ever-continuing westward movement.

A good history is William E. Wilson, *Indiana: A History* (1966). Other good histories are Logan Esarey, *History of Indiana* (1915); and Jon B. Martin, *Indiana: An Interpretation* (1947).—R. S.

Indian Affairs, Bureau of. The Bureau of Indian Affairs is the official agency for the United States government's dealing with American Indians. Most federal bureaus, such as the Office of Economic Opportunity, which deals with poverty, or the Soil Conservation Service, which deals with erosion, concentrate on a limited area of governmental activity or service. The Bureau of Indian Affairs is unique in that it deals with all aspects of Indian life except medical services—and this exception

dates only from 1955, when the United States Public Health Service took over that responsibility from the bureau. Among the activities that fall into the bureau's purview are education, employment assistance, police forces, welfare, agricultural assistance, credit, forestry management, industrial development, real property management, road construction and maintenance, and real estate appraisal. To handle these responsibilities, the bureau runs ten administrative area offices, sixty Indian agencies and major installations like boarding schools and irrigation projects, and over four hundred minor posts such as urban relocation centers. In the extent of its jurisdiction and control over the people with which it is concerned, the Bureau of Indian Affairs is much closer kin to the colonial offices of imperial Britain than to any other organization within the governmental structure of the United States. As a consequence of the bureau's omnipresence in Indian matters, it has throughout its history been a focus for dispute and criticism from Indians and white alike.

The origin of the bureau can be traced to 1789, when Congress created the Department of War. Among its duties was specified "all those relating to Indian Affairs." It was not until 1824, however, that the War Department created a particular bureau for Indian affairs. The first chief of the bureau was Thomas L. McKenney, who from 1816 to 1822 had been superintendent of Indian trade. McKenney's primary role was to administer finances and examine claims arising out of "laws regulating intercourse with the Indian tribes." In 1832 Congress created the office of commissioner of Indian affairs, appointed by the president and confirmed by the Senate, and directly responsible to the secretary of war. The commissioner was charged with the "direction and management of all Indian affairs and all matters arising out of Indian relations." Two years later an additional act defined the internal organization of the bureau, establishing a system of subagencies and regulating the employment of personnel and the disbursement of funds for supplies and annuities. With subsequent modifications this law of 1834 is the organic act for the bureau as it exists.

By the 1840s, with the passing of Indian military resistance east of the Mississippi and the removal of the surviving tribes to the West, the feeling developed that Indian affairs were misplaced under the jurisdiction of the War Department, and in 1849 the bureau was transferred intact to the newly created Department of the Interior. When war developed with the Indians of the trans-Mississippi region in the years 1850-90, a considerable public debate resulted over whether the bureau should be transferred back to the War Department. It was argued that the division of responsibility between the army, which was charged with subduing "hostiles" and moving them onto reservations, and the bureau, whose responsibility was their care, feeding, and containment once they got there, was both impractical and ineffective. Military leaders and westerners generally favored the return of the bureau to the War Department, while eastern humanitarians and congressmen who feared the loss of patronage opportunities, preferred the bureau to remain under civilian control. Although the military position often had a great deal of support, particularly whenever a new spate of hostilities would break out, Congress never voted on the issue

An issuing agent of the Bureau of Indian Affairs stands at the center of a circle of Indians waiting to draw rations at Camp Supply, Indian Territory, in 1871. (National Archives)

and the bureau remained in the Interior Department.

Throughout the nineteenth and early twentieth centuries, the Bureau of Indian Affairs was not seen as a policy-making, or even a policy-recommending, body in any sense of the term. Its activities merely reflected the policies of successive administrations. The post of Indian commissioner became an entirely political appointment from the start, and administrative continuity within the bureau was almost totally lacking. Between 1834 and 1907 there were twenty-two commissioners of Indian affairs, none of whom served more than eight years. A large percentage of commissioners were incompetent party hacks, receiving the office as a patronage reward. With patronage came corruption, and the bureau was notorious for encouraging chicanery and graft in the rewarding of contracts for reservation supplies. It has been estimated that of all the funds appropriated by Congress between 1834 and 1890 for the purpose of providing for Indian subsistence, education, and land payments, more than eighty-five percent was absorbed within the bureau by padded administrative costs, overpricing of supplies, and outright graft. There can be no doubt that the corruption within the bureau was a major cause of the failure of many well-intentioned and well-founded federal policies and laws, and that Indian hostility toward whites was thereby exacerbated to a great degree.

As a result the bureau was continually the target of reform lobbies and the political party opposed to whichever president was in office, and there were recurring efforts to "clean up the Indian mess." The most notable nineteenth-century effort was made by President Grant, who appointed Ely Parker, a full-blooded Seneca Indian, as commissioner of Indian affairs and instituted a PEACE POLICY of appointing Indian agents from the ranks of churchmen. His program was short-lived. Politicians resentful of the loss of patronage succeeded in discrediting Parker through trumped-up charges of malfeasance in office, and he resigned. The church-nominated field agents proved as susceptible to corruption as other men. And Grant's own brother became involved in a scandal involving kickbacks for Indian traders' contracts. Carl Schurz, secretary of the interior under Grant's successor, Rutherford Hayes, had some degree of success in tightening the bureau's administrative structure and eliminating the most blatant excesses in the Washington central office, but the general pattern of incompetence and corruption persisted into the twentieth century.

With the final subjugation of the Indians by 1890, and the passage of the Dawes Severalty Act (1887)—which intended the breakup of reservations and absorption of Indians into the American mainstream—the public and Congress came to see the bureau as an institution of diminishing importance. During the years 1900-30 appropriations for Indian affairs progressively decreased, and the bureau was primarily engaged in the mechanics of administering the implementation of the severalty act and its subsequent corollaries. During the 1920s, however, the deterioration of Indian life and the glaring inequities of the severalty program became increasingly apparent. A widespread movement of Indian rights organizations, led by social theorist and reformer John COLLIER, began calling for a new approach to Indian affairs. With Collier's appointment as commissioner of Indian affairs by Franklin Roosevelt, and the subsequent enactment of Collier's program for the regeneration of Indian society as embodied in the Indian Reorganization Act (1934), the Bureau of Indian Affairs was institutionally regenerated and for the first time became the source of innovative policy.

The efforts of Collier and his successor, William Zimmerman, during the 1930s and 1940s were to a large degree successful in restoring the reservations' land base and promoting the preservation of remaining Indian culture. But growing appropriations for the bureau upset many congressmen, and during the 1940s committees of both the Senate and the House accused the bureau of spending too much time and money on trying to "recapture ancient, worn-out cultures" instead of helping to "make the Indian a citizen." As part of a general economy drive and reaction against the governmental activism of the 1930s and 1940s, Congress passed a series of resolutions in 1950, 1952, and 1953 that accused the bureau of promulgating "welfarism" among Indians. It urged a speedy termination of all special relationships between Indians and the federal government. The Eisenhower administration fully supported these positions, and during the 1950s Indian commissioner Dillon Myer reversed the direction of the bureau's activities by cutting back on expenditures and helping to push through termination legislation for a number of tribes. Disastrous economic consequences were immediately apparent in those tribes, particularly the Klamath and Menomini, and the bureau's field reports began to urge a slowdown in the withdrawal of federal supervision. On the positive side, the "termination" policy triggered the "INDIAN POWER" movement.

Reappraisal of federal policy during the Democratic administrations of the 1960s by Indian commissioners Philleo Nash and Robert Bennett led to an emphasis on economic development on reservations, and increased Indian involvement in the administration of federal programs. Self-sufficiency and independence of government ties was to be a distant rather than immediate goal. By 1971 "termination" had become such a hated term among Indians that President Nixon formally disavowed it as a policy, while affirming the ultimate goal of economic independence for Indian tribes.

The early 1970s were a period of crisis and change for the Bureau of Indian Affairs. Caught in a squeeze between legislators who still saw it as wasteful and ineffective in solving the problems of reservation and urban Indians, and the increasingly militant attitude of Indians who always viewed it as the instrument of white oppression, the bureau endeavored to bring Indians into positions of authority within the administrative structure, eliminate waste and redundancy, and make its efforts toward economic development of Indian resources more in tune with Indian lifeways. The question remains, however, of how well both Indians and whites can overcome two centuries of antagonism to cooperate in a common cause.

For the history of the bureau and its organization up to the 1920s, see Lawrence F. Schmeckbeier, *The Office of Indian Affairs* (1927). For a history since the 1920s, see William Brophy and Sophie Aberle, eds., *The Indian: America's Unfinished Business* (1966); and Theodore Taylor, *The States and Their Indian Citizens* (1972). In addition, the bureau is the subject of continuous evaluation and commentary in the numerous na-

tive American newspapers and periodicals.—P. R. M.

Indian-captivity narratives. One of the greatest fears experienced by the westward-moving pioneer was that of being captured alive by Indians. Modern fans of the frontier are familiar with the terse order, usually delivered to women, to "save the last bullet for yourself." Notwithstanding such instructions, many frontier people, beginning in earliest colonial times, were taken by Indians and yet managed to survive to tell the tale. And tell it they did, creating one of the most extensive and fascinating subcategories of American literature.

The oldest Indian-captivity account is *La Relación* of Alvar Núñez CABEZA DE VACA, first published in 1542, which describes his shipwreck, his capture by Texas Indians in 1528, and his subsequent wanderings throughout the Southwest. More familiar is John Smith's famous tale of capture and then salvation by the fair Pocahontas in Virginia of 1607, a story that also has the dubious distinction of probably being the first fictitious captivity narrative. The development of captivity narratives as a large body of literature began among the Puritan pioneers of early New England. Theirs are essentially religious documents, wherein the narrator describes a sort of pilgrim's progress through capture, torture, removal to Canada, temptation by Jesuits, and finally redemption, which demonstrates God's inscrutable wisdom and divine mercy. Excellent examples are John Williams' *Redeemed Captive Returning to Zion* (1707) and Mary Rowlandson's *Sovereignty and Goodness of God* (1682), the latter going through fifteen editions by 1800.

It was not long, however, until purely religious concerns became incidental. As conflict intensified between the English colonists and the French and Indians, writers began emphasizing the cruelty of their captors and attempted to inspire hatred of the enemy. William Flemming's *Narrative of the Sufferings* (1750) contains blood-and-thunder advice for campaigning against the French and attributes Indian barbarities to the teachings of Roman Catholic priests. The narratives also became literary and stylized, often reworked by a genteel editor before publication. In Ann Eliza Bleeker's *History of Maria Kittle* (1797), the Indian who has just slaughtered most of the family says, "Maria, be not afraid; I have promised to protect you, you shall live and dance around the fire with us in Canada; but you have only one small incumberance, which if not destroyed, will much impede your progress thither." He then kills, presumably in good taste, her infant child. By the middle of the eighteenth century the captivity narrative was a mainstay of the printer's trade, and journalistic hacks began turning out scores of tales that were pure gory sensationalism. Their factual basis is slim, and many, such as *The Affecting History of the Dreadful Distresses of Frederic Manheim's Family* (1793), are nothing but collections of choice bits culled from several earlier narratives. They were the dime novels of their day.

Serious narratives continued to appear and were usually accompanied by affidavits and depositions attesting to their validity. Some of these, like Edwin James's *A Narrative of the Captivity and Adventures of John Tanner* (1830), are most useful to scholars and interested laymen (see John TANNER). Of course, the fictionalizers were soon fictionalizing affidavits, and in some cases it is difficult to determine today which accounts are factually based and which are not, although most imitations are easy to spot. For example, in Phillip M'Donald and Alexander M'Lead's *A Surprizing Account* (1794), the two heroes are captured in Ohio, then escape and reach the Pacific coast in two weeks. There they discover an island inhabited by people speaking purest Hebrew, and eventually return home via Russia after six years. Their absence is historically verifiable, but one wonders what their wives thought of their story.

The popularity of the captivity narratives was often used by Indian-haters like polemicist Hugh Henry Brackenridge, to whip up support for their proposals of Indian extermination. His editing of Knight and Slover's verifiable *Narrative of a Late Expedition* (1783) was intended to induce Americans to realize that the Indians were subhumans and that "extirpation of them would be useful to the world, and honorable to those who can effect it."

The popularity of the captivity narratives was basically an eighteenth-century phenomenon, and by 1815 they were rapidly losing their widespread public appeal. Before that time, white farmers had advanced directly into the Indian country, and most Indian battles had been fought by the settlers themselves. After the War of 1812 nearly all Indian wars occurred in advance of actual permanent settlement, and fighting was done mainly by the army. The threat of Indian capture was consequently more remote, and the captivity narrative lost its immediacy for the reading public. The West was more and more seen as a place of romantic adventure instead of horror, and scientific explorations and studies had also removed much of the ignorance upon which many narratives were based.

Captivity tales from the Far West continued to be published, but their circulation was much reduced. Pieces like Nelson Lee's *Three Years Among the Comanches* (1859) and Fanny Kelly's *Narrative of My Captivity Among the Sioux Indians* (1871) tended to be more factual and less sensationalistic. Still, some, like E. D. Eastman's *Seven and Nine Years Among the Comanche and Apache* (1874), happily ignored known facts, described Aztec architecture in Texas, and plagiarized other writers. His motives were revealed when he described a miracle drug he had discovered among the Indians that was "a tonic, a diuretic, a nervine, and gentle laxative."

With the passing of the Indian wars the captivity narrative disappeared from popular literature, except for the tales of Daniel Boone and Andy Burnett, which still thrill countless school children. Today the great quantity of narratives are preserved only in university libraries, where they are consulted on infrequent occasion by students of literature and the frontier. In recent years, however, the narrative of Indian captivity has reemerged in quite a different form. Several well-received novels and films such as *A Man Called Horse* and *Little Big Man* have sought to use Indian captivity as a device to show that the Indian way of life was meaningful in ways Americans have hitherto ignored and to demonstrate the inequities of America's treatment of its native peoples. The success and popularity of these efforts indicate that the captivity narrative is a form flexible enough to survive radical changes in its premises as well as in the social environment, and that it will retain a measure of usefulness as long as Americans remember their frontier.

Roy H. Pearce, "The Significance of the Captivity Narrative," *American Literature* (March 1947), is the best account of the evolution of the form. An alternative analysis is Phillips Carleton, "The Indian Captivity," *American Literature* (May 1943). R. W. G. Vail, *The Voice of the Old Frontier* (1940), covers captivity accounts from 1542 to 1800. Two recent anthologies of selected captivity narratives are Frederick Drimmer, ed., *Scalps and Tomahawks: Narratives of Indian Captivity* (1961); and H. H. Peckham, ed., *Captured by Indians: True Tales of Pioneer Survivors* (1954). See also C. C. Rister's *Border Captives: The Traffic in Prisoners by Southern Plains Indians, 1835-1875* (1940).—P. R. M.

Indian languages. In pre-Columbian times there were at least 200 distinct Indian languages in America north of Mexico and approximately 2,000 in the Western Hemisphere as a whole, accounting for about one third of the languages of the world. In the modern United States and Canada there still survive nearly 150 Indian languages, the number of speakers ranging from a mere handful for some California tongues to the 80,000 native-speaking Navaho of New Mexico and Arizona. While some Indian languages are similar to one another or have developed from a common origin, they do not form a single historically interrelated stock, as do, for example, the Indo-European languages.

As the variety and complexity of Indian languages have been increasingly studied during the past century, it has become apparent that the form and evolution of their languages can tell much about the culture and historical development of Indian tribes and ethnic groupings. Through analysis of how language expresses basic cultural assumptions and perceptions of reality, linguists have revealed much that was previously unknown or misunderstood about the Indians' conceptions of matters such as religion, land tenure, and political power—matters that had crucial impact in the long conflict between Indians and whites. In a particularly striking example, linguistic analysis of the Navaho has demonstrated a cosmology in which man is completely subordinate to the forces of the universe and must keep himself in an ordered relationship to those forces. This fundamental belief explains much about the disharmony and bitterness that resulted when the Navaho were forced into interaction with nineteenth-century Americans, in whose worldview man was the master of nature.

In other cases, comparative language study has been used to explain specific features of culture within a single tribe. The Crow Indians are the only Plains tribe with matrilineal descent, a pattern that makes no functional sense in an otherwise male-dominated society where prestige is measured by hunting and fishing prowess. Genetic language classification has explained this seeming anomaly, revealing that the Crow language is most closely related to Hidatsa, in the Siouan language family. In the historic period the Hidatsa lived in large villages on the Missouri River in the Dakotas, obtaining about half their food from agricultural products raised only by women on plots owned by those women. They practiced matrilineal descent. If, as archaeological evidence suggests, the Crow and Hidatsa both practiced agriculture at the time (five hundred to one thousand years ago) when they spoke a common language and shared a common culture, then the matrilineal descent of the Crow during the nineteenth century was a survival from an earlier time when women were more important in society.

By employing sophisticated techniques to determine how much a language has changed through time, linguists have also been able to demonstrate genetic connections between Indian groups previously thought separate, and to discover how far back in time offshoot groups and tribes split off from a parent stock. Such study is revealing much about the prehistoric migration patterns and cultural evolution of the Indian peoples. It has been shown, for example, that the Paiute of the Great Basin, who evolved one of the simplest New World cultures, spoke a language that can be genetically related to that spoken by the culturally complex Aztec, indicating that both groups trace their origins to a common ancestry.

The first comprehensive classification of the Indian languages north of Mexico was published in 1891 by John Wesley Powell. It was based on comparison of vocabularies. Powell recognized fifty-eight separate language stocks, or families, a figure later revised to fifty-three. Subsequent scholars, notably A. L. Kroeber, refined Powell's classification by studying language structure, and discovered new connections between groups. Edward Sapir then began applying techniques developed in the study of European languages, and in 1929 proposed a regrouping of Powell's language stocks into six major genetically related divisions, or phyla. At the same time Sapir advanced a theory about the interactive relationship between language and culture, which was then elaborated upon by B. L. Whorf. Since that time work on Indian languages has been primarily directed at refining Sapir's classifications and at further testing the Sapir-Whorf hypothesis. Their studies have revealed that languages change very slowly even when the speakers migrate great distances and experience vast cultural changes. Apparently, language is much more stable than culture; and concurrently, those abstract cultural concepts most closely dependent on language, such as religious perceptions, are the parts of culture most resistant to change.

In recent years the number of Indian linguistic studies has rapidly increased, and henceforth it will be impossible to understand the American Indian experience without incorporating linguistic knowledge.

The following table presents a genetic outline of Indian languages spoken north of Mexico, based on a revised Sapirian classification published in 1966 by C. F. and F. M. Voegelin. It is divided into three levels: phyla, family, and individual language. The phyla and family levels can be seen as hypothetical parent language stocks from which the languages contained under them all evolved. When there is only one language to represent a family, it is called a language isolate. Tribes or dialects connected by hyphens should be considered to be mutually intelligible. All the numbered languages are mutually *un*intelligible.

PHYLUM I
American Arctic-Paleosiberian

A. Eskimo-Aleut family
   1. Central-Greenlandic Eskimo
      (Transarctic Eskimo)
   2. Alaskan Eskimo
      (Kuskokwim Eskimo)

   3. Eastern Aleut
      (Unalaskan)
   4. Western Aleut
      (Atkan, Attuan)
B. Chukchi-Kamchatkan family
    (in Siberia)

PHYLUM II
Na-Dene

A. Athapascan family
   1. Dogrib-Bear Lake-Hare
   2. Chipewyan-Slave-Yellowknife
   3. Kutchin
   4. Tanana-Koyukon-Han-Tutchone
   5. Sekani-Beaver-Sarsi
   6. Carrier-Chilcotin
   7. Tahltan-Kaska
   8. Tanaina-Ingalik-Nabesna-
      Ahtena
   9. Eyak
   10. Chasta Costa-Galice-Tututni
   11. Hupa
   12. Kato-Wailaki
   13. Mattole
   14. Tolowa
   15. Navaho
   16. San Carlos Apache
   17. Chiricahua-Mescalero Apache
   18. Jicarilla
   19. Lipan
   20. Kiowa Apache
B. Tlingit language isolate
C. Haida language isolate

PHYLUM III
Macro-Algonquian

A. Algonquian family
   1. Cree-Montagnais-Naskapi
   2. Menomini
   3. Fox-Sauk-Kickapoo
   4. Shawnee
   5. Potawatomi
   6. Ojibwa-Ottawa-Algonquian-
      Salteaux
   7. Delaware
   8. Penobscot-Abnaki
   9. Malecite-Passamaquoddy
   10. Micmac
   11. Blackfoot-Piegan-Blood
   12. Cheyenne
   13. Arapaho-Atsina-
       Nawathinehena
B. Yurok language isolate
C. Wiyot language isolate
D. Muskogean family
   1. Choctaw-Chickasaw
   2. Alabama-Koasati
   3. Mikasuki-Hitchiti
   4. Muskogee (Creek)-Seminole
E. Natchez language isolate
F. Atakapa language isolate
G. Chitimacha language isolate
H. Tunica language isolate
I. Tonkawa language isolate

PHYLUM IV
Macro-Siouan

A. Siouan family
  1. Crow
  2. Hidatsa
  3. Winnebago
  4. Mandan
  5. Iowa-Oto
  6. Omaha-Osage-Ponca-
    Quapaw-Kansa
  7. Dakota, or Sioux (Santee-Yankton-
    Teton)
B. Catawba language isolate
C. Iroquoian family
  1. Seneca-Cayuga-Onondaga
  2. Mohawk
  3. Oneida
  4. Huron (Wyandot)
  5. Tuscarora
  6. Cherokee
D. Caddoan family
  1. Caddo
  2. Pawnee-Arikara
  3. Wichita
E. Yuchi language isolate

PHYLUM V
Hokan

A. Yuman family
  1. Upland Yuman (Walapai-
    Havasupai-Yavapai)
  2. Upriver Yuman (Mohave-
    Maricopa-Kavelchadom-
    Halchidom-Yuma)
  3. Delta River Yuman (Cocopa-
    Kohuana-Halyikwamai)
  4. Southern & Baja California
    Yuman (Diegueno-Kamia-
    Akwa'ala-Kiliwa-Nyakipa)
B. Seri language isolate
C. Pomo family
  1. Coast Pomo
  2. Northeast Pomo
  3. Western Clear Lake
  4. Southeast Clear Lake
D. Palaihnihan family
  1. Achumawi
  2. Atsugewi
E. Shastan family
F. Yanan family
G. Chimariko language isolate
H. Washo language isolate
I. Salinan family
J. Karok language isolate
K. Chumashan family

PHYLUM VI
Penutian

A. Yokuts family
  1. Yokuts, Foothill North
  2. Yokuts, Foothill South
  3. Yokuts, Valley
B. Maidu family
  1. Southern Maidu
  2. Northwest Maidu

  3. Mountain Maidu
  4. Valley Maidu
C. Wintun family
  1. Patwin
  2. Wintun
D. Miwok-Costanoan family
  1. Sierra Miwok
  2. Coast-Lake Miwok
  3. Costanoan
E. Klamath-Modoc language isolate
F. Sahaptin-Nez Percé family
  1. Nez Percé
  2. Sahaptin
G. Cayuse language isolate
H. Molale language isolate
I. Coos family
J. Yakonan family
  1. Alsea
  2. Siuslaw-Lower Umpqua
K. Takelma language isolate
L. Kalapuya family
  1. Santiam-Mackenzie
  2. Yonkalla
M. Chinookan family
  1. Upper Chinook
  2. Lower Chinook
N. Tsimshian language isolate
O. Zuñi language isolate

PHYLUM VII
Aztec-Tanoan

A. Kiowa-Tanoan family
  1. Tiwa (Taos-Picuris-
    Isleta-Sandia)
  2. Tewa (San Juan-Santa Clara-
    San Ildefonso-Tesuque-
    Nambe-Hano)
  3. Towa (Jemez)
  4. Kiowa
B. Uto-Aztecan family
  1. Mono
  2. Northern Paiute-Bannock-
    Snake
  3. Shoshoni-Gosiute-Wind River-
    Panamint-Comanche
  4. Southern Paiute-Ute-
    Chemehuevi-Kawaiisu
  5. Hopi
  6. Tubatulabal
  7. Luiseno
  8. Cahuilla
  9. Cupeno
  10. Serrano
  11. Pima-Papago
  12. Pima-Bajo
  13. Yaqui-Mayo

PHYLUM VIII
Families and Language Isolates with
Undetermined Phylum Affiliations

A. Keres language isolate
B. Yuki family
  1. Yuki
  2. Wappo
C. Beothuk language isolate

D. Kutenai language isolate
E. Karankawa language isolate
F. Chimakuan family
    1. Quileute
    2. Chimakum
G. Salish family
    1. Lillooet
    2. Shuswap
    3. Thompson
    4. Okanagon-Sanpoil-Coville-Lake
    5. Flathead-Pend d'Oreille-Kalispell-Spokane
    6. Coeur d'Alene
    7. Middle Columbia-Wenatchi
    8. Tillamook
    9. Twana
    10. Upper Chehalis-Cowlitz-Lower Chehalis-Quinault
    11. Snoqualmi-Duamish-Nisqualli
    12. Lummi-Songish-Clallam
    13. Halkomelem
    14. Squamish
    15. Comox-Sishiatl
    16. Bella Coola
H. Wakashan family
    1. Nootka
    2. Nitinat
    3. Makah
    4. Kwakiutl
    5. Bella Bella-Heiltsuk
    6. Kitamat-Haisla
I. Timucua language isolate
J. Tarascan language isolate

A notable feature of the linguistic situation shown above is the preponderance of languages on the Pacific slope of the continent. Of Powell's original listing of families, thirty-seven were in the Pacific drainage and twenty-two actually on the coast, while only seven bordered the Atlantic and ten the Gulf of Mexico. It is believed that wide distribution of a few major languages is a development of comparatively recent times, and that in the early stages of cultural evolution a great number of languages flourished, each confined to a small population and limited geographic area. If true, this would indicate that cultural evolution occurred with more speed and complexity east of the Rockies, where large language families with wide distribution were found; and that on the West Coast, particularly California, cultural development remained relatively static over a very long period of time. High cultural development need not require linguistic similarity, however, as the case of the multi-language Pueblo cultures shows.

In terms of population, more than seventy percent of the pre-Columbian Indian population north of Mexico was represented by eight language families. These, with their estimated populations, were: Algonquian 192,000; Eskimo-Aleut 89,700; Siouan 88,500; Iroquoian 71,700; Muskogean 66,500; Uto-Aztecan 63,100; Athapaskan 60,500; and Salish 57,900. The remainder of Powell's classification consisted of eighteen families with an average population of 12,000, while twenty-nine were spoken by only from 500 to 5,000 persons. A brief sketch of each of the eight largest families follows.

Algonquian. It embraces a large number of languages spoken along the Atlantic Coast from eastern Quebec and Cape Breton south to the Carolinas, in interior Labrador, the northern St. Lawrence drainage, the area of the upper Great Lakes and upper Mississippi valley, and west onto the Plains from Saskatchewan to Colorado. This is the largest geographic area occupied by any language family on the continent. The tongues constituting the Algonquian family are comparable in their degree of relationship to the Romance or Germanic languages of Europe. The spread of Algonquian speakers has been generally from east to west, and it is estimated that the Blackfoot, the westernmost Algonquian group, emerged from the woodlands onto the plains about A.D. 1200. The cultural range embraced by the Algonquian speakers is large, from the semisedentary agriculturalists of New England to the nomadic buffalo-hunting Cheyenne and Arapaho. Most of the individual Indians renowned in American colonial and early national history were Algonquian—Powhatan, King Phillip, Pontiac, and Tecumseh, for example. Of the Indian practices and vocabulary absorbed by white Americans, the greatest part is of Algonquian origin. The first Bible printed in the colonies (1663) was in an Algonquian language.

Eskimo-Aleut. It includes Eskimo dialects ranging from east Greenland west to southern Alaska and East Cape Siberia, and the Aleut speakers of the Alaska peninsula and the Aleutian Islands. The degree of relationship between Eskimo and Aleut is comparable to that between English and Russian, and it is estimated that the two were a single language up to about four thousand years ago. Among Eskimo speakers, there are two languages. A speaker of Greenland Eskimo can make himself understood, with some dialect difficulties, through Labrador, the Canadian Arctic coast, and north Alaska. In the remainder of Alaska and east Siberia, however, the language is about as different as English from Dutch. Within this second type of Eskimo, the dialect differences are greater than in the more widespread first, indicating that the second language has been in use in west Alaska for a long time, and that there has been a fairly rapid spread of the other Eskimo language east from Alaska during the last few centuries. The culture of the Eskimo-Aleut family is more uniform than that of most large language groups, perhaps partly due to the small variation permitted by the Arctic climate.

Siouan. It is found in four separate regions: an eastern group in Virginia and the Carolinas, a small fragment in southern Mississippi, another in Wisconsin, and a large population in the Missouri River valley and Great Plains, where they are the dominant and most populous linguistic stock. Anthropologists believe that the original proto-Siouan people resided in the lower Ohio or central Mississippi valleys, but were broken up and dispersed by yet unknown forces. Fragmentary groups then drifted toward their historically known locations, sometimes recombining or assimilating with other language stocks along the way. Like the Algonquians, the cultural variety of the Siouans is great, ranging from the agricultural Catawba of the Carolinas through the prairie Winnebago of Wisconsin to the archtypical Plains nomads, the Teton-Dakota (Sioux).

Iroquoian. It originally was spoken in three disconnected areas: the lower Great Lakes, upper New York region (Iroquois, Huron, and minor tribes); eastern Virginia and North Carolina (Tuscarora); and the Smoky Mountains area of the southern Appalachians (Cherokee). The widest linguistic cleavage is between the Cherokee and all the rest. It is estimated that the Cherokee split from the rest more than 3,500 years ago. Tuscarora split off from the northern languages about 2,000 years ago, and the languages of the Iroquois Five Nations diverged at least 1,200 years ago, at about the time archaeologists can first recognize classic Iroquois culture. For many years it was believed that the Iroquoian family had in early prehistoric times migrated eastward up the Ohio valley, intruding upon an Algonquian culture area, and that the Cherokee split off somewhere along the way. Recent studies, however, combining archaeologic, linguistic, and conventional anthropologic methods, have definitely shown that Iroquois culture developed indigenously to the Ontario-New York region, and that the Cherokee and Tuscarora are very early offshoots that drifted south. There is a relatively high degree of cultural similarity among Iroquoian speakers, largely because they all inhabit eastern woodlands. They are most noted for their high degree of political development, the Iroquois and Huron having evolved large intertribal confederacies and the Cherokee a complex form of democracy.

Muskogean. It occupied the Gulf region from the Mississippi River east to Florida and Georgia and north to Tennessee and Kentucky, and was dominant in the southeastern culture area. This linguistic stock evidently developed indigenously in its homeland, although Muskogean is genetically related to Algonquian, and there is evidence of strong meso-American culture influence among Muskogean tribes. The relationships among Muskogean speakers, their linguistic ancestry and development, are exceedingly complex, and scholars have not yet been able to posit generally accepted theories to explain them.

Uto-Aztecan. It extends in a long irregular tract from southern Idaho to central Mexico, and beyond as far as Panama in scattered pockets. Including the population south of the Mexican border, this was probably the largest single language group in pre-Columbian North America. These languages are thought to have been a single parent tongue about 5,000 years ago and to have spread from a central homeland in southern California and western Arizona. The presence of three closely related Uto-Aztecan languages in the Great Basin indicates a relatively recent spread into the area, probably within the last 2,000 years. The Comanche, the easternmost Uto-Aztecan tribe, reached Texas about A.D. 1700. The Aztecs reached the Valley of Mexico only about 350 years before the Spanish conquest. Uto-Aztecan speakers display the greatest cultural divergence of any language family. It is theorized that the Paiute and Shoshoni of the Great Basin experienced a degenerative process in their movement from southern California to the even less hospitable environment of the Nevada and Utah deserts, while the proto-Aztec rapidly evolved toward the more complex cultures that preceded them in Mexico.

Athapaskan. It is composed of more than fifty distinct idioms and distributed in three separate geographic regions. The largest group occupied the whole of interior Canada and Alaska northwest of the Churchill River. The Pacific Coast Athapaskans included sixteen languages spoken in southwestern Oregon and northern California. The third group consisted of seven tongues spoken by the Navaho and Apache of the southwestern states and northern Mexico. The northern languages are more diverse than either the Pacific Coast group or the Apache, indicating that the original Athapaskan homeland lay in the North, and that the two southern groups were migrants from the Canada-Alaska area. Study has determined that the proto-Athapaskan community began to break up about 200 B.C. and that the movements southward started around 400 years later. This short time explains why, in spite of the great geographic distance, the difference between northern and southern Athapaskan is so small, hardly more than that between German and English. Cultural divergence, on the other hand, was great. The northern Athapaskan remained wholly subarctic. The Pacific group became so completely acculturated to their neighbors that even experts cannot distinguish the artifacts of the Athapaskan Hupa from those of the Ritwan-speaking Yurok or the Hokan-speaking Karok. The Navaho and Apache demonstrate varying degrees of acculturation with the Pueblo peoples.

Salish. It occupies a continuous area in southern British Columbia and northern Washington, Idaho, and northwest Montana. There are also detached groups along the Pacific coast as far south as Oregon. There were substantial structural differences between the coastal and interior Salish languages, divided at the Cascade Range. A cultural dichotomy closely paralleled the linguistic division, with the coastal peoples belonging to the Northwest Coast complex, and the interior tribes to the Plateau culture. Absence of recent studies makes further conclusions about the history and internal relationships of the Salish stock impossible.

Excellent introductions to the importance and study of American Indian languages can be found in most general anthropologic texts on Indians, particularly Harold E. Driver, *Indians of North America* (2d ed. rev. 1969), and R. F. Spencer, J. D. Jennings, and others, *The Native Americans* (1965); both have bibliographies for more extensive study. A few of the classic analyses are Franz Boas, *Race, Language, and Culture* (1940); R. B. Dixon and A. L. Kroeber, *Linguistic Families of California* (1919); J. W. Powell, *Indian Linguistic Families of America North of Mexico* (1891); Edward Sapir, *Selected Writings*, ed. D. G. Mandlebaum (1949); L. Spier, A. J. Hallowell, and S. S. Newman, eds., *Language, Culture, and Personality* (1941); C. F. Voegelin, "Relative Chronology of North American Linguistic Types," *American Anthropologist*, vol. 47 (1945); and C. F. Voegelin and F. M. Voegelin, *Map of North American Indian Languages* (1966).—P. R. M.

Indian-Negro relations. See NEGROES ON THE FRONTIER.

Indian painters. Although little material production has survived to the present, it is reasonable to suppose that the prehistoric inhabitants of North America were chiefly concerned with making utilitarian or ceremonial objects, and that artistic activity among them derived from a sense of pride in manufacture, as in the decoration of weapons and apparel, or from the larger need to express ideas through various, related art forms. Established artistic traditions were radically altered as a result of the Anglo-European conquest. As late as the latter half of the nineteenth century, the Department of the Interior continued to impose a basically alien way of life upon the Indian population, with a corresponding suppression of all nationalist or ethnic activity. In the first decades of the twentieth century, this policy was revised to some extent, and proposals to revive aspects of an almost forgotten culture were put forward by such agencies as the Indian Arts and Crafts Board. Its emphasis on the production of marketable items tended to discourage more serious artistic efforts. Nevertheless, there arose at this time a number of potters, weavers, sculptors, painters, and printmakers whose works, expressive of traditional themes and subjects, earned for them a place in the contemporary art world.

In 1931 the largest exhibition of Indian art assembled to that time opened in New York City. Included in this show were the paintings of several Kiowa youths who had received wide public notice three years before when they were represented at an international art festival in Prague, Czechoslovakia. Having earlier come to the attention of the field matron at the Kiowa Agency in Anadarko, Oklahoma, these young Indians had been encouraged to pursue art careers, enlisting in time the interest of Professor Oscar Brousse Jacobson at the University of Oklahoma's department of art. Jacobson subsequently invited them to live in Norman, Oklahoma, and to work at the university under his private supervision. A member of the Oklahoma state legislature prompted oilman Lew Wentz of Ponca City, Oklahoma, to provide the funds that enabled these artists to devote their full time to painting.

First to arrive in Norman in 1927 was Spencer Asah (1905-57), descendant of a distinguished line of Kiowa medicine men, who later produced historical and decorative murals for a federal building in Anadarko and the Oklahoma State Historical Building in Oklahoma City. After him came Jack Hokeah (1902-   ) who, under the auspices of the WPA in the 1930s, painted murals at the United States Indian School in Santa Fe, New Mexico, and exerted considerable influence upon young Pueblo artists studying there. Stephen Mopope (1898-   ), whose inspiration in painting derived from his knowledge of Indian rituals and traditions, was the next to join this association, later producing murals for the Artillery Museum at Fort Sill, Oklahoma, and federal buildings in Anadarko and Muskogee, Oklahoma. Mopope was joined at the university by Monroe Tstaoke (1904-1937), son of a Kiowa army scout, and James Auchiah (1906-   ), grandson of the Kiowa war chief Satanta. Auchiah devoted a long career to the depiction of the tribal and ceremonial life of the Plains Indians, and with Mopope was commissioned in 1939 to execute murals for the Department of the Interior building in Washington, D.C. Lois Smoky, grandniece of Appiatan, last of the great Kiowa chiefs, was the only girl to join the Kiowa artists group, but she later abandoned art for marriage and a family. As in the case of Jack Hokeah, few of Smoky's individual works are extant, but examples of the works of all the above-named artists were reproduced in *Kiowa Indian Art* (1929), by C. Szwedzicki. Other artists from Oklahoma include Acee BLUE

EAGLE, Woodrow CRUMBO, Willard STONE, and Walter WEST.

In the Southwest, several painters achieved national prominence, among them Harrison Begay (1917-   ), born on a Navaho reservation in Arizona. Begay studied art at the United States Indian School in Santa Fe in the 1930s. He was later instrumental in organizing Tewa Enterprises, which made quality reproductions of contemporary Indian art available to the public. Gerald Nailor (1917-1952) also studied at the Indian School in Santa Fe, and later produced many works expressive of Navaho life and thought. During his student days he shared a studio with Allan Hauser, grandson of Apache leader Geronimo, and with Hauser illustrated at least one book, *I Am a Pueblo Indian Girl* (c. 1937).

Many Indian painters work independently in developing respective, personal styles. Fred Beaver (1911-   ), a Creek artist from Eufaula, Oklahoma, retired in 1960 from twenty-five years of service with the Bureau of Indian Affairs to devote his full time to art. Blackbear Bosin (1921-   ), a Kiowa-Comanche painter born at Anadarko, Oklahoma, achieved success with little formal training and was the only Indian artist represented in the White House Arts Festival in 1965. Juan Martinez (1917-   ), a San Ildefonso Pueblo artist and son of the famous potter Maria Martinez, became noted for his distinctive style of representation. Solomon McCombs (1913-   ), from Vivian, Oklahoma, has perpetuated the strong narrative traditions of the past in many historically based works and was chosen by the International Educational Service in 1955 to tour Africa, the Near East, and India on a good will mission with a series of exhibits and lectures.

Several painters abandoned traditional styles of representation, if not Indian themes and subjects. One of these was Pawnee illustrator Brummett ECHOHAWK, feature writer for the *Tulsa World* and staff artist with the *Chicago Times* and *Sun Times*. Born in Pawnee, Oklahoma, Echohawk studied at the Chicago Art Institute before pursuing a successful career as a commercial artist, painter, and writer. Still others devoted themselves almost entirely to teaching, such as Al Momaday (1913-   ), Kiowa painter from Mountain View, Oklahoma; and Fred Kabotie (1900-   ), a Hopi born at Shungopovi, Second Mesa, Arizona, and for many years a field representative of the Indian Arts and Crafts Board.

See Jeanne O. Snodgrass, *American Indian Painters: A Biographical Dictionary* (1968).—D. C. H.

Indian pottery. See POTTERY, SOUTHWESTERN INDIAN.

Indian Power movement. On Thanksgiving Day 1970, a ceremony was held at Plymouth Rock, Massachusetts, by two hundred Indians from twenty-five tribes, who proclaimed that henceforth the holiday ought to be a national day of mourning. In honor of the Wampanoag Indians who had taken part in the first Thanksgiving, 350 years before, the state Department of Commerce invited the remnants of the tribe to send a spokesman to the ceremonies. The tribe designated Frank James (Wamsutta), a high school music teacher and direct descendant of the Indians who had welcomed the Mayflower. His speech was banned by state officials, for Wamsutta said that the welcoming of the Pilgrims was his forefathers' "greatest mistake." "We forfeited our country. Our lands have fallen into the hands of the aggressor. We have allowed the white man to keep us on our knees," Wamsutta said in the speech he did not deliver. "We're standing not in our wigwams, but in your concrete tent. We stand tall and proud and before too many moons pass we'll right the wrongs we have allowed to happen to us. This is only the beginning of the American Indian, particularly the Wampanoags, to regain the position in this country that is rightfully ours."

The "incident at Plymouth Rock" is symbolic of the spiritual rebirth of the modern tribes, known variously as the Red Power, Indian Power, or New Indian movement. Within a generation many centuries-old tribal beliefs have been revived, American history has been rewritten, the stereotypes of Indian life have been challenged, and a cultural and political awareness has stirred the reservations and urban ghettos, where from one million to one million and a half American Indians (by 1970 estimates) have long lived in historical eclipse.

The New Indian movement began in the halcyon years after World War II, when the advance of technology and demise of rural sectionalism ended the isolation of the reservation tribes. W. R. Zimmerman, head of the Bureau of Indian Affairs (see INDIAN AFFAIRS, BUREAU OF), in 1947 advocated the "termination" of federal responsibilities to the "advanced" tribes and the entry of Indians into what he called the "mainstream." In that year the Hoover Commission recommended "rapid integration [of Indians] into American life." An official policy of termination of federal responsibilities to the tribes was inaugurated by the Eisenhower administration. In 1953 Congress passed Public Law 280, which permitted states to assume legal jurisdiction on reservation lands, without tribal consent. The attempt was made to terminate at least a dozen tribes and to "relocate" the Indians in urban life.

On the reservations there was great resistance to these termination policies. The nationwide opposition of the tribes was successful. Every national administration since has disavowed termination and instead has urged "self-determination" in Indian affairs. For the first time since the tribal federations of Tecumseh and Sitting Bull, the diverse and sometimes warring tribes united to counter the initiatives of the dominant society.

Within a few years there were scores of national and regional intertribal groups: the National Congress of American Indians, at its zenith in the early 1960s, representing 104 tribes in Washington, D.C.; the National Indian Youth Council, a group of university Indian clubs founded by Clyde Warrior and others, which participated in the Poor People's March and the Fish-Ins; the United Native Americans, an urban movement claiming five thousand members; the United Sioux Tribes, representing nine Lakota (Sioux) bands, which in 1963 defeated state jurisdiction in South Dakota; the American Indian Movement (AIM), based in the Midwest and Great Lakes region, which in the 1970s reached a membership of fifty thousand; the North American Unity Convention, a religious and traditionalist group whose yearly powwows have been attended by thousands of Indians from eighteen nations in North and South America; the Indians of All Tribes, who occupied Alcatraz in 1969; and numerous federations of Indian prison inmates, urban Indian centers, professionals, and tribal chiefs.

The Tuscarora (Iroquois) tribe of upstate New York was the first to achieve national recognition for this new spirit when in 1959 it turned back the crews of the state power authority, who had sought to convert reservation land into the Niagara Power Project reservoir. Led by Chief Clinton Rickard and a young traditionalist, Wallace "Mad Bear" Anderson, the tribe routed the linemen of then "power czar" Robert Moses.

On the reservations the demand for tribal control of tribal affairs spread across the country. It basically altered the hundred-year-old policies of the Bureau of Indian Affairs. In the Zuñi Pueblo (New Mexico) the tribe sought, and was granted, nominal control of several governmental programs. The Taos Pueblo won a sixty-four-year fight for the return of its sacred Blue Lake in 1969, when Congress passed, and President Nixon signed, a bill returning 47,000 acres of land to the tribe. In the Black Hills of South Dakota, the Lakota (Sioux) bands of the Pine Ridge, Rosebud, and Cheyenne River reservations occupied a United States forest ranger station, atop a sacred peak, claiming the land in the name of their tribal religion. In northern California a band of Pit River Indians occupied land on which the Pacific Gas and Electric Company had built a plant, claiming that both the land and the plant were legally theirs by virtue of a United States Indian Claims Commission ruling. Along the Nisqually and Puyallup rivers in Washington, Indian fishermen claimed the right to net salmon freely, a right accorded them by the Treaty of Medicine Creek in 1854. When the state supreme court ruled against the tribes, dozens of Indian fishermen were arrested, fishing camps were raided and destroyed by game wardens, nets were seized, and Fish-In leader Hank ADAMS was shot in 1971 by unidentified vigilantes. Since 1964 the Indian fishermen have cast their nets "illegally" each spring, when the salmon begin their run.

Education of Indians had consistently been the poorest in the country. The Navaho, Sioux, Cherokee, Passamaquoddy, and other tribes have urged that the schools offer tribal history and culture, revise the curriculum and textbooks, and teach in the native languages, especially in the early grades. At the Rough Rock Demonstration School (Arizona), an all-Navaho school board has instituted many of these educational reforms. Tribal community colleges have been established by the Navaho during the tribal chairmanships of Raymond NAKAI and Peter MACDONALD, and by the Sioux. Indian studies courses have been instituted in many universities.

The literature of the American Indian has achieved national prominence. *Custer Died for Your Sins* (1969) and *We Talk, You Listen* (1970), by Vine DELORIA, Jr., a Standing Rock Sioux, offer a critique of tribal and national affairs. *Bury My Heart at Wounded Knee* (1971), by Dee BROWN, tells the story of the Plains Indian wars from the Indian viewpoint and in so doing has revised the history of the West. *House Made of Dawn* (1968), by N. Scott MOMADAY, a Kiowa, was awarded the Pulitzer Prize for fiction.

Indian beliefs, Indian religions, Indian ecology, and pseudo-Indian fashions became nationwide bywords. In Hollywood a new Indian image was projected (by non-Indians) in films such as *Little Big Man* (1970), *Tell Them Willie Boy Is Here* (1969), and *Flap* (1969). A bumper sticker proclaimed: "Indians Are In."

Some have seen these cultural changes as the result of the Indian Power movement. But to tribal traditionalists, they are the fulfillment of ancient prophecies that foretold "rebirth of the Great Spirit," when the "circle of life" was made whole once more. To the younger, "new Indians," the meaning of the change was succinctly expressed in an editorial comment in *Akwesasne Notes*, a newspaper of the Mohawk nation: "Enough 'pride in my heritage.' I *am* my heritage." Caustically another tribal newspaper said, "All we have left is our culture. You have stolen everything else. Now, you are trying to steal that too."

In political response to the Indian Power movement, President Richard Nixon, in his message to Congress in July 1970, wrote: "The time has come to break decisively with the past and to create conditions for a new era in which the Indian future is determined by Indian acts and Indian decisions." Louis R. BRUCE, of Mohawk descent, appointed commissioner of Indian affairs in 1969, declared this new national policy long overdue. Henceforth, the Bureau of Indian Affairs (BIA) would be transformed, he said, from a management to a service organization. Young Indians were brought into high-level policy positions, and federal programs were announced to give tribes more power in determining their future.

In the spring of 1971 tribal discontent became vocal once more. Unemployment on the reservations, estimated at 40 to 75 percent, was not appreciably decreased, the average tribal family income of fifteen hundred dollars yearly was barely increased, and the school dropout rate of Indian children, from 40 to 100 percent, was still the worst in the nation. "By every standard, Indians receive the worst education of any children in the country," declared a study by the Harvard Center for Law and Education and the NAACP Legal Defense Fund. The newly appointed Indian director of BIA Community Services, Ernest Stevens, an Oneida, resigned in protest because the new policies were tied up in bureaucratic red tape (or, as one Indian leader dubbed it, "white tape").

In the autumn of 1972 the tribes across the nation, urban Indians, college students, and religious traditionalists joined in the "Trail of Broken Treaties" to protest what they termed another betrayal of government promises. Caravans of several thousand Indians journeyed to the nation's capital. In an unprecedented act they seized the Washington building of the Bureau of Indian Affairs and held it for one week. The conflict led to the Interior Department demoting and finally dismissing Commissioner Bruce and the young tribal leaders he had appointed.

Led by the young Indians of AIM, and at the invitation of the Sioux traditionalists, the protesters moved onto the Dakota prairies that winter. In the spring of 1973 they occupied Wounded Knee, South Dakota, the site of the massacre of one hundred years before, and militarily held the village for two months under the guidance of Indian veterans from Vietnam.

One of the Indian Power campaigns that gained wide support in the early 1970s coincided with the popular concern for the country's ecology. The Navaho's and Hopi's battle to save their sacred Black Mesa from strip mining and electric power plants brought about Senate hearings. In Idaho the Shoshoni-Bannock tribes on the Fort Hall reservation banned aerial spraying of pesticides. Puget Sound tribes in Washington protested the killing of millions of salmon in the Columbia River by chemical pollution.

"We always have been ecologists," said Taos Pueblo leader Paul Bernal. "We believe all life is sacred. We cherish all life. We can teach that to the white man, if he will listen."

As early as the 1950s a few scholars and tribal prophets foresaw the spiritual rebirth of what they termed a "pan-Indian revivalist movement." From the white man's perspective, the Indian movement was more than a fad but less than a genuine revival of concern. The white nation turned toward the Indian out of its own moral malaise; but it was not prepared really to understand the Indian way of life and thought, nor was it prepared for the political and cultural effects of the Indians' spiritual resurgence.

See Henry W. Hough, *Development of Indian Resources* (1967); Stuart Levine and Nancy O. Lurie, eds., *The American Indian Today* (1968); Stan Steiner, *The New Indians* (1968); Steiner and Shirley Witt, eds., *The Way: An Anthology of American Indian Literature* (1972); Virgil J. Vogel, ed., *This Country Was Theirs: A Documentary History* (1972); Wilcomb E. Washburn, *Red Man's Land, White Man's Law* (1971) and (ed.) *The Indian and the White Man* (1964); and Edmund Wilson, *Apologies to the Iroquois* (1959).—S. S.

Indian Rights Association. This humanitarian organization, the most prominent of the several groups whose appearance in the 1880s signaled the revival of public interest in Indian affairs, was formed by Herbert WELSH, a wealthy Philadelphian. Although it was dedicated to arousing public opinion, the association failed to reach the magnitude that Welsh had envisioned. It never had more than one thousand five hundred members, many of whom were from the same families, and donations never exceeded $10,000 in any year. Yet it was the strongest organization in what was a flaccid reform movement, in part because it employed a full-time lobbyist in Washington.

The association was instrumental in the passage of the DAWES SEVERALTY ACT of 1887 and in the introduction of civil service rules to the Indian Service in the 1890s. Beyond these two policies, however, the association showed little originality and even less flexibility. It steadily supported the idea of assimilating the Indian into American life, but its primary interest in efficient administration blinded it to the obvious failure of the Dawes Act to accomplish this objective. From its early creative role in working for citizenship, law, and land-in-severalty, it declined at the turn of the century to one of carping at the activities of the Indian Bureau. Despite the increasing distress of the Indians, the association had no new policies to propose, and its influence declined in proportion to the rise in authority of the Indian Bureau over the affairs of Indians.—E. A. G.

Indian rugs. See NAVAHO RUGS.

Indians, Christian. See PROTESTANT MISSIONARIES; ROMAN CATHOLIC MISSIONARIES.

Indians and white diseases. Diseases carried to the Western Hemisphere from Europe caused more deaths and were more destructive of Indian culture than any other single factor—and probably more than all the Indian wars and removals combined. These diseases, most terribly smallpox, measles, and cholera in epidemic form, spread throughout the aboriginal population in advance of actual white colonization and settlement, passing from tribe to tribe or carried by roaming explorers and traders. European disease spread so quickly that often whole Indian populations were destroyed before white men penetrated the region. The full extent of this phenomenon is only now beginning to be studied and will probably never be completely known, since some Indian groups were totally exterminated. It has already become apparent, however, that traditional estimates of the pre-Columbian population may have to be revised drastically upward.

The effects of European disease were clearly apparent to the first colonizers. When the Pilgrims landed at Plymouth harbor in 1620 they found that the New England Indians had been devastated some four years earlier by a "pestilential sickness"—probably measles or bubonic plague—which had destroyed at least seventy-five percent of the native population from Maine to Connecticut. It had been contacted from European fishermen who were frequenting the coasts. The survivors were too few to bury the dead, and Puritan travelers found large portions of the countryside literally carpeted with the skeletons of victims. The New Englanders seized upon this event as particular evidence of God's favor upon their enterprise, Governor John Winthrop remarking that the natives were "neere all dead, so as the Lord hath cleared our title to what we possess."

Smallpox, which was to prove the greatest single scourge of the Indians, began sweeping west soon after the colonists landed. By 1637 traders in the New England hinterlands reported that the disease was raging "as far to the west as any Indian plantations are known," and that trade was nearly impossible because so much of the population was dead. The situation was similar in the other colonies. Two epidemics of smallpox had reduced the Indians of the Delaware valley before the founding of Pennsylvania in 1681, and the early chroniclers of Virginia reported how after the first English exploring parties passed through the Indian villages, "a greate sickness came on the salvages, and dyed in vaste numbers." The fact that the Indians were nevertheless able to mount such bitter resistance to the English, as occurred in Virginia in 1622 and in New England in 1637 and 1675, indicates how different history would have been had the colonists been confronted by the natives in all their strength.

It was not long before the whites put to use their perception that disease-stricken tribes were the tribes that gave way easily before white advance. Following the French and Indian War, Lord Jeffrey Amherst, British military commander in America, instructed his subordinates to determine if "could it not be contrived to send the Small Pox among the dissatisfied tribes," and germ-laden blankets were in fact distributed among Ohio valley and Great Lakes Indians. Similar occurrences of deliberate infestation are recorded throughout the advance of the frontier, well into the nineteenth century.

Premeditated germ warfare was not necessary for the propagation of disease, however. The smallpox frontier reached the upper Missouri River valley by the 1770s, well in advance of even the fur-traders, and destroyed more than two-thirds of the population of the agricul-

tural river tribes, thus contributing to the rise of the horse-nomad culture that moved into the resulting power vacuum. A second, larger epidemic of smallpox, initially carried up the Missouri by traders' boats in the 1830s, swept through nearly every tribe from the Dakotas to the Pacific Coast, eventually spreading across Alaska and into the Arctic. This particular epidemic, stretching across five thousand miles of the continent, ranks among the most terrible plagues of human history and is on a par with the Black Death of medieval Europe. In just two of its instances, the Mandan, a Missouri River tribe, were reduced from 1,600 to 31 in a single winter; and the Blackfoot, long the most feared and powerful tribe on the northern Plains, were reduced by three fourths and were never again able to resist successfully encroachment from either Indian or white enemies.

Cholera, carried onto the middle and southern Great Plains by the Oregon-California immigrant caravans of 1849-51, had a large effect on those Plains tribes that, because of their dispersal and meager contact with whites, had avoided the greater earlier ravages of smallpox. Nor was the spread of European diseases confined to Anglo-America as as a point of origin. The Indians of the Southwest and California had since the sixteenth-century Spanish explorations been subject to periodic epidemics radiating out of Mexico, and the establishment of permanent settlements only worsened the situation. The early mission period of California was marked by a wholesale reduction of the native population through a variety of illnesses, particularly in the San Joaquin valley, where the zone of biologic influence of the missionaries extended far beyond their religious and cultural influence.

The effect of these epidemics on the form of native culture is almost impossible to exaggerate. Apart from instances of total extermination, many groups were reduced below the threshold of biologic population maintenance and so were forced to combine with other stronger groups, or with several small groups, to form a new cultural unit. Organizational and trading units and interdependencies were interrupted, and political confederacies of high structural level—like the Natchez of the lower Mississippi—completely disappeared. A blurring of hitherto clear cultural, even linguistic, distinctions was an inevitable result. Even those Indian groups that retained their basic integrity often suffered severe losses of prominent individuals, so that traditional lines of authority and ritual practice weakened and new patterns emerged that might never have otherwise developed. As a result, most of our present conceptions of aboriginal Indian life reflect only a brief period of disorganization and tentative reconsolidation following severe cultural trauma. It immediately preceded the appearance of white observers but was not understood by them.

The emotional impact on the Indians of such sudden, unexplainable wholesale death is hard to determine, given the immense variety of Indian culture. In general, however, it appears that in those cases where the disease was associated with whites, it was attributed to white magic. This belief enhanced fear and awe of white power while at the same time contributing to antagonism and hatred. Unresolved frustration increased, with the impulse to revenge the loss of loved ones restrained by the fear of prompting greater disasters. Such frustrations and antagonisms often led to the failure of well-intentioned white policies and to outbreaks of sudden violence.

The final subjection of Indian culture to white dominance and the beginning of the modern, or reservation, period of Indian history brought no respite from the effects of white diseases. Crowded and unsanitary conditions on many reservations, coupled with malnutrition resulting from the loss of traditional subsistence and lack of an adequate substitute, left Indians highly susceptible to endemic debilitations like tuberculosis, trachoma, and venereal disease. Special health problems developed as an adjunct to the emotional and cultural limbo of reservation existence, such as widespread alcoholism and spiritual anomie leading to suicide. Unhealthy reservation conditions were responsible for many of the so-called uprisings of the early reservation period, such as the escape of the Winnebago in 1863 from the disease- and starvation-ridden Crow Creek reserve in South Dakota and the famous flight of the Cheyenne from Oklahoma to Nebraska in 1878-79.

The health of reservation Indians remains a problem in the present. Information released in 1970 by the Indian Health Service of the Department of Health, Education, and Welfare reveals that infectious and communicable diseases are still more prevalent among Indians than non-Indians. The death rate from tuberculosis, though declining, is approximately six times greater for Indians than whites. And the average life-expectancy of an Indian baby born in 1970 is six years less than a white baby's. Government and private organizations are continually working to erase the conditions indicated by these statistics, but until such a time arrives, the era of white conquest and subjugation of the Indian cannot be said to be over.

There are no inclusive studies of the impact on Indians of European diseases, but references, generally to smallpox, can be found in practically all histories or descriptions of any Indian group. Some good statistics on the effect of smallpox can be found in J. R. Swanton, *The Indian Tribes of North America* (1952). Native diseases and medical practices, on the other hand, receive excellent coverage in J. G. Bourke, *Medicine Men of the Apache* (1892); and V. J. Vogel, *American Indian Medicine* (1970). Other useful works are S. F. Cook, *The Conflict Between the California Indians and White Civilization* (1943); Alfred W. Crosby, *The Columbian Exchange* (1972); B. Knollenburg, "General Amherst and Germ Warfare," *Mississippi Valley Historical Review*, vol. 41 (1954); E. B. Leacock and N. O. Lurie, *North American Indians in Historical Perspective* (1971); W. C. MacLeod, *The American Indian Frontier* (1928); and Alden Vaughan, *New England Frontier* (1965).—P. R. M.

Indian sign language. Communication across language barriers through signs made by the hands and arms is universal among mankind, but only among the Plains Indians of North America did sign language reach the level of a fully developed language. The Plains sign language was understood commonly by all tribes regardless of the differences of their spoken languages. There were some regional variations in the system, akin to dialect differences in speech, but a Blackfoot from Saskatchewan had no difficulty in understanding the signs of a Texas Comanche. Nearly any concept expressible in speech could be conveyed by the sign language,

from the complexities of treaty negotiations to the abstractions of a religious myth or the mundane details of daily events. The Indian system was distinct from that of deaf-mutes, in that the Indian practice involved expansive use of the arms and body for visibility at a distance, while the deaf rely primarily on finger signs for face-to-face communication. In fact, the Indian system should more accurately be called a gesture language instead of a sign language. Other aids to long-distance communication—such as riding patterns on horseback, stirring of dust clouds, and smoke signals—were but extensions of the Indian system; they were not separate from it.

The Indians had no specific idea of the origin of the language except for a belief that it had come out of the South. They regarded the Kiowa as the great developers of the system. Most nineteenth-century white scholars believed the language grew out of the necessities for communication among potentially hostile nomadic tribes of different spoken languages. More recent scholars feel that the sign system developed from the need of members of the same tribe to communicate with each other across the vast flat distances of the Plains, where the eye reaches much farther than the ear. Information about the presence of enemies or the movement of game could thus be quickly relayed. Instructions could likewise be passed quickly along, and white military observers were often amazed at the signal drill of Plains war chiefs who at distances of hundreds of yards could instantly maneuver large and rapidly moving bodies of horsemen by the movements of an arm or mirror flashes. These techniques were picked up by white cattle-drovers and wagon-masters. Dr. Albert Myer, first chief of the army signal corps, developed the semaphore and other innovations in military communications after observing the sign and signal language of the Comanche.

The best illustrated guide of sign language is in William Tomkins, *Universal Sign Language of the Plains Indians of North America* (1927). Detailed analyses of the system based on first-hand observations in the nineteenth century are William Clark, *The Indian Sign Language* (1885), and Garrick Mallery, *Sign Language Among North American Indians* (1881). The best brief description of the history and development of the language is in Walter Prescott Webb, *The Great Plains* (1931).—P. R. M.

Indian silverwork. See SILVERWORK, SOUTHWESTERN INDIAN.

Indians of California. At the time of white settlement the Indian population of California consisted of seven main language families, with more than one hundred and twenty distinct dialects. California includes a wide variety of climatic and geological settings, and the various peoples adapted themselves in unique ways to local conditions. Some 250,000 Indians lived in more than five hundred small village-states, each politically and territorially independent. There were wide differences among these peoples, and few generalizations can hold for them all.

Most Californians were blessed with plentiful natural resources, which provided little incentive for the development of agricultural skills; they remained a hunting, fishing, and gathering people. Nineteenth-century Anglo invaders, struck by the primitive nature of this small-scale, stone-age society, interpreted it as backward and degenerate, its members as slovenly and slavish "Diggers." The concentration of attention on material culture blinded Anglos to the rich social and religious life of the Indians. The northernmost peoples, including the Modoc, Shasta, and Yurok, had much in common with the celebrated tribes of the Pacific Northwest, especially in the value they placed on money payment, around which they built an elaborate ritual and practical life. But, unlike their northern neighbors, the northern California Indians shared with their southern compatriots an aversion to war. This was a general characteristic of the Californians, related to their focus on the village. The villages were nearly in perfect harmony with the environment; there were few expansionist pressures and, consequently, little intervillage conflict. This was even more true of peoples like the Miwok, Yokuts, and Salinan, who inhabited the great central valleys and the slopes of the Sierra Nevada. The religions of these central peoples found their cosmology in the local ecology, thus reifying their village orientation and helping to produce a gentle, quiet, and introspective character. It was this gentle aspect of California Indian culture that Anglos characterized as slovenly, and that made these peoples an easy target for military adventurism.

In the southern part of the state lived the Gabrielino, Serrano, Luiseño, and Dagueno, among others. They were much like the northern peoples, but with an even more varied culture. Remaining artifacts and accounts testify to their exquisite mastery of basket-making and ground-painting, their development of a solar-lunar calendar system, and their highly stratified social structure. Here, in the south, centered the "toloache" cult based on the psychedelic effects of the jimson weed. The cult spread north throughout the state, underlining the highly mystic nature of these peoples.

Finally, along the Colorado River lived the desert Mojave, Yuma, and Kamia, the only peoples in California to develop a real tribal, supravillage society. The pressure from the nomadic southwestern peoples to the east forced these riverine villages together for protection and encouraged the development of warlike values in their culture. The requirements of the harsh desert environment pushed them to develop a rudimentary agriculture. They varied most from the California prototype and are sometimes not considered of this Indian group, but their existence on the fringe of California aboriginal society acted as a protective barrier for their more pacifistic California compatriots.

European encroachment did not begin until the late eighteenth century, but after less than one hundred years of Spanish, Mexican, and Anglo cycles of conquest, the aboriginal setting was all but destroyed. Beginning in the 1770s, the Spanish pushed north from present-day Mexico with their mission system as a protective reaction to fears of Russian and French expansion. They planned a conversion of the aboriginal population to Spanish ways, thereby expanding the area of Spanish control without costly colonization. By design, then, the mission system involved the destruction of autonomous Indian culture and the enforced adaptation by California peoples to European civilization. The mission system was, in this sense, a massive failure. Although the mission environment is a matter of some

historiographic controversy, most contemporaries described the missions in terms more befitting concentration camps than happy, pastoral retreats. While few Franciscan missionaries were brutal toward the mission Indians, the system was brutal, for the relocation from village to mission complex and the imposition of nearly new sets of cultural and material standards were profoundly demoralizing for the Indians. Within the coastal areas of their dominance, the most outstanding effects of the mission were a genocidal population decline due to disease, malnutrition, and a plummeting birth rate, the combined effects of which reduced the population from about 150,000 in 1500 to 98,000 by 1832 and accomplished a near total destruction of the southern and mid-coastal peoples' cultural integrity.

The absence of tribal organization and the Spanish effort to destroy the village structure worked against any mass Indian rebellion. Only in the south, among tribal riverine peoples, did organized, mass resistance to Spanish rule take place. On the other hand, individual flight, rebellion, and despondency were common forms of resistance by all mission Indians. They and the alarming population decline exposed the futility of the mission system by the early years of the nineteenth century.

With the secularization of the missions in 1834, the bondage of the Catholic church was replaced by the peonage of the ranchos, which now dominated the pastoral economy and, like the mission, depended upon the Indians for the labor necessary for production (see CALIFORNIA RANCHO SYSTEM). Southern and coastal Indian organization had been destroyed, but under the peonage system cultural restraints were loosened and former mission Indians were allowed to recongregate in local rancherias, where an indigenous Spanish-mestizo culture developed. In the great fertile central valleys, however, where the Spanish had only rarely penetrated, rancheros now regularly raided nonmission Indian villages to procure needed workers. This Mexican encroachment, and some earlier Spanish attempts to extend control into the hinterland, had little demographic effect on the interior and northern Indians, but it did encourage the evolution of new social and cultural patterns of defensive warfare among these previously gentle peoples. By the mid-1840s the California peoples living on the fringes of Mexican settlement had begun to take the offensive in a war against the invaders.

The discovery of gold brought a cataclysmic change for these Indians. Gold-searching Anglos poured into precisely those areas where the Spanish and Mexicans had failed to penetrate. Hispanic culture had envisioned a society exploiting Indians, but native peoples had no place whatsoever in the Anglo conception of California. Without any program for the inclusion of Indians into Anglo society, each cultural conflict tended to escalate to genocidal proportions. But while massacres offered frequent and dramatic evidence of Anglo intent, the most serious disruption of Indian society came through the elimination of food supply by the heavy Anglo use of the valleys and hillsides for mining and, later, farming. There was literally no place for the Indians. After fifty years of Anglo domination, only 15,000 Indians survived.

California's Indenture Act of 1850 established a form of legal slavery for the Indians; throughout the decade this system was supplemented by illegal trafficking in kidnapped Indian children, sold as slaves to farmers and rancheros. But even these brutal attempts to integrate the Indian into the political economy were ended by the success of the free labor movement culminating in the Civil War. A somewhat more humane attempt to come to terms with the Indian "problem" was made by federal commissioners, who negotiated eighteen treaties with representatives of various village and tribal groups in 1851, promising reservations of 8.5 million acres. But intense lobbying by official and public Anglo California resulted in defeat of the treaties by secret session of Congress in 1852, and they were hidden away in federal archives, unrevealed until 1905. As a result, reservation policy in California suffered from no overall plan and was carried out without even the slightest pretense of agreement from the California peoples themselves; those Indians who could be concentrated were removed, beginning in 1853, to inhospitable military reservations. Legal battle over the original disputed treaties began in 1928, and only after forty years of litigation did the federal government agree to minimal compensation for the remaining Indians.

For those Indians who survived this onslaught, there were really only two methods of accommodation. In the southern desert and the northern watershed, Indians fled to the interior, maintaining primitive, backland enclaves against the Anglos. The other, more typical, reaction was for Indians to enter the free labor economy of the state as individual men and women.

While mission rancho systems had allowed some retention of social organization, the Anglo system forced the nearly total destruction of native society. Completely isolated from each other, Indians drifted into the urban areas of the state, taking the lowest menial jobs available. Today California has the fourth largest Indian population among the states, but only a small number live on reservations in Indian patterns. They are, predominantly, an urban people. In the years since 1849 California's first residents have become the poorest and most devastated of all California's ethnic minorities.

For anthropological and ethnographic analysis of the California Indians, the classic study is Alfred L. Kroeber, *Handbook of the Indians of California* (1925). It should be supplemented with the articles in R. F. Heizer and M. A. Whipple, *The California Indians: A Source Book* (rev. ed., 1971). Kroeber and Heizer provide a valuable summary and scores of beautiful photographs in *Almost Ancestors: The First Californians* (1968). For the interaction between the Indians and the Spanish, Mexican, and Anglo invaders, see Sherbourne F. Cook, "The Conflict Between the California Indians and White Civilization," in *Ibero-Americana*, nos. 21-24 (1943), and "The California Indian and Anglo-American Culture" in Charles Wollenberg, ed., *Ethnic Conflict in California History* (1970).—J. F.

Indians of the Great Basin. The Great Basin lies between the Sierra Nevada and the Rockies and between the uplands of eastern Oregon, Washington, and Idaho and the deserts north of the Colorado River. It is the focus of interior drainage from the east and west and was in previous times the site of many large shallow lakes and marshes. Today only a few such places exist, none of them large. The area is generally arid and warm in the

summer and often cold in the winter. During the period of western migration it was considered a wasteland, and today only some parts of the eastern and western fringes have been settled, making it one of the most sparsely settled regions in the United States.

Because of the rugged environment the Indians of the region, until relatively recently, suffered less interference with precontact cultural patterns than have Indians in many parts of the West. Samuel Barrett's fieldwork in the early 1900s found Washo Indian families still dependent on the annual hunting and gathering rounds and using flint-tipped arrows. The last of the Washo "bunches" to give up the traditional mobile life did not do so until the late 1920s, perhaps even a few years later. This situation has permitted the collection of more firsthand knowledge of the workings of aboriginal society than has been the case in any other area in the United States.

Because the culture of the Basin Indians displayed little for white men either to fear or admire, as compared with that of the flamboyant, warlike tribes of the Plains and the East, it received relatively little attention from early explorers or travelers. Almost universally described as destitute and often compared with animals, Basin peoples, along with a number of peoples in California, were generally referred to as "Diggers," a reference to their pursuit of roots and other plant foods and perhaps to the semisubterranean houses used by some of them in the winter. In the north, Diggers were differentiated from the "Snakes." These appellations have no basis in ethnology and were applied across cultural and linguistic lines by early travelers. Essentially, Snakes were those tribes in the plateau and northern basin that adopted the horse and for a brief time a modified form of Plains culture. Diggers retained a prehorse culture, which appears to be a continuation, almost to the present day, of an ancient and persistent adaptation during the Pleistocene called Desert Culture, postulated as the cultural base for many later developments and adaptations in the West.

Virtually all Great Basin peoples were of one or another branch of the Uto-Aztecan language family. Broadly divided, the linguistic affiliations of the Basin were Shoshoni and Paiute, further divided into northern and southern branches. The Shoshoni-speakers were affiliated with peoples to the north in the plateau and in the Wind River country of Wyoming and ultimately with the Comanche, themselves a branch of the Shoshoni. To the south, Shoshoni affiliations extended into California. The Paiute-speakers tended to be more concentrated to the south of Shoshonian groups and extended into the Southwest, where the Southern Paiute mingled with and acculturated to Navaho culture, becoming in the present time both bilingual and bicultural. In the south and east, extending into the Rockies, were the Ute.

Among both the Paiute and the Shoshoni, bands, or "bunches," were identified with specific areas, distinctions that have sometimes been adopted in standard discussions; others, however, are seldom used. Among these bands are the Chemehuevi of the extreme southern Paiute area and the Kaiabab of the northern rim of the Grand Canyon. Western Colorado and southeastern Utah Shoshoni are often referred to as Gosiute. Northern Paiute- and Shoshoni-speakers in the Basin are less frequently differentiated with band names except in technical ethnological discussions.

In the extreme west of the Basin, extending from Lake Tahoe in the Sierras to the first low ranges of piñon-covered hills on the western edges of the Basin steppe, there are the Washo, who have been identified recently as having remote Hokan-Siouan affiliations after being considered for several decades as a separate and independent language stock.

Basin peoples and culture can be said to have occupied that area south of the plateau extending to the edges of the true desert bordering the Colorado. The means of subsistence was generally the same although marked by variations in local conditions. Pronghorn antelope inhabited the southern portion of the area from California into Nevada and through the northern half of the Basin; even in the zone in between, at least small bands of antelope were common prior to the introduction of firearms. Mule deer were plentiful in the mountains. The few year-round streams and shallow lakes provided some fishing, but in general this food source was most exploited by groups with access to the bordering mountains. The western hare or jackrabbit was ubiquitous. Cottontail rabbits, ground squirrels, tree squirrels, raccoons, wildcats, and ground hogs also served as game animals when necessity demanded. Insects, particularly grasshoppers and locusts, were considered delicacies, as were certain grubs. Game birds were taken in areas they frequented. The standard hunting weapon was the bow. Deer were generally taken by stalking, although group drives and fire drives were not infrequently used. Although often throwing-sticks were used for rabbits, the most rewarding method for rabbit hunting was a large-scale drive using the combined nets of a number of families so that hundreds of animals could be taken in a single day to be eaten fresh or air-dried for storage. Sun-drying was the only other method of preserving fish and game. Antelope were taken in elaborate drives utilizing a corral or pen. These drives were the foundation of the most elaborate expression of social and political organization to be found in the Basin.

Plants played an even more important role in the basic subsistence of the Basin. The nut of the piñon pine was the almost universal staple of the region. The quantities were so great in many areas that surplus supplies usually remained in the spring as other food stuffs became available. A wide variety of grass seeds, tubers, and roots were also regularly collected, almost always by women, along with a variety of leafy plants and berries when available. Some people, notably the Washo and the westerly Paiute, sent parties into California to collect acorns on the western slope of the Sierra Nevada. It was common, but not universal, to burn off grasslands in the fall to assure heavier crops in the spring. Some groups are reported to have sown grasslands with excess seeds to improve the yield, and in the extreme west one is reported to have diverted streams to irrigate natural meadows and assure a constant plant yield. For a time ethnologists debated whether irrigation was learned from the whites or had been independently invented by the Indians themselves.

The Washo have been characterized by A. L. Kroeber as possessing the simplest culture of any people in North America. From the material point of view this description might well be extended to all the Basin peoples.

Although shockingly inhospitable to the white man, the Basin provided an adequate living for a sophisticated desert steppe dweller. Such a living required mobility, the ability to seize short-lived opportunity, and flexibility in social and cultural patterns. In accommodation to the environment, nowhere did Basin tribes build anything resembling permanent houses. Small bands on hunting and gathering rounds used temporary windbreaks of brush in favorable locations and small houses of brush tule or cattail. Winter housing, to be abandoned in the spring, was usually constructed of branches, bark slabs, brush, or tule and covered with earth. In the nineteenth century, the eastern bands of Shoshoni and some of the Northern Paiute bands adopted the tepee from the Plains. In the extreme West, at least one group of Washo borrowed the large semisubterranean house for ceremonial and recreational uses. Clothing in prewhite times was scanty to nonexistent. Men often went naked during the summer, and mature women's costumes were usually limited to a fiber apron or a hide kilt. In winter, robes of bearskin were highly prized and quite common after the introduction of firearms. More common and still being produced in the 1960s were rabbitskin blankets made by weaving strands of rabbit hide into a light and warm robe for wear and sleeping. Hard-soled hide moccasins were made and in earlier times fiber sandals. Pottery was generally not made, nor would it have been useful in this mobile setting. Basketry, on the other hand, was well developed, but nowhere in the Basin did the skill of weavers equal that of the tribes of central California. The flat *mano* and *metate* grinders were used to grind grass seeds, and in some areas mortars were used for crushing seeds and dried meat or fish. Mano and metate grinders were often carried by moving families. Mortars were usually fashioned in large boulders near a stream, at often-used camp sites. The bow and arrow was used for hunting and fighting. Clubs of wood or with stone heads were used as weapons or tools. A number of points, blades, and scrapers were made from flint and perhaps bone, and a number of different types of arrowheads were made for different purposes. Musical instruments were largely rattles of seedpods or deer hooves and a notched stick scraped with another stick. The skin drum penetrated the area from the East in historic times. Among those tribes that fished, harpoons and hooks were made of wood or bone. Fish weirs were also constructed in streams. Long nets and net bags were woven for rabbit drives. Perhaps the outstanding technical achievement was the antelope corral, made large enough to contain a number of antelope and usually having wings extending away from the entrance. If there was an aboriginal public architecture, this was it. It was also semipermanent in the sense that the corral would remain for years and need only periodic repair before use. Art was limited to rather simple and conventional designs woven on baskets; personal decoration for social and ceremonial occasions consisted of paint, feathers, and jewelry.

With a population density in some places of only one person for every forty square miles, perhaps nowhere exceeding ten per square mile, large groups of people seldom congregated for more than a few days. Thus, social organization seldom transcended that of a small band seldom exceeding thirty or forty people usually related by blood and by marriage. Kinship was reckoned bilaterally. Such groups usually were under the leadership of an older male, but sometimes a woman. The leader had little more than advisory and admonitory power. Membership in such groups was fluid, with individuals and families leaving at will or because immediate resources would no longer support the group. Similarly, groups might expand if they were located in areas of abundance. Each band tended to be identified with certain camping spots during the yearly gathering rounds. Not infrequently, one band leader would have a degree of ascendancy over others in the same general area—a position, if it can be called that, that became associated with the title "captain." Several bands might combine for antelope or rabbit drives or to defend themselves against enemies, but no one was obligated to join these group efforts. Even linguistic lines were blurred; there existed bands composed of Paiute and Washo and of Paiute and Shoshoni. Territory was weakly held but specific resources might be defended against strangers.

No recognized political roles existed in aboriginal times. Those men credited with the power to locate and charm antelope herds were accorded a degree of authority to direct both practical and ritual actions during an antelope drive. But this authority ended with the end of the drive. Similar but lesser authority seems to have been accorded those accredited with powers to attract and capture rabbits. Certain individuals in historic periods are credited with wide influence over large areas but had little real authority. One such was the Paiute Winamucca. Generally their prestige was derived from the assumption that they possessed some special but often undefined supernatural power. Even in the most provident areas, the demands for mobility prevented all but the most rudimentary development of village life. Nothing approaching tribal organization even to the limited degree it existed in California could be described in the Basin.

General patterns familiar among all western Indians can be discerned in the Basin religion, but like the other aspects of culture, these were weakly developed. A general belief in personal power or medicine was shared by all Basin people. However, power was seldom sought and nothing resembling the Vision Quest of the Great Plains can be found. Individuals obtained power by accident and often viewed its possession and use as dangerous. Among some groups, exercise of antelope power, for instance, was thought to cause a death within the group. Curers obtained their power directly from the spirits, who would cause a person to become sick if he or she rejected the gift. However, once a person had recognized being thus singled out, a period of apprenticeship under an experienced curer was required. "Prayers" were persons who were felt to have some ability to shape events through chanting or offering prayers. These persons often assumed some authority during gatherings in the fall before piñon collecting. The most important religious ceremony celebrated the appearance of a girl's first menstrual period.

The spirits of the dead were always seen to be vindictive and dangerous, and every effort was made to break ties between the deceased and his survivors. A dead person's property was buried or destroyed. If death occurred in a house or shelter, the structure was usually burned and the family left the area for at least a year. A belief in the afterlife perhaps existed, but informants have been so influenced by Christian thought that it is difficult to be certain.

From the Basin originated two major religious movements of American Indians. The GHOST DANCE of 1870 began near Pyramid Lake and was taken up by most of the tribes of California. It left permanent marks on California Indian religions in the form of dances and songs long after the nativistic aspect of the movement had been forgotten. Jack Wilson, or Wovoka, also of Pyramid Lake, the grandson of the founder of the 1870 cult, founded in 1889 a new nativistic movement also known as the Ghost Dance. This had little impact in the Basin but spread throughout the Plains tribes from Canada to Texas and culminated in the massacre at Wounded Knee in 1890.

Early relationships between Indians and white trappers, explorers (beginning about 1820), and the Mormon settlers of the Salt Lake region and in the extreme west of Nevada (beginning about 1840), were generally peaceful and without conflict. Even though grazing and farming tended to upset the gathering and hunting patterns of Basin peoples, the resources provided by the white settlements in the form of cast-off material goods, food, and wage labor for tasks similar to those of the aboriginal pattern tended to minimize potential struggles over resources. Too, the Indians could become prostitutes and beggars. In the north, however, both the Paiute and Shoshoni adopted a modified form of Plains life, based on horses. They used Plains clothing and ritual styles, the cone-shaped tepee, and other surface manifestations of Plains culture. These mounted Indians reshaped their social organization into what has been termed "mounted raiding bands," and for a brief period maintained themselves by a modified hunting and gathering round supplemented by raiding other Indians and whites and occasional forays into the Plains after buffalo. This new style was briefly successful, and the Paiute succeeded in soundly defeating a white volunteer force sent against them from the mining communities in Nevada. However, they quickly collapsed before federal troops under General George Crook in the late 1850s. The paraphernalia of Plains culture is still spreading among modern Basin peoples, partly because of its appeal to the Indians and partly because of its appeal to tourists.

Containment on reservations was never complete, and many Indians lived as wanderers, seasonal laborers, and squatters around white communities well into the twentieth century. Because these communities had less need for cheap wage labor, the Indians became something of an embarrassment and small colonies were set up in various parts of the Basin, particularly Nevada. Some Indians established claims on their holdings through homestead and squatters-rights laws. One group of Washo was deeded a forty-acre plot by a concerned white rancher named Dressler. An Indian agency and school was established in Carson City to oversee the affairs of these scattered peoples.

The degree of adjustment to modern times varied from complete detribalization and successful assimilation into white life to utter social and personal disorganization. In the 1920s and '30s the Peyote religion (see PEYOTISM) entered the region and made many converts.

Peyote congregations formed the basis for many new social arrangements.

Many of the Nevada peoples have demonstrated in recent years a growing ethnic awareness and a degree of militancy. One of the earliest of Indian newspapers of the recent period was published by a multitribal group in Nevada.

See Myron Angel, ed., *History of Nevada* (1958), a reproduction of the same title by Thompson and West in 1881; J. F. Downs, *Two Worlds of the Washo, An Indian Tribe of California and Nevada* (1966); A. L. Kroeber, *Handbook of California Indians*, Bureau of American Ethnology Bulletin No. 78 (1925), and *Cultural and Natural Areas of Native North America* (1948); and Julian H. Stewart, *Basin-Plateau Socio-Political Groups*, Bureau of American Ethnology Bulletin No. 120 (1938). —J. F. D.

Indians of the Northwest Coast. Occupying a narrow strip along the Pacific from southeastern Alaska through British Columbia into Washington and Oregon, the Northwest Coast Indians represent one of the most distinctive of New World cultures. Little is known of the early historical development of these Indian groups, and in the absence of archaeological evidence of antiquity it is believed that the characteristic culture of the area is of recent origin. Unlike nearly all other native culture areas of North America, the Northwest Coast owes little or nothing to the strong cultural influences radiating from Mexico. On the other hand, influences from eastern Asia *are* noticeable—particularly in matters of apparel and the use of armor made from rods and slats, like that of the medieval Japanese. But as a whole the area is unique, and anthropologists believe that it represents the most elaborate nonagricultural culture in the world.

There were many tribal and linguistic divisions in the Northwest Coast, all sharing basic cultural features. Regional variations in the development of some of these features, however, have led to a classification into three major geographic sectors. The classic Northwest culture reached its highest concentration and integration in the northern area, centering in what is now the mainland and islands of the Alaska panhandle. The major tribes and their locations were: the Tlingit, occupying most of the coast and islands from Yakutat Bay south to Prince of Wales Island; the Haida, almost entirely located on the Queen Charlotte Islands; and the Tsimshian, on the lower course of the Skeena River and neighboring coast and close islands. The central area was dominated by the Kwakiutl, on both sides of Queen Charlotte Sound and northern Vancouver Island; and the Nootka, on the rest of Vancouver Island and the north coast of the Olympic Peninsula. The southern area, from Puget Sound down along the coast and interior valleys, included among others the Quinault and Chinook of Washington, the Tillamook and Tolowa of Oregon, and perhaps marginally the Hupa, Karok, and Yurok of northwest California.

Cultural orientation and ethnic groupings were well-defined in the northern and central zones. The southern area, however, poses difficulties of classification. The sector, although culturally affiliated with the northern centers, in general suggests more of a marine variation of a predominately Plateau culture, and there is little of the vitality so characteristic of the Northwest

Coast in its classic form. This is partly because of geographic variation. Along the Alaska and British Columbia coasts, rugged mountains make access to the interior impossible, which led the aboriginal inhabitants of the region to turn almost entirely toward the sea and prevented contact with inland cultures. South of Puget Sound the coastal mountains are lower and the interior valleys easily accessible, which permitted a high degree of interaction and movement between seaboard and inland peoples.

The economy of the Northwest Coast depended almost entirely upon fish, mainly salmon, although every available kind of sea mammal, shellfish, seaweed, and bird was also used. Foods from the land were used to a lesser degree. There were no cultivated crops, but the abundance of marine foods was so great that subsistence was never in doubt, and the search for food did not require nearly as much time or effort as in the other American Indian cultures. The natural abudance was a primary factor in the kind of cultural development that occurred. Utilization of the salmon run as the main food resource led to generally permanent residences and settlements and a clearly defined group territory, even though men did go afield for other kinds of hunting. Harvesting salmon also meant that labor was seasonal, when total community effort for a short period of time would produce a longterm supply of food. So intensively was salmon hunted that the density of population was greater in the Northwest Coast than in any other part of pre-Columbian America north of Mexico. The knowledge of abundance, and therefore surplus, became translated into a concept of wealth, and this concept was the defining characteristic of all the societies in the area. The food pattern also allowed long periods of freedom from basic economic activity, and the human energies thus released moved the culture toward a high degree of complexity.

Wood, the most readily available raw material, was used to build large and solid plank houses, great dugout canoes, food vessels, watertight containers for storage or cooking, and in carving masks, religious objects, and the characteristic symbol of Northwest culture, the totem pole. Their sculpture and painting rivals the best of African and Indonesian achievements, and is paralleled in America only by the Maya and Inca. Clothing and other fabrics were made of the inner bark fiber of spruce and cypress, which was combined with mountain-goat wool to produce yarn for weaving blankets and robes. The central region tribes became great seafarers, paddling out of sight of land in their canoes to hunt deep-water whales.

Social and political organization was a function of kinship and was centered on the individual village rather than tribe or language group. Descent was matrilineal, and the individual gave his primary group loyalty to his mother's lineage. Lineages were hierarchically ranked according to wealth. The senior lineage chief in each village was automatically head chief, but political decisions were by consensus. Among some ethnic groupings in the Northwest, larger kinship units—clans and moieties—played varying roles in social organization. Marriage was uniformly exogamous regardless of the kinship unit in question. Warfare and feuding were important parts of the culture, and fights between lineages, villages, or tribes were continuous. Captives

The interior of a Chilkat chief's house; the Chilkat group belonged to the Tlingit tribe. (Culver Pictures)

taken in war were slaves, were the total chattel property of the captor, and lived or died at his sufferance. Children of slaves were also slaves, and freedom could only come by being ransomed. Slavery was a large part of Northwest Coast life, as indicated by the fact that twenty to thirty percent of the population at the time of white contact were slaves.

The most noted characteristic of Northwest culture was the development of a concept of status based on inheritable wealth and the almost complete ordering of society to correspond to that status. The relative status of individuals, lineages, or even whole villages was determined by the elaborateness of the *potlatch*, a word meaning "giveaway" in the Chinook trade jargon. Though each tribe or ethnic group had its characteristic version, there were common general features. The affair was highly ceremonial with strong religious connotations, and ritual formalities were observed in inviting guests, speechmaking, and the distribution of goods according to the rank of the recipient. The size of a potlatch reflected the rank of the donor and often included guests from a wide territory. Great feasts and lavish hospitality accompanied the ceremony, and the kin group of the donor helped to maximize the display, since the proceedings gave wide publicity to the status of the donor and his people. Nonfunctional prestige goods

were most commonly given away, although useful property was also given in quantities far beyond normal needs.

Potlatches were given by heirs to assert and validate their new status and for other important occasions like marriage, but even a baby's first haircut could serve as a justification. Among the Tlingit the potlatch centered around the mourning of a chief's death. For the Haida and Tsimshian it memorialized a chief and established his successor. The Kwakiutl and Nootka potlatched for these reasons, but more frequently to affirm and reaffirm social rank. They gave face-saving potlatches to erase lapses in dignity, like falling out of a canoe, and competitive potlatches, where rivals for social station vied for status by destroying property till only one had any left. Preparation for a major potlatch took several years, and it was the most absorbing institution of Northwest culture—both for the participants and for white observers.

Because of the unattractiveness of their territory for white settlements, most of the Northwest Coast Indians escaped being evicted from their homelands and still hold traditional locations. Since their way of life was marine-oriented, the important contacts of the Indians were not with land-hungry settlers, but with the maritime elements of white expansion. The Russians, who began to hunt sea otter and coastal fur-bearing mammals in the middle of the eighteenth century, practiced large-scale Indian slavery for labor, with the result that conflict was bitter from the beginning. In 1802, three years after the Russian American Company founded Sitka, Alaska, the local Indians rose and destroyed it, only to be destroyed themselves when the Russians returned in force two years later. Frequent small-scale outbreaks continued throughout the period of Russian control of Alaska, but the fragmented and local political organization of Northwest culture made effective resistance impossible. A large population reduction from smallpox occurred in 1836-40, putting the Indians even more at the mercy of whites, and afterward they were drawn steadily into the role of laborers and low-return markets for Russian, British, and American traders.

Since the 1860s the Northwest Coast Indians have experienced the same quota of disease, alcoholism, and economic deprivation that has accompanied white domination in the rest of the continent, but much of their cultural identity has survived. Potlatches were still being given in the 1960s and the salmon run was still the food source. Many Indians now work in canning factories.

There is no ethnohistorical account of the Northwest Coast Indians as a whole or of any particular tribe. The best introductory material, with good bibliographies for further study, can be found in Helen Codere, *Fighting With Property* (1950); P. Drucker, *Indians of the Northwest Coast* (1955); and E. H. Spicer, ed., *Perspectives in American Indian Culture Change* (1961).—P. R. M.

Indian Territory. See OKLAHOMA.

Indian wars. *1789-1865.* The end of the American Revolution did not settle problems between the United States and the Indians in the Old Northwest, and an aggressive Indian policy, which was not backed by an army of corresponding strength, hastened conflict (see INDIAN-WHITE RELATIONS: *United States Indian policy, 1775-1860*). When diplomacy failed and western pressure increased, General Josiah HARMAR was authorized to punish the Indians. The Harmar expedition of 1790, however, was an inauspicious beginning, for his army of 1,453 men suffered a series of defeats. A second expedition of 1791 also failed. Governor Arthur ST. CLAIR started late and moved slowly, pausing to construct forts along his route. When he camped near the upper Wabash on November 3, he was unprepared for an attack. The Indians surprised the camp the following morning and put his ill-trained militia to flight, killing more than 600 and wounding 260 in one of the worst defeats ever suffered at the hands of the Indians. In 1794, after negotiations had again failed, General "Mad" Anthony WAYNE led a third expedition against the Indians. His victory at FALLEN TIMBERS on August 20 demonstrated the value of training, discipline, and a superior supply system. Although casualties were minimal, it was a major psychological victory, for the British refused to support the Indians. In JAY'S TREATY the British abandoned the Northwest posts, and in 1795 the Indians ceded most of present Ohio in the Treaty of GREENVILLE.

Wayne's victory was merely a palliative, for the desire of the government to clear Indian title to lands east of the Mississippi, along with the advance of white settlements, caused renewed tensions and contributed to the rise of the Shawnee TECUMSEH and his brother TENSKWATAWA. Indian discontent alarmed Governor William H. HARRISON of Indiana Territory, although his land purchases had antagonized the Indians. In November 1811, while Tecumseh was in the South seeking support from the FIVE CIVILIZED TRIBES, Harrison moved against the Prophet's village at TIPPECANOE. Harrison's victory at Tippecanoe resulted in heavy losses on both sides and insured widespread Indian support for the British during the WAR OF 1812. During that conflict the western Great Lakes fell to the British and Indians, although the death of Tecumseh at the battle of the THAMES on October 5, 1813, and the Treaty of GHENT placed the tribes of the Old Northwest at the mercy of the Americans. During the War of 1812, also, Andrew JACKSON broke Indian resistance in the South with his victory over the hostile Creek at HORSESHOE BEND in 1814.

The removal policy of the 1820s and 1830s brought the peaceful removal of most eastern tribes to the trans-Mississippi West, although there was a brief flurry in 1836 known as the Creek War. More unfortunate was the BLACK HAWK WAR of 1832, which was caused in part by treaty violations by settlers. Several skirmishes were fought; volunteer troops killed warriors under a white flag; and about 150 Indians were killed in the Bad Axe Massacre despite attempts by the Indians to surrender. Even more serious was the second SEMINOLE WAR (1835-42), in which the regular army suffered more than 1,400 deaths. About 10,000 regulars and 30,000 volunteers served in Florida during this period, and estimates of the cost of the war range from between $30 to $40 million.

During the 1850s the scene of Indian hostility shifted to the trans-Mississippi West. The Rogue River War, Yakima War (see YAKIMA INDIANS), and the campaign of 1858 crushed the Indians of the Oregon country. In the latter campaign, Lieutenant Colonel Edward J. Steptoe was defeated by portions of the Spokane, Coeur d'Alene, and Palouse Indians, but Colonel George Wright defeated them at the battles of Four Lakes and Spokane Plain, both in 1858. In the Southwest, however, the army was less successful. During the 1850s battles were also fought with most of the major tribes of the Great Plains, although the limitations of American power in the region dictated that conflict should be avoided. Fighting with the SIOUX INDIANS began in 1854 when Lieutenant John Grattan made an issue of a stray cow and caused the extermination of his thirty-man command (see the GRATTAN MASSACRE). The government retaliated by sending Colonel William S. HARNEY against the Sioux. Harney believed that negotiations must be preceded by a sound whipping, and he defeated the Brulé and Miniconjou at Ash Hollow in September 1855. Both whites and Indians were to blame for difficulties with the CHEYENNE INDIANS, which quickly escalated to warfare, and in 1857 Colonel Edwin "Bull" SUMNER attacked and defeated them on the Solomon River. Bitter hatred between Texans and COMANCHE INDIANS caused continued conflict on the southern Plains, and in 1858 and 1859 regulars led by Earl Van Dorn defeated the tribes. By 1860, therefore, the United States had engaged the major Plains tribes even though American power was not commensurate with such an aggressive posture.

Warfare in the West was renewed with the Sioux MINNESOTA UPRISING in Minnesota in August 1862. Although the fighting was of short duration, between 400 and 800 whites were killed; military posts and towns were attacked; and much of the frontier was abandoned. By the end of September the Sioux had been defeated, and eventually some were executed; the remainder were removed from the state. In the following year, under the direction of John POPE, generals Henry Hastings SIBLEY and Alfred SULLY, whose combined forces totaled nearly 4,000 men, attempted a pincer movement against the Sioux in eastern Dakota Territory, and while they won victories at Big Mound, Dead Buffalo Lake, Stoney Lake, and Whitestone Hill, the Sioux had not been chastised. General Sully with 2,200 men moved against the Sioux west of the Missouri River in 1864 and defeated a force he estimated at 6,000, but which the Sioux later claimed consisted of 1,600 warriors.

The brutal SAND CREEK MASSACRE of the Cheyenne on November 29, 1864, which was part of the CHEYENNE-ARAPAHO WAR, brought retaliatory raids that halted travel on the Platte route and caused the temporary abandonment of Julesburg, Colorado. However, the end of the Civil War released thousands of men for service on the Plains, and a large, coordinated campaign was planned to conquer the Sioux and Cheyenne. The POWDER RIVER INDIAN EXPEDITION against RED CLOUD failed, and although regulars replaced the volunteers in 1866, hostilities continued.

Military campaigns in the Southwest in 1862-64 were somewhat more successful. The United States inherited Indian hostility in 1846, and between 1846 and 1861 there were more than a dozen major offensives against the APACHE, NAVAHO, and UTE led by officers such as Colonel Alexander DONIPHAN (1846), Lieutenant Colonel John Washington (1849), Colonel Sumner (1851), Colonel Thomas Fauntleroy (1855), Colonel Benjamin BONNEVILLE (1857), and Colonel E. R. S. Canby (1860). Military campaigns and Indian Bureau diplomacy failed to bring peace, and when the California Volunteers arrived in New Mexico, General James Henry CARLETON sent them against the Apache and Navaho. By 1863 the Mescalero had been placed on a reservation in the Pecos valley, and during 1863 and 1864 Kit CARSON and others forced the bulk of the Navaho to surrender and accept a similar fate. Expeditions in the Gila country were less successful, although MANGAS COLORADAS was murdered by soldiers. Nor can Carson's 1864 campaign against the Comanche be considered a success, for he barely escaped defeat at the battle of Adobe Walls.

See Henry P. Beers, *The Western Military Frontier* (1935); Averam B. Bender, *The March of Empire* (1952); Francis Paul Prucha, *Sword of the Republic* (1969); and Robert Utley, *Frontiersmen in Blue* (1967), and *Frontier Regulars* (1973).—R. N. E.

1865-1891. The Indian wars of the post-Civil War period were episodic in nature, yet possessed unity as the military phase of the last stage of white investiture of the continent. Basically, the army's mission was to clear the way for settlement and transportation by forcing Indians onto or back onto reservations. As a continuation of the conquest that had begun before the Civil War, the wars between 1865 and 1891 are nonetheless distinctive in that most of the fighting resulted from efforts to clear the Great Plains, which had once been considered the permanent home of the American Indian. As a result, the army met the full force of the well-mounted, well-armed, warlike, and mobile Plains Indians. Moreover, the fighting was complicated by the fact that the Indians often received arms and ammunition for hunting from the Indian Bureau and then turned those better weapons against the army, whose weapons sometimes were inferior. The tradition-bound organization of the army, which was not suited to Indian warfare in the West, reduced the effectiveness of troop operations. However, the army had a happenstance ally in the buffalo hunter, who decimated the herds on which Plains Indian civilization was based, and, hence, hastened the conclusion of the Indian wars.

The regular army—reorganizing and readjusting after the Civil War—inherited a turbulent frontier when it replaced volunteers at western posts (see ARMY ON THE FRONTIER and FORTS). The war of 1864-65—waged by the Cheyenne and Arapaho against whites in, and transportation routes to, Colorado—came to a close in the fall of 1865, but Southern Plains Indians remained in an angry mood. In spite of treaty cessions of land, many considered the land to be their own, for individualistic Plains Indians did not consider themselves bound by decisions of tribal leaders. Although the Sioux had continued attacks on the Oregon Trail into 1865, the government decided in that year to maintain the BOZEMAN TRAIL and established forts for its protection in 1866. The Sioux kept up a steady pressure of attacks—resulting in the FETTERMAN MASSACRE (December 21, 1866) and the Wagon-Box Fight (August 2, 1867), among other engagements—and the army abandoned the area when a new treaty was concluded with the Sioux in 1868.

Overlooking its setback at the hands of the Sioux in 1866-68, the army recognized twelve major campaigns between 1865 and 1891 when, in 1905, it authorized the Indian campaign badge for any soldier who had participated in any of the following campaigns:

In southern Oregon and Idaho and northern parts of California and Nevada, 1865-68. Under the direction of Lieutenant Colonel George CROOK, companies and detachments ferreted out small bands of Snake and Paiute Indians who had disrupted transportation routes to the Idaho mining camps. Engagements were small and scattered, the major one being the battle of Infernal Caverns on the south fork of Pit River in California, September 26-27, 1867. When the campaign ended in August 1868, Crook reported that eight hundred Indians had surrendered.

Against Cheyenne, Arapaho, KIOWA, and Comanche in Kansas, Colorado, and Indian Territory, 1867-69. On the basis of rumors that the Cheyenne planned to attack in Kansas, the army sent an expedition commanded by Major General Winfield Scott Hancock onto the Kansas plains in 1867. The HANCOCK CAMPAIGN did little more than frighten the Indians into flight and stir up controversy.

Tribal leaders agreed in the Treaty of MEDICINE LODGE of 1867 to accept permanent lands within Indian Territory. But warriors refused to give up the Kansas hunting grounds and ravaged the Saline and Solomon valleys in the late summer of 1868. Small troop units fought scattered engagements in a defensive policy laid down by Major General Philip SHERIDAN, who knew that he did not have enough troops to hunt down free-roaming Plains Indians during the summer. Meantime, Sheridan planned a winter campaign that would catch the unsuspecting Indians in permanent winter camps and force them to move onto a new reservation at Fort Cobb. In November 1867, Sheridan took the field with three columns converging on what is now northwestern Oklahoma, from Fort Bascom, New Mexico, Fort Lyon, Colorado, and an advance base at Camp Supply in Indian Territory. On November 27, 1868, Lieutenant Colonel George Armstrong CUSTER commanded what was the major engagement of the campaign, the battle of the WASHITA. The Indians scattered, and the command moved to Fort Cobb and then to a new post that came later to be named Fort Sill. In operations extending into the summer of 1869 and ranging from Kansas to Texas, troops forced most of the four tribes onto the reservation, for the time being.

MODOC WAR, 1872-73. In resisting efforts to force them to return to the Klamath Reservation in southern Oregon, a small band of Modoc under CAPTAIN JACK retreated to the fastnesses of the Lava Beds in northern California. In January 1873 about fifty Modoc held off a force of about four hundred regulars and volunteers. The federal government then intervened, ordering peace talks rather than war. In the course of fitful peace negotiations, the Modoc treacherously attacked the peace commissioners on Good Friday, April 11, 1873. Mounting a retaliatory attack, troops drove the Modoc from the Lava Beds and hunted down small bands until they captured Captain Jack on June 1, 1873. Tried by a military commission at Fort Klamath for the murder of peace commissioners E. R. S. Canby and J. E. Thomas, Captain Jack and three others were hanged in October 1873; two others were sentenced to life imprisonment.

Against the Apache of Arizona, 1873. With the failure of government attempts to persuade all Arizona Apache to move onto a reservation, signified by the continued raiding of small bands, Crook—by then a colonel and commanding the Department of Arizona—mounted an offensive using many "buffalo soldiers" (see NEGROES ON THE FRONTIER). In operations extending from November 1872 until April 1873, he sent five columns to hunt down small bands in the Tonto Basin. The principal engagements, each small, occurred at Salt River Canyon and Turret Butte. Most Apache thereafter were on a reservation, but not yet permanently.

Against Kiowa, Comanche, and Cheyenne in Kansas, Colorado, Texas, Indian Territory, and New Mexico, 1874-75. The RED RIVER WAR destroyed the military power of the southern Plains Indians. After a major outbreak in 1874, the War and Interior departments agreed that all Indians not answering to regular roll calls at their agencies were to be considered hostile, that the army was to hunt down the hostiles and force them back to the reservations and there dismount and disarm them, and that leaders of the war parties were to be imprisoned. Resulting military operations extended from July 1874 to April 1875. The army sent six converging columns against western Indian Territory and the Texas panhandle, to which the Indians had fled. Troopers fought several engagements, the most impor-

tant being an attack by Colonel Ranald Slidell MACKEN-ZIE on a large village in PALO DURO CANYON. By constant attack and harassment, the army forced the hostiles to return to their agencies, where arms and mounts (but not all) were taken from them. A number of ringleaders were sent to Fort Marion, Florida, for imprisonment. The campaign ended on June 1, 1875, with the surrender of the Kwahadi Comanche under QUANAH PARKER.

Against Northern Cheyenne and Sioux, 1876-77. Similarly, this campaign destroyed the concentrated military power of the northern Plains Indians. In precipitate action, the government decided to clear the Wyoming-Montana and Black Hills regions of Sioux and Northern Cheyenne. In November 1875 the Indians were given until January 31, 1876, to move to reservations or be turned over to the army. Few complied. The Indians who flaunted the ultimatums were "irreconcilables," with CRAZY HORSE and SITTING BULL as their best-known leaders. Crook—by then a brigadier general and commanding the Department of the Platte —sent a column northward from Fort Fetterman, Wyoming, in March 1876, which attacked an Indian village on Powder River; most of the Indians fled.

Sheridan—commanding the Military Division of the Missouri from Chicago—ordered a three-prong advance, with troops taking the field in May and June and converging on the Big Horn-Yellowstone region. Crook moved north from Fort Fetterman; Brigadier General Alfred Howe TERRY moved west from Fort Abraham Lincoln, across the river from Bismarck; Colonel John Gibbon moved east from Montana posts and joined Terry. Indian agents had estimated that the hostile Indians included only about five hundred warriors, but the soldiers advanced toward what was perhaps in truth the largest concentration of northern Plains Indians ever known, with several thousand warriors ready to fight. Crook and Terry each had about one thousand troops.

The soldiers fought two major battles. Crook met Crazy Horse in the battle of the ROSEBUD on June 17, 1876, but both forces withdrew after several hours of fighting. Crook retired to a camp near present Sheridan, Wyoming, to await reinforcements. Meantime, Terry had advanced toward the same area, sending Custer and the Seventh Cavalry on a mission that resulted in the battle of the LITTLE BIG HORN on June 25. When reinforced, the two commands continued their advance in August, met and operated jointly for a brief time, and then separated to search for Indians. Crook made the wearing Horsemeat March from Heart River to the Black Hills, in the course of which his men attacked the village of AMERICAN HORSE at SLIM BUTTES. Crook terminated his campaign in the Black Hills in September, and Terry withdrew about the same time, also without positive military results.

Troops left at cantonments in Wyoming and Montana carried out a winter campaign against dispersed bands. Mackenzie broke up a Cheyenne village on the Powder River in November. Colonel Nelson A. MILES harried Sitting Bull and Crazy Horse until the former fled to Canada. Crazy Horse surrendered at Red Cloud Agency, Nebraska, in May 1877. The vanquished were dismounted and disarmed, and only a few small "outlaw" bands remained.

NEZ PERCE WAR, 1877. When the government

peremptorily ordered the nontreaty Nez Percé to move onto the Nez Percé reservation in Idaho, in June 1877, angry young braves forced war by killing several settlers in the Salmon River valley. Pursued by forces under Brigadier General Oliver Otis HOWARD and encountering other troops in Montana (see the battle of BIG HOLE), a band of 750 men, women, and children fled to join Sitting Bull in Canada. After a tortuous flight across the Lolo Pass, south to Yellowstone National Park, and north through Montana they were attacked by Miles in the Bear Paw Mountains, within thirty miles of the international boundary. CHIEF JOSEPH, their principal leader, surrendered on October 5. An entire community with all its remaining property had traveled more than one thousand seven hundred miles, battled a total of two thousand troops, and had won or escaped from all but the last of eighteen engagements.

Bannock War, 1878. A short-lived outbreak from June to September 1878 resulted in small-unit actions, extending from Oregon to Wyoming, that brought small groups of BANNOCK and other Indians under government control.

Against Northern Cheyenne, 1878 and 1879. Having been transferred against their will to the Cheyenne reservation in Indian Territory, a band of about three hundred under DULL KNIFE fled to their northern homeland in the fall of 1878, fighting off two army attempts to intercept them. One group, under LITTLE WOLF, split off and reached Montana, where they later enlisted as army scouts. Others, who had remained with Dull Knife, were virtually imprisoned at Fort Robinson, Nebraska, from which they escaped on the night of January 10, 1879. Most were killed, including women and children, in the ensuing pursuit.

Against Ute in Colorado and Utah, September 1879 to November 1880. En route to maintain order at the White River Agency of the Ute at present Meeker, Colorado, a force of about 150 army troops was pinned down from September 29 to October 6, 1879. Meantime, the Ute attacked the agency, killing agent Nathan Meeker and his white assistants. By the time the troops reached the agency, the government ordered peace negotiations, and the troops bivouacked there through the winter.

Against Apache in Arizona and New Mexico, 1885 and 1886. Grueling guerrilla warfare resulted in the final surrender of GERONIMO.

Against the Sioux in South Dakota, November 1890 to January 1891. The Indian wars came to an end with the WOUNDED KNEE MASSACRE, the most controversial of all Indian fights. The GHOST DANCE, and what it signified to the Sioux, caused the Pine Ridge agent to call for troops in November 1890. Sitting Bull, who had returned to the United States from Canada, was killed "resisting" arrest. On December 29 army troops, having intercepted Indians fleeing to the Bad Lands, demanded surrender of their arms, and fighting broke out. Other skirmishes occurred before the Sioux were returned to the reservation that winter.

All engagements between the army and Indians were not included within the army's list of major campaigns, such as Mackenzie's operations in West Texas in the early 1870s and the intermittent warfare against the Apache. Similarly, the Indians—conducting war against whites in general and not just those in blue—tangled

with Texas Rangers and civilians throughout the West.

An official army compilation showed 1,065 engagements between 1866 and 1891, but the record does not purport to be complete; it also includes some fights between civilians and Indians. Of 930 recorded fights between soldiers and Indians, 592 were fought by small units, and only 70 engagements involved five companies or more. (The Indian characteristically attacked only when he had superiority of numbers.) Fighting reached a peak in 1867-69, with the largest number of engagements, 140, occurring in 1868. Army casualties were 932 killed and 1,061 wounded between 1866 and 1891, but total Indian casualties are unknown. Estimates for individual engagements generally are unreliable.

The total cost of the Indian wars has not been calculated, but Secretary of War Robert T. Lincoln estimated that Indian campaigning cost $223,891,264 between 1872 and 1882.

The causes of the various outbreaks are embedded in a tangled skein of cultural conflict, mismanagement by the Indian Bureau, corrupt Indian agents and traders, vindictiveness, unrealistic policies ordered by easterners who did not understand the situation in the West, broken promises on both sides, white acquisitiveness, and other factors. (See INDIAN-WHITE RELATIONS: *United States Indian policy, 1860-present*.)

The extensive literature of the Indian wars will lead one into predominantly topical accounts, many of them antiquarian in approach. Among the better general surveys are Fairfax Downey, *Indian-Fighting Army* (1941); Oliver Knight, *Following the Indian Wars* (1960); Don Rickey, *Forty Miles a Day on Beans and Hay* (1963); and Paul I. Wellman, *Death on Horseback* (1947). Regional surveys include Ralph K. Andrist, *The Long Death: The Last Days of the Plains Indians* (1964); Alvin M. Josephy, *The Nez Percé Indians and the Opening of the Northwest* (1965); William H. Leckie, *The Military Conquest of the Southern Plains* (1963); Keith A. Murray, *The Modocs and Their War* (1958); W. S. Nye, *Carbine and Lance* (1937) and *Plains Indian Raiders* (1968); and Dan L. Thrapp, *Conquest of Apacheria* (1967).—O. K.

Indian-white relations. *British Indian policy, 1763-1775*. The British colonies in North America had long controlled their own relations with the Indians. They placed restrictions upon the fur trade and established licensing systems, but competition between colonies for the trade and the impossibility of adequate control along the extensive frontier resulted in ineffective regulation. Corruption and fraud in the trade caused Indian resentment and led to Indian outbreaks. Eventually steps were taken to give imperial direction to Indian policy. In 1755 Sir William JOHNSON, longtime friend of the Iroquois, was appointed superintendent of Indian affairs for the northern district, and in the following year Edmond ATKIN was given a similar post in the South, to be replaced in 1762 by John STUART. (The northern district embraced the tribes north of Maryland and the Ohio River, while the southern district covered the tribes south from there to Spanish Florida.) The superintendents were to have full charge of the political relations between the British and the Indians, and they exercised what control they could over the fur trade, but to a large extent the management of the trade still remained in colonial hands. Attempts were made, too, in the 1750s to ease the Indians' concern about their lands by restricting the purchase of Indian lands by private individuals. PONTIAC'S REBELLION in 1763, however, showed the inadequacy of these measures to prevent conflicts between the Indians and the whites. In the same year the treaty of AUGUSTA was made with southern tribes to prevent a duplication of the northern rebellion.

A new policy in Indian affairs was promulgated by the Proclamation of 1763, issued by George III on October 7 (see BRITISH ADMINISTRATIVE POLICY). The proclamation drew a line between the lands of the Indians and those of the whites, prohibited the colonies from surveying or granting lands beyond the line, and forbade private purchase of land from the Indians and any settlement in Indian country. The emergency line, specified as the crest of the Appalachians, was replaced by one surveyed and laid out in detail, and by 1768 a boundary line extended from Canada to Florida, determined by solemn agreements with the Indians in the treaties of FORT STANWIX (1768), HARD LABOR (1768), and LOCHABER (1770).

The confusion in colonial trade regulations, however, was not removed by the Proclamation of 1763, and the Board of Trade in 1764 proposed a plan that would have set up an imperial department of Indian affairs independent both of the military commander in America and of the colonial governments. According to the plan, Indian trade was taken completely out of the hands of the colonies and vested in imperial superintendents. The fur trade was declared open to all British subjects, but clearly defined districts were set up and fixed points for the trade were designated. Licenses were required for trade and fines and imprisonment decreed for violators. No trader could sell or supply the Indians with rum or other liquor, with swan shot or rifled guns. Credit could not be extended to Indians beyond the value of fifty shillings, and new prohibitions were placed on the purchase of Indian lands.

This plan of 1764 served as a guide for the superintendents, but it was never formally adopted. The costs of administering the plan were too great, and in 1768 attempts at imperial control over Indian trade were abandoned, although the superintendents were retained. The important matter of regulating the fur trade thus reverted to the very governments that had been so ineffective before. The results were what might have been expected. The boundary line alone did not restrict the settlers, and failures among the colonies to enact necessary legislation to control the fur trade caused restlessness among the Indians. The problem was too intricate for the colonists to handle without some closer union than then existed.

The continual encroachment on Indian lands and the failure of the colonies to agree on general trade regulations led to intolerable conditions in the West. One last attempt, therefore, was made to provide unified control. By the Quebec Act of 1774 the western areas were placed under the governor of Quebec. Although the freedom of the fur trade for all His Majesty's subjects was again enunciated, the need for fixed times and places for trade, for tariffs for goods and furs, and for prohibition of the sale of liquor was realized. The governor received a copy of the Plan of 1764 to serve as his guide in drawing up necessary rules. This return to the earlier plan for imperializing the West came too late.

The American Revolution and ensuing independence ended British responsibility for the trans-Appalachian West, and the new United States government was forced to take up the problems that had not been solved by Great Britain.

An excellent recent account of British Indian policy appears in Jack M. Sosin, *Whitehall and the Wilderness* (1961). Sosin's book criticizes, but does not entirely supersede, Clarence W. Alvord, *The Mississippi Valley in British Politics*, 2 vols. (1917). John Alden, *John Stuart and the Southern Colonial Frontier* (1944), treats of Indian affairs in detail. Less useful is Helen L. Shaw, *British Administration of the Southern Indians* (1931).—F. P. P.

United States Indian policy, 1775-1860. During the American Revolution the Indians became the pawns in the military game between the rebelling colonies and the mother country. The British had the better position and in large measure retained the allegiance of the Indians. Superintendent John Stuart in the South and numerous British agents in the North made use of their authority and influence with the Indians to prevent them from following the colonists in opposition to the king.

Individual colonies sent commissioners to the Indians, but the Indian problem of the united colonies could not be handled adequately by disparate provincial practices; furthermore, settlers lusting after land took treaty-making privileges upon themselves as in the Treaty of SYCAMORE SHOALS (1775). On July 12, 1775, the Continental Congress inaugurated a federal Indian policy. Three departments were established and special commissioners appointed for each. The commissioners were to treat with the Indians "in the name, and on behalf of the united colonies"; they were to work to preserve peace and friendship with the Indians and "to prevent their taking any part in the present commotions." That Benjamin Franklin, Patrick Henry, and James Wilson, the able delegate from Pennsylvania, were appointed commissioners for the middle department is an indication of the importance attached to the matter.

The British imperial experiment in the unified management of the Indians had made its mark on Congress. Although there was some opposition to central control of Indian affairs, especially on the part of South Carolina, the Articles of Confederation declared: "The United States in Congress assembled shall also have the sole and exclusive right and power of . . . regulating the trade and managing all affairs with the Indians, not members of any of the States, provided that the legislative right of any State within its own limits be not infringed or violated." The concept of a boundary line between Indian lands and those of the whites, initiated by the Proclamation of 1763, was continued. Indian country was that territory lying beyond the boundary lines and forbidden to settlers and to unlicensed traders; it was also the area over which federal authority extended. Congress, however, had to reassert its ascendency and unique authority in regard to Indian affairs in the face of action by the separate states that controvened that authority.

The Indians were not a party to the Treaty of Paris (1783) and many who had been allies of the British remained hostile. A policy for dealing with them was established in 1783 and 1784. A new boundary line was to be drawn, which would provide lands as bounties for revolutionary soldiers. The Indians (considered to share the defeat of Great Britain) would be granted peace only if they agreed to the boundaries. Treaties were negotiated with the northern Indians at FORT STANWIX (1784), Fort McIntosh (1785), and Fort Finney (1786), in which the commissioners dictated the boundary lines and offered no compensation for ceded lands. The Indians objected to this high-handed arrangement, for they refused to be treated as conquered peoples. Furthermore, although the lands west of the boundary lines were guaranteed to the Indians and the United States promised to restrict the encroachment of the whites, white aggressions continued to cause great trouble. The government seemed powerless to hold back the onslaughts of advancing whites, and by 1786 the northwest Indians, out of disgust with the whole policy of the United States, were ready to repudiate all the arrangements made with them since the close of the war. Treating with the Indians on the basis of the right of conquest then gave way to a new policy of paying for ceded lands, and in 1789 treaties at Fort Harmar paid for the lands given up by the northern Indians in the earlier treaties.

In the South the difficulties were even greater because of the tenacity with which the Indians held on to their lands, the mounting pressure of the white settlers on the lands, the history of the hostility of the tribes against the whites, and the serious interference by state officials in the federal government's handling of Indian affairs. In 1785 and 1786, however, treaties were concluded at Hopewell, South Carolina, with the Cherokee, Choctaw, and Chickasaw, which fixed boundaries for the Indian country.

Because it was imperative for the new nation that the Indians remain at peace, the government had to promote a policy of justice toward the Indians and protect their rights and property against unscrupulous traders and avaricious settlers. For this purpose Congress on August 7, 1786, enacted the Ordinance for the Regulation of Indian Affairs. It reasserted again the exclusive right of Congress to deal with the Indians and established a southern and a northern department with a superintendent responsible to the secretary of war in charge of each. Trade was restricted to United States citizens and licenses were required to enter Indian country. But neither this ordinance nor the Northwest Ordinance of 1787, which included a fine statement about the protection of Indian rights, was effective in restraining white encroachment on Indian lands.

The Constitutional Convention had little discussion on Indian matters, but the Constitution gave Congress the power to regulate commerce "with the Indian tribes." Through this brief statement, together with the treaty-making power, Congress exercised plenary power in dealing with Indian tribes.

Beginning in 1790 Congress enacted a series of laws "to regulate trade and intercourse with the Indian tribes," which were periodically renewed and augmented. Continuing the pattern set in the Ordinance of 1786 and earlier colonial legislation, the law of 1790 provided for the licensing of traders and established penalties for trading without a license; it declared invalid the purchase of land from the Indians except through treaty with the United States; and it made provisions to punish crimes committed by whites against Indians in Indian country. The law of 1796 specified in detail the line between the whites and the Indians, the first designation of Indian country in a statute law, and it strengthened the provision restricting whites in Indian lands. In 1802 a still stronger law was enacted, which stayed in effect until 1834, when it was replaced by a new codification of legislation governing Indian relations. The enforcement of these laws was entrusted to the territorial governors, who were *ex officio* superintendents of Indian affairs, and to Indian agents appointed for the various tribes. Force to back up the agents was supplied by the regular army troops on the frontier.

It was the hope of President Washington and his secretary of war, Henry Knox, who were the first architects of this policy, that the treaties and the intercourse laws would insure peace. Such was not the case. The Treaty of NEW YORK did not bring peace to the Creek frontier. The Northwest Indians, determined to make the Ohio River the northern boundary of the whites and aroused by white settlers moving onto their lands, would not be pacified. The pressures for war became too strong to resist, as reports of Indian incursions and atrocities poured in from the West, and the War Department authorized campaigns against the tribes (see ARMY ON THE FRONTIER; and INDIAN WARS: *1789-1865*). The expeditions of General Josiah HARMAR in 1790 and of General Arthur ST. CLAIR in 1791 were defeated by the Indians, whose victories emboldened them in their resistance to American advance. In 1794, however, General Anthony Wayne's defeat of the Indians at the battle of FALLEN TIMBERS crushed the Indian will to resist, for the British failed to succor the Indians, whom they had encouraged in their hostility. In the Treaty of GREENVILLE (1795) that followed, the Indians ceded much of Ohio and a portion of Indiana. But within a dozen years the old tensions had returned. British agents again encouraged the Indians to resist American advance, and the appearance of the Shawnee leaders TECUMSEH and his brother TENSKWATAWA, who preached an Indian confederation to protect their lands, led to new conflicts. Although the Indians were defeated by troops under William Henry Harrison at the battle of TIPPECANOE (1811), hostility continued, and white-Indian conflicts on the frontier merged into the WAR OF 1812.

In the South aggressions by white settlers into Indian lands caused comparable conflicts in Georgia and Tennessee with the Creek and Cherokee, although protection of the white settlements rested upon militia rather than regular army troops.

In an attempt to remove evils resulting from unscrupulous private traders and to gain the friendship of the Indians, the federal government in 1795 entered the Indian trade itself, with a series of government trading houses known as factories. After some initial success, the factory system (see FUR TRADE) was attacked by private traders, and in 1822 Congress abolished it.

The federal government also adopted positive measures for civilizing the Indians, for it was generally believed that the Indians could be educated to white ways and thus assimilated into white society. It was hoped that the Indians would realize the advantages of private property and of agriculture over the chase. Livestock, agricultural implements, spinning wheels, and looms were given to the Indians, and teachers were supplied to instruct them in their use. In 1819 Congress provided a Civilization Fund, money from which was used to encourage missionary groups to set up schools for the Indians, and considerable success was attained, especially among the southern tribes.

There had been a continuing process of extinguishing Indian land titles in the West to satisfy the land hunger of westward-moving pioneers. In treaty after treaty, negotiated by special commissioners of the United States with chiefs of the various tribes, the Indians had parted with parcels of land, getting in return annuities of goods or money. Much of the Old Northwest was thus cleared of Indian title and opened to the whites. But in the South, where the Cherokee, Creek, Choctaw, and Chickasaw held vast areas in Georgia, Alabama, and Mississippi, the tribes resisted alienation of their lands. Some of the members of these tribes had advanced rapidly in the white man's way of life with well-developed farms and formal political organization, and they were an obstacle to the expanding whites. Georgia, especially, demanded that the United States government remove the Cherokee from the state.

The 1820s thus brought a crisis in Indian affairs, for the states were calling for removal of the Indians and the Indians refused to migrate. The federal government adopted a policy, first proposed by Thomas Jefferson in 1803, of inducing the Indians to exchange their lands in the East for lands west of the Mississippi. President James Monroe formally proposed the policy to Congress in a special message of January 27, 1825, and it was accepted by John Quincy Adams, his successor. Monroe emphasized the advantages to the Indians in moving to an area where there would be no state jurisdictional claims and where they could establish a government to protect their interests.

President Andrew Jackson, who believed that the Indian tribes should not be treated as independent nations but should be subject to federal regulation, strongly endorsed the removal policy. On May 30, 1830, after bitter debate in Congress and in the public press, Congress passed the Removal Bill, which authorized the president to negotiate removal treaties with the tribes. Jackson and his supporters looked upon removal as the only solution to the Indian problem and the only safety for the Indians, who would otherwise be destroyed by contact with the whites. Jackson urged liberal terms in the removal treaties as an inducement to Indian agreement. Removal costs were to be borne by the government and support would be provided for the Indians while they got settled in the West. Vociferous opposition to the policy came from missionary groups in New England and from others, who pointed to the ancient rights of the Indians to their lands and to guarantees made to the Indians in previous treaties.

Jackson's administration was able to negotiate removal treaties with the southern FIVE CIVILIZED TRIBES, although in some cases only by disregarding the large antiremoval elements among the Indians. The Treaty of DANCING RABBIT CREEK with the Choctaw (1830), treaties with the Chickasaw and Creek (1832), and the Treaty of NEW ECHOTA with the Cherokee (1835) allotted strips of land west of Arkansas (in the present state of Oklahoma) to these tribes in exchange for their holdings east of the Mississippi. Opposition to removal among the Creek, however, led to the brief Creek War

(1836), and many of the Cherokee had to be rounded up by military troops to be sent to the West. Treaties with the Seminole in Florida in 1832 and 1833 were resisted by the Indians, leading to the long second SEMINOLE WAR (1835-42), in which troops eventually killed or removed to Oklahoma the bulk of the Seminole.

Meanwhile the smaller northern tribes, too, were relocated in the West, some at first in Iowa and Minnesota and then in the region west of Missouri or Arkansas. These Indians migrated with little resistance except for a band of Sauk and Fox led by BLACK HAWK, who insisted on returning to lands in Illinois that they had signed away in 1804. In the BLACK HAWK WAR (1832) the Indians were crushed. Defense plans for the western frontier were drawn up in an attempt to protect the emigrating Indians from white encroachment and from the warlike Indians of the Great Plains, and military FORTS were established in western Indian country. No government such as that envisaged by President Monroe was established, however.

The region west of Arkansas and Missouri, which had been considered a permanent home for the Indians, was not long immune to white probings. The Santa Fe trade, which had begun in 1821, cut a deep channel through Indian country, and military escorts were periodically provided for the wagon trains to protect them from Indian attack. And in the 1840s and 1850s migrations to Oregon and California were the beginning of serious attrition on Indian lands, which was met by occasional Indian warfare.

The addition of Texas, Oregon, New Mexico, and California to the United States greatly increased the Indian problem. These new, vast regions gained protection from new military posts set up to control or subdue hostile tribes who objected to the swarms of migrants, settlers, and miners passing through or taking over their lands. The Treaty of FORT LARAMIE (1851) was supposed to bring peace to the Plains. Outbreaks in KANSAS, OREGON, and WASHINGTON in the 1850s presaged the warfare of the post-Civil War period. In California, where the simple Indian societies were no match for aggressive miners, the tribes were quickly decimated and the remnants forced onto reservations, which set a pattern for later Indian policy (see INDIANS OF CALIFORNIA).

Indian relations, nevertheless, were not entirely a military matter, and in 1849 the responsibility for Indian affairs was removed from the War Department, where it had resided since the founding of the nation, and given to the newly created Department of the Interior (see INDIAN AFFAIRS, BUREAU OF; and INTERIOR, DEPARTMENT OF THE). Controversy arose over whether soldiers or civilians were best suited to manage Indian affairs, and competition between the two departments added a new complication to Indian policy that was never quite satisfactorily resolved.

Two scholarly, detailed studies of early United States Indian policy are Reginald Horsman, *Expansion and American Indian Policy, 1783-1812* (1967); and Francis Paul Prucha, *American Indian Policy in the Formative Years: The Indian Trade and Intercourse Acts, 1790-1834* (1962). A more extensive study is George D. Harmon, *Sixty Years of Indian Affairs: Political, Economic, and Diplomatic, 1789-1850* (1941), but its topical arrangement makes it difficult to follow the development of Indian policy. William T. Hagan, *American Indians* (1961), is a very brief but competent survey. The frontier setting in which Indian-white relations occurred can be seen in two books dealing with the military frontier: Francis Paul Prucha, *The Sword of the Republic: The United States Army on the Frontier, 1783-1846* (1969); and Robert M. Utley, *Frontiersmen in Blue: The United States Army and the Indian, 1848-1865* (1967).—F. P. P.

United States Indian policy, 1860-present. For the American Indian, the century since 1860 has been one of rapid, bewildering, and painful change. Not that the Indians' experience was uniform. In 1860 the Comanche were still nomadic buffalo hunters at the height of their power, while the former mission Indians of California were dejected and decimated. In virtually every instance, however, the Indian was reacting to the white population. If any organization can be imposed on this history, it must be in terms of the Indian response to white occupation of the West and to white attempts to convert the Indian into the white man's image of himself. From this perspective certain arbitrary chronological periods can be employed to tell the story of Indian-white relations: subjugation of the warriors, 1860-90 (see INDIAN WARS: *1865-1891*); imposition of another culture, 1860-1920; new policies, 1920 to the present.

What happened to the Indians between 1860 and 1890 is largely the story of American occupation of the West in that period. Enough settlers entered the region for ten states to be created, and in 1890 the Census Bureau could document the end of the frontier era. During this period precious metals lured prospectors into every nook and cranny in the West, the buffalo were destroyed, the cattleman and the small farmer arrived, and five transcontinental railroads were constructed.

Standing before a flood of whites backed by the weight of the United States Army, the Indian tribes were powerless. Wars would take place, but no one doubted the outcome. The Indians had no more chance than any other people faced by a more numerous, better organized population equipped with a superior technology. For the Plains Indians, the destruction of the BUFFALO only removed the temptation to escape the reservations on which they had been incarcerated.

Between 1860 and 1886, not a year passed without some clash between Indians and the United States Army. The following is an attempt to summarize only the most important campaigns.

In 1862 some elements of the Santee SIOUX INDIANS, presumed well along the road to civilization, vented their anger and frustration over inept agency administrators and grasping traders and settlers by attacking settlers in southern Minnesota. Perhaps seven hundred whites lost their lives before the MINNESOTA UPRISING was quelled in a campaign led by John POPE. Thirty-eight Sioux were the victims of drumhead courts and were hanged simultaneously from a huge scaffold on December 26, 1862. The surviving Sioux, innocent as well as guilty, were forced from Minnesota, their home for several generations.

When the United States acquired New Mexico in 1848 it also acquired the responsibility for protecting the Mexican and Pueblo communities from the ravages of the NAVAHO INDIANS. In the first fifteen years numerous councils and punitive expeditions failed to eliminate the Navaho threat. In 1863 and 1864, however, the Navaho were finally subdued in a well-organized and persistent campaign of James H. CARLETON, featuring the invasion of the Navaho heartland, Canyon de Chelly, by a column led by Colonel Kit CARSON. More than six thousand Navaho were relocated under Carleton's military control at Bosque Redondo on the Pecos River, where they remained until 1868. When an ambitious program of forced civilization foundered in the sands of Bosque Redondo, the Navaho were returned to civilian control and repatriated to a reservation in their old haunts, where they demonstrated remarkable resilience and recuperative powers in the next century.

Efforts to locate the Plains Indians on reservations produced their share of violence, as in the CHEYENNE-ARAPAHO WAR of 1864-65. By a treaty signed at Fort Wise in 1861 the Southern CHEYENNE AND ARAPAHO INDIANS had agreed to settle on a reservation. But the next three years saw them and the other tribes of the Southern Plains charged with many robberies and murders. On November 29, 1864, Colorado troops under Colonel John M. CHIVINGTON perpetrated the infamous SAND CREEK MASSACRE, a brutal attack on Chief Black Kettle's Cheyenne, who had presumed they were camping under a flag of truce. The attack enraged the Cheyenne, COMANCHE, and KIOWA, and the tribesmen retaliated with another wave of attacks on wagon trains, stagecoach lines, and isolated ranches before a lull fell over the Southern Plains.

To the east of the Southern Plains, the Five Civilized Tribes were being drawn into the Civil War. Because of their southern origins and slaveholding traditions, their natural sympathies were with the Confederacy, although there were pro-Union elements in each tribe. With initial Confederate successes in the area, however, each of the tribes concluded a treaty with the Confederacy. Though most Indians were not actively engaged on either side, the war was a disaster for them. The always fragile tribal governments were torn by dissension and their territories were the prey of lawless elements, such as escaped convicts, murderers, and rapists. With the victory of the Union, the Five Civilized Tribes were further punished in a new round of treaties forced upon them. By these negotiations land was extorted from them to provide homes for tribes of Kansas, who were being evicted from their homelands.

The expansion of the mining frontier helped set the stage for the Sioux War of 1865-67. A flood of miners into the region had led to demands for government roads and to the survey in 1865 of the BOZEMAN TRAIL (Powder River Road). In 1865 the army campaigned against the Indians in the POWDER RIVER INDIAN EXPEDITION.) To further intimidate the Teton Sioux and Northern Cheyenne, through whose hunting grounds the trail would run, the army constructed in 1866 Fort Reno, FORT PHIL KEARNY, and Fort C. F. Smith. From the day construction began, the troops were under constant threat of attack, and numerous skirmishes were fought. The Indians under RED CLOUD enjoyed one signal success, the FETTERMAN MASSACRE, when they wiped out a detachment of eighty-one troops from Fort Phil Kearny on December 21, 1866. In another attack near the same fort, they were beaten off in the Wagon-Box Fight (August 2, 1867). The construction of a railroad to Salt Lake City provided an alternate route to the mining fields, and in 1868 troops were withdrawn from the Bozeman Trail and the Indians enjoyed one of their rare triumphs. However, the negotiations closing the Bozeman Trail also provided for the location of the Sioux on a large reservation in Dakota Territory, with only hunting rights in the area through which the trail had run.

To the south the incidence of difficulties between the whites and the Indians had increased to the point that the term war could be again employed. Despite the HANCOCK CAMPAIGN and new treaties (such as MEDICINE LODGE in 1867) providing for their location on reservations, most southern Plains Indians led by TALL BULL and ROMAN NOSE, still pursued their nomadic life, with all the opportunities it provided for friction with the whites. As the complaints of outraged whites mounted, three columns of troops were sent into the field in the summer of 1868, resulting in the Black Kettle War and the battle of BEECHER'S ISLAND. Cheyenne, Arapaho, Comanche, and Kiowa were the targets, but they eluded all but glancing blows until the battle of the WASHITA on November 27, 1868. Then a column under Colonel George A. Custer surprised Black Kettle's Cheyenne, who had gone into winter camp. They were the victims of a growing belief among certain army circles that winter campaigns, when the Indians were immobilized, were more fruitful than chasing the nomads during their hunting seasons. Even with the advantage of surprise, Custer barely eked out a victory, and the Cheyenne and their allies were only temporarily chastened.

While the southern Plains Indians frustrated efforts to make reservation inhabitants of them, farther west the Modoc were being driven to the point of resisting the same policy. Natives of southern Oregon, they had been coerced into ceding their land and settling on a reservation with a related tribe, the Klamath. One Modoc faction of fewer than a hundred warriors plus dependents, led by CAPTAIN JACK, fled the reservation for the lava beds along the California border. In the ensuing MODOC WAR, lasting from November 1872 to June 1873, troops suffered heavy casualties in dislodging the Modoc from this rough terrain, and General Edward Canby was killed when the Indians violated a flag of truce. For this latter action several Indians were court-martialed and Captain Jack and three others were hanged. The survivors of Jack's band were exiled to Oklahoma.

While the Modoc were being sent to the Quapaw Reservation in northeastern Oklahoma, complications at two agencies, the Kiowa-Comanche at Fort Sill and the Cheyenne-Arapaho at Darlington, were about to give rise to the RED RIVER WAR, in 1874-75. Treaties in 1867 had provided for the location of these tribes on reservations. But with the absence of any real political structure capable of controlling all the members of a tribe, some bands, particularly among the Comanche, either never set foot on the reservation or came in only to collect annuities. Other Indians, driven to desperation by the buffalo-hide hunters and the prospect of a dreary reservation existence, slipped away to join them. When the number of incidents increased sharply in the early summer of 1874, the army sought and received permission to enter reservations to punish the guilty, and the war was under way. Again columns crisscrossed the Plains, seldom able to do more than force a band to flee so rapidly that it lost camp equipment or a portion

of its horse herd. But the relentless pursuit, which came to a climax at the battle of PALO DURO CANYON, and the decline in the buffalo population took their toll, and in the spring of 1875 the last bands reported to their agencies to be disarmed and dismounted. Seventy-five warriors from the most recalcitrant bands were shipped to prison in Florida. The Red River War had ended, and with it, major military operations on the Southern Plains.

To the north the scene was being set for the final clash of the army and the Plains Sioux and Cheyenne. Again, the tribes had presumably been located on reservations, but bands were continually fleeing to the Plains. An influx of miners, lured by strikes in the Black Hills, provided the final ingredient for the Sioux and Cheyenne war, 1876-77. The failure or inability of bands to respond to an order to report to the agency in the dead of winter, at the risk of being stigmatized as hostile for noncompliance, subsequently was used to justify columns of troops combing the area. On June 17, 1876, the army and Cheyenne and Sioux clashed in the battle of the ROSEBUD. Then, on June 25, a column commanded by Colonel George Armstrong CUSTER located a large Sioux encampment, including the bands of such famous chiefs as GALL, CRAZY HORSE, and SITTING BULL. The luck that had ridden with Custer in a similar attack at the battle of the Washita deserted him now, at the battle of the LITTLE BIG HORN. Within a few hours Custer and nearly half of his command were dead. This was the principal engagement of the war, although some fighting occurred into the spring of 1877. Sitting Bull and Gall escaped to Canada, Crazy Horse died in a scuffle with a guard after being captured, and AMERICAN HORSE died in the battle of SLIM BUTTES. An uneasy peace settled over the great Sioux reservation. The Cheyenne, led by LITTLE WOLF and DULL KNIFE, attempted to return north to their homeland and thus alarmed the army and white population again.

The NEZ PERCE WAR (1877) fits the pattern already encountered. The NEZ PERCE INDIANS had been forced to settle on an Idaho reservation, but they yearned to return to their native Oregon. An onrush of settlers further antagonized them, clashes occurred, and troops moved in. Although at peace for many years, these Indians, under the leadership of Looking Glass, White Bird, Toohoolhoolzate, and CHIEF JOSEPH, were able to carry out a retreat of almost two thousand miles before being overtaken and defeated only thirty miles from the Canadian border.

The Ute War (1879) also fits the pattern. A people who lived by the hunt, the UTE INDIANS had signed the usual treaty. One group was located on a reservation administered by N. C. Meeker, an agent noted for his arbitrary ways. When he called in troops to back his commands, the Ute ambushed the detachment and then attacked the agency, killing Meeker and others. Fresh troops soon forced the Indians to capitulate, and several Ute charged with raping white women were sent to a penitentiary.

South of the Ute, several Apache bands were the last Indians to hold out against American power. For more than twenty years the APACHE INDIANS resisted efforts to locate them on reservations. Seldom could the bands committing depredations be identified, and even the number of hostiles was consistently exaggerated. Rarely did these bands include more than fifty warriors, and Geronimo had only twenty during the last phase of the Apache wars. Relying on speed and deception, and ranging deep into Mexico, the Apache terrorized Mexican and American settlers and outwitted and outfought the soldiers on numerous occasions. But continual warfare took its toll. COCHISE was forced to surrender after twelve years of resistance and died in 1874. VICTORIO was killed by Mexican troops in 1881 after six years of frustrating the troops and punishing the whites. GERONIMO surrendered in 1886 to Nelson A. MILES after a decade of intermittent resistance. Apache scouts played a major role in his final defeat, typifying the fatal inability of the Apache, as with other Indians, to maintain a common front against the whites. It is doubtful if at any given time in the more than twenty years of Apache wars that a majority of the Apache were hostile.

The GHOST DANCE uprising (1890) was not a real Indian war. A blundering effort to disarm religion-intoxicated Indians did lead, however, to the WOUNDED KNEE MASSACRE on December 29, 1890. The slaughter thoroughly disillusioned any Indians still nursing hopes of successful resistance.

Wars were a product of the Indian policies pursued by the government during this era, but genocide was not an objective. After the fears of Spanish and British intervention in Indian affairs faded in the 1820s and 1830s, most Americans remote from the frontier applauded efforts to civilize the Indians and save them from the extinction that threatened. Because the cost of maintaining troops and installations in the West was mounting, and because of an increasing public revulsion, inspired by casualties of both white and Indian noncombatants in the Plains wars, Congress created a "peace commission" in July 1867.

The commission's chief work was two sets of treaties (Medicine Lodge in 1867 and Fort Laramie in 1868) designed to force the Plains Indians onto reservations, a strategy favored by "hard-liners" William T. SHERMAN and Philip H. SHERIDAN. It also persuaded Congress to drop the treaty as an instrument for negotiating with Indian tribes, replacing it with agreements that required the approval of both houses of Congress.

Under a new president, Ulysses S. Grant, the eastern humanitarians made a major innovation, the Quaker or PEACE POLICY. Originating in conversations between Grant and Quaker leaders, the plan provided that Quakers designate nominees for superintendencies of two Indian agencies and that other religious groups assume such responsibility elsewhere. Unfortunately, the practice failed to live up to expectations. There were quarrels about which churches should nominate which agents, and the technique failed to uncover enough people who not only meant well but had the rare combination of qualities necessary for success in this very difficult administrative position. By the beginning of William Henry Harrison's administration the glamour had worn off that experiment, and few protests were heard when the selection of agents was returned to the politicians.

Another innovation, the Board of Indian Commissioners, lasted until 1934. In 1869 Congress created the board after some prominent Quakers and Episcopalians proposed a nonpartisan group to oversee disbursement of Indian funds. Ten distinguished philanthropists serving without pay constituted the Board of Indian Commissioners. They had the power to investigate and to recommend, but after a few years they carried little weight against the entrenched bureaucracy of the Indian Service.

For the Indian, the reservation system seemed productive of little good, and when the agent was incompetent or dishonest it could be a disaster. The scandal of corrupt agents had helped initiate the peace policy and it also had outlived it. Agents did everything from hiring incompetent relatives as teachers and clerks to padding payrolls and taking bribes from businessmen. The financial opportunities were so great and the chances of conviction so slim that many succumbed to temptation. And it was the Indian who suffered: his rations fell to below subsistence levels, his money purchased shoddy goods, his land was mined and farmed and grazed by those whites with the right connections. It is not surprising that the Indians so frequently fled reservations when some chance remained of returning to their old, free life.

The tribulations of the tribesmen produced an Indian rights movement as well as the peace policy and the Board of Indian Commissioners. Some of the energies that had gone into the abolition movement surfaced in the 1880s in new organizations. Herbert WELSH and Henry Pancoast were leading figures in the INDIAN RIGHTS ASSOCIATION founded in 1882, and Alfred Meacham and T. A. Bland were prime organizers of the National Indian Association in 1885.

To coordinate the efforts of the friends of the Indian, Albert K. Smiley began in 1883 the practice of inviting them to his Lake Mohonk resort in New York for conferences. These took place for thirty years and helped develop among the reform groups a consensus on Indian policies. For the average reformer the same formula for civilization that had been arrived at early in the nineteenth century seemed efficacious: agriculture, private property, education, and Christianity, applied in a segregated reservation environment until the Indian was ready for absorption by the greater society. An exception was the National Indian Defense Association, which persisted in seeing merit in aboriginal cultures.

Farming was then the occupation of most Americans, and scholars equated hunting with barbarism, agriculture with civilization. Thus, only by giving up their wandering and resorting to tilling the soil could the Indians hope to survive. Likewise, private property was an essential to progress. A number of treaties had already incorporated provisions for land allotment when it was enshrined as public policy in the DAWES SEVERALTY ACT of 1887. Although the Indians could not see its virtues, few whites challenged the wisdom of this policy. To the eastern humanitarian, communal ownership of property had deprived Indian society of the self-interest that was the root of individual advancement. Westerners for once were in agreement with them, because after the standard 160-acre allotment to the Indians a substantial portion of the reservation could be opened to white occupancy. Of the approximately 138 million acres in Indian hands in 1887, about two-thirds, including most of the best land, had passed into white possession by 1934.

Education and Christianity still went hand in hand.

That the Indians could be civilized and remain pagan was unthinkable. Government policy had always been to support mission activity, and the peace policy had made unprecedented use of church groups. A Christian education was a natural corollary to missionary operations, and most reservations boasted at least one mission school. Until the late 1890s these were subsidized by the tribes by rent-free tracts and by the government by payment of tuition for Indian pupils. Reservation boarding schools were preferred to day schools because they separated the child as far as possible from his home environment. This led in turn to the off-reservation boarding school, which might put several hundred miles between the child and the corrupting influences of home and tribe. The CARLISLE INDIAN SCHOOL founded by Richard Henry PRATT carried this approach to its logical extreme. Selected students were placed with white families near Carlisle, Pennsylvania, for total submersion in white society. But whether in Pennsylvania or on the reservations, the curricula varied little. The manual-labor school was still the model, and the object was to instruct the boy in farming and some of the trades, the girl in those skills that would make her a good housekeeper and farmer's wife, and both in the fundamentals of reading, writing, and arithmetic—all flavored with substantial doses of Christianity.

The one new element in the "civilization" formula was an experiment with Indian policemen and judges, one of the few successful policy innovations. In May 1878 Congress approved an amendment to the Indian appropriation bill, providing $30,000 to employ 480 Indian policemen on the several reservations. For some time agents such as John P. CLUM and George CROOK had been experimenting with the idea. It finally won Congress's approval, since the police could fill many needs. Interior Department officials endorsed the idea because it offered an alternative to calling upon soldiers to maintain order on reservations. Agents liked having police who could build bridges, act as truant officers, detect intruders and malcontents, apprehend criminals, and perform a multitude of other chores. The Indians themselves found this policy relatively palatable because many of the tribes had had soldier societies that performed quasi-police functions.

The appointment of Indian judges stemmed from the concern of Secretary of Interior Henry M. Teller with the persistence of certain practices such as the scalp dance and SUN DANCE. The Courts of Indian Offenses operated under guidelines established in April 1883, and not only discouraged those "heathenish" practices that alarmed Secretary Teller, but also provided a tribunal for minor criminals apprehended by the Indian police. Together, the courts and police forces contributed measurably to effective reservation administration. Their peak of activity came in the late 1890s, but within ten years most of them had ceased to function, because reservations were allotted and county and state authorities assumed the burden of law enforcement.

For most American Indians the old closed reservation ceased to exist early in the twentieth century. Proposed as a temporary training ground for a native population threatened by extinction, the reservation system's record was not good, and the deliberate efforts to eradicate tribal cultures had not succeeded. Concentrating the Indians had freed most of the country for white settlement, but it had done little for the Indian. The typical Indian emerged from the reservation period impoverished and ill-equipped to compete for a livelihood in a white society.

By the 1920s the bankruptcy of Indian policies, pursued with such optimism for half a century, was apparent. Although on June 2, 1924, Congress had given citizenship to all Indians, the act did not reflect the successful fulfillment of the civilization program. Rather it appeared that the program had crippled one way of life without replacing it with anything as satisfactory to the people involved.

As the trust period lapsed on the land allotments, many Indians disposed of the land to which they now had complete title and squandered the proceeds, which left them landless as well as penniless. A "New Policy" inaugurated by Commissioner Cato Sells, which was designed to end the government's guardianship of Indian land, only expedited the above process and aroused concern. Exposure of an effort by white ranchers to acquire land cheaply from gullible Pueblos led to the formation of the Committee of One Hundred·in 1923, which further publicized the plight of the Indians. Secretary of the Interior Herbert Work authorized a survey of the situation by a group headed by Dr. Lewis Meriam and financed by the Rockefeller Foundation. The chief contribution of the Meriam Report, appearing in 1928, was to document the need for change. It was particularly critical of allotment and of health services.

Herbert Hoover in 1929 appointed as commissioner and assistant commissioner of Indian affairs two friends of the Indian, Quakers Charles J. Rhoads and J. Henry Scattergood. Under their administration Indian education and health programs were improved markedly and a new look was taken at the allotment program. The depression, which hit shortly afterward, simply underlined the failure of the government's programs to turn the tribesmen into self-sustaining citizens.

The time was ripe for a new approach to Indian affairs when Franklin D. Roosevelt entered the White House. To head the Interior Department he chose Harold Ickes, who was well acquainted with Indian affairs, but his most significant appointment was John Collier as commissioner of Indian affairs. Collier had been a critic of the government's policies for many years and was a warm admirer of Indians and their culture.

The Indian New Deal that followed is best exemplified in the Wheeler-Howard (Indian Reorganization) Act of June 1934 (see John COLLIER). It stopped allotment and enabled tribes to purchase additional land. Loans were made available for tribal business ventures and civil service regulations were redrawn to give Indians preference in employment. Perhaps most important was a provision permitting tribes to draft constitutions that could then serve as a basis for self-government. It was a deep disappointment to Commissioner Collier that, although 172 tribes accepted it, 73 tribes including the most populous Navaho rejected the Wheeler-Howard Act. But all Indians benefited from a new attitude in Washington, which gradually worked its way through the bureaucracy. Indian cultures enjoyed a new respect and Indians were to be given a larger voice in their own affairs. On the reservations infant mortality was dropping, food and fiber production were increasing; and the Indian land base was expanding.

During Roosevelt's second term, the Indian New Deal suffered from the rising chorus of conservative protest. Not even the shift of interest to international affairs with the outbreak of World War II completely stilled the critics of John Collier. In 1943 a Senate committee echoed past policies by recommending the curtailment of federal Indian programs and the ultimate dissolution of the Bureau of Indian Affairs. In March 1945, Collier resigned; he had achieved much, but not the revolution for which he had aimed.

In the post-World War II era of reaction, Indian programs seemed to be a politically safe place to retrench. "Termination," or "getting the government out of the Indian business," became the order of the day, as was made clear by House Concurrent Resolution 108, which Congress passed in 1953. The Wheeler-Howard Act was not repealed; it was gutted. Loan funds dried up. County and state governments were persuaded to assume a larger role in Indian health and education. A program was launched to subsidize relocation of reservation Indians to urban centers. In 1953 Congress enacted Public Law 280, which authorized the transfer —without consent of the Indians involved—of responsibility for law and order on reservations to state governments. Only a few thousand Indians, among them the Menomini and the Klamath, actually had their connections with the federal government dissolved, and the mixed results of these termination proceedings did not encourage further efforts along these lines.

But the urge to terminate had a curious by-product. In 1946 Congress created the Indian Claims Commission to settle tribal claims against the government so as to pave the way for dissolution of the tribes. About six hundred suits were filed by the Indians, and with nearly four hundred of these adjudicated, judgments for more than $200 million have been rendered in their behalf.

By 1960 the ardor for termination had waned, and both political parties disavowed it in the presidential campaign of that year. Nevertheless, the "Indian problem" remained. Their population on reservations was increasing, but their land base was not, and in an age of affluency the conditions in which most Indians lived qualified them for the dubious distinction of being the most depressed American minority.

During the decade of the 1960s, termination was replaced by self-determination as the goal of government policy. A commitment to Indian social, economic, and political development was made by the Kennedy administration, but not until President Lyndon B. Johnson launched his war on poverty did Indians on and near reservations begin to receive substantial aid. To dramatize the attention his administration was giving Indians, Johnson created the National Council of Indian Opportunity. Richard M. Nixon, as a candidate, indicated his sympathy with the concept of Indians pursuing "a useful and prosperous life in an Indian environment."

To provide substance for the rhetoric, appropriations for Indian programs doubled in the 1960s and continued to increase in the early 1970s. To implement self-determination, the first tentative steps were taken to turn over federal programs on Indian reservations to Indian control. Real efforts were made to attract tourists

and light industry to the reservations. Under President Nixon's commissioner of Indian affairs, Louis Bruce, Indians were appointed to a majority of the policy-making positions in the Bureau of Indian Affairs. Nevertheless, much yet needs to be done. The Indians still constitute not only the most economically deprived minority in American life, but also the one whose political and economic existence is most restricted by government control.

See INDIAN POWER MOVEMENT.

See William A. Brophy and Sophie D. Aberle, *The Indian: America's Unfinished Business* (1966); Henry E. Fritz, *The Movement for Indian Assimilation, 1860-1890* (1963); Lawrence G. Kelly, *The Navajo Indians and Federal Indian Policy, 1900-1935* (1968); and Alan L. Sorkin, *American Indians and Federal Aid* (1971).—W. T. H.

Industrial Army movement. An organized protest movement of the unemployed. The Industrial Army movement represented one of the more dramatic and well-publicized responses to the severe depression that followed the 1893 economic collapse. The idea originated early in 1894 when Jacob S. Coxey, a wealthy Ohio businessman and a prominent urban spokesman of the Populist movement, led a group of approximately one hundred unemployed men on a march from Massillon, Ohio, to Washington, D.C. Coxey's "Army" aimed at persuading the national government to assume responsibility for immediate and direct action to relieve unemployment. His so-called "petition with boots on," which enlisted about five hundred participants by the time it reached the nation's capital, was an immediate failure, but the example had far-reaching effects. The idea caught on and attracted a wide variety of malcontents. Perhaps as many as seventeen "armies," originating largely in the West, headed for Washington in 1894. Several of these were much larger than Coxey's; those that originated on the West Coast may have numbered together around five thousand men at their strongest. California contributed the largest single contingent; Texas also produced a significant group. Their trips across the country caused much turmoil. Trains were commandeered, the press had a field day, and whole towns were panicked.

These armies, which owed what little support they did receive to the Populists, were, of course, highly reprehensible to the influential conservative power structure. So strong was the reaction that the phrase "Coxey's Army" was passed down by oral tradition through the years to serve as a synonym for a ragged "aggregation of disreputables" and was frequently used by individuals who had not the slightest idea of its historical origin. As a matter of fact, it was a symbolic synonym which, for anti-Populists, would do equally well to describe Populists per se.

See Donald L. McMurry, *Coxey's Army: A Study of the Industrial Army Movement of 1894* (1929).—O. G. C.

Industrial Workers of the World. Radical labor union. The Industrial Workers of the World (IWW) was founded in Chicago in June 1905 by a coalition of radicals headed by William D. HAYWOOD of the Western Federation of Miners (WFM), socialists such as Daniel DeLeon and Eugene V. Debs, and disgruntled American Federation of Labor (AFL) members. Haywood called the Chicago meeting the Continental Congress of the working class.

The IWW was created as an all-inclusive industrial union, called "One Big Union" by its members. The latter were by 1914 (and perhaps earlier) nicknamed Wobblies; the origin of the term *Wobbly* is obscure, but one version is from a supposed Chinese distortion of IWW into "I wobbly wobbly." The IWW's motto was Solidarity, and its long-range goal was working-class revolution. Although it gained a violence-smeared reputation, the IWW's actions were primarily nonviolent and often devoted to such prosaic objectives as better wages, hours, and working conditions. Unlike the rival AFL, the IWW in ideals and rhetoric uncompromisingly rejected the capitalist system. This, along with its "direct action" tactics, accounted for the fear and revulsion it aroused among businessmen and industrialists. In its direct-action mode the IWW concentrated on strikes, free-speech fights, petty sabotage, and its innovative slowdown, or "strike on the job."

In the history of the IWW distinctive eastern and western phases may be noted, although the greatest impact was in the West. In the East the IWW led several notable strikes: the McKees Rocks, Pennsylvania, steel strike (1909); the Lawrence, Massachusetts, textile strike (1912); the Paterson, New Jersey, silk strike (1913); the Akron, Ohio, rubber strike (1913); and the Detroit, Michigan, automobile strike (1913). Despite much publicity, the eastern organizing effort (except among Atlantic seamen) was essentially a failure except for the McKees Rocks and Lawrence strikes, and their gains were transitory. In the West the IWW began piling up a succession of remarkable triumphs in its free-speech campaigns from 1909 to 1916. Most of its twenty-six free-speech fights took place in Washington, Oregon, and California. The IWW's first important victory was gained in Spokane, Washington (1909-10), where a drive against exploitative employment agencies allowed the IWW to perfect its free-speech tactics. The plan was for IWW members to flood a city and mount soapboxes in exercise of their claim to free speech. This was in defiance of restrictive municipal ordinances with the result that hundreds of arrests clogged the courts and jails. As expenses and confusion mounted, the city authorities gave in and conceded free speech to the ebullient Wobblies. The colorful, indomitable free-speech campaigns caught the public fancy and did much to foster the image of the IWW cardholder as a rugged frontier individualist. Another major free-speech success came at San Diego, California, in 1912, but a campaign in Everett, Washington, in 1916 triggered a vigilante attack that erased five IWW lives. Eventually, however, the IWW won at Everett, as it did in all of its free-speech fights.

The IWW in the West was especially active in organizing itinerant agricultural workers, lumber workers, and dock workers. An attempt at local organization of migrant workers ended in bloodshed and failure on the Durst hop ranch in Wheatland, California, in 1913, but this tragedy was overshadowed by Great Plains success, where in 1915-16 the IWW organized eighteen thousand harvest workers in the aggressive Agricultural Workers Organization (AWO), one of the IWW's key constituent unions. A similar organizing triumph was achieved in the Pacific Northwest in 1916-17 by the IWW's Lumber Workers Union, which did much to alleviate the oppressive, squalid conditions in the logging camps.

The IWW was also forging a reputation of bumptious grass-roots radicalism. Contributing to the reputation were such phenomena as the "Overalls Brigade" of nineteen Wobblies, who in 1908, attired in black overalls with IWW buttons, left Portland, Oregon, in an empty freight car bound for the annual IWW convention in Chicago. The Overalls Brigade literally sang its way across the country, holding thirty-one meetings and selling IWW literature and song sheets. With its "Little Red Song Book," *I.W.W. Songs to Fan the Flames of Discontent*, the IWW soon became known far and wide as a singing organization. It even had its own bard, troubadour, and martyr in the person of Joe Hill. A bluff, handsome Swedish immigrant, Joe Hill (born Joel Hagglund in 1879 and known first as Joe Hillstrom in America) joined the IWW in 1910 and composed many of the Wobblies' favorite songs, among them "The Preacher and the Slave," with its ironic refrain of "pie in the sky." Hill's life as a radical songster came to an end in 1915 when a Utah firing squad executed him after his conviction on a charge of murdering two Salt Lake City policemen in a grocery store robbery. Scholars still debate Hill's guilt or innocence, but his telegram to Haywood just before his execution ("Don't waste any time in mourning. Organize.") sealed his place in the pantheon of American radical heroes.

The IWW was often torn by factional disputes, but by 1916 "Big Bill" Haywood (who in 1907 had been frozen out of leadership in the rightward trending WFM) was the dominant figure in the organization. Assisting him was Ralph Chaplin, the talented editor of the incisive IWW journal, *Solidarity*. From 1919 to 1923 IWW membership peaked at from 58,000 to 100,000. Ironically, while the size of the membership climbed in the World War I era the IWW received a series of fatal blows stemming from the war and the ensuing antiradical hysteria, from which it never recovered. Two defeats occurred in the vital western copper-mining industry. An Arizona copper strike in 1917 collapsed after vigilantes at Bisbee deported 1,200 strikers into the desert. Far to the north, in Butte, Montana, another copper strike led to the vigilante lynching of IWW organizer Frank Little. More violence came in Centralia, Washington, in 1919. Previous threats against the Centralia IWW by the local American Legion had made the southwestern Washington lumber center tense, and on Armistice Day, when a Legion parade passed the Wobbly hall, shooting broke out. Three Legionnaires were killed, and the IWW found another martyr in the young World War I veteran Wesley Everest, who was castrated and lynched.

The Bisbee, Butte, and Centralia troubles were symptomatic of the times, but what led to the irreversible decline of the IWW was a federal and state legal campaign against it. In the federal drive, 105 IWW leaders were tried for sedition in 1918 in Chicago, of whom 92 (including Haywood and Chaplin) were convicted. The sedition convictions shattered the leadership of the IWW, and it never rebounded. State governments attacked the IWW from 1920 to 1923, with more than five thousand arrests in California, Oregon, Kansas, Oklahoma, and Idaho. They used the ubiquitous state "criminal syndicalist" laws, which were passed in 1917 and after. By the late 1920s the IWW was moribund. It still exists, but only as a token of its former self.

Despite many reverses, IWW agitation had some effect in bringing about an improvement in the workingman's lot in the often brutal extractive industries of the early twentieth-century West. Miner, logger, and harvester were better off as a result of IWW militance. Melvyn Dubofsky has noted that, although the IWW never solved the dilemma of whether precedence should be given to its long-range target of revolution or to immediate gains for its members, IWW radicalism nevertheless induced labor reform which had the paradoxical effect, in the long run, of making workers less radical. Perhaps even more significant has been the rich legacy of spirit and example bequeathed by the Wobblies to the American radical tradition. At the heart of the IWW mystique is the archetypal Wobbly as the personification of the egalitarian, antiauthoritarian western radical tradition—an ethos most skillfully evoked by John Dos Passos in his fictional trilogy *U. S. A.* (1930-36).

See Paul F. Brissenden, *The I.W.W.: A Study of American Syndicalism* (1919); Joseph R. Conlin, *Bread and Roses Too: Studies of the Wobblies* (1969); Melvyn Dubofsky, *We Shall Be All: A History of the Industrial Workers of the World* (1969); Philip S. Foner, *History of the Labor Movement in the United States: The Industrial Workers of the World, 1905-1917* (1965); and Joyce L. Kornbluh, ed., *Rebel Voices: An I.W.W. Anthology* (1964).—R. M. B.

Interior, Department of the. The Department of the Interior was established by Congress on March 3, 1849, to administer bureaus that were misplaced in other departments or had no departmental affiliation. These included the General LAND OFFICE in the Treasury Department, the Indian Office in the War Department, the Patent Office in the Department of State, the Pensions Office in the Navy and War departments, and the Census Bureau, a minor independent agency. The new department had practically no functional unity. It was called, at first, the Home Department. Western politicians anticipated that after 1849 the General Land Office would be less influenced by eastern attitudes and more friendly to the West. In general, this expectation proved to be correct.

The Department of the Interior grew steadily as the years passed. In 1869 the Office of Education was assigned to the department. In 1879 the United States GEOLOGICAL SURVEY was created to bring the functions of surveying, map-making, and geological research into a single bureau. Under the leadership of John Wesley POWELL, the colorful one-armed scientist-explorer, this new agency became one of the leading scientific institutions in the United States in the late nineteenth century. The Reclamation Service, under Frederick H. Newell, was set up in 1902 to plan and execute RECLAMATION AND IRRIGATION in the West. In 1910 Congress established the Bureau of Mines to supervise mine safety and undertake mining research. The NATIONAL PARK SERVICE, authorized in 1916, gave the NATIONAL PARKS AND MONUMENTS coordinated administration for the first time and institutionalized preservationist values in the federal establishment.

During the New Deal the Department of the Interior expanded rapidly, assuming a wide range of new func-

tions. Secretary Harold L. Ickes, in addition to his other duties, served as administrator of the Public Works Administration (PWA). The department cooperated fully in the work of the Civilian Conservation Corps (CCC). It housed, either permanently or temporarily, the Soil Erosion Service, the Oil Commission, the Subsistence Homestead Division, the United States Housing Authority, the Division of Territories and Island Possessions, the Bituminous Coal Commission, and the Bonneville Power Administration. Established bureaus, such as the National Park Service and the Bureau of Reclamation, grew dramatically during these years. In 1934, following passage of the Taylor Grazing Act, the Division of Grazing was established to manage and regulate 142 million acres of range land on the public domain. In 1939 the Fish and Wildlife Service came into existence, uniting the Bureau of Fisheries from the Department of Commerce and the Biological Survey from the Department of Agriculture. Capitalizing on the crisis of the Great Depression, Ickes attempted to remake the Interior Department into a Department of Conservation by bringing all of the federal conservation agencies into a single administrative group. The Forest Service opposed Ickes' plan, preferring to remain in the Department of Agriculture, which had been its home since the days of Gifford Pinchot at the beginning of the twentieth century. In the end, Ickes failed in his reorganization efforts, but he committed the Department of the Interior to an emphasis on conservation that has continued to the present time.

Since World War II, the department has continued to expand. The Bureau of Land Management was established in 1946, consolidating the Division of Grazing and the General Land Office. The Southwestern Power Administration, created in 1943, the Southeastern Power Administration, established in 1950, and the Alaska Power Administration, set up in 1967, joined the Bonneville Power Administration in the task of marketing the electrical power generated at federal reservoirs and power plants. The Office of Minerals Mobilization grew out of the Korean emergency in 1950. In 1962 Secretary Stewart L. Udall created the Bureau of Outdoor Recreation to coordinate national recreational planning. The regulation of petroleum exploration and drilling on the continental shelf has become an important function of the secretary of the interior in recent years.

From time to time, bureaus were transferred out of the Department of the Interior. In 1903 the Census Bureau was moved to the newly established Department of Commerce and Labor. The Patent Office was shifted to the Department of Commerce in 1925. The Veterans Administration took over the Pensions Office in 1930. The Bureau of Mines was transferred to the Department of Commerce when Herbert Hoover was secretary of commerce in the 1920s but was returned to the Interior Department under Ickes. The Soil Erosion Service was moved to the Department of Agriculture in 1935 and renamed the Soil Conservation Service. The Subsistence Homestead Division was assigned to the Resettlement Agency in the Department of Agriculture later in the 1930s. The Office of Education went to the Federal Security Agency in 1939.

Traditionally, the secretary of the interior has been a westerner or a man of considerable sympathy for the

West. Thomas Ewing was the first man to hold the job. The first outstanding secretary of the interior was Carl SCHURZ, who filled the position from 1877 to 1881. Schurz, a former senator from Missouri, was a dedicated reformer. He jousted vigorously with the War Department over Indian policy in the West, staving off efforts by the army to reclaim jurisdiction over the Indians. Under Schurz, the Department of the Interior instituted a system of merit promotions for the first time. James A. Garfield, Theodore Roosevelt's secretary of the interior from 1907 to 1909, played an important part in initiating the Roosevelt-Pinchot conservation program on the public domain, a program that called for scientific planning, regulation, and coordinated development of natural resources. Ickes, an old Bull Moose Progressive from Chicago, presided over a vast expansion of the department during the New Deal and focused its programs mainly on conservation. From 1961 to 1969, Stewart L. Udall, who ranked with Ickes in his commitment to conservation and in effective administrative leadership, guided the affairs of the department. Under his supervision, the department took the lead in identifying and publicizing the ecological crisis of the 1960s.

Controversies have rocked the Department of the Interior at intervals throughout its history. Political battles over western land policy and Indian affairs occurred intermittently after the Civil War. The controversy between Richard A. Ballinger and Gifford PINCHOT in 1910, involving charges of alleged corruption leveled at Ballinger, the secretary of the interior, aroused national interest. At heart, the battle was over administrative values and conservation priorities rather than corruption. Ballinger had seemed determined to reverse recently established policies for the planned, regulated development of the public domain. In the 1920s, the Teapot Dome scandal again brought the Department of the Interior under suspicion. Secretary Albert B. FALL was indicted for accepting bribes in return for opening the Naval Oil Reserves to commercial exploitation. Fall was convicted and sentenced to a year in prison. The oil men who allegedly bribed him escaped conviction. Historians have pointed out that Fall, though not blameless, initially came under attack for largely the same reason that Ballinger had been condemned, namely, that conservationist groups feared he would reverse or undermine established management policies on the public lands. The political struggle over Dinosaur National Monument in the 1950s called attention to the internal clash of objectives that had plagued the Department of the Interior from the beginning. The Bureau of Reclamation proposed to construct two irrigation reservoirs in Dinosaur as part of the Colorado Basin Project. The National Park Service and preservationist organizations, such as the Sierra Club and the National Parks Association, opposed the plan. Secretary of the Interior Oscar L. Chapman was caught in the middle. Finally, after a prolonged fight in Congress, the preservationists managed to block the construction of the reservoirs.

For the first fifty years of its history, the Department of the Interior was a citadel of developmental values. Its main function was to dispose of the public domain and to expedite the development of natural resources in the West. In the twentieth century, the department began to change as its policies gradually reflected urban, industrial attitudes more than frontier values. Resource development and management continued to be important. The gigantic multiple-purpose reclamation projects constructed in the 1930s and 1940s, particularly Hoover Dam, Grand Coulee Dam, and the Central Valley Project in California, were in the scientific, utilitarian tradition of Powell and Pinchot. The regulation of oil exploration, grazing, and mining on the public domain is still among the department's most important functions. In the 1920s, however, the National Park Service became a stronghold of aesthetic conservation and served as a spokesman for the preservationist viewpoint within the department. In the 1960s Secretary Udall took the lead in proclaiming "America's new conservation," asserting the overriding significance of environmental quality rather than developmental considerations in national policy. The department's priorities have changed greatly since 1849.

The Department of the Interior now has more than sixty thousand employees. Its annual budget is almost $2 billion. It has custody of approximately 750 million acres of public land. It has become, as Ickes intended, the main coordinating and policy-making arm of the federal conservation program.

See Department of the Interior, *Annual Report of the Secretary of the Interior*; especially useful is *The Third Wave: America's New Conservation*, Conservation Yearbook for 1966 (1966); and *A Century of Conservation, 1849-1949*, Conservation Bulletin 39 (1950), which contains a brief summary of departmental programs over the past century. *The Secret Diary of Harold L. Ickes*, 3 vols. (1953-54), offers considerable insight into departmental affairs during the New Deal. No general scholarly study has been made of the Department of the Interior.—D. C. S.

Interior Low Plateau. See PHYSIOGRAPHY OF THE UNITED STATES.

internal improvements. The boldness of New York State in undertaking in 1817 the construction of a 363-mile canal to connect the Hudson River at Albany with Lake Erie at Buffalo was quickly repaid by the large volume of freight and passenger traffic that developed even before construction was completed in 1825, and by the rapid growth of the area north and south of the canal and of numerous cities and towns along the route. Other states wished to emulate New York's experience in tapping the trade of the Middle West and in opening up previously isolated areas to settlement. Internal improvements such as roads, canals, railroads, and the dredging of rivers and harbors were all proposed, primarily to be constructed at government expense (see CANAL ERA and NATIONAL ROADS). In the older and well-established commonwealths, the state was the entrepreneur, though it was sometimes possible to secure supplementary federal aid, as with the Chesapeake and Delaware Canal and the Dismal Swamp Canal. But across the Alleghenies the states and territories were sparsely settled, their tax base limited, and their credit not the best. In their midst were great blocks of federal land whose attraction would be immensely increased if they could be made accessible by roads, canals, or railroads. From the outset the residents of those areas favored using a portion of the public lands to aid in developing such projects.

Members of Congress, having foreseen the need for government aid to internal improvements, had inserted in the acts of 1802 and 1803 providing for the admission of Ohio into the Union stipulations setting aside five percent of the net returns from the sale of public lands for building roads to and within the state. Appropriations from this fund made it possible to begin the construction of the Cumberland, or National, Road, which was to extend from Cumberland, Maryland, across the mountains to Wheeling, Virginia, on the Ohio River. It reached that point in 1818 and then was pushed on to Columbus, Ohio; Indianapolis, Indiana; and Vandalia, Illinois.

Before the National Road was built to Indianapolis, canals were replacing roads as routes for immigrants going west with their goods and for produce-seeking eastern markets. In the year before the Erie Canal was completed, Ohio, with less than half the population and wealth of New York, took upon itself the building of 341 miles of canals to extend from Portsmouth on the Ohio to Cleveland on Lake Erie and from Cincinnati to Dayton. Like New York, it failed to secure federal aid and yet succeeded in completing construction in 1832 and 1833, and, as in New York, the canals raised land values, hastened settlement of their hinterland, provided facilities for shipping east the surpluses of grain, whisky, tobacco, beef, and pork which Ohio's farmers were producing, and led to the establishment of numerous towns along the routes. Other sections of the West drafted plans to construct spurs to the Ohio and Miami canals, and to extend the Miami Canal to Lake Erie, to connect Lake Erie with the Wabash River and Lake Michigan with the Illinois River. To each of these trunk-line canals Congress granted in 1827 and 1828 five alternate sections of land through a strip ten miles wide for each mile of canal, as a subsidy. Since the lands would not sell until construction was assured and indeed underway, other sources of capital had to be found. Not until the 1830s were the states of Ohio, Indiana, and Illinois able to borrow these funds and to start construction. By then the new western states were afire with excitement about internal improvements and were preparing larger programs that, when completed, would gridiron them with a network of roads, canals, and railroads. But where was the money to come from?

Henry Clay, as part of his AMERICAN SYSTEM, had a partial answer: distribute to the states the growing surplus in the federal treasury, which came almost entirely from the tremendous increase in public land sales. In this way Clay thought he could outmaneuver those who advocated either reducing the tariff or the price of public land, or both, as a means of avoiding the surplus and he believed he could win support in the West for a measure that would provide new states with millions of dollars for internal improvements. President Andrew Jackson's veto of the distribution bill in 1833 temporarily spiked that gun, although Clay kept it before Congress persistently until 1841. In the place of distribution, John C. Calhoun brought forth in 1836 another proposal: to deposit the surplus with the states for use as they saw fit. Though not substantially different in its effect from distribution, Jackson found it expedient to sign the deposit bill, and $28 million was thus made available for the states, mostly to be used for internal improvements.

The West was now growing mightily, and state governments were able to borrow from eastern and European capitalists some $75 million for their projects. Unfortunately, most of the projects were unwisely planned and were extravagant ventures that only a mature society could support. There was much mismanagement in carrying them out, and some persons charged with selling the securities of the states disobeyed instructions, causing large losses. The crash of 1837, the closing of banks, and the tightening of credit brought the era of expansion to an abrupt halt. Few projects were completed and there was little financial return from them. The heavy debts and interest obligations proved more than the states could carry. Seven states defaulted on their obligations: Florida, Mississippi, Arkansas, and Indiana in 1841 and Illinois, Michigan, and Louisiana in 1842. Four states repudiated their debts outright and others effected compromises with their bondholders. As part of the compromises, Indiana and Illinois permitted their canals and land grants to pass to the bondholders, who finished the construction of the Wabash and the Illinois and Lake Michigan canals. Efforts to get the United States to assume the defaulted and repudiated debts of the states failed.

The West was not yet content with the amount of federal aid for internal improvements. In 1841, in the Distribution-Preemption Act, Congress was persuaded to grant a half million acres for internal improvements to each public land state that had not previously received such a grant. The West thought it a bitter pill to have to accept Clay's distribution section with these grants, for it was based on population and the older states would receive far larger sums out of the land revenues than the new states. However, the West had won preemption; distribution was halted in 1842 because of an amendment that President John Tyler had insisted on, which provided that when the tariff rates were raised distribution should end. The half-million-acre grant was used by some states to complete their canal projects and by others to aid the building of railroads, on which attention was increasingly focused. In 1850 Congress began to offer RAILROAD LAND GRANTS in the public land states by granting alternate sections of land within a strip twelve miles wide for a railroad from Chicago to Mobile, thus beginning another and more lavish period of subsidization for transportation improvements.

See Paul W. Gates, *History of Public Land Law Development* (1968); and George Rogers Taylor, *The Transportation Revolution* (1951).—P. W. G.

Iowa. The frontier period in Iowa history began with the explorations of the Frenchmen Jacques Marquette and Louis Jolliet, who visited the Iowa shore of the Mississippi River in 1673. Other exploring and trading expeditions passed by or through Iowa in the next century, but no white men established permanent settlements until after France had ceded the region in 1762 to Spain, which held it until Napoleon forced its return to France in 1800. During the Spanish period three men secured land grants in present-day Iowa. Julien DU-BUQUE, a French-Canadian, got permission from the Mesquakie (Fox) Indians to mine lead near the present town of Dubuque in 1788, and the Spanish governor confirmed the grant to Dubuque in 1796. Upon Dubuque's death in 1810, the Indians destroyed his home and took over the mines, which they controlled until

1832. Two other Frenchmen, Louis Tesson in 1799 and Basil Giard in 1800, received grants from the Spanish in the present Lee and Clayton counties. In 1803 Napoleon sold Louisiana to the United States, which issued a patent to the assigns of Tesson in 1839 and to Giard's heirs in 1844, but denied the claims of Dubuque's assigns on the grounds that he only held a lease from the Indians.

Though the expeditions of Meriwether Lewis and William Clark in 1804-06 and Zebulon Pike in 1805 passed by Iowa, the United States government showed little immediate interest in the area. Indeed, before whites could settle in the region, the Indians had to be dispossessed. There were conflicting tribal claims to the area because of the displacement of eastern Indians by whites. By 1820 the Iowa Indians had been pushed west to the Platte River valley, and four major groups claimed what is now Iowa. The Winnebago claimed part of the northeast, the Sioux the north and west, and the Potawatomi the southwest. The most important tribes in Iowa history, the allied Sauk and Mesquakie, dominated central and eastern Iowa and northwestern Illinois. The latter tribe had received a second name when some French met a band of Mesquakie about 1650 and confused a clan name, Fox, for that of the whole tribe. The so-called Fox and their allies, the Sauk or Sac (Ousaukie), had arrived in the Iowa country by 1750, having been forced from the Detroit area by the French. Remnants of the two tribes lived in the same region yet remained separate political entities, although the United States government tried to treat them as one tribe. During the 1830s the Sauk under BLACK HAWK most actively resisted white advance, while KEOKUK, his foe, led the peaceful faction.

By 1800, there were about two thousand Mesquakie living in several villages in present eastern Iowa and four thousand Sauk, mostly on the Illinois side of the Mississippi River. In the summer they planted corn and hunted on the Plains; in the winter they moved into the various Iowa river valleys to trap. They resisted American efforts to make them into full-time farmers; in fact, they became less agriculturally proficient as dependence on trade goods forced them to spend ever more time traveling farther afield to trap enough of the decreasing game to pay for supplies. Each succeeding year saw a decline in the area under cultivation.

By 1824 there was sufficient white demand to force land cessions from the Mesquakie and Sauk in what is now Iowa. The first cession, known as the "Half-breed Tract," was in the southeast corner. At the close of the BLACK HAWK WAR in 1832, the tribes ceded to the United States a strip about fifty miles wide along the west bank of the Mississippi. The inevitable next cession came in 1837, followed by the cession in 1842 of central and southern Iowa. By 1845, with the last of their lands gone, the Sauk and Mesquakie had removed to Kansas. In a short time the Potawatomi (1846), the Winnebago (1848), and the Sioux (1851) ceded the last federally recognized Indian lands in Iowa.

During the frontier period the United States established eight forts for short periods of time to control or protect the Indians and discourage white trespassers: Fort Madison (1808) in the southeast, which had to be abandoned when attacked in 1813; the first Fort Des Moines (1834-37) in the southeast; Fort Atkinson (1840-

49) in the northeast; Fort Croghan (1842-43) on the Missouri River in the southwest; Fort Sanford (1842-43) part way up the Des Moines River; the second Fort Des Moines (1843-46) farther up the Des Moines River; Fort Dodge (1850-53) in north-central Iowa; and Fort Defiance (1862-64) in the north, as a response to the Sioux uprising in Minnesota.

There were no major battles between Indians and whites in Iowa, the only notable incident being the Spirit Lake Massacre. In 1857 a band of Sioux attacked isolated settlements in the northwest part of the state in retaliation for the murder of members of the chief's family by a white trader three years before. The pillage, murder of about fifty people, and abduction of some white women greatly excited the state; however, rescue parties did not succeed in catching the Indians, and the two surviving captives had to be ransomed.

Far more significant for the future was the reestablishment of an Indian community within Iowa after the last land cessions. This singular event in Indian-white relations came about in 1852 when some Mesquakie who had been removed to Kansas, along with some who had never really left the state, gathered in eastern Iowa in Tama County, where they purchased eighty acres of river-bottom land. They posed no threat to whites; indeed, the local economy welcomed the income from the Indians' purchases made with the annuity money they received from the 1842 treaty. Because of legal questions about non-citizen Indians holding clear title, Governor James W. Grimes took a deed to the property in trust for the Mesquakie in 1857. Over the years the tribe bought more land so that by 1895 several hundred Indians held more than 2,800 acres in common and had succeeded in living among the whites while remaining culturally independent. The next year the state transferred its trust position to the federal Bureau of Indian Affairs, which still carries out some functions within the Mesquakie settlement.

The first whites in the Iowa region marveled at the richness and beauty of the prairies, described in the novels of John Herbert QUICK, and the "salubrious" climate. The gently rolling prairie land of approximately 80 percent of the state represented about 25 percent of the first-grade soil in the present United States. Yet there was usually some timber not too far away in one of the many stream valleys and water was plentiful. These were rich promises that attracted many whites even before it was legally possible to settle in the politically unorganized area.

In 1804, political jurisdiction of the Iowa region passed to the District of Louisiana, under the control of the governor of Indiana Territory. In 1805 the District of Louisiana was renamed Louisiana Territory, which became Missouri Territory in 1812. When the state of Missouri was admitted to the Union in 1821, what became Iowa was cast adrift without any political organization. Thus it stayed until 1834, when it became part of Michigan Territory.

By 1828 a few cabins had appeared in the southeast on the west bank of the Mississippi and by 1834 settlers had named the community Keokuk. After the Indian cessions, whites began to cross the river in numbers so that the towns of Dubuque, Fort Madison, Burlington, and Davenport sprang up. As usual on the frontier, settlers overran the region before federal land surveyors began work in 1836. There were already ten thousand people by then and more were coming quickly. Once begun, surveys proceeded quickly. By 1837 at least twenty-four survey parties were in the field and by 1843 one fourth of Iowa Territory was surveyed. Iowa even experienced a land rush when the cession of 1842 was opened on May 1, 1843. Five years later half of the state was surveyed, and by 1858 most of the work had been finished.

The first public land sale took place at Dubuque in November 1838, and a second sale followed at Burlington a few weeks later. By the end of 1840 more than one million acres had been sold and more land was put on the market each year. Within thirty years almost all of Iowa had passed out of the hands of the federal government. By 1890 only five thousand acres of public land remained. Of the 36 million acres the Indians ceded to the United States, 14 million were traded for military bounty warrants, 12 million were sold for cash, 4,360,000 were given for railroad construction, 4,200,000 were given to the state for such purposes as education and swamp drainage, 902,000 were given away as homesteads, and 259,000 were claimed for other states through the land grants for agricultural colleges provided for by the Morrill Land Grant Act of 1862.

Considerable concern arose over the extent of speculation that attended the sales of public land. To protect squatters' rights, the CLAIM ASSOCIATION was formed. Using group intimidation, the clubs prevented outsiders from making competitive bids at the government sale on land claimed by a club member. In this way, clubs could also aid speculation by allowing members to claim more land than they could use or by allowing into the club nonresident members, all in hopes of selling excess land or whole claims to latecomers.

Regardless of the source—federal, state, or private holdings—there was sufficient land available to attract settlers quickly. In 1840 there were 43,112 Iowans; by 1850 the population had soared to 192,214. In the early years, the majority migrated from the southern states, but after 1845 more and more came overland from the East and overseas. Population had increased to 674,913 in 1860, of which about 15 percent were foreign born: Germans, the most numerous, 38,000; Irish, 28,000; English and Scottish, 14,000; Scandanavians, 5,600; Dutch, 2,600; Swiss, 2,500; and French, 2,400. About 28 percent of the population had been born in Iowa and about the same number were born in the Old Northwest, while only 8 percent had been born in the South. There were only 1,069 blacks in the state, which is not surprising because the territorial and state governments discouraged black settlers.

Political development quickly followed settlement, but for the first few years politicians from Michigan Territory concentrated on urging Congress to create a separate Iowa Territory. In 1836 Congress attached the region to Wisconsin Territory, but two years later Iowa Territory was formed. After General Henry Atkinson declined the honor of being the new territory's first governor, Robert Lucas, a Jacksonian Democrat from Ohio, accepted, and established his temporary capital at Burlington. The next year a commission chose Iowa City as the capital and the legislature moved there in 1842.

The first legislature, controlled by Democrats, met in Burlington in November 1838 and busied itself with adopting laws, organizing counties, and arguing with the governor over vetoes of appropriation resolutions.

Iowa, like many other new territories, had a boundary dispute with its neighbor, Missouri. In 1839 both governors called out their militia briefly to try to enforce conflicting claims to their common border, arising from ambiguous language in the Missouri Enabling Act of 1820. The United States Supreme Court finally settled the bloodless contest in Iowa's favor in 1849.

The transition from territory to statehood took longer than many politicians desired, but the voters refused to authorize constitutional conventions twice—in 1840 and in 1842—before agreeing in 1844. The proposed constitution of 1844 was typical for the time, providing for low salaries for officials, a $100,000 limit on state debt, and restrictions on banks and corporations. However, since Congress and Iowa could not agree on boundaries, statehood had to wait two years. The new constitution of 1846 had many provisions of the previous document but prohibited banks and locally issued paper money and established the present boundaries of the state. Congress admitted Iowa as the twenty-ninth state in December 1846.

In state as in territorial politics, the Democrats usually triumphed, generally electing senators and representatives sympathetic to the southern position in the national party. However, as the slavery issue became more important and the southern percentage of Iowa's population declined, divisions appeared in the Democrats' ranks. By 1854, with the election of James W. Grimes as governor on a Whig-Free Soil coalition ticket, the Democrats lost control of the state; and two years later, with the disintegration of the Whig party, the new Republican party rose to the position of dominance it generally maintained from then on.

The development of the economy and the changing political character of the state did not harmonize with the Constitution of 1846. The banking provisions were against Whig and Republican principles and restricted economic development, so in 1857 the Republicans proposed a new constitution that allowed the establishment of banks. Voters accepted it, and, though amended, it still serves the state. That same year, the legislature moved the capital to Des Moines in the central part of the state.

During the pioneer period the economy of the state rested solidly on agriculture, although the trade with Indians and lead mining were important at times. Farmers raised corn, wheat, oats, barley, potatoes, cattle, and hogs in abundance, though crop failures did occur in 1843, 1851, and 1858. In early years, Iowa had a ranching economy, but soon farmers found it more profitable to convert the prairies into cornfields and to feed the corn to large numbers of cattle and swine concentrated in feedlots. The demands of new immigrants, as in many growing regions, created the first major market outlet for the early farmers, but soon transportation developments and commercial connections made it possible for farmers settled in eastern Iowa to send produce on the rivers toward the South. Interior farmers, however, suffered from the lack of markets. In an effort to stimulate the economy, the state obtained a federal land grant in 1846 in a fruitless effort to improve navigation on the Des Moines River. California-bound immigrants provided a temporary market in 1850, 1851, and 1852, but the great boon to economic growth was the railroad. The Chicago, Rock Island, and Union Pacific Railroad reached the Mississippi River opposite Davenport in 1854, bridged the river, and pushed on to Iowa City by 1856. The Civil War briefly interrupted construction of the four major railroads in the eastern quarter of the state and caused a depression in the southeast by cutting off the southern market, but farmers resumed shipping produce east on the railroad. During the war years the economy expanded as men opened new farms, even though eighty thousand Iowans served in the Union army. In 1867 the first railroad, under the supervision of engineer Grenville Mellen DODGE, reached to the Missouri River, connecting western Iowa to eastern markets.

Iowa, like other frontier regions, hosted various distinct groups of settlers. The Mormons established a few settlements in southeast Iowa in 1839 across from Nauvoo, Illinois. In 1846 and 1847, the main group of Mormons crossed southern Iowa on their exodus from Illinois to Utah. Their famous handcart brigades started from Iowa City at the end of the railroad in the 1850s. Some Mormons, however, stayed in southern Iowa after 1852 and helped found the Reorganized Church of Latter-day Saints. In 1847 more than eight hundred Dutch Free Calvinists founded Pella. And in 1855 a group of German Pietists founded the communitarian AMANA COLONIES. There were at least four smaller utopian settlements within the state and an Amish community as well (see AMISH, IN IOWA). Generally Iowans welcomed anyone, but free Negroes were a notable exception. In 1850 the legislature forbade free blacks to settle in the state and blacks who had pioneered in Iowa did not get political rights until after the Civil War.

There were the usual attempts to improve life through organizations. At least fifty academies and colleges were founded between 1838 and 1850. Wesleyan College, founded in 1842, is the oldest college. Farmers organized the State Agricultural Society in 1852 and a state fair in 1854. The legislature had chartered a state university in 1847, but the state University of Iowa did not offer instruction until 1855. An agricultural college, now Iowa State University of Science and Technology, was founded in 1858 with the help of Benjamin F. GUE, a member of the Iowa legislature. The great moral issues of the time were slavery and the temperance question. Not until 1854 did political leaders adopt an antislavery position. The next year the state prohibited the manufacture and sale of hard liquor which was not reversed for more than forty years.

The 1850s also saw another frontier phenomenon in Iowa—the formation of vigilantes or "regulators." Horse stealing and murder in eastern Iowa had provoked the formation of private groups intent on enforcing the law; before they were stopped they had killed several innocent men as well as a few criminals.

By the end of the Civil War the general character of the state could no longer be considered frontier even though the northwest was still open for settlement. The 1,194,020 residents of 1870 turned their attention to the problems of a maturing state in the deflationary economy of the late nineteenth century.

Iowans were in the forefront of the Granger movement (see GRANGER LAWS), which sought to regulate railroads and supported various programs—for paper money and silver coinage—to inflate the currency. Iowan James B. WEAVER ran for president on the Greenback ticket in 1880 and on the Populist ticket in 1892. Many Iowans abandoned their usual Republican political loyalty in the bad times of the 1890s to support the Populists, but returned to their old party after 1896. During the Progressive era and the good times, which lasted until the end of World War I, the state enjoyed prosperity and voted Republican. Two Iowa Republican senators, Albert Cummins (1908-26) and Jonathan Dolliver (1900-10), were leaders in the Progressive movement, and James WILSON, as secretary of agriculture, enlarged the role of his department to the advantage of farmers. With the collapse of farm prices in the early 1920s, Iowans joined the movement to try to force the federal government to aid the farmers, and they were helped by Henry Cantwell WALLACE, an Iowan who was appointed secretary of agriculture in 1921, and by his son, Henry Agard WALLACE, secretary of agriculture under Franklin Delano Roosevelt. By 1932 times were so desperate that Iowa farmers intimidated judges at foreclosure proceedings, withheld produce from market, and disrupted mortgage foreclosure sales. In 1933 the governor declared martial law in some of the western counties to control the farmers' protests. The state voted for the Democrats in 1932 and 1936, but by 1940 the effects of the depression had lessened and voters returned to supporting the Republican party, sending Bourke Blakemore Hickenlooper to the Senate for three consecutive terms.

World War II and the postwar years brought prosperity again, but also brought some problems. Mechanization and inflation made smaller farm units less efficient, hastening the trend toward fewer but larger farms. At the same time the state was becoming more industrial. By the 1960s more than 94 percent of Iowa land was still in farms, the value of agricultural product sold was second only to California, and the four major products were corn, soybeans, cattle, and hogs. However, market value of manufactures was three times that of agricultural products. Although much of that value lay in processed agricultural goods, the state was also a large producer of farm machinery, radio equipment, washing machines and dryers (dating from 1907, when Frederick Louis MAYTAG started production of hand-powered washing machines), chemicals, rotary pumps, and sheet aluminum. Most manufacturing was concentrated in six urban centers. The 1970 population was 2,825,041, of which 57.2 percent were urban dwellers and less than 1½ percent were nonwhite. Des Moines was the largest city with 200,000 people, Cedar Rapids was second with 110,000, and there were five other cities each with more than 50,000 inhabitants. In politics the state has become less solidly Republican, electing a Democrat governor in 1957, 1959, 1963, 1965, and 1967.

See Benjamin F. Gue, *History of Iowa*, 4 vols. (1903); Edgar R. Harland, *A Narrative History of the People of Iowa*, 5 vols. (1931); Roscoe L. Lokken, *Iowa Public Land Disposal* (1942); William J. Petersen, *The Story of Iowa*, 4 vols. (1952); and Robert P. Swierenga, *Pioneers and Profits* (1968). See also various issues of *Annals of Iowa* (1863-   ), *Iowa Journal of History and Politics* (1903-1960), and *Palimpsest* (1920-   ).—J. W. W.

Irish immigration. The traditional interpretation of the history of the American Irish places them in an eastern industrial setting. The Irish arrived from a famine-racked country, impoverished and physically weak, and for three generations remained trapped in urban slums. They rose to middle-class status through politics, civil service, law, labor unionism, and the RO-MAN CATHOLIC CHURCH. Historical reflections upon the Irish in the West seldom have strayed far beyond rail-road construction or mining. This eastern picture has been generally accepted as a national synthesis even though it rests on a large but still distinctly regional base. As a generalization this is, with individual and dramatic exceptions, rather accurate as far as it goes. Of the millions of Irish residents of the nation in 1900 a full eighty-nine percent did live in the Northeast. Their American experience, however, was not similar to that of their clansmen in the West.

Even though the experience of the Irish immigrant in the West has not been examined as closely as that of his eastern cousin, sufficient evidence exists to suggest that his life has varied significantly from that of the tradi-tional Irish-American.

Even before the United States had obtained the Mexi-can cession, Irishmen appeared in the Far West, not as forerunners of later immigrants but rather as solitary adventurers. They adjusted readily to life on the ran-chos. These few were unique among the Irish not only because of the distance they placed between themselves and the tenement slums at so early a date but also for having chosen an agricultural way of life. Even though the immigrants worked the soil in Ireland, they showed little inclination for turning to it in America. Those few who did can be explained as having acted from accident rather than choice. No thirst for free land and a fresh start on a homestead of their own brought them west. Population figures have continued to display a definite pattern which skirts farming areas. The persistent Irish choice, even in the West, was urban rather than rural life. This pattern remained in spite of late-nineteenth-century efforts of energetic Catholic prelates who estab-lished colonization bureaus designed to relocate their Irish coreligionists on farms.

The mammoth Irish immigrant population stretched only as far as Illinois, where it abruptly trickled off to follow railroad construction lines west. It hesitated at pockets of nonprecious metals but became significant only in California. Through the century starting in 1860 California led other western states and territories as the destination of the Irish immigrant. When that century began, 33,147 Irishmen called California home while only 1,266 lived in Oregon. Utah attracted but 278. By 1900 California's Irish population had inched up to 44,476, the majority living in San Francisco and its near-by counties. San Francisco in fact became the Irishman's point of orientation. For the archbishop to transfer an Irish priest away from the city was equal to banishment. The humiliated cleric was then forced to receive his mail from Ireland at a provincial address. Only recently has the Irish-born population in the Los Angeles area come to rival that of San Francisco, each hovering at about 41,000 in 1960.

Gold and other metals brought Irish immigrants west. Some struck it rich; a few even held on to their wealth and established their families in local society. This group provided the first link in an enduring chain that stretched to Ireland. One common response to inquiries as to why an Irishman came west revolves not around the qualities of the region but relates instead to the geographical location of the person who sent him his ticket. Subsequent immigrants came west because an older brother or maiden aunt brought them there. This leapfrog system goes back to the gold rush and the accompanying expansion of economic opportunity. At that point the Irish came for the same reasons as other Americans, as is also true of the post-World War II migration.

The Irish immigrant in the West had a different ex-perience from his clansmen elsewhere in America even though he often joined the unskilled urban work force. When he arrived society was still rather open and fluid. In this western setting he was not cowed by dominating cultural elites. He was healthy, confident, and aspiring as an individual. Within organizations he displayed gall and aplomb. When one association of millowners locked out Irish union labor, the Irishmen retaliated by build-ing their own mill with union funds and then, in a sense of devilment, demanded and obtained admission to the very employers' association that had locked them out. The western opportunities to satisfy rising expectations also provided a salutary political effect. The Irish have enjoyed political success in the West too, but never at the cost of surrendering their subculture to a Tammany-like machine or a charismatic chieftain. Having never been obsessed by politics in the past, the contempo-rary Irish in the West face an easier adjustment to the eclipse of old political forms and the creation of new forces.

Except for those entrapped in company towns, the strenuous efforts of Irish immigrants in the West have been rewarded with material success and social accept-ance. Their identity crested in 1919, the year San Fran-cisco granted Eamon de Valera freedom of the city and then jeered at the pro-British Woodrow Wilson. Since that time Republican Ireland has won independence and the Catholic church has entered into a state of transition. Both factors suggest an acceleration of the assimilation process. At present the western Irish still enjoy their ethnic identity and cultural heritage while simultaneously experiencing free access to ongoing American life. To prevent their threatened absorption into an amorphous Anglo society the Irish are con-sciously attempting a cultural renaissance.

For more on the immigrant West see Moses Rischin, "Beyond the Great Divide: Immigration and the Last Frontier," *Journal of American History* (June 1968). For the Irish West see James P. Walsh, "American-Irish: West and East," *Eire-Ireland* (summer 1971), and "Father Peter Yorke of San Francisco," *Studies: An Irish Quarterly Review* (spring 1973).—J. P. W.

Iroquoian language. See INDIAN LANGUAGES: *Iroquoian*.

Iroquois confederacy. The Iroquois confederacy, or League of the Iroquois, was a confederation of five (later six) Indian tribes occupying most of upstate New York until the American Revolution. The five con-stituent tribes were the Mohawk, occupying several vil-lages in the Mohawk River valley; the Oneida, not far from Oneida Lake; the Onondaga, whose one village near modern Syracuse served as capital of the confederacy; the Cayuga, to the east of Cayuga Lake; and the Seneca, the largest group, who maintained a number of villages in the vicinity of the Genesee River. To these tribes a sixth, the TUSCARORA, was added in 1722, after large numbers of that kindred group had migrated from North Carolina. All spoke related dialects and were connected linguistically to such other Iroquoian-speaking tribes as the Huron, Erie, and Susquehanna.

The origins of the Iroquois proper, or Five Nations, are uncertain; there is even a myth, the HIAWATHA LEGEND, explaining the confederation's formation. It is reasonably clear that the Cayuga and Seneca moved into their historic homes after a long trek from the Southwest. The three eastern tribes—the Mohawk, Oneida, and Onondaga—or their predecessors may have come from the same direction, or possibly from the northern shores of the Great Lakes. When these migrations occurred is unknown, but one theory has the eastern tribes moving into New York from the St. Lawrence valley as late as the sixteenth century. The league may date from this time, or it may be older. A more recent theory indicates that the Iroquoian peoples may have developed indigenously to the St. Lawrence valley from earlier, prehistoric groups. Linguistic and other evidence indicates a particularly close relationship between the Seneca and Cayuga and between the Mohawk and Oneida.

Social and political organization was more highly developed among the Iroquois than among most of their neighbors, the confederacy representing the greatest degree of intertribal unity north of Mexico. But it is easy to exaggerate this unity. By European standards Iroquois government was extremely primitive and lacking in effective control over the individual members of society. Each tribe had a body of chiefs, or sachems, chosen by the women from a number of hereditary candidates. The sachems of all the tribes met together from time to time to administer league affairs, but in both tribal and league concerns their authority was limited. The responsibility for organizing and leading war parties, for example, lay with individual warriors, who were essentially free agents. Their zeal for revenge or glory frequently nullified the diplomatic efforts of the chiefs and prevented the tribe from pursuing a consistent policy for any length of time.

Within each tribe the village was often the most significant unit in decision-making. The confederacy was more important as a means of keeping peace among the member tribes than as a force for united action by all of them. Every tribe was free to make war or peace, negotiate treaties, and conduct its domestic affairs as it saw fit. Evidences of collaboration among two or three of the tribes are very common; but almost never did the league as a whole pursue any significant policy requiring united action. By preventing warfare and minimizing hard feelings among the constituent tribes, however, the league was a source of great strength.

Iroquois population figures for the seventeenth and eighteenth centuries must rest on conjecture, but almost certainly they were never higher than fifteen thousand from the coming of the white man until very recent times. An estimate of 1660 gives the Mohawk no more than five hundred warriors, the Oneida less than one hundred, the Onondaga three hundred, the Cayuga three hundred, and the Seneca a maximum of one thousand, nearly half of the whole number of warriors in the league. The league never seems to have had a fighting force of more than twenty-five hundred, and this number was never in the field at once. If the numbers of warriors are multiplied by five to arrive at the total population, the entire league numbered no more than eleven thousand persons. Iroquois population was never constant; disease and warfare could wipe out hundreds in a single year, and family vacancies were commonly filled by adopting captives or tributary groups from outside the league.

The Iroquois economy was basically agricultural but heavily supplemented by hunting and fishing. The main crops, raised by the women in plots around the villages, were corn, beans, pumpkins, melons, and by the late eighteenth century, even orchard fruits. Fishing, also primarily women's work, occupied most of the warm months. Hunting was a male pursuit, the main season falling in the winter. The men commonly ranged many miles from home collecting game from the tribal hunting grounds, which were clearly delimited in most cases from those of other tribes in and out of the confederacy, and which occupied the bulk of the tribal domain. After the white man's arrival, the beaver became more highly regarded than before, as it constituted the staple of the northern fur trade. Iroquois hunters first traded with the Dutch at Albany in the 1620s and then with the English after they expelled the Dutch from New Netherland in 1664. By 1640 they had virtually exhausted the beaver supply in their own territories in what is now upstate New York. They began to invade hunting lands of French-allied tribes to the north and west, completely routing the Huron in 1649-50 and extending their hunting and fighting activity by 1680 as far as the Ottawa and Illinois countries. They also plundered western fur shipments heading toward Montreal and, on occasion, even raided French settlements. This desire to conquer new hunting lands is almost certainly the primary cause of Iroquois warfare and imperialism in the seventeenth and eighteenth centuries, which made them a terror to tribes as remote as Maine, South Carolina, and Illinois.

The Mohawk, when the French and Dutch first encountered them soon after 1600, were at war with their closest neighbors, the Mahican of the upper Hudson valley, as well as with the Algonquian Indians of the St. Lawrence. A generation later Mohawk war parties were penetrating deep into New England and terrorizing both the French settlers around Montreal and the lower Hudson valley bands near New Amsterdam. At the same time their western confederates, especially the Seneca, defeated and dispersed the Huron tribe around Georgian Bay by 1650, the Neutral Nation along the Niagara River by 1651, and the Erie tribe, living south and east of Lake Erie, by 1655. They then moved southward against the Susquehanna tribe of Pennsylvania, defeating it by 1676. In 1680 Seneca warriors destroyed villages of the Illinois Indians and invaded the territories of the Ottawa near the Straits of Mackinac. Warriors of the central tribes meanwhile were raging southward behind Maryland and Virginia, fighting minor engagements with the local Indians and occasionally even attacking English settlers. Many of these forays were conducted by small parties on their own responsibility, often regardless or in defiance of the policy of the sachems. But others, especially those to the west, were the products of tribal policy and involved hundreds of warriors from two or three tribes. Their causes were often obscure, particularly when privately inspired, but Indian warfare tended to be self-perpetuating. Young men sought to prove themselves by martial exploits, and every raid brought casualties that had to be avenged. Peace treaties painstakingly arranged by the sachems, often with colonial assistance, were sometimes broken before the ink was dry.

So far as tribal policy dictated warfare, the traditional motivations were supplemented by economic and political factors which had hardly existed before the advent of the white man. These included European imperial rivalries, with the Iroquois caught in the middle, and the benefits to be gained from the colonial fur trade. The Iroquois both profited and lost by the European intrusion into North America. Although they risked being crushed in the conflict between the English and French, their power by 1690 was also a direct result of their commanding position in the western fur trade and the armaments supplied them by the Dutch and then the English. When the English developed imperial ambitions after 1680, they sought to use the Iroquois as a means of penetrating the interior and eventually dislodging the French. What had originated as a lax willingness to sell guns to insistent Indians became a deliberate policy of arming military allies through annual subsidies.

In the three-cornered power struggle that lasted from the 1620s to the 1760s, the Iroquois affiliated primarily with the Dutch and English of New York. The reason for this alliance is clear. Iroquois policy was to control as much of the western fur supply as possible and carry it to the best eastern market. At Albany the Dutch and (after their expulsion in 1664) the English were consistently able to provide better trading goods at a cheaper price than were the French at Montreal. Too, they were totally dependent on the Indians to bring them furs. Unlike the French, neither the Dutch nor English sent traders into the interior; their few attempts to do so were rebuffed by the Indians and the French. In the case of the Mohawk and Oneida at least, proximity was also a factor. The three western cantons had pro-French factions which occasionally prevailed temporarily, but New York could do more for them economically while French policy usually dictated a closer relationship with the fur-rich western tribes such as the Huron, Ottawa, Miami, and Illinois, who were the objects of Iroquois aggression. The result was sporadic warfare with Canada, which never entirely ended until the French were driven from North America. Iroquois war parties occasionally harassed settlements around Montreal and disrupted the trade with the western tribes on which the French colony subsisted. The French in turn invaded the Iroquois country on several occasions between 1666 and 1696, destroying villages and corn supplies.

These hostilities reached their climax in King William's War, in 1689-97 (see COLONIAL WARS). In this contest the Iroquois suffered extremely, always hoping that with English help they could drive the French from Canada altogether. But English participation in this war was so limited and the French proved so durable that the sachems made peace with Canada in 1701 (after the English had already done so without them) and settled

on a policy of neutrality. In the subsequent Anglo-French conflicts, which broke out anew the next year, the Iroquois managed to pursue this policy most of the time. Only when British preparations against Canada seemed to promise an ultimate French defeat did the Five Nations temporarily abandon their neutrality to join military expeditions against Canada. The French defeat came at last with the fall of Quebec (1759) and Montreal (1760), climaxing a war in which Iroquois braves helped the British to capture Fort Niagara and other French strongholds on the fringes of Canada.

By this time the Iroquois had given up their imperial ambitions of the 1680s and settled for more modest benefits. They made a more or less durable peace with the western tribes, permitting them continued hunting on the lands that they had already conquered around the eastern Great Lakes. They also permitted the western tribes to trade directly with the British at Oswego after 1721. Their colonizing activities became centered in Pennsylvania and the upper Ohio valley, where the Seneca in particular established villages and for a time reduced local tribes such as the Delaware and Shawnee to tributary status. Iroquois relations with the British, which were centered at Albany in the seventeenth century, broadened after 1700 to include Pennsylvania and Virginia, whence Iroquois diplomatic missions went more and more often.

Ironically the French defeat for which the Iroquois had wished so long was a major factor in terminating their power. With the English now planted at Montreal and paying the same prices as at Albany and Oswego, the western fur trade gravitated to the St. Lawrence. And the English, no longer fearing Iroquois defection to the French, felt less need to subsidize them with armaments and other gifts. The Iroquois thus lost their strategic significance just at the time when colonial population began to engulf their territories. For generations Iroquois power had combined with other circumstances to prevent much white settlement in their New York homeland. Dutch settlement by 1664 extended only to Schenectady, at the fringe of the Mohawk country. A hundred years later the frontier reached far up the Mohawk valley to Fort Stanwix (Rome), threatening particularly the Mohawk and Oneida with inundation.

Iroquois independence was eventually doomed in any event, but the American Revolution terminated it abruptly. When the conflict began, the Iroquois sided overwhelmingly with the British, owing in part to the effective diplomacy of Sir William JOHNSON, the British superintendent of Indian affairs. But in larger measure it sprang from the knowledge that American westward colonization rather than the British crown was the biggest threat to their tribal and territorial integrity. The Oneida and Tuscarora remained neutral, but the other tribes contributed hundreds of warriors to British military operations and to combined Indian-Tory frontier raids like the Wyoming and Cherry Valley massacres of 1778, led by Mohawk Joseph BRANT. The American reply to these activities was the SULLIVAN-CLINTON CAMPAIGN of 1779, which destroyed the villages of the Onondaga, Cayuga, and Seneca. Forty villages and 160,000 bushels of corn went up in smoke, and with them most of the Iroquois' capacity for further resistance.

Many of the Iroquois fled to Canada at the end of the American Revolution and eventually settled on the Six

Nations Reserve near Brantford, Ontario. The others, as a defeated power, were required to give up nearly all their lands in a succession of treaties, and were confined to several reservations that progressively shrank in size. Even the neutral Oneida were induced to sell out, and moved to Wisconsin by 1832. A Seneca faction under CORNPLANTER moved to Pennsylvania, and other tribal fragments also moved west.

The bulk of the Iroquois in New York and Canada settled down with more or less success as farmers while a tide of white population came to surround them. As the white community grew and became urbanized, jobs opened in nearby cities, to which increasing numbers of Indians have commuted from the reservations. The Mohawk in particular have taken high-paying jobs in structural steel work in New York City and elsewhere, but in general the Iroquois, like other Indians, have remained very selective in their acceptance of white men's ways. Traditional political organization has been retained with modifications both in New York and Canada. Traditional languages, ceremonies, and customs are also consciously preserved, although these inevitably have eroded as the Indians embraced larger parts of the surrounding material culture. Although a large proportion of the Iroquois have adopted Christianity, many others follow the teachings of RED JACKET and Handsome Lake, a Seneca prophet whose visions in 1799 led to a religious movement. Iroquois population, after falling in the eighteenth and nineteenth centuries, has increased in recent decades to about twenty thousand, nearly equally divided between Canada and the United States.

The Iroquois confederacy is one of the most studied and written about of all American Indian groups. Some of the more useful and interesting works are G. E. Hyde, *Indians of the Woodlands: From Prehistoric Times to 1725* (1962); L. H. Morgan, *League of the Ho-dé-no-sau-nee, or Iroquois*, 2 vols. (1851); F. G. Speck, "The Iroquois," *Bulletin of the Cranbrook Institute of Science*, vol. 23 (1945); Edmund Wilson, *Apologies to the Iroquois* (1960); and A. W. Trelease, *Indian Affairs in Colonial New York: The Seventeenth Century* (1960), and "The Iroquois and the Western Fur Trade: A Problem in Interpretation," *Mississippi Valley Historical Review*, vol. 44 (1962). See also G. T. Hunt, *Wars of the Iroquois* (1920); and G. P. Murdock, *Ethnographic Bibliography of North America* (1960).—A. W. T.

irrigation. See RECLAMATION AND IRRIGATION.

Irvine, William C. (1852-1924). Wyoming cattleman and politician. Born in Carlisle, Pennsylvania, Irvine moved in 1872 to the Sandhills of Nebraska, where he was employed by Bosler Brothers, a Carlisle firm that had established a large range-cattle outfit on Blue Creek, north of Ogallala. He soon was made one of the foremen of the outfit. Having gained much experience in the ranching business, he left the Boslers in 1876 and went to Texas, where he purchased four thousand head of cattle, which he located on a ranch near Fort Fetterman on the North Platte River in Wyoming. His brand was the Jay Y. Through skill and good management he had doubled the size of his herd by 1878.

Three years later Irvine joined forces with others in organizing the Converse Cattle Company. About 1884 he sold out his livestock interests and returned to Pennsylvania. But the call of the open range brought

him back to the West two years later to serve as range manager of the Converse outfit. In December 1887 he resigned that position to accept the general managership of the Ogallala Land and Cattle Company, which ran about thirty-two thousand head of cattle. From 1899 to 1905 he was general manager of the U Cross outfit located near Buffalo, Wyoming.

Always a staunch supporter of the Wyoming Stock Growers' Association, Irvine served as a member of the executive committee (1882-85 and 1903-07), trustee (1884-85 and 1903-07), president (1896-1911) and treasurer (1912-24).

Irvine was also a political leader, first as a Democrat, later as a Republican. He was a member of the Wyoming constitutional convention and a signer of the state constitution in 1890. He served two terms in the state legislature (1913 and 1915) and as state treasurer from 1903 to 1907. He was director of the first company organized to build the Cheyenne Northern Railroad, and, with Senator Joseph Maull Carey, was one of the promoters of the Wheatland irrigation project. During World War I he was the state director of war finance.—R. B. W.

Irvine Ranch. Midway between Los Angeles and San Diego is Irvine Ranch, one of California's largest unified landholdings remaining from the nineteenth century. It was created as a composite of three Spanish-Mexican ranchos, the Santiago de Santa Ana, the San Joaquin, and the Lomas de Santa Ana. As a result of droughts of the 1860s and continuing claim battles, the Mexican owners of these vast tracts had been reduced to easy prey for land speculators. A holding company of four men bought up these three ranchos piecemeal after 1864. The four—James Irvine, Llewellyn Bixby, and Thomas and Benjamin Flint—had come during the gold rush and stayed in northern California to make money in mercantile and sheep-raising pursuits. In 1876 Irvine bought out his partners' southern California land interests for $150,000 and thus created the Irvine Ranch.

Irvine, a Scotch-Irish Presbyterian, traveled to California on the same ship as Collis Huntington, a man not dissimilar in aggressive business sense. Huntington's Southern Pacific Railroad later challenged the Irvine land claims in order to get not only the right-of-way to San Diego but also the alternate-section land grants from the government. At one point in 1887, railroad construction gangs fought off Irvine's land with guns, and the issue was only settled when Irvine forged a more congenial right-of-way agreement with a subsidiary of the rival Santa Fe.

Originally devoted to sheep, the ranch was diversified with cattle herds and farming by the time of its founder's death in 1886. Some initial failures with grapes and olives were followed by successes with beans, sugar beets, walnuts, lemons, and oranges; the latter two became primary crops after the turn of the century.

During the leadership of the second James Irvine, the ranch was incorporated in 1894. At that time, the ranch covered 103,000 acres, approximately one third of Orange County. Land development became increasingly important under the direction of Myford Irvine, president from 1947 until his death in 1959. On January 20, 1961, the company deeded one thousand acres for the Irvine campus of the University of California. Coincidentally, master plans were drawn up for all surrounding land. Urban development of the ranch is now accompanied by the gradual transfer of cattle operations to holdings in Montana and agriculture to company land in the Imperial Valley of California.

See Robert Glass Cleland, *The Irvine Ranch* (1962), rev. with epilog by Robert V. Hine.—R. V. H.

Irving, Washington (1783-1859). Essayist and historian. Irving, born in New York City, began to read law in 1801, but though he was admitted to the bar he never practiced the profession seriously. In 1815 he went to England to take over the management of the Liverpool branch of the family's hardware firm. While in England he moved in literary circles, lionized because of the *Sketch Book* (1819-20) and *Bracebridge Hall* (1822), both of which were popular successes in England. When the family business went into bankruptcy in 1818, rather than become a lawyer, Irving decided to make his living as an author, gambling on his ability to repeat the earlier American success of his pseudonymously published Diedrich Knickerbocker's *History of New York* (1809). His gamble was a good one; until his death the earnings from his writings enabled him to live the leisured life he preferred of a country gentleman. Upon his return to America in 1832 Irving lived quietly at his villa "Sunnyside" near Tarrytown, New York, except when he served as minister to Spain (1842-45).

When Irving returned from Europe he seriously attempted to understand the immense changes that American life had undergone during his long stay in England. A trip to the Southwest in 1832 suggested to him the possibility of using various aspects of western life for literary subjects. Many critics have been rather harsh with Irving for not seeing the deeper significance of the American western experience, and for shamelessly romanticizing western life and history. Although this may be true, his subject was simply not what the modern reader considers fraught with significance. As a gentlemanly romantic he was interested primarily in reporting straightforwardly, if superficially considered, the curious facts of the strange life he found about him. He was, in short, fascinated by what the eighteenth century had called "the picturesque," and of this he found more than enough to satisfy both himself and his readers. *A Tour on the Prairies* (1835), a colored account of his own trip, is not filled with accounts of hardship or peril but rather with descriptions of scenery and, more importantly, of colorful character types, new to him and equally new to his audience. *The Adventures of Captain Bonneville* (1837) is put together in much the same way. It is ostensibly an autobiographical account of the adventures of Benjamin L. E. de BONNEVILLE, as told by him to Irving, whose contributions to the narrative are only editorial. This is undoubtedly true; yet Irving conceived of his editorial role in a broad sense, and *The Adventures* as a result are stories of privation interspersed with exciting accounts of Indian battles and picturesque descriptions of trappers, Indian life, and all the colorful miscellany of the American West in the early 1830s.

Astoria (1836), Irving's most famous work of western writing, is the only one that attempts a historical account of the significance of the western experience, although the anecdotal nature of the particular history of the colony of Astoria gives this book a superficial resemblance to Irving's two other books about the West. And again, Irving's account of the significance of Astoria is quite different from the modern. The villains of his tale, in addition to the troublesome British, are often the colonists of Astoria themselves, who do not understand, and sometimes consciously subvert, the plans of John Jacob Astor, whose family, incidentally, commissioned the piece. It is Astor's purpose, as Irving tells the story, not only to control the immense wealth of the western fur trade but to pioneer the settlement of the western territories. Where a modern writer would concentrate on the spoliation of the wilderness through the civilization represented by Astor's infant settlement (as does A. B. Guthrie, whose novel *The Big Sky* (1947) is almost an inverse *Astoria*), Irving concentrates upon the blessings of civilization that will follow inevitably in the train of his pioneering enterprise. Irving, like most of his contemporaries, believed firmly in the beneficent effect of civilization on the wasteland of the West.

The Works of Washington Irving, in twenty-one volumes, were collected in 1860-61 and reprinted many times since; an excellent one-volume selection entitled simply *Washington Irving* was made by H. A. Pochman in 1934. See also Laura Benet, *Washington Irving, Explorer of American Legend* (1944); Lucy L. Hazard, *The Frontier in American Literature* (1927); and Stanley T. Williams, *Life of Washington Irving*, 2 vols. (1935). —J. K. F.

Italian immigration. Only slowly did Italian immigrants follow after the priests (see ROMAN CATHOLIC MISSIONARIES), explorers (such as Henri de TONTI, Count Paolo Andreani, Giacomo Constantino Beltrami, and the eccentric Count Leonetto Cipriani, who in 1853 mounted an expedition with more than a thousand animals across the Great Plains from Missouri to California), and traveling journalists. Yet from the 1840s onward, Italian names crop up—in the mining pits of Arizona and New Mexico, in the lumber camps of Colorado and the Northwest, and in the vineyards of California. The gold rush attracted many of them to San Francisco. There Domenico Ghirardelli founded a chocolate factory that still stands. He was followed by sausage makers with names like Gallo and Molinari. In San Francisco, Denver, Seattle, and other cosmopolitan centers the Italians established foreign-language newspapers, churches, schools, and lodges. For a time Italians in San Francisco were publishing as many as five newspapers simultaneously, of which *La Voce del Popolo* was the most important prior to World War I. Many cultural groups also existed, such as the Figli d'Italia, La Garibaldina, and Il Cenacolo, a social circle.

Settling throughout the twenty-two states west of the Mississippi River, Italians born abroad numbered 20,233 in Louisiana (1930), 15,204 in Missouri (1930), 14,375 in Colorado (1910), and 13,121 in Washington (1910). The largest concentration was in California, where 107,249 people had settled by 1930. These figures are not totally accurate because census takers missed a good many persons, especially illiterates. Nevertheless, they did and do not begin to match the concentration of Italians in the East.

In 1920, when first-generation Italians in California numbered more than 80,000 and only about 8,000 in Texas, more than 500,000 Italians were living in New York, more than 200,000 in Pennsylvania, and more than 300,000 in Rhode Island—this many despite the decline in the quota of immigrants allowed into the United States as determined by the several immigration acts. Between 1901 and 1910 more than two million Italians entered the United States, but during the next decade that figure was cut in half. The law of 1924 further reduced the annual Italian quota to only 5,500 persons. Yet the restriction of immigration may have helped to increase social homogeneity.

How many Italians came from a rural or an urban background cannot be determined. In Italy a *contadino* ("peasant") frequently tended a plot of land in the countryside while living in a nearby town. Of the 880,908 Italians who migrated to the United States in the period 1891 to 1910, more than half—or 452,059—were farmers. In contrast to those who settled in the large cities of the East, numerous north Italians (Piedmontese,

Genoese, Venetians, and Lombards) entered agriculture. The majority of them did not end up on farms, but some did, particularly in the California vineyards and in truck farming and dairying. The Di Giorgio and Maggio families became especially prominent in California. Italians were successful in other areas as well, notably A. P. GIANNINI in banking, Louis Martini in viticulture, Joe Di Maggio in sports, Alex Perino in the culinary field, and Joseph Alioto and Anthony CAMINETTI in California politics.

See Paul Radin, *The Italians in San Francisco* (1935); Andrew Rolle, *The Immigrant Upraised: Italian Adventures and Colonists in an Expanding America* (1968); and Giovanni Schiavo, *Four Centuries of Italian-American History* (1952).—A. R.

J

jackrabbit. *Jackrabbit* is the common name given to large North American hares (genus *Lepus*). It has long hind legs and long ears and lives in the open grasslands, brushlands, and deserts of the West.

There are four species of jackrabbits. By far the most common and best known is the black-tailed jackrabbit (*Lepus californicus*), also called the California jackrabbit. This species can be found throughout the short-grass prairie, Great Basin (or high desert), and hot (or low) desert areas. It is also common throughout Nebraska and Texas and west to California and southern Oregon (except in the high mountains above twelve thousand feet). It is usually grayish brown with white patches on the forehead, around the eyes, and behind the ears, and a black stripe on the tail and the tips of the ears. When this jackrabbit runs, he keeps his tail pointed downward. Black-tailed jackrabbits have a gestation period of forty-one to forty-seven days, averaging about forty-three days. They have three to four litters a year with one to six young per litter.

The next most common species is the white-tailed jackrabbit (*Lepus townsendii*). Although its range overlaps that of the black-tailed jackrabbit in the short-grass prairie and Great Basin to the northern edge of the hot desert, the white-tailed jackrabbit is most often found farther north in the open high-plateau areas of Wyoming, Montana, Idaho, and Washington. Where the habitats of the white-tailed and the black-tailed do overlap, the former tends to occupy the foothills and higher elevations and the latter tends to occupy the valleys. Its distinguishing feature is its white tail. It is also a larger animal than the black-tailed jackrabbit. In the northern parts of the range the white-tailed jackrabbit becomes white in winter. This species may have only one litter a year, averaging three to six young.

The antelope jackrabbit (*Lepus alleni*) is found in the deserts of south-central Arizona. It is generally larger with lighter ears and tail than its relative, the black-tailed jackrabbit, which lives in the same area. This species reportedly has three to four litters a year with one to five young per litter.

The Gaillard jackrabbit (*Lepus gaillardi*) is found in the desert grasslands of southwestern New Mexico. It is easily distinguished from the black-tailed jackrabbit by its white flanks. Little is known of its breeding habits.

Contrary to common belief, the jackrabbit is not a true rabbit. Being a hare, it has longer ears and hind legs than a rabbit and does not construct elaborate fur-lined nests. The young jackrabbit is born out in the open, covered with fur, and mobile almost immediately after birth. Rabbits, on the other hand, bear young which are naked, blind, and helpless.

The jackrabbit, particularly when frightened, can travel at a rate of forty miles an hour or more and can leap twenty feet at a time. Its ears often constitute one third of its body length. The large ears are important in keeping the jackrabbit alert to what is happening around him and in acting as a heat-regulating device during the hot summers. On the hottest days, jackrabbits sit in any available shade, which cools the blood running through the large ear surfaces and allows them to act as heat dissipators. The jackrabbit is well adapted to life in the semi-arid country, for it feeds on almost every kind of vegetation and, drawing moisture from these plants, can go long periods of time without fresh water. It occupies a significant position in the western wildlife chain, serving as the basic food for the coyote, and constituting part of the diet of most of the intermediate predators, such as the bobcat and golden eagle.

The number of jackrabbits (once a significant food item for the Indians and early settlers), especially the black-tailed ones, varies greatly from year to year. In those years when they are particularly numerous and feeding heavily on the farmers' crops, such as alfalfa and grain, jackrabbits are considered pests and every effort is made to eliminate them. They may also carry diseases affecting man, such as tularemia. Often the measures used are somewhat indiscriminatory. Sometimes local residents will organize massive drives by men and dogs. Other times jackrabbits are pushed into wire pens and slaughtered and quite often are used as targets for the casual shooters coming into the area. All too often, they have been eliminated not because they were actually damaging a significant portion of the agricultural crops or constituting a health threat to the area, but rather because they were numerous. Studies such as those conducted by the Department of the Interior's Jack Rabbit Research Center in Idaho are now under way to develop effective and humane population control methods that can be used when it becomes necessary to cut back the number of jackrabbits.

See E. R. Hall and K. R. Kelson, *The Mammals of North America*, vol. I (1959); and L. G. Ingles, *Mammals of California and Its Coastal Waters* (1954).—M. J. P.

Jackson, Andrew (1767-1845). Lawyer, soldier, and politician. Jackson's personality epitomized the westward movement. Although a frontiersman only part of his life, he came to be a hero of the whole frontier and a vigorous spokesman for all sorts of people who were caught up in the great rush to settle across the continent. Measured in terms of formal schooling, Jackson was almost an illiterate. He often revealed an uncultivated and raw nature in his personal demeanor, even resorting to sharp physical means to assert himself. He apparently did not know what fear meant, and his fiery temperament sometimes made him appear fiercer than he really was in fact.

Jackson was born in the "Garden of the Waxhaws," South Carolina, just below the present North Carolina line. His parents were Irish immigrants who had moved into the South Carolina backcountry. The exact spot of his birth, even the precise state, has long been a point of controversy, but the fact really has no significant meaning in the history of the man. Before he emigrated west to Tennessee, he was associated with both the Carolinas. Jackson himself seemed to believe he was born in South Carolina.

Jackson's father died just before he was born of an injury resulting from overstraining himself in lifting a log. Left in straitened circumstances, Elizabeth Jackson resolved to keep her family together. She did not live, however, to bring her children to maturity. Andrew received the meagerest sort of schooling in a classroom, but the raw frontier, with its extrovert society, was a kind of schooling that remained with him all his life. As a youth he was associated with rowdy frontier types who accepted the challenges of nature on a no-holds-barred basis.

The "Garden of the Waxhaws" was in direct line of British activities in the late summer of 1780. With Lord Rawdon and Cornwallis pushing up from Charleston to Camden and Knobkirk's Hill and Banastre Tarleton pushing southward from North Carolina, the natives of the sandhill region were caught in a squeeze. On August 1, 1780, there occurred the battle of Hanging Rock in which Jackson participated. He and his brother, Robert, were captured in a skirmish about the Waxhaw Church.

Robert died, and Andrew received a sword wound when he refused to black an officer's boots, a wound that was to engender deep Irish hatred and the seeking of tenfold revenge.

Equally as biting to Jackson was the fact that the revolutionary war had brought an end to his mother's life. Having volunteered to go aboard a prison ship in the Charleston harbor, she was overworked and contracted prison fever, from which she died. Her remaining son, Andrew, was fourteen years of age and was now left footloose. He inherited a small sum of money and went to Charleston, where he was attracted to the Jockey Club's race meetings. The reckless lad spent his patrimony quickly and was penniless. He turned back to the up-country of Salisbury, North Carolina, with the intent of studying law. How much law Jackson learned is highly speculative. In Salisbury, as in Charleston, he frolicked away much of his time. By considerable luck and perhaps even more charity, he was admitted to the practice of law before the court in Guilford County, North Carolina, on November 12, 1787. His prospects for clients in the beginning year were slimmer than for most fledgling lawyers. By this time he was twenty-two years old and fancy free. No specific geographical spot had a hold on him.

In 1788 he rode over the Blue Ridges with John McNairy intending to visit in the Mero District of the Middle Tennessee country. McNairy was on his way to preside over the court at Nashville, and Jackson was keeping him company. Tennessee at that moment was in an important formative period. Within two years the Southwest Territory was to be formed under the authority of the federal government. This was country where an attorney practiced one part law and about nine parts political management and a demonstration of personal courage. His visit became a residence, and the young Carolinian was chosen in 1791 to be attorney general for the Southwest Territory. He also found private clients in protesting merchants who had lost money as a result of the political actions involved in extending United States authority to the area and by negotiations with the Indians. Sometime in 1791 or 1792, Jackson became solicitor in McNairy's district, and the two were again associated in riding a rugged court circuit out of Nashville.

There occurred in these years a social and legal fiasco that was to haunt Jackson the rest of his life. He boarded at the home of Mrs. John Donelson, widow of the famous John Donelson who had brought settlers around Muscle Shoals to settle in central Tennessee in 1779-80. Donelson quickly became a central figure in the new western settlement. His daughter, Rachel, was one of the belles of the new community. In 1785 she married Lewis Robards of Mercer County, Kentucky, and went to Harrodsburg to live. The Robards family were Kentucky pioneers who had succeeded in laying a firm economic foundation by the acquisition of a large holding of fertile bluegrass land. Difficulty arose between husband and wife because of Robards' jealousy of Peyton Short, and in 1790 he left her. When Rachel returned to Nashville she met Jackson. In a short time Robards made a jealous scene over Rachel and Jackson, and again he left her after a temporary reconciliation. Rachel, however, returned to Harrodsburg, but it was impossible to patch up her marriage with Robards. In

July 1790 she finally left Kentucky in company with Jackson. This was the beginning of a long and unhappy episode. Robards sought a divorce of the Virginia general assembly through his brother-in-law, Colonel Jack Jouett of revolutionary war fame, but governmental red tape (in which Robards was given permission to sue for a divorce in the supreme court of the district of Kentucky) delayed granting of a final decree. In the meantime, in August 1791, Jackson and Rachel Robards were married in the Gayoso Mansion near Natchez. Technically, Rachel's divorce from Robards had not been granted and the marriage was illegal, and in years to come Jackson's political enemies were to make capital of this.

In the years between 1790 and 1796 Jackson played an active role in the formation of the new state of Tennessee both in a legal and military manner. He settled his bride on the Poplar Grove Plantation and in the next few years traveled frequently back and forth between the central and eastern settlements of the district. In 1796 Jackson was elected a delegate to the constitutional convention and played an active role in the creation of the independent state. He had been a forceful advocate of the unification of the settlements into a compact union. Perhaps as a reward, he was elected the first representative from Tennessee to Congress, arriving in Philadelphia on December 5, 1796, to present his credentials. As a member of the House of Representatives, he supported the Jeffersonian cause and was no doubt disappointed when his favorite was defeated by John Adams. As a speaker he was turbulent if not explosive, but in expressing his views privately he was calm. He hardly distinguished himself as a legislator, largely because his term of service was not long enough to give him seasoning to become an effective statesman. Too, the cloud of William Blount's abortive plan to conquer Spanish Florida and subsequent expulsion from the United States Senate had a decided bearing on Jackson's career. He was sent to the United States Senate as a successor to Blount, but in 1798 he returned to Tennessee to straighten out his entangled personal affairs.

Jackson led a double life really. As politician he was active in the formation of Tennessee; as congressman and then senator he represented that state nationally. As a private citizen he was a trader, land speculator, merchant, farmer, lawyer, and sportsman. His success as the master of Poplar Grove Plantation and as a merchant was indifferent. His personal life was further complicated by a financial transaction he made with John B. Evans and Company through the manipulations of a speculator and rascal named David B. Allison. Allison signed a promissory note for nearly $1,500, a sum that seemed even larger in the face of a biting financial panic caused partly by the Bank of England suspending specie payments. As endorser of the Allison note, Jackson was caught in a precarious situation that caused him to lose his store and 3,300 acres of prime land. He was now faced with the hard challenge of recouping his fortunes while at the same time carrying on a public career.

In 1798 Jackson was elected judge of the supreme court of Tennessee, a position he held until 1804. In the last year of his service on the bench he became embroiled with the old frontier hero John Sevier. There had been ill feelings between the two men for some time over various causes arising from issues in the emerging state. On one particular occasion, October 1, 1803, Jackson overheard Sevier addressing a crowd on the courthouse steps in Knoxville about his service to the people. Jackson spoke up and said he too had rendered service. Sevier then committed the unpardonable act of referring to Jackson's marriage confusion. Jackson then challenged Sevier to a duel, which was averted only by entreaties of friends. This, however, did not end the affair. Later the two men faced each other with drawn pistols at Southwest Point in the Cherokee country. In this comic Gilbert and Sullivan confrontation, a frightened horse ran off with Sevier's pistols, and friends again averted an open fight by persuading Sevier to leave the field. Behind this was more than an insult to Rachel Jackson; the two men were rivals in deeply involved political and land speculative affairs.

Jackson was to become involved in the BURR CONSPIRACY. Aaron Burr reached the Cumberland on May 29, 1805, where he was welcomed by the citizens of Nashville. At a public dinner Jackson drank a hearty toast to the late vice-president of the United States and the victor in the duel with Alexander Hamilton. Burr was to win Jackson's support of his schemes, no doubt without the latter understanding fully what it was he was supporting. Before this episode ended, Jackson had become more deeply involved than he wished to be and later asked in a hot letter for an explanation of Burr's activities. The letter was in effect a withdrawal of Jackson's support, although he did lend Burr a couple of boats. A communication about Burr's intent from President Jefferson upset the people of Nashville, and in a feverish attempt to stop Burr, Jackson became involved in a frantic but fruitless attempt to protect the republic against a traitorous attack.

In the six-year period between the end of the Burr fiasco and the outbreak of the War of 1812, Jackson was engaged in various activities, among them recouping his ever-sagging fortune, developing his Hermitage Plantation, trading, and politics. During these years he had time to indulge his interest in horseracing. There was, however, a disturbing interlude in the fairly even tenor of Jackson's life as farmer and merchant. Charles Dickinson, a fashionable young man of Nashville, had on one occasion insulted Rachel, but had apologized. Later Jackson heard of his repeating the remark; there was also a misunderstanding over the exchange of some promissory notes. Their quarrel grew larger because it was egged on by various persons who had political or economic associations with the adversaries. Dickinson wrote in the Nashville *Review* that Jackson was "a worthless scoundrel, a poltroon and a coward." There followed the famous duel on May 30, 1806, just across the Tennessee line on the bank of the Red River in Kentucky, in which Jackson killed Dickinson. With the exception of this episode, this was the only period in which Jackson came close to enjoying a quiet, domestic life.

With the outbreak of the War of 1812 Jackson entered upon a new career as a military commander. He was caught up in a new and turbulent stream of activities that was to hurl him to national fame and destiny. The Tennessean volunteered for service in the war and was willing to go to any area the War Department ordered him. He met with disappointment, however, at not receiving a command. Late in 1812 Governor William Blount signed a commission making Jackson a major general of volunteers. By January 1812 Jackson had already raised a command of twenty-five hundred men and had personally given notes for equipping them. On January 7 one contingent under the command of Colonel John Coffee headed for the lower South. Jackson himself followed later with the rest of the Tennesseans. A month later, however, Jackson was ordered by James Wilkinson to dismiss his troops in Natchez and to return home. Refusing to do this, he marched his troops back to Nashville, where they were discharged on home grounds. In the interim period, May to November, the frustrated Jackson became involved in an argument that had arisen between his inspector, William Carroll, and Lieutenant Littleton Johnson. When Carroll refused to fight Johnson, he was challenged by Jesse Benton, and Jackson found himself forced into serving Carroll as a second. In the duel Jesse Benton stooped over and was shot in the buttock, which was humiliating to him. Because of this Jackson was involved in a subsequent physical encounter with Jesse Benton and his brother Thomas Hart Benton, in which he received a wound that was to cause him an enormous amount of suffering in the future.

In November of that year Jackson once again collected an army of Tennessee volunteers to quell troubles in the Creek country to the south, where inhabitants of Fort Mims had been massacred by Indians. Jackson and John Coffee prepared to invade the woodlands of central Alabama. In a strenuous march Jackson's command pushed forward almost without benefit of supply lines or waystations through the wilderness. On the way south they established bases in Alabama named Fort Recovery, Fort Strother, and Fort Williams. Coffee made the first strike against the Indians near Fort Strother, killing men, women, and children. A second move was made to free the Talladega village from siege, where again the Creek were surrounded and threatened with annihilation. Only a slip-up in troop placement allowed some of the Indians to escape.

The Tennessee army was troubled by an overextension of its line, failure to receive supplies, and Jackson's illness, incurred in the Benton encounter. Because of these handicaps Jackson had to delay his forward movement, which threatened his expedition with failure. His men were disgruntled, and the Creek were assembling large numbers of warriors. It was not until March 1814 that the volunteers could resume their march.

On the morning of March 27 the militiamen were in Horseshoe Bend of the Tallapoosa River, Alabama, reaching this place before the Creek had fortified their line of defense. The ensuing battle was formulated on the surrounding tactics that had been used successfully at Fort Strother and Talladega. By three o'clock in the afternoon eight hundred Indians were dead and approximately three hundred women had been taken captive. The battle of HORSESHOE BEND, or Tohopeka, was a complete victory, not only because of its immediate rout of the enemy, but because it broke the back of Indian resistance in this area of the South.

Following the battle of Horseshoe Bend, Jackson pursued the Indians southward toward the Gulf in a drive to break Spanish-Indian collaboration. For Jackson and his volunteers, the Alabama campaign was a triumph of arms and human endurance. It was also to have far-reaching political and economic importance. Jackson's personal position was now firmly solidified in Tennessee. In dealing with the Indians he was a hard bargainer. In the great council at Fort Jackson on August 1, 1814, he prescribed sweeping terms that gave the Americans virtual domination of both Indians and land in the area of Alabama. In recognition of his accomplishment the government commissioned him as a major general in the regular army.

Once the Indians along the upper reaches of the Alabama River were subdued, Jackson shifted his scene of operation to the neighborhood of Mobile, where he remained until the latter part of November 1814, all the time keeping an eye on the Creek and their allies. When he received word that he was urgently needed in New Orleans, he left a part of his command with General James Winchester and headed for the Mississippi. On December 1 he arrived in New Orleans and engaged himself in reconnoitering the area east and south of the city, locating three lines of defense, building a fortified front, gathering men and supplies, and fighting off British preliminary assaults. Early in the morning of January 8, 1815, the main thrust of the British against the New Orleans front occurred. This was the main battle of NEW ORLEANS, and it resulted in a clear victory for the Americans. General Jackson had been as successful against the British as against the Creek. He emerged from the Plains of Chalmette both as a frontier and national hero.

Jackson's southern campaign in the War of 1812 was a battle against almost insuperable odds. He lacked men, supplies, and transportation facilities and was almost without communication. For an extended period after the British withdrew, it was necessary for him to maintain a state of martial watchfulness on the Mississippi. This embroiled him in a contempt of court charge with Judge Dominick Hall. Judge Hall had ignored the martial law imposed on the city, and Jackson charged that the judge had aided the enemy. Jackson was fined $1,000, but refused to allow his friends to pay it. On April 7 Jackson left New Orleans to operate in a much broader field.

On February 15, 1815, Jackson arrived home in Tennessee and suddenly found himself transformed from the status of a local country squire to that of national hero. His world had changed. For the first time he was out of debt, and already his admirers were speaking of an even more glamorous future. Rest and pleasure at being back with his family and his horses promised a moment of peace. This calm was not to endure for long. There remained the tumultuous Indian-Spanish border along the Gulf, but unlike the Creek troubles in the Alabama country, the international territory of East Florida was involved. In this area the United States had to deal with two Indian groups and the Spanish and British. So far, American military forces had been unsuccessful in quelling threats to American expansion and trade in the coastal country.

By the time James Monroe was inaugurated president of the United States, Jackson had become involved in an argument with the War Department and with John Adair and the Kentuckians. His dispute with the War Department arose over an attempt to reassign Jackson's officers to other, less pleasing, duties. After an exchange of letters he took it upon himself to order his men to ignore War Department orders. His dispute with John

Jackson's popular image was nurtured by a profusion of engravings based on such sentimental anecdotal paintings as Christian Schussele's portrayal of Jackson's confrontation with Judge Hall. (Bettmann Archive)

Adair and the Kentuckians arose over charges of failure and cowardice on the west bank of the Mississippi during the battle of New Orleans.

The newly appointed secretary of war, John C. Calhoun, ordered Jackson south to the southern Georgian frontier on December 26, 1817. This was the beginning of a long and bitter controversy. Jackson wondered if patrolling the border would lead only to slaughter. Or did the administration have in mind a more comprehensive and aggressive policy? General Edmund Pendleton Gaines, Jackson's immediate predecessor, had operated under defective orders. Reading Calhoun's instructions, Jackson undertook to clarify the objectives of his mission. His own wishes were to seize East Florida for the United States. He asked for some official intimation that this would be desirable, if not a formal communication then perhaps word through Congressman John Rhea.

By February 1818 Jackson's command had arrived in southern Georgia, where he received the much disputed "Rhea Letter." Monroe had been ill and had not responded to Jackson's request for instructions through this source. Jackson jumped to the conclusion that Rhea had written him with full presidential knowledge. It is not now possible for historians to recite with full assurance all the precise official facts in this case. It seems, however, that Congressman Rhea wrote more than he knew and that General Jackson read into his letter more than the letter actually said. Anyway, it was unofficial. The military facts are that early in March the Americans invaded Florida in what became the Seminole War. At St. Marks they captured the Scottish trader Alexander

Arbuthnot, who had long-standing amicable relations with the Seminole and Creek, and two Indian chiefs. The latter were hanged at the outset. Arbuthnot was tried and executed. Robert C. Ambrister, a young Englishman, fell into the Jacksonian net and was tried and executed on grounds that he had incited the Indians to fight. In the process of the court-martial Jackson was made technically responsible for the hangings.

Jackson's Florida campaign aggravated an already brittle relationship with the Creek refugees and the Seminole and stirred a conflict that was not to end until the closing of the Seminole War. Of even greater importance was the fact that the border campaign led to acute bitterness between Spain and the United States and to the negotiation of the Adams-Onís treaty (1819), by which Spain ceded East Florida to the United States upon payment of $5 million.

In April 1820 Jackson was appointed territorial governor of Florida, a position he held until October 5, 1821. The Florida episode was to involve the general in a running debate for the rest of his life. His opponents used issues growing out of it in three presidential campaigns. In the campaign of 1828 they published the famous "Coffin Pamphlet," which dragged in the hanging of Arbuthnot, Ambrister, and other victims. Congress voted down anti-Jackson resolutions but not without a show of considerable strength against General Jackson's strong-armed actions on the Gulf. Jackson believed conditions in Florida demanded strong and direct action, and this was the policy he pursued with marked success. This campaign, however, was not to add luster to his growing reputation.

The name of Jackson is associated indelibly with American frontier expansion in the nineteenth century. It is unlikely that any historian will ever be able to say with satisfactory assurance what his full influence upon the frontier was. The debate will continue as to whether Jackson was made by the frontier, or whether he was highly influential in shaping the turn of events of his period. It is more likely that he was distinctly a product of his age and that, as chief executive of the United States, he was in a position to influence the making of broad frontier and national policies.

Jackson was not a frontiersman in a comparable sense with Daniel Boone, Simon Kenton, Isaac Shelby, John Sevier, James Robertson, or the later explorers and mountainmen. He was never a trailbreaker, an Indian scout, a cabin builder, or a common foot militiaman. Yet his background and life experience to 1828 was that of a frontier lawyer and southern planter, advancing from the backwoods settlements to become a successful farmer, militia officer, and politician. Jackson personified his era for hundreds of thousands of Americans. He was a personality to whom they could personally relate. If they felt deprived of education, they could recall that he was not educated; if their attitude toward the Indians was challenged, they could refer to Jackson's attitudes and actions. If they were afraid of getting themselves involved in costly internal improvement projects, they could refer to his reactions. Jackson was a strong nationalist, and so were the American frontiersmen in the expanding West. Even though Jackson's attitude toward banking and monetary policies left much to be desired, people of the frontier shared his suspicions. They did not understand money, banking, or government fiscal policies, and perhaps Jackson himself was not much better informed.

At no level of society was the age and influence of Andrew Jackson more keenly felt than in the area of frontier politics. Obviously the Jacksonians did not invent rotation in office, fierce partisanism, or an abiding sense of egalitarianism, but they became accepted facts with Jackson. It is an open question whether the common man gloried in a spirit of aggressive egalitarianism more in the age of Jackson than in preceding decades, but frontiersmen practiced this belief with marked intensity.

As president of the United States Jackson favored frontier interests in at least four major issues: Indian removal, removal of government deposits from the Bank of the United States, the Maysville Veto, and a frugal federal tax policy. No doubt most frontiersmen agreed wholeheartedly with the president's actions in the famous nullification controversy, which arose between the South Carolinian and the federal government over tariff policies. Certainly they shared his deep sense of nationalism and the central idea of a strong Union.

The Removal Act of 1830 cleared several areas of the frontier of Indians and opened to settlement large blocks of fresh public lands. No more than a handful of common yeoman backwoodsmen either read or knew anything about the long history of United States Indian policy or even read the stern messages of the president on this subject; nevertheless they knew about the removal of the eastern Indians to lands west of the Mississippi. Most of them did not, however, partake in Jackson's lip service to humanitarian interests. Jackson's personal attitudes and beliefs about the Indians reflected the racial and cultural arrogance prevailing in the nation, and particularly the West, during his times. He saw them primarily as an obstacle to the economic and political development of the land. Like his contemporaries, it is doubtful that it ever occurred to him to consider the Indian as a human. He classed them along with escaped slaves in his hierarchy of values, referring to his quarry in the Florida campaign of 1818 as "parti-colored banditti." Jackson did not "hate" Indians; neither did he hate the wild animals that he might hunt in the wilderness.

It is difficult to explain why partisans of the Ohio valley country and the South supported Jackson's opposition to the Maysville Road Bill, except to say that this was a politically charged issue that involved personalities more than it did the fundamental issue of internal improvements. Although frontier acceptance of the veto was within itself an economic and political anomaly, it appealed to people who had an ingrained fear of taxation for any purpose. The Maysville Veto was in many ways one of the major disasters of the rapidly expanding American frontier of the 1830s. It delayed for almost three quarters of a century the opening of adequate public roads to keep up with both demand for transportation facilities and the production and distribution of frontier goods. Jackson's actions gave considerable strength to the arguments of anti-internal-improvement partisans in the state legislatures.

Jackson's war with Nicholas Biddle and the Bank of the United States involved too many subtleties for many frontiersmen to understand. They did understand, however, that banks could be both exploitative and risky. Bank issues involved constitutional delegates and legislators in endless debate. Before Jackson reached Washington the banking question was a full-blown issue. He only gave these arguments against banks a dramatic national standing.

In other respects the age of Jackson was reflected in the bringing to full fruition of the folk mind and culture. Since the middle of the seventeenth century frontiersmen had been building themselves into heroic proportions as individuals who performed numerous feats of superior human adventure, which lifted them above the rank of their fellows. This was an age when folk-yarn spinners found publishers for their tales, when the roads and steamboats brought travelers to view backwoodsmen and their homes, and when newer generations of Americans were charmed by the stories of their heroic forebears. Despite all its bustle and fermentation, the Jacksonian age was the first time the early waves of settlers found leisure and security enough to sit down and reminisce about their exploits. This aspect of frontier culture became so intimately interwoven with contemporary political activities that the latter took on the sacrosanct aspects of the self-sacrificing fight against all odds necessary to make settlement. Jackson had been a colorful personal part of the past, and he was a willful arbiter of the present. He, too, had reached the time in life when the past evoked a glow of hardship, a call for courage, a rising national pride, and the thrill of bare-knuckle personal politics. Now the American dream of continental expansion seemed certain of eventual realization, and Jackson's expansionist policies gave support and substance to that dream.

It mattered not to the Jacksonians that much of the expansionism of their age had little or no direct connection with their politics. The building of the first railroads, the digging of canals, opening of mills and mines, the rise of cities, the development of a merchant marine, the development of public schools, the rise of institutions of higher learning, and the establishment of insane asylums would have come as a matter of fact, but they came in this age. Artists, scientists, editors, authors, and inventors all contributed to the color and substance of the age. Only at a few periods in American history did so many forces of so revolutionary a nature converge to shape an era as in the Jacksonian period. All these gave impetus to the westward movement. Many of the changes of this age were attributed by the simple bit actors on the great national stage to their central hero, Andrew Jackson. As John W. Ward has said, he personified for the frontiersmen three massive American emotions: the forces of nature, providence, and human willpower.

The bibliography pertaining to Jackson is extensive. The best single source is John Spencer Bassett, *The Life of Andrew Jackson*, 2 vols. (1911). An interpretive study is Harold C. Syrett, *Andrew Jackson: His Contribution to the American Tradition* (1953). Marquis James, *Andrew Jackson, the Border Captain* (1933), closely parallels the Bassett account and is more colorful. Frederick A. Ogg, *The Reign of Andrew Jackson* (1921), is a brief interpretive account. Standard of the older accounts is James Parton, *The Life of Andrew Jackson*, 3 vols. (1860).—T. D. C.

Jackson, Helen [Maria Fiske] Hunt (1830-1885). Novelist and poet. Jackson was born in Amherst, Massachusetts, where she was a neighbor and schoolmate of Emily Dickinson, who remained a lifelong friend. Her first marriage, to Edward Hunt, an army engineer, ended tragically when he was killed in an accident in 1863. One of their sons had previously died in 1854, and the other died in 1865. Completely bereft, Jackson moved to Newport, Rhode Island, where her husband had once been stationed and where she met the writer Thomas Wentworth Higginson, who encouraged her interest in literature. In 1872 she moved to California. While spending the winter of 1873-74 in Colorado Springs, she met William Jackson and married him a year later.

Although a nostalgic interpreter of an idealized western past, Jackson's view of the present was neither sentimental nor particularly sanguine. Nederland, Colorado, for example, she once summarily dismissed as "that dismal little mining town," and her most famous nonfiction work, *A Century of Dishonor* (1881), proved to be an effective propaganda tool in arousing public concern over the plight of the American Indian.

Nevertheless, *Ramona* (1884), her best-known work of fiction, clearly betrays Jackson's weaknesses as well as indicates her strengths. Conceived as a fictional counterpart to *A Century of Dishonor*, *Ramona* lacks the force of the former book. Social commentary shades into sentimentality, and the plight of the Indian heroine is too easily lost sight of amidst the nostalgic never-never-land of a romantic California past that never existed. Too great allegiance to the conventions of sentimental literature prevent *Ramona*, as well as Jackson's other imaginative writing, from achieving real literary excellence. —J. K. F.

Jackson, Sheldon (1834-1909). Alaska promoter and missionary. Jackson, a native of New York State, was educated at Union College and Princeton Theological Seminary before ordination by the Presbytery of Albany, New York. His earliest service was among the Choctaw Indians; then he worked in Minnesota before receiving an appointment in 1870 as superintendent for the Board of Home Missions of the Rocky Mountain District. The district included Montana, Wyoming, Utah, Colorado, New Mexico, and Arizona. For a decade, until 1882, he edited the *Rocky Mountain Presbyterian* and roamed and organized his giant parish. His administrative ingenuity and incredible energy were disguised by a short stature, weak eyes, and an unimpressive physique.

In 1877 he visited Alaska and established in Wrangell a mission directed by Mrs. Amanda McFarland, whose frustrated attempts to formalize social relations on the frontier he publicized widely. Through his friend John Eaton, United States commissioner of education, Jackson obtained federal funds to help finance Alaska's mission schools. The educational and missionary work was shared by several Christian denominations on the basis of informal jurisdictional agreements. Jackson himself became in 1885 general agent of education in Alaska. He was perhaps Alaska's most effective Washington lobbyist during the nineteenth century. His friendship with prominent political figures, especially Senator Benjamin Harrison of the Committee on Territories, and his ability to arouse public opinion helped to promote passage of Alaska's earliest Organic Act and other legislation supporting the territory. A former Presbyterian minister, John G. Brady, served as Alaska's "first noncarpetbag governor" (1897-1906), thanks to Jackson's lobbying. Jackson also directed the transplantation of domesticated reindeer from Siberia, in order to supplement the food supplies of Alaskan Eskimos, and during the gold rush he toured the Yukon River for the Department of Agriculture.

The Presbyterian hierarchy's influence did not go unchallenged within Alaska. Not surprisingly, the missionaries came out "in favor of sobriety and chastity" and honest officials, thereby alienating a segment of the population. Jackson was on one occasion arrested. Despite opposition, his record of concern for the natives and for home rule has led Professor Ted Hinckley to conclude that Jackson was a positive force in the early history of American Alaska.

See Ted C. Hinckley, "The Presbyterian Leadership in Pioneer Alaska," *Journal of American History* (March 1966), and "Sheldon Jackson and Benjamin Harrison," *Pacific Northwest Quarterly* (April 1963); and Robert L. Stewart, *Sheldon Jackson* (1908).—M. B. S.

Jackson, William Henry (1843-1942). Photographer and painter. Born in Keeseville, New York, Jackson received no formal art training. Best known today for his photographs of the West, he accompanied a wagon train across the continent to California in 1866 and later was employed as a photographer with the Hayden geological survey of the Yellowstone region in 1871. He settled in Denver and set up a photographic studio. Commissioned by *Harper's Weekly*, he made photographic reports of many sections of the West and produced a number of paintings illustrative of his western experiences. His *California Crossing*, in the collection of the Thomas Gilcrease Institute of American History and Art, Tulsa, Oklahoma, is an excellent example of his untutored style and incorporates many details of the activities attending the crossing of the South Platte River by a large body of immigrants. A collection of his watercolors was utilized as illustrations in *Picture Maker of the Old West*, published in 1947 by his son, Clarence S. Jackson. Most of his paintings are in private hands.

See Clarence S. Jackson, *Picture Maker of the Old West* (1947), and *The Diaries of William Henry Jackson*, edited by LeRoy R. Hafen and Ann W. Hafen (1959). —D. C. H.

Jackson, W. Turrentine (1915-　　). Historian. Born in Ruston, Louisiana, Jackson attended the University of Texas at El Paso and the University of Texas at Austin, where he worked under Walter Prescott Webb, a prominent western historian who analyzed the influence of environmental factors in western history, especially on the Great Plains. An enthusiastic teacher of western history, Jackson joined the University of California at Los Angeles in 1940, moved to Iowa State University in 1941, and on to the University of Chicago in 1947. In 1949 he was a visiting professor at the University of Glasgow and in 1950 joined the University of California at Davis, where he remained for more than two decades.

An active researcher, Jackson wrote about various phases of western economic history. His first book was *Wagon Roads West* (1952), an account of the role of the United States Army Engineers and their road-building projects in the trans-Mississippi West. Meanwhile, Jackson had also authored various articles about the cattle industry in Wyoming and Colorado and collaborated on a study of the cattle business in nineteenth-century Colorado, *When Grass Was King* (1956). During the succeeding decade Jackson increasingly focused his energies on mining development in the trans-Mississippi region, especially the role of foreign investors in the years after the Civil War. One phase of this interest, concerned with mining development in Arizona, was addressed in *Treasure Hill* (1963). Five years later appeared Jackson's comprehensive work on the activities of Scottish investors in western mining, *The Enterprising Scot* (1968), a detailed scholarly account that did much to clarify the role of European influences on western growth in the later nineteenth century.—G. D. N.

Jackson family. Virginia and West Virginia politicians. George Jackson (1757-1831), lawyer and legislator of western Virginia, led the successful opposition to confirmation of the colonial Indiana Company's extensive claims to northwestern Virginia land. At the same time, Jackson acquired upward of 60,000 acres of land in the same region, while his brother, Edward (1759-1828), a surveyor and Virginia assemblyman, acquired 72,867 acres in his own right and 51,936 in partnership with others. From these two men descended western Virginia's most prominent and powerful family.

George Jackson served in the Virginia federal convention of 1788, in the Virginia and Ohio legislatures, and in Congress. Among his descendants, his sons John George (1777-1825) and Edward Brake Jackson (1793-1826) followed him to Congress and also served as the first judge and clerk, respectively, of the federal district

court of western Virginia. John George Jackson's grandson, John Jay Jackson, Jr. (1824-1907), was appointed by Lincoln to the same judgeship in 1861 and held it for thirty-four years, during which time he rendered important decisions affecting Reconstruction politics and labor union activities in the West Virginia coalfields. General John Jay Jackson, Sr. (1800-77) held local and legislative offices and was prominent among those western Unionists who opposed both secession and the creation of West Virginia. His two younger sons, James Monroe (1825-1901) and Jacob Beeson Jackson (1829-93), served, respectively, as a West Virginia jurist and congressman and as governor of West Virginia.

The descendants of Edward Jackson, the surveyor, formed a large and locally prominent cadet branch of the family whose best-known members were Thomas Jonathan "Stonewall" Jackson (1824-63), the Confederate military leader; and William Lowther Jackson (1825-90), a Virginia jurist and lieutenant-governor and a Confederate officer in his cousin's command.

Apart from entries in biographical compendia and a book by George W. Atkinson and Alvaro F. Gibbens, *Prominent Men of West Virginia* (1890), Stonewall Jackson's biographers provide the best source of information on his large and "very clannish" family. See especially Roy Bird Cook, *The Family and Early Life of Stonewall Jackson* (1924); and Mary Anna Jackson, *Memoirs of "Stonewall" Jackson by His Widow* (1895). —J. A. W.

Jacobs, Wilbur S. (1918-　　). Historian. Born in Chicago, Illinois, Jacobs received his education at the University of California at Los Angeles. After teaching at Stanford University from 1947 to 1949, he joined the history department at the University of California in Santa Barbara, where he remained for the next two decades. Meanwhile, he was a frequent lecturer at many universities, including Indiana University, the University of Colorado, the Claremont Graduate School, and the University of California at Los Angeles.

Jacobs had varied interests. His first book, *Diplomacy and Indian Gifts* (1950), examined in depth British policies in regard to Indian tribes on the frontier during the eighteenth century. Jacobs continued this theme in *Indians of the Southern Colonial Frontier* (1954), which also included an analysis of Anglo-Spanish rivalry. In succeeding years he increasingly turned his attention to the historiography of frontier history. He edited *The Letters of Francis Parkman* (1960) and then—aided by several fellowships from the Henry E. Huntington Library and Art Gallery—focused on Frederick Jackson Turner. Some of his research in the Turner manuscripts at the Huntington Library found its way into *Frederick Jackson Turner's Legacy* (1965), an analysis of diverse aspects of the frontier hypothesis. Jacobs followed this study with *The Historical World of Frederick Jackson Turner* (1968), a work designed to reconstruct the context within which Turner developed many of his major ideas. By 1970 Jacobs became increasingly concerned with the history of ecological imbalance and natural resource conservation and wrote several articles pleading with historians to investigate these subjects more intensively.—G. D. N.

James, Edwin (1797-1861). Explorer and scientist. Dr. James's fame rests upon his report of the Long expedition of 1820 (see Stephen H. Long). It was cautious and was not well received by an expansion-minded America. Following this task he became a surgeon in the army. Resigning in 1830, he continued his study of Indian languages, did some writing, and eventually settled down as a farmer in Iowa. In later years James became an eccentric, a recluse, and also an abolitionist.

See James obituary by C.C. Parry in *American Journal of Science and Arts* (May 1862).—R. A. B.

James, Jesse [Woodson] (1847-1882) and **[Alexander] Frank[lin]** (1843-1915). Bank robbers, train robbers. Frank and Jesse James were legends in their own time and occupy a place of preeminence in the folklore of western outlawry. In the role of an American Robin Hood, forced into crime to protect the poor and the weak, Jesse James and his brother Frank have won praise and admiration for their criminal activities. The ballad of Jesse James told the story in a few words: "Jesse James was a lad who killed many a man. / He robbed the Glendale train. / He took from the rich and he gave to the poor. / He'd a hand and a heart and a brain." Any account of Jesse and Frank James must take into consideration the benevolent mantle of folklore that surrounds them and must take care not to be swept away by the appealing character of the legend, for the truth is that Jesse and Frank James were thieves and murderers. Even the argument that they were driven to lives of crime falls apart in the light of hundreds of their neighbors who lived out their lives respectably even though they were spawned by the same environment and circumstances that produced the James boys.

America's most famous outlaws were born in Clay County, Missouri, to the Reverend Robert James and his wife, Zerelda. Jesse was only three when his father left for California. The Reverend James died there, and Mrs. James married Dr. Reuben Samuel in 1855. The James boys grew up in an atmosphere of sectional conflict. When the Civil War came, Frank joined William Clarke Quantrill's guerrillas. Quantrill soon became notorious as a plunderer and murderer, but in 1864, Jesse followed his brother's lead by joining the guerrillas under "Bloody Bill" Anderson. Jesse participated in the Centralia massacre when twenty-four unarmed Union soldiers were ruthlessly shot. In the spring of 1865 Jesse attempted to surrender under a white flag, but being a guerrilla, was shot at and seriously wounded by Union soldiers.

After Jesse's recuperation, the James boys apparently launched their careers of crime at Liberty, Missouri, on February 13, 1866, when they robbed a bank and killed a bystander. Other bank robberies were attributed to them and their friends the Youngers, but not until the robbery of the bank at Gallatin, Missouri, in 1869 were they clearly identified. The Gallatin bank job was followed by others from Iowa to Alabama. The James boys expanded their operations to include stages and trains and were blamed for many other crimes. They were audacious and impudent. Once they robbed a bank while a political rally was in progress. On the way out of town Jesse reined up and told the crowd that he thought something was wrong at the bank. On another occasion they robbed the box office at a Kansas City fair in the middle of a crowd of ten thousand people. Such exploits gave rise to a romanticized view of Jesse James and launched a Robin Hood legend that conveniently ig-

nored the little girl who was wounded at the Kansas City fairgrounds and the other innocent, if not youthful, people who died at the hands of these desperadoes. But the sensational stories rolled off the presses and made the James boys celebrities as well as criminals.

One popular legend has always blamed Jesse's outlawry on corrupt legal officials and the railroads that allegedly forced his family off their land. Casting the railroad as villain was not difficult in the 1870s, but the truth is that Frank and Jesse were criminals long before they robbed a train. Nevertheless, the legend persists and is usually connected with a real tragedy that won sympathy for the Jameses throughout Missouri. The efficiency of the gang in robbing trains was so great that in 1874, Pinkerton detectives were hired to hunt them down. On the night of January 5, 1875, two unidentified men, later rumored to be Pinkerton men, tossed a "bomb" (actually a flare) into the Samuel house. Jesse's young half-brother was killed, and his mother's arm was blown away. The incident gave credence to the claim that Frank and Jesse were the victims of railroad harassment. Jesse took advantage of the incident, increasing his depredations with full awareness of public sympathy for him. So great was public anger that the state legislature came very close to voting amnesty for the entire James gang.

Then, in 1876, Jesse made a mistake. He and Frank joined forces with the Younger gang to rob the bank at Northfield, Minnesota. The robbery became a death trap. Three men were killed, the Youngers were captured, and Jesse and Frank barely escaped. For three years the James boys lived under assumed names in Nashville, Tennessee. But in October 1879 they struck again with a new gang by robbing a train at Glendale Station in Missouri. After two men were murdered by the James boys in 1881, the state of Missouri offered rewards of $5,000 each for Jesse and Frank. The reward proved too great a temptation for two members of Jesse's gang. They made a deal with Governor Thomas Crittenden to assassinate Jesse.

On April 3, 1882, Jesse James was shot dead in his home at St. Joseph, Missouri, by Robert Ford, as the outlaw leader stood on a chair straightening a picture. Jesse James's career of robbery and murder was over, but the headlines of the Kansas City *Journal*—"GOODBYE JESSE"—heralded the beginning of a legend in the tradition of Robin Hood.

A few months later Frank James gave himself up. He was tried first in Missouri on a charge of murder and found not guilty. Next he was tried for robbery at Huntsville, Alabama, and found not guilty. The authorities returned him to Missouri for trial on yet another charge of armed robbery. Again, he was released. Frank James was a free man. That is a measure of public sentiment in Missouri in one sense, but it is also true that the state could not put together a single case against him that the authorities believed would stick. Frank James lived a quiet, retiring life until his death in 1915.

See William A. Settle, *Jesse James Was His Name* (1966).—G. L. R.

James, Will[iam Roderick] (1892-1942). Novelist, short-story writer, and illustrator. According to the story he was later to tell in *Lone Cowboy* (1930), James was born near Great Falls, Montana. Orphaned at an early age, he was adopted by a French trapper named

Jesse James after death. (National Archives)

Frank James as he appeared in 1898. (National Archives)

Jean Beaupre. He spent his youth traveling over the West until, when he was about fourteen years old, the trapper died. The bereaved James continued his life on the range as a solitary lone cowboy.

In sober fact, however, Will James was born Ernest Dufault in the town of St. Nazaire de Acton, in the Canadian province of Quebec, of respectable and moderately successful parents. When he was fifteen Ernest Dufault left Quebec for the Canadian West, appearing in Montana about 1910 complete with the name of Will James and a legend to account for his possession of it. After 1910 James worked as a cowboy for various ranches in the United States and Canada, captured wild horses in Nevada, entered rodeo competitions, and was a stunt rider for a number of Hollywood western films. His varied experiences on the range form the factual basis of his fiction. He never considered himself solely an author, and at the time of his death owned and operated a large ranch near Billings, Montana.

James is primarily remembered now as the man who wrote *Smoky* (1926), one of the all-time favorite animal stories for children. Since *Smoky* is read today almost entirely by juveniles, James has been somewhat unjustly relegated to the status of a child's author. This is not quite fair; in fact, *Smoky* is the only one of his stories to have been written primarily for children. The rest of his novels and stories are pure adventure fiction, with a strong anecdotal base in James's own biography or in stories he had heard during his checkered career on the range. In addition to his fiction James also wrote an entertaining description of life in the cattle country, *Cowboys North and South* (1923).

James is interesting literarily as one of the few cowboy authors who claimed—believably—to have been totally insulated from books and bookishness until a series of riding accidents laid him up and made him turn his hand to literature. While many cowboy authors tend to write a mannered prose, James wrote in a swift-moving, colloquial western idiom, closer to spoken than to written English. His style, though often technically incorrect, is compelling and curiously moving; and it is generally free from the dependence upon literary stereotype that mars so much western writing.

James's autobiographical *Lone Cowboy* cannot be trusted as an accurate account of his own life, though it does contain—along with *The Drifting Cowboy* (1925) and *All in a Day's Riding* (1933)—many excellent vignettes of day-to-day life on the range at roughly the turn of the century. Anthony Amaral's *Will James: The Gilt Edged Cowboy* (1967), which also contains a bibliography of James's writing, must be used to set James's biographical record straight.—J. K. F.

About 1920 James began to study art in San Francisco, where he soon was producing illustrations for *Sunset* magazine. Having earlier visited Reno, Nevada, he returned there in the 1920s and began to write and illustrate stories about western life for *Scribner's Monthly*, the *Saturday Evening Post*, and other magazines. Some of these illustrations were later used in such books as *Cowboys North and South*, *The Drifting Cowboy* (1925), and *Cow Country* (1927), all nonfiction. *Smoky* was also illustrated with his pen-and-ink drawings. When James died, he had achieved a wide reputation in America as a chronicler of cowboy life. His paintings and drawings are widely scattered in private and museum collections.—D. C. H.

Japanese-Americans. The majority of the Issei, the "first generation" of immigrants from Japan, located in California; 10,151 Japanese resided there in 1900 and 71,952 in 1920. In these two census years the national total of Japanese residents amounted to 24,326 and 111,010 respectively. The states on the West Coast benefited from their proximity to Japan, with Washington having attracted 5,617 Japanese in 1900 and 17,387 in 1920 and Oregon 2,501 in 1900 and 4,151 in 1920. Montana, Idaho, Utah, and Wyoming led the mountain states at the turn of the century in the number of Japanese residents, while Colorado showed the greatest increase, from 48 Japanese in 1900 to 2,464 in 1920. At the turn of the century Seattle was the urban center of Japanese immigration with 2,990 residents, followed by San Francisco (1,781) and Portland (1,189).

Within the following two decades, three fifths or more of the Japanese in California took up farming, and the new centers of Japanese immigration reflected the major economic activity of the newcomers. In 1920, Sacramento County (5,800) and Fresno County (5,732) outranked San Francisco (5,358) in size of their Japanese population, but the Los Angeles area outdistanced them all as the number of its Japanese residents increased from 204 in 1900 to 19,911 in 1920. In Washington, Seattle kept its position as a center of Japanese life with 7,874 inhabitants in 1920, as did Portland in Oregon, despite a slight decrease of the city's Japanese population to 1,715 inhabitants.

By 1920 the steady drift of Chinese from the rural sections of the West to the cities had left the Japanese as the largest Oriental group engaged in agriculture. In 1920, of the total of 111,010 Japanese in the United States, 25,657 were occupied in agriculture, forestry, and animal husbandry. The census of that year recorded one fifth of the Japanese residents in the category of domestic and personal service occupations, particularly as restaurant and hotel keepers, laundrymen, janitors, and barbers. Although permanently excluded by law from becoming United States citizens, and seriously limited by alien land acts in their ability to acquire agricultural and residential property, forty thousand Issei nevertheless managed to gain a recognized position in the wholesale distribution and retailing of fruits and vegetables in the West. Despite their handicaps, they had decided to remain and raise their children in the United States.

Some of the seventy thousand Nisei (second generation), composed of American-born children of Japanese immigrants, were reluctant to follow their parents into agriculture because of discriminatory land laws. In increasing numbers they prepared themselves to enter business, clerical jobs, and the professions. These young adults had achieved a degree of acculturation which made them indistinguishable from other Americans of their generation in speech and apparel as well as attitudes and ideals. About twenty thousand of them had been to Japan, mostly for brief childhood visits or a little schooling. Fewer than nine thousand, usually the older brothers and sisters in a family, were actual Kibei, who

were born in the United States but educated in Japan. Most of them had rejected the way of life in the land of their ancestors, and only a small number of Kibei identified themselves with it.

When the Japanese attacked Pearl Harbor in 1941, about 127,000 people of Japanese descent were living in the United States, more than 112,000 on the Pacific Coast. The month of stress and strain accompanying the Japanese conquests in Southeast Asia eroded the fine distinction between caution and hysteria and resulted in a series of measures intended to remove all persons of Japanese ancestry from the West Coast. Eventually, most Japanese-Americans were taken to ten barracks camps in California, Arizona, Idaho, Utah, Wyoming, Colorado, and Arkansas under the control of the War Relocation Agency. Private hostility and public harassments, including the virtual requirement that they sell their property at great loss, made such an impact that in January 1945, when the army ended the policy of mass expulsion and began to close the relocation camps, only two thirds of the Japanese-Americans at first chose to return.

In 1960, 473,170 Japanese-Americans lived in the United States, 408,048 of them in the West. Hawaii (203,876) led the states in the number of residents of Japanese ancestry, followed by California (157,317). These figures are strongly influenced by the practice of the Bureau of the Census that classifies children of mixed racial parentage according to the race of the nonwhite parent.

See Leonard J. Arrington, *The Price of Prejudice* (1962); Morton Grodzins, *Americans Betrayed: Politics and the Japanese Evacuation* (1949); Yamato Ichihashi, *Japanese in the United States* (1932); Harry H. Kitano, *Japanese Americans: The Evolution of a Subculture* (1969); Eliot Grinnell Mears, *Resident Orientals on the American Pacific Coast* (1928); H. Brett Melendy, *The Oriental Americans* (1972); Bradford Smith, *Americans from Japan* (1948); and Dorothy Swaine Thomas, *Japanese-American Evacuation and Resettlement* (1946-52).—G. B.

Japanese immigration. The trickle of Japanese newcomers to the West swelled to a stream in the first decade of the twentieth century. The increase of Japanese immigration followed social and economic changes in Japan set in motion by Commodore Matthew C. Perry's reopening of Japan to Western influences and by the Meiji Restoration. Another reason for the rise in immigration was the West Coast's need for cheap labor after the Exclusion Act of 1882 suspended immigration of Chinese laborers. In 1880 the census counted 148 Japanese in the United States, 2,039 in 1890, 24,326 in 1900, and 72,157 in 1910, the majority of them in California.

The opening of direct shipping between San Francisco and Japan in the 1850s had brought a few travelers and, toward the end of the 1860s, also a few settlers. Most publicized among the early colonists was a group led by J. H. Schnell, a German who had lived in Japan under the name of Matsudaira Takebe, and his Japanese wife. Their attempt to raise tea and silk at Gold Hill in Eldorado County failed, and the colonists dispersed. In the later decades of the nineteenth century, the importation of Japanese contract laborers into the kingdom of Hawaii facilitated the increasing flow of Japanese immigrants to the West. The sugar planters were seeking substitutes for Chinese workers who had entered business and commerce after the expiration of their terms of service, and in the 1880s, when the Japanese government officially sanctioned the recruiting of contract laborers, Hawaii became the destination of the first large-scale Japanese oversea emigration in modern times.

The contract laborers were recruited deliberately from impoverished sections of southwestern Japan in order to get experienced, hardy, and docile laborers. The chief motive of the contract workers was to make money on the plantations to better the position of their families and to return to Japan. Most of them, however, soon forgot that they had migrated only to earn the means to finance a better life in Japan and instead embarked on a new life in Hawaii, where by 1894 they were the backbone of the plantation labor force. The number of Japanese residents in Hawaii increased from 116 in 1884 to 61,111 in 1900. With the beginning of the emigration to the United States, people from the same areas in southwestern Japan, conditioned to transpacific migrations, contributed the greatest share of Japanese immigrants to the United States.

Anti-Oriental sentiment in California, fostered by the state's experience with the Chinese, soon shifted to the Japanese newcomers. In 1906 the San Francisco School Board crisis brought worldwide attention to the problem. When the Board of Education—under pressure from the Asiatic Exclusion League, founded in 1905 by labor leaders—ordered all Japanese and Korean pupils to join the Chinese in the Oriental school, protests from the Japanese government led to a diplomatic crisis between the United States and Japan. President Theodore Roosevelt worked out a compromise with San Francisco officials about the Japanese children and in turn arranged a clause in the gentlemen's agreement in which Japan promised not to issue passports for the continental United States to skilled and unskilled laborers. While the Labor and Progressive parties continued to attach to the Japanese the cultural stereotypes that had been employed earlier against the Chinese, after 1908 the changing concentration of the Japanese population shifted the focus of the anti-Japanese movement to rural areas, culminating in the Alien Land Act of 1913. The law provided that aliens ineligible for American citizenship (the Japanese fell into this category through the Naturalization Act of 1790) could not own land in California, or lease it for more than three years. Without openly saying so, it applied almost exclusively to Japanese aliens, but its chief effects were political and emotional, rather than economic. The Japanese-Americans transferred the land titles or leases to their American-born children or to corporations with a majority of the stock entrusted to American-born Japanese.

The conservative triumph of the 1920s and the elevation of anti-foreignism to a patriotic stance aided the continuing discrimination against Japanese newcomers. The Immigration Act of 1924, which contained a clause excluding from entry all aliens not eligible for citizenship, made Japanese exclusion the law of the land for twenty-eight years. Under the provisions of the Immigration and Nationality Act of 1952 (McCarran-Walter Act), Japan, with an annual quota of 185, contributed 4,973 immigrants between 1955 and 1964. The national origins quota was eliminated by the Immigration Act of 1965.

See Roger Daniels, *Politics of Prejudice* (1962); Yamato Ichihashi, *Japanese in the United States* (1932); Harry H. Kitano, *Japanese Americans: The Evolution of a Subculture* (1969); Eliot Grinnell Mears, *Resident Orientals on the American Pacific Coast* (1928).—G. B.

JA Ranch. In 1876 Charles GOODNIGHT founded the first ranch in the Panhandle of Texas. Born in Illinois, Goodnight had come to Texas with his parents in 1845. In 1855, en route to California, he and a friend were given a job tending cattle, for which they would later be given shares; thus he started his own herd. At the end of eleven years he and his partner had more than six thousand head of cattle. In 1866 Goodnight took his share of the cattle farther west in Texas near present-day Throckmorton. Shortly thereafter, he briefly trailed cattle with Oliver LOVING into New Mexico, selling them to the army. After successful ventures in Colorado and New Mexico, Goodnight returned to Texas in the fall of 1876 and established the predecessor to the JA Ranch in Armstrong County in the Palo Duro Canyon (near present-day Amarillo). Originally consisting of corrals and picket houses, Goodnight's ranching operations grew to encompass 700,000 acres. In 1878 he sold an interest in his ranch to John G. Adair, a gentleman financier from England. Before Adair's death in 1885 they built one of the largest ranches in Texas. By 1888 the ranch had forty thousand head of cattle on its 700,000 acres of land. As an advocate of herd improvement, Goodnight developed outstanding cattle by mixing Herefords and Longhorns; he also owned a herd of domesticated buffalo. In 1880 he helped found the Panhandle Stockmen's Association. The ranch was still in existence during the 1960s. Goodnight managed the ranch until 1889, when he sold his interest in it and moved into the area north of his old place to begin a ranch he would control completely. He died in 1929.

See Harley T. Burton, *A History of the JA Ranch* (1928).—J. A. S.

Jayhawkers. Kansas guerrilla movement during Civil War. The term *Jayhawker* was first applied in 1858 to antislavery, free-state-minded Kansas guerrillas. The origin of the name is clouded in controversy. One theory is that it was first used by Illinois emigrants to California in the 1849 gold rush. It may have been adopted by Kansas settlers in reference to the predatory habits of the blue jay.

The Kansas usage of *Jayhawker* was soon associated with the career of "Doc" Charles R. Jennison. Jennison, a sinister person in his late twenties from New York, surfaced in Kansas on the eve of the Civil War. Under a pose of abolitionism that fooled many, the unscrupulous, opportunistic Jennison was more dedicated to banditry than black freedom. In the summer of 1861 he led his Jayhawkers, operating at first without formal designation but soon to be known as the Independent Mounted Kansas Jayhawkers (Seventh Kansas Regiment), on a campaign of murder, looting, and theft in western Missouri that lasted until early 1862. The Jayhawkers struck their first major blow in July 1861, when they pillaged Harrisonville, Missouri, a pro-southern center. The Jayhawkers scored again in December 1861, in their brutal occupation of Independence, Missouri, during which they robbed the residents wholesale, burned houses, and beat and killed inhabitants. So undiscriminating were the Jayhawkers in their forays, that the loyal Unionists of Missouri began to protest vigorously against the actions of Jennison's troop. This led to the ouster of Jennison as commander of the Seventh Kansas in 1862, which thereafter served east of the Mississippi. Jennison stayed behind in Kansas as did most of the Jayhawkers. The Jayhawkers reemerged in 1863 as the Red Legs, an organization of irregulars with distinctive red leggings. Under the command of Jennison henchman George Hoyt, they flayed western Missouri with plundering raids that were similar to the Jayhawker exploits early in the war.

Back East the Seventh Kansas, reformed and purged of the bad habits of its Jennison phase, popularized the term so that after the Civil War all Kansans—regardless of wartime or political preferences—were called Jayhawkers. Since then Kansas has been known as the Jayhawk State, and the athletic teams of the University of Kansas have been nicknamed the Jayhawks.

See Richard S. Brownlee, *Gray Ghosts of the Confederacy: Guerrilla Warfare in the West, 1861-1865* (1958); Albert Castel, *A Frontier State at War: Kansas, 1861-1865* (1958); William A. Lyman, "Origin of the Name of 'Jayhawker,' and How It Came to Be Applied to the People of Kansas," *Collections of the Kansas State Historical Society*, vol. XIV (1915-18); and Mitford M. Mathews, ed., *A Dictionary of Americanisms on Historical Principles* (1951).—R. M. B.

Jay's Treaty (1794). Jay's Treaty (signed in 1794 but not implemented until 1796) relieved a genuine crisis in the relations between the United States and Great Britain. The crisis arose in early 1794, when the news of two unconnected "outrages" by Britain arrived almost simultaneously in the American capital. First, there was the disclosure of a cabinet order by authority of which the Royal Navy had begun to capture American ships that might be suspected of hauling goods for Britain's enemy, France. Second, there came to Philadelphia reports of a speech by Lord Dorchester, governor-general of Canada, clearly encouraging the Indians of the Great Lakes region to make war on the United States. In response to a public demand to "do something" about these outrages and out of a desire to head off a possible war with Britain, President George Washington sent Chief Justice John Jay to London to seek an overall settlement of Anglo-American differences.

One of these differences that particularly concerned the future of the West was the matter that Dorchester's speech brought sharply into focus: the control of the frontier between the United States and Canada. The United States's original treaty with Britain, the Treaty of Paris of 1783, had defined the boundary with precision but without full regard for the actual occupation of territory. Thus such strategically located posts as Oswego, Niagara, Detroit, and Michilimackinac were transferred to American ownership, even though the British army held them at the end of the American Revolution. And, indeed, redcoats continued to occupy these "northwest posts" for another decade, until the 1794 crisis and beyond. At first the British delay in surrendering the posts seemed merely incidental, rather like the unhurried evacuation of New York City. But as time passed, a British intention to retain the posts

indefinitely became unmistakable. When the weak Articles of Confederation government eventually complained, the British conceded the American title to the posts but refused to give them up until the Americans honored all of *their* obligations from the peace treaty—specifically the obligation to pay British creditors. Occupation of the posts gave the British, then, a kind of leverage for insuring that the terms of the peace treaty would be carried out.

In addition, the northwest posts assumed great importance in the thinking of British administrators in Canada, who worried about military attack from the United States, especially after the adoption of the new constitution and the inauguration of George Washington as president in 1790. For Lord Dorchester and his ambitious lieutenant in Upper Canada, John Simcoe, British possession of the posts, coupled with alliances with the frontier Indians, was the only feasible way of maintaining a "thin red line" of British authority in the wilderness of North America. To these colonial officials and to British merchants engaged in the highly lucrative fur trade (half of which came from below the border), the military campaigns of America's new federal government against the frontier Indians presented both a threat and an opportunity. If the Americans continued to lose battles to the Indians, as in 1790 and 1791, perhaps they would accept British mediation and a settlement that would include the erection, on American soil, of an Indian buffer state. At the time, one Britisher on the scene wrote: "I wish our peace makers of '83 had known a little more of this country . . . perhaps this is the important moment in which the unfortunate Terms of that Peace may be altered: perhaps this Moment will never return." In Philadelphia, however, Washington's administration declined the British offer of mediation and, instead, outfitted a new expedition against the Indians to be conducted by General Anthony Wayne.

As Wayne marched into the Indian country, Dorchester ordered the establishment of fortifications at Fort Miami to intercept the American force before it could reach Detroit. Thus the British in 1794 were not only preserving their old strongholds on American soil but were also moving southward to secure a new one. In August of that year, several days after a decisive victory over the Indians in the battle of FALLEN TIMBERS, Wayne's expedition pulled up outside Fort Miami. This was the climax of the frontier crisis. When the commander inside the fort received Wayne's request to withdraw, he declined, explaining that he was under military orders only and that the legality of the presence of British troops on American soil was a question for diplomats. Happily, Wayne decided against forcing compliance with his request. He stated that he too was willing to await the outcome of the diplomats' deliberations.

In those deliberations Jay found that the officials in London, preoccupied with their war in Europe, were much cooler than Dorchester and Simcoe to the notion of war with the United States. Consequently, the foreign secretary, Baron Grenville, despite his unwillingness to make any concessions on maritime questions (because they related directly to the European war), speedily agreed to evacuate the posts and drop his proposal for "rectifying" the boundary by bending it southward to touch the Mississippi River. Acceptable as these western provisions of Jay's Treaty were to Americans, the maritime provisions of the document were so objectionable that long and acrimonious debate ensued before the Senate approved and the president ratified it. But at last the treaty went into effect in 1796, and this time the British actually did relinquish the northwest posts. They did so, in fact, with considerable style. When Wayne took charge of Detroit he discovered that he was out of food. He was compelled to send across the Detroit River to borrow fifty barrels of salt pork from the British commander before he could proceed north to receive Michilimackinac, the last of the posts to be handed over.

See Samuel Flagg Bemis, *Jay's Treaty* (1923); and Bradford Perkins, *The First Rapprochement: England and the United States, 1795-1805* (1855).—W. B. F.

Jefferson, Thomas (1743-1826). Statesman, scholar, and third president of the United States. When Jefferson designed his dream house, Monticello, he included a broad porch and terrace facing west, toward the Blue Ridge, beyond which lay an immense wilderness awaiting exploration and settlement. Although Jefferson never penetrated the interior any further than the Shenandoah valley, the idea of an unspoiled West haunted his imagination and shaped his public policies throughout his life. He had early developed a passion for the land under the influence of his father, Peter Jefferson, a planter, burgess, and militiaman who had pushed up the James River in the 1740s and founded his estate, Shadwell, in Goochland (now Albemarle) County, Virginia, where Thomas was born. The influence was twofold. First, the elder Jefferson, a man of great intellectual as well as physical strength but of scant formal education, had cultivated his mind as assiduously as he had the soil, becoming thereby the embodiment of self-reliance, discipline, the democratic spirit, and a host of other virtues that his son would forever associate with the rural life. Second, Peter Jefferson gave Thomas his early education and his introduction to the classics. The writings of the French physiocrats and of John Locke, as well as the classics, have been variously cited as the source of Thomas Jefferson's agrarian views; but Jefferson, a brilliant graduate of the College of William and Mary and a voracious reader, would scarcely have drawn upon any single source.

Jefferson was little concerned with the commercial and speculative uses of land; rather, he esteemed land as the basis of a kind of society—the rural and agrarian— that seemed to produce men uniquely fitted for citizenship in the Republic. The values of the yeoman farmer, as typified by his father, were to Jefferson the only sound foundation for an uncorrupted republican government. This belief occasioned fears that as soon as the majority of the nation's population ceased to live by agriculture, turned to manufacturing, and congregated in cities, honest government would disappear. "The mobs of great cities," he warned, "add just so much to the support of pure government as sores do to the strength of the human body." After seeing Europe in the 1780s, he became even more convinced that individual liberty went hand in hand with frontier, or at least rural, conditions—a line of thinking similar to Benjamin Franklin's and foreshadowing by a century that of Frederick Jackson Turner. In Europe commerce and industry had tended to divide society into the rich and the poor, with power falling to the rich. And to Jefferson "the general prey of the rich upon the poor" was nothing less than tyranny. Convinced that "those who labor in the earth are the chosen people of God," he could only hope that most Americans would be given their own pieces of land to work. But an expanding population and future generations would require new lands, and so, quite logically, Jefferson looked to the West.

Jefferson's earliest opportunity to thwart the entrenchment of the aristocratic, European landholding system in America presented itself during his years in the Virginia legislature (1776-79). He successfully fought for abolition of entail, the restriction of a bequest of property to a stipulated line of descent, and pressed for abolition of primogeniture (achieved in 1785), the right of a firstborn son to inherit his father's estate. It was hoped that the abolition of both would forestall the accumulation of large tracts of land by any individual and thereby encourage the development of a society of small landowners.

Between 1781 and 1784 Jefferson was instrumental in persuading Virginia to deed its vast landholdings beyond the Appalachians to the nation, thus laying the foundations of the national domain. In 1784, as a member of the Congress of the Confederation, he wrote an ordinance proposing that the OLD NORTHWEST be carved into ten states, each with a democratic government. The ordinance was especially notable because it included a clause forbidding slavery in the proposed states. After each of the states passed through three easy stages of settlement and development, each was to be admitted to the Union on an equal footing with the original thirteen states. After rejecting the ten-state and antislavery clauses, Congress passed the ordinance but made its implementation contingent on the cession by all states of their western lands; it never did go into effect, because it was superseded by the NORTHWEST ORDINANCE, or Ordinance of 1787. In modified form, Jefferson's ideas about the admission of new states to the Union and his proposals for the rectilinear survey of western lands were included in the Land Ordinance of 1785 and the Northwest Ordinance; the latter, written in part by Jefferson's close friend James Monroe, established the unique American TERRITORIAL SYSTEM, by which more than twenty western territories were governed between 1788 and 1912.

As president, Jefferson procured in 1804 a relaxation of the land-purchase requirements imposed on settlers in the Northwest Territory. The Land Act of 1800, or Harrison Land Act, required that land, then selling at two dollars per acre, be sold in units of a minimum of 320 acres. The Jefferson administration reduced the minimum to 160 acres, and Jefferson himself fought back attempts to overturn the prevailing easy-credit policy. Abuse of the deferred-payments privilege by settlers led to the passage of the Land Act of 1820 during Monroe's presidency; this act lowered the price of land to $1.25 per acre but required immediate payment. This trend to ever-increasing democratization of land sales, which was to culminate in the Homestead Act of 1862, was in large measure the practical outcome of Jefferson's visionary agrarianism.

Jefferson's attention was also directed westward by his subscription to the ideals of the age. Enlightenment thinkers declared that order was sacred and that science made order possible. To this Jefferson added a strong utilitarian streak in his belief that all activity must serve a useful purpose. The unknown, the chaotic wilderness, thus constituted a fascinating challenge to his mind. His only book, *Notes on the State of Virginia* (1784), reveals a keen scientific interest in the geography, botany, and anthropology of the West.

As early as 1781 Jefferson showed an interest in finding an American water route to the Pacific Ocean—a variation of the idea that a legendary Northwest Passage led from the Atlantic to the Pacific. At the close of the Revolution he invited George Rogers Clark to explore western regions, but Clark declined. While Jefferson was in France as the American ambassador, John Ledyard, a Connecticut adventurer who had visited the Pacific Northwest in 1778 as a member of Captain James Cook's third voyage, was a frequent guest at Jefferson's hospitable table. To his host he proposed to cross Russia on foot, sail from Siberia to the Northwest Coast of North America, and then hike eastward across the continent to become the first person to circumambulate the globe. Jefferson responded to Ledyard's plan with enthusiasm and—even though Catherine the Great of Russia denied Ledyard permission—blessed his departure in 1788. Regrettably Ledyard got only as far as central Russia before being stopped by the Russians and returned to Europe. While in France, Jefferson also collected information on Spanish Louisiana, both for scientific and expansionist reasons. He confided to the American minister in Madrid that he hoped Louisiana would remain in Spanish hands, for since Spain was a weak power, that condition would benefit the United States.

Ledyard's failure only banked the fires of Jefferson's enthusiasm for exploring the West. In 1792, as secretary of state, Jefferson proposed sending the French botanist André Michaux up the Missouri and thence to the Pacific Ocean. A friend of the Jefferson family, Meriwether LEWIS, begged to go along, but Jefferson felt that Lewis, at eighteen, was too young for the undertaking. Eventually the question became academic, since Michaux became embroiled in French-American politics and the plans for his trip were abandoned.

A decade later, Jefferson, now president, revived the idea of a transcontinental expedition. He believed that the nation needed to assert its claim to the fur-rich Pacific Northwest; indeed, American vessels were already carrying furs collected by the Russians from the Pacific Northwest to China. In the spring of 1804, fifty men left St. Louis under the leadership of the now-mature Lewis and William CLARK bound for the Pacific Ocean. "The object of your mission," Jefferson wrote to them, "is to explore the Missouri River" and its tributaries in search of "the most direct and practicable water communication across this continent for the purposes of commerce." So little was then known about the trans-Mississippi West that Jefferson thought that perhaps the Missouri and Columbia rivers either flowed from the same source or were close enough for easy portage between the two. Along with economic and political considerations, Jefferson underscored the scientific importance of exploring the West. He ordered Lewis and Clark to make careful records of the soils, animal and vegetable life, minerals, and geography of the region they traversed. To his friend Caspar Wistar he lamented in 1803 that Lewis did not have "a perfect knowledge of botany, natural history, mineralogy and astronomy" but was pleased that the explorer had qualified himself for making astronomical observations by special training in Philadelphia.

Two years and more than seven thousand miles later, the LEWIS AND CLARK EXPEDITION returned from the wilderness with a wealth of information. The party had ascended the Missouri, had crossed the Continental Divide in western Montana, had followed the Lolo Trail to the Clearwater, Snake, and Columbia rivers, and ultimately had seen the Pacific. Jefferson was disappointed to learn that there were no easy portages between the Missouri and the Columbia rivers, but the information that the expedition provided and the news that the Missouri and its tributaries were teeming with fur-bearing animals delighted him.

In 1803, shortly before Lewis and Clark departed, Robert Livingston, Jefferson's minister to France, and special envoy James Monroe succeeded in buying the province of Louisiana from France for $15 million. The explorers would now be investigating American territory. Anxious to learn about other regions of Louisiana, Jefferson dispatched two expeditions up the Red River even before Lewis and Clark returned. The Red River expeditions did not succeed, but Jefferson wrung additional funds from Congress to launch Zebulon Pike on a trip to the headwaters of the Mississippi River. In 1806, Pike followed the Arkansas River to the front range of the Rocky Mountains, tried to climb the peak that bears his name, was captured by the Spanish army, and eventually returned with reports of country no American had previously seen.

To Jefferson the acquisition of Louisiana meant that he had at last secured enough land to make the United States a magnificent agrarian empire of hardy yeoman farmers. Privately troubled by the fact that the Constitution did not provide for the acquisition of new territory, he justified the LOUISIANA PURCHASE in his own mind on the grounds that the purchase would increase the stability of the Republic, for—like Madison—he believed that large republics would endure longer than small ones, because the great national concerns of the large would swallow up the factionalism that characterized the small. It was not Jefferson's intention, however, to populate the newly purchased territory immediately; the westward movement of the American people was to be a gradual and orderly extension of society at a pace just quick enough to prevent the population density of the eastern states from increasing to the point where their essentially rural character would be destroyed. Jefferson assumed that it would take hundreds of years for the American people to push the frontier to the Pacific and, thus, proposed that the lands west of the Mississippi be made an Indian reservation until the nation had extended its borders to the river, a process, he estimated, that would take at least half a century. The slow westward growth of society—as distinct from the haphazard intrusion of isolated settlers on the wilderness—would have created a West far different from that which was to be.

The immediate cause of the purchase of Louisiana was the desire to rid the West of the threat posed by the presence there of foreign powers and, more specifically, to remove control of the Mississippi, the major commercial artery of the West, from European hands. There remained, however, the British in the Northwest and the Spanish in the Southwest. American claims to the Northwest had, as noted, been a consideration in the launching of the Lewis and Clark expedition, but Jefferson offered a more direct challenge to British hegemony in the area by his support of the Northwest ventures of John Jacob ASTOR. (Ironically, Astor's enterprise was the juggernaut before which fell the government's system of fur-trading posts, which Jefferson had so carefully nurtured.) Jefferson's attitude toward the Spanish was expressed in a letter written in Paris on January 25, 1786, to his friend Archibald Stuart:

> Our confederacy must be viewed as the nest from which all America, North and South, is to be peopled. We should take care too not to think it for the interest of that great continent to press too soon on the Spaniards. Those countries cannot be in better hands. My fear is that they are too feeble to hold them till our population can be sufficiently advanced to gain it from them piece by piece.

The real importance of this letter is, of course, in its articulation of Jefferson's unquestioning belief in the justice of American territorial ambitions.

Both as inquiring scholar and public figure, Jefferson was fascinated with the American Indian, whom he liked and respected, arguing that Indians were on a "level with whites in the same uncultivated state." In his *Notes on the State of Virginia*, he attacked the French naturalist Buffon's argument that New World plants, animals, and peoples were weaker and less advanced than those of Europe. He studied reports on the archaeological remains of the Hopewell Indian culture of southern Ohio, and he asked Lewis and Clark to collect as much data as they could on the western tribes. Yet Jefferson felt that the Indian would have to become a farmer if he were to survive, and while he sought justice for the Indian, it was never at the price of holding up American expansion. He supported the military campaigns of Generals Harmar, St. Clair, and Wayne against the tribes of the Old Northwest during the 1790s when treaty-making failed, and he did not hamper William Henry Harrison's ruthless acquisition of tribal lands. Jefferson repeatedly told the many tribal delegations that came to Washington between 1801 and 1809 to abandon the hunt and turn to agriculture. Jefferson's reasoning, as Reginald Horsman has observed, was ambivalent: Farming would bring the Indian into the fold of civilization, where he could intermarry and become a regular American citizen, but at the same time the Indian would give up large tracts of wild land needed for white farmers. To carry out his policy Jefferson proposed settling the whites all around the tribes remaining east of the Mississippi so that the Indians would be forced to accept an agricultural life. He even suggested that trading houses be located near the tribes to make them dependent on the white man's goods and felt that if they became debt-ridden they would more speedily accept an agrarian life-style. If that did not work, he was prepared to recommend removal to the west bank of the Mississippi, a policy that was eventually adopted by Andrew Jackson. Jefferson was fully aware of white injustice and violence toward the Indian, yet he constantly persuaded himself that the end result would be a happy racial amalgamation and mutual respect. In this instance Jefferson's capacity for self-deception was painfully evident.

Ironically, Jefferson died knowing that the West, which held such promise, might well be the rock on which the union would founder. The extension of slavery into the territories, particularly into Missouri, triggered a crisis in 1820, and Jefferson knew that it was a harbinger of tension to come. "Like a fire bell in the night," the debates over Missouri's admission to the union as a slave state filled Jefferson with apprehension over the future of a West he had done so much to secure and explore. In the year of his death he also began to fear for the purity of "my favorite western country," for by then the Old Northwest had become a market for the commercial East, while the East had begun to import the agricultural surplus of the Northwest via national roads and the Erie Canal. In this instance, as in others, it is clear that Jefferson never understood that Americans were as much a commercial as an agricultural people and that urban and industrial development were inevitable. Nevertheless, it was Jefferson who doubled the size of the Republic, who identified democratic ideals with the West, and who provided the ideological basis for a social approach to land use, which climaxed in the passage of the Homestead Act of 1862. While the United States never became the agrarian "empire of liberty" he espoused, the concept itself was a powerful stimulus to American democratic thought and policies, and survives even today in a persistent belief in the social value of small farms, limited government, rugged individualism, and western egalitarianism.

The most comprehensive biography is Dumas Malone, *Jefferson and His Time* (1948-   ). A useful one-volume account is Merrill D. Peterson, *Thomas Jefferson and the New Nation: A Biography* (1970). Jefferson's works are being edited in a massive project under Julian Boyd, ed., *The Papers of Thomas Jefferson* (1961-   ). Jefferson's agrarian ideas and their national impact are brilliantly portrayed in Henry Nash Smith, *Virgin Land: The American West as Symbol and Myth* (1950). See also John Bakeless, *Lewis and Clark* (1947); Robert Berkhofer, Jr., "Jefferson, the Ordinance of 1784, and the Origins of the American Territorial System," *William and Mary Quarterly*, vol. 29 (1972); Bernard De Voto, *The Journals of Lewis and Clark* (1953); William H. Goetzmann, *Exploration and Empire* (1966); Reginald Horsman, *Expansion and American Indian Policy, 1783-1812* (1967); and Roy Harvey Pearce, *The Savages of America* (1965).—R. N.

Jefferson Barracks. Located approximately ten miles south of St. Louis, Missouri, Jefferson Barracks was built in 1826 to replace Fort Bellefontaine, which stood at the junction of Coldwater Creek and the Missouri River, four miles from where the river empties into the Mississippi. First occupied in July, it received its official designation in October, honoring the revered former president, who had just died.

From its inception through the end of the Mexican War, Jefferson Barracks stood as the most important military installation west of the Mississippi. During the westward expansion of the 1840s it was the largest post in the country. Because of its central location it served as the outfitting and training headquarters for much of the military effort in the western United States. Occupying fourteen hundred acres, it could house twenty-two companies.

The rosters of those located there before the Civil War indicate that most of the prominent military figures of the conflict, on both sides, had served there at one time or another. Abraham Lincoln received some training there during the Black Hawk crisis, and it was to Jefferson Barracks that the young Lieutenant Jefferson Davis brought the old warrior and other Indian leaders at the conclusion of that same war. When the Civil War broke out, the Union established a military hospital there. By April 30, 1864, it had accommodated 11,434 patients. Its post cemetery was designated as a national military cemetery in 1867, and today ranks second in size only to Arlington.

After the Civil War Jefferson Barracks continued to play an important role in the training of frontier armies. In subsequent wars it served as a recruiting center of considerable importance in its area. But by the close of World War II it had become outmoded and was deactivated in 1946. Only three structures remain from the frontier period: a laborer's house built in 1851, the stables constructed that same year, and the powder magazine erected in 1857.

More detailed accounts may be found in Ruth Layton, *The Story of Jefferson Barracks and the Story of the 6th Infantry* (1961), and Harry E. Mitchell, *History of Jefferson Barracks* (1921).—W. E. P.

Jeffords, Thomas J. (1832-1914). Indian agent. Jeffords was born in Chautauqua County, New York. He helped survey the road from Leavenworth, Kansas, to Denver, Colorado, in 1858. A year later he moved to Taos, New Mexico. In 1862 he worked for the United States Army as a scout and during the Civil War helped guide General James H. Carleton and his California Column in New Mexico. When the war ended in the Southwest, Jeffords drove a stage and ran a line in southeastern Arizona through Central Chiricahua Apache territory. Meanwhile, COCHISE had begun his raids against white men. When fourteen of Jeffords' employees were killed by Cochise's band in 1867, Jeffords elected to meet him personally to resolve the problem. After their meeting, in which Jeffords confronted Cochise alone, the two became fast friends. The friendship continued, even though at times Jeffords—whom the Chiricahua called Sandy Whiskers—served as an army scout against the Apache.

Jeffords' efforts coincided with the new peace policy toward Indians during the Grant administration, when Indians were put on reservations and, where possible, were placed under the jurisdiction of religious groups. In Arizona, Jeffords' friendship with Cochise became crucial in forwarding the peace policy.

In the autumn of 1872, Jeffords accompanied General Oliver O. HOWARD into Cochise's camp, where Howard negotiated an informal treaty with Cochise. Jeffords was again an emissary between Cochise and the army when he accompanied John G. BOURKE and a few other men to see him. The result of these meetings was the formation of the Chiricahua Indian reservation and the appointment of Jeffords as its Indian agent, with headquarters at Apache Pass. The reservation lasted only from December 14, 1872, to October 30, 1876.

When Cochise died in 1874, it was Jeffords who saw to it that no other non-Indian knew the precise place of burial, thus forever protecting Cochise's remains from vandals and curiosity-seekers.

Jeffords spent the final years of his life tending some mining property about fifteen miles from Red Rock in Pinal County, Arizona. He was buried in Tucson when he died. Since his death, Jeffords has become a symbol of the white man who came to understand and respect the "wild Indians" and their way of life.

See Thomas E. Farish, *History of Arizona*, vol. II (1915).—B. L. F.

Jennings, William (1823-1886). Mormon businessman. Born in Yardley, England, Jennings arrived in America at the age of twenty-four. He married a young Mormon woman a few years later in St. Joseph, Missouri, and traveled with her to Utah, where he later became a Mormon. Always aware of business opportunity, Jennings freighted a large supply of goods to Utah and sold them at a profit in the Salt Lake valley. He went to Carson Valley, Nevada, in 1856 as part of a settlement mission but was recalled the following year when Mormondom was threatened with war.

Entering into the grocery and meat business in Salt Lake, he soon branched into other areas. He was one of the organizers of the Utah Central Railroad and later was one of its directors and vice president. He was also the president of the Utah Southern Railroad and an officer of the Deseret National Bank.

When the church instituted cooperative general stores, Jennings' department store, the Emporium, formed the primary basis for Zion's Co-operative Mercantile Institution. He was its superintendent and vice president at the time of his death. In his day he was the wealthiest Latter-day Saint and contributed generously to the church's programs.—L. J. A.

Jerome, Arizona. Mining town. Located in Yavapai County, Jerome was the site of one of the richest mining areas in the West. Prior to their closing in 1953, the mines of Jerome had produced nearly $800 million in copper, gold, and silver. Copper was discovered on Mingus Mountain in 1876, but Jerome's mining boom did not get fully under way until 1882 when the Atlantic and Pacific Railroad came into the region and the United Verde Copper Company was formed. To a great extent, United Verde *was* Jerome, for the fortunes of this mining concern determined those of the town that grew up around its mines. The town was named for Eugene Jerome, a New York financier who invested in United Verde.

In 1888 William A. Clark of Montana bought United Verde and moved to Jerome to take over control of the mining operations. Under Clark's control United Verde enjoyed great success and was sold to Phelps Dodge in 1935 for a reported $20,800,000. The mines operated until 1953, and their closing left Jerome a near ghost town.

Jerome is literally built on the side of a mountain; its top layer of buildings is fifteen hundred feet higher than its lowest. Following a dynamite explosion in 1925, the town began to slowly slip down the mountainside at the rate of several inches annually. Many of the vacant buildings have been upended, and the old jail has moved three hundred feet down the side of the mountain.

The town has been trying to make a comeback as a

tourist attraction, and the state has helped by establishing Jerome State Historic Park nearby.

See Nell Murbarger, *Ghosts of the Adobe Walls* (1964); and Muriel S. Wolle, *The Bonanza Trail* (1953). —R. B. W.

Jesuit missions. See ROMAN CATHOLIC MISSIONARIES.

Jesup, Thomas Sidney (1788-1860). Soldier. Jesup was born in Virginia and entered the army in 1808. During the War of 1812 he was on General William Hull's staff and participated in the battles of Chippewa and Niagara. From 1818 to 1860 he was brigadier general and quatermaster general, a position that permitted him to reform and modernize the quartermaster department.

In Indian warfare, Jesup was involved with southern tribes who were resisting removal to lands west of the Mississippi River. In 1836 he directed operations in Alabama against the Creek Indians and in December of that year was sent to FLORIDA to direct operations against the Seminole. He has been described as the most important white individual in the Seminole War; his harsh language and threats, although apparently never meant seriously, and his seizure of Osceola and other Indian leaders certainly made Jesup the most controversial figure of the conflict. His military procedure was to divide the area into war zones and establish a chain of forts. He tried both large- and small-scale operations as well as negotiations. Jesup recommended that the Seminole be permitted to remain in Florida, but he also seized Osceola and other leaders under a flag of truce, thinking that only their capture would end the bloodshed. Within eighteen months he captured about twenty-nine hundred Indians, but, having failed to bring peace to Florida, he was discouraged and in 1838 was relieved at his own request.

See Erna Risch, *Quartermaster Support of the Army: A History of the Corps* (1962).—R. N. E.

Jewish immigration. Jews first entered the American West in large numbers as part of the wave of European immigration that followed the great discoveries of gold, silver, and copper. Between 1849 and 1870 Jews left their homelands in Bavarian Germany, France, and central Europe and came to the West where the majority of them engaged in the retail and wholesale merchandising of food, clothing, tobacco, and hardware. A few are known to have engaged directly in mining and related enterprises.

San Francisco was the port of entry for these immigrants, and many who came (e.g., M. J. Brandenstein, Isaac and Joseph Magnin, Adolph Sutro, and Levi Strauss) settled in the towns and cities of the Bay area and opened mercantile establishments. Others engaged in merchandising or in small businesses in remote towns and mining camps of the California and western mineral rushes (Anthony and Marks Zellerbach; Aaron Fleishhacker; Sigmund, Ignatz, and Frederick Steinhart) before settling in San Francisco or cities that became commercial centers of other regions. The Michael Goldwater family later settled in Arizona; and the Seligmans—Jesse, Henry, Leopold, and Abraham—became investment bankers in New York. David May of Colorado became a department store magnate as did Frederick, Samuel H., and Theodore Auerbach in Salt Lake City, Utah; Nicholas Ransohoff in Salt Lake City and San Francisco; and Aaron Meier, who founded Meier and Frank Company in Portland, Oregon. To a few, fame came in ways other than in merchandising. Ben Selling, whose family had lived in Sonora, California, became famous in politics in Oregon and for his philanthropy; Bailey Gatzert, a merchant in Nevada City, California, became mayor of Seattle, Washington; Albert Michelson, who was brought to Murphy's Camp, California, in his youth and attended high school in Virginia City, Nevada, was the first Jew to win a Nobel Prize. Otto Mears was a prominent road and railroad builder in Colorado. Still other early merchants in the West were younger brothers or nephews of well-established wholesale merchants in San Francisco who had been brought from Europe to work the retail establishments the family had founded earlier in remote mining communities.

Jews also entered government and politics. Five were members of the California Supreme Court (Solomon Heydenfeldt, Henry Lyons, Marcus Sloss, Mathew Tobriner, Stanley Mosk); Lyons was chief justice in 1852. Milton Badt was chief justice of the Nevada Supreme Court intermittently between 1951 and 1966. Julius and Florence Prag Kahn represented San Francisco in Congress for almost forty years. Six Jews have been governors in the West: Edward Salomon (Washington Territory, 1870-72); Moses Alexander (Idaho, 1915-19); Simon Bamberger (Utah, 1917-21); Arthur Seligman (New Mexico, 1931-33); Julius Meier (Oregon, 1931-35); and Ernest Gruening (Alaska Territory, 1939-53). United States senators have included Joseph Simon (Oregon, 1898-1903); Richard Neuberger (Oregon, 1955-60); and Ernest Gruening (Alaska, 1956-69). Solomon Hirsch was Oregon state senator and United States minister to Turkey (1889-92).

By 1876 there were 21,465 Jews in the eleven western states and territories, excluding Alaska and Hawaii. The religious and cultural institutions they established were, for the most part, synagogues, benevolent societies (B'nai B'rith, Kosher Shel Barzel, local societies), and cemeteries. In smaller cities the extent of Jewish communal organization was the establishment of a cemetery and a benevolent society that maintained the cemetery and dispensed charity. Jewish cemeteries are still extant in towns where only a few Jewish families reside today: Nevada City, Grass Valley, Placerville, Jackson, Mokelumne Hill, Sonora, Shasta, Marysville, Oroville, Folsom, and Visalia, California; Albany and Jacksonville, Oregon; Olympia, Washington—towns and cities that formerly had active Jewish communities. In these small towns in the nineteenth century, individual Jews joined nonsectarian lodges, became naturalized citizens, engaged in local politics, voted, served on juries, sponsored dances and other entertainments, and advertised in the newspapers.

With the decline of the mining economy around 1880, Jews left rural mining areas and opened businesses in larger cities. By the turn of the century, Jewish communities were established in Victoria, British Columbia; Seattle; Portland; Sacramento; San Francisco; Oakland; Stockton; San Jose; Los Angeles; San Diego; Salt Lake City; Helena; Reno; Denver; Albuquerque; El Paso; and other cities.

About the same time, the Jewish population of the West, and of the United States, was augmented by a great migration from Russia and eastern Europe. The majority of these immigrants were orthodox in their faith, in contrast to the earlier immigrants, whose ritual practices had become liberalized and reformed. In addition to differences in ritual practice, the Jewish community was also divided according to one's place of origin. On Yom Kippur 1849, two services were conducted in San Francisco, one by Germans and the other by Poles, which resulted in the formation of Congregations Emanu-El and Sherith Israel, respectively.

Immigrants of eastern European origin engaged in small businesses and merchandising but were almost wholly urban and lived in close-knit communities near their institutions of worship and culture. Some, however, turned to farming. Although the several Jewish agricultural colonies throughout the West that existed between 1880 and 1920 failed, individual Jews succeeded in agricultural pursuits, especially in Petaluma, California, and in the California central valleys.

One group of Jewish immigrants to the Pacific Northwest around the turn of the century were Sephardim from the Isle of Rhodes. They brought with them a form of worship, culture, and even cooking that differed from the customs of the dominant eastern European community. Today, there are Sephardic congregations in Seattle, Portland, San Francisco, and Los Angeles.

The center of today's western American Jewry is Los Angeles. More than 500,000 Jews live there, attracted by the climate, the aerospace and scientific research industries that proliferated after World War II, and new opportunities in businesses and professions. Since the earliest days of the entertainment industry in Hollywood, Jews have been closely related with all phases of motion pictures, radio, recordings, and television. From the era of silent pictures until the present time, the names of the Warner brothers, Louis B. Mayer, Samuel Goldwyn, Irving Thalberg, William Fox, Jesse Lasky, David O. Selznick, Harry Cohn, Carl Laemmle, and Adolph Zukor stand out. And the roster of Jewish radio and recording artists is legion. Today, there are more than one hundred congregations and branches of the three largest American rabbinical seminaries in the Los Angeles vicinity, as well as regional offices of most national Jewish fraternal and philanthropic societies. More than 100,000 Jews live in the Greater San Francisco Bay area.

As is true of most cities in the United States, the dispensing of charity and the unifying force of the Jewish community is the Jewish Welfare Federation. Local branches, numbering twenty-four in the West, are professionally staffed and serve to coordinate the fundraising efforts and activities for Jewish institutions, including religious schools—both after-public-school-hours and all-day schools—homes for the aged, summer camps, Jewish community centers, and Israel. The majority of these federations publish Jewish community newspapers that bring items of importance in the community to individuals and their families. Seven such federations in California organized the Jewish Public Affairs Committee, which represents these communities before the state legislature on matters of Jewish interest. Congregations, however, are independent of federations and are usually affiliated with national synagogue organizations (orthodox, conservative, reform), according to the desires of a majority of the membership.

See Martin A. Meyer, *Western Jewry* (1916); Bernard

Postal and Lionel Koppman, *A Jewish Tourist's Guide to the U.S.* (1954); Union of American Hebrew Congregations, *Statistics of the Jews of the United States* (1880); Max Vorspan and Lloyd P. Gartner, *History of the Jews of Los Angeles* (1970); and Michael Zarchin, *Glimpses of Jewish Life in San Francisco*, 2nd ed. (1964).—R. E. L.

Jicarilla Indians. See APACHE INDIANS.

Jogues, Isaac (1607-1646). Jesuit missionary. Jogues was born in France and was professor of literature at the college in Rouen. In 1636 he was a Great Lakes missionary and was tortured by Mohawks in 1642. He was honored for his heroism at French and papal courts. Jogues then returned to America and was again tortured and this time killed at the Iroquois Confederation's headquarters near Auriesville, New York. Jogues was canonized in 1930.

See Francis X. Talbot, *Saint Among Savages* (1935). —R. I. B.

Johannsen, Robert (1925-   ). Historian. Johannsen was born in Portland, Oregon and was educated at Reed College in Oregon and the University of Washington. He began teaching at the University of Washington in 1953, moved to the University of Kansas in 1954, then joined the University of Illinois at Urbana in 1959, where he rose through the ranks to become professor.

Johannsen's first book, *Frontier Politics: The Pacific Northwest on the Eve of the Civil War* (1955), developed a neglected aspect of western history. In this study he analyzed the views of leading political figures and parties in the Pacific Northwest on the sectional issues dividing the North and South. He demonstrated how this newly emerging area of the West was beginning to exert a significant influence in the development of sectional antagonisms that were to result in the Civil War. The growth of the Pacific Northwest within the trans-Mississippi region sharpened the conflict between the older sections as the interests of the Pacific Coast increasingly coincided with those of the North. After the appearance of this work, Johannsen increased his interest in Stephen A. Douglas and the Old Northwest in the pre-Civil War era. In 1961 he edited *The Letters of Stephen A. Douglas* and in 1973 published a widely praised biography of Douglas.—G. D. N.

Johnson, Eastman (1824-1906). Painter. Born in Lovell, Maine, Johnson spent his youth in Augusta, Maine, and in 1816 went to Boston, where he was employed for a year in a lithographic shop. Turning to crayon portraiture, he worked from 1841 to 1849 as a portraitist in Augusta; Cambridge, Massachusetts; Newport, Rhode Island; and Washington, D.C. In 1849 he went abroad to study, spending two years under Emanuel Leutze at Düsseldorf and traveling in France and Italy, after which he studied for about four years at The Hague, where he was offered a post as court painter. Returning to the United States in 1855, he made several trips to the Great Lakes area, the first in 1856 to visit a sister living at Superior, Wisconsin. During this and subsequent visits, he became interested in the activities of the Chippewa Indians of that vicinity and recorded their appearance and customs in charcoal and oil. Many of these scenes presently are in the possession of the St. Louis County Historical Society in Duluth, Minnesota.

Returning to the East, Johnson painted in Cincinnati and in Washington, D.C., before settling permanently in

New York City in 1859. Painted in Washington, his *Old Kentucky Home* won him election to the National Academy of Design in 1860. During the Civil War he followed closely the movements of various campaigns and painted a number of scenes from selected battlefield sites. Johnson began to make regular visits to Nantucket Island in the 1870s, and after about 1880 he began to produce genre subjects with a somewhat romantic view of everyday life.—D. C. H.

Johnson, Frank Tenney (1874-1939). Painter. Born in Big Grove, Iowa, Johnson studied art in New York City and maintained a studio there before moving to Denver and then to Alhambra, California, in 1920. He became best known for his paintings illustrative of the life of the American cowboy. He was elected an associate of the National Academy of Design in 1929 and a full member in 1937. Johnson's paintings are represented in collections in the United States, Europe, and New Zealand.—D. C. H.

Johnson, Hiram Warren (1866-1945). California politician. Johnson was born in Sacramento and attended the state university at Berkeley for two years. He studied law in the office of his father, Grove L. Johnson, a leading supporter of the SOUTHERN PACIFIC political machine in the state legislature. Political and personal quarrels with his father led him to move from Sacramento to San Francisco in 1902. He assisted Francis J. Heney in the San Francisco graft prosecution, and when Heney was shot and seriously wounded during the main trial of "boss" Abe Ruef, Johnson took Heney's place and secured Ruef's conviction. Elected governor on the Republican ticket in 1910, Johnson not only carried out his famous campaign promise to "kick the Southern Pacific Railroad out of politics," but also sponsored a program of progressive reforms, which Theodore Roosevelt praised as the best that any state had accomplished (see CALIFORNIA). In 1912 Roosevelt chose him as the vice-presidential nominee of the Progressive party. Hoping to extend his own brand of progressivism to national politics and ultimately to be president, he was elected senator in 1916 and resigned as governor the following March. From 1919 onward, his hostility to President Woodrow Wilson's League of Nations and to any foreign entanglements often overshadowed and obscured his interest in domestic reform, though during the 1920s he did lead the fight for federal construction of Hoover (Boulder) Dam, and successfully fought the opposition of private power companies. In 1920 he declined Warren G. Harding's offer of the vice presidency, and in 1924 he lost the Republican presidential nomination to Calvin Coolidge. In the 1930s, like many other old progressives, he became an opponent of the New Deal. He was elected five' times as senator from California.

Johnson's gubernatorial and senatorial papers, and his senatorial journal in the form of letters to his sons, are in the Bancroft Library of the University of California at Berkeley. George E. Mowry, *The California Progressives* (1951, 1963), and Spencer C. Olin, Jr., *California's Prodigal Sons: Hiram Johnson and the Progressives, 1911-1917* (1968), tell the story of his governorship. —W. B.

Johnson, Richard Mentor (1780-1850). Soldier and politician. Johnson was the son of pioneer parents, who had migrated to the Old Southwest from Virginia in the early years of that area's settlement. Born at Beargrass, Kentucky, a struggling settlement on the site of present-day Louisville, Johnson had few educational advantages, but he took advantage of every available opportunity and managed to learn enough Latin to enable him to enter college. He studied law at Transylvania University and was admitted to the bar in 1802. In 1804 he was elected to the state legislature as a Democrat and two years later found himself seated in the United States House of Representatives, a position he occupied until 1819.

The War of 1812 was a great boon to Johnson's career. An avid war hawk, he rushed home from Congress to form a regiment of Kentucky riflemen to fight the British. He led the regiment in the battle of the Thames and was severely wounded. During this battle he was reputed to have killed the great Indian chief Tecumseh, an allegation that was to serve him well in later political campaigns.

Following the war Johnson returned to politics. He was elected senator from Kentucky in 1819 and served until 1829 when he was defeated in a bid for reelection. He returned to the House in 1829 as a supporter of Andrew Jackson, although his personal views were closer to those of fellow Kentuckian Henry Clay. Jackson rewarded Johnson's sycophancy with nomination as Martin Van Buren's vice-presidential running-mate. Despite the engaging campaign jingle, "Rumpsey, Dumpsey, Colonel Johnson killed Tecumseh," Johnson failed to secure a majority of the electoral vote and became the only vice president elected by the Senate.

His term was inconspicuous, and in 1841 he returned to Kentucky to retire. Two weeks before he died, Johnson ended his political career as it had begun: winning a seat in the Kentucky legislature.—R. B. N.

Johnson, Robert Ward (1814-1879). Arkansas politician. Born and educated in Kentucky, Johnson opened a law office in 1835 in Little Rock, Arkansas, where his father, Benjamin, a brother of Richard Mentor Johnson, was a federal judge, and where his brother-in-law, Senator Ambrose Sevier, was a powerful politician. Johnson went to Congress in 1846, serving three terms in the House and one in the Senate. He secured land grants for Arkansas railroads, and though a southern sectionalist he supported the Homestead Bill. He represented Arkansas throughout the Civil War in the Confederate Senate and after the war, losing his Arkansas property, practiced law in Washington, D.C., with Albert Pike. Returning to Arkansas in 1878, he ran unsuccessfully for the Senate.—W. L. B.

Johnson, William (1715?-1774). Diplomat. Johnson was the dominant figure on the New York frontier from the 1740s until the eve of the American Revolution. Born in County Meath, Ireland, Johnson came to America in 1737 or 1738 and took charge of an estate in the Mohawk valley belonging to his uncle, Admiral Sir Peter Warren. Here there were plentiful opportunities for him to trade with the Indians and to speculate in land. Over the years Johnson became the largest fur trader in the colony, dealing with the neighboring Mohawk Indians and other tribes in the Iroquois confederacy. By the time of his death he had accumulated one of the largest landed estates in British America, with its seat at Johnson Hall, near modern Johnstown, New York. His dealings with the Indians generated an understanding of them and a mutual friendship which no other man of his wealth and position could equal. He was adopted into the Mohawk tribe and took at least two successive wives or mistresses from the tribe, including Molly Brant, sister of Mohawk chief Joseph Brant, who bore him several children.

Johnson's major importance lay in the political and military sphere, where the good will he had won by his dealings with the Indians proved invaluable to colonial and imperial authorities. Johnson demonstrated his influence early in King George's War (1744-48) when he was instrumental in persuading the Iroquois not to side with the French. For this service Governor George Clinton of New York appointed him provincial superintendent of Indian affairs in 1746, the first time such an office had been vested in one man. In this capacity he held numerous conferences with the Indians, distributing presents and assuring them of British support in return for the service of Indian war parties. In 1748 Johnson was also given command of the militia companies, which were raised for the protection of the New York frontier.

With the coming of peace in 1748 Johnson returned to trading, farming, and land speculation. From 1750 until his death he was a member of the provincial council and one of the most potent political figures in the colony. He resigned as superintendent of Indian affairs in 1751, despite Indian protests, but continued to use his good offices informally until the outbreak of the French and Indian War in 1754. A year later, by appointment of General Edward Braddock, Johnson became superintendent of British relations with the Iroquois and their allies. He also received a commission as major general in command of an intercolonial force organized to attack the French stronghold at Crown Point on Lake Champlain. Johnson met and defeated the French at Lake George, eliminating the danger of their further advance and obscuring somewhat his failure to capture Crown Point. He was rewarded with a baronetcy by the king. Between 1755 and 1759 Johnson did much to solidify the Iroquois alliance, getting the Iroquois to supply war parties in support of colonial military operations. In 1759 he commanded a joint colonial and Indian force that captured Fort Niagara, and in 1760 he participated in the successful attack on Montreal.

With the return of peace after 1760, Johnson's major concerns were to impose some order and control over the fur trade and over the expansion of white settlement into the interior. His policy of restricting the Indian trade to designated places was only partially upheld by the authorities in England, but his idea of a boundary line to separate white settlements from Indian hunting lands was realized when he concluded the Treaty of FORT STANWIX (1768) with the Indians. He also devoted much time to keeping the Indians at peace with one another, as well as friendly to the British. His diplomacy was certainly a factor in keeping most of the Iroquois loyal to the British during the American Revolution, which broke out in 1775, a year after his death.

See J. T. Flexner, *Mohawk Baronet: Sir William Johnson of New York* (1959); Arthur Pound, *Johnson of the Mohawks* (1930); and J. Sullivan and A. C. Flick, *The Papers of Sir William Johnson*, 13 vols. (1921-62).
—A. W. T.

Johnson County War (1892). Wyoming cattle war.

For many years cattle "kings" of Wyoming had been losing cattle to rustlers. The greatest concentration of thieves appeared to be in Johnson County, 250 miles northwest of Cheyenne. Cowboys would leave the employment of big outfits, take up homesteads, and with rope and branding iron build herds at the expense of their former employers. The courts protected the big cattlemen inadequately. Evidence was hard to get and jurors showed more sympathy for the little fellows than for the big ones, particularly since the latter were often wealthy absentees. Failing to get justice in the courts, the big cattlemen hired detectives, some of whom ambushed suspects. But assassinations (such as of Jim Averill and CATTLE KATE) of this kind only stirred up more animosity toward the big cattlemen, and rustling continued. So some of the big cattlemen laid plans for an invasion of Johnson County. They would go in force and surprise and shoot down some of their tormentors, whom they hoped to catch one or two at a time. Over a period of months they gathered a list of condemned men. The members of the Wyoming Stock Growers' Association were invited to send nominations to the association secretary, and the executive committee of the association decided which nominees should go on the final list. It was later asserted that ninety percent of the listed men were fugitives from the law in other states, and no doubt many of them were. Although it was never admitted that the project was an official function of the Wyoming Stock Growers' Association, the involvement of that prestigious organization was considerable.

Forty-six vigilantes (sometimes referred to as Invaders or Regulators) led by Frank Wolcott and Frank H. CANTON boarded a special Union Pacific train at the state capital, Cheyenne, on April 5, 1892, at the conclusion of the annual spring meeting of the Stock Growers' Association. In addition to nineteen cattlemen and five of their stock detectives, there were twenty-two hired gunmen, one from Idaho and the others from Texas. Six observers, including two newspaper reporters, went along. Members of the expedition occupied three passenger cars while three baggage cars held horses, wagons, and gear. At Casper, within a hundred miles or so of their scattered quarry, the Invaders had to leave their special train and travel the rest of the way on horseback.

The Invaders surprised and shot to death two men who were high on their list, but thereafter the hunters became the hunted. While the two suspected rustlers, Nate Champion and Nick Ray, were being murdered at the KC ranch, officials in the county seat, Buffalo, forty-six miles to the north, got wind of the fracas. Citizens rallied to the sheriff's call for a posse. Two hundred strong, the posse surrounded the Invaders at a ranch thirteen miles south of Buffalo.

Although the Invaders had cut the telegraph wires, word of their predicament soon got to Acting Governor Amos Barber in Cheyenne. With the aid of Senators Francis E. Warren and Joseph M. Carey, the governor obtained the intervention of a troop of cavalry in time to prevent further casualties. Two of the Texas mercenaries suffered accidental wounds, from which they later died.

Johnson County authorities demanded surrender of the Invaders for trial in Buffalo. Instead, the cavalry gave them protective custody and escorted them to

Cheyenne, where able attorneys headed by Willis Van Devanter, later to become associate justice of the United States Supreme Court, skillfully prepared the defense. After various delays trial was set for January 1893 in Cheyenne, where the Invaders had more friends than elsewhere. Impaneling a jury proved to be extraordinarily difficult. Then when all appeared ready for the trial to begin, the prosecution moved for dismissal. Two considerations caused this surprising turn of events. One was that two trappers who had witnessed the killing of Champion and Ray and whose testimony was crucial could not be found. They had been spirited out of the state and kept in hiding by friends of the accused. The other consideration leading to dismissal was financial. Johnson County already owed $18,000 in connection with the case, and the treasury was empty.

Although the Invaders thus went free, traces of fallout from their foolhardy expedition lingered for years. The affair split the state, with most people, especially the lower class, taking the side of Johnson County. The "war" became the major issue in the political campaign of 1892. Democrats and Populists succeeded in persuading a majority of the voters that "the Republican Ring Gang of Cattle Barons of Cheyenne" was responsible for the invasion, although both Democrats and Republicans had participated in it on a completely nonpartisan basis. Fusion between the weak Democratic party and the weaker Populist party made possible the derailment of the Republican machine. A Democratic governor was elected. But with five Populists holding the balance of power in the legislature, no senator could be elected, leaving a vacancy for the next two years.

The invasion and its aftermath cost the participants and their friends more than $100,000, a large sum in the depressed 1890s. Paying the piper was painful. Some of the Invaders quarreled over apportionment of the costs. Johnson County refused to pay the $18,000 bill for feeding and prosecuting the Invaders; ultimately in 1899 the legislature made an appropriation, and so the state picked up the tab.

For a few months after the invasion it was open season on property in Johnson County belonging to the Invaders. Twelve troops of cavalry were sent into summer encampment in Johnson and neighboring Converse counties, and a bit later a federal marshal arrived with a posse to look for the lawless element. The posse frightened some of the rustlers into leaving the state. In time lawlessness declined, the G.O.P. got back on the main track, and the Invaders lived down their folly. In the many subsequent accounts of the conflict, the only hero to emerge is Nathan Champion, who after his partner Nick Ray had been killed, held off almost fifty marksmen by himself for twelve hours before they burned him out and shot him.

See T. A. Larson, *History of Wyoming* (1965); Asa S. Mercer, *The Banditti of the Plains* (1894); and Helena Huntington Smith, *The War on Powder River* (1966). —T. A. L.

Johnston, Albert Sidney (1803-1862). Soldier. Johnston was born in Washington, Kentucky. He received his education at Transylvania University and at West Point, where he was a classmate of Jefferson Davis. He was graduated in June 1826 and was stationed at Sackett's Harbor, New York, and Jefferson Barracks, Missouri.

After fighting in the Black Hawk War, he resigned his commission on April 24, 1834, to farm near St. Louis.

Two years later Johnston came to Texas and enlisted in the upstart Texas army as a private. On August 5, 1836, he was named adjutant general, and on the following January 31 he became senior brigadier general in command of the army to replace Felix Huston. Huston felt that Johnston's appointment was a blow to his honor and challenged him to a duel. To everyone's surprise—since Huston was an acknowledged expert with a pistol, while Johnston's weapons were rapier and rifle—Johnston chose pistols. He had not fired a pistol since leaving Jefferson Barracks. However, neither man showed much ability as a marksman on that morning of February 5, 1837, and only after five or six exchanges did Huston manage to hit Johnston in the hip. As a result, Johnston was unable to take command. During the administration of Mirabeau B. Lamar, president of Texas, Johnston served as secretary of war and in December 1839 led an expedition against the Cherokee in East Texas. During the Mexican War he was colonel of the First Texas Rifle Volunteers and later was inspector general of Monterrey, Mexico. On December 2, 1849, Johnston became paymaster of the United States Army assigned to the Texas frontier. Later as colonel of the Second Cavalry in the middle 1850s and then as brevet brigadier general from 1858 to 1860, he served in Utah and in California.

When the Civil War broke out, Johnston refused the federal government's offer of a command and returned to Texas. Confederate president Jefferson Davis appointed Johnston a general in command of the western department. He captured Bowling Green, Kentucky, and then began to try to enlarge his army and improve its efficiency. In February 1862 he moved his army to the vicinity of Nashville, Tennessee, and then on to Corinth, Mississippi. On April 6, 1862, he was killed at the battle of Shiloh in a Pyrrhic victory for the Confederacy. The body was buried in New Orleans but later removed to the state cemetery at Austin.

See William Preston Johnston, *The Life of General Albert Sidney Johnston* (1878); and Charles P. Roland, *Albert Sidney Johnston: Soldier of Three Republics* (1964). —J. B. F.

Jolliet, Louis (1645-1700). Native-born Canadian explorer who, with Father Jacques MARQUETTE, discovered the upper Mississippi. Jolliet established a trading post at Sault Ste. Marie in 1670. With Father Marquette and five companions he pushed off from St. Ignace, near the Straits of Mackinac, on May 17, 1673, in search of the "great river." They entered the Mississippi from the Wisconsin on June 17, 1673. After floating southward nearly to the mouth of the Arkansas, the party returned to New France. Jolliet remained active as a fur trader and hydrographer.

See Jean Delanglez, *Life and Voyages of Louis Jolliet (1645-1700)* (1948). —R. A. B.

Jones, John Percival (1829-1912). Nevada politician and financier. Born in Herefordshire, England, Jones came to the United States as an infant, his family settling near Cleveland, Ohio, where he attended school. He joined the rush to California in 1850 and for the next few years had indifferent luck as a miner in the gold fields. After serving as deputy sheriff and then sheriff of Trinity County, Jones was nominated in 1867 by the

Republicans to run for lieutenant governor of California but was defeated in the election. That same year, through the influence of Alvinza Hayward, a director of the Bank of California, Jones was made superintendent of the Kentuck mine on the Comstock. In 1870 he became superintendent of the Crown Point mine and the next year struck a bonanza in that mine which made him a multimillionaire. Jones decided to stand for the United States Senate and in 1872 spent lavishly to get a sympathetic legislature elected. The following year the legislature selected him to replace James W. Nye as senator from Nevada. He was reelected to that post four times, retiring in 1903 after thirty years of service, the longest of any Nevadan. His most important work in the United States Senate was his extended effort to achieve the remonitization of silver. Allen Weinstein calls him the first bimetallist and notes that Jones played a pivotal role in making silver a national issue in 1876. His position on silver derived more from his political goals than from principles of economics and it paid off in making him popular in Nevada. By 1875 his investments were directed more toward real estate and land development than silver mining. He founded Santa Monica, California, in 1875.

There are Jones papers in the Huntington Library, San Marino, California, and the library at the University of California, Los Angeles. Harry M. Gorham, *My Memories of the Comstock* (1939), has useful material, and Allen Weinstein, *Prelude to Populism: Origins of the Silver Issue 1867-1878* (1970) has an excellent chapter on Jones's role in the silver issue.—R. R. E.

Jones, Thomas ap Catesby (1790-1858). Naval officer. Jones, who was orphaned in childhood in his native Virginia, became a naval midshipman when he was fifteen years old. For the next half-century the navy was the stage upon which he acted out his eccentric life, until finally a general court-martial suspended him from active duty. Three different times he served as the commander of the navy's Pacific squadron. In that role he became the model for the commodore in Herman Melville's *White Jacket* (1850).

Remote from Washington and operating under very general instructions, Jones exercised American authority in the eastern Pacific virtually without check. When, therefore, in 1842 at Callao, Peru, he chose to believe the rumor of war between the United States and Mexico, he was able to plan and execute the occupation of Monterey, California, without interference from superiors. He did seek advice, however, from his officers, who also believed the war rumor; in their deliberations the officers cited the 1823 annual message of President Monroe as justification for seizing Monterey or other California points that, in case of war, might fall to a European power.

Jones's force of two ships descended on Monterey on October 19, 1842. Within twenty-four hours the bloodless conquest was complete. But within forty-eight hours Jones learned that his country was not at war with Mexico after all. The American flag came down, the Mexican flag went back up, and American and Mexican guns boomed salutes at each other. To satisfy the Mexican government, Jones was transferred to another command. But privately the secretary of the navy praised Jones, and five years later he was reinstated as commander of the Pacific squadron. By that time war with

Mexico was undisputably real, and all of California was in American hands.

See G. M. Brooke, Jr., "The Vest Pocket War of Commodore Jones," *Pacific Historical Review*, vol. 31 (1962).—W. B. F.

Joseph, Antonio (1846-1910). New Mexican politician. Joseph was born in Taos, New Mexico. His father was a Portuguese immigrant who came to the United States in 1837, and his mother a native American of Spanish and French descent. Six years before Joseph's birth, his parents moved to New Mexico. He attended Lux's Academy in Taos, Bishop Jean Lamy's school in Santa Fe, Webster College in St. Louis, Missouri, and Bryant and Stratton's Commercial College in St. Louis. After completing his commercial courses, he undertook a business career, becoming an owner of hotels and extensive lands in New Mexico. Between 1878 and 1880, Joseph served as county judge of Taos County, New Mexico. He then moved to Ojo Caliente, New Mexico, and in 1882 became a member of the territorial legislature. A Democrat and elected territorial delegate in 1884, Joseph served in the House of Representatives from 1885 to 1895, being reelected to the four succeeding Congresses.

Joseph's first election as delegate was partly attributable to a split in the Republican party, and also to a national Democratic trend. Moreover, he was endorsed by the powerful Colonel José Francisco Chaves. Joseph had been nominated instead of the incumbent, conservative Francisco Manzanares. In 1886 he easily won reelection on the Democratic platform, which belittled the question of land fraud in the state. Joseph was accused in New Mexico of not promoting the cause of statehood during his first two terms in Congress, but by 1890 he was more established as a promoter of admission, and this aided his reelection. In 1889 he spoke in Congress for statehood, arguing for early admission on the basis of the Treaty of Guadalupe Hidalgo. After New Mexico had been dropped from the Springer Omnibus statehood bill, Joseph in 1889 introduced two bills for statehood, but Congress took no action on either. After the 1889 constitutional convention in New Mexico, Joseph was one of many Democrats who urged defeat of the constitution at the polls. He had long been concerned with the question of land grants, and felt that the 1889 constitution was unfair in that large land-grant holders would escape taxation. He accused the convention delegates of "economic motives," and his statehood bills in 1889 reflected an implicit negation of the 1889 constitution. Speaking in Congress, he compared New Mexico favorably to Idaho and Wyoming (which had been admitted) on the basis of population, property values, education of the people, and agricultural prospects through irrigation.

Known as a good speaker, Joseph introduced in Congress on March 11, 1892, another bid for New Mexico statehood. Joseph's bill was passed three times by the House but on each occasion was passed over by the Senate. Joseph won reelection in 1892 over powerful Republican Thomas Benton Catron, largely on the question of statehood. During his final term as delegate he introduced another statehood bill, again passed by the House but ignored by the Senate. Catron came back in 1894 to defeat Joseph, probably because Joseph had been unsuccessful in gaining statehood for New Mexico and because Catron's protectionist policies were favored by the northern wool growers. Joseph's strong advocacy of the coinage of silver also hurt his cause in Congress.

Returning to Ojo Caliente, Joseph served for two years (1896-98) in the territorial senate. He remained interested in statehood and became a member of the nonpartisan statehood league after the turn of the century. He was closely identified with Spanish-speaking New Mexicans throughout his life, and his advocacy of statehood and better educational opportunities through federal resources are a reflection of his concern for their well-being.

Howard R. Lamar, *The Far Southwest: 1846-1912* (1966), and Robert W. Larson, *New Mexico's Quest for Statehood, 1846-1912* (1968), mention Joseph in the context of territorial politics of the 1880s and 1890s. A biographical sketch is contained in R. E. Twitchell, *The Leading Facts of New Mexican History* (1912).—J. R. V.

Joseph, Chief. See CHIEF JOSEPH.

Joset, Joseph (1810-1900). Jesuit missionary. Joset was born in Switzerland and was in the Rocky Mountains from 1844 to 1900. He is especially identified with the Coeur d'Alene and was a peacemaker in the 1858 and 1877 Indian wars.

See Robert I. Burns, *The Jesuits and the Indian Wars of the Northwest* (1966).—R. I. B.

Joslyn Art Museum. When the Joslyn Art Museum, in Omaha, Nebraska, opened in 1931, the collections consisted chiefly of gifts from generous local collectors and reflected turn-of-the-century taste in pastoral and genre painting. Since then more varied acquisitions have broadened the collections, both by gift and by purchase. Major acquisitions were made possible from estate funds following the death in 1940 of Sarah H. Joslyn, who had donated the building to house the museum in memory of her husband, George A. Joslyn. These additions included works by such masters as di Credi, Titian, Veronese, and Rembrandt. With money allocated especially for the purchase of winning paintings at Midwest exhibitions, works by regional artists have been added regularly. Examples of nationally and internationally known twentieth-century artists round out the collections.

The museum's policy is to present a comprehensive survey of man's artistic achievements from all regions and all ages with a special interest in preserving and presenting the development of regional art.

In 1954, the one hundredth anniversary of the founding of the Territory of Nebraska and of Omaha City, as it was then called, the Joslyn Art Museum opened an exhibition called Life on the Prairie. The cost was underwritten by the National Society of Colonial Dames of America in the State of Nebraska, whose members were also active in seeking gifts and purchasing suitable paintings, prints, maps, and household furnishings for the display.

Life on the Prairie covers the first one hundred years of white settlement on the Great Plains—the early arrivals by wagon, the steamboat traffic on the Missouri, the building of the railroad, the cattle drives, and the cowboy era. Small period interiors depict the full-blown prosperity of Victorian decor. Introductory exhibits survey earlier epochs of exploration and fur trading and touch briefly on the geologic history of the land itself

and the Indian tribes who preceded the European settlers.

The scene is re-created visually with displays of original, handcrafted utensils and useful tools, examples of folk art that are at times better proportioned than the decorative arts pieces cherished by pioneer housewives as keepsakes from "back home."

The then new art of photography comes into play by using enlargements of early photographs as backdrops to exhibits. Such recognition of the first generation of photographers is especially appropriate since one of the most prominent, William Henry Jackson, maintained a studio in Omaha from 1867 on while he roamed the West as an official photographer of government surveying parties.

Contemporary pictorial material in Life on the Prairie exhibits includes documentary paintings by local primitive artists, especially George Simons; romanticized prints published by Currier & Ives; and illustrations from the popular weeklies *Leslie's* and *Harper's*, whose commissioned reporter-artists spread the word of the Oregon Trail, Indian raids, discoveries of gold, and the building of the transcontinental railroad. The gold-framed landscapes by Albert Bierstadt, acquired by prospering early residents as parlor pictures, are tangible proof that the vastness and grandeur of the American West had been recognized and made generally known by artists of the day.

Among other artists whose works tell the Great Plains story are John Mix Stanley, Seth Eastman, Charles (or Carl) F. Wimar, Thomas Moran, Frank Tenney Johnson, E. W. Gollings, William R. Leigh, and Frederic Remington. A large oil, *Staging in California*, by J. Gutzon Borglum, notes the Borglum family's early residence in Omaha. His brother, Solon Borglum, is represented by a small bronze sculpture, *On the Trail*.

Other bronzes are Remington's *Bronco Buster* and the Mormon sculptor Avard Fairbanks' *Winter Quarters*. Numerous bronzes by Charles M. Russell, on loan from a local collector, are used throughout Life on the Prairie. Prints by Karl Bodmer and George Catlin and by Alfred Jacob Miller present a capsule acknowledgment of the great contribution made by these artists in the 1830s. They are also represented by complete collections in other parts of the museum.

In 1958 another new exhibit featured artwork of American Indians, shown both as regional cultures and as examples of skilled techniques in sculpture, pottery making, weaving, and drawing. Paintings by Oscar Howe, Richard West, Solomon McCombs, and other contemporary artists represent the twentieth-century school of Indian art.

The greatest number of western paintings has come through long-term loans of collections acquired by the Northern Natural Gas Company of Omaha. In 1962 the company purchased the Maximilian-Bodmer and Stewart-Miller collections, which with a loan of thirty-five Catlin oils from the National Collection of Fine Arts in Washington, D.C., have made possible a separate exhibition called Age of Exploration, Artist-Explorers of the 1830s.

The Maximilian-Bodmer collection contains more than 400 superb sketches and watercolors by Karl Bodmer and the original diaries and other manuscripts of Prince Maximilian of Wied covering his 1832-34 scientific expedition to America. The Stewart-Miller collection consists of 113 field sketches by Alfred Jacob Miller that were executed when he accompanied the sportsman William Drummond Stewart to the Rocky Mountains in 1837. The Joslyn Art Museum also owns eight oil paintings by Miller, including one of the large scenes painted for Stewart's home in Scotland, Murthly Castle.

In 1967 the Northern Natural Gas Company brought to Omaha a third collection of eighty-six works by thirty-seven artists of the frontier. Among the artists are Bierstadt, F. O. C. Darley, Eastman, James Earle Fraser, Paul Kane, William Tylee Ranney, Stanley, Worthington Whittredge, and N. C. Wyeth. The artists were explorers, military men, war correspondents, landscape painters, and illustrators. Some pictured the scene with meticulous accuracy; others sought its poetry and romance. As illustrators, others created a believable myth of western lore, which has now achieved a reality of its own.—M. G.

Joy, James Frederick (1810-1896). Lawyer and railroad executive. Joy was closely associated with John Murray FORBES and other Boston capitalists in the construction and acquisition of midwestern railroads. He was born in Durham, New York. First in his class at Dartmouth College and a graduate of the Harvard Law School in 1836, Joy settled in the frontier community of Detroit, where he rapidly prospered as a railroad lawyer.

Joy arranged the sale of the state-owned Michigan Central Railroad to the Forbes group and in the following years pursued an energetic policy of expansion, which ultimately resulted in a divergence between his methods and the more conservative policies of the Bostonians. He sought to build a transcontinental route, but the "Joy system" of roads, based on the Hannibal and St. Joseph (a trans-Missouri line soon to become part of the Burlington system), never coalesced into a stable enterprise.

In later years Joy was an associate of Jay Gould, when Gould sought, also unsuccessfully, to build a transcontinental system. See also BURLINGTON NORTHERN RAILROAD.

Arthur M. Johnson and Barry E. Supple, *Boston Capitalists and Western Railroads* (1967), and Richard C. Overton, *Burlington Route, A History of the Burlington Lines* (1965), discuss Joy's contribution to western railroad development.—A. M.

Judah, Theodore Dehone (1826-1863). Engineer and railroad builder. Judah was cheated by an early death of a prominent place in the history of the CENTRAL PACIFIC RAILROAD. He was the son of an Episcopal clergyman of Bridgeport, Connecticut. After studying engineering at Rensselaer Polytechnic Institute and working on the New York and New Haven and Connecticut Valley railroads, Judah planned and built the Niagara Gorge Railroad. From the moment he arrived in California in 1854 to supervise the building of the Sacramento Valley Railroad, Judah became an ardent proponent of a transcontinental railroad. He served as delegate to the Pacific Railroad Convention in Washington in 1859 and the following year discovered a practical route through the Sierras.

It was his calculations of the profits to be made from a road over this route that encouraged the "Big Four," Collis P. HUNTINGTON, Leland STANFORD, Charles CROCKER, and Mark HOPKINS, to invest in the project that made them multimillionaires, and his lobbying activities in Washington that helped secure the aid of the Pacific Railroad Act of 1862. "We have drawn the elephant," he wired his partners from Washington; "now let us see if we can harness him up." But it was Judah himself who refused to be harnessed to the profit-minded policies of the Big Four. As an engineer he wanted to build well, but the others recognized that a mile of quickly built line would qualify just as readily for the government subsidy. Judah sold his interest to the others, taking back an option to buy their interests at the same price, $100,000 each, and hurried East to seek new backers. In his haste he chose the unhealthy route across the Isthmus of Panama, and a week after arriving in New York he was dead of yellow fever. The Central Pacific remained a project of western capitalists. (See also RAILROADS.)

Judah's short career is summarized in Oscar Lewis, *The Big Four* (1938). Stuart Daggett, *Chapters on the History of the Southern Pacific* (1922; repr. 1966), is still useful.—A. M.

K

Kaiser, Henry J. (1882-1967). California industrialist. Kaiser was born in rural New York and dropped out of school at thirteen to help support his family. His first great successes came as a builder of highways, in the Pacific Northwest and California from 1914 to 1926 and in Cuba from 1927 to 1930. Then he became chairman of the executive committee of the Six Companies, Inc., which constructed Hoover (Boulder) Dam. He was also one of the principal builders of the San Francisco-Oakland Bay Bridge, and of Bonneville, Grand Coulee,

and Shasta dams. For Shasta he built a mammoth cement plant at Permanente, California. During World War II, though new to shipbuilding, he constructed seven shipyards, six on the West Coast and one on the Atlantic, and in fewer than four years they turned out 1,490 vessels. His shipyard at Richmond, California, produced a 10,500-ton "Liberty ship" in four days and fifteen hours. Construction went so quickly because Kaiser developed prefabrication techniques. For these ships he built the Pacific Coast's first completely integrated iron and steel plant, at Fontana, California. His only major failure was a venture into automobile production just after the war. Through the Permanente Foundation, later called the Kaiser Foundation, he pioneered in prepaid group medical care provided by independent partnerships of doctors in self-sustaining hospitals. Originally established for his own employees, it was later opened to other groups of workers and ultimately covered more than 1,250,000 people in California, Oregon, Washington, and Hawaii. His relations with labor were so exemplary that in 1965 he became the first industrialist to receive the Murray-Green award of the AFL-CIO, the highest honor bestowed by organized labor. Always bustling, and usually smiling, he worked an average of sixteen hours a day. From 1921 the headquarters of his vast enterprises were in Oakland, California. In his last years his greatest interest was in the development of real estate in Hawaii.—W. B.

Kamiakin (1810?-1877). Yakima Indian leader. Kamiakin was born in the Yakima valley, Washington, and was recognized as early as 1840 as a leader of the Yakima Indians, although his enemies resented the nontribal origins of Ki-yi-yah, his father, a Nez Percé. Kamiakin was not educated in a formal sense, but the Catholic priests whom he had invited to establish the Ahtanum mission near his home gave him some information of the non-Indian world.

Kamiakin was leader of the peaceful faction of the Yakima. He counseled neutrality during the Cayuse War of 1847-48, which followed the massacre of missionary Marcus Whitman. But later events made it impossible for Kamiakin to maintain peaceful relations with white men. The invasion in 1853 of Captain George B. McClellan's military party to survey a possible route for a railroad through Naches Pass with neither prior notice to the Yakima nor any request to cross their land alarmed the Indians. At the Walla Walla treaty council of 1855, Governor Isaac Ingalls Stevens announced that he wanted to buy the Yakima's land and threatened violence if they refused to sell. Kamiakin signed the treaty, but the Yakima were embittered. He, too, then turned against the whites, and in September 1855 his Indians began to attack soldiers and trespassers in what became the Yakima War (see YAKIMA INDIANS). Kamiakin next attempted with partial success to develop an anti-American confederacy of Northwest Indians under the leadership of the Klickitat band, the most powerful of the Yakima.

Following the Indian defeat in 1858, Kamiakin exiled himself to Canada but returned quietly to southeastern Washington in 1861. He died at Rock Lake, Washington.

See A. J. Splawn, *Ka-mi-akin: The Last Hero of the Yakimas* (reissued in 1944); Frances Fuller Victor, *The Early Indian Wars of Oregon* (1894); and Hubert Howe Bancroft, *History of Washington, Idaho, and Montana, 1845-1889* (1890).—K. A. M.

Kane, Paul (1810-1871). Painter. Born in Mallow, County Cork, Ireland, Kane emigrated to what is now Toronto at the age of eight. Desiring to gain formal instruction in art as a young man, he left Canada for the United States in about 1836 and worked at various jobs in Detroit and New Orleans until he had earned enough money to sail for Europe in 1841. After four years

abroad, he returned to Toronto determined to fulfill his earlier ambition to go West and paint Indian life. With the support of patrons such as Sir George Simpson, governor of the Hudson's Bay Company, and a Mr. George W. Allan, who commissioned him to paint one hundred Indian paintings for his private collection, Kane spent the next three years (1845 and 1846-48) sketching in the Canadian West from Sault Ste. Marie to Fort Vancouver on the Pacific coast. His experiences, illustrated by himself, appeared in his *Wanderings of an Artist Among the Indians of North America* in London in 1859. Kane died in Toronto, his reputation secure as the pioneer of Canada's western artists.

The paintings produced for Allan now reside in Toronto's Royal Ontario Museum of Archaeology. The Stark Foundation in Orange, Texas, owns more than two hundred of Kane's paintings and annotated field sketches, which are reproduced in *Paul Kane's Frontier* (1971), edited by J. Russell Harper.—D. C. H.

Kansa Indians. See SIOUAN TRIBES, SOUTHERN.

Kansas. Kansas became the thirty-fourth state on January 29, 1861, with an area of 82,276 square miles, about one third smaller than the Territory of Kansas. The native vegetation of this two-hundred- by four-hundred-mile rectangle was grass, the taller grasses in the more humid east and low, creeping buffalo grass in the west, where the average rainfall is below twenty inches. Two to three percent of the original area was forested, lakes were few, and rivers and streams had a leisurely flow. The lowest elevation above sea level was about seven hundred feet along the east and southeast border, while the greatest elevation along the western border was in excess of four thousand feet.

The first recorded history of this area was made by the Spanish chroniclers of the Francisco Vásquez de Coronado expedition. They set out from the Rio Grande to visit a region in the present central part of the state they identified as Quivira. On this trip in the summer of 1541 they found the soil to their liking and capable of growing all the products of Spain. The Indians, also, were described as physically attractive, but they lived in grass houses and possessed no gold, the primary object sought by the Coronado party. Friar Juan de Padilla returned to Quivira the following year as a missionary to the Indians and he was martyred by those he sought to convert.

The Kansa Indians, native to the northeastern part of the Kansas region, lived in large earthen lodges and depended on their gardens and on hunting for their food. They and the neighboring Osage Indians to the south lived a seminomadic life, whereas Indians making use of the western Plains region were nomadic, depending on the buffalo for food, shelter, and clothing. The Indians first seen by the Spanish in the Kansas area were too few in number to be easily exploited under the colonial system of relying on masses of servile natives. Furthermore, the lack of precious metals and the great distance from areas of other Spanish interest resulted in little attention being paid to the region during the remainder of the sixteenth century.

Early in the next century Spain began colonizing the area around Santa Fe and Juan de Oñate led a well-equipped force northeastward to spy out the region near the area of Quivira, but the Spanish had interests elsewhere and did not locate settlements there. Instead, by the early eighteenth century, the French, as claimants to the Mississippi valley, were exploring westward and visiting the region along the Missouri River that became Kansas. Etienne Venyard, sieur de Bourgmont, led one of these expeditions early in the eighteenth century. A few years later Claude Charles Du Tisne brought another party into the area. Trade, on a minor scale, was attempted by Paul and Pierre Mallet between the Mississippi River valley and Santa Fe in 1739. With so much area to exploit along the Mississippi River and in the Great Lakes region, the French spent little energy in using the resources of Kansas. Like the Spanish, they penetrated the region many times, making friends with the Indians and claiming the land for their king, but they made little permanent impression on the region.

During mid-eighteenth-century wars, Spain and France became allies and in 1763 the Spanish acquired French claims to all of the lands west of the Mississippi. During the Napoleonic wars of a generation later, Spain was forced to cede the area back to France and a few years later, in 1803, the United States purchased the Louisiana Territory; the purchase included most of the area which later became the state of Kansas. The territory acquired by the United States was assumed to be the watershed region draining eastward into the Mississippi River and that area included all of Kansas. But in 1819 in a treaty with Spain defining the international boundary, about 7,500 square miles of the southwestern corner of what was to become Kansas was transferred to Spain.

The United States had earlier expressed interest in the trans-Mississippi area and plans were formulated for exploration there even before the Louisiana Purchase. Three army expeditions exploring some part of the future state were led by Meriwether Lewis and William Clark, by Zebulon Pike, and by Stephen Long. Lewis and Clark traveled along the northeast border region near the Missouri River in 1804 and 1806. Pike's journey across Kansas from east to west was in the late summer and fall of 1806. Long's major party traveled around the future state in 1820, but during the previous August a small detachment had penetrated the northeast portion and in 1820 another group descended the Arkansas River.

These explorations, particularly those led by Pike and Long, were to have a profound influence on American understanding of the area during the first half of the twentieth century. Pike reported all manner of wild animals in the grassland but he could not visualize it as a future farmland. As an army officer he looked upon the region as advantageous to the United States for he felt that the country could not be attacked easily across the grassland. Pike's report emphasized aridity but it was Long, a few years later, who defined the western part of the grassland as the GREAT AMERICAN DESERT, a term that conjured up visions of blowing sand and the absence of water or vegetation.

While Pike and Long may possibly have explored the area during a period when it was drier than the period of Coronado's expedition of two and a half centuries earlier, that would not be a sufficient explanation for the differences in their reports. Coronado was a product of dry and subhumid Spain and Mexico. He visited Quivira after passing through desert and dry country. His brief residence in Quivira, during late June, July, and early

August, came in months when rainfall is usually abundant and vegetation lush. Moreover, the chroniclers of the Coronado expedition, who had to report so much failure elsewhere, may have been interested in emphasizing the advantages they saw in the soil of Quivira.

Pike and Long had experiences almost totally related to forested country and they were indoctrinated with the typical American view that fertile land could be found only where big trees grow. Their explorations also traversed the grassland from east to west, thus the increasing aridity was obvious to them. Pike's expedition arrived late in the year and he passed through when the normal vegetation was brown and dry. In any case their reports prompted the identification of the area as "Indian Country" and plans were soon initiated for removal of Indians located east of the Mississippi to a new haven in the West.

In the meantime, men engaging in commerce, fur trappers, and missionaries were gaining increased knowledge of the region that was to become Kansas. As unofficial explorers they marked out travel routes, recorded their experiences in diaries and journals, and helped to enlarge the scanty information about the area. Typical was William Becknell, who left central Missouri in September 1821 with a small party carrying goods on pack animals. His plan of trading with Indians on the upper Arkansas was diverted to trading in Santa Fe, located on the northern fringe of newly independent Mexico. So successful was this venture that Becknell repeated his trip the following year with loaded wagons and inaugurated the commercial use of the Santa Fe Trail, extending across the future state, which was to become a vital link in transportation from the Missouri River to Santa Fe for the next fifty years.

Fur trappers, seeking the elusive beaver, by the 1820s were blazing an overland trail westward that was soon to be identified as the Oregon Trail. This route, cutting across the northeast portion of the future state, became an important emigrant trail in the 1840s and later.

Missionaries arrived in the Indian country in increasing numbers after the Indian Removal Act of 1830, under which eastern Indians were sent into the Kansas region. Newly relocated tribes included the Shawnee, Delaware, Potawatomi, Kickapoo, Ottawa, Miami, Iowa, Sauk and Fox, Wyandot, and a number of smaller tribes. They were given reservations with precise boundaries carved out of country formerly claimed by the Kansa and the Osage. Exploration and boundary delineation by missionaries added to the early information about the future state of Kansas.

Exploring parties of the 1840s, such as those led by John C. Frémont, and movement of troops during the Mexican War resulted in reports generally more optimistic than Pike's and Long's, for they believed that farming would be successful in that great empty land. William Gilpin, who was with Frémont on several expeditions, viewed the area already known as the Great American Desert as a Pastoral Region or Great Plains. With increased exposure after 1848, when large numbers of emigrants headed to gold country over trails passing through the region, much of the mystery of the grassland was untangled. People living along the eastern border of Indian country, as well as some within the region, were anxious to open the area to settlement, and politicians in Washington were responding to that interest.

The twin territories of Kansas and Nebraska were created by the Kansas-Nebraska Act of May 30, 1854. This law was a product of the sectional issues engulfing the nation in the mid-nineteenth century. To avoid a clash over slavery, the act provided that the future status of these territories be decided not by Congress, but by the settlers there; thus the idea of POPULAR SOVEREIGNTY came into being. Senator Stephen A. Douglas, ardent proponent of the law, may have been motivated also by a desire for organization of Indian country through which a central railroad route to the West could be constructed.

The long debates in Congress over the Kansas-Nebraska Act (see KANSAS-NEBRASKA ISSUE) widened the breach between North and South and brought into being a new political organization, the Republican party. The struggle to decide the slave issue had been transferred to the territories; in Kansas, but not in Nebraska, this issue took violent forms. (See John BROWN.)

An indication of the confusion in the Territory of Kansas can be seen in the office of the territorial governor. These governors were appointed by the president to four-year terms and the men who received these positions were generally of high caliber. But, in the six and a half years of territorial status, Kansas had six appointed governors and four others who held the office on a temporary basis. Most governors were forced to resign because they were unable to satisfy the president that their administration was handling the slave issue properly. Presidents Franklin Pierce and James Buchanan were apparently committed to the view that Kansas must be a slave state, but their governors in the territory were unable to get the issue settled in favor of slavery.

There were four constitutional conventions in Kansas in the same period. A convention sponsored by the Free-State party drafted a constitution at Topeka in 1855. At Lecompton, in 1857, a proslavery constitution was prepared and presented to Congress. Another Free-State constitutional convention convened at Leavenworth in 1858 but it was unable to draft a constitution. Finally, in 1859, at Wyandotte, a constitutional convention was held which for the first time in territorial history had delegates from both major parties—by that time the Democratic and Republican parties. Defeat of the slavery issue was no longer in doubt, and it was recognized that Kansas would become a free state. This convention also set new western boundaries for Kansas at 25 degrees west of Washington, thus lopping off about one third of the area included in the territory.

Kansans had to wait about one and a half years before Congress would accept the Wyandotte constitution, which was not approved until several of the southern states had seceded from the Union. In achieving statehood on the eve of the Civil War and having been the scene of a violent struggle involving free state and proslavery factionalism, many Kansans proclaimed that the Civil War had actually begun in Kansas. In reality, at least half of the two hundred or so violent deaths that occurred in territorial Kansas were not a product of the free state-proslavery struggle but were the result of other issues of a nonpolitical character. But the attention of the nation was drawn to "Bleeding Kansas" in the late 1850s and whenever violence occurred it was magnified by the emotions evoked by the slavery issue. With statehood, Kansans barely had time to get their state government under way before the nation was overwhelmed by the tragedy of a fratricidal civil war.

Many Kansans, or JAYHAWKERS, were involved in the war, primarily on the Union side (see NEGROES ON THE FRONTIER). Only one battle, at Mine Creek, took place in Kansas. However, the raid led by a confederate guerrilla captain, William C. Quantrill, on Lawrence in August 1863, left 150 dead and many buildings in smoldering ruins. More died by the hand of QUANTRILL'S RAIDERS than all the violent deaths from partisan conflict in "Bleeding Kansas," but coming as it did shortly after the massive bloodletting at Vicksburg and Gettysburg, the raid on Lawrence lacked the impact of earlier slaughter.

The federal census of 1860 showed 107,206 people in the area that was to become Kansas and about 35,000 people in the mountain area of western Kansas Territory around Denver, where gold discoveries in 1859 attracted miners. Most of the people in Kansas at the time of statehood had come from Missouri and the states along the Ohio River. James H. LANE, one of the first United States senators, was an example of the Ohio valley immigrant. Relatively few immigrants came from the middle Atlantic states and only about one percent of the population was from New England. Charles ROBINSON, the first governor, and Samuel C. Pomeroy, the other early United States senator, were both from Massachusetts, and other Yankees were a sort of leaven in the business, teaching, and ministerial professions, exerting influence far greater than their numbers. The number of foreign-born residents in the state remained small, and while never rising above fourteen percent of the total, they made important contributions in various areas.

There is great drama and some extravagance about the settlement era of any region, and Kansas was no exception. Between 1855 and 1888 there were 106 (later dropped to 105) counties organized in the state. Each county, upon organizing, selected a county seat and "wars" between rival communities to gain control of the courthouse produced high emotion, some humor, and some tragedy. Farms were carved out of the prairie grassland; trees and orchards were planted. Transportation facilities were constructed and they in turn were influenced by existing villages, towns, and cities and at the same time were responsible for new communities in the state. The impact of new railroad lines was immense. By law public roads were built on almost every section line. Mines and quarries were opened, businesses developed and some flourished. Simple manufacturing plants were built to meet local needs. Schools, churches, and fraternal groups were organized to satisfy the desire of Kansans to build up their local community. All of this immense activity involved a huge capital outlay, some of which was invested in enterprises that failed. However, a feeling of progress was associated with each new activity; new construction was looked upon with pride, and optimism flowered.

But the climate did not always cooperate with the farmer, and the resulting economic ups and downs had their influence on Kansas enterprise. For example, 1860 was the driest year ever and the whole area suffered. The grasshopper year, 1874, was notorious and stories tended to exaggerate the devastation. The dry years beginning in 1888 brought boom times to an abrupt halt and many Kansans left the state. The droughty 1930s (see DUST BOWL) brought disaster to many farmers and only in that decade did Kansas show a reduction in the population figures recorded by the federal census. The major panic years, nationally, had influence in Kansas, although the Panic of 1857 had little local effect. The Panic of 1873 and particularly the Panic of 1893 greatly curtailed new economic activity, especially railroad construction, and slowed the influx of farmers seeking land. The Great Depression of the 1930s brought in a whole new attitude toward governmental responsibility for hard times, and the national government therafter had greater involvement in the internal affairs of states.

Kansas was to reach almost one million in population by 1880 and the second million was added by 1954, the territorial centennial year. The 1970 population of 2,249,071 allows for five members of the House of Representatives in Congress. Congressional seats for Kansas numbered eight from 1892 to 1932 with a decline since then because Kansas population growth has not kept pace with the nation. The internal movement of Kansas population has been important. An overwhelming proportion of Kansans in the nineteenth century were farmers or members of farm families. By 1920 two thirds of all Kansans were still residents of farms and small towns. The migration from the farm has been so rapid since then that by 1970 the urban population of Kansas had become almost two thirds of the total. In that year the state's largest cities were Wichita, established in 1870 and named for the Indians who inhabited the town site in south-central Kansas during the Civil War; Kansas City, the state's largest city in the late nineteenth and early twentieth centuries; and Topeka, an Indian word descriptive of the land in this Kansas River valley community. Farming has remained important in the Kansas economy but income from manufacturing employment in these cities took the lead away from farming in the 1960s, and by the end of that decade farmers numbered less than ten percent of all employed persons in the state.

The problems facing new settlers in Kansas in the early days of statehood were the same as those encountered on other frontiers; the immediate concern for secure shelter, for water, food, and fuel, and the long-range desire for a productive livelihood. In the eastern part of the state the early settlers built log cabins and many later constructed substantial stone houses. In the central and western part of the state the first homes were usually a dugout or a SOD HOUSE. After a few years in such warm but primitive structures, houses often were built of wood imported from northern or western forests. Surface water was inadequate at first, and lucky was the settler who found a spring on his land. Hand-dug wells was the next step for water in many areas, and eventually the drilled water well capped by a pump and windmill provided the needs of the farmer and his livestock. Early settlers expected to plant corn and a garden, hunt wild game, and catch fish. After the country began to fill up, the buffalo herds were killed off and settlers had to rely on the produce of their fields and gardens. In the eastern part of the state there was sufficient wood to supply the fuel needs of settlers. Elsewhere, buffalo chips, prairie grass, sunflower stalks, and corn cobs pro-

vided an inefficient but plentiful fuel source. New farmer settlers might take as many as fifteen years to get their land into full production. These were frequently exhausting years, involving hard physical labor, low income, and disappointment. After the promising advertisements of bountiful land in Kansas, the business of putting land into production was disillusioning.

The central location of Kansas provided the state with a geographical advantage as a route for major transportation lines. The early trails to Santa Fe and to Oregon passed through the region. The first transcontinental railroads across the state were the Kansas Pacific (later part of the UNION PACIFIC) and the ATCHISON, TOPEKA AND SANTA FE. A product of the development of these two railroads was the "long drive" of Texas Longhorns from southern Texas to Kansas railheads for shipment to northern feed lots and packinghouses (see CATTLE TOWNS). Later railroads with significant mileage in the state were the Missouri, Kansas, and Texas (Katy); the MISSOURI PACIFIC; the CHICAGO, ROCK ISLAND, AND PACIFIC; and the St. Louis and San Francisco. High-speed paved highways have carried immense volumes of vehicular traffic since the mid-twentieth century, and transcontinental airlines crisscross the state. The transportation net also includes hundreds of miles of underground pipelines that transport an enormous tonnage of petroleum, natural gas, and various refined products from the oil fields and refineries of Kansas.

Manufacturing in the early days of Kansas history was limited primarily to the gristmill, the sawmill, and the blacksmith. Products of the Kansas soil became the basis for manufacturing in later years with vast increases in flour mills, in meat packinghouses, and in food processing. In addition petroleum and natural gas resources, little exploited before the twentieth century, provide the basis for a refinery and chemical industry. Skilled Kansas workmen also are employed in metal fabrication industries, such as airplane manufacturing at Wichita (see AEROSPACE INDUSTRY). World Wars I and II and the Korean War greatly stimulated the growth of war-related industries in Kansas.

Kansas remains in the top ten states agriculturally, with cattle and wheat providing the bulk of cash sales made by the Kansas farmer. As the nation's top producer of wheat, Kansas normally harvests one fourth to one sixth of the total crop (see WHEAT PRODUCTION). Wheat produced on Kansas farms is known as hard winter wheat. It is sown in the fall, germinates and grows until cold weather sets in, begins growth again in the spring, heads, and is harvested in late June or July. More than one fourth of the fifty million acres of Kansas farmland has been sown to wheat in a single year, but seedings in the 1960s and early 1970s have been closer to nine million acres. Cattle on Kansas farms by 1970 exceeded six million, a figure larger than the total number traveling up the Chisholm Trail to Kansas cattle towns in the twenty years after the Civil War. Cattle sales bring more money to Kansas farmers than wheat. Other products resulting in sizable income for Kansas farmers are sorghums, which have become the alternate crop to wheat; corn, showing increased production under irrigation; hay; and hogs. By 1970 the number of Kansas farms was 86,000, down from 177,000 in 1935. The average Kansas farm in 1970 was 581 acres, or about seven eighths of a section one mile square, but the variation in the state is large. In central western Kansas the average farm is two sections or more, while in central eastern Kansas the average farm is a half section or less. With labor demands for Kansas farms down, it is little wonder that they are highly mechanized and electrified for more efficient production.

Kansas was advertised nationally during the "Bleeding Kansas" era of the 1850s and during the agitation of the Populist party of the 1890s. In the interval between, Kansas was regarded as the land of homesteading opportunity—as the place to tickle the soil and raise a bounteous crop. That period was a time of trial and experimentation on Kansas farms and slowly it became evident that wheat was a more reliable crop under Kansas conditions than corn and by World War I wheat was the ranking crop in the state. Sorghums have displaced corn as the number two crop since World War II.

The agitation and seemingly radical proposals of the Populists of the 1890s did not seem so extreme when similar programs were advanced by Kansas Progressives in the early twentieth century. Kansas was a leader in supporting prohibition, woman suffrage, direct election of United States senators, the direct primary, the initiative and referendum, and the use of a legislative reference service. But in the twentieth century the typical Kansan is most likely to be considered a conservative, whereas the typical Kansan of the nineteenth century was thought of as a liberal. The nation was rural in the nineteenth century but is under urban domination in the twentieth, and Kansas did not shift its population base as quickly. The rural-oriented Kansans prided themselves on their isolationist sentiment between the two world wars and on their ardent support of their fighting men when war was declared. On domestic problems, they favor a humane solution to human ills, but are suspicious of big government serving as the agency to supply the solutions.

In statewide politics, Kansas traditionally has been dominated by the Republican party. Of thirty-five elected governors (1861-1970), twenty-six were Republican, seven were Democratic, and two were Populists, elected in the political upheaval of the 1890s (see PEOPLE'S PARTY, KANSAS). Several governors have gained national recognition, among them John P. St. John (1879-83), who was the presidential candidate of the Prohibition party in 1884; Arthur CAPPER (1915-19), who served in the United States Senate for thirty years (1919-49); and Alf Landon (1933-37), who was the Republican candidate for president in 1936. Other Kansans who became well-known United States senators were Lane (1861-66); his successor, Edmund G. Ross (1866-71), who voted for acquittal in President Andrew Johnson's impeachment trial; Samuel C. Pomeroy (1861-73), who was not reelected to a third term because of sensational charges of scandal; John J. Ingalls (1873-91) who, due to the influence of Populist Mary Elizabeth LEASE, lost out after three terms, including four years as *president pro tem*; and Charles Curtis (1907-13, 1915-29), a part Indian who was Herbert Hoover's vice president; William Allen WHITE, though never elected to office, became Kansas' "senator-at-large" through his newspaper editorials. Other Kansans served in presidential cabinets, on the Supreme Court, in federal administrative departments, as generals and admirals in the military service, and on foreign assignments. Kansan

Dwight D. Eisenhower (1953-61) served two terms as president.

See John D. Bright, *Kansas: The First Century* (1956); Nyle H. Miller, *Kansas: A Students' Guide to Localized History* (1965); and William F. Zornow, *Kansas, A History of the Jayhawk State* (1957).—H. E. S.

Kansas-Nebraska issue. Because it reopened the question of slavery in the territories, the passage in 1854 of the Kansas-Nebraska Act probably did more than any other issue in the 1850s to exacerbate sectional antagonism between North and South. Subsequently, the turbulent process of settling the Kansas Territory gave the new Republican party, which arose in opposition to the act, an issue that greatly strengthened it in the North and consequently aroused fears in the South.

On January 4, 1854, Stephen A. Douglas reported out of the Senate Committee on Territories a bill that would organize a Nebraska Territory in an area from which slavery was prohibited by the Missouri Compromise of 1820 and allow states formed out of that territory to enter the Union "with or without slavery, as their constitution may prescribe at the time of admission." Historians disagree about Douglas' complex motives for introducing the bill, but one reason was his sincere interest in removing Indians from the Platte region and encouraging "a continuous line of settlements to the Pacific Ocean." Douglas' motives, however, are in a sense unimportant, for the final form of the Kansas-Nebraska Act, which produced such widespread indignation in the North, was substantially different from Douglas' bill and was the result of political maneuvers and pressures by certain southern senators of both parties. The final bill created two territories, declared the Missouri Compromise void, and applied popular sovereignty to the territories, although it was unclear when the people could make the decision on slavery. This popular sovereignty formula thus opened to possible slavery expansion an area, adjacent to populated states, from which it had been prohibited by law for more than thirty years.

Public antagonism to the bill in the North was vehement even before its passage in May 1854. Northern outrage was both fomented and shaped by the "Appeal of the Independent Democrats," which was sent out to the public by the most prominent antislavery men in the Senate. This appeal asserted that the bill was part of "an atrocious plot" by southern slaveholders to exclude immigrants and small farmers from the area and to reserve it for planters and slaves. Hostility to the act in the North cut across party lines. Sincere antislavery men abhorred the possible extension of an immoral institution; white Free-Soilers were anxious to keep out both planter competition and Negroes, free or slave; many simply deplored the violation of the Missouri Compromise as an aggression on northern rights by a slave-power conspiracy. For years abolitionists had warned of a plot by slaveholders to expand slavery, and the Kansas-Nebraska Act seemed concrete proof of that charge. In any case, it was northern denunciations of the South and not any initial interest in the bill or Kansas that aroused southerners to support the act.

The issue of slavery in western territories had a significant impact on political developments in 1854. Grass-roots anti-Nebraska coalitions of Free-Soilers, Whigs, and Democrats mushroomed throughout the North and especially in the Midwest, where people had the most direct interest in moving to Kansas or Nebraska. In some places these parties quickly took the name Republican. In all areas of the North, however, politicians could agitate the issue against the Democratic administration, which sponsored the act, to great effect. The Democrats suffered disastrous defeats in the congressional elections of that year, but the Kansas-Nebraska issue was not solely responsible for those losses. Nativism, anti-Catholic sentiment, the temperance movement, and other factors also contributed to those results.

The Kansas-Nebraska issue remained a potent political force after 1854, although national attention focused almost exclusively on Kansas. Settlers from proslavery Missouri as well as from adjacent free states rushed into Kansas. Antislavery men in New England and other northern areas formed Emigrant Aid Societies to raise money and arms to send northerners there and make sure it became a free state; southerners in Alabama and Georgia followed suit. Free-state men and proslavery men established separate and hostile territorial governments. There was some violence between the two sides. The so-called Wakarusa War, in which a posse of Missouri men marched on Lawrence, Kansas, involved no fighting, but murder committed by John BROWN of five southerners along Pottawatomie Creek in May 1856 and the subsequent battle of Osawatomie produced bloodshed.

Because of these events contemporary politicians and later historians portrayed everything that occurred in Kansas as a struggle between North and South, between freedom and slavery. Actually the amount of violence, the corrupt elections, and the chaos in Kansas differed little from that found during the settlement of other frontier areas. The Missourians and free-state men who poured into Kansas were more interested in land than in slavery or national issues. Many Missourians were anti-Negro, not proslavery. Turmoil resulted from conflicting land claims, competition for government contracts and the location of county seats, and struggles for the patronage available in the new territory. If Missourians crossed the border into Kansas to carry the territorial elections, Iowans did the same in Nebraska. By 1860 there were only two slaves in the entire Kansas Territory. Republican propagandists, however, exaggerated the amount of bloodshed and blamed it on southern aggressions against free-staters. "Bleeding Kansas" was a major issue with which Republicans tried to align indignant northern opinion behind their party in the presidential election of 1856.

After 1856 the internal situation in Kansas remained confused, but the application for statehood under the Lecompton constitution brought Kansas back into the national spotlight. The maneuvers behind the constitution are complex. In 1857 the proslavery legislature called for an election of delegates to a convention at Lecompton to write a constitution under which Kansas would apply for statehood. The census to register voters omitted fifteen of thirty-four counties in the territory. Free-state men refused to vote for delegates because the proslavery legislature called the election, and less than a fourth of the eligible voters participated. The convention then wrote a proslavery constitution that protected the right to hold slaves already in Kansas, but it refused to submit the entire constitution for popular ratifica-

tion. It allowed the voters only a choice between a clause allowing future entry of slaves and a clause prohibiting such entry. In the referendum the free-staters again abstained, the provision for allowing more slaves carried by about six thousand to six hundred, and the Lecompton constitution with that clause was forwarded to Congress. Meanwhile free-state men had gained control of the territorial legislature because Governor Robert J. Walker had thrown out fraudulent proslavery returns. This legislature called another referendum on the entire Lecompton constitution, and in this election, in which free-staters participated and proslavery men abstained, more than ten thousand votes were cast against Lecompton. Despite this evidence that the majority of settlers in Kansas opposed the constitution, President James Buchanan emphatically endorsed it and demanded that the Democratic party push it through Congress in 1858.

Douglas, whose popular sovereignty doctrine was based on local majority rule, revolted and led several Democrats and the entire Republican party in opposition to the bill. Though the Lecompton constitution passed the Senate, anti-Lecompton Democrats in the House imposed on the Senate a compromise bill, which in effect resubmitted the entire Lecompton constitution to the people of Kansas. They rejected it by an overwhelming majority and thereby delayed their admission as a state.

Kansas ceased to be a national issue after 1858. But because the Lecompton constitution split the leadership of the Democratic party and caused a substantial number of anti-Lecompton Democrats to bolt the party in subsequent elections, the Kansas-Nebraska issue contributed significantly to the victory of the Republicans in 1860, just as it had to the founding of the party and its strength in 1856.

See Eugene H. Berwanger, *The Frontier Against Slavery: Western Anti-Negro Prejudice and the Slavery Extension Controversy* (1967); Avery Craven, *The Coming of the Civil War* (1957); Paul W. Gates, *Fifty Million Acres: Conflicts over Kansas Land Policy, 1854-1890* (1954); James C. Malin, *John Brown and the Legend of Fifty Six* (1942); Allan Nevins, *Ordeal of the Union*, 2 vols. (1947); and Roy F. Nichols, "The Kansas-Nebraska Act: A Century of Historiography," *Mississippi Valley Historical Review*, vol. 43 (1956).—M. F. H.

Kansas Pacific Railroad. See UNION PACIFIC RAILROAD; Henry VILLARD.

Kearney, Denis (1847-1907). California labor agitator. Born in Ireland, Kearney went to sea at the age of eleven and in 1868 settled in San Francisco. Four years later he was able to purchase a draying business. He educated himself by reading widely and became a voluble speaker by attending a Lyceum of Self-Culture on Sunday afternoons. As economist Henry George remarked, the temperance that Kearney "practiced and preached as to liquor and tobacco did not extend to opinions or their expression." After the anti-Chinese riots in the summer of 1877, Kearney was a member of the "pick-handle brigade" organized by William T. COLEMAN and made up largely of employers. But for reasons that are uncertain he suddenly changed sides, and after a series of demagogic speeches on the "sand-lot" opposite the city hall, he became the leader of the newly formed Workingmen's party of California. Union labor in general did not support the party; its strongest supporters were the unemployed, and its consistent demand was for expulsion of the Chinese. Kearney was repeatedly arrested for inciting violence and repeatedly acquitted. After some brief and limited successes in electing Isaac S. Kalloch as mayor of the city and a large minority of the delegates to the state constitutional convention in 1878, the party disintegrated and Kearney returned to obscurity.

The chapter "Kearneyism in California" in James Bryce, *The American Commonwealth* (1893), is a classic account.—W. B.

Kearny, Stephen Watts (1794-1848). Soldier. Born in Newark, New Jersey, Kearny attended Columbia College and served as an officer in the Thirteenth Infantry during the War of 1812. Transferred to the Second Infantry, he was sent west in 1819 to assist in exploring the trans-Mississippi country. An excellent disciplinarian, inflexible and stern, he succeeded to command of the dragoon regiment and in 1837 published *Carbine Manual of Rules for the Exercise and Maneuvering of U.S. Dragoons*. He made the dragoons an elite group. At the outbreak of hostilities with Mexico in 1856, Kearny was ordered to raise an army to conquer New Mexico and California. In August he entered Santa Fe with sixteen hundred men, declared the province a United States territory, and formed a provisional government. He then hastened west along the Gila River with a dragoon detachment, crossed the Colorado; was attacked by and held off a Mexican force at San Pasqual, California, on December 6; and eventually reached San Diego. There he combined forces with Commodore Robert Field Stockton, who had tried to create a provisional government in southern California but had been driven from the coastal towns by Mexican forces. Stockton and Kearny won battles near the San Gabriel River on January 8-9, 1847, and captured Los Angeles. When Stockton appointed Captain John C. Frémont to succeed him as governor and then departed, Kearny claimed that Stockton's government had never actually functioned and the delegation of authority to Frémont was invalid. On March 1 Kearny formed his own civil government and declared himself governor but was unable to get Frémont to vacate his position or obey him. Returning east with Frémont accompanying him, Kearny charged the junior officer with insubordination and mutiny. A court-martial found Frémont guilty, and he resigned from the army. In the early summer of 1848 Kearny was briefly military governor at Veracruz and Mexico City. Brevetted a major general, he died in St. Louis from the ravages of yellow fever while commanding the Sixth Military Department.

See Dwight L. Clarke, *Stephen Watts Kearny* (1961). —H. P. H.

keelboat. See TRANSPORTATION ON THE MISSISSIPPI RIVER SYSTEM.

Keeler, William Wayne (1912-   ). Cherokee businessman and tribal chief. Keeler was born in Dalhart, Texas. He began his career in the oil industry when he was sixteen years old, working during summer vacations in the engineering department of Phillips Petroleum, the company he served from 1968 as chairman of the board and chief executive. Keeler worked his way up in the oil business and worked in many capacities, including research, chemistry, engineering, and in the

oil fields. During World War II he was on several committees of the Petroleum Administration for War and since then has been the head of other government petroleum agencies.

When the Cherokee Nation's formal government in Oklahoma was abolished in 1949, President Truman appointed Keeler principal chief of the Cherokee, a position he continued to hold by virtue of reconfirmation by every succeeding president. Keeler in turn appointed an executive committee to run tribal affairs. In 1961 the Cherokee were awarded nearly $15 million in compensation for a strip of land taken in 1853. The money was distributed in $280 per capita payments, but more than $2 million was "left over" because of unclaimed and fractional shares. Keeler used this as seed money to begin a reconstruction of an eighteenth-century Cherokee village and cultural center, Tsa-La-Gi. Also constructed was a tribal headquarters (which houses administrative offices, an arts and crafts center selling Cherokee handcrafts, Restaurant O' the Cherokees, and a gas station) on a forty-acre tribal plot outside of Tahlequah, Oklahoma.

Despite this impressive record, Keeler received much criticism in his role as principal chief because of the continued low standard of living of the tribe and the appointive nature of tribal government. The fact that more than ten thousand Cherokee fullbloods live without a voice in tribal—or any—government in the hills of northeastern Oklahoma, with family incomes averaging less than $2,000 per year, has been, to put it mildly, a sore point. These people live in tarpaper homes. About ten percent have indoor plumbing and pure-water supplies; thirty-five percent have electricity.

Ninety miles or so from Tahlequah, in Bartlesville, Oklahoma, Keeler was a prominent businessman and civic leader, and he held important positions in several national organizations within the petroleum industry as well. He was appointed a member of the National Advisory Board of the War on Poverty by President Johnson in 1965, and in 1968 Governor Walter J. Hickel appointed him chairman of a task force to recommend "ways to use native labor" in Alaska. In 1957 he was named outstanding Indian of the year and in 1963 was given the Indian Council Fire Achievement Award. —C. C.

Keith, William (1839-1911). Painter. Born in Aberdeenshire, Scotland, Keith emigrated in 1850 to New York City where he served an apprenticeship as an engraver. In 1859 he moved to California and established an engraving shop, also devoting himself to portrait and landscape painting. Traveling to Düsseldorf in 1869 for further study, he returned to California in 1871. He resided for an indefinite period in New Orleans in the 1880s and in 1893 made another trip to Europe, where he studied in Munich and traveled in Spain. Keith is best known today for his California landscapes.—D. C. H.

Keleher, William Aloysius (1886-1972). Historian and attorney. Born in Lawrence, Kansas, Keleher moved to New Mexico at an early age. He was employed at thirteen as a telegraph operator, copying "pony" Associated Press reports in Western Union offices for newspapers in the territory. Keleher later worked as a reporter and city editor for the Albuquerque *Journal* and Albuquerque *Herald*. After studying law at

Washington and Lee University in Lexington, Virginia, he returned to New Mexico to practice law in 1915. In 1928 the politically active Albuquerque attorney served as chairman of the Democratic State Central Committee and in later years served in other organizations as well.

In later life Keleher became one of the most prominent historians of New Mexico's long and colorful territorial period. In 1943 he published the *Maxwell Land Grant: A New Mexico Item*, an interesting, readable account of the intricate history of perhaps the most famous Mexican land grant. Two years later his *The Fabulous Frontier: Twelve New Mexico Items* was published. In it he described briefly the functions and makeup of the mysterious Santa Fe Ring, having connected this politically potent ring with the struggle to gain control of the Maxwell Grant in his earlier volume. In 1952 he published *Turmoil in New Mexico, 1846-1868*, and in 1957 his *Violence in Lincoln County: A New Mexico Item* appeared.

Keleher's approach to writing history is reminiscent of the great Francis Parkman. In preparing his *Turmoil in New Mexico*, he not only consulted the available papers and documents but also visited the ruins of the military forts and the Civil War battlefields about which he wrote. In order to get a better perspective about the tragic forced march of the sorrowful Navaho Indians to the Bosque Redondo reservation in 1863, he rode horseback through the Navaho reservation in the Four Corners area, often visiting Indians living far off the beaten path.—R. W. L.

Kelley, Hall Jackson (1790-1874). Promoter of Oregon settlement. A Harvard-educated New Englander, Kelley surveyed, taught school, and wrote school books in his early years. His interest in the unsettled lands of the Northwest began in 1818, and he soon became the leading advocate of migration to the Oregon country, which at the time was claimed jointly by Great Britain and the United States. Although Kelley knew Oregon only second hand, he did not hesitate to extol its virtues in speeches, pamphlets, circulars, and petitions. In the 1820s it is safe to say that Oregon was known to New Englanders largely through his work.

In 1829 Kelley organized the American Society for Encouraging the Settlement of the Oregon Territory. He proved adept at transmitting enthusiasm but less talented as an actual entrepreneur of exploration and settlement. When his hopes for federal financing did not materialize, Kelley's plan to lead settlers to Oregon in 1832 collapsed. Nathaniel J. Wyeth's success in a similar venture in 1832 and again in 1834 underscored Kelley's failure.

Undaunted, Kelley continued as Oregon's foremost booster until the 1850s. Only once, in 1832, did he personally visit the land of his dreams, only to encounter considerable hostility from the Hudson's Bay Company, which had preceded the American settlement. But the interest in Oregon that Kelley helped arouse in the East did much to overcome such opposition to America's Northwest expansion.

Kelley's career may be traced in his works, such as *A Geographical Sketch of that Part of North America called Oregon* (1830) and *Manual of the Oregon Exploration* (1831). The only biography is Fred W. Powell, *Hall Jackson Kelley—Prophet of Oregon* (1917). Powell has also edited most of Kelley's writings in *Hall J. Kelley on Oregon* (1932).—R. N.

Kelley, Oliver H. (1826-1913). Minnesota farm organizer. Kelley migrated west from Boston by way of Peoria, Illinois, and Muscatine, Iowa. He stepped off a steamboat at St. Paul in June 1849. Within a few weeks he had joined Minnesota's first Masonic Lodge and had gotten involved in local politics. In 1850 he settled in Itasca, upriver from St. Paul. This settler from Boston shrewdly recognized that the future of Minnesota lay not in the Indian trade but in the land. He turned to agriculture with surprising enthusiasm for a city-bred man. Since he had received a better-than-average education and had no rural background to draw upon (his father was a tailor), Kelley became a confirmed "book farmer." He campaigned for more experimentation, advanced methods, and exchange of information among farmers. On his farm he built one of the first frame barns erected north of St. Paul and sowed the first timothy hay in Minnesota. He experimented with everything from buckwheat to apples, from melons to asparagus. Hard-pressed by the drought of 1863, he installed an elaborate irrigation system and became the Minnesota agent of J. D. West's patented pumps. He is also said to have owned the first mechanical reaper in the state.

As a practical farmer Kelley was moderately successful, moving steadily away from grain and stock raising and in the direction of horticulture, vegetable gardening, and the nursery business, as nearby city markets became more accessible. Yet there always remained in him a strong flair for promotion, politics, and journalism. He began to write columns on agriculture in newspapers in and outside of Minnesota. In 1864 he received through his old patron, Governor Alexander Ramsey, a job as clerk under the commissioner of agriculture in Washington. It was during a southern tour in 1866 that the idea of a national farmers' organization began to develop in Kelley's mind. Still a dedicated Mason, he found himself accepted as a brother member by Masons throughout the South despite the general antagonism southerners exhibited toward northerners. Why not develop a similar organization among the nation's farmers, he wondered. Such an organization would bring men of the North and South closer together, and farmers of both sections would have a channel through which to cooperate in working for their common good. From this dream sprang the GRANGER LAWS and a Populist agrarian movement that in a few short years was to shake the social and political foundations of the Midwest.

Kelley worked throughout 1867, busily filling in the outlines of his grand scheme. Caroline Hall, his niece, contributed many ideas, among them the inclusion of women in the organization on an equal basis with men. Kelley took into his confidence a select circle of sympathetic friends, mostly other federal employees. Six of them, with him, became founders of the Order of the Patrons of Husbandry, better known as the Grange, which was formally established on December 4, 1867. He served as secretary for its first eleven years of existence.

See Solon J. Buck, *The Granger Movement* (1913); and Rhoda R. Gilman and Patricia Smith, "Oliver Hudson

Kelley: Minnesota Pioneer, 1849-1868," *Minnesota History* (Fall 1967).—R. W. F.

Kelly, Milton (1818-1892). Idaho newspaper editor and lawyer. A native of Onondaga, New York, Kelly taught school and farmed prior to his admission to the bar in Wisconsin in 1845. He moved to California in 1861 and to Oregon in 1862. Later in 1862 he moved from an Oregon mining camp to Placerville in present-day Idaho and in 1863 went on to Rocky Bar. He served in the first session of Idaho's territorial legislature and as an associate justice of the Idaho Supreme Court from 1865 to 1870. From 1872 to 1889 he published the *Idaho Statesman* in Boise, where he became a senior member of the influential (but not corrupt, as it was alleged to be) Boise ring. Retiring from the *Statesman*, he developed a major resort at Kelly's Hot Springs near Boise.

Kelly was so active in beating down projects to parcel out Idaho Territory to surrounding states and territories that much of the credit for Idaho's admission as a state in 1890 belongs to him—M. W.

Kelly, New Mexico. Ghost town. In Socorro County, Kelly and its nearby sister town Magdalena prospered for nearly sixty years as the center of a rich lead and zinc mining area in central New Mexico. The area produced nearly $30 million worth of valuable minerals, and Kelly managed to postpone until 1931 the early death that came to most mining towns. Today all that remains of Kelly is a few broken buildings, and Magdalena survives as a picturesque anachronism.

See Ralph Looney, *Haunted Highways: The Ghost Towns of New Mexico* (1968); and Muriel S. Wolle, *The Bonanza Trail* (1953).—R. B. W.

Kendrick, John Benjamin (1857-1933). Wyoming politician. Born in Texas, Kendrick drove a herd of Longhorns to northeastern Wyoming for a wealthy Texas cattleman in 1879. After establishing his credentials as a foreman and ranch manager, he married his wealthy employer's daughter and himself acquired large ranch properties near the east slope of the Big Horn Mountains in Wyoming and Montana. He became a millionaire.

Not having gone to school beyond the seventh grade, Kendrick later taught himself with some help from his schoolteacher wife. He entered politics late, when he was drafted to run for the Wyoming senate in 1910. Once involved, he learned fast and remained in political office until he died. A conservative Democrat, he was elected governor of Wyoming in 1914 and United States senator in 1916, 1922, and 1928.

In line with the wishes of his state's livestockmen, farmers, and raw-materials producers, he consistently favored high tariffs, low railway freight rates, aid to homesteaders, federally aided reclamation, and other legislation calculated to benefit his constituents. While president of the American National Live Stock Association in 1919 he began vigorously promoting regulation of the meat-packing industry, achieving his goal in 1921.

Although of a different political party and representing a different kind of livestock, Kendrick found it easy to cooperate effectively with Wyoming's senior senator, the woolgrower Francis E. Warren, who was chairman of the Senate Appropriations Committee in the 1920s. Kendrick and Warren were both millionaires and had much in common.

It was Kendrick who opened the Teapot Dome controversy at the instigation of a few independent oilmen in Wyoming. The Senate adopted his resolution calling upon Secretary of the Navy Edwin Denby and Secretary of the Interior Albert B. Fall to advise whether negotiations were in progress for the leasing of the Teapot Dome Navy oil reserve without competitive bidding. He was seeking to protect the rights of his constituents and his state's royalty rights and had no idea that he was lighting a fuse that would lead to the great Teapot Dome scandal (see Albert B. FALL).

Tall, rugged, and unassuming, Kendrick personified for his constituents the spirit of the western frontier and enjoyed immense popularity. He was plain "John" to many Republicans as well as Democrats.

See T. A. Larson, *History of Wyoming* (1965). —T. A. L.

Kenedy, Mifflin (1818-1895). Steamboat captain and Texas rancher. Kenedy was born in Pennsylvania of Quaker parents. In 1834 he shipped to India as a sailor. From 1836 to 1842 he was a clerk and acting captain on Ohio and Mississippi river steamers. He then worked on Florida waters to 1846, where he met Captain Richard King, later his partner in ranching and other enterprises. (King was the founder of the famous King Ranch in Texas.) In 1850 Kenedy, King, Charles Stillman, and James O'Donnell became partners in a firm engaged in Rio Grande transport and trade. Kenedy and King later bought out the other two partners. During the Civil War they aided the Confederacy by shipping cotton around the Union blockade of the Texas coast. Before it was dissolved in 1874, the firm had built or bought more than twenty boats.

Kenedy's first venture into ranching was in 1854, when he took Merino sheep from Pennsylvania to Texas and established ten thousand head in Hidalgo County. He sold them after losses in 1856. After King started his ranch one hundred and twenty miles to the north, Kenedy started running cattle at Brownsville. In 1860 the two joined forces, King putting up land and cattle and Kenedy cattle and cash. The partnership was dissolved in 1868 after a ten-month roundup and division of 58,644 head of cattle, 4,400 horses, and many sheep, goats, and mules.

That same year Kenedy bought twenty-six leagues of the Laureles grant, east of King's Santa Gertrudis ranch. Kenedy ranched there until 1882, when he sold the ranch, which had grown to 242,000 acres, to a Scottish syndicate. He then moved south to present-day Kenedy County, Texas, where he formed La Parra Ranch, which covered 390,000 acres at the time of his death.

In 1876 he and King were principal backers of the "Tex-Mex" railroad from Corpus Christi to Laredo, and in 1885 he helped build the San Antonio and Aransas Pass road. Kenedy and King also shared the first fenced range of any size west of the Mississippi. In 1868, before barbed wire had come to the plains, the two men used creosoted cypress posts and Louisiana pine planks to lay thirty miles of fence across the peninsula, which formed Laureles Ranch. Kenedy presided at the creation of the Stock Raisers' Association of West Texas in 1870 and was named its first president. In 1874 he successfully crossed Brahma cattle from India with native stock. —H. R. L.

Kensington Rune Stone (Minnesota). The rune stone was unearthed near Kensington in Douglas County,

Minnesota, in 1898. Bearing the date 1362, the runic characters on the stone tell of a journey of exploration from "Vinland" westward by twenty-two Norwegians and eight Goths.

For three quarters of a century the rune stone has been the subject of intense controversy. Its authenticity has had its defenders, but it has been seriously challenged by runologists and historians. No one has proved beyond doubt either its genuine or fraudulent character, but most scholars suspect that the stone was implanted and inscribed by jokesters.

See Theodore C. Blegen, *The Kensington Rune Stone: New Light on an Old Riddle* (1968); Aslak Liestol, "The Runes of Bergen: Voices from the Middle Ages," *Minnesota History* (Summer, 1966); and Erik Wahlgren, *The Kensington Stone: A Mystery Solved* (1958).—R. W. F.

Kenton, Simon (1755-1836). Frontiersman. Born in Fauquier County, Virginia, Kenton fled to the upper Ohio River frontier under the mistaken impression that he had slain a rival in love. That was the beginning of a forty-two-year career in the Old Northwest states of Kentucky and Ohio as one of America's greatest frontiersmen. Kenton was in Lord Dunmore's War; joined the American Revolution in the frontier theater; fought against the Shawnee with Daniel Boone (whose life Kenton saved in 1777 when the Shawnee raided Boonesboro; the Indians felled Boone in front of the fort, but Kenton carried him inside to safety); survived a harrowing Indian captivity in 1778; led "Kenton's boys" (a self-defense band in Kentucky in the late 1780s and early 1790s); and, finally, performed as a fifty-eight-year-old scout under Isaac Shelby at the battle of the Thames during the War of 1812. By the time of his death near Zanesville, Ohio, Kenton had become a living American legend.

See Patricia Jahns, *The Violent Years: Simon Kenton and the Ohio-Kentucky Frontier* (1962); and Edna Kenton, *Simon Kenton: His Life and Period: 1755-1836* (1930). —R. M. B.

Kentucky, settlement of. Between 1740 and 1774 the area that is now Kentucky was visited by various persons. There were Indian captives such as Mary Ingles who were brought into the area as unwilling visitors. Hunters and traders sent by George CROGHAN came this way. In 1750 and 1751 Dr. Thomas Walker and Christopher GIST came land-spying for the Loyal and Ohio land companies. In the early 1760s a man named John Swift was in the region, and a persistent legend has it that he found a rich lode of silver. It was not until the advent of the long hunters in the years after 1765, however, that visitations actually began to open the region to prospective settlement.

Between 1773 and 1785 Kentucky was opened to a constant stream of settlers coming from Pennsylvania, Maryland, Virginia, the Watauga settlements, and North Carolina. They came by way of the Ohio River from Pittsburgh, and by way of CUMBERLAND GAP and the WILDERNESS ROAD. The first permanent settlement was begun in June 1774, when James HARROD and his party began building Harrod's Town, but this venture was disrupted by LORD DUNMORE'S WAR (1774). In the early spring of 1775 Harrod and his party were back at their settlement, and the Transylvania Company, led by Richard HENDERSON, Daniel BOONE, and others, had begun building Fortress Boonesboro. Soon there were settlements begun all across the central BLUEGRASS REGIONS.

Kentucky settlements were begun in the most bitter years of the American Revolution. The years 1776-82 were a period of constant raiding by Indians and the British from above the Ohio. In February 1778 Daniel Boone and a party of salt makers were captured at Blue Licks and taken as prisoners across the Ohio to the British post at Detroit. Early in the spring Boone escaped and returned to Boonesboro to prepare the fort for certain assault from the British and Indians. In 1777 George Rogers CLARK returned to Virginia to make plans for a campaign against the Indians and British beyond the Ohio at the posts of Kaskaskia, Vincennes, and Detroit. These plans were made in Fort Harrod, although the Northwest expedition began from Corn Island just above the Falls of the Ohio. This expedition set out down the Ohio on June 24, and by July 4 was before Fort Kaskaskia.

In spite of the dangers of war and the tremendous pressures against the Kentucky settlements, they held out to the end of the war. By 1781 the roads from Cumberland Gap and down from the Ohio and the mouth of Limestone Creek were filled with incoming settlers. They were for the most part yeomen who sought out small landholdings and opportunities to escape debt and oppressions caused by the revolution. Many were revolutionary veterans who came with Virginia land warrants entitling them to land claims under the famous Virginia land law of 1779 (see LAND SYSTEM, SOUTHERN).

By 1784 the population of Kentucky had expanded to the point where settlers began to complain to Virginia about its official shortcomings, and most of all about the confusions that had arisen over conflicting land claims; in time, literally hundreds of petitions were sent east of the mountains. In 1784 a meeting was called in Danville for the purpose of discussing the greatest problem of all, the Indian menace. Although raids against the settlements ceased in August 1782, in the battle of the Blue Licks, the threat along the Ohio was as serious as ever.

The meeting at Danville in 1784 was the first of ten conventions that led to the formation of the independent Commonwealth of Kentucky. The process of separation involved many issues, among them protection of land titles, the sharing of Virginia's debts, and the entry of Kentucky into the Confederation. After 1787 one of the most important issues was the opening of the Ohio and Mississippi rivers to free use by Kentucky farmer-boatmen.

The conventions in Danville were to involve a considerable number of personalities, among them Benjamin Logan, George Nicholas, John Brown, Thomas McDowell, Caleb Wallace, David Rice, Isaac SHELBY, and James WILKINSON. None was so troublesome as Wilkinson. On his famous visit to the Spanish officials in New Orleans in 1787, he reached an agreement that doubtless boded ill for the struggling young territory. Neither Wilkinson nor the SPANISH CONSPIRACY prevailed, and the process of separation went on its uncertain course. In May 1792 delegates to the tenth, or constitutional, convention, drafted and sent away to Congress a satisfactory document. Despite all the discussion in the separation conventions and the Danville Political Club, Kentucky's first constitution revealed no originality and no departures from the established pattern of state constitutions. Shelby was elected governor.

Admission to the Union ended the frontier period of Kentucky. There were still raw and unorganized fringes in the state, but the pioneering period was ended. Kentucky had been a testing ground for settlers moving west of the mountains. Its people had made adjustments to the hard demands of the land, withstood the attacks hurled against them in the American Revolution, built homes, opened farms, and had begun the organization of towns. LEXINGTON, for instance, was by the end of the pioneer period the chief town on the old frontier and LOUISVILLE, a chief port. At least four church bodies had established themselves in the West, John Bradford had begun publication of the *Kentucky Gazette*, the Fayette County legal bar already had distinguished members practicing in the courts, and Kentuckians were beginning to exercise some considerable political influence nationally.

The process of pioneering in Kentucky was never of a single period. Central Kentucky and the Bluegrass underwent a remarkably short period of primitive living. Rich lands and a growing trade greatly shortened the years of pioneering. In the Green River settlements and around the Appalachian Plateau the process was to continue for at least a half-century more. These latter areas were truly log cabin frontiers.

Kentucky's pioneer period left a strong impression on the state's history. Persons who crossed the mountains in this era were truly the founders, and their deeds were heroic. Out of the vast army of settlers who came were Daniel Boone, Simon Kenton, George Rogers Clark, Benjamin Logan, Isaac Shelby, Jacob Sandusky, John Floyd, James Harrod, and Hugh McGary.

Kentucky in its pioneering period became closely allied with interests in the Ohio valley. Well before it achieved independent statehood, boatmen were drifting farm products to the New Orleans market. They reacted vigorously against the proposed Jay Treaty, which would close the Mississippi River to Americans, and later against the federal tax on distilled liquors. Most important of all, Kentucky was to become a major staging area for the continuing westward movement.

See Thomas D. Clark, *History of Kentucky* (1937); Lewis Collins, *History of Kentucky*, 2 vols. (1874); W. E. Connelley and E. M. Coulter, *History of Kentucky*, 5 vols. (1922); Robert S. Cotterill, *History of Pioneer Kentucky* (1917); and Humphrey Marshall, *History of Kentucky*, 2 vols. (1824).—T. D. C.

Kentucky frontier stations. Beginning with the founding of Harrod's Town in 1774 in Kentucky, numerous forts, blockhouses, and stations were established in the central part of the state. Generally these were strong log houses that could be used as places of refuge from Indian attacks. Some of them were surrounded by puncheon walls, and in the fortresses proper there were strong logs or blockhouses along the walls. Some of the best-known stations were McClelland's, Ruddle's, Bryan's, Harmon's, and Whitley's. In all, there were more than two hundred. Most of the stations became the centers of farmsteads, and some of them, such as the ones at Danville, LOUISVILLE, LEXINGTON, and Harrod's Town, grew into towns.

The early Kentucky station was an excellent center from which land hunters and settlers could work. They could leave their property and families at these places with some sense of security while they located sites for homesteads and stations of their own. Whitley's Station on the fork of the Wilderness Road near the Crab Orchard in eastern Kentucky was famous as a place of arrival and departure for emigrants traveling to central Kentucky. However, many of these stations were subjected to severe Indian attacks; the most damaging occurred at Estill's Station, Bryan's Station, Ruddle's Fort, and Hingston Blockhouse, while McClelland's Station had to withstand more than one raid.

See W. E. Connelley and E. H. Coulter, *History of Kentucky*, 5 vols. (1922), and Humphrey Marshall, *The History of Kentucky*, 2 vols. (1824).—T. D. C.

Kentucky rifle. The gun called Kentucky rifle was not of Kentucky, but of Pennsylvania origin. The term refers to the fact that this long rifle was used by pioneers who crossed the Appalachians and who fended off the Indians along the Ohio River. These backwoods defenders and hunters brought fame to the firepower and accuracy of the guns. The first rifle of the long-barreled muzzle-loading type was produced in 1728, and by 1800 almost as many manufacturers were producing guns as there were rifles. Most rifles used in the frontier were supplied by German gunsmiths about Lancaster, Pennsylvania, and there is no doubt that the American gun was a modification and adaptation of European guns, which earlier were shipped to Philadelphia and New York.

Generally there were four basic types of Kentucky rifles, the variations being in the length of barrels and the type of percussion or fuses in use. The most primitive were the flintlocks that fired into a priming pan and transmitted fire through a powder hole to the chamber of the rifle. The later types used a percussion cap fitted over a tube or fuse plug. The Kentucky rifle was largely a handmade gun produced by gunsmiths using highly primitive tools, but using them with deftness and accuracy. The boring and rifling was done on a gun lathe in which the bore and "rifles" in the barrel were cut according to the size and shape of the tool used. The heavy octagonal barrel was mounted in a long sheath of curly maple or burled walnut, and individual owners decorated them according to their own fancy. Necessary accouterments to the rifle were a large powder horn, a smaller priming horn, a patch pocket, flints, channel picks, and a stout but slender ramrod.

The long rifle early became the symbol of pioneering, and use of the rifle by frontiersmen was a mark of great personal pride. Local gunsmiths all across the expanding frontier kept up with needs for rifles until the Kentucky type was finally supplanted by commercially produced guns. (See GUNS.)

See John G. W. Dillin, *The Kentucky Rifle* (1924). —T. D. C.

Keokuk. (c. 1790-1848). Sauk tribal leader. Born at Saukenuk, the great Sauk town at the confluence of the Mississippi and Rock rivers, Keokuk (known also as the Watchful Fox) became prominent for his political skill, loyalty to the Americans, and complaisance in serving American authorities. A member of the Fox clan, he could not claim the proper hereditary title to civil authority among the Sauk because his mother was half French. But his audacity and courage, combined with a restless ambition and oratorical skill, gained him recognition as a war chief and member of the Sauk council during the War of 1812. Subsequently he challenged the leadership of the veteran BLACK HAWK, placing himself at the head of a faction of the Sauk and Fox tribes that sought to accommodate to American demands. His influence was recognized and his favor courted by American officials; and with his considerable abilities as an orator, Keokuk's apparent success in negotiations increased his popularity among the Sauk and Fox.

The rivalry between Keokuk and Black Hawk culminated in the BLACK HAWK WAR of 1832. Keokuk led the peace party and was given charge of his old rival after Black Hawk's capture and release from imprisonment. The humiliation of Black Hawk was completed when federal treaty commissioners officially installed Keokuk as civil chief of the Sauk and Fox—a dubious authority that he nevertheless accepted and exercised until his death.

After the Black Hawk War, Keokuk led the Sauk and Fox in Iowa and later, after signing additional treaties of land cessions, presided over the tribes' removal to Kansas. His cupidity and favoritism, particularly in the handling of tribal annuities, caused friction and lost Keokuk popularity during these years, while his overfondness for whiskey further undermined his people's confidence in his leadership. Following a drunken episode, he died of dysentery in 1848. His title as civil chief passed to his eloquent son, Moses Keokuk. For his services to the United States, Keokuk's fame is perpetuated by a bronze bust in the national capitol.

The most detailed information on Keokuk is in William T. Hagan, *The Sac and Fox Indians* (1958). —K. N. O.

Kern, Edward Meyer (1823-1863). Painter and draftsman. Born in Philadelphia, exhibited for the first time at the Artists' Fund Society in 1841. From about 1845 to 1847 he served as a topographer with John C. Frémont's third expedition to the Southwest and during the war with Mexico served under Frémont's command in California. During the fall and winter of 1848-49, he and his two older brothers, Benjamin and Richard, accompanied Frémont on his fourth expedition to the Rocky Mountains in Colorado and in 1849 Edward also served as topographer with J. H. Simpson's expedition into the Navaho country of southwestern Colorado, Utah, and Arizona. From 1853 to 1856, Kern was an official artist with the Ringgold exploratory and surveying expedition to the North Pacific, and after a brief period in Washington, joined the navy's expedition to chart a route from California to China between the years 1858 and 1860. Kern served again under Frémont during the first year of the Civil War but was discharged in November 1861, returning to Philadelphia, where he died.

Kern's work appeared in the *Reports of the Secretary of War with Reconnaissances of Routes from San Antonio to El Paso* and *Report of J. H. Simpson of an Expedition into Navaho Country*, published for the first session of the thirty-first Congress as Senate Document 64 in 1850. He was also a contributor of illustrations for other official published reports and is represented in Henry R. Schoolcraft's six-volume *Information Respecting the History, Conditions, and Prospects of the Indian Tribes of the United States*. Kern is also represented today in the collection of the Office of Naval Records and the National Collection of Fine Arts, Smithsonian Institution, in Washington, D.C., the United States Naval Academy Museum in Annapolis, Maryland; the Henry E. Huntington Library and Art Gallery, San Marino, California; and the Thomas Gilcrease Institute of American History and Art, Tulsa, Oklahoma.

See John C. Ewers, *Artists of the Old West* (1965); and Robert Taft, *Artists and Illustrators of the Old West, 1850-1900* (1953).—D. C. H.

Kern brothers. Artists, scientists, and explorers. The Kern brothers were of a genteel Philadelphia family whose eldest son, John, was a successful art teacher. Edward KERN and Richard Hovendon Kern (1821-53) in particular shared an interest in art and science throughout their careers. Their attention was turned toward the West when Edward first accepted a position as artist for the third expedition of John Charles Frémont in 1845.

The expedition left Westport Landing, site of present-day Kansas City, on June 23, 1845, intending to map and explore the central road to California and to be on hand should hostilities commence with Mexico. Edward sketched the route, made scientific drawings of botanical and zoological specimens, and along the way learned further the skills of astronomy and topography. After the party left Bent's Fort on the Arkansas River he was assigned increasing responsiblity for the topography of the expedition. When the party split to take two paths across the Great Basin along the Humboldt River, Edward was placed in charge of topography for his segment. After leaving Walker's Lake, Kern, with Joseph Reddeford Walker continuing as guide, mapped the route southward around the southern Sierra Nevada through Walker's Pass into the San Joaquin valley. There they were to meet the other part of the expedition under Frémont at a stream they knew simply as the lake fork of the Tulare. They missed one another because they camped on different rivers and thereby discovered the distinction between the present King's River and the Kern River. Frémont assigned Edward's name to the latter, his most enduring memorial.

When the Mexican War broke out in 1846, the Frémont expedition became merged into the California Battalion, in which Edward was commissioned first lieutenant on July 4, 1846. During the Bear Flag Revolt against Mexico in June Frémont had placed Kern in charge of the prisoners at Sutter's Fort, and during the remainder of the war he commanded that place. Kern also organized the relief from Sutter's Fort for the Donner Party early in 1847. In April the California Battalion was disbanded, but due to illness Edward did not leave the area until November, when he sailed for Philadelphia.

Richard had meanwhile been engaged in teaching art and making scientific illustrations, while Benjamin Jordan Kern (1818-49) had begun the practice of medicine. When Frémont proposed his fourth expedition to test the central Rockies in winter to prove the feasibility of an all-season railroad route, Edward convinced both Richard and Benjamin to accompany the expedition. Leaving Westport Landing in October 1848, the three brothers, all of whom were now members of the Philadelphia Academy of Natural Sciences, worked as scientific collectors, sending back specimens and sketching the route. They proceeded to the headwaters of the

Rio Grande in the San Juan range, one of the most impenetrable regions of the southern Rockies. With Old Bill Williams as guide, Frémont was determined to force the expedition through. But the winter proved extraordinarily harsh and they lost their direction. Frémont refused to retreat, however, until they became almost hopelessly stranded. On the desperate return down the mountains, Frémont abandoned his men and in various broken groups they straggled back to Taos. The three Kerns survived, but one third of the expedition, eleven men, perished. The Kerns blamed Frémont and refused to accompany the expedition farther. A cache of possessions and papers had been left in the mountains, and Ben Kern and Old Bill Williams returned for them when the first snows melted. On March 13 or 14, 1849, Ben and Williams were killed by an enraged band of Ute, probably mistaken for part of an army detachment that had attacked a Ute village the day before.

Edward and Richard were now stranded in New Mexico. For a two-year period their skills as artists and scientists were engaged in a series of tasks by the Army Topographical Corps. They accompanied Lieutenant James H. Simpson on the 1849 punitive expedition against the Navaho, including the first official penetration of Canyon de Chelly. In 1850 they were hired for topographical work by Lieutenant John Pope and Lieutenant John Parke. In 1851 Richard was engaged under Lieutenant Lorenzo Sitgreaves on an exploration of the Little Colorado River. That same summer Edward accompanied Pope on a topographical search for a better route between Santa Fe and Fort Leavenworth. On these various assignments, the Kerns added substantially to their knowledge of southwestern archaeology, sketching and measuring pueblo ruins and making major discoveries in this field. Their field contributions aided the scholarship of such easterners as Henry Schoolcraft.

Richard was next hired for one of the Pacific Railroad surveys with John W. Gunnison along the thirty-eighth parallel. Richard and Captain Gunnison were killed by Ute Indians on October 25, 1853.

Edward, sole survivor of the threesome, sailed on June 11, 1853, on the North Pacific exploring expedition commanded first by Captain Cadwalader Ringgold and later by Commander John Rodgers. This expedition provided the scientific counterpart of Commodore Matthew Perry's opening of Japan. The Ringgold-Rodgers party mapped the Japanese shores and harbors for American shipping and returned to San Francisco on October 13, 1855. Kern then joined Lieutenant John M. Brooke in a survey of the sea lanes between California and China including coaling stations and guano deposits. He left San Francisco aboard the U.S.S. *Fenimore Cooper* on September 26, 1857, and returned on March 17, 1860.

Reconciled with Frémont, Kern enlisted under him as a captain of topographical engineers and served in Missouri on scouting missions. When Frémont was relieved of his command of the western department by President Lincoln in 1861, Kern's commission was also revoked. Edward returned for the last time to Philadelphia, spent his remaining days as an art teacher, and died of an epileptic attack on November 23, 1863.

Edward and Richard Kern were both accomplished artists, having exhibited in the important galleries of Philadelphia. As scientists, Edward's specialization tended to be in botany and zoology, while Richard did more work in ethnology and archaeology. Although Ben was sober and restrained, the other two were known as buoyant spirits full of zest and good humor. Their essential tragedy lay in the shortness of Benjamin and Richard's lives and in Edward's epilepsy, which brought him also to an early death.

See the Fort Sutter Papers at the Huntington Library, San Marino, California, which are basically the papers of Edward Kern; and Robert V. Hine, *Edward Kern and American Expansion* (1962).—R. V. H.

Kerr, Robert S. (1896-1963). Oklahoma politician and business leader. Born in a log cabin near Ada, Oklahoma, Kerr was one of seven children of a tenant farmer and schoolteacher. He attended local public schools, East Central State College, and the University of Oklahoma Law School, where he studied for one year, completing his legal education in the law office of an Ada attorney. During World War I Kerr was commissioned a second lieutenant of field artillery, but he saw little action, commenting that "the only powder he smelled was face powder." After the war he returned to Ada and began his law practice.

In 1925 Kerr turned to drilling oil wells with a single small rig. With the gambler's instinct, he took a share of production from each well drilled rather than a fixed fee and invested in additional drilling equipment. During the early 1930s his company was a leader in bringing in the Oklahoma City field. From oil and natural gas production Kerr moved to refining and distribution, expanded exploration in the western states and offshore tidelands, the production of chemicals, and the exploration, production, and processing of minerals, including uranium. He also established a sixty thousand-acre ranch, stocked with Aberdeen Angus cattle, near Poteau. Kerr consolidated his many enterprises under the aegis of Kerr-Magee Industries Inc.

Ambitious politically, Kerr developed an Oklahoma power base that included the Southern Baptist Convention in which he maintained long service as a lay leader and benefactor, and the American Legion, serving a term as state commander. Kerr's special talent as a fund raiser and his earthy, frontier-style oratory made him a valuable asset for the Democratic party. He won election as governor of Oklahoma in 1942 and provided sound state leadership during the war years. His reputation as a stirring orator won for him assignment as keynote speaker at the 1944 Democratic convention. In 1948 he was elected to the Senate and became an articulate spokesman for oil and gas interests, industrial dispersion, and conservation. Kerr soon surfaced as a leader and was acknowledged by many to be "the uncrowned king of the U.S. Senate." For years he dominated and influenced Senate actions from his strategic positions as chairman of the aerospace committee, public works committee, and ranking Democrat on the Senate finance committee. His compelling goal was to effect the Arkansas Basin Project, a series of dams and locks on the Arkansas River and its tributaries to provide flood control, power generation, and navigation.

See Malvina Stephenson, ed., *Land, Wood, and Water* (1960).—A. M. G.

Kesey, Ken (1935-   ). Writer. Born in La Junta, Colorado, and raised in the Willamette valley of Oregon, Kesey had a meteoric career. His two novels, *One Flew Over the Cuckoo's Nest* (1962) and *Sometimes a Great Notion* (1964), are set in the modern West but are not westerns in the tradition of Ernest Haycox or Max Brand; rather, both novels are to a degree examples of what critic Leslie Fiedler calls the "new western," a form that exploits the old western with irreverence and pleasure, especially in its treatment of the Indian. Moreover, Kesey was a kind of cultural hero taking off from the earlier generation of North Beach "beats." He toured West to East in a psychedelic bus freighted with Merry Pranksters and advertising not snake oil, soft soap, and minstrelsy (like some old-time western medicine show), but marijuana, LSD, and hard rock.

Kesey grew up in a logging community in a family in which physical prowess was encouraged and respected. But the boy had a bookish bent that ran to writing poetry and reading Edgar Rice Burroughs, Zane Grey, comic books, and science fiction. At the University of Oregon, Kesey's taste in literature began to mature, and under the influence of James Hall he moved toward a literary career. In 1957 Kesey entered Wallace Stegner's creative writing program at Stanford University, where Malcolm Cowley's encouragement helped Kesey gain confidence in his own competence. At Stanford Kesey also participated in perhaps the first controlled experiments in the use of LSD. A group gathered around Kesey in California, and for a year or two their leader and his disciples, the Merry Pranksters, formed the leading edge of what came to be called a counter-cultural revolution.

Both of Kesey's novels deal with the search of the individual for freedom, identity, and dignity. In *Cuckoo's Nest* one of the two dominant figures is Chief Bromden, an American Indian, trapped on the ultimate reservation: an Oregon mental institution. The chief moves toward sanity and freedom with the aid and at the expense of R. P. McMurphy, a kind of new westerner. In a startling reversal of roles, the white westerner dies and the Indian lives to flee the asylum and return to the remnants of his tribe.

Sometimes a Great Notion is more experimental, more complex, less tightly knit than the earlier book. Although the Indian role in *Sometimes a Great Notion* is reduced to the pathetic, sodden, sexually depraved figure of Indian Jenny, other regional themes are much more evident than in *Cuckoo's Nest*, with the logger cast in a heroic mold reminiscent of the cowboy in the familiar formula western. In this novel Kesey betrays his ambivalence about the region. His view of the environment is sometimes jaundiced, as when he describes Oregon's rain-rotten winters, and sometimes loving, as in his vignette of an Oregon October. But out of recognition of complexity and ambiguity, paradox and pain, and through long and intimate experience with land and river and climate, Kesey reveals a fierce emotional commitment to the Pacific Northwest that is convincing and healthy. To read Kesey's second novel is to catch a measure of that commitment.

The most convenient commentary on Kesey is Tom Wolfe, *Electric Kool-Aid Acid Test* (1968). Gordon Lish conducts an engaging interview of Kesey in *Genesis West* (Fall 1963).—E. R. B.

Kickapoo Indians. The Kickapoo are a branch of the Algonquian linguistic stock, in a special group with the Fox and Sauk. The word *Kickapoo* is from the Algonquian *Kiwigapawa*, which means "he moves about, standing now here, now there," a most appropriate name for this nomadic people.

The Kickapoo resided originally in Wisconsin. In about 1765 they moved south into Illinois and Indiana. The tribe fought against the United States in the War of 1812 and the Black Hawk War. In 1837 a hundred Kickapoo were engaged to assist the federal government as mercenaries against the Seminole.

Continually on the move in the face of white encroachment on their lands, the Kickapoo moved to Missouri and then to northeastern Kansas. About 1852, a large band migrated to Mexico. They were such a nuisance to border settlers, however, that in 1873 most of them were returned to the United States and settled on a reservation in what is now Oklahoma.

All their tribal lands having been opened to white settlement in 1895, the remaining members of this proud and independent tribe live on individual government allotments in Oklahoma.

See Arrell M. Gibson, *The Kickapoo: Lords of the Middle Border* (1963).—R. B. W.

Kidder, Alfred Vincent (1885-1963). Archaeologist. Kidder was probably the most highly regarded American archaeologist during most of his lifetime, both as a man and as a scientist. Born at Marquette, Michigan, his family moved east when he was still quite young. He went to private schools in Cambridge, Massachusetts, until 1901, and when his family moved to Europe, he went to school in Switzerland. In 1904 he enrolled in Harvard College intent on a career in medicine. Anthropology courses from Roland B. Dixon and Alfred Tozzer and a journey to the Southwest in 1907 changed the course of his life. The journey took him to Mesa Verde in southern Colorado and to ruins in neighboring New Mexico. His companions were fellow students John Gould Fletcher, who later became a writer, and Sylvanus Morley, later the dean of Mayan archaeology. Their director was Edgar L. Hewitt of the Archaeological Institute of America.

After his graduation in 1908, Kidder returned to the Southwest. After receiving his Ph.D. from Harvard in 1914, he revolutionized southwestern archaeology by introducing the carefully controlled stratigraphic techniques of Egyptologist George A. Reisner to the area. He also developed his own ceramic typological systems to enable him better to interpret single-period sites.

Kidder published 186 books, monographs, articles, and reviews, including his reprinted and justly famous *An Introduction to the Study of Southwestern Archaeology* (1924). His efforts at Pecos, New Mexico, and elsewhere in the Southwest made him preeminent in the field. In the late 1920s and during the 1930s he became involved in Mayan research through his position with the Carnegie Institution of Washington. He excavated at Kaminaljuyu in Guatemala in the mid-1930s.

Kidder's contributions to the understanding of the prehistory of the Southwest are transcended in importance by his contributions to American archaeology generally. When he retired from the Carnegie Institution in 1950, the American Anthropological Association announced the establishment of the Alfred V. Kidder award, the highest honor that can be bestowed on any American archaeologist.

See Robert Greengo, "Alfred Vincent Kidder, 1885-1963," *American Anthropologist*, vol. 70 (1968); A. V. Kidder, "Reminiscences in Southwest Archaeology," *The Kiva*, vol. 25, (1960); and Robert Wauchope, "Alfred Vincent Kidder, 1885-1963," *American Antiquity*, vol. 31 (1965).—B. L. F.

Kieft's War (1643-1645). A conflict between the Dutch and Indians around New Amsterdam. Kieft's War was a major event in the establishment of European control along the Atlantic seaboard. In New Netherland as elsewhere Indian relations deteriorated as colonists began to settle in numbers, taking up lands that Indians used for hunting and regarded as their own. In the 1630s in what is now the New York metropolitan area, a host of minor frictions developed between Dutch settlers and Indians over trade, trespass, and the liquor traffic, as well as land ownership. Offenses were committed on both sides, culminating in murders and retaliatory forays after 1640.

Governor Willem Kieft had contributed to the troubles by trying to tax the Indians in 1639. He initiated a full-scale war in February 1643 by authorizing the massacre of some peaceful tribesmen who had fled to Dutch settlements for protection against northern Indian enemies. As a result, at least ten bands of Indians in northern New Jersey, the lower Hudson valley, and Long Island took the warpath, raiding and destroying outlying Dutch settlements. Most of the colonists fled to New Amsterdam, where they were under virtual siege for months. They sent out military forces that attacked and destroyed Indian villages, but pitched battles were rare. The most spectacular battle involved the destruction of a Westchester Indian village and the death of more than five hundred of its occupants in March 1644. The Indians lacked the firepower to contest the Dutch on even terms, and they were poorly coordinated among themselves. They lost perhaps a thousand lives altogether. Gradually, one or two bands at a time, they made peace by August 1645 and were forced to recognize that the Europeans were there to stay. But Kieft had come close to destroying his colony, and was shortly recalled to Holland in disgrace.

See A. C. Flick, ed., *History of the State of New York*, vol. I (1933); and Allen W. Trelease, *Indian Affairs in Colonial New York: The Seventeenth Century* (1960).—A. W. T.

Kimball, Jonathan Golden (1853-1938). Mormon humorist and ecclesiastic. Born in Salt Lake City, Utah, Kimball became a Mormon folk hero. Plain-spoken and jocular, his stories and remarks produced both laughter and consternation in Mormon circles. The folksy expressions in his sermons were products of his varied work experiences as a mule-skinner, cellar-digger, rock-hauler and, eventually, contractor. When Kimball discovered that contracting was also a losing occupation, he and his brother Elias moved to Meadowville, Rich County, Utah, to take a squatter's claim in 1876. Slack times found the two brothers working in nearby logging camps.

In 1881 Karl G. Maeser, the principal of the Brigham Young Academy in Provo, Utah, inspired Golden to study there. In 1883 he went on a proselyting mission to the southern states, but contracted malaria and returned home. He next tried ranching in the Bear Lake area of northern Utah, during which time he married (1887). Then he attempted to speculate in real estate in

Logan, Utah, but lost money. In 1889 Kimball was called to be president of the Southern States Mormon Mission and in 1892 became a member of the First Council of Seventy of the Church. Making his home in Salt Lake City, he became the secretary of the Seventies (1900-22). At the time of his death in an automobile accident near Fallon, Nevada, he was the senior president of the Seventies.

The anecdotes and comical sayings of Kimball are legion. Although a general authority of the church, Kimball sometimes used indelicate expressions, even at the pulpit. When someone once suggested that he might be excommunicated for his language, he is said to have replied, "They can't cut me off the Church; I repent too damn fast." On another occasion an apostle criticized him for upsetting the audience during a sermon, and Kimball responded, "Well, you see, Brother ———, you talk to send them to sleep and I have to talk to wake them up." Kimball was much like the rough frontier leaders of Mormon pioneer folklore. Stanch in the faith, he endeared himself to the Mormons of the twentieth century who felt estranged from their less urbane heritage of the nineteenth century. He was the uncle of the president of the Mormon church, Spencer W. Kimball.

See Thomas E. Cheney, *The Golden Legacy: A Folk History of J. Golden Kimball* (1973); Austin and Alta Fife, *Saints of Sage and Saddle* (1956); Claude Richards, *J. Golden Kimball: The Story of a Unique Personality* (1934); and Wallace Stegner, *Mormon Country* (1942). —D. M. Q.

King, Charles Bird (1785-1862). Painter. Born in Newport, Rhode Island, King received his first instruction in painting at an early age from Newport artist Samuel King. He later studied under Edward Savage in New York City and under Benjamin West in London from about 1805 to 1812. King began his professional career in Philadelphia and later moved to Washington, D.C., where he made his reputation in the 1820s painting the portraits of Indian chiefs visiting the nation's capital for Thomas L. McKenney, head of the Bureau of Indian Affairs. These formed the heart of McKenney's projected National Indian Portrait Gallery, later transferred to the Smithsonian Institution. Nearly all of King's work for this project was destroyed by a fire at the Smithsonian in 1865. King made a few replicas for his own collection, however, and may have distributed smaller copies of some of his portraits among the Indians themselves.

The collection, left to the Redwood Library in Newport upon King's death, has since been sold at auction. A few other examples are to be found at the Smithsonian and the White House in Washington, D.C.; the Thomas Gilcrease Institute of American History and Art, Tulsa, Oklahoma; the Philadelphia Museum of Art; Yale University; and the National Museum of Copenhagen, Denmark, which received a gift of nine King portraits from President Andrew Jackson during his term of office. Lithographic reproductions of many of the lost portraits were featured in Thomas L. McKenney and James Hall's *History of the Indian Tribes of North America* (1837).

See John C. Ewers, "Charles Bird King, Painter of Indian Visitors to the Nation's Capital," *Smithsonian Report for 1953* (1954), and *Artists of the Old West* (1965); and Frederick Webb Hodge, *The Indian Tribes of North*

America, with Biographical Sketches and Anecdotes of the Principal Chiefs, 3 vols. (1933).—D. C. H.

King, Clarence (1842-1901). Geologist and writer. King was the "geologist in charge" of the United States Geological Exploration of the Fortieth Parallel and the first director of the United States GEOLOGICAL SURVEY. He was born in Newport, Rhode Island, and was reared by his widowed mother. In 1862 he graduated from the Sheffield Scientific School at Yale, and with his friend James Terry Gardner went to California and joined Josiah Whitney's California Geological Survey.

In 1867 King went to Washington and, although a very young man without a Civil War record, obtained his own organization (the United States Geological Exploration of the Fortieth Parallel), subject only to the administrative jurisdiction of the Army Corps of Engineers. He gathered a competent staff of young men, went into the field, and for the next decade was occupied with this survey. In the course of his work he exposed the GREAT DIAMOND HOAX in extreme northwest Colorado in 1872. He was also a key figure in the creation of the United States Geological Survey (1879) and he was its first director before stepping down after one year to make way for John Wesley Powell.

The remainder of King's life was anticlimactic. He possessed literary ability and was a close friend of Henry Adams. Although a dilettante, his *Mountaineering in the Sierra Nevada* (1872) is a charming collection of essays. But when King died he had obtained neither the riches he had so diligently pursued in the last two decades of his life nor a professional reputation that was as secure as that of some of his contemporary geologists.

The Fortieth Parallel Reports are in *Professional Papers of the Engineer Department*, No. 18, in seven volumes and with an atlas (1871-80). See also Richard A. Bartlett, *Great Surveys of the American West* (1962); Thurman Wilkins, *Clarence King* (1958).—R. A. B.

King, Richard (1824-1885). Steamboat captain and Texas rancher. King, founder of the world-famous KING RANCH of south Texas, was born in New York of poor immigrant Irish parents. While only a small boy he was apprenticed to a jeweler. At age thirteen the youngster left New York on a steamer bound for Mobile, Alabama, serving as a cabin boy. He became a Gulf Coast river boatman and progressed from the rank of deckhand to that of pilot and captain. In 1847, during the Mexican War, he piloted a Rio Grande steamer in support of General Zachary Taylor's expedition into northern Mexico. After the war King formed a partnership with Captain Mifflin Kenedy in a Rio Grande steamship company. Between 1850 and 1874, when the firm was dissolved, the firm built or bought more than twenty steamers and did an immense trade in cotton. During the Civil War the firm acted as a cotton agent for the Confederacy, circumventing the Union blockade by transshipping cotton into Mexico.

In 1853 King bought 15,500 acres of the Santa Gertrudis Spanish grant, and seven years later he and Kenedy formed a ranching partnership that lasted until 1868. King eventually accumulated 1.27 million acres, on which were located 40,000 cattle, 1,200 sheep and goats, 6,600 horses, and 500 jacks and jennets. In 1884 King sent nearly 4,000 beeves up the trail to Dodge City. Early in his ranching career he began to upgrade Longhorns with superior British breeds. King's descendants,

the Klebergs, carried to success the development of the first American breed of beef cattle, the Santa Gertrudis, essentially a mixture of five-eighths Shorthorn and three-eighths Brahma.

See Tom Lea, *The King Ranch*, 2 vols. (1957).—R. B. W.

King George's War. See COLONIAL WARS.

King Philip's War (1675-1676). Indian war. The growth in the white population, the incursion of whites into Indian territory, and the inevitable decline in the power and prestige of individual sachems increased friction between Indians and whites in New England after 1650 and led to open warfare in June 1675. Since 1643, when the colonies of Massachusetts, Plymouth, Connecticut, and New Haven formed the United Federation of New England Colonies to defend themselves against the Indians, the colonies had practiced a divide-and-conquer technique by setting tribe against tribe, but this policy backfired: jealousy of the favoritism shown the Mohegan tribes prompted the rebellion of King Philip (Metacomet), chief of the Wampanoag tribe and the son of Massasoit, who had befriended the Pilgrims.

The war began with sporadic attacks by the Wampanoag tribe upon the white settlers of Plymouth Colony who lived in the little village of Swansea, lending support to the thesis that the war was probably not a well-planned conspiracy. More likely, a number of young braves were trying to force the Wampanoag sachem, King Philip, into war with the white settlers. Most of the evidence suggests that King Philip would have preferred to delay the war until he could establish a network of alliances with other tribes in New England. In the ensuing war he did receive assistance in varying measure from the Narragansett, the Nipmuck, and the Pocumtuck. But most of the tribes probably remained neutral, while some—including the Mohegan, Pequot, Nauset, Massachusett, and some River tribes—allied with the whites.

Even though all tribes did not participate, the war devastated the frontier settlements of New England from Saco, Maine; across southern New Hampshire; and down the Connecticut valley. It was, in fact, the bloodiest Indian war of the seventeenth century and claimed the lives of one thousand New England colonists. Through a series of blunders by whites, including an unwise attack on the semineutral Narragansett, the Wampanoag were able to continue the conflict and spread it throughout southern New England. By July 1675 the war had reached the Connecticut River valley, and until the spring of 1676 the Wampanoag and their allies held a decided advantage. After the battle of Peskeompskut in May 1676, in which a small force of whites slaughtered Indian men, women, and children and burned crops, Connecticut troops and friendly Mohegan Indians drove the enemy tribes into New Hampshire in June. In August an Indian friendly to the Puritans killed Philip, and Indian resistance was crushed.

After 1676 the Indians of New England were a broken people. They had experienced heavy casualties, the women and children suffering from starvation, and they quickly lost their remaining lands. Some tribal remnants fled west to join other tribes; others were placed on reservations, and some were made servants to the settlers. But the white settlers also paid a fearful price. The war destroyed crops at the very moment that refugees from the frontier were crowding into the coastal settlements and creating a food shortage. The white death rate was so great that Douglas E. Leach, the foremost authority on the war, has noted that "in proportion to population, King Philip's War inflicted greater casualties upon the people than any other war in our history." To survive, the colonists had to adopt the Indian techniques of stalking and ambushing. Southern New England was won for the white man at last, but at the expense of large-scale social dislocation, trauma, and physical damage.

The authoritative work on this subject is Douglas E. Leach, *Flintlock and Tomahawk* (1958).—E. W. K.

King Ranch. On July 25, 1853, Richard KING purchased Juan Mendiola's Spanish land grant of approximately 75,000 acres in the area of the present Nueces County, Texas, on the Santa Gertrudis Creek (near present-day Kingsville, the ranch headquarters). Seven years later Mifflin Kenedy, an associate from King's steamboating days, bought a fifty percent interest in the ranch. The partnership was dissolved in 1868, but King retained the Santa Gertrudis Creek area. The ranch's famous Running W brand appeared sometime in the 1860s. King died in 1885, but his wife continued to run the gigantic enterprise until her death in 1925. Thereafter the ranch was incorporated and run by descendants of the family.

The ranch crossbred Brahman cattle with Shorthorns, and the result was the famous Santa Gertrudis cattle. The ranch also practiced advanced methods of mineral feeding and, after 1912, conservation techniques. That year the ranch began programs to preserve wild game. The ranch experimented with grass-improvement techniques, land clearing, and other programs to increase the quality of the cattle and the productivity.

The business prospered and grew in size until it reached more than 1.25 million acres in southern Texas. By 1947 Humble Oil and Refining Company had developed nearly four hundred producing wells on the property. The King Ranch, like other great ranching enterprises, owned fattening lands in other states and overseas. In the middle of the 1970s the ranch had foreign holdings of 10 million acres in Australia and about 1 million acres scattered through Argentina, Brazil, Venezuela, and Morocco.

See Tom Lea, *The King Ranch*, 2 vols. (1957).—J. A. S.

Kings Canyon National Park. See SEQUOIA AND KINGS CANYON NATIONAL PARKS.

Kings Mountain, battle of (1780). The battle of Kings Mountain was part of an extensive plan by the British to overwhelm the southern states in the American Revolution. Late in 1779 British troops under the command of Lord Cornwallis began a drive north from the coast at Charleston. This drive was two-pronged, with one force striking up the Savannah River and the other into the upper Piedmont of South Carolina. In the upper coastal sandhills area Cornwallis was successful in his attack on Camden and encamped for the winter at Winnsboro.

In the Piedmont area there was constant skirmishing between Whigs and Tories (or royalists), and between Whigs and British regulars. Cornwallis dispatched Major Patrick Ferguson, an experienced officer, to deal with the resisters on his western flank. Ferguson, with a thousand-man force of Carolina loyalists, moved quick-

ly up the inland river complex to the old Trading Post Ninety Six and then veered northeast toward Charlotte, North Carolina, by way of Fair Forest, just skirting Spartanburg, and Gaffney to Kings Mountain.

News of Ferguson's advance reached the western country in early summer 1780 and stirred frontiersmen to immediate action. In the Watauga, Nolichucky, and southwestern Virginia settlements, militiamen were recruited under the leadership of William Campbell, Isaac Shelby, John Sevier, and Charles McDowell. Crossing through the narrow defiles of the Great Smokies, meeting in a rendezvous at Abingdon, Virginia, and then crossing the Blue Ridges, the frontiersmen joined forces with James Williams' North and South Carolinians, creating an army of fifteen hundred men.

Confronted by this American force when he reached Quaker Meadows on the Catawba River, Ferguson retreated south across the headwaters of the Broad River. On October 6, 1780, he sighted the dome-like ridge of Kings Mountain rising above a sixteen-mile shoulder of the easternmost Appalachian chain. The plateau, or top, of this ridge formed a natural table of approximately 600 by 250 yards. Because of the nature of the ridge and its steep shoulders, it seemed that it would be physically impossible for an attacking force to scale the ridge, let alone attack forcibly a well-equipped and securely encamped British command of approximately eleven hundred men.

On October 5 and 6 the chief officers of the frontiersmen worked out a careful plan of attack based on rather precise and timely knowledge of the terrain before them, and of Ferguson's strength, location, and organization of his encampment. William Campbell was placed in command with Isaac Shelby, John Sevier, Joseph Winston, Benjamin Cleveland, and a group of officers of lesser rank to carry out his commands. Tactfully, the less capable Charles McDowell was maneuvered into a less sensitive position. The mountaineers, numbering nine hundred picked men, began the assault against the British in mid-afternoon October 7, 1780. Their initial drive came as a surprise, and there then followed a rocking tactic in which militiamen on one side of the ridge fired and fell back while those on the opposite shoulder rushed up and fired. The cross firing on Ferguson's camp was deadly, despite the fact his command gave a good account of itself. In approximately an hour and fifteen minutes the British were cut to pieces. Ferguson was killed, and when his troops surrendered it was difficult to stop the frontiersmen from firing. Some troops were killed needlessly in this way, and nine were hanged after the battle. Cornwallis had sent Banastre Tarleton to the rescue, but he was too late in arriving. The battle of Kings Mountain no doubt blunted Cornwallis' western campaign and perhaps delayed his drive northward. Success in the battle brought great satisfaction to the frontiersmen, and it was to produce an abundant crop of frontier heroes.

See John R. Alden, *The South in the Revolution, 1763-1789* (1957); and Lyman C. Draper, *Kings Mountain and Its Heroes* (1929).—T. D. C.

Kings River. Not large when matched by the mighty Sacramento or the San Joaquin rivers, which form the master streams of the Central Valley of California, the Kings is still an important river in the California scheme of things. It has cut a canyon spectacular enough to be set aside as a national park and has built its alluvial fan across the Central Valley, creating a basin of interior drainage. The Kings River fan is known to most students of land forms and is one of the notable agricultural districts of the San Joaquin Valley.

The river rises near the crest of the highest part of the Sierra Nevada, where water from melting snow and glaciers at elevations near 14,000 feet feed the headwater streams. Three forks flow together to form the main stem of the stream in the High Sierra, and the river flows westerly down the slope of the mountain until it reaches the apex of its fan. Before the stream was controlled by Pine Flat Dam in 1954, flood flows of the Kings poured both northward into the San Joaquin and southward into Tulare Lake.

The name given to the river in 1805 by its discoverer, Gabriel Moraga, was El Rio de los Santos Reyes ("The River of the Holy Kings"). Concerned with their coastal settlements, the Spaniards and Mexicans did not explore or make use of the waters of the Kings. It yielded beaver to the mountain men, but miners searching its bed for gold were disappointed. It was not until farmers began diverting its waters in the 1860s and 1870s that its value was truly appreciated. By 1875 irrigation canals carried its waters to thousands of acres of land in the southern part of the Central Valley, and it was not long before more land was being farmed. The ensuing long series of battles over water rights were finally settled by litigation that led to the appointment of a water master in 1911, and the formation of a water user's association in 1927. In 1954 Pine Flat Dam, a large flood control and irrigation project, was completed. It made possible the building of additional hydroelectric facilities upstream. Today the Kings supplies water for almost a million acres of farmland and is fully developed for the production of electricity.

For map, see CALIFORNIA.

See California Department of Water Resources, *The California Water Plan* (1957); S. T. Harding, *Water in California* (1960); and Lawrence R. McDonnell, ed., *Rivers of California* (1962).—R. W. D.

King William's War. See COLONIAL WARS.

Kinkaid, Moses Pierce (1856-1922). Nebraska politician. A native of Monongalia County, West Virginia, and a graduate of the University of Michigan (1876), Kinkaid practiced law in Illinois and South Dakota before moving to O'Neill, Nebraska, in 1880. He was a member of the state senate in 1883 and from 1887 to 1900 was a Nebraska district court judge. A Republican, Kinkaid was elected to Congress from the "Big Sixth" District of northern and western Nebraska in 1902 and held this position until his death.

Kinkaid was the author of a 1904 statute that permitted the homesteading of tracts of 640 acres, as opposed to the traditional 160 acres, in thirty-seven counties in western Nebraska. The Kinkaid Act was intended to provide a workable land unit for small ranchers and farmers in the semiarid portion of the state. The law did stimulate the settlement of Nebraska's last frontier in the decade after its enactment, yet it did not in the long run prevent the domination of that area by large landholders.

See Addison E. Sheldon, *Land Systems and Land Policies in Nebraska* (1936).—H. A. D.

Kino, Eusebio Francisco (1645?-1711). Roman Catholic missionary and explorer. Kino was born near Trent, Italy, but entered the German Jesuit order in 1665, specializing in astronomy and mathematics. In 1678 he left Genoa to become a missionary in the New World, but did not reach Mexico until 1681. Kino's activities were many and diverse. The cattle industry of the American Southwest dates in large measure from the ranchos established by him throughout a belt 250 miles in width. At the missions he founded, Kino introduced many varieties of livestock and European grains as well as such fruits as grapes and pomegranates. He has also been credited with making the first astronomical observations in western America.

Kino's study of cartography implemented the Spanish advance northward. He explored the Altar, Sonora, Santa Cruz, and San Pedro rivers, in addition to the lower Gila and Colorado. In 1683 he was appointed royal cosmographer of an expedition commanded by Admiral Isidro de Atondo y Antillon, which unsuccessfully tried to colonize Baja California. During the period 1698-1701 Kino prepared maps, ultimately printed in Paris, proving for the first time that California was not an island. He also made major improvements in mapping Spain's North American empire from the Colorado River to the Gulf of Mexico.

Kino's explorations on horseback and foot, conducted over a period of twenty-five years, put Pimería Baja (in northern Mexico) and Pimería Alta (in southern Arizona) on the map. He made some fifty journeys of one hundred to one thousand miles in length, including six trips to the Gila River, two to the land of the Yuma Indians on the Colorado River, and one into what was then called "California." Traveling from twenty-five to seventy-five miles per day, Kino was indeed the "padre on horseback" that his biographer, Herbert Eugene Bolton, once called him. He has been described as "merciful to others but cruel to himself." At least twenty southwestern cities owe their origins to this indefatigable traveler.

During the years 1687 to 1711, Kino established some twenty missions in Greater Sonora. After founding Nuestra Señora de los Dolores on the San Miguel River, he built an important mission system on the Magdalena and Altar rivers. In the present-day United States the most important of these was SAN XAVIER DEL BAC, now a national munument near Tucson (see GUEVAVI and TUMACACORI). As the first person to attempt colonization of Baja California, Kino was an explorer, astronomer, cartographer, mission builder, ranch man, cattle king, dispatcher of packtrains to mines he helped open, and defender of the frontier. In total, the "Apostle of Arizona" traveled some twenty thousand miles and founded twenty-four missions. He died in the mission village of Santa Magdalena, which he had founded.

In 1965 Kino's statue was unveiled in the United States Capitol in Washington, a symbol of the numerous Blackrobes who contributed their learning, and in some cases their lives, to Spain's empire. Without their contribution to knowledge about the approach routes to California and the Southwest, it would have taken decades longer to occupy.

See Herbert Bolton, *Rim of Christendom* (1960); and Ernest Burrus, *Kino and the Cartography of Northwestern New Spain* (1965).—A. R.

Kiowa-Apache Indians. See APACHE INDIANS.

Kiowa Indians. The Kiowa are of Uto-Aztecan stock and linguistically are related to the Taos. In the sixteenth century they lived on the Three Forks of the Missouri River in southwestern Montana. According to their tradition, the tribe split into two groups in a power struggle between two chiefs, the Kiowa group moving off to the southeast through Wyoming and eastern Colorado to the Arkansas River. No trace has been found of the other group.

About the time that the southward-moving Kiowa reached eastern Colorado they secured horses and moved out onto the Plains to become buffalo-hunting nomads. There they fought for a time with the Comanche before a lasting peace was made between the two tribes. The Kiowa then established themselves just to the east of the Comanche, roaming from the Arkansas River across Oklahoma and deep into Texas. In this position they acted as a buffer between the Comanche and the Siouan tribes (the Osage and Ponca) to the east and the Caddoan people (the Pawnee and Wichita) to the northeast. They fought for many years with the Cheyenne and Arapaho to the north and made occasional raids across the Rocky Mountains into Ute territory.

Kiowa depredations against the whites occurred mostly along the Texas frontier to the south. Their biggest fight with soldiers was in 1864, when a large Kiowa force joined with the Comanche to attack Kit Carson and his three hundred New Mexico volunteers at Adobe Walls on the Canadian River in the Texas panhandle.

Culturally the Kiowa were more like their northern enemies, the Cheyenne and Arapaho, than their Comanche allies. They had strong social organizations and held a large sun dance each year. At an early date they learned how to use metal, chiefly silver, for jewelry and to decorate their horse trappings.

Although no major travel route passed through their lands, the Kiowa suffered greatly from cholera in 1849, smallpox in the winter of 1861-62, and measles in 1877.

The scandals in the Indian Bureau following the Civil War brought such a wave of protests from friends of the Indians, especially from the Society of Friends (Quakers), that President Ulysses S. Grant decided to make some changes in the federal administration of the Indian (see PEACE POLICY). The Quakers maintained that a great deal of the Indian troubles were the direct results of the mismanagement of Indian affairs by dishonest and incompetent agents. They believed that if Grant would appoint honest Christian agents who would treat their charges like humans, most of the troubles would be ended.

In 1869 government officials decided to give the Quakers a chance to prove their point by putting them in charge of the Kiowa, for those who followed SATANTA were notoriously the most troublesome of all the reservation tribes, who were on a portion of the Comanche reservation. To the surprise of the officials, the Quakers, by their intelligent and sympathetic approach to Kiowa problems, soon had the tribe engaged in farming and ready to enter into more peaceful relations with their former enemies. In 1871 a lasting peace was made between the Kiowa and Pawnee.

When the southern tribes rose in defense of their buffalo lands in 1874 in the RED RIVER WAR, the Kiowa joined the hostile forces, but after the defeat at Anadarko in 1875, they returned to their reservation. Hunting parties continued to have fights with the Texans until 1879.

In the summer of 1890 the Kiowa attempted their last great SUN DANCE, but it was not a success and the formal ritual was not completed. Friendly Arapaho who had come south from Wyoming for the sun dance then taught the Kiowa the songs and ritual of the new GHOST DANCE. Some of the Kiowa accepted the new teaching enthusiastically and danced a great deal that fall, but by spring, after the news of the slaughter of the Sioux ghost dancers at Wounded Knee reached the Kiowa, the new religion was abandoned. Most of the Kiowa then joined the Comanche in the peyote religion (see PEYOTISM).

The Kiowa portion of the reservation shared with the Comanche was lost in 1906 when the reservation was ended. Each Kiowa received an allotment of 160 acres as his private property.

See Hugh Corwin, *The Kiowa Indians: Their History and Life Stories* (1958), and *Comanche and Kiowa Captives in Oklahoma and Texas* (1959); Alice Marriott, *The Ten Grandmothers* (1945); and Mildred P. Mayhall, *The Kiowa* (1962).—F. H.

Kittson, Norman Wolfred (1814-1888). Fur trader. Canadian-born Kittson served an apprenticeship with the American Fur Company and in 1842 became a trader at Fort Snelling on the upper Mississippi River in Minnesota. In 1844 he established a trading post at Pembina in the northern Dakota country, for the American Fur Company. He and his partner, Henry Hastings Sibley, bought furs from the Indians, which they had smuggled across the Canadian border. The Indians were paid in cash and then bought goods. Because of a disastrous flood in 1851, the partners moved their headquarters to St. Joseph (present-day Walhalla) near Pembina.

Although Kittson and his partner thus contributed to ending the monopoly of the Hudson's Bay Company over the fur trade in the Red River valley, they could not compete with it. The Indians demanded high prices for furs, buffalo hides, and pemmican. The Hudson's Bay Company did not purchase large quantities of the latter two items, but the company's trading posts stocked the trade goods that the Indians most desired and for a lower price. Kittson and Sibley therefore bought goods from the Indians but did not always sell to them. In 1854 they gave up their operation.

Because Kittson was familiar with the Indians, especially the Chippewa, he was hired by steamboat interests to command one of their vessels, the *International*, which traveled on the Red River of the North. The Indians of the area disliked the new mode of transportation because it disturbed fish and game. Kittson worked toward conciliating the Indians.

In 1864 Kittson, acting for the Hudson's Bay Company, his former rival, bought out the owners of the *International*, which thereafter carried only company goods. Because of increased competition on the Red River, Kittson expanded his operation to that of a common carrier. In 1872 he and James J. Hill, his competitor, merged to form the Kittson Red River Transportation Line. Kittson later became involved in the railroading activities of Hill in North Dakota.—D. J. T.

Klamath Indians. See MODOC AND KLAMATH INDIANS.

Klamath River. The Klamath River, extending from Oregon through northwestern California, has an annual flow exceeding twelve million acre-feet, almost as much as the virgin flow of the Colorado. In contrast to the Colorado, however, most of its water reaches the sea without being used for any other purpose than the generation of electricity. And about three fourths of its flow occurs between December and May.

The basin of the river encompasses an area of 15,600 square miles, of which one third lies in Oregon and two thirds in California. It begins in Oregon in Lower Klamath Lake at the confluence of the Wood, Williamson, and Sprague rivers. Shortly before entering California the river flows at elevations of four to five thousand feet before it drops from the plateau region of southeastern Oregon and enters the deep and winding canyon that carries its water 235 miles to the ocean. The Klamath flows generally southwestward after entering California and is joined by the Shasta, Scott, Salmon, and Trinity rivers, most of which flow in broad flat valleys like that of the upper Klamath before plunging into canyons leading to the main river.

Much of the upper Klamath flows across a lava plateau, while the course in California is for the most part through an old mountain mass, the Klamath Mountains, composed of modified sedimentary rocks of ancient age. Many of the broad, flat valleys are grass-covered and offer excellent forage for livestock. The mountain slopes are heavily timbered with pine and fir, and lumbering and recreation represent the principal use of the canyons and mountain slopes.

The climate of its basin is similar to that of other Pacific Slope locations. Winter rains from storms originating off the Aleutians drop eighty or more inches of precipitation along the west-facing slopes near the ocean. Inland, some areas in eastern Oregon lying in the rainshadow of high mountains receive as little as six to eight inches of rain. In general, most of the region receives moderate to heavy amounts of rain and snow. Coastal locations and higher mountain regions are cool, but summer temperatures in many of the broad valleys of the interior are relatively high.

The Klamath was explored by Jedediah Smith in May and June of 1828 and by other fur trappers who preceded and followed him. On early maps of the West it is shown as Smith's River, but the name Klamath, derived from the Indians living in the headwater area, soon became the one used—probably because John C. Frémont used that name on his official maps.

Following the discovery of gold on the Trinity in 1848, the banks of the Klamath and its tributaries bustled with activity, with Trinidad City and later Eureka on the coast serving as the port of debarkation for the trip to the mines. Large quantities of gold were derived from the Klamath, but as elsewhere in California, gold mining declined in the late 1850s.

The principal irrigation project on the river is the Klamath project of the Bureau of Reclamation, which diverts and distributes water for over 200,000 acres of land in Oregon and California. Downstream from the Klamath project, the Pacific Power and Light Company operates seven hydroelectric plants. On the Shasta River, Dwinnel Reservoir stores water for irrigation in Shasta valley. By far the largest dam and reservoir are near the headwaters of the Trinity River. There, Clair Engle Lake holds 2,438,000 acre-feet of water to be used for the generation of power; about a million acre-feet of this water is diverted into the Central Valley of California for use there.

Although large quantities of the water in the river are utilized for the development of electricity and for irrigational agriculture, the primary use of water over most of the region is for recreation. In the summer months fishermen may be found along almost every quiet stretch of the river. The upper basin is the principal western resting place for waterfowl migrating along the Pacific Coast flyway. Four game reserves are maintained in the area by the Fish and Wildlife Service.

For map, see CALIFORNIA.

See California Department of Water Resources, *Klamath River Basin Investigation* (May 1960); S. T. Harding, *Water in California* (1960); and Lawrence R. McDonnell, ed., *Rivers of California* (1962).—R. W. D.

Kluckhohn, Clyde Kay Maben (1905-1960). Anthropologist and teacher. Possibly the single most outstanding student of Navaho Indian culture, Kluckhohn acquired "an obsessive fascination" for the Southwest when he was sent by his family to a ranch at Ramah, New Mexico, when he was just seventeen. He learned to speak Navaho and five other languages (in addition to English) fluently, graduated from the University of Wisconsin in 1928, taught anthropology at the University of New Mexico from 1932 to 1934, and received his Ph.D. in anthropology from Harvard in 1936.

Although Kluckhohn spent his entire formal academic career after 1935 teaching at Harvard and although he is known for his studies in culture and personality, his first love was the Navaho Indians. He either authored or coauthored *Navaho Witchcraft* (1944), *The Navaho* (1946), *Children of the People* (1947), *Navaho Means People* (1951), and *Navaho Material Culture* (1971), not to mention dozens of articles on the subject.

Kluckhohn also organized and directed the Comparative Study of Values in Five Cultures Project, which was carried out in the Ramah area from 1949 to 1953 by thirty-seven fieldworkers and which involved comparative studies of the neighboring Ramah Navaho, Zuñi, Spanish-Americans, Mormons, and Texan homesteaders. He died of a heart attack while writing an article in a small cabin on the upper Pecos River near Santa Fe, New Mexico.

See Talcott Parsons and Evon Z. Vogt, "Clyde Kay Maben Kluckhohn, 1905-1960," *American Anthropologist*, vol. 64, no. 1 (1962).—B. L. F.

Know-Nothing party. The Know-Nothing, or American, party enjoyed spectacular, if ephemeral, political success between 1853 and 1857. Originally a secret fraternal society, it grew out of the xenophobic Order of the Star-Spangled Banner. Its name derived from the practice of members when asked if they belonged to the order to reply, "I know nothing." Anti-Catholic and antiforeign in principles, the society became a force in politics in early 1854 when its lodges secretly chose candidates from the slates of already existing parties and pledged members by oath to vote for them. The party opposed office-holding by anyone but native-born Protestants, and it also sought to increase the naturalization period of aliens from five to twenty-one years or to abolish naturalization altogether to prevent immigrants from voting and to stem immigration. The party grew fastest in cities rather than rural areas, where nativism is traditionally supposed to flourish, and was much stronger east of Ohio than west of Pennsylvania.

A combination of factors caused the rise of the Know-Nothings in such strength in the mid-1850s. In the North, especially the Northeast, many middle- and working-class native-born Protestants resented job competition from the immigrants pouring into the country in the late 1840s. They also feared what they regarded as a Catholic conspiracy to subvert American institutions. Concrete grievances against the Catholics in 1852 and 1853 as well as resentment of the increased political participation in those years by immigrants whose five-year naturalization periods had expired do much to explain the timing of the party's rise. It was large-scale political activity by immigrants that initially drove the Know-Nothings to political action. On the other hand, the intense nationalism of the American party just when sectional antagonisms were exacerbated by the Kansas-Nebraska issue, and the appearance of the seemingly radical Republican party attracted conservatives who had nowhere else to go because the Whig party was disintegrating. This latter motive particularly explains the strength of the party in the South. Although the party emerged in western states, there it was fairly quickly absorbed by the Republican party. In this instance, nativism was not a rural or western phenomenon.

The Know-Nothing party disappeared almost as quickly as it rose. The party showed considerable strength in all areas in 1854 and 1855, and in many parts of the North nativism as much as anti-Nebraska sentiment contributed to Democratic defeats in those years. But even in 1855 the national party convention split over slavery, and most northern delegates stormed out of the national Know-Nothing convention in 1856 when it refused to call for prohibition of slavery expansion. This group held a North American convention in June 1856 and then merged with the Republicans behind John C. Frémont. The remaining Americans, primarily conservatives from the North and South who were concerned with unionism more than nativism, ran Millard Fillmore for president in 1856, but he managed to carry only twenty-five percent of the popular vote. On the state level, the failure of Know-Nothing legislators to pass restrictive legislation and a growing hostility to the party's secrecy lost it support. Know-Nothingism ceased to be an important national political force after 1856, but the ethnic and religious antagonisms that caused its rise continued to affect voting behavior long after the party's demise.

The best accounts of the Know-Nothings are Ray A. Billington, *The Protestant Crusade, 1800-1860* (1938); Allan Nevins, *Ordeal of the Union*, vol. II (1947); and Joel Silbey, *The Transformation of American Politics, 1840-1860* (1967). For an account that differs with these, see Michael F. Holt, *Forging a Majority: The Formation of the Republican Party in Pittsburgh, 1848-1860* (1969). —M. F. H.

Kroeber, Alfred Louis (1876-1960). Anthropologist. Born in Hoboken, New Jersey, Kroeber grew up in New York City and could speak German, English, Latin, and Greek before he entered Columbia College at the age of sixteen. He earned his M.A. degree in English in 1897, but influenced by Franz Boas, who taught at Columbia starting in 1896, and by field trips in 1899-1900 to the Arapaho, Ute, Shoshoni, and Bannock Indians, Kroeber switched from English to anthropology, writing his dissertation on Arapaho art.

In 1901 Kroeber went to the University of California at Berkeley, where for the next forty-five years he built a department and museum of anthropology preeminent in the field. By the end of 1961 there had appeared 532 publications, many of them major books and monographs, under his authorship. More than seventy items, including his *Handbook of California Indians* (1925), concern the ethnology of California, and even more were involved with the linguistics of native Californians. His other fieldwork involved the Zuñi and Plains Indians as well as trips to Mexico and Peru. His *Cultural and Natural Areas in Native North America* (1939) continues to influence North American Indian studies.

His legacy of substantive data and theoretical conceptions is virtually beyond measure. He was regarded by many of his colleagues as the undisputed dean of American anthropology. He touched all bases of his discipline—physical anthropology, archaeology, cultural anthropology, and linguistics—as evidenced in his long-used text, *Anthropology*, first published in 1923 and revised for the final time in 1948. He was also a philosopher of history and had more than a passing acquaintance with the fields of sociology, psychology, music, and art.

See Theodora Kroeber, *Alfred Kroeber: A Personal Configuration* (1970); and Julian H. Steward, "Alfred Louis Kroeber, 1876-1960," *American Anthropologist*, vol. 63, no. 5 (1961).—B. L. F.

Kruttschnitt, Julius (1854-1925). Railroad executive. Kruttschnitt was born in New Orleans, Louisiana, where his father had come in the late 1840s as the German consul. His maternal uncle was Judah P. Benjamin, the Confederate secretary of state. A graduate civil engineer, Kruttschnitt worked on Southern Pacific's lines east of El Paso, Texas, rising rapidly in the company.

In 1901 Edward H. Harriman, who had acquired control of the railroad, made him assistant to the president. When the Union Pacific-Southern Pacific merger was dissolved in 1913, he assumed the position of chairman of the board of the Southern Pacific.

A leading expert on railroad economics, Kruttschnitt bitterly opposed the repressive rate policies of the Interstate Commerce Commission during the Progressive era and warned that the government's entry into management-labor negotiations meant that in the future railroad labor would look to the government, not the companies, for the granting of subsequent demands. He worked energetically during the period of voluntary coordination of the railroads' war efforts, but refused any official role during the period of government operation.

Harriman and Kruttschnitt were referred to as the "Napoleon and the Von Moltke of transportation," reflecting the fact that Harriman was the last of the tycoons and Kruttschnitt the prototype of the professional, twentieth-century executive.—A. M.

Kurz, Rudolph Friedrich (1818-1871). Painter and draftsman. Kurz, born in Switzerland, came to America at the age of twenty-nine after having spent the early part of his life traveling and studying art in Paris and elsewhere. Between 1847 and 1852 he traveled in the West, principally along the Mississippi and Missouri rivers, spending time at Council Bluffs, Iowa; St. Joseph, Missouri; and Fort Union on the upper Missouri waters. He arrived at the latter post on horseback from Fort Berthold in 1851 and made many sketches of the Mandan, Arikara, and other tribes in that vicinity, making a side trip up the Yellowstone and spending the winter of that year in and about the fort. Kurz returned to St. Louis in April 1852 and shortly thereafter made his way back to Europe. The five years spent on the American frontier were devoted almost entirely to the production of art work, and when he sailed for home he took nearly everything with him. Residing in his native Bern, Switzerland, for the remainder of his life, Kurz continued to paint and teach art, turning to his earlier American studies for inspiration.

A single watercolor by Kurz is preserved at the Peabody Museum at Harvard, and a sketchbook of his drawings was divided into separate leaves and sold by a New York art dealer in 1946. With the exception of these and a collection of eighteen watercolor and pen-and-ink studies in the collection of the Thomas Gilcrease Institute of American History and Art, Tulsa, Oklahoma, the bulk of Kurz's work remains in Bern.

See J. N. B. Hewitt, *Journal of Rudolph Friedrich Kurz* (1970); and John Francis McDermott, "Rudolph Friedrich Kurz, A Swiss Artist on the American Frontier," *American Scene*, vol. 8, no. 3 (1967).—D. C. H.

Kwakiutl Indians. See INDIANS OF THE NORTHWEST COAST.

Kyle, James Henderson (1854-1901). South Dakota politician. Kyle served as a Congregational minister at Aberdeen, South Dakota, and as state senator from Brown County. As a political independent he attacked corporations, wealth, and monopolies, calling himself an "Indecrat." He sat with the Democrats, worked with the Knights of Labor, supported women's suffrage, and promoted the initiative and referendum. A combination of Republicans, Populists, and Democrats kept him in the United States Senate from 1893 until his death. —D. J. T.

L

La Barge, Joseph. See RIVERMEN.

labor movement. The earliest labor union organizing activity in the West occurred in the streets of San Francisco and in the mining camps. In San Francisco the printers first organized in 1850, and other crafts formed unions soon thereafter. San Francisco thus emerged as the strongest labor-union city in the West, a distinction it held from the gold-rush era to the 1860s (the molders' and boilermakers' strike of 1864), to the 1870s (the Workingmen's party movement of Denis KEARNEY), past the turn of the century (the City Front Federation of 1901, which gave rise to the Union Labor party), and down to the 1930s (which saw the rise of the longshoremen leader Harry R. Bridges in the great strike of 1934). The first miners' union appeared in Virginia City, Nevada, in 1863, with other early miners' unions springing up in Butte, Montana (traditionally a strong union center); Lead, South Dakota; Globe, Arizona; and Leadville and Aspen, Colorado.

The great national railroad strike of 1877 spread into the West with walkouts in Omaha and San Francisco. More railroad strikes came in 1885-86 when the Knights of Labor led men out on the southwestern railroads controlled by Jay Gould. At first the Knights were successful against Gould, but in 1886 the southwestern movement failed when the railroad spurned a compromise and as violence occurred in Parsons, Kansas; Fort Worth, Texas; and East St. Louis, Illinois. Another wave of railroad strikes came in 1893-94 on the heels of the 1893 founding of the American Railway Union (ARU) headed by Eugene V. Debs. The ARU's successful strike against the Great Northern Railroad in 1893 instilled a hunger for greater gains among the rank and file. The result was the massive Pullman strike of 1894. In sympathy with Pullman Company workers, 60,000 western members of the ARU went on strike. Federal intervention doomed the walkout. First, a United States court injunction forbade union officials to obstruct the movement of the mails over the railroads by their leadership of the strike. This judicial crackdown on the ARU was powerfully supported by President Grover Cleveland when he followed Attorney General Richard Olney's advice to deploy federal soldiers against the strikers. These actions led to a total defeat of the union, which died from the blow. The defeat of the ARU is said to have given rise to the railroad "boomer," a former ARU member who was blacklisted by the railroad companies and so roved from job to job throughout the West under various aliases.

With the demise of the Knights of Labor and the ARU, western railroad workers in the twentieth century settled down to membership in the less radical brotherhoods—independent and American Federation of Labor (AFL)-affiliated unions of engineers, firemen, conductors, brakemen, and nonoperating employees. The vast but thinly populated western states were crisscrossed with railroads, and the large number of railroad workers constituted a significant element in the western labor movement as a whole. In 1916-17 the threat of a strike by the railroad brotherhoods resulted in the Adamson Act, which provided the eight-hour day for railroad workers.

Strikers at the Ludlow, Colorado, tent colony. (State Historical Society of Colorado)

Concurrent with labor-union activity among railroad workers in the late nineteenth and early twentieth centuries was the rise of two key organizations: the WESTERN FEDERATION OF MINERS (WFM) and the INDUSTRIAL WORKERS OF THE WORLD (IWW). Meanwhile the early twentieth-century labor movement was undermined by four traumatic events: the dynamiting of the Los Angeles *Times* building in 1910, the Ludlow Massacre of 1914, the Tom Mooney case of 1916, and the sedition case against William D. HAYWOOD in 1918. While San Francisco was notable for its militant labor tradition, Los Angeles had established an iron-clad open-shop movement, led by the powerful, aristocratic publisher of the *Times*, Harrison Gray Otis. The interdict on union organizing activity was challenged by, among others, the AFL's Bridge and Structural Iron Workers union. For the destruction on the *Times* building (which took twenty-one lives on October 1, 1910), two brothers in the union's leadership, John J. and James B. McNamara, went on trial, pleaded guilty, and drew long prison terms in what was a tremendous defeat for the western labor movement. Labor's trusting, all-out support of the McNamaras was totally discredited when the two brothers reversed their initial denials of guilt to confess their atrocious crime. An event of equal violence occurred in the Ludlow Massacre of 1914. This event was an outgrowth of a 1913 strike by the United Mine Workers in the coal fields of southern Colorado, where the dominant company was the Rockefeller-controlled Colorado Fuel and Iron Company. The climax to what proved to be an unsuccessful strike came on April 20, 1914, when militia killed eighteen in an attack on a union tent camp at the little mining town of Ludlow. The Ludlow carnage triggered a guerrilla war between strikers and militia and a total of seventy-four were killed in a matter of weeks before federal intervention brought peace. The Tom Mooney case stemmed from the bombing of the San Francisco Preparedness Day Parade of July 22, 1916, which resulted in ten fatalities. Amid charges of a frame-up, a dynamic, young California labor organizer, Tom Mooney, was tried and sentenced to death for the explosion. Even after the commutation of his sentence to life imprisonment and until his full pardon in 1939, the Mooney affair was a *cause célèbre* in western labor history.

While defeats outnumbered victories in the efforts of the WFM, IWW, railroad unions, and other labor organizations, a new era of union success dawned with the election of President Franklin D. Roosevelt in 1932. The mine, mill, and smelter workers' union, a lineal descendant of the WFM, revived and went on to greater successes. Under the charismatic leadership of Harry R. BRIDGES, the emergent longshoremen's union won a big Pacific Coast maritime strike in 1935 and gained supremacy on the West Coast docks. Whereas the five-day general strike in February 1919 in Seattle in behalf of shipyard workers had been crushed, the July 15-19, 1934, San Francisco general strike in support of the maritime effort was a key episode in the eventual victory of the workers. The New Deal saw, at last, the permanently successful organization of the loggers and lumber-mill workers of the Pacific Northwest, in contrast to an earlier failure by the IWW. The IWW's temporarily successful Lumber Workers Union had been supplanted by the Loyal Legion of Loggers and Lumbermen, an industry-dominated union that had been organized during World War I by the army to negate the power of the IWW. Labor resurgence in the Pacific Northwest began with a large strike in 1935. Victory for the AFL's United Brotherhood of Carpenters and Joiners ultimately led to the establishment of a competitor union, the International Woodworkers of America (IWA) of the Congress of Industrial Organizations (CIO). A number of strikes flared as the IWA and its AFL opponent, reconstituted as the Lumber and Sawmill Workers Union (LSWU), fought for dominance, but by 1942 the situation was stabilized with the two unions sharing a peaceful coexistence.

See Graham Adams, Jr., *Age of Industrial Violence: 1910-15* (1966); Irving Bernstein, *Turbulent Years: A History of the American Worker: 1933-1941* (1970); Gerald C. Eggert, *Railroad Labor Disputes: The Beginnings of Federal Strike Policy* (1967); and Philip Taft and Philip Ross, "American Labor Violence: Its Causes, Character, and Outcome," in Hugh D. Graham and Ted

R. Gurr, *The History of Violence in America* (1969).
—R. M. B.

Laclède, Pierre (1729-1778). French fur trader and
founder of St. Louis. Born at Bedous, France, Laclède
was educated at the Military Academy of Toulouse and
reportedly received some commercial training. In 1755
he came to New Orleans in the hope of making a fortune. Little is known of his years here, but some time
later he became a partner in the trading firm of Maxent,
Laclède, and Company, which obtained an eight-year
monopoly grant to the trade of the Missouri country in
July 1763.

While located at New Orleans, Laclède established a
liaison with Marie Thérèse (Bourgeois) Chouteau,
whose son René Auguste CHOUTEAU went with him as
his clerk when he ascended the Mississippi River in
August 1763. Laclède took one boat with a carrying
capacity of thirty to fifty tons. The boat required a crew
of at least twenty and would ordinarily take three
months to complete its journey. Arriving on November
3 at Ste. Genevieve, which was the only settlement on the
west bank of the Mississippi at that time, Laclède found
it impossible to secure adequate storage there for his
goods. Three days later he arrived at Kaskaskia, where
the local commandant offered him facilities at Fort
Chartres, which he accepted.

Sometime the following month Laclède crossed the
river with young Chouteau to seek a site for a trading
post. They determined to use the rocky, shelving bluff
where downtown St. Louis now stands in order to place
the operation well above flood stage. Chouteau returned in February 1764 with thirty workmen to lay out
the village. In the absence of hostile Indians, no stockade was needed until 1780. Laclède arrived in April with
a specific layout and named the new community for
King Louis IX.

When word reached the settlements on the east bank
that spring that they were now in British territory, Laclède persuaded many of the French settlers there to
move to his new village. Within a year forty to fifty
families had settled there, and the town had become
firmly established when the news came that Spain would
be the new master.

Meanwhile French authorities at New Orleans had
been receiving numerous complaints against the monopoly of Maxent, Laclède, and Company that led to its
cancellation early in 1765, although Laclède probably
did not learn of it until October. By that time he was well
in his way to establishing a strong corner on the Missouri
trade by his personal skill in dealing with the Indians
and his prestige as founder of St. Louis. In May 1769
Laclède bought out Maxent's interests, and their company was dissolved.

Thereafter Laclède acted independently or in concert
with his stepson Chouteau and young Sylvestre Lab-
badie, who had married into the Chouteau family. His
financial affairs became tangled, and while in New Orleans on one of his frequent visits he fell ill. En route
back up river he died near the mouth of the Arkansas
and was buried on shore.

The best brief account of Laclède's activities is to be
found in John Francis McDermott, "Myths and Realities
Concerning the Founding of St. Louis," in his *The French
in the Mississippi Valley* (1965).—W. E. P.

Ladd, Edwin Fremont (1859-1925). Chemist,

educator, and North Dakota politician. Ladd was born
on a farm in Maine. He graduated from the University
of Maine and worked for a time as a chemist for the New
York Agricultural Experiment Station in upper New
York. Arriving at the North Dakota Agricultural College at Fargo in 1890, Ladd taught chemistry and supervised the chemical work at the new experiment station.
His experiments included testing the suitability of sugar
beets as a North Dakota crop, discovering the flour-
making qualities of lower grades of wheat and the value
of screenings as stock feed, and numerous tests on food,
paint, and fertilizer sold in North Dakota. In terms of
the number of experiments conducted, the North Dakota Agricultural College was the leading experiment station in the United States by 1899.

In 1902 Ladd published a pamphlet on adulteration
of wholesale commodities in the state. Earlier he had
edited and published a circular entitled *North Dakota
Farmer and Sanitary Home*. His work convinced the
North Dakota legislature, which passed several laws
against adulteration of consumer goods. The 1903 an-
tiadulteration law of North Dakota made it the duty of
the experiment station to analyze foods and beverages
suspected of adulteration and to furnish, twice a year,
each county auditor with a list of such foods for publication by official newspapers.

Ladd won an international reputation for his efforts
in this field. In 1916 he became president of the agricultural college and in 1920 helped found the farm bureau
in North Dakota. In 1920 he was also elected to the
United States Senate, with the endorsement of the progressive Nonpartisan League. He formed a natural alliance with such other reformers as Robert M. La Follette and George Norris to oppose legislation for the
benefit of vested interests. Because of his independence
he was dropped from the Republican Steering Committee in the Senate.

Ladd was killed in an automobile accident.—D. J. T.

La Farge, Oliver [Hazard Perry] (1901-1963). Novelist and anthropologist. La Farge was born in New York
City. He received a B.A. from Harvard in 1924 and an
M.A. in 1929 and from 1926 to 1928 was an assistant in
ethnology at Tulane University. He made three archaeological expeditions to New Mexico for Harvard,
and two to Mexico and Guatemala for Tulane. His trips
to New Mexico introduced him to Navaho life and culture and gave him the specific material for his novel
Laughing Boy (1929), which won a Pulitzer Prize. His
interest in Indian life was lifelong. From 1930 La Farge
was associated with various branches of the American
Association on Indian Affairs and other organizations
concerned with various aspects of Indian life. In 1931 he
became a research associate in anthropology at Columbia University, a position he held until 1933. Later in
his life he moved to Santa Fe, New Mexico, where he
died.

Though many western authors have discussed the
"Indian problem" in some form or other, La Farge is
almost the only one to have written about Indian culture
from the Indian point of view. Whereas typical treatment of Indian themes has been either to focus on the
Indian as "the enemy" or to handle him as an unreal,
quasi-allegorical figure, La Farge attempts to write
about Indian life from the standpoint of an Indian living
in a culture that is remote from whites. The measure of

his success is his ability to create believable Indians with whom the reader can identify and sympathize but who are nonetheless truly Indian in their values, rather than romanticized and sentimentalized noble savages. La Farge's intimate firsthand knowledge of Indian life enables him to portray Indians who are recognizable as human beings while at the same time clearly different in their values from the whites into whose society they are thrown.—J. K. F.

La Flesche, Francis (1857-1932). Ethnologist. La Flesche was the son of "Chief Joseph" La Flesche, a half-French and half-Omaha leader of the Omaha, and an Omaha mother. His early schooling at the Presbyterian Mission School in Bellevue, Nebraska, was later recorded in *Middle Five* (1900), a classic bit of native American literature. In spite of his Presbyterian training, young La Flesche participated in Omaha buffalo hunts and ceremonials. La Flesche went to work in the Office of Indian Affairs while attending National University, where he earned a law degree in 1893.

In 1903 anthropologist F. W. Hodge brought La Flesche into the Bureau of American Ethnology, where he remained until his retirement in 1929. He spent his last three years among his people in the Omaha Indian community near Macy, Nebraska.

It is to La Flesche that subsequent generations owe much of their knowledge of the Osage and Omaha Indians. He was principal collaborator with Alice Fletcher in the compilation of *The Omaha Tribe* (1911) and alone published *A Dictionary of the Osage Language* (1932) and seventeen articles. In 1926 the University of Nebraska awarded La Flesche an honorary doctorate.

See Hartley B. Alexander, "Francis La Flesche," *American Anthropologist*, vol. 35 (1933).—B. L. F.

Lahontan, Louis-Armand de (1666?-?1715). French explorer. When Lahontan was seventeen, in 1683, he came to Canada with a company of marines. He appears to have enjoyed the life and year by year extended his geographical knowledge, so that by 1688 he was as far afield as Mackinac. In that year he claimed to have explored west to the Mississippi and up that stream to a "River Long," which he then ascended for many leagues. He also claimed to have visited the nations of the "Eokoros, Esanapes, and Gnacsitares" and to have heard of a river far to the west that emptied into a salt lake three hundred leagues in circumference. On July 9, 1689, so he said, he arrived back in Montreal.

Subsequently, Baron Lahontan rose to fairly high estate, fell into disgrace, and became an exile, publishing in Holland his *New Voyages in North America* (1703). It was successful and, save for Letter Sixteen, which tells of his improbable voyage up the "River Long," constitutes an interesting source on the social history of New France in the late seventeenth century.

See Lahontan, *New Voyages to North America*, Reuben Gold Thwaites, ed. (1905).—R. A. B.

Lake Bonneville (Utah). Prehistoric inland sea. Lake Bonneville existed sometime during the Pleistocene Epoch, which began about one million years ago. This epoch was marked by the rise and recession of continental ice sheets. Consequently, Lake Bonneville's level rose and fell depending on precipitation and aridity. It left behind distinctive fossil beaches (now benches) on the Wasatch Mountains. At one point, the lake reached depths of one thousand feet and covered approximately half of present-day Utah. The Great Salt Lake, Utah Lake, and Lake Sevier are modern remnants of the once-great inland sea.

The lake is named after explorer Benjamin Lewis Eulalie de Bonneville because it was under his direction that a map was published in 1837 showing the Great Basin as an area without external drainage. He named only the Salt Lake "Bonneville," but that name has been applied to the larger prehistoric lake. Bonneville himself probably never saw the area that the lake covered.

Lakes Erie, Huron, Michigan, Ontario, and Superior. See GREAT LAKES, MEN OF THE; and TRANSPORTATION ON THE GREAT LAKES.

Lamar, Mirabeau Buonaparte (1798-1859). Politician. Lamar was born near Louisville, Georgia, the son of a plantation owner. Educated at several academies, he professed an early interest in literature and art. After beginning his career as a merchant, he became secretary for Governor George M. Troup. In 1828 he established the Columbus *Enquirer*, a journal favorable to Troup's policies. He was elected state senator in 1829 but withdrew from the race for reelection because of his wife's death.

In 1835 he accompanied James W. Fannin, Jr., who later died in the Goliad massacre, to Texas to gather historical information and decided to remain. Lamar joined the Texas army, immediately distinguishing himself in the battle of San Jacinto, and served as secretary of war for the provisional government. In 1836 he was elected vice-president of the Republic of Texas under Sam Houston and in 1838 defeated Houston's candidate for the presidency.

During his term the independence of Texas was recognized by major European powers. Lamar opposed annexation of Texas by the United States, believing instead that Texas should extend her lands to the Pacific. He was responsible for establishing the new capital at Austin, designating land for public schools and two universities, carrying on an aggressive campaign against the Indians, and encouraging the unsuccessful Santa Fe expedition—costly measures at a time when the government was near bankruptcy. In 1841 Lamar retired from politics. He served in the army during the Mexican War and in 1847 was elected to the state legislature. In 1857 he was named United States minister to Costa Rica and Nicaragua. Twenty months later he returned to Texas, where he died at his Richmond plantation.

Lamar is generally accepted as the father of public education in Texas; his words (from a message to the Texas congress) "A cultivated mind is the guardian genius of democracy" became the motto of the University of Texas. Considered an effective poet and a considerable orator, he inspired fanatical loyalty among his supporters and an almost equally fanatical opposition from the adherents of Sam Houston. To a considerable degree his reputation as an impractical visionary (he was bitterly criticized for his grandiose schemes) is the result of his being a man of large ideas who unfortunately found himself president of an infant nation with a narrow, uncertain present and small immediate prospects.

See Asa K. Christian, *Mirabeau Buonaparte Lamar* (1925); and Herbert M. Gambrell, *Mirabeau Buonaparte Lamar, Troubador and Crusader* (1934).—J. B. F.

L'Amour, Louis Dearborn (1908-). Novelist.

L'Amour, who was born in Jamestown, North Dakota, left high school at the age of fifteen and pursued his education as a ranch hand, seaman, and longshoreman during the Great Depression. Returning from World War II, in which he had served as an officer in a tank corps, he began writing short stories and novels. By the mid-1970s he had written sixty-two books, with total sales of over fifty million copies, causing him to be called "probably the most prolific, best-selling and most highly rated Western writer in the country today." Four of his novels have sold a million copies each: *Burning Hills, Guns of the Timberland, Shalako,* and *Silver Canyon.* His works have provided the stories for thirty-three movies, including *Hondo* and *How the West Was Won.*

L'Amour celebrates the strength and endurance of the men of the American West. "When you open a rough, hard country," he has said, "you don't open it with a lot of pantywaists." Using historical research to insure authenticity, L'Amour concentrates on action, considering such things as the depiction of sexual encounters and the use of dialect to be beyond his literary limits. His lack of official recognition he attributes to the general critical lack of respect for the western novel: "If you write a book about a bygone period that lies east of the Mississippi, then it's a historical novel. If it's west of the Mississippi, it's a Western, a different category." L'Amour believes that the opening of the West was an event of such fundamental importance in the history of the United States that it deserves major attention by novelists and historians.—P. L. N.

Lamy, Jean Baptiste (1814-1888). Roman Catholic missionary. A Frenchman, Lamy was active in frontier Kentucky and Ohio. As vicar-apostolic he reorganized the church in Arizona, New Mexico, and eastern Colorado from 1850, an area that became Santa Fe diocese in 1853. The first Roman Catholic bishop of the Southwest, he labored prodigiously among Anglos, Mexicans, and Indians. His principal task in New Mexico was the reform of a religious establishment that had been allowed to stagnate and grow corrupt through neglect by the clergy. He removed several priests from their posts and unfrocked them, among them padres José Manuel Gallegos and José Antonio Martinez. Those disciplined by Bishop Lamy were often members of the most important families in New Mexico, and in a spirit of vengeance some entered politics in an effort to gain power that might be turned against Lamy. Ex-padre Gallegos, for example, representing anti-Lamy forces, won election as territorial delegate to Congress in 1853.

In the mid-1870s Lamy, now archbishop, was again drawn into politics by the need to oppose a bill of the Territorial Assembly that would have curtailed the Roman Catholic church's dominance over New Mexico's educational system. Largely through his influence this legislation was defeated.

Willa Cather immortalized Lamy in her novel *Death Comes for the Archbishop.*

See Paul Horgan, *Lamy of Santa Fe* (1975).—R. I. B. and M. S.

Lancaster, Treaty of (1744). This treaty, agreed to on July 4, 1744, was the result of a great Indian conference held at Lancaster, Pennsylvania, to discuss many problems that had arisen between the western Indians and settlers in Pennsylvania, Maryland, and Virginia. There was an urgency to please among the whites at this gathering, for the colonies were then involved in King George's War against the French, and the outcome in America depended in great part on whether the French or the English received the loyalty of the Iroquois Confederacy—the Six Nations. Present were representatives of the Six Nations, with the exception of the Mohawk. Jason Lee represented the Ohio Land Company, there were personal representatives of two colonial governors, and Lieutenant Governor George Thomas of Pennsylvania was there in person. Conrad Weiser acted as interpreter and was mainly responsible for the conference's success.

The Treaty of Lancaster actually outlined Indian policy on this part of the frontier for some time to come. In back of it was the whole problem of settler expansion into the hinterland. Land company activities had been one of the disturbing elements and was a major subject of discussion. Both settler and speculator had been encroaching on the Indian lands along the Susquehanna River and about the headwaters of the Ohio. The Seneca claimed, for instance, that illegal sales had been made to Thomas Cresap on October 11, 1736. And in 1742, Lieutenant Governor Thomas had been forced by the threat of an Indian war to issue a proclamation requiring intruders on the Juniata River and elsewhere in the territory to remove themselves by May 1743.

Maryland and Virginia were involved in the same issue. Virginians, it was said, had crossed the Blue Ridge and had taken up lands of four tribes of the Six Nations. As a result there had been a skirmish between settlers and Indians. There were cited incidents of trader irregularities and murder that had gone uncorrected. The bigger stake, however, lay in cementing friendship between the English and the Six Nations because of the war with France. After discussions lasting from June 22 to July 4, a treaty was signed wherein Virginia and Maryland paid £700 in gold for Iroquois claims within colonial territory, and the Iroquois promised to strictly manage their unruly Delaware vassals and to be true to their English friends. By thus allying the Six Nations to the British, the Lancaster treaty was one of the most crucial Indian agreements of the colonial period. It did not, however, completely extinguish the Iroquois's western land claims, which remained unsettled until the Treaty of FORT STANWIX (1768).

See Charles P. Keith, *Chronicles of Pennsylvania from the English Revolution to the Peace of Aix-la-Chapelle, 1668-1748* (1917); C. H. Sipe, *The Indian Wars of Pennsylvania,* 2nd. ed. (1931); and C. Z. Weiser, *The Life of (John) Conrad Weiser, The German Pioneer, Patriot, and Patron of Two Races,* abridg. ed. (1899).—T. D. C.

land claims, private. Those areas of the public domain acquired by the United States from Great Britain, France, Spain, and Mexico brought with them serious land title problems, some of which were not settled for more than half a century. As recently as 1967, the problem flared up in New Mexico and culminated in the Tierra Amarilla Court House raid, led by Reies TIJERINA. The predecessor governments had made a variety of grants and concessions for tracts of land ranging all the way from the equivalent of a fee title to life leases and simple occupancy rights. Altogether some thirty thousand claims for a total area larger than the state of Wisconsin were to be filed for confirmation. They ranged in size from residence lots in Detroit, Vincennes,

Mobile, New Orleans, and San Gabriel to tracts of many square leagues (a square league is 4,428 acres), granted on condition of colonization, the erecting of sawmills, tanneries, distilleries, ropewalks, or for development as cattle ranches. In addition to desirable sites for towns and cities the grants included the alluvial land along both sides of the lower Missouri and Mississippi rivers, the Tombigbee, Alabama, and Arkansas rivers, and practically all the better coastal valley lands in California.

Throughout the nineteenth century, Congress, the state legislatures, and state and federal courts were all deeply involved in adjudicating these grants and concessions and determining their boundaries. The task was complicated because officials of the predecessor governments had been vague in defining the boundaries of the grants, imprecise as to the nature of the title being granted, and careless in maintaining records of the transactions. Also, as time neared for the transfer of the territories, it became apparent that land previously having had little or no value would, when it came under American control, become sought after. Grants were speeded up in anticipation of the transfer and, as the courts were later to find, many were rushed through at the last moment, while others were fraudulently antedated. In fact, nearly every official of Mexican California was later found to have participated in these postmidnight grants.

Congress early set about adjudicating these numerous grants whose owners had been promised confirmation of their property rights. Commissioners were set up to investigate the claims, scrutinize the documentary evidence, and report to Congress whether they were outright grants or conditional grants, and, in either case, whether the conditions had been fulfilled; or whether the grants were mere occupancy rights. Members of Congress showed a marked willingness to approve claims up to 640 acres, later 2,000 acres, but larger grants were examined more carefully. Land claims on the Detroit River in Michigan, at Vincennes on the Wabash in Indiana, and at Cahokia on the Mississippi in Illinois were the first to be adjudicated. The anticipated rise in land values which followed American control unfortunately led to an unseemly scramble to buy up these claims on the part of territorial governors, judges, and other officers, members of their families, and some of the well-to-do French residents. Their attorneys resorted to "incredible forgeries, fraud, subornation and perjuries" to advance the claims of their clients, according to Dean Francis S. Philbrick in *The Laws of Indiana Territory, 1801-09.* From the outset it seemed almost impossible to separate complete grants from questionable claims, and the evidence suggests that numerous questionable claims were confirmed and possibly some sound claims were struck down.

Most critical for the development of the states in which they were located were the private land claims in Missouri, Louisiana, Mississippi, Florida, California, and New Mexico, though some excellent farm and city property was included in claims in Michigan, Illinois, Alabama, and Arkansas. Until the legality of the claims was settled and their boundaries clearly established and surveyed, it was impossible to open to settlement the immediately surrounding land. Yet settlers, accustomed to regarding unimproved land on the frontier as subject to squatting and preemption, not only took possession

of the lands surrounding the claims but also took up residence upon undeveloped portions of the larger claims, anticipating that such large and still unused tracts would not be confirmed. In this way a conflict of interest developed between the claimants, whose attorneys asked for the greatest leniency in interpreting the claims they represented, and the squatters, whose representatives demanded not only the strictest tests to determine validity but actually advanced the view that claims larger than the claimant could utilize had no justification and should be struck down. The state legislatures were somewhat influenced by the squatters and were disposed to validate the rights of occupants who had even a color of title, but the practice of the courts in the days of John Marshall, Roger B. Taney, and Stephen J. Field was to expand conditional grants, or grants with reservations, into outright grants and to deal harshly with squatters' claims. A California law conceding occupants making improvements on land claims, a negotiable right, was invalidated by the state supreme court.

Outstanding leaders in American political and financial circles acquired interests in these claims and many of the greatest lawyers of the day were retained to defend them, while the men defending the government's interest, as members of the claims commissions, district attorneys, and high-ranking officials in the Department of Justice, were, generally speaking, men of mediocre talents. Among the well-known men who acquired claims were William Henry Harrison, Aaron Burr, John Slidell, Stephen Girard, Edward Livingston, Captain (later General) Henry W. Halleck, John C. Frémont, and Commodore Robert F. Stockton, and among the well-paid attorneys defending their claims before the courts were Daniel Webster, Thomas Hart Benton, Hugh Lawson White, S. S. Prentiss, David L. Yulee, Caleb Cushing, and John G. Carlisle. Well-known members of Congress actually appeared before the Supreme Court in behalf of private claimants while serving in Congress. Since the ablest and best-paid legal talent was generally on the claimants' side where fees were high, it is understandable that the courts were persuaded to confirm borderline claims that might have been rejected if the government's case had been better presented. Only during the Buchanan administration, when Jeremiah S. Black was attorney general and Edwin M. Stanton a special attorney, was the case against questionable claims that had been confirmed by the lower courts effectively presented by the government.

In the bay area of California, where disappointed gold-seekers had moved upon the large but wholly undeveloped claims, the prolonged litigation over titles got into politics, with the settlers' party exercising considerable influence in the state legislature. Local and state courts were unfriendly, however, and serious confrontations occurred between large mobs of settlers and posses sent out to dispossess them, keeping the state in turmoil for years. It was the concentration of land ownership in California and the agrarian warfare it produced that contributed to Henry George's indictment of English-American land laws and tax policies.

The most scandalous part of the adjudication of private land claims occurred in New Mexico, where one claim that could not have originally included more than 97,000 acres was finally confirmed after much legerdemain for 1,714,764 acres, the largest ever to be patented. This claim of the Maxwell Land Grant Com-

PANY amounted to five percent of the total acreage confirmed—33,440,482 acres in 28,492 grants.

Texas, having retained the public lands within its borders, had its own problem in adjudicating the many grants made by the predecessor Spanish and Mexican governments, but it does not appear that confirmation of claims was as long delayed or as troublesome as in other states.

See Paul W. Gates, *History of Public Land Law Development* (1968).—P. W. G.

land companies. From the beginnings of English and Dutch settlement in America, land and trading companies provided much of the leadership and capital that made possible the recruitment of settlers, their transportation to the New World, and their subsidization for the initial period of dependency. Thus, the London and Plymouth companies and the Dutch West India Company invested substantial sums in efforts to establish settlements that would produce minerals, furs, and other commodities in demand in the mother countries. In addition to dividends from their stock, investors could acquire large tracts of land as manors from which rental income would be expected (see LAND POLICY: *in the colonies, 1607-1775*).

Virginia had its beginning under the London Company, but its corporate rights were surrendered in 1624 after seventeen years of mismanagement and turmoil (see VIRGINIA, SETTLEMENT OF). The investors received little or no return on their capital though some took land that, in one instance, developed into the Fairfax holding of a million acres in the Northern Neck of Virginia. The Plymouth Company was replaced by the Council for New England, which in turn made grants to five colonies: Plymouth, Massachusetts Bay, Maine, New Hampshire, and Connecticut. Dutch capitalists, in their zeal for profits from trade and piracy, neglected their New Netherlands colony. Its small and discontented population was easily taken over by the British. Aside from a small Dutch population and numerous place names, the principal heritage of the Dutch period of New York was the huge Van Rensselaer landholding, which was to survive for two hundred years.

Though these land companies were unsuccessful in producing large returns for their investors from trade, preying upon the commerce of other nationals, or developing rent-producing estates, it had become the pattern for governments to charter land and settlement companies liberally provided with land grants and government powers. Influential individuals and groups of proprietors sought similarly generous grants of millions of acres of land from the English crown and undertook extensive emigration promotion activities to settle their tracts. Most successful was William Penn in developing the Commonwealth of Pennsylvania. Maryland, the Carolinas, and Georgia were also first developed by individual or group grantees.

In the eighteenth century, western land investments seemed to offer a profitable and rapid turnover of capital. New land companies came into existence; some were strictly local like the Susquehanna Land Company, which consisted of Connecticut investors, but companies in which both English and colonial capital was invested were more common.

Colonial charters, with their vague, uncertain, and unsurveyed boundaries, led to serious intercolonial disputes, one of the most threatening being the dispute over the right of Connecticut to extend its control through the Wyoming valley of northeastern Pennsylvania. Connecticut's sea-to-sea charter of 1662 was the basis of its claim to this region, though the claim was not asserted until 1753. Then, disdaining Pennsylvania's claim to the area and with the approval of the Connecticut legislature, the Susquehanna Land Company organized and bought from the Iroquois confederacy of Six Nations the Wyoming valley for the settlement of its expanding population. Hundreds of Yankees with titles from the company settled in the valley, bringing with them their Congregational church, their marked acquisitive instinct, their rugged honesty and self-righteousness, and willingness to fight to preserve the titles they claimed. There followed years of conflict between settlers claiming rights to land from the Susquehanna Land Company and those claiming rights from Pennsylvania. Clashing interests, turbulence, and uncertainty of titles culminated in a compromise whereby Pennsylvania issued to 1,745 Connecticut claimants certificates of title and gave its own grantees land elsewhere. In contrast to other contemporary land companies, the Susquehanna company had succeeded in settling what quickly grew into a thriving development in the Wyoming valley.

In the meantime, less homogenous groups of investors, consisting of men of capital in England, Quaker merchants of Philadelphia, and influential planters of Virginia and Maryland, were brought together in a number of land companies organized to acquire large tracts of land west of the mountains for development and sale. Already there had developed in the older colonies men who, by virtue of their official positions or because of their investments, had acquired thousands of acres they were either selling, renting, or improving with indentured servants or slaves. Few could deny that land was the source of all, or almost all, wealth, and the scramble to share in its distribution came to absorb the attention of public officials of the colonies and of the imperial administration, as well as planters, traders, and merchants, in the years just before the American Revolution.

Among the companies being formed to speculate in land were the Transylvania Company (see Richard HENDERSON), the Wabash, the Indiana, and the Vandalia land companies, all of which tried to secure grants from the British Board of Trade to sanction their purchases from Indian tribes. Their maneuvers for preference became the theme of Clarence Alvord's *Mississippi Valley in British Politics*, which shows how ministries were made and broken in part as the result of the schemes of land companies. All such trans-Appalachian land-company proposals, though they had obtained Indian approval and for a time imperial preference, failed in the end. Among the reasons for the failures were the jealousy of the different colonies, Virginia's desire to retain control of the huge area its charter had granted it, and Great Britain's conviction that the creation of new colonies with legislative assemblies would produce additional disputes with the imperial government and that activities of private groups negotiating with the Indians for land would result in Indian wars and add to the expenses of the mother country. (After independence was achieved, some of these land companies, assuming that they had acquired valuable rights, flooded Congress with petitions for relief and compensation for losses they had sustained, but none was successful. Investors in land-company schemes played a part in shaping the attitudes of Virginia, Maryland, and Pennsylvania toward the proposed cession of western lands to the central government.)

The war for independence halted all these speculative schemes and forced the contraction of the frontier line of settlement, but with peace, proposals for land-company purchases were again advanced for every section of the frontier from Maine to Georgia. Tracts were sold ranging from 1 million or 2 million acres in Maine to 30 million acres in Georgia (to four companies), and extensive promotional work was undertaken to attract settlers. Most important of these companies were the Ohio Company, organized by Massachusetts speculators who undertook to purchase from the United States 1.5 million acres in southeastern Ohio; and the John Cleves Symmes group of New Jersey entrepreneurs who tried to buy a large tract in southwestern Ohio. To win the approval of Congress for their purchase, the Ohio associates had to include some members of Congress and form an enlarged Scioto Company, which proposed to purchase 5 million acres. The Scioto Company failed to carry out its plans, but the Ohio Company did succeed in settling many people from Massachusetts in the vicinity of Marietta. The Symmes group, through poor planning and inadequate financial resources, succeeded only in paying for and settling an eighth of the area it had hoped to acquire, but it did contribute much to the development of the region between the Great and Little Miami rivers, soon to become the backcountry for the swiftly growing city of Cincinnati. Notwithstanding the low cost of the two purchases (one dollar an acre but payable in depreciated currency and revolutionary war bounty land warrants that reduced the original investment to just a few cents an acre), there is little evidence that the investors in these companies profited substantially from their enterprise. They did, however, direct emigration to their tracts and their leaders provided much of the leadership in the political, economic, and social life of the territory. They were also influential in persuading Congress to adopt the Northwest Ordinance, which provided the structure of territorial government through the three steps to statehood.

In contrast to the record of the Ohio companies, the Yazoo land companies never actually acquired any land and did nothing to encourage migration and settlement but, like some of the late colonial companies, they played an important role in politics and constitutional development. Georgia sold its western lands lying along the Yazoo River in present Mississippi and Alabama in 1795 to four companies very cheaply in what was one of the most flagrantly corrupt actions taken by any legislative body. The next legislature repudiated the sale. But in the meantime, securities of the companies had passed into innocent hands (thereafter spoken of as "widows and orphans") who sought redress in the court for their losses. In 1810 John Marshall declared for the Supreme Court in *Fletcher* v. *Peck* that the original sale was a contract and that Georgia had violated the contract clause of the Constitution in repudiating it. Georgia,

when it had ceded its western lands to the United States in 1802, required that the latter should assume responsibility for any claims rising under the sale of 1795. John Randolph fought hard to prevent Congress from making an appropriation for relief, but in 1814, when he was temporarily out of Congress, $4.7 million was voted to the shareholders of the four companies.

Other states with western land claims ceded them either wholly or in part to the federal government or sold them to land companies. Massachusetts sold its entire tract in New York, roughly the area west of Seneca Lake and amounting to 6 million acres, for the equivalent of three cents an acre, to Phelps & Gorham and their associates. Phelps & Gorham could not carry the investment and portions were sold through Robert Morris to a group of Scottish capitalists called the Pulteney associates, another part to Dutch capitalists organized as the Holland Land Company, and a third to the Wadsworth brothers of Connecticut. Agents of all three groups devoted much of their time and a great deal of capital to developing their areas by constructing roads, establishing towns, and extensively advertising their lands for sale on long credit at modest prices. The efforts of these men and their agents to sell their lands to people who would create farms, the aid they gave them in times of adversity by extending longer credit and taking produce in place of cash, and their willingness to rent improved land to those lacking capital for development is wholly different from the sheer speculation of Robert Morris and the buyers of the Yazoo lands. The Holland Land Company and the Ohio Company created the pattern of land colonization later to be expanded upon by the land-grant railroads.

Speculation in public lands reached its high points in 1818-19, 1835-37, and 1854-57, when many millions of dollars were invested in the purchase of wild lands on the frontier, away from transportation facilities and not likely to be made into farms for years to come. Individuals and land companies borrowed heavily to finance their purchases, overestimating their ability to carry their holdings. When the inevitable crash came, many were forced to liquidate their holdings and fell into bankruptcy. Greatest of these companies was the American Land Company, incorporated in 1835 with a capitalization of a million dollars and soon the owner of more than 300,000 acres, much of it prospective cotton land in Arkansas and Mississippi. There is little evidence that this company—and dozens of other companies and individual land speculators—planned to invest capital in improving and settling their holdings as the Dutch capitalists and the Pulteney associates had done. The contrast between the two types of land companies and individual speculators is marked: the one withheld land from settlement and improvement while waiting for the unearned increment that incoming population would give it, and as a result brought about the widespread dispersion of settlers; the other stimulated and directed immigration, allowed settlers to use its capital for improvements, accepted livestock and grain for payments, and showed marked leniency when crop failures or other catastrophes struck.

For a time, the later land-grant railroads, beginning with the Illinois Central in 1851, were as much concerned about the sale and settlement of their extensive holdings as they were about building their lines and running trains. Like the Holland Land Company, they were true empire builders. They looked for financial returns both from the sale of their lands and from the traffic the new settlers would provide. Such was the case, for example, with the Northern Pacific (see BURLINGTON NORTHERN RAILROAD). Another type of land company is that which developed its holdings sometimes through tenants but more often with workers having no equity in the land. Such a company had no intention of selling its land, which it regarded as a permanent investment. Perhaps best known of this type of land company is the Kern County Land Company of California.

See Paul D. Evans, *The Holland Land Company* (1924); Shaw Livermore, *Early American Land Companies: Their Influence on Corporate Development* (1939); and A. M. Sakolski, *Great American Land Bubble* (1932).—P. W. G.

Land Grant Act of 1862. See COLLEGES AND UNIVERSITIES.

land-grant college. See COLLEGES AND UNIVERSITIES.

Land Office, General. The General Land Office was established in the Treasury Department in 1812 to administer the public lands, which then amounted to 756 million acres and were held at a minimum sale price of two dollars an acre. The chief officer, who held the rank of commissioner, examined the monthly reports of the registers and receivers of the individual land offices in the West (105 of them by 1883) and of the surveyors general (16 in 1883). He passed upon all contested land claims submitted by local officers, made recommendations to the secretary of the treasury for improvements and changes in policies, and reported, in increasing detail, the operations of the land system. In 1849 the General Land Office was transferred to the Department of the Interior (or Home Department) along with the Bureau of Indian Affairs, the Bureau of the Census, the Pension and Patent offices and a number of minor agencies. The many surveying contracts and patronage appointments to be granted in the western states made the office of commissioner much sought after by ambitious politicians, among them Abraham Lincoln. Some commissioners were honest and in a few cases reform-minded, but more commonly they had a bias in favor of large companies and capitalists who solicited favors from them.

After 1891, when national forest reserves were being created out of the public lands, the G.L.O. was required to administer great areas of land along the lines of modern conservation principles while at the same time to dispose of the public lands to private owners and tolerate destructive timber cutting on public lands not within the national forests. This ambivalence led President Theodore Roosevelt to transfer control of the national forests to the Forest Service in the Department of Agriculture in 1905 on the urging of Gifford Pinchot. The withdrawal of other public lands from entry for national parks and monuments and the adoption of the Taylor Grazing Act of 1934 virtually halted further transfers of public lands to private ownership, except for tracts on which some equitable claims had already been established. The Grazing Service, created in 1934 to manage the 140 million acres of grazing lands, was joined with the old G.L.O. in 1946 to form the Bureau of Land Management, which, in addition, administers the rich Douglas fir lands of the forfeited Oregon and California Railroad in Oregon and the mineral rights to many millions of acres of public land in fifteen western states.

See Paul W. Gates, *History of Public Land Law Development* (1968); and Malcolm J. Rohrbough, *The Land Office Business* (1968).—P. W. G.

land policy. *in the colonies (1607-1775)*. English companies and proprietors interested in settling seventeenth-century America quickly learned that land was their most valuable resource. Land served both as a means to promote immigration and as a way to underwrite the initial costs of colonization. Outside the Puritan colonies, the common method of granting land in this period was the HEADRIGHT SYSTEM, a guarantee that any man who paid for the transportation to America either of himself or some other person would receive a stipulated amount of land. The promise of land lured hundreds of thousands of Englishmen to the New World, many of whom served willingly as indentured servants in anticipation of becoming freeholders themselves.

The Puritan colonies of Massachusetts, Connecticut, and Rhode Island developed an orderly and unique system for distributing land. The rulers of colonial New England granted townships to groups of men called town proprietors, who in turn divided the acreage among the individual settlers. The seventeenth-century proprietors were not speculators who sold their land for profit. Their chief responsibility was to see that lots were given only to those people who met the community's moral standards. The early Puritans determined the size of a man's holdings by "the rule of persons and estates," a process that took into consideration his wealth, his social standing, and his family's needs. The town proprietors generally awarded each man a house lot in the center of the village and several acres for farming in some other part of the settlement. In many villages a large piece of land called the commons was set aside for the benefit of the entire community. The remainder of a town's ungranted land was held by the proprietors until they decided that it was time for a second or third division of acreage among the settlers. New Englanders held their lands free from feudal dues, and the quitrents that were collected in the other colonies were rare in the Puritan commonwealths. The New England system may well have influenced the legislators who later passed the important Land Ordinance of 1785, which divided the Northwest Territory into carefully surveyed townships (see TERRITORIAL SYSTEM).

The founders of many of the other American colonies advanced plans for the orderly distribution of land, but their elaborate, often feudal, schemes seldom worked. Lord Baltimore, the proprietor of Maryland, proposed establishing large manors of several thousand acres, each possessing "all such royalties and priviledges, as are usually belonging to Mannors in England." The seventeenth-century proprietors of Carolina hoped to avoid the dangers of "a numerous democracy" when they issued the Fundamental Constitutions of 1669, a document calling for the creation of a hereditary nobility supported by huge grants of land. The abundance of cheap land in America doomed these early plans to failure. English immigrants crossed the Atlantic in anticipation of becoming freeholders and were not interested in reproducing the manorial system in the New World. With the exception of New York's Hudson valley, large-scale tenancy was rare in the colonies. Most of the governments outside New England required a quit-rent from landowners as a nominal recognition of fealty to the king. Virginia, for example, demanded a payment of two shillings for each hundred acres. Quitrents were generally not a burden on the settlers, however, and in many areas their collection was ignored.

In the colonies in which the headright system pre-vailed, settlers frequently staked out claims wherever they pleased. In Virginia and in South Carolina, new arrivals rushed to seize lands with river frontage, be-cause they knew the importance of water transportation in the sale of tobacco and other staple crops. In contrast to the orderly development of the New England towns, southern plantations were usually scattered throughout the backcountry, and villages were extremely rare. In many cases claims were poorly surveyed, and the validity of land grants was often challenged. The situation was so bad in Virginia that the government ordered all freeholders to recheck the boundaries of their land ev-ery four years for the "preservation of friendshipp among neighbors." If a colonist was not qualified to receive a land grant and did not have enough money to purchase a lot, he could still get acreage by becoming a "squatter." The Ulstermen, who settled in Pennsylvania, squatted wherever they could find a place, and when authorities questioned their action, they explained sim-ply that it was "against the laws of God and nature that so much land should lie idle." In the later colonial period, frontier farmers sometimes defended their land claims by what they called corn rights, which gave a man a hundred acres for every acre he planted. Even though the preemptive corn rights had no basis in the law, many colonial communities accepted them as evidence of ownership.

During the eighteenth century, the sale of land re-placed grants as the principal means of acquiring ac-reage. In New England the laying out of townships became a speculative venture, and any man was allowed to settle in a community if he could afford to purchase a share from the proprietors. In Virginia wealthy planters who enjoyed the governor's favor were able to engross great tracts of land, which they resold for substantial profits. It is estimated, for example, that William Byrd II owned 100,000 acres, while Robert Carter left an estate of more than 300,000 acres. Another Virginian, George WASHINGTON, made a fortune on western lands. But historians have discovered that, despite the extraor-dinary success of a few planter-aristocrats, most colonial farms were of small or medium size. Land prices varied from area to area, but until the middle of the eighteenth century, they seldom were high enough to prohibit pur-chase by men of moderate means. With the exception of western Virginia, land companies were not a significant factor in the settlement of America during the pre-Revolutionary period, and most buyers dealt directly with the colonial governments.

Scholars who have studied patterns of settlement dur-ing the colonial era have discovered several important trends. One historian has found that the average size of the New England farm decreased from between one hundred and two hundred acres in the seventeenth century to between forty and fifty acres in the late eigh-teenth century. Moreover, by the Revolutionary period, less fertile, marginal lands were being cultivated for the first time. After 1750 the value of land rose significantly.

This rise apparently was not the result of inflation, for the price of other goods, such as furniture, tools, and clothing, showed long-term stability. This evidence sug-gests that Revolutionary America was an overcrowded society—that the colonists were competing for old lands located near the Atlantic coast. Kenneth Lockridge has written that New England "was rapidly becoming more and more an old world society; old world in the sense of the size of farms, old world in the sense of an increasing-ly wide and articulated social hierarchy, old world in that 'the poor' were ever present and in increasing numbers."

In general, colonial farmers exploited the land through poor agricultural methods. The tobacco plan-ters of the Chesapeake region systematically ruined the soil. By failing to rotate crops properly, they sapped the land of vital nutrients. By cultivating only the surface of the land, they exposed valuable topsoils to quick ero-sion. No care was taken to fertilize the fields, and live-stock was allowed to roam free so that the manure needed to restore the land was lost. As a result of these poor techniques, it was an accepted agricultural axiom in Virginia that good tobacco could not be grown on the same field for more than three seasons. In New En-gland, farming techniques were little better than those of the South. With the exception of Jared Eliot, one of the first men in America to make scientific agricultural experiments, few men in Massachusetts and Connec-ticut paid attention to crop rotation. The German set-tlers who populated the mid-Atlantic colonies were the exception to the rule, for they were excellent farmers who knew how to protect the soil. They penned their livestock, plowed deeply, and rotated their crops. One Pennsylvania writer explained in 1753 "how much we are indebted to the Germans for the Oeconomy they have introduced and how serviceable they are in an infant colony."

Of the many studies of this subject, some of the best are Percy W. Bidwell and John I. Falconer, *History of Agriculture in the Northern United States, 1620-1860* (1925); Lewis Cecil Gray, *History of Agriculture in the Southern United States to 1860*, 2 vols. (1941); Kenneth Lockridge, "The Evolution of New England Society," *Past and Present*, no. 39 (1968); and Richard Shyrock, "British Versus German Traditions in Colonial Agricul-ture," *Mississippi Valley Historical Review*, vol. 26 (1939).—T. H. B.

1780-1896. Between 1781 and 1802 the United States came into the possession of 225 million acres of public land under the terms of the Treaty of Paris of 1783 and by cessions to the national government by the states of their western land claims. It thus was necessary for the new national government to draft policies for the ad-ministration and disposal of its public domain. The Con-gress of the Confederation gave much thought to the matter and after long discussion adopted two measures: the Land Ordinance of 1785 (see TERRITORIAL SYSTEM), which established some of the basic organizational fea-tures followed thereafter, and the NORTHWEST ORDI-NANCE of 1787, which provided for the structure of government for the territories prior to their admission as states. In the deliberations leading to these measures, representatives of the thirteen states were deeply influ-enced by the experience of their own governments, were quite aware of those policies that had worked well on the whole and those that had not, and showed considerable familiarity with the experience of governments other than their own.

In the southern colonies there had been no government surveying system, and owners of rights or grants were privileged to make their selections and run their boundaries as they wished, provided they did not encroach upon the land of others. In the middle colonies large manorial grants were not uncommon. In the southern New England colonies titles were held without quitrent obligations in the form of township grants made by the legislature to responsible groups, and tracts were surveyed in a rough way. Thus the tangle of overlapping claims that came out of the southern system was avoided (see LAND SYSTEM, SOUTHERN). It was also common to reserve one section in each township for the church and one for schools. In both systems it was common to award land to individuals, but as time passed there was an increasing tendency to sell portions of the ungranted lands.

Members of the Congress of the Confederation borrowed features from the land system of both sections. Distressed at the low standing of public credit and the heavy debt with which the American Revolution had burdened the young republic, the Confederation decided to sell the lands and to encourage competitive bidding for them at well-advertised public auctions at a minimum price of one dollar an acre. At the same time, veterans of the Revolution were to be allowed to locate their bounty land warrants in a military tract located in the center of Ohio Territory. Before the public sale, the lands were to be surveyed into townships six miles square, each containing thirty-six sections of 640 acres, and settlement was to be permitted only on land purchased or entered with the military bounty warrants. Surveys were to be extended slowly to assure compact and orderly settlement comparable to the controlled advance of settlement in New England. Surveying was to be in the charge of the geographer of the United States assisted by a surveyor from each state. Religious differences prevented the adoption of a provision for the reservation of a glebe lot in each township for the church, but one section was to be reserved for common schools. Thus were basic policies early established, some to be retained into the twentieth century, others to be gradually modified: public lands were to be surveyed and offered for sale at public auction, and settlement or squatting upon them was forbidden until they were purchased; a relatively high minimum price was established; a reserve for military bounties was set aside; and one thirty-sixth of the lands were reserved for the support of common schools. Having established the rudimentary outline of a national land system, Congress proceeded to breach it by selling for a few cents an acre great tracts in southern Ohio to John Cleves Symmes and to the Ohio Company, which was composed of New England capitalists and speculators in securities. A number of other large speculative purchases applied for were not sanctioned, however.

An act of 1796 further outlined land policies. Alternate tiers of townships were to be sold in quarter township lots (5,760 acres) at the national capital, and the other townships were to be sold in sections (640 acres) at either Pittsburgh or Cincinnati; the minimum price was raised to two dollars an acre; and credit of one year was to be granted. Sales continued to be few because the price was altogether too high for unimproved land, and a credit of one year was insufficient for anyone to be able to make out of the land the balance owed on it. Moreover, only speculators needed or could buy land in such large quantities.

Until 1800, growth in the Ohio country was largely concentrated in the districts being settled by the Ohio Company, the Symmes associates, the Connecticut Land Company in the Western Reserve, and the two military tracts reserved for the holders of revolutionary war bounties; the public lands held directly by the United States were being avoided. In that year William Henry Harrison, Ohio's territorial delegate, persuaded Congress to liberalize the land system by extending credit for parts of the purchase price for two, three, and four years; allowing a discount of eight percent a year for advance payments; reducing the smallest unit that could be purchased to 320 acres; creating four land districts; and establishing a local land office in each to be presided over by a register, who had charge of sales, and a receiver who cared for the payments. With this measure the government's income from public land sales picked up, reaching four percent of its total income in 1805, ten percent in 1814, and thirteen percent in 1819.

Advocates of selling the public lands to produce revenue could well have been pleased, but a growing number of people in the new states and territories of the West were dissatisfied with the system of land disposal, maintaining that the minimum price was too high, that credit permitted, indeed encouraged, speculators to buy up and withhold large tracts from settlement, and that squatters—i.e., settlers who had moved upon land before they had title and had begun their improvements— were being brutally treated and ejected from claims which they were planning to purchase with their savings. Furthermore, the large number of buyers of government lands who were in arrears was becoming a source of major concern to Congress.

Some of these complaints were met in 1820 when Congress abolished the credit system for all future sales, showed leniency in extending the time for outstanding payments, reduced the base price of land to $1.25 an acre, and made the smallest tract that could be sold eighty acres. Left unsatisfied, however, was the desire of thousands of actual settlers to be privileged to roam over the public lands to select whatever land they wished, and to improve and live upon it for a number of years before they would be compelled to purchase it. Moreover, they wished to be entitled to buy at the minimum price without having to worry about speculators forestalling them. This preferential right, called preemption, had generally existed in the southern colonies, and when Virginians and North Carolinians penetrated into Ohio or Alabama they expected to enjoy the same right there.

In the absence of this preferential right, westerners devised a system that gave them some protection against large capitalistic speculators. They organized claim associations of all the squatters on land announced for public sale, massed their strength at the sale, and intimidated speculators from bidding against them. The CLAIM ASSOCIATION existed on all frontiers throughout most of the nineteenth century as an extralegal device, so far as federal land law was concerned, but it was recognized and actually sanctioned by state and territorial laws and generally succeeded in preventing competition where settlers' claims were involved. However, like most of the land laws, the claim associations became subject to abuse, sooner or later, being used by petty capitalists to select and hold small tracts they could sell to later settlers at a nice profit without any investment. But settlement upon public lands before the public auction was illegal, and troops were sometimes used to eject intruders. Congress time after time was asked for and did enact limited measures that forgave intrusions and granted settlers already on public land in specified areas the right of preemption, but the West wanted a general and prospective preemption measure that would sanction squatting anywhere on surveyed public lands. It was over this question that Henry Clay destroyed much of his potential western support by the bitterness with which he opposed preemption and the sharpness of his criticisms of squatters. In 1841 the West won prospective preemption on surveyed lands and in the 1850s had its victory extended to apply to unsurveyed lands.

Victory with preemption only whetted the appetite of western land reformers. Their major animus was the large capitalist speculators who roamed the West looking for lands, not to develop or even rent, but to purchase and hold until they had appreciated in value and could be sold at a large profit. In the years just preceding 1819 and 1837, many millions of acres of land were bought and withheld from development, becoming "speculators' deserts." Would-be settlers coming into such areas had to bypass them and spread more widely over the frontier. It was the speculators' purchases that induced the government to hasten its surveys until it had surveyed and offered at public sale huge areas in which settlement remained thin. As the surveyors moved farther west, they left behind not only the "speculators' deserts" but also millions of acres of less attractive lands, which settlers would pass by in their search for those more promising. The LAND REFORM MOVEMENT wished the government to curb speculative purchasing by reserving the public lands for actual settlers and reducing the minimum price, especially for those areas passed over by earlier waves of settlers. Finally, land reformers were coming to believe that the costs and burdens of farm making, whether in the timbered areas of southern Indiana, the canebrakes of Louisiana, or the prairies of Illinois and Iowa, were so great that wild and unimproved land on the frontier had no value and should be given to the actual farm maker as a reward for his part in making America.

In 1854 Thomas Hart BENTON, senator from Missouri, a state in which the greatest amount of land had been available for sale for many years without success, got Congress to adopt the graduation measure. It reduced the price of land in proportion to the length of time it had been on the market, the lowest price being twelve and a half cents an acre. Eight years later the HOMESTEAD ACT, which had been taken up by the Republican party, was passed with its promise of 160 acres of public lands free to any person who would settle upon and develop it for five years, the only cost to him being modest fees. Revenue, however, as a basic policy, was not abandoned; lands continued to be sold to speculators, lumbermen, and other groups.

When carefully considered it will be realized that the victory of the West in gaining free homesteads in 1862 was something less than complete. No legal obstacles

were placed in the path of the land speculator, as reformers had wished. Also at the time the act was adopted, Congress was giving away huge grants of land to aid in the construction of railroads, which soon amounted to 174 million acres. It was also giving to the states a total of 72 million acres of the PUBLIC DOMAIN for agricultural COLLEGES AND UNIVERSITIES, as well as for other public institutions and buildings, and was moving toward the allotment of Indian reservations, a policy that would ultimately transfer 75 million acres to private ownership through sales by the allottees. None of the land so granted or allotted would come within the Homestead Act.

The Homestead Act was passed at the time when settlement was approaching the less humid areas of the Great Plains, where more than 160 acres might be required for a profitable economic unit. By entering a preemption claim settlers could acquire an additional 160 acres. After 1873 they could acquire a third 160-acre tract by fulfilling the requirements of the TIMBER CULTURE ACT: setting out trees on 40 acres (later reduced to 10 acres) and maintaining the improvement for ten years. Next came the Desert Land Act of 1877, whereby individuals could acquire 640 acres of desert land for a small sum if they could show that they had improved it by conducting water to it for irrigation. These new laws gave the land system more flexibility and adapted it to the drier regions, but at the same time they became subject to gross abuse by the cattlemen, lumbermen, speculators, and, indeed, by the settlers who were as willing to take advantage of the loopholes in the laws as were other interests. It was easy for men with some capital to employ others as dummy entrymen, who would then make entries under these laws under the guise of creating farms, commute their homesteads to a cash entry or preempt the tracts as soon as the law allowed, and then transfer the land to their employers.

Notwithstanding the abuse of the public land laws, the census figures show that actual farm makers in the new West were acquiring ownership of land, and it is clear that the Homestead Act was a major factor in achieving that objective. The great giveaway, a term that some have applied to the law, contributed more than anything else to making the area to which it applied a region in which small owner-operated farms existed as well as large cattle ranches.

Meantime, the land-grant railroads with their vast areas needing settlers had succeeded through their extensive advertising in drawing westward a flood of land-seekers who were swiftly transforming the western third of America, creating new commonwealths, and bringing to an end the American frontier. In contemplating these changes, the CONSERVATION MOVEMENT was asking questions about traditional policies that had permitted the timber, mineral, and ranching resources of the country to pass into "monopolistic" hands and to be despoiled in the process of exploitation for the benefit of a few men. What of the future, when these resources would approach exhaustion? Should consideration be given to the unique and superlative beautiful natural phenomena in Yellowstone, Yosemite, and Grand Canyon? In the 1870s voices were raised in behalf of retaining public ownership of such scenic spots and also great forest areas for future generations. Carl SCHURZ, secretary of the Department of the INTERIOR under President

Rutherford B. Hayes, was familiar with what European governments had done to preserve and develop their natural resources. He called for the preservation of whole sections of the redwoods of the California coast and the giant sequoias of the Sierra Nevada.

In 1872 Congress withdrew two million acres of public lands for the first national park at Yellowstone. Seven years later it authorized the appointment of a Public Land Commission (the first of three ultimately to be created), which was to report on a system of classifying the public lands; to propose a new procedure for surveying the public lands to replace the existing one, which was poorly adapted to the mountain region; and to make plans for future disposal and protection of the public lands. The commission was loath to recommend the legislative action that the testimony presented to it in western meetings seemed to call for, and aside from the publication of Thomas C. Donaldson's huge *The Public Domain*, with its great collection of land data, it achieved little. President Grover Cleveland's commissioners of the General Land Office were well in advance both of Congress and of the land commission in recommending administrative reforms that might have eliminated or at least reduced corruption on the part of local land officers and perhaps the influence of lobbyists in the Washington office. Carl Schurz even earlier had fought hard to prevent the widespread timber plundering on public lands and to get Congress to appropriate funds for the appointment of a sufficient number of timber agents to bring indictments against the thieves. Congress did not respond to the early conservationists' warning about the rapid depletion of the standing forest cover; in fact, Congress denounced the timber agents for persecuting men "trying to make an honest dollar." By 1891, however, public opinion made itself felt sufficiently that Congress was persuaded to authorize the president to withdraw forest lands from purchase by private interests. This was the beginning of the national forest policy, which since has led to the creation of the United States Forest Service, one of the great administrative agencies protecting and utilizing along scientific lines the resources under its jurisdiction. At about the same time, Mount Rainier, Yosemite, Kings Canyon, and Sequoia national parks were created out of the public lands. Conservation seemed to have made considerable progress by the close of the century, but the public forests were still being plundered, rangelands were being overgrazed, and many areas of superlative natural beauty were being despoiled.

See Paul W. Gates, *History of Public Land Law Development* (1968), and *Landlords and Tenants on the Prairie Frontier* (1973); and John Ise, *Our National Park Policy* (1961).—P. W. G.

land reform movement. At the close of the American Revolution the United States was faced with a heavy war debt, no direct taxing power, and disinclination on the part of the individual states to honor the requisitions for funds made upon them by the central government. In this plight it was natural for the government to look upon the public lands of the West, which England had surrendered to it and over which the individual states were ceding their claims, as a potential source of revenue. In the Land Ordinance of 1785 and subsequent legislation, the public lands were pledged for the payment of the debts, and sale of these lands for the purpose of raising revenue was established as the basic feature of public land policy. This was quite in contrast to the earlier land distribution policies of most of the colonies with their headrights and free grants.

Though the pledge may have strengthened the government's credit, the lands did not become an important source of revenue for many years, yielding less than ten percent of the government's annual receipts until 1817, after which they rose to twelve and thirteen percent in 1819. Revenues from the lands then declined to less than ten percent of the government's income until the middle 1830s when sales boomed, raising land revenues to forty-eight percent of the nation's income by 1836. Thereafter they fell away rapidly and never again were to be a truly important source of revenue. By that time the government debt had been retired and the need for revenue could no longer be used as an excuse for a high land price, though people who preferred to hold the public land for a high price to deter the movement of population from the East to the West thought otherwise. Henry Clay had yet another motive for keeping up the price of western lands, and that was to assure a treasury surplus that might be distributed among the states on the basis of their population, a plan the older states warmly approved.

It was at this time that the land, or national, reform movement got under way. It was based on the doctrine of natural rights: man's right to life, with its corollary the right to land as the basis of his living. From this basic proposition it followed that there should be no monopoly in land, that all should be able to obtain it in farm-sized units, and that these homesteads should not be subject to foreclosure for debt. George Henry Evans, a leader in the labor movement, argued that free land in the West would draw off surplus labor from the cities and improve the bargaining power of employees. Evans' SAFETY VALVE THEORY was pure agrarianism, owing much to Tom Paine and Thomas Jefferson. It called for free land in small tracts for the actual settler, limitation on the amount of land individuals could acquire or own, and exemption of the worker's household from debt collection.

National, or land, reform was preached widely in the *Working Man's Advocate* and in other journals and tracts read by workingmen, and was sufficiently attractive as an ameliorative program promising to improve their lot to win the acceptance and full support of Horace Greeley. It was not socialistic but sprang from doctrines Americans had early espoused. It promised to rid the eastern cities of their redundant population, to elevate the condition of the workingmen, and to bring about the development of commonwealths of landowners in the new western states.

Greeley's conversion to land reform was Evans' chief success, for as time passed it became clear that the eastern workingmen and their journals were not having much effect upon public opinion or upon the representatives of the older states. Only when the West took up the cry for free land was there hope for its adoption. Greeley, soon to become America's most influential editor, had in 1841 established the *New York Tribune*—a combination of two earlier papers he had edited. At first he was drawn to Fourierism, whose adherents advocated the creation of communal societies, but he came to see its weaknesses and in its place advocated land reform as the panacea for labor's problems. To the public land states of the upper Mississippi valley—Illinois, Wisconsin, and Iowa, and later Kansas, Colorado, and California—and to their settlers, towns, railroads, and government institutions, he gave an inordinate amount of space, while neglecting significant developments in the older states. His concern for the welfare of the growing West became second only to the many problems of his own city. It was this wide coverage which the *Tribune* gave to the West and its problems, combined with Greeley's advocacy of free lands and later his opposition to the extension of slavery in the territories, that made his paper the most widely circulated outside its immediate environment. Equally important, it was the *Tribune* that greatly increased western support for free lands.

Donations of land to settlers on the frontier had been advocated by some members of Congress well before Evans' national reform brought the issue more concretely to the fore. Between 1842 and 1854 free grants were offered in more remote territories, but the areas that were most attractive to settlers, like Kansas and California, were denied this boon. National reformers were not interested in directing settlers to out-of-the-way places or to slave territory but wished public lands to be made free in those regions offering the most to settlers: Illinois, Wisconsin, Iowa, and, a few years later, Minnesota and Kansas. That land reform was gaining ground was shown by the emergence of the FREE-SOIL PARTY of 1848, which declared for free land, and even more by the Free-Soil Democrats of 1852, who called for free land and the withholding of the public lands from corporations and speculators.

In the 1850s land reformers were more concerned with halting the growing "monopolization" of the public lands by railroad companies, which had received large grants to aid in the building of state and intersectional railroads, and by speculators. Individual speculators and land companies had acquired many millions of acres of public lands in the booming days of the middle 1830s and were operating on an even larger scale in the 1850s. Some of these large purchasers were developing their lands with hired hands or tenants and were not simply withholding their lands for resale at a profit, but land reformers were almost as much opposed to BONANZA FARMING done by armies of laborers or tenants as they were to undeveloped absentee ownerships. Greeley and his land reform followers, and Evans before him, wanted safeguards to prevent further "land monopolization" and development of landlord estates, and were convinced that limitation of ownership was most important—as was freedom of small homesteads from foreclosure for debt.

Southern hostility to the growth of free-soil areas delayed the adoption of a homestead act of any kind for a time. When, however, the southern congressmen and senators withdrew from Congress in 1861 they enabled the North to adopt such a measure. The North was now well convinced that free land—without the emphasis on natural rights, without the inalienability clause, and without restricting further acquisitions by corporations, land companies, and individual speculators—was both safe and conservative for all interests. The HOMESTEAD ACT of 1862 was not national reform, but at least it held

out the possibility of ownership to every adult citizen or person intending to become a citizen of a quarter section of land after five years of residence upon it and the making of certain minimum improvements. Carelessly framed and poorly administered, the Homestead Act permitted the accumulation of large ownerships through the use of dummy entrymen and the clause allowing outright purchase of homesteads after six months with cash. Yet, in spite of such abuses of the law, the measure was most important in the development of owner-operated farms in the Middle West and far western states.

After free homesteads were made available, land reformers continued to work for preserving the remaining public lands for actual settlers only. They induced Congress to close southern public lands to all but homesteaders; obtained settler clauses in the last of the railroad land-grant measures requiring that the railroad land be sold only to settlers in small tracts at $2.50 an acre; got further grants to railroad corporations halted in 1871; and began a movement demanding forfeiture of unearned grants and grants whose conditions had not been fulfilled which led to several forfeitures and in 1890 to a general act requiring the forfeiture of all unearned grants. William A. J. Sparks, the only settler-oriented land commissioner (1885-87), succeeded in returning to entry many millions of acres which had been withdrawn from homesteaders for years while waiting for companies to which they had been promised to earn them. The reformers reached their greatest strength in 1888-91 when they reenacted the southern Homestead Act, which had been repealed in 1876; ended unlimited purchase; made 320 acres the maximum that individuals could acquire under all United States laws; repealed the Preemption and Timber Culture acts, which had become subject to extensive abuses; and placed additional safeguards in other measures to prevent land accumulation by individuals and companies. Two twentieth-century measures reflected the antimonopoly views of land reformers: the NEWLANDS RECLAMATION ACT of 1902, which provided that water from federally sponsored projects should be made available to farmers for only 160 acres, no matter how much more they owned and might wish to irrigate; and the recovery by judicial process of the remaining 2,891,000 acres of the richly timbered Oregon and California grant for failure of the railroad company to sell them in small tracts as the law required.

After 1890 a new type of reformer calling himself a conservationist (see CONSERVATION MOVEMENT) looked toward the preservation of the remaining public lands for scientific management of the forests; controlled and efficient use of the minerals; development of highly scenic and recreational areas for national parks; and the halting of destructive overgrazing on the livestock ranges, which had reduced their carrying capacity and caused the silting of reservoirs and irrigation ditches and had endangered public water supplies.

See Benjamin H. Hibbard, *History of the Public Land Policies* (1941); and Helene S. Zahler, *Eastern Workingmen and National Land Policy, 1829-1862* (1941). —P. W. G.

land surveys. In the Land Ordinance of 1785, which set forth the fundamental principles of the American land system, the Congress of the Confederation provided for the survey of public lands before settlement was to be permitted on them—a feature borrowed from the land systems of the New England states. A base line was to be run west from the Pennsylvania-Ohio border. North and south of that line, ranges of townships six miles square were to be laid out. The boundary between Ohio and Pennsylvania was to be the north-south meridian. Thus the first township north of the base line and west of the boundary, or meridian, was township one north, range one west, and that south of the base line was township one south, range one west. New meridians (altogether thirty-four) and base lines were established as the surveys were extended into new territories. The ordinance, as subsequently amended, provided that each township was to be divided into thirty-six sections of one square mile, each of which was to be numbered from one to thirty-six in a prescribed pattern. As later provided, each section was to be divided into quarter sections and quarter quarter tracts of forty acres, the smallest unit of sale except for town lots. Thus, the northeast quarter of the northeast quarter of section six in township one north, range one east of the third principal meridian could be easily identified with no other location given.

Surveying was done on a contract basis under the surveyors general, who were appointed usually to cover one or two states. Payments for surveying ranged from two to sixteen dollars per linear mile depending on the nature of the terrain. The right to appoint their own staff and to award surveying contracts gave the surveyors general much patronage to dispense, and as a result such jobs were much sought. Political henchmen and business associates were favored, and surveys were frequently poorly or fraudulently done. Complaints that lines did not meet and that corners had been improperly or inadequately marked with wooden stakes or mere blazes on trees forced the General Land Office to maintain a staff of inspectors to examine both the reports and the surveys in the field and frequently to withhold compensation, and, if payment had already been made, to sue for recovery on the bonds surveyors were required to give.

Surveying in wooded areas was best done in the winter, when the leaves were off the trees, and least satisfactorily during the spring thaw. Dangers from lurking Indians, wild animals, and mosquitoes carrying malarial germs, and the burden of transporting equipment and supplies through the trackless wilderness, made surveying a difficult and at times a dangerous task. It was not uncommon for surveyors to default on their contracts when their compensation proved inadequate to cover costs, especially in the higher mountain areas and when floods, sickness, and Indian troubles delayed the completion of their tasks. Surveyors in the pineries of the lake states and in the redwood and Douglas fir lands of the Pacific Coast states who kept careful notes of sections that were heavily covered with valuable trees could sell those notes to lumbermen for substantial gratuities.

The original surveyor records descriptive of the forest and grass cover, possible minerals, drainage, streams, and soil quality, now in the National Archives, are valuable to students of ecology and have been used extensively by land appraisers in determining the value of land cessions made by the Indians well before white settlers reached their country.

The great compilation of information relating to the public lands and their surveys, Thomas C. Donaldson's *The Public Domain* (1884), contains a surveyor's plat of a Utah township with descriptions of types of land, many pages of detailed notes kept by the surveyors, a list of all surveyors' general offices to 1884, and the instructions sent out to all surveyors.—P. W. G.

land system, southern. The southern land system might well be called no system at all. Its genesis is to be found in the feudal or parish and manorial systems of England, and partly in the nature of the country into which land claimants entered early in the seventeenth century. Boundaries to claims were established on the basis of "metes and bounds." This meant that no established pattern of survey was followed. Land claimants began their boundaries at such landmarks as a tree, a large rock, a certain place in a stream, or along a road or trail. By 1730 expansion into the western country gained momentum, and by 1750 speculative fever was high. Lacking an official colonial plan of survey of the new lands, every claimant, large or small, was left free to establish his own boundaries.

By the outbreak of the American Revolution the western land system south of the Ohio River was in hopeless chaos. In 1778 and again in 1779 the Virginia assembly enacted laws designed to bring some order out of the confusion. The law of 1779 created a land court or board of commissioners and provided that prior claimants could establish their ownership if they had built a cabin and planted a patch of corn prior to January 1, 1778. Beyond this the claimant had either to meet with the land commissioners and verify his claim and have it registered in the certificate book, or secure a warrant and register the warrant with the county clerk at the time he produced a surveyor's plat. The result was wholesale overlapping, conflicting claims, and endless litigation. As a specific instance, a great majority of the first cases brought before the Kentucky Court of Appeals after 1792 had to do with land disputes. This same condition prevailed in eastern Tennessee, to a large measure in the Piedmont area of North and South Carolina, in western Virginia, and even in the Virginia revolutionary lands area of Ohio.

There were constantly before several of the legislatures demands for revisions of land laws that would disentangle the snarls that had been developed. Because of the carelessness with which surveyors and landowners marked their boundary lines, and the wanton destruction of landmark trees, stones, and other objects, land-ownership problems continued to multiply. In 1792 Virginia transferred Kentucky District land records to the state government of Kentucky. Kentucky then began a process of registration and revision of land laws. Between 1816 and 1873 it issued its own land warrants in attempts to cede all the open lands to private ownership. In the meantime, the general assembly enacted at least three adverse possession laws, attempted to speed up by legislation the making of decisions in disputed land cases, and tried to strengthen occupancy laws. This led to the classic case of *Green* v. *Biddle* in 1824, in which official Kentucky to all intents and purposes ignored a decision of the United States Supreme Court in a land dispute case.

Both historians and land lawyers have regarded the Virginia land law of 1779 as a calamitous one. Instead of establishing an orderly system of land surveys and land registry, it simply opened the West to irresponsible exploitation by yeoman claimants and large land speculators. Even the "cabin and corn patch" evidence was either faked or based on the flimsiest kind of conformity with the intent of the law. Because of the terms of the Virginia law and the requirement of registry, many of the earliest pioneers lost the lands on which they settled. Perhaps the most important effects of this chaotic condition were the formulation of the rectilinear system of the Ordinance of 1785, and the forcing of emigration farther westward to escape the woes of confused land claims in the older settlements of Kentucky, West Virginia, and eastern Tennessee.

See Thomas Perkins Abernethy, *Western Lands and the American Revolution* (1959); Willard Rouse Jillson, *The Kentucky Land Grants*, 2 vols. (1925); Humphrey Marshall, *The History of Kentucky*, 2 vols. (1824); and Samuel M. Wilson, *The First Land Court of Kentucky, 1779-1780* (1923).—T. D. C.

Lane, James Henry (1814-1866). Kansas politician. Lane, one of the outstanding political leaders of the territory and early state of Kansas, settled near Lawrence in 1855. His birth in Indiana Territory, his political education there, his service as a commanding officer of two Indiana volunteer regiments in the Mexican War, and his election on the Democratic ticket as lieutenant governor of Indiana (1849-53) and as a member of Congress (1853-55) were unusual credentials for his career on the Kansas frontier.

Lane was a flamboyant, energetic, tireless, magnetic personality, whose oratory could sway any audience. He was tall, lean, unkempt in clothes and appearance, an impressive figure in frontier political activities. Purportedly he went to Kansas Territory to help organize the Democratic party, but he soon gravitated to the antislavery cause, helped to establish the Free-State party, and became a dynamic leader. A perennial opponent of Charles Robinson, he nonetheless worked closely with that emigrant-aid leader in defense of Lawrence and in promoting free-state causes. Lane was chairman of the Topeka constitutional convention, which was sponsored by his party, and formed free-state military forces throughout the territory. In 1858 in a feud over a land claim, Lane killed a neighbor and retired temporarily from politics.

When Kansas became a state in 1861, Lane, by then a Republican, was elected to the United States Senate. He arrived in Washington just as the Civil War began and organized a "Frontier Guard" to protect the White House; thus an intimate friendship developed with President Lincoln. While senator, he was appointed a brigadier general of volunteers. This led Governor Robinson to appoint a new senator, on the grounds that Lane had given up his elective office. Lane used his influence to discredit Robinson, who was not reelected. In Washington, Lane favored emancipation of slaves and westward expansion by supporting the homestead and railroad bills. He strongly backed Lincoln and was the chief Kansas spokesman for Lincoln in the 1864 election. At the end of the war, Lane supported the reconstruction programs of Lincoln and President Andrew Johnson and deserted the radical Republican

plans. Many Kansans responded harshly to Lane's conservatism and in despondency he shot himself on July 1, 1866, and died ten days later. Ever a controversial figure and agitator, Lane was a devoted Kansan, and Kansans of his day loved him.

See John Speer, *Life of Gen. James H. Lane* (1896); and Wendell H. Stephenson, "The Political Career of General James H. Lane," *Kansas State Historical Society Publications*, vol. 3 (1930).—H. E. S.

Lane, Joseph (1801-1881). Oregon politician. Lane was born in North Carolina. Beginning his career as a Democrat in Indiana, Lane was first elected to that state's lower house in 1822; he served in its senate from 1844 to 1846. Following service in the Mexican War, during which he was brevetted major general, he was sent by President Polk to Oregon Territory to be governor, where he became the linchpin of the early Oregon Democratic party.

In 1850 Lane won the friendship and respect of Oregonians by courageously subduing an angry group of Rogue River Indians without violence. In 1853 he led in the making of the Treaty of Table Rock with the same tribe. When Samuel R. Thurston died in 1851, Lane was elected the territory's second delegate to Congress, a position to which he was repeatedly reelected until Oregon statehood in 1859.

While Asahel Bush puffed and touted Lane in the influential *Oregon Statesman* and held county Democrats in line, Lane saw to it that federal patronage was awarded as the party directed. This balance of interests and loyalties, precarious even in quiet times, withstood neither the national havoc of the 1850s nor the clash of Lane's personal ambitions with those of Bush supporters. Local discipline and organization was so good and Lane was so popular that Democrats demanded more patronage and more reward for Lane's repeated success at the polls than his large electoral majorities required him to give. Boosted for the presidency by Indiana's Democrats in 1852 and by Bush in 1856, Lane was a national personage. A man more consistent than logical and more pro-southern than Oregon Democrats could tolerate in principle or policy, Lane ran for vice-president on the Breckenridge ticket in 1860. This completed the rift in the local Democratic party between the Bush and Lane factions and brought to an end both Lane's political career and the Democratic party in Oregon.

Lane, once the most popular of Oregonians, returned from the East in 1859. Instead of the smiles and fanfare he had grown used to upon his arrival from Washington, D.C., he was greeted by silence. His former friends deserted him. Lane spent the rest of his days as a farmer and died a hermit.

Collections of the Lane papers are on deposit at the Oregon Historical Society, Portland, and in the Lilly Library, R. S. Ellison Collection, Indiana University, Bloomington. Much has been written about Lane, of which James E. Hendrickson, *Joe Lane of Oregon* (1967), is the most recent monograph.—R. J. L.

Langer, William (1886-1959). North Dakota politician. Born on a farm near Casselton, North Dakota, Langer graduated from the University of North Dakota Law School and from Columbia University. He began his political career in 1914 as a state attorney in Morton County, where by fighting the bootleggers and the

Northern Pacific Railroad he became a controversial figure. In 1916 he became attorney general on the Non-partisan League ticket. For political reasons he turned against the league in 1919 and was defeated for governor in the 1920 primary.

During the 1920s Langer practiced law and laid the groundwork for a political machine. His years of waiting paid off in 1932, when North Dakotans elected him governor. He pursued a daring, aggressive course to fight the depression, using his authority as governor to stop foreclosures on farms and placing embargoes on wheat in an attempt to raise the price. In July 1934 he was removed from office because he was convicted on charges of soliciting and collecting money for political purposes from federal employees; he was later vindicated. In 1936 he was again elected governor and in 1938 attempted to unseat veteran senator Gerald P. NYE.

In 1940 Langer was elected to the United States Senate, where he served until 1959. An isolationist, he voted against the United Nations, the Marshall Plan, the North Atlantic Treaty Organization, and all foreign-aid bills. He continually called for a reordering of priorities that would strengthen domestic programs. Extremely popular in North Dakota, Langer was reelected in 1958 without campaigning in the state.

The William Langer papers are in the Orin G. Libby Manuscript Collection at the University of North Dakota.—D. J. T.

Langlade, Charles Michel (1729-1801). Wisconsin fur trader and Indian military leader. Langlade was born in Mackinac, Michigan. His father was a fur trader of French extraction, and his mother was of the Ottawa tribe. Educated by Jesuit missionaries, he held military office under French, English, and American governments. With his father, he founded a fur post at Green Bay about 1745. He led the western tribes at Braddock's defeat in 1755, and at Crown Point, Lake Champlain, and Quebec in the French and Indian War; and he supported the British in the American Revolution. He was pensioned by the British and given a land grant for his service "in 99 battles," according to him, and spent most of his days at Green Bay after 1764. By founding and settling that post, he has some claim to the title of "father of Wisconsin." A Wisconsin county is named in his honor.

See Louise P. Kellogg, *The French Regime in Wisconsin and the Northwest* (1925).—W. D. W.

languages. See BLACK ENGLISH; CHINOOK JARGON; ENGLISH LANGUAGE AND THE WESTWARD MOVEMENT; FRENCH DIALECTS IN THE MISSISSIPPI VALLEY; HAWAIIAN PIDGIN ENGLISH; INDIAN LANGUAGES; PENNSYLVANIA GERMAN; and SPANISH LANGUAGE IN THE SOUTHWEST.

La Paz, Arizona. See GILA CITY, ARIZONA.

Larkin, Thomas Oliver (1802-1858). United States consul in Mexican California. A Massachusetts Yankee, Larkin settled in California in 1832 and became the most important merchant in Monterey. His were the first children born in California whose parents were both from the United States. He became consul in 1844 and filled his official reports with suspicions of British designs on California based on rumors that he mistakenly believed to be true. In October 1845 Secretary of State James Buchanan gave him an additional appointment as "confidential agent" with instructions to work

for a peaceful secession of California from Mexico and its adherence to the United States. This would probably have been accomplished had it not been forestalled by the filibustering activities of John C. FREMONT, the BEAR FLAG REBELLION, and the outbreak of the Mexican War.

The Larkin Papers, George P. Hammond, ed., 10 vols. (1951-64), forms an important source not only on Larkin but also on the history of California in the Mexican and early American periods.—W. B.

Larpenteur, Charles (1807-1872). Fur trader and memoirist. Born near Fontainebleau, France, Larpenteur migrated with his family to the United States in 1818 and settled on a Maryland farm. He then moved on to Missouri, working as an overseer for famous Indian agent Major Benjamin O'Fallon.

Although the fur trade had already reached its peak by 1833, the small, wiry Frenchman was so determined to pursue a career in it that he went as a laborer with William Sublette and Robert Campbell on their annual expedition. At the 1833 rendezvous Larpenteur found himself tending bar in the whiskey tent. From the Green River he and Smith and Campbell moved north to the Yellowstone to build Fort William almost in the shadow of Fort Union, bastion of the American Fur Company. After a winter of cutthroat competition for furs and buffalo robes, his employers sold out to the American Fur Company—much to Larpenteur's disgust. Kenneth McKenzie, Fort Union's able factor, spotted the hardworking, lively, and intelligent Larpenteur and appointed him clerk and trader. For nearly a decade Larpenteur worked tirelessly for the company. In addition to his fort duties he made dangerous winter trips, some of them into Saskatchewan, to Indian camps, in order to beat his competitors to the furs. When the company failed to give him a post of his own, Larpenteur tried to establish his own post in the Flathead country. Delays and the unusually harsh winter of 1848-49 frustrated his efforts, however, and he suffered a minor breakdown and returned east for a year.

Larpenteur's movements in the next two decades echo the desperate search for new furs as the business went into decline. He took charge of the old Vermillion, South Dakota, fur post in 1850, but trade was so poor he gave it up and in 1852 took over Peter Sarpy's post on the Niobrara River, also to no avail. Then he settled on an Iowa farm but stayed there only briefly, for trading was in Larpenteur's blood. In 1859 he returned to the Missouri to take charge of Fort Stewart, located some thirty-five miles above Fort Union. Later he joined other traders erecting a post at Fort Berthold, North Dakota, and a second on the Poplar River in Assiniboine country. In furnishing these posts he broke with tradition by hauling his goods in carts nine hundred miles overland from St. Paul, Minnesota. But again bad luck and harsh weather crippled his enterprises. He then agreed to work for LaBarge, Harkness and Company at its Fort Galpin post, but both he and his Indian clients nearly starved so scarce were both food and furs.

Larpenteur realized a long ambition of sorts in 1864, when the army and the American Fur Company placed him in charge of Fort Union to handle the supplies sent there for General Alfred Sully's campaign against the warring Sioux. After Fort Union was sold and the army had built Fort Buford, he ran a successful store nearby, until a new federal law prohibited private traders at an army post. He then returned to Iowa to farm. There he completed his valuable journal, *Forty Years a Fur Trader on the Upper Missouri: The Personal Narrative of Charles Larpenteur, 1833-1872* (1898), one of the best firsthand accounts of the business side of the fur trade, for Larpenteur was observant, literate, and accurate. His descriptions of the 1837 smallpox epidemic and the wild sprees that ensued when a cask of whiskey was broached at an Indian camp are unforgettable.

Larpenteur's life was marked by personal tragedy. His first two wives, both Indians, died, the first in the Fort Union smallpox epidemic and the second at the hands of raiding Omaha, who mistook her for a Sioux. Seven of his children also died early. His third wife, Rebecca Bingham, apparently survived him.

Larpenteur's journal is available in two editions, one edited by Elliot Couesin 1898 and a second by Milo M. Quaife in 1933. See also Louis Pfaller, "Charles Larpenteur," in LeRoy R. Hafen, ed., *The Mountain Men and the Fur Trade of the Far West*, vol. I (1965).—G. B. D.

Larrazolo, Octaviano A[mbrosio] (1859-1930). New Mexican politician. Larrazolo was born at Allende, Chihuahua, Mexico. Until 1870, when he accompanied Bishop Jean Baptiste Salpointe to Tucson, Larrazolo lived in Mexico. When Salpointe in 1875 became archbishop of Santa Fe, he was again accompanied by the young Larrazolo. He first planned to enter the priesthood but later turned to the study of law. Larrazolo briefly taught in Tucson and was from 1879 to 1884 a high school principal in El Paso County, Texas. While there he was admitted to the bar and twice elected district attorney for western Texas. In January 1895 he returned to New Mexico to open a law office.

Larrazolo was an unsuccessful Democratic candidate for delegate to Congress in 1900, 1906, and 1908, but in the last two elections he lost by only a few hundred votes. Although not an official delegate to the New Mexico constitutional convention in 1910, he championed the rights of Mexican-American citizens and was instrumental in having safeguards against disfranchisement and discrimination written into the state constitution. Thereafter he actively campaigned for the election of Mexican-Americans to state offices.

In 1911, stating that the Democratic party had not given a significant place to native citizens in strongly Democratic counties of New Mexico, Larrazolo became a Republican. That fall he nominated a Spanish-American for governor at the Republican convention, but his candidate did not carry the convention. In 1918, as a Republican, Larrazolo was elected governor of New Mexico, the first person born in Mexico to serve as a governor in the United States. He was the second, and to date last, Spanish-American governor of New Mexico. During his term he advocated federal aid to farmers and stockmen. Although Larrazolo was not renominated in 1920, he remained active in politics and was nominated in 1924 for justice of the state supreme court. Defeated for the court, he was elected in 1928 to the United States Senate, where he served only briefly before his death in Albuquerque.

See references in R. E. Twitchell, *The Leading Facts of New Mexican History* (1912).—J. R. V.

Larson, T. A. (1910-   ). Historian. Born in Wakefield, Nebraska, Larson attended the University of Colorado, the University of Chicago, and the University of Illinois. In 1936 he joined the history department at the University of Wyoming, where he taught for more than thirty-five years. During World II he served in the navy and in 1950-51 was a visiting professor at Columbia University.

Much of Larson's interest was devoted to the history of Wyoming. In 1954 appeared his *Wyoming's War Years, 1941-1945*, a competent narrative based largely on contemporary newspapers. Meanwhile, Larson was engaged on a comprehensive history of the state and wrote his *History of Wyoming* (1965), one of the best one-volume surveys available at the time. He also edited *Bill Nye's Western Humor* (1968), which includes some of the best examples of Nye's yarns. In his later career Larson became increasingly interested in the history of women in the West and authored "Dolls, Vassals and Drudges—Pioneer Women in the West," *Western Historical Quarterly* (January 1972).

During 1970-71 Larson was president of the Western History Association.—G. D. N.

La Salle, René Robert Cavelier, Sieur de (1643-1687). Explorer. René Robert Cavelier, known as La Salle from his family name, was born in Rouen, a town in Normandy. He received a good education from the Jesuits, but being very independent and strong-willed, did not choose to become one of their number. Instead he sailed for Canada and in 1666, at the age of twenty-three, received a seigneury (a grant of land) through family connections. In the next three years he mastered the Iroquois and Algonquian dialects. Then in 1669 he began his explorations, probably discovering the Ohio and possibly the Illinois by the year 1673.

In 1674 La Salle returned to France, where he won royal esteem as well as financial backing. Returning to North America, he built Fort Frontenac, near present Kingston, Ontario. He had trouble with his creditors and rivals, however, and was in France once again in 1677. This time he received from the king a royal patent to explore and occupy the Mississippi country, which was deemed to be close to Mexico and the wealthy silver mines there.

From his return in 1678 until his death, La Salle was concerned with his business interests in the Mississippi fur trade. He demonstrated the feasibility of using sailing vessels on the Great Lakes by using the forty-five-ton vessel *Griffin* on those waters (see TRANSPORTATION ON THE GREAT LAKES). Leaving his fur business in the hands of his subordinates, he and his men pushed into the Illinois country in January 1680. Hardships and business reverses continued to plague him, but finally, in April 1682, La Salle reached the mouth of the Mississippi and christened the entire valley Louisiana in honor of his king. Returning upstream, he built Fort St. Louis near present Ottawa, Illinois.

A last trip to France in 1683 resulted in La Salle's final expedition. He led colonists by water to Matagorda Bay, where he erected Fort St. Louis of Texas. After two unfortunate years there, he and some of his men started for the Illinois country for supplies. The men were dejected and in a starving condition, while La Salle's actions had assumed psychotic qualities. Somewhere in east Texas he was murdered by his own men.

A new and definitive biography of La Salle is much needed, but it could never surpass the literary qualities of Francis Parkman, *La Salle and the Discovery of the*

Great West (1910). See also E. B. Osler, *La Salle* (1967).
—R. A. B.

Lassen Volcanic National Park. Lassen Volcanic National Park is a relatively small park (106,934 acres) in nothern California, near Redding. It is characterized by a remarkable variety of volcanic formations, including sulfur springs, steam vents, mud pots, cinder cones, lava flows, and an active volcano, Lassen Peak (10,457 feet). The park was established by Congress on August 9, 1916, shortly after a spectacular eruption of Lassen Peak. Clouds of steam and cinders could be seen as far away as Sacramento, California, about 150 miles to the south. The symmetrical Cinder Cone, the Painted Dunes, and the black lava field in the northeastern corner of the park were used as landmarks by early pioneers crossing the Sierra Nevada into the northern Central Valley of California. At the lower elevations there are beautiful forests of white fir, ponderosa, Jeffrey, and sugar pines. The park contains excellent backcountry trails.—D. C. S.

Las Vegas, Nevada. The name *Las Vegas* (the Meadows) was given to the valley and springs by the Mexicans who used the site as a stop on the Old Spanish Trail. On May 10, 1855, an official mission of the Church of Jesus Christ of Latter-day Saints was sent to Las Vegas under the direction of William Bringhurst. The party arrived at Las Vegas spring on June 14. Although the mission was mainly a religious one, it was hoped that its establishment would provide a rest stop for travel between Salt Lake City and Los Angeles. Attempts by the Mormons to develop a nearby lead mine, the Potosi, led to difficulties and early in 1857 the members of the Las Vegas mission were released from their assignment. The site of the old mission became the O. D. Gass ranch; Gass later sold the property to Archibald Stewart. As in the case of Reno, the completion of a railroad transformed the area into a city. Senator W. A. Clark, while building his railroad from Los Angeles to Salt Lake, had purchased eighteen hundred acres of the Stewart ranch with the intention of developing a division stop at the site. Thus, on May 15, 1905, railroad officials auctioned lots for the new community and Las Vegas, the town, came into being. Las Vegas benefited slightly from the Tonopah-Goldfield boom but its population was just 945 persons in 1910. Completion of Boulder Dam in the early 1930s, the building of the Basic Magnesium plant at Henderson in 1941, and the entrance of the United States into World War II stimulated a tremendous development in southern Nevada, jumping the population from 5,165 in 1930 to 24,624 in 1950. Additional developments in southern Nevada since 1950, including the establishment of the Nevada test site some sixty-five miles northwest of Las Vegas, further stimulated growth. By 1960 Las Vegas had become the population center of Nevada and one of the great entertainment cities of the world. In 1970 its population was listed as 124,161; Clark County, where Las Vegas is located, recorded 270,045 people, and for the first time had more than half of the state's population.

See also GAMBLING, NEVADA.—R. R. E.

Lathrop, [Austin Eugene] "Cap" (1865-1950). Alaska businessman. Lathrop, Alaska's only resident millionaire during the first half of the twentieth century, began his career in construction and transportation—both local drayage and long-distance shipping. He then built his business empire not on the gold, fish, and fur for which Alaska was famous, but on those service industries that made life easier for the remote territory's small population.

Lathrop was born in Lapeer, Michigan, and in 1889, the year of a big fire in Seattle, he established a reconstruction business in that city. From the Panic of 1893 he salvaged only his credit, and with it purchased the 110-foot schooner *L. J. Perry* in 1896. Lathrop and his partner shuttled freight and prospectors up and down Cook Inlet for several years. Soon after the turn of the century, reports of petroleum seepages on the Alaska Peninsula moved Lathrop to begin drilling for oil on the site; the wells were sunk but were capped when new fields were discovered in California and when federal conservationists began to curb exploitation of Alaska's resources. The unsuccessful oil venture was followed by a move to Cordova on Prince William Sound, where Lathrop reentered the drayage business and built a movie theater and an apartment house. As mayor he played a central role in the "Cordova Coal Party" of 1911, in which citizens of the town dumped Canadian coal into the bay to protest federal action preventing the exploitation of local coal resources.

In 1915 Lathrop was in Anchorage, construction headquarters for the new federal Alaska Railroad. The Cordova pattern was repeated: Lathrop established a transfer service and built a movie house and an apartment building. In Fairbanks, the northern terminus of the railroad, he eventually added a bank, a radio station, a newspaper, and a bowling alley to still more movie houses and real-estate investments. He pioneered in the construction of large concrete buildings in the cold interior of Alaska. Earlier, he acquired the Healy River Coal Corporation at Suntrana, south of Fairbanks. The mine produced a soft coal for the local market. It became his special interest in later life.

A strong, active man outdoors and on the job, Lathrop was killed at the age of eighty-four in a mine accident at Suntrana.

See Ernest Gruening, *The State of Alaska* (1954); and J. A. Ray, "Cap Lathrop," *Alaskana* (December 1971).
—M. B. S.

Latter-day Saints. Commonly known by the nickname **Mormons**. The Church of Jesus Christ of Latter-day Saints (LDS) was organized on April 6, 1830, in Fayette, Seneca County, New York State, under the leadership of Joseph Smith, Jr. With headquarters at Salt Lake City, Utah, it has a world membership of four million. Of this number, about forty-five percent are concentrated in the western United States. The LDS church is led by a president who is revered by the membership as "prophet, seer, and revelator." The presidents of the LDS church have been: Joseph SMITH, Jr. (1830-44), Brigham YOUNG (1848-77), John TAYLOR (1880-87), Wilford WOODRUFF (1889-98), Lorenzo Snow (1898-1901), Joseph Fielding SMITH (1901-18), Heber J. GRANT (1918-45), George Albert Smith (1945-51), David O. McKAY (1951-70), Joseph Fielding Smith (1970-72), Harold B. Lee (1972-73), and Spencer W. Kimball (1973-   ).

The organization of the LDS church in 1830 was proclaimed by Joseph Smith as a fulfillment of revelations received by him as early as 1820. In that year, according to his official history, his religious inquiries were answered by a direct revelation: God the Father and his Son, Jesus Christ, appeared to him and commissioned him to be a prophet through whom the true Church of Christ would be restored on the earth. This restoration was necessary, he claimed, because there had been a total apostasy of the church following the deaths of the apostles of Jesus. In a subsequent revelation reportedly given him by an angel named Moroni, Smith was commissioned to translate a history of ancient inhabitants of the western hemisphere, which, he said, was written on plates of gold. Following two years of interruptions, Smith completed his translation in 1829. Because these ancient plates had been entrusted to him by the angel, he was prohibited from showing them to the public. Before their permanent return to the angel, however, the golden plates were reportedly shown to three men by Moroni and to eight other men by Smith. The publication of the Book of Mormon in 1830 brought Smith considerable notoriety.

The Book of Mormon is a narrative of supposedly two distinct groups of ancient inhabitants of the western hemisphere. One group, the Jaredites, traveled by boats to the western hemisphere shortly after the Tower of Babel experience. The other group, traveling from Jerusalem to the western hemisphere by sailing ships, arrived about 600 B.C. under the direction of a prophet named Lehi. Nearly five hundred pages of the present edition concern the descendants of Lehi's sons, Nephi and Laman. The narrative ends in A.D. 421, when the Lamanites, a darker skinned people, destroyed the Nephites, the keepers of the records. The book is named after Mormon, one of the last prophets of the Nephites. He compiled and abridged nearly all of his people's thousand-year history.

theology. Far more important to the LDS church than the narrative line of the Book of Mormon, however, is its doctrinal content. Such questions as salvation, redemption, sanctification through the atonement, infant baptism, the judgment, the relationship between the Father and the Son, free will, the Law of Moses, and mercy versus justice were purportedly discussed by these ancient inhabitants of America. Because of its religious content, the Book of Mormon is regarded by the LDS church as scripture on an equal basis with the Old and New Testaments.

The Book of Mormon is not the only LDS addition to the canon of scripture. A collection of revelations received by Smith from 1823 to 1843, plus one revelation to Brigham Young, and some miscellaneous writings are published as the *Doctrine and Covenants* (first edition, 1835), a book regarded in LDS theology as having greater applicability to modern conditions than either the Bible or the Book of Mormon. The last book in the LDS canon of scripture is the *Pearl of Great Price* (1851), which contains a translation of some writings of Abraham, a revelation purporting to duplicate a lost revelation given to Moses, a revision of the twenty-fourth chapter of Matthew, an autobiography of Smith from his birth in 1805 to 1838, and the "Thirteen Articles of Faith," the closest approximation in the LDS church to a formal creed. Although these four books constitute the "Four Standard Works" and official scriptures of the LDS church, they are regarded in LDS theology as being static and therefore subordinate to the current revelations of the living president of the church.

Central to the role of the LDS prophet and the organization of the church is the LDS concept of authority. Smith taught that the authority to act for God and to perform the necessary ordinances of Christ's Church was a literal authority entrusted to "the Priesthood," which was conferred by ordination through the laying on of hands. This priesthood, Smith taught, had been given by God to Adam and was passed from Adam directly to his descendants. Whenever there is a break in this chain of ordination, this priesthood has to be restored by an angel or by God directly. Such a restoration occurred during the life of Jesus Christ, when as Son of God he ordained twelve of his disciples to be apostles, to act both as special witnesses of Christ and as the earthly foundation for the priesthood and church. According to LDS theology, God designed that there should always be apostles on the earth with the same authority as the original twelve apostles. When the apostles were all killed and no others ordained in their place, the foundation of the Church of Christ collapsed, and confusion, false doctrine, and a final Great Apostasy entered the church. The effect of the apostasy, according to Mormon Theology, was the loss of the priesthood authority from the earth and therefore an end to the legitimacy of the ordinances taught and practiced in the early Christian church.

Smith taught that this Great Apostasy continued from the first century of the Christian era until his own "First Vision," in which God and Jesus Christ appeared to him and commissioned him as a prophet. Even this epiphany, however, was not sufficient to give Smith the priesthood. He did not claim to have received that authority to act for God until he was translating the Book of Mormon in 1829. On May 15, 1829, according to Smith, his inquiry about baptism led to the appearance of John the Baptist, who ordained Smith with the authority to baptize. He claimed that some time later the ancient apostles Peter, James, and John returned to the earth and conferred upon him the authority of the apostles. Less than a year later Smith organized a church, originally called the Church of Christ, subsequently to be called the Church of the Latter-day Saints, and finally in 1838 to receive its present official name. From the publication of the Book of Mormon in 1830, however, the church received the shorter and more memorable nickname Mormon church.

As soon as the membership of the church warranted it, Smith "by revelation" organized a hierarchy. One of his revelations authorized two counselors to assist the prophet, forming the First Presidency of the Church, the highest authority in the church structure. Some of the presidents of the church, including Smith himself, have had more than two counselors at one time, but two counselors has been the rule. In 1835 he organized the Quorum of the Twelve Apostles. In accordance with Mormon theology, there may be more than twelve apostles, but only twelve men at one time constitute this governing body of the church. Next in authority are the seven presidents of the First Quorum of Seventy, a body of men who preside over those who have a proselyting responsibility. Also under the direction of the presidency are the presiding bishop and his two counselors. The presiding bishop directs the affairs of the thousands of bishops who preside over the local congregations ("wards") throughout the world. Another position is the patriarch to the church, an office without counselors and restricted to members of the Joseph Smith family, generally the direct descendants of his brother and fellow martyr, Hyrum Smith. In the twentieth century, the burgeoning membership and activities of the LDS church resulted in the establishment of Assistants to the Quorum of the Twelve, usually from twelve to fifteen men. These offices, all but the latter instituted by Smith, constitute what are known as the General Authorities of the church.

The theology of Smith was complex and subject to frequent refinements through official revelations. For example, the Book of Mormon, presumably of ancient origin, actually reflects only a fraction of the theology taught by Smith during his fourteen-year leadership of the church.

The most fundamental doctrine is the belief in the need for and the actuality of present-day revelations of the character usually associated with the Old Testament prophets. The LDS concept of the Deity emanates from this premise of modern revelation. Smith claimed that God and Jesus Christ appeared to him as two distinct personages in the form of men. He later refined this description by adding that God the Father and Jesus Christ are not only distinct personages, but that they both have glorified bodies of flesh and bone. In LDS theology, the Holy Ghost is a spirit in the form of man, lacking the substance of flesh and bone.

This very personal concept of God suggests that God is intimately involved with man. Men and women, according to Mormon theology, are not created things, but have had existence as spiritual children of God before mortal birth. The ultimate purpose of mortality is to attain the natural heirship of the Eternal Father—literally to become God-like. Because of differences in obedience and disobedience, there must be varying degrees of reward and punishment after the physical death. Although the shades of difference are infinite, the Mormon rejection of heaven and hell is not total. There are three divisions of reward—celestial, terrestrial, and telestial—with levels of reward within each division. They are governed respectively by God the Father, Jesus Christ, and the Holy Ghost. The lowest kingdom, the telestial, is for murderers, adulterers, liars, and other willful sinners who have suffered sin and guilt and have become reconciled to Christ. Having experienced this "hell," they nevertheless enjoy a limited influence of God. Failure to attain one's highest potential as a child of God is the greatest punishment. Those who attain the highest reward in the Celestial Kingdom are married to each other for eternity. The throne of Godhood is therefore restricted to glorified husbands and wives.

The attainment of these rewards, though a potential of all mankind as God's children, is no automatic thing. Salvation in LDS theology is at once restricted and unconditional. Man is a dual being: offspring of God and sinning mortal. So that God's children may transcend corruptible mortality, Mormons believe, God sent his first-born spirit son to earth as a savior. Christ's resurrection from the dead assures the resurrection of every mortal, whether good or evil, but the Atonement of Christ is conditional. One must accept Christ as Savior and demonstrate faith by obedience to all the commandments, both anciently and currently revealed. No one can obey all the commandments, but the grace of Christ claims those seeking to "endure to the end." And here emerges the role of the prophet and the church. The prophet, as God's spokesman on earth, not only interprets the revelations and scriptures of the past, but adds to the canon of revelation in order to assist the individual in his understanding of himself and his relation to God. The church provides the fellowship and community in which individuals can progress collectively toward the LDS concept of salvation. To guide this progress, there are many commandments: the ten commandments, the law of love, tithing, a health code ("The Word of Wisdom," which requires abstinence from coffee, tea, alcohol, tobacco, and all immoderation, including the unwise use of drugs), baptism by immersion, confirmation of the Holy Ghost, attendance at specified meetings, service to others, and finally a total commitment to follow the spiritual direction of the living prophet. The course of Mormon history is inseparable from implications of this theology.

Joseph Smith period (1830-44). The Joseph Smith period is a series of hegiras, great and small. A year after the organization of the church in New York, Smith led a small exodus of several hundred church members ("Saints") to Kirtland Mills in the Western Reserve of Ohio, there to establish the temporal headquarters of the church. Nevertheless, the revelations received by Smith pointed toward a future spiritual community of the Saints to be called the New Jerusalem or the City of Zion. Although the revelations were at first vague concerning the location, they soon indicated that it was to be established in Jackson County, Missouri. Hundreds of Saints traveled there to settle. Kirtland was the official headquarters of the church, but the settlements of the Saints in and around Independence, Missouri, were the focal point of the LDS millenarian aspirations. Smith had abolished a communal "family" he found operating among the Saints in Kirtland, but he inaugurated the Law of Consecration in the chosen land of Missouri. The Saints deeded all property to the Lord's steward and then received according to their individual needs property and goods that they were to increase for their own benefit, the surpluses to be rededicated to the Lord through the church. Although not very successful in practice and disbanded later by Joseph Smith, the economic cooperation fostered by the Law of Consecration contributed to the conflicts between the Mormons and the older settlers of Missouri. Not only did the Mormons have different beliefs, restrictive economic and social cohesiveness, and a penchant for regarding Missouri territory as their special inheritance, but they were predominantly from the North and had too liberal attitudes toward Negro slaves. An article titled "The Free People of Color" in the Mormon newspaper in Missouri led to the forcible expulsion of the Mormons from Jackson County in 1833. The expelled Mormons were given refuge in adjoining counties of Missouri, and Kirtland became the center of the church's activities, even though hopes to "redeem Zion" continued.

In the meantime, Kirtland had grown to such prominence that Smith began to erect an imposing temple there. Completed in 1836, the temple was used primarily as a meetinghouse and schoolhouse, but visionary manifestations and the administration of such ordinances as anointing the head with oil and the symbolic washing of feet presaged a significance of LDS temples to be developed at a later date. The apparent tranquility and prosperity of the Kirtland headquarters deteriorated irretrievably in 1837 when Smith's Kirtland Anti-Banking Society Bank collapsed amid the national panic of that year. General dissatisfaction with the economic decline in Kirtland plus rumors that Smith had introduced polygamy caused widespread disaffection and apostasy, even among some leaders of the church. Smith sent the apostles on a proselyting mission to England while he and his loyal followers left Kirtland and went to the settlements in Missouri.

The former difficulties in Missouri, however, were repeated within a year. All the causes for friction were acerbated by a certain bravado and belligerence on the part of some Mormon leaders. Virtual civil war was the result: mobs terrorized the Mormon settlements by burning, raping, pillaging, and murdering. Some influential Mormons responded by organizing a vigilante band, variously called the Daughters of Gideon, the Sons of Dan, or Danites. The state militia entered the conflict more in sympathy with the older residents, and the church officially established its own defenses, regarding the militia as an organized mob. Smith repudiated the Danites, but Governor Lillburn W. Boggs became convinced that the Mormons were the aggressors and issued an order that all Mormons were to leave Missouri or suffer extermination. When the Mormon stronghold of Far West, Missouri, was surrounded by the militia, Smith and the other LDS leaders in Far West surrendered to avert a massacre of their followers. Rape and pillage were the result. Narrowly escaping summary execution, Smith and other leaders were accused of treason and imprisoned, while thousands of Mormons were driven from Missouri. After six months of imprisonment, Smith and his associates were apparently allowed to escape. Though driven from Missouri, Smith still envisioned the creation of a temporal community and kingdom for the Saints.

In Illinois, he established such a community. Rejecting advice to let the Saints settle wherever they might, Smith purchased land on the Mississippi River north of Quincy, Illinois, and established a new gathering place in 1839. He called the new city Nauvoo, which he derived from a Hebrew word for "beautiful." Becoming mayor of Nauvoo in 1842, Smith also was appointed lieutenant general of the Nauvoo Legion by the governor of Illinois. He ordered the construction of a grand temple, which he announced would be used not only for meetings but also for some very special ordinances, such as the sealing of husbands and wives for eternity and the giving of certain "endowments." He encouraged the immigration of Mormons from England and the gathering of all Mormons to Nauvoo, which increased the population from less than a thousand in 1839 to more than ten thousand in 1844. In 1841, he instituted baptism for the dead, so that all could have benefit of LDS baptism. In the ultimate development of Mormon theology, Smith announced in 1844 that the potential of man was to become like God, who himself had once been a mortal on another planet. Moreover, because his hopes for an LDS community of power had long implied a fusion of political, economic, and ecclesiastical authority, he organized in the spring of 1844 a parapolitical body (the Council of Fifty) to help build that Kingdom of God on earth. Within a month, he had publicly announced himself as a candidate for the presidency of the United States. At Nauvoo, Smith arrived at an apex of power, both ecclesiastical and temporal.

Nevertheless, evidences of growth for Nauvoo, the church, and Smith were undermined. Smith was a fugitive from Missouri, and repeated attempts to kidnap him caused him to surround himself with bodyguards. Nauvoo's growth in economic and political power resulted in animosity on the part of surrounding towns and cities. Rumors that POLYGAMY was being practiced in Nauvoo, though repeatedly denied, increased anti-Mormon feeling. Recognizing that Nauvoo might suffer as did the Missouri enterprises, Smith prepared for an exodus to the Rocky Mountain region, commissioning men to scout the area.

By 1844, Smith's career seems to have reached a crescendo, but he did not survive the year. When some disaffected members of the church issued a newspaper with the intention of exposing polygamy and other secret developments in Nauvoo, Smith ordered it destroyed as a public nuisance. He was then imprisoned at Carthage, Illinois, on charges of arson, treason, and polygamy. Before his case came to trial, a mob entered the jail on June 27, 1844, and murdered him and his brother Hyrum, patriarch to the church, and seriously wounded apostle John Taylor. The death of Smith ended the formative era of the Mormon church.

Brigham Young period (1844-77). Within two months of Smith's death, the apostles had effectively convinced the majority of the church, including many of the Smith family, that the right of succession lay with the Quorum of the Twelve Apostles. Brigham Young, who had led the defense of Smith during the troubled days in Kirtland and who had held the church together during his Missouri imprisonment, was the president of the apostles and became the head of the church. His first efforts were to complete the Nauvoo temple. As mob violence increased, Young and his associates prepared to effect the great exodus to the unsettled West, which Smith had anticipated. An uneasy truce with the mobs, which had allowed completion of the temple, deteriorated; many homes were burned and lives were threatened. After nearly the entire population of Nauvoo deserted the city in the winter of 1846, mobs bombarded the city with cannon and forced the remaining inhabitants and recent arrivals in Nauvoo to surrender. The temple was desecrated, later set afire by an arsonist, and finally destroyed by a tornado.

Young now set out to accomplish in a wilderness what Smith had failed to do in settled America—establish a permanent sanctuary and kingdom for the Saints. Despite great loss of life from illness and lack of adequate food and shelter, thousands of Mormons followed Young in 1846 on the MORMON TRAIL to a temporary shelter at Winter Quarters (near Omaha, Nebraska), from which he led the first wagon company to the Salt Lake valley in July 1847. Prior to this, he had provided five hundred men to serve as a battalion of the United States Army in the Mexican War, a war that was to make the Great Basin, to which he looked for sanctuary, a part of United States territory. Whether Young actually uttered the apocryphal words, "This is the place," is not certain, but he unquestionably decided that the Salt

Lake valley was to be the refuge and capital of the Saints (see SALT LAKE CITY). This determination was to make the history of the LDS church inseparable from the history of UTAH and much of the West during the next fifty years.

During its first years of existence as part of the United States, Utah was a theocracy outwardly and inwardly. Civil positions were staffed by men prominent in LDS leadership who were appointed by Young or elected by LDS communities. Theocracy in an absolute sense, however, was neither possible nor, in all probability, anticipated by Young. After the Treaty of Guadalupe Hidalgo (1848), the Great Basin and its Mormon sanctuary at Salt Lake were a part of the United States. The influx of gold-seekers in 1849 brought the Basin not only vital economic benefits but also the beginning of a permanent non-Mormon ("Gentile" in LDS parlance) population. However, if the Saints were to be spared the mobbings and expulsions of the past, they would have to be the dominant force in population, as well as in the political, economic, and military structure of the area.

Brigham Young's program to establish a secure sanctuary for the Saints was necessarily multidirectional. Hundreds of men were called with their families to go to wilderness areas to build towns and cities. By 1877 more than 360 settlements were established in what are now the states of Utah, Idaho, Arizona, Nevada, and California—a vast area Young called the State of DESERET. One difficulty in settling the Basin with Mormons was building up the population rapidly enough to support such a vigorous colonizing effort. With the population in the Great Basin at only six thousand in 1849, Young and his associates incorporated the Perpetual Emigration Fund and HANDCART COMPANIES to encourage emigration to Utah from Britain and the rest of Europe. By 1852 there were twenty thousand inhabitants in the Great Basin, and by Young's death in 1877, more than one hundred thousand. To facilitate mail service, Young organized the BRIGHAM YOUNG EXPRESS & CARRYING CO. in 1856. In economic terms, the goals were to build economic independence without encouraging a large influx of Gentiles. Until 1868 Young encouraged local manufactured goods in preference to goods made in the East. With the arrival of the railroad and the end of economic isolation, he instituted a program of church cooperatives throughout every settlement, called the ZION'S COOPERATIVE MERCANTILE INSTITUTION. It was formed primarily out of a store owned by William JENNINGS, a wealthy Mormon. In the winter of 1873-74, he turned his efforts to reestablishing the plan of economic cooperation revealed by Smith (see UNITED ORDER OF ENOCH). Also, Young at various times urged the boycott of Gentile businesses and opposed the development of mining in an effort to discourage Gentiles from settling in the Deseret refuge.

As in the past, these efforts antagonized non-Mormons in Utah and in the nation at large. Contrary to previous experiences with local non-Mormons, the misunderstandings and difficulties did not result in anti-Mormon mobbings. Young had been too successful in establishing the unquestioned domination of the territory by the church. Success in preventing mob action, however, led to a very different conflict with federal officials, who feared and opposed the establishment of the theocratic commonwealth within the Union. National suspicion and antagonism toward the Mormons was increased by the 1852 public announcement of Orson PRATT that polygamy, long a secret practice, was a fundamental tenet and practice of the church. Public avowal made it easy for federal officials and the public to believe that the Mormons were capable of gross immorality. To Mormons, polygamy was a holy practice, commanded by the Lord as a part of the restoration of all things through Joseph Smith. To non-Mormons and members of the RLDS church (see LATTER-DAY SAINTS, REORGANIZED), it was evidence of private lust and public lawlessness. This was to be a contributing factor to half a century of conflict.

The major conflict with the federal government during Young's administration of the church occurred during the years 1857-59. Convinced by the complaints of federal appointees in Utah and public clamor that Young and the Mormons were guilty of lawlessness and rebellion, President James Buchanan sent an expedition to Utah to suppress the alleged rebellion. In addition, he removed Young as governor of Utah Territory, a position to which he had been consistently reappointed, even after the 1852 announcement of polygamy. Learning of the expedition, the Mormons assumed that the troops were sent to annihilate them. Unfortunately, the news of the expedition came at the height of a religious revival among the Mormons known as the Reformation, in which emotions had already been incited against the forces of evil. The impending arrival of armed troops seemed like only one more persecution, and inflammatory rhetoric and war fever swept the territory.

In this atmosphere occurred one of the most regrettable events in the history of the West. A wagon train of non-Mormon emigrants was ambushed in August 1857 by Indians at Mountain Meadows in southwestern Utah. Unsuccessful in their initial assaults on the emigrant train, the Indians demanded that the Mormon residents in the area help them destroy the train, or the Indians would attack the Mormon settlements. In the war hysteria in these isolated southern settlements, some of the LDS leaders decided that destroying the train would be preferable to fighting the Indians at a time when war with federal troops seemed imminent. Therefore, Indian agent John D. Lee and several other prominent Mormon leaders in the southern settlements organized a detachment of the militia to assist the Indians. Pretending to rescue the emigrants, Lee and the militia shot down the men and the wounded, while the Indians murdered the women and children. About 120 persons died in the massacre (subsequently called the Mountain Meadows Massacre). The enormity of this treachery can only be explained in terms of mass hysteria. Young had urged the southern colonists to leave the emigrant trains in peace and at first was given a false report of the massacre by Lee. When Young later learned the truth, rather than implicate the men of an entire community, he merely encouraged civil authorities to investigate the matter without giving them much assistance. Subsequently, he excommunicated several of the prominent leaders of the massacre, including Lee, who was tried and executed by the federal government twenty years after the massacre.

The outcome of the Utah expedition, or "Utah War," fell short of actual war. Although at first Mormon leaders indicated they would oppose the troops by armed force, Young soon decided to avoid actual bloodshed and to cut off the supplies of the troops to prevent their advancement. If unsuccessful in halting the progress of the troops, he had ordered preparations for a southward exodus and destruction of Salt Lake City. The Mormons burned the trading posts of Fort Bridger and Fort Supply, destroyed military supply trains, and burned the forage in front of the advancing troops. Influential friends of the Mormons, such as Thomas L. Kane, assisted in obtaining a reconciliation with the federal government, including a pardon for alleged Mormon offenses, a pardon accepted by Young on June 12, 1858. Two weeks later United States troops passed through the deserted Salt Lake City to establish Camp Floyd forty miles away. This last reminder of the Utah War was abandoned at the outset of the Civil War.

Following this conflict, the period of Young's presidency was one of continued consolidation and growth for the LDS community. Missionary and colonizing efforts, interrupted by the Utah War, were resumed with increased vigor. LDS converts continued to emigrate to "Zion" in large numbers, a pilgrimage made easier by the completion of the transcontinental railroad at Promontory, Utah, in 1869. The LDS church entered into the local railroad business. Polygamy, despite the 1862 Morrill Act, which prohibited it in the territories, was allowed to develop virtually unmolested into an entrenched social and religious institution. A judicial attack by federal judge James B. McKean upon the LDS church and Young was ended in 1872 by a United States Supreme Court decision. In 1874 Young's secretary, George Reynolds, began a test case against the constitutionality of antipolygamy laws, a case the Mormons felt assured of winning under First Amendment guarantees. Young's death in 1877 occurred at a a time when the LDS dreams of community and Kingdom had reached their apex.

conflict with the nation (1877-90). Ostensibly, the source of conflict between the Mormons and the federal government was the persistent practice of plural marriage in violation of federal laws. But central to the struggle was the influence of the church over its members and therefore over Utah, and to a lesser extent IDAHO, as a territory and future state. To the federal government, the LDS church domination in the territory represented a direct challenge to the separation of church and state. In 1879 the Supreme Court upheld the constitutionality of antipolygamy laws, and the decision gave the federal government the weapon with which to attack the power of the church. The assumption of federal authorities was that if the church would yield to pressure against its practice of polygamy, then LDS political and economic domination could also be broken. Leading the opposition to these federal efforts was John Taylor, the successor of Young. Taylor's attitude was that compromise with the government was impossible, since polygamy was divinely commanded and therefore superior to any legislation or Supreme Court decision. These apparently irreconcilable positions developed into a conflict that became acrimonious and, for the LDS resistance, increasingly hopeless.

After the 1879 Reynolds decision, the antipolygamy crusade began. Congress in 1882 enacted the Edmunds law against polygamy, making plural marriage a misdemeanor, disfranchising polygamists, and establishing a federally appointed commission of five men to supervise all registration and election proceedings in Utah Territory. In 1882 polygamist George Q. CANNON was expelled from Congress and was replaced by John Thomas CAINE. When the arrests for unlawful cohabitation became frequent, the Mormons continued to resist and John Taylor and most of the other LDS leaders went into hiding. Congress increased the pressure in 1887 with the Edmunds-Tucker Act, which disincorporated the LDS church, escheated its real and personal property, and abolished woman suffrage in Utah. The effect of this law and the increasing arrests struck at the Mormons ecclesiastically, socially, economically, and politically. In exile and dying, Taylor assented to one concession: making polygamy a misdemeanor in the 1887 proposed constitution and petition for Utah statehood. Congress, unsatisfied with this compromise, rejected this sixth petition for statehood.

Assuming the leadership of the church after the death of Taylor in 1887 was Wilford Woodruff. For a time he also continued a resistance, though less vociferous, against federal authority. But a series of setbacks for the church in 1889 and 1890 led to the inevitable resolution of the conflict. In 1889, federal judges began refusing to naturalize LDS immigrants merely because of their belief in polygamy. In the spring of 1890 the Supreme Court upheld the constitutionality of the Edmunds-Tucker Act and also a provision of the Idaho state constitution that disfranchised all members of the church whether or not they were polygamists. Moreover, in the summer of 1890 progress was being made in Congress to enact the Cullom-Strubble bill, which would disfranchise all Mormons. The church had lost its judicial struggle and faced virtual destruction because of polygamy, a practice entered into by not more than ten percent of the married LDS males in the West. Finally, on September 25, 1890, Woodruff as president of the church issued the Manifesto urging all members of the church to comply with the laws of the land regarding marriage. The Manifesto, announced to be a result of revelation, was adopted by the church the following October. This action signaled the virtual end of the conflict and the beginning of the accommodation of the LDS church to the national community.

transition into the American community (1890-1907). The Manifesto of 1890 ushered in an "era of good feeling" between the Mormons and the nation. Although more than a thousand men had been imprisoned for plural marriage or "cohabitation" during the previous ten years, after the 1890 Manifesto scores of indictments were quashed and sentences commuted. Only cursory efforts were made to enforce laws affecting the polygamous relations entered into prior to 1890. The next step taken by the church was to encourage the national party system in Utah Territory, since for decades Utah politics had been dominated by the church-sponsored People's party and the anti-Mormon Liberal party. The People's party was dissolved in 1891, and after some suspicious hesitation the Liberal party dissolved in 1893. Presidential amnesties to the pre-1890 polygamists were granted in 1893 and 1894, and the escheated real property of the church was returned following Utah's admission to the Union in 1896.

As with all transitory periods, however, there were evidences of the past intermingled with signs of a new era. Some of the former anti-Mormans in Utah were unwilling to forget the past, and the traditionally anti-Mormon newspaper, the Salt Lake *Tribune*, continued its invective until World War I. Moreover, there were Mormons, even among the LDS General Authorities, who regarded former concessions as only temporary in nature and who worked for church domination of local politics and economics and also toward a restoration of polygamy. In general, these underlying instances of recidivism were resolved locally, but in two instances the time-worn "Mormon problem" returned to national prominence.

In 1898 Brigham H. ROBERTS, a polygamist and member of the First Council of Seventy, was elected Utah representative to Congress. To Congress and much of the nation, it was an unspeakable affront for a practicing polygamist to flaunt his family relations and rekindle the polygamy issue only eight years after the Manifesto. The House of Representatives responded in 1900 by overwhelmingly excluding Roberts.

Three years later, an apostle, Reed SMOOT, was elected to the Senate. Although he was not a polygamist and few questioned his personal eligibility for the office, a formal protest was lodged against him because of his leadership and ultimately his membership in the LDS church. A Senate investigation began in March 1904 and continued until 1907, in which the LDS church more than Smoot was under scrutiny. As a direct result of this investigation, another manifesto threatening excommunication for entering into new polygamous marriages was adopted by the LDS church on April 6, 1904, and two years later two apostles were deposed for refusing to comply with the ban on polygamy. The church had demonstrated its firm intention to comply with the norms of United States society. When the Senate in 1907 voted to confirm Smoot's eligibility, it represented the final acceptance of Mormons and the LDS church itself into America's pluralistic society.

1907-present. LDS leaders, having finally gained a degree of acceptance in American society, conscientiously worked to enhance the public image and influence of Mormonism. To demonstrate their sincerity in rejecting the continuation of polygamy, LDS presidents since 1910 have disciplined and excommunicated persons advocating or entering into polygamy, a policy that has resulted in these polygamists ("Mormon Fundamentalists") forming a small schismatic movement. In 1929 the Mormon Tabernacle Choir began weekly broadcasts on national radio networks and since that time has become internationally renowned. In the 1930s the LDS church, which had long emphasized the importance of education, turned over three of its academies to the state of Utah and concentrated on building up Brigham Young University. Forty years later, the LDS authorities had to limit enrollment at BYU to twenty-five thousand. In 1936 the church began a welfare program for the benefit of its unemployed and needy members. By establishing a program especially for American Indians at BYU and through its Indian Placement Program, the church has worked since 1954 to help the Indians achieve social equality in America. The extent to which twentieth-century Mormons have become accepted in American society is indicated by the fact that prominent LDS leaders, including an apostle, have been appointed members of presidential cabinets.

The LDS church has become far more international during the twentieth century. In 1919 the first LDS temple was constructed outside the continental United States, in Hawaii. Since then LDS temples, reserved for special ordinances rather than for Sunday worship, have been constructed in Canada, Switzerland, England, New Zealand, Brazil, Mexico, and Japan. In 1921 LDS leaders discontinued their previous encouragement of emigration to the headquarters of the church and urged foreign members to remain in their respective countries. Although the church had proselyted outside the United States almost from its organization, the visit in 1946 by the apostle Ezra Taft Benson to war-ravaged Europe signaled the beginning of a vigorous effort to make Mormonism international in scope. In the following decades, LDS world membership increased phenomenally, with as many as one hundred thousand converts in a single year and membership doubling or tripling in parts of Europe, Latin America, and the Far East. The church established elementary and secondary schools in the South Pacific and Latin America and began giving more of the responsible leadership positions to local members rather than to missionaries from the United States. The internationalization of the church progressed sufficiently that in 1971 the General Authorities began a program of holding foreign conferences of the stature of its own traditional semiannual General Conferences at Salt Lake City.

The Church of Jesus Christ of Latter-day Saints has grown from a despised sect on the American frontier to a respected and influential church in the international community of religions. It has survived the martyrdom of its founder, the persecutions of its enemies, the repressions of the United States government, the schisms of its apostates, and the strains of its accommodation to the non-LDS community. Its history is inseparable from the history of the American frontier and West, but its development now transcends the confines of its origins.

See Nels Anderson, *Desert Saints: The Mormon Frontier in Utah* (1942); Lenoard J. Arrington, *Great Basin Kingdom: An Economic History of the Latter-day Saints, 1830-1900* (1958); Thomas F. O'Dea, *The Mormons* (1957); Brigham H. Roberts, *A Comprehensive History of the Church of Jesus Christ of Latter-day Saints: Century I*, 6 vols. (1930); and Joseph Fielding Smith, *Essentials of Church History* (1922).—L. J. A.

Latter-day Saints, Reorganized. The murder of Joseph Smith, Jr., on June 27, 1844, created a succession crisis for the Church of Christ of Latter-day Saints. Claims were made by Sidney Rigdon as surviving counselor, by Brigham Young as president of the apostles, by James J. Strang as secretly designated successor, and ultimately by Joseph Smith III as son of the prophet, and heir of his ecclesiastical prerogatives. These conflicting claims for succession threatened to splinter the Mormons into a multitude of warring sects. The situation of the Mormons in 1844, however, demanded a unified position (see LATTER-DAY SAINTS). In August 1844 a general assembly voted to sustain the claim of Young that he and the other apostles had the lawful authority to direct the church.

Those Mormons who could not accept Young's leadership or who could not accept doctrines and practices they felt had been introduced after the death of Smith did not join Young on the westward migration to Utah in 1846. Instead they turned to the secondary leadership of those LDS congregations that had been the hinterland of the church during the years of Smith's leadership. It was in this manner that LDS congregations and leaders in the Great Lakes area rose to prominence.

In Michigan James J. STRANG proclaimed himself the successor of Smith by right of special appointment and on Beaver Island established a kingdom that attracted many Mormons east of the Mississippi. Strang, however, repelled other Mormons by his polygamy and other practices associated with Young. In Wisconsin the leaders of two separate congregations sought divine guidance, since they were unwilling to follow Young, Strang, or any of a host of existing splinter movements. On November 18, 1851, Jason W. Briggs at Beloit, Wisconsin, received a revelation indicating that God wanted a son of Joseph Smith, Jr., to lead the true church. About the same time, Zenas H. Gurley at Yellowstone, Wisconsin, received a similiar instruction.

On June 12, 1852, the followers of these two men held a conference at Beloit, Wisconsin, and made resolutions to accept no one as a leader except a descendant of Joseph Smith, Jr., to discontinue connection with any other claimant, to accept the ordinations of all those before the death of Smith, and to affirm that the church organized by Smith in 1830 still existed and would always continue as long as there were six true believers. In January 1853 Gurley received a revelation repudiating polygamy; and on April 6-8, 1853, at Zarahemla, Wisconsin, the church was officially organized and the Quorum of Twelve Apostles formed. No descendant of Smith accepted its leadership, and Briggs became president of the newly appointed Quorum of the Twelve Apostles. Once reorganized, the church languished for seven years in anticipation of leadership by a son of Smith.

Joseph Smith III had been designated to Briggs and Gurley as the spiritual heir apparent of the prophet, but the young man remained aloof. Born November 6, 1832, "young Joseph," as he was called by most Mormons, had been only eleven years old at his father's murder and was only twenty when the church was reorganized by Briggs and Gurley. When they visited him at Nauvoo in November 1856 to urge him to assume leadership of the reorganization, young Joseph stormily refused to discuss the matter, saying he would discuss any subject but religion.

As he matured, however, Joseph Smith III began to consider the claims of his father's alleged successors. Repelled by polygamy, he could not seriously consider joining Brigham Young, Strang, Lyman Wight, or even his uncle William Smith, all of whose groups practiced some form of polygamy. In the fall of 1859 the young man received a revelation indicating that the group at Zarahemla, Wisconsin, was the only faction of the church acceptable to God. In April 1860 at a conference at Amboy, Illinois, Joseph Smith III was sustained by the membership as the president and prophet of the Reorganized Church of Jesus Christ of Latter-day Saints. At that time the membership of the church was less than five hundred persons.

The first decades of the RLDS church were primarily a reaction against the Mormon church in Utah. Through the columns of its official organ, the *True Latter-Day Saints' Herald* (established in 1860), the RLDS church attacked the Utah Mormons for their alleged betrayal of the truths and practices espoused by Joseph Smith, Jr. The center of the controversy was polygamy, but it included a plethora of other differences in practice and interpretation. As polygamy declined and eventually died as a practice among Utah Mormons, the RLDS church's activities became less defensive.

Moving toward the twentieth century, the RLDS Church began the completion of its internal organization. In 1897, after a lapse of more than fifty years, the office of presiding patriarch was reinstituted with the appointment of Alexander H. Smith, son of Joseph, Jr. In 1901 the first stakes (wards comprising several local congregations) of the church were organized at Lamoni, Iowa, and Independence, Missouri. The capital of the RLDS church varied for several years. In 1881 Lamoni became the capital, but at the same time Independence was developing into a second capital. Dual capitals continued until 1920, when Independence became the official headquarters. While Lamoni was the capital, the RLDS church established Graceland College there in 1895.

The presidents of the RLDS church have been Joseph Smith III (1860-1914), Frederick M. Smith (1915-46), Israel A. Smith (1946-58), and W. Wallace Smith (1958-   ). The latter three were sons of Joseph Smith III, and in each case the RLDS president has designated his successor prior to his own death.

See Inez Smith Davis, *The Story of the Church* (1948); Francis W. Holm, Sr., *The Mormon Churches: A Comparison from Within* (1970); Russell F. Ralston, *Fundamental Differences Between the Reorganized Church and the Church in Utah* (1963); Joseph Smith III, *Joseph Smith III and the Restoration*, Mary Audentia Smith Anderson and Bertha Anderson Hulmes, eds. (1952); and Joseph Smith III and Herman C. Smith, eds., *History of the Church of Jesus Christ of Latter-Day Saints*, 4 vols. (1896-1903). —D. M. Q.

Lavender, David (1910-   ). Writer. Lavender was born in the Colorado gold-rush town of Telluride in the San Juan Mountains. He attended schools in Denver, the Mercersberg Academy in Pennsylvania, and was graduated from Princeton in 1931. Turning from the prospect of a career in law after a year at the Stanford Law School (1931-32), Lavender worked at the old Camp Bird gold mine above Ouray, Colorado, and then was a rancher and Denver advertising writer before 1943, when he became head of the English department at the Thacher School of Boys near Ojai, California. Just before starting at Thacher, Lavender wrote *One Man's West* (1943), a remarkably interesting autobiographical account of Colorado ranching and mining. Two western novels, *Andy Claybourne* (1946) and *Red Mountain* (1963), are based upon that personal experience. Lavender's other books on the West include *The Big Divide* (1948); *Bent's Fort* (1954); *Land of Giants* (1958); *The Great West* (1965); *The Rockies* (1968); and *California, Land of New Beginnings* (1972). *The Fist in the Wilderness* (1964) is a history of the American Fur Company. *The Great Persuader* (1970) is a colorful biography of Collis P. Huntington, based upon analysis of a large mass of documentary material at the Huntington Library. Much of Lavender's literary talent and research has been incorporated into a new textbook, *The Story of California*, accepted for use in the elementary schools of California.—W. R. J.

La Vérendrye, Pierre Gaultier de Varennes, Sieur de (1685-1749). Fur trader and explorer. La Vérendrye spent his youth in Quebec and at the age of twelve joined the French army to fight on the New England frontier in King William's War. His military career took him to Europe, where he fought in several major battles in the struggle between England and France for control of the New World.

Upon his return to Canada he entered the fur trade and in 1727 was placed in charge of the post on Lake Nipigon, north of Lake Superior, on the periphery of New France. He and his sons explored the surrounding territory and established forts along the canoe route from Lake Superior to Lake Winnipeg and along the Red River of the North.

With the backing of French merchants and a grant from the French government of Canada for a monopoly of the fur trade in the area he was to explore, La Vérendrye and his party set out in 1731 to search for an overland route to the Pacific. The stories from Cree and Assiniboin Indians of a westward-flowing river (the Missouri) and a tribe (the Mandan) that lived nearby so intrigued him that he planned another expedition into the area. His party set out in 1738. The Assiniboin, who had traded with the Mandan for several decades, acted as guides. La Vérendrye kept a journal of his exploits and observations. His descriptions of the Mandan earth lodges, physical characteristics, clothing, and trade constitute the earliest known written record of Indians in North Dakota.

His sons visited the Mandan area again in 1742 but failed to discover a water route to the western sea. Despite their disappointment, La Vérendrye and his sons were the first white men to explore Manitoba, the Dakotas, and possibly Montana. They were also the first to travel on the Assiniboine River and the Red River of the North and to see the Missouri River.—D.J.T.

law and order. The American West has always been described as an area of lawlessness and violence; yet the distinguishing feature of western settlement has been the triumph of law and order in previously violent regions. American frontiersmen used firearms for hunting and self-defense and readily resorted to their fists, knives, and pistols to settle disputes; but it was American environmental and social conditions as much as willful lawlessness that prevented an easy establishment of law and order in the West. Settlers moved west ahead of regular courts of law and peace officers and were beyond the reach of any government. Indian tribes, often with cultures that glorified war, raids, and acts of revenge, naturally resisted white encroachment, while the whites themselves practiced the right of self-defense and exhibited their own European traditions of revenge and feuding—practices that they applied to their white neighbors almost as readily as they did to the Indians. With no one to restrain the lawless minority of violent youths, outlaws, criminals, and bullies who also migrated west, frontier violence was inevitable.

The first agents of frontier law and order, besides the law-abiding settlers themselves, were army or militia detachments and Indian agents, both of whom were charged with keeping peace between Indians and whites. Three centuries of violent conflict between the two groups should not obscure the fact that both the British and the American governments sought to keep peace on the frontier by regulating tribal bounds, the purchase and occupation of land, trade, and the sale of whiskey and firearms.

White settlers coming to a wilderness region often devised their own systems of law and order. The famous Mayflower Compact of 1620 was, in effect, a set of rules for the infant colony at Plymouth. Religious and utopian groups, such as the Rappites at New Harmony, Indiana, set up well-regulated colonies on the frontier with a complete absence of violence. Ignoring all colonial laws, a group of Presbyterians on the Appalachian frontier formed the Watauga Association and adopted codes by which to govern themselves. In 1775 land speculators in the Transylvania Company attempted to set up their own proprietary government in frontier Kentucky. Throughout the history of the West, land speculators or special-interest groups sought to create agencies of law and order that would benefit themselves rather than the general public. This special-interest approach was responsible for much of the conflict between settlers in the frontier period.

In general, however, frontier settlers imitated forms of government they had known earlier. Westward-moving New Englanders continued to found townships with appropriate peace officers, while pioneers from the middle and southern states created county governments with justices of the peace and sheriffs as the basic units of local government. Practically speaking, pioneers did not create new forms of law and order; rather they continued to use two ancient English institutions: the justice court, headed by a justice of the peace; and a county, or high, sheriff with powers to collect taxes, deputize citizens, and form a posse.

The average frontier justice of the peace often had no formal training, generally possessed little knowledge of the law, and often had no copy of the statutes available for use. Since justices depended upon fees in lieu of a salary, they naturally looked after their own self-interest when assessing fines. Between 1760 and 1775 the settlers of western North Carolina found that corrupt judges, land agents, and sheriffs were charging such exorbitant quitrents, taxes, and legal fees that a group of protesting citizens formed the "Regulation" to force them to behave. Meanwhile, on the frontier of South Carolina there were so few peace officers that armed citizens, or Regulators, took the law into their own hands in order to drive out horse thieves and outlaw bands. They also punished individuals whom they considered shiftless or immoral. Both forms of VIGILANTISM appeared in various guises on all subsequent frontiers from the Mississippi valley to California.

Unfortunately, many writers have focused too much attention on these brief periods of violence or on colorful western characters such as Judge Roy BEAN of Texas, who among other things once fined a corpse for carrying a concealed weapon. Charles Howard Shinn observed that most of the judges of the early California mining camps were respected men who relied more on honest judgment and common sense than upon specific points of law. Wayne Gard, another authority on frontier justice, points out that however much their decisions might be open to question, untrained judges frequently established precedents for subsequent decisions: "They showed that disputes could be settled with-

In Rawlins County, Kansas, a dispute over water rights between the Berry and Dewey families ended in bloodshed rather than in a court of law. (Kansas State Historical Society, Topeka)

out the use of the six-shooters and that crimes could be punished without resort to vigilante hanging ropes."

After various states ceded their western land claims to the United States during the 1780s, Congress passed the Northwest Ordinance of 1787, which provided a basic framework of government for western territories. Thereafter, most western states passed through a territorial period before entering the Union as a state. In this period federal laws, laws borrowed from older state codes, and territorial laws provided courts and peace officers for the territories.

County, district, and federal courts in newly settled territories and states experienced many problems in establishing law and order. Jails were either nonexistent or so primitive that it was relatively easy for criminals to escape. Most courthouses were crudely constructed and not infrequently destroyed by fires. This was especially true in early Texas, where fires were sometimes set to intimidate the judges and to destroy criminal records. In addition, honest jurors were difficult to find and some were notoriously lenient on friends and neighbors or even in collusion with the defendants.

Although better trained than local officials, judges of higher courts were almost as informal in basing their decisions on common sense rather than on strict interpretation of the law. Many were overworked and had to ride long distances in a manner similar to frontier circuit-riding preachers. Others were known to let financial favors influence their decisions, especially in the mining regions of the Far West.

Generally the most efficient and least subject to the whims of local politics were the federal judges, one of the most famous of whom was Isaac C. PARKER. Presi-

dent Grant appointed Parker to preside over the Western District of Arkansas and he eventually became known as the Hanging Judge because of the severity of his sentences in homicide cases. Parker soon brought to his court—the jurisdiction of which included Indian Territory—considerable respect for law and order where none had previously existed. During twenty-one years on the bench (1875-1896), Judge Parker sentenced 168 men to be hanged (only 88 were, however). He was also noted for his fairness in a district where more than sixty federal law officers met death in the discharge of their duties.

As an area became better organized, responsibility for law enforcement rested more and more upon federal, territorial (or state), and local officials. Slowly the offices of public prosecutor, territorial attorney general, and United States district attorney became full-time jobs. Many a western governor and congressman got his start by riding circuit and serving as a public defender. United States marshals and deputy marshals served under the jurisdiction of federal district courts and were chiefly concerned with violation of federal laws such as mail robberies. In Indian Territory, however, their responsibilities were much broader when dealing with white outlaws (see MARSHAL, FEDERAL).

On the county level, the sherriff and his deputies were charged with enforcing local laws including the collection of taxes. As in colonial days the western sheriff was entitled to supplement his salary by various fees, a practice that he frequently abused in pursuit of personal gain. Frontier counties often were very large, and the population sparse and scattered. Thus, the sheriff's job of law enforcement and the capture of criminals was a

difficult one. One of the most common duties of a frontier sheriff was to enforce laws against dueling, carrying
concealed weapons, or wearing guns in towns. At first
these laws seemed impossible to enforce. Peace officers
in the Mississippi valley before the Civil War found their
task especially difficult, for a large number of river
pirates, riverboat gamblers, counterfeiters, horse
thieves, highwaymen, murderers, and kidnappers of
slaves congregated there. The entire nation experienced periods of violence after the Mexican War and
Civil War.

Throughout the nineteenth century, Americans continued to settle many of their "affairs of honor" privately
and often violently, while others, understandably impatient with horse thieves, cattle rustlers, robbers, and
claim jumpers, formed vigilante groups or claim associations. Many frontier leaders and businessmen were
convinced that without law and order their area would
never prosper, while others seized control of territorial
and state legislatures as tools to forward their own interests. In Wyoming, for example, a powerful cattle association saw to it that laws passed benefited the cattle
grower rather than the farmer. Later, railroads and
mining interests dominated the lawmakers in other
states and territories.

In the trans-Mississippi West the most famous peace
officer was the frontier marshal, whose role has been
popularized by the legendary careers of Wild Bill
HICKOK and Bat MASTERSON in the Kansas cattle towns
and by Wyatt Earp (see EARP BROTHERS) in Tombstone,
Arizona. Western towns hired marshals and deputies to
enforce ordinances, while larger places depended upon
uniformed police forces. The enforcement of laws
against the carrying of a concealed weapon, public
drunkenness, gambling, and prostitution constituted
the typical duty of town marshals. His job could frequently be dangerous, but he was seldom a very romantic or glamorous individual. As western towns grew, the
marshal's office evolved into that of the chief of police or
he himself became a deputy United States marshal.

Law officers and judges found their problems considerably more complex in areas where some outlaw gangs
were held in high esteem. This was particularly true in
communities where memories of the Civil War and Reconstruction remained fresh and bitter and the myth of
the "lost cause" had crystalized. In postwar Missouri, for
example, many people regarded members of the Jesse
James gang more as heroes than as criminals. Similarly,
in the Kansas cattle towns, fellow Texans looked upon
rowdy cowboys as fun-loving individuals letting off
steam at the expense of the Yankee merchants who were
fleecing them; others saw the troublemakers as uncivilized and unreconstructed rebels, who lacked respect
for decency and authority.

Some territories and states were forced to create special bodies to assist in law enforcement. As early as 1823
Stephen F. Austin's infant Texas colony created a
"watch" to guard the community. In 1844 the Republic
of Texas created a force of rangers under Captain John
C. ("Jack") Hays, a former sheriff, to guard the frontier
against marauding Mexicans and Indians. Reconstituted in the 1850s, and again after the Civil War, the
Texas Rangers have continued down to the present as
the oldest state police system in the United States. In
1853 California created a special ranger force to control
bands of Mexican highwaymen. At the turn of the century, Arizona and New Mexico territories each created
companies of rangers or special mounted police to assist
local officials in maintaining law and order. Although
they were disbanded after a few years, ranger organizations were precedents for the state police system now
common in the United States.

Special police forces also existed on Indian reservations. By the time the Five Civilized Tribes had moved to
Indian Territory, they had their own sheriffs and deputies, or "light horsemen," to keep order. In 1874 John
P. Clum, Indian agent to the San Carlos Apache, created
a police force of Indians to keep order on the reservation. The idea spread until Indian police and special
Indian courts became a part of the reservation system.
By 1900 some nine hundred Indian police handled
routine matters and individual lawbreakers. Eventually
they and the special courts were replaced by local police
and regular courts, although special Indian police exist
on some reservations today. Still, Indian protection
from white violence was never notable, and other
minority groups, such as Mexicans, Chinese, Japanese,
and blacks, suffered from both irate mobs and intolerant police and courts throughout the West.

Meanwhile, western Americans became more confident than ever that they were competent to establish
territorial and state governments on their own. Using
the concept of "popular sovereignty," they set up their
own republic in Texas (1836-46), formed a provisional
government in Oregon, and organized California as a
state. During the 1850s extralegal pro- and antislavery
groups attempted to rule Kansas, while in 1859 the Pikes
Peakers created their own squatter Territory of Jefferson. In a unique exercise of popular sovereignty the
Mormons created their own theocratic State of Deseret
in Utah in the 1840s.

Between 1849 and 1890 gold and silver rushes in the
Far West created special law-and-order problems. The
scores of camps and towns that sprang up overnight
lacked any law-enforcement agencies. To fill the need,
miners held meetings to adopt codes of mining law for
their camp or district, which, among other things, limited the size of claims and appointed a recorder of
claims. These informal codes, often a crude amalgam of
Spanish mining law and American land law, were eventually accepted as law in regular courts in California and
elsewhere. Indeed, the philosophy of the local codes was
embodied in the federal mining law of 1866 even
though the codes bore little relation to the problems of
the industrial mining systems that soon replaced individual mining operations. Miners' meetings also appointed constables and judges and created courts to
hear civil and criminal disputes. When the rough elements or outlaw gangs began to harass western mining
towns, informal "peoples' courts" tried and often
hanged wrongdoers, or else citizens formed vigilante
committees to restore order.

Even after regular law agencies took over in the mining areas of the West, business firms discovered they
had to provide their own extralegal police system. Wells
Fargo hired guards to protect their gold shipments as
well as detectives to catch highwaymen. The Union
Pacific and other railroads maintained railway guards
and detectives, and when large-scale mines developed,
owners hired Pinkerton detectives to spy on labor or-

A wooden jailhouse in Wyoming Territory (1893). (National Archives)

ganizers. In Texas and Wyoming, cattle associations employed stock inspectors to spot stolen cattle at railroad yards and detectives to catch rustlers. In the Great Plains, claim associations sometimes punished claim jumpers by hanging. These extralegal efforts to achieve law and order often provoked, rather than prevented, violence.

Generally speaking, frontier violence was as much a result of the lack of law-enforcement agencies as it was an expression of lawlessness. That lack, combined with the romantic ideas of rugged individualism and personal defense of one's honor, the presence of criminals, and intense racial hatreds hindered the establishment of law and order. Further, considering the problems of early western courts, untrained officials, rugged terrain, scattered population, poor communication, and frequent public indifference, it is understandable why law and order, once achieved, was so difficult to maintain. In his two-volume *Popular Tribunals* (1887), Hubert Howe Bancroft concludes that under the circumstances, it was miraculous that mob law and failure of justice in the California gold fields were as infrequent as they were. The same may be said of the West as a whole.

See Wayne Gard, *Frontier Justice* (1949); John D. W. Guice, *The Rocky Mountain Bench* (1972); W. Eugene Hollon, *Frontier Violence: Another Look* (1974); Philip D. Jordan, *Frontier Law and Order: Ten Essays* (1970); and Frank R. Prassel, *The Western Peace Officer* (1972). —W. E. H.

Lea, Tom (1907-   ). Illustrator, painter, and writer. Born in El Paso, Texas, Lea received his first formal instruction in painting at the Art Institute of Chicago, where he enrolled in 1924. Making a brief trip to Europe for further study in 1930, he moved in 1933 to Santa Fe, New Mexico, where he worked as a part-time staff artist at the Laboratory of American Anthropology. In 1936, following the death of his first wife, Lea returned to El Paso and during World War II was active as an artist-correspondent for *Life* magazine. A folio of drawings illustrative of his war experiences was published in 1945 under the title *Peleliu Landing*. A friend and longtime associate of author J. Frank Dobie, Lea illustrated several of Dobie's books as well as his own novels *The Brave Bulls* and *The Wonderful Country*. Other illustrations appeared in numerous publications later, including a reprint edition of Charlie Siringo's *A Texas Cowboy* and Lea's own history of the King Ranch. Lea is represented by murals in the Federal Court House in El Paso and at the El Paso public library. He also designed the masthead for the University of Texas Press, and a number of his paintings of Texas cattle and cowboy life may be seen at the Dallas Museum of Fine Arts.

Lea's first novel, *The Brave Bulls* (1949), is the story of a Mexican bullfighter. Lea also wrote a history, *The King Ranch* (1957), and a novel of the conquistadores, *The Hands of Cantú* (1964). His best novel, however, is *The Wonderful Country* (1952), a superb story of the border country he knows well, written in the idiom of the conventional western, complete with Apache, cavalry patrols, *bandidos*, and Texas Rangers. The novel is a brilliant example of the way in which a gifted author can transform the staple clichés of western fiction into a superb analysis of cultural differences. The basis of the novel is the often discussed "international theme," and its resolution describes how its hero, Matthew Brady, learns that he cannot live both in Texas and Mexico, but must choose one or the other.—D. C. H. and J. K. F.

Part of the Homestake works in Lead, South Dakota, in 1889. (Library of Congress)

Lead, South Dakota. Mining town. Lead has avoided the fate of most western mining towns, for the gigantic Homestake Mine on which the prosperity of the town has rested since 1878 continues to produce gold. The Homestake is the largest producing gold mine in the Western Hemisphere. Through 1970 it had produced over 30,933,744 ounces of gold from over 107,627,954 tons of ore, and most of the $500 million in gold produced in the Black Hills since 1875 has come from this single mine. The rich deposits of the mine were discovered by Moses and Fred Manuel in 1876, and since that time the history of Lead has been the history of the Homestake Company.

The original business district of the town is no more. Where the town once stood is now a grassy meadow, and next to it is the awesome open cut from which Homestake miners gouged out an estimated forty-eight million tons of rock. Lead's early businessmen unwisely located their townsite on mineral property, and by the end of World War I the city's buildings had been undermined by so many tunnels and workings that the business district had to be abandoned and razed and a new town center built.

The fortunes of Lead have fluctuated with the price and production of gold. Labor troubles plagued the town in the early twentieth century, highlighted by the Western Federation of Miners strike of the Homestake from November 24, 1909, to March 2, 1910. World War I brought inflation and the crumbling destruction of many of the town's most famous buildings. Unlike most of the United States, Lead prospered in the 1930s as the Homestake expanded and modernized. Reconstruction of the city acted as a further hedge against depression. However, World War II brought disaster when the federal government suspended gold mining in October 1942. After the war, production resumed, and the town regained a measure of prosperity, though this prosperity still rests on an uncertain foundation of gold.

See Lambert Florin, *Ghost Town Trails* (1963); Albert M. Williams, *The Black Hills* (1952); and Muriel S. Wolle, *The Bonanza Trail* (1953).—R. B. W.

lead mining. Two principal areas of frontier lead mining were developed in the Mississippi valley during the eighteenth and nineteenth centuries. The southernmost area, termed by geologists the Southeast Missouri Lead District, is located about seventy miles south of St. Louis, centering upon the "Old Lead Belt" around the town of Flat River in St. Francois County. It is one of the world's largest lead mining districts, having produced more than 9 million tons of pig lead since it was opened to large-scale production after 1800. The second area, the Upper Mississippi Valley Lead-Zinc District, is more extensive though less rich, encompassing a region of northwestern Illinois, southwestern Wisconsin, and eastern Iowa that spreads over seven counties. Principal towns in this area, all brought to life by the lead mines, include Dubuque, Iowa; Galena, Illinois; and Platteville and Mineral Point, Wisconsin. This district has produced an estimated 821,000 tons of pig lead since the late eighteenth century. In both areas the principal lead ore is galena dolomite, dating geologically from the Cambrian age. The Upper Mississippi Valley District is further distinguished because it lies within a region bypassed by the last advance of glacial ice, leaving the mineral veins more openly exposed to discovery and surface mining.

Both the Southeast Missouri and Upper Mississippi lead deposits were known to the native peoples of these regions prior to white contact, and it was their accounts that first brought Europeans to begin working the surface ores. Pierre Lemoyne, Sieur d'Iberville, and his brother Jean Baptiste, Sieur de Bienville, the founders of French Louisiana, were early interested in the possibilities of the Missouri mines for silver or other precious metals. After reports by other French explorers, a major speculative venture was launched in 1719 by Philippe Renault, who came from France to New Orleans and then to the Illinois country, bringing along two hundred experienced French miners and an additional five hundred black slaves purchased in Santo Domingo. Renault carried out the first systematic mining efforts at the Mine La Motte and the Mine à Breton, producing lead for the local trade and exporting a surplus to New Orleans and Europe during the next twenty years. Fort Chartres, Kaskaskia, and Ste. Genevieve all developed as centers of French settlement on the middle Mississippi by the 1740s, in large part stimulated by lead mining and the commerce it induced.

Despite this early attention, the Missouri mines remained productive only on a limited scale during the period of Spanish rule and through the early decades of American sovereignty. Among other notable figures, Moses Austin and William H. Ashley were both interested in these mines, but no great fortunes were made from Missouri lead strikes during the frontier era. In 1864, however, the St. Joseph Lead Company began operations with modern milling techniques, open-pit mining, and subsequently deep-shaft mining.

Meanwhile the Upper Mississippi District had rapidly come into production. The efforts of Julien DUBUQUE, a French-Canadian entrepreneur, were most important in opening this district. Dubuque began operations west of the Mississippi in 1788, at the site of modern Dubuque, Iowa. Before his death in 1810 he was also directing mining crews on the Fever River—later renamed the Galena River—and adjacent sites east of the Mississippi. Equally important, Dubuque encouraged the Sauk and Fox Indians of that country to take up mining and smelting, trading with them for the crudely smelted ore they produced by working open veins of lead.

Dubuque's activities prepared the way for American advances into the Upper Mississippi region following the War of 1812 (see WISCONSIN). After various preliminary ventures, a sizable American invasion began during the 1819 season, and by the mid-1820s the Fever River and Mineral Point areas were in the midst of a frontier mining boom that exhibited many characteristics found later on the gold and silver mining frontiers of the Far West. The town of Galena, founded in 1821, became the chief commercial center and supply-point for these areas (see ILLINOIS, SETTLEMENT OF). A continued influx of miners, merchants, and tradesmen were attracted to the region through the 1830s and the 1840s, while the Upper Mississippi District remained the major lead-producing area in the United States. But the best of the deposits were becoming exhausted by the late 1840s, and mining was already on the decline when news of the California gold strikes launched a mass exodus from the region. Many of the lead miners were from Ireland; others, experienced in tin mining, came from Cornwall. Thereafter the Irish and Cornish miners were found in California, in the Colorado silver and lead mines, and in every other western mining area.

Mississippi valley lead mining had important effects upon the development of the mining frontier throughout the Far West. In 1849 a large and experienced body of lead miners joined the other argonauts in California, and with their skills helped train thousands of gold-seekers by example. In addition to their knowledge of basic mining techniques, they were experienced with a type of locally adopted, extralegal miners' codes that became a model for the creation of local mining districts and the growth of miners' law in the gold regions. Moreover, the federal government's unsuccessful administration of a land-leasing and mine taxation system had brought about an important policy change on the eve of the gold rush. In 1848 Congress abolished the reservation of mineral lands and threw open the public domain freely to every prospector and miner. Certainly this change hastened the expansion of western mining after the discovery of gold in California.

In the Far West, lead became a significant by-product of silver. Particularly in Colorado silver was often found in argentiferous lead ores. The smelters at Leadville, Colorado, in the forefront of mining technology for their day, used improved methods of extracting silver from lead carbonate and reducing both minerals. By 1879, two years after the first smelter was built at Leadville, lead production in the district already totaled $1,775,000. A similar development occurred in other mining regions: where rich silver deposits could be found in lead-bearing ores, both minerals were soon brought into production. Eureka, Nevada, and the Coeur d'Alene region of northern Idaho also became centers for profitable lead and silver mining in the 1880s, and continued as primary producing areas in the twentieth century.

Another lead region contributed largely to lead production after 1900, the Tri-State District of southwestern Missouri, southeastern Kansas, and northeastern Oklahoma. Found in this district were many scattered, shallow deposits of lead sulfide (galena) closely mixed with zinc sulfide (blende) ores, notably free of silver or other mineral impurities. These deposits were being worked on a limited basis in southwest Missouri before the Civil War, with the first blast furnace built near Neosho in 1852. The city of Joplin, Missouri, founded in 1862, became the smelting, marketing, and supply headquarters for the Tri-State District in the postwar period. Large-scale operation began in the 1870s, when a number of mine operators from southeast Missouri took an interest in the region. But the geology of the district, with ore deposits typically scattered and shallow, and most mines short-lived, brought ruin to their attempts to introduce heavily capitalized, industrial mining techniques. The district remained a "poor man's camp," left to small-scale operators who risked their labor and lives, but little capital.

The most productive period in the history of the Tri-State District came between 1900 and 1930. With more highly mechanized methods, the district was producing weekly some fifteen thousand tons of lead and zinc by 1926. After 1930, however, no new fields were discovered, and the remaining ore deposits became increasingly marginal. By 1962, the centennial of Joplin, the historian of the Tri-State District could conclude that the rich mineral lodes were exhausted, and mining had ceased.

Today lead is still produced in combination with silver in a few districts of Idaho, Utah, and Colorado. The Southeast Missouri Lead District, however, continues to be the largest producing area, and St. Joseph, Missouri, remains an important mining center. The Old Lead Belt in that district is now near exhaustion, but the Viburnum Lead Belt, fifty miles to the west, promises to develop reserves as large as the older area. The one remaining pioneer firm, the St. Joseph Lead Company, has dominated mining in the district since the 1930s; but the Missouri Lead Operating Company, a joint venture of American Metal Climax and Homestake Mining Company, has recently developed the Buick mine, which became the nation's top producer in 1971. Total United States mine production of recoverable lead in 1971 amounted to 578,500 short tons, compared with 352,800 short tons in 1955, and a historic high of 684,000 short tons in 1925. Of the total domestic production, Missouri provided 74 percent in 1971, followed by Idaho with 12 percent, Utah 7 percent, and Colorado 4 percent.

See also MINING, METAL.

A comprehensive modern history of the lead mining frontier remains to be written. Available accounts include T. A. Rickard, *A History of American Mining* (1932); Joseph Schafer, *The Wisconsin Lead Region* (1932); and R. G. Thwaites, "Early Lead Mining in Illinois and Wisconsin," *Annual Report of the American Historical Association, 1893* (1894). James E. Wright, *The Galena Lead District* (1966), provides a sketchy study of the federal leasing system, while Arrell M. Gibson, *Wilderness Bonanza: The Tri-State District of Missouri, Kansas, and Oklahoma* (1972) contains a comprehensive summary of mining in that region. For an early appraisal of Colorado mining, see Samuel F. Emmons, *Geology and Mining Industry of Leadville* (1886). Geological information and modern production summaries are available in John D. Ridge, ed., *Ore Deposits in the United States, 1933-1967* (1968). Latest production data is published by the United States Bureau of Mines, *Minerals Yearbook, 1971*: vol. I, *Metals, Minerals, and Fuels* (1973). —K. N. O.

Leadville, Colorado. Mining town. Located at an altitude of 10,188 feet in the Colorado Rockies, Leadville is reputed to be the highest incorporated city in the United States. Leadville and vicinity have been one of the most productive mining areas in the West since 1860, when placer mining began in nearby California Gulch. With the discovery of huge beds of silver carbonate in 1877, the city became the silver capital of America, and since that time the mines surrounding Leadville have produced nearly $700 million in gold, silver, lead, zinc, copper, iron, bismuth, manganese, and molybdenum.

The boom years of the town were from 1878 to 1881. In 1880 the population reached 40,000, many of whom were millionaires. Most notable of these was Horace TABOR, who parlayed his Leadville holdings into an empire that extended throughout the state. By 1880 the monthly mining payroll in Leadville reached an astounding $800,000, and the city began to take on all the trappings of civilization: five banks, three newspapers, department stores, seven churches and schools, and, according to one local newspaper, 120 saloons, 110 beer gardens, 118 gambling halls, and 35 seraglios. In 1879 Oscar Wilde stopped at Leadville and, holding a single white lily in his hand, lectured the miners from the stage of the Tabor Opera House on the "Ethics of Art." Three railroads, the Denver and Rio Grande, the Santa Fe, and the Denver and South Park, battled one another fiercely for the right to service the city's transportation needs,

with William J. Palmer's Denver and Rio Grande winning the contest in 1880.

The fortunes of Leadville declined steadily in the 1880s. Mining capitalists were plagued by labor troubles and were unwilling to forgo the immediate gains of wholesale exploitation of existing lodes for a more secure program of long-range exploration and development. The repeal of the Sherman Silver Purchase Act in 1893 dealt the decisive blow to Leadville's prosperity. The town revived somewhat in the late 1890s on the strength of James J. Brown's gold strike. Although this boom was short-lived, it did bring to prominence two remarkable curiosities—Brown's wife, Unsinkable Molly Brown, and the Ice Palace, a huge castle of solid ice constructed for the town's Crystal Carnival in 1895.

Leadville slept peacefully until the 1930s when the molybdenum mines at nearby Climax were opened. This guaranteed the city's future, but it is a shadow of the booming town of millionaires of the 1870s. Many of the relics of Leadville's boistrous history remain for visitors to observe, including the Augusta Tabor house, the Matchless Cabin, where Tabor's mistress, Baby Doe, lived the last thirty years of her life, and the Tabor Opera House.

See Phyllis Dorset, *The New Eldorado* (1970); Don L. and Jean H. Griswold, *The Carbonate Camp Called Leadville* (1951); and Rodman Paul, *Mining Frontiers of the Far West* (1963).—R.B.W.

Lease, Mary Elizabeth (1853-1933). Populist orator. Born in Pennsylvania of Irish immigrant parents, Mary Elizabeth Clyens went to Osage Mission, Kansas, in 1870 to teach school. In 1873 she married Charles L. Lease and they moved to a homestead in Kingman County, where grasshoppers and hard times drove them off the farm to Denison, Texas. In the 1880s another try was made at farming in Kansas and in 1884 the Leases moved to Wichita. With the responsibility to help support four growing children, she took in laundry, began reading law, and was admitted to the bar.

Interested in self-education, Lease helped organize a ladies' club and her quick intelligence and forthright tongue attracted attention. She gave public speeches on behalf of Irish freedom and on other public issues to Greenbacker and Knights of Labor audiences. Nominally a Republican, she held Democrats responsible for the death of her brothers in Civil War combat and her father at the Andersonville prison.

Her support of Union Labor candidates in 1888 led her to the Farmers' Alliance movement and the Peoples party in the early 1890s. In the frenzied campaign of 1890 she gave 160 speeches throughout Kansas, and even larger crowds than usual turned out to hear her, believing that she had said, "What you farmers need is to raise less corn and more hell!" Victorious Farmers' Alliance members, as a majority of the Kansas legislature in 1891, refused to support United States Senator John H. Ingalls for reelection, and Lease was given much of the credit. In 1892 she campaigned nationally for the Populist candidates and with victory in Kansas was appointed chairman of the state Board of Charities. In 1896 she opposed Populist-fusionist leadership and refused to support William Jennings Bryan's candidacy for president. She moved her family to New York City in 1896. Her last years were spent on a farm near Callicoon, New York.

Recent works on Lease are Carleton Beals, *The Great Revolt and Its Leaders* (1968); Katherine B. Clinton,

"What Did You Say, Mrs. Lease?" *Kansas Quarterly* (Fall 1969); and Richard Stiller, *Queen of Populists: The Story of Mary Elizabeth Lease* (1970).—H. E. S.

Lecompton constitution. See KANSAS-NEBRASKA ISSUE.

Lee, Andrew Erickson (1847-1934). South Dakota politician. Born near Bergen, Norway, Lee emigrated with his family in 1851 to Dane County, Wisconsin, where he attended public schools. He engaged in mercantile work at McGregor, Iowa, and Madison, Wisconsin, for eight years before settling at Vermillion, South Dakota, in 1867. In 1869 he formed a partnership in a mercantile firm that continued in operation for fifty years.

Lee's political career began in 1892, when he was elected to a seat on the Vermillion city council. He served as mayor for two terms. He entered the gubernatorial race on the Populist ticket in 1896 and won. He was reelected in 1898, but the remainder of the ticket was defeated. He ran for governor as a Democrat in 1908 and was defeated. He then devoted his attention to the operation of his many farms until his death. —D. J. T.

Lee, Ann. See SHAKERS.

Lee, Jason (1803-1845). Oregon missionary and pioneer. Lee was the leader of the first American settlement in the Oregon country and the first missionary to bring Christianity to the Indians of the Pacific Coast. Traveling overland with Nathaniel Wyeth's second expedition, Lee, his nephew Daniel, Cyrus Shepard, and two secular helpers arrived at Fort Vancouver on September 15, 1834. Lee took his baggage from the *May Dacre*, which docked the next day, and in less than two weeks he made one of his many controversial decisions. Instead of heading northeast to the Flathead Indians of Montana, Lee followed the advice of the Hudson's Bay Company's John McLoughlin and settled on the banks of the Willamette River ten miles north of present-day Salem. Here the Willamette resembled the countryside of the small Massachusetts town of Wilbraham where Lee attended school in 1829 and 1830, and the tall evergreen forests looked very much as they did in Stanstead, the southern Canadian border town where he was born. The Chinook Indians of the Willamette, some with flattened heads, were a dying people, and Lee was not optimistic for their collective conversion. Yet their conversion as individuals, and the conversion of the half-breeds, the French-Canadians, and of all others, was of very great concern to Lee. He was singlemindedly devoted to the rise and spread of Methodism throughout the world, but he was incapable of organizing such a vast pioneering enterprise. Nevertheless he set out to Methodize Oregon. He left for the East (1838) in search of more financial support and for that righteous breed of settler only New England could supply. In 1840 Lee returned to Oregon on the *Lausanne* with fifty-one more settlers. He soon sprinkled the country with his New Englanders. With money from church donations Lee provided them with capital and goods. His purpose was to lay a moral foundation such as that provided by the Hudson's Bay Company for the time when the company's influence would be weakened by the inevitable influx of American settlers and by the final determination of the boundary line. Oregon's history suggests that Lee succeeded, but the mission board in New York dismissed Lee in 1843 on the grounds that his mission had grown too secular. His ministerial cohorts in the field deserted him, and he returned to his home in Stanstead to die. He was exonerated before his death and achieved legendary stature following it. Lee was neither an ordinary man nor an especially talented man, but was an authentically average man who expressed in his efforts some of the deepest themes of his times.

The Oregon Historical Society has a collection of Lee materials and his diary, which has been published in the *Oregon Historical Quarterly*, vol. 17 (1918). The *Quarterly* has published other documents relating to Lee and his mission from the society's archives. See also C. J. Brosnan, *Jason Lee: Prophet of the New Oregon* (1932), which contains some Lee correspondence now lost, and Robert J. Loewenberg, *The Idea of Equality in Ante-Bellum America* (1976). Other Lee papers are in the Collins Library, University of Puget Sound, and in the Washington State Historical Society, both in Tacoma, Washington; at the Rosenbach Foundation, Philadelphia; and scattered throughout the pages of the *Christian Advocate and Journal*, the leading Methodist paper of Lee's day.—R. J. L.

Leidesdorff, Alexander. See NEGROES IN THE FAR WEST.

Leigh, William R. (1866-1955) Illustrator, painter, and writer. Born in Berkeley County, West Virginia, Leigh studied art at the Maryland Institute in Baltimore in 1880-83 and at the Royal Academy in Munich, Germany, in 1883-87 and again in 1891-92. Returning to the United States in 1896, he worked as an illustrator for various New York publishers and made his first trip to the Southwest ten years later, courtesy of the Santa Fe Railroad. Thereafter he continued to make annual excursions to New Mexico, Arizona, Colorado, and Wyoming and produced a great many paintings depicting life in the West at his New York City studio. In 1926-27 he accompanied the Carl Akeley expedition and in 1928 the Carlisle-Clark expedition to East Africa for the American Museum of Natural History, serving as master painter of the backgrounds for the African habitat groups on display at that institution.

One of the most accomplished draftsmen in America, Leigh made exhaustive pictorial and photographic studies of the subjects to be incorporated into his finished work. His pencil and small oil renderings of human and animal forms are among the finest examples of his skill. He considered himself a realist in the photographic sense, although many of his finished paintings appear to be somewhat "overworked," his lively sense of the dramatic overwhelming the more matter-of-fact details in his pictures. Many of his historical canvases are quite romantic in retrospect.

Leigh's awards were many over the years. He also authored several plays, magazine articles, and books, notably *The Western Pony* (1933) and *Frontiers of Enchantment* (1938), relating to his African experiences. Collections of Leigh's work may be seen at the Thomas Gilcrease Institute, Tulsa, Oklahoma; the Adventurers' Club, New York City; and the Woolaroc Museum, Bartlesville, Oklahoma.

See Donnie D. Good, "W. R. Leigh, the Artists Studio Collection," *American Scene*, vol. 9, no. 4 (1968); David C. Hunt, "W. R. Leigh, Portfolio of an American Artist," *American Scene*, vol. 7, no. 1 (1966); and Paul Rossi and David C. Hunt, *The Art of the Old West* (1971).—D. C. H.

Leland, Alonzo (1817-1891). Oregon and Idaho pioneer. Moving from his native Vermont to Oregon in 1850, Leland became a leading citizen of Portland. He had a conspicuous part in establishing the school system, was a postmaster, and launched the first three daily newspapers in Portland and the Pacific Northwest. The last of them he used to promote the Idaho mines and joined the Idaho gold rush himself in 1862. Settling in Lewiston in 1862 (after losing a mine in Florence to claim jumpers), he had a versatile career as a surveyor, attorney, journalist, and member of the Idaho legislature. He worked tirelessly to develop North Idaho, which was geographically cut off from the rest of Idaho Territory, by bringing saw mills and stamp mills to the mining country and interesting his community in railroads and Snake River navigational improvements. Leland's main ambition, very nearly realized, was to persuade Congress to establish a new territory for North Idaho, eastern Washington, and adjacent Montana, or, lacking that, to have North Idaho removed from Idaho Territory and returned to Washington Territory. He served as a leading member of the Washington constitutional convention of 1878, representing North Idaho. But after more than twenty years of trying to rework boundary lines to North Idaho's advantage, Leland's effort was nullified when Washington and Idaho came into the Union as states in 1890.—M. W.

Lemke, William (1878-1950). North Dakota politician. Born in Minnesota, William Lemke graduated from the University of North Dakota and studied law at Georgetown and Yale universities. He was one of the founders of the Nonpartisan League, an organization that advocated socialist reforms. In 1920 he ran for attorney general and won but was recalled along with Governor Lynn J. Frazier in 1921 on charges of being communistic and corrupt. A supporter of La Follette for president in 1924, he headed the liberal wing of the Nonpartisan League.

Lemke served in the United States House of Representatives from 1932 until his death, with the exception of one term. He championed the cause of the farmer and was the author of the Frazier-Lemke Farm Bankruptcy Act of 1934, which would have protected farmers from foreclosure but was found unconstitutional by the Supreme Court. A revised, constitutionally acceptable version of the act was passed in 1935. In 1936 Lemke became the presidential candidate of the Union party, carrying no states and winning only thirteen percent of the presidential vote in North Dakota.

See Edward C. Blackorby, *Prairie Rebel: The Public Life of William Lemke* (1963).—D. J. T.

Leonard, Zenas (1809-1857). Fur trapper and trader and memoirist. Born in Clearfield, Pennsylvania, Leonard was a free trapper working out of St. Louis from 1831 to 1833. He then joined Captain Benjamin Bonneville's expedition and was with Joseph Walker as a clerk on his expedition to California via the Humboldt River. After retirement from the fur trade, he became a retailer, Indian trader, and steamboat operator in Sibley, Missouri. His *Narrative of the Adventures of Zenas Leonard* (1839) covers his adventures from 1833 to 1835 and points to California as a place for the workings of United States destiny. Lively and well written, the volume suggests that Leonard was an intelligent and observant explorer-trapper.—G. B. D.

leone. See MOUNTAIN LION.

Leopold, Aldo (1886-1948). Ecologist. Leopold's passion for the natural world began among the bluffs and bottom lands of the Mississippi River near Burlington, Iowa, where he was born. He graduated from Yale in 1908 and obtained graduate training at the Yale Forest School, then the sole producer of professional foresters in the United States. In 1909 Leopold began to work for the United States Forest Service in Arizona and New Mexico. At first he thought in the traditional terms of utilitarian resource management. Under this philosophy the environment exists to serve man's material needs; thus, for example, mountain lions, bears, and wolves are predators and must be eliminated. But gradually Leopold came to understand that the environment is not a commodity that belongs to man but a community to which man belongs. The community, moreover, is delicate, built on intricate harmonies and balances among all living things and the physical staffs of life. This "ecological consciousness," as Leopold termed it, leads one to a sense that, as the yielder of enormous and potentially disruptive technological power, man has the primary responsibility for maintaining environmental health. Ultimately, Leopold believed, such responsibility should be assumed because it is ethically right, not because it is economically expedient. The "land ethic" of Leopold synthesized science and morality. Articulated in a series of brilliant essays in the 1920s, 1930s, and 1940s, Leopold's philosophy was collected in 1949 in *A Sand County Almanac*.

As an ecologically undisturbed environment, wilderness occupied a central position in Leopold's life and thought. Before 1920 he took the lead in advocating wilderness preservation in the United States Forest Service. Heretical as this idea was to the traditional utilitarian foresters, it gradually made headway as the Forest Service was forced to compete with the dramatic gains in popularity of the preservation-minded National Park Service. In 1924 Leopold had the satisfaction of seeing the first wilderness reserve established on national forest land as the result of his own recommendation. Although the designation of a wilderness area in the Gila National Forest in New Mexico was administrative policy, not congressional law, it marked a significant departure from former management principles.

Leopold left the Forest Service in the late 1920s and embarked on a new career as a professor of wildlife management at the University of Wisconsin. There he developed one of the first programs of applied ecology. His life was cut short in mid-stride while fighting a brush fire along the Wisconsin River. His teachings have steadily gained momentum, and the present generation of environmentalists regards Leopold as the prophet of a new era in man's relationship to the land.

A chapter on Leopold appears in Roderick Nash, *Wilderness and the American Mind* (1967).—R.N.

Leslie, [Nashville] Frank[lin] (1842-?). Gunman. "Buckskin" Leslie's youth is shrouded in mystery; it is not even certain that his real name was Leslie. At times he claimed to be a Texan and other sources say he was born in Kentucky. There is evidence that he had some training in medicine or pharmacy as a young man, and he once declared that he had studied medicine in Europe. In the 1870s he was an army scout against the Plains Indians and later was in the Apache campaigns.

In 1878 he turned up in San Francisco, but the boom-town lure of Tombstone, Arizona, soon drew him there, and in 1880, he opened the Cosmopolitan Hotel in Tombstone. In June 1880 he killed Mike Killeen in a quarrel over Killeen's wife, and in August he married Killeen's widow. During the Earp-Clanton feud, during which Tombstone reached its height of violence, Leslie remained aloof, although he was friendly with the Clan-ton crowd. Yet his reputation was bad enough eventual-ly to get him into trouble in the town. He was frequently a drinking companion of gunman John Ringo, and when Ringo was found dead in July 1882 some believed Leslie to be the killer. One of those people was Billy Claiborne. He called Leslie out one morning, and Leslie killed him. After that, he scouted for a while and worked as a customs inspector.

In 1887 Leslie was divorced and took up with Mollie Williams. Two years later he killed her in a drunken rage. Leslie went to prison for the murder but was paroled in November 1896. He then went to the Klon-dike during the gold rush and apparently made money there; at least he showed up in San Francisco in 1904 with a sizable roll. After that, however, Leslie's life took a downward turn. He worked as a bartender in a variety of saloons in California and operated a poolroom be-tween 1913 and 1922 in Oakland, California. Then he vanished. Rumors suggest that he worked as a janitor in saloons and pool halls. The persistent story that he com-mitted suicide has not been proven. He simply vanished into the mists of time, as obscure in death as in the details of his youth.

See Colin Richards, *"Buckskin" Frank Leslie: Gunman of Tombstone* (1964).—G. L. R.

"Levi's." See COWBOY CLOTHING.

Lewis, Andrew. (1720-1781). Virginia frontiersman and soldier. Of western Virginia, Andrew Lewis was the son of John Lewis, an early (1732) and influential settler o: the Valley of Virginia. With his father and three brothers, and with eastern Virginia speculators such as George Washington and Dr. Thomas Walker, Lewis took an active interest in frontier lands. Through sever-al western expeditions, he helped to locate and open to settlement the most attractive regions of present south-west Virginia and southern West Virginia. As a colonel of the frontier militia, Lewis participated in the cam-paigns of the French and Indian Wars, including the Washington (1754), Braddock (1755), and Forbes (1758) expeditions against Fort Duquesne (Pittsburgh). He represented Virginia in the Indian diplomacy that followed the Proclamation of 1763 and helped to negotiate westward extensions of the proclamation line that were favorable to the Loyal and Greenbrier land companies, in which he was interested.

Lewis' best-known achievement was at the Battle of Point Pleasant, October 10, 1774, when eight hundred Virginians under his command defeated approximately the same number of Shawnee warriors under Cornstalk. This bloody engagement, the major encounter of LORD DUNMORE'S WAR, secured much of southwestern Vir-ginia from further Indian incursions and quieted the entire frontier during the initial years of the American Revolution. Subsequently, Lewis commanded the forces that expelled Governor Dunmore from Virginia in 1776-77. Through Washington's influence, the Conti-nental Congress made him a brigadier-general, but he

resigned the commission in 1778 in favor of a Virginia command, which he held until his death on the eve of the siege of Yorktown.

Lewis' role in Indian warfare and diplomacy and in frontier land speculation is discussed in Thomas P. Abernethy, *Western Lands and the American Revolution* (1937); and Otis K. Rice, *The Allegheny Frontier: West Virginia Beginnings, 1730-1830*. Alexander Scott With-ers, *Chronicles of Border Warfare* (1831; 2nd ed., 1903), and John P. Hale, *TransAllegheny Pioneers: Historical Sketches of the First White Settlers West of the Alleghenies* (1886, 1931), provide interesting, although not always reliable, accounts of frontier warfare in northwestern and southwestern Virginia, respectively.—J. A. W.

Lewis, Meriwether (1774-1809). Soldier, explorer, and politician. Lewis was born at Locust Hill, his family's plantation in Albemarle County, Virginia. Although his father, an army officer in the American Revolution, died when he was only five years old, Lewis spent a carefree childhood in Virginia and, for a short time, in Georgia, where his mother moved with her second hus-band, John Marks.

Lewis was a soldier most of his life. In 1794 he enlisted in the Virginia militia to help suppress the Whiskey Rebellion in western Pennsylvania. In May of the follow-ing year, he was appointed an ensign in the regular army and by the end of 1800 was a captain and paymaster in the First United States Infantry Regiment. Through extended service on the western frontier he learned much about the wilderness and its aboriginal inhabitants.

Early in 1801, President-elect Jefferson invited Lewis to become his private secretary, probably with a view to naming him to command a transcontinental exploring expedition. Jefferson had planned such an undertaking several years earlier, and Lewis, although then only eighteen years old, had volunteered for it, but had been rejected in favor of a more mature and better qualified person. Soon after becoming Jefferson's secretary, Lewis, under the president's direction, began to plan and prepare for his western journey. He obtained some scientific and technical training from members of the faculty of the University of Pennsylvania, selected and collected equipment and supplies of various kinds, and gathered information of his proposed route. Following congressional approval of the enterprise and his defi-nite designation as its commander early in 1803, Lewis invited William Clark, whom he had known since they had served together in the army in 1795-96, to be its coleader. Although on the LEWIS AND CLARK EXPEDITION itself Lewis and Clark acted as equals, Lewis was the official commander of the expedition. Of the two men, Lewis was the better trained scientifically and the more literate, authoring most of the scientific information contained in the expedition's journals.

Following Lewis' return from the Pacific, on March 3, 1807, President Jefferson appointed him governor of Louisiana Territory. Detained in the East by business related to the expedition and to the Burr conspiracy, he did not actually assume the post until a year later. Un-suited by temperament and experience for the office, the governor quickly ran into difficulties. He quarreled with Frederick Bates, the territorial secretary, and soon became unpopular with many of the inhabitants of the territory. Lewis communicated only infrequently with his superiors in Washington and failed to consult them on his policies and plans, especially with regard to the management of Indian affairs. He, consequently, fell under their severe criticism, and it is not unlikely that he would not have been reappointed to a second term of office had he lived out the first.

Lewis served as governor of Louisiana for only about a year and a half. In September 1809 he left St. Louis for the national capital in order to explain some of his acts as chief executive and to renew his efforts to secure the publication of the expedition's journals. On the way, while stopping overnight at a tavern on the Natchez Trace about seventy miles southwest of Nashville, Tennessee, he died in a mysterious and violent manner. The evidence as to whether he was murdered or committed suicide is still inconclusive. Thus at the age of thirty-five tragically ended the life of this moody, introverted, and extremely serious young man, who has been called "undoubtedly the greatest pathfinder this country has ever known."

The best biography of Lewis is Richard Dillon's *Meriwether Lewis: A Biography* (1965). John Bakeless' *Lewis and Clark: Partners in Discovery* (1947) also contains a good account of his life. The subject of Lewis' death is fully explored in Vardis Fisher's *Suicide or Murder? The Strange Death of Governor Meriwether Lewis* (1962). —J. L. L.

Lewis and Clark expedition (1804-1806). Lewis and Clark and their companions were the first white men to cross the western half of North America within the present limits of the United States. Their exploration was the concluding act in the long and fruitless search for a water route through the continent, a Northwest Passage, that had begun soon after Columbus discovered the New World.

The author of the exploration was Thomas Jefferson. He had first thought of such an undertaking about the time the United States achieved its independence in 1783, and during the succeeding decade he twice tried unsuccessfully to have a transcontinental exploring party sent out. Not until assuming the presidency in 1801, however, was Jefferson in a position to have his plan properly implemented.

On January 18, 1803, President Jefferson asked Congress for authorization, and an appropriation of $2,500, to send a military expedition to explore up the Missouri River to its source in the Rocky Mountains, then down the nearest westward-flowing stream to the Pacific. Jefferson gave two purposes of the proposed mission: to prepare the way for the extension of the American fur trade to the tribes throughout the area to be explored; and to advance geographical knowledge of the continent.

When he sent his message to Congress, none of the territory Jefferson wanted explored lay within the United States. The area between the Mississippi and the Rocky Mountains, called Louisiana, belonged to France, while the Pacific Northwest was claimed by England, Spain, and Russia, as well as by the United States. At the very moment he was maturing his plans for the transcontinental exploring expedition, however, the president was also conducting negotiations with the government of Napoleon Bonaparte that resulted, at the end of April, in the purchase of Louisiana. Thus, in ascending the Missouri the expedition would be exploring Ameri-

can territory, while, by completing the journey to the Pacific, it would be strengthening the United States claim to the region beyond the mountains.

To command the expedition, Jefferson chose his private secretary, Captain Meriwether LEWIS of the First United States Infantry Regiment. With the president's concurrence, Lewis then invited his old friend, William CLARK, to be coleader. Clark quickly accepted. The two men had become friends while serving together in the army in the 1790s. Clark had resigned his commission in 1796, however, and had gone home to Kentucky to manage the family plantation. Although commissioned only a second lieutenant in the corps of artillerists, on the expedition Clark was treated as a captain, equal in every respect to Lewis.

After making initial preparations in the East and receiving final and detailed instructions from the president, Lewis set out for the West on July 5, 1803. Traveling overland to Pittsburgh, he then descended the Ohio River by keelboat, picking up Clark and and several recruits for the expedition as he passed the Falls of the Ohio, at Louisville, Kentucky. From the mouth of the Ohio, the little party ascended the Mississippi to Wood River, Illinois, opposite the mouth of the Missouri River, and encamped. Lewis and Clark spent the next five months at Camp Wood River recruiting and training their men, gathering additional supplies and equipment, and collecting information about the Missouri from traders and boatmen who had been some distance up the river. On April 1, 1804, they chose the members of the permanent exploring party. In addition to the two officers, it included twenty-seven young, unmarried soldiers; a half-breed hunter and interpreter named George Drouilliard; and Clark's Negro slave, York. Besides these men, a corporal and five privates and several French boatmen were to accompany the expedition the first season and then return with its records and scientific specimens.

The "Corps of Discovery" began its historic journey on May 14, 1804. It started up the Missouri in a 55-foot keelboat and two pirogues, or dugout canoes. Averaging about fifteen miles a day, by the end of October it reached the villages of the Mandan and Minnetaree Indians near the mouth of Knife River in present North Dakota. There the explorers built a log fort and went into winter quarters. During the long, frigid winter at Fort Mandan, Lewis and Clark made copious notes in their journals, drew maps of their route, and counseled with numerous Indian visitors. From the Minnetaree especially, they obtained invaluable information about the course of the Missouri and the country through which it ran. The contributions of these and other Indians to the success of the exploration cannot be exaggerated.

On April 7, 1805, the expedition resumed its journey. The party now numbered only thirty-three persons. It included, besides the permanent detachment, an interpreter named Toussaint CHARBONNEAU, his young Shoshoni squaw, SACAGAWEA, and her papoose. Passing through country never before visited by white men, the expedition reached the navigable limits of the Missouri on August 17.

Leaving their canoes at the second fork of the Jefferson, the exploring party began the portage of the Rockies. With Sacagawea's help, they purchased horses from her people, who lived nearby, and crossed the Continental Divide through Lemhi Pass. Turning northward, they proceeded along the Lemhi and Salmon rivers, up over Lost Trail Pass, and down the Bitterroot valley. At the mouth of Lolo Creek, Montana, about ten miles southwest of present-day Missoula, the expedition again faced west and crossed the rugged Bitterroot range on the Lolo Trail. It was the most difficult part of the entire journey. Completing the mountain portage by September 22, the explorers entrusted their horses to a friendly Indian tribe and in five small canoes descended the Clearwater, Snake, and Columbia rivers to the Pacific. "Men appear much Satisfied with their trip beholding with estonishment . . . this emence Ocian," wrote Clark laconically in his journal on November 18, 1805.

Having decided to winter near the coast in order to enjoy the mild climate and to replenish its salt supply by evaporating seawater, the Corps of Discovery erected and occupied a post on the south side of the Columbia River. Lewis and Clark named it Fort Clatsop for the nearest Indian tribe. As during the previous year, they spent the winter gathering and recording much information concerning the surrounding country and its aboriginal inhabitants.

After a winter made very disagreeable by rainy weather, thieving Indians, and a scarcity of edible game, on March 23, 1806, the explorers started for home. Retracing their route to the mouth of Lolo Creek, in early July the party split. Lewis, with nine men, went directly across country to the Falls of the Missouri. Before descending the Missouri, he explored up Marias River as far as Cut Bank Creek, in northern Montana. Clark and the rest of the party returned to the Three Forks of the Missouri, whence they crossed over to the Yellowstone and went down that river. The two parties were reunited a few miles below the mouth of the Yellowstone on August 12. Stopping at the home of the Mandan only long enough to persuade one of the chiefs and his family to return with them for a visit to the United States, the explorers hurried on down the Missouri. They arrived in St. Louis on September 23, 1806. Having long since been given up for lost by nearly everyone but Jefferson, the little band of explorers was greeted with great rejoicing.

Warren L. Cook, in *Flood Tide of Empire: Spain and the Pacific Northwest, 1543-1819* (1973), casts an interesting sidelight on the expedition: General James WILKINSON, Aaron Burr's ambitious fellow conspirator, alerted Spanish authorities to the American venture, which Jefferson had tried to keep a secret. Between August 1804 and August 1806 four Spanish expeditions were sent out to stop Lewis and Clark, but each was forced to turn back by hostile Indians and, in one case, by the high number of deserting troops. The fourth expedition reached the region of Red Cloud, Nebraska, coming within 140 miles of the American party without either group knowing it.

The Lewis and Clark expedition accomplished its mission with remarkable success. During an absence of more than twenty-eight months it covered more than eight thousand miles. On that entire journey only one man, Sergeant Charles Floyd, lost his life, probably of a ruptured appendix. Although encountering thousands of Indians, the explorers had only one violent encounter

with them, which occurred while Lewis was high up the Marias River and resulted in the death of two Indians. The total expense of the undertaking, including the special congressional appropriation of $2,500, was something less than $40,000. At this small cost Lewis and Clark and their companions took the first giant step in opening the trans-Mississippi West to the American people. Their achievement has well been called the most perfect of its kind in the history of the world.

Two good secondary accounts of the Lewis and Clark expedition can be found in John Bakeless, *Lewis and Clark: Partners in Discovery* (1947), and Richard Dillon, *Meriwether Lewis: A Biography* (1965). An excellent work on the scientific and technical aspects of the expedition is Paul R. Cutright, *Lewis and Clark: Pioneering Naturalists* (1969). Reuben G. Thwaites, ed., *The Original Journals of the Lewis and Clark Expedition, 1804-1806*, 7 vols. and with an atlas (1905), and Donald Jackson, ed., *The Letters of the Lewis and Clark Expedition* (1962), are major publications of primary materials.—J. L. L.

Lexington, Kentucky. No mention was made of the central bluegrass area about Lexington, Kentucky, until 1775. A party of hunters and land spies came out from Harrod's Town in the spring of that year under the leadership of Robert Patterson. On or about June 5, they encamped near the heart of the present city. This party helped William McConnell to build a cabin to substantiate his claim to the land on which Lexington was to be built. Tradition has it that when news of the battle of Lexington reached the Patterson party, they gave the spot of McConnell's cabin the name Lexington in honor of the outbreak of the American Revolution.

The actual beginning of the frontier town of Lexington was the building of a blockhouse by Robert Patterson on the north bank of Town Creek. About this blockhouse was established the circular puncheon wall that became Lexington Station. In 1780 the tiny settlement was made the seat of sprawling Fayette County. The Fayette County Court was to attract at an early date many bright young lawyers who came from Virginia to engage in land law practice. By 1800 the town had developed into a rich farming market town; the seat of the Transylvania-Lexington Public Library, TRANSYLVANIA SEMINARY, and several private academies; a famous tavern town; and the place where the Kentucky state government was organized in June 1792. Quickly outgrowing its frontier beginnings, it became a place of some sophistication, a political and legal center, and the mecca of almost every traveler who visited the western country. Until 1820 Lexington enjoyed the distinction of being the chief town on the Ohio frontier below Pittsburgh.

See W. H. Perrin, ed., *History of Fayette County, Kentucky* (1882); George W. Ranck, *History of Lexington, Kentucky* (1872); and Charles R. Staples, *The History of Pioneer Lexington, 1779-1806* (1939).—T. D. C.

Libby, Orin Grant (1864-1952). Historian. A native of Wisconsin, Libby prepared the classic *Geographical Distribution of the Vote of the Thirteen States on the Federal Constitution, 1787-8* (1894) under Frederick Jackson Turner. After arriving at the University of North Dakota in 1903, he did pioneer work in studies of the origin of American political parties and in quantification methodology. He wrote about La Vérendrye's explorations in

Dakota country and recorded Indian narratives of Custer's last expedition.

Libby was a founder and fourth president of the Mississippi Valley Historical Association and an organizer of the State Historical Society of North Dakota (1903), of which he was secretary and editor until 1944.

See Robert P. Wilkins, "Orin G. Libby: His Interests, Ideas, Opinions," *North Dakota Quarterly* (Summer 1956).—D. J. T.

Lincoln, Abraham (1809-1865). President. Few presidents have been more closely identified with the frontier and the West than Abraham Lincoln. Yet the portrait of him as "Honest Abe," the rail-splitting frontiersman, is vastly overdrawn. Lincoln's life was influenced by the frontier, but in no sense can he be considered a frontiersman.

Born in a log cabin three miles south of Hodgenville, Kentucky, Lincoln was a child of the second frontier, the frontier of the mobile homesteader. During his first twenty-one years, his father, Thomas, moved the Lincoln family first to the Knob Creek area of Kentucky, then to Spencer County, Indiana, then to Macon County, Illinois, and finally to Coles County in the same state. In 1859 Lincoln recalled that Indiana "was a wild region, with many bears and other wild animals still in the woods." While living in Indiana, he received all of his formal schooling—which totaled less than one year. He spent most of his time working on his father's farm, clearing trees, and splitting the proverbial fence rails. But all the while he harbored an intense dislike for farming. In 1842, when a friend asked Lincoln for some advice about a farm problem, he replied: "As to your farm matter, I have no sympathy with you. *I* have no farm, nor ever expect to have; and, consequently, have not studied the subject enough to be much interested with it. I can only say that I am glad *you* are satisfied and pleased with it." He was also not interested in the frontier pastimes of fishing and hunting, and though he spent his youth in a rural area, he developed no apparent love of nature.

In 1831, after coming of age, Lincoln turned his back on the rural agricultural life for good and moved to the small village of New Salem, in Sangamon County, Illinois, where he worked as a merchant, surveyor, postmaster, and jack-of-all-trades. He remained in Sangamon County until he moved to Washington in 1861. Settled in one county for thirty years, he can hardly be considered representative of the nomadic frontiersman. Shortly after Lincoln moved to New Salem, he was caught up in the excitement of the Black Hawk War of 1832 and was elected captain of the local volunteer company. More than a quarter century later he described that election as "a success which gave me more pleasure than any I have had since." He also recalled that during his eighty days in the army he never "saw any live, fighting Indians . . . ; but I had a good many bloody struggles with the musquitoes [sic]; and, although I never fainted from loss of blood, I can truly say I was often very hungry."

Deeply interested in a political career, he returned home to run unsuccessfully for the legislature in 1832. He won election in 1834, however, and held his seat until 1841. In New Salem, Lincoln studied law independently and gained admission to the bar in 1836.

New Salem was hardly the place for an ambitious lawyer and politician. Nearby, rapidly growing Springfield, which became the state capital in 1836, was much more likely to prove the fulfilling setting for such a man's needs. In moving to Springfield in 1847, Lincoln, like thousands of others, participated in the post-frontier movement to towns and cities. One of the most prominent examples of the rapid growth of cities in the West was to be found in northern Illinois. In 1830 only a few settlers lived on the site of what would become Chicago; in 1860 Chicago was a thriving city with more than 110,000 inhabitants.

While living in Springfield, Lincoln was befriended by the cultured, well-educated men of the town. When he married Mary Todd of Kentucky in 1841, he became a member of one of the town's leading families. When he sought the Whig nomination for Congress in 1843, he was "put down here as the candidate of pride, wealth, and arristocratic [sic] family distinction." Lincoln was also a member of the town's intellectual elite; in 1838 he addressed the Young Men's Lyceum of Springfield on the subject of law and order.

Lincoln's relationship to the frontier is displayed clearly in his legal career. His years as a lawyer traveling the circuit on horseback have been chronicled fully, but the impact of this experience on his life has been exaggerated. It does appear that he enjoyed riding the circuit. Circuit-riding enabled him to keep in touch with voters, make political speeches, and regale his listeners with stories drawn from his inexhaustible fund of frontier yarns. And it was on the circuit that Lincoln perfected the techniques of frontier politics. However, only a portion of Lincoln's legal work was done on the circuit. More important were his cases in the state appellate courts and in the federal circuit court. Unlike most of the itinerant lawyers, Lincoln invariably attended court at every county seat. It would not be too much of an overstatement to call Lincoln a railroad attorney; he represented the Illinois Central, the Rock Island, and other railroads. Banks and manufacturing concerns were also numbered among his clients. At the same time he represented clients in suits against railroads and corporations. By the time Lincoln was elected president he had become one of the leading attorneys in Illinois; he was certainly much more than a country lawyer.

Lincoln's first love was politics, not law. After his fourth term in the state legislature, he turned his eyes to Washington and began his one-term congressional career in December 1847. In the House Lincoln faced an issue of primary concern to his constituents in Illinois and to other westerners, the Mexican War and territorial expansion. As a loyal Whig, Lincoln joined his party's attack on President James K. Polk's conduct of the war. In response to Polk's claim that the war began because Mexicans had killed Americans on American soil, Lincoln introduced resolutions demanding that Polk show the exact spot where American blood was first shed. These "spot" resolutions earned Lincoln the nickname of "Spotty" Lincoln but did not endear him to his constituency. Unlike most residents of the Mississippi valley, Lincoln was not an ardent expansionist and gave only lukewarm support for the annexation of Texas. To Lincoln the phrase "Young America" meant that America should spread democracy, freedom, and equality not by territorial expansion, but rather by moral example. Lincoln's constituents in the normally Whig seventh district rebuked him in 1848 when they elected a Democrat as his successor.

At the end of Lincoln's term, the recently installed Whig president, Zachary Taylor, offered Lincoln the governorship or secretaryship of Oregon Territory. He rejected the offer to move to that overwhelmingly Democratic territory and returned to Springfield.

In 1854 a question of policy toward the territories shook the foundations of Illinois politics. Under the parliamentary direction of Senator Stephen A. Douglas of Illinois, Congress passed the Kansas-Nebraska Act. The act repealed the Missouri Compromise of 1820, which had prohibited the introduction of slavery into that part of the Louisiana Purchase that lay north of the 36°30' line. The new act allowed the white people of Kansas and Nebraska to decide for themselves whether or not they wanted slavery. Thus slavery was free to expand into land that had been closed to it for thirty-four years.

The repeal of the Missouri Compromise aroused opposition among thousands in the North, including Abraham Lincoln. He declared that he had been losing interest in politics until the repeal of the compromise galvanized him. Northern opposition to the expansion of slavery was heightened by the Supreme Court's Dred Scott decision of 1857, which declared that the Missouri Compromise was unconstitutional and that Congress had no authority to exclude slavery from the territories. Lincoln's position on slavery in the territories may be seen most clearly in his debates with Douglas during the senatorial contest of 1858, when he ran as the candidate of the new Republican party against the "Little Giant," and the numerous speeches he made during 1859.

While many Republicans opposed the expansion of slavery because they wanted the territories reserved exclusively for free white labor, Lincoln opposed it mainly because he believed slavery to be wrong. In late 1859 he warned a Chicago audience: "Never forget that we have before us this whole matter of the right or wrong of slavery in this Union, though the immediate question is as to its spreading out into new Territories and States." Lincoln saw slavery as "a moral, social, and political evil," a "monstrous injustice." He contended that the founding fathers had viewed slavery in a similar way and had sought to put it "in course of ultimate extinction" by providing for the abolition of the African slave trade and by the Northwest Ordinance of 1787, which prohibited slavery in a portion of the land ceded by Virginia to the central government. Congress further limited slavery when it passed the Missouri Compromise in 1820. According to Lincoln, the issue excited little interest until 1854 because the public believed that slavery was gradually dying. The Kansas-Nebraska Act destroyed that belief by repealing the compromise and by opening up all the territories to slavery. Lincoln argued that by limiting the area into which slavery could spread, the Missouri Compromise represented a moral condemnation of the peculiar institution. By opening the territories to slavery, Lincoln argued, the Kansas-Nebraska Act substituted an amoral attitude toward slavery, best expressed by Stephen Douglas when he said, "I don't care if slavery is voted up or down." The act was the first step, Lincoln contended, toward the expansion of slavery throughout the nation. Next came the Dred Scott decision. Its purpose, combined with "the Nebraska

doctrine . . . is to *educate* and *mould* public opinion, at least *Northern* public opinion, to not *care* whether slavery is voted *down* or voted *up*." If people had no moral objection to slavery in the territories, Lincoln asked, what objection could they have to the expansion of slavery elsewhere? The moral shield that protected the North against the nationalization of slavery would be removed. Once the North no longer had any moral objection to slavery the stage would be set for the Supreme Court to declare unconstitutional all *state* laws prohibiting slavery. But as long as northerners believed slavery a moral wrong, opposed its expansion, fought for the repeal of the Kansas-Nebraska Act and the Dred Scott decision (and incidentally elected Republicans to office), all would be well.

Intense public interest in the Lincoln-Douglas debates of 1858 established Lincoln as a prominent member of the Republican party, and in 1860 the tall gaunt Illinoisan was elected president.

Lincoln's presidency was focused on the Civil War, but in 1862 he and his fellow Republicans attained one of their party's goals when he signed into law a congressional bill prohibiting slavery in all the territorial possessions of the United States. Other congressional measures critical to the development of the West were enacted under Lincoln's administration. Congress organized the remaining West into territories, passed the Homestead Act, and provided for the building of a transcontinental railroad, the Union Pacific and the Central Pacific. But Lincoln's role in the passage of these measures was passive. Although numerous Indian tribes engaged in rebellions during the war years, there is little evidence to suggest that Lincoln took an active interest in the formulation of Indian policy.

Lincoln's writings and speeches are collected in Roy P. Basler, ed., *The Collected Works of Abraham Lincoln*, 8 vols. (1953-55). The best one-volume biography of Lincoln is Benjamin Thomas, *Abraham Lincoln* (1952). The fullest account of his pre-presidential years is Albert J. Beveridge, *Abraham Lincoln, 1809-1858*, 2 vols. (1928). The best account of the presidential years is James G. Randall and Richard N. Current, *Lincoln the President*, 4 vols. (1945-55). Don E. Fehrenbacher, *Prelude to Greatness: Lincoln in the 1850's* (1961), provides a penetrating analysis of the Lincoln-Douglas debates. Harry V. Jaffa, *Crisis of the House Divided: An Interpretation of the Issues in the Lincoln-Douglas Debates* (1959), is a superb analysis of the political thought of Lincoln and Douglas.—M. W. K.

Lincoln County War (1878-1881). New Mexican political and economic violence. The Lincoln County War is remembered today largely as the range war that served as a backdrop for the career of Billy the Kid. Yet the troubles in Lincoln County, New Mexico, cannot properly be called a range war or a blood feud, and their significance transcends mere individuals, however legendary they have become. In perspective Billy the Kid seems almost incidental, a minor figure in a drama that had elements of range war and bitter personal hatreds but that was far more complicated. Lincoln County was a remote section of New Mexico with a reputation for lawlessness that antedated the Lincoln County War by at least a decade. Nevertheless it was an area that attracted men like John Chisum, a cattleman who pushed his herds into the Pecos valley in the early 1870s and began to preempt government lands there, and Lawrence G. Murphy, a hard-nosed businessman who saw the future of the area in terms of profits for his mercantile business.

Control of the area depended in large measure upon government contracts for beef and other provisions. Thus, at its simplest level, the Lincoln County War was a struggle for economic supremacy between two factions of entrepreneurs. Murphy acquired control of government contracts for the region through the patronage of a powerful political clique in Santa Fe. The Santa Fe Ring was a nebulous political group composed of prominent Republicans who sought to control the economic and political life of New Mexico. Although the ring's very existence was denied by Republicans, their opponents insisted that it was very real. The ring supported Murphy and his associates in Lincoln County, James J. Dolan, Emil Fritz, and James H. Riley, even though they were Democrats, because Murphy's operations constituted a virtual monopoly in Lincoln County, and the monopoly permitted Murphy to control the population. That fact had a political payoff. The economic dominance of the House of Murphy provided an effective lever for insuring political control as well. Public officials, especially in law enforcement positions, were controlled by the Murphy group; as a result, legal controversies were usually decided in their favor.

Against these forces, the cattle baron John Chisum stood almost alone until 1875. Unlike Murphy, who owned virtually no cattle and depended on his economic control of small ranchers, Chisum owned vast herds. He sought government contracts directly and threatened Murphy's position. In 1875 a lawyer named Alexander McSween arrived in Lincoln. Initially he worked for Murphy, but he gradually became disenchanted with the association. The next year John Tunstall, an Englishman, established a ranch in Lincoln County. Together McSween and Tunstall aligned themselves with Chisum and set up a rival mercantile company in Lincoln.

By that time Murphy had pulled out, selling his interests to Dolan and Riley, who found themselves losing business to the new firm. Competition threatened Dolan's domination, and loss of economic supremacy threatened political collapse as well. In retaliation, Dolan and his friends used their political connections to apply legal and economic pressure on Tunstall, McSween, and their supporters. A haggle over the estate of Emil Fritz heightened the antagonism between the two groups, and the small ranchers, farmers, and businessmen gradually took sides behind the two factions.

As John Chisum preempted more and more public land in the Pecos valley, he aroused the opposition of numerous smaller ranchers who now gave their support to Dolan. Other citizens of the county were lashed to Dolan by credit and patronage. On the other hand, many saw Tunstall's store as an opportunity to wrench free of the political and economic exploitation of the "House." Small farmers, ranchers, and a strong element of Spanish-speaking citizens rallied to McSween and Tunstall. Under Dolan and Riley, the House of Murphy had grown increasingly arrogant toward its customers, and rumors were rife that Dolan was dealing in stolen cattle to fill his contracts. These factors contributed still other supporters to the McSween-Tunstall faction.

But Dolan still controlled law enforcement in the area,

and he applied more legal pressure against Tunstall. Writs of attachment were filed against him, and the Englishman was subjected to constant harassment. On February 18, 1878, Tunstall was murdered by a posse of Dolan supporters, and Lincoln County suddenly exploded into a bloody shooting war. The courts and law enforcement agencies were too partisan to restrain the violence. Sheriff William Brady and District Attorney William L. Rynerson were supporters of Dolan. The governor, Samuel B. Axtell, was himself a partisan of the Santa Fe Ring and, therefore, the Dolan faction.

After Tunstall's murder, Brady arrested Fred Waite and Billy the Kid, both employees of Tunstall, but refused to arrest the murderers of Tunstall even though warrants had been issued for their arrest. Supporters of the McSween faction then concluded that they could expect no help from the legally constituted authorities. Upon his release, Billy the Kid returned to Lincoln with five men for the purpose of protecting the wives and children of the McSween group. Billy and the others had just arrived in town when they saw Brady and a group of Dolan men walking toward them. They hid behind a fence and opened fire, killing Brady and wounding George Hindman. Other murders followed. A. L. "Buckshot" Roberts was killed by McSween partisans, but not before Roberts killed Dick Brewer, a small farmer who worked as Tunstall's foreman and now led the McSween fighters. With Brewer's death, Billy the Kid became a leader of McSween's partisans. In July 1878 the feud was climaxed by the "five-day battle" in Lincoln. The Murphy-Dolan faction lay siege to the McSween home. Troops from Fort Stanton arrived, but the commander showed marked partiality toward the Dolan faction. Ultimately, the McSween home was set on fire. Under withering fire Billy the Kid and his friends made their escape from the burning house, but McSween and four other men were killed.

The violence seemed to subside after that, and nominally that was the end of the conflict. Axtell was replaced by Lew Wallace as governor, Pat Garrett was elected sheriff of Lincoln County, and there was talk of amnesty for the Kid. But fresh violence and more murders followed. Harassment of McSween's followers continued. Outlaws like John SELMAN took advantage of the unsettled state of affairs, and Billy the Kid, angered by John Chisum's failure to pay him for his support of Tunstall and McSween, turned to stealing cattle from the big ranchers. The Kid was soon involved in more murders that can be linked to the earlier troubles, and only after his death at the hands of Garrett in 1881 could the governor of New Mexico report with confidence that Lincoln County was in "a state of quiet." But the hatreds roused by the trouble were not completely extinguished even then. In 1884 Juan Patron, leader of the Mexican-Americans in Lincoln County, was murdered, and his support of the Tunstall-McSween faction was believed to be the reason. That same year John Chisum died, and gradually peace returned to Lincoln County.

See William A. Keleher, *Violence in Lincoln County* (1957); and Robert N. Mullin, ed., *Maurice Garland Fulton's History of the Lincoln County War* (1968).—G. L. R.

Linn, Lewis Fields (1795-1843). Physician and Missouri politician. Linn was born near Louisville, Kentucky, and orphaned at an early age. Determined to study medicine, he saw service as a surgeon with Colonel

Henry Dodge's Mounted Rifle Volunteers in the War of 1812 and then went to Philadelphia to complete his medical studies.

In 1816 he set up practice at Ste. Genevieve, Missouri, where he seemed to thrive on the life of a frontier physician. Amiable and personable, he built up a large practice and became an authority on Asiatic cholera, which wracked the river country on two different occasions.

Although strongly interested in Democratic politics and a staunch Jacksonian, Linn declined public office when urged to run—until he spent one term in the Missouri Senate. In 1833 he served as commissioner to settle French land claims. That same year Governor Daniel Dunklin appointed him to fill the vacancy created by the death of United States Senator Alexander Buckner. Staunchly representing the expansionist interests of his frontier constituents, he was rewarded in 1837 and 1843 with reelection.

During his second term Linn served as chairman of the committee on territories and actively sought the protection of developing American interests in Oregon. Although unsuccessful in securing legislation in his lifetime, Linn's efforts were recognized by the Oregon settlers with their naming of a county in his honor.

Conventional biographies are J. M. Greenwood, *Lewis Fields Linn* (1900); E. A. Linn and N. Sargent, *Life and Public Services of Dr. Lewis F. Linn* (1857); and W. F. Switzler, *The Father of Oregon* (1899).—W. E. P.

Lipan Indians. See APACHE INDIANS.

Lisa, Manuel (1772-1820). Fur trader. Born in New Orleans or Cuba of Spanish parents, Lisa was reared in Louisiana and settled in St. Louis about 1790. After several fur-trading ventures in the lower Missouri region, Lisa in 1807 went upstream and established a post at the mouth of the Big Horn River. The prospects for developing the fur business in this area seemed bright, and in 1809 Lisa, in partnership with other St. Louis traders, formed the MISSOURI FUR COMPANY. Trouble with the Indians ensued and with the coming of the War of 1812 British traders temporarily dominated the upper Missouri basin.

This disruption of trade restricted the Missouri Fur Company to the lower reaches of the river, and internal disputes led to a reorganization of the firm in 1812. In that year, Lisa established a fur post, Fort Lisa, on the Missouri River north of present-day Omaha. He became the leading figure in the early Nebraska fur trade and made his post the center of traffic with the Omaha, Oto, and Pawnee tribes. A sharp competitor, Lisa knew his business and enjoyed amicable relations with the Indians. Largely through his influence, the tribes in eastern Nebraska developed cordial relations with the United States government, which proved enduring.

See Walter Bond Douglas, *Manuel Lisa*, ed. by A. P. Nasatir (1964); and Richard E. Oglesby, *Manuel Lisa and the Opening of the Missouri Fur Trade* (1963).—H. A. D.

lithography. See PRINTS.

Little Arkansas, Treaty of the. See CHEYENNE-ARAPAHO WAR.

Little Big Horn, battle of the (1876). This battle was the culmination of the vacillating policy of the United States government toward the Indians of the Great Plains. The policy consisted of alternately "loving the Indian to death" and "beating him to death," neither of which was followed long enough for it to be effective.

When in 1876 governmental ineptitude and scandal and Indian intransigence had forced matters to a crisis, army troops were ordered sent against the Sioux and Northern Cheyenne who were concentrated in the Powder River country in Montana. One column, which was to march from Fort Abraham Lincoln, was commanded by Brigadier Alfred Howe TERRY and consisted largely of the Seventh Cavalry under Lieutenant Colonel George Armstrong CUSTER. Because of a combination of politics and bad weather, the column was late in starting and did not reach the Powder River until June 7, where U. S. Highway 12 now crosses that stream.

Here, in an attempt to locate the enemy, General Terry sent Major Marcus A. Reno with six companies to scout up to the forks of the Powder. Then, after exploring the tributaries of both streams, they were to move west to the Tongue River and come down that stream to the Yellowstone. In a technical violation of his orders, Reno went as far west as Rosebud Creek, where he found the remains of a large Indian village and evidence that a large number of Indians had lately moved up that stream. He then returned to the Yellowstone, where the remainder of the regiment was waiting.

In the meantime General Terry had met and concerted plans with General John Gibbon, whose command had been patrolling the north bank of the Yellowstone. It was arranged that Gibbon, who had both infantry and cavalry, would move to the Big Horn River, and then up that stream to the confluence with the Little Big Horn, where it was expected that the hostiles would be found. Custer was to march up the Rosebud and follow the trail discovered by Major Reno. He was not to hasten his march, and if the trail was found to lead west across the Little Wolf Mountains into the Little Big Horn valley, he was not to follow. In order to give Gibbon's slower-moving infantry time to get into position, Custer was to move farther south before turning west, and then to move north in what has been called a hammer-and-anvil operation.

Custer's command moved out shortly after noon on June 22. By late afternoon of June 24 they were near the present town of Busby, Montana, where they noticed increasing indications that large numbers of Indians—larger numbers than they had previously thought—were ahead. Here the trail turned west, but Custer, ignoring Terry's order, embarked on a night march in order to get close to the summit of the Little Wolf Mountains before daybreak. On the morning of June 25 the regiment was camped near the summit on the eastern slope. Scouts sent ahead reported a large Indian village in the valley below. Custer professed not to believe this, but on learning that the presence of his command had been discovered and fearing that the village, if indeed there, would begin to scatter, he decided to move forward and to do something almost without precedent in Indian warfare: attack in the middle of the day. (In Indian warfare it was almost standard procedure to attack at dawn.)

The regiment crossed the divide at almost precisely noon. Soon after, Custer divided the regiment: Troop B was detailed to protect the pack train, which could not be expected to keep up with the rest of the command; a battalion of Troops H, D, and K, under command of Frederick W. BENTEEN, the senior captain, was sent on a scout to the left. The precise reason for this is unknown, but it was possibly to protect the command from a surprise attack from that direction. Troops M, A, and G formed another battalion under Major Reno; Custer kept the remaining five troops under his personal command.

Benteen's battalion soon disappeared from sight on the left, and the pack train dropped behind as the Custer and Reno commands rode down the valley of present Reno Creek. About three or four miles from the river they saw a group of about fifty warriors riding downstream. Fearing that the village was already in flight, Custer ordered Reno and his battalion to pursue the Indians and bring them to battle. Reno was told that he would be supported by "the whole outfit." Reno then led his command down to the Little Big Horn, crossed it, and rode down the valley toward the village. As he was crossing the river it was noted that some of the Indians were advancing to meet him, possibly to fight a holding action and permit the village to escape. One of the scouts went back to inform Custer of this new development.

As Reno rode toward the village the number of Indians increased. Uncertain of what was ahead, he halted the command and dismounted to fight on foot, every fourth man being detailed to hold the horses. The Indians, by now in large numbers, began to get around the line, which was forced back into a patch of timber along the stream. But the Indians soon infiltrated this position, and seeing no sign of the promised support, Reno decided to withdraw and try to regain the bluffs across the river. There was a great deal of confusion; Reno seems to have panicked temporarily and the retreat became a disorganized rout. The bluffs were gained with the loss of about one third of the battalion just as Benteen's three troops approached. They had found nothing on their scout and the commander had decided to go in the direction taken by the remainder of the regiment.

In the meantime, Custer, hearing that the Indians were coming up to meet Reno, had turned downstream hoping to take the enemy in flank. He had seen the great numbers of the enemy from the edge of the bluffs, and messengers were sent back to the pack train and to Captain Benteen, urging them forward. Then the five companies started down Medicine Tail Coulee toward the river. From that time on the events concerning Custer's command are conjecture and controversy. Some historians think that a part of the command crossed; others say that no part of the five companies reached the stream before being forced back a long and dusty ridge paralleling the Little Big Horn, where their bodies were later found in what may or may not have been battle lines.

Major Reno, after being joined by Benteen's battalion, was waiting for the pack train with the reserve ammunition to arrive. There was considerable disagreement as to what to do, but finally Captain Thomas B. Weir started downstream on his own initiative, followed at first by Benteen and ultimately by all of the command. The presence of the wounded made the advance slow and tedious. The Indians, having destroyed Custer's command, now swarmed against the advancing troops and drove them back to the original position on the bluffs. Here, the remnant of the regiment fought in entrenched position until the evening of June 26, when the Indians withdrew. The next forenoon, General Gibbon's command, accompanied by General Terry, reached the scene and rescued the survivors.

See *Field Diary of Lieutenant Edward Settle Godfrey at the Battle of the Little Big Horn* (1957), edited by Edgar I. Stewart; see also the bibliography for Custer.—E. I. S.

Little Crow (Taoyateduta) (c. 1810-1863). Chief of the Kapozha band of Mdewakanton Sioux. The last in a line of Kapozha chiefs called Little Crow, Taoyateduta was born in the band's village on the east bank of the Mississippi River, some fourteen miles below the mouth of the Minnesota River. His father, Chetanwakanmani, also known as Little Crow, was prominent in early relations between the Santee Sioux and the Americans. The elder Little Crow signed the first treaty between the Sioux and the United States with Lieutenant Zebulon Pike in 1805, and after aligning with the British during the War of 1812, he took a leading part in the general peace council of 1825 at Prairie du Chien. The younger Little Crow, already known as a scapegrace, assumed the headship of the Kapozha upon the death of his father, probably in 1834.

As the result of a cession treaty signed in 1837, Little Crow's band moved across the Mississippi, and during the next decades attempted to put their feet on the white man's road while living among other Mdewakanton bands along the lower Minnesota River. According to the later account of General Henry H. Sibley, who bore the man no good will but gives a reliable account, Little Crow during these years was distinguished as a drunkard and a liar. In public life he assumed a posture of uneasy, weak-willed compliance with the demands of American officials. At the Mendota council of 1851, after originally protesting and then being bullied by the American commissioners, he was the first to give way and sign the critical land-cession treaty that provided a small reservation on the upper Minnesota River for the lower Santee bands. He volunteered warriors in 1857 to campaign against Inkpaduta's renegade band following the Spirit Lake massacre. In 1858 he led a Santee delegation to the national capital, where further treaty demands were made by Indian Commissioner Charles Mix. Little Crow resisted throughout an extraordinary nightlong conference, but finally, at seven in the morning, after being hectored steadily by Mix, he reluctantly put his name on a paper that authorized the division of reservation lands in severalty.

Starvation was the reward Little Crow's people had for his cooperation with the Americans. When annuity payments were delayed in August 1862, with conditions already extremely tense, a trivial and foolish incident led four young Mdewakanton men to murder five white settlers near the reservation. When they returned to their village, there seemed general consensus that war with the whites was inevitable. As they discussed the matter, the other Santee leaders turned to Little Crow, seeking his support. He argued, it is said, the futility of war against the whites, but as it became clear that all others were determined to have war, Little Crow placed himself at the front of the hostile party.

A, a war leader and strategist of the ensuing MINNESOTA UPRISING, he urged an immediate attack upon Fort Ridgely, before it could be reinforced. Unfortunately for Santee success, his strategy was overruled, and younger men first led an unsuccessful attempt to capture the nearby town of New Ulm. Little Crow then directed a series of hard-fought assaults upon the reinforced garrison at Fort Ridgely, only to have his forces driven back by devastating artillery fire. With this defeat and the failure of a second attack on New Ulm, the momentum of the campaign was lost. Little Crow continued to stage assaults against outlying settlements, even while dissension began to divide the Santee councils. On September 23, 1862, Little Crow's warriors were decisively defeated by General Sibley's command at the battle of Wood Lake, and Little Crow fled westward with a remaining few supporters to the Devil's Lake region.

After a winter of hardship, Little Crow unsuccessfully sought British aid at Fort Garry in May 1863. Then he and his few followers returned south and carried out a number of small raids in the area of McLeod and Meeker counties. Picking raspberries with his son on the evening of July 3, he was discovered and shot down by two white settlers, also a father and son. His body was discarded as offal, but his scalp became a trophy in possession of the Minnesota State Historical Society.

The most detailed and accurate information on Little Crow's life and times appears in Roy W. Meyer, *History of the Santee Sioux* (1967).—K. N. O.

Little Rock, Arkansas. The state capital and the seat of Pulaski County, Little Rock lies on the south bank of the Arkansas River near the center of the state. Here the river drops from the highlands of the northwest into the coastal plain of the southeast, and the city got its name from the rock exposed in the banks of the river at the site, a natural crossing place on the Arkansas. A local legend has it that the French explorer Bernard de la Harpe, who visited the site while exploring the Arkansas River in 1722, named the smaller rock in the south bank Little Rock and the tall rock bluff on the north bank Big Rock. Early American hunters, travelers, and land claimants probably followed local tradition in giving the site its unusual name. The town of Little Rock was plotted in 1821 and it was designated the territorial capital the same year. It was incorporated as a town in 1831 and chartered as a city in 1836. Little Rock and Pulaski County were strongly Whig in early statehood days when most of the state was Democratic. The city opposed secession and was bitter when state authorities seized the United States arsenal there on February 8, 1861. But after Fort Sumter was fired on, its people supported Arkansas's decision to secede and join the Confederacy. General Theophilus H. Holmes, commander of the South's trans-Mississippi department in 1862-63, established his headquarters in the city but evacuated it in September 1863 when threatened by a superior force. On September 10, 1863, it was occupied by Union troops commanded by General Frederick Steele, who early in 1864 helped organize a loyal state government in preparation for readmission to the Union.

Little Rock became important as a railroad center and cotton market in the 1880s, though it was surpassed by St. Louis, Memphis, and New Orleans. Railroads brought industrial growth, especially in large railroad shops, lumber, furniture, bauxite, and cotton-oil mills, but it was World War II that launched the chief industrial growth of the city. Little Rock is noted for its three capitols. One is the Territorial Restoration. The Old State House, on Markham Street, capitol from 1836 until 1912, is a fine example of antebellum classical architecture. The present state capitol stands west of the downtown business district, and from its eminence looks eastward down Capitol Avenue into the heart of the modern city. Built of marble, part of which came from Arkansas, the building is copied from the national capitol.

The city made national and international headlines in 1957-58 when Governor Orval E. Faubus, defying a federal court order, used state military forces to block admission of nine Negro children to all-white Central High School. President Dwight D. Eisenhower federalized the state troops, sent in United States Army troops, put the school off-limits to obstructionists, and enforced the court order. The nine black students attended school that year protected by federal troops, but the next year, 1958-59, all the public high schools remained closed in an attempt at massive resistance led by Faubus and Little Rock segregationists. Finally, in 1959, the people voted to reopen the public high schools on an integrated basis. In the decade that followed, token integration of all the public white schools was accomplished. An exodus of white families to the suburbs saw former all-white Central High School become increasingly black with new suburban high schools having only token integration. The city's population in 1970 was 132,483.—W. L. B.

Little Turtle (1752-1812). Miami war chief. A man of outstanding abilities both on the battlefield and in the council house, Little Turtle first gained fame as leader of the Miami force that defeated General Josiah Harmar's expedition at the Miami River in 1790. To oppose the American invaders, he favored the Miami policy of alliance in a general tribal confederacy that the British and the Iroquois promoted after the American Revolution. He was in command of the confederated Indian army that crushed the expedition of General Arthur St. Clair at the battle of Mississinewa, November 4, 1791. This battle, though less renowned than many other frontier engagements, cost the American force 632 lives—the single most costly defeat for United States forces in the history of Indian warfare.

With his prestige at a peak, Little Turtle then became a principal figure in the councils of the Northwest Confederacy. Though failing to secure British aid, he directed the warriors of the confederacy against General Anthony Wayne's army in 1793-94. After he led an impetuous, unsuccessful attack upon Fort Recovery, June 30-July 1, 1794, Little Turtle resigned his command and headed only a small Miami contingent at the battle of Fallen Timbers. Wayne's victory in that engagement convinced Little Turtle that further Indian military resistance was doomed to failure. He became an advocate of peace and took a leading role in negotiation of the Treaty of Greenville (1795).

Subsequently he cooperated with American officials at virtually every turn in efforts to keep the peace. He accepted an annuity and other benefits for aiding the United States in dealing with the northwestern tribes. On several eastern trips he was consulted by President George Washington and other eminent personages, his opinions were sought by the French philosopher Volney, and his portrait was painted by Gilbert Stuart. By his steadfast advocacy of peace and accommodation with the Americans, Little Turtle is credited in his last years with preventing the Miami from joining Tecumseh's antiwhite confederacy. A leader to the last, enjoying the highest prestige among his own people, he died at Fort Wayne.

William Bridgewater provides a full sketch of Little Turtle in the *Dictionary of American Biography*, citing earlier authorities. More detailed information on his military and diplomatic accomplishments is contained in Bert Anson, *The Miami Indians* (1970).—K. N. O.

Little Wolf (?-1904). A chief of the Bowstring Soldiers, a Cheyenne military society. Known in his youth as Two Tails, Little Wolf was one of the ablest tacticians the Cheyenne produced. By the end of the 1850s he had earned a reputation for bravery in conflicts with the Kiowa, the Comanche, and the United States Army. He was probably present at the Fetterman Massacre in 1866 and was a participant in the battle of the Little Big Horn in 1876. He has been given credit for putting the torch to Fort Phil Kearny after its evacuation in 1868.

Sent to an Indian Territory reservation after making peace in 1877, Little Wolf was joined by Dull Knife and some three hundred other Cheyenne men, women, and children in the famous march back to their old homeland in the north in 1878. Although Little Wolf had announced a peaceable intention, the countryside was thoroughly alarmed. Despite a series of attacks by military forces, the chief's skillful defensive tactics kept Cheyenne casualties at a minimum. After crossing the North Platte, the group divided, and Dull Knife led his band into Fort Robinson. Little Wolf and his followers continued their march north into Montana, where in the spring of 1879 the chief was overtaken by his friend Captain W. P. Clark, who persuaded him to surrender. Little Wolf then served briefly as a scout with General Nelson A. Miles, but soon disgraced himself by killing one of his tribesmen, thereby forfeiting for the rest of his life any official influence or standing within the tribe.

George Bird Grinnell treats the military career of this "greatest of modern Cheyennes" in *The Fighting Cheyennes* (1915), while other aspects of his life are described in Grinnell's *The Cheyenne Indians* (1923).—J. T. K.

Livingston, Edward (1764-1836). Politician and diplomat. Born at Livingston Manor, New York, Livingston was the younger brother of Chancellor Robert R. Livingston. A 1781 graduate of the College of New Jersey (Princeton), he represented New York in the United States House of Representatives from 1795 to 1801 as a stanch follower of Aaron Burr and Thomas Jefferson. His loyalty to Jefferson in the disputed election of 1800 won him appointment in 1801 as federal attorney for the district of New York and as mayor of the city of New York. In 1803 he was discovered to be delinquent by almost $50,000 in his returns to the federal government. Declaring bankruptcy, he resigned his positions and removed to the city of New Orleans, where he immediately identified with the native population against Governor William CLAIBORNE, became legal counsel to the Laffite privateers, and rose to eminence as a leader of the bar.

His career in state politics was capped by his coauthorship with Louis Moreau-Lislet and Pierre Derbigny of the scholarly 1825 Civil Code of Louisiana, which still serves as the basis of the state's civil law jurisprudence, unique in the United States. His greatest legal achievement, a criminal code, was rejected by Louisiana but won him international acclaim and description by Sir Henry Maine as the "first legal genius of modern times" because of his highly advanced and humane proposals for penal reform. Service in the House of Representatives (1823 until 1829) led to his election to the Senate in 1829, where he supported Andrew Jackson, whom he had first served as aide-de-camp at the battle of New Orleans (1814-15). When President Jackson dissolved his cabinet in 1831 because various of its members refused to accept the wife of the secretary of war, Mrs. John Eaton, into their social circle because of her supposed sexual immorality, Livingston was brought to the post of secretary of state, in which his chief contribution was to help shape the president's vigorous proclamation against the doctrine of nullification in 1832. Sent to Paris as United States minister (1833-35), Livingston failed in his attempts to settle claims against France for naval spoliations committed during the Napoleonic wars. He died at his country home, Montgomery Place, New York.

See William B. Hatcher, *Edward Livingston* (1940); and Charles H. Hunt, *Life of Edward Livingston* (1864).—J. G. T.

Lochaber, Treaty of (1770). When northern district Indian superintendent Sir William Johnson negotiated the Treaty of Fort Stanwix in November 1768, in which the Iroquois surrendered claim to the lands south of the Ohio River, a division line between the southern colonies and the Cherokee Indians had already been ratified in the Treaty of HARD LABOR. In North Carolina and Virginia this boundary ran from a point on Reedy River to Tryon Mountain, thence to Chiswell Lead Mine, and on to the mouth of the Kanawha River at the Ohio. The purpose of this boundary was to contain settlement above this line and to leave the Cherokee country unmolested.

Settler movements into the upper valley of Virginia were too rapid, however, and Virginia's desire to expand into the territory ceded by the Iroquois at Fort Stanwix exerted too much pressure against the Hard Labor line for it to stand. On December 22, 1770, at Lochaber, South Carolina, southern district Indian superintendent John Stuart negotiated a second agreement with the Cherokee by which a new line would be surveyed, this time west along the Virginia-North Carolina border to "Steep Rock," then to a point six miles east of Long Island in the Holston River, and thence northward to the mouth of the Kanawah River, leaving Long Island in Cherokee territory. The intention of this negotiation was to include all the Virginia settlements that had been made over the original line both east and west of the Appalachians, and to extend the Virginia land authority to this new area.

The Cherokee had no objection to the surrendering of a bigger slice of land, but they were adamant about retaining possession of Long Island to prevent its fortification. They felt that the sale of another three hundred square miles was a reasonable exchange for an end to the long-standing boundary problem. But their expectations were futile, for even while the treaty was being negotiated white settlers were pushing across the new line in defiance of both the Indians and the orders of the British government.

See John R. Alden, *John Stuart and the Southern Colonial Frontier, 1754-75* (1944); Louis De Vorsey, Jr., *The Indian Boundary in the Southern Colonies, 1763-1775*

(1966); and J. G. M. Ramsey, *The Annals of Tennessee to the End of the Eighteenth Century* (1853).—T. D. C.

Lockwood, [Francis] Frank C[ummins] (1864-1948). Educator and author. Lockwood was born in Mount Erie, Illinois, received a doctorate in philosophy at Northwestern University, trained for the ministry, and in 1902 received an M. A. in English from Wesleyan University (Connecticut). Active in the Anti-Saloon League, Lockwood ran unsuccessfully in 1914 for Congress on the Prohibition party ticket, while teaching at Allegheny College in Pennsylvania. Two years later he joined the faculty at the University of Arizona and in World War I was a Y.M.C.A. overseas secretary. Returning to the University of Arizona, Lockwood held numerous positions—director of the Extension Division, dean of men, dean of the Liberal Arts College (1921-30), and interim university president in 1922. While working with the Extension Division, he became deeply interested in Arizona history and spent most of his time thereafter researching, visiting historic places, and interviewing old-timers. Of the ten books Lockwood published, most of them focused on Arizona personalities and were written for a general audience. Among his better-known works are *Arizona Characters* (1927), *Tucson—The Old Pueblo* (1930), and *Pioneer Days in Arizona* (1932). In 1941 Lockwood retired from the University of Arizona.

See John Bret Harte, "Frank C. Lockwood, Historian of the Southwest," *Arizona and the West* (Summer 1967).—H. P. H.

Logan, James (1674-1751). Pennsylvania politician and scholar. Logan was born of English ancestry in County Armagh, Ireland. The son of a Quaker schoolmaster, he continued his education until 1697 and retained scholarly habits all his life. In 1699 he was employed as the private secretary of William Penn and accompanied him to America, becoming friend and counselor to the Penn family for the next half-century. With their patronage Logan achieved responsible and honored position in Pennsylvania, acting as the proprietor's agent and guiding the Penns' financial affairs. Politically loyal to the proprietary conservative faction, he served as secretary of the province and clerk of the Provincial Council from 1701 to 1717, becoming a full member in 1702 and finally the council's president until his retirement in 1747. He was elected an alderman of Philadelphia in 1717 and mayor in 1722 and also held office as justice of the peace, judge of common pleas, and chief justice of the Provincial Supreme Court.

As Pennsylvania's commissioner of property and receiver general, Logan supervised the advance of frontier settlement and managed the colony's Indian affairs. He always maintained amicable relations with the natives, particularly the Iroquois, although he was not adverse to cheating them if he could. Logan's background negotiations were instrumental in binding the Six Nations to the English through the Albany Treaty of 1722 and the Treaty of Lancaster in 1744. During the "boundary war" with Maryland in 1736, he successfully persuaded the Iroquois to cede most of their lands west of the Susquehanna River to Pennsylvania, and in 1737 he engineered the notorious Walking Purchase, by which the remnants of the eastern Delaware Indians were conned out of 1,200 square miles of land. Aided by his official position, Logan became rich through land investment and the fur trade and is credited with coining the term "Conestoga" to describe the heavy freight wagons he used to transport goods to and from his posts in the Conestoga valley. Although a devout Quaker, he recognized the value of military power, and in 1741 recommended that all Friends who could not in conscience support frontier defense measures withdraw from government.

Natural science, particularly botany, was Logan's abiding interest. He experimented with electricity and astronomy and corresponded with many of the learned authorities of the times. Several of his scientific papers were published, and Linnaeus was so impressed with Logan's experiments on the pollination of corn that he named an order of plants in Logan's honor. At the time of his death from a stroke, he was preparing a philosophical treatise called *The Duties of Man Deduced from Nature*. An eclectic yet stanchly conservative personality, Logan typified the intellectual aristocracy so striking in the English colonies of the eighteenth century.

See I. J. Cooper, *Life and Public Services of James Logan* (1921); Wayland Dunway, *A History of Pennsylvania* (1948); F. B. Tolles, *James Logan and Culture of Provincial Pennsylvania* (1957); and A. G. Zimmerman, "James Logan, Proprietary Agent," *Pennsylvania Magazine of History and Biography*, vol. 7 (1954).—P. R. M.

Logan, James or **John** (1725?-1780). A chief of the Mingo—those Iroquois who had located in the Ohio country. Logan was born probably at Shamokin, now Sunbury, Pennsylvania, where his father, Shikellamy, and brother were sachems. In his early years he associated closely with the provincial authorities of Pennsylvania and was known as a friend of the white man. But about 1770 he moved to the Ohio country and by 1774 was leading raids against white settlements, which were beginning to push across the Appalachian mountains. The turning point for Logan seems to have been the Yellow Creek massacre of April 1774, in which some of his family were killed by whites. Logan and his followers were leading participants in LORD DUNMORE'S WAR of 1774, a conflict between Virginia and the Shawnee, Mingo, and other Indian allies, and he refused to be reconciled after the Indians were defeated at Point Pleasant. On this occasion he expressed his feelings so movingly to a Virginia emissary—or at least they were so reported—that his words gained wide currency in colonial newspapers and were later incorporated by Jefferson into his book *Notes on Virginia* (1781).

During the American Revolution Logan continued, with British encouragement, to attack the frontier settlements, taking both prisoners and scalps. As he grew older he fell prey to alcoholism and was given to ferocious rages. In 1780 he was killed by a relative, apparently as a result of a drunken quarrel.

See W. M. Beauchamp, *Shikellamy and His Son Logan* (1916).—A. W. T.

Logan, Utah. Located in Cache valley, which straddles Utah and Idaho, Logan does not receive intense summer heat, as do the desert valleys to the west. In fact, the early Mormons, aware of the valley's altitude of 4,535 feet, were slow to settle for fear of the cold temperatures. In 1859, however, they began to arrive in numbers, naming the townsite after Logan River, which was named for Ephraim Logan, a fur trapper in the area in

1820. Incorporated in 1866, Logan soon became the marketing and distribution center for northern Utah and southern Idaho. A land-grant college was started in 1888 and today is Utah State University.

Cache valley and Logan are known for grain, sugar beets, dairy products, and stock breeding. Industry has been arriving in recent years, however, and in 1970 the city had a population of twenty thousand. The town is the site of a classic Mormon temple built in 1884.
—L. J. A.

log cabin. The design of the log cabin as commonly used on the American frontier was of Scandinavian origin. Nevertheless English, French, and Spanish pioneers used this type of housing. The English at Jamestown used logs in upright construction, but as the Anglo-American settlers moved deeper into the frontier they adopted the horizontal type of log construction. In western Pennsylvania, the Valley of Virginia, the Piedmont area of the western Carolinas, and in Georgia, the log cabin became the standard type of building.

There was no set pattern or design for the log cabin, but the nature and availability of logs and the skill of the builders were decisive in shaping the structure. Cabins were usually constructed on a plan of ten by ten to twenty by twenty feet. Walls were made of medium-sized poles or square-hewn logs. The most desirable position for the cabin was to have the sides facing east and west, and the ends north and south. A fireplace and chimney were built on one end. The chimney was constructed of a variety of materials, ranging from mud-rolled grass cats or bats to stone construction. Usually a door and a window penetrated one side wall and a window the other. Floors were either hard-packed clay or puncheon, and roofs were made of hand-riven shakes or boards. In the earliest cabins glass was unknown, and slit openings were closed with solid shutters and sometimes with greased paper.

The housing capacity of the log cabin was increased by the addition of a loft and a shedroom or lean-to across the back. It was the large central room, however, which served as kitchen, living room, workroom, and bedroom. Here it was that the family stored all sorts of tools, weapons, clothing, food, and seeds. Pegs were driven into the walls on which the occupants hung everything from guns to harnesses.

Walls of the cabins were chinked with wooden fillers, daubed with clay. If hewn logs could be fitted closely together with carefully notched ends, the seams were sealed with clay alone. In historical chronology, the pole cabin made of sapling logs preceded the much more substantial hewn-log structure, largely because it took more skilled labor and time to construct the latter.

See R. C. Buley, *The Old Northwest: Pioneer Period, 1815-1840,* vol. I (1950); Daniel Drake, *Pioneer Life in Kentucky* (1870); and Baynard Rush Hall [Robert Carlton], *The New Purchase* (1916).—T. D. C.

Logstown, Pennsylvania. Logstown was located approximately eighteen miles down the Ohio River from the confluence of the Allegheny and Monongahela rivers on the north bank of the river. Its founding is known to have been sometime between 1745 and 1750. Logstown was in the center of activities for the Mingo, Shawnee, and Delaware Indians but was also a gathering place for members of other tribes. The town was closely associated with the Mingo chief Scruniyatha, shortened by traders to Half-King. By the middle of the eighteenth century Logstown had become a center of both English and French trading and diplomatic activities. It was to this town that George Washington went in 1753 to begin his mission to the French posts up the Allegheny. In April 1748 George Croghan and others were able to negotiate a treaty agreement here with the Shawnee, Miami and some of the Iroquoian Six Nations over trading matters relating to fairness in prices and the robbing practices of the Indians. Specifically, Logstown was major point of contact from 1745 to 1763 between the Indians on the upper Ohio and the British colonials.

See Lawrence H. Gipson, *The British Empire Before the American Revolution*, vol. IV: *Zones of International Friction: North America, South of the Great Lakes Region, 1748-1754* (1939); A. T. Volwiler, *George Croghan and the Westward Movement, 1741-1782* (1926); and Nicolas B. Wainwright, *George Croghan, Wilderness Diplomat* (1959).—T. D. C.

Lomax, John Avery (1867-1948). Folklorist and folksong collector. When Lomax was two years old his family moved by covered wagon from Mississippi to Bosque County, Texas. Lomax heard his first cowboy songs while growing up on a farm by the Chisholm Trail, and before he was twenty, he had begun writing them down. He went to Granbury College in 1887 and taught school before entering the University of Texas in 1895. After he graduated in 1897 he held several jobs at the university. In 1903 he went to Texas A. & M. University to teach English. In 1906 he received a scholarship to Harvard, which enabled him to work under Barrett Wendell and George L. Kittredge, two well-known English scholars. Kittredge encouraged Lomax to take up again seriously the collection of western ballads that he had begun as a youth. With Harvard providing financial support, Lomax began his task and by 1910 had completed his first book, *Cowboy Songs and Other Frontier Ballads.* The book represented the first comprehensive compilation of cowboy ballads (preceded only by N. Howard "Jack" Thorp's privately printed little paperback volume *Songs of the Cowboys,* which appeared in 1908) and was an immediate success.

At this point in his life Lomax regarded song collecting as only a hobby and for the next two decades other pursuits drew his attention. In 1910 he became secretary of the Ex-students Association of the University of Texas. Except for a brief period during World War I when he sold government bonds in Chicago, Lomax remained with the association until 1925, at which time he became vice-president of the Republic National Company, a banking concern in Dallas. During the next twenty years Lomax limited his folk-song interests to the preparation of one book, *Songs of the Cattle Trail and Cow Camp* (1919), which supplemented his earlier book, and providing assistance to Harry Yandell Benedict in the preparation of *The Book of Texas* (1916).

In 1931 Lomax was beset with misfortune. His wife had died, and he suffered a partial physical breakdown, became depressed, incurred severe financial reverses, and, finally, lost his banking post. Thinking that a leisurely folk-song lecture tour might help him recover his health and perhaps even bring in a few needed dollars, he decided to tour America. Accompanied by his son

John, Jr., Lomax spent the next year traveling around the country and lecturing to various groups. The tour yielded him over one thousand dollars and the recovery of good health. He never returned to the business world, preferring, instead, to devote the rest of his life to collecting and publishing folk songs.

Together with his son Alan, Lomax visited all the penitentiaries in the southern states in order to listen to the inmates sing. Impressed with the talent and style of one named Huddie "Lead Belly" Ledbetter, Lomax persuaded the governor of Louisiana to pardon the inmate and took Ledbetter on tour and, eventually, wrote a book about him entitled *Negro Folk Songs as Sung by Lead Belly* (1936). Lomax and his son also wrote *American Ballads and Folk Songs* (1934) and *Our Singing Country* (1941). Shortly before his death he completed his autobiography, appropriately entitled *Adventures of a Ballad Hunter* (1947).

Cow-country historian J. Frank Dobie wrote that Lomax was "a man who more than any other made the cowboy songs and Negro songs a part of the inheritance and folklore of the world." Lomax was one of the organizers of the Texas Folklore Society, a member and president of the American Folklore Society, and president of the Modern Language Society.

See J. Frank Dobie, "John A. Lomax," *The Sunny Slopes of Long Ago* (1966); and *Handbook of Texas*, vol. II (1952).—J. C. D.

London Company, The. See VIRGINIA, SETTLEMENT OF.

Long, Ellen Call (1825-1905). Florida civic leader, writer, and planter. Long was reputedly the first white child born in Florida's frontier capital, Tallahassee. The first child of Richard Keith Call, a governor of Florida, and Mary Letitia Kirkman, she was pampered and precocious. At the age of nine she was enrolled in a school for young ladies in Franklin, Maryland, and was there when her mother died in 1836. At seventeen she came home to her father in Tallahassee bearing a love for him little short of adoration. In 1844 she married Medicus A. Long, a leading Democrat who was to be a presidential elector in 1856. Four children were born to them, but only two survived childhood. In 1858 Medicus moved to Texas and did not return. In 1851 Call had deeded his Tallahassee mansion, The Grove, to Long and she resided there the remainder of her life.

The Civil War profoundly disturbed both Long and her father, for both opposed secession vehemently. At the war's end she dedicated her energies to restoring the South to the Union and to facilitating the adjustment of whites to the new role of the freedmen. Postwar governors often used Long's talents. She is said to have known every governor from Andrew Jackson to N. B. Broward and got along with all of them—Democrat, Whig, or Republican, southerner or "carpetbagger."

In 1874 she became Florida secretary of the Philadelphia Centennial Exposition and worked against hostility and apathy to stir Floridians to support that anniversary of independence. In 1875 Governor Harrison Reed named her regent for Florida of the Mount Vernon Association to preserve Washington's home. Governor Marcellus Stearns sent her as Florida's delegate to the 1876 Centennial Exposition and Governor William Bloxham appointed her to represent Florida at the New Orleans World Exposition of 1884. In 1889 Governor E.

A. Perry sent her to France to represent Florida at the Paris Exposition. In 1881 Governor Reed had wished to nominate her postmaster of Tallahassee, but she declined in favor of William G. Stewart, a black Methodist minister.

Meanwhile, as Long's financial resources dwindled, she sold property, mortgaged her home, and looked for new money crops. Her experiments in silk producing were described in *Silk Farming in Florida* (1883). The project was not profitable, however. Unsuccessfully she also tried to market her writings on her father and on Florida. The result of these efforts was a rambling book, *Florida Breezes; or, Florida New and Old*, published in 1883. Probably her most lasting contribution, the book is uneven, grandiloquent, and redolent of moonlight and magnolias. Yet it is a valuable source for frontier social history, for she saw not only the mansions and slave cabins but also the yeoman farmers and the "poor white trash," and descriptions of them give her book enduring value.

As the new century began, debts seemed to overwhelm her and, health broken, she died after a lingering illness.

The facsimile edition of *Florida Breezes; or, Florida New and Old* was published in 1962 and has an invaluable introduction by Margaret Louise Chapman.—H. J. D.

Long, Huey P. See LOUISIANA, STATE OF.

Long, Stephen Harriman (1784-1864). Army engineer and explorer. Major Long is best known for his western expedition of 1820. The official report of this exploration, which appeared under the signature of Dr. Edwin JAMES, the expedition's physician (probably because Long and his family were ill and James did most of the work), included Long's map, which labeled the area east of the Rockies as the GREAT AMERICAN DESERT (see also KANSAS).

This was but one event in a military career that spanned nearly half a century. Long was born in Hopkinton, New Hampshire, and graduated from Dartmouth in 1809 with membership in Phi Beta Kappa. He received his appointment as second lieutenant in the Corps of Engineers in 1815, taught mathematics at West Point for a year, and was then brevetted major in the Topographical Engineers. From 1816 until 1824 he was engaged in exploration along the upper Mississippi and the lower Arkansas. He instigated the ill-fated Yellowstone expedition of 1819-20 by suggesting to President James Monroe that the upper Missouri be explored with a steamboat.

Long supervised the construction of the faulty steamboat named the *Western Engineer* and assembled an exploring party that included Titian Ramsay Peale and Thomas Say. All kinds of difficulties marred this expedition; for example, many men died of scurvy while wintered at "Engineer Cantonment" near Council Bluffs. When this project was abandoned it was immediately replaced by Long's western tour, described above. In 1823 he led an exploration of the Red River of the North, the forty-ninth parallel, and the Rainy Lake district.

The remainder of his life was concerned with railroad surveys, dredging of rivers, construction of marine hospitals, and other assignments that fall to the lot of a civil engineer. Long retired at the age of seventy-eight.

See Richard G. Wood, *Stephen Harriman Long, 1784-1864* (1966).—R. A. B.

Longhorn. See CATTLE INDUSTRY.

long hunters. Fur trappers who lived off the land. In the latter half of the eighteenth century, particularly in the decade 1760-70, fur trappers and traders from the Appalachian Mountain section of Virginia, North Carolina, and Tennessee traveled westward to the Appalachian Plateau. Men such as Timothy Demunbreun, John Finley, and Daniel Boone, engaged in either trapping, trading, or land speculating, went on "long" expeditions living off the countryside. Their journeys opened up Kentucky and Tennessee, particularly the valleys of the Kentucky, Green, and Cumberland rivers, for settlement during the 1770s and 1780s.—G. B. D.

Longley, William Preston (1851-1878). Gunman. The bitterness of the Reconstruction period has been used to explain Longley's murderous career in frontier Texas, but the ease with which he took human life strongly suggests that the argument is specious. He was born in Austin County, Texas, and before he was twenty several men were the victims of his guns. Negroes were supposed to be among his favorite targets, and his hatred of blacks was matched by their terror of him. He was a tall, quick-tempered man whose murders were generally in response to some supposed insult. The authorities forced him to leave Texas for a time, and although there are conflicting reports of his wanderings, it is evident that he pursued a pattern of violence wherever he went.

Once, it is reported, Longley was hanged along with a horse thief, but as the hangmen departed they fired a volley at the dangling bodies, a bullet cut the rope suspending Longley, and he survived. Other reports say that he rode with outlaw Cullen Baker, that he served time for murder, and that he lived among the Ute Indians. In any case, by 1875 he was back in Texas, living under a variety of aliases. The story there is familiar—more murders, more escapes, and more aliases. His victims included an unarmed man named Thomas, who made the mistake of arguing with Longley over a card game, and a minister named Roland Lay. After he killed Lay he left Texas, but in 1877 he was captured in Louisiana. Several murder warrants existed for Longley, but he persuaded the authorities to turn him over to the Lee County sheriff. Longley was wanted there for the murder of Wilson Anderson, and since the evidence against him was slight he thought he could beat the charge. However, he was convicted of killing Anderson. While awaiting execution he wrote numerous letters about his life, confided to the sheriff that he had actually killed only eight men (six whites and two blacks), and accepted the Catholic faith. On October 28, 1878, he mounted the gallows smoking a cigar. He delivered an oration on the consequences of a life of crime, said that God had forgiven him, and declared that his punishment was just. He then kissed the sheriff and the priest, said good-bye to the crowd, and was dropped to eternity. Unfortunately for Longley the rope slipped so that his knees touched the ground. The hangmen lifted him up, adjusted the rope, and watched eleven minutes before he was declared dead.

See Ed Bartholomew, *Wild Bill Longley: A Texas Hard-Case* (1953).—G. L. R.

Lord Dunmore's War (1774). Although the treaties of Fort Stanwix (1768), Hard Labor (1768), and Lochaber (1770) had technically disqualified Indian titles to lands south of the Ohio River and east of the negotiated line from the point of Hard Labor to the mouth of the Kanawha River, the whites were not satisfied with these limits and began pushing into the Kentucky and southern Ohio region. While no tribe actually inhabited Kentucky, both the Cherokee of Tennessee and the Shawnee of Ohio hunted and fought there. When the white long hunters caused a serious depletion in the area's game, and when Virginia land speculators made a series of surveys along the Ohio and Kentucky rivers in 1772-74, marking off extensive claims and establishing towns such as Harrodsburg, an expectable conflict arose. Lawless frontiersmen started the fighting by isolated attacks on friendly and defenseless groups of Shawnee. Until the spring of 1774 the Shawnee showed restraint in their reaction, hoping that the Pennsylvania Quakers could find a peaceful solution to the Virginia claims, but the murder of two boys, Israel Boone and Henry Russell, just east of Cumberland Gap in 1773, was a potent sign of Indian dissatisfaction and unrest.

Lord Dunmore (John Murray), colonial governor of Virginia, and his western agent, Dr. John Connolly, were the prime movers behind Virginia's expansion. Early in 1774 Dunmore forcibly seized possession of western Pennsylvania and the Kentucky region under the 1609 Virginia Charter claims. Dr. Connolly, anxious to get his hands on Kentucky land, issued a proclamation urging all frontiersmen to defend themselves against the Indians, which was tantamount to a declaration of war. To this end, Dunmore ordered held as hostages, if not prisoners, from December 1773 to April 1774, a party of Shawnee chiefs who had gone to Pittsburgh to plead for peace. When they were attacked after their release by some of Connolly's "troops," Shawnee patience broke and warriors massacred thirteen whites at Baker's Cabin on Yellow Creek on April 30. This in turn led to a bloody assault by a band of white hoodlums upon the peaceful Mingo family of Chief John Logan. This attack was said to have been led by Daniel Greathouse, and in years to come it was to involve even Thomas Jefferson in a highly emotional political argument. Dunmore had gotten his war.

Dunmore's next act was to secure the safety of his surveying parties, and he sent Daniel Boone and Michael Stoner to find them. The neutrality of the Cherokee, Iroquois, and Delaware was then secured by the efforts of James Robertson, Sir William Johnson, and George Groghan, and Dunmore turned to the conquest of the Shawnee, who were left to fight alone. A two-pronged assault on the Shawnee villiages on the Scioto River was mounted, with Dunmore approaching from Pittsburgh while Colonel Andrew Lewis led a southwest Virginia militia force from the south via the Kanawha River. Lewis' force was attacked at Point Pleasant near the mouth of the Kanawha on October 10 by a Shawnee party led by Chief Cornstalk. Also engaged in the fight were some Mingo, Huron, Delaware, and Ottawa warriors. It is still an open question as to who actually won the battle in a military sense. The Indians, however, withdrew from the field, and the militiamen claimed the victory. Hearing of the fight while marching up the Hocking River, Dunmore moved directly on the Shawnee town of Chillicothe to threaten the Indian homes and families. Caught between two white armies, the Shawnee sued for peace. Lewis, who had continued his advance, was ordered to return his troops to Point Pleasant without further engagement of the Indians. Because Dunmore's order engendered great anger, it was necessary for the governor to leave the treaty ground to check in person that the militiamen from the western settlements had obeyed him. At the reassembling of the peacemakers at Dunmore's Camp Charlotte near Chillicothe village, John Logan delivered an eloquent oration in which he charged the whites with willful murder of his people. Acknowledging no responsibility, Dunmore forced the leading chiefs to sign the Treaty of Camp Charlotte, wherein the Shawnee agreed to give up all claim to Kentucky, to stop hunting there, and to stop molesting traffic on the Ohio River. Dunmore's War opened the way for the settlement of the Ohio valley, but the embittered Indians would continue to resist white settlement every inch of the way.

See Temple Bodley, *George Rogers Clark, His Life and Public Services* (1926); Thomas Jefferson, *Notes on the State of Virginia* (1856); Reuben Gold Thwaites and Louise Phelps Kellogg, eds., *Documentary History of Dunmore's War* (1905); and Dale Van Every, *Forth to the Wilderness: The First American Frontier, 1754-1774* (1961).—T. D. C.

Lorenz, Richard (1858-1915). Painter. Born in Voigtstadt, Thuringia, Lorenz was sent at fifteen to a preparatory art school in Weimar and at eighteen years of age was enrolled in free evening classes in life drawing at the Royal Academy in that city under Heinrich Albert Brendel, noted animal painter. In 1886 he came to the United States and settled in Milwaukee, Wisconsin, at the urging of a former Weimar comrade, Otto von Ernst. Ernst was the son-in-law of Frederick Pabst, Milwaukee shipping and brewing tycoon, and had arrived in America only the year before with a group of German artists hired specifically to paint religious and historical panoramas. Lorenz soon joined this group, specializing in the depiction of horses in action, and worked on a number of panoramas depicting Civil War battle scenes. In 1887 he went to San Francisco to assist in the installation of a panorama in that city and remained in the West for several months, during which time he traveled widely in California, Arizona, Colorado, and Texas. He returned to Milwaukee in 1888 to teach in the newly organized Milwaukee School of Art, producing a number of finished paintings from sketches executed during his western travels.

Lorenz visited the West again in the 1890s, traveling in the Dakotas, Montana, and Wyoming. He painted his first Indian subjects at the Crow reservation in Montana about 1889 and that same year attended the Indian Conference associated with the Trans-Mississippi Exposition in Omaha, Nebraska. By 1912 he was exhibiting western works in the galleries of the Milwaukee Art Society and became noted for his landscapes and Wisconsin snow scenes. An advocate of outdoor painting, he was greatly influenced by the Impressionist movement and distinguished himself as a nature and genre painter, as well. He was preoccupied somewhat with the more dramatic aspects of rural and frontier life, as characterized in such canvases as *The Wolf Pack, Only One Came Back, Pursued by Wolves, Roundup in the Southwest*, and *Farewell to Shoshone*. His painting *End of Day* won first

prize in the genre category in the 1896 nationwide competition held by the Osborne Art Company of New York, and his *Impulses of Spring* won in 1906. Both are reproduced with the works of other prizewinners in the Osborne Company's annual calendars for those years. —D. C. H.

Los Angeles, California. The urban sprawl of the Los Angeles area has come to be regarded as one of the vanguards of a new way of life. As the "Sea-Coast of Iowa" or "Six Suburbs in Search of a City," a generation ago Los Angeles seemed just a much-publicized paradox, but its continuing efforts to reconcile its ambitions as a megalopolis with its notions of a good community not only illuminate much of its immediate past but also suggest some of the alternatives available to American cities in the future. In the first hundred years of its existence Los Angeles merely "grew." In its second century Los Angeles has typified the "land of magical improvisation." It built its harbor without moving to San Diego, brought water from distant mountains for future millions, and altered the ecology of its semidesert environment. The sequence of booms was sustained by the high points in the sale of real estate, which occurred approximately twenty years apart—in 1887, 1906, 1923, 1946, and 1963. The constant upsurge of population modified the downswings of the cycle. There were 11,183 inhabitants in 1880, 102,479 in 1900, 576,673 in 1920, 1,504,277 in 1940, and 2,479,015 in 1960. The city outgrew itself so extensively that the actual administrative boundaries lost their meaning and faded away before the more revealing designation, the Los Angeles area. Although the change from Mexican to American California relegated the city for half a century into a secondary position, it became characteristic of Los Angeles to be able to live in the future, one step ahead of the coming change.

Founded in 1781 as one of several *pueblos* ("towns") to help colonize the most recent addition to the Spanish empire, Los Angeles emerged as the only settlement in California that was occasionally called *ciudad* ("city") in official records. Although it was by far the largest town in Mexican California, Los Angeles enjoyed only limited social and economic significance in a society revolving around *haciendas* and based on the economic autonomy and social self-sufficiency of the rancheros and their Indian servants. The district of Los Angeles contained 2,228 people in 1836 and 2,497 in 1844, exclusive of Indians. At the end of the Mexican rule, the town itself housed 1,300 people. The first federal census for 1850, taken after the American influx at the height of the Sonoran trek to the gold mines in northern California, enumerated 1,610 residents, 895 men and 715 women. Within two decades after the Mexican War, the American way of life and natural catastrophes had destroyed the pastoral economy that sustained Los Angeles during the Mexican era. The effects of the gold rush, the legislation requiring validation of Mexican land titles, and the flood and drought of the 1860s sapped the economic strength of the native Angelenos. However, the Latins together with the westernized Indians, another "Spanish" group, remained in the numerical majority until the 1870s. The social contact of Americans, who, although in the minority, controlled government and business, helped to lay the foundation of the modern community. The city turned to agriculture and railroads to catch up with the change.

Los Angeles as it appeared in 1857.

The breakup of the large ranchos brought a diversified farm agriculture into existence, with the need and opportunities for numerous communities. The development of the Los Angeles metropolitan area began in the 1870s and 1880s when the construction of transcontinental railroads placed climate and scenery within reach of settlers and tourists. During the land boom of the 1880s railroads influenced the location of town sites; when the countryside began to fill up with settlements they stimulated community growth. The interurban and street railways linked the emerging towns to Los Angeles, helped to transfer farm land and orchards into marketable real estate, placed beaches and mountains at the door steps of the Angelenos, and offered housing developments as an alternative to tenement districts in Los Angeles. Between 1859 and 1951, through 121 annexations, the territory of Los Angeles increased from 28.01 square miles to 453.5 square miles. Pasadena, Long Beach, and Glendale grew to be the most active suburban cities in the Los Angeles area.

Having learned to boom on agriculture, railroads, and climate, Los Angeles could boom again with the coming of the automobile. And the city, used to booms, was ready to keep booming on commerce and industry (oil, motion pictures, aerospace) with the aid of the motor vehicle. The climate helped too, making the utmost use of the innovation possible. In the early decades of the twentieth century, when most automobiles were open, passenger traffic in southern California differed only seven percent between summer and winter. Because of their rural origins, Angelenos readily accepted the horseless carriage as a variation of the horsedrawn carriage, in both of which the driver personally controlled speed and direction of the movement. Urban dwellers in the East, who had been removed from the farm for more than one generation, still conceived of movement in transportation facilities as outside their control. The Angelenos' acceptance of the motor vehicle spurred the growth of an automobile civilization thriving on the increased physical and social mobility of its members. Workers were no longer compelled to live within walking distance of their jobs or chained to the lines of public transportation systems, but free to range over a wide area in search of better jobs and housing.

In 1923, Los Angeles counted a total of 430,000 passenger cars, one to every two and nine-tenths persons, the largest percentage of automobile ownership in the world. In 1952 Los Angeles County had one automobile for approximately every two persons, a total of about 2 million cars, and in 1967 its 7 million residents shared 3.7 million automobiles. In the first migration of the automobile age in the 1920s, one of the great internal migrations in the history of the American people, 1.3 million people moved into Los Angeles County. Within two decades the number of inhabitants in Los Angeles surged from 319,198 in 1910 to 1,238,048 in 1930.

Since the 1920s, experimentation with advanced problems of urban life in the automobile age has epitomized Los Angeles. Hollywood or Watts, the expanding empire of the Los Angeles *Times*, the enclave of the Henry E. Huntington Library and Art Gallery in San Marino, the race track at Santa Anita, or the universities and colleges from U.C.L.A. to the California Institute of Technology at Pasadena are actually less characteristic of Los Angeles than is the city's urban experimentation. Its imprint gives face and vitality to a community that had not yet developed features of its own when the technological standards and societal fashions accelerated the trend to uniformity. Master planning has affected public administration and social services, and indeed most areas of life and death, from the arteries of the gigantic freeway system to the Los Angeles approach to burial cultivated at Forest Lawn.

Residence in the laboratory of social change produces problems more complex than air pollution and traffic congestion. In a world where such elementary references to norms as distances measured in miles are discarded for distances measured in minutes, politics seems to be one area of life in which old, reactionary creeds are reiterated even though an intensified urban technology exists. Mobility has obliterated communal contacts at a moment when the complexities of the megalopolis have left people craving for direct relationships and simple settings. The constant reduction of time distances brought vast numbers of people physically closer to each other but increased the mental separation of individuals, ethnic groups, and races. At the same time, however, Los Angeles is groping to channel its vitality into bridging the chasms dividing white and black Angelenos, Japanese, Chinese, Filipinos, Indians, and Mexican-Americans.

See Robert Fogelson, *The Fragmented Metropolis* (1967); Richard Gilbert, *City of the Angels* (1964); Remi A. Nadeau, *Los Angeles: From Mission to City* (1960); Christopher Rand, *Los Angeles, the Ultimate City* (1967); W. W. Robinson, *Los Angeles, A Profile* (1968); and Francis J. Weber, *El Pueblo de Nuestra Senora de los Angeles: An Inquiry in Early Appellations* (1968).—G. B.

Los Angeles County Museum of Natural History. The Los Angeles County Museum of Natural History opened in 1913. Since that time the original building in Exposition Park has been greatly enlarged. Today the museum houses important collections in earth sciences, life sciences, and history.

Of the earth science collections, that in vertebrate paleontology is the largest and probably most important. The fossils from the tar pits of Rancho La Brea in Los Angeles form a large part of this collection. The museum excavated at La Brea between 1913 and 1915, recovering nearly half a million fossils. In 1915 G. Allen Hancock gave Rancho La Brea to the county, and the museum has continued its excavations at La Brea, renamed Hancock Park, ever since. The La Brea fossils are extremely important for the study of the prehistoric flora and fauna of the southwestern United States. The collection in vertebrate paleontology also consists of fifty thousand fossils acquired from the California Institute of Technology in 1967. The Cal Tech and La Brea collections together with the museum's other collections in vertebrate paleontology constitute probably the most extensive body of fossils from southern California and the southwestern United States in existence.

The collection in invertebrate paleontology includes fossil shells, plants, and insects and is most complete for fossils from the Pleistocene and Pliocene epochs. The sizable gem and mineral collection of the museum is developing through purchases and gifts.

The life science category covers nine areas— anthropology, archaeology, botany, entomology, herpetology, ichthyology, invertebrate zoology, ornithology, and mammalogy. The two largest and most complete collections are in entomology and ichthyology, containing respectively 2 million and 1.7 million specimens. The collections of mammals and birds, also important, are weighted with specimens from Africa and the New World.

Because of the museum's location, the collections tend to represent most fully western North America, then the whole of North America, then Central America, South America, and finally the rest of the world. The marine zoology collections are excellent for the Pacific east of Hawaii. The museum is also the repository for the Antarctic expeditions of the University of Southern California and has the world's finest collection of Antarctic marine life. In anthropology and archaeology, the museum has good collections in African and pre-Columbian Central and South American Indian ethnology. It also has good material on the Indians of western North America.

The history collection spans the length of man's existence, but most of the emphasis is on the history of the American West, particularly California. The Charles J. Prudhomme Collection and the del Valle Collection contain a wealth of artifacts, documents, photographs, and paintings from the families of most of the major names in the history of southern California. The collections cover a period from 1750 to 1900 and contain items from almost every facet of life. In addition, both collections have many *carte-de-visite* views. During the early years of photography, these small card-photos were used as calling cards. They are important because they allow us to see people as they wanted their friends to see them around 1860.

The Antonio F. Coronel Collection contains more than four thousand items detailing the history of Los Angeles. It also includes many types of artifacts, costumes, paintings of early California life, and some of the only remaining copies of books printed by Augustin V. Zamorano, the first printer in California.

The museum has an extensive photo collection. Besides excellent photographs of early California life in the Coronel Collection, the del Valle Collection contains many photographs taken by Honore Penelon and V. Wolfenstein, early southern California photographers. In the Adam Clark Vroman Collection are more than two thousand glass photographic plates made by Vroman between 1895 and 1905 of Pasadena, the missions, Yosemite, and Indian agencies.

In motion-picture photography, cameras, projectors, film clips, and costumes from the early days of movies up to the present time provide a basis for a history of the movies in Hollywood.

Other important collections are the Colonel and Mrs. George J. Denis Collection of military memorabilia, covering the years between 1795 and 1900; the William B. Honeyman Collection of awards and medals; and the Edwin Deakin paintings of California missions. The Samuel K. Rindge Collection and the General Harrison Gray Otis Collection are important parts of the museum's arms collection.

Documentary materials include maps and prints from the Shearman Collection and mission records from the Thomas Workman Temple II Collection. These history collections make the museum an important research center for any study of the American West, particularly for the study of southern California history.—M. K.

Lost Dutchman's Mine. Legendary gold mine. No legend excites more public interest than that of the Lost Dutchman's Mine in Superstition Mountain, east of Mesa, Arizona. No evidence of gold has been reported, but lavish tales about the mine and its riches persist to the present day.

One story is that the mine was discovered in 1840 by a Mexican boy hiding out from an irate *hidalgo*, father of the lad's paramour. The youth stumbled onto a nest of gold nuggets. The ranchero's Indian slaves killed him and turned over the gold to the patron, who later exploited the mine. Apache then wiped out all the people on the ranch except three Mexicans, who returned to work the diggings. The three miners foolishly showed their claim to a homicidal Dutchman, Jacob Waltz, who killed them, dropped their bodies into a crevice, and took over the mine. Occasionally the Dutchman spent his gold dust in nearby towns, where he made drunken brags about his bonanza. In one version of the tale, the old murderer killed four greedy men who trailed him in hopes of discovering his secret.

Years later, when the ailing old Dutchman lay dying, he told a friend about killing eight men and surrendered a map showing where to find the rich mine. This friend and many others have continued fruitless searches for the lost gold of the Superstitions.

See Oren Arnold, *Ghost Gold* (1967); Estee Conatser, *The Sterling Legend* (1972); Edwin Corle, *The Gila, River of the Southwest* (1951); and Joseph Miller, *Arizona: The Last Frontier* (1956).—B. W. A.

Lottinville, Savoie (1906-   ). Publisher and teacher. Born in Hagerman, Idaho, Lottinville received his education in the public schools of Tulsa, Oklahoma, and the University of Oklahoma. As editor of the school paper, he discovered several writers of future note, including George Milburn, who produced a regular column for Lottinville. After graduation from the university, he was selected as a Rhodes scholar.

After his return from Oxford in 1932, Lottinville worked as a reporter for the Oklahoma *Times*. The following year he joined the University of Oklahoma Press, where he remained until his retirement in 1967. In 1938 he was appointed director of the press and became a leader in scholarly press circles, serving a term as president of the Association of American University Presses (1948-51). While director of the press, Lottinville expanded two established series, the Civilization of the American Indian Series and the American Exploration and Travel Series, and inaugurated two new ones, the Western Frontier Library and the Centers of Civilization.

Lottinville himself wrote a good deal about western history, producing *The Life of George Bent* (1968) and contributing to *Probing the West* (1962) and *Three Men in Texas* (1967).

In 1966 the University of Oklahoma awarded Lottinville the Distinguished Service Citation for national leadership in scholarly publishing. He was invited to serve as chairman of the Oklahoma Advisory Committee to the United States Commission on Civil Rights, became a member of the Advisory Committee of the National Foundation for the Arts and Humanities, and was made a member of the Oklahoma Hall of Fame. In 1967 the University of Oklahoma made him the Regents Professor of History.—A. M. G.

Loucks, Henry Langford (1846-1928). Farm leader in the Dakotas. As president of the Dakota Territorial Farmers' Alliance during the 1880s, Loucks supported joining the Southern Farmers' Alliance and served as its national president. Upon the establishment of statehood for North and South Dakota in 1889, Loucks organized the farmers as pressure groups in the constitutional conventions. In 1890 he ran as an independent candidate for governor of South Dakota but was not elected. As editor of the *Dakota Ruralist* his support of Populism was well known throughout the Dakotas. Unable to maintain control of the Populist party, in 1898 he returned to the Republican fold.—D. J. T.

Louisiana, District of. See LOUISIANA TERRITORY.

Louisiana, state of. George Washington Cable once reported that when the tricolor of France was lowered to be replaced by the Stars and Stripes in the Place d'Armes of New Orleans on December 20, 1803, the citizens wept. But there is really no sound evidence to indicate that the French Louisianians truly opposed becoming part of the American Union. The Act of 1804 creating the Territory of Orleans did affront them, however, because it created a government wholly appointive and separated Orleans from the District of Louisiana, which lay north of the thirty-third parallel (see LOUISIANA TERRITORY). Citizens of the Territory of Orleans were also infuriated by attempts to make English the official language of the community and to replace the French and Spanish legal system with the common law. Equally offensive were the government's refusal to honor certain clauses in the Louisiana Purchase Treaty giving preferential import-duty status to New Orleans and its imposition upon the territory of a slave-trade policy more restrictive than that allowed in other parts of the nation. Some of these resentments were eased by the Territorial Act of 1805, which established an elective legislature, the first governmental body ever chosen by popular ballot in the history of the region.

The governor of the Territory of Orleans, William C. C. CLAIBORNE, who had come to New Orleans in 1803 to act with General James Wilkinson as one of the commissioners to receive transfer of the Louisiana Purchase, was handicapped by his ignorance of French and by the deep ethnic antagonisms in the population. The community was divided into three major groups: the French-speaking *ancienne population*, which traced its origins back to colonial days; the "Americans," a loose assemblage of migrants from the Anglo-Saxon regions of the country and their cousins from Ireland and Scotland; and the "Foreign French," refugees from continental France and the West Indies. (There has been much confusion about ethnic terms in Louisiana: the word "creole," frequently used today to identify the group properly called the *ancienne population*, was actually employed by early Louisianians to designate anyone native-born to the region, be he French, Anglo-American, black, or white. "Cajuns" are the descendants of the Acadian refugees expelled from Nova Scotia by the British in the 1750s, who settled in Spanish Louisiana in the 1760s, generally along the bayous of southwestern Louisiana such as the Teche. In the early nineteenth century, they were clearly part of the *ancienne population* and, as natives, were equally accepted as "creoles." Present usage tends to insist upon the pure white, Latin character of "creoles" and to confine that term to non-Cajun descendants of Louisianians whose ancestors were continental French, but the distinction is historically unsound.) The three ethnic factions, with the *ancienne population* and the "Foreign French" generally allied, contested bitterly for control of the territory and eventually the state. The turbulence thus occasioned may well explain Aaron Burr's apparent belief that Orleans would rally to his support in 1806, but again there is little evidence that his assumption was correct, and betrayal of the BURR CONSPIRACY by General James WILKINSON prevented its being tested.

Despite its lack of the 60,000 free inhabitants required by the Act of 1805, Orleans was permitted to enter the Union as the state of Louisiana in April 1812. Presidents Jefferson and Madison had always maintained that the LOUISIANA PURCHASE had included West Florida from the Mississippi River on the west to the Perdido River on tht east, and when the inhabitants of the region around Baton Rouge expelled their Spanish masters in 1810,

Madison ordered Governor Claiborne to occupy the area. Congress, in the 1812 act creating the state of Louisiana, joined to the original Territory of Orleans that segment of West Florida which lay west of the Pearl River, a portion of the state known even today as the "Florida Parishes."

Invasion by the British in December 1814 saw the native population hold true to the United States, despite the suspicions of them harbored by General Andrew Jackson, who repelled the invaders on the Plains of Chalmette some ten miles below New Orleans, with major assistance from Jean Laffite's privateers and other Louisianians. Although the climactic engagement of the campaign was fought on January 8, 1815, after the signing of the Treaty of Ghent in December 1814, there is no validity to the frequent assertion that the battle of New Orleans was fought after the end of the war, for the treaty specifically called for hostilities to continue until ratification of the pact, which did not come until February 1815.

The constitution of 1812, under which the state was admitted to the Union, was rigidly conservative, with suffrage limited to taxpayers and office-holding to property owners, and was geared to insure extended political control of the state by the French-speaking element of the community. Louisiana's political battles of the antebellum period were thus waged on two distinct levels, one for domination of the internal affairs of the state, pitting the French against the "American" faction, and the second on the more general plane of competition between national political parties in congressional and presidential campaigns, in which ethnic group identifications played little part. Until 1845, local control remained largely in the hands of representatives of the French faction who happened to be Whigs, while Jacksonians carried the presidential campaigns. Under this arrangement Louisiana maintained its French civil code and its unique system of parish rather than county units in local government, institutions that remain operative even today. Growing numbers of upland yeoman "American" cotton farmers in northern Louisiana eventually combined with New Orleans clerks and laborers and Irish and German immigrants to outweigh conservative sugar planters of the southern and southwestern regions and to replace the constitution of 1812 with a more liberal one in 1845, which embraced white manhood suffrage and shifted local control to the "American" faction, symbolized by removal of the state capital from New Orleans to Baton Rouge in 1849. (Donaldsonville had served briefly as the seat of government in 1830.) The 1850s were "flush times" in Louisiana. The plantation economy, based on sugar and cotton, dominated the area and explains the more-than-fifty-percent-black composition of its population. Steamboat traffic on the Mississippi made New Orleans the nation's second-largest port and the financial and commercial center of the South. Black-belt domination of politics was highlighted by adoption of the constitution of 1852, which provided for legislative representation based on total parish population, slave as well as free. Louisiana was now firmly in the Democratic party camp, represented by such leaders as John Slidell, Pierre Soulé, and Judah P. Benjamin, a Whig until the slavery issue dissolved his party after 1854 and forced him into the Democracy. Democratic monopoly in Louisiana was contested thereafter only by the ineffective American party, an offshoot of the Know-Nothings and not to be confused with the older American party faction.

In the crisis of 1860, largely because of the influence of Soulé, the state cast more votes for the moderate pro-Union candidates, Stephen A. Douglas and John Bell, than for the radical John C. Breckenridge, but the division of the ballots gave Breckenridge the plurality and the state's electoral vote. The strong nationalist tradition in Louisiana, compounded of old Whig elements and some New Orleans commercial interests sensitive to eastern and northern ties, briefly held fast against the rising passion for secession, but even such moderates as Soulé were eventually reduced to championing united southern political action rather than individual state declarations of independence. These "cooperationists" vied with the direct secessionists in elections for membership in a state convention to be assembled in January 1861, and the results gave seats to eighty secessionists, forty-four cooperationists, and six undecided delegates. The issue was thus decided, and on January 26 Louisiana seceded from the Union under the leadership of Governor Thomas O. Moore. After a few months as an independent state, she joined the Confederacy on March 21, 1861. Among her most distinguished sons in the military service of the South were generals P. G. T. Beauregard, Richard Taylor, Braxton Bragg, and Leonidas Polk, the last also Episcopal bishop of Louisiana. Of her two United States senators in 1860, Judah P. Benjamin served as Confederate attorney-general, secretary of war, and secretary of state, while John Slidell became Confederate commissioner to France. While en route to his post, Slidell and the commissioner to England, James M. Mason, were seized from the British mail packet *Trent* by Captain Charles Wilkes of the U.S.S. *San Jacinto* on November 8, 1861, and returned to the United States. British indignation reached near war fever and was dissipated only by the release of the two men by Secretary of State William Seward, who acknowledged that their removal had been in violation of international law.

As part of the Federal campaign to divide the Confederacy by gaining complete control of the Mississippi, Admiral David Farragut seized New Orleans in April 1862. The city was then occupied by the troops of General Benjamin F. Butler. Butler's ruthless suppression of opposition included the hanging of William Mumford for removing the federal flag from the old New Orleans mint and his famous "General Order No. 28," which required that any female insulting an officer of the United States be "treated as a woman of the town plying her avocation." This earned him the sobriquet "beast," while his supposed avaricious appetite for collecting New Orleans flatware tagged him as "silver spoons." But he did maintain order and bring surprising cleanliness to a notoriously dirty city by the unprecedented assignment of two thousand commandeered New Orleanians to a steady scouring of the streets of the metropolis. Baton Rouge fell in May 1862, and Port Hudson in 1863 after Grant's victory at Vicksburg. In 1864 General Nathaniel P. Banks, Butler's successor, launched his Red River campaign aimed at Shreveport, where Confederate governor Henry W. Allen had removed his seat of government from its temporary location in Opelousas. Banks's advance was blocked by General Richard Taylor's resistance at the battles of Mansfield and Pleasant Hill, which ended most of the fighting in the state. Surrender of the trans-Mississippi West to the Federals in New Orleans on May 26, 1865, marked the capitulation of the last Confederate troops and the end of the Civil War.

Reconstruction lasted longer in Louisiana than in any other state, getting a fitful start under President Lincoln's mild program with a moderate new constitution in 1864, which was rejected by a vengeful radical Republican Congress after Lincoln's assassination. Under radical reconstruction, Louisiana was joined with Texas in the military district of General Philip Henry Sheridan, and a new constitution of 1868 gave political power to Radical Republican supporters at the expense of ex-Confederates and anti-Negro forces. Readmitted to the Union under this constitution, Louisiana became the battleground for opposing Radical Republican factions, the most successful being that of Henry Clay Warmoth, governor from 1868 to 1872, whose administration was a mixture of long-remembered corruption and soon-forgotten solid reforms in education and expansion of civil rights. By 1872 excesses of carpetbag rule, disaffection of Negroes disappointed by their lack of real power under the Radicals, gradual enfranchisement of ex-Confederates, and division in the ranks of the Republicans themselves led to a revival of Democratic strength. William Pitt Kellogg and his Democratic rival, John McEnery, both claimed victory in the gubernatorial contest of that year, and only the presence of federal troops made good Kellogg's claims. The election of 1876 led to an identical conflict of claims to office by the Republican S. B. Packard and the Democrat Francis T. Nicholls, but this time the outcome was determined by the dispute over the electoral count in the presidential race between Rutherford B. Hayes and Samuel J. Tilden. Reconstruction ended in Louisiana in 1877 when the Republican party withdrew federal troops from the state in return for the state's electoral votes. Hayes went to the White House and Nicholls to the governor's mansion.

The new Democratic governor was typical of a succession of "Bourbon" leaders, masters of the state's landed and capital wealth. Under them white supremacy was gradually restored by such devices as the "grandfather clause" of the constitution of 1898, which restricted Negro suffrage. This was followed by imposition of more and more stringent patterns of racial segregation. The late nineteenth century saw gradual expansion of sharecropping and tenant farming and a general decline in river commerce, which was only partly offset by James B. Eads's successful opening of the frequently silted-over mouths of the Mississippi by construction of his ingenious jetties. The "Louisiana Lottery" was a major force in state politics until its dissolution in 1893. Considerable economic relief came to the state in the twentieth century with the development of its rich mineral deposits, particularly oil, gas, salt, and sulphur. The great scourge of yellow fever, which almost annually had taken its toll of Louisianians, never more viciously than in the epidemic years of 1832-33 and 1853, was finally conquered by the genius of Walter Reed and his associates in Cuba. "Bronze John" paid his last call to Louisiana in 1905.

Even the reactionary rule of the Bourbons began to yield to relatively progressive political leadership under Governor John M. Parker (1920-24), but not quickly enough to restrain the rise of the Louisiana "Kingfish," Huey Pierce Long, who swept to power in 1928 on promises to crush the rule of the Bourbons and to end domination of the state by the vested interests such as the railroads and Standard Oil. His many accomplishments, ranging from expanded welfare programs to free schoolbooks, improved roads, a great Charity Hospital in New Orleans, and a much expanded state university in Baton Rouge, were at the price of widespread corruption and political dictatorship. An attempt to impeach him in 1929 failed, and he resigned his post to take a seat in the United States Senate in 1931, where he soon shifted his support from Franklin D. Roosevelt to mount his own candidacy for president with a "Share Our Wealth" platform and the slogan "Every Man a King." His assassination in 1935 led to reconciliation between his lieutenants in Louisiana and the Roosevelt administration, labeled by its critics the "Second Louisiana Purchase." Revelation of gross corruption among his party leaders sent many of them to jail in 1939. A "reform" governor, Sam Jones, was chosen in 1940, but the Long tradition has been kept alive by Earl K. Long, Huey's brother, who served as governor in 1948-52 and 1956-60, and by Huey's son Russell, a United States senator since 1949. "Uncle Earl," a flamboyant figure in his own right and self-proclaimed "Last of the Red Hot Pappas," maintained the Long "populist" approach and, like Huey, disdained exploitation of racial bigotry as part of his program.

Economically, the state continued to profit from its agricultural and timber production, rich seafood and fur resources, and mineral wealth (see OIL INDUSTRY), and from the extensive development of industry along the Mississippi from Baton Rouge to New Orleans. A new ship channel to the Gulf stimulated New Orleans trade and facilitated the manufacture of huge rocket boosters for the Apollo moon launches at the Michoud assembly plant on the fringe of the city. The state is still divided at the Red River into a basically conservative Anglo-Saxon Protestant north and a relatively more liberal Gallic Roman Catholic south, a partition that greatly affects its political personality.

See E. A. Davis, *Louisiaia: A Narrative History* (1961); Federal Writers Project, *Louisiana: A Guide to the State* (1941); Alceé Fortier, *History of Louisiana*, 4 vols. (1904); Charles E. A. Gayarré, *History of Louisiana*, 4 vols. (1965); Fred B. Kniffen, *Louisiana: Its Land and People* (1968); T. Lynn Smith and Homer L. Hitt, *The People of Louisiana* (1952); and T. Harry Williams, *Huey Long* (1969).—J. G. T.

Louisiana Purchase (1803). The Louisiana Purchase, which doubled the territory of the United States, was a result of both frontier and European pressures. The frontier pressures were mostly upon the government of the United States in Washington, for the settlers in the trans-Appalachian territories on both sides of the Ohio River dramatically increased their numbers in the decade 1790-1800 and looked forward to using the Mississippi to transport their produce, via the Gulf and the Atlantic, to the east coast and also to Europe. The population of Kentucky rose from 73,677 to 220,955 in the ten years between the first and second national censuses. The estimated non-Indian population of the entire Northwest Territory in 1790 was 3,000, but by 1800

Ohio alone had a population of 45,365. By the end of the century there was fear in the West that the Spanish, in possession of Louisiana, might refuse access to the great river and to a place of deposit, despite the guarantees of the Treaty of the San Lorenzo of 1795.

Meanwhile, with the unfolding of the French Revolution, the European picture was changing with great rapidity. By the turn of the century Napoleon was in power as "first consul." At the outset he seems to have favored a scheme of his foreign minister, Talleyrand—the creation of a new French empire in the New World. When the European war momentarily halted with the Treaty of Amiens in 1802, Napoleon actively commenced organizing an expedition to reinforce the beleaguered French troops in Haiti and to occupy New Orleans. By this time, he had obtained the retrocession of Louisiana from the government of Spain, first in the secret Treaty of SAN ILDEFONSO of October 1, 1800, and then in the Godoy-Lucien Bonaparte treaty of March 21, 1801.

It was news of the latter treaty and actual possession of its text (the British government gave it to the American minister in London) that stirred President Thomas JEFFERSON to action. Minister to Great Britain Rufus King's letter of November 20, 1801, enclosing the text of the Franco-Spanish treaty of 1801, arrived in Washington on February 18, 1802. Precisely two months later—time perhaps did not seem unduly important to Jefferson, ensconced in the executive mansion in the little village of Washington in the American woods—the president sent a now-famous letter to Minister Robert Livingston in France through the agency of the French economist Pierre Samuel du Pont de Nemours, his longtime friend and correspondent and an advocate of the purchase. In this letter, which du Pont was allowed to read before delivering it into Livingston's hands personally, the president remarked that "The day that France takes possession of New Orleans, fixes the sentence which is to restrain her forever within her low-water mark. It seals the union of two nations who in conjunction can maintain exclusive possession of the ocean. From that moment, we must marry ourselves to the British fleet and nation."

This threat was more idle than serious, for if there was one nation Jefferson distrusted more than France, it was Great Britain, the enemy of the American Revolution. In subsequent months Jefferson put his faith in negotiation far more than in threats. At first he worked through Livingston, apparently without result. Then early in 1803, when news arrived in Washington that the Spanish intendant in New Orleans had revoked the right of deposit, contrary to the Treaty of SAN LORENZO, Jefferson sent his young Virginia friend James Monroe to Paris to assist Livingston.

By this time the European international scene had changed. The imminence of a renewal of war between France and Britain was persuading Napoleon to sell Louisiana to the United States before the British might capture it, and Monroe arrived in Paris just as Livingston was consummating the sale. Livingston was astonished at the offer of Louisiana, for at Jefferson's direction he had been dickering only for the so-called island of New Orleans and the Floridas, East and West. Talleyrand one day asked with a flashing directness, "What will you give for the whole?" After considerable parleying, in which Monroe joined Livingston, the United States purchased the vast territory for $11,250,000 in a treaty dated April 30, 1803. By a separate claims convention the American government assumed the debts owed by France to American citizens for spoliations during the recent wars, a sum of $3,750,000, making $15 million the total price for Louisiana. On May 15, little more than two weeks after the Louisiana treaty, Great Britain declared war on France.

The meaning of the Louisiana Purchase has occupied historians to the present day. Among the many results of the purchase, it provided a vast new area for agriculture and stimulated a declining fur trade; it initiated an expansionist psychology among the American people; it set a precedent for the new government under the Constitution to acquire land by purchase; it allowed for Indian removal; it created problems of territorial government; and it ended the presence of strong powers on the western frontier.

See Francois Barbé-Marbois, *The History of Louisiana* (1830), a classic account by Napoleon's minister of the treasury; Edward Channing, "The Louisiana Procurement," in *Federalists and Republicans* (1917); and E. Wilson Lyon, *Louisiana in French Diplomacy: 1759-1804* (1934).—R. H. F.

Louisiana Territory. Louisiana Territory embraced all of the area included in the Louisiana Purchase of April 30, 1803, that lay north of the thirty-third parallel of north latitude. It comprised most of the western half of the Mississippi valley and extended as far north as the present state of Montana. (The area south of the thirty-third parallel included in the purchase, designated the Territory of Orleans, was administered separately. In 1812 the Territory of Orleans, along with a portion of West Florida, became the state of LOUISIANA.)

Under the Spanish, Louisiana Territory was called Upper Louisiana. Originally claimed by France, the territory had been ceded to Spain by the Treaty of Fontainebleau in 1762.

Although retroceded by Spain to France by the Treaty of San Ildefonso of 1800, the territory continued to be run by Spanish officials. Napoleon then sold it to the United States in 1803 as part of the Louisiana Purchase. On March 9, 1804, Captain Amos Stoddard of the United States Army received Louisiana Territory as commissioner for France, and on the following day assumed control as civil commandant for the United States. At the time of the transfer the territory had a population of a little more than ten thousand, of whom three fifths were Anglo-Americans and about 1,300, slaves.

Stoddard was civil commandant of Upper Louisiana, as it was still called, until October 1, 1804. During this period the old Spanish officials (except for the lieutenant governor) continued to administer Spanish laws and customs, while Stoddard's principal duty was to preserve public order.

The new government that took effect on October 1 was established under the Louisiana Government Act of March 26, 1804. By its terms Congress formally divided the Louisiana Purchase area, making the area south of the thirty-third parallel the Territory of Orleans and that north of the line the District of Louisiana. For governmental purposes, the District of Louisiana was attached to Indiana Territory. Indiana's governor, William Henry Harrison, became chief executive of the district, and he and the territory's three judges drew up a body of laws for its government. They retained the five administrative districts into which the Spanish had divided the territory but with more carefully defined boundaries. For each of these divisions Harrison appointed a commandant and other local officials, and courts were established in each.

Many Louisianians were unhappy with the Act of March 26, 1804, and stated their objections to the law in a memorial to Congress. Not only did they dislike being attached to Indiana Territory, but they also were opposed to the provisions of the law authorizing the president, as part of the Indian removal policy, to exchange the lands of Indians living east of the Mississippi for lands west of the river, and voiding virtually all lands grants made by the Spanish after October 1, 1800.

By an act of March 3, 1805, Congress detached the District of Louisiana from Indiana and organized it as a territory effective July 4. President Jefferson appointed Brigadier General James WILKINSON, the ranking officer of the army, as first governor of the territory. He named Joseph Browne of New York, a brother-in-law of Aaron Burr, secretary, and John B. C. Lucas, John Coburn, and Rufus Easton, judges. Even though he was a controversial chief executive and soon after assuming the post became involved in the Burr conspiracy, Wilkinson retained the confidence of the Jefferson administration. It was while serving as governor of Louisiana that he sent Zebulon M. Pike on his exploring expeditions up the Mississippi and into the Southwest. In the spring of 1806, Wilkinson was ordered to the territory of Orleans to handle the boundary dispute with Spain along the Sabine River. With his departure, Browne became acting governor of Louisiana, but because of his family connection with Burr he was replaced on April 1, 1807, by Frederick Bates as secretary and acting governor.

In the meantime, on March 3, Meriwether LEWIS had been appointed governor of the territory, replacing Wilkinson, as a reward for his services as coleader of the Lewis and Clark expedition. At the same time, William CLARK, Lewis' exploring partner, became principal Indian agent for Louisiana and brigadier general of its militia. Since Lewis did not arrive in Louisiana until a year after being named governor, Bates served as chief executive. With Clark's assistance, he reorganized the militia and tried to improve relations with the Indians and to reduce British influence among them. Bates also played a major role in the preparation and publication of a new code of laws for Louisiana and in trying to settle the land claims based upon Spanish and French grants.

Lewis assumed the active governorship of Louisiana in March 1808. He was not a successful chief executive, however, quarreling with Bates, making numerous enemies by his ineptitude as a politician, and failing to consult his superiors in Washington concerning his plans, especially those dealing with Indian affairs. In September 1809 Lewis left St. Louis for Washington in order to explain to federal officials some of his actions as governor. He died en route to the capital on October 11.

Benjamin Howard, a representative in Congress from Kentucky, became governor of Louisiana in the spring of 1810 but spent little time in the territory. For nearly two years, Bates again served as acting governor. During this period, his main concerns were to strengthen the militia, improve relations with the Indians, and prevent the illegal engrossment and exploitation by whites of the valuable lead mines of the territory.

Following the admission of the Territory of Orleans to the Union as the state of Louisiana in April 1812, Congress changed the name of the Louisiana Territory to Missouri Territory on June 4, 1812. Although the territory's area remained the same, its government was raised to the second stage with a bicameral legislature and a congressional delegate. In 1821 MISSOURI was admitted to the Union as a state.

Good sources of information on Louisiana Territory are Louis Houck, *A History of Missouri*, and Thomas M. Marshall, ed., *The Life and Papers of Frederick Bates*. Important documentary material is contained in Clarence E. Carter, ed., *The Territorial Papers of the United States*, vols. XIII (1948) and XIV (1949).—J. L. L.

Louisville, Kentucky. Louisville is located opposite the Falls of the Ohio. Long before Anglo-American settlers appeared in the Ohio valley, this spot was known to the Indians and later to the Frenchmen. The actual move toward American settlement was begun in 1773, when Captain Thomas Bullitt surveyed lands in the area, but activities about the falls were disrupted by Lord Dunmore's War (1774). Not until 1778 was another move made to plant a settlement there. In the latter year George Rogers Clark landed his command of Northwest troops on Corn Island and established a fort. Soon after Clark's departure for Kaskaskia on June 24, 1778, settlers moved over to the mainland and began building cabins on the site of present-day Louisville. In May 1780 the Virginia general assembly enacted a law establishing the town of Louisville.

Because of its favorable location on the main artery of western navigation, and because nearly all boat traffic on the Ohio had to stop at the town, Louisville grew into an important port and later into a major supply center for the western and southern country. Many of the adventures onto the western frontier, including the Lewis and Clark expedition, gathered men and supplies in the town. By 1820 the steamboat had made Louisville an important commercial center for both the West and the lower South.

See Benjamin Casseday, *The History of Louisville, from Its Earliest Settlement till the Year 1852* (1852); Reuben T. Durrett, *The Centenary of Louisville* (1893); and Henry McMurtrie, *Sketches of Louisville and Its Environs* (1819).—T. D. C.

Loving, Oliver (1812-1867). Trail driver and cattleman. Born in Kentucky, Loving settled in Lamar County, Texas, in 1845. A year later he moved to Collin County, where he raised cattle, farmed, and freighted from both Houston and Shreveport. In 1855 he moved his herds to Palo Pinto County and three years later made the first of his long trail drives, to the Chicago yards—the first recorded movement of Texas cattle to that terminal market.

During the Civil War Loving supplied the Confederate army with beef and after the war became associated with Charles Goodnight in filling contracts for army and Indian beef. In 1866 they drove a herd from the Fort Belknap area across the Pecos to Fort Sumner, New Mexico, then on to the mouth of Crow Creek on the South Platte River north of Denver. The trail they marked became known as the Goodnight-Loving trail and was long in use. Loving also pioneered or laid out other trails, including the Shawnee trail from Texas to Chicago and a route to Denver that later became the Western Trail.

Loving was wounded by Indians while he and Goodnight were trailing a herd in 1867 and died three weeks later at Fort Sumner, New Mexico. His last remark is reputed to have been, "Don't leave me in foreign soil—take me back to Texas."

The towns of Loving, Texas, and Lovington, New Mexico, are named for this pioneer trailblazer. —R. B. W.

Lowe, Joseph (1846?-1899). Saloonkeeper. "Rowdy Joe" Lowe made his dubious reputation in Kansas as a brawling, quarrelsome saloonkeeper and procurer. Historians have searched in vain for redeeming characteristics, and he apparently deserved the odium that attaches to his name. Virtually nothing is known about his early life except that he was born in Illinois. Some sources say that he rode with William Clarke Quantrill's Confederate guerrillas in Missouri and Kansas during the Civil War. Other sources place him in the Texas Rangers in 1866 fighting Indians with W. G. O'Brien's company. Later he turned up in Denver, where he probably acquired his nickname. Dave J. Cook, the Rocky Mountain lawman and detective, recalled in later years that he once stopped a saloon fight between Lowe and another man. He demanded that the two combatants apologize to each other, whereupon Lowe said to his adversary, "Come here. I want to kiss and make up." Then he seized the man and bit off the end of his nose. After that "Rowdy Joe" was a mild enough sobriquet.

In the late 1860s Rowdy Joe opened the U. S. Saloon and Dancehouse in Ellsworth, Kansas, a disreputable gambling hall and brothel frequented by soldiers from Fort Harker. In July 1869 Lowe and another man robbed a man outside the saloon, whereupon a group of well-meaning citizens asked Joe to leave the country for his health and theirs. He may have worked as a gambler in Houston, Texas, the following winter, but he was back in operation at Ellsworth by midyear. Late in 1870 he was at Wichita long enough to steal a mule and win an acquittal when the only witness against him failed to appear in court.

In 1871 Lowe and his wife, "Rowdy Kate," moved to Newton, Kansas. Again his place, known as the "swiftest joint in Kansas," was regarded as a dive in a town full of dives. Violence frequently punctuated the festivities at Joe's saloon, and in the spring of 1872, Joe himself shot and killed a rival named Jim Sweet, who paid too much attention to Kate. After that, the Lowes left Newton and set up their operations in West Wichita (or Delano). Joe apparently left Wichita long enough to visit Denison, Texas, late in 1872, but he soon returned. Not long after, he became embroiled in a personal feud with E. T. "Red" Beard, another saloonkeeper. The feud reached a climax in a bloody gunfight in which Beard was killed. The testimony at the trial was so confused that Joe was found not guilty. New warrants were sworn out against him on lesser charges, and he took a ,ast horse out of Wichita. In 1874 he was reported killed by Indians in Dakota Territory, but in 1875 he was back in Ellsworth. In 1876 he was in Fort Worth, Texas, operating a gambling hall. In the years that followed he turned up in

Fort Griffin, Texas; Dodge City, Kansas; Tombstone, Arizona; and several boom camps. He was reported to have visited Dodge again in 1883 during the Dodge City War. Lowe's last years were spent on a ranch near Denver, but in 1899, he was murdered in a Denver saloon by ex-policeman E. A. Kimmel, who held a personal grudge against him.

See Nyle H. Miller and Joseph W. Snell, *Why the West Was Wild* (1963).—G. L. R.

Lowie, Robert H. (1883-1957). Ethnologist. Born in Vienna, Lowie was brought to New York while still a child. After graduating in 1901 from the College of the City of New York, he flirted with the idea of becoming a chemist, but after meeting anthropologist Franz Boas, he decided to spend the rest of his life as an ethnologist. From 1908 to 1921 he was with the American Museum of Natural History, under whose aegis he made field trips to the Plains Indians. He then spent thirty years teaching at the University of California at Berkeley in the company of anthropologist Alfred L. Kroeber.

Although perhaps best known for his contributions to the theoretical body of cultural anthropology, Lowie is remembered as author of *Indians of the Plains* (1954) and for his many publications concerning the Crow, Northern Shoshoni, Comanche, Hidatsa, Washo, Mandan, Kiowa, and Ute Indians. He also had more than a passing acquaintance with the Hopi Indians of Arizona. When he died, he left behind a bibliography of nearly five hundred books, monographs, articles, and reviews.

See Paul Radin, "Robert H. Lowie: 1883-1957," *American Anthropologist*, vol. 60, no. 2 (1958)—B.L.F.

Luhan, Mabel Dodge (1879-1962). Writer. Luhan was born in Buffalo, New York. After extensive travels in the United States and Europe, she eventually arrived more or less by chance in New Mexico in 1918. There she became enraptured of the Indian life in Taos, which seemed to her more profound than the presumably sterile existence she had left behind in the East. Her fourth husband, Antonio Luhan—three prior marriages had ended in divorce—whom she married in 1923, was an Indian of the Taos pueblo.

Luhan has been identified almost entirely with the artists' colony at Taos, of which she was the most detailed reporter. The preponderance of her literary work, notably *Winter in Taos* (1948) and *Taos and Its Artists* (1948), is reminiscent of Taos and its inhabitants. Her account of New Mexican Indian life and its personal meaning to her may be found in the fourth volume of *Intimate Memories* (1933-37), *Edge of Taos Desert* (1937).

Luhan's precise relationship to the Taos art colony is difficult to analyze exactly. She was not the first to arrive there, and she publicly disclaimed association with the artistic hangers-on, whom she saw as making up a pretentious pseudoartistic "colony." Nonetheless, she did hope to develop a poetic voice for hitherto mute New Mexico and to that end was instrumental in bringing D. H. Lawrence and other writers to Taos. Her attempt at calling forth a native New Mexican muse was unsuccessful, perhaps, as her detractors always insisted, because it was too self-consciously "artistic."—J. K. F.

lumber industry. The lumber industry of the United States has had a history marked by repeated migrations. Depletion of timber stands and changing patterns of demand have necessitated opening new areas of production and made it possible to speak of a lumberman's

Cutting timber in California's redwood forests. (Library of Congress)

frontier. Yet, in spite of what one might deduce from the frontier label, the industry has never been exclusively western.

In colonial times, with forests near to hand and lumber expensive to ship because of its bulk and the poorly developed systems of transportation, production was widely scattered east of the Appalachians. However, by the end of the colonial period loggers and farmers had removed the timber from large portions of the region. As the anonymous author of *American Husbandry* noted in 1775, even firewood had become scarce along much of the Atlantic seaboard and had to be imported from Maine. Indeed, upper New England's white pine forests were not only supplying much of the domestic demand for lumber but also sizable markets in the West Indies and elsewhere. By the early nineteenth century, Bangor, located on the Penobscot River in Maine, had become the largest lumber manufacturing center in the world. It was, as Stewart Holbrook put it in *Holy Old Mackinaw* (1938), "the fair and fullest flower of the Eastern lumber industry."

As it became necessary to push ever farther into the backcountry of New England to find untapped stands and as demand increased in inland areas of the United States, more and more lumbermen moved westward. By 1840 expanded production in western Pennsylvania and upstate New York had pushed those two states into the lead in the manufacture of lumber. Four years later James H. Perkins, who had moved from New Hampshire to Pennsylvania, built a large boom for collecting logs at Williamsport on the Susquehanna River. Logging on the river's upper West Branch expanded rapidly to supply sawmills that sprang up near the boom. Fifty

mills were active at Williamsport during its heyday as a lumber town.

Most migrating lumbermen moved even farther west. Some went all the way to the Pacific Coast, but the majority transferred their operations to the lake states. In 1845 Isaac Stephenson, who had started his career in New Brunswick, moved from Bangor to Wisconsin, where he soon rose to preeminence. The pattern was common. Of 131 leaders in the lumber industry of the lake states, more than four fifths were born either in the Northeast or eastern Canada. Laborers from New England's stagnating lumber industry also found fresh opportunity in the lake states, as did numerous French-Canadian and Scandinavian immigrants. Residents of the older areas were distressed. A congressman from Maine complained in 1852 that "the stalwart sons" of his state were "marching away by the scores and hundreds to the piny woods of the Northwest."

Beginning in the 1850s the lumber industry of the lake states expanded rapidly. Much of the white pine of this area went into building the cities of the Midwest, but railroad construction was also consuming large quantities. During the last decades of the century railroads consumed nearly one fourth of all the lumber produced in the United States. By 1880 Michigan had vaulted into first place in production, its cut worth twice that of second-place Pennsylvania. Michigan had fewer mills than Pennsylvania, but they included several far larger than any in the older center. Saginaw, with over seventy mills, was now the premiere city among lumber centers. Not all its cut was consumed in the West. Huge quantities of forest products from Michigan passed out to market via the Erie Canal. As the receiving point at the eastern end of the canal, and from areas nearer to hand, Albany became a vast emporium for lumber.

As timber in the Saginaw area disappeared, millmen moved on to Michigan's Upper Peninsula—where Robert Dollar first rose to prominence as a sawmill operator—and to WISCONSIN and Minnesota—where Frederick Weyerhaeuser and his associates had been cutting since the 1860s. Much of the timber felled in these states was sawed to the south. Rafts of logs, at first simply driven along by the current, then longer and maneuvered by steam-powered sidewheelers, floated down the Mississippi and its tributaries to mills at Rock Island and other centers. As far south as St. Louis practically every town along the Mississippi had its sawmill.

In time, even the extensive pineries of the lake states became depleted. With their passing some of the area's lumbermen began cutting hemlock or hardwoods, but most either gave up or moved on. Those who migrated went in many directions. Some crossed into Canada to tap stands north of lakes Huron and Superior; others went to the pine forests of the South or to the stands of Douglas fir, redwood, and pine in the Far West. Both Dollar and the Weyerhaeuser interests followed the latter course.

Lumbermen from the lake states arrived in the South and Far West to find that others had long been sawing there. Small operations had existed in the South since colonial times, cutting primarily for local consumers. In the Far West production antedated by many years the dominion of the United States. Scattered settlements of woodsmen in Hispanic California and the Hudson's Bay Company in the Pacific Northwest had cut lumber for local consumption as well as for export. With the gold

Hauling logs of the big trees of the Sierra Nevada over a trestle (c. 1902). (Library of Congress)

rush in California, production on the West Coast expanded rapidly. Some firms established during these flush times survived beyond them, most notably those of A. M. Simpson and Pope & Talbot. Gradually others established firms to compete with the survivors from the gold-rush years. These early firms dispatched scores of shiploads of lumber from their coastal mills to San Francisco and other ports of the Pacific. Sailing vessels taking on lumber were a familiar sight in the ports of British Columbia, Washington, Oregon, and northern California. Significantly, most of the owners of the West Coast's pioneer mills were transplanted New Englanders, many with more experience in maritime trade than in lumbering.

Lumbermen arriving from the lake states during the late nineteenth and early twentieth centuries reoriented the industry in the South and Far West. Rail connections between these regions and the rest of the nation were improving, freight rates declining. Already familiar with the markets in the Midwest and East, the newcomers built mills near rail lines and continued serving them. With the addition of these new markets for their cut, the production of the South and Far West expanded rapidly. By 1899 the South had passed the lake states as the leading lumber-producing region, while the Far West had become a serious challenger, not only to the South's leadership in output but also to the domination of it and the lake states in many midwestern markets. The keen competition that developed in the early twentieth century between lumbermen of the South and Far West continues to this day.

The history of the lumber industry is marked by technological change as well as by migration. As capital, experience, and the fruits of ingenuity accumulated, milling techniques became increasingly sophisticated. Eventually nearly every phase of sawmill operations was mechanized. Most basic were changes to the head rig, the main saw in a mill. At first sawyers worked in pairs, one above a log and one below it in a pit, and cut planks by hand with a long saw with handles on each end. In time waterpower replaced manpower as the saw's driving force, and the muley saw came into being. Up-and-down sawing continued with various modifications until the advent of the much faster circular saw. This in turn survived with modifications for a considerable period, but was eventually superseded by the band saw—a giant, toothed loop of flexible steel strung tightly between paired flywheels above and below the log carriage. Each type was superior to its predecessor but also required more investment capital to install. Some mill owners hesitated to risk the capital necessary to make such improvements, but as one of the industry's leaders put it, the only way to remain competitive with progressive rivals "is to go and do as they do." Those who could not or would not fell by the wayside.

Changes in organization accompanied changes in the sawing of lumber. Mill owners pushed both the vertical and horizontal integration of their holdings. In addition to logging and mill operations, they engaged in the transporting, wholesaling, and retailing of lumber and numerous by-products and entered into numerous subsidiary activities. During the period 1900-14 members of the Weyerhaeuser family held an interest in forty-eight forest product companies, which, in turn, had various subsidiaries. For example, the Weyerhaeuser

Timber Company, their major enterprise in the Pacific Northwest, held shares in twenty-seven other corporations in 1914. Subsidiary operations sometimes became of major importance. The steamship company Robert Dollar established to haul the cut of his far western mills grew into one of the nation's largest maritime enterprises. It survives today as the American President Lines.

The increased size and efficiency of sawmills put a premium on improved logging techniques. Numerous innovations resulted. In New England loggers had felled trees in winter, skidded logs over the snow to the banks of streams, and then floated them out of the woods on the floods that came with the spring thaw. The coming of a log drive was a signal event for communities downstream. As Stewart Holbrook recalled, "the distant drumming of the logs" heralded the coming of a drive. "Then came the advance guard—slim, easy-riding logs that somehow managed to break away and get miles ahead. . . . Soon the logs began coming thicker until you scarcely could see the water between them. The river became a mass of sluggish bodies, rolling this way and that, grumbling all day and all night. No door could shut out the noise." When lumbermen from New England migrated to the lake states they continued to utilize the log drive, but to keep up with demand they developed a giant two-wheeled device so logs could be moved to the waterways in summer as well as winter. Known simply as Big Wheels, this contrivance had an axle so high above the ground that logs could be pulled over brush, stumps, and rocks with little difficulty.

Other new devices and techniques appeared. Loggers built splash dams on small streams in the Rocky Mountain and far western states to stop their flow until a head of water accumulated that was sufficient to sluice logs gathered behind the dam and along the watercourse below out to where they could be handled by more conventional means. Bitter struggles between splash-dam operators and riparian landowners downstream often developed, but millions of feet of logs were washed from the woods by this method. Loggers also erected flumes, sometimes miles in length, to carry logs out of areas where there were no large streams. In 1876 a single firm owned 156 miles of flumes in California's Sierra Nevada. Even more important were the steam donkey, the first in a series of power equipment for yarding logs, and the logging railroad. Both were widely adopted during the 1880s and 1890s. Taken together these innovations largely freed loggers from the old pattern of seasonal harvest, opened vast new areas to the profitable harvesting of timber, and helped encourage the building of new and even more efficient mills.

Stimulus for change in woods operations also came from the expansion of lumbering into new regions. Nowhere was this more evident than in the redwood and Douglas fir forests of the Far West, where logs were too large and the ground too muddy during much of the year to make practical the adoption of techniques used in the lake states and Northeast. The pioneer loggers of the West Coast avoided problems created by log size and mud by cutting only those trees that could be felled or easily rolled into waterways, but a more productive approach was necessary if a major industry were to develop in the area. It was provided by the skid road.

Loggers learned to clear paths through the forest across which they half-buried small logs every few feet. The center of each crosspiece had a notch cut in it to serve as a guide for the logs that were to pass over it. Using teams of oxen for power, workers skidded logs over these "roads" to the water's edge. Before each run a "grease monkey" dashed ahead and daubed each notch with grease so the logs would slide more easily. Skid roads made it practical to log as far as two miles back from waterways as well as during periods when mud made logging by other means totally impossible. They served as the main means of getting logs out of the forests of the Pacific Coast until the widespread adoption of steam donkeys.

Conditions on the West Coast led to other innovations besides the skid road. Because the bases of many trees were greatly enlarged, and often pitchy and useless, timber fallers devised the springboard. They inserted short boards into notches they had cut into the base of the tree and then stood upon them while cutting above the swollen base. Fallers in the Far West also adapted the crosscut saw to the felling of timber. Elsewhere the crosscut had been used to buck trees into lengths once they were down, but felling itself had been done with the ax. However, timber species of the Pacific Coast forests grew so large that felling by ax alone was impracticably slow. Fallers continued to make their undercut with the ax, but came to use the much faster crosscut for the rest of the operation. In doing so they helped to point the way to power saws, which appeared during the twentieth century and further reduced the time required to fell a tree.

As logging moved farther back into the hinterlands of the Far West, the land became rougher. This led to the replacement of logging railroads with logging trucks, which were more versatile. This opened previously inaccessible portions of the Coast Range and Cascades and vaulted Oregon into the lead among lumber-producing states. Increasingly rugged country also brought about high-lead logging. Instead of pulling logs along the ground, lumbermen now began to use engines to hoist logs into the air and pull them overhead to yards for loading on rail cars or trucks. High-lead logging made possible the logging of steep hills and rugged terrain and gave rise to the "high climber." High-lead logging required spars—that is, tall trees limbed and topped so blocks could be hung high above the ground and cables run through them. Someone had to go up the tree and remove its branches and top. As Murray Morgan put it in *The Last Wilderness* (1958), no "sight in the woods is more thrilling than that of the high climber working on a great spar—the tiny man against the giant. . . ." The climactic moment came when the top finally went crashing to the ground and set the spar into sudden, violent motion. Then, "while the spar jerks and vibrates . . . the high rider, as often as not, waves his free hand like a bronc rider or climbs the last few feet of the still-quivering bole and stands on his head."

While the great centers of commercial lumber production were shifting and modes of operation changing, lumbermen in the older areas continued to turn out forest products, and old-fashioned means of production continued to be used. The industry was dominated by the intensively competitive mills that cut for major mar-

Logs being loaded onto flatcars. (Library of Congress)

kets, usually far removed from the millsites, but a host of small mills remained. The latter cut lumber for use in their own vicinity and entered into competition with the industry's giants only infrequently or indirectly. For the small areas they served and the small, marginal stands of timber these mills tapped, old methods of logging and milling continued to be profitable long after they had ceased to be so for major producers. Indeed, the large investments required by modern operations could hardly have been justified for operations such as these.

Continued production in old areas and the repeated opening of new areas had created an industry of immense size by the beginning of the twentieth century. In 1909 the industry set a production record that still stands: 44,509,761,000 board feet of lumber—to say nothing of enormous quantities of railroad ties, shingles, poles, and other forest products. Since 1909 the industry has become increasingly static, dominated by the necessity of coming to terms with the facts that there are no great new forested frontiers to exploit and that production cannot be maintained at the level of 1909 without endangering the industry. Today lumbering is concentrated in the West and South, for that is where most of the remaining stands of sawtimber are located, but it has ceased to be a cut-and-run activity and has become instead a permanent part of the economy of those areas where it is carried out. The adoption of sustained yield timber management has been the hallmark of the transition. Forest nurseries and tree farms are now common.

As the industry became increasingly stationary much of its frontier flavor was lost; as old-timers put it, the timber beasts and sawdust savages became domesticated. Louie Blanchard, who logged on the Chippewa between 1886 and 1912, shared their feeling of nostalgia. According to Walker D. Wyman, who related Blanchard's story in *The Lumberjack Frontier* (1969), one poem in particular caught Blanchard's feelings about the old operations. It concludes:

> Everyone was a sturdy pioneer so jovial and kind
> And they called themselves the lumberjacks while driving down the line.
> Those good old loggin' days are past and we'll never see them more.
> All I have left is memory of the logging days of yore.

Yet, compared to other major industries, lumbering remains decentralized, competitive, and individualistic—as President Nixon's Price Commission learned in seeking, with limited success, to hold down the price of lumber. Many factors contributed to this pattern for the industry: the scattered resource base on which lumbermen draw and markets they service; the necessity of carrying out milling near the source of raw materials; federal and state laws that, for all their loopholes, hindered massive concentration of timber ownership; the fact that the economies of scale available through increased mill size are too limited to justify centralizing operations to the degree they have been in other industries; and perhaps even the failure of the industry's leaders to display the vision and leadership, if not the ruthlessness, that allowed John D. Rockefeller to win control over the equally competitive and unstable oil-refining industry. The result is a lumber industry closer to the economic state of perfect competition than any other major manufacturing industry in the United States. With a good deal of justification, lumbermen continue to describe themselves as rugged, self-reliant individualists. If the measure of an industry's westernness is how closely those engaged in it accept the values of the westerner of popular stereotype, then the lumber industry continues to be as western as any in the country. (See LUMBERJACK.)

For general reading, the best, most enjoyable single volume on the lumber industry is Stewart H. Holbrook, *The American Lumberjack* (1962), originally published as *Holy Old Mackinaw* (1938). Also useful are James E. Defebaugh, *History of the Lumber Industry of America* (1906-07); Agnes Larson, *History of the White Pine Industry of Minnesota* (1949); and Frederick W. Kohlmeyer, "Northern Pine Lumbermen," *Journal of Economic History* (December 1956). Excellent company studies include Ralph W. Hidy, Frank Ernest Hill, and Allan Nevins, *Timber and Men: The Weyerhaeuser Story* (1963), and Edwin T. Coman and Helen M. Gibbs, *Time, Tide and Timber: A Century of Pope and Talbot* (1949). Numerous other articles and references are found in *Forest History*, the quarterly journal of the Forest History Society.—T. R. C.

lumberjack. Not all North American loggers have considered themselves lumberjacks. As Walter McCulloch points out in *Woods Words* (1958), *lumberjack* is a "genteel term used by fiction writers who should have said logger if they mean[t] a man working in the western woods." Properly the term should be used only in referring to those employed in logging the white pine forests of the Northeast and lake states, but in popular usage it means loggers working anywhere. Used in this broader way, it has become an accepted part of the American vernacular.

If the term *lumberjack* is fully established, so too is the popular Paul BUNYAN image of the lumberjack as a rambunctious, self-reliant, ax-wielding giant, usually of French-Canadian or Scandinavian descent. Stewart Holbrook described his classic history of the lumberjack, *Holy Old Mackinaw* (1938), as the story of "the lad who ranged three thousand miles through the forest from Maine to Oregon, steel calks in his boots, an ax in his fist, and a plug of chewing handy. The lad who at intervals emerged from the dark savage woods for purposes of calling on soft ladies and drinking hard liquor." In short, his account was a chronicle of the "timber beasts" who manned logging camps until well into the twentieth century.

Clearly, the image is an exaggerated stereotype. Shocked Victorians who saw lumberjack life firsthand left accounts that were hardly unbiased. Similarly, the selective memories of nostalgic old-timers, including Holbrook, contributed to the distortion. Recent works have supplied an antidote. George Blackburn and Sherman L. Ricards, Jr., in their study of Manistee County, Michigan, have suggested that the promiscuity, carousing, and violence of those who worked in the lumber industry have been overdrawn. While Ralph W. Hidy, Frank Ernest Hill, and Allan Nevins have noted in *Timber and Men* (1963) that "lumberjacks and 'river pigs' were young physically tough men who knew their jobs, avoided risks, and in general took care of themselves. . . ." Such men were fairly typical in the industry and a far cry from the celebrated Jigger Johnson, who

proudly announced: "I can run faster, jump higher, squat lower, move sidways quicker, and spit further than any son of a bitch in camp" and who lived a life that gave credence to the boast.

Yet the popular image of the lumberjack has some basis in fact. In *The Concept of Jacksonian Democracy* (1964), Lee Benson compared the voting records of nineteenth-century lumbering and farming communities. His statistical analysis lent support to the view that lumber towns were centers for what Benson, with scholarly restraint, called non-puritan values. Vernon Jensen, in *Lumber and Labor* (1945), acknowledged that the lumberjack's "spontaneous rowdyism" has often been exaggerated, but argued that it was none the less real. Loggers lived a transient life, without a sense of security and belonging. Emotionally starved, they "emerged from a monotonous winter in the isolated camp," seeking satisfaction "for long-inhibited desires." Moreover, logging called for spurts of exertion under conditions of great physical danger rather than the daily routine of most occupations. Falling branches (loggers called them widow makers), rolling logs, and the rapids and logjams of the drives exacted a heavy toll. "If death was lurking so close," Jensen asked rhetorically, "why not yell for another drink? If a man was soon to be penned up again in the distant woods all winter until the spring and the log drive, why not have a fling with the bottle and the women?"

Settlers felled trees from the beginning of European colonization in North America, but the lumberjack as a distinct type emerged only gradually. When he did, it was New England that furnished the archetype. As Joseph Malone demonstrated in *Pine Trees and Politics* (1964), New England loggers engaged in a running battle with agents of the British crown from the beginning of the eighteenth century until the outbreak of the Revolution. Under the so-called Broad Arrow policy, pine trees over twenty-four inches in diameter were reserved to insure a supply of masts for the Royal Navy. Only those with influence in London could obtain contracts to cut and ship masts to the naval yards. Colonial lumbermen lacked such leverage, but they felled the trees anyway and quickly sawed them into planks to destroy the evidence. They intimidated and harrassed agents of the crown who attempted to enforce the regulations. Through such tactics, they were able to maintain a lucrative lumber trade with the West Indies. The ruggedly independent lumberjack was sprouting, but at this point those who worked in the woods and those who worked in the mills were the same men. Timber beasts and sawdust savages were not yet differentiated.

New England supplied the lead in more than self-reliance. Even after the primary centers of production had shifted westward, ideas and management influences from Maine predominated. The early camps and many of the early tools were modeled after those down East. Most notable among these tools was the peavey, a pole with a hinged hook and spiked tip, which was invented in 1858 by Joseph Peavey, a Maine blacksmith. It remained the logger's primary instrument for moving logs throughout the industry's many migrations.

From New England to the lake states the pattern of life in the lumber camps was the same. During the early fall some of the crew would ready the camps. With the arrival of the others, falling would begin and continue through the long, cold winter to the spring thaw. After the last trees had been cut and pulled to landings along the waterways, the big drives began with the spring runoff. In the fall the cycle would begin again.

During the winter months the logging camp was the center of the lumberjack's world. It was said that lumberjacks lived in trees. The comment was facetious, but the first bunkhouses—crude log dwellings with a roof of logs or bark—were not much better. In the center of the roof, a hole let out the smoke from the cook's fire. Floors were "corduroy," consisting of close-placed poles. The bunks, made of planks and covered with boughs, were double- or triple-decked and placed side by side along the walls so that one could get in only over the end. Muzzle loaders, the men called them. They complained that the horses and oxen had superior accommodations. Perhaps they were right; teamsters slept in the hovels, or barns, apparently from choice.

Bunkhouses gradually acquired plank floors and shingle or tar-paper roofs. Stoves replaced the open fires in the center of the room. One thing did not change, however: bunkhouses continued to be festooned with drying clothes every night. Louie Blanchard, who logged on the Chippewa during the heyday of Wisconsin's lumber industry, recalled it vividly. As he put it in *The Lumberjack Frontier* (1969): "Everybody's clothes got wet from the snow every day and so we needed a lot of racks for drying. When the socks begun to send off steam at night, you sure knowed you was in a logging camp. When you mix the smell of wet socks with the smell of baked beans and chewing tobacco, you have a smell that a lumberjack never forgot even if he lived as long as Methuselah."

Separate cookhouses appeared early. Salt pork, salt cod, baked beans, bread, and tea were staples from the beginning. Only with the coming of the Norwegians and Swedes did coffee become a standby. Loggers considered eating a serious business, not a social occasion, and consumed prodigious quantities in silence. Employers viewed a good cook as a tremendous asset. One later recalled that when he hired a woodsman, "I couldn't make a better pitch than to tell prospects Tom Brackett was cooking." Other cooks earned reputations for non-culinary reasons. Dirty Joe Boulay was the classic example. One old-timer recalled Boulay as "the most desperately unclean, slovenly, soiled, and unkempt character ever seen in these woods. . . ." But, as Stewart Holbrook observed, Boulay's food apparently tasted all right if you could avoid looking at him.

Crews spent ten to twelve hours, six days a week in the woods. The work was hard as well as long. Production was the single goal. Camp foremen and head choppers strained to exact the maximum from the men. Generally there was an excess of woodsmen available, but pride and competitive spirit drove most loggers as surely as abuse from the foreman or fear of losing one's job. In the 1880s and 1890s, as the crosscut replaced the ax in the felling of trees, sawyers replaced choppers as the key man in a logging operation. Previously it took four men to fell and buck into lengths twenty thousand feet of timber in a day. With the adoption of the crosscut to felling, the output doubled.

Felling the trees was only the first step in getting out logs. Once a tree was on the ground it was bucked into lengths. Then a chain tender barked one side of the log

so it would slide more easily, put a chain on the log, and helped hoist the butt onto a go-devil, a primitive sledlike device made from the crotch of a hardwood tree to which a crossbar had been attached. The butts of two or three logs were placed on the crossbar; the other ends were left to drag on the snow. Horses or oxen were then hitched to the go-devil and the logs pulled to a skidway, where they were piled prior to being loaded on sleds. The skidder and swamper pulled the logs onto a pair of tamarack skids and from there onto the sleds. One skidder might follow two fallers and skid seventy-five logs a day.

Once on the sleds, logs were pulled over skidways to landings beside the streams that would be used in the spring drive. At first horses or oxen supplied the motive power; later steam log haulers became common. In the fall, before cutting began, crews went into the woods to clear and level the skidways, which stretched up to five miles into the woods from the waterways. While hauling was under way, the sled tracks were kept icy with nightly applications of water from a sprinkler sled. A road monkey, usually a boy or old man, ran along the road and shoveled manure out of the ruts and chopped lumps from the ice.

Changes gradually came to logging operations in spite of the persistence of the old New England pattern. Log carriages with a single pair of giant wheels appeared in the woods of the lake states during the late nineteenth century. With these it was possible to pull logs over obstructions and thus log in summer as well as winter. Production jumped. Even greater changes occurred as the lumber industry moved into the forests of the South and Far West. Indeed, conditions were so different in the South that the lumberjack as a type was almost unknown. Southern woods workers were less migratory than their northern counterparts, their life more akin to that of the poor sharecropper tied to the land through indebtedness. The lumberjack existed in the Far West, but west of the Cascades winter brought rain and mud, not snow. Summer was the season for falling timber and getting the logs from the woods, and a whole host of new techniques and devices emerged as adjustments to the change.

Wherever they went, lumberjacks lived beyond the bounds of polite society. A rough camaraderie developed when they gathered, whether it was along the original skid road (not skid row) in Seattle, on Muskegon's Sawdust Flats, or around Bangor's Haymarket Square. There they fought, drank, and whored, but such things were expected. Had life in the logging camps been better, these violent releases might have been less common, but conditions improved very little with the passage of time.

Not every lumberjack remained a lumberjack. As Frederick W. Kohlmeyer has demonstrated, the lumber industry had remarkable upward mobility during the nineteenth century. Of 131 men who became leaders in the lake states' industry, seventy-eight percent had only a common school education. Most came from poor backgrounds; the parents of over half were farmers. The typical lumber baron was a self-made man who had started at the bottom in the woods or mill. Simon Benson, for example, arrived in the United States as a penniless immigrant lad, worked hard, saved and reinvested his money, and twice started over, undaunted after disaster wiped out his holdings. In the end he became one of the leading lumbermen of the Pacific Coast. Only his success in building ocean-going log rafts, which he sent 1,100 miles from the Columbia River to a mill in San Diego, and his quixotic attempt to wean Portland's loggers from liquor by installing drinking fountains on the city's streets, set him apart from many another millman who rose to preeminence. Indeed, Vernon Jensen suggests, the gamble or dream of quick wealth was part of what drew lumberjacks into the woods and gave their labor a special appeal in their own minds and in the minds of others.

In spite of the success of some lumberjacks, a gradual decline in their social position set in. In New England and the lake states the hearty lumberjack was admired, however grudgingly, but by the beginning of the twentieth century woodsmen in the Far West were being referred to as "bindlestiffs"—a term equated roughly with bums—because they wandered from job to job with a bedroll, or bindle, containing all their worldly possessions. The possibility of quick wealth seemed gone forever.

Perhaps their reputation suffered as much from middle-class fears as from middle-class contempt. Management opposed early attempts at unionization with a unanimity rarely shown on other occasions. They beat down pioneer unions and, in the process, insured that woodsmen did not win even the limited gains of others in the industrial work force. When the INDUSTRIAL WORKERS OF THE WORLD moved into the forests of the West after 1905, they found ready recruits among the bindlestiffs. Organized violence erupted in the woods and mills on a scale not seen before or since. Although at least as much of the violence came from management as from the IWW, in the end the Wobblies, like their predecessors, were crushed, and the loggers gained only a further erosion of their image. They now seemed not just vagabonds, but in a period of growing nativism, dangerous and un-American to many "good" citizens of the West.

The changing image of woods workers partially resulted from changes in the industry's work force. As Kohlmeyer's study reveals, those lumberjacks who succeeded in rising to leadership came overwhelmingly from English-speaking stock. For the French-Canadians, Scandinavians, Finns, and Germans, who supplied more and more of its workers as the industry moved west, opportunity was less real. By the time people in the Pacific Northwest were speaking contemptuously of bindlestiffs, woodsmen as a group resembled more closely a permanent drifting proletariat than the lumberjacks of yore. At the same time, the country's growing nativism added to the problems of these workers trapped in jobs that led nowhere.

Holbrook and others have argued that the lumberjack disappeared in the 1890s because mechanization eliminated the need for many of his skills and because improved transportation made it possible to commute from town to woods. These changes sealed the doom of the whole camp system that had been central to the lumberjack's life. These interpreters were only half right. The lumberjack was evolving into something quite different *before* those changes occurred. What mechanization and modern transportation killed was *new*, a way of life with far less to recommend it than the

life of the old-time lumberjack who had cut his way across the continent and who, because there had always been virgin forests still untapped, had dreamed of and sometimes experienced upward mobility in the industry. Technology did not destroy the lumberjack, but the bindlestiff.

Once the bindlestiff disappeared, the old image of the lumberjack began to reemerge. Myth and reality blended to create the romantic stereotype of today. It is an exaggerated, but basically accurate conception. The dreary hopelessness that fueled the protests of the IWW was the dominant reality only toward the end of the nineteenth century and the beginning of the twentieth. And yet, though the lumberjack has long since vanished, his heritage is still strong in the industry. Ken Kesey's semiautobiographical novel *Sometimes a Great Notion*, set in the woods of Oregon in the 1950s, and the uninhibited annual meetings of the Pacific Logging Congress powerfully demonstrate that the old attitudes, values, and behavior have not completely disappeared. (See also LUMBER INDUSTRY).

Two enjoyable narratives are Stewart H. Holbrook, *Holy Old Mackinaw* (1938, reprinted as *The American Lumberjack*, 1962), and *Yankee Loggers* (1961). More dependable is Robert E. Pike, *Tall Trees, Tough Men* (1967). Louie Blanchard's reminiscences appear in Walker D. Wyman, *The Lumberjack Frontier* (1969). Especially good on the twentieth century is Vernon Jensen, *Lumber and Labor* (1945). Also valuable are George Blackburn and Sherman L. Ricards, Jr., "A Demographic History of the West: Manistee County, Michigan, 1860," *Journal of American History* (December 1970); Frederick W. Kohlmeyer, "Northern Pine Lumbermen: A Study in Origins and Migrations," *Journal of Economic History* (December 1956); and various articles and references found in *Forest History*, the quarterly journal of the Forest History Society.—T. R. C.

Lummis, Charles F[letcher] (1859-1928). Editor, anthropologist, and historian. Lummis was born in Lynn, Massachusetts. He entered Harvard in 1881, but soon left. After editing a newspaper in Ohio (1882-84) he decided quite literally to follow Horace Greeley's famous advice and in 1884 walked by a roundabout route from Cincinnati to Los Angeles, a distance that he computed to be 3,507 miles and that took him 143 days to cover. For most of the rest of his life he lived in Los Angeles, though he interrupted his residence there in order to spend long periods elsewhere on the American continent as an explorer. In later life Lummis would say that he had explored the continent from Canada to Chile, and though this is certainly true it does give a slightly false impression. His greatest historical and ethnographic interest lay always in the American Southwest and in its Indian and Spanish inhabitants. He lived for five years in the Indian pueblo of Isleta, New Mexico, mastering the native language and collecting folk tales and legends, many of which he was later to include in his books about the Southwest. In 1894 Lummis founded *Out West* magazine, a periodical dedicated to the study of western life, and served as its editor until 1909. In 1895 he was one of the founders and the first president of the now famous Landmarks Club, an organization dedicated to the preservation of California buildings of historic interest, and in 1903 was one of the founders and the first secretary of the Archaeological Institute of

America's Southwest Society. He was instrumental in preserving the famous mission of San Juan Capistrano and other remains of Spanish California, and his studies of the Spanish in America earned him a knighthood from the king of Spain in 1915. He died in Los Angeles.

Lummis wrote verse all his life. His first volume, *Birch Bark Poems* (1879), was privately printed on real birch bark and is now, needless to say, extremely rare. In 1928, the year of his death, he published a representative collection of his verse entitled *A Bronco Pegasus*. He is best remembered, however, as a prolific reporter of anecdotes of all kinds about New Mexico, which he published in a number of collections, beginning with *The Land of Poco Tiempo* (1893). Most of his nonhistoric writing is more ethnographic than imaginative and concerns itself almost entirely with the early legendary history of New Mexico or with the folk beliefs of the Pueblo Indians.

Lummis' writing is in a sense derivative from the earlier American tradition, stretching back at least to Emerson, of philosophical inquiry into subjects of topical interest. The unique quality of his work is to be found quite simply in the fact that his topics themselves were almost totally fresh, particularly when written for a popular audience. And this forms the strength of his work, even today. For Lummis was a popularizer of New Mexican life in the best sense of the word; he discovered the difficult trick of writing for a mass public without writing down to them.

See Edwin R. Bingham, *Charles F. Lummis, Editor of the Southwest* (1955).—J. K. F.

Luna, Solomon (1858-1912). New Mexican politician. Luna was born in Los Lunas, New Mexico. At the time of his birth, Luna's ancestors had lived in New Mexico for well over a century. He was tutored privately and was graduated from St. Louis University, Missouri. From 1892 on he held many offices in his native county of Valencia and was a member of the Republican National Committee from New Mexico from 1896 until his death. On March 16, 1901, the territorial legislature created Luna County in honor of his name. Deeply involved in the business life of Albuquerque, Luna was the wealthiest sheep owner in the territory at the time of the 1910 convention and was vice president of the First National Bank of Albuquerque.

As an example of his prominence in the Republican party in the territory, Luna went with Governor Miguel A. Otero in 1903 to the White House to argue for statehood before President Theodore Roosevelt. He had helped Governor Otero organize the most effective grass-roots support any governor had known in the territory's history. Successor to Colonel José Francisco Chaves as the "patron" or political leader of Valencia County, Luna was the most prominent member of the Republican majority at the 1910 New Mexico constitutional convention. For the previous half century, the Luna family had made Valencia County of critical importance in New Mexico politics. Luna himself was a primary representative of New Mexico's native Spanish-speaking citizens and sought the maintenance of their traditional language and way of life. He was also regarded as a key member of the old guard leadership of the Republican party in New Mexico. Along with Holm Bursum, Luna is credited with responsibility for the "protective" clauses in the state constitution. In 1911 he

was the apparent choice for the Republican nomination for governor, but he supported Bursum for the post instead. Had he sought the nomination for the United States Senate in March 1912 he probably would have been chosen on the first ballot. In any case, Luna died suddenly five months later on one of his large ranches in western Socorro County.

Jack E. Holmes, *Politics in New Mexico* (1967), examines Luna's political importance in New Mexico. See also a biographical sketch and useful references in R. E. Twitchell, *The Leading Facts in New Mexican History* (1912).—J. R. V.

Lungkwitz, Carl Hermann Frederick (1813-1891). Painter. Born in Halle an der Saale, Saxony, Lungkwitz as a youth attended an art academy in Dresden, where he became friends with Richard Petri, artist and student revolutionary whose sister eventually became Lungkwitz's wife. Following the political upheavals in Germany in the late 1840s, both Petri and Lungkwitz came to America, settling in Indianola, Texas, in 1851. Primarily interested in landscape painting, Lungkwitz also produced many views of early Texas settlements and operated a photographic studio in San Antonio for a time in partnership with Carl G. von Iwonski. In 1870 another brother-in-law, Jacob Kuechler, became commissioner of the General Land Office at Austin and the following year offered Lungkwitz a position as official photographer for the reproduction of maps. Residing in Austin, the artist also taught drawing and painting and later accepted a position at the Texas English and German school. Remembered today for his landscapes, he also produced a number of views of life in old San Antonio, some of which were reproduced as lithographic prints.

See Pauline A. Pinckney, *Painting in Texas in the Nineteenth Century* (1967).—D. C. H.

Lytle, John T. (1844-1907). Trail driver and Texas cattleman. Lytle was born in McSherrystown, Pennsylvania, but in 1860 he moved with his family to Bexar, Texas, where he worked on a ranch owned by his uncle. Lytle joined the Thirty-second Texas Cavalry in 1863 and served with it until the end of the Civil War. Two more years of work on his uncle's ranch convinced Lytle that he should get into the cattle business on his own, and so, in 1867 he bought a ranch in Frio County. In 1857 he sold the ranch and began to lease pasture for his cattle on a large scale, but he soon became a ranch owner again, with spreads in Frio, Maverick, and Collingsworth counties. In these and other enterprises he formed partnerships at various times with John W. Light, T. M. McDaniel, and Charles Shreiner, among others; his SL and LM brands became famous throughout the Southwest. (Lytle's operations included sheep as well as beeves.)

In 1871 Lytle embarked on the enterprise for which he would become most famous: he became a trail driver and a sort of middleman between Texas cattlemen and buyers at northern railheads. He spent the fall and winter traveling all over Texas, lining up prospective sales, and then in the spring rode north to arrange for the purchase of the cattle. Having completed the arrangements, he rode south to meet the cattle on their trek northward. Between 1871 and 1887 he handled investments totaling nine million dollars and drove over 450,000 cattle up the trail.

In 1887 Lytle became associated with the American Cattle Trust and provided it with 27,000 head of cattle before it failed nine years later. Most of his later years were spent on his Medina County ranch, to which he had moved in 1879; then, as throughout his career, he was active in various cattlemen's associations, especially the Texas Cattle Raisers' Association.

See Ramon F. Adams, ed., *Prose and Poetry of the Livestock Industry of the United States*; and J. M. Hunter, ed., *The Trail Drivers of Texas.*—H. R. L.

M

McCarran, Pat[rick A.] (1876-1954). Nevada politician. Born near Reno, Nevada, and educated in Nevada schools, Pat McCarran was elected to the state assembly from Washoe County in 1902 and served one term. He was admitted to the Nevada bar in 1905 and that same year moved to Tonopah and Goldfield during the new mining boom. He served one term as district attorney of Nye County before returning to Reno. In 1912 he was elected to a six-year term on the state Supreme Court. McCarran was defeated in the Democratic primary campaign for United States senator by Key Pittman in 1916 and by Ray T. Baker in 1926. However, he ran unopposed in the Democratic primary in 1932 and went on to defeat Tasker L. Oddie in the general election. Once in the Senate, McCarran began to mold a political machine that placed him in command of the Democratic party in Nevada after Pittman's death in 1940. Although he gained a reputation for being anti-New Deal, he seldom opposed New Deal measures that benefited his home state. McCarran won acclaim in Nevada for opposing President Franklin D. Roosevelt's plan to "pack" the Supreme Court. He gained additional support for his unrelenting fight against Communism. Seniority brought him the chairmanship of the Senate Judiciary Committee and important subcommittee assignments. McCarran was responsible for a great deal of important national legislation including the Civil Aeronautics Act, the Internal Security Act of 1950, and the McCarran-Walter immigration act. He died of a heart attack in Hawthorne, Nevada, just after completing a speech on Communism. His campaign to that point, during the off-year elections, was in support of the entire Democratic ticket, including Pittman's brother, Vail, which was a reversal of his usual role as a "lone wolf" in the party.

See Sister Margaret Patricia McCarran, "Patrick Anthony McCarran," *Nevada Historical Society Quarterly* (Fall-Winter 1968 and Spring 1969); and Gilman M. Ostrander, *Nevada, The Great Rotten Borough, 1859-1964* (1966). The McCarran papers are in the Nevada State Archives.—R. R. E.

McCarty, Henry. See BILLY THE KID.

McClintock, James Harvey (1864-1934). Editor, soldier, and historian. The preeminent historian of Arizona until his death, McClintock was born of pioneer California parents in Sacramento. In June 1879 he settled in Phoenix, Arizona, where his brother, Charles, was then publishing the Phoenix *Herald*. There he met another new arrival, William O. "Buckey" O'Neill, who was destined to become a close friend of McClintock's and a comrade-in-arms during the Spanish-American War.

McClintock worked as a newspaperman with papers in Phoenix, Tucson, Prescott, Globe, and Tempe. In Tempe he was justice of the peace at the early age of twenty-two. He was additionally a teacher, an official with the normal schools of Arizona, and a member of the territory's Republican party organization. At the time of the campaign against Apache leader Geronimo, McClintock was an employee in the adjutant general's office at Whipple Barracks, Prescott.

Just prior to the war with Spain in 1898, McClintock was running a news bureau in Phoenix. Along with his old friend Buckey O'Neill (then mayor of Prescott) and Alexander O. Brodie, McClintock worked with Myron McCord, governor of Arizona Territory, in enrolling a regiment of volunteer cavalry troopers for the Cuban campaign. Although only two troops from Arizona were selected for the First United States Volunteer Cavalry Regiment (the ROUGH RIDERS), McClintock was named captain of one of them and O'Neill captain of the other. Brodie was put in command of the Arizona squadron.

McClintock was seriously wounded in the first land engagement of the Cuban campaign, at Las Guásimas on June 24, 1898, his leg shattered by three enemy Mauser bullets. He recovered and was discharged the following November.

In the years following the war, McClintock served as colonel of the First Arizona Infantry (1902-10); president and historian of the Rough Riders Association; postmaster of Phoenix (1902-14 and 1928-33); state historian (1919-23); and Republican candidate for the United States Senate (1922). He was author of a number of historical works including a three-volume work, *Arizona: Prehistoric, Aboriginal, Pioneer, Modern* (1916).

See Charles Herner, *The Arizona Rough Riders* (1970). There is also a valuable file of McClintock papers in the Phoenix Public Library.—D. L. W.

McClure, Jake (1903-1940). Rodeo cowboy. Born near Amarillo, Texas, McClure migrated to New Mexico, where he grew up on a ranch near Lovington. By the time he was fifteen McClure, who had learned calf-roping while still a child, was competing in rodeos. In 1924 he began his career as the premier calf-roper in major rodeos throughout the country. McClure's trademark was the small loop he used (called the McClure loop), as well as the fast action and coordination between himself and his horse. In 1930 he was declared all-around Champion at Pendleton, Oregon, and again in 1937 at Phoenix, Arizona. He was given the Arizona state championship cowboy award in 1932 and declared championship rodeo winner at Houston, Texas in 1939. McClure's horse, Silver, won accolades as "the world's best calf-roping horse."

McClure was killed in a freak accident; he was thrown from his horse and struck his head on the saddle horn, causing a fatal concussion.—R. B. W.

McCormick, Richard Cunningham (1832-1901). Journalist and Arizona politician. McCormick was born in New York City, received a private school education, and turned to journalism. An active Republican in New York, he ran unsuccessfully in 1862 for Congress, but was appointed chief clerk in the Bureau of Agriculture. When the Territory of Arizona was created in February 1863, McCormick was appointed the territorial secretary and accompanied Governor John N. Goodwin to Arizona. A small dapper man with red hair and boundless energy, McCormick quickly became the dominant figure in Arizona politics. He suggested the name Prescott for the newly established capital city, launched a newspaper (the *Arizona Miner*), and invested heavily in real estate and mining claims. He designed the first territorial seal, sold his small personal library to the territory as a nucleus for a library department, and gave talks and published articles in the East on Arizona's resources. Appointed governor on April 10, 1866, McCormick soon afterward became interested in running for territorial delegate to Congress. He gained political support in southern Arizona by encouraging the transfer of the capital from Prescott to Tucson in 1867, and in 1868 won the coveted delegateship. He was accused of forming a loosely organized "ring" in Tucson while the capital was there, made up of both federal and territorial officials, who profited from the manipulation of government contracts for military and Indian supplies. Founding the Tucson *Arizona Citizen* to maintain his influence, McCormick was reelected delegate in 1870 and 1872. He lived in the East after 1874 but continued to promote various mining properties in Arizona. McCormick accepted the position of assistant secretary of the treasury in 1877, was elected to Congress from New York City in 1894, and was active in local civic and banking enterprises. He died in Jamaica, New York.

See Howard R. Lamar, *The Far Southwest, 1846-1912: A Territorial History* (1966).—H. P. H.

McCoy, Joseph G. (1837-1915). Entrepreneur and cattleman. McCoy was born on a farm in Sangamon County, Illinois. He gained prominence in the late 1860s, after he had made Abilene, Kansas, the principal shipping point of Texas cattle bound for the packinghouses in the East and Midwest, by laying out the Chisholm Trail, along which great trail drives moved thousands of cattle to the town's rail head. Between 1867 and 1871 Abilene grew from "one dozen log huts" into a boom town so boisterous that "Wild Bill" Hickok was hired to keep the peace. McCoy was elected the first mayor of Abilene in 1871.

In 1873 McCoy moved to Kansas City, Missouri, where he organized his own livestock sales company. In 1874 he wrote *Historic Sketches of the Cattle Trade of the West and Southwest*, considered one of the better treatments of the subject.

A man of diverse business pursuits, McCoy was at one time or another a grocer, real estate agent, stockman, speculator, proprietor of a flour and feed store, wrought-iron fence salesman, author, cattle inspector, livestock broker, and treasury department narcotics agent. He died at Wichita, Kansas. Most observers feel the Chisholm Trail should really have been named for McCoy.

McCoy's *Historic Sketches of the Cattle Trade* has been edited and reprinted under its original title in Ralph B. Bieber, ed., The Southwest Historical Series, No. 7 (1940); it contains an excellent essay on McCoy's life.—J. B. F.

McCraken, Tracy Stephenson (1894-1960). Wyoming publisher. For many years McCraken controlled seven of Wyoming's ten daily newspapers and exerted powerful behind-the-scenes influence on affairs of the state. He was called "Wyoming's Mr. Big" by *Time* magazine in 1954.

Born and reared in Illinois, McCraken graduated from the University of Wyoming in 1917. He began his newspaper career as a reporter on the *Laramie Boomerang*. A conservative Democrat, he was an aide to Governor William B. Ross and to Senator John B. Kendrick, then resumed newspaper work as publisher of the *Wyoming Eagle* (Cheyenne) in 1926. The Great Depression, which ruined less opportunistic entrepreneurs, worked the other way for McCraken, making it possible for him to absorb the newspapers of his Republican competitors in both Cheyenne and Laramie. Thereafter one success led to another, and he became a millionaire with interests in radio, television, banking, construction, and real estate.

Although he never ran for elective office, McCraken was a confidant of senators Kendrick and Joseph C. O'Mahoney and of Governor Leslie A. Miller. As Democratic national committeeman, 1942-60, he maintained his state organization's cautious, conservative image. For many years he was the dominant member of his alma mater's board of trustees, devoting his energies equally to promoting winning football teams and good academic instruction.

See T. A. Larson, *History of Wyoming* (1965).—T. A. L.

McCulloch, Hartnell and Company. The first commercial firm established in California. The company began operations with the arrival of the British traders Hugh McCulloch and William E. P. Hartnell at Monterey in 1822. They came from Lima, Peru, on the *John Begg*, the first foreign ship to be openly welcomed by California authorities after the newly independent government of Mexico had opened the ports of Monterey and San Diego to foreign trade. The firm obtained a contract to buy cowhides from the missions at the bargain price of one dollar each. The partners became so commonly known in California as "Macala y Arnel" that they often signed their names in that hispanicized form. Hartnell became a permanent resident of Mexican California and one of its most distinguished citizens. For a time he operated virtually the only school in California, and as administrator of the missions he made a valiant though unsuccessful effort to bring some sort of order to the process of secularization.

See Susanna Bryant Dakin, *The Lives of William Hartnell* (1949).—W. B.

McCumber, Porter James (1858-1933). North Dakota politician. The Illinois-born McCumber spent his adult life living in, and working for, the state of North Dakota. From 1881 to 1900 he was a member of a law firm at Wahpeton. He served in the lower house of the Dakota territorial legislature from 1885 to 1889. When North Dakota entered the Union in 1889, he was elected to represent the new state as one of its United States senators. He was reelected to the Senate four times. Although he was backed by Alexander McKenzie's Republican political machine in North Dakota, he was not a mere puppet for that organization. During the wave of progressive reform legislation in the early twentieth century, McCumber altered his conservatism to sponsor a much-needed grain-grading law.

He advocated strict neutrality prior to World War I, but after the United States entered the war, McCumber was active in supporting President Wilson's war aims. In 1916 he introduced a resolution in the Senate asking for the United States to take a lead in forming an international peace organization and in 1919 fought hard for the Senate's acceptance of the League of Nations. He was the only Republican senator who voted for joining the league both with and without reservations.

After his senatorial defeat in 1922, McCumber returned to private law practice until his death.—D. J. T.

McDermott, John Francis (1902-   ). Historian. McDermott was born in St. Louis, Missouri, and educated at Washington University. He joined the university's history staff upon receipt of his A.M. degree in 1924 and remained there until 1963, when he moved to Southern Illinois University, Edwardsville campus. During World War II he saw service as an army air corps intelligence staff officer in Europe and the Caribbean.

A prolific writer and editor with forty-one books and numerous articles to his credit, McDermott made major contributions to the history of the West and especially the early development in the Mississippi and Missouri valleys. His *Old Cahokia* (1949) and *The Early Histories of St. Louis* (1952) are important documentary collections in this regard. He edited the proceedings of a symposium on the Edwardsville campus, *The French in the Mississippi Valley* (1965), an excellent picture of their life and contributions. McDermott wrote two notable biographies of important western artists: *George Caleb Bingham, River Portraitist* (1959) and *Seth Eastman, Pictorial Historian of the Indian* (1961). The latter supplemented an earlier study, *The Art of Seth Eastman* (1959). In addition, he edited the diaries and journals of several other western artists.

MacDermott was a Newberry Library Fellow in Midwestern Studies in 1947-48 and held a Guggenheim Memorial Fellowship in 1954-55. He was named Chevalier de L'Ordre National du Merite by the French government in 1970 and Miembro Titular at the Instituto de Cultura Hispanica at Madrid that same year.—W. E. P.

MacDonald, Peter (1928-   ). Navaho businessman and tribal chairman. Born in Teecnospos, Arizona, and reared in a traditional Navaho home, MacDonald was a school dropout for a while. But he went back, won two scholarships, and completed his education at the University of Oklahoma and the University of California at Los Angeles. He was in the marine corps from 1944 to 1946, in the Pacific and China. After the war he worked as a project engineer for Hughes Aircraft Corporation, winning an award for a cost improvement program.

Although he did very well in private industry, MacDonald decided to enter public service. As executive director of the Office of Navaho Economic Opportunity, he administered a large tribal program and was a member of the New Mexico Governor's Economic Development Board, the Navaho Reservation Development Committee, and the National Congress of American Indians. He was called before many House and Senate subcommittees for testimony. His election in 1970 as tribal chairman of the Navaho gave him an opportunity to use his experience to lead the largest tribe in the United States.—C. C.

McDougall, Alexander. See GREAT LAKES, MEN OF THE.

McDowell, Ephraim. See DOCTORS.

McGillivray, Alexander (1759-1793). Creek leader. McGillivray was born the son of a Scots trader, Lachlan McGillivray, and Sehoy Marchand, a half-breed Creek princess, at Little Tallassie village on the Coosa River in east central Alabama. He was raised by his mother as a natural son of the Creek Indians until he was fourteen years of age, when he was sent away to school in Charleston, South Carolina. There he was tutored by a relative, the Reverend Farquhar McGillivray. He learned much of the manners of the aristocratic whites of Charleston and how to use the English language to good advantage.

Back in the Georgia-Alabama wilderness, the Creek Indians were caught in an international struggle for control of North America, which prevailed between 1754 and 1818. In the early years of European activities in this region, the Creeks were associated with Spanish and French authorities and traders. In the years after the middle of the eighteenth century Anglo-American colonial traders had ventured into the territory. At the outbreak of the American Revolution Lachlan McGillivray, an ardent loyalist, was forced to leave America for fear of being harmed by American patriots. He returned to England, while his son went back to the western woods and his home with the Creek. Once back with his people, Alexander McGillivray quickly rose to a position of power. The British made him a colonel and depended upon him to maintain the support of the Creek. This experience prepared him to engage in larger actions in future years, even though Creek activities in the American Revolution were of only minor importance.

As the American settler frontier expanded up the Savannah River and moved inland across Georgia, and as land speculators moved in from the Tennessee River valley, the Creek perceived more distinctly the meaning of the revolutionary struggle and England's loss of power. This was especially true after 1783, when international relationships were revised under the terms of the Treaty of Paris. England's withdrawal from the Southwest left the Indians caught between the Americans on one side and the Spanish on the other. This was a situation that called for management if not full-scale diplomacy on the part of McGillivray and his people.

The Creek were dependent upon the Gulf coastal towns, especially Mobile and Pensacola, for trade. A persuasive influence in the area was William Panton of the famous trading partnership of Panton, Leslie, and Company. It was to this company's best interest to draw the Creek into the Spanish orbit. McGillivray conferred with Spanish officials in the months following the Treaty of Paris, and on June 1, 1784, the Creek and Spanish signed a treaty outlining conditions of conducting the Indian trade. McGillivray's Scotch shrewdness showed through to good advantage and he drove a favorable bargain with both the Spanish and Panton, Leslie, and Company.

On the eastern and northern borders McGillivray played a coy game. He refused to attend the Augusta and Savannah treaty conferences. Nevertheless United States Indian agents continued to court his favor. He proved difficult to woo; in fact, he consistently refused to attend conferences or to support the efforts of the Indian agents to come to terms with the Creek at Galphinton settlement on the Ogeechee River in 1785. As the drive by Indian agents to secure the support of the southern Indians increased, McGillivray's situation became more complex. In May 1786, he visited New Orleans, where he secured supplies of ammunition and arms for his people along with other forms of presents for them. At this moment the Creek enjoyed their most amicable trade relations with the Spanish. Their friendship was further solidified when the Indians refused to make concessions to Georgia land commissioners in negotiating a land dispute.

By 1786 McGillivray had become the most powerful personal influence among the Creek, and perhaps in the whole Gulf coastal area. He had an Achilles' heel, however, in his heavy dependence upon the Spanish and free-lance English traders for support. By the end of the decade 1780-90, the Creek were subjected to heavy pressures from the Georgia land speculators and especially from those interested in the speculative Yazoo land-grabbing ventures.

In the summer of 1789 the new government of the United States concerned itself with the Creek problem. Early in 1790 Colonel Marinus Willett was sent to the Creek nation to confer with the Indians. He persuaded McGillivray and a group of Creek Indians to visit New York to confer with President George Washington. After an extended period, made more extensive by McGillivray's illness, the Treaty of NEW YORK was signed on August 7, 1790. The treaty outlined boundary and land agreements and undertook to silence the dispute with Georgia. McGillivray was given a secret commission as a brigadier general and a salary of one hundred dollars a month. The treaty failed, however, to accomplish its main objective of settling the Georgia dispute, nor did it ease international rivalries.

McGillivray continued to use his influence and power to trade American and Spaniard off against each other. In 1790-92 he reached the height of his power. His death, at the home of William Panton in Pensacola, left the Creek without strong leadership, and they were finally overwhelmed by American encroachment on their territory.

See Jane M. Berry, "The Indian Policy of Spain in the Southwest, 1783-1795," *Mississippi Valley Historical Review*, vol. 3 (1917); John W. Caughey, *McGillivray of the Creeks* (1938); Albert J. Pickett, *History of Alabama and Incidentally of Georgia and Mississippi From the Earliest Times* (1896); and Charles C. Royce, "Indian Land Cessions in the United States," in Bureau of American Ethnology, *Eighteenth Annual Report, 1896-97* (1899).
—T. D. C.

McKay, David Oman (1873-1970). Mormon leader. Born on an alpine farm in Huntsville, Utah, McKay graduated from the University of Utah's elementary school in 1896 and almost immediately thereafter left for Scotland on a gospel mission for the Mormon church. Returning to Utah in 1899, he took a teaching position at Weber Academy in Ogden. While attending the University of Utah in Salt Lake City, he boarded with the Riggs family and in 1901 married Emma Ray Riggs, a graduate in music. Their marriage became an idealistic model for several million Latter-day Saints.

In 1906 McKay was called to be a member of the church's Quorum of the Twelve Apostles. For many years he was a leader in the church's Sunday school organization and in 1919 was named commissioner of education for the church. A leading influence in the development of education in Utah, McKay is the only person to have been on the board of regents of the University of Utah, Utah State University, and Brigham Young University. He ultimately was granted honorary doctorates by all three schools.

An active and effective missionary, McKay was president of the European Mission of the church (1921-24) and often visited the church's foreign missions. He became a member of the First Presidency of the Church in 1936 and president of the Latter-day Saints in 1951, serving until his death. Under his presidency the church experienced its greatest growth. Schools, churches, and temples were built in many new locations. He had a worldwide view and worked toward a universal organization. His sermons were most commonly directed toward strengthening the home and family.

See Jeanette M. Morrell, *Highlights in the Life of President David O. McKay* (1966).

Mackay, John W. (1831-1902). Nevada miner and financier. An immigrant from Ireland, Mackay went to the United States in 1840, to California in 1851, and to the Comstock in 1859. He worked his way from hardrock miner to the most powerful figure on the Comstock. He is often cited as the most important member of the "Big Bonanza" firm of Mackay, Fair, Flood, and O'Brien, although some writers maintain that Fair was the engineering brains of the firm.

The millions made by Mackay on the Comstock were more than doubled by investments in other than mining, particularly in the organization and development of the Postal Telegraph. His activities in this area started when he and James Gordon Bennett founded the Commercial Cable Company in 1883 and laid two submarine cables to Europe the following year. In 1886 Mackay organized the Postal Telegraph Cable Company, which soon developed into a major competitor of Western Union. Mackay was engaged in laying a cable across the Pacific as part of the overall Postal Telegraph system when he died.

His son, Clarence, and his wife left millions of dollars to the University of Nevada in his name. Some of the money was used to build the Mackay School of Mines, the Mackay Science Building, Mackay Stadium, and the Mackay Statue by Gutzon Borglum.

There is no adequate biography. The following works, however, are useful: Oscar Lewis, *Silver Kings: The Lives and Times of Mackay, Fair, Flood and O'Brien, Lords of the Comstock Lode* (1947); and Ethel Manter, *Rocket of the Comstock: The Story of John Mackay* (1950). —R. R. E.

McKenzie, Alexander (1851-1922). North Dakota politician. McKenzie was born in the London District, Ontario, Canada, of Scottish parents. In 1868 he came to Dakota on a wagon train carrying supplies to Fort Rice. In 1873, McKenzie settled in Bismarck, Dakota Territory, after having worked on a construction crew for the Northern Pacific Railroad. The following year he was elected sheriff, a position that he held for the next twelve years. He also became the political agent for the Northern Pacific Railroad. The railroad, banking, and grain interests in Minneapolis-St. Paul controlled Dakota Territory as though it were their colony, and McKenzie well represented their interests and his own.

One of his first political coups was the removal of the Dakota territorial capital from Yankton to Bismarck, on the main line of the Northern Pacific. By dispensing patronage and helping incoming settlers, he built a powerful political machine that received the loyal support of Republicans and foreign-born immigrants. McKenzie was most interested in using his influence to elect men to the United States Senate who could then protect the powerful interests he represented. Because he spent much of his time in the Twin Cities, it was said that they were really the capitals of North Dakota, politically and economically.

His days as political boss came to an end with the growth of Progressivism. The North Dakota legislature adopted the direct primary election in 1906, and this took away his control over nominations. In that year his machine lost the governorship and control of the lower house of the legislature. To make matters worse for McKenzie, he was jailed for illegal gold-mining operations in Alaska. By 1910 he had lost most of his control over state politics, and many progressive reforms were added to the statute books, further weakening his position.

McKenzie's career has been fictionalized in Rex Beach's *The Spoilers* (1906).—D. J. T.

Mackenzie, Donald (1783-1851). Fur trader and explorer. In 1800 Mackenzie left the Highlands of Scotland, where he was born, for Montreal. Entering the fur trade as a clerk for the North West Company, he then joined John Jacob Astor's Pacific Fur Company in 1809 and spent the fall of 1811 exploring a long stretch of the Snake River on his way to Astoria. He set out in the spring of 1812 to explore Willamette valley and had a winter post at Lewiston later in 1812. With the complete failure of Astor's enterprise during the War of 1812, he left the Northwest. Returning with the North West Company in 1816, Mackenzie organized the annual Snake country expeditions, which continued until 1832. In the process he laid the foundations for developing the Snake country fur trade.

In 1822 he left the Northwest and soon assumed one of the most important posts in the service of the Hudson's Bay Company, managing operations in the region around Winnipeg. Both as an explorer and trader, Mac-

kenzie played a leading part in the beginnings of white occupation of much of the Pacific Northwest and in establishing peaceful relations with the Indians.—M. W.

Mackenzie, Kenneth (1797-1861). Fur trader and merchant. Mackenzie was born in Rosshire, Inverness, Scotland, but in his teens went to Canada, where he worked as a clerk for the North West Company. When that firm amalgamated with the Hudson's Bay Company in 1821, Mackenzie crossed the border to join the Columbia Fur Company, which operated in the Great Lakes region, along the headwaters of the Mississippi, and westward to the Missouri River. A man of extraordinary ability, Mackenzie assumed the presidency of his firm in 1825. He and two partners, William Laidlaw and Daniel Lamont, were so successful in the fur trade on the Missouri that they consistently outtraded the Western Department of the American Fur Company, with the result that the latter proposed a merger virtually on Mackenzie's terms in 1827.

The agreement placed Mackenzie in charge of the Upper Missouri Outfit, the name of the American Fur Company's branch for the region, and allowed him to run it as he saw fit. Mackenzie proceeded to carry out a grand strategy by building a large fort on the Missouri above the mouth of the Yellowstone. Originally named Fort Floyd, it soon came to be called Fort Union and was the most important post in the entire upper Missouri region. Mackenzie's purpose was as ambitious as it was obvious: he hoped to control the Missouri River trade west of Fort Union while using the fort itself as a base from which to penetrate the Rocky Mountain stronghold of the independent trappers to the south. To achieve this his men moved up the Yellowstone to build Fort Cass on the Bighorn River. Refusing to be bound by the traditional system of stationary forts favored by the American Fur Company, Mackenzie imitated the independent trappers by sending his own fur brigades into the wilderness to trap. To capture the Crow Indian trade he sent Etienne Provost among that tribe to deflect furs to Fort Union. He also made overtures to the hostile Blackfoot by building Fort Mackenzie in their territory and sending the talented James Kipp to develop the trade there. Meanwhile, Mackenzie maintained Fort Clark and Fort Tecumseh (later Fort Pierre) along the lower Missouri. He also hired mountain men, notably William H. Vanderburgh and Andrew Drips, to shadow the Rocky Mountain Fur Company brigades in order to discover their sources of fur.

Mackenzie did not succeed without a challenge. In 1833 William and Milton Sublette and Robert Campbell built an "opposition" fort at the mouth of the Yellowstone, only four miles from Fort Union, and established their own string of posts further down the river. Mackenzie paid such high prices for furs, however, that the opposition was forced to sell out, although the American Fur Company did agree to stay out of the mountains for a year if Sublette and Campbell would leave the river. Thereafter Mackenzie was indeed the "King of the Upper Missouri Outfit."

Mackenzie's only major mistake in an otherwise brilliant career was to import a still to manufacture whiskey at Fort Union, a practice strictly forbidden by the American government. When his activities were reported to government authorities, the American Fur Company nearly lost its trading privileges on the Missouri. Mackenzie traveled in Europe until matters quieted down; but although he returned to the river trade, he soon moved to St. Louis, where he made a fortune in the supply business as an importer of whiskey and spirits. Several business reverses greatly reduced his wealth, however, before he died.

Mackenzie's success was in part the result of his incredible energy and an authoritarian manner. Some said he was so ruthless that profits meant more to him than lives. Others branded him an aristocratic martinet, an understandable comment, since Mackenzie lived grandly on the frontier and always wore a uniform. Nevertheless, his subordinates admired and respected him, and contemporaries noted that his talents for diplomacy in the trade were impressive. Chittenden has called Mackenzie the ablest trader that the American Fur Company possessed, an opinion echoed by Bernard De Voto.

While at Fort Union, Mackenzie fathered a half-breed son, Owen, but upon his return to St. Louis, he married Mary Marshall of Tennessee, who bore him two daughters.

See Annie H. Abel, ed., *Chardon's Journal at Fort Clark, 1834-1839* (1932); Hiram M. Chittenden, *The American Fur Trade of the Far West* (1902); Bernard De Voto, *Across the Wide Missouri* (1947); Ray H. Mattison in LeRoy R. Hafen, ed., *The Mountain Men and the Fur Trade of the Far West*, vol. II (1965); and Erwin M. Thompson, *Fort Union: Trading Post* (1968).—H. R. L.

Mackenzie, Ranald Slidell (1840-1889). Soldier. After distinguished Civil War service, Mackenzie became the scourge of the Comanche and Kiowa after he took command of the Fourth Cavalry at Fort Concho, Texas, in 1871. He found the key to sustained policing of the Staked Plains when, in leading a column to Fort Bascom, New Mexico, and back (July 28-August 31, 1872), he found water holes at intervals, which made troop operations feasible. Previously, the army had considered military operations impossible on the southern Staked Plains. On September 29, 1872, he struck a Comanche village of 262 tipis on the North Fork of the Red River, taking 124 captives whom the government held prisoner until Mow-way's band settled on the Fort Sill reservation. Before he could strike the Comanche again, Mackenzie's regiment was transferred to the Rio Grande to deal with Mexican Kickapoo who were raiding Texas ranches. (The Kickapoo originated in the Great Lakes region, but one group had migrated to Mexico.) Apparently under secret orders, Mackenzie crossed into Mexico and destroyed a Kickapoo village on May 18, 1873. He captured about forty women and children, whom the government used as lures to bring the Kickapoo to a reservation in Indian Territory. Returning to the north, he dealt the Comanche a catastrophic blow when he attacked a village in PALO DURO CANYON on September 28, 1874, destroying the lodges, a winter food supply, and about one thousand ponies. Left destitute, most of the fleeing Indians straggled into the Fort Sill reservation. As commander of Fort Sill, Mackenzie forced Quanah Parker's Kwahadi, the last of the southern Plains hostiles, to surrender on June 2, 1875.

During the Sioux War of 1876-77, Mackenzie scattered Dull Knife's Cheyenne when he destroyed their village on Powder River, November 25, 1876. He then went to Washington at President Ulysses S. Grant's request to command troops in case a national emergency should result from the disputed Hayes-Tilden election. Ordered again to the Rio Grande to pursue cattle thieves, he crossed the border in June 1878 and faced down a Mexican commander who tried to turn him back; the expedition was barren of results. In 1881 he used a threat of force to effect the removal of the Ute from the Los Pinos Agency in Colorado to a new reservation in Utah, commanded all troops in New Mexico and Arizona in another in the long series of Apache wars, and commanded the District of New Mexico.

Promoted to brigadier general in 1882, Mackenzie assumed command of the Department of Texas in 1883. Just before he was to have been married in 1883, he became mentally ill and was transferred to Bloomingdale Asylum in New York City. There he was pronounced insane and was retired from the army in 1884.

The only study of Mackenzie is Ernest Wallace, *Ranald S. Mackenzie on the Texas Frontier* (1965). For eyewitness accounts written by an officer who served with Mackenzie, see R. G. Carter, *The Old Sergeant's Story* (1926) and *On the Border with Mackenzie* (1935).—O. K.

McLaughlin, James (1842-1923). Indian agent. James McLaughlin was born in Avonmore, Ontario. Until 1871 he and his Sioux mixed-blood wife lived in Minnesota, where he pursued his trade as a blacksmith and engaged in various other business ventures. In 1871 he was hired to become the general overseer and blacksmith for the Devils Lake Indian Agency in Dakota Territory. By 1876 he had risen to the position of agent at Devils Lake. His fairness and record of progress led to another promotion in 1881, when he was transferred to the larger Sioux agency at Standing Rock. McLaughlin, who spoke Sioux, promoted Indian education and practical agriculture. He improved Indian living conditions and encouraged Indians to work for a living.

McLaughlin is most widely known for his conflict with SITTING BULL, which resulted in the death of the Indian leader when he and some followers resisted the arrest ordered by McLaughlin. He felt that Sitting Bull was a "demoralizing" influence on his people. As inspector for the Bureau of Indian Affairs he negotiated numerous treaties between the United States government and Indian tribes. He was also a troubleshooter for the government in its relations with the Indian, and his work eventually took him to agencies all over the United States. His recollections, published in 1910, are entitled *My Friend the Indian*.—D. J. T.

McLoughlin, John (1784-1857). Fur trader and physician. As chief factor for the Hudson's Bay Company in the Columbia District (Oregon Territory) from 1824 until 1845, McLoughlin ruled the Pacific Northwest in the final years of its joint occupancy by Great Britain and the United States. A man large in both size (six feet, seven inches) and spirit, the "White-Headed Eagle" extended a helping hand to all those who asked.

McLoughlin was born at Rivière-du-Loup, Quebec. His mother was formerly Angélique Fraser of the famous Fraser clan who were engaged in the Canadian fur trade. Her brothers, McLoughlin's uncles, included Alexander and Simon Fraser. Alexander was a wintering partner of the North West Company. Simon was one of the best Canadian physicians of his day. Under their influence young McLoughlin began to study medicine at the age of fourteen, but no sooner had he received his license to practice (in 1803) than he was attracted to the frontier service of the North West Company. His first wilderness years were spent at Kaministikwia (Fort William) as a company physician. McLoughlin's medical talents appear to have been average. But the doctor took up fur trading on the side and quickly showed ability to control the Indians and reap a good profit. Such were his talents that McLoughlin could successfully demand that he be made a partner in the North West Company as a condition for his reemployment in 1811. Upon the North West Company's merger with the Hudson's Bay Company, McLoughlin was made a chief factor under British Governor George Simpson. From 1822 to 1824 McLoughlin was in charge of the American border district of Lac la Pluie. McLoughlin's abilities convinced Simpson to appoint him to the general superintendency of the vast Columbia District in July 1824. McLoughlin traveled west and took over command in 1825, retaining this position of responsibility for twenty years.

From his headquarters at Fort Vancouver on the Columbia River, McLoughlin controlled a territory larger than Great Britain. His goal was to make the Oregon country both a fief of the Hudson's Bay Company and a productive and profitable supplier of furs for European markets as well as a supplier of foodstuffs for local consumption. This task was a hard one. The area was jointly occupied by Great Britain and the United States. McLoughlin had no legal control over American citizens coming into the Oregon Territory and could not force them to obey Hudson's Bay Company regulations. But his high moral sense would not allow him any disreputable alternatives.

McLoughlin's first problems were directly related to the fur trade. In the Snake country, Peter Skene Ogden's trading party for the company met American competition under Jedediah Smith in 1824, resulting in desertions of Ogden's men to the Americans and a considerable loss of furs. Despite these losses, McLoughlin determined to continue trapping in the area. He persuaded his superiors in London to make company employment more attractive to trappers and convinced the traders under him to compete vigorously with the encroaching Americans. When Nathaniel Wyeth came to Oregon hoping to set up a trading company of his own, McLoughlin dealt politely but firmly with the Bostonian. By 1834, when Wyeth sold Fort Hall to the Hudson's Bay Company, it appeared that McLoughlin had secured the interior of Oregon Territory against outsiders and was at least holding his own along the borders. However, 1834 also marked the arrival in Oregon of Jason Lee and his Methodist missionary party. It was these missionaries who brought rapid changes to the status quo in Oregon.

The American missionaries had come to evangelize Oregon's Indians. Lee's party was the first to arrive, followed in 1836 by Marcus Whitman and Henry Harmon Spalding of the American Board. Lee's group was persuaded, possibly by McLoughlin, to settle on the Willamette River. This location was away from any real missionary work but south of the Columbia River border, which McLoughlin expected would mark the final boundary between the United States and British North America. Whitman and his group, however, remained true to original plans and settled in the interior. In addition to working with Indians, both groups were soon sending back glowing reports of Oregon's agricultural promise to their countrymen. Ironically, it was the example of McLoughlin's successful agricultural and cattle-raising enterprises that impressed the American missionaries. As a sincere Christian, McLoughlin felt it his duty to support these missionaries as much as possible. He gave both Lee and Whitman use of Hudson's Bay Company facilities and even contributed his own funds to them, although he was a Roman Catholic. This was a generous but serious error, for the reports of the missionaries' successful settlement induced massive migration of Americans to Oregon (whom McLoughlin also had to save with gifts of food and loans). Thereby was destroyed the Hudson's Bay Company's monopoly on the region.

McLoughlin nevertheless remained determined to maintain the company's foothold in what is now the state of Washington. Yet his determination seriously worsened his relations with Governor Simpson and other company officials, who all felt after about 1841 that it was prudent to remove the company's base of operations to a northern position such as Vancouver Island. Such disagreements and the fact of declining revenues from the Columbia District resulted in McLoughlin's retirement after 1845 to land he owned in Oregon City.

The best short account of McLoughlin's life is William R. Sampson's introduction to *John McLoughlin's Business Correspondence, 1847-1848* (1973). See also W. Kaye Lamb's introduction in E. E. Rich, ed., *McLoughlin's Fort Vancouver Letters* (1941-44). A definitive biography is yet to be written.—G. B. D.

McMurtry, Larry (1936-   ). Novelist. McMurtry was born in Archer County, Texas, where his family had been ranchers for three generations. He attended North Texas State University at Denton, Rice University, and Stanford University, where he studied writing under Wallace Stegner. He then joined the department of English at Rice University.

McMurtry's Archer County reappears in his fiction, all of which is intensely regional. His attitude toward Texas is not uncritically favorable, as he makes clear in *In a Narrow Grave: Essays on Texas* (1968). The author of three Western novels—*Horseman, Pass By* (1961, filmed as *Hud*), *Leaving Cheyenne* (1963), and *The Last Picture Show* (1966), made into a successful movie—his constant thematic concern is the encroachment of change upon the semimythical world of the "cattle kingdom." *Horseman, Pass By,* his most successful novel, movingly tells the story of the passing of the old order through the eyes of a boy who must grow up in a new world. Yet McMurtry's view of history is not nostalgic. Most emphatically the good times are *not* all gone, and his heroes learn to accept their places in the world of the future.—J. K. F.

McNelly, Leander H. (1844-1877). Lawman. McNelly was a frail, soft-spoken man who won respect throughout Texas as a fearless and uncompromising officer of the law. When seventeen he joined the Confederate army in Texas, serving with distinction in the New Mexico campaign and later in Louisiana. In 1870 McNelly was appointed a captain in the Texas State Police by the Reconstruction governor in spite of his disagreement with Reconstruction policy, and he managed to serve honorably in an organization that enjoyed an unsavory reputation.

In 1874 the Texas Rangers were reorganized and McNelly was given command of a "Special Force." He recruited a tough band of Rangers, who followed him with a devotion bordering on fanaticism. His first assignment was to restore order in De Witt County, the scene of a long-standing feud between the Sutton and Taylor families. It was a hopeless assignment. The feud dated back to 1867-68 when Creed Taylor's boys ran afoul of Union troops and managed to spark a blood feud when one of them was killed by William Sutton. In the unsettled atmosphere of Reconstruction Texas, the feud flared and smoldered until 1875, when Jim Taylor's death left one faction without a leader. McNelly's efforts in 1874 managed only to restrain the violence until the spring of 1875, when he was called away from De Witt County for a bigger assignment.

He was given the unenviable task of ending outlawry along the Mexican border in the area known as the Nueces Strip. The Strip was not only plagued by American rustlers and outlaws like King Fisher and his followers, but was also constantly harassed by Mexican bandits under the leadership of Juan Nepomuceno Cortina. McNelly moved effectively in all areas, winning the confidence and support of the people of the area and making life miserable for outlaws in general.

In one daring episode, McNelly led his Rangers across the Rio Grande into Mexico and brazenly attacked a Cortina stronghold. Confronted by superior forces, the Rangers retreated to the Rio Grande and dug in on the Mexican side. American troops had arrived on the scene by that time and, fearing that McNelly's force would be slaughtered, crossed the river. The Mexicans withdrew and the officer in command of the American forces demanded that McNelly return to Texas. McNelly calmly informed the army that he would cross the river at his discretion, concluding, "Give my compliments to the secretary of war, and tell him United States troops may go to hell." After additional raids on the Cortinistas, the Ranger captain turned his attention to King Fisher, but before he could accomplish all his objectives, bad health forced him to turn his command over to Lee Hall. McNelly suffered from tuberculosis and had directed the Rangers from a wagon bed much of the time. He died a few months later.

See O. C. Fisher and Jeff C. Dykes, *King Fisher: His Life and Times* (1966); N. A. Jennings, *A Texas Ranger* (1899); and Walter Prescott Webb, *The Texas Rangers* (1935).—G. L. R.

McSween, Alexander. See LINCOLN COUNTY WAR.

Magoffin, James Wiley (1799-1868). Businessman and diplomat. Of all the men who played significant roles on the southwestern frontier in the years immediately before and after the Mexican War (1846-48), perhaps none was more intelligent and economically successful than pioneer merchant Magoffin. He was born in Harrodsburg, Kentucky, and as early as 1825 he began developing a profitable mercantile business in northern Mexico while serving as American consul at Saltillo. By 1836 he had moved to Chihuahua, where he entered the Santa Fe trade. Through his Mexican wife, command of Spanish, and liberality, he soon gained influence in the social and economic life of the northern provinces. With his family he established himself in Independence, Missouri, in 1844, raising mules and with

his brothers Samuel and William maintaining two wagon trains to Santa Fe.

When President James K. Polk two years later cast about for a man knowledgeable of north Mexican affairs, Senator Thomas Hart Benton of Missouri recommended Magoffin. With special presidential instructions, he preceded General Stephen Watts Kearny's army to Santa Fe and, in secret conference with Governor Manuel Armijo, a cousin of his wife, he helped pave the way for a peaceful occupation of New Mexico by American forces. Attempting to play the same role in Chihuahua, he was arrested as a spy and released after nine months' captivity.

In 1849 Magoffin founded a sumptuous hacienda and a freighting business at El Paso, but much of the fortune he accumulated was lost when he gave full support to the abortive Confederate invasion of New Mexico during the Civil War. Retreating to San Antonio with southern troops in 1862, he maintained his residence in that city until his death.

Magoffin's life is described in Rex W. Strickland, *Six Who Came to El Paso* (1963). Adding much helpful information is the diary of his sister-in-law, Susan Shelby Magoffin, *Down the Santa Fe Trail and Into Mexico* (1962).—M. Sɪ.

mail service. See TRANSPORTATION, OVERLAND.

Maine, settlement of. Excited by reports of abundant fish and furs, the Plymouth Company dispatched a small group of settlers to the coast of Maine in 1607. These men established a base called Sagadahoc on the Kennebec River, but poor planning and an "extremely unseasonable and frosty" winter so discouraged the colonists that they soon returned to England. After this experience the Plymouth Company gave up all efforts to develop the area, and over the next decade only fishermen showed interest in Maine.

In 1620 the Council for New England, led by Sir Ferdinando Gorges, took over the claims of the moribund Plymouth Company. Nine years later the council granted the land north of the Merrimack River to Gorges and his associate, Captain John Mason. These two men in turn divided the territory—Maine going to Gorges and New Hampshire to Mason. In 1639 Charles I issued a charter making Gorges absolute lord and proprietor over the "Province of Maine." However, Gorges' dreams of a great feudal principality in the New World were frustrated by the confusion of the English Civil War and by the aggressiveness of the Bay Colony. The leaders of Massachusetts assumed that their charter gave them authority over the settlements in Maine, and in 1652 they incorporated these communities into the county of York. Despite the generous terms offered by the Bay Colony, many of the Maine colonists were not happy about becoming part of the Puritan commonwealth. In fact, it was not until 1658 that Scarborough and Falmouth finally joined with Wells, Cape Elizabeth, and Saco in submitting to the government of Massachusetts.

After the English Restoration in 1660 the heirs to Gorges' title tried to have the actions of Massachusetts declared illegal. In 1677 an English court restored Gorges' full rights both to the soil and to the government of Maine, but to everyone's surprise, Gorges (Ferdinando's grandson) immediately sold all his rights to the Bay Colony. Maine remained part of Massachusetts until

1820, when it became the twenty-third state of the Union. During most of the colonial period the population of Maine was under constant threat of attack by the French and Indians, and, as a consequence, the area retained its frontier character long after the rest of New England had matured.

See Charles M. Andrews, *The Colonial Period of American History*, 4 vols. (1934-38); and Marion Jaques Smith, *A History of Maine, From Wilderness to Statehood* (1949). —T. H. B.

Majors, Alexander (1814-1900). Freighting expert. Majors was born near Franklin, Simpson County, Kentucky. He grew up on a Kentucky farm and worked in his father's saw and flour mills. In 1834 he married Katherine Stallcup and began farming on his own. To supplement his income and support his growing family, he transported a wagonload of Indian trade goods to the Pottawatomie reservation on the Kansas River in 1846. Two years later he entered the freighting business with six wagons, transporting goods from Independence, Missouri, to Santa Fe, New Mexico, along the Santa Fe Trail. This first venture, taking ninety days for the round trip, produced a profit of $1,500. By 1850, Majors undertook the transportation of military supplies under contract with the government. The next year he supervised a freight train of twenty-five wagons taking merchandise for businessmen to Santa Fe and returned in time to make another trip to Fort Union, the military headquarters for the United States Army in New Mexico. Henceforth, most of his freighting experience was for the War Department, although occasionally he delivered for private parties. According to his memoirs, *Seventy Years on the Frontier* (1893), Majors was a strict disciplinarian in the conduct of his freight trains. He refused to travel on Sunday and required his teamsters to take a pledge not to swear, drink, gamble, or mistreat animals, but to behave like gentlemen.

In December 1854 Majors went into a partnership with William H. Russell and William B. Waddell in the freighting business, a firm sometimes known as Majors & Russell and after 1858 as RUSSELL, MAJORS AND WADDELL. Majors was responsible for all the road operations, while Russell handled promotion and government contracts, and Waddell dealt with office matters. The partnership made a $300,000 profit in 1855-56, but soon overextended itself in making exclusive freighting contracts to deliver military supplies to Utah during the Mormon War (1857). Through the activities of his partner Russell, Majors became involved in stagecoach operations in 1859 and the Pony Express in 1860, both of which meant additional financial loss. The firm of Russell, Majors and Waddel collapsed in 1862, and Majors pledged his personal estate to assist in liquidating the indebtedness. He continued in the freighting business on his own until 1866, then worked on the Union Pacific Railroad, and later prospected for silver in Utah, where he maintained a residence in Salt Lake City between 1869 and 1872. Majors died in Chicago, Illinois.

See Arthur Chapman, *The Pony Express* (1932); Raymond W. Settle and Mary L. Settle, *War Drums and Wagon Wheels* (1966) and *Saddles and Spurs: The Pony Express Saga* (1955); and Henry Pickering Walker, *The Wagonmasters* (1966).—W. T. J.

Malin, James Claude (1893-   ). Historian. Malin has an acknowledged reputation as a prolific author, teacher, and leading authority on Kansas history. Jared Malin, his father, was a mobile settler, typical of the late nineteenth century; over a period of almost twenty years he migrated from Illinois to Kansas, returned to Illinois where he married, moved to North Dakota, where Malin was born, and in 1903 returned to Kansas. The family moved frequently between farms and small towns.

Malin took his first degree from Baker University in 1914. During the next seven years, he obtained two graduate degrees from the University of Kansas, taught high school in three different communities, and served briefly in World War I. He was appointed to the University of Kansas faculty in 1921 and received emeritus status in 1963.

One of the most original thinkers of his generation, Malin made an impact on American history through his writings. While he was a good teacher, his insistence on high standards of student achievement made him unpopular. His first decade of research and writing on topics of general American history brought much success and recognition. In the early 1930s, after difficulties with the university chancellor concerning the accuracy of the history of Lawrence and with publishers in getting a long manuscript accepted, he turned his exceptional energy toward local and regional history. He aided in the creation of the *Kansas Historical Quarterly* and in building the state historical society. Among his thirteen books, eighty articles, and innumerable book reviews are the well-known *John Brown and the Legend of Fifty-Six, The Nebraska Question,* and *The Grassland of North America.*

Always a stern proponent of objectivity, Malin opposed relativism. He courageously, calmly, and carefully broke down images created by earlier historians who were less rigorous in their search for truth. He challenged the traditional slavery view of the Kansas conflict, for example, and replaced it with a broader interpretation involving geography, communication facilities, and the force of man's creativity. He adhered to no school of historical inquiry and in his methodology frequently borrowed from other disciplines.

After World War II Malin's ideas were denied a broader circulation because of his distrust of editors and publishers. Most of his longer monographs from that period were reproduced from typescript, and at great personal expense he served as his own editor and publisher. Few people found Malin easy to appreciate, know, or understand, but his total contribution cannot be ignored.—H. E. S.

Mandan Indians. The Mandan Indians were a semisedentary agricultural tribe that formerly inhabited the Missouri River valley in the Dakotas. Because many Mandan possessed lighter skin and finer features than most Indians, the origins of the tribe have been a popular mystery. Still-current theories claim the Mandan to have descended from Phoenician traders, Viking explorers, and even Welsh royalty. In reality they were a Siouan offshoot tribe, closely related linguistically to the Winnebago and Tutelo, and among the first peoples to separate from the ancestral proto-Siouan body. Early Mandan groups, not then a unified tribe, began drifting into the Missouri valley from the Southeast about A.D. 1200, settling in many small village clusters of about two hundred people and scattered over a large area. Archaeological evidence indicates that they lived in large earth lodges, they were skilled in pottery-making, and their economy was evenly balanced between agriculture and hunting.

About 1500 the Mandan began to coalesce into fewer and much larger villages and developed an elaborate system of social control and integration. By 1738, when La Vérendrye visited the tribe, the entire Mandan population of at least ten thousand people was concentrated in nine fortified villages within twenty miles of each other near the Heart River. This cultural concentration was characteristic of all northern Plains agricultural tribes in that period and was intensified by the introduction of European trade goods, influx of displaced eastern tribes, and the appearance of equestrian nomads from the Southwest.

During the period 1700-50 Mandan culture was at the peak of its development. Their economy had become primarily agricultural, and they traded surplus corn to Assiniboin and Cree middlemen in exchange for European metal tools. Politically, each Mandan community was an independent entity, but the villages were bound closely together through kinship and ceremonial linkages. Social organization was based on thirteen matrilineal, exogamous, nontotemic clans grouped in two moieties. Religion was also connected with kinship, since ceremonial practices were based on clan ownership of tribal ritual objects. Membership in a clan owning important objects was a primary determinant of individual social class and opportunity for tribal leadership. Both men and women also belonged to a series of secular societies through which age groups moved progressively from youth to old age. Each society was charged with specified tribal duties according to the age of its membership. There was a strict sexual division of labor, the women being entirely responsible for agriculture. Because of a surplus of females, polygyny was the marital norm, and Mandan women were later renowned among white traders for their wonderful availability.

The Mandan had acquired both guns and horses by 1750, neither of which disrupted their cultural pattern except to facilitate already-established practices of hunting and warfare. For a time their villages and those of the neighboring Arikara and Hidatsa were an impregnable barrier to territorial expansion by either the equestrian tribes to the west or the Sioux pressing in from the east. In the 1770s, however, a series of devastating smallpox epidemics reduced the Mandan population to about 1,500. The Sioux drove them from their homes north toward the Knife River, where they resettled in two villages adjoining the surviving Hidatsa. Cultural dominance on the northern Plains then passed to the Sioux and other nomads, who nonetheless acquired many customs and practices from the Mandan and associated river tribes.

In 1804-05 the Lewis and Clark expedition wintered among the Mandan, and early-nineteenth-century travelers and fur traders along the Missouri seldom failed to visit their villages. Some, like Chardon, Prince Maximilian, and the artist George Catlin, made detailed records of their observations. All whites who came in contact with the Mandan were uniformly impressed with their unfailing courtesy, dignity of manner, and spectacular costumes and ceremonies. In 1837, however, one more plague of smallpox was carried up the Missouri by the American Fur Company's annual steamboat. By spring of 1838 there were only 130 Mandan left alive. These joined with the remnants of the Arikara and Hidatsa and became entirely dependent on the United States government for support and protection. Even then they labored to preserve their valued tribal and cultural integrity, and it was not until after the establishment of a permanent agency for them at Fort Berthold in 1868 that white influences finally overwhelmed their traditional way of life. Merging with the two other tribes, the Mandan became culturally extinct, and today it is impossible to identify any separate Mandan identity among the Fort Berthold Reservation Indians.

See Edward M. Bruner, "Mandan," in E. H. Spicer, ed., *Perspectives in American Indian Culture Change* (1961); A. E. Goplen, "The Mandan Indians," *North Dakota History*, vol. 13 (1946); and M. T. Newman, "The Blond Mandan," *Southwestern Journal of Anthropology*, vol. 6 (1950).—P. R. M.

Manfred, Frederick (1912-   ). Novelist. Manfred, who wrote under the pseudonym Feike Feikema from 1944 to 1951, was born of Frisian parents near Dune, Iowa. He received a B.A. in 1934 from Calvin College in Michigan. A reporter for the Minneapolis *Journal* from 1937 to 1939, he devoted most of his life to writing. He was writer in residence at Macalester College, Minnesota, from 1949 to 1952.

Manfred's western writings include, among other books, *This Is the Year* (1947), *Morning Red, A Romance* (1956), and *Lord Grizzly* (1954). Very different in subject matter, they are similar in that all take place in a region Manfred calls "Siouxland," that area where South Dakota, Minnesota, Nebraska, and Iowa meet. Manfred dedicated *Morning Red* to William Faulkner, and though the comparison between the two makes little specific sense, it is an intriguing idea. Each writer exhaustively explored a semimythical county, essentially a product of his own mind, however close it may be to some real geographical area; and the theme of both men's work is the exploration of the American character as it expresses itself within the boundaries of this region. For both, the world is best seen from the vantage point of home, and general considerations are best explored in terms of a particular place.—J. K. F.

Mangas Coloradas (1795?-1863). Indian chief. Mangas Coloradas ("Red Sleeves" or "Roan Shirt") was a chief of the "Red Paint People," or Eastern Chiricahua Apache. Born probably somewhere in southern New Mexico, he grew into a giant of a man—about six-and-a-half feet tall with proportions to match—among medium-statured people. He raided from the Navaho country in the north to Durango, Mexico, and from western Texas to eastern Arizona. During the 1840s his raids into Mexico terrorized the people of the northern Mexican states all along the eastern flank of the Sierra Madre.

Until 1861, as revenge for wrongs done to his close relatives and people, Mangas Coloradas had carried out raids and warfare only against Mexicans. In 1846, when General Stephen Watts Kearny was en route to California from Santa Fe, Mangas Coloradas met him along the Gila River trail and pledged his friendship with the Americans. He even offered to take an active part with the Americans in their war with Mexico, an offer that Kearny respectfully declined.

In 1852 Mangas Coloradas continued to profess friendship with Anglos, and he agreed to terms of a treaty proffered by Major John Greiner, superintendent for Indian Affairs in New Mexico. His raids against Mexicans and Mexican settlements, however, were unrelenting. He also harassed miners of any ethnic background who worked in the area near modern Silver City, New Mexico. In 1861, when COCHISE began warring with North Americans, Mangas Coloradas sided with his fellow Apache, to whom he had given his eldest daughter in marriage.

Soon after the outbreak of the Civil War in April 1861, United States troops withdrew from Arizona. Mangas Coloradas, Cochise, and other Apache mistakenly assumed they had something to do with the withdrawal. After a brief occupation of southern Arizona by Confederate forces in June 1862, the Union "recaptured" the territory through General James S. Carleton and his California Volunteers. In July 1862 a contingent of the First Infantry of California Volunteers under Captain Thomas L. Roberts—including 126 soldiers, 242 animals, and 21 wagons—moved into Apache Pass at the northern end of the Chiricahua Mountains. Mangas Coloradas and Cochise and their men, who commanded the heights above the pass, attempted an ambush. The combination of howitzers and reinforcements in the form of mounted cavalry proved too much for the Indians, and so, they were routed.

During the fight Mangas Coloradas was shot from his horse by an army private. The Apache took him to Janos in Chihuahua, Mexico, where they forced a Mexican doctor to tend to Mangas Coloradas' wound. He recovered, but in January 1863 he was captured near Pinos Altos, New Mexico, and taken prisoner to abandoned Fort McLane, New Mexico. Although there are at least four printed versions of what happened to Mangas Coloradas at Fort McLane—the official army version is that he was killed while trying to escape captivity—the most probable is that he was murdered when he angrily objected to the soldiers who were burning his legs and feet with heated bayonets. One of Mangas Coloradas' non-Indian contempories asserted that his life was characterized by "the most atrocious cruelties, the most vindictive revenges, and widespread injuries ever perpetrated by an American Indian." But on the Apache-Anglo frontier, it was not always easy to separate victim from criminal.

See John C. Cremony, *Life Among the Apaches* (1868); Lee Myers, "Mangas Colorado's Death," *New Mexico Historical Review*, vol. 41, no. 4 (1966); and Dan L. Thrapp, *The Conquest of Apacheria* (1967).—B. L. F.

manifest destiny. Manifest destiny is not a unique American phenomenon. Similar attitudes can be found in the history of every powerful nation or empire since ancient times. In the United States manifest destiny is a verbal banner attached to the moods, motives, and rationalizations of nineteenth-century territorial expansion. The phrase refers primarily to the expansion of the 1840s: the annexation of Texas, the acquisition of Oregon, and the purchase of California and the Southwest from defeated Mexico. It is also attached to the abortive midcentury movements for the acquisition of all Mexico, Cuba, the Dominican Republic, and Canada.

The annexation of Hawaii and the Philippines in 1898-99 is frequently termed a product of a "new manifest destiny."

The phrase has multifarious connotations. The core concept is that Americans are destined by divine providence to expand their national domain. The roots of the idea of a special mission, talent, and opportunity for expansion go back to the colonial period. The concept was fully expressed, for example, by Benjamin Franklin. Variations on the idea appeared with increasing frequency in political discourse after the War of 1812 and reached a crescendo in the mid-1840s. The precise phrase was first used by the widely read editor John L. O'Sullivan in the *Democratic Review* in July 1845. O'Sullivan supported the annexation of Texas as a response to foreign interference, which, he said, exists "for the avowed object of . . . checking the fulfillment of our manifest destiny to overspread the continent alloted by Providence for the free development of our yearly multiplying millions."

Manifest destiny was not a repository for sharply defined ideas, but rather a slogan expressive of vague and inchoate emotions, the symbol of a rambunctious national mood. Albert K. Weinberg, for example, discovered fifteen different aspects or arguments in support of the nation's manifest destiny to expand: (1) natural right, (2) geographical predestination, (3) God's injunction that the soil be used intensively by agricultural settlers rather than nomadic hunters, (4) extension of the area of freedom, (5) the assignment of the "true title" by God, (6) the mission of regeneration, (7) natural growth, (8) political gravitation, (9) inevitable destiny, (10) the White Man's Burden, (11) paramount interest, (12) political affinity, (13) self-defense, (14) the responsibility to exercise an international police power, and (15) world leadership. Frederick Merk, the other principal historian of the concept, attempts to distinguish between the selfish, aggressive aspects of manifest destiny to acquire land and the altruistic, idealistic sense of mission to improve the lives of others. He sees the latter as the true foundation of American national character. Merk's distinction, like Weinberg's categories, is too theoretical. Even those supporters of manifest destiny judged by posterity to be most contemptuous of the rights of others believed they were acting idealistically and that what was ordained for the special benefit of Americans was good for all mankind.

Cries of "manifest destiny" survive in diplomatic and political documents—wherein, for example, Secretary of State John Quincy Adams argues American rights against Spanish, British, or Russian rights; President James K. Polk does the same against Mexican and British rights; and a host of exuberant congressmen cry "54°40' or Fight" or agitate for all of Mexico. Such men and the publicists who echoed them went to elaborate lengths to justify what the nation and its population were doing.

Most exponents of manifest destiny exaggerated the hostile intentions and capabilities of European nations. Using the MONROE DOCTRINE, they argued for the acquisition of Canada, the Floridas, the Mississippi valley, Texas, Oregon, and California on the grounds the present or potential enemies were about to use these regions to undermine the security of the United States. Most exponents were imbued with an unquestioning sense of American superiority. They ignored or denied that the Indians living on or claiming title to lands coveted by Americans had legitimate rights. All extolled the spread of American democratic institutions, but few defined those institutions with clarity or recognized a conflict between democracy and slavery. Some dwelled on the advantages other people would enjoy when placed under American jurisdiction, but once a piece of territory was acquired little further thought was devoted to altruism.

The exponents of manifest destiny were challenged on occasion: the Jefferson administration by the Federalists over the Louisiana Purchase; the Polk administration by antislavery elements over the annexation of Texas and the war with Mexico; and the McKinley administration by anti-imperialists who argued that America's mission was to improve the lot of her own people, not conquer others. Sometimes the expansionists of one generation survived to become the opponents of manifest destiny in another. This was the case with Albert Gallatin and John Quincy Adams, who opposed southwestern expansion in the 1840s.

Manifest destiny was a result and an accompaniment of expansion, not a cause. Given the absence of significant opposition by other nations, a nearly empty continent, a life-supporting environment, a high American birthrate, innovations in transportation and communication (the railroad and telegraph), and specific objectives pursued by political leaders, expansion would have taken place with or without the many doctrines that swarmed around the concept of manifest destiny. There was no single overriding material motive behind the rhetoric. Some expansionists sought land for military security; others stressed room for agricultural expansion or access to natural resources in timber and ore; a few were interested in the Pacific Coast as an outlet for the CHINA TRADE.

The lasting importance of manifest destiny lies in the legacy of American self-confidence and sense of superiority over other peoples. Expansion was the result of a fortunate and fortuitous conjunction of international political circumstances, geography, and technology. Americans, however, instinctively attributed success to special moral superiority awarded them by God. Those who stood in the way of America's mission were perceived as agents of wickedness.

Manifest destiny as an expression of territorial expansion faded with the nineteenth century. As an expression of a special mission to exercise power and influence over other people and regions, it continued. The fulfillment of that mission, however, was not as easy as acquiring and settling the West. The shock of failure, after a heritage of seemingly inevitable triumph, affected American diplomacy and domestic politics throughout the twentieth century. The failures to fulfill the modern version of manifest destiny were at first attributed to bad or incompetent men—for example, senators who rejected Woodrow Wilson's League of Nations or "communist sympathizers" who "sold out" to the Soviet Union—but by the 1960s Americans were beginning for the first time in their history to question the existence of a special manifest destiny. The frontier that helped produce the original manifest destiny disappeared, according to the census taker's estimate, in 1890, but an altered form of manifest destiny has survived.

See Norman A. Graebner, *Empire on the Pacific: A Study in American Continental Expansion* (1955), and (ed.) *Manifest Destiny* (1968); Frederick Merk, *Manifest Destiny and Mission in American History* (1963); Julius W. Pratt, "The Origin of 'Manifest Destiny,' " *American Historical Review* (July 1927); and Albert K. Weinberg, *Manifest Destiny: A Study of Nationalist Expansionism in American History* (1935).—G. G. S.

Manzanares, Francisco [Antonio] (1843-1904). New Mexico politician. Manzanares was born in Abiquiu, New Mexico. Although his early schooling was in Spanish under Father Antonio José Martínez, he later studied English and in 1863 and 1864 attended St. Louis University in Missouri. He operated a wholesale grocery in Las Vegas, New Mexico, beginning in 1866. A conservative Democrat, Manzanares was elected to both branches of the New Mexico legislature and was an Indian agent for the Ute and Apache. In the territorial delegate election for the Forty-eighth Congress, Tranquilino Luna of Valencia County was first declared the winner; however, Manzanares successfully contested the election and served as delegate from March 5, 1884, to March 3, 1885. The election of 1882 had demonstrated the factionalism of the Republican party in New Mexico, and Manzanares, although the acknowledged leader of the New Mexico Democratic party, had been the choice of many Republican voters. He declined renomination in 1884 and served in 1896 and 1897 on the Board of County Commissioners in Las Vegas, New Mexico, where he died.—J. R. V.

mapmaking. See CARTOGRAPHY.

Marcy, Randolph Barnes (1812-1887). Soldier, trailblazer, and mapmaker. A native of Greenwich, Massachusetts, Marcy graduated from West Point in 1832 and was commissioned a brevet second lieutenant. A few months later he married Mary Mann of Syracuse, New York, and the young officer and his bride went to their first frontier assignment—Fort Howard, at Green Bay, Wisconsin. Although he arrived too late to participate in the Black Hawk War, for the next fifty years he led an active military life, most of it on the frontier.

Traveling as extensively as any other nineteenth-century explorer, Marcy never achieved the fame of Lewis, Clark, Pike, Long, and Frémont. Yet he conducted five major expeditions through the West and was the first to trace the Red River to its source (1852), an accomplishment that eluded both Pike and Long. In addition, he drafted the first reasonably accurate maps of the Southwest and his advice led to the establishment of a chain of "Cross Timbers" forts from eastern Oklahoma to western Texas. Included in these was Fort Sill, today one of the nation's major military installations. Marcy also located several small Indian reservations in the Southwest, participated in the campaign against the Seminole Indians (1857) in Florida, and during the government's expedition to bring the Mormons in Utah back under federal authority (1857-58), he led a dramatic march over 634 miles of snow-covered mountains to New Mexico to obtain relief supplies for isolated Fort Bridger, Wyoming.

Captain Marcy saw action at Palo Alto and Resaca de la Palma in the Mexican War (1846-48) before returning to the East on recruiting duty. During the Civil War his son-in-law, General George B. McClellan, appointed him his chief-of-staff. When President Lincoln removed

McClellan as commander of the Army of the Potomac, Marcy's role in the war naturally diminished, but he remained a professional soldier until retiring in 1881.

Marcy is remembered today primarily because of three autobiographical and entertaining books: *Prairie Traveller* (1859), *Thirty Years of Army Life on the Border* (1866), and *Border Reminiscences* (1872).

See Grant Foreman, *Adventures on Red River* (1937), and *Marcy and the Gold Seekers* (1939); and W. Eugene Hollon, *Beyond the Cross Timbers: The Travels of Randolph B. Marcy* (1955).—W. E. H.

Marquette, Jacques (1637-1675). Jesuit missionary and French explorer. Marquette was born in Laon, France, came to Quebec in 1666, and founded the Mission of St. Mary at Sault Ste. Marie, Michigan, in 1668. He moved it to the present Ashland, Wisconsin, on Lake Superior the next year and then to St. Ignace, Michigan in 1670.

When Louis Jolliet was sent out by Comte de Frontenac, vice regent for Louis XIV, in search of the great river flowing into the unknown Western or Southern Sea, Marquette accompanied him. With five *voyageurs*, they left St. Ignace in canoes on May 17, 1673. Armed with a map based on Indian lore, they traveled via Green Bay, up the Fox River, and portaged to the Wisconsin River and down it. Indians warned them of dangerous tribes ahead who would show them no mercy, of monsters that would devour both canoes and men, of a demon "who barred the way, and who swallowed up all who ventured to approach him," and, finally, of heat ". . . so excessive in those countries that it would inevitably cause our death." When the party arrived at the Mississippi on June 17, they were the first Europeans to traverse the river route across Wisconsin. They were welcomed by Indian tribes as they descended the Mississippi, one chief saying that "Never has the earth been so beautiful, or the sun so bright, as today . . . never has our tobacco tasted so good, or our corn appeared so fine, as we see them now . . ." The Indian offered them a slave and a "mysterious calumet," or pipe. When they reached the present Arkansas City, Arkansas, they decided that the Mississippi did not flow into either Virginia or California, so they turned back via Illinois River and Lake Michigan to St. Ignace.

Marquette served other Jesuit missions until his death. His bones rest in the chapel at St. Ignace. Marquette is one of the two Wisconsinites in Statuary Hall of the United States Capitol.

See Joseph P. Donnelly, *Jacques Marquette, S. J., 1637-1675* (1968).—W. D. W.

Marsh, Grant. See RIVERMEN.

Marsh, John (1799-1856). California ranchero. After graduation from Harvard in 1823, Marsh took an appointment as a tutor on the Minnesota frontier. There, as a result of his marriage to a French-Sioux woman, he became closely involved with the Sioux Indians. After the Black Hawk War (1830-32) Marsh was accused of having Indian sympathies, and following the death of his wife in 1833, he fled the territory of the United States, embittered and despondent. Arriving in Mexican Los Angeles in 1836, he set up a medical practice based on skills he had learned from a Minnesota friend. Within two years he was able to parlay his virtual monopoly of medical knowledge into a large and growing rancho in the San Joaquin Valley. In 1856 he built an imposing villa, called the Stone House, on the ranch. The building survives today. In the early 1840s Marsh encouraged the first of the overland migrations to California with a series of letters published in the eastern press extolling California virtues. But to Mexicans and Anglos alike he was disliked as a hard, miserly, embittered man. In 1856 disgruntled *vaqueros*, complaining about poor wages, murdered him.

See George D. Lyman, *John Marsh, Pioneer* (1930). —J. F.

marshal, federal. The federal marshal occupies a unique position in the history of the West. When the United States came into being under the Constitution, dual sovereignty to the state and the republic created a problem for law enforcement. Since the federal establishment included its own judiciary, specially designated officers were required for realization of the authority inherent in United States courts. In order to provide for limited national law enforcement, Congress turned in 1789 to English admiralty precedents and created appointive positions of federal marshals. These officers possessed jurisdictions corresponding to those of United States district courts, a pattern that has endured to the present.

While federal marshals and their deputies served throughout the formative years of the republic, it was not until expansion of national power and the Civil War that the judiciary's own police came into prominence. This generally corresponded in time to the establishment of giant territorial systems west of the Mississippi River. Acts of original organization for future states normally included provisions for a federal marshal, appointed directly by the president of the United States and empowered to execute all orders and processes of the courts.

The post of federal marshal, with duties often extending over tens of thousands of square miles, became hotly contested political rewards. Persons with close connections to high office naturally enjoyed the greatest likelihood of selection, and commands routinely changed with different national administrations. Only on rare occasions, such as the appointment of Thomas Jefferson Carr in Wyoming, did professional lawmen obtain these coveted positions. Rather, they went to an assortment of politicians, merchants, lawyers, and others of regional note. With disturbing frequency these men became embroiled in charges of fraud and embezzlement, such as filing false claims. Still, the federal marshal enjoyed a romantic aura. His wide jurisdiction and formal allegiance directly to the United States provided a partial insulation from purely local problems and pressures. Meanwhile, he helped fill a vacuum in law enforcement.

Federal marshals had to rely upon their deputies for actual performance of duties. In this aspect, also, political patronage played a major role. Many of the West's most famous peace officers were chosen to fill available positions, but it should be pointed out that some of the best known never held a federal commission. Not all marshals were federal marshals; they could be town marshals appointed by the mayor or city council, as are today's police chiefs. The community lawmen functioned purely as local police, while those with national authority worked essentially for United States courts. "Wild Bill" Hickok, for example, earned his reputation as town marshal of Abilene, while Wyatt Earp gained fame in a similar position at Dodge City.

The number of deputy federal marshals varied markedly by district and time. A quiet portion of the East might require only two or three posts, while a large western territory could have scores of officers at work. A marshal appointed as many deputies as he and the district judge saw fit.

Deputy federal marshals fell into two regular categories. Office assignments could reasonably be filled by individuals with clerical or business backgrounds. Field duties, on the other hand, went to those with practical law-enforcement experience. The geographic immensity of many districts forced marshals to scatter their men widely. Consequently, field deputies had to be capable of independent and sometimes courageous action.

When territories first opened, some marshals had to act in the stead of local policemen. Although the popular image of deputies maintaining order in trail and mining communities has little foundation in fact, isolated instances of such responsibility undoubtedly did occur. Ordinarily, however, town or county officers performed such tasks.

Federal marshals and their deputies, even on the frontier, spent most of their working time on routine functions related to civil and criminal court activity. They issued and served subpoenas, gathered jurymen, conducted property sales, located witnesses, and executed countless writs and warrants. Criminal investigations and captures of outlaws constituted only a fraction of duties performed.

Deputies originally earned their living through fees for specific legal services, payments for expenses, and infrequent rewards. The fees were paid by those who filed suit. A great many deputies obtained supplemental income from other jobs. Some worked as stage guards; others ran saloons! The fee system eventually became controversial. Supporters proclaimed that fees were an incentive for individual effort and initiative. Critics contended that they led to overzealous enforcement or entrapment. Reform finally won and in 1896 regular annual salaries were authorized.

Fees continued to be charged after 1896, however, with the money flowing into general funds. Most districts operated with considerable profit, although certain operations were expensive and had to be funded through additional means. Marshals, especially in Arizona and New Mexico, maintained large territorial prisons with public monies. Inmates were frequently leased to private interests for labor, a practice that contributed to the terrible reputations acquired by some institutions.

Many of the problems confronted by federal marshals involved prisoners. The shortage of satisfactory facilities on the frontier added to difficulties of transport and confinement. Deputies resorted to chaining prisoners to trees and wagons, particularly when moving through unorganized regions.

In time of unusual demand or need, federal marshals issued "special" commissions. These permitted rapid expansion of available forces for limited periods and purposes. During the widespread railroad strikes of 1922, for example, hundreds of emergency deputies were placed on duty.

One highly significant legal principle developed through actions of a special officer. Special Deputy Marshal David Neagle was appointed to protect United States Supreme Court Justice Stephen Field. While acting as bodyguard, Neagle killed an assailant in 1889 and was accused of murder by California authorities. The Supreme Court of the United States ruled in 1890 that deputies possess implied power to preserve the peace and, when acting in line of duty, are beyond state jurisdiction.

Activities of federal marshals reached a high point on the closing frontier, in the Oklahoma and Indian territories. Scores of them operated throughout the undeveloped regions, among them Leo F. Bennett, Thomas B. Needles, and Evett D. Nix. Working far from established courts or sizable communities, these officers provided the only significant and available form of law enforcement. Dealing with a wide assortment of Indians, former slaves, white settlers, and fugitives from other sections, the deputies faced unprecedented difficulty, resentment, and danger. A considerable number of black men, including Bass Reeves, held commissions from federal marshals. Together with special deputies representing Indian nations, they left a distinguished heritage in the era preceding Oklahoma's admission as a state.

A great deal of information concerning federal marshals on the frontier can be found in the *Annual Reports of the Attorney-General of the United States.* The National Archives has available a comprehensive microfilm "Index to Names of United States Marshals, 1789-1960." *Cunningham* v. *Neagle*, 135 U.S. 1 (1890), is the landmark decision on legal authority. No definitive secondary source exists dealing specifically with federal marshals, but see Frank R. Prassel, *The Western Peace Officer: A Legacy of Law and Order* (1972).—F. R. P.

Martin, Anne (1875-1951). Nevada politician and leader of women's suffrage movement. Born in Reno, Nevada, Martin was graduated from Stanford University. She accepted a position at the University of Nevada, becoming the first head of the department of history, a post she held from 1897 to 1901. She left the field of education to devote her time, money, and energy to the women's suffrage movement. She participated in that fight in England in the years from 1909 to 1911 under the tutelage of Mrs. Emmeline Pankhurst. Returning to Nevada, she was elected president of the Nevada Equal Franchise Society in 1912. The suffrage amendment had already passed its first legislature in 1911 but had to survive passage through the 1913 legislature and a vote of the people in the following general election. Martin gave successful leadership to this campaign and the suffrage amendment passed both these hurdles, the latter in 1914. She was elected first national chairman of the National Women's party at its national convention in 1916, and was the first woman to run for the United States Senate. Although she was defeated in 1918 and again in 1920, her campaigns were strong efforts and may well have influenced the ultimate choice in each instance.

A large collection of Anne Martin papers are in the Bancroft Library, University of California, Berkeley. See also Anne Martin, "The Story of the Nevada Equal Suffrage Campaign," Austin E. Hutcheson, ed., *University of Nevada Bulletin* (August 1948).—R. R. E.

Martínez, José Antonio (1793-1867). Priest and New Mexico politician. The most enigmatic figure of nineteenth-century New Mexico was Father Martínez, an ambitious power-seeker, an uncompromising individualist, and a man of intellect in an intellectual wasteland. The son of aristocratic and wealthy Don Severino Martínez, he was born in the village of Abiquiu in northern New Mexico. In 1804 the family moved to Taos (in present New Mexico), which except for brief periods was Martínez's base of activity thereafter. In 1817 he began studies for the priesthood at a seminary in Durango, Mexico; and after what he himself described as a brilliant academic career was ordained as a presbyter (honorary title for priests of exceptional merit) in 1822. For the next several years he served in various New Mexican parishes, becoming curate of Taos in 1830. Active in politics, he was a deputy in the territorial legislature during 1830 and 1831 under the system created by the Mexican republic. A sizable estate inherited from his father was expanded through his own business acumen, adding to his stature as one of the most influential men in the Rio Arriba, or northern country. From his wealth he made generous contributions to the state, to charity, and to promising young men of his parish studying for the priesthood. For a while he owned a printing press and briefly in 1835 published a small periodical, *El Crepúsculo de la Libertad.*

Father Martínez apparently played a significant role in the New Mexican civil disturbance of 1837, which resulted in the death of Governor Albino Pérez, although his precise part remains speculative. Likewise he may have been involved in the Taos revolt of 1847, following occupation of the territory by American forces. Governor Charles Bent, who was assassinated on this occasion, was a bitter foe of Martínez and previously had stated, "He is more sincerely devoted to Bacchus than any of the other gods," and "The priest will spare no means to injure me." Again, though, the part Martínez played in this event remains obscure.

What emerges with clarity are the priest's moral imperfections. With no attempt at secrecy, he maintained a harem and fathered several children, one of whom later became a Presbyterian minister. This conduct in no way lessened his popularity among the people, however, and he was elected president of a convention that convened at Santa Fe in 1848 to petition Congress to replace military rule of the territory with a civilian government. When a legislative assembly was convoked in 1851, he was a prominent member.

Father Martínez met his match when reform-minded Jean Baptiste Lamy became New Mexico's first bishop in 1853. A prolonged struggle between the two powerful churchmen brought about Martínez's excommunication in 1858, causing a schism in the Taos parish. When he died at the age of seventy-four, he was buried by a faithful protégé, Father Mariano Lucero. Martínez's grave lies near that of Kit Carson in the Taos cemetery.

An account of Martínez's early career in his own words is translated by Cecil V. Romero in "Apologia of Presbyter Antonio J. Martínez," *New Mexico Historical Review*, vol. 3 (1928). A new interpretation of his controversial activities appears in E. K. Francis, "Padre Martínez: A New Mexican Myth," *New Mexico Historical Review*, vol. 31 (1956).—M. Sı.

Martínez, María Montoya (1881?-   ). Potter of San Ildefonso Pueblo in northern New Mexico. Martínez is credited not only with great artistic skill but with having spirited the revival of exceptionally fine quality pottery among potters in her own and other pueblos of the Southwest.

In 1908 archaeologists of the school of American Research found some unshaped, prehistorically prepared pottery clay in a cave in the Rito de los Frijoles. The clay was given to María (or Po-vi-ka, as she is known to her neighbors) and her husband, Julian, to see what they could do with it. Using a method popular in the first decade of the twentieth century, they made a few pieces of pottery with highly successful results. This success apparently inspired María and some of the other potters of area to try for bigger and better things.

According to Alice Marriott, an Oklahoma anthropologist, Martínez discovered accidentally the technique for making her now precious black-on-black ware (matte black-on-polished black). The first black pieces produced by María and her husband were the result of an inadvertent smothering of the fire with fine particles of manure toward the end of the burn. The heavy black smoke that was produced penetrated the vessels inside and out, making them a dense black. At a later date, sometime in 1918 or 1919, Julian, on a whim, painted a design on one of María's polished pots. After firing, the design appeared as a dull black (matte) on the highly lustrous black background. Since that first pot was made, María and Julian consistently strove toward higher quality and excellence of design. After Julian's death, María worked with her daughter-in-law, Santana, then her son, Popovi Da, and her grandson, Tony Da. Today, the results of their labor are works of art that, accordingly, command high prices.

Martínez's skill brought her many awards and honors, including an award from the American Institute of Architects, the prestigious *Palmes Academiques* awarded to her by France, and an honorary doctor of fine arts degree from New Mexico State University.

See Alice Marriott, *María: The Potter of San Ildefonso* (1948).—B. P. D. and M. L.

Maryland, settlement of. George Calvert, first Lord Baltimore (1580?-1632), was a man of vision and energy. In the early years of the seventeenth century, Calvert concluded that an American colony might fulfill two dreams that had always been close to his heart. He hoped that a settlement would become both a refuge for his fellow Catholics persecuted in England and also a great feudal seigniory bringing wealth and power to his family. During the late 1620s he personally attempted to establish a colony in southern Newfoundland, called Avalon, but unfortunately he found that "from the middle of October to the middst of May there is a sadd face of wynter upon all this land." Leaving Newfoundland to the local fishermen, Calvert asked the crown for a grant south of Virginia. Instead, he received a charter in 1632 for ten million acres named Mary Land in honor of Charles I's Catholic wife. The location of the grant was determined in part by England's desire to block Dutch expansion in the New World. Whatever his motives, Charles I thought he was being generous by offering Lord Baltimore all the land between the fortieth parallel and the "first fountain" of the Potomac River, and it was only when people later discovered that the river curved northward that they realized that Maryland was one of the smaller American colonies.

The Maryland charter was an anachronism. It made Baltimore absolute lord and proprietor in the manner of a fourteenth-century bishop. His powers were immense. He owned the land, controlled the government, appointed the officials, laid out the towns, established the courts, and drafted the laws. This autonomy suited the proprietor's plans well, and there is evidence that he himself may have written the charter.

Cecilius Calvert, second Lord Baltimore (1605?-75), who directed the colony after his father's death in 1632, hoped to create a feudal pattern of settlement, placing the majority of the population under tenurial obligation to a small group of manor lords. Any man who transported five people to Maryland was promised two thousand acres and the right to erect a manor "with all such royalties and privileges as are usually belonging to manors in England." Liberal headrights were granted to individual settlers, but all colonists, regardless of status, had to pay a quitrent to the proprietor. This feudal system, so neat on paper, was the source of contention in Maryland for more than a hundred and fifty years.

Despite Baltimore's plans, Maryland's society looked more like Virginia's than that of a medieval seigniory. In fact, when Robert Beverley wrote his famous *History of Virginia* in 1705, he observed, "I shall be talking about Virginia, though you may consider at the same time that there cannot be much difference between this and Maryland." In both colonies tobacco was king. Small plantations, relying on slave labor, were scattered throughout Maryland, and by 1660 the county court, not the manor, had become the dominant form of local government. Maryland was never as prosperous as Virginia, however. A study by Aubrey C. Land has revealed that during the 1690s more than seventy-five percent of the estates in Maryland were worth less than one hundred pounds—a sum barely sufficient to sustain a marginal existence. As in other colonies, there were a few very wealthy men who dominated politics as well as commerce.

During the early years of settlement, Baltimore tried to maintain absolute control over Maryland, but the colonists stubbornly, often violently, challenged both his religious and government policies. Baltimore hoped that Protestants and Catholics could live in peace in the New World, and he instructed his first governor, "suffer no scandall nor offence to be given to any of the Protestants." In 1649 the second Lord Baltimore, now proprietor, drafted the Toleration Act, giving freedom of worship to anyone who believed in the Trinity. However, neither the Catholics nor the Protestants saw the virtue of tolerance. In 1641 the proprietor was forced to curb the Jesuits, and in 1652 a group of Puritans, led by William Claiborne, seized the entire colony, holding it until 1657. Maryland's government was another source of conflict. Baltimore's charter stated that he, as the proprietor, had to ask the colonists' "advice and consent" before making laws. Baltimore interpreted this requirement to mean that he had the right to initiate all legislation and that the freeholders could only accept or reject what was presented to them. But the representatives of the freemen who formed the lower house of the legislature thought they deserved a larger voice in colonial affairs. In 1658, after a decade of quibbling, the

Maryland delegates declared themselves the "highest court of Judicature" and "without dependence on any other Power in the Province." Only the king's timely intervention preserved Baltimore's full charter powers.

In the years following the Restoration, the second Lord Baltimore attempted to strengthen his control over Maryland by appointing his own family to important government positions, especially to places on the governor's council. The proprietor had reluctantly given up his plan for a feudal society, and his main concern was with the money that came from the collection of quitrents and the sale of land. The members of the lower house, however, continued to demand a greater degree of self-government. In 1669 they submitted a list of grievances, mostly economic, to Baltimore, and although he ignored these complaints, the delegates were not easily discouraged. Minor insurrections occurred in 1676 and 1681, and in 1689 there was a full-scale rebellion. The leader, John Coode, organized a group called the Protestant Association and seized power. The rebels protested the inadequate defenses against the Indians, the low tobacco prices, the number of Catholic officeholders, and the proprietor's high quitrents. English administrators, tired of the confusion in Maryland, declared the province a royal colony in 1691. The third Baltimore's loss was not as great as it might appear, however, for he retained ownership of the land.

Benedict Calvert, fourth Lord Baltimore, regained the government of Maryland in 1716 by becoming a Protestant and by supporting the new king, George I. He quickly discovered, however, that proprietary rule was as unpopular as it had ever been. The historian Charles A. Barker explained, "At no time in the eighteenth century, from the restoration of proprietary government to the Revolution, was there even an interval of real political peace in Maryland." It is important to note that these political battles were not fought between eastern and western interests, or between democrats and aristocrats, but between the wealthiest planters in Maryland and the Calvert family.

On the early years of Maryland history, see Charles M. Andrews, *The Colonial Period of American History*, vol. III (1936), and Wesley Frank Craven, *The Southern Colonies in the Seventeenth Century, 1607-1689* (1949). For the later period, see Charles A. Barker, *The Background of Revolution in Maryland* (1940), and Aubrey C. Land, "Economic Base and Social Structure: The Northern Chesapeake in the Eighteenth Century," *Journal of Economic History*, vol. 25 (1965).—T. H. B.

Mason-Dixon line. The surveying of the Mason-Dixon line was the result of a dispute that arose between Cecilius Calvert and William Penn in 1681 over the exact location of the boundary between their respective grants in the neighborhood of 40 degrees north latitude. This argument continued between the families for more than a century with a considerable amount of surveying, petitioning, and argument before the Lords Committee of the Privy Council. Throughout the remainder of the seventeenth century the argument was carried on in a series of conferences, and in 1718 a conference occurred between Governor John Hart of Maryland and Governor William Keith of Pennsylvania. This dispute was passed on from father to son until the two factions signed an agreement in which the Calverts of Maryland acknowledged the rights of the Penns to the lower counties on the Delaware River. Before this happened the situation between the colonies had become so aggravated that the Privy Council prescribed a set of conditions for its settlement.

An established boundary line was now surveyed. Between 1763 and 1768, Jeremiah Dixon and the astronomer Charles Mason located 233 miles of boundary from an agreed point east of the Delaware River to a point just west of the Monongahela River. This survey was confirmed by the king in council on January 11, 1769. In 1779 the issue of extending the Mason-Dixon line westward arose between Virginia and Pennsylvania, and in 1784 it was extended 5 degrees of longitude farther west. Contrary to popular reference, the Mason-Dixon line had no implication of dividing slave and free territory.

See Lawrence H. Gipson, *The British Empire Before the American Revolution*, vol. XI: *The Triumphant Empire: The Rumbling of the Coming Storm, 1766-1770* (1965), and John E. Potter, "Pennsylvania and Virginia Controversy," *Pennsylvania Magazine of History and Biography*, vol. 38.—T. D. C.

Mason Valley Ranch. The Mason Valley Ranch located in Lyon County, ten miles north of Yerington, Nevada, was started in 1860 as a modest spread by N. Henry A. Mason, a native of Tennessee who had lived briefly in California before settling in an area eventually known as Mason Valley. In 1871 he began buying ranches to expand his ranges. By 1880 he owned more than thirty thousand head of cattle, more than ninety thousand acres, and operated the largest ranches in Nevada. The great drought and the severe winter of 1889-90 threw him deeply into debt, and he sold out in 1890 to Henry Miller, a California cattle king.—J. A. S.

Massachusetts, settlement of. Captain John Smith's *A Description of New England* (1616) was the first English publication to use the name Massachusetts, a Natick Indian word for "At the Great Hill." He wrote of the region in glowing terms: "the Countrie of the Massachusets . . . is a Paradise of all those parts. For, heere are many Iles all planted with corne; groves, mulberries, savage gardens, and good harbors." Despite Smith's enthusiasm, interest in Massachusetts developed slowly. In 1620 the English king granted all New England to forty aristocrats who called themselves the Council for New England, and this body in turn issued patents to various groups for land and commercial rights. One such patent went to the Dorchester Adventurers, a small company that in 1623 tried unsuccessfully to establish a fishing community at Cape Ann. The company's most energetic promoter, the Reverend John White (1575-1648), was not discouraged by the failure, and during the 1620s he continued to praise the area, especially among people of Puritan leanings. Although White never moved to the New World, a contemporary correctly described him as "one of the chief founders of the Massachusetts Colony."

The founding of Massachusetts is a chapter in the story of the English Reformation. By 1620 a large group of Englishmen, whom their detractors called Puritans, had become convinced that the ecclesiastical reforms begun under Henry VIII and Elizabeth had not gone far enough toward scriptural purity. They regarded the nation's failure as a serious matter, for they believed that

God had formed a special covenant with England. The Puritans explained that the Lord expected a covenanted people to obey his commandments and would punish them if they disappointed him. As they looked around them, they concluded that the country was growing worse, not better, which they interpreted as the Lord's increasing displeasure everywhere. There was a major depression in the woolen industry. Charles I took a Catholic for his queen. Public morality seemed as low as anyone could remember. But what worried the Puritans most was that none of the leaders of church and state were attempting to curb the spread of corruption or to establish God's law. The crisis came to a head in 1629, when Charles decided that he would rule without Parliament. John Winthrop, future governor of Massachusetts, declared, ". . . I am veryly perswaded, God will bringe some heavye Affliction upon this lande, and that speedylye."

These seventeenth-century Puritans were not the pleasure-hating fundamentalists that H. L. Mencken and others have described. Winthrop and his friends loved their women, liked strong drink, played games, wore colorful garments, and respected the powers of human reason. The Lord had created things like women and drink for man to enjoy. But the Puritans were always conscious of a higher purpose—the glorification of God—and they thought that sin occurred only when earthly pleasures became ends in themselves. The Puritans recognized God's omnipotence and accepted the fact that they were helpless to alter the fate that he had predestined for them.

In 1628 a group of Puritans formed the New England Company and took over the rights of the moribund Dorchester Adventurers. This new commercial venture obtained a patent from the Council for New England, which served until March 1629, when the company received a more secure charter directly from Charles I. This grant gave the stockholders control over the land between the Merrimack and the Charles rivers and from sea to sea. The Massachusetts Bay Company, as the venture was now called, had full authority to "establishe all manner of wholesome and reasonable orders" as long as they were not contrary to the laws of England. There was a curious omission in the charter, however, for unlike other corporations founded in this period, the Massachusetts Bay Company was not required to hold its meetings in London. This omission was probably no clerical accident, for in August 1629 twelve leading Puritans, including Winthrop and Thomas Dudley, signed the Cambridge Agreement, promising to move to America if the charter went with them. The company's stockholders, fearful that the Anglican archbishop, William Laud, would get wind of the project, quickly voted to transfer to the New World. The king's commercial patent was about to become a civil constitution for a Puritan commonwealth.

The Puritans of Massachusetts did not leave England to escape persecution or to search out new commercial opportunities. They believed that they were engaged in the Lord's work; they were on a mission. The Separatist Pilgrims who had landed at Plymouth in 1620 maintained that the Church of England was far too corrupt ever to be saved, but the men who settled in Massachusetts a decade later disagreed. They thought that the church was in bad shape, but it was not beyond reform. They argued that a small group—a "saving remnant"—could establish the type of church that God demanded and that this example would serve as a model for other Englishmen to follow. As the Puritans sailed in 1630 they issued a statement protesting their loyalty to the Church of England, "our deare Mother." In mid-Atlantic, Governor Winthrop reminded the colonists of their special purpose: "wee shall be as a Citty upon a Hill, the eies of all people are uppon us." These non-separating Puritans intended to fulfill the English Reformation in the New World, aware that if they failed, "wee shall be made a story and a by-word through the world." As the historian Perry Miller has explained, the Puritans' sense of mission influenced their attitudes about America and about themselves for well over a century.

In June 1630 the first large group of Puritan settlers landed at Salem, where an advance party under the direction of John Endecott (1589?-1665) had already built some homes. This was the beginning of the decade-long Great Migration, during which time some twenty thousand English Puritans settled in the Massachusetts Bay Colony. Winthrop thought that Salem was not a suitable site for a populous plantation, and he led most of the colonists south to the area around Boston. Only a few of the men who arrived with Winthrop had been shareholders, or "freemen," in the Massachusetts Bay Company, and technically, it would have been possible for a small clique to control the colony's government. But Winthrop realized that there could be no meaningful civil obedience without voluntary consent, and during the first year he opened the freemanship to many persons who could never have afforded to become part of the original company. After 1631 only adult male church members were accepted as freemen, but still, the franchise in Massachusetts was proportionally larger than that of England. The voters annually selected a governor, a deputy governor, and a group of assistants (often called magistrates). By 1634 the freemen had grown far too numerous to attend meetings of the General Court, and they began to elect deputies in the various towns to represent their legislative interests. A decade later a fight between the deputies and the magistrates caused the General Court to split into two separate houses.

Massachusetts possessed a large electorate, but it was not a "democracy"—at least, not in any modern sense of that word. The people selected their magistrates, but those magistrates were responsible to God, not the voters, for their actions in office. Winthrop promised the freemen that "we shall govern you and judge your causes by the rules of God's laws and our own, according to our best skill," but as governor, he would not tolerate criticism of his policy decisions. While this government was arbitrary, it was. not oppressive, for most of the citizens were Puritans and thus shared common notions about the nature of the civil state.

The CONGREGATIONALISTS of Massachusetts tried to avoid the ecclesiastical errors made in England. Each Puritan congregation was an independent body, controlled by the decisions of its own membership. Gone were the bishops with authority over individual churches; gone too were the ecclesiastical courts, which had silenced puritan ministers in the mother country. The American Puritans believed that church member-

ship should be restricted to persons who could prove that they had been selected by God for salvation, that they were "visible saints." Many English Puritans were bothered by the exclusive membership of the Congregational churches, declaring that the church sacraments should be open to everyone, but the colonists insisted that they had taken a great step toward scriptural purity. The churches of Massachusetts were strong, but Massachusetts was not a theocracy. Not only were all church officials barred from civil posts, but also no church censure, including excommunication, could affect a man's civil rights. It was the magistrates, not the ministers, who banished Roger Williams and Anne Hutchinson from the Bay Colony.

Puritans settled in compact units, and as Perry Miller has observed, "The lone horseman, the single trapper, the solitary hunter was not a figure of the Puritan frontier." The General Court granted townships to groups of men called town proprietors, who in turn distributed this acreage among individual families. Since most adult males were also proprietors during the seventeenth century, this system worked harmoniously. It was not until the next century, when Massachusetts began to sell townships to absentee proprietors for speculative purposes, that friction developed between the settlers and the proprietors. Villages were usually built around a meetinghouse, which served both as a church and a town hall. Most communities set tracts of land aside, called the commons, for future needs. Studies by Kenneth Lockridge and Philip Greven have shown that there was very little geographic mobility within the Bay Colony before 1700, and if a family moved at all, it generally went to a neighboring village. The wilderness to the west apparently had very little attraction for the Puritan, and one typical minister explained, "People are ready to run wild into the woods again and to be as Heathenish as ever, if you do not prevent it."

During the 1630s the colonists prospered by selling their agricultural surplus to new immigrants, but when the Great Migration stopped in 1640, the Puritan commonwealth was forced to find new commercial opportunities. The sea held the answer. Boston merchants soon discovered markets in Spain and the West Indies for the fish, foodstuffs, barrel staves, and livestock that the Bay Colony produced. By the end of the seventeenth century, the ships of Massachusetts were visiting ports on four continents. Nevertheless, the overwhelming majority of the colonists were farmers.

Edmund S. Morgan once wrote that it could be argued that we "know more about the Puritans than sane men should want to know." There are excellent studies on almost every aspect of the history of early Massachusetts. Some of the best are George L. Haskins, *Law and Authority in Early Massachusetts: A Study in Tradition and Design* (1960); Perry Miller, *The New England Mind: From Colony to Province* (1953); Edmund S. Morgan, *The Puritan Dilemma, The Story of John Winthrop* (1958); and Samuel Eliot Morison, *Builders of the Bay Colony* (1930). Also see Philip J. Greven, Jr., "Family Structure in Seventeenth-Century Andover, Massachusetts," *William and Mary Quarterly*, vol. 23 (1966); Alan Heimert, "Puritanism, The Wilderness, and the Frontier," *New England Quarterly*, vol. 26 (1953); and Kenneth Lockridge, "The Population of Dedham, Massachusetts, 1636-1736," *Economic History Review*, vol. 19 (1966). For information of Winthrop, see the *Winthrop Papers* (1929-   ) and James K. Hosmer, ed., *Winthrop's Journal "History of New England," 1630-1649* (1908). —T. H. B.

Masterson, Bat [Bartholomew] (1853-1921). Gambler, lawman, and newspaperman. Masterson was neither plaster saint nor dapper fop. He was simply a man who did good things and bad, won a reputation as a good lawman, and outlived his time. He was born on a farm in the Province of Quebec, Canada, and christened Bartholomew Masterson, a name which he later changed to William Barclay Masterson for reasons never explained. He grew up in a large family on farms in New York, Illinois, and Kansas. In 1872 he and his older brother Ed left the family home in Wichita for a more exciting life. They worked for the Santa Fe Railroad as graders that year and collected their wages at gunpoint the following spring after the contractor skipped out without paying them.

Bat was a buffalo hunter in 1873 and 1874, operating out of Dodge City, Kansas. When the hunters penetrated restricted Indian lands in 1874, he went with them and was present at the battle of Adobe Walls when the hunters were attacked by Comanche and Kiowa. Later that year he enlisted as an army scout and served during the Red River War with the Southern Plains tribes.

When his enlistment as a scout expired, Masterson remained in Texas until January 1876, when a bloody confrontation changed the direction of his life. At Sweetwater (later Mobeetie), he was critically wounded in a gunfight with Corporal Melvin A. King over the affections of Molly Brennan, a dance-hall girl. The soldier and the girl died in the fight. When Masterson recovered, he went to Dodge City, where he was briefly a policeman. In the fall of 1876, he was on the move again, but by 1877 he was back in Dodge with enough money to invest in a saloon. In June 1877 he was arrested for interfering with the arrest of a noted frontier vagabond named Bobby Gill, but he was soon appointed undersheriff of Ford County by Charles Bassett. In October of that year he was elected sheriff by only three votes.

Bat's term as sheriff proved to be a busy one. Ford County was large and so was the job. He chased train robbers in the early spring. His brother Ed, now the town marshal, was killed by Texas cowboys in April. Ed's death deeply affected Bat, but stories that he was the man who killed Ed's murderers are doubtful. In September, Dull Knife's Cheyenne passed through Ford County on their flight north from Indian Territory and in October, Bat led the posse that captured the killer of Dora Hand, a well-known Dodge City personality. In January 1879 he was in Colorado chasing a horse thief. Before the month was out he added a commission as a deputy United States marshal to his credentials. The next month he was delegated to bring seven Cheyenne prisoners to Dodge for trial for depredations committed during the Dull Knife raid. In March he took time off to head the forces of the Santa Fe Railroad in its war with the Denver, Rio Grande and Western Railroad.

By the time the election for sheriff rolled around that year, some of Bat's popularity had worn off in spite of his rather impressive record. For one thing, people thought he had spent too much money as sheriff, particularly on the Cheyenne trial, which had netted few results. For another, Bat faced opposition from the area outside of Dodge and local opposition from the so-called reform element in Dodge, which felt that Bat was too close to Mayor James H. "Dog" Kelley's city administration, known locally as "the Gang." Masterson was defeated by George T. Hinkle. Bat let everyone know how he felt in explicit terms and, when his term was up, shook off the Kansas dust and headed for Leadville, Colorado, where he spent his time gambling.

After Dodge, Bat's life seemed rather tame, and when he was asked to help Billy Thompson, the troublesome younger brother of his friend Ben Thompson, Bat responded. Billy had been shot in a gunfight at Ogallala, Nebraska, and Ben feared he would be lynched. Bat went to Ogallala and spirited Billy out of town with the help of Buffalo Bill Cody, who lived nearby. After Thompson was safely out of Ogallala, Bat visited his old stomping grounds at Dodge City. In February 1881 he followed Wyatt Earp and Luke Short to Tombstone to work with Wyatt at the gambling tables at the Oriental Saloon. But in April he was called back to Dodge by his brother James, who was in trouble with his partner, A. J. Peacock, and with Al Updegraph. Bat's arrival in Dodge sparked a gunfight in which Updegraph was wounded. Bat was fined ten dollars and costs.

Masterson was in and out of Dodge after that, but he lived in Colorado, serving for a time as a deputy sheriff at Las Animas, Colorado. In 1883 he was instrumental in preventing the extradition of Doc Holliday from Colorado to Arizona. Doc had just arrived in Denver after fleeing Arizona with Wyatt Earp when he was arrested on trumped-up charges designed to hold him in custody until he could be extradited to Arizona to stand trial for murder. Bat interceded with the governor of Colorado and convinced him that Doc could not receive fair trial in Arizona. The governor refused to grant extradition.

The next year, Bat was called to Dodge City by his friend Luke Short. Short had been run out of Dodge City by the reform element and felt that he had been unfairly treated. He asked Masterson to help him reestablish himself in Dodge. Bat and Luke called on the governor of Kansas and presented Luke's case. Then Bat wired Wyatt Earp, Doc Holliday, and an assortment of other gunmen, who moved into Dodge quietly. Under the pressure, Luke Short was reinstated in Dodge City and the Dodge City War came to an end. The next year, Bat decided to become a newspaperman, but his paper, the *Vox Populi*, published a single issue. In 1886, in a move that shocked everyone, Bat suddenly became a prohibitionist and renounced demon rum. Even more incredible, he was appointed a special officer, and he closed the Dodge City saloons. His advocacy of prohibition did not last, however, and the following year he turned up in Fort Worth, Texas, working with Luke Short at the White Elephant Saloon. He was there when Short killed Jim Courtright. But these excursions were only visits. Bat had become a resident of Denver. Occasionally he wore a badge and apparently served as marshal of Creede, Colorado, in 1892, but mostly he gambled and basked in his reputation as a sporting man. For a time he was associated with prominent and respectable gambling houses. Unfortunately he began to drink heavily and became involved with some unsavory gamblers. The whole gambling fraternity was losing its respectability by the turn of the century, and in 1902 Bat was asked to leave Denver.

Turning his back on the West, Masterson went to New York City. He had his troubles there too, until Theodore Roosevelt appointed him a deputy United States marshal for the southern district of New York. He was later removed by President Taft. Masterson made numerous acquaintances among New York's social set, including the writer Alfred Henry Lewis, who turned the gambler into a newspaperman. Lewis wrote numerous stories about "Mr. Masterson," as he invariably called him, and published a novel called *The Sunset Trail* about him. At Lewis' insistence, and in an effort to help his friend out of financial straits, Masterson was persuaded to write a series of articles about his gunfighter friends for *Human Life Magazine*. The series of articles included sketches of Luke Short, Wyatt Earp, Doc Holliday, Bill Tilghman, Ben Thompson, and William F. Cody, under the title "Famous Gun Fighters of the Western Frontier." In the articles, Bat reminisced about his days on the frontier and commented on the qualities that made a man a good gunfighter. In time Bat became a rather prominent journalist. He became sports editor of the New York *Morning Telegraph*. He was acknowledged as a leading authority on boxing, and his columns were frequently interesting and pungent. Once he was convicted of contempt of court when he opined in his column that a certain criminal had not received justice.

In his last years Bat Masterson was a crusty old man who drank too much and still managed to get into trouble occasionally. The West was something he tried to forget. He had little patience with the people who were constantly pestering him, and once he sued a fight manager who had called him a murderer and a bad man. But in spite of the troubles, Masterson achieved a kind of respectability that most of his frontier contemporaries only dreamed of. In October 1921 he had a heart attack at his desk and died. There was a touch of tragedy in the cynical words found written on a sheet of paper on the desk: "There are many in this old world of ours who hold that things break about even for us. I have observed, for example, that we all get about the same amount of ice. The rich get it in the summer-time and the poor get it in the winter."

The only biography is Richard O'Connor, *Bat Masterson* (1957), which leaves much to be desired. See also Dale T. Schoenberger, *The Gunfighters* (1972); and George G. Thompson, *Bat Masterson: The Dodge City Years* (1943). A handy reference is Nyle H. Miller and Joseph W. Snell, *Why the West Was Wild* (1963). —G. L. R.

Masterson, Louis. Pen name of **Kjell Hallbing** (1935-). Novelist. Masterson followed a banking career until he began to write western novels. Masterson, who still lives in his native Norway, completed sixty-two western novels by 1972, when he was thirty-seven, without ever having visited the United States. He is Norway's most widely read author, having sold over fifteen million books about his fictional western hero Morgan Kane. Since 1970 his novels have begun to appear in English translation and have been immensely popular in the British Commonwealth countries. His prolific output is the result of the short time he spends on writing his novels, which he claims take between four days and four weeks to write. In reaction to conventional Ameri-

can western fiction, he became one of the first western novelists to describe his hero's sex life.—P. L. N.

Matador Ranch. The Matador Ranch, located in Motley County about three miles south of Matador, was actually founded in 1879 when H. H. Campbell and A. M. Britton bought from a buffalo hunter the range rights to a large area in the Texas Panhandle. These men then purchased about eight thousand head of cattle and operated the ranch until 1882, when they sold the entire investment to the Matador Land and Cattle Company of Dundee, Scotland. Under the management of Murdo Mackenzie, the Matador became one of the largest of the Texas ranches. The Scottish investors capitalized their enterprise at $2.5 million and by 1884 owned more than 375,000 acres and seventy-five thousand head of cattle. The ranch grew rapidly; by 1891 it included 540,000 acres of deeded land and nearly 200,000 of leased land in the more northern ranges. The ranch covered parts of several counties, including Motley, Cottle, Dickens, and Floyd. By 1925 the company owned 830,000 acres and held leases to more than 700,000 additional acres in South Dakota and Montana. In 1951 the business was sold to an American syndicate and subdivided. The core of the old ranch is still in operation.

See N. M. Pearce, *The Matador Land and Cattle Company* (1964).—J. A. S.

Mather, David (1845-?). Gambler, lawman, and outlaw. Mather, remembered by a contemporary as "a very wicked man," was a direct descendant of Cotton Mather, Puritan patriarch and theologian. He was born in Connecticut. Beyond that, little is known of him before 1873, when he reportedly rode with cattle rustlers in Arkansas. He was on the buffalo range in 1874 and inevitably drifted into the cattle town Dodge City. He stayed on as a gambler and sometime peace officer. Not long after his arrival in Dodge, Mather had a fight with another gambler who nearly killed him with a knife. After he recovered, he became a leader of a vigilance committee organized to deal with horse thieves. One of the most popular stories about Mather's sojourn in Dodge City involved his encounter with a traveling evangelist. He was persuaded by pranksters, one of whom was Bat Masterson, to attend a service. The preacher devoted his best efforts to the salvation of Mather's soul. In the end Mather announced that he was converted. Pulling his revolver, he declared that he was ready to die and invited the minister and deacons to join him. As his gun roared, the churchmen departed unceremoniously through the windows.

In 1878 Mather was in Mobeetie, Texas, where he and Wyatt Earp operated a con game, selling "gold bricks" to gullible cowhands. The next year he went to Las Vegas, New Mexico, where he divided his time between wearing a badge and running from it. He was accused of robbing a train late in 1879, but the charges were dropped for lack of evidence. On the side of the law in January 1880, Mather accompanied Marshal Joe Carson into the Close and Patterson Saloon to disarm the Henry gang, who were wearing guns in defiance of local ordinances. In the melee that followed Marshal Carson was killed by Tom Henry. Mather killed one of the gang and critically wounded another. Three days later he killed another man in a gunfight. In February the two surviving killers of Marshal Carson were captured and returned to the Las Vegas jail to join their wounded friend. Mather was in the mob that dragged them from the jail and lynched them.

Criticized by the local papers for "promiscuous shooting," Mather left Las Vegas in March 1880 and spent the rest of the year drifitng from New Mexico to Kansas, Colorado, and, finally, Texas. In 1881 he became assistant marshal of El Paso. That did not last long. He quarreled with the city fathers about his salary and resigned in a huff. He next tried pimping for a while and nearly got himself shot by a prostitute when he skipped town with "the wages of her shame," as the Las Vegas *Gazette* put it. In 1883 Mather returned to Dodge City, where he was appointed assistant marshal and deputy sheriff. In February 1884 he lost his job as assistant marshal when the city administration changed. He was soon embroiled in a quarrel with his successor, Tom Nixon, over business affairs and his attention to Nixon's wife. On July 18, 1884, Nixon took a shot at Mather and missed. Three days later Mather shot Nixon dead, but he was acquitted.

In May 1885 Mather was involved in another shooting, which left one man dead and three, including himself, wounded. This incident grew out of a card game. Mather was arraigned for murder and released on bail. But when it was reported that he had a list of men he intended to kill in Dodge, Marshal Bill Tilghman forced him to leave Dodge, this time for good.

Mather's trail is obscure after that. He was reported to be city marshal of New Kiowa, Kansas, briefly and was in Long Pine, Nebraska, in 1887. But then he simply vanished. One tale says he served in the Canadian Northwest Mounted Police, and another claims he died in Alberta, Canada, in 1916, but neither story has been confirmed.

See Colin Rickards, *Mysterious Dave Mather* (1968). —G. L. R.

Mather, Samuel Livingstone. See GREAT LAKES, MEN OF THE.

Mathews, Alfred Edward (1831-1874). Topographical artist, painter, and lithographer. Born in Bristol, England, Mathews was brought to the United States as an infant and grew up in Rochester, Ohio. Before the Civil War he traveled about the country as a bookseller and painter and served with the Union army during the war, producing a number of battle sketches later incorporated into a panorama of the campaigns in the South. Immediately after the war he went into the West, established a studio in Denver, Colorado, and for several years devoted himself to the production of lithographic views of the western scene. Many of these were issued separately and others in book form, including his *Pencil Sketches of Colorado* and *Pencil Sketches of Montana*, both published in 1866, and *Gems of Rocky Mountain Scenery* in 1869. From about 1869 to 1872, he was engaged in promoting the settlement of Canon City, Colorado, and later visited southern California.

See Robert Taft, *Artists and Illustrators of the Old West, 1850-1900* (1953).—D. C. H.

Maxwell, Lucien Bonaparte (1818-1875). Landowner in Southwest. Maxwell was of French and Irish ancestry. From his birthplace in Kaskaskia, Illinois, he early went west to join the American Fur Company on a two-year trapping expedition. In 1842, while serving John C. Frémont, he became a friend and confidant

of Kit Carson. After trapping in the Sangre de Cristo Mountains, Maxwell settled in Taos, New Mexico, where he married María de la Luz Beaubien in 1844. From his father-in-law, Carlos Beaubien, he acquired an interest in the huge Beaubien-Miranda land grant east of Taos, and by buying up the rights of other heirs after Beaubien's death, he became sole owner by 1865. This tract, set at about 97,000 acres in 1869, extended from present Springer, New Mexico, northward into Colorado. Indeed, he became the largest individual landowner in the United States.

Maxwell built a lavish mansion at Cimarron, east of Taos, to serve as headquarters for his vast estate, and his largess and hospitality to travelers became legendary. To his extensive ranching, farming, and mercantile interests was added mining when gold was discovered in the western part of the grant in 1867. Sale of real estate and business ventures in the new boom camp of Elizabethtown further augmented his fortunes. But pressures of administering such extensive operations finally induced Maxwell to sell his entire interest in the grant to a group of capitalists in 1870 for the sum of $1,350,000, and thus began the complicated history of the MAXWELL LAND GRANT COMPANY.

Maxwell dissipated the money from the sale through poor investments, so that he had to return to ranching, purchasing old Fort Sumner and adjacent lands from the federal government. Here on the Pecos River in southern New Mexico he died, his reputation secure as one of the most respected and enterprising businessmen who contributed to land development in the Southwest.

Two significant volumes treat Maxwell's career: William A. Keleher, *Maxwell Land Grant: A New Mexico Item* (1949); and Jim Berry Pearson, *The Maxwell Land Grant* (1961).—M. Si.

Maxwell Land Grant Company. Northern New Mexico and southern Colorado have been the scene of persistent attempts by visionary capitalists to build a regional empire. One of the most important phases of this imperial enterprise was speculation in Spanish land grants, which reached a peak in the 1870s and 1880s. The complex history of the Maxwell Land Grant Company readily reveals the grandiose dreams, shady maneuvers, political intrigue, and violence that characterized this exercise in empire-building.

The grant was originally awarded in 1841 by Mexican governor Manuel Armijo, himself a speculator in land grants, to Carlos Beaubien, a prominent Taos merchant, and Guadelupe Miranda, the collector of customs for New Mexico. Following Beaubien's death in 1864, Lucien Bonaparte Maxwell, his son-in-law, bought out the claims of his relatives as well as the land owned by Miranda. Maxwell established himself as a virtual prince on his extensive holdings, which were set at 22 leagues (roughly 97,000 acres) in 1869 under the terms of the Colonization Law of 1824. Maxwell was alerted to the great value of his land, as well as to its potential dangers, when gold was discovered in 1867 and prospectors swarmed onto his estate without regard for his claim to ownership. Maxwell saw an opportunity to make a fortune by selling the grant, and by 1869 word of the land's availability had reached four groups of investors—two American and two European.

The two groups of American investors were centered in Denver and Santa Fe, and their collaboration demonstrated the meaninglessness of political borders for the farsighted developers of the region. The Colorado group was headed by Jerome B. Chaffee, a wealthy mine owner, and the New Mexicans were led by Stephen B. Elkins. In 1869 Maxwell granted an option to buy to Chaffee and Elkins, and a year later the purchase was concluded for $1,350,000. The buyers formed the Maxwell Land Grant and Railroad Company and set about immediately to gain a return on their investment.

The purchasers, well aware of the vagaries of the land-grant title, sought to increase their holdings by having the grant surveyed as a 2,000,000-acre plot rather than the 97,000 acres to which Maxwell had been limited in 1869. Before confirmation of this enlarged survey was received, the grant was sold in April 1870 to English purchasers, who in turn persuaded a group of Amsterdam financiers to handle the mortgage. Stock was issued for $5 million, and William Jackson Palmer, then superintendent of the Kansas Pacific Railroad, was elected president of the company.

In 1871 the company suffered the first of its many difficulties when Secretary of the Interior Columbus Delano ruled that the grant covered only 97,000 acres. Faced with disaster, the company turned to political influence in Congress to secure its claim. Chaffee became delegate from Colorado Territory in 1871, and Elkins, running on an unbeatable platform of statehood and settlement of land claims, was elected delegate from New Mexico in 1872. In order to exert the tremendous influence necessary for a favorable solution of the land question, Elkins and his fellow investors needed a well-oiled organization of legal, political, financial, and journalistic talent. Out of this need emerged the Santa Fe Ring, a diverse group of men united by an interest in the exploitation of the area's resources.

Despite an impressive campaign to secure confirmation of the enlarged survey, the company was faced with bankruptcy in 1875. It sold its claim to cover a tax debt, but after a series of smooth legal and financial maneuvers the claim ended up in the hands of Thomas B. Catron, a close friend and former law partner of Elkins. The bankruptcy little altered the structure of the company, for the Dutch bankers managed to regain control from the New Mexican promoters.

Not all of the company's problems were of a strictly financial nature, for several groups opposed the influence of the corporation in general and of the Santa Fe Ring in particular. The Maxwell Company's claims encroached on the lands of settlers who had entered the Cimarron country unaware that they were on private property. This company-squatter conflict was exacerbated by the claims of the gold miners centered at Elizabethtown, which was on company land. Texas ranchers valued the grazing land of the area. In addition, a group of local investors led by Frank Springer opposed the control of the company by the Santa Fe Ring, led by Robert Longwill, probate judge of Colfax County. The conflicts between these contentious factions made for a highly volatile situation, which finally erupted in the Colfax County War.

The "war" was in reality a series of assassinations. The first to go was Rev. T. J. Tolby. The Methodist minister was ambushed in September 1875 by two thugs, Cruz Vegan and Manual Cardenas. They were purportedly hired by Longwill and his associates, M. W. Mills, Pancho Griego, and a man named Donahue. During the course of the next two years Vega was hanged by a mob, Cardenas was ambushed on the way to his trial, Griego was killed by Texas gunman Clay Allison, and Longwill fled to the safer environs of Santa Fe. The troubles did not end here, however, for the anti-Ring standard was picked up by Rev. Oscar P. McMains, a vengeful, violent preacher who appointed himself Tolby's avenger. McMains led the mob that lynched Cruz Vega and continued to plague the Maxwell Company for a decade.

The significance of the Colfax County troubles went deeper than the personalities involved. As Howard R. Lamar has remarked, the conflict was between men who held different conceptions of the frontier. On one hand were the settlers, ranchers, and miners who held an "American" or public-domain concept of the frontier. Pitted against them was an organization that saw the region in Spanish-Mexican terms—that is, as private property.

The scene brightened for the Maxwell Land Grant Company in 1879 when United States land commissioner James A. Williamson ruled that court decisions based on a surveyor's recommendation would determine the size and validity of a claim rather than the Colonization Law. The company received a favorable decision based on a new survey done by Elkins and received patents for 1,714,764 acres. In 1887 the company's patent was validated by a Supreme Court decision. Under the control of the Dutch bankers the Maxwell Land Grant Company thrived until well into the twentieth century, parlaying land, cattle, and mining investments into the profitable empire its founders envisioned. The company retired from northern New Mexico in the 1960s, its vast land holdings sold to a diverse group of investors that included Texas oilmen, Phelps-Dodge, and the Boy Scouts of America.

The best history of the grant and the company is Jim B. Pearson, *The Maxwell Land Grant* (1961). William A. Keleher, *Maxwell Land Grant: A New Mexico Item* (1949), and F. Stanley, *The Grant That Maxwell Bought* (1952) are also useful. The best study of the interaction between the potential of the grant and the Santa Fe Ring is in Howard R. Lamar, *The Far Southwest* (1966). Some interesting comments on the role of assassination in New Mexican politics are found in Richard M. Brown, "Historical Patterns of Violence in America," in Hugh D. Graham and Ted R. Gurr, *The History of Violence in America* (1969).—R. B. W.

May, Karl Friedrich (1842–1912). Novelist. May was born in Ernstthal, a small town in the German state of Saxony, the fifth of fourteen children of a weaver family living in extreme poverty. Shortly after his birth he lost his sight, presumably because of malnutrition. But when he was five, a physician succeeded in restoring his eyesight. The young May turned out to be gifted, eager for knowledge, and imaginative. Supported by the church and by his family, which had suffered grave hardships in order to aid him, he entered a teachers' training college in 1857. He passed the final examinations in 1861, thus becoming a candidate for a teacher's post.

May's professional career was terminated, however, before he could become a teacher. After having been convicted in 1862 of the theft of a watch, he spent most of the next thirteen years of his life in prison. Embittered by what he regarded as an unjust court verdict, which closed to him forever the possibility of a teaching career, May came to consider himself an outcast from society. By his own later account he resolved to revenge himself on society and committed during the next years a series of frauds and swindles. He used a variety of assumed names, including that of the Greek god of thieves, Hermes, and false identities, such as that of an official of the Leipzig secret service. In 1865 he was sentenced to four years imprisonment but was released in 1868. In 1870 May was again convicted and this time received four years' penal servitude.

After his release in 1874, May began a new career as a writer. Initially as an editor of various family magazines, then as a free-lance author, he turned out a vast quantity of writing, the quality of which varied greatly. He wrote village tales, short novels, humorous sketches, dime novels, adventure novels, and, at the end of his life, novels in which he employed symbolism. The third edition of his collected works, still in print, comprises seventy volumes.

May gained his fame as a writer for the common people. He had a lasting impact on generations of young Germans through his adventure novels, which were set in the Orient and the American West of the mid-nineteenth century. Between 1887 and 1900, with the aid of atlases, encyclopedias, dictionaries, geographical and ethnological studies, and an inexhaustible imagination, May published numerous adventure novels. Of his more than twenty novels on the American West, the most successful have been *Winnetou, Old Surehand,* and *Der Schatz im Silbersee.* He usually used the form of first-person narrative. Almost every German schoolboy knows the heroic figure of May's American Wild West, Old Shatterhand. A German by birth, Old Shatterhand is strong as a bear and invincible, and constantly proclaims Christian principles. Just as well known is his friend and companion Winnetou, the melancholy and handsome "red gentleman," who has a presentiment of the inevitable decline of the Indians and who, when dying, embraces Christianity. Old Shatterhand is the charismatic leader of a group of white "westmen" such as Old Surehand, Old Firehand, Old Wabble, and Sam Hawkins, whose goal it is to create a just order of Christianity, charity, and humanity in the "Wild West." Although they are armed to the teeth, trigger-happy, and continuously involved in violent actions, the deeds of this group allegedly serve this aim. In constantly changing situations, which follow the same basic pattern, May's "westmen" have ample opportunity to pursue their goal: in the vast expanses between the Mississippi and the Rocky Mountains they fight endless battles against white and red scoundrels.

The Indian tribes in May's novels are aggressive and cruel, but only as a result of circumstances, not because of any inherent wickedness. Driven to the defensive by the white man and by the policies of the railroad companies, they commit their greater crimes only when manipulated by whites for the latter's own selfish purposes. Winnetou, Old Shatterhand's friend, stands between the opposing groups. He has adopted in part the values of the "westmen" without really wanting to become one of them. On the other hand, he is no longer regarded by the Apache as a full member of their tribe,

although he is still their chief. Winnetou recognizes his situation and accepts it silently and in loneliness.

Following the publication of the first volumes of his *Collected Travel-Novels* in 1892, May's popularity grew as quickly as his bank account. He had difficulties in answering the quantities of mail he received from his devoted admirers. Then he made a crucial mistake. Hesitantly at first, then with increased boldness, he began to identify publicly with Old Shatterhand and with Kara Ben Nemsi, the hero of his Oriental novels. Everything which he had described in his novels, he claimed, he had experienced himself. Pictures of May dressed as Old Shatterhand or Kara Ben Nemsi were sent to his admirers. His recently acquired villa was filled ostentatiously with souvenirs from all over the world. With the help of intermediaries, he secured an honorary doctorate from a "Universitas Germana-Americana" in Chicago, finally legitimizing a title which he had used beforehand. In 1899 he traveled for eighteen months in the Orient, allegedly to visit "old friends."

After his return to Germany, the whole fiction crashed. Because of the financial success of May's adventure novels, a reprint of the rubbishy dime novels of his early writing career was published illegally. Personal enemies and journalists became more and more interested in his past. In 1904 his prison sentences were revealed; the press had a delicious new scandal, and a series of subsequent actions for defamation of character ruined May's reputation. In vain he tried to escape from this miserable situation by means of a three-month journey, his first, to the United States in the fall of 1908. His travels, however, did not lead him to the Wild West, but rather to New York, Albany, Buffalo, and Toronto. After his return he was again involved in new lawuits, which detracted still further from his reputation.

The lawsuits have not impaired the enduring success of the works of May. The sales of his books have constantly increased over the past sixty years. Over 45 million copies have been sold in Germany, and his works have become popular in other north European countries. Though often labeled as "trivial literature" by literary critics, his works, especially his adventure novels, met the approval of such diverse men as Albert Schweitzer, Albert Einstein, Adolf Hitler, Hermann Hesse, and Carl Zuckmayer.

May's novels have given rise to numerous plays, movies, and radio programs. More than 100,000 of his admirers attend each year the annual Karl May Festival in Bad Segeberg (Schleswig-Holstein), held since 1952. At last the news of his popularity has reached the Indians in the United States. According to *The New York Times* of January 4, 1971, the United Sioux Tribes, in cooperation with May's publisher in Bamberg, Germany, planned to lure European tourists to visit famous tribal areas in the now not so Wild West, thus providing jobs for thousands of Indians.—D. J.

Mayflower Compact. See PLYMOUTH COLONY.

Mead, Elwood (1858-1936). Irrigation expert. Elwood Mead is best known as the director of the Bureau of Reclamation (1924-36), under whose supervision Hoover Dam was built. He was born on a farm near Patriot, Indiana. A bucolic childhood implanted in his mind a lifetime determination to preserve a saving remnant of America's agrarian society and led him to pursue a career in civil engineering. As a land-surveyor and schoolteacher, he was able to work his way to a B.S. degree at Purdue University in 1882. Then he served in the Army Engineers for several months and secured his engineering degree from Iowa State College and an M.S. degree from Purdue in 1883. Meanwhile he was teaching at Colorado State Agricultural College and in 1885 became professor of irrigation engineering, the first such appointment in an American university.

When Wyoming undertook a program of economic development, Mead was selected in 1888 for the newly created post of territorial engineer and was largely responsible for drafting the farsighted water code provisions of Wyoming's new state constitution. The code provided for a hydrological survey of total water resources available for surface streams, stated that applications for water rights could not exceed water available, and set up an administrative body of engineers to determine conflicts and administer the code. The "Wyoming idea," as these provisions were termed, worked so admirably in eliminating vexatious litigation that Mead launched a campaign under the aegis of the state engineers to secure uniform water laws in America's "arid domain."

Mead's conception of the role of the federal government in irrigation development was as partner to, rather than controller of, the states.

As early as 1889 he proposed a measure by which arid federal lands would be ceded to the states in the West. His proposal was the inspiration for the inauguration of the Irrigation Congress movement in 1891 and for the CAREY ACT. Not only would private enterprise be encouraged by land grants, so Mead foresaw, but speculation would be eliminated when state governments controlled both water and land and could prevent monopolization of either. Wyoming Senator Francis Warren's cession bills found little support in Congress, but the Carey Act was passed by Congress in 1894. Mead drafted a statute for Wyoming's acceptance of the act's million-acre grant, and Mead's statute was imitated by other states. He next worked through the American Society of Irrigation Engineers as well as the Irrigation Congresses for reform of the public-land laws and federal cession of irrigable and grazing lands for homesteaders in arid states. Mead's last effort to devise an alternative to reclamation under federal control was formulated in the state engineers' plan, which was submitted to Congress in 1901, when Francis Newlands' bill for national reclamation was under consideration. Mead's bill would permit federal construction of reservoirs but would ensure continued state control of water rights and the distribution of water to homestead settlers.

In 1899 Mead was appointed expert in charge of the Department of Agriculture's Irrigation Investigations Office. Cooperative programs with state engineers and experiment-station personnel worked to achieve water-law reform and acquainted farmers with the special features of irrigation agriculture. Mead soon became the acknowledged authority on irrigation institutions, delivered lectures at Harvard University and elswhere in the East, was appointed professor of the Institution and Practice of Irrigation at the University of California, wrote extensively for the engineering press and journals of opinion, and produced the widely respected book *Irrigation Institutions* (1903).

Mead's vision that agrarian society could be reconstituted through government reclamation was perfected during the years (1899-1907) he headed the irrigation work for the Department of Agriculture, though rivalry with the more pretentious Reclamation Service circumscribed his efforts. Fulfillment came when Mead was called to head an Australian colonization project, the Victoria State Rivers and Water Commission, between 1907 and 1915. He learned the crucial role that government must play in advancing credit, screening settlers, supplying expertise in irrigation agriculture, and providing the essentials for community organization. He returned in triumph to the University of California and soon persuaded California to embark upon a colonization program. In 1917 he was put in charge of a land settlement board, which founded and administered the two model colonies of Durham and Delhi in California's Central Valley. Until 1924, when Mead left for Washington, the Durham colony was a notable success, its fame spreading through the publication of Mead's *Helping Men Own Farms* (1920). The Delhi community told a different tale, for with the depression of 1921 and the waning of enthusiasm for the back-to-the-land movement, a third of its acreage was never taken up. Poor planning in choice of land and crops and financial stringency enforced by hostile public opinion meant that over the long run both projects were accounted failures.

Paradoxically, at the very time when Mead's California colonies were coming under critical public scrutiny, his personal reputation as the national authority on reclamation soared. His services were in demand as a consultant by foreign governments, he wrote extensively for national publication, and the Coolidge administration in 1923 appointed him to the Fact Finders Committee to investigate the Bureau of Reclamation. The report of the Fact Finders team was largely of his authorship, and he accepted appointment as commissioner of the Bureau of Reclamation in 1924 to see if he could bring about the reorganization he had recommended. It was well-known that he had been critical of the reclamation projects since their inception, but he was convinced that scientific management and a humanitarian concern for settler interests would solve the bureau's problems in his ten-year program of reorganization. He immediately won disfavor in the West by placing a limit on the opening of new projects. He scaled down the operations on existing projects so that construction costs covered only productive land. Water-user associations took over the actual management of projects.

Mead was the first bureau chief to balance the books, but the Great Depression undercut these advances. Unperturbed by the opposition of the farm belt and Department of Agriculture toward further expansion of reclamation, Mead mounted a national campaign to have the bureau undertake the construction of the Hoover Dam and Grand Coulee projects, both of which had been in the planning stages for years. Mead brought the Bureau of Reclamation to the pinnacle of national prestige with the Depression-induced program of high-dam construction, a program of flawless engineering. With its generated power available to the public, the dams more than paid for themselves. The waters impounded by Hoover Dam have been named Lake Mead.

Elwood Mead, *Helping Men Own Farms* (1920) recounts the author's experiences with reclamation project colonization in Australia as well as the California colonies. The emphasis is upon correct principles of colony administration. Donald C. Swain, *Federal Conservation Policy, 1921-1933* (1963) relates Mead's role with the Fact Finders Committee as well as his achievements as commissioner of the Bureau of Reclamation. It offers a balanced treatment. Swain's "The Bureau of Reclamation and the New Deal, 1933-1940," *Pacific Northwest Quarterly* (July 1970), offers an objective description and evaluation of Mead's final years in the Bureau of Reclamation. And his "Dr. Elwood Mead, Commissioner of Reclamation, Dies," *Reclamation Era,* (February 1936), especially valuable for "Chronological Events in Life of Elwood Mead" and an extensive Mead bibliography.—L. B. L.

Meagher, Michael (1844?-1881) **and John** (1844?-?). Lawmen, saloonkeepers. When Timothy Meagher (pronounced Meer) left his native Ireland for a home in frontier Kansas, his twin sons, Mike and John, were already young men. The family settled in Sedgwick County near Wichita in 1868 or 1869 and were soon respected members of the community. Both Mike and John were soon involved in local affairs, particularly law enforcement matters, and in time the twins moved into places of responsibility. Mike, in particular, had the aptitude for law enforcement and was soon recognized as one of the most efficient lawmen in Kansas history.

Mild-mannered Mike was appointed city marshal of Wichita in April 1871 and held that position for five of the next six years. John was his assistant at first, and the brothers did such an effective job that John was elected sheriff in the fall of 1871. He served one term and did a good job but then decided that the life of the frontier gambler was more inviting than the life of a sheriff. Wichita was a fast-growing town with all the problems that implied, but Mike got his first real test when the town became the hub of the Texas cattle trade. He was equal to the responsibility. In 1874 Bill Smith replaced him as city marshal, and Mike drifted into the Indian Territory for a while. That summer southern Kansas was the scene of Indian trouble and he was appointed a deputy United States marshal to deal with white horse thieves, who had contributed to the outbreak. When the attacks became serious, he also served as first lieutenant in a militia company.

The following spring he was elected city marshal of Wichita again. One of his deputies that year was Wyatt Earp. Again Meagher ran an efficient office, so efficient in fact that the size of the police force was reduced. Mike was reelected in 1876 in spite of a preelection fight between policeman Earp and Bill Smith, the opposition candidate for marshal who had made some disparaging remarks about Meagher and Earp. On January 1, 1877, Mike Meagher killed a man named Sylvester Powell when he resisted arrest and shot the marshal. Perhaps that is why Mike decided not to seek reelection in 1877. He had built an admirable record during the difficult years of the cattle boom, and in all that time he had killed only one man. But Sylvester Powell was one too many.

As the cattle trade had shifted west to Dodge City, Wichita began to settle into a quiet community. Men like the Meaghers grew restless and sought new opportunities. In 1879 Mike and John moved to Caldwell,

Kansas, a boistrous, rowdy town near the border with Indian Territory. The railroad was coming to Caldwell, and the town seemed sure to boom. Within a short time Mike was elected mayor. But Caldwell was no Wichita. It was a town with a history of violence, and the influx of Texas cattlemen merely added another explosive element to the assortment of frontier types gathered there. Tinhorn gamblers, prostitutes, thieves and killers who used the Indian Territory as a sanctuary, and other riffraff rubbed shoulders in Caldwell's numerous saloons and brothels. Caldwell was soon lost in a wild, bloody fling as a cowtown. Murders were frequent, and when Mike and his entire police force were arrested for the murder of a former lawman named George Flatt, Mike Meagher knew that his effectiveness as mayor was ended. He was shortly released for lack of evidence against him, but he did not run for reelection.

Other murders followed, and the townsfolk asked Mike to accept the job as marshal. Instead he opened a saloon and wore a badge only when there was a particular need for his services. Several times he was asked to be marshal, but he always turned down the job. John Meagher soon departed Caldwell for greener fields in Arizona, but Mike stayed.

Then a group of cowboys led by one James Talbot, alias James Sherman, arrived with a cattle herd, stayed on after the cattle were sold, and let it be known that Meagher was their quarry. Talbot spent a lot of time with George Flatt's friends, and his men were deliberately provocative in their contact with local lawmen. On December 17, 1881, the town marshal called on Mike Meagher to help him stop a disturbance with the Talbot crowd. A wild battle erupted on the streets of Caldwell, and Mike Meagher was killed. Why he was murdered remains a mystery. Some said that Talbot was related to the man Meagher killed in Wichita. Others saw Mike's death as a revenge murder for the death of George Flatt. Whatever the truth, his death had all the earmarks of a premeditated murder. In 1895, James Sherman was arrested in California and returned to Kansas for trial. Too many years had passed. Too many witnesses were dead. Sherman was acquitted and returned to California. A few months later he was mysteriously murdered.

After leaving Caldwell, John Meagher went to Tombstone, Arizona, where he acquired an interest in the Alhambra Saloon. In 1881 he posted bond for Doc Holliday when Doc was arrested for attempted robbery and murder. He was considered a partisan of the Earp faction. He left Tombstone about the same time the Earps did and followed the gambler's circuit for a while. Eventually, he dropped from sight. He was reported living in Oklahoma at one time, and he visited old friends in Wichita in 1908. That is the last know record of him.

The brothers Meagher have not found a biographer. The most reliable source is Nyle H. Miller and Joseph W. Snell, *Why the West Was Wild* (1963).—G. L. R.

Mears, Otto (1840-1931). Road and railroad builder. Born in Russia, Mears was orphaned at an early age, and when he was ten years old he left his native land for America. Arriving in San Francisco, he held various odd jobs and was employed in California and Nevada mining camps. During the Civil War he was a member of the First Regiment of California Volunteers, serving for a time under Kit Carson in the Navaho war. After his discharge he went first to Santa Fe and then to Conejos, Colorado, where he established a sawmill and gristmill in partnership with Lafayette Head. He later moved to Saguache, Colorado, and finding no roads to markets in mining camps to the north, he built a toll road over Poncha Pass to the Arkansas valley near present Salida, the first of his numerous road-building projects. After rich mineral deposits were found in the San Juan Mountains, Mears built hundreds of miles of roads, thereby earning his nickname, "Pathfinder of the San Juans." He was also instrumental in drafting the Brunot treaty with the Ute Indians in 1873 by which they ceded a large rectangle of land in the San Juans that contained the mines, thus legally opening the region to prospectors. His newspapers in Saguache and Lake City helped to promote the area. After the Meeker Massacre in 1879, Mears helped rescue the women held captive by the Ute, and was a member of the commission that negotiated another treaty with the Ute by which most of the tribe was eventually removed to Utah. Although Mears was charged with bribing the Ute to obtain their consent, he was later exonerated by the secretary of the interior.

Turning to railroads, Mears built the Rio Grande Southern and the Silverton Northern railroads in the San Juan region. In 1884 he was elected to the Colorado legislature, where he served for many years. He was also a member of the State Capitol Commission. Although much of the fortune he had accumulated was lost in the Panic of 1893, he later built the Chesapeake Beach Railroad in Maryland. Moving to California in 1920, Mears had interests in ranch and hotel properties there prior to his death.

See Sidney Jocknick, *Early Days on the Western Slope of Colorado and Campfire Chats with Otto Mears* (1913). —M. B.

Medicine Lodge, Treaty of (1867). Indian treaty. The Treaty of Medicine Lodge marked a fundamental turning-point in the history of United States Indian policy. In the half-century before the close of the Civil War the Great Plains had been seen by white policy-makers as "one big reservation," where all Indian peoples would be located and where they could continue their traditional way of life. But the Indians had by 1865 become a threat to lines of communication and transportation across the Plains, and white agricultural advance into Kansas and Nebraska made it apparent that a different program was required. Consequently, in 1867 a federal "peace commission" was formed and charged with negotiating treaties with the Plains Indians to remove them from the path of white settlement and to "establish a system for civilizing the tribes."

In the autumn of 1867 this peace commission met with several leading representatives of the Southern Plains tribes—Comanche, Kiowa, Cheyenne, Arapaho, and other, smaller groups—on Medicine Lodge Creek near present Medicine Lodge, Kansas. Sporadic hostilities had been dragging on in the region for several years, and the Indians appeared willing to negotiate and accept white proposals, although it is extremely doubtful that they had any sense of the true implications of the commission's program, or that the chiefs were seeking any more than a temporary respite from fighting. In the treaty provisions agreed to on October 21 and 28, the "one big reservation" concept was abandoned forever. Instead, the Southern Plains tribes were allotted reservations in the western part of present Oklahoma and forbidden to occupy territory outside their bounds. On the reservations, to which the tribes were required to move immediately, the Indians were to be provided with schools and resident farmers to teach them white cultural practices and agricultural techniques.

The actual peacemaking effect of the Treaty of Medicine Lodge, like the similar treaty negotiated the following year with the Northern Plains tribes at Fort Laramie, was practically nonexistent. Most Indian bands and groups of warriors simply ignored it and refused to abandon their accustomed hunting grounds. Violent encounters across the width of the frontier continued. The United States Congress, embroiled in an appropriations wrangle, refused to ratify the peace commission's treaties for several years, and in the interim those amenable Indian bands that did try to move onto the designated reservations were left without sustenance and were often attacked by army patrols who found it too difficult to track down actual hostiles. Notwithstanding this inauspicious beginning, however, the principles of Indian assimilation and cultural elimination, first embodied in the Treaty of Medicine Lodge, continued as the foundation of Indian policy for nearly three quarters of a century to come.

See H. E. Fritz, *The Movement for Indian Assimilation, 1860-1890* (1963), and D. C. Jones, *The Treaty of Medicine Lodge* (1966), for the policy aspects of the treaty. For the immediate aftermath on the Plains, see Dee Brown, *Bury My Heart at Wounded Knee* (1971). —P. R. M.

Meek, Joseph L. (1810-1875). Mountain man and Oregon politician. Born in Virginia, Meek fled to Missouri (it is said, to escape a strong stepmother), where he joined two of his brothers, Hiram and Stephen. In 1829 he entered Sublette's service as a Rocky Mountain trapper and attended the multiple rendezvous of that year. For the next eleven years Meek, later joined by his brother Stephen, trapped in the vast region from the Snake River to southern Utah. The brothers traveled to California in 1833 with Joseph R. Walker and his exploring party, crossing the Sierra near Yosemite and going on to the settlements in search of adventure, supplies, horses, and furs. Walker and his party were not welcome, however, and they returned to the famous Bear River fur-trading rendezvous of 1834, where the Rocky Mountain Fur Company was dissolved.

Meek's years as a trapper were studded with adventures and tragedy: he hunted in the dangerous Blackfoot country with Kit Carson and Robert Newell; was nearly killed in an Indian ambush in the Yellowstone Lake region; and experienced a fight with a grizzly bear. After a group of Bannock Indians killed his Indian mate Umentucken, he married the daughter of a Nez Percé chief. In 1839 Blackfoot murdered his partner as they trapped in the Tetons.

The decline of the fur trade forced Meek to make Fort Hall—by then an important way station for Oregon immigrants—the center of his operations. When his friend Newell agreed to pilot a wagon train to Oregon in 1840, Meek and his Indian wife and family joined the party and settled on a farm in the Willamette valley. Marcus Whitman, Meek, and Newell were among the first to use wagons on the Oregon Trail.

Meek was a great storyteller, and his exaggerated

accounts of Indian fights and wild sprees in the mountains had the unmistakable quality of the frontier tall tale. This talent, plus courage, understanding, and a hospitable nature, led him into Oregon politics. He served as sheriff under the Oregon provisional government, was elected to the legislative assemblies of 1846 and 1847, and later was marshal of Oregon Territory. In 1848 he was sent to Washington to notify President Polk, whose wife was Meek's cousin, of the Whitman massacre and to urge territorial organization for Oregon. Obviously capitalizing on his connections with Polk, Meek ran for territorial delegate in 1849 but lost. After that he held minor political and military posts. In return for his services in the 1855 Yakima Indian War he was promoted to the rank of major.

A fervent Unionist in the Civil War, Meek helped found the Oregon Republican party. Although his final years were embittered by poverty and the fact that white Oregonians ostracized his half-breed children, Meek's honesty, directness, irrepressible nature, and flair for turning his adventures into great stories persisted.

See Harvey L. Tobie, *No Man Like Joe* (1949); and Frances Fuller Victor, *River of the West* (1870).—G. B. D.

Meeker Massacre. See COLORADO; and UTE INDIANS.

Menard, [Antoine] Pierre (1766-1844). Fur trader, Indian agent, and political leader. Little is known about Menard's early life except that he was born at St. Antoine, Quebec, grew up near Montreal, and apparently received an ordinary education. He appeared in Vincennes, Indiana, in 1786 in the employ of Colonel Francis Vigo, a well-known Indian trader.

Four years later Menard moved to Kaskaskia in Illinois country, which remained his home for the rest of his life. Opening a store in partnership with Toussaint DuBois, he prospered and rose to a position of prominence in that area. The partners handled goods for the Indian trade as well as building supplies, tools, and other equipment needed by a growing frontier community. Menard received an appointment as major in the local militia when it was organized in 1795. In February 1801 Governor William Henry Harrison placed him on the Randolph County Court of Common Pleas, where he remained for ten years. In the interim he also served in the Indiana territorial legislature and in 1806 was promoted to lieutenant colonel and designated commander of the county militia.

That same year Menard married Angelique Saucier (his second wife), whose sister was the wife of Jean Pierre Chouteau. He also formed a partnership with Manuel Lisa, a well-known trader, and William Morrison, another Kaskaskia merchant, to exploit trading and trapping opportunities in the area from which Lewis and Clark had just returned. The two Kaskaskia merchants, deciding not to accompany the expedition Lisa headed, designated George Dourillard, who had just left government service, as their agent. The adventure proved a financial success and forced the Chouteaus and other St. Louis merchants, who had previously been reluctant, to organize the St. Louis Missouri Fur Company in partnership with Lisa, Menard, and Morrison in 1809. Menard accompanied the new company's first expedition to the upper Missouri. One group of trappers, under his leadership, reached the Three Forks of the Missouri on April 3, 1810, marking the first time that such an outfit had penetrated that far in any organized

fashion. Meeting fierce opposition from the Blackfoot Indians, the group broke up, and Menard returned to his home at Kaskaskia.

Menard now turned increasingly to politics as the Illinois country moved toward statehood. He served as president of the legislative council (senate) from 1812 until statehood was achieved six years later and became the new state's first lieutenant governor, retiring after one term to spend his remaining years overseeing his business and charitable enterprises. During this period he was twice called upon to serve as Indian commissioner with the tribes of that region.

A thorough sketch of Menard's career may be found in William S. Merrill, "Pierre Menard of Illinois," *Mid-America* (July 1931). A valuable source for his role in the western fur trade is Richard E. Oglesby, *Manuel Lisa and the Opening of the Missouri Fur Trade* (1963).—W. E. P.

Menéndez de Avilés, Pedro. See FLORIDA.

Merk, Frederick (1887-   ). Historian and teacher. Merk was born in Wisconsin and graduated from high school in Milwaukee. In 1911 he received his B.A. degree from the University of Wisconsin, where he studied under Frederick Jackson Turner; and then accepted a position as a manuscript editor with the Wisconsin State Historical Society. Various published articles on state and local history were helpful in securing for him the Edward Austen Fellowship in 1916. Entering Harvard University, young Merk renewed his studies under Turner in pursuit of a Ph.D. in western history; in 1921 he was appointed a member of the Harvard faculty.

Academic promotions at Cambridge followed a normal course as Merk concentrated most of his energies on teaching rather than publishing. Among his contemporaries were Samuel Eliot Morison and Arthur M. Schlesinger. He and Schlesinger shared teaching the basic undergraduate course taken by several generations of Harvard students, "The Growth of the American Nation." But his fame rested primarily upon the more advanced "Westward Movement," which graduate students referred to as "Wagon Wheels." The content of this course underwent constant refinement and covered the broad sweep of historical movement from the earliest settlements along the Atlantic Coast to the Pacific—with all its relative problems, issues, and social and political developments.

Although he possessed a slight figure and a thin voice, "Harvard's Mr. Chips" quickly cast his spell over his classrooms with his eloquent phrases and whimsical humor. In 1931, at the age of forty-four, he married one of his graduate students, Lois Bannister, an instructor at Wheaton College. Merk was elevated to the distinguished chair of Guerney Professor of History and Political Science in 1936, a position he retained until becoming professor emeritus twenty-one years later.

Merk's career resembled that of his mentor and good friend Turner in that he first established a national reputation through the publication of scholarly articles rather than prize-winning books. Although he did publish two or three monographs, he resisted pressures by colleagues, students, and university officials to commit his lectures to permanent form until he was ready. His best-known works during these years were *Fur Trade and Empire: George Simpson's Journal, 1824-1825* (1931) and *Albert Gallatin and the Oregon Problem* (1950). After

The Cliff Palace in Mesa Verde National Park. (Library of Congress)

his retirement in 1957 he published three significant studies: *Manifest Destiny and Mission* (1963); *The Monroe Doctrine and American Expansionism, 1843-1849* (1966); and *Essays in Anglo-American Diplomacy and Politics* (1967).—W. E. H.

Mesa Verde National Park. Mesa Verde National Park, in southwestern Colorado, is rich in Indian history and archeology. The park consists of a high, forested mesa and many steeply walled canyons. On both the mesa top and in the canyons, prehistoric Indian ruins have been found. They are among the best preserved Indian pueblos in North America.

The Indians of Mesa Verde went through four developmental periods. In the Basket Maker period, which lasted until about A.D. 400, the Indians lived in small caves or in rude shelters on the mesa top. They made baskets but had no pottery. They could not build houses. The Modified Basket Maker period lasted from 400 to about 750. During this period, the Indians built pit houses and began to use pottery. They learned to use the bow and arrow, and their villages spread over a wide area now known as the Four Corners region, where New Mexico, Colorado, Arizona, and Utah meet. They were farmers. In the developmental period from 750 to 1100, the Indians experimented with more complicated architectural forms. They developed masonry construction techniques, erecting clusters of houses around open

courtyards. These became communal habitations. Pottery and basketry improved as art forms. The pit houses became *kivas*, or ceremonial rooms. The highest level of the cliff dwellers' culture was reached during the Great, or Classic, Pueblo period, from 1000 to 1300. The masonry work became functional and beautiful. The Indians designed jewelry, made pottery and decorated it artistically, and wove intricate designs in their fabrics. They developed a complex social structure and elaborate religious rituals. About 1200 they moved from the top of the mesa to inaccessible, easily defended ledges or caves in the canyon walls because of marauding Indians, possibly the ancestors of the Navaho. It was in these locations that the most beautiful pueblos were built. The Cliff Palace in Mesa Verde National Park is a good example. A twenty-five year drought, beginning about 1275, finally drove the Indians off the mesa. They were the ancestors of the present Pueblo Indians of the Southwest.

Mesa Verde became a national park by act of Congress on June 19, 1906. The mesa was first explored by a United States government party in 1874. The first thorough scientific investigation of the area was by Gustaf Nordenskjöld in 1891. The entrance to the park's 52,074 acres is near Durango, Colorado.—D. C. S.

Mescalero Indians. See APACHE INDIANS.

Mesquakie Indian settlement. The home of Iowa's

only surviving Indian tribe. Today's Mesquakie are descendants of early-day Fox Indians who lived in IOWA before the coming of the white man. During the 1840s the federal government moved the tribe to Kansas, but many were unhappy with Plains life and eventually wandered back to Iowa. The Indians purchased land near Tama, and Congress recognized them as a separate tribe—the Mesquakie. In 1896 the Tama Reservation was established for them, but the name was later changed to "settlement" as the Indians gradually purchased the land on which they lived. The settlement today contains about 3,600 acres.

Each year in late August the Mesquakie stage a five-day powwow when they perform ceremonial dances and exhibit their craft work and native costumes. Through their dances and ceremonies they tell the story of their early life and history.

The Indians' annual celebration is highlighted in "Tama Pow Wow," *Palimpsest* (July 1967).—D. S.

Methodists. John Wesley was a priest of the Church of England. After preaching as a missionary in Georgia in 1738, he founded the first societies of the "People called Methodists" in Bristol and London in 1739. Wesley considered his movement to be within the Church of England, despite the fact that his new organization was characterized by its own centralized authority and rigorous rules for the activities of the hierarchy of teachers and preachers that he brought into being. Wesley set forth the rules that governed the movement from the highest officers down to the communicant in the pew in what he called the "Discipline." The migrating Methodists brought the "Discipline" with them to the American colonies.

In 1766 the first Methodists landed on American shores and numbered about fifteen thousand when the American Revolution ended in 1783. Most of them lived south of the Mason-Dixon line. The leaders at that time, with the exception of Francis Asbury, whom Wesley sent to the New World in 1771, were young Americans imbued with the philosophy of the American Revolution. None were ordained ministers. The severance of ties with the Church of England, which came with national independence, made it impossible for American Methodists to depend upon the Anglican Church for the sacraments. To meet the situation Wesley sent the clergyman Thomas Coke across the Atlantic in 1784. Coke ordained Asbury, thus giving him proper ecclesiastical status. Wesley appointed Coke and Asbury to be joint superintendents "over our brethren in America." Coke, ill fitted to cope with the crude life-style and the illiteracy of the scattered backwoods settlements where Methodism sought to expand, soon returned to England. A conference made up of preachers was then held in Baltimore in December 1774. It formulated a constitution for the independent Methodist Episcopal Church. The name reflected the fact that the constitution provided that the highest official in the new church be called a bishop and, hereafter, be elected by a conference. Asbury, as head of the church, changed his title from superintendent to bishop. With foresight, complete commitment, and vast energy, he set about expanding the church in the South, the North, and the West.

The frontier of settlement moved westward after the close of the American Revolution irregularly and without plan. Methodism's push into the West got fully under way with the Great Revival of 1800 and its spirit of REVIVALISM. The Methodist institution of the circuit rider provided the key to the extraordinary success of the denomination on the moving frontier. Bishop Asbury himself was the greatest of them, traveling on horseback along the roads and trails from New England to Georgia. He selected, ordained and sent into the field other circuit riders, among them Peter CARTWRIGHT. In Tennessee, Kentucky, and the Ohio valley the circuit rider would recruit and organize Methodists in an unchurched area. Visiting a settlement, he would find a place where he might preach, usually a farmer's house. After collecting a company of communicants and leaving one of their number to serve as preacher, he would ride, often on forest trails, to the next settlement. In time he would establish a rough circle of stations so spaced that he could visit each about once a month. He carried in his saddlebags a Bible, a volume of sermons by John Wesley, and the "Discipline." The latter told him what to do at a wedding or a funeral and set forth his obligations to his bishop and the flock he served. It also detailed the organization in the local community. Here a local unordained preacher or exhorter, usually a farmer, carried on religious services and activities between visits of the circuit rider. In such communities the communicants were organized into class meetings of about twelve persons each. A leader headed each class meeting and assumed the responsibility to see that none backslid from the faith or escaped admonition when they broke the sabbath or engaged in frivolities or other sins discountenanced by the church. Authority, moving down through channels and spelling out in detail procedures and responsibilities in the "Discipline," prevented variations in the life and worship of local churches in diverse communities.

In the early decades of the nineteenth century, when the primitive character of communication emphasized the isolation of new settlements, the circuit rider became more than a religious pioneer seeking new stations in which to preach, more than a presiding elder encouraging and supervising the usually unlettered local preachers in his circuit. He brought with him on each visit a sheaf of news from a wider world. For three months after December 16, 1811, his most exciting news concerned recurring earthquakes in the central Mississippi valley. The riverbank at New Madrid caved in, carrying the better part of the town into the Mississippi. Farther downstream a quake completely destroyed Cauthersville. Violent changes in elevation of the water level frightened people who lived near its banks. These convulsions of nature seem to have affected profoundly communities in which ignorance and illiteracy were common phenomena. In the year of the quakes, 1812, the reported Methodist membership west of the Appalachians jumped by a third, to a figure above forty-four thousand. In the same year the church counted a national membership of a little under two hundred thousand. Although the disturbances and distractions of the War of 1812 caused a momentary setback in recruiting, the western churches grew until they reached approximately one hundred thousand by 1822. That figure was approximately one third of the national count.

The itinerant Methodist preachers followed the

march of Americans across the continent. They scattered churches across Missouri. They came early to the march of Americans across the continent. They scattered churches across Missouri. They came early to the Red River valley. Crossing the border of the nation, one of them preached in Austin's colony in Texas within three years of its establishment. Going west as a missionary to Indians, Jason LEE founded the first American settlement in the Willamette valley in Oregon. Invariably, they were men of the people, speaking the vernacular of the people and dressing in homespun or even buckskin. Many had a native eloquence that gave them mastery over the congregations seated before them. Their authority derived from the Bible, the literal word of God. They preached hellfire and the rewards of a heaven whose golden streets echoed to the music of harp singing. But the gospel of the circuit rider was a democratic gospel. God had prepared salvation for all men. The individual sinner, man or woman, could achieve it by meeting the divine requirements. All men had an equal opportunity before God; all had an equal responsibility to abandon and to contend against sin. The Methodist came to see the saloon as the chief symbol of evil in communities threatened always with a lapse into barbarism. The growing armies of the faithful became a powerful force for social stability and for civilization.

The story of Methodism in Nebraska illustrates the genius of the denomination and its impact on the life of the broad interior of the nation. The Kansas-Nebraska Act of 1854 brought the territory into being. For many years Nebraska was a sod-house frontier. Practically from the beginning of white settlement circuit riders carried their work of ministry and organization to the scattered settlements moving westward from the Missouri River. Their stipends were pitifully small. Camp meetings held in groves furthered their work of evangelism. In time church buildings with walls of sod provided material evidence that work in the vineyard was bearing fruit. Railroads after the 1860s caused the population to spread over the state and brought into being rapidly growing villages and cities. As the crude conditions of the frontier passed, the circuit rider dismounted and became the presiding elder. He supervised the work of local churches in which an increasing number of pastors had theological training, Sunday schools flourished, and young peoples' organizations were important. In 1890, with six Protestant denominations carrying on significant work in Nebraska, the Methodists had 649 organized congregations. The second-place Lutherans, mostly recent immigrants from Europe, had 387. Accepting the responsibilities of leadership, the Methodists in the last two decades of the nineteenth century founded Nebraska Wesleyan University, established a hospital in Omaha, and created an important home for homeless children. They carried on the old war against the saloon in an unwavering support of prohibition.

In 1844, when slavery became a moral and political issue that could not be ignored in the councils of Methodism, the church divided and the Methodist Episcopal Church South came into existence. As formerly, the southern church counted large numbers of blacks among its communicants, but after the close of the Civil War the blacks withdrew from the white-dominated church to form the Colored Methodist Episcopal Church. This organization later merged with the African Methodist Episcopal Church, which had been founded in Philadelphia in 1787.

As in other large denominations, many factors made for division among the Methodists in the nineteenth century. There were disagreements as to the interpretation of the "Discipline." There were theological differences and diverse attitudes toward polity and ritual. At the end of the first quarter of the twentieth century separate white organizations numbered eight. At that time the blacks, feeling their way toward a denomination of their own, counted ten distinct organizations. In the middle decades of the century the ecumenical movement triumphed among both white and black organizations. In 1970 only two small splinter groups, the Free Methodist Church of North America and Wesleyan Methodist Church of America, maintained separate existence among the whites. Three important branches of Methodism united in 1939: the Methodist Episcopal Church, the Methodist Episcopal Church South, and the Methodist Protestant Church. The United Methodist Church came into being in Dallas, Texas, in 1968 with the union of the Methodist Church and the Evangelical United Brethren Church. It counted a membership in 1970 of just over 11 million people. In that year the African Methodist Episcopal Church had a membership of more than 1,166,000 and the African Methodist Episcopal Zion Church numbered around 1,100,000.

See Sidney E. Ahlstrom, *A Religious History of the American People* (1972); H. E. Luccock and P. Hutcheson, *The Story of Methodism* (1926); and W. W. Sweet, *Methodism in American History* (1933).—R. H. G.

Mexican-Americans. Mexican-Americans are citizens of the United States whose ancestors can be traced to Mexico. Many are descendants of people who lived on lands ranging from St. Louis on the Mississippi River to Florida on the Gulf of Mexico and then westward to Texas, New Mexico, and California, long before the United States came into existence in 1776 and in some cases before Jamestown was settled. Most Mexican-American families, however, do not date from this early period but from the years following the United States conquest of the Southwest in 1848, and the majority of those from the period following the Mexican Revolution of 1910.

Although most Mexican-Americans are United States-born, a stream of new immigrants enters from Mexico all the time. Those who come illegally are usually called wetbacks, alluding to earlier times when they presumably crossed the Rio Grande to avoid detection. According to length of residence in the United States, Mexican-Americans may be identified as Spanish-empire Mexican-Americans (c.1550-1820), Mexican-republic Mexican-Americans (1824-48), United States Mexican-Americans (1848 to the near present), and recent immigrants. Recent figures suggest that it is among recent immigrants, most of them illegal, that the Mexican-American population growth rate is the greatest.

Mexican-Americans can also be described by racial stock or cultural heritage. Most are *mestizo*, of mixed stock. As long as a European immigrant could establish good Catholic standing, he and his family could gain entrance legally into the vast Spanish empire. Thus mestizos may be a mixture of Indian and any European stock, but most are of Spanish and Indian stock.

Even then, they are as different culturally and physically as are the Spanish who came to Mexico. Some barely consented to obey the Spanish crown. The Andaluz from southern Spain, the Gallego from the northwestern parts, the Basque and the Catalan of the northeast, and the Valenciano were often rather different physically and culturally. Generally, those from the northern parts of Spain were lighter in skin and taller, while those from the southern parts were darker and shorter.

The Castilians from the north-central plateau of the peninsula came to rule Spain during the time of Ferdinand and Isabella, who through marriage joined their separate kingdoms into a common inheritance for their successors. The Castilian language and customs of Isabella gained prominence because of the prestige that the discovery of America gave her. The Castilian form of Spanish became the language of the court and became synonymous with a new standardized form of Spanish. In time Spanish characteristics were mainly of Castilian origin.

Indians also varied greatly at the time of the Spanish conquest of Mexico. History has concentrated on the Aztec and the Maya, but there were many other groups who spoke different languages and had different cultures and physical characteristics. Even today more than a dozen major Indian languages survive in Mexico. Sometimes recent Mexican immigrants bring these languages to the United States; for them Spanish is a second language and English, a third.

In parts of Mexico that touch on the Gulf of Mexico are another important group of Mexicans, black people from Africa who descend from colonial-era slavery. In time, the Catholic church gave certain social and religious protection to Africans (*negros*), as it did to Indians. Legal obstacles to intermarriage between Europeans and Africans were not raised by the church and crown; instead, a limited degree of legal rights was extended to slaves and African freemen. The church opened its doors to their membership and tried to encourage marriage among common-law unions. Children born out of wedlock (*hijos naturales* or "natural children") could gain the legal name of their father.

Some anthropologists have called Mexicans *la raza cosmica*, referring in part to their complex racial and cultural background. The chart below summarizes the sorts of racial mixtures Mexican-Americans may represent:

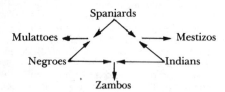

Mexican-Americans have been called and have called themselves many names during their long history. The names used by others and the names they have used to call themselves have changed according to regional preferences and in response to new conditions. The history of this group is evident in the names that apply to it. The following breakdown of terms used to call Mexican-Americans is helpful:

Terms used by Mexican-Americans	Terms used by other Americans	Terms used by Mexicans
Formal	*Formal*	*Formal*
Mexicano	Mexican	Mexico-American
Latino-Americano	Mexican-American	Mexicano
Latino	Latin	Latino
Hispano	Latin American	Hispano
	Spanish-surnamed	
Colloquial	*Colloquial*	*Colloquial*
la raza	beaner	pocho
Chicano	greaser	
	wetback	
	spic	

Colloquial terms abound according to regions and groups, but most of them are derogatory to some extent. Lately, *la raza* and *chicano* have been redefined into a positive usage. Indeed, some Spanish-Americans who would oppose the use of Mexican-American are willing to call themselves la raza or chicano. In areas of New Mexico and Colorado live Mexican-Americans of mostly pure Spanish background. They are Mexican-Americans only in the technical sense (their ancestors were Mexican citizens for a time) and may choose to be called Hispanos or Spanish-Americans.

Estimates of Mexican-American population range from five million to eight million. The 1970 census put the number at about seven million, but this figure is open to challenge because of the difficulties in nomenclature and the reluctance of some Mexican-Americans to be counted. Certainly, there are hundreds of thousands of illegal residents. Efforts by some to "pass" also helps explain the undercount in census data. In recent years, however, the tendency of Mexican-Americans successful in business and the professions to change their names or move out of the *barrios* has declined. This, in turn, changes the views held about the group. All told, Mexican-Americans are the second largest minority group, after black Americans. The population increase, by about three million over the 1960 estimate, is relatively great. Because its numbers tend to be young, there will be a continued increase over the years ahead; in such areas as California the growth will be explosive. Clearly, Mexican-Americans are not going to disappear into the mainstream as other national minority groups have done.

Most Mexican-Americans live in the Southwest, but by 1970 there was a combined total of more than one million in Washington, Idaho, Wyoming, Kansas, Illinois, and Michigan. Work on the railroads and the agricultural migrant streams took Mexican-Americans everywhere in the country, and more and more they have stayed there after their seasonal work. Over the long run they will become a national minority group, as are the blacks. With the appointment of Romana Banuelos as treasurer of the United States in 1971 Mexican-Americans formally gained national recognition.

Mexican-Americans came into existence after 1848, when the United States forced Mexico to accept the Treaty of Guadalupe Hidalgo. By this treaty the war between Mexico and the United States came to an end, costing Mexico about one half of its national territory and terrible destruction from several invading United States armies. Citizens of Mexico became citizens of the United States simply by choosing to remain within new United States territory, which stretched from Texas to the California border with Oregon. The Treaty of Guadalupe Hidalgo is a sore point among Mexican-Americans because, they charge, those of its features designed to protect their interests have been ignored, as has happened with treaties with Indian nations. Most Americans know little about the treaty, and their accounts of the war stem from highly pro-United States accounts that place Mexicans in a poor light. Mexican-Americans had to carry on their shoulders the overwhelming military defeat of Mexico. Americans often saw them as offspring of a conquered "race," lucky enough to be citizens of "their" country without making demands on their conquerors.

Within one generation, between the 1820s and 1840s, two peoples came to blows in the Southwest. Their history up to the clash suggests to some that war was inevitable. Others feel that war was rather the product of certain forces turned loose by certain groups and individuals. By the 1820s manifest destiny was on the rise. Americans seemed to believe that their religious, cultural, and political institutions were so superior to those of the Mexicans that any means were justified to gain control over choice Mexican territory.

After Mexico became a republic, she opened her doors to new citizens and welcomed American colonists into Texas during the 1820s. Free land under the EMPRESARIO SYSTEM and tax benefits attracted immigrants from many lands, but most of the new settlers were Americans. Moses Austin and others received generous grants of choice land in order to build up Mexico's northern frontier. Some political figures in Mexico City feared the ambitions of American colonists, such as Stephen F. AUSTIN, Moses' son; others believed that with safeguards Americans would serve as a buffer to others and protect Mexico's interests. Young Austin and the early colonists helped their new motherland against such Americans as Haden and Benjamin Edwards, leaders of the FREDONIAN REBELLION. Early prospects for Mexican and American contacts were mixed, as a result. By 1830 new American-Mexicans comprised the majority of residents in Texas, which was part of the state of Coahuila.

In Washington the annexation of Texas had always been an issue (see TEXAS, ANNEXATION OF), but now territorial expansionists spoke out more frequently about America's manifest destiny to stretch control from sea to sea. Senator Thomas Hart Benton pushed for federal support to chart new roads and trade routes to Santa Fe, New Mexico, and other places. Furthermore, Benton argued, the United States should do this even without the support of the Mexican government, if need be. Such hostile statements alarmed Mexican government officials. The United States already had a bad reputation for grabbing territory one way or another, as Mexicans saw it. Too, American colonists in California, Texas, and New Mexico frequently voiced the desire that these lands be made part of the United States.

The Mexican government cooled toward American immigrants after 1830. In 1828 Mexico had suppressed a Spanish insurrection in which several top officials were

implicated. Mestizos were slowly coming into power, and they often mistrusted Spanish-Mexicans, for Spain had not recognized Mexico's independence since 1824. In California and New Mexico, Mexican government officials were known to collaborate with American contraband traders. Many of these Mexican officials were of Spanish background and got along better with Americans than they did with mestizo Mexicans. In Texas relations between Mexican officials and American-Mexicans also cooled. Thus *Tejano* (Texan) efforts to gain separate statehood status within Mexico failed. Such status was practical, but some Mexican officials feared it might be a prelude to American separatist actions. Finally, proslavery feelings among Texans were common at a time when Mexico was trying to eliminate the vestiges of slavery.

After the threat of a pro-Spanish revolt in 1828, Mexico was threatened by a Spanish naval force gathered in Cuba. A Liberal party now dominated Mexican politics, dedicated to greater equality for all citizens, freer economic activity, and nationalism. Everywhere in Mexico reform was in the air. In California the vast mission system was broken down, and the mission land was given to Indians who soon lost most of it at the hands of clever cheaters. New tax-reform measures promised more efficient government, but these only displeased wealthier people in California and New Mexico. American immigrants in Texas did not get the attention they sought from a government preoccupied with these other national concerns.

Americans in Texas declared independence from Mexico in March 1836. They had good reason to believe support and annexation to the United States would be forthcoming. Mexico then prepared to put down the insurrection. The outcome surprised everyone.

General Antonio López de Santa Anna, president of Mexico, was reorganizing the government into a virtual monarchy in disguise. He saw the insurrection in Texas as a good opportunity to look strong and patriotic. But his military campaign against Sam Houston was a great failure, and at the battle of San Jacinto (1836), Santa Anna was soundly defeated by a smaller Texan force. He managed to save his reputation to some extent by a trip to Washington, D.C., before returning to Mexico City upon his release by Houston after the battle of San Jacinto. The trip gave rise to suspicions that he was not loyal to Mexico, though this charge is disputed by his supporters.

In gaining independence in 1836, Texas acquired a deep hatred for Mexican soldiers because of the execution of Texans captured in the battle of the Alamo in San Antonio. For their part, Mexicans saw the terrible act in different ways. Some believed it was no worse than Texan violence against Mexicans; others saw it as an execution of traitors who would not surrender. The new Republic of Texas aroused patriotism by reminding its people of Mexican atrocities, and this helped produce further hostility between Texans and Mexicans.

Between 1836 and 1846 Mexico and the United States prepared for war. Mexico was in a poor position to regain its territory because of civil wars at home. The United States finally annexed Texas, which Mexico took as an open act of aggression. The ensuing MEXICAN WAR was all one-sided. The United States was prepared with naval forces in the Gulf of Mexico and off the coast of

California. Its agents there and in New Mexico were busy buying off Spanish-Mexican officials. In April 1846 President James K. Polk ordered American forces to occupy the sandy stretch between the River Nueces and the Rio Grande to the south, which Mexico was now willing to call the border with Texas. Mexican forces fought with the Americans and forced them to surrender. This incident, which set off the war, gave the United States an opportunity to claim it had been invaded. Quickly, it invaded Mexico in several places on land and on sea. In California American residents seized Mexican officials who had been entertaining them as guests (see BEAR FLAG REBELLION). In Santa Fe the Mexican governor cooperated with the American overland expedition. Mexico itself was invaded by three armies and one naval assault from the Gulf of Mexico. The defeat for Mexico was complete and humiliating; indeed, the signing of the Treaty of Guadalupe Hidalgo had to wait until a semblance of a provisional government could be established. The reluctant Mexican signers of the treaty said that failing to agree to American terms would leave all Mexico free to grab, for nothing was left to stop the Americans.

In light of this series of events, the morale of Mexican-Americans was low after 1848. How many went across the border into Mexico is not certain, but most appear to have stayed in the lands joined to the United States. Mexican-Americans have never fully recovered from the tragic way in which they became part of the United States. A hundred years later, the war still comes to life and raises questions about Mexican pride, self-respect, and hostility toward the victors, while the victors have commonly viewed Mexican-Americans as a conquered people, like Indians.

The period from the end of the war to the Mexican Revolution of 1910 was very difficult for Mexican-Americans. Although they were numerically the majority in many counties and towns, they lost what political influence their numbers might have gained. In parts of California and Texas they were soon swamped by newcomers and became a numerical as well as a social minority. Their position was generally above Indians, but in some ways below, for they lived among Americans. They were part of the English-speaking, European-oriented society in that they practiced agriculture, were Catholic, and had an urban-centered life. But proximity to the Anglo-Americans aggravated hostility. They often stood in the way of Anglo-American newcomers because they held desirable land.

Conditions for Mexican-Americans varied in the Southwest after 1848. Resistance to American control was strongest in Texas, and hostility was common between the two groups. although some intermarriage took place. Generally, however, Mexican-Americans were called by derogatory names and were suspected of wanting revenge. The Texas Rangers began their history as a unique police force on horseback by earning a terrible reputation among Mexican-Americans for their violence and disrespect. Likewise, some Mexicans drove out Anglos and plotted separation from Texas; others, such as Juan Cortina and Gregorio Cortez, fought against the *gringos* (as Mexican-Americans often called Anglos). Although the historian Walter Prescott Webb set a pattern in which such men appeared as crude outlaws, Mexican-Americans saw them as heroes. Mexican resistance was futile in politics; its only outlet lay in physical actions.

Gradually the Mexican-Americans and Anglo-Americans reached an accommodation. In this arrangement Anglos had all the legal, political, and social advantages. Generally Mexican-Americans were better off living apart from Anglos, and most withdrew into life in their own neighborhoods, farms, and towns. If Anglos and Mexican-Americans lived in the same towns ghettos gradually developed, with the older parts of towns comprised of Mexican-Americans, Indians, blacks, and poor whites. In the barrio Mexican life was protected and preserved.

In New Mexico Territory (present-day New Mexico and Arizona) life for Mexican-Americans was very distinctive. The seizure of the territory was accomplished with almost no violence, and as a result Mexican-Americans got along better with the newcomers. Although many felt betrayed by high Mexican government officials, American control over New Mexico was not burdensome as compared to Texas. More intermarriage and cross-cultural relations took place. Thus, many older families in New Mexico are part Mexican and part Anglo, and the Hispanic and Mexican cultural heritage has survived. Nevertheless, what little political influence Mexican-Americans had could be expressed only through cooperation with the newcomers, for officials appointed from Washington ruled completely. By the time New Mexico and Arizona were made states (1910 and 1912, respectively), the Anglo-American population controlled government at the state level by manipulation of democratic processes. Only in some counties and towns of Texas and New Mexico did Mexican-Americans have a real voice in government.

California was the great prize of the Mexican War. President Polk had made his intentions to take California very clear. Thus secret missions and undercover agents were sent to buy or seize the territory by any means that would appear acceptable to public opinion. The small and scattered numbers of "Californios," as the Mexicans there were called, were not a violent people and their leaders were disunited over loyalty to Mexico. Careful planning and deceit on the part of the Americans and disunity among Californian provincial leaders led to the loss of the vast region. Soon California became a state, as did Texas.

The great gold rush changed California. As thousands of people poured in to get rich at any cost, Indians and Mexican-Americans suffered most. Their lands were often seized and they suffered violence. A new wealthy class emerged from the mining industry and agriculture. Money attracted talent, ambition, and Anglo cultural institutions quickly. The Mexican-Americans, deprived of leadership that could cope with the aggressive and violent newcomers, were simply overrun in California. Some combined with the new powerful groups in business and through marriage, but most withdrew to their dwindling lands and barrios. When more peaceful immigrants came from the East, a pattern of Mexican-American subordination and isolation was established. Although they and Anglos were economically interdependent, they lived their lives pretty much apart.

Between 1848 and 1910 Mexican-Americans were nevertheless vigorously preserving their cultural heritage. Many newspapers and magazines were printed in the Southwest, and novels and other published works from Mexico were common, although Mexican litera- ture has escaped study by Anglo-American scholars. Mexican-American cultural societies, insurance groups, and religious life were also vigorous.

With construction of railroads and telegraph lines, Mexican-Americans began to travel far from their bar- rios to work on railroads, drive cattle, and join the new groups of farm workers who lived on the move. Refrig- erated trains opened a new phase in winter crop agricul- ture in the Southwest. Mexican-Americans supplied much of the labor force and skills in mining, ranching, and agriculture. They were commonly used as a cheap source of labor, as were the Chinese.

A great flood of Mexican immigration changed Mex- ican-American life after 1910. The first wave came be- tween 1910 and 1917, during the Mexican Revolution. Most of the lawyers, doctors, engineers, and other pro- fessionals who fled Mexico planned to return but stayed on. Poor people fled for fear of recruitment and because their farms were ravaged by soldiers of both sides. These refugees tended to settle where relatives were already living. During the Roaring Twenties great pros- perity created a labor shortage. About the time that peace returned to Mexico, American labor recruiters ranged over Mexico hiring people to fill labor ranks in the United States. Immigration officials looked the other way as thousands of Mexicans crossed the border. During World War I many new jobs had opened for Mexican-Americans, and now labor shortages made them highly valued. Many barrios almost exploded with the newcomers. Housing was scarce and segregation kept most Mexican-Americans close to their barrio. Conditions became worse as a result of crowding, and the government did not usually provide paved streets, water supplies, schools, parks, and other public services. Too, tensions arose between the established Mexican- Americans and the newcomers.

The Immigration Act of 1924 for the first time re- stricted immigration to the United States in order to preserve its racial and/or ethnic composition. (Race is often confused with nationality and culture.) Fear of Mexican immigration motivated some of the supporters of this legislation, yet despite the law, Mexican immigra- tion continued until the early 1930s, when the labor market disappeared. Only then did immigration offi- cials try to stop the influx. Now Mexicans were undesir- able for employers as well as racists. Even then, however, Mexicans continued to sneak across the border, some- times with the help of officials and employers who pre- ferred illegal Mexican workers to Mexican-Americans, for wetbacks accepted lower wages and had no legal protection.

During the Great Depression life for Mexican- Americans, as for most minority groups, was harder than for others, for they were generally the last to be hired and the first to be fired. Many immigrants re- turned to Mexico and some Mexican-Americans chose to emigrate. A hundred years after the war between the two neighbor republics, Mexican-Americans still had relatives back in Mexico with farms or a business to which they could go if faced with starvation in the South- west. Some states and counties tried to ship Mexican immigrants back to Mexico by paying their travel costs.

The repatriation programs worked differently, but usu- ally various forms of pressure, such as police harass- ment, were put on Mexicans to leave, especially in south- ern California barrios.

American sociologists discovered Mexican-Ameri- cans during this time. Most of the literature presents them as a cause of problems in public health, jobs, edu- cation, and crime. To the racist literature of the nineteenth century, such as the popular dime novels, and the early twentieth century, sociological literature now added its voice. In few places could one read about the Mexican-American in a positive, or even neutral, light.

World War II changed that picture and, ironically, gave Mexican-Americans a new lease on life. Although Indians and blacks were still segregated in the military branches, Mexican-Americans got their first chance to compete with others on a democratic basis. Their service in technical and skilled areas, such as in the air forces, shattered the myths that they were good only with their hands. Outstanding valor in battle laid to rest the myth that they were docile or cowardly. Many died in the war after having volunteered for dangerous duty in the tank corps and marines, and barrios commonly displayed gold stars in the windows.

The GI generation of Mexican-Americans came home with greater vigor and pride. In greater numbers they would not stand for Anglo racism any more than enemies in the field. New veterans' groups in Texas, New Mexico, and California tried to open up housing to veterans, get better schools, and widen job oppor- tunities. New skills learned in the military were useful, and experience gained away from the barrios gave the veterans a broader viewpoint.

Thousands took advantage of the GI Bill of Rights, creating a new generation of businessmen and profes- sionals. More politically aware than their parents, most of these young people took advantage of new laws that discouraged prejudice and used the judicial system to their own ends.

The children of the GI generation became more like other young people due to the influences of the mass media. They still preserved much of the Mexican cul- ture, but fewer could read or speak Spanish. Their veteran parents had fought to gain use of the word "Mexican-American," rather than plain Mexican. Now some opposed the use of the hyphen because it seemed to imply inequality. Some took up words like *la raza* (those of Hispanic-American background) to kindle new pride in their cultural heritage. Others took up the word *chicano*, which has a negative meaning in Mexico, "country hick." They gave it a positive meaning and tried to gain common use of it as a badge of pride in Mexican heritage. By 1970 "Chicano" was in common use everywhere, despite some misgivings among older and more traditional Mexican-Americans. We are now in the Chicano generation. See CHICANO LIBERATION MOVEMENT.

See also SPANISH LANGUAGE IN THE SOUTHWEST.

See Rodolfo Acuna, *Occupied America* (1972), Carey McWilliams, *North from Mexico* (1948); Julian Nava, *Vi- va La Raza* (1973); and Cecil Robinson, *With the Ears of Strangers* (1963).—J. N.

Mexican War (1846-1848). On May 13, 1846, the United States declared war on the Republic of Mexico.

The failure to pay American claims, the desire to acquire the north Mexican provinces, and a boundary dispute precipitated the decision. The drift toward war had begun a year earlier, following the annexation of Texas, when the Mexican government, refusing to recognize the independence of Texas or the Rio Grande as an international boundary, had severed its diplomatic ties with the United States. Anticipating trouble, President James K. Polk had ordered Brigadier General Zachary TAYLOR to move a force from Louisiana to the Nueces River in Texas and, in a last-minute effort to settle differences, sent John Slidell to Mexico. When Slidell's mission failed, Taylor advanced to the Rio Grande, and on April 25, 1846, General Mariano Arista crossed the river and attacked the Americans. Receiving news of the hostilities, Congress in mid-May declared war, authorized the president to call up 50,000 volunteers for twelve months' service, and voted $10 million for an invasion of Mexico. The regular army was increased from about 7,200 to 15,540. The first call for volunteers was for 20,000 men to be raised in the states bordering the Ohio and the Mississippi valleys; by the fall of 1846 they had been mustered and were in Mexico. The total number of men who served in the war was about 90,000—31,000 regulars and 59,000 volunteers.

Americans volunteered for service eagerly, giving little thought to the distances involved, the problem of supply, or the dreaded *vomitó*. General in Chief of the Army Winfield Scott and his advisers proposed that two American armies be sent into Mexico: one army should move from the Rio Grande south through Monterrey and capture Mexico City; a second should strike west, seizing New Mexico and California. Simultaneously, American warships would blockade the principal Mexican seaports.

Even before he learned that war had been declared, Taylor fought two battles north of the Rio Grande. On May 8, near Palo Alto, and the following day, at Resaca de la Palma, he won victories over a superior Mexican force. Crossing the Rio Grande to Matamoros, Taylor marched upriver to Camargo and established a military depot. He then moved inland and in mid-September captured Monterrey and declared an eight-week armistice. Extending his defense line east to the coast, Taylor moved his headquarters west to Saltillo. On February 22, 1847, General Santa Anna with about twenty thousand men attacked Taylor at Buena Vista, seven miles south of Saltillo. The American army, which included the forces of Brigadier General John E. WOOL, numbered about four thousand eight hundred men. During the heavy fighting on the second day, Santa Anna turned the American left flank, but Taylor, who had been to Saltillo to check its defenses, arrived on the field with fresh troops and saved the day. His legions decimated by Taylor's light artillery, Santa Anna ended the battle and retreated to San Luis Potsi. The battle of Buena Vista, which has been called the most important engagement of the Mexican War, ended Taylor's campaign in Mexico. Within ten months he had fought and won four battles and gained control over the three Mexican states of Coahuila, Nuevo León, and Tamaulipas.

Meanwhile, Brigadier General Stephen Watts KEARNY had marched from Fort Leavenworth in June 1846 with about one thousand six hundred men—dragoons, Missouri Volunteers, and artillerymen—for New Mexico. He entered Santa Fe without opposition in mid-August, attached the province to the United States, established civil government, and selected territorial officials. Kearny then divided his forces, instructing Colonel Alexander W. DONIPHAN to march for Chihuahua, and Captain Philip St. George COOKE to open a wagon road through northern Sonora to California. By early October Kearny with one hundred dragoons was en route west to join the American forces struggling to conquer California.

Kearny's lieutenants executed their missions well. Doniphan moved south with five hundred men, defeated a Mexican army at El Brazito on the Rio Grande, and occupied El Paso in December; the following spring he entered Chihuahua, broke through an enemy force on the Sacramento River, and captured Chihuahua City. By midsummer his men had reached the Gulf Coast and had been shipped to New Orleans for discharge. Cooke left Santa Fe in October with the Mormon Battalion and a few wagons, headed southwest across New Mexico into Sonora, and struck the headwaters of the San Pedro. Heading north, then west across present-day southern Arizona, Cooke reached Tucson in mid-December. Marching north to the Gila, he again faced west, crossed the Colorado River, and joined Kearny's forces in California in late January 1847.

Upon reaching California in December, Kearny found the conquest incomplete. Commodore Robert F. STOCKTON, whose forces included Captain John C. Frémont's Bear Flag contingent, had seized Los Angeles but was soon driven out. Combining their forces, Stockton and Kearny on January 8-9, 1847, defeated the Mexican army at Los Angeles. On March 1 Kearny established civil government in California.

Because Taylor's victories had not been decisive, President Polk in November 1846 ordered General Winfield SCOTT to land an army at Veracruz and capture Mexico City. In March 1847 Scott put nearly twelve thousand men ashore near Veracruz, seized the town, and moved inland. Flanking Santa Anna's defenses at Cerro Gordo Pass, he eventually halted at Puebla, where reinforcements for his army arrived. With ten thousand effectives, Scott in August swung south of the capital, seized the towns of Contreras and Churubusco, and on August 24 declared an armistice. When Nicholas P. Trist, Polk's commissioner, failed to negotiate a peace, Scott launched an attack, stormed Molino del Rey and the fortress of Chapultepec, and marched into the Grand Plaza of Mexico City. On September 14, 1847, for the first time in United States history, the American flag was raised over a foreign capital.

At the village of Guadalupe Hidalgo, a few miles north of Mexico City, Trist on February 2, 1848, finally concluded a treaty and sent it to Washington, where despite opposition the agreement was approved (see GUADALUPE HIDALGO, TREATY OF). In July 1848 the American forces withdrew from Mexican soil.

The war had far-reaching effects. By the Treaty of Guadalupe Hidalgo, the United States acquired a vast western territory stretching from Texas to the Pacific and north to Oregon. Within a decade rich mineral strikes occurred, a large Spanish-speaking population known as MEXICAN-AMERICANS began adjusting to American institutions and society, a series of Indian wars broke out, and the clamor for transportation development to tie the new region to the East and provide ports to world markets reached back to Congress. At the same time, however, the Mexican acquisition renewed the debate over the extension of slavery and hastened the day when a civil war would tear the Union asunder.

See K. Jack Bauer, *The Mexican War, 1846-1848* (1974); Robert S. Henry, *The Story of the Mexican War* (1950); George L. Rives, *The United States and Mexico, 1821-1848,* 2 vols. (1913); Otis A. Singletary, *The Mexican War* (1960); and Justin H. Smith, *The War with Mexico,* 2 vols. (1919).—H. P. H.

Miami Indians. The Miami were an Algonquian tribe, known to themselves and the English colonists as Twightwees. At least part of the tribe was living near Green Bay, Wisconsin, in the mid-seventeenth century, but they moved about considerably in following years: to the lower end of Lake Michigan in Indiana by 1700, then to the vicinity of the Miami River in Ohio, and after 1763 back into Indiana.

The Miami were an important part of the western fur trade and alliance system that the French built up in the seventeenth century. As such they were frequent objects of Iroquois aggression before 1700, since the Iroquois wanted a share of the western fur trade and were allies of the English. When English colonists began to encroach upon their territories in the later eighteenth century, the Miami under LITTLE TURTLE joined the nearby Shawnee, Delaware, and other tribes in armed resistance, which was not fully broken until 1815.

Most of the Miami were removed to Kansas by 1827, and later to northeastern Oklahoma, where they still live. Numbering perhaps forty-five hundred in 1650, they were reduced to about fifteen hundred a century later, and only a few hundred survived into the twentieth century.

See F. V. Hodge, ed., *Handbook of American Indians North of Mexico,* 2 vols. (1907-10); and W. V. Kinietz, *The Indian Tribes of the Western Great Lakes* (1940).—A. W. T.

Michelson, Halvor. See GREAT LAKES, MEN OF THE.

Michigan, settlement of. There are two or three theories regarding the origin of the word *Michigan*, the most commonly mentioned being the Chippewa *nicigama,* meaning "large river." The state of Michigan borders on four of the five Great Lakes and is divided into an upper and lower peninsula by the Straits of Mackinac, which link Lakes Michigan and Huron. The peninsulas were originally occupied by the Ottawa, Potawatomi, Miami, Wyandot, and Chippewa Indians and such lesser tribes as the Menomini, Sauk, Huron, and Fox. Most of these Indians lived in villages along the shores of lakes and inland streams and made their living by gardening, hunting, fishing, and gathering, before the early white traders introduced the fur trade.

The first European to examine the area was, perhaps, Etienne Brulé, whom Lieutenant Governor Samuel de Champlain sent from Quebec about 1620 on an exploring expedition. Other early visitors from New France included Jean Nicolet, who sailed through the Straits of Mackinac in 1634; Father René Ménard, a Jesuit who established a mission at Keweenaw Bay in 1660; and Father Jacques Marquette, who eight years later founded Sault Ste. Marie, Michigan's first permanent settlement. Within a short time the Michigan region had been thoroughly explored and mapped by such famous

Frenchmen as Louis Jolliet; René Robert Cavelier, Sieur de La Salle; and Antoine de la Mothe Cadillac, founder of the future city of Detroit. But the French were more interested in developing the fur trade and in converting the Indians to Christianity than in encouraging settlements. Otherwise, they had made little progress by the time the British took over.

The British occupied all the former French forts in the Great Lakes region following the end of the French and Indian War and the signing of the Treaty of Paris in 1763. In that same year Indians massacred the entire garrison at Fort Michilimackinac and killed many of the settlers and soldiers at other Michigan forts. They were less successful under the Ottawa leader, Chief Pontiac, at Detroit and abandoned efforts to destroy the fort after a five months' siege. Once PONTIAC'S REBELLION was brought under control, British agents continued the French practice of exploiting the Great Lakes region for its furs. In 1774 Michigan became a part of the Province of Quebec and provided sanctuaries during the American Revolution for Indian and white parties raiding frontier settlements.

When Michigan became a part of the United States in 1783 its boundaries still had not been formed. Indeed, the British did not evacuate the military fortifications and trading centers of the region until thirteen years later. Meanwhile, the future twenty-sixth state formed part of the Northwest Territory, but few Anglo-Americans were acquainted with its geography and resources. When Indiana Territory was created in 1800 it included the western half of the Lower and the eastern half of the Upper Peninsula. Two years later Congress added the remainder of both peninsulas to Indiana. In 1805 it organized the Territory of Michigan and approved the appointment of William Hull as its first governor (see OLD NORTHWEST).

The population of the new territory grew very slowly and was still below five thousand at the outbreak of the WAR OF 1812. Most of the people lived in the vicinity of the capital at Detroit and were ill-prepared for defense against the British and Indian attacks that followed. The American fort at Mackinac Island fell in July 1812, and one month later Canadian forces under General Isaac Brock captured Detroit. They evacuated the settlement the next year following Oliver Hazard Perry's victory on Lake Erie, but they held on to Mackinac Island until the Treaty of Ghent in 1814.

Lewis CASS became govenor of the territory in 1813 and served until 1831. During that time the Indians gave up their claims throughout the region and ceased to be a threat to white settlement. But inadequate roads made it difficult for immigrants from the East to reach Michigan. Moreover, its false reputation as a land of swamps and barren soil discouraged homeseekers from entering the area in large numbers until after 1830. The federal census that year, incidentally, placed the territory's entire population at approximately thirty-two thousand—most of whom lived in Detroit and surrounding communities.

Several things combined almost overnight to change Michigan from a lethargic wilderness to a bustling frontier state. The opening of the Erie Canal in 1825 provided easy access to Great Lake ports for those who wanted to migrate westward, and six years later steamers from Buffalo began depositing immigrants at Detroit. Soon afterward the Eastern press and writers of guidebooks began featuring the news that Michigan contained millions of acres of rich soil and luxurious forests.

By 1836 Detroit boasted a population of ten thousand inhabitants, a theater, museum, public gardens, schools, churches, libraries, lighted streets, and an efficient water and sewer system. It also had become the gateway to such rich farming communities as Pontiac and Rochester in the Clinton River valley, Ann Arbor and Ypsilanti on the Huron River, and Monroe, Tecumseh, and Adrian along the Raisin River. Because of the Erie Canal and the newly completed Chicago and Territorial Road, the rolling hills, level plains, and fertile soils of Michigan were no longer isolated from land-hungry immigrants.

During the 1830s speculators laid out and developed new cities such as Kalamazoo, Saginaw, Grand Haven, and Grand Rapids. By the middle of the decade the territorial population was large enough to apply for admission to the Union as a state. But there was a two-year delay, until January 26, 1837, because of a boundary dispute with neighboring Ohio. Congress finally awarded the "Toledo Strip" to Ohio and placated Michigan by giving it the entire Upper Peninsula. It eventually became apparent that the rich iron and copper deposits in the Upper Peninsula were ample compensation for the initial loss. Except for the northern section, the state by 1850 had passed from the frontier stage.

According to the official census, more than a third of the total population of 400,000 in 1850 were native-born. The largest number of residents, or approximately forty percent, had migrated into Michigan from the eastern states of New York, Pennsylvania, and New Jersey. The rest had come from Europe (fifteen percent), New England (eight percent), Old Northwest (five percent), and the South (one percent). Lumbering and agriculture were the principal industries until long after the Civil War. Before the end of the century water and rail transportation and the development of great mineral resources made Michigan one of the most populous and industrialized states in the Union.

See Frederick C. Bald, *Michigan in Four Centuries* (1961); Willis F. Dunbar, *Michigan Through the Centuries*, 4 vols. (1955); Bert Hudgins, *Michigan: Geographic Background in Development of the Commonwealth* (1961); and Milo M. Quaife and Sidney Glazer, *Michigan, from Primitive Wilderness to Industrial Commonwealth* (1948).—W. E. H.

middle border. Coined by novelist Hamlin GARLAND, the term *middle border* was both a place—the advancing frontier of the trans-Mississippi West—and a way of life. As a youth, Garland and his family followed the middle border, moving from Wisconsin to Minnesota and then to Iowa. Recalling his childhood in *A Son of the Middle Border* (1917), Garland wrote that his family "set toward the west, bound once again to overtake the actual line of the middle border." After Garland had left home and was beginning his literary career, his family settled in South Dakota. "The border line had moved on," wrote Garland, "and my indomitable Dad was moving with it."

The middle border was more than just a geographical delineation to Garland, however. As described in his novels and short stories, it also meant hardship; growing old before one's time; endless days of toil and boredom; the sometimes cruel and sometimes beautiful prairie; and—occasionally—good times, friendship, and laughter.

In addition to the books by Garland, see Carl O. Sauer, "Homestead and Community on the Middle Border," in Howard W. Ottoson, ed., *Land Use Policy and Problems in the United States* (1963).—D. J. T.

Miles, Nelson Appleton (1839-1925). Soldier. Born in Massachusetts, Miles was a clerk in a crockery store before he began his military career. He joined the army in 1861 and by 1865 had been wounded four times, fought in almost every important battle of the Army of the Potomac, and had been promoted to the rank of major general of volunteers. In 1892 he received the Congressional Medal of Honor for his bravery at Chancellorsville in 1863. Miles went to the frontier as an infantry officer and was a primary field commander in the Red River War (1874-75) against the Kiowa, Comanche, and Southern Cheyenne Indians. His winter campaign on the Northern Plains in 1876-77 brought several victories over the Sioux and forced many to surrender, and in 1877 he made a forced march to intercept the fleeing Nez Percé and forced their surrender.

In May 1886 General Miles replaced General George Crook as commander of the Department of Arizona and was charged with the responsibility of capturing GERONIMO and his small band, whose most recent flight from the Apache reservation had been in March 1886. Miles relied on white troops rather than on Apache scouts, whom Crook had used in dealing with the Indians. The burden of the campaign was placed on Captain Henry Lawton. He pursued a band of about forty Apache through the Sierra Madre, Mexico, although he rarely had a trail to follow. Within a period of four months—from May to September 1886—he traveled more than three thousand miles. Only Lawton and a surgeon, Leonard Wood (later commanding general of the army), served throughout the entire campaign, and Lawton became so discouraged at their failure to find and defeat Geronimo that he said he would "cry if it would do any good." Miles eventually sent Lieutenant Charles Gatewood and two Apache scouts to contact Geronimo. Gatewood did meet Geronimo and arranged negotiations that led to his surrender, but Miles never credited him for this work. Miles had been instructed to obtain an unconditional surrender, but unable to defeat Geronimo outright, he eventually violated his orders and negotiated a surrender with terms, whereby Geronimo and his band were sent to confinement on a Florida reservation. He also sent to Florida the reservation Chiricahua and the Apache scouts, who had not only been loyal to Miles but were also enlisted men in the United States Army.

When the Ghost Dance uprising developed on the Sioux reservation in South Dakota in 1890, Miles was commander of the vast Military Division of the Missouri. A leading expert on Indians, Miles directed the concentration of troops in South Dakota and worked vainly for a peaceful solution to the Sioux disturbances. He favored military control over the Sioux both before and after the battle of Wounded Knee in 1890 and wanted to bring the Sioux into the agencies and disarm them.

After the battle he aggressively sought to implement his policies for the Indians.

Miles was in charge of the troops sent to quell riots rising out of the Pullman strike in 1894 and a year later became commander-in-chief of the army. During the Spanish-American War, however, he was not permitted to lead the expeditionary forces to Cuba, because at the time he was involved in a bitter public quarrel with Secretary of War Russell A. Alger and was officially censured by President Theodore Roosevelt for his involvement in a controversy with the navy. His expedition against Puerto Rico went almost unnoticed. He retired a lieutenant general in 1903.

Miles was an extremely able officer who combined aggressiveness and boldness with imagination. He was also vain, pompous, and dogmatic (Theodore Roosevelt called him a "brave peacock"), and his primary concern was usually his own advancement. His criticism of most other officers caused many to dislike him. He was particularly critical of those who had been to West Point, believing that training there gave officers an unfair advantage in promotions. In addition to his other quarrels, Miles was engaged in a long feud with General George CROOK concerning the confinement of Apache in Florida and argued with General Oliver Oits Howard over the honors from the capture of the Nez Percé.

Miles left his own record of his career in *Personal Recollections of Nelson A. Miles* (1897) and *Serving the Republic* (1911). See also Virginia W. Johnson, *The Unregimented General: A Biography of Nelson A. Miles* (1962).—R. N. E.

Miller, Alfred Jacob (1810-1874). Painter. Miller was born in Baltimore, Maryland, the son of a grocer. Showing a marked talent for drawing as a youth, he studied for a while under Thomas Sully and in 1833 went to Paris, where he studied for a year at the Ecole des Beaux-Arts. After Paris and a visit to Rome and Florence, Miller returned to the United States in 1834 and set up a studio in Baltimore. He was not very successful at this time, however, and later moved to New Orleans, where he attempted making a living at portrait painting.

It was during his first year in New Orleans that Miller met former British officer and sportsman Sir William Drummond Stewart, who was about to embark upon one of his periodic hunting expeditions into the Far West. Impressed with young Miller's work, Stewart retained him as artist for the proposed trip, which, in the company of a caravan of wagons and men of the American Fur Company, was made in the summer of 1837 along the Oregon Trail to Fort William on the Laramie River in present-day Wyoming. The journey took Miller through the territories of many Indian tribes and eventually across the Rockies to the fur company's rendezvous on the Green River in Oregon. After the expedition Miller returned to Baltimore and produced a number of pictures from the sketches he had made during the summer's trip. He then sailed for Europe in 1840 to visit Stewart at Murthly Castle and painted a number of western scenes for his patron's hunting lodge.

Miller returned to Baltimore two years later and continued for the remainder of his working life to paint Rocky Mountain landscapes and hunting scenes for his eastern audiences. When he died, he left a large volume of work illustrative of his single western experience.

Ignored by most contemporary critics and forgotten altogether by art historians in the years since, Miller's paintings have received attention recently because of their documentary value in relating the details of the life of the Indian and the Rocky Mountain fur trapper of his day.

The largest collections of Miller's work are at the Stark Museum of Art, Orange, Texas; the Walters Art Gallery, Baltimore; the Joslyn Art Museum, Omaha, Nebraska; and the Thomas Gilcrease Institute of American History and Art, Tulsa, Oklahoma. A few of his western scenes were reproduced as salable prints in the 1850s and others appeared in book publications. A manuscript annotating 166 of his western studies, collected together under the title "Rough Drafts to Notes on Indian Sketches," is preserved in the library of the Gilcrease Institute. It is believed to have been compiled by Miller sometime after 1859 to serve as the text for a proposed printing.

See Bernard DeVoto, *Across the Wide Missouri* (1947); Marvin C. Ross, *The West of Alfred Jacob Miller* (1958); and Paul Rossi and David C. Hunt, *The Art of the Old West* (1971).—D. C. H.

Miller, Geroge L. (1831-1920). Nebraska editor. Miller was born in Booneville, New York, and graduated from the College of Physicians and Surgeons in New York City in 1852. After practicing medicine in Syracuse, he moved to Omaha, Nebraska Territory, in September 1854. Miller soon abandoned medicine and became active in real estate development and politics. He was elected to the territorial House of Representatives in 1855 and from 1857 through 1859 served in the territorial council. For a brief time Miller edited the St. Joseph (Missouri) *Gazette* and from 1861 to 1864 was post trader at Fort Kearny, Nebraska. In the latter year he won the Democratic nomination for territorial delegate to Congress, but was defeated in a campaign marked by the hostile passions of the Civil War.

In October 1865 Miller established the Omaha *Herald*, which, despite its Democratic partisanship, quickly attained success. No person exceeded Miller in promoting the development of Nebraska and, most especially, Omaha. Recognizing the importance of railroads to Omaha's growth, he maintained close relations with leading officials of the Union Pacific. In 1868 he helped convince leaders of the railroad that a Missouri River bridge should be constructed at Omaha, rather than at a point downstream. This decision may well have been crucial to the continued growth of the city.

Since his paper was often quoted in the eastern press, Miller used the *Herald* to preach the virtues of Nebraska's agricultural opportunities. As an advocate of progressive agricultural practices, he often published articles of technical advice for Nebraska farmers. In the 1890s University of Nebraska scientists discovered that Turkey Red winter wheat was superior to spring wheat in rust- and drought-resistance. Accordingly, Miller worked with Burlington Railroad officials to encourage Nebraska farmers to plant winter wheat in preference to the spring variety, which they traditionally had grown. Soon after 1900 the state's grain-growers made this transition and Nebraska became a major wheat-producer.

Miller sold the *Herald* to John A. McShane, an Omaha businessman, in 1887 and two years later Gilbert M.

Hitchcock acquired the publication. Hitchcock merged the *Herald* with his *World*, thus forming the Omaha *World-Herald,* which remains a major regional newspaper.

See Wallace Brown, "George L. Miller and the Struggle Over Nebraska Statehood," *Nebraska History*, (December 1960); and "George L. Miller and the Boosting of Omaha," *ibid.* (Fall 1969).—H. A. D.

Miller, Henry (1827-1916). Rancher. Miller was born in Württemberg, Germany. His family name was Kreiser. He emigrated as a young man to New York with that surname, but when he booked passage from New York, where he had been a butcher, to San Francisco, he bought a ticket already made out to a man named Henry Miller. Young Kreiser took not only Miller's ticket but his name as well.

Miller soon became a successful butcher in San Francisco. His business mushroomed when he went into partnership with Charles Lux, an Alsatian-born butcher who had been Miller's chief competitor in the booming city. An expansive, persuasive man, Lux was at home with the business leaders and gold millionaires of San Francisco and from them raised funds for Miller to invest in ranches. In 1863 Miller bought the Rancho Sanjon de Santa Rita in the San Joaquin valley and launched the firm of Miller & Lux, which eventually became the largest ranching enterprise on the Pacific Coast. More than fifteen ranches came under their famous "Double H" brand. By the 1890s their range lands stretched into Oregon, where Miller bought the properties of Todhunter and Devine, and into Nevada, where Miller purchased the holdings of N. H. A. "Hock" Mason, who had been the largest rancher in that state. Many ranches not bearing the "Double H" brand were actually financed by Miller and were usually absorbed by him if the rancher proved unproductive. At one point a herd of 100,000 cattle grazed on Miller & Lux lands along forty miles of the San Joaquin River, and a total of a million cattle were to be found on all of their holdings.

Perceiving the farming possibilities of the San Joaquin valley, which the firm dominated, Miller built storage dams and irrigation systems and began to produce vegetables and farm produce on some 500,000 acres. His ruthless efforts to control the local water rights led to many bitter court and legislative battles with settlers and the state, but he was usually successful in his fight. Many of the court cases set important precedents for the water laws of California. When Lux died in 1887 Miller engaged in a twenty-year court fight with Lux's heirs before ownership of the enormous property-holdings was settled. Miller reorganized his holdings as the Pacific Livestock Company before his death at the age of eighty-nine.

See George F. Brimlow, *Harney County, Oregon, and Its Range Land* (1951); and Giles French, *Cattle Country of Peter French* (1964).—H. R. L.

Miller, James P. (1866-1909). Professional killer. "Deacon Jim" Miller attended church regularly and never drank, cursed, or smoked, but he killed for money. He was born in Van Buren, Arkansas, and the next year moved to Texas. After his parents died, he lived with a married sister until he shot his brother-in-law to death for some mysterious reason in 1884 and was arrested for murder. He was convicted, but on appeal won a new trial and, eventually, freedom. Later, he showed up in Run-

nels County, Texas, where he met Manning Clements, a crusty old trail driver related to outlaw John Wesley Hardin. When Clements was killed by Joe Townshend, the local marshal, Miller bushwhacked the marshal with a shotgun. He later married Clements' daughter and became a close friend of his son, Mannie.

In 1890 Miller opened a hotel in Pecos, Texas, and began to cultivate the respectable part of the community. He was convincing in his role as a good citizen, and Sheriff G. A. ("Bud") Frazer appointed Miller a deputy sheriff. For a time it appeared to be a good appointment, but people grew suspicious in 1892 when Miller killed a Mexican prisoner in his charge. Eventually, Frazer learned that Miller was involved in cattle stealing. Once Miller knew that Frazer suspected him, he was determined to kill the sheriff. Frazer, told of Miller's intentions in May 1893, apparently contacted the Texas Rangers, and Miller was arrested in July on a charge of mule theft. Miller was released on bail, and the case was eventually dismissed. Miller's release unnerved Frazer, who decided to protect himself by killing Miller. In December 1893 and again in May 1894 the frightened ex-sheriff shot Miller without inflicting fatal wounds. Following the second shooting, charges were filed against Frazer, but the case was not heard until May 1896, when Frazer was acquitted. In September 1896, Miller found Frazer playing cards in a Toyah, Texas, saloon and killed him with a shotgun blast. Miller was arrested, but his trial ended in deadlock; a second trial resulted in a verdict of guilty, which, however, was set aside on appeal. In the meantime, Miller was at large. Several deaths are attributed to him during those months, but Miller emerged unscathed. Incredibly, he even served as a Texas Ranger for a time.

During the next few years, Miller killed several other men in Texas and Oklahoma, these times for money. It was in this period that he gained his reputation as a professional killer. At least seven men died at Miller's hands between 1896 and 1907, and there are rumors of more. He was probably the man who in 1908 killed Pat Garrett, the lawman who had killed Billy the Kid, although another man took the blame. The next year Miller was hired to kill an ex-lawman named A. A. "Gus" Bobbitt. Bobbitt was shotgunned from ambush but lived long enough to suggest the man responsible. Based on that Miller was eventually captured. On the night of April 13, 1909, Miller and three others were dragged from the jail at Ada, Oklahoma, and lynched in a barn.

See Colin W. Rickards, *How Pat Garrett Died* (1970); and Glenn Shirley, *Shotgun for Hire* (1970).—G. L. R.

Miller, Joaquin [Cincinnatus Hiner] (1839-1913). Poet. Miller was born in a covered wagon as it crossed from Indiana into Ohio, so he later claimed. His parents, though respectable farmers, were incorrigible wanderers, and most of his early years were spent in aimless travels among the settlements of the middle border. In 1852 his parents decided to try their luck in the recently opened territories of the Pacific Northwest and set out for Oregon, which they were to reach seven months later. In 1856 Miller left his parents' Oregon home for the Klamath River settlements just below the Oregon-California border, an area in which he stayed until 1859. There he went to work as an odd-job helper of the local gold miners, became involved in a nebulous

Joaquin Miller, poet of the West. (Library of Congress)

plan to establish an Indian republic in the locality, and adopted the name Joaquin in honor, or so he avowed, of the famous California bandit Joaquin Murieta, whom he was later to memorialize in verse. The facts of this period of his life are difficult to establish, partly because documentary evidence is lacking and partly because Miller consciously falsified the impression of himself that he gave out for public consumption. He claimed to have fought with the Indians against the whites, an assertion that is in all probability untrue, and to have accompanied the American adventurer William Walker on his filibustering expedition to Nicaragua, a statement that is demonstrably false. In 1861 Miller became an express rider between Walla Walla, Washington, and the newly opened mines at Millersburg, Idaho, and in 1863 was for a short time the editor of the Eugene, Oregon, *Democratic Register*. His editorial sympathies were secessionist and made him extremely unpopular in Oregon, which was strongly Unionist in its loyalties. He left Eugene for San Francisco the same year, where he married a mysterious "Minnie Myrtle," a young lady with whom he had been in correspondence, whom he was to immortalize in his verse, and who later divorced him.

His rather cool reception as a harmless eccentric by San Francisco literary circles drove him back once more to Oregon. He lived there until 1870, when he went to Europe. In London he affected "western" clothing of the sombrero and cowhide boot variety and was adopted by literary society as an authentic American genius, an unrefined, though doubtless valuable, nugget from the gold fields of California. He found especially congenial

spirits among the London Pre-Raphaelite Brotherhood and began to see himself in Byronic terms as a kind of Childe Joaquin nursing a mysterious sorrow while he pursued his destiny in the romantic capitals of the world. In 1871 he returned briefly to the United States, but in 1872 set off again for Europe by a roundabout route through South America and the Near East. In 1876 he was again in the United States, living in various cities until 1886, when with his second wife he once again went to California. There in San Francisco he settled into yet another role, as the grand old man of western letters. This role is less anachronistic than it sounds, since by the 1880s California had changed immeasurably from the rough-and-ready frontier society of the days of '49, of which Miller liked to consider himself a typical representative. His new role seemed authentic at least to the New York *Journal*, which sent him to cover the Klondike gold rush of 1897-98 as a special correspondent. In 1898 he returned to San Francisco, where he lived until his death, a notorious if scarcely respected "character."

Miller's poetic achievement is almost entirely forgotten today. He wrote too much and revised too little, and his volumes of western poetry—including *Joaquin, et al.* (1869), *Songs of the Sierras* (1871), *Fallen Leaves* (1873), *By the Sun-Down Seas* (1873), and *Shadows of Shasta* (1881)—are generally unknown even in the heavily excerpted posthumous collection *The Poetical Works of Joaquin Miller* (1923). Moreover, much of the interest his contemporaries felt in Miller was clearly attributable, even at the time, to his eccentricity, and after his death interest in his poetry waned. The English critics who saw in him an authentic American genius, a new poetic voice sounding—with Whitman—a "barbaric yawp," were quite simply mistaken. Miller's verse is conventional in the extreme, and though he shared Whitman's passion for self-publicity, his writing is strident rather than original, bombastic rather than profound.

See O. W. Frost, *Joaquin Miller* (1967); M. M. Marberry, *Splendid Poseur* (1953); Martin S. Peterson, *Joaquin Miller, Literary Frontiersman* (1937); and Stuart Paul Sherman, Introduction to Joaquin Miller, *The Poetical Works*, edited by Sherman (1923).—J. K. F.

mining, metal. By universal usage, the word *mining* has been made to cover remarkably varied activities, ranging from simple work with a shovel and pan, as in the traditional picture of the forty-niner PROSPECTOR, to the creation of a vast underground maze of chambers, passageways, and shafts on the Comstock Lode, or to the stripping of thousands of tons of copper ore per day by steam shovels at Bingham Canyon. In the West each of these types of mining—and several others besides—was dominant for a period and served as the economic base upon which ambitious men built their individual careers and upon which western society as a whole created towns, cities, transportation facilities, and a wide spectrum of dependent industries and social activities (see MINING TOWNS). As a step toward simplicity, this discussion will divide western mining history into two general periods—an era of almost exclusive interest in precious metals, and a subsequent era in which base metals became the principal concern, even though production of gold and silver continued.

Rich superficial gold placers—the least demanding species of mineral deposit in terms of technological un-

Hydraulic mining. (Library of Congress)

derstanding and capital investment required—first introduced the West to mining. During the preceding rule of Spain and Mexico, discoveries of minerals had been made at several locations, such as gold placers in New Mexico, silver in Arizona, copper in Arizona and New Mexico, and quicksilver in California, but exploitation had been very limited, quite local in its influence, and intermittent. With the unexpected discovery of gold at Sutter's Mill in 1848 (see John A. SUTTER), so soon after the conquest from Mexico, a totally different situation broke upon the West, as people with all kinds of vocational backgrounds and from almost all parts of the world came hurrying to California (see GOLD AND SILVER RUSHES).

The relatively simple requirements to work superficial placers, and the more complex means of beginning operations on veins, were met by hasty borrowing from the technology that had been developed in classical and medieval times and codified during the Renaissance in that most admirable of mining manuals, *De re metallica* (1556), written by a Saxon who called himself Agricola. Spanish-Americans, the heirs to this great European tradition, were often the medium through which Anglo-Americans learned fundamentals. Indeed, some Anglo-Americans had already been in contact with Spanish-Americans while working primitive gold mines in Georgia and North Carolina during the two decades before Sutter's Mill. In the Illinois country, LEAD MINING also had been instructive. For guidance in underground operations, however, Americans learned to seek out Cornishmen, who had acquired their knowledge and skills during generations in the tin mines of the old country and who sometimes had had further experience in the copper mines of the Great Lakes region before coming to California.

Much of the Americans' effort during the first quarter century of precious metal mining was essentially an attempt to adapt to their own needs Spanish methods of surface mining and ore treatment, and Cornish methods of underground mining—plus Welsh smelting techniques and a little metallurgy and chemistry from Germany. In each case the American tendency was to do things on a bigger scale and more quickly and to replace human and animal labor with some other source of power—water or steam.

At the start of the gold rush, with the emphasis on placer mining, the pick and shovel, prospecting pan, rocker, "long tom," and sluice were the principal implements employed. With them was used quicksilver, which will amalgamate with gold to the exclusion of worthless material. (The mercury and gold can then be separated by heating in a retort.) A beginning toward solving the more difficult problem of how to free gold that was encased in veins or lodes was made by copying some of the traditional devices for crushing gold-bearing rock, such as the arrastra, which was a circular pit in which heavy stones were dragged over partly broken ore, or the stamp mill, in which heavy, iron-shod stamps rose and fell as if they were a huge mechanized pestle and mortar.

The years 1848-59 constitute a subperiod within the precious-metal era of mining history. During those years activities were confined mostly to California, with attention centered at first on the famous Mother Lode, a belt of 120 miles of mining country on the western slope of the Sierra Nevada, although soon miners became aware of the rich deposits in the Sierra Nevada just north of the Mother Lode, and of the less attractive diggings in the Californian northwest. Some mining spilled over into southern Oregon and the western fringes of southern Arizona and central Nevada. In type of mining, simple placers lost their appeal in the middle 1850s, when exhaustion of the more accessible deposits forced men to turn to elaborate cooperative efforts to divert present-day rivers from their courses, so as to expose the auriferous beds, or to try to reach the deeply buried channels of prehistoric rivers, which were hidden beneath layers of accumulated debris.

For this last operation a method of removing masses of low-paying material had to be devised, and for it Californians developed one of their most notable innovations, hydraulic mining, which means washing down deep gravels with quantities of water shot out of a cannon-like nozzle under very high pressure. Hydraulic mining, in turn, made it necessary to create reservoirs high up in the mountains and bring water through flumes and ditches for very long distances to the scene of operations.

As this perhaps suggests, much of the Californians' contribution to the ancient art of placer mining lay in the field of engineering, where the size and audacity of Californian damming projects, aqueducts, and lines of sluices won worldwide attention. Much the same was true when Californians turned to vein, or lode, mining. The basic implement, the stamp mill, was centuries-old in concept; what the Californians did was to adapt it to modern steam power, increase its size and strength, and devise a series of mechanical improvements for the stamp mill itself and for handling the crushed ore after it came from the stamps. While progress in mechanical engineering was rapid, Californians were relatively slow in seeking greater knowledge of metallurgy and chemistry, on the one hand, and underground development, on the other. There was a pronounced tendency to rely on German or British specialists for the one and Cornishmen for the other. Nor had Californians discovered the need for careful control of operating costs or equally careful study of the percentage of gold saved by their machinery and processes.

By the opening of a new subperiod in 1859, one could hardly say that Californians had lifted lode mining up to a level of mature effectiveness, yet they had gone far enough to be able to provide the leadership when veins of silver were discovered in that year on the Comstock Lode of NEVADA, near VIRGINIA CITY. With a typically American extravagance, operations on the Comstock were quickly enlarged to unprecedented dimensions. The Comstock became internationally famous for its huge stamp mills, vast underground workings, and very large plants for treating the crushed ore. The problem of how to keep underground chambers from caving in was solved by one of the most notable Comstock innovations, the "square-set" pattern of underground timbers, devised by Philip Deidesheimer, a German-born engineer from California. It was copied throughout the West. Pumping out the quantities of underground water was handled by an old and proven device, the Cor-

nish pump, with its characteristic long wooden pump rod.

A high degree of efficiency in saving precious metal and keeping down costs was never achieved. Furthermore, with the relatively unfamiliar device of the incorporated company, which divorced ownership from control, managerial dishonesty became all too possible. Nevertheless, the output of precious metal from the Comstock was immense—perhaps $300 million from 1859 to the early 1880s. Equally important, the Comstock created individual fortunes that were soon seeking investment elsewhere, as in the cases of George Hearst and John P. JONES. It also created a large class of experienced and resourceful mining men of every category, from owner and manager down to the "muckers" who loaded the ore cars. Soon these "graduates" of the Comstock school of mining were at work throughout the West.

While lode mining was thus advancing, the Californian precedent was also inspiring pioneering. Starting in 1858 and 1859, men who had learned something about mining in California set off as prospectors and participants in rushes to all parts of the Far West. Most sought placer gold initially, and in the 1860s they found it in abundance in Idaho and Montana, less so in Colorado, and much less so in Arizona, New Mexico, and Utah. Their searches extended up into British Columbia and down into Mexico.

Chinese laborers sluicing for gold. (National Archives)

A cross-sectional view of the Comstock mine in 1876. (Bancroft Library)

In Colorado, after its initial placer boom, at several points in Montana, and throughout the Great Basin, mining men soon turned to the task of freeing gold and silver ores from solid rock. They found that the California and Comstock experiences offered only limited guidance. The relative simplicity of Comstock silver ores had been misleading; many silver ores in the Great Basin and Rocky Mountains were silver-lead, which required smelting and involved production of lead as a by-product. Until railroad transportation became available in the 1870s, it was economically impossible to ship out the lead or to bring in the large amounts of fuel, fluxes, and supplies needed for smelters. Equally difficult technical and economic problems were encountered in Colorado gold lodes, where once the veins had reached even moderate depth, the gold proved to be in chemical combination with sulphides, thus constituting what miners called "sulphurets" or "refractory" or pyritic ores.

The decline of simple placer mining, the complexities of "hard-rock" mining, and the increasing need for sophisticated, heavily capitalized operations made the late 1860s and the early 1870s a difficult era of transition. Factors that favored an ultimate solution were the advent of railroad transportation, a somewhat more favorable level of other costs, including wages and interest on capital, and a steadily growing technical compe-

tence. The latter benefited especially from the presence of a small but growing and highly significant number of professionally trained engineers from European and eastern schools (see MINING ENGINEER).

One such European-trained mining engineer, August R. Meyer, was sent into California Gulch, Colorado, in 1876, where he correctly determined that reported silver ores were silver-lead carbonates. The town of Leadville in COLORADO, located at 10,000-feet altitude, thus boomed into existence in 1877, soon had railroad service, and soon became a great producer of silver, a major source of lead, and a center of effective smelting operations. Slightly earlier in time and less dramatic in volume, Eureka, Nevada, achieved a similar output of silver and lead. A gold rush to the remote Coeur d'Alene region of northern Idaho in the early 1880s led to the discovery of silver, lead, and zinc ores and the creation of still another major center of mining, ore treatment, and smelting of both base and precious metals.

The most remarkable instance of this kind occurred at Butte, MONTANA, where Marcus DALY, once a penniless Irish immigrant, persuaded three newly rich tycoons of San Francisco, including the veteran mining man George Hearst, to back him in developing what he believed to be a silver mine. In 1882 Daly notified his partners that in buying the Anaconda they had unwittingly acquired one of the richest copper mines in the world. The elements present at Butte were characteristic of the new era of the 1880s and 1890s: a shift to copper; management by Daly, a self-made product of Nevada and Utah mines; financial backing by well-to-do absentee owners; a large initial capital investment, said to have been $4 million prior to realizing a return; creation of a new company town (Anaconda) that soon had a population of two thousand and housed a crew of thoroughly professional miners and smelter men, many of whom were immigrants; participation in an international syndicate to "corner" the world copper market; and ultimate ownership by eastern interests that included the "Standard Oil crowd" and the head of the National City Bank of New York.

The new age that opened during the 1880s and 1890s came to maturity only in the twentieth century. It stressed technological innovation and the application of newly acquired scientific understanding and thus needed the services of professionally trained engineers, metallurgists, chemists, and geologists who could keep abreast of and adapt to local needs some of the infinitely varied technical advances then being achieved throughout the thoroughly international world of mining. In 1900 Anaconda Copper Mining Company was persuaded to establish the first resident geological staff to be employed by a mine. The new mines, or the rejuvenated old ones, became massive industrial undertakings in which there was a constant searching for ways to reduce operating costs per unit handled and ways to retain a higher percentage of the valuable content of any mineral processed. Viewed in this light, the gold rush to the Yukon, Klondike, and Nome in ALASKA at the turn of the century seems an anachronism, a last romantic adventure.

Far more typical of the new age was the revolutionary implication of the new cyanide process for use with gold tailings and gold ores. Introduced to the world through patents obtained by three researchers in Glasgow, Scotland, in 1887, it was first tried commercially in New Zealand and then was applied in South Africa with sensational success before being adopted in the United States during the 1890s and the opening years of the twentieth century. Through its use, mines with low-grade gold ores that had not hitherto paid the cost of production could now count on as much as twenty to twenty-five percent more income from the same ores.

Equally important for COPPER MINING and ultimately also for zinc was the flotation process, developed in Britain and tested in Australia under a series of basic patents granted between 1894 and 1905. First tested experimentally in the United States with lead-zinc ores at Butte, beginning in 1911, it was soon shifted to copper ores in Arizona and at Butte, and during trial operations in 1913-16 proved to be a highly effective agent for increasing the percentage of copper "recovered." The flotation process made it economically feasible to exploit immense bodies of low-grade copper ore in ARIZONA, Utah, Nevada, and Montana. While the main use of the new process was in the burgeoning copper industry, successful experimentation soon established it as essential also to the much smaller western lead-zinc operations. It is no exaggeration to assert that the introduction of cyanidation for gold and flotation for copper and zinc revolutionized those great branches of western mining.

The new emphasis on copper reflected the obvious circumstance that with the introduction of electricity a constantly expanding market for copper was opening. The old monopoly of the Great Lakes states was broken, partly by the simple fact of the huge output of the new western mines, and partly by the development in Britain of the electrolytic method of refining copper, which permitted the western mines, starting with Montana in the 1890s, to produce a refined copper that was high enough in quality to compete with the remarkably pure native copper that the Lake states had long been marketing. Electrolytic extraction of zinc came much more slowly because the early experiments, conducted mostly in Europe, produced unsatisfactory results. Successful development came only under the stimulus of high zinc prices during World War I.

Electricity played a major role also in one of the central preoccupations of mine managers at the end of the century: how to bring power less expensively to the mountainous sites in which mines were often located, and how to transmit power down into the mine itself. Power had usually meant steam engines, which raised serious questions as to fuel supply, even after western coal began to be available. Steam engines, again, were sufficient for operating hoists, pumps, and mills, but were ill-suited to use underground or to any purpose that required transmission of power for any distance, because of the inefficient system of belts. The need was great for some means of introducing power underground, for such fundamental purposes as operating drills and hauling ore cars. Late in the nineteenth century, good results were obtained from the use of compressed air, despite the unavoidable clumsiness of running air lines and hoses underground. The highly successful North Star gold mine at Grass Valley, California, was an example of a mine that relied upon compressed air for many years, starting in 1895. Its compressors were driven by a huge Pelton waterwheel.

But nothing could rival the potentialities of electricity. Electricity could be generated at some point convenient to fuel supplies or water power and conveyed to even the most inaccessible mines, while within the mine wires could supply power for all kinds of uses that would replace human and animal labor underground and would permit a much more rapid and more massive exploitation. The first use of an electric motor in western mining is believed to have been at Aspen, Colorado, in 1888, when a streetcar motor was used to haul ore cars. At the Virginius mine in Ouray, Colorado, engineers calculated that the total cost of installing their electric power plant was no more than they would have spent each year for fuel for a steam engine.

Perhaps the most remarkable instance of what the new industrial technology could do was at Bingham Canyon, Utah. There preliminary studies indicated that very low-grade porphyry copper ore was disseminated through literally millions of tons of material. The percentage of copper in this huge mass was believed to be only one to two percent. Elaborate promotional efforts and financial maneuvers finally united the support of the Guggenheims and the American Smelting and Refining Company ("the smelter trust") in accordance with an agreement reached in 1905. Under the driving leadership of a young engineer, Daniel C. Jackling, the property was organized on what was genuinely a mass-production basis. Steam shovels stripped off the "dirt" and loaded it onto railroad dump cars that traveled over the mine's own railroad en route to a very big mill and the world's largest copper smelter, built nearby especially to serve this mine. The mine is still functioning. It has removed more than 16 billion pounds of copper worth $5 billion in present-day values, in addition to large values of molybdenite, silver, and gold.

Mining for precious metals did not cease suddenly when base metals began to take over western mining. By the 1870s most of the superficial gold placers, except those in Alaska, had long been abandoned by white miners in favor of Chinese, who were willing to work for a small return. But in California the growing size and effectiveness of hydraulicking brought large annual placer yields until the 1880s. In 1884 hydraulic mining was enjoined by the courts because it turned loose tons of debris that the winter rains flooded down onto the valley farms below. A federal statute (the Caminetti Act of 1893) sought to encourage the revival of hydraulicking under expensive safeguards, but proved insufficient to inspire a general return to activity.

Rather than abandon all forms of placer mining, Californians introduced from New Zealand the floating gold dredge, which proved to be about as destructive to the landscape as hydraulicking. Floating on an artificial pond, the dredge tore up masses of alluvial deposits with an endless chain of buckets. First tried successfully in California in 1898, the dredges went through many successive improvements that enabled them to continue operating until well into the 1960s. While introduced into several other states, notably Alaska, gold dredges, like hydraulicking, achieved their greatest development in California, where there was the right combination of natural conditions, ambitious promoters and operators, and ingenious equipment manufacturers eager for business. On the eve of World War I, fifty-six "boats" were at work in California, as compared with about thirty-five in Alaska.

Lode mines of gold and silver were subject to the inevitable pressures of increasing cost with increasing depth. The better-managed mines continued in operation until World War II. In order to divert manpower to more militarily valuable minerals, the War Production Board issued the famous order L-208, which suspended all gold mining for the duration of the war. Most gold mines never reopened, and those that did found themselves fighting inflationary costs while the price of their only product, gold, was fixed at the level set by President Franklin D. Roosevelt in 1934. By 1960 the great Homestake mine in the Black Hills of South Dakota claimed to be the only major gold mine still operating in the whole nation. High efficiency, a completely integrated, self-contained pattern of operation, and the support of a huge capital investment all combined to keep this vast enterprise going.

Significantly, by the 1960s the great copper operations at Bingham were able to claim that they had become the second largest producer of gold; in other words, the once noble metal, gold, had become a by-product of copper production. The same had long been true of silver. Even before World War I, a large part of the silver was essentially a by-product of lead and copper operations (and later also of zinc). Less hurt by wartime suspension, the silver industry nevertheless was slow to

The copper mine at Bingham Canyon, Utah. (Bettmann Archive)

resume production and soon found itself struggling with economic difficulties.

Almost as soon as mining began to operate in large industrial units, it began to have what contemporaries termed "labor troubles." The first unions were formed on the Comstock Lode in 1863-64 and soon were engaged in a dispute to maintain wages. Reorganized in 1867, the Comstock union ultimately succeeded in both wage and hour demands. Just as the Comstock Lode was a training ground for mining techniques, so it became what one authority has called "the training center of hard-rock miner unionism." The Comstock's example, or perhaps the activities of a few Comstock veterans, directly inspired the formation of miners' unions in the California lode mines; in Butte, Montana; in Globe, Arizona; and in the Coeur d'Alene region in IDAHO. By what was perhaps independent action, other unions were formed at Leadville and at Eureka, Nevada (see LABOR MOVEMENT).

After a bitter strike in the Coeur d'Alenes, representatives of fifteen unions met at Butte in 1893 to form the WESTERN FEDERATION OF MINERS. Affiliated for a short time with the American Federation of Labor, and in bitter rivalry at another time with the Industrial Workers of the World, the Western Federation and its successor organization led an uneasy, strife-torn existence for decades.

Repeatedly, between the late 1870s and the 1930s, there were fierce strikes, such as the CRIPPLE CREEK STRIKES in Colorado, in which both sides used armed force and the workers resorted to dynamite. Most of the mine owners and managers, while often paternalistically benevolent, were dogmatically opposed to unions and collective action by labor. With so many miners living in company towns in isolated localities, dependent on company stores, company medical service, and company kindness, the employers had the odds in their favor. The fact that the workers came from increasingly varied national backgrounds made unity among the miners inherently difficult. To these advantages the employers could usually add the influence of the state governments and the use of the militia and at times federal troops. It is little wonder that industrial peace was so slow in coming to the larger mines, or that mutual distrust persisted for so many years after actual violence had largely ceased.

The future of western mining rests with the base metals and the rare and "strategic" metals—molybdenum, manganese, tungsten, lithium, silicon, and URANIUM—that became so important during and after World War II. Production of these metals has taken place under conditions that do not in any way resemble circumstances during the gold and silver era. Whether the new enterprises will prove more permanent than their predecessors is conjectural. After all, mining is based on the deliberate depletion of resources. But in the meantime the new types of mining not only establish payrolls, buy supplies and services, and diversify the western economy, as the chambers of commerce like to stress, but, like the gold and silver mines that preceded them, they create new skills and new technological understanding that presently will find new uses elsewhere, just as veterans of the earlier mining eras went from California and the Comstock Lode to open new mines. A study of western mining history convinces one that the people involved are more enduring than any one era of the industry itself.

See Leonard J. Arrington and Gary B. Hansen, *"The Richest Hole on Earth": A History of the Bingham Copper Mine* (1963); Vernon H. Jensen, *Heritage of Conflict: Labor Relations in the Nonferrous Metals Industry up to 1930* (1950); Rodman W. Paul, *Mining Frontiers of the Far West, 1848-1880* (1963); Thomas Arthur Rickard, *A History of American Mining* (1932); and T. H. Watkins, *Gold and Silver in the West* (1971).—R. W. P.

mining engineer. Like every other industry, metal mining depends heavily upon the skilled technician—in this case, the mining engineer. Prior to the mid-1870s mining engineers were either trained by experience or educated abroad, usually at Freiberg in Germany or the Ecole des Mines in Paris. Later, many attended the Columbia School of Mines, which by 1892 had produced nearly half of the M.E.'s in the country, and after the turn of the century, the University of California, although numerous other engineering schools trained a significant numbers of graduates.

Once graduated, fledgling mine engineers often acquired experience in other fields before turning to mining proper; they built railroads, improved rivers and harbors, and designed irrigation projects. Many took government positions of various types, the most popular being with the United States Geological Survey, which came to be regarded as "a great graduate school of instruction" for them. During much of the nineteenth century, "book larnin'" engineers—men with theory but little practice—were met with considerable public skepticism, but they soon won their battle for recognition and pushed the old-time practical mining man into the background.

A gold dredge. (Bettmann Archive)

This field, wrote one practitioner, was "the most polyglot of all the professions. . . . Geologist, surveyor, lawyer, mechanic, chemist, metallurgist, mineralogist, electrician, this was the mining engineer of the old school." At least until World War I, the engineer tended to be a general practitioner, a jack-of-all-trades in the mining world, although time pushed him increasingly toward specialization. Often he was in charge of both mine and mill, which meant that he was not only concerned with locating, developing, exposing, measuring, and removing ore from the ground, but also with the reduction and marketing of the metal itself. As mine or mill manager, he often designed and installed equipment; planned and built roads, flumes or aerial tramways; handled accounts and contracts; and served as a diplomat in dealing with directors and shareholders and in the supervision of a large labor force. As a consultant, the engineer dispensed advice on the potential value of mineral property or on its working to whomever purchased his services—owner, vendor, promoter, stockholder, or manager. Mine examination was at best a difficult task, for even with increasingly sophisticated techniques, the inspecting engineer could not see into the bowels of the earth nor predict the fluctuations in market, labor costs, or other expenses that might spell the difference between success and failure.

In the courts, the mining engineer helped to shape MINING LAW and its application through his work as an expert witness in controversies over title, especially those stemming from the vexing "apex law," which permitted a locator to follow a lode downward to any depth beyond the sidelines of his location, provided its top or "apex" came within its endlines. Yet at the same time, it was the engineer who saw the waste and folly of apex litigation and who took the lead in unsuccessful efforts to revise the statutes. Often, too, the mining engineer was a hardheaded businessman whose success came more from his ventures in prospecting, leasing, promoting, or investing or speculating in mines than from his engineering income. But the financially successful—men like John Hays Hammond, Herbert Hoover, and Daniel Jackling—were by no means typical. The average mining engineer fell somewhere in the middle to upper-middle income bracket.

Often, even in the nineteenth century, the engineer specialized at different times in his career, jumping perhaps from mine examination to management to the erection of machinery, or moving from one mineral to another, like Frederick Bradley, who went from deep-level gold to silver-lead production to dredging and eventually to antimony. Rossiter W. Raymond, the foremost expert on the "apex law," was a specialist in both coal and iron as well as the precious metals. Some focused on a particular mineral—gold, lead, or phosphate; others on a specific type of mining—deep-level, hydraulic, dredging, or low-grade copper. Yet as technology advanced, increasing specialization became part of the picture, with large corporations dominating and seeking specialists in mine management, metallurgy, petroleum, or geological engineering, leaving room for few of the old-style general practitioners in the field.

The American mining engineer was a nomad. His work took him all over the world and by the 1890s he was recognized as the elite of international mining experts.

He supervised the exploitation of the deep South African mines in the 1890s; he carried new processes into Latin America and China; in prerevolutionary Russia, he was responsible for introducing American-built gold dredges—modified from New Zealand models—into Siberia. As he practiced his profession around the globe, the American mining engineer became in the process an instrument for the diffusion of technological advance, and ideas or equipment sent abroad often came back improved and modified.

The engineer lived a life of contrasts. One week his work might take him mule-back into the wilds of Idaho, the next into sophisticated financial circles of New York. He was called upon to perform rugged, outdoor work, and at the same time he was also concerned with theory and often with culture, for his experience was cosmopolitan and his outlook frequently eclectic. Locally he was a man of stature and social prestige, and while not especially a political animal, he did important governmental work in wartime and sometimes served as legislator, governor, or in Herbert Hoover's case, as chief executive.

As an articulate and skillful writer of his own experiences and of the problems of mining, he advertised American resources and spread technical ideas on a global scale. As an inventor or introducer of new methodology and equipment, the engineer led the way in innovation. He adapted whatever was useful wherever he found it, introduced more expert and judicious management, and provided additional protection for capital and the investor. Certainly he was influential in helping to shape the western legal, cultural and economic base, and through him the American mineral industry made an indelible imprint on mining around the globe.

See also MINING, METAL.

A detailed study is Clark C. Spence, *Mining Engineers and the American West* (1970). Significant accounts by engineers are found in *The Autobiography of John Hays Hammond*, 2 vols. (1935); and Thomas A. Rickard, *Retrospect* (1937).—C. C. S.

mining law. The California gold rush began at a time when there was great uncertainty as to American mining law and the legal status of mining lands. There had never been an occasion for the United States to develop a real code to govern mining operations, and Congress's attempts to lease rather than sell the mineral-bearing parts of the public domain had recently been acknowledged to be unenforceable. Nor did Congress respond to the new conditions in California by passing legislation that would assert the government's ownership of the mineral lands and stipulate conditions for using (that is, exploiting) them.

Left to their own devices, the forty-eighters and forty-niners assumed, by a kind of universal tacit agreement, that they were free to work any deposit found on the public domain—and that included virtually all the land on the slopes of the Sierra Nevada save for John Charles Frémont's Mariposa grant. But where the paramount owner (the federal government) was silent, and the occupiers (the miners) were mere users, who was to decide how much mineral land any one individual might appropriate, and under what conditions he might continue to hold it? And who was to adjudicate disputes between rival claimants?

The Americans among the gold-rush population

were accustomed to a high degree of local self-government and to settling their own problems in informal ways when external authority was absent. In one locality after another miners took the initiative by summoning their fellows to mass meetings. Each meeting, in turn, elected a presiding officer, declared its particular area a mining "district" with specified boundaries, and appointed a committee to draft a code of "laws" regulating ownership of claims. For example, at Jackass Gulch, five miles from Sonora, California, a district was organized in 1848 with a code of laws that seems to have been only verbal at first but later was revised and written down and by 1851 was in print. The code declared "that these rules shall extend over Jackass and Soldier gulches and their tributaries." According to the codes, the discoverer of a gold deposit must post a notice and begin work within a stipulated number of days. By right of occupation and continued use, each miner in the district in 1848 was permitted to hold a claim not larger than ten feet square. When yields declined, as the mineral land was worked and reworked by successive occupants, the limits were extended, so that by 1851 a claim might be as large as one hundred feet square. Except in cases of illness, a miner's right to a claim was forfeited if he were absent from work for more than five days. A jury of five was to settle disputes. A recorder was to keep a record of all claims in the district.

The earliest codes were relatively simple because they dealt with placers, gold that had been eroded out of the primeval rock and transported and abraded by streams before being dropped on sandbars or in crevices, where it was found in the form of flakes, dust, or tiny pieces. More complex legal problems developed when miners became interested in what they variously termed quartz, vein, or lode claims, meaning claims in which the gold was still encased in solid rock, so that the vein had to be traced underground.

Legal scholars have found many similarities between provisions of the California codes and those of the well-matured mining ordinances of Spanish America, Britain, and Germany. Just as they borrowed mining techniques from those older countries, so the gold-rush pioneers seem to have drawn upon these ancient codes that reflected the common experience of miners everywhere.

When first used, the codes were enforced only by the collective will of the local population, but in 1851 the California legislature, at the urging of Stephen J. FIELD, the future chief justice of California and associate justice of the United States Supreme Court, passed a statute that asserted:

> in actions respecting "Mining Claims," proof shall be admitted of the customs, usages, or regulations established and in force at the bar, or diggings, embracing such claim; and such customs, usages, or regulations, when not in conflict with the Constitution and Laws of this State, shall govern the decision of the action.

In short, the California legislature accepted the local mining codes as constituting a kind of customary law for the mines, which would be governing whenever cases were shifted over to the regular state courts. The California Supreme Court confirmed this in a classic case in 1864, and the United States Supreme Court upheld it a year later.

When Californians began hurrying to all parts of the Far West during the twenty years of gold and silver rushes that began in 1859, they carried with them this habit of relying on local rules that were drafted by local assemblies and given general sanction by state or territorial legislatures and courts. The number of independent districts and codes in the West must have totaled several thousand. A confusing diversity as to details inevitably developed, even though the major principles were fairly standardized. Some of the newer territories, such as Arizona and Idaho, sought to enact territorywide provisions, and there was a tendency to substitute the county for the smaller and more informal district.

For their own day and their own population, the local mining codes worked reasonably well, and they had the great advantage of providing a means for quick and inexpensive settlement in the presence of an assembly of local men who knew the local rules. But as the years passed, the local men became careless about keeping records, careless about amending the codes to adjust to new conditions, and forgetful as to just what had happened on some distant day when two miners had asserted rights to the same piece of ground that much later developed an unexpected value. When transferred to the regular courts, disputes based on the local codes often became a costly maze of mutually contradictory testimony, altered or missing records, and confusing questions of interpretation.

Much trouble could have been avoided if the early Californians had stuck more closely to their Spanish precedents in regard to lode claims. With only a few exceptions, Spanish (and also British) precedents specified that the underground boundaries of a lode claim were simply the downward extension of the surface boundaries. Realizing that a claimant might easily misjudge the course of his vein after it disappeared beneath the surface, the early Californians adopted the principle that a claimant might follow the vein, including all its "dips, spurs, angles, and variations," wherever it might lead, even though this might mean penetrating under a neighbor's claim. Because of the difficulty of determining whether a vein was continuous, this provision became a prolific source of expensive legal disputes.

After years of neglect, in 1866 Congress finally passed a federal statute to govern lode claims, in 1870 a statute concerning placer claims, and in 1872-74 a series of revisions and codifications. These several statutes specifically recognized and accepted the binding force of the existing local codes, continued most of their principles, and established rules by which miners could henceforth obtain United States patents (that is, titles) to claims on the public domain. In an attempt to preserve the California rule concerning lode claims, Congress passed the famous Apex Law of 1872, which proved to be a stimulus to expensive and confusing litigation, since it made the success of lawsuits hinge upon the identification of the top, or "apex," of a vein, an identification upon which no two opposing expert witnesses ever seemed to agree. The Apex Law stated that a claimant must fix his surface boundaries in such a way as to embrace the apex of his vein. If he succeeded in doing so, the claimant could pursue his vein for an indefinite distance through the vertical downward extension of the side limits of his rectangular claim, but not through

Creede, Colorado, boomed when silver was discovered in the region, but its prosperity was soon to prove short-lived. (Denver Post)

the extension downward of the end limits of that claim. If trial and error subsequently demonstrated that the claimant had missed the apex when he located his boundaries, then he lost the right to follow the vein. In terms of litigation, this meant that the right to work mineral ground of great potential value would be determined by the geologically uncertain question of where the apex was situated.

See Curtis H. Lindley, *A Treatise on the American Law Relating to Mines and Mineral Lands Within the Public Land States and Territories*, 3 vols. (1914); Rodman W. Paul, *Mining Frontiers of the Far West, 1848-1880* (1963); Robert W. Swenson, "Legal Aspects of Mineral Resources Exploitation," in *History of Public Land Law Development* (1968); and Gregory Yale, *Legal Titles to Mining Claims and Water Rights, in California, Under the Mining Law of Congress of July 1866* (1867).—R. W. P.

mining towns. Mining rush towns have been a phenomenon of the West, with the exception of such isolated cases as the boomtowns of Dahlonega and Auraria, Georgia, in the Appalachian gold field (1799-1847) and the lead-mining metropolis of Galena, Illinois (1820s). The typical western mining town started as a tatterdemalion collection of frame shacks and houses, with an occasional brick or stone structure. Usually on a mountainous site that was arid and bleak, wind-blown the year round, baked in summer heat, buried in winter snowdrifts, and often hidden by a pall of mine or smelter smoke, the mining town was distinctly unattractive in appearance.

Men were drawn to mining communities by their po-

tential for individual gain, and out of that motivation developed the hectic life cycle of the mining town. The first phase was that of a rough mining camp in the throes of a frantic boom. The boom characteristically lasted from one to six years. The next stage was either a depression followed by a revival paced by technological advance and capital investment—a revival that might assure the existence of the town for decades—or a slow decline to ghost-town status. Those towns that survived the boom stage underwent a transition from frontier America (the mining camp) to modern, industrial America (the mining town). Unionization of labor, corporate ownership and management, and the predominance of foreign workers became true of mining towns such as Butte, Montana, and Virginia City, Nevada, no less than of the industrial communities of the East. The change from a dismal mining camp of tents and hovels to a cosmopolitan, modern city was speedy. The great silver- and lead-mining boom began at Leadville, Colorado, in 1877. By 1880 Leadville had a population of fifteen thousand, twenty-eight miles of streets, gas light, a water works, thirteen schools, five churches, and three hospitals in support of its fourteen smelters and thirty mines. In the transition to industrial status, however, the frontier strain was not altogether lost, and mining-town existence retained the strenuous, bustling character of pioneer life.

A notch above the hundreds of ephemeral mining camps such as Red Dog and Rough and Ready, California, were the substantial but small towns like North San Juan, California, where hydraulic operations for mining

On June 5, 1892, Creede suffered the fate of many another mining town when fire swept through its hastily built wooden structures. (Colorado State Museum)

gold were conducted. In 1859 North San Juan, population one thousand, had eight brick buildings on a main street and boasted a school, church, three hotels, two restaurants, a brewery, several sawmills, an iron foundry, and about forty stores or shops. There was a library of six hundred books, Masonic and Odd Fellows lodges, a mutual relief society, and a Welsh temperance association. Neat cottages and gardens were a feature of this prosperous town, but there was an unsavory side, too. In addition to twenty liquor dealers there were a number of houses of prostitution, while on the fringe of the settlement were about forty ramshackle Chinese huts. Typical of the medium-size mining towns was the silver camp of Eureka, Nevada, which had a population of six thousand in the early 1880s. In contrast to the well-watered location of North San Juan, Eureka was on an arid, bleak mountain site. As in many western camps, water was ordinarily a problem, and a visitor to Eureka in 1879 noted only four or five grassy front yards and a scattering of trees. From the beginning of its boom in 1870-71 Eureka had suffered the usual run of mining-town ordeals: two unexpected mountain flash floods, two big fires, and a smallpox epidemic. But in spite of all, the Eureka of the early 1880s was a thriving town with two daily newspapers, an imposing courthouse, several churches, and a number of blocks of brick shops and warehouses. During the fourteen years of its prosperity Eureka's yield was bountiful: $40 million in silver, $20 million in gold, and 225,000 pounds of lead.

The mining towns that survived their boom periods developed social structures similar to their industrial counterparts in the East. At the apex was an elite of mine owners, managers, engineers, and supervisors. Next were the leading merchants and the more prepossessing doctors, lawyers, editors, and ministers. Forming the core of the town was its ethnically diverse laboring population of skilled and unskilled workers. While management positions were monopolized by native Americans, immigrants were prominent among the miners. Most skilled among the hard-rock deep miners were the Cornish, who brought with them expertise developed over the centuries in the tin and copper mines of Cornwall. Completing the social "pecking order" were the Irish, Welsh, Germans, Italians, and Serbo-Croats (derisively called Bohunks by others).

The strain and hazard of deep mining and the isolation of mining-town life in the 1850-1900 period took the miners to the ubiquitous SALOON. GAMBLING and PROSTITUTION were equally important. The genteel patronized the local opera house—an ornament of the more prepossessing towns —or theater, where lectures, comedies, dramas, and musicals were well attended. Mining-town newspapers featuring the sort of salty personal journalism made famous by Mark Twain and Dan DeQuille in Virginia City, Nevada, gained an attentive readership. Many miners joined the Masons, Odd Fellows, and other fraternal lodges. Management in the mining towns was generally unsympathetic to labor, and with growing industrialization miners unions, such as the WESTERN FEDERATION OF MINERS, sprang up. In the often lawless early years miners' courts and vigilante movements antedated and sometimes paralleled the functioning of the regular system of law and order.

The mine-rush era of the West, from 1849 to 1904, produced many famous BOOM TOWNS, which later became famous GHOST TOWNS. Among the leading gold-rush towns were COLUMBIA, SONORA, PLACERVILLE, BODIE, and many others in California, 1849-60 (see also GOLD-RUSH TOWNS OF CALIFORNIA); VIRGINIA CITY and BANNACK, Montana, beginning in 1863; DEADWOOD and LEAD in the Black Hills of South Dakota, 1876-79; CRIPPLE CREEK, Colorado, beginning in 1892; and TONOPAH and GOLDFIELD, Nevada, 1900-1904. Important silver-rush towns were VIRGINIA CITY, Nevada, beginning in 1860; LEADVILLE and ASPEN, Colorado, beginning in 1878; and Coeur d'Alene, Idaho, beginning in 1885, with Virginia City also emerging as a significant gold producer.

A feature mainly of the twentieth-century West has been the "company town"—a mining town wholly owned or dominated by one large corporation. In a study of 191 western company towns, James B. Allen found that 114 were mining towns—largely in the realms of coal and copper. The company towns, exemplified at their worst by the Rockefeller-dominated Colorado Fuel and Iron Company coal-mining towns of southern Colorado early in the century, were often characterized by a stifling oppressiveness. In such towns the company owned everything—houses, stores, saloons, schools, churches, and clubrooms—and paid the salaries of ministers, teachers, and others. Dedicated to the maximization of profits by the imposition of low wages and squalid living conditions on the miners and their families, the companies rigidly controlled all aspects of community life and harshly opposed the efforts of union organizers to break the iron hold of the company on the workers. Conditions were considerably better in the paternalistic Union Pacific coal-mine towns in Wyoming and the Kennecott Copper Corporation (McGill, Nevada, and elsewhere) and Phelps Dodge (Morenci, Arizona, and elsewhere) copper mine and smelter towns of the Southwest. In recent years company towns have waned as mines have closed down, and some companies (for example, Kennecott in 1955) have sold their town properties. One of the few important company towns that still exist is Lead, South Dakota, site of the gigantic Homestake gold mine.

See James B. Allen, *The Company Town in the American West* (1966); William S. Greever, *The Bonanza West: The Story of the Western Mining Rushes, 1849-1900* (1963); W. Turrentine Jackson, *Treasure Hill: Portrait of a Silver Mining Camp* (1963); George S. McGovern and Leonard F. Guttridge, *The Great Coalfield War* (1972); Rodman W. Paul, *Mining Frontiers of the Far West: 1848-1880* (1963); Duane A. Smith, *Rocky Mountain Mining Camps: The Urban Frontier* (1967); and Tom H. Watkins, *Gold and Silver in the West: The Illustrated History of an American Dream* (1971).—R. M. B.

Minitari Indians. See HIDATSA INDIANS.

Minneapolis. See TWIN CITIES, MINNESOTA.

Minnesota. The central geographic position of Minnesota was fundamental in determining the course of its history. The state occupies the Lake Superior highlands, a portion of the prairie plains, and the upper limits of the Mississippi valley. It looks eastward through the Great Lakes, northward down the RED RIVER OF THE NORTH to Canada, and southward along the MISSISSIPPI RIVER, serving as the northern gateway to the western United States and to central Canada. Minnesota is the crest of the Midwest and the approximate geographic center of the continent. More than eleven thousand lakes are Minnesota's most distinctive feature. Its waters flow into three great systems: the many-branched Mississippi; the Red River of the North; and the Great Lakes-St. Lawrence River system.

The first white visitors found the network of streams and lakes bordered by coniferous and deciduous forests or flowing through a generous expanse of prairie country. Northern Minnesota was endowed with a great belt of evergreen forest—white pine, spruce, fir, tamarack, and cedar—that ran diagonally from northwest to southeast and constituted a paradise for lumbermen. It deepened into what the pioneers called the Big Woods in the central and southeastern parts: a region some hundred miles long and forty miles wide of hardwood—oak, maple, and ironwood—for building and fuel. To the farmer the area offered difficulties in clearing the land for crops, but west, southwest, and south lay the prairie, a treeless, grass- and flower-covered land. Here farmers plowed the tough turf, which they also used to build sod shanties.

The earliest known inhabitants of this fertile land were Indians (see MINNESOTA MAN AND BROWNS VALLEY MAN). At a very early time they discovered ways of shaping stones to their use by grinding stone against stone, pecking or pounding both hard and soft materials. Among the latter were pipestone, slate, and even copper—a metal they mined to depletion in an island of Lake Superior later known as Isle Royale. Indian mounds help to elaborate the story of the Woodland era from about 1000 B.C. to the coming of the white men. Modern man has dealt harshly with the mounds, and few remain, although it is estimated that there were once more than ten thousand in the state. The largest of those remaining is at Laurel, near International Falls on the northern border, where interesting finds of bone and copper have been made. Effigy mounds, once common, have disappeared.

The two great Indian "families" of major importance in Minnesota history were the SIOUX, or Dakota, and the Chippewa, or OJIBWA. The Sioux occupied most of Minnesota when white explorers and traders first saw the region in the seventeenth century. Just how long the Sioux had lived here or what their relationship was to the primitive folk of the postglacial era, no one can say. They were a tall, vigorous, gifted, warlike people organized in seven tribes of "council fires." The largest of these, the Teton, as well as the Yankton and Yanktonai, lived on the Plains. The other four tribes (the Santee Sioux) were primarily Minnesotan, and of these the Mdewakanton—meaning the "people of the spirit or holy lake"—occupied a place of central importance. The "spirit or holy lake"—Mille Lacs—was long regarded as the very center of the allied Dakota tribes.

It was the fate of the Sioux to be driven from much of their domain, not by the white men, but by a tribe of red men. About the middle of the seventeenth century the Ojibwa—a nation of Algonquian stock—was forced from its homeland in the St. Lawrence valley by Iroquois. They found respite and homes about the Sault Ste. Marie at the eastern end of Lake Superior. In this land of peace and plenty their numbers multiplied greatly, and in their search for additional hunting grounds, it was inevitable that they would reach still farther west into the lands controlled by the Sioux. By 1785 Minnesota was divided between the Ojibwa in the wooded northern canoe country and the Sioux in the hills, valleys, and plains of the south and west. The Ojibwa had already been influenced by the white man: they possessed firearms, objects of tin, iron, steel, and brass, and blankets. Even their eating and drinking habits were in transition: they had flour, pork, molasses, and tea, although they preferred rum and whiskey when available. Both tribes faced an extraordinary revolution in a period infinitesimally brief compared with the centuries of their occupation of primeval lands.

The Indian population of the area early in the nineteenth century is not known with precision, but the number probably ran between 10,000 and 15,000. Today there are some 25,000 Indians, mainly Ojibwa, in Minnesota, almost evenly divided between the Twin Cities and outstate communities, including seven Ojibwa reservations.

Two Frenchmen, Pierre Radisson and his brother-in-law, the Sieur des Groseilliers, seem to have been the first white men to record a journey to Minnesota. On their first voyage, in 1654, they may have reached Prairie Island in the Mississippi River below Hastings. On their second, in 1660, they apparently skirted the shore of Lake Superior and traveled some distance into the interior. They returned to Montreal with sixty canoes filled with furs secured in trade from the western Indians.

In 1678 Daniel Greysolon, Sieur du Lhut (or Duluth), had been sent to make peace between the warring Sioux and Ojibwa. The spring of 1679 found him near Sault Ste. Marie. After holding a council not far from the site of the city that now bears his name, he and his men pushed on to the Sioux villages at Mille Lacs. There Duluth asked for the Indians' friendship and claimed possession of the area for Louis XIV. Then he set out on a vain search for a fabled lake far to the west whose waters, he was told, were not good to drink—the western ocean, he was sure. Duluth's route from Lake Superior led him in 1680 up the Brule River and down the St. Croix to its junction with the Mississippi. There some Sioux told him of the three captive white men, including the Belgian friar Louis Hennepin. Duluth called the Indians into council at the Mille Lacs villages and forced them to release the white men, whom he then conducted safely back east.

In 1686 Nicolas Perrot, in command of the French in the West, established the trading post Fort St. Antoine on the east side of Lake Pepin. Here in 1689, he proclaimed the sovereignty of Louis XIV over the lands of the Sioux. In 1695 Pierre Charles Le Sueur established a post on Prairie Island and in 1700 he led an expedition up the Minnesota River to the great bend where the city of Mankato now stands. There, at the mouth of the Blue Earth River, he built Fort L'Huillier and spent the winter. In 1731 Pierre Gaultier de Varennes, Sieur de LA VERENDRYE, started on a journey that took him deeper into the West than any of his fellow Frenchmen had yet penetrated. He reached Grand Portage and the following year built Fort St. Charles on Lake of the Woods. During the next fifteen years La Vérendrye's men

traveled far into the Dakota plains and built a chain of forts into the Saskatchewan valley. During the French and Indian War, however, the French empire crumbled piece by piece, and its control of the Northwest was broken by 1760. When a British officer arrived at the Sault Ste. Marie in 1762, he found a single trader in charge of the post. That same summer a few British soldiers accompanied some traders to Grand Portage, planting the British flag for the first time on Minnesota soil. (See GRAND PORTAGE NATIONAL MONUMENT.) In 1766 Major Robert Rogers, superintendent of Indian affairs for the British in the Northwest with headquarters at Mackinac, sent an expedition under Captain James Tute to search for a Northwest Passage, a short all-water route to the Orient. As mapmaker for the expedition, and to win the friendship of the Indians in the Mississippi valley, Rogers sent along a Connecticut Yankee named Jonathan Carver. During the winter of 1766-67, Carver lived among the Sioux along the Minnesota River. He saw the Falls of St. Anthony and discovered the famous cave at present-day St. Paul that bears his name. In the spring of 1767 he won from the Indians an agreement to trade with the British. Carver's party then traveled northward toward Lake Superior, but when the expedition reached Grand Portage they found that Rogers, busy defending his position at Mackinac, had failed to send fresh supplies. Disheartened, they returned to Mackinac.

At the close of the American Revolution, Great Britain acknowledged the sovereignty of the United States over the region east of the Mississippi River, but the new nation was too feeble to govern the area effectually. Whatever law and order existed was administered by the British fur-trading companies, then at the zenith of their power. From 1783 until after the War of 1812, the North West Company was in practical control of the Minnesota country, with at least twenty-four posts. The most important were those at Grand Portage (western headquarters for the whole British trade), Fond du Lac, Sandy, Leech, Cass, and Red lakes. Nevertheless, American exploration was under way, beginning with the Lewis and Clark expedition (1804-06). In addition, Lieutenant Zebulon M. PIKE was dispatched to explore the upper Mississippi valley. Pike arrived in the Minnesota country in September 1805 and went into camp on an island at the mouth of the Minnesota River still known as Pike Island. Here for the first time the United States flag was raised on Minnesota soil, and, at a council, Pike persuaded the Sioux to cede land at the mouth of the St. Croix River and at the junction of the Minnesota and Mississippi rivers for army posts. Although the season was well advanced, Pike continued his journey up the Mississippi. In the face of incredible difficulties, he made his way to the North West Company fur posts at Sandy and Leech lakes. He was cordially received, but when he found the British flag flying over the Leech Lake post he ordered his men to shoot it down and hoist the American flag in its place.

Up to this time, the only white settlement had been temporary and incidental to the fur trade. In 1811, however, Lord Selkirk, a Scottish nobleman, began an experimental settlement of agricultural workers in the Red River valley near Fort Garry (present-day Winnipeg, Canada). By 1814 the colony contained more than two hundred persons. The establishment of this colony so close to American soil and the fall of American garrisons in the Northwest during the War of 1812 caused the United States government to hasten its occupation of the northern lands. A treaty with the Sioux was concluded at the Portage des Sioux, near St. Louis, on July 19, 1815, by which the Indians agreed to resume friendly relations with the United States and to acknowledge the president as their only Great Father. It was a first step toward protecting American citizens lawfully engaged in the fur trade. The following year Congress passed a law prohibiting all but Americans from trading with the Indians on American soil and established the first three of a contemplated chain of forts on the frontier—Fort Armstrong at Rock Island, Illinois; Fort Howard at Green Bay, Wisconsin; and Fort Crawford at Prairie du Chien, Wisconsin. In 1819-20 the post first known as Fort St. Anthony, later as FORT SNELLING, was established at the junction of the Minnesota and Mississippi rivers with Lawrence TALIAFERRO as its Indian agent. For a generation it remained the northwesternmost military and civil post in the United States, and around it developed the fur trading center of the region.

Missionaries were alert to follow the expansion of American authority in the Minnesota country. As early as 1818 Father Sévère Dumoulin was working among the Ojibwa Indians at Pembina (see ROMAN CATHOLIC MISSIONARIES), and before long, representatives of the various Protestant churches were also on the scene. In 1829 Jedediah Stevens was with the Ojibwa of the St. Croix valley. In the early 1830s Frederick Ayer established a school at Sandy Lake, and soon Edmund F. Ely and William T. Boutwell were also in the field. Boutwell, after accompanying Henry R. Schoolcraft to the headwaters of the Mississippi in 1832, built a mission and school at Leech Lake. American missionaries were also active among the Sioux. In 1834 the brothers Gideon and Samuel POND began their long careers by helping the Indians of Kaposia break ground for gardens. They then established themselves among the Sioux at Lake Calhoun, and from there they went to the Lac Qui Parle Mission, where they worked with Dr. Thomas S. Williamson and Stephen R. Riggs.

An unusual achievement of these men of the church was their success in devising alphabets for the Indian languages and reducing the spoken languages to writing. Among the Sioux, the Pond brothers and Dr. Williamson were the leaders in this work. Among the Ojibwa, the Catholic missionaries Father Georges A. Belcourt and Father Frederic Baraga devised excellent dictionaries, while the Protestant teacher Frederick Ayer compiled a spelling book.

In 1818 the jurisdiction of Michigan Territory was extended to the Mississippi River. Its governor, Lewis Cass, attempted to find the source of the Mississippi in 1820. In 1823 extensive explorations of the Minnesota and Red River valleys were conducted by Major Stephen H. LONG and, subsequently, by others: Henry R. Schoolcraft, who discovered Lake Itasca, the source of the Mississippi, in 1832; George Catlin, whose journey of 1836 took him to the famous pipestone quarry; Joseph N. NICOLLET, whose tours of the late 1830s resulted in the first accurate map of the region; and Major Samuel Woods, who explored the Red River valley in 1849.

These explorers gave publicity to the Minnesota country, which in 1820 was isolated indeed. It took from thirty to forty days to make the journey from St. Louis to Fort Snelling by keelboat, and when winter set in the area was practically shut off from the rest of the world. The first step toward closer contact with the outside world was taken in 1823, when the steamboat *Virginia* overcame the obstacles to navigation in the Mississippi River and triumphantly steamed upriver to Fort Snelling. The practicability of navigation on the upper Mississippi encouraged the development of commerce and led to increased activity in the fur trade. The journey of the *Virginia* was also viewed with hope by the people in the little Selkirk colony in the Red River valley because it promised to give these struggling colonists a new route to market.

The lure of furs—the gold of the Northwest—had drawn many men to Minnesota in the century and a half since white men reached the upper Mississippi valley. The events of the early nineteenth century prepared the way for the last big, although short-lived, spurt of the buisiness. After the War of 1812 forced the British to withdraw, the AMERICAN FUR COMPANY gradually gained control of the trade in the Minnesota country. Its headquarters were at Mendota, on the Minnesota River opposite Fort Snelling. In 1834 Henry Hastings SIBLEY was appointed to manage the company's business in the upper Mississippi valley in partnership with Hercules L. Dousman of Prairie du Chien. Operating as the "Sioux Outfit," Sibley and Dousman handled the trade with those Indians in the Northwest. Sibley's success was immediate, but after 1837 the fur trade declined in importance, in part because of the depletion of fur-bearing animals, but more importantly because of the encroachment of settlement. In 1842, under the impact of the disastrous Panic of 1837, the American Fur Company went into bankruptcy, and its reign in the Northwest ended. Sibley continued his fur-trading business, however, using the RED RIVER CART as a means of transporting furs.

As early as the 1820s, men looked with covetous eyes at the rich stands of white pine in the valley of the St. Croix and wondered about the farming possibilities of the area. But except for the Fort Snelling military reservation, on and around which a nucleus of white settlement appeared, the Indians held title to the entire Minnesota region. In 1837 the federal government negotiated treaties with the Sioux and Ojibwa whereby they gave up their lands in a triangle bounded by the St. Croix and Mississippi rivers and by a line drawn eastward from the mouth of the Crow Wing River. As soon as the treaties of 1837 were concluded, lumbermen moved into the region, and settlements rapidly grew up at Stillwater and St. Paul (see TWIN CITIES). By the federal census of 1850 the territory had 6,077 inhabitants, most of whom lived east of the Mississippi or along the Red River in the extreme northwest. Treaties negotiated in 1851 with the Sioux opened to settlement the greater part of the land in the territory west of the Mississippi; and treaties with the Ojibwa in 1854 and 1855 extinguished the Indian title to nearly two thirds of the northern half of the state. The ensuing unparalled rush to the new lands brought the 1857 census to 150,037. The lumbering business was booming and building up the towns of Stillwater and St. Anthony. St. Paul, at the head of navigation on the Mississippi, became the commercial center of the territory. Other river towns proved prosperous ports of entry for settlers who trekked to the interior, sometimes individually, sometimes by whole transplanted colonies.

Pamphlets describing Minnesota's attractions were printed in French, Flemish, and German for distribution in Europe. Under this stimulus such settlements as the German town of New Ulm and Swedish communities in Chisago County came into being. In 1860 Minnesota had a total population of about 172,000, of which the largest foreign-born groups were 18,400 Germans and nearly 12,000 Scandinavians. An overwhelming majority of the people, however, was native-born, from New England, New York, Pennsylvania, Ohio, Indiana, and other states of the Midwest. In some eastern communities colonies were formed to establish settlements. From New York came the Western Farm and Village Association, which sought to establish a colony at Rollingstone, near Winona. Zumbrota was founded by the Strafford Western Emigration Company, a group of New Englanders. In Northampton, Massachusetts, prospective settlers organized a colony influential in the development of Faribault and the communities about Lake Minnetonka in Hennepin County.

The greatest influx of settlers came between 1854 and 1857, at which time the boom collapsed when a financial panic swept the East. With immigration came agitation for statehood, beginning in 1854. In 1849 the bill organizing the Territory of Minnesota had been passed by Congress, and Alexander RAMSEY, a Pennsylvania Whig, was appointed governor. The first territorial legislature met in St. Paul on September 3, 1849. In 1857 Congress passed an enabling act, and the next task was to draw up a constitution. On July 13, 1857, two elected delegates from each district in the territory assembled in St. Paul after a highly partisan campaign. On the very first day the convention split into two hostile and intransigent groups, one dominated by the Democrats and the other by the vigorous new Republican party. So bitter was the enmity between the two that they refused to meet together. As a result, two constitutions were drawn up, and a committee was appointed to iron out the differences between them. Even then, it was impossible to get the representatives of the two parties together, for members of one group refused to sign a document signed by the other. Consequently, two copies had to be made. Although every effort was made to keep them identical, inaccuracies in copying occurred. As a result, Minnesota today has two slightly different, but equally authentic, constitutions. Although Minnesota voters accepted the constitution and elected state officers, members of the judiciary, and three representatives to Congress in October 1857, Congress dramatically kept Minnesota standing before its portals until the question of "Bleeding Kansas" was settled. Finally, on May 11, 1858, the president signed the bill that admitted Minnesota to the Union. The news reached St. Paul two days later, and on May 24 the state officers were formally inducted into office.

Problems of transportation and communication were of concern to most Minnesotans during the 1850s. Men had come to depend on steamboats, but Minnesota was isolated during the long months when the Mississippi was frozen. With the quickening of the tide of immigration pioneer Minnesotans undertook to open wagon roads over which stagecoaches and freight sleighs could operate when navigation was closed. Congress appropriated huge sums of money to build a network of roads in Minnesota, and the people themselves opened trails leading to future sites of the inland communities, which soon dotted the southern part of the state.

As early as 1850 the navigability of the Minnesota River as far as Mankato was demonstrated, and thereafter steamboats plied the lower river regularly. That same year, too, steamboats were built to navigate the Mississippi from the Falls of St. Anthony to St. Cloud and, occasionally, to points farther upstream. Meanwhile the number of steamboats in use on the Mississippi from downstream points to St. Paul and St. Anthony increased from five in 1850 to sixty-two in 1858. During the latter year the wharfmaster recorded 1,090 boat arrivals at St. Paul.

Though busy with the conquest of the frontier, Minnesotans had time to engage in the bitter political conflicts that were driving a wedge between the North and the South. By the close of the 1850s the young Republican party had gained so much strength in Minnesota that it had displaced the Whigs and threatened the rule of the once secure Democratic party. Under the militant leadership of men like Alexander Ramsey, who was elected governor in 1859, and with sharp-tongued spokesman like Jane Grey SWISSHELM, editor of a newspaper in St. Cloud, the Republicans took up the antislavery cause with enthusiasm. When the crisis arrived in the election of 1860, the Republicans carried the state with 22,000 votes for Lincoln to 12,000 for Douglas. Minnesota provided 22,000 men for the Union armies during the Civil War. Ramsey, the young state's war governor, was in Washington, D.C., in April 1861 when Fort Sumter fell to the Confederacy. He at once offered 1,000 troops to President Lincoln, who readily accepted them. The state of Minnesota, less than three years old, was first to volunteer soldiers to defend the Union.

Sixteen months later—in August 1862—Minnesota faced a war within the larger war, this one within its own borders. When the Santee Sioux bands gathered in the spring of 1862 to elect a speaker, LITTLE CROW was defeated by Traveling Hail, the former having fallen into disfavor with many of his people who felt he was too friendly with white fur traders and public officials in treaty negotiations. As Indian grievances against the whites piled up—loss of ancestral lands, dissatisfaction with reservation life, crop failures, starvation, delay on the part of the government in paying overdue annuities —Little Crow joined other Sioux leaders in appealing to the Indian agents at the Lower and Upper Sioux agencies for food. Their appeals were met with indifference. Wanton murders of five white settlers by four young Sioux on August 17, 1862, provided the fuse that ignited the bloody and tragic MINNESOTA UPRISING throughout the Minnesota River valley.

The warlike faction of Sioux turned to Little Crow. Initially, he opposed an armed revolt, but when accused of being a coward he slowly shifted his position. He led an assault on the Lower Sioux Agency the following day, capturing it. The weeks that followed in southern Minnesota were scenes of death, burning, looting, horror, confusion, and panic. Little Crow's forces twice mounted fierce attacks upon Fort Ridgely and New

Ulm, which they correctly regarded as the gateways to the lower Minnesota valley. The Sioux triumphed at Birch Coulee but were defeated at Wood Lake. With a small band of followers, Little Crow fled to Canada but later reappeared in Minnesota. While picking berries with his son near Hutchinson, on July 3, 1863, he was shot and killed by two white settlers.

Two hundred and sixty-nine white captives were released with the aid of a number of Sioux chiefs who had resisted the war. Many Sioux fled into the Dakota country. Expeditions under generals Henry H. Sibley and Alfred Sully in 1863 and 1864 drove other bands of Sioux beyond the Missouri. Thus ended the tragic Sioux Uprising in Minnesota—only to be fought again farther west a number of times over the next three decades. Virtually all of the Sioux were expelled from Minnesota. Thirty-eight were hanged at Mankato on December 26, 1862. Five hundred to eight hundred white settlers and an unknown number of Indians were destroyed in the short space of thirty-eight days.

The war rolled back the frontier at least a hundred miles and for a time resulted in white emigration from the state. Its tragic aftereffects kept the northwestern frontier in a turmoil throughout the Civil War. By 1869, however, the tide of westward immigration resumed. In western Minnesota, Hutchinson, Glencoe, and Litchfield were growing rapidly. Up the Minnesota River, Mankato and a rebuilt New Ulm were thriving. On the Mississippi River above the Falls of St. Anthony, settlement had passed beyond St. Cloud to Little Falls, and up the valley of the Sauk River, Sauk Center and Alexandria were stockaded settlements in the wilderness. There were even a few settlers in the Red River valley, and an isolated island of settlement had formed at Duluth, at the head of Lake Superior.

In the north the forests began to be felled under the organized attack of lumber companies. Agricultural conditions revived after a massive invasion of grasshoppers had destroyed many crops in the late 1850s, railroads were being built, and the basis was laid for steady growth in the following decades. In 1861 the Milwaukee and Waukesha Railroad (later part of the CHICAGO, MILWAUKEE, ST. PAUL AND PACIFIC) managed to build about fifteen hundred feet of track, an amount sufficient to run its lone locomotive from a steamboat wharf to the roundhouse the company had erected. In the spring of 1862 the firm pushed its work with such vigor that in early July it opened service over the first ten miles of its line, from St. Paul to St. Anthony (present-day Minneapolis). By 1865 there were 210 miles of railroad in operation in the state. Two years later Minnesota achieved a major goal, an all-rail link with Chicago. By the end of 1872 fifteen companies had built almost two thousand miles of track, covering the settled portions of the state. The tracks of the Northern Pacific (see BURLINGTON NORTHERN) and the Milwaukee and St. Paul (the old Milwaukee and Waukesha) reached into the wilderness itself. The main outlines of Minnesota's present railroad system were already discernible, but in the next thirty years almost five thousand miles of additional track was laid. So rapidly were the lines extended that the tracks often preceded settlement. The railroad firms became great land offices, offering their lands for sale under generous terms to induce settlement within reach of the tracks and thus create revenue-producing

traffic. They even sent agents abroad to encourage immigrants to settle along their lines.

The state also assisted the land-hungry. In 1867 a board of immigration was established with Hans Mattson, a Swedish immigrant and a veteran of the Civil War, as its secretary. As was done in the preceding decade, the board published pamphlets about Minnesota in many foreign languages and set agents to New York and abroad to encourage immigration. Private individuals also entered the race to bring settlers to the state; the Irish "Sweetman colony" at Currie in Murray County is an outstanding example. Even the churches participated, and Bishop (later Archbishop) John Ireland was very active in promoting settlements of Irish Catholics in the state.

The Yankee, German, Norwegian, Swedish, Irish, Czech, Welsh, and other settlements that took root in the 1850s expanded dramatically after the Civil War. Waves of migration richly diversified the state's population. The state census of 1865 showed a population of 250,000; the federal census of 1900, 1,751,394. In 1880 the state had a population of 780,773; of these, 267,676, or roughly thirty percent, were foreign-born. More revealing of the complexion of the people is that by 1880, seventy-one percent of the total "represented European blood of the first and second generations." The largest single immigrant group in 1880 was German-born, contributing 66,592 to the total. The Scandinavians numbered 107,768: 62,521 Norwegians, 39,176 Swedes, and 6,071 Danes. The third largest immigrant group were the English-speaking peoples (Irish, English, Scots, and Welsh), who totaled 38,504. In addition, 29,631 Minnesotans traced their ancestry to British America.

In 1858, for the first time, wheat was shipped commercially from the state. A year later wheat exports exceeded furs in value, and the wheat crop increased from 2 million bushels in 1860 to 19 million in 1870, 34 million in 1880, and 95 million in 1890. Minnesota farmers devoted sixty-six percent or more of their acreage to wheat. Wheat was king, and it was shipped by rail and boat to markets all over the East and Europe. Because repeated planting of this grain exhausted the soil, a kind of wheat frontier moved across the state. By 1890 it had reached the Red River valley.

As the wheat frontier moved on, farmers turned their attention to other crops. Milk, butter, and cheese were produced from the beginning, but it was not until the 1880s that dairy products took a leading position in the state's agricultural economy. One factor in this growth was the invention of the cream separator in 1878. It was found occasionally in Minnesota as early as 1885, and by 1890 it was in use in many farm homes. With the growth of dairying came an increased emphasis on stockraising, particularly cattle and hogs. This in turn enhanced the need for forage crops, and oats and corn soon became important. Minnesota agriculture swung toward a balanced crop program as early as 1900. By that year even the farmers in the Red River valley were beginning to talk of crop diversification to conserve the soil, so that they might continue to raise big crops on the acres that wheat was gradually wearing out.

In 1884 the mining of iron ore was begun on the Vermilion Range, and in 1890 and 1891 the much larger deposits of the Mesabi Range were discovered.

The ore was shipped from DULUTH, on Lake Superior. With the opening of the Cuyuna Range in 1911, Minnesota became the primary source of United States iron ore. Minnesota still leads the nation in the production of iron ore. With the depletion of its high-grade ore in sight, considerable research in recent years has been devoted to the utilization of low-grade ores and taconite. The taconite industry, involving both mining and manufacturing, is now well developed on a commercial scale, is growing substantially, and has given new economic life to northeastern Minnesota.

Lumbering and flour milling were also major forces affecting Minnesota's economy in the nineteenth century. But other factors were also involved. The combination of agricultural products and fine transportation facilities led to the growth of South St. Paul and Austin as meat-packing centers. The quarries of the St. Cloud area contributed to the growth of the "Granite City." International Falls manufactured paper as a by-product of the lumber industry.

Because Minnesota was an agricultural and industrial center, it had an unconventional political history. While the Republican party dominated during much of the state's history, a vigorous liberal tradition nurtured a number of third parties. Liberalism can be traced to the cooperative social and economic ideas imported by Scandinavian immigrants, to a strong labor tradition forged in the lumber and mining camps as well as in the cities, to recurring economic depressions in the midwestern farm belt, and to a remarkable series of farm-protest leaders who articulated the keenly felt grievances of the Minnesota farmer. Oliver H. KELLEY founded the Patrons of Husbandry in 1867. Ignatius DONNELLY fostered a third-party movement during the last third of the nineteenth century, which achieved significant success in the first half of the twentieth century as well. Prior to World War I, the Progressive movement in Minnesota was led by Congressman Charles A. Lindbergh. In 1915 Arthur C. TOWNLEY, a native of Browns valley, organized the Nonpartisan League, and for several years it wielded a powerful influence in the politics of the Midwest and West. Most successful of all was the Farmer-Labor party, which grew out of the league, captured the governorship in 1930, and remained in power under governors Floyd B. Olson and Elmer A. Benson until 1938. Thereafter, third-party fortunes merged with those of the Democratic party, officially in 1944.

In the twentieth century, Minnesota became an urban, industrial commonwealth, the metropolitan center for the upper Midwest. Its industrial power, once closely tied to its varied natural resources, continued to develop but was diversified by the introduction of "brain" industries—electronics, adhesives, and abrasives. In 1860 less than one Minnesotan in ten lived in St. Paul, St. Anthony, and Minneapolis. St. Paul's population, the largest, was only 10,401. By 1970 one half of the 3,800,000 people in Minnesota lived in the seven-county area surrounding Minneapolis and St. Paul.

The most comprehensive history of Minnesota is William W. Folwell, *A History of Minnesota,* 4 vols. (1956-69); and the best documentary history is Philip D. Jordan and Theodore C. Blegen, eds., *With Various Voices: Recordings of North Star Life* (1949). See also Blegen, *Minnesota: A History of the State* (1963); Blegen and

Theodore L. Nydahl, *Minnesota History: A Guide to Reading and Study* (1960); Russell W. Fridley, *Minnesota: A Students' Guide to Localized History* (1966); and Carl H. Chrislock, *The Progressive Era in Minnesota, 1899-1918* (1971). *Minnesota Heritage: A Panoramic Narrative of the Historical Development of the North Star State*, edited by Lawrence M. Brings (1960), is an anthology of uneven quality but includes several good articles. Rhoda R. Gilman and June D. Holmquist compiled a collection of the best articles from *Minnesota History* in *Selections from "Minnesota History": A Fiftieth Anniversary Anthology* (1965).—R. W. F.

Minnesota Man and Browns Valley Man. Prehistoric skeletons. The foremost evidence of human habitation in Minnesota in prehistoric times are two skeletons unearthed in the Red River valley in the 1930s. In 1931 a skeleton called Minnesota Man was unearthed in Otter Tail County some nine or ten feet below the surface in layers of silt laid down under glacial Lake Pelican. With it were a dagger shaped from an elk antler and a conch shell ornament. Archaeologists regard the finds as proof that man was in Minnesota some ten or twelve thousand years ago and that he traded over a wide area, since the conch shell presumably could not have come from a source nearer than the Gulf of Mexico.

Another skeleton, the Browns Valley Man, was found in Browns Valley in 1934 in a gravel bar of a once-great river that flowed out of glacial Lake Agassiz. Here, too, important objects came to light: flaked stone points, knives, and sandstone abraders. Browns Valley Man lived and hunted in primeval Minnesota some seven or eight thousand years ago. By that time the region had cast off the cold of the glaciers, and men were adjusting to an environment that may not have differed much in its essential character from that of historic times.

See Elden Johnson, *The Prehistoric Peoples of Minnesota* (1969).—R. W. F.

Minnesota (Sioux) Uprising (1862). Indian war. During the summer of 1862 the discontentment of the Santee Sioux, comprising the Mdewakanton, Wahpeton, Wahpekute, and Sisseton tribes, created an extremely volatile situation in the Minnesota valley. For nearly a half-century, white settlers had been invading Santee territory, and government pressure had forced the Indians to cede most of their lands, restricting them to limited reserves along the Minnesota River. Dependent on annuity issues as the game vanished, the Santee were subject to incredibly corrupt and insensitive practices by federal Indian agents and supply contractors. During July 1862 the Santee were near the brink of starvation, but agent Thomas Galbraith refused to distribute the large store of supplies the contractors had delivered, because he feared he might not get his customary kickback money if he gave out the food before the traders received their payment from Washington. When the Santee appealed for help at a council at Redwood agency on August 15, Galbraith's trader friend Andrew Myrick replied that if the Indians were hungry they could eat grass or their own excrement. The Santee chiefs left the council without reply, but the Indian rage and frustration exploded two days later when four young warriors, seemingly without provocation, murdered five white settlers. On August 18 a large force of Mdewakanton and Wahpekute led by LITTLE CROW attacked the Lower Agency, killing twenty men and taking a dozen women captives. One of the dead was trader Myrick. The Indians left his body with its mouth stuffed full of grass.

All of southern Minnesota was soon involved in the war. A relief force from nearby Fort Ridgely was ambushed, with twenty-four men killed, and the fort itself was unsuccessfully attacked on August 20 and 22. The settlement of New Ulm was attacked on August 19 and 23, and although the defenders drove off the Indians, thirty-four men were killed and sixty wounded, and most of the town was destroyed. Fort Abercrombie, to the north, was attacked several times in September and was under siege for almost two months. Thirteen men were killed and forty-seven wounded at Birch Coulee on September 2 when the Indians surprised a force under Major Joseph Brown.

Following the initial shock, General Henry H. Sibley defeated the hostiles at the battle of Wood Lake (actually Lone Tree Lake) on September 23, recovered many captives, and caused many of the Santee to surrender. On December 26, thirty-eight Santee who had been convicted of rape and murder were executed, and the Santee were later removed from Minnesota to the Crow Creek and Sisseton reservations in present-day South Dakota. From four hundred to eight hundred settlers and soldiers were killed in the uprising, much of the Minnesota-Dakota frontier was abandoned, and expeditions were sent against the Sioux in Dakota Territory in the following years. (See also MINNESOTA.)

See Kenneth Carley, *The Sioux Uprising of 1862* (1961); and Roy W. Meyer, *History of the Santee Sioux* (1967).—R. N. E.

missions, California. See (in order of founding) SAN DIEGO DE ALCALA; SAN CARLOS BORROMEO; SAN ANTONIO DE PADUA; SAN GABRIEL ARCANGEL; SAN LUIS OBISPO DE TOLOSA; SAN FRANCISCO DE ASIS; SAN JUAN CAPISTRANO; SANTA CLARA DE ASIS; SAN BUENAVENTURA; SANTA BARBARA; PURISIMA CONCEPCION, LA; SANTA CRUZ; NUESTRA SENORA DE LA SOLEDAD; SAN JOSE DE GUADALUPE; SAN JUAN BAUTISTA; SAN MIGUEL ARCANGEL; SAN FERNANDO REY DE ESPANA; SAN LUIS REY DE FRANCIA; SANTA INES, VIRGIN Y MARTYR; SAN RAFAEL ARCANGEL; and SAN FRANCISCO SOLANO.

Mississippi, state of, to 1860. When Mississippi was admitted into the Union in 1817, the Choctaw and Chickasaw still held two thirds of the 30,438,240 acres that comprised the total acreage of the state. In 1801, 1803, 1805, and 1816 the Indians had ceded the first third of their lands to the white settlers, and it was this area that was the settled portion of the state in 1817. The Natchez District (a region ten to forty miles wide, extending along the Mississippi River from the Louisiana line to the Yazoo River, a distance of a little more than a hundred miles) comprised sixty percent of the total population and seventy-five percent of the total slaves of the state, but only about eight percent of the total area of the state. Indians were not counted in the census schedules, but it has been estimated that there were about 5,000 to 10,000 Choctaw and 2,000 Chickasaw in the state in the 1700s. The Pearl River region, with three times the area of the Natchez District, had a population of only 10,000, of which not more than 2,000 were slaves. The Tombigbee region, separated from the settled part of the state by some two hundred miles of

wilderness, had a population of only 2,721, of which 521 were slaves.

In the cessions of 1820 and 1832 the Choctaw surrendered 15,592,918 acres. In 1832 the Chickasaw surrendered 6,283,804 acres. Thus, the Indians were eliminated as landowners in Mississippi by the 1830s. Settlers rushed in to occupy these new lands. Indeed, the greatest population increase in the history of the state—about 175 percent—occurred between 1830 and 1840. The total population figures for the state between 1820 and 1860 show a steady growth: 1820—75,448; 1830—136,- 621; 1840—375,651; 1850—606,526; 1860—791,305. Most of the white population was of British descent, and Negroes were more numerous than whites after 1840.

At the time of statehood, fourteen counties had already been organized. By 1860 there were sixty counties. After the mid-1830s, when the representatives of the new Choctaw and Chickasaw counties in central and northern Mississippi were admitted into the legislature, the preponderance of political power passed from the old to the new section of the state.

Mississippi in the 1830s was a place of abundant opportunities, somewhat akin to the spirit of California during the gold rush. Land was easy to obtain and available. In an expansionist economy, fortunes were accumulated quickly. One bought land and slaves to plant cotton. With the profits one bought more land and slaves to plant more cotton.

Sharp party divisions began to emerge in Mississippi after the adoption in 1832 of the most democratic constitution for whites in the history of the state. For most of the antebellum period Mississippi was the scene of two-party politics—Democrats versus Whigs—for the first and only time in the history of the state. Both the Whigs and the Democrats defended and desired to preserve the institution of slavery, but they differed widely on the expedience of secession as a means of preserving the state's social and economic system. The Whigs drew their strength from wealthy mercantile and planter groups, and also from political leaders and their followers disenchanted with Jackson's stand against nullification and the Bank of the United States. The Whigs also attracted some voters opposed to President Martin Van Buren, to the handling of patronage matters by the Democrats, and to the repudiation of the Union Bank bonds.

In 1860, Mississippi produced 1,202,507 bales of cotton, one fourth of the nation's crop. During the 1850s there was also a substantial increase in the production of wheat, rye, corn, tobacco, peas, beans, Irish potatoes, orchard products, market garden products, wines, and livestock. Although Mississippi was basically an agricultural state, industrial production doubled between 1850 and 1860. Mississippi was not a poor, debt-impoverished state. In real and personal property it was tenth in the nation with a total of $754,000,768. Per capita wealth was $4,525.48 in aristocratic Adams County as against $694.41 for the nation. Yet many of its potential agricultural resources were still undeveloped in 1860.

Mississippians spent money on private tutors, academies, and local private schools, but not on public schools. Private academies were the dominant forces in Mississippi's educational life of the early years. Numerous colleges were established before the Civil War. Surviving from that period to the present day are Mississippi College, denominational and chartered in 1826, and the University of Mississippi, state-supported and chartered in 1844.

With its Anglo-Saxon background, it is not surprising that Mississippi was from the beginning Protestant in religion. By 1860 there were 1,441 churches in the state: 606 Methodist, 529 Baptist, 148 Presbyterian (plus 60 Cumberland fundamental Calvinist groups), 25 Episcopal, 24 Christian, 17 Roman Catholic, and 9 Lutheran.

One usually thinks of Mississippians before 1860 as living in two-story mansions with columns across the front and a cupola on the roof, but the majority of the people lived in the traditional dogtrot houses or log huts. The capitol building in Jackson (now a museum) was completed and occupied in 1839. The Governor's Mansion, as it was called, was first used in 1842 and still is the official residence of the governor. Both of these buildings are of classical design but were poorly furnished at first.

Mississippians were fond of reading, keeping diaries, and corresponding. Prominent writers were Joseph Holt Ingraham, the one Mississippi novelist who achieved national fame; Henry Hughes, the first American sociologist; Dr. John Wesley Monette, an outstanding scientific writer; Benjamin Leonard Covington Wailes, diarist, historian, and scientific writer; and John Francis Hamtramck CLAIBORNE, historian.

Mississippi was not and never has been an urban state. Natchez, established in 1716 and the oldest settlement in the state, had 6,612 inhabitants in 1860. In 1798 the town had no serious rival in population or commerce (or, indeed, infamous reputation; see NATCHEZ-UNDER-THE- HILL) between New Orleans and Cincinnati, but by 1860 it had fallen far down the list of southern municipalities in size and trade activity. It was still, however, the largest urban center in Mississippi. Vicksburg, the port rival of Natchez on the Mississippi River, had a population of 4,591 in 1860. Jackson was a frontier village inhabited by about a dozen families at the time of its incorporation in 1823. Its only real importance after its founding arose from its being the state capital. It had only 3,191 inhabitants according to the 1860 census.

Mississippi's population was not stabilized by the time of the Civil War; the influx of settlers from the eastern seaboard states continued, and a considerable number of residents of Mississippi were moving farther west. The majority of Mississippi's leaders migrated to the state: for example, Jefferson DAVIS came from Kentucky; John Anthony QUITMAN came from New York; Henry Stuart FOOTE, David HOLMES, and George POINDEXTER came from Virginia; Albert Gallatin BROWN came from South Carolina, William Lewis SHARKEY came from East Tennessee; Jacob THOMPSON came from North Carolina; and Robert John WALKER came from Pennsylvania.

During the 1850s the secessionists increased their influence. The Union victory in the 1850-51 secession crisis over the acceptance of the COMPROMISE OF 1850 proved to be short-lived. Governor Henry Stuart Foote, the architect of that victory, left the state in 1854 when the "fire-eaters," or secessionists, gained control of state politics.

The group advocating secession in Mississippi believed that there was greater danger to the state's social system in the Union than out of it. Mississippians opposed to secession regarded secession as a doubtful remedy and as a hazard to the social order if it should lead to violent revolution. The secessionist strength came from the country editors, lawyer-politicians, and small planter-farmer groups. Those opposing secession were the men of property or old-line Whigs. However, these conservative forces, especially in the Natchez area, lacked strong leadership in the decade preceding the Civil War.

With the election of Abraham Lincoln as president in November 1860, Mississippi took steps to secede from the Union. On December 20, 1860, voters elected delegates to a convention to be held on January 7, 1861, to consider the state's future role in the Union. The forces of immediate secession won at the convention by a vote of eighty-four to fifteen. On January 9, 1861, Mississippi seceded from the Union, and another period in her history began.

See John K. Bettersworth, *Confederate Mississippi* (1943); Arthur H. De Rosier, Jr., *The Removal of the Choctaw Indians* (1970); D. Clayton James, *Ante-Bellum Natchez* (1968); William D. McCain, *The Story of Jackson*, 2 vols. (1953); Richard A. McLemore, ed., *A History of Mississippi*, 2 vols. (1973); Edwin A. Miles, *Jacksonian Democracy in Mississippi* (1960); John H. Moore, *Agriculture in Ante-Bellum Mississippi* (1958); Percy L. Rainwater, *Mississippi, Storm Center of Secession, 1856-1861* (1938); John Ray Skates, Jr., *A History of the Mississippi Supreme Court, 1817-1948* (1973); Charles S. Sydnor, *Slavery in Mississippi* (1933); and Herbert Weaver, *Mississippi Farmers, 1850-1860* (1945).—J. E. G.

Mississippi River. The Mississippi, "Father of Waters," has its source in Lake Itasca in north-central Minnesota (see MISSISSIPPI RIVER, SOURCE OF). It flows almost straight south for more than 2,350 miles, gathering up the runoff of more than a third of the conterminous United States before emptying into the Gulf of Mexico. Some of its western tributaries, such as the Missouri and the Arkansas, rise among the snowcapped peaks of the Rockies, but the Mississippi is a lowland river; Lake Itasca lies at 1,463 feet. Its flow through central Minnesota can be traced from one lake to another, now and then cutting through glacial debris at points where the names of cities indicate the nature of its flow. Grand Rapids, Little Falls, and Sauk Rapids are places where the river descends abruptly. At points such as these and where it plunges over a ledge of limestone at the Falls of St. Anthony in Minneapolis, the water power was harnessed early to cut the timber that grows abundantly throughout the area.

Below Minneapolis and St. Paul the river valley widens out considerably, and the stream gradient decreases appreciably. This change in the nature of the valley is attributable to the fact that from this point on the river acted as the major spillway for the continental ice sheet to the northwest and northeast. The Minnesota River, which joins the Mississippi River in the Twin Cities area, drained ancient Lake Agassiz; the St. Croix, the west end of Lake Superior; the Rock River, the Green Bay lobe of ancient Lake Michigan; and the Illinois River, the southern end of ancient Lake Michigan. Nowhere now does the river occupy all of its channel, except perhaps only in Lake Pepin, where the delta of the Chippewa River draining western Wisconsin has acted to dam the flow of the Mississippi. Other wide sections of

Mississippi River

sion of sedimentary rocks has created some spectacular scenery. Farther downstream, after being joined by the Missouri and the Ohio, the Mississippi truly becomes a great river, almost a mile in width. Of this flow, almost sixty percent is derived from the Ohio and less than twenty percent from the Missouri.

Below its juncture with the Ohio, the gradient of the Mississippi is very slight, and it meanders a distance of more than 1,500 miles to reach the Gulf; the airline distance is 600 miles. For much of this stretch of the river the flow is confined between levees maintained by the Corps of Engineers. The major tributaries are the Arkansas and the Red River of the South, which reach the Mississippi from the west. The delta section begins at its confluence with the Red. The land becomes low and swampy and the stream divides to form distributaries, locally known as bayous.

For the Indians and the first white men to reach it from the north and east, the Mississippi River and its tributaries represented a broad road on which they could travel easily within the interior of the continent by canoe, raft, or boat. Although it was Spaniards who first reached the Mississippi basin, it was Frenchmen who knew the craft of building boats and canoes and of traveling on water that floated downstream. Thus it was that Marquette and Jolliet crossed over from Green Bay on Lake Michigan to the waters of the Wisconsin and thus into the upper Mississippi drainage in 1673. La Salle, the man most responsible for the exploration of the Mississippi, was essentially a fur trader who envisioned a series of trading posts up and down the river and a fleet of boats operating on it to carry trade goods in one direction and furs in the other. Soon other parties of French traders and missionaries penetrated other parts of the basin and established themselves at such places as St. Louis and New Orleans, later destined to become great cities. Even after Louisiana passed into Spanish hands in 1763 and became part of the United States in 1803, French cultural influence remained strong, especially along the lower river.

The river continued to be the main north-south avenue of travel under the Americans; its tributaries, the Ohio and Missouri, carried most of the westward-bound explorers and settlers of the early nineteenth century (see TRANSPORTATION ON THE MISSISSIPPI RIVER SYSTEM). Eventually, many towns and cities grew up on sites along the river, in most cases occupying sites on the bluffs overlooking the river in order to escape the floods that frequently ravaged the lowlands. Many of them had been established as trading posts; others grew at river crossings or where the Mississippi steamboats of Mark Twain's era stopped to discharge passengers and freight and to take on fuel and provisions. As time went by, portions of these towns crept down onto the floodplain, and with each major flood came the cry for protection.

As early as 1837 the Corps of Engineers became interested in the management of the river, and in 1852 it was given $75,000 to improve the channel at its mouth. The Civil War intervened, however, and progress on river improvement ceased. A convention to discuss the improvement of the river was held in St. Louis in 1873 and shortly thereafter a system of jetties was built through the delta area. The jetties permitted ocean-going vessels to reach the wharves of New Orleans and that city jumped from eleventh place to second place

the river are found where locks and dams have been built to permit barge traffic to reach Minneapolis and St. Paul.

In the area where Minnesota, Iowa, and Wisconsin meet, the Mississippi flows through the Driftless Area, a portion of the northern United States that was untouched by the glaciers. In this section differential ero-

among American ports in tonnage of freight handled.

The Mississippi River Commission was established in 1879, but it was not until after the great flood of 1927 that a massive program to control the flow of the river was put into effect. The river was straightened, floodways were created, and improvements to navigational features were made. Today the Mississippi River is widely used by pleasure craft, and massive barge trains pushed by powerful tugboats move petroleum, coal, and other cargoes up and down the river. Most of the people living along the river no longer live in fear of the spring floods.

See Ben Lucien Burman, *Big River to Cross* (1940); Willard Glazier, *Down the Great River* (1893); Pare Lorentz, *The River* (1938); Gerard H. Matthes, "Paradoxes of the Mississippi," *Scientific American* (April 1951); John F. McDermott, *The Lost Panoramas of the Mississippi* (1958); Willard Price, *The Amazing Mississippi* (1962); Lyle Saxon, *Father Mississippi* (1927); Timothy Severin, *Explorers of the Mississippi* (1968); and Mark Twain, *Life on the Mississippi* (1883).—R. W. D.

Mississippi River, source of. The source of the Mississippi River was an elusive goal of a number of explorers. David Thompson, the renowned surveyor and trader of the British North West Company, believed he found the origin of the great river at Turtle Lake (near present-day Bemidji, Minnesota) when he visited there in 1798. Seven years later, one of Lieutenant Zebulon M. Pike's major objectives was to "ascend the main branch of the Mississippi to its source." Undaunted by the cruel Minnesota winter, Pike arrived at Leech Lake, which he considered to be the "main source of the Mississippi," and to upper Red Cedar Lake (Cass Lake), which he described as the "upper source of the Mississippi." Another expedition sponsored by the United States government was that of Lewis Cass, governor of Michigan Territory, in 1820. He agreed in part with Pike, declaring Upper Red Cedar Lake the "true source of the Mississippi." Another explorer who sought to discover the "true source" was a romantic Italian, Giacomo C. Beltrami. After he had wandered through the wilds of the northern Minnesota country in 1823, an Indian guide led him to a heart-shaped lake situated between Red and Cass lakes. He named it Lake Julia, the "most southern source of the Red River and the most northern source of the Mississippi." It remained for Henry R. Schoolcraft, mineralogist on Cass's expedition in 1823, to finally unlock the geographical mystery in 1832. With a well-equipped party he penetrated the wilderness at Fond du Lac, followed the St. Louis River, crossed the Savanna Portage to Sandy Lake, and entered the Mississippi. An Ojibwa at Cass Lake guided him to the actual source of the Mississippi. With the help of a missionary, William T. Boutwell, Schoolcraft named the lake "Itasca," from the Latin *veritas caput.*

See Bertha L. Heilbron, "How the Source of the Mississippi Was Found," *Gopher Historian* (1958); and William J. Petersen, "Veritas Caput: Itasca," *Minnesota History* (June 1937).—R. W. F.

Mississippi Territory. The old Southwest, the area now largely included in the states of Mississippi and Alabama, was settled first by the French. Part of it then became the province of British West Florida. At the end of the American Revolution, Spain and Georgia claimed the area. With the settlement of the Spanish claim in 1795 (see SAN LORENZO, TREATY OF), the way was paved for the organization of Mississippi Territory.

On March 6, 1798, Congress passed a bill creating Mississippi Territory, which included the later-formed ALABAMA TERRITORY. By an act of April 9 the territory was defined by a line drawn east from the mouth of the Yazoo River near the Walnut Hills to the Chattahoochee River on the east, southward down the eastern shore of that river to the 31st degree north latitude, thence west to the Mississippi River, and up that stream to its beginning. When Georgia surrendered her claims in 1804, the area north to the 35th degree parallel was added. The district between the Pearl and Perdido rivers south of the 31st degree, claimed as part of the Louisiana Purchase of 1803, was added in 1813 during the War of 1812. Thus between 1798 and 1813 all the lands lying within the present boundaries of the states of Alabama and Mississippi became a part of Mississippi Territory.

Government in the territory was patterned after that of the Northwest and Southwest territories. Winthrop SARGENT of Massachusetts was appointed governor, and a court of four judges was established.

Population of the new territory was concentrated about Natchez and the Walnut Hills on the Mississippi. Before Sargent arrived in the territory to assume his duties, Peter B. Bruin acted as governor. The new territory was beset by a complexity of problems, many of them centering about Spanish intrigue and armed threats. It was necessary for the acting governor to take some immediate steps.

Until there was a population of twenty-five thousand, legislative powers were exercised by the governor and two or three judges. Some of the major issues dealt with by this committee were Indian relations, Spanish pressures, law and order, and relations with the agents of the Georgia land companies, especially Zachariah Cox. Governor Sargent appointed committees of conservators of the peace late in 1798, an act that created internal political friction. Need for these committees was reflected in the fact that the first public building erected in Natchez was a jailhouse.

Population of Mississippi Territory increased rather rapidly. The boundary issue was on the way to settlement by 1799, and other sources of irritation with the Spanish were slowly being resolved. New counties were created and a code of laws adopted, but not without serious internal bickering. On May 10, 1800, Congress approved a second stage of territorial government by permitting the holding of a popular election. On May 25, 1801, William C. C. CLAIBORNE, a Jeffersonian appointee, succeeded Sargent as governor. In succeeding years Mississippi Territory experienced numerous disturbances, most of them resulting from friction along the Spanish border. The Kemper "revolution" (1804), an attempt to assert American over Spanish authority, caused trouble, and so did the BURR CONSPIRACY.

The invention of the cotton gin in 1793 and the establishment of cotton as a staple crop hastened the maturing of the territory. By 1810 its total population had reached 40,352. The first attempt at statehood for the entire territory failed. The War of 1812 then turned the attention of Congress to more pressing matters, and further consideration of admission was delayed until the end of the war. Congress finally decided in 1817 to divide the territory into two states, but the problem was to find an acceptable dividing line. Congress accepted the argument of those favoring a north-south line, giving each state access to the Gulf of Mexico.

An enabling act of March 1, 1817, gave the inhabitants of the western part of Mississippi Territory the privilege of forming for themselves a constitution and a state government and assuming a state name as they deemed proper. They chose Mississippi. The sessions of the first constitutional convention were held in the territorial capital of Washington during the summer. Elections were held in September and October 1817. On December 10, 1817, President James Monroe declared Mississippi the twentieth state of the United States. Two years later the eastern part of the territory became the state of Alabama.

See Thomas Perkins Abernethy, *The Formative Period in Alabama, 1815-1828* (1965); and Dunbar Rowland, *History of Mississippi*, vol. I (1925), and *Encyclopedia of Mississippi History*, 2 vols. (1907).—T. D. C. and J. E. G.

Mississippi valley: French and Spanish periods. The first Europeans to occupy the American midcontinent were the French. In the European rivalry for empire in North America, the French expanded from their colonized areas in the St. Lawrence River valley westward to the Great Lakes and then down into the Ohio and Mississippi valleys, while the English moved west from the Atlantic coast and the Spanish moved north from Mexico (see FRENCH HERITAGE).

French expansion was motivated by a desire for a water route to the Pacific and Asia; for economic windfalls from the fur trade and untapped markets for French goods; and for the Christianization of "heathen" populations (see EXPLORATION, FRENCH). The expedition (1673-74) led by Louis JOLLIET, a trader, and Jacques MARQUETTE, a missionary, is representative of these forces in action during the early French advances into the Mississippi valley. It was the Sieur de LA SALLE, however, who developed the idea that the Mississippi should be the center of French America. In 1682 he sailed the full length of the river, named the area, and took possession of the whole valley in the name of the king of France. La Salle, a fur trader and explorer, envisioned a settlement at the mouth of the Mississippi that would serve not only as a center for trade and colonization but would also be a vantage point from which to mount expeditions against the Spanish to the west. But it remained for the sons of the Canadian pioneer Charles Lemoyne, the sieurs de IBERVILLE and BIENVILLE, to establish a strong French foothold in Lower Louisiana (the designations Upper Louisiana and Lower Louisiana are explained in LOUISIANA TERRITORY). Meanwhile, operating in the Illinois country and possessing a royal patent to explore and build forts in exchange for a fur-trade monopoly, La Salle and his successors, such as Henri de Tonti, Father Louis Hennepin, Pierre Charles Le Sueur, the Sieur Duluth, and Nicolas Perrot, began the work of exploration and alliance-building among the Indians.

La Salle himself met with frustration and disaster. Given permission to plant a colony in the Mississippi delta region, he set sail from France in 1684. Unfortunately he missed the mouth of the Mississippi and landed instead on the coast of Texas. Establishing his colony on Garcitas Creek on the western side of Matagorda Bay, La Salle attempted to contact his partner, Tonti,

who was to have descended the river from the north. Tonti achieved this goal and founded a small fort in Arkansas. He tired of waiting for his partner, however, who on his fourth attempt to reach the Mississippi was murdered by his own men. Interest in the area on the part of individual French traders did not wane, for fabulous tales of mineral wealth in New Spain (Mexico) and half-mythical notions of a water link to the Pacific led such men as Mathieu Sagean and Baron de Lahontan to continue the work of expansion. Before the end of the seventeenth century, French traders had probably reached the Rio Grande and were among the Missouri and Osage tribes.

The Spanish, jealously guarding their own claims in the Gulf of Mexico and fearful of any advances being made on their mines in New Spain, founded Pensacola, Florida, to forestall the French. Forced to go further west, the Lemoyne brothers established their first colony at Biloxi, Mississippi, and in 1702 set up headquarters at Mobile, Alabama. The colony was placed under a government similar to that of Canada, with Bienville in charge. In addition to the Spanish in Florida and on the Texas-Louisiana frontier, Bienville had to contend with the English influence among various tribes in Alabama and Tennessee. There were, moreover, insuperable personal quarrels and endemic hazards such as hurricanes and strange diseases, and so, the colony did not prosper. In 1712 the French government, deeming Louisiana too heavy a liability, granted Antoine Crozat a fifteen-year trade monopoly in the vast area between Illinois and the Gulf of Mexico in exchange for a promise that he would colonize and develop the region. The governor was Antoine de la Mothe Cadillac, who encouraged the growth of Detroit in the north. Crippled by the paternalistic regulations of the mother country, by Crozat's monopoly, and by low prices for furs, Louisiana barely survived. Crozat gave up after five years, and Louisiana was taken over by John Law's Company of the West (Company of the Indies after 1719). Granted full political and commercial powers, Law centered his great speculations in the area of present-day Louisiana and Arkansas. His schemes, however, were such colossal failures that they have been referred to since as the Mississippi Bubble. During this time some immigration to Louisiana did occur, especially from Germany. Perhaps the one bright spot was that the able Bienville was reappointed governor of Louisiana. It was he who established a new capital at New Orleans (1718).

Wars in Europe reverberated in America, and inevitably hostilities broke out between the "children colonies." When France and Spain went to war in Europe (War of the Spanish Succession, 1701-14), fighting erupted on the Louisiana-Florida frontier. Mobile and Pensacola were each captured and recaptured. Hostilities also flared up on the Louisiana-Texas frontier. Louis Juchereau de St. Denis explored and opened the Red River route to Texas and Santa Fe, and in 1713 he founded the frontier post of Natchitoches and began making new excursions to Texas, where he parleyed with Indian groups already hostile to the Spanish. The Spanish reacted to these invasions and those of French traders coming all the way from the Illinois country by sending out expeditions of their own. That of Pedro de Villasur in 1720 ended in destruction at the hands of Indians supplied with French guns.

Meanwhile, Bienville had established Fort Toulouse on the Alabama River, to control English influence. Indian troubles such as the NATCHEZ WAR and the Fox wars proved costly, but under Bienville's guidance Louisiana's prosperity and population slowly began to increase. When the Company of the Indies withdrew in 1731, Louisiana became a royal colony. Bienville was again appointed governor, and a superior council was established. Bienville was continually hampered in this period (until 1743) by English-inspired conflict with the Chickasaw and Choctaw nations.

Throughout the middle decades of the eighteenth century individual French traders and explorers carried on trade with the western tribes. The French furnished the Plains Indians with guns in exchange for Spanish horses. The Spanish policy forbade guns to the Indians. Working out of New Orleans, Opelousas, Natchitoches, and Caddodacho, the last mentioned founded by Bénard de la Harpe, the French penetrated, and expanded their influence into, Texas. They traded with the Hasinai and Caddo Indians in the very shadows of Spanish posts. By 1750 the Red River region and northeastern Texas were virtually under French control. The way to western Texas and the upper Red River was barred by the Apache, and in 1753 Governor Kerlerac proposed a breakthrough. From their Arkansas post, French traders engaged those tribes living in the Arkansas River valley. A breakthrough to distant Santa Fe had already occurred, for in 1739 the Mallet brothers reached the isolated Spanish provincial capital.

Throughout the years before the French and Indian War, successful incursions westward were made from Illinois. Claude Du Tisné explored the Missouri and Osage rivers and won the allegiance of the Pawnee. Later Etienne de Bourgmont founded Fort Orléans and made peace between the Comanche and other tribes. Inter-Indian rivalry, however, prevented the French from reaching Santa Fe with any regularity. Those who did were always uncertain of their fate, for often they were met with imprisonment and harassment. Fort Cavagnolle was established among the Kansa, and peace was effected between the Comanche and their eastern enemies, thereby lessening the difficulty of a previously troublesome route. Throughout this period the Spanish acted primarily in response to French gains. Unable to establish permanent footholds in eastern Texas, they founded San Antonio as a halfway station between Coahuila and eastern Texas. However, after being driven out, they occupied eastern Texas in 1721 by founding Los Adaes, forty-five miles from the French outpost of Natchitoches.

The nature of all these borderland struggles changed drastically when the French were defeated by the British and their allies in the Seven Years' War. After ceding Canada to Great Britain and Louisiana to Spain in the Treaty of Paris of 1763, France retired from the mainland of North America. While the British willingly assumed control of the Ohio and Illinois country, Spain's Charles III was not anxious to take the "white elephant" of Louisiana off French hands; indeed, Charles III turned down the offer at first but came to see that Louisiana could serve Spain as a buffer colony against the English.

The news of the cession caused consternation and protest among the Louisiana colonists. The first governor appointed under Spanish rule was Antonio de UL-LOA, who was given only ninety soldiers and told that he could expect the enlistment of the French militia. Ulloa never entered New Orleans. He sent out some exploratory parties and made some visitations; but resentment, poor economic conditions, and unpopular acts, including his marriage to a Peruvian princess on board his boat anchored at La Balize, caused the New Orleans French to cut his moorings. Next, an efficient and loyal military officer, Alejandro O'REILLY, was then sent with twenty-six hundred soldiers to put down the so-called Revolution of 1768. Dealing sternly with the leaders of the revolt, he received the sobriquet "Bloody O'Reilly."

Ironically it was under Spanish rule that Louisiana finally began to achieve some degree of long-awaited prosperity. Spanish administrative law was instituted in conjunction with the prevalent *coûtume de Paris* (i.e., French law). The economy expanded under relatively lax Spanish rule. Lieutenant governors of French extraction were appointed for the Texas frontier and Illinois. Officials such as Balthazar de Villiers, Athanase de Mézières, Don Zenon Trudeau, and Charles de Hault de Lassus, made great strides in stabilizing conditions in the provinces. O'Reilly was succeeded by such able governors as Luís de Unzaga y Amezaga, and Bernardo de GALVEZ. In 1771, Louisiana was attached to the captaincy general of Havana for military purposes and to the *audiencia* of Santo Domingo for judicial purposes.

The major problems of the period for the Spanish were English competitors along the Indian trade routes and smugglers along the Gulf Coast. New Orleans, Natchitoches, Arkansas Post, and St. Louis became the main trading and administrative centers. To control the Indians, the Spaniards adopted French ways and used French traders rather than the mission system, which had prevailed in the northern provinces of Mexico. The licensing of traders and the giving of presents were the mainstays of the French policy. De Mézières succeeded in turning the former Indian allies of the French into allies of the Spanish. The troublesome Osage were finally brought under some semblance of control by the Chouteau family of St. Louis. Some difficulties arose, though, from the fact that Louisiana was administered by Havana, and Texas by New Spain (Mexico) and the Provincias Internas. The differing policies of these two administrative districts allowed contraband activities to thrive.

The American Revolution also raised difficulties. Bernardo de Gálvez, always ready to oppose the English, strictly enforced Spanish neutrality by stopping and confiscating English vessels while winking at the Boston ships, thus permitting supplies and money to reach the Americans in the West. Preparing for what he thought would be an eventuality, Gálvez was ready to drive the British from the lower Mississippi valley and Florida when Spain declared war on England in 1779. He accomplished his task with lightning speed. The Spanish did not try to attack the British along the borderlands of Upper Louisiana where French fur traders were already in competition with British traders from Canada. As a result the merchants and traders of Upper Louisiana suffered from English competition and depredations for a number of years.

Trailblazing also continued under the Spanish regime. Chief among the pathfinders was Pedro VIAL, a Frenchman who, as the discoverer of routes between Santa Fe and St. Louis and between Natchitoches and both San Antonio and Santa Fe, ranks among the truly great, but unsung, early western frontiersmen.

After the American Revolution, Spain tried to check the westward advance of the youthful United States through border intrigue, control of the Indians on the American frontiers, and international diplomacy. The American westerners, feeling at times that their own government had let them down or was too weak to gain free navigation of the Mississippi, were often willing to engage in intrigue with the Spaniards. Spain built up a pension list of "friends" and gave special advantages to favored American traders. Spain also tried countercolonization to hold back the expanding Americans; but ironically the only colonists who came were American citizens whom the Spanish trusted. Before the end of the century scores of Americans had crossed the Mississippi to settle in Spanish Louisiana: George Morgan and his colony; Moses Austin; the famous Kentucky frontiersman Daniel Boone; and many others. Realizing that Spanish imperial needs were hopelessly undercut by the realities of American westward expansion in Missouri and elsewhere, Spain gave in and in 1795 signed the Treaty of SAN LORENZO, by which the Americans were allowed to use the Mississippi River.

During the last decade of the eighteenth century, Spanish colonial officials also made a final attempt to counteract the British influence in their borderland regions. By exploiting and encouraging the initiative of the French merchants of St. Louis, backed by their lieutenant governor, Zenon Trudeau, and the governor of Louisiana, Hector Carondelet, Spain hoped to drive the British traders out. Three costly expeditions failed, but aided by the internal dissension among Canadian fur-trading companies and by JAY'S TREATY (1794), the French Creoles made some gains along the Missouri. Nevertheless, Jacques Clamorgan's Missouri Company and the efforts of the Missouri traders James Mackay, John Evans, and Andrew Todd eventually failed because of quibbling and selfish speculation. The merchant groups of Upper Louisiana did eventually dominate the troubled borderlands regions but only after Spanish imperial boundaries had contracted by virtue of the secret Treaty of SAN ILDEFONSO in 1800, which stipulated that Spain cede Louisiana back to France.

When the United States purchased Louisiana from France in 1803, Spain fell back again to her old Texas and New Mexico frontiers. By the opening of the nineteenth century, the population of Spanish Louisiana had reached fifty thousand, five times that achieved under France. Generally speaking, the region was on the threshold of a new vitality with a local population ready to expand the fur trade and open new areas to settlement. The reestablished French empire lasted but forty days when Napoleon, faced with rebellion in Haiti and war clouds in Europe, decided to sell the colony to the Americans.

See John Francis Bannon, *The Spanish Borderlands Frontier, 1513-1821* (1970); Henri Folmer, *Franco-Spanish Rivalry in North America* (1953); Charles Gayarré, *History of Louisiana,* 4 vols. (1903); Noel Loomis and A. P. Nasatir, *Pedro Vial and the Roads to Santa Fe* (1967); John F. McDermott, ed., *Frenchmen and French Ways in*

the Mississippi Valley (1969) and *The Spanish in the Mississippi Valley, 1762-1804* (1974); A. P. Nasatir, *Spanish War Vessels on the Mississippi, 1792-1796* (1968) and (ed.) *Before Lewis and Clark,* 2 vols. (1952).—A. P. N.

Missouri. To 1850. By 1700 Europeans were living in the lower Missouri River valley. Frenchmen began to extract lead from the eastern Ozark highlands by 1715, and they came to settle premanently at Ste. Genevieve by 1735. In this quiet little hamlet on the Mississippi, about sixty miles south of present-day St. Louis, they refined the ore taken from the hills, bartered for furs with the Indians, and traded with their kinsmen living across the Mississippi in Illinois.

After being licensed by the governor of Louisiana to trade for more furs, a company of merchants sent its agents up the Mississippi from New Orleans to find a site for a trading post. In 1763 Pierre LACLEDE, an adventurer from the Pyrenees, selected a limestone bluff on the west bank of the river, about fifteen miles south of the confluence of the Mississippi with the Missouri. During the next year the company's workers constructed a trading post on the site, which they called St. Louis.

Unknown to them, France had ceded the west-bank lands to Spain in 1763, but Spain did not send a garrison to occupy the place until 1770. Settlers came, most of whom were French, while life remained fairly tranquil except for Indian attacks and floods. The Spanish governors of the region, known as Upper Louisiana, established their capital at St. Louis. They discovered that Protestant Americans were crossing the Mississippi to squat on the lands of the king and that there was nothing they could do to exclude the intruders effectively. Spain returned Louisiana to France in 1800, and Napoleon sold it to the United States in 1803. The return as well as the sale were acknowledged simultaneously on March 10, 1804, in a ceremony of transfer at St. Louis.

Congress provided a government for Upper Louisiana in October 1804, and it became the LOUISIANA TERRITORY in 1805 with its own governor. In 1812 Congress changed the name of Louisiana Territory to Missouri Territory, giving its inhabitants a legislature. Within six years the Assembly requested admission to the Union. Congress enacted the MISSOURI COMPROMISE in 1820, which permitted slavery within Missouri's boundaries, but excluded involuntary servitude in western lands lying north of Missouri's southern boundary. In 1820 David BARTON led Missouri's constitutional convention, and in 1821 Missouri was admitted to the Union with a population of about sixty-seven thousand.

Americans possessed Missouri before they owned it, for the frantic efforts of its former Spanish governors had failed to keep out the Americans. By 1804 more than half of Missouri's inhabitants were native Americans, among them the families of Daniel Boone and Moses Austin. It was not until 1815, after the peace with Britain, that the great rush of Americans into Missouri Territory began, however. Frenchmen remained in scattered places in the lower Missouri valley, but most clustered together in the towns along the Mississippi. Some of the St. Louis French, most notably the CHOUTEAU FAMILY, made fortunes from the fur trade. Farmers from the upper South occupied the grass plains and Missouri River bottomland in central Missouri. Kentuckians and Virginians brought southern ways and slaves to such towns as Boonville, Franklin, and Lexington, established in 1819, 1817, and 1822 respectively. Men from New England and western Pennsylvania came, too. The diversity of the state's population was complicated even more by the arrival of many Germans after 1830. Most of them settled near St. Louis; by 1850, one third of that city was German. People came to the Ozark hills as early as the 1830s, but settlement continued there after the Civil War. By 1860 nearly every part of the state except the Ozarks was settled.

French merchants and more recently arrived American entrepreneurs, notably William GILPIN, realized that Missouri lay on the path west, and they were determined to exploit the good fortune their strategic location might bring them. A thriving commerce developed, particularly at St. Louis, although also at the towns of INDEPENDENCE (established about 1827) and WESTPORT LANDING (founded 1833 and later called Kansas City). St. Louis fortunes were made quickly by the sale of lead and furs extracted from the Missouri backcountry, but as more Americans began moving up the Missouri River to homes in the West, a substantial trade developed in supplying tools, capital, and transportation to the migrants. St. Louis craftsmen made plows, rifles, wagons, and leather goods for those moving west. A major customer was the United States Army, which maintained one of the West's largest military posts nearby at Jefferson Barracks. The Bank of the State of Missouri, founded in 1837 in St. Louis, provided the soundest bank notes west of the Wabash; its issue was coveted as far west as the Pacific Coast. From St. Louis to Independence, Missourians sold those notorious beasts, the Missouri mules, to any brave enough to buy. The levee at St. Louis became a depot for steamboats on the Mississippi and the Missouri. Five thousand of these river palaces docked at the city in 1860, when the steamboat traffic was at its peak. As for railroads, St. Louisans were slow to bring them to the state. Railroad conventions were held in 1836 and 1849, but financial catastrophe, fire, and cholera hindered plans for making that city the terminus of a Pacific railroad. Entrepreneurs in western Missouri profited from the Santa Fe trade and stagecoach lines, however. The Russell, Majors and Waddell line at Lexington was probably the greatest of the mid-nineteenth-century freight lines.

The national spokesman for the commercial interests of the state, and western America as well, was Thomas Hart BENTON, a United States senator from 1820 until his defeat in 1850. He came to St. Louis from North Carolina in 1815, ingratiating himself with the old French families by defending their land titles. He crusaded for rapid development of the West by small freeholders with the aid of federally stimulated internal improvements and hard money. When Benton opposed war with Mexico and the extension of slavery into the West, the Missouri Democrats, who profited from both, deserted him in 1850. Benton's less bombastic colleague, Senator Lewis Fields LINN of Ste. Genevieve, proposed the establishment of Oregon territory in 1837 and campaigned with Benton for homesteads.

See William Nisbet Chambers, *Old Bullion Benton* (1956); Glover Moore, *The Missouri Controversy* (1937); and James Neal Primm, *Economic Policy in the Development of a Western State: Missouri, 1820-1860* (1954). —K. W. K.

Since 1850. Although Missouri had evolved in French and southern traditions, by the 1850s the area had begun to receive major infusions from other outside sources. Immigrants from the northern states and abroad came in sufficiently large numbers during the decade that by 1860 they outnumbered the southern-born within the state's population for the first time. While the older settlers had concentrated in the fertile lands along Missouri's river systems, the northerners tended to move into the southwest prairies and the more fertile Ozark regions, the upper tier of counties beyond the recently completed Hannibal and St. Joseph Railroad (see ST. JOSEPH), and the St. Louis area. Though the foreign-born centered almost entirely around St. Louis, they also spread out along the Missouri River as far west as Cole County. They could also be found in considerable numbers in Marion County in the northeast, Buchanan and Platte counties at the opposite end of the state, and Cooper and Lafayette counties in west-central Missouri. The vast majority were German and Irish, with the former outnumbering the latter two to one. Although these newcomers were not in a position to effectively challenge the existing political superstructure, they still had to be reckoned with, particularly at the local level. By the end of the Civil War they would emerge as the backbone of the newly formed Radical Union party, which would dominate state politics for five years.

Missouri's economic patterns were also slowly shifting. With the inching of railroad tracks south and west across the Illinois prairie, more and more freight traffic found its way east rather than south along the rivers. The bridging of the Mississippi near Davenport, Iowa, in 1856 and the completion of the Hannibal and St. Joseph Railroad early in 1859 helped divert considerable trade from the Missouri River line to the advantage of that growing lakeside community, Chicago. St. Louis poured several millions of dollars into railroad development during the decade, and the state contributed nearly $25 million in bonds. Lines slowly reached out from the metropolis toward the western and north-central borders of the state (these would not be completed until 1865 and 1868). St. Louis interests also stretched a line into the mineral region around Iron Mountain to tap the resources there in the late 1850s.

The lead industry in the Iron Mountain area was revitalized in 1853 with the discovery of a new ore-reducing method by John B. Valle, and by the end of the decade this source was supplemented increasingly by new mines in southwest Missouri. Several pockets of cannel coal were discovered, which became an important economic enterprise over the next several decades. Iron continued to be a principal product with the heaviest concentrations around Pilot Knob, located southwest of St. Louis.

The 1850s also marked a shift in emphasis for Missouri agriculture from subsistence to commercial concerns. The number of acres of land in use doubled, while crop and livestock production tripled. Norman J. COLMAN had begun preaching the wonders of applied scientific agriculture through the pages of his *Valley Farmer* and countless fairs and expositions. By 1860 Missouri's farmers were divided roughly into two groups representing somewhat contrasting interests: those who produced the staple crops of hemp, tobacco, some cotton and cereals and relied on slave labor to a considerable extent; those who raised livestock, corn, wheat, and occasionally tobacco using few if any slaves. The latter found their economic interests tied increasingly to the eastern rather than the southern traffic pattern.

Missourians greatly increased the amount of capital plowed into manufacturing. Much of this centered around St. Louis, but forty percent of the monetary value of finished goods came from small factories scattered about the state. Most of these were concentrated in the older and more populous river counties. For all these developments, however, Missourians by 1860 had barely begun to scratch the surface of their state's potential wealth. The postwar decades would bring considerable expansion in all areas.

Although local economic concerns were not overlooked, Missouri politics tended to be dominated by the same divisive issues that were rending the nation in the 1850s. The proslavery wing of the Democratic party managed to oust Thomas Hart Benton from his Senate seat in 1851, ostensibly because of his refusal to accept the doctrines of John C. Calhoun on slavery extension. Thereafter it managed to stay in power at Jefferson City although its hold on the legislature was sometimes tenuous. One of its leaders, Senator David R. ATCHISON, pushed congressional repeal of the Missouri Compromise and then played a prominent role in trying to turn the new Kansas Territory into a slave state. Although Missourians crossed the border in considerable numbers—some to stay, others merely to vote—they lost the struggle for control of that region as it filled increasingly with immigration from the North and East. The enmities engendered would reverberate along the border throughout the Civil War as guerrilla activity plagued the state.

An obscure army captain, who saw service in Kansas throughout the difficulties, was destined to play a major role in determining the course Missouri would follow in the Civil War. Nathaniel Lyon arrived at Jefferson Barracks in the midst of the secession crisis and quickly joined hands with Francis BLAIR and others to prevent any precipitate action by state officials to take Missouri out of the Union. A "Connecticut Yankee" with decidedly antislavery, pro-Union views, Lyon moved decisively during the first half of 1861, as occasion warranted, to assert strong Union control over the state. Matching wits with him was Governor Claiborne F. Jackson, elected in 1860 on the Douglas Democrat ticket but long a power in the proslavery wing of his party. Jackson and his lieutenant governor, Thomas C. Reynolds, believed strongly that Missouri should enter the Confederacy and worked strenuously toward that end. But they found themselves checked initially and effectively by the majority of Missourians, who, through their votes for a state legislature and a state convention, indicated their strong desire for neutrality within the Union.

The legislature approved the calling of a convention to weigh the secession issue but refused to reorganize the state militia along lines demanded by Jackson. The convention, when it met in early March 1861, decided that Missouri had no cause to leave the Union, and that indeed it would be detrimental to her interests to do so. A showdown came when Lyon moved against a state militia encampment, which had ostensibly gathered for training exercises at St. Louis, and forced its surrender on May 10. This became known as the Camp Jackson affair. A month later he drove the Jackson administration from its capital after failing to reach a compromise on the extent of federal authority in Missouri. The state convention met again in July to depose Jackson, Reynolds, and the state legislature. It then established a provisional government under Hamilton R. Gamble, which remained in power until January 1865.

Jackson and his military commander, Sterling PRICE, retreated with their followers into southwest Missouri. Success at the battles of Wilson's Creek (where Lyon was killed) and Lexington, coupled with a quick and reassuring trip to Richmond, prompted the governor to call the legislature into special session at Neosho in October 1861. Although a quorum was probably not in attendance, those present approved a secession ordinance. A month later the Confederate Congress accepted Missouri as a full partner and admitted her representatives. Driven into Arkansas by the end of the year, the Jackson-Reynolds regime maintained a shadow government, cooperating with the Confederacy, throughout the war. Sterling Price, accompanied by Reynolds, returned to Missouri in September 1864 on a daring raid to the Missouri River but met continuing military disaster at every turn. In the interim the state had been wracked by internecine guerrilla warfare from one end to the other.

Out of the holocaust of this internal conflict the Radical Union party rode the whirlwind to victory in November 1864. Made up of budding entrepreneurs and antislavery men, it swept into control of a newly commissioned state convention as well as the regular governmental machinery. The new body emancipated Missouri's slaves in January 1865 and then wrote a new constitution under the leadership of Charles D. Drake, defeating the efforts of a group led by Abraham Lincoln's former attorney general Edward BATES. While this reflected highly progressive tendencies, including full civil rights short of suffrage for the Negro, it also contained stringently proscriptive regulations against political and professional participation by anyone even remotely sympathetic with the Confederate cause.

During the next five years the Radicals worked hard and successfully to attract new immigrants and capital to Missouri. Although the 1870 census figures are somewhat unreliable, they show a gain of forty-five percent in Missouri's population over the decade—a particularly healthy increase considering wartime losses. Investments in agriculture, mining, and industry showed strong advances. The state's basic rail network was completed after several failures and considerable financial manipulation in the legislature. The Radicals placed the state's educational system on a strong foundation and tried to make certain that the blacks enjoyed their fair share of its advantages. An attempt to secure Negro suffrage failed in 1868; but with the passage of the Fifteenth Amendment two years later, Missouri's blacks, led by J. Milton TURNER, encountered little difficulty in exercising their newly gained privilege.

In the end, however, the Radicals' vindictiveness against their conservative opponents proved their undoing. The party split over the issue of reenfranchisement in 1870, giving birth to the Liberal Republican movement. Two years later the Democrats elected Richard P. BLAND to Congress and regained full power over the state government, which they retained for the rest of the century. They combined Union and Confederate elements in a successful coalition that saw the spoils of office divided to the satisfaction of both groups. A new convention rewrote Missouri's constitution in 1875, producing a generally more conservative document whose predominant note was the restriction of state and local governmental units in the areas of finance and taxation.

In the turbulent postwar era many of the disfranchised turned to lawlessness and crime. Foremost among them was the Jesse JAMES gang, which created havoc in Missouri for fifteen years after the Civil War. Ultimately Governor Thomas T. Crittenden brought outlawry to an effective halt through the judicious use of reward money, much of it furnished by the railroads, who were especially hard hit by this activity.

Missouri ushered in the twentieth century with the Louisiana Purchase Centennial Exposition, held at St. Louis in 1904. A magnificent extravaganza, it attracted 20 million visitors from all parts of the world. Among its features, heralding greater things in the new century, were a display of one hundred automobiles, including one driven under its own power all the way from New York City, and the sale on "The Pike" of the first ice cream cones.

While work on the fair went forward in 1902 and 1903, an effort of a different sort was also taking place in St. Louis. A vigorous young prosecuting attorney, Joseph W. Folk, was in the process of exposing graft and corruption in the municipal government, having secured thirty-two grand-jury indictments. Before he had finished Folk revealed a pattern of "boodling" that reached into the state legislature. In 1904 he rode the wave of resentment into the governor's chair. There he helped move Missouri on to the Progressive bandwagon with the enactment of a statewide primary election law, the initiative, and the referendum. Folk, a Democrat, was succeeded in 1909 by his trust-busting attorney general, Herbert S. Hadley, a Republican, who continued to push for needed improvements. Hadley in turn gave way in 1913 to yet another Progressive, Democrat Elliott W. Major. These three men did much to help keep Missouri abreast of needed change as she entered the new century.

With the entry of the United States into World War I in 1917, Missourians rallied to the war effort and geared their production efforts in mining, manufacturing, and agriculture to meet increased demands. The postwar years brought three successive Republican governors to the mansion—Arthur M. Hyde, Sam A. Baker, Henry S. Caulfield—for the only time in Missouri's history. These men were generally progressive in their outlook, and some moderate reforms were accomplished. The coming of the Depression brought a return to Democratic rule; and, with the exception of the 1941-45 term, Missouri had a Democratic governor right up to 1972. In the midst of World War II a constitutional convention met and provided Missouri with a new working document—its first in seventy years.

One of the major accomplishments in the 1930s was the damming of the Osage River by the Union Electric Light and Power Company to create the Lake of the Ozarks. One of the largest artificial lakes in the world, it has approximately fourteen hundred miles of shoreline and has made Missouri a strong tourist and recreational area. Its dam at Bagnell also provides an important source of electric power for the St. Louis area.

The post-World War II years brought enormous growth as Missouri kept step with an expanding nation. Manufacturing, agriculture, and mining have all grown apace to keep a good balance in the state's economy. Agriculture, which until 1940 continued to dominate the scene, has long since been surpassed by manufacturing as the principal employer of labor and chief source of wealth in the state. Of particular note is the development of the aerospace industry.

The best general history of Missouri is David D. March, *The History of Missouri*, 4 vols. (1967). An older but still useful set is Floyd C. Shoemaker, *Missouri and Missourians: Land of Contrasts and People of Achievement*, 5 vols. (1943). A good one-volume treatment is Duane Meyer, *The Heritage of Missouri* (1963). The 1850s are well covered in Perry McCandless, *A History of Missouri*, vol. II (1972). For a more detailed treatment of the Civil War and Reconstruction periods, one should consult Richard S. Brownlee, *Gray Ghosts of the Confederacy: Guerrilla Warfare in the West, 1861-1865* (1958), and William E. Parrish, *Turbulent Partnership: Missouri and the Union, 1861-1865* (1963) and *Missouri Under Radical Rule, 1865-1870*, 2 vols. (1965). The economic growth and development of the state's two principal cities is well covered in Wyatt W. Belcher, *The Economic Rivalry Between St. Louis and Chicago, 1850-1884* (1947); and Charles N. Glaab, *Kansas City and the Railroads* (1962). Aside from a few biographical studies and an occasional monograph on a highly specialized topic, little of book length has been written on late nineteenth-century and early twentieth-century Missouri. The *Missouri Historical Review* contains many fine articles on various topics of these and other periods, however. Two good political studies on twentieth-century Missouri are Lyle W. Dorsett, *The Pendergast Machine* (1968); and F. D. Mitchell, *Embattled Democracy: Missouri Democratic Politics, 1919-1932* (1968).—W. E. P.

Missouri Compromise (1820). The Missouri Compromise was the first sectional compromise on the problem of slavery extension into western territory. By the end of 1818 there were an equal number of free and slave states in the nation; then Missouri applied to Congress for admission as a slave state. On February 13, 1819, James Tallmadge, Jr., a New York representative who considered slavery morally intolerable, introduced an amendment to the Missouri enabling bill that prohibited the further introduction of slaves into the state of Missouri and provided that, after its admission, all children born of slaves within the state would be freed at the age of twenty-five. The amendment passed the House by a sharp sectional vote but was defeated in the Senate. It set off a full-scale congressional debate on slavery that continued into the 1819-20 session.

The Missouri debates were a microcosm of the entire sectional controversy over slavery in the antebellum period. Almost every economic, political, constitutional, religious, and moral argument voiced later appeared in these debates. When northerners denounced slavery as a sin, southerners sprang to its defense as a benign institution. While some northerners opposed slavery on moral grounds, others resented the political power the

South gained from the constitutional clause allowing three-fifths of the slaves to be counted for purposes of congressional apportionment. Whatever the reasons, northern congressmen were unified in their hostility to the admission of another slave state that would upset the sectional balance. Because of the intensity of the debates, action on Missouri stalled.

Eventually a compromise was reached that entailed two essential parts. Because Maine was also applying for statehood, Congress maintained the sectional balance by admitting Maine as a free state and Missouri as a slave state, without the Tallmadge amendment. The second part of the compromise, an amendment introduced by Senator Jesse Thomas of the new state of Illinois, prohibited slavery from the remaining area of the Louisiana Purchase north of the line 36°30'. South of that line slavery would be permitted, but not guaranteed, in the territorial phase. With the defection of several northerners, the Missouri Compromise solution passed Congress in March 1820.

The best accounts of the Missouri Compromise can be found in George Dangerfield, *The Era of Good Feelings* (1952); and Glover B. Moore, *The Missouri Controversy, 1819-1821* (1953).—M. F. H.

Missouri Fur Company. Impressed by the reports of Lewis and Clark, Manuel LISA organized with William Morrison and Pierre MENARD a fur-trading expedition in keelboats on the upper Missouri in 1807. Lisa commanded the field party and built FORT RAYMOND on the Yellowstone at the mouth of the Bighorn River. In 1809 Lisa and his associates enlarged their partnership to form the St. Louis, Missouri Fur Company. Lisa sent out numerous trapping expeditions to the northern Rockies that added greatly to geographical knowledge. John COLTER made his lone exploration of portions of present-day Wyoming and Montana. George Drouillard, the famous hunter of the Lewis and Clark expedition, was able to compile a map of his explorations of the Bighorn and Yellowstone rivers that was utilized by William Clark. Ezekial Williams discovered the central Rockies.

The company, hampered by the mutual mistrust of the partners and attacks by the Blackfoot, was forced into reorganization in 1812. Now referred to simply as the Missouri Fur Company, the organization was forced into further reorganization in 1814 by the War of 1812 and was further reshaped in 1817 and 1819. Lisa was appointed Indian subagent (1814-16) in this troubled era and was officially recognized for his services in retaining the loyalties of the western tribes, especially those of the Ponca, Omaha, and Sioux.

At Lisa's death he had opened up the mountain fur trade, dispatched men who had added greatly to geographical knowledge, and planted several key trading posts along the Missouri and its tributaries, which obviated the necessity of relying on an annual seasonal expedition from St. Louis. Lisa awakened the interest of St. Louis businessmen in the northern fur trade—and even attempted to reach the Spanish Southwest from St. Louis and Fort Raymond—and gave St. Louis the impetus to its future importance in the trade. After Lisa's death, Joshua PILCHER became president of the company, which did well until a party led by Robert Jones and Michael Immell was massacred by the Blackfoot. The company became defunct in 1825, never overcoming this disaster and the competition of William H. Ash-

ley and his successor companies and that of the American Fur Company.

See Hiram M. Chittenden, *The American Fur Trade of the Far West* (1902); and Richard E. Oglesby, *Manuel Lisa and the Opening of the Missouri Fur Trade* (1963). —G. B. D.

Missouri Pacific Railroad. The Missouri Pacific Railroad, incorporated as the Pacific Railroad of Missouri in 1849, bid fair to be one of the first transcontinental railroads, but foundered on the indifference of St. Louis businessmen and the complex financial manipulations of Jay Gould. Senator Thomas Hart Benton had championed a transcontinental line to run from St. Louis to California, crossing the Rockies by one or another of two passes that John C. Frémont was thought to have discovered. State aid was granted in 1851, but lack of funds stopped the railroad just thirty-seven miles west of St. Louis at a place forlornly named Pacific. By 1865, however, it had managed to reach Independence, Missouri, near Kansas City. For ten years it was repressed by the Atlantic and Pacific, the St. Louis-San Francisco ("Frisco") Railroad's transcontinental affiliate, but after Gould gained control in 1879, construction was pressed rapidly. Omaha was reached in 1882 and Pueblo, Colorado, in 1887. Originally planned as an East-West system, the "MoPac" became more of a southwestern system when Gould acquired the St. Louis, Iron Mountain and Southern Railroad and the International-Great Northern Railway in 1880. Two years later he took control of the Texas and Pacific, which extended the Gould lines through Little Rock, Arkansas, and Dallas and Fort Worth, Texas, to El Paso and a junction with the Southern Pacific.

Gould left his railroad empire to his son, George, at his death in 1892, but only ten years after the latter had embarked on his grandiose plan to build a true transcontinental railroad, the empire had begun to fall apart (see DENVER AND RIO GRANDE WESTERN RAILROAD). In 1911 the MoPac elected its first board without a Gould in over thirty years, but protracted financial malnutrition had left the system in bad shape, while much of the country through which it ran was as poor as ever. In receivership by 1915, the line was reorganized, fresh capital was raised, and extensive improvements were made during the 1920s as the Southwest generally prospered. Throughout the Depression, however, the MoPac was in receivership. Revitalized by World War II prosperity, the railroad was strengthened in the postwar period by an aggressive policy of cutting costs and dropping unprofitable branch lines and passenger service. —A. M.

Missouri River. The principal tributary of the Mississippi and the longest river in North America (2,464 miles), the Missouri River begins at the point where the Gallatin, the Madison, and the Jefferson (the main headstream) join in southwestern Montana at Three Forks. Flowing out of the Rocky Mountains and across the Great Plains, it joins the Mississippi just north of St. Louis. Along its course it passes through the states of Montana, North Dakota, and South Dakota and forms parts of the boundaries of Nebraska, Kansas, and Iowa. In doing this the Missouri picks up the waters of a number of significant tributary streams, among them the Milk, Yellowstone, Grand (in South Dakota), Little Missouri, Cheyenne, White, Niobrara, James, Big

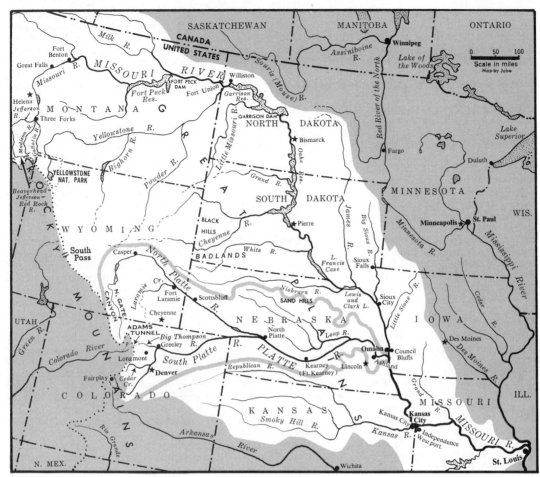

Missouri River

Sioux, Little Sioux, Platte, Kansas, Osage, and Grand (in Iowa and Missouri).

In spite of the length of the river and the size of its drainage basin (528,000 square miles), the Missouri's flow of 40 million acre-feet is comparatively small, being less than that of the Columbia, Ohio, and Tennessee rivers. This is because much of its course flows through arid and semiarid land, and its tributary streams carry much water only during the spring floods.

The western margin of the Missouri basin lies in the Rocky Mountains along the Continental Divide, where snow accumulates in the long cool winters and melts in late spring and summer. The mountain slopes are covered with relatively slow-growing conifers and shrubs, among which are open grassy mountain meadows known locally as "parks." In the mountain foothills and out on the Great Plains, precipitation amounts decrease, and the Missouri and its tributaries have cut broad trenches into the land. Only light snowfalls occur during the long cold winters, which are interrupted briefly by warm chinook winds that keep average temperatures in the western Great Plains somewhat warmer than farther east. Only sparse bunch grasses cover the Plains, and trees grow only along the riverbanks. The wind blows

almost constantly. The Central Plains section through which the Missouri flows is of great climatic instability. Average precipitation is about fifteen inches, but amounts both much higher and much lower than that are to be expected. Much of the total precipitation occurs in late spring and summer in the form of showers. Winters are extremely cold and the short summers are hot. Temperature ranges are the greatest found in the conterminous United States. Here again, the almost constant movement of air increases the loss of surface moisture. Before the coming of the white man, short grasses covered the upland surfaces, while the green foliage of deciduous trees marked the courses of the streams hidden below the level of the Plains.

The eastern margins of the Missouri basin mark the transition zone from the High Plains to the lowlands of the Mississippi. The climate is more humid, and the streams no longer cut so deeply into the land. The original grass cover was taller and grew more densely. Spring and summer storms bring large amounts of rain in short periods of time. Hail, floods, and tornadoes are problems, but drought occurs with less frequency than farther west.

The fact that much of the basin is sparsely covered by

vegetation and that much of the precipitation occurs in the form of sudden downpours accounts for another one of the characteristic features of the "Big Muddy," as the Missouri River is called. The river contributes more sediments and has a higher concentration of sediments than any other tributary of the Mississippi. In flood years the sediment load is five times that of normal flow years.

The Missouri River was a pathway of commerce long before Lewis and Clark ascended it in 1803. Indians from both sides of the Continental Divide raided and traded with Indians living along this transmontane route. French voyageurs had penetrated to the foothills of the Rockies in the late eighteenth and early nineteenth centuries in their search for furs. However, it was the Lewis and Clark expedition that opened up the territory for the fur traders and trappers. Because the river was navigable, the expedition was able to travel far upstream until it had to abandon canoes at the two forks of the Jefferson River. Not that travel for Lewis and Clark was easy. Sandbars and driftwood and the constantly changing channel impeded thier progress. On some days they managed to move only a mile or so. And the innumerable meanders made the going even slower. As Clark relates, "In pursuing some game in an eastern direction, [we found ourselves] at a distance of 370 yards from the camp, at a point on the river where we had come twelve miles." In winter, ice was a problem. In the upper reaches of the river many portages were necessary.

The trappers and traders who came after Lewis and Clark followed the tributaries of the Missouri to their headwaters. One of the first, Manuel Lisa, erected a fort at the mouth of the Bighorn River in 1807. From it John Colter, who had been a member of the Lewis and Clark expedition, reached the area of Yellowstone National Park. Steamboats were introduced on the river as early as 1819, and in 1832 the American Fur Company steamboat ascended the river as far as the Yellowstone River. Thus it became possible for easterners to ride down the Ohio onto the Mississippi and up the Missouri as far as Fort Benton, Montana. However, the main stream of traffic left the Missouri a short distance upriver from St. Louis. With the opening up of the Oregon country and with the discovery of gold in California, it became more practical to leave the Missouri where the river turned northward and then go overland along the Republican River across to the Platte and up the Platte to South Pass in Wyoming. With the building of railroads following the Civil War, steamboat traffic declined precipitously. (See TRANSPORTATION ON THE MISSISSIPPI RIVER SYSTEM.)

As the Plains Indians were subdued and fell back before the onslaught of cattlemen and soldiers, livestock ranching came to dominate much of the drainage basin of the Missouri. With the building of dams irrigational agriculture has become important.

See Abraham P. Nasatir, *Before Lewis and Clark* (1952); Robert Osborn, "The Nation's Greatest River Basin," *Fortune* (August 1960); Marian E. Ridgeway, *The Missouri Basin's Pick-Sloan Plan* (1955); Rufus Terral, *The Missouri Valley* (1943); and Stanley Vestal, *The Missouri* (1945).—R. W. D.

Mitchell, John Hipple (1835-1905). Oregon politician. Mitchell, born John Hipple, was a talented and affable lawyer who went to Portland, Oregon, in 1860,

leaving a wife and two children in Pennsylvania. An opportunist, he thought it would be well to add to his own name his mother's maiden name, Mitchell, not troubling himself to make either the name change or the separation from his wife matters of legal notice. In 1862 he married Mattie Price of Oregon City and in 1874, under political attack, made legal his change of name and divorced his first wife.

Admitted to the Pennsylvania bar in 1856, Mitchell began a law practice with Joseph N. Dolph in Portland. As counsel to Ben Holladay's Oregon and California Railroad and to the Northern Pacific, the firm prospered. Mitchell was elected to the state senate in 1862 and made president of that body in 1864. In 1872 he defeated businessman Henry W. Corbett for the United States Senate, and his value to Oregon's only organized political party, the Republicans, grew accordingly. He was reelected in 1885, 1891, and 1901.

Exploiting his use of "senatorial courtesy," Mitchell aided the efforts of post-Civil War Republicans to build up the Republican party in Idaho Territory. Lewiston, Idaho, located on the Snake River, was geographically dependent on Portland, and Mitchell, making use of this leverage, did all he could to see that Lewiston became a political dependent as well. With his "colleagues from the Pacific Coast," writes historian Earl Pomeroy, he "exercised a sort of guardianship" over Idaho Territory.

Though Mitchell was not as corrupt as he was made to appear by H. W. Scott, editor of the *Oregonian* and an aspirant to Mitchell's senatorial seat, the senator was sufficiently tainted to become a target of Oregon's Progressive reformers. It was Mitchell's habit to support men and measures that kept him in office. In 1903 he was faced with the dilemma of having to support a popular Progressive measure for the use of the preferential primary in the nomination of United States senators. As a product of the party legislative caucus, the power the preferential primary was trying to destroy, Mitchell spoke in favor of the measure while acting to nullify its impact by excusing state legislators from nominating the men chosen by the voters. William S. U'Ren took brilliant advantage of such an open disdain of voter opinion by instituting a device ("Statement Number One") that held legislators to the voters' primary choices. Mitchell's efforts in a land grab provided reform-minded Oswald West with political leverage to win election to the governorship and to get some landmark conservationist legislation passed.

Mitchell died pending an appeal of his conviction for land fraud, and died, according to one supporter, of "a broken heart." The Senate, for its part, waived its customary practices in the matter of deceased members and neither adjourned nor sent a delegation to Mitchell's funeral.

See William H. Galvani, "Recollections of J. F. Stevens and J. H. Mitchell," *Oregon Historical Quarterly* (September 1943).—R. J. L.

Modoc and Klamath Indians. The ancestors of the Modoc and Klamath peoples drifted into the lakes district of southern Oregon and northern California in the 1600s.

The Modoc traditionally lived to the south and east of Upper Klamath Lake, while the Klamath lived to the north and west. Their common language, classed as a divergent form of Shahaptian and included within the

Penutian language family, indicates that upon arrival they were one people. During the eighteenth century they separated into the two groups known today. There is a folk tradition that the separation took the form of a rebellion on the part of the Modoc, but the two groups remained in loose political association for perhaps another century. By the time white men entered the area the Modoc-Klamath relationship was based on trade alone, and when the Modoc and Klamath were moved onto a common reservation in 1864, friction between the two peoples was such that their separate settlements had to be kept at a considerable distance from one another. The Bureau of Indian Affairs today uses the term *Klamath* to refer to Modoc and Walapai Snake persons as well.

Modoc-Klamath culture cannot be strictly identified as either a Plateau, Basin, or California type, but rather shares characteristics with all three culture groups. Both peoples were hunter-gatherers, the Klamath placing more emphasis on fishing and the Modoc on hunting. During the summer both groups wandered over extensive ranges, following deer, antelope, and mountain sheep. In winter they returned to their lakeside villages, clusters of semisubterranean circular earth lodges, which were entered through a hole in the center of the roof. Traveling in dugout canoes or rafts made of tules, they fished the lakes and streams in spring and gathered their staple vegetable, the seed of the *wocus,* a pond lily. Most of their tools were made of the volcanic rock found in the area. They made their clothing of grass or tule fibers, which were also used for baskets.

Neither Modoc nor Klamath society had a strong sense of tribal unity. The village-band was the important social unit; the tribelet, formed of numerous villages, was the major political unit. While no political leader represented the entire nation, specific leaders were assigned in both Modoc and Klamath society to the areas of religion, warfare, and domestic life. The religious leader, or shaman, wielded more power than the war chief or the domestic headman, whose title was simply "leader." A war chief, if he wished to lead a raid or an attack, announced his plan but each man could decide whether or not to join him. The leader, who was responsible for keeping peace within the group he represented, addressed his people several times a year in formal sermonlike speeches. He reminded men, women, and children of their respective roles and the virtues proper to each and urged industriousness and ambition. He could only cajole his followers, however, and had no power of enforcement beyond his moral authority.

Contact with Indians to the north who were involved in the fur trade in the late eighteenth century changed many aspects of Modoc-Klamath culture. By 1835, both groups were participating in the international trade fairs held at The Dalles, Oregon. They took immediately to the horse, which they acquired by trading slaves to the northern Indians who had already adopted the horse. Raiding weaker tribes for captives, though common before contact with the "horse Indians," now increased considerably; later, white emigrants were raided for stock and captives. The horse, along with its counterpart, the gun, became a new index of prestige in a wealth-conscious society.

Changes in the economy produced changes in political institutions. A domestic leader did not usually participate in war activity, but he was expected to be a rich man; but when the horse and gun, indirect products of the raid-attack, became the new currency, the leader was forced to become a warrior. Large-scale raiding placed a new emphasis on military affairs in village life. The functions of the war chief and the domestic leader became inseparable, and by the 1860s a single position of authority had evolved. The new "chief" was all the more powerful because the political unit he represented increased in size. Where tribelets were formerly self-contained units, they now consolidated for increased effectiveness in raiding. In several cases, leaders who had acquired power during this era became white-appointed chiefs on the reservation.

Reservation life began in 1864. With the notable exception of CAPTAIN JACK and others who participated in the MODOC WAR of 1872-73, most Modoc and Klamath accepted the new situation. The American values of materialism and industriousness were not new to them. Many took up cattle-raising and logging successfully. The breaking up of reservation land into individual allotments after the Dawes act of 1887 brought more economic and social changes, which led toward a dissolution of the tribal framework. In 1961 most of the 2,133 residents of the Klamath reservation ceased to be wards of the federal government and became subject to the same laws and privileges that affect other citizens in Oregon. In 1974 the remaining members of the tribe received $49 million from the United States government for the tribal lands.

One might begin a study of the Modoc-Klamath with Luther S. Cressman, *Klamath Prehistory: The Prehistory of the Culture of the Klamath Lake Area, Oregon* (1956). Leslie Spier, *Klamath Ethnography* (1930), and Verne Ray, *Primitive Pragmatists: The Modoc Indians of Northern California* (1963), are the products of fieldwork conducted on the Klamath reservation in the 1930s and are thorough ethnographic accounts. The reservation era up to the 1960s is covered in Theodore Stern, *The Klamath Tribe: A People and Their Reservation* (1965). —J. E. S.

Modoc War (1872-1873). The Modoc War originated in a struggle for land. Settlers who entered the northern California-southern Oregon country during the gold rush were attracted to lands in the Lost River valley. The area was occupied by a subdivision of the Modoc Indian nation; the group's leader in the 1850s was Keintpoos, called CAPTAIN JACK by whites. A treaty signed in 1864 removed all Modoc, together with the Klamath of southeastern Oregon, onto a reservation carved out of Klamath lands. In 1865 Captain Jack led his band back to Lost River, having left the reservation in anger because the agent there chose to recognize Old Schonchin, a more powerful leader, as the chief of the entire Modoc people. The group was persuaded to return in late 1869 through the efforts of Alfred Meacham, Indian superintendent for Oregon. But the Klamath, who regarded the Modoc as intruders on their land, made life unpleasant for all of them. So the next spring Jack led another exodus from the reservation, accompanied this time by those led by Old Schonchin. Eventually Old Schonchin led most of his followers back to the reservation. Jack's people, however, reverted to their former life-style of hunting and gathering. Jack favored peaceful coexistence with the white man, and so his group traded at the California mining town of Yreka.

Nevertheless, settlers who had moved onto the Modoc lands in Oregon while Jack was on the reservation were alarmed by the prospect that the Indians might never be made to leave. By 1872 the state of Oregon, the Department of the Interior, and the War Department were agreed that Captain Jack's band had to be removed, but interagency rivalry and failures in communication led to an outbreak of violence. Thus, when T. B. Odeneal, who had replaced Meacham as superintendent, was told by the Indian Office to remove the band, he attempted to do so with a force of forty men and without the authorization of the commanding officer of the Department of the Columbia, General Edward R. S. Canby. The troops entered Jack's camp on Lost River on the morning of November 29, 1872. While the Indians were being disarmed a Modoc and a soldier fired at each other simultaneously and a skirmish ensued. The army lost several men, while Jack's people escaped unharmed. They fled to the Lava Beds south of Tule Lake and entrenched themselves in this perfect natural stronghold.

Jack was joined there by a party from his band who, led by a power-seeking shaman named Curley-Headed Doctor and his son-in-law, Hooker Jim, had killed fourteen settlers on their way. The Hot Creek Modoc, a small band that had separated from Jack after 1870, arrived soon after. Curley-Headed Doctor and Hooker Jim knew that they would be hanged if caught by the settlers. The Hot Creek had barely escaped a lynching and also had an idea of what they might expect at the hands of the whites. These two factions now joined forces to prevent Jack, who was disposed to keep peace with the settlers, from surrendering. For almost six months they succeeded in holding their leader in check while repelling the government's attempts to capture them. On January 17, 1873, Lt. Col. Frank Wheaton's 309 men were defeated by 50 Modoc warriors. President Grant endorsed Alfred Meacham's suggestion for a new, peaceful approach, and the War Department replaced Wheaton with Canby, who had experience in dealing with Indian affairs. For three months the army lay idle while a commission, including Meacham, Canby, and Methodist preacher Eleasar Thomas, attempted to negotiate with the Modoc. Jack was inclined toward conciliation, but the pro-war faction prevented him from capitulating. The war party, hoping to disperse the army by removing its leader, finally forced Jack to agree to kill Canby. On April 11, under a flag of truce, Jack shot and killed the general; other Modoc killed Reverend Thomas, and Meacham narrowly escaped.

The murder of Canby, a Civil War hero and the only general ever killed by Indians, provoked national outrage. The army resumed hostilities immediately. The Indians continued to use psychological warfare and their familiarity with the terrain to their advantage. It was not until late May that the army gained the upper hand and won an engagement at Dry Lake. Demoralized by their first real defeat, the war party separated from Jack and surrendered on May 22. Four members agreed to lead the army to the rest of the band. Jack was captured on June 1, and the Modoc prisoners of war were moved to Fort Klamath, Oregon. The United States attorney general ruled that a military commission would try only those directly responsible for the deaths of Canby and Thomas. Captain Jack and five others were found guilty of murder and were sentenced to death. Two of the sentences were later changed to life imprisonment at Alcatraz. Captain Jack, Schonchin John, Black Jim, and Bogus Charley were hanged on October 3, 1873. The rest of the Modoc captives were moved to the Quapaw agency in Oklahoma, but after 1909 were permitted to return to the Klamath reservation. The seven-month Modoc War cost the government more than $500,000 and struck a mortal blow to the Grant administration's so-called Indian peace policy.

A thorough military history of the conflict is Keith A. Murray, *The Modocs and Their War* (1958). Jeff C. Riddle, son of the Modoc woman Toby (Winéma) and her white husband, who were interpreters during the war, tells the Indian version in *The Indian History of the Modoc War and the Causes That Led to It* (1914). Alfred Meacham's recollections of the event are in his *Wigwam and Warpath* (1875).—J. E. S.

Moffat, David Halliday (1839-1911). Colorado businessman. Born in Washingtonville, New York, Moffat left home at the age of twelve for New York City, where he became a messenger boy at the New York Exchange Bank and eventually rose to the position of assistant teller. He later engaged in banking in Iowa and Nebraska before coming to Denver in 1860, where he opened a book and stationery store with C. C. Woolworth. In 1867 he was named cashier of the First National Bank and was its president from 1880 until his death. He was one of the largest mining operators in Colorado, either owning wholly or with others more than one hundred mines. He had numerous investments in mining properties with Jerome B. Chaffee, including the Little Pittsburg Consolidated Mining Company near Leadville, and he also had substantial real estate interests, particularly in the southern part of the state.

Moffat was also involved in many railroad enterprises, cooperating with John Evans and others in building the Denver Pacific and the Denver, South Park and Pacific, and constructing the Florence and Cripple Creek. From 1887 to 1891 he was president of the Denver and Rio Grande (see DENVER AND RIO GRANDE WESTERN RAILROAD). Moffat long dreamed of building a railroad through the mountains from Denver to Salt Lake City and developing the northwestern portion of Colorado, and he ultimately poured all his fortune into the Denver, Northwestern and Pacific, incorporated in 1902. He did not live to see the completion of this project, but, although high operating costs initially caused severe financial difficulties, the famous Moffat Tunnel through the Continental Divide, finished in 1928, eliminated the greatest problems. Moffat confined his attention primarily to his business affairs, rather than to politics, but he did serve as territorial treasurer of Colorado (1874-76) and was adjutant general during John Evans' governorship of Colorado Territory (1862-65).

There is no full-scale biography of Moffat, but for a good account of his railroad, which contains biographical information, see Edgar C. McMechen, *The Moffat Tunnel of Colorado: An Epic of Empire*, 2 vols. (1927) —M. B.

Mogollon, New Mexico. Ghost town. Mogollon, in

Catron County, was the center of a rich gold, silver, and copper mining area that produced $15 million worth of ore during its heyday in the early years of the twentieth century. The town's last big year was 1926, after which Mogollon settled down to the sleepy existence of a semi-ghost town. Today many of the old buildings remain, and the town is seeking to make a comeback as a tourist attraction.

See Ralph Looney, *Haunted Highways: The Ghost Towns of New Mexico* (1968); and Muriel S. Wolle, *The Bonanza Trail* (1953).—R. B. W.

Mohawk Indians. See IROQUOIS CONFEDERACY.

Mohegan Indians. The Mohegan tribe was an offshoot of the Hudson valley Mahican (both names are variants of the Algonquian word for wolf) and later of the Pequot tribe. The Mohegan-Pequot apparently emigrated eastward and southward down the Connecticut River valley in the late sixteenth century, settling eventually in eastern Connecticut. A warlike people, they managed to conquer and subordinate a number of neighboring bands who had tried to resist their intrusion, as well as some of the Long Island Indians. They were united as the Pequot tribe under the sachem Sassacus until 1637, when part of the tribe under Uncas seceded and resumed the Mohegan name. This occurred at the time of the bloody PEQUOT WAR, in which Uncas and his followers joined the English against their fellow tribesmen. The Pequot proper were destroyed as a tribe, and many survivors were absorbed by the Mohegan.

They remained for some years the most powerful tribe in Connecticut and confirmed allies of the English. But as white settlement expanded, most of the Mohegan gradually gave up their lands and moved away, chiefly to New York, losing their tribal identity in the process. Their population of 2,000 to 2,500 in 1643 had dwindled to 750 in 1705 and to 206 in 1774. Only a remnant of mixed-bloods has survived into the twentieth century, at Mohegan on the Thames River in eastern Connecticut.

See H. Bradstreet, *The Story of the War with the Pequots, Re-Told* (1933); and M. Spiess, *The Indians of Connecticut* (1933).—A. W. T.

Mojave Desert. See VEGETATION: *deserts*.

Momaday, N[avarre] Scott (1934-   ). Novelist. Momaday was born in Oklahoma. A Kiowa Indian, he spent his youth on Indian reservations in the Southwest. He received his B.A. degree from the University of New Mexico and his M.A. and Ph.D. degrees from Stanford University. He was appointed professor of English and comparative literature at the University of California.

Momaday's first novel, *House Made of Dawn* (1968), received a Pulitzer Prize. It is the story of a young Indian man trapped between the world of his Indian heritage and the white world of the mid-twentieth century. *The Way to Rainy Mountain* (1969), in part an expanded treatment of material in the earlier book, is an account of the legendary history of the Kiowa people, interspersed with Momaday's own reminiscences of the landscape of his youth.—J. K. F.

Monaghan, Jay [James] (1891-   ). Historian. Monaghan was born in West Chester, Pennsylvania. Reared in a Hicksite Quaker community, educated at the Friends Central School in Philadelphia; at Swarthmore College, from which he received his bachelor's degree in 1913; and at the University of Pennsylvania,

where he took his master's degree in 1918, he was awarded the Litt.D. degree by Monmouth College in 1947. Monaghan's numerous books on the West are based upon solid documentary research, but much of the pioneer spirit that fills his writings stems from his years as cowboy, rancher, and herder of sheep, and from such experiences as living with renegade Ute Indians and service as a teamster with the Fourth Cavalry on the Mexican border. Monaghan was editor and state historian of the Illinois State Historical Library (1939-51) and in 1953 became consultant for the Wyles Collection of Lincolniana and Western Americana, University of California, Santa Barbara. Monaghan's writings on Lincoln as frontiersman have been published in many languages, including Korean and Vietnamese. His *Bibliography of Lincolniana* (2 vols., 1943-45) is a prized reference work, and his study of Lincoln, *Diplomat in Carpet Slippers* (1945) is still in print. *The Great Rascal: the Life and Adventures of Ned Buntline* (1952) tells the story of the origins of the dime novel, and his *Life of George Armstrong Custer* (1952) brings to life the man whom Custer-haters hate and Custer-lovers love. Among Monaghan's many other contributions to the literature of the West are *The Overland Trail* (1947); *The Civil War on the Western Border* (1955); *Australians and the Gold Rush* (1966); *The Book of the American West* (1963), and *Chile, Peru, and the California Gold Rush of 1849* (1973).—W. R. J.

Mondell, Frank Wheeler (1860-1939). Wyoming politician. One of five children born to a poor hotel-keeper in St. Louis, Missouri, Mondell was orphaned at seven and spent most of his early years with a Congregational minister's family on a homestead in northwestern Iowa. Discouraged from becoming a farmer by the plenitude of grasshoppers, Mondell at sixteen moved to Chicago and two years later to Colorado, where he worked briefly in a sawmill and as a rodman before obtaining employment with Kilpatrick Brothers, a railroad construction company. He worked as teamster, timekeeper, corral boss, and commissary clerk. Horatio Alger would have been impressed by this extraordinarily eager, diligent, and well-behaved youth. From a host of temporary employees he was selected to become a part of the company's permanent cadre and received progressively more important assignments. In 1887 Kilpatrick Brothers sent him to northeastern Wyoming to locate coal required for a projected Burlington railroad extension. He found the coal at Cambria and settled down as his company's local manager.

In 1888 Mondell was elected mayor of the new town of Newcastle, then two years later was drafted to serve in the state's first legislature. In 1894 he won his state's lone seat in the House of Representatives, where he remained until 1923, except for a two-year break (1897-99).

In Congress Mondell was a conservative Republican, primarily interested in bringing development to the West through private enterprise (aided when necessary by the federal government). In time he gained recognition as a congressional authority on matters related to settlement and disposal of public lands, mining, reclamation, and forestry administration. Having succeeded in dry-farming experiments near Newcastle, he introduced and got passed the 320-acre homestead law of 1909. He was instrumental in getting provision for the surface use of reserved mineral lands for agriculture.

He fought much of the Pinchot conservation program, and pressed for high tariffs on coal, wool, hides, and sugar.

Scrupulous economy characterized his approach to problems on the House Appropriations Committee. He slipped into rare insurgency when his state's interest dictated.

Mondell was majority floor leader, 1919-23, and was in line to become Speaker of the House when he made the mistake of running for the Senate in 1922 against John B. Kendrick, Wyoming's invincible "cowboy senator."

See T. A. Larson, *History of Wyoming* (1965); and Frank W. Mondell, "My Story," published serially in the Cheyenne *Wyoming State Tribune* (August 1, 1935-February 4, 1936).—T. A. L.

Monroe Doctrine (1823). Although subject to several interpretations over the years, the Monroe Doctrine has been consistently useful to the United States government as a defense or security policy. The doctrine's central sentiment—that European influence should be removed from the neighborhood of the United States—manifested itself in the nation's actions well before President James Monroe put the sentiment on paper in 1823. By then experience had shown that a capital way of reducing the influence of European states was to annex their American territories to the United States.

For example, in 1811 President James Madison came to worry that as a by-product of the Napoleonic wars West Florida was about to pass from the ownership of enfeebled Spain to either France or Great Britain. In the hands of either one of these great powers West Florida could easily become a base of operations against Georgia, Mississippi Territory, or the further reaches of the recent (1803) Louisiana Purchase. Congress, therefore, at Madison's request declared its opposition to any transfer in title to a foreign power and empowered the president to use the army and navy to occupy the area until future negotiation could settle its fate. In 1819 Secretary of State John Quincy Adams completed a treaty with Spain (Adams-Onís treaty) that obtained all of Florida for the United States.

At the same time Adams acquired Spanish claims to the Pacific Coast north of the forty-second parallel (the present northern border of the state of California). Russia and Great Britain also maintained claims in this ill-defined "Oregon country," and the possibility that their claims would become actual settlements was very much in the mind of Adams as he helped formulate the Monroe Doctrine. Consequently, the noncolonization clause of the doctrine banned the planting of any new European colonies, not only on the northwest coast but throughout the New World. But the moratorium on expansion applied specifically to European nations and not to the United States. A sure indication of this meaning of the noncolonization clause was the refusal of Monroe and Adams to join Britain at the time in a mutual pledge not to seek the ownership of any remnants of the disintegrating Spanish-American empire. Clearly Adams' aim in trying to seal off the hemisphere from European politics was to make the continent a preserve for the secure and leisurely expansion of the United States.

Two decades later President James Polk belligerently rephrased Monroe's message and applied it to his daz-zling program of continental expansion; manifest destiny was in its heyday. His program included the annexation of Texas (recently authorized by Congress), the establishment of a definite boundary in the Oregon country, and the acquisition of California, ardently desired by Polk himself. In the process of successfully pursuing these territorial objectives, Polk formed an exaggerated impression of a determination by Britain and France to hem in the United States. He interpreted an 1845 speech by the French prime minister to mean that France wanted a balance of power in North America and would support Mexico against the United States. Similarly, he felt Britain was trying to prevent the addition of Texas and California to the United States and attempting to make them her puppets instead. Polk reacted by warning the European powers, in his first annual message (1845), to stay out of his dispute with Mexico. Citing Monroe, he vowed that he would not stand for any "future European colony or dominion" in North America. Again in 1847, after American troops had occupied California but before the war with Mexico had ended, Polk pointed to the Monroe Doctrine as justification for urging the immediate incorporation of California into the Union. To delay might allow the Mexicans to deed over California to a European state; and California in European hands would eventually mean war, Polk predicted.

Subsequent years would again witness the invocation of the Monroe Doctrine by expansionists who would sound the theme of defense or security. But the use of the argument for continental expansion ended with the Polk administration.

See Dexter Perkins, *A History of the Monroe Doctrine* (1955).—W. B. F.

Montana. Who first went to Montana is still unknown, but the Old North Trail from Asia through Alaska and south may have been the discovery route. The first written record is apparently that of the La Vérendryes from Canada, who saw "shining mountains" on January 1, 1743. The Louisiana Purchase in 1803 led to the Lewis and Clark expedition of 1804-06, and their magnificent journals report their discoveries and the first exploration of Montana.

A highly profitable fur trade between 1830 and 1860 resulted in the thorough exploration of the area. The first posts were erected in 1807. The trade centered at Fort Union at the mouth of the Yellowstone River, built in 1830 by Kenneth McKenzie, and at Fort Benton, built in 1846 by Alexander Culbertson and developed by Andrew Dawson. Missouri River steamboats, which reached Fort Union in 1832 and Fort Benton in 1860, greatly accelerated Montana's development. Canada's David Thompson built Salish House in 1809 near Thompson Falls for the North West Company, and Angus McDonald transferred activities to Fort Connah south of Flathead Lake in 1846, which he operated for the Hudson's Bay Company until it was abandoned in 1854.

Favorable reports of the area led to a survey in 1853 by Isaac I. Stevens for a transcontinental railway route. The Mullan Road from Fort Benton to Fort Walla Walla was a result of this survey. Then emigrants discovered gold deposits, which were among the richest in the world's history.

François Finlay's discovery of gold in the lower Deer

Lodge valley in August 1853 was the first to be publicized. Four large discoveries were made early in the 1860s—at BANNACK on July 28, 1862; Alder Gulch, May 26, 1863, which later became VIRGINIA CITY; Last Chance Gulch, later Helena, on July 14, 1864; and Confederate Gulch, also called Diamond City, in January 1865. For a decade these and lesser camps produced more than $10 million in precious metal annually.

The great gold camps resulted in an influx of people, in road building, commercial enterprise, and agricultural production in nearby valleys. The formation of the Vigilantes to stop the depredations of a bandit gang led by Henry PLUMMER gave rise to organized government. This resulted in the creation of Idaho Territory on March 3, 1863. However, the territory was so large that it was difficult to provide effective control from the capital city, Lewiston, and a second territory, Montana, was formed on May 26, 1864. Sidney Edgerton was its first governor. The first capital city of Montana Territory was Bannack, but the government moved within a year to Virginia City, and in 1875 Helena was made the capital.

Unrest among the Indians because of this mass invasion by whites resulted in the construction of a number of small frontier military forts. The earliest included Camp Cooke on the Missouri River and Fort C. F. Smith on the Bozeman Trail, both built in 1866, followed in 1867 by Fort Shaw on the Great Falls-Helena Road and Fort Ellis in the Gallatin valley. Montana's worst Indian wars were between Indians from other areas and pursuing military detachments. National attention was attracted to the overwhelming defeat of General George A. Custer at the battle of the Little Big Horn on June 25, 1876. This was followed in 1877 by the retreat of the Nez Percé from their homelands in Idaho across Montana, and their spectacular outmaneuvering of three military detachments before they were captured. These wars hastened the building of larger forts—Fort Missoula, Fort Custer, Fort Assiniboine, and Fort Maginnis. Montana has seven major Indian concentrations: the Flathead, the Blackfoot, the Gros Ventre, the Assiniboin-Sioux, the Rocky Boy-Cree, the Cheyenne, and the Crow.

Transportation in the fur trading era was largely by river. Hand craft and steamboats were used in the mining period. Land travel prevailed after the opening of the Northern Overland or Montana-Minnesota Road in 1853. The route to the southeast, the Bozeman Trail, was charted by John Bozeman and Jim Bridger in 1863 and 1864. The Mullan Road westward was opened in 1860. The Whoop-up Trail to Canada, north from Fort Benton, was easy to travel and much used. The busiest trail, the Virginia City-Corinne Road leading to the Mormon settlements, was well marked by 1860.

Early Montana had excellent railroad service because its long, fertile valleys lead to the lowest passes in the northern Rockies. Its location midway between the Great Lakes and the Pacific Coast and the need for the government to transport large amounts of supplies to the Indian reservations and military forts were not unimportant factors. The railroads followed closely the major highway routes. First was the Utah Northern from Salt Lake City to Butte, completed on December 21, 1881. The golden spike for the Northern Pacific, a land-grant railroad, was driven near Garrison on September 8, 1883. The James J. HILL railroad, the Great Northern, was extended from western North Dakota to Havre and Great Falls in 1877, the fastest construction ever attained on the continent. It was completed to Seattle in 1893. The Burlington connected Billings with Omaha and Denver in 1894. The Milwaukee also drove a golden spike near Garrison when its transcontinental connection was completed between Chicago and Seattle on May 14, 1909. The consolidation of the Northern Pacific, the Great Northern, and the Burlington as the BURLINGTON NORTHERN took place March 2, 1970.

Montana's enormous range livestock industry had its beginnings in 1846 when St. Mary's Mission reported having forty head of cattle. Philip Poindexter and William C. Orr in 1865 apparently made the first cattle drive from California, and their brand, the Square and Compass, was the first one registered. This ranch became well known as the P & O, and it sent out one of the first large drives to the Canadian prairies in Alberta. By 1870 the western valleys were crowded with herds which met the demands of the mining camps for beef. After the Piegan massacre on January 23, 1870—in which 173 Piegan Blackfoot men, women, and children out of a total of 219 were set upon and shot to death in their undefended camp on the Marias River by a United States Army cavalry command—the stockmen moved to the vast plains ranges east of the mountains. Nelson Story drove the first herd up the Texas Trail to the Yellowstone valley in 1866. After Custer's Little Big Horn battle in 1876 the Yellowstone became a popular range.

Missionaries apparently brought the first sheep, some three hundred, to winter near St. Peter's Mission in 1867. John Bishop trailed about fifteen hundred from The Dalles in Oregon to the Beaverhead valley in 1869. Since many of the eminent stockmen, Bishop, Robert Ford, Conrad Kohrs, John Bielenberg, T. C. Power, and the Fergus Brothers, James and Andrew, raised both sheep and cattle, the traditional conflict between the sheepmen and the cattlemen was avoided.

Fabulous profits attracted investors from the East and England and Scotland as well. An overcrowded range developed by 1886, a dry year, and the grass was depleted. Then the severe storms of the "Hard Winter of 1886-87" caused losses of up to seventy-five percent. A consolidation of the depleted herds by local residents returned the industry to Montana ownership.

The livestock industry constantly adjusted to meet changing conditions. The coming of homesteaders and their barbed wire was a disaster. The cattlemen first attempted to "fence out" intrusion by fencing around their home ranches and water holes. This led to the branding and roundup system to identify and control the still free-ranging but increasingly crowded stock. The intrusion of larger numbers of homesteaders forced the purchase or lease and the "fencing in" of great private landholdings and brought a sudden end to the open range.

Statehood was delayed for twenty-five years following the creation of the territory in 1864, even though a first constitutional convention was held in 1866. The next convention was held in 1884, at a time when the political party balance was so even that national approval was not possible. Finally, five years later, on November 8, 1889, Montana became a state.

Severe party conflict in the new state prevented the first session of the legislature from organizing. Nevertheless, each party chose two senators for the national Congress, and since the Senate had a Republican majority, it voted to seat Republicans Wilbur F. Sanders and Thomas C. Power. Governor Joseph K. Toole was forced to improvise for state funds until the legislature began functioning.

Typical of the several problems inherited by the state was the location of the capital. The constitutional convention had directed that this be decided by the people in the election of 1892. Seven cities entered the race and Helena and Anaconda received the highest votes. In 1894, with "copper kings" Marcus DALY promoting Anaconda and William A. CLARK supporting Helena, an exciting election favored Helena to retain the capital.

Conflict between the leading mining magnates (Daly, Clark, Samuel T. HAUSER, and Clark A. BROADWATER), known as the "War of the Copper Kings," kept Montana in a turmoil from the mid-1880s until 1906. Clark, immensely wealthy and politically ambitious, was pitted against Daly, who was creating the gigantic Anaconda Copper Mining Company and feared government curbs upon its management. Both men became apprehensive over the sudden rise in popularity and affluence of the dynamic young mining engineer Frederick Augustus HEINZE, who threatened Clark's political ambitions by his influence with the voting public and Daly's copper mines by his "apex" theory, which held that the owner of a mineral vein at its surface—where it "apexed"—could follow the vein and mine it wherever it led, even into the richest ore lodes of a neighbor's mine. All three were Democrats and party politics became thoroughly confused.

One of the numerous battles of the "war" centered on Clark's burning desire to be a United States senator. In 1899 he was elected under strained circumstances, and he accused Daly of the bribery that was evident. Daly thereupon provided financial assistance for a Senate investigation. Clark resigned before the Senate report, which accused him of fraud, was made.

The "war" came to an end slowly with the resolution of its various points of conflict and with Daly's death in 1900. Clark won election to the Senate without bribery in 1901. The Amalgamated Copper Company, a holding company for the Anaconda, took much of the policy-forming power to New York in 1900, and in 1906 it purchased the Heinze interests in Butte. The Amalgamated was dissolved in 1915.

The continuing narrow political balance between the Democrats and Republicans posed the threat that political victory might be won at any time by a sudden thrust of power by the Progressives, the Fusionists, corporation interests, the stockmen, and other influences. A point of friction from 1894 until 1959 was the ownership by the Anaconda company of a large majority of the newspapers of the state. A new economic and political dimension was added in 1912 when John D. RYAN, president of the Anaconda, consolidated a number of small electric power companies in the Butte vicinity, forming the Montana Power Company. It increased rapidly in wealth and influence.

Major progressive legislation resulted from the work of Joseph M. Dixon (1867-1934), who started his political career as a conservative Republican. He became a liberal leader during his term in the United States Senate to which he was elected in 1906. He was defeated for reelection while serving as national chairman for Theodore Roosevelt's Bull Moose campaign in 1912. As governor of the state from 1920 to 1924, Dixon outlined a highly progressive program of government reorganization and tax reform. This included a constitutional amendment for a graduated metal mines tax, which the mining interests opposed. The schizophrenia often apparent in Montana's politics ("It sends its liberals to Washington and its conservatives to Helena") was evident when the amendment was approved but Dixon was defeated.

In spite of its tense political climate, Montana came within five votes of being the first state to adopt woman suffrage in 1889. The state sent the first woman, Jeannette Rankin (1880-1973), to Congress in 1916 and again in 1940. Rankin worked for women's and children's rights, especially their working and health conditions, at the state and national level. An ardent peace advocate, she voted against United States entry into both world wars. She was the only person to vote against war with Japan in 1941. The "war of the copper kings" led to the adoption of the eight-hour day for mining, well ahead of other states, and Montana adopted the first old-age pension law in the nation in 1923. Major economic interests naturally still maintained a close scrutiny of political activity, but a situation prevailed in which such progressive legislators as senators Thomas Walsh (1859-1933), Burton K. Wheeler (1882-1975), and Mike Mansfield (1903-) attained national and international recognition. Both Walsh and Wheeler were involved in investigations of Secretary of the Interior Albert Fall and the ensuing Teapot Dome scandal. As chairman of the powerful Interstate Commerce Committee, Wheeler secured laws regulating the railroads. Closely connected with railroad labor, the farmer-labor group, and the Great Plains Nonpartisan League, Wheeler was a natural choice for the vice-presidential candidate of the Progressive party in 1924.

Montana's population has always been sparse—4.7 persons per square mile in 1970—a reflection of its arid and mountainous characteristics. Its slow but steady growth reversed in the 1920s when it lost 2.1 percent in population. In 1970 it had 694,409 people, a 2.9 percent gain over 1960. Among its larger cities, Billings, with a 16.5 percent decade gain to 61,581 people, took first place over Great Falls with its 60,091. Missoula was in third place with a drop to 29,497 persons, while Butte lost 16.2 percent in a decade, occupying fourth place with 23,368. Bozeman showed a 39.7 percent gain in a decade, the largest in the state, giving it sixth place, following Helena in fifth.

Yellowstone County, in which Billings is located, is also the most populous county with 87,367 people. The extremes of losses and gains in population often reflect federal programs. Valley County lost 32.8 percent in a decade because of the disengagement of the large Strategic Air Command base near Glasgow. Lincoln County gained 44.1 percent because of construction of the Libby Dam.

The population is 92 percent native white, with 4.4 percent foreign born. Of the nonwhites, 18,739 are Indians and 1,460 are Negroes. Numerous interesting ethnic groupings dot the state, such as the southern

Europeans in Butte, the Russian concentration near Plentywood, the Finns of Milltown, and the Dutch agricultural colony near Bozeman. During the 1960s, urban population showed a 9.5 percent growth while the rural areas lost 3.7 percent. In 1970 some 53.4 percent of the people lived in urban areas as compared to 50.2 percent in 1960.

Montana's efforts are directed at the careful use of its resources. The wise use of its land was severely threatened during the "homestead era," 1910-22, when forty-two percent of the entire state, 90 million acres, was filed upon for farming purposes, although at least eighty percent was unfit for this use. The Agricultural Experiment Station and Extension Service, pressured by a severe drought in the 1920s and another in the 1930s, pioneered in new methods, new crop varieties, and a whole new way of living on arid lands.

Many of Montana's resources are of an extractive nature (see COPPER MINING), and the opening of new sources of wealth holds great promise. Development is proceeding with 222 billion tons of coal, one of the largest deposits in the world. The first petroleum field, Elk Basin near the Wyoming border, was opened in 1915. In 1919 Gordon Campbell began a long career of developing new oil fields. The discovery of petroleum in the Williston Basin in 1951, and in the Bell Field near Broadus in 1966, together with the construction of refining plants, particularly in Billings and Laurel, have made oil a major industry.

The arid state has an increasing concern for the wise use of its water resources. With the help of the federal government it is making considerable progress. In 1902 construction was begun on one of the nation's largest irrigation projects, that on the Milk River. Montana has some of the largest dams in the nation, conserving water and producing power from such stations as Fort Peck, Hungry Horse, and Yellowtail. Construction on the Libby Dam began in 1968. These, together with a large network maintained by the Montana Power Company, provide an impressive resource. The forests of the state also assist in the preservation of its water. About one fourth of Montana, 22,354,000 acres, is forested. Of this the state has eight forests with six hundred thousand acres, while the eleven federal forests comprise 9 million acres. There are 1.2 million acres in Indian reservations and public-domain areas.

Montana is reassessing all of its resources for use in its newest industry, tourism, which economically is in third place, bringing in an income of over $100 million annually. The state's natural and artificial lakes, scenic plains and mountain areas, historical landmarks, ghost towns, Glacier and Yellowstone national parks, state parks, museums, art galleries, and summer rodeos and winter snow fields are being meshed for availability and use. All, when implemented, will provide for a higher quality of living for visitor and Montanan alike.

See *Montana, the Magazine of Western History*; M. G. Burlingame and K. R. Toole, *A History of Montana*, 2 vols. (1957); J. M. Hamilton, *History of Montana*, 2d ed. (1970); J. K. Howard, *Montana, High, Wide and Handsome* (1943); R. R. Renne, *Government and Administration of Montana* (1958); K. R. Toole, *Montana, An Uncommon Land* (1959); and Ellis L. Waldron, *Montana Politics Since 1864* (1958).—M. G. B.

Montez, Lola (1818-1861). Actress and dancer. Montez, with her beautiful figure and mercurial temper, cut one of the most picturesque figures on the San Francisco stage.

Montez came to California after a tempestuous career in Europe and a cold reception of her talents on the American East Coast. She was born in Limerick, Ireland, of obscure parents (she claimed to be a daughter of Lord Byron) and was baptized Marie Dolores Eliza Rosanna Gilbert. "Lola" was the diminutive of Dolores; she used "Montez" to authenticate her standing as a Spanish dancer. At nineteen she eloped with a dashing young British army officer. Shortly thereafter she had an affair with another army officer. She then moved on to Spain to study dancing in the proper "atmosphere" but was a total failure in her 1843 debut on the English stage. Undaunted, Montez decided to make her name and win fame in Europe. She was a lover to Franz Liszt and Alexandre Dumas, among others. In Bavaria in 1846, she became the mistress of King Ludwig I until the 1848 uprising forced her to flee. She then toured Spain, Italy, and Greece with a second, newly acquired husband but found no appreciation of herself. Leaving her second husband behind, Montez moved on to New York in 1851, went up and down the East Coast in search of an audience that understood her talents, and finally arrived at San Francisco in May 1853.

The secret of Montez' San Francisco success (at the American Theatre) was not her acting ability as much as it was a suggestive performance of her own *La Tarantula*, the Spider Dance. She would pretend to be attacked by spiders and swiftly try to free herself. Or she would be attacked by just one spider hidden somewhere on her person and would then try to find the spider. Or she might portray the spider itself. Within a month after the spunky lady's arrival in San Francisco, however, her novelty had worn thin and her acting had been so poor it was parodied by other actresses. She gave benefit performances to aid the city fire department and the charity of the Hebrew Benevolent Society, but only twenty-five days after arriving in California she had a final benefit herself at the American Theatre and left San Francisco.

Montez's career from that point forward was bleak. In Sacramento rotten eggs and apples were thrown at her. She tried to settle in Grass Valley with a third husband, Patrick Purdy Hull. (There Montez discovered Lotta Crabtree, later a nationally famous actress.) With advancing years, her figure lost its charm and left her few resources except her undauntable courage. In June 1855 she left California to try a comeback in Australia. Failing, she was again in San Francisco by late summer, 1856. There she auctioned off her jewelry to support the children of a man who had jumped ship on the return voyage. But when she performed on stage, she found no one interested in her limited abilities, now not even enlivened by the Spider Dance. Montez finally left the West in October 1856. She died in a room on 17th Street, New York City.

See G. R. MacMinn, *The Theater of the Golden Era in California* (1941), for the best account of Montez in California. Good biographies include Amanda Darling, *Lola Montez* (1972); and Ishbel Ross, *The Uncrowned Queen* (1972).—R. S.

Mooney, James (1861-1921). Ethnologist. Born in Richmond, Indiana, Mooney worked for a Richmond newspaper, all the while reading to become a self-taught expert on American Indian life. He met Major John W. Powell, founder of the Bureau of American Ethnology, who hired him for the bureau in 1885. From then until his death, he was an ethnologist with the bureau.

No one concerned with the history and culture of Sioux Indians or with the phenomenon of nativistic revivals can afford to overlook Mooney's *The Ghost-Dance Religion and the Sioux Outbreak of 1890*, published in 1896 as part of the Fourteenth Annual Report of the Bureau of American Ethnology. It has become the baseline study for the understanding of messianic movements and is one of the most important monographs ever written on the Sioux.

Mooney also became the acknowledged authority on the Kiowa, publishing *Calendar History of the Kiowa Indians* in 1898, and was a leading scholar of Cherokee Indian culture. His more than sixty publications further attest to his knowledge of Cheyenne and other tribes of the trans-Mississippi West, in addition to Indians of the eastern United States.

See Ione L. Mooney and anonymous coauthor, "James Mooney," *American Anthropologist*, vol. 24, no. 2 (1922).—B. L. F.

Moran, Thomas (1837-1926). Painter. Born in Bolton, Lancashire, England, Moran came with his family to the United States in 1844. Apprenticed to a wood engraver in Philadelphia, he studied painting in France, Italy, and Germany from about 1866 to 1870. Back in America in 1871, he made his first trip into the West with a government-sponsored geological expedition under the leadership of Dr. Ferdinand V. Hayden to the relatively unexplored region of the upper Yellowstone River. The following year he ventured into Yosemite Valley, California, making numerous sketches of the scenery in those parts. In 1873 he was with Major John Wesley Powell in southern Utah and Arizona and in 1874 penetrated the wilderness of central Colorado in search of the Mountain of the Holy Cross.

After his travels Moran produced a number of large landscapes, of which *The Great Canyon of the Yellowstone* and *Chasm of the Colorado* were purchased by Congress for the Capitol in Washington, D.C. A series of Moran's watercolor studies of the Yellowstone area, executed to supplement the reports of Professor Hayden, are believed to have had a definite influence upon the government's decision to set aside that portion of the West as a national park in 1872. Other of his favorite sketching sites were declared national parks or monuments during his lifetime, and the National Parks Service considers him to have been a pioneer in the conservation movement through his much publicized portrayals of the scenic wonders of the Far West.

Moran produced an enormous amount of work over the years and at the age of seventy still was at his easel. He traveled from Maine to Florida and was often in the West, making occasional trips to England, Scotland, and Italy. An admirer of the work of the British painter J. M. W. Turner, Moran produced in later years a number of canvases suggestive of the older master's style. He was elected an associate member of the National Academy of Design in 1881 and a full member in 1884. When he died, he was regarded by contemporaries as the venerable "dean" of America's landscape artists.

Moran's wife, Mary Nimmo Moran (1842-89), born in Strathaven, Scotland, also was an artist, noted particu-

larly for her etchings. His brothers, Edward and Peter Moran, his son, Paul Nimmo Moran, and his nephews, Edward Percy Moran and Leon Moran, all were active painters or engravers. The largest inventory of his assembled works is owned by the Thomas Gilcrease Institute of American History and Art, Tulsa, Oklahoma, numbering in excess of eight hundred pieces. There is also an important collection of western studies in the possession of the United States Parks Service.

A selection of Moran's views of the Yellowstone region was reproduced by L. Prang and Company of Boston as a series of chromolithographs in 1876. Today the number of this striking folio in its complete and original form is possibly only one or two.

See Paul Rossi and David C. Hunt, *The Art of the Old West* (1971); Robert Taft, *Artists and Illustrators of the Old West, 1850-1900* (1953); and Thurman Wilkins, *Thomas Moran, Artist of the Mountains* (1966).—D. C. H.

More, J. Marion (1827?-1868). Idaho miner. A resident of the Pacific Coast after 1850, More came from Tennessee. He joined the Clearwater country gold rush in present-day Idaho and was elected in 1861 to represent the miners in the Washington Territory legislature. Unlike other eastern Washington farming and mining members, he favored establishing a new territory for the Idaho miners. Following a major gold discovery in Boise Basin on August 2, 1862, he led the party that founded Idaho City on October 7. Returning to Olympia for another session of the Washington legislature, he again found himself alone among the eastern delegation endorsing a territory that would represent the miners' interests. But his new settlement in Boise Basin—more than five hundred miles from Olympia—was growing so rapidly that Olympia leaders could afford no more delay, and Idaho Territory was established in spite of the opposition of the other mining members.

With new gold discoveries across southern Idaho, More developed substantial mining interests in most of the major camps. He generally could be relied upon to bring in stamp mills or to construct major ditch systems necessary for large-scale mining. But then his good fortune changed. In Owyhee, his overextended empire collapsed financially on August 30, 1866. More escaped blame for this disaster, but had worse luck at Silver City a year and a half later. One of his properties was then contested in the Owyhee "war"—a mine claim dispute fought mainly underground in 1868. Within a few days the deputy marshal imposed a settlement. But on April 2, 1868, a victory celebration turned into a drunken brawl, shooting broke out, and More wound up the leading casualty of the war.—M. W.

Morés, Antoine Amedee Marie Vincent Manca de Vellombrosa, Marquis de (1858-1896). Entrepreneur. The Marquis de Morés came from his native France to the United States in 1882 after marrying Medora von Hoffman, the daughter of a wealthy New York banker. In 1883 he journeyed to the Badlands of Dakota, where he purchased land at the junction of the Northern Pacific Railroad and the Little Missouri River. Here at his newly founded town, which he called Medora, he organized the Northern Pacific Refrigerator Car Company and built a slaughterhouse. His objective was to slaughter cattle on the Great Plains and ship dressed meat to the shops of the East by refrigerator car. He established a chain of icehouses and cold-storage facilities along the Northern Pacific Railroad line and began operations in the fall of 1883. Although at first he sold only wholesale products, by 1885 he realized that selling on the retail market would eliminate the middleman. In early 1886 he formed the Northwest Dressed Beef and Land Company, which was to set up retail meat shops in New York City. By the end of the year, however, the plan failed. New York butchers organized against him and drove down the price of meat, ruining the marquis' scheme. In 1887 he left Dakota, having lost in the neighborhood of $1-2 million, most of which had been put up by his father-in-law.

While in Dakota, however, the Marquis de Morés entered several other businesses. He established a freight route between Medora and Deadwood, two hundred miles to the south, and promoted his road as the best way to ship goods to and from the Black Hills. When this failed, he organized his own company, the Medora Stage and Forwarding Company. Within six months the company folded. The Marquis also attempted to ship salmon from the Pacific Northwest to New York City. This too failed. A highlight of his stay in the West was his trial for the murder of one of three men who had ambushed him. He was acquitted after a colorful trial.

From Dakota the marquis went to India to join other French nobility in a tiger hunt. In 1888 he became involved in a scheme to build a railroad through French Indochina to the Chinese interior, but the French government refused to give him a concession.

From 1889 to his death in 1896, when he was assassinated in North Africa by anticolonialists, he was at the center of stormy French politics. He waged a harsh campaign against the Jews and was one of the founders of the modern anti-Semitic movement in Europe (he blamed his failure to get the Indochina concession on Minister of the Interior Ernst Constans, who was a Jew). At the same time, he espoused socialism and championed such ideas as credit for workers and public housing. His name is indelibly imprinted on Dakota of the 1880s and on the France of the 1890s.

See D. Jerome Tweton, *The Marquis de Morés: Dakota Capitalist, French Nationalist* (1971).—D. J. T.

Morgan, Dale L. (1914-1971). Historian. Had Morgan not lost his hearing at the age of fourteen because of meningitis, he probably would be less well known today. A descendant of Orson Pratt, who was a member of the original Quorum of Twelve Apostles in the Church of Jesus Christ of Latter-day Saints, Morgan was born in Salt Lake City and ultimately became one of the West's most important scholars in the fields of history, biography, and cartography. His father died when Morgan was four, leaving a widow to support several children on a modest schoolteacher's salary. Later the psychological readjustment in overcoming severe physical and emotional handicaps as a result of his deafness was painfully accomplished through the help of patient tutors and an understanding mother.

Fortunately an obsession for reading compensated considerably for the oppressive loneliness young Morgan experienced. An early interest in language, form, and color led to specialization in art and English at the University of Utah, from which he graduated in 1937. Although his formal training in history was extremely limited, he demonstrated a latent talent for research and editing when he was employed on the Work Projects Administration's Historical Records Survey in Utah. From 1938 to 1940 he was a historical editor of the survey and during the next two years was supervisor of the Utah Writer's Project. His work in these programs resulted in *Utah, a Guide to the State* (1941), which some historians have proclaimed to be the most useful yet written about the state.

Morgan also wrote or edited the following books during this period: *A History of Ogden* (1940); *Origins of Utah Place Names* (1941); and *Provo, Pioneer Mormon City* (1942). Through these works on Mormon history, he developed an interest in the fur trade and western exploration, which led to the first extensive biography of Jedediah Smith, *Jedediah Smith and His Opening of the West* (1964).

From 1942 to 1954 Morgan was engaged in a variety of research and writing activities. These included three years during World War II in the Office of Price Administration in Washington, D.C., followed by five years at the Utah Historical Society in Salt Lake City. In January 1954 he joined the Bancroft Library at the University of California as editor of the Guide Program of Manuscripts. He continued to write voluminous articles, reviews, introductions, and monographs until his retirement in 1970 because of poor health.

A partial list of Morgan's various publications compiled in 1965 filled three single-spaced manuscript pages. In addition to books previously mentioned, his major works include *The Humboldt: High Road of the West* (1943); *The Great Salt Lake* (1947); *Santa Fe and the Far West* (1949); *Life in America: The West* (1952); and *The West of William H. Ashley* (1964).—W. E. H.

Morgan, Lewis Henry (1818-1881). Anthropologist. Morgan, often characterized as "the father of American anthropology," was born near Aurora, New York. After graduating from Union College in 1840, he read law, was admitted to the bar, and then moved to Rochester, where he coupled a legal and political career with his anthropological research and writing. During the 1860s he served several terms as a Republican state assemblyman and state senator. He is known primarily for his work on the Iroquois confederacy and for his book *Ancient Society* (1877).

Morgan's interest in the Iroquois developed early, partially because their traces were still fresh around his boyhood home and partially through the influence of his friend Ely S. Parker, a Seneca Indian who later became a general in the Union army and commissioner of Indian affairs. In 1851 Morgan published his masterful and delightfully written book *League of the Ho-dé-no-sau-nee, or Iroquois*. Although superseded at some points and supplemented at many others, this book is still the main point of departure for Iroquois studies and represents the first scientific investigation of an Indian tribe. Morgan became particularly interested in the Iroquois kinship system and extended his research on this subject to other tribes. Beginning in 1859 he traveled as far as the upper Missouri and the Hudson Bay country collecting information on more than seventy tribes. Concluding that all American Indians followed similar kinship systems, he produced in 1870 a massive treatise called "Systems of Consanguinity and Affinity of the Human Family," published by the Smithsonian Institution.

Under the influence of Darwinian evolutionary theory, Morgan advanced the idea that all races of men have a common origin and have passed through successive evolutionary stages from savagery to civilization. These ideas became the thesis of his *Ancient Society.* Although modern anthropologists have questioned his application of evolutionary theory to primitive society, it was widely supported at the time, among others by Marxists who found that it supported their own theories concerning primitive society.

Morgan's other major works are *The American Beaver and His Works* (1868), long considered a classic on the subject, and *Houses and House-Life of the American Aborigines* (1881), published just before his death.

See Carl Resek, *Lewis Henry Morgan, American Scholar* (1962); and B. J. Stern, *Lewis Henry Morgan, Social Evolutionist* (1931).—A. W. T.

Mormons. See LATTER-DAY SAINTS; LATTER-DAY SAINTS, REORGANIZED; UTAH.

Mormon Trail. The early history of the Mormons, members of the Church of Jesus Christ of Latter-day Saints, was largely a story of migration from New York to Ohio, west to Missouri, and back again to Nauvoo, Illinois. There they encountered resentment from their neighbors because of clannishness, economic success, and political influence, and violence broke out. Convinced that they could not be assured protection within the United States, the Mormons resolved to move again. Real estate was sold and the proceeds converted into wagons and teams to haul personal possessions to a new Zion. Brigham Young, chosen to lead his people, organized the migration effectively even though he had little knowledge of the geography of the West beyond the Great Plains and no specific location for the new settlement in mind.

The first major problem was to plan for a mass evacuation from Nauvoo. In February 1846 sixteen hundred Mormons crossed the Mississippi River on the ice in sub-zero weather to reach temporary quarters at Sugar Grove, Iowa. Expecting to make the western trek by stages, Young selected the first major stopping place on the Missouri River opposite Council Bluffs. An advance group went forward to determine the route across southern Iowa, select camping sites, which were improved by digging wells, and on occasion to build log cabins and plant a crop of corn so that those who followed might be adequately housed and fed. The first group of Mormons reached the Missouri River in June 1846, and throughout the summer months various parties, including the very young and the very old, followed behind, their journey made easier by the advance preparations. By fall, twelve thousand Mormons were encamped at Winter Quarters, not far from present Omaha.

Although the Mormons suffered from the cold during the winter—they were ill-housed and poorly fed, and outbreaks of malaria and scurvy took a toll of six hundred—planning for the western migration progressed without delay. Young displayed exceptional administrative ability in keeping the able-bodied at work building semipermanent structures, such as a mill and a council house, that would serve immigrants expected to come later. Encouraged by the success of the Iowa crossing, he once again planned for another "Pioneer Band" made up of volunteers that he would lead to

mark the route and determine the final destination for the main group. Throughout the winter the able-bodied were instructed in the most efficient ways of Plains travel. Young planned a more structured organization of the Mormon migration than had been used by the earliest parties on the Oregon Trail by dividing his followers into hundreds, fifties, and tens with a leader assigned to supervise each in semimilitary fashion. Instructions were issued concerning wagon formation in the field, procedures for driving stock, and the formation of corrals for camping each night. A daily schedule was outlined for weekdays, including morning and evening prayers. The Sabbath was to be observed as a day of rest. Most important, Young insisted that a record be kept of the direction and distance traveled each day, with the camping places clearly marked to assist those who might follow.

The Mormons had hoped to obtain financial support from the United States government to build way stations along the Oregon Trail as they moved westward. However, the nation's interest shifted from the Northwest during 1846 to the Southwest, where a war with Mexico had developed. Recruiting agents from Stephen W. Kearny's Army of the West arrived at Winter Quarters, and the Mormon Battalion was organized to accompany that force to New Mexico and California. This incident was a godsend in providing a soldier's pay and an advance for a clothing allowance that could be used to support the destitute. On the other hand, many able-bodied men who were needed to complete the long and difficult journey ahead were taken from the group. Those who were married had to trust the security and well-being of their families to others, hoping to rejoin them later at an undisclosed destination.

The Pioneer Band of 148 persons set out in April 1847, with a year's provisions and agricultural implements packed into 72 wagons and a large herd of cattle. Rather than follow the south bank of the Platte as the earlier travelers to Oregon had done, the Mormons blazed a new route along the north bank of the stream, which became known as the Mormon Trail. They reached Fort Laramie early in June, and from this post their route to Fort Bridger was identical with that of the Oregon Trail. The migration had been conducted with great efficiency, averaging twenty miles a day to the South Pass. Once in the mountains, some members of the party contracted spotted, or mountain, fever. Jim Bridger warned Young that a mountain barrier lay to the west of his fort and that beyond was a barren desert and urged him to follow a different route. However, the Mormons wanted isolation as well as a productive land and pressed on over the Uinta and Wasatch ranges. When Young first caught a glimpse of the Great Salt Lake valley, he announced that this was the place for which he had been looking.

Brigham Young returned East to organize the migration for 1848. Not far from the Great Salt Lake he met the major Mormon company of more than 1,500 driving 3,500 head of livestock that had followed behind the Pioneer Band. Approximately 1,600 Mormons made the trek in 1847. Young returned to Utah by September 1848, bringing with him 2,500 additional emigrants. In 1849 the Perpetual Emigration Fund was started to assist poverty-stricken converts to migrate to Utah with the understanding that loans would be repaid to assist those who came later. When these funds proved inadequate, the Mormons introduced a new plan whereby emigrants constructed handcarts of hardwood at the point of departure on their overland journey to transport their essential possessions. Between 1856 and 1860, ten different HANDCART COMPANIES comprised of 2,962 immigrants pushed or pulled 655 handcarts as they walked 1,300 miles to the Promised Land. This was without question one of the most remarkable experiments in western travel.

A major concern with all the handcart migrations was to start the westward march early enough to arrive in Utah before the storms of winter came. The first three parties of 1856 made as good time as those that had traveled by wagon. The last two, getting a late start, were caught in snowy blizzards not far from the Devil's Gate in Wyoming. Rescue parties were sent forth from Salt Lake City, but not before fifteen percent of one party and twenty-five percent of a second had lost their lives. Improvements in organization were introduced for the annual migrations of the next three years, including the allocation of a limited number of supply wagons to accompany the handcart brigades. Although migration over the trail declined in the 1860s, it was used continuously until the completion of the Pacific Railroad in 1869.

An offshoot of the Mormon Trail was the Mormon "corridor." In 1849 the Mormons launched a program to establish a "corridor to the sea" at San Diego, California, along the general route first traversed by the fur trader and mountain man Jedediah Smith. As an initial step, a series of communities was organized between the Great Salt Lake and the southern border of Utah Territory: Provo, Fillmore City, Parowan, and Cedar City. In 1851 a group of colonizers were sent to establish a colony near the Cajon Pass, gateway to California, and succeeded in founding San Bernardino. From this outpost, the route to San Diego was well known. The string of settlements was connected by a trail well used by Mormon pioneers in the 1850s.

Wallace Stegner, *The Gathering of Zion: The Story of the Mormon Trail* (1964), is unquestionably the most readable single-volume account of the migration of the Mormons into the Great Basin. Daniel Tyler, *A Concise History of the Mormon Battalion in the Mexican War* (1964), clearly delineates the relations of the Mormon pioneers to the military campaign of the Army of the West in the Mexican War. LeRoy R. Hafen and Ann W. Hafen, *Handcarts to Zion: The Story of a Unique Western Migration, 1856-1860* (1960), provides the documentation of the most dramatic sequence of events on the early overland migrations of the Mormons.—W. T. J.

Morrill Act. See COLLEGES AND UNIVERSITIES.

Morris, Esther (1814-1902). Suffragist. After spending most of her life as a milliner and housewife in her native New York State and in Illinois, Morris in 1869 followed her second husband, John Morris, to Wyoming Territory, where the year before he had opened a saloon in a remote gold mining camp, South Pass City.

Later in 1869 a legislator from South Pass City introduced the bill that, when enacted, made Wyoming Territory the first political unit in the world to give women full rights to vote and hold office. Under the new law the acting governor, an ardent suffragist, appointed three female justices of the peace, of whom only

Esther Morris. *(Denver Public Library, Western History Department)*

Mrs. Morris qualified: she was an American citizen, was bonded, and was willing to serve. She was hailed as the first woman judge in the world. Since her appointment was to fill out the term of a man who had resigned, she served only nine months, during which time she handled twenty-six cases. She retired in November 1870, sought no other public office, wrote nothing, made no public addresses except a few brief remarks, and when consulted in later years, advised women to leave the suffrage movement to the men. Nevertheless, her brief career as justice of the peace in a village of 460 people gave her the distinction of being the only woman in public life in twenty years of Wyoming Territory's history.

When eastern suffrage leaders thought of Wyoming, they thought of Mrs. Morris, first woman judge. In 1890 one of her sons in his Cheyenne newspaper began calling her the "mother of woman suffrage." Suffragists accepted the term. Then in 1918, an old man recalled that the man who had introduced the woman suffrage bill in 1869 had done so at Mrs. Morris's suggestion. Supporting evidence is inconclusive. Also, a letter written by one of Mrs. Morris's sons in 1869 gives reason to believe that she did not meet the bill's sponsor for the first time until after the legislative session. Nevertheless, as "first woman judge" and "mother of woman suffrage," Mrs. Morris easily won designation in 1955 as the state's outstanding deceased citizen. Bronze statues of her were placed in Statuary Hall in Washington, D.C., and in front of the state capitol building in Cheyenne.

See Grace Raymond Hebard, "How Woman Suffrage Came to Wyoming" (1920); T. A. Larson, *History of Wyoming* (1965); and *The Revolution* (January 13, 1870).

See also Docket of Esther Morris, Justice of the Peace, Sweetwater County, Wyoming Territory, in the Wyoming State Archives, Cheyenne.—T. A. L.

Morton, J[ulius] Sterling (1832-1902). Nebraska agriculturalist, journalist, and politician. A native of Adams, New York, Morton was reared in Michigan. After completing his studies at the University of Michigan and working for the Detroit *Free Press*, he moved to Nebraska in November 1854. He established the Nebraska City *News* and served two terms in the territorial legislature. Morton was a constant advocate of the interests of the South Platte region in its struggle against the ambitions of Omaha, and as a conservative Democrat he unsuccessfully opposed the chartering of wild-cat banks. In 1858 President Buchanan appointed him secretary of the territory and for a brief period (December 1858-May 1859) he was acting governor of Nebraska.

For the three decades after 1860 Morton was Nebraska's most outstanding Democrat but, although he frequently ran for public office, he could never overcome the dominant Republican position in the state. During these years he worked for the Burlington Railroad as a publicist and was also a stanch promoter of Nebraska's agriculture. Through his efforts to encourage tree-planting on the prairies, the Nebraska legislature in 1885 declared April 22, Morton's birthday, as Arbor Day.

Morton was an early supporter of William Jennings Bryan, but when Bryan espoused free silver, Morton broke with him. In 1893 Morton became President Cleveland's secretary of agriculture, an office to which he brought his strong belief in economy in government. After four years in Washington, Morton returned to Nebraska and published a political journal, *The Conservative*. His home and its surroundings have been preserved as Arbor Lodge State Park.

See James C. Olson, *J. Sterling Morton* (1942). —H. A. D.

Moses, Phoebe Ann. See Annie OAKLEY.

Mossman, Burton C. (1867-1956). Rancher. Mossman was one of the few ranchers with the cow sense and business ingenuity to survive disasters associated with bad weather, falling prices, and rustling—triple plagues that often forced ranchers into bankruptcy. Backed by cool courage and a fast gun, he timed his surprise attacks to catch rustlers before they had time to dispose of stolen horses, cattle, or freshly butchered beef and tell-tale green hides.

Mossman was born in Aurora, Illinois. At age twenty-one he ramrodded his first spread in New Mexico; when thirty, he was superintendent of the two-million-acre Hash Knife ranch in northern Arizona, with its 60,000 cattle.

In 1901 Arizona governor Nathan Oakes Murphy persuaded Mossman to serve as the first captain of the Arizona Rangers, newly organized to rid the country of cattle-rustlers and other outlaws flourishing in the territory. A gritty manhunt, unequaled in western history, occurred when Mossman rode alone into Mexico and finessed the arrest of murderer Agostine Chacon, guilty of killing fifteen United States citizens and thirty-seven Mexicans. With the help of Burt Alvard, Arizona peace officer turned outlaw, Mossman lured Chacon with the promise to help the Mexican steal a number of prize horses from the San Rafael ranch in southern Arizona.

When they reached the United States border, Mossman arrested Chacon, who later was hanged.

Mossman later assumed his ranching career and owned or was a partner in cattle operations in Sonora and Chihuahua, Mexico, and in New Mexico, South Dakota, and Montana. A million cattle wore his brand before he hung up his saddle in 1944 and shaded up on the comfortable porch of his ranch in Roswell, New Mexico.

See Frazier Hunt, *Cap Mossman* (1951); James R. Jennings, *Arizona Was the West* (1970); Joseph Miller, *Arizona, The Last Frontier* (1956); and Jay J. Wagoner, *Arizona Territory 1863-1912* (1970).—B. W. A.

motion picture industry. *Hollywood* and the *motion picture industry* are almost inseperable terms. Yet the two were born on opposite sides of the continent, and in the first fifteen years of their existence neither had heard of the other.

Hollywood was founded in 1887 as a temperance town devoted mainly to attracting retired midwesterners. In 1904 the city still had a law limiting the number of horses, cattle, sheep, and hogs that could be driven through town and another law that prohibited a horse from taking a corner faster than six miles per hour. This quiet, restricted town might well have remained so for years to come, except for events already underway on the East Coast.

In the earliest days of the motion picture industry several small, poor companies were formed in New York, Chicago, and Philadelphia. Somehow the owners obtained, legally or illegally, but always ingeniously, a camera that they pointed at anything that moved and a projector that could show the movement to anyone who would pay a nickel to watch. There was always an audience, particularly in the working-class districts of the big cities, and from the beginning the movies made money.

The movie-makers, however, were hampered by the winter weather in the East and easily exhausted much of the scenery in their own area. Stock companies made up of a director, a cameraman, a leading man and leading lady, and a handful of jacks-of-all-trades, began to travel the United States looking for places to make pictures. These companies had to keep moving because Thomas Edison, who claimed he held the patents on the entire process of making movies, was continually trying to put them out of business.

Director Francis Boggs of the Selig Polyscope Company passed through California in 1907. He stayed only long enough to film some water scenes for *The Count of Monte Cristo*, but in March 1909 he arrived in Los Angeles to establish a permanent studio. It was now possible for the company to settle permanently, since William Selig, the owner, had reached an agreement with Edison. Edison, realizing the futility of fighting all the other companies, had joined with them to form the Motion Picture Patent Company. Selig later said that his decision to move to the West was based entirely on the climate. Producers also wanted to use realistic scenery for westerns which already were becoming a major ingredient in any company's stock of pictures (see FILMS, WESTERN).

Most of the other companies soon followed Selig's lead. Within a few months Biograph—with its great director, D. W. Griffith—arrived, and by early 1910 almost every major company—Lubin, Kalem, Pathé,

Vitagraph, New York Motion Picture—had sent movie-makers to Los Angeles. Studios were established in downtown Los Angeles, Glendale, Pasadena, Santa Monica, and even as far afield as Orange, San Diego, and Santa Barbara.

It was this search for a location that made David Horsely almost accidentally the founder of the first Hollywood studio. Horsely, in 1911, decided that his Nestor films needed a California studio. He rented a tavern, abandoned because of a prohibition ordinance, at the corner of Sunset and Gower in Hollywood and began production.

At first, having a studio in Hollywood was no different than having one in any other outlying district of Los Angeles. The suburbs, however, had begun to make it clear that the movie industry was not welcome. Hollywood could not do the same, since it was no longer an independent city. Faced with the lack of a sufficient water supply, Hollywood had disincorporated and become part of the city of Los Angeles in 1909. The studios, therefore, were free of harassment by local ordinances and were also out of the high-rent district of downtown Los Angeles.

Film-makers quickly followed Horsely to Hollywood. William Fox brought Fox Films to Sunset Boulevard; Carl Laemmle and his Imp Company took over the Nestor studio; Vitagraph moved down from Santa Monica; and even Essanay, which had defied movie custom by making its pictures near San Francisco, opened a studio in the center of Hollywood.

The quiet, suburban nature of Hollywood quickly disappeared under the onslaught of the movie-makers. Large, barnlike studios were built for interior scenes, while exterior shots were filmed in the middle of the street. Particularly evident in Hollywood and all over Los Angeles were the comics, mostly from Mack Sennett's studio. They pushed their way into parades or any other public event that met their fancy and raced cars through the city, oftentimes hosing down the streets to cause sensational skids.

By 1912 the center of production had shifted from New York to California, but the coming of the motion pictures to Hollywood did very little in itself to attract attention to the area. Hollywood's fame came out of the war between the monopolistic Motion Picture Patent Company and the independents. These companies, most notably that of Carl Laemmle, defied the trust by distributing their own pictures. They also began to search for the magic ingredient that would bring audiences to their theaters.

Out of this search came longer and more expensive pictures. A film that a few years before would have cost well under a thousand dollars cost $20,000 by 1915. One of the major events in winning widespread attention for the movies was the opening in 1915 of D. W. Griffith's *Birth of a Nation*. Griffith spent $100,000 on the film and combined and refined all the techniques he had learned at Biograph.

The audience also began to change. At first most theaters were in working-class districts and the pictures themselves were filmed against a similar background. As the movies became big business and as bigger pictures became available, downtown theaters began to appear and the audience base was broadened to include the middle class. The interests of that class were first reflected in movies made by Cecil B. DeMille, who translated them into a series of sophisticated comedies, such as *Why Change Your Wife* (1920) *Forbidden Fruit* (1921), and *Adam's Rib* (1923). Most of Hollywood followed DeMille's lead, so that the new pictures were inhabited almost exclusively by a leisure class. Too, the independent producers, again looking for a means of attracting audiences, began advertising their players, and the star system was born.

The immediate result was a sensational rise in fame and income for those who became stars. In 1910, say, the standard salary for actors was $5 a day. Mary Pickford, by 1914, was receiving $1,000 a week and a year later signed a contract for $104,000 a year. An English comedian named Charlie Chaplin joined Mack Sennett in 1913 at a salary of $150 a week. A year later he went to Essanay at $1,250 a week; a year after that to Mutual for $10,000 a week plus a $150,000 bonus; and finally in 1917 to First National, where he was given $1 million to make eight pictures in the next eighteen months.

Actors who had shunned the movies now came to Hollywood to seek their fortunes; would-be actors arrived to await the "big chance"; even tourists came to at least see the studios and, hopefully, some of the stars.

Others, however, attacked Hollywood, both its inhabitants and the movies they acted in, for being another Sodom and Gomorrah. In the early 1920s, with the aid of sensational news stories concerning the stars, they were given added ammunition by the divorce of Mary Pickford, the manslaughter charge brought against Fatty Arbuckle in the death of actress Virginia Rappe, and the murder of director William Desmond Taylor. Movie content itself was relatively mild, but since it was more easily controlled than the private lives of the stars, the industry decided to attack it by forming its own censorship body, the Motion Picture Producers and Distributors of America. Will Hays, former postmaster general of the United States, became president. The code itself was naïve and may have contributed to the naïveté of motion pictures for years to come. Certainly, it taught many directors and producers to use their ingenuity to get around the code's provisions.

One reason for forming a self-governing group was the fear of government censorship. Far more important, however, was the fact that motion pictures were now big business with a large investment to protect. Bigger audiences meant bigger revenues, and this in turn attracted eastern investors, who by the end of World War I were willing to finance the movies in exchange for control of the companies. Throughout the early 1920s Wall Street invested and consolidated. Small companies disappeared, while a handful of large ones began to dominate the industry. Typical of this concentration was the formation of Metro-Goldwyn-Mayer in 1924. The company was organized out of several smaller ones by Loews, Inc., a theater chain, and had such extensive financial backing from the Chase National Bank that money for production was almost unlimited.

Louis B. Mayer was hired to supervise the entire studio operation in Hollywood. Mayer had left his father's junk business to purchase a small theater in 1907 and eventually became a film distributor. In 1918 he came to California to open his own studio. As the head of MGM's Hollywood studio until 1951, he was the prototype of a Hollywood movie mogul. Mayer brought

Irving Thalberg to MGM as supervisor of production. Thalberg, not quite twenty-five at the time, remained in this position until his death in 1937. Although his name rarely appeared on the screen, he was the organizational force behind the studio's entire schedule of pictures. Many who worked with him considered him a genius in finding and correcting the flaws in both scripts and finished pictures.

Eastern investors brought not only consolidation, but efficiency experts, who were sent to Hollywood to end wasteful procedures. Gone was the free-wheeling practice of making pictures anywhere with suitable scenery. Instead, production companies retreated behind locked studio gates and shot interior scenes on the stages and exterior scenes on the back lot. In many instances the efficiency movement was badly needed, but in some cases it attacked those whose major sin was nonconformity rather than inefficiency. One victim was Erich von Stroheim, who believed in thorough detail in costume and setting even though it might never appear on the screen. Von Stroheim built a critical reputation with such pictures as *Foolish Wives* (1921), *Queen Kelly* (1928), and *The Wedding March* (1928), but also became known as an extravagant and wasteful director. By the end of the 1920s he was finished as a director in Hollywood, although he survived as an actor for years to come.

No sooner had studios been consolidated, organized, and made efficient than sound was introduced. There was considerable opposition in Hollywood, mainly from those successful in silent movies. Warner Brothers, however, had not shared in this success and at times had almost collapsed because of a lack of financing. Since only the big companies were making money, Warner Brothers decided to expand. They obtained a loan from Goldman, Sachs and Company, built theaters in New York and Hollywood, and purchased the Vitagraph Company in order to obtain a Hollywood studio for production. They also reached an agreement with Western Electric, which owned several sound patents, in which Warner Brothers would introduce sound pictures in exchange for a royalty on all Western Electric sound devices that were sold.

In 1926 *Don Juan*, an all-singing picture, opened. It was followed by *The Jazz Singer* (1927), in which Al Jolson not only sang but spoke a few words, and *The Singing Fool* (1928), which had a considerable amount of talking. Critics were almost unanimous in denouncing both the quality of the sound and the quality of the drama. The public, however, was impressed, and by 1929 a successful picture had to have sound.

Talking pictures changed the way of making movies. The range of early microphones was only a few feet, and old cameras were so noisy that they had to be isolated in sound-proof booths. Many directors, particularly those brought in from Broadway, felt that sound movies should have nonstop talking. Consequently, movies retreated, at least temporarily, to the earliest days when they were little more than filmed stage plays.

The new methods also caused a change in Hollywood personnel. Silent-film directors like D. W. Griffith and Rex Ingram disappeared almost overnight, and many silent stars, notably John Gilbert, left for good after one or two sound pictures, because they had heavy accents or vocal deficiencies. When the spoken word became essential in the 1930s, many writers went to Hollywood: William Faulkner, Dorothy Parker, F. Scott Fitzgerald, Moss Hart, and Lillian Hellman, among others. The presence of such recognized, or soon-to-be-recognized, talents was to occasion a new and more penetrating criticism of the Hollywood machine than that directed at it in the 1920s and 1930s by moralists who denounced the "vileness" of life in Hollywood and of its films. The evils of power and its stultifying effect on creative talent became the new critical theme, especially among novelists, in the late 1930s, and the glamorous image of Hollywood began to pall.

Budd Schulberg in *What Makes Sammy Run* (1941) and Robert Carson in *The Magic Lantern* (1952) portrayed the Hollywood czar as a ruthless man who fought his way up the Hollywood ladder by trampling on those below and conning those above. The same theme was developed, although with more sympathy, by F. Scott Fitzgerald in his unfinished novel, *The Last Tycoon* (1941). Fitzgerald himself was the hero of another Schulberg novel, *The Disenchanted* (1950), in which Hollywood is seen as the home of the crude, uneducated studio boss, interested only in making money and continually unperceptive and unappreciative of true creative talent.

In many cases the novels were overdrawn, but it is true that by the 1930s individuality in pictures had given way to a "studio look." Each major studio had its own stable of stars, directors, and producers whose talents were coordinated by studio executives. Each studio produced pictures in its own image, from the sentimental, family movies of MGM to the fast-paced, hard-nosed dramas of Warner Brothers.

If Hollywood was artistically poor, it was monetarily rich. While the rest of the United States struggled through the Depression, Hollywood was involved in its most successful decade. Just how successful was demonstrated in 1939 with the opening of *Gone With the Wind*, released by MGM. The picture, based on Margaret Mitchell's best-selling novel, was beset by numerous problems in casting, writing, and directing, but when it was finished, it represented the full flowering of the studio system in all its virtues and faults. It was the biggest money-maker up to that time, and each subsequent reissue has only added to its reputation.

Ironically, just after the success of *Gone With the Wind* and just as the rest of the country began to come out of the Depression, the movie industry slumped. The coming of World War II in Europe closed the overseas market and income declined sharply. Also, in 1945 the federal government began a suit against eight major motion picture companies. This suit eventually banned the practice of forcing exhibitors to take pictures in large blocks without seeing them, and also required the companies to get rid of their affiliated theater chains. Then it began to appear that the much-predicted collapse of the motion picture industry had been a false alarm. Throughout World War II revenue continued to mount, and in 1946 the movies had their most profitable year. Once again, however, the slump returned, this time with more force and with more permanence.

In 1947 the industry was faced with several problems all at once. A long series of labor troubles, including an eight-month strike in 1945, had forced the studios to substantially raise salaries. At the same time England passed laws providing for stiff taxes on all movies imported from Hollywood. Once again economy measures were taken, with an estimated twenty-five percent of the working force being laid off. Hollywood was also badly frightened by the House Un-American Activities Committee's investigation into the political affiliations of movie-makers. Suddenly several anti-Communist pictures appeared to establish the loyalty of the movie industry. A longer-range effect was the creation of a blacklist of those considered dangerous and no longer welcome on studio payrolls.

By the end of the 1940s even prewar Hollywood's basic institution, the studio with its all-powerful boss, was threatened. Warner Brothers had stopped production; Universal had merged with International; and RKO, faced with financial difficulties, was taken over by Howard Hughes. This last move forced Dore Schary to leave as head of production at RKO and take the same position at MGM. This, in turn, brought on a clash of personalities resulting in the resignation, in 1951, of Louis B. Mayer, the symbol of the big studio czar.

It was into this already-nervous Hollywood that television was introduced. Local television had been popular since the end of the war, but the network relay that brought nationwide programming was not completed until 1951. Faced with this competition, Hollywood at first refused to allow stars to appear and refused to sell old movies. But it soon became evident that television and movies were natural allies, for television badly needed skills that were available only in Hollywood. Thus as early as 1951 Columbia Pictures established a subsidiary, Screen Gems, to make half-hour programs, and several small companies began to make television commercials.

The breakthrough for a major studio came in 1954 when Disney Studio went on television with an hourlong program. From a producer's standpoint the format was ideal. Most of the time was spent advertising forthcoming Disney movies, and it was all paid for by sponsors (see Walt DISNEY). Within a few years every major studio was involved in television, either in producing its own shows or in selling off its old stock of movies.

Yet television seriously cut into the number of moviegoers. Hollywood, therefore, stressed the limited size of the television screen by expanding the size of the movie screen. In 1952 Cinerama was introduced, but because it needed three projectors and a curved screen it was restricted to specially equipped theaters. Another vogue of the 1950s was 3-D movies, which required the audience to wear special glasses with red and green lenses. The eventual winners were those processes, such as Cinemascope, that gained the wide-screen effect with larger negatives and special enlarging lenses, thus avoiding complicated Cinerama equipment.

The wide screen meant that the narrow confines of the sound stages and back lots were no longer suitable. More and more directors left the studios to shoot their pictures on location. Indeed, many companies left the United States as well. Large assets could not be taken from foreign countries into the United States because of foreign governmental regulations. If, however, money was spent in making a picture, the picture could be shown in the United States and at least some of the money extracted. Cheap labor was another factor, as

was the desire of many stars to seek income-tax breaks by working abroad.

Income-tax problems also did much to end the control of the studios. As actors began to free themselves from the long-term studio contracts of the 1930s and 1940s, they formed their own independent companies for tax purposes. With the stars now free to pick their own roles, producers were forced to change their methods. No longer was it possible for a production chief to obtain a story and assign it to the appropriate director and stars on the studio roster. Instead, a producer bought a story, interested a director in it, then used the story and director to sell actors on doing the picture. Most of the new producers had little connection with the studios, and when the time came to shoot, they went on location or rented someone else's facilities. So thorough was the flight from California that by the end of the 1960s only one picture in six was made in a Hollywood studio.

Symbolically, the end of the old Hollywood came in 1969, when investor Kirk Kerkorian took control of MGM. He immediately announced that all but a few acres of the studio would be sold to developers. Furthermore, MGM's entire collection of props and costumes, including Charleton Heston's chariot from *Ben-Hur* and Judy Garland's red slippers from *The Wizard of Oz*, were to be turned over to an auction house. In May 1969 the physical effects that had seen service in MGM films for more than forty years were sold in a studio sound stage, which itself had been converted to an auction gallery for the occasion.

See Lewis Jacobs, *The Rise of the American Film* (1939); Arthur Knight, *The Liveliest Art* (1957); Richard Dyer MacCann, *Hollywood in Transition* (1962); and the International Film Guide series.—R. B.

mountain lion. The mountain lion (*Felis concolor*) is a large cat with the characteristic beauty and grace of the feline family. Naturalist Ernest Thompson Seton described the mountain lion as "lithe and splendid beasthood. His daily routine is a march of stirring athletic events that not another creature—in America, at least—can hope to equal." Russet or tawny to gray in coloration, males range in weight from 140 to 200 pounds in the northern parts of their range, while females are considerably smaller, averaging about 100 pounds. In Mexico and Central and South America they are smaller in size. Capable of living in habitats ranging from tropical jungles to deserts to subalpine types, the lion can exist on a diet of small rodents or animals the size of elk. They are extremely shy and secretive and seldom are seen in their natural habitat. They shun contact with man and are of negligible danger to humans; even years ago, when lions were more numerous, attacks on humans were almost unheard of. Indeed, the lion was revered rather than feared by early inhabitants of South and Central America, and Indians inhabiting Lower California utilized portions of the lion's unconsumed prey.

Because of its secretive habits, the mountain lion is perhaps the most mysterious and misunderstood of all the world's large carnivores. This is evident from the many names applied to this great cat throughout its range: *puma,* the Inca term; *painter,* a local North American colloquialism; *cougar,* a French corruption of a Tupi Indian word widely used in the Northwest;

A mountain lion poised for the kill grips a kid with its forepaws. (Library of Congress)

panther, the Greek word for *leopard; catamount,* a New England expression; *léone,* used in much of Central and South America. Most adaptable of all the large cats, it once had the widest distribution of any mammal in the western hemisphere, and perhaps the world. It ranged over both American continents, from the east to the west coasts, and from central British Columbia south to Patagonia—a total of more than 100 degrees of latitude. Authentic records of mountain lions are available from forty-seven of the forty-eight contiguous states—Indiana is missing—and from the District of Columbia. Similar records exist for Canada from the east to west coasts, with the possible exception of the province of Manitoba. It is likely that lions inhabited every part of the United States in which food and cover could be found, from sea level to high mountain slopes. In Central and South America, lions occur in tropical jungles and subtropical grasslands and have even been recorded above fifteen thousand feet in the Andes.

Mountain lions originally were abundant on both continents but now exist only in greatly reduced numbers. As the white man populated North America, lions vanished from much of their range. They now occur in sizable numbers only in the western and southwestern states, in unsettled areas of Central and South America, and in parts of British Columbia and Alberta. A population of undetermined size exists in the Florida Everglades, and recent information suggests there are a few in New Brunswick in eastern Canada.

With the settling of the New World, the mountain lion was subjected to indiscriminate killing. Because it sometimes killed livestock, early settlers regarded the big cat as an enemy to be destroyed at every opportunity. Even Theodore Roosevelt, an avid conservationist, described the mountain lion as a "big horse-killing cat, the destroyer of the deer, the lord of stealthy murder, facing his doom with a heart both craven and cruel." This

attitude has persisted to recent times in many quarters, and indiscriminate killing, aggravated by a now-disfavored bounty system, has taken a fearful toll. The New York Zoological Society, in 1964, estimated the total in the western United States at between 4,000 and 6,500—and there is evidence that the number may be dwindling even further.

Despite thoughtless and callous persecution, the mountain lion has survived in the western United States in inaccessible mountainous regions and in broad expanses of desert. Although deer is probably the mainstay of the lion's diet throughout its range, many other species are eaten as well, including elk, bighorn sheep, mountain goats, porcupines, rabbits, rodents of all kinds, and, in fact, any animal life available. Other carnivorous species, such as coyotes, bobcats, and skunks, are taken without hesitation. Lions also eat certain insects and grasses, illustrating that they, like most predators, eat what is most easily obtainable.

Mountain lions are strictly solitary, males and females exhibiting social tolerance only during the brief breeding period. (Females, of course, remain with the young during the long period of juvenile dependency.) Lions are capable of breeding at any season of the year, similar to the domestic cat. In the northern parts of their range, however, breeding is limited largely to winter and early spring. A male and female will pair and remain together for two weeks or perhaps longer. They then part and the male plays no further role in the family life.

The spotted young are born after a gestation period of about ninety days. Litter size ranges from one to six. They are born in a cave, under a rock ledge or windfall, or some similar site. Helpless at birth, they grow quite rapidly. In addition to providing milk, the mother carries meat to them. At approximately two months of age they leave the den in which they were born, thereafter utilizing different temporary dens and caves while the mother hunts for food.

Young lions remain dependent on the lioness for a long period. Although they possess certain inherent abilities, they must learn specific killing techniques crucial in bringing down such large prey as deer and elk. The female trains her young in the art of killing, then leaves them on their own when they are eighteen to twenty-two months of age. The litter may remain together for a short period but soon breaks up, each young lion going his own way.

Mountain lions are territorial, each individual staking out a sector in which it usually confines itself. The size of these territories varies with the availability of food, the terrain, types of vegetative cover, and other factors. Males may inhabit a home range or territory of fifteen to fifty square miles in size or more; females' areas are normally smaller.

This territorialism, or spacing, acts to limit the size of any given population of lions. When an individual establishes itself firmly on a territory, other lions respect that individual's property rights. The resident animal regularly marks the boundaries of its range with markings called scrapes or scratches. The lion scrapes together leaves, twigs, or conifer needles into mounds four to six inches high, then urinates or defecates on them to make sight and scent markers delineating its territory.

Intensive studies of the interaction of lions and their

prey species have shown that predation by lions is beneficial in wilderness and semiwilderness environments. Rather than decimating herds of desirable big game animals such as deer and elk, predation by lions tends to keep these herds within the limits of their food resources and lessens the frequency of extreme fluctuations in population growth. Grazing animals tend to increase in numbers to the point of eating themselves out of food. When this occurs catastrophic die-offs result. Many years are required to restore the vegetation and, in turn, the animal populations.

Americans are becoming increasingly appreciative of all forms of wildlife and are demanding a halt to the persecution of many species. Practically all states and Canadian provinces in which mountain lions live now have some form of protective legislation. Further restrictions on the killing of lions in the absence of objective data and knowledge are certain. It appears that an enlightened human society will make provisions for the continued existence of the mountain lion—one of America's truly spectacular animals.

See V. H. Cahalane, *Cougar, Grizzly and Wolf in North America*, New York Zoological Society Monograph (1964); M. G. Hornocker, *An Analysis of Mountain Lion Predation upon Mule Deer and Elk in the Idaho Primitive Area*, Wildlife Monograph No. 21 (1970); W. L. Robinette, "Notes on Cougar Productivity and Life History," *Journal of Mammalogy* (1961); and S. P. Young and E. A. Goldman, *The Puma, Mysterious American Cat* (1946).—M. G. H.

Mountain Meadows Massacre. See LATTER-DAY SAINTS: *Brigham Young period.*

Mount McKinley National Park. Mount McKinley National Park, located in central Alaska, is a vast and formidable wilderness, including huge glacier fields, great stretches of tundra, incomparable lakes, and Mount McKinley (20,320 feet), the highest peak in North America. The Indians who lived in the shadow of the mountain called it Denali. The Russians, during their ownership of Alaska, referred to it as Bulshaia. Gold prospectors called it Densmore's Peak or Mount Allen. W. A. Dickey, the leader of a small expedition up the Susitna River in 1896, viewed the mountain and named it Mount McKinley in honor of the Republican nominee for president. When William McKinley won the election of 1896, Dickey's name took precedence over the others in official usage. The mountain defied climbing until 1913, when Hudson Stuck and Harry Karstens reached the summit of the south peak.

In 1906 Charles Sheldon, a noted naturalist, made a detailed scientific study of wildlife in the Alaska Range, concentrating on the Dall sheep. He was captivated by the scenery and the animals. In the next decade he led a campaign for federal legislation to protect the natural beauty of Mount McKinley. The wildlife of the region is, in fact, almost as spectacular as the landscape. The hulking Toklat grizzly is found throughout the park. The Alaska moose thrives in its forests and marshes. Every year large herds of caribou trek across the park on the way to their summer range. Dall sheep, timber wolves, and animals that are becoming extinct elsewhere inhabit the area. Congress established the park on February 26, 1917. It contains 1,939,493 acres and is, except for Yellowstone, the largest of the national parks. Fairbanks, Alaska, is the closest city of significant size.—D. C. S.

Mount Rainier National Park. Mount Rainier National Park is located about fifty miles south of Tacoma, Washington, on the western slope of the Cascade Range. The main feature of the park is Mount Rainier itself, a commanding volcanic cone (14,410 feet) that dominates the landscape of the region. The mountain is one of the best-known landmarks of the Pacific Northwest. It towers over neighboring mountains and in clear weather may be seen from the Puget Sound region. Its slopes contain the largest single-peak glacier system in the United States.

Indian tribes from eastern Washington traditionally came to Mount Rainier's high meadows in the summer and fall. Early settlers in the Puget Sound country used the region around the mountain for hunting and fishing. Longmire Springs, at the base of the peak, was the site of the earliest tourist accommodations in the area. There was grazing, mining, and lumbering in the region. The mountain was first scaled by Hazard Stevens and P. B. Van Trump in 1870. In the 1880s some of the leading citizens of Seattle and Tacoma initiated a political drive to have the mountain set aside as a scenic preserve. President William McKinley signed an act establishing Mount Rainier National Park on March 2, 1899.

The park has many scenic delights. It is famed for its forests of western hemlock, Douglas fir, and red cedar and for its wildflowers, which grow in great profusion in July and August. It contains dozens of alpine lakes and streams fed by the melting glaciers on Mount Rainier. The Wonderland Trail, ninety miles long, completely encircles the mountain and takes hikers through a variety of forest and mountain terrain. The park may be entered via the Nisqually gate on the southwest, the White River entrance on the east, or the Ohanapecosh gate on the south. It contains 241,782 acres. —D. C. S.

Muir, John (1838-1914). Writer and naturalist. A Scot by birth, Muir grew up on the central Wisconsin frontier in the 1850s. Unlike most pioneers, he formed a love of the wilderness that led him on a thousand-mile hike to the Gulf of Mexico and, in 1868, to California's Sierra Nevada. This "range of light," as Muir called the Sierra, became the focal point of his exploration, writing, and conservation activities.

Intellectually, Muir was a disciple of the Transcendentalists, particularly Ralph Waldo Emerson, whom he met in Yosemite Valley in 1871, and Henry David Thoreau. To Muir, nature, especially wild nature, was a "window opening into heaven, a mirror reflecting the Creator." It followed that protecting wilderness was an act of worship, and Muir plunged into the battle with the intensity of a religious fanatic. In 1892 he and a group of like-minded San Franciscans organized the SIERRA CLUB. The organization, which Muir served as president for twenty-two years, dedicated itself to "exploring, enjoying and rendering accessible the mountain regions of the Pacific Coast." Wilderness outings of up to several weeks' duration were a central feature of the Sierra Club program. Muir expressed the philosophy of the club in 1901 when he wrote: "thousands of tired, nerve-shaken, over-civilized people are beginning to find out that going to the mountains is going home; that wildness is a necessity; and the mountain parks and reservations are useful not only as fountains of timber and irrigating rivers, but as fountains of life."

By 1900 Muir's genteel, enthusiastic essays had given him a national reputation as the foremost publicizer of wilderness values. In the next decade he came into sharp conflict with the utilitarian wing of the American conservation movement, led by Gifford Pinchot. Muir believed that Pinchot was nothing more than an exploiter in conservationist's clothing. Pinchot, on the other hand, felt Muir's definition of "conservation" was narrow, impractical, and selfish. The men clashed over the purpose of the national forests—were they timber farms or wilderness preserves? They also locked horns on the Hetch Hetchy issue. Muir worked feverishly from 1908 to 1913 to prevent this spectacular wild valley in Yosemite National Park from being granted to San Francisco as the site of a dam and municipal reservoir. Pinchot supported the city's application as the "highest use" of the region, and ultimately his view prevailed. For Muir this was not only wrong but evil. "These temple destroyers," he raged, "devotees of ravaging commercialism, seem to have a perfect contempt for Nature, and, instead of lifting their eyes to the God of the mountains, lift them to the Almighty Dollar." Although Muir died discouraged a year after the Hetch Hetchy defeat, he laid the basis for the dramatic rise of the wilderness preservation movement in subsequent decades. Representative of Muir's writings are his *Our National Parks* (1901) and *The Yosemite* (1912).

Muir's life is the subject of Linnie Marsh Wolfe, *Son of the Wilderness* (1945). Roderick Nash, *Wilderness and the American Mind* (1967), puts Muir's thought and activity in the context of three centuries of changing attitude toward wild country. Muir's own books are available in many editions, and his journals have been edited by Linnie Marsh Wolfe under the title *John of the Mountains* (1938). William F. Badè has edited *The Life and Letters of John Muir*, 2 vols. (1923).—R. N.

mule. What is a mule? It is an "outrage upon nature, a monstrosity, a combination of the donkey and the horse, with qualities of neither." It is a "puzzle of the brutes"— undoubtedly the "incarnation of sum-total of quadrupedal deviltry." It stands alone in its nature and qualities, "unapproachable in devilment, fathomless in cunning, born old in crime, of disreputable paternity, and incapable of posterity, stolid, imperturbable, with no love for anything but the perpetration of tricks, no dexterity in aught save the flinging of his heels, no desire for anything but rations—stolen if possible and by preference—and no affection at all." It is "haf horse, haf jackass," kicks with uncanny skill, and gives evidence of "malace aforethought." There is neither a fence that will hold it nor a system that will train it into "staid and respectable barn-yard habits." There is nothing more pitiful than a "stalwart mare, whose ears are clean-cut and sharp, and whose veins stand out over her glossy skin, looking affectionately over her shoulders at the little dun-colored, fuzzy, impish monstrosity who tugs at her udders." One would think she would run away and "abandon it to starve, if indeed, a young mule can be starved." But the mare never does, and "it goes far to show how poor judges mothers are of their own children." The best way to put a "jarhead" in a stall is to hire someone else to do it. Thus spoke some nineteenth-century westerners on mules in general.

Yet most of these men probably spoke with tongue in cheek, because they realized that this "hybrid beast," with all its supposedly unlovely characteristics, played a central role in settling the American West. Mules were empire builders. They pulled a majority of immigrant wagons; they transported civilian and military staples and supplies; and they became the chief draft-farm animals in the West.

Although the mule's origin cannot be accurately determined, the practice of breeding the animal is at least three thousand years old. By the late fifteenth century the popularity of mules had spread throughout western Europe and breeding centers had been established in France, Italy, and Spain. During the eighteenth century the French province of Poitou had become the chief European center for buying mules.

No doubt the first breeders of donkeys and horses learned early that mating a stallion to a female donkey created an inferior animal, the hinny. This creature, usually too small for strenuous labor, rarely was produced intentionally. Only by breeding a male jack to a solidly proportioned mare could they get the tough, surefooted, hard-skinned mule. Despite the fact that the genetic principles have not been fully explained, the mule evidently obtains its size and body from the mare and its feet, head, and tail from the donkey. Early breeders also discovered that although male mules are sterile, the females could produce, occasionally, an offspring when mated with a stallion.

Not only did the Spaniards introduce the horse into the New World, they also introduced the less glamorous and more dependable mule. In fact, this hybrid became the chief draft animal of Spanish America. The mule needed less grain, and was able to carry heavier loads over more difficult terrain than any other beast of burden. Colonizers used packtrains of mules almost exclusively to transport supplies from the coastal to the interior regions. The most famous of the early trains crossed the Isthmus of Panama from Nombre de Dios on the Atlantic to Panama City on the Pacific. Throughout the colonial period the Spanish shipped gold eastward and grain, leather hides, and meat westward—all on the backs of mules.

One of the reasons the Spanish early relied so heavily on mules was that there was a surplus of them in Spain. In 1494 Ferdinand reissued an edict first proclaimed by Alfonso X in 1248 stating that only clergy and women could ride mules. If any man were caught riding one, the animal would be killed. Ferdinand had resorted to this measure when he found out that more than 100,000 Spaniards preferred riding mules to the clumsy, high-spirited horses then being bred and that the nation could muster no more than 12,000 horses for use in battle against the Moslems.

When the Spaniards began exploring what later was to become the western United States, they began to rely on mules. Only one hybrid was listed on the Coronado muster roll, but at this time breeding for the animals was only beginning in northern Mexico. Most available mules were being utilized in the mines, and horses were most easily obtainable for packing purposes. Later expeditions, however, did use mules to carry supplies.

In 1598, when Juan de Oñate's expedition went to settle New Mexico, the settlers took with them more then one hundred riding, pack, and harness mules and several jacks for future breeding purposes. Although most of the wagons and carts accompanying the pioneers were drawn by oxen, the mule gradually replaced the ox for this task. *Mayordomos* (wagon masters) learned that even though oxen in equal numbers pulled heavier loads, particularly through muddy and sandy terrain, they tired more easily than mules and tended to weaken on the highland diet of short, dry grass. New Mexicans relied heavily on mules. Some local traders used small packtrains to bring luxury goods to the settlements and to trade with the Indians and the Americans. In Santa Fe, mules, not horses, were used to draw carriages and coaches. A large number of citizens preferred riding the animals. Poor settlers rose in community esteem when they were able to replace their small burros with mules.

Missionaries became the primary breeders and suppliers of mules throughout the borderlands. When sent out from parent missions, they inevitably took with them a few Christian Indians, a small herd of cattle, a mare, a stallion, and a jack. If a missionary were lucky, he also rode a mule. This was true of the Jesuits in Sierra Madre and Pimeria Alta and of the Franciscans in New Mexico and Texas. When Father Junipero Serra and his Franciscan brothers began advancing into Alta California in 1768, they appropriated mules at every mission in Baja California; otherwise, they declared, they would have starved had it not been for mule meat.

By the time Americans pushed into Mexican domains, mules were numerous throughout the settled portions of the West. The "gringos" were not especially surprised at seeing the hybrids, for mules had also become popular in parts of the United States. Before the American Revolution the farmers of Narragansett Bay and the Connecticut valley bred mules. Louisiana planters had periodically carried on illegal business with Santa Fe mule traders, as did early settlers in Upper Louisiana around the old fur-trading station. St. Louis began to acquire mules from the same source. George Washington's and Thomas Jefferson's attachment to, and advocacy of, the use of mules is well known. By the nineteenth century, mules had become popular draft animals in the North and even more so in the South. Between 1850 and 1860 alone the number of mules in the United States increased one hundred percent.

What did astonish some Americans, however, was the smaller size of the Mexican mule and its agility and strength. It could carry a load almost equal to that of its heavier American counterpart and could endure longer. According to some early intruders, it acted more like a mountain goat. There was hardly a trail that one of these animals could not traverse.

As settlers moved into the tier of states immediately west of the Mississippi River, they first depended on the animals they had brought with them for draft stock. But as their animals wore out, they relied on whatever mules they could illegally purchase from New Mexican traders. During the initial settlement of Missouri, draft stock was at a premium, and even Mexican mules were hard to obtain. The stock remained scarce until the beginning of the Santa Fe trade. Every caravan during the initial years of the trade brought back mules. The 1823 Cooper expedition returned to Missouri with more than four hundred jacks, jennets, and mules. But as more mules arrived, more were demanded by the settlers.

Missourians soon discovered that reexporting these Mexican mules to the South was as profitable as the Santa Fe trade. As a result mules remained scarce and enterprising Missourians began breeding their own animals. Within a decade they had developed one of the largest mule-breeding centers in the nation. The breeders early learned that the size of the jackass alone made relatively little difference in mating for a sturdier mule. Rather it depended primarily on the mare. By breeding good-sized Mexican and Portuguese jacks to large draft mares, they developed superior mules. Missouri mules always brought high prices. In Howard County, in 1854, 120 mules sold for $13,000, an average of $110 a piece. A large majority of the draft and harness mules used by western farmers and shippers came from Missouri.

The Santa Fe trade serves as an excellent example of the use of harness mules in the West. Of the various routes that traders traveled, none was more grueling on both men and animals than the Santa Fe Trail. On the initial expeditions horses were used more frequently because of the scarcity of mules. But by 1829, with mules easily obtainable in Santa Fe and Missouri, most seasoned traders had discarded their draft horses for the superior pulling mules. Even when Major Bennet Riley's four companies of the Sixth Regiment escorted the caravan in 1829 and used oxen to pull the army supply wagon, thereby introducing oxen to the trade, mules nevertheless held their own. Although oxen pulled heavier loads—an important consideration to any trader—mules did not have to be shod, required less time to recuperate in Santa Fe before beginning the return trip, were less susceptible to disease and sunburn, and traveled much faster. Indeed the merits of each animal were such that traders in general after 1829 remained undecided as to which animal was best. Thereafter, on the yearly caravans, according to Josiah Gregg, mules pulled half the wagons and oxen the other half.

Nor was the Santa Fe trade the only example of mules being used as transporters. Butterfield's Concord coaches used three pairs on the desolate, rough stretches across the Unorganized Territory and Texas. Wells, Fargo & Co. used mules almost exclusively. As late as 1875, more of America's freight was hauled by harness and pack mules than by railroads. Until the late 1920s, small communities located several miles off the railroad lines were furnished supplies by wagons pulled mainly by mules.

Not only did civilian transporters depend heavily on mules, but the United States Army did also. As the American settlers moved westward, particularly after the Mexican War, troops naturally followed, setting up post after post throughout the West. To supply these distant stations, the army—partly for convenience but mainly for economy—provided as much of its own transportation as possible. It relied on wagon trains pulled by harness mules. Six-mule "jerk-line" wagons weighing 1,950 pounds carried from 3,000 to 3,300 pounds of cargo. Two- and four-mule "escort" wagons carried from 1,200 to 1,400 pounds. The official army wagon train was made up of 36 men, 112 wagon mules, 6 riding mules, and 28 wagons. Some trains, however, were much larger. For example, between May and September 1849, a train of 275 wagons and 2,500 animals traveled from San Antonio to El Paso. The next year 267 wagons pulled by 1,068 mules transported 767,000 pounds of subsistence stores between the same two locations. In 1854-55, 70 wagons pulled by 750 mules traveled from Fort Leavenworth to California. According to the assistant quartermaster, Captain Rufus Ingalls, he neither lost nor abandoned anything on the way, and the mules were in fine condition at the conclusion of the journey. Even with the construction of the transcontinental railroads after the Civil War, posts were still largely supplied by wagon trains, since most of the posts were miles from even a feeder line.

After the Civil War when western troops left their posts to campaign against the Indians, they relied heavily on mules. For any extended expedition over rugged terrain, a packtrain usually consisting of sixty-four mules and fourteen men traveled at the end of the column. In using these trains the army had adopted almost completely the Spanish method of packing. It used the *aparejo*, a stiff, well-padded blanket contrivance with small wooden bibs that kept weight evenly distributed on a mule's back. It further adopted the Mexican bell-mare method of driving. Mexican packers learned that the mule is by nature a herd-bound animal and that it also has acute hearing. They also discovered that horses and especially mares tend to dominate mules; the mare with a bell around her neck therefore leads her followers. All experienced packers rode mules; they did not want more than one leader among the animals.

Whenever possible, army officers acquired the smaller Mexican mule for packing. In 1873 M. C. Meigs, the quartermaster general of the army, asked officers in the field to comment on the advisability of using Mexican pack mules. The officers replied almost unanimously that the small, short-legged, barrel-bellied Mexican mule from thirteen to fourteen hands high was by far the best animal.

Throughout the West, mule trains performed feats that seem almost unbelievable. In 1881 a company of Indian scouts and one packtrain marched eighty-five miles in twelve hours under the summer sun of New Mexico. This same train, a few days later, marched sixty miles in one day's time. From San Carlos Agency, Arizona, in 1882, a packtrain loaded with 200 pounds to the mule made a forced march of 280 miles in three days.

Whether purchasing saddle, wagon, or pack mules, the army set high standards, which were usually adhered to after 1870. Wagon mules had to be of dark color, sound in all particulars with full flesh and good condition, well broken and square trotters in harness, from four to ten years old, and not less than thirteen and a half hands high. Pack mules thirteen hands high were acceptable as long as they weighed at least 850 pounds. No pack mule was to have ever been in harness, and all were to be of "even disposition" and possess no blemishes. Saddle mules had to meet the same requirements as pack mules and, in addition, be extremely bridle-wise and agile.

Although mules played a significant role in civilian and military transportation, they played at least an equally important role in western agriculture. Until 1930 these animals were the dominant draft animals on the farms throughout the South, the Midwest, and the West. Whether bred in Missouri, in Mexico, or locally,

mules performed most of the farmers' strenuous chores. It was the combination of mules and steel plows that enabled western farmers to plow the deep furrows so necessary for dry farming in the Great Plains. Mule power was required to pull the large combines and harvesters. After harvesting, farmers used mules to transport their crops to market. If the legend of the West's dependence on the horse had not survived so long and if the truth were known, most farmers hitched mules, not horses, to their wagons.

Most agriculturalists became very attached to their mules. As one old-timer stated, these animals could pull two-thirds their own weight, they were "long livers," and "faithful and enduring laborers and friends." Even though they cost more than a draft horse, mules usually stayed healthier, lived twice as long, and were less expensive to maintain.

Because of mechanization, the mule has been steadily declining in popularity. In the census of 1920 the mule population was almost five and a half million. The mule's peak year in the 1920s was in 1925 when just over six million were used in agriculture and industry. By 1930, however, the number had fallen off almost one million and began to decrease steadily each year. World War II brought about a brief revival of the mule. With farm machinery and parts scarce, mules were used again on the smaller farms, and some were used by American troops in Italy and Burma. But by 1954 their number had dropped to below two million.

Today the mule has become a curiosity. Only in a few isolated communities is it used for draft purposes. No doubt it is headed for extinction in the United States. Ironically, this most successful hybrid animal helped to produce a mechanized civilization that made it obsolete. (See also BURRO, WILD.)

See Averam B. Bender, "Military Transportation in the Southwest, 1848-1860," *New Mexico Historical Review* (April 1957); John J. Boniface, *The Cavalry Horse and His Pack* (1903); W. H. Daly, *Manual of Pack Transportation* (1917); Emmett M. Essin III, "Mules, Packs, and Packtrains," *Southwestern Historical Quarterly* (July 1970); Josiah Gregg, *Commerce of the Prairies*, 2 vols. (1845); Robert Byron Lamb, *The Mule in Southern Agriculture* (1963); Max L. Moorhead, "Spanish Transportation in the Southwest, 1540-1846," *New Mexico Historical Review* (April 1957); Theodore H. Savory, "The Mule," *Scientific American* (December 1970); W. D. Smithers, "Mule Packs and Wagon Trains," *Western Horseman* (February-April 1965); James W. Stelle, *Frontier Army Sketches* (1969); Gary Webster, "Unsung Empire Builder—The Mule," *Natural History* (March 1956); and Harvey Wiley, *A Treatise on the Mule* (1867).—E. M. E.

Murieta or **Murrieta, Joaquin** (c. 1830-1853 or c. 1878). Bandit, or revolutionary. In the hidden history of the West there rides a mythological horseman—"The Ghost of Sonora," or Joaquin Murieta. Was he a man or a myth? Was he a "Napoleon of banditry," as an officer of the California Rangers charged, or was he a "great liberator" of La Raza, the Mexicans of California, as his descendants have declared? Some historians have called the legend of Murieta a folk tale. Some historians doubt that he ever existed at all.

In the spring of 1853, when The Ghost of Sonora reigned over the San Joaquin valley and terrorized the gold-rush camps, even the authorities did not know who he was. The California legislature, in establishing the state's rangers, ordered the capture of not one, but five, "Joaquins": Joaquin Valenzuela, Joaquin Ocomorenia, Joaquin Carrillo, Joaquin Botellier, and—the closest they came to naming the man they were after—a Joaquin Muriati.

The legend of Murieta begins with his baptismal paper, dated 1830 and located in the old church of Alamos, a city in Sonora, Mexico. The document says he was the son of "Joaq. y Rosalia Murieta," who worked in a silver-mining camp of Mayo Indians near Varoyeca, fifteen miles to the south. His mother was a descendant of the Rubios of Cadiz, Spain; it was said that her father, Jorge Hipolito, had Moorish blood. About the boy's father little is known. In the mountains the villagers believe he was a Mayo Indian, a light-skinned tribe that still lives in the Sonoran highlands.

At thirteen, Murieta studied in the Jesuit school of Alamos. His schooling in guerrilla warfare began much earlier, however, for Sonora was in a constant state of rebellion against Mexico. The Mayo and Yaqui Indians, who worked in the mines, had revolted in 1825 and fought almost unendingly in the mountains until the invasion of Mexico by the United States Army in 1846. While a teen-ager Murieta married the daughter of a mule skinner for the mines, and in 1848 the young couple joined the trek of thousands of Sonorans to California, seeking to escape from the war-ravaged province.

Gold had been discovered in the hills of Los Angeles by a local ranchero owner, Francisco Lopez, in 1841. In 1848, when John Marshall found gold in the tracer of Sutter's Mill, the thousands of Sonoran miners who were already in California rushed to the Sierra Nevada. In that first year, the Sonorans mined at least half of the gold taken from the mother lode.

On coming to California Murieta worked as a ranch hand. He herded wild horses near Stockton until 1850, when he was arrested in that city on suspicion of robbery, kept in jail, and then released as innocent. He sought refuge in the California town of Sonora, named for the large population of his countrymen who lived there. At Saw Mill Flat, up river, he built a cabin and staked a small claim, but Yankee miners were said to have raped his wife and driven him away.

In the mining camps the vigilantes had begun an "engine of terror" to drive out the Mexicans. By passing in 1850 the Greaser Act (its official title) and the Foreign Miners Tax, the California legislature reflected the hysteria of the Yankee miners in regard to the Sonorans.

The journals of the old forty-niners refer to Murieta's attacks on these miners as "acts of revenge." Caleb Dorsey, the district attorney of Tuolumne County and sometimes called the "only Harvard man in the gold rush," described the would-be highwayman as quiet and a gentleman—a reluctant revolutionary. Murieta's attempts at robbery were at first amateurish and unsuccessful. Within a few months, however, he had gathered a band, then several bands, of dispossessed Sonoran miners, renegade Yankees, and ordinary thieves. By the summer of 1853 Murieta's bands raided up and down the length and breadth of the San Joaquin valley. His horsemen were aided and hidden on the estates of some of the oldest and wealthiest California dons, who had lost much of their land grants to the invaders. One of his hideouts was on the ranchero of the former governor of California, don Carlos Antonio Carrillo. "Insurrection!" was the cry raised against Murieta on the floor of the legislature.

Although it was believed that Murieta was beheaded by the California Rangers in July 1853, and although his raids did cease at that time, there is growing evidence that the Ghost of Sonora escaped his captors. He was reported in northern Sonora in the late 1870s, ranching in Arispe. In the village of Cucurpe, high in Sierra Madre, the Indians claim he was buried in the old Jesuit cemetery.

Major Horace Bell of the California Rangers wrote of Murieta years later:

In any country in America except the United States, the bold defiance of the power of the government, a half year's successful resistance, a continuance conflict with the military and civil authorities and the armed populace—the writer repeats, in any country in America except the United States—the operations of Joaquin Murieta would be dignified by the title of revolution, and the leader with that of rebel chief.

The final eulogy to Murieta was given by Robert Richards, née Rodriquez, his second cousin, in 1932: "To the Mexicans he was a great liberator, come out of Mexico to take California back from the hands of the gringos. They did not call his 'looting' and 'killing' banditry. They called it war." In the barrios of California, there are those who still call him El Patrio—The Patriot.

See Yellow Bird (John Rollin Ridge), *The Life and Adventures of Joaquin Murieta* (1854, repr. 1955); Walter Noble Burns, *The Robin Hood of El Dorado* (1932); *The Life of Joaquin Murieta*, printed by the California Police Gazette (1859, repr. 1932); Margaret Hanna Lang, *Early Justice in Sonora* (1963); Leonard Pitt, *The Decline of the Californios* (1966); and Horace Bell Hebberd, *Reminiscences of a Ranger* (1927).—S. S.

Murrell [Murrel, Murel], John A. (1804-?). Outlaw. Famous in his own time for his alleged leadership of what seems in retrospect to have been a spurious plot for an enormous combined rebellion of lower Mississippi valley white outlaws and black slaves, Murrell was born in Williamson County, Tennessee, and taught to steal by his mother. He was first jailed in Tennessee for riot, gambling, and horse stealing, with the last conviction bringing a one-year sentence in 1826. After his year in prison Murrell forsook single banditry for membership in a criminal organization. According to his accuser, Virgil A. Stewart, who claimed to have infiltrated Murrell's band, Murrell was the leader in the creation of an interstate organized-crime combine. At this time Mississippi valley criminal activities were often carried on by gangs that operated across several state lines in the interest of horse stealing, counterfeiting, and—in the lower part of the valley—the kidnapping of free and slave Negroes, who were then illegally sold to slave owners. These gangs were large and well organized, with their leaders sometimes carrying on a façade of respectable life. Murrell, a product of the rural underworld life of the old Southwest, contributed, apparently, to the rationalization and expansion of the scope of the nether element that nurtured him.

One of Stewart's charges, which was generally believed by his contemporaries, was that Murrell and his "clan" of a thousand planned a gigantic lower Mississippi valley uprising that would find white outlaws and black slaves coalescing to overturn the existing social structure. Historians doubt that such a plot existed, and Murrell's actions may well have been restricted to little more than the offense of Negro-stealing, for which a Jackson, Tennessee, court convicted him in 1834. Yet Stewart's bizarre accusations against Murrell in 1834 were widely credited, and a notable result was the hysterical vigilante-type suppression of an alleged white-led plan for a slave uprising in Mississippi in 1835 (which seemed to echo the charges against Murrell). The main point, however, is not whether Murrell and his henchmen really were conspiring for a great social upheaval—it is almost certain that they were not—but that Murrell's career was symptomatic of a banditti group so pervasive in the lower Mississippi valley that citizens felt threatened, culturally and materially, by its existence and were increasingly obsessed with fears of a slave uprising.

After enduring a ten-year term for his Jackson, Tennessee, sentence, Murrell was released from prison in 1844. He died of tuberculosis several years later (the exact year is unknown) in Pikesville, Tennessee.

See Robert M. Coates, *The Outlaw Years: The History of the Land Pirates of the Natchez Trace* (1930); H. R. Howard, ed., *The History of Virgil A. Stewart* (1836); and Edwin A. Miles, "The Mississippi Slave Insurrection Scare of 1835," *Journal of Negro History,* vol. 42 (1957). —R. M. B.

Murrieta, Joaquin. See Joaquin MURIETA.

Museum of Navaho Ceremonial Art. See TL'AH HASTIIN.

Museum of New Mexico. The theme of the Museum of New Mexico, located in Santa Fe, is man in the Southwest. The old PALACE OF THE GOVERNORS was designated by the territorial legislature in 1909 to house the museum. Today the palace has exhibits on the history of the palace itself, the state of New Mexico, and the prehistory of New Mexico from twenty thousand years ago until the Spanish conquest. In the Hall of the Modern Indian are exhibits of modern southwestern Indians, their ways of living, and their artifacts.

West of the palace is the Fine Arts building, built in 1917 in the style of New Mexico's mission churches (substantially a replica of the New Mexico State Building exhibited in the 1915-16 Panama-California Exposition in San Diego). The Fine Arts permanent collection consists primarily of work done by regional artists, such as Robert Henri, Ernest L. Blumenschein, Randall Davey, John Sloan, Joseph H. Sharp, and William P. Henderson. Here one of the finest collections of post-Spanish Indian art is housed, including displays of pottery and blankets.

Special exhibits include competitions, invitationals, retrospectives, and a Southwest biennial exhibit. St. Francis Auditorium, a replica of a mission church interior, is used for the performing arts and public functions.

Two miles south of the plaza is the Museum of International Folk Art, the newest unit of the state museum. The Laboratory of Anthropology, located next to the Museum of International Folk Art, is built in pueblo style. Here, staff archaeologists and ethnologists study the prehistory and contemporary cultures of southwestern peoples. The laboratory also salvages archaeological sites endangered by the construction of highways, dams, and pipelines.

The museum administers a number of state monuments at major archaeological ruins. Quarái, a Tiwa Indian Pueblo, settled originally in A.D. 1250, located north of Mountainair, New Mexico, was proclaimed a state monument in 1935. It contains the mounds of the pueblo and the ruins of two seventeenth-century Franciscan mission churches. The site was abandoned after Apache raids and crop failures during the 1670s. It was designated a national historic landmark in 1962.

Another museum responsibility is San Gregorio de Abó, located ten miles west of Mountainair, which was established in the 1620s as a Franciscan mission and *convento* (friar house). It stands on the remains of a thirteenth-century pueblo three stories high. Although the thirty-foot-high walls of the red sandstone church have been reduced by neighboring people, who used the stones to build houses, the ruins are still beautiful and imposing, with the Manzano Mountains as a backdrop. Abandonment occurred about the same time as that of Quarái and for the same reasons. Abó became a state monument in 1938 and was designated a national historic landmark in 1962. The Jémez state monument, so designated in 1935, is located in the Jémez Mountains and consists of the Franciscan mission church and monastery of San José, founded in the first quarter of the seventeenth century, and the ruins of a thirteenth-century Towa Indian site, *Giusewa* ("Pueblo at the Boiling Waters"). The museum has excavated only part of the pueblo, which in its time probably housed about eight hundred inhabitants. In 1922 alfresco murals on the east and west walls of the church's nave near the altar were uncovered, showing handsome floral patterns and Indian motifs in blues, yellows, greens, reds, black, and white. Apparently the oldest fired bricks used in the state of New Mexico were laid as paving in the mission's entryway.

Another well-known site administered by the museum is the Coronado State Monument, proclaimed in 1940. In 1540 Francisco Vásquez de Coronado and his expedition arrived in the Rio Grande valley near Albuquerque and during the winter of 1540-41 camped at a Tiwa pueblo near Kuaua. The pueblo, first settled in the late twelfth or early thirteenth century, was abandoned before 1680. About twelve hundred small ground-level rooms, part of terraced house blocks built of coursed adobe mud that faced open plazas, covered nearly a quarter of a mile north and south and an eighth of a mile east and west. In the open plazas were circular and rectangular *kivas* (underground ceremonial rooms). Not all of the pueblo was constructed or inhabited at one time.

In the large south plaza, the walls and altar of a kiva were painted in successive layers with multicolored murals of ceremonial figures, symbols, birds. animals, and religious paraphernalia. The museum removed these murals for preservation and study. After excavation, the kiva was reconstructed, and accurate reproductions of the paintings were placed on its walls, where they may be viewed today.

The museum also administers the ruins of Fort Sumner, a military post of the 1860s that was used as a nightmare reservation for captive Apache and Navaho from 1863 to 1868. The post, built along an Indian pathway in 1862, is situated east of the present-day town of Fort Sumner. After abandonment as a reservation in 1869, the buildings were sold in 1871. The cutting of the Pecos River and a major flood in 1914 reduced the adobe walls to the mere outline seen today. Celebrating a century of progress since those dismal days, the Navaho held a year of commemorative observances in 1968. Among these was a reenactment of the trek to Fort Sumner. The post was made a state monument in 1968 and dedicated in 1970.

See Wesley L. Bliss, "Preservation of the Kuaua Mural Paintings," *American Antiquity* (January 1948); Ely Dittert et al., *New Mexico Historic Sites* (1967); Bertha P. Dutton, *Let's Explore: Indian Villages Past and Present* (1970) and *Sun Father's Way: The Kiva Murals of Kuaua* (1963); Edgar L. Hewitt, "Prehistoric Frescoes in the Rio Grande Valley," *Papers, School of American Research* (1938); Edgar L. Hewitt and Reginald G. Fisher, *Mission Monuments of New Mexico* (1943); Paul Reiter, *The Jémez Pueblo of Unshagi* (1938); Julia K. Shishkin, *An Early History of The Museum of New Mexico, Fine Arts Building* (1968); John L. Sinclair, "The Story of the Pueblo of Kuaua," *El Palacio* (1951); and Paul A. F. Walter, *The Cities That Died of Fear* (1931).—B. P. D. and M. L.

museums of anthropology. The history of ethnological collecting in the West may be said to have begun when Melchior Diaz, the Spanish commander of Culiacan in New Spain, found and sent to the viceroy a "long colored wig from the hair" of some animals like large Spanish hounds, which some southwestern Indians, possibly Zuñi, were said to shear.

Although the Spaniards moved into the Southwest in the sixteenth century and plied the Pacific Coast with their ships, whatever anthropological and natural-history collecting they may have done was so incidental to their main purposes as to make it insignificant. It was the eighteenth-century scientific expeditions of a Frenchman, the Count of Péruse, and a Spaniard, Alejandro Malaspina, in California and the Pacific Northwest that inaugurated systematic investigation of western Indians. James Cook's landing among the Northwest Coast Indians in 1778 and the opening there of trade in otter pelts ultimately brought New England trading ships to northwestern shores. Their captains gathered ethnological specimens and took them home to rest in the Museum of the East India Marine Society, today the Peabody Museum of Salem, Massachusetts.

Various scientific, exploratory, and cartographical expeditions in the first half of the nineteenth century collected archaeological, ethnological, and natural-history materials incidental to their main purposes. In the second half of the century, and especially with the creation of the Bureau of American Ethnology within the Smithsonian Institution in 1879, the gathering of museum materials relating to American Indians gained full federal sanction.

Today's student of the aboriginal West has at his disposal several large collections of native American material culture, most of it dating from the nineteenth century and much of it originating east of the Mississippi River. The National Museum of Natural History, part of the Smithsonian Institution, has an outstanding collection of ethnological materials and archaeological specimens from virtually every section of the West. The Textile Museum, in Washington, D. C., has good American Indian materials, and the Indian Arts and Crafts Board of the Department of the Interior, also in Washington, has a small museum of contemporary arts and crafts.

The two most important collections in New York City are at the HEYE FOUNDATION, MUSEUM OF THE AMERICAN INDIAN, and the American Museum of Natural History. Both have large holdings in ethnological and archaeological materials, and both thoroughly cover the western United States. The Brooklyn Museum has American Indian collections, as does the Museum of Primitive Art.

In Massachusetts the two principal repositories of western anthropological materials are the Peabody Museum of Archaeology and Ethnology at Harvard University in Cambridge and the archaeology and anthropology museum of the Robert S. Peabody Foundation for Archaeology in Andover. The Peabody Museum of Salem and its Northwest Coast collections has already been mentioned. In New Jersey there is another fine Northwest Coast collection at the Princeton University Museum of Natural History.

Chicago's Field Museum of Natural History is the great Illinois repository, while the Museum of the University of Michigan at Ann Arbor has important archaeological and ethnobotanical holdings. In eastern Canada, the National Museum of Canada in Ottawa and the Royal Ontario Museum in Toronto have both archaeological and ethnological specimens relating to western North America.

In the West itself most states have collections representative of at least their immediate area. In California the major anthropological holdings are at the Lowie Museum of Anthropology at the University of California at Berkeley, the Southwest Museum in Los Angeles, the LOS ANGELES COUNTY MUSEUM OF NATURAL HISTORY, also in Los Angeles, and the San Diego Museum of Man in San Diego. The H. M. de Young Memorial Museum in San Francisco's Golden Gate Park has a good, if small, collection of prehistoric and historic southwestern Indian textiles.

In Washington the Thomas Burke Memorial Washington State Museum in Seattle is the largest. The Portland Art Museum in Oregon boasts the Rasmussen collection of northwestern tribal art. In western Canada there are the Provincial Museum of Natural History and Anthropology in Victoria, British Columbia; the Museum of Anthropology of the University of British Columbia in Vancouver; the Glenbow-Alberta Institute in Calgary, Alberta; and the Museum of Natural History in Regina, Saskatchewan.

Arizona has four museums with major archaeological and ethnological holdings: the Arizona State Museum in Tucson; the Amerind Foundation, Inc., at Dragoon; the Heard Museum in Phoenix; and the Museum of Northern Arizona in Flagstaff. New Mexico has its MUSEUM OF NEW MEXICO, Institute of American Indian Art, School of American Research, and Museum of Navaho Ceremonial Art (see TL'AH HASTIIN), all in Santa Fe; and the Maxwell Museum of Anthropology in Albuquerque. In Colorado are the University of Colorado Museum in Boulder, the Denver Art Museum and Denver Museum of Natural History, and the TAYLOR MUSEUM in Colorado Springs.

Rounding out the picture for the Far West are the Utah Museum of Natural History at the University of Utah in Salt Lake City; the Nevada State Museum in Carson City; the Wyoming State Museum in Cheyenne; the Sioux Indian Museum and Crafts Center in Rapid City, South Dakota; and the Museum of the Plains Indian and Crafts Center at Browning, Montana.

Oklahoma has the Southern Plains Indian Museum and Crafts Center at Anadarko; Woolaroc Museum at Bartlesville (see Frank PHILLIPS); Stovall Museum of Science and History at the University of Oklahoma in Norman; and Tulsa's Thomas Gilcrease Institute of American History and Art and the Philbrook Art Center (see Thomas GILCREASE). There are at least a half-dozen additional museums in this state devoted to particular Indian tribes.

Large collections in Texas can be found at the Texas Memorial Museum in Austin and at the AMON CARTER MUSEUM OF WESTERN ART in Fort Worth.

Many western Indian tribes are developing museums of their own. In Arizona, for example, the Navaho, the Hopi, the Pima, the Colorado River tribes (Mohave and Chemehuevi), and the Western Apache on the Fort Apache reservation have different kinds of museums and "culture centers." The National Park Service is responsible for the administration of large numbers of prehistoric Indian ruins as NATIONAL PARKS AND MONUMENTS throughout the West, especially in the Southwest. For the student interested in learning the prehistory and history of American Indians through a study of their material culture, there is an abundance of data. —B. L. F.

music, western. Music in the West was primarily for entertainment or diversion. It had basic themes: the cowboy, the miner, the Mormons, the homesteaders, and even the buffalo hunters. All the songs and music carry Anglo musical characteristics. The tunes were usually those brought from the home state of the singer.

The music first heard in the West was that of the American Indian, followed by Spanish and Mexican music. Indian music had no influence on western music, and even though the Spanish-Mexican culture was the most dominant factor in determining the dress, tools, working knowledge, and terminology of the cowboy, it made very little impact on his musical expression. The vaquero songs were as popular among the Spanish-American-Mexican as were the cowboy songs among the Anglos, but they required singing and playing techniques that were and are difficult to master if one has not been reared in the tradition.

A trail driver once wrote that "it was a poor cow outfit that did not have in its equipment at least one fiddle or banjo, and a man who could play the same. Some played well, and others not so good." The popular image of a guitar-playing cowboy is without nineteenth-century foundation: the banjo and fiddle were the popular instruments of the cowboy. They were both small and could be carried more easily than a guitar. In addition, they were traditional instruments of the South, the original home of most of the cowboys. Both instruments were good for dances, a popular form of entertainment for the cowboy. If no instrument was available, he clapped his hands and stomped his feet. No matter what

the source of the rhythm, he danced—alone if necessary. And he sang.

The fiddle was the musical instrument of the frontier. Normally it was a rhythm, solo instrument, rather than an instrument used to accompany a singer. The fiddle was the dance band; many frontier dances were centered around it, along with clapping hands and stomping feet. This relationship with dancing caused the more fundamental church members to name the fiddle "the devil's instrument." Condemnation of "dancin' " and "fiddlin' " came with the arrival of churches and settled communities.

One cowboy wrote that he learned to play the fiddle when he was young, and that there were two tunes that he could play "to perfection, one of which was 'Seesaw,' the other was 'Sawsee.' " This is an indication of the cowboy's fiddling style, "sawin' on the fiddle," that is, playing a simple melody by fingering and bowing on one string at a time. Actually, the bowing technique was only the more obvious characteristic of the style. The short movement of the bow over one string, the stiff bowing arm and wrist movements, breaking the sound with each note, the placement of the fiddle more on the chest than under the chin, and the strict adherence to the melody line were what created the "sawin' " fiddling style. The western-swing style of the twentieth century is almost a complete reversal: the bowing arm and wrist are used with a heavy, continuous swing movement, the fiddle placement and fingering is in the style of the violinist, the method of bowing two strings for harmonic notes is common, and a rapid flowing movement of the bow is necessary. Also, the degree of melodic improvisation— almost to the extreme of not recognizing the tune— shows the skill of the modern swing fiddler.

Rosin for the bow, necessary for a good tune, was hard to obtain on the frontier, so the fiddler let the rosin accumulate on his instrument. When he needed more rosin for the bow, he simply ran the bow beneath the strings over the rosin on the fiddle. Also, it was believed that rosin on the fiddle improved the sound, a belief doubtlessly derived from the practice of rosin economy. Although in recent times rosin has become easily obtainable, it is still not uncommon to see old-time fiddlers with white powdered rosin accumulated just above the bridge of the fiddle.

The most popular fiddle tune on the western frontier was "The Arkansas Traveler," which, though it had a strong dance rhythm, was often performed as a humorous talk number. Following a run through the melody, the fiddler would stop and usually speak about Arkansas. The dialog was between a stranger and an Arkansas farmer, and the jokes exchanged were ageless. The most widely spread joke was when the stranger asked the farmer, "Why don't you fix your roof?" The farmer responds, "Can't when it's rainin'. Don't need it when it's dry."

Other typical fiddle tunes were "Dinah Had a Wooden Leg," "Shake That Wooden Leg," "Give the Fiddler a Dram," "Turkey in the Straw," "Sugar in the Gourd," and "Irish Washer Woman." The names of fiddle tunes, such as "Hell Among the Yearlings," "Tulsy Waltz," and "Fort Smith Rag," as well as the words to ballads, were often changed locally or influenced by occupation as they traveled across the country.

The other popular instrument of the West, the banjo,

was of southern mountain origin. It was used more as the seconding or accompanying instrument to the fiddle or the voice, however, than as a solo instrument.

The songs of the cowboys were those that were popular in the South prior to the Civil War. Since the cowboy usually was a southern product, his musical heritage was southern. Ballads such as "Barbara Allen" and "Green Grow the Lilacs" were popular. Most were adaptations of old ballads and popular songs of English, Irish, and Scottish origin.

As the cowboy occupation developed and expanded following the Civil War, cow-country music slowly grew. The songs of the late 1860s, such as the "Chisholm Trail" and "The Cowboy's Life Is a Very Dreary Life," dealt specifically with the cowboy's life and work. They were usually rather simple with a personal point of view. The cowboy often set his stories to traditional tunes; an example is the ballad "Streets of Laredo," or "The Cowboy's Lament," which was derived from "The Unfortunate Rake," a British broadside.

Although the ballads were more for cowboy camp entertainment than for singing to the cattle (as has so often been written by the second generation of cowboys), many songs were sung to accompany the cowboy's labors. These were usually the night herders' songs, which quieted the restless cattle at night. Church songs and hymns were popular for cattle songs, and occasionally a fiddle would be played to quiet or soothe the cattle and let them know that a cowboy was nearby. Daytime work, in spite of romanticized concepts, was hard, dusty work that did not encourage singing. The exception was daytime guarding of the herd or slow riding away from the cattle. Songs sung during the day were often loud yells that would stir up lazy cattle and keep them moving. Roundup, branding, trail driving, and other cowboy tasks were hard, unrhythmical, and unromantic jobs. The bunkhouse, the cow camp, the bars, and guarding the cattle provided opportunities for singing.

Obscene songs were popular among the cowboys. Most cowboys who wrote about their music and most collectors of cowboy songs subtly mention that the words would scorch the paper if they were printed. The romanticized cowboy is never depicted as being vulgar. The working cowboy was. When an old-time singer of cowboy songs was asked if he ever sang dirty songs to the cattle, he indignantly replied, "No! We sang church songs to the cattle. Those ugly songs were sung to men in bars and after stag dances."

The romanticized attitudes and songs were based on reminiscences and stories told by sons of the first cowboys long after the trail drives and hardships of the early range-cattle industry were over. In the late 1800s work was still hard and the traditions of the first generation endured, but it was also a time that allowed some retrospective contemplation. Many songs were written during this period that were quickly absorbed into range-cattle industry lore, but only after the industry had matured.

The composers of many ballads are known. Charles Badger CLARK, Jr., D. J. O'Malley, N. Howard "Jack" Thorp, Larry Chittenden, and Curly Fletcher were among cowboy songwriters. Thorp wrote "Little Joe the Wrangler," one of the most popular ballads. In 1898 Thorp was trailing cattle from Chimney Lake, New Mexico, to Higgins, Texas; one night by the lonely light of the campfire he wrote on a paper sack the story of

"Little Joe." It had just enough sentimentality to appeal to all cowboys, and many remembered Little Joe or someone like him and the event or an event just like the one that killed Little Joe. Thorp collected nineteen cowboy songs and wrote five others that were published in a small paperback volume, *Songs of the Cowboy* (1908). This was the first published book of cowboy songs and included some of the best traditional songs, such as "Sam Bass," "Zebra Dun," and "Cowboy's Lament."

In 1910 John A. LOMAX had his collection published as *Cowboy Songs and Other Frontier Ballads.* He included as traditional songs some written by Thorp. The Lomax book was so popular that many singers learned or polished their songs to the versions published in his volume.

Cowboy themes and rhythms were as varied as the background of the industry. Cattle, horses, roping, and riding, the bases of "cowboying," were the heart of the songs and ballads. Outlaws, lost love, death on the Plains, and occasionally Indians were additional topics.

"I Ride An Old Paint" is a slow, calm ballad that supposedly was sung to the walking gait of the horse while the cowboy soothed the cattle. In contrast to the slow songs were the bronc-riding songs: "The Zebra Dun," or "Z-Bar Dun," represented the bronc rider in the form of a learned man who was placed on the meanest horse. The cowboys expected him to be thrown:

> But the stranger he was growed there just like the camel's hump;
> The stranger sat upon him and curled his black mustache,
> Just like a summer boarder waiting for his hash.

"The Zebra Dun" typifies the practical joke that the cowboy would play on a greenhorn. His humor was rough and dangerous; only the strong and determined man could withstand it, much less the work.

Another riding song of later vintage is "The Strawberry Roan." The poem, written in the 1920s by cowboy poet Curly Fletcher, was quickly set to music and accepted by the cattlemen as an old cowboy song. Recordings were made and Gene Autry sang a variation in his movie of the same title. This song was parodied into a rodeo "bull-riding" ballad, "The Flying U Twister," or "The Bad Brahma Bull." The theme is the same in both versions; only the setting changes. The cowboy with confidence sets out to ride the horse or bull that looks easy to ride only to be treated to the wildest ride of his career:

> I figure I'm ridin' the hurricane deck
> of a cyclone and tornado havin' a wreck;
> He's the worst bucker I've seen on the range,
> He'll land on a nickel and give you the change.
>
> . . . . . .
>
> Well, I turns over twice and I comes back to earth,
> And I sets there a'cussin' the day of his birth.
> But I says there's some horses that I cannot ride,
> There's some of them livin', boys, they haven't all died.

The rodeo is an extension of the range-cattle industry, with the lore, traditions, and songs of the industry changed to fit the arena and event. Rodeo songs, however, are not as well known as the industry songs. Roping songs do not seem to be as prevalent as riding songs, probably because the excitement and action are not as obvious and spectacular as bronc riding, and the cowboy did not have the same relationship with the cattle that he had with his horse. "Windy Bill," or "The Black Steer," is about the bragging cowboy who could rope and tie any steer. The other cowboys knew a black steer, "a sort of an old outlaw." Bill threw his loop and made his catch around the steer's horn, but the saddle cinches broke from the steer's strength.

Bill landed in a big rock-pile;
His hands and face were scratched;
He 'lowed he always could tie a steer
But guessed he'd found his match.

The rodeo version was adapted to Bob "Wild Horse" Crosby in 1947 by Ray Reed. While the theme, action, and results remained the same, this time it was written as a tribute to the greatest of all steer ropers.

With his Crosby bit and his Crosby tree,
His chaps and spurs to boot,
And his old nylon tied hard and fast,
Bob swore he'd get the brute.

Death always confronted the cowboy: a rattlesnake, a prairie dog hole, a blizzard, a stampede, a shoot out. Death and a lonely prairie burial were realities. Many of the songs of the West reflected the cowboy's concern.

I wish to be laid where a mother's care
And a sister's tear can mingle there;
Where friends can come and weep o'er me;
Oh, bury me not on the lone prairie.

"The Dying Cowboy," or "Oh, Bury Me Not On the Lone Prairie," was an adaptation of the popular song "The Ocean Burial," written by Edwin H. Chapin in the late 1830s. It is another example of parody or adaptation from one setting to another and of how time, tradition, and travel condense and smooth a song into simple and easily remembered verses.

Sacrificial heroic death appealed to the romantic nature of the cowboy, and the story "Utah Carroll," concerning a young cowboy who died under the hoofs of a stampeding herd as he saved the boss's daughter, "Lenore," from being trampled to death, was popular.

I rode into the circle and I knew his life
    She was o'er,
But still I hears him a-cryin', 'Lay still,
    I'll get you, Lenore.'

Outlaws and badmen were all too often cowboys, who as victims of changing times had gone bad. After the range-cattle industry changed from open range and trail herding traditions to fenced ranches, those cowboys who could not adapt to the new ways often became outlaws. While this is probably more fiction than fact, the cowboy did protect the law breakers through his willingness to give each man another chance, a practice that is still observed. They were friends and the cow-

puncher enjoyed singing about them. "Sam Bass," "Jesse James," and "Billy the Kid," written by Thorp, were among the most well-known.

Since Indians and cowboys were usually enemies, not many ballads mention Indians; not with favor that is. One, "Billie Vanero," tells the story of a cowboy who rides to warn his sweetheart and neighboring ranchers about Apache raids. He is wounded and writes a note:

From a branch, a twig he broke
Then he dipped his pen of oak
In the warm blood that was spurting
From a wound below his heart.

"Beware before it is too late
Apache warriors lie in wait."
Then he tied himself to the saddle
And gave his horse the rein.

They were warned in time, but Billie Vanero "was asleep" and "Poor Bessie could not wake him, if she tried forever more."

It was the singing cowboy who preserved the song about the buffalo hunter. This short-lived occupation was far from being romantic, and its participants were rough, tough men. Often cowboys joined a hunt in order to earn fast money. One of the greatest ballads to come from the West was "The Range of the Buffalo," or "The Buffalo Skinners," originally a lumber chantey that had undergone several occupational transitions, the best version being the buffalo-hunter adaptation. In the summer of 1873 a group agreed to hunt buffalo with "a man by the name of Crego." The dangers, the work, the food, and the lack of wages were too much for the crew.

The season being near over, old Crego he did say,
The crowd had been extravagant, was in debt to him
    that day.
We coaxed him and we begged him and still it was no
    go—
We left old Crego's bones to bleach on the range of the
    buffalo.

The miners' songs spoke of the dangers of travel, the history of the period, and the occupation of placer mining. When the gold fields changed from panning to hard-rock mining, the songs reflected the hazards of hard-rock mining. Parody for entertainment, not work songs, was the source of most of the material. The miner put his words to the popular, familiar songs of the day that he brought with him. Three songs that emerged from the days of the forty-niners and continue in oral tradition are "Joe Bowers," "The Days of '49," and "Sweet Betsy from Pike."

"The Days of '49" was humorously composed and sung a few years after the time that is described, and the words represent the memories about the early reckless days of a man who is happy to be "a bummer" and of the wild friends made during 1849.

Old Tom Moore they call me now
A relic of bygone days.
A bummer too they call me now
But what I care for praise.

. . . . .
There was windy Jake the butcher boy;
He was always getting tight.
When he'd fill up on red eye
He was longing for a fight.

. . . . .

"Sweet Betsy from Pike" was written by John A. Stone, who experienced the problems of the day and committed them to song. He published a collection of his songs, *Puts' Original California Songster* in 1855; "Sweet Betsy" appeared in the second edition in 1858. The song is a humorous account of the problems faced by those who traveled overland; it continues to enjoy popularity.

"Joe Bowers" was a legend in song. A typical miner who left home in Pike County, Missouri, to find a fortune in the gold fields, Bowers left the girl he loved behind. He worked hard and saved his gold for his "Sally," only to be told that she had proved to be untrue and had married a redheaded "butcher." This popular theme was an occupational hazard for the adventuresome man who was willing to risk all for the chance of unlimited success on the frontier.

The religious fervor that drove members of the Church of Jesus Christ of Latter-day Saints westward away from persecution proved to be the wellspring of their musical heritage. This same religious fervor, however, brought musical ridicule from the critics and enemies of the faithful. Another theme expressed in the songs was the hardships experienced in establishing their mecca in Utah. Mormon music is both secular and religious, and much history is narrated through it.

One of the most traditional songs of faith is "Come, Come, Ye Saints," written in the late 1840s by William Clayton, secretary to Brigham Young. It was set to the music of the popular religious song "All Is Well," and it provided the renewal of faith that helped the Saints complete their westward trek.

Come, come, ye Saints, no toil nor labor fear,
But with joy wend your way,
Though hard to you, this journey may appear,
Grace shall be as your day.
'Tis better far for us to strive
Our useless cares from us to drive.
Do this and joys your hearts will swell,
All is well, all is well!

"The Handcart Song" tells of the movement of impoverished European immigrants and converts who, with the direction of Brigham Young and with the help of experienced guides, pushed and pulled handcarts across the continent to the Great Salt Lake. Other songs spoke about Brigham Young, polygamy, and tragedy. "The Mountain Meadows Massacre" narrated the massacre of the Fancher emigrant train in 1857 near Cedar City, Utah, where Mormons killed approximately 125 people in the train. It condemned the massacre and gained traditional acceptance by Mormons and Gentiles throughout the West.

The songs that ridiculed the Mormons were usually Gentile songs, but not always, for the Mormons were able to see humor and mistakes among themselves. Those critical, usually humorous, songs were most often sung about the male ratio to and relationship with wom-

en. Obscene variations were rarely printed, but often sung. One such song which is still in oral tradition is "The Mormon Cowboy," the story of a woman who did not find a "real man" until she met and married a Mormon cowboy. It describes the physical characteristics and abilities of the Mormon cowboy with the terminology of the rough frontiersman. Mormon music provides one of the greatest sources of song in the entire history of the United States.

Another source of western songs was the farmer. When the western lands were opened to homesteaders, the farmers moved with the sounds of their traditional music. From their experiences came songs such as "Starving to Death on a Government Claim" and "The Little Old Sod Shanty on My Claim."

I'm looking rather seedy now while holding down my claim,
My victuals are not always of the best;
And the mice play shyly round me as I nestle down to rest,
In my little old sod shanty on my claim.

The music of the farmer was based on the same familiar traditional songs and hymns that set the pattern in cowboy music. Farm music was not work music, with the exception of that sung on cotton farms by the field hands, who were often migratory and carried southern musical traditions.

As mechanization began to displace field hands, the migratory farm laborer became less and less important. Little collecting of traditional lore has been done among these people. However, one voice sang out about the troubles of the migratory people in the 1930s. Woody GUTHRIE was born near Okemah, Oklahoma, in 1912, and in 1929 moved to Pampa, Texas. There he experienced the hard years of the Dust Bowl and wrote many songs about the times. Although Guthrie and the migrants blamed their plight on the dust and drought, their problems were far more complex and probably stemmed from the collapse of the cotton economy.

In 1937 Guthrie migrated to Los Angeles, California, and sang his Dust Bowl songs and migrant songs over station KFVD. His music was and is the only voice to speak for the migrant farm laborer. Guthrie was the best-known American folk-song composer. He was a poet of the people who set his poems to traditional tunes, and he was the leading influence in the urban folk revival of the 1960s.

Cowboy songs and western music changed during the early decades of the twentieth century. The written ballads gained traditional status through the efforts of Thorp and Lomax, and in the 1920s the recording industry introduced many singers and new songs. While traditional cowboy songs and singing are not dead, they have been changed by the recording and radio industries. The Sears Roebuck catalog had tremendous impact on the music of the West; by simply looking through the catalog, any rural citizen could purchase his own records, song books, radios, guitar instruction books, and guitars.

RCA Victor recorded numerous western songs and singers during the 1920s, including such old favorites as Vernon Dalhart, Jules Verne Allen, Eck Robertson, Carl T. Sprague, and Harry "Mac" McClintock. Their records were popular and helped stabilize the words to many songs.

Commercial radio stations were established in the early 1920s. The first such station west of the Mississippi was 5XT in Oklahoma City. In 1924 KFRU in Bristow, Oklahoma, started broadcasting and became commercial in 1925. In 1928 the station moved to Tulsa as KVOO and became a leader in broadcasting western music. One of the early western bands to broadcast over the station in 1924 was Otto Gray and His Oklahoma Cowboys. The popularity of this Stillwater, Oklahoma, cowboy band was so great that soon it was broadcasting out of Kansas City. The letters were numerous and the air coverage was extended throughout the Midwest and Southwest. Otto Gray then toured the nation for ten years playing western songs.

In 1929 Gene Autry made his first recording, and a new influence on western music was introduced. Born in Tioga, Texas, he later moved with his family to a ranch in southern Oklahoma and as a young man worked as a telegrapher in various Oklahoma railroad towns. In 1928 and 1929 Autry performed over KVOO in Tulsa as "Oklahoma's Singing Cowboy." He went to Chicago and sang for the WLS "Barn Dance," where he starred from 1930 to 1934. He was soon recorded on the Sears label, and the Sears catalog began advertising a Gene Autry guitar.

Autry's first recordings were blues songs in the style of Jimmie Rogers, whose influence in country-western music was immense. In 1933 Autry recorded western songs, and in 1934 he sang in a Ken Maynard film. This western movie kicked open a new door for him; soon Republic Studio had made him into a singing cowboy star. Western music and the cowboy guitar for many fans became the songs and style of Gene Autry.

Ken Maynard was the first cowboy star to sing western traditional songs on the screen. In 1930 he played his first fiddle and sang in *Songs of the Saddle*, but it was really the Autry movies that set the pattern for the musical western on the screen. Roy Rogers, Tex Ritter, Eddie Dean, Jimmy Wakely, and Johnny Bond were a few of the other cowboy movie singers who followed Autry.

Supporting musical groups were too numerous to mention, but two well-known groups attracted viewers to the movies: the Sons of the Pioneers and Bob Wills and His Texas Playboys. Although most bands were organized for a specific movie, gained no fame or following, and were disbanded as soon as the filming was completed, these two groups remained stable and popular.

In 1929 the most important influence to appear in country-western music was a black-face fiddler in a traveling medicine show around Fort Worth, Texas. Bob Wills was born in Limestone County, Texas, and grew up in Hall County. He was the son and grandson of old-time fiddlers. After unsuccessfully working at a variety of occupations he joined the medicine show. During one show he met and teamed up with Herman Arnspiger, who as a Texas farm boy had learned to play the guitar from a Sears catalog guitar book. The two played for house parties and dances around Fort Worth as the Wills Fiddlin' Band. They were joined by a cigar salesman turned singer, Milton Brown. As the Alladin Laddies the three men played over WBAP, Fort Worth.

In the fall of 1930 W. Lee O'Daniel of the Burrus Mill and Elevator Company sponsored them; on January 1, 1931, as the Light Crust Doughboys they went on the air over KFJZ, Fort Worth, and western-swing music was given birth.

Milton Brown left the group in 1932 and formed his own band, Milton Brown and His Musical Brownies. Wills left in 1933 and with his brother, Johnnie Lee, Tommy Duncan, and three other musicians organized the Playboys in Waco, Texas. In 1934 they moved to WKY in Oklahoma City and played five programs before O'Daniel bought the air time and forced them out. They traveled to Tulsa, and on February 9, 1934, they broadcast their first program over KVOO. Bob Wills and His Texas Playboys were on the air.

Wills's music was dance music. It had a strong rhythm for dancing and was patterned after the swing-jazz bands of the late 1920s. He used a forceful swing sound on the fiddle that is heard in most country music today. It is not unusual to hear "old-time" fiddlers play the fiddle tunes exactly as Wills recorded them or played them over KVOO. Wills introduced drums to country-western music, and he used brass and woodwind instruments as he constantly worked at improving and changing the sound of his band. Western-swing fiddling differs from other styles in its dependence on a strong rhythm section to carry the rhythm while the fiddler embellishes the tune. Other types of fiddling are characterized by the fiddler setting and maintaining the rhythm while the back-up instruments follow the tune.

Tommy Duncan, vocalist for the Playboys, sang with a phrasing style that is now heard in the singing of many country, western, and popular singers. The Wills band added many songs to the repertory of western music, including "San Antonio Rose." And the steel guitar became prominent through the playing of Leon McAuliff, who joined Wills in 1934. The Texas Playboys' influence on the sounds of country-western music has been greater than any other performer or group.

Wills took some of the Playboys to Hollywood in 1940 for a movie career, and in Tulsa Johnnie Lee and His Boys continued the KVOO daily noon broadcast under the sponsorship of General Mills until 1958. It was the longest regularly broadcast weekday radio program in the nation, having remained on the air for twenty-five years.

Wills did not use fancy clothes as did other groups. This influence came from eastern ideas about western dress, and it was seen more frequently in country-music groups than among western musicians.

Cowboy singing-fiddle playing evolved into western-swing, which by 1955 had passed as a popular musical form for dancing. Other swing musicians were Spade Cooley, Tex Williams, Leon McAuliff, and Pee Wee King.

Black musicians in the West were more influential in style than in song. Black cowboys were contributors to the growth and transmission of cowboy songs, but it was in blues and jazz that their significant influence developed.

Many of the traveling swing and jazz bands stopped over or broke up in Oklahoma City during the late 1920s and early 1930s, and the young black musicians in the community were greatly influenced by these "stranded" professionals. During the same period black students were being inspired and taught in the classical music tradition by Zelia Breux, an Oklahoma City schoolteacher, who with her devotion to music and young people influenced many outstanding black musicians. These musicians combined their formal training with the informal influence and training of the jazz men. In the late '20s a band was organized as the Blue Devils, which developed such nationally known singers and instrumentalists as Jimmy Rushing and Harry Youngblood. Many of the Blue Devils merged with Benny Moten's band in Kansas City, which, after Moten's death in 1935, became the world-renowned Count Basie band. It was this group that ultimately exerted local influence on changing musical styles.

The greatest single contribution came from jazz guitarist Charles "Charlie" Christian, who was born in Bonham, Texas, in 1919. Shortly after his birth, the Christian family moved to Oklahoma City, were he learned music from his parents, brothers, and the community musicians. His two older brothers, Edward and Clarence, were excellent instrumentalists on the piano and bass; Edward had been one of the original Blue Devils. After trying various instruments, Christian settled on the guitar. He worked at making the guitar a solo instrument, not just a rhythm instrument. His style was built around melodic chord progressions combined with single string notation for solo instrumentation. Also, he amplified his guitar, a jazz innovation. By the age of eighteen, Christian was being mentioned in jazz circles around the nation. Benny Goodman, following the advice of Mary Lou Williams, invited Charlie to join his band in 1939. For the next three years, Christian's guitar style was heard primarily through the Goodman Sextet, during which time he experimented with melody improvisation. Christian died of tuberculosis in 1942. Today jazz guitar techniques are expansions of the Christian style; in 1956 the "Musicians' Musicians Poll" elected him as the greatest jazz guitarist ever.

Western music is the music of the nation. Its background was primarily the music of the Anglo-Saxon world, and its counterinfluence changed the musical tastes of the country. (See also MUSIC ABOUT THE WEST.)

The study of cowboy ballads should start with N. Howard "Jack" Thorp, *Songs of the Cowboys* (1908), reprinted with commentary in 1966. The collection was expanded and published under the same title in 1921. Thorp's *Pardner of the Wind* (1945) is also an important source. Although John A. Lomax is as important to cowboy ballads as is Thorp, Lomax's influence extends to all American folk-music studies. See Lomax, *Cowboy Songs and Other Frontier Ballads* (1910), revised and enlarged in 1916; *Songs of the Cattle Trail and Cow Camp* (1919); and John A. Lomax and Alan Lomax, *Cowboy Songs and Other Frontier Ballads* (1938), a joint revision of the earlier volume. The publications of Austin E. Fife and Alta S. Fife are excellent studies and collections about Mormon lore and cowboy lore. See their *Saints of Sage and Saddle* (1956); *Songs of the Cowboys by N. Howard Thorp* (1966); *Heaven on Horseback* (1970); and *Cowboy and Western Songs* (1969). See also Jules Verne Allen, *Cowboy Lore* (1933); Margaret Larkin, *Singing Cowboy* (1931); and Richard E. Lingenfelter, Richard A. Dwyer, and David Cohen, *Songs of the American West* (1968).

Periodical articles by J. Frank Dobie, Austin Fife, John I. White, and many other scholars are available in two Texas Folklore Society Publications, *Journal of the American Folklore Society* and *Western Folklore*.

Other books of interest that deal with specific subjects include Eleanora Black and Sidney Robertson, *The Gold Rush Song Book* (1940); Richard A. Dwyer, Richard E. Lingenfelter, and David Cohen, *The Songs of the Gold Rush* (1964); Woody Guthrie, *American Folksong* (1947); Bill C. Malone, *Country Music U.S.A.* (1968); and Robert Shelton and Burt Goldblatt, *The Country Music Story* (1966).

There are many excellent recordings. Some of the best can be purchased from the Library of Congress, including field recordings of old-time cowboys collected by John A. Lomax and Alan Lomax. Available from other sources are "Authentic Cowboys and Their Western Songs"; Kenneth Goldstein, ed., "The Unfortunate Rake"; Woody Guthrie, "Dust Bowl Ballads"; L. M. Hilton, "Mormon Folk Songs"; and Henry Jackson, "The Cowboy: His Songs, Ballads, and Brag Talk."—G. L.

music about the West. The frontier experience has furnished important thematic material for music, ranging from operas and symphonies to popular and folk songs. Sometimes the themes have reflected the frontier process itself—moving westward, settling in the wilderness, breaking new land, and creating a new society. In other instances, they deal with types of life and work in the West. But since life in the West was often inseparable from the frontier process, musical treatments of the West can be considered as expressions of the frontier environment.

Western themes are most often associated with music for the theater—opera, light opera, musical theater, and dance. "Program music," or symphonic music that tells a story, also frequently employs frontier motifs. Music for the stage has concentrated largely on three western topics: mining, agriculture, and Indians.

By far the most famous opera based on life in a mining camp is Giacomo Puccini's *La Fanciulla del West (Girl of the Golden West*, 1910), adapted from David Belasco's play of the same name. Minnie, the eponymous heroine, embodies the hardy self-reliance of the frontier woman in her various roles as saloonkeeper, Bible-class teacher, gambler, and horsewoman. The story concerns her love for a highwayman and her saving him from lynching. When she persuades the mob to exercise Christian charity, the redeemed lover rides off with Minnie into the golden West.

Puccini adorned this plot with music that captured the flavor of the mining West. He emphasized the masculinity of mining communities by assigning sixteen of the eighteen solo roles to men—ten to baritones and basses. The all-male chorus sings entirely in octaves or in unison, underscoring the primitive nature of the miners. Puccini simulated the rawness of setting and action with such musical directions as *allegro feroca, allegro brutale, allegro incisivo, come gridi* ("like shouts"), *con strazio* ("tearing"), and *rubusto*. In addition, he used authentic folk tunes and composed original themes in the folk vein. For Wowkle, the squaw, Puccini created a lullaby based on a text of original Indian words.

The American composer Douglas Moore also chose a mining theme for an opera. His *The Ballad of Baby Doe* (1956) rivals Puccini for musical excitement and surpasses him in authenticity. It is based on the life of H. A. W. Tabor and his wife, Baby Doe. It incorporates the dramatic story of the silver strike at Leadville, Colorado;

Tabor's divorce from the prim Augusta; his marriage to Baby Doe; the collapse of silver; Bryan's 1896 campaign; and Tabor's unshaken faith that silver would rebuild their fortune. The opera's language is mining-camp dialogue, and both the melodies and harmonies evoke the primitive strength of the mining frontier.

A musical from the celebrated team of Alan Jay Lerner and Frederick Loewe, *Paint Your Wagon* (1951), recounts the trials of an itinerant miner. The plot also deals with such typical frontier themes as racial prejudice against Mexicans and distaste for Mormon polygamy. Vigorous cancan dancing and the consumption of great quantities of whiskey lend authenticity to the mining camp atmosphere. "I Was Born Under a Wandering Star" and "They Call the Wind Maria" have an unmistakable western spirit.

The most famous Broadway musical with an agrarian setting is *Oklahoma!* (1943), by Richard Rodgers and Oscar Hammerstein. This creation, with its totally integrated story, music, and dancing, was a watershed in that it transcended the genre of musical comedy to establish a new and compelling art form, best described as musical theater. Based on the play *Green Grow the Lilacs* by Lynn RIGGS, *Oklahoma!* deals with the simple farmers and ranchers of the Southwest. Its lyrics abound with the folk idiom, and although the score never employs authentic folk tunes, it captures their ebullience and optimism. Few can forget the thundering refrain of the title song, "We know we belong to the land, and the land we belong to is grand!"

No aspect of the West has inspired more operatic composition than the Indian, yet no Indian opera has attained permanent success. Certainly, no American subject has more innate drama than the white man's conquest of Indians, and few themes would offer composers more opportunity to employ native melodies and other exotic effects. Consequently, this remains a musical field where significant creative work may still be done. Among those who have composed Indian operas are Victor Herbert (*Natoma*, 1911) and Charles W. Cadman (*Shanewis*, 1918). Cadman also devoted a considerable amount of his creative energy to incorporating Indian themes in his other music. His "Four American-Indian Songs" (1909) includes the famous "At Dawning" and "From the Land of the Sky Blue Water," and his orchestral *Thunderbird Suite* (1914) was inspired by his study of an Omaha Indian reservation.

In the field of symphonic music, such American composers as Aaron Copland, Virgil Thomson, and Roy Harris have incorporated western themes into their work. Copland's *Appalachian Spring* (1944) embodies folk tunes of the mountain pioneers, and his ballet scores or *Billy the Kid* (1938) and *Rodeo* (1942) evoke western atmosphere with jaunty rhythms and harmonies that suggest the openness and rawness of the region. Thomson's *The Plow That Broke the Plains* (1936), drawn from his score for Pare Lorentz's documentary film, uses musical themes associated with farmers as they moved westward to cultivate the Great Plains. Harris was born in a log cabin in Oklahoma, and grew up on a farm in California. His symphonic music has always suggested the virility and harshness of frontier life, especially his *Folk-Song Symphony* (1939). Although a Czech, Anton Dvorák, who served as head of the National Conservatory of Music in New York City (1892-95), was able to invest the melodies and rhythms of his Symphony no. 9 in E minor ("From the New World," 1893) with an unmistakably American quality without actually quoting folk music.

American folk and popular music have celebrated various aspects of the western experience through the years (see MUSIC, WESTERN). The California gold rush's "My Darling Clementine" typified that event, as "The Streets of Laredo" expressed the universal quality of the trail driver's loneliness. That songs about the cowboy have penetrated to the core of the national consciousness was documented when President Franklin D. Roosevelt called "Home on the Range" his favorite song. Other popular cowboy songs that express the western desire for elbow room, openness of the country, and a sense of isolation include "Don't Fence Me In," "Tumbling Tumbleweeds," and "Bury Me Not on the Lone Prairie." A Mormon hymn recounts the Saints' westward flight from persecution and so typifies the impact of the West on their collective experience: "We'll find a place which God for us prepared/ Far away in the West; Where none shall come to hurt or make afraid;/ There the Saints will be blessed."

See H. Wiley Hitchcock, *Music in the United States: A Historical Introduction* (1969); and Walter Rundell, Jr., "The West as an Operatic Setting," in K. Ross Toole, ed., *Probing the American West* (1961).—W. R.

Muskogean language. See INDIAN LANGUAGES: *Muskogean.*

mustang. See HORSE, WILD.

N

Nahl, Charles C. (1818-1878). Nahl was born into a family of artists in Kassel, Germany. With his half-brother, Hugo, he studied art in Paris and in 1849 emigrated to the United States. After a brief sojourn in New York City, the two brothers traveled to California and worked in the gold fields for a few months before resuming their professional pursuits in San Francisco. Between the years of 1850 and 1867 the Nahls worked as commercial photographers and illustrators, producing a few paintings of historical interest on the side. In 1867 Charles secured the patronage of Judge E. B. Crocker, for whom he executed a number of large canvases. During the 1870s his pictures enjoyed a local popularity and at the time of his death Nahl was regarded as one of the leading painters of pioneer life in California.

See Robert Taft, *Artists and Illustrators of the Old West, 1850-1900* (1953).—D. C. H.

Nakai, Raymond (1918-   ). Navaho tribal chairman. Born and raised on the Navaho reservation in Lukachukai, Arizona, Nakai was educated at Fort Wingate and Shiprock Indian schools. He was in the navy during World War II, in the South Pacific.

Nakai was a disk jockey and radio announcer when he ran for tribal council chairman in 1963. As chairman he administered a budget of several million dollars for the 120,000 Navaho, the largest tribe in the United States. Under his administration, several irrigation systems were installed, a hotel-motel-restaurant started, and nine tribal parks, patrolled by Navaho rangers, established. The tribe also started the Navaho Community College, where courses are taught in Navaho and English. The tribal scholarship fund (for attendance at any accredited school) was raised to more than $10 million under Nakai's leadership. Silversmithing and weaving tribally produced wool were encouraged by the Arts and Crafts Guild, and radio broadcasts in Navaho began to be heard even on the transistor radios of sheepherders in the hills.

The production of timber, uranium, crops, and livestock increased under Nakai's administration. So did that of coal, gas, and oil, but they have been the center of great controversy because of pollution, erosion of sacred and other land, and lack of jobs and fair royalty payment for Navaho and Hopi for use of their land. Many industries opened plants on the reservation, including a modern sawmill and forest products factory and a division of a camera company. There was some concern in this instance, too, because in a few of the plants women were hired, and were moved from their families to dormitories for up to two weeks at a time, leaving husbands at home to care for children. Although building factories and "industrial parks" away from towns and villages prevented some pollution in the communities, the effects on family life were bad. If the problems of rapid industrialization can be overcome, the program of economic expansion together with encouragement of tribal values, customs, and arts begun by Nakai can be continued and enlarged.—C. C.

Nana (1815?-?1895). Indian chief. Nana (also known as Nanay) was one of several famous leaders among the Eastern Chiricahua, or Warm Springs Apache. In 1877 Nana, as well as Loco, VICTORIO, and GERONIMO, was moved from the Warm Springs reservation in New Mexico to the San Carlos reservation in Arizona by John P. Clum. Later that same year, Victorio, Nana, and other Warm Springs Apache fled the San Carlos reservation and returned to the Warm Springs reservation, where they remained for two years; when the army tried to return them to San Carlos, they fled once more. This time they attacked ranchers, travelers, and virtually every non-Apache they could find, devastating the country east to the Rio Grande and south to Mexico.

In October 1880, Mexican troops all but annihilated Victorio's band in the Tres Castillos mountains in northern Chihuahua. Victorio was killed, and Nana, who was not with the band at the time, became the leader. Although already elderly and lamed from many wounds suffered in battles with non-Indians, for the next six years he burned his name permanently into the history of the Southwest.

Taking the lead of the survivors, including some Navaho as well as Apache, Nana terrorized parts of Texas, southwestern New Mexico, and northern Chihuahua. In six weeks from mid-July to the end of August 1881, the old warrior and his thirty or forty men rode over more than a thousand miles of New Mexico; killed from thirty to fifty Americans; fought a dozen skirmishes with troops, winning most of them; captured two women and two hundred horses and mules; and successfully eluded the hot pursuit of a thousand soldiers and several hundred civilians.

Nana allied himself with the Southern Chiricahua fighting in Mexico. In 1883, however, he surrendered to General George Crook and went with his people to San Carlos once more. He broke out again in 1885, this time with Geronimo, but he was recaptured along with the families of Geronimo and Nachez early in 1886. Thereafter he was sent to Fort Sill, Oklahoma, where he lived out his days.

See Eve Ball, *In the Days of Victorio* (1970); Jason Betzinez and Wilbur S. Nye, *I Fought with Geronimo* (1959); and Dan L. Thrapp, *The Conquest of Apacheria* (1967).—B. L. F.

Narváez, Pánfilo de (c. 1478-1528). Spanish explorer of Florida. The significance of Narváez lies more in the fame of the survivors of his expedition than in his own accomplishments. One first hears of him in Cuba, in connection with a protest made by the priest Bartolomé de Las Casas against Narváez's cruelty to the Indians there. A few years later Narváez, in Mexico under orders to stop Hernán Cortés in his conquest of Mexico, was attacked by that able commander and taken prisoner. Narváez lost an eye in the process. Ultimately he returned to Spain, testified against Cortés, and received from the king a commission to conquer and colonize Florida.

In 1527 he left Spain with six hundred men. His poor leadership caused so many desertions in Santo Domingo and Cuba, however, that he had not more than four hundred with him when he landed at Tampa Bay on the west coast of Florida in April 1528. It is also possible that a hundred of them stayed behind on the ships.

Narváez led his men north to Apalachee, in the big bend of Florida, treating the Indians with cruelty and receiving their arrows in return. When his ships failed to appear, the survivors constructed crude boats and set out for the Mexican port of Pánuco, which they hoped to reach by sailing westward along the Gulf Coast.

The last episode in Narváez's life known to historians took place somewhere west of the mouth of the Mississippi, where he refused to give aid to another boat, telling the men to save themselves. Of the men finally shipwrecked on Galveston or nearby San Luis Island, only four survived the expedition, of whom CABEZA DE VACA and the black slave Estevanito are best known.

See Morris Bishop, *The Odyssey of Cabeza de Vaca* (1933); Cleve Hallenbeck, *Alvar Núñez Cabeza de Vaca*

(1940); and F. A. Kirkpatrick, *The Spanish Conquistadores* (1962).—R. A. B.

Nashville, Tennessee. Long hunters from 1772 on visited the region on the Cumberland River and about the site of present-day Nashville. This part of the Cumberland valley was lined with salt and sulphur licks. In 1775 Captain De Mumbrunne hunted about Nashville and established his cabin near the present town at a place called Eaton's Station. In 1778 a trading post was established at the "bluffs" on the Cumberland. In 1779 James Robertson led a party of settlers out from the Watauga settlements and established a camp about the French Lick and planted a field of corn. While Robertson and his companions were beginning a settlement, a second party of Wataugans, under the leadership of John Donelson, set out in flatboats, chief of which was the *Adventure*, down the Tennessee River to reach the Cumberland. They left the Watauga Fort on December 22, 1779, and arrived at the bluffs of the Cumberland on April 24, 1780.

In the expeditions of 1779 and 1780 three hundred settlers came to the Cumberland, and in a short time seven stations had been built in the region. The "Bluff Fort" had been established on the high ground overlooking the Cumberland. Eaton's Station was nearby on the north bank of the river, and Freeland's Station was to the west of the lick. The fertile lands about the young settlement were quickly brought into production, and Nashville became a trading and political center for the western part of Tennessee. Here it was that Andrew Jackson came as a fledgling lawyer in 1788. In 1812 the Tennessee legislature met for the first time in the town, but it was not until 1825 that Nashville became the permanent capital of the state.

See Thomas Perkins Abernethy, *From Frontier to Plantation in Tennessee* (1932); Harriette Arnow, *Flowering of the Cumberland* (1963); W. Woodford Clayton, *History of Davidson County, Tennessee* (1880); and James Phelan, *History of Tennessee* (1888).—T. D. C.

Natchez Indians. See NATCHEZ WAR.

Natchez Trace. This famous road through the southwestern wilderness extended approximately five hundred miles from Nashville on the Cumberland River to Natchez on the Mississippi. It passed diagonally across Middle Tennessee, the northwest tip of Alabama, and all the way across Mississippi. At the time it was opened much of the way lay in Choctaw and Chickasaw Indian country. Ostensibly, the road was planned as a land route to the Natchez District and the southwest corner of the republic. General James Wilkinson was charged with the responsibility of negotiating agreements with the Indians to permit this crossing of their territories.

There was signed with the Chickasaw on October 24, 1801, the Treaty of Chickasaw Bluffs, and two months later on December 17, 1801, the Treaty of Fort Adams with the Choctaw. Anticipating that these treaties would be signed, the Mississippi territorial assembly provided for the location and opening of the trace. Commissioners located the road in 1802 south of Natchez to Pinckneyville near the Mississippi, but it was not until after Congress appropriated $6,000 on April 21, 1806, that the northern section of the road was located and opened. Between this date and 1820 building and rebuilding of the road took place. Much of it passed through boggy swamp ground, and nearly all of it through heavy virgin forest.

At Nashville the Natchez Trace connected with the Louisville and Nashville Boatroad, and indirectly over it with the Limestone, or Maysville, Road and Zane's Trace. When the Natchez Trace was opened it was used by all sorts of travelers, but the most numerous were flatboatmen-farmers who returned from their river journeys each year to the New Orleans market. Because these travelers usually carried money with them they were often prey to highwaymen and sharpers. Occasionally there was some friction with the Indians. In time the trace was to develop a highly romantic and legendary history.

Some of the famous landmarks on the Natchez Trace were Doak's Stand, Grindstone Ford, French Camp, and Colbert's Ferry. The trace's major historical significance lay in the fact that it was a main commercial, military, and emigrant artery of travel into the Southwest.

See Julian Bretz, "Early Land Communications with the Lower Mississippi Valley, *Mississippi Valley Historical Review*, vol. 13 (1927); Jonathan Daniels, *The Devil's Backbone* (1962); Ross Phares, *Reverend Devil* (1941); Dunbar Rowland, *Mississippi*, vol. II (1902); and Charles C. Royce, "Indian Land Cessions in the United States," in Bureau of American Ethnology, *Eighteenth Annual Report, 1896-97* (1899).—T. D. C.

Natchez-under-the-Hill, Mississippi. Mississippi River port. Natchez has always had two sections. Above the bluff overlooking the Mississippi River was the more prosaic section of town, though not without its moments of violence. Below the bluff in a narrow strip about three quarters of a mile long was the raucous waterfront district known as Natchez-under-the-Hill. Along Silver Street, its main stem, straggled the wild taverns, gambling dens, and brothels that as early as the 1790s were giving Natchez-under-the-Hill an infamous reputation. American and foreign visitors were shocked by what they saw. Typical was traveler John Bradbury's reaction, who in 1810 observed that "for the size of it there is not perhaps in the world a more profligate place." Giving Natchez-under-the-Hill its roistering, violent ambience were the thousands of boatmen who passed through and the gamblers, prostitutes, wagoners, fishermen, and frontier adventurers. Among the most colorful leaders of the low life were the tough tavern proprietor, Jim Girty, and his legendary paramour, Marie Dufour, a bluff, blonde Titaness who ran a high-class house of prostitution. The two were a redoubtable pair: the bearded Jim reputedly was so rugged that he had no ribs but an all-bone chest which was impenetrable to knife or bullet; Marie, hotly in love with Jim, was a crack shot and famed for her ability to open a bottle with her teeth. Yet, Jim and Marie were proven merely mortal when Girty— who had ribs after all—was killed in an ambush and Marie, in a torrent of grief for her fallen man, did away with herself by a gun shot in the mouth.

At the center of social and economic life was the boat trade. In 1808, for example, as many as 150 New Orleans-bound flatboats and keelboats could be found at the port on peak days of river commerce. In 1824 a total of 229 steamboats and 542 flatboats tied up at the town. By the 1830s, Natchez-under-the-Hill bars and whorehouses were giving way to an increasing number of storage and commercial facilities. In 1835 Natchez followed the example of its sister city of Vicksburg, Mississippi, and by vigilante action expelled the professional gamblers who were so prominent a part of the scene. In time the gamblers returned, but after 1840 gambling was muted.

Violence and immorality were Natchez' man-made plague, but the town as a whole suffered repeated natural disasters much more costly in human life. Yellow fever epidemics were common in late summer and early fall, and from 1823 to 1853 five bad epidemics took 1,654 lives. Mississippi River floods were a menace to the lower town, with the worst overflows occurring in 1811, 1815, 1828, and 1840. To cap it all a tornado in 1840 left three hundred fatalities along its path. By 1860, with the Civil War and the waning of the steamboat era both at hand, Natchez-under-the-Hill had seen its wildest years.

In the violent temper of its life, old Natchez-under-the-Hill had much in common with such famous American frontier boomtowns as Dodge City, Deadwood, and Tombstone, but more precisely it represented the marine frontier of bustling river, lake, and ocean ports. It flourished in the lively, lethal tradition of San Francisco's Barbary Coast, Memphis' Pinch Gut, and the Swamp of New Orleans.

See D. Clayton James, *Antebellum Natchez* (1968); and Harnett T. Kane, *Natchez on the Mississippi* (1947). —R. M. B.

Natchez War (1729-1730). In 1716 Fort Rosalie, one of the administrative units of the French speculative John Law Company in Louisiana, was established in the heart of the Natchez Indian country at present-day Natchez, Mississippi. The Natchez Indians were concentrated in the Mississippi and lower Yazoo river country in nine villages, and they numbered approximately 1,200 warriors. They were a Muskogean-affiliated people who had previously been the dominant element in a large Indian confederacy in the lower Mississippi valley. Although they had declined in power during the seventeenth century, they were still the strongest tribe in the area when the French settlers appeared. The Natchez were strictly organized into hierarchical classes and practiced an eleborately ritualized form of sun worship with human sacrifice. They were proud Indians who held aloof from other tribes and viewed the arrival of the French with misgivings. Governor Antoine Cadillac had been tactless in ignoring a Natchez gesture of hospitality in 1714, and there arose friction over trade goods. In succeeding years the pressure of new arrivals at Fort Rosalie and Fort St. Peter caused additional anxiety among the Indians, especially when Frenchmen abused their women. Arbitrary and despotic actions by the French administrators led to serious outbreaks. The Sieur de Bienville attacked the Natchez in 1723, and the Indians planned a rebellion in 1728, which failed to come off.

Commandant Chepart, Père du Poisson, made public plans at Fort Rosalie in 1729 to remove the Natchez from the region. The Indians' resistance grew, and on November 29, 1729, they fell in force on the French settlements. The attack was disastrous for the French, with possibly as many as 300 people killed and 400 or more taken captive. In the months that followed, French troops pursued the Indians across the Mississippi coun-

try. The Natchez were supported by the Yazoo tribe, but the French mounted a campaign of extinction and destroyed the Natchez villages in 1730. The tribe was dispersed and nearly 450, including the Great Sun Chief, were sold into West Indian slavery. The remainder amalgamated into other tribes and became culturally extinct by 1743.

See D. Clayton James, *Antebellum Natchez* (1968); and J. W. Monette, *History of the Discovery and Settlement of the Valley of the Mississippi* (1848).—T. D. C.

Nation, Carry A. (1846-1911). Temperance champion. Carry Amelia Moore was born in Kentucky into a slave-owning family. She was early influenced not only by the psychotic illness of her mother but by the religious intensity of the Negroes. Although her family moved a dozen times within Kentucky and to Texas and Missouri during her childhood, she received a better than average education. The end of the Civil War found the family in Texas, where her father was ruined financially. They relocated in Missouri, and in 1867 she married Dr. Charles Gloyd, a Union army veteran and physician from Ohio. Gloyd was an alcoholic and the young bride sought to reform him. Their marriage broke up, Gloyd died, and a daughter was born. She then taught school, and in 1877 married David Nation, nineteen years her senior. Although he was a minister, lawyer, and editor, their years in Texas were financially fruitless. By 1889 the Nations were located in Medicine Lodge, Kansas, near the Oklahoma border, where David ministered to a church.

Although Kansas, in 1880, had approved a constitutional amendment providing for the prohibition of alcohol, there was open defiance of the law. Carry Nation worked for temperance in Medicine Lodge and campaigned to expel the saloons, but without immediate success. In 1900, impelled by "visions," she broadened her attack on saloons, based on the idea that since saloons were illegal, it was the responsibility of any citizen to destroy not only illegal liquor but saloon property as well. Her commanding presence—she was a muscular 175-pound woman almost six feet tall—and the fierceness of her attacks with her ever-present hatchet intimidated saloonkeepers and many closed down their "joints." The Kansas towns she invaded included Kiowa, Wichita, Enterprise, Winfield, Topeka, and Leavenworth; she carried her campaign outside the state too. Usually her violent destruction of property brought charges against her of "disturbing the peace" and she was jailed.

Nation's attacks on the open saloon received widespread support; often her fines were paid by friends. She sold souvenir hatchets, went on extensive lecture tours, and made stage appearances. To further expand her movement she published several short-lived journals, including *The Smasher's Mail*. Although she actively sought martyrdom, she died of old age, worn out by a decade of intense activity. The long-term effects of her work were slight; probably she influenced Kansas to enforce its prohibition laws more stringently. The advent of national prohibition in 1920 found her virtually forgotten.

Two recent biographies are Carleton Beals, *Cyclone Carry: The Story of Carry Nation* (1962); and Robert Lewis Taylor, *Vessel of Wrath: The Life and Times of Carry Nation* (1966).—H. E. S.

National Cowboy Hall of Fame and Western Heritage Center. The National Cowboy Hall of Fame, located at 1700 Northeast Sixty-third Street atop Persimmon Hill in Oklahoma City, Oklahoma, is one of the newest and largest of the growing number of museums devoted to the history of the American West. The idea of a cowboy hall of fame dedicated to prominent men and women associated with open-range ranching and the cattle industry and honoring the American pioneer spirit was the brainchild of the late Chester A. Reynolds of Kansas City. At his urging, representatives from seventeen western states met during the 1950s to choose the site and approve a dramatic architectural design for the buildings that employed the shapes of tents and the camp circle. The idea of a hall of fame was enlarged to include a western heritage center honoring pioneer men and women generally. In 1957, although still not completed, the museum was declared a national memorial by Congress. It was formally dedicated June 26, 1965.

Each year the board of trustees elects a number of men and women to the Cowboy Hall of Fame. Such prominent historical figures as Lewis and Clark, Sacagawea, Theodore Roosevelt, and Will Rogers have been chosen honorees at large, while others are elected to represent the individual western states. Western businessmen, leaders, and writers have also been elected, among them Collis P. Huntington and Otto Mears, railroad builders; A. P. Giannini, founder of the Bank of America; Pedro Altube, patron of the Basques in the West; Lynn Riggs, the Oklahoma playwright; and J. Frank Dobie, noted authority on the West. Scientists and academicians who have contributed to the development of improved cattle breeds have also been named to the Cowboy Hall of Fame.

The museum early recognized that the cowboy—epitomized by the career of Will Rogers—was as much a part of western movies, show business, and the rodeo as he was of the cattle industry and sought to portray all aspects of the cowboy's varied life. Each year the trustees elect one honoree and one All-Around Champion to a Rodeo Hall of Fame. Here one can find pictures and accounts of such rodeo immortals as L. E. "Ed" Bowman of Colorado, Bob Crosby of New Mexico, Bill Linderman and Oral Zumwalt of Montana, or learn that Jim Shoulders held the title of All-Around Champion for four years (1956-59) and Dead Oliver of Idaho (1963-65) and Larry Mahan of Oregon (1966-68) each held it for three years. The Rodeo Hall of Fame contains displays of the five major rodeo events: bareback bronc-riding, saddle bronc-riding, bull-riding, calf-roping, and steer-wrestling. The museum also has a Hall of Fame of Western Actors and Actresses, which includes both movie and television film stars.

The Western Heritage Center houses a vast electronic relief map of the West, displays of famous guns and saddles, and life-sized exhibits of Indian, pioneer, and cowboy life. These are supplemented by selected paintings, bronzes, and illustrations by Frederick Remington, Charles M. Russell, and other artists. Actively supported by the seventeen sponsoring western states, the National Cowboy Hall of Fame and Western Heritage Center is still growing. It has become a major tourist and educational center attracting many thousands of visitors and schoolchildren annually. Since the cowboy, in all his

roles, continues to be the primary American folk hero, the museum's importance as an expression of American values and interests would be difficult to exaggerate. —H. R. L.

national parks and monuments. In the trans-Mississippi area of the United States are a large number of national parks, monuments, and historic sites, administered by the National Park Service. All have some bearing on the evolution of the West. Many have played a central role in the natural history of western North America and have figured in the discovery and exploration of the area. Others bear a central relation to the understanding of the culture of the American Indians in the West and to the coming of the Spanish and Anglo-American people to the region.

Alaska. Glacier Bay National Monument. This 2,274,248-acre monument, established near Juneau in 1925, features the great tidewater glaciers that once covered much of the western United States and still exist farther north. Also included in the area are several rare species of wildlife and an exhibit of the early stages of postglacial forests.

Katmai National Monument. Located near the northern end of the Alaskan peninsula and established in 1918, Katmai is known primarily for its numerous dying volcanos. The 2,697,590 acres include the Valley of Ten Thousand Smokes, the scene of violent volcanic eruption in 1912. The monument is also the home of the world's largest carnivore, the brown bear.

Sitka National Monument. This monument in SITKA, ALASKA, marks the site of an Indian stockade, where in 1804 the Kik-Siti tribe made its last stand against the Russian settlers. The monument features an exhibit of totem poles.

See also MOUNT MCKINLEY NATIONAL PARK.

Arizona. Canyon de Chelly National Monument. Within this national monument can be seen four periods of Indian culture, dating from A.D. 348 to 1300. The earliest known Indian occupants of the canyon were the Basket Makers, who constructed sunken circular structures (see PUEBLO INDIANS). They were followed by the Anasazi, or Pueblo, culture. This society is responsible for the apartment-style cliff dwellings built on the level above the canyon floor between A.D. 1100 and 1300. Hopi Indians, also a Pueblo people, sporadically occupied the canyons after the fourteenth century. Presently the monument contains the summer house of over three hundred Navaho, who use the canyon floor for peach orchards, farming, and grazing.

Casa Grande Ruins National Monument. Casa Grande ("Big House") is one of the foremost examples of the construction techniques of the early Indian. Although in partial ruin, the four-story earth building has withstood the elements for about six hundred years. The real purpose of the structure is unknown, but it may have served as a watchtower, a fort, an apartment house, or a temple. The main structure is surrounded by the vestiges of several prehistoric villages.

The area surrounding Casa Grande was settled by the Hohokam Indians as early as 400 B.C. These people developed an extensive system of irrigation canals which enabled them to farm the arid deserts of the Gila and Salt River valleys. They built Casa Grande and used it for approximately a century before abandoning it about 1450. The first white man to visit the site was Father

Eusebio Kino, who performed mass in the ruin in 1694.

Chiricahua National Monument. Also known as the "Wonderland of Rocks," this 10,480-acre monument is located in southeastern Arizona high in the Chiricahua Mountains and features giant monoliths of volcanic rock that have been eroded by wind and water into fantastic formations. These include a totem pole 137 feet high and only a yard thick; a mushroom; Punch and Judy; Thor's Hammer; and a balanced rock.

The Chiricahua country was the stronghold of the Apache Indians under Cochise during the latter half of the nineteenth century. The area was also the scene of the one-man raids of "Big Foot" Massai. The monument was established in 1924.

Coronado National Monument. This 2,745-acre site, located in southeastern Arizona east of Nogales, commemorates Francisco Coronado's exploration in 1540-42, and provides a view of part of the route by which the expedition entered what is now the United States. The memorial, established in 1952, grew out of the four-hundredth anniversary celebration of the expedition that paved the way for exploration and settlement of the Southwest.

Fort Bowie National Historic Site. Established in 1862, Fort Bowie was the focal point of the military operations against Geronimo and his band of Apache. The ruins of the fort which remain today are not open to the public.

Hubbell Trading Post National Historic Site. The sixty-year-old trading post and 152-acre site illustrates the part played by Indian reservation traders in the settling of the West. Juan Lorenzo Hubbell settled on the Navaho Indian Reservation in 1871 as a pioneer trader, and his descendants have remained prominent traders in the Navaho country to this day.

Montezuma Castle National Monument. Built by the Pueblo Indians during the thirteenth and fourteenth centuries, Montezuma Castle is one of the best-preserved cliff dwellings in the United States. The building is forty-three feet from top to bottom with about thirty feet of cliff overhanging. Each unit of this twenty-room communal house was built and occupied by a family or group. The castle also served as a perfect natural fortress, inaccessible except by ladders.

Navaho National Monument. Included in this national monument are three of the largest and most elaborate of known cliff dwellings in the Southwest. Each of these ruins—Betatakin, Keet Seel, and Inscription House—dates from the thirteenth century. They are completely surrounded by the Navaho Indian Reservation.

Organ Pipe Cactus National Monument. This monument, located in Southern Arizona west of Tucson, was established in 1937 to preserve an outstanding section of the Sonoran desert and certain rare species of plant and animal life. These include the organpipe cactus, one of the most spectacular of the native cacti. Other interesting plants in the 328,691-acre monument are the giant saguaro, palo verde, ironwood, and ocotillo. Among the more interesting animals which inhabit the area are the collared peccary and the desert bighorn sheep.

Father Kino, a Jesuit missionary, visited the region in 1698 and established the route that came to be known as Camino del Diablo (Devil's Highway) in 1700.

Petrified Forest National Park. This park, located in eastern Arizona east of Holbrook and established in 1962, gets its name from the petrified coniferous trees which lie scattered across the Painted Desert. It is believed that many of the trees grew where they lie today. About 190 million years ago the area was a swampy basin near sea level. Streams flowing into the basin from surrounding highlands carried in sediments of volcanic ash which eventually buried the dead logs which the streams picked up and carried from the low hills surrounding the lowlands. Gradually the wood of the logs was impregnated with silica, which eventually filled in the wood cells until the logs were virtually solid stone. The silica was stained by iron oxide and other minerals, giving the logs their brilliant rainbow colors. The park encompasses 94,189 acres.

Pipe Spring National Monument. Pipe Spring is a tribute to the Mormon pioneers who were instrumental in exploring, settling, and developing the region. This site preserves Winsor Castle, a fort built in 1871-72 as protection against the Indians, and two buildings that were used as quarters.

In 1858 a Mormon missionary party led by Jacob Hamblin camped here. A member of the party, William (Gunlock Bill) Hamblin demonstrated his sharpshooting ability by shooting the bottom out of a clay pipe which he had laid on a rock near the spring. Thus, the spring was christened Pipe Spring.

Saguaro National Monument. This 60,988-acre monument, located in southeastern Arizona near Tucson and established in 1933, is dedicated to the saguaro cactus, one of the greatest cacti. The habitat of this cactus is limited to southern Arizona and northern New Mexico. A saguaro may live over 200 years and averages between 25 and 36 feet in height. The flower of the saguaro is the state flower of Arizona, and the fruit that the cactus bears is eaten by the Papago and Pima Indians.

Sunset Crater National Monument. The cone of Sunset Crater, an extinct volcano, dominates this 3,040-acre national monument, which also includes fields of cinder dunes, lava squeeze-ups, spatter cones, and inactive hot springs. The peculiar coloring of the volcano creates the illusion that the mountain is always in the rays of the setting sun. Dark at the base, the cone becomes rosy, then shades to various hues of yellow. The monument, located in northern Arizona near Flagstaff, was established in 1930.

Tonto National Monument. These well-preserved cliff dwellings were occupied in the fourteenth century by the Salado Indians who farmed in the Salt River valley. The ruins include a two-story adobe and rock house built in a natural cave.

Tumacacori National Monument. This historic Spanish Catholic mission stands near the site of the village of Tumacacori, which was visited by the pioneer Jesuit missionary Father Eusebio Kino in 1691. The church itself, a massive adobe structure, was begun about 1800 and never completed. Apache raids, Mexican neglect, and a terrible winter contributed to its final abandonment. By the 1850s the mission was already in partial ruins.

Tuzigoot National Monument. The forty-two acres of this national monument contain at least three pueblos, which in turn have a total of more than 110 rectangular rooms. Only part of the complete dwelling area has been restored. Archaeologists estimate that Tuzigoot was inhabited from the tenth through the fourteenth centuries. Evidences of the high degree of culture attained by the inhabitants can be seen in the pottery, bead work, mosaics, and implements on display in the museum at the monument.

Walnut Canyon National Monument. Walnut Canyon contains the remains of more than three hundred prehistoric cliff dwellings built under the outward-sloping canyon walls. Instead of the usual communal type, these houses were apparently built for separate families. They were inhabited by the Sinagua Indians from about A.D. 1100 to 1275.

Wupatki National Monument. Comprised of more than eight hundred ruins of red sandstone prehistoric pueblos, Wupatki is thought by many scholars to be the home of the ancestors of the Hopi Indians of today. Perhaps the most impressive of the ruins is the "Tall House," which consists of more than one hundred rooms.

See also GRAND CANYON: NATIONAL PARK.

Arkansas. *Arkansas Post National Memorial.* With the erection of a fort in 1686, the 221-acre Arkansas Post became the first permanent white settlement in the lower Mississippi valley.

Fort Smith National Historic Site. One of the first United States military posts in Louisiana Territory, FORT SMITH was from 1817 to 1890 a point of civilian authority for the untamed regions to the west. The site covers thirteen acres.

Pea Ridge National Military Park. Pea Ridge was the scene of one of the biggest engagements of the Civil War west of the Mississippi. The battle of Pea Ridge, fought on March 7-8, 1862, was of great importance because it secured the Mississippi River for the Union. (See CIVIL WAR.)

See also HOT SPRINGS NATIONAL PARK.

California. *Cabrillo National Monument.* This monument was erected in honor of Juan Rodriguez CABRILLO, discoverer and explorer of the West Coast, who landed on Point Loma (near present-day San Diego) in 1542. The monument also includes a historic lighthouse, first lighted in 1855.

Channel Islands National Monument. These islands, covering 18,166 acres off southern California, serve as an isolated haven for unique plant and animal life. The species that inhabit the islands are quite different from those of the mainland. One of the islands is a major sea lion rookery, while the other is a nesting colony for California brown pelicans and Farallon cormorants. Both islands contain fossils and examples of ancient volcanism. They were established as a national monument in 1938.

Death Valley National Monument. Death Valley gained its name and reputation in the winter of 1849 when a group of emigrants started across the barren valley, straddling eastern California and southwestern Nevada, believing it to be a shortcut to the California gold fields. Lack of food and water caused a panic that resulted in the splitting up of the band into several frantic parties which stumbled through the valley before a few survivors made their way to safety.

Later prospectors followed the forty-niners into the valley, and although some precious metal was found, it was the discovery of borax that opened the area to large-scale mining. The first roads were built in the 1880s, and over them the famous twenty-mule teams drew their wagonloads of borax from the desert.

The valley ranges from less than four miles to about sixteen miles in width; is about one hundred forty miles in length; and covers 1,879,088 acres. Death Valley is one of the hottest regions in the world. The maximum temperature in summer can be as high as one hundred twenty degrees for several days in succession. A high of one hundred thirty-four degrees was once recorded. It was established as a national monument in 1933.

Devils Postpile National Monument. The central feature of this 798-acre national monument, located in central California southeast of Yosemite, is a sheer wall of symmetrical blue-gray basaltic columns which rise as high as sixty feet. Devils Postpile is a remnant of a lava flow which was worn smooth by glacial action. A trail leads to the top of the columns where the surface resembles a tile inlay. It was established as a national monument in 1911.

John Muir National Historic Site. This nine-acre site, commemorating the contributions of John MUIR to conservation and literature, includes the John Muir House and the adjacent Martinez Adobe. It is located in Muir Woods National Monument.

Joshua Tree National Monument. The 504,720-acre monument, located in southeastern California near Indio, abounds with many varieties of desert flora, but the most spectacular is the Joshua-tree (*Yucca brevifolia*). This member of the lily family grows to a height of 10 to 40 feet and produces greenish-white blossoms which grow in clusters 8 to 14 inches long. The trees are usually at their best from March through May. The monument was established in 1936.

Lava Beds National Monument. Centuries ago the volcanoes of northern California northeast of Mount Shasta poured forth masses of molten lava which, when cooled, formed a unique region of rugged terrain. This 46,238-acre area, incorporated into a monument in 1925, includes cinder cones, deep chasms, collapsed tunnels, and more than two hundred caves. Some of the caves contain rivers of solid ice and in others are pictographs recording Indian life.

Muir Woods National Monument. The 485-acre monument, located near Mill Valley (or San Francisco), was established in 1908 in honor of John Muir. It is one of the most beautiful and accessible of the famous California redwood groves. The woods feature the *Sequoia sempervirens*, the tallest of all tree life. Though not as large in girth as the giant sequoias of the Sierra country, these trees are just as beautiful and more graceful because of their comparative slenderness and lofty height.

Pinnacles National Monument. The 13,618 acres of this monument, located in southern California south of Hollister, feature numerous precipitous bluffs, spires, and crags of colorful volcanic rock. The pinnacle spires from which the area derives its name are located on a ridge 1,000 feet above the canyon floor. Many of the spirelike formations themselves are over 1,000 feet high.

The monument, which was established in 1908, also has an abundant bird population, a wide variety of wildflowers, and numbers of deer. In addition, the finest example of Coast Range chaparral in the National Park System thrives in the monument.

See also LASSEN VOLCANIC NATIONAL PARK, SEQUOIA and KINGS CANYON NATIONAL PARKS, and YOSEMITE NATIONAL PARK.

Colorado. *Bent's Old Fort National Historic Site.* As the principal outpost of civilization on the southern Great Plains and a rendezvous for the Indians of the region, BENT'S FORT, 178 acres near La Junta, was one of the most significant fur-trading posts of the West. The fort has been restored and is open to the public.

Black Canyon of the Gunnison National Monument. The 13,034-acre monument, located in southwestern Colorado near Montrose, contains ten miles of the deepest and most scenic portion of the gorge of the Gunnison River. It is one of the most spectacular geological displays in the West. The gorge reaches a maximum depth of 2,425 feet and narrows to a minimum width of 40 feet at the bottom of the canyon. The name Black Canyon comes from the dark color of the Precambrian rock of the sheer canyon walls. It was established as a national monument in 1933.

Colorado National Monument. Colorado National Monument is an excellent display of the power of erosion. The 17,607-acre area, in western Colorado near Grand Junction, is seamed with numerous canyons and many giant monoliths. The most fantastic of these sandstone shafts is the 500-foot Independence Monument. Fallen Rock, Coke Ovens, and Window Rock are also prominent formations. The monument, established in 1911, has a forest cover of juniper and pinon pine, and in the spring and summer wildflowers abound.

Great Sand Dunes National Monument. Located in Colorado's San Luis valley southwest of Alamasa, this 34,980-acre monument contains some of the highest and largest sand dunes in the United States. In some places the crests of the dunes rise to a height of 700 feet. One of the unique features of the monument is Medano Creek, which disappears among the great dunes only to reappear again five miles away in the form of an immense spring. The monument was established in 1932.

Hovenweep National Monument. Hovenweep comprises six groups of prehistoric towers, pueblos, and cliff dwellings (two in Utah and four in Colorado). All the ruins date from the Great Pueblo Period of A.D. 1100-1300. They are the work of the same Pueblo group that built the great cliff dwellings found in Mesa Verde National Park.

Mesa Verde National Park. The ruins at MESA VERDE NATIONAL PARK are the most notable and best-preserved cliff dwellings and other works of early man in the United States.

Yucca House National Monument. Yucca House consists mainly of the unexcavated ruins of a large prehistoric Indian pueblo. This monument is not open to the public.

See also ROCKY MOUNTAIN NATIONAL PARK.

Hawaii. City of Refuge National Historical Park. This site commemorates the sacred ground where vanquished Hawaiian warriors, noncombatants, and taboo-breakers fled for refuge from death. The park includes prehistoric house sites, royal fishponds, coconut groves, and spectacular shore scenery.

Haleakala National Park. Looming over this 17,130-acre national park, located on Maui, is the world famous 10,023-foot Haleakala volcano. This dormant volcano has one of the largest and most colorful craters known and is the home of many varieties of plant and animal life, including a species of the rare silversword. The park was established in 1961.

Hawaii Volcanoes National Park. This 198,549-acre park, the scene of the most impressive active volcanism on the island of Hawaii, contains luxuriant vegetation at the lower levels and many rare plants and animals. It was established in 1911.

Idaho. Craters of the Moon National Monument. This area, located in south-central Idaho, contains more volcanic features than any other area of similar size in the continental United States. Although the last eruptions occurred about 1,600 years ago, volcanic activity in the region dates back over a million years.

During these eruptions lava charged with gas was thrown hundreds of feet into the air and wind currents caused this frothy lava to form giant cinder-cones. Many other volcanic phenomena, such as spatter cones, lava trees, sinks, and hornitos, were also created. Massive liquid lava rivers flooded the countryside, resulting in the weird formations which compose a surface comparable to telescopic views of the moon.

One remarkable feature of the 48,004-acre monument, which was established in 1924, are the lava tubes or caves. Two of them are over thirty feet in diameter and several hundred feet long. Inside these tubes are fantastic lava stalactites and ice formations.

Nez Percé National Historical Park. The first decentralized park in the nation, established in 1965, Nez Percé National Historical Park coordinates twenty-two widely separated and dissimilar sites in northern Idaho. Together comprising 124 acres, each section in some way reflects the culture of the NEZ PERCE INDIANS and the emergence of white domination with the advent of the fur trader, the missionary, the gold miner, the lumberman, and the homesteader.

Iowa. Effigy Mounds National Monument. The Effigy Mounds are mounds of earth built in the shape of animals and birds by a prehistoric Indian society that lived in the area more than one thousand years ago.

Herbert Hoover National Historic Site. This site in West Branch, Iowa, includes the birthplace, boyhood home, and burial place of President Hoover. Adjacent to the forty-two-acre site is the Herbert Hoover Library.

Kansas. Fort Larned National Historic Site. The 406-acre FORT LARNED, which was one of the most important posts on the Santa Fe Trail and the Indian frontier from 1859 to 1882, has not been restored, and its sandstone buildings remain unchanged.

Fort Scott Historic Area. Pre-Civil War conflicts typical of the "bleeding Kansas" period were heavily concentrated in the vicinity of Fort Scott. The fort, originally established in 1842, was reactivated to quell the disturbances. Many of the old military buildings are still standing.

Minnesota. Pipestone National Monument. Within this national monument are the famous pipestone quarries from which the Plains Indians quarried the red pipestone for their ceremonial pipes. Here, as Longfellow put it in *The Song of Hiawatha,* the mighty "Gitche Manito," the Great Spirit, called on the tribes to "Break the red stone from this quarry,/ Mould and make it into Peace-Pipes." The monument protects the remainder of this raw material, the use of which is reserved to Indians of all tribes.

See also GRAND PORTAGE NATIONAL MONUMENT.

Missouri. Jefferson National Expansion Memorial National Historic Site. This memorial commemorates the territorial expansion of the United States and the persons connected with that expansion. It includes the 630-foot-high stainless steel Gateway Arch designed by Eero Saarinen.

Wilson's Creek National Battlefield Park. This 2,728-acre park, established in 1965, marks the site of one of the early battles of the Civil War, fought on August 10, 1861, for control of the Missouri.

Montana. *Big Hole National Battlefield.* This monument commemorates the battle on the BIG HOLE River fought on August 9-10, 1877, when a force of United States troops aided by local civilian volunteers staged a surprise attack against a band of Nez Percé Indians led by Chief Joseph.

Custer Battlefield National Monument. The famous battle of the LITTLE BIG HORN is commemorated by this monument. The battle, a confrontation between the Seventh United States Cavalry and the Sioux and North Cheyenne Indians, was fought on June 25-26, 1876, and resulted in the death of Lieutenant Colonel George A. CUSTER and about 260 of his men.

See also GLACIER NATIONAL PARK.

Nebraska. *Agate Fossil Beds National Monument.* These world-renowned quarries, covering 1,970 acres near Scotts Bluff, Nebraska, contain numerous, concentrated, well-preserved Miocene mammal fossils. These fossils represent an important chapter in the evolution of mammals.

Chimney Rock National Historic Site. Towering over five hundred feet above the North Platte River valley, Chimney Rock was a prominent landmark and campsite on the Oregon Trail.

Homestead National Monument of America. This monument comprises the first quarter-section (160 acres) of land claimed under the Homestead Act of 1862. Daniel Freeman, who filed this claim and settled on it after the Civil War, was the first of over one million homesteaders whose contributions to the settlement of the West are commemorated by this monument.

Scotts Bluff National Monument. Named for Hiram Scott, a fur trapper who died in the vicinity about 1828, Scotts Bluff was a landmark on the Oregon Trail.

Nevada. *Lehman Caves National Monument.* This 640-acre monument, located in eastern Nevada near Ely and established in 1922, includes an illuminated limestone cave. The cave has a variety of interesting and colorful formations, including thirty-foot columns and curious formations shaped like shields or palettes.

New Mexico. *Aztec Ruins National Monument.* This monument preserves one of the largest of the prehistoric towns built by the Pueblo Indians. Built of masonry and timber in the twelfth century, the town has been largely excavated and stabilized. The greatest of the pueblos was built about A.D. 1100 and contained five hundred rooms.

Bandelier National Monument. Some of the dwellings found in this monument are unique among the various types of abodes adopted by prehistoric man in North America. They consist of man-made cave rooms hewn out of the soft tuff rock. The most accessible ruins include the cave rooms, houses built on talus slopes, and a large circular community house.

Capulin Mountain National Monument. The extinct volcanic cone on this 680-acre monument, located in northeast New Mexico east of Raton, is one of the most symmetrical to be found in the United States. Capulin Mountain rises 8,215 feet above sea level. It was formed when the pressure of steam and gases caused a volcanic vent through which lava was blown high into the air and, with ashes and cinder, fell to earth to pile up around the vent in a conical hill. Indications are that this activity occurred about 7,000 years ago. The cup-shaped crater is 1,450 feet in diameter and 415 feet deep. The monument was established in 1916.

Carlsbad Caverns National Park. Carlsbad Caverns are a series of enormous rooms, covering about 45,847-acres, which form one of the world's largest caves. The caverns, located in southeastern New Mexico in the foothills of the Guadelupe Mountains, were formed in a limestone reef by percolating ground water, a process estimated to have begun some three to five million years ago. Stalactites hang from the ceiling of the caves while stalagmites and other masses of limestone in grotesque shapes are found on the cavern floor. Helictites, small and delicate growths that resemble plants, are also found on the walls of the caves.

One of the most remarkable attractions of the park, which was established in 1923, is seen each evening at dusk from May through October when bats emerge from the uppermost chamber of the caverns in search of food. When insects are plentiful, more than a million bats may make this exodus.

Chaco Canyon National Monument. Chaco Canyon contains the ruins of thirteen major cities and many smaller villages, representing the highest point of prehistoric Pueblo culture. One of these ruins, Pueblo Bonito, contained about eight hundred rooms and thirty-seven ceremonial chambers before its abandonment in the twelfth century.

El Morro National Monument. The central feature of this national monument is "Inscription Rock," a soft sandstone monolith on which are carved hundreds of inscriptions. The first carvings were Indian petroglyphs dating back many hundreds of years. The first legible inscription was left by Don Juan de Oñate, governor and colonizer of New Mexico. Emigrants making their way westward added their names and dates of stopovers.

Fort Union National Monument. This monument consists of the ruins of this key fort that shaped the destiny of the Southwest from 1851 to 1891. On the Santa Fe Trail, FORT UNION was a major base for both military and civilian ventures.

Gila Cliff Dwellings National Monument. These cliff dwellings contain groups of small, yet interesting, prehistoric structures in six natural cavities in the face of a grayish-yellow overhanging cliff which is about 150 feet high.

Gran Quivira National Monument. Gran Quivira stands as a monument to the Spanish mission system that swept over New Mexico in the seventeenth century and partially succeeded in Christianizing the Indians. The Franciscans exercised influence over the Indians until drought, crop failure, and Apache raids brought about permanent abandonment in 1672. Two mission churches are preserved, as well as several Indian pueblos dating from the fourteenth century.

Pecos National Monument. This 341-acre monument includes pueblo ruins and the crumbling walls of the old Pecos Mission, erected by the Franciscans around 1707. The pueblo served for over six hundred years as a great trading center between the Pueblo and Plains Indians.

White Sands National Monument. This 140,247-acre monument, established in 1933, is part of the largest of rare gypsum deserts, the White Sands of New Mexico's Tularosa Basin. The desert is formed when the waters from rain and malting snow carries tons of gypsum from the mountains into Lake Lucero. Dry winds evaporate the lake and whirl the gypsum particles into the surrounding area. In some spots giant sand dunes are formed which rise ten to forty feet above the valley floor.

The first atomic bomb was detonated just outside the monument on July 16, 1945. The spot, Trinity Site, is located on a military reservation and is closed to the public except in October.

See also MUSEUM OF NEW MEXICO.

North Dakota. *Fort Union Trading Post National Historic Site.* The ruins of FORT UNION, the principal fur-trading depot in the upper Missouri River region from 1828 to 1867, are under excavation, and part of the stockade is to be restored. This 104-acre site is not open to the public.

Theodore Roosevelt National Memorial Park. This 70,436-acre park, in the Badlands of North Dakota along the Little Missouri River, pays tribute to the contributions made by Theodore ROOSEVELT toward the conservation of the country's natural resources. Roosevelt first came to the Badlands in 1883 to hunt bison and other big game. He became interested in ranching and acquired a ranch in the area. The park, part of Roosevelt's Elkhorn Ranch, was established in 1947.

Plateaus, buttes, and conical hills give the area great scenic appeal. The Little Missouri has carved the countryside into many weird and brilliantly colored formations. A variety of wildlife inhabits the multidimensional landscape of the park.

Oklahoma. *Platt National Park.* In contrast to its barren surroundings, Platt National Park features approximately 900 acres of woods, streams, and small waterfalls. The park, established in 1906, is recognized for the purported curative properties of its mineral waters. There are numerous fresh, sulphur, and bromide springs within the park.

Oregon. *Fort Clatsop National Memorial.* Fort Clatsop was the winter encampment of the Lewis and Clark expedition in 1805-06. The memorial features a replica of the log fort built by the explorers.

McLoughlin House National Historic Site. Dr. John McLOUGHLIN lived in this house from 1847 to 1857. Often called the Father of Oregon, McLoughlin was a premier figure in the early development of the Pacific Northwest.

Oregon Caves National Monument. Located in the heart of Mount Elijah in southwest Oregon, this 480-acre monument consists of several magnificent caves which nature has carved out of a bed of marble. These Marble Halls of Oregon feature an ever-changing display of pillars, stalactites, and canopies of limestone. The monument was established in 1909.

See also CRATER LAKE NATIONAL PARK.

South Dakota. *Badlands National Monument.* The area known as the Badlands is located between the White and Cheyenne rivers in the southwestern part of South Dakota. It contains some of the most spectacular examples of weathering and erosion in the world. Formations resembling pinnacles and towers, cathedral spires and castles, were carved by streams from the layers of sediment washed from the Black Hills. This process is estimated to have begun about forty million years ago. Every rain washes away a little bit of the sediment, gradually reducing the size of the Badlands.

The 100,000-acre area is rich in fossil remains. At one time, when vegetation was plentiful, such species as the titanothere (a prehistoric grass-eater), the saber-toothed tiger, the three-toed horse, and early ancestors of the hog, camel, and rhinoceros roamed the Badlands. The monument was established in 1939.

Jewel Cave National Monument. Jewel Cave, located in southwestern South Dakota near Hot Springs, consists of a series of subterranean chambers and limestone galleries. The cave is particularly noted for the dogtooth calcite crystals lining the walls. The 1,275-acre monument was established in 1908.

Mount Rushmore National Memorial. Carved from the solid granite face of Mount Rushmore are the colossal heads of George Washington, Thomas Jefferson, Abraham Lincoln, and Theodore Roosevelt. Created under the direction of Gutzon Borglum, it is one of the largest pieces of sculpture ever completed. Each face is between sixty and seventy feet high and is carved with a perfection of detail that is remarkable in sculpture of such size.

Wind Cave National Park. Comprising about 28,000 acres of the Black Hills in southwestern South Dakota and established in 1903, this national park features Wind Cave, a large limestone cavern carved out of the vast limestone layers which underlie much of the park area. Changes in atmospheric pressure cause strong currents of wind to blow in and out of the cave.

Tom Bingham, a local pioneer, is credited with the cave's discovery in 1881. While deer-hunting, Bingham heard a strange whistling sound that led him to the cave entrance. The South Dakota Mining Co. was responsible for the exploration of Wind Cave and the discovery of many of its rooms and passageways. Alvin McDonald, the leading explorer of the cave, is buried near its entrance.

Texas. *Alibates Flint Quarries and Texas Panhandle Pueblo Culture National Monument.* These quarries, covering approximately thirteen hundred acres, provided the agatized dolomite which prehistoric Indians used to fashion projectile points, knives, scrapers, and other tools for more than one thousand years. This monument is not open to the public.

Chamizal National Memorial. This fifty-five-acre site memorializes the peaceful settlement by the Chamizal treaty (1963) of a one-hundred-year boundary dispute between the United States and Mexico. The memorial, located on Cordova Island in the Rio Grande, is not open to the public.

Fort Davis National Historic Site. Established in 1854 to protect travelers on the Overland Trail, FORT DAVIS was a key post in the defensive system of western Texas during the Indian wars. More than fifty adobe and stone buildings constituted the fort at the time of its abandonment in 1891. The site covers 447 acres.

Guadalupe Mountains National Park. This 77,500-acre mountain mass rising out of the desert in western Texas contains portions of the world's most extensive and significant Permian limestone fossil reef. The park also features a tremendous earth fault, lofty peaks, unusual flora and fauna, and a colorful record of the past. This park, established in 1966, is not open to the public.

San José Mission National Historic Site. Regarded as one of the finest Spanish missions in North America, San José Mission was established in 1720. It is an outstanding example of the frontier Spanish missions that stretched across the Southwest in the eighteenth century.

See also BIG BEND NATIONAL PARK.

Utah. *Arches National Park.* This park, located in eastern Utah near Moab, derives its name from the windows that erosion has carved into hundreds of vertical redrock slabs. The 34,250-acre park is divided into three tracts, the Windows, Devil's Garden, and Delicate Arch, where the basic geology of the arches can be studied. Landscape Arch, in the Devil's Garden section, is believed to be the longest arch in the world with a span of 291 feet and a height of 105 feet. The monument was established in 1929 and became a national park in 1972.

Canyonlands National Park. The terrain of this park, which is located near Moab, Utah, varies from high plateaus and mesas to basin lands along the cliff-rimmed Green and Colorado rivers. Among the features of the 257,600-acre area are the multicolored rock spires of the Needles section and the finlike formations of the Land of Standing Rocks, which rise to a height of 1,000 feet. The park was established in 1964.

Capitol Reef National Park. The name of this 36,115-acre park, in southern Utah, is derived from its reeflike cliffs capped by white, dome-shaped Navaho sandstone formations. Capitol Reef's exposed multilayered and multicolored rockbeds furnish a graphic illustration of the way in which the earth's surface was built, folded, and eroded in this region. The monument was established in 1937, and became a national park in 1972.

Cedar Breaks National Monument. Cedar Breaks, located in southwestern Utah near Cedar City, is a gigantic coliseum-shaped natural amphitheater eroded to a depth of 2,000 feet by water and other natural forces. The 6,172-acre amphitheater displays an amazing variety of colors caused mainly by iron oxides in the limestone cliffs. Orange predominates, but it is blended with white, cream, purple, yellow, brown, red, green, and many more. These tints are constantly changing with each new angle of the sun's rays. The monument was established in 1933.

Dinosaur National Monument. Straddling northeastern Utah and northwestern Colorado, this monument contains the most remarkable remains of dinosaurs ever found. Twenty-four complete skeletons have been removed from this fossil quarry, including that of an allosaurus which is considered to be the most perfect in existence.

Among the exceptional features of the 184,900-acre monument, established in 1915, are the spectacular canyons that slice into the wilderness. The gorges are narrow and deep, with sheer, strangely carved, and brightly tinted sandstone cliffs. Visitors to the area can view dinosaur bones in their original positions. The fossils have been uncovered in high relief rather than removed.

Golden Spike National Historic Site. This site, located at Promontory Point, Utah, commemorates the completion, in 1869, of the first transcontinental railroad in the United States. Each year on May 10, the "driving of the golden spike" is reenacted at exactly 12:47 P.M. The original spike is in the Stanford Museum, Palo Alto, California.

Natural Bridges National Monument. Of particular interest among the many eroded formations that comprise this 2,650-acre monument, in southeastern Utah near Blanding, are three large, natural rock bridges. Owachomo Bridge, the smallest of the three, spans a distance of 180 feet. Kachina Bridge, the largest bridge, spans 206 feet and is 93 feet thick at its smallest point. Sipapu Bridge is the longest and best-proportioned of the three. The span of this bridge is 268 feet. The monument was established in 1908.

Rainbow Bridge National Monument. Rainbow Bridge, located in southern Utah, is the greatest of the known natural bridges of the world. It has not only an enormous and almost perfectly formed arch below, but also a curved surface above, giving the effect of a rainbow. The arch is 309 feet above the streambed and 278 feet wide. It was established as a national monument in 1910.

Timpanogos Cave National Monument. These scenic caverns, designated as a national monument in 1922, are located on the rugged north slope of Mount Timpanogos in northern Utah. Most of the interior formations of the 250-acre cave are lemon yellow in color and include spectacular helictites and aragonite crystals. The cave is electrically lighted.

See also BRYCE CANYON NATIONAL PARK and ZION NATIONAL PARK.

Washington. *Fort Vancouver National Historic Site.* From 1824 to 1846, FORT VANCOUVER was the center of the fur-trading empire of the Hudson's Bay Company. In 1849 it became the first United States military post in the Pacific Northwest and remained the seat of political and military authority for the area. The seventy-five-acre site was designated a national monument in 1954.

San Juan Island National Historical Park. This 472-acre park memorializes the struggle for possession of San Juan Island by British and American settlers, a dispute that culminated in the "Pig War" of 1859. The "war" centered around a pig owned by the Hudson's Bay Company which was shot by an American settler when he found it rooting up his potato patch. Both nations organized garrisons on opposite ends of the island, but no fighting actually occurred. In 1872, after twelve years of joint military occupation, the dispute was finally arbitrated, sustaining the American claim. In 1966 it was designated a national historical area.

Whitman Mission National Historic Site. Established by Dr. Marcus WHITMAN and his wife in 1836, this mission was one of the first institutions of its kind in the Northwest. It operated until 1849 when the Whitmans and eleven others were massacred by the Cayuse Indians.

See also MOUNT RAINIER NATIONAL PARK and OLYMPIC NATIONAL PARK.

Wyoming. *Devil's Tower National Monument.* Devil's Tower, a huge monolith resembling a colossal stone tree-stump, is the most conspicuous landmark in northeastern Wyoming. It rises to a height of 865 feet and is about 1,000 feet in diameter at the base. The sides are symmetrical and almost perpendicular.

In certain lights the many subdued shades make an awe-inspiring effect which lead the Indians to attribute supernatural powers to the tower. It was established as a national monument in 1906.

Fort Laramie National Historic Site. This site includes the surviving buildings of the principal military fort FORT LARAMIE, which guarded covered-wagon trails to the West between 1834 and 1890.

See also GRAND TETON NATIONAL PARK and YELLOWSTONE NATIONAL PARK.

See Devereaux Butcher, *Exploring Our National Parks and Monuments* (1969); and John Muir, *Our National Parks* (1901).—R. B. W.

National Park Service. A bureau of the Department of the Interior, the National Park Service was established by Congress in 1916 to coordinate and administer the national park system. Conservationists and park enthusiasts, including Stephen T. Mather, Horace M. Albright, Frederick Law Olmsted, J. Horace McFarland, and Robert Sterling Yard, helped draft the authorizing legislation and lobbied successfully for its passage. The act directed the National Park Service "to conserve the scenery and the natural and historic objects and the wildlife" in the parks and to provide for their public use "by such means as will leave them unimpaired for the enjoyment of future generations." Tension between use and preservation has marked the bureau's administrative policies from the beginning.

Stephen T. Mather became the first director of the National Park Service, and Horace M. Albright served as his chief assistant. Working together, they organized the bureau, established its administrative style, participated in every aspect of its program, and encouraged preservationist and developmental values. In the 1920s, they launched an extensive publicity campaign to advertise the scenic western parks and increase the number of park visitors. As tourism increased, appropriations for the management and protection of the parks increased. Private entrepreneurs, regulated by the Park Service, were counted on to develop tourist facilities in the parks. Albright succeeded Mather as director in 1929, continuing the administrative values and basic polices of the Mather era. He headed the bureau during Herbert Hoover's administration, and guided it through the first hundred days of the New Deal. He resigned in August 1933 and was replaced by Arno B. Cammerer, another Mather man, who directed the bureau during Franklin D. Roosevelt's first two terms.

The most dynamic period of expansion in the history of the National Park Service occurred during the New Deal. In the 1930s, the bureau consolidated its control over all of the NATIONAL PARKS AND MONUMENTS and historic battlefields, some of which had previously been administered by the War Department and the Department of Agriculture. New national parks were established, including Olympic, Isle Royale, the Everglades, and Kings Canyon. Other national parks were significantly enlarged. Responding to the crisis of the Great Depression, the National Park Service cooperated with the Civilian Conservation Corps (CCC), the Works Progress Administration (WPA), and the Public Works Administration (PWA) to put unemployed men to work in the parks. The bureau also enlarged its historic preservation program and took a leading part in formulating national recreational policy. By 1940, after eight years of rapid expansion and functional diversification, the National Park Service came under heavy criticism from wilderness preservationists, who charged that the

scenic western parks were being neglected. Newton B. Drury's appointment as director in 1940, replacing Cammerer, was the beginning of a swing away from the Mather tradition in National Park Service affairs.

During World War II, resource developers made serious attempts to gain access to timber and other valuable natural resources in the national parks. A plan to cut the Sitka spruce in Olympic National Park, for example, almost succeeded. But the National Park Service resisted these demands and kept the national park system largely inviolate in spite of reduced budgets and a shortage of manpower. The bureau went through a period of retrenchment during the war years and in the immediate postwar era. It was revitalized in the 1950s by the Mission 66 Program, an ambitious plan to expand the parks and build new campgrounds and tourist facilities in the parks and national monuments. Proposed and carried out under Conrad L. Wirth, the Mission 66 Program came in response to massive public demand for new outdoor recreational facilities. Public use of the national park system was intense during these years, and the need for additional park and recreational lands became more and more apparent. Point Reyes, Redwood, Canyonland, and North Cascades national parks were established in the 1960s, a decade that, like the 1930s, produced rapid expansion in the National Park Service.

In 1970, the bureau administered 278 separate scenic, historic, and recreational units, a vast domain that totaled 29,508,288 acres and accommodated almost 200 million visitors. Overcrowding has been a problem in some of the parks and monuments since 1945 and restricting public access may soon be necessary.

See also entries on individual western national parks.

See John Ise, *Our National Park Policy* (1961); Robert Shankland, *Steve Mather of the National Parks* (1954); and Donald C. Swain, *Wilderness Defender: Horace M. Albright and Conservation* (1970).—D. C. S.

national roads. With remarkable foresight Congress included in the enabling acts of 1802 and 1803, which provided for the admission of Ohio into the Union, a provision setting aside three percent of the net proceeds from the sale of public lands in that state for its use in "laying out, opening and making roads" and two percent to be used by the federal government in constructing roads leading to Ohio. By 1806 a small but promising fund had accumulated, and Congress authorized surveys for a proposed national road from Cumberland, Maryland, across the mountains to Wheeling, Virginia, on the Ohio River. The Army Corps of Engineers and later the Corps of Topographical Engineers of the War Department were given charge of the surveys and later of construction. There thus came into existence two features of United States policy toward the West of far-ranging importance: a continually growing fund for road construction, because the three-and-two-percent clause was included in later enabling acts; and army bureaus, staffed with skilled engineers capable of surveying for roads, canals, and railroads—regardless of whether they were later to be developed for private profit. Many hundreds of miles of roads primarily intended for military purposes were built by the army engineers, and they proved to be of equal or greater value for nonmilitary purposes.

Construction of the Cumberland Road was not begun

until 1811 and was slowly pushed westward, reaching Wheeling, a distance of about 130 miles, in 1818. Well before its completion, the traffic—including stagecoaches, carriages, heavy freighters, and large droves of cattle, sheep, and hogs—proved greater than had been anticipated. Repair and maintenance costs loomed large. The route proved an immense success and demands were voiced that it be extended across the Ohio to Columbus, into Indiana and Illinois and on to Columbia, Missouri. Surveys were authorized in 1820 for the western extension—the National Road—and in 1825 the first appropriation for construction was voted. The route roughly followed Zane's Trace from Wheeling to Zanesville for which Congress had granted three sections of land in 1796, and continued to Columbus, which it reached in 1833. As the National Road was pushed westward it won some new support, though the great excitement about its expected results was dying down. Canals were now drawing the chief attention. The road was completed in finished form to Indianapolis in 1850, but only through private aid because federal funds were being used for other purposes. From Indianapolis to Vandalia it was only graded and bridged. The National Road was later turned over to the states in which it was built.

By the 1830s the scattered population in Michigan, Wisconsin, and Indiana were calling for aid in the building of roads, and the government responded by providing land grants to aid in the construction of three such roads. It was in the territories beyond the Mississippi that military roads were extensively constructed: one from Fort Snelling at the junction of the Mississippi and Minnesota rivers to Fort Bent in present-day Colorado, one from Fort Smith, Arkansas, to Albuquerque and the Colorado River, and one from San Antonio, with two gaps, to San Diego. Forts had already been established to warn Indians against raiding parties of emigrants and to provide the emigrants following these routes with some prospect of aid. In 1861 the Emigrant Overland Escort Service was established to strengthen that protection. One of the best known and extensively used of these military roads was constructed by Lieutenant John Mullan, running from Fort Walla Walla on the Columbia River across the continental divide to Fort Benton, the head of navigation on the Missouri River in Montana Territory, a distance of 624 miles through desert and high mountains. It was much used during the gold rushes into that northwestern area. Another road that had been planned by the Topographical Engineers was the Powder River route along the Bozeman Trail from Fort Laramie, Wyoming Territory, to Virginia City, Montana Territory. Difficulty with the Sioux Indians, the Fetterman Massacre, and jurisdictional disputes with the Department of the Interior forced its abandonment. Instead, the department was given the task of building a road to Virginia City; it also built roads from Memphis on the Mississippi to Fort Yuma on the Colorado and another from Fort Leavenworth by way of South Pass to California. The work was marked by mismanagement, fraud, political interference, and bureaucratic rivalry with the War Department, an unsavory record.

Most inexcusable was the grant of 2.5 million acres for the building of "military" roads in Oregon. The term *military roads* was a legal fiction, the construction was indifferent if not outright fraudulent, and the only result was that another large chunk of public lands had passed to speculators and lumber interests. (See ROADS AND HIGHWAYS.)

See John F. Due, "Dangers in the Use of the Subsidization Technique: The Central Oregon Wagon Road Grants," *Land Economics* (May 1970); Forest G. Hill, *Roads, Rails, and Waterways* (1957); and W. T. Jackson, *Wagon Roads West* (1952).—P. W. G.

Native American Church. See PEYOTISM.

Navaho (Navajo) Indians. Linguistically and culturally related to their Apache Indian neighbors in the Southwest, the Navaho speak an Athapaskan language that is intelligible to many speakers of Apache as well. The most recent archaeological and ethnohistorical data available suggest that the Navaho, like other Apachean groups, came into the Southwest from the Plains in the sixteenth century. Since the early seventeenth century, by which time they had become farmers, hunters, and gatherers, living in widely scattered local groups, the Navaho's homeland has been in the high plateau country of northeastern Arizona, northwestern New Mexico, and southeastern Utah.

The basic unit of social and economic support was the biological family, composed of a man, his wife, and their unmarried children. Some Navaho practiced polygyny, and it was not uncommon for a man to have two wives who were sisters. Each biological family occupied its own fork-stick or six-sided house, the *hogan*.

Because many tasks required more people to perform them than provided by a single family, Navaho traditionally lived together in camps of loosely grouped hogans made up of members of an extended family. The extended family included husband, spouse, unmarried children, married daughters, sons-in-law, and unmarried grandchildren. Beyond the extended family groupings there were larger family clusters, or "outfits," composed of kinsmen whose hogans were out of sight but who nonetheless could be counted on for economic or social support when needed. The Navaho, like the Apache, also had nonlocalized matrilineal kin groups called clans. In former times there were more than sixty such clans.

The Navaho "tribe" as a political entity is a modern phenomenon. In the old days Navaho headmen were the leaders of independent outfits. Each outfit had its war leader and its peace leader, and each outfit made its decisions independently of those of other Navaho. It is not surprising, therefore, that to non-Indians who dealt with them in the nineteenth century, it often appeared that Navaho were breaking the terms of settlement agreements. Whites failed to realize that a single leader could be spokesman for only a rather small group of people.

As Navaho in increasing numbers moved into the Southwest in the sixteenth century, it was inevitable that they would come into conflict over land and resources with people already there—Ute, Pueblo Indians, and Spaniards. The Navaho fell into the Apachean pattern of raiding for goods and waging desultory revenge warfare. In 1622 Navaho even forced the abandonment of one of the New Mexico pueblo settlements from which the people of the modern Jémez Pueblo are descended. Between 1630 and 1700 they acquired horses and sheep, and people who had been sedentary farmers,

Before a hogan, Navaho women clean, card, and spin the wool for a blanket woven on an upright loom. (New Mexico Department of Development)

hunters, and gatherers became increasingly raiders, travelers, and stockmen. As their territory grew, so did their enmity with neighboring Hopi, Zuñi, and other Pueblo Indians, but especially with the former two tribes.

In the eighteenth century, attempts by Spanish Franciscans to Christianize Navaho and to establish missions among them ended in failure. By the early nineteenth century, the Navaho had become a veritable scourge in the eyes of their neighbors. The northern frontier of New Spain was in a state of collapse; after 1821, when New Mexico became part of the Mexican republic, Mexican troops on the frontier were equally incapacitated, being too few and short on supplies. Navaho attacked the Hopi village of ORAIBI in 1837 and nearly depopulated it.

Three months after the United States declared war on Mexico in May 1846, General Stephen Watts KEARNY entered Santa Fe, New Mexico, and proceeded to claim most of the Southwest in the name of the United States. Lieutenant Colonel Alexander DONIPHAN led the first American expedition into Navaho country. He and his 350 troops met with 500 Navaho near Bear Springs, New Mexico, where they negotiated a peace treaty. This was in the winter of 1846.

Between 1846 and 1849, when Lieutenant Colonel John Washington negotiated a second treaty with the Navaho, United States troops were forced to send five expeditions against the persistently marauding Indians. The treaty between John Washington and the Navaho, negotiated at the mouth of Canyon de Chelly in Arizo-

na, was formally ratified by the United States Senate, the first to be thus approved.

But in spite of ratification, some of the Navaho outfits continued their raids and had numerous clashes with United States troops. In 1863 Colonel Kit CARSON, backed by Ute Indian scouts and allies, went on a search-and-destroy mission through the very heart of Navaho country, ruining crops and capturing or killing livestock wherever he found them. In early 1864 large numbers of Navaho began to surrender. Before long some eight thousand of them were taken on the brutal "long walk" of three hundred miles from Fort Defiance, Arizona, to Fort Sumner at Bosque Redondo on the Pecos River in New Mexico. They were held here as prisoners until a treaty between the Navaho and the United States was approved in 1868.

The Navaho treaty of 1868—and the Navaho are the only Indians living today in Arizona and New Mexico who have a treaty negotiated and ratified by both sides—gave them a reservation of 3.5 million acres. Subsequently, fourteen major additions were made to the reservation, either by executive order or act of Congress, bringing it up to its present size—15,132,143 acres. Today there are more than one hundred thousand Navaho living on the reservation. Thus, in terms of population and land, the Navaho tribe is by far the largest in the United States.

During the 1960s many Navaho referred to their reservation as the "land of the sleeping giant." And that sleeping giant is awakening. The first stirrings of modern Navaho political organization came in 1923 when the first tribal council was elected. This was followed in 1927 by the creation—through the urging of United States Indian agents—of local institutions known as chapters. Each of the present-day ninety-six chapters elects its own president and is responsible for administering its purely local affairs.

In the early 1930s grazing districts and grazing district committees were established, again at the urging of the Bureau of Indian Affairs, this time to combat the problem of overgrazing and deterioration of the rangeland. Since the 1800s the Navaho had been acquiring ever larger herds of sheep, goats, and horses. so that by the twentieth century the entire tribe had been converted from farmers, hunters, and gatherers to pastoralists who supplemented their income and subsistence from livestock with more traditional means of making a living. Non-Navaho in the 1930s viewed overgrazing as a critical threat to the Navaho's future; grazing districts, which became politically potent segments of tribal organization, were one result.

The tribe is also divided into seventy-four Navaho Tribal Council districts, and there are nineteen district tribal councils in addition to the chapter organizations. The modern result is what is now proclaimed verbally on letterheads and in all tribal publications as the Navajo Nation. It is comprised of an enormously complex bureaucracy and is becoming increasingly sophisticated in the management of all of its own affairs.

The tribe operates its own tribal utilities, police, ground water development, public works and housing, and a host of other activities and has departments to oversee leases involving mining and industrial development. In 1969 the Navaho became the first reservation tribe in the United States to found their own college, the Navajo Community College, a two-year school that offers an Associate in Arts degree. In 1974 a new campus was opened at Tsaile, Arizona, and plans were under way to start a Navaho medical college.

Although the public image of the Navaho, reflecting history, continues to be that of the colorful desert shepherds who excel in silversmithing and the weaving of fine rugs, saddle blankets, and other woolen textiles, it does not accord with present realities. Sheep camps and remote trading posts still exist, but so do supermarkets, paved highways, and rapidly growing reservation urban centers, such as those at Window Rock, the capital, and Tuba City, Fort Defiance, and Shiprock. Shiprock, in New Mexico, is the home of a large Fairchild electronics plant. Window Rock, in addition to housing the tribal offices and United States governmental offices, has its own bank, museum, tribal arts-and-crafts store, motels, an FHA housing development, fairgrounds, restaurants, and modern community building, which serves as both sports arena and concert hall. It is also where the *Navajo Times*, the most widely read tribal newspaper in the country, is published. Its sometimes controversial reservation competitor, *Diné Baa-Hané*, is published in Fort Defiance.

The Navaho also have their own corps of legal aid people. Dinebeiina Nahiilna Be Agaditahe ("Lawyer Contributing to the Revitalization of Navajos' Economic Well-Being"), known more simply as DNA, operates on funds provided by the Office of Navajo Economic Opportunity. Beginning in 1967, DNA completed more than fifteen thousand cases in the first two years of operation. By 1970 it had an annual budget of a million dollars and employed fourteen attorneys and ninety additional personnel. Government, both Navaho and federal, has become the largest income source on the reservation. Tribal income is derived from various kinds of mineral and industrial leases and from a multiplicity of tribal business enterprises and investments. The 1971-72 tribal budget was more than $18 million.

For all of its spectacular growth and in spite of its high annual budget, the Navaho continue to be beset with problems of poverty and unemployment. The present estimated rate of unemployment is about sixty-five percent; about twenty-three thousand Navaho required welfare assistance through the Bureau of Indian Affairs during 1970.

There is no question, however, that the prognosis for the Navaho future is good. The people have retained their language and innumerable aspects of their native culture and continue to find ways to combine the best of all worlds. Their native religion and mythology, which borrows heavily from Pueblo Indian religion, including such elements as the famous SANDPAINTINGS, are probably as important to the Navaho as they have ever been. They make up part of the curriculum of Navajo Community College. Navaho weavers are probably among the best known in the world, and their rugs, which are really of tapestry quality, of TL'AH HASTIIN are among the most prized possessions of the museums and collectors who own them. Navaho silversmithing, which began in the nineteenth century, is also known today throughout the world and continues to be an important source of income for many of the people (see SILVERWORK, SOUTHWESTERN INDIAN). The Navaho are a spirited and nationalistic tribe, a group whom other Indians will doubtless come to emulate in the future.

See Henry F. Dobyns and Robert C. Euler, *The Navajo People* (1972); Lawrence C. Kelly, *The Navajo Indians and Federal Indian Policy, 1900-1935* (1968); Clyde Kluckhohn and Dorothea Leighton, *The Navaho* (1946); Ruth Roessel, ed., *Navajo Stories of the Long Walk Period* (1973); Ruth M. Underhill, *Here Come the Navajo!* (1953); and Aubrey W. Williams, Jr., *Navajo Political Process* (1970).—B. L. F.

Navaho rugs. Today, the terms Indian rug and Navaho rug are interchangeable, for the Navaho are the only Indians of the Southwest who still weave rugs. The Pueblo long ago switched to less tedious pursuits, although Hopi men still weave a few blankets. The Navaho may have known the rudiments of weaving before settling in the Southwest, but they gleaned additional knowledge from the Pueblo and adopted the use of their vertical loom. The Pueblo Indians were great weavers of native fibers and cotton cloth and garments before the Spaniards came to the Southwest in the sixteenth century. The craft gradually deteriorated among the Pueblo, probably because the Spaniards demanded a large sum in the form of textiles as a tribute to the crown and the accessibility of European cloth provided a much easier way for the Indians to produce their attire.

The Navaho, always quick to absorb from the culture of others, took to the loom with great enthusiasm. Although the technique and the loom itself were those of the Pueblo, the designs were Navaho. The Pueblo Indians are hidebound by traditional ceremonial patterns even today, in their limited production of belts, headbands, and garters. A Navaho, on the other hand, sits down at a loom with a vision or idea—a product of imagination—and begins to develop the design.

The conceptual freedom afforded the Navaho gradually evolved into certain regional styles of design. These styles were encouraged and promoted by traders of different areas, so that today regional styles are quite distinctive.

A Navaho weaver, almost always a woman, sets about her craft using the same crude methods and implements employed since the Navaho first started weaving blankets about 1700. It all begins with the sheep, which must first be grazed and cared for. The wool is clipped, washed, carded, and spun. The family helps with shearing the sheep, but washing, carding, and spinning is the weaver's responsibility. She also gathers the materials from which the dyes are made. This is a time-consuming job and subject to seasonal limitations, for many of the dyes used are made from native plants. Spinning the yarn is still accomplished by using a primitive spindle and whorl arrangement. This is a polished slender stick about two feet long that is pushed through a wooden disk about four or five inches in diameter. After the yarn has been spun it is dyed in the desired colors. Then, the loom is prepared by attaching two stout upright poles and two crossbars that are used to string the warp (the lengthwise threads opposed to cross threads, or woof) of the rug. The weaver begins to weave using crude implements made from sticks of various shapes and sizes. The only manufactured utensil used by the contemporary Navaho weaver is the commercial card, with metal teeth, used for combing the fibers straight before spinning.

A weaver works from the bottom of the loom up, putting the wefts as far across as she can reach without changing her position. Because of this, the finished rug may show faint diagonal lines where the joints have been made. These lines have been dubbed the "lazy line" because of the Navaho woman's refusal to change position until absolutely necessary. Since Navaho adhere strictly to their rule "to avoid excesses," a Navaho weaver generally will not weave for more than two hours at one time; thus, even a small rug is weeks in the making. The final product, however, is usually a creation of great beauty, unique style, and of such quality that it will give the possessor pleasure for many years.

Probably the most famous and certainly the most precious of those regional styles are those Navaho rugs of the Two Grey Hills, located midway between Shiprock and Gallup, New Mexico. These rugs are frequently more costly than a Persian rug of similar size, and the intricacy of the geometric designs is just as busy. These rugs invariably are bounded by a black border and rarely incorporate other than natural colors, brown, black, and white. Sometimes the brown and black wools are carded with white to produce tan and grey or perhaps with a bit of native yellow or commercial turquoise. Two Grey Hills rugs are exceptionally finely woven, frequently with more than fifty weft threads to the inch. Outstanding examples produced by Esther Manulito count more than eighty wefts to the inch, and by Daisy Taugel-chee as many as one hundred ten to an inch. Obviously such finely woven material is more appropriately used as a blanket or wall hanging than as a rug.

Teec Nos Pos rugs, developed west of Shiprock, New Mexico, in the northeastern corner of Arizona, are recognized by outline designs that date back to the 1890s, in which each geometric figure or zigzag is outlined with a narrow row of contrasting color. Although a somewhat swimming effect is produced, it is pleasant and gay. Other geometric patterns are utilized, some similar in design to the Two Grey Hills. However, commercial chemical dyes are used extensively, and commercial yarns are on the increase.

Wide Ruins and Pine Springs, located at the southeastern edge of the Navaho reservation in Arizona, are the homes of the Revival style, so-called because these rugs are borderless and the designs simple. The use of both natural color and vegetal-dyed homespun yarn in soft pastel shades of green, gray, yellow, and pink and a generous use of white creates a muted harmonious effect soothing to the eye.

Crystal rugs, from the Crystal Springs area of western New Mexico, are distinctive for their wavy stripes created by alternating two or three weft picks (a pick up of two or three weft threads) of contrasting colors. The simple straightforward patterns are generally woven in dark vegetal dyes of black, green, tan, yellow, and rust. These rugs are well woven and simple.

Another identifiable regional style is the Ganado, which features black, white, and red geometric designs. The deep red tone so prized by this region came to be known as "Ganado red." Rugs of the Kayenta region frequently employ black, gray, and red on a background of white, utilizing a large serrated diamond or the "storm pattern." The Shiprock, Lukachukai, and Upper Greasewood regions are major producers of the *yei* rugs, characterized by stylized figures and often mistaken for ceremonial rugs by the uninitiated.

Many other fine styles are representative of the Chinle, Black Mountain, Steamboat, Rock Point, and Nazlini regions.

See Charles A. Amsden, *Navajo Weaving* (1949); Noël Bennett and Tiana Bighorse (Butler), *Working with the Wool—How to Weave a Navajo Rug* (1971); Bertha P. Dutton, *Navaho Weaving Today* (1970); Mary Kahlenberg, Mary Hunt, and Anthony Berlent, *The Navaho Blanket* (1972); Kate P. Kent, *The Story of Navaho Weaving* (1961); Gilbert S. Maxwell and Eugene L. Conrotto, *Navajo Rugs: Past, Present and Future* (1964); and Harry P. Mera, *Navajo Textile Arts* (1948).—B. P. D. and M. L.

Neagle, David (1847?-1926). Lawman, miner, and saloonkeeper. Neagle was born in Boston, but San Francisco has the surest claim on this short, left-handed member of the six-shooter gentry. He grew up in the Bay area and went to school there. In 1860 he dropped out of school and departed for the mining camps of the Pacific Slope. For the next two decades he frequented the toughest camps in the Far West as miner, gambler, saloonkeeper, lawman, and small-time politician. In 1880 he arrived in Tombstone, Arizona, as the foreman of a mine and was a deputy sheriff in Tombstone during the troubled period of the Earp-Clanton fued. Although his superior, John Behan, was very much involved in the difficulties between the Earps and the "Cow-Boys," Neagle managed to maintain a reputation for fairness on both sides. He was elected city marshal of Tombstone in January 1882 but was defeated in his bid for the sheriff's star that year and soon departed for other boomtowns. By the mid-1880s he was back in San

Francisco, where he dabbled in politics and became a deputy sheriff, clerk, and deputy marshal.

In 1888 Neagle became involved in one of California's most celebrated legal battles, the Sharon case, growing out of the alleged marriage of Sarah Althea Hill to Nevada's millionaire senator, William Sharon. The court fight continued even after Sharon's death and Sarah Hill's marriage to David Terry, one of her attorneys and a former member of the California State Supreme Court. The Terrys were a volatile pair, and when a federal court decided against Mrs. Terry in a climactic decision in the fall of 1888, a courtroom brawl ensued. Mrs. Terry was removed forcibly from the courtroom, and her husband drew a knife and attempted to break through the crowded hallway to his wife. Neagle was on the scene and helped authorities subdue him. The judge in the case was Stephen J. Field, associate justice of the United States Supreme Court and an old political adversary of Terry.

In the months that followed the Terrys repeatedly threatened Field, and when Field returned to California the following year, Neagle was hired as a deputy marshal to protect him from Terry's threats. On August 14, 1889, Neagle shot and killed Terry in the railroad depot at Lathrop, California, after Terry accosted Field in the dining room. Neagle was arrested for murder but was released after a *habeas corpus* hearing. Field then presented Neagle with a gold watch for his act.

In releasing Neagle, the presiding judge at the hearing applied a broad interpretation of the word *law*, maintaining that Neagle had acted under the law as a deputy marshal even though no federal statute specifically authorized marshals to protect judges. California appealed the decision. The state's argument was that, under the state's homicide statutes, California had jurisdiction in the case. The subsequent proceedings resulted in the landmark Supreme Court decision, *In re Neagle*, which has been called the most relevant utterance of the court on the extent of executive authority under the Constitution. In the decision the court upheld the lower court's interpretation of the word "law," asserting that "any obligation fairly and properly inferable" from the Constitution "is a 'law' within the meaning of the phrase." The statement gave the executive branch extensive authority and has been cited as the direct source of Theodore Roosevelt's "stewardship" theory of the presidency.

Neagle remained in San Francisco and was mentioned frequently in the newspapers in the 1890s, but his last years are obscure.

Stacy W. Osgood, "The Life and Times of David Neagle" and "More on David Neagle," both published in *The Westerners Brand Book* in 1962, are currently the best sources.—G. L. R.

Nebraska. The name *Nebraska* originated in the Omaha Indian term "Nibthaska," meaning "flat water." This was an apt description of the broad, shallow Platte River, which flows eastward across the state from the Rocky Mountains. Physical environment did much to shape Nebraska's development. The Missouri River was a natural highway to the West, as was the valley of the unnavigable PLATTE RIVER. The rich alluvial bottomlands adjoining these rivers and their tributaries have played a part in Nebraska's agriculture far disproportionate to their relatively small area. Well-watered loess

soils, which cover the eastern half of the state, were suited to traditional agriculture, while the semiarid high plains of western Nebraska required land use of a nontraditional character. The Sandhills region of north-central and northwestern Nebraska comprises almost one quarter of the area of the state and has long been recognized as an outstanding cattle-grazing district.

Even before 8,000 B.C. Nebraska was the home of various prehistoric peoples. The historic Indian tribes of east and central Nebraska were semisedentary and included the Iowa, Missouri, Omaha, Oto, Pawnee, and Ponca. The Omaha lived along the Missouri River from the Platte to northeastern Nebraska, and the Ponca lived immediately to the northwest. The Iowa, Missouri, and Oto dwelt along the Missouri south of the Platte, and the Pawnee occupied central Nebraska. The Pawnee spoke a Caddoan tongue, but the other tribes were part of the Siouan language family. Most numerous and powerful of these peoples were the Pawnee who had a population of approximately 10,000 in 1780. Like the other semisedentary peoples, they used horses, resided in earth lodges in villages, and practiced various crafts, such as pottery-making. The livelihood of the Pawnee was based upon corn and two annual buffalo hunts. Sharing many of the traits of the Pawnee, the Omaha were second in importance among the semisedentary tribes and in the late eighteenth century numbered some 2,800 persons. The Ponca were closely akin to the Omaha, but numbered only about 800 in 1780. The Iowa, Missouri, and Oto were the least viable of the semisedentary peoples.

Although Arapaho, Cheyenne, and Comanche sometimes visited western Nebraska, the principal nomadic Indians were the Brulé and Oglala branches of the western Dakota (Sioux). These hardy peoples roamed over central and western Nebraska and adjacent areas, posing a frequent threat to their linguistic kin along the Missouri River and to the Pawnee as well. Highly mobile hunters, the Sioux were well adapted to the semiarid conditions of their homeland.

Francisco Coronado, seeking gold for Spain, reached modern Kansas in 1541, but not until the early eighteenth century did white men enter the area that became Nebraska. By then, France had gained control of the mouth of the Mississippi River and from this base in Louisiana claimed the region drained by that stream. As early as 1714, Etienne Veniard de Bourgmont, a Frenchman, explored the lower reaches of the Missouri. Hoping to thwart any French ambitions in the interior of the continent, the Spanish authorities in Santa Fe sent a military expedition under Pedro de Villasur to the northeast in 1720. On August 13, near the confluence of the North and South Platte rivers in western Nebraska, Villasur and most of his party met death at the hands of the Pawnee. France did not in fact have any great interest in the region, although in 1739 Pierre and Paul Mallet sought to establish trade relations with Spanish New Mexico. In their westward journey to Santa Fe they quite by error traversed the Missouri valley and much of eastern Nebraska.

In 1763 title to the region west of the Mississippi passed to Spain. The Spanish made no haste to exploit the Missouri valley, but by the 1790s St. Louis-based fur traders were operating as far north as the Dakotas. In 1800 Spain secretly ceded the trans-Mississippi region to

Omaha City was the capital of Nebraska Territory when this engraving of the city appeared in Frank Leslie's Illustrated Newspaper *in 1858.*

France, and on April 30, 1803, France sold Louisiana, which included the Nebraska region, to the United States.

In the summer of 1804 the Lewis and Clark expedition spent seven weeks along the Nebraska section of the Missouri River, during which time they carried on amicable relations with the local Indians. Following the War of 1812 the United States government adopted a policy of establishing a line of military posts strategically located in the West. In 1819 Colonel Henry M. Atkinson was sent up the Missouri and established a base some ten miles north of modern Omaha. The next year his military encampment on the river bottoms was moved to high ground, where Fort Atkinson was established. Until its abandonment in 1827, this fort was the army's most westerly garrison.

In the meantime, Major Stephen H. Long of the Army Engineers had ascended the Platte valley to the Rocky Mountains, returning east by way of the Arkansas River. The official report of the Long mission proclaimed that the Plains region was desolate and ill-suited to white settlement, a judgment similar to one rendered by Lieutenant Zebulon Pike, who crossed the area in 1806. These negative commentaries gave rise to the concept of the trans-Missouri plains as the "Great American Desert," a notion that endured until the actual settlement of the land.

Soon after 1800 the Missouri River became the natural route in the northern Plains fur trade. The early leader in this business was Manuel Lisa, who in 1809 organized the Missouri Fur Company in partnership with other St. Louis traders. In 1812 Lisa, owing to difficulties with the Indians and British in the upriver country, established Fort Lisa, north of contemporary Omaha. Other firms, most notably John Jacob Astor's American Fur Company, operated in the area, and by 1823 trading was being carried on at a site named Bellevue, just above the mouth of the Platte. In later years the American Fur Company dominated the

Missouri River trade, and its Bellevue post became an important point in this commerce. The Missouri, however, was not the only artery to the western fur traffic, for in the 1820s the Platte valley became a useful route to the Rocky Mountain trade. Until the demise of the fur trade in the 1850s, Nebraska, while the scene of some of this business, served primarily as a path to the rich fur areas in the Rockies and northern Plains.

By the mid-1830s a few missionaries were ministering to the Indians of eastern Nebraska, but it was not until the next decade that Nebraska achieved importance in America's westward expansion. In the spring of 1841 a small group went up the Platte valley, bound for California and Oregon. From 1843 onward, the Platte valley became a portion of the Oregon and California trails as thousands of persons journeyed from Independence, Missouri, toward the South Pass in search of new homes or wealth in the Far West. In the summer of 1846 the Mormons, fleeing from Nauvoo, Illinois, reached the west bank of the Missouri at a point in modern Omaha and established a camp they called Winter Quarters. The following spring Brigham Young and a small band of the faithful went west through the Platte valley to the Great Salt Lake. In the next two decades some 80,000 Mormons made the trek through the Platte valley and across Wyoming to the new Zion.

By the 1840s some men saw the desirability of constructing a railroad to the Pacific. Governmental organization of the trans-Missouri region was a necessary prelude to such action, for it would bring about control of the Plains Indians. As early as 1844, Stephen A. Douglas of Illinois, hoping to make Chicago the eastern end of a railroad to the Pacific, introduced legislation in Congress to create a territory of Nebraska. Through Douglas' leadership, the adoption of the Kansas-Nebraska Act of May 30, 1854, was a key step in promoting a railroad utilizing a central route across the continent. Moreover, the statute was intended to satisfy speculators in western Iowa and Missouri who saw railroad construction and townsite development in the adjacent area as a boom that would come with the legal opening of the region to settlement. The act created the Territory of Kansas between 37 and 40 degrees and the Territory of Nebraska between 40 and 49 degrees north latitude, with both territories extending from the Missouri River to the continental divide. The new law repealed the portion of the Missouri Compromise of 1820 that had barred slavery north of 36° 30' in the area west of the state of Missouri. In providing that the people of the new territories would determine the fate of slavery, the Kansas-Nebraska Act brought internal strife to Kansas and led the nation toward civil war, although Nebraska was out of the mainstream of this controversy.

Even before the creation of Nebraska Territory, the government had extinguished Indian title to the lands along the Missouri. This enabled town promoters to move quickly in establishing paper metropolises at Bellevue, Brownville, Nebraska City, Plattsmouth, Florence, and Omaha City. A census taken late in 1854 showed that two thirds of Nebraska's population lived along the Missouri River south of the Platte. Ignoring protests from the people of this area, acting governor Thomas B. Cuming, who was associated with Iowa interests promoting the development of OMAHA, established the seat of government at that community, located well to the north of the Platte. For many years the Platte River was a major divisive force, for the stream was too shallow and quicksand-laden to ferry, and bridge construction was too costly.

Like other frontiersmen, early Nebraskans devoted much time to land speculation and other forms of promotionalism. Since the territory had not developed sources of cash income, the legislature chartered banks with the power of note issue. These unregulated wildcat establishments collapsed in the wake of the Panic of 1857, a fate that befell the entire speculative economy of the territory. Yet as the 1850s ended, Nebraska was beginning to develop a productive economy. Political leaders such as J. Sterling MORTON and Robert W. FURNAS promoted agriculture, and farming became increasingly important in the counties along the Missouri River. Nebraska City and Omaha became important terminals for freight and passengers arriving on Missouri River steamboats. Overland freight and stage companies, using the Platte valley as their route to the settlements and army posts of the West, advanced the economy of these river towns. Along the Platte, outposts such as Columbus, Grand Island, and Kearney City sold goods and services to westward-bound emigrants, as did road ranches at various points in the valley.

In December 1863 President Lincoln established a point opposite Omaha on the Iowa side of the Missouri River as the eastern terminus of the transcontinental railway. With the completion of the Union Pacific in 1869 and the opening of a railroad bridge across the Missouri in 1873, due to the persuasiveness of George L. MILLER, Omaha attained a primacy in Nebraska that it never relinquished. In 1869 the Burlington and Missouri River Railroad (later the Chicago, Burlington and Quincy) began to build west from Plattsmouth and in the next decade moved across southern Nebraska toward Denver. The Union Pacific and Burlington, as well as smaller lines, received federal and state land grants that amounted to more than sixteen percent of the total

area of Nebraska. The construction of the railroads gradually destroyed the steamboat, wagon-freighting, and stagecoach businesses—and also the metropolitan aspirations of all Missouri River communities except Omaha.

In 1864 Congress authorized Nebraska to devise a state government, but later that year the voters rejected statehood on grounds that it would increase taxes. Yet the pressures for admission mounted, and in June 1866 the electorate voted by a slim margin in favor of statehood. On March 1, 1867, Nebraska, greatly reduced from its 1854 dimensions, became the thirty-seventh state.

The chicanery through which the territorial capital had been located at Omaha still rankled many Nebraskans. In June 1867 the legislature thus voted to relocate the seat of government. A special commission later that summer established the capital at the village of Lancaster, on the open prairie some fifty miles southwest of Omaha. A major consideration in the selection of Lancaster—renamed Lincoln—was its proximity to some salt deposits. (As it turned out, they never became economically significant.) In order to assure the success of Lincoln's initial development, the capital commissioners, including Governor David Butler, misused state funds. Edward ROSEWATER then led a successful movement in the legislature to indict and remove Butler from office.

In the early 1870s Nebraska doubled in population. In 1870 a majority of the people still lived near the Missouri, but in the next few years the interior grew rapidly. Although the Arapaho, Cheyenne, and Sioux had offered sporadic resistance to the whites on the frontier through the 1860s, army posts and the reservation system now eased the trepidations of the sod-house pioneers. Far more burdensome than Indians were the difficulties of living in a SOD HOUSE, depression, and grasshoppers. As the national Panic of 1873 swept westward, swarms of Rocky Mountain locusts devoured the crops of the entire Plains region from 1874 through 1876. Private charity and federal funds provided relief for the destitute farmers.

When recovery came, Nebraska's population rose from 452,402 in 1880 to 1,058,910 in 1890—the most rapid numerical increase in its history. Many European immigrants, especially Swedes, Irish, and Bohemians, came to the state. By far the most numerous were the Germans, who in 1890 numbered 72,000 out of a total foreign-born population of 202,244.

In the 1880s corn production tripled; the oat yield increased over sixfold; and outstanding gains were recorded in hay, rye, potato, and swine production. Nebraska's range-cattle industry, which had made a good start in the 1870s, almost tripled its output as John BRATT and many other stockmen recognized the merits of the Sandhills area. Related to the growth in the livestock industry was the development of Omaha as a major packing center. Other businesses developed in the city, including a smelting works that was reputedly the largest in North America. With a population of 30,000 in 1880, Omaha became a city of over 102,000 ten years later. Other communities, particularly Beatrice, Grand Island, Hastings, Kearney, Lincoln, and Norfolk, grew rapidly during the boom years of the '80s.

Real estate speculation was common to all of Nebraska's cities.

Prosperity was more apparent than real, however, and as the 1880s ended Nebraska farmers faced the paradox of good crops bringing poor prices. Moreover, rural grievances against the railroads multiplied, for rate regulation under the state constitution of 1875 had been ineffective. The Farmers' Alliance became the voice of agrarian dissent and in July 1890 took the leadership in forming a People's Independent (Populist) party. Chief among the Populist demands were the reduction of freight rates to the level prevailing in Iowa and a drastic increase in the currency supply for the benefit of the debt-ridden farmers. Drought, crop failures, and the depression of 1893 later added to this reform impulse. Moreover, Judge Elmer DUNDY of the United States District Court in 1893 barred the implementation of the recently passed Newberry Act, which was designed to establish maximum railroad rates in Nebraska.

Recognizing that the farmers were no longer playing their traditionally passive role in politics, the Democrats and Republicans began to liberalize their platforms to meet the Populist challenge. Advocating free and unlimited coinage of silver as the remedy for the limited money supply, William Jennings BRYAN, encouraged by Populist senator William Vincent ALLEN, seized control of the Nebraska Democratic organization from a conservative old guard—a major step toward his presidential nomination in 1896. The Populists accepted fusion with the Democrats as a necessity, albeit a grim one. In 1897 a fusionist legislature, although failing to adopt railroad-rate legislation, enacted statutes controlling grain elevator company combines, telephone and telegraph firms, and stockyards, and also passed other reform measures.

After 1898 the Populists faded from the scene. Fusion with the Democrats had divested the party of its identity, and the return of prosperity made agrarian radicalism untenable. Yet in the early twentieth century Nebraska experienced a vigorous Progressive movement that in part may have been a legacy of the Populist revolt. In 1907 a Republican state government passed railroad regulatory measures, an anti-child labor statute, a primary election law, and other reforms. Later Democratic legislatures added to the list of Progressive accomplishments.

As the twentieth century began, the frontier disappeared. The railroads had sold their lands and only semiarid tracts remained available under the homestead statutes. By 1910 title had been awarded to 95,998 Nebraska settlers, or forty-eight percent of those initially filing, under the HOMESTEAD ACT (1862) the TIMBER CULTURE ACT (1873) of Phineas W. HITCHCOCK, and the Kinkaid Act (1904) of Moses P. KINKAID. Although the era of cheap or free land was gone, there were some new dimensions to Nebraska agriculture. Alfalfa, sugar beets, and winter wheat became vital to the economy, while DRY FARMING and irrigation grew in importance. Such University of Nebraska scholars as Samuel Avery, Charles E. BESSEY, E. A. Burnett, and Lawrence Bruner did much to make pure and applied science relevant to rural life. In 1910 the average value of Nebraska farms ranked fourth in the nation. World War I brought extremely high commodity prices, a condition that re-

sulted in a significant increase in crop acreage, soaring land prices, and mortgage indebtedness.

The bonanza ended sharply in 1920, and throughout the next decade the agricultural economy stagnated, only to collapse completely in the Great Depression. Drought, dust storms, and record-breaking heat merely added to the debacle confronting farmers and city-dwellers alike. The situation was improved somewhat by the millions of dollars Franklin D. Roosevelt's New Deal provided for farm recovery and aid to the unemployed. The Rural Electrification Administration did much to modernize farm life, while loans from the Public Works Administration laid the groundwork for the creation of a statewide, consumer-owned power system. Partly as an economy measure, and in response to the reform pleading of Senator George W. NORRIS, the voters in 1934 approved the establishment of a one-house, nonpartisan state legislature. The "Unicameral" first met in 1937 and, although the nonpartisan aspect remained controversial, this unique parliamentary body has functioned reasonably well. As the Depression passed, conservatism came to typify the political life of Nebraska, and leaders such as Senator Kenneth S. WHERRY emerged as vociferous foes of federal involvement in the state's economy.

In the thirty years after the coming of World War II, urban and rural Nebraskans enjoyed unparalleled prosperity. As had been the case since 1890, the population of the state continued to rise very slowly, reaching 1,483,791 in 1970. Although the growth rate was well below the national average, there was a drastic population shift within Nebraska from the rural to urban areas. With increased mechanization in agriculture and a highway system that provided easy access to the cities, employment opportunities on the farms and in the small towns steadily decreased. At the same time job opportunities in metropolitan Omaha, Lincoln, and other cities increased. Agriculture remained vital to the state's prosperity, yet Nebraskans were increasingly a part of urban America.

An excellent survey of the history of the state is James C. Olson, *History of Nebraska*, 2nd ed. (1966), which has a good bibliography. *Nebraska History*, a quarterly journal, is indispensable.—H. A. D.

Needham, James (?-1663). Explorer. Needham and Gabriel Arthur were sent in 1662 into the western woods by Major General Abraham Wood on an exploring expedition. They traveled southward from the headwaters of the James River to the Yadkin valley, where they were captured by Indians. Needham was murdered by an Occaneechi Indian known as "John," whom they had hired to guide them. His companion, Arthur, was spared to wander over a vast territory as an Indian captive. Whatever General Wood had in mind for these scouts on this venture, their expedition was a failure so far as it added any immediate information as to the nature of the western country, since Arthur did not return to Virginia to tell his tale until 1674.

See Clarence W. Alvord and Lee Bidgood, *The First Explorations of the Trans-Allegheny Region by the Virginians, 1650-1674* (1912); and W. E. Connelley and E. M. Coulter, *History of Kentucky*, vol. I (1922).—T. D. C.

Negroes in the Far West. There were persons of African descent in the West from the days of the earliest explorations of the Spanish. Black Estevanito, the shipwrecked colleague of Cabeza de Vaca, spent seven years in the Southwest, and his reports stimulated settlement of California by the Spanish. One result was the Coronado expedition of 1540, which explored part of the Colorado River and, incidentally, included several black neophyte padres in its company.

The first Afro-Americans to settle in the West came with the first settlers to Los Angeles in 1781. They were among the poor of the Sinaloa-Sonora provinces in Mexico, who were brought to California to stabilize that region for the Spanish. The only Afro-Americans in the West prior to the Los Angeles settlement were in Baja California, and they arrived early in the eighteenth century. One authority on the Spanish period of settlement concluded that by 1790 the settlers and soldiers of the Californias were about twenty percent of African or part African descent. Most of these people tended to disappear into the general Mexican population with the passage of time. A few, however, became prominent in Alta California during this period, the Tapia and Pico families being the best known.

In the years prior to the 1849 gold rush, a few English-speaking Negroes arrived and remained in California. They were mostly deserting sailors. Other English-speaking black men were associated with the fur hunters who found their way across the Sierra to California. Peter Ranne accompanied Jedediah Smith into California in 1826 and Jim BECKWOURTH, one of the most famous mountain men, explorers, and western guides, spent many years in and out of California. However, none of these men remained permanently in the Far West.

The most prominent black of this origin was Allen B. Light, who arrived in 1835 and became a Mexican citizen. His knowledge of otter hunting earned him an official appointment from Governor Juan Bautista Alvarado as "comisario general," which made him responsible for suppressing illegal otter hunting along the Santa Barbara coast.

The best-known Afro-American of the Mexican period was Alexander Leidesdorff, who was born in the Virgin Islands of a father who was Danish and a mother who was a Virgin Island black. He lived in California from 1841 to 1848 and became a prominent San Francisco buisnessman. He also owned and introduced the first steamship on San Francisco Bay. Just before the American conquest of California, Leidesdorff was appointed a United States vice consul. He died one year before the California constitution of 1849 was ratified, which, ironically, would have disfranchised him because of his part-African ancestry.

The gold rushes of 1848 and 1849 not only overwhelmed the racially tolerant California society but also sharply increased the number of Negroes in the West. In 1848 deserting black sailors joined deserting white sailors to rush to the gold fields when their ships anchored in San Francisco Bay. By 1849 many more Afro-Americans had arrived in California, some as slaves of gold-seeking Southerners and others who sought material improvement either as miners or in the shorthanded menial and service occupations. By 1850 there were 962 Afro-Americans in California, which constituted approximately one percent of the non-Indian population. In the early years of the gold rush they tended to concentrate in the mother-lode areas, Sacramento and San Francisco. As the gold rush waned toward the end of the 1850s, blacks and whites drifted toward Sacramento and San Francisco and many of the Negroes developed communities in Marysville, Grass Valley, and Stockton, California. In this period, only a handful lived in the Oregon and Washington territories, which was partly the result of hostile legislation.

California's 1849 constitution made it a free state, but the law was hostile to Negroes in its failure to provide suffrage, education, or equal rights with regard to testifying in the courts. For most blacks this was a familiar situation, but many New England-born Negroes had by 1849 experienced some democratic rights. Hundreds of Afro-Americans had come to California by the end of 1849 as slaves and many of them achieved freedom through self-purchase and remained in the state. But many, perhaps most, of them went back to slavery when their masters returned with them to the slave states. A courageous handful attempted to flee slavery while in California, and some succeeded. Through the rest of the 1850s Negroes continued to come to California, and by 1860 there were more than four thousand Afro-Americans in the West. This number was still about one percent of the non-Indian population.

During the early unsettled days of the gold rush the color line in California was a bit blurred, but as stability developed, the eastern patterns of discrimination and segregation emerged in the West. Independent churches, however, were organized very early in the 1850s. By the mid-1850s there were "colored" Methodist and Baptist churches in the largest black communities, such as San Francisco and Sacramento. By 1860 black churches were also organized in Marysville, Stockton, and Grass Valley. "Colored" schools, however, were established in the 1850s, not by choice, but through the racist neglect of local and state officials. At first the Negro churches set up schools in their meager quarters, but by the end of the decade, they were getting some financial support from local boards of education, largely through the work of the devoted black teacher-minister Jeremiah B. Sanderson. It required a number of state supreme court struggles to completely integrate these schools just before the beginning of the twentieth century.

Discrimination in the court system produced a civil rights movement in the 1850s that was called the Colored Convention. Its major objective was to obtain equal testimony rights. The denial of these rights made a black man defenseless in the protection of his person and property in the absence of white witnesses to a violation. This California Colored Convention movement was organized by some of the most talented and well-educated black men of the century, many of them with prior organizational experience in the eastern states. Three colored conventions, held before the Civil War, inaugurated statewide petition campaigns to democratize the testimony laws. In spite of thousands of white signers to these petitions, the intensely prejudiced Democratic-controlled state legislature rejected these appeals. Not until 1863, when the Republican party became a force in state politics and the Emancipation Proclamation had been issued, did the testimony laws become democratized for Negroes. However, blacks in California did not get the vote until 1870 when the Fifteenth Amendment made it mandatory. State legislation never provided it voluntarily.

In spite of racist obstacles, many blacks gained material wealth before the Civil War. They tended to be predominant in the culinary fields and were found in many occupations in the state. Through the efforts of the convention leadership, they published a newspaper, the *Mirror of the Times*, which appeared between 1855 and 1857.

In the years after the Civil War the growth of the western black population was slow. They comprised only a minute portion of southern California's total population. In 1870, when San Francisco had more than a thousand black citizens, Los Angeles County had a little more than one hundred. In the same year the black populations of Oregon and Washington were more than three hundred and two hundred, respectively.

At the turn of the century the black population grew slightly in California, mostly in southern California. While San Francisco and Sacramento Negro communities remained stationary, there was some movement toward Alameda and Oakland. Small, totally black communities, such as Allensworth, emerged in the San Joaquin Valley as a result of the coming of the railroad and flights from the terror of the southern states following collapse of Radical Reconstruction. By 1910 the trickle of black immigrants had become a flow: California's black population reached more than 21,000, nearly half of which resided in Los Angeles. While San Francisco had 1,600, Alameda across the bay had 3,600. The Oregon and Washington black populations reached more than 1,400 and 6,000, respectively.

During the second half of the nineteenth century the black communities of all three Pacific states, including a small émigré group in British Columbia, maintained contact through two Negro newspapers published in San Francisco, the *Pacific Appeal* and the *Elevator*, the latter brilliantly edited by a remarkable New York-born Negro, Phillip Bell, who was associated with the very first effort at Afro-American journalism in 1827. These papers failed to survive the end of the century and were replaced by a series of local journalistic efforts of lesser importance. When the Negro journalists of the Bass family published the *California Eagle* in Los Angeles in the early twentieth century, the black community once more had a stable press. It continued to publish for a half century.

Denials of opportunity in the South, the opening of opportunity—especially in railroad work—in the Los Angeles area, and the growth of industry in World War I increased Negro migration to southern California. This movement was partly inspired by Negro press reports of a relatively high degree of home-ownership by blacks around Los Angeles. These migrants were coming increasingly from the southeastern states, a development that became predominant in the years between the two world wars and after.

While a very small professional and business class emerged in the black communities at this time, the majority of Negroes were in the menial and domestic services. In the first quarter of the century, although the skilled and artisan blacks grew even fewer in number as organized white workingmen squeezed them out, black workers increased somewhat in the growing, but unorganized, industries of the state. Negroes found one interesting form of employment available to them in the film industry, but most of this work was only in mob scenes or in exotic roles portraying other types of non-Caucasians. As the years passed, Negroes were offered parts as buffoons or musical entertainers in this California industry. Not until the 1960s were dignified roles available to Negroes.

It was the racist and historically distorted film *Birth of a Nation* that gave the Los Angeles branch of the young National Association for the Advancement of Colored People (NAACP) its first important work. This film, completed in Hollywood in 1915, depicted black people as stupid, arrogant, and lecherous unless they were totally subservient to whites. It presented the period of Radical Reconstruction as a complete political disaster and did not indicate that during this period the first fumbling steps toward democracy in the South were taken. The film also made heroes of Ku Klux Klansmen. The Los Angeles branch of the NAACP protested the film's appearance and alerted its national organization, then only six years old, to broaden the fight. By 1914 this earliest civil rights organization of the twentieth century already had six chapters in the West. They were in Los Angeles and Oakland, California; Portland, Oregon; and in Tacoma, Walla Walla, and Seattle, Washington. Under the influence of Booker T. Washington, by 1914 four locals of the National Negro Business League were organized, three in southern California and one in Oakland, California.

Between the world wars the partial segregation of California blacks, intensified by the white society's continued job discrimination in the better-paying positions, began to turn Negro communities into ghettos and slums. The mass migration of blacks to California as a result of wartime industry deepened the process. It was most noticeable in the Los Angeles area and in the East San Francisco Bay communities of northern California. The post-World War II period saw no letup in the black westward migration, and by 1960 there were nearly 465,000 blacks in the Los Angeles area, making it the sixth largest black urban community in the United States. The San Francisco Bay area had nearly 239,000. By this time the black population was 5.6 percent of California's citizenry. In the same year the black population in Washington was 48,738, or 1.7 percent of that state's population. In Oregon the statistics were 18,133, or 1 percent of the population.

During the 1930s the California Negro voter moved en masse into the Democratic party, as did blacks in the rest of the country where they had the franchise. The first black assemblyman in California was Augustus Hawkins, a Democrat from the Los Angeles area who represented his district from 1935 to 1962. In 1962 he was elected to Congress, the first black congressman from California. In 1970 he was joined by Democrat Ronald Dellums, who was elected from the Oakland area. In 1972 a black woman, Yvonne Braithwaite Burke, was elected from the Los Angeles area and became the third black in the California congressional delegation. Other elective positions held by blacks in California as of 1969 were fifteen city council seats, five state assembly seats, one state senate seat, and two mayoralties. The third and most unusual of the mayoral victories for California blacks came in 1973, with the election of Thomas Bradley, a former Los Angeles city councilman, over Samuel Yorty in Los Angeles, where whites constitute a majority. In that same year, a black woman, Doris Davis, was elected mayor of Compton. The first black state superintendent of education, Wilson Riles, was elected in 1970. Much of this political achievement was undoubtedly the result of the existence of seven successful Negro newspapers in the state.

However, in spite of some political gains, the masses of blacks in California found themselves increasingly ghettoized and experiencing de facto segregation in the schools because of their general inability to afford improved housing (see CALIFORNIA). Those who could afford better housing discovered that "gentlemen's agreements" by realtors effectively blocked implementation of the Fair Housing Act. White Californians revealed their prejudices in 1964 when they passed Proposition 14, which eliminated the Fair Housing Act. In 1966 the state supreme court declared Proposition 14 unconstitutional, and this decision was upheld the following year by the United States Supreme Court. Resentment over the majority white vote for this proposition, added to a long history of black hostility toward the Los Angeles police, erupted in August 1965 in the West's most violent racial outbreak, in Watts, California. With the slogan "Burn, baby, burn," the largely black community of southeastern Los Angeles exploded into a mile-square conflagration in which hundreds were involved and thirty-five people, mostly black, were killed.

Within a year of the Watts riot, and not unrelated to it, the Black Panther party was organized among Oakland black youth by Huey P. Newton and Bobby Seale. The party's tenets, originally only to bear arms in defense of residents in black communities where its organizers charged police harassment, expanded until by the end of the 1960s the Black Panther party described itself as a Marxist-Leninist party. It published a weekly called the *Black Panther*, which became a national publication when the party established membership in the eastern and midwestern states. In early 1971 the major activity of the Black Panther party was a nationwide effort to gain the release of all blacks from the nation's prisons; the party considers all black prisoners to be political prisoners. Central to this objective in California was the freeing of Angela Davis, a member of both the Black Panther party and the Communist party, who was charged with complicity in killings that resulted from an abortive effort to free three black convict witnesses from the Marin County Courthouse. Since 1972 the Panthers have concentrated on electoral politics. Such activity reached a high point in the 1973 candidacy of Bobby Seale for mayor of Oakland: he received one third of the vote.

See Delilah Beasley, *The Negro Trail Blazers of California* (1919); Eugene H. Berwanger, *The Frontier Against Slavery* (1967); Lawrence B. de Graaf, "The City of Black Angels: Emergence of Los Angeles Ghetto, 1890-1930," *Pacific Historical Review* (August 1970); Jack Forbes, *Afro-Americans in the Far West*; and Rudolph M. Lapp, "Negro Rights Activities in Gold Rush California," *California Historical Society Quarterly* (March 1966).—R. M. L.

Negroes on the frontier. Most Americans until recently would have accepted the dictum of the Pulitzer Prize-winning historian James Truslow Adams that Negroes did not play a significant role on the American frontier. Adams asserted that the Negroes brought to the West possessed many excellent qualities, including "even temper, affection, great loyalty, . . . imitativeness, willingness to follow a leader or master," but they were not the qualities of frontiersmen. He further maintained that the entire institution of slavery had made Negroes ill-suited to founding communities on the frontier.

The facts are considerably different. Although most Negroes were handicapped by their legally imposed servile condition, and free Negroes by discrimination, during nearly four centuries they were active, and in some cases disproportionately significant, on almost every American frontier.

Because these frontiers, particularly in their earlier phases, drew racial lines between Indians and "civilized" peoples rather than between blacks and whites, because of the special need for an able and industrious frontier population, and because of the almost incessant border warfare that caused the warring peoples to seek allies, free Negroes, runaways, and even slaves on various frontiers sometimes had the opportunity to display qualities of intelligence, courage, initiative, and endurance and to advance from the lowly status of servile laborer to that of explorer, trader, interpreter, prospector, soldier, scout, cowhand, and, if free, even prosperous landowner or capitalist.

The frontier of exploration preceded, sometimes by centuries, the frontier of settlement and, often, even the fur-trading frontier. Negroes were members of many exploring expeditions. Although principally slaves initially intended as body servants and unskilled laborers, they frequently, under the exigencies of frontier life, displayed special personal qualities and abilities.

Estevanito, "an Arabian black," was one of the four survivors of the expedition of Pánfilo de Narváez, which was shipwrecked in 1529 on the Texas coast. During years of wandering among the Indians he distinguished himself as a medicine man and linguist. When the little party finally reached the Spanish settlements of northern Mexico, the viceroy sent Estevanito as leader of an advance party on an expedition northward. Although his march was at first triumphantly successful, the people of the Zuñi pueblo of Cíbola in New Mexico put him to death.

Negroes also accompanied the French explorers of the eighteenth century and the Anglo-American explorers of the nineteenth. York, who accompanied the Lewis and Clark expedition as Captain William Clark's body servant, was also a popular entertainer, expert swimmer, skillful hunter, and even on occasion served as interpreter. Jacob Dodson, a youthful free Negro, accompanied John Charles Frémont on his second and third expeditions (1843-46) as body servant and developed skills as a hunter, boatman, Indian-fighter, rider, and roper.

Fur traders closely followed and sometimes preceded the official explorers. Negroes were active in the fur trade from the Carolinas in the early eighteenth century to the Rocky Mountains in the mid-nineteenth. They occupied all positions, from servant, packhorseman, voyageur, cook, and hunter; through trusted and responsible employee (particularly interpreter); to independent trader. At least two men of Negro ancestry were among the overland Astorians in 1811: one was the notorious Edward ROSE, of white, Cherokee, and Negro ancestry, who served as interpreter, hunter, and guide to many fur-trading and government expeditions; the other was Francois Duchouquette.

The best-known Negroes in the fur trade were Jean Baptiste Point-au-Sable, a French mulatto who in 1778 married a Potawatomi Indian woman and a little later established a trading post on the site of present-day Chicago; the Bongas, descendants of a couple who during the 1780s were slaves of the British commandant at Fort Michilimackinac, who intermarried with the Chippewa and served in all ranks of the fur trade as voyageur, interpreter, and independent trader; and Jim BECKWOURTH, a Virginia-born and Missouri-raised mulatto who became a mountain man in 1824.

Colonel James Stevenson of the Bureau of Ethnology may have exaggerated somewhat when he asserted that "the old fur traders always got a Negro if possible to negotiate for them with the Indians ... because ... they could manage them better than white men, with less friction," but the Negro's lesser racial arrogance may indeed have given him an advantage. Negroes, moreover, were readier than whites to marry Indian women and to maintain permanent or semipermanent associations with their tribes. The virtual nonexistence of white women in the fur-trading world reduced tensions and the pressures of prejudice from the whites, for, as Danial Boorstin has pointed out, "the making of social distinctions was woman's work."

Although Negro slaves had been with all the early sixteenth-century Spanish explorers and conquistadores, the score of Africans who arrived at Jamestown in 1619 were the first of their race on the Anglo-American agricultural frontier. Treated at first merely as servants, the African servant was transmuted into the Negro slave not long after mid-century. By the middle of the eighteenth century, Negro slavery had been established in all the British colonies.

From the beginning of European settlement to the final termination of Amerindian resistance more than three centuries later, almost every frontier was to some extent a military frontier, on which settlers of European descent were intermittently engaged in an armed struggle with the native inhabitants and, in some cases, with the forces of rival European powers. The roles of Negroes on these military frontiers varied according to circumstances, especially the character of their servitude (if slaves), their relative numbers, and their proximity to the territory of powerful Indian tribes and of nations unfriendly to Great Britain or the United States; their role, of course, changed drastically after emancipation.

Slavery on the early Anglo-American frontier existed in essentially one of two forms. Where slaves were numerous and worked in gangs under an overseer, there was little opportunity for them to develop any sense of identity with, or loyalty to, their masters. And when, as in South Carolina, the frontier of settlement was also a military frontier beyond which runaway slaves could find refuge, they were potential enemies. Yet, paradoxically, it was on this frontier that Anglo-American authorities used Negro slaves as a regular part of the military establishment. A South Carolina law of 1708 required each militia captain to enlist, train, and bring into the field for each white "one able Slave armed with gun or lance." These slave-militiamen were actually used in the field on only one occasion—in the Yamasee-

Creek War of 1715. They served well, but Negro slaves on the southern Anglo-American frontier were never again used extensively as armed militiamen, because of their large numbers, the Spanish authorities' active efforts to encourage South Carolina slaves to join runaways in Florida, and the consequent danger that armed slaves would turn on their masters. The South Carolina government soon accepted the principle adduced by General James Oglethorpe of Georgia: "As many slaves ... so many Enemys. ..." Slaves, however, continued to appear on South Carolina militia rolls and served on military expeditions as servants, wagoners, and "pioneers."

Where, on the other hand, slaves were comparatively few—in the backcountry of New England and the middle colonies and states, west and south to the Virginia and North Carolina backcountry (including Kentucky and Tennessee), and on into Missouri and even parts of Texas—their roles were frequently much the same as those of white employees. They felled trees, plowed the soil, tilled and harvested the crops, and did the usual chores—working side by side in field and shop and kitchen with their masters and other members of their families. The Negro men were frequently skilled in various crafts, and some were experienced woodsmen. Humanely treated domestic slaves of this type often identified their interests with those of their masters much as if they were white indentured servants.

Although on such Anglo-American frontiers Negro slaves were involved in struggles with hostile Indians principally as noncombatants, from western Virginia to Texas domestic slaves frequently wielded ax, hoe, club, and even firearms against Indians in defense of their own and their masters' homes and families; sometimes they lost their lives, as did the slave London, who was killed in single combat with an Indian outside the Boonesborough palisade when his gun misfired.

Free Negroes with useful skills, and especially Negroes of mixed ancestry, sometimes enjoyed opportunities and privileges on the frontier that a more settled community might have denied; some attained positions of prestige. Such free Negroes—including runaways able to pass as free—were found in the back settlements from Virginia, the Carolinas, and Florida all the way across the continent.

Free persons of color participated in the resistance to and expeditions against Indian raiders. In fact, a special category of free Negroes developed on the frontier. They were usually mulattoes, sometimes with an Indian admixture, who as hunters and traders had become acquainted with various Indian tribes and who served as interpreters, guides, and experienced fighting men on military and quasimilitary expeditions. A "bold quadroon mulatto named Evans" who was killed in the Red Stick War, Ben Wiggins of Florida, the mountain men Rose and Beckwourth, Jack Ivy of the Red River frontier of Texas, "Old Jefferies" of Fort Leavenworth—all are antebellum examples.

More typically, however, the free Negro on the frontier was a skilled farmer or craftsman—sometimes both.

In 1753 the only blacksmith near Staunton, Virginia, was a free Negro from Pennsylvania with a Scottish wife; in the same community was a runaway, a literate Negro farrier. Even in early South Carolina the need for able and industrious settlers sometimes caused the authorities to allow, and even encourage, the settlement of free persons of color. Governor Robert Johnson in 1731 permitted Gideon Gibson, a "colored" carpenter and landowner from Virginia—with seven Negro slaves, a white wife, and several sons, all with white wives—to settle on the Santee. In 1751 another free Negro carpenter from Virginia, John Chevis, with a family of nine children, applied for and apparently received a land grant, although the following year Matthew Chavous (note the similarity of names), a free Negro who had been in the colony for twelve years, was denied such a grant.

Free Negro farmers, stock-raisers, and craftsmen were attracted to the Texas frontier by the Mexican republic's racial tolerance and freehanded land policy and managed to remain despite the Texas republic's racist laws. William Goyens (or Goings), a free Negro man with a white wife and several Negro slaves, was settled as early as 1821 at Nacogdoches, where he operated a large blacksmith shop employing slave, free black, and white labor, speculated in land, served as an interpreter to the Cherokee Indians, and enjoyed the confidence and respect of Sam Houston. The Ashworth clan of free Negroes, whose progenitors had settled in Texas before its revolution, were by 1850 the largest cattle-raisers in Jefferson County.

Missouri—perhaps in part because of an atmosphere still somewhat tinged by French traditions of racial tolerance—furnished opportunities to various prosperous farmers and skilled craftsmen. The Negro Hiram Young, in the days of the Santa Fe and Overland trails, was one of the largest manufacturers in Independence, Missouri, operating with both white and slave labor a large blacksmith shop and one or more wagon-manufacturing establishments that produced hundreds of wagons and thousands of ox yokes. George BUSH, a freeborn mulatto who had settled in Missouri, was by 1844 a prosperous stock-raiser with a white wife and five sons. George Washington, the Virginia-born son of a white mother and a Negro slave father, was brought up in Missouri by a white family and early developed remarkable skills as a farmer, tanner, tailor, distiller, gristmiller, and sawmiller. James Milton TURNER, born a slave in St. Louis County, was a leader in the Negro suffrage movement in Missouri after the Civil War.

Both Bush and Washington joined the rush from Missouri to the Oregon country. Bush went out in 1844 and, on learning of the provisional government's passage of an anti-Negro law, settled on Puget Sound, where he farmed with great success, helped build the region's first American-owned gristmill and sawmill, and introduced the first mower and reaper. His son, William Owens Bush, carried on his father's tradition as a master farmer and also served during the first two terms of the Washington state legislature. George Washington also settled in Washington as a farmer in 1851, became a wealthy man for the time and place, and in 1872 founded the town of Centerville (now Centralia). Both men were highly regarded for their ability, industry, and generosity.

The American frontier had at least two sides. Confronting the Anglo-American frontier was the Indian frontier and, sometimes, a French or Spanish frontier. Negroes were found among Indians, Spanish, French, and, later, Mexicans, confronting and sometimes attempting to resist the Anglo-American advance. The more relaxed racial mores of these peoples made it possible for free Negroes and runaway slaves from the Anglo-American frontier to settle among them as individuals and families and even to establish Negro communities—the latter an impossibility on the preemancipation Anglo-American frontier. Although nearly all frontier settlements were, in a sense, on a military frontier, this was particularly true of Negro settlements, which were exposed not only to the relentless official encroachments of Great Britain and the United States but also to frequent unofficial or semiofficial raids by Anglo-American slavers and filibusters. These Negroes thus were under a particular necessity to be prepared and equipped for military action.

Not all slaves, even domestic slaves on Anglo-American frontiers of small Negro population, were well treated, and even if well treated, not all were contented. Frontier slaves often escaped to the Indians, French, or Spanish. In 1712, during the Tuscarora War in North Carolina, a runaway Negro named Harry helped the Tuscarora to plan a formidable fort, which required a long siege supported by artillery to subdue; when it capitulated, Harry "was cut to pieces immediately." A runaway slave named Pompey was active among the hostile Shawnee on the Kentucky frontier until killed during the siege of Boonesborough while sniping from a tall tree.

The preemancipation frontier on which Negroes were most prominent, active, and formidable was the southern frontier bordering on, and including, Spanish Florida. The comparatively large numbers of Negroes in South Carolina, the proximity to Spanish territory, the existence of several powerful Indian tribes, and a state of almost incessant border warfare combined to give the Negroes unusual importance. Soon after the establishment of South Carolina, slaves began to escape to Florida, where they received Catholic baptism and were given land and arms; runaway Negroes accompanied Indian allies of the Spanish on border raids; and in 1738 the governor of Florida established a Negro military colony, protected by a fort, north of St. Augustine. Negro emissaries encouraged plots among South Carolina slaves to seize arms and fight their way to Florida; one such plot, in 1739, culminated in a bloody insurrection. Oglethorpe's invasion of Florida in 1740 encountered resistance from numerous Negroes, including refugees from South Carolina, and the Spanish force that unsuccessfully counterattacked in 1742 included a regiment of Negroes and another of mulattoes. Runaway Negroes also operated effectively among the Creek Indians as agents for the French and Spanish.

Although the cession of Florida to Great Britain in 1763 temporarily terminated these runaway-slave settlements, the outbreak of the American Revolution, followed in 1783 by the retrocession of Florida to Spain, restored its importance as a refuge for slaves from South Carolina and Georgia. Negro slaves, or runaway Negroes who were accepted as "vassals and allies" of the Indians, had also become important among the Five Civilized Tribes of the South. But although all these tribes possessed Negroes, the full-blooded Creek of Alabama and, still more so, their Seminole kinfolk in Florida exerted comparatively little control over the Negroes among them, whether legally purchased slaves, runaways, or captives. The Seminole country, in particular, became a refuge for runaways, who settled in separate villages, under the protection of chiefs to whom they paid a moderate tribute, and whose industry and prosperity astonished all beholders. These Negroes gained great influence among the somewhat isolated Seminole, who, lacking any important half-breed element, largely depended on Negroes for their knowledge of the white man's language and ways.

The existence of Negro villages was always precarious, even on Spanish soil, and their inhabitants had to be constantly prepared to fight in their defense. In 1811 when the United States decided to take possession of East Florida by encouraging an uprising by American settlers and an invasion by adventurers from Georgia, only the determined resistance of Florida Negroes prevented the plan's early success. The free Negroes and the runaways among the Indians feared that Florida's annexation to the United States would mean reenslavement for them, while the slaves dreaded the stricter slave code of the southern United States. The Spanish authorities armed the local Negroes and brought in Negro troops from Cuba, while the Negroes living with the Seminole stirred up the Indians against the invaders and instigated American-owned slaves in Florida and Georgia to leave their masters and join the resistance forces. The Negroes and Indians badly defeated the invaders in two actions—in one of which a Georgia officer reported of the Seminole that the Negroes were their best soldiers—raised the siege of St. Augustine, and were able temporarily to maintain the comparatively beneficent Spanish rule.

The invasion of Florida in 1812 inaugurated thirty years of intermittent warfare in which Negroes were allied with Creek and Seminole Indians in the ultimately hopeless resistance to the Anglo-American advance. A raid by vengeful Tennesseans early in 1813 destroyed the Indian and Negro villages on the Alachua savanna and drove their inhabitants west to the Suwannee. Negroes were active in the uprising of the Creek Red Sticks in Alabama, which Andrew Jackson crushed in 1814. During their invasion of the South in the War of 1812, the British recruited extensively in Florida among refugee Creek and runaway Negroes; and when, after the Treaty of Ghent, they departed, they left a garrison of runaway Negroes at a well-equipped fort on the Apalachicola River in Florida. About one thousand runaways settled under the fort's protection, their fields and grazing grounds extending fifty miles along the river. But Andrew Jackson, recognizing the threat of such an establishment and settlement to the slaveowners of the border, ordered its destruction and the restoration of the Negro garrison and other property "to their rightful owners." The fort was invested by land and water, by troops, gunboats, and slave-hunting Creek; and after some skirmishing, on July 27, 1816, a red-hot shot in the magazine blew up the fort and killed nearly the entire garrison.

The few survivors and the numerous Negroes from the Apalachicola settlement fled to the Suwannee villages, vowing vengeance. "Old Hickory," however, was determined to put an end to all such settlements of armed runaways. In 1818 he took advantage of an outbreak of border warfare between Georgia settlers and dispossessed Creek to invade Florida, destroy nearby Indian and Negro villages, and then march his army for several days overland to attack the Suwannee villages. The outnumbered Negroes fought a brief delaying action on April 16, 1818, to cover the flight of their families, and suffered heavy casualties; they also lost many captives to Jackson's slave-hunting Creek allies. Those who escaped sought refuge elsewhere on the peninsula and even in the Bahamas.

The Negroes had suffered so heavily at the fort and on the Suwannee that neither they nor their Indian allies offered the slightest resistance to the United States annexation of the Floridas in 1819-21. And yet, in spite of a decade of harassment and dislocation, prosperous Negro villages of well-built log cabins, with fields of corn, cotton, and vegetables and herds of cattle, horses, and swine, survived into the period of United States rule and up to the great Seminole War, which began in 1835.

The last and perhaps most important military action by Negro settlers on the southern frontier was in resistance to the United States program of removing the Seminole to the Indian Territory west of the Mississippi River. Seminole Negroes, most of them runaway slaves or their descendants, feared that assemblage for removal would mean enslavement. They urged on Indian resistance, laid in supplies of ammunition, and prepared the plantation slaves of the St. Johns River to rise up in arms whenever war should break out, as it did in late December 1835. This war, which is usually referred to as the most protracted and costly "Indian war" in United States history, was described by the general in command during its most crucial period as "a negro, not an Indian war." A well-informed officer commented: "The negroes . . . have, for their numbers, been the most formidable foe, more bloodthirsty, active, and revengeful, than the Indians." And in some actions, Negro fighting men—Seminole Negroes and rebel slaves—were reportedly at least as numerous as Indian warriors. Not until the generals commanding in Florida gave the Negroes effective assurance that if they "came in" they would be granted freedom and permitted to go west with the Indians, did Negro resistance dwindle.

Although the Florida promise of freedom to Negroes who would surrender was declared invalid and although half-breed Creek insisted that the Negroes should be treated as slaves and kept under close supervision, the Seminole Negroes in the Indian Territory continued as best they could their tradition of independent villages and industrious farming and stock-raising. Wewoka, county seat of Seminole County, was originally a Seminole Negro village. But kidnapping and other harassment caused many of the independent-spirited Seminole Negroes to seek other havens of refuge.

Negroes had from early years participated in the northward advance of the Mexican frontier, and free "colored" people there encountered comparatively little racial discrimination. More than half of the forty-six men, women, and children from Mexico who in 1781 founded Los Angeles were to some extent of Negro ancestry. In 1829 the Republic of Mexico had outlawed slavery. In 1849, consequently, a couple of hundred Seminole, Creek, and Cherokee Negroes commanded by John Horse, and a similar number of discontented Seminole Indians under Wild Cat, left the Indian Territory, crossed Texas, and received from the Mexican government grants of land as military colonists. Their trailing and fighting ability helped greatly to reduce Comanche and Apache raids, and they also aided Mexican troops in repelling slave-hunting filibusters from Texas. After Wild Cat's death in 1857 most of the Indians filtered back to the territory, but the Negroes remained behind in fear of slavery and continued their operations against *los indios barbaros* until the end of Indian warfare in that part of Mexico. Several hundred descendants of these Negro settlers are still living as farmers and stock-raisers at Nacimiento, Coahuila.

The various mining frontiers of the United States overlapped chronologically and geographically with other frontiers—of exploration, the fur trade, agriculture, and stock-raising. Negroes, although often harassed by discriminatory laws, were present, active, and often successful.

Negroes in the greatest of all gold rushes—to the California mines—numbered almost a thousand in 1850 and more than four thousand by 1860. Some of them were slaves whose masters had brought them to assist in mining operations, sometimes with the promise of freedom for faithful service; a few slaves were even permitted to go to California on their own to work out their freedom. White miners often objected to competition with slave labor and forced slave-owning miners and their Negroes to remove. Other Negro prospectors either were legally free or were runaway slaves. Negroes sometimes banded together for more efficient operations and for mutual protection; others belonged to racially integrated companies. The success of Negro companies and of individual Negroes is betokened by such "names on the land" as Nigger Gulch, Nigger Hill, Nigger Creek, and Nigger Bar. Some observers believed that Negroes were unusually lucky, but probably their successes merely attracted more attention. The history of the Negro in the California gold rush was repeated in large measure on other mining frontiers, but only in California was the slave-miner important.

Negroes, however, tended to move from the mines into the cities, where probably in the long run they profited as much as they would have in a continued search for gold. Barney Ford, for example, a runaway mulatto who worked his way from Chicago to Denver in the early 1860s only to discover that a territorial law barred Negroes from filing on mining claims, turned first to barbering and then to the operation of restaurants and hotels, at various times owning one of the leading hotels in Denver and the principal hotel in Cheyenne.

The Civil War was the most important development in American Negro history since the establishment of slavery. An important contribution to the defeat of the Confederacy, with its avowed basis in human slavery and racial inequality, was what may be regarded as a slave uprising in support of the increasingly antislavery government of the United States. Before the war was over, more than 200,000 Negroes in the armed forces of the Union had contributed to its victory. Negroes on the frontier were the first of their race to take up arms on behalf of the Union and their own freedom.

Although early in the Civil War the Confederacy succeeded in negotiating treaties of alliance with all of the Five Civilized Tribes, those treaties did not represent the real wishes of many Cherokee, Creek, and Seminole Indians. The Negroes of the Civilized Tribes were virtu-

ally unanimous in their support of the Union; they could readily see that assimilation into the Confederacy would ultimately mean the hardening of the comparatively lenient system of servitude among the Cherokee, Creek, and Seminole—which among the Seminole was hardly slavery at all. When the old Creek chief Opothlayahola late in 1861 organized resistance to the Confederacy and prepared to fight his way north to Union territory, his army of about a thousand warriors included two or three hundred Negroes. The Union Indians and Negroes twice defeated the pursuing Confederates, but in a third action the outnumbered Unionists were broken and scattered, suffering terrible hardships from cold, hunger, and Confederate harassment before they reached a haven in Kansas. There they were organized into Union regiments in which the Negroes served as equals.

These Union Indian and Negro regiments saw action along with Kansas Negro regiments, largely raised among runaway slaves from the Missouri border. The exigencies of frontier warfare, including the danger of attacks from Missouri-based partisans, caused free-state Kansans to minimize racial distinctions and disregard strict legality. Long before the United States government legally authorized Negro enlistment, Negroes were serving in Kansas volunteer regiments. Although the first regiment of freed slaves was not officially mustered into the Union army until November 1862 in South Carolina, two Kansas Negro regiments had been organized the previous month and a detachment from one of them had fought an action against Confederate irregulars—the first action of the Civil War involving "colored" troops as distinguished from the Indian Negro warriors who had fought under Opothlayahola.

Kansas Negro regiments, frequently in association with Indian-Negro and white regiments, were thereafter engaged in savage no-quarter border warfare. Their greatest victories were at Cabin Creek and Honey Springs, or Elk Creek, in the Indian Territory; their greatest disaster was at Poison Spring, Arkansas, where a Texas regiment, which had been driven from the field at Elk Springs, wreaked vengeance on the outnumbered First Kansas by shooting and bayoneting the wounded—an atrocity for which the Second Kansas retaliated with the bayonet at Jenkins Ferry.

The Negro soldiers of the Indian and Kansas frontier regiments were not, for the most part, former plantation slaves inured to gang labor under constant supervision, but farmhands, handymen, and sharecroppers, accustomed to some independence in using their own intelligence. In a "Black Flag" war in which guerrilla bands gave quarter to no one and Confederate troops frequently refused to take Negroes prisoner, they successfully met some of the most severe tests that soldiers in this bloodiest of American conflicts ever confronted.

The Civil War and emancipation inaugurated a new era in American Negro history, which dramatically manifested itself on the western military frontier. Negro cattlemen—now representatives equally with their white counterparts of a sedentary pastoral and agricultural civilization—participated in expeditions against, and resistance to the raids of, the nomadic tribes of the Southwest. Such Negroes as Charley Tyler and Britton Johnson won spectacular reputations as Indian fighters before dying in action at the hands of the Paiute Indians of

Soldiers of the Ninth U.S. Cavalry's black regiment. (Library of Congress)

California and the Kiowa and Comanche of western Texas.

The most important Negro Indian-fighters, however, were those who served in the regular army—the "buffalo soldiers," as the Indians called them, because of the texture of their hair. After the Civil War, when the United States Army was reduced to a permanent peacetime establishment of ten cavalry and twenty-five infantry regiments, primarily for service against the hostile Indians of the western plains, deserts, and mountains, two cavalry regiments, the Ninth and Tenth, and two infantry, the Twenty-Fourth and Twenty-Fifth, were composed of Negro privates and noncommissioned officers, under white commissioned officers. For a quarter century these regiments fought against hostile Cheyenne, Comanche, Kiowa, Apache, Ute, and Sioux Indians, and against Mexican outlaws and border desperadoes in nearly two hundred engagements. More than once, detachments from these regiments came to the aid of beleaguered white troops. For months and even years at a time the garrisons of many frontier posts consisted of detachments from Negro regiments. The campaigns against the Apache chiefs Victorio and Nana—actually more important than those against the more publicized Geronimo—were conducted almost entirely by Negro troopers. The quality of their services is indicated by the fact that between 1870 and 1890 fourteen Negro soldiers were awarded the Medal of Honor.

A principal problem in coping with the hostile Indians, particularly those in the Southwest who often operated in small bands of hit-and-run raiders, was in following their trails and locating their camps. Expert scouts were indispensable to an effective campaign. The most effective scouting organization in the United States Army was recruited from the Seminole Negro military colonists of northern Mexico. Operating both independently and with detachments from regular Negro and white regiments, they have been given major credit for having freed west Texas from Indian raids. Although never at any one time numbering more than fifty, four of the scouts won the Medal of Honor. Between their last Indian fight in 1881 and their final disbandment in 1914 they had a generation of more routine activity on the Texas-Mexican border, principally against bandits and horse thieves.

A few individual scouts, guides, and interpreters to the Indian-fighting army who were of Negro or part-Negro ancestry included Isaiah Dorman, who was killed in the battle of the Little Big Horn; Frank GROU-ARD, also active in the Sioux country; and Sam Bowman, prominent in the 1880s in the Apache country.

A few Negroes, however, even after emancipation, were involved in continued resistance to the advance of the Anglo-American frontier. Cattlemen and soldiers, both white and black, sometimes found themselves opposed to hostile bands in whose ranks were Negroes, sometimes in positions of leadership. Some of these Negro outlaws were doubtless of a definitely criminal type, but others may have been of too independent a spirit to endure their subordinate position in a white-dominated society.

Between 1866 and 1890 the buffalo soldiers of the Negro regiments helped clear the buffalo-hunting Indians from the Great Plains to make way for cattle ranches and, later, for sod-busting farmers.

Negro vaqueros, both slave and free, had been active on the northward-moving Mexican frontier as early as the mid-sixteenth century, and Negro "cattle hunters" were numbered among South Carolina slaves in the early eighteenth century. Seminole Negroes in Florida, the Indian Territory, and Mexico were devoted to stock-raising, as were free Negroes in Texas, where slaves also worked as cowhands. The heyday, however, of Negroes in the cattle country was the generation after the Civil War, when great herds of southern Texas cattle were pushed north to railheads, Indian reservations, and fattening grounds in Kansas, Wyoming, and elsewhere. Of the cowhands who participated in these "long drives," approximately a fourth were Negroes, ranging in importance from the lowly wrangler through ordinary hands and top hands to the authoritative cook. Racial prejudice, however, inhibited the use of Negroes as trail bosses and ranch foremen, except in the few cases of all-Negro or Negro and Mexican outfits (see COWBOY).

Negro cowhands were numerous in terms of the Negro population of the counties from which the trail herds emanated, and they were also frequently of outstanding ability. The chuckwagon or ranch cook, who ranked next in authority to the trail boss or foreman, was frequently a Negro. Negro cooks were not only celebrated for culinary ability; they were frequently also noted riders and ropers, fiddlers, banjo-strummers, and guitar-pickers, and widely versatile handymen. "Nigger Add," Matthew "Bones" Hooks, "Bronco Sam" Stewart, and others were legendary horsebreakers, some of whom also had great roping skills. Bob Lemmons was noted for his ability to "walk down" a band of wild horses and eventually lead them into a corral by convincing them that he was really "one of them." Some Negro cowhands turned their riding and roping skills to extra profit as rodeo contestants or members of Wild West shows. Perhaps the most important rodeo figure of all time was Bill Pickett (see RODEO). He invented "bulldogging"—the now lost art of throwing a steer by gripping its lip or nostrils with the teeth.

Although Negroes never reached prominence in the cattle business any more than they did in the fur trade, a number of cowhands—such as Daniel Webster Wallace, known as "80 John," and Jess Pickett, both of Texas—saved their wages, bought little spreads, and eventually became prosperous ranchers. Possibly the racial barrier to becoming a ranch foreman caused ambitious Negro cowhands, who might otherwise have been willing to settle for a position as top employee on a big ranch, to turn to independent ranching—to their ultimate benefit. They settled not only in the Texas cattle country but also as far away as Alberta, to which Texas cattle were taken by Negro trail drivers.

Antebellum free Negroes and runaways frequently throve as farmers from Florida and the Carolinas to the Oregon country, but they were less attracted to the postbellum frontier of the Great Plains—the "sodhouse frontier," so-called because its early buildings were characteristically built of blocks of sod. Although much of the soil of the Great Plains was deep and fertile, the terrain was also semiarid, treeless, and blizzard-swept. Negroes recently emancipated from plantation slavery who had tried to support themselves as landless sharecroppers usually preferred—if they decided to leave their profitless tenant farms—to seek urban employment rather than to pioneer on government or railroad land in the West.

Nevertheless, some Negroes did seek—and sometimes achieved—success on the sodhouse frontier, occasionally as individual settlers but often as members of usually short-lived colonies. "Exodusters"—as those Negroes called themselves who went out from the Egypt of the post-Reconstruction South to what they hoped would be the Promised Land of Kansas—frequently got no farther than the towns and cities of eastern Kansas, but hundreds and perhaps thousands pushed out onto the Great Plains. Of the Exoduster settlements, Nicodemus, in Graham County, northwest Kansas, was the most successful and permanent. Its settlers accomplished this success through great courage, energy, and perseverance in conquering apparently insuperable obstacles. Their vanguard reached the projected site in the autumn of 1877, too late—like the Pilgrims of 1620—to plant crops, but they homesteaded land on the "high black prairie," burrowed into hillsides for shelter, and grimly stuck it out until spring—when they confronted the task of breaking the heavy prairie sod for planting. They had only three horses among them, so one man plowed with a milk cow while others broke the stubborn sod with grubbing hoes, mattocks, and spades and managed thus to plant several acres of corn per family. White settlers came to their aid with men and teams. By the autumn of 1880 it was reported that there were eight hundred in the colony and all were doing well.

Despite periodic droughts and crop failures, Nicodemus throve. Some members of the community pushed on to the Cimarron valley of Oklahoma Territory and to southern Colorado. Although Nicodemus has suffered the decline characteristic of rural communities in sparsely populated regions, descendants of the original settlers still own most of the land in the township.

The history of Negroes on the American frontier has no well defined terminal point. An episode of the early twentieth century is, however, significant historically and symbolically. While the cattle frontier was being pushed north and west, partly by Negro soldiers, scouts, and cattlemen; while Negro prospectors on the mining frontier of the Black Hills were thriving at Nigger Hill, Nigger Creek, and Nigger Gulch; while Exodusters were pitting their strength and determination against the stubborn soil and hostile climate of the Great Plains—Negroes in the Indian Territory were participating in the affairs of what were still independent Indian nations. In the Creek and Seminole nations particularly, Negroes enjoyed political and, to a large degree, social equality. They had achieved this position partly because they had traditionally allied themselves with the most intransigent elements of these tribes in their resistance to Anglo-American encroachments on their freedom and independence.

In the Indian Territory, cleavages developed between Indian full-bloods, who for the most part were reluctant to relinquish their old culture entirely, and half-breeds or full-bloods under half-breed influence, who sought acceptance from the whites by attempting to bring their tribes fully into the orbit of white culture, including the white man's pattern of slavery and racial discrimination. Negroes naturally supported the full-bloods, who, without being Negrophiles, had a more relaxed and tolerant racial attitude than the "progressive" half-breeds. Negroes supported the full-bloods in opposition to the Confederacy and in various factional disputes in the Creek nation, which sometimes became small-scale civil wars.

The admission of Indian Territory and Oklahoma Territory to the Union in 1907 as the state of Oklahoma was disastrous for the full-bloods and their Negro allies. Tribal independence was conclusively ended, and the Indians were subjected to a white-dominated state government, while the Negroes experienced southern-type segregation and discrimination. When a full-blooded Creek and Union veteran, Chitto Hajo (Crazy Snake), led a movement for the restoration of tribal government, he drew much of his support from disgruntled Creek and Seminole Negroes. The Negro-Indian frontier alliance against racist white domination was making its final, futile stand. In late March 1909, with a few sputters of rifle shots—not, however, without casualties—the century-old attempt by allied frontier Negroes and Indians to defend by force of arms their claims to self-government, equality, and dignity came to an end.

But the very month before the "Crazy Snake Rebellion," on the anniversary of Abraham Lincoln's birthday, Negroes and whites had issued a call for the founding of an organization to be named the National Association for the Advancement of Colored People. Its purpose was to fight in the courts and legislatures against the racism that the Creek and Seminole Negroes on Oklahoma's Hickory Ground were preparing to protest, ineffectually, through the muzzles of their Winchesters. One of the organization's first triumphs was a United States Supreme Court decision invalidating Oklahoma's racially discriminatory "grandfather clause."

The American frontier of "free land" had vanished. Henceforth, the frontier, for both whites and Negroes, was the entire United States. The weapons and tools for its conquest were no longer the rifle, the ax, and the plow, the pick, the shovel, and the gold-pan, but political and economic organization for the common benefit.

See Kenneth Wiggins Porter, *The Negro on the American Frontier: Select Preliminary Studies* (1971).—K. W. P.

Neihardt, John G[neisenau] (1881-1973). Poet. Neihardt was born near Sharpsburg, Illinois, but spent most of his childhood in Kansas and, later, in Wayne, Nebraska. As a child he read Tennyson and Browning, both of whom influenced his own later poetry, and Homer and Virgil. After graduating from the Nebraska Normal College in Wayne in 1897, he worked at various odd jobs until 1901, when he became an assistant to the

Indian agent at the Omaha Indian reservation near Bancroft, Nebraska. He lived on the reservation until 1907, familiarizing himself with Indian customs and history and maturing in his mind the desire to become a poet. During this time his published poems and stories had been favorably received and, in 1908, he gave up his career, determined to live by writing. He immersed himself in the study of western history and, in 1912, began work on a cycle of epic poems about the American West, which he was to consider his masterpiece. In 1921 he was made poet laureate of Nebraska and in 1923 was appointed to an honorary chair of poetry at the state university. In 1926 he became literary editor of the St. Louis *Post-Dispatch*, a position he held until 1938. From 1944 until 1948 he worked with the Office of Indian Affairs and was later poet in residence and lecturer in English at the University of Missouri.

Though Neihardt considered himself to be primarily a poet, contemporary readers, with different expectations from his own toward epic verse, will find his western epics disappointing. His versification is conservative—the epics are written in heroic couplets—and his style owes too much to the conventions and heroic posturings of Victorian verse, particularly in diction, which is too often consciously archaic and "literary." Moreover, two of the epics, *The Song of Three Friends* (1919) and *The Song of Hugh Glass* (1915), are fairly straightforward anecdotes of the American fur trade; they probably strike the modern reader as trivial rather than epic in nature.

As a writer of prose, however, Neihardt has long been unjustly ignored. His *The Lonesome Trail* (1907) and *Indian Tales and Others* (1926) are almost forgotten short-story collections of first-class quality, many dealing with supernatural themes. He also wrote, among other things, an interesting history of the early fur traders, *The Splendid Wayfaring* (1920), and ghostwrote the autobiography of an Oglala Sioux medicine man, *Black Elk Speaks* (1932).—J. K. F.

Nelson, Aven (1859-1952). Botanist and educator. A son of Norwegian immigrants, Nelson grew up on an Iowa farm. From devout, hard-working parents and the McGuffey *Readers* series he absorbed the Protestant ethic. In his old age he was still quoting from McGuffey's *Third Reader*:

> The lark is up to meet the sun
> The bee is on the wing,
> The ant his labors has begun,
> The woods with music ring.
>
> Shall bird and bee and ant be wise
> While I my moments waste?
> Oh, let me with the morning rise
> And to my duties haste.

Young Nelson taught in public schools and at Drury College, Missouri, and then was hired to teach English at the University of Wyoming the year it opened, in 1887. When it was found that another member of the faculty of six was better prepared to teach English, Nelson was assigned classes in biology and calisthenics. Since he lacked formal college training in science, he learned with his students. In summertime he collected plants, studied them, and began writing papers for botanical journals. He earned a master's degree at Harvard in 1902 and a Ph.D. at Denver University in 1904.

Collecting systematically at every opportunity, often in virgin territory, Nelson gradually put together the best herbarium in the Rocky Mountain West. His "Rocky Mountain Herbarium" and scholarly publications brought recognition from his peers and election to the presidencies of the Botanical Society of America, the American Society of Plant Taxonomists, and the national honorary society Phi Kappa Phi. Partway through his scholarly career he accepted a draft to become president of the University of Wyoming (1917-22), then voluntarily withdrew from administration to devote the last thirty years of his life to botany.

See W. O. Clough, *A History of the University of Wyoming, 1887-1937* (1937); and Ruth Ashton Nelson, "Dr. Aven Nelson," *University of Wyoming Publications*, vol. 2, no. 1 (1944).—T. A. L.

Nevada. Nevada, ranking seventh in physical size and forty-seventh in population among the fifty states, is an excellent example of a political unit formed without reference to its natural physical features. Its history, consequently, has been a constant struggle to establish an economic base to justify its political existence.

The present area of Nevada except for the northeastern corner, which belongs to the Columbia River drainage system, and the southeastern corner, which belongs to the Colorado River drainage system, lies within the land which John C. Frémont in 1845 called the Great Basin in order to identify it as a land of interior drainage.

Four main native groups occupied the area at the time of the first white intrusion: the Northern Paiute, the Southern Paiute, the Washo (see INDIANS OF THE GREAT BASIN), and the SHOSHONI INDIANS. Of these, the Northern Paiute are, perhaps, the best known. Their ancestral home included most of western Nevada, particularly the area from PYRAMID LAKE to Walker Lake. The Southern Paiute occupied the present Clark and Lincoln counties. The Shoshoni ranged mainly along the Humboldt River from present Winnemucca eastward, touching the Northern Paiute on the west and the Southern Paiute on the south. The Washo, the smallest of the four main Nevada Indian tribes, centered around the Carson and Washoe valleys, the Truckee Meadows, and Lake Tahoe. All Nevada Indians were forced by the Great Basin environment to a nomadic, material culture, a culture remarkably adapted to hostile natural forces that was almost completely disrupted · by the white intrusion.

Trappers opened the area beginning in 1826 and were its first explorers. Jedediah SMITH, part owner of the Rocky Mountain Fur Company, led a small party across the southern tip of the present state in 1826 and the next year on his return from California crossed the entire state roughly along the present Highway 6. Peter S. Ogden and a Hudson's Bay party, entering the state from the north, discovered the Humboldt River in 1828 and the following spring followed that stream from its source to the "sink," the point where the river disappeared into the sands. Although both Ogden and Smith identified the land as nearly worthless for furs, a third major trapping expedition crossed Nevada in 1833-34. This party, under the leadership of Joseph R. Walker, not only demonstrated the usefulness of the Humboldt

River as a highway between the Great Salt Lake and the Pacific Coast, but also blazed the trail that connected the Humboldt River route with the Oregon Trail and thereby provided a main link in the later emigrant route to California. Between 1829 and 1831 another group of trapper-traders, operating from New Mexico and including Ewing Young, Antonio Armijo, William Wolfskill, and George C. Yount, established a trail across the southern tip of Nevada as a part of the Old Spanish Trail.

The first official exploring party into Nevada was led by John C. Frémont in 1844. Returning from his second expedition to the Pacific Coast, Frémont entered Nevada from Oregon, moved south to discover Pyramid Lake in January and then led his party west across the Sierra Nevada mountain barrier at what became Carson Pass. The following year Frémont led another expedition to the Great Basin, crossing into Nevada directly west from the Great Salt Lake over a vast salt desert. Near the Ruby Mountains he divided his force, sending the larger contingent, under Joseph Walker, westward along the Humboldt River; the smaller group under his own command crossed the Ruby Mountains at Harrison Pass, then proceeded southwest across the central part of Nevada via Diamond valley and the Big Smoky valley to the rendezvous point at Walker Lake. At Walker Lake Frémont again divided his party, sending the larger group southwest into California and across the Sierra at Walker Pass. Frémont and the smaller contingent moved north and west from Walker Lake, met the Truckee River near Wadsworth and followed it to the mountains, crossing the Sierra at Donner Pass.

Although Frémont marked new travel routes in northern and central Nevada, his was not the first white party to cross the Salt Lake Desert nor was it the first across the Donner Pass. The first passage of the salt desert was accomplished by a remarkable group of emigrants organized by John Bidwell, who traveled from the Missouri River to California in 1841. This party was probably the first white group over Sonora Pass. An emigrant party also was the first to open the Truckee River route across the Donner Pass into California. This party, guided by Elisha Stevens, not only crossed this difficult Sierra barrier in 1844 but took wagons with them. Additional trails were blazed in Nevada as a result of emigrant travel, including the Applegate Trail, which was established in 1846 as an alternate route to Oregon via the Humboldt River; the Lassen Road, which used part of the Applegate Trail before turning into northern California; the Beckwourth Trail, which cut off from the Truckee River route near Sparks and then went north and west to the northern gold fields; and the Nobles Road, which left the Applegate Trail to cut almost directly west to the Honey Lake region of California.

Emigrant travel across the Great Basin to California was noticeably slowed after the Donner tragedy of 1846, in which forty of eighty-seven emigrants lost their lives when an early and heavy snowfall blocked their passage over the Sierra Nevada. Two events that occurred in 1848 effectively erased the memory of that disaster and turned the Humboldt River route into a highway west for the thousands of emigrants seeking fame, fortune, and homes in California. The first of these events was the discovery of gold in California in January 1848, and the second was the signing of the Treaty of Guadalupe Hidalgo under which California, Nevada, and other western lands were transferred to the United States.

The heavy emigrant travel led inevitably to temporary and then permanent supply centers along the trail through Nevada. The first such post was built at GENOA, formerly Mormon Station, in June 1850 by a group of men from Salt Lake City under the leadership of Captain Joseph DeMont, with Hampton S. Beatie serving as clerk. This temporary post became Nevada's first permanent settlement when John Reese, with another group of settlers from Salt Lake, purchased the Beatie site and constructed a permanent building there in 1851. By November 1851, some one hundred settlers were in western Utah Territory demanding more government than the Utah authorities were able to provide. Included in this number were a few miners in nearby Gold Canyon working a placer field that had been discovered in the spring of 1850 by William Prouse.

From 1850 to 1861 the Utah territorial government exercised official control of the present state of Nevada but was able to maintain effective control for only two years, from 1855 to 1857. During the rest of the period Utah and federal officials vied for control with vigilante groups or with "squatter" governments. The squatter movements on three different occasions, in 1851, 1857, and 1859, led to the establishment of governments with elected officials. The most sophisticated of these movements was that in 1859 when a constitutional convention was held, a provisional territory established, and Isaac Roop elected as its first governor. Although the discovery of the Comstock Lode in June 1859 disrupted the movement, it placed additional pressure on the federal government to provide the area with a separate territorial government. The secession of a number of southern states from the Union, followed by the formation of the Confederate States of America in February 1861, paved the way for territorial status for Nevada on March 2, 1861. Appointments to the new territory by President Lincoln, including James W. NYE as governor, Orion Clemens as secretary, and John W. North as surveyor-general, insured early Republican domination of the territory. Pressures from within the territory, coming mainly from ambitious politicians and from dissatisfaction with the territorial judiciary, and pressures from Lincoln and the Congress for new, Republican-controlled states, provided Nevadans with an opportunity to seek early statehood. A constitutional convention, authorized only by the territorial legislature, met in November 1863. The constitution they wrote was voted down in January 1864. In spite of this defeat, pressure for statehood continued and an enabling act was passed by Congress and signed by the president on March 21, 1864. A second convention met from July 4 to July 27, producing a constitution that was accepted by the voters on September 7. Nevada was proclaimed the nation's thirty-sixth state on October 31, 1864.

Nevada before it came into the Union was somewhat smaller in size than it is today. Its western boundary was the eastern boundary of California from the 42nd parallel on the north to the 37th parallel on the south; its original boundary to the east was the 116th west meridian. Antagonism in Washington toward the Utah government enabled Nevada to gain two additional degrees of territory to the east, to the 115th meridian in 1862

and to the 114th in 1866. In 1867 the Nevada legislature took advantage of a congressional act of 1866 to obtain the southern tip of territory, then belonging to Arizona Territory, from the 37th parallel to the point where the Colorado River intersects the 35th parallel. Nevada's boundary on the north was, from the beginning, the 42nd parallel.

From 1864, when it became a state, until the decade of the 1930s, Nevada's history centered around two major mining booms. The first boom resulted from the discovery of the Comstock Lode. It was first uncovered in January 1859 by James Finney and others; in June 1859, Peter O'Riley and Patrick McLaughlin uncovered what became the Ophir mine. The Comstock Lode stands by itself in the history of metal mining and GOLD AND SILVER RUSHES. As the first major gold-quartz ledge developed in the United States, the Comstock challenged men to new mining and reduction techniques, including the "square-set" timbering devised by Philip Deidesheimer and the Washoe Pan Process of amalgamation attributed to Almarin B. Paul. The combined problem of water in the mines and excessive heat and poor ventilation in the underground passages led to an amazing engineering feat, the Sutro Tunnel. The builder, Adolph SUTRO, struggled against great odds from October 1869 to July 1878 to complete this four-mile tunnel into the side of Mount Davidson. Unfortunately, its completion was late, by at least five years, since the boom days of the Comstock were closing when the final connection of the lode with the tunnel was made at the Savage mine. (See MINING, METAL.)

VIRGINIA CITY, "Queen" of the Comstock, was an interesting combination of industrial city and frontier town. Its industrial face could be identified particularly by its foundries, railroad yards, lumber mills, its mine and mill buildings, and the large immigrant population, which supplied not only the basic labor for the mines, but also many of the city's merchants, engineers, politicians, and financiers. Its prosperity brought it a sophistication rivaling that of San Francisco. During its heyday the city could boast of hotels, restaurants, private clubs, and theatrical entertainment equal to the best in the latter city. Yet, throughout its history, the community maintained its frontier flavor, mirrored in the rows of gambling houses, saloons, and "red light" districts.

The importance of the Comstock to the history of Nevada transcended mere physical experience. Its mineral wealth built hotels, foundries, banks, railroads, and residential areas in California, particularly in San Francisco, and created some of the great American fortunes. It was a major factor in bringing territorial status in 1861 and statehood to Nevada in 1864 and it dominated the state economically, politically, and socially in the years from its discovery until 1900 and has dominated its historiography since. No greater indication of its importance to Nevada can be noted than to record the twenty-year depression in the state that followed the mineral decline.

From 1880 to 1900 Nevadans struggled, without success, to regain the prosperity of the Comstock period. Mineral activity was encouraged and although numerous mineral discoveries were made, neither alone nor collectively could they balance the declining production of the Comstock. Francis NEWLANDS tried to promote reclamation, but the lack of water and financial support limited such attempts. Many politicians then directed attention to the Central Pacific, charging that the railroad was "milking" the state of needed support through unfair charges and lobbying activities that kept assessments low. It appeared that the railroads might have to pay additional taxes when a Board of Equalization was established by legislation in 1891; the power of the railroad lobby was indicated when the law establishing the board was repealed in 1893.

By this time Nevadans were hitting at the cause of the mineral depression: the coinage act of 1873. This act had omitted the silver dollar from the list of minted coins and had demonetized silver, causing the price of the metal to decline rapidly and thus close most of the silver mines. If the cause of the depression was so simple, it seemed reasonable to the silver supporters that prosperity would return with repeal of the act—which they called the "Crime of '73"—and the restoration of the bimetallic standard. The silver issue soon dominated Nevada politics and created a new party, the Silver party, in 1892. National efforts to restore silver were revitalized with the formation of the People's party, which included in its platform a plank calling for the free and unlimited coinage of silver at the ratio of 16:1, i.e., sixteen units of silver being legally equivalent to one unit of gold. Four years later the national Democratic party adopted a similar plank. At the urging of William Morris STEWART and others, the Nevada Democrats then "fused" with the Silver party. The combination was sufficient to control Nevada politics through the election of 1906. Although the silver issue proved to be a successful one for winning elections in Nevada, it failed to achieve results nationally and the price of silver continued to decline.

By 1900 the population of Nevada had slipped to only 42,335 persons; it was suggested by one national newspaper that since the state's silver mines were exhausted, Nevada should be deprived of its statehood. It was obvious that the state needed economic activity, not political nostrums. Finally, in May 1900, the long-looked-for mineral discovery was made. The initial find was made at Tonopah in southwestern Nevada by a transplanted Californian named Jim Butler. From the Tonopah area prospectors spread out and soon additional bonanzas were found: at Goldfield in 1902; at Rhyolite in 1904; and at dozens of other sites in the next few years. The 1900 mining revival included the development of an extensive body of low-grade copper ore (see COPPER MINING) in eastern Nevada near an old gold camp named Ely. The copper boom began when two young miners, David Bartley and Edwin Gray, optioned some claims in September 1900. The claims became the Ruth mine when Mark Requa purchased them in 1902. With New York capital provided by the Guggenheim brothers, Requa started the construction of a short-line railroad and the building of a reduction plant. By 1920 the Ruth copper mines had produced as much as both Tonopah and Goldfield combined; copper had replaced silver as Nevada's important metal.

Nevada's second mining boom repeated the story of its first. The entire economy of the state received a major boost, population boomed, cities were built and politicians from the new boom camps—men like Key PITTMAN, Tasker L. ODDIE, and Pat McCARRAN—replaced their predecessors of the Comstock era in posi-

tions of power. The most powerful political figure of the new era, however, was George WINGFIELD, who preferred to remain behind the scenes and to control the state through a powerful bipartisan machine. As in the Comstock boom, the labor supply was provided by large numbers of immigrants. This time, however, it was the "new immigration" that moved to the new areas—Greeks, Serbs, Croats, and other central and southern Europeans. A sizable number of Japanese were also employed in the copper mines at Ruth and at the reduction plant at McGill.

The history of Nevada since the 1930s has been, very largely, the story of the ability of the state and individual billionaires such as Norman BILTZ and Howard HUGHES to take advantage of the great westward flow of population and of the increasing affluence and mobility of the American people. To accomplish this, Nevadans turned to a multifaceted industry labeled "tourism" (see TOURIST TRAVEL), which has as its main ingredient legalized gambling (see GAMBLING, NEVADA). Gambling, which had been outlawed in the state October 1, 1910, was again legalized on March 19, 1931. Its growth during the following decade was not impressive but the advent of World War II brought large defense industries and additional military installations to the Pacific Coast and thus brought hundreds of thousands of people within effective range of Nevada's growing gambling industry. The continued movement of population to the western states in the 1950s and 1960s and the state's ability to attract thousands of people made gambling the major industry. The extent of its growth and its domination of the economy is reflected in the following statistics: in 1972, while agricultural products brought in a revenue of $110,520,000 and mining production reached $181,702,000, gross revenue from gambling was $804,200,000. It is apparent, also, that gambling and its related services have been responsible for a major population growth, from 91,058 in 1930 to 481,882 in 1970. With gambling, Nevadans found the economic base necessary to justify the state's political existence.

Nevada's economy today, while centering around the gambling industry, is marked by a much greater diversity than ever before. While mining and agriculture remain basic industries, others such as warehousing and manufacturing have been encouraged. Recreational activities apart from those associated with gambling, such as hunting, fishing, skiing, boating, hiking, gem- and bottle-hunting, and visiting former boomtowns AURORA, GOLDFIELD, RHYOLITE, and TONOPAH bring thousands of visitors to the state annually. In addition, federally supported projects such as Boulder Dam, the Basic Magnesium plant built during World War II, and the Hawthorne Naval Ammunition Depot have been complemented by other programs connected with the defense and space programs. Government activities associated with the NEVADA PROVING GROUND in southern Nevada not only have stimulated the economy with the millions of dollars of government funds expended, but the location in Nevada of Atomic Energy Commission and National Aeronautics and Space Administration facilities has encouraged the entrance of their prime contractors.

The booming population and the emphasis on gambling and tourism have created many problems: overcrowding in schools and inadequate educational facilities, welfare problems, a growing crime rate, pollution, and most of all, the delicate problem of gambling control.

The most recent history of Nevada from its beginnings to the present is Russell R. Elliott, *History of Nevada* (1973). Another useful history is the brief volume written for use as a high school text by James Hulse, *Nevada Adventure* (1969). Useful as an interpretation of Nevada is Richard Lillard, *Desert Challenge* (1972). The basic history for the years to 1880 is Myron Angel, ed., *History of Nevada* (1881 repr. 1958). Also important is Russell R. Elliott and Helen J. Poulton, *Writings On Nevada: A Selected Bibliography* (1963).—R. R. E.

Nevada City, California. Mining town. Nevada City has been a gold-mining center for more than a century. It is the seat of Nevada County, whose lode and placer mines have yielded more than half of California's total gold production. When major placer-deposits of gold were discovered in September 1849 at a camp known as Deer Creek Diggings and Caldwell's Store, some ten thousand people rushed to the area and soon established Nevada City, which boasted a population of two thousand and four hundred buildings. A fire gutted much of the town in 1851, but the residents, with great ¡aith in the future, rebuilt with brick and stone buildings. They still stand today along the town's winding hillside streets, making it one of the really charming gold-rush cities.

After the original placers were panned out, Nevada City declined until quartz and hydraulic mining techniques gave the city new life in 1856. In 1880 the town still had a population of more than four thousand. Among the buildings still extant are the assay office, the National Hotel, and Firehouse No. 1, which houses the Nevada County Historical Museum.

See Remi Nadeau, *Ghost Towns and Mining Camps of California* (1965); and Muriel S. Wolle, *The Bonanza Trail* (1953).—R. B. W.

Nevada Proving Ground. In December 1950 the Atomic Energy Commission designated the area of Frenchman's and Yucca flats, about sixty-five miles northwest of Las Vegas, as the Nevada Proving Ground for atomic testing. The first atomic device was detonated there on January 27, 1951, and for the next six years aboveground tests were conducted. The government began shifting to underground testing in 1957, making such testing a fixed policy in 1962. In 1956 the Nevada test site was selected for the development of nuclear reactor engines for spacecraft and rocket propellants. The Nuclear Rocket Development Station occupies the southwest corner of the test site. The twin programs of research and testing of nuclear propulsion systems for spacecraft and of nuclear weapons have made the test site an important part of the defense and space programs, and have resulted in great economic benefit to Nevada.—R. R. E.

Newberry, Oliver. See GREAT LAKES, MEN OF THE.

New Echota, Treaty of (1835). The United States government had by 1835 determined to coerce the final removal to Oklahoma of all Cherokee remaining in their eastern homeland. After refusing several government proposals as unfair, the full Cherokee council was ordered to gather at New Echota, Georgia, to negotiate a treaty. The Cherokee were informed that those failing to appear would be counted as in favor of any treaty made. Then the treaty commissioners had the Cherokee's principal leaders arrested and held without charges, and their tribal newspaper was suppressed. With less than a fourth of the tribe in attendance, an agreement was prepared at New Echota on December 29, 1835. Representing the United States government as commissioners were William Carroll and Reverend John F. Schermerhorn. Among the participating Cherokee were "Major Ridge," John Ridge (Major Ridge's son), James Starr, and Elias Boudinot.

It was agreed that the United States Senate would consent to pay $5 million for the lands. The Cherokee in turn would surrender all their lands east of the Mississippi. In turn, the Indians would be given a specified territory along the Arkansas, Grand, and Canadian rivers, bounding on lands of the Osage and Seneca Indians. In case this cession was insufficient, additional lands would be ceded from the lands just west of Missouri in the Osage tract, and the United States would quiet the claims of the Osage. Lands ceded to the Cherokee were to be held in perpetuity, and the United States would finance the Cherokee removals and subsist them for one year after their arrival. Funds were to be invested for the Indians on a pro rata basis. Certain pensions were to be made. Finally, the Indians agreed to removal within two years after ratification of the treaty.

Cherokee leaders immediately submitted to Washington petitions and resolutions from eighty percent of the tribe. denouncing the methods used and pointing out that the treaty was illegal. But the Senate ratified it, and President Andrew Jackson replied that the treaty would be executed as written, that no Cherokee council would be permitted to discuss the treaty, and that no further communication would be held with the now-extinct eastern Cherokee nation. Accordingly, during the next three years the Cherokee were, first individually and then en masse, evicted from their homes and herded west over the infamous "Trail of Tears." The Treaty of New Echota is considered to be one of the most reprehensible Indian treaties in United States history.

See Grant Foreman, *Indian Removal: The Emigration of the Five Civilized Tribes of Indians* (1932); Charles C. Royce, "Indian Land Cessions in the United States," in Bureau of American Ethnology, *Eighteenth Annual Report, 1896-97* (1899); Emmet Starr, *History of the Cherokee Indians and Their Legends and Folklore* (1921); and Thurman Wilkins, *Cherokee Tragedy: The Story of the Ridge Family and of the Decimation of a People* (1970).—T. D. C.

Newell, Robert (1807-1869). Oregon trapper and pioneer. Newell, one of Oregon's more famous mountain men, was born in Ohio and arrived in the Willamette valley in December 1840. He was the first person to travel the entire Oregon Trail, driving wagons from Fort Boise on the Missouri River to Walla Walla on the Columbia, and was the first person to take a wagon into the Willamette valley.

Newell was influential in the formation of Oregon's famous provisional government in 1843, "an organization . . . [made] in case of a misunderstanding with the Indians" as he described it. His account of the Champoeg meetings of 1843, written in 1866 in response to the *History of Oregon*, written by William Gray, is an important primary source for those events.

In 1829 Newell began a trapper's life, setting out for

the Rocky Mountains from St. Louis with the firm of Smith, Jackson and Sublette. He earned little in the way of a fortune, but a moderate success in backwoods medicine won him the title of "doctor." He kept memoranda of his mountain experiences in prose rarely imprecise though frequently misspelled.

Newell's life is marked by conspicuous service to his community, and by his evenhanded friendship with Indians, French-Canadians, Hudson's Bay men, and missionaries. Following the Whitman massacre in 1847 (see Marcus WHITMAN), Governor George Abernethy made Newell, H. A. G. Lee, and Joel Palmer peace commissioners to the Cayuse Indians. In 1852 Newell, together with André Longtain, plotted the Champoeg townsite. His first two wives bore him sixteen children; he died five months after marrying his third wife, the widow of a Methodist missionary. He was at his best in small groups where his kind of leadership, relying on wit and personal contact and not on any ability to command, could prevail.

Letters written by Newell to the Oregon *Herald* in 1866 are in several collections, including those of the Oregon Historical Society in Portland and the Beinecke Library at Yale University. Other Newell correspondence is in various collections in the two libraries and in the papers of the Provisional and Territorial Governments of Oregon at the Oregon Historical Society. D. O. Johansen edited Newell's *Memoranda* (1959).—R. J. L.

New England, settlement of. New England owes its name to the famed Virginia adventurer Captain John Smith. In 1616 Smith published a popular little book entitled *A Description of New England*, which contained a remarkably accurate map of the area. Although Smith bore the grand title Admiral of New England, the future of the region lay with other men. In 1620 James I gave a charter to all land between the fortieth and the forty-eighth parallels to a group of aristocrats called the Council for New England. This proprietary body in turn awarded patents to people who wanted to fish or to settle within the boundaries of their grant. The council issued a patent in 1628 to the New England Company, a Puritan organization.

The leaders of the New England Company persuaded Charles I to give them a charter of their own in 1629, and they renamed their enterprise the Massachusetts Bay Company. The next year the Great Migration began. For a decade thousands of English Puritans emigrated to the colonies, bound together by a sense of religious mission. Governor John Winthrop captured the spirit of this movement when he reminded the first settlers, "wee shall be as a Citty upon a Hill, the eies of all people are upon us."

The major colonies of seventeenth-century New England—Plymouth, Massachusetts, Rhode Island, Connecticut, and New Haven—often regarded each other with suspicion, stressing small theological differences. The population of the region, however, was far more homogeneous than the early Puritans were willing to admit, and it is possible for historians to write of the "New England way." Three of the more important elements of this system were a Congregational Church polity, "covenanted" communities that allowed broad participation in government affairs, and a deep sense of the value of education in human society. These colonies tried to solve some of their common problems in 1643 by

forming the Confederation of the United Colonies of New England—"a firm and perpetual League of Friendship and Amity for offense and defense, mutual advice and succour upon all just occasions." Although the confederation was allowed to die during KING PHILIP'S WAR (1675-76), its establishment represented America's first experiment in regional cooperation. During the 1680s English administrators made an effort to bring all these colonies under a single government called the Dominion of New England. But the colonists had other ideas, and in 1689 they demonstrated their support of the Glorious Revolution and William III by shipping the dominion rulers back to London.

Colonial New England never developed a staple crop, such as tobacco or sugar, to support her economy. The sea, not the land, was the source of the region's wealth. By the second half of the seventeenth century, New England ships were trading in three continents. They carried fish and barrel staves to Portugal, horses and slaves to the Sugar Islands, and food to other American colonies. During the eighteenth century the prosperity of New England came to depend much more heavily on rum, and in 1763 there were more than 150 distilleries in the area. Merchants traded rum for slaves in Africa, and they in turn were exchanged for molasses in the Caribbean. The commercial cycle was complete when the molasses became rum in Boston, Newport, or New Haven. By the time of the American Revolution, New England merchants were known throughout the English colonies as "Yankees," as men who always drove a hard bargain.

During the seventeenth century, people from Massachusetts moved south to Rhode Island, New Haven, and elsewhere in Connecticut for a mixture of religious and economic reasons. It was not until the next century that large groups of colonists began to populate Maine, Vermont, and western Massachusetts. Many of the men who established towns in this period were looking for better land. Others, however, were seeking religious purity, and they moved because they could not tolerate the beliefs of their former neighbors. After the American Revolution, thousands of settlers carried the "New England way" west to New York, Ohio, and Pennsylvania.

More has been written about early New England than any other topic of colonial American history. A few of the best studies are Perry Miller, *The New England Mind: From Colony to Province* (1953), and Bernard Bailyn, *The New England Merchants in the Seventeenth Century* (1955). Also see Lois K. Mathews, *The Expansion of New England* (1909).—T. H. B.

New Hampshire, settlement of. In 1629 the Council for New England granted the land north of the Merrimack River to Sir Ferdinando Gorges and Captain John Mason, and these two gentlemen in turn divided the territory—New Hampshire going to Mason and Maine to Gorges. But it was the Massachusetts Bay Colony, not Mason, that exercised actual control over New Hampshire during most of the seventeenth century. The rulers of Massachusetts construed their northern boundary as a line "three miles northward of the most northerly part or branch" of the Merrimack River. This broad interpretation gave the Bay Colony authority to govern New Hampshire's four towns, Hampton, Dover, Exeter, and Portsmouth. Most of the people in New

Hampshire were Puritans who preferred the government of the Bay Colony to Mason's proprietary rule. Moreover, the settlers looked to the larger colony for protection from the Indians.

The Mason family resented the loss of New Hampshire, but they were helpless to do anything until the restoration of Charles II in 1660. After 1660, when the English Puritan regime had been defeated, the family's interests were aggressively put forward by Robert Mason, heir to the proprietary title. He informed English administrators that the people of New Hampshire were unhappy as part of the Bay Colony. A more telling point, however, was his claim that Massachusetts had ignored the Navigation Acts. In 1679 the Lords of Trade ordered all Bay Colony officials to leave New Hampshire. Mason recovered title to the colony's land, but he had no control over the appointed council and elected assembly that governed New Hampshire. Few of the settlers had wanted to separate from Massachusetts, and they made it clear that they were going to obstruct Mason's attempts to collect land rents. In fact the assembly insisted on copying the actions of the Bay Colony legislators. One of Mason's lieutenants wrote in frustration, "Surely it would not please his Majesty that we should cast off obedience to the jurisdiction of Massachusetts, and yet yoke ourselves inseparably under its laws."

Mason quickly realized that he would receive no profits until the government was changed. In 1683 his lobbying led to the appointment of Edward Cranfield as the first royal governor of the colony. But this move to strengthen the proprietor's authority backfired, for, according to historian Herbert Osgood, Cranfield entered on "the most reckless and tyrannical course of policy which was ever followed by an appointee of the Crown in the American continental colonies." Mason finally sold his claims in 1691.

Well into the eighteenth century, New Hampshire remained a weak, sparsely populated colony, its frontier being subject to constant attacks by the French and Indians. New Hampshire's only valuable export during this period was naval stores. Unfortunately, most of the settlers did not benefit from the commerce in white pines, since the best timber was monopolized by a powerful oligarchy under the leadership of Governor Benning Wentworth. Between 1741 and 1767 this group, with the support of influential English administrators, controlled the political life of New Hampshire.

See Jeremy Belknap, *The History of New Hampshire* (1784-92); Jere R. Daniell, "Politics in New Hampshire under Governor Benning Wentworth, 1741-1767," *William and Mary Quarterly*, vol. 23 (1966); and Herbert Osgood, *The American Colonies in the Seventeenth Century*, 3 vols. (1907), and *The American Colonies in the Eighteenth Century*, 4 vols. (1924).—T. H. B.

New Haven Colony. In 1638 a group of more than two hundred and fifty London Puritans, led by the Reverend John Davenport and Theophilus Eaton, founded Quinnipiac (New Haven, Connecticut). These colonists had originally left England intending to settle in the Massachusetts Bay Colony, but when they arrived in Boston, they discovered that the commonwealth was bitterly divided over religious issues and that the best sites were already occupied. After preliminary exploration, Davenport and Eaton decided that the territory

bordering on Long Island Sound would answer their needs, since it appeared to offer good harbors and easy access to the Indian trade. The Puritan settlers purchased rights to the area from the local Indians, but unfortunately, they possessed no formal claim to the land, such as a royal charter or a patent from the Council for New England. The lack of a charter put the people of New Haven at a great disadvantage when dealing with their aggressive neighbors in Connecticut and the New Netherlands, and the Dutch even referred to the plantation as "a pretended colony."

Soon after New Haven was established, other towns were planted in the area: Milford, Guilford, Stamford, Fairfield, Greenwich, and Branford. At first these scattered communities were independent, bound together only by their common commitment to the Congregational religion. In 1643 they formed a loose federation that took the name New Haven Colony, after the largest member of the group. The towns decided that only church members would be allowed to participate in elections or to hold civil offices. Contemporaries regarded New Haven as the strictest of the Puritan settlements, and the records of the government reveal the magistrates' great fear lest Satan invade their jurisdiction.

The New Haven Colony was probably doomed to failure from the start. It was cut off from the best fur trade by Connecticut to the north, and its soil was of poor quality. In 1653 one disconsolate settler wrote that we "are confined and straitened, the sea lying before us and a rocky rude desert, unfit for culture and destitute of commodity, behind our backs, all convenient places for accomodations on the sea coast already possessed and planted." Leading New Haven merchants attempted to stimulate the colony's faltering economy by purchasing lands on the Delaware River, but these efforts were frustrated by the Swedes and the Dutch, who had prior claim to the area. After the Restoration, Connecticut received a charter from Charles II that gave it control over all the New Haven Colony. The people of New Haven felt that they had been cheated, but they were unable to alter the crown's grant. New Haven resisted surrender until 1664, when the threat of seizure by the duke of York, proprietor of New York and Charles II's brother, forced the colonists to choose rule by Connecticut as the lesser of two evils. Fortunately, the duke did not press his claims, but some unreconciled individuals moved to Newark rather than give up their dream of a perfect godly commonwealth.

See Charles M. Andrews, *The Colonial Period of American History*, vol. II (1936); and Isabel M. Calder, *The New Haven Colony* (1934).—T. H. B.

New Helvetia. See John Augustus SUTTER.

New Indian movement. See INDIAN POWER MOVEMENT.

New Jersey, settlement of. During the first half of the seventeenth century, the Dutch owned the territory between the Hudson and Delaware rivers. The Dutch West India Company had possessed neither the funds nor the colonists needed to develop the area, however, and with the exception of a few Dutch farmers at Bergen, the region was uninhabited by Europeans. In 1664 the English launched a secret attack against the New Netherlands. In fact, Charles II had granted the entire colony to his brother, the duke of York, months before the Dutch had realized that they were in danger.

The duke's proprietary governor, Richard Nicolls, thought the acreage west of the Hudson, which he called Albania, was the most valuable part of the former Dutch possessions, and he encouraged English colonists to move there. Nicolls stated that any group that cleared a title with the local Indians and that promised to settle as a community could apply for a land grant. Moreover, he guaranteed religious freedom and an elected government. Nicolls was vague about what the settlers would owe the duke of York in return. Two groups of Long Island Puritans quickly complied and received the Elizabethtown and the Monmouth grants in the northeast section of the province. For almost fifty years these two grants were a source of unrest in the colony, for the Puritans believed they had been given rights denied to them by the later New Jersey proprietors.

Before Nicolls had arrived in America, the duke gave New Jersey to two of his old friends, Sir George Carteret and Lord John Berkeley, through an instrument known as a deed of lease and release. Nicolls was furious when he heard the news, and he correctly explained, "if the duke will improve this place to the utmost, neither the trade, the river, nor the adjacent lands must be divided from this colony but remain entire." The duke ignored this sound advice, however, and both New York and New Jersey suffered economically as a consequence.

Carteret and Berkeley, who were also involved in the Carolina project, hoped that New Jersey would yield large returns without requiring a large investment. Neither man intended to go to the New World. Instead, they planned to act as land agents, selling acreage and collecting rents from persons who immigrated to New Jersey from established English colonies. To promote interest in the region, the two proprietors issued the "Concessions and Agreements" in 1665. This document, originally drafted as a description of conditions for settling in Carolina, promised liberal headrights (grants of free land), freedom of religion, and an elected assembly. It also announced that after 1670 colonists would have to pay a quitrent to the proprietors. This requirement angered the Elizabethtown Puritans. They were familiar with the land policies of New England, where individuals were not required to pay rents or feudal dues, and they regarded the proprietors' claim as an unjust innovation. The civil government, which the proprietors set up in 1665, sparked another long controversy. Under English law the duke of York had no authority to transfer the powers of government without the crown's consent, but both the duke and his friends acted as if he possessed that right. The Puritans refused to play this game, however, and during the entire period of proprietary rule, they insisted that their government rested on an illegal foundation.

New Jersey brought Carteret and Berkeley few profits and many problems. Their appointed governor, Philip Carteret, arrived in Elizabethtown in 1665. It was quickly apparent that many colonists were in a rebellious mood. The Puritans living on the two grants that Nicolls had made claimed the right to hold their own legislature. Moreover, they announced that they had no intention of paying quitrents. The unrest came to a head in 1672, when the Puritans called an assembly and elected John Carteret, arrant son of the proprietor, as president. Sir George Carteret and the duke of York supported the governor, however, and told John to leave

New Jersey. The proprietors declared that henceforth no settler could participate in government affairs until he had sworn an oath to the proprietors and paid his quitrents. This tough response temporarily quieted the Puritans, but the source of the trouble remained.

In 1674 a discouraged Lord Berkeley sold his interests in the proprietorship to two London Quakers. Until 1702 the colony was divided into two parts—East Jersey and West Jersey—each having its own governor and proprietors. The Quakers who bought West Jersey may have envisioned a haven for their coreligionists who were persecuted in England and Scotland. In any case William Penn and other Quaker leaders soon became involved in West Jersey. In 1677 the Quaker trustees issued a second "Concessions and Agreements," a liberal document guaranteeing religious freedom and broad participation in government. The authors declared, "... we lay a foundation for after ages to understand their liberty as men and christians, that they may not be brought in bondage, but by their own consent; for we put the power in the people." West Jersey did not prosper, and after 1681 most Quaker immigrants preferred the newly founded Pennsylvania. In 1687 an Anglican courtier, Dr. Daniel Coxe, purchased the proprietary rights to West Jersey and in 1692 sold out to a group of forty-eight investors called the West Jersey Society. Few people complained when the crown finally took over the colony's confused affairs in 1702.

The story of East Jersey during the proprietary period was equally complex. In 1682 a group of Quakers purchased Carteret's rights over the area, but the new proprietors were no more successful than Carteret had been in controlling the Puritans. These settlers stubbornly refused to pay quitrents or to relinquish the grants that Governor Nicolls had given them. To make matters worse the proprietors fought among themselves over the proper way to distribute land, while they allowed the civil government to drift in confusion.

In 1702 the proprietors of East and West Jersey happily surrendered "all their pretences to the said powers of Government." The entire area became a royal colony ruled by a governor, council, and assembly. Until 1738, however, New Jersey's governor was also the governor of New York. Unfortunately the proprietors did not give up their rights to the lands of the colony, and throughout the eighteenth century they tried to collect quitrents and to defend their claim to all ungranted acreage. Their policy of holding land off the market to keep the price high irritated the small freeholders, who could not understand why such an anachronistic body should control the colony's landed wealth. Riots over the land were frequent, but the government was totally incapable of bringing peace to New Jersey. Only after the American Revolution did the state's deep political and social divisions begin to heal.

There are several good books on the history of colonial New Jersey. Two general accounts are Richard P. McCormick, *New Jersey from Colony to State 1607-1789* (1964), and Wesley Frank Craven, *New Jersey and the English Colonization of North America* (1964). John E. Pomfret deals with the proprietary period in *The Province of West New Jersey 1609-1702* (1956) and *The Province of East New Jersey 1609-1702* (1962).—T. H. B.

Newlands, Francis Griffith (1848-1917). Conservationist and Nevada politician. Newlands has an enduring reputation in the West associated with his authorship of the Reclamation Act (1902). His subsequent role as a legislator contributed epochal landmarks in Progressive era legislation. Concern for the public interest, however, did not characterize his early years. Newlands was born near Natchez, Mississippi, and knew genteel poverty as a youth in Quincy, Illinois, occasioned by the death of his father when he was three and the business reverses of his stepfather following the Panic of 1857. His mother inspired his ambitions for educational and cultural advancement and insisted on the special tutoring that brought his admission to Yale University at the age of sixteen. His schooling at Yale came to an end in the middle of his junior year when he had to return to the support of his family, now in Washington. While working in the Treasury Department he studied law at night at the future George Washington University and was admitted to the District of Columbia bar on his twenty-first birthday.

From Yale associations Newlands learned of the opportunities for a young lawyer on the Pacific Coast, and he moved to San Francisco in 1870. He achieved an exceptionally successful practice in a few years and also made his way in the *nouveau riche* society of San Francisco, where as a handsome young man with the cultured manners of eastern society he was much in demand. Soon he was courting the daughter of William Sharon, millionaire partner of William C. Ralston of the Bank of California. Newlands' marriage to Clara Adelaide Sharon in 1874 freed him forever from dreaded poverty and gave him a new career associated with administering and protecting great wealth. He became the confidant of his father-in-law in the reorganization of Bank of California assets after the Panic of 1875. The defense of Sharon properties in and out of court also earned him the position of sole trustee for the estate of William Sharon at the time of the latter's death in 1885.

A combination of circumstances between 1878, when nervous exhaustion forced him to seek rest in Europe, and 1888 brought a reordering of his social values and a desire to seek public office in Congress. His wife died in 1882. On top of this sorrow came an increasing personal revulsion for his father-in-law's predatory activities. The measures deemed necessary to protect the Sharon estate in the celebrated litigation growing out of the marriage claims of Sharon's mistress, Sarah Althea Hill, brought Newlands and his new wife's removal to Nevada in 1888.

Newlands' entrance on the Nevada political scene was made possible through the especial assistance of Senator William Stewart, who suggested reclamation as a means to restore the sagging mining economy of Nevada and win wide public backing for launching a political career. (Newlands had attempted to win the Democratic nomination for senator from California in 1887 but failed in competition with Senator George Hearst.) Newlands' venture in irrigation promotion, 1889-91, demonstrated the difficulties facing private enterprise without government support. He hired experts in hydrology, water law, and civil engineering, and invested a quarter of a million dollars in reservoir sites and demonstration ranch lands. But when he sought state legislative backing to place water rights and reclamation institutions on a systematic basis, the legislature repudiated this experi-

ment. This, as well as a downturn in the economy, forced the zealous young millionaire to seek political preferment more directly by joining with Senator Stewart and others in the rising silver movement. Although Newlands did not openly advocate unlimited coinage of silver until its universal popularity as a national program was demonstrated in 1895, he was elected to Congress in 1892 because of his sympathy for the silver movement. He spurned the Populist program associated with the silver forces in Nevada, however, but became active in the formation of the National Silver party and gave his support to the Bryan ticket in 1896.

The break between Stewart and Newlands finally came in the 1898 election when the younger man cast aside his silver associates and sought Stewart's Senate seat, unsuccessfully. In the meantime, Newlands had invested heavily in Washington, D.C., real estate, and had won a circle of friends including career scientists and conservationists as well as influential members of Congress. As a congressman, Newlands served on the Foreign Affairs Committee and introduced the joint resolution for annexation of Hawaii, but his name is not associated with any notable legislation until passage of the Reclamation Act in 1902.

The NEWLANDS RECLAMATION ACT was of surpassing significance to the West, ushering in a whole new era of economic development. It was momentous as well for the political career of Newlands. After he was elected to the Senate in 1903, he assumed an even more important role as a champion of conservation measures. His detailed analysis of legislative problems revealed that western irrigation needs and eastern waterways development were all part of the same problem requiring comprehensive national planning and construction of public works. He adopted the multipurpose approach developed in the Geological Survey by Marshall Leighton and popularized by Gifford Pinchot's friend, W. J. McGee. Their program would bring flood control and improved navigation to river basins, increased forest yield and agricultural productivity, and the conservation of resources generally through the construction of dams at the headwaters of major streams. What was called for was a body of experts analogous to the Reclamation Service, who were freed from congressional supervision and the piecemeal approach dictated by traditional politically oriented rivers-and-harbors legislation. Newlands' advocacy of waterways legislation between 1907 and 1917 clearly marked him as the principal Democratic conservationist in Congress.

Unlike his western colleagues in Congress, Newlands supported Roosevelt administration public-lands policies, and for this he was appointed to the Inland Waterways Commission. He participated actively in the promotional venture, which included a much-celebrated voyage down the Mississippi River, and introduced the enabling legislation in 1907 to give the commission permanency. Minding the precedent of the 1902 reclamation statute, he provided for an independent Inland Waterways Fund of $50 million that would free the proposed waterways board from annual congressional appropriations. Formidable opposition by the Corps of Engineers, whose chief concern was improvement of navigation and the construction of levees, prevented the Newlands bill from enactment.

The Senator's famous legislative tenacity finally won out with the passage of a token waterways commission bill in 1917. But with President Woodrow Wilson's preoccupation with the war effort and the death of Newlands in December 1917, the Engineers were able to block its implementation. The concept of multipurpose river-basin development later became the core principle of the New Deal's T.V.A. program.

Newlands left a record of Progressive legislation outside the areas of reclamation and conservation. With respect to the principal problems of transportation, the tariff, and industry, his solution involved using national powers and politically independent commissions staffed with experts. Long advocating a tariff commission, Newlands saw this device incorporated in the Payne-Aldrich tariff (1909). He recognized the shortcomings of antitrust action by politically motivated attorney generals and drafted the bill that created the Federal Trade Commission (1914), designed to produce continuity in protecting the public from unfair competitive practices of American business. But it was in the area of railway regulation that Newlands soon became the leading congressional authority and that he made his largest contribution. As early as 1905 he had authored a measure of considerable originality calling for the federal incorporation of railroads so that all of their operations, including capitalization, rate-setting, taxation, and labor relations, would be determined by one national authority, the Interstate Commerce Commission. He was friendly to organized labor and was in the thick of the action as railway labor became restive prior to American entrance into World War I. He wrote a mediation-and-conciliation amendment to the Interstate Commerce Act in 1913, and expedited passage of the Adamson Eight-Hour Act in 1916. At the time of his death, he was chairman of a longstanding joint congressional committee investigating all aspects of the railroad problem, and many of this committee's recommendations found their way into the Transportation Act of 1920.

The factors accounting for Newlands' success are apparent. His dedication to the general welfare came from his reaction to the acquisitive society of William Sharon. His great wealth not only gave him freedom from the influence of vested interests in Washington, but enabled him to mount promotional campaigns for his own proposals. His strong financial position brought him control of the Democratic party in Nevada. While scorned as the Great Rotten Borough, Nevada offered its senior senator a political base of electoral security without exacting much in return. In consequence, Newlands devoted his primary effort to solving national problems, though he contributed far more to his constituents' welfare than had any previous Nevada senator. He shared with westerners their passion for growth, but his affection for the methods of the engineer and his attachment to eastern conservation values set him apart from the exploitative temper prevalent in the West. He sought to give the federal government an important role in fostering homestead settlement in the West and in protecting western natural resources. At the same time he endeavored to achieve social justice throughout the whole nation by placing federal agencies in the position of arbiters between conflicting economic interests.

Franklin K. Lane, "Senator Newlands: An Apprecia-

tion," *New Outlook* (January 9, 1918), is an insightful view of Newlands' contributions by a close friend and public official. Mary Ellen Glass, *Silver and Politics in Nevada: 1892-1902* (1969), describes the foundations of Newlands' political career. Her *Water for Nevada: The Reclamation Controversy, 1885-1902* (1964) charts Newlands' reclamation experience in Nevada, which led to his leadership in the national reclamation effort. The introduction in Newlands, *The Public Papers of Francis G. Newlands*, ed. by Arthur B. Darling, 2 vols. (1932), provides the only published biography of Newlands. Gilman M. Ostrander, *Nevada, the Great Rotten Burough, 1859-1964* (1966), provides perspective for Newlands' highly successful political career.—L. B. L.

Newlands Reclamation Act (1902). The Newlands Act, named for its principal author, Congressman (later Senator) Francis G. NEWLANDS, authorized the secretary of the interior to construct federal reclamation reservoirs in the West, such projects to be financed by a newly created Reclamation Fund derived from public land sales in eleven western states and territories. The Department of the Interior reserved public lands in the projects exclusively for settlers in tracts not to exceed 160 acres under the Homestead Act. Water-users were to pay water charges and construction costs in ten annual payments. They would gain title to their irrigated land in three years and would share in the management of the project when the government had been reimbursed for the initial cost. This was truly an innovative statute that achieved unprecedented reservation of the public domain and federal bureaucratic control in the states in an endeavor to conserve natural resources. Furthermore, the program was initially self-supporting through the Reclamation Fund. Perhaps this feature commended it to Congress and explains why so much discretion was given to the secretary of the interior in locating the projects and administering the program.

At the outset, the Hansbrough-Newlands bill contained too many novel features to be readily accepted when first submitted to the two houses of Congress in January 1901. Favorable public opinion in the East was achieved through the skillful advertising campaign launched by a prominent publicist and lobbyist, George Maxwell, on behalf of a national reclamation policy. His National Irrigation Association dominated the organized irrigation movement and his press releases and speakers bureau carried the message to industrial and civic groups as well as labor bodies. Both major political parties urged federal reclamation in their 1900 campaign platforms. Frederick H. Newell, chief hydrographer of the United States Geological Survey, and Gifford Pinchot, United States forester, worked closely with Newlands and Maxwell at congressional hearings and interviews with the president. Western congressional leaders were hesitant to accept this national program and looked with favor on bills introduced by Senator Francis Warren of Wyoming and others that authorized federal reservoir construction but insisted on state control in order to protect state water-rights.

The succession of Theodore Roosevelt to the presidency was the single most important factor in the struggle to achieve national reclamation. He shared with Newlands an attachment for the American agrarian ideal and wanted to open up a new homestead frontier through federal reclamation. Furthermore, he savored western political support and gloried in a truly national program of conservation. White House pressure brought the measure to a vote in the Senate and helped Newlands secure House leadership acceptance. The National Reclamation Act was signed by the president on June 17, 1902. It was the first truly Progressive statute of the Roosevelt administration, incorporating the principles of nationalization, executive independence from Congress, and scientific solutions for natural resource problems. The program was soon inaugurated under Frederick Newell's direction, and the Reclamation Service's large dam-and-reservoir-construction achievements quickly brought renown to this national program. (See also RECLAMATION AND IRRIGATION.)

John T. Ganoe, "The Origins of a National Reclamation Policy," *Mississippi Valley Historical Review* (June 1931), the first scholarly presentation of the national reclamation movement, is particularly good in tracing legislative maneuvers leading to adoption of the Newlands Act. Paul W. Gates, *History of Public Land Law Development* (1968), describes the passage of the Reclamation Act in terms of the movement that preceded it. William Lilley III and Lewis L. Gould, "The Western Irrigation Movement, 1878-1902: A Reappraisal," in *The American West: A Reorientation*, ed. Gene M. Gressley (1966), is valuable for its interpretation of the eastern influence in passage of the Newlands Act. William E. Smythe, *The Conquest of Arid America* (1969), includes an account of the legislative history of the Newlands Act.—L. B. L.

New Mexico. In New Mexico vestiges of frontier America remain today more clearly in evidence and more numerous than in any other state. Here three vigorous cultures, Indian, Spanish, and Anglo, met and coalesced, forming a life-style and undergoing a frontier experience that was wholly unique. The PUEBLO INDIANS, because they were a relatively advanced and tightly knit society, and the NAVAHO and the APACHE, because they were isolated and among the last to be subdued, have held closely to traditional ways, preserving their identity even amidst the conforming pressures of twentieth-century America. For 250 years the Spaniards clung tenaciously to their colony in New Mexico; beset by enemies, removed from all but the most tenuous contact with the outside world, they wrested a precarious existence from sparse rangeland and a fertile, albeit poorly watered, soil. And although Spain no longer rules, the Iberian heritage remains firmly fixed upon the land and the people. Finally the latecomers, the Anglo-Americans, brimming with self-confidence and aggressively devoted to change, introduced railroads, drained oil from the Permian rocks, built ever-larger cities as reservoirs for the eastern overflow of population, and at last detonated the world's first atom bomb—at White Sands, July 1945.

Within New Mexico occur tremendous variations in topography and physiography. Elevation varies from the highest point, Wheeler Peak in the north at 13,151 feet, to the lowest at 2,850 feet, where the Pecos River crosses the southern boundary into Texas. The basic topographic structure is that of a high plateau tilted toward the south with numerous mountain ranges rising above the level of the surrounding country. The principal river, the RIO GRANDE, roughly bisects the state from north to south. It has always drawn to its

valley the largest concentrations of human population, for here water has always been found for irrigation, and the mountainside windbreaks provide a modicum of shelter from intemperate winters.

The date of man's first appearance in New Mexico has not been definitely established, although it may have been as long as thirty to forty thousand years ago. First evidence of Ice Age man in America was unearthed in 1925 at Folsom, in the northeast corner of the state. Subsequent discoveries at Clovis, Sandia, and elsewhere have greatly enlarged our knowledge of the big-game hunters who roamed the southern Plains and produced superb projectile points, far superior to anything known from the Old World. Other peoples settled into permanent villages about the beginning of the Christian era and, borrowing agriculture and ceramics from their neighbors in Mexico, laid the groundwork for the development of Pueblo culture during the first millennium A.D. The Pueblo Indians built impressive cliff cities, ruins of which may still be seen at Mesa Verde National Park (Colorado) and Bandelier National Monument west of Santa Fe. But they also erected on open sites large apartment-like structures of stone and adobe. Ladders, which could be pulled up in time of war, gave access to the terraced upper levels. It was this kind of communal building the Spaniards encountered in 1540, since the cliff dwellings had long since been abandoned. Surrounding the Pueblo and alternately warring and trading with them were the Athapaskan-speaking Navaho and Apache, who may have entered the Southwest from the north about A.D. 1400. It was they, as obdurate foes of the Spaniards, who kept the southwestern frontier in turmoil for much of the colonial era.

Beginning in 1519 Spanish expeditions from Jamaica explored the Texas coast and made an abortive attempt to found a colony at the mouth of the Rio Grande. Had this been successful, the European approach to New Mexico might have been from the east across the Texas plains. As it was, penetration of the interior came from the south, where Hernán Cortés had secured a firm base by vanquishing the Aztec empire. Enticed by rumors of treasure-laden kingdoms, including the mythical Seven Cities of Cíbola, Francisco Vásquez de Coronado in 1540 assembled a glittering host of adventurers and noblemen and embarked for the north (see EXPLORATION, SPANISH). Guided by a Franciscan padre, Fray Marcos de Niza, who claimed to have viewed the Seven Cities from a distance, Coronado traveled up the west coast of Mexico, across southern Arizona, and through virtually the entire Pueblo province of New Mexico. All proved a disappointment since the Indian towns, except for some turquoise, were devoid of treasure. Nor did a similar quest through the Texas Panhandle and into southern Kansas for another legendary kingdom, Quivira, produce more fruitful results. The legends of the north had been exploded. Yet there clung an aura of mystery for another hundred years, until the last corners of this frontier had been explored. The Spaniards referred to the country as the other Mexico or the new Mexico, thereby expressing their vain hope that it would someday prove as rewarding as the old Mexico conquered by Cortés.

In the years 1581 to 1591 several small expeditions visited Pueblo land, but other than renewing Spanish interest in this area they had no permanent results. In 1598, however, Juan de ONATE, a member of a wealthy mining family of northern New Spain, led a colonizing force of 130 families to the upper Rio Grande valley, where he established the town of San Gabriel adjacent to the Tewa Pueblo of San Juan. Riding out both a rebellion among the Acoma Indians, in which his nephew was slain, and a mutiny among his own settlers, Oñate laboriously laid the foundations for the Spanish kingdom of New Mexico. Nevertheless, when he resigned his governorship in 1607, the colony was in feeble condition and would have been abandoned had not the king decided to maintain it at royal expense as a missionary province. The conversion of several thousand Pueblo by Franciscan missionaries was the one signal achievement of these early years.

Oñate's successor was Don Pedro de Peralta, who founded the provincial capital of SANTA FE in 1610. It was during his tenure as governor that the first serious disharmony developed between civil and ecclesiastical officials over the supremacy of jurisdictions. In following decades the conflict often broke into open strife, dividing the colony into bitter factions and weakening respect for Spanish institutions among the Pueblo Indians. Savage attacks by Apache, drought in the early 1670s, and repeated smallpox epidemics added to the colonists' woes. All this paled, however, before the disaster that befell New Mexico in August 1680. The Pueblo, strained by the heavy burden of Spanish rule and by assaults of the missionaries on their religion, united in common cause under the leadership of Popé of San Juan. They ravaged the entire province, killing Franciscans and colonists, destroying churches and ranches, sacking Santa Fe, and sending the wretched survivors scurrying south to El Paso. It was one of the worst defeats ever sustained by Spain in her overseas empire and proved a damaging blow to her pride and military prestige.

General Diego de VARGAS reconquered New Mexico in the period 1692 to 1694, an event still commemorated annually in the Santa Fe fiesta, and instituted the rebuilding of the province. Before the century's end, the villa of Santa Cruz near modern Española was founded, and Albuquerque was established in 1706. These, together with the capital and El Paso del Norte, formed the chief urban centers. The majority of the population, however, was dispersed in widely scattered farms and haciendas throughout the Rio Grande valley, up the Rio Chama basin, and in the district around Taos. Aside from the sedentary Indians, most of the people were mestizos, or mixed bloods, with a sprinkling of full-blooded Spaniards among the leading families, clergy, and government officials. By the opening of the nineteenth century, in spite of steady immigration from the south, the province could show a population of scarcely more than twenty-three thousand, exclusive of Indians.

During later colonial times the Spaniards displayed a more enlightened policy toward the Pueblo Indians, drawing them close as friends and allies. By contrast, they experienced serious difficulties with the Navaho and Apache and two groups of newcomers, the Ute and Comanche who unleashed murderous raids on the exposed and vulnerable settlements. Soldiers at the single presidio in Santa Fe, numbering only 125, appeared powerless to check these incursions, but Governor Juan Bautista de ANZA put together a strong force of regular troops, a citizen militia, and Pueblo auxiliaries and attacked a large Comanche camp in southern Colorado, killing the head chief, Cuerno Verde ("Green Horn"). This victory, followed by Anza's artful diplomacy, won a permanent peace with the Comanche as well as other tribes, leaving only the most refractory Apache bands still at war.

In addition to the Indian menace, the movement of French traders across the plains from Louisiana posed a grave concern for Spanish officials. Pedro de Villasur and forty-five soldiers scouted northward from Santa Fe in 1720 to check on foreign presence among the Plains Indians. When they neared the junction of the North and South Platte rivers, they were overcome and slain by the Pawnee, who seem to have been inspired by the French. The Mallet brothers, Frenchmen from Illinois, reached Santa Fe in 1739 and disposed of a quantity of trade goods before they were expelled by the governor. The danger from this quarter subsided, however, when Spain acquired Louisiana in 1763; but when she returned it provisionally to France and when France yielded it permanently to the United States, a new threat from Anglo-American pioneers loomed on her northern boundary. Lieutenant Zebulon Montgomery Pike, sent to explore the headwaters of the Arkansas and Red rivers in 1806, either by design or chance entered New Mexican territory and was arrested as a spy. Reports of other Americans wandering on the Plains as well as the appearance of traders in Santa Fe kept royal officers in a continual state of alarm through the ensuing decade. The real danger to the colony, however, was not from without, but rather from within, as became evident in 1821 when Mexico, including the province of New Mexico, achieved independence from Spain.

Don Pedro Bautista Pino, the only New Mexican ever to serve as deputy in the Spanish *cortes* (parliament), wrote a treatise published in 1812 in which he detailed the problems his province experienced as a result of its isolation, economic poverty, Indian troubles, and the inferior quality of its political administration. The bleak picture he painted at the end of the colonial period was destined to change but little during the twenty-five stormy years of Mexican rule (1821-46). The one bright note for the humble citizen was the growth of trade with Missouri over the Santa Fe Trail, which allowed the introduction of an abundance of cheap manufactured goods (see SANTA FE AND CHIHUAHUA TRAIL). In 1824 Yankee merchants realized a three hundred percent profit on $35,000 worth of wares sold in New Mexico. But these men held little respect for their customers and in their journals wrote of them in disparaging terms, noting especially their poverty and apparent deficiencies as soldiers. Thomas James in the early 1820s, for example, referred to the Santa Fe militia as "a gang of tatterdemalions and a troop of scarecrows." When the Americans impugned the bravery of the New Mexicans, however, they flew wide of the mark, for these simple farmers, often reduced to fighting with bows and arrows because they lacked firearms, had proved their mettle and powers of endurance during two centuries of border warfare.

In the years immediately following independence, only a series of depredations by the Navaho disturbed

New Mexico's tranquility. The outbreak of civil conflict in 1837, however, resulted in the beheading of Governor Albino Pérez and the emergence of a half-breed buffalo hunter from Taos, José Gonzalez, as provisional governor. The rebels, composed mainly of poor people opposed to new tax levies, were defeated at La Cañada by wealthy and ambitious Manuel ARMIJO of Albuquerque, who executed Gonzalez and installed himself as chief executive in 1837. He dominated provincial politics thereafter until the opening of the Mexican War in 1846.

Another serious incident occurred in 1841 as a result of the Texan-Santa Fe expedition. The new Republic of Texas, desirous of partaking in the profitable Santa Fe trade and perhaps asserting its vague claim to eastern New Mexico, sent an expedition of merchants and soldiers westward under General Hugh McLeod. Armijo chose to interpret this as a hostile invasion. When the Texans reached the Pecos River, weakened by privations endured crossing the Staked Plain, they were arrested and disarmed. After suffering brutal treatment, the captives were sent to Mexico City and finally released. Armijo received a medal for his part in the affair, but the hostility engendered between Texas and New Mexico was long in abating.

When the United States declared war against her southern neighbor in 1846, Brigadier General Stephen Watts Kearny was entrusted with detaching the north Mexican provinces. Departing from Fort Leavenworth, Kansas, "with a fluttering of banners," he marched to Santa Fe without opposition and proclaimed the annexation of New Mexico. Apparently, the peaceful occupation had been eased by the prominent trader James Wiley MAGOFFIN, who had urged Governor Armijo not to oppose the invaders. In any event Armijo had fled south, leaving the leading citizens of Santa Fe in heated debate over the wisdom of demolishing the churches in order to prevent their being converted into barracks by the barbarous American soldiers. Of the latter, Lieutenant W. H. Emory wrote, "Here all persons from the United States are called *Americans*, and the name is extended to no other race on the continent."

Neglect by their former government and a quarter century of close business relations with the Missouri traders had prepared most New Mexicans to accept the change of political fortunes with grace. Hastening to organize a new government for the territory, General Kearny appointed Charles Bent (see BENT BROTHERS) as governor; Donaciano Vigil, secretary; and Carlos BEAUBIEN as judge of the superior court. A legal structure created at the general's behest became known as the Kearny Code. All elements of the population, nevertheless, were not reconciled to the new order. In January 1847 Governor Bent, while visiting his home in Taos, was murdered and scalped by a mob of Indians and Mexicans, and other Americans met death at nearby Turley's Mill and Mora. The uprising was subsequently put down by Colonel Sterling Price, and the ringleaders were executed.

By the Treaty of Guadalupe Hidalgo (1848), New Mexico was ceded to the United States, but not until 1851 was a formal territorial government organized. In ensuing years political sentiment became polarized around a statehood party, led by such men as James S. Calhoun and Manuel ALVAREZ, and a territorial party,

prominent in whose ranks were Ceran ST. VRAIN and Thomas Cabeza de Vaca.

A boundary dispute with Texas was resolved when Congress agreed to pay the Lone Star State $10 million to surrender its claims, and a problem with Mexico over the international boundary was settled by the Gadsden Purchase (1853), which provided the United States with a convenient railroad route to California through southern New Mexico. The territory of Arizona was organized out of western New Mexico in 1863.

By 1849 a regular stage line was in operation over the Santa Fe Trail, and nine years later John Butterfield's famous Overland Mail Company was serving the southern part of the territory on its run from St. Louis to San Francisco. But this service was discontinued with the outbreak of the Civil War. Although most of the military officers on duty in New Mexico as well as new pioneers and traders were southerners, popular feeling favored the Union cause. Beginning in July 1861 Lieutenant Colonel John R. Baylor of Texas occupied southern New Mexico and proclaimed it the Confederate Territory of Arizona with Mesilla as capital (see ARIZONA: *Confederate Arizona*). Early the following year General H. H. Sibley won an engagement against Union forces at Valverde near Fort Craig and marched northward to take Albuquerque and Santa Fe. In late March, however, his army was defeated at the battle of Glorieta Pass east of Santa Fe by troops from Fort Union and the Colorado Volunteers, and he was obliged to withdraw back into Texas. The Confederate design to acquire New Mexico as a springboard for a march against California was thus frustrated.

The most serious threat to New Mexican security in the post-Civil War period was posed by continuing Indian hostilities. In 1863 and 1864 Kit CARSON directed a roundup of hostile Mescalero Apache and Navaho, who were confined to the Bosque Redondo reservation at Fort Sumner. In the late 1860s and 1870s a series of campaigns broke the spirit of the Plains Indians. But renegade Apache under Geronimo contined to terrorize the southwestern frontier until 1886, when General Nelson A. Miles caused them to give up the fight. The territory witnessed further disorder with the flare-up of the infamous LINCOLN COUNTY WAR, which pitted rival groups of cattlemen and merchants and involved the young desperado BILLY THE KID.

Scarcely less disruptive was the tumultuous course of territorial politics. Manipulation of ballots, political patronage, the statehood issue, and rivalry between parties for the Spanish-American vote created bitter partisan feuds and kept New Mexico in turmoil. Territorial delegates elected to serve in Congress were usually from old families and included such prominent men as the ex-priest José Manuel GALLEGOS, the elder Miguel A. OTERO, Francisco MANZANARES, and Antonio JOSEPH. After the Civil War a group of powerful Republicans under the leadership of Thomas Benton CATRON formed the "Santa Fe Ring," which sought to gain economic advantage through control of politics and land (see MAXWELL LAND GRANT COMPANY). Three of Catron's associates were L. Bradford Prince, who became territorial governor in 1889, Stephen B. ELKINS, a territorial and federal attorney, and Pedro PEREA, a wealthy sheep baron who lost his bid for the governorship in 1897 to the younger Miguel A. OTERO.

Economic development in the early territorial years was rapid and impressive. Five thousand freight wagons traveled across the Great Plains in 1866, but this mode of traffic was made obsolete by the arrival in 1880-81 of the Santa Fe, Southern Pacific, and Denver and Rio Grande railroads. Sheep raising since late Spanish times had predominated over cattle, and the old aristocratic families, such as the Bacas, Lunas, Luceros, and Pereas, whose flocks had once been counted by the scores of thousands, continued to dominate the industry. The coming of the railroads gave rise to a cattle boom, however, and there appeared an occasional "cattle king" such as John CHISUM, Holm Olaf BURSUM, and Charles M. O'DONEL.

The change in New Mexico's social complexion was less marked, for well into the twentieth century native Hispanos outnumbered Anglos. The Catholic clergy exercised a preponderant influence over the people and exerted pressure on territorial politics. One well-known priest, Antonio José MARTINEZ of Taos, was a man of wealth and ambition who ruled his community with an iron hand, even after suffering excommunication by New Mexico's first bishop, Jean Baptiste LAMY. Padre Martínez, as well as others in public life, drew support from the much publicized brotherhood of Catholic laymen known as the Penitentes, or BROTHERHOOD OF PENITENTS. Chapters of this association are still to be found in many rural communities, but most of their severe practices, such as self-flagellation with cactus whips and the crucifixion of members on Good Friday, have been moderated.

Reform-minded Bishop Lamy gradually removed clerical influence from the political arena, but his work was largely offset by the emergence of powerful cliques in Santa Fe that attained a stranglehold on government and manipulated territorial affairs for their own profit until statehood in 1912.

Following statehood in 1912, some Spanish-Americans, notably Octaviano A. LARRAZOLO, distinctly emphasized racism in their political appeals, and this approach helped elect Democrat Ezequiél CABEZA DE BACA as governor in 1917. Others, such as prosperous rancher Solomon LUNA, preached harmony and played down the racial issue. In recent decades no Spanish-American has served as governor, although several have been elected lieutenant governor.

Today New Mexico is the only area within the United States where the Spanish cultural tradition has continued unbroken since colonial times. Revival of many old crafts and folk practices, strong support for traditional fiestas and religious observances, and new programs in schools and universities that emphasize the Iberian contribution to the state help maintain pride of ancestry and culture among the Spanish-speaking population. As a result, feelings of inferiority and loss of cultural identity are far less acute in New Mexico than among Mexican-Americans elsewhere in the Southwest. In no other region does a minority group show so many members as leaders in politics, business, education, and other spheres of social activity. Outstanding names include the late Senator Dennis CHAVEZ, Santa Fe Mayor George González, noted historian and poet Father Angélico Chávez, educator-author Sabine Ulibarrí, and folklorist Peter Ribera Ortega. A discordant note in recent years was provided by a fiery ex-preacher from Texas, Reies TIJERINA, who is involved with the CHICANO LIBERATION MOVEMENT. He organized rural folk in claiming thousands of acres under old Spanish land grants. A series of violent episodes culminated in the now famous raid on the Tierra Amarilla courthouse in 1967.

As the importance of subsistence agriculture and stock raising declines, Hispanos increasingly desert their rural homes to seek jobs in Albuquerque, Santa Fe, or urban centers outside the state. Development of uranium mining since the 1950s; expansion of the oil industry, particularly in the San Juan basin; continuing atomic research at Los Alamos and Albuquerque; and the growth of small manufacturing firms have served to diversify the state's economy and provide new jobs for all sectors of the population. Perhaps nothing is more incongruous, yet more typical, of New Mexico than the situation of the San Ildefonso Indians, who travel daily from their ancient adobe pueblo to work among the scholars and scientists at nearby Los Alamos. In this one corner of the country, the past has not fully relinquished its hold on the present.

A comprehensive, up-to-date survey history of New Mexico is still lacking. An older standard reference is Ralph Emerson Twitchell, *The Leading Facts of New Mexican History* (repr. 1963). The Spanish and Mexican years are covered in Cleve Hallenbeck, *Land of the Conquistadores* (1950). A provocative and well-researched account of the territorial period may be found in Howard R. Lamar, *The Far Southwest, 1846-1912* (1966). Readers should also consult Lyle Saunders, *A Guide to Materials Bearing on Cultural Relations in New Mexico* (1944).—M. Si.

New Mexico missions. When Juan de ONATE failed to find the rich gold and silver deposits that he believed would make colonization of Spanish NEW MEXICO a highly profitable venture, most Spaniards were prepared to abandon the harsh deserts and rugged mountains of the province to the Indians. But the Franciscans, playing upon the piety of Philip III, reminded the king of the spiritual profit to be gained from the preservation and extension of their missionary efforts among the Indians. The stratagem worked, and thus was the continued Spanish presence in New Mexico assured.

It has been estimated that between 1598 and 1700 the Spanish crown spent the equivalent of two million gold pesos or more to maintain the missions of New Mexico. During this period some two hundred and fifty Franciscans labored at more than forty missionary posts, most scattered unevenly along the Rio Grande from the vicinity of El Paso north to Taos, with others as far east as Pecos and as far west as the isolated Hopi pueblos of present-day Arizona. Efforts to congregate the seminomadic peoples who ranged over the neighboring mountains and plains—bands of Western Apache, Navaho, and sundry Plains tribes—failed consistently. With the single exception of Nuestra Señora de Guadalupe de los Mansos, built on the site of present-day Ciudad Juárez, Mexico, the friars founded their missions in or near existing communities of the sedentary town-dwelling natives who came to be called the PUEBLO INDIANS.

Like the Indians of central Mexico, the twenty to thirty thousand Pueblo were agricultural peoples living in compact, several-storied earth-and-stone apartment complexes. The obvious advantage to the missionary of ready-made congregations was lessened by two factors. Unlike the Indians of central Mexico, the Pueblo were not joined in larger political groupings; each community acted independently. Neither did they possess a lingua franca, speaking instead a variety of mutually unintelligible languages and dialects.

Most Pueblo communities passively accepted a friar. From the time of Coronado they had seen what destruction the invaders were capable of working on peoples who openly defied them. Most Pueblo permitted the missionary to preach, to baptize their children, and to lead them in the external motions of the new cult. On occasion they stood by while the missionary destroyed the objects of their own sacred ceremonial life. They built a mission church of unfamiliar dimensions and a *convento* (living quarters) for him; they learned to use new tools; they planted wheat and herded the mission's stock. At his insistence they paid tribute in kind to an *encomendero*, an armed colonist who was supposed to protect them from the enemies of the colony. One of their number let himself be elected *gobernador*, representative of the people in their dealings with the missionary and the Spanish civil authorities. Thus, on the surface the missions of New Mexico seemed to an early seventeenth-century observer well on the way to achieving the twin goals of Spanish colonialism—the transformation of a pacified native population into a "civilized," productive province and the conversion of a pagan land to the Roman Catholic church.

The Pueblo did not abandon their old religion, the very fabric of their closely integrated daily existence; rather, they took it underground. To oblige the missionary, they adopted the externals of Roman Catholicism: images of saints, processions, and polyphonic chant. The ruse did not always work. When the traditional ceremonial leaders were caught practicing "paganism and idolatry," they were flogged and publicly humiliated or even executed. Pueblo ceremonial chambers (kivas) were invaded and destroyed and secret caches of sacred objects put to the torch. Sometimes the people in outlying areas, pushed beyond the limit of their tolerance, rebelled, martyred their missionary, and fled, as at the Zuñi pueblo of Hawikuh in 1632, at the Hopi pueblo of Awátovi in 1633, and at Taos in 1639. For the most part, however, the Pueblo Indians endured, held to their old ways in secret, and bided their time.

From beginning to end, the Spanish missions of New Mexico were a monopoly of the Franciscans. By 1616 the friars had founded ten permanent establishments. That same year the order's general chapter elevated the New Mexico field to the status of a semiautonomous administrative district, the Custody of the Conversion of Saint Paul. Ordinarily a custody became in time an independent province within the order, but the New Mexico custody did not. Indian wars, quarrels between missionaries and civil officials, and the lack of a seminary to train novices combined to keep the frontier custody subordinate to the Mexican Province of the Holy Gospel for two centuries and more.

The golden age of the New Mexico missions, if it can properly be called that, was between 1630 and 1660. Its herald was a propagandist par excellence, Fray Alonso de Benavides. Sent out in 1625 as Franciscan prelate, or *custos*, the energetic native of the Azores gave great impetus to missionary outreach. He presided over the founding of ten new missions, laboring in the vineyard himself among the Piro, the Jémez, and the Gila Apache. As an agent of the Inquisition, Benavides was empowered to investigate cases of crimes against the faith by Spaniards (Indians were exempt from prosecution by the Inquisition), to gather evidence, and to arrest and deport the accused to Mexico City for trial before the tribunal of the Holy Office. Still, his greatest service to the New Mexico missions he performed after he had departed the custody in the fall of 1629.

Fully intending to return, Fray Alonso found himself instead aboard a ship bound for Spain. His superiors had dispatched him as a lobbyist to the court of Philip IV. He was a natural. Presenting to the king his *Memorial* of 1630, Benavides, with pious exaggeration, graphically protrayed the New Mexico apostolate. He lamented the grievous shortage of workers for so great a harvest and set forth the many "wonders and miracles" indicative of God's special concern for these missions. As a result of his pleas the Franciscans received more funds.

While still in Spain, Benavides traveled north to Agreda to interview María de Jesús, a nun who claimed to have been mystically transported in her blue cloak to New Mexico, where she preached the Gospel to the natives in their own tongues. After an intense examination, Fray Alonso publicly verified her assertion. It made grand publicity for the order. And it did not end there. Apparently in honor of María de Jesús of Agreda and the doctrine of the Immaculate Conception, the Franciscans of the Province of the Holy Gospel changed the color of their own habits from gray to blue. In later years word of "the Lady in Blue" would turn up again and again from Texas to the Colorado River. As for Benavides, he wanted to be bishop of New Mexico. Instead, after presenting a revised version of his *Memorial* to Pope Urban VIII, he received appointment as auxiliary bishop of Goa in Portuguese India. He never returned to New Mexico.

If any one conspicuous feature characterized seventeenth-century New Mexico, it was the bitter, mutually destructive conflict between church and state, between the missionaries and the royal governors. Because New Mexico was first and foremost a missionary colony, the friars wielded unusual power, both social and economic. Because they were the only clergy, they held a formidable spiritual monopoly over all of society, from governor to muleteer. The local Franciscan prelate sat as the only ecclesiastical judge in the colony. Often he doubled as agent of the Inquisition. Because the see of Durango, which claimed jurisdiction over the church in New Mexico, lay seven hundred miles to the south, no bishop restrained the friars. A majority of them had come out from Spain, which meant that they enjoyed an elevated status in colonial society. As a class, they were by far the best-educated persons in New Mexico. They had charge of the colony's only regular freighting service, the periodic mission supply caravans. Combined, the economic resources of the missions—land, crops, livestock, and Indian labor—at times exceeded those of the entire Hispanic community.

For their part, New Mexico's royal governors, too often mercenary, self-seeking troublemakers, exercised such broad civil and military powers that they readily became tyrants. The failure of the crown to define clearly the respective authority of church and state in New Mexico made conflict inevitable. And because appeal to the viceroy regularly took a year or longer, contending friars and governors fought it out on the spot, too often literally, to the obvious detriment of the colony.

In 1613 the Franciscan superior excommunicated the governor, branding him "a Lutheran, a heretic, and a Jew"; a shooting incident followed; the friars and their partisans fortified the mission of Santo Domingo and later cast the governor into solitary confinement for nine months. In 1640 Governor Luis de Rosas bloodied the heads of two friars on the streets of Santa Fe, calling them "liars, pigs, traitors, heretics, schismatics," and the like. Less than two years later Rosas was murdered under sordid circumstances.

Although the missionaries never ceased to represent their actions as consistent with the legitimate privileges of the church and the well-being of souls and although the governors loudly proclaimed the king's rights as patron of the church in his empire, at base the struggle turned on a less theoretical issue—competition for the colony's prime resource, Pueblo Indian labor. As wards of the church, said the friars, the Indians should be attending catechism, building churches, and looking after mission fields and flocks. As vassals of the king, said the governors, the Indians should be paying tribute, laboring on public works, and serving the colonists. Ordered to do one thing in the name of God and another in the name of the king, exploited by the minions of both, the Pueblo Indians lost all respect for their quarrelsome masters.

Other factors contributed to the colony's unhappiness. Periodic epidemics of smallpox, typhus, and other infectious diseases ravaged the populace. One unnamed plague in 1640 carried off an estimated three thousand Pueblo Indians. Often provoked by hostile Spaniards marauding for slaves, Apache and Navaho raiders, ever more formidable as they adapted their culture to the horse, took an increasing toll of livestock and human life, including at least two Franciscans. It was a vicious circle. Spanish "punitive" expeditions retaliated by burning native rancherias and taking more slaves. The Pueblo too began to stir under the oppression of the missionary and civilian regimes. Word of Indian conspiracies brought down on suspected leaders public sentences of whipping or hanging. During the 1660s one Esteban Clemente, evidently a mixed-blood, laid plans for a general uprising. He too was caught and hanged. But perhaps the most menacing factor of all was the weather. Beginning about midcentury a dry spell set in. With it came crop failure, famine, and starvation. As a direct result, the hungry remnants of half a dozen towns, the Saline pueblos (so called because of the nearby salt lakes), abandoned their homes, leaving the colony's southeastern frontier open to Apache invasion. Thus, by the mid-1670s the stage was set for tragedy.

It began routinely enough in 1675 when the superstitious old missionary at San Ildefonso accused his people of having bewitched him. As a result, forty-seven Tewa Indians were brought to Santa Fe for trial; four were hanged and the rest whipped and released. One of the latter, a San Juan leader known as Popé, began plotting a massive purge of everything Spanish. In a kiva

at Taos, far from the prying eyes of the oppressors, he worked out the details, perhaps with the aid of a mysterious and vengeful mulatto, Domingo Naranjo, whom historian Fray Angélico Chávez sees as the real mastermind.

On August 10, 1680, in one great spree of killing, slashing, looting, and desecration, the Pueblo Indians rose en masse. Twenty-one missionaries died agonizing, humiliating deaths. Of the colony's Hispanic community, numbering perhaps 2,400, some 380 perished while the rest fought for their lives. Governor Antonio de Otermin, besieged in Santa Fe with the survivors from the north, boldly broke out and retreated down the Rio Grande, overtaking en route his fleeing subjects from the south. Not till they reached the El Paso area did the governor stop to take inventory. In less than seven weeks the Spaniards had been cast out of an entire colony. Behind them the Pueblo were celebrating.

Still, no matter how many images of saints they smashed or mission orchards they uprooted, the Pueblo Indians could not erase the Spaniards' eighty-year program of acculturation. The very way Popé swaggered was Spanish. His effort to perpetuate the revolution in a confederation of tribute-paying pueblos was doomed to failure. When the bold and strutting Spanish reconqueror Diego de VARGAS reoccupied the colony in 1692-93, he was able to divide and conquer. The Pueblo's united front had collapsed. By the end of the century—despite one last revolt by the northern pueblos and five more martyred friars—a majority of the missions had been reestablished.

The fundamental shift in emphasis that occurred in New Mexico between the seventeenth and eighteenth centuries reflected changes of much broader scope. The eighteenth was avowedly a more secular century. The Enlightenment reigned. It was also the great century of colonial rivalry in America between England, France, and Spain. New Mexico, primarily a missionary colony in the seventeenth century, became in the eighteenth an imperial outpost of defense first and foremost. Never again did the missionaries regain their awesome powers.

To the dismay of the friars, three bishops of Durango actually carried out personal visitations of New Mexico—Benito Crespo in 1730, Martín de Elizacoechea in 1737, and Pedro Tamarón in 1760. Bishop Crespo installed Santiago Roybal as his vicar at Santa Fe, an opening wedge intended to break the Franciscans' clerical monopoly. From time to time secular priests served the Hispanic communities of Santa Fe (founded in 1610), El Paso (1680), Santa Cruz de la Cañada (1695), and Albuquerque (1706). More and more of the missionaries were American-born (*criollos*). Although a majority were selfless and dedicated priests, the overall quality of the clergy declined. Within the Franciscan order, missionary momentum shifted from the provinces to the newly formed missionary colleges whose gray-robed friars (the provinces still wore blue) pushed into Texas and California and replaced the Jesuits of Arizona-Sonora.

No longer did the missionaries of New Mexico control the supply line of the colony. Although they still received an annual allowance from the crown (*sínodo*), the mission payroll was several times less than that of the military. In 1763 thirty-four Franciscan priests received 330 pesos each, and one lay brother, 230, for a total of

11,450 pesos, whereas 32,065 pesos were allotted the Santa Fe presidial garrison. The missions' combined wealth also declined in proportion to that of the expanding Hispanic community. The Pueblo Indian population leveled off at around ten thousand, while the non-mission population grew to twice that number. Now when Franciscans and royal governors quarreled, as they continued to do, the friars could no longer intimidate their adversaries with the threat of a dreadful journey in chains to the Inquisition dungeons in Mexico City. The eighteenth century had tamed the Inquisition.

Nowhere is the contrast between the pious expectations of the seventeenth century and the scabby reality of the eighteenth more vividly drawn than in the writings of Fray Francisco Atanasio Domínguez, inspector of the New Mexico missions in 1776. Charged to report in detail on the spiritual and economic state of the custody, Domínguez, a painfully conscientious, earnest, and witty observer, was so frank that he earned the enmity of missionaries and superiors alike. Along with his incredibly thorough architectural descriptions, inventories, and assessments of people, customs, and things, he laid bare the deterioration of the missions.

It could hardly have been otherwise. The colony was chronically impoverished. Comanche, Apache, Navaho, and Ute threatened from all sides. Frontier technology had not begun to conquer drought or pestilence. As a result, the missionary establishment contracted. The deserted Saline pueblos were never refounded. A single mission served the Zuñi. After the Hopi rose in 1700 and destroyed Awátovi, the friars never did win them back, despite the fear that the Jesuits of Sonora might. All efforts to set out missions for the Navaho and the Apache failed as before. While the famous trek of Father Domínguez and Fray Silvestre Vélez de Escalante through the Great Basin in 1776 was a remarkable feat of exploration, it did not result in missionary expansion (see EXPLORATION, SPANISH). To their credit, the friars in New Mexico hung on. Although their missions and their authority declined in the eighteenth century, they still ministered to the vast majority of the colony, under the most trying circumstances.

From the last years of Spain's dominion in America, through the period of Mexican sovereignty, up to the arrival of Vicar Apostolic Jean Baptiste LAMY in 1850, observers resorted again and again to the same word to describe the state of the New Mexico missions—neglect. In 1812 Pedro Bautista Pino counted twenty-two Franciscans and only two secular priests for twenty-six Indian pueblos and one hundred and two Hispanic settlements. Twenty years later lawyer Antonio Barreiro wrote of "the most pitiful neglect, since only five of the pueblos have missionary fathers." By the early 1840s they had all retired or died. With them died the venerable 225-year-old Franciscan custody of New Mexico.

Ironically, Bishop José Antonio Zubiría of Durango, who made visitations in 1833, 1845, and 1850, tried to revive the defunct custody in 1845 by inviting Fray Mariano de Jesús López to come to New Mexico with the title of custos. Alone, a superior without subjects, López lived at Isleta, ministering as well to Laguna, Acoma, and Zuñi. But he died in 1848, the year in which New Mexico passed by treaty to the United States.

As for the missions themselves, they suffered too. "The churches," wrote Barreiro in 1832, "are in near ruin, and most of them are really unworthy to be called temples of God." The annual government subsidy expired in the economic and political chaos following 1810. Secularization—the transfer of missions from religious order to secular clergy—proceeded fitfully in New Mexico, where a diminishing number of friars and a handful of diocesan priests intermittently served Indian pueblos and Hispano communities alike. With the creation in 1853 of a diocese of New Mexico—the intent of Father Benavides more than two centuries before—Bishop Lamy gradually recruited clergy, repaired or rebuilt the churches, and brought the surviving missions of New Mexico into the diocesan structure. Today, despite the inroads of Protestants and bureaucrats, an overwhelming majority of Pueblo Indians remain Roman Catholics.

Seventeen living Pueblo communities, excluding the El Paso district of Texas and the Hopi pueblos of Arizona, embrace Spanish missions. Some, like Acoma, have survived relatively unaltered. Others, like Nambé and Jémez, have collapsed or been rebuilt in the twentieth century. Of the mission sites associated with ruined pueblos, two are national monuments (Gran Quivira and Pecos) and three are state monuments (Guisewa, Abó, and Quaraí). Built of the earth and stone of the region, wrought in a functional architecture combining Hispanic and Indian elements, preserved and copied by Anglos, the Spanish missions of New Mexico are among the West's richest legacies.

The New Mexico missions are too numerous, and their histories too varied, to be described in detail here. The following outline lists only the most important of the missions, grouped according to Pueblo language or region.

El Paso district. Between 1657 and 1659 Fray García de San Francisco y Zúñiga established Mission Nuestra Señora de Guadalupe on the Rio Grande at the site of present-day Ciudad Juárez, Mexico, to minister to the seminomadic Manso and Suma Indians. In 1682 four missions were founded just downstream to serve Indians uprooted by the Pueblo revolt of 1680: San Lorenzo del Realito; San Antonio at Senecú del Sur; San Antonio (Corpus Christi) at Isleta del Sur; and Nuestra Señora del Socorro at Socorro del Sur.

Hopi. Fray Francisco de Porras set up Mission San Bernardo de Awátowi in 1629. Soon thereafter the Franciscans were in residence at Mission San Bartolomé in Shungopovi and at Mission San Miguel in Oraibi, with *visitas* (secondary stations) in Walpi and Mishongnovi. Virtually nothing remains of the Spanish presence among the Hopi.

Keres, Eastern. The principal eastern Keresan-speaking pueblos, each with its own mission, are Santo Domingo, Cochití (Mission San Buenaventura), San Felipe, Santa Ana, and Sia (Mission Nuestra Señora de la Asunción). Before the Pueblo revolt Mission Santo Domingo, founded between 1600 and 1610, served as headquarters for the Franciscan custody of New Mexico.

Keres, Western. The pueblo of Acoma was visited by Fray Gerónimo de Zárate Salmerón during the mid-1620s, but no missionary came to stay until 1629, when Fray Juan Ramírez founded Mission San Esteban. Laguna, one of New Mexico's few artificially congregated pueblos (*congregaciones*), grew out of the Indian unrest of the 1690s; Mission San José de la Laguna began to minister to the refugee Keres gathered there by Fray Antonio de Miranda in 1699. Laguna now has about twice the population of Acoma.

Piro. In 1626 Benavides inaugurated missionary work among the Piro and, with Fray Martín de Arvide, set up Mission Nuestra Señora del Socorro. San Antonio de Senecú and San Luis Obispo de Sevilleta followed in 1629 and Santa Ana del Alamillo during the next decade. The Piro did not take part in the 1680 revolt; instead, they migrated to the El Paso district. With the exception of Sevilleta, archaeologists still have not found the sites of these pueblos.

Saline pueblos. In 1613 Fray Alonso de Peinado founded Mission La Natividad de Nuestra Señora at Chililí, northernmost of the Saline group. Within ten years a beginning was made at Abó, but Mission San Gregorio did not thrive until the arrival in 1629 of the hard-working Fray Francisco de Acevedo, who not only built the church there but also the smaller churches at the pueblos of Tabirá (Pueblo Blanco) and Tenabó. Between 1629 and 1631 Fray Francisco de Letrado founded short-lived Mission San Isidro at Pueblo de las Humanas (or Gran Quivira, a name first used in the eighteenth century as a bad joke on a treasure-hunter); when Fray Diego de Santander arrived there in 1659, he renamed the mission San Buenaventura. At Quarái, a mission had been set up by 1628, and during the 1630s it served as residence of Fray Esteban de Perea, agent for the Inquisition in New Mexico. The last of the Saline missions, none of which survived the 1670s, was San Miguel at Tajique, founded by the early 1640s.

Tano (Southern Tewa). Mission Santa Cruz at Galisteo, set out by 1612, was the principal Tano mission, with San Cristóbal (before 1620) its visita. San Marcos, mentioned as a visita of Santa Cruz as early as 1616, had San Lázaro and La Ciénega as its visitas. The Pueblo revolt dispersed the Tano, but in 1706, Galisteo was refounded and dedicated to Nuestra Señora de los Remedios. It fell to ruin by 1800.

Tewa. Because Juan de Oñate settled in their midst, the Tewa were the earliest Pueblo converts: San Juan had its church by 1598; San Gabriel, by 1600; and San Ildefonso, by 1601. Thereafter, missions were established at Nambé (Mission San Francisco, 1613), Santa Clara (1625-30), Tesuque (Mission San Diego), and Pojoaque (Nuestra Señora de Guadalupe).

Tiwa, Northern. Fray Pedro de Ortega had great difficulty establishing Mission San Gerónimo at Taos between 1622 and 1625, the Northern Tiwa being the most belligerent of the Pueblo (it was at Taos that Popé planned the Pueblo revolt). At Picurís, Fray Martín de Arvide endured much between 1621 and 1625 in attempting to found a mission; but it was left to his successor, the zealous Fray Ascencio de Zárate, to make Mission San Lorenzo a reality. Only ruins of the Taos mission church remain, but Picurís has a church dating from the 1770s.

Tiwa, Southern. Fray Esteban de Perea founded a mission at Sandía soon after his arrival in 1610. After the upheaval of 1680 many Tiwa took refuge with the Hopi and did not return to Sandía until 1748. The Tiwa at Isleta, where Mission San Antonio had been founded by Fray Juan de Salas in 1612-13, removed to the El Paso district after the revolt; the mission was refounded as

San Agustín in 1710 with Tiwa refugees from various places. Sandía's present church dates from the 1890s, but Isleta's incorporates much of the 1613 original.

Towa. The present-day pueblo of Jémez is all that remains of some ten villages. In one of these pueblos Fray Alonso de Lugo had built a church by 1601, the year he left the colony. Not for twenty years was the Jémez ministry revived; then in 1621-22 Fray Gerónimo de Zárate Salmerón founded San José at Giusewa and another he called La Congregación, near present-day Jémez. The latter burned in 1623 but was restored by Fray Martín de Arvide five years later and renamed Mission San Diego. The Jémez scattered during the Pueblo uprising but were returned by 1706 to form the pueblo now called Jémez.

The pueblo of Pecos was visited by the Franciscans as early as 1542, but not until about 1617 did they found Mission Nuestra Señora de los Angeles de Porciúncula. Under Fray Andrés Juárez the mission thrived. Between 1622 and 1625 Juárez supervised construction at Pecos of the Mexico's largest church. Following the 1680 rebellion, internal dissension, disease, and hostile Plains Indians contributed to the pueblo's decline. The last survivors abandoned Pecos in 1838.

Zuñi. Chief among the six Zuñi pueblos, which the Spaniards first sought as the fabled Seven Cities of CIBOLA, was Hawikuh. Here, in 1629, Fray Roque de Figueredo built the first Zuñi mission, La Purísima Concepción. Apache or Navaho raiders swept through Hawikuh in 1670, killing its missionary and destroying its church. The pueblo never recovered. At Hálona, on the site of present-day Zuñi, one of Figueredo's companions had set up Mission Nuestra Señora de la Candelaria about 1630. The rebellious Zuñi took to the mountains in 1680 and did not return until nineteen years later, at which time Fray Juan de Garaycoechea rededicated the mission at Hálona to Nuestra Señora de Guadalupe. The mission church has since been restored.

See Eleanor B. Adams and Fray Angelico Chavez, eds., *The Missions of New Mexico, 1776: A Description by Fray Francisco Atanasio Domínguez* (1956); Frederick Webb Hodge, George P. Hammond, and Agapito Rey, eds., *Fray Alonso de Benavides' Revised Memorial of 1634* (1945); Henry W. Kelly, *Franciscan Missions of New Mexico, 1740-1760* (1941); George Kubler, *The Religious Architecture of New Mexico* (4th ed., 1972); Ross Gordon Montgomery, Watson Smith, and John Otis Brew, *Franciscan Awátovi* (1949); and France V. Scholes, *Church and State in New Mexico, 1610-1650* (1937), and *Troublous Times in New Mexico, 1659-1670* (1942).—J. L. K.

New Netherland. See DUTCH IN AMERICA.

New Orleans, Louisiana. The largest city in Louisiana, New Orleans is located in the southeastern corner of the state. Its location on a great bend of the Mississippi River earned New Orleans the nickname "Crescent City." The city ranks second only to New York among United States ports in the value of its foreign commerce. Two bridges span the Mississippi here and the world's longest overwater highway links Jefferson parish on the city's outskirts with St. Tammany parish across Lake Pontchartrain to the north. The city's great harbor stretches along fifty-one miles of frontage on both banks of the Mississippi, as well as along the eleven-mile Industrial Canal linking the river with the lake, and the installations on the seventy-three-mile tidewater ship channel to the Gulf opened in 1963. A heavy concentration of industry, especially in petrochemicals, has developed on the Mississippi between Baton Rouge and New Orleans, and at the NASA Michoud Assembly Plant in the lower limits of the city were produced the rocket boosters that propelled the Apollo flights to the moon.

None of this would be the least surprising to the city's founder, Jean Baptiste Le Moyne, Sieur de BIENVILLE. From the moment in 1699 when he first gazed on the Indian portage linking the mighty river to the lake that gave onto the Mississippi Sound and the open sea, he recognized its position as one of the potentially great trading centers of the world. Finally governor of all of Louisiana in 1717, the next year he planted his city and commissioned his engineer, Adrian de Pauger, to lay out its boundaries. The new proprietor of the colony, John Law, had already christened it to honor his patron the Duc d'Orleans, regent of the little Louis XV. Beginning in 1721, Pauger fashioned the new settlement on the great crescent bend along a gridiron pattern, six squares deep, eleven long, with a spacious center paradeground fronting on the river and called the Place d'Armes (now Jackson Square). Thus was born the Vieux Carré or "French Quarter," which remained the legal extent of the town until the nineteenth century and which today still keeps alive the aura of its past. Made the capital of Louisiana in 1727, for most of the eighteenth century New Orleans slumbered as a quiet colonial village. Secretly transferred to Spain along with the rest of the Isle of Orleans and Louisiana west of the Mississippi by the Treaty of Fontainebleau in 1762 prior to the signing of the Treaty of PARIS of 1763, it housed such Iberian governors as Esteban Miró, who began the "Western Conspiracy" against the United States as protest against resented sections of the Peace of Paris of 1783. By this plot Miró hoped to induce Tennessee and Kentucky to withdraw from the United States and join Spanish Louisiana, their reward to be access to the navigation of the Mississippi River. When he closed the Mississippi to United States trade in 1784, trans-Allegheny backwoodsmen began to recognize the supreme importance of New Orleans to their economic survival. The Treaty of San Lorenzo (1795) ended the "conspiracy," opened the river trade, and allowed the United States the right of deposit at New Orleans. Immediately the city began to stir.

For a short twenty days, November 30-December 20, 1803, New Orleans was once again part of the French colonial empire as a result of Napoleon's Treaty of San Ildefonso (1800) with Spain. With the LOUISIANA PURCHASE all barriers were down, and New Orleans began to receive the rising flood of produce of the Mississippi valley and the Anglo-American and foreign settlers come to profit by it. *Faubourgs* ("suburbs") expanded from the Vieux Carré. The "Americans" clustered in one of them upriver from the old quarter, with a Lafayette Square to balance the Place d'Armes, a James Gallier City Hall to challenge the original section's Cabildo, and a St. Patrick's Church to minister to the hordes of Irish immigrants as the St. Louis Cathedral on the Place d'Armes served the old community. Farther up the river beyond Tivoli Circle (new Lee Circle), the Americans had developed by the 1850s a neoclassic section called the "Garden District," still one of the distinctive residential areas of the nation. The Louisiana Purchase also brought conflict between the *ancienne population* and the newly arrived "Americans." (The term *ancienne population* identifies white Louisianians who traced their ancestry back to the colonial period and is the correct designation for the class frequently but mistakenly described as "creoles." Historically, "creole" in Louisiana meant simply native-born and was applied to black and white, slave and free.) There were bitter quarrels as to political domination, language, and social customs, but the two groups did not isolate themselves from each other as is so frequently claimed. Rather, they joined in business and marriage and contined to quarrel. Together they fought against the British at the BATTLE OF NEW ORLEANS in 1814-15, and together they exploited the great steamboat trade, which had begun on the river in 1812 and by 1830 had made New Orleans the busiest export center of the nation. The steamboat era was at its peak in the 1850s, but soon withered as railroads diverted the Mississippi valley commerce to an east-west axis. The Civil War brought capture by Admiral Farragut in 1862 and occupation by the hated General Benjamin F. Butler. Even the end of Reconstruction in 1877 failed to restore the city's verve, for by then its vital artery, the river, was silting over at its mouth and threatening to cease its commercial existence. But this problem was overcome by James B. Eads and his jetties in 1879, and the river continued to sustain the city into the period of its present prosperity.

Much of the *ancienne population*'s joy in the sensate life continues to shape the spirit of New Orleans, which clings to its love of music, THEATER, the arts, and good food and drink. "Creole" cuisine, an artful blend of French genius with the indigenous produce of the region, particularly herbs, spices, and seafoods, has given New Orleans some of the truly distinguished restaurants of America. Here in the early nineteenth century were produced many of the first American performances of famous operas (see OPERA). And here too was born the American musical expression of jazz, eventually carried to all parts of the world by such New Orleans ambassadors as Louis Armstrong.

Always notorious as a den of wickedness, fed by the roistering life of its waterfront, New Orleans has preserved a relaxed acceptance of mores and behavior often identified elsewhere as immoral if not illegal. The unique color and character of the city have stimulated a whole literature by native sons and daughters, including novelists George Washington Cable and Robert Tallant, historians Charles Gayarre and Grace King, and playwright Lillian Hellman. The seductive charm of its easy, gracious, and, above all, tolerant, way of life has also attracted many other creative spirits, such as the playwright Tennessee Williams and novelists Lafcadio Hearn, William Faulkner, Sherwood Anderson, and Roark Bradford.

See Federal Writers Project, *Guide to New Orleans* (1952); Joy Jackson, *New Orleans in the Gilded Age* (1967); Harnett Kane, *Queen New Orleans* (1949); John S. Kendall, *History of New Orleans*, 3 vols. (1922); Henry A. Kmen, *Music in New Orleans* (1966); and Robert Tallant, *The Romantic New Orleanians* (1950).—J. G. T.

New Orleans, battle of (1814-1815). During the War of 1812, there were five engagements in the battle for New Orleans. The first occurred on December 14, 1814, when the British made a surprise appearance on Lake

Borgne and captured the tiny American fleet under the command of Lieutenant Thomas ap Catesby Jones. The second fight was at Villeré's Plantation well above the English Turn on the Mississippi River, on December 23-24. The American schooner *Carolina* was blown up on December 27, and the British struck again on New Year's Day at Andrew Jackson's thin left flank near Lake Borgne, disabling the U.S. corvette *Louisiana*. The major British push came up the level Plains of Chalmette on January 8, 1815.

Late in November 1814, Andrew Jackson had moved from Pensacola, Florida, to New Orleans after having prepared Fort Bowyer for defense at the head of Mobile Bay. His arrival in New Orleans preceded the British appearance in the lower Mississippi and along the Gulf Coast at the mouth of Lake Borgne. In command of this large force were Admiral Sir Alexander Cochrane, General Sir Edward Pakenham, Major General John Keane, and Sir Thomas Picton. There were in the British armada 10,000 seamen, 1,500 marines, and 9,600 infantry troops. Most of them came fresh from attacks on Bladensburg, Maryland, and Washington, D. C.

Upon his arrival in New Orleans in December, Jackson was confronted with the stupendous problems of making a careful survey of the territory below the city, organizing his forces, establishing a skeleton naval force, and placating the natives. By January 6 he not only had made a thorough exploration of the area, but had firmly entrenched his forces along the Rodriguez Canal. With the aid of the pirates Dominque You and Jean Laffite he kept himself informed as to British movements and was able, within limits, to choose the ground on which he would fight. (Until now, the British had had this advantage.) The success of the Americans in stemming the British assault on January 1 proved to be a major factor in the protection of New Orleans. By the time the enemy had fairly well revealed his strategy, Jackson had gained vital time in which to strengthen his main line of fortification and to establish a secondary line of defense west of the river. By the morning of January 8, Jackson's line was solidly entrenched, his major guns were strategically placed, and there were on the defense in the main line thirty-five hundred men, while another thousand reserves waited in the rear. When the British did strike, the choice of battle timing was largely with the Americans.

West of the Mississippi, eight hundred militiamen under the command of General David Morgan formed only a slender line of defense. Four hundred of General John Adair's Kentuckians on this line were without adequate arms and had little choice in the face of heavy fire but to fall back or die.

At about 6:00 A. M. on January 8 the British command concentrated its main thrust against Jackson's left flank. The dawn was a misty one and was further befogged by heavy cannonading. This created a protective shield for Jackson's line, which was favored by moments of lifting fog and smoke. Just as the British units, marching in full ranks, came within rifle range they were exposed to savage fire, and Lord Pakenham, Major General Keane, and Major General Sir William Gibbs were cut down. By 8:00 A. M. the battle on the east bank before the Rodriguez parapets was largely ended, with a quick and cheap victory for the Americans. Across the river on the west bank, the British, under the command of Colonel William Thornton, were successful in driving the Americans back, thus causing General Jackson to rush relief troops across the river above New Orleans to strengthen the line of General Morgan. By this time, however, the British were through fighting. Out of 3,400 troops sent into battle, 291 were killed, 1,262 were wounded, and 484 were missing. Pakenham and Gibbs were killed, and Keane was seriously wounded. American losses were remarkably light, with 13 killed, 39 wounded, and 19 missing. The American victory, if not complete, was most impressive. It decided nothing in fact so far as the diplomatic outcome of the War of 1812 was concerned. Nevertheless, it did set off lingering speculation as to what the British might have done along the lower Mississippi had they been victorious. To American frontiersmen the victory at New Orleans was enormously satisfying, both from military and political viewpoints, and it made Andrew Jackson president.

See Francis F. Bierne, *The War of 1812* (1949); Reginald Horsman, *The War of 1812* (1969); Marquis James, *Andrew Jackson, the Border Captain* (1933); and Glenn Tucker, *Poltroons and Patriots*, 2 vols. (1954). —T. D. C.

New York, settlement of. In March 1664 Charles II granted his brother, the duke of York, a charter making him absolute proprietor over the New Netherlands, a territory that was then still in the hands of the Dutch. England's seizure of this colony was motivated in part by the fact that Holland was her most formidable commercial rival. Moreover, the location of the New Netherlands had blocked the expansion of New England, while Dutch merchants had monopolized the most lucrative fur trade. No doubt the duke also hoped that profits from the New World would restore his own fortune, depleted by the English Civil War. His charter gave him full authority to make laws, fill offices, and establish courts. Richard Nicolls (1624-72), one of the duke's friends and an extremely able administrator, was in charge of the military operations, and in the summer of 1664, supported by troops from Connecticut, he ordered Governor Peter Stuyvesant to surrender. The Dutch colonists offered no resistance. The Articles of Capitulation guaranteed that all Dutch citizens would become free inhabitants and enjoy full liberty of conscience under the new government. Nicolls believed that the region between the Hudson and the Delaware rivers was potentially the duke's most valuable possession, and he was therefore extremely disappointed when he learned that his patron had split the area into two by deeding New Jersey to Sir George Carteret and Lord John Berkeley. A later governor understandably complained that New York was "cooped up" between New England and New Jersey. The Dutch recaptured the colony in 1673, but their brief rule, lasting only fifteen months, had little effect on New York's development.

Deep ethnic, religious, and economic differences divided the society of seventeenth-century New York. The Dutch influence, for example, remained strong after 1664. The Dutch Reformed Church was long the colony's most powerful denomination, and for more than a century after the conquest many New Yorkers continued to speak the Dutch language. The majority of Long Island settlers were Puritans, most of whom had emigrated from New England. These people found the duke of York's government intolerably autocratic, for they had come from colonies that encouraged greater popular participation in civil affairs. The historian Wesley Frank Craven has explained, "Not only were New York's inhabitants few in number; they were also sharply divided and remarkably lacking in social cohesion. Partly Dutch, partly English, and partly a wide variety of other peoples, they gave their first loyalty to the lesser communities to which they belonged." The duke's economic policies exacerbated the tensions already present within the colony. Albany was given a monopoly over the fur trade, while the city of New York controlled all overseas commerce. As time passed, the Dutch and Puritan farmers in outlying districts became increasingly resentful of these special privileges.

The charter of 1664 did not mention a legislative assembly, and in the early years a governor and council appointed by the proprietor ruled New York. Richard Nicolls, the colony's first governor, recognized that this arbitrary system of government would anger the Long Island Puritans as well as discourage fresh emigration from New England. In 1665 he therefore drafted the Duke's Laws, a code based upon the laws of Massachusetts, Connecticut, and England. This code provided for the election of certain local officials, the continuation of religious liberty, and the establishment of trial by jury. The Long Islanders were not satisfied with this partial measure, however. They demanded a voice in taxation, and some of them even declared that they were "inslav'd under an Arbitrary Power." But the duke resisted, noting that nothing was "more knowne than the aptness of such bodyes to assume to themselves many priviledges which prove destructive to, or very oft disturbe, the peace of government." When tax revenues declined, however, the proprietor reversed himself and instructed Governor Dongan (1683-88) to call for the election of delegates. In 1683 the first assembly passed the Charter of Liberties and Privileges, which spelled out the rights that New Yorkers claimed as Englishmen. Unfortunately, the duke of York repudiated this document soon after he became James II. Not until William and Mary took the English throne did the New York assembly develop into a powerful and regular part of the colony's government.

New York's land system was quite different from that of the other American colonies. Before the conquest, the Dutch had attempted to establish huge feudal estates along the Hudson River valley called patroonships, but with the exception of the Van Rensselaer manor, all these projects failed. Most of the great estates associated with the New York "aristocracy" were laid out after 1664. The colony's entire land policy invited fraud. Prospective landlords were required to obtain preliminary authorization to buy land from the governor. The purchaser then cleared his title with the Indians and paid to have the claim surveyed. After these formalities had been completed, the governor and council awarded a permanent patent for the land. Most of the grants went to influential favorites. Robert Livingston, for example, was able to acquire 160,000 acres from the proprietary government. Although these practices caused some complaint, Governor Fletcher (1692-99) and Governor Cornbury (1702-08) continued to grant their friends large Hudson River manors. Almost nothing was demanded in return, for as one historian has discovered, "the quitrent in proprietary New York . . . was

more a formality, honoring tradition, than a burden actually imposed upon the settlers." The leading families of New York seldom sold their land to small farmers. It was far more common for them to rent acreage to tenants, and throughout the history of colonial New York, there were arguments—often violence —over leases and rents. The population of New York lagged behind what it should have been, chiefly because Americans preferred to own their own land. New settlers knew that they could buy farms on easy terms in Massachusetts, Vermont, and Pennsylvania, and they therefore avoided the Hudson River valley almost to the time of the American Revolution.

Throughout the seventeenth century the Dutch and the English relied upon the IROQUOIS CONFEDERACY to bring beaver pelts to Albany. (see FUR TRADE: *in the colonies*). It was not until 1684, however, that the New Yorkers made a formal alliance with the Iroquoian Five Nations. The duke's governor, Thomas Dongan, explained to the Indians that the treaty placed them under the protection "of the great sachem Charles that lives over the Great Lakes." Dongan and other officials were worried by the aggressive French efforts to divert the fur trade from Albany to Montreal. This commercial rivalry created constant tension along the entire New York frontier, and in 1690 a combined French and Indian force leveled the town of Schenectady. The Iroquois, who formed a buffer between New York and Canada, suffered heavy losses during these years, and in 1701 they announced their neutrality in the conflict between the two European powers. The English had one insurmountable advantage over the French in the Indian trade; they could produce and merchandise better goods at lower prices. By the turn of the century, certain Albany merchants had built up a flourishing, but technically illegal, business with Montreal. The New Yorkers provided manufactured items that the French in turn sold directly to the Indians. In 1730 one New York official claimed "that Canada could not have subsisted had it not been supplied from Albany." By the 1740s, however, relations with the Iroquois were strained by the push of land speculators into the traditional Indian territory of the Mohawk valley.

See Charles M. Andrews, *The Colonial Period of American History*, 4 vols. (1934-38); Wesley Frank Craven, *The Colonies in Transition, 1660-1713* (1968); Oscar Handlin, "The Eastern Frontier of New York," *New York History* (1937); Lawrence Leder, *Robert Livingston, 1654-1713, and the Politics of Colonial New York* (1961); Herbert Osgood, *The American Colonies in the Seventeenth Century*, 3 vols. (1907); and Allen W. Trelease, *Indian Affairs in Colonial New York: The Seventeenth Century* (1960).—T. H. B.

New York, Treaty of (1790). Early in the summer of 1790 the Creek Indian chief Alexander McGILLIVRAY and a party of Creek representatives were persuaded by Colonel Marinus Willett to visit President George Washington and Secretary Henry Knox in New York to review the major problems of Georgia-Creek relations in the Old Southwest. Because the Creek had a respect for the newly formed national government, and hoped to capitalize on American-Spanish diplomatic tensions in the Creek country, they were willing to make this journey, and along the way presented an interesting pageantry of Indian color and manners.

Negotiations were rather long-drawn-out because of the illness of McGillivray, and it was not until August 7, 1790, that the Treaty of New York was finally signed. This agreement defined in more or less precise terms the boundaries separating the Creek nation's lands from those claimed by the Georgians. It was based to some extent on earlier agreements on this subject. The line began at an old point in the Creek boundary on the Savannah River and followed it to a point on its headwaters at Keowee, South Carolina, thence along a northeast line to the top of Occenna Mountain, then southwest to Tugaloo River, thence along a line to the top of Currahee Mountain, thence to the main source of the Oconee River, down the middle of that stream to the confluence with the Ocmulgee, to the Altamaha, down the middle of that stream to the old Creek line, and southward to a junction with the St. Marys River. This territory included more than half of the modern state of Georgia.

The Treaty of New York succeeded in affecting cordial relations between the new federal government and the Creek, but it increased diplomatic and frontier tensions. Georgians were resentful because the established Indian boundary was not as far west as hoped, and settlers casually disregarded it. The Spanish were worried that the Creek were becoming allied with the United States and worked against this possibility by supplying guns and agitating the Indians against American settlers. These intrigues were in part responsible for the Cumberland War the Creek carried on in 1792 and for renewed hostilities on the Georgia frontier.

See John W. Caughey, *McGillivray of the Creeks* (1938); and Charles C. Royce, "Indian Land Cessions in the United States," in Bureau of American Ethnology, *Eighteenth Annual Report, 1896-97* (1899). —T. D. C.

Nez Percé Indians. The Nez Percé belong to the Shahaptian branch of the old Penutian language group that came down the west coast of North America and up the Columbia River more than thirteen thousand years ago, as has been shown by the excavations of old campsites. Originally they were a small fishing tribe along the Snake River and its tributaries, located in the southeast corner of Washington, the northeast corner of Oregon, and in northern Idaho. They comprised about three thousand people scattered in fifty or so small villages on the riverbanks. The Nez Percé depended on the annual run of salmon for about eighty percent of their food needs and secured the rest from game animals, upland birds, waterfowl, berries, and various plants, particularly the bulbs of the camas and the the roots of the kouse. A village was usually comprised of three to five extended families, each consisting of parents, their sons, and the sons' families. Their lodges, fishing grounds, and camas grounds were community property. Well protected by mountain barriers on all sides, they lived a peaceful, sedentary life.

About 1720 the Nez Percé secured their first horses in trade from the Shoshoni in the Boise valley to the south. Their country was well suited for raising horses on the open range and soon the tribe had more horses than could be used, so they began trading off several hundred each year to their neighbors. This culling of the herds, coupled with the gelding of some of their stallions, kept the quality of the Nez Percé horses at a high level, and they are credited with developing the famous Appaloosa breed.

After they became horsemen, the Nez Percé extended their travels to include visits to other tribes and to the big trading center near Spokane Falls (now Spokane, Washington), where they met Flathead from Montana with buffalo robes. The two tribes soon became friends and the Nez Percé opened up Lolo Trail along the mountain ridges to connect with the Flathead trail across Lolo Pass to the upper Lochsa fork of the Clearwater River. Small parties of Nez Percé then traveled the new trail every year to the Montana buffalo country, where they hunted with the Flathead. There they were attacked by the Blackfoot moving south from Alberta, and bitter fighting raged between the two groups until 1855.

The first white men to reach Nez Percé country were those in the Meriwether Lewis and William Clark expedition party. They came across the Lolo Trail in September 1805 and left their horses in care of the tribe while they continued to the coast in dugout canoes. The following spring they returned and spent six weeks with the Nez Percé, establishing a strong friendship that endured for seventy years.

Fur traders who first came to the Nez Percé country in 1812 learned that the Indians would neither trap for them nor allow trappers on tribal lands. They had enough horses to trade for all their needs and were adverse to trapping, but they remained friendly to the trappers and from them learned a smattering of white culture. As a result, the Nez Percé sent to St. Louis for teachers, probably expecting that the new learning would furnish them with strong "medicine." The delegation reached St. Louis in October 1831, and a highly colored account of their quest, published in several church papers along the Atlantic Coast in 1833, sparked a strong missionary movement that brought Henry and Eliza Spalding to Lapwai on the Clearwater River in 1836, where they founded a mission that lasted eleven years.

The Indians who flocked to the mission school created social problems, which led the whites to induce the Nez Percé to elect twelve chiefs who were to have some authority over all the Indians. The mission was closed following the massacre of Marcus Whitman and his missionary group by the Cayuse in 1847, but the pattern of elected tribal chiefs was retained.

When the wagon trains of settlers bound for Oregon began to travel the Oregon Trail in 1843, the friendly Nez Percé met them on the east slope of the Blue Mountains in northeastern Oregon, bringing fresh horses to trade for footsore cattle and horses, and fresh meat from the hills, fresh salmon from the rivers, and flour from the mission gristmill to exchange for cloth and hardware. The Nez Percé were also helpful in treaty-making, as when Governor Isaac Stevens met with the Columbia Basin tribes in a great treaty council in the Walla Walla valley in 1855. This council established the Nez Percé reservation in present-day Idaho. The following year, during the Yakima War, the Nez Percé supplied Governor Stevens with a company of cavalry, a company of mounted scouts, and a large number of horses. Although these horses were legally purchased, the federal government later refused to pay for them. In 1858 the Nez Percé again furnished mounted scouts for a campaign, this time for Colonel George Wright, who fought the Coeur d'Alene and Spokane.

When gold prospectors overran many of the Indian lands, the Nez Percé placed guards on the trails to their reservation to bar the miners, but a few got through and found gold on Orofino creek in 1860. Although the resulting series of gold rushes endangered the Indian lands, at first the Nez Percé were not greatly alarmed; they even furnished horses, pack trains, and supplies to the camps. Then federal officials intervened, but instead of protecting the Indians' rights, they purchased land, thereby drastically reducing the size of the reservation to exclude the gold fields, against strong objections from several Nez Percé bands. The resulting treaty of June 1863 split the Nez Percé into two groups. The larger group, sedentary Indians living on the reduced reservation, favored the new treaty and the increased payments. The smaller group, about a fourth of the tribe and mostly stockmen and buffalo hunters, were losing their grazing lands and opposed the treaty.

Following the death of Colonel George A. Custer at the hands of the Sioux in 1876, army officials and Indian agents brought heavy pressure on all the nontreaty Nez Percé bands to force them onto the reservation. Such a move would have forced the bands to give up buffalo hunting and reduced the size of their herds of stock. CHIEF JOSEPH tried to resist white encroachment with diplomacy, but to no avail. This pressure finally brought on the NEZ PERCE WAR of 1877, in which a small band of fighting men, never more than 145 in number, and burdened with about 500 noncombatants, fought off the soldiers in several battles. Caught by surprise in camp on three separate occasions, at Whitebird, Clearwater, and BIG HOLE, and attacked by superior numbers of soldiers, they nevertheless beat off each attack and escaped. Finally, after a chase of about twelve hundred miles across the wilds of Idaho, Montana, and Wyoming, they succumbed to a large force of cavalry under Colonel Nelson A. Miles near the Bear Paw Mountains in northern Montana.

In their long, hopeless struggle against great odds, the Nez Percé had the sympathy of many Americans. They took no scalps, killed no prisoners, and harmed very few noncombatants. Many influential people deplored their plight and brought pressure on the government to secure better treatment for the captives, who were finally returned to the northwest, about half of them to the Nez Percé reservation in Idaho, the rest to Nespelem in northern Washington.

In 1895 the federal government terminated the Nez Percé reservation, giving each Nez Percé a farm plot and taking the rest of the land for white settlers. The money paid for these lands was divided among the tribal members. In addition, when the Bonneville Dam was built on the Columbia River, the tribe received more than $3 million to relinquish their fishing rights at Celilo Falls, which was inundated by the new dam. In 1959, after a series of lawsuits, the tribe was paid $7,450,000 for the land ceded in 1863 and for the gold taken by miners from tribal lands.

The Nez Percé tribe still has about three thousand members, almost all of them with a mixture of white blood. Many members of the tribe have learned skilled trades and professions; some are college graduates and several have advanced degrees. These people have moved away and blended into American communities where they are well received, thus depriving the tribe of what white men describe as their best leaders. As a result, the Bureau of Indian Affairs still supervises and guides tribal affairs.

See Mark Brown, *The Flight of the Nez Percé* (1967); Francis Haines, *The Nez Percé* (1955); and Lucullus Virgil McWhorter, *Yellow Wolf* (1940).—F. H.

Nez Percé War (1877). The threat that the Nez Percé would lose their hunting land and be forced onto a reservation was the issue that brought trouble with these peaceful Indians, who boasted that they had never killed a white man. But in the tense days of June 1877 young warriors killed some whites. Troops under Captain David Perry were then soundly defeated at White Bird Canyon on June 17, and thirty-four men were killed. On July 11, General Oliver Otis Howard surprised the Indians, who were now trying to escape to Canada, on the Clearwater but failed to defeat them despite superior forces. The Nez Percé headed east, crossing the mountains by Lolo Pass, and bypassed "Fort Fizzle," manned by volunteers from Montana. On August 9, Colonel John Gibbon surprised the Indians in the battle of BIG HOLE and killed an estimated eighty-nine but failed to capture the remainder. The flight continued through Yellowstone Park, where General William Tecumseh Sherman was vacationing. The Indians then swung north, crossing the Missouri and approaching Canada. On October 5, 1877, after a flight of more than a thousand miles, the small band of Nez Percé surrendered to Colonel Nelson A. Miles in northern Montana.—R. N. E.

Nicolet, Jean (1598-1642). First known European in Wisconsin. Born in Cherbourg, France, Nicolet came to Quebec in New France in 1618. He spent several years living with Indian tribes, learning their languages and ways of life as part of Samuel de Champlain's policy of expanding the French fur trade and empire. Champlain sent him west in 1634 to quiet Indian unrest and to gain information of a water route through North America to the Orient. He was to seek particularly the Winnebago, whom the French called "People of the Sea." Nicolet and his seven native companions traveled via Georgian Bay, the north shore of Lake Huron, through the Straits of Mackinac to Lake Michigan, and then to Green Bay. His exact landing place is unknown, but markers are located at both Menasha on Lake Winnebago and at Red Banks, northeast of the city of Green Bay. Expecting eventually to meet the emperor of China, Nicolet wore "a grand robe of China damask, all strewn with flowers and birds of many colors. . . ." The Winnebago welcomed him, called him "the wonderful man," and at one feast "served at least sixscore beavers."

After returning to Canada, Nicolet married and settled down as a fur trader and Indian agent at Three Rivers, Quebec. He was drowned in an accident on the St. Lawrence River.

See L. P. Kellogg, *The French Regime in Wisconsin and the Northwest* (1925), and *Narratives of the Northwest, 1634-1699* (1917).—W. D. W.

Nicollet, Joseph N[icolas] (also known as **Jean N. Nicollet**) (1786-1843). Scientific explorer of the upper Mississippi and Missouri rivers. Nicollet was a native of Savoy. His intellect attracted the notice of a priest, who made it possible for the boy to obtain an education.

Nicollet then went to France, became a French citizen, and established himself as an astronomer and mathematician. When he emigrated to the United States in 1832 he had already established his reputation as a leading scientist. Proud of the heritage of French exploration, he determined to renew the memory of these accomplishments by conducting geographical explorations on his own. Having been welcomed by the French people and the Catholic clergy of New Orleans, St. Louis, and Baltimore, he had already made a successful exploration of the headwater country of the Mississippi when he accepted employment by the Topographical Engineers. Accompanied by young Lieutenant John Charles FREMONT, Nicollet made an extended exploration into the vast prairies between the Mississippi and the Missouri rivers south of the Canadian boundary. On this expedition of 1839-40, and in his subsequent scientific work in Washington and Baltimore, he trained and befriended Frémont.

See John Charles Frémont, *Memoirs of My Life*, vol. I (1886); and Allan Nevins, *Frémont: The West's Greatest Adventurer*, vol. I (1928).—R. A. B.

noble-savage concept. Primitivism—the belief that other, simpler societies are more fulfilling, more virtuous, and happier than one's own—was popular among European intellectuals during the eighteenth and early nineteenth centuries. The American Indian was usually portrayed as the epitome of all that the primitive man should be: brave, honorable, innately fair and dignified, graceful in movement and manners, and perfect in bodily form—a "noble savage." Such a state of existence was held to be a desirable alternative to the discontents and debilitations of contemporary European society.

White Americans of that era, however, were unwilling or unable to share that benevolent and frankly admiring view of the Indian and his way of life. The seventeenth-century English colonists believed it was their duty to extend Christianity and civilization to the Indians, but it soon became apparent that the Indians were not very impressed with "civilization" and tended to resist the white advance at every opportunity. As contact between Indians and whites became increasingly a struggle for survival and conquest, Americans came to perceive the Indians not as noble savages but as vicious, cunning beasts, barbarians at best, at worst inhuman and demonic creatures worthy only of destruction. Yet at the same time Americans were conscious that Indians did possess some virtues, such as an undeniable nobility in their fight to preserve their homeland and way of life. These contradictory attitudes in the American mind were reconciled during the eighteenth century by the development of a belief that Indians represented an earlier stage in human evolution, a stage that had survived beyond its time in America and that was inevitably destined to disappear before the advance of white Anglo-American civilization. This earlier state of being, called savagery, had both noble and ignoble qualities, but the nobility of the savage was the nobility of the hunter and nomad and would have to give way before the superior nobility of the farmer and city-dweller.

This rationale enabled Americans to justify their extermination of the Indian while recognizing his noble qualities. Combined with an increasing certainty of the moral superiority of American society and its historic destiny, it was the foundation of the United States's policies and attitudes toward the Indian throughout the nineteenth century and well into the twentieth. The American idea of the noble savage was thus quite different from the European. Although the same qualities of Indian life were seen as virtues by both points of view, in the European concept these qualities made the Indian better off than civilized man, while the American saw these qualities as the virtues of childhood, which must necessarily give way to maturity. Accordingly, although Americans admired the bravery with which the Indians resisted white advance, the peak of savage nobility was personified by the Indian who willingly, albeit unhappily, made way for the triumph of civilization, a viewpoint clearly demonstrated by the fates of nineteenth-century literary Indian heroes in poetry like Longfellow's *The Song of Hiawatha* and novels like Cooper's *Leatherstocking Tales*.

As the zone of Indian-white conflict moved westward, a regional division developed in the American concept of the Indian. The Indians' noble qualities were increasingly appreciated in those eastern parts of the nation where Indians were no longer a danger, and the East became critical of the harsher attitudes and actions of the West. This division widened during the nineteenth century and was reflected in bitter arguments over reform of government Indian policy, wherein westerners accused easterners of sentimental dreaming and easterners accused westerners of inhumanity and cruelty.

After the end of the Indian wars and the reduction of the remnants of separate Indian culture to semi-invisibility, the American concept of the noble savage continued to evolve. In recent years it has become much more like the eighteenth-century European view. The new attitude is reflected in historians' reevaluations of the westward movement, which no longer view the destruction of Indian culture as having been morally imperative; in current literature and entertainment media, which portray Indians as heroes in their own right; and in the back-to-nature movements, which are often exact reflections of eighteenth-century primitivism. As discontents with urban-industrial life have increased, the Indian and his way of life have become increasingly positive images. Such a reconceptualization of the Indian and his past is probably more desirable than what went before, but the new noble savage is as much a myth as the old and is a better reflection of the shape of white society than Indian.

The definitive statement on the image of the Indian in the eighteenth and early nineteenth century is Roy Harvey Pearce, *Savagism and Civilization: A Study of the Indian and the American Mind* (rev. ed., 1965). An excellent work dealing with specific aspects of the savage image is Lewis Saum, *The Fur Trader and the Indian* (1965). The image of the Indian in the late nineteenth and twentieth century has not yet been the subject of a detailed study.—P. R. M.

Noland, Charles Fenton Mercer (1810-1858). Humorist and sportsman. Noland was an Arkansan who contributed the famous stories of the southwestern frontier, signed "N. of Arkansas" and "Pete Whetstone of Devil's Fork," to William Trotter Porter's *Spirit of the Times*, a sporting magazine. By the 1850s he was known nationally as Pete Whetstone. A Virginian who flunked out of West Point, "Fent" Noland migrated to Arkansas in 1826, studied law, acquired large landholdings, built a stable of blooded racehorses and made the track circuits, served briefly in the army (1833-36), and became a prominent Whig politician. He began writing for the *Spirit of the Times* in 1836 and continued until his death. His stories describe, in humorous but realistic vein, life on the southwestern frontier—hunting, racing, dancing, and politicking. A sportsman with a zest for the life he depicted, Nolan's writings have a vibrancy caught by few of the frontier authors of the age. His home until 1855, when he moved to Little Rock, was at Batesville on White River. See Ted Worley and Eugene A. Nolte, *Pete Whetstone of Devil's Fork* (1957).—W. L. B.

Nonpartisan League. See AGRARIAN MOVEMENTS; and Arthur C. TOWNLEY.

Nootka Indians. See INDIANS OF THE NORTHWEST COAST.

Nootka Sound controversy. The controversy between Great Britain and Spain in 1789-90 over the right of British traders to establish a post at Nootka Sound on the west side of Vancouver Island. The controversy traced back to the division of territories in the New World between Spain and Portugal sanctified by the bull of Pope Alexander VI in 1493. Ever afterward the Spanish considered that they had an original right to all the territory in the Americas, with the exception of Brazil, although they grudgingly recognized other nations' holdings. When British traders appeared at Nootka in 1789 a Spanish ship broke up the settlement, taking some Britishers to Mexico in irons. William Pitt the Younger, then prime minister of the London government, sent an ultimatum, which the Spanish accepted. Meanwhile President Washington had asked Gouverneur Morris, then in Europe, to go to England as the first presidential executive agent in what was to be a long line of such representatives. Morris was to determine if the British would make a commercial treaty with the United States, and by luck discovered Pitt in the midst of the Nootka Sound crisis. If one may believe Morris, the American envoy used the occasion to talk roughly to the young prime minister about American rights. At home the Washington administration debated the possibility that the British might try to conquer Spanish Louisiana by crossing American territory—the first cabinet debate over an issue of foreign policy by the new government under the Constitution of 1787. Then the whole affair blew over. The long-range effect of the Nootka crisis was that the Spanish thereafter began to lose interest in the Pacific Northwest and by the time of the Adams-Onís treaty in 1819 had virtually left the area to the British and the Americans.

See W. R. Manning, "The Nootka Sound Controversy," *Annual Report of the American Historical Association: 1904* (1905).—R. H. F.

Norbeck, Peter (1870-1936). South Dakota politician. By aligning with progressive Republicans, Norbeck, a successful businessman of Redfield, South Dakota, became lieutenant governor in 1914 and won the governorship in 1916 by almost twenty thousand votes. Progressivism reached high tide during his governorship: loans were extended to farmers, a state hail insurance program was begun, and wildlife conservation was promoted. He called for a state-owned coal mine and grain terminals, waterpower sites on the Missouri, and workmen's compensation but opposed the Nonpartisan League because he believed it to be too radical. He was elected as a Republican to the United States Senate in 1920. Attempts to unseat him in 1926 because his rural credit program was in trouble failed, and in 1932 Norbeck became the first South Dakota senator to be elected three times. The lifelong progressive died in office. —D. J. T.

Norris, [Benjamin] Frank[lin] (1870-1902). Novelist. Norris was born in Chicago, but in 1885 moved to San Francisco, the setting of most of his later fiction. He attended boarding school there until his father decided that his artistic inclinations warranted study in Paris. After two years abroad he returned to California with a taste for Emile Zola, probably the most important single influence on his later writing, and a determination to become a novelist. He spent a year at Harvard as a special student of writing.

As a war correspondent for the San Francisco *Chronicle*, Norris was sent to South Africa to cover the Boer War. He reached Johannesburg just in time to be captured by the Boers, who deported him as soon as he recovered from African fever. Upon his return to California he joined the staff of the literary periodical *Wave*, to which he contributed between 1896 and 1898 a number of essays and stories, posthumously collected in *Frank Norris of "The Wave"* (1931). A recurrence of African fever drove him to New York, where he worked as a reader for a publishing house. At the age of thirty he married and returned to California, where he bought a ranch.

Despite his early death, Norris was one of the most prolific of American "naturalist" writers. Although most of his writing is set in and around San Francisco, it cannot really be called western writing. Even *McTeague* (1899), by critical consensus one of his two best works, which is placed primarily in San Francisco and ends with a famous chase through Death Valley, uses a western setting as background for basically nonwestern concerns. Norris' western writing, as such, is primarily confined to *The Octopus* (1901), the first, and best, of his never-completed epic trilogy of "the wheat." Of this trilogy *The Octopus* tells the story of the growing of wheat in the San Joaquin valley of California, *The Pit* (1903) describes the machinations of the grain speculators in Chicago, and *The Wolf*—which exists only as scattered notes, since Norris died before he could write it—would have told of the distribution of the wheat to the starving masses of Asia.

The Octopus is one of the last and most successful attempts to write, at least in a traditional form, the "great American novel." It is based, at one remove, on the so-called Mussel Slough affair, in which blood had been shed when the Southern Pacific Railroad had attempted to evict a group of squatters from California land that both claimed as their own. As Norris tells the story the squatters have been metamorphosed into powerful wheat ranchers struggling against the chicanery of the Pacific and South Western Railroad—the "octopus" of the novel's title—which is slowly squeezing the people of the state to death. Norris' attempt to give significance to a relatively unimportant historical event by making all the characters larger than life-size has uniformly been regarded as the novel's greatest weakness; it forces him into attempting to give a pseudoprofundity to his work by insisting on the importance of size alone, and weakens the novel stylistically by compelling him to write in an imitation eighteenth-century style, complete with capitalized abstractions, which at its worst deteriorates into empty rhetoric.

The great strength of *The Octopus* is to be found in Norris' transformation of the expectable clichés of his novel into something considerably more profound. The Mussel Slough affair could be the perfect vehicle for telling a basically sentimental story about the destruction of the poor but honest members of nature's nobility by the unfeeling cruelty of rapacious industrialism—the plot, after all, of Upton Sinclair's muckraking novel *The Jungle* (1906). By emphasizing not the differences but the similarities between the ranchers and the railroad, Norris has turned *The Octopus* into something more profound. The ranchers are capitalists like the railroaders and are interested in making a quick and immensely profitable "killing"; like the railroaders, whose methods they ostentatiously disapprove of, the ranchers hope to achieve their goals by bribery and political corruption. *The Octopus* is ultimately a study in the ironies of beating somebody at his own game, in a world where winner takes all and the ends justify the means.

The posthumously published ten-volume edition of *The Complete Works of Frank Norris* (1928) contains all of Norris' major writing. It may be supplemented by Oscar Lewis' edition of his newspaper writing, *Frank Norris of "The Wave"* (1931), and Donald Pizer's edition of *The Literary Criticism of Frank Norris* (1964). See also Warren French, *Frank Norris* (1962); Ernest Marchand, *Frank Norris: A Study* (1942); Donald Pizer, *The Novels of Frank Norris* (1966); and Franklin Walker, *Frank Norris: A Biography* (1932).—J. K. F.

Norris, George William (1861-1944). Nebraska politician. Norris was born near Clyde, Ohio. Owing to the death of both his father and only brother in 1864, Norris spent part of his youth working for neighboring farmers and teaching school. In 1883 he received an LL.B. degree from Northern Indiana Normal School (Valparaiso) and in 1885 started practicing law in Beatrice, Nebraska. Seeking greater opportunities, he soon moved westward in the state to Beaver City and in 1900 to McCook, his home at the time of his death. As a frontier lawyer Norris acquired an extensive and varied practice and served as prosecuting attorney of Furnas County. Beginning in 1895 he was twice elected a district judge, serving until 1903, when he resigned following his election as a Republican to the United States House of Representatives. After five terms in the House, he ran successfully for a seat in the Senate in 1912, where he also served five terms.

As a congressman, Norris was relatively insignificant until 1910, when he played a leading role in the overthrow of "Cannonism." In that year Norris successfully introduced the resolution that removed from the speaker of the house the power to appoint members of the all-important Rules Committee, a power some congressmen deemed dictatorial. The term *Cannonism* derives from the arbitrary practices exercised by Joseph G. Cannon, who was speaker from 1903 to 1911. In the Senate Norris was one of a small group who opposed American participation in World War I and the Versailles peace treaty. He also opposed most of the policies and many of the appointments proposed by business-dominated Republican administrations in the 1920s. He favored aid to agriculture that directly benefited the

farmer and not the middlemen who served him. He championed multiple-purpose development of river valleys, including federally owned and operated installations to provide facilities for flood control, irrigation, improved navigation, hydroelectric power, recreational opportunities, and other practices to promote the use of natural resources in the widest public interest. While his attention focused on the Tennessee River and the properties at Muscle Shoals, his interests included the multipurpose development of rivers in Nebraska and throughout the western regions. In the 1930s, during the New Deal years, his vision became a reality with the creation of the Tennessee Valley Authority and the construction of a "little TVA" system in Nebraska.

For many years Norris was the recognized leader of the liberal element in Congress. An outspoken advocate of the necessity of relief for agriculture, he also proclaimed the rights of labor, sponsoring legislation restricting the use of injunctions and outlawing the "yellow dog" contract. He called for the abolition of the electoral college and the direct election of presidents and was the author of the Twentieth (Lame Duck) Amendment to the Constitution, the only amendment that resulted almost exclusively from the efforts of one man. He was the Senate sponsor of the act creating the Rural Electrification Administration and the farm-forestry act, both New Deal measures.

In 1928 he supported Alfred E. Smith and in 1932, 1936, and 1940 he endorsed Franklin D. Roosevelt. His campaigning helped elect Progressives and greatly aided these presidential candidates in the western states where his efforts were generally directed. In 1936 Norris was reelected as an independent, dropping his Republican party label. In 1942, after announcing his intention to retire, he decided to seek reelection and was defeated. He returned to McCook, where he spent his remaining days. Earlier, in 1934, he played a major role in securing the adoption of the amendment to the Nebraska constitution that established a unicameral legislative system.

His record of constructive statesmanship and the courage, independence, and undeviating honesty characterizing his career made Norris one of the outstanding figures in American public life in the twentieth century. Best described as a Progressive, he first stressed efficiency and economy as the desired route to achieve reform. By the time he reached the Senate Norris began to see government operation of utilities as an effective way of battling powerful, self-seeking corporations and also of promoting wider service in the public interest. As a senator he plunged into areas where few Progressives previously had traveled. He battled throughout the 1920s and 1930s with a moral fervor characteristic of the earlier movement and won victories that in some instances could serve as a capstone of Progressivism. In other instances he went beyond the regulation favored by Progressives and called for outright government operation and management of sectors of the economy, particularly as they affected resource development.

Although of western rural background, Norris was more a national than a western spokesman, in part because he viewed his constituents not exclusively as Nebraska farmers but as citizens involved in a larger network that included underpaid producers, overcharged consumers, and exploitative middlemen. Combining his concern for both the producer and the consumer, Norris waged battles against the improper use of inordinate wealth and political power. These battles placed him in the main currents of American political life throughout his forty years of service on Capitol Hill.

See Richard Lowitt, *George W. Norris: The Making of a Progressive, 1861-1912* (1963), and *George W. Norris: The Persistence of a Progressive, 1913-1933* (1971); and George W. Norris, *Fighting Liberal* (1945). See also George W. Norris Papers, Library of Congress.—R. L.

North Carolina, settlement of. During the reign of Queen Elizabeth, Sir Walter Raleigh financed a settlement at Roanoke on the coast of what was later known as North Carolina. After the Roanoke colonists mysteriously disappeared in the late 1580s, Englishmen turned their attentions to the more promising lands around the Chesapeake Bay. It was not until 1663 that Charles II granted eight court favorites, led by Sir John Colleton, title to the unexplored region south of Virginia. Two years later the crown issued a second charter expanding the Carolina territory so as to include all of Albemarle Sound. The king's patent gave the proprietors complete control over the entire region, but in the northern half of the grant, called "the province of Albemarle," their authority rested lightly. The Carolina proprietors spent most of their limited resources developing the land around Charles Town and generally ignored the needs of Albemarle.

The proprietors had good reasons to be discouraged about the prospects for northern Carolina. During the 1650s several hundred Virginians had drifted south and settled in the area around Albemarle Sound. The region they populated, however, was almost inaccessible by either water or land. Coastal sandbars made it impossible for all but the smallest vessels to enter the sound, and during most of the colonial period, only a few New England captains were willing to take the navigational risk. The land journey to Albemarle was even more difficult, for miles of dense pine forest and dangerous swamps separated the Carolinians from their nearest Chesapeake neighbors. Because of its commercial isolation, the Albemarle settlement remained poor, and, according to the historian Wesley Frank Craven, "Taken together, the inhabitants of Albemarle undoubtedly formed as poverty-stricken a community of Englishmen as could be found anywhere in North America." There were no towns in northern Carolina during the seventeenth century, only scattered small farms producing tobacco and pine products. The proprietors further retarded the economic development of the colony by refusing to lower their high quitrents, even though local settlers asked to hold their land upon the same terms that the inhabitants of Virginia held theirs.

Perhaps because of their poverty, the people of North Carolina were often ridiculed by visitors. In his classic essay *History of the Dividing Line Run in the Year 1728,* urbane William Byrd wrote, "Surely there is no place in the world where the Inhabitants live with less Labour than in N. Carolina. It approaches nearer to the Description of Lubberland than any other, by the great felicity of the Climate, the easiness of raising Provisions, and the Slothfulness of the People."

Turbulence characterized North Carolina politics during the entire period of proprietary rule. In fact, in the years before 1712 three different rebellions occurred within the colony. The first clash, called Culpeper's Rebellion, took place in 1676. A group of leading Albemarle planters, led by George Durant, refused to obey the English Navigation Acts and jailed the men who had been appointed to enforce them. Fearing the consequences of an official investigation, the Carolina proprietors protected the "Rebellious Rable" from punishment but, at the same time, moved to quell the disturbances. The plan was to send one of the proprietors—"a sober, moderate man"—to the divided colony. But the person they chose, Seth Sothel, who arrived in 1682, turned out to be a petty autocrat whose arbitrary seizure of property angered everyone. In 1689 the colonists forced Sothel to renounce his governorship and to leave Albemarle. A third crisis, known as Cary's Rebellion, developed during the first decade of the eighteenth century. The proprietors' governor tried to make the Church of England the established church of North Carolina, but the Quakers and other dissenting groups that composed a large part of the colony's population naturally resisted the move. After a series of comic-opera battles that pitted the forces of "Governor" Cary against those of Governor Hyde, political peace was established. No sooner had the religious problems been settled, however, than the Tuscarora Indians devastated the North Carolina countryside. In 1729 the discouraged Carolina proprietors surrendered their charter to the crown. As Charles M. Andrews has explained, "There can be no doubt whatever that under the proprietors North Carolina, irreligious, unrestrained, and resentful, was a poor and neglected colony, without a sound and settled government."

Under royal government political controversy continued, but it was of a less violent nature. During the early decades of the eighteenth century colonists pushed north from South Carolina and carved out plantations in the region around the Cape Fear River. This area, which was growing much more rapidly than the older Albemarle territory, soon demanded equal representation in the assembly with the northern counties. While the request was fair, the people of Albemarle would hear none of it, and from 1746 to 1754, they boycotted the assembly rather than accept a reduction in their allotment of delegates. Conflicts over land speculation added to the contention. Local planters who had received legally questionable land grants from the proprietors fought to protect their acreage against the rival claims of such influential Englishmen as Henry McCulloh and Arthur Dobbs. Governor Gabriel Johnson (1734-54), a clever politician with an eye for his own advantage, usually drew criticism from both factions. According to Charles G. Sellers, Jr., the men who formed the leadership in North Carolina before and during the American Revolution were "native politicians, intent on controlling the colony to the advantage of their own class and impatient of increasing restrictions by the mother country."

There is no outstanding work on the colonial history of North Carolina. Charles M. Andrews, *The Colonial Period of American History* (1937), and Wesley Frank Craven, *The Southern Colonies in the Seventeenth Century* (1949), provide a good introduction to the subject. A fine account of the importance of land speculation during the eighteenth century is Charles G. Sellers, Jr.,

"Private Profits and British Colonial Policy: The Speculations of Henry McCulloh," *William and Mary Quarterly*, vol. 3 (1951). William Byrd, a wealthy eighteenth-century planter, gives one of the first pictures of the American frontiersman in his *History of the Dividing Line Run in the Year 1728.*—T. H. B.

North Dakota. When North Dakota was formed from part of DAKOTA TERRITORY to become a state in 1889, its population was 190,983. Its vast rolling plains and prairie country, covering 70,665 square miles, was only partially settled. Its cool, semiarid grassland was ideal for the raising of wheat and cattle. At the time of statehood, North Dakota was tied economically to the Twin Cities of Minneapolis and St. Paul, Minnesota, and was peopled largely by immigrants from Norway, Canada, Germany, and Russia (see GERMAN RUSSIAN IMMIGRATION). It was dominated politically by the Republican machine of Alexander McKENZIE, the political ally of the railroads and the grain trade.

North Dakota history falls naturally into three periods: the completion of settlement, 1889-1915; a time of troubles, 1915-45; and a period of revolutionary change and adaptation, 1945-70.

After the slow growth of the depression years of the 1890s came a time of spectacular expansion: some 250,000 latter-day pioneers entered the state from 1898 to 1915. Homesteading in North Dakota reached its peak in 1906. By the census of 1920, the first after the completion of settlement, foreign stock (the foreign-born and their children) made up 66.7 percent of the population; 26.1 percent were of Scandinavian origin, and 22.1 of German.

North Dakota became the leading producer of spring wheat (see WHEAT PRODUCTION). Exploitation by the monopolistic combination of the railroads and the grain trade stimulated discontent among the wheat farmers, which led to the election of Eli C. D. SHORTRIDGE, a Populist, as governor in 1892. John BURKE, a Democratic governor elected in 1906, 1908, and 1910, overthrew the McKenzie machine and enacted much progressive legislation. Important reformers were Edwin Fremont LADD, a professor of chemistry at the North Dakota Agricultural College and later United States senator; George B. Winship, editor of the Grand Forks *Herald*; and Charles Fremont AMIDON, a federal district judge and a friend of Theodore Roosevelt.

The great turning point in North Dakota history was in 1915, when settlement gave way to emigration from the state, so that the population actually declined from 680,845 in 1930 to 617,761 in 1970. A total of 450,746 persons born in North Dakota were residing in other states in 1960.

The uprooting was one aspect of the troubled time from 1915 to 1945. Another was the agrarian radicalism that reached a climax when the Nonpartisan League (see AGRARIAN MOVEMENTS), led by the talented agitators Arthur Charles TOWNLEY and William LEMKE and utilizing traditional Republican loyalties by operating within the Republican party, gained control of the state government in 1919. The league enacted a program of state socialism (a state-owned bank and a state-owned flour mill and grain elevator), opposed American entry into World War I, and adopted socialistic war aims, including conscription of wealth as well as of men. Many North Dakotans thought war meant profits for Wall Street, a symbol of the state's outside exploiters, but the state's conservatives fought the league's socialism, called its leaders pro-Germans, and drove them from office; indeed, Governor Lynn J. FRAZIER was recalled from office.

To such turmoil was added postwar deflation. The value of North Dakota farm property fell by more than a half billion dollars from 1920 to 1925, and more than five hundred banks failed in the 1920s. In the 1930s the worst drought in the state's history coincided with the worst depression in the nation's history. Late in 1936 half of the North Dakota population was on relief. In these bitter years the Nonpartisan League returned to power under the leadership of William LANGER, William Lemke, and Usher L. BURDICK. North Dakotans opposed the drift of the nation toward participation in another world conflict. It was North Dakota's United States Senator Gerald P. NYE who conducted the munitions-industry investigation that strengthened the national isolationist sentiment of the 1930s. The World War II years, however, with good rains, high prices, and record crops, brought North Dakota its greatest prosperity.

Prosperity restored optimism and triggered the revolutionary changes of the years after 1945. The changes—adaptations to the nature of the country—had begun earlier, but they were now carried forward more rapidly than ever before. More automobiles, trucks, tractors, and combines greatly increased mobility—a key adaptation aided by a boom in highway construction. The mechanization of agriculture increased the average size of farms from 590 acres in 1945 to 1,024 acres in 1970 and decreased their number from a peak of 86,000 in 1933 to 41,000 in 1970. Consequently, the rural population (persons living in the country or in towns under 2,500) declined from 510,012 in 1940 to 344,093 in 1970.

At the same time, rural electrification, automobiles, and television were erasing the differences between rural and urban living. Thus, agrarian radicalism declined, the North Dakota Farmers' Union lost some of its crusading zeal (its cooperatives had been growing rapidly), and the political temper of the state became more conservative.

With the conservative trend, the Nonpartisan League, the instrument of agrarian radicalism, was no longer able to control the state Republican party, and in 1956 it moved over to the Democratic party. The realignment led to the repeated election of William Lewis Guy, a Democrat, as governor and of Quentin Northrop Burdick, a Democrat, as United States senator. North Dakota was no longer a one-party state.

Although the 1950s and 1960s were politically conservative, they were socially innovative. They saw the beginnings of social institutions to serve large areas—large school and public health districts, county and multicounty libraries, and multicounty social service and mental health centers. Such institutions are an essential adaptation to the state's sparse population—less than nine persons per square mile.

See Elwyn B. Robinson, *History of North Dakota* (1966).—D. J. T.

Northern Pacific Railroad. See BURLINGTON NORTH-
ERN RAILROAD; and Henry VILLARD.

Northern Securities Company. See BURLINGTON
NORTHERN RAILROAD.

Northwest Coast Indians. See INDIANS OF THE
NORTHWEST COAST.

North West Company. Canadian fur company. Or-
ganized in 1784 as a rival to the HUDSON'S BAY COMPANY,
the North West Company fought its competitor
throughout Rupert's Land until the British government
forced the two companies to merge in 1821. North West
Company explorers such as Simon Fraser, Alexander
Mackenzie (see EXPLORATION, ENGLISH), Alexander
ROSS, and David THOMPSON explored much of North
America including regions later part of the United
States—for example, the lower Columbia River and the
Snake country. Many of its former employees were
numbered in the ranks of John Jacob Astor's fur
companies.

See Gordon C. Davidson, *The North West Company*
(1918); and Frederick Merk, ed., *Fur Trade and Empire*,
2nd ed. (1968).—G. B. D.

Northwest Ordinance (1787). In the years immediately following the passage of the Ordinance of
1784 (see TERRITORIAL SYSTEM) many Americans gave
thought to the operation of government in the western
lands. To some, the provision that the settlers should
establish self-government when the territory had a minimal population was too liberal and did not afford
enough control over the settlers. To many westerners,
the plan to create up to sixteen states from the territory
was unwise because there would be too many states with
artificial boundaries; the westerners preferred fewer,
larger states with natural features for boundaries.
Further, it was provided that the 1784 law would not
become effective until all states had ceded their western
lands to Congress. North Carolina and Georgia, under
pressure from land speculators, delayed their cessions
until after 1789.

As a result, by early 1786, Congress felt it necessary to
provide some government for the settlements that were
developing north of the Ohio River at Detroit, Vincennes, Kaskaskia, and Cahokia. A committee chaired
by James Monroe drew up an ordinance on May 10,
1786, which provided for congressional government
until the 1784 law went into effect. During months of
intermittent debate, a group of New Englanders, mostly
revolutionary war veterans, organized a land company,
the Ohio Company of Associates, to purchase lands in
the Ohio country and to collect on military bounty warrants. By spring 1787 Ohio Company agents were
negotiating a land purchase with the central government. The company officers, concerned about the lack
of government for the Ohio country, directed their
agents to work with Congress for a remedy. Also in May
1787, the Constitutional Convention was meeting in
Philadelphia. The prospects of a new constitution, or
revision of the Articles of Confederation, influenced the
development of a new law for western government.

The bill proposed by Monroe's committee was presented for a third reading on July 9, 1787. This bill
amended the Ordinance of 1784. However, new pressures led Congress to recommit it for further revisions.
During the next two days the bill was completely re-
drafted. The committee spent time in discussion with
Nathan Dane and the Reverend Manasseh Cutler of the

Ohio Company, and both of these men contributed
greatly to the ordinance. The new bill, which was reported out on July 11 and passed on July 13, contained
ideas drawn from the 1784 ordinance, suggested by the
committee and by Dane and Cutler. It repealed the
older ordinance. Monroe, who chaired the committee
throughout, wrote to Thomas Jefferson explaining that
"it is in effect to be a colonial government similar to
which prevailed in these States previous to the
revolution."

The "Ordinance for the government of the territory
of the United States North west of the river Ohio" (see
OLD NORTHWEST) passed on July 13, 1787, and was
reenacted on August 7, 1789, under the new constitution. It provided not only for the government but also
for the civil rights of the settlers. The first paragraph
provided that the temporary government should be established in one district, although Congress could establish two districts if necessary. Congress made provision
for the conveyance of real property, for the making of
wills, and for the settlement of estates of persons dying
intestate, in the second paragraph.

The executive branch of territorial government was
to be headed by a governor appointed by the president
of the United States for a three-year term. He was required to live in the territory and own a one-thousand-
acre freehold within the territory. As commander-in-
chief of the militia, he appointed all junior officers,
while the president appointed general officers. The
magistrates and other civil officials in the territory were
appointed by the governor, although the general assembly had the power to describe the duties and powers of
such officials. Until the organization of the legislature
the governor had power to lay out counties, townships,
and other civil divisions. He also had the right to convene, prorogue, or dissolve the general assembly as he
saw fit and had an absolute veto over acts of the
assembly.

The secretary of the territory was also appointed by
the president, for a term of four years. He had to own a
freehold of five hundred acres within the territory,
where he was required to reside. The primary duty of
the secretary was "to keep and preserve" the acts and
laws of the legislature, the public records and executive
proceedings of the governor, and other public records.
Every six months he was required to transmit "authentic
copies" of the records to the secretary of state. He served
as governor in the latter's absence from the territory.

Three judges appointed by the president composed
the judicial branch. Any two could form a court and
their jurisdiction was that of common law. Their commissions extended in force throughout their good behavior. Each was required to own a five-hundred-acre
freehold within the territory.

The legislative branch during the early period of territorial development consisted of the governor, secretary, and judges sitting together, a majority of whom
constituted a quorum. They were authorized to "adopt
and publish" criminal and civil laws from existing states
as necessary for the proper governance of the territory.
Following organization of the second-stage general assembly, the full legislature could alter these laws.

When a census showed five thousand free males of
"full age" residing in the territory, these men were to
elect representatives to the lower house of the general
assembly and second-stage government would begin.

The initial apportionment was one representative for every five hundred free males until the number of representatives reached twenty-five. At that time the general assembly could regulate the number and apportionment of election districts. To qualify to vote, a man had to own a fifty-acre freehold and be a resident of the territory. A representative had to own a two-hundred-acre freehold and be a resident of the territory. Each representative had a term of two years, and vacancies were to be filled by special election.

The legislative council, or upper house, of the general assembly was to have five members, all of whom had to be resident in the territory and own freeholds of five hundred acres. The governor and lower chamber were to meet together and nominate ten men, and from this list the president would appoint five for terms of five years. Vacancies during the five-year period were to be filled by a similar procedure.

The general assembly had authority to enact any laws necessary for the territory that were not repugnant to the Constitution of the United States. The governor had an absolute veto. The council and lower house meeting in joint session had the right to elect a delegate to the United States Congress. The delegate had the right to participate in debates but not to vote.

The second part of the Northwest Ordinance consisted of a solemn compact between "the Original States and the People and States in the said territory." The compact guaranteed to the people of the territory religious freedom, the writ of habeas corpus, trial by jury, a representative legislature, judicial proceedings under common law, and many other civil rights commonly expressed in the state bills of rights of the time. Schools were encouraged, and Indians were protected in their rights and lands from encroachment or injustice. Slavery was prohibited and provision made for extradition of fugitive slaves or convicted criminals.

The territory was to remain forever a part of the United States. The inhabitants were held responsible for their share of the federal debt and government expenses, although their taxes were to be levied by their territorial or state legislatures. The territories or states could not interfere with the disposal of the public domain nor tax the property of the United States. Navigable waters and portages were to be regarded as common highways and open to all people.

Under the compact, the United States provided that no less than three nor more than five states would be created from the territory. The ordinance established boundaries for three states and gave Congress authority to change these boundaries and to create one or two more states if it should deem it expedient. The new states were guaranteed republican government and admission to the Union with a status equal to that of the original states.

The Ordinance of 1787, or Northwest Ordinance, was one of the great achievements of the United States under the Articles of Confederation. It provided a constitution for the territories, instituted an orderly method of government, and guaranteed the basic civil rights of all residents. Because the authors were familiar with colonial government, they instituted provisions that alleviated many problems. The work of territorial delegates and the guarantee of eventual statehood assured the peaceful development of future states. The

ordinance has stood as the basis for temporary government of territories that have become thirty-two states, one commonwealth, and one republic.

See John Porter Bloom, ed., *The American Territorial System,* National Archives Conferences, vol. 5 (1973); Max Farrand, *Legislation of Congress for the Government of the Organized Territories of the United States, 1789-1895* (1896); and Merrill Jensen, *New Nation* (1950).—J. T. B.

Northwest Passage. Name given to a short, all-water route to the Orient, uniting the Atlantic and the Pacific. The concept of a Northwest Passage—a dream almost identical with the myth of the Strait of Anian, which was believed to be somewhere in the vast regions to the north of Mexico and the Gulf—was predicated upon the ignorance in the sixteenth and seventeenth centuries of the breadth of North America and of the existence of a continent there. Conversely, it was believed that the cold polar seas were open save for icebergs and occasional islands. The possibility of a short Northwest Passage or a Strait of Anian connecting East and West therefore seemed reasonable, and, based upon these geographical premises, the economic rewards to the West European nation that discovered it could have been tremendous.

It was the search for this Northwest Passage that prompted the voyages of the Cabots, which established England's claim to North America (see EXPLORATION, ENGLISH). The search by others led to the French claim to North America (see EXPLORATION, FRENCH), and led Jacques Cartier and Samuel de Champlain and his "young men" into the interior. Henry Hudson discovered both the river and the bay that bears his name in the pursuit of this elusive water highway. Spanish and Portuguese explorers, among them Juan Rodríguez CABRILLO, searched along the Pacific Coast for this shortcut. It is interesting to note that not until 1905 was an all-water crossing actually accomplished, by the Arctic explorer Roald Amundsen; and in 1960 the American nuclear submarine *Seadragon* crossed the Atlantic to the Pacific via the Arctic also. In 1969 an American tanker, the U.S.S. *Manhattan,* became the first commercial vessel to run the passage.

The belief in the existence of the Northwest Passage was, then, a contributing factor in the exploration of the northwest Atlantic coast, the interior of Canada, and the upper Mississippi-Great Lakes region. Similarly, much of the western part of North America was explored in hopes of finding the Strait of Anian.

See John Bartlett Brebner, *The Explorers of North America* (1933); and Nellis M. Crouse, *In Quest of the Western Ocean* (1928).—R. A. B.

Northwest Territory. See OLD NORTHWEST.

novel, western. The one truly indigenous American literary art form, the western novel, was not so much a response to peculiarly American concerns as it was to a general European fascination with the continent to the west. Although the first novel in English specifically placed in the American West is *Francis Berrian, or The Mexican Patriot* (1826), by Timothy FLINT, clear prefigurations of western themes in American writing are to be found much earlier than this, going back at least to J. Hector St. John de Crèvecoeur's *Letters from an American Farmer* (1782) and, less specifically, to the preoccupation of eighteenth-century European primitivists with the moral value of life in a state of nature, removed from the pressures and corruption of civilized society. American western literature may specifically be traced to a response to a call articulated in Ralph Waldo Emerson's essay "The Poet" (1844) for a literature dealing with native American themes in general and with "the western clearing" in particular. The newness of the American experience translated itself, in literary terms, into explications of peculiarly American habits of life and into a search for artistic expression that would be exclusively American, not only in form but in subject matter. The first American writer to achieve widespread success as a writer of western themes was James Fenimore COOPER. Cooper's importance to the general development of subsequent western literature cannot be overemphasized, but the modern "western" can be traced specifically to Owen WISTER, whose famous novel *The Virginian* (1902) established the form of subsequent writing in this genre.

A proper, simple definition of western fiction is difficult to arrive at partly because of the amorphous nature of much western writing and partly because of the ever-changing historical definition of the American West itself. For example, though Flint wrote the first western to take place in the Southwest, the fictional locale of most of his stories is the Mississippi valley. The same is true of James HALL and Cooper, all of whose *Leatherstocking Tales* except *The Prairie* (1827) take place on the New York frontier of the late eighteenth century. A working definition, however, may take account of the fact that western writing tends to concern itself with two quite different aspects of western life. On the one hand stands the "frontier novel," a clear descendant of Cooper's stories of wilderness adventure. The frontier novel is primarily about frontiersmen's encounters with various wilderness perils; hostile Indians and wild animals are the most easily recognizable, though by no means the only, examples. The "novel of pioneering," in contrast, focuses its attention primarily on the settler and developer, rather than the explorer, of the newly discovered wilderness and his difficulties in a hostile environment. The novel of pioneering is more closely related to "local color" fiction than is the frontier novel and is in general more overtly concerned with the facts of pioneer life.

These two kinds of western writing reflect a constant debate about what western fiction should be. From the time of Cooper to the present the frontier novel has been accused of forsaking the facts of western life to take refuge in a world of romantic escape and of using the West only as a convenient never-never land, where the facts of actual life can safely be suspended. The novel of pioneering has been accused of being too factual, of losing sight of the significance of the western experience by its too great concentration on the minutiae of daily life and the often trivial anecdotes of the social history of colonization.

Moreover, this debate itself reflects a still wider American debate about what the significance of the West actually is. For the West, like the fiction written about it, cannot be fitted into a simple definition. In one sense the West is a geographical entity; but it is also an idea, an almost mythical region in which abstractions can be personified and talked about concretely and particular historic characters can be universalized into respectable philosophical generalizations.

The perennial fascination of Americans with western literature has a universal, rather than purely historical, source. For like all mythical literature, western literature can be made relevant to many kinds of social concerns without being confined by them, as, for example, *The Ox-Bow Incident* (1940), by Walter Van Tilburg CLARK, and the *Leatherstocking Tales*, which latter, for all their apparently dated quality, provide a fresh view of the problems not only of the prerevolutionary frontier in New York but of man in any society that, by its very nature, must ask compromises of him. Much western fiction deals with the tragedy of people who discover that their ideal of western life does not square with its reality, and the debate at the heart of most western literature over how best to develop a newly discovered territory into an ideal society almost perfectly mirrors the American debate over the proper destiny for America. On the surface nostalgic and escapist, the western novel on examination becomes much more profound; it is like a dream in which important concerns masquerade in apparently absurd and irrelevant disguises.

See DIME NOVELS and HUMOR.

Most studies of the western novel have concerned themselves primarily with discussion of the differences between the western experience and its literary expression. Lucy L. Hazard, *The Frontier in American Literature* (1927), is a still valuable study of the frontier experience and its reflection in American letters. E. Douglas Branch, *The Cowboy and His Interpreters* (1926), documents the difference between the real-life cowboy and his literary imitations, a line of research continued by Joe B. Frantz and Julian Ernest Choate, Jr., in *The American Cowboy: The Myth and the Reality* (1955). Henry Nash Smith, *Virgin Land: The American West as Symbol and Myth* (1950), and Edwin Russell, *Frontier: American Literature and the American West* (1965), have concerned themselves primarily with the West as a symbol to the American imagination. Robert Edson Lee has suggested reasons for the failure of a great literature to rise out of the western experience in *From West to East: Studies in the Literature of the American West* (1966). James K. Folsom, *The American Western Novel* (1966), has attempted a discussion of the literary implications of the western story more or less divorced from its historic basis. —J. K. F.

Nuestra Señora de Guadalupe de los Nacogdoches. See SAN FRANCISCO DE LOS TEJAS.

Nuestra Señora de la Candelaria. See SAN XAVIER RIVER MISSIONS.

Nuestra Señora de la Purísima Concepción de Acuña. Spanish mission. Originally located in East Texas near the Angelina River, La Purísima Concepción de los Ainai, as it was then known, was one of six Franciscan missions that the Spanish established in the summer of 1716 as a counter to French expansion into Texas from Louisiana. Concepción served as the headquarters of Governor Don Martín de Alarcón when he visited East Texas in 1718. Father Gabriel Vergara, who was in charge of the missions, had barely begun work among the friendly Hasinai Indians, however, when war broke out between France and Spain in 1719. All the East Texas missions, which at that time were little more than brush shelters and log huts, were abandoned until 1721, when the Spanish reoccupied the region. This time Dolores presidio, which was located near the Concepción mission, promised added protection for the fathers.

Neither the Concepción nor the other East Texas missions ever really prospered. The Indians of the region already knew how to farm, preferred to live in their own scattered villages rather than in mission compounds, and frequently went off on hunting expeditions. In 1730 the Concepción and two other Querétaran missions, SAN FRANCISCO DE LOS TEJAS (or Neches) and San José de los Nazonis, were moved to the Colorado River of Texas, but when it was discovered that the site lacked an adequate water supply and lands suitable for farming, they were moved to the fertile east bank of the San Antonio River in 1731. There the new Concepción was located between San Antonio de Valero (the ALAMO) and SAN JOSE Y SAN MIGUEL DE AGUAYO missions and was built of stone and adobe. It was at this time that the mission took on the name of the incumbent viceroy, Juan de Acuña, the Marqués de Casafuerte.

While Concepción mission was never as large or as famous as its two neighbors, Valero and San José y San Miguel, 250 Indian neophytes were in residence in 1739 when a smallpox epidemic reduced the number to 120 persons. But by recruiting converts from more distant tribes, the numbers again rose to more than 200.

As was the case at the other missions on the San Antonio River, the Indians were taught Christian doctrine daily and learned to farm and to herd cattle and sheep. An irrigation canal, the "Concepción ditch," brought water both for the mission and for crops. Since the missions were supposed to be temporary enterprises, lasting only as long as it took to teach the Indians Christianity and the Spanish way of life, after 1768 both royal officials and local settlers began to press for the secularization of the San Antonio missions. As a result, Concepción's lands and herds were turned over to the Indian families there in 1794. The mission's remaining properties were administered by the fathers from nearby San José y San Miguel until February 1824, when the Concepción mission, along with San José y San Miguel, SAN JUAN CAPISTRANO, and SAN FRANCISCO DE LA ESPADA were completely secularized by order of the Mexican government. For Espada the mission period came to an end. After 1824 even its religious duties were taken over by the local parish priest.

Concepción's role in Texas history was far from ended, however. On October 25, 1835, shortly after the Anglo-Texans began to rebel against Mexican authority, Colonel James Bowie, Captain James W. Fannin, and ninety men were surprised and surrounded while at the mission by a large number of Mexican troops. Although heavily outnumbered in the ensuing battle, the Texans won. In 1841, after independence was achieved, the independent Republic of Texas deeded the Concepción and other missions to the Roman Catholic church authorities in Texas. Bishop John Mary Odin then persuaded the Brothers of Mary to establish a school in the buildings. Later the mission was used as a seminary and an orphanage. Today it serves as the site for a seminary for the Diocese of San Antonio.

The Concepción mission's massive, severe church, with walls of stone and adobe nearly four feet thick, reflect Moorish and Romanesque styles. The best preserved of the Texas missions, it now has a Spartan quality, but it was once decorated with bright colors by the fathers and the Indians. The church itself is dominated by twin towers and a Moorish dome.

See John Francis Bannon, *The Spanish Borderlands Frontier, 1513-1821* (1970); James Wakefield Burke, *Missions of Old Texas* (1971); Carlos E. Castañeda, *Our Catholic Heritage in Texas*, vol. II (1938); and Dorman H. Winfrey et al., *Six Missions of Texas* (1965).—H. R. L.

Nuestra Señora de la Soledad. Spanish Franciscan mission. Appropriately named for Our Lady of Solitude, the thirteenth of California's Franciscan missions was never a popular place. Father Fermín de Lasuén founded it on October 9, 1791, probably to provide a point of rest between San Carlos Borromeo and San Antonio de Padua. If he had another reason, it is hard to imagine, for Soledad never achieved much success in its sparsely settled valley. At its high point in 1805 it had only 688 Indian neophytes in residence. Because it was extremely hot in the summer, chillingly damp in the winter, and extremely isolated, Soledad was shunned by most Franciscan fathers. Such was the difficulty in obtaining missionaries for it that in 1828 the father-prefect of the missions, Vicente Francisco Sarría, personally took over duties there. When Alfred Robinson visited Soledad in 1829, he said it was the "gloomiest, bleakest, and most abject-looking spot in all California." Sarría, who died from exhaustion and starvation in 1835, was the last Franciscan to reside at the mission. By then it had been united with San Antonio de Padua by the secularization decree of 1834. From that time forward, it was abandoned. Not notable for its architecture, which resembles that of La PURISIMA CONCEPCION, Soledad remained untouched until 1954, when restoration of the chapel was begun.

For a history of the mission, see Kurt Baer, *Architecture of the California Missions* (1958); and John A. Berger, *The Franciscan Missions of California* (1941). —R. S.

Nuestra Señora del Espíritu Santo de Zuñiga. Spanish mission. Espíritu Santo was founded on Matagorda Bay in 1722, near the presidio of Santa Maria de Loreto de la Bahía del Espíritu Santo; since Matagorda Bay was then called La Bahía del Espíritu Santo, both mission and fort eventually were referred to as La Bahía. The mission was built to convert the fierce coastal tribes of Karankawa Indians and the Bahía presidio was designed to protect the mission and to fortify the Gulf Coast against French invasion. Both mission and fort owed their existence to the Marqués de Aguayo, a devoted servant of the Spanish crown who had been ordered to improve the defense of Texas in 1719. Assisted by the able Father Antonio Margil de Jesús from the Franciscan College at Zacatecas, Mexico, he restored the missions and presidios in East Texas (see SAN FRANCISCO DE LOS TEJAS); strengthened the presidio at San Antonio de Béjar; allowed Margil to found there a second mission, SAN JOSE Y SAN MIGUEL DE AGUAYO; and initiated the coastal mission and fort.

Four years later, difficulties with the local Indians persuaded authorities to move the Bahía complex inland to the banks of the Guadalupe River, near the modern city of Victoria. Then in 1749 it was relocated on the San Antonio River, on the site of the present-day town of Goliad, Texas. Under the wise direction of Father Francisco López, who was soon to head all the mission enterprises in Texas, Espíritu Santo began to prosper. The mission built up herds of cattle, horses, sheep, goats, burros, and oxen; the mission cattle may well have been the progenitors of the vast herds of wild cattle for which Texas became famous in the nineteenth century. In its early years on the San Antonio, Espíritu Santo must have looked more like a frontier fort of the Old West than a mission, for it was protected by a wooden stockade, and its rude corrals and houses were made of palings bound together with strips of hide.

The Franciscans at Espíritu Santo dreamed of repeating the success story of San Antonio de Béjar upriver, where five missions flourished in close proximity and where in 1731 a civilian colony of Canary Islanders had formed the nucleus of the future city of SAN ANTONIO. Thus, in 1754 a second mission, Nuestra Señora del Rosario, was founded four miles west of Bahía presidio and placed under the control of Father José Escovar. Both Espíritu Santo and Rosario prospered between 1760 and 1780, but both lacked the water supply needed for raising crops and were forced to depend on San José y San Miguel for their food supply. The two missions also suffered frequent attacks by Apache raiders who would run off the mission stock and abuse the Christian Indians and the fathers. By 1781 Rosario was already in decline, and despite efforts to revive the mission during the 1790s, it had been abandoned by 1807. Yet because the two served as outposts against the Apache, neither was secularized when the San Antonio missions were, in 1794. The priests at Espíritu Santo also argued that the Indians there were still so backward that they were not ready to take over the lands and herds according to the provisions of the secularization law.

At the very moment that the mission effort was being repressed elsewhere in Texas, the Franciscans persuaded authorities to let them establish one last mission. In 1793 Nuestra Señora del Refugio was founded south of the San Antonio River, almost opposite present-day Goliad. Refugio's function was to attract the runaway Indians from Espíritu Santo and Rosario. Like them, Refugio was protected by the garrison at the Bahía presidio. The original site of Refugio proved to be so inhospitable that in 1794 both mission and presidio moved to the site of the modern town of Refugio, where, because of continuous Comanche raids, the mission led a precarious existence until Mexican authorities secularized it in 1830.

After 1800 Espíritu Santo also declined in importance and was heavily damaged by a storm in 1818. By 1820 it was probably more important as a school for the families of soldiers and settlers than as a mission. Indian attacks became so frequent that all movable mission property had to be stored within the walls of the presidio. In 1830 the mission was finally closed by order of the Mexican government, despite the heroic efforts of Father Diaz de León to keep it open. After the American conquest of Texas the mission buildings housed Aranamus College, a Presbyterian school, until that, too, was closed when all the students enlisted in the Confederate army at the outbreak of the Civil War. Later the buildings were destroyed by fire.

Events surrounding the Mexican struggle for independence in 1810-1821 and the coming of the Anglo-Americans to Texas meant that the Bahía presidio, which occupied a commanding position on a hill on the opposite riverbank from the mission, would become a focal point of events. In November 1812, José Bernardo Gutiérrez de Lara and Augustus W. Magee seized the Bahía presidio from loyalist forces and held it until January 1813. Four years later Henry Perry, a Connecticut adventurer, tried to take the fort, but he and his men were eventually captured. In 1821 a Mississippi filibuster, Dr. James Long, also tried to take the presidio, but he was defeated and imprisoned in Mexico City.

At the outbreak of the Texas revolution in 1835, Captain George M. Collingsworth took the presidio, now commonly called Goliad, from Mexican soldiers and issued the first declaration of Texan independence there in December 1835.

Both the Bahía mission and presidio have been restored and are part of the state park at Goliad. The mission church has a simple, clean, and attractive façade, decorated only by carved stonework around the arched doorway and a statue above. The roofline of the façade is curved, suggesting a Moorish design, and is surmounted by a cross. The belfry, topped by a pointed roof is of simple, but sturdy, Romanesque design. A short distance away the Bahía chapel, made of rough river stone and mortar and almost devoid of outside ornamentation, suggests the enduring strength of one of the most important Spanish outposts in Texas.

See John Francis Bannon, *The Spanish Borderlands Frontier, 1513-1821* (1970); James Wakefield Burke, *Missions of Old Texas* (1971); Carlos E. Castañeda, *Our Catholic Heritage in Texas*, vols. II and III (1936-38); Marion A. Habig, *San Antonio's Mission San José* (1968); Dorman H. Winfrey et al., *Six Missions of Texas* (1965); and Robert S. Weddle, *San Juan Bautista: Gateway to Spanish Texas* (1968).—H. R. L.

Nuestra Señora de los Dolores de los Ais. See SAN FRANCISCO DE LOS TEJAS.

Nunis, Doyce Blackman, Jr. (1924-   ). Historian. A native of Georgia, Nunis received both his undergraduate and graduate educations in California. His twenty-year teaching career, divided between the University of California at Los Angeles and the University of Southern California, was devoted to the fields of education and history.

California's romantic events and mixture of racial cultures caught the attention of the young southerner, and, as the years went by, Nunis became increasingly interested in the history of his adopted state. Accordingly, almost all his magazine articles and all his books examine some phase of either California or far western history.

In 1960 he produced *Andrew Sublette, Rocky Mountain Prince, 1808-1855*, a biography of a famous mountain man. This was followed by *The Letters of a Young Miner* (1964), the adventures of Jasper Smith Hill during the 1849-52 gold rush, edited and annotated by Nunis; and *The Trials of Isaac Graham* (1967), a legal-documentary biography of a mountain man tried for treason by the Mexicans in June 1841. He also edited *The Hudson's Bay Company's First Fur Brigade to the Sacramento Valley* (1968), Alexander McLeod's journal of his 1829 expedition, and *The San Francisco Vigilance Committee of 1856, Three Views* (1971), the Silver Anniversary publication of the Los Angeles chapter of The Westerners, an international organization of western history buffs. He also contributed several biographical sketches to the series *The Mountain Men* as well as numerous book reviews to professional journals and quarterlies and to popular western history magazines.

Nunis became a member of a number of professional societies, including the Western History Association, the Western Literature Association, and the Los Angeles chapter of the Westerners.—J. C. D.

Nute, Grace Lee (1895-   ). Historian. Nute was born in North Conway, New Hampshire, and attended the Fryeburg Academy in Maine. After graduating from Westfield State Normal School in Massachusetts, she entered Smith College in 1914 to study for a B.A. degree in English. When she enrolled in Radcliffe College in September 1917, she came under the influence of Frederick Jackson Turner and under his guidance received her M.A. degree in 1918 and Ph.D. in 1921.

Until this time Nute had not been out of New England, but when a position opened in the manuscripts division of the Minnesota Historical Society, she obtained the appointment upon Turner's enthusiastic recommendation. Minnesota then became her home and the subject of most of her writings. She was curator of manuscripts (1921-46) and research associate for the society (1946-58), professor of Minnesota history at Hamline University (1927-60), and a visiting professor and lecturer at various times at the University of Minnesota and at Macalester College.

During her long and active career, Nute made three or four research trips to Europe, developed a close friendship with the family of Charles Lindbergh, and produced several books distinguished by stylistic writing. Her first major work, *The Voyageur* (1931), is now a rare collector's item. Among her other books are *Caesars of the Wilderness* (1943), which won a prize offered by the American Historical Association; *The Voyageur's Highway* (1941); *Lake Superior* (1944); and *Rainy River Country* (1950). In addition, she edited numerous books and contributed scores of articles to scholarly and popular journals.—W. E. H.

Nye, Bill [Edgar Wilson] (1850-1896). Humorist. Nye won fame writing newspaper columns in Laramie, Wyoming, from 1876 to 1883. After reporting for the *Laramie Sentinel* he edited the *Laramie Boomerang*, named after his mule, which was so named "because he has such an eccentric orbit and no one can tell just when he will clash with some other heavenly body."

Born in Maine and brought up in Wisconsin, Nye had done only limited reporting of local items for Wisconsin newspapers before moving west. In Laramie, a town of two thousand people, he found circumstances appropriate for developing his talent as a rural philosopher. Freedom to write as he pleased and a new, exciting environment gave fresh stimulus to his imagination.

Nye often commented on local and national news items. At other times he related anecdotes involving picturesque frontier characters—some real, some imaginary. He took delight in deflating the pompous and in poking fun at eccentrics, but he soon learned that unless the targets were remote it was safer to laugh at himself, as he often did. Between jobs on the *Sentinel* and the *Boomerang* he tried gold mining, read some law, passed the Wyoming bar, and practiced law. He served also as justice of the peace, United States commissioner, and postmaster. Changing occupations gave him new

information and insights for use in literary exposition.

Neither muscular nor belligerent, Nye normally reflected rather than shaped the opinions of western readers. He ridiculed Indians, carpetbagger officials, Mormons, and bumptious tenderfeet. He used devices common to nineteenth-century humorists, particularly homely details, exaggeration, incongruities, anticlimax, and foreign phrases in wrong context.

To recuperate from an attack of spinal meningitis, Nye moved back to Wisconsin in 1883. Later he made his home in New York City and near Asheville, North Carolina, while supplying long syndicated columns for the New York *World*. Besides his regular contributions to the *World* he lectured extensively and also published fourteen books under twenty titles. His best books are *Bill Nye and Boomerang* (1881), *Forty Liars and Other Lies* (1882), *Baled Hay* (1884), and *Remarks by Bill Nye* (1886). His burlesque *Bill Nye's History of the United States* (1894) sold five hundred thousand copies. Nye's activity in the 1880s and 1890s, which bordered on the frenzied, made him the nation's best-known humorist but also brought a heart attack and death at the age of forty-five. (See HUMOR.)

See T. A. Larson, ed., *Bill Nye's Western Humor* (1968); and Frank Wilson Nye, *Bill Nye: His Own Life Story* (1926).—T. A. L.

Nye, Gerald P. (1892-1972). North Dakota politician. A native of Wisconsin, Nye was editor of the Griggs County (North Dakota) *Sentinel-Courier* in Cooperstown. He was also an ardent champion of the progressive Nonpartisan League and edited for a time the *Nonpartisan* in Bismarck. In 1925 Nye, then a political unknown in North Dakota, was appointed to fill the United States Senate seat left vacant by the death of Edwin F. Ladd. He was elected to the Senate in his own right in 1926, 1932, and 1938. His isolationist record was the campaign issue in 1944, when he lost to Democratic governor John Moses.

Nye was best known as a skilled conductor of senatorial investigations. As a leading Republican isolationist and as chairman of the Senate committee to investigate the manufacturers of arms and munitions, he set about to prove the isolationist belief that America entered World War I because of the machinations of these manufacturers. As a result of the Nye committee's findings, many Americans accepted the thesis, and Congress passed a series of laws in the late 1930s designed to insure American neutrality.

See Wayne S. Cole, *Senator Gerald P. Nye and American Foreign Relations* (1962).—D. J. T.

Nye, James W. (1814-1876). Nevada politician. Born in DeRuyter, New York, Nye trained as an attorney and was elected probate judge of Madison County at the age of thirty. Named county judge three years later, he was elected a master and examiner in chancery in 1851, serving two terms in that post. Nye joined the Republican party in 1856 and served as William H. Seward's campaign manager in the latter's attempt to gain the nomination of that party for the presidency in 1860. When Abraham Lincoln won the nomination, Nye campaigned strongly for the Republican candidate and was rewarded with the appointment as the first governor of Nevada Territory. He arrived in Carson City on July 8, 1861, and in the next few weeks, through a series of proclamations, organized the new territory. Nye was successful in obtaining an enabling act for the territory and after Nevada became a state on October 31, 1864, he and William M. Stewart were chosen as the state's first United States senators. After serving a short term of two years, he was reelected in 1866 to a six-year term. Without money and becoming senile, Nye was shunted aside by his party in 1872 and when the state legislature met in 1873 his name was not presented. He spent his last years in a hospital in Flushing, New York.

See Effie M. Mack, "James Warren Nye, A Biography," *Nevada Historical Society Quarterly* (July-December 1961).—R. R. E.

O

Oakland (California) Museum. The Oakland Museum, located at the south end of Lake Merritt in Oakland, California, is a unique regional museum and municipal facility, reflecting and interpreting the land and people of California through exhibits of art, history, and natural science. The selective California theme collections and the Archives of California Art research program began in 1955; the museum opened as a public institution in 1969.

Enclosed by a wall around a four-block area, the museum is a three-tiered complex of galleries, courts, pools, lawns, and exhibition areas. Facilities include 100,000 square feet of exhibition space, a 300-seat theater, a 100-seat lecture hall, classrooms, a restaurant, a 200-car garage, and a bookstore. The building, an architectural landmark of international significance, was designed on a new concept by Kevin Roch, John Dingaloo and Associates.

Three museum divisions are housed in their own tier; each has a major exhibition gallery and a smaller gallery. A fourth major gallery, the Great Hall, houses a variety of changing exhibitions drawn from regional, national, and worldwide sources.

The fourth department, the Department of Education and Special Exhibits, provides opportunities for community involvement and makes presentations related to both the permanent collections and temporary shows. The "Museum on Wheels" takes exhibitions into the classrooms of the Oakland public schools; the schools also participate in study schedules within the museum.

In the Hall of California Ecology the display "A Walk Across California" reflects the varied geography of the state—from Pacific tidepools to Nevada deserts—and demonstrates the ecological balances of these environments. The Cowell Hall of California History, funded in 1968 by a donation from the S. H. Cowell Foundation, provides a visual account of man's experience in California since prehistory—from Maidu Indian handwork to the first generation of computers.

The Gallery of California Art displays a panorama of paintings, sculpture, crafts, graphics, and photography, from the art of the explorers to the arts of today. The collection contains more than fifteen thousand items; the works of more than two hundred artists are on view in the major gallery. The smaller gallery exhibits six to eight one-man or group shows annually. The Oakes Art Observatory, adjacent to the main gallery, offers a multi-media presentation and houses the graphics, prints, and photography collections.

Displays representing the various periods are arranged in bays of the main gallery. The Gold Rush bay features Currier & Ives color lithographs, Charles Christian Nahl paintings, and the works of other professional artists, along with scenes by primitive artists whose depictions are of historic interest. In the marine section are coastal views of San Francisco Bay, the Golden Gate, and shipwrecks along the Pacific shore by James Hamilton, Charles Dorman Robinson, and other painters. Among views of California towns are paintings by Ferdinand Richardt, Edwin Deakin, Albertis Del Orient Browere, and Albert Bierstadt. The William Keith Collection was the 1957 gift of the Keith Art Association, bequest of Elizabeth Keith Pond.

The California Decorative School, corresponding with Art Nouveau, is revealed by the works of Arthur Mathews and his followers. In 1965 the Concours d'Antique of the Art Guild of the Oakland Museum Association purchased the Arthur F. and Lucia K. Mathews Collection of 1,977 items in paintings, pastels, drawings, manuscripts, and furniture designed by Mathews.

Illustrations of the various group-styles and wares of individual painters active from 1915 through the 1960s are displayed in the other half of the main gallery. Impressionists and Postimpressionists are represented. Works by the Social Realists of the 1930s include those of Diego Rivera and Anton Refregier. Among the works of Abstract Expressionists are those of Clyfford Still, Hassel Smith, Frank Lobdell, and Robert Hultberg; changes in their styles, in some cases, have resulted in some of their work being displayed with the Bay Area Figurative painters of the 1950s and 1960s who include Richard Diebenkorn, David Park, Elmer Bischoff, and Nathan Oliviera.

Paintings and sculpture of the 1960s and 1970s offer a visual documentation of Contemporary Realism, Pop Art, Funk, Hard Edge, Post Figurative Abstraction, and Technological Art. Displays include works by Wayne Thiebaud, Mel Ramos, William Wiley, Bruce Conner, Fred Martin, Tom Holland, Ron Davis, and Tony De Lap.

Sculpture from all periods is displayed in the gallery

and outdoor areas. Arthur Putnam, Sargent Johnson, Beniamino Bufano, David Gilhooly, Jeremy Anderson, George Rickey, and Manuel Neri are among the sculptors whose works are on view. A Peter Voulkos one-ton sculpture in cast bronze was the major acquisition of 1970, presented by the Concours d'Antique of the Art Guild, the Oakland Museum Association.

In 1965 the Kahn Foundation, established by members of the pioneer merchant Kahn family, funded the Kahn Collection of more than one hundred nineteenth-century paintings, including portraits by William Smith Jewett, genre scenes by William Hahn, landscapes by Albert Bierstadt, a California neoclassic allegory by Domenico Tojetti, 1849 watercolors by Alfred Sully, and a rare painting of San Francisco's Seal Rocks by Martin Johnson Heade.

Significant images of California and the West in the graphics collection range from early views in drawings and daguerreotypes to the contemporary work of Ansel Adams. Among the major landmarks in photography are the studies of Yosemite and figures in motion by Eadweard Muybridge. Of the five thousand items, a substantial number are the works of Dorothea Lange, whose pictures of the rural-urban shift of the 1930s and 1940s are in negative and print form. Financial support has been obtained through Paul S. Taylor, D. B. and Mrs. D. Bell, Dr. and Mrs. Stanley Truman, and the Oakland Museum Association.

The display of crafts by California artists is a survey of the development of crafts, ranging from the art pottery of the late nineteenth century through each decade of the twentieth century. Noteworthy individual collections are the Esther Torosian Fuller Collection in Memory of Fenner Fuller, the Yvonne Greer Thiel Collection, and the Dorothy Wright Liebes Collection.

Outstanding exhibitions are "Tropical—Tropical Scenes by the Nineteenth-Century Painters of California"; "The Arrested Image," demonstrating the influence of the camera on contemporary multi-media work; "Mathews: Masterpieces of the California Decorative Style"; "The Society of Six"; and "A Period of Exploration, San Francisco, 1945-1950."—M. A.

Oakley, Annie. Stage name of **Phoebe Ann Moses** (1860-1926). Markswoman. Phoebe Ann Moses was born in Darke County, Ohio. Her father died when she was six. She learned to shoot at eight and soon contributed to the family support with money earned from supplying game to a Cincinnati hotel. Its owner set up a match for her against Frank Butler, who did exhibition shooting between acts of a stock company show. She won and the following year, in 1876, married Butler. It was then that she adopted the professional name Annie Oakley. (She had previously altered her family name to Mozee.) While appearing at a St. Paul theater in 1884 Oakley was acclaimed by Sitting Bull, who dubbed her *Watanya cicilia* ("little sure shot"). That winter the Butlers were with the Sells Brothers Circus during the Cotton Exposition at New Orleans and offered their services to "Buffalo Bill" Cody's Wild West show, also playing there.

For seventeen years Annie Oakley was peerless wing and rifle shot for Buffalo Bill's Wild West. She would hit a cigarette being smoked by her husband or a dime held in his fingers. After two clay pigeons had been released, she would leap over a table, pick up a gun, and bring down both targets. Her shooting of card targets gave rise to the slang term "Annie Oakley" for a pass or complimentary ticket, commonly punched full of holes for identification. In rifle competition she scored 943 out of 1,000 glass balls tossed in the air and 4,772 out of 5,000 in nine hours with a shotgun. The show's engagement at Queen Victoria's Golden Jubilee in 1887 brought her world fame, and she left the show for a solo tour of European capitals. She also toured with Pawnee Bill's Wild West and in the melodrama *Deadwood Dick* before rejoining the Buffalo Bill show in 1889 for a tour that included France, Spain, Italy, Austria, and Germany. One of the show's greatest seasons was at the World's Columbian Exposition in Chicago in 1893.

At the close of the 1901 season the show train had a head-on collision with a freight train, and Oakley suffered severe internal injuries. After several operations she recovered slowly; white-haired after the wreck, she never recovered her old-time vigor, but her shooting skill returned. In 1902-03 she appeared in the melodrama *The Western Girl* and toured with the Young Buffalo Wild West, 1911-13. In 1915 the Butlers joined the staff of the Carolina Hotel, Pinehurst, North Carolina, where they taught and demonstrated rifle, shotgun, and skeet shooting. During World War I they toured army camps giving exhibitions and instruction. She was crippled in an auto accident in 1921 and went back to Darke County, where she died on November 3, 1926. Frank Butler died twenty days later.

It was showmanship as well as skill that made Oakley "America's sweetheart" and her name a household word. Small and pretty—she weighed about one hundred pounds—she was personality in movement. Offstage, however, she was puritanical. Her other great skill was needlework and embroidery. She was quiet and sedate, little like the brash, extroverted heroine depicted in comic books, movies, television sequences, and the Irving Berlin musical *Annie Get Your Gun* that perpetuated her fame. Although she was never west of Ohio except on tours, she came to typify the western girl.

Courtney Ryley Cooper, *Annie Oakley, Woman at Arms* (1927), is contemporary to the subject matter; Cooper was a press agent for shows in which she appeared. Some errors on the personal side are corrected by Oakley's niece, Annie Fern Swartwount, in *Missie, An Historical Biography* (1947). Walter Havighurst, *Annie Oakley of the Wild West* (1954), is based on extensive research.—D. R.

Occaneechi Trading Path. This famous trail led from Bermuda Hundred on the James River by way of Fort Henry at the falls of the Appomattox to the Indian town of Occaneechi on the Roanoke River. From the latter place it led down across western North and South Carolina to the Savannah River at a point near present-day Augusta, Georgia. It crossed through the hunting grounds of both the Catawba and Cherokee. It also crossed the valleys of the Broad, Congaree, and Savannah rivers.

Like most Indian trails, the origin of this one is obscured in Indian antiquity. During the latter part of the seventeenth and first half of the eighteenth centuries the path was a route of penetration to the frontier for the explorers who went out from Colonel Abraham Wood's Fort Henry. When settlers began moving into the Piedmont in the eighteenth century many of them moved along the old trading path into the interior. Even today, major highways in the Piedmont follow the general directions of the old trail.

See William E. Meyer, "Indian Trails of the Southeast," in Bureau of American Ethnology, *Forty-second Annual Report, 1924-25* (1928).—T. D. C.

Ochoa, Esteban (1831-1888). Businessman. A native of Chihuahua, Mexico, Ochoa was sent to Kansas City as a youth to study English and mercantile practices. Becoming a naturalized citizen, he established a prosperous firm in Mesilla, New Mexico, and later in partnership with Pinkney R. Tully opened branch stores in Arizona. The two men also engaged in freighting and operated a stage line from Yuma and Tucson, Arizona, to Santa Fe, New Mexico, by which they amassed a considerable fortune. Headquarters for the firm became Tucson, from which Ochoa was expelled during the Confederate occupation for refusing to take an oath of allegiance to the South. With the triumph of Union forces, he returned and recovered his property.

Ochoa suffered greatly from Apache raids. In one instance Indians drove off all his draft oxen, slaughtered them, and dried the meat on a butte near the Salt River, known thereafter as Jerked Beef Butte. With railroad development in the early 1880s, his freighting business collapsed and he was said to have suffered a personal loss of over $100,000. He was active in the foundation of public education in Arizona, donated land for the first school in Tucson, and served one term as mayor of that city. When he died, Ochoa was regarded as a leading spokesman for Spanish-Americans in southern Arizona and New Mexico.

A brief biography of Ochoa appears in James H. McClintock, *Arizona*, vol. II (1916). His business activities are summarized in Howard Lamar, *The Far Southwest, 1846-1912* (1966).—M. Si.

Oddie, Tasker L. (1870-1950). Nevada politician and mineowner. Born in Brooklyn, New York, Oddie trained for the law. He went to Nevada in 1898 as a personal representative of the wealthy Anson Phelps Stokes, who owned property in central Nevada. Oddie decided to stay in Nevada and opened law offices at Austin and at Belmont. In 1900 he became associated with Jim Butler in the development of a number of mines in the new boom camp of Tonopah in Nye County. Oddie entered politics in Nevada when he was elected to the state senate from Nye County in 1904. He filed to run for governor on the Republican ticket in 1910 and shortly thereafter announced that he was a "Progressive or Insurgent Republican" like Hiram Johnson of California. His lack of funds forced him to conduct a "shoestring" campaign by automobile throughout the state. His campaign not only won him the election but gave him a deep appreciation of the need for a good highway system. In 1912, since he was not running for election, he refused to commit himself to Theodore Roosevelt's Progressive party although he earlier had indicated his sympathy for Roosevelt. He was defeated for reelection as governor in 1914 and in 1918. However, he was elected to the United States Senate in 1920 and reelected in 1926. He was defeated by Pat McCarran in 1932. His most important work as a senator was obtaining the location of the federal Hawthorne Naval Ammunition Depot in Nevada and the

passage of the Oddie-Colton bill, which provided extensive highway benefits for Nevada and other western states.

There is a substantial collection of Oddie papers at the Huntington Library, San Marino, California, and a less important collection at the Nevada Historical Society Library in Reno, Nevada. The best—and only full-length—biographical treatment is Loren Chan, *Sagebrush Statesman: Tasker L. Oddie of Nevada* (1973). —R. R. E.

O'Donel, Charles M. (1860-1933). New Mexico cattleman. O'Donel was born in County Mayo, Ireland, and graduated from Britain's famed Sandhurst Military College. After service in the first Boer War and Zulu War, he decided to resign his captain's commission and emigrate to the United States. In 1885 he came to the Texas Panhandle as a cowhand and began learning the ranching business from the bottom up. He then moved to New Mexico, where he became manager of the large, eastern-owned Bell Ranch in San Miguel County. There he developed a herd of finely bred Herefords that in time became famous throughout the Southwest. By 1900 O'Donel was running cattle on one million acres. Despite poor health he remained in charge of the Bell Ranch until a year before his death.

Although O'Donel was a formal and reserved man, he believed that the livestock industry could be greatly helped by organized activity, and willingly served as president of the New Mexico Cattle and Horse Growers' Association for two terms and as an officer in the American National Livestock Association. By the time of his death O'Donel had also collected a library of more than three thousand books.—H. R. L.

O'Fallon, Benjamin (1793-1842). Indian agent and trader. O'Fallon was born in Lexington, Kentucky, son of Dr. James O'Fallon, the notorious land-speculator. Left fatherless in early childhood, he and his brother John were reared and educated in St. Louis by their maternal uncle, Governor William Clark, the famous explorer. Benjamin began independent trade with the Sioux in 1816 and, through the patronage of his uncle, became Indian agent at Prairie du Chien in 1817, making treaties with the Oto and Ponca tribes. In 1819 he was appointed Indian agent for the upper Missouri and accompanied Major Stephen H. Long's Yellowstone expedition as far as Council Bluffs, where he made his agency headquarters. During 1821 he took a group of Pawnee on a celebrated tour of eastern cities and in 1825 was part of General Henry Atkinson's expedition to overawe the Indians of the upper Missouri, concluding fifteen treaties with the tribes of that region. O'Fallon was an effective agent, possessing sympathy for Indian sensibilities and a knack for their style of oratory.

Resigning his agency post in 1827, O'Fallon in the later years of his life became active in Missouri politics as a Jacksonian and increased his interests in the Indian trade. He was a principal of the Missouri Fur Company and was responsible for the relative friendship of the Indians to that organization. Throughout his life, O'Fallon's own talents were substantially aided by his family connection with the Clarks, whose informal dynasty largely controlled Missouri politics and trade in the early nineteenth century.

See J. S. Morton et al., *Illustrated History of Nebraska*, vol. II (1906); and J. C. Parrish, "The Intrigues of Dr.

James O'Fallon," *Mississippi Valley Historical Review*, vol. 17 (1930).—P. R. M.

Ogden, Peter Skene (1794-1854). Fur trapper and explorer. As an employee of the Hudson's Bay Company, Ogden explored much of the West, including the Snake River region, the Oregon country, the Great Salt Lake, the Bear River drainage system, and most of northern California. In 1828 he also discovered and traced the entire course of the Humboldt River. Ogden's accomplishments rank him with Jedediah Smith as a major explorer of the fur-trade period.

Born in Quebec City, Canada, of American loyalist parents, Ogden grew up in Montreal where his father was assigned to a judgeship. Entering the fur trade before he was twenty, he worked briefly for John Jacob Astor's American Fur Company in the Great Lakes region before joining the vigorous North West Company at a time when it was engaged in fierce competition with the Hudson's Bay Company. Ogden proved to be so lawless and brutal to his competitors, however, that he was sent to the Pacific Northwest in 1818 virtually as an outlaw and was dropped by the North West Company in 1820-21. After the merger of the North West Company and the Hudson's Bay Company Sir George Simpson hired Ogden to run the Spokane House district and in 1824 placed him in charge of the Snake country fur brigade. Simpson ordered Ogden to trap the interior ruthlessly in order to create a fur desert that would seal off the Americans from the more valuable Columbia River grounds.

Ogden's first Snake River expedition (1824-25) took him as far east as the Bitterroot River and then south to Bear River and the Cache valley, Utah. Though he arrived a year after James Bridger's party first saw Great Salt Lake, Ogden's party was the first to make a contemporary record of its existence. While in Utah Ogden encountered a party of American free trappers under Johnson Gardner. Gardner ordered him to leave, claiming that the Canadian was on American soil (both were actually trespassing on Mexican soil), and offered such high prices for beaver skins that twenty-five of Ogden's trappers were persuaded to abandon the Hudson's Bay Company and work for the Americans.

Ogden's second expedition (1825-26) took him south from the Columbia to the Deschutes River in Oregon and east over the Blue Mountains into the Snake River country. This time he succeeded in making a magnificent catch of beaver and other furs. On his third trip (1826-27) Ogden traveled south from Walla Walla (Fort Nez Percé) to the headwaters of the Deschutes, and then to Klamath Lake, and perhaps as far as the Pit River in northern California. It was on this trip that he saw Mount Shasta. The next year Ogden was back on the Snake River competing with American trappers. In 1828-29 he moved into Utah, explored the northern edge of Great Salt Lake, and was the first white man to locate and trace the Humboldt to its sink in Nevada. Ogden's discovery helped end a persistent rumor that the mythical Bonaventura River flowed from Great Salt Lake to the Pacific.

Ogden's last expedition was in many ways both his most significant and his least known. Designed as a trip to the Gulf of California, he traveled south from Oregon through the Great Basin to the Colorado River. Although suffering great hardships and a full-scale attack

Peter Skene Ogden. (Library of Congress)

by the Mohave, he did reach the Gulf of California and became the first man to make the gruelling north-south trip. Ogden then crossed the Sierra at Tehachapi, or Walker Pass, and explored the San Joaquin and Sacramento valleys of California. While trapping there, he and Ewing Young's party met and traveled together for a time. Ogden then took the now familiar trail that led him from the Pit River back to the Oregon country. Tragedy struck on the last leg of the journey, when Ogden lost nine men and his precious journals while crossing the Columbia. The careful reports and maps made by Ogden and his assistant, William Kittson, illuminated the geography of the West. Their findings were so significant they were incorporated into the illustrious maps of Aaron Arrowsmith in Britain and A. H. Brué in France.

The harsh life of a fur brigade was such that Ogden himself said it "makes a man sixty in a few years." So, after completing his six expeditions, he went north to manage Fort Simpson. He was then sent to the Stikine River near the Alaskan coast to build a new outpost, but the presence of a stronger, if illegal, Russian fort on the Stikine forced him to abandon the effort. In the diplomatic controversy that followed, the British managed to exact advantageous trading privileges on the Alaskan coast from the Russians. In 1835 "M'sieu Pete," as his workers called Ogden, became chief factor of the New Caledonia district for nine years. Then, after sharing the management of Fort Vancouver for a time, he became chief factor from 1845 until 1852.

Obviously the short, dark, tough, joke-loving youth— whom Ross Cox once described as "the terror of the Indians and the delight of all gay fellows"—had matured into a wise and diplomatic servant for the Hudson's Bay Company. After the Whitman massacre at Walla Walla in 1837, it was Ogden who successfully negotiated the return of nearly fifty white captives held by the Indians. Wealthy in his later years, Ogden traveled to Europe and New York, but he preferred to live in the West. He died at the home of a son-in-law in Oregon City with his common-law Indian wife at his side. A year later his *Traits of American Indian Life and Character. By A Fur Trader* (1855) appeared.

See E. E. Rich, ed., *Peter Skene Ogden's Snake Country Journal, 1824-25 and 1825-26* (1950). Ogden's other journals, edited by T. C. Elliott, are in the *Quarterly of the Oregon Historical Society* (1909-13). See also Ted J. Warner, "Peter Skene Ogden," in L. R. Hafen, ed., *The Mountain Men and the Fur Trade of the Far West*, vol. III (1966).—G. B. D.

Ogden, Utah. The second largest city in Utah, Ogden is located on a delta formed by the Weber and Ogden rivers as they flowed into prehistoric Lake Bonneville in Weber valley, thirty-five miles northwest of Salt Lake City. Immediately east of the city lie the rugged Wasatch Mountains. Named after Peter Skene Ogden (1794-1854), a Britisher who trapped in the rivers and streams in 1825, the site was first settled in 1846 by Miles Goodyear. Goodyear built a stockade called Fort Buenaventura but sold out in 1847 to the Mormons. Captain James Brown of the Mormon Battalion settled the new property, and for a time the town was called Brownsville. The name Ogden was reassigned by the State of Deseret in 1850. The town was incorporated in 1851.

The advent of the transcontinental railroad in 1869 transformed Ogden from an agricultural community into an important western rail center. Still a major distribution center, Ogden is the location of missile plants, canneries, stockyards, and government manufacturing and storage plants. It is also the location of Utah's reformatory for boys, Utah's institution for the deaf and blind, and Weber State College, founded in 1889.

See Earl T. Pardoe, *Lorin Farr: Pioneer* (1953). —L. J. A.

Ohio, settlement of. The first European to visit Ohio probably was the French fur trader Louis Jolliet, who was in the area of Lake Erie in 1669. About the same time René Robert Cavelier, Sieur de La Salle, supposedly discovered the Ohio River. English fur traders traveled to the Mackinac region by way of Lake Erie in 1685 and within a few years traders from Carolina, Virginia, and Pennsylvania were strengthening British claims to the Ohio country. At the same time the British continued their competition with the French for the friendship of the local Indians. The major tribes of the region were the Miami, Shawnee, Wyandot, and Delaware. Some of America's most famous chiefs and warriors lived in the area: Tecumseh, Blue Jacket, and Cornstalk (Shawnee); Tarhe or Crane (Wyandot); Little Turtle (Miami); and Pontiac (Ottawa).

Both France and England remained interested in Ohio, principally because of its rich supply of furs. Thus a clash between the two European powers soon became inevitable. When France ordered Pierre Joseph de Céloron de Blainville down the Ohio in 1749 to bury leaden plates claiming French ownership, the British followed the next year by sending Christopher Gist into the same

area. His visit stimulated apprehension by the Indians and made them increasingly hostile toward English traders. It also intensified fears of the French and caused them a short time later to attack the English settlement at Pickawillany. Young George WASHINGTON of Virginia carried out Lieutenant Governor Robert Dinwiddie's orders in 1753 and warned the French against erecting forts near the Forks of the Ohio.

When the French refused to leave the area Dinwiddie ordered the construction of Fort Pitt, but before it could be completed the enemy seized the fortification and renamed it Fort Duquesne. The commander of the strategic post then sent a detachment after Colonel Washington's retreating forces and defeated them on July 3, 1754, at Great Meadows. This series of events triggered the French and Indian War in America, which did not end until the Treaty of Paris in 1763 when France surrendered its claims to Canada and all its land north of the Ohio River.

British problems in the Northwest were far from over, for Chief Pontiac and other Ohio Indians were soon laying siege to former French forts and settlements between present-day Pittsburgh and the Great Lakes (see PONTIAC'S REBELLION). The turning point came at Detroit when the British successfully withstood a five months' Indian siege. Soon afterward the British created a new problem with the Proclamation of 1763, which temporarily forbade the American colonists to settle west of the Alleghenies. Various land companies already had projected settlements for the Ohio country and were far from happy over the development. Resentment on the part of the colonists intensified in 1774 when the British government made the area north of the Ohio River and east of the Mississippi part of the Province of Quebec.

Frontier encroachment by whites and Indian retaliations that same year quickly produced Lord Dunmore's War, in which Lord Dunmore, governor of Virginia, took the field against the Ohio Indians and successfully drove them out of the Kentucky country. During the American Revolution, which followed, Ohio became the scene of invasions and counterinvasions from the British headquarters in Detroit and the American stronghold at Fort Pitt. The results proved inconclusive and the Indian menace continued long after the Treaty of Paris (1783), when the Northwest theoretically became a part of the United States. In addition, land claims to the Ohio country made by several states needed resolving and the British were refusing to evacuate key military and fur-trading posts in the area.

Meanwhile, New York and Massachusetts surrendered all their Ohio lands, but Virginia kept its Military District to satisfy soldier bounty claims. Connecticut held on to the Western Reserve in order to extend grants to citizens whose property had been destroyed by Tory raids during the American Revolution. In preparation for large-scale immigration, Congress under the Articles of Confederation enacted the Land Ordinance of 1785 to provide for the survey of the Old Northwest into townships and sections. The famous Northwest Ordinance of 1787 further provided for a framework of government and the ultimate creation of three to five new states.

In 1786 a group of New England veterans known as the Ohio Company of Associates obtained title to a large tract of land beyond the Ohio. General Rufus Putnam arrived at the mouth of the Muskingum River two years later with the first group of settlers. When the new governor of the Northwest Territory, Arthur ST. CLAIR, arrived early in July 1788 to set up the territorial government, the general already had laid out the capital city, Marietta. As more settlers arrived from New England and the middle states, additional towns sprang up throughout southwestern Ohio. It was about this time also that a group of New York speculators organized the Scioto Company and laid plans to colonize a large area north and west of the Ohio Company grant. The project collapsed, however, after the company failed to meet its payments.

Governor St. Clair moved the territorial capital down the Ohio River to Losantiville, the site of Fort Washington, in 1790 and renamed the town Cincinnati. Before the end of the decade the British had evacuated the northwest forts, the important settlements of Chillicothe, Cleveland, and Steubenville had been founded, and several frontier battles had been fought to secure the settlements against the Indians. American forces under General Josiah Harmar suffered a disastrous defeat in 1790 in the vicinity of present-day Fort Wayne, and one year later various Ohio tribes ambushed a sizable army led by St. Clair in present-day Mercer County. Finally on August 20, 1794, General Anthony Wayne avenged the defeat at FALLEN TIMBERS. Little Turtle and other important chiefs signed the Treaty of GREENVILLE the next year, whereby they agreed to abandon most of their Ohio lands to white settlement.

Wayne's victory paved the way for rapid immigration and by 1800 Ohio boasted a population of more than 45,000 people. By now it had achieved representative government in accordance with the Ordinance of 1787 and was looking forward to statehood. Governor St. Clair's strong Federalist beliefs caused him to delay action as long as possible. Republican leaders such as Thomas Worthington and Edward Tiffin secured the help of President Thomas Jefferson in getting the Ohio Enabling Act through Congress (April 30, 1802). The thirty-five delegates who assembled at Chillicothe on November 1, 1803, took only twenty-five days to draft a state constitution. Ohio entered the Union on March 1, 1803, as the seventeenth state, and for the next several years its politics were strongly dominated by Jeffersonian Republicans.

Thomas Worthington and John Smith were elected Ohio's first United States senators, along with Edwin Tiffin as governor and Jeremiah Morrow as representative to Congress. Before the capital was permanently located in the center of the state at Columbus, in 1816, it had been moved from Chillicothe to Zanesville and back to Chillicothe as a result of considerable political chicanery.

See John D. Barnhart, *Valley of Democracy: The Frontier Versus the Plantation in the Ohio Valley, 1775-1818* (1953); Randolph C. Downes, *Frontier Ohio, 1788-1802* (1935); Eugene R. Roseboom and Francis P. Weisenburger, *A History of Ohio* (1967); and Carl F. Wittke, ed., *The History of the State of Ohio*, 6 vols. (1941-44). —W. E. H.

Ohio River. See PHYSIOGRAPHY OF THE UNITED STATES: *Central Lowland;* RIVERMEN; and TRANSPORTATION ON THE MISSISSIPPI RIVER SYSTEM.

oil industry. During the twentieth century petroleum has become by all odds the West's most important mineral, far outstripping in value and significance the precious metals that earlier had brought such glamour to so many western areas. This rise of the West to national oil prominence was abrupt. At the turn of the century, the western states and territories were still a relatively inconsequential source of oil. Except for California, where earnest efforts to develop an oil industry had been going on since the middle 1860s, crude oil production elsewhere—Texas, Colorado, Kansas, Oklahoma Territory, and Wyoming—was indeed meager. Ohio, West Virginia, and Pennsylvania, in that order, were the leading oil states in 1900. That year California ranked fifth and the West's contribution to national production amounted to only about 9 percent of a total output of 63,621,000 barrels. In 1911, the year the Supreme Court dissolved the Standard Oil Trust, the West's share had grown to more than 72 percent of a national total of 220,449,000 barrels. Three of the five most prolific oil states—California, Oklahoma, and Louisiana—were west of the Mississippi River, and Texas was a close sixth. By 1968 the West was providing more than 95 percent of a national production of 3,320,000,000 barrels. Texas, Louisiana, and California were responsible for approximately 70 percent of this huge flow, but all of the trans-Mississippi states except Hawaii, Washington, Oregon, Idaho, Minnesota, and Iowa were at least marginal contributors.

The vast surge in the West had a profound effect on the national oil scene. As new oil field followed new oil field, particularly in the midcontinent, along the Gulf Coast, and in California, the soaring production gradually laid to rest an opinion common among petroleum scientists prior to World War I that the nation's oil resources would soon be exhausted and oil would be a mineral known only historically by about the middle of the twentieth century. One reason for setting up two naval oil reserves on public lands in Elk Hills and Buena Vista, California, in 1912, and at Teapot Dome, Wyoming, a little later, was to try to insure a supply of this more efficient fuel to the modern oil-burning navy against the prospect of future shortage.

Soaring western production also contributed to the decline of the dominance of the Standard Oil Trust over the national petroleum industry. The share of crude oil production controlled by the Trust declined from a little more than 85 percent in 1900 to less than 65 percent at the time of the dissolution decree. The new flush fields of flowing oil wells offered so many opportunities that not even the giant Standard Oil organization could respond speedily and effectively to all of them. In some cases, it chose not to respond; in others, its response was too slow to be effective; in still others, it was hampered by a hostile political climate, notably in Texas.

Standard was most active in California and in the midcontinent fields. In California it purchased in 1900 a small pioneer firm, the Pacific Coast Oil Company, which it redesignated the Standard Oil Company (California) in 1906. By 1911 the California subsidiary had become the leading oil enterprise in the Far West and was purchasing or producing 29 percent of the state's oil. This important subsidiary engaged in all aspects of the oil business except for producing and marketing overseas.

Standard's venture into the midcontinent was somewhat more complex. In 1895 one of the Trust's oil-producing subsidiaries, the Forest Oil Company, acquired leases in Kansas and Oklahoma Territory to seven hundred thousand acres of likely oil land, which were transferred in 1900 to the Prairie Oil & Gas Company, a large and newly organized subsidiary empowered to produce, buy, store, pipe, and refine petroleum. Prairie connected such flush fields of valuable light oil as the Glenn pool in Oklahoma with Standard's refineries as far away as the East Coast, and long before 1911 the company was taking the bulk of the highly prized midcontinent production. In 1909 the Trust organized another new subsidiary, the Standard Oil Company (Louisiana), to receive and refine midcontinent crude oil at Baton Rouge. Shortly the Louisiana company was producing, piping, storing, and marketing oil and oil products in its territory in addition to refining.

Standard was least active in the new oil region along the Texas Gulf Coast. Except for the surreptitious financing of the Security Oil Company, a major early-producing concern (later absorbed by the Magnolia Petroleum Company), Standard left the Gulf Coast fields largely to others. The well-known public antipathy to the Trust in Texas because of the flagrant behavior of its marketing affiliate, the Waters-Pierce Oil Company, probably was one reason, but another, surely, was the less attractive character of the heavy gravity, sulfurous Gulf crude oils.

Thus Texas offered the best opportunity for new competitors of Standard Oil to emerge. And emerge they did. Following the historic gusher at Spindletop near the Gulf Coast in 1901, two important oil enterprises known today as Texaco, Inc., and the Gulf Oil Corporation were organized. Currently, they rank among the ten largest American industrial corporations. A third important competitor, the Sun Oil Company, had earlier been active in the Lima-Indiana field, which originated in Lima, Ohio, and ran over into Indiana. After Spindletop, it transferred much of its energies to Texas. In each case, the expertise for operating these companies was brought in from the older oil regions, and their capital was also supplied largely from eastern and midwestern sources. The Mellons of Pittsburgh, who were well acquainted with the oil industry in western Pennsylvania, soon became dominant in the predecessor of the Gulf Oil Corporation; another family with Pennsylvania oil experience, the Laphams, who controlled the United States Leather Trust, and John W. Gates, the maverick capitalist, were the leading investors in the predecessor of Texaco, Inc.; the Pew family of Philadelphia and western Pennsylvania controlled the Sun Oil Company.

When production of the fields along the Gulf Coast sharply declined after 1905, two of Standard's new rivals, the predecessors of Texaco and Gulf, sought to offset this decline by building pipelines to the midcontinent fields. In competition with Prairie Oil & Gas, they quickly reduced Prairie's share of purchased production. A decade later the position of the Standard Oil companies in the midcontinent fields was further eroded by the growth of another series of oil firms—Sinclair Oil & Refining Corporation, Phillips Petroleum Company (an outgrowth of the Phillips Gas and Oil Company founded by Thomas Wharton Phillips), Cities

Service Company, and the Skelly Oil Company, among others.

In California, too, Standard was experiencing the competition of an increasing number of powerful oil firms. The oldest of these, the Union Oil Company, had been incorporated in 1890; like the new competitors in Texas, it had drawn essential oil skills and capital primarily from Pennsylvania. Another, the Associated Oil Company, was formed in 1901 by a large group of producers in the lower San Joaquin valley. Within a few years Associated came under the control of the Southern Pacific Railroad, which also set up a subsidiary, the Kern Trading & Oil Company, to produce oil on its railroad land grants. Similarly, the Santa Fe Railroad turned to oil development on its land grants. Another competitor, the General Petroleum Company, was put together by a group of prominent western entrepreneurs, representing shipping and utility interests, shortly before the dissolution of the Standard Oil Trust. And in 1913 Standard's worldwide rival, Royal Dutch Shell, invaded the California industry by acquiring rich oil lands at Coalinga in the San Joaquin valley after having begun to sell gasoline from Sumatra on the West Coast during the preceding year. The invaders soon built a refinery on San Francisco Bay connected by pipeline with Coalinga. Almost simultaneously, through another subsidiary, the Roxana Petroleum Company, Shell began putting together a second oil enterprise in the midcontinent fields.

The emergence of so many new and strong competitors for Standard Oil even prior to the antitrust decision in 1911 reduced markedly the importance of that decision. After 1900, the great growth and rapid geographic spread of the oil industry throughout much of the West made it impossible for even an organization as large as Standard Oil to hope to maintain its former dominance.

In passing, it can also be noted that the sequence of events leading to the antitrust suit were western in origin. In 1905 embattled Kansas producers prevailed on the Kansas attorney general to file suit against Prairie Oil & Gas, Standard's chief midcontinent subsidiary. At about the same time Congress asked the federal Bureau of Corporations to investigate Standard's operations in the Kansas oil fields. The bureau soon extended its inquiry to all phases of oil activity throughout the nation, with particular attention to the newer oil regions. Its voluminous reports led directly to the filing in November 1906 of a federal antitrust suit against Standard in the United States Circuit Court for the Eastern District of Missouri. The suit was fought to a decision adverse to Standard three years later. The Trust appealed the verdict only to have the Supreme Court deliver a confirming judgment in 1911.

The dissolution decree contributed thirty-three independents of varying sizes and functions to the changing shape of the industry. West of the Mississippi, the Standard Oil Company (California) and Prairie Oil & Gas were the two largest of the newly independent companies. Several of the independent companies with headquarters east of the Mississippi, notably the Standard Oil Company (New Jersey), the holding company for the old Trust, and the Standard Oil Company (Indiana), also had important investments in the West, particularly in and adjacent to the midcontinent fields.

During the early years of the century the oil industry was being changed not only in its competitive structure but also in its product market. The West contributed no less to the one than to the other. Prior to 1900 kerosine was the oil industry's chief money product. After 1900 the industry's "age of illumination" yielded to the "age of fuel," and after 1910 to the "age of motor fuel," in the nomenclature of the eminent Texas oil geologist Everette Lee De Golyer. The extent of the industry's growing importance in supplying the nation's energy needs may be indicated statistically. In 1900 petroleum and natural gas supplied a little more than 8 percent of the nation's energy, compared to nearly 90 percent for coal; today the oil industry's share has grown to approximately 75 percent of the national total.

There had always been residuum from the refining process that could be sold for fuel. What was new after the turn of the century, however, were huge stocks of heavy crude oil in the West, little suited for refining, which could provide cheap and abundant fuel in competition with costly imported coal. Well before 1900 local oil companies in California were looking to brewers, vintners, power companies, sugar beet refineries, iron and steel firms, cement companies, and brick and pottery works as outlets for their fuel. As output shot upward, the oil industry found important new fuel uses in powering railroad locomotives and ocean vessels. Indeed, during World War I railroads and steamships were burning more than half of California's oil for fuel. Crude oil from the midcontinent fields was usually too light and valuable for fuel uses, but the residuum after refining was available for such purposes. The heavy crude oils of the Texas Gulf Coast, by contrast, like those of California, found their primary market early in the century as cheap fuel.

Midcontinent crude oils and the refinable crude oils of California and Texas were increasingly highly prized after 1910 for their gasoline content. The number of motor vehicles, less than one hundred thousand in 1905 and less than five hundred thousand in 1910, jumped nearly twenty-fold in the following decade, making gasoline, a volatile and formerly lightly regarded by-product of the refining process, a Cinderella product for the oil industry. Crude oil that might have been sold directly for fuel prior to 1910 was thereafter much more likely to have been "topped" in simple refineries to save its gasoline fraction. Much of California's crude oil was exceptionally rich in high octane hydrocarbons, giving the gasoline of that state a naturally high octane rating.

The geographic conjunction of cheap fuel and gasoline had a substantial influence on the process of urbanization in communities near major oil fields. Cheap fuel helped foster industrialization in such new cities as Los Angeles and Houston. The ubiquitous motor car also gave them a sprawling character, as members of the middle class and, later, blue-collar workers roamed ever more widely seeking less crowded, more pleasant environments for their homes. The new western cities with their broad boulevards and vast suburban tracts were a striking contrast to the more congested urban East.

These booming years of oil production in the West can be viewed in another perspective consequential both to the oil industry and to the nation. During the first two decades of this century, applied scientists trained in

colleges and universities began to make their way toward positions of leadership in many industries for the first time, thus supplanting their more limited "on-the-job-trained" rivals of an earlier era. Within the oil industry, the new, more sophisticated leadership had much to do with the great increase in production. Such surface indications as oil seeps, which had served drillers of an earlier day, had already been largely explored; many of the prolific new fields of the West were to be found associated with anticlinal or other geologic structures that could be most readily discerned by a professional geologist. Once an oil field was discovered, skilled petroleum engineers could usually bring about a larger recovery of the oil than traditional methods permitted.

This movement toward scientific leadership in oil production was particularly marked in California. Fully one third of the more than two hundred professional petroleum engineers at work in the United States prior to 1920 were trained either at Stanford or at the University of California. This number was about as large as that for thirty-four colleges and universities east of the Mississippi and in Europe, and two and a half times as large as that for nineteen other schools west of the Mississippi, including the University of Southern California and the predecessor of the California Institute of Technology. The training of specialists in oil production has continued to take place primarily in the West, but since World War I it has been less highly concentrated, as a larger number of institutions, particularly in the midcontinent and Texas, have developed strong programs.

There are at least two reasons why Californians were so prominent in this rise of applied science within the oil industry. Both Stanford and the University of California were important centers for training specialists in the mining industries. Also, the boom in petroleum production following the turn of the century offered graduates of mining curricula alternatives to employment in gold and silver mining, which had long been declining in the Far West, and copper mining, for which the growth curve was no longer so steep.

Two California enterprises, the Union Oil Company and the Southern Pacific Railroad, were pioneers in the later 1890s in hiring professional geologists. Union's William W. Orcutt, a member of Stanford's first graduating class, became the key figure in his company's surging advance as a producer in several major California fields. Edwin T. Dumble, a former state geologist of Texas, was hired by the Southern Pacific and organized oil producing subsidiaries for the railroad in both Texas and California. He used geologists not only for exploration but also to bring about efficient production of the oil after discovery. The resident geologist (petroleum engineer) in the oil field was responsible for determining the location of new wells and the depth at which the casing should be set in order to keep water from seeping into and diminishing the value of the oil sands. Numerous young geologists and petroleum engineers from both Stanford and Berkeley served their apprenticeships with Southern Pacific companies and, later, their California, Texas, and midcontinent competitors.

One of these young technologists, Roy P. McLaughlin, left private enterprise to return to the California State Mining Bureau, where he lobbied for and then administered an effective statute to deal with the serious water problem in several of California's oil fields. This statute, passed in 1915 and signed by Governor Hiram Johnson, provided for a petroleum and gas department in the California State Mining Bureau staffed by technically trained specialists and headed by an oil and gas supervisor. The effect of this law was to make competent technical advice available to operators who might feel they could not afford the expense of a geologist which in turn upgraded and standardized oil field practices.

The influence of these technically trained young Californians ran outward from their home state to appropriate federal scientific agencies and to other oil regions. A few were engaged in surveying far western oil lands for the United States Geological Survey. Two of their monographs provided the scientific basis for President William Howard Taft's withdrawal of potential oil lands from the public domain in California in 1909, thus bringing to an end the long period in the West of easy transfer of public oil lands into private ownership.

Another federal agency, the recently created Bureau of Mines, was staffed to a far greater extent by the young Californians. Organized in 1910 to promote the conservation and development of the nation's mineral resources, it set up a petroleum division in 1914. The first four men to head this division were Stanford-trained. In 1917 the division opened a national petroleum experiment station at Bartlesville, Oklahoma. Five of the first six in charge of that important facility were also Californians.

In addition to spreading information concerning more effective practices in oil production, the bureau carried on numerous pioneering studies. One important subject for research was the conservation of natural gas, which ignorant operators allowed to blow away by drilling far too many closely spaced wells in an at times frantic fight for oil. The bureau's research studies pointed to the role of gas as a lifting agent and the larger recoveries of oil that gas made possible if it was not dissipated by unwise drilling. Indeed, as far back as 1916, James O. Lewis, the first head of the Bartlesville station and later of the petroleum division, was advocating the unitized operation of oil fields for the mutual protection of their multiple contesting owners. The next year he published a trail-blazing bulletin that ultimately led to the widespread injection of gas or water into the underground reservoirs to bring about renewed production after the original gas supply had been exhausted.

As the national oil industry increasingly recognized the economic value of the work of these young scientists, new opportunities opened up for them outside government either as consultants or on company payrolls. Nowhere did they find a more cordial reception than in the Cities Service Company and its subordinate units in the Henry L. Doherty organization. Doherty, a brilliant self-taught engineer, had followed closely the work of the petroleum division and highly esteemed its technical reports. During the 1920s he was the most prominent—and, at times, somewhat lonely—industrial leader crusading for sounder conservation practices.

Almost simultaneous with this concern for a larger recovery of crude oil from its underground reservoirs, and thus a reduction in "physical waste," was a conjoined concern for "economic waste" when flush fields spilled their plenty wildly over the surrounding landscape, breaking the market and causing the price of oil

to drop precipitously. An early significant effort to deal with the problem of economic waste occurred in Oklahoma in 1915. Legislation was passed empowering the state's corporation commission to fix production quotas within fields in order to reduce the supply of crude oil to an amount no greater than could be handled by existing transportation and marketing facilities and to an amount that did not exceed "reasonable market demand." This legislation, enacted when production in the great Cushing and Healdton fields was running wild, was of little effect at the time, but it pointed the way to more efficient procedures later on.

Economic waste again became a live issue in Oklahoma in 1927 and 1928 when the roaring production of the prolific Seminole and Oklahoma City fields revived memories of Cushing and Healdton a dozen or more years earlier. In the fall of 1928 the Oklahoma Corporation Commission took the drastic step of trying to limit statewide production to less than 700,000 barrels daily. But the greed of many operators, combined with uncertainty as to the commission's legal powers, reduced sharply the effectiveness of this and other attempts to prorate production and to limit the drilling of new wells.

Moreover, economic waste was not a matter that could be handled within the boundaries of a single state. By the end of 1931 this had become abundantly clear when production in the mammoth East Texas field, largest in the nation's history, drove oil prices down to less than 10 cents per barrel. Extensive litigation and martial law followed before a new statute, the Market Demand Act, was passed in 1932. Under its authority, the Texas Railroad Commission began the exhausting task of trying to restrict production through prorationing on an equitable basis. Try though it did, the commission's efforts were undermined by a large flow of "hot oil" produced in violation of its orders which frequently found a market outside Texas. This weakness was one contributing factor to the idea of an Interstate Oil Compact. However, such an agreement, supported by the federal government, was not reached until the summer of 1935.

Meanwhile, it had appeared for a time that the federal government might become the agency for bringing order out of the chaos in the oil industry. During the summer of 1933, under the aegis of the New Deal's National Recovery Administration, the oil industry drew up a code authorizing the federal government to issue permits for drilling and to fix production quotas. Administration of the code was delegated to the Secretary of the Interior, Harold Ickes. By executive order, he gradually curbed the flow of hot oil from Texas. But adverse court decisions, culminating in the Supreme Court case in May 1935 which declared the NRA unconstitutional, and the industry's fears that Ickes would try to convert oil into a public utility persuaded industry spokesmen to seek a new means of control. This control was provided by the Interstate Oil Compact of 1935.

During its early months, the Interstate Oil Compact regulating production was signed by six major oil states (later joined by most others, except California) and was ratified by Congress in August. Previously, in February of that year, Congress had passed the Connally "Hot Oil" Act to stop interstate shipments of oil in excess of quotas prescribed by state regulatory boards or commissions. And still earlier, in 1933, the federal government had provided one other essential support for the new plan. At that time, the Department of Interior's Bureau of Mines had begun the practice of making monthly forecasts of refinery demand, on the basis of which the state members of the compact could agree on appropriate production quotas. Thus a formerly chaotic industry was reduced to order and a more efficient rate of production established. There is no question that the new pattern of cooperation between states and with the federal government has encouraged a more rational development of the nation's oil resources, but there is a lurking suspicion in some quarters that (as in the case of the oil depletion allowance) this regulatory pattern, further supported by federally enforced quotas on foreign oil imports, may be too favorable to the domestic oil industry.

Prompted by the growing and seemingly insatiable demand for an increasing range of oil products, including petrochemicals and diesel and jet fuels, the search for oil has gone on unceasingly throughout the West. It has been carried on with various degrees of success in the coastal region north of Los Angeles, the Los Angeles basin area, and the San Joaquin valley in California, almost statewide across Texas from the long Gulf Coast and eastern Texas to the Panhandle and western Texas, spilling over into New Mexico, Louisiana, Oklahoma, Kansas, Arkansas, Montana, Wyoming, and Colorado, and in the Williston basin area of North Dakota. Particularly from the 1930s onward, the industry has been more and more attracted by the possibilities for oil offshore, especially along the coasts of Louisiana, Texas, and California, and, in the 1960s, by the enormous potential of Alaska.

Offshore drilling occurred at Summerland on the Santa Barbara Channel in California as far back as 1894 and at Black Duck Bay in Texas as early as 1917, but systematic efforts awaited an improved technology, which gradually emerged in the 1930s. Later exploration of the tidelands was caught up in the swirling controversy over their ownership between the states and the federal government. The matter was not finally settled until 1953 when federal legislation gave the states title for three miles offshore on the Atlantic and Pacific coasts and for three marine leagues into the Gulf of Mexico. Beyond these limits, the federal government retained ownership, offering the possibility of two different lessors, depending on the attractiveness of the submerged lands and their distance offshore. None of the offshore lands have proved more productive than those adjacent to the Louisiana coast; in 1968 wells on these lands yielded almost 900,000 barrels per day, which was approximately 10 percent of the nation's total production of crude oil. Offshore wells in Texas and southern California have been providing a lesser increment.

Exploration for oil in Alaska has gone on since before the turn of the century, but the development of a modest commercial oil production in that great and remote state, principally in and around Cook's Inlet in southern Alaska, has been largely a story of the 1960s. Then, in January 1968 there occurred the vast discovery on Alaska's frozen North Slope, near Prudhoe Bay, the precise extent of which is still a matter of some conjecture. It seems likely, however, that the North Slope may hold beneath its frozen surface from 25 to 60 billion barrels

of oil, far surpassing Texas and at least doubling the current known oil reserves in the United States. It has touched off an oil boom that promises to make the earlier Klondike boom appear like a search for small change. Nine major oil companies, either singly or in various combinations, paid the Alaskan government more than $900 million for the right to explore approximately 1,300 square miles along the North Slope. Construction of a trans-Alaska pipeline to deliver the North Slope oil to the ice-free port of Valdez was held up for several years because of environmental concerns. These were swept aside late in 1973 by legislative action in the wake of the energy crisis. The 789-mile pipeline was ready for operation in 1977.

These and other major oil companies have been the result of a trend toward growth and consolidation that has been going on steadily for decades. The domestic production of these companies has been found, inevitably, almost wholly in the West, while their sales outlets have gradually expanded to encompass all of the fifty states, which provide the world's largest and most secure market for oil products. Over recent decades, many important companies have been acquired or merged. Thus the largest American oil company, Standard Oil Company (New Jersey), in 1919 acquired a half-interest and later sole ownership of the Humble Oil & Refining Company, a prominent Texas concern. Also in 1919 the Standard Oil Company (Indiana), a leading producer in Louisiana and Arkansas, bought the Dixie Oil Company, and within four years thereafter completed the purchase of the Midwest Refining Company, which controlled the bulk of Wyoming's crude oil production. A little later, in 1925, the Standard Oil Company (New York), today the Mobil Oil Corporation, purchased the Magnolia Petroleum Company in Texas and the General Petroleum Corporation in California. The Associated Oil Company, freed from the Southern Pacific Railroad in the 1920s in an antitrust suit, for many years was linked to the Tidewater Oil Company on the East Coast before its marketing facilities were sold to the Phillips Petroleum Company in the middle 1960s. The Standard Oil Company of California, which had acquired in 1926 the remaining oil lands of the Southern Pacific, invaded the eastern United States under its Chevron hallmark after World War II and in 1961 moved deep into the south Atlantic states by purchasing the Standard Oil Company (Kentucky). Meanwhile, using its own resources, Texaco by 1930 had extended its producing and marketing facilities to California. During the 1950s the Gulf Oil Corporation also moved to the Pacific after purchasing a small California firm, the Wilshire Oil Company. In the following decade the Union Oil Company leaped from the West to the East Coast by acquiring the historic Pure Oil Company, while the Atlantic Refining Company made a countermove west by purchasing the Richfield Oil Company.

These evidences of growth depending domestically on a resource today almost wholly western in origin might be taken as an evidence for optimism concerning the economic future of much of the trans-Mississippi West. And indeed it can. In 1968 the value of crude oil and natural gas produced in the West amounted to more than $13 billion, exclusive of additional increments accruing from the processing and transportation of these raw materials. In contributing to the western economy, the black gold of the twentieth century is a notable successor to the more glamorous precious metals of an earlier day.

But in its effects the oil industry in recent years has proven to be a mixed blessing. If in conjunction with the automobile it has increased the options as to the kind of life most of us choose to live, it has also led to highway slaughter and air pollution. The production and transportation of crude oil has also given rise to widespread concern. A tanker rupture or collision, or an offshore well run wild, as in the Santa Barbara Channel or along the Gulf Coast, means miles of fouled beaches and threatened bird and marine life. Such accidents are intolerable for a society learning to treasure its increasingly scarce natural and recreational resources. A great debate in planning to unlock Alaska's huge oil resources along the North Slope is the effect an eight-hundred-mile heated pipeline will have on the delicate ecological balance of that vast wilderness.

The standard history of the oil industry is H. A. Williamson et al., *The American Petroleum Industry*, 2 vols. (1959, 1963). The best sources of petroleum statistics are *Minerals Yearbook*, published annually by the Bureau of Mines of the U.S. Department of the Interior, and the American Petroleum Institute, *Petroleum Facts and Figures* (1967). The best bibliography is E. B. Swanson, *A Century of Oil and Gas in Books* (1960). Other useful company, regional, or technical histories include the following: American Petroleum Institute, *History of Petroleum Engineering* (1961); Kendall Beaton, *Enterprise in Oil: A History of Shell in the United States* (1957); D. J. Chasan, *Klondike '70: The Alaska Oil Boom* (1971); K. K. Landes, *Petroleum Geology of the United States*, 2nd ed. (1970); Henrietta Larson and Kenneth Porter, *History of Humble Oil and Refining Company* (1959); C. C. Rister, *Oil!: Titan of the Southwest* (1949); Francis W. Schruben, *Wea Creek to El Dorado: Oil in Kansas, 1860-1920* (1971); and G. T. White, *Formative Years in the Far West: A History of the Standard Oil Company of California and Predecessors Through 1919* (1962).—G. T. W.

Ojibwa (Chippewa) Indians. The Ojibwa Indians are a northern Algonquian people who in the eighteenth and early nineteenth century occupied the entire northern Great Lakes region. Their territory stretched from the north shore of Lake Huron west across Lake Superior and Minnesota as far as the Turtle Mountains of North Dakota, and from upper Wisconsin and Michigan in the south to Lake Winnipeg and James Bay in the north. When first contacted by Jesuit missionaries in 1640, they were reported to be inhabiting a comparatively small region around Sault Ste. Marie, but during the period of the French fur trade they rapidly expanded their territory. This expansion has generally been explained by the military advantage the Ojibwa possessed by ready access to firearms from French traders, but recent study indicates that the importance of early firearms in intertribal warfare has been much overrated, and that most of the new Ojibwa territory was vacant or taken from tribes too weak to resist in any case. Ojibwa groups moved into the Huron country after the Iroquois had destroyed that tribe in 1649. When the Ojibwa drove the Fox from northern Wisconsin in the eighteenth century, that tribe had already been reduced by a war with the French. And while the Ojibwa have been credited with expelling the Sioux (Dakota) from

northern Minnesota and pushing them out onto the Plains after a bitter war, most of the Sioux had already moved from the region before the Ojibwa arrived, and only scattered remnants put up resistance.

The prehistoric origins of the Ojibwa are undetermined. Among the southern bands there is a strong tradition, as well as some anthropological evidence, of a late prehistoric migration from the eastern seaboard in company with ancestral Ottawa and Potawatomi peoples, who split off and formed separate tribes when reaching the Straits of Mackinac. In historic times these tribes and the Ojibwa formed a loose confederacy known as the League of the Three Brothers or Three Fires. The northern Ojibwa groups, on the other hand, were so closely connected with the Cree and Maskegon as to be indistinguishable to most observers, and archaeological evidence points to Ojibwa presence north of Lake Superior from earliest prehistoric times.

The Ojibwa were one of the most populous Indian groups on the continent. Their numbers are estimated as having been approximately 35,000 in 1650, but they were so diffused and had so many associated units that a precise determination is impossible for any period. At no time were the Ojibwa a politically unified people. Their traditional organization was that of extended kinship units living in small local bands, and it is more accurate to refer to the Ojibwa as an Indian ethnic group, instead of as a "tribe." They did speak a common language, shared a general though regionally varied uniformity of customs, and thought of themselves as one people. "Ojibwa" is their native name and refers to the characteristic puckered seam of their moccasins. "Chippewa" is a white corruption of the term.

Their social organization was based on exogamous, patrilineal, totemic clans, twenty-three of which have been identified. Polygamy was common. Originally a woodlands people, the Ojibwa cultivated fields of corn, beans, and squash, but as they expanded westward and associated more with prairie people, hunting became the dominant source of subsistence. Wild rice, gathered from the lakes abounding in their country, was the primary vegetable food, and continues so among many modern Ojibwa. They lived in semipermanent villages of round bark lodges, though skin tepees were commonly used among western bands. Their religious practices followed the general Algonquian pattern, based on a general pantheistic animism. The Ojibwa were more strongly resistant to missionaries than most Indians, and Christianity did not much affect them until the twentieth century. The modern pan-Indian peyote religion is widespread among the Ojibwa.

The Ojibwa were friendly with the French traders who began to come among them during the 1640s, and the economic bond was sealed by a large number of interracial marriages by the Canadian *voyageurs* and *coureurs de bois*. When British officials replaced the French in Canada after 1763, the Ojibwa resented the newcomers' racial arrogance and joined in Pontiac's futile attempt to expel them from the frontier. But British trade soon became as essential as the French had been, and as American settlement approached the edges of the Ojibwa country after the American Revolution, the Ojibwa supported the Confederacy of Tecumseh and sided with the British during the War of 1812. Their distance from the centers of fighting kept Ojibwa participation in these conflicts at a low level, and after the peace of 1815 they did not again resist the American advance.

The subsequent peacefulness of United States relations with the Ojibwa was due to the remoteness of their homeland from the main thrust of white expansion and to the slowness with which white settlers advanced across their country when they did arrive. The Ojibwa had the time to adapt slowly to the domination of white culture, time that was denied to most American Indians. Not that the Ojibwa fate was any happier thereby. Beginning with the Treaty of Prairie du Chien in 1825, the Ojibwa throughout the nineteenth century were required to gradually cede their lands and were gathered on small reservations where they experienced the full measure of misery, disease, and starvation with which the government compensated them. None, however, were ever removed from their homeland except for two small bands and scattered families, who went to Kansas in 1839 and were settled among the Cherokee in Oklahoma in 1866.

During the 1960s the Ojibwa constituted one of the largest remnants of the native population of the United States. In 1962 the Bureau of Indian Affairs reported 13,000 Ojibwa living on or near reservations in Michigan, Wisconsin, Minnesota, North Dakota, and Montana. On approximately five times as many reservations in Ontario, Manitoba, and Saskatchewan are nearly 20,000 Canadian Ojibwa. Oddly enough, the Ojibwa have become noted to white America not because of their large numbers or their nonresistance to frontier advancement, but through the immense popularity of Longfellow's *The Song of Hiawatha* (1655). This poem, although it confusingly mixes Iroquois hero legends with Ojibwa mythology, gave to American literature its first Indian love saga and achieved for the Ojibwa a romantic fame unparalleled among American Indians.

For an introduction to Ojibwa history and culture, see H. Hiskerson, *The Southwestern Chippewa* (1962); F. W. Hodge, ed., *Handbook of American Indians North of Mexico*, 2 vols. (1907-10); and M. C. Levi, *Chippewa Indians of Yesterday and Today* (1956).—P. R. M.

O.K. Corral shootout. See EARP BROTHERS.

Okies. The depression of 1929 hit the Great Plains with two fists—a one-two combination of economic and natural disaster. By the mid-1930s small farmers throughout eastern Colorado and New Mexico, western Kansas and Texas, and Oklahoma were confronted by depressed prices and farm foreclosures on a massive scale. At the same time a dry-weather cycle resulted in swirling dust storms, creating the DUST BOWL. Approximately 300,000 to 400,000 local farmers gave up and fled to the golden state of California to find work. These were the Okies, migrant workers who squatted in ramshackle shantytowns in the great agricultural valleys, hoping to find enough work to keep their families alive. Most of the Okies remained in California and were absorbed into the state's cities during the war boom of the 1940s.

The term *Okie* was brought into common usage through John Steinbeck's novel *Grapes of Wrath* (1939). The Nobel Prize-winning author painted a vivid picture of a family of Okies, the Joads, forced off their land by choking dust and impersonal corporations. The novel also inspired a prize-winning film of the same name.

The erosion of peoples and lands in the 1930s is the subject of many other books, of which Stuart Chase, *Rich Land, Poor Land* (1936); Carey McWilliams, *Factories in the Field* (1939); and Paul B. Sears, *Deserts on the March* (1935), are the most notable. The Okies are also the partial subject of an excellent photographic essay by Dorothea Lange and Paul Schuster Taylor: *An American Exodus* (1940). See also Walter J. Stein, *California and the Dust Bowl Migration* (1973).—R. B. W.

Oklahoma. The word *Oklahoma* is a combination of the Choctaw *okla*, meaning "people," and *humma*, meaning "red." The area became part of the United States in 1803 with the Louisiana Purchase, but its boundaries were indefinite until 1819 when Spain and the United States agreed on the Red River and the 100th meridian as the international border. Early explorers maintained that the area was unsuited to white colonization but that it would make an excellent home for the eastern Indians.

Indian removals began as early as 1817; in the ensuing years the federal government put increasing pressure on the FIVE CIVILIZED TRIBES of the South to surrender title to all their lands east of the Mississippi River in exchange for a "permanent" home west of the 96th meridian. In 1824 army engineers completed construction on Fort Towson near the Red River and Fort Gibson on the Arkansas River in preparation for the arrival and protection of all the Cherokee and Choctaw. A treaty with the first group called for their relocation in the northeastern corner of the present state of Oklahoma. A similar agreement with the Choctaw in 1830 stipulated that they were to settle in the southeastern corner. Soon afterward the federal government signed treaties with the Creek, Chickasaw, and Seminole whereby these Indians accepted reservations along the western borders of the Cherokee and Choctaw lands.

Meanwhile, many members of the Five Tribes refused to honor the commitment to move westward and the federal government—acting under authority of the Indian Removal Act of 1830—resorted to force. The subsequent suffering and heartbreak endured by the Indians constitute one of the blackest chapters in the history of the United States. Of the thirteen thousand Cherokee driven along the "trail of tears," at least four thousand died of privation and exposure. And of one group of one thousand Choctaw emigrants, only eighty-eight survived. The Creek removal was almost as grim, while many Seminole chose to fight and die rather than evacuate their Florida lands. Two full-scale campaigns were directed against them by the United States Army before they surrendered. Only the Chickasaw escaped major disaster or partial annihilation before 1846, when the removals finally ended.

The Five Civilized Tribes were relocated in the eastern half of present Oklahoma on lands claimed by various southwestern bands. The Osage, Comanche, and Kiowa especially opposed the arrangement and the army finally sent Colonel Henry Dodge to settle the matter. At Camp Holmes in 1834 he obtained agreements from various Plains tribes not to molest the new arrivals. Thus, the Five Tribes in time were able to develop their governments, improve their farms and livestock, and even educate their children at mission schools established by eastern church groups. By 1860 the federal government had built additional forts at five or six

Members of the Seger colony heading into Oklahoma Territory (c. 1900). (National Archives)

points, ostensibly to protect against raids by the Plains Indians and incursions by white settlers.

The steady progress of the Five Civilized Tribes in Oklahoma ended abruptly with the outbreak of the Civil War. Although most of them, under the influence of Stand WATIE, cast their lot with the Confederacy, a large number sympathized with the Union, and a third group tried to remain neutral. All suffered. Thousands were killed or died of starvation, and many more were left destitute—their government torn by strife and dissension, their homes burned, cattle stolen, and their lands grown up in weeds and grass. After the war the federal government imposed harsh punishment on each nation without regard to individual wartime loyalty. Indians were forced to grant rights-of-way to railroads and to cede western lands for reservations for tribes being moved from other sections of the Great Plains. Some tribes, such as the Southern Cheyenne, Arapaho, Kiowa, Apache, Wichita, and Caddo, eventually received large holdings in the former hunting grounds of the Five Civilized Tribes—the western half of present Oklahoma. And in 1872 the Osage settled in the vast area known as the Outlet, immediately west of the Cherokee Nation and south of the Kansas border.

With the arrival of additional tribes the federal government moved its line of forts farther west and garrisoned them heavily. But it proved difficult to keep the Plains Indians under control, and intermittent wars occurred. By 1875 the Southern Cheyenne, Arapaho, Kiowa, and Comanche warriors were so thoroughly chastised and reduced in number that they had no alternative but to remain on the reservation in a hopeless effort to "follow the white man's road." A systematic program of locating still more displaced Indians in Oklahoma soon got under way. Sixteen small reservations were opened: seven in the extreme northeast corner of the Cherokee Nation, five more in the Old Cherokee Outlet immediately west of the Osage, and four in lands between the Arkansas and Canadian rivers that formerly belonged to the Creek and Seminole nations.

Into these small reservations were moved such minor groups as the Kickapoo, Sauk and Fox, Kaw, Seneca, and Wyandot. By 1885 representatives of some fifty Indian tribes had settled on the lands once promised to the Five Civilized Tribes for "as long as the grass grows and water runs." With the exception of a heartshaped district between the Canadian River and the southern boudary of the Outlet known as the "unassigned lands," all of Oklahoma had been allocated. The western half of the Outlet was still claimed by the Cherokee and re-

mained unoccupied, although ranchers from Texas and Kansas continued for several years to pasture their cattle on its lush grass.

For a full generation after the Civil War the Five Civilized Tribes maintained governments independent in name only. From time to time they tried to draw up a union that would exclude the federal government, but no such plan was ever accepted by Congress. The Indians realized why. "Boomers" from Kansas, Texas, and Arkansas were casting covetous eyes on the fertile unoccupied heartland, and cattlemen were moving their herds onto the empty ranges, sometimes paying lease money and sometimes not.

This was also the period of railroad construction. Construction of the Missouri, Kansas, and Texas was begun south from Kansas across Indian Territory, and in 1872 the road was completed at Sherman, Texas. The Atlantic and Pacific, later known as the Frisco, was built from east to west a short time later. And in 1887 the Atchison, Topeka, and Santa Fe came south from Wichita, crossed the center of the unassigned lands, and extended to Fort Worth and beyond. There were other railroads, but their names have disappeared. Each brought in thousands of workers, hundreds of unpainted section houses, and dozens of dingy depots that remained a permanent part of the landscape.

As Texas ranchers drove their herds northward to the Kansas railheads and more and more whites became acquainted with the Indian lands of Oklahoma, the pressure increased to open them to settlement. Men like C. C. Carpenter, David L. Payne, and William C. Couch openly violated United States law by encouraging white encroachment into the territory. The activities of these and other "boomers" were curtailed wherever possible and the violators arrested, but public sympathy for their cause precluded punishment. Congress enacted legislation in 1885 that paved the way for purchases of unused lands from the Indians, and two years later the Dawes Severalty Act made white settlement of Indian Territory a certainty.

President Benjamin Harrison in 1889 authorized the opening of the unoccupied lands to white settlement and the first of several "runs" occurred on April 22 of that year. Estimates of the number of white immigrants on that day range from 50,000 to 60,000, and almost overnight towns such as Norman, Oklahoma City, Kingfisher, Edmund, and Guthrie sprang to life. Most of the newcomers settled on town lots, while the rest staked out quarter-section claims on the approximately two million acres of farm lands available. A few months later Congress created the Territory of Oklahoma out of these lands and the Panhandle—formerly known as No Man's Land. Guthrie was the capital of the territory and George Steele the first governor.

Soon further demands for the opening of still more Indian lands for white settlements were made. The Dawes Commission and the Jerome Commission eventually negotiated with various tribes for extinguishing their titles in return for grants in severalty of approximately 160 acres for each man, woman, and child. This threw millions of acres open for homesteading and paved the way for the greatest "run" of its kind in history. This event took place in 1893; 100,000 people participated in the opening of the Cherokee Outlet and in the disposal of six million acres of land. Other runs and lotteries followed until 1905, when all the surplus Indian holdings were gone.

By this time the present "Sooner State" consisted of two territories, Oklahoma on the west and Indian Territory on the east, with a combined population of approximately one million people. Both territories clamored for statehood but neither particularly desired being a part of the other. From time to time they held separate conventions and sent petitions to Congress, but they received little attention. When it became evident that statehood could be achieved only by combining, the two territories did so and applied to Congress, which passed the necessary enabling legislation in 1906.

At the constitutional convention held at Guthrie that year some 112 delegates attended—55 from Oklahoma Territory, 55 from Indian Territory, and 2 from the Osage country. William H. ("Alfalfa Bill") Murray, a white citizen of the Chickasaw Nation who had an Indian wife, presided over the convention and later played a prominent role in state politics. The constitution eventually submitted to the people for approval was largely the work of Kate BARNARD and reflected many of the Populist ideals of the day. It prohibited the sale of liquor in the state, a provision that was not repealed for more than half a century, and established the initiative and referendum. In addition, it limited the governorship to a single four-year term—a restriction that remained in effect for sixty years—and provided for strong county government, an eight-hour work day for public employees, and strict regulation of the railroads and other corporations.

Oklahoma officially entered the Union on November 16, 1907, as the forty-sixth state. Democrats, led by Thomas P. GORE and Robert L. OWEN, quickly gained control of the government and moved the capital from the Republican stronghold of Guthrie to Oklahoma City. It has remained there since 1910. Meanwhile, the state has gradually shifted from an agricultural to a business and industrial economy and from progressive Populism to political conservatism.

The 1920s was a decade of particularly immature and volatile politics for the Sooner State. Two governors were impeached on grounds of general incompetence and misuse of power. The situation improved little with the election of Alfalfa Bill Murray in 1931. For the next four years his demagogic antics provided much amusement but added little to the state's luster. Indeed, Oklahomans were a long time overcoming the memory of the rustic governor as well as the "Okie" image created by John Steinbeck's *Grapes of Wrath* (see DUST BOWL). The political picture has not been all bad, however.

Robert S. KERR and Roy J. Turner were able governors who gave the state eight years of efficient leadership (1943-51). Kerr went on to become one of the most powerful United States senators of the post-World War II period. Oklahoma moreover has sent such national leaders to Washington as Senators Mike Monroney and Fred R. Harris and Representative Carl Albert, Speaker of the House. But since the early 1960s the state has grown considerably more conservative. Henry Bellmon was elected the first Republican governor in 1962 and six years later defeated the liberal Monroney for the Senate seat. An even more conservative Republican, Dewey Bartlett, succeeded Bellmon as chief executive in 1967 and then went to the Senate. Democrats were elected to the governorship in 1971 (David Hall) and 1975 (David L. Boren).

The Great Depression of the 1930s devastated the economy of Oklahoma at a time when the state was becoming one of the great petroleum-producing regions of the world (see OIL INDUSTRY). (It still ranks fourth among the states in oil and gas production.) Industrial expansion, military installations, and massive federal subsidies in the form of the Arkansas River Project and other water development programs have revitalized the economy and helped reverse the trend of a declining population. (The population in 1970 approximated 2,500,000 and represented a gain of more than 200,000 since 1950.) Even so, the state government is burdened with the support of eighteen colleges and universities, an unusually large proportion of citizens on welfare and pensions, an antiquated tax structure, and a state constitution that has long been a relic of an earlier age.

See Edward E. Dale and Jesse L. Rader, *Readings in Oklahoma History* (1934); Grant Foreman, *The Five Civilized Tribes* (1934); Arrell M. Gibson, *Oklahoma: A History of Five Centuries* (1965); Roy Gittinger, *The Formation of the State of Oklahoma* (1939); Edwin C. McReynolds, *Oklahoma: A History of the Sooner State* (1964); and Muriel H. Wright, *A Guide to the Indian Tribes of Oklahoma* (1951).—W. E. H.

Old Northwest. In 1787 the United States Congress created the "Territory Northwest of the River Ohio," a political entity that included all of the present states of Ohio, Indiana, Illinois, Michigan, Wisconsin, and a small part of Minnesota. According to the organizing act, three to five states were to be created from the vast area and admitted to the Union after passing through a period of territorial government (see TERRIT.CRIAL SYSTEM and NORTHWEST ORDINANCE).

In summer 1788 Governor Arthur ST. CLAIR and Secretary Winthrop SARGENT arrived in Marietta, Northwest Territory, to inaugurate the first territorial government in the United States. The territorial capital was moved to Cincinnati soon afterward and brought the government closer to the population, which was spread from the Ohio country west to Kaskaskia and north to Michilimackinac and Green Bay. During the early 1790s Indian wars occupied the government and discouraged immigration, but following the Treaty of GREENVILLE in 1795 more people took up lands within the territory, rapidly populating what was known as the Ohio country (see OHIO, SETTLEMENT OF). Land-speculating groups in the territory were deeply involved in politics and began to press for advantages when an elected legislature was organized. The first territorial delegate to Congress, William Henry HARRISON, successfully secured division of the territory in 1800, giving the Northwest Territory approximately the present boundaries of the state of Ohio. The remaining portion of the territory was renamed Indiana Territory (see INDIANA, SETTLEMENT OF), and Harrison was appointed first governor. The Northwest Territory continued to argue over the respective capitals and delegates, but in 1802 the process of securing statehood began. Ohio was made a state in 1803.

In Indiana Territory, Harrison was supported by a strong proslavery group that wished to introduce slavery into the territory by repealing the prohibition in the Northwest Ordinance. This movement failed after a few years. In 1805 the Territory of Michigan (including present-day Wisconsin) was formed (see MICHIGAN, SETTLEMENT OF), leaving Harrison with only the Indiana and Illinois countries to govern. He was also superintendent of Indian affairs and spent a great deal of time making treaties. The first delegate, Benjamin Parke, supported the governor's administration, while the second delegate, Jesse Thomas, worked to secure further division of the territory, a move that was successful in 1809 when Illinois Territory was created. In 1811 a small Indian war broke out and Harrison defeated the Indian forces at the battle of TIPPECANOE. He resigned as governor and was succeeded by Thomas Posey. The last delegate from Indiana Territory, Jonathan Jennings, served from 1809 to 1816 and actively opposed Harrison's administration even after Harrison's departure from the territory. The major political split was between Harrison and the southern migrants who early supported slavery on the one hand, and, on the other, the New England and Quaker settlers in the southeast who supported Jennings and opposed slavery. Immediately following the War of 1812 Jennings urged statehood and, in 1816, the state of Indiana joined the Union with Jennings as its first governor.

The Territory of Michigan was organized in 1805 under the governorship of General William Hull. The main settlements were at Detroit, Raisin River, Green Bay, and Michilimackinac and consisted largely of French-Canadian fur traders and their families. Following the organization of the territory more Americans migrated to Detroit and the fur trade slowly came to be dominated by Americans. After 1825 the lead-mining region in the southwest had a rush of settlers and the administrative problems multiplied. Increased immigration led to the election of a delegate in 1820 even though full second-stage government was not granted until 1823. William Woodbridge, the first delegate, was territorial secretary and judge for fourteen years. Solomon Sibley participated in the political structure of the Northwest Territory as well as Michigan Territory, serving the latter as delegate and judge. The third territorial delegate, Father Gabriel Richard, was the first Roman Catholic priest to serve in Congress. Lewis CASS, who succeeded Hull in 1813, was governor longer than any man in Michigan. In 1831 he became secretary of war and was succeeded as governor by George B. Porter, Stevens T. Mason, and John S. Horner. One of the most important debates during the territorial period concerned the "Toledo Strip." Ohio constantly agitated for possession of the whole of Maumee Bay although Michigan had been granted most of it. In 1836 a congressional compromise ceded the Toledo Strip to Ohio and gave Michigan the Upper Peninsula as compensation. In 1837, when Michigan became a state, Mason served as its first governor.

The population in Illinois Territory, which was created in 1809, increased as migrants settled fertile lands in the southern part of the territory (see ILLINOIS, SETTLEMENT OF). Governor Ninian Edwards worked through his Kentucky friends to secure second-stage government in 1812. Although the War of 1812 brought threats of Indian raids and agitated the settlers, little damage was done and the population steadily increased. Following Indiana's admission to the union, Illinois began pressing for similar status. Nathaniel Pope, the Illinois delegate and brother of Senator John Pope (later governor of Arkansas Territory), worked diligently to achieve an enabling act. At this point political factionalism began to develop as various groups worked to secure control of the new state government. Governor Edwards had almost no opposition as territorial governor and did not run for state governor. When the enabling act was passed in 1818, Pope had added two important provisions. First, the northern boundary was moved north from the original boundary at the southern tip of Lake Michigan to a point north of the Chicago River, allowing access for the projected Illinois River canal route from the lake to the Mississippi River. This provision also meant that Chicago was located in Illinois, not Wisconsin. The second and more innovative provision designated that three percent of the money received from land sales in the state would be allotted to the support of education, particularly a university, in Illinois. Another two percent was used, as in other states, for road building. With a satisfactory constitution and enabling act, Illinois became a state in 1818.

In establishing WISCONSIN Territory in 1836, Congress attached to it an extensive region—present-day Iowa, Minnesota, and a small area of the Dakotas—most of which had not been a part of the original Northwest Territory. The rapid growth of population in lead-mining areas of the Iowa country (similar to that in southwestern Wisconsin) had produced a vexing problem of a vacuum in legal jurisdiction, which was thus solved. Iowa Territory was established two years later, however, and included the Minnesota country until Iowa attained statehood in 1846, when Minnesota reverted to Wisconsin's jurisdiction, although in fact remaining somewhat in a condition of limbo. When Wisconsin became a state in 1848, and Minnesota a territory in 1849, their common boundary was established in such a way that the latter retained the portion of the old Northwest Territory lying between the St. Croix and Mississippi rivers.

The governors of Wisconsin Territory were Henry DODGE (1836-41, 1845-48), James D. DOTY (1841-44), and Nathaniel P. Tallmadge (1844-45). Dodge had climaxed a frontier military career by widely publicized success in the Black Hawk War of 1832, and seemed fitted by popularity, personality, and experience to preside over a rough frontier community. Doty, his bitter political and personal enemy, was less successful as governor, because of his own excessive cleverness and his wracking quarrels with the legislative assembly. Dodge and Doty alternated as territorial delegates in Congress, the former serving there from 1841 to 1845, and returning in 1848 as one of the first United States senators from Wisconsin. Doty was delegate from January 1839 to March 1841, having replaced the first delegate, George Wallace Jones, in a disputed election. Henry H. Sibley (son of Solomon Sibley) from Mendota enjoyed the interesting distinction of being seated in Congress in January 1849 as delegate from Wisconsin Territory after Wisconsin had attained statehood. He continued as delegate from Minnesota Territory when that jurisdiction was created later in 1849.

See Beverley W. Bond, Jr., *The Foundations of Ohio* (1941); R. C. Buley, *The Old Northwest: Pioneer Period, 1815-1840*, 2 vols. (1950); and Francis S. Philbrick, *The Rise of the West, 1754-1830* (1965).—J. P. B. and J. T. B.

Old Shasta, California. Ghost town. Located six miles west of Redding, Old Shasta is a true ghost town and one of California's most romantic. The town mushroomed following the discovery of gold in the spring of 1849, flourished through the middle years of the century, and died in the 1880s when the gold placers were worked out and the major transportation routes bypassed the city. Today, Shasta is being restored as a state historical monument, and its famous rows of brick buildings rise once again from the ruins. Among the outstanding landmarks are a museum, the courthouse and jail, and the Masonic Hall.

See Remi Nadeau, *Ghost Towns and Mining Camps of California* (1965).—R. B. W.

Old Southwest. The term *Old Southwest* is an imprecise one, and scholars have used rather wide latitude in defining the area. This area was bounded by heavy stands of deciduous and pine forests. Its terrain is marked by the lower spine of the Appalachian range and by the bottoms or deltas of numerous rivers. The latter drain into the Atlantic and the Gulf of Mexico.

The opening of the Southwest began with the advance of long hunters and then settlers who moved into the upper valleys of western Virginia and eastern Tennessee. The upper end of this region was part of the territory covered by the king's Proclamation of 1763. With the spread of settlement across the mountains after 1768, the Old Southwest came clearly into focus. Subsequently the settlement of KENTUCKY after 1774 gave further impetus to the opening of the region. With the settlement of the Cumberland River area about NASHVILLE, an important central island of Anglo-American civilization was established.

It was not until the signing of the Treaty of Paris of 1783 that the Old Southwest had a political definition. This treaty ceded to the United States the area east of the Mississippi north of a line drawn eastward along the thirty-first parallel to the Chattahoochie River, down this river to the mouth of Flint River, then due east to the upper St. Marys River, and along it to the Atlantic. Much of the territory involved in this cession was wild virgin forest, thinly populated in most places by Indians. There were in fact four major Indian tribes along with several subgroups concentrated in the area. The major tribes were the Cherokee, Creek, Chickasaw, and Choctaw (see FIVE CIVILIZED TRIBES), and all four had sprawling tribal boundaries that earlier served to block free trading and land-hunting activities. Especially important was the fact that speculators found the lands of the Indian territories especially inviting. In time such well-known frontiersmen as John SEVIER, James ROBERTSON,

John Donelson, William BLOUNT, and scores of others sought to establish claims to lands located in such strategic spots as the big bend of the Tennessee River, northern Alabama, and western Tennessee.

Indian traders of several nationalities carried on an active commercial intercourse in the Old Southwest, some of them coming from as far away as Florida and Mobile. From 1775 on, political and commercial rivalries kept the territory in a turmoil.

In 1789 North Carolina ceded its claim to the transmontane territory, and so did South Carolina and Georgia. By act of Congress there was established the "Territory South of the River Ohio" (see SOUTHWEST TERRITORY), and James WHITE was elected to Congress. Theoretically, a territorial government was established in the area that is now TENNESSEE, but in application it embraced a broad land pattern. In 1796 the political Southwest Territory as established by the federal government ceased to exist in theory.

There were at least three major incidents outside the boundaries of Tennessee that contributed to the turmoil in the Southwest Territory. The first of these was the political commotion that arose over the Yazoo lands, which Georgia had sold in 1789 to several private companies (see LAND COMPANIES). Again in 1795 the Georgia assembly compounded its felony by selling a large block of land in present-day Alabama and Mississippi to four companies for $500,000. This so-called Yazoo Fraud stirred up a bitter court litigation, resulting in the famous *Fletcher* v. *Peck* decision rendered by the United States Supreme Court.

The second major incident was the division of Tennessee into three sections. They were ultimately drawn together into a single state, but not without stirring up personal, economic, and political rivalries that exerted an influence on the national political scene. Out of these struggles came William Blount's veiled proposal of a filibuster against Spain, which led to his dismissal from the United States Senate; the rise of the Jacksonian political party; and the intense interest in the future in the southwestern campaigns of the War of 1812.

The third incident was the activities of the French conspirators who appealed to Kentuckians and Tennesseans for assistance to reestablish themselves in the Mississippi valley. Then there was the long-drawn-out matter of establishing the southern boundary between the United States and Spain from the Mississippi to the Saint Marys. The Treaty of SAN LORENZO (1795) opened the New Orleans port to the deposit of goods that were sent down the Mississippi River from American settlements. Finally, there was the concluding act of the signing of the Treaty of DANCING RABBIT CREEK on September 27, 1830, which opened the way to Indian removal from western Alabama and the southern half of Mississippi. Since the opening of trade down the Mississippi, farmers from Kentucky, Tennessee, and the Old Northwest had crossed Choctaw country on their return north from New Orleans. Following 1830, the Choctaw country was opened to settlement by restless frontiersmen in search of good cotton lands.

The Old Southwest produced a stubborn, tenacious, restless, and politically-minded frontiersman. Bitter land speculating and political rivalries between Tennesseans, for instance, reflected these facts. Sectionalism throughout the entire Old Southwest was also strong, as evidenced in the types of culture the area produced. Eastern Tennesseans, land- and river-locked, became provincial and isolated Appalachian highlanders. Settlers in the Cumberland valley developed a bluegrass society of some sophistication. Those in western Tennessee and northern Mississippi were yeoman backwoodsmen who reflected much of the greenness and ignorance of isolated frontier America. Unlike the Northwest, cultural and social institutions of importance were a long time in developing in the Southwest. Despite this, the region exerted perhaps an undue amount of influence in settlement east of the Mississippi.

See Thomas Perkins Abernethy, *From Frontier to Plantation in Tennessee* (1932); Harriet Arnow, *Seedtime on the Cumberland* (1960) and *Flowering of the Cumberland* (1963); John P. Brown, *Old Frontiers* (1938); John Haywood, *The Civil and Political History of the State of Tennessee* (1891); Archibald Henderson, *The Conquest of the Old Southwest* (1920); and Constance Lindsay Skinner, *Pioneers of the Old Southwest* (1921).—T. D. C.

Old Spanish Trail. The Old Spanish Trail remains one of the least known of the pioneer thoroughfares that once threaded their way across the western United States. It began at Santa Fe, New Mexico, ran northwestward up the Rio Chama valley to the village of Abiquiu, and thence in the same direction over the Continental Divide through southwestern Colorado and across the Grand (now Colorado), Green, and Sevier rivers in Utah. It then traversed the Great Basin and finally dropped through Cajon Pass to Los Angeles. The long swing to the north avoided the forbidding terrain surrounding the Grand Canyon, but even so this short-lived trail could be negotiated only by pack animals.

The origins of the eastern stretch of the trail from Santa Fe as far as the country of the Ute Indians go back at least to 1765, when Juan María de Rivera explored to the Gunnison River. Ranging farther was the expedition of two Franciscans, Fray Vélez de Escalante and Fray Athanasio Dominguez, who in 1776 attempted to blaze a way to California but were turned back by heavy snows in southwestern Utah. In succeeding years Spanish traders made frequent visits to the Ute to barter for pelts and slaves, but no further effort was made to reach California from New Mexico, and the two provinces remained unlinked at the end of the colonial period.

The first expedition known to have reached Los Angeles from Santa Fe was that of Mexican trader Antonio Armijo in the winter of 1829-30. Ewing YOUNG with a trapping party out of Taos may have followed the trail at about the same time. In 1830-31 William WOLFSKILL proved that the trail could be used for pack trains, and for a dozen years a brisk trade flourished, the New Mexicans making annual trips to California to secure Chinese goods and mules for the Missouri market. The last large pack caravan made the round trip in 1848, and thereafter the Old Spanish Trail rapidly fell into disuse.

The first significant study of this subject was J. J. Hill, "The Old Spanish Trail," *Hispanic American Historical Review*, vol. 4 (1921). A comprehensive treatment, including a translation of Armijo's brief diary, may be found in LeRoy R. Hafen and Ann W. Hafen, *Old Spanish Trail, Santa Fe to Los Angeles* (1954).—M. Si.

Old West. The term *Old West* applies to that area of the Appalachian valley and trans-Appalachian frontier lying largely along the Tennessee and Ohio rivers. The region was opened to Anglo-American settlement by an extended and complex series of events. In the seventeenth century both French and American explorers and traders visited the region. Robert Sieur de LA SALLE and Celeron de Blainville came to the area from the Great Lakes frontier, and from the outlying Virginia posts came Gabriel ARTHUR and James NEEDHAM into TENNESSEE, and John Peter Salling, Thomas Batts and Robert Fallam. In the first half of the eighteenth century a host of traders and adventurers came from Virginia, Maryland, and Pennsylvania.

During the eighteenth century the Ohio valley became the scene of an intense commercial and diplomatic rivalry between the French and the English, and between the English and the Spanish on the southeastern border. The French established themselves along the Mississippi-Wabash-Great Lakes frontier, and the Anglo-Americans penetrated the region through the Mohawk, Ohio, and Tennessee passways. The treaties of LANCASTER, Logstown, STANWIX (1768), HARD LABOR, and LOCHABER helped to open wider the region to settler penetration.

The traders of the various colonies, especially those of Pennsylvania, Maryland, Virginia, and the Carolinas, ranged far into the West. The French and Indian War (see COLONIAL WARS) and LORD DUNMORE'S WAR (1774) quickened the movement of pioneers to the frontier, and between 1768 and 1785 the westward movement of settlers on the various segments of the sprawling frontier was phenomenal. They crossed the mountains from North Carolina and Virginia to settle along the headstreams of the Tennessee, as at the HOLSTON RIVER SETTLEMENT (see also the WATAUGA ASSOCIATION). They pushed into the Shenandoah and Susquehanna valleys, and up the Monongahela River to Fort Pitt and then down the Ohio. In 1774-75 settlement was begun in KENTUCKY, first at Harrod's Town (see James HARROD) and then at Boonesboro. During the American Revolution a constant stream of settlers crossed the mountains to Kentucky.

Early in 1778 George Rogers CLARK located his base of operations for his Northwest campaign at the Falls of the Ohio, and in 1779-80 John Donelson and James ROBERTSON began the settlement of the Cumberland valley about NASHVILLE. Along the south bank of the Ohio from Pittsburgh to south of the Falls of the Ohio there developed a fringe of settlement that in time thickened into backcountry communities.

The end of the American Revolution quickened the flow of settlers to the West by way of the Ohio and through CUMBERLAND GAP over the WILDERNESS ROAD. Immediately there was a growing sense of political interest in the region, which resulted in the organization of numerous counties, the state of FRANKLIN, and the beginning of a long series of conventions to effect the separation of Kentucky from Virginia. Because of their isolation and dependence upon political and diplomatic policies of the East before 1790, westerners developed a sensitivity about the freedom and use of the rivers, protection from Indian raids, and the fiscal policies of the newly formed United States government.

See Temple Bodley, *Our First Great West in Revolutionary War, Diplomacy and Politics* (1938); John P. Brown,

Old Frontiers (1938); Thomas D. Clark, *The Rampaging Frontier* (1939); and Daniel Drake, *Pioneer Life in Kentucky* (1948.)—T. D. C.

Olive, [Isom Prentice] Print (1840-1886). Cattleman. Olive was a Texan, the oldest son of a pioneer rancher. When he came home from the Civil War, he and his brothers expanded their cattle holdings and fought doggedly to maintain them against the rustlers who infested Texas during Reconstruction. Olive was a hardworking man, and under his leadership the Olive brothers faired well. By the 1870s the clan was wealthy and decided to increase their holdings by moving northward to lands along the Platte River in Nebraska. By 1877 the Olives were firmly entrenched in Custer County with herds numbering twenty-five thousand head and claim to a vast region of territory. Unfortunately for Print Olive's plans, Custer County was rich, black earth, perfect for farming, and he suddenly found himself confronted with homesteaders.

Although an honest man, Olive had a fierce temper and could not compromise. Committed to the open range, he threw his full weight into a desperate effort to protect it. But Nebraska took the side of the homesteaders. Olive had taken the law into his own hands before, and now he fought again with the same ferocity he had used against the Texas rustlers. He cut fences and destroyed crops and pushed his cattle across plowed fields. Two homesteaders, Ami Ketchum and Luther Mitchell, retaliated by killing Olive cattle. Print's hotheaded brother Bob, who was wanted by the Texas Rangers, secured a position as deputy sheriff, tried to arrest Ketchum and Mitchell, and got himself killed for his trouble. The two homesteaders were arrested, but before any formal hearing could be held Print Olive kidnapped them and lynched them. Later, two of Olive's hands doused the bodies with whiskey and set them on fire. Sources do not agree on Olive's role in this part of the affair, although it appears that he had no part in the burning. Nevertheless, the incident outraged the community and won for him the reputation of "Man Burner." Feeling ran so high in the case that when his trial was held, federal troops were called out to prevent an attempted rescue by cattlemen. Olive and one of his hands were convicted of murder in the lynching of Ketchum and Mitchell and sentenced to prison for life. Two years later they were released by order of the Nebraska Supreme Court because the original trial was not held in Custer County, where the crime had been committed. A new trial was ordered but never held. Print Olive was free.

Olive tried to make a comeback as a rancher, but he lost much of his holdings in the blizzards of 1880-81. In 1882 he moved his decimated herds south into Kansas. His efforts there won respectability and success until the blizzards of 1885-86 put an end to the open-range cattle industry. Olive grimly accepted the facts. With the little money he had left, he purchased property in a new boomtown called Trail City in eastern Colorado. In the summer of 1886 he was murdered there by Joe Sparrow, a former hand who owed him ten dollars.

See Harry E. Chrisman, *The Ladder of Rivers* (1962); and Richard Crabb, *Empire on the Platte* (1967).—G. L. R.

Olmsted, Frederick Law (1822-1903). Landscape architect and conservationist. Olmsted was born in Hartford, Connecticut, and educated at Yale. In the 1850s he traveled extensively in Europe and the southern states. His published observations of the latter, *The Cotton Kingdom* (1861), comprise one of the most valuable factual records of southern social and economic life on the eve of the Civil War. In 1858 Olmsted and Calvert Vaux submitted the winning plan of design for New York City's Central Park. Subsequently Olmsted became the park's chief superintendent. A pioneer endeavor in municipal planning, Central Park led to other opportunities for Olmsted. In thirty years of practice as a landscape architect he made the public park a significant factor in American urban life. Boston, Chicago, Detroit, and Baltimore all bear the imprint of his ideas.

Olmsted's contact with the American West began in 1863 when he visited California. Yosemite Valley in the Sierras particularly excited him, and in September 1864 he received an appointment as commissioner to manage the valley, which had been granted in June 1864 by Congress to the state of California "for public use, resort, and recreation." Sensing the significance of the grant, Olmsted prepared a report in 1865 that discussed the values of the new state park. It opened with a commendation of the preservation idea, which prevented spectacular natural scenery from becoming private property. Olmsted next launched a philosophical defense of scenic beauty: nature has a favorable influence on "the health and vigor of man" and especially on his "intellect." There is a need, Olmsted continued, for civilized man occasionally to slough off the tensions and cares of civilization. If areas like Yosemite were not provided, serious mental disorders might well result.

Although Olmsted returned to the East in 1865, he remained a friend of Yosemite. In 1890, when the campaign to establish Yosemite National Park was at a critical stage, John Muir called on Olmsted's prestige and national reputation to lend strength to the national park movement. The landscape architect gladly consented, and his words have been frequently quoted in defense of Yosemite and other national parks. Olmsted's son, Frederick Law Olmsted, Jr., succeeded to his father's place as a leader in the field of environmental design.

The Frederick Law Olmsted Papers are in the Library of Congress. His 1865 Yosemite report has been published in *Landscape Architecture*, vol. 43 (1952). Secondary discussions appear in Hans Huth, *Nature and the American* (1957); Holway R. Jones, *John Muir and the Sierra Club* (1965); and Roderick Nash, *Wilderness and the American Mind* (1967).—R. N.

Olympic National Park. Olympic National Park in Washington was established on June 29, 1938, after a long struggle between the Department of the Interior, which argued that the proposed park should be preserved unspoiled because of its great natural beauty, and the Forest Service, whose supporters contended that the dense forests and mineral deposits in the area should be open to commercial development. The main issue came to be the size of the proposed scenic preserve. Part of the disputed acreage had been set aside by President Theodore Roosevelt in 1909 as a national monument. The skillful lobbying of Secretary of the Interior Harold L. Ickes and Congressman Monrad C. Wallgren of Washington was instrumental in obtaining the authorizing legislation for the park. President Franklin D.

Roosevelt was also actively involved, visiting the Olympic Peninsula in 1937 and taking the lead in working out a political compromise between the warring factions. Governor Clarence Martin, of Washington, had maintained that the park was too big and that it needlessly hampered the lumber industry of his state. His successors continued until recently to make this argument. The original park contained 680,000 acres. In spite of intense political opposition, Roosevelt enlarged it to 835,411 acres in 1940, an action that was in accordance with the establishing legislation. About 60,000 acres were added later. By the mid-1950s, opposition to the park had begun to disappear, but many lumbermen in Washington continued to grumble that the park had unnecessarily "locked up" natural resources.

Olympic National Park is administered as a primitive area. It has few roads. Its dense rain forests in the west contain the largest Douglas fir, western red cedar, and western hemlocks in the United States. The rare Olympic elk live in the forests. The glaciated peaks of the Olympic Mountains, dominated by Mount Olympus (7,965 feet), contain rugged, unspoiled vistas. Explorers in the late eighteenth century viewed the Olympic Mountains from the ocean and the straits to the north, but the Olympic Peninsula was not well explored until the late nineteenth century. It is still sparsely populated. The park is approximately fifty miles northwest of Tacoma, Washington.—D. C. S.

Omaha, Nebraska. Located on the west bank of the Missouri River, Omaha, Nebraska, is the product of the interaction of geography and human ambition. The city derives its name from the Maha or Omaha Indian tribe. The word *Omaha* means "upstream," an "upstream people," or "above all others upon a stream."

The Lewis and Clark expedition passed the site of modern Omaha in 1804, and shortly thereafter fur traders were operating in the area. From 1820 to 1827 the army maintained Fort Atkinson at a point immediately north of contemporary Omaha, and after 1823 fur trading was carried on at Bellevue, a few miles south of Omaha. In the 1830s Bellevue became a government Indian agency and the seat of missionary activities. The Mormons, fleeing from Nauvoo, Illinois, in 1846, established what they called their Winter Quarters on the west side of the Missouri. This community of dugouts, houses, tents, and wagons, the temporary home of some 3,500 persons, was on the site of what became Florence, now part of Omaha. Death was a constant reality at Winter Quarters, for approximately six hundred persons succumbed to the harsh environment. Yet in 1847 and after, the camp served as the major point of departure for the great Mormon migration to the Salt Lake.

The westward movement of the Mormons and the forty-niners gave birth to a town on the Iowa side of the Missouri known as Kanesville, soon renamed Council Bluffs. Certain residents of that community recognized the potential for speculative activity if Nebraska were opened for settlement, and in 1853 they organized the Council Bluffs and Nebraska Ferry Company. In March 1854 the Omaha Indians ceded their land to the United States government, and after the creation of Nebraska Territory in May, the land adjacent to Council Bluffs was opened to settlers. The Iowa promoters quickly platted a town of 320 blocks to which they gave the name of the departing natives.

To assure the success of its venture, the Council Bluffs and Nebraska Ferry Company erected a building in Omaha for use by the territorial legislature as a capitol. In October 1854 Francis Burt, the recently appointed governor, arrived at Bellevue. Burt intended to convene the legislature at Bellevue, Omaha's only serious rival for the seat of government, but the governor died soon after reaching Nebraska. The secretary of the territory, Thomas B. Cuming, a young man whose ambition exceeded his scruples, became acting governor. After deciding that his personal fortunes rested with Omaha rather than Bellevue, Cuming proclaimed that the legislature would meet at the former settlement. The acting governor also apportioned the representation in the legislature in such a fashion as to protect the interests of Omaha.

Omaha remained the capital until 1867, when the town of Lincoln, especially founded for the purpose, became the seat of government. The state penitentiary and the University of Nebraska were also located at Lincoln and for years many Omahans took a churlish attitude toward the capital city and its institutions. Yet Omaha's future was not contingent upon Nebraska politics. In 1855 Congress appropriated funds for the construction of a 180-mile wagon-road from Omaha to Fort Kearny. This thoroughfare, completed in 1858, helped make Omaha an important transfer point for passengers and freight arriving by steamboat and proceeding west through the Platte valley by stage or wagon. By the late 1850s Omaha had scheduled stage service to Fort Kearny and other points. The Colorado gold rush and United States military operations in the West stimulated Omaha's economy and that of Nebraska City, a rival community downstream. In the mid-1860s Nebraska City was the leader in overland wagon freighting with sixty-four operators, including the famous firm of Russell, Majors, and Waddell. Omaha had twenty-four freighting companies, the largest of which were owned by Edward Creighton and William Paxton.

In December 1863 word came from Washington that Omaha would be the eastern terminus of the Union Pacific Railroad. Yet governmental decrees did not dispel Nebraska City's dreams of greatness. Not until 1866 did the construction of the Union Pacific move ahead rapidly, but when this occurred, Omaha easily won the race to become Nebraska's leading city. By the late 1860s the Burlington and Missouri, the Rock Island, and the St. Joseph and Council Bluffs railroads were also serving Omaha, and the completion of a railroad bridge across the Missouri in 1873, spurred on by Omaha booster George L. MILLER, added greatly to the city's importance as a transportation center.

The population of Omaha reached 16,083 in 1870. Like other frontier communities, Omaha was raw, lusty, and highly materialistic. As the Nebraska hinterland was settled in the period between 1870 and 1890, Omaha's trade area grew accordingly and the population of the city rose over sixfold. In 1884, through the efforts of Alexander H. Swan, a Wyoming cattleman, William A. Paxton, an Omaha businessman with large ranching interests, and others, the Union Stockyards Company was established in South Omaha. By means of a donation of land, money, and part-ownership in the Union

Stockyards, the Omaha entrepreneurs induced Gustavus Swift to start meat-packing operations in the city. For a time, Sir Thomas Lipton was in the Omaha packing business but soon sold his interests to the Armour-Cudahy Packing Company. By 1890 Omaha was the nation's third largest packing center. In the meantime other industries, including a huge smelter that processed gold, silver, and lead, a large linseed oil plant, breweries, and a distillery were established. The dynamic growth of banking, real estate business, and wholesale trade reflected Omaha's regional importance.

Industrial growth led to labor-management discord. In 1880 workers at the smelter went on strike and in 1882 laborers employed in a landfill project for the Burlington Railroad also struck. In both instances, management successfully thwarted the modest wage demands of the workers. Although the threat of violence was minimal in both cases, Omaha's civic leaders prevailed upon the governor of Nebraska to secure federal troops to vindicate the rights of private property. The primacy of capital over labor in Omaha was not seriously challenged until the middle of the twentieth century.

Employment opportunities brought many people of diverse origins to the city, and in 1890 almost one third of Omaha's population was foreign-born. Germans were most numerous, but there were also many Scandinavians and Irish. In the early years of the twentieth century Omaha became the home of Bohemians, Greeks, Italians, Poles, Russians, and Jews of various nationalities. By then, the city had the beginnings of what became a sizable Negro ghetto.

By the 1890s the development of paved streets, electric illumination, an electric trolley system, and gas, water, and telephone service demonstrated that Omaha's frontier quality was passing. An art gallery, an opera house, and a public library were important local cultural attractions; the city was developing a modern, well-planned park system. The Edward and John Creighton families provided for the establishment of Creighton University, a Jesuit institution, in 1878. Three years later the Omaha Medical College was established, which in 1902 became the University of Nebraska College of Medicine. The University of Omaha (now the University of Nebraska at Omaha) was founded in 1908.

The boom conditions of the 1880s, which had made Omaha one of the leading cities of the West, gave way to depression in the 1890s. As the agricultural economy of the region faltered, Omaha suffered from the problems afflicting its trade area. In July 1892 the city hosted the Populist national convention. The "Omaha platform" of the Populists not only voiced the agrarian protest of the moment, but proved to be a great charter for reform in modern America (see POPULISM). In 1895 a number of civic leaders, hoping to dispel the atmosphere of depression that hung over the area, formed an organization known as the Knights of Ak-Sar-Ben (reverse spelling of "Nebraska"). This group continues to the present day to stress the interdependence of Omaha and the agricultural heartland. As a further promotional effort organized in large part by Edward ROSEWATER, Omaha sponsored the Trans-Mississippi and International Exposition in 1898. This fair, with its impressive plaster-of-paris buildings and its exhibits from across the nation and abroad, drew a total attendance of 2,613,508 and brought Omaha businesses a good return on the investment.

With the turn of the century, prosperity returned to the city and its hinterland. In 1903 local businessmen formed the Omaha Grain Exchange, an enterprise that was moderately successful. At this time corrupt boss rule and a progressive reform movement flourished side by side in Omaha. In 1912 the private waterworks came under public ownership, as did the gas company eight years later. The commission form of municipal government was adopted in 1912 (retained until 1956) and public services were greatly expanded. Yet Tom Dennison's Third Ward political machine ran a gambling, saloon, and prostitution operation that made Omaha a "wide-open" town, despite the efforts of the evangelist Billy Sunday and others to bring virtue to the community. James C. Dahlman, an ex-cowboy who was mayor from 1906 to 1918 and from 1921 to 1930, was a colorful leader who, while not profiting financially from boss rule, had a close political association with the Dennison machine. The adoption of statewide prohibition in 1916, long an issue that aggravated the relations between Omaha and rural Nebraska, weakened Dennison's position. The defeat of "Cowboy Jim" Dahlman in the face of reform forces in 1918 also demonstrated that boss rule was fading, although the stigma of corruption marked Omaha's government until the 1930s.

On March 23, 1913, a tornado struck Omaha and left 174 persons dead. Yet nature was not responsible for all of the violence in Omaha during this period. In 1919 it experienced the same racial tension that gripped other northern cities. On September 28 a black man, charged with attacking a white girl, was taken by a mob from the Douglas County courthouse in downtown Omaha and lynched. The reform mayor narrowly escaped the same fate when he sought to halt the violence.

Prosperity in the 1920s gradually gave way to the Great Depression. In August 1931 the five state-chartered banks in the city failed, although the national banks endured. In 1932-33, members of the Farmer's Holiday Association tried vainly to raise dairy prices by forceably preventing milk trucks from entering the Omaha-Council Bluffs market. By 1935, jobs in manufacturing in Omaha numbered only three fourths of their 1929 figure, and in 1937 seven of the ten railroads serving the community were bankrupt.

Although New Deal agencies made a major effort to assist the needy, the entrance of the United States into World War II brought a return of prosperity to Omaha and the midlands. After the war military spending remained important to the local economy, for in 1948 Bellevue, adjoining Omaha to the south, became the headquarters of the Strategic Air Command of the United States Air Force. Despite a movement toward decentralization in the meat-packing industry, Omaha remains the world's largest livestock market. The processing of food accounts for almost one half of the industrial activity in the city. Omaha is the fourth largest rail center in the United States and in the 1960s became a major center for commercial air traffic. As the population grew from 251,117 in 1950 to 347,328 in 1970, the suburbs spread for miles across the hills to the west of the old community near the river.

There is no comprehensive history of Omaha based

upon modern scholarship. Pioneer accounts include J. T. Bell and James W. Savage, *History of the City of Omaha, Nebraska* (1894); Arthur C. Wakely, *Omaha: The Gate City, and Douglas County, Nebraska* (1917); and Alfred Sorenson, *The Story of Omaha From the Pioneer Days to the Present Time*, 3rd ed. (1923). A useful summary of the history of Omaha to 1920 is Howard P. Chudacoff, " 'Where Rolls the Dark Missouri Down,' " *Nebraska History* (Spring 1971). Chudacoff has also written *Mobile Americans: Residential and Social Mobility in Omaha, 1880-1920* (1972). George R. Leighton, *Five Cities: The Story of Their Youth and Old Age* (1939) traces the development of the city through the 1930s, but is journalistic and unbalanced.—H. A. D.

Omaha Indians. See SIOUAN TRIBES, SOUTHERN.

O'Mahoney, Joseph Christopher (1884-1962). Wyoming politician. O'Mahoney was born in Chelsea, Massachusetts, to Irish immigrant parents. When both parents died, he went to New York City to live with an older brother and entered Columbia University in 1904 to study under such scholars as Charles A. Beard, James Harvey Robinson, and Max Eastman. He interrupted his education in 1908 to take a tubercular younger brother west and soon found a job as reporter for the *Boulder* (Colorado) *Daily Herald*. As a strong admirer of Theodore Roosevelt, O'Mahoney was chosen president of the local Young Republicans in 1912. The following year he returned briefly to Massachusetts to marry Agnes Veronica O'Leary.

In early 1916 he became city editor of the *Cheyenne* (Wyoming) *State Leader*, a Democratic newspaper controlled by Governor John B. Kendrick. After Kendrick's election to the Senate that fall, O'Mahoney spent three years as his secretary in Washington while obtaining a law degree at Georgetown University. In 1920 he entered private practice and became active in Wyoming politics, assuming the job of vice-chairman of the State Democratic Committee, running unsuccessfully for his party's senatorial nomination in 1924, and finally becoming Democratic national committeeman in January 1931. As an early booster of Franklin D. Roosevelt for president, he attracted the attention of party boss James A. Farley and, after serving as vice-chairman of the National Campaign Committee in 1932, joined Farley's staff as first assistant postmaster general. Following Kendrick's death in November 1933, O'Mahoney was named to fill the Senate vacancy and continued to serve until his narrow defeat in the Eisenhower landslide of 1952. The death of Wyoming's other senator, Lester Hunt, in 1954, induced O'Mahoney to make one final race, which he won.

Long before that O'Mahoney had become a figure of regional and even national stature. He played a major part in defeating President Roosevelt's "court packing" plan in 1937 (all the more significant because of his previous reputation as a "100 percent New Dealer") and authored the Senate Judiciary Committee's famous adverse report on the court bill. After striving to reestablish good relations with the White House, he was named chairman of the Temporary National Economic Committee in 1938 and spearheaded that massive investigation of the concentration of economic power. The TNEC's final recommendations included a plea for federal licensing of corporations engaged in interstate commerce—a proposal always close to O'Mahoney's heart—

and the facts produced by the study helped shape the Full Employment Act of 1946.

Just as noteworthy was O'Mahoney's reputation as an effective spokesman for Wyoming and the West. Throughout his Senate career he was active in shaping sugar legislation; he considered development of natural resources vital to the nation's economy and promoted drilling for oil and gas on the public domain; and in 1952 the National Wool Growers Association named him "Mr. Wool" for his efforts on their behalf. He understood the tremendous importance of water resources to the West and was an able proponent of reclamation, flood control, and public power projects. At the same time, O'Mahoney always considered himself a friend of organized labor and worked closely with Wyoming's railroad brotherhoods and mine workers.

In 1948 he was widely discussed as a vice-presidential running mate for Truman but was vetoed by Truman's advisors, who anticipated that Truman would be defeated and feared that the defeat would be blamed on O'Mahoney's Catholicism. By the early 1950s, O'Mahoney had become one of the most powerful senators. Although stripped of seniority by his 1952 defeat, he played an important role as elder statesman during his last term. In 1957 he was a pivotal figure in engineering the "jury trial amendment" compromise that facilitated passage of the first federal civil rights act since Reconstruction. Two years later he vigorously opposed confirmation of Lewis Strauss as secretary of commerce because of Strauss's earlier involvement in the Dixon-Yates affair, in which private companies received government contracts through patronage. In the process, O'Mahoney suffered a crippling stroke. By the spring of 1960 he was able to return to his Senate duties but declined to seek reelection.

O'Mahoney was, in jurist Thurman Arnold's words, a "born advocate," but would be remembered most of all as a foe of monopoly. His epitaph could well be the declaration he appended to the autographs he signed: "There can be no permanent political liberty without economic freedom."

See Gene M. Gressley, "Joseph C. O'Mahoney, FDR, and the Supreme Court," *Pacific Historical Review* (May 1971); T. A. Larson, *History of Wyoming* (1965); Carl Moore, "Joseph Christopher O'Mahoney: A Brief Biography," *Annals of Wyoming* (October 1969); and Julian Snow, "Joseph C. O'Mahoney: 'His Answer to the Enigma,' " in J. T. Salter, *Public Men In and Out of Office* (1946). The voluminous O'Mahoney papers are in the William Robertson Coe Library at the University of Wyoming in Laramie.—F. A. C.

Oñate, Juan de (c. 1549-1624?). Colonizer of New Mexico. If any man deserves the titles Father of New Mexico and Founder of Spanish Civilization in the Southwest, it is Oñate. His origins are obscure, although it is believed he was born about 1549 in the province of Nueva Galicia in western Mexico. His father, Cristóbal de Oñate, was a prominent soldier and government official and one of the discoverers of the rich Zacatecas mines. In his youth Oñate distinguished himself in several expeditions against hostile Indians. At an undetermined date he married Doña Isabel de Tolosa, a descendant of Cortés.

In 1595 Oñate received a contract from the Spanish king to colonize the upper Rio Grande valley and introduce Franciscan missionaries to convert the Pueblo Indians (see EL PASO). By late 1598 he had entered New Mexico with some 230 men, many with their families, and had established the first Spanish settlement in the Southwest, San Gabriel, near the Indian pueblo of San Juan on the Rio Grande. Prospecting expeditions eastward to the Plains and as far west as the Gulf of California failed to discover gold or silver lodes, which Oñate had been relying upon to finance his colony. A revolt by Acoma pueblo, suppressed with much bloodshed, and a mutiny among the disillusioned Spaniards added to his trials. By 1607 he tendered his resignation as governor of New Mexico, although he remained in the province for another two years. Later he was brought to trial for mismanagement of his office but was cleared on most of the charges. In the early 1620s, he was in Spain petitioning the crown for recognition of past services, and there he evidently died after 1624. In founding New Mexico, Oñate ruined both his health and the family fortune but gained for his labors a secure niche in history.

The most readable work on Oñate is George P. Hammond, *Don Juan de Oñate and the Founding of New Mexico* (1927). Spanish documents on the subject have been translated by the same author and Agapito Rey in *Don Juan de Oñate, Colonizer of New Mexico, 1595-1628*, 2 vols. (1953).—M. SI.

Oneida Indians. See IROQUOIS CONFEDERACY.

O'Neill, [William Owen] Buckey (1860-1898). Lawman, editor, and Rough Rider. It was only natural that the irrepressibly ambitious O'Neill would be written about in superlatives. Gambler, lawyer, newspaperman, miner, explorer, sheriff, politician, irrigationist, soldier—he fulfilled William McLeod Raine's description of him as "the most many-sided man Arizona ever produced," cramming several lifetimes of hectic activity into his short life of thirty-eight years. Even in death, as one of the chief heroes of the ROUGH RIDERS, correspondent Edward Marshall said he was "the biggest, handsomest, laziest" officer of the regiment.

The first of four children of Irish-born parents, O'Neill was raised in Washington, D. C., where his father (a Civil War veteran who was lamed from wounds received at Fredericksburg) was an employee of the Treasury Department.

Making his way westward in 1879, O'Neill first worked as a typesetter on the Phoenix *Herald* and served as occasional deputy for city marshal Henry Garfias. It was in the faro games in Phoenix, "bucking the tiger," that O'Neill earned his famous sobriquet (which he used himself in letters to friends, always spelling it with an "e").

After a stint as editor of the Phoenix-based *Arizona Gazette*, and an equally brief period as reporter for John Clum's Tombstone *Epitaph*, O'Neill moved to the territorial capital of Prescott in 1881 where he became, in typically rapid succession, editor of the Prescott *Miner*, court reporter, and owner-editor of the cattleman's newspaper *Hoof and Horn*. In 1886 he married and was elected probate judge.

In 1888 O'Neill was elected sheriff of Yavapai County. His most famous exploit as a lawman was the six-hundred-mile, three-week search for four men who robbed a railroad safe at Diablo Canyon, east of Flagstaff. Sheriff O'Neill and his posse ran the bandits to bay in Wah Weep Canyon, in southern Utah. All four were returned to serve prison terms in the Yuma Territorial Prison.

In the years between 1890 and the outbreak of the Spanish-American War, O'Neill became moderately wealthy from his investment in an onyx mine near Prescott; explored the Grand Canyon; uncovered copper deposits on the Coconino Plateau near the canyon's South Rim; and became a pioneer developer of the famed Bright Angel Trail and of a railroad link to the canyon. Always politically ambitious, he ran as the territorial Populist candidate for Congress in 1894 and 1896, losing both races after energetic campaigns. The next year he campaigned even more vigorously for the office of mayor of Prescott and was elected January 1, 1898. A month later, the United States battleship *Maine* exploded and sank in Havana harbor, ushering in a war against Spain.

Along with Major Alexander O. Brodie of Prescott and James H. McClintock of Phoenix, O'Neill is credited with the swift organization of Arizona volunteers that became a part of the First United States Volunteer Cavalry Regiment, the Rough Riders.

As captain of Troop A of "Teddy's Terrors," Buckey O'Neill took part in the skirmish at Las Guásimas on June 24, 1898 (during which both Brodie and McClintock were wounded) and, on July 1, at the battle of San Juan Hill.

With his troopers crouched in the high jungle grass below Kettle Hill, one of a series of rises known collectively as San Juan Hill, O'Neill, standing up and puffing his ever-present brown-paper cigarette, was struck in the mouth by a sniper bullet and instantly killed.

On May 1, 1899, after his body had been identified and removed from its temporary grave where he had fallen, O'Neill was buried with full military honors in Arlington National Cemetery. Nine years after his death, a Rough Rider Monument, in the Remington style, was unveiled in the plaza at Prescott (the sculpture was executed by Solon Borglum, brother of the Mount Rushmore artist), which commemorated the Arizona Rough Riders and, particularly, Buckey O'Neill.

Theodore Roosevelt developed a strong liking for O'Neill and wrote of him often in *The Rough Riders* (1899). Ralph Keithley, *Buckey O'Neill* (1949), remains the only biography. A more recent book, Charles Herner, *The Arizona Rough Riders* (1970), is a thoroughly documented study containing much new and valuable information on O'Neill. An important file of papers relating to O'Neill are in the James H. McClintock Collection at the Phoenix Public Library.—D. L. W.

Onondaga Indians. See IROQUOIS CONFEDERACY.

Opechancanough (1545?-1644). Chief of Powhatan Confederacy. Opechancanough was a brother of Chief Powhatan and succeeded him in 1618 as ruler of the Powhatan Confederacy, although another brother, Opitchapan, was the nominal head chief. He lived within the region of the York River early in the seventeenth century, but seems to have ranged widely over the eastern Virginia complex of streams emptying into Chesapeake Bay. In 1607 he and three hundred warriors trailed Captain John Smith's small exploring party of Englishmen and Indians toward the headwaters of the Chickahominy River. Smith's white companions were caught asleep by their campfire and slaughtered. Fortunately, Smith was absent with his Indian companions, hunting for game. Upon finding the rest of the explorers, Opechancanough and his warriors forced Smith into the mud of a creek, and after an endurance contest the Englishman threw down his gun and surrendered. Opechancanough showed kindness to the captive, especially after he showed them a compass and explained as best he could the rotundity of the earth. Smith's captors took him to Pamunkey River, and at the residence of Opechancanough the Indians practiced their magic on Smith and decided he was good medicine. They then took him to Powhatan, who would have had him beheaded had it not been for "the loue [love] of Pocahontas," who, according to Smith's famous tale, threw herself across his body and begged his life from her father the chief.

Opechancanough's amiable attitude toward Smith changed when the Englishman a few months later decided that the Indians were not sufficiently respectful of the colonists and went to Opechancanough's camp on the pretext of buying food, seized him by the hair and marched him off as a prisoner at pistolpoint. Opechancanough was ransomed by his people but never forgave the English for turning the tables on him. After Powhatan's death in 1618, Opechancanough prepared a war to drive out the whites. On March 22, 1622, a general attack was made along the whole frontier. Over three hundred colonists were killed and every settlement destroyed except Jamestown itself, where warning had come just in time. A fourteen-year period of bitter war followed, marked by duplicity and treachery on both sides. The greatest battle was in 1625, when Governor Wyatt defeated over a thousand Indians at Uttamussick village on the Pamunkey. Opechancanough made a reluctant peace in 1636, which lasted until 1644, when he tried to take advantage of internal dissensions among the whites and strike once more. Nearly a hundred years old, the chief was borne into battle on a litter as the Indians fell on the settlements on April 18 and killed nearly five hundred persons. When the Indian attack stopped suddenly for as yet unexplained reasons, Opechancanough was captured and taken to Jamestown, where one of the whites detailed to guard him murdered him instead. The Powhatan Confederacy broke up following his death, and eastern Virginia was never again threatened by the Indians.

See Samuel G. Drake, *The Aboriginal Races of North America* (1880); F. W. Hodge, ed., *Handbook of American Indians North of Mexico*, 2 vols. (1907-10); and John Smith, *The Generall Historie of Virginia, New England & the Summer Isles* (1632).—T. D. C.

opera. Almost by definition, opera has been an urban phenomenon. Consequently, its production in the trans-Appalachian West has occurred only where enough people have gathered to form some kind of city. The surprising fact is that many western cities began having operas soon after their founding, while the frontier wilderness was yet close at hand. Moreover, the first opera to be heard in the United States was in New Orleans, far away from the cities that would later develop into the nation's cultural centers.

It is impossible to document exactly when New Orleans began having operas, for the demarcation between opera and other forms of vocal entertainment is unclear. The first opera of record was André Grétry's *Sylvain* in 1796, but there were apparently earlier performances. In the first two decades of the city's operatic life, the favorite operas were those that could also be seen in Paris. New Orleans' enthusiasm for the lyric art obviously stemmed from the city's close ties with France and its own French heritage. Of great significance was the fact that until John Davis' New Orleans opera company began touring the Northeast in 1827, that area had not yet heard French and Italian operas. By the 1830s New Orleans' musical tastes were so well developed that it supported three theaters presenting opera to a populace of approximately sixty thousand. In the week of April 18-24, 1836, an opera goer could choose from fourteen performances of nine different operas.

Among the American premieres staged in New Orleans were Rossini's *Barber of Seville* (1823), Meyerbeer's *Robert le Diable* (1835) and *Les Huguenots* (1839), Bellini's *Norma* and *Il Pirata* (1836), Donizetti's *Lucia di Lammermoor* (1841), Lalo's *Le Roi d'Ys* (1890), Massenet's *Hérodiade* (1892) and *Don Quichotte* (1912), and Saint-Saëns' *Samson et Dalila* (1893). Despite this glorious heritage, which rested on the firm support of loyal audiences, opera began to lose favor with New Orleanians around World War I. Production costs mounted and patrons drifted away. Part of the problem was that the war severed the opera's close ties with France, but the larger problem was that Creole culture no longer dominated the city. Jazz supplanted opera as the chief musical ornament of New Orleans. Although the city still produces a few operas each year, they can only evoke memories of a once-flourishing operatic center.

The history of opera in Chicago, while recalling a glorious past, can still record some solid triumphs of the present. The city heard its first opera in 1850, when it numbered only 28,000 people. In that decade itinerant troupes presented largely the standard Italian fare. In 1865 Crosby's Opera House opened and gave Chicago its first proper theater for opera, only to perish in the holocaust six years later. The dynamic, bustling spirit of the Windy City would not be content without a great theater, and in 1885 Ferdinand W. Peck began planning the legendary Auditorium Building. One of the architects he engaged was Louis Sullivan, whose apprentice was Frank Lloyd Wright. The 4,250-seat theater, called simply the Auditorium, proved acoustically perfect at its dedication late in 1889. The great tenor Enrico Caruso later called it the best theater he ever sang in. For twenty-five years it was the scene of performances by many fine opera companies, and most of the world's great artists sang there. But only in 1910 did Chicago inaugurate its own resident company to grace its superb Auditorium. The Chicago Grand Opera Company was something of a spin-off from the settlement between the Metropolitan and Oscar Hammerstein's Manhattan Opera Company. The Chicago opera got most of the latter's productions, plus its great luminary, Mary Garden. She introduced to Chicago the roles for which she had become famous—Melisande, Louise, Thaïs, Salomé, Marguerite, Carmen, and the juggler (de Notre Dame).

Despite bankruptcy in 1914 and reorganization in 1915 as the Chicago Opera Association, the company retained most of the same officers, repertoire, and singers. A brilliant addition, Amelita Galli-Curci, who came completely unheralded in 1916, enlivened the Chicago operatic scene for eight years with her superb coloratura singing. In 1921 an event unparalleled in the annals of opera occurred when Mary Garden, the leading soprano, was elected general director of the company. That Garden was a great artist is beyond question; that she was fiscally irresponsible was equally indisputable. But in the process of bankrupting the company during 1921-22, Garden presented Chicago with some spectacular opera.

The new Chicago Civic Opera began in 1922 with Samuel Insull, the utilities tycoon, as president. Insull's notable contribution was building the new opera house at 20 North Wacker Drive, where Chicago's operas are still presented. The Great Depression, which wiped out Insull, also doomed the company in 1932. Various operatic organizations struggled along through the depression and World War II, but only in 1954 did resident opera return to Chicago. In that year Carol Fox began the Lyric Theater of Chicago, which subsequently became the Lyric Opera. By introducing to America such artists as Maria Callas and Renata Tebaldi, the Lyric has performed a notable service. Many other great singers have made their American debuts with this company. Just as important, the Lyric has balanced its seasons with new works, revivals of neglected scores, and standard offerings.

In San Francisco opera followed hard upon the heels of the gold rush. In 1851, only three years after gold was found at Sutter's Fort, the city heard *La Sonnambula*, *Norma*, and *Ernani*. Many troupes presented the standard Italian and French operas during the 1850s and 1860s and in the 1870s the city built two suitable theaters, the Grand Opera House and the Tivoli. Although the latter was famous for light opera, the former attracted many touring companies, including the Metropolitan Opera. This organization was playing in San Francisco at the time of the 1906 earthquake, which destroyed both theaters. Although no singers were injured, the Metropolitan sustained heavy losses of costumes, instruments, and scenery. After the earthquake, the city could furnish only improvised theaters for visiting troupes, including the Chicago Opera at its artistic zenith.

Another visiting company, the San Carlo Opera from Italy, numbered Gaetano Merola among its conductors. He had been to San Francisco many times prior to the 1921 tour, but it was then that he conceived the idea of creating a resident opera company. His vision materialized when the San Francisco Opera Association was organized in 1923, thus making it the second oldest company in continuous existence in the United States. Merola followed a conservative path, presenting operatic staples that resulted in box-office success. By the time the War Memorial Opera House was ready for occupancy in 1932, the company was well established. The depression and World War II inclined Merola to continue serving the public the established repertoire, usually borrowing artists from the Metropolitan. During these years the company suffered from its imitative practices and lack of innovation, despite the fact that many productions were of admirable quality.

When Merola died in 1953, Kurt Herbert Adler became manager and injected new life into the company. He has introduced many singers to America who have become reigning stars, such as Birgit Nilsson and Leontyne Price, and his innovations in repertoire have

created a dynamic, vigorous organization. Adler has presented American premieres of Orff's *Carmina Burana*, Strauss's *Die Frau ohne Schatten*, Honegger's *Jeanne d'Arc au Bucher*, Shostakovich's *Lady Macbeth of Mtsensk*, and Dello Joio's *Blood Moon*. To insure the continuing health of opera on the West Coast, the company conducts annual auditions and awards scholarships to develop regional talent.

Like Chicago's Lyric, the Dallas Civic Opera invited Callas to inaugurate its first season (1957). Lawrence Kelly and Nicola Rescigno formed the Dallas company after they broke with Carol Fox of the Lyric. For two more seasons Callas created her own special operatic excitement in Dallas with performances in *Medea*, *Traviata*, and *Lucia*. Since then the company has vigorously maintained its policy of mounting productions imaginatively, striving to create artistic unity. Although some innovations have misfired, no presentations have been dreary and shopworn.

One of the real pioneers has been the Santa Fe Opera Company, founded and directed by John Crosby. The open-air theater began its summer seasons in 1957. It has offered operatic favorites but has gained fame for such successful ventures as Igor Stravinsky's *The Rake's Progress*, Alban Berg's *Lulu*, Carlisle Floyd's *Wuthering Heights*, Douglas Moore's *The Ballad of Baby Doe*, and Marc Blitzstein's *Regina*.

A general survey is Ronald L. Davis, *A History of Opera in the American West* (1965). More detailed accounts are Davis, *Opera in Chicago* (1966); and Henry A. Kmen, *Music in New Orleans: The Formative Years, 1791-1841* (1966).—W. R.

Ophir, Utah. Ghost town. Ophir was founded by soldiers under the command of Colonel Patrick E. Conner, who rushed into the area when they heard that Indians were mining lead, gold, and silver from the canyons of the Oquirrh Mountains. The soldiers staked out the St. Louis lode, and the rush to Ophir was on. During the period 1870-1948 the Ophir mines produced an estimated $40 million worth of ore, combining the production of gold, silver, copper, zinc, and lead. Today Ophir is but a shadow of its former self. A few families continue to live in the town and work the mines, but most of the town's dwellings are deserted.

See Nell Murbarger, *Ghosts of the Glory Trail* (1956); and Muriel S. Wolle, *The Bonanza Trail* (1953). —R. B. W.

Oraibi, Arizona. Hopi Indian town. Located in Navaho County in the Four Corners area of northeastern Arizona, Oraibi may well be the oldest continuously occupied town in the United States. Archaeological evidence indicates that an original town, now called Old Oraibi, was inhabited as early as A.D. 1150. It was visited in 1583 by the members of the Espejo expedition, who described it as the largest of the Hopi (or Moqui) towns. Old Oraibi contained at least half of the Hopi population of four thousand, but declined because of drought, white diseases, and dissension between factions. The dispute led to the rise of newer towns, Hotevilla and Bakabi, nearby. Lower, or New, Oraibi is at the foot of the mesa on which the original pueblo was located.

Oraibi is remarkable not only for its age but for the fact that the Hopi Indians, who were of Shoshonian stock, were so isolated from the Spaniards that they managed to preserve their culture intact perhaps longer than any other Pueblo group. The old and new towns are now in the heart of the Hopi reservation, which is, in turn, embraced by the Navaho reservation. (See NEW MEXICO MISSIONS.)

See Byrd H. Granger, *Arizona Place Names* (1960); and Mischa Titiev, *Old Oraibi: A Study of The Hopi Indians of the Third Mesa*, Papers of the Peabody Museum of American Archaeology and Ethnology, Harvard University (1944).—H. R. L.

Ordway, Nehemiah (1829-1907). Dakota Territory politician. At the time of his appointment by President Rutherford B. Hayes to the territorial governorship of Dakota, Ordway was a member of the New Hampshire state senate. His appointment in 1880 was supposedly brought about by the influence of New Hampshire businessmen on investments in Dakota. Shortly after his arrival in the territory, he formed an alliance with Alexander MCKENZIE and was in on the plan to move the territorial capital from Yankton to Bismarck. Bismarck was on the main line of the Northern Pacific Railroad, which McKenzie represented. Governor Ordway refused to sign bills unless the legislature voted for the bill to transfer the capital and confirmed his son's appointment as territorial auditor. Yankton businessmen were not pleased with the legislature's acquiescence and levied charges of corruption against Ordway. He was removed from his office in 1884 by President Chester A. Arthur.

Ordway did not return to New Hampshire; rather he became a lobbyist for the Northern Pacific Railroad, which opposed statehood for Dakota. The plan presented by Ordway for the antistatehood interests was to create one large state of the whole territory. This plan was defeated by the Democrat-controlled Congress, as the railroad, grain, banking, and eastern investors had hoped it would be. Not until 1889, under a Republican administration, did the territory achieve statehood, and then as two separate states.—D. J. T.

Oregon. Oregon first came to the attention of Europeans in the sixteenth century when Spanish sailors sighted its coast and thus laid Spain's earliest claims to the Pacific Northwest. In 1579 Sir Francis Drake sailed north along the continent's Pacific coast and claimed the area for England, but that country's major claim was based on Captain James Cook's landing in 1778. With Cook was the American John Ledyard. He watched in amazement as Cook's men bought furs from the Chinook Indians along the coast at six pence each and then sold them in Canton, China, for one hundred dollars each. Fired with plans for an American fur trade, Ledyard pressed his views with the postwar minister to France, Thomas Jefferson, and in September 1787 two ships were launched from Boston under captains John Kendrick and Robert Gray.

While Cook claimed Oregon for England and Gray claimed it for America in 1791, Russia asserted in 1810 that it claimed the Pacific Northwest to the mouth of the Columbia River. In 1819 Spain settled on a boundary with the United States at the forty-second parallel, in the Adams-Onís treaty. Russia ceded its pretensions south of 54°40′ to the United States in 1824 and to Britain in 1825, leaving Americans and Englishmen to strike a boundary between themselves. Conventions in 1818 and 1827 failed to produce agreement and the area

remained "free and open" to both until 1846, when a boundary was finally drawn at 49°. During this uncertain period a de facto boundary at the Columbia River was observed, with the British to the north and the Americans to the south. The OREGON CONTROVERSY focused upon what is now the state of Washington, west of the Columbia River.

The promise that Ledyard saw in the Pacific Northwest was first realized by New England shippers who dominated the maritime fur trade in the Pacific until 1812. The famous Lewis and Clark expedition (1804-06), authorized by Thomas Jefferson, was an attempt, among other things, to find a suitable overland route to the Pacific. Captain Nathan Winship of Boston made a try at constructing a depot forty miles up the Columbia in 1810 as part of a sophisticated plan of trade, but the threat of Chinook hostility forced him to abandon the attempt. A far more ambitious plan was that of John Jacob ASTOR, who hoped to link the interior trade of the Columbia valley with his fur monopoly in the Great Lakes and Missouri valley. Representatives of Astor's Pacific Fur Company, arriving on the *Tonquin* in 1811, erected a fur post and were joined by Wilson Price Hunt's overland party from Montreal the following year. The War of 1812 brought news of an advancing British warship, and Astor's erstwhile partners sold out hastily to the North West Company of Canada. Although Astoria was returned to the United States after the war, the fort and the fur trade of the Oregon country remained in British hands until they became unprofitable.

At first the absence of a boundary worked in favor of Britain's fur-trading monopoly, the HUDSON'S BAY COMPANY. After its merger with the North West Company in 1821, the company's governor in British North America, George Simpson, turned the entire Oregon country into a company preserve. The company's main depot was Fort Vancouver on the north side of the Columbia, one hundred miles inland and just to the east of the Willamette River flowing in from the south. The depot's chief factor, John MCLOUGHLIN was benevolent despot to traders, settlers, and Indians for more than twenty years.

But the company's favored position did not last. As the beaver dwindled and as American settlers began trickling into the rich alluvial valley of the Willamette, the company looked to Whitehall for a boundary line. But Englishmen, unsympathetic to the monopoly's interests and unsure of their own, did nothing. The government's indecision forced company officials in the field into unaccustomed roles as diplomats and public relations men who, ironically, assisted American settlement in the Willamette valley. This assistance, nobly and willingly dispensed by McLoughlin, was required not only as a matter of good policy but by humanitarian considerations as well. The company could not legally chase Americans away, and any attempt to do so would have further aroused the friends of Oregon in the United States Congress to press their plans to occupy the Columbia. McLoughlin advised immigrants to settle in the Willamette valley to insure their dependence on Fort Vancouver, while realizing that any settlement was bound to grow and to develop a degree of independence with a thirst for more. The situation was further complicated by the company's contradictory impulses for secure and rational boundaries on the one hand and the need to show profits on the other.

America's policy of what Senator John C. Calhoun of South Carolina called "masterly inactivity" proved more than a match for Britain's inertia. The American settlers kept coming until British honor seemed to compel negotiations. Although the Americans were located south of the Columbia, Britain found itself quite willing to accept the original United States claim to 49°.

The first American immigrants to Oregon were Methodist missionaries from New England led by Jason LEE. They arrived in 1834. Lee had come in response to what the eastern evangelical establishment willingly believed was a call for the "white man's Book of Heaven," made by a delegation of Nez Percé Indians. Nathaniel J. WYETH, a jovial and courageous ice-cutter from Cambridge, Massachusetts, had brought Lee and his party across the Great Plains in his second attempt to begin a business in either fur or salmon. But for a second time McLoughlin foiled Wyeth's hopes, and Lee was directed south to the Willamette valley, where a number of Astorians and retired company employees, mostly French-Canadians, had begun settlements in the last years of the 1820s. The hub of these settlements was a clearing on the east bank of the river about eighteen miles above the Willamette Falls at a place called Champoeg. Lee settled about a dozen miles to the south, moving yet ten miles farther south in 1841 to Chemeketa, now Salem. McLoughlin assisted Lee on the same terms as the others, lending cattle, advancing seed, and selling farm tools.

In 1836 more Protestant missionaries came from the East, including Marcus WHITMAN, Henry Harmon SPALDING, and William H. GRAY of the American Board of Commissioners for Foreign Missions. Spalding's mission among the Nez Percé at Lapwai, near present Lewiston, Idaho, has been considered the most successful of the Protestant missions. Whitman, who helped pilot the immigrants of 1843 from St. Louis, was murdered along with his wife, Narcissa, and twelve others at the mission in 1847 near present Walla Walla (see CAYUSE INDIANS), touching off the first of several Indian "wars." Catholic priests François N. Blanchet and Modeste Demers arrived in the Willamette valley in 1838 in response to the earnest petitions of the French-Canadian population. Missioners of the Jesuit order entered the Oregon country in 1840 led by Pierre Jean De Smet (see ROMAN CATHOLIC MISSIONARIES).

The Indians whom the missionaries came to Christianize were importantly different from the Indians Americans had previously known. While eastern Indians were strongly tribalized by the early nineteenth century, INDIANS OF THE NORTHWEST COAST lived in villages that were just emerging into tribal organizations. At the eastern edge of the Oregon country, in present western Montana, lived the Flathead, with the Nez Percé to the west. Northward in what is now Idaho dwelt the Coeur d'Alene, Pend d'Oreille, and Kalispel. Around the eastern rim of the junction of the Snake and Columbia rivers lived the Spokane, Cayuse, and Umatilla, with the Yakima, Klickitat, Molala, and others to the west and south. The coastal Indians west of the Cascade Mountains, called Chinook, lived luxuriously on nature's bounty. At the start of the nineteenth century the Pacific Northwest was an Indian world on which the world of the trapper was only lightly superimposed. By midcentury the Indians were squeezing into cores and pockets that the oncoming whites had not yet reached. When Jason Lee arrived in 1834 the Indians of the Pacific Coast were already well launched along the path of physical deterioration, the victims of white diseases and epidemics that struck them periodically and with devastating effect.

No sooner was Lee settled than the mountain men and independent settlers began coming in on the OREGON TRAIL, starting their farms to the west of existing settlements. The first of them was Ewing Young, dashing Indian fighter and fur trader. Robert NEWELL, Joseph MEEK, and others came in 1841 to settle on the Tualatin plains. Recruits for the Lee mission in May and September 1837, and the Great Reinforcement of more than fifty persons in June 1840 swelled the Methodist population of Oregon and dotted the landscape with "mission families" from The Dalles on the Columbia to Nisqually at the southern tip of Puget Sound. Elijah White left the Lee establishment in disgrace in 1841 when he was accused of immoral conduct, but returned in 1842 with over one hundred immigrants and a commission as Indian subagent. White thus became the first United States official assigned to the Oregon country. American naval officers had been directed to look in on Oregon—Lieutenant William Slacum in 1837 and Lieutenant Charles Wilkes in 1841 (see WILKES EXPEDITION). By 1843 the white male population south of the Columbia was approximately sixty French-Canadians and one hundred American and independent British.

When Ewing Young, the wealthiest resident in the Willamette valley, died intestate, the "civil community," as Jason Lee called the scattering of inhabitants, set up a court of probate to administer the estate. A semblance of government was inaugurated when Ira L. Babcock, a New Yorker and lay member of the Methodist mission, was made "supreme judge." The next two years were much occupied with efforts by various individuals and groups to disavow or to reaffirm, depending on their bias, the legitimacy of Babcock's "appointment." At length the internal pressures of a growing population that faced increased danger from Indian attack provoked the establishment of a provisional government. It was ratified in a meeting on July 5, 1843, attended, so tradition has it, by about one hundred men—thirty-seven percent of the American males and approximately half the French-Canadians in the area, although almost surely fewer actually attended.

Long viewed as a contest between French-Canadians and Americans, the provisional government was instead a compromise among several groups in the Willamette valley. The issues dividing contemporaries were more economic and local than national. One group favored a strong local government. In this group were individuals who were willing to see a national boundary at the Columbia River if only it would eliminate the Hudson's Bay Company as a competitor. Another group wanted merely an understanding among the whites about how to act in case of an Indian attack.

A third group, led by Jason Lee and the Methodists at the Falls (Oregon City), opposed the provisional government as a threat to their land claims and favored instead an immediate extension of American territorial jurisdiction. Like the group favoring a strong local government, the Methodists at the Falls were less concerned with the location of a boundary line and more interested in simply seeing one drawn. The Methodists were also interested in diminishing the economic power of the Hudson's Bay Company. An alliance between the Methodists at the Falls and the strong local government advocates was prevented by the Methodists' fear, justly entertained, that a local government might eventually become independent of the United States. This would endanger the mission's land claims and even more, since the mission's secular concerns were but the visible side of an overarching evangelical purpose in Oregon. Independence, or even a strong interim local government would, they feared, have given their adversaries, the Catholic missionaries, an equal chance in converting the Indians. The Methodists reasoned that an equal chance to the Catholics amounted to putting the Methodists at a disadvantage because they insisted that Catholics used unfair means to make Indian converts.

The fall of 1843 saw the Great Migration of about nine hundred persons (among them, Jesse APPLEGATE), and they rewrote the organic law of July 1843 to suit their purposes. In 1844 came another twelve hundred people, who again altered the organic law in spring 1845. Both sets of immigrants came mostly from Missouri and Illinois—born and reared there if young (about eighty percent) and originally from the Atlantic states if middle-aged. The Midwest was the "crucible in which the population of the Pacific Northwest was molded," historian Jesse S. Douglas wrote, and Oregon has continued to attract large segments of its population from the Midwest. The compact of 1845 provided for participation in the government in Oregon by both British subjects and American citizens without prejudice to the national allegiance of either, and the Hudson's Bay Company joined the settlers' government. George Abernethy, once Lee's chief accountant, was the provisional government's only governor.

President James K. Polk signed the bill making Oregon a territory on August 14, 1848, and appointed Joseph LANE, a hero of the Mexican War, to the governorship. Lane reached Oregon on March 2, 1849, and declared the territorial government in operation the following day, thus beginning ten of the most fiery years in Oregon's political history. Typical of territorial governments since the formation of Ohio in 1799, there was a fight for the location of the territorial capital, with Oregon City winning out over Salem in 1850. There was also a typical struggle between "foreign" appointees (that is, nonresidents of Oregon appointed in Washington, D.C.) and "home rule" appointees, championed by local politicos who affected revolutionary rhetoric, seeing themselves as the American patriots and the federal government as King George reincarnate. The drama led ultimately to a demand for statehood. When President Zachary Taylor's appointee to the governorship, John P. Gaines, arrived in Oregon—Abraham Lincoln having refused the job—the battle was on. Gaines was neither a corrupt nor a bad man, but he was a poor choice politically. His high-toned whiggery was of service largely in the formation and solidification of the Democratic party machine in Salem. The Salem Clique, directed by Asahel BUSH, editor of the *Oregon Statesman*, which he founded in 1851, had within its ranks the brightest legal light in the territory, Matthew P. DEADY;

the grandest orator, Delazon Smith; the surest vote-getter, Lane; and a host of able jurists, among whom R. P. Boise, L. F. Grover, B. F. Harding, and J. W. Nesmith were the steadiest.

Those who favored making Oregon City the capital, including "soft" Democrats, potential Whigs, and others, were led by editor Thomas Dryer of the Portland *Oregonian*, founded in 1851. While editors attacked each others' policies and personalities in venomous prose, the power of the Democratic machine in Salem was unable to effect its objective, a vote in favor of a constitutional convention and statehood. The measure was defeated at the polls in 1854, 1855, and 1856, but was finally accepted in 1857 by an overwhelming majority. Although there were various reasons why statehood was thrice rejected, including the opposition of disorganized Whigs and others to a Democratic-controlled statehouse and the disinclination to support a state government, the real conundrum was why statehood was so abruptly approved. The reason lay with Oregon's immersion in the history and politics of the nation. Oregon's constitution was to mark the end of an ambiguous and complex process that began with the Virginia constitution of 1776 and with the march of people into Kentucky and Tennessee after the American Revolution.

The election of James Buchanan as president in November 1856, followed by the Supreme Court decision in Dred Scott's case on March 6, 1857, made it plain to Oregonians that the doctrines they most cherished—POPULAR SOVEREIGNTY, the characteristic, traditional consensualist democracy Americans revered, and the slavery prohibition of the Northwest Ordinance written into the organic law of 1843 and the Oregon territorial bill of 1848—had now been overruled. According to the Dred Scott decision, the Constitution was said to declare territorial laws on slavery to be an interference with national authority, or rather with "freedom"; the Dred Scott decision had redefined congressional powers so that federal legislators were prevented from deciding the question of slavery in the territories while required to disallow any territorial legislation against slavery. The national debate on states' rights and slavery had come full circle, it seemed. Oregon's constitution and a cluster of events surrounding it represented the culmination, in miniature, of the several contradictions that underlay the coming, and the passing, of the Civil War.

The theory of popular sovereignty was, in a rough way, the antislavery side of the states' rights doctrine. Dred Scott did not destroy the right of a *state* to determine citizenship. It was possible that the citizens of one state might not be considered, or even eligible, for citizenship in other states. Implicit here, and perhaps this is even more important than the well-known Civil War issues of state versus national powers and rights, was the consensual basis of American polity, as it stood in ominous conflict with a new, emergent, pluralistic model associated with the forces of "nationalism." Of course, the question of citizenship was hardly to be considered a mere abstraction, since free Negroes, citizens in some states, were unwelcome in others. But until the adoption of the Oregon constitution in 1857, and its subsequent congressional acceptance in 1859, no state had excluded Negroes on other than statutory grounds. This anomalous "dual" citizenship quite literally put the union of the states in doubt.

In fact, a revolutionary alteration of ideas was taking place in America, specifically touching the idea of equality and the ideals depending upon it for meaning. The course of the revolution was marked out along the path of constitution-making beginning in Virginia in 1776 and ending in Oregon in 1857. Oregonians, voting to outlaw slavery and Negroes in their basic law, made rights the consequence of compact. This reversed the logic of Virginia's constitution, wherein natural or inalienable rights were held to be antecedent to the compact. The earlier document, written, as its preamble states, for "the good people of Virginia," did not distinguish *the* people from *a* people and consequently did not stipulate the exclusion of undesirables, although reserving certainly the right to do so by statute.

In the years intervening between the first state constitution and the thirty-third, the structural bases of American life had changed radically in almost every measurable way. Less readily measurable consequences of such change are suggested by the differences of language in these two public documents. Virginia's constitution reflected a series of realities no longer obvious in 1857 when the Oregon constitution was written. Even while the words and ideals used and implied in both documents were on everyone's lips as the Civil War approached, the realities were no longer the same. Moreover, and of much greater significance, the older referents were either destroyed or reshaped beyond recognition. Oregon's constitution, accepted by the United States Congress in 1859, saved the old words, which congressional acceptance, the product of compromise, ratified. How much the Civil War and the Fourteenth Amendment, granting national citizenship, would temper the transition reflected by the Virginia and Oregon constitutions remained (and perhaps still remains) to be seen. Strangely, it seemed the denial of federalism would mean the denial of freedom to Negroes and federalism encroaching upon state authority involved a limitation of the fundamental principle of the consent of the governed. For certain southern theorists of sovereignty in 1861, states' rights was a doctrine of power, not of law. But for Oregonians, and for earlier Americans, "states' rights" was shorthand for "democracy."

The thirty-third state entered the post-Civil War period after a tortured four years of ideological chest-thumping and confused loyalties. The Democrats made a significant if feeble effort to rescind the state's ratification of the Fourteenth Amendment, which took from the states precisely that power Oregon asserted in the constitution of 1857, namely the power to confer citizenship. The Republicans, who were soon to dominate the state's politics, declared that their party was "for the Union without condition. We are for it, if the administration is pro-slavery, democratic, popular sovereignty democratic, or republican." The Democrats were ideologically replaced, not superseded, by the Republican party. Matthew Deady symbolized the process by becoming, in 1861, as rabid a Union man as he had been a proslavery, states' rights man in 1857, when chairman of the constitutional convention. His fondness for the Middle Ages and his affection for agricultural pursuits were replaced by an attachment to laissez-faire and a commitment to substantive due process—the use of the Fourteenth Amendment to protect property against

state interference. Deady, who had insisted on a "pure white" commonwealth in 1857, struck down a state Chinese exclusion law in 1872. What was sectionalism and patriotism before the Civil War had become parochialism and subversion following it. This was one of the ways the theme of popular sovereignty lived on into the twentieth century.

The first amendment to Oregon's constitution in 1902 was for the purpose of adding the nonpartisan measures of initiative and referendum, advocated by Progressives William S. U'Ren and Jonathan Bourne and, later, Oswald WEST. The initiative and referendum were political procedures intended to give voters direct participation in law-making. In 1908, the recall was adopted, giving the electorate the power to remove elected officials from office before their terms expired. Whatever the functional merits of these measures— known as the "Oregon System"—may be, they were based upon the same popular sovereignty idea, as were the constitution and the Republican-party credo. The assumption was that when power was taken from the legislature and given to the electorate, the "people's will" would prevail, a result that could be expected only when "the people" is a homogeneous aggregate, that is, nonpartisan. Since Oregon has both a popular sovereignty tradition and an extraordinarily homogeneous population, along with a traditional civility and tolerance bred of more than a century of truly consensus politics, the problems of this Oregon System, like the earlier problems of state sovereignty versus nationhood, will remain invisible until some form of dissonant heterogeneity makes differences stark and strong state parties necessary.

Though the Democratic party has grown in Oregon— more than fifty percent of registered voters in 1960—its orientation has been largely national in scope. Political "pull" in Oregon is centrifugal, against centralization, and unfavorable to organization. In Oregon parties serve personalities, and personalities do not, as the adage would have it, come to the aid of their party. Just as it was no contradiction for laboring men to show a preference, before World War I, for industrial unionism and the Industrial Workers of the World, and then, after the war, to join the Ku Klux Klan and other nativist groups, so it was not unnatural that the New Deal should be well received or that President Franklin D. Roosevelt should have carried the state four times. Some Oregonians liked Roosevelt, and many required the type of aid— development of hydroelectric power and irrigation— that his New Deal program offered. But in 1938 Republicans won back the state House of Representatives from the Democrats—who had taken it in 1932, the first time since 1878—just as soon as the Bonneville Dam was completed and the debate over public or private control of hydroelectric power could be returned safely to local disputants.

Oregon is not the only state in which popular sovereignty has had an active and influential history, but it is perhaps the best example of the type. Predictably and ironically, given their historical backgrounds, such states tend to be "nationalistic." The state's early physical and economic isolation was also a factor affecting its political development. Unlike California with its spectacular gold rush of 1849 (Oregon had minor rushes) or later its oil and real-estate booms, Oregon has been able to exploit the tendency of American migrants to seek destinations where like-minded people reside. Oregon, until very recently, has been able to attract a population highly compatible with its existing population. From a time in 1850 when Portlanders turned away business developers from out of state to Governor Tom McCall's apparently successful efforts to curb immigration and tourism, Oregon has tried to regulate her enterprise and her population, even when such regulation meant, as in these two cases, an economic loss.

Oregon experienced three large booms (1880-90, 1900-10, and 1940-50) when population, property values, and production rose markedly. The first boom followed the completion of the transcontinental railroad connections in the 1880s. The second represented Oregon's share of America's last migration of agricultural peoples from the Midwest, urged west by real estate and railroad land company promoters and by an extravagance of boosterism of which Portland's Lewis and Clark Exposition of 1905 was the high point. The third boom occurred during World War II when some four hundred thousand laborers came to Oregon.

Portland, laid out in 1845, is the leading city in the state and among the larger cities in the country. In 1860 Portland became the emporium for the state and for Idaho and parts of Washington Territory. As the West's principal exporter of wheat, Portland tied valley growers, and eventually those of the interior, to its export trade by means of a city-based steamship monopoly, the Oregon Steam Navigation Company (see Simeon G. REED), and by the California and Oregon Railroad.

Large-scale timber operations began in 1900 when Frederick Weyerhaeuser purchased 900,000 acres. The lumber industry soon became the state's dominant industry, and by 1938 Oregon was the largest producer of wood products in the country. Forest-based industry accounts for more than fifty percent of the Beaver State's industrial productivity.

The best text on Oregon is Dorothy O. Johansen and Charles M. Gates, *Empire of the Columbia: A History of the Pacific Northwest* (2d ed., 1967). Johansen's presidential address at the Pacific Coast Branch of the American Historical Society, "A Working Hypothesis for the Study of Migrations," *Pacific Historical Review* (February 1967), is also significant. A specialized study is Jesse S. Douglas, "Origins of the Population of Oregon in 1850," *Pacific Northwest Quarterly*, vol. 41 (1950). The file of the *Oregon Historical Quarterly*, beginning in 1900, is the greatest single source of published documentary materials readily available. Howard McKinley Corning, *Dictionary of Oregon History* (1956), is useful, as is Charles H. Carey, *A General History of Oregon Prior to 1861*, 2 vols. (1935). Robert I. Burns, *The Jesuits and the Indian Wars of the Northwest* (1966), is excellent for students interested in a general view of Indian-missionary relations. The relevant portions of Earl Pomeroy, *The Pacific Slope* (1965), are highly informative on current political questions. See also Robert J. Loewenberg, *The Idea of Equality in Ante-Bellum America* (1975).—R. J. L.

Oregon controversy. There was more than fifty years of controversy (1789-1846) over the grand question of the ownership of Oregon before the United States in a treaty with Great Britain on June 15, 1846, took all of Oregon up to the forty-ninth parallel. The dispute commenced with the NOOTKA SOUND CONTROVERSY in 1789, in which the British maintained their position in the Northwest against Spanish claims. Three years later occurred the fateful discovery of the Columbia River by Captain Robert Gray, who named the river after his ship; Gray's discovery gave the United States a claim to the territory, although it would be many years before the government would push that claim into an argument with the British. John Quincy Adams as secretary of state in 1819 arranged in the Adams-Onís treaty with the Spanish to draw a line by rivers and parallels out to the Pacific by way of the forty-second parallel, the southern boundary of present-day Oregon. Five years later the American government concluded a treaty with Russia that set the southernmost boundary of Alaska at the later famous parallel of 54°40'; the Russians asked for that line because they wished to include Prince of Wales Island within Alaska. The next year, 1825, the British concluded a similar treaty with the Russians. A definition of the extent of the Oregon country was thus established, from 54° 40' all the way down to the parallel the Americans had drawn with Spain in 1819—and which by 1825 paralleled the land of Spain's former colony, now independent, Mexico. Meanwhile a treaty between Britain and the United States in 1818 had agreed to make the Oregon country "free and open" for a period of ten years. In 1827 another Anglo-American treaty continued that arrangement indefinitely, subject to notice of one year.

Nothing much happened with the Oregon dispute until the presidency of James K. Polk, whom the Democrats had elected on the platform of the "reannexation of Texas and the reoccupation of Oregon." The Texas part of the slogan referred to the Democratic claim that John Quincy Adams in the Adams-Onís Treaty had lost Texas (a claim that Adams hotly disputed for the rest of his long life). The reoccupation of Oregon seemed to say that the territory always had been American but ought to be certified as such.

The position of Polk in all of this is of some considerable interest. Polk was willing enough to possess the entire Oregon territory, but disliked the idea of a conflict with Great Britain at the very time that American-Mexican relations were on the verge of war. His essential willingness to compromise the Oregon issue at the forty-ninth parallel is the key to his Oregon policy in 1845-46. He was not unwilling to bluff the British, if he could, but he was reasonable on the issue. It was for him, of course, a tricky position, for he had to be extremely careful of any surrender or apparent surrender of American rights in Oregon. All the Oregon extremists—the "Fifty-four Forty or Fight" enthusiasts (the slogan became popular in 1845, rather than in the campaign of 1844)—were Democrats, members of his own party. There was indeed a hot party feeling by the congressmen from the Old Northwest that Polk, a southerner from Tennessee, might give in to the southern desire for Mexican lands while compromising the other side of the expansionist program, Oregon.

In advancing his arguments with his countrymen and the British, Polk pursued a Byzantine policy, and in retrospect one must admire the care with which he moved, as well as the good fortune that enabled him to secure the treaty he desired. He made a quiet offer to the British minister of a line extending the forty-ninth parallel to the sea, but the minister foolishly turned it down without consulting his home government. The president then stiffened and seems to have "unleashed" the Fifty-four Forty men. A great debate began in Congress late in 1845, which ran on for nearly five months before its end on April 23, 1846, in which one after another of the expansionists invoked the deity, Greek and Roman mythology and history, the rights of Americans, the entire history of the world, to prove that the United States needed all Oregon. Polk knew, of course, and so did even the Oregon men, though they were not fond of remembering it, that about the only part of Oregon the United States rightfully could claim by settlement was the area below the Columbia River, the present-day state. Above that river in the year 1845 there were exactly eight Americans; seven of them had come in October of that year, and the eighth was an Americanized Englishman. Eventually Polk indirectly sought to bring some sense into the congressional debate, which circled around the question of what form of notice should go out to the British government in accord with the treaty of 1827, and appears to have persuaded his old college roommate, Senator William H. Haywood, Jr., of North Carolina, to come out for the forty-ninth parallel. This maneuver led Senator Edward A. Hannegan of Indiana to say that if Polk favored the forty-ninth parallel then "so long as one human eye remains to linger on the page of history, the story of his abasement will be read, sending him and his name together to an infamy so profound, a damnation so deep, that the hand of resurrection will never be able to drag him forth."

All the while the government of Great Britain was preparing to settle at the forty-ninth parallel. The British in the past had tended to stick for the area north of the Columbia River, but when the Hudson's Bay Company made known its intention of moving its principal Oregon trading post north from the Columbia to Vancouver Island, the British cabinet gave in. After taking precautions with Lord Palmerston, the audacious Whig who seemed likely to make trouble with any government that dealt kindly with "Brother Jonathan," the cabinet of Sir Robert Peel, which was about to give way to Lord John Russell and the Whigs, arranged for its minister in Washington to sign a treaty giving the Americans the forty-ninth parallel, while preserving the right of navigation on the Columbia River below 49 degrees to the Hudson's Bay Company, and the protection of the property of the company and of British subjects in the territory thus made American. A line delimiting the boundary between the islands in Juan de Fuca Strait was drawn after an arbitration by the German emperor in 1872.

The definitive account is by Frederick Merk, *The Oregon Question* (1967). This volume reprints an earlier account by Merk, *Albert Gallatin and the Oregon Problem* (1950). See also Edwin A. Miles, " 'Fifty-four Forty or Fight': An American Political Legend," *Mississippi Valley Historical Review*, vol. 44 (1957-58).—R. H. F.

Oregon Trail. The Oregon country for many years was an area of international rivalry as Spanish, British, Russian, and American explorers and fur traders competed for control. The British fur-trading companies emerged from the struggle dominating the region north of the Columbia River. OREGON then became a missionary frontier. The Oregon missionaries were instrumental in making the United States aware of the Pacific Northwest through published books on their travels, speaking tours in the eastern states, correspondence in the religious press, and conversations with politicians. The economic potential of Oregon as a veritable agricultural paradise was also proclaimed in a flow of books and articles and a barrage of popular lectures from the lyceum platform by Hall J. KELLEY and other Oregon enthusiasts. Official explorers for the United States Navy and Army confirmed the impressions of Oregon traders and missionaries. The WILKES EXPEDITION reported on the region in 1841. The explorer-hero John C. FREMONT provided the greatest contribution to the publicity campaign by a report of his second exploring expedition for the United States Army in 1843. His precise and accurate description of the route to Oregon in his official account of the exploration provided a handbook for immigrants.

The overland migration of pioneers intending to settle permanently in Oregon, primarily to farm, did not begin until 1841. A pioneer band, numbering seventy persons, left Independence, Missouri, in May expecting to follow the route westward along the PLATTE RIVER, through the SOUTH PASS, and northwest to the Columbia River, portions of which had been made known by the mountain men and fur traders. During the 1840s this route was to become known as the Oregon Trail. Starting at Westport Landing, Independence, or other Missouri frontier towns, with the adult males riding on horseback or driving covered wagons loaded with precious household possessions and transporting wife and children, these pioneer parties traveled in a direction north of west to Fort Kearny on the southern bend of the Platte River. Following the south bank of this stream, they forded the river at a convenient crossing near the confluence of its southern and northern branches and traveled on to the outpost of Fort Laramie, a distance of 667 miles as measured by some parties. At this fort most immigrant trains paused long enough to rest, to exchange broken-down livestock for healthy animals, to repair wagons, and to replenish their supply of flour and other foodstuffs. From Fort Laramie the route followed the North Platte in a counterclockwise direction toward the north, across present Wyoming to the mouth of its tributary, the Sweetwater. This winding mountain stream was ascended in a westerly direction to its source at the foot of the South Pass, known as the gateway to Oregon. By this time, emigrants had traversed 947 miles. Leaving the South Pass, the trail crossed the Green River valley southwest to Fort Bridger, 1,070 miles out, and then turned abruptly northwest by way of Soda Springs, Idaho, to Fort Hall on the Snake River, the total distance from Missouri now being 1,283 miles. Following along the Snake River, past Fort Boise, pioneers traversed the Grande Ronde valley, across the Blue Mountains to Whitman's mission on the Columbia, having come 1,835 miles. From there they moved down the Columbia River to the mouth of the Willamette River and turned southward down the Willamette valley to seek a home in the fertile lands in the vicinity of Lee's mission. It was a long trail of approximately two thousand miles, taking from four to six months to travel.

In 1842 a larger group of approximately one hundred persons and eighteen wagons were guided over the Oregon Trail by Dr. Elijah White, a former missionary heading for his new post as an Indian agent for Oregon. This party brought the news that the Presbyterian missions were to be discontinued in the Pacific Northwest. Marcus Whitman, unwilling to accept this, returned to the East and obtained a reversal of the decision, after pleading with political leaders to take a more active interest in the region. He returned to Oregon in 1843, guiding what has been described as the Great Migration. Many factors conspired to bring about the sizable movement of 1843. The Middle West had been in the grips of an economic depression for several years following the Panic of 1837. Many residents suffered from malaria and pulmonary complaints in the humid river valleys. In contrast, Oregon appeared a land of opportunity both for the adventurous and the ambitious seeking new lands and markets. The flood of propaganda from fur traders, missionaries, and government servants fell on willing ears. Peter H. Burnett was elected captain by the one thousand men, women, and children who gathered in the early spring of 1843 in western Missouri, having come from Ohio, Indiana, Illinois, Kentucky, and Tennessee. The train comprised more than a hundred wagons with a herd of oxen and cattle, estimated as high as five thousand head, bringing up the rear.

In traversing the Great Plains, the physical obstacles were comparatively unimportant except for the river crossing, where a wagon might be upturned on the banks approaching a ford or be swept downstream in the river current. Departure had to be timed so that the livestock could feed off the grass of the Plains when it was in prime condition. Caravans getting a late start had to leave the well-traveled route if vegetation was scarce. Travelers learned to reduce baggage to a minimum, and frequently precious possessions had to be abandoned en route. Oxen were preferable to horses as draft animals and were not nearly so attractive to the Indians. As protection from the ever-present threat of attack by hostile Indians, the emigrant wagons were drawn into a circle, the tongue of one placed under the body of the next to make a corral or a stockade. If an Indian raid on stock grazing outside this enclosure was suspected, or in cases of severe storm, a rope was placed around the outside of the wagons and the cattle were driven into the enclosure. At night families made preparation for the next day's travel. The captain of the train engaged in counsel with the heads of families; guards were posted to watch the grazing cattle and for any signs of Indian attack. Actually, the danger from Indians proved greater in imagination than in reality, for little blood was shed. As a rule, Indians hesitated to attack a large, well-organized caravan. The route was well marked to Fort Hall, but beyond that point it was a pack trail over very difficult and rocky terrain, across hills, and through dense forests alternating with stretches where grass and water were uncertain.

The annual migration of 1844 was smaller than the previous season, the travelers got a late start as a result of an unusually wet spring, and they arrived at their destination late and somewhat disconsolate. In 1845 an estimated three thousand migrants traveled to Oregon. This season there was not one great caravan, but many smaller ones, composed of a dozen or two wagons, which were scheduled for departures at time intervals that would permit the grass to be replenished along the route

after each passage. Migration on the road to Oregon now became an annual event. In 1847 an estimated four to five thousand people traveled along the trail.

Of all the overland trails, the Oregon Trail remained in use the longest time. Until the Oregon Short Line was constructed by the Union Pacific Railroad between 1882 and 1884 along the general route from Granger, Wyoming, to Portland, Oregon, travelers continued to use the Oregon Trail into the Northwest. The trail also served for eastward cattle and sheep drives. In 1880 an estimated 200,000 head of northwestern cattle were reported to have traversed this route into the Great Plains. Between 1885 and 1890 flocks of sheep were driven along the trail from the midwestern feeding grounds to the stockyards in Omaha and Kansas City for slaughter.

David Lavender, *Westward Vision: The Story of the Oregon Trail* (1963) is a history of the Pacific Northwest with the Oregon Trail serving as a focal point. Two brief, reliable accounts are W. J. Ghent, *The Road to Oregon* (1929), and Jay Monaghan, *The Overland Trail* (1947). A classic account of the 1843 immigration is Jesse Applegate, *A Day With the Cow Column* (1934). —W. T. J.

O'Reilly, Alejandro (1725-1794). Administrator of Spanish Louisiana. O'Reilly was responsible for the suppression of the "Revolution of 1768," in which French Louisianians rejected transfer to Spain, and for firmly establishing Spanish authority in the colony. A native of Ireland, O'Reilly fled his homeland to escape poverty, finally settling in Spain. His service in the military was crowned by a successful suppression of an insurrection in Madrid, during which he personally saved the life of Charles III. His reward was to become the monarch's favorite military commander. Arriving in New Orleans in 1769 with 24 ships and 2,600 troops to take possession of the province, O'Reilly arrested twelve leaders of the rebellion, executed five of their number by firing squad, and sent the remainder to prison terms in Morro Castle. These "Martyr Patriots" became enshrined in Louisiana folklore, which has also remembered their executioner as "Bloody" O'Reilly. In fact, O'Reilly's record as administrator of Louisiana is most impressive. He followed the executions with full amnesty for all who chose to remain as Spanish subjects in Louisiana, replaced the old Superior Council with the Spanish *cabildo*, established admirably clear and equitable legal procedures, introduced the first scientific land surveys to minimize confusion in titles, created the Louisiana Regiment as a militia force under native Louisianians, and abolished Indian slavery in the colony. In 1770 he turned over a pacified and orderly Louisiana to the governorship of Don Luís de Unzaga.—J. G. T.

Orleans, Territory of. See LOUISIANA, STATE OF.

Osage Indians. See SIOUAN TRIBES, SOUTHERN.

Osceola (1800?-1838). Seminole Indian leader. Osceola was of the Red Stick faction of the Upper Creek (see FIVE CIVILIZED TRIBES) and was born on the Tallapoosa River in Alabama. Neither born nor selected a chief, he emerged as the leader of resistance to removal of the Seminole Indians from FLORIDA during the SEMINOLE WAR. Some accounts maintain that his mother was a Creek but that his father was an Englishman, William Powell. He was sometimes called by the whites Billy Powell or simply Powell. Some writers maintain that Powell was Osceola's stepfather and that his true father was a Creek.

After Andrew Jackson crushed the Creek in 1813, Osceola and his relatives moved into Florida, probably to a British trading post on the Apalachicola River. About 1815 they moved to the St. Marks region, remaining there until 1818. The band in which Osceola moved was among those that kept the Florida frontier in turmoil until Jackson's 1818 punitive expedition. Osceola was among those captured by Jackson in Florida on the Enconfina River but he was held only briefly. His group then moved to a spot south of Tampa Bay. During the 1820s Osceola is said to have been one of several braves used by the United States Indian agent for police work, notably to apprehend Indians straying beyond reservation limits.

Osceola's wedding date is unknown but at the time of his capture in 1836 he had two wives and two children. His residence in the 1830s was about seven miles southwest of present-day Ocala.

Nine years after the Treaty of Moultrie Creek of 1823, which had established the Seminole reservation, a council was held at Payne's Landing to get Seminole consent to move to the trans-Mississippi West. Though present, Osceola did not speak nor affix his mark to the treaty, so small was his influence. During 1833-34 resentment over the removal agreement spread, Osceola encouraging and stimulating it. In council in 1834 the agent warned them to be ready to move in the spring, but Osceola urged resistance to removal upon the assembled chiefs. Next day they informed the agent that the Moultrie Creek treaty still had seven years to run and that the Treaty of Payne's Landing was a fraud. Osceola at this council assumed the role of principal spokesman.

On President Jackson's orders a very large council was held in April 1835, and military officers made it clear to the chiefs that they must move or be taken by force. A document reiterating the promise to emigrate was presented and sixteen chiefs made their marks. An old story persists that Osceola pinned it to the table with his knife, proclaiming that to be the only mark he would make, but Indian agent Wiley Thompson's accounts make no mention of this. In November Charley Amathla, a chief who had agreed to emigrate, was murdered by Osceola and his followers and in December they killed Thompson and an army lieutenant near Fort King (Ocala). Organized hostilities ensued in which Osceola was prominent. By the spring of 1837 most of the chiefs had consented to move, gathering at Fort Mellon and at Tampa Bay. Osceola appeared at Fort Mellon in May, but rather than preparing to emigrate, he organized a coup in which the more docile chiefs at Tampa Bay were seized and their followers scattered.

In late summer of 1837 several important chiefs were captured in East Florida by militia. Coacoochee, the son of one of them, conferred with militia forces under a flag of truce and announced that Osceola and a band of followers were desirous of a conference. In October militia General J. M. Hernandez went to Osceola's camp and after a brief talk Osceola, thirteen other chiefs, and seventy-one warriors were seized in accord with plans laid by General Thomas S. Jesup. Imprisoned in St. Augustine in the Castillo de San Marcos, Coacoochee and nineteen others escaped in November but Osceola

scorned to do so. Thereafter, the remaining Indians were moved to Fort Moultrie in Charleston, South Carolina, where Osceola died on January 31, 1838. An army doctor said that he died from an acute attack of quinsy. Other observers believed that he had willed his own death out of deep melancholy at having been tricked into leaving his people leaderless. In a belated and rather meaningless gesture of atonement, Osceola was buried at Fort Moultrie with full military honors.

See *Florida Historical Quarterly* (January-April 1955).—H. J. D.

Osgood, Ernest S. (1888-   ). Historian. Osgood was born in Lynn, Massachusetts. Graduating from Dartmouth College in 1912, Osgood did not embark upon graduate studies in history until twelve years later, when he enrolled at the University of Wisconsin. His entire teaching career in the ensuing three decades was spent at the University of Minnesota, where he taught courses in western history and trained graduate students in the field. Among his students were historians such as Reynold M. Wik, who traced the influence of steam power on western farmers; Robert G. Athearn, a prominent railroad historian; and Clark C. Spence, a specialist in western mining. After his retirement in 1957, Osgood continued to lecture about frontier history for more than a decade at the College of Wooster in Ohio.

Osgood's reputation was based on quality rather than on quantity. His only book was *The Day of the Cattleman* (1928), an authoritative analysis of the rise and fall of the cattle industry in the trans-Mississippi region during the second half of the nineteenth century. Distinguished by breadth as well as by depth, this work was for many years considered one of the definitive works on the subject. —G. D. N.

Otero, Miguel A[ntonio] (father) (1829-1882). New Mexican politician and businessman. Born in Valencia, New Mexico, Otero attended private and parochial schools and St. Louis University in Missouri. He was graduated from Pingree's College, Fishkill, New York, where he also was a member of the faculty. Although his parents wanted him to enter the priesthood, Otero studied law in New York City and in Missouri under Governor Trusten Polk and was admitted to the bar in St. Louis in 1851. Returning to New Mexico, he began a law practice in 1852 and in the same year was elected to the territorial legislature from Valencia County. With the support of Bishop Lamy, Otero in 1855 defeated "Padre" José Manuel Gallegos for territorial delegate. The election was decided by contest, and Otero did not take his seat until July 23, 1856. He was reelected delegate in 1857 and 1859.

During his first term as delegate, Otero married Mary Josephine Blackwood of Charleston, South Carolina. Otero's marriage enhanced his political ties with the South, and he wanted New Mexico to cooperate with southern views of slavery. Thus in 1859 he was instrumental in the passage of the "slave code" by the territorial legislature, which restricted Negroes in the territory. He later supported the Crittenden Compromise, which would have extended slavery to New Mexico, but when it was defeated Otero suggested in Congress a confederation of Pacific states that would be aligned with neither the North or South.

A Democrat and a delegate to the 1860 Democratic

convention in Charleston, where he supported Stephen A. Douglas for the presidency, Otero's electoral power in New Mexico was eroded by a national Republican trend. On April 18, 1860, Otero delivered a well-publicized speech in the House in which he sought a "regiment of New Mexican mounted volunteers . . . for the suppression of Indian hostilities in the Territory of New Mexico." Referring to the laxity of the territorial governor in Indian affairs and "the blood of my own relatives spilled upon the soil of my own country," Otero declared: "We thought when we became a part of this great republic, that our condition would have been bettered; we had the right to expect it if your promises were sincere."

Otero declined the appointment as minister to Spain offered in 1861 by President Lincoln. Lincoln then appointed him in 1861 territorial secretary and acting governor, but his nomination was not confirmed by the Senate. From 1861-64 he was engaged in mercantile businesses in Kansas City and in 1864 he went to Leavenworth, Kansas, where he was involved in merchandising. Having in 1858 called New Mexico an isolated "territorial isle," Otero was involved until 1877 in the extension of railroads into the territory. He was director of the Maxwell Land Grant and Railroad Company and helped to organize the New Mexico and Southern Pacific Railroad. Also engaged in banking, Otero was a founder and the first president of the San Miguel National Bank of Las Vegas. He was an unsuccessful candidate for delegate in 1880, losing to Tranquilino Luna of Valencia County, and died in Las Vegas, New Mexico.

See extensive references in R. E. Twitchell, *The Leading Facts in New Mexican History* (1912); and, for briefer mention, Howard R. Lamar, *The Far Southwest: 1846-1912* (1966) and Robert W. Larson, *New Mexico's Quest for Statehood, 1846-1912* (1968). Otero's speech in the House on April 18, 1860, concerning the raising of a New Mexico volunteer regiment, was reprinted by H. Polkinhorn (1860).—J. R. V.

Otero, Miguel A[ntonio] (son) (1859-1944). New Mexican politician and writer. Born in St. Louis, Missouri, Otero was the son of the then Democratic territorial delegate of the same name. He received a classical education at the University of St. Louis and at Notre Dame. From 1873 to 1881 Otero was employed by his father's mercantile firm and later held various local posts in New Mexico.

President McKinley, whom Otero had met in 1892 when a delegate to the Republican National Convention, in 1897 appointed him to a four-year term as governor of New Mexico. Otero, then a worker in the Republican party, had sought appointment only as federal marshal. Soon called the "little governor," Otero's inaugural ceremonies were perhaps the most elaborate in territorial New Mexico. His appointment angered the Republican old guard, eroded the power of Thomas Benton Catron, who previously had dominated the Republican party in New Mexico, and led to a feud between Catron and Otero. With the aid of Pedro Perea—whom Otero later opposed during Perea's term as delegate—José Francisco Chaves, and Solomon Luna, Otero organized grass-roots native support for his administration, previously unrealized by New Mexico's governors. He thereby immensely increased the impor-

tance of the governorship in New Mexico politics.

As governor, Otero gained the support of all the Republican National Committee and forty-five of forty-seven members of the territorial Republican Central Committee. He successfully opposed the construction of an international dam between El Paso, Texas, and Ciudad Juárez, Mexico, thus reserving the waters of the Rio Grande for agricultural development in New Mexico. He was reappointed by President McKinley on June 15, 1901, and, after McKinley's assassination, by President Roosevelt on December 18, 1901.

Although largely satisfied with the territorial status of New Mexico during his first term as governor, Otero became a proponent of statehood at about the turn of the century. Having helped Theodore Roosevelt to recruit Rough Rider regiments in New Mexico, in 1899 Otero received Roosevelt's pledge of support for statehood. Otero called a statehood convention to meet in Albuquerque on October 15, 1901, and was successful in gaining passage of resolutions for statehood. By 1901 the statehood issue had transcended the earlier rivalry between Catron and Otero. Moreover, by 1901 Pedro Perea, with whom Otero had often disagreed on such issues as the coinage of silver, was no longer delegate. Otero opposed joint statehood (by which New Mexico and Arizona would enter the Union as one state) as early as 1903. In 1905 strife in the Republican party in New Mexico led Roosevelt to request Otero's resignation. Looking back on his governorship, Otero in 1940 wrote: "I prided myself on giving New Mexico a businesslike administration." He was especially pleased with the expansion of the railroads in New Mexico during his administration.

From 1909 to 1911 Otero was treasurer of New Mexico and president of the state board of penitentiary commissioners. He was president of the New Mexico parole board (1913-17) and United States marshal of the Panama Canal Zone (1917-21). Having switched to the Democratic party after 1905, Otero was chairman of the New Mexico delegation to the Democratic national conventions of 1912 and 1916, a member of the Progressive party National Committee in 1916, and chairman of the Canal Zone delegation to the Democratic national conventions of 1920 and 1924. Between these latter years he was also a member of the Democratic National Committee.

Among Otero's publications are *Conquistadors of Spain and Buccaneers of England, France and Holland* (1924), *My Life on the Frontier, 1864-82* (1926), *My Nine Years as Governor of the Territory of New Mexico* (1940), and *The Real Billy the Kid* (1936). Otero, who at the age of nine had known Wild Bill Hickok in Hays City, at age twenty-one met Billy the Kid after he had been captured by Marshal Garrett. He rode with Garrett and Billy the Kid on the train to Santa Fe and visited Billy frequently in jail. Subsequently he collected material on Billy the Kid and wrote the biography in which he describes him as "a man more sinned against than sinning."

R. E. Twitchell, *The Leading Facts in New Mexican History* (1912), discusses at length the administration of Otero. Otero's voluminous official papers are deposited in the Official Governor's Files of New Mexico. A valuable, succinct account of Otero's changing views on the question of statehood is contained in Marion Dargan,

"New Mexico's Fight for Statehood, I," *New Mexico Historical Review* (January 1939).—J. R. V.

Ouachita Province. See PHYSIOGRAPHY OF THE UNITED STATES.

Oury brothers. Arizona pioneers. As a Virginia-born Texas patriot, Texas Ranger, Mexican War veteran, gold-miner, Arizona cattleman, Indian fighter, stage agent, mayor, newspaper editor, sheriff, and politician, William Sanders Oury (1817-1887) epitomizes the pioneer American from eastern greenbelts who conquered the harsh southwestern environment and helped make it habitable for Anglo-Americans. Oury made his transition from East to Southwest with a historic stopover in Texas. A volunteer at the Alamo in 1836, he was sent away from the fort by William Travis as courier to Gonzales, Texas, for help, and therefore escaped death. Oury participated in the battle of San Jacinto (1836) that followed and later joined the Texas Rangers. In December 1842 he became a member of the ill-fated Mier expedition captured by the Mexicans. He was one of the lucky ones who drew a white bean from a lottery bottle and gained freedom. (Those who drew a black bean from the bottle were shot by the Mexicans.) Next he joined Texas volunteers and participated in several border battles in the Mexican War (1846-48).

Oury began his Arizona career as an overland stage agent and newspaper editor. A man with a fiery disposition and steel nerve, he killed two men in duels, thus establishing his reputation for self-preservation. When Tucson was incorporated in May 1864, Oury was its first mayor. Soon after, he became a cattle rancher and introduced Shorthorn cattle to upgrade local Spanish stock.

Apache preyed upon white settlements continually, and Oury was an active member of the local volunteer army of Indian fighters.

Toward the end of his checkered career, Oury was elected first president of the Arizona Pioneers' Historical Society in Tucson and was appointed Tucson's deputy collector of customs.

Congressman, Arizona chief justice, and delegate to the Confederate Congress, Virginia-born Granville H. Oury (1825-1891) took a lively interest in Arizona Territory legislative matters. While overshadowed by the illustrious accomplishments of his brother, Granville made significant contributions in his own right. One of the petitioners to the Congress for territorial status for Arizona, he later served two terms as speaker of the house in the Arizona legislature, 1873-75.

Granville espoused the southern cause at the outbreak of the Civil War and was elected territorial delegate to the Confederate Congress in Richmond, Virginia. Arrested in Arizona as a secessionist, his United States citizenship later was reinstated. He became a Democratic party stalwart and served in the United States Congress from 1880 to 1884.

See Cornelius C. Smith, Jr., *William Sanders Oury, History-maker of the Southwest* (1967), and Jay J. Wagoner, *Arizona Territory 1863-1912* (1970).
—B. W. A.

overland guidebooks. See EMIGRANTS' GUIDEBOOKS.

Overland Mail Company. Persistent demands for a through mail service to the Pacific Coast culminated in the authorization of an overland mail service by a congressional act of March 1857. The service was to be

semiweekly, with the trip taking a maximum of twenty-five days. The government subsidy was $600,000 a year. The postmaster general awarded the contract to a joint stock company, known as the Overland Mail Company, organized by men having substantial financial and managerial interest in the major express companies: American, National, Adams, and Wells, Fargo & Co. Among the directors were John Butterfield, William G. Fargo, and William B. Dinsmore. The Post Office located the route starting at both St. Louis and Memphis, converging at Fort Smith, Arkansas, and then by a circuitous way through Preston and El Paso, Texas, Tucson and Yuma in Arizona, and on to Los Angeles and San Francisco. This indirect route was almost two thousand eight hundred miles in length. The founders were allowed up to a year to survey and improve the route, build way stations, purchase stagecoaches, and stock the line. The first stages left at opposite ends of the line on September 15, 1858, and made the trip in slightly more than twenty days. The company had invested more than a million dollars before the first mail was delivered.

The aggressive spokesman for the company was its president, John BUTTERFIELD, and the line was often referred to in its early years as the "Butterfield Overland Mail," although his name was never incorporated in the official title nor did it appear on the side of the Concord stagecoaches making the run. The service was exceptionally well maintained between stations located at ten- to fifteen-mile intervals. In isolated areas or hostile Indian country guards were quartered at the stations and sometimes rode with the driver to protect the passengers. The Concord coaches, made by Abbott-Downing Company, were mounted on the running gear by leather thoroughbraces in lieu of springs. Three seats inside the coach were designed for nine passengers but many more often rode on the outside, some preferring the dust and open air to the crowded interior. Mail and packages were placed in a boot at the rear of the stage or on top of the coach. Passengers paid cash, usually $200, for their transportation and were allowed forty pounds of luggage. On the other hand, government mail was carried at a flat rate, and when the stagecoach was overcrowded, mailbags were often left at wayside stations to give passengers preference.

A stagecoach trip was not a pleasurable excursion. The stages rolled along both day and night on the three-week trip and passengers found all attempts to sleep periodically interrupted by the jolting of the coach on the rough roads. An alternative was provided by stopping at one of the "home stations" to sleep, but one risked being unable to resume his journey if the next stage that came along was overcrowded. Travelers complained constantly about lack of toilet and bathing facilities, the miserable and expensive food, the extensive use of whiskey both by fellow passengers and stage attendants, and the drunken and profane stage drivers. In spite of the inconvenience, the organization and effectiveness of the Overland Mail Company was not seriously criticized, but the long "ox-bow" route was the object of continuous complaint.

Stagecoach service was developed on the central route directly west from Missouri to Denver and Salt Lake on to the California border in the hope of obtaining the overland mail contract. The Pony Express was introduced by Russell, Majors and Waddell to publicize the shortness and superiority of a central route to the more southerly mail line. Butterfield proposed to meet the challenge by establishing a rival pony express, but Wells, Fargo & Co., directors on the board of the Overland Mail Company, blocked this action. To conduct their business with speed and efficiency, Wells, Fargo & Co. utilized the Pony Express on the central route and did not wish to subsidize a competing service that could not meet a comparable schedule. Dissension had already developed between Wells, Fargo & Co. and the Overland Mail Company because the latter could not meet the payments on loans advanced to launch the enterprise. Next to Butterfield, the three largest shareowners in the Overland Mail Company were directors of Wells, Fargo & Co. To forestall foreclosure, the board of directors of the mail company was reorganized in April 1860 to give the directors and large shareholders in Wells, Fargo & Co. the majority of the seats. Butterfield was removed from the presidency and William B. Dinsmore, of Adams Express Company, was elected.

With the outbreak of the Civil War, the Overland Mail route through Texas had to be abandoned and operations transferred to the central route. In March 1861 a contract for the delivery of a daily overland mail both by stagecoach and Pony Express was awarded to the Overland Mail Company. Russell, Majors and Waddell, disappointed in the outcome, were granted a subcontract whereby their Central Overland California and Pike's Peak Express Company operated the stage and Pony Express line east of Salt Lake City. A year later Ben Holladay purchased the assets of this firm at a foreclosure sale to protect the loans he had made, and from 1862 to 1864 he fulfilled their mail contract.

In 1864 the contracts for the overland mail service were divided between Holladay's Overland Stage Line—carrying the mail from St. Joseph, Missouri, to Salt Lake City—and the Overland Mail Company—operating from Salt Lake to Carson City and Virginia City, Nevada. The Overland Mail Company made a subcontract with the Pioneer Stage Company to deliver the mails from western Nevada to Folsom, California, an arrangement that had been in effect since 1861. Only the mails were to be carried by stagecoach under the terms of the 1864 contract with the Post Office, with newspapers and documents being carried to the Pacific Coast by sea.

In 1866 all transportation and mail facilities west of the Missouri became the responsibility of Wells, Fargo & Co., which had consolidated the interests of the express companies, the Holladay lines, the Pioneer Stage Company, and the Overland Mail Company. In 1868, when the date for contract bidding arrived, Wells, Fargo & Co. was the only organization financially able and equipped to handle the mail service. The Post Office awarded the contract to the lowest bidder who defaulted. Wells Fargo at first refused to carry the mails after the expiration of its 1864 contract, but finally agreed to transport them between the railroad termini for $1,750,000 subject to pro rata reduction for every mile of railroad completed. The completion of the transcontinental railroad on May 10, 1869, automatically canceled the last overland mail contract.

The pioneering study, *The Overland Mail, 1849-1869* (1926), was written by LeRoy R. Hafen. Roscoe P. Conkling and Margaret B. Conkling, *The Butterfield Over-land Mail, 1857-1869* (1947), is a scholarly and definitive treatment of the subject. Lyle H. Wright and Josephine M. Bynum have edited a valuable and entertaining account by Waterman L. Ormsby, *The Butterfield Overland Mail* (1955). He traveled on the first westbound stage on the overland mail route.—W. T. J.

Owen, Robert L. (1856-1947). Oklahoma politician. Born in Lynchburg, Virginia, the son of Robert Latham Owen and Narcissa Chisholm Owen, a Cherokee woman, Owen was educated in Virginia private schools and at Washington and Lee University. Following graduation, he taught school for a year at Baltimore and then moved to Indian Territory and settled among his kinsmen, the Cherokee. He taught at the Cherokee Orphan Asylum, served as secretary of the Cherokee Nation Board of Education, studied law, and was admitted to the bar at Tahlequah in 1880. He edited and published the *Indian Chieftain*, a daily newspaper at Vinita, and held appointment as United States agent for the Five Civilized Tribes (1885-89) with headquarters at Muskogee. In 1890 Owen established the First National Bank of Muskogee, serving as its president for ten years. He was a leader in the formation of the Indian Territory Democratic party and became widely known over the territory as a public official, civic leader, and public speaker.

With the advent of Oklahoma statehood in 1907 Owen became a candidate for the United States Senate. He was victorious and continued in the Senate until his retirement from politics in 1925. As a senator Owen concentrated on monetary questions and Indian affairs. He served as chairman of the Senate committee on banking and currency and was largely responsible for framing the Federal Reserve Act of 1913 and the Federal Farm Act of 1916. As a reformer Owen urged adoption of laws improving the status of the United States Public Health Service, child labor legislation, and woman suffrage. He was a principal Senate spokesman for the ratification of the League of Nations Convenant.

Following retirement, Owen practiced law in Muskogee and Washington, D.C. His varied interests were reflected in his service as president of the National Popular Government League, which promoted the preferential primary, short ballot, and direct election of senators; president of the Sound Money League, which advocated a government-owned central bank; president of the National Monetary Conference; and president of the World Language Foundation, which offered a phonetic alphabet for a universal language.—A. M. G.

Owens, Commodore Perry (1852-1919). Lawman. Owens was born in East Tennessee on the anniversary of Commodore Perry's victory on Lake Erie during the War of 1812, a fact of history that his parents insured he would always remember. As a child he lived in Indiana and, like many other young men, headed for Texas in the 1870s. He drifted throughout the Southwest, developed dexterity with guns, and established a reputation for honesty and courage. By the time he rode into Apache County, Arizona, in 1881, he was already an experienced gunman. Of medium height, he sported shoulder-length hair, a broad-brimmed hat, and a Colt revolver butt-forward on his left side. He worked as a cowboy for the big ranchers in the area and later as a wrangler for a stage line, fighting against Navaho horse thieves. Still later he homesteaded a small place in

Apache County. In 1886 his reputation for honesty and his popularity won the sheriff's office for him, but he modestly had little to say about the whole affair.

Apache County was a rowdy area in those days. Big cattle outfits like the Hash Knife brought drovers into the towns in large numbers, who caroused and shot up the saloons. Occasionally, the Navaho acted up. And the Graham-Tewksbury feud was warming up in 1886. In spite of the obstacles, Owens was a good sheriff. He brought a new measure of law and order to St. Johns and Holbrook, but his biggest challenge was the blood feud between the Grahams and the Tewksburys. Inevitably he was drawn into their troubles.

Among the partisans of the Graham faction was a young tough named Andy Blevans, alias Andy Cooper, who was wanted for stealing horses. On September 4, 1887, Sheriff Owens rode into Holbrook to arrest Blevans, but when Owens ordered him to surrender on the front porch of the Blevans home, a gunfight erupted that left Andy and two other men dead and a fourth man wounded. Owens was unscratched. The incident at Holbrook made Owens a legend, but its bloody consequences replaced some of the community's admiration with fear. After all, he had killed three men and wounded another in less than a minute. His relationship with the county officials paled after that, and he eventually retired as sheriff almost a decade later.

During his last years as sheriff, Owens was a reminder to the community of its violent past, and the new attitude affected him deeply. He became more sullen, and some say he drank too much. He spent his last years as a saloonkeeper until his mind began to fail him. Owens died of general paresis and was buried at Flagstaff, Arizona.

See Will C. Barnes, *Apaches and Longhorns* (1941); and Earle R. Forrest, *Arizona's Dark and Bloody Ground* (1936).—G. L. R.

Ozark Plateaus. See PHYSIOGRAPHY OF THE UNITED STATES.

P

Pacific Border Province. See PHYSIOGRAPHY OF THE UNITED STATES.

Pacific Fur Company. See FUR TRADE: *in the United States*.

Pacific Mail Steamship Company. California's remoteness had been a great deterrent to its development during the period of Spanish and Mexican occupation. A spirit of separatism made political control and administration difficult. When the province became a part of the United States in 1850, Congress resolved to improve communication and transportation by means of a mail subsidy. The overland routes from Missouri were difficult because of geographic obstacles; the voyage around Cape Horn was both long and hard. The development of the route across Panama appeared to be the logical solution to the problem. In addition to feeling concern for the Pacific Coast settlements, Congress recognized that commercial steamships could be converted into auxiliary vessels for the navy. When the Post Office Department was unable to find a contractor for the mail service under legislation of 1845 and 1847, the Navy Department was authorized to act. William H. Aspinwall organized the Pacific Mail Steamship Company, incorporated in New York in April 1848 with a capital of $500,000, to carry out a federal government contract for passenger and mail service between Panama and Oregon on a monthly basis. The annual subsidy was $199,000. At the same time the UNITED STATES MAIL STEAMSHIP COMPANY accepted a contract to deliver the mails semimonthly between New York and New Orleans to Chagres on the Isthmus for an annual subsidy of $290,000.

The Pacific Mail Steamship Company operated three well-known vessels, the *California*, the *Panama*, and the *Oregon*. These steamers were entirely inadequate to carry all the travelers who arrived in Panama at the time of the gold rush demanding passage to San Francisco. The original fare from Panama to San Francisco had been set at $250 for a cabin passage and $100 for steerage. There was considerable resale of tickets, and on the first voyage of the *Oregon* and the *Panama*, steerage accommodations went for $1,000. The Pacific Mail Steamship Company attempted to meet the demands for passage by purchasing additional vessels, such as the *Tennessee* and the British steamer *Unicorn*, and placing them in service. The *Frémont* was purchased and sent to the Pacific to supplement the *Columbia* on the Oregon run, and a new steamer, the *Golden Gate*, was built. The company instituted sailings between San Francisco and Panama at fortnightly intervals; a semimonthly mail service was also provided between Panama and Astoria, Oregon. The company prospered and as early as 1850 had increased its capital stock to $2 million. In July 1850 a fifty percent dividend was paid.

Competition developed from such profits. A short period of bitter competition with the United States Mail Steamship Company for passengers and express terminated in an agreement whereby they would divide this business as long as their mail contracts were held. A monopoly appeared imminent, but Cornelius Vanderbilt opened a competing service through Nicaragua in 1851. Within the year he sold his seven steamers for $1.2 million cash and an additional $1.5 million payable within the year to the Accessory Transit Company,

The Palace of the Governors in Santa Fe, New Mexico. (New Mexico Department of Development)

previously concerned only with the crossing of the Isthmus. Shortly thereafter Vanderbilt reentered the business by organizing the Independent Line and began cutting rates. Sharp competition continued until 1856. For the next three years the Nicaragua Transit Company cooperated with the Pacific Mail Steamship Company and the United States Mail Steamship Company to undermine the influence of Vanderbilt. Between 1856 and 1859 the Pacific Mail company paid him $40,000 a month and then $56,000 a month to stay out of the business.

In 1859 the original mail contract expired and the United States Mail Steamship Company withdrew from the Isthmian service. Both Pacific Mail and Vanderbilt attempted to get the new contract, and "Commodore" Vanderbilt was successful. At this juncture, the Panama Railroad, completed in 1855, joined forces with Pacific Mail to put steamers on the Atlantic route between New York and Aspinwall, now Colón, Panama, to compete with Vanderbilt. In 1860 the expensive competition ended in a truce whereby Vanderbilt agreed to operate only in the Atlantic and Pacific Mail only in the Pacific. Vanderbilt purchased a large interest in the Pacific Mail Steamship Company and consolidated his various operations into the Atlantic and Pacific Steamship Company.

In contrast to the United States Mail Company, the Pacific Mail Steamship Company fulfilled all its government contracts satisfactorily in delivering passengers and mails during the first decade of the Panama service. The company was reasonably prosperous, paying semiannual dividends of ten percent for 1853, from twenty-five percent to thirty percent annually between 1856 and 1858, and ten percent in 1859. In 1865 Pacific Mail purchased Vanderbilt's Atlantic fleet and took over the entire route. The company undertook a major expansion of capital to open up a steamship service to China. After the completion of the transcontinental rail-

road in 1869, the Far Eastern routes were emphasized. However, as late as 1874 the steamers between Panama and San Francisco were carrying crowds of passengers on every trip. The fare from New York to California via Panama was about half what it was by rail, and less affluent travelers continued to use the steamship service.

Two authoritative studies are John H. Kemble, *The Panama Route, 1848-1869* (1943); and Raymond Rydell, *Cape Horn to the Pacific: The Rise and Decline of an Ocean Highway* (1952). Arthur Hamilton Clark, *The Clipper Ship Era, 1843-1869* (1910), provides ample dramatic detail.—W. T. J.

painter. See MOUNTAIN LION.

Paiute Indians. See INDIANS OF THE GREAT BASIN.

Palace of the Governors. El Palacio, the Palace of the Governors in Santa Fe, New Mexico, facing the town plaza, is the oldest public building in the United States. It is probably the oldest European-built structure of any kind in the country. Because Pueblo Indians burnt the earliest palace archives, and an American governor sold the later Spanish and Mexican records for scrap paper, no known written documents on the laying of its cornerstone remain. But the Archives of the Indies, in Seville, Spain, contains a copy of the orders given in March 1609 to Don Pedro de Peralta, New Mexico's third Spanish governor, telling him to establish a new capital in the province. The officials were to "designate . . . one block of streets, for the erection of the Royal Houses."

The Royal Houses, constituting the residence of the governor, the stronghold and arsenal, would have priority over any other construction except, possibly, a temporary church. It is, therefore, reasonably certain that by the winter of 1609-10 Governor Peralta was adequately roofed and walled in.

The palace was built of heavy adobe bricks and plastered with mud. In Mexican and European archives, mention is made of new apartments added by later governors (dressing rooms, drawing rooms, and a shop where one governor sold chocolates, hats, and shoes).

By 1680, when the long-suffering Pueblos rebelled and overthrew the Spanish, the great walled and fortified "Royal Houses" were large enough to hold "more than a thousand persons, five thousand head of sheep and goats, four hundred horses and mules, and three hundred head of beef cattle without crowding."

In 1692, when Captain-General Don Diego de Vargas reconquered Santa Fe, the palace and royal houses had been transformed into a high-walled multi-storied pueblo. The chapel had been converted neatly into a *kiva*, an Indian underground ceremonial chamber. His successors in office just let the massive walls and towers gradually erode and slump down (as adobe is wont to do when neglected). Various royal governors complained wearily through the years of leaking roofs, falling plaster, and general decay after it became a civil and domestic establishment.

When Mexico won independence from Spain in 1822, a large room was designated as the meeting hall of the New Mexico deputies. In 1847, with the American flag flying over it, the palace was readied for the first session of the territorial House of Representatives.

In 1866 the busy Americans, with their passion for change, tore down a third of the building to the west with its tower where gunpowder was stored and the jail. The east end was rebuilt, the outbuildings torn down and rebuilt, reducing the patio to one half its size, and, of course, the planting was torn out, leaving only a dead cottonwood.

In 1878 the front portal of peeled logs and dirt roof was replaced by a proud new Midwest Victorian porch, which was replaced, in its turn, by a Spanish-style portal in 1913.

Except for the thirteen years as an Indian pueblo and two months as a Confederate stronghold, the palace never ceased to be the official residence and office for Spanish, Mexican, and American civil and military governors from 1610 to 1900. In 1909 the palace was turned into the MUSEUM OF NEW MEXICO. In 1940 it was designated a state monument, and in 1970, as El Palacio, was named a national historic landmark.

See Bruce T. Ellis, *The Historic Palace of the Governors* (1968).—B. P. D. and M. L.

Palladino, Lawrence (1837-1927). Jesuit missionary. Palladino was born in Italy. An educator as well as a priest, he served Indians and settlers in the Pacific Northwest, especially Montana, for about sixty years, beginning in 1863. He is the author of *Indian and White in the Northwest* (1894).

See Robert I. Burns, *The Jesuits and the Indian Wars of the Northwest* (1966).—R. I. B.

Palmer, William Jackson (1836-1909). Soldier and railroad builder. Palmer was born in Leipsic, Kent County, Delaware. He learned railroad operations while serving as secretary to J. Edgar Thompson, president of the Pennsylvania Railroad, from 1858 to 1861. During the Civil War Palmer organized and led the Fifteenth Pennsylvania Cavalry at Antietam, Missionary Ridge, Chickamauga, and Atlanta, retiring from the service as a brigadier general of volunteers.

In 1865 he became treasurer of the Kansas Pacific Railroad, soon to become Union Pacific's eastern division, and surveyed the western portion between Sheridan, Wyoming, and Denver, Colorado. Recognizing that Denver, having been bypassed by the main line of the Union Pacific, needed rail facilities of its own, he concentrated on the Denver and Rio Grande Railroad, which linked the city with connections to the South and West. Palmer and the Rio Grande survived the depression of the 1870s, and the line was completed to Salt Lake City, Utah, in 1883. Despite fierce opposition by the Santa Fe Railroad, which almost degenerated into open warfare, Palmer saw the western and eastern segments of the Rio Grande merged in a reorganization in 1889.

"Cultured, intelligent, and likeable," Palmer took a deep interest in the development of the city of Colorado Springs, Colorado College, and Hampton Institute. For his service during the Civil War he received the Congressional Medal of Honor in 1894. By then the Denver and Rio Grande and its Royal Gorge route through the canyon of the Arkansas River had become one of the most popular with western tourists.

A relatively unknown figure in western railroad history, Palmer's monument is the DENVER AND RIO GRANDE WESTERN RAILROAD, whose story is well told in Robert G. Athearn, *Rebel of the Rockies: A History of the Denver and Rio Grande Western Railroad* (1962).—A. M.

Palo Duro Canyon, battle of (1874). With the outbreak of the RED RIVER WAR on the southern Plains in 1874, six strong columns from Texas, Kansas, Indian Territory, and New Mexico Territory were sent against the hostile Kiowa, Comanche, and Southern Cheyenne. After skirmishing with the Indians on the eastern edge of the Llano Estacado in West Texas in September, Colonel Ranald S. MACKENZIE, operating out of Fort Concho, Texas, made a rapid march northward to Palo Duro Canyon, Texas, where he found a large encampment of hostiles. On the morning of September 28 his men found a trail and descended to the valley floor seven hundred feet below. In the fighting that followed the Indians abandoned their villages, leaving them and their horse herd in Mackenzie's hands. He destroyed the village and slaughtered 1,048 horses. Few Indians were killed, but the battle at Palo Duro Canyon and the relentless pursuit that followed helped bring the Red River War to a rapid and successful conclusion with few casualties on either side.—R. N. E.

Panama: Isthmian diplomacy since 1850. The isthmus between North and South America has naturally had a considerable importance for settlement of the American West. That importance was at its height during the years immediately after the gold strike in California, when during the 1850s tens of thousands of Americans traveled from east to west via the isthmus. Most of the travelers passed through Nicaragua, not Panama, for the latter was a pestilential place and it proved possible to construct the Panama Railway only after the loss of many lives. The Nicaraguan route was far better. It was indeed almost a picnic excursion, as passengers from New York and New Orleans landed at Greytown, proceeded in boats of light draft up the San Juan River to Lake Nicaragua, crossed the lake in steamers to a point on the west shore called Virgin Bay, and from there were conveyed in carriages over a macadamized road to San Juan del Sur and the steamer for San Francisco.

As the Nicaraguan route became lucrative, the Accessory Transit Company, an American enterprise, sought to protect itself from the volcanic animosities of Nicaraguan politics by setting up an individual named William Walker as president of the country, which office he retained for several years. Walker was a notorious filibuster from California, and his downfall owed partly to the fact that he sought to take over the Transit company and thereby ran afoul of that company's part owner, Commodore Cornelius Vanderbilt. The latter fomented a rival Nicaraguan revolution that expelled *El Presidente* Walker in 1857. The former president made two attempts to regain office, and during the second a British captain arrested him on the coast of Honduras and handed him over to unfriendly Hondurans, who shot him.

The taking of the Canal Zone by the United States in 1903 had little connection with the American West, other than the fact that part of the rationale for an interoceanic canal was to cut the cost of transporting goods by rail across the West. The other part of the rationale was to enable the American fleet to transit from Atlantic to Pacific easily, rather than going around Cape Horn as the battleship *Oregon* had done in 1898. The American government felt that its vessels making the East-West crossing and carrying domestic cargo deserved to be exempt from the tolls of the canal, and in the election of 1912, held on the eve of the opening of the canal, all three candidates—Woodrow Wilson, President Taft, and former President Theodore Roosevelt—championed exemption of American coastwise shipping. A law was passed to this effect. The British government took deep offense at what it deemed a change of the arrangements set out in the Hay-Pauncefote Treaty of 1901, which had abrogated the Clayton-Bulwer Treaty of 1850; according to the instrument of 1901 the cargoes of all nations were supposed to receive equal treatment. President Wilson in 1913-14 then changed his mind on the issue of exemption of coastwise cargoes and arranged the repeal of the 1912 tolls law just before the canal opened in 1914.

On William Walker, see Lawrence Greene, *The Filibuster: The Career of William Walker* (1937); and W. O. Scroggs, *Filibusters and Financiers* (1916). For the canal tolls issue, see Arthur S. Link, *Wilson: The New Freedom* (1956).—R. H. F.

Panamint City, California. Ghost town. Panamint City was the center of a copper and silver boom that began in 1872. The boom was short-lived, however, and in the summer of 1876 the town was destroyed by a flash flood. Today Panamint is a true ghost town. Floods still roar through the canyons surrounding the town, and its remains are best reached by jeep or truck.

See Nell Murbarger, *Ghosts of the Glory Trail* (1956); Remi Nadeau, *Ghost Towns and Mining Camps of California* (1965); and Muriel S. Wolle, *The Bonanza Trail* (1953).—R. B. W.

panther. See MOUNTAIN LION.

Papago Indians. See PIMAN INDIANS.

Paris, Treaty of (1763). Termination of French and Indian War (1756-63). The New World territorial arrangements of the Treaty of Paris of 1763 were of crucial importance for the success of the American Revolution, for they inspired the government of France with an intense hatred of the British government, leading the French to look for an opportunity for revenge. It was not the custom in the eighteenth century for governments, upon conclusion of wars, to take great territorial indemnities. The British, however, under the leadership of William Pitt the Elder, had obtained a vision of empire during the Seven Years' War (in America, the French and Indian War), and even though Pitt was no longer a member of the government at the conclusion of the war, the ministry in power saw to it that the peace settlement against France and Spain was rigorous. Canada passed from France to Britain, and Spanish Florida also went to Britain. The French hastily gave the Spanish the territory of Louisiana, ostensibly because Spain was losing territory to Britain. Actually, France wanted to be rid of a white elephant; the administration of Louisiana was a nuisance to the French, because the huge colony did not pay its way. Nonetheless, the loss of Canada was a severe blow. The loss of prestige to the French court was even more severe, and it was shortly after the Seven Years' War that the French began to send a series of agents to the New World to observe the temper of the American colonials, to see if there might be colonial unrest and, perhaps, serious trouble for the hated British.

See Max Savelle, *Origins of American Diplomacy* (1967).—R. H. F.

Paris, Treaty of (1783). Termination of the American Revolution. Like most important treaties of peace, the instrument ending the war between the United States and Great Britain had a long history of complex negotiation prior to its signature on September 3, 1783. From the revolution's beginning, Americans looked forward to peace and so did the British government and people. With the Declaration of Independence in 1776, peace became more difficult, since the government of George III was not inclined to grant absolute independence. There followed an effort to negotiate, which involved the sending of a British commission to the United States to present the Congress in the New World with an acceptable compromise that would allow virtual autonomy if the Americans would but rejoin the empire. The Carlisle Commission of 1778 failed; besides, the Americans had already chosen an alliance with the French government, signed on February 6, 1778. Among other provisions, this alliance recognized American independence. Gradually—as several European powers became involved in a subsequent war with the British government—the obdurate monarch of Great Britain came to see that he too would have to recognize the independence of the Americans. Lord North resigned as prime minister in March 1782. George III drew up a message of abdication, but relented.

The French-American Alliance explicitly forbade America to enter into separate negotiations with Britain. The negotiations by which the United States did, in fact, conclude virtually a separate peace with the British government were inspired on the American side by suspicion and by a divination of the true feelings of the French foreign minister, Charles Gravier Comte de Vergennes. During the war the Americans had not always been certain of the intentions of their French ally. For example, the French government in 1779 had signed an alliance with the Spanish government, bringing that regime into the war, promising as a quid pro quo that France would assist Spain to regain Gibraltar, a possession lost to the British in a previous conflict. The war for Gibraltar indirectly pledged the American government, bound in alliance to the French, to continue fighting according to this new Spanish condition. There were other instances or supposed instances when French national interests seemed to point to a loose construction of the alliance with the United States, certainly to the possibility that, should France find herself in a straitened position, the government of Louis XVI might overlook some of its pledges to the Americans. But when the war for Gibraltar began to prove far more difficult than the Spanish and perhaps even the French had anticipated, the French foreign minister, Vergennes, became uncertain of the advantage of his Spanish pledge. Vergennes had only entered the war to humiliate the British because of France's defeat in the Seven Years' War (1756-63), and that object he had accomplished, even without the capture of Gibraltar. He began to yearn for peace, and at this juncture the American negotiators in Paris—Benjamin Franklin, John Adams, and John Jay—anticipated him.

It was a complicated politique. When Jay arrived in Paris from Madrid to act in concert with Franklin and Adams in negotiation of a peace treaty, he was strongly suspicious of the Spanish, who had not treated him well during his mission in Madrid, and on his own responsibility he opened a negotiation with a representative of the British cabinet then in Paris, a onetime slave trader named Richard Oswald. John Adams was extremely suspicious of the French court and supported this move. Franklin, acting less from suspicion than from a belief that Vergennes would not object to an initiation of negotiations, agreed to go along with his colleagues in talks with Oswald. The latter gentleman quickly proved a complaisant negotiator, and at one point in the discussions was willing to allow the Americans the possession of Canada, although for this imprudence he was properly reprimanded by the British foreign office. In other respects the negotiation proved not difficult, and soon a "preliminary treaty"—not a formal treaty, for that would have violated the letter of the alliance with France—was arranged. Franklin informed Vergennes of this treaty the night before the Americans signed it.

The preliminary instrument of November 30, 1782, gave the Americans almost everything they could have desired. Britain recognized American independence; set the Canadian-American boundary at the St. Croix River dividing Maine and Nova Scotia, the St. Lawrence-Atlantic watershed divide, the forty-fifth parallel to the St. Lawrence and then to the Great Lakes and their connecting waterways to the Lake of the Woods and the Mississippi; recognized an American "liberty" to fish in the territorial waters of British North America; stipulated the evacuation of American soil and waters by British forces "with all convenient speed"; affirmed all debts due creditors of either country by citizens of the other; and asked that Congress recommend to the state legislatures a restoration of loyalist rights and property.

The debatable aspect of this preliminary treaty was, of course, its virtual breaking of one of the engagements of the French alliance. Vergennes seems not to have been too disturbed, however, for American bad faith must have helped him to move the Spanish into a frame of mind more agreeable to peace. Some days after the signing of the preliminary treaty the foreign minister

scolded Franklin in a letter inquiring into his conduct. The shrewd American answered slyly that, although he and his colleagues perhaps had been guilty of a slight impropriety, they trusted that the British government would not learn of this disagreement between two allies. In the same letter Franklin asked for another loan of funds to the new government of the New World, which request Vergennes granted.

At once, the powers engaged in war with Great Britain—France, Spain, and the Netherlands—set about arranging separate treaties of peace with America, which were signed on September 3, 1783.

See Richard W. Van Alstyne, *Empire and Independence* (1965); E. S. Corwin, *French Policy and the American Alliance of 1778* (1916); and especially Samuel Flagg Bemis, *The Diplomacy of the American Revolution* (1935), the definitive account. For the arranging of the peace, see Richard B. Morris, *The Peacemakers* (1965). —R. H. F.

Parker, Bonnie. See BONNIE AND CLYDE.

Parker, George Leroy. See Butch CASSIDY.

Parker, Isaac Charles (1838-1896). Politician and famous "hanging judge" of Arkansas. Born and educated in Ohio, Parker moved to Missouri, where he practiced law. He served as a Republican congressman from Missouri from 1871 to 1875. The latter year President Grant sent him to serve as federal judge of the corrupt court of the Western District of Arkansas, at Fort Smith, which also had jurisdiction over the crime-ridden Indian Territory. In twenty-one years he sentenced 168 persons to death, of whom 88 were actually hanged. At the same time, sixty-five of his deputy marshals, "the men who rode for Parker," were slain in line of duty. He was a friend of the Indian tribes, a civic-minded supporter of good schools and good city government at Fort Smith, and a man whose sympathies lay with the victims and their families rather than with the criminals. A book published two years after Parker's death, *Hell on the Border*, written by S. W. Harman, a publicity-seeking defense attorney of the judge's court, is chiefly responsible for Judge Parker's undeserved reputation as a sadistic enforcer of law and order. Dime novels, western pulp magazines, and Hollywood and television have added to his much-maligned image. His restored courtroom and a replica of his hanging gallows, which could accommodate up to six criminals at a time, are a part of the Fort Smith National Historic Site.—W. L. B.

Parkman, Francis (1823-1893). Historian. Parkman was born in Boston. His father, a Unitarian minister, passed on to his son an inheritance that made him financially independent. The young historian was educated at a Boston preparatory school and at Harvard College, where he received his bachelor's degree in 1844 and also studied law. Most of Parkman's college years were spent in preparation for what he conceived to be a lifelong task, writing the history of "the Old French War." His commencement oration, "Romance in America," was an early indication of the romantic coloration the writings of Sir Walter Scott were to give to Parkman's later work. At the same time he was intensely practical about his preparations, studying, for example, Joseph François Lafitau's *Moeurs des Sauvages*. An early Jesuit, Lafitau concluded that his study of living Indians would throw light on cultures of antiquity. Parkman's decision to spend a summer on the Plains in 1846 with mountain man Henri CHATILLON to study the Sioux in order to understand the Iroquois society of the colonial era was based on Lafitau's research principles, now considered basic for the field ethnologist. Parkman's history, entitled *France and England in North America*, published in nine volumes in 1892, was the result of his large collection of data from a number of sources—not only the personal observation of Indians, pioneers, and historic sites and the examination of original manuscripts and rare books, but also from his study of nature and human character. He was a longtime scholar of French civilization before he became the historian of New France.

Parkman's historical works followed close upon the publication of his personal narrative, *The Oregon Trail* (1849), an account of his visit to the Great Plains Indian country in 1846. *The Conspiracy of Pontiac* (1851), a history of the Anglo-French wars leading up to the Ottawa chief's uprising, was a prelude to Parkman's other volumes. His *Pioneers of France in the New World* (1865) was followed by *The Jesuits in North America* (1867); *La Salle*, revised after its first publication in 1869; *The Old Regime in Canada* (1874); *Count Frontenac* (1877); *Montcalm and Wolfe* (1884); and *A Half-Century of Conflict* (1892). The *Half-Century*, like all Parkman's other works, is an artistic masterpiece encompassing economic, social, and institutional history all woven into a dramatic narrative. All these works, including *The Oregon Trail*, were part of the nine-volume *France and England in North America*. The Frontenac Edition of this work, published in 1907, includes Parkman's last revisions of his text.

There is evidence in Parkman's correspondence to show that an illness in his mature years that he called "the enemy" (semi-blindness and arthritis, heart trouble, and insomnia) could be traced to a neurosis. Critics of Parkman's writings have argued that his illness influenced his work. They accuse him of Anglo-Saxonism and have noted his tendency to give heroic individuals a commanding role in key historic events. Yet he remains one of the greatest historians, an imaginative writer who demonstrated that narrative history can be both captivating to the reader and historically accurate.

A short biography of Parkman, including a discussion of his mysterious illness, is in *The Letters of Francis Parkman*, W. R. Jacobs, ed., 2 vols. (1960). Two excellent biographies are Howard Doughty, *Francis Parkman* (1962), which includes the best account of Parkman's literary techniques, and Mason Wade, *Francis Parkman, Heroic Historian* (1942), which stresses Parkman's formative years. Wade is also the editor of the *Journals of Francis Parkman*, 2 vols. (1947). Further analysis of Parkman's literary talents is in David Levin, *History as a Romantic Art: Bancroft, Motley, Prescott, and Parkman* (1959); and Jacobs, "Francis Parkman's Oration, 'Romance in America,' " *American Historical Review* (April 1963), and "Some of Parkman's Literary Devices," *New England Quarterly* (June 1958).—W. R. J.

Parrington, Vernon Louis (1871-1929). Historian and educator. Parrington was born in Aurora, Illinois. His father was principal of an Aurora high school and captain of a Negro regiment during the Civil War. In 1877 the family moved to Americus, Kansas, not far from Emporia, and took up two quarter sections of nearby farmland on the virgin prairie. After some

rather unsuccessful farm years, the family settled in Emporia when the father was elected probate judge on the Republican ticket. There Parrington attended the new Academy and then College of Emporia. He graduated in 1891 and entered Harvard College as a junior in the class of 1893.

After graduation he taught English literature and French at Emporia College (1893-97) and then moved to the University of Oklahoma at Norman as professor of English literature and modern languages (French and German). In 1901 he married Julia Williams and in 1903-04 traveled and studied for fourteen months in England and France.

When Oklahoma became a state in 1907, the newly elected governor—in political alliance with southern Methodists—reorganized the university, dismissing fourteen of the faculty, among them Parrington, and replacing them with his political allies. Parrington was invited to join the English department at the University of Washington, Seattle. From 1908 until his death he was with that university.

At the University of Washington he began studies and courses in American literature, an innovation there as in many American colleges at that time. In 1913 he started his book originally entitled *The Democratic Spirit in American Literature, 1620-1870*. The first two volumes, retitled *Main Currents in American Thought* at the publisher's request, came out in 1927 and was awarded the Pulitzer Prize for history the next year. The third volume, with the subtitle *The Beginnings of Critical Realism in America*, incomplete at the time of his death in England, was published from the available manuscripts in 1930. *Main Currents* gained favorable recognition both in England and the United States. It influenced students of literature and historians even after it was attacked in the 1940s chiefly for its political radicalism, its aesthetic bias and shortcomings, and its antipuritanism.

The formative influences of the frontier West on Parrington are evident in *Main Currents*. His sympathy with western Populism stems from his life in Emporia, while the influences of two colleagues at the University of Washington, J. Allen Smith, a political scientist, and Edward McMahon, a United States history professor, and the frontier interpretations of Frederick Jackson Turner were decisive in Parrington's interpretation of American thought. Admittedly a Jeffersonian, he thought the frontier, particularly the western one, a democratizing influence. A chapter in volume two of *Main Currents*, "The Romance of the West," and two chapters in volume three, "Hamlin Garland and the Middle Border" and "A Democratic Economics—Henry George," are eloquent testimony to western influence. He thought his own boyhood experience on a Kansas homestead remarkably parallel to that of Hamlin Garland as described in his *A Son of the Middle Border*.

Perhaps even more decisive was his experience with Populism while a student and then teacher at Emporia. He attended the 1897 Kansas convention of the Populists as chairman of the Emporia delegation and remained sympathetic with agrarianism, even though he later admitted it was a lost cause. Some of his admiration for William Morris can be attributed to that writer's criticism of industrialism. The general drift of Parrington's interpretations away from a belletristic to an economic base certainly derives from Morris' socialism. Further stimulus in that direction came from his closest colleague at the University of Washington, J. Allen Smith, whose *The Spirit of American Government* influenced Parrington's political and economic interpretations. This was reinforced by Charles A. Beard's *Economic Interpretation of the Constitution*.

The third strand of his interpretation, while closely related to the two foregoing ones, might be called antipuritan or—from a slightly different angle—antigenteel, since Parrington considered the "genteel" not only snobbish elitism but puritanism gone to seed. George Santayana's "The Genteel Tradition in American Philosophy"; his own experiences with Fundamentalism while at Oklahoma; his earlier liberation from Calvinism by reading Herbert Spencer and Henry Drummond's *The Ascent of Man*; and the H. L. Mencken-Van Wyck Brooks attacks on puritanism all influenced Parrington's thought. Fundamentally his interpretations are moralistic, but they are also reactions to the narrowness of the puritan ethic.

Parrington's reaction against the formal pedagogy he encountered at Emporia and Harvard led to innovations in teaching methods which made him a most successful and popular teacher at the University of Washington. He broadened the curriculum, introduced American literature and contemporary writers, liberalized the ancient language requirements, and encouraged student argument rather than the formal lecture.

Undoubtedly Parrington saw himself as a cosmopolitan liberal who had escaped puritan parochialism and frontier regionalism. Still his experiences in Kansas and Oklahoma, his favorable portrayal of Thomas Jefferson and of Populism, his acceptance of Turner—evident in both his writing and his teaching—led some to identify him with the West. His influential role as teacher and educator at the University of Washington made him a prominent figure in that state. Essentially a national figure, Parrington and his views have been accepted sympathetically by the region in which he lived.

See Richard Hofstadter, *The Progressive Historians* (1968); Robert A. Skotheim, *American Intellectual Histories and Historians* (1966); and Robert A. Skotheim and Kermit Vanderbilt, "Vernon Louis Parrington: The Mind of a Historian of Ideas," *Pacific Northwest Quarterly*, vol. 53 (1962).—E. H. E.

Parsons, Elsie Clews (1875-1941). Ethnologist. Born in New York and trained at Barnard College, Parsons took her first trip to the West to Zuni, New Mexico, in 1915. Throughout her life she conducted intensive fieldwork and published voluminously on the Zuñi, Hopi, Acoma, Laguna, Isleta, Jémez, and various Tewa groups of the Southwest.

Parsons annotated the *Hopi Journal of Alexander M. Stephen* (1936) and capped dozens of publications and her twenty-five-year-long interest in the subject with the classic *Pueblo Indian Religion* (1939); she also found time for important work among the Kiowa and in the Mexican states of Oaxaca and Puebla. *Mitla, Town of the Souls* (1936) concerns itself with Spanish acculturation of Zapotec Indians and is a landmark study in anthropology.

See Leslie Spier and A. L. Kroeber, "Elsie Clews Par-

sons," *American Anthropologist*, vol. 45, no. 2 (1943). —D. L. F.

passage to India. See CHINA TRADE.

Pattie, Sylvester (1782-1828), father of **James Ohio Pattie** (1804?-?1851). Fur trappers. James and Sylvester Pattie were both born in Kentucky and in 1812 moved to Missouri. In 1824 they began trading along the Missouri and later that year traveled to Taos and Santa Fe. In 1826 Sylvester became manager of a copper mine in southwestern New Mexico, while James joined a trapping party led by Ewing Young near present-day Phoenix. Young's group made a remarkable journey, the extent of which remains disputed. James claimed its route proceeded down the Gila to the Colorado, along the Colorado to the Grand Canyon, northward to the Bighorn and Yellowstone rivers, and back to Santa Fe in 1827. In 1828 the Patties trapped on the Gila and eventually went down the Colorado to its mouth and overland to San Diego, where they were jailed by the Mexican governor. Sylvester died in this prison in 1828. James won his release and reached the United States in 1830. In the same year he dictated his colorful reminiscences to the writer Timothy Flint in Cincinnati, who published them in 1831 under the title *The Personal Narrative of James O. Pattie of Kentucky, During an Expedition From St. Louis, Through the Vast Regions Between That Place and the Pacific Ocean*. The book became a famous source, although its value is marred by the vague description of the journey of 1826-27. One of the forty-niners, James disappeared in the Sierra Nevada in the winter of 1850-51.

See LeRoy R. Hafen, ed., *The Mountain Men and the Fur Trade of the Far West*, vol. IV (1966).—G. B. D.

Pattullo, George (1879-   ). Novelist and short-story writer. Pattullo was born in Canada and educated at the University of Toronto, after which he went into newspaper work in London, Montreal, and Boston until 1908. He then moved to Texas. There he learned the rudiments of the cattle industry and began to write stories in the western idiom, taken from the life around him. The southwestern stories in *The Untamed* (1911) and many of those in *A Good Rooster Crows Everywhere* (1939) date from this period, as does *The Sheriff of Badger* (1912), usually considered to be his best western work. During World War I he was a special European correspondent for the *Saturday Evening Post*, and shortly after the end of hostilities he moved to New York City.

For some reason Pattullo's western fiction has never achieved the widespread recognition it deserves. Though he has always had a following among western Americana buffs, his fiction has failed to attract the larger audience of the more popular western writers. This is probably because Pattullo's fiction is less sensational and less anecdotal than most other western writing. It is more psychological in its concerns than the typical adventure story and consequently focuses more upon how a character thinks than on what he does. Though at its weakest Pattullo's fiction is didactic and slow-moving, at its best it draws an insightful inner picture of a world that is usually conceived only externally.—J. K. F.

Paul, Rodman Wilson (1912-   ). Historian. Born in Villanova, Pennsylvania, Paul was educated at Harvard University (B.A., 1936; Ph.D., 1943), where he was a student of Frederick Merk. After teaching at Harvard and Yale universities, he joined the faculty of the California Institute of Technology in 1947.

Paul's major scholarly interest was the western mining industry. He devoted attention both to technology and to the men who organized and developed the mines. His book *California Gold, 1848-73* (1947) argues that the techniques of western mining were not developed solely in California but came from all over the world. The stamp mill was copied from European models, the diamond drill came from France, and dynamite was a Swedish import. The California gold rush was thus an "international movement." Paul also found that in the period between 1848 and 1873 the mining industry changed from the "flush times" of the amateur miner with pan, pick, and shovel, to the "maturity" of university-trained experts using one-thousand-foot sluices, diamond drills, and dynamite. The author expanded the California study to include other western states in *Mining Frontiers of the Far West, 1848-80* (1963). He found the pattern of California mining repeated in other states and concluded that western mining had been unified by the migration of miners carrying similar techniques from one camp to another and by the influence of equipment distribution centers such as San Francisco and St. Louis.

Other books by Paul include *The Abrogation of the Gentlemen's Agreement* (1936), *Roughing It* (1953), *Mining Camps* (1965), and *California Gold Discovery* (1966). —J. S. W.

Paxson, Edgar Samuel (1852-1919). Painter. Born in East Hamburg, New York, Paxson early acquainted himself with life in the American West. He worked as a lumberjack in Wisconsin, was a hunting guide in Minnesota, and finally signed as a driver with a freight caravan destined for Wyoming Territory in 1876. Arriving in Montana Territory in 1877, Paxson was employed briefly as a driver with the Overland Stage Company. Following action in the Philippines during the Spanish-American War, Paxson settled in Montana.

Noted for his paintings of frontier characters and western activity, Paxson produced many excellent watercolors and meticulous oil portraits, some of which were done from photographs, others from memory. His most ambitious undertaking was the monumental canvas *Custer's Last Stand*, completed at his studio in Butte in 1899 and now at the Whitney Gallery of Western Art in Cody, Wyoming. Paxson is also represented by murals in the state Capitol in Helena and another mural series in the Missoula County Courthouse depicting episodes in the history of the Lewis and Clark expedition. He also contributed illustrations for several local publications, including *Old Timer's Hand Book, A Story of Butte* (1897), E. J. Stanley's *Life of the Rev. L. B. Stateler, A Story of Life on the Old Frontier* (1907), and Kate Hammond Fogarty's *Story of Montana* (1916). Other of his works are widely scattered.—D. C. H.

Paxson, Frederick Logan (1877-1948). Historian. Although not associated with any new hypothesis or concept, Paxson ranks among the ten or twelve outstanding scholars on the American West during the first half of the twentieth century. This position is based primarily upon his reputation as an outstanding teacher, and the ability in his writings to synthesize historical events and relate them to one another. During his forty-four-year academic career, he directed more than sixty doctoral

dissertations and published three major works and twenty-four scholarly articles on subjects relating directly to the frontier. His *The Last American Frontier* (1910), *The History of the American Frontier, 1763-1893* (1924)— for which he received the Pulitzer Prize—and *When the West Is Gone* (1930) represented pioneering efforts at the time. His other major publications include *The New Nation* (1925), *Recent History of the United States* (1921), and the three-volume *American Democracy and the World War* (1936-48).

Paxson was born of Quaker parents. Except for two years of graduate work at Harvard University, he obtained all of his formal education in his native city of Philadelphia. Upon receipt of a Ph.D. in diplomatic history in 1903 from the University of Pennsylvania, he accepted a position at the University of Colorado. Since primary materials then available in the local library did not range much beyond state and regional material, Paxson's first ten or twelve scholarly articles related to Colorado subjects. The publication of his first book in 1910 brought an immediate invitation to teach at the University of Wisconsin. He remained at that institution until 1932 and devoted fifteen of the twenty-two years as chairman of the history department.

Like several Wisconsin colleagues with distinguished records in teaching and writing, Paxson moved on to the University of California. From 1932 until his retirement in 1947 he occupied the chair of Margaret Byrne Professor of History at the Berkeley campus and maintained an arduous schedule of writing and lecturing. At the time of his death he had filled eighty drawers with carefully cross-referenced historical notes, which are now a part of the manuscript collection of the Bancroft Library.

Paxson's many students remember him as a warm and friendly individual with qualities of dignity, good taste, and a sly sense of humor. He constantly updated his material, and, as Ira Clark wrote, gave his students "a sense of participating in his exploration of the past" and of "contact with living men and problems rather than narrative." He was an active member of numerous historical societies and was president of the Mississippi Valley Historical Association (1917), the American Historical Association (1938), and the Pacific Coast branch of the American Historical Association (1942). In addition, he was for many years curator of the State Historical Society of Wisconsin, a member of the managing committee of the *Dictionary of American Biography*, on the board of editors of the *Pacific Historical Review*, and on the advisory committee of the Franklin D. Roosevelt Library.

See Ira G. Clark, "Frederick Logan Paxson, 1877-1948," *Arizona and the West* (Summer 1961); and Earl Pomeroy, "Frederick L. Paxson and His Approach to History," *Mississippi Valley Historical Review* (March 1953).—W. E. H.

peace policy. Federal Indian policy. The approach to Indian affairs that characterized the administration of President Ulysses S. Grant (1868-76) was known as the peace policy. It acquired this name because one of its central tenets, according to the treaty commission in 1869, was "the hitherto untried policy in connection with Indians, of endeavoring to conquer by kindness." The foundations of the peace policy were established soon after the close of the Civil War. Before the war, government response to Indian resistance of westward expansion had generally been to remove offending tribes to the Great Plains, a region believed to be of no possible use to white men, where the Indians could have "one big reservation" and be left substantially alone. White encroachment onto the Plains and adjacent desert regions during the war years and immediately afterward made this practice obsolete, as it became apparent that there was no place on the continent whites would not eventually want. Policy makers were then faced with two alternatives: either assimilate the Indian into white society or exterminate him. The more peaceful course had much appeal to a nation which in the late 1860s was tired of war and bloodletting.

The first important manifestation of the new policy was the treaty commission sent out in 1867 to negotiate with certain Plains tribes that had been sporadically hostile for several years. The resultant treaties of MEDICINE LODGE (October 1867) and Fort Laramie (May 1868) embodied themes that characterized the subsequent policy. The Indians were to be concentrated on two reservations, the northern Plains tribes in the western half of the Dakotas and the southern tribes in the western part of Indian Territory in present-day Oklahoma. This would remove Indian pressure from the Kansas and Nebraska region, where the white push westward was strongest. Once on these reservations the Indians were to be taught white practices and assimilated into white culture through a system of elementary education for children, education in agricultural techniques taught by resident farmers, and guaranteed annuities to replace traditional subsistence until the Indians could become self-supporting in the white manner.

The initial response of the tribes involved was favorable, and the commission urged Congress to make speedy and substantial appropriations so that the reservations could become as attractive as possible to those wild nomadic bands who remained reluctant to abandon the swiftly diminishing buffalo herds. But Congress allowed the treaties to languish without ratification or appropriation. Meanwhile, peaceful Indians moved onto reservations that did not legally exist and, as in the case of Chief Black Kettle's Cheyenne on the Washita River in November 1868, were attacked there by soldiers who found it too difficult to track down real hostiles.

When President Grant took office in 1869 his new administration consequently found Indian policy in a confused state. The treaty commissioners had laid the groundwork for a peaceful removal of the Indian barrier, but a Senate-House dispute over the treaty-making power and appropriations had paralyzed Indian affairs. Reformers were clamoring for an end to corrupt and inhumane treatment of the Indian. The generals, led by William T. Sherman, were fearful of further reductions in military strength and urged a larger army role and Indian assimilation at bayonet point. Western representatives and newspapers demanded Indian extermination, and politicians sought continued patronage and spoils.

Even though Grant's sympathies lay with the military, his first actions regarding Indian policy were balanced and sound. For secretary of the interior he appointed J. D. Cox, a noted advocate of civil service reform, and as

commissioner of Indian affairs Ely Parker, a full-blooded Seneca Indian of considerable attainments. Through the pressure of the administration and reform lobbies, Congress broke its deadlock over the Indian treaties in April 1869 by appropriating the undistributed sum of $2 million for Indian affairs and by authorizing the formation of a citizen Board of Indian Commissioners to supervise the disbursement of funds jointly with the Department of the Interior. In June the president by executive order expanded the board's watchdog powers and appointed ten philanthropic members who had been recommended by various religious denominations.

Church organizations and moral reformers, many of whom were former abolitionists, had for several years been interested in Indian affairs. Spurred on by the efforts of such men as John Beeson, a sometime Quaker who was outraged by white barbarity in Oregon's Rogue River War of 1855, and Henry B. Whipple, the Episcopal bishop of Minnesota whose account of agency corruption leading to the Santee outbreak of 1862 had received wide publicity, these groups lobbied tirelessly for a humane and peaceful Indian policy. In the summer of 1869 the president responded to these reformers by placing the Hicksite Friends in charge of the Central Superintendency, which included Kansas, Nebraska, and Oklahoma. Grant reportedly remarked that if the Indians could be made into Quakers it would take the fight out of them. He viewed the appointments as an experiment, filling the rest of the agency posts with unassigned army officers in accord with his military loyalties. When Congress in July 1870 made it illegal for military personnel to hold civil office, the president was persuaded by Secretary Cox to refuse to make the vacant agencies patronage appointments and instead to extend the concept of religious administration to cover the whole Indian Bureau. Agencies were distributed among Christian denominations, excluding Mormons, on the basis of missionary work already done among respective tribes and the church's ability to participate in the program. The final distribution was as follows:

American Board of Commissioners for Foreign Missions (one agency for 1,500 Indians): Dakota Territory—Sisseton Agency.

Baptist (five agencies for 41,000 Indians): Indian Territory—Cherokee and Creek agencies; Nevada—Paiute and Walker River agencies; Utah Territory—special agency.

Christian (two agencies for 8,200 Indians): New Mexico Territory—Pueblo Agency; Washington Territory—Neah Bay Agency.

Congregational (three agencies for 14,500 Indians): Minnesota—Chippewa of the Mississippi Agency; Wisconsin—Chippewa of Lake Superior and Green Bay agencies.

Episcopalian (eight agencies for 26,900 Indians): Dakota Territory—Cheyenne River, Fort Berthold, Ponca, Red Cloud, Upper Missouri, Whetstone, and Yankton agencies; Wyoming Territory—Shoshoni Agency.

Friends, Hicksite (six agencies for 6,600 Indians): Nebraska—Great Nemaha, Omaha, Otoe, Pawnee, Santee, and Winnebago agencies.

Friends, Orthodox (ten agencies for 17,700 Indians): Indian Territory—Kiowa, Osage, Quapaw, Sauk and

Fox, Shawnee, Upper Arkansas, and Wichita agencies; Kansas—Kaw, Kickapoo, and Potawatomi agencies.

Lutheran (one agency for 300 Indians): Iowa—Sauk and Fox Agency.

Methodist (fourteen agencies for 54,500 Indians): California—Hoopa Valley, Round Valley, and Tule Lake agencies; Idaho Territory—Fort Hall Agency; Michigan—Michigan Agency; Montana Territory—Blackfoot, Crow, and Milk River agencies; Oregon—Klamath, Siletz, and Warm Springs agencies; Washington Territory—Quinault, Skohomish, and Yakima agencies.

Presbyterian (nine agencies for 38,000 Indians): Arizona Territory—Moquis Pueblo Agency; Idaho Territory—Nez Percé Agency; Indian Territory—Choctaw and Seminole agencies; New Mexico Territory—Abiquiu, Mescalero Apache, Navaho, and Tularosa agencies; Utah Territory—Uintah Valley Agency.

Reformed Dutch (five agencies for 8,000 Indians): Arizona Territory—Camp Grant, Camp Verde, Colorado River, Pima and Maricopa, and White Mountain agencies.

Roman Catholic (seven agencies for 18,000 Indians): Dakota Territory—Devil's Lake and Grand River agencies; Montana Territory—Flathead Agency; Oregon—Grand Ronde and Umatilla agencies; Washington Territory—Colville and Tulalip agencies (see ROMAN CATHOLIC MISSIONARIES).

Unitarian (two agencies for 3,800 Indians): Colorado Territory—Los Pinos and White River agencies.

The president appointed as agents those candidates recommended by each denomination. This extensive official participation by churches in Indian administration was the distinguishing feature of the peace policy. Politicians and the patronage lobby fought vigorously for the return of agency appointments to their control, but throughout his administration Grant refused to yield the issue.

Religious and reformist principles were not the only ingredients of the peace policy. As conceived by Grant, Secretary Cox, and Commissioner Parker, it was a realistic political compromise incorporating military personnel and western proposals as well as the more humanitarian interests of the East. The churchmen had final authority on the reservations, where they could try their philosophy of kindness, but Indians refusing to remove to or remain on a reservation were put under the jurisdiction of the military and either driven to the reservation by force or eliminated in the process. This suited western opinion since it freed more land for white settlement and legitimatized whites' racial antagonism.

Despite its auspicious beginnings and theoretical plausibility, the peace policy foundered. It was deprived of good leadership almost before it was begun. Blocked by party regulars in his efforts to reform the civil service, Secretary Cox resigned in October 1870. Commissioner Parker departed in February 1871 under a cloud of false accusations of fraud brought by politicians seeking to discredit the new order. The new interior secretary, Columbus Delano, was politically loyal but a nonentity, and Francis Walker, Parker's successor, was a brilliant economist and statistician but more interested in the census than in Indians. Delano's resentment of what he viewed as outside interference from the citizen Board of Indian Commissioners led to the resignation of all its

original members by 1874, and the board became an impotent body. The president did not sustain his initial interest and involvement in Indian affairs, and the Indian Bureau gradually reverted to its previous corrupt and uncoordinated state.

In the West, where the policy became practice, the memory of a generation of bad faith and violence kept many Indians away from the reservations and threw them into conflict with the military and the advancing settlements. Resultant tales of atrocity and massacre made Congress loath to appropriate much money for reservations, which were described in western newspapers as havens and supply depots for savage murderers. Without sufficient funds agents were unable to keep the few Indians they had from starvation, much less make the reservation an attractive alternative to the nomadic life. The meager funds that were granted were largely soaked up by continually venal traders and contractors. More than a few church-nominated agents, forced to live on an annual salary of only $1,500, became corrupt. Even honest agents did little to benefit the Indian or preserve peace. Several reservations were torn by interchurch quarrels over the right of different denominations to establish missions, and most missionaries believed it was more important to teach the Bible than to teach how to farm. Continuing hostilities gave rise to a renewal of efforts by westerners and the military lobby to return the Indian Bureau to the War Department, where it had been before 1849. The administration successfully resisted this pressure, but the conflict between the military and civil elements of the peace policy made its success an impossibility. In national politics the obvious disparity between the peace rhetoric of the church agencies and the violent reality of events like the Canby murder (April 1873) and the Custer debacle at the Little Big Horn (June 1876) made the peace policy a front issue in the presidential campaign of 1876. Although Grant's successor, Hayes, was a Republican, the Democrats won control of Congress in the election, marking the end of the peace policy.

During the eight years that the peace policy was nominally in effect, more lives were lost to Indian depredations, more money was spent on Indian campaigns, and soldiers fought more engagements against Indians than in any comparable period in the nation's history. And when the Indian barrier was finally removed, it was done not by friendly persuasion but by the coercive operations of an army that often blundered but was ultimately effective. After Grant left office official church participation in agency administration ceased, and the peace policy was discredited. In an ironic sense, however, the complete subjugation and humiliation of the Indian during the 1870s made possible later reforms by permitting the rise of a sympathetic public opinion, which could not have been sustained while Indians were a potential threat to white supremacy in the West.

Subsequent Indian policy rested on many practices and attitudes developed during the Grant administration. The first appropriations for federally administered native education were made in 1870. Congressional abolition of the Indian treaty system (March 1871) and passage of the Indian Homestead Act (1875) were at the time politically motivated and generally ineffective but represented attempts to encourage individual Indian responsibility to the government and to promote agricultural practices. As first embodied in the work of the treaty commission of 1867, the principles underlying the peace policy were basic to the movement for Indian assimilation, which finally reached statutory fulfillment in the DAWES SEVERALTY ACT of 1887 and continued to determine Indian affairs until the Wheeler-Howard Act of 1934 (see John COLLIER and INDIAN-WHITE RELATIONS: *United States Indian policy, 1860-present*).

See H. E. Fritz, *The Movement for Indian Assimilation, 1860-1890* (1963); G. W. Manypenny, *Our Indian Wards* (1880); R. W. Mardock, *The Reformers and the American Indian* (1971); L. B. Priest, *Uncle Sam's Stepchildren* (1947); L. F. Schmeckebier, *The Office of Indian Affairs* (1927); and R. L. Utley, "The Celebrated Peace Policy of General Grant," *North Dakota History*, vol. 20 (1953).—P. R. M.

Pecos River. The Pecos, one of the main tributaries of the Rio Grande, has its source in the Truchas Mountains, almost due east of Santa Fe. From wooded, scenic areas at elevations of over 11,000 feet it flows generally south across New Mexico and Texas toward the Mexican border. In the first part of its course it is entrenched in a canyon over a thousand feet below the general level of the land, with the southern fingers of the Rocky Mountains to the west and the Llano Estacado to the east. Below Fort Sumner the river valley opens up a bit and a series of dams impound water for irrigation agriculture. In Texas the valley widens and the stream frequently disappears into its bed, reappearing at times of heavy runoff.

The Pecos drains a basin of about 35,000 square miles and has an annual flow of about 400,000 acre-feet of water. One of the major tributaries, the Rio Hondo, passes through Roswell, New Mexico, before emptying into the Pecos, adding 21,000 acre-feet of water to the flow of the main stream. The only other tributary contributing any significant water is the Rio Penasco, with a flow of 4,000 acre-feet annually.

Like many other southwestern streams, the Pecos is almost dry at times and subject to violent floods at others. The land it flows across is sparsely covered with vegetation and the rock material is poorly consolidated. Thus, the river is highly laden with sediment and the water quality is extremely poor because of the large quantity of dissolved minerals it contains.

Early Spanish explorers found the Pecos a barrier to be traversed. It was probably crossed by Cabeza de Vaca in the 1530s as he wandered westward across Texas. Coronado's men discovered Pecos Pueblo on their way to the plains of Kansas in 1540, and later Spanish explorers forded the river at this point also. The merchant explorer Antonio de Espejo was the first to follow the valley southward to its juncture with the Rio Grande. In 1583 he traversed the route to be made famous later as the Loving-Goodnight cattle trail.

Spanish settlers moved into the upper Pecos River country from their core settlements around Santa Fe, building villages and establishing ranches as they went. San Miguel del Bado, at the site where the Santa Fe Trail crossed the Pecos, became the largest settlement on the upper river. Though troubled by Comanche raiders, the Spanish grazed their flocks of sheep over extensive areas. Their spread downriver was eventually stopped by the establishment of Fort Sumner and its Indian reservation.

In 1866 Oliver Loving and Charles Goodnight led the first large herd of Texas cattle across their lands, and the long-lasting feud between the Mexican settlers and the Texas cattlemen began. The steers in the Loving-Goodnight herd were sold at Fort Sumner to feed the soldiers and the Indians quartered there and the cows and calves were driven north to Denver and were sold to the settlers in the mining camps of Colorado.

Soon other cattle herds were moving northward over the trail and competing with the flocks of sheep belonging to the Mexican-American settlers of the area. Texas cattlemen began acquiring large landholdings. John Chisum acquired holdings for one hundred and fifty miles along the Pecos River in New Mexico and established his headquarters at Fort Sumner.

During this period cattle rustlers, train robbers, and assorted bad men were forced into West Texas by the activities of the Texas Rangers. The law west of the Pecos was enforced by Judge Roy Bean in his courthouse-saloon in Langtry, Texas.

Following the arrival of the Southern Pacific Railroad in 1881, programs for irrigational agriculture were developed. In the 1890s the Pecos Irrigation and Investment Company built three dams in New Mexico and irrigated what had formerly been range land. In the same decade, deep-well irrigation techniques were being developed and land away from the river was farmed. By 1900 there were over eight thousand people in the valley and agricultural production of sugar beets and orchard crops had begun. However, none of this was easily done. Floods constantly harassed the settlers and in 1904 washed out all of the dams along the stream. These were later rebuilt by the Bureau of Reclamation and form the basis for agriculture in the valley today. Alamogordo Reservoir (132,000 acre-feet), McMillan Reservoir (38,660 acre-feet), and Red Bluff Reservoir (307,000 acre-feet) are the main reservoirs on the river.

Discovery of the rich Yates pool of oil in the Pecos valley of Texas in 1926 brought a new wave of settlers and a new source of income to the area. Today agriculture, ranching, and the oil industry form the economic basis of life for a majority of the people who live in the Pecos River valley.

For map, see RIO GRANDE.—R. W. D.

Peffer, William Alfred (1831-1912). Kansas editor and Populist politician. A Pennsylvanian by birth, Peffer left his native state in the 1850s to farm and teach school, at intervals, in Indiana, Missouri, and Illinois. When the Civil War began, he enlisted to fight with an Illinois regiment. During his army service he studied law and at the war's end practiced for a time in Clarksville, Tennessee. In 1870 he established himself in Fredonia, Kansas, where he practiced law and gradually developed an interest in journalism, becoming editor of the Fredonia *Journal*. Peffer was elected in 1874 to the state senate as a Republican, the party that had received his support from its inception. In 1876 he became the publisher and editor of the *Journal* in Coffeyville, Kansas, remaining at that position until 1881 when he took over the editorship of the Topeka *Kansas Farmer*, the state's most influential agricultural weekly.

As editor of the *Farmer*, Peffer developed a deep interest in the many problems then confronting agriculture, and when the farmer's predicament became extraordinarily difficult, after 1887, with the collapse of the western boom, he gradually was drawn into and championed the Populist movement. He became one of the party's most learned authorities on the issues of transportation and finance. The kind of thought that went into *The Farmer's Side* (1891), his major work, made him the first Populist senator in 1891. His appearance (whiskers that flowed to his waist) made him a symbol of Populist radicalism, but he was a level-headed and clear-thinking reformer whose record in the Senate from 1891 to 1897 reflected a determination to force a lethargic government to meet the responsibilities for problems in an age of economic revolution.

See Peter H. Argersinger, *Populism and Politics: William A. Peffer and the Republican Party* (1974). See also O. Gene Clanton's *Kansas Populism: Ideas and Men* (1969) for a treatment of his position as a Populist leader. —O. G. C.

Pelzer, Lewis (1879-1946). Historian. Born in Griswold, Iowa, Pelzer—a "gifted son of the Middle Border," as one of his colleagues described him—enjoyed a distinguished career as teacher, author, editor, and authority on the West. Except for brief visits out of state for professional reasons, Pelzer spent his entire life in Iowa. Following receipt of his bachelor's degree in history from the University of Iowa in 1906, he stayed on in Iowa City as a graduate student for three more years and received his Ph.D. During that time he was appointed by Dr. Benjamin F. Shambaugh as a research assistant in the State Historical Society of Iowa.

In his sophomore year at the university, the *Iowa Journal of History and Politics* published Pelzer's first scholarly article, "The Negro and Slavery in Early Iowa," the first of many studies that he subsequently submitted to the *Journal*. As a young man he had the further distinction of reading a paper at the organizational meeting in 1908 of the Mississippi Valley Historical Association. Following a brief sojourn at Montana State Normal College, Pelzer returned to his alma mater in 1911 as an assistant professor of history.

Meanwhile, he had already published two full-length biographies, *Augustus Caesar Dodge* (1908) and *Henry Dodge* (1911), and eight more articles. Another book, *Marches of the Dragoons in the Mississippi Valley* (1914), and seven or eight additional scholarly articles followed. By the time he obtained the rank of full professor in 1925, he had perfected the technique of lecturing in polished sentences that contained dramatic and descriptive phrases, and concise, factual, and pertinent information. His seminars in western history attracted large numbers of students from various disciplines who received rigid training in the use of documents, archives, newspapers, and the art of composition.

Pelzer's most outstanding contribution was *The Cattleman's Frontier, 1850-1890* (1936). More than any other, this exhaustively researched publication established his reputation as one of the leading western historians. He also became widely known in the profession through his service on almost every important committee of the Mississippi Valley Historical Association from 1912 until his death. He was also president of the association in 1935-36, a member of the board of editors from 1936 to 1939, and editor of the *Review* from 1941 until his death.

See Louis Bernard Schmidt, "Louis Pelzer, 1879-1946," *Arizona and the West* (Winter 1960).—W. E. H.

Pembina, North Dakota. *Pembina* is derived from the Chippewa word *anepeminan*, meaning "summer berry." This red berry, known to whites as the highbush cranberry, grew in abundance along the banks of the river, which flowed north—hence also the name Red River of the North.

The settlement of the area around Pembina began with the fur-trading activities of such companies as the North West Company and Hudson's Bay Company. Trading posts were established in the vicinity during the winter of 1797-98. In 1801 Alexander Henry of the North West Company built a fort at the confluence of the Pembina River and the Red River of the North, from which he began to open up the valley to the south for the fur trade. Except for a few years between 1823 and 1840, Pembina has been occupied continuously from 1801 to the present. The first white families to settle at Pembina came in the winter of 1812-13. They were Scottish and Swiss colonists from the Selkirk community around present-day Winnipeg, Canada.

Until the United States and Great Britain agreed to a boundary, the area was considered British. When Major Stephen H. LONG arrived to stake the international boundary, the Pembina settlement was found to lie south of the border (except for one cabin). Employees of the Hudson's Bay Company and several of the Selkirk settlers then withdrew to the north.

The town grew slowly. In 1823 Major Long estimated the population to be around 350, mostly métis (French-Indian half-breeds). In 1836 a trading party passed through the area and saw no one. During the 1830s the Hudson's Bay Company paid the American Fur Company not to trap the area, but it was a smuggler's rendezvous during those years. By 1844 the monopoly of the British fur company was broken and the American Fur Company established a large general merchandise store there. Pembina soon became the center for the fur trade between Canada and St. Paul. Furs, buffalo hides, pemmican, and other trade goods were carried by canoe, dogsled, and the practical Red River cart.

In 1870 the federal government located a fort at Pembina. The population of northern Dakota Territory at this time was estimated to be 2,405, with most of it concentrated in the Pembina area. In 1890 the census revealed a population of 670. In 1970 the town was only slightly larger, with 741 residents. Despite its size, Pembina was an important crossroads for the fur trade and an advertisement for the rich lands of the Red River valley.—D. J. T.

Pennsylvania, settlement of. The Dutch had explored the Delaware River rather thoroughly by 1623, but the first Europeans to live in Pennsylvania were Swedes, who began a settlement on Tinicum Island, near the Schuylkill River, in 1643. The Dutch seized New Sweden in 1655, and in 1664 the English took the area from the Dutch.

The region that the English took was the last large land area near the coast and was relatively free of population. (About five hundred people lived in Pennsylvania in 1680, some of whom were Quakers.) Charles II gave the lands west of the Delaware between the fortieth and forty-third parallels of latitude as a proprietorship to the Quaker William Penn (1644-1718) in 1681. Charles had owed Penn's father money and paid off the debt with this grant of land. In 1682 Penn got the title to present-day Delaware from the duke of York. Penn began planning a "holy experiment," hoping to create in the newly granted land a peaceful refuge for men persecuted by the established church of England for their religion. He made ambitious plans for its economic development and publicized it in Europe to attract immigrants. A joint-stock company, the Free Society of Traders, was formed to promote settlement, and Penn gave it twenty thousand acres of his lands for its work. The proprietor drafted the Frame of Government in 1682 that granted generous liberties to settlers, including toleration of all religions, and then composed a set of humane fundamental laws for the provincial assembly's approval. His surveyors laid out the province's well-planned capital, called Philadelphia, in 1682. Penn had little difficulty in attracting settlers, and he even visited Germany and Holland to recruit them. Pacifist German and Dutch Mennonites and Baptists (called Dunkers), mystics, and Welsh and English Quakers responded to his invitation by coming shortly after 1682.

To Penn's dismay, those who came soon began to contend with each other and with the persons Penn named to administer the province in his absence. (Penn visited Pennsylvania only twice, from 1682 to 1684 and from 1699 to 1701.) The proprietor's choices of surrogates were often poor ones, and frequently the assembly resisted their efforts to govern. Penn was entitled to quitrents (one shilling per one hundred acres owned) from his settlers, and when financial embarrassments caused him to ask for them, Pennsylvanians tried to avoid payment. Pennsylvania remained a financial liability until the end of his life. Land titles were often carelessly drawn, and people questioned the rights of the Free Society of Traders to its land, too. To soothe tempers in the turbulent province, Penn returned in 1699 with James LOGAN to present the assembly with a new scheme of government, the Charter of Privileges (1701), which it approved. The charter remained the fundamental law of Pennsylvania until the American Revolution.

In 1683 Penn agreed in a treaty with the Delaware Indians to purchase all lands the colony needed from the tribes and to remain at peace. Fortunately, the amicable relations Penn established with the Delaware preserved the quarrelsome province from serious violence until 1754. After Penn's death in 1718, his heirs became Anglicans and ruled the province casually. Their difficulties with the Quakers were compounded by boundary controversies with adjacent colonies. In the notorious WALKING PURCHASE of 1737, they swindled the Indians out of lands Penn had given the tribes, thus undermining the Indian's trust of the white man's ways.

Pennsylvania attracted a diverse collection of immigrants, some of whom scoffed at the Quakers' pacifism. The last communities of religious pacifists to come were the German Schwenkfelders, who arrived after 1734, and the Moravians, or United Brethren, the founders of Bethlehem in 1741. The newcomers included Germans who were not adherents of peace sects, but who were members of the Lutheran and Reformed churches. They moved west of Philadelphia, Bucks, and Chester counties, where most Quakers lived, to the Piedmont between the coastal plain and the Susquehanna. They kept to themselves, for few English inhabitants understood their language. The Germans brought with them agricultural techniques learned in Europe, which they

quickly applied to their new farms. After seeing the Germans' thoroughly cleared lands, huge stone barns, and hardworking women, contemporaries concluded they were the most efficient farmers in America. Thanks to their labor, Pennsylvania quickly became an exporter of food to other colonies. The Germans also perfected the Conestoga wagon and an early version of the Kentucky rifle.

Presbyterian immigrants from Ulster, Ireland, proved more troublesome to the Quakers, for many of them insisted upon moving to the edge of settlement, trespassing upon lands Penn had assigned to the Indians. These SCOTCH-IRISH, as Americans called them, went to the Cumberland Plateau, the northern Shenandoah Valley, and to trans-Allegheny Pennsylvania. Many moved near the new settlement of Pittsburgh after 1764. When the French began establishing forts in the upper Ohio valley after 1750, they incited the Indians against the colonists (see COLONIAL WARS and PONTIAC'S REBELLION). When pacifism was no longer possible on the frontier, Presbyterian settlers demanded military protection from the provincial government, which the assembly refused to supply. When the Quakers seemed to scorn their pleas for defense against the tribes, the Presbyterians became enraged. Quakers could not in good conscience support the violent measures the province took against the Indians, so many began to abstain from public office after 1756, when Pennsylvania declared war against the Delaware. Quaker influence was not broken in Pennsylvania until the Revolution, however.

Because devout Quakers, Mennonites, and Moravians felt it necessary to abstain from office-holding during the American Revolution, western Pennsylvanians, long inadequately represented in the Assembly, moved into power. They allied themselves with Whig merchants in Philadelphia and made a new constitution for the commonwealth in 1776. The Assembly was reapportioned, the lands of the Penn family were seized in 1779, and new counties were created in the west. But western Pennsylvanians suspected their mercantile allies, who included the land speculator Robert Morris, so east-west animosity within the state continued after independence. In 1787 much antifederal sentiment in the state appeared in the west.

Credit must also go to the city folk for taming Pennsylvania's frontier. The American Philosophical Society and Philadelphians such as Benjamin FRANKLIN, Tench Coxe, Benjamin Rush, and James Wilson aroused much interest in the West and its settlement, and they encouraged entrepreneurs to develop it. The perplexing diversity, physical size, and rapid economic growth of Pennsylvania sustained its political turbulence long after its first century of settlement.

Helpful accounts of this complicated province are Gary B. Nash, *Quakers and Politics* (1968); and Frederick Tolles, *Meetinghouse and Countinghouse* (1948) and *James Logan and the Culture of Provincial America* (1957). —K. W. K.

Pennsylvania German. Pennsylvania German is the correct name for the dialect commonly known as Pennsylvania Dutch, a middle Franconian dialect spoken by the descendants of German immigrants who settled in the southeastern part of Pennsylvania and the northwest corner of Maryland during the period 1683-

1775. The word *Dutch* in the common name for the dialect reflects the older meaning of the word, since it originally designated all the Germanic languages spoken in Austria, Germany, Switzerland, and the Low Countries. A majority of the immigrants came from the Rhenish Palatinate and adjacent areas, although a considerable number were Swiss; and one contingent, the Moravian Brethren, originated in Saxony and Silesia, while another was made up of Low-German Mennonites. The chief causes of the European exodus, which was initiated by William Penn during two visits to Germany, were religious persecution, economic insecurity, and the general social turmoil engendered by the ravages of the Thirty Years' War and subsequent disasters. By the time the migration ended in 1775, because of hostilities in Europe and America, about 110,000 German-speaking people had established their homes in an area more than twice the size of Massachusetts. It has been estimated that almost ten million Americans trace their ancestry back to these colonists.

From 1683 until 1727 the majority of German immigrants were members of religious sects. Among the sects that have, in varying degrees, maintained their identities to the present are the Amish, Dunkers (Church of the Brethren), Mennonites, the Moravian Brethren, and the Schwenkfelders. After 1727 most of the German colonists were members of the Lutheran and Reformed churches, which had originated in the Reformation and eventually became the "official" churches of the Protestant areas of Europe. Relatively few were of the Catholic or Jewish faiths. Because of their characteristic dress, their picturesque buggies, and their defiance of state laws regarding compulsory school attendance, the Amish attract attention, and consequently they are often equated with Pennsylvania Dutch, although in reality the "plain people" comprise only a small minority of the Pennsylvania Germans.

The religious diversity among the Pennsylvania Germans has had a significant impact on education and music in this country since each religious group founded its own colleges, theological seminaries, and musical conservatories. As early as 1807 the Moravians, for instance, had founded a men's and a women's college as well as a seminary in Bethlehem, Pennsylvania, and they were also instrumental in establishing the world-famous Bach Festival there.

As the frontier was pushed west, groups of Pennsylvania Germans followed in the wake of the Scotch-Irish. Their westward progress is traced by the numerous "Swiss" barns and well-kept farms that dot the countryside from the Allegheny Mountains to the Dakotas, Nebraska, and Kansas. In this tier of states, the Pennsylvania-German Mennonites were joined by coreligionists from German settlements along the Volga River, many of whom spoke similar dialects. Less conspicuous than their barns but by no means less important are the numerous church-related institutions of higher learning founded by the Pennsylvania Germans in Ohio, Indiana, Illinois, Iowa, and other states of the Midwest.

The Pennsylvania Germans were an important stabilizing force along the frontier; their role in the struggle between the English and the French for power in North America, into which the Indians were drawn, often has been overlooked. It would have been almost impossible for the English colonies to have survived the attacks of the French had it not been for the support of the German-speaking Pennsylvanians under the leadership of Conrad WEISER. A German by birth and a Mohawk by adoption, Weiser was instrumental in maintaining the neutrality of the Six Indian Nations and their tributaries, whose lands extended from Canada to the Carolinas and from the Atlantic to the Mississippi. He also intervened to maintain or restore peace between the Six Nations and several colonies; for example, in 1743 he persuaded the Iroquois not to go to war against Virginia in retaliation for an unprovoked attack by colonists in the Shenandoah Valley. Consequently only renegade Indians and tribes joined the French in their assaults on the English colonies, the brunt of which was borne largely by the Germans living on the frontier.

When the American Revolution began, a number of royalist German families left for Ontario, where their descendants still speak the Pennsylvania-German dialect. Others, like the pacifist Moravians, refused to bear arms, but supported the colonists by caring for the sick and wounded. The great majority of them, however, aligned themselves with the colonists against England. The most famous of the German soldiers in this war was Conrad Weiser's eldest grandson, General John Peter Gabriel Muhlenberg ("there is a time to pray and a time to fight"), who served on George Washington's general staff. One of the most important contributions of the Pennsylvania Germans were the so-called Kentucky rifles, which were manufactured in Lancaster, Pennsylvania.

The Pennsylvania-German dialect is remarkable for its persistence. In 1870 roughly one million Americans spoke this dialect as their native tongue, not only in the Pennsylvania "homeland" but also in scattered speech islands on the East Coast, in Canada, and far and wide throughout the Midwest. In 1970 about 250,000 persons still used the dialect as their chief means of oral communication, and an additional 250,000 individuals understood the dialect even though they could not speak it well. In general, Pennsylvania German has persisted most tenaciously in rural areas, especially in speech islands in which the dialect is closely identified with religion. As a literary vehicle, the dialect has been used most successfully in nostalgic and humorous verse, in folk songs, and in anecdotes and plays of a comical nature. Radio broadcasts in Pennsylvania German were popular from about 1940 to 1960, and weekly newspaper columns in the dialect flourished for decades. Attempts to delay the inevitable demise of Pennsylvania German by teaching it as a college subject were not successful.

In phonology, morphology, and basic vocabulary, Pennsylvania German corresponds closely to the dialects of the eastern Palatinate. Whereas these dialects often differ markedly from village to village, Pennsylvania German is remarkably homogeneous with only slight regional variation. As is usually the case in colonial speech islands, the amalgamation process was rapid. As early as 1742 the word *Pennsylvanisch* was used to differentiate the dialect from the speech of later immigrants, and when the dialect first appeared in print in 1830, it had essentially the same linguistic features as it has today. During the leveling process practically all distinctively Swiss and Swabian phonological features were lost, despite the fact that a substantial number of immigrants were natives of Württemberg and Switzerland.

Of special interest to the historical linguist is the fact that Pennsylvania German has preserved sounds and forms that have largely or entirely disappeared in German. Most striking is the pronunciation of all short vowels that occur before *r* followed by a consonant as a vowel sound similar to that in English *hot*—a phonological phenomenon that was widespread in and around the Palatinate during the period of emigration, but has been retained only by Pennsylvania-German and a few other Palatine dialects spoken until recently in eastern Europe. Thus the dialect equivalents of German *dort* ("there") and *Wort* ("word") are pronounced *dot* and *vot*. In western Germany this pronunciation occurs only sporadically in a few words and in relatively remote areas.

Pennsylvania German shares a number of phonetic features with the Palatine dialects as opposed to standard German. Thus the German words *Leute* ("people") and *heute* ("today") are pronounced in these dialects like the English words *light* and *height*. That is, the German sound *oi* is represented in the dialects by the sound of *I*. The dialect equivalent of the German sound *I* is *ay* as in English *day*, so that German *Bein* ("leg") and *klein* ("small") sound somewhat like English *bay* and *clay*. As can be seen from these examples, the slurred vowel *-e* and final *-n* are regularly dropped in these dialects. Furthermore, vowels that are pronounced with puckered lips in the standard language are produced without lip-rounding, so that German *Mühle* ("mill") and *Hölle* ("hell") sound like the English *meal* and *hell*.

The consonant system in the Palatine dialects and Pennsylvania German is almost identical with that of the standard language except that the dialects have the sound of *p* when German has the sound combination *pf*. Thus German *Pfanne* ("pan") is pronounced like the English *pun*, and *Apfel* ("apple") is pronounced *oppel*.

Whereas the phonology, morphology, and inflections of Pennsylvania German have remained unchanged, the speakers of this dialect, for reasons of necessity or convenience, have borrowed numerous words from English. Such loan words are always pronounced according to the sound patterns of the dialect, so that *job*, *rag*, and *jump* are often misunderstood by speakers of English as *chop*, *rack*, and *chump*. Such possible misunderstandings are a rich source of bilingual humor. Borrowed nouns are assigned genders according to a complicated set of rules. *Pie*, for example, is given the masculine definite article *dah*, probably because it is associated with the masculine noun *der Kuchen*. Loan words are also inflected exactly like native words. Thus the English word *to mix*, when used in the dialect, has the past participle *gemixed*, which is formed by adding a native prefix and suffix to the stem of the word.

Loan phrases and translated idioms are also common, such as *sell iss oof tsoo deer* ("that is up to you"), an expression that would be meaningless to German speakers. Frequently too a dialect word takes on the meaning of a related English word, as when *droovel* comes to mean "trouble" instead of "turmoil."

Stronger than the influence of English on the dialect is the influence of the dialect on English, since Pennsylvania-German English is spoken with the intonation and articulation patterns of the dialect. Palatine dialects are regarded as "singing" dialects, and their intonation patterns are quite as distinctive as those of Italian or Swedish. In the speech of many educated Pennsylvania Germans the accent is confined to the intonation patterns, and in speech islands west of the Missouri River even this "singsong" tone may be lacking. Sometimes the Pennsylvania German can be detected only by certain semantic borrowings such as "ground" for "soil" or "salad" for "lettuce," or by translated idioms such as "to wait on" in the sense of "to wait for." Among the Pennsylvania-German contributions to the American vocabulary are "Christmas tree," "Christmas gift," "Easter egg," "Easter rabbit," "sawbuck," "bake oven," and "waffle iron." And George Washington was known as *Landesvater* among the Pennsylvania Germans long before the translation, "Father of his country," became popular. Sportswriters are fond of "dunk" and "hex," and cowboys in western stories sometimes wear a jacket called a "wommes" or "warm-us," the latter form (as attested in the *Dictionary of Americanisms*) obviously a popular etymology. The Palatine form is *Wammes*, Standard German *Wams* ("jacket").

Pennsylvania German and Netherlandish are not mutually understandable, but Pennsylvania Germans can communicate without difficulty with Palatines, and verse in their dialect appears from time to time in Palatine publications.

A. F. Buffington and P. A. Barba, *A Pennsylvania German Grammar* (1954), is an introduction to the dialect with exercises, reading selections, and glossary. C. E. Reed, *The Pennsylvania German Dialect Spoken in the Counties of Lehigh and Berks: Phonology and Morphology* (1949), is a thorough descriptive and historical analysis. O. Springer, "The Study of the Pennsylvania German Dialect," *Journal of English and Germanic Philology* (1943), is a critical survey of completed research and a program for future study; it has an excellent bibliography. See also M. B. Lambert, *A Dictionary of the Non-English Words of the Pennsylvania-German Dialect* (1924).—P. S.

People's party. See POPULISM.

People's party, Kansas. Drought, hard times, and economic unrest led Kansas Populists, under the name of the People's party, to organize in June 1890 with delegates from the Farmers' Alliance and other rural organizations. Their candidates swept the election for the state House of Representatives in 1890, giving them the power to elect William A. PEFFER to the United States Senate. The national People's party was formed soon after (see POPULISM), and Kansas led an active campaign in the elections of 1892. Kansans sent to the national House of Representatives by the Populists included William Baker, Jeremiah D. Botkin, Benjamin H. Clover, John Davis, William A. Harris, T. J. Hudson, Nelson B. McCormick, John G. Otis, Mason S. Peters, E. R. Ridgely, "Sockless Jerry" SIMPSON, and W. D. Vincent. Harris also served in the Senate as a Democrat. Best known nationally were Simpson, who served three terms in the House, and Annie DIGGS and Mary Elizabeth LEASE, who gained reputations as Populist orators. Populists also elected two governors during the 1890s, L. D. Lewelling (1893-95) and John W. Leedy (1897-99). The party declined in the late 1890s and few Populists won election after 1898.

For additional information, see O. Gene Clanton, *Kansas Populism: Ideas and Men* (1969); Walter T. K. Nugent, *Tolerant Populists: Kansas Populism and Nativism* (1963); and the special issue devoted to Populism of *Kansas Quarterly* (Fall 1969).—H. E. S.

Pequot War (1636-1638). Indian war. The Pequot War was the first serious Indian war in New England. It was also one of the bloodiest and most destructive for the Indians involved and resulted in the opening of much of southern New England to white settlement. The Pequot Indians, originally part of the Mahican tribe of New York, seem to have migrated in the late sixteenth century from the upper Hudson valley into eastern Connecticut. A warlike people (their name meant "destroyer"), numbering about seven hundred warriors in 1637, they conquered and dominated many neighboring Indian bands, including some on Long Island.

It is hard to say who bore major responsibility for the conflict. The Pequot apparently killed nine English traders in 1634, whose conduct may have invited this fate. In 1636 they harbored two Indians of another tribe accused of a similar offense. When they refused to surrender the culprits, Massachusetts took it upon herself to punish this tribe, which lived outside her borders, by sending a punitive force under John Endecott that unnecessarily destroyed and looted a Pequot village. In 1637 the Pequot retaliated in kind against the new Connecticut settlements, which had reluctantly cooperated with Massachusetts. Neighboring Indians such as the Narragansett and the Mohegan under Uncas, fearing the Pequot more than the English, actively joined the latter. In May a Connecticut and Indian force under Captain John Mason invaded the Pequot country. In a surprise attack they destroyed a fortified Pequot village near the Mystic River and massacred its several hundred occupants, who lacked the armament to resist effectively. The Pequot, demoralized by this defeat, fled in all directions. By August most of them had been hunted down and either shot or captured by the English and other Indians. Pequot casualties totaled more than seven hundred and the remaining tribesmen made peace in 1638. But the Pequot were utterly destroyed as a tribe. The survivors were parceled out among other tribes or enslaved by the English, who appropriated most of their lands. Such exemplary punishment was not lost on other Indians, who refrained from challenging English supremacy in this area for nearly forty years.

See H. Bradstreet, *The Story of the War with the Pequots, Re-Told* (1933); H. M. Sylvester, *Indian Wars of New England* (1910); and A. T. Vaughan, *New England Frontier: Puritans and Indians, 1620-1675* (1965).—A. W. T.

Perea, Pedro (1852-1906). New Mexican politician. A cousin of J. Francisco Perea, territorial delegate from New Mexico to the Thirty-eighth Congress, Pedro Perea was born in Bernalillo, New Mexico. He attended St. Michael's College in Santa Fe, Georgetown University in Washington, D.C., and was graduated from the St. Louis University in 1871. One of the wealthiest sheep ranchers in New Mexico and a bank president, Perea was a preeminently powerful Spanish-American leader in the Republican party in New Mexico. In 1889, at the New Mexico constitutional convention, he was joined by his friend Thomas Benton Catron in defeating a school amendment that was opposed by much of the Spanish-speaking population. In that year, as well as in 1891 and

1895, Perea was a member of the council of the New Mexico legislature. In 1896 he was a delegate to the Republican National Convention, which nominated McKinley. He was, therefore, a possible appointment of McKinley as governor of the territory and was supported for that post by Catron. In 1898 he was elected delegate to Congress, but did not seek reelection.

During his term as delegate, Perea's disagreements with Governor Miguel A. Otero no doubt impeded the fight for statehood. Moreover, he introduced only one statehood bill in Congress, and it was not reported out of committee. He later supported Delegate Smith's efforts for statehood.

In 1900 Perea returned to New Mexico, where he was involved in banking and raising stock. He died shortly after being appointed in 1906 as territorial insurance commissioner.

Perea's slight role in the statehood movement and his relationships with Catron and Otero are mentioned in Howard R. Lamar, *The Far Southwest, 1846-1912* (1966); and Robert W. Larson, *New Mexico's Quest for Statehood, 1846-1912* (1968), and "New Mexico's Fight for Statehood, I," *New Mexico Historical Review* (January 1939).—J. R. V.

Perkins, Charles Elliott (1840-1907). Railroad executive. Perkins was primarily responsible for extension of the BURLINGTON NORTHERN RAILROAD west of the Missouri River into Nebraska. Born in Cincinnati, Ohio, he was a young cousin of John Murray Forbes, leader of the Boston capitalists who developed the Burlington. By 1873, after twenty-three years of advancement through the ranks, Perkins was appointed general manager of all of the system's lines west of the Mississippi River, and became president when Forbes retired in 1881. Forbes, who had usually remained in the company's Boston headquarters, and Perkins, who was the chief operating officer on the spot, comprised one of the most successful teams in the early history of big business. Their solutions to organization and procedural problems form much of the basis for modern railroad management practice. Like many of the newer breed of railroad managers, Perkins combined a striking physical presence with the courteous, affectionate manner of one whose power derives not from property but from professional ability.

Richard C. Overton, *Burlington Route, A History of the Burlington Lines* (1965), covers Perkins' career.—A. M.

Perrigo, Lynn (1904-   ). Historian. Perrigo was born in Delphi, Indiana. After attending Ball State Teacher's College in Muncie, Indiana, he moved west in 1933 to the University of Colorado, where Colin B. Goodykoontz was teaching popular courses in the development of the trans-Mississippi West. In 1938 Perrigo began teaching at the University of Kansas City. He spent another year with the University of Colorado, then in 1947 became chairman of the history department at New Mexico Highlands University in Las Vegas, New Mexico, where he stayed until his retirement in 1971.

Perrigo's interest in the Spanish borderlands and the Southwest was reflected in several articles and books. In addition to collaborating on a textbook on Latin American history in 1944, he published *Our Spanish Southwest* (1960). This work, also intended as a textbook, was distinctive in attempting to survey the history of the Southwest as a region. Although Perrigo did not develop a conceptual framework for regional analysis, he did discuss the history of California, Arizona, New Mexico, and Texas comparatively, treating individual states as components of the larger region. Though this general work did not arouse much attention at the time of its first publication, increasing awareness of cultural diversity in the Southwest during the 1960s led to its republication in 1971.—G. D. N.

Perrot, Nicolas (1644-? 1718). French explorer and founder of French fur trade in Wisconsin. Born in France, Perrot came to Canada at an early age and lived among several tribes to learn their languages and to attach them to the French empire. In 1667 he and a partner came to Wisconsin, hoping to break the trade monopoly of the Ottawa Indians over the western tribes. Welcomed by the Potawatomi near Green Bay—as "one of the chief spirits, since thou usest iron," said one chief—he offered them French friendship and guns, knives, needles, and other metal things of interest to a stone-age people, in exchange for furs. Traveling among the various Algonquian tribes between 1667 and 1670, he may have been the first Frenchman to see the Mississippi River. After returning to Montreal with valuable furs, he came back to Green Bay in 1671 to rally the Indian allies for the formal ceremony at Sault Ste. Marie, in which St. Lusson took possession of the West for the French. Over the years he became the dominant French leader in the West, probably built three posts on the Mississippi at Prairie du Chien and Lake Pepin, and extended the trade among the Sioux west of the river. He formally took possession of the upper Mississippi region for France at Fort St. Antoine on Lake Pepin on May 8, 1689. When the French government revoked all fur-trade licenses in 1696, Perrot returned to Canada financially ruined and spent the rest of life writing his memoirs.

Perrot State Park on the Mississippi River in Wisconsin is named in honor of the founder of the French fur trade west of Lake Michigan.

See Louise P. Kellogg, *Narratives of the Northwest, 1634-1699* (1917).—W. D. W.

Perry, Oliver Hazard. See GREAT LAKES, MEN OF THE.

Pershing, John Joseph (1860-1948). Soldier. After nearly four decades of military service, Pershing, General of the Armies of the United States, came to symbolize "the professional soldier." In campaigns against the Indian, the Spaniard, the Mexican, the Moro, and the German in World War I, Pershing became the American counterpart of England's Lord Kitchener—a symbol of national firmness, fearlessness, discipline, and self-confidence.

Born near Laclede, Linn County, Missouri, Pershing, after a brief career as schoolteacher, entered West Point and was graduated in 1886. The same year he was assigned to the Sixth Cavalry at Fort Bayard (New Mexico), an old and hallowed regiment, which had taken the brunt of the Geronimo campaign. As a new shavetail, Pershing's first duties involved locating a line of heliograph stations in the Apache country between Bayard and Fort Stanton.

Pershing was to spend nearly six years in the western Indian wars. He scouted, hunted down Geronimo's renegade Apache, and pursued Zuñi out of Fort Wingate. He participated in the merciless police action in the badlands of the Dakota-Nebraska border and com-

manded a troop of Sioux scouts in patrolling parts of the Pine Ridge Agency, looking for Indians with "bad hearts" and preventing gun-running. He rode on the fringes of the bloody campaign against the Sioux, hunting bands of hostiles and chasing rumors in the freezing winter months, that culminated in the battle of Wounded Knee in 1890. His last Indian assignment came when he spent a year (1895-96) commanding the Tenth (Negro) Cavalry at Fort Assinniboine (Montana Territory), rounding up Cree Indians, who were adept at cattle rustling and petty thievery, for deportation across the Canadian border.

After a stint as instructor at the University of Nebraska and at West Point, Pershing rejoined his Tenth Cavalry troopers in the spring of 1898 for the Cuban expedition of the Spanish-American War, participating along with the ROUGH RIDERS in the famous assault on San Juan Hill and winning a Silver Star for his services there. His command of the Negro troopers in Montana and Cuba, and his lifelong respect and admiration for the black soldier, earned him the nickname "Black Jack." Coupled with his reputation for hard-nosed discipline and his outwardly granitic and emotionless personality, the name was especially appropriate.

From 1899 and for the better part of the next fourteen years, Pershing worked in the Philippine jungles, attempting to pacify the fearsome Moros. In 1906, the year after his marriage to the daughter of Senator Francis E. Warren of Wyoming, he was jumped an unprecedented four grades in rank, from captain to brigadier general, over 862 senior officers, by President Theodore Roosevelt.

In 1913 Pershing returned from the Philippines and was immediately ordered to Fort Bliss (El Paso, Texas) to protect the border from the depredations of Mexican rebels. (The great tragedy of Pershing's life occurred while he was stationed there. On August 27, 1915, he was notified that his wife together with their three daughters had perished in a fire that swept through their home at the Presidio in San Francisco. Only one child survived, his only son, Warren.) In the spring of 1916, Pershing led a punitive expedition of twenty thousand men against the rebel soldiers of Francisco "Pancho" Villa, who had attacked the New Mexico border town of Columbus on March 9, killing several soldiers and civilians. With the permission of the Mexican government, Pershing and his troops (approximately ten thousand by the end of the expedition) crossed the Rio Grande to chase Villa and his *banditti*. Although the Americans fought some rearguard actions against the Mexican rebels, Villa was never sighted and the campaign ended indecisively. Villa, however, attempted no further depredations on the American side of the border. Pershing returned from the indecisive campaign in February 1917. Three months later he was selected to command the American Expeditionary Force to be sent to France for the European war.

The contributions of the A.E.F. to ending the "Great War" were considerable. German Field Marshal Paul von Hindenburg told correspondent George Seldes that "the American infantry won the World War in the battle of Argonne." Pershing's role in the ultimate success of the A.E.F. was critical. Demonstrating a single-mindedness of purpose, he adamantly refused to allow his Doughboys to be melded into the French forces on the battle line (feeling that the Americans fought better under their own officers and flag), developed a resolute plan to break the Hindenburg line in the Argonne battle, and made the A.E.F. into an effective fighting unit. Captain B. H. Liddell Hart, the noted English military historian, said of him that there "was perhaps no other man who would, or could, have built the American Army of the scale he planned. And without that army the war could hardly have been saved and could not have been won."

After the war ended Pershing attended the Peace Conference in Paris and participated in framing the military terms of the Treaty of Versailles. On September 3, 1919, by a special act of Congress, he was raised to the permanent rank of "general of the armies of the United States." (Pershing was the only general of the armies in our history. It was a congressional title presented to him in recognition of his work as the commander of the A.E.F. and the American contribution to the eventual victory in France. The significance of this title is its uniqueness.)

The general retired in 1924 after three years as chief of staff of the army. In 1938 he suffered heart, artery, and kidney failures and became an invalid. From 1941 until his death he lived in seclusion at Walter Reed Army Hospital in Washington, D.C., seldom appearing outside his room.

"Self-confidence was the keystone of his career," wrote Pershing's biographer Richard O'Connor, in *Black Jack Pershing* (1961), a fair and modern appraisal. Donald Smythe, *Guerilla Warrior: The Early Life of John J. Pershing* (1973), the definitive work to date, is to be followed by an additional volume or more on Pershing's later career. See also Frank E. Vandiver, *John J. Pershing* (1967), which contains a large section of autobiographical material from Pershing's unpublished memoirs plus a valuable photographic section and chronology of the general's life. The Pershing papers are deposited in the Library of Congress.—D. L. W.

Peterson, Helen W. (1915-   ). Dakota Oglala in race relations work. Peterson was born on the Pine Ridge reservation in South Dakota. She began working her way through Nebraska teachers college by giving music lessons and using her land-allotment money. She later worked for Nelson Rockefeller's Office of Inter-American Affairs as the director of its Rocky Mountain Council, located in Denver. Next, Peterson set up the Colorado Inter-American Field Service Program, which was concerned with the interests and problems of Spanish-speaking people in Colorado. She helped organize twenty Latin American Community Service Clubs, which in time became the Latin American Education Foundation.

Appointed director of the Denver Mayor's Commission on Human Relations in 1948, Peterson set up that agency for the city. In 1949 she was sent as an advisor to the United States delegation to the Second Inter-American Indian Conference in Cuzco, Peru, where an Indian education resolution she wrote was passed. Between 1943 and 1961 Peterson was executive director of the National Council of American Indians and in 1962 was reappointed director of the Denver Commission on Community Relations. In 1970 she was named assistant commissioner for the Bureau of Indian Affairs.

Peterson belonged to many other organizations dealing with Indian affairs, education, and race relations. In 1968 she was named the "outstanding American Indian" at the American Indian Exposition at Anadarko, Oklahoma.—C. C.

petroleum industry. See OIL INDUSTRY.

Pettigrew, Richard Franklin (1848-1926). South Dakota politician and businessman. After spending his early childhood in his birthplace of Ludlow, Vermont, Pettigrew moved to Wisconsin. He attended Evansville Academy, Beloit College, and, briefly, the University of Wisconsin. Summer work as a surveyor took him to Dakota Territory in 1869, and he decided to settle there permanently a year later.

Opportunistic and shrewd, Pettigrew speculated in land and promoted railroads with striking success until 1890. He pursued a political career at the same time and used his commitment to Dakota statehood, his economic resources, and natural guile to win dominance within the Republican party. He served in the upper house of the legislature between 1877 and 1880, went to Congress as a delegate from 1881 to 1883, and returned to the legislature in 1885. From all these offices, Pettigrew advocated statehood and maneuvered for a Senate seat when admission came. In 1889 he became South Dakota's first senator, the climax to two decades of what his biographer called "unscrupulous and ambitious" activity.

Once in the Senate, Pettigrew found his constituents turning toward the protest doctrines of the Farmers Alliance and the western Democratic call for the free and unlimited coinage of silver as currency to ease the monetary and credit plight of the farmer and settler. His business interests also faltered under the impact of his own overexpansion and a depressed economy. These developments eroded his allegiance to the Republicans, who wanted to maintain the gold standard, made him a champion of the white metal, and even caused him to question the values of capitalism. In 1896 he left the party to join the Populist party and to endorse William Jennings Bryan. Two years later he opposed American expansionism. By 1900 his intemperate personal attacks on his Senate colleague Mark Hanna made Pettigrew a special target in the presidential campaign. The disappearance of his political base and Hanna's effective speaking tour ended his slim hopes for reelection in 1901.

During the last quarter century of his life, Pettigrew indulged his cranky radicalism in letters to national figures, vain attempts at a comeback within the Democratic party, and books such as *Imperial Washington* (1922). A critic of American involvement in World War I, he survived government harassment and died a confirmed opponent of the economic system to which he had devoted himself fifty years earlier. Pettigrew's rise to power was a case study in the deft manipulation of the territorial system for personal advancement. His decline into obscurity provides evidence of the turbulent politics that characterized the newer western states in the 1890s.

See the Pettigrew Papers, Pettigrew Museum, Sioux Falls; and Kenneth E. Hendrickson, Jr., "The Public Career of Richard F. Pettigrew of South Dakota, 1848-1926," *South Dakota Department of History Report and Historical Collections* (1968).—L. G.

Peyotism. Indian religion. Peyote (*Lophophora williamsii*) is a spineless cactus native to northern Mexico and the southwestern United States. For centuries it has been used by the Indians of that region for its curative and hallucinogenic qualities. The medically active principle in peyote is mescaline, an alkaloid drug. Peyotism has taken two major forms. As an aspect of early Indian cultures, peyote was used primarily as a medicine and to bring visions to individuals seeking supernatural power. It also figured in tribal dancing rites that intended to induce a trance state in the participants. The origins of these practices are unknown, but peyote is mentioned in the surviving Aztec codices, and sixteenth- and eighteenth-century Spanish documents report its use from Yucatan to northern New Mexico and Oklahoma. Remnants of the old peyotism still exist in remote parts of Mexico.

In its second major form, peyotism has since the late nineteenth century become the foundation of a religion that is playing a large role in the modern resurgence of Indian cultural awareness. The peyote religion is a blend of Christian and native spiritual precepts. Although there are ritual and experiential variations among different tribal groups, the basic form is constant. The religion is an organization for practicing a rite of supplicative prayer, singing, and silent contemplation centering around peyote as the sacrament of the spirits being worshiped and the embodiment of their power. Peyote cannot be smoked. It is eaten, and the visions and discomforts induced by it during the religion's characteristic nightlong rituals are viewed as a means of opening a communion with God and native spirits. It is a strong and viable faith, reinforcing the traditional Indian belief in individual access to supernatural power while at the same time enhancing a feeling of group identity.

The religion's present form developed among the Mescalero Apache and the Kiowa and Comanche of Oklahoma during the 1870s. Peyotists maintain that Quanah Parker, the famed Comanche half-blood, developed the rite after having been cured of an extreme spiritual melancholy through use of the drug. Following the collapse of the Ghost Dance religion in the early 1890s, the quieter peyote belief spread across the Plains and into tribes from every part of the nation. Some of the most effective agencies of its dissemination were the government Indian schools, which brought together young people from many tribes. White missionaries and government officials tried to suppress the religion, claiming its rites were sexual orgies and arresting suspected peyotists under a variety of vaguely written and loosely applied antidrunkenness laws. Aided by the noted white Smithsonian Institution ethnologist James Mooney, the peyotists responded to persecution by incorporating in 1918 as the Native American Church, which was chartered by the state of Oklahoma.

In the 1960s the church had branches in every state and claimed 200,000 members. Verification is difficult, for many groups are underground to avoid continuing legal problems, and most peyotists officially list their religion as another Christian denomination. By 1970 several states, including most western ones with large reservations, had amended their laws to permit the use of peyote in religious services, and court cases in some others have effectively legalized it.

Peyote is still highly controversial. Medical authorities disagree about the effects of its longterm use, and the legal issue is entangled in the whole drug problem of the midtwentieth century. Notwithstanding such problems, the religion is apparently still growing. Many young Indians see peyotism as an affirmation of their cultural identity and a denial of white domination.

The best brief account of modern peyotism is in Hazel W. Hertzberg, *The Search for an American Indian Identity: Modern Pan-Indian Movements* (1971). Weston La Barre, *The Peyote Cult* (rev. ed., 1969), and J. S. Slotkin, *The Peyote Religion: A Study in Indian-White Relations* (1956), are the definitive ethnological studies. See also David Aberle, *The Peyote Religion Among the Navaho* (1966), and Alice Marriott and Carol Rachlin, *Peyote* (1971). —P. R. M.

Philip, [James] Scotty (1857-1911). Freighter, scout, and cattleman. Philip emigrated from Scotland to the United States when he was sixteen years old. Traveling west, he paused briefly in Kansas before continuing on to Colorado and Wyoming, where he became a freighter. In 1876 he was lured to South Dakota by tales of the discovery of gold in the Black Hills. Although Philip never found any gold, he decided to remain on the rough range land and in 1877 began working cattle near Running Water, Wyoming. A year later he became an army scout and quickly made friends with the Cheyenne and Sioux; in 1879 he wed a Cheyenne woman by whom he had ten children. The family ranched near the Pine Ridge agency on White Clay Creek.

Freighting into the Black Hills to supplement his small ranch operation from 1882 to 1896, Philip began large-scale ranching with outside capital in the Bad River country, where a town was named for him. With establishment of the famed 73 Ranch near Fort Pierre, he became one of the West's big cattlemen. For a quarter of a century he was known from the Black Hills to the Mexican border. He ran from fifteen thousand to twenty-three thousand head of cattle. His long friendship with the Indians helped him get grazing rights on the lower Brule reservation to add to his own corporate holdings.

Fearing that the buffalo were about to be killed off, he acquired five captive calves, converted the Fort Pierre ranch to a sixteen-thousand-acre pasture, and built the herd to nearly one thousand head. The Dakota zoo herds of today are descended from the buffalo stock Philip maintained on his Fort Pierre ranch.—R. B. W.

Phillips, Bert G. (1868-1956). Painter. Born in Hudson, New York, Phillips studied at the National Academy of Design in New York City and the Art Students League. He opened up a studio in New York in 1894 and afterward traveled to Paris, where he met fellow American artists Joseph Henry Sharp and Ernest L. Blumenschein. Returning to New York in 1896, Phillips shared a studio with Blumenschein before the two of them, at Sharp's earlier suggestion, ventured westward to Taos, New Mexico, in 1897. Here Phillips elected to remain, becoming one of the founders of the Taos Society of Artists. He maintained his home and studio in Taos until his death, painting many scenes illustrative of Pueblo Indian life, which are now included in the collections of the Fine Arts Museum, Santa Fe, New Mexico; the Thomas Gilcrease Institute of American History and Art; the Philbrook Art Center, Tulsa, Oklahoma; and numerous other museums.

Phillips was instrumental in protecting the Taos Indian Sacred Mountain and surrounding forests from exploitation by commercial mining interests and encouraged the federal government to set this area aside as a national preserve, which it did in the 1930s.

See Ven Deren Coke, *Taos and Santa Fe: The Artist's Environment* (1963); and Mabel Dodge Luhan, *Taos and Its Artists* (1947).—D. C. H.

Phillips, Frank (1873-1950). Financier and art collector. Born in Scotia, Nebraska, Phillips grew up near Creston, Iowa, and entered the banking business. In 1903 he moved to Bartlesville, Indian Territory, where he soon became involved in the booming petroleum industry. With a younger brother, Phillips organized the Phillips Petroleum Company in 1917. He became its first executive officer, holding this position throughout most of his life.

Interested in the preservation of America's western heritage, Phillips created in the 1920s near Bartlesville a wild-game preserve he named Woolaroc, stocking it with native elk, deer, and buffalo. At about this time he began to collect Indian relics, pioneer artifacts, and other mementos of western life. Also an aviation buff, Phillips engaged Art Goebel to pilot a small monoplane called the *Woolaroc* in a race between Oakland, California, and Honolulu, Hawaii, in the same year that Lindbergh made his famous trans-Atlantic flight. Following Goebel's winning of the Pacific race, the plane itself was returned to Woolaroc Ranch, where Phillips built a small museum to house and display it. In time this building was greatly enlarged to hold Phillips' growing collection of guns, paintings, sculptures, and other memorabilia. Through the University of Oklahoma, whose excavations of prehistoric Indian mounds Phillips had supported, he secured the services of a professional museum director in 1941. Today the Woolaroc Museum houses one of the largest private collections of its kind in the Southwest and displays numerous works by such western artists as O. E. Berninghaus, Frank Tenney Johnson, William R. Leigh, Robert Lindneux, and Joseph Henry Sharp. The former Tulsa estate of Waite Phillips, another of Phillips' brothers, serves as the Philbrook Art Center, host to the nation's American Indian Artists' Annual.

See Aline B. Saarinen, *The Proud Possessors* (1958).—D. C. H.

Phoenix, Arizona. About 1867 Jack Swilling, a Wickenburg prospector, saw the possibilities of opening farms in the Salt River valley to supply nearby Fort McDowell, organized the Swilling Irrigating Canal Company, and erected several adobe buildings. Yavapai County established an election precinct there, and Darrel Duppa, an English adventurer, named the area Phoenix, after the mythical bird. By the early 1870s local promoters had laid out a regular townsite west of the Swilling settlement as the seat for newly created Maricopa County. Incorporated in 1881, Phoenix boasted a population of more than one thousand seven hundred and had thirty thousand acres under irrigation. The Southern Pacific constructed a railroad line from the junction at Maricopa Wells, and in 1889 Phoenix was designated the territorial capital. Various canal companies developed a vast acreage along the Salt, and Arizona ranchers began sending their cattle to the valley for winter feeding. The completion of Roosevelt Dam in 1911 solved the problem of water storage and control in the valley and assured the growth of the city. The state's constitutional convention was held in Phoenix, which in 1912 became the state capital. Manufacturing (aircraft parts and electronic equipment) was brought to the valley by World War II, and within a decade it ranked with agriculture (cotton, citrus fruits, grains), retirement centers, and tourism as a major local industry. By 1970 the largest concentration of population in Arizona was in the Salt River valley, and Phoenix was the largest city in the state, with more than 580,000 people.

See *Arizona: A Guide to the Grand Canyon State* (1966); and Herb and Dorothy McLaughlin, eds., *Phoenix, 1870-1970, in Photographs* (1970).—H. P. H.

photography. Photographs of the West were being taken a very few years after the process was discovered in 1839. The earliest photographers, daguerreotypists, came to the West in the 1840s, and soon their "mirrors with a memory" began to reveal the believable truth of this little-known territory. Formerly, descriptions of the West had been couched in mystery. Potential colonizers and settlers, as well as other outsiders interested in what was taking place west of the Mississippi, had always been dependent on artists, writers, explorers, and "tall-tale" tellers for information about the new territory. Unfortunately, more often than not they were presented with a distorted image of the West. The frontier came to be perceived as a land of romance, of mythical beauty and mystery, peopled by fierce Indians and wild beasts. This misconception was enhanced by the relative isolation of frontier life, the restricted opportunities for travel between one section of the country and another, and the primitive stage of communication existing at the time.

With the advent in 1839 of the daguerreotype (a photograph produced on a silver-coated copper plate), a "true-to-life" view of the West at last became possible. Brilliant in their clarity, precise in their rendering of detail, and utterly faithful to their subject, these first photographs were easily fitted to play a decisive role in presenting a believable West to a waiting world. Hailed as a "mirror with a memory," the daguerreotypes were quickly and widely accepted as accurate documents. Their first major test as visual news recorders was to document the California gold rush, a task they fulfilled admirably.

In 1851 Robert H. Vance, a leading San Francisco daguerrean artist, brought to an exhibition in New York City some three hundred daguerreotype views of San Francisco: the mines, miners, California Indians, and portraits of leading Californians. The collection was received with enthusiasm and did much to excite interest in the California region. During the Mexican War a few enlisted American army typesetters made daguerreotype views of Major General John Ellis Wool's Saltillo campaign. A mere handful survive in the Beinecke Library at Yale University. The sales potential for photographs of the West's varied people attracted scores of daguerrean artists. Views of Indians and their camps, western rivers, army forts, early settlements, river steamboats, and the incredible western landscape all were recorded. Sadly, few of these earliest photographs remain.

In the late 1840s and early 1850s many western exploring expeditions attempted daguerrean documentation of their efforts. Solomon Nuñes Carvalho accompanied John Frémont's fifth exploring expedition in 1853 as artist and daguerrean; John Mix STANLEY made many daguerreotypes as a member of Governor I. I. Stevens' 1853 exploring party, one of several surveys undertaken to choose a transcontinental rail route; and Captain F. W. Landers in 1853 reported photographers at work with his survey team, laying out a proposed road from Salt Lake City over the South Pass eastward. Most of these activities, which met with mixed success, came to an end with the outbreak of the Civil War and the discontinuance of major exploratory expeditions.

Major improvements in the new photographic process followed one another swiftly. With the successful development of the wet-plate collodion glass negative and the paper print in 1851, duplicate prints were possible for the first time, opening another horizon for western photography. Although still a precise and time-consuming process, the new glass negatives allowed faster exposures. Speedier chemical emulsions made photography easier than daguerreotyping and permitted much wider latitudes in photographing out-of-doors and in poorly lit circumstances.

The problem of suitable transport to carry the heavy equipment used in early-day photography was solved with the introduction of horse-drawn darkrooms. This useful device allowed the frontier photographer to penetrate areas of interest and natural beauty never previously shown to audiences in the East. The increased mobility of horse-drawn photography shops encouraged amateur use of the medium by those already moving westward. A "seeding" of photographers across the western plains was the happy result. These tyros produced fine pictures and often stayed where they settled, reappearing as the photographers of a newly built western town. Groupings of itinerant as well as permanent photographers soon dotted the country from St. Joseph, Missouri, to San Francisco, California. In their struggle to make a living as photographers, they often doubled as the town's apothecary, bookseller, notions merchant, and optician.

These vigorous years evidenced a crop of able professionals and some gifted and dedicated amateurs, all of whom photographed the events taking place in the mid-nineteenth century. Alfred A. Hart (1816-?) and Captain Andrew J. Russell (1831-76) recorded on glass plates the building of the first transcontinental railroad, the Central Pacific east from Sacramento, California, the Union Pacific west from Omaha, Nebraska, and the joining of the rails at Promontory Point, Utah. Timothy O'Sullivan (1840-82), John K. Hillers (1843-1925), Jim Fennemore (1849-1941), and E. O. Beaman accompanied the two great exploring expeditions of the Grand Canyon of the Colorado River in the 1870s. O'Sullivan also joined Clarence King's explorations of the Rocky Mountains in 1867, 1868, and 1869. William Henry JACKSON, dean of frontier photography, created a superb visual record of Ferdinand V. Hayden's tireless penetration of the West in the 1870s. Alexander Gardner (1821-82), of Civil War fame, left a valuable 1867 photographic view of the emerging Kansas frontier.

Throughout this twenty-five-year period there were steady attempts, successful and unsuccessful, to preserve a photographic record of the many Indians of the West. Early daguerreotypes left a brilliant heritage of

Indian views, sparse as it is at present. The wet-plate photographers who superseded them left an equally important legacy of their work: William Henry Jackson's exhaustive catalog of Indian portraits and encampments; the newly discovered portraits of the Southern Plains Indians at Fort Sill in Indian Territory (1869-74) by William S. Soule, an extremely rare visual record; W. H. Illingworth's work with General George A. Custer's Black Hills expedition of 1874; and V. T. McGillicuddy's in the same Black Hills area in 1875. Other photographers, like L. A. Huffman (1854-1931), F. Jay Haynes (1853-1920), and David F. Barry (1858-1934), did significant work among the Indians of the Northern Plains. This area of interest culminated with the multivolume work on the North American Indian by Edward S. CURTIS.

The work of John K. Hillers among the Paiute, Mojave, and Havasupai Indians has yet to be surpassed for its ethnological importance. Camillus Fly and Henry Beuhman, from Arizona, recorded the transition of the Spanish-American frontier into late nineteenth-century America, recalling the languor, ferocity, and primitive dusty torpor of that transition. The Pueblo, Navaho, Hopi, and Zuñi Indians, the tribes of the Rio Grande, and the indomitable Apache, as well as the lesser tribes, all passed before the cameras of A. F. Randall, Ben Wittick (1845-1903), and the sensitive humanitarian A. C. Vroman (1856-1916).

Many unknown photographers left small pockets of revealing images detailing the many struggles to operate mines, build railroads, irrigate the desert, create towns, extend lines of communication and transportation, and establish schools, churches, saloons, and brothels. The great cattle drives over the Texas, Oklahoma, and Kansas plains live in the photographs of Erwin Smith, G. F. Swearingen, and William S. Prettyman (1858-1932). A poignant view of the settlers' West is preserved in the images of Solomon Butcher, who photographed his immigrant sod-shanty neighbors on the cold Nebraska plains. Testimony to the labor, skill, and resolution of Pacific Northwest lumbermen is found in the glass plates of Darius Kinsey (1871-1945), some as large as twenty inches by twenty-six inches. Wilhelm Hester (1870-1947), a German immigrant, captured the drama of Puget Sound sawmills and the sailing ships that carried their lumber to impatient markets around the world. Stanley J. Morrow (1843-1921), trained by Mathew B. Brady, photographed around Yankton, Dakota Territory, in the 1870s. His images of river steamboats, army forts, and Indian faces and his coverage of the Custer battlefield at the Little Big Horn in 1876 are incomparable. Charles R. Savage (1832-1909), who photographed from the Mississippi to the Pacific until the turn of the century, faithfully filmed each day another facet of the many-sided, grueling effort that finally built Salt Lake City.

Counterparts of such men existed in the many cities that grew in the West. John A. Sherriff, Charles P. Fessenden, Henry Payne, the Parker brothers, and Herbert R. Fitch vividly traced in their photographs almost one hundred years of the growth of San Diego, California. The roster of San Francisco's important nineteenth-century photographers is long and distinguished. Widely recognized then and now, they include the industrious whaleman turned photographer I. W. Taber; Ead-

A Union Pacific photographic car near Point of Rocks, Wyoming, about 1867. (Library of Congress)

ward Muybridge; Carleton E. Watkins, the lover of Yosemite Valley, most of whose work was almost entirely destroyed in the San Francisco fire; George Fiske; William Henry Rulofson, San Francisco's peerless portrait photographer; the waterfront photographers of San Francisco's maritime heyday Messrs Swadley, Morton, and Waters; and Arnold Genthe, who gained wide recognition by photographing the Chinese in San Francisco with a sensitive, romantic eye.

Great landscape photographers abound: Watkins, Fiske, and Muybridge of California; Jackson of Colorado; F. J. Haynes of Montana and Wyoming; Asahel Curtis of Washington Territory; A. C. Vroman of the Southwest; and many others. All of these men found and presented their own West to the city dwellers who were so anxious to possess it. Through their efforts the beauty, difficulty, and the opportunities of the West took on visual life. This record provided needed knowledge and the sense of security that was so important in an attempt to understand western living. It offered clear proof that many of the problems were solvable or had been solved. Such photographs satisfied the need to believe that a viable life was possible. It popularized a West that was in the daily process of being built by plain people. It proved to be effective propaganda.

The problems of these photographers were similar to their neighbors. In newly settled country towns there was the never-ending battle against nature and boredom. Periodic economic distress was their common lot, as was the difficulty of communication. A dependable supply system for their professional needs was speculative. Professional contact was uncertain and often of dubious value. Aesthetic and intellectual support for their efforts was infrequent and hard-won. The photographers fought these problems as well as their circumstances allowed. Their inventiveness, determination, and loyalty to a profession whose economic future was uncertain, and their unbelievable energy, daring, and

enthusiasm mark them as men and women of character and ability.

The photographer moved about with approximately eighty pounds of bulky equipment. Finding a suitable vantage point from which to photograph and setting up the camera and lens firmly on a heavy tripod was only the start of a long process. Crouching underneath a spread light-tight cloth, the photographer had to balance a plate of clean and polished glass on his outstretched fingers; coat it evenly with syrupy chemical solutions; place the coated wet plate into a lightproof, wooden plate holder; rush out to the camera; and then expose the plate to the waiting sun. Once exposed, the plate was rushed back underneath the black cloth, there to be developed in additional chemical solutions. Each picture required this same process, an immense amount of work. William Henry Jackson did just that countless times over, high in the unexplored snow-covered Rocky Mountains. So it is easy to sympathize with this sober comment on his ninetieth birthday. Having received a 35-mm Leica camera as a birthday gift, he hefted it lightly in his weather-beaten hand, turned to the donor, and said: "My God, this little thing makes a sport of our labors."

The impact of western photography was startling. The United States Congress was stimulated to create national parks of the scenic areas because of photographic albums presented to them, among them Jackson's photographs of Yellowstone. These albums provided visual proof of the need to preserve the areas as public parks. Western photography also played a role in creating a deeper sense of nationhood and unity in a people confined for a long period of time to east of the Mississippi. The western photographer helped more than almost any other "communicator" to transform the mythical West into reality, habitable and exploitable.

The photographer's quick success coupled with the discovery of colored photolithography assured the growth of the colored postcard business. The profit potential in this new business was so great that new channels for mass distribution were quickly generated. The photographer's ability to present the "real" West was now within the reach of anyone who possessed a copper penny. The market and the product were joined in mutual success. One could examine views of the land, the many different peoples at work, the developing life, the myriad opportunities for new arrivals, and the many "strangers" in the West. (These "strangers" were, of course, the Indians, Mexicans, Chinese, Japanese, Filipinos, and Hawaiians.)

New trades and newly found skills in the booming West were also quickly added to the storehouse of popular knowledge. The know-how for ranching, mining, cowpunching, citrus agriculture, and even the bringing in of a gushing oil well were soon appreciated by all Americans. Western photographers captured this excitement on film, and visitors to the West carried these photographs all over the world. Prize-winning western photographers soon became known in international photographic exhibitions. In time the photographed reality came close to creating its own new fantasy.

No branch of the government was without its official photographer. Early survey parties employed Timothy O'Sullivan, Hillers, and Jackson. Much later the federal Farm Security Administration employed Dorothea Lange (1895-1965) to document the tragic Dust Bowl period. These photographs still appear from time to time in popular magazines, and her work is now housed permanently in the Library of Congress and the Oakland Museum in California.

Every western industry and almost every western community of any size has by now created a photographic archive of the many facets of western development. Major depositories include the Bancroft Library; the Huntington Library; California Historical Society; Los Angeles County Museum of Natural History; University of Oregon; Washington State Historical Society; San Francisco Maritime Museum; Denver Public Library; Colorado State Historical Society; University of Wyoming; and the Arizona Historical Society. These archives embrace the full range of man's capabilities and abilities. The triumph of the completed transcontinental railroad is captured on a glass plate, as is the wanton outrage of the Wounded Knee Massacre. The deep satisfaction of water brought to a parched land rests on film in the same archives alongside the pictorial record of the shameful Japanese-American internment during World War II.

Two of the best contemporary western photographers turned once more to natural grandeur for their creative sustenance. Edward Weston (1886-1958) and Ansel Adams (1902-   ) were both drawn inexorably to the diminishing natural beauty of the West. Their rendering of its wilderness splendor is matchless. Adams continued to make dramatic images of the western land, lending both his eloquent work and his untiring self to conservation efforts. Imogen Cunningham (1883-   ), a western photographer of enduring fame like Lange before her, found great strength and creative impulse in the daily lives of western men and women.

There is, of course, no one West; there are many, each reflecting a geographical area, a time span, a particular form of economic development, an ethnic center, or even a personal point of view. The frontier photographers' task was to reproduce each one of them. The fruit of their labors lies in the multiplicity of brilliant and evocative images of those many facets of the West we possess today. And their successors are offering once again to the world the vision of a West that must be redeemed if it and its inhabitants, both animal and man, are to grow and survive.

See Beaumont Newhall, *The History of Photography from 1839 to the Present Day* (1949) and *The Daguerreotype in America* (1961); Robert Taft, *Photography and the American Scene: A Social History, 1839-1889* (1938); Freeman Tilden, *Following the Frontier with F. Jay Haynes, Pioneer Photographer of the Old West* (1964); Russell F. Belous and Robert A. Weinstein, *Will Soule, Indian Photographer at Fort Sill, Oklahoma, 1869-74* (1969); LeRoy R. Hafen, *The Diaries of William Henry Jackson, Frontier Photographer* (1959); Wesley R. Hurt and William E. Lass, *Frontier Photographer, Stanley J. Morrow's Dakota Years* (1956); James Horan, *Timothy O'Sullivan, America's Forgotten Photographer* (1966); William Webb and Robert A. Weinstein, *Dwellers at the Source* (1973); David Phillips and Weinstein, *The West, An American Experience* (1973); A. D. Coleman and T. McLuhan, *The North American Indians of Edward S. Curtis* (1973); Joanna Scherer, *Indians* (1973); Joan Paterson Kerr and Oliver Jensen, *American Album* (1968); and Don D. Fowler, ed., *John Hillers' Diaries* (1972).—R. A. W.

physiography of the United States. The North American continent has more varied and abundant resources useful to mankind than any other continent, and the United States occupies the most favored part of the continent. These resources are the result of geologic history.

The rich resources existed before Columbus arrived, but most of them had not been used. Settlement of the land and development of the resources were an outgrowth of the efforts of the migrating Europeans, and they came in large part because of the richness of the resources as well as the favorable physiography. Availability of land was not the only attraction; there was land elsewhere, as in the tropics and the Arctic regions. North America offered more than merely land.

The prehistoric archaeological record and the historical record combine to show that environment does not make man, but neither can it be supposed that man could have made the United States what it is today without the wealth of water, mineral, agricultural, and other resources—as well as the land—that were waiting to be discovered and used.

In order to consider the physiography of the United States, students divide the land into physiographic provinces (Fig. 3). These are the structural elements of the nation's part of the continent; each province had a distinctive geologic history, which controlled the formation of the land, its topography, soils, water, minerals, and other resources. One half of the land is plain, one quarter is mountain, and one quarter is plateau (Fig. 1). Some physiographic units are large-scale and others are small-scale.

The largest unit is the continent, North America, which is a slab of granitic rock having a maximum thickness of about twenty-five miles and thinning toward its rim to less than five miles thick (Fig. 2). This slab floats like a raft on a denser layer called the mantle. The continent divides into its smaller structural elements, the provinces.

The provinces, in turn, are further divided into parts that have differing environments and resources. A sandy coast, for example, can include offshore, nearshore, onshore, and backshore environments, each with a different ecosystem and use. A mountainous area can include fertile valleys as well as high summits and steep mountainsides.

The central part of the continental slab of granitic rock is called the *shield*, or more specifically the Canadian Shield to distinguish it from the similar central parts of the other continents. The Canadian Shield, centering around Hudson Bay, includes all of eastern Canada and extends westward to the Mackenzie River. The south end extends into the United States at Lake Superior and includes the northern parts of Minnesota, Wisconsin, and Michigan.

This central part of the continent is composed of ancient, greatly altered (metamorphosed) Precambrian rocks (see Table 1), which are more than 600 million years old, with some as old as 3.5 billion years. If theories about early earth history are approximately correct, this part of the crustal slab began forming as solid crust 4.6 billion years ago; the formation of that earliest solid crust is considered to be the beginning of geologic history. The date is based on radiometric age determinations of meteorites and lunar rocks and on astronomical calculations. Earlier earth history is in the domain of astronomy and predates geologic history.

Bordering the Canadian Shield, particularly on the south and west, is a broad, stable platform of Precambrian rocks that stabilized as long ago as 600 million years, before the beginning of the Paleozoic era. During that era the platform was repeatedly submerged, but shallowly, and during those times marine and coastal plain sediments were deposited on it. During the 375 million years of Paleozoic time, the sediments accumulated to an average thickness of about five thousand feet. During this time, the continental slab slowly sank into the mantle, but the kinds of sediments deposited show that the surface never was deeply submerged below sea level. At the times when coastal plain sediments were deposited on it, the surface was slightly higher than sea level.

Since the continent sank 5,000 feet in 375 million years, the average rate of sinking was only 1 foot in 75,000 years. This illustrates an important geologic principle, namely, that earth processes operate exceed-

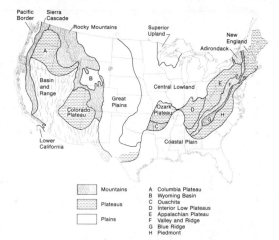

Figure 1. Half of the United States is plain, a quarter is plateau, and a quarter is mountainous. (From C. B. Hunt, Geology of Soils, copyright © 1972, W. H. Freeman and Co.)

ingly slowly, but they have literally all the time in the world in which to operate and so accomplish great changes. Even a foot of uplift in 1,000 years is hardly an exciting rate of earth movement; many parts of the country are moving at a livelier rate than that at the present time. But the rate of movement of one foot in 1,000 years continued for 10 million years—which is not very long geologically speaking— can produce a mountain range 10,000 feet high.

The stable platform ended southeastward at an unstable edge of the continental slab that gradually bent downward during the Paleozoic era to form a deep trough, known as a geosyncline (Fig. 2). A similar geosyncline formed along the unstable western edge of the platform at the site of the Canadian Rockies and southward across western Montana, Idaho, and central Nevada. Both the eastern and western geosyncline became flooded by mediterranean seas, and the sediments deposited in them accumulated to a thickness of forty thousand feet—eight times the thickness of the sediments deposited on the platform. The seas were never that deep. In fact, both the shellfish preserved as fossils and the kinds of sediments that were deposited reflect

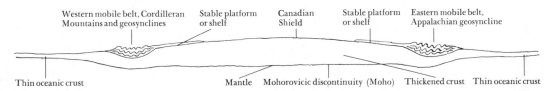

Figure 2. Diagram illustrating the principal structural elements of North America. The continent is a thickened slab of rock with density about that of granite floating on the denser mantle with density about that of basalt. The central part of the slab, the Canadian Shield, exposes Precambrian rocks. Bordering this is a stable platform or shelf that was intermittently shallowly submerged and now is capped by thin marine formations of Paleozoic and/or Mesozoic age. Bordering the platforms are mobile belts that were deep troughs (geosynclines) during the Paleozoic and/or Mesozoic; the marine formations that accumulated in these troughs are many miles thick and are much folded and faulted. Under the oceans the crust is thin. (U.S. Geological Survey)

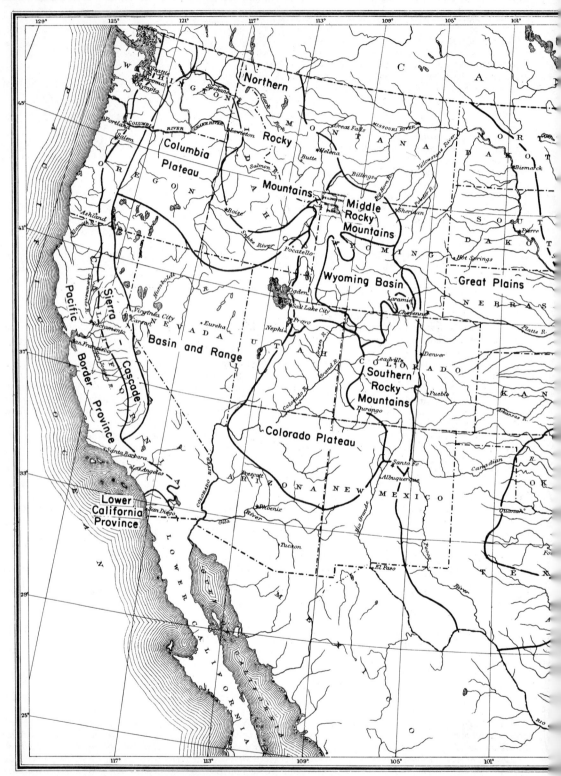

Figure 3. *Physiographic provinces of the United States. Basically these are the structural members of the country;*

each is distinctive. (From C. B. Hunt, Physiography of the United States, copyright © 1967, W. H. Freedman and Co.)

Table 1. Geologic time scale

Era	Period	Epoch	Estimated ages of the time boundaries, in millions of years
Cenozoic (age of mammals)	Quaternary	Holocene Pleistocene	
			2-3
	Tertiary	Pliocene Miocene Oligocene Eocene Paleocene	
			65
Mesozoic (age of rep-tiles, notably dinosaurs)	Cretaceous		
			135
	Jurassic		
			190
	Triassic		
			225
Paleozoic (age of inver-tebrates which were abundant and varied; first fishes, amphibians, and land plants)	Permian		
			280
	Pennsylvanian		
			320
	Mississippian		
			345
	Devonian		
			395
	Silurian		
			440
	Ordovician		
			500
	Cambrian		
			570
Precambrian (primitive forms of life; algae etc.)			
			4,600

Astronomical History

comparatively shallow water environments. The rate of sinking of the geosynclines was about one foot every one thousand years.

At various times during the Paleozoic, while the troughs gradually deepened, the sediments were squeezed between the sides of the troughs and became folded. At the end of the Paleozoic they were severely folded and uplifted to form the ancestral Appalachian Mountains in the eastern United States and some of the mountains in the West. Incidentally, this accounts for the occurrence of seashells on mountaintops. The seas never were that high; rather, the fossil-bearing marine formations have been uplifted to the positions in which they are found.

The Continental Divide separating the two geosynclinal troughs was along a structural ridge trending southwestward across the stable platform from Lake Superior to the southwestern part of New Mexico. The shallow seas that intermittently flooded the platform frequently submerged the divide, but it persisted at least as the shallowest part of the sea. This structure is referred to as the Transcontinental Arch and its effects are still obvious.

During the first part of the Mesozoic era, in the Triassic and Jurassic periods (Table 1), a geosyncline developed along the western edge of the continent west of where the Paleozoic geosyncline had been. No such trough is known along the Atlantic Coast, although one may be concealed under the outer part of the continental shelf—that submerged part of the plain extending eastward along the Atlantic seaboard. During the latter part of the Mesozoic, in the Cretaceous period, the unstable belt along the western edge of the continent became uplifted and eroded. A geosynclinal trough also developed along the valley of the Rio Grande and extended northward across the Transcontinental Arch and along the site of the Rocky Mountains. It extended all the way across Canada and connected the Gulf of Mexico with the Arctic Ocean. This mediterranean sea received sediments eroded from the mountains that had formed from the Triassic and Jurassic geosynclines.

At the end of the Cretaceous, roughly 65 million years ago, this geosyncline became folded and uplifted. The Rocky Mountains rose from what had been the axial and deepest part of the trough, and they continued to rise and be folded and faulted during the Tertiary. The Sierra Nevada, Cascade, and Coast ranges are Tertiary mountains.

Clearly the systems of mountains developed where there had been geosynclines and thick accumulations of marine sediments. What went down eventually had to come up, and there is a critical limit of somewhere from 40,000 to 50,000 feet of sediments that could be received in the geosynclines before they reversed their direction of movement. Whatever the mechanics, the mountain ranges coincide with the ancient troughs that contained mediterranean seas.

Although the mountains of North America are impressive in their height—almost four miles, Mount McKinley being 20,320 feet—this relief is only one sixth as great as that across the bottom of the crustal slab. In fact, to keep perspective, the roughness of the land surface should be compared proportionally with the roughness of a billiard ball.

The structural members of the continent, the physiographic provinces, are considered from east to west, not for physiographic reasons but because historically this was the direction of progress of exploration, settlement, and development.

New England Province. New England and the bordering Maritime Provinces of Canada are part of the Appalachian Mountain system and constitute a hilly to mountainous, glaciated terrain composed of metamorphosed, geosynclinal, sedimentary formations of Paleozoic age. The rocks are very much folded and faulted and intruded by Paleozoic granite. Mantling these complexly deformed old rocks are the young glacial deposits of sand and gravel deposited during the Pleistocene epoch by the glaciers that originated in Canada and moved southward to Long Island, Martha's Vineyard, and Nantucket. Some of the mountaintops of old rocks are more than 5,000 feet in altitude, Mount Katahdin, Maine, being 5,268 feet, Mount Washington, New Hampshire, 6,288 feet. The Adirondack Mountains—with Mount Marcy, 5,344 feet, the highest peak—also are a Paleozoic uplift although its rocks are

Precambrian and closely related to those in the nearby Canadian Shield.

The Connecticut River valley is a structural trough, a fault valley containing rock beds of Triassic age. With the red sedimentary rocks are sheets of basaltic rock forming the prominent Holyoke Ridges and East and West Rocks at New Haven. This valley provided easy access to interior New England.

North America has been tilted northeastward, and as a consequence the north end of the Appalachian system of mountains is partly submerged, and the hilly or mountain valleys are embayed by the sea. The saltwater bays are separated by rocky headlands. Southward along the Atlantic Coast, the Appalachians are separated from the sea by the Coastal Plain Province, but this flat plain, like the mountains, tilts northeastward, and it passes below sea level at Long Island, Martha's Vineyard, and Nantucket.

During Pleistocene time, when New England was weighed down with glacial ice, the land was submerged even more than it is today. As a result, marine Pleistocene deposits are found far inland from the coast in Maine, indicating that the land there has risen faster than has the sea level. The glaciation blanketed the ground with boulders and, with sand and gravel transported southward by the ice. Later, when the land was farmed, the fields had to be cleared of stones, which were laid in walls. These stone walls are as typical of New England as cod and so are the glacial erratics, e.g., Plymouth Rock. Another effect of the glaciations was to deposit gravel and sand in rounded, elongated hills known as drumlins. Bunker Hill is one, and there are many others in Boston Basin. The sand and gravel left by the ice was deposited irregularly in ways that disrupted the drainage and formed innumerable lakes and ponds, including Thoreau's Walden Pond.

The vast amounts of water released by the melting ice caused the sea level to rise. The land, relieved of its extra load, also rose. At first the land rose faster than the sea; later the sea rose faster. A prehistoric fishweir (c. 2500 B.C.) in Boston harbor shows that sea level has risen 16 feet in about 4,500 years. At the present time sea level is rising, apparently about 6 inches a century.

The rocky headlands and islands were and still are shipping hazards, and the early history of lighthouses, the beginning of a coast guard, began at Boston harbor in 1716. The drowned valleys provided good harbors, but the rivers could not be navigated far inland because of rapids just beyond the limit of tidewater. Those rapids, though, provided waterpower that led to the construction and development of mills of all kinds in New England, and this in turn spurred the invention and development of various kinds of manufacturing machinery.

Off the New England coast the submerged coastal plain, or continental shelf, at Georges Bank and farther east is one of the world's rich areas for finfish, especially herring, mackerel, perch, and cod. The shores yield abundant clams and lobsters. Whaling was a major activity too during the colonial period, but declined after the Revolution because of overkill. Shipping the dried fish to the West Indies and Europe led to a demand for salt, and evaporation pans were established—at Piscataqua in 1623, at Beverley in 1638, and at Cape Cod.

The maritime environment led to shipbuilding because of the ready availability of the right kinds of lumber in the northern hardwood forests and in the spruce-fir forests farther north. The forests yielded the type of lumber needed for structural forms, boarding, masts, and finishing. They also provided naval stores, that is, the resins and turpentine needed in building wooden ships. In New England an oak vessel could be built for two thirds the cost of building it in England, and by 1775 two thirds of the ships under British flag had been built in America.

The forests also provided the materials needed for the construction of homes and mills and for fuel. Until the middle of the nineteenth century, wood provided three quarters or more of the country's energy requirements, not only in New England but all over the country. Wood ashes were used as a source of potash. After the middle of the nineteenth century, coal became the dominant source of energy.

Agriculture, the first and basic industry during the colonial period, required clearing the forests, which was done by girdling the trees or killing them with fires around their bases. With the trees defoliated and the underbrush cleared, sunlight came through, allowing maize—Indian corn—and flax to be planted before the stumps were cleared. Berries and squash also grew locally, and soon potatoes and grains, especially rye and buckwheat, were introduced.

Cold winters and cool summers control the kinds of forests in New England; they also favor animals with fur, and furs very early became a major industry in New England, especially beaver, otter, and black fox. It quickly spread from there and the Maritime Provinces of Canada, all the way westward across southern Canada and northern United States. The cold climate of New England, resulting partly from latitude and partly from proximity to the cold Labrador Current, also prompted a need for warm clothes. An important part of every New England home was the spinning wheel for drawing out carded wool and flax for weaving.

Except as a source for building stone, especially granite and marble, New England's mineral resources did not play a major role in its early history. Later there were found deposits of the kind associated with metamorphic and granitic rocks—titaniferous magnetite, talc from serpentine, and graphite and mica. One might expect precious metals in such rocks, but none have been found. With no precious metals being mined there could be no coinage, and the small amount of money brought by the colonists was soon returned to England to pay for manufactured goods or for other purposes. Commodities were used as money, at values fixed annually by the local governments. Wampum—Indian beads—served as change as long as it was accepted in Indian trade for beaver hides.

The hilly and mountainous terrain, having a topographic grain oriented roughly from north to south, did not encourage large landholding or large-scale migrations westward. In general, settlement progressed up the valleys, and only the Connecticut River was navigable far inland. This isolation by the terrain apparently aided the impetus to the first union of the English colonies (1643 to 1684), partly out of fear of the Dutch. The isolation also has been the butt of many jokes about the extent of western travel by the people of Boston; the jokes are rooted in the physiography.

Atlantic and Gulf Coastal plains. The broad plain extending along the coast from New York harbor southward to Georgia and Florida and west around the Gulf of Mexico is as wide as three hundred miles in some places, and almost all of it is below five hundred feet in altitude. The plain continues seaward for another one hundred to two hundred miles, forming the continental shelf, which ends at a depth of about six hundred feet at the rim of a steep continental slope, falling off to the abyss under the ocean. Both the continental shelf and its landward continuation, the Coastal Plain, are underlain by poorly consolidated sandy and clayey formations of Cretaceous, Tertiary, and Quaternary age. The formations are mostly of marine origin and represent uplifted sea floor. In Cretaceous time (Table 1) the shore was along the inner edge of the Coastal Plain Province.

The formations underlying the Coastal Plain and continental shelf are nearly flat but dip gently seaward (Figs. 4 and 5). They were deposited on a stable platform that developed across what had been the unstable eastern part of the Paleozoic geosyncline.

Despite the simplicity of the geologic structure of the Coastal Plain formations, the shorelines vary along different sections of the coast, chiefly because of crustal warping. We have seen that the northeastward tilting of North America has partly submerged the Appalachians, forming the New England Province. The northern part of the Coastal Plain, from Cape Hatteras to New York, also is partly submerged. River valleys there are drowned, like that of the Susquehanna River which forms Chesapeake Bay and that of the Delaware River forming Delaware Bay. The drowning of the Hudson River has extended tidewater as far inland as Albany. East of the Hudson only the highest hills protrude as islands, and east of Nantucket the plain is wholly submerged.

From New York to Cape Hatteras is the Embayed Section of the Coastal Plain. The brackish tidal water in the bays extends to the falls of the rivers—the so-called Fall Line, where the streams tumble from the Piedmont Plateau to sea level at the inner edge of the Coastal Plain.

South of the Embayed Section, from Cape Hatteras to Cape Romain, the shoreline is cuspate with four prominent capes—Hatteras, Lookout, Fear, and Romain—separated by three broadly arcuate indentations. This part of the Coastal Plain is the Cape Fear "arch"; it has been uplifted. South of it, along the coast of South Carolina and Georgia, is the Sea Islands Section, where many islands along the shore seem to reflect downwarping of the land and flooding by the sea. The flooding is so recent that oak trees killed by salt water can still be seen.

As suggested earlier, the rise of sea level along the Atlantic Coast because of water freed by the melting ice caps averages about six inches per century. This would mean a rise of almost two feet since the earliest colonial settlements. On such gently shelving shore, a two-foot increase in sea level can make a considerable difference in the position and configuration of the shoreline. But because of earth movements, some parts of the coast have been submerged faster than the average, and some parts more slowly, hence the variation in the configuration of shorelines along the various sections of the coast.

The Florida peninsula is an uplifted area like the Cape Fear "arch." The Atlantic side has long, straight,

sandy beaches; the Gulf side is more irregular with some cliffs of limestone. At the south are coral beaches.

Both the east and west Gulf Coastal Plains have long, straight barrier-beaches backed by lagoons. At the delta of the Mississippi River, a constructional rather than erosional feature, the shore has a very irregular bird's-foot outline.

The role played by the bays and harbors of the Embayed Section of the Coastal Plain in the history of the United States can hardly be overestimated. They attracted early settlement because they provided protection against storms. Chesapeake Bay was charted by John Smith, and his publication in 1612 provided a basis for the grant to Lord Baltimore in 1634. The bays favored experiments with sailing, and later with steam vessels, and fostered the evolution in form and size from the Indians' log canoe to the seagoing Baltimore clippers. The bays provided shellfish and finfish; writer H. L. Mencken described Chesapeake Bay as an immense protein factory that enabled Baltimoreans to "eat Divinely." Chesapeake Bay oysters seem not to have been attractive to the early settlers, although the Indians had gathered them, but they had become the basis of a major industry by the middle of the nineteenth century. And the bay is wintering ground for ducks and geese.

The heads of the bays—at the head of the tidewater and the foot of the falls on the rivers—were settled first. Even today the Fall Line is part of the most densely populated area of the United States. Trenton, Philadelphia, Chester, Wilmington, Baltimore, Washington, Richmond, and Petersburg all are Fall Line cities. This belt, with the New England coast as far north as Boston, is a modern megalopolis with a substantial percentage of the nation's population.

The flat terrain between the bays was easy to farm and easy to travel on, but was settled and developed more slowly than the heads of the bays and western shores. The eastern shores were accessible only by stub roads, because the only feasible places for crossing the rivers was at the Fall Line or farther inland. The first through road crossed the Delaware River at Trenton, the Schuylkill at Philadelphia, the Susquehanna near Lancaster, and the Potomac above Harpers Ferry. The road did not return eastward to the Coastal Plain until it reached South Carolina. By 1800 the main road south was along the Fall Line, as it is today. Shortly after independence was achieved, canals were built connecting the bays—the Dismal Swamp Canal in 1794, the Chesapeake and Delaware Canal in 1829, and the Delaware and Raritan Canal in 1834.

Generally the climate of the Coastal Plain is mild, for it is moderated by the ocean. In Florida it is subtropical. In the southwestern section of the plain, in Texas, temperatures average high enough relative to precipitation so that the climate there is semiarid. In early times as today the coast was subject to hurricanes; the Rio Grande was navigable upstream for one hundred miles until its channel was changed by a hurricane in 1874. But in the early days there was little reason to build on exposed beaches, and property damage by hurricanes was slight despite the lack of modern warning systems. The most damaging effects came later when the nation had become weatlhy enough to use and develop the beaches by building on them. Although several national and state seashores have been created, most of the ocean fron-

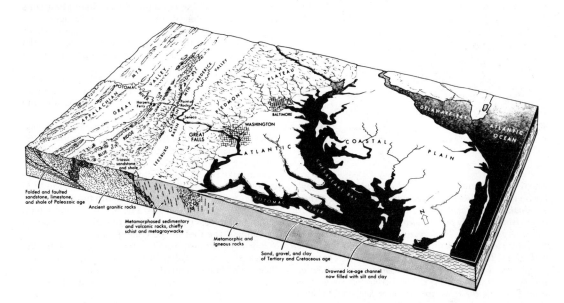

Figure 4. Block diagram of the Chesapeake Bay and Potomac River region, showing the physiographic provinces and the flat-lying formations of the Coastal Plain resting on a platform of older metamorphic and igneous rocks forming the higher ground to the west. (U.S. Geological Survey)

tage—about ninety-eight percent—is privately owned, although publicly protected against erosion.

Most of the southern Coastal Plain is forested with pine, and it is one of the principal lumber producing areas in the country, surpassed only by the Douglas fir forests of the Pacific Northwest. In the early days the southeastern pine forests were important producers of naval stores and were a source for fuel as well as lumber for construction.

The flatlands favored large landholdings and extensive farms, a factor that contributed to slavery in the United States. The distribution of slavery along the Atlantic seaboard—and later, inland—clearly reflected the physiography. Slavery was not economical in New England. In the Embayed Section of the Coastal Plain in 1760, about a quarter of the population was slave; farther south about half the population was slave. The chief export crop was tobacco, and along the many navigable rivers the plantations were large enough for each to have its own wharf. The poorly drained lands of the Sea Islands Downwarp were used early for growing rice.

Tobacco crops grown repeatedly year after year exhausted the soil, and slavery might have died out but for a technological development, the invention of the cotton gin in 1793. Cotton could be grown in most of the southern Coastal Plain and, like tobacco, could be grown on large plantations. This created new interest in the slave trade. Despite its many physiographic advantages, the southern Coastal Plain has never fully recovered from the error of using slave labor.

Mineral resources on the Coastal Plain are those that would be expected in sedimentary rock formations that originated in shallow coastal waters. They are the kind

that do not glitter and with minor exceptions were little used until the last hundred years. Bog iron supplied colonial forges; sand for manufacturing glass was developed early at Jamestown and may have been the first industrial mineral. Clay formations supplied material for manufacturing brick, but with one notable exception there was no building stone. The exception is the sandstone near Aquia, Virginia, that was used beginning in 1795 for constructing the White House and the central section of the Capitol in Washington, D.C. Not until much later was there a demand for and development of the tremendous petroleum resources and the salt and sulfur deposits of the Gulf Coastal Plain and the phosphates for fertilizer in the Florida peninsula.

See also GULF COASTAL PLAIN.

Piedmont Plateau. Next inland from the Atlantic Coastal Plain and extending from the Fall Line to the Blue Ridge is the Piedmont Plateau (Figs. 4 and 5). This is hilly country, fifty to two hundred miles wide and a few hundred feet higher than the Coastal Plain. Altitudes are mostly between five hundred and one thousand feet in the south and between sea level and five hundred feet in the north.

The underlying bedrock formations and their structure are like those in New England. In large part they are geosynclinal rocks of Paleozoic age, greatly folded, faulted, intruded by granite, and metamorphosed. They are much older and much harder than the rock formations of the Coastal Plain, but this difference is not immediately apparent because the rocks on the Piedmont are deeply weathered to red and yellow clay. Both the colors and textures of this weathered residuum resemble Coastal Plain formations, which were derived in large part by the erosion of such residuum on the Pied-

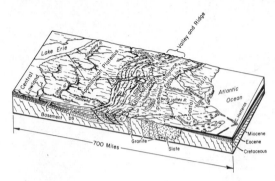

Figure 5. Structural framework of the Appalachian High-lands and Coastal Plain. At the west, bordering the Central Lowland, are the Appalachian Plateaus, which are composed of flat-lying or gently folded Paleozoic formations west of the Paleozoic geosyncline. The formations thin where they overlap the stable platform bordering the Canadian Shield (north of Lake Erie). The Valley and Ridge and Blue Ridge provinces are where the geosyncline was located; the formations there are greatly thickened and tightly folded. Farther east, in the Pied-mont Province, the rocks are still more folded and faulted, intruded by granite, and strongly metamorphosed. These great-ly altered rocks, mostly of Paleozoic age, form the stable plat-form under the much younger and flat-lying Coastal Plain formations. (From C. B. Hunt, Physiography of the Unit-ed States, *copyright © 1967, W. H. Freeman and Co.)*

mont Plateau and on the mountains farther west. This weathering altered the hard rocks to clay; granite, for example, becomes so clayey that it can be sliced with a knife. In places the residuum is one hundred feet deep.

The hard rocks that are the parent material for the weathered residuum can be seen where streams have cut deeply enough to reach the bedrock, such as has oc-curred near the Fall Line. Great Falls of the Potomac River, part of the national park system, is an example. This falls is formed by steeply dipping ribs of very hard rocks, and the falls accordingly does not retreat, al-though in time it is reduced in height. The more familiar Niagara Falls is formed by water crossing horizontal beds of resistant rock; this type of falls retreats in time without being reduced in height. Great Falls of the Potomac typifies the falls of the Fall Line.

The hard rocks of the Piedmont Plateau provided plenty of building stone for canal walls, mills, factories, and railroad viaducts. Although these rocks are rather like those in New England, there are major differences both in the landscapes and kinds of ground because the Piedmont lies south of the limit of glaciation. The re-siduum on the Piedmont Plateau was formed by weath-ering that occurred before the last glaciation; any such mantle that formerly existed on the New England rocks was eroded by the ice. The rocks in New England are not weathered; the soils there are young. The equally hard rocks on the Piedmont Plateau are deeply weathered, and the soils there are old.

One of the most significant features of the Piedmont Plateau that greatly affected settlement and develop-ment is the series of large streams that cross it and then continue eastward across the Coastal Plain. A dozen

large rivers draining from the Appalachian Mountains are spaced at intervals of about fifty miles across the plateau. Collectively they discharge a volume of water about one fourth that of the Mississippi River and ten times that of the Colorado River, which collects drainage from an area twice as large.

Many of the large rivers are navigable for consid-erable stretches, and they were an open invitation to build canals around the falls at the Fall Line. One of the first canals (1795) bypassed the falls on the James River at Richmond. The Chesapeake and Ohio Canal, which bypassed Great Falls of the Potomac, was begun in 1828. The Susquehanna and Tidewater Canal, connecting the navigable parts of the Susquehanna River with Chesapeake Bay, was built in 1840. The Schuylkill Navi-gation Canal was built along the Schuylkill River in 1825 and connected via the Union Canal with the Susquehan-na near Harrisburg in 1828. The Schuylkill and Union canals had to pass through ridges of bedrock and did so by tunnels, the first in the United States.

Basins of Triassic rocks, quite like those along the Connecticut River valley in New England, occur in the Piedmont Plateau. With the red sedimentary formations are lava flows and intrusive sheets of basalt, known as sills, forming such well-known topographic features as the Palisades of the Hudson, the Watchung Ridges in northern New Jersey, and Cemetery Ridge at Get-tysburg.

Topographic relief on the Piedmont Plateau is low enough to allow as easy entrance and settlement as the Coastal Plain, and as riparian rights along the valleys became taken up, the rounded uplands were farmed. Until 1700 settlement was concentrated along the Fall Line, the shores of the bays in the Coastal Plain, and the New England coast. The contrast between Piedmont Plateau and Coastal Plain along the Fall Line is indicated in the pattern of land use, even in today's world. At all the Fall Line cities, suburbia is on the rolling hills of the Piedmont Plateau, while the flat Coastal Plain has been used mostly for industry and transportation lines.

At first, travel on the Piedmont Plateau was by pack train along Indian trails that led inland. Later, as roads were built, wagons were utilized and a Conestoga wa-gon, which was developed on the Piedmont Plateau and pulled by six horses, could move five times as much load as six pack animals. Canal boats, pulled by only one or two horses, could move ten times as much as a Conesto-ga wagon. Later came the railroads and more recently the airlines, trucklines, and pipelines. Each in turn has protested its disadvantages as it became superseded.

The mineral wealth of the Piedmont Plateau is rather like that of New England, because of the similar geologic histories. One notable difference though is the occur-rence of gold in the central and southern part of the Piedmont Plateau. Gold production was important enough during the first half of the nineteenth century to warrant establishing mints in 1838 at Charlotte, North Carolina, and at Dahlonega, Georgia.

Blue Ridge Province, Valley and Ridge Province, and Reading Prong. Westward travel across the Piedmont Plateau was easy, whether by boat along the rivers and canals or by wagon roads along the uplands. But at the Blue Ridge and Reading Prong, the most easterly of the Appalachian ridges, barriers were encountered, and west of them lay another half dozen or dozen parallel mountain ridges about as high but not so long as the Blue Ridge and Reading Prong.

The Blue Ridge Province extends five hundred miles from Georgia to southern Pennsylvania, and in this distance it is broken by only three watergaps—at the Potomac, James, and Roanoke rivers. In addition, between the Potomac and the James rivers there are a few windgaps, topographic saddles where rivers formerly crossed the ridge but were subsequently diverted around it. Another important pass is Saluda Gap that gave access to the French Broad River, the Holston, and the rest of the Tennessee River valley. Altitudes along the Blue Ridge range from about 500 feet at the water gaps to a maximum of 6,684 feet at Mount Mitchell in the Great Smoky Mountains.

A similar ridge, the Reading Prong, extends from the Schuylkill River at Reading, Pennsylvania, northward to the Hudson River where it forms the Highlands of the Hudson—one of the grandly scenic places in the country. East of the Hudson River the Highlands merge with the mountains of New England. Other watergaps besides that of the Hudson River are along the Delaware River below Easton, Pennsylvania, and along the Ramapo River, which is the route used by the Erie-Lackawanna Railroad and the New York Thruway.

West of the Blue Ridge Province and the Reading Prong is a belt fifty to one hundred miles wide of valleys and ridges, the Valley and Ridge Province. The ridges are short compared with the Blue Ridge or Reading Prong, but most of them are about as high and are narrow and steepsided. Their crests are amazingly level.

The valley floors are mostly between five hundred and one thousand feet in altitude. They are wide and flat bottomed. Settlement was along the valleys, especially those having the larger streams, and travel for the most part was around the ends of the ridges or through watergaps. At a few places trails or wagon roads crossed ridges at windgaps.

The rivers wind among the valleys between the parallel ridges and have a distinctly trellis pattern, as does the network of roads. This pattern shows very conspicuously on a road map of Pennsylvania. The parallel system diagonally crossing the central part of the state contrasts with the highly irregular network on the Piedmont Plateau and on the Allegheny Plateau to the west.

The parallelism of the valleys and ridges is caused by the rock formations having been folded when the Appalachian geosyncline was uplifted at the close of the Paleozoic era. This physiographic province is the classic area in the world for illustrating fold mountains (Figs. 4 and 5). The rock formations were deposited as sediments to a thickness of forty thousand feet or more in the geosyncline along that edge of the continent. This geosyncline ended at the close of the Paleozoic when the sea was expelled and the two flanks of the trough were pushed together. This folded the sedimentary beds like the folds in a bundle of papers. The shortening, including that in the Piedmont Province, amounts to about one hundred miles and brought the site of Washington, D.C., that much closer to the site of Pittsburgh.

Many of the formations are limestone, and in a humid climate such as that in the Appalachians, limestone erodes readily by solution. The limestone formations are mostly along the valley floors, and their solution has produced numerous well-known caverns. The weather-ing of the limestone has produced a deep red clay, terra rosa, and a typical valley floor has red clay with ledges of gray limestone sticking through it. The ridges are mostly of resistant rocks such as quartzite and sandstone.

Another feature of the humid climate is the broadleaf oak forest, although originally the limestone valleys seem to have been mostly grassland. On the highest mountain ridges are found the northern hardwoods and even some spruce. Animal life in the north provided furs, and in the south, skins. Still another climatic feature of this part of the country is its cloudiness.

Trails that had been used by the Indians led the early settlers to the hinterland. One of these, the Mohawk Trail, was across New York along the site where the Erie Canal was later built. Another, the Kittanning Path, followed the Juniata River across the Valley and Ridge Province, climbed the Allegheny Front at the west edge of the province, and then descended the rivers westward to the Forks of the Ohio at the site of Pittsburgh. Still a third trail followed the easternmost of the valleys, known as the Great Valley because of its width and great length. This trail was the route of the first wagon road (1774) connecting Philadelphia and Charleston, South Carolina. The Great Valley, extensively settled by 1776, figured prominently in the campaigns of the Civil War.

The increased folding of the formations eastward is reflected in the mineral resources. Shale formations toward the east are metamorphosed to slate, and a great deal of that stone has been produced. Coal toward the east is metamorphosed to anthracite (see below). This is a cleaner coal than the more crumbly bituminous coal, but has less heat value because of lower volatile content. In fact, anthracite was developed slowly because it was difficult to burn; at first some was mined for road metal. Other mineral resources include glass sand, refractory clay, hematitic iron ores (the Clinton beds, which extend from New York to Alabama), zinc (Franklin Furnace, New Jersey), and copper (Ducktown, Tennessee).

Appalachian Plateaus. The first great barrier to colonial expansion inland from the Atlantic seaboard, the Appalachian Plateaus—ranging in width from fifty to two hundred miles and ruggedly dissected—constitute the next physiographic unit west of the Valley and Ridge Province. In the north are the Catskill Mountains, reaching altitudes of more than four thousand feet, overlooking the tidewater in the Hudson River valley. South of these mountains is the Pocono Plateau in northeastern Pennsylvania, and to the west of the Pocono is the Allegheny Plateau (also called the Allegheny Mountains). Both are rough and neither was very hospitable for settlement, although the Wyoming Valley section of the Susquehanna River was settled early. Farther south, in West Virginia, is the still rougher Kanawha Section, and south of it is the Cumberland Plateau, crossed at Cumberland Gap.

Travel and settlement were impeded also by dense oak forests. Perhaps if the skies had been sunny, the rough terrain and the forests would have seemed less formidable, but these forested, rough plateaus are one of the cloudiest and foggiest parts of the United States. Areas of the plateaus average fewer than eighty clear days per year. Moreover, the growing season averages sixty to ninety days shorter than it does east of the Blue Ridge Province.

Except at the north, the plateaus are formed of late

Paleozoic sandstone and shale containing numerous thick coal beds. Toward the north the formations are older and non-coal bearing. Throughout the plateaus the formations are almost horizontal or in broad gentle folds parallel to those in the tightly folded Valley and Ridge Province. The landscape generally is that of a dissected plateau with flat uplands commonly around three thousand feet in altitude. The valleys, five hundred to one thousand feet deep, are steep-sided and V-shaped in cross section. Where the valleys are widely spaced, as in the north, settlements and roads are mostly on the flat uplands; where the valleys are closely spaced, as in the Kanawha Section, settlements and roads are mostly along the valley bottoms.

The plateaus end northward at an escarpment extending westward from Albany and overlooking the Mohawk valley. At the Helderberg Escarpment, southwest of Albany, the escarpment turns south along the west side of the Hudson River past the Catskill Mountains and Pocono Plateau. It winds across the anthracite fields in northern Pennsylvania and after crossing the Susquehanna River near Scranton it becomes the Allegheny Front, which extends to Tennessee as a bold, nearly straight mountain front facing the westernmost valley of the Valley and Ridge Province. Except for the valleys of the New River and West Branch of the Susquehanna River, this is an almost unbroken escarpment a thousand feet high and six hundred miles long. It is one of the most persistent topographic features in the country.

Although the escarpment is high and persistent, it is not too difficult to cross, but west of it for fifty to two hundred miles is rough country with deep, winding valleys. But for a quirk of physiography, this mountainous plateau barrier might have greatly modified the nation's history. In an effort to prevent expansion westward, George III decreed the Proclamation Line of 1763, barring settlement beyond "the sources of the rivers which fall into the sea," meaning the divide between drainage eastward to the Atlantic Ocean and westward to the Ohio River. On a planimetric map this line looks reasonable, but the divide does not follow the structural members; rather, it cuts diagonally across them. The divide between the two watersheds begins at the south in the eastern part of the Blue Ridge, crosses that province and the Valley and Ridge in southern Virginia, then follows the Allegheny Front to south-central Pennsylvania where it turns north into the Allegheny Plateau, much of which drains into the Susquehanna River. Had the Proclamation Line been designated as the Allegheny Front and its counterparts farther north, enforcement might have been possible, sufficient at least for the British government to have prevented the colonists from expanding into the Ohio and Mississippi River valleys.

The cause of the structural and topographic differences between the Appalachian Plateaus and the Valley and Ridge Province goes back to the Paleozoic era. The plateaus are just west of what had been the Appalachian geosyncline and are at the southeastern edge of the stable platform bordering the Canadian Shield. Folding of the formations in the geosyncline ended westward at the edge of the platform where the formations were subject to warping but not to tight folding. At the western edge of the plateaus the basement rocks are only

about five thousand feet deep; under the Allegheny Front the depth is more like twenty thousand feet and increases eastward.

The plateaus end westward where the late Paleozoic formations, greatly thinned, outcrop in an escarpment that overlooks the Central Lowland to the west. The erosion of the formations has left knobs capped by resistant beds, and this terrain is known as the Knob Belt.

The northern part of the Appalachian Plateaus was glaciated, and the valleys there were deepened and rounded by glacial scour—like the beds of the Finger Lakes in New York. Hills and ridges of gravel and sand deposited in the valleys by the ice and its meltwaters disrupted the drainage, and at many places streams were diverted because the valleys were blocked, first by ice and later by the debris dumped in them by the melting ice. An example is Pennsylvania's "grand canyon" along Pine Creek at the Leonard Harrison State Park.

The Erie Canal, and later the Mohawk Turnpike and New York Central Railroad, went around the north end of the Appalachian Plateaus. To compete with the Erie Canal, Pennsylvania business interests developed the canal system that crossed the Piedmont Province and linked Philadelphia with the Susquehanna River. Other canals extended up the Susquehanna and connected with the Erie. A canal to the west followed the Juniata River and crossed the Allegheny Front at Hollidaysburg, Pennsylvania. This required building the Allegheny Portage Railroad to cross the front and descend to the Conemaugh River, which could then be followed to Pittsburgh at the Forks of the Ohio, where the Allegheny and Monongahela rivers join. The railroad, first using horses and later steam locomotives to pull the cars, was completed in 1834 and joined the two sections of canals that had been completed a few years earlier. This canal system was less subject to freezing and was open a month longer than the Erie.

The vast deposits of coal contained in the Appalachian Plateaus are the carbonized remains of tree-like ferns that grew in the marshes and swamps on the deltas that were built westward across the Paleozoic geosyncline. Where ground is saturated with water, oxygen is excluded, and the plant matter is preserved as peat. During burial, water is squeezed from the peat, and easily decomposable fractions alter to volatile hydrocarbons which escape. The mass alters to brown coal, or lignite, and as more volatiles and water are lost the lignite alters to subbituminous and then to bituminous coal, like that in the Appalachian Plateaus. Farther east, the same coal measures were involved in the tight folding of the Valley and Ridge Province, and there the shearing and high pressures accompanying that folding drove off more volatile matter and converted the bituminous coal to anthracite, which has only half as much volatile matter as bituminous coal.

Development of the coal resources on the plateaus was greatly accelerated by technological developments during the early part of the nineteenth century. Gas obtained from coal was used for city lighting in Baltimore in 1817 and in New York in 1823. For a hundred years lamplighters were employed to make their evening rounds in the eastern seaboard cities.

Paleozoic platform deposits also include salt beds, which were deposited when bays extending westward from the geosyncline became partly closed and evaporation caused precipitation of the salts. Seepage from the salt brines gave rise to numerous salt licks, used first by animals, then by Indians, and later by explorers. First production from the salt brines, which are "fossil" Paleozoic seawater, was in 1778 in Onondaga County, New York. Later, deposits along the Kanawha River, West Virginia, and at Saltville, Virginia, became important contributors to the early economy.

America's first oil well, the Drake Well at Titusville, Pennsylvania, was drilled in 1859 as a result of the discovery of the oil while digging and drilling for salt brines. The Paleozoic formations under the Appalachian Plateaus are important sources for natural gas and toward the west they contain oil. Petroleum is scarce in the geosynclinal formations but abundant in the formations on the platform to the west, which were spared the natural distillation caused by the folding and faulting of the geosynclinal formations. The era of long-distance transportation of petroleum by pipeline began in 1878 when construction began on a pipeline across the Allegheny Front to the tidewater.

Central Lowland. Once the migration westward had surged across the barrier of the Appalachian Mountains, it spread rapidly and widely across the vast plain—much of it open grassland prairies—which forms the central part of the continent.

The Central Lowland (Fig. 3) descends from the western foot of the Appalachian Plateaus, at an altitude of about one thousand feet, to less than five hundred feet in the area where the MISSISSIPPI RIVER is joined by the Ohio River and MISSOURI RIVER. From there the lowland rises again westward about fifteen hundred feet in five hundred miles to the edge of the Great Plains at an altitude of about two thousand feet near the 100th meridian.

The Central Lowland is blessed with great lakes and rivers, rich soil, hardwood forests, and grassland prairies, and, very important, warm, rainy summers that compensate for cold, harsh winters. The great rivers are too muddy for many fish, but they and the Great Lakes provided low cost water transportation. About the only real natural obstacle was the Falls of the Ohio at Louisville, Kentucky, but in 1830 a canal was built around them. The flat land favored construction of roads and railroads as well as farming. The rich soil on the easily cleared prairies and the warm summer rains made possible abundant agricultural produce. The combination of these physiographic features quickly made this region one of the richest in the world.

The Central Lowland is built of nearly flat-lying Paleozoic formations, mostly of marine origin, which were deposited in the Paleozoic seas that overlapped the continental platform west of the Appalachian geosyncline and south of the Canadian Shield. As already noted, these formations average only about five thousand feet thick. The principal physiographic features of the Central Lowland derive from this geologic structure, but many other important features are the result of the glaciations during the Pleistocene epoch.

The Mississippi River valley is a broad trough extending southward down the center of the continent, and the Pleistocene ice sheets moved far down this trough to the Ohio River in the east and Missouri River in the west. The original course of the Ohio River, known to geolo-

gists as Teays, was across central Ohio and Indiana. Streams as far west as the Kentucky River flowed north to Teays, but the glaciers pushed this drainage southward to a small valley at the present position of the Ohio River, heading near Madison, Indiana. The original preglacial course of the Missouri River had been northeastward from Montana to Hudson Bay, but the glaciers turned that river southward. Flowing southward along the front of the ice, the river cut a deep gorge across the Dakotas—the Missouri Trench—to discharge onto the Central Lowland in Nebraska. It may be noted that the Missouri Trench has no tributaries from the east. The tributaries from the west formerly continued northeastward, but like the preglacial course of the Ohio River, they have been filled with glacial detritus and the surface smoothed. The mighty Mississippi-Missouri River system is young geologically speaking, probably younger than most of the lesser valleys in the Appalachians and elsewhere south of the glacial border.

Lobes of ice occupied the basins of the Great Lakes and deepened them by scour. Around the southern ends of the lakes during stillstands of the glaciers, gravel and sand were deposited in hummocky ridges along the ice front, forming parallel sets of marinal ridges that curve around the west end of Lake Erie, the head of Saginaw Bay, and the south end of Lake Michigan (Fig. 6).

Where drainage was ponded at the ice front, lakes were formed. Among these were the ancestral Great Lakes. One of the most extensive, known as Lake Agassiz, occupied the basin of the RED RIVER OF THE NORTH when the front of the glacier had receded to the vicinity of Lake Winnipeg. Drainage northward was blocked by the ice, and there resulted the vast Lake Agassiz that overflowed southward by way of the Minnesota River valley. Today there is only a small stream in the big

Figure 6. During the Pleistocene period the Great Lakes region was entirely covered by glacial ice moving southward into the United States from Canada. The lake beds were deepened by glacial scour; where the ice advanced onto the Appalachian Plateau in New York, it scoured the beds of the Finger Lakes. When the ice front receded, lobes of ice in lakes Erie, Huron, and Michigan melted slowly enough to deposit arcuate ridges of sand and gravel around the west end of Lake Erie, the head of Saginaw Bay, and the south end of Lake Michigan. Structurally those lakes are in the shale valleys behind the Niagara Escarpment, which is a ridge of lower Paleozoic formations extending from Rochester, New York, to Milwaukee, Wisconsin. (From C. B. Hunt, Geology of Soils, copyright © 1972, W. H. Freeman and Co.)

valley. The bed of Lake Agassiz became a vast level plain of rich lake bottom sediments, and this terrain made possible farms covering many square miles, some as large as one hundred square miles.

The big farms in turn spurred inventions and technological developments of farm machinery for mass production. Among these were the steel plow, perfected in 1833, and the McCormick Reaper, patented in 1834.

Ponds and lakes are not numerous on the bed of Lake Agassiz except along the hilly sides, both to the east and west. One of these, to the east, is Lake of the Woods, where the boundary between the United States and Canada makes a curious bend to the north. This has been described as a "politico-geographical curiosity of a boundary"; it arose because the boundary originally was defined in 1782 with reference to the lake, but the position of the lake proved to be incorrectly shown on the maps of the time.

Perhaps the most important feature of the Central Lowland attributable to the Pleistocene glaciations is the wind-deposited silt, known as loess, that blankets most of the plain. The loess represents dust that was blown out of the riverbeds when they dried after being desolated by floods discharging down the valleys each time the ice thawed. Flood control along the rivers of the Central Lowland continues to be a major problem, but the Pleistocene floods make modern floods seem like dwarfs. Winds then as now were from the west, and the dust was blown eastward onto the uplands. The loess blanket thins and becomes finer grained eastward from each of the rivers that had discharged glacial meltwaters. This loess is the parent material for the rich soils in the agricultural heart of America.

An important physiographic feature that speeded early exploration and settlement are the low divides separating the Great Lakes from the Wabash, Illinois, and other tributaries of the Ohio and Mississippi rivers. The St. Lawrence River and Great Lakes enabled the early explorers to reach the center of the continent, and the low divides at the south made for easy portage to the Mississippi and Ohio rivers. By these portages travelers on the Great Lakes were easily connected with rivers draining to the Gulf of Mexico. In the seventeenth and eighteenth centuries the ring of water around the west and north of the English colonies was held by the French and defended by their military outposts, such as the one at Ste. Genevieve, Missouri. This water ring was a natural barrier to westward expansion by English colonists. When the outposts passed to the British government, it might have succeeded in its efforts to contain the rebellious colonists east of the Appalachians, had the Proclamation Line of 1763 been more realistic.

Rich agricultural production and inexpensive transportation in the Central Lowland are supplemented by a wealth of mineral resources, and the combination has resulted in a balanced economy of agriculture and industry. Deposits of the fossil fuels, coal, oil, and gas, are extensive and provide inexpensive sources of energy for manufacturing, steam transportation, and the generation of electricity. There are also deposits of salt, fluorite, lead, and zinc. Until about 1850 the three big salt-producing areas were upstate New York, the Kanawha valley of western Virginia, and Saltville, Virginia. Salt producers formed one of the first trusts in restraint of trade in an effort to maintain prices in the face of in-

creasing supplies. The competition was aggravated by discovery of SALT LICKS and production from the newly-found brines in Ohio, Kentucky, Michigan, and Illinois. These salt springs lent the word "lick" to many place names in those states, e.g., Salt Lick and Mays Lick in Kentucky.

Interior Low Plateaus, Ozark Plateaus, and Ouachita Province. South of the Central Lowland and between the Appalachian Plateaus and the Mississippi River are the Interior Low Plateaus, mostly below one thousand feet in altitude and little if any higher than the Central Lowland. The plateaus are early Paleozoic formations, largely limestone, that were deposited on the stable continental platform as were the formations of the Central Lowland. At the west are coal-bearing, deltaic, coastal plain deposits of late Paleozoic age. Principal streams are the Tennessee and Cumberland rivers.

West of the Mississippi River and just south of the Central Lowland are the Ozark Plateaus, also composed of early Paleozoic formations and also in large part limestone. Altitudes are higher, averaging about fifteen hundred feet. On both the Interior Low and Ozark plateaus the limestone is deeply weathered to the red clayey soil known as terra rosa, like that in the Great Valley of the Valley and Ridge Province.

Both the Interior Low and Ozark plateaus, being so largely of limestone, have numerous caverns, and in both provinces the underground streams emerge in large springs. Drainage off the Interior Low Plateaus has a dendritic pattern; drainage off the higher Ozark Plateaus is radial.

The Ouachita Province differs structurally and topographically from both plateaus. It consists of geosynclinal formations tightly folded like those in the Valley and Ridge Province and has similarly parallel ridges and valleys. This province is drained by the Arkansas River and the drainage system has a trellis pattern.

The south end of the Ouachita Province has important deposits of bauxite, an ore of aluminum. Coal beds in the Ouachita Province, like those in the Valley and Ridge, are altered to anthracite. Coal in western Kentucky is bituminous. The Ozark Plateaus have lead-zinc deposits at the Tri-State District in the southwest corner of the plateaus and at the Ste. Genevieve area in the northwest. All three provinces originally were covered with oak forest.

Superior Upland. Part of the Canadian Shield, the Superior Upland lies north of the Central Lowland and forms the central, stable part of the continent. The shield is composed of ancient Precambrian rocks that originally were partly of igneous origin and partly of sedimentary origin and subsequently were greatly folded, faulted, and metamorphosed, more so than the rocks of New England or of the Piedmont Province. Prior to the beginning of Paleozoic time these hard rocks and their complicated structures had been reduced by erosion to form a low hummocky area. This was overlapped by shallow seas during the Paleozoic, but most of the sediments deposited there have since been removed by erosion.

The surface on the Precambrian rocks, exhumed from beneath the Paleozoic formations that covered it, is blanketed by gravel and sand deposited by the Pleistocene glaciers. These deposits are young enough (less than ten thousand years old) to retain the original hummocky forms they had when dropped by the ice and its meltwaters. Such built-up topography is constructional, not erosional. Through streams are few; lakes and ponds are numerous.

Most of the upland is conifer forest, with pines toward the south and spruce-fir toward the north. The climate is subhumid, yet these forests have experienced some of the worst fires in United States history. In 1871, twelve hundred persons died as a result of forest fire at Peshtigo, Wisconsin; in 1894, four hundred died in a forest fire at Hinckley, Minnesota, and in 1918, four hundred in a forest fire at Cloquet, Minnesota.

The region first produced furs. Later, as industrialization progressed, its wealth of metallic minerals was developed. The Precambrian rocks of the shield contain huge deposits of iron, copper, nickel, cobalt, and uranium.

Great Plains. The plains of the central United States continue westward another five hundred miles from the Central Lowland to the foot of the Rocky Mountains. These are the Great Plains, where the West begins. They rise westward from about two thousand feet at the edge of the Central Lowland to about five thousand feet along the foot of the Rocky Mountains. A step on the state capitol building at Denver, Colorado, is 5,280 feet above sea level, from which Denver took its slogan, "The Mile High City." Above Denver tower the Rocky Mountains.

The Great Plains are semiarid and are what John Wesley Powell termed "the lands in the arid west." The plains also have been referred to as the "GREAT AMERICAN DESERT." Here the badlands begin. Semiaridity or aridity characterize the country west of the 100th meridian, which is sometimes called the semiarid line. On the Great Plains annual precipitation averages less than twenty inches; annual runoff averages less than one inch and this amount is not enough to create throughflowing streams. There would be no streams but for the runoff from the comparatively high rainfall watersheds in the lofty Rocky Mountains.

During the Paleozoic era the site of the Great Plains was a structural platform like the Central Lowland, and the Paleozoic formations, like those in the lowland, are mostly marine sediments deposited in the shallow seas that overlapped from the geosynclines onto the Precambrian platform. The Transcontinental Arch diagonals southwestward across the central part of the Great Plains, and the Paleozoic seas overlapped it from the east and from the west edges of the continent.

The platform persisted, largely emergent, during the early Mesozoic. Overlying the Paleozoic formations are marine deposits laid down in the eastern part of the geosyncline, formed during the Cretaceous period, that crossed the Transcontinental Arch and extended northward along the site of the Rocky Mountains. The Rocky Mountains were uplifted at the end of the Cretaceous and during the Tertiary, and as the mountains rose during the Tertiary, sediments eroding from them were washed eastward onto the Great Plains. The deposits formed huge alluvial fans extending to what now is the eastern edge of the Great Plains.

The Tertiary history of that part of the country is recorded by those deposits. During the Paleocene and Eocene epochs, drainage off the newly formed Rocky Mountains collected in extensive basins, like the Powder River Basin in northeastern Wyoming. By Oligocene time the basins became filled and began to overflow and build fans eastward. During the Miocene and Pliocene the fans were built farther and farther eastward as the drainage was collected in fewer and fewer channels. During the late Pliocene and Pleistocene epochs the drainage became concentrated in very few channels and was able to reach the Mississippi River. In Pliocene time, prior to the glaciations, as already noted, the Missouri River discharged northeastward to Hudson Bay.

A consequence of this geologic history is that the ground is increasingly sandy and increasingly permeable westward. This, combined with low rainfall, results in scarce water supplies except along the main streams. The parallel drainage system eastward on the Great Plains provided the natural routes westward for the fur traders and explorers during the 1820s and 1830s and later for the Mormons and forty-niners. The Missouri River, incised into an upland known as the Missouri Plateau and navigable as far as Fort Benton, Montana, below Great Falls, was used by Meriwether Lewis and William Clark during their expedition in 1806. Later the river was used for hauling buffalo hides back to St. Louis.

The Great Plains, as the name implies, are mostly plains. Rising above them in the north are isolated mountains—the Black Hills, Judith Mountains, Bearpaw Mountains, Sweetgrass Hills, and others. The hills are wooded; the plains are mostly grassland—grazing land that once supported huge herds of buffalo and later would support huge herds of cattle.

Again, technological advances met new needs. During the 1870s, the need to fence in cattle led to the invention of barbed wire; the shipping of beef carcasses rather than live cattle led to the development of refrigerator cars for trains, and the long distances to be traveled led to the invention of the comfortable Pullman cars.

Uplands on the Great Plains are treeless and subject to very strong winds. Homes there need to be protected by windbreaks. The grasses, notably the grama grass, are short with shallow roots in contrast to those of the Central Lowland, where grasses are tall with long roots. The change in grasses coincides with the line of semiaridity and with a change in the soils. In most of the Central Lowland the soils are acid; there is sufficient water to pass all the way through the ground to the water table and this leaches the soluble elements like the alkalis. On the Great Plains, though, the soils are alkaline, for there is not enough water to pass through the ground. The water is held in the soil openings where it evaporates and there precipitates the soluble elements. A chracteristic feature of the soils of the Great Plains and elsewhere in the arid west is the occurrence of a layer of calcium carbonate (caliche) in the subsoil.

The streams draining eastward across the central and northern Great Plains had plenty of water for travelers moving west. The principal trails started at Kansas City or Independence, Missouri, which were accessible by boat. Some began at Omaha. The most used route, that of the Mormon, California, and Oregon trails, was via the Platte and North Platte rivers, passing through the Wyoming Basin and going around the north end of the Southern Rocky Mountains. The Santa Fe Trail headed for the south end of the Rocky Mountains by crossing the Great Plains in a diagonally southwesterly direction. Streams farther south, such as the Canadian and RED RIVER OF THE SOUTH, provided less dependable water supplies and were less used for westward travel.

Among the valuable mineral deposits on the Great Plains are the mineral fuels in the Cretaceous and early Tertiary formations, rock salt in Kansas, and potash salts in late Paleozoic formations in southeastern New Mexico and the Texas Panhandle. The Homestake Mine in the Black Hills is one of the world's important gold mines. It was discovered by trespassers on land that had been reserved for Indians. The Indians protested violently, but the United States government sent troops to dispossess the Sioux, Cheyenne, Oglala, and Arapaho in order to develop the gold.

There are few large towns and no large cities on the Great Plains. Urban settlement has preferred the rivers east of the Plains or at the foot of the Rocky Mountains.

Rocky Mountains. The name of the Rocky Mountains derives from the great extent of bare rock there, far more than in the Appalachians. Soils are shallow and stony. The Rockies are so varied (Fig. 7) that they are divided into the Southern Rockies, the Middle Rockies and Wyoming Basin, and the Northern Rockies. The latter continue far northward as the Canadian Rockies.

The Southern Rocky Mountains, which extend from northern New Mexico across Colorado into southern Wyoming, rise abruptly from the Great Plains to altitudes greater than fourteen thousand feet. The Continental Divide is along the summit; this area is properly called the Great Divide. The mountains were and still are a formidable barrier to westward travel. Early migrants had to go around them.

These mountains developed at the end of the Cretaceous period and during the Tertiary by uplift of the Precambrian rocks that had been the basement under the Cretaceous geosyncline (Fig. 7D). Cretaceous and older formations are turned up steeply along the foot of the mountains; the turned-up edges of red Paleozoic formations form the Garden of the Gods near Colorado Springs and the Red Rocks Theater west of Denver. When uplift started, the land was near sea level. Subsequently, in addition to more anticlinal uplift and upward faulting, the entire region was elevated so that the mountain base today is a mile above sea level. Volcanism in southwestern Colorado built a tremendous volcanic pile on an uplift at the San Juan Mountains. The Southern Rocky Mountains are young compared to the Appalachians; they still may be growing.

The mountains were glaciated during the Pleistocene epoch, and some of the most spectacular scenery there (e.g., Rocky Mountain National Park) is the result of ice sculpture. The glaciers did not extend far down the valleys—only about halfway to the base—but their meltwaters deposited thick fills that now form gravel terraces along the rivers where they leave the mountains.

The mountains collect much snow and rain and are the source of five rivers, three draining east—ARKANSAS RIVER and South Platte and North Platte rivers (see PLATTE RIVER)—one draining south (RIO GRANDE), and one draining west (COLORADO RIVER). These rivers and their tributaries provide almost all the water for the southwestern quarter of the United States. When John Wesley Powell pointed out the limited water supply in the area, many people and most western politicians ob-

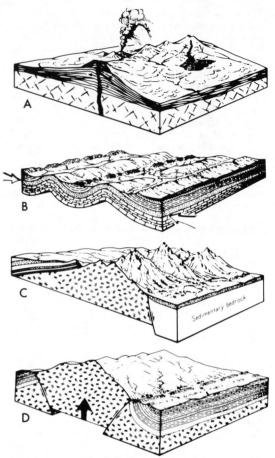

Figure 7. Mountains are of many kinds. Some are volcanic piles, such as the High Cascades (A); others are caused by folding, such as the Valley and Ridge Province in the Appalachians (B); others are block mountains that are faulted on one side and tilted, such as the Teton Range in the Middle Rocky Mountains (C); and still others are anticlinal uplifts, in part accompanied by faulting as at the Front Range (D). (U.S. Geological Survey)

jected and he was attacked politically. The hard fact is being realized as the West outgrows its supply of water.

Urban settlements developed around the base of the mountains as centers of supply for mining and lumbering activities in the mountains and for ranching on the plains. Mining in the Southern Rocky Mountains began in the late 1850s when gold was discovered in the glacial gravels in the streams near the base of the mountains. This led to exploration of the valleys and the discovery of rich lode deposits of gold and of lead and silver. Mining towns were built in the mountains and narrow gauge railroads built to them.

Rocky Mountain forests, including those in the Middle and Northern Rockies, are mostly conifer forests, and the number of species is small compared to the number in the broadleaf forests of the central and eastern United States (see VEGETATION: *mountains*). This difference may be due partly to differences in climate, but partly it is due to differences in the age of the landscapes. Landscapes in the central United States and in the Appalachians have been evolving since the end of the Paleozoic, that is, during the last 225 million years. Landscapes and forests on the Rocky Mountains, on the other hand, have been evolving less than 60 million years. The landscape and vegetation on the Great Plains is in large part a constructional surface on Pliocene alluvial deposits and can be no more than about 10 million years old.

The Middle Rocky Mountains, which consist of several mountain ranges that are separated from each other, are a much less formidable barrier to westward travel than are the Southern Rockies. The Wyoming Basin provided the corridor through the mountains and became the route for the Mormon, Overland, and Oregon trails. This route was shorter and easier than the Santa Fe Trail around the south end of the Southern Rockies and became the principal route for the forty-niners and later emigrants to the Pacific Coast. Before that, the route had been used by fur traders and had been followed by the Mormons to the valley of Great Salt Lake. Overland travel via the North Platte generally was preferred to travel by boat up the Missouri.

The Wyoming Basin is a structural as well as topographic basin. When the individual ranges of the Rocky Mountains were uplifted, a large land area that became the Wyoming Basin sagged behind. It is not one but several basins that developed gradually during the Tertiary (and may still be developing) while the individual mountain ranges, such as the Big Horn, Uinta, Wind River, and Teton mountains (Fig. 7C), were being uplifted. The Wyoming Basin, however, participated in the late Tertiary uplift that raised the base of the Rocky Mountains a mile above sea level. The Basin is about the altitude of the high parts of the Great Plains.

Most of the Wyoming Basin is desert with less than ten inches of precipitation annually, so water is scarce except along the streams discharging from the mountains. Travel in winter can be hazardous even today because of ground blizzards, which are strong winds blowing the light snow in a layer just above the ground surface. Visibility in a ground blizzard may be near zero.

Vegetation, except along the streams, is mostly sagebrush. Along the streams are cottonwood, willow, rabbit brush, and greasewood, a tough, alkali-tolerant shrub.

The trail west to "greener pastures" beyond the Continental Divide was along the North Platte around the north end of the Laramie Range. It continued west along a tributary, the Sweetwater River, which provided a route with water around the south end of the Wind River Range, crossed the Continental Divide at South Pass, which is low, and gave easy access to the Green River flowing southward across the Bridger Basin. This route crossed the Green River, then turned up Blacks Fork and through the Middle Rockies via Bear River to the Snake River Plains in Idaho. Later, the Union Pacific Railroad found another route, a low pass across the Laramie Range at Cheyenne and via the Laramie Basin around the north end of the Medicine Bow Mountains. It then turned west across the Washakie Basin and southern part of the Bridger Basin to the head of Weber River, which provided a route through the Middle Rockies to the valley of Great Salt Lake at Ogden, Utah.

Geologically the Northern Rockies are a complex of different kinds of mountains. In central Idaho they are of granite and are without linear trends. Southwestern Montana, at the corner with Wyoming and Idaho, on the other hand, consists of north-trending block mountains of Paleozoic formations marking the eastern edge of the geosyncline that was along the west edge of the continent, the counterpart of the Appalachian geosyncline.

These Paleozoic rocks have had a complex history. They were folded and faulted at least four times—in the late Paleozoic, again during the Jurassic and Cretaceous, again during late Cretaceous and early Tertiary time when the Rocky Mountains were developed, and finally in the late Tertiary period they were block faulted to produce the linear trends that characterize that part of the country. During the Cretaceous period these rocks formed the mountains that were eroded to provide the sediments deposited in the geosyncline that was at the site of the Rocky Mountains.

The block faulting is continuing. In 1959, at Hebgen Lake, Montana, just west of Yellowstone National Park, earth movement tipped the lake bottom twenty feet toward the northeast, and half that displacement was taken up by a fault that displaced roads, fences, and buildings by ten feet. The resulting earthquake and the damage it caused provide a classic example of how mountains grow—by small increments of movement repeated over long periods of time.

The Northern Rockies like the Southern Rockies were sculptured by the Pleistocene glaciations, beautifully so at Glacier National Park and farther north in Canada as at Banff. Those glaciers descended eastward to the Great Plains where they bumped into the continental ice sheet moving southwestward from its source on the Canadian Shield.

The Continental Divide, which is along the eastern part of the Northern Rockies, could be reached by ascending the Missouri River, by boat as far as Fort Benton and by packtrain or wagon from there. Lewis and Clark traveled up the river to the divide, backtracked to the Clark Fork, and then found their way to the Spokane and Columbia rivers on the western slope.

The mountains are very well watered. The main stems of the Missouri and Yellowstone rivers each are larger than the combined flow of the streams draining eastward off the Southern Rockies, which are higher. Both the Clark Fork and the Spokane rivers, which drain the western slope, have more water than the Colorado River. This difference is attributable to variations in movement of air masses over the continent; in the Northern Rockies, precipitation averages higher and evaporation averages lower than in the Southern Rockies. Moreover, a greater amount of the precipitation falls as snow, from which water infiltrates slowly and helps maintain stream discharge. The land is used chiefly for grazing; hay is raised along some valley bottoms.

Mineral resources in the Northern Rocky Mountains include one of the country's large copper mines, at Butte, Montana, which started as a gold mine and then became important chiefly for its silver, and finally in the 1890s produced chiefly copper. At Coeur d'Alene, Idaho, another major mining center, mining for silver and lead was first; later this became a major producer of lead and zinc.

Colorado Plateau. West of the Southern Rocky Mountains and south of the Middle Rockies and Wyoming Basin is the Colorado Plateau (Fig. 1), averaging about five thousand feet above sea level, the nation's highest plateau and named for the Colorado River that crosses it. Along its western edge are the High Plateaus of Utah, ten thousand feet or more above sea level; they are among the highest plateaus of the world. They cast a rain shadow to the east across the canyon lands of the Colorado River where precipitation averages less than six inches annually.

Thus, the canyon lands are desert. Some are shale desert with barren, rounded hills known as badlands "badder" than those at Badlands National Monument— so bad, some would say, that they are not fit to be a monument. Some areas are sand desert with dunes. Much of the plateau is beautifully multicolored bare rock. Twenty-five national parks and monuments are on the Colorado Plateau, which is an indication of the grandness of the scenery.

Total relief is about the same as in the Rockies, with altitudes ranging from about 2,500 feet along the Colorado River in Grand Canyon to more than 10,000 feet on the High Plateaus and more than 12,000 feet on some of the isolated mountains.

The plateau is built mostly of flat-lying Mesozoic formations. Paleozoic rocks are exposed along the southwest rim of the plateau and in Grand Canyon (Fig. 8). Precambrian rocks are seen in the bottom of Grand Canyon. The Paleozoic also is exposed in the cores of some broad asymmetrical anticlines such as the Circle Cliffs, San Rafael Swell, and Monument Upwarp. Tertiary formations are on the surface of the Uinta Basin along the north and northeastern edges. Generally the upland is a flat surface made up of gently dipping formations, but the flat plateau is interrupted in several ways.

Along the steep flanks of asymmetrical folds on the plateau, the formations are turned up in hogbacks forming colorful rock ridges one thousand to two thousand feet high. One of the better known and longer ones is the Waterpocket Fold, so named because depressions in the sandstone are natural cisterns and an important source of water for travelers in that desert. A similar hogback, crossed by Interstate 70, is along the east flank of the San Rafael Swell; a third, Comb Ridge, extends across the San Juan River at Monument valley.

The flat plateau surface also is interrupted by isolated mountains five thousand to seven thousand feet higher than the plateau. Some of these are Tertiary volcanic cones, notably Mount Taylor in New Mexico and the San Francisco Mountains in Arizona. Farther north are similarly isolated but less conical mountains formed by igneous intrusions (laccoliths) that dome the Paleozoic and Mesozoic formations.

The greatest interruption to the plateau surface, though, is provided by the canyons, the best known of which is GRAND CANYON. The canyon lands extend all across the plateau along the Colorado and Green rivers and their tributaries. The canyon lands were a roadless primitive area until the uranium rush of the 1950s.

The effectiveness of the canyons as barriers may be illustrated by the experience of Padre Escalante in 1776 in trying to find a route from Santa Fe to Monterey, California. He had almost circled the plateau before he finally turned back and crossed the Colorado River near the Crossing of the Fathers.

The canyons, one thousand to five thousand feet deep with precipitous walls, have been referred to as "mountains inside out." They can be crossed even today at only a few places. The canyons first became well known as a result of John Wesley Powell's exploratory trips down the Green and Colorado rivers, which began in 1869.

The plateau is drained by the Colorado, Green, and San Juan rivers, but these streams are in canyons far below the surface of the plateau. As a consequence, water is scarce and the land is used mostly for grazing. The population is small; cities are few and none is large. Vegetation is sparse and mostly shrub land of Upper Sonoran forms. In a humid climate, the principal resource of the plateau—its scenery—would be lost.

The Colorado Plateau was the home of one of the most advanced prehistoric Indian cultures in the United States—that ancestral to the Pueblo Indians. Their horticultural communities were scattered over the plateau around the Four-Corners area, but a drought at the end of the thirteenth century seems to have caused the loss of their crops, which, according to some, were stolen by their more aggressive nomadic neighbors, the Navaho and the Apache. Consequently most of the Pueblo Indians moved to the Rio Grande valley, the Hopi and Zuñi remaining.

This shift of population because of the effects of climatic change occurred in other areas on a smaller scale. At several places the geology of the alluvial and eolian deposits combined with archaeological evidence indicates a shift of population upstream as if in response to decreasing stream flow. It is not known whether the diminution of flow resulted from climatic change or from land use. But the same types of changes happened again during the period when water tables dropped because of erosion by arroyo cutting, which began soon after white men settled on the land and began ranching and farming. How much of the changes is attributable to land use and how much to climatic change remains unresolved.

One of the ancestral Pueblo Indian villages is buried under volcanic ash. A twelfth-century eruption at Sunset Crater, Arizona, buried a Pueblo village. One eruption, near the ancient pueblo of Wupatki, occurred in the volcanic field of the San Francisco Mountains south of Grand Canyon.

Before the Cretaceous period, the Colorado Plateau was part of the stable platform west of the Transcontinental Arch and east of the Cordilleran geosynclines. Jurassic and older formations are thin. At Grand Canyon, for example, one can see the Precambrian basement rocks of the platform in the inner gorge, and from there to the rim are Paleozoic formations ranging in age from Cambrian to Permian and reaching only four thousand feet thick. One hundred miles west, at Death Valley in the Basin and Range Province where the Paleozoic geosyncline was located, the equivalent formations are about forty thousand feet thick. The difference in land form between the Colorado Plateau and the Basin and Range Province to the west is very largely inherited from structural differences in the crust dating back to Paleozoic time.

Figure 8. View east across Grand Canyon at Point Sublime. The Colorado Plateau typically has flat-lying formations, which account for the flat plateau surface. This view shows the 4,000-foot section of Paleozoic platform deposits; in the bottom of the canyon the Precambrian basement is exposed. On the skyline at the right are volcanic cones of the San Francisco volcanic field, the highest peaks of which rise above 12,000 feet. The canyon bottom is below 3,000 feet, and the plateau surface here lies at 7,500 to 8,000 feet. (U.S. Geological Survey)

Mineral deposits on the Colorado Plateau are mostly fuels—coal, oil, gas, and the huge but controversial oil-shale deposits. They are controversial because it is not known how to develop the oil shale without turning upside down substantial areas of three states. In addition to the fossil fuels, there are valuable uranium deposits, mostly in the Triassic and Jurassic formations.

Basin and Range Province. South and west of the Colorado Plateau is the Basin and Range Province, composed of nearly parallel block-faulted mountains and valleys. This is another province with valleys and ridges but it differs from others because its valleys are structural, not erosional. Some of the valleys are below sea level, such as Death Valley and the Salton Sea in Imperial Valley. Other valleys are five thousand feet in altitude. Some of the mountains reach heights of more than ten thousand feet.

This is even more of a desert than the Colorado Plateau. The western part is in the rain shadow of the Sierra Nevada; the southern part is continuous with the Sonoran Desert of Mexico.

The mountains are asymmetrical fault blocks, having been uplifted by faulting along one side and tilted toward the other. Usually a steep escarpment marks the faulted front, whereas the other side has a long gentle slope. Death Valley is an example (Fig. 9). The block faulting occurred during the middle and late Tertiary period and in many places is continuing. Tiltmeters on fault blocks in the vicinity of Death Valley show active earth movement there. Lake Mead has also tilted measurably toward the southwest in the last twenty-five years. There has been historic faulting like that at Hebgen Lake, Montana, and prehistoric faulting recent enough to leave fresh fault scarps. Belts of active

earthquake centers are located along the western valleys near the Sierra Nevada, along the foot of the Middle Rockies from Salt Lake City to Montana, and along the Basin and Range stretches of the Rio Grande.

Around the bases of the mountains are gravel fans, some of them several miles long and many hundreds of feet high, built of debris washed from the mountains. At the valley bottoms, the fans terminate at playas (dry lake beds) or alluvial floodplains along streams, most of which are usually dry. Gravel fans on the faulted sides of the mountains generally are short; those sloping from the gently dipping side are long. This is due in part to the short drainage lines off the faulted fronts, and in part because the valley floors are also being tilted and the lower parts of the fans along the faulted fronts have been lowered and buried by the playa or floodplain deposits.

The playas are bare mud flats. Some of them are encrusted with salt, such as the Great Salt Lake Desert, Searles Lake, and Death Valley. Many have springs around their edges where groundwater seeping through the gravels is checked by the relatively impervious, fine-grained sediments under the playa.

Throughout, the Basin and Range Province is characterized by these three major types of environments. The mountains are largely bare rock with cliffs and crags, especially in limestone formations. The fans are stony, being covered by gravels partially rounded during their transport from the mountains. Parts of many fans have an amazingly smooth surface, known as desert pavement because of its smooth layer of stones resting on from one to six inches of silt. Playas flooded by storms become cracked mud flats when they dry.

Based on present topography and on pre-Cretaceous

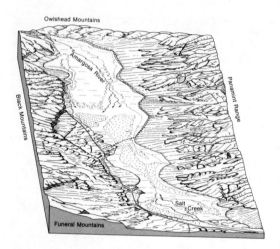

Figure 9. Diagram of Death Valley, California, a landscape typical of the Basin and Range Province. The mountains are bare and rocky. Sloping from them are gravel fans. Such fans are short along the faulted fronts of the block faulted mountains, as along the front of the Black Mountains in this diagram, but they are long on the sides toward which the mountains were tilted. The middle parts of the valleys are playas, or dry lake beds, some of which are bare mud flats, while others are crusted with salts. These three kinds of environments are typical of the basins and ranges. (From C. B. Hunt, Geology of Soils, *copyright © 1972, W. H. Freeman and Co.)*

history, geologists divide the Basin and Range Province into two parts. Western Utah and Nevada are referred to as the Great Basin because almost no exterior drainage occurs there. It is an area of closed basins including Great Salt Lake at the northeast, Carson Sink and the lakes north of Reno in the northwest, Mono and Walker lakes at the west, and Death Valley at the south (see GREAT BASIN STREAMS). Southern Arizona and New Mexico form the other section of the Basin and Range Province.

During the Pleistocene the Great Basin had closed basins containing huge lakes, fed by a climate that was rainy and by meltwaters from glaciers in the mountains. Great Salt Lake is the residue of the Pleistocene lake LAKE BONNEVILLE, which was one thousand feet deep and covered most of western Utah. Lakes in western Nevada are the remains of another large Pleistocene lake, Lake Lahontan. Even Death Valley contained a lake six hundred feet deep.

The Great Basin has few exposures of the Precambrian basement rocks. The Paleozoic and early Mesozoic rocks are thick because they represent the geosynclinal deposits lying along the western edge of the continent. Moreover, those formations were much folded and faulted in the late Paleozoic and Mesozoic; during the late Tertiary period these rocks became block faulted to form the block mountains and structural valleys.

The second part of the Basin and Range Province developed from the platform across the Transcontinen-

tal Arch and its southeastern flank in southern Arizona and southwestern New Mexico. Here, unlike the Great Basin, Precambrian basement rocks are extensively exposed, whereas the overlying Paleozoic and Mesozoic formations are thin. The Cretaceous geosyncline that extended northward along the site of the Rocky Mountains crossed the eastern part of the Basin and Range Province. Today, the desert valleys in this part of the Basin and Range Province are connected by throughflowing streams—the GILA RIVER and Rio Grande and their tributaries. Except at San Augustin, New Mexico, there were no large Pleistocene lakes in this area.

Extensive areas in the Basin and Range Province receive less than five inches of precipitation annually. Streams with running water are few, the largest being the Humboldt, Colorado, Gila, and Rio Grande. At one time there was another, the Mojave River, which crossed the Mojave Desert to join the Colorado. The river's course was disrupted by faulting and other earth movements, and the drainage now ends in a series of closed basins.

Throughout the Basin and Range Province water supplies are scanty. Springs are numerous but small; much of the surface water is excessively saline or alkaline. As a consequence, water is being mined from many of the desert valleys and the water tables are being lowered. When those supplies are exhausted, another chapter of American history will be closed.

Only a few of the higher mountains in the province are forested. Most are covered by shrubs or sparse woodland. Gravel fans support stands of shrubs, sagebrush in the north and varieties of creosote bush in the south. The southern and southeastern parts also are characterized by the abundant and picturesque cacti, yucca, and other exotic plants representative of the Sonoran Desert and Mexican Highland (see VEGETATION: *deserts*).

Except for scarcity of water and high summer temperatures, travel is not difficult because the valleys are connected by low passes. The mountains can be bypassed; it is not necessary to cross them. One of the rivers, the Humboldt, provided a water-level route and the water supply for the forty-niners and other migrants moving westward across the Great Basin. Thus, this small river played an important part in the nation's history.

Similarly, the Rio Grande not only provided the water needed by the agricultural Pueblo Indians in northern New Mexico, but also was a corridor northward from El Paso through which the Spanish extended their influence to Santa Fe.

Mineral deposits in the Basin and Range Province are considerable and varied. Of principal importance at the present time are the several huge deposits of copper, the so-called porphyry copper ores. The copper in these deposits is finely disseminated through igneous rocks, so fine, in fact, that the copper content is only one half of one percent. Nevertheless, that metal, and others occurring only in trace amounts, can be recovered economically by moving vast quantities of the mineralized rock even though such a great percentage of the mined rock is waste.

Mining in the West not only affected world politics and the national economy, but contributed many sagas to the history of the American West. Among the important mineral deposits were those of silver at the Comstock Lode at Virginia City, Nevada, and gold and silver at Tombstone, Arizona. Nevada silver production caused such a drop in the price of silver that monetary policies in the United States and Europe were affected. The borax mined in Death Valley in the 1880s was hauled out by twenty-mule teams, a well-advertised episode in transportation history. The Basin and Range Province still produces quantities of salts of various kinds. It also manufactures a large number of purple bottles made of glass colored by photochemical alteration. This glass, though, which is concentrated at abandoned mining camps, is rapidly being used up.

Columbia Plateau. The Columbia Plateau is unique among this nation's plateaus in that it is composed almost entirely of basaltic lavas and it is unique among deserts in that it has two of the country's largest rivers, the COLUMBIA RIVER and the SNAKE RIVER. Altitudes are approximately two thousand to three thousand feet, but they range from below five hundred feet along the Columbia River where it leaves the plateau at The Dalles to more than ten thousand feet in the Blue Mountains.

Both the desert climate and the rivers are the result of exterior influences. The desert is created by the rain shadow extending eastward from the High Cascades. Parts of the plateau are as desert as the Basin and Range Province. The rivers reach the plateau from the Rocky Mountains, where they collect runoff from a well-watered segment of the Rockies five hundred miles long and two hundred miles wide in western Montana and eastern British Columbia. Crossing the Columbia Plateau, the rivers are in deep canyons, and their water generally has not been available for agriculture. In the last several decades, however, a large number of dams and reservoirs have been built, and extensive areas are being irrigated. The dams have interfered with one important resource of that region, the salmon, which formerly came up the rivers in large numbers to spawn.

Much of the surface of the lavas is covered with loess, and this land is highly productive agriculturally where water has been brought to it. Desert shrub, the original vegetation of the Columbia Plateau in the west, is replaced eastward by grass and, in the mountains, by forest.

The Columbia Plateau lavas have been estimated to total about 100,000 cubic miles. The lavas began accumulating early in the Tertiary and have been accumulating ever since. At Craters of the Moon National Monument in Idaho, on the Snake River Plains, the lavas are so recent that their surfaces are still as bare and rough as when the lavas flowed onto the surface. These may have erupted as recently as 1492. At the east end of the lava field, at Yellowstone National Park, the ground at shallow depth still is hot enough to produce hot springs and geysers.

The lavas in some places are known to be more than two miles thick. They were erupted in a gradually subsiding basin as highly fluid flows that could spread widely. Streams entering the basin from the bordering mountains, the ancestral Cascades and Northern Rocky Mountains, deposited gravel and sand in fans and as lake beds around the sides of the basin, and these deposits are interbedded with the edges of the lava, which thins toward the sides of the basin. In southeastern Oregon the lavas are slightly different in composition and mode of eruption from those in the Columbia River

Basin; that part of the plateau experienced numerous violent, explosive eruptions that blanketed the countryside with cinders and volcanic ash as well as lavas. In general the older lavas are in the Columbia Basin, younger eruptives are to the south and to the east, along the Snake River Plains.

One part of the Columbia Plateau is not composed of volcanic rocks; this is at the Blue and Ochoco mountains in northeastern Oregon. The rocks are Paleozoic and early Mesozoic and represent geosynclinal deposits like the rocks to the south in the Great Basin in Nevada. Presumably these two sets of geosynclinal rocks connect with one another under the Cenozoic lavas in southeastern Oregon.

Some of the lavas in the Columbia River basin have had the loess stripped from their surfaces, and such ground is known as scabland. The loess was eroded by floods, which were one of the most spectacular episodes of Pleistocene history. This happened when the glaciers moved southward into the Rocky Mountain valleys in western Montana and dammed Clarks Fork. The ice dam produced a lake a thousand feet deep, known as Pleistocene Lake Missoula, and this lake, repeatedly overflowing because of glacial meltwaters, could rapidly cut through the edge of the ice dam, which would give way catastrophically and discharge tremendous floods down the Spokane and other rivers of eastern Oregon. The canyon of the Columbia River was filled with ice, and the flood spread across the plateau surface. The floods eroded the loess, cut huge canyons, such as Grand Coulee, with waterfalls as high as Niagara, and left behind giant bars of sand and gravel.

Along the Snake River, where it forms the boundary between Oregon and Idaho, is Hells Canyon, which is deeper than Grand Canyon. It was cut as a result of repeated uplift at the eastern end of the Blue-Ochoco mountain barrier. Each increment of uplift would dam the Snake River, and pond it, causing lake beds to be deposited upstream from the barrier, but each time that the lake rose to the height of the uplifted canyon, it could again overflow via the old canyon route and cut it deeper.

The Oregon Trail crossed the Columbia River via the Snake River Plains across southern Idaho, but had to leave the river where it entered the defile at Hells Canyon. The trail climbed across the Blue Mountains and, on the north side, descended to the Columbia River to pass through the High Cascades.

Sierra Nevada and Cascade Range. The Sierra Nevada and Cascade Range are very different geologically and topographically, yet they form a linear mountain barrier one thousand miles long extending from southern California to Canada. They nearly isolate the Pacific Coast from the rest of the country. The Sierra Nevada is a block of granite and older rocks sloping north and west; northward it is buried by lavas and these rise northward to form the Cascade Range. The sag between the two sets of mountains is crossed by the Pit River and KLAMATH RIVER; no river crosses the Sierra Nevada and only one, the Columbia, crosses the Cascades.

The Sierra Nevada (Fig. 10A) is a segment of the granitic batholith that extends along the western edge of North America from Baja California to Alaska. The granite formed during the Jurassic and early Cretaceous periods. It intruded older Jurassic and Paleozoic formations and became uplifted and exposed to erosion during the early Tertiary. Some of the gravels deposited during that erosion concentrated placer gold and were the object of considerable interest in 1849; in fact, those Tertiary gold deposits triggered the principal mass migration westward across America.

In late Tertiary time the granite was faulted on the east, uplifted, and tilted westward (Fig. 10B). This uplift and tilting may still be continuing, as is suggested by the severe Owens valley earthquake in 1872 and the belt of active earthquake epicenters along the eastern foot of the Sierra.

As a consequence of the faulting and westward tilting, the summit, which is up to fourteen thousand feet in altitude, is crowded toward the east side of the moun-

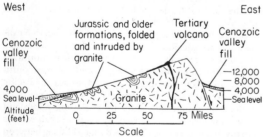

Figures 10. Diagram of the Sierra Nevada, Central Valley, and Coast ranges of California (A, top) and a cross section illustrating the general structure of the Sierra Nevada (B, bottom). The Sierra is a block of granite faulted on the east and tilted west, a block mountain (compare Figure 7 C). (From C. B. Hunt, Physiography of the United States, *copyright © 1967, W. H. Freeman and Co.)*

tains, and long, deep, parallel canyons drain the western slope. They discharge into the Central valley of California at an altitude of around five hundred feet. During the Pleistocene, glaciers descended the canyons about halfway to the base of the Sierra Nevada, cutting deep U-shaped valleys, such as Yosemite valley and Kings Canyon, formed by KINGS RIVER.

The fault block was tilted north as well as west, and the lowest passes are at the north. FEATHER RIVER heads in a windgap at an altitude of 5,218 feet. At one time the Humboldt River may have continued westward via this gap and crossed the Sierra Nevada when it was lower. If so, the drainage became disrupted by one of the later episodes of uplift of the range, and the Humboldt became permanently ponded in the Basin and Range Province.

The next lower gap across the mountains in the south is at Donner Pass, at an altitude of slightly more than seven thousand feet. This was a favorite pass for early travelers because it is located opposite the Nevada lakes near the sink at the terminus of the Humboldt River, which was the route across the Great Basin. Donner Pass was the scene of one of the tragedies of western migration in 1846 when a party of would-be settlers was caught there by early winter storms. Thirty-six of the eighty-one perished.

The Cascade Range rises northward from the sag separating it from the Sierra. This is a volcanic ridge surmounted by tremendous volcanic cones (Fig. 11), such as Mounts Baker, Rainier, Adams, St. Helens, Hood, Jefferson, and Loughlin, the Glacier and Three Sisters peaks, and Crater Lake. At the south end, in California, are Mounts Shasta and Lassen. These peaks are twelve thousand to fourteen thousand feet in altitude; passes between them are about five thousand feet.

To the east is the vast sea of basaltic lava forming the Columbia Plateau. Similar lavas constructed broad low volcanoes along the axis of the ancestral Cascades, forming what are called shield volcanoes. In late Tertiary and Quaternary time the mode of eruptions changed, and the volcanoes along the Cascades became explosive. The large quantities of fragmental material ejected violently from the craters collected in conical heaps around the orifices and built the conical peaks that form the High Cascades.

Several of the volcanoes have been active recently. Mount Lassen erupted in 1915. Eruptions during the relatively recent Holocene epoch spread ash deposits far east of the Cascades. At Crater Lake, a Holocene eruption blasted the top of the volcanic cone, creating a structural subsidence known as a caldera. Crater Lake occupies it. The ancestral pre-Crater Lake volcano is referred to as Mount Mazama.

A single watergap, that formed by the mighty Columbia River, provides the only corridor through this barrier. The gap is at least as old as middle Tertiary because lavas of that age discharged through it. As the lava ridge was uplifted and built upward by additional lava flows, the river was repeatedly ponded east of the range but each time overflowed its old canyon and cut it downward to form the gorge used by the Oregon Trail and used today for both railroads and highways.

The Sierra and Cascades are kept well watered by the moisture they wring from air drifting eastward from the

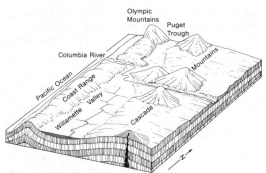

Figure 11. Diagram of part of the High Cascades, which are composed of high volcanic cones (mounts Rainier, St. Helens, Adams, Hood, and Jefferson) built on an anticlinal arch of older lavas. West of the Cascades is a structural trough forming the Willamette Valley and Puget Trough. The Coast Ranges west of the trough are folded lavas and sedimentary rocks. The Columbia River is in a canyon across the Cascade and Coast ranges. (From C. B. Hunt, Geology of Soils, copyright © 1972, W. H. Freeman and Co.)

Pacific. The north end of the Cascades is one of the wettest places in the forty-eight conterminous states. Precipitation averages more than one hundred inches annually. On the high parts of the Sierra Nevada, precipitation averages more than sixty inches annually. As a result large rivers cascade down the western slopes of these mountains. Not much moisture is left in the air that continues eastward across the Columbia Plateau and Great Basin.

The growth of the Cascades with resulting increased aridity to the east is recorded very completely in the fossil vegetation in the John Day Basin of the Columbia Plateau. During the early Tertiary the vegetation and soils of the basin were subtropical and quite like that growing to the west along the coast, for there was no Cascade Range. By middle Tertiary time, the effects of the rising mountains began to show in differences in vegetation on the two sides. Forests to the east include broadleaf, temperate-zone species like some of our eastern oak forests. By late Tertiary time, as the Cascades rose higher, the number of species became greatly reduced, and this further changed to the typically shrub vegetation of the present climate.

The high peaks of the Cascades extend considerably higher than timberline and in fact retain glaciers. The highest forests are Englemann spruce and Alpine fir. Next below this on the western slope and continuing westward to the Coast Ranges is a forest of Douglas fir, white fir, and lodgepole pine, one of the principal lumber-producing areas in the United States. The drier eastern slopes have Ponderosa pine and this gives way eastward to sagebrush on the Columbia Plateau at the foot of the mountains.

The dry eastern slope of the Sierra Nevada also has Ponderosa pine and this grades to a woodland of piñon and juniper, which gives way to sagebrush in the arid Great Basin. On the western slope is Sequoia, and at the western foot of the Sierra is evergreen oak and digger pine.

In terms of mineral resources, the Sierra are best known for the gold that caused the rush there in 1849. The gold was discovered in a mill race along the AMERICAN RIVER, and this led to the discovery of the placer gold deposits, which in turn led to discovery of the Mother Lode. As a result of these discoveries, United States gold production jumped fiftyfold, and gold became an exportable commodity.

At the site of the Cascades, during the early Tertiary before those mountains had developed, the scenery was that of a low deltaic plain. Marshes on that plain accumulated peat that gradually was altered to lignite and later to coal. The deposits are not large, but they were an important source of fuel before the Columbia and other rivers in the region were harnessed for their hydroelectric power.

Pacific Border Province. West of the Sierra-Cascade barrier is a variety of terrain collectively referred to as the Pacific Border or Pacific Coast Province. The topography resembles a series of links of a chain. The center of the north link is the structural valley at the Puget Trough in Washington and the Willamette valley in Oregon, cut out by the WILLAMETTE RIVER. The structural and topographic depression forming the Central valley of California is the center of the middle link. The center of the south link is the depression at Salton Sea and the Gulf of California. These structural valleys are below five hundred feet in altitude. As they subsided they were kept filled with sediments washed there from the bordering mountains. The floors of the valleys are extensive, flat floodplains. At the north they are well watered and heavily forested; southward they become arid and originally were shrub land but now are irrigated farmland.

The mountains of the Pacific Coast Province are young, many of them even younger than the Sierra and Cascades. The oldest, the Klamath Mountains, are like the Sierra in being composed of Paleozoic and Jurassic formations that were uplifted, folded, faulted, and intruded by granite. The history of the Klamath Mountains is very much like that of the Sierra Nevada; they may be part of the same geologic structure connected under the north end of the Central valley.

The Coast Ranges of California north of San Francisco Bay are Jurassic geosynclinal rocks, tightly folded, faulted, and metamorphosed and generally older than the granitic intrusions in the Klamath Mountains and the Sierra. The general structure is brought out by the parallel courses of the Mad, EEL, and Russian rivers. The Coast Ranges south of San Francisco Bay and those in Oregon and Washington are composed of late Cretaceous and Tertiary formations younger than the Sierra Nevada granite and composed of sediments eroded from that granite. The deposits in California accumulated in rapidly subsiding basins; in places the thicknesses exceed twenty thousand feet. In Oregon and Washington, as already noted, the earliest Tertiary formations were laid down as deltaic deposits.

The Pacific Coast is not at all like the Atlantic Coast, for it is mountainous. There is almost no coastal plain and almost no continental shelf. Sandy beaches are a rarity. There are harbors at Puget Trough, San Francisco, and San Diego; the port of Los Angeles is more of a roadstead than harbor. Until it was developed as a naval base, San Diego harbor did not figure prominently in Pacific Coast history despite its being the first California settlement. It was almost abandoned during the 1860s.

San Francisco Bay, though, is one of the world's great harbors. It is a natural terminus for overland travel, being located where the SACRAMENTO RIVER, SAN JOAQUIN RIVER, and Central valley reach the coast, and it is advantageously located near the Great Circle route from Panama to eastern Asia. How and when the bay came into existence is uncertain. A submarine canyon off Monterey Bay and the lack of one off San Francisco Bay has led some to suggest that the original course of the Sacramento River was southward past San Jose to Monterey Bay, where it would have joined the SALINAS RIVER. If so, the passage to the Pacific at the Golden Gate is a recent geological development, resulting from earth movements along the San Andreas fault or its branches.

The San Andreas fault is the best known of a series of faults trending about northwest along the southern Coast Ranges of California and along the coast north of San Francisco Bay to Cape Mendocino. These are high-angle faults thought to extend to the base of the crust, which is much thinner under the Coast Ranges than under the Sierra Nevada. The crustal blocks west of the fault are moving northwestward relative to the blocks east of the fault. This movement, going on at the present time, can be detected by accurate surveys, by displacement of conduits, railroad tracks, and even buildings that lie across the fault.

In 1906, at the time of the San Francisco earthquake, strain on the two blocks, which were being held together by friction, became excessive and the rocks slipped as much as twenty feet past each other. Highways, orchards, ditches, and fences were displaced by an equal distance. A secondary result was that fires burned out of control because water lines were disrupted.

At many places where stream courses cross the faults, they bend to the right as much as a thousand feet. These obviously displaced courses represent a series of episodes of displacement like the one that occurred in 1906. Some of the older rock formations are displaced scores of miles, and there is some suggestion that over the life of the fault there has been a total of perhaps three hundred miles of displacement. Whatever the total amount, it is considerable and occurred as repeated small episodes of faulting. These episodes will continue to occur.

The coast of southern California is semiarid, with precipitation about 15 inches annually. One of the finest observatories in the United States was built on the San Gabriel Mountains because of the clear atmosphere. Precipitation increases northward to 60 inches in the California Coast Ranges, 100 inches along the Oregon coast, and 140 inches at the Olympic Mountains. Vegetation and land use reflect these differences. At the south is irrigated farmland; originally it was shrub or chaparral on the Coast Ranges. North of San Francisco the coast forests are redwood, and along the coasts of Oregon and Washington, at the rear of a narrow coastal belt, are forests of Douglas fir.

The present climate poses real problems for Californians. The rains occur mostly during the winter. On the young but locally rugged Tertiary formations, which are as poorly consolidated as those along the Atlantic Coastal Plain, the runoff can cause severe damage by flooding, landsliding, and mudflows. Conversely, during the summer, which is the growing season, there is little rain. Crops must be irrigated; mountainsides become dry as tinder and disastrous brush fires break out.

California is a land of extremes. It has some of the sunniest and some of the foggiest skies, some of the driest and some of the wettest climates, and, depending on the season, mud and tinder-dry dust create problems. That the benefits outweigh the hazards, however, seems indicated by the fact that this is the most populous state, a population that is crowded into half the area of the state.

Mineral resources in the Coast Ranges are mostly mineral fuels, oil and gas in southern California and coal in Washington. A major deposit of mercury occurs at New Almaden, a deposit that figured prominently in the gold rushes because mercury was needed for amalgam in order to concentrate the gold.

The foregoing is adapted largely from Charles B. Hunt, *Physiography of the United States* (1967; repr. as *Natural Regions of the United States and Canada*, 1974). Some other general references are W. W. Atwood, *The Physiographic Provinces of North America*, with a map by Erwin Raisz showing landforms in the United States (1940); Isaiah Bowman, *Forest Physiography* (1909); N. M. Fenneman, *Physiography of Western United States* (1931) and *Physiography of Eastern United States* (1938); A. L. Kroeber, *Cultural and Natural Areas of Native North America* (1947); F. B. Loomis, *Physiography of the United States* (1938); J. H. Paterson, *North America: A Regional Geography* (1963); W. E. Powers, *Physical Geography* (1966); and W. D. Thornbury, *Regional Geomorphology of the United States* (1965).—C. B. H.

Pickett, William. See RODEO.

pidgin English. See HAWAIIAN PIDGIN ENGLISH.

Piedmont Plateau. See PHYSIOGRAPHY OF THE UNITED STATES.

Pierce, Elias Davidson (1824-1897). Prospector. Pierce came from his native Northern Ireland to Virginia in 1839 and to Indiana in 1844. There he became an attorney before serving in the Mexican War and joining the California gold rush in 1849. A prospector and itinerant trader rather than a miner, he served in the California legislature in 1852. Later that year, he joined a retired Hudson's Bay Company trapper on a trip to the Nez Percé country. The area, he decided, could be developed into a gold-mining empire. Returning to California, he made the first ascent of Mount Shasta in 1854, but he never lost his ambition to discover the Nez Percé mines. Early in 1860, he finally managed to smuggle a prospecting outfit into the camp of his Nez Percé friend, Wislanaeqa. Favorable results, while out gold hunting with Wislanaeqa, led Pierce to drop his disguise as a trader. But unable to interest the Indians in letting whites mine their reservation, he managed to sneak a prospecting party into the Nez Percé lands in August. Commercial gold discoveries on September 30, 1860, induced a band of miners to return to found Pierce City on December 3. While Pierce worked on other projects, thousands of fortune-seekers rushed to the new Idaho mines, and in less than two and one half years, a new mining territory of Idaho was established as a result of Pierce's find. Most of the Nez Percé's lands were taken away.

In 1865-66, Pierce joined in a stage-line venture from

Sacramento valley to southwestern Idaho, but Indian opposition ruined that enterprise. Then in 1869, Pierce heard that his girlfriend back in Indiana (to whom he had been engaged for twenty years but whom he had not seen during that time) was getting restless; he hurried back, got married, and returned to settle in Oakland, California. There, and in Calistoga, he participated in California quartz-mining projects. Finally in 1884, he retired to his old hometown in Indiana.—M. W.

Pierce, [Abel Head] Shanghai (1834-1900). Cowman. Pierce, the man primarily responsible for the introduction of the Brahman breed of cattle into the United States, spent his childhood years in the East. While serving as an apprentice in his uncle's general store in Virginia, he became restless for adventure and sneaked aboard a schooner bound for Indianola, Texas. Quickly discovered, the stowaway worked as a cargo handler for the remainder of the trip. Shortly after reaching Texas, Pierce began working on a ranch. Although he was only twenty years old, he decided that ranching would suit him as a career, and set to work registering a brand (AP) and acquiring cattle. His younger brother, Jonathan, joined him in 1860. The Pierce brothers together served in the Confederate army, married sisters, and, as soon as the war ended, established the Rancho Grande in Wharton County, Texas. Chárlie Siringo, the well-known western author, worked as a cowhand on the ranch and wrote of "Old Shang" (Pierce) in his autobiography, *The Texas Cowboy* (1885).

Although the ranch itself was a success, Pierce became involved in the hanging of some rustlers and quietly sold all his stock. Taking the profits of the sale, he went to Kansas to allow things to settle down. Upon his return, one and one half years later, Pierce formed a partnership with Daniel Sullivan and established the Pierce-Sullivan Pasture Company. The company was enormously successful, acquiring 250,000 acres of land, sending thousands of cattle up the northern trails, and shipping thousands of others by rail.

The dreaded Texas fever was taking a severe toll on the livestock, however. Concluding that the fever was carried by cattle ticks, Pierce began experimenting in ways for removing them (this was before "dipping" was introduced). After searching throughout Europe for a breed of cattle that might be immune to the fever, he finally decided that the Brahman breed of India might answer his purpose. His plans for importing a small herd were interrupted by his death but were completed by his favorite nephew and namesake, Abel Pierce Borden. Pierce's Brahman cattle were to become the foundation stock for the now numerous herds found throughout America.

Six-foot-four with a big booming voice, Pierce once told a new clerk at one of his favorite hotels: "I am Shanghai Pierce, Webster on cattle, by God, Sir."

See Chris Emmett, *Shanghai Pierce, a Fair Likeness* (1953).—J. C. D.

Pierpont, Francis Harrison (1814-1899). A founder of West Virginia. A lawyer and small businessman in Fairmont, (West) Virginia, Pierpont pursued his career into middle life uneventfully except for occasional public activities in behalf of Virginia's moribund Whig party. But as the sectional crisis deepened in 1859, Pierpont attracted regional attention with a series of newspaper letters criticizing slavery and emphasizing northwestern Virginia's grievances against the existing Virginia regime. As the state moved toward secession in 1861, he helped through mass meetings and printed appeals to mobilize western resistance to the Richmond government and to launch the West Virginia statehood movement. In this enterprise he adopted a middle course between advocates of immediate separation from Virginia and advocates of delay. As a result, the Second Wheeling Convention (June 11-25, 1861) elected Pierpont governor of a "restored" Virginia government designed to reestablish civil authority and to provide constitutional sanction for the eventual dismemberment of the state. Federal authorities promptly recognized the restored government and, following West Virginia's admission to the Union in 1863, sponsored its transfer to Alexandria and then to Richmond in 1865. Here Pierpont could find no middle way amid the contending forces of Reconstruction. After three disillusioning years in Richmond as governor of Virginia, he returned to West Virginia, where subsequent defeats in the state at large and within his own Republican party soon returned him to his former obscurity. After his death, however, West Virginia authorities memorialized Pierpont as "the father of West Virginia" in the United States Capitol's Statuary Hall.

Most accounts of the West Virginia statehood movement concentrate on other leaders following Pierpont's elevation to the governorship, but Charles H. Ambler, *Francis H. Pierpont, Union War Governor of Virginia and Father of West Virginia* (1937), places his preparatory and supportive role in a better perspective (except for an overly generous estimate of Pierpont's abilities). See also Richard O. Curry, *A House Divided: Statehood Politics and the Copperhead Movement in West Virginia* (1964); and George E. Moore, *Banner in the Hills: West Virginia's Statehood* (1963).—J. A. W.

Pierre, South Dakota. Pierre was developed by the Chicago and Northwestern Railroad as the site where the rails would cross the Missouri River. It was located on the east bank of the river, just opposite Fort Pierre. The first train reached the settlement in the autumn of 1880.

Pierre became a freighting center for the mining country of the Black Hills until it was replaced by Rapid City in 1886. An attempt to remove the capital of Dakota Territory from Bismarck to Pierre in 1885 failed, but it became the capital on a temporary basis in 1889 and permanently in 1890.

The town's population in 1890 was 3,235. Despite fluctuations, it has trebled in size; the 1970 census showed a total of 9,699 residents.—D. J. T.

Pierre's Hole, battle of (1832). At the close of the fur-trade rendezvous in 1832 at Pierre's Hole (in present-day Wyoming), the party of fur traders Milton Sublette and Nathaniel Wyeth encountered about two hundred Gros Ventre Indians on July 17. One of the Flathead Indians allied to the trappers murdered a Gros Ventre chief carrying a flag of truce, and the battle commenced. After defending themselves in an impromptu fort, the Gros Ventre melted away, having killed five whites and seven Indian allies at the cost of ten killed on their side.

See Dale L. Morgan, ed., *The West of William H. Ashley* (1964).—G. B. D.

Pierson, George Wilson (1904-   ). Historian. Born

in New York City, Pierson was educated at Yale University, where he was a student of Ralph Gabriel and Charles M. Andrews. He then taught at Yale, becoming professor of history in 1944. In 1946 he was appointed Larned Professor of History.

Pierson's scholarly interests centered on the development of American character. He first explored this interest in a study of the American voyage of Alexis de Tocqueville and Gustave de Beaumont and published *Tocqueville and Beaumont in America* (1938). His interpretations of Tocqueville's experiences on the American frontier led him to believe that Frederick Jackson Turner's frontier thesis was "too narrow, too nationalistic and too contradictory and confusing." Pierson's critique of Turner was expounded in two major articles, "The Frontier and Frontiersmen of Turner's Essays" (*Pennsylvania Magazine of History and Biography*, October 1940) and "The Frontier and American Institutions" (*New England Quarterly*, June 1942). Pierson criticized Turner for not making exact definitions of the terms "democracy" and "individualism" and for not considering whether American individualism differed from individualism in other cultures, particularly that of the French. Pierson was equally distressed with Turner's repetition of his thesis in the twelve essays written between 1893 and 1914, published as *The Frontier in American History* (1920). Pierson thought Turner resorted to dogmatic statements and exaggerated his thesis when he should have endeavored to prove it with the accumulation of hard evidence and comparative techniques.

Pierson's critique of Turner influenced him to study the factor of mobility in American society. He wrote a number of articles on the subject, including "The Moving American" (*Yale Review*, Autumn 1954), "The M-Factor in American History" (*American Quarterly*, vol. 15, Summer supplement, 1962), and a comparative study, "Mobility" (*The Comparative Approach to American History*, edited by C. V. Woodward, 1968). The last study was one Pierson thought Turner should have made.

Pierson also published a two-volume history of Yale, *Yale College: An Educational History, 1871-1921* (1952) and *Yale: The University College, 1921-37* (1955). He also wrote a statistical study of the college background of prominent Americans from the American Revolution to the present in *The Education of American Leaders* (1969).—J. S. W.

Pike, Albert (1809-1891). Arkansas author, lawyer, soldier. Pike was born in Boston and educated in Newburyport, Massachusetts. He taught school, wrote poetry, and, in 1831, traveled via Tennessee and St. Louis to Santa Fe, where he clerked in a trading post. In 1834, his book *Prose Sketches and Poems Written in the Western Country* was published, an account of his travels to Santa Fe, of his impressions of the Santa Fe Trail and New Mexico, and of his trip across Texas in 1832 to Fort Smith, Arkansas. In Arkansas he taught school, went to Little Rock to edit the anti-Jackson newspaper, the *Arkansas Advocate*, read law and became one of the Southwest's ablest lawyers, helped found and lead Arkansas' Whig party until 1852, published his "Hymns to the Gods"— eight long poems in the classical style—in the prestigious *Blackwood's Edinburgh Magazine* in 1839, reported the decisions of the Arkansas supreme court in 1840-45, led

a squadron of Arkansas mounted troops during the Mexican War and participated in the battle of Buena Vista, and, returning home in 1847, fought a bloodless duel with his regimental commander John Selden Roane, who was later governor of Arkansas. Pike won prominence in the 1850s for his advocacy of the South's building its own Pacific railroad, for his promotion of the Know-Nothing party, and for his prosecution of the claims against the United States by the Choctaw and Creek Indians. In 1861 he negotiated Confederate treaties of alliance with the slaveholding Indian tribes of present-day Oklahoma and, in 1861-62, commanded, as a brigadier general, the department of Indian Territory. After the Civil War he owned and edited the *Memphis Appeal* briefly, moved to Washington, D.C., in 1868 to practice law with Robert Ward Johnson until about 1878, and devoted himself to research and writing for the Scottish Rite of Freemasonry. From 1859 until his death, Pike was sovereign grand commander of the Scottish Rite Supreme Grand Council, Southern Jurisdiction, which included the South and all the states west of the Mississippi. He did much work organizing the bodies of the Scottish Rite in the West, revising the rituals of the order, writing *Morals and Dogma of the Ancient and Accepted Scottish Rite of Freemasonry*, published between 1872 and 1905, and administering the work of the council. He died in Washington. —W. L. B.

Pike, Zebulon Montgomery (1779-1813). Soldier and explorer. Born in Lamberton (now a part of Trenton), New Jersey, Pike enlisted in the army at the age of fifteen and saw service in the Old Northwest with General Anthony Wayne, at times being attached to the company of his own father, Zebulon Pike, a veteran of the American Revolution. In 1799 he was made a lieutenant and in the following years was assigned to various frontier river posts—Fort Allegheny, Fort Washington, Fort Knox, and Kaskaskia, among them.

Pike's formal education was meager but he was alert and courageous and a leader of men. His attention to duty was unremitting. Determined to win fame as a soldier, he not only read widely on military tactics but taught himself Spanish, French, mathematics, and elementary science.

The opportunity he coveted came when General James Wilkinson ordered him to make a reconnaissance of the upper Mississippi. Pike left St. Louis with twenty soldiers on August 9, 1805, in a seventy-foot keelboat with orders to explore the headwaters of the Mississippi if he could do so "before the waters are frozen up" (which would have prevented his return), to collect information on the furs, minerals, and population of the region, to purchase sites for future military posts, and to invite important Indian chiefs who had not been to St. Louis to pay Wilkinson a visit. The keelboat was left at Prairie du Chien and the expedition continued on in smaller craft. Pike abandoned the idea of returning in the fall, made a winter encampment for most of his men near present-day Little Falls, Minnesota, and proceeded by sled up the main branch of the Mississippi (the true source, Lake Itasca, is at the extremity of the branch that Pike did not take).

The expedition was only moderately successful. Few chiefs visited St. Louis, and the United States Senate failed to ratify the treaty he negotiated with the Sioux whereby the present St. Paul-Minneapolis area was acquired; however, his map and journal provided the first real cartographic portrayal of the upper Mississippi.

Pike returned from his Minnesota expedition on April 30, 1806; less than three months later—July 15—he was on his way west, again under orders of General Wilkinson. He escorted fifty-one Osage captives to their homes in western Missouri and continued to a Pawnee village on the Republican River in Nebraska for the purpose of effecting peace settlements with the tribes of that region. He traveled across present-day KANSAS and from there proceeded to explore the headwaters of the Arkansas, which took him into Colorado, where on Thanksgiving Day he and his cotton-clad men tried unsuccessfully in snow and zero temperatures to reach the peak that ultimately came to bear Pike's name. After wandering about searching for the Red River, he crossed the Sangre de Cristo Range and reached the Rio Grande, which he believed to be the elusive Red River. Early in February he built a stockade on the Conejos, a western affluent of the Rio Grande, and it was there that he was taken into custody by a Spanish patrol, conducted first to Santa Fe and then to Chihuahua, and finally escorted by a circuitous route to the United States boundary near Natchitoches, Louisiana, where he arrived on June 30, 1807.

Undoubtedly Pike had been lost, but undoubtedly, too, he wanted to be captured in order to further his mission of obtaining information on the territory around Santa Fe. Upon his return there was some suspicion that he might have been connected with the Aaron Burr conspiracy or involved in a private connivance with the rogue Wilkinson, but there is no evidence of the former and the steadfast loyalty to his general appears more naïve than sinister.

Pike's poorly organized narrative of his travels was published by C. & A. Conrad & Co. in Philadelphia in 1810, and British, French, Dutch, and German editions followed. They brought the explorer some recognition although no money, but his reputation as an efficient officer was recognized in his promotion to brigadier general during the War of 1812, shortly before he was killed by the explosion of a British magazine in April 1813 when he led the attack on Toronto.

For a biography and an edition of the journals and correspondence (with excellent notes, maps, and map commentaries), see the following: Eugene Hollon, *The Lost Pathfinder* (1949); and Donald Jackson, ed., *The Journals of Zebulon Pike*, 2 vols. (1966).—M. L. S.

Pilcher, Joshua (1790-1843). Fur trader and superintendent of Indian affairs. Pilcher was born in Culpepper County, Virginia, but his family moved to Kentucky when Joshua was quite young. Pilcher was a merchant in Kentucky and Tennessee before moving to St. Louis in 1815. He was a partner in the new Missouri Fur Company founded by Manuel Lisa in 1819. After Lisa's death he became head of the company. With sixty of his men he accompanied Colonel Henry Leavenworth as Indian subagent in the military expedition against the Arikara in the summer of 1823, but he refused to draft a treaty with the Indians, because he thought that Leavenworth had been too lenient with the tribes. Pilcher's opinion may have been influenced by the fact that hostile Indians had wiped out one of his brigades on the

upper Missouri a short time before. Leavenworth subsequently charged Pilcher with firing the Arikara villages without authorization; in turn, Pilcher denounced Leavenworth as an ineffective officer.

Pilcher's own efforts to better the fortunes of the ailing Missouri Fur Company met with frustration, and in 1825 the firm failed. Pilcher blamed the failure on the losses suffered by the company when one of its parties led by Robert Jones and Michael Immell was wiped out by the Blackfoot in 1823. He formed a new company and between 1828 and 1830 penetrated the Northwest all the way to Fort Vancouver, where he offered his services to the Hudson's Bay Company but was rebuffed. Pilcher wrote a valuable report that pointed out that the Oregon country would be attractive to American farmers, ranchers, and shipbuilders and suggested that the overland trip via South Pass was easy enough to allow migrants to bring their household goods and cattle. Pilcher's report was printed by Congress and revealed, as William H. Goetzmann has observed, that he had an "explorer's sense of national mission" that was as keen as that of Jedediah Smith and William H. Ashley.

Yet Pilcher's northwestern travels and his pioneering efforts to develop the Platte River trade (1827-30) did not bring financial success. By 1833 he had joined the American Fur Company, and that same year he accompanied Prince Maximilian of Wied-Neuwied and Karl Bodmer, the artist, on their western tour. He then served as Indian agent on the upper Missouri (1834-38), and upon the death of William Clark, he became superintendent of Indian affairs for two years (1839-41), a post that his friend Thomas Hart Benton probably secured for him. Pilcher worked earnestly at his new job to inform himself about the Indians under his jurisdiction and to help them as best he could. Serious and hardworking, Pilcher spent his life performing duties. He never married and died of lung trouble at the age of fifty-three.

See LeRoy R. Hafen, ed., *The Mountain Men and the Fur Trade of the Far West*, vol. IV (1966); and John E. Sunder, *Joshua Pilcher, Fur Trader and Indian Agent* (1968).—G. B. D.

Pilgrims. See PLYMOUTH COLONY.

Piman Indians. The Piman Indians of southern Arizona and northern Sonora, Mexico, are North America's desert dwellers par excellence. Their prehistoric and present homeland is in the lower Sonoran Desert of Arizona and Sonora; they worked out unique environmental adjustments as means of wresting a living from their sparse surroundings.

The Piman—which include the modern Pima and Papago Indians—speak an Uto-Aztecan language fairly closely related to that spoken by the Aztec Indians of ancient Mexico. Before the coming of Europeans there were essentially three groups of Piman. The first consisted of the hunting, gathering, and fishing peoples living in the lower Colorado vegetation zone of southwestern Arizona and northwestern Sonora who were called Sobas by the Spanish and who have been known in more recent times as Sand Papago or Areneño. They traveled in small groups throughout an area bounded by the Gila and Colorado rivers, the Ajo Mountains in Arizona, and the head of the Gulf of California in Sonora.

Their immediate eastern neighbors, the Papago proper, lived in the riverless expanse of desert south of the Gila River, west of the Santa Cruz River, north of the rivers in Sonora, and east of the Ajo Mountains. These people maintained two villages. One fairly permanent village was in the mountain foothills, where springs provided a steady source of water. The second was built in the intermontane valleys, near the mouths of arroyos, where it was possible to farm during the summer by damming the mouths and irrigating fields with water collected from flash floods. This "two-village" people supplemented its small amount of farming by hunting and gathering.

The third group of Piman lived along the riverine perimeters of this vast desert area. Known to Spaniards as the Sobaipuri, Pima, and Gileños, depending on the particular group or groups, their modern descendants include the Pima Indians of the Gila River Indian Reservation south of Phoenix, Arizona; the Papago living on the San Xavier Indian Reservation near Tucson, Arizona; and a few Papago living in settlements in northern Sonora.

All Piman refer to themselves as the *o'odham*, "the people." Aboriginally they lived in small groups and had no political connection with one another. The hunting and gathering bands of western Sand Papago gave way to related villages, or "rancherias," of Papago in the central desert. Houses were dome-shaped brush huts. The Piman on the rivers, where the water supply was permanent, lived in fixed villages and farmed for much of their subsistence. Two or more of these settlements might be related, but again, there was no leadership beyond that of related villages.

Father Eusebio Kino became the forerunner of European influence on the Piman. In 1687 he established a mission, Nuestra Señora de los Dolores, at the southern perimeter of their territory. It was also he who founded Mission SAN XAVIER DEL BAC. Until his death in 1711 he worked among the Piman to introduce a new religion, cattle, new kinds of crops (including wheat), and other elements of non-Indian culture. Although the Piman fought against Spaniards in the 1690s and again in the 1750s, they were never involved in armed conflict with the United States. The Pima and Papago of Arizona fell under United States jurisdiction in June 1854, with ratification of the Gadsden Purchase by the United States Senate.

A reservation was set aside for the Pima in 1859. The Gila River Indian Reservation (371,933 acres) became the first in Arizona. In 1874 the San Xavier reservation (71,095 acres), which surrounds the old mission, was established for the Papago; the Gila Bend reservation (10,337 acres) was created in 1882, also for the Papago; the Ak Chin reservation (21,840 acres) was set aside for Pima in 1912; and in 1916 the Papago Indian Reservation, the second largest in the United States (2,773,357 acres), became a reality through an executive order signed by President Woodrow Wilson. The Pima also live on the 46,624-acre Salt River reservation, which dates from 1879.

Although some groups of the Piman revolted against Spanish rule in 1695 and again in 1751, their record of relationships with non-Indians is largely that of allies against the Apache. As early as 1782 the Piman were enlisted as soldiers in the Spanish army in Sonora, and throughout the last half of the nineteenth century the Pima and the Papago fought with Anglos against Apache Indians, sometimes on temporary enlistments and sometimes purely as volunteers. The Papago, in fact, did most of the killing at the CAMP GRANT MASSACRE. Not once did the Pima and Papago fight against United States citizens.

The Papago organized in 1937 under the terms of the 1934 Indian Reorganization Act, and today they are divided into eleven voting districts: one each at San Xavier and Gila Bend and nine on the Papago reservation proper. Each district sends two representatives to Sells, Arizona, the tribal capital, to speak for them on the tribal council. The council elects the tribal chairman. Additionally, each district has its own council to handle local affairs.

For their livelihoods the Papago are largely dependent today on income from mineral leases, cattle, employment by tribal or federal agencies, wage labor in mines or on farms, and welfare payments. Of the approximately twelve thousand Papago—most of whom continue to speak their native language—there are about eight thousand on the reservation at any given moment. Others live in Tucson and Phoenix in Arizona and in California urban centers.

The Pima, nearly eight thousand of them, organized as the Gila River Pima-Maricopa Community in 1936. The Maricopa, originally from the Colorado River, settled near the Pima in the mid-nineteenth century. The Pima at Salt River and Ak Chin operate under their own tribal councils. Modern Gila River reservation activities, in addition to farming, include a wide range of federally sponsored programs, including Model Cities, as well as a large number of leases to industrial and service firms. Tribal headquarters are at Sacaton, Arizona.

The Pima also operate a tribal restaurant and arts-and-crafts center on their reservation. In very recent years there has been a small revival in Pima basketmaking; Papago Indian women have never ceased to make baskets in large quantities, and today they make more of them for sale than any other Indian tribe in North America.

Pima and Papago children are attending school and finishing high school in ever-increasing numbers. In the distant future, it is likely that most on-reservation affairs will be administered by the Piman in their own behalf.

See William H. Kelly, *Indians of Arizona* (1953); Frank Russell, *The Pima Indians* (1908); Ruth Underhill, *Social Organization of the Papago Indians* (1939); and Thomas Weaver, *Indians of Arizona: A Contemporary Perspective* (1974).—B. L. F.

Pinchot, Gifford (1865-1946). Conservationist and politician. Born to a wealthy family of French descent, Pinchot studied at Yale and at the French Forest School in Nancy. Returning to the United States in the early 1890s with the concept of managing forests as a renewable crop (the "sustained yield" idea), Pinchot found little demand for his abilities. Most Americans still acted under the influence of the frontier-bred myth that resources were inexhaustible. At length Pinchot found employment in Biltmore, the huge North Carolina estate of the Vanderbilt family. In 1898 he accepted an appointment as chief of the federal Forestry Division (later the United States Forest Service), and as chief he controlled the forest reserves (later called the national forests). When Theodore Roosevelt, a personal friend of Pinchot, became president in 1901, the stage was set for the rise of both Pinchot and conservation.

Pinchot claimed to have coined the term *conservation* in 1907 to designate the concept of managing the whole environment efficiently for the long-term good of all the poeple. In 1908 he organized the White House Conservation Conference to launch the movement. Although more than a thousand national leaders including the governors of the various states attended, the conservation movement became hampered by political infighting and lack of funds. The headline news was Pinchot's battle with Secretary of the Interior Richard A. Ballinger, who had allegedly aided private interests in acquiring Alaskan coal lands. Pinchot contended that the principles of both conservation and democracy had been violated. In January 1910 he overtly challenged Ballinger and was immediately fired from the Forest Service by an outraged William Howard Taft. The Ballinger-Pinchot controversy subsequently helped split the Republican party and culminated when Theodore Roosevelt returned from a safari in Africa to challenge Taft on an independent ticket in the election of 1912. Recent scholarship has shown that Ballinger was not technically guilty of abusing the power of his office and that Taft had no alternative but to dismiss the unyielding Pinchot. Political realities, rather than conservation policy, determined the outcome of the Ballinger-Pinchot controversy.

During his tenure as chief forester, Pinchot was also challenged by John MUIR and the preservationist wing of the American conservation movement. Accusing Pinchot of being no better than a scientific exploiter, Muir and his colleagues called for the complete protection of federal forest lands. In 1913 Pinchot pushed his utilitarian position through in the case of Yosemite National Park's Hetch Hetchy Valley, which San Francisco wanted as the site for a dam and municipal reservoir. Muir regarded the invasion of wilderness as sacrilegious and branded Pinchot a heartless disciple of the dollar.

After his dismissal from the Forest Service, Pinchot maintained his presidency of the National Conservation Association and began to dabble in elective politics. Unsuccessful in a bid for the Senate from Pennsylvania in 1914, he persevered and captured that state's governorship in 1922 and again in 1930. In these years Pinchot's name occasionally entered the discussion of presidential possibilities. He could not hide an interest in the top office, but he never advanced beyond the Republicans' smoke-filled rooms. His last years were spent in advising various state and federal agencies on the conservation movement he had done so much to create.

Pinchot's life is well documented in Martin L. Fausold's *Gifford Pinchot, Bull Moose Progressive* (1961); and M. Nelson McGeary, *Gifford Pinchot* (1960). Harold T. Pinkett, *Gifford Pinchot: Public and Private Forester* (1970), is the most recent study. An autobiography, *Breaking New Ground* (1947), is extremely useful as a source of Pinchot's ideas, as is Pinchot's *The Fight for Conservation* (1910). The voluminous Gifford Pinchot Papers are excellently indexed in the Manuscripts Division of the Library of Congress.—R. N.

Pinckney's Treaty. See SAN LORENZO, TREATY OF.

Pine Bluff, Arkansas. Pine Bluff lies southeast of Little Rock and is the seat of Jefferson County. Situated on the south bank of the Arkansas River, the settlement was first called Mount Marie but was renamed Pine Bluff after the giant pines located at the site. It was chartered as a town in 1835 and as a city in 1839. A Union force occupied it in September 1863, and in October repulsed a Confederate counterattack. In 1873 a Negro branch of the University of Arkansas was founded in Pine Bluff; it is now integrated. The city is a railroad center and cotton market, and in recent decades has become a manufacturing center for farm machinery, lumber and wood products, textiles, chemicals, and electric products. The Arkansas River Navigation Channel furnishes barge transportation to the Gulf of Mexico. The city's population in 1970 was 57,389. —W. L. B.

Pinkerton Detective Agency. Allan Pinkerton was born in Glasgow, Scotland, in 1819 and migrated to the United States at the age of twenty-three. He soon settled in Kane County, Illinois, and worked as a cooper until he accepted an appointment as deputy sheriff. In 1850 he moved to Chicago and served briefly as the city's first police detective until establishing his own private agency. (Following Allan's death in 1884, his sons, William and Robert, took charge of the New York and Chicago offices, respectively.) He soon became an ardent abolitionist and allowed his home to be used as a stop on the underground railroad. In 1859 John Brown and eleven runaway slaves hid out at the Pinkerton residence until money could be raised to transport the blacks to Canada.

The founder of the famous agency was the first to devise what became the forerunner of today's "rogues' gallery." He insisted upon a detailed description of known criminals, including physical characteristics, background, companions, and hideouts. His organization never closed a case until the individual was officially declared dead.

Pinkerton gained fame just before the Civil War by thwarting a plot to assassinate Lincoln on the trip to Washington for his first inauguration and later for directing secret-service operations for General George B. McClellan. After the war Pinkerton agents played major roles in several clashes between workers and management, the most famous of which involved the Molly Maguires in 1874-75 and the Homestead strike in Pittsburgh in 1892. The Pinkertons gained a dubious reputation as strikebreakers, and their battles were invariably bloody and the aftereffects long and bitter. Organized unions naturally hated them with a passion, but their reputation fared better in the West after they had successfully scattered several outlaw bands.

In March 1874 a Pinkerton detective was killed while trying to infiltrate the James gang. A few days later another agent, Louis J. Lull at Chicago, and Sheriff Ed Daniels of Osceola, Missouri, died of wounds sustained in a shootout with two of the notorious YOUNGER BROTHERS. John Younger also died, and Jim sustained severe wounds. By January 1875 agents came upon a cabin thought to be the hideout of the James boys. Unaware that the James boys had already escaped, the detectives poured a volley of bullets into the cabin and killed the outlaws' eight-year-old half-brother and wounded their mother. Jesse James's hatred for Allan Pinkerton became an obsession, and on one occasion he went to Chicago to kill the noted detective and trailed him for several months. He ultimately failed in his mission but allegedly reported to a close friend that "I know God some day will deliver Allan Pinkerton into my hands."

The Texas and Pacific Railroad retained the agency in 1878 to go after Sam BASS, who had robbed several of their trains and express offices. But before the Pinkertons could catch up with the gang, one of Bass's men betrayed him and a company of Texas Rangers subsequently shot him down in Round Rock, a few miles north of Austin. Another Texas outlaw gang, led by Rube and Jim Burrows, was broken up in 1888 when Pinkerton detectives shot and killed the two brothers and arrested their three companions. By this time business had become so good that the agency had opened branch offices in Denver, Kansas City, and Seattle. In March 1896, J. C. Frazier, an agent from the Denver office, joined Pat Garrett at Las Cruces in an attempt to solve the murder of a prominent New Mexico political leader, Colonel Albert Jennings Fountain, and his eight-year-old son. Unfortunately, the mystery of who the killers were remains unsolved to this day.

Another famous episode involving Pinkerton detectives in the West centered on their persistent pursuit of the Wild Bunch. They eventually chased the gang out of Montana and Wyoming into New Mexico. From there Butch CASSIDY, the Sundance Kid, and their female companion, Etta Place, fled to New York and finally to South America, where agents continued to harass them. Etta soon returned to the United States, and soldiers eventually killed the two men at San Vicente, Bolivia, in 1909.

While the West was being plagued by outlaw gangs, it also was experiencing violence from the labor wars that spread across Texas, Colorado, Utah, Nevada, and Idaho. Management frequently employed Pinkerton agents who did not hesitate to promote violence in order to discredit the labor movement and frame and convict union leaders. Jay Gould used several dozen spies to break up the 1888 strike on his Texas and Pacific Railroad. Six years later agent Charles SIRINGO went to Coeur d'Alene, Idaho, to inform on mine workers. He joined the union and eventually became recording secretary. When the miners learned his true identity, Siringo narrowly escaped from an angry lynch mob of strikers.

In 1905 former Governor Frank STEUNENBERG of Idaho was killed in a bomb explosion, apparently in retaliation for having called in federal troops to control striking miners. Pinkerton agents soon obtained a confession from Harry Orchard, who in turn implicated officials of the Western Federation of Miners. A jury found Orchard guilty of having planted the bomb and sentenced him to life in prison but acquitted the other defendants on the grounds of insufficient evidence.

The Pinkertons' willingness to spy in behalf of management was based on their belief that unionism did the workers more harm than good, a view conditioned by their early experiences with the most violent elements of a tactically unsophisticated labor movement. The agency, however, fell behind the times and did not officially abolish its industrial division until 1937, after a resolution by Congress declared spying unfair and illegal.

See James D. Horan, *The Pinkertons* (1967).—W. E. H.

Pitalesharo (1787?-?1832). Skidi Pawnee warrior, noted for his role in ending human sacrifice among his people. The son of Lachelesharo (Knife Chief), chieftain of the Skidi, Pitalesharo (Man Chief) by 1817 ranked first of his tribe's young warriors in bravery and honor. The event on which rests his fame occurred in the spring of that year, when he made a daring rescue of an Ietan Comanche girl who was about to be killed in a ritual sacrifice to the Skidi's Morning Star deity. Halting the ceremony abruptly, he cut the girl free from the scaffold on which she was bound, set her on a waiting horse, swiftly escorted her from camp, and after several days' journey westward sent her on homeward to rejoin her own people. In this dramatic act he was encouraged by his father, who had determined to abolish the Morning Star sacrifice after visiting St. Louis to confer with Indian superintendent William Clark.

Reports of Pitalesharo's deed were soon published, and in 1821, when he traveled east from central Nebraska with a Pawnee delegation, the youthful war chief was publicly honored with the award of a silver medal bearing the legend "To the Bravest of the Brave," presented by the young ladies of a Washington, D.C., female seminary. His heroism was further perpetuated in John Bell's account of Major Stephen Long's 1820 expedition to the Rocky Mountains.

Pitalesharo died between 1825 and 1833, probably in the smallpox epidemic of 1832, which carried off his father and half the Skidi tribe.

The most reliable account appears in George E. Hyde, *Pawnee Indians* (1951), which rectifies errors in earlier accounts based upon the information of J. B. Dunbar. —K. N. O.

Pittman, Key (1872-1940). Nevada politician. Born in Vicksburg, Mississippi, Pittman passed a university entrance examination before reaching his fifteenth birthday and spent three years attending Southwestern Presbyterian University in Clarksville, Tennessee. On impulse, before graduation, Pittman decided to go west and arrived in Seattle, Washington, in 1890. He was admitted to the Washington state bar in 1892 but practiced only five years before leaving for the Klondike, arriving at Dawson in September 1897. He moved to Nome in 1899, participated in the formation of a "consent," or "squatter," government, and was appointed its first district attorney. Pittman left Alaska in the autumn of 1901, going first to San Francisco and the next year moving to Tonopah in southern Nevada during the new mining boom. Immediately successful there as an attorney, he moved into politics and in 1910 was nominated by the Democrats to run for United States senator against the Republican incumbent, George Nixon. In the November election, the Democrats won the state legislature but Pittman had agreed to a popular referendum which gave Nixon a 1,105 vote victory. However, Nixon died in 1912 and Pittman was elected by the state legislature in January 1913 to fill the unexpired term. He was reelected to the Senate four times.

In the Senate Pittman spent a great deal of his time, along with other western senators, fighting to raise the price of silver to a point where silver mining in Nevada and other states would be encouraged. For a number of years before World War I the silver price had averaged about sixty cents an ounce, a price that was much too low for any but the most efficient producers. However, war conditions, particularly Great Britain's use of silver to purchase war matériel in India, forced the silver price to more than $1 an ounce. By the early part of 1918, Britain had exhausted its silver supply and called upon the United States for financial assistance. The emergency measure, authored by Pittman and often called the Pittman Act of 1918, which provided for a loan of silver bullion to Great Britain, in effect guaranteed the American silver miner a minimum of $1 an ounce for at least four years. He also was author of the Silver Purchase Act of 1934.

Pittman's seniority on the Foreign Relations Committee ultimately projected him into the chairmanship of the committee when Franklin D. Roosevelt took office in 1933. His lack of training in this field, his isolationist viewpoint, and his growing alcohol problem brought severe criticism of his role as chairman of that committee.

See Fred L. Israel, *Nevada's Key Pittman* (1963). The Pittman papers are in the Library of Congress.—R. R. E.

Placerville, California. Mining town. Placerville was the first big gold camp after the discovery of gold at Coloma and was the boisterous gateway to the goldfields that sprouted up throughout central California. The original camp, called Old Dry Diggings, was renamed Hangtown after residents there hanged several men accused of robbery. It became Placerville in 1851. Although the surface gold in the immediate Placerville area had played out by 1851, the town continued to thrive as a transportation and commercial center. The telegraph, the Pony Express, and several stage lines ran through the town. Later it served as a supply center for the Comstock Lode operations in Nevada. Among the town's early merchants were Mark Hopkins, Phillip D. Armour, and John M. Studebaker. Today lumbering has replaced mining as the town's principal industry, and most of the old buildings are camouflaged with plaster, paint, and advertising.

See Remi Nadeau, *Ghost Towns and Mining Camps of California* (1965); and Muriel S. Wolle, *The Bonanza Trail* (1953).—R. B. W.

Plant, Henry Bradley (1819-1899). Southern railroad builder and developer. Born near Branford, Connecticut, Plant was of a prosperous farm family. After the death of his father, when Plant was six, his mother remarried and moved first to Martinsburg, New York, and then to New Haven. Plant was a bright boy who so impressed his grandmother that she offered to send him to Yale to become a minister. Desiring a different kind of life, he refused, and at age eighteen he became a cabin boy on a small steamer operating between New Haven and New York. He later transferred to the Adams Express Company and after a few years headed the New York office. In 1852 he was put in charge of all the company's operations south of the Potomac and Ohio rivers.

In 1853 his wife was forced to go south for her health and he spent several months in Jacksonville where he noted the opportunities for development that the region offered. As the Civil War approached, Adams Express divided their properties to prevent confiscation. All southern operations were turned over to Plant as the Southern Express Company, incorporated in Georgia. The company acted as a fiscal agent for the Confederate government. In 1863 his health failed and Plant went to Europe for a rest.

After the Civil War southern railroads were disorganized and bankrupt. Plant saw in this state of affairs the opportunity to build a rail empire. In 1879 he began purchasing railroads in the southern Atlantic region. In 1882, with the assistance of Florida businessmen Henry M. Flagler, M. K. Jesup, and William T. Walters, he organized the Plant Investment Company to manage his various properties. Standardizing and reconstructing his roads, he built them into a system that gave speedier service between Florida and the North. Making Tampa the southern terminus of his system, he built the palatial Tampa Bay Hotel in a Moorish architectural style. He operated a line of steamships from Tampa to Havana. At his death his transportation empire included two thousand one hundred miles of track, fourteen railroad companies, a number of hotels, and several steamship lines. In his will he attempted to prevent the division of his properties, but his widow, Margaret Loughman, contested it successfully. Thereafter, the Plant System was merged with the Atlantic Coast Line Railroad.

See G. Hutchinson Smyth, *The Life of Henry Bradley Plant* (1898).—H. J. D.

plantation system. The southern plantation system was an important factor in expansion across the frontier of the Old West and the coastal Southwest (see AGRICULTURAL EXPANSION). *Plantation* may be defined in several different ways. First, it may be considered in the elementary terms of acreage. There was no rigid agreement on this point. A plantation could vary from five hundred to fifty thousand acres. Anything under five hundred acres was regarded most likely as a yeoman farm. A second criterion was the kind of labor system involved. Generally both indentured and chattel Negro slaves were employed. Third was the matter of capitalization, and finally the kinds of crops grown. There was a tendency for southern planters to produce semitropical crops, such as tobacco, rice, sugarcane, cotton, and indigo.

By no means was the plantation system of agriculture of purely southern origin or confined only to North America. English, Spanish, and French planters operated plantations in the West Indies and South America. Nevertheless, the availability of vast expanses of cheap western lands was highly conducive to expansion of this mode of agricultural operation into the fresh lands acquired from the southern Indians in the 1830s. Planters operated plantations in Virginia, Maryland, the Carolinas, and Georgia, and after 1785 in the bluegrass regions of Kentucky and Middle Tennessee. Following the War of 1812 and the rapid expansion of the growing and machine processing and manufacture of cotton, the lower southern plantation-slave system was extended rapidly and broadly into the Gulf coastal area and the lower Mississippi valley.

Essentially, the plantation system demanded a rather high degree of economic specialization. The early Virginia plantations along the James River and in eastern Maryland were engaged largely in the production of tobacco, grain, and livestock. In time the repetitive planting of these crops leeched the thin sandy soils of their nutrients and necessitated either the opening of fresh lands from nearby forests or removal to the western frontier in search of better soils. In the tidewater areas field crops shared interest with the exploitation of the virgin pine forests for naval stores, mast timbers, and lumber and shingles.

To the south and along the Carolina coast the tidelands were devoted to the growing of the highly specialized crops of rice, indigo, and sea island cotton. Rice especially was a fairly satisfactory crop, which could be readily adapted to both the use of slave labor and extensive methods of cultivation. Certainly it was highly adapted to the capitalistic mode of planter economics. Almost all the way around the Atlantic and Gulf coasts in the eighteenth century both English and Latin planters engaged in some kind of capital form operation, whether it be growing rice, sugarcane, small grains, livestock, or the harvesting of forest products.

The old specialized crops were severely limited as to their adaptations to broad expansion, either by nature of climate and soil or by credit availability and productive facilities. Before the end of the eighteenth century the beginnings of the expansion of the short staple cotton belt, made possible by the invention of the cotton gin in 1793, opened both a new landed and capital plantation frontier. Short staple cotton, unlike all other specialized crops, could be grown on a wide variety of lands and under considerably variable conditions of climate and modes of cultivation.

In many ways cotton was one of America's most hardy crops (see COTTON CULTURE). Between 1794 and 1815 the cotton plantation system was in a formative period. It was confronted with problems of organization, of procuring supplies on credit terms, and of securing a sufficient amount of labor. Equally important was the perfecting of processing machines, development of a market, and expansion of a factorage system. By the end of the War of 1812 cotton planters were poised and ready to penetrate the southwestern frontier at four different points: the Black Belt of Alabama and Mississippi, the great bend region of the Tennessee River, the lower Mississippi valley, and the Yazoo Delta and West Tennessee.

As the British markets for American raw materials were again opened and there was demand for cotton, southern planters opened the second phase of plantation history by multiplying the numbers of new plantations, the importation from the upper South and Africa of additional slaves, and by the rapid increase of cotton production. The third period was the years 1830-60, when further expansion led to the removal of the eastern Indian tribes. Hardly had the last word been uttered on the Dancing Rabbit Creek treaty ground before cotton planters crowded onto the Choctaw lands of Alabama and Mississippi. Production of cotton rose steadily, the number of Negro slaves increased, and the capitalistic system of land acquisition and productive credit was intensified. This was especially true of the old colonial factorage system, which was both adopted and expanded to meet the growing needs of the plantation economy. This factorage procedure served a supply, credit-granting, and marketing function. It enabled planters without readily available cash assets to operate a plantation on future crop expectations. By 1840 the plantation frontier had advanced west of the Mississippi as far away as Texas and as far north as southwest Missouri, and was particularly involved in the growing of cotton and sugarcane.

Because of its highly specialized nature of crops grown, the use of slave labor, the location of the major markets, and the nature of capital needs, it was inevitable that the plantation system would find itself caught up in such major political and social crises as the War of 1812, the Missouri controversy, banking and tariff issues, social controversy over slavery, and a sharp sectional division of political points of view. The plantation played a tremendously important role in advancing the frontier westward. It influenced attitudes toward Indian occupation of the land, toward the modes of land use and legislation, military policy, the use of the western rivers and natural arteries of transportation, and internal improvement policies. Likewise, planter interests were influential in shaping reactions to many national issues.

See Charles S. Davis, *The Cotton Kingdom in Alabama* (1939); Clement Eaton, *A History of the Old South* (1949); Lewis C. Gray, *History of Agriculture of the Southern United States to 1860*, 2 vols. (1933); U. B. Phillips, *Life and Labor in the Old South* (1929); and Charles S. Sydnor, *Slavery in Mississippi* (1933).—T. D. C.

plants. See VEGETATION.

Platte River. The Platte has been described as "a thousand miles long and six inches deep"; according to another observer, "At times it is almost dry, and may be forded in particular places with almost dry feet; while at others, it is difficult to conceive of the volume of water that seeks a level, with astonishing rapidity, through its wide cut channels." Its name is derived from the French word for broad, flat, or shallow.

Although these descriptions are true of the course of the river across the Plains, its headwaters do rise in the Rockies. The North Platte River originates in north-central Colorado, flows into Wyoming through Northgate Canyon, and continues northward through mountainous country to a point near Casper, Wyoming, before turning southeasterly through eastern Wyoming and western Nebraska. At North Platte, Nebraska, it is joined by the South Platte River to form the main stem of the Platte.

The South Platte rises about fifty miles southwest of Denver on the eastern slopes of the Continental Divide northwest of Fairplay, Colorado. Its headwater area is backed by a 10,000-foot mountain wall; down it pours torrents of water from time to time. The river emerges from the mountains about fifteen miles south of Denver and flows northward through that city toward Greeley, where it makes an eastward bend and flows across the Plains to join the North Platte River. Along its 442-mile course, the river's gradient varies greatly. Near its source, the slope is more than 1,000 feet per mile, but as it reaches the Plains, the slope decreases to 15 feet per mile and then to less than 8 feet per mile at its juncture with the North Platte.

The main stem of the Platte is a meandering, sandy, island-studded stream fed mostly by underground and surface flows from the north. In many places the stream has no permanent channel but follows any one of several channels for a period of time before changing to another. Today, the flow in some sections is extremely erratic because of diversions for irrigation and the generation of power. The channel of the stream downstream from the city of North Platte is relatively wide and flat until the stream enters the gorge leading to the Missouri River at Ashland, Nebraska.

The largest tributary of the Platte is the Loup River, which flows out of the sandhills of Nebraska in a well-defined valley that is incised to depths 100 to 200 feet below the level of the plain. Much of the flow is derived from seepage from the sandhills, which act as sponges to soak up the moisture that falls on the area.

Most of the water supply in the basin originates in the Rocky Mountains of Colorado. Its flow is augmented by Colorado River water brought in a tunnel through the mountains to the Platte. Melting snow in the spring months brings peak flows from April to mid-July; at this time water is needed for crops and large quantities of water are diverted for irrigation on both the North and South Platte. Thus, streamflows at the mouths of these streams are greatly affected by irrigation diversions upstream.

Spaniards may have been the first to reach the Platte River as they traveled northward across the Plains from Quivira, but it was French *voyageurs* who explored and opened the Platte basin for trade in the early eighteenth century. In 1738-39 an expedition led by Pierre and Paul Mallet and six other Canadians went south from the Missouri and then up the Platte before turning south on their way to Santa Fe. Because of the strength of the Plains Indians, no settlements were made.

The movement to the Oregon country and later to the California gold fields established the Platte as the main highway to the West (see OREGON TRAIL). The river offered a fairly direct route leading from the points at which immigrants collected along the frontier to the main opening through the Rockies, known as South Pass. Water and grass were available along the route for horses and cattle, and trees and shrubs were available at places along the river bottoms for use as fuel. When wagons began rolling alongside the river in great numbers in the early 1840s, the Platte River route was simply a broad path cut across a wide expanse of grazing land on which thousands of head of buffalo roamed. It consisted of two strands, one on each side of the river, that were essentially independent of one another. Useless for navigation because of the braided nature of its bed, the Platte also formed a barrier to those wanting to cross it.

The northern strand originated near Council Bluffs and Omaha, crossed the Platte near its mouth, and then proceeded westward along the north bank of the river. The southern strand left the Missouri near Independence and Westport and moved up the Republican River before cutting northwest to the Platte at Fort Kearny. Both strands led to other outposts of American settlement, the fur-trading posts in the Rockies. The most important was Fort Laramie, established in 1834 at the juncture of Laramie Creek and the North Platte. It then became a military base from 1849 to 1890. From Fort Laramie the route led up a relatively easy gradient to South Pass, across the Continental Divide, and on to the Pacific. Following the discovery of gold in California thousands of wagons used the route, and the trail soon became a series of ruts that can still be followed in places today.

The Platte River and the land along it have seen many changes since the gold miners trudged along its banks. It continued to be a major thoroughfare leading from the Missouri westward—followed by the overland stages carrying passengers and mail, the Pony Express, the railroad built west from Omaha, and finally by one of the major transcontinental highways. In places where immigrants let their horses and cattle graze, irrigated fields now produce bountiful crops.

In the early days settlement along the route had been confined to places near military posts, but as the Plains Indians were gradually brought under control, individuals established additional way stations to provide for the needs of travelers. Some established farms to grow feed for livestock and built corrals to keep cattle to fatten, for the once lush grasslands had deteriorated badly under heavy use.

The discovery of gold near Denver in 1858 had two immediate effects on the basin of the Platte. It brought cattle northward from Texas to mingle with eastern cattle abandoned on the Plains by westward-bound miners. It also stimulated the development of irrigational agriculture along the South Platte to provide vegetables for the miners. Water that had been used to wash gravels for gold was reused to provide food. As a result streams such as Clear Creek became muddy, and the flow of the South Platte diminished further.

The railroads further stimulated settlement, especially along the South Platte in the 1870s. The most notable of the new settlements were at Longmont and Greeley. The growth of the sugar-beet industry around the beginning of the twentieth century further aided agricultural development of the region.

The land along the North Platte remained relatively undeveloped until after the Bureau of Reclamation was established in 1902. The North Platte project, authorized for construction in 1903, was one of the bureau's first projects and provides water for extensive farmlands in eastern Wyoming and western Nebraska. Settlements along the Lower Platte depended originally on water from the river but since the early 1940s have been sustained by pumped groundwater. The basin today supports almost two million people, with agriculture giving way to industry and commerce.

For map, see MISSOURI RIVER.

See Alexander R. Crabb, *Empire on the Platte* (1967). —R. W. D.

Pleasant Valley War. See GRAHAM-TEWKSBURY FEUD.

Plenty Coups (1848-1932). Crow Indian chief. Aleek-chea-akoosh, meaning "many accomplishments," or Plenty Coups, was born near Billings, Montana. At about the age of fourteen he traveled to the Crazy Mountains in southern Montana to receive the revelation of his "medicine." This revelation usually consisted of a dream in which the animal, bird, or object which dominated it was considered to be the guardian or the protective medicine of the dreamer. For Plenty Coups his medicine was the chickadee, and his unusual dream when interpreted by the Indian council predicted success for the Crow if they remained friends with the white man. He became chief of a major subgroup at age twenty-five. Plenty Coups assisted in obtaining Crow Indians as guides for General George A. Custer in his disastrous march in 1876 and for the army in pursuit of Chief Joseph and his Nez Percé band in 1877. He quieted a threatened uprising among the Crow in 1887. When an envoy to Washington was needed, Plenty Coups's knowledge of English made him a logical choice. The

Northern Pacific and Burlington railroads welcomed his negotiating skills when claims for building across the Indian lands were being settled. In World War I he urged young Indians to serve in the military in order to acquire experience and desirable skills. He represented all the Indians of the nation at the dedication of the Tomb of the Unknown Soldier in 1921, speaking simply but eloquently:

> For the Indians of America I call upon the Great Spirit of the Red Men with gesture and chant and tribal tongue that the dead should not have died in vain, that war might end, that peace be purchased by the blood of Red Men and White.

In 1928 at the age of eighty he gave forty acres of his ranch "to be used in perpetuity for the Crow people and used as a public park by them and others irrespective of race and color." It is now a state park. When Plenty Coups died, the Crow honored him by passing a resolution to the effect that the term *tribal chief* should never be used by future leaders.

See Frank B. Linderman, *American: The Life Story of Plenty Coups* (1930); and Norman B. Wiltsey, "Plenty Coups, Crow Chief," *Montana, The Magazine of Western History*, vol. 13 (1963).—M. G. B.

Plummer, Henry (1837?-1864). Outlaw. Originally from the East (probably Connecticut or New York), Plummer turned up in the California mining region in 1852. For about a decade he dabbled in politics, served as a law officer (killing a man along the way), and swept ladies off their feet—a pattern of life that was to be repeated in Plummer's more famous Montana career. Plummer escaped punishment for his California sins, but after ten years his reputation as a fighter, killer, and jail breaker made it wise for him to head north in 1861 to Washington Territory and then on to Idaho, where he secretly led a murderous band of robbers. By 1862 Plummer was in present Montana in the era of its great gold rush.

Handsome, well spoken, upright in bearing, and generally ingratiating, Plummer attracted people to him. This was a key factor in his success as a *sub-rosa* bandit chief. The Montana pioneers took to Plummer as had those of California and Idaho. Settling in Bannack, it was not long before he was elected sheriff—his killing of his brutal former henchman, Jack Cleveland (for which he was acquitted in trial), notwithstanding. Plummer's office of sheriff was the perfect cover for his other role: that of secret leader of an infamous gang of road agents that spread terror throughout southern and western Montana with their robberies and murders. Primarily a gang of youngsters led by a still-young man, the Plummer crew operated with an almost juvenile fervor. So great were the depredations—more than one hundred were robbed or murdered—that the settlers of Bannack and Virginia City rose as vigilantes and wiped out the gang in one of the notable lynch-law campaigns in American history. Plummer himself was hanged in Bannack on January 10, 1864.

Plummer's outlaw career and its ultimate denouement was given wide publicity in contemporary newspapers and in Thomas J. Dimsdale's widely reprinted classic with a strong pro-vigilante viewpoint, *The Vigilantes of Montana* (1866). It seems probable that Plummer's devious history was the original for more than a century of stories, novels, movies, and television dramas that have taken for their theme the villainous western sheriff—the apparently honest and brave law officer who (it is learned in the last chapter or the last reel) is in truth the covert head of the nefarious outlaw band.

See Hoffman Birney, *Vigilantes* (1929); and Nathaniel Pitt Langford, *Vigilante Days and Ways* (1890).—R. M. B.

Plymouth Colony. The colonial scholar Samuel Eliot Morison once lamented what he called the "flapdoodle about the *Mayflower* and the Pilgrim fathers," for he observed quite correctly that the popular myths about the settlers landing on Plymouth Rock, building log cabins in the wilderness, and hunting turkeys with blunderbusses only confused the true history of the Plymouth Colony. The Pilgrims' story began in 1607 when a group of Separatists, including William Bradford, William Brewster, and the Reverend John Robinson, formed a small church at Scrooby in Nottinghamshire, England. These men believed that the practices of the Church of England had become so corrupt that good Christians could no longer remain a part of it. In fact, God expected them to break away immediately— "without tarrying for any." But local Anglican magistrates had other ideas and harassed the Separatists. In 1608 the Scrooby Congregation departed for Holland, moving first to Amsterdam and then on to Leyden, where it was allowed to worship in peace.

Despite Holland's religious toleration, many of the Pilgrims were unhappy in Leyden. Some found it difficult to master the Dutch language; others were forced to take up unfamiliar trades. Moreover, as the children of the Scrooby Congregation were assimilated into the new culture, they began to lose interest in the theological issues that had driven their fathers from England. When it was rumored that Catholic Spain might seize Holland, the Pilgrim leaders decided it was time to transfer to the New World. They received a patent from the London Company for land in Virginia, but since the Pilgrims were so poor, they were unable to pay for the transportation and supplies that were required. Thomas Weston, an unscrupulous London merchant, offered to underwrite the costs of colonization if the Pilgrims would form a joint-stock company with a group of Weston's associates. The two parties—the Pilgrims and the merchants—agreed that at the end of seven years the profits and property of the colony would be distributed equally among the shareholders. Until the division the company was to control all commercial ventures, including agriculture and trade. In practice the agreement proved unworkable, and Weston deserted the Pilgrims when it became clear that the enterprise was not going to yield large returns.

In the early years almost everything seemed to go against the Pilgrims, and a people of less faith and courage would probably have given up the attempt to settle America. The Pilgrims landed near Provincetown late in 1620, poorly equipped to meet the challenge before them. In addition they possessed almost no knowledge about the geography of New England and spent valuable time searching out a suitable site for their community. Plymouth was eventually selected for its harbor and easy access to fresh water. During the first winter dozens of underfed, disheartened colonists died. The London merchants, who were supposed to have provided Plymouth with supplies, did not fulfill their bargain, dumping new settlers but no food on the struggling colony. In 1627 the colonists decided to buy out their English partners, but this purchase created a huge debt that took seventeen years and a great amount of personal sacrifice to pay off. If the Pilgrims had been better businessmen their story might well have been happier.

The Pilgrims had no legal right to settle in New England, for their patent from the London Company had been for lands in Virginia. In the absence of a charter, some of the settlers (Bradford called them strangers) claimed that "none had power to command them." In order to avoid civil contention, Pilgrim leaders drew up the Mayflower Compact, a temporary covenant signed by forty-one persons in 1620. The signers, Pilgrims as well as non-Pilgrims, agreed to "Covenant and Combine ourselves together into a Civil Body Politic, for our better ordering and preservation. . . ." They promised "due submission and obedience" to any officers elected by the freemen of Plymouth. The signers then chose John Carver as their governor. Although the Mayflower Compact had no legal force the settlers appear to have accepted it as the basis of their government until 1621, when they received a new patent.

American historians have assigned the Mayflower Compact far greater importance than it deserves. George Bancroft, the great nineteenth-century scholar, called it "the birth of popular constitutional liberty." This interpretation, however, was based on a misunderstanding of seventeenth-century political theory. The Pilgrims had no intention of setting up a democracy in the American wilderness, and in 1623 Governor Bradford specifically denied rumors that Plymouth was a democracy or that everyone had the right to vote. The Pilgrim settlers believed that it was their responsibility to choose magistrates of superior wealth, education, and piety. Once such officers had been selected, the people had no right to question the decisions of government.

In 1621 the Council for New England awarded the Pilgrims a new patent. The government that evolved in Plymouth was similar to that of Massachusetts and Connecticut. The freemen, persons who had met a property qualification, chose a governor, a council of assistants, and representatives from each of the towns. Bradford was selected governor of Plymouth after John Carver died in 1621 and was reelected thirty times. He possessed broad discretionary powers, but he seems to have used them fairly and wisely. As governor, Bradford always hoped to obtain a royal charter for Plymouth, but his efforts were unsuccessful. This failure probably made it inevitable that the larger, more populous Massachusetts would eventually annex the Pilgrim colony.

The Pilgrims had originally planned a fishing community, but they quickly discovered that they did not know much about fishing. They then turned to furs, establishing trading posts from the Kennebec to the Connecticut River. These ventures never prospered, however, and it was soon apparent that Plymouth's economy would have to rely on its own agriculture. The colony flourished during the Great Migration to Massachusetts, since the new Puritan settlers purchased grain and livestock at inflated prices from the Pilgrims. During the second half of the seventeenth century,

Plymouth became an economic satellite of the Bay Colony, producing crops that Puritan merchants carried to the West Indies. It was not until Plymouth became part of Massachusetts in 1691 that a thriving shipbuilding industry developed within the old Pilgrim colony.

The earliest account of Plymouth Colony is Bradford's *History of Plymouth Plantation*, written between 1630 and 1650; in a simple but forceful style, he related how the Pilgrim community fit into God's plan. A 1952 edition of the *History* has been edited by Samuel Eliot Morison. The fullest account of the colony is George D. Langdon, Jr., *Pilgrim Colony, A History of New Plymouth 1620-1691* (1966). On the colony's economy, see Darrett B. Rutman, *Husbandmen of Plymouth* (1967). Of special interest are Samuel Eliot Morison, "New Light Wanted on the Old Colony," *William and Mary Quarterly*, vol. 15 (1958), and John Demos, "Notes on Life in Plymouth Colony," *Ibid.*, vol. 22 (1965).—T. H. B.

Poe, Orlando M. See GREAT LAKES, MEN OF THE.

Poindexter, George (1799-1853). Mississippi politician. Historian J. F. H. Claiborne probably summed up Poindexter's career accurately when he wrote: "The history of his career is, in fact, the history of the Territory and the State, so closely and prominently was he connected with everything that occurred." Born in Virginia, Poindexter came to Mississippi Territory in 1802, and from that time until his defeat by Robert John Walker in the 1835 United States senatorial election he was active in Mississippi politics. He held almost every major office in territorial or state government it was possible to hold and also represented Mississippi in the United States House of Representatives as well as the Senate.

Originally a Jeffersonian Republican, Poindexter soon moved away from Jeffersonianism except in such intellectual phases as religious toleration and freedom of expression. Poindexter wanted to construct a society based on planters, not small farmers. He supported Andrew Jackson during "Old Hickory's" first administration but became his greatest critic during the second administration. Poindexter's actual break with the administration resulted from a local matter—the dispensation of patronage. Poindexter fought unsuccessfully the appointment of Samuel Gwin to the office of register of the Land Office at Clinton, Mississippi. But the bank question was the major issue. Of the Mississippi delegation in Congress, only Poindexter sustained the bank in its fight for recharter. All during Jackson's second administration he was one of the leaders in the fight against Jackson's banking policy. Poindexter's defeat in his bid for another term in the Senate in 1835 can be attributed to Jackson's continuing popularity in the state, prosperity, and Walker's able campaign as a Jacksonian against him.

From 1831 to 1835 Poindexter's story is as much a part of American history as it is of Mississippi history. The principal contributions he made to the state's history, however, were in his roles as "father" of the state's first constitution and the first codifier of the laws of the state.

In 1835 Poindexter moved to Lexington, Kentucky, to practice law, later practicing law in Jackson until his death.

See Mack Swearingen, *The Early Life of George Poindexter, a Story of the First Southwest* (1934).—J. E. G.

Point, Nicolas (1799-1868). Roman Catholic missionary and topographical artist. Father Point, born in France, went into the upper Missouri River country with Belgian missioner Pierre De Smet in 1841 to build a mission station among the Flathead Indians in the Bitterroot valley. After the founding of Sacred Heart Mission he ventured in 1845 among the Blackfoot and the Nez Percé of the Northwest, remaining in that country until 1847. Little else is recorded of his subsequent life or missionary service in the field, but the Jesuit Provincial House in St. Louis, Missouri, sponsor of the early missionary venture, retains more than one hundred of Father Point's sketches produced during his experiences among the Indians of the West. Other sketches formed the basis for lithographic illustrations in Father De Smet's published journal, *Oregon Missions and Travels Over the Rocky Mountains in 1845-46*.

See Nicolas Point, *Wilderness Kingdom* (1967). —D. C. H.

Pokagon, Leopold (1775-1841). Jesuit missionary. Pokagon was an Ojibwa captive, his Indian name being Pugegun ("Rib"), who became high civil chief of the Potawatomi. He was devoted to the memory of those Jesuits who had worked the area a half-century earlier, before the French king and later the pope suppressed the order. Thus at a time when Jesuit work was supposed to have disappeared, men such as Pokagon were keeping the work of this order alive. In 1830 he secured Stephen Badin as missionary to the Potawatomi.

Pokagon's son, Simon (1830-99), was educated at Notre Dame and Oberlin. He was highly regarded for his education and was also a noted speaker, especially at the World Exposition in 1893 in Chicago. Through his speaking and writing he influenced the public, Congress, and several presidents for the Indian cause.

See C. Buechner, *The Pokagons* (1933).—R. I. B.

polygamy. In dictionary terms, polygamy refers to a state in which men and women have two or more wives, husbands, or mates at the same time. In the West the term has generally been used to describe "plural marriage" practiced by the Latter-day Saints, under which the Mormon church sanctioned plural marriage for men only—technically polygyny but popularly known as polygamy.

The Mormons first engaged in plural marriage during the 1840s in Nauvoo, Illinois, although some sources date the practice as far back as 1831. Evidence suggests that by 1841 Joseph Smith, in accordance with supposed revelation, began to marry additional wives. His revelation on plural marriage was written down on July 12, 1843. Within a year many of the Apostles and other prominent men had secretly married plural wives. The revelation not only implied that plural marriage was right when men were so commanded, but also became the basis for the Mormon doctrine that marriage is an eternal union when performed by proper authority.

Like other Americans and European immigrants, the Mormons were members of a society based on monogamy. Because of this morality the new commandment to live polygamously met with resistance. Many Mormons fell away and some joined splinter groups (see LATTER-DAY SAINTS, REORGANIZED). A few men tried to take advantage of the revelation and entered into additional marriage contracts without Smith's or the church's permission. Some of them, when confronted

with chastisement or excommunication, became antagonistic and wrote bitter exposés. One such man, John C. Bennett, a confidant of Joseph Smith, was accused by the church of immoral practices. Following his excommunication in 1842, Bennett wrote a series of letters stating that he had infiltrated the Mormon church in order to expose its inner secrets. His lurid accusations, the publication of the inflammatory *Nauvoo Expositor*, and that paper's destruction by Nauvoo leaders as a community nuisance, were prominent among the factors that led to the murder of Joseph Smith and his brother Hyrum in 1844. Aside from exciting the local non-Mormons to mob violence, the anti-Smith writings unofficially announced Mormon plural marriage to the world.

In 1852, five years after Mormon Church headquarters had been moved to the Salt Lake valley and its members had achieved a certain security in their isolation, Apostle Orson PRATT officially and openly confirmed that plural marriage was, and had been, a church doctrine.

Not all Mormons were allowed to take part in "the new and everlasting covenant of celestial marriage." Only those who had demonstrated their worthiness, both spiritually and economically, were approved to practice "the principle of plurality." Even then, the ancient order of plural marriage that Smith claimed had been restored under the direction of God could only be contracted with permission from the church president. One further deterrent was the consent that each man needed to receive from his first wife. How many people participated in plural marriage is not known; percentages varied from five to fifteen percent of the married men in most Mormon communities.

Just why the Latter-day Saints turned to polygamy is uncertain. They felt, of course, that it was a commandment of God, but their biblical and modern arguments in defense of the custom were not persuasive to nineteenth-century non-Mormon Americans. Much of the agitation and persecution against the LDS church came about because of its practice (see LATTER-DAY SAINTS: *conflict with the nation*). The Mormons maintained that polygamy was needed in order to establish a royal priesthood before Christ's return. Polygamy would facilitate providing bodies for righteous spirits that were waiting to come to earth (see LATTER-DAY SAINTS: *theology*). Latter-day Saints also believed that if ancient Jews and early Christians had plural wives, so also should Mormons, as part of the "restoration of all things" in latter days. Mormon writers further declared that polygamy prevented adultery and prostitution. Monogamy had created immorality, and monogamists who secretly and without God's sanction lived promiscuously were living in sin. They also argued that men would acquire wisdom and women unselfishness through plural marriage. Generally speaking, Mormon polygamy was a religious principle by which Latter-day Saints hoped to redeem the human family, produce an elite of righteous people, and build the kingdom of God. But all the various justifications for polygamy were secondary to the belief that God had commanded it through his prophets. Moreover, none of these considerations was sufficient to persuade more than a relatively small percentage of Mormon men to marry plural wives.

When John C. Frémont ran for president of the United States in 1856, the Republican platform called for an end to "the twin relics of barbarism," slavery and polygamy. In the years that followed a number of congressional acts were designed to punish practitioners and discourage its practice.

When the United States Supreme Court in 1890 upheld the constitutionality of the Edmunds-Tucker Act, which had disincorporated the LDS church and escheated its property, Mormon president Wilford Woodruff issued the "Manifesto," which directed members of the church to forego further plural marriages. For a brief period Mormon colonists in Mexico and Canada continued to sanction plural marriages, but all such possibilities were officially closed in 1904. Small groups of excommunicated "Fundamentalists" have continued the practice in recent years in some remote areas of southern Utah and northern Arizona.

See Stanley S. Ivins, "Notes on Mormon Polygamy," *Western Humanities Review* (Summer 1956); and Kimball Young, *Isn't One Wife Enough?* (1954). —D. M. Q.

Pomeroy, Earl S. (1915-   ). Historian. Pomeroy was born in Capitola, California. He was educated at San Jose State College and the University of California at Berkeley, where he worked under Frederick L. Paxson, one of the prominent historians of his day. Pomeroy began teaching in 1940 at the University of Wisconsin. In 1942 he moved to the University of North Carolina, in 1945 to Ohio State University, and in 1949 to the University of Oregon, where he remained for more than two decades, after 1961 as Beekman Professor. He also was lecturer at the Bologna Center of Johns Hopkins University in 1963-64 and as Coe Visiting Professor at Stanford University in 1967-68. In 1975 he left Oregon to accept a professorship at the University of California, San Diego.

In his various writings Pomeroy continuously urged his colleagues to broaden their outlook and perspectives and to place the field of western history within the mainstream of American history. His first major book, *The Territories and the United States, 1861-1890* (1947), won the Albert B. Beveridge Award of the American Historical Association. In this provocative volume Pomeroy focused attention on an important but much neglected phase of western history, the administration of the territories conceived as part of a far-flung colonial system. The book opened up a hitherto obscure subject for students of the West. He developed his theme in *Pacific Outpost: American Strategy in Guam and Micronesia* (1951). In various articles in the *Mississippi Valley Historical Review* and in essays Pomeroy then pleaded with western historians to extend their conceptual frameworks beyond the frontier theories espoused by Frederick Jackson Turner. He urged them to adapt new methods and concepts from the social sciences and to delve into unexplored aspects of western history, especially social and cultural trends, and the entire history of the region during the twentieth century.

Pomeroy himself attempted to follow his own prescription. His *In Search of the Golden West: The Tourist in Western America* (1957) dealt with a significant but little-studied aspect of western history. In *The Pacific Slope: A History of California, Oregon, Washington, Idaho and Utah* (1965), Pomeroy attempted to emphasize unity amidst the diversity of their development. Thereafter Pomeroy

turned his attention to studies of the twentieth-century West.

Pomeroy was a frequent speaker at professional meetings and before historical societies. He was also an active teacher and trained an able group of young frontier historians in his seminars at the University of Oregon. Many honors have come to Pomeroy, including a Senior Fellowship of the National Endowment for the Humanities in 1968 and the presidency of the Pacific Coast branch of the American Historical Association in 1970.—G. D. N.

Ponca Indians. See SIOUAN TRIBES, SOUTHERN.

Ponce de León, Juan (1460?-1521). Spanish explorer of Florida. In 1513 Ponce de León, who had been governor of Haiti and Puerto Rico, received a patent to explore and exploit the islands of Bimini to the north of Cuba. It was rumored that there was a fountain of youth there, as well as great wealth. Ponce de León landed a few miles below the mouth of the St. Johns River and named the land *Pascua Florida*, for it was discovered at the time of the Feast of the Flowers (April 2 to 8, 1513). He then coasted southward, landed briefly south of Cape Kennedy, examined Biscayne Bay, sailed along the Florida Keys and the Tortugas (which he named), and then turned north to the central west coast area. This brought him to Charlotte Harbor or a little north of it. He landed on Pine Island off Carlos Sound and lost a man there in a skirmish with the Indians. By October 1513 he was back in Puerto Rico.

In 1521 he returned to Florida, which he still considered an island, and attempted colonization. Landing at Charlotte Harbor, he was attacked by the Indians and his settlement was abandoned. Ponce de León returned to Cuba to die of his wounds.

See T. Frederick Davis, "History of Juan Ponce de León's Voyages to Florida," in *Quarterly Periodical of the Florida Historical Society* (July 1935).—R. A. B.

Pond, Peter (1740-1807). Fur trader and explorer. Pond was a Yankee fur trader who participated in the exploration of the Canadian Northwest. In the French and Indian War he joined the British and engaged in four campaigns, receiving a commission in 1760. By the age of twenty he was a seasoned war veteran who could command men.

In 1765 Pond began to trade in the country around Detroit, and in ensuing years he established such a good reputation that in 1772 he entered into partnership with a successful trader named Graham to carry on trade from Michilimackinac. Successful in this, Pond became an independent trader as well as something of a peacemaker among the Indians, particularly the Yankton Sioux. However, in 1775 he left the upper Mississippi country to trade and explore in the Canadian Northwest. He is credited with discovering the Athabasca River and Lake Athabasca and developing a lucrative trade there. He was also the first to cross the Methye Portage into the Mackenzie River drainage basin, and he produced the first map of the Canadian Northwest (1785). Pond died in poverty.

See H. A. Innis, *Peter Pond, Fur Trader and Adventurer* (1930).—R. A. B.

Pond, Samuel (1808-1891) and **Gideon** (1810-1878). Missionaries. The Pond brothers, from Connecticut, arrived on the upper Mississippi in 1834 to convert the Sioux. They developed missions at Lake Calhoun, Lake

Harriet (present-day Minneapolis), and Lac qui Parle. Their major contribution was to transliterate the spoken Dakota (Sioux) language into a written language. At the Lac qui Parle mission, Gideon and three others translated the Bible into the new Dakota language. Together, the Pond brothers contributed a number of published works in Dakota—including a newspaper, catechism, and grammar.

Initially, they were independent and not ordained. They soon were taken under the wing of the American Board of Commissioners for Foreign Missions (representing the Congregational, Presbyterian, and Dutch Reformed churches). In 1837 Samuel was ordained a Congregational minister; in 1848 Gideon was ordained a Presbyterian minister.

See Theodore C. Blegen, ed., "Two Missionaries in the Sioux Country," *Minnesota History* (March, June, and September 1940).—R. W. F.

Pontiac's Rebellion (1763-1765). Pontiac was a member of the Ottawa tribe that in the mid-eighteenth century inhabited the eastern half of Michigan and adjoining parts of Ohio and Ontario. The date of his birth is unknown but was certainly sometime in the latter half of the first quarter of the century. Pontiac was tall, physically strong, light-skinned, possessed of an air of command, easily offended, and proud of manner. His tribe was closely associated with the Potawatomi, Ojibwa, and Huron, and with the French traders in the region. The Ottawa were highly competitive, a quality that involved them in rivalry with the Iroquois over the fur trade. By the 1760s the Indian situation in the Great Lakes region was disturbed both by French policies and by the French and Indian War. The Ottawa were inevitably drawn into the struggle, favoring the cause of the French, with whom they had the closest trading ties. Ottawa warriors were present at General Edward Braddock's defeat, and Pontiac himself may have been there. They gave strong support at the French Fort Duquesne, and even went as far east as the Lake Champlain frontier. Failure of the French to check English control of America in the war proved a bitter disappointment to most of the Great Lakes Indians, and Pontiac's absence from the peace conference with the Indians, which took place August 20, 1759, at Croghan Hall, reflected his personal animosity.

Although the Ottawa had never been friendly toward the British, a more immediate cause of Pontiac's Rebellion lay in the administration of Lord Jeffrey Amherst's austere Indian policy (see BRITISH ADMINISTRATIVE POLICY), and in new trading arrangements. Amherst hated Indians, and asked Colonel Henry Bouquet, British military commander in the West, if "could it not be contrived to send the Small Pox among those dissatisfied tribes?" Bouquet replied that he would distribute germ-ridden blankets, and that he wished he could employ dogs to hunt Indians down instead of wasting good men fighting them. In 1762 Amherst reduced the Indian department's appropriation by forty percent and ordered a halt to the practice of distributing presents to insure the loyalty of chiefs. The Indian reaction to such attitudes and policies was not surprising. A secret council was held at an Ottawa village on the Detroit River in the summer of 1762. The role of Pontiac in this council is not clear. At this time, the Great Lakes Indians were also influenced by the teachings of a Delaware mystic

prophet who traveled among them teaching a new era for the western tribes. Too, a few French agents talked of opposition to the English on several grounds, most of which the Indians were unable to appraise accurately. Pontiac no doubt was influenced by all these factors. As the head chief of three Ottawa villages near Detroit, he determined to organize a general Indian attack on British posts. He planned an immediate drive against Detroit, and then possibly an ever-widening series of attacks against other posts. Detroit was highly vulnerable, despite the capability of its commander, Major Henry Gladwyn.

On May 1, 1763, Pontiac and a band of forty or fifty braves visited Fort Detroit on a reconnaissance mission, but ostensibly to hold a dance. On May 5, 1763, a band of approximately three hundred braves were admitted to the fort, only to find it armed and alert. Major Gladwyn had been informed of Pontiac's intent by an unidentified person. Again on May 8, the Indians were back at the fort with Pontiac and three chiefs attempting to throw Gladwyn off guard. On the afternoon of May 9 the Indians crossed the Detroit River in large numbers to make a frontal attack on the fort. They were thwarted in this attempt, and there followed an extended siege that lasted until October 30. In time almost a thousand warriors were gathered in Detroit. Pontiac's hard core of followers were drawn principally from the Ottawa, Potawatomi, Ojibwa, and Huron, but segments of many other tribes were involved in the conflict as the news of the attack on Detroit spread across the frontier. The Shawnee and Delaware laid siege to Fort Pitt in late May. Mackinac was captured on June 7 when a force of Ojibwa, who were playing lacrosse beneath the walls of the fort, rushed inside after a ball and turned on the garrison. Forts Presqu' Isle, Le Boeuf, Sandusky, St. Joseph, and Ouiatanon were also taken by the Indians. By late July, the British had lost the West.

Amherst sent two expeditions to relieve the besieged posts. The first, under Captain James Dalyell, resupplied Detroit on July 29. The second, led by Bouquet, broke the siege of Fort Pitt by defeating the Indians at the bloody battle of Bushy Run in August. Discouraged by the failure of the French to give him support, and with his fickle followers melting away, Pontiac in October arranged a truce at Detroit that allowed him to retire to the Illinois country, where he hoped to reorganize for another offensive. Most of the tribes were ready for peace, however, and answered Sir William Johnson's call for a peace conference at Fort Niagara in the summer of 1764. Those that didn't (primarily Delaware and Shawnee) were crushed by expeditions under Bouquet and Colonel John Bradstreet, who marched through the Ohio country in July and August, burning every village they encountered. Pontiac himself concluded a treaty of peace through the mediation of George Croghan in May 1765, and visited Johnson at Oswego in 1766, professing allegiance to Britain. His intention was only to buy breathing space in which to rearm and reunite the Indians, but he found that the tribes were more interested in trade than war, and that his dealings with Johnson had destroyed his prestige among those warriors who were willing to fight. No longer respected or feared, Pontiac was murdered by an Illinois Indian at Cahokia in April 1769.

See Randolph C. Downes, *Council Fires on the Upper*

Ohio (1940); B. Knollenburg, "General Amherst and Germ Warfare," *Mississippi Valley Historical Review*, vol. 41 (1954); Francis Parkman, *History of the Conspiracy of Pontiac*, 4th rev. ed. (1868); Howard Peckham, *Pontiac and the Indian Uprising* (1947); and Dale Van Every, *Forth to the Wilderness: The First American Frontier, 1754-1774* (1961).—T. D. C.

Pony Express. The trans-Missouri Pony Express was inaugurated on April 3, 1860, between St. Joseph, Missouri, and Sacramento, California. The service was sponsored and financially supported by RUSSELL, MAJORS AND WADDELL, a well-known freighting firm that had also organized the Central Overland California and Pike's Peak Express Company to operate a mail and passenger service along the central route. An intense rivalry had developed between this organization and the OVERLAND MAIL COMPANY which delivered the mail under a government contract along a semicircular route from Missouri to Fort Smith, Arkansas, then southward through Texas, New Mexico, Arizona, into southern California, and north to San Francisco. Senator William M. Gwin of California, an ardent supporter of government aid to transportation, persuaded William H. Russell that a speedy mail delivery service on horseback would advertise the superiority of the shorter central route and might result in a lucrative mail contract. Gwin also agreed to seek financial reimbursement from Congress for the experiment. Alexander Majors and William B. Waddell doubted that a pony express was a sound business venture, but they reluctantly agreed to the experiment. Public announcement that the Pony Express would deliver letters for five dollars an ounce from Missouri to California within ten days, half the time necessary on the Overland Mail route, created a great excitement in business circles. Russell established 190 way stations between ten and fifteen miles apart and selected both horses and men known to have physical stamina. The mail was wrapped in oiled silk to protect it from the weather and placed in a leather mochila that fitted over the saddle.

Most trips of the ponies were confined to the distance between Fort Kearny, Nebraska, and Fort Churchill, Nevada, the terminals of the telegraph under construction. The crucial test for the service came in the winter of 1860-61, when a schedule of thirteen days was maintained between the ends of the telegraph lines and seventeen or eighteen days between St. Joseph and San Francisco. Although a dramatic success, the Pony Express was a financial failure, costing Russell, Majors and Waddell somewhere between $100,000 and $200,000, a loss they could ill afford. Moreover, the partnership did not get the anticipated mail contract. The Overland Mail Company, forced to abandon its route through Texas upon the outbreak of the Civil War, was reorganized and transferred its stagecoach service to the central route. On March 2, 1861, the government signed a contract with this company providing for a daily overland mail and a semiweekly Pony Express on the central route with an annual compensation of $1 million a year. Thus, during the last third of its eighteen-month existence, the Pony Express enjoyed a government subsidy, but, while the Overland Mail Company awarded Russell, Majors and Waddell a subcontract to carry both the Pony and stage mail on the line eastward from Salt Lake City, mounting losses and indebtedness of the latter

Pony Express rider Frank E. Webner (1861). (National Archives)

firm forced it into bankruptcy the following year. The Pony Express service came to an end in October 1861, with the completion of the overland telegraph.

Arthur Chapman, *The Pony Express* (1932), was for many years accepted as the standard book on the subject. Raymond W. Settle and Mary L. Settle, *Saddles and Spurs: The Pony Express Saga* (1955), places heavy emphasis upon the role of Russell, Majors and Waddell in inaugurating and operating the Pony Express in the initial months. Roy S. Bloss, *Pony Express—The Great Gamble* (1959), emphasizes the Wells, Fargo & Co. contribution, through the Overland Mail Company, in keeping the system going.—W. T. J.

Pope, John (1822-1892). Soldier. Pope was born into a politically prominent Illinois family and graduated seventeenth in his class from West Point in 1842. He received brevet ranks in the Mexican War, but most of his early career was spent as a surveyor in Minnesota and in the Southwest, where he experimented with artesian wells and participated in the Pacific railroad surveys. In the Civil War he won victories at New Madrid and Island No. 10 in 1862 and commanded the army of Virginia until his defeat at Second Bull Run.

In September 1862 Pope took command of the new Department of the Northwest and directed the campaign against the Santee Sioux, who had risen in August. He sent large forces against the Sioux in Dakota Territory in 1863 and 1864, and his administrative ability caused General Ulysses S. Grant to appoint him to the new Divison of the Missouri, which included most of the Plains country. Pope organized the unsuccessful Powder River campaign of 1865 against the Sioux and Cheyenne and briefly commanded the Department of the Missouri and the Third Military District in the South before returning to the West in 1870.

From 1870 to 1883, Pope commanded the Department of the Missouri and sought to control the tribes of the southern Plains. Several columns operated under his command in the Red River War (1874-75), and he was deeply involved in efforts to control the Apache in New Mexico. He directed the troop movements against the Ute (1879-81) and attempted to keep the land-hungry "Boomers" out of Indian Territory. From 1883 until his retirement in 1886, he commanded the Division of the Pacific.

By 1886 Pope had exercised command over all of the trans-Mississippi West except Texas and during that time was one of the most vocal critics of federal Indian policy. He favored military control of Indian affairs, but he also encouraged missionaries to work with the Indians, insisted that Indians on the reservations be well-treated, and shared with humanitarians the goal of assimilating the Indians into white society.

See Richard N. Ellis, *General Pope and the U.S. Indian Policy* (1970).—R. N. E.

popular sovereignty. Popular sovereignty, which in general means the right of the people to self-determination, referred in the antebellum period to a specific solution to the problem of slavery in national territories. Often called "squatter sovereignty" by southerners, it meant that slavery should not be established in or banished from a territory by congressional statute. Rather, the people of the territory should determine by majority rule through their elected political bodies whether or not they wanted slavery. Precisely when they could make this decision—during the territorial phase or in writing a constitution to apply for statehood—was an unclear and often hotly debated point.

Sectional divisions within the Democratic party played an important role in the emergence of the principle. It first gained prominence during the controversy over the Wilmot Proviso, which would prohibit slavery in land ceded by Mexico to the United States. Western Democrats such as Lewis Cass in his Nicholson Letter of December 1847 and then Stephen A. Douglas offered the doctrine as a compromise position between congressional prohibition of slavery from the territories and the demand by John C. Calhoun and his southern followers that slavery be allowed to go into any federal territory. By removing the decision on slave extension from Congress, popular sovereignty was a way to reduce sectional tension and preserve party unity. In the election of 1848 Cass, the Democratic candidate, fell back on the doctrine to unify his party. When the territories of Utah and New Mexico were organized as part of the Compromise of 1850, popular sovereignty was applied. Not only could the people of those territories decide whether they wanted to enter the Union as free or slave states, but the territorial legislatures were explicitly given the right to legislate on the issue in the territorial phase.

The most controversial application of the doctrine to territories came in the Kansas-Nebraska Act of 1854, which repealed the Missouri Compromise prohibition of slavery. (Douglas argued that it had been superseded by the principles of the Compromise of 1850.) Northern and southern settlers poured into Kansas, and a struggle for control of the territory ensued. The new Republican party denounced popular sovereignty because it condoned the possible extension of slavery; nevertheless, the Democratic party in its national platform of 1856 endorsed the formula as the official party solution to the problem of slavery in the territories. The Democrats could do this because the meaning of popular sovereignty was ambiguous. Northern Democrats argued that a territorial legislature could prohibit slavery from a territory, while southern Democrats maintained that no decision could be made until the territory was ready to apply for statehood.

The aftermath of two developments in 1857 destroyed the viability of popular sovereignty as a compromise solution. In 1857 the Supreme Court ruled in the Dred Scott decision that Congress could not prohibit slavery from a territory; the implication was that Congress could not delegate this authority to a territorial legislature, as the northern interpretation of popular sovereignty asserted. Faced with Republican charges that his doctrine could no longer keep slavery out of the territories, Douglas argued in the summer of 1857 that while a territorial legislature could not legally prohibit slavery it could keep slavery out of a territory by refusing to pass positive slave codes, which were necessary for the establishment of the institution. Thus Douglas announced in 1857 what became the famous Freeport Doctrine of the Lincoln-Douglas debates in the following year.

Also in 1857, the Lecompton constitution was adopted against the wish of the majority of settlers in Kansas. When President James Buchanan attempted to force Congress to accept that proslavery constitution, Douglas split with him and opposed it as a palpable violation of popular sovereignty. In August 1858 the people of Kansas rejected the Lecompton constitution and statehood as a slave state by a large majority. This vote as well as Douglas' opposition to Lecompton and his interpretation of the impact of the Dred Scott decision on popular sovereignty turned southern Democrats against his doctrine as an acceptable solution to the slave expansion problem. By 1859 some of them were demanding positive federal protection of slavery in the territories. At the same time Lecompton had persuaded many northern Democrats that popular sovereignty was not an effective way to stop slave expansion.

See OREGON.

The best general account of the history of the doctrine can be found in Allan Nevins, *Ordeal of the Union*, 2 vols. (1947), and *The Emergence of Lincoln*, 2 vols. (1950). For Douglas' relation with the Democratic party, see Don E. Fehrenbacher, *Prelude to Greatness: Lincoln in the 1850's* (1962); and Roy F. Nichols, *The Disruption of American Democracy* (1948).—M. F. H.

Populism. Populism was the major third-party movement of the 1890s. Until recently, Populism was considered by historians as the culmination of a quarter-century of western and southern agrarian unrest triggered by the passing of the frontier. Increasingly, studies have demonstrated that the movement accommodated greater diversity of thought than was once supposed and that its origins embraced more than was usually conveyed by the frontier explanation. Although its dominant agrarian orientation has not been questioned, the party did appeal to and win, with varying degrees of success, some support from the laboring and small-business elements of the towns; the party was also led, to a significant extent, by less provincial, middle-class, nonagrarian reformers whose backgrounds were predominantly rural. As a result, the party became the vehicle by means of which a traditional agrarian-oriented politics was coupled with a more broadly based and sharply focused criticism of the new industrial society that had emerged in the Gilded Age (for an example, see the INDUSTRIAL ARMY MOVEMENT).

American society in the 1880s and 1890s felt the full impact of the many dislocations produced by the great nineteenth-century economic revolution, and the Populist movement, although perhaps premature, was, on the whole, a progressive and instructive response to those changed conditions. By all means, Populist criticism of the new industrial society owed much to two preceding decades of thought and agitation sparked by the profound changes that had transformed the United States into the world's foremost industrial power by the last decade of the nineteenth century. In this highly transitional period a multitude of forces were at work, pulling American society first one way and then the other. The value structure of the older agrarian society was seriously affected; agriculture and industry were effectively revolutionized and mechanized; the transportation revolution accelerated at a fantastic pace; vast segments of the West were thoroughly and rapidly populated; the urbanization process was intensified remarkably; and vast new problems came into being for which there appeared to be no ready solutions.

In the 1870s the nation's farmers effectively began the search for new arrangements to cope with the novel conditions confronting American society. Initially, this response was excessively influenced by the self-centered and, in retrospect, retrograde aim of reestablishing the position of agriculture as the primary factor in the nation's economy. In any case, an organization movement among farmers was well under way by the 1870s, and it expressed itself in such efforts to regulate railroads and grain elevators as was promoted by the National Grange (see GRANGER LAWS) and subsequently advocated by such independent political organizations as the GREEN-BACK PARTY and Union-Labor party, which embraced a wide spectrum of reform proposals.

During the late 1870s and early 1880s, a variety of farmer organizations came into being (see AGRARIAN MOVEMENTS). In the former Granger strongholds of the Northwest and Middle West, the National Farmers' Alliance and the Farmers' Mutual Benefit Association joined the Grange in competing for the support of farmers; in the Northwest there was also the Farmers' League; in the South there evolved the National Farmers' Alliance and Industrial Union (formed out of several state and regional alliances), the Colored Farmers' Alliance, and the Agricultural Wheel. Among these organizations, the National Farmers' Alliance (Northern Alliance) and the National Farmers' Alliance and Industrial Union (Southern Alliance, which absorbed the Wheel) became the most important. Membership in both organizations grew with astonishing speed in the late 1880s. By 1890 the Southern Alliance claimed anywhere from one to three million members,

with another million and a half in a Negro affiliate, while the Northern Alliance claimed to have over a million.

The Populist or People's party was decidedly the political product of a cross-fertilization of these organizational drives and grievances among farmers and the culmination of several decades of reform thought and energies that were not confined to any single region or economic endeavor. The plight of the farmer, however, very largely sustained the movement and made it a force to be reckoned with. What it owed to the frontier environment has, indeed, been overstated, but this by no means precludes a debt. It was on the frontier that some of the worst features of a highly speculative, ruthlessly competitive brand of industrial capitalism manifested themselves; it was there too that one found, paradoxically perhaps, a strong representation, in the agrarian setting, of the democratic ideal of equal opportunity and justice for all—circumstances that helped mightily to make the West a crucible of contention. It was also along the frontier line of the 1880s—extending down through the Dakotas, Nebraska, Kansas, and Texas—that the collapse of the latest in a series of booms in 1887 set in motion the train of events that led to the organization of the People's party.

The Alliances—the northwestern wing of the Southern Alliance in particular—were highly instrumental in the creation of the third party. Contrary to proclaimed intentions, both gradually assumed a political orientation. An effort was launched in 1889 to unite the two regional Alliances, which resulted in the meeting of the two in St. Louis, Missouri, in December 1889. Except for Kansas, North Dakota, and South Dakota, states that had converted to the Southern Alliance, the consolidation effort failed. At the St. Louis convention, however, both national Alliances adopted a set of reform demands that reflected a unity of purpose and pointed the way to a real political change.

Initially, the Alliances attempted to achieve their ends by capturing political power at the state level. In the South the aim was to gain control of the Democratic party, which held the power in every state, and by 1890 this strategy was well under way and had met with some success; in the Northwest the alliance flirted for a time with a similar tactic but with the Republican party as the object of their efforts. The Alliance in several western states, however, Kansas in particular, resolved at an early stage to make their effort a third-party fight. In Kansas, Citizens' Alliances were organized early in 1890 to work with the Farmers' Alliance, Single-Tax Clubs, Bellamy Nationalist Clubs, the Knights of Labor, and other organizations, to produce the first state People's party by June 1890 (see PEOPLE'S PARTY, KANSAS). The designation won increasing acceptance thereafter, and "Populist" and "Populism" were seemingly natural derivatives.

The 1890 election results testified to the effectiveness of the third-party strategy. In no state did the new party win complete control, but in four, Kansas, Nebraska, South Dakota, and Minnesota, it made itself a force to be reckoned with. In the South, Alliance victories, won through the mechanism of the Democratic party, were most impressive. Alliance gubernatorial candidates won in North Carolina, South Carolina, and Georgia, and eight southern legislatures were successfully captured by the Alliance. The movement also made an impression on Congress. Two Populist senators, William A. PEFFER of Kansas and James H. KYLE of South Dakota, claimed seats for the opening session of the Fifty-second Congress. Counting third-party men and Alliance men together, perhaps as many as forty-four congressmen were to be included in the Alliance camp. Among Southern Alliance congressmen, however, only Thomas E. Watson of Georgia proclaimed his independence of the Democratic party.

Third-party sentiment was rampant in the Northwest after 1890, and it seemed only logical to the enthusiasts of the area that the next step should be the creation of a national party. Southern Alliance men, apparently much less influenced by nonfarmer, radical third-party elements, were not sympathetic to the creation of a third party. The Alliance in the southern states had the special problem of whether to break with a one-party system that had been used so successfully to maintain white supremacy. In addition to the racial bugaboo, there was some reason to believe that the Alliance in the South could work effectively on the state level within the Democratic party.

The opposition of the Southern Alliance to the third-party idea, which was manifested strongly at the Ocala, Florida, meeting early in December 1890, did not restrain the third-party ardor of northwestern enthusiasts. Long-time third-party leaders, who had been content to work quietly and inconspicuously within and behind Alliance lines before the 1890 elections, began soon thereafter to work diligently to organize a national party. Leading Kansas Populists, working closely with other prominent northwestern leaders, took the initiative in arranging a series of conventions, beginning at Cincinnati in May 1891, where a National People's Party committee was created, and which culminated with a nominating convention at Omaha, Nebraska, in July 1892.

The Populist Omaha platform, written largely by the versatile and imaginative Minnesota reformer, Ignatius DONNELLY, was indeed a remarkable document. Although the party was meant to be a coalition of workingmen of farm and factory, the platform reflected the fact that the movement was sustained largely by several decades of agrarian discontent, with significant support from a variety of lower-middle-class Americans who had been affected by the displacement influences of the economic revolution. The platform called for changes that appealed strongly to elements of both groups, but the plight of agriculture was paramount, and it was among the nation's distressed farmers that the appeal was most intense. Their call for government ownership of the nation's railroad, telegraph, and telephone systems was aimed, realistically, at improving the farmers' competitive position by democratizing the control of these networks and by alleviating the high cost of transportation and communication. The demand for a "national currency, safe, sound, and flexible," through the use of gold, or silver, or paper, or all three, to counter the deflationary trend of the period, was legitimately expected to contribute to an increase in the price of farm products. The proposal for a subtreasury system, whereby the creation of national warehouses would enable farmers to obtain government loans on stored crops, was included to meet the farmers' need for easier credit. The demand for a graduated income tax would

lighten the tax load on property and redistribute the national wealth in a more equitable fashion. They demanded also that all public lands which had been granted "in excess" of "actual needs" to "railroads and other corporations" be returned to the government, as well as all land held by aliens, to be "held for actual settlers only."

Clearly these proposals were aimed primarily at farmers, but they struck sympathetic chords elsewhere. Several other favorably mentioned reforms must have had a broader appeal: among these was a call for postal savings banks, shorter hours for labor, the Australian ballot, the initiative and referendum, the direct election of United States senators, and a single term limitation on presidental and vice presidential officeholders.

In retrospect, the Populists symbolized a break with the conventional wisdom in a far broader sense than the details of their platform. Their belief that the object of government was "to protect the weak from the oppressions of the strong" constituted the primary significance of their movement and contributed mightily to their undoing: "We believe that the powers of government—in other words, of the people—should be expanded . . . as rapidly and as far as the good sense of an intelligent people and the teachings of experience shall justify, to the end that oppression, injustice, and poverty should eventually cease in the land." Their aim of eliminating poverty was especially noteworthy; few major-party politicos accepted the idea that the national government was anything more than a "benign policeman" who, at best, promoted business prosperity and law and order at home, and commerce and peace abroad. The Populists were assailed bitterly for taking this stand, but after their threat was put down, a broader governmental responsibility for the welfare of all the nation's citizens became a much less heretical tenet of democratic social thought.

A good showing was just about all the Populists hoped for in the ELECTION OF 1892; they managed that feat. James B. WEAVER, the 1880 Greenback-Labor party candidate for president, headed their ticket, and the party became the first third party since the Civil War to win electoral votes.

Populists were confident their movement would continue to grow and that a victory of the "people" over the "plutocrats" in the 1896 contest would be assured. Subsequent circumstances were such, however, that the great victory failed to materialize. Populism, as an independent and radical force, without the benefit of fusion with the Democratic party in the Northwest and West and the Republican party in the South, had gone just about as far as it could go by 1894. It was still at that point a minority party, even in the states where it was strongest, and fusion with one or the other of the old parties became a practical necessity that subjected the party and its original program to tremendous strains. The election of a Democratic president and Congress in 1892, the onset of a severe depression beginning in 1893, and President Grover Cleveland's ill-advised and inane focus upon the Sherman Silver Purchase Act as the cause of the depression and its repeal as the cure all combined, in a most complex pattern, to undermine the Populist movement (see SILVER ISSUE). In seeking and winning a repeal of the Sherman Silver Purchase Act, Cleveland divided his party along sectional lines and made of the silver issue a far more important issue than it deserved to be. In the South and West, where silver sentiment crossed party lines, the tendency to seek common ground on this one issue was irresistible. The end result was an even more intense polarization of the nation along sectional and rural-versus-urban lines; a repudiation of President Cleveland's leadership by his own party and a declaration of Democratic support for silver; and the nomination of the Nebraska silverite William Jennings Bryan for president in 1896 by both the Democratic party and the People's party. After Bryan's defeat in the ELECTION OF 1896, fusion was widely practiced and the Populist party was gradually and discordantly dismantled throughout the country.

A wide variety of discontent did, indeed, momentarily congeal in the 1890s, especially after the economic collapse of 1893, and Populism aptly reflected this development, not only in its appeal but in its internal dissensions. Because of this, it would be most ahistorical to attempt a *rigid* definition of Populism—even in its unadulterated form, before fusion tactics became the order of the day. And despite a glib tendency in recent years to label some disparate political figures Populist, perhaps there never was a fixed Populist ideology. Certainly one must take note of its regional variations and internal polarities, and the term should be used with utmost caution, if at all, in the generic sense. In its historic context, however, perhaps a Kansas Populist captured its positive essence most succinctly:

Populism demands the enactment of new laws based on the natural rights of men, and not limited by precedents and accepted theories in relation to property, when such precedents and accepted theories do not meet the requirements of modern life. Populism does not necessarily mean "to nationalize all the essentials of existence. . . ." It does mean, however, that the power of law shall control and prohibit the centralization of land titles. That labor shall be provided with all necessary legal machinery to protect itself against the unjust demands of aggregated wealth. That not only the means of transportation, but all public utilities, shall be subject to public control, and when necessary, public ownership. That money of all kinds shall be issued direct by the government, and its legal tender value regulated by law, and not by foreign bankers and money-lenders.

In the 1890s this bold philosophy created much controversy, which has been rivaled to an extent, in recent years, by the historiographical debate among Populism's interpreters; both are testimony to the complexity and dynamism of the movement, as well as an indication of the degree to which the Populists challenged prevailing attitudes. Certainly there was much that was viable in Populism; above all, Populists contributed to an expansion of the conventional wisdom in a manner that was, eventually, conducive to a much more creative social dialog. Even historian Richard Hofstadter, the party's most-noted recent critic, conceded that it "was the first modern political movement of practical importance in the United States to insist that the federal government has some responsibility for the common weal; indeed, it was the first such movement to attack seriously the problems created by industrialism."

John D. Hicks, *The Populist Revolt: A History of the Farmers' Alliance and the People's Party* (1931), remains the only general history of Populism. Richard Hofstadter, *The Age of Reform: From Bryan to F.D.R.* (1955), is an interpretive and highly critical revisionist study that has done much to reopen the whole subject. Norman Pollack, *The Populist Response to Industrial America: Midwestern Populist Thought* (1962), is a direct response to Hofstadter's revisionism, which contends that Populism was an even more radical movement than Hicks had suggested. Since Pollack's work, several excellent studies have appeared to shed light on the many interpretive issues generated by the revisionist and counterrevisionist dispute; of these, two of the more pertinent studies are O. Gene Clanton, *Kansas Populism: Ideas and Men* (1969); and Michael Paul Rogin, *The Intellectuals and McCarthy: The Radical Specter* (1967).—O. G. C.

Porter, Kenneth Wiggins (1905-   ). Historian. Like many of the older generation of historians of the West, Porter was truly a product of his time and place. Born near Sterling, Kansas, to parents who had come to western Kansas—his mother by covered wagon—in the sodhouse frontier days of the mid-1880s, he witnessed at close range drastic changes in western life. Porter was graduated from Sterling College in 1926 and a year later obtained an M.A. degree in European history from the University of Minnesota. From then on his scholarly career followed a varied course and covered a wide range of interests: business history, poetry, religion, minority groups, particularly in the West, and folklore.

Porter arrived at Harvard in 1927 and worked intermittently as a research assistant in business history until he eventually received the Ph.D. in 1936. One of his teachers was Frederick Merk. He then returned to his native Kansas as an assistant professor of history and political science at Southwestern College in Winfield. Two years later he accepted a position at Vassar College and remained at that institution until 1948.

Among his other appointments were senior associate of the Business History Foundation (1948-51, 1952-53), principally in Houston, Texas; visiting professor at the University of Oregon (1951-52); Fulbright lecturer at Melbourne University, Australia (1954); and professor at the University of Illinois (1955-58). In 1958 he became professor of American history at the University of Oregon.

He wrote four significant books: *John Jacob Astor: Business Man*, 2 vols. (1931); *The Jacksons and the Lees: Two Generations of Massachusetts Merchants, 1755-1844*, 2 vols. (1937); *History of Humble Oil & Refining Company: A Study in Industrial Growth*, with H. M. Larson (1959); and *The Negro on the American Frontier* (1971). He also wrote three volumes of verse, whose subject matter varies from religious themes to the High Plains, plus numerous articles in historical and folklore journals, mostly about Indians and blacks on the frontier. —W. E. H.

Posey, Alexander (1873-1908). Writer and educator. Posey was born on a ranch near Eufaula, Indian Territory. Family tradition relates that until the age of twelve Posey spoke only his mother's native tongue, Muscogee (she was of the Creek Harjo family). Then his father engaged a tutor who taught him to read, write, and speak English. Posey attended the tribal public school at Eufaula and Indian University (Bacone) at Muskogee.

In college he developed his talent for writing by working on the school paper, writing under the name of Chinnubbie Harjo, a figure in Muscogee mythology. His first published poem, written at the age of nineteen, "The Comet's Tail," set in verse a Creek tradition describing the first Europeans to reach America.

In 1895 Posey entered Creek Nation politics by winning election to the House of Warriors, the tribal legislative body. The following year he married a teacher from Fayetteville, Arkansas. Concerned about the many unlettered members of his nation, Posey and his wife became involved in education. Their assignments included the supervision of the Creek Orphan Asylum at Okmulgee and Creek Nation schools at Eufaula and Wetumpka. In 1898, Posey became superintendent of public instruction for the Creek Nation. He was elected delegate from the Creek Nation to the Sequoyah Convention, a statehood movement for Indian Territory, which met at Muskogee in 1905, serving as secretary of the convention and contributing to the constitution which resulted from the deliberations. When the Creek Nation was allotted land, he worked with the Dawes Commission to watch over and protect the landed property interests of his people.

Posey's nationwide fame came from his literary work as poet, editor, and satirist. Throughout his public career he regularly retired to his rural home near Vivian to write poetry. He also edited the *Indian Journal*, published at Eufaula, and excelled in satire. His series, the "Fus Fixico Letters," a broken Creek-English dialog between Fus Fixico, Wolf Warrior, and Hot Gun, consisted of humorous discussions of white man's politics and ways.—A. M. G.

Poston, Charles Debrille (1825-1902). Arizona pioneer and government official. Born on a farm near Elizabethtown, Kentucky, Poston worked as a newspaper apprentice, studied law, and in 1851 secured employment in the Customs House in San Francisco. Hired in 1854 by a railroad-mining syndicate, he investigated the possibility of a railroad terminus at Guaymas, Sonora, gauged local feelings about annexing that Mexican state to the United States, and examined mines in the Santa Cruz valley and at Ajo in southern Arizona. Across from Fort Yuma he and Herman Ehrenberg, a German-born mining engineer, surveyed a townsite that later became Yuma. Poston's reports stimulated interest in the Arizona mines, and the Sonora Exploring and Mining Company was organized in Cincinnati, Ohio, to work the silver mines in the Santa Cruz. In the late summer of 1856 Poston arrived at Tubac from Texas with a wagon train, supervised the Sonora company's mining operations in the vicinity, and functioned as deputy county clerk of Dona Ana County, New Mexico. When the Civil War forced the mines to close, Poston returned to Washington and lobbied for the creation of the Territory of Arizona; at its formation on February 24, 1863, he was appointed the first Arizona superintendent of Indian affairs. Although elected the first territorial delegate, Poston was defeated for reelection; he went abroad for several years and then held a variety of jobs, government and otherwise. In financial straits in 1899, Poston was voted a pension by the Arizona legislature but died in squalor in Phoenix.

See B. Sacks, "Charles Debrille Poston, Prince of Arizona Pioneers," in Tucson Corral of the Westerners, *Smoke Signal No. 7* (Spring 1963).—H. P. H.

Potawatomi Indians. The Potawatomi Indians are an Algonquian tribe having close historical connections with the linguistically related Central Algonquian Indians of the Old Northwest: the Shawnee, Miami, Sauk and Fox, and Kickapoo. Potawatomi traditions of origin, however, separate them from these peoples and indicate that in very early times the proto-Potawatomi, along with ancestral Ojibwa and Ottawa groups, migrated from the éastern seaboard because of pressure from Iroquoian tribes. Near the Straits of Mackinac they separated into three tribes, although maintaining an alliance known as the League of the Three Brothers or Three Fires. The Potawatomi crossed into the lower peninsula of Michigan, where they were first encountered by French explorers in the early 1600s. Westward expansion of the Iroquois Confederacy, equipped with firearms, during the mid-seventeenth century temporarily drove the more poorly armed Potawatomi and Central Algonquian tribes out of Michigan and Ohio and into Wisconsin. By 1750, however, the increase of white trade and the waning of Iroquois military superiority allowed the Potawatomi and their associates to spread southeastward around the southern end of Lake Michigan and back into the Ohio valley. The Potawatomi occupied the territory from the Milwaukee River to the Grand River in Michigan, and south across a large area of Illinois and Indiana. The tribe had four principal divisions, known to whites by their respective locations as the Potawatomi of the St. Joseph in Michigan, the Potawatomi of the Huron in Michigan, the Potawatomi of the Wabash in Indiana, and the Prairie Bands in Illinois and Wisconsin. Their total population was about 2,500 in 1750-1800.

Potawatomi culture was transitional between the characteristic woodland pattern and the nomadic forms of the Plains. An indeterminate number of generally autonomous village-bands were only loosely united through a tribal council and a selected village chief, who was nominally chief of the whole tribe. Social organization was based on a system of patrilineal, exogamous, totemic clans, which also functioned as ceremonial units and acted as an integrating force within the whole tribe. Among the western sections of the Potawatomi, economic activity was seasonally divided between agriculture and hunting. In summer the Prairie Bands occupied semipermanent bark-house villages along rivers, the women tending fields of corn, squash, and pumpkins, while the men hunted the vicinity. After the late summer harvest the bands moved onto the prairies, set up winter camps of skin lodges in stream bottoms, and sent small parties out on extended hunts that might last all winter. In spring there was a communal buffalo hunt and then a return to the fields. The eastern sections of the tribe were not as dependent on hunting, fishing being a major activity and a communal spring fish-catching their largest annual gathering.

The Potawatomi played a subsidiary role during the French and Indian War (1754-63), living too far west to be actively affected by the whites' territorial contests. They were supporters of the French, however, due to the long tradition of trade with them. Potawatomi warriors participated in Braddock's defeat (1755) and raided outlying British posts during the course of the war. After the British victory the Potawatomi joined with Pontiac in his attempt to expel all whites from the Old Northwest (1763-64), and continued loyal to his cause even after his defeat. When the fugitive Pontiac was killed by an Illinois Indian at Cahokia in 1769, the Potawatomi and their allies carried war into the Illinois country and nearly exterminated the disease-weakened tribes of that region. During the American Revolution the Potawatomi first took the side of the British, whose posts had replaced the French as the Indians' trade suppliers. The tribal leaders soon decided, however, that their people could only lose by becoming involved on either side of any white war, and the Potawatomi withdrew from active participation in the conflict, except for those younger warriors who could not resist the opportunity for a good fight. With the war's end the Potawatomi and the Central Algonquians realized that the Americans meant to take over their country, and with British backing attacked settlers along the Ohio. The tribes were defeated at the battle of Fallen Timbers (1794) and forced to cede most of present Ohio by the Treaty of Greenville (1795). The Potawatomi's territory was not affected by this cession, but as the eastward tribes were forced to move in with them and the American demands for land continued, the Potawatomi joined in the confederacy of Tecumseh for a final attempt to block the white advance. The defeat of the confederacy at the battle of Tippecanoe (1811) and American frontier victories during the War of 1812 broke the Potawatomi strength and will to resist.

During the remainder of the nineteenth century Potawatomi culture rapidly disintegrated under pressure for removal of eastern Indians to beyond the Mississippi and the occupation of their lands by white farmers. Tribal cohesion, never centralized, disappeared as some groups accepted United States government proposals for removal while others attempted to retain part of their homeland. Many Potawatomi families and small groups scattered and joined with other displaced tribes. Even those who accepted white domination peacefully and tried to live in accord with whatever program was invoked for them found no solution, for the government did not seem to be able to make a final decision on what to do with these unhappy refugees. The bulk of their lands were ceded piecemeal in forty-seven different treaties between 1820 and 1841. A large group of Indiana Potawatomi refused to cede and were evicted by force in the 1830s, most escaping to Canada and settling on Walpole Island in Lake St. Clair. The Prairie Bands were removed to Missouri in 1833, then to southwest Iowa in 1837, and in 1846 were settled in Kansas and united with those eastern parts of the tribe (called "Potawatomi of the Woods" or "Mission Band" by whites) who had been removed from Indiana and Michigan in 1840. Most of the Mission Band in 1861 took land in severalty but by 1868 had sold their individual tracts to white speculators and were moved to a new reservation in Oklahoma, becoming known as the Citizen Band. Parts of the Prairie Bands have since managed to regain some land in Wisconsin, and the Potawatomi of the Huron have kept a small tract in Michigan. In the 1960s there were small Potawatomi reservations in Wisconsin, Kansas, Michigan, and Oklahoma, with a population totaling 1,642.

Material on the Potawatomi is extensive, although not cohesive. A survey of their history and customs can be gained from Charles Callender, *Social Organization of the Central Algonkian Indians* (1962); V. B. Deale, "The History of the Potawatomies Before 1722," *Ethnohistory*, vol. 5 (1958); F. W. Hodge, ed., *Handbook of American Indians North of Mexico*, 2 vols. (1907-10); Ruth Landes, *The Prairie Potawatomi* (1970); and P. V. Lawson, "The Potawatomi," *Wisconsin Archeologist*, vol. 19 (1920). —P. R. M.

pottery, southwestern Indian. Latest dating methods indicate that the art of pottery making came to the Southwest from Mexico about 500 B.C. Sherds, indestructible broken bits of the potter's craft (for pottery never disintegrates into the earth), litter this country and lead the way to knowledge of the ancient cultures that fashioned them.

The earliest potters of southeastern Arizona and southwestern New Mexico were the descendants of farmers living more than four thousand years ago. Wandering peoples had no need to carry fragile pottery on their travels. The craft was only practicable when the people became sedentary. It was through the Indians of southwestern New Mexico that pottery making finally diffused, probably through traders, up to the Four Corners region where Arizona, New Mexico, Colorado, and Utah join.

Six thousand years ago in the Old World the potter's wheel was invented. Pottery making became a trade that could supply all of the vessels needed in a whole village. Men took it up and supplied the housewives, who paid for it in goods. In the New World, wheels for potters or machines were never invented (all were introduced in historical times; although, oddly, some children's toys were equipped with wheels. Each woman made her own pottery, building it, decorating it, and polishing it before firing. Much of our knowledge of ancient cultures comes from the designs women painted on their ware.

The ingredients that go into making a vessel are clay, tempering material, water, and patient skill. Clay beds may be near a pueblo but potters will travel long distances to dig the color and quality they want. Red, white, blue-gray, and brown with mica particles are now in use. Tempering material, such as fine volcanic sand, ground basaltic rock, or ground potsherds, is used to prevent the raw clay from shrinking and cracking in drying and in firing. The clay and temper are moistened and kneaded together to a consistency like putty—just dry enough to crack when pinched. If there is too much temper, the clay becomes "short" and brittle and will not retain its shape while being molded.

A *puki* is used as a base in which to start building a vessel. In very early times the women started their pots in a basket base, but now the puki is a rounded piece of broken pottery or a dish. The interior is sprinkled with fine ashes or temper to prevent the clay from sticking. A pancake of clay paste is pressed into the puki, then the walls of the vessel are built up by the coiling process: ropes of clay laid one upon the other. A dried smoothed gourd rind is used to rub away finger marks, the junction between the clay coils, and any irregularities that may appear at the lip and rim.

Next the vessels are set in the sun to dry. If any cracks appear, the potter grinds up the vessel to be used later. When the pottery has dried, it is scraped with a tin can lid or a knife and a wet cloth or with sandpaper. The scraping, originally done with shaped potsherds or animal bones, removes the marks left by the puki and the gourd and thins the sides to reduce the weight. The exterior is softened by wiping it with a wet rag; scraping is done while the surface is wet. The interiors are never scraped.

Slipping comes next. This is the application of a very thin layer of clay to the pot's surface to produce a smooth texture and to act as a sizing. It may be the only decoration, or it may serve as the background for painted designs. Slips are usually red, dark red, orange-red, white, or yellow. Several coats, one after another as they dry, are spread on with a cloth mop dipped in the liquid slip. As the slip dries, it leaves the vessel dull. It must now be polished with a stone. Because the slip cannot dry out too much before the polishing, usually only parts of the vessel are slipped at one time. The polishing process must be done speedily and yet in the most exacting manner to achieve luster and to apply the decoration smoothly.

Decorative motifs are peculiar to each pueblo, and individual potter's works can be distinguished. Either chewed cuds of yucca leaf slivers or commercial paintbrushes are used for decorating. Paints are made from iron oxides (red from hematite, yellow from limonite) and from the Rocky Mountain bee plant. The bee plant (*guaco*) paint is black. It is boiled in cooking pots until it thickens, then it is cooled and stored in cakes for a year. When it is to be used, a chunk is broken from the cake and dissolved in water, making a syrupy solution. The painter's hand is uncannily steady as she paints from memory or a conceived design. Men sometimes assist in vessel painting.

Firing is the most critical part of the potter's craft. No permanent kiln is used. Flat cakes of sheep manure are laid around and over the pots in a domed structure. The ground is first heated by a wood fire. The pots are arranged in an inverted position on an improvised grate of, for example, broken bed springs or iron pipe and laid over the coals. The vessels are protected from the burning dung by flat pieces of old sheet iron or tin that are laid across them before the fuel is added. The dung burns with intense heat for about an hour, reaching a temperature of approximately seven hundred degrees centigrade. When the heat becomes endurable, the sheet iron is removed, and the pots are lifted from the grate with sticks and placed on the ground to cool. The brownish guaco paint is a deep black, white slip is a creamy buff, and red clay is a deeper red. The ash is then removed with a greasy cloth, and the pots are ready for use.

Today's pottery making, the result of more than two thousand years of tradition, is again attaining great beauty and high quality, following a period of decline in quality and decoration. Fine examples of contemporary work can be found in many New Mexico pueblos and in the Hopi villages of Arizona.

The Picurís and Taos pueblos, in northern New Mexico, are noted for micaceous pottery (so named because the clay from which it is made contains mica and gives the resulting pot a sparkling quality). The pottery produced by these pueblos is primarily for cooking and serving. It is generally well shaped, thin walled, well fired, and largely undecorated. The Picurís are particularly envied for their marvelous bean pots of which it is

said, no bean tastes quite so good as that cooked in a Picurís pot.

San Ildefonso Pueblo sprawls out over the prairie north of Santa Fe, New Mexico. Probably the best known and the most highly prized decorative pieces are the ones that were produced by María MARTINEZ and her son Popovi Da. This pottery is noted for its lovely high-luster black embellished with dull black, or matte black on polished black, with simple formalized designs almost modernistic in appearance. Many different forms are made, including platters, vases, bowls, boxes, trays, ashtrays, and candlesticks. Other equally fine and lovely pottery types are made at San Ildefonso; polychrome, distinctive for geometric linear and curvilinear designs in combinations of black and red on white or cream background; and a recently developed sienna, featuring black at the base with a burnt sienna tone in the upper portion on which highly polished flowing designs are executed. Some of these are life forms, and some are set with turquoise.

Potters at Santa Clara Pueblo, in northern New Mexico, make highly polished black ware, similar to that made at San Ildefonso, and polished red ware. The fine black ware of Santa Clara either carries no decoration at all or the subtle impression of a bear claw. The polished red ware is frequently distinguished by intricately carved designs on a matte tan background. A variation in style was originated by Lela and Van Gutierrez and was carried on by Lela's son Luther. They execute very small geometric designs in pastel shades of green, blue, and yellow on a cream background. Graceful, well-executed pieces have been the result.

The pottery made at San Juan Pueblo, located just north of Española, New Mexico, is so similar to that of San Ildefonso, and particularly to that of Santa Clara, that it generally cannot be distinguished by the untrained eye. The most notable exceptions are the incised pieces derived from prehistoric ware made as early as A.D. 1450. The late Regina Cata was responsible for reviving this ancient form about 1930. In these vessels simple geometric line designs are cut into the clay. These cuts are then painted or filled with micaceous slip. The upper band around the vessel may be left in the natural buff clay color, while the lower portion is frequently slipped with red and polished. This lends a simple dignity to the overall effect of the finished piece.

Acoma Pueblo, also in New Mexico, produces the thinnest and finest walled pottery made by southwestern Indians. A snap of a finger on the side of an Acoma vessel will always produce a resonant ping. The smooth curve of an Acoma jar provides a surface that lends itself to continuous designs that flow evenly over the entire vessel. Geometric designs, birds and berries, and flowers and leaves are favored themes. Reds, yellows, blacks, browns, and oranges are applied effectively to form the design on a very white or cream-colored base. Acoma ware tends to chip or flake because of improper preparation of the clay or impurities in it.

The Hopi villages located on three mesa tops in western Arizona are still famous for their excellent pottery. Their large storage jars and cooking vessels are graceful, simple, rough, unslipped, undecorated, and beautifully fired. Their famous decorated wares, produced primarily at first mesa, are made in the tradition of

Nampeyo, who, it is said, was inspired by the potsherds recovered from Sikyatki, a prehistoric site of the Hopi. These early designs encouraged Nampeyo to improve her own pottery decorations. The distinctive style that she created has been passed down from her daughter to her granddaughters and to many other Hopi women of the first mesa.

Hopi jars and bowls are distinguishable by their shape and decoration. The bowls may be deep or shallow with walls that are incurving, almost straight, or outcurving. The Hopi jar is shallow, has an incurving rim, and a flattened shoulder. Hopi painters excel in the careful execution of balanced geometric patterns, swirls, and scrolls. Bowls feature a central design on the interior and banded symmetrical designs on the exterior. Hopi jars are usually recognized by either a continuous band on which unusually joined elements such as a scroll or wing pattern are painted, or by a symmetrically broken band of four, six, or more equal sections on which identical patterns are repeated. Hopi decorations are pleasing and feature a rhythmical balance of colors: black on buff, sometimes relieved by muted rose; black alone, or with white, on a red base; and black with soft touches of red on buff.

Tesuque Pueblo, located north of Santa Fe, New Mexico, has been heavily influenced by the lure of tourists' dollars and their corresponding lack of knowledge. This pueblo, lamentably, is noted for its poster-red pots and animals, ashtrays, and other trinkets painted in psychedelic colors that fade and smudge as the eager, moist hands of their owners fondle them.

See Ruth Bunzel, *The Pueblo Potter* (1929); Kenneth M. Chapman, *The Pottery of San Ildefonso Pueblo* (1971); Bertha P. Dutton, *Indians of the Southwest* (1965); F. H. Harlow, *Historic Pueblo Indian Pottery* (1967); F. H. Harlow and J. V. Young, *Contemporary Pueblo Indian Pottery* (1965); Majorie F. Lambert, *Pueblo Indian Pottery: Materials, Tools, and Techniques*, Popular Series Pamphlet, no. 5 (1966); and Michael B. Stanislawski, "The Ethnoarchaeology of Hopi Pottery Making," *Plateau* (Summer 1969).—B. P. D. and M. L.

Powder River Indian Expedition (1865). This military effort was organized to stop Sioux and Cheyenne Indian raids against whites on the roads through the Indians' hunting grounds, and to open a new road to the Montana gold fields. Commanded by General Patrick Edward Connor, a Californian whose reputation had been made in the battle against hostile Bannock and Shoshoni Indians at Bear River in 1863, the expedition was an expensive failure that emboldened rather than discouraged the Indians. Plans for a cooperating command under General Alfred Sully were canceled at the last moment, and the expedition itself was hampered from the beginning by supply and equipment shortages, inaccurate maps, mutinous soldiers and inexperienced officers.

Connor divided his expedition into three columns and, with the left column, marched from Fort Laramie along the Bozeman Trail, detached some troops to build Fort Connor, and continued to the Tongue River, where he found and attacked a village of Arapaho Indians, who until then apparently had not been hostile. The right column, under Colonel Nelson Cole, marched from Omaha to the Black Hills, where it met Lieutenant Colonel Samuel Walker's center column, which had

come from Fort Laramie. Together the two columns marched uncertainly toward a planned rendezvous with Connor on the Rosebud River, fighting off several Indian attacks and eventually running out of supplies. The campaign came to an ignominious end when some of Connor's Pawnee scouts found the starving, tattered right and center columns and led them back to Fort Connor.

The best general coverage of the expedition is in Robert M. Utley, *Frontiersman in Blue* (1967). LeRoy R. Hafen and Ann W. Hafen, *Powder River Campaigns and Sawyers Expedition of 1865* (1961), is an excellent collection of source materials. The Indian point of view is presented in George Bird Grinnell, *The Fighting Cheyennes* (1915).—J. T. K.

Powell, John Wesley (1834–1902). Explorer and conservationist. Powell was born at Mount Morris near Palmyra, New York. His father was a Methodist exhorter who had removed his family from England to America in 1830. While the family stopped for a number of years on a farm in Jackson, Ohio, on their westward trek, the youthful Powell found an alternative to his father's theology when he was taken on as a special student by a self-taught, elderly naturalist, George Crookham, who introduced the boy to elementary natural science. As the eldest son, whose circuit-riding father was often away from home, he willingly assumed the laborious farm chores to support his seven brothers and sisters as new farmsteads were cleared in Walworth County, Wisconsin, and later in Illinois. He left home, however, at the age of sixteen. By dint of self-instruction, which so characterized his future advancement, and attendance at public schools in Janesville, Wisconsin, he made up his deficiencies in basic subjects and by 1852 was teaching elementary school. His preoccupation, however, was with the natural world.

During the next seven years Powell followed his own counsel as he pursued the various branches of natural science in and out of colleges: Illinois College, Wheaton, and Oberlin. He also taught country school from time to time as a source of livelihood. More significant for the future were his extended solitary rambles on water and field along the Mississippi River and its tributaries. These expeditions, for the most part carried on during summer months from 1855 to 1858, developed in him fortitude and self-sufficiency and expanded his scientific horizons as he added specimens to the herbarium he maintained at the family residence at Wheaton, Illinois. He also became famous for his specialized knowledge and collection of mollusks, and thereby was drawn into the orbit of the Illinois Natural History Society. He was secretary of the organization, curator of the society's conchology museum section, and was well-known among the state's scientists before the Civil War broke out.

Powell abhorred slavery and naturally enlisted after the attack on Fort Sumter. Characteristically, he became a self-taught army officer through mastery of manuals of tactics and engineering and came to the attention of General Grant. He was an artillery battery commander at Shiloh, where he lost his lower right arm. Fortunately his bride of one month, Emma Dean Powell, was with the army and nursed her husband back to good health after a few months. Promoted to major, he distinguished himself at the siege of Vicksburg and subsequent operations until hostilities were concluded in the West.

Returning to civilian life in 1865, Powell taught science at colleges in Illinois, but after a few years his vision was lifted to the far-off Rockies, where he combined exploration with fieldwork for some of his advanced students and prominent local amateur scientists in 1867 and 1868. The 1868 expedition, which took in a congressionally authorized reconnaissance of the Grand and Green rivers was a prelude to the Grand Canyon voyage of 1869. He also laid the groundwork for the soon-to-be-realized geological and geographical survey of the Rocky Mountain region. In Washington he sought congressional and bureaucratic support for scientific exploration, while in the field he performed his preliminary geological survey of the Uinta Mountains and made his first systematic ethnological observations.

Powell's first canyon voyage of 1869—in which ten men in four small boats navigated the churning rapids of the Green and Colorado rivers, losing themselves in the cavernous depths of the Grand Canyon and emerging a thousand miles downstream three months later as conquerers of the unknown—made Powell something of a folk hero. If this expedition was launched out of a spirit of adventure and a craving for national acclaim, it was equally a scientific enterprise. Its leader, however, though something more than an amateur, did not rank with the professionals with eastern and European degrees. In keeping with the spirit of his age and his own genius, Powell determined to become a scientist of commanding stature and prove that his topographical work and geology were superior to that produced by the surveys of Clarence King, Ferdinand Hayden, and Lieutenant George Wheeler, all of whom were competing for public funds. Before he launched his second expedition down the Colorado in 1871, he took satisfaction in having won the coveted government appropriation of $12,000 for mapping the Colorado Plateau region. He also used the opportunity thus afforded to study the arid region drained by the Colorado River in all its ramifications. In so doing, he became a self-taught geologist and ethnologist, a public-lands reformer, and an expert on irrigation institutions for this vast region. Finally, the canyon voyages and reconnaissance convinced him that the pursuit of science under federal auspices must be rationalized and that he, as the self-appointed entrepreneur of government science, was the person to do it.

Powell displayed a canny ability to influence the course of events to his advantage in Washington and lead his 1871 survey to scientific renown. His friendships with those in administrative and congressional circles after his removal to Washington, D.C., in 1873 are attested to by the continued appropriations for the Powell Survey. These funds were substantially less than the other surveys garnered, but the Powell Survey findings were largely confined to geology. The survey operated with about seven or eight professionals in the field annually. Powell's brother-in-law, Almon Thompson, no professional, learned the art of topographical surveying the hard way, but his maps soon displayed technical proficiency. Professional geologists such as Grove K. Gilbert and Clarence E. Dutton complemented Powell's insightful studies with distinguished reports on the Henry Mountains and Grand Canyon district in Utah.

Powell himself was in the field in 1874 and 1875 studying the geology of the Uinta Mountains, but after that administrative duties and political considerations confined him to Washington.

Powell had lectured and published fragmentary sketches of the canyon voyages but was hesitant to turn out full-fledged reports until the quality of the survey's scientific techniques were suitably advanced. Finally, at the urging of his friend Congressman James A. Garfield and in order to win wide public approbation for his emerging role in centralizing government scientific work, the Smithsonian Institution published his *Exploration of the Colorado River* in 1875. The first part of the monograph consisted of the journal of the 1869 voyage, based upon his diary and records drawn from both voyages. It has long been considered a classic, thrilling its readers then and now. Unfortunately, history was distorted in the narrative, because events were introduced from the second voyage without explanation and little credit was given to the valiant members of the 1871-72 expedition.

Powell's reputation as a scientist is largely based upon two treatises: his geological description of the Colorado River Plateau country, appearing as part two of *Exploration*; and *Geology of the Uinta Mountains* (1876). The observations and conclusions rendered in the latter introduced for the first time the principal subject matter of a new branch of geology, geomorphology. His principal focus was on land forms and the genesis of surface features. He concentrated on the effect of stream flow in the wearing down of mountains and introduced principles still in good repute among geologists descriptive of types of river valleys. This self-made geologist was nationally recognized by 1876, when he entered the political arena to seek unification of governmental science agencies.

Powell played an important if behind-the-scenes part in the consolidation of the western surveys into the United States GEOLOGICAL SURVEY in 1879. He had spoken for merger of the surveys in his testimony favoring civilian control before a congressional investigating committee in 1874. The advent of the reform-minded Hayes administration along with the business recession of 1877 influenced Congress to think in terms of consolidation. Powell's demand for land classification, appearing in his 1878 *Arid Lands Report*, envisioned a single governmental agency that could classify and dispose of public lands on the basis of a thorough geological reconnaissance. Representative Abram Hewitt, a close friend of both Clarence King and Powell, was instrumental in guiding through Congress the bill supported by the National Academy of Sciences creating the U. S. Geological Survey. Powell was content to head up the newly established Bureau of Ethnology, while his friend, King, became director of the U.S.G.S. at its inception. Subsequently President Garfield appointed Powell director when King left the Geological Survey in 1881.

During his thirteen years as head of the Geological Survey, Powell's principal accomplishment was to make government science respectable. He lectured Congress and addressed the public on the necessity for recruitment of scientists and government support of research and publication effort. He gathered the budgetary controls of the U.S.G.S. firmly into his own hands, and his control over operations as well as complete fiscal integrity was the result. He gave his young scientists and engineers, "Powell's Boys," paternalistic encouragement and bureaucratic protection and set them problems to solve. He fostered his agency's needs by superbly informed testimony before congressional committees and won the backing of leading universities and the states by hiring professors as specialists for summer projects and executing cooperative contracts for state geologic mapping. The nation's geologists were won over to the work of the U.S.G.S. by its systematization of map symbols and the increasing accuracy of the map sections for the mammoth program of mapping the entire area of the nation. Even the mining industry finally recognized the serviceability of the survey's mining studies in the 1890s. Powell's personal prestige soared with that of his institution, and he became the leader of a richly endowed scientific community in the nation's capital. In the prolonged struggle to change federal public-land policies, Powell mustered the full force of this prestige and even gambled the future of his beloved Geological Survey as he did battle against western opponents of conservation.

As early as 1874, in testimony to Congress, Powell revealed the practical orientation of his scientific thinking. He sought the collection of scientific data about the West, but he also looked to its long-term development. He thus advocated a program of land reform that would make possible agricultural settlement in the "arid domain." His *Report on the Lands of the Arid Region of the United States* (1878) was a realistic portrayal of the opportunities that irrigation made possible for balancing the predominantly mining economy of the West. But first land-settlement laws and their administration had to be drastically reformed to prevent corporate engrossment of western resources. And inevitably, a host of western enemies massed against his proposals during the years 1879-94. They included mining, cattle, and timber corporate interests who feared that a change in the land laws would end their era of exploitation. Railroad and agricultural promoters charged that Powell was selling the West short in denying that a vast realm could be successfully irrigated. The 1878 report, apart from its strikingly descriptive passages disclosing the area and condition of the arid domain, provided prescriptive measures in two categories. One demanded reform of the land laws and their administration in general terms; the other described the nature of legal institutions essential to successful irrigation agriculture.

Congress did not share Powell's vision. Even the Public Land Commission, of which he was a member, did not accept his plan for abandonment of the rectilinear survey system, and the commission's recommendations for classifying the public domain and permitting entry on enlarged pasturage homesteads did not receive the mandate of Congress. It was not until 1888 that Congress gave Powell authority to implement the irrigation provisions of his *Arid Lands Report*. In it, he had noted that only two to three percent of the vast arid region could be made irrigable with the water available. He anticipated that the next stage of irrigation development must be the construction of reservoirs and the reservation of irrigable public lands to encourage maximum homestead settlement. When the Geological Survey embarked upon its extensive hydrographic survey

in response to congressional authorization, Senator William Stewart of Nevada and others soon became alarmed over Powell's proposed withdrawal of public lands on such a large scale, and the hydrographic survey was terminated in 1890. The western bloc in Congress then combined with other enemies of the "autocratic" Powell and threatened the regular operations of the Geological Survey with reduced appropriations until he resigned in 1894 as director.

Powell continued scientific work through the Bureau of American Ethnology, which he had guided since 1879, and also began to commit to writing a lifetime of philosophical musings that blended his optimistic faith in humanity and his positivistic reliance on science. Powell's vision of scientific, ordered western development was finally vindicated before his death when the NEW-LANDS RECLAMATION ACT (1902) authorized the federal government to build reclamation projects and reserve irrigable land for homestead settlers in the arid domain.

At the time of his death, Powell was honored as a soldier, teacher, explorer, geologist, and anthropologist, and judgment was rendered that his career in directing scientific institutions in the federal government outweighed his personal contributions to scientific knowledge. In the West he is known as the father of the reclamation movement. While his achievements as a scientist and promoter of government science have recently been reassessed, one cannot avoid stressing also the breadth of his contribution to the conservation movement. He was in the vanguard of the twentieth century's demand for a rational use of resources. Through his survey, special commissions, and the Geological Survey and Bureau of American Ethnology, he revealed the limits of western resources and warned that section of the harsh necessity to classify and develop legal institutions for the conservation of this resource base.

Richard A. Bartlett, *Great Surveys of the American West* (1962), is a balanced presentation of the Powell surveys as part of a larger study of the geological surveys that were united as a government agency. William C. Darrah, *Powell of the Colorado* (1951), is the definitive biography of Powell. W. M. Davis, "Biographical Memoir of John Wesley Powell, 1834-1902," *National Academy of Science Biographical Memoirs* (1915), is a well-balanced biography. A. Hunter Dupree, *Science in the Federal Government* (1957), describes and evaluates Powell's role in shaping the U. S. Geological Survey. Everett W. Sterling, "The Powell Irrigation Survey, 1888-1893," *Mississippi Valley Historical Review* (December 1940), offers the best description of Powell's irrigation survey program and the political ramifications following therefrom.—L. B. L.

Powhatan (?-1618). Indian chief. Powhatan was the founder and chief of the Powhatan Confederacy of eastern Virginia Algonquian tribes that was prominent in the early colonial period. The name "Powhatan" means "falls in a running stream" and was originally the name of one small tribe. There is no precise record of Chief Powhatan's birth. Captain John Smith said his true name was Wahunsonacock, and that he ruled as "an Emperor ruleth over many Kings or Govenours. . . . He hath as many women as he will, wherof he lieth on his bed, one sitteth at his head, and another at his feet, but when he sitteth, one sitteth on his right hand

and another on his left." He was a tall and well-proportioned man, of sour expression, with a thin beard and a graying head. He seemed to be approximately sixty years of age at the time Smith first saw him. In his youth Powhatan had become chief of his own tribe and seven loosely associated others. Through a campaign of conquest he had by 1607 brought twenty-two other tribes consisting of over two hundred villages under his dominion.

When the white colonists first appeared, Powhatan remained aloof. He had good reason to be suspicious of his English neighbors, who were contemptuous of the Indians and demanded they furnish food to keep the colony from starving. As John Smith was to learn, Powhatan could be stern in his punishments of both Englishmen and Indian enemies who fell into his clutches. When Smith was captured while hunting near Powhatan's village, the chief would have had him executed except for the famous intercession of Powhatan's daughter Pocahontas. Powhatan was unpredictable in temperament, and only the marriage of Pocahontas to John Rolfe modified his actions against the whites and ended the petty warfare that had plagued the Jamestown colony's early years. When he died in 1618 control of the tribes passed to his brother, Opechancanough, who hated the whites utterly.

Powhatan's significance in frontier history lies in the fact that his people were the first Indians with whom the English settlers came in contact on landing at Jamestown in 1607. The relationships of the two peoples were to reflect some of the problems that American settlers would confront the rest of the way across the continent. Too, Powhatan and Pocahontas added a touch of romance and color to the opening of the first Virginia frontier.

See F. W. Hodge, ed., *Handbook of American Indians North of Mexico*, 2 vols. (1907-10); C. W. Sams, *The Conquest of Virginia*, 4 vols. (1916-39); and John Smith, *The Generall Historie of Virginia, New England & the Summer Isles* (1632).—T. D. C.

prairie dog. In September 1804, Lewis and Clark noted "barking squirrels" along the upper Missouri River in what is now South Dakota. Zebulon Pike in 1806 and Edwin James in 1820 described "prairie dogs" in "villages." Such dog towns occur on the short-grass plains that extend from eastern Montana to western Texas. The plump, tawny, ground squirrels (*Cynomys ludovicianus* or "dog-mouse of Louisiana Region") with short black-tipped tails may weigh two pounds. The entrances to their burrows, which are about five inches in diameter, are spaced roughly a dozen yards apart. Around each entrance an earthen mound, sometimes butted into a cone, forms a watchtower and dike. During the winter the dogs do not hibernate deeply, although they may stay underground for days. They mate underground and, a month later, bear young, about four per litter. The pups, born in March and April, remain in nest burrows for six weeks, then, after weaning, emerge to feed on surface plants greened by early rains.

On summer days the dogs spend hours on their mounds or feeding afar. Often when two meet they kiss, nose each other's rear, or playfully chase and wrestle. At a sharp alarm bark, all dash to the burrows. Then, as fright subsides, some emerge and call *ee' ko* as they quickly extend their bodies erect and point their noses

skyward, as if to signal "all clear." During the summer the town populace may divide into social groups, each with a dominant male. Aided by other members, he chases, threatens, and sometimes fights alien dogs that enter the group territory of about one acre.

Spring births may double or treble the winter population of about five dogs per acre. Crowding then stimulates the digging of new holes at the outskirts of the town, so that the town may double in area. Sometimes towns remain static in size for a number of years. Others often become "ghost towns" through natural depopulation by adverse weather, food shortages, diseases, or predation. The rare black-footed ferret pursues dogs in their galleries. A nesting pair of golden eagles can take hundreds of dogs during a few months. Badgers dig out dogs and catch others on the surface. Coyotes also catch them, as wolves probably did. In some dog towns, hundreds of prairie rattlesnakes den in winter and emerge hungry in the spring, when inexperienced pups abound.

Dog burrows are also homes to Plains cottontails and, as James noted, burrowing owls. But the tale that the owl, rattlesnake, and prairie dog lived in communal bliss was rightly labeled "pure bosh" by naturalist Elliott Coues in 1874. On preserves today, pronghorns and bison gather on dog towns to feed, rest, and wallow.

Most towns are located on gently sloping, deep, alluvial soils, rarely including sandy or rocky areas, hilltops, or wet bottoms. Older burrows may be more than thirty feet long and ten feet deep and have several entrances. Average towns usually contain twenty-five burrows per acre. On adequate cattle range, burrow mounds and surrounding bared soil amount to about three percent of the area, but where plant cover has been depleted through heavy grazing the proportion is greater and the dogs may speed erosion. Prairie dogs help soil formation by raising deep earth to the surface and by allowing air and water to penetrate. Further, they incorporate feces, grass, and, finally, their own bodies.

Feeding habits vary seasonally. On winter days, even after snowfall, some dogs come out to nibble cactus, saltbush, or tubers. With the coming of spring all feed heavily on green herbage. During summer, as weeds and grasses grow tall, the dogs cut them low, as if to clear their field of vision. Locally they eat cutworms and grasshoppers. Then, as plants dry in the fall, the dogs turn to hard seeds and short grasses. Dogs that fail to fatten in the fall may not reproduce or survive the winter. Although the dogs eat cattle forage, they do not, contrary to common beliefs, remove nutrients from the land but, rather, speed their recycling in the ecosystem.

By clipping the seedlings and young sprouts of tumbleweeds and shrub, prairie dogs aid stockmen. Many southwestern ranchers attribute the spread of spiny mesquite trees to the poisoning of range rodents. Over long periods, selective feeding by prairie dogs tends to increase the short perennial grasses, blue grama and buffalo grass, which form their favored habitat. Thus, a dog town range may appear "like a bowling-green in fine order," as Lewis and Clark noted. To a degree, bison and prairie dogs form a symbiotic association, each tending to produce habitat favorable to the other.

Man continually alters the Plains habitat. The horse, introduced by Coronado in the mid-1500s, made efficient bison hunters of the Indians. The addition of firearms led to the destruction of the buffalo herds before 1880. Railroads stimulated rapid settlement and a boom in sheep and cattle ranching. Fences and windmills led to destructive grazing and, by 1900, an increase in prairie dogs. To reduce them, poisoned grain was scattered annually over huge areas, under a federal program. World War I needs for grain led to the excessive plowing of range sod, which was followed by abandonment and dust storms. Land misuse favored a greater increase of "animal weeds" such as prairie dogs, and range poisoning intensified. Efficiency of the kill increased with the introduction of Compound 1080, a persistent chemical that secondarily killed coyotes and other animals that had eaten dead rodents. The resultant complex long-term effects of poisoning on animal, plant, and soil communities are largely unknown. Black-tailed prairie dogs still survive in limited areas of ten states, and dog towns are prized exhibits in government preserves.

For additional ecological data, consult C. B. Koford, *Prairie Dogs, White Faces, and Blue Grama,* Wildlife Monograph No. 3 (1958). For behavioral details, see J. A. King, *Contributions Laboratory Vertebrate Biology* (1955).—C. B. K.

Prairie du Chien, Treaty of (1825). Indian treaty. The Treaty of Prairie du Chien grew out of the centuries-long feud between the Ojibwa and Sioux (Dakota) Indian peoples, which by the early nineteenth century was involving neighboring tribes and threatening the advance of white settlement into the upper Mississippi valley. In 1824 an Indian delegation went to Washington to ask that the federal government mediate and establish tribal boundaries. Accordingly, the following year William Clark, former governor of the Missouri Territory, and Governor Lewis Cass of Michigan Territory headed a commission that met with the tribal leaders of the Santee Sioux, Ojibwa, Sauk and Fox, Winnebago, Potawatomi, and Iowa in Prairie du Chien, Wisconsin. The tiny garrison of Fort Crawford was detailed to preserve order among the gathered Indians, who numbered over a thousand, but the peace of the conference was due entirely to the Indians' determination to put an end to internecine war. After lengthy discussions, during which Cass nearly broke the hearts of the assembled chiefs by pouring all their gifts of whiskey on the ground in a gesture of temperance, the Indians on August 19, 1825, agreed to specific boundaries and swore perpetual peace to each other and to the white man. Although no land cessions were made in the Treaty of Prairie du Chien, it paved the way for agricultural advancement into the upper Midwest by eliminating most of the intertribal warfare and creating an attitude of respect toward the white government. This attitude aided immeasurably in the long series of piecemeal cessions and evictions of Indians that occurred in following years.

See B. E. Mahan, *Old Fort Crawford and the Frontier* (1926); F. P. Prucha, *Broadaxe and Bayonet: The Role of the United States Army in the Development of the Northwest, 1815-1860* (1953); and P. L. Scanlan, *Prairie du Chien: French, British, American* (1937).—P. R. M.

prairies. See VEGETATION.

prairie schooner. The prairie schooner—or steamboat of the Plains, as the freight wagon of the trans-

Mississippi frontier was called—received its appellation from its boatlike shape. The body of the wagon flared out, the wheels were out-turned, and a tarpaulin upheld by bows covered the top, thus giving the wagon "a jaunty boatlike air." The forerunner of this wagon was the CONESTOGA WAGON, built by the Pennsylvania Dutch during colonial times. The Conestoga wagon was modified for use in the Middle West and Far West, but the basic design was not altered drastically. Prairie schooners were four-wheeled vehicles and could carry several thousand pounds of freight. The price of a well-built wagon ran as high as $1,500.

Prairie schooners followed several trails. The starting points were usually river and ocean ports or towns where the rail lines were temporarily halted. A wide variety of goods was carried by the wagons, ranging from mining equipment and farm machinery to grocery items, liquor, and tobacco, to firearms and ammunition. Scattered military outposts, mining camps, and farm communities relied on these shipments to meet the requirements and amenities necessary to sustain life on the frontier. The wagons usually made the return trip empty. The heyday of wagon freighting, the 1850s to 1870s, was short-lived, because railroads pushed ever westward, following the frontier line.

See Oscar Osborn Winther, *The Transportation Frontier: Trans-Mississippi West, 1865-1890,* (1964), Histories of the American Frontier, Ray Allen Billington, ed. —D. J. T.

Pratt, Orson (1811-1881). Mormon leader. Born in Hartford, New York, Pratt was the younger brother of the noted Mormon preacher and publicist, Parley P. Pratt. Converted and baptized by his brother in 1830, Orson began the most remarkable missionary effort in Mormon history. Between 1830 and 1867, he served varying types of missions to New York; Ohio; all the other eastern states; Canada; England; Washington, D.C.; Scotland; and continental Europe. In all, he crossed the Atlantic sixteen times.

Intertwined with proselyting are Pratt's accomplishments as a mathematician and writer. He was editor of *The Latter-day Saints' Millennial Star* (Liverpool, 1848-51) and *The Seer* (Washington, D.C., 1852). He was one of the first Mormons to enter the Salt Lake valley in 1847. Often a member of the Utah territorial legislature, Pratt was a seven-term speaker of the house.

Made an apostle in 1835, he was the last of the original twelve chosen by Joseph Smith. He was temporarily excommunicated in 1842 because he rebelled against the secret practice of polygamy. He later became a strong advocate of polygamy, being the man who announced it officially in an 1852 discourse. Pratt became historian and recorder for the church in 1874, and in 1878, while in that position, he divided the Book of Mormon and *Doctrine and Covenants* into verses.

See Andrew Jenson, *Latter-day Saint Biographical Encyclopedia* (1901).

Pratt, Richard Henry (1840-1924). Indian educator and soldier. Born in Rushford, New York, Pratt grew up in Logansport, Indiana. His father's death caused Pratt to end schooling at age thirteen and apprentice himself at the tinner's trade in order to support his family. In 1861 he enlisted in the Union army. He saw action in several major battles and earned the rank of first lieutenant before he was mustered out in May 1865. He married Anna Laura Mason on April 12, 1864, and together they reared four children.

Unsuccessful in civilian life, Pratt reenlisted in March 1867 as a second lieutenant. He was assigned to a Negro regiment in Indian Territory and given command of the Indian scouts. For the next seven years his duties kept him in close contact with these two great minority races of the country. In 1874 the army ordered Pratt to search out the Indians responsible for recent depredation around Fort Sill, Oklahoma, and later to escort seventy-two of these suspects as prisoners to Fort Marion in St. Augustine, Florida, where they were to pass an indefinite exile.

Once at Fort Marion (May 1875), Pratt began to experiment in educating his prisoners, enlisting financial help and teaching assistance from residents of the town when he received no official encouragement. The army approved the release of the Indians in the fall of 1877, and Pratt, encouraged by their rapid progress, asked to continue the schooling of some in the East. Again denied governmental support, he persuaded General S. C. Armstrong of Hampton Institute to take seventeen Indians into his all-Negro training school, and Pratt himself taught there.

The progress of the Indians at Hampton in the following year brought praise from officials in Washington, including President Rutherford B. Hayes, but it did not dissuade the army from demanding Pratt's return to military duty. Under the threat of recall, Pratt appealed to Secretary of the Interior Carl Schurz for permission to establish a governmental Indian school at the abandoned army barracks in Carlisle, Pennsylvania. The cooperation of Secretary of War George McCrary led to the opening of the CARLISLE INDIAN SCHOOL in October 1879, with eighty-two children recruited from the Sioux tribes in Dakota Territory, and with Lieutenant Pratt as superintendent.

Pratt served at Carlisle for the next twenty-five years. In addition to reviving public interest and confidence in the idea that Indians could become more like whites by means of education, he made an original contribution to educational policy with his concept of the eastern boarding school. He argued that the only way to get the Indian into the mainstream of American life was to isolate him from the tribal environment and put him into contact with educated white men. Although his central idea of an *eastern* location for the schools was never adopted, boarding schools were widely introduced on and near the reservations in an attempt to realize these objectives.

The issue of location gradually forced Pratt to oppose the Indian Bureau and humanitarian organizations interested in the Indian. He was convinced that assimilation could only be accomplished by the physical integration of the Indian; governmental policy, unfortunately, served to continue the segregation of the race on increasingly squalid reservations. Pratt's forceful personality and his candid opinions, considered by some to be evidence of an unbalanced mind, finally led to his forced retirement from the army on February 17, 1903, and his dismissal from Carlisle for insubordination on June 30, 1904. Pratt continued to argue his point of view for two more decades while in retirement, but without success.—E. A. G.

Presbyterians. Among the European migrants who settled in the English colonies were several different groups who got their doctrine from Calvin but who preferred the Presbyterian form of church organization—English Puritans, Scottish and Scotch-Irish Presbyterians, French Huguenots, and adherents to the Reformed churches of Switzerland, Germany, and Holland. A request from a member of the Governor's Council of Maryland to the Presbytery of Laggan in Ireland led to the ordination there of Francis Makemie and to his service in North America as a roving missionary. In the 1680s his labors helped to create several Presbyterian churches in Maryland and in 1706 he organized the first presbytery in the New World. It included seven churches in Maryland, Delaware, and Philadelphia. By 1716 it included churches from New Jersey and Long Island and transformed itself into a synod. The ministers from Philadelphia and the North were mostly of New England origin; those in Delaware and Maryland were Scottish or Scotch-Irish.

Persecutions following the Restoration of Charles II in 1660 and again after the Test Act of 1713 in Ireland caused a large migration of Presbyterian Scottish and, more importantly, Scotch-Irish settlers. They established themselves, for the most part, in the back-country of the Middle Colonies. The isolated settlements of these cabin dwellers were stirred in the third and fourth decades of the eighteenth century by the Great Awakening. Gilbert Tennent, of New Brunswick, New Jersey, together with a neighboring pastor, Jacob Frelinghuysen of the Dutch Reformed Church of Raritan, first lighted revivalistic fires, which ultimately spread from Georgia to New England. Tennent had been trained at an academy at Neshaminy, Pennsylvania, established by his father, William Tennent, in 1736. The elder Tennent, a graduate of the University of Edinburgh, sensed that aspirants to the ministry in the Middle Colonies were impeded by the requirement of the General Synod, created in 1716, that they must have been educated abroad or at Yale or Harvard in distant New England. William Tennent, an effective teacher, instructed his students in the theology of the Westminster Confession and imbued them with his evangelistic impulse. His work, which lasted from 1736 to 1745, stimulated the founding of other academies. Its importance is also suggested by the fact that a quarter of the first board of trustees of the College of New Jersey, founded in 1746, were William Tennent students as was also an early president, Samuel Finley. Conservative pastors of churches in older settlements looked upon revivalism with a jaundiced eye and dubbed Tennent's school "log college," a designation that, in time, became an accolade.

In 1768 the trustees of the College of New Jersey called John Witherspoon from across the Atlantic to the presidency. As tension between the colonies and the mother country grew, Witherspoon championed the cause of American rights and liberties. Witherspoon led his fellow Presbyterians, most of whom were Scotch-Irish, in support of the Patriot effort and became the only clergyman to sign the Declaration of Independence. National independence prepared the way for the national organization of the Presbyterian Church. In 1788 the General Assembly, the supreme authority, came into being. It was made up of delegates elected from four synods. At the time the denomination had 177 ministers, 111 probationers, and 419 churches. An educated ministry, the wide distribution of its congregations, an effective national organization, and the prestige of its unquestioned patriotism combined to make the Presbyterians the most influential religious body in the new nation.

Presbyterian leaders, many reared in the back-country of the original thirteen states, sensed the challenge of the rapidly moving frontier west of the Appalachians. At a time when New Englanders were streaming into the West, the Presbyterians teamed with the Congregationalists in a Plan of Union of 1801. The agreement made it possible for newly gathered western congregations to belong to both denominations, an arrangement which, in the end, worked to the advantage of the Presbyterians. The General Assembly created in 1802 a Standing Committee of Missions (later the Board of Missions), which sent missionaries to unchurched communities in the continental interior. Often they rode circuit, spreading the spirit of REVIVALISM and scattering churches over a vast nation. Because they held fast to the requirement of an educated clergy, the Presbyterians achieved no such numerical triumphs as did the Methodists and the Baptists.

The stories of Presbyterian origins on two remote frontiers suggest the assignments and the conditions faced by the missionaries. In May 1833 a sailing ship dropped anchor off the mouth of the Chicago River at the southern end of Lake Michigan. It brought from Sault Sainte Marie two companies of soldiers under the command of a major who had been ordered to relieve the commandant at Fort Dearborn. (Chief Black Hawk's war in Illinois and Wisconsin the year before had caused the army to reorganize its frontier defense.) The Reverend Jeremiah Porter also came on the ship along with some members of the small congregation he had gathered in his short stay in Sault Sainte Marie. Young Porter from Williams College was two years out of Princeton Theological Seminary when the ship's long-boat took him ashore.

He looked out over a low-lying, swampy prairie. Outside the fort a cluster of log cabins housed the families of traders, trappers, carters, and artisans—perhaps three hundred persons when the garrison of the fort was added. Just beyond the cabins Porter saw the prairie schooners of the Hoosiers from the Wabash valley, who had brought their products to trade for salt, groceries, and other goods. Some of the "praying men" who stood for decency and order in a rowdy community where whiskey flowed freely left with the ship. Others of the community welcomed the young missionary and the new commanding officer, who had been a member of Porter's congregation in the north. The major immediately ordered the fort's carpenter shop to be cleared and made ready for worship services. As the young missionary walked from his rooming house on the following Sunday to preach his first sermon in the carpenter shop, he passed some Indians sitting in front of a French dram shop playing cards while white loungers looked on.

The congregation that Porter quickly gathered soon set about to build a church. The men gave their labor and skills as well as money. The women made and raffled off quilts to raise funds. In the January after Porter's arrival the minister and congregation dedicated their church with the thermometer reading fifteen below zero. It was the largest hall in the community and served as schoolhouse, town hall, a place for debates and concerts, and, on one occasion, a courthouse for the circuit court. The membership grew rapidly. The missionary board that had sent Porter to Sault Sainte Marie had commissioned him to explore the shores of Lake Michigan for settlements where the gospel might be preached. He looked no farther than Fort Dearborn.

In the spring of 1834 two young brothers, Presbyterian ministers, traveled from Galena to Fort Snelling on the upper Mississippi River. Acting on their own volition, they proposed to teach the Dakota Indians the gospel and the ways of civilization. In spite of the law forbidding the entry of whites into the Indian country, the commanding officer of the fort allowed them to remain and appointed them to instruct the Indians in farming. Other missionaries came the following year. They organized a church in the fort. Men of education, they began the task of mastering the language of the Dakota Indians. Within four years they had produced a dictionary of the language, which was published by the Smithsonian Institution. They also translated into Siouan the Gospel of St. Mark and Christianized a number of tribesmen.

Treaties made in 1837 opened a large area of Minnesota for white settlement. Improved transportation by canal and by steamboat on the lakes and the Mississippi River made the rich lands of Minnesota accessible. Congress organized in 1849 the Territory of Minnesota. In the same year a Presbyterian missionary organized a church in St. Paul. The sanctuary was the first Protestant church building in the territory. The Presbyterians attracted persons of education, substance, and social standing, who came in increasing numbers to the Minnesota frontier. A demand for higher education led to the founding of Macalester College in 1874. It was made possible by a large gift from a Philadelphia philanthropist, who responded to an appeal from an old friend, one of the pioneer missionaries who came to Minnesota.

Education is the most striking contribution to the life of nineteenth-century frontier communities by Presbyterians working in cooperation with Congregationalists. In the early decades "log" colleges like that of William Tennent sprang up in Kentucky and Tennessee. Combined Presbyterian and Congregationalist labors scattered colleges over Ohio, Indiana, and Illinois. A story of dedication and zeal lies behind the founding of Illinois College in 1829 in Jacksonville. The Reverend John Mills, while working in that community under the auspices of the American Home Missionary Society, published in a letter to the *Home Missionary Journal* his hopes that a seat of higher learning might be established in the region of his mission. Challenged by the letter, six students at the new Yale Divinity School mutually pledged themselves on the completion of their theological training to devote their lives to missionary and educational work on the Illinois project. J. M. Sturtevant of the "Yale Band" became the first instructor at Illinois College. The others did equally significant work elsewhere on the frontier. Before the United States divided in war in 1861 the Presbyterians with the aid of the Congregationalists had contributed to the life of the nation forty-nine colleges and universities located in twenty-one of the then thirty-four states.

If the nineteenth century was a time of expanding

Presbyterianism, it was also a time of division and splintering. Disputes arose concerning the interpretation of the constitution of the denomination. Theological differences caused heresy trials and also the creation of dissident groups, such as the DISCIPLES OF CHRIST. The issue of slavery caused the main body of the church to break into separate entities. In the first quarter of the twentieth century nine distinct bodies called themselves Presbyterian. But the middle decades of the twentieth century saw marked progress toward the union of diverse groups. In 1970 the Cumberland Presbyterian Church, organized in Tennessee in 1810, reported a membership of something more than 88,000. The Presbyterian Church in the United States, which dates from 1861, had a membership a little in excess of 960,000. The United Presbyterian Church in the United States of America came into existence in 1958 with the union of the United Presbyterian Church of North America and the Presbyterian Church in the United States of America. Its membership in 1970 exceeded 3,268,000.

See Sidney E. Ahlstrom, *A Religious History of the American People* (1972); J. B. Scouller, *History of the United Presbyterian Church, North America* (1894); G. J. Slosser, ed., *They Seek a Country* (1955); and L. J. Trinterud, *The Forming of an American Tradition* (1949).—R. H. G.

Prescott, Arizona. The setting for the mile-high city of Prescott is a lush pine-forested valley with Granite Creek bending through it. Granite Peak, Spruce Mountain, and Mount Tritle form crested eminences on a range that encircles the town on three sides.

In 1863 Joseph Reddeford Walker's party of gold-seekers were the first white campers on Granite Creek. The next immigrants came the following year from California and New Mexico, among them a Joseph Ehle and family. They left New Mexico with two hundred head of cattle, but upon reaching Prescott, only four head remained; the others had been lost or stolen by Apache.

The original Camp Whipple, named for Brigadier General A. W. Whipple, was established in 1863 in the Chino valley, more than seventeen miles north of Prescott. It served as headquarters for two companies of California Volunteers. Fearful of a Confederate takeover in Arizona in 1863, Congress and President Lincoln made Arizona a territory. The following year Governor John N. Goodwin arrived in Camp Whipple from the East with an entourage of Washington-appointed subordinates. Shortly after the new governor moved Fort Whipple and the territorial government to Granite Creek. The new location was named Prescott, to honor the historian William Hickling Prescott. A handsome pine-log Capital building was constructed to house the state legislature until 1867, when the seat of state government was transferred to Tucson. The capital came again to Prescott in 1877 but was permanently located in Phoenix in 1889.

Prescott boomed in 1870 when more modern machinery simplified and cheapened the cost of metal recovery from ore. Miners flocked in, and many struck paydirt in rich lodes yielding gold, silver, copper, lead, and zinc. Cattle and sheep were introduced to supply meat for Fort Whipple and miners; today they represent the major source of ranch income. The coming of the Atchinson, Topeka and Santa Fe Railway in 1893 helped with cheaper transportation and increased net income.

Still a mining, lumbering, and livestock center, Prescott is also a mecca for tourists, retired people, fishermen, and hunters. In 1970 it had a population of 13,000.

See Pauline Henson, *Founding a Wilderness Capital: Prescott, Arizona Territory, 1864* (1965); and Jay J. Wagoner, *Arizona, A Guide to the Sunset State* (1940) and *Arizona Territory 1863-1912* (1970).—B. W. A.

Preuss, Charles (1803-1854). Topographer and artist. Preuss, born in Germany, began his professional career as a surveyor for the Prussian government. He immigrated to the United States in 1834 and was hired by the United States Coast Survey under Ferdinand Hassler. In 1841 Hassler introduced him to John Charles FREMONT, and Preuss was thereafter engaged for the first two Frémont expeditions to Oregon and California. Preuss did the map and numerous sketches for the important report of the second expedition. His map has been called by Carl Wheat "a monument of Western cartography."

Resentful and irritated with Frémont, Preuss did not join the third expedition (1845-46) but was persuaded to embark on the disastrous fourth expedition (1848-49), an attempt to cross the Colorado Rockies in winter. In that effort, which cost the lives of eleven men, Preuss blamed the guide, Old Bill Williams, for the failure.

The expedition left Preuss in California, where he engaged in various surveying jobs until he suffered a sunstroke in 1850 and returned to Washington. In 1853 he was invited to accompany Frémont again, but he refused and joined instead R. S. Williamson on one of the Pacific Railroad surveys. On his return to Washington, he fell ill and in desperation hanged himself from a tree on September 1, 1854. The suicide probably was related to what his translator, Erwin Gudde, has called a morose and melancholy strain in his personality. Preuss always disliked the hardships of the trail and vented his unhappiness toward Frémont in his private diaries, written in German.

See Erwin G. and Elisabeth K. Gudde, eds., *Exploring with Frémont: The Private Diaries of Charles Preuss, Cartographer for John C. Frémont on his First, Second and Fourth Expeditions to the Far West* (1968).—R. V. H.

Priber, Christian Gottlieb (?-c.1743). Socialist missionary to the Cherokee. Priber was a German utopian socialist who, after being expelled from his homeland because of his radical philosophy, settled in 1736 among the Cherokee Indians of western Carolina and began instructing them in his theories. Adopting Indian dress and rapidly learning their language, this odd Enlightenment *philosophe* was befriended by the British puppet emperor, Moytoy, and was soon styling himself "His Cherokee Majesty's Secretary of State." Envisioning a communistic Indian republic that would embrace the Cherokee, Catawba, Creek, and Choctaw, Priber preached community ownership of property, communal marriage, equality of sexes, and state custody of children.

Surprisingly popular among the Cherokee, he was considered a harmless little lunatic by British trading agents until he taught the Indians how to check for honest weights and measures. Priber was then suspected of French sympathies, and when he called for an independent Indian state that would maintain neutrality and trade with both the British and French, the Carolinians were convinced he was a Jesuit. Needing Cherokee loyalty in the tightening conflict with the French, the South Carolina governor made two attempts to arrest Priber, but both times his emissaries were threatened by the outraged Indians and made it safely back only through Priber's intercession. In 1743, however, he was captured by British traders while journeying to French Fort Toulouse. Taken to Frederica, Georgia, for examination, Priber soon died in what was charitably termed confinement, and the Cherokee remained loyal to England during King George's War.

See R. S. Cotterill, *The Southern Indians* (1954); Verner Crane, "A Lost Utopia of the First American Frontier," *Sewanee Review*, vol. 27 (1919); and C. J. Milling, *Red Carolinians* (1940).—P. R. M.

Price, Clayton S. (1874-1950). Illustrator and painter. Born on a ranch at Bedford, Iowa, the third of eleven children, Price spent his early years working as a cowhand in Wyoming and filling notebooks with sketches of horses, cattle, and ranch life. In 1905 he spent a year at the St. Louis School of Fine Arts, the only formal training he was to receive. Although he returned to ranching for a time, his real interest was art.

From 1908 to 1910 he lived in Portland, Oregon, serving as illustrator for the *Pacific Monthly*, a literary and promotional magazine, and then he moved to San Francisco. During these years he painted in the western manner much like the cowboy artist Charles Russell, whom he had met in St. Louis. Soon thereafter, however, while visiting the 1915 Panama and Pacific International Exposition in San Francisco, Price was exposed to modern European painting and, between 1918 and 1927, developed a style that identified him as a "modernist."

In 1928 Price returned to Portland, where he remained until his death, and in 1933 joined the federal Works Progress Administration (WPA) Art Project. Much of his work during this period was allocated to public buildings and collections in Portland and Washington, D.C. In the 1940s the artist, working alone, matured and won growing recognition on the national scene. His work was displayed in the Portland Art Museum, the Detroit Institute of Arts, and in the Valentine Gallery, the Museum of Modern Art, and the Willard Gallery in New York.

Like some of his contemporaries, John Sloan, John Marin, George Luks, and Edward Hopper, Price was a "regionalist," but with a difference. By 1940 he had attained a mystic and symbolic expressionism that linked him with a younger generation of painters and had come under formative influences from such diverse sources as Rouault, Byzantine frescoes, oriental art, and the art of the Pacific Northwest Indians. As a matter of choice Price never traveled east of the Mississippi, yet he fought free of the artistic provincialism of his beginnings to achieve a rendering of commonplace western subjects, such as cattle, wolves, and horses, that transcended traditional representational treatment and resulted in a profound symbolic statement of his understanding of the West.

See *C. S. Price, 1874-1950: A Memorial Exhibition* (1951), with reproductions of the artist's work and commentaries by Harris K. Prior and Priscilla Colt; and Frank H. Hurley, "Fifty Years with C. S. Price," *Oregon Journal* (1950).—E. R. B.

Price, Sterling (1809-1867). Missouri politician and Confederate officer. Price was born in Prince Edward County, Virginia. After a year at Hampden-Sydney College he studied law with the well-known Virginia jurist Creed Taylor. When his parents migrated to Missouri in 1831, he went with them and eventually settled on a farm in Chariton County, where he remained until the Civil War.

Price served three terms in the Missouri General Assembly (1836-38, 1840-44) and was named speaker his last four years. Elevated to the United States Congress in 1844, he failed to be renominated two years later. Disgusted, he resigned in August 1846 to accept appointment as colonel of one of the Missouri regiments bound for New Mexico. Shortly after his arrival there, he assumed the military governorship of Chihuahua and vigorously crushed uprisings by the Pueblo Indians and Mexicans. At the close of the Mexican war, he returned to Missouri with the brevet rank of brigadier general, a solid reputation, and a strong feeling for things military.

For the next several years Price again devoted his efforts to his tobacco plantation and politics. In the political turmoil of the 1850s in Missouri he sided with the proslavery, anti-Benton wing of the Democratic party, which rewarded him with the state's governorship in 1852. As chief executive he looked with favor upon the attempts of Missourians to make Kansas a slave state, although he took no official action in behalf of the "border ruffians."

Price favored conciliation in the crisis of 1860-61 and chaired the Missouri secession convention that decided against the need for leaving the Union. However, after the Camp Jackson affair in May 1861, in which Union Commander Nathaniel Lyon seized state troops, he was afraid that the Union sought to coerce the state from following a neutral path, and decided to accept command of the reorganized Missouri state guard. His subsequent victories over Union forces at Wilson's Creek and Lexington captured for him a popularity among southerners and his own men that failed to die—even in the face of later reverses and quarrels with Confederate officials.

Following the Confederate defeat at Pea Ridge, Arkansas, in March 1862 most of his state guard was integrated into the southern army, and Price himself accepted a Confederate commission as major general. He fought with little success in Mississippi and Arkansas for the next two years. Then in September 1864 he led a futile raid back into Missouri to gather recruits and divert Union strength from General William T. Sherman, who was located outside Atlanta. When the war ended shortly thereafter, Price beat a retreat to Mexico, where he remained in exile for a year and a half.

His health broken, Price returned to St. Louis in January 1867 to enter business. He died shortly thereafter.

The best standard biography of Price is Robert E. Shalhope, *Sterling Price: Portrait of a Southerner* (1971). Price's Civil War career is well analyzed in Albert Castel, *Sterling Price and the Civil War in the West* (1968). —W. E. P.

prints. In the years before the invention of photography, pictures had to be printed, with very few experimental exceptions, from wood, engraving on metal, or lithography. By the last half of the nineteenth century these techniques, particularly wood engraving and lithography, had gained widespread popular acceptance and were a conspicuous part of American daily life. Innumerable illustrations in papers and journals, pictorial advertising, posters, trade cards, dime novels, and popular prints created an incredible circus of graphics reflecting the life of the period. Altogether, these prints were a manifestation of a new democracy in the arts and provide a highly colorful and fascinating pictorial chronicle of the era.

Life in the early West is particularly well portrayed in this genre of popular prints. Feeling is sometimes more important than fact in many of the prints, but a casual disconcern with historical accuracy does little to detract from their human appeal and historical flavor. The unmistakable spirit of the early barroom West is quickly communicated in the lusty if primitive woodcuts in contemporary issues of the *California Police Gazette*. The anonymous designer of such lively scenes as "Panic in a Brothel During the San Francisco Earthquake" and "A Lively Row at the National Brewery, in Virginia City, Nevada" entered into the spirit of the moment with such zest that he clearly was a habitué of the scene rather than any visiting dude artist. No less vivid were the illustrations in the popular dime novels of the period, which almost always had similarly vigorous woodcuts. The stylistic family likeness of the illustrations in dime novels was the result of consistently dreadful Victorian typography, the frequent full-page woodcut on the cover (sometimes beautifully printed in color), and, in the literary style, obsessive alliteration in titles. The woodcuts to illustrate "Roaring Ralph Rockwood the Reckless Ranger" and "Deadwood Dick's Diamonds" are only slightly more sophisticated than those of the *California Police Gazette* and are representative of the prevailing style of book illustration in the last half of the nineteenth century, both in America and abroad. It is a style equally familiar to readers of certain cheap editions of Jules Verne, temperance tracts, and tabloid newspapers. The melodrama and mood of such literature was well captured by this style of popular illustration, but it was more the result of mediocre taste and hack engraving than artistic intention.

More enlightened taste and better-trained hands at engraving were found in another great popular success of the late nineteenth century, the picture magazine. The *Illustrated London News, Harper's Weekly,* and *Frank Leslie's Illustrated Magazine* were full of original wood engravings of excellent quality for this period. A new love of pictorial journalism demanded that professional artists on the scene provide drawings for the paper. These had to be translated into wood for printing. The resulting news picture thus represented several talents. The artist's original design was directly drawn, copied, or pasted onto fruitwood (or preferably endgrain boxwood) in preparation for cutting by the engraver. Since such blocks were available in only small sizes, large wood engravings had to be made up of several small blocks bolted together in the back. Both the front and back of an original four-piece wood block by William J. Linton (1812-1897) are illustrated to show the extraordinary

technical skill developed by certain engravers to supply the great popular demand for printed pictures. Eye fatigue—if not blindness—caused by the work on thousands of such finely detailed prints, often by gaslight, for the picture magazines, was an occupational hazard. Nevertheless, scores of craftsmen made highly successful lifelong careers of wood-engraving. The best examples demonstrate the technical proficiency of these men who translated the fine Civil War drawings of Winslow Homer and the splendid western landscapes of Frederick Church into wood-engraved prints artistically respectable in their own right.

Even more representative of American social history was the rise, in the back pages of these same picture magazines, of advertising art. Here, in full riotous splendor, were the beautifully detailed wood engravings depicting all the consumer products of a growing America. Corsets, patent medicines, farm machines, false teeth, soap and firecrackers, rococo pianofortes and Gothic organs, cough syrups and hair restorers, were represented in surreal juxtaposition, and were an appropriate precursor of, the "pop-panorama" that is advertising's contribution to a more civilized West.

Lithography also was an important technique in the reproduction of early western American prints. This relatively new process relied on special lithography presses and heavy lithographic stones, so that itinerant work in this medium was impractical. The excessive popularity of Currier & Ives in the East and the advantage of direct transfer of an artist's drawing from the stone resulted in the proliferation of lithographic firms in America. Among the published prints of Currier & Ives are found all the favorite Victorian subjects: biblical—"The Prodigal Son"; sentimental—"The Soldier's Farewell"; and morally edifying—"The Ages of Man." But in addition to these and other familiar themes there are some other lithographic prints of historical interest. These rare pictorial documents of western American history often have an unmistakable feeling of firsthand observation. A more tangible reality than any literary account of Mormonism is conveyed in such rare lithographic protraits as "The Two Martyrs Joseph and Hyrum Smith, Murdered at Carthage, Ill., June 27, 1844." The spiritual pride of the Mormons in their naïve but aspiring architecture is also to be found in such rare lithographs as "The Great Mormon Temple at Nauvoo" (c. 1848).

The Mormons suffered their share of caricature, if not graphic persecution, in certain lithographic prints. The abundant contemporary satire of their practice of polygamy is seen in a series of lithographs, published in England by one E. Smith, delineating the possible bedroom crises of the Mormons' bearded prophet, Brigham Young, and his many wives.

The California gold rush, perhaps the most famous single event in the history of the West, is also richly documented in early popular lithographs. Britton & Rey, who were known as the "Currier & Ives of San Francisco," produced a considerable number of prints depicting in unsparing detail daily life in the gold camps. In addition to the usual subjects of prospecting, gambling, and hangings, Britton & Rey created a number of domestic scenes of the frustrations of bachelors and men without women, including scenes of clothes washing, cooking, and button sewing.

Some of the rarest and most entertaining lithographs of the gold rush were made by two itinerant Cuban artists, José Baturone and August Ferrán. Their *Album Californio* (Havana, 1849) contains a series of *Typos Californios*, long-haired and disheveled, who could easily be the original street-people of San Francisco's Haight-Ashbury section.

Two artists famous for their book illustrations and prints are Felix Octavius Carr DARLEY and Charles NAHL. The two have many stylistic qualities in common. They attended European art schools in their youth, and their smooth, clean, often elegant draftsmanship betrays this early academic discipline. Darley's Indians are highly finished academic studies of the male nude, incapable of really scalping or burning white men. His "Life of an Indian" (1843) recalls John Flaxman's neoclassic illustrations of Homer and Virgil. Nahl's illustrations of California prospecting life, while extremely charming, also have an academic tidiness that does not ring true for the hard quality of the early West. His California prospectors are attractive, well-shaven types, and his gold-camp scenes are beautifully composed and delineated, suggesting the domestication of a Tyrolean village rather than the more real, unkempt wildness that was a part of the frontier.

Graphic documentation with more of the grit of reality is found, surprisingly enough, among the antique graphic memorabilia of Victorian scrapbooks. A rich graphic potpourri of such printed ephemera as old valentines, advertising trade cards, dance programs, tickets, and *cartes de visite* is part of Victorian America's parlor albums. These albums, plush marvels of bad taste in binding, contain orgies of chromolithographed nostalgia but also often include real treasures of delicate printmaking (as in the early valentines) and historical documentation. Along with the dreary relics of dried flowers and locks of hair are found such valued rarities as early clipper-ship cards. These cards, now true collector's items, announced the sailing schedules to California from the East, and were always embellished with appropriate and fine color woodcuts. Other small treasures in printed ephemera are such unexpected graphics as playing cards made by American Indians, Currier and Ives trade cards, and lithographed vigilantes' certificates.

Also rare and coveted by collectors are early copper-engraved or lithographed sheet-music covers. It is easy to associate these elaborate cover designs with the fancy scroll-saw music racks of the reigning symbol of Victorian cultural status: the pianoforte. And who can say how much of the West was won with such gently civilizing persuasion as four-hand piano arrangements of "The Yellow Rose of Texas" or Indian medleys for piano, like the "On-ka-hye Waltz"?

More somber popular graphic Americana is seen in the strange romantic taste for funereal prints. Full of weeping willows, tombs, and angels, these black-edged lithographs still invoke much of their original melancholy.

A general Victorian taste for black is also seen in the unusual popularity of silhouette artists. The celebrated American portraitist in black-paper cutouts, Auguste Edouart, made no less than 3,712 recorded shadow profiles of Americans in the decade 1839-49. These and countless other silhouettes are an interesting phase of popular portraiture in the nineteenth century, which evolved from miniatures and Physiognotrace portraits (a popular precursor of photography, which used a camera-lucida device to trade the outline of the sitter's profile) to the daguerreotype and the early photograph. The black-paper silhouette cutouts were often pasted on special lithographed background scenes, graphic descendants of the colonial limner's prepainted settings.

Finally, and impossible to forget, are the posters and printed broadsides of the late nineteenth century. These splendid forerunners of contemporary supergraphics papered the walls of post offices and the sides of barns throughout rural America. A Barnum and Bailey philosophy permeated this ultimate popular art, and posters for the circus, theater, and cure-all medicines alike offered incredible promises in the most sensational possible printing in sectional chromolithography and wood-types. American wood-types, typically printed in the most richly riotous and even joyful way in these posters, are intimately a part of their times. It is impossible to separate the image of the frontier from these boldly carved wood-types proclaiming WANTED: DEAD OR ALIVE, and similar terse bannerlines advertising the latest Buffalo Bill Wild West show or the next public hanging.

Popular prints of the early West, despite their once commonplace role, their crudity and naïveté, are still able to awaken some of the youthful excitement, vigor, and optimism of a still young nation. Their great appeal may rest in their easy honesty of expression and undevious simplicity, qualities often lacking in later, more sophisticated art and life.

See Alice Van Leer Carrick, *Shades of Our Ancestors* (1928); William Dunlap, *A History of the Rise and Progress of the Arts of Design in the United States* (1918); Sinclair Hamilton, *Early American Book Illustrators and Wood Engravers, 1670-1870* (1958); Bella C. Landauer, *Early American Trade Cards* (n.d.); Harry T. Peters, *America on Stone* (1931); and David McNeely Stauffer, *American Engravers Upon Copper and Steel* (1907).—D. R. R.

Proclamation of 1763. See BRITISH ADMINISTRATIVE POLICY (1763-1775).

Proctor, Alexander Phimister (1860-1950). Sculptor. Born in Bozanquit, Ontario, Proctor spent his youth in Canada, Michigan, Iowa, and Colorado. He was interested at an early age in sketching people and animals and received his initial instruction from itinerant Denver illustrators. In 1885 he sold a homestead property and went to New York to study at the National Academy of Design and later at the Art Students League. He returned for brief visits to the West as often as possible to hunt, prospect, and make studies of wild animals.

Proctor's first important commission was to produce several monumental animal sculptures for the World's Columbian Exposition in Chicago in 1893. While studying at the Académie Julien in 1893-94, he was approached by Augustus St. Gaudens to model a horse of St. Gaudens' proposed equestrian statue of General John A. Logan, which was installed in Grant Park, Chicago. Proctor collaborated with St. Gaudens on other equestrian pieces and produced numerous decorative sculptures for various public buildings and monuments in New York City and Washington, D. C. He became an associate member of the National

Academy of Design in 1895 and that same year visited the Blackfoot Indian Reservation in Montana to obtain studies of the Indians in that area. Commissions followed in rapid succession: for the American Pavilion at the Paris International Exposition of 1900, the Pan American Exposition at Buffalo, New York, in 1901, the Louisiana Purchase Exposition in St. Louis in 1904, and others. With Alden Sampson, he built a studio in New York City and continued to travel widely throughout the West.

A friend of naturalist William T. Hornaday, architect Stanford White, and art collectors H. C. Frick and George Pratt, Proctor became known internationally for his animal and American Indian sculptures. Always on the move, he finally settled with his growing family in Seattle in the 1940s but continued to visit New York and California until his death. His public sculptures are in Washington, D. C.; New York; Kansas City, Missouri; Denver, Colorado; and Austin and Dallas, Texas. His more notable works are the *Bronco Buster* (1918) and *On the War Trail* (1920) at the Civic Center Plaza in Denver; *The Rough Riders* at Roosevelt Park, Minot, North Dakota (1920); *Pioneer Mother*, Kansas City, Missouri (1923-27); and *General Robert E. Lee and a Young Soldier*, Dallas, Texas (1935). One of his last important commissions was a group of seven plunging wild horses entitled *Mustangs*, commissioned at the urging of historian J. Frank Dobie, who considered Proctor to be America's outstanding western sculptor. This work was placed at the University of Texas campus in Austin in 1948.

See Proctor's autobiography, *Alexander Phimister Proctor*, with an introduction by Vivian Paladin (1971). —D. C. H.

pronghorn. The pronghorn (*Antilocapra americana ord*) evolved during the Pleistocene epoch and is endemic to North America. Coronado and his men saw pronghorns on the plains of Kansas in 1535, but it was the reports of Lewis and Clark and a specimen collected by them that made the animal known to science and led George Ord to describe and name it in 1818.

Before the arrival of the white man, pronghorns—often called antelope—roamed a great expanse of prairie and semidesert west of the Mississippi River from central Mexico into the prairie provinces of Canada. They apparently equaled or even surpassed the buffalo (*Bison bison*) in numbers. It has been estimated that there were once 40 million pronghorns in North America. Subsequent to 1870, the white man's occupation of the open range depleted the herds. By the early 1900s, only about 30,000 remained, and extinction of the species seemed imminent. Protection from hunting halted the decline, but increases were slow until the early 1940s, when transplanting programs returned pronghorns to many suitable but unoccupied ranges. By the late 1950s, it was estimated that 400,000 pronghorns again roamed the West. Hunting regulations were liberalized and the population was stablized or reduced slightly. The tolerance of ranchers and the policies of the Bureau of Land Management will determine, to a great extent, how many pronghorns can be maintained.

Five subspecies of pronghorn are generally recognized. The animals farthest north tend to be the largest, while those farthest west tend to be the darkest in color. Pronghorns are not large animals, the largest does usually weighing between 100 and 110 pounds and the bucks between 120 and 135 pounds. The basic body color is cinnamon buff with black and white markings on the head and neck. The face of the buck is black, and a black line that distinguishes the male at all ages outlines the edge of the lower jaw below the ear. The black on the face of the doe is confined to the nose. In both sexes the belly and lower sides are creamy white. The short tail is surrounded by a large, white rump patch. Hairs of the rump patch can be erected at will and apparently serve as a visual signal to other animals in the vicinity. Rump glands release a pungent odor when the rump patch is erected. A mane, which can be erected, is present along the back of the neck. The eyes are large, black, and lustrous with heavy, jet-black eyelashes that act as sunshades. In summer the hair of the pronghorn is smooth and flexible, but as winter approaches it lengthens, and each hair, composed of many air cells, becomes thick and spongy. The hair is so loose and brittle that it falls out or breaks off at the least pressure.

Pronghorns are the only hoofed animals in America that do not have dewclaws; their absence is an adaptation for fast running in open country. These animals do not hide; they remain in open country, relying on eyesight and speed for protection. Their eyesight has been compared to a man with eight-power binoculars, and they have been clocked at speeds up to sixty miles per hour. A highly developed sense of curiosity prompts the pronghorn to investigate anything unusual in its territory. Before the advent of long-range rifles, hunters often took advantage of this characteristic.

Pronghorns feed on a seemingly endless variety of plants. Studies have shown that forbs and browse, especially sagebrush, are the principal food during summer and winter, respectively. Grass is consumed in quantity only during spring "green-up." Cacti are usually eaten in substantial quantities where they are available. Other strange preferences include many weeds and even plants that are poisonous to livestock. Pronghorns feed extensively on wheat and barley shoots and, to some extent, on the ripe grain. Few farmers object to the amount of grain these animals eat, but a large herd running through a field of ripe grain can do extensive damage.

During spring and early summer, bucks may be found alone or in small herds. The breeding season is short, beginning in early September and reaching a peak during the middle of the month. Groups of does are collected by individual bucks, with the number of each harem depending on the aggressiveness and vigor of a particular male. Fighting is most prevalent prior to the breeding season, when supremacy is determined. In late fall and early winter, pronghorns gather into large herds that generally migrate to areas where snow depths are not extreme and browse is readily available. Does often become solitary when kids are dropped in the spring but band together in small groups shortly after the youngsters are old enough to follow. Newly born fawns generally weigh from five and one half to nine pounds and somewhat resemble their parents in color, but are more drab. They begin walking less than an hour after birth and can outrun a man when they are several days old. The greater portion of their first two weeks of life is spent hidden; they rise only to nurse.

Rivers and small mountain ranges are not barriers to pronghorns. They can pass under or through many barbed wire fences, but woven wire topped with barbed wire or seven-strand barbed wire fences, constructed with the bottom close to the ground, form barricades that pronghorns are unable to cross. A modification of a cattle guard, called an "antelope pass," has been developed and shows considerable promise for allowing pronghorns to cross fences on migrations or to get to water. Their movement appears critically curtailed in some areas because highway rights-of-way are being fenced. Some herds may have to be reduced to levels that would allow a particular range to be adequate for both summer and winter use.

Pronghorns have a number of unique characteristics. Their common name is derived from the best known of these, the branching or "pronged" horns. These are true horns composed of keratinized epithelial cells forming a black outer sheath over a bony core. Both sexes have horns; those of mature bucks average about a foot in length, while those of the does range from one to five inches in length and usually do not have prongs. About one third of the does do not have horn sheaths, even though small nipple-like cores can be felt under the skin. The outer sheaths of the bucks' horns are shed annually, usually in November. Those of the does are shed but not at a definite time of year. Early authors reported that the horns were made of hair. A great deal of hair, which may lend considerable structural support, is indeed embedded in the keratinized epidermis.

Another unique characteristic involves the female's reproductive cycle. While twin births are the rule, three to seven ova are commonly ovulated, fertilized, and begin embryonic development. At one stage in early development, the fetal membranes become long and thread-like. The "threads" of several embryos may knot and tangle, causing the death of some embryos when their membranes are "strangled" and disintegrate. When more than two embryos survive the "thread stage," the two that implant closest to the center of the uterus grow fastest and usually force the other embryos and their membranes to the tips of the uterine horns, where they perish. Pronghorns have an unusually long gestation period for their size—about 250 days or eight months. Females usually breed at the age of about sixteen months. Occasionally a four- to six-month-old female will breed and produce fawns at slightly over one year of age. On a good range, where food is plentiful, adult does produce twins about ninety-eight percent of the time, but fewer first births involve twins.

More than 50,000 pronghorns are now being harvested annually. They provide the only prairie hunting available to many American big-game hunters. Stalking these beautiful animals on the open range is fine sport, but unfortunately, many hunters pursue pronghorns with vehicles or "flock-shoot" them at long range.

See W. Hepworth and Floyd Blunt, "Research Findings on Wyoming Antelope," *Wyoming Wildlife* (June 1966); G. J. Mitchell, "Minimum Breeding Age of Female Pronghorn Antelope," *Journal of Mammalogy* (August 1967); and Bart W. O'Gara, "Unique Aspects of Reproduction in the Female Pronghorn (*Antilocapra americana ord*)," *American Journal of Anatomy* (June 1969).—B. W. O.

prospector. The prospector's job is to find mineral deposits of economic value and remove them from the site of natural deposit. The deposits are then exploited by the miner or his technological counterpart. The values broken out and hoisted are then concentrated and refined by mill men. At every stage, the prospector works under the direction of a trained supervisor, after 1860 usually a specialist engineer.

In the West two general methods of removing minerals were commonly used by the prospector. The first was placering, which involved the separation by air-blast or moving water of the naturally milled particles of heavy mineral from the alluvium in which they were deposited by natural erosion. The other was mining, conducted either in open-cast "glory holes" or quarries, or in underground workings. Placering is always distinguished from mining, the former usually being less costly, using much less complex equipment, and requiring less capital and knowledge to pursue. Settlements devoted to placering were often called "diggings," whereas "mining camps" as an expression persists to this day in reference to such communities west of the Great Plains.

Prospecting itself is an age-old art, at times crude and at times remarkably subtle and complex. On the far western frontier after 1849, prospecting for precious metals, or values, was practiced systematically and intensively by a class of men who soon evolved into a type as characteristic of their profession as the fur trappers and cowboys. First to penetrate new mineral districts were usually bands of placer prospectors, organized both for cooperative gold-washing and to fend off attacks. Shortly after such a district became reasonably secure appeared the solitary, nomadic hard-rock prospector, who searched for the upstream mineral lodes from which the placer values had been eroded. Although the first-comers were inclined to work the placers themselves, the locator of a mineral lode usually sold his location as soon as possible to a mining syndicate, since the promotion and operation of a mining development was seldom within the means and ability of the "desert rat."

American prospectors of the period 1849-60 were frequently natives of Georgia, where placering and shallow lode-mining of gold had been an established industry since 1800. Southeastern techniques were reportedly introduced to the California diggings by Isaac Humphreys of Georgia, who probably popularized the flat-bottomed pan and later the rocker or cradle-type of gold-saving equipment. Colorado gold was found successively by John Beck, William G. Russell, and John H. Gregory, all of whom came from the southern Appalachian gold regions. The Irishmen Peter O'Riley and Patrick McLaughlin played a crucial part in the discovery of the Comstock silver bonanza, while such Germans as Henry Wickenburg in Arizona, and August Rische and George F. Hook in the Leadville district of Colorado, prospected successfully. The Australian E. H. Hargraves, educated in gold-finding in California, returned to find the first gold in the diggings of New South Wales. The first hints of mineralization in a given district, inciting its systematic investigation, were occasionally supplied by Indians who had brought in nuggets or native metal, as did the Red River métis François Finlay, in the Montana placers. Oddly enough, the Cornishmen who virtually monopolized American mining from 1830 to 1880 were not greatly attracted to prospecting, probably because of their conservative and sedentary outlook.

Hispanic contributions to the American mineral frontier were in some cases noteworthy. Spanish milling and reduction techniques were widely imitated. Yet the relative absence of Spanish technical phraseology and the inapplicability of their mining methods suggests that the numerous Mexican and Chilean *gambusinos* of the Southwest exercised less influence than did the Georgians or the Cornishmen: indeed, the American mining vocabulary is far more Cornish in etymology than is that of the British Commonwealth. The classic mining textbook favored by the Spanish, Georg Bauer's (pen name, Georgius Agricola) *De re metallica*, was virtually unknown to Americans until its popularization in the Herbert Clark Hoover translation, published after the frontier had passed. Nonetheless, Mexicans prospected widely in the desert Southwest, penetrating as far northwest as California (Secundio Robles at New Almaden), north to Nevada (Ignacio Parades at Gold Hill), and northeast to the San Juan River of Colorado. The world's second school of mines after the Bergakademie at Freiburg, Saxony, was the Colegio Real de Mínera, established at Mexico City in 1783, considerably antedating the founding of the Columbia University School of Mines in 1864. The inability of Mexicans to retain and expand their southwestern mineral strikes must be ascribed more to the effect of conditions in metropolitan Mexico than to any lack of experience or enterprise on the part of individuals.

The American prospector typically worked as a teamster, quartz mill hand, or carpenter until he accumulated a grubstake of food, equipment, and pack animals sufficient for a season of exploration. Failing this, he might enter a grubstake agreement by offering to divide the ownership of any discovery claim with his backer. Perhaps for this reason, the first discoverer of a new mineral district was permitted under the common law to peg two claims instead of the customary one. Horace A. W. TABOR of Leadville, Colorado, for example, was not a prospector, but a groceryman whose business enabled him conveniently to finance others. Such a venturesome assayer as Richard Gird speculated at Tombstone, Arizona, by offering to do the necessary assay work in exchange for half-equities in promising locations. Noah S. Kellogg, who made the great Bunker Hill-Sullivan silver-lead strike in the Coeur d'Alene region of Idaho, reputedly had the most miserly grubstake agreement of all: He was loaned seventeen dollars' worth of food and the use of a pack burro. Although litigation over dishonored grubstake agreements was not unknown (for that matter, all rich discoveries were subject to much litigation), most prospectors strictly honored these informal, often verbal, contracts with their backers.

Apart from James Wilson Marshall's original discovery of gold in California, very few major mineral strikes were made by accident, coincidence, or through the traditional intervention of a pack-animal. Quite to the contrary, major strikes were usually the product of intensive and prolonged search by experienced prospectors who had a fair idea of what they were after and a very good idea of where it ought to be found. Perhaps the most prolonged search was that of the cowboy Robert Womack, who required twelve years to find gold at Cripple Creek, Colorado, although he lacked the art to pursue his strike to a personally profitable conclusion; Winfield Scott Stratton, who was experienced, learned of Womack's discovery, and in less than six months found real *bonanza* less than a mile distant from Womack's prospect pit. Edward S. Schieffelin required more than a year to locate the complex and deceptive lodes of Tombstone, Arizona. John H. Gregory's discovery of the pyritic gold lodes of the Colorado Front range was a model of systematic and intelligent search. Although some degree of luck was obviously essential, the skilled and persistent prospector would usually find values if values existed, and could even relocate deposits that had been deliberately concealed by some earlier finder. Since thousands of such men ransacked virtually every inch of the West before 1908, the probability of finding new high-grade bonanzas or rumored "lost mines" is very slight. To be sure, many men found one mineral while searching for another, but since the values of a primary lode deposit are composed of highly variable percentages of metals and metallic compounds, this is no reflection upon their ability.

An experienced desert rat continually swept the terrain with his eyes, seeking such promising formations as black-stained strata, "rusty" outcrops, quartz dikes, or other anomalies that suggested possible mineralization. If nothing specific met his gaze, he checked the gravels of watercourses by panning for heavy mineral, invariably following upstream whichever fork showed the

A prospector cradling for gold. (National Archives)

Oldtimers panning gold in the Dakotas. (Library of Congress)

most "color." If at some point the colors abruptly ceased, he knew that he had just passed the lode of origin. The throats of gorges, alluvial bars, upturned slate strata, and the point at which one type of country rock abruptly gave way to another were always carefully investigated. He was deeply interested in the brilliant shades of color produced by metallic salts: green and blue of copper, rust-red to brown of iron, lilac of cobalt, yellow or white of lead, dead black of manganese, or the metallic glint of pyrites and newly fractured silver-lead. He was on the alert for spongy-looking bits of maroon-stained quartz in stream beds. Such a rock had once contained mineral and was called "float," and half the prospector's life was devoted to tracing promising float upward to its point of origin.

When found, a lode was subjected to field assay by a variety of tests, all of which began with detaching chips across its face, pulverizing them in the sawed-off lower part of a mercury flask, which served as a mortar, and panning out the heavy residues. Gold and silver could be checked by amalgamation with mercury in the pan. The pellet of amalgam was roasted at moderate heat to drive off the mercury, and the remaining bead of gold-silver was recovered by estimation of value. Nitric acid could give determinations for gold, silver, lead, and copper. Reduction with a charcoal block by blowpipe was the most recondite of field-assay methods, but it was also the most informative, since the behavior of a great many common metals was characteristically peculiar under the blowpipe flame. Rough calculation gave an approximation of the values per ton of the surficial rock. If this seemed sufficient, the prospector set his boundary monuments and performed the ten days' work upon the claim sufficient to make good his application for a common law or statutory patent.

It is a peculiarity of nature that atmospheric action tends to concentrate high values in the surfaces of low-tenor, or physically meager, mineral lodes. This made prospecting comparatively easy, but such deposits were said to lie "big end up" and often contained no more than a few tons of milling ore. Frequently old prospectors, suspecting that their locations "wouldn't stand blasting," were inclined to leave them alone in the hope that a naïve purchaser would assume that the surficial values persisted to depth. Purchasers soon learned that it was wiser to option, rather than to buy outright, any location on which sufficient development work had not been done prior to acquisition. On the other hand, many prospectors preferred to "sink on their ore" in the hope that a lode of substantial size and tenor lay beneath. If successful, they would obtain a higher price, and if unsuccessful could recoup their expenses with the wagonload or two of milling ore they had hoisted during such development.

Very few of the successful prospectors save Schieffelin, Winfield Scott Stratton, and Thomas F. Walsh became rich or even moderately prosperous from their discoveries, nor did this well-known fact discourage others. The adventurous life, the excitement of the search, and the possibility of a memorable spree following success seem to have been their chief attractions. Most prospectors came from very humble circumstances, had little or no formal education, and disliked the restrictions of settled life. Their worst professional vice was the temptation to "salt" attractive but otherwise low-grade prospects by such devices as firing a shotgun loaded with gold dust into the face of the outcrop, or by pouring gold or silver solutions into the crevices. The samples thus treated would assay much higher values, and accordingly enhance the sale price. This deceit was practiced by only a few. They also had a tendency to "float," or illegally sidle, their location monuments to an area they thought to be the more profitable, but for the most part their deceptions were the products of their optimism and their ignorance of geology. For an unaccountable reason, many failed to demand shares in the developments founded upon their own discoveries, preferring to surrender their claims in return for lump sums.

Mineral claim law was originally fairly simple. The discoverer of mineral had a common-law right to the placer or lode he had found, irrespective of the rights or desires of the landowner of record. He was entitled to peg a claim of fixed dimensions about the apex of the lode, and he could not be denied access to this location. After building proper location monuments and doing a fixed amount of "location work" roughly equivalent to the expense of one hundred dollars, he could register his claim at the appropriate seat of justice and work it or sell it as he pleased. Annual "assessment work" to the same value would continue his possession, but failure to conform to these requirements was regarded as abandonment. The location could be then relocated in the same manner by the next-comer, or would revert to the original holder. Since a mineral location was traditionally one thousand feet in length, shares in such a development were sold as so many "feet," and costs and assessments were divided pro rata on the basis of the fraction of one thousand which the purchaser held.

Prospecting in the frontier period was completely empirical, and so prospectors tended to draw false conclusions regarding the genesis and extent of mineralization. This was abetted by promoters and journalists, so that much of the economic history of frontier mining concerns the squandering of capital on developments that scientifically trained engineers had minimized or even dismissed. Though prone to leave a modestly profitable claim in order to join the latest rumored excitement, the prospector of wide parts was expert at his profession. He possessed a soldier's eye for terrain, an artist's sensitivity for color, and a gopher's ability to dig. His equipment was crude and minimal, but with it he could make remarkably accurate field assays, often discovering values in formations that displayed no outward signs of their contents. He learned and assimilated a host of "signposts" to the values he sought, embodying them in such proverbs as "Iron rides a gold horse" or "Gold wears an iron hat" (gold is often associated with iron-stained formations), and "a copper penny will stain a mile" (a minute amount of copper will produce enough blue or green "blossom" to instill unjustified hopes in the inexperienced). Proud of his craft, he was fond of teaching it to others, for the professional esprit of hard-rock prospectors and miners was and remains remarkably high.

One of the most important side contributions of the prospector and placer man was in the enlargement and extension of the common law, particularly as it applied to mineral locations (see MINING LAW), water rights, and the conduct of human relations. Far removed from any normal law-giving body, the nomadic mineral-seeker lost no opportunity to organize in body politic, enacting and enforcing legislation that proved remarkably uniform and equitable. Although schooled scientists and engineers criticized the untutored desert rat, most ob-

servers ended by admitting that within the prospector's unpolished head lurked shrewd, enterprising, and perceptive brains. See also GOLD AND SILVER RUSHES; MINING, METAL.

See Eliot Lord, *Comstock Mining and Miners* (reissue ed., 1959); Watson Parker, *Gold in the Black Hills* (1966); Thomas Arthur Rickard, *History of American Mining* (1932); and Otis E Young, Jr., *Western Mining* (1970). —O. E Y.

prostitution. Along with gambling, drinking, shooting, and other easy virtues, prostitution is part and parcel of the myth of the rugged West. The saloons with their brightly dressed girls and the parlors with their kindly, wise madams make prostitution, or at least a particular form of it, a trademark of the ribald West of yesteryear. At the same time, it is an aspect of the western past that is more often than not brushed over in respectable histories. Upright citizens never accepted prostitution, even when they had to endure it. In respectable circles it was either ignored or actively crusaded against. As a result, prostitution is one of the least well understood phenomena in the West. It is either regarded as an insidious corrupter of western virtues, or as just plain, honest fun that the men-folk had with their colorful female friends.

Prostitution was regarded as a very disreputable profession for American girls but a fitting one for females of other nationalities. Many Americans passing through Sante Fe on their way to the California gold fields noted with pleasure the easy virtue of the local girls. Indians were equally regarded as creatures with low morals, ready to sell their favors for a few trinkets. Blacks were considered fair game. Many of the prostitutes in San Francisco from the 1860s on were Chinese women who were forced into the profession by the Chinese tongs (see CHINESE-AMERICANS). In short, social attitudes made the nonwhite, non-Anglo-Saxon out to be immoral and equated prostitution with a status of human inferiority.

There were four general levels of prostitution. At the bottom of the ladder was the streetwalker, who was the most obvious and the least secure of the ladies. A step up were the saloon girls, who plied their trade one floor above the bars and in the dance halls. Next on the ladder were the cribs, in the larger cities filled with upward of a hundred women of all colors and origins, whose chief trade was the business in out-of-town transients. Most august of all were the parlor houses, which catered to the exclusive, local clientele and often referred to themselves as the girls' boardinghouses. Not every western town had all four types of prostitution. Indeed, the parlor houses were in only the very large and prosperous cities, such as Denver, San Francisco, and Seattle, or in wealthy mining towns such as Virginia City, Nevada, and Cripple Creek and Leadville, Colorado. However, it was the rare location that did not have its saloon, while most medium-sized towns had at least one embarrassingly well-known brothel. Towns with army posts had their "hog farms."

Prostitution was more visible in the West than in the East. The Denver board of aldermen once passed an ordinance requiring that prostitutes wear yellow ribbons on their arms to show their shame. The Denver madams had their girls wear not only yellow armbands, but yellow everything—from shoes on their feet to bonnets on their heads—with such dramatic effect that the ordinance was soon repealed. In Seattle a local writer expressed the common western attitude that, while eastern vice was "silent, muffle-footed, velvet-gloved, masqued-faced," the western variety went about "openly, unclad, unpolished, open-handed." Prostitution could go about openly because it was a necessity; the ratio of males to females was very unbalanced. California is a characteristic case in point. In 1847 San Francisco had a population of 459 persons, of whom 138 were females. But when the gold rush struck, the migration of 1849 brought in about 65,000 men and only 2,500 women. The ratio did not improve rapidly, either. In 1880 only one out of every three immigrants was a woman. This meant that most men could not marry until the local births produced a more balanced population. Seattle was founded as a logging camp, and the state of Washington had few women for many years. Denver and Leadville received their inhabitants through the lure of gold, the lure being primarily for men. In 1880 Leadville had a bordello for every 148 inhabitants. The Kansas cattle towns, such as Dodge City and Abilene, were predominantly male for the first years of their existence. In fact, the rule is made even more conspicuous by the exception: Salt Lake City. There was no prostitution in that Mormon town until the United States Army established a nearby post and brought in outsiders. But the Mormon migration differed from the others by the relatively even number of women and men it contained.

Being ineradicable, prostitution had a somewhat open relation with the law; which made possible the establishment of red-light districts. The idea behind them was to better control prostitution by limiting it to certain areas. San Francisco had its Barbary Coast, Portland its Skidroad, Denver its Market Street, and so on. Most of these tenderloin districts had legally established boundaries. Seattle set aside a very large red-light district, as did Denver. Smaller towns tried to make sin support the city coffers. Ellsworth, Kansas, for example, more than paid for all its municipal expenses out of the taxes collected on saloons, gambling houses, and, of course, prostitution. The Topeka *Commonwealth* stated in an editorial comment about Ellsworth,

> The city realizes $300 per month from prostitution fines alone. . . . The city authorities consider that as long as mankind is depraved and Texas cattle herders exist, there will be a demand and necessity for prostitutes, and that as long as prostitutes are bound to dwell in Ellsworth it is better for the respectable portion of society to hold prostitutes under restraint of law.

Prostitution as a source of municipal revenue typified the uneasy truce of coexistence between respectable citizens and prostitutes.

Who, then, were the prostitutes? There were perhaps fifty thousand of them between Kansas City and San Francisco in the second half of the nineteenth century, most of whom were immigrants. Coming from very poor families, often unable to speak English, and considered inferior because of race, creed, or color, the majority of the prostitutes did not lead easy lives. The streetwalkers, being least desirable, had difficulty finding enough customers in most times except the very flush. Girls in the cribs had to rent rooms at high rates, as much as one thousand dollars a month in San Francisco. The majority of prostitutes were in debt to somebody, either to the madam who boarded and clothed them or to the vice lord who owned the madam. Existence was a hardship, and many women took their own lives to end the sorrow. Scarcely a week would go by in Denver without two or three swallowing poison. Most prostitutes did not eventually settle down and raise families. The same social and economic forces that brought them to their trade prevailed throughout their lives. They died in the poorhouse if old, or by violence and disease.

There are a few famous names, however, that bring thoughts of glamour and excitement: Mammy Pleasant and Madame ATOY of San Francisco, Julia Bulette (the Queen of the Comstock), Mattie Silks and Jennie Rogers of Denver, and CATTLE KATE of Wyoming. CALAMITY JANE of Deadwood was possibly a prostitute for a while, employed on E. Coffey's "hog farm" near Fort Laramie in 1875. With each of these names is associated a host of stories, some true and all exciting. The romantic image of these madams is still present, though in bowdlerized form, in most of the modern westerns of television and the movies. The present conceptions of these madams are not totally incorrect. The women who ran the parlor houses were very intelligent in the operation of their businesses. They had their coteries of admirers. And in towns with limited outside contact, the ladies at the top of their profession provided a lot of grist for the local gossip mills. In some respects, the madams can be compared to the Hollywood starlets who portray them today.

As an open and boisterous trade, western prostitution could not go on forever. By the turn of the twentieth century, the forces of reform had marshaled enough strength to make serious inroads into the freewheeling affairs of the red-light districts. The cow towns banned prostitution soon after their hectic days as railheads were over. San Francisco's Barbary Coast was burned down in the fire of 1906. Seattle cracked down on prostitution in 1911. And Denver's red-light district was forced underground forever in 1915. Prostitution did not end in the West after the turn of the century, however; rather, it came to resemble more its eastern counterpart. The only state that now allows legal prostitution is Nevada, and even it made the venerable profession illegal for a period during and after World War II. Prostitution remains a social problem in the West, just as it is one in the rest of the country. Lacking nowadays is the sense of slightly jaded excitement that western prostitution once had.

The most adequate general history of prostitution is Harry Sinclair Drago, *Notorious Ladies of the Frontier* (1969). Some interesting anecdotes about Rocky Mountain prostitution are in Forbes Parkhill, *The Wildest of the West* (1957). San Francisco's story is well told in Curt Gentry, *The Madams of San Francisco* (1964).—R. S.

Protestant churches. One of the truly unique characteristics of the American experience is the manner in which different religious groups have learned to live together in reasonable harmony. No Thirty Years' War, no St. Bartholomew's Day massacre, no *Kulturkampf* between church and state appeared in America. In large part, the success of peaceful disestablishment emerged from the frontier. The ingredients for this success story were ample space, so that nobody felt unduly cramped or unable to move on to fresh ground; a general consensus among the people that they wanted to be freed from the constant religious bickering of the mother countries; the realization that freedom of worship for each body could best be achieved by allowing the same privilege to every other group; the harsh demands of the frontier environment, showing by daily necessity the need for cooperation for mutual survival; and a bent of mind emphasizing down-to-earth solutions rather than insistence on maintaining pure doctrine and Old World liturgical practices.

Out of this blend appeared the recipe for the successful solution of the age-old dilemma of what was Caesar's and what was God's. To be sure, bitter and even violent hostility toward religious and racial minorities among frontiersmen did break out periodically. Petty denominational jealousies consumed valuable time. Often something less than the Golden Rule was demonstrated toward Catholics, Mormons, and Jews. And not all Protestant frontiersmen were enthusiastic about the emancipation of the slave. But between 1607 and 1900 the Protestant churches found the means for establishing their ministries.

From the very outset, the Protestants who came to America represented a wide variety of religious positions. This diversity prevented any one body from becoming ascendant in more than localized areas. Some groups, such as the Anglicans in Virginia, received financial support from England, but most became self-supporting. In general outline, the denominational makeup of the colonies was as follows: Puritans in Massachusetts Bay and Connecticut; Separatists in Rhode Island; Dutch Reformed in New York and New Jersey; Quakers and Presbyterians in Pennsylvania; and Anglicans in Virginia and Maryland.

Puritan Christianity (see MASSACHUSETTS, SETTLEMENT OF) exerted a greater influence on society than did any other religion. While not wanting to extend freedom of religious practice to all settlers, the Puritans by hard experience slowly were forced to grant grudging toleration by the early 1800s. Yet their zeal for Christian living was maintained; from the New England frontier came the impulse for replanting higher learning on the moving frontier, the impetus for church-led abolition of slavery, and the momentum for foreign missionary work and for revivalism.

In New Netherlands (New York) the Dutch Reformed church was dominant. Its leaders made no strong efforts to enforce religious uniformity, and as a result the colony soon attracted a wide variety of church bodies. Commercial enterprises rather than theological activities dominated public interest; hence, New York became a proving ground, showing how mutual respect could succeed.

New Jersey also attracted Dutch Reformed settlers, but like New York, it also welcomed all Protestant bodies. Quakers and Lutherans found congenial religious and economic opportunities in that colony, adding to its diversity and hence to its religious stability.

Pennsylvania, meanwhile, was founded, in William Penn's words, as a "holy experiment." Penn established there a haven for religious dissenters in the 1680s. In this colony, Penn and his followers made a carefully planned effort to put Christian ideals into practice in every phase of life; thus, the Quakers negotiated with, and paid for, their lands from the Indians. All religious minority groups were welcomed with guarantees that no state church would be established. The appeal of this colony was widespread and to it came a variety of small groups, most of whom had known persecution in their mother countries. Quakers were the most numerous immigrants, but substantial numbers of the pietist sects, generally Anabaptists of Germany, came to the eastern part of the colony. One could also find Mennonites, Swiss Brethren, Dunkers, Baptists, Presbyterians, Lutherans, and Moravians. Generally, each group collected its strength in one town or one county. Pennsylvania attracted a greater variety of sects and churches than any other colony.

The oldest colony of all, Virginia, was primarily Anglican. In contrast to Massachusetts and Pennsylvania, its settlers were motivated far more by economic interest than by religious ones; hence, the religious life of Virginia was more subdued and ceremonial in character. While the government attempted to re-create a fully established Church of England, complete with general tax revenue used to support Anglican ministers, it did not prohibit dissenters from moving into its frontier regions. Along the edge of settlement by the mid-eighteenth century one found Moravians, Waldensians, Huguenots, rather large numbers of Quakers, Baptists, and Lutherans. This diversity was significant mainly because the mutual toleration that developed in Virginia was the kind of evidence used later by Thomas Jefferson and James Madison when they wrote into both the state constitution and the United States Constitution the guarantee of the separation of church and state.

In Maryland, Roman Catholics occupied more positions of leadership than in any other colony, but full religious diversity was as evident there as it was in the two Carolinas and Georgia. This toleration was accentuated by the periodic outbursts of REVIVALISM everywhere on the frontier, beginning with the Great Awakening of the mid-eighteenth century. While some pioneer churches broke up over differences of opinion regarding revivalist techniques, a far more lasting result was achieved by the strong nondoctrinal emphasis of the revivals, which stressed personal experience and inner conviction rather than denominational loyalty as the chief aim of religious understanding. The revivals strengthened the ecumenical character of the frontier churches, creating common experiences that the mobile pioneers could share with one another regardless of sectarian membership.

By way of statistical summation, Edwin Scott Gaustad in the *Historical Atlas of Religion in America* (1962) shows the following: in 1660 there were 41 Anglican churches, 4 Baptist, 75 Congregational, 13 Dutch Reformed, 4 Lutheran, 5 Presbyterian, and 12 Roman Catholic. In 1780 the figures were 406 Anglican churches, 457 Baptist, 749 Congregational, 328 Reformed, 240 Lutheran, 495 Presbyterian, 56 Roman Catholic, and 200 Quaker. (Gaustad's carefully prepared maps give precise geographical locations for each of these bodies.)

In the great migration of peoples over the Appalachians and to the Pacific Coast after the founding of the new republic, the motive of religious freedom was not dominant for more than a tiny number of pioneers, such as the LATTER-DAY SAINTS. Indeed, the economic motive so dominated the developing frontier throughout the nineteenth century, with but few exceptions, as to place the religious development in the West in a secondary position. This did not mean the American frontiersman was not concerned about religion; it meant that he was by now so accustomed to toleration and disestablishment that he found the ideal of religious freedom a virtually accomplished fact. To be sure, much of this was simple indifference; one can be magnificently tolerant about another's strongly felt convictions if one has no interest in them. This kind of freedom and its attendant indifference largely explain why the organized Protestant churches made such apparent little statistical progress in the West in the eighteenth century.

For the frontiersman who was sure of his faith and his good standing in the eyes of God, the principal concern was ethics rather than theology. He believed he could best express his faith by putting it into practice. Primary among the Protestant pioneer's concerns was an interest in formal education on all levels. The frontier clergyman was the foremost agent in promoting the creation of the dozens of hilltop centers of higher learning in the trans-Appalachian West. Needing educated clergymen and laymen and knowing they were free from any governmental regulation, the major Protestant bodies carried out the program of building colleges first started by their ancestors on the seventeenth-century frontier. By 1800 there were three Congregational colleges (Harvard, Yale, and Dartmouth) and two Anglican (William and Mary and King's, now Columbia). Now with the rapid movement westward, the college fever caught hold. William Warren Sweet, in *Religion in the Development of American Culture 1765-1840* (1952), presents the statistical evidence: before 1830 the Presbyterians founded sixteen permanent colleges and the Congregationalists five; the Baptists four and the Catholics one. Between 1830 and 1860—the boom time—the Presbyterians added thirty-three more permanent colleges, the Methodists thirty-four, the Baptists another twenty-one, the Congregationalists another eighteen, Episcopalians nine more, the Lutherans added six, Disciples of Christ five, German Reformed and Universalists four each; Quakers and Unitarians two each, the Dutch Reformed and United Brethren one each. During the same period some twenty-seven semi-state and municipal colleges and universities were founded. They were staffed largely by ministers.

When the westward movement crossed over into the Great Plains after 1860, the total number of new church-related colleges diminished rapidly. Most of the new schools were state-supported and vocation-oriented.

Obviously the demand for seminaries grew along with that for colleges. Generally the practice was to add such institutions to the more wealthy colleges, such as Harvard, Yale, or Princeton. On the frontier by 1860 two seminaries were making their influence felt: Lane and Oberlin, both in Ohio. But some denominations were deeply suspicious of learned ministers and hence contributed little to this phase of education.

A second educational enterprise of importance was the development of the Sunday school. Varying in degree from place to place, this institution became a prime instrument of the frontier churches for conversion and

for transmitting the knowledge of the Christian faith to the next generation, which would carry it even farther westward. In *Frontier Mission* (1966), Walter Brownlow Posey shows that formal schooling over a long time span came to be more important among most churches than the earlier emphasis on the revivalist experience.

The frontier Protestants showed little interest in the conservative, traditional liturgical practices common in Europe and in some eastern seaboard cities. The pastoral duties were reduced to the basics: baptizing, celebrating communion, officiating at weddings and funerals, preaching, and instructing. Little interest developed, even among the highly confessional Lutherans, in strict adherence to vestments, extensive observation of church festivals, trained choirs, and ornate church interiors. On the other hand, the frontier church's insistence on baptisms, weddings, and funerals conducted by clergymen served not only the obvious religious needs of the parishoners but made the churches the centers of community activity. The monotony, loneliness, and hardship of isolated farm life was gladly broken for the joyous celebration of a birth or a wedding; funerals in turn served as pointed reminders of the transitoriness and solemnity of life.

The Protestant churches in the West provided other services for their communities. The momentum for public regulation of the enormously widespread use of alcoholic beverages was usually sponsored by the local ministers. The Methodists were the leaders in temperance work and spent considerable energy and funds on educating the public about the abuse of alcohol. Posey, in *Frontier Mission*, presents the statistical evidence: before the Protestant churches became involved, the annual per capita consumption of hard liquor rose from two and a half gallons in 1792 to seven and a half gallons in 1823; after concerted church work was carried out, consumption dropped to two and a half gallons by 1840.

The pioneer churches also tried to establish some control over the use of tobacco. The leaders were also the first and often the only persons working to curb gambling, dance halls, prostitution, street fighting, and similar practices that they felt degraded the individual. While most of these efforts obviously fell far short of their goals, at least the churches had taken upon themselves the responsibility for trying to improve the moral quality of life in their respective communities.

The following presents more tangible evidence of religious activity in terms of the size, location, and mobility of the major denominations in the West.

The BAPTISTS, fragmented and scattered everywhere, were especially concentrated on the southern frontier after 1800. The exact number of Baptists by 1850 can only be estimated; Gaustad shows that the national membership increased from 60,000 in 1790 to more than 300,000 in 1830. This figure increased greatly after the emancipation of the black slaves.

The CONGREGATIONALISTS, historically centered in New England, did not populate the frontier in large numbers. As late as 1830 ninety percent of their congregations were still in New England. There were no Congregationalists in measurable numbers in the South or in border states. When they did migrate after 1800, it was primarily to Ohio, Illinois, Michigan, Wisconsin, or Iowa. The Congregationalists were not as well equipped as, say, the Baptists or Methodists for the strenuous life of the West. Not willing to compromise on the educational level of the clergy and being of the high socioeconomic class of society, the denomination found its chief strength still lay in the East after 1860.

A more indigenous Protestant group on the frontier was the DISCIPLES OF CHRIST, founded by Alexander Campbell in the 1820s in Ohio. Based primarily on local autonomy, a rejection of formal creeds as prerequisites for membership, and a dedication to recapturing the purity of the New Testament church, the Campbellites, as the Disciples were sometimes known, found a congenial response throughout the Middle West and the border states. By 1850 some 200,000 members were claimed by the founder. Flexible in polity and priding itself on equalitarian membership, the Disciples' success was evidence of how the frontier could encourage so innovative a religious institution.

The EPISCOPALIANS were not plentiful in frontier communities before 1830. Then, as small cities appeared in the West, this body tripled its membership by 1853, most of it centered in towns. Not as devoted to revivals and evangelizing as were its rivals, the Episcopalians offered a more liturgically oriented option. The church's influence was limited greatly, however, by the fact that by 1852 it had only 152 ministers in the field.

By contrast, the METHODISTS enjoyed substantial growth and influence in all sections. Of the many transplanted European denominations the Methodists were perhaps the best suited to America, and so, Methodism spread steadily throughout the post-1800 period. Its legendary circuit riders were a rare breed of evangelists, bringing the church into remote areas untouched by other churches. Its revivalism, its emphasis on piety rather than doctrine, and its willingness to adapt its polity to existing conditions all helped the Methodists take hold of the changing society of the West. Its geographical strength was concentrated in the Middle West, the border states, and small, but dense, areas of the Deep South. Gaustad estimates that in 1800 there were some 64,894 Methodists; fifty years later this had risen to 511,153. There were more Methodist churches in America than of any other denomination. They led in twenty states, while the Baptists led in seven, the Congregationalists in three, and the Roman Catholics in one, California.

The PRESBYTERIANS, also divided and scattered throughout the West, became one of the important church bodies. Perhaps the most evangelistic-minded of the groups discussed here, they brought a tremendous amount of energy and practicality to winning souls. Their internal history was marred by bitter disputes over mission policy and social outreach, but in the more sparsely settled regions of the frontier, the Presbyterians were as active and involved as any other denomination. Geographically they were strongest in western Pennsylvania, Ohio, and the border states. The best estimate of their membership would be around 750,000 by 1860.

There is always a danger in claiming too much importance for the influence of the West on American Protestantism and vice versa. This is especially true after 1860, when church influence on the remaining frontier started to dwindle to a very low point. In many communities, no church at all appeared until well into the twentieth century. Some practical considerations help to explain this decline. Small congregations were not able to raise adequate funds; ministers often showed little enthusiasm for working in remote areas; and farmers found the great distances separating them to be detrimental to building a sense of community organization. Educational institutions, especially colleges, simply did not appear on the Great Plains, and what little moral emphasis the churches had established in earlier years was nonexistent in the last stages of the frontier. Revivals were fewer in number, although some dedicated circuit riders did carry on the work of the Kingdom despite these problems, and no uniquely American religious groups (such as the Mormons and Disciples) appeared on the scene after 1860. Eventually the churches of the East found their way to the Great Plains. But it is interesting to note that, in contrast to the buildings east of the Mississippi River, the highest edifice in a Plains town is the grain elevator, not the church steeple.

All of these developments did not, obviously, spell the end of the church in the West. It simply meant that the churches had some catching up to do in terms of new programs, new outlooks, and new priorities.

As Martin E. Marty has shown in his study of American church life, *Righteous Empire* (1970), this transformation came about very slowly and almost imperceptibly. In broadest terms, American churches moved from actively creating a spiritual empire that would shape the nation's ethos, manners, and laws to a more passive defense of the status quo. In the West this took place in the early twentieth century. Experimentation and innovation gave way to the churches' frequent identification with the social mores of the communities.

With the exception of the Roman Catholic church and some Lutheran bodies, most churchgoing westerners sent their children to the public schools rather than to parochial institutions. Parents who wanted their children to attend the denominational college of their choice sent the young people to the established eastern schools rather than erect their own. Most churches actively involved themselves in the civic activities of the community, such as Boy Scouts, charities, or educational associations.

One major exception developed in this respect. The area of greater Los Angeles became in the 1920s and thereafter a spawning ground for new, usually esoteric forms of religious expression. Dozens of groups, such as Aimee Semple MacPherson's Gospel movement, focused attention usually on one specific theme: spiritualism, diet, faith healing, speaking in tongues, or the imminent end of the world. Even today Los Angeles serves as the nursery for those who choose to seek religious understanding outside traditional sources. But generally the churches in the West today show no significant signs of difference from those across the nation.

Although one of the favorite parlor games among church membership statisticians seems to be disclaiming the accuracy of each other's figures, some general estimate of the strength of the Protestant churches west of the Mississippi River can be made, based on a comprehensive report by the National Council of Churches in 1956, the last time such a study was made. Two counteracting tendencies since the study was made may suggest that its figures have not changed considerably;

obviously population is up, but church membership is declining somewhat. In any event, here are the 1956 statistics: Baptists, 4,840,000; Congregationalists, 564,000; Disciples of Christ, 154,200; Episcopalians, 630,000; Lutherans, 2,654,600; Methodists, 3,681,600; Presbyterians, 1,620,000, and Mormons, 732,000.

For information in addition to the titles mentioned in the text, one should consult the official denominational histories of each of the churches. Also see Sydney Ahlstrom, *A Religious History of the American People* (1972); and Kenneth Scott Latourette, *Three Centuries of Advance* (1936) and *The Great Century* (1941). Easily the most helpful interpretation of American church life is Sidney Mead, *The Lively Experiment: The Shaping of Christianity in America* (1963).—E. J.

Protestant missionaries. Of the many instruments of technology and culture used to harness the undeveloped frontier, the Protestant churches and missionaries, in retrospect, seem to have played a secondary role. Indeed, most historians of the American frontier would attribute to the cattle trade, land-distribution policies, or Indian policy a greater influence on the shaping of the West than they would to organized churches. This ranking should not surprise the reader. As the line of advance settlement moved westward, the pioneer usually faced a survival situation; his basic physical needs demanded his full attention. The churches and the missionaries often accompanied the advance guard of settlement but found that settlers assigned to their religious needs a role secondary to the need to earn a living.

Yet, a considerable degree of organized, often well-financed missionary work was carried out during the frontier years of American history. Settlers came to the wilderness and remained there for the express purpose of carrying out what to them was the most important task of all: "Go ye therefore, and teach all nations, baptizing them in the name of the Father, and of the Son, and of the Holy Ghost, teaching them to observe all things whatsoever I have commanded you. . . ." This, the Great Commission from the Book of Matthew, furnished the motivation to those who, in their Protestant faith, believed they must give their lives to propagation of the Gospel. Ever since Martin Luther had restored the Bible to its place at the heart of the Christian message, in opposition to Roman Catholic loyalty to the teachings and discipline of the visible church, Europeans and then Americans had created missionary movements for carrying on this work. As early as Elizabethan England they saw the New World as a land of boundless opportunity for missionizing. Here was open land waiting for the Gospel; here were Indian aborigines, none of whom had heard the tidings of salvation; here was a rich land beckoning Protestants to develop it and thus turn back the "papal plots" of the hated Spanish and French rival colonists. Here indeed could the Gospel be planted on fresh soil for all the world to see.

The first and most obvious group for evangelizing in America was the Indian. By 1612 Alexander Whitaker of Virginia had sent to supporters in England a sermon of his that pointed out the great opportunity for missionary work among the natives. Later he converted Pocahontas; her subsequent visit to England, sponsored

by Anglican prelates to promote a fund-raising drive, assured the Indian princess of at least historical immortality. However, all plans for the future collapsed in 1622 when an Indian massacre of whites on the Virginia frontier disparaged further missionary efforts. No new work was carried out in that colony for the next seventy-five years.

In New England, enthusiasm ran very high for converting the aborigines. The first charter of the Massachusetts Bay Colony expressly stated that the chief object of the colony was the conversion of the Indian. However, as Lawrence Cremin shows in his magnificent study *American Education: The Colonial Experience* (1970), membership in a Puritan congregation demanded not only acceptance of minimal practices, such as baptism and adherence to Puritan morality, but also a thorough knowledge of the Bible and an extended knowledge of Puritan theology. New Englanders also expected all converts to accept their dress and behavior codes. For those reasons they won few converts in their first two decades in America.

In 1649 Parliament created the Society for Propagation of the Gospel in New England. Financed primarily by wealthy Puritan merchants and dedicated to supporting both evangelizing and educational mission work, the society provided badly needed funds (between 1660 and 1689 its average annual budget was £440).

Thereafter, missionary efforts improved dramatically, aided by two remarkable Puritan ministers, Thomas Mayhew of Martha's Vineyard and John Eliot of Roxbury. Working directly with nearby tribes, Mayhew used his first converts to help win others, drawing on the principle of encouraging the Indians to do as much of the teaching as possible. By 1652 he claimed 283 converts.

The specific work among the Indians in New England was supervised by a board, the Commissioners of the United Colonies; this agency allocated the funds to the fieldworkers. Before the outburst of violence in King Philip's War of 1675, which ended their work, the missionaries had established day schools, attempted to create a college for Indians at Harvard, distributed food in hardship cases, and, perhaps most important, financed the translation of the Bible by Eliot into the Algonquian tongue. It became the primary instrument in conversion efforts.

Eliot also contributed another remarkable innovation, the Indian "praying villages." In 1651 he obtained two thousand acres of land along the Charles River, about eighteen miles north of Boston; there he and his converts founded Natick. The Indians and Eliot laid out the town, assigned lots for housing and farms, prepared the land for farming, and established a village constitution based on Old Testament models. Within fourteen years at least thirteen other such villages sprang up in the area populated exclusively by converted Indians.

By 1675 some 2,500 Indians, representing about twenty percent of the native population in New England, had been converted. The outbreak of war in that year ended missionary work for a few years, but within the decade Eliot was able to rebuild his ministry. The results of the total experience since 1630 are obviously impossible to measure from a spiritual standpoint. But from another viewpoint we can see tangible evidence of the impact of each culture on the other. The Indians taught the Puritans how to plant corn, trap fur-bearing animals, and utilize local building materials. In turn, the Indians learned something of the rewards of participating in a growing capitalist society. This pattern would appear over and over again on the American frontier.

In each of the other colonies, Protestants launched missionary programs comparable to those of the Puritans. Often funds and fieldworkers were in short supply, but the work went ahead with some spectacular successes in some areas but generally with disappointing results. In New York, Henry Barclay of Albany established a highly successful mission among the Mohawk. Active work was also carried out with the Iroquois before the American Revolution. One of the most successful programs was that of William Penn and his fellow Quakers in Pennsylvania. Following their convictions about warfare, the Quakers preserved peace with the Indians well into the eighteenth century. They also paid the natives for the land they occupied.

In the other colonies, especially in the South, missionary efforts were generally small in scope and meager in results. This was largely the result of a lack of leadership among church members, the widely dispersed tribes, and apparently a belief that the Indians were no more capable of understanding Christianity than were the growing number of Negro slaves in the region. By 1776, as historian Kenneth Scott Latourette points out, very little missionary work was being conducted among the slaves. Some Christians held to a medieval belief that to convert a black meant that he would have to be freed. In most slave-owning colonies a sincere effort was made by a few missionaries to work among the transplanted blacks, but the resistance was simply too great among slave-owners, many of whom feared that slaves instructed in the Golden Rule and exposed to the Bible's persistent references to freedom might seek to gain their own freedom.

The small number of actual converts by the end of the seventeenth century persuaded mission-minded Englishmen and colonists to rethink their entire program. The immediate result was the formation of two missionary societies, both of which were to a great degree the brain children of the industrious Anglican clergyman Thomas Bray. The first, the Society for Promoting Christian Knowledge (S.P.C.K.), was founded by Bray in 1699 with the stated purpose of providing books to clergymen sent to the colonies. Its libraries were to be found not only in the colonies but in the British ports from which clergymen embarked for America. (Its later activities took it to other parts of the empire.) The second organization, the Society for Propagation of the Gospel in Foreign Parts (S.P.G.), was chartered, at the instigation of Bray, in 1701; it sought to increase the number of Anglican clergymen and teachers in the colonies. Although the S.P.G. undertook work among slaves and Indians, its most intensive efforts were directed at unconverted white colonists. Dedicated to propagating not only the Gospel but the Anglican definition of the Gospel, the society yet learned over the next few decades to share its work with other denominational bodies with the same general aims. In some colonies it remained High Anglican, but by 1763 many of its workers were cooperating with Congregationalists, Lutherans, and Huguenots.

The first missionary of the organization was a Scots-man, George Keith. He ministered in the northern colonies, concentrating on the sparsely settled areas. On his recommendation the society soon sent out other missionaries and organized congregations on the frontier in all thirteen colonies. Oftentimes the society's representatives were ignored by the established clergy, but they persisted and increased their numbers from three in 1718 to thirty in 1761. Among other accomplishments, the society founded several schools as a means of preparing future ministers and distributed prayer books and tracts. By the time of the Treaty of Paris in 1783, after which the S.P.G. of course suspended its activities in the former colonies, the society had established at least 169 missionary stations embracing all sections of the thirteen colonies.

These preachers made special efforts to work among friendly Indian tribes but made little headway. Most natives by the later eighteenth century were apparently suspicious of white settlers who preached brotherhood but practiced something else. Enthusiasm in England among financial supporters was flagging badly, because converts were not made, and new recruits for work on the farthest frontiers were not found. Also those whites such as fur traders, who used the Indians for their own economic purposes, wanted to maintain complete control over the Indians rather than risk missionaries coming in to divide native loyalties.

The society made courageous forays into black society in both the North and the South. Records of this venture are very rare, and only scattered information is available. Apparently most enterprises consisted of day schools for the young people in the cities. Very little missionary work was done on the frontier plantations among the slaves.

Cremin points out that these efforts failed because of unbridgeable cultural gaps. The Indians and blacks found they might be able to understand the basic teachings of Christianity but could not accept the racism or demands for accepting white behavior that almost always accompanied missionary effort.

As the population increased in frontier communities and as the churches found new opportunities for growth among white settlers as well as Indians, the mission-minded Protestants drew upon the experiences of the S.P.G. and the S.P.C.K. to start organizing comparable denominational agencies for winning souls. These were especially numerous in New England and the middle colonies among Congregationalists, Presbyterians, Baptists, Dutch Reformed, and Methodists. At first the agencies were local in scope, concentrating on converting the nearby Indians. Then, as new funds and leaders appeared, the churchmen organized agencies on a colonywide basis and later, around 1800, on a regional basis. Using periodicals, itinerant preachers, and revival meetings (see REVIVALISM) as their primary instruments, they expanded their evangelistic programs to reach the large numbers of white Americans who had heretofore shown little interest in the life of the spirit.

The first interdenominational agency to coordinate Protestant missionary work on the frontier after independence was the American Home Missionary Society, created in 1826. It consisted primarily of contributing members from the major denominations, especially Congregational, Methodist, and Presbyterian. The society saw its work as educational and, indeed, made a significant contribution through its vigorous support of colleges and schools, a program that brought a more learned clergy to the edge of settlement. By 1835 it was employing 719 representatives, of which 481 were located on the frontier. Two decades later some 1,032 Protestant missionaries were working in the West. Shortly after 1826 other large denominations founded their own home mission societies, carrying on the same kind of work.

The frontier offered unlimited opportunities for the mission-minded. Neither state, church nor hostile government stood in their way as they joined the westward movement of population in the nineteenth century. In ,act, the presence of the churches helped reenforce in the pioneer the concept of manifest destiny—that the Americans had a special mandate from God to occupy the best parts, if not all, of North America, there to make available the benefits of democratic government and Protestant religion. In some areas, especially Oregon, missionaries such as Jason LEE, Marcus WHITMAN, Henry H. SPALDING, and William H. GRAY were among the first settlers. Men such as Daniel Lee in 1834 sent back glowing reports of the economic opportunities available to Americans headed westward. In that manner churchmen contributed to the means by which the West was populated.

Although conditions varied greatly from one region to the next, a general pattern of missionary work developed in the trans-Appalachian West by 1840. Most communities of fifty families or more supported at least one mission church. The preachers were usually circuit riders, tending flocks in vast areas. This limited their ministry to preaching, revivals, and brief attempts at educating the youth.

No one denomination dominated the West as it stretched to the West Coast by midcentury. The METHODISTS were perhaps the most energetic, the BAPTISTS the best organized, the CONGREGATIONALISTS the most devoted to education, and the PRESBYTERIANS the most fond of the annual revival. With the exception of the independent-minded Baptists, their ministers were sponsored by the American Society or by their own denominational board, and the funds came more from the East Coast than from local congregational sources.

Obviously it would be impossible to measure the effectiveness of the Protestant missionary effort among fellow countrymen. Formal church membership statistics show that overall only fifteen to twenty percent of Americans held membership in churches before 1850. That figure must be seen in context, however, since no frontier church kept careful membership records. Many frontiersmen may well have been faithful participants but not formal members. The physical mobility of frontiersmen meant that the size of a parish was always in flux. And finally, some pioneers lived long distances from any church facilities. What we do know is that churches were built and related educational programs did go on.

Missionary work among the Indian tribes in the trans-Appalachian West, however, was visible and the results more apparent. The one element in nineteenth-century Indian missionary work different from earlier work was the full cooperation of the federal government with the interested church bodies. The government wanted to teach the Indians the civilizing arts of agriculture and related crafts as well as formal literacy. The missionary societies were asked to cooperate in this effort by conducting the schools and helping to teach agriculture. The missionary agencies generally responded with great enthusiasm. In 1819 there were three such schools, and by 1835, thirty-eight. The government's interest resulted in a direct subsidy, and it virtually remade the entire missionary effort among the natives. To be sure, the established churches contributed more funds than the government; historian William Warren Sweet estimates the ratio in 1825 as being something like $13,620 from the government to seven times that from the churches. But the program had started, and the missionaries had the support and protection of the federal government for its work.

A drastic new change took place in the 1830s when federal officials started the removal program, which took Indians from their lands east of the Mississippi, now coveted by whites, and placed them on reservations west of that river. This policy soon made these Indians direct dependents of the government by depriving them of their hunting grounds and exposing them to the worst habits of the whites, such as drinking and gambling.

As the Indians were settled on new reservations, they found both government agents and missionaries there ready to teach them white ways. As Robert Berkhofer shows in *Salvation and the Savage* (1965), most missionaries not only taught the Bible and worked for conversions but used the opportunity to persuade the Indians to accept all of the white man's culture, such as private property and white codes of law. The general rejection of this culture by the natives was interpreted by the whites as proof of the Indian's biological inferiority. Hence, the missionary experience, contrary to its original design, helped to contribute to racial prejudice rather than brotherly understanding between the races.

Other missionary work in the 1830s and 1840s, off the reservations, was less spectacular but often constructive in certain areas. Perhaps the most successful were the Quakers, who had long been concerned with correcting the injustices shown the Indians. Through the nineteenth century they worked actively among the tribes from New York to Alaska, concentrating on teaching literacy and useful skills rather than working for conversions. In 1869, as the federal government revamped its welfare policy toward the Indians once again (see PEACE POLICY), the Quakers were given the prime responsibility for selecting Indian agents to carry out the actual fieldwork; many Quakers became field agents for this purpose. At the same time, a national agency calling itself the National Indian Association, created in 1881, worked both with the government and independently to help protect the legal rights of Indians in treaty negotiations and to promote educational, medical, and religious activities among the tribes.

The federal government, by both warfare and peaceful means, had placed almost every Indian on a reservation by 1900. Missionaries thus found their work more geographically concentrated and more controllable, since their wards were living so closely together. The larger Protestant bodies, especially the Baptists (both Northern and Southern), Methodists, Presbyterians, and Episcopalians, were the most active contributors to these missions. In 1908, under the direction of the newly created Federal Council of Churches, these programs were coordinated under the leadership of the Home Missions Council for conducting church-sponsored work among the reservation Indians. The creation of this body, in effect, ended the frontier stage of Protestant missionary activity among the natives; now the work was coordinated by this agency located in New York.

The effect of the Protestant enterprise can be summarized as follows. In 1913 Indian communicant church members totaled 31,815; occasional participants totaled about 35,000. This was about the same total number of converts as announced by Roman Catholic missionaries on the frontier. Kenneth Scott Latourette concludes that for many of these converts the choice of Christianity meant very little; the Indians had joined a church just as they had become American citizens. Little visible difference was made in their lives. But for some, Latourette points out, a striking difference in spiritual and moral outlook was visible after conversion. For instance, the converts rejected their drug-oriented peyote religion. Other Indians voluntarily accepted training to become missionaries themselves. Some Indian congregations were self-supporting; the Bible in many languages was distributed.

Latourette also reminds us that the white missionary often was able to protect the Indian against legal or economic exploitation by land-hungry whites; they also conducted much philanthropic, educational, and medical work. Many of them worked hard to convince the American public of the plight of these original citizens and attempted to combat the generally held notion that Indians were hatchet-wielding, scalping-minded savages who were good only when dead. In these areas, then, the Protestant mission work contributed constructive programs for the American Indians.

Yet today with the presence of the militant Indian, or the Red Power movement, one can understand that the missionary enterprise produced negative results as well. Along with the general white population, the missionaries made little protest to the government in its removal policies of the Indians onto the reservations; they accepted the manifest destiny claim of whites to the lands of the frontier; many sought to teach the Indians white culture as well as the Christian faith. Not until the later nineteenth century did the mission boards and agencies protest the means and goals of the federal government's policy of reducing the integrity of Indian nationhood to one of subservience. That the church-related groups were the first to protest was to their credit, but by that time there was no turning back from the policy of exploitation and subjection.

Today most church bodies are trying to atone in some measure for the guilt of their predecessors. In the middle of the twentieth century, missionary work among the Indians came to be limited primarily to educational programs on the reservations. The emphasis was no longer on evangelistic soul-winning but on preparing young people for a vocation and for citizenship in the outside world (for those who choose to leave the reservation). Indeed, many of the policies of the early part of the century have been virtually reversed. Now the missionaries are trying to help the Indians develop a sense of pride and accomplishment in their traditional culture. Young Indians call for Red Power (see INDIAN POWER MOVEMENT), in order to hold on to tribal culture and to help reeducate the general American public

about the true role and accomplishments of the Indian in American history. The movement is small because funds are so drastically limited. But the new perspective suggests that, in its own way, the missionary effort among the Indians has been willing to recognize past mistakes and accept the new realities of Indian life in America. However, the church-minded white reformer, like his secular colleague, has some distance to go.

Two authors round out in factual detail what has been sketched out here. Kenneth Scott Latourette, in *Three Centuries of Advance* (1936) and *The Great Century* (1941), is reliable and clear. William Warren Sweet, the great historian of American religion, contributed two very useful studies: *Religion in the Development of American Culture, 1765-1840* (1952) and *Religion in Colonial America* (1943). More specialized but definitive is Colin Brummitt Goodykoontz, *Home Missions on the American Frontier* (1939).—E. J.

Provo, Utah. Named after Etienne Provost (1782-1850), who explored and trapped in Utah in 1824, Provo was first colonized by the Mormons in 1849 and was the second largest city in Utah until the railroad propelled Ogden into the place in 1869. Standing between shallow Utah Lake and the encompassing Wasatch Mountains (12,000 feet), Provo is a city of trees and gardens—its beauty enhanced by its mild climate. Brigham Young University, founded as Brigham Young Academy in 1875, has had a strong influence on the community. Steel mills constructed in 1923 and 1943 have also influenced the area.

See Jens M. Jensen, *History of Provo, Utah* (1924).

Provost, Etienne (1782-1850). Fur trader and guide. Provost was born in Montreal but in 1815 migrated to St. Louis, where he soon joined August Pierre Chouteau and Jules De Mun's two-year expedition to the upper Arkansas. In 1817 Provost and the rest of the party were captured by the Mexicans and imprisoned in Santa Fe. Rather than responding hostilely to his captors, Provost made his home in New Mexico after Mexican independence and, in partnership with one Le Clerc, led expeditions to hunt in the Colorado Rockies (1823-24) and over the mountains to trap in the Green River-Uintah Basin region. In the course of his travels in the Great Basin he may have been the first white man to discover the Great Salt Lake.

In the spring of 1825 Provost encountered Peter Skene Ogden and his Hudson's Bay Company trappers in Weber Canyon, in the Wasatch Mountains. A few weeks later he met William H. Ashley in the Uintah Basin and joined Ashley at the first fur-trapping rendezvous in the Rockies that year. Provost's presence marked the convergence of three separate fur-trading frontiers in the Rockies as well as the existence of a north-south route from Taos to the northern trapping grounds.

It is known that Provost's fortunes rose and fell, but his activities are sometimes difficult to follow. Some authorities suggest that his partner Le Clerc, about whom nothing is known, may have been a stabilizing influence, but that once Le Clerc disappeared from view, Provost ceased to be an important figure. Provost was sometimes an independent trader and sometimes an employee of the American Fur Company until retirement in 1848. He accompanied the Fitzpatrick expedition (which included Alfred Jacob Miller, the artist) in

1837, the Nicollet-Frémont expedition in 1839, and the Audubon expedition of 1843. Provo, Utah, is named for him.

Older histories of the fur trade describe Provost as an employee of William H. Ashley and as being one of the party that rediscovered South Pass in 1823, but recent studies indicate that these assertions are erroneous. Greatly respected by his men, the portly Provost was described by Bartholomew Berthold as "the soul of the trappers in the mountains." Had Provost's men kept written records of their explorations and adventures the accounts would undoubtedly establish him as one of the major figures in the Rocky Mountain fur trade.

See LeRoy R. Hafen, ed., *The Mountain Men and the Fur Trade of the Far West*, vol. VI (1968); Dale L. Morgan, *Jedediah Smith and the Opening of the West* (1953); and David J. Weber, *The Taos Trappers, 1540-1846* (1971). —G. B. D.

Prowers, John Wesley (1838-1884). Colorado trader, politician, and cattleman. Prowers was born near Westport, Jackson County, Missouri. When he was eighteen years old, he crossed the Plains with Robert Miller, an Indian agent, and located at Bent's New Fort on the Arkansas River in southern Colorado. For a short time he worked in Miller's agency selling goods to the Kiowa, Comanche, Apache, Cheyenne, and Arapaho. In 1857 he entered the service of Colonel William Bent, the famous Indian trader now located at the same post. During his seven-year stint with Bent, Prowers made twenty-two trips across the Plains: ten trips in charge of wagon trains bringing supplies from the Missouri River to the trading post; several trips to Fort Union, New Mexico; and one to Fort Laramie, Wyoming. Prowers then left Bent and went to Old Fort Lyon, where he managed the sutler's store. From 1865 to 1870 he freighted government supplies from Leavenworth, Kansas, to Fort Union.

In 1861 Prowers was married to Amy, daughter of the Cheyenne chief Ochinee. In 1868 he began to farm at Boggsville, Colorado. When Bent County was organized, its county seat was located at Boggsville, which then became an important business center. Prowers became one of the first county commissioners, initially by gubernatorial appointment but later by popular election. In the fall of 1873 Prowers moved to the newly founded town of West Las Animas, where he spent the rest of his life in merchandising. Prowers was elected to the state legislature as an Independent in 1873 and reelected in 1880. He was the originator of the reapportionment act that came to be called the Sliding-Scale Bill.

Prowers was also well known as a large and successful stock raiser and dealer. A firm believer in the superiority of Hereford stock, he was one of the first to introduce the breed into southern Colorado. In 1871 he bought the cow known as Gentle the Twelfth from Frederick William Stone, of Guelph, Canada; her offspring during a ten-year period netted Prowers $10,800. The foundation of his general herd consisted of cows shipped in the late 1860s from Missouri; they were crossed first with purebred Shorthorns and then with Herefords. Prowers fenced eighty thousand acres of land as one unit and owned forty miles of river frontage, controlling 400,000 acres of range. In 1882 he was offered $775,000 for his herds and ranches. In 1880

Prowers opened and began operating a modern slaughterhouse in Las Animas and started shipping meat to the East.—H. R. L.

Prucha, Francis Paul (1921-   ). Clergyman, author, and historian. Prucha was born in River Falls, Wisconsin. He received his B.S. degree from Wisconsin State College at River Falls in 1941. A tour of duty in the United States Air Force (1942-46) interrupted his academic career. Returning to school, he received an M.A. degree from the University of Minnesota in 1947, a Ph.D. from Harvard in 1950, and an S.T.L. from St. Louis University in 1959. In 1960, Prucha became assistant professor of American history at Marquette University and, in 1966, a full professor and chairman of the Department of History.

Prucha received a faculty research grant from the Social Science Research Council (1959) and a Guggenheim Fellowship (1967-68). He was a member of the American Historical Association, the Organization of American Historians, and the American Catholic Historians Association.

Prucha specialized in the western military frontier and in federal Indian policy. His publications on the military include *Broadax and Bayonet* (1953), a study of the United States Army in the Northwest before 1860; *A Guide to the Military Posts of the United States, 1789-1895* (1964); and a basic, comprehensive survey, *The Sword of the Republic: The U.S. Army on the Frontier, 1783-1846* (1969). He also edited George Croghan's *Army Life on the Western Frontier, 1826-1845* (1958). On Indian affairs, he outlined the background of, and precedents for, government policy in *American Indian Policy in the Formative Years, 1780-1834* (1962), and found fewer flaws and failings in government policy than have the many scholars who have criticized the federal role in Indian affairs. He also edited two important sources: *Americanizing the American Indians: Writings by the Friends of the Indian, 1880-1900* (1973) and D. S. Otis' *The Dawes Act and the Allotment of Indian Lands* (1973). —P. L. N.

public domain. *Public domain* is the term applied to government-owned lands. The United States acquired lands from foreign nations by treaty, through cession of land claims of several of the original thirteen states, and as a result of the annexation of Texas. Treaties with Great Britain in 1783 and 1846 resulted in the acquisition of lands lying between the Appalachian Mountains and the Mississippi River, and the Oregon country south of the forty-ninth parallel, respectively; with France in 1803 of the Louisiana Territory; with Spain in 1819 of Florida; with Mexico in 1848 and 1853 of the great Southwest and the Gadsden Purchase, respectively; and with Russia in 1867 of Alaska. Claims that some of the original states had to lands in the trans-Appalachian country were surrendered to the federal government between 1781 and 1802. The annexation of Texas in 1845 brought no public domain to the United States, for Texas, like the original thirteen states, was permitted to retain all its public lands. However, being heavily burdened with the debt it incurred to gain its independence in 1836, Texas agreed in 1850 to cede to the United States 78,842,880 acres of its western lands in present New Mexico, Oklahoma, Colorado, Kansas, and Wyoming for $10 million. All of these acquisitions brought to the United States a total of 1,778,615,000 acres of public domain. Some 35 million acres of this land was claimed by individuals as grants from predecessor governments. Though these private claims had to be tested for their validity, the land was a part of the public domain until the titles were confirmed, but the usual rectangular surveys were not extended over them. Upon the annexation of Hawaii in 1898, the government and crown lands, amounting in 1904 to 1,720,000 acres, were ceded to the federal government. They were administered by the territorial authorities for the benefit of Hawaii. On its admission to the Union as a state in 1959 these lands were retroceded to the Hawaiian state government.

After independence the public domain was regarded as a national treasure that would produce revenue for the new nation by sale of the lands at relatively high prices (see LAND POLICY: *1780-1896*). In those early days there was no thought of permanently retaining any part of the public lands, though it was not long before the oak forests in the Gulf territory were reserved to provide timber for ship building. The western states and territories, whose influence in Congress became increasingly powerful during the nineteenth century, were never happy with the revenue policy. They gradually persuaded Congress to modify it, to reduce the price of land from $2.00 an acre to $1.25 in 1820, and to abandon efforts to induce competitive bidding at auction sales. Squatters were granted rights to settle upon public land in advance of the sales and surveys and to enter the land of their choice at the minimum price after one or two years of free use. Prices of lands long on the market were reduced to as little as twelve and one half cents an acre, and free homesteads were promised to anyone who would settle upon them and improve them for five years. The revenue policy was never completely abandoned, but the Homestead Act of 1862 made it no longer necessary for the pioneer farm maker to worry about raising the two hundred dollars previously needed to purchase his quarter section.

On the admission of Ohio in 1803, the first state carved out of the public domain, Congress gave it a small share of the public lands within its borders for the support of public schools, the establishment of a state university (see COLLEGES AND UNIVERSITIES), and the management of salt springs. None of these objectives was specifically authorized by the Constitution, but Congress was finding that it could vote lands for objectives for which it could not directly vote funds. As new states were admitted, additional objectives for granting lands were found and the share the states received became larger. The common-school grant was originally one section in each township or one thirty-sixth of the land; in 1850 new states were given two sections, and beginning in 1896 the last contiguous states were given four sections in each township. Grants were also made for public buildings and other public institutions. Under the swamplands act of 1850, swampy and overflowed lands unfit for cultivation were given to each state wherein they were located to induce the states to drain them. The act did not apply to states entering the Union after 1860. Generous grants were given for agricultural colleges and for the building of roads, canals, and railroads. Florida received the largest proportion of its land, sixty-five percent, from federal grants; Louisiana received thirty-six percent; Arkansas, thirty-five per-

cent; Michigan, thirty-two percent; and Minnesota, thirty percent. Alaska on admission was given the privilege of selecting 102,550,000 acres or 27 percent of the unreserved land within its boundaries; the privilege of making its own selection made the grant unique, for no other state had been so privileged. Nevada, in return for surrendering a part of its school grant, was allowed to select the balance from the best of the remaining nonmineral lands. It thus received the smallest portion but had the selection privilege. The most valuable donation to the states was that of the tidelands and navigable riverbeds with their great oil reserves by an act of 1953.

In 1872 what is now Yellowstone National Park was set aside from the public domain, and in 1890 three additional parks were set aside in California. To these beginnings Congress has slowly added new parks, monuments, and historic sites, withdrawing them from the public domain and opening them to the public. For many years national parks were created only on the public lands, which meant there were none in the eastern states. Finally in 1916 wealthy philanthropists led by John D. Rockefeller, Jr., purchased and gave to the United States six thousand acres, including Mount Cadillac on Mount Desert Island, in Maine for the Acadia National Park. Since then Great Smoky National Park and a number of others have been created from donations made by states.

The National Forest Reservation Act of 1891 marked an even more drastic change in the underlying policy toward the public lands, for it authorized the withdrawal of valuable timber stands, not to lock up these resources but to assure that they would be administered under the best scientific management policies by government foresters. In 1911 Congress took another step in pushing the federal government into the administration of the natural resources of the country by authorizing it to purchase forest land on the watershed of streams subject to destructive flooding, thereby enabling the government to reforest and thus protect cutover areas where private owners could not.

Seeing the grazing capacity of the open rangelands of the West progressively decline because of overgrazing and lack of administrative management, Congress in 1934 ordered their withdrawal from public-domain status and placed them under the management of the Grazing Service, later the Bureau of Land Management in the Department of the Interior. Thus, for all practical purposes, Congress ended land sales and homesteading and applied bureaucratic grazing control to the withdrawn lands similar to that already practiced in the national forests.

Congress was as slow to develop clear-cut and easily interpreted laws for regulating mineral lands as it had been for other valuable lands. Theodore Roosevelt used his executive authority to withdraw large areas of coal and oil lands. Under the Mineral Leasing Act of 1920 these lands were opened to leasing with a prospect of some return to the public. Of the proceeds from leasing, fifty-two and one half percent was to go into the reclamation fund for development of irrigation projects in the semiarid states of the West, thirty-seven and one half percent to the states in which the lands were located for road-building, and the remaining ten percent to the United States Treasury. Other revenue-sharing measures required that most of the income from public lands should be either shared largely with the states where the funds originated or spent within them.

See Paul W. Gates, *History of Public Land Law Development* (1968); and Benjamin H. Hibbard, *History of the Public Land Policies* (1924).—P. W. G.

Pueblo Indians. The Pueblo of New Mexico and northern Arizona represent one of the best preserved native American cultures remaining in the United States. The name derives from the Spanish word *pueblo*, meaning "village," and was applied by the conquistadores to those people who dwelled in large multistoried apartments of stone or adobe and who shared, if not a common language, at least a common culture based on intensive agriculture and a rich religious ceremonialism. Extensive research, which began about 1880 with the work of archaeologist-historian Adolf F. BANDELIER, has to date produced an enormous body of information on the prehistory, history, and ethnology of these people.

The Pueblo cultural tradition had its beginnings about the opening of the Christian era. As far back as late Pleistocene times, however, early man had hunted the mammoth, camel, horse, ground sloth, and giant bison on the lush savannas and along the fringes of lakes in eastern New Mexico. Important archaeological excavations that have unearthed finely worked projectile points and other remains of these big-game hunters are found at Folsom, Clovis, and Sandia. The Clovis site, including the famous excavations at Blackwater Draw, has yielded artifacts that seem to provide a link with the upper Paleolithic age in Siberia.

Another early tradition, usually referred to as the Desert Culture, was concentrated west of the Continental Divide and was characterized by an economy based upon the gathering of wild food products and the hunting of small game. In southern New Mexico and Arizona the local manifestation of this tradition has been labeled the Cochise Culture, the beginnings of which are placed at about 8000 B.C., or contemporaneous with Folsom man. The end of the last Ice Age was followed by a prolonged period of desiccation, culminating in the altithermal stage about 5000 B.C. The severe climatic changes resulted in the disappearance of both the large mammals and the men who hunted them. The Cochise gatherers adapted to the new environment, however, and in so doing furnished the base from which Pueblo farming cultures developed.

The origins of agriculture in the Southwest, as is true elsewhere in the New World, are obscure. Excavations beginning in 1952 at Bat Cave in west-central New Mexico brought to light Cochise artifacts in the same archaeological level with small primitive ears of corn. They date between 2000 and 3000 B.C. Until this discovery there had been no proof of the practice of agriculture in the United States before the Christian era. It is supposed that this earliest corn, along with squash and the gourd, represented a diffusion from Middle America, and that later diffusions brought beans, other crops, and finally pottery. These innovations worked a transformation in the simple Cochise way of life, so that by 100 B.C. a new, more sophisticated southwestern tradition had emerged. The earliest stage of this phase was represented by the Mogollon people, who were centered in the southern uplands along the present border of New Mexico and Arizona. In the first centuries after Christ, the Mogollon were the cultural leaders in the Southwest, living in pit-house villages, farming mesa tops and stream valleys, and producing creditable and distinctive ceramics.

Mogollon influence seeped into the deserts of southern Arizona, affecting other descendants of the old Cochise gatherers. Combining with new influences from Mexico, it ultimately produced the culture known as the Hohokam (from a Pima word meaning "those who have vanished"). These people remain best known for their skillfully engineered canals and irrigation works in the drainages of the Salt and Gila rivers.

It is to the northern neighbors of the Mogollon, the people now called the Anasazi (Navaho for the "ancient ones"), that the ancestors of the modern Pueblo Indians may be traced. Anasazi is an inclusive term referring to the prehistoric to historic Basket Maker-Pueblo continuum. Because of the spectacular cliff and open-site ruins left by the later Anasazi, archaeologists have devoted the bulk of their attention to this culture, and only in recent decades have the Mogollon and Hohokam been identified as separate and distinct traditions. The first attempts at establishing chronological stages for Anasazi development were made in 1927 at a conference at Pecos Pueblo led by Dr. Alfred Vincent Kidder. Stratigraphy and cross-dating of pottery types initially provided the basis for identification of archaeological periods, although shortly afterward dendrochronology (tree-ring studies) and carbon-14 dating offered more accurate help in determining culture sequences.

The earliest Anasazi have been termed Basket Makers for the profusion of finely woven baskets left behind in dry caves. They apparently advanced in a manner similar to the Mogollon, but at a later time. By the end of the Basket Maker era (A.D. 700-800) agriculture and pottery were well established, setting the stage for Pueblo development. The transition was marked by a shift from pit-house living, characteristic of the Basket Makers, to aboveground, multi-roomed masonry structures or the distinctive apartment-like dwellings, which were to give Pueblo culture its name.

In the years from A.D. 800 to 1100 the Pueblo moved toward a cultural summit as farming became more intensive through effective utilization of water resources; as ceremonial practices, especially those related to weather control, assumed more elaborate forms; and as ceramics reached new heights of excellence. The Great Pueblo Period, sometimes called the Classic, extended from the eleventh through the thirteenth centuries and witnessed the rise of three large population centers at MESA VERDE, Colorado (now a national park), Chaco Canyon, New Mexico, and Kayenta in Arizona. The most impressive construction on an open site occurred in Chaco Canyon, where a massive communal dwelling sheltering twelve hundred people was raised at Pueblo Bonito.

A severe drought in the Pueblo country between 1276 and 1299 contributed to the decline of the large centers, as did perhaps pressure from hostile nomadic tribes and increasing incidence of infectious diarrhea. Some of the Pueblo drifted south, founding new towns and becoming the ancestors of the modern Zuñi and Hopi Indians. Others, probably the majority, migrated eastward where climatic conditions were more favorable, and settled alongside their rustic country cousins on the Pajarito Plateau and in the valleys of the Rio Grande and its tributaries. Here they were situated, prosperous and secure, at the opening of the Spanish period.

Pueblo society and culture made a strong impression on the first Spaniards because it contrasted so sharply with that of the primitive tribes of northern Mexico. One soldier wrote of the Pueblo in 1581, "For a barbarous people, the neatness they observe in everything is very remarkable." Yet, in spite of admiration for the architecture, agriculture, and crafts of the Pueblo, the Spaniards found much that appeared repugnant, particularly in native religion. Especially onerous to them were the snake dances, once common to all villages but today confined to the Hopis, in which rattlesnakes and other serpents were charmed by priests and then released to carry messages to the gods.

Religion formed the core of Pueblo life and was manifested in an ancient and rich ceremonialism, much of which centered on the *kiva*, or underground ritual chamber. The entire social fabric was woven about the single theme of achieving harmony with the gods of nature to insure an abundance of crops. The religious hierarchy, composed of native priests, directed all phases of village life, acting through clans or, in some cases, medicine societies. An important feature of religion was the *katcina* cult, largely concerned with rainmaking. It was strongest among the western Pueblo, who had little water available for irrigation, and weakest among the Rio Grande villagers. The *katcinas* were regarded as ancestral spirits, impersonated in ceremonies by elaborately costumed and marked men who bore invocations to the gods for moisture, good health, and general well-being. Some scholars believe the *katcinas* may be an offshoot of the Tlaloc rain cult of central Mexico, which penetrated the Southwest after A.D. 1300. Evidence may also be found that in colonial times the Pueblo incorporated Catholic saints into their religion as *katcinas*.

At the time of the Spanish conquest, each pueblo, surrounded by its farmlands, composed an independent political unit. No shadow of governmental superstructure existed to connect even villages of the same language with any kind of league or confederacy. Communal autonomy was in fact jealously guarded, and there were frequent instances of open conflict between towns. Pueblo society, marked for its absence of social classes, emphasized conformity and cooperation with the community. Monogamy was the rule and women enjoyed higher status than in most other Indian groups.

Ceramics and weaving were the most advanced arts of Pueblo material culture, and basketry was widespread though inferior to that produced by some California tribes. The economy was based on agriculture, the principal field crops being maize, beans, squashes, tobacco, and native cotton. The Spaniards introduced wheat; orchard fruits such as peaches, apricots, and apples; alfalfa; and probably chile. In prehistoric times, the Pueblo possessed only the dog, although they kept turkeys, eagles, and macaws for feathers. After the conquest, cattle, horses, burros, sheep, and goats became an important part of their economy. Agriculture was supplemented by the hunting of wild game, and excursions were made seasonally to the plains for buffalo. Abundant use was made of wild plants for food, dyestuffs, herbal remedies, and ceremonial purposes. Salt lakes, particularly those east of the Manzano Mountains and

south of Zuñi, were visited frequently with much ritual surrounding the extraction of the salt. All in all, the Pueblo made efficient use of an environment whose aridity and temperature extremes rendered meager gifts to man.

The record of Pueblo history commenced with the expedition of Francisco Vásquez de Coronado in the years 1540 to 1542. A chronicler of the expedition, Pedro de Castañeda, left a brief, albeit valuable, account of the Pueblo in which he listed a total of seventy-one villages with an estimated population of twenty thousand men. Historian France V. Scholes has suggested the population numbered about thirty-five thousand at the end of the sixteenth century.

At the time of the Spaniards' arrival, the Pueblo were distributed along the Rio Grande from the area near present Socorro northward to Taos, with outlying settlements to the west at Jémez, Acoma, Zuñi, and Hopi and to the east at Pecos Pueblo, the villages beyond the Manzano Mountains, and those in the Galisteo Basin. The conduct of the members of the Coronado expedition set the pattern for Spanish-Indian relations for the next 150 years. Submission of the Pueblo to the authority of the king of Spain was demanded and swift retaliation visited upon any that refused it. Usually the destruction of a village or two in any given area was sufficient to enforce obedience, as Coronado proved with the defeat of the Zuñi town of Háwikuh and two Tiwa pueblos near Bernalillo. Once the Indians were reduced to peace, the Spaniards levied tribute in the form of blankets and bushels of maize, and initiated efforts to convert them to Christianity. Coronado's stay in New Mexico was brief and the few missionaries he left behind were killed, so that except for several small and ephemeral expeditions that followed, the Pueblo remained relatively untroubled to the end of the century.

In 1598, however, permanent colonization of the upper Rio Grande valley was initiated by Juan de ONATE, and the Indians came to feel the full weight of European rule. The motive behind Spanish expansion into this area was ostensibly a missionary one, based on the desire to convert the last large body of sedentary, agricultural Indians remaining in the Viceroyalty of New Spain. The colonists who came with the Franciscan friars, however, were more interested in prospecting for gold and silver, and when mineral riches failed to materialize they turned to exploitation of the native people. The Pueblo were parceled out among the leading settlers in grants of *ecomienda*—that is, a trusteeship arrangement whereby the Spaniards agreed to protect and supervise their charges in exchange for annual tribute. Although the Indians in theory had certain legal protection, the system in practice cloaked all manner of abuses.

The missionary program, expanding rapidly after 1610, saw large churches and friaries constructed in the majority of the pueblos, and within another decade a priest, reporting upon the success of his brethren, claimed more than thirty thousand baptisms. Although the zealous friars acted to shield their neophytes from mistreatment by the colonists, they themselves imposed heavy demands upon Indian labor in the building of churches and meted out stern punishment for infractions of ecclesiastical discipline. Equally disquieting to the Pueblo were the persistent efforts on the part of the

The north group of New Mexico's Taos pueblo. (Library of Congress)

friars to destroy all forms of native religious practice and ceremonialism. Periodically the churchmen, with support of Spanish soldiers, raided the *kivas* where they collected sacred objects and carried them to the plaza for burning. Such attacks on religion had the effect of disturbing the entire web of Pueblo life. One result of this persecution was that much of the ritualism that had once been public was now performed in secret, and is so done to the present day.

The clumsy attempts to smother Pueblo religion were not only futile, but kindled bitter hatred toward the friars and all Spaniards. This enmity culminated in a general Indian revolt that broke forth in early August 1680. Within a short time twenty-one Franciscans and more than four hundred colonists were slain, and the surviving Spaniards were forced to abandon the province. More remarkable than the relative ease that attended victory was the unity achieved by the Pueblo. This was effected through the leadership of a Tewa Indian from the village of San Juan named Popé, who had striven tirelessly to forge an alliance against the common enemy. It should be noted, however, that a church historian, Fray Angélico Chavez, has come forward with the hypothesis that a mulatto named Naranjo posing as the devil was the true mastermind behind the revolt.

With the expulsion of the Spaniards, the Indians set about to remove all vestiges of alien rule. European livestock was slaughtered, fruit trees pulled up, and the people waded into the rivers to wash away the taint of baptism. It is thus thought that the revolt represented, in anthropological terms, a nativistic movement—the rejection of foreign domination and the revival and reaffirmation of traditional culture. In any case, the event may be regarded as the most successful Indian revolt ever to occur within the limits of the United States.

The Pueblo held firm to their independence for twelve years, but the old particularism and suspicion of one village toward another gradually reasserted itself, so that when the Spaniards under Diego De VARGAS returned in the period 1692-94 a united front could not be mustered. Several of the northern towns were defeated in bitter fighting, the Spanish governor reoccupied Santa Fe, and the Pueblo, except the Hopi who remained independent, again found themselves under the white man's yoke.

The Spaniards, however, had learned much from the sad experience of 1680, and hereafter their conduct toward the Indians improved accordingly. The *encomienda* was not reestablished, fewer demands were made upon Indian labor, and, most significantly, the missionary program, founded anew, desisted from attacks on Pueblo religion so long as its practice was kept discreetly in the background. The Pueblo folk, in fact, became an important part of colonial society, and their warriors, joining with Spanish forces, played a major role in turning back attacks of Comanche, Navaho, and Apache. A royal grant of four square leagues of land was made to each village so that its community base was secure, and a public defender was provided by the government to protect Indian rights and carry their legal cases to court.

Yet the presence of the Spanish took its toll. By 1750

the Pueblo population was reduced to scarcely more than twelve thousand and the number of villages to about forty, the result of raids by nomadic enemies and frequent epidemics of smallpox, measles, and other European diseases. By the time of independence from Spain (1821), the population had decreased further to approximately nine thousand.

The story of the Pueblo Indians in the nineteenth century is chiefly one of neglect, first on the part of the Republic of Mexico, which governed New Mexico for twenty-five years, and then on the part of the United States, which assumed jurisdiction in 1846. The territorial Supreme Court in 1869 did confirm Pueblo citizenship and possession of tribal lands, but Special Indian Agent William F. M. Arny, who toured the Pueblo in 1870, reported that they were suffering greatly from lack of official attention. Previous agents had been either disinterested or dishonest, and there was almost a complete dearth of schools. At Zuñi, which was typical, Arny found only one literate person out of a population of 1,530. He wrote that the Zuñi "begin to think that because they do not steal, the Government does not give them anything, but if they steal like the Navaho they would get something."

By the end of the century, the government had swung around from an attitude of neglect to a policy of close supervision of Indian affairs, the aim of which was to enforce speedy assimilation into the white man's world. The boarding-school program, vigorously supported from the 1890s to the 1930s, carried many Pueblo children away from their villages for the first time, and a flood of Protestant missionaries undertook to wean older people from their traditional religious observances, which had survived three centuries of Spanish persecution. The multiplicity of Christian denominations led one bewildered Indian to sum up the problem as one of "Too many Jesuses." Founded by Oklahoma Indians in 1918, the Native American Church, which utilizes peyote, has made minor inroads among the Pueblo, particularly at Taos, but traditional practices and a superficial layer of Catholicism continue to dominate the religious lives of the majority of the people. In recent years many Pueblo have been torn by intense factionalism over the issue of how much change should be tolerated by the community.

Each pueblo today remains essentially an autonomous unit, preserving as much as possible of its ancient heritage while confronting the problems of twentieth-century America. The lands of each village are inalienable, although the federal government reserves the right to intervene in their management. A governor, elected annually by the people, serves both as secular leader and spokesman for the religious hierarchy, the real power in all pueblos. A tribal council maintains law and order, handles funds, and establishes ordinances with approval of the secretary of the interior. An All Pueblo Council, first organized in 1922, now meets periodically at Santo Domingo, New Mexico, to consider matters of wider concern and provide unity of action.

See ADOBE ARCHITECTURE; NEW MEXICO MISSIONS; POTTERY, SOUTHWESTERN INDIAN; SAND PAINTING; and SILVERWORK, SOUTHWESTERN INDIAN.

A standard text on prehistory is John C. McGregor, *Southwestern Archaeology* (2nd ed., 1965). Oakah L. Jones, Jr., offers a sound treatment of the Pueblo during

Linguistic Affiliation and Population (1970)

Language Families	Languages	Pueblos	Population
Tanoan	Tiwa:	Taos	1623
		Picurís	183
		Sandía	261
		Isleta	2527
	Tewa:	San Juan	1487
		Santa Clara	1119
		Nambé	328
		San Ildefonso	358
		Tesuque	259
		Pojoaque	107
	Towa:	Jémez (including Pecos remnants)	1765
	Tano:	Extinct except for remnant at Hano	
	Piro:	Extinct	
	Dialects		
Keresan	Eastern:	Cochiti	779
(Queres)		Santo Domingo	2311
		San Felipe	1632
		Santa Ana	472
		Zia	534
	Western:	Acoma	2861
		Laguna	5086
Zunian		Zuñi	4869
Uto-Aztecan (Shoshonian)	Hopi:	12 villages	4857

colonial times in *Pueblo Warriors and Spanish Conquest* (1966). Ruth Underhill, *Workaday Life of the Pueblos* (1954), is a popular account of society and culture. Indispensable is Edward H. Spicer, *Cycles of Conquest: The Impact of Spain, Mexico, and the United States on the Indians of the Southwest, 1533-1960* (1962). Edward P. Dozier, a leading anthropologist and a Pueblo himself, provides an up-to-date survey of the subject in *The Pueblo Indians of North America* (1970).—M. SI.

Pullman, George Mortimer (1831-1897). Industrialist. Pullman, the man chiefly responsible for the development of the sleeping car that made comfortable long-distance travel in the United States possible, was born in Brocton, New York. He learned mechanics from his father and cabinetmaking from a brother, two crafts which he was to put to good use later. Arriving in Chicago in 1855, he accumulated his first capital by successfully contracting to raise buildings in the business district above the flood level.

Realizing the need for a practical railroad sleeping car, Pullman invested in a demonstration car, which the Chicago and Alton Railroad put into experimental service in 1858. It was not a success, but by 1865 Pullman and a partner had patented a convertible coach seat that would make up into lower and upper berths for sleeping. Investing in an experimental car, designed from the ground up to embody the invention, Pullman placed the Pioneer in service in time for it to serve as President Abraham Lincoln's funeral coach. It was a remarkable success, and the Pullman Palace Car Company, founded in 1867, grew rapidly.

The interior of Car No. 9, the first Pullman sleeper. (Library of Congress)

At the "model" town of Pullman, now a part of Chicago, the company produced thousands of railroad passenger cars of constantly increasing size and luxuriousness—sleeping, dining, parlor, and lounge cars—to which were applied such Pullman innovations as the enclosed vestibule and the reclining seat. Determined to provide sleeping accommodations equalling those of a first-class hotel, Pullman formed a separate operating company to see to it that the service was up to his high standards; all the railroads had to do was haul the cars and collect the fares. By the time of his death the Pullman company had beaten out all competitors and imitators. But Pullman, for all his foresight and practical genius, was a failure in his relations with his workmen. The model town was a dismal failure, due in no small measure to autocratic policies the men resented; his stubborn refusal to bargain collectively with his men (Mark Hanna said such a man was a fool) led to the tragic strike of 1894 with which Pullman's name is permanently associated (see LABOR MOVEMENT).

Lucius M. Beebe, *Mr. Pullman's Elegant Palace Car* (1961), profusely illustrates Pullman and other makes of railroad passenger cars from the golden age of rail travel. Stanley Buder, *Pullman, An Experiment in Industrial Order and Community Planning* (1967), has just about the last word on this subject, which has fascinated three generations of social scientists. There is no biography of Pullman.—A. M.

puma. See MOUNTAIN LION.

Pumpelly, Rafael (1837-1923). Mining engineer and archaeologist. Pumpelly was born in Oswego, New York, and studied engineering in Hanover, Germany. Employed as a mining engineer by the Santa Rita Company, he rode many dusty furlongs in stagecoaches to the booming mines in Tubac, Arizona, prior to the Civil War. Engaging privately in mining ventures near Santa Rita, Arizona, Pumpelly lost his holdings during ferocious Apache raids, when Union soldiers were withdrawn from frontier garrisons at the beginning of the Civil War. Indians had whites on the run, and Pumpelly and Charles D. Poston, an Arizona pioneer, escaped westward through the arid Papago Indian reservation on their difficult trek to safety in California.

Pumpelly later was a mining engineer in Japan, China, Russia, and the Gobi Desert and headed an archaeological expedition into central Asia and Russian Turkestan in 1903-04. A hardy, enthusiastic explorer, his book *Across America and Asia* (1870) is a classic story of adventure and travel for those interested in Arizona, mining, and Southwest history.

See *Pumpelly's Arizona* (1965), an excerpt from *Across America and Asia*, edited with an excellent introduction by Andrew Wallace.—B. W. A.

Purísima Concepción, La. Spanish Franciscan mission. La Purísima Concepción (the Immaculate Conception) was the eleventh link in the Alta California mission chain. Father Fermín de Lasuén dedicated it on December 8, 1787, but the actual construction did not commence until March 1788. Situated in the fertile valley of the Rio Santa Inés, the mission was near an Indian village—as were all the missions—whose population was the source not only of its neophytes but of its labor for building the mission, tending its herds, and growing its crops.

The first buildings were poorly constructed and soon succumbed to torrential rains, but by 1802 a new compound, including an adobe and tile-roofed church, had been erected. The earthquake of December 21, 1812, struck with such violence that it ruined almost the entire mission. After living in makeshift huts that winter the Franciscan fathers and the Indians decided to abandon the original location, on the site of the present-day town of Lompoc, and move four miles northeast. Father Mariano Payers, then president of the California missions, undertook the difficult task of rebuilding. The new facilities consisted of three simple rectangular structures in a row. The church was a large room in the main mission house. The Indian revolt of 1824, begun at Santa Inés Mission, so seriously disrupted life at Purísima Concepción that the mission, which was already declining, never recovered. The buildings fell into ruin soon after the Mexican secularization law of 1834. Thus things remained until the Union Oil Company purchased the site and donated it to California. La Purísima Concepción was the object of extensive restoration in the 1930s and is today a lovely state park.

For a history of the mission, see John A. Berger, *The Franciscan Missions of California* (1942); and Rexford Newcomb, *The Old Mission Churches and Historic Houses of California* (1925).—R. S.

Puritans. See CONGREGATIONALISTS; and MASSACHUSETTS, SETTLEMENT OF.

Pushmataha (c.1764-1824). Choctaw chief. Pushmataha was born at one of the Choctaw Six Towns in present Noxubee County, Mississippi. He was probably orphaned in early childhood, and the circumstances of his birth, family history, and youth were subjects of speculation in his own lifetime. Aware of the political value of mystery and supernaturalism among his people, Pushmataha himself shielded his origins, saying often, "I had neither father nor mother nor any kinsman. The lightning rent the living oak, and Pushmataha sprang forth."

Pushmataha rose to prominence as a warrior in intertribal warfare between the Choctaw and their trans-Mississippi enemies, the Caddo and Osage. By 1805 he had become an elected chief. An ambitious man, Pushmataha foresaw the futility of resisting the Americans, who by that time were pushing into Choctaw country. He sought to increase his personal power and prestige by becoming the leader of the Choctaw faction that sought a policy of alliance and conciliation with the whites. At Mount Dexter, in 1805, he signed a treaty ceding Alabama and Mississippi lands, and for his efforts was rewarded a gift of $500 and a government salary of $150 a year for as long as he remained chief. He adamantly opposed the Shawnee leader Tecumseh's efforts to form an Indian confederacy against the whites, and his prestige and oratory were instrumental in the failure of Tecumseh's visit to the South in 1811.

During the Creek War (1813-14) Pushmataha, with the aid of federal interpreter John Pitchlynn, persuaded the Choctaw to join the United States. Leading five hundred warriors to support Andrew Jackson's forces, Pushmataha was made a brigadier general and given a full-dress uniform, which he wore throughout the campaign. After the war, he was party to two or more treaties of cession in 1816 and 1820.

By 1824, however, Pushmataha had become alarmed at the rapacity of white demands for land and opposed a government proposal for a further cession. Invited to Washington with several other chiefs for treaty negotiations, he was lavishly entertained while discussions were extended by the government, which hoped to soften his resistance. Before these tactics could take effect, however, Pushmataha contracted a throat infection and suddenly died. The government arranged a spectacular official funeral, and he was buried in the congressional cemetery after a great procession viewed by thousands, musical accompaniment by the marine band, and numerous volleys of cannon. A large stone monument was erected over his grave. Government negotiators during the subsequent era of Indian removals continually referred to Pushmataha as the sterling example of what rewards awaited "good Indians."

See Anna Lewis, *Chief Pushmataha: American Patriot* (1959); and Gideon Lincecum, "Life of Apushimataha," Mississippi Historical Society *Publications*, vol. 9 (1906). —P. R. M.

Pyramid Lake, Nevada. The largest water remnant of prehistoric Lake Lahontan, Pyramid Lake was named by John C. Frémont when the explorer first saw it on January 10, 1844. The lake has an inlet, the Truckee River, but no outlet. Consequently, when the Newlands project diverted some of the waters of the Truckee River to form the reservoir behind Lahontan Dam, the natural drying-up process of the lake was speeded. Recently, the Pyramid Lake Indians, who held the lake as the main asset of the Pyramid Lake Reservation, have been fighting to restore the flow of the Truckee River to Pyramid Lake. They have achieved only limited success to the present but have enlisted powerful friends who may well turn the balance in their favor in the future.

See Samuel G. Houghton, "Pyramid Lake—An Ancient Remnant," *Nevada Highways and Parks* (Winter 1967), and Alvin M. Josephy, Jr., "Here in Nevada a Terrible Crime . . ." *American Heritage* (June 1970). —R. R. E.

Q

Quaife, Milo Milton (1880-1959). Historian. Few scholars have ever accumulated a more impressive record of publishing and editing in the fields of American history and the American West than Quaife. A list of his books, articles, reviews, and commentaries that was compiled four years before his death filled a fifty-two-page booklet.

Like most historians of his generation, Quaife was born in a small town—Nashua, Iowa. He attended Iowa College (now Grinnell College) and received a B.A. degree in 1903 before enrolling in graduate school at the University of Missouri. He took his M.A. degree in American history there and then entered the University of Chicago for his doctorate. From 1908 to 1914 he taught history at the Lewis Institute of Technology, following which he transferred to Madison as superintendent of the Wisconsin State Historical Society. Quaife was editor of the society's publications for eight years, and in 1924 moved to Detroit as editor of the Burton Historical Collection. He retired from that position in 1947 to devote full time to his many research and writing projects.

Meanwhile, he enjoyed a long and close relationship with the Mississippi Valley Historical Association, the present Organization of American Historians. As managing editor of its *Review* from 1924 to 1930, he maintained a high standard for articles and book reviews and enlivened the publication with news and frequently colorful comments. He had previously served on the editorial board and as a member of the executive committee of the *Review* and one term as president (1919-20) of the association.

Beginning in 1910, with the publication of his doctoral dissertation and the four-volume edition of *The Diary of James K. Polk During His Presidency*, he edited six other major works and six volumes of the *Wisconsin Historical*

Collection. During the next five decades he wrote at least six significant books relating to the history of the Wisconsin-Michigan-Chicago region; more than two hundred scholarly articles, book reviews, and commentaries; and edited forty volumes in the Lakeside Classics of the Western Americana series.—W. E. H.

Quaker policy. See PEACE POLICY.

Quanah Parker (c. 1845-1911). Comanche chief. Quanah was the son of white captive Cynthia Ann Parker and Comanche chief Peta Nocona. His early years were spent on the southern Great Plains, but in May 1875 he reported to Fort Sill with one of the last groups of Comanche to give up nomadic life under pressure from the army. At this time, he added the name Parker to his Indian name of Quanah. Identified immediately as a mixed-blood and manifesting a willingness to adapt to the white man's way of life, Quanah rose rapidly in the reservation political structure. A favorite of the agents and of the Texas cattlemen who grazed their herds on the reservation ranges, he became the principal Comanche chief by 1890 and also the possessor of considerable property. The progressives (pro-assimilation faction) of the tribe accepted him as their leader; the conservatives (adherants to traditional culture) denounced him as a half-breed in the pay of the cattlemen. When the Jerome Commission (created in 1889 to apply the principles of the Dawes Act to Indians in Oklahoma) negotiated with the Comanche in 1892 for the dissolution of their reservation, Quanah did not oppose the agreement but did work to get the best possible bargain. Later he tried to postpone land allotment of the reservation.

Quanah was a progressive in economic matters, but he was sufficiently conservative in other areas to suit the most reactionary members of the tribe. He was slow to use his influence to back educational programs, showed no interest in Christianity, and was one of the most persistent users of mescal and peyote. In fact, modern peyotists honor him as the founder of their religion. Quanah was also a polygamist, and had a total of eight wives over the years. In 1897 his polygamy cost him his judgeship on the reservation's Court of Indian Offenses. In his declining years, Quanah was a local celebrity, and his fine home near Cache, Oklahoma, was a showpiece for visiting dignitaries.

See William T. Hagan, *Indian Police and Judges* (1966); Clyde L. Jackson and Grace Jackson, *Quanah Parker: Last Chief of the Comanches* (1963); and A. Marriott and C. Rachlin, *Peyote* (1971).—W. T. H.

Quantrill's Raiders. A Confederate guerrilla movement in Missouri and Kansas. The guerrillas' leader, William Clarke Quantrill (1837-1865), was born and raised in Ohio, taught school for a time in Ohio and Illinois, made a trip to Utah, and finally settled down in Lawrence, Kansas, in 1859-60. Adopting the alias of Charles Hart to mask his checkered background, Quantrill became involved in shady dealings and fled to Missouri, where he joined the proslavery faction. By Christmas 1861 this young man of twenty-four, possessed of blonde good looks rendered sinister by cold, heavy-lidded eyes, emerged as the leader of a Confederate irregular force of ten men that harried Union soldiers and sympathizers at every opportunity and skirmished with Kansas Jayhawkers raiding into Missouri.

After taking part in the capture of Independence,

Missouri, in August 1862, Quantrill and his men were taken into the Confederate regular army, with Quantrill gaining the rank of captain. The change in official status of Quantrill's force made no difference in its tactics, which remained in the classic guerrilla style. Quantrill's group knew the country well and, riding fluidly in many small troops, they easily ambushed larger enemy forces. Mounted on the best horses, they thrived on the active support of an admiring civilian population. Quantrill's baleful career reached its peak on August 21, 1863, when he led a troop of 450 on a murderous raid against the abolitionist center of Lawrence, Kansas. In the brutal attack on Lawrence, at least 150 male civilians were killed in a general massacre and much of the town was burned. A lesser massacre occurred two months later when Quantrill's band slaughtered seventeen federal noncombatants captured after a battle near Baxter Springs, Kansas. The ebullient members of Quantrill's troop were hard even for him to control, and eventually the band broke up into smaller units headed by Quantrill's equally ferocious lieutenants: "Bloody Bill" Anderson, George Todd, and David Pool. Quantrill himself was fatally wounded on a raid into Kentucky in May 1865.

With the Missouri-Kansas border region bitterly divided between Confederate and Unionist sympathizers, conditions were ideal for the rise of savage guerrilla warfare. Reared in a frontier style of life where riding and shooting came naturally, the young men of Missouri and Kansas flocked around the guerrilla leaders of their choice—Senator James H. Lane for the Unionists and Quantrill for the Confederates. Quantrill and his lieutenants showed a genius for molding high-spirited youths, such as Frank and Jesse James and Cole and Jim Younger, into a fearsome, mounted fighting array (armed primarily with Colt revolvers) that struck hard and often against federal forces. Paul I. Wellman has contended that from Quantrill's Raiders was bred a postwar generation of southwestern outlaw gangs (the James-Younger, Belle Starr, Dalton, Doolin, Jennings, and Cook gangs) whose members adapted to bank and train robbery the technique of mounted hit-and-run attack they learned so well under Quantrill's tutelage.

See Richard S. Brownlee, *Gray Ghosts of the Confederacy: Guerrilla Warfare in the West, 1861-1865* (1958); and Paul I. Wellman, *A Dynasty of Western Outlaws* (1961).—R. M. B.

Quapaw Indians. See SIOUAN TRIBES, SOUTHERN.

Quechan Indians. See YUMA INDIANS.

Queen Anne's War. See COLONIAL WARS.

Quick, John Herbert (1861-1925). Writer and Iowa politician. Quick grew up on the prairie near Grundy Center in the north-central part of Iowa. The rugged existence his family harvested from their small farm stamped him with thorough-going agrarianism, reinforced by his quasi-religious conversion to the single-tax theory of Henry George in the mid-1880s. Quick maintained a granite-like devotion to the single tax for his entire adult life.

At age twenty, Quick left the farm and taught school. Then he studied law and passed the state bar examination in April 1886. Four years later, following his marriage, he set up a law practice with a Sioux City legal firm. When the Panic of 1893 hit Sioux City its real-estate boom crashed. Chicanery in both county and municipal governments was obvious, and a citizens' committee was organized to investigate. Quick was its general counsel. The notoriety he gained in that capacity led to his election as Democratic mayor of Sioux City in 1898. From that office he grew to leadership in the Democratic party of Iowa during the next decade.

Quick began writing in 1901. His first effort of consequence was *Aladdin & Co.* (1904), a novel in which an ever-present love story winds through a setting of real-estate speculation in an Iowa frontier boom town. *The Broken Lance* (1907) tells the tragedy of a single-tax clergyman and his martyrdom, while *The Brown Mouse* (1915) campaigns for progressive rural education. *We Have Changed All That* (1928), written in collaboration with a Russian emigré, is a jaundiced portrayal of the chaos created in Russia by the Bolshevik revolution. It is drawn primarily from Quick's stint in Vladivostok with the American Red Cross in 1920.

The author's magnum opus was his trilogy of Iowa frontier and smalltown life: *Vandemark's Folly* (1921), *The Hawkeye* (1923), and *The Invisible Woman* (1924). These three works established Quick as a novelist of stature and contain some of the best descriptive prose ever written about the Iowa prairie and its people.

In 1908 Quick became the associate editor of *La Follette's Weekly Magazine*, a position he left seven months later to serve as editor of *Farm and Fireside*, a national farm magazine. In 1916 he was appointed a charter member of the Federal Farm Loan Board, on which he served for three years. Following his subsequent trip to Vladivostok, where he lost his health, Quick retired to his estate at Berkeley Springs, West Virginia. Quick died in the middle of a speaking tour on agricultural finance.—F. G. M.

Quinault Indians. See INDIANS OF THE NORTHWEST COAST.

Quitman, John Anthony (1798-1858). Mississippi planter and politician. Quitman came to Mississippi in the 1820s from New York after a brief sojourn in Ohio. His marriage into a very prominent and wealthy Natchez planter family converted him to the cotton economy, and he became one of the leading "fire-eaters," or secessionists, in the South. He held numerous state offices; his only national political office was in the House of Representatives, where he served from 1855 until his death.

When the controversy over the right of South Carolina to nullify the tariff in 1832 arose, it was Quitman who led in the formation of the State Rights party in Mississippi. By the spring of 1834, however, the issue of nullification was of little interest to Mississippians. The Nullifiers then joined forces with the National Republicans to form the Whig party in the state. Quitman led the Whigs in the fight against Jackson's banking policy. By 1840 he had decided that the internal rivalry in the Democratic party was more important than the Democratic-Whig struggle. He joined forces with Jefferson Davis, Jacob Thompson, and Albert Gallatin Brown to lead the radical state-rights wing of the Democratic party. Quitman led the fight against the acceptance of the COMPROMISE OF 1850 by the state of Mississippi by campaigning unsuccessfully in 1851 for both a secession convention and the governor's office.

His popularity was at its height after his military victories in the Mexican War. Quitman was a strong believer in Manifest Destiny and thought that the United States should annex all of Mexico in 1848 and should liberate Cuba in the 1850s. He died contented that the secessionists were in control in Mississippi and was buried on the grounds of his plantation Monmouth near Natchez.

See J. F. H. Claiborne, *Life and Correspondence of John A. Quitman, Major-general, U. S. A., and Governor of the State of Mississippi*, 2 vols. (1860).—J. E. G.

R

radio and television, westerns on. Although the first western star on radio, Gene Autry, started his career as "Oklahoma's Yodeling Cowboy" on a Tulsa station in 1929, it was three more years before a real "western" drama appeared. *Death Valley Days*, an anthology created by writer Ruth Cornwall Woodman with no continuing characters—except for the host, the "Old Ranger," played by several actors—consisted of dramatizations from history and personal accounts. Throughout its long history (it holds the record for longevity), it has had only one sponsor, the Pacific Coast Borax Company, whose historic "twenty-mule team" became an introductory trademark for the series, which made the transition to television.

One year later *The Lone Ranger* was aired on stations in Detroit, Chicago, and Newark. The creation of Bruce Beemer and writer Fran Striker, neither of whom had had any connection with the West, the "masked rider of the plains," with his horse "Silver" and his trusty scout, the Indian "Tonto," was an instant hit, first on radio, then in television, motion pictures, and comics. The program, patterned on Douglas Fairbanks' *Mark of Zorro*, was in turn copied by many others and, with the *William Tell* Overture theme and the call "Hi-yo, Silver! Away!" became nationally famous.

The *Tom Mix Show* also appeared in 1933. Mix was the first star to move at the height of motion picture fame to radio. His program was created by advertising man Charles Claggett, who, with writer George Lowther, perfected a format copied by many others, featuring "Tony the Wonder Horse," the "Old Wrangler" sidekick, and two young wards. The action took place in the present on a modern ranch owned by Mix, who was supposedly just living his normal life as a rancher-movie star. Mix himself was impersonated by an actor. The show initiated the craze for boxtop premiums and the giveaway comic-book versions of its stories. Similar programs soon followed, with an airplane replacing Tony in *Sky King* and Autry and Roy Rogers playing themselves on their "singing cowboy" programs.

Other prewar radio shows, among them *The Range Rider, Red Ryder, The Cisco Kid,* and *Sergeant Preston of the Yukon*, had formats that were similar and usually included the ever-present sidekick, who was usually comic, always ineffectual, but always there when needed, helping the hero describe in dialogue what was taking place.

Although these "B" formula westerns all survived World War II, the intense and realistic programs originated during the war doomed them to children's fare and set the stage for more mature westerns. The first adult western appeared on radio in 1952 when *Gunsmoke* was aired on CBS. Dissatisfied with stereotyped characters, oversimplified plots, and stock action, writer-editor John Meston and producer-director Norman Macdonnell tried to bring to life the real West of history. While keeping some standard ingredients, the heroic marshal, Matt Dillon (played by William Conrad), and the faithful sidekick, Chester Good (played by Parley Baer), *Gunsmoke's* creators broke new ground with the introduction of a more realistic heroine, the saloon and "dance-hall" proprietress Kitty (played by Georgia Ellis). The new format, soon copied by others, was semianthological with one or more of the regulars involved in the problems of the many characters drifting through Dodge City during the 1870s. It relied more on character and mood than on action; even Dillon's heroism was toned down. The program attracted better writers than the action-only westerns and within one season was the most popular program on the radio.

Gunsmoke's only rivals in presenting serious and authentic westerns were *Fort Laramie* (1955), a cavalry-western created by Meston and Macdonnell, and *Death Valley Days*. Together they influenced the new programs beginning to appear on the new medium of television.

With wartime restrictions lifted and expansion possible, television began its phenomenal growth. Early network creative staffs had held the "horse opera" in low esteem, and they were never seen on television except as "fillers" on local stations that ran old western films. But within the first half of the 1950s most of the radio westerns made the transition to television.

Among the first was Autry's show. While most Hollywood stars and business heads ignored this threatening medium, Autry, who had become head of his own "Flying A" Production Company and owner of a number of radio stations, added television stations to his holdings and transferred his own program to television (1951). He also began filming other cheaply made western episodic serials, such as *The Range Rider* (1951), *Annie Oakley* (1958), *Buffalo Bill Jr.* (1955), and *The Adventures of Champion* (1955), featuring his own horse. Another star to take advantage of the trend was William Boyd, of *Hopalong Cassidy* fame, who bought up the television rights to these now-obsolete films and leased them as reruns on television in (1951). He then pro-

duced a new series especially suited to the medium; soon "Hoppy" was a favorite of millions of children.

Other early transfers, such as *The Lone Ranger*, (1952), *Sky King* (1953), and the *Roy Rogers-Dale Evans Show* (1952), were soon joined by new cheaply-made and children-oriented programs, such as *Wild Bill Hickok* (1951) and *Kit Carson* (1952). But by 1955 the adult western had already created a demand, and CBS brought out a television version of *Gunsmoke*, using film-trained actors rather than radio veterans; Dillon was played by James Arness, Chester by Dennis Weaver, Kitty by Amanda Blake, and Doc Adams by Milburn Stone. It was an immediate success and for several years held a high spot in weekly ratings.

Preceding *Gunsmoke*, however, was the outstanding though short-lived western *Frontier* (1955), produced by Worthington Miner. Created by David Friedkin and Morton Fine, who had taken part in early abortive attempts to work out radio's *Gunsmoke*, the anthological format took the same tough, realistic approach to the West and provided a wide range of material. Another high-quality production with realistic stories was *The Life and Legend of Wyatt Earp* (1955), based on the often-criticized stories in Stuart Lake's admiring biography of the controversial Earp.

A number of other excellent half-hour westerns appeared in the next few seasons, including the *Zane Grey Theatre* (1956), featuring stories taken from the writer's books, and *Broken Arrow* (1956), based on the Tom Jeffords-Cochise friendship as related in Elliott Arnold's novel *Blood Brother* (1947), and the motion-picture version, *Broken Arrow* (1950). Arnold himself supervised the scripts, which frequently related actual incidents during the time Jeffords was Indian agent for Cochise's Chiricahua band and were generally sympathetic toward the Indians. Other Indian-oriented series followed, including *Brave Eagle* (1956), and *The Law of the Plainsman* (1959). None were very successful.

Another attempt to overthrow the cliché western and take a starkly realistic approach was made in 1960 with Sam Peckinpah's *The Westerner*, starring Brian Keith and featuring an antihero, a drifter, who with his dog and a few possessions simply wandered the West, taking an odd job whenever he felt the need. Unfortunately, like most of the series concepts preceding it, the formula became routine and repetitive, and the script finally took on an air of unreality.

Meanwhile, in 1954 Walt Disney Productions released for television its first *Davy Crockett* film, aired in weekly one-hour segments. Aside from launching Fess Parker's career and initiating a craze for coonskin caps, Disney had started a new trend. The one-hour format gave greater scope in using scenery, which was to become of prime importance with the advent of large-screen color television sets, and allowed better characterizations and more complex plots. In the fall of 1955, ABC aired the first *Cheyenne*. The move to longer form was on.

Soon came a flood of one-hour shows, many of them successful. *Wagon Train* (1957)—whose wagonmaster was played first by Ward Bond and then by John MacIntire—with its near-perfect format combining the best of both the anthology and the continuing-character series, told stories of the historic "westering" movement. So, too, did *Rawhide* (1958), with much the same natural freedom of material and appeal of a close and realistic look at a major historical force, in this case the cattle trade. There were others. Then in 1959 came *Bonanza*, the first one to be filmed in color, which took full advantage of the scenic values of the "Ponderosa" country around Lake Tahoe while relating the story of a rancher, played by Lorne Greene, and his four sons.

If one-hour formats were better, then why not ninety minutes? In 1958 CBS tried it unsuccessfully with *Cimarron Strip*. Finally, in 1962 it was done successfully with *The Virginian*, the story of a Wyoming rancher, his family, and his hired hands, led by the Virginian (James Drury) and Trampas (Doug McClure), based on Owen Wister's novel. Little remained of Wister's original portrayals, but the show still achieved success.

By 1958-59 the western was at its height, with as many as thirty-seven in production, and writers had to comb history for new ideas. There were shows based on such diverse historical figures as Daniel Boone, Bat Masterson, Judge Roy Bean, and Custer. Institutions like the Texas Rangers, the Pony Express, and the railroad served as inspirations, as did colorful locales in such programs as *The Dakotas* (1963), *The High Chaparral* (1967), and *The Big Valley* (1965). Even animals in western settings furnished subject matter, with Lassie, Fury, Rin Tin Tin, and Flicka popular among children.

Westerns were rarely attempted on live television, and the only performances of note were two *Playhouse 90* productions: Rod Serling's *A Town Has Turned to Dust* (1958) and Aaron Spelling's *The Last Man* (1957).

Documentaries have gained in popularity as Americans have become increasingly interested in the history of the West. In 1961 Gary Cooper effectively narrated *The Real West*, a program that relied almost entirely on archive photographs and old paintings of the West as it really was. Other superb programs were Project 20's *The American Indian* (1969), narrated by Henry Fonda, and *The West of Charles Russell* (1970), narrated by Milburn Stone, and Public Broadcasting System's *The Black Frontier* (1970), a four-part series prepared by the University of Nebraska under a Ford Foundation grant.

By the late 1950s the air was glutted with cowboys, and a reaction set in. As late as 1967, there were still fifteen western shows on the production schedule, but by 1970 they had shrunk to six, and by the 1973 season, only *Gunsmoke* survived to begin its nineteenth year on television, its twenty second year of life. *Death Valley Days* succumbed during this period but continued in reruns.

The indication for the future is that the western, with its roots deeply imbedded in the American consciousness, will continue to be a television staple, though never in profusion as during the 1950s.

See Erik Barnouw, *A History of Broadcasting in the United States* (1966); William K. Everson, *A Pictorial History of the Western Film* (1970); George N. Fenin and William K. Everson, *The Western* (1962); Jim Harmon, *The Great Radio Heroes* (1967); and Ron Lackmann, *Remember Television* (1971).—J. D.

railroad land grants. Congress early began granting public lands to states for purposes for which appropriations of public funds could not, in the opinion of rigid constitutionalists, be justified. The rationalization justifying such grants was that they increased the value of the remaining public lands. Early grants to states for public buildings, schools, and universities were followed in the 1830s by grants for roads and canals. It was the practice in these grants to give a broad right-of-way

through the public lands and alternate sections of land within a belt from two to ten miles wide on either side. The intervening sections retained by the government were required to be sold at double the minimum price, thus assuring that from half the land the government could receive as much as if it had made no grant.

The first grant in aid of railroads was made by Congress in 1850 to Illinois, Mississippi, and Alabama. It consisted of alternate sections of public lands within a strip twelve miles wide with a right-of-way through the reserved sections for a railroad from Chicago and Galena, in northern Illinois, by way of Cairo to Mobile, Alabama. The grant was a major factor in attracting English capital to the Illinois portion of the projected line and enabled the Illinois Central Railroad to complete construction of its seven hundred miles by 1856. Before completion, the railroad was advertising throughout the East and in northern Europe its prairie lands at prices from six dollars per acre upward, depending on their location and quality. So widespread was this advertising campaign that it has been said that scarcely a literate person north of the Mason-Dixon line could have avoided seeing one or more of the colorful advertisements describing the high productivity of lands in the Prairie State. Following construction and the emigration promotion campaigns, thousands came to Illinois looking for land and, within a year after completion of the road, one half of its 2,595,000 acres had been sold at more than ten dollars an acre. Some of this was speculative purchasing and had to be canceled later, but it was good evidence that the Illinois Central was fairly certain to recover, as it actually did, the full cost of construction from land sales. Residents of other states now joined in a concerted demand for land grants for railroads.

Though strict constructionists were firmly in control of Congress and in the leadership of the Democratic party, the effect of railroad building upon real-estate values and population growth was too much for the followers of John C. Calhoun. A series of measures was adopted providing land grants for railroads in Michigan, Wisconsin, Minnesota, Iowa, Missouri, Arkansas, Louisiana, Mississippi, Alabama, and Florida, all on the alternate-section plan with the price of reserved lands within the primary grant area increased from the minimum sale price of $2.00 an acre to $2.50 an acre. Altogether during the administrations of Presidents Millard Fillmore and Franklin Pierce, 27,876,000 acres were granted to aid in building 7,500 miles of railroad.

Peace with Mexico in 1848 and the acquisition of California and Oregon brought a demand for a transcontinental railroad to connect the West Coast with the Great Lakes or the Mississippi River. It was clear that to build such a line largely through undeveloped territory, government aid would be needed, and the army did in fact make several TRANSCONTINENTAL RAILROAD SURVEYS. Sectional differences over the location of the route and its eastern terminus, however, made it impossible for Congress to act until the South seceded from the Union. Then between 1862 and 1871 Congress abandoned all caution and granted aid for the construction of four railroads to be built to the coast, at first ten sections (6,400 acres) of land for each mile of road, then twenty sections, and finally forty sections. Altogether 174 million acres of public lands, or an area greater than

New England, New York, Pennsylvania, and Ohio combined, were offered to the four transcontinentals and numerous additional lines in the Middle West to aid their construction. This extraordinary generosity meant that the railroads became major land-administering agencies in the West almost on a par with the federal government. Greatly stimulated by the grants and the prosperity of 1862-73, railroad building was rapidly pushed, and though construction was slowed by the Panic of 1873 it revived in the late 1870s.

Since the western railroads were constructed in advance of settlement, most of the railroad companies became true empire builders. They had to stimulate, organize, and direct emigrants to their land to produce the grain and livestock to be hauled to market, because without freight and passenger traffic they would not survive as transportation companies. Borrowing from the promotional activities of the Illinois Central Railroad but conducting their operations on a far grander scale, they sent agents through the rural areas of the older states and the British Isles, Germany, Norway, and Sweden to distribute handbills, put up posters, distribute illustrated pamphlets, and make public addresses calling attention to the superior soil of, and the high returns on, farming in Dakota, Kansas, Montana, Washington, and California. The land and colonization departments of the railroads also sought to ease the immigrants' paths to success by encouraging the drainage of wet land; giving subsidies to agricultural fairs; supporting farmers' papers; and distributing information about new crops, methods of tillage, and improved livestock. They worked closely with the state agricultural departments in various ways to improve the lot of the farmers and the returns on their labor.

There was another side to the story of the western railroads. The high prices they charged for land deprived settlers of funds needed for farm improvements, kept them in debt when commodity prices were low and interest payments had to be met, forced people without resources to search far afield for land, and kept much land from development and off the tax rolls for years. As a rule the railroads paid no taxes on unsold lands, thereby placing the cost of local government on farmers. Too, the farmers thought that their rate-making practices seemed to favor the big commercial shippers. Not only were large areas of land withdrawn from settlement for years because they had been set aside for companies that failed to build and to earn their grants, but a few companies actually withheld their grants from sale in the anticipation of higher returns in the future. At first westerners approved of giving lands, so as to bring railroads to their communities. But when they saw that, although the lands had returned all or a good part of the cost of construction, the railroads were pursuing monopolistic, unfair, and some thought extortionate practices, western sentiment turned hostile. Hostility led to the GRANGER LAWS and POPULISM. The Grangers and Populists demanded that no further land grants be made and that railroad lands be taxed and sold at moderate prices or be forfeited. Some unearned grants were forfeited and one, the Oregon and California, was revested in the United States because of failure to sell in small lots as the law required.

Land-grant railroads were required to carry government traffic at a lower rate than was charged commercially in return for the government subvention. This was not of great importance until World War I, when the volume of government traffic was enormous and the savings from land-grant rates large. The major western lines then launched a campaign, which ended successfully in 1945, to have the reduced rates abolished.

See Paul W. Gates, *History of Public Land Law Development* (1968); and Richard C. Overton, *Burlington West* (1941).—P. W. G.

railroads. Railroads were the most important factor in the rapid settlement of North America. Still the most efficient and versatile of all forms of inland transportation, the railroad was indispensable in the settlement of most of the West. The earliest incentive for building railroads, however, was the need of seaport towns to maintain trade connections with the interior. The striking success of the Erie Canal revealed to cities like Philadelphia and Baltimore that they would lose much interior trade to New York unless they established better transportation facilities. Philadelphia chose to imitate, and in her "main line" system of canals, railroads, and inclined planes, by which she sought to reach Pittsburgh, she lost a critical decade in her development, for the system was a failure. Baltimore chose to innovate and gave the United States its first common carrier of goods and passengers, the Baltimore and Ohio Railroad, chartered in 1828 and first operated by steam two years later. Completed to its original goal, the Ohio River at Wheeling, in 1852, the Baltimore and Ohio set the pace for nearly a century of railroad development in the United States. In the next decade railroads were built from tidewater into the hinterland throughout the Northeast and, to a much lesser extent, in the South.

By the 1840s the railroad fever had reached the Midwest, soon to become the jumping-off point in the post-Civil War westward movement. The Chicago and Rock Island, first to reach the Mississippi River in 1854, bridged that broad stream two years later and on the eve of the war was spreading throughout Iowa (see CHICAGO, ROCK ISLAND AND PACIFIC RAILROAD) as were the Chicago, Burlington and Quincy, the CHICAGO AND NORTHWESTERN, the Chicago, Milwaukee and St. Paul, and many other railroads.

By the time the first transcontinental was completed in 1869, four midwestern railroads were ready to connect it with the East. Short lines began to be knit into integrated systems as early as the 1850s. Several railroads between Albany and Buffalo became the New York Central Railroad, while in Pennsylvania the businessmen of Philadelphia, disgusted with the "main line" public works, completed their own, all-rail route to Pittsburgh in 1854. In view of the fact that Sir Henry Bessemer invented his steel-making process only four years later, the opening of Pittsburgh to rail transportation must rank as one of the most important events in the history of American economic growth.

While southern railroads, skimpy and undermaintained, added little to the Confederate war effort, those of the North were a leading factor in victory. They served to knit together northern industries and for the first time were utilized in military strategy, notably the long-distance movement of entire divisions.

By 1873, which marked the beginning of a twenty-five-year period of rapid expansion of railroad mileage and declining transportation costs, four fully integrated trunk-line railroads (the New York Central, Erie, Pennsylvania, and Baltimore & Ohio) linked the expec-

When in 1869 A. J. Russell photographed this steam shovel at Echo Canyon, Utah, such machines were still rare; most railroad construction work was done by immigrant laborers. (Oakland Museum)

tant West with the East at Chicago, St. Louis, and numerous less important points.

An all-rail route across the nation to the Pacific had been the dream of many persons, most notably Asa WHITNEY, since the 1840s (see CHINA TRADE). Congress finally authorized five TRANSCONTINENTAL RAILROAD SURVEYS to be undertaken during the 1850s: the forty-fifth, forty-second, thirty-seventh, thirty-fifth, and thirty-second parallels (later the routes of the Northern Pacific, UNION PACIFIC/CENTRAL PACIFIC, MISSOURI PACIFIC DENVER AND RIO GRANDE WESTERN/WESTERN PACIFIC, Santa Fe, and SOUTHERN PACIFIC railroads, the last utilizing, in part, land acquired in the Gadsden Purchase). In 1862 Congress passed the first Pacific Railroad Act, which designated the forty-second parallel the initial transcontinental route, authorized huge grants of public lands to the enterprise (see RAILROAD LAND GRANTS), and promised loan subsidies.

Progress was nil at first and then agonizingly slow, because of the scarcity of capital and a host of unprecedented construction problems—vast mountain ranges, severe winter weather, and increasing Indian hostility. After eastern money and entrepreneurship became available, the Union Pacific, the eastern half of the route, was pushed ahead rapidly. On May 10, 1869, at Promontory Point, Utah, it joined with the Central Pacific, built eastward from Sacramento, California, by a syndicate headed by Collis P. HUNTINGTON.

Many more transcontinentals were built in the following two decades. In 1881 the Atlantic and Pacific Railroad (an affiliate of the ATCHINSON, TOPEKA AND SANTA FE) joined with the Southern Pacific at Deming, New Mexico; and two years later Jay Cooke and Henry

VILLARD completed the Northern Pacific between Minneapolis-St. Paul and Seattle. Huntington meanwhile had beaten Thomas A. SCOTT in the race to build the southernmost transcontinental and by 1885 controlled a line from New Orleans to Los Angeles. The Santa Fe, originally planned to join Kansas City with the old trading post of Santa Fe, New Mexico, expanded in both directions. It reached Los Angeles and, ultimately, San Francisco and was extended from Kansas City to Chicago by quickly and efficiently building its own line between those major cities. From 1887 to 1909, when the Milwaukee road completed its West Coast extension, the Santa Fe was the only railroad operated from Chicago to the Pacific Coast entirely on its own rails.

The most spectacular developments, however, occurred in the Northwest. In 1878 James J. HILL, an obscure St. Paul businessman, persuaded a group of associates to buy a decrepit railroad and transform it into an all-rail link between the Twin Cities and Winnipeg. Expanding slowly but shrewdly, Hill made his St. Paul, Minneapolis and Manitoba the dominant railroad in the Northwest. It was better built, more efficient, and thus more profitable than the Northern Pacific. In 1889 Hill renamed it the Great Northern and extended it to the Pacific Coast. By the turn of the century he had all but merged the Great Northern, the Northern Pacific, and the Burlington route into one of the most efficient transportation systems in the world (see BURLINGTON NORTHERN RAILROAD). Profits were enormous, yet the average charge to ship a ton of freight a mile over the Great Northern fell from 2.88 cents in 1881 to 0.77 cents in 1907. The last transcontinental to be built was the route formed by the Missouri Pacific, Denver and Rio

Grande, and the Western Pacific—the last a railroad completed early in the twentieth century by George Gould, son of Jay GOULD—and the CHICAGO, MILWAUKEE, ST. PAUL AND PACIFIC, which extended its lines from South Dakota to Seattle in 1909.

That the railroad would open the West to settlement for the growing of marketable surpluses of agricultural products was obvious from the beginning. In the early 1850s a railroad writer estimated that Illinois' annual produce would net farmers $40 million if produced in upstate New York, but without cheap transportation they would realize only $12 million. Recognizing that the coming of the railroad would greatly increase the value of adjoining farmlands and that such gains might well be the only source of profit for a railroad for some years, Congress adopted a land-grant policy that ultimately conveyed some 130 million acres of land to railroad companies. Although this eventually became a controversial issue (see LAND-REFORM MOVEMENT), it is doubtful that the railroads actually got something for nothing after deducting the special rates accorded government shipments until 1947 and in view of the restrictions under which they operated as recipients.

As the largest land mass in the world located in a latitude conducive to intensive economic development and enjoying government by a single sovereignty, the United States had impatiently awaited the arrival of a practical system of inland transportation. To such a nation, handicapped with a poor system of navigable rivers (the most important of which "ran the wrong way"), the impact of the railroad was immeasurable. Even in the older areas, settled before the coming of the railroad, the effects were dramatic: the iron and coal industries were greatly stimulated, a burgeoning post-

Civil War industry was speeded up, and sectional differences dwindled in the face of a vastly increased volume of travel. But the railroad's greatest impact was in the undeveloped sections (see, for example, WYOMING and DAKOTA TERRITORY). The Old Northwest, with its rich prairies, and the Great Plains, with their even more fabulous if less hospitable grain-growing areas, rapidly filled up with people from the East and immigrants from the half-starved lands of Europe. The productive efficiency of the people grew at a prodigious rate. Young men of the Jacksonian era who had seen a thin stream of goods hauled by wagon on the National Road for several dollars a ton-mile were not yet old by the time the cost of shipping freight had dropped to less than a cent a ton-mile. During the 1870s beef cattle driven over long Texas trails to CATTLE TOWNS were shipped via rail to northern feedlots. The postal service blossomed from a luxury service delivering a single tissue sheet only four hundred miles for thirty cents to a vital national service carrying a torrent of letters, newspapers, magazines, and other reading material across the continent for a few cents. The railroad remained virtually the only form of transportation in America for nearly one hundred years. By the time the automobile, the truck, and the airplane arrived, the trains already had made America into an economic, social, and political unit.

This unification was not accomplished without costs. Especially in the West, still wild and untamed well into the 1870s, the quality of life was altered irrevocably and beyond recognition. The Indian and the buffalo, if they did not altogether disappear, lived after the railroad came only on the white man's suffrage and, indeed, largely on his charity. But the quickened pace of life, harbinger of the close of the agrarian phase of Ameri-

Ceremonies attending the completion of the first transcontinental rail line at Promontory Point, Utah, on May 10, 1869. (Oakland Museum)

can civilization, was noted in the East as well. James Whitcomb Riley, complaining that the railroad trestle had destroyed the seclusion of his childhood swimming hole, could not have known that a hundred years later similar romantics would sadly mark the passing of the steam locomotive, whose engineer had waved at three generations of naked little boys. Not the automobile, but the railroad, which made possible the modern industrial society that could create the automobile, changed the quality of American life in its most fundamental aspects. It was bound to occur; any practical, low-cost, versatile, ubiquitous mode of transportation would have brought it about. But it was in the railroad that Americans found embodied what the vast majority had demanded—an instrument of rapid growth and profound change.

As the dominant factor in nineteenth-century American life, the railroads quickly became and remained a center of national controversy: constantly annihilating distances and disrupting settled trading centers and transportation patterns; allegedly over-charging farmers when crop prices were low; corrupting venal legislators to win special favors, as in the CREDIT MOBILIER scandal; and discriminating between shippers in fixing rates (see GRANGER LAWS and AGRARIAN MOVEMENTS). The old historical treatment based on the cliché of the "public welfare versus private interests," however, was naïve. Although the Granger movement of the 1870s, for example, had begun as a demand by farmers for lower long-distance rates, such charges had already begun to fall rapidly, as they would continue to do until the end of the century. In fact, these low long-distance rates, which deprived New York and many smaller cities—especially in the Mississippi River valley—of their traditional role in controlling interior trade, generated the most pressure for federal regulation.

By 1885, when Congress began seriously to consider a railroad regulatory law, most of the contending interests had come to realize that fixing of maximum rates was

unnecessary and infeasible; that low long-distance rates, even where they resulted in absolute "discrimination" between short and long hauls over the same route, were fundamental to the American economic structure; and that rate differentials between routes and between terminals were also economically sound.

The degree of sophistication concerning railroad economics had grown considerably since the days of Granger agitations and New York State's Hepburn Committee in the 1870s. It had come to be realized by many that rates bore little relationship to how far freight was hauled. This was not only because most of the costs of handling freight were "fixed" (being present whether freight was hauled a short distance, a long distance, or indeed, hauled at all), but also because the most fundamental factor in rate-making was the "value of the service." Thus, if the value of the service was high, as in the case of costly manufactured goods, the rate per hundredweight would be high even if the distance involved was only a few miles. If the value of the service was low, as in the case of agricultural products, whose market price was only a few dollars per hundredweight, rates might result that were only slightly above the "out-of-pocket" or "direct" costs of haulage, even if the distance involved was a thousand miles or more. This principle, which railroad men considered to be beyond their control, was enunciated as "*what* the traffic will bear," an unfortunate expression quickly corrupted to "*all* the traffic will bear." Rates, of course, tended to be sticky; they did not seem, at least to farmers, to go down as fast nor as far in bad times as did the prices of the commodities they had to sell. Even so, by 1885 such diverse groups as railroad executives, shippers, and state railroad commissioners had come to realize that the economics of railroading led to rate wars and consequent instability of rates and would continue to do so until the government found some way to support pooling of traffic among railroads. (The corporate consolidation of railroads had not yet begun, and thus pooling of freights by railroads held out the only promise of stability.) Despite strong sentiment for legalized pooling, the intransigence of Texas congressman John H. Reagan, who regarded pooling as morally wrong, resulted in an antipooling clause in the Act to Regulate Interstate Commerce of 1887. Three years later Congress passed the Sherman Anti-Trust Act, which was soon interpreted as prohibiting simple agreements between railroads to support rate schedules.

Victorian railroad regulation was therefore an empty exercise. From 1887 to the onset of the depression of the 1890s, rates declined under controlled competition, and after a short-lived effort by J. P. Morgan to set tariffs jointly, rates were as unstable as ever. Railroad after railroad sank into receivership, including such important western lines as the Northern Pacific, the Union Pacific, and the Santa Fe. (For a discussion of the fate of much of Northern Pacific's properties, see BONANZA FARMING.) Then began one of the most impressive movements in the concentration of economic power in United States history. By 1900 most of the important railroad systems were gathered into some six or seven "communities of interest." Concentration was perhaps heaviest in the West, where James J. Hill, in the north, and Edward H. HARRIMAN, in the south, gained control of virtually all important lines. Although repeated efforts were made to break up such power concentrations,

Grading the Central Pacific; the cut at Owl Gap, in Placer County, California. (Library of Congress)

Dormitory cars for railroad construction crews in the 1880s. (Library of Congress)

the American railroad industry continued to demonstrate George Stephenson's maxim, "where combination is possible, competition is impossible," a maxim which would have been demonstrated by American railroads sooner or later, even if government regulation, ironically, had not hastened the day.

The years 1890-1917 form one of the most important periods in American railroad history. Traffic grew prodigiously in this intensely prosperous era, especially in the West. Prices rose by roughly fifty percent and wage rates almost as much, while railroad rates rose only about seven percent from 1897 to 1906 and then fell under the pressure of new and stronger government regulation. At the same time, the American railroad network was essentially rebuilt: more capital was poured into the system than had been invested in the entire period 1828-90. Systems were thoroughly re-engineered, again most notably in the West. Hill made the Northern Pacific as efficient a railroad as his Great Northern. Edward P. RIPLEY and Victor Morawetz of the Santa Fe made that jerry-built railroad into one of the nation's strongest. The Union Pacific was double-tracked every foot of the way from Council Bluffs to Ogden.

At the height of these improvement programs government policy toward the railroads, under the pressures of insurgent Republican politics, became intensely repressive, if not actually self-destructive. Congress had already given the Interstate Commerce Commission (I.C.C.) power to fix maximum rates in the Hepburn Act of 1906. By 1910 legislative leaders, such as Senators Albert B. Cummins of Iowa and Robert M. La Follette of Wisconsin, noting that the railroads were able to and inclined to raise rates jointly for the first time, demanded amendments to ward off all increases. In 1910 the Mann-Elkins Act gave the commission power to suspend a rate increase and to deny it altogether upon investigation. Meanwhile, greatly strengthened railroad labor unions began a campaign to increase wages (see

LABOR MOVEMENT). Despite repeated efforts by railroad men to raise rates because of rapidly rising costs, the I.C.C. on notice from Cummins and La Follette that pro-railroad commissioners would be opposed for reappointment, denied all such applications. Although the need for capital improvements continued, the money was unavailable from either retained profits (disappearing by 1917) or the capital market. From 1906 to 1917 the deficiency in the flow of investment funds into the railroads was roughly $5 billion. World War I placed extraordinary demands on the carriers, which were prohibited by antitrust laws from pooling their resources, despite serious deficiencies in equipment, especially locomotives. Takeover of the railroads by the government proved the only practical solution.

Since 1920, when the railroads were returned to private control, they have passed through four distinct phases. In the 1920s the carriers experienced moderate prosperity, but saw the beginnings of truck transportation, which, despite the railroads' efforts to retain their high-rated traffic, they could not fight effectively under the archaic regulation practiced by the I.C.C. The Depression made all but the strongest railroads wards of the federal government—the Santa Fe, the Southern Pacific, and Hill's lines escaped receivership—but the prosperity of World War II quickly resuscitated them. The record of the railroads during that war is perhaps their most striking: despite fewer employees and less equipment than before the Depression, and a near-tripling of freight volume and a quadrupling of passenger traffic, the carriers hauled ninety percent of all inland freight and carried ninety-eight percent of all men traveling on military orders, without serious problems.

In the first postwar decade billions of dollars were invested in modernization, notably the replacement of steam by diesel motive power and installation of centralized traffic control on many miles of heavily used lines. But the trend away from rails to highly subsidized

Laying tracks in Arizona Territory, c.1898. (National Archives)

highway and inland waterway carriers was resumed, a development that was inevitable because of a government rate policy that forbids competitive cutting of rates and that was greatly hastened by construction of the new interstate superhighway system. Passenger service, which had long been unprofitable, was dealt a death blow by the advent of cut-rate air fares in the early 1950s and the jet airplane. By 1971 rail passenger service had been cut to the bare bone, and most of what was left was being operated at huge losses by Amtrak, the national rail passenger corporation. Eastern railroads, the least adaptable of all to the new role which American society was forcing upon its railroads, were in critical financial condition by 1970, when the Penn Central, formed several years before from the New York Central and the Pennsylvania, fell into bankruptcy. By 1972 the railroads had joined with common-carrier truck lines (themselves feeling the pinch of high wage costs and loss of freight to private truck carriers) in a campaign for government-guaranteed, low-interest loans to provide them with the improvement capital they could no longer raise in the competitive money market.

With some exceptions the western transcontinental railroads fared best under these conditions. With their long hauls and the relatively greater growth rate of the West, some (like the Santa Fe, the Union Pacific, and the Southern Pacific) remained strong, viable businesses. Others, like the Hill lines (the Northern Pacific, Great Northern, and Burlington), while equally strong, sought to prepare for an unpromising future by formal merger to permit the lines to be operated with the utmost efficiency as a single system. Withal, the railroads—even the eastern lines—remain the carriers with the lowest true costs, the least polluting, and the most versatile. Whether by modernization of archaic regulatory practices, which for fifty years had encouraged the growth of inefficient modes of transportation, or by permanent government subsidy, it seems inevitable that a growing United States will become more dependent on its railroads than ever before.

Since no one has ever attempted to write a definitive railroad history, John F. Stover's necessarily superficial *American Railroads* (1961) will have to do. John Moody's classic *The Railroad Builders* (1921) remains valuable for the insights of one who knew his subject very well. Michael Robbins, *The Railway Age in Britain and Its Impact on the World* (1965), is excellent for its broad viewpoint. The best recent work on western railroads is found in Julius Grodinsky's two excellent books *Transcontinental Railway Strategy* (1962) and *Jay Gould: His Business Career 1867-1892* (1957). G. R. Taylor and I. D. Neu, *The American Railroad Network* (1956), is basic. The railroads also have received the attention of the left and the "new" economic historians—with rather bizarre results—in such widely noted books as Gabriel Kolk, *Railroads and Regulation* (1965), and Robert W. Fogel, *Railroads and American Economic Growth* (1964). More useful are the number of books that abandoned the "private interests versus the public welfare" cliché for a more pragmatic approach. Among the best are Lee Benson, *Merchants, Farmers and Railroads* (1955); K. Austin Kerr, *American Railroad Politics* (1968), which outlines the evolution of post-World War I policy; Albro Martin, *Enterprise Denied: Origins of the Decline of American Railroads, 1897-1917* (1971); and George H. Miller, *Railroads and the Granger Laws* (1971).—A. M.

Rainer, John C. (19??-   ). Taos Pueblo teacher and civic leader. Rainer was born at Taos Pueblo, New Mexico, which is very conservative and traditional. Rainer did not learn to speak English until he was thirteen, and when he decided to become a teacher, there was bitter opposition from the tribe. When his parents supported his decision, they were virtually ostracized. Rainer stood fast and went on from Santa Fe Indian School to Bacone Junior College and University of the Redlands. He began teaching at Dulce and Zuñi Pueblo and then became principal at Santa Domingo and Santa Ana Pueblo. Finally he was able to return to his home village as principal of its school.

In 1950 Rainer was appointed executive secretary of the National Congress of American Indians in Washington, D.C. Scholarships enabled him to pursue special studies in adult education. Then he was appointed director of the rehabilitation program for the Ute mountain tribe and was elected representative of the 22,000 Indians of the New Mexico pueblos at a conference in Washington, D.C., concerning state and civil jurisdiction over these pueblos. Secretary of the All Pueblo Council for several years, he was nominated for the chairmanship and won, despite the initial strong opposition of one of the Taos leaders.

Rainer was active in the National Congress of American Indians and other such organizations, the United States Civil Rights Advisory Board for New Mexico, and school and business groups in Taos. He ran a mercantile store in Taos for many years and had a cattle ranch. —C. C.

Ralston, William Chapman (1826-1875). California capitalist. Ralston was born in Ohio and went to San Francisco as a partner in a steamship company in 1854. Ten years later, with Darius Ogden Mills and others, he organized the Bank of California. It became the most highly regarded financial institution in the Far West, and Ralston was often regarded as the leading citizen of San Francisco. He financed many of the city's major buildings, notably the huge and lavish Palace Hotel, and committed his own funds and those of the bank to a remarkably wide panoply of enterprises—factories, mills, a theater, the city's principal water company, and even a salted "diamond mine" into which two swindling old prospectors inveigled him. His largest area of investment was the Comstock Lode in association with William Sharon, his representative in Virginia City. But he overinvested in mines that proved unproductive and so involved the bank in this and other unwise ventures that a run forced it to close its doors temporarily on August 26, 1875. The next morning the directors asked for and received his resignation as president. A few hours later, after he had gone for his accustomed daily swim in the bay, his body was found, a victim of drowning. Whether he died by accident or suicide is not known.

See George D. Lyman, *Ralston's Ring: California Plunders the Comstock Lode* (1937).—W. B.

Ramsey, Alexander (1815-1903). Minnesota politician. Ramsey, a Whig from Pennsylvania, became Minnesota's first territorial governor in 1849. He arranged for the cession of southern Minnesota by the Sioux Indians to the United States government, thus opening the area to white settlement. Defeated by Henry Hastings Sibley in the first election for governor of the state of Minnesota in 1857, Ramsey was successful in 1859, serving as governor during the Minnesota Uprising (1862) and much of the Civil War. He also served as United States senator and as secretary of war for President Rutherford B. Hayes (1879-81).

See John Haugland, "Politics, Patronage, and Ramsey's Rise to Power," *Minnesota History* (September 1960).—R. W. F.

ranches of California. See CALIFORNIA RANCHO SYSTEM.

Randsburg, California. Ghost town. Randsburg, together with its neighboring camps in the Mojave Desert, was the scene of a mining revival in California in the 1890s. Gold was discovered in 1893, and the mines in the area continued to produce well into the twentieth century. The remains of this once-large camp are very well preserved and the area is filled with old mine shafts. The Desert Museum contains artifacts of the town's glory days.

See Remi Nadeau, *Ghost Towns and Mining Camps of California* (1965).—R. B. W.

Rankin, Jeanette. See MONTANA.

Ravalli, Anthony (1812-1884). Jesuit missionary. Ravalli was born in Italy and beginning in 1844 was in the Pacific Northwest. He served as a peacemaker among Flathead, Coeur d'Alene, Kettle, and other tribes. Ravalli was especially skilled in medicine and architecture.

See Robert I. Burns, *The Jesuits and the Indian Wars of the Northwest* (1966).—R. I. B.

Raynolds expedition. On April 13, 1859, Captain William F. Raynolds (1820-1894) of the United States Army Corps of Topographical Engineers received orders from the War Department to organize and conduct "an expedition for the exploration of the region of country through which flow the principal tributaries of the Yellowstone River, and of the mountains in which they, and the Gallatin and Madison forks of the Missouri, have their source." As was the case with most topographical expeditions Raynolds was to report on the climate and resources of the region, estimate the numbers, culture, and location of Indian tribes, and ascertain suitable routes for roads. In this instance the location of roads was undoubtedly uppermost in the government's mind, for Raynolds was to explore the possibilities of wagon routes between Fort Laramie and the Yellowstone River, between Fort Laramie and Fort Benton, between the Yellowstone River and the South Pass, and between the headwaters of the Wind River and the headwaters of the Missouri. The route to Fort Benton was seen as especially important since it would connect with the Mullan Road to Walla Walla, Washington, and thence to the Pacific Coast.

With a well-equipped party of seven experts (one of whom was Ferdinand V. Hayden), thirty soldiers, and the noted mountain man and guide Jim Bridger, Raynolds left Fort Pierre on the Missouri on June 28, heading west along the Cheyenne River to find a new route from the Missouri to the valley of the Platte.

The expedition reached the north fork of the Cheyenne River on July 15, went around the Black Hills and reached the Powder River on July 26. After proceeding to within fifty miles of the mouth of the Powder, it struck off to the west and arrived at Fort Sarpy on the Yellowstone on August 29. Here Raynolds paused briefly for refitting before setting out again. At the mouth of the Bighorn River on September 2 the expedition divided, one party under Lieutenant Henry E. Maynadier ascending O'Fallon's fork for surveying purposes. The remainder, under Raynolds, pushed up the Bighorn to Richard's trading post in the valley of the Platte. Reaching there October 11, the expedition soon went into winter quarters near the Platte road where it remained until May 1860.

On May 23 Raynolds divided his command once more, taking part of it with him up the Wind River. Meanwhile Lieutenant Maynadier descended the Bighorn and turned westward to the Three Forks of the Missouri. After numerous difficulties and delays, the parties rejoined at this point on July 3. Raynolds then detoured north to Fort Benton for the purpose of descending the Missouri River by boat while Maynadier proceeded directly to Fort Union via the Yellowstone River.

From Fort Union the two halves of the expedition began the final stage of their journey. Leaving Maynadier to continue down the Missouri by boat, Raynolds marched southeast by the overland route to Fort Pierre. There the two rejoined on September 7, over fourteen months after they had first set forth. The expedition disbanded formally at Omaha on October 14.

In the course of its explorations the Raynolds expedition traveled over 2,500 miles by land and water, and charted an area almost 250,000 square miles in size. In addition to the surveys, it provided the government with valuable information concerning the local Indian tribes, the area's agricultural and mineralogical resources, its navigable streams, and the routes by which expansion might be best effected. Baffled by late snows and formidable terrain, Raynolds failed to penetrate and explore the Yellowstone Park area, but he did accept as true Jim Bridger's fantastic descriptions of boiling springs, large lakes, and geysers.

The expedition also allowed Hayden to fill in the last major void concerning geological knowledge of the West by constructing a stratigraphical map of the Dakota-Montana-Idaho area. From information collected on the Raynolds and previous expeditions, Hayden was able to write his important *Geological Report of the Yellowstone and Missouri Rivers* (1860), a study which historian William H. Goetzmann has termed in many ways "the most important work of the Topographical Engineer period."

Raynolds himself pointed up the impracticality of developing road systems along the routes which he had explored, although a line of forts and a trail along the front of the Bighorn Mountains were built. Raynolds also noted that scant rainfall would limit agricultural development but that valuable minerals were present. His *Report*, published in 1868 and accompanied by a useful map (published in 1864), was both a scientific summary and a serious literary effort punctuated by flashes of dry humor. The importance and significance of this last major exploration by the Topographical Engineers has been overshadowed by the coming of the Civil War and by the fact that it was the Washburn expedition of 1870 which actually explored and described the spectacular region of Yellowstone Park.

See William H. Goetzmann, *Army Exploration in the American West, 1803-1863* (1959); *Report of Brevet Brigadier General W. F. Raynolds on the Exploration of the Yellowstone and the Country Drained by that River*, 40th Cong., 2nd Sess., Sen. Exec. Doc. 77 (1868); and Raynolds Papers, Yale University Library.—E. H. S.

Reading Prong. See PHYSIOGRAPHY OF THE UNITED STATES.

Reagan, John H. (1818-1905). Politician. Reagan was born in Sevier County, Tennessee, where he received a limited college education and studied law. He moved to Texas in 1839, began practicing law, served as deputy surveyor of public land, was elected to the state house of representatives in 1847, and became a district judge in Palestine in 1852. From 1857 to 1861 he served in Congress as a Democrat. After participating in the secession convention in 1861, Reagan was chosen postmaster-general of the Confederate states and, later, acting-secretary of the Confederate treasury. Imprisoned in Boston for a few months after the war, he wrote to Texans urging that they acknowledge the extinction of slavery and offer certain civil liberties to the Negro in order to avoid military rule imposed from the North. His request was unpopular and misunderstood by his constituents.

After he had returned to Texas, Reagan participated in drafting the short-lived constitution of 1866 and the constitution of 1875. He served in the United States House of Representatives from 1875 to 1887 and in the Senate until 1891. As chairman of the House commerce committee Reagan introduced a bill establishing the Interstate Commerce Commission. He was a proponent of states' rights, low tariffs, and economy in government.

From 1897 until 1903 he was the first chairman of the Texas Railroad Commission.

See Ben H. Procter, *Not Without Honor: The Life of John H. Reagan* (1962).—J. B. F.

Reavis, James Addison (1843-1914). Swindler. A debonair crook, Reavis nearly hoaxed Arizona land owners on the Salt and Gila rivers out of twelve million acres of land. Jittery mining companies, railroad owners, ranchers, and businessmen paid him thousands of dollars for an alleged "quiet title" to their lands before his grandiose swindle was exposed.

In late 1882 Reavis boldly put into operation the theft of the Peralta Spanish land grant by stealing a questionable title to the vast area. He supplemented this claim by forging records in Mexico and Spain in an attempt to provide faked proof that his Spanish-American wife was a lineal descendant of the original grantee and bonafide heiress to the land grant. Mrs. Reavis, duped and charmed by her eloquent husband, remained loyal to him and actually believed herself to be the legitimate heiress.

Thousands of dollars were spent in litigation by Reavis and the opposition.

One of the opposition lawyers, Severo Mallet-Prevost, a shrewd Spanish-American, finally uncovered the clues to the crafty deception. Some of Reavis' hired witnesses then caved in and admitted their part in the fraud—claims Reavis denied. Unimpeachable evidence was uncovered by the same lawyer, who learned that the original Spanish-grant records in both Spain and Mexico had been amateurishly forged in favor of Mrs. Reavis. Also, the Spanish archivist reported that Reavis had inserted new documents unrelated to the original. On June 30, 1886, a judge sentenced the swindler to two years in jail and fined him $5,000.

See Hubert Howe Bancroft, *History of Arizona and New Mexico, 1530-1888* (1889); and Donald M. Powell, *The Peralta Grant* (1960).—B. W. A.

reclamation and irrigation. In American history the terms *reclamation* and *irrigation* have been inextricably associated in the public mind because the greatest unoccupied area of the country that required reclamation was in the "arid domain" west of the 100th meridian, and irrigation was the agency by which desert soil could be made to grow crops. Furthermore, reclamation has been a significant factor in the development of the West chiefly through the national program inaugurated in 1902 with the Newlands Act. Under this law the Bureau of Reclamation developed a vast complex of high-level dams and reclamation projects that added significantly to irrigation farm acreage in arid America. More importantly, these dams provided mushrooming urban-based populations with industrial and domestic water supplies, hydroelectric power, flood control, recreation, and conservation values. It has been one of the ironies of history that a program to spur agriculture brought in its wake booming urban metropolises.

Individual and group efforts had made impressive headway in capturing the water from running streams for irrigation purposes by 1880. It is estimated that one million farm acres were thus irrigated. The efforts required in the necessary next phase of irrigation development—the construction of storage reservoirs— were large-scale and dictated a federal program of funding. A favorable public opinion in support of the requisite legislation had to be manufactured. It is this campaign that inaugurated the irrigation movement and that resulted in passage of the NEWLANDS RECLAMATION ACT of 1902, sponsored by Francis G. NEWLANDS. Friends of forest and water conservation became allies. Under the widely held "stream flow" hypothesis of the time, protected forest cover slowed down the run-off from storms and snow melt, prevented destructive floods, and allowed a greater amount of the run-off to be captured behind high dams and their reservoirs, thus providing augmented water supples for summer irrigation. Ironically, today the dam-builders and the conservationists have parted company.

Federal assistance for irrigation began in 1888, when Congress authorized the Geological Survey, led by John Wesley POWELL, to make irrigation surveys. Prior to that date the federal government had published studies of irrigation enterprise abroad, had appropriated funds for an investigation of irrigation prospects in California's Central Valley (1874), and had attempted to foster irrigation ostensibly via the small farmer or rancher through the misguided Desert Land Act (1877). The Powell survey was envisioned by its promoters, senators William Stewart of Nevada and Henry Teller of Colorado, as a measure to usher in the reservoir stage of reclamation and to forestall speculative aggrandizement of irrigable land, so characteristic of operations under the Desert Land Act. The survey called for the marking out of all possible reservoir sites and the withdrawal from public land entry of these sites and surrounding irrigable land. The West, however, was not ready for an arbitrary reservation of public lands by visionaries such as Major Powell, whose designs for an ordered economic development of western hydrographic basins would have curbed private enterprise. The Geological Survey's funds were drastically reduced in 1890 in response to the outcry from the West, and the reservation provision was repealed. Hydrographic surveys were continued on a reduced basis, however; engineers such as Frederick H. Newell and Arthur Powell Davis received future valuable training; and Powell's vision of western reclamation survived in the minds of his successors in the survey.

The irrigation movement's first goal then became cession of land. A proposal for cession of federal public lands to western states received national attention when Elwood MEAD, Wyoming state engineer, presented the subject to Senator Stewart's Irrigation Committee on tour in the West in the summer of 1889. The proposal to cede public lands to the states in which they were located had a long and respectable history associated with sectional demands of the Jacksonian Era. But Mead envisioned cession as a device for federal funding that did not entail federal financing or control. It was pushed during the irrigation boom period, 1887-93, when private enterprise was promoting irrigation ventures as a phase of economic development through agricultural expansion, with the added incentive of speculative profits. The principal vehicle for the movement, the Irrigation Congress, was launched at Salt Lake City in 1891 under the sponsorship of such notables as Senator Stewart, Senator Francis E. Warren of Wyoming, Congressman Newlands of Nevada, and Governor Arthur Thomas of Utah. It adopted cession as its principal goal for national legislation. William E. SMYTHE, journalist

and founder of *Irrigation Age*, became secretary of the Irrigation Congress and spearheaded the ensuing propoganda effort with truly evangelical effort. Subsequent meetings of the congress at Los Angeles in 1893 and Denver in 1894 trumpeted cession as the solution, but the onset of the Panic of 1893 removed the local business support for cession, and subsequent congresses were won over to the proposal of federal construction of reclamation dams at the various reservoir sites the Geological Survey had located.

In the meantime, in 1894, Senator Joseph M. Carey of Wyoming had won passage of the CAREY ACT, still in effect today, which constituted a substitute for the all-embracing cession plan. It authorized the donation of a million acres of public lands to each of the arid states and territories. Depressed business conditions and the lack of effective state implementation made this worthy law largely ineffective. Only in Wyoming, where irrigation was considered absolutely vital to the transformation of the pioneer economy, was there a concerted effort to launch a state-sponsored program that offered an alternative to federal reclamation. State engineer Mead feared that with the combination of state water rights and federally owned lands speculators would produce a Pandora's box of litigation and block effective utilization of reclamation opportunities. In concert with Carey and Warren, he saw that Wyoming took full advantage of the Carey Act and worked with other state engineers on a proposed federal bill that would preserve state control over water rights and encourage homestead settlement, while still securing federal reservoir construction. Mead's alternative to national reclamation lost out to Senator Newlands' bill in 1902.

The Newlands Reclamation Act was a departure from previous policy with respect to western development. It came about as the result of a gigantic promotional effort undertaken by George Maxwell, starting in 1896. Maxwell, a California lawyer with a background in that state's tangled water-rights history, became converted to a plan of federal financing of reclamation projects. With a real flair for promotional undertakings, Maxwell single-handedly turned the Irrigation Congress around in 1896. He created his own auxiliary National Irrigation Association, notably backed by the financial support of five of the major western railroads and leading business associations in eastern cities. Maxwell and his growing band of influential followers believed that only the federal government could solve the problem of water rights on interstate streams. Also, federal construction of storage reservoirs would offset the tendency toward land monopoly endemic to state operations. Most importantly, it alone could provide the financial resources for an ambitious program of public works. Maxwell's efficient lobbying organization achieved the adoption of favorable resolutions by both national party platforms in 1900. He worked closely and tirelessly with Congressman Newlands and Frederick H. Newell of the hydrographic branch of the Geological Survey, sharpening up legislative proposals and lobbying in Congress.

President Theodore Roosevelt had early been won over to the idea of national reclamation when conservationist Gifford Pinchot introduced him to Newell. In fact, the Newlands bill passed in Congress largely because of the president's support. By equating federal dam construction in the West with federal river-and-harbor improvements in the East and South, Roosevelt persuaded many opponents in Congress to support the bill. Also, the provision opening reclamation projects to Homestead Act entrymen, written in at Newlands' insistence, appealed to a universal theme, the agrarian ideal, which helped to assure the measure's passage. Finally, the adoption of the Reclamation Fund device, with its income derived from western land sales, satisfied those eastern members of Congress troubled over the financial burden the program might entail for the treasury. The Reclamation Act proved of innovative significance comparable only to the Homestead Act of 1862 in the development of the West.

The program measured its successes during its first three decades primarily in terms of its engineering achievements. Newell, in charge of the Geological Survey's hydrographic work since its inception in 1888, now headed up the administration of the Reclamation Act. Although Newell had wide-ranging scientific interests and was one of the principal architects of the national conservation movement, his first concern in reclamation was the dam-building phase of the program. He marshaled an extremely capable force of civil engineers who turned from measuring stream flow and locating reservoir sites to planning and supervising the construction of high-level dams. The program was not free of politics. Some twenty-two reclamation projects completed during the first three decades of operation were located at sites dictated by political pressures and in accord with a provision of the statute that dictated distribution to states or territories where the most land sales occurred. The influence of Senator Newlands, George Maxwell, with Arizona interests, and James J. Hill of the Great Northern Railroad was all too apparent. Engineering feasibility was not the major consideration, but there is no evidence, as later charged, that sites challenging the latest technical skills of the engineering profession were purposely chosen.

The first projects were those on the Salt River in Arizona, the Truckee-Carson rivers in Nevada, the Minidoka in Idaho, and the Milk River in Montana. Some of these spectacular dams rose in canyon gorges from 220 feet (Roosevelt Dam) to 350 feet (Arrowrock Dam on the Snake River) and backed up as much as two million acre-feet of water in giant reservoirs. Much of this pioneering construction work also involved building rail lines, cement factories, power-generating facilities, and camp cities for employees. It gave the Bureau of Reclamation needed experience for building the behemoth projects of the Depression era and afterward: Hoover, Grand Coulee, Shasta, and Glen Canyon dams.

While the construction phase of reclamation projects proved on balance to be outstandingly successful despite the political pressures, the economics of reclamation agriculture were little understood from the beginning. Neither Newell nor Arthur Powell Davis, who followed him as director of the Reclamation Service in 1914, ever turned the reclamation projects into self-sufficient producing-units. While both men were dedicated to the family-sized farm and to the expansion of reclamation agriculture, they found the arbitrary provisions of the Newlands Act restrictive and the manifold social and economic problems arising on each site incapable of ready solution. Some problems could not have been

foreseen, because they related to specifically agricultural problems, such as drainage, soil conditions, and crop selection. If the work of the Department of Agriculture's irrigation investigation branch had been conjoined with the Bureau of Reclamation from the beginning, the lot of the pioneers on the projects would have been easier. Other complications related to the speculative engrossment of land within the projects, so that there was relatively little Homestead Act settlement. Then too, settlers incurred so much initial private debt in paying speculative land prices that they found it difficult to pay off their project debt for the cost of the dam and appurtenances. Other problems surfaced respecting conflicts in water rights, premature settlement, and delays in disposing of project lands. All problems in the end, however, were reduced to a question of finances—the inability of projects to meet their payments so that the federal government's Reclamation Fund could be reimbursed and the program expanded.

The financial plight of the program came to Congress' attention as early as 1910, and remedial legislation followed at least until the end of the 1930s. Congress first authorized a loan of $20 million in 1910 to replenish the finances of the Reclamation Fund. At the same time it required the secretary of the interior to prevent people from making application for government land and Homestead Act tracts until water was actually available. Homesteaders could obtain title to their tracts after only three years' residence, even if they had not paid off their indebtedness. In 1914 settlers were given an extension to twenty years to pay off the project construction costs, which along with maintenance costs were incorporated into their water charges. In the 1920s, following the recommendations of the so-called Fact Finders Commission, Congress gave the commissioner of the Reclamation Bureau discretionary authority to adapt payment requirements to the conditions of each project, and the total period for repayment was extended to forty years. Relief acts exempting settlers from water charges during certain years in the 1920s and 1930s produced a needed cushion for the hard-pressed settlers. Such liberality on the part of the government produced a continuing demand in the West for a moratorium or cancellation of debts, but Congress on recommendation of the bureau refused such political pressures.

The Depression, while threatening to demolish the reclamation program, really enabled Congress to arm Commissioner Elwood Mead with the means to solve all problems, scatter reclamation's enemies, and push the bureau into the peak of construction activity. Mead had been called to head the Reclamation Bureau in 1924 because of the wealth of his experience in irrigation law, agricultural engineering, and reclamation colonization in Australia and California. He won the confidence of water-user associations, to whom he turned over projects management, and faced down the opposition of the Department of Agriculture and its clientele, who opposed the expansion of reclamation because of the problem of crop surpluses. Mead cultivated the support of Presidents Hoover and Roosevelt and organized a national reclamation association of western economic interests, whose assistance brought congressional approval for new projects even in the depth of the Depression. More important than any other development for the future of reclamation was the bureau's undertaking of the Boulder Canyon Project. This multipurpose river-basin development was the harbinger of the Grand Coulee, the Central Valley Project in California, the Upper Colorado Basin, and other large-scale projects.

The Depression, World War II, and cold war years assured the triumph of national reclamation. The success with which the Bureau of Reclamation launched the Boulder Canyon work suggested to the Roosevelt administration that the bureau should carry out all of the public works reclamation activities in the West. The multipurpose approach of the bureau gave it the edge over the Army Corps of Engineers, and the generation of electric power especially commended itself to Congress. Congress realized that electric power, at that time a little exploited by-product of high-dam construction, could be used to pay off Reclamation Fund deficits and carry the full burden of future reclamation construction.

Since World War II western economic interests have become increasingly dependent on electric power and the water resources of the giant reclamation projects as industry and urban population were growing. Hoover Dam (built 1931-35), costing as much as all previous reclamation projects, might be characterized together with subsequent multipurpose projects as a contributing factor in inducing the take-off period in midcentury western economic growth. In 1968 the Bureau of Reclamation provided about 2 million acre-feet of water for municipal, industrial, and nonagricultural use and served the needs of 14 million people. Bureau of Reclamation projects generated over 33 billion kilowatt-hours of electricity for western urban areas.

The sustained growth in western agriculture has also been spearheaded by the national reclamation program. In 1906 there were about 22,300 irrigated acres with crops yielding a value of $244,900 on reclamation projects of the bureau. The latest figures (1970) disclose 8.5 million acres under irrigation supplied by Bureau of Reclamation reservoirs, representing a total crop value of almost $2 billion realized by 140,505 farm units. The leading states benefited by federal reclamation were California, Washington, Idaho, Colorado, and Arizona. The chief crops produced on these irrigated acres were sugar beets, cotton, oranges, potatoes, and alfalfa.

The financing of these projects came to be paid by the general treasury as well as the Reclamation Fund, to which electric power revenue contributed handsomely. Selection of project sites as well as qualified applicants has improved over the years. Lessons have been learned in irrigation agriculture and new project openings for settlers have continued, but on a limited basis. The chief problem not yet solved is the question of "excess lands." The law, with some exceptions, places a clear obligation on Bureau of Reclamation management to force a sale of lands in excess of 160 acres owned by agricultural producers who receive waters from Bureau of Reclamation projects. These owners could sell excess land back to the government at "pre-water" prices or could put the land up for sale in the general market, but the law states that land in excess of 160 acres for a single owner (320 acres for man and wife) would not get Bureau of Reclamation water. The directors have never successfully enforced this proviso as a general policy. Such enforce-

ment might make more meaningful the intentions of the original reclamation law, that homesteader- and family-sized farms be favored on federal projects.

In the 1970s the Bureau of Reclamation found itself the target of the "new conservationists." In its search for new sites for high-level dams, it was thwarted by the wilderness movement in the Echo Park (Dinosaur National Monument) controversy in the mid-1950s and the Bridge Canyon (Grand Canyon National Park) defeat of the mid-1960s. The bureau in league with privately owned utilities also faced the wrath of environmentalists who opposed their gigantic coal-burning electric-generating plants in the Four Corners area, where Arizona, New Mexico, Utah, and Colorado met. In its perennial search for more electric power capacity, the bureau may exploit geothermal energy sources as well as atomic reactors. Thus reclamation is now everybody's business, city denizen as well as rural dweller.

The most helpful books are Paul W. Gates, *History of Public Land Law Development* (1968), which contains an excellent chapter that surveys the manifold operations of federal reclamation law down to the 1960s; Samuel P. Hays, *Conservation and the Gospel of Efficiency* (1959), which gives adequate emphasis to the irrigation movement as a pioneer expression of federal conservation; William E. Smythe, *The Conquest of Arid America* (1969), which offers a primary account of the irrigation movement and whose introduction furnishes biographical insights into Smythe's career; and Donald C. Swain, *Federal Conservation Policy, 1921-1933* (1963), the best treatment of Bureau of Reclamation operations in the 1920s. See also the following articles: John T. Ganoe, "The Origins of a National Reclamation Policy," *Mississippi Valley Historical Review* (June 1931), the first scholarly presentation of the national reclamation movement; Lawrence B. Lee, "William Ellsworth Smythe and the Irrigation Movement: A Reconsideration," *Pacific Historical Review* (August 1972), which presents a historiographical examination of reclamation history; and Everett W. Sterling, "The Powell Irrigation Survey, 1888-1893," *Mississippi Valley Historical Review* (December 1940), which places John Wesley Powell in the forefront of the irrigation movement.—L. B. L.

recreation. See GAMBLING; RODEO; SPORTS AND PASTIMES.

Rector, Henry Massey (1816-1899). Arkansas politician. Born in Kentucky, Rector settled in Arkansas in about 1835 to look after his family's extensive claims to land at Hot Springs. In 1877 he lost a forty-year legal battle for possession of the United States reservation of Hot Springs. A relative of the Conways and a Democrat, Rector wished to succeed Elias Conway as governor in 1860 but was shunted aside when Richard H. Johnson, the brother of Senator Robert Ward Johnson, was nominated. Angry, Rector ran as an independent Democrat in defiance of the Conway-Johnson clique, and, with the aid of politician Thomas Hindman, beat Johnson. As governor, he proved inept politically, alienated Hindman, and quarreled with Confederate officials. Defeated for reelection in 1862, he retired to his plantation. In 1874 he was a delegate to the state constitutional convention.—W. L. B.

Red Bird (1788?-1828). Winnebago chief. Relations between Red Bird and white men were generally good.

However, when the settlement of southeastern Wisconsin by lead miners began around 1825, Red Bird and his people, who occupied much of central and southeastern Wisconsin, feared encroachment on their lands. A rumor that two Winnebago prisoners had been executed at Fort Snelling, Minnesota, for a murder they did not commit further increased the uneasiness. Red Bird and three companions decided on revenge and on June 28, 1827, entered a home and murdered Registre Gagnier and Solomon Lipcap and scalped Gagnier's infant daughter. Two days later a band of Winnebago attacked the *Oliver Perry*, a keelboat on its way up the Mississippi, killing two crew members. The militia of the lead-mining district in Wisconsin and federal troops were sent into Wisconsin territory. To prevent a general Indian war, Red Bird dressed in white deerskin, carrying a pipe of peace and one of war, and wearing a preserved red bird as an epaulette, dramatically surrendered at the portage between the Fox and Wisconsin rivers, expecting to be put to death. He died in prison at Prairie du Chien, Wisconsin. This surrender, which prevented war, inspired paintings, stories, and at least one play.

See Wisconsin State Society Collection, vol. V (1868). —W. D. W.

Red Cloud (Makhpíya-Lúta) (c.1822-1909). Sioux warrior. Red Cloud was a war leader and headman among the Oglala subtribe of the Teton Sioux. The details of his character and career are uncertain and the subject of much controversy. He was born near the forks of the Platte River. His father evidently died soon after Red Cloud was born, and he was raised as an orphan in the camp of his maternal uncle, Chief Smoke. Red Cloud began going on war parties at an early age and quickly gained a reputation for cunning and cruelty in raids against the Pawnee and Crow. A highly ambitious youth, he became involved in a long-standing feud between Smoke and the most powerful Oglala chief, Bull Bear, and during a confrontation near Fort Laramie in 1841, shot and killed his uncle's rival. This assassination divided the Oglala for fifty years, and while it gained Red Cloud a measure of popularity among Smoke's people, he lost any potential chance to attain overall leadership of the Sioux. Even so, his prestige as a war leader continued to grow. By 1865 Red Cloud was generally recognized by the Oglala as their most fierce fighter, and though he was not made a chief, he had a large following of warriors who looked to him for leadership.

When the government in 1865-66 determined to open the Bozeman Trail through the Indians' Powder River hunting grounds, Red Cloud and the vast majority of the Sioux were vehementaly opposed and refused to recognize the so-called treaty of 1866 by which the army was granted the right to guard the route. During the resulting Powder River Indian Expedition of 1865-66, Red Cloud was a principal architect of Sioux tactics, including the trap that annihilated Captain William J. Fetterman's command. Such victories led the federal peace commission of 1867 to think Red Cloud was the foremost Sioux chief, and attempts to end the hostilities were based on that assumption. After difficult negotiations at Fort Laramie, Red Cloud in November 1868 agreed to peace in exchange for the army's abandonment of the Powder River forts and promised to try to keep his people out of war.

The government's satisfaction with the Fort Laramie treaty was unwarranted, for Red Cloud was still only a leading warrior to most of the Sioux. The tribe's suspicion of his personal ambitions was increased by his claiming of credit for the war's success and his associations with the whites, including a celebrated trip to Washington and New York in 1870. When in 1871 he settled at the agency that the Indian Bureau had established in his name, Red Cloud could muster less than a fifth of the Sioux population to accompany him. As time passed, however, increasing numbers of Sioux were compelled to move to the reservation, and Red Cloud spent the rest of his life there, striving to meet the fickle demands of the whites and to conciliate his unsatisfied tribesmen without alienating either. As a result he was completely trusted by no one and was forced to maintain an unpopular position of compromise in all the major crises confronting the Sioux after 1870: the cession of the Black Hills and the 1876-77 war, the reduction of the reservation in 1889, and the Ghost Dance crisis of 1890. Still, his name retained its formidable aura, and he obstructed the erosion of Sioux culture whenever he could. Perhaps more than that of any other Indian leader, Red Cloud's life points up the weaknesses of the United States officials' understanding of Indian society, and the immense difficulties faced by the Indian when forced to change from a traditional to a white-dominated way of life.

See George Hyde, *Red Cloud's Folk* (1937) and *A Sioux Chronicle* (1956); James C. Olson, *Red Cloud and the Sioux Problem* (1965); and Robert M. Utley, *The Last Days of the Sioux Nation* (1963).—P. R. M.

Red Jacket (Sagoyewatha) (c.1756-1830). Seneca chief and leader of the anti-Christian "pagan party" among the New York Iroquois. Born into the Wolf clan of the Seneca nation and a nephew of the Seneca prophet Handsome Lake, Sagoyewatha (his Iroquois name) first gained public attention in 1777 as a spokesman for the Seneca policy of neutrality during the American Revolution. When this policy was rejected by the warriors of the Six Nations, he followed Cornplanter, Joseph Brant, and other Iroquois war chiefs in taking up the British hatchet against the Americans. He acquired the name Red Jacket during this war, since British officers garbed him in scarlet coats when he was assigned duty carrying dispatches.

During the critical years after the American Revolution Red Jacket became the official spokesman for the Seneca council and served on occasion as the speaker for the Six Nations. Hence he was required to interpret and express the views of the Seneca and the Iroquois confederacy. His success in this role made him appear inconsistent and even perfidious to those outsiders, Indian and white, who did not understand the workings of Iroquois diplomacy. Moreover, the failure of the Six Nations' foreign policy and the breakup of the Iroquois confederacy during the 1780s and 1790s further marred his reputation. But even while the larger Iroquois strategies fell to the ground, Red Jacket and Cornplanter may be credited with salvaging, at the least, a series of concessions from the American authorities that secured minimum guarantes of reservation lands, technical assistance, and legal rights for the New York Iroquois. Yet in 1797, at the Treaty of Big Tree, both Red Jacket and Cornplanter—as well as other trusted men—succumbed to petty bribery, chicanery, and perhaps moral exhaustion when they sold off the bulk of the remaining Seneca lands west of the Genesee to the agents of Philadelphia financier Robert Morris.

Red Jacket in his later years made his home at Buffalo Creek on Lake Erie, one of the eleven small reserves left to the Seneca after 1797. There he became the spokesman for an anti-Christian policy, though opposing the religious movement led by Handsome Lake, inspired by his visions beginning in 1799. In 1801, while still holding the position of speaker for the Seneca nation, Red Jacket was accused of witchcraft by Handsome Lake. These accusations damaged his standing, and while he was later exonerated in council, the suspicions roused by Handsome Lake blocked his advance to the dignity of sachem. The rise of the Handsome Lake religion on the one side and the growth of Christian missionary influences on the other kept Red Jacket involved in political intrigue and traditional Iroquois religious advocacy during the last decades of life.

It was during these years, from 1801 until his death in 1830, that Red Jacket gained his widest fame among Anglo-American observers as an exponent of anti-Christian doctrines. With an oratorical brilliance well preserved in contemporary accounts, he repeatedly urged the right of his people to maintain their separate beliefs and forms of worship while consistently criticizing the extremes of Iroquois cultural nationalism put forward by younger followers of Handsome Lake. Nevertheless Red Jacket came to represent in white opinion the most intransigent resistance to moral progress and enlightened Christian policies among the Seneca. Repeatedly he demonstrated a willingness to accept the technical benefits of Anglo-American culture, but he would not tolerate the overbearing religious racism of the ministers of Christian denominations sent among the Iroquois.

As religious divisions became more extreme among the Seneca, Red Jacket emerged in the 1820s as the recognized leader of a traditionalist, anti-Christian faction that carried the label of the "pagan party." At the peak of its success, his party managed to expel all Christian missionaries from the Seneca reserves in 1824. Thereafter, however, the prestige of Red Jacket and his party began rapidly to decline. No stranger to the whiskey-trader's jug, his personal demoralization made him an easier target for the Christian party's efforts to destroy his influence. The deciding stroke came when his second wife, his stepchildren, and a great number of his neighbors at Buffalo Creek converted to Christianity. Red Jacket died abject and an alien in a world he had not fashioned. His wife gave him a Christian burial in a Christian cemetery.

As a counsel of perfection, the Iroquois say a great leader must be beyond moral reproach and have a skin seven thumbs thick. Too human, Red Jacket never fulfilled these conditions. George Catlin, who painted his portrait in 1826, found him a vain man. The Seneca accepted him as a great orator, unfortunately weak in moments of crisis, and still a person whose memory should not be lost.

Details of Red Jacket's life are preserved in the account by J. N. B. Hewitt in F. W. Hodge, *Handbook of American Indians North of Mexico* (1910). More precise information regarding his military career and religious

views are in Barbara Graymont *The Iroquois in the American Revolution* (1972); and Anthony F. C. Wallace, *The Death and Rebirth of the Seneca* (1970). In his work Wallace also points out the credit due to Red Jacket and Cornplanter for gaining concessions from the American negotiators during the difficult period after the American Revolution.—K. N. O.

Red Power movement. See INDIAN POWER MOVEMENT.

Red River cart. The Red River cart was used extensively from 1839 to 1869 for overland freighting in the Northern Plains. Its origin is uncertain, but it was probably developed by French-Canadians or French-Indian half-breeds, called métis. The cart trains traveled on one of three routes, all of which ran on the Mississippi River from St. Paul or Mendota, Minnesota, to the north on either side of the Red River of the North into Canada. Pembina, in northern Dakota Territory, was an important stop on the trails, and the carts usually wintered there.

The two-wheeled, wholly wooden carts were drawn by oxen. Occasionally, wet rawhide was wrapped around the hub and rim for added strength and endurance. The wheels were very large, so that the cart rode high and could more easily forge streams. The out-turned (dished) wheels were never greased; thus, a train of carts could be heard from some distance away because of the piercing screech of wood turning on wood. The high, fencelike sides of the cart could be piled with from 700 to 1,000 pounds of goods. These sturdy vehicles were inexpensive, costing from five to fifteen dollars.

The carts were organized into trains of seventy-five to one-hundred vehicles. Five to ten carts were joined into a brigade by leather strips between cart and ox. Métis accompanied each train; two or three walked with each brigade. Goods commonly carried on the southbound trip from Canada included buffalo hides, furs, and pemmican. On the return trip from Minnesota, general merchandise, ammunition, trade goods for the Indians, and sometimes even the United States mails were carried. Red River carts were ultimately replaced by shallow-draft steamboats and railroads.

See Lauren C. Post, "Red River Carts," *Brand Book No. 1* (1968).—D. J. T.

Red River of the North. The headwaters of the streams that join to make the Red River rise among the lakes of central Minnesota only 270 miles from the Red River's mouth in Canada. The Red River is said to begin at the confluence of the Otter Tail and Bois de Sioux rivers near Breckenridge, Minnesota, and is one of only a few rivers in the United States to have a northerly course. It forms the boundary between North Dakota and Minnesota, enters Canada at Emerson, and flows through Winnipeg before emptying into Lake Winnipeg.

Its headwater streams flow through rolling hill country formed from young glacial deposits dropped as the last continental ice sheet melted away ten thousand years ago. Their courses meander from one lake to another before reaching the bed of ancient Lake Agassiz. At this point, the Red River turns north to flow through a broad fertile valley formed by the deposits of the ancient lake.

The valley was first reached and occupied by Canadian fur trappers before the middle of the eighteenth

Red River of the North

century, and the first agricultural settlement was sponsored by the fifth earl of Selkirk, Thomas Douglas, who obtained a grant of land called Assiniboia. The first settlers arrived in Manitoba, Canada, in 1812, but permanent settlement was not made until 1816. This agricultural settlement was opposed by the fur-trading companies, and conflict occurred. The treaty of 1818 with England gave all of the territory south of the forty-ninth parallel to the United States.

Following the establishment of Fort Snelling (near the site of present-day Minneapolis) in 1820, Stephen H. Long led an expedition up the Minnesota to the Red River and down that river to Lake Winnipeg, thus establishing the trade route that tied settlements in the Red River valley to the advancing American frontier. The completion of railroads through Minnesota in the early 1870s brought floods of Scandinavian settlers to farm the rich prairie grass soils of the valley. The twin cities of Fargo and Moorhead on either side of the river and Grand Forks farther north on the Dakota side developed as the main market and service towns in what became the leading spring-wheat area of the United States. Today the basin continues to provide the nation with grain, but agriculture has become diversified and some industrial development has occurred.—R. W. D.

Red River of the South. A number of small, intermittent streams rising on the High Plains section of Texas join to form the Red River of the South, which then flows south and east for 1,300 miles before entering the Mississippi River. The Red River, so called because it carries a load of red clay soil eroded from the Plains of Texas and Oklahoma, forms the boundary between Texas and Oklahoma and for a short distance the boundary between Texas and Arkansas. In this portion of its course the river flows through hilly, forested terrain before turning south and east to meander across Louisiana to its juncture with the Mississippi River.

Although first explored by members of the expedition led by Hernan de Soto in the early 1540s and by La Salle in the late seventeenth century, the Red River

country was not settled until the middle of the eighteenth century, when French colonists moving northward out of the mother colony at New Orleans established settlements along the streams in the bayou country of Louisiana. After the acquisition of the Louisiana Territory by the United States, exploration of the river became important, because the Red River marked a portion of the southwestern boundary of the newly acquired territory. The expeditions of Sibley (1803), Sparks (1806), Zebulon Pike (1806), and Stephen Long (1820) sought to determine the source and true course of the river, and their published reports focused attention on the basin. When cotton farming extended to the rich alluvial soils of its floodplains, additional settlements were made. Shreveport became the head of navigation for the steamboats that served the needs of the territory. Established in 1834, Shreveport became the capital of the state of Louisiana in 1863. The discovery of oil and natural gas in the lower basin early in the twentieth century added greatly to the wealth of natural resources of the basin and added to the number of people living there.

For map, see ARKANSAS RIVER.—R. W. D.

Red River War (1874-1875). Indian wars. During the Civil War era the Comanche, Kiowa, and related tribes on the Southern Plains fought continually against the advancement of white settlement into western Texas. To stop their depredations and as part of a new approach to Indian relations, the Treaty of Medicine Lodge was negotiated in 1867. One provision of the treaty located the Comanche and Kiowa with the Cheyenne and Arapaho on lands in western Indian Territory (present-day Oklahoma), and reserved the Staked Plains area of the Texas Panhandle for their hunting grounds. Many bands, however, did not feel bound by the treaty, and congressional delay in appropriating funds for reservation development worsened the situation. The Kwahadi Comanche, led by Quanah Parker, stayed in the Staked Plains area, refusing to register at the Fort Sill agency. The Kiowa, led by Satanta, Kicking Bird, and Lone Wolf, settled on the reservation, but warrior bands continued to raid into the Texas settlements.

The whites in the area were as divided in their view of the situation as were the Indians. The regional army detachments, commanded by the fiery Phillip Sheridan, were in conflict with the Quakers, who under President Grant's peace policy had been assigned to administer the Indian Territory reservations. In Washington, General-in-Chief William Tecumseh Sherman and the civilian Indian Bureau were trying to separate fact from fantasy in the contradictory reports from their subordinates. The Texans were disturbed because under the terms of the 1845 annexation Texas retained control of its public lands, but the federal peace commissioners at Medicine Lodge had assigned a portion of these lands as hunting grounds, apparently ignoring the Texas claim. White buffalo hunters, who by 1870 had already greatly reduced the herds, were still another irritation. The slaughter of the buffalo not only increased the Indians' suspicion of the government's sincerity, but led off-reservation bands to prey upon white stock and goods for basic subsistence.

In May 1871 a band of Kiowa and Comanche, frustrated in their attempts to find buffalo, slipped across the Red River to raid in Texas. The target they selected was a group of freighters carrying corn to Fort Griffin. On May 17 the raiders, led by Satanta, Big Tree, and Tsatangya, attacked the wagon train between Fort Belknap and Fort Richardson, killing six of the teamsters and capturing forty mules. Coincidentally, General Sherman was then at Fort Richardson, inspecting the Texas frontier to see for himself if the area was in as much danger as had been reported. To Sherman, this incident proved the military's case, and he personally organized the search for the Indians responsible. The leaders were captured and two were eventually tried for murder under Texas law, in a rare exception to the general policy of federal jurisdiction over Indian "crimes."

Sherman further authorized Sheridan to gather all wayward tribes onto the reservation. Aggressively carrying out his orders, Sheridan in 1874 despatched Colonels Nelson Miles, George Buell, J. W. Davidson, and Ranald S. MACKENZIE and Major William Price into the Staked Plains. The major incident of this campaign occurred in September when Mackenzie attacked and destroyed a large Comanche-Kiowa camp in the battle of PALO DURO CANYON, killing their horses and burning their supplies. The surviving Indians scattered onto the Plains, but winter and the loss of their equipment forced them to return to the reservation between February and May 1875.

The Red River war broke the strength of the Comanche and Kiowa. Twenty-six of their leaders were shipped to prison in Florida, and Indian resistance on the Southern Plains was ended. A wider consequence was that Sherman's attitude toward Indians as a whole hardened, reinforcing the military's subsequent harsh Indian policy throughout the West.

For other views and details of the incidents, see Dee Brown, *Bury My Heart at Wounded Knee* (1971); and C. C. Rister, *The Southwestern Frontier, 1865-1881* (1928). A complete account of the raid into Texas in May 1871 and its aftermath is in Benjamin Capps, *The Warren Wagontrain Raid* (1974).—R. F. M.

Reed, Simeon Gannett (1830-1895). Oregon businessman. Born in East Abington, Massachusetts, Reed arrived in Oregon with his wife, Amanda, in 1852 and was soon in partnership with merchant William S. Ladd, a former Vermonter. In 1858 Reed invested in three Columbia River steamers while Ladd opened a bank that helped to launch Oregon's most successful enterprise, the Oregon Steam Navigation Company, in 1860, with Reed as vice-president and manager. Formed with the assets of competing steamer companies ($172,000), the business was in operation in time to take advantage of the Idaho gold rush. In two years the company was recapitalized at $2 million. By 1867 its stock was owned by three men, one of whom was Reed. The other two were Captain John C. Ainsworth and Robert R. Thompson. The trio had just won an internal company struggle with another group of stockholders who were eager to see less reinvestment of money in business projects and more dividends (the company paid about $5 million in dividends over twenty years).

With the expansionists in control, the company purchased ships and built portages, bought out competitors, and was soon roundly disliked as a powerful monopoly with, apparently, a preference for rate fixing. When Washington Territory attempted to legislate

against the company, Reed got Congress to abrogate the territorial legislation. "That Territory will be reminded," he gloated, "that there is a 'power above them.'"

Reed used his earnings from the company to invest in mines in eastern Oregon and to engage in livestock breeding with Ladd. Together they owned almost twenty farms in the Willamette valley. In 1879 the navigation company sold out to the Villard syndicate for $5 million.

Reed's interest in the arts and in nonsectarian philanthropy provoked him to will instructions to his childless wife that she endow at her death some "suitable" cultural endeavor. When Amanda Reed died in 1904 she left $3 million toward the founding of Reed College in Portland, which opened in 1911.

Reed's papers are deposited with the Reed College Library, Portland.—R. J. L.

Refugio. See NUESTRA SENORA DEL ESPIRITU SANTO DE ZUNIGA.

Regulators of North Carolina. Throughout American history, frontier citizens who felt they were suffering from absentee government, corrupt officials, or unfair taxes have organized armed protests against their oppressors. One of the most important of these citizens organizations appeared on the Appalachian frontier a decade before the American Revolution. Its members were drawn from the backcountry of North Carolina and called themselves Regulators. The people of the Piedmont, complaining of inadequate representation in the assembly, unfair taxation, corrupt officials, scarcity of land, and the seizure of property for the inability to pay taxes, vented their frustrations and grievances against the most prosperous coastal regions in much the same manner as Nathaniel Bacon of Virginia had in 1676 and as Daniel Shays of western Massachusetts was to do in 1786. The Regulators, who eventually numbered more than two thousand men, in several instances roughed up county officials and unpopular lawyers and prevented courts from meeting.

Matters reached a climax on May 16, 1771, when a large body of farmers encountered several companies of militia on the Alamance River. The militia fired upon the untrained Regulators, killing one or two of their members and forcing the others to flee for their lives. The troops pursued the Regulators and captured fifteen prisoners, six of whom were later hanged for treason. The colonial governor then extracted an oath of allegiance from every male inhabitant of the Piedmont area in exchange for the promise of legislative reforms. The assembly subsequently passed some remedial laws but not enough to satisfy the former Regulators. As a consequence, most of the dissidents abandoned the region during the Revolution; most of them moved still further out onto the frontier, to Kentucky and Tennessee.

See William S. Powell et al., eds., *The Regulators in North Carolina* (1971).—W. E. H.

Reid, Hugo (1810-1852). California ranchero. Scottish-born and Cambridge-educated, Reid left England at eighteen for a trader's life in South America. In 1834 he settled in Mexican Los Angeles, where he operated a successful trading company. Three years later he fulfilled a dream of becoming a *haciendado* by marrying the adopted Indian daughter of a local ranchero family. The couple's Rancho de Santa Anita, on former Mission San Gabriel lands, prospered through 1846, but after the American conquest, partly as a result of his neutrality in the struggle, he was stripped of his lands. In the years before his death he became a champion of Indian welfare, arguing unsuccessfully for their civil rights at the state constitutional convention in 1849, and two years later writing a series of excellent articles exposing their genocidal treatment at the hands of the Spanish, Mexican, and Anglo invaders.

Helen Hunt Jackson's *Ramona* was inspired in part by Reid's marriage, but it is highly distortive if read as a history of the Reid family.

See Susanna Bryant Dakin, *A Scotch Paisano: Hugo Reid's Life in California* (1939).—J. F.

Reid, Robert Raymond (1789-1841). Florida politician. Born in Prince William Parish, South Carolina, Reid was schooled in Augusta, Georgia, at South Carolina College in Columbia, and returned to Augusta to read law.

In 1816, at age twenty-seven, Reid was named to the Superior Court of Georgia in Burke County. He went to Congress in 1818 and served two terms. There he opposed the restriction upon slavery contained in the Missouri Compromise. He returned to the Georgia bench in 1821, serving until 1825. From 1827 until 1832 he sat as the city judge of Augusta. In 1828 he was named a presidential elector from Georgia and, identifying with the old Crawford faction, he cast his vote for Andrew Jackson. In 1832 President Jackson appointed him United States judge for East Florida, to hold court in St. Augustine. There he associated with politicians of all stripes but gravitated toward those who formed Florida's Democratic party. One of its leaders, David Levy Yulee, studied law under Reid in St. Augustine.

At the Florida constitutional convention in 1838-39 Reid was chosen president in a contest largely drawn on Whig-Democratic lines and participated in 1839 in the formal organization of the Democratic party. Late in the same year President Martin Van Buren, at the solicitation of Yulee, named Reid governor of Florida, removing Richard Keith Call, who had become a bitter critic of the administration. Reid fell heir to all the problems of his predecessor, chief of which was the Seminole War. Though he had little confidence in General Zachary Taylor, the federal commander, Reid followed a conciliatory policy toward the administration. In 1840, however, when General Walker K. Armistead came into command, relations between the governor and the general reached the breaking point over the question of the use of the militia in the war. In the fall of 1840 Whig William Henry Harrison was elected president and Florida Whigs agitated for Reid's removal. In March 1841 he was turned out and Call was reinstated. On June 30, at his home near Tallahassee, Reid suddenly died of a fever.

There is no readily available biography of Reid. A typescript copy of his diary is in the Florida Historical Society Library, Tampa, Florida.—H. J. D.

Reifel, Benjamin (1906-   ). Dakota Brulé politician and government official. Reifel was born in Rosebud, South Dakota, and studied dairy science and chemistry in that state. His first of many positions with the United States Indian Service (now Bureau of Indian Affairs) was farm agent. Under provisions of the 1932 Indian Reorganization Act, he helped Indian groups form business councils and later was superintendent of his home reservation. After World War II service Reifel returned briefly to the Indian Service as tribal relations officer at Billings, Montana. He then decided to return to school, earning a Ph.D. at Harvard. In 1955 Reifel was appointed director of the Aberdeen (South Dakota) area office of the Bureau of Indian Affairs.

In 1960 Reifel ran for Congress from South Dakota, defeating two strong opponents in the primary and going on to win the election for five terms, by larger pluralities each time until 1970, when he decided to resign. In the House, Reifel served as ranking minority member of the Appropriations Subcommittee and as a member of the Interior and Related Agencies Subcommittee (the Bureau of Indian Affairs is part of the Department of the Interior) and the Legislative Subcommittee.—C. C.

Remington, Frederic (1861-1909). Illustrator, writer, painter, and sculptor. Remington was born in Canton, New York. Among the first to enroll at the Yale School of Fine Arts in 1878, he later studied at the Art Students League in New York City and early in his career became rather widely known as a reporter of life in the West, where he went initially for the sake of his health in 1880. He sold his first folio of western sketches in Kansas City in 1884 and almost immediately returned to New York to marry Eva Caton, his college sweetheart. Back in Kansas City with his bride, Remington spent the next two years visiting frontier military posts and traveling about with the cavalry on several southwestern campaigns. The first picture to be published under his full name appeared on the cover of *Harper's Weekly* in 1886. Thereafter ensued a period of increasing popularity

Bronco Buster *by Frederic Remington. (Thomas Gilcrease Institute)*

and frequent sales, promoted mainly by the owner-editor of *Outing* magazine. Exhibition honors and publications in leading magazines added to Remington's fame, and numerous assignments from New York publishers sent him westward again and again to secure material of interest to eastern readers.

Observing the soldier in combat in the West and as a war correspondent during the Spanish-American War, Remington achieved a lasting reputation for his portrayals of the United States cavalry in action. His characterizations of the American Indian, the cowboy, and other frontier types likewise earned him a great deal of praise from such western enthusiasts as Owen Wister and Theodore Roosevelt. During the last twenty years of his life he produced more than 2,700 paintings and drawings, his illustrations appearing in 41 different periodicals and 142 books. In 1893 he held his first one-man show in New York City and in 1895 attempted his first bronze sculpture, *Bronco Buster*. He also authored several volumes of stories, including *Pony Tracks* (1895), *Crooked Trails* (1898), *Sundown LeFlare* (1899), and *John Ermine of Yellowstone* (1902). His twenty-fourth and last sculpture, *Caught in a Stampede*, was cast by Roman Bronze Works, New York City, within a year following his death of acute appendicitis near Ridgefield, Connecticut.

The largest collections of Remington's work are at the Remington Art Memorial, Ogdensburg, New York; the Thomas Gilcrease Institute of American History and Art, Tulsa, Oklahoma; and the Whitney Gallery of Western Art in the BUFFALO BILL HISTORICAL CENTER, Cody, Wyoming. Other collections of his paintings or bronzes are displayed at the Art Institute of Chicago; the Amon Carter Museum of Western Art, Fort Worth, Texas; the National Cowboy Hall of Fame, Oklahoma City, Oklahoma; and the Stark Museum of Art, Orange, Texas.

See Peter Hassrick, *Frederic Remington* (1973); Harold McCracken, *The Frederic Remington Book: A Pictorial History of the West* (1966); Paul Rossi and David C. Hunt, *The Art of the Old West* (1971); and Robert Taft, *Artists and Illustrators of the Old West, 1850-1900* (1953). —D. C. H.

rendezvous system. See FUR TRADE: *in the United States.*

Renne, Roland Roger (1905-). Educator and agricultural economist. Born in New Jersey, Renne was graduated from Rutgers University in 1927 and received a master's degree in 1928 and a Ph.D. in 1930 from the University of Wisconsin. He then became assistant professor of Agricultural Economics at Montana State College. In 1942 he was named president of the college, at the age of thirty-seven the youngest in the institution's history. He served until 1964, the longest term in its history. Between 1930 and 1942, while engaged half-time in research with the Montana Experiment Station, he wrote many influential bulletins on land economics, taxation, and local government. Those on school districts and county organization resulted in effective changes. He played an important part in the adoption and retention of the county manager form of government in Petroleum County, the smallest county in the United States with this type of government.

Renne took leaves of absence to accept such foreign assignments as chief of the Mutual Security Agency's Economic Mission to the Philippines from 1950 to 1953 and chief of the Agricultural Survey Mission to Peru made by the Joint International Bank in 1958 and to serve with a land development mission in Ethiopia in 1960. He served on national boards for Indian affairs and forest and land resources and on President Harry S. Truman's Water Resources Policy Commission in 1950 and 1951. During another leave in 1963 and 1964, Renne was assistant secretary for agriculture for international affairs.

He resigned from the post in 1964 to run for governor of Montana. The campaign was hectic since, during his long term as president of Montana State College, he had exerted strong influence on the entire state university system and had alarmed many tax-conscious groups who were concerned with its expense. In addition, while serving as assistant secretary for agriculture for international affairs, he had aroused fear among Montana stockmen with his support for reduced import tariffs on certain types of beef even though this did not include Montana's fresh or "red meat" type of beef. Renne was narrowly defeated in the election.

From 1964 to 1969 he was director of Water Resources Research in the Department of the Interior, where he was among those who early recognized and warned about the rapid deterioration of the nation's water resources. He was named professor of agricultural economics at the University of Illinois in 1969 and later took a leave of absence to accept a foundation contract post as an economic advisor in agricultural studies and research at Panth Nagar University in India.

He was given honorary degrees by Rutgers University and by the national universities of the Philippines, Ethopia, Peru, and Paraguay. Renne also served as president of the Western Farm Economics Association and vice president of the Farm Economics Association. He wrote *Montana Citizen* (1937); *Land Economics* (1947); and *Government and Administration of Montana* (1958).

See Louis True, "Roland R. Renne," *Montana Collegian* (April 1963), and "R. R. Renne," *Montana Education*, News Ed. (March 5, 1964).—M. G. B.

Renner, Frederic G. (1897-). Art expert, writer, and conservationist. Born in Great Falls, Montana, Renner spent his first twelve years there and on the family ranch located on the Missouri River, west of Great Falls. Legend has it that Charles Marion Russell, the then fledgling cowboy artist, once worked as a cowboy on the Renner ranch. Later, seeing Russell on the streets of Great Falls, Renner became much intrigued with his "breed" sash (used by Canadian half-breeds, hence the name), which he wore in lieu of a belt.

In 1922, after serving in the army during World War I and completing his education at several western universities, Renner became a grazing assistant for the United States Forest Service in New Mexico. In 1936 he began his twenty-five-year task as chief range conservationist for the newly organized United States Soil Conservation Service. He played a major role in changing the face of America, recruiting and training the range staff and developing the procedures and techniques for the first technical assistance provided owners and operators of private range lands.

Renner's reputation as a range conservationist was international; he headed a land-use study group in

Greece in 1946 and participated in grassland management conferences in Sweden, England, Argentina, Australia, and New Zealand. During his career he prepared a number of articles on grass and range management for technical magazines and government publications, including the best technical bibliography available, *A Selected Bibliography on Management of Western Ranges, Livestock and Wildlife* (1938), containing over 8,200 entries.

During his conservation years, Renner began collecting original works by his childhood hero, Russell, as well as books and magazines the artist had illustrated, and visited Russell's widow and friends. Retirement allowed Renner's hobby to become a vocation, and he quickly became the recognized authority on Russell's work. His collection, including oils, watercolors, pen and ink drawings, illustrated letters, models, and bronzes, is believed to be the largest and most representative in private ownership. It is supplemented by a notable library, a complete collection of Russell prints and over twenty-five hundred black-and-white photographs and several hundred transparencies.

In 1948 Renner contributed articles to Karl Yost's *Russell Bibliography*. His own *Rangeland Rembrandt* (1948) was soon followed by a number of other books, including *Paper Talk: Illustrated Letters of Charles M. Russell* (1962), *Charles M. Russell Paintings, Drawings and Sculpture in the Amon G. Carter Collection* (1965), and, again with Yost, the *Russell Bibliography* (1971), the most comprehensive work on any American artist-illustrator to date. In addition, he cataloged over thirty-five hundred original Russell pieces, including all the major public and private collections and many minor holdings.

Renner was appointed the Russell consultant to the C. M. Russell Gallery in Great Falls, the Montana Historical Society's Russell Memorial Collection in Helena, and the Amon Carter Museum of Western Art at Fort Worth, Texas. As one of the Old Bookaroos, a group of four men who produce the column "Western Book Roundup," printed monthly in a number of western magazines, Renner wrote numerous book reviews. —J. C. D.

Reno, Marcus A. See LITTLE BIG HORN, BATTLE OF THE.

Reno, Nevada. The emigrant crossing at the Truckee River, known first as Fuller's and then as Lake's Crossing, became the new town of Reno when the Central Pacific Railroad auctioned lots there on May 9, 1868. The town was named by Charles Crocker in honor of General Jesse Reno, a Union officer killed at the battle of South Mountain in 1862. The arrival of regular trains from Sacramento in July 1868 immediately established Reno as a distribution center for the Comstock Lode, western Nevada, and eastern California. The town grew slowly but steadily during the Comstock era and continued to prosper during the long depression in Nevada following the Comstock's decline. By 1900 Reno had become the largest city in the state and its most important banking and trading center. Nevada's second major mining boom, which began with the discovery of Tonopah in 1900 and Goldfield in 1902, reemphasized Reno's new status and nearly tripled its population by 1920. Since World War II Reno has been able to use its attractive location and several permissive state laws—a six-week residency requirement for divorce, legalized

gambling, its free port law, i.e., property passing through Nevada from one state to another is exempt from Nevada property taxes so long as it is warehoused in the state—to take advantage of a number of national trends, including a massive and seemingly continuous westward movement of population, a recreation and transportation revolution, and a rising tide of prosperity, to become the center of a multifaceted tourist industry.

The law requiring six weeks of legal residence for divorce was signed by Governor Fred B. Balzar on March 19, 1931, but did not become effective until May 1 of the same year. Nevada, particularly the city of Reno, entered the field of easy divorce as a result of the publicity given to the divorce of William E. Corey, president of United States Steel Corporation, in 1906, when the state had the relatively brief residency requirement of six months. The divorce business was stimulated further when the well-known actress Mary Pickford obtained a divorce from her film-star husband, Owen Moore, in 1920. The resulting publicity benefited Nevada so much that the state legislature in 1927 reduced the residency requirement to three months. The possibility of losing its status as a divorce capital to competing states led the legislature in 1931 to pass a new act requiring only a six-week residency. It had the desired effect and Reno in the 1930s became the divorce capital of the United States. The recent easing of divorce laws in neighboring states, particularly California, has caused a noticeable decline in divorces in Nevada.

Although its population growth since 1940 has been phenomenal—from 21,317 in that year to 72,121 in 1970—Reno gave up its status as Nevada's largest city in 1960 when the census of that year showed Las Vegas with 64,405 people while Reno could count only 51,470. Reno is the site of the Reno campus of the University of Nevada, the Nevada State Historical Society Museum and Library, and the Desert Research Institute with its Water Resources Building and the unusual Atmospherium-Planetarium.

See Richard G. Lillard, *Desert Challenge: An Interpretation of Nevada* (1942).—R. E.

Reorganized Church of Jesus Christ of Latter-day Saints. See LATTER-DAY SAINTS, REORGANIZED.

reptiles. When the western United States was settled by Europeans there was no doubt about which reptile attracted the most attention and caused the greatest concern. It was, of course, the snake that carried on the tip of its tail a noisemaking structure and used two hypodermic needlelike teeth to inflict bites that were sometimes fatal to man and beast. No snake just like these lived in the Old World, and the fame of rattlesnakes grew rapidly. In the early days this fame was spread by those who met rattlesnakes but did not study them. Folklore student J. Frank Dobie wrote a book of stories entitled *Rattlesnakes*, and the late Laurence M. Klauber, perhaps the foremost student of rattlesnakes, wrote a 1,476-page monograph with the same title that includes much additional folklore. Although scientific, most of Klauber's monograph can be understood by any educated person.

The early arrivals had no way of knowing that many of them were approaching the evolutionary home of rattlesnakes: the southwestern United States and northern Mexico. Arizona may be taken as the heart of rattle-

The ability of the snake to unhinge its jaw allows it to swallow creatures larger than itself, in this case a lizard. (Library of Congress)

snake country, for in that state alone eleven species occur; only one additional species is known in the western states, and the total for the United States is but fifteen. Rattlesnakes are found over the entire West except near the tops of the highest, coldest mountains and in a few other limited areas. Thus there was ample opportunity for travelers and settlers to become acquainted with them, person by person.

Two common beliefs are worthy of note. One is that the age of an individual snake can be told by counting the segments of the rattle. This is wrong for two reasons: a segment is added every time the skin is shed, and rattlesnakes shed more than once a year; and the endmost segments wear off in a few years. (Several individual rattlesnakes have been known to live nineteen years.) The second belief, that the rattler is a "gentleman" because it gives warning, is too anthropomorphic to appeal to the scientific mind. The sounding of the rattle no doubt enables the snake to avoid many a conflict.

In the West no one had to bother about venomous snakes without rattles, since among these there is only the Arizona coral snake. It is rare and secretive and confined to central and southern Arizona and the southwestern tip of New Mexico. This snake never seems to bite anybody.

The most conspicuous harmless snake of the West is probably the gopher snake or bullsnake. Its general distribution rivals that of the rattlesnakes, and it has a pattern that makes it slightly resemble some rattlers. Moreover, when annoyed, it vibrates the tail and produces in dry leaves a sound often mistaken for the rattling of a rattler. The gopher snake is large and highly beneficial in areas where destructive rodents abound; it devours countless numbers of these. The Hopi Indians of Arizona include many of these snakes in their dance for rain. Although the main attraction of the dance is the use of rattlesnakes, gopher snakes and racers also appear in considerable numbers along with the deadly species.

A group of five related species, the whipsnakes and racers, constitute another element of the western snakes. The largest of these, which, like the gopher snake, may be somewhat over eight feet in length, is the coachwhip. The slender body and tail and the appearance of the scales give it the name. It is a nervous, fast-moving reptile seen less often than the gopher snake because it does not wait around to be examined. The coloration is variable but there are no stripes along the body. The racer, somewhat smaller and brown or olive above (spotted when young), is also very active. The three remaining species of this group have stripes extending along the body. Like the rattlers and gopher snake, the whipsnakes and racers feed largely on rodents and are therefore of economic value. There are many fables supposedly illustrating the speed of the slender snakes, but they seldom crawl faster than the rate of three or four miles per hour, and eight miles per hour is probably their maximum.

In the mountains of southwestern Washington southward through California a beautiful snake, the California mountain kingsnake, occurs. The black, white, and red bands across the back and down the sides give this species a striking appearance. Another species, similarly colored, the Sonora mountain kingsnake, is found in Utah and Arizona, and, in the latter state, can be easily confused with the venomous Arizona coral snake. However, the white snout of the harmless species contrasts with the black snout of the other. More widely distributed than these tricolored species is the common kingsnake, which usually has alternating bands of plain black (or dark brown) and white (or pale yellow). The milk snake, a close relative of the kingsnake, rarely enters the West. The kingsnakes are popular as pets and protected by most people because they sometimes devour rattlers. Their disposition is calm and they are easy to handle.

No snakes are more abundant and conspicuous in both East and West than the garter snakes. They are encountered everywhere in the East, but in the West they tend to avoid the drier areas. Among the several species in the West two are widely distributed, the common garter snake and the western terrestrial garter snake. Garter snakes have a characteristic look that is largely due to a combination of stripes and rows of small spots along the body; in a few species the spots are lacking. Garter snakes are inoffensive except that when first handled they produce a strong, unpleasant odor; many are reluctant to bite. They are not economically very valuable, although they do devour insects; many frogs and other small animals are also eaten. Large broods of young are born ready to fend for themselves.

One small, slender snake, the ringneck, with an olive or bluish back, an orange or yellow band crossing just behind the darkened head, and a yellow-orange to red belly, deserves mention. The ringneck is entirely inoffensive, and is especially common in moist areas of western Washington and California. When caught they have a quaint habit of coiling the end of the tail in a tight spiral, turning it upward, and waving it about. The brightly colored bottom of the tail probably serves to divert attention or to intimidate predators. Finally, two miniature boas should also be mentioned, since many people have no idea that boas live in this country. The rubber boa, which ranges widely over the northern and central parts of the West, grows to be a little more than two feet long, and has a blunt tail shaped much like the head. The rosy boa, in the southern part of the West, does not have such a blunt tail and grows to be three and a half feet long. Both of these docile snakes eat rodents and other small animals.

Just as the rattlers stand out among the western snakes, the Gila monster is the most spectacular of the lizards. As the only venomous lizard of the United States, and one of only two reptiles with venom glands in the lower rather than the upper jaw, the Gila monster has a claim to fame. Moreover, it is a venomous reptile protected by Arizona law. Gila monsters harm few people who do not handle or play with them. Though a big one is two feet long, the species is not aggressive and will not attack. In contrast to the rattlesnakes, it has a limited range, which extends from extreme southern Nevada southeastward through Arizona to the southwestern corner of New Mexico. Broad rocky canyons and arroyos with permanent or intermittent streams are its favorite haunts. The scales of the Gila monster suggest beads and the gaudy pattern is a mixture of black and pink, orange or yellow.

The second largest lizard of the West is the chuckwalla, which may be sixteen inches long, and has a range much like that of the Gila monster. Chuckwallas have loose folds of skin on the neck and sides and are perfectly harmless. Arid, relatively barren, rock-strewn slopes are the haunts of this reptile. When alarmed it retreats into rocky crevices and inflates the body so that it is tightly wedged in place and cannot easily be removed.

The western lizards that may almost rival the Gila monster in popularity are the so-called horned toads, which are more properly known as horned lizards. These unmistakable reptiles have wide, spiny bodies, large legs, and a crown of long, sharp projections set in a row around the back and sides of the head, the "horns." One or more of seven species may be found in almost every part of the West. Being well camouflaged, they are not readily seen. Occasionally one, when annoyed, will squirt a fine stream of blood from the eye. Horned lizards are popular as pets but do not live well in captivity. They feed on ants. The body of an adult is only about three or four inches long and the tail is short.

The two largest groups of lizards in the West are the spiny lizards and the whiptails. Spiny lizards may be found over nearly all western country, but the whiptails do not occur in Montana and Washington. The spiny lizards are great climbers and often prefer rocky areas. There they are seen in plain view until alarmed, when they rapidly disappear into crevices. Some males have blue patches on the belly and the throat, and the scales of the back in all the species are pointed and project more or less upward, giving a spiny appearance. In contrast, the whiptails dash over the ground and it is impossible to see that the back is covered with granular scales, the belly with eight longitudinal rows of squarish plates. Whiptails are always on the move and are incredibly hard to catch. The reproductive habits of some species are indeed unusual: there are no males, the females reproducing by parthenogenesis. Only a few other lizards of the world do this.

The collared lizard is robust and has a massive head and long tail. It lives in the dry areas east of the Rocky Mountains and southward toward Mexico but does not occur in Washington, Montana, or Wyoming. It has a conspicuous black and white collar, and the body is more or less clearly spotted. The collared lizard is a great runner, and, when pushed, may run on its hind legs. The leopard lizard, a close relative, lacks the collar but has more conspicuous spotting. The zebra-tailed lizard lives in dry areas from Nevada southward and has a slender tail with black bars under it. When running rapidly this lizard curls the tail upward and forward, bringing the black bars into view. The alligator lizard has a remote resemblance to a young alligator, and can be recognized by the deep fold along each side of the body. They are found north and west of the Rocky Mountains and in the relatively moist forests of southeastern Arizona and extreme southwestern New Mexico.

The western United States is not turtle country; in fact, a whole section of the central part of the West is virtually devoid of turtles. There are only three kinds that might be called truly western. One of these is the western pond turtle of the western parts of Washington and Oregon, and most of California; it is also found in a tiny corner of western Nevada. In ninety-eight percent of its range no other turtle lives, therefore recognition of it is easy. The next truly western species is the Sonora mud turtle of Arizona and the southwestern corner of New Mexico. It is an aquatic, woodland reptile. The third truly western species is the desert tortoise of extreme southern Nevada, extreme southeastern California, and western Arizona. It is so attractive that it is protected by law. Desert tortoises are often picked up by travelers to take home for pets, but this practice might only result in their extermination now that roads cross the deserts in all directions.

One species, the painted turtle, found over nearly all of the eastern United States, extends its range northwestward through Montana and adjacent areas on to Washington and extreme northern Oregon. It is thoroughly aquatic and may be recognized by the smooth olive or black upper shell, the front edge of which is bordered with yellow; sometimes there is a network and stripe of yellow on this shell. A few other species of turtles enter the southern part of the West, but their ranges are limited.

The largest of turtles, the marine leatherback, occurs off the coast of California, Oregon, and Washington. The shell is covered with smooth, leathery skin.

See J. Frank Dobie, *Rattlesnakes* (1965); Laurence M. Klauber, *Rattlesnakes: Their Habits, Life Histories, and Influence on Mankind*, 2 vols. (1956); and Robert C. Stebbins, *Amphibians and Reptiles of Western North America* (1954) and *A Field Guide to Western Reptiles and Amphibians* (1966).—C. H. P.

Republican party, 1856-1896. Republican party policies toward and its popularity in the West changed markedly between 1856 and 1896. The free-soil and economic programs of the early party in the 1850s had great appeal in western states and territories, but the impact of those programs once put into law was disillusioning. And after 1865 the Republican party became identified increasingly with eastern positions on issues that concerned the West.

Plans for the future development of the West played a crucial role in the formation of the Republican party and its initial triumph in 1860. A diverse coalition, the

Republicans nevertheless agreed on opposition to the extension of slavery into the western territories, a position that was popular in the free states of the West where free-soil sentiment was strong. Promised economic programs—federal aid to a Pacific railroad, rivers and harbors improvements, and free homesteads to heads of families—augmented the appeal of the party in that section.

Once in power during the Civil War, the Republicans enacted many of their promised programs and thereby disposed of much of the public domain. The Homestead Act of 1862 offered 160 acres to heads of families after five years of continuous residence. The Morrill Land Grant College Act of 1862 granted loyal states thirty thousand acres for each senator and representative for the purpose of endowing at least one agricultural college. The Civil War Congress also chartered the Union Pacific, Central Pacific, and Northern Pacific railroads and gave them vast land grants to help finance construction. The net result of these programs, however, proved disappointing to farmers and laborers. Few eastern workers could take advantage of the Homestead Act, and it benefited speculators and large landholders, not small farmers. Railroad grants contained much of the choicest land and prevented settlement of much of the rest. Corporations and monopolies, not the individual farmer, benefited most from Republican programs.

Between 1865 and 1896 the giveaway continued. Land grants to railroads stopped in 1871, but by that time Republican-dominated governments had given 134 million acres directly to the roads. In the 1880s and 1890s railroad ownership of land was a major target of agrarian protest (SEE AGRARIAN MOVEMENTS). Republicans were also in part responsible for the Desert Land Act of 1877 and the Timber and Stone Act of 1878, which helped cattle barons and timber magnates monopolize public lands. Thus the land policies of the Republican party after 1865 identified it with monopolists and diminished its popularity among western agrarians.

Other Republican policies between 1865 and 1896 seemed to serve the East at the expense of the West. Republicans favored high tariffs, which most western consumers disliked. Laborers in California and other states wanted to restrict Chinese immigration, but until 1882 Republican presidents foiled any such move. By 1884, however, Republicans were openly advocating Chinese exclusion.

After 1873 the currency question was of greatest interest to western agrarians faced with falling prices, and Republican policy on that issue was unacceptable to the West. Westerners wanted inflation after 1873, at first with greenbacks, but increasingly after the mid-1870s through the free coinage of silver (see SILVER ISSUE). The latter remedy won additional support from western silver miners interested in a government market for their product. From the western point of view, Republicans could be blamed for currency contraction after the Civil War, pledging the payment of the national debt in gold, the demonetization of silver and thus the adoption of the gold standard in 1873 (the notorious Crime of '73 as westerners later called it), the veto of an inflation bill in 1874, and the Specie Resumption Act of 1875, all of which seemed deflationary. Republicans were also responsible for the National Banking System, which favored the East at the expense of the South and West.

Moreover, Republicans defeated efforts to get free silver by severely limiting the amount of silver to be purchased by the government in the Bland-Allison Act of 1878 and the Sherman Silver Purchase Act of 1890. In 1896, when the free silver crusade reached an apogee in the West, the Republicans pledged themselves to the gold standard. This action caused western silverites to bolt the party. Together, Republican currency and land policies helped weaken the popularity the party had won in the West before and during the Civil War. Indeed, their policies played a major role in the rise of the Populist party there.

See ELECTIONS OF 1856-1896.

George Mayer, *The Republican Party, 1854-1966* (1967), is a general history of the party. The popularity of the Republican free-soil position in the West is discussed in Eugene Berwanger, *The Frontier Against Slavery: Western Anti-Negro Prejudice and the Slavery Extension Controversy* (1967). The best discussion of the impact of Republican land policies is still Fred A. Shannon, *The Farmer's Last Frontier: Agriculture, 1860-1897* (1945). A lucid analysis of the currency question can be found in Walter T. K. Nugent, *The Money Question During Reconstruction* (1967).—M. F. H.

revivalism. Revivalism, a phenomenon of Protestantism, appeared first in the English colonies of North America in the Great Awakening of the early eighteenth century. It crested in the United States in the first half of the nineteenth century and continued, with declining importance, far into the twentieth century. Revivalism stemmed from the Reformation emphasis on the priesthood of all believers. It was an aspect of pietism, a type of religious expression that emphasized the feelings in contrast to insistence upon the acceptance of formal creeds. The salvation of men and women in the eternal life provided the central theme of pietism. The preaching in pietism sought in the hope of salvation to bring persons to a conviction of sin and to repentance.

The cresting of revivalism began with the Second Awakening, which got under way in the 1790s and continued past the turn of the century. The Second Awakening had two different but related aspects. East of the Appalachian Mountains it took the form of a quickening of life and an enlargement of membership in existent churches. West of the mountains a spectacular and famous episode called the Great Revival brought organized religion to the unchurched communities of a forest frontier, especially to Kentucky and Tennessee.

The eastern manifestation of the Second Awakening represented a pendulum swing away from religious indifference. The preoccupations and disruptions of the American Revolution had prevented any significant advance of organized religion. The conflict lessened the influence of the Church of England in America, established originally in the southern colonies and represented by prominent congregations in northern seaports, for some Anglican clergy and parishioners had espoused the Loyalist cause. At the same time American intellectuals were profoundly affected by the deistic rationalism of the Enlightenment. Contact with French officers during the American Revolution, but more especially the outbreak of the French Revolution, gave popularity to the Parisian idea of setting up a "Goddess of Reason." Rationalism became a fad on college campuses. The number of undergraduates willing to make a profession of Christianity dropped to a small minority. But the shocking executions of the Reign of Terror caused a reaction against the French Enlightenment. When Timothy Dwight became president of Yale in 1794, he began through weekly sermons and in classroom sessions a determined attack upon deistic rationalism. Mingling in his sermons rational argument and emotional appeal, as his grandfather, Jonathan Edwards, had done, Dwight brought quiet revivals to Yale. Such revivals, carefully guarded against extremism, spread widely in New England. In Pennsylvania and Virginia the reaction against popular deism centered in three colleges of Presbyterian origin in the backwoods frontier of those states: Hampden-Sidney, Washington College (now Washington and Lee), and Jefferson College (now Washington and Jefferson). In these institutions student revivals produced committed preachers who carried a quiet Presbyterian revivalism to the frontier west of the Appalachians.

At the turn of the century the scattered backwoods settlements of Tennessee and Kentucky were characterized by rareness of books, rudimentary development of schools, widespread illiteracy, ignorance, uncouthness, and violence. In 1801 the institution of the camp meeting came into being as an adjustment to a society of scattered settlements and often lonely cabins. This now famous revival meeting was held in August 1801 in Cane Ridge, Kentucky. Thousands of backwoods folk traveling in wagons, on horseback, or on foot came to it. Some brought tents. All brought food, for the meeting would last several days. Presbyterian, Methodist, and Baptist preachers also came to Cane Ridge. They exhorted from several rough platforms set up in clearings opened for the occasion. Several preachers in different parts of the campground addressed the crowds at the same time all through the summer days and, by the light of great fires, far into the nights. The people sang simple and sometimes improvised hymns characterized by a lively rhythm, appeals to fight "old Satan," and glimpses beyond the pearly gates of heaven. The prolonged and intense emotionalism of the great crowds produced extraordinary hysterical phenomena. The revival also produced a great company of recruits for the emerging frontier churches.

Peter Cartwright, most famous of the early Methodist circuit riders, described the Cane Ridge camp meeting in his *The Backwoods Preacher: An Autobiography* (1858). "Ministers of almost all denominations flocked in from far and near. The meeting was kept up by day and night. Thousands heard the mighty work, and came on foot, on horseback, in carriages and wagons. . . . As Presbyterian, Methodist, and Baptist ministers all united in the blessed work of this meeting, when they returned home to their different congregations, and carried news of this mighty work, the revival spread rapidly throughout the land. . . ." Cartwright added with a touch of denominational pride: "Time rolled on, population increased fast around us, horse thieves and murderers were driven away and civilization advanced considerably. Ministers of different denominations came in and preached through the country; but the Methodist preachers were the pioneer messengers of salvation in these ends of the earth."

Cane Ridge was never duplicated on the frontier in the size of the crowds or the number of converts. But it set a pattern followed for many years. While Mrs. Anthony Trollope was a guest of an English lady who lived in the Ohio valley in the late 1820s, she visited a camp meeting in "the backwoods of Indiana" (and described it in her *Domestic Manners of the Americans* (1832). The ladies arrived at the campground shortly before midnight and found most of the frontier people crowded in tents singing and praying after the exhortations heard earlier in the evening. "At midnight a horn sounded through the camp . . . and we presently saw them flocking from all sides to the front of the preachers' stand." She thought there were some two thousand persons in the crowd. "One of the preachers began in a low nasal tone, and . . . assured us of the enormous depravity of man as he comes from the hands of his Maker, and of his perfect sanctification after he has wrestled sufficiently with the Lord. . . . The admiration of the crowd was evinced by almost constant cries of 'Amen! Amen!' 'Jesus! Jesus!' 'Glory! Glory!' and the like." The preacher then issued what had become the traditional invitation to come forward to what he called "the pen," an open space immediately below the stand. "The crowd fell back. . . . The preachers came down from their stand and placed themselves in the midst of it [the pen], beginning to sing a hymn, calling upon the penitents to come forth." Gradually the crowd joined in the singing of the chorus. "It is certain that the combined voices of such a multitude, heard at dead of night, from the depths of their eternal forests . . . the lurid glare thrown by the altar fires on the woods beyond, did altogether produce a fine and solemn effect . . ." Then "above a hundred persons, nearly all females, came forward, uttering howlings and groans, so terrible that I shall never cease to shudder when I recall them." They all fell on their knees, "but this posture was soon changed for others that permitted greater scope for the convulsive movements of their limbs. . . . They threw about their limbs with such incessant and violent motion, that I was every instant expecting some serious accident to occur. . . . Hysterical sobbings, convulsive groans, shrieks and screams the most appalling, burst forth on all sides. I felt sick with horror." Mrs. Trollope and her friend fled to their carriage about 3 A.M. and spent the rest of the night there. "At day-break I saw the whole camp as joyously and eagerly employed in preparing and devouring their substantial breakfasts as if the night had been passed in dancing . . ."

The appeal of the camp meeting was a thrill in the here and now and the pleasure of escape from the loneliness of the isolated farmstead. But the preachers backed by the authority of the Bible, the very words of God, brought large numbers into the fold. On the western frontier revivalism, either as practiced in the camp meeting or in the much more limited "protracted meetings" in a single church, provided the standard technique for recruiting church membership.

Charles G. Finney, in the years from 1824, when the St. Lawrence Presbytery licensed him to preach, to 1835, when he began to lecture on theology at Oberlin College, became the greatest and most famous evangelist America had produced. He came from upstate New York, "the burnt-over district," so named because of the succession of revivals that had flamed across the region. As preacher and counselor he displayed hypnotic power. He invited persons who attended his great meetings

and who came under conviction of sin to come forward
to the "anxious bench." In the followup small prayer
meetings, he challenged a sex taboo of the times by
encouraging women to pray in the presence of men. His
meetings sometimes produced hysterical phenomena,
and his direct attacks from the pulpit on the evils of a
particular community brought retaliatory persecutions.
But in many cases he effected lasting changes. Finney's
revivals in the middle and eastern states made him a
national figure. They also made revivalism an urban as
well as a rural phenomenon. In 1835 he summed up his
experience and techniques in a book that went through
many editions and was widely read abroad.

As the United States became increasingly industrialized and urbanized, Finney's chief successors—
Dwight L. Moody in the last quarter of the nineteenth
century, Billy Sunday in the early decades of the twentieth, and Billy Graham in the middle decades—
followed his lead in directing their crusades to the
people of the cities. After Horace Bushnell's powerful
attack on revivalism in *Christian Nurture* (1847), however, American Protestantism emphasized more and
more education in Sunday schools and young peoples'
activities as the method for maintaining and increasing
membership in the churches.

See Timothy L. Smith, *Revivalism and Social Reform in
Mid-nineteenth Century America* (1957); Harvey Wish,
Society and Thought in Early America (1950); and Louis B.
Wright, *Culture on the Moving Frontier* (1955).—R. H. G.

Rhode Island, settlement of. Rhode Island was
founded by people whose religious views made them
unwelcome in the Massachusetts Bay Colony. When Puritan civil authorities threatened to arrest the outspoken
Roger Williams in 1635, he fled south and purchased
from the Indians land that he named Providence in
recognition "of God's merciful providence unto me in
my distress." The Indians living in the area respected
Williams, perhaps because he was one of the few who
understood the Algonquian tongue, a "barbarous rockie
speech." In 1643 he completed *A Key into the Language of
America*, a dictionary and discussion of the local Indians. Williams was able to put his friendship to diplomatic use. In 1636 he successfully discouraged a dangerous alliance between the neighboring Narragansetts and
the warring Pequots of Connecticut—a negotiation that
nevertheless caused him to dream nightly of the Pequots' "bloody knives at my own throat."

In 1638 another group of Massachusetts exiles, led by
Anne Hutchinson and William Coddington, settled at
Portsmouth on the island of Aquidneck in Narragansett
Bay. Internal disputes, however, soon divided this new
community, and in 1639 Coddington established his
own town on the southern tip of the island, called New-
port. The next year Portsmouth and Newport were
forcibly joined under a common government, which
Coddington hoped would form the basis of a separate
New England colony. A fourth village was founded by
Samuel Gorton, an eccentric individual who was expelled from Portsmouth and Providence, as well as from
Boston, for his "bewitching and bemadding" beliefs.
Thus, by the early 1640s there were four independent
communities within the Rhode Island territory, each
having little or no interest in the welfare of its neighbors.
The rest of New England looked with disdain upon the
whole region, and one man once graphically explained,

"Roade Island is (pardon necessity's word of truth) a
rodde to those that love to live in order,—a road, refuge,
asylum to evil livers."

The leaders of both Massachusetts and Plymouth
realized that the Rhode Island settlements did not possess a formal English charter for their lands, and in the
early 1640s, they were apparently planning to annex the
entire Narragansett area. In any case the people of
Rhode Island saw it as an ominous sign that they were
not invited to join the New England Confederation, a
military alliance formed in 1643, and they quickly dispatched Roger Williams to England in order to defend
their interests. Although the mother country was in the
midst of civil war, Williams was able to obtain a patent
from Parliament confirming Rhode Island's right to
exist. This document, issued in 1644, joined the four
towns under the title Providence Plantations, but
nowhere did it state the exact form of government that
these communities should adopt. No steps were taken to
work out the details of central government until 1647,
when a meeting of freemen was called at Portsmouth. It
was decided that the colony would be ruled by an elected
president, a council of assistants, and a representative
assembly, which was to meet in each of the towns in
rotation. These "acts and orders of 1647" also created a
judicial system. But despite these efforts at unification,
Rhode Island remained divided. Newport and Portsmouth stubbornly maintained their own independence,
while Coddington continued to scheme for a charter of
his own. It is not surprising that Williams complained
bitterly in 1654 of the "divisions and disorders within
ourselves." The colonial historian Charles M. Andrews
has written, "It is a remarkable fact in the history of New
England that such a colony as Rhode Island should have
emerged from its unpromising beginnings and developed in later times into a well compacted and united
state."

When reports from England of the Puritan Commonwealth's downfall and of the Stuart Restoration reached
Rhode Island in 1660, the colonists immediately
realized that their parliamentary patent might be in
danger. They sent Dr. John Clarke to London in order
to petition for a new, more secure charter, but they
failed to supply him with the funds that were necessary
to win friends at court. While Clarke was waiting for a
hearing, he learned that the Connecticut charter of
1662 had awarded that colony half of Rhode Island's
territory—all of the land west of Narragansett Bay.
Ironically, the man who engineered this land grab, John
Winthrop, Jr., soon came to Rhode Island's assistance,
persuading royal officials to grant the colony a charter
similar to Connecticut's. The Rhode Island charter of
1663 essentially sanctioned the system of government
that had been established in 1647. A governor replaced
the president, but all the colony's rulers continued to be
elected by the freemen. Unlike most of the other American provinces, Rhode Island's laws were not subject to
English review. The charter also confirmed the long-
standing policy of religious toleration, stating that "noe
person within the colonie, at any time hereafter shall be
in any wise molested, punished, disquieted or called in
question for any difference in opinions in matters of
religion." The people of Rhode Island were pleased
with their charter, but they were determined to resist
their neighbors' land claims with all their resources. For

more than sixty years, the colony was locked in bitter boundary disputes with Connecticut, Plymouth, and Massachusetts. Although Rhode Island held its own in these battles, the constant litigation drained money and energy that the poor agricultural colony could have used better elsewhere. With great wisdom, Williams observed that the unity of New England was being destroyed by "a depraved appetite after the great vanities, dreams and shadows of this vanishing life, great portions of land, land in this wilderness . . ."

There is no satisfactory account of early Rhode Island. The best are Charles M. Andrews, *The Colonial Period of American History*, vol. II (1936), and Herbert L. Osgood, *The American Colonies in the Seventeenth Century*, vol. I (1904). On the land disputes, see Richard S. Dunn, "John Winthrop, Jr., and the Narragansett Country," *William and Mary Quarterly*, vol. 13 (1956). The two best accounts of Williams' life are Edmund S. Morgan, *Roger Williams: The Church and the State* (1967); and Ola E. Winslow, *Master Roger Williams* (1957). See also Mauro Calamandrei, "Neglected Aspects of Roger Williams' Thought," *Church History* (1952).—T. H. B.

Rhodes, Eugene Manlove (1869-1934). Novelist and short-story writer. Rhodes was born in Tecumseh, Nebraska, and, in 1882, moved to Engle, New Mexico, where he was later to work as a cowboy. Rhodes' schooling was informal, except for two years' study at the University of the Pacific, in San Jose, California. He was, however, always an avid reader, and constantly referred to the Bible, Shakespeare, and the classics of English literature in his writing. In 1899 he traveled to New York, where in the same year he married May Davison Purple, a widow with whom he had previously carried on a literary correspondence. After returning to New Mexico for several years, the couple lived in New York where, Rhodes said humorously, he was snowed in for twenty years. In 1926 he and his wife returned to New Mexico, but moved again, in 1931, to California because of Rhodes' worsening health. Rhodes was buried in the San Andres Mountains of New Mexico, near his old ranch, under a stone marked with the simple epitaph *pasó por aquí* ("passed by here"), taken from one of his own stories.

Rhodes is one of the relatively few writers about the West who was a westerner himself, and the only cowboy author who achieved a widespread reputation, due largely to the efforts of William Henry HUTCHINSON. Rhodes returned to New Mexico constantly in his fiction, much of which is very highly particularized. Many of the people whom Rhodes knew in New Mexico appear in his books, some under their own names, as do places that he had lived in or visited and cattle companies for which he had worked. His writings include eight novels: *Good Men and True* (1910), *Bransford in Arcadia* (1914), *West Is West* (1917), *Stepsons of Light* (1921), *Copper Streak Trail* (1922), *The Trusty Knaves* (1933), *Beyond the Desert* (1934), and *The Proud Sheriff* (1935); several novelettes, of which one, "Pasó por Aquí" (1926), has often been singled out as Rhodes' masterpiece; and a number of short stories and articles.

Rhodes' firsthand experience of the West enabled him to avoid the obvious anachronisms and impossibilities of much pulp western fiction. The weakness of many of his stories may also be traced to his biography, for on occasion his fiction deteriorates into a tedious recapitulation of anecdotes from his own life coupled with rather snobbish special pleading for the moral superiority of cowboys and those who adhere to a sentimentalized western code. Though at its worst Rhodes' fiction is didactic, at its best it is evocative of an intangible but very real western spirit. Rhodes' sense for the physical presence of the Southwest sets him apart from the generality of western writers, for whom the West is often little more than a picturesque backdrop to a melodramatic story.

The only easily accessible samples of Rhodes' work are in *The Best Novels and Stories of Eugene Manlove Rhodes*, edited by Frank V. Dearing, and *The Rhodes Reader* (1957), edited by W. H. Hutchinson. See also Edwin W. Gaston, Jr., *Eugene Manlove Rhodes, Cowboy Chronicler* (1967); W. H. Hutchinson, *A Bar Cross Man* (1956), and *A Bar Cross Liar* (1959); and May Davison Rhodes, *The Hired Man on Horseback* (1938).—J. K. F.

Rhyolite, Nevada. Ghost town. Rhyolite underwent an unusually short lifespan, even for a western mining town. The town was laid out in 1905 following a series of gold strikes in 1904 and reached its peak in 1906 when the population climbed to sixteen thousand; but by 1911 the town was dying with the depletion of the mines of the district. In this short period the diggings in the Rhyolite area produced over $3 million in gold. Today an elaborate railroad station, ruins of stone and steel office buildings, and a house built of bottles are the only remainders of a once-prosperous mining community.

See Nell Murbarger, *Ghosts of the Glory Trail* (1956); and Muriel S. Wolle, *The Bonanza Trail* (1953). —R. B. W.

Ribault, Jean (1520?-1565). French explorer and colonizer. Ribault was born in Dieppe and became a Huguenot. A sailor of skill, he became one of the most competent of Admiral Gaspard de Coligny's captains. Early in the 1560s, Coligny planned to establish in the New World a refuge for the Huguenots, which would also extend the French empire at the expense of Spain and unite Frenchmen against the Spaniards. Ribault was his choice to head the expedition with René de Laudonnière as second in command. In 1562 they set sail with three ships and one hundred and fifty colonists and on May 1 entered the St. Johns River, which Ribault called the River of May. A stone column was erected and the land claimed for France.

The expedition sailed north along the coast and planted a small colony at Port Royal, South Carolina. Ribault then returned to France to seek aid for the new colony. Religious civil war, which had erupted meanwhile, detained Ribault, and his colony was abandoned. Fleeing to England to seek aid, he was asked to collaborate with the establishment of an English colony in North America. Upon refusing he was imprisoned.

In the meantime, a second Huguenot expedition, under Laudonnière, had founded Fort Caroline near the mouth of the St. Johns River. Securing his release in 1565, Ribault set out to reinforce the colony with a fleet of seven ships. About the same time a Spanish force under Pedro Menéndez de Avilés arrived to drive out the French. He organized a settlement at St. Augustine, which Ribault set out to attack. The French fleet was scattered and wrecked by a storm, however, as Menéndez advanced against the French fort overland. After destroying it and most of its garrison, Menéndez returned to St. Augustine and learned of the French marooned to the south of him. Judiciously taking advantage of their separation, Menéndez dealt with them in three groups. Although most of the last group were returned to Europe, most of the persons in the first two groups were slaughtered. The second group, in which Ribault was found, was put to the knife at Mantanzas Inlet on October 12, 1565.

Despite his sudden and bloody end, Ribault made a lasting contribution to Florida history in the narrative of his discovery. To it "we owe more of our knowledge of the ancient inhabitants of Florida than to the sum total of Spanish sources," said anthropologist John R. Swanton.

See Jeanette Thurber Connor, *Jean Ribaut: The Whole and True Discouerye of Terra Florida* (1927); see also a facsimile edition published in 1964 with a valuable introduction by David L. Dowd. Historians have differed over the spelling of Ribault, but in 1928 the dispute was resolved when French archivist Charles de La Roncière found a receipt for artillery signed "Ribault," dated May 21, 1565.—H. J. D.

Rich, Charles Coulson (1809-1883). Mormon leader. Rich, a native of Kentucky, rose to· prominence as a Mormon leader not long after he entered Joseph Smith's new church in Illinois in 1832. He traveled over the country as a missionary for several years before joining a new Mormon community in Missouri early in 1838. After hostilities between the Saints and the anti-Mormons broke out on election day in nearby Gallatin, Rich took command of the Mormon forces during an emergency in the battle of Crooked River, October 24-25, when the state militia renewed the fight. After this clash, the Mormons had to evacuate to Illinois, where they founded Nauvoo. There he soon became a brigadier general in the Nauvoo Legion, and by 1844 he stood second to Joseph Smith in command of the Mormon army.

Rich held a position of responsibility during Mormon removal to Salt Lake and in 1849 he became a member of the Quorum of Twelve Apostles. Two years later he and Amasa M. Lyman founded San Bernardino, California, to give the Mormons a base near the Pacific Coast. In 1860 he went on a European mission; in 1863, he founded the Mormon Bear Lake valley settlements, which unexpectedly turned out to be mostly in Idaho rather than Utah. With a substantial family of six wives and fifty children, Rich was the most conspicuous early Idaho Mormon leader. Unembarrassed by his Idaho residence, he continued to serve in the Utah legislature as well as in the highest policy-making body of his church, symbolizing the close Mormon connection between Utah and adjacent southeastern Idaho.

See Leonard J. Arrington, *Charles C. Rich* (1974); and John Henry Evans, *Charles Coulson Rich: Pioneer Builder of the West* (1936).—M. W.

Richardson, Rupert N. (1891-   ). Historian. Born in Caddo, Texas, Richardson studied at Simmons College (later Hardin-Simmons) in Abilene, Texas, the University of Chicago, and the University of Texas. In 1917 he began teaching at Hardin-Simmons College, where he remained until his retirement in 1953, serving as the institution's president from 1945 until 1953. Always active in local and regional historical societies, Richardson also served as president of the Southwestern Social Science Association in 1936.

Much of Richardson's published work dealt with Texas history. One of his first books was *The Commanche Barrier to Plains Settlement* (1933), which reviewers found to be a most useful contribution to the history of Indians in Texas. He also made an attempt to use a regional approach in *The Greater Southwest* (1934), which emphasized economic, social, and cultural developments. Meanwhile, he authored one of the most widely used textbooks on the history of Texas, *Texas: The Lone Star State* (1941), a survey of the history of the state from its early beginnings until the eve of World War II.

Despite his increasing administrative responsibilities, Richardson continued his research into various phases of Texas history. In 1963 he produced *The Frontier of Northwest Texas, 1846-1876* and the following year wrote a shorter work about President Woodrow Wilson's confidante, *Colonel Edward M. House, the Texas Years.*—G. D. N.

Richter, Conrad (1890-1968). Novelist. Richter spent most of his life near the small town of Pine Grove, Pennsylvania, where he was born. His formal education ceased with high school, though he has been the recipient of two honorary degrees. In 1951 Richter received the Pulitzer Prize for *The Town* (1950) and in 1961 a National Book Award for *The Waters of Kronos* (1960).

Richter's ability to breathe life into the hoary clichés of western fiction remains his most significant attribute. Even *The Sea of Grass* (1937), his best-known novel, is almost defiantly unoriginal. Its plot is the well-worn story of the conflict between the cattlemen and the "nesters" for control of the open range. *The Light in the Forest* (1953) is equally derivative from the long series of stories concerning the plight of whites captured by the Indians. But Richter was able, partly by his style and partly through his attitude toward his material, to transform his stories into something unique. They have the quality of reminiscence (in fact, *The Sea of Grass* is written from the point of view of a doctor remembering his youth) or beloved family anecdote, worn smooth through constant retelling, nostalgic, and somewhat sad.

See Edwin W. Gaston, Jr., *Conrad Richter* (1965). —J. K. F.

Riegel, Robert E. (1897-   ). Historian. Riegel was born in Reading, Pennsylvania. He secured his education at Carroll College in Waukesha, Wisconsin, and the University of Wisconsin, where Frederick L. Paxson, a leading western historian in the Turnerian tradition, aroused his interest in frontier history. Riegel's entire teaching career was spent at Dartmouth College in Hanover, New Hampshire, where he served from 1922 until his formal retirement in 1964. During these years he taught popular courses on frontier history and was a frequent guest lecturer at other institutions. From 1964 until 1967 he was H. Y. Benedict Professor at the University of Texas at El Paso.

Riegel showed an aptitude for generalization in the field of western American history quite early. His first book, *The Story of Western Railroads* (1926), was widely hailed at the time—and by later critics—as the best available summary of the subject, and it was widely used for many years after its first appearance. A few years later he wrote a textbook, *America Moves West* (1930), designed for college courses. The volume surveyed the history of the West from its beginnings until the late nineteenth century. During the three decades after its first initial appearance it was one of the most popular and widely used textbooks in the field and established Riegel as one of the more articulate spokesmen about the history of the frontier. After 1930 Riegel turned his research interests in other directions, focusing on the social history of the Jacksonian era.

Riegel's main contributions to western history were to synthesize skillfully the development of railroads on the nineteenth-century frontier, and to provide one of the best introductory surveys of the entire scope of western frontier development.—G. D. N.

Riel, Louis [David] (1844-1885). Leader of the western Canadian métis. Riel was born at St. Boniface, Red River Settlement (present-day Manitoba). In his youth he was sent to Montreal to study for the priesthood but was not of suitable temperament for that vocation and returned to the West. When in 1869 the Hudson's Bay Company surrendered Rupert's Land to the British crown and preparations were begun to transfer the territory to Canadian jurisdiction, the métis (people of mixed French-Canadian and Indian ancestry) of the Red River Settlement became greatly agitated and fearful that their land rights and semibarbaric way of life would not be respected. Under Riel's leadership they organized the Comité National des Métis, which in October 1869 prevented the Canadian governor-to-be, William MacDougal, from entering the territory and in November seized Fort Garry.

Enlisting the support of many English settlers in the area who were also reluctant to come under Canadian governmental authority, the métis established a provisional government with Riel as president and opened negotiations with the Canadian commissioners. Terms were agreed upon by which the Red River Settlement became the province of Manitoba in 1870, but a peaceful disposition of the issue was prevented when some Canadian sympathizers were executed by a métis courtmartial. Denied amnesty after this act, many rebellious métis withdrew to the Saskatchewan River settlements. When a military expedition under Colonel Garnet Wolseley was sent in August 1870 to maintain order in Manitoba, Riel fled Fort Garry. His local popularity undiminished, Riel was elected representative from Provencher district to the federal parliament in 1873 and 1874 but was denied his seat and banished from Canada in 1875. Between 1876 and 1878 he was confined to mental asylums in Quebec. After he was released he went to Montana, where he became an American citizen under the name David Riel and taught for several years in the Jesuit mission school at Sun River.

In 1884 the métis on the Saskatchewan were again threatened by advancing agricultural settlement and by the Canadian Pacific Railway's surveys across their lands. When the Canadian government failed to grant them land reserves or guarantee their rights, the métis appealed to Riel, who returned to Canada to lead a peaceful protest movement in the Saskatchewan valley. During the early spring of 1885, however, Riel became increasingly provocative and erratic. He eschewed constitutionally permissible protest and began to see conspiracies developing against him, even among his old friends. Some of his statements indicate he was seeing

himself in messianic terms. Supported by his radical followers, he broke with the Catholic Church, established another métis provisional government, and attempted to enlist the Indians to his cause. After incidents of violence at Frog Creek and the defeat of a Mounted Police force by métis at Duck Lake in March, the government sent an expedition under General Middleton that defeated Riel's army at Batoche on May 12. Riel was captured and tried for treason before an English-speaking jury at Regina. He repudiated his counsel's plea of insanity and was convicted. After several postponements Riel was hanged on November 16, 1885. His execution set off a nationwide political uproar. Whether he was sane or not is still a matter of controversy, but to the métis Riel remains a hero whose memory yet intrudes upon the uneasy relations between Canadians of English and French descent.

See Hartwell Bowsfield, ed., *Louis Riel: The Rebel and the Hero* (1971); A. G. Morice, *A Critical History of the Red River Insurrection* (1935); G. H. Needler, *Louis Riel* (1957); and G. F. G. Stanley, *The Birth of Western Canada* (1936).—P. R. M.

rifles. See GUNS; and KENTUCKY RIFLE.

Riggs, Lynn (1899-1954). Poet and playwright. Born near Claremore in the Cherokee Nation of Indian Territory (present-day Oklahoma) Riggs was the son of a cattleman and banker. In 1917 Riggs graduated from Eastern University Preparatory School at Claremore and began a writing career, which included stints as reporter for the *Wall Street Journal*, the Tulsa *Oil and Gas Journal*, and the Los Angeles *Times*. Three years later Riggs entered the University of Oklahoma and began spending his summers touring the West as a singer with a Chautauqua quartet. While at the university, Riggs wrote and produced his first play, *Cuckoo*.

He was attracted to the literary-artistic community at Santa Fe and Taos, New Mexico, and in 1925 his *Knives from Syria* was staged by the Santa Fe players. The following year he moved to New York, where he contributed poems to *The Nation* and *Poetry* and published his collected poems, *The Iron Dish* (1930). A Guggenheim Fellowship enabled Riggs to study and write in France. There he composed his play *Green Grow the Lilacs*, a nostalgic sketch of his childhood in Oklahoma set in the Indian Territory in the early 1900s. The Theater Guild presented the play, and it ran for sixty-four performances on Broadway, then went on tour, and was rated one of the ten best plays on Broadway in 1931. Critics praised Riggs's creative use of western folklore. Later Richard Rodgers and Oscar Hammerstein adapted *Green Grow the Lilacs* to *Oklahoma*.

His success obscured by the more famous Rogers and Hammerstein production, Riggs worked in Hollywood as scenario writer and was guest author and director on the faculties of Baylor University, Northwestern University, and the University of Iowa. Later plays included *Russet Mantle* (1936), *Cherokee Night* (1936), and *World Elsewhere* (1947).—A. M. G.

Rindisbacher, Peter (1806-1834). Painter. Rindisbacher received only a limited amount of schooling before coming with his family from Switzerland to America in 1821 to join a party of settlers destined for the earl of Selkirk's Red River Colony near present-day Winnipeg. Traveling overland from Hudson's Bay to Fort Douglas, fifteen-year-old Rindisbacher made many sketches of the Indians and animals of the northern wilderness and throughout the next five years contributed in small portion to the family's support through the sale of his drawings and watercolors. In 1826 and 1827 many of the settlers abandoned the Red River site and migrated south into Wisconsin Territory. Others, including the Rindisbachers, settled finally at St. Louis, Missouri, where in 1829 Peter established a studio and began contributing sporting scenes to the *American Turf Register*. He was beginning to make a name for himself as an illustrator of frontier life when he died at the age of twenty-eight.

Surviving examples of Rindisbacher's work are relatively scarce; collections in the United States are at the United States Military Academy at West Point; the Thomas Gilcrease Institute of American History and Art, Tulsa, Oklahoma; and the Peabody Museum, Harvard University. At least ten lithographic reproductions of his paintings are known to have appeared in the *American Turf* magazine and a portfolio of six others, entitled *Views in Hudson's Bay*, was issued in London before his death. Yet another of his pictures was selected as the frontispiece for volume one of Thomas L. Mc-Kenney and James Hall's *History of the Indian Tribes of North America* (1837).

Forty watercolors depicting the journey from Hudson's Bay to Fort Douglas and views of life in and around the Red River settlement are preserved in the Public Archives of Canada. Considered to be the earliest paintings to document English settlement in western Canada, these are probably the first genre works by any artist in the interior of North America. They are primitive in style, with more emphasis on detail than on aesthetic expression.

See Bernard DeVoto, *Across the Wide Missouri* (1947); A. M. Josephy, Jr., *The Artist Was a Young Man* (1970); and Harold McCracken, *Portrait of the Old West* (1962).—D. C. H.

Ringo, John (1844?-1882). Outlaw. Ringo was a mysterious, silent man. Since only scattered records on the facts of his life are available, he is more image than reality. Ringo emerges from the past as the idealized embodiment of the gentleman outlaw. Stories of his courage, honesty, and chivalry were common even in his own time. He was lionized by some who knew him in Tombstone, Arizona, and their recollections have dominated history's view of him. From these sources Ringo is characterized as an intellectual, a reserved and morose man who drank too much, an educated man obsessed with violence yet possessed of a sense of honor straight out of Sir Walter Scott. Some claim that his real name was really John Ringgold, that he hailed from California, and was college-educated. Others, presumably more reliable, insist that his name was indeed Ringo and that, while he attended school until age fourteen, he never made it to college. Missouri and Texas are suggested as possible birthplaces by still other observers, while some argue that he had family ties to the Youngers, Daltons, and Jameses. An accurate view of Ringo's early years seems unlikely until family papers reported to exist are finally released.

The first concrete record of Ringo is in Mason County, Texas, in 1875, where he was a cronie of Scott Cooley during the "Hoodoo War," one of Texas' numerous feuds. The feud began when a large body of citizens lynched four men for rustling cattle, and it grew into two full years of murder and mayhem. Ringo was involved in two murders, shooting one man down after his victim had invited Ringo and a companion to eat with him. Ringo was arrested for murder but escaped from jail in Lampasas. He was jailed at Austin later, released, and reported dead when he vanished from Texas. To that point in his career, at least, there is little evidence to support the romantic image.

He surfaced again in Galeyville, New Mexico, where he worked as a cowboy and was involved with Curly Bill BROCIUS and the Clanton-McLaury crowd in cattle-stealing excursions into Mexico. He was regarded as a loner, drank too much, and was feared as a deadly man with a gun. In December 1879 he shot a Louis Hancock in the neck when the man refused to drink with him. He was soon known in southeastern Arizona as "the king of the cowboys" and was involved in a number of barroom incidents. Lawman and outlaw alike feared and respected him; at least that is what old-timers insist.

On another occasion Ringo lost heavily in a poker game, left the room, and then returned to relieve the players of all their money at gunpoint. He later returned the money, calling the incident a joke. A deputy sheriff was sent out to arrest him, but Ringo promised the deputy he would report to the sheriff later. He came in as he promised and was shortly released. The Ringo legend maintains that this incident was evidence of his sense of honor, but many Tombstone residents regarded it as evidence of too much friendship between the sheriff and a local badman.

Although he was clearly identified with the Brocius-Clanton element in Cochise County, Arizona, he managed to steer clear of most of the Earp-Clanton troubles until after the OK Corral incident in 1881. There is strong evidence, however, that he was very much involved in the vendetta against the EARP BROTHERS. In January 1882 Ringo confronted Doc Holliday, an Earp supporter, on the streets of Tombstone and offered to shoot it out with him, but both men were promptly arrested before violence occurred. Wyatt Earp suspected that Ringo was a party to the murder of his brother Morgan in March 1882, although no real evidence was ever produced to prove it. Ringo was a member of the sheriff's posse that pursued the Earps when they left Tombstone for the last time shortly afterward.

In July 1882 Ringo grew despondent and began drinking heavily. On July 14 he was found dead, apparently a suicide. Some accounts insist that Frank Leslie, a drinking companion of Ringo's, killed him, but Wyatt Earp left a manuscript account detailing how *he* killed Ringo. So Ringo's death as well as his life is still plagued by unanswered questions.

What history lacks in the way of facts, old-timers and folklore have provided, with a portrait of a brooding, tragic figure, the prototype of the educated, fatalistic loner, with a past shrouded in mystery.

See Jack Burrows, "Ringo," *American West*, vol. 7 (1970).—G. L. R.

Rio Grande. The Rio Grande, the "great river," is anything but that over most of its course. Although it rises in the snow-capped peaks of Colorado in a zone of abundant precipitation, the Rio Grande is frequently shrunken by drought or bled thin by the irrigation

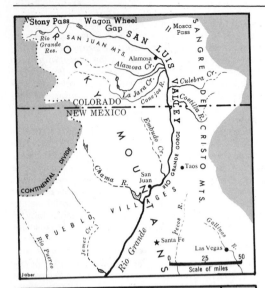

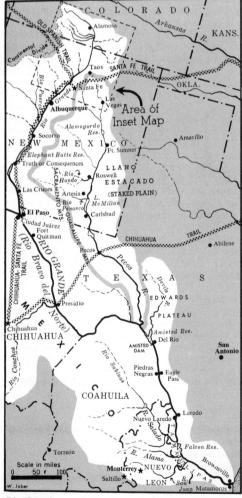

Rio Grande

ditches that lead its flow off to adjacent lands. Sometimes it ceases to be a river at all, and its bed lies baked in the sun. At other times torrents of water fill its channels; before the building of dams, water overflowed the banks and flooded the countryside. It has been a difficult river for men to manage although the Pueblo Indian tribes used its waters for irrigation before the Spanish appeared. Its flow is undependable and reaches a peak in late spring and early summer. It has been a barrier to east-west traffic, for in many places it flows in canyons or in broad, shallow, and sandy channels, making it difficult to ford and difficult to bridge. Man has also contributed to the set of problems. Through overuse and misuse of the land he has increased the sediment load and caused changes in the flow rates and characteristics of the stream.

Some of the most difficult management problems are associated with the international character of the stream. The limited water resources of the basin must be divided among the people of three American and four Mexican states—none of which are completely satisfied with the arrangements that have been made for dividing the meager quantities of water available in the stream. Along half its length the Rio Grande forms a part of the border between the United States and Mexico, with El Paso, Laredo, and Brownsville on the Texan side and Cindad Juárez, Nuevo Laredo, and Matamoros on the Mexican side. One of the problems with using it as a boundary is that no one is quite sure where the Rio Grande will be flowing next year. In the El Paso and Brownsville areas it has shifted its course appreciably since the border was first set by the International Boundary Commission in 1854. Additionally, most of the water flowing in the lower portion of the river comes from Mexican tributaries; out of the 185,000 square miles that comprise its watershed, more than 80,000 square miles lie in Mexico. Agreement with Mexico on the allocation of its waters was not reached until 1944.

The river rises near the summit of Stony Pass, Colorado, at an elevation of 12,584 feet, in one of America's most beautiful alpine regions in the San Juan Mountains. Here, melting snow and perpetual springs join to form a brook destined to flow some 1,800 miles into the Gulf of Mexico. The minute stream is soon joined by other tributaries rising under similar conditions through forty miles of beautiful mountain scenery. At an elevation of about 9,000 feet the valley broadens. Natural meadows provide feed for livestock, and the first permanent settlements appear. About thirty miles farther downstream the river flows through Wagon Wheel Gap and enters the San Luis Valley. Along the way its flow is augmented by water from Conejos and Alamosa rivers and La Jara, Culebra, and Costilla creeks. Trout abound in these waters and the area is a sportsman's paradise. However, most of the water is used for irrigating farmlands. Just below the border with New Mexico the river plunges into a spectacular canyon, the Rio Grande Gorge, and for about seventy-five miles flows through a region of lava flows. Then, just before it is joined by the Chama, the valley of the Rio Grande broadens out and irrigated fields appear again. It was here that the Spanish located their first capital, San Juan de los Caballeros, as they moved upstream from Chihuahua. From this point to just below El Paso portions of the floodplain support scattered agricultural oases—many of them farmed by Pueblo Indians who are continuing the ways of their centuries-old ancestors.

In this section the Rio Grande is joined by a number of small tributaries. Many of them are ephemeral, for much of the precipitation occurs in the form of summer thunderstorms. The main tributaries joining the river in New Mexico are the Rio Taos, Embudo Creek, Rio Chama, Jemez Creek, Rio Puerco, and Rio Salado. Ground water is pumped to supplement the water available from the river.

Below Fort Quitman, Texas, which marks the division point between the upper and lower Rio Grande, the river flows through dry, mountainous, and dissected plateau country as it passes through the Big Bend. The principal tributaries in this section are the Rio Conchos from Mexico and the Pecos and Devils rivers from Texas. After receiving the waters of the Pecos, the Rio Grande turns southeastward and flows across the Balcones Escarpment and through hilly, undulating country before reaching its delta section. In this part of its basin the Rio Grande receives its largest tributaries and has the greatest volume of water available for use. The Mexican rivers Salado, Alamo, and San Juan contribute the bulk of the flow used to irrigate thousands of acres of rich agricultural land in the Brownsville section of Texas and near Matamoros, Mexico.

Long the home of Pueblo Indians who built their villages along the river and its tributaries in New Mexico, the Rio Grande was the first of the western rivers to be seen by Europeans. However, they were in no shape to record their observations or map their locations. Shipwrecked on the coast of Mississippi, they had worked their way westward only to be captured by Indians along the Texas coast. From this point they were passed from tribe to tribe before finally reaching Culiacan on the northwestern frontier of New Spain in 1534. Their stories of seven "golden cities" generated a period of Spanish exploration. Though the Spanish found no golden cities, the knowledge they gained resulted in further exploration and eventual settlement in 1598. In that year Juan de Oñate named the river the Rio Grande. Before that it was known as the Rio de las Palmas, Rio del Norte, or Rio Bravo in its lower course. After 1598 Spanish settlers moved from their bases at El Paso and Santa Fe into the many small tributary valleys of the middle section of the Rio Grande, tending sheep and cattle and raising vegetables and fruits. Many of these small agricultural villages perched on the slopes above the irrigated valleys can still be seen today, relatively unchanged.

A few American traders and trappers penetrated into the agrarian locale, only to be expelled or imprisoned by the Spanish. In 1806 an American exploring party commanded by Lieutenant Zebulon Pike crossed Mosca Pass in the Sangre de Cristo Range and made winter camp at the confluence of the Conejos and Rio Grande rivers in the San Luis Valley. Pike's account of the region was enough to send a number of parties to Santa Fe in an effort to initiate trade with the Spanish. However, not until Mexico became independent of Spain in 1821 were these trading ventures welcomed, but even then it was the United States rather than Mexico that profited. From then until the Southwest became part of the United States in 1846, the SANTA FE AND CHIHUAHUA TRAIL was lined with wagons carrying manufactured goods to

be sold in the northern provinces of New Spain. The logistics that led to Yankee supremacy in this trade are simply explained. Goods from the eastern part of the United States could be carried down the Ohio and up the Missouri to Franklin, Westport, or Independence and carried less than eight hundred miles across the prairie by wagon. The journey from the port of Vera Cruz in Mexico to Chihuahua northward to Santa Fe was not only longer but more difficult.

The ensuing trade to the California settlements occurred as a natural extension of the trading patterns that developed. Santa Fe, and to a greater extent, Taos, also became the centers from which mountain men fanned outward through the Southwest seeking beaver pelts and carrying American ideas and goods as baggage. It was they who pioneered the Gila River and Old Spanish Trails along which the commercial traffic moved and along which Americans hurried to reach the gold fields of California.

Americans came to the Rio Grande country in numbers with the commencement of hostilities with Mexico in 1846. They came again in numbers when the railroad was built through the San Luis Valley, but the region from the southern part of the valley, where Spanish-speaking settlers came in 1852, to the delta near Brownsville remains predominantly Hispanic and Indian, and the landscape bears the impact of their culture. Only Albuquerque, with its massive freeway system and extensive business section, shows the heavy-handed imprint of the American way.

See Allan Vaughan Elston, *Rio Grande Deadline* (1957); Laura Gilpin, *The Rio Grande, River of Destiny* (1949); Paul Horgan, *Great River: The Rio Grande in North American History*, 2 vols. (1954); Norris Hundley, *Dividing the Waters* (1966); and Ross A. Maxwell, *The Big Bend of the Rio Grande* (1968).—R. W. D.

Ripley, Edward Payson (1845–1920). Railroad executive. Born in Dorchester, Massachusetts, Ripley was so successful as New England agent for a number of western railroad lines that he was hired by the traffic department of the Burlington railroad system. By 1888 he was general traffic manager and, after several years as a vice president of the Chicago, Milwaukee and St. Paul Railroad, was offered the presidency of the SANTA FE RAILROAD, which had just emerged from bankruptcy in the early 1890s. During the next two decades Ripley converted the decrepit line into one of the most efficient and prosperous railroads in the nation, while more than doubling its total mileage.

The major rebuilding program which Ripley carried out on the Santa Fe is a good example of the thorough-going transformation of American railroads in the two decades before World War I. Ripley supported the Hepburn Act of 1906, believing that the government should have the power to fix maximum railroad rates when carriers and shippers could not agree on what was reasonable. In the historic rate case of 1910, when the railroads jointly sought general increases in the face of rampant inflation and vastly increased demands on the systems, Ripley represented the western railroads before the Interstate Commerce Commission. At first dismayed and eventually disgusted by the repressive rate policy and pro-labor stance the government followed in railroad affairs from 1910 onward, Ripley finally turned his back on the role of industry statesman. Long accustomed to having a free hand as long as they produced results for their employers and the public, the men of Ripley's generation never understood or accepted the political role in which the railroads were cast after 1906.

Ripley's work on the Santa Fe is discussed in Lawrence L. Waters, *Steel Trails to Santa Fe* (1950).—A. M.

Rister, Carl Coke (1889-1955). Historian. If ever an individual could rightfully be called "a product of his time and place," it would be Rister. Born in the small town of Hayrick during the period when western Texas was still frontier country, Rister grew up in a strict Baptist family. His father was a fundamentalist preacher and, although in later life the younger Rister had many honors and established himself as a leading historian, scholar, and writer of the West, his "Puritan conscience" determined his philosophy and guided his conduct. He remained conservative in politics, dress, speech, and mannerism. When an older colleague once observed, "I never discuss sin with Carl since he obviously does not believe in it," he was not being entirely facetious.

Virtually all of Rister's scholarly writings deal with the Southwest when debauchery and violence seemed to have been its chief characteristics. Subjects involving frontier saloons, outlawry, Indian raiders, tinhorn gamblers, and prostitutes receive realistic treatments. Yet Rister's religious background inhibited him in the use of the word "whore" (it generally came out as "soiled dove"), and he considered drinking and gambling almost as bad as murder and rape. If some found him prudish and rigid, no one ever accused him of insincerity or hypocrisy. Indeed, he was the embodiment of kindness, always helpful and patient with students and generous in his praise and encouragement of younger colleagues.

Rister obtained his B.A. degree in American history from Hardin-Simmons University in Abilene, Texas, in 1915. The next year he married a classmate who became his assistant in many research projects. During World War I the Risters lived in Washington, D.C., where he worked as a civil-service employee and attended graduate school at George Washington University. In 1920 he received his M.A. degree and accepted a position teaching history at Hardin-Simmons. He remained in Abilene, Texas, until 1929, meanwhile completing the work for his Ph.D. from George Washington. His first book, *The Southwestern Frontier, 1865-1881*, came out in 1928 and subsequently earned him an appointment as assistant professor at the University of Oklahoma.

During the twenty-two years on the Norman campus, Rister produced approximately a dozen books, either singly or with co-authors. Among these were *The Greater Southwest* (1934); *Western America* (1941); and *Oil: Titan of the Southwest* (1950). The last-mentioned work was made possible by a $30,000 grant from the Standard Oil Company of New Jersey and eventually won the Texas Institute of Letters Award. Rister's other honors and distinctions included election as president of the Mississippi Valley Historical Association (1949-50); and service as chairman of the department of history and eventually appointment as research professor of history at Oklahoma. He returned to his native state in 1951 to accept a chair as distinguished professor of western history at Texas Technological College in Lubbock, where he maintained his heavy writing and research schedule.

Although not an outstanding stylist, Rister was a meticulous researcher, tireless worker, judicious collector of western Americana, and careful in the use of documentary evidence. He rarely engaged in broad interpretations, believing that the facts should speak for themselves. Yet his lectures could be exciting and students often marveled at his command of information and his ability to deliver polished discourses without benefit of notes.—W. E. H.

rivermen. The pioneering efforts of many men developed TRANSPORTATION ON THE MISSISSIPPI RIVER SYSTEM:

Bixby, Horace (1826-1912). Steamboat pilot. Bixby began his river career at eighteen as "mud clerk" on a steamboat out of Cincinnati. Endowed with a tenacious memory and instant judgment, he became a "lightning pilot," taking big packets between St. Louis and New Orleans. In 1857-58 he taught Mark Twain the art and science of piloting.

Blair, Walter (1856-?1930). Raft pilot. A schoolteacher in Iowa river towns during the winters, Blair piloted the *Silver Wave* and other towboats, pushing log rafts down the Mississippi River from the northern pine woods. His colorful book, *A Raft Pilot's Log* (1909), recreates the era of rafting on the upper river.

Burns, Tom (1836-1890). River pilot and steamboat inspector. For thirty years Burns worked as pilot for the Minnesota Packet Company between St. Louis and St. Paul. Later he served as United States local inspector of steamboats under Presidents Cleveland and McKinley.

Cramer, Zadok (1773-1813). Writer. Cramer wrote *The Navigator*, a guide book to the Ohio and Mississippi rivers. It was first published in Pittsburgh in 1801. By the time of the final (twelfth) edition the little book included strip maps of the rivers as well as a mile-by-mile manual of the unmarked channels.

Devol, Jonathan (1756-1824). Pioneer shipbuilder. A veteran of the American Revolution, Devol directed building in 1788 of the barge *Mayflower*, which brought the first settlers down the Ohio to Marietta. In 1801-03 he built a rigged ship, two brigs, and a schooner, all of which carried Ohio produce to Cuba and Atlantic coastal ports.

Eads, James B. (1820-1877). River engineer. After a few seasons as mud clerk on the St. Louis-Galena run, Eads developed a diving bell for salvaging wrecked vessels. In 1874 he completed construction of the famous Eads bridge across the Mississippi at St. Louis. His crowning achievement was to open the Mississippi mouth at the Gulf of Mexico by a system of jetties that controlled river currents and sediment. (See entry on EADS.)

Ellet, Charles R. (1810-1862). Civil engineer. In 1848, for improvement of the western rivers, Ellet urged a system of dams and reservoirs, a plan that led to the slack-water system of locks and dams eventually realized by the Corps of Engineers. During the Civil War he built a ram fleet that broke the Confederate blockade on the lower Mississippi.

Fink, Mike (1770-1823). "King of the keelboatmen." During three decades on the Ohio and Mississippi rivers Fink was known from Pittsburgh to New Orleans. In St. Louis in 1822 he joined General William Ashley's fur brigade and went to the Yellowstone country, where he was shot in a quarrel over an Indian woman. Called the

"Snag" and the "Snapping Turtle," he became the subject of extensive folklore. An archetype of the reckless, roistering early rivermen, his legend survives in frontier mythology. (See entry on FINK.)

Harris, Daniel Smith (1808-1891). Steamboat captain and owner. With his brother, R. Scribe Harris, an engineer, Harris built and operated a succession of fine steamers, culminating in the *Grey Eagle* (1857), the largest and fastest boat on the upper Mississippi.

Howard, James (1814-1876). Steamboat builder. After apprenticeship to a Cincinnati boatwright, Howard established his own boatyard in Jeffersonville, Indiana. His son and grandson succeeded to the business. By 1890 nearly five hundred steamers had come from the Howard yards.

Hunter, Walter L. (1868-1962). Towboat captain. After bringing the last log raft down the upper Mississippi in 1915, Hunter turned to towing coal barges. He then saw the river dammed and locked, with diesels replacing steamboats in the towing trade.

La Barge, Joseph (1815-1899). Steamboatman. At sixteen La Barge signed as clerk on the pioneer fur trade steamer *Yellowstone*. As pilot and master for the American Fur Company and later for the federal government, he navigated the hazardous Missouri for half a century.

Lisa, Manuel (1772-1820). Fur trader. In 1807 Lisa led a keelboat expedition up the Missouri River to establish trading posts for his MISSOURI FUR COMPANY. Between 1807 and 1820 he logged more than 25,000 miles on the Missouri. (See entry on LISA.)

Marsh, Grant (1834-1916). Steamboat captain. At twelve Marsh shipped as cabin boy on a Pittsburgh steamer. In 1864 he began navigating to Missouri and was employed by the government during the Sioux wars. As master of the *Far West* in 1876, he brought out the wounded from Custer's battle of the Little Big Horn.

Roosevelt, Nicholas J. (1767-1854). Inventor and engineer. In 1809 Roosevelt became associated with Robert Fulton and in Pittsburgh directed building of the steamer *New Orleans*. As commander of that vessel he made the first steamboat trip down the Ohio and the Mississippi.

Sellers, Isaiah (1802?-1864). Mississippi pilot. In 1844 Sellers made a record four-day run from New Orleans to St. Louis on the *J. M. White*. Under the name Mark Twain he wrote letters for New Orleans newspapers. Samuel L. Clemens took the pseudonym and made it famous.

Sire, Joseph A. (1795-1854). Steamboat captain. Sire began employment with the American Fur Company in 1836 in St. Louis. For a decade he commanded the annual boat that served fur posts on the upper Missouri.

Shreve, Henry M. (1785-1851). Steamboat builder and captain. In 1815 at Wheeling Shreve built the famous *Washington*, the first steamboat with shallow hull and engines on the main deck. As superintendent of river improvements from 1827-1841, he built steam snagboats that cleared the channels of the Ohio, Mississippi, Arkansas, and Red rivers.

Tobin, John W. (1834?-1888). Steamboat owner and captain. After youthful adventures in the California goldfields, Tobin built some of the finest steamboats on the Mississippi. Most splendid was the third *J. M. White*, launched in 1878. This packet could carry ten thousand bales of cotton, though railroad competition kept it from ever loading a full cargo.

Twain, Mark. Pen name of **Samuel L. Clemens** (1835-1910). Mississippi pilot and writer. During 1857-61 Twain served as an apprentice pilot and licensed pilot on Mississippi steamboats. The Civil War blockade of the lower Mississippi ended his river career, but his later books made his years on the Mississippi known to readers around the world. "Mark Twain" is an old river term, the leadsman's call for a sounding of two fathoms. It meant safe water. (See entry on TWAIN.)—W. H.

roads and highways. The historic western trails were in no way roads in the modern sense. The pioneers set out in the general direction of their goal—to New Mexico, Oregon, or California—usually following a river valley so as to avoid deserts and badlands. Settlers followed with wagon trains, establishing tracks through the grass and marking the trail. The lowest mountain passes in the Rockies and the Sierra Nevada were sought out, but road building consisted only of rolling aside rocks and other obstacles in the path. Both the Pacific Wagon Road program and the railroad surveys of the federal government in the 1850s attempted to shorten and improve these routes.

By 1890, lands far from the routes of the transcontinental railroads had been settled, and farmers began to demand roads that could be traveled all year round. About the same time the bicycle suddenly became a popular fad. Local organizations of wheelmen were formed to promote bicycle use, and these groups combined, in 1880, to form the League of American Wheelmen. Several million wheelmen, through articles written for popular magazines and periodic conventions, called loudly for smoother roads so they could enjoy their rides in the countryside. Farmers and bicyclists joined forces in a nationwide movement for improved highways. In 1892 the National League for Good Roads was founded in Chicago, and shortly thereafter the National Good Roads Association. The federal government took cognizance of the movement in 1893 with the establishment of the Office of Road Inquiry in the Department of Agriculture. Its responsibility was to study the methods of road making, publish information on the subject, and construct pilot projects.

There were about two million miles of rural highways in the United States in 1890, most of them dirt roads, with 100,000 miles with surfaces that could be used year round. Most of the improved roads were surfaced with gravel or crushed stone, but concrete was being tried by 1893. Both methods were too expensive. The first step away from purely local financial support came when New Jersey began to provide state aid to its counties for road building in 1891. Eight states had similar programs by 1900.

The introduction of the automobile made the expansion and improvement of roads imperative. The Duryea brothers built the first gasoline automobile in 1893. Seven years later there were eight thousand automobiles in the United States, and by 1925 there were twenty-four million motor vehicles on the nation's roads and streets. Between 1900 and 1915 thirty-eight states entered the field of planning, construction, and maintenance of highways. The "good roads" movement was in full swing. Up to this time the federal government had assumed no responsibility, but in 1916 the Federal Aid

Road Act was passed to provide matching funds for those states that established a program whereby the funds could be used effectively. Federal appropriations were distributed among the states on the basis of their comparative area, population, and mileage of rural mail routes. The states made the surveys, planned the improvements, and supervised the construction. The Bureau of Public Roads in the Department of Commerce acted for the federal government. In 1921 a system evolved whereby state roads were welded into a national network.

During World War I the value of motortruck transportation was recognized, while the use of passenger cars was transformed in the next decade from a Sunday-afternoon recreational activity into a business necessity. There was no expansion in rural roads after 1920, but the surfaced mileage was increased from approximately 400,000 miles in 1921 to one million miles in 1941. As speeds increased and trucks became bigger and carried heavier loads, highways had to be rebuilt to provide more durable surfaces and multilanes, and to eliminate curves. Around the congested urban communities, both East and West, the tremendous volume of traffic necessitated the establishment of expressways and parkways. Traffic lights and cross streets were eliminated, entrance and exit was provided only at specific places, and the highways were divided by a strip or barrier to separate the cars going in opposite directions.

Nowhere was the modern highway more important than in the trans-Mississippi West, where great distances had to be crossed, where tourists visited the scenic wonders of the national parks, and where motortruck service bound the Pacific Slope with the Great Basin and Rocky Mountain region. The modern economy of the American West was totally dependent upon improved transportation and communication. In 1967 the federal government was constructing a series of interstate highways, east and west, north and south, that followed in general the routes established by the pioneer trail makers. Running east and west, Interstate 94 was constructed by way of Fargo and Bismarck, North Dakota, to Billings, Montana, where it was joined by Interstate 90, running by way of Sioux Falls and Rapid City, South Dakota, and Buffalo, Wyoming. The combined route traversed Montana to Coeur d'Alene, Idaho, via Spokane into Seattle, Washington. Across the central portion of the West, Interstate 80 crossed Iowa to Council Bluffs, on to North Platte, Nebraska, provided alternate routes into Denver and Cheyenne, and crossed southern Wyoming into Salt Lake City. From here one alternate followed, in general, the route of the old California Trail across Nevada, over the Sierra, and into Sacramento and San Francisco. Another alternate headed toward the Northwest, along the Snake valley route of the old Oregon Trail, terminating in Portland. Interstate 70, running west from Kansas City to Denver, continued on to Grand Junction, Colorado, and across central Utah, before joining the north-south Interstate 15 into Los Angeles, passing through Las Vegas, Nevada, and San Bernardino, California. This route of travel was first made famous by the Mormons. Interstate 40 traversed the trans-Mississippi West by way of Oklahoma City, Amarillo, Albuquerque, Flagstaff, and into California generally along the thirty-fifth parallel route worked out for wagon roads and railroads in the 1850s.

The most southern interstate is provided by the junction of Interstate 20, from the Fort Worth-Dallas area in Texas, with Interstate 10, from San Antonio in the trans-Pecos River country, on to El Paso, Tucson and Phoenix, Arizona, and west. Travelers headed for San Diego can leave Interstate 10 between Phoenix and Tucson, and go west just north of the Mexican border on Interstate 8. These east-west arteries are connected by three interstates running north and south: Interstate 25 from El Paso, through Santa Fe, New Mexico, to Denver, Colorado, Casper, Wyoming, and joining Interstate 90 in Buffalo, Wyoming; Interstate 15 from Los Angeles to Salt Lake, north to Pocatello, Idaho, Butte and Helena, Montana, to the Canadian border; Interstate 5 connecting San Diego, Los Angeles, and Sacramento, California, and northward through Portland and Seattle to the Canadian border. (See NATIONAL ROADS.)

Oscar O. Winther, *The Transportation Frontier: Trans-Mississippi West, 1865-1890* (1964), includes a valuable chapter on the "good roads" movement. Two volumes attempting to survey the entire subject are Jean Labatut and Wheaton J. Lane, eds., *Highways in Our National Life* (1950); and J. W. Gregory, *The Story of the Road from the Beginning to the Present Day* (1938).—W. T. J.

Roberts, Brigham Henry (1857-1933). Mormon leader and historian and Utah politician. Born in Lancastershire, England, Roberts migrated to Utah in 1867 with his older sister. An orphan, he began life as a humble farmhand and apprentice blacksmith. He obtained very little formal schooling but completed the University of Deseret's elementary school courses in 1878. He taught school and plied his trade as a blacksmith until 1880, when he was sent on a proselyting mission to the midwestern states. In 1883 he was called as the president of the Southern States Mission and from there went on yet another mission to England, where he was editor of the *Latter-day Saints' Millennial Star* (1886-88). Shortly after his return to Salt Lake City, he was made a member of the Mormon church's First Council of Seventy, eventually becoming senior president of that body. Between 1890 and 1893 he traveled among the Mormons of the Pacific states and assisted apostle Francis M. Lyman in opening the church's mission in southern California.

A former member of the People's party (the official party of the Mormon church), Roberts joined the Democrats in 1891 when Utahans began to align themselves with the two national parties. He was a member of Utah's state constitutional committee of 1895, distinguishing himself by his unrelenting opposition to female suffrage. In 1895 he also became a candidate for the United States Congress. He was defeated, as was the entire Democratic ticket that year, but he ran again in 1899 and was victorious. Congress, however, challenged his right to the seat because he was a polygamist. A brilliant orator, Roberts defended himself in a speech that lasted four days. Despite his impassioned plea, he was excluded from the House of Representatives.

Roberts was always concerned with the common man and became known for his work in behalf of labor. His most notable experience in this area was as mediator in the Salt Lake City streetcar strike of 1907. He was also a member of the State Board of Equalization in 1917. When the United States declared war in 1917, Roberts volunteered for service as chaplain with the 145th Field Artillery.

In 1930 Roberts published a six-volume work, *A Comprehensive History of the Church of Jesus Christ of Latter-day Saints: Century I*. Other writings include *The Gospel* (1888), *Life of John Taylor* (1892), *Outlines of Ecclesiastical History* (1893), *New Witnesses for God* (1895), *Mormon Doctrine of Deity* (1903), and *Defense of the Faith and the Saints* (1907). He also edited the seven-volume *History of the Church* by Joseph Smith (1902).

Roberts, Oran Milo (1815-1898). Jurist and politician. Roberts was born in South Carolina. He studied at the University of Alabama, was admitted to the bar in 1837, and then served a term in the state legislature. In 1841 he moved to San Augustine, Texas, where he served as district attorney, district judge, and president of the board of trustees and law professor for the University of San Augustine. From 1857 to 1861 he served as associate justice of the state supreme court.

An avid secessionist, Roberts was instrumental in calling the secession convention of 1861 and was chosen as its president. He organized a regiment and served as its colonel until 1864, at which time he was appointed chief justice of the state supreme court for the duration of the war. He again served as chief justice from 1874 to 1878. During his term as governor of Texas (1878-1883) state indebtedness was diminished and the University of Texas founded.

Roberts was organizer and first president of the Texas State Historical Association and the author of several publications, including *A Description of Texas, Its Advantages and Resources* (1881) and *Our Federal Relations, from a Southern View of Them* (1892). He lectured at the University of Texas Law School from 1883 to 1893.
—J. B. F.

Robertson, James (1742-1814). Tennessee frontiersman. Robertson was of Virginia birth, but moved south to North Carolina. There is some dispute as to the year that he moved on west to the upper Tennessee valley, but 1770 seems to be approximately correct. Riding west on horseback, he first appeared at the pioneer Honeycutt's cabin on the Holston River. As he said in later years, the Watauga country seemed like the promised land. Robertson spent his first summer in Tennessee land-scouting and then returned to North Carolina through the highland wilderness, becoming lost for fourteen days. In 1771 he organized an emigrant party and set out to make his home in the West.

Back in the Watauga settlements, Robertson became a major figure in the new country and has been called by local historians "the Father of Tennessee." Closely associated with John Sevier, William Bean, Evan Shelby, and others, he was active in the defense of the new settlements against Indian attacks. He even acted as a goodwill agent to the Cherokee towns in the face of an impending attack early in 1774. In October of that year he went with Colonel Andrew Lewis' militia army to fight in the battle of Point Pleasant in Lord Dunmore's War.

In subsequent years Robertson played a supporting role in backing up the Kentucky settlements in the American Revolution with frontier militia forces. He engaged in western land speculations and took an active part in eastern Tennessee politics, including the formation of the State of Franklin. He also served as a member of the North Carolina legislature and was an Indian agent. Possibly Robertson's explorations of the great bend of the Cumberland and his leadership role in establishing the Nashville settlement in 1779 were among his most notable accomplishments.

Robertson found himself in later years politically aligned with Andrew Jackson in the famous Jackson-Sevier feud in matters of land and Indian policies. He was not only a political supporter of William Blount, but he was his Indian and land agent. No other Tennessee pioneer played a more active role in the settlement of that state than Robertson.

See Thomas Perkins Abernethy, *From Frontier to Plantation Tennessee* (1932); J. G. M. Ramsey, *The Annals of Tennessee* (1853); and Samuel Cole Williams, *Dawn of Tennessee Valley and Tennessee History* (1937).—T. D. C.

Robidoux brothers. Fur traders. Six members of this family of French Canadian ancestry were participants in the fur trade: Antoine (1794-1860); Joseph (1783-1868); François (1788-1856); Louis (1796?-1862); Michel (1798-?) and Isidore (?-?). The most prominent was Antoine, who was involved in the Santa Fe trade in 1822 but by 1824 had turned to fur trapping in the Southwest. In 1829 he took out Mexican citizenship. He also married into a New Mexican family. Using Santa Fe and Taos as his bases of operations Antoine and various of his brothers exploited the Colorado country. He built Fort Uncompahgre, a trading post, on the Gunnison River in southwestern Colorado, possibly as early as 1828, and Fort Uintah, or the Robidoux Rendezvous, on the Uintah River in northeastern Utah in 1837. In 1844, shortly after Antoine introduced whiskey to the Ute on the western slope, the tribe attacked Fort Uintah, and it was abandoned in 1845. Robidoux's Fort Uncompahgre was burned by the Ute in 1846-47. Facts concerning the year-by-year activities of the Robidoux brothers are lacking, but Antoine dominated the trade of the area between northern Utah and southern Arizona. He and his brothers also succeeded in maintaining an important north-south supply line both along the western slope of the Rockies and on the High Plains east of the Rockies until Fort Laramie and Bent's Fort created ruinous competition.

At the outset of the Mexican War in 1846, Antoine served as an interpreter for General Stephen W. Kearny, who occupied New Mexico. Antoine continued with Kearny on his march to California. He was badly wounded at the battle of San Pascual but recovered and returned to St. Joseph, Missouri, to live. Eight years before his death he became blind.

Joseph, the eldest of the Robidoux brothers, began his career in the fur trade as an employee of Bernard Pratte and Company along the Missouri River. A wily businessman, he financed trading outfits that were sometimes in competition with those of his own employer. In 1824, or possibly earlier, he sent trade goods to Santa Fe in care of his brothers François and Isidore. Joseph also appears to have spent some time trapping in the northern Rockies until he was paid by Kenneth McKenzie of the American Fur Company to stay out of the mountains for two years. In 1831 he established a post in the Blacksnake Hills from which evolved St. Joseph, Missouri.

François liked the Southwest so much that he settled in Taos, where he married a New Mexican girl. His frequent disputes with New Mexican authorities about licenses and customs fees allow the historian to trace many of his movements, but the activities of his brothers Michel and Isidore remain obscure.

Louis Robidoux operated a grist mill and iron works (probably for making beaver traps) in Santa Fe, while Antoine maintained a store there. Since they were naturalized Mexican citizens, they could hold public office, and, indeed, both served as first alcalde and as alderman in Santa Fe. Able and ubiquitous, the Robidoux brothers were counted among the most influential merchant-politicians who lived in New Mexico in the decade before American conquest.

The often confusing and obscure careers of the Robidoux brothers are carefully explained in David J. Weber, *The Taos Trappers, 1540-1846* (1971). See also Dale L. Morgan, ed., *The West of William H. Ashley* (1964); and *Dictionary of American Biography*, vol. XVI.—G. B. D.

Robinson, Charles (1818-1894). Kansas politician. Robinson was born in Massachusetts. After a year and a half at Amherst College, he withdrew and began the study of medicine. In 1843 he began medical practice at Belchertown, Massachusetts, moved to Springfield in 1845 and the following year to Fitchburg, Massachusetts, where his wife died. Attracted by the gold rush to California in the spring of 1849 he set out for an overland trip to the gold fields. Robinson soon abandoned the mines, however, and started a boardinghouse in Sacramento. He became actively interested in politics and was wounded severely during a fight on behalf of squatters. He recovered and was elected to the state legislature. In mid-1851 he returned to Massachusetts, married Sara T. D. Lawrence, resumed his practice of medicine, and took charge of a weekly newspaper.

The agitation over popular sovereignty and the Kansas-Nebraska Act resulted in Robinson's leading the first party of the New England Emigrant Aid Company to locate in Kansas at Lawrence. He was an active townbuilder, an ardent "free-stater," and a leader in the antislavery movement. His feud with Kansas politician Jim Lane detracted from his political effectiveness, but he was elected governor on the Republican ticket in anticipation of statehood. As the state's first governor, he set precedents for the functioning of the state government. Backers of Lane had Robinson impeached in 1862 on the grounds of illegally selling state bonds, but he was acquitted. He changed political parties a number of times in later years and served the state in minor offices. In the last three decades of his life he never regained the respect he had commanded in the first decade of Kansas settlement.

The official biography is Frank W. Blackmar, *The Life of Charles Robinson: The First State Governor of Kansas* (1902). See also G. R. Gaeddert, *The Birth of Kansas* (1940).—H. E. S.

Robinson, Edgar Eugene (1887-   ). Historian and educator. Born in Oconomowoc, Wisconsin, Robinson attended the University of Wisconsin during the last years Frederick Jackson Turner taught there. He received his bachelor of arts degree in 1908 and master's degree in 1910 from that institution. Joining the faculty of Stanford University in 1911, Robinson became professor of history in 1923 and was made Margaret Byrne Professor of American History there in 1931. While Robinson's main interests were politics and government, his course on the history of the American West made him one of the most popular teachers at Stanford.

Robinson had a deep interest in undergraduate education and headed a number of committees to revise the curriculum at Stanford. In 1922 he devised an interdisciplinary course on citizenship and later developed Stanford's noted course "The History of Western Civilization." He pioneered the Independent Study Plan and published the results of his effort in *Independent Study at Stanford University 1931-37* (1937).

His books include *The Foreign Policy of Woodrow Wilson* (1917), *Evolution of American Political Parties* (1924), *The Presidential Vote, 1896-1932* (1934), *American Democracy in Time of Crisis* (1934), *The Presidential Vote* (1936), *The New United States* (1946), *They Voted for Roosevelt* (1947), *The Roosevelt Leadership, 1933-45* (1955), and *Powers of the President in Foreign Affairs, 1955-65* (1966).

After the death of Ray Wilbur, president of Stanford from 1916 to 1943 and secretary of the interior in the Hoover administration, Robinson became coeditor of *Memoirs of Ray Wilbur 1875-1949* (1960). He received the Freedom Foundation's Award in 1950.—J. S. W.

Rocky Mountain Fur Company. The company was the successor to Smith, Jackson, and Sublette, having bought out that firm on August 4, 1830. Its partners— Thomas FITZPATRICK, James BRIDGER, Milton Sublette of the famous SUBLETTE BROTHERS, Henry FRAEB, and Jean Baptiste Gervais—were all experienced mountain traders. In spite of its successful predecessors and its able field men, the Rocky Mountain Fur Company was not viable. Its downfall is attributable chiefly to two factors: the lack of business aptitude of its members, and competition from John Jacob Astor's American Fur Company. In 1831 no supplies reached the company's fur-trading rendezvous, and the trappers had to begin their fall hunt without the goods and without means of getting their furs back to the St. Louis market. In order to extricate themselves from their financial problems, the partners were forced to make an agreement in late 1831 with William Sublette for the supplies for the succeeding year. This agreement, amplified in a contract of July 1832, made Sublette the dictator of the company's finances for the balance of its existence.

The company's partners also struggled against numerous rivals in the field. Four were relatively insignificant: the Bean-Sinclair party (1830-32), the Gantt-Blackwell Company (1831-32), Nathaniel Wyeth (1832-34), and Captain Benjamin Bonneville (1832-35). The American Fur Company, however, in 1832 began a new and hated technique that resulted in tragedy. Since the Rocky Mountain Fur Company men were paramount in their knowledge of fur conditions, an American Fur Company brigade under the leadership of Andrew Drips and William H. Vanderburgh dogged their footsteps throughout the mountains, trapping the animals discovered by their unwilling guides. Enraged by this pursuit, Fitzpatrick and Bridger, whose party was being followed up the Three Forks of the Missouri, decided to lure Vanderburgh and Drips to their death. In October the Rocky Mountain Fur Company moved up the Madison River, and Vanderburgh naturally followed. Vanderburgh and his men then moved to the junction of the Shoshone River and Alder Creek, where they were assailed by a party of Blackfoot. Vanderburgh was killed.

At the rendezvous of 1833 the two rivals each possessed about the same number of beaver packs, although the Rocky Mountain Fur Company had only one half as many men in the field as American Fur Company. At this meeting the Rocky Mountain Fur Company contracted with the independent Nathaniel Wyeth to receive his annual supplies from him at the rendezvous of 1834. But shortly thereafter the company sustained a loss when the American Fur Company induced the hitherto friendly Crow Indians to rob them of their skins and horses. The coup de grace for the company came at the rendezvous in the Green River region in 1834. William Sublette crushed the company by demanding that it pay its debt to him; it was thus unable to purchase its supplies from Wyeth, who accordingly constructed Fort Hall on the Snake River. William Sublette then bought out the Rocky Mountain Fur Company.

See Don Berry, *A Company of Scoundrels* (1961); and Hiram M. Chittenden, *The American Fur Trade of the Far West* (1902).—G. B. D.

Rocky Mountain National Park. Rocky Mountain National Park in Colorado was created by congressional action on January 26, 1915. For many years before that, Enos A. Mills, a gifted author and publicist, had written about the grandeur of the scenery near Estes Park, Colorado. He earned the title of "Father of Rocky Mountain National Park." The park is about sixty-five miles from Denver and three miles from Estes Park. It contains 260,018 acres of forests, streams, and mountain peaks. Its scenery is perhaps unmatched anywhere on the eastern slope of the Rocky Mountains. Its elevation ranges from a low point of approximately 7,800 feet to the 14,256-foot summit of Longs Peak, which is the highest point in northern Colorado. A number of peaks in the park exceed 13,000 feet. The Continental Divide angles through its boundaries, and the headwaters of the Colorado River originate in this vicinity. Trail Ridge Road, which traverses the park, reaches an elevation of 12,183 feet and offers spectacular views of the stark, rocky pinnacles and valleys carved mainly by glacial action. The lower slopes of the mountain are thickly forested, sheltering large numbers of American elk and Rocky Mountain muledeer. Bighorn sheep and mountain lions may be seen in the more remote regions of the park.

The Colorado-Big Thompson project, a plan to bring irrigation water from the Grand Lake region to Colorado's arid eastern slope, involved the park in controversy beginning in the mid-1930s. The plan called for a lengthy tunnel under the park to transport water over the Continental Divide to the farmers and ranchers who needed it. Proponents of the Colorado-Big Thompson project, including the Bureau of Reclamation, claimed that no damage would be done to the park. The National Park Service opposed the plan, fearing that it would establish a precedent for further reclamation work in the parks. The Sierra Club, the National Parks Association, the National Audubon Society, and other conservation organizations joined in opposing the project. Secretary of the Interior Harold L. Ickes sided with the National Park Service. But after a loud contest, the reclamationists won congressional authorization of the plan in 1937. The Colorado-Big Thompson project, including a thirteen-mile tunnel under the Continental Divide, was constructed by the Bureau of Reclamation. Every effort was made not to mar the scenery of the park. As a result of this controversy, preservationist groups became deeply suspicious of the reclamation program, and the stage was set for the battle over Dinosaur National Monument, in the 1950s, in which the conservationists blocked two proposed reservoirs that would have encroached on the national monument. —D. C. S.

Rocky Mountains. See PHYSIOGRAPHY OF THE UNITED STATES; and VEGETATION: *mountains*.

rodeo. The word *rodeo* stems from the Spanish *rodear*, meaning "to go round" or "to surround or encircle." The cowboy pronunciation is "roh'dee-oh": to say "rohday'oh" is a clear indication to a cowboy that he is speaking to an eastern dude. The original rodeo activities and terminology were of Spanish-American origin.

The range-cattle industry competitions were not known as rodeos but as Frontier Days Celebrations, Roundups, Stampedes, or some other title related to a day of celebration, a practice that is still common. It was the WILD WEST SHOW that used the term *rodeo* for cowboy competition and exhibitions. As the range-cattle industry and the Wild West shows disappeared, the rodeo, as we know it today, emerged. From 1915 to 1925 *rodeo* slowly became the word for this developing form of entertainment.

The rodeo cowboy as a participant in the sporting world carries with him the traditions of the past. His sport is the only major American sport to emerge from an industry, the range-cattle industry. He is an extension of the range cowboy, and he maintains some of the characteristics of the cowhand—independent, rough and rugged, clannish, and proud. The rodeo cowboy, however, has the added characteristic of showmanship; he enjoys the action, drama, and excitement of the arena show that is staged not only for prize-winning competition but also for spectator enjoyment. The rodeo cowboy is first and foremost an entertainer. Although events in roping and riding perpetuate the everyday activities of the range-cattle roundup and cow-camp entertainment, many rodeo cowboys are graduates of rodeo schools and know nothing about ranching or the cattle industry.

The rodeo cowboy has become a major sports figure. There are more than 3,120 members of the Rodeo Cowboys Association, and in 1970 there were 547 rodeos. Prize money for 1970 totaled $4,115,021. And the RCA shows and cowboys represent only a part of the rodeo world. The exact number is impossible to determine, for there are shows with no affiliation and cowboys with no membership in any organization. (There were at least seventy-six non-RCA rodeos in California in the first eight months of 1971.) The International Rodeo Association has many affiliated shows and members (amateur rodeos, Future Farmers of America and 4-H rodeos, junior rodeos, high school rodeos, collegiate rodeos, and all-female rodeos) which are too numerous to estimate. In addition, small local competitions attract a faithful following that cannot be counted.

Many communities proudly claim to be the site of the "original" rodeo, without evidence to support their claims. Since the rodeo is a range-cattle industry product and since Texas was the heart of the development of the range-cattle industry, it is logical to speculate that the first rodeo was staged in Texas. The site and date that is usually given is Pecos, Texas, on July 4, 1883. The local merchants penned Longhorn steers in the courthouse square and invited the local cowboys to rope and to ride on the main street. The Fourth of July was a popular day of celebration in the Southwest, and the Pecos event was an attempt to provide an outlet for the celebrating cowhands and entertainment for the townfolks, as well as to determine which cowboy and cow camp was the best.

The community of Prescott, Arizona, claims the distinction of having awarded the first trophy, a silver mounted medal, to a rodeo winner. On July 4, 1888, the Prescott Frontier Days Celebration presented the award to Juan Leivas. In addition, Prescott has since claimed to have the "oldest continuous annual rodeo." Payson, Arizona, however, claims to stage the "oldest consecutive annual" rodeo, for their "August races," which became the Payson Annual Rodeo, started in the early 1880s. By 1884 the community was sponsoring a rodeo, and as the area had many citizens from Texas, roping competition was added to the racing. Later the Payson Rodeo became widely known for its "street" show. Its main street became the arena in the day and the entertainment area at night. This street celebration continued into the 1930s, at which time Payson built an arena with spectator seating facilities. The Main Street nighttime entertainment is still observed and becomes a wild celebration when the sun goes down each evening after the rodeo. Caldwell, Kansas, staged a "grand cowboy tournament" on May 1, 1885. Charles Siringo, cowboy and historian, wrote that he won "a fine silver cup" in the steer-roping event, three years earlier than Prescott's claim.

The first known reference to cowboy competition was in a letter written by Captain Main Reid on June 10, 1847, in which he described a "round-up" in Santa Fe. He wrote that it was "a Donneybrook fair" in which they "contest" for "the best roping and throwing" along with "horse races and whiskey and wine," and that "there is much dancing on the street." The rodeo atmosphere has not changed.

The influence of the Wild West show on the rodeo cannot be minimized, for steer wrestling and the rodeo's international popularity resulted from the traveling Wild West show. The first Wild West show to be organized and to "take the road" in 1883 was Buffalo Bill's Wild West organized by William F. "Buffalo Bill" CODY and W. F. Carver. Within a few years Gordon W. "Pawnee Bill" Lillie launched a successful series of shows, and in 1905 the Miller Brothers' 101 Ranch Wild West Show was successfully produced. Although each show enjoyed much success in its early years, popularity slowly waned until each financially failed. The death of these Wild West shows was slow, however. In 1931 the Millers' 101 Ranch show, the last of the great shows, folded.

It was the 101 Ranch show that introduced bulldogging (now known as steer wrestling) through the showmanship of Bill Pickett, a cowboy from Texas of black and Indian descent. As a special attraction, Pickett on his horse, Spradley, would ride alongside a Longhorn steer, drop to the steer's head and twist the head slowly toward the sky. He would then bite the steer's upper lip, which would control the steer in any manner Pickett chose. Bulldogs, when used as cattle dogs, were known to bite the lip and subdue cattle, so Pickett's method was called "bulldogging." The lip biting was dropped as the event became popular with rodeo cowboys. Pickett's act not only created a new contest event but also made him an immortal rodeo figure. He died in 1932, at the age of seventy, from injuries received while working some horses at the 101 Ranch. His grave is on the old 101 Ranch property near Ponca City, Oklahoma. When a former rodeo cowboy was asked if he knew any stories about Pickett, he replied negatively, adding that he and a friend had recently shared a fifth of whiskey while they sat on Pickett's grave and recalled old rodeo stories. Pickett was selected the 1972 honoree of the National Rodeo Hall of Fame in recognition of his contribution to the sport.

The roping and bronc-riding events are activities of those in the range-cattle industry, but bull riding originated as an entertainment function. It is possible that range cowboys rode steers for laughs and recreation, but it was the wild steer-riding exhibition of the Wild West shows that finally evolved into Brahma-bull riding —the most exciting arena event. Bull riding requires a bullfighter to pull the bull away from the rider. The bullfighter became the rodeo clown who provided humor as well as protection. The skill of the clown determines the mental attitude of the contestant, for a rider knows that he has a chance to avoid injury when a good clown is working the bulls.

"Red" Sublett was a Wild West show performer with an unusual ability for bronc riding, but in the 1920s he turned to bullfighting and clowning. Sublett was possibly the greatest rodeo clown. Hoyt Hefner and John Lindsey were two of the best clowns and bullfighters of the 1930s and 1940s. Lindsey is remembered not only for his skill with bulls, but also for his famous trained bull, Iron Ore. Lindsey and Iron Ore entertained the rodeo fans with their "End of the Trail" act, in which Iron Ore would break a leg and Lindsey would have to shoot his "faithful steed." This was a humorous version of the famous contract act by Hardy Murphy, who with his horse, brought tears to the eyes of the fans with two acts, "The End of the Trail" and "The Last Roundup."

The contract act is the modern-day Wild West show act. The performers are contracted to entertain the rodeo crowd while the officials and contestants prepare for the next contest event. The acts are many and varied, but for years the most popular were trick and fancy riding and roping. (Trick roping involves catching a man or an animal in an unusual way; rope spinning is the trick of rope twirling in a variety of ways.) The Wild West show's best-known trick-roping artist was Will Rogers.

He could throw three ropes at one time and catch a horse and rider as they galloped past him; one loop would catch the rider, one would catch the horse's neck, and one would catch the horse's front legs. His exhibition has never been excelled by any other roper. And he was equally as good at rope spinning. Rogers' skill can be seen in his classic silent movie, "The Roping Fool."

The rodeo circuit's most famous trick and fancy roper was Chester Byars, who was elected to the National Rodeo Hall of Fame in 1969. Another great trick roper is Jim Eskew, Jr., and the best calf roper, Jake McCLURE. The acts usually include such tricks as spinning three ropes simultaneously, one held in each hand and one held with the teeth, and moving the body through spinning loops in a variety of ways; embellishment is added by performing the tricks while standing on a saddled horse. Trick roping is usually combined with spinning-rope techniques. A performer might skip through the rope and with continued movement of the rope catch a rider and horse as they gallop by. The showmen will call their catch: a front leg catch; both front legs catch; neck catch; rider catch; rider and horse catch; horse's body catch; or hind legs catch. The experts make the catch that they call.

The Wild West show trick and fancy riding was an exhibition of maneuvering over a running horse during a fight with Indians. It represented a make-believe way of dodging arrows and bullets. This type of showmanship, combined with a natural tendency to show off on horseback, created trick riding as a contract act. One early form of the rodeo act was the Roman riding style, where a rider would stand with each foot on the back of a different horse; the team would race other teams or put on a jumping exhibition. Trick riding evolved into an exhibition skill that requires a specially constructed saddle with hand holds and other aids for the hands, legs, and feet. The acts include the head stand, going under the horse's body and back to the saddle, holding the saddle horn and vaulting the body from one side of the horse to the other, and many other acrobatic skills performed while the horse is running. Some of the great trick riders were Dick Griffin, Bernice Taylor, Nancy Bragg, Don Wilcox, and Buff Brady, Jr.

The bronc-riding events are modifications of the cow-camp activities and include both bareback and saddle bronc riding. While not as exciting to the spectators as bull riding, these events have killed their share of rodeo cowboys. Pete Knight was one of the greatest bronc riders and was world champion in 1932, 1933, 1935, and 1936. On May 23, 1937, he was kicked by the bronc Duster after completing his ride. A broken rib punctured his spleen and within minutes he was dead at the age of thirty-three. Knight is an honoree of the National Rodeo Hall of Fame.

Another famous rider was Samuel Thomas "Booger Red" Privett, who thrilled crowds during the early 'Stampedes' and 'Frontier Days' shows. Booger Red was lucky enough to live for sixty-one years, during which time he was a working cowboy as well as a rodeo performer. It has been claimed by some old-time cowboys and journalists that "he rode 82 horses in one day" and that "he must have averaged at least two a day for fifty years and that makes about 40,000." He died of Brights' disease in 1925.

Famous bucking horses are as well remembered as the men who rode or tried to ride them. Two such horses were Midnight and Five Minutes to Midnight. Midnight was born in 1916 and died in 1936. During his rodeo career only five cowboys, including Pete Knight, rode him. Frank E. Studnick rode him twice, but only one ride is officially recorded. Midnight was buried in Denver. In May 1966 Dean Krakel, director of the National Cowboy Hall of Fame and Western Heritage Center in Oklahoma City, disinterred Midnight's remains, took them to the center, and buried them south of the build-ing. Old-timers from the rodeo circuit came from all over the West for the service, which included eulogy, prayers, and songs. Five Minutes to Midnight came forth as Midnight's replacement. During twenty-three seasons he threw more than two thousand riders. On his tombstone was written "He was the bronc they couldn't break." His remains have also been moved to the Western Heritage Center.

It is often stated that riders are from northwestern states and ropers from southwestern states. This is based on the idea that the cold northwestern climate does not allow the cowboy as much time to practice in order to develop his roping skill, therefore he rides more. However, there is little to support this contention, for many top cowboys from both regions compete and win in the events for which climatically they supposedly are not suited. The warmer states do provide more practice time for roping, but Dean Oliver, three-time All-Around Champion from 1963 through 1965, is a world champion roper from Boise, Idaho. Jim Shoulders, five-time All-Around Champion, first in 1949 and then from 1956 through 1959, is a world champion bull rider and bronc rider from Henryetta, Oklahoma.

Roping events are more closely related to the work of the range-cattle industry than any of the other events, and there are more "ranching" cowboys, such as Ed BOWMAN, who enter roping contests than enter other events. *Ranching cowboy* is the term used to separate the modern ranch hand who participates in amateur shows and Sunday afternoon "ropings" from the professional rodeo follower. Some ranchers will not hire a young rodeo professional as a ranch hand, for it is believed that they will run the stock too much. Many top professional rodeo cowboys are successful ranchers, however, and many work satisfactorily as hired ranch hands in the off season.

Roping events usually allow a man more years of active participation in the arena than do riding events. As in many competitive sports, the rodeo cowboy usually terminates his role as a competitor, especially as a rider, during his early thirties. An exception is Freckles Brown, who at the age of forty-nine still wins as a bull rider. It is in roping, however, that a cowboy finds age less important as a competition factor.

The most colorful roper to enter the arena was Bob "Wild Horse" Crosby from Kenna, New Mexico. He was billed and respectfully recognized as the King of the Cowboys. He was the world champion roper and a rough, tough man who was either well liked or thoroughly disliked. He competed with injuries that would have hospitalized most men. Crosby was a rancher who turned to the arena to earn money to save his ranch during a severe drought in New Mexico in the early 1920s. The excitement of the rodeo captured him, and each season he would return to the arena to compete or to work as a judge, pick-up man, or in some other capacity. As a competitor he won over $150,000 in the arena, but he paid a high price with injuries for his earnings. Not all of that money was profit, for, like all rodeo cowboys, he had to pay his own transportation, living expenses, hospitalization and medical bills, and entry fees. Crosby was the only man to win the Roosevelt Trophy three times, which entitled him to keep it permanently. The trophy was awarded each year by the Roosevelt Hotel in New York City to the cowboy who won the highest total points at the Cheyenne and Pendleton rodeos. The winner of the trophy was declared World Champion Cowboy. Crosby was champion for the years 1925, 1927, and 1928.

Crosby's life was an odyssey of injuries, and most of the stories that continue to be told about him pertain to these injuries. One legend is that he broke his leg with the bone breaking the skin. The break was set, but gangrene developed. The doctors wanted to amputate the leg but Crosby would not let them. Instead, he went to his ranch, tied his Levi's at the ankle, and stuffed manure around the leg. The manure drew the poison, and some say that it hardened and served as a cast for the leg.

The problem with his leg was the result of a series of events that started at a steer-roping contest in Wilcox, Arizona, in 1929. A steer rammed a horn through his leg below the knee. He poured kerosene on a rag and with a nail forced it through the wound. Since he refused to let a doctor treat it, it did not heal properly. Then in 1930 at the Prescott show, he broke the same leg and again refused to let the doctors pin the bone. The leg would not heal, so he went to the Mayo Clinic where they advised amputation. He immediately left and returned to Roswell where a local doctor opened the leg and cut out the infected tissue. This was done often. He tried the cow manure cure with no success, and he tried letting flies blow the leg, or deposit eggs, so that the maggots which would hatch could eat the infected tissue. He started working the rodeos again, not as a competitor but as a judge. During the Omaha, Nebraska, show a man approached him with an offer to cure his leg. A doctor in Omaha operated and eventually cured him.

It is a rodeo cowboy belief that accidents occur in threes. At the Salt Lake City rodeo in 1925 Crosby was faced with this superstition. Two accidents had occurred in the same arena: the first one occurred one year earlier when a cowboy was shot and killed; the second one had been when a cowboy's horse was jerked down and the man's brains were spattered all over the place. Many cowboys withdrew, but Crosby chose to compete. He was bulldogging, and the steer ran its horn up Crosby's nostril and punched the eyeball from its socket. As it did not sever the optic nerve, he did not lose the eye. After a successful operation and with adequate bandaging, Crosby showed up the next afternoon at the arena and continued to compete. He went on to be the top money winner at the Salt Lake Roundup. Even his critics admired his physical endurance and courage. Another superstition of Crosby's was that his old, worn-out black hat brought him good luck. He was wearing it when he won the Roosevelt Trophy, and never entered the arena again without wearing it. It was a trademark that fans looked forward to seeing.

Those who disliked Crosby based their criticisms on his "fighting" tendencies and on his harsh treatment of animals. Even many of his friends and admirers were critical, particularly about his rough handling of horses, but he justified his method by saying that "A hoss is like a woman. . . . They'll mind yuh a little from love, but a lot more from fear. Of course, it's a heap easier to get a hoss afraid of yuh than a woman." His horses were well trained. And this beginning was reflected in his success as a champion steer roper. He was as hard on himself as he was on any animal. Crosby was killed when he was

fifty years old in a jeep accident near his ranch at Roswell, New Mexico, in 1947. He is an honoree of the National Rodeo Hall of Fame, where the Roosevelt Trophy and his old black hat are on display.

Another champion, who later turned to producing rodeos, is Jim Shoulders from Henryetta, Oklahoma. Shoulders is the all-time high money winner with approximately $400,000. Until 1967, when Larry Mahan won $51,996, Shoulders was the all-time high winner for a season with $43,381, which he won in 1957. His circuit was a typical cowboy's circuit. He traveled over seventy-five thousand miles each year in order to participate in forty to fifty rodeos. His expenses were his own, and he had no guarantee. Unlike other professional sportsmen, he was not paid if he stayed out of competition in order to let an injury heal. He thus competed often with broken bones. His speciality was bull riding; during one ride he was hit in the face by the bull and suffered seventeen fractures of the face. He went on to win that event. On another ride his collarbone was fractured; the other collarbone already had a pin in it. He completed the ride, however, rode another bronc to win the purse, and rode a Brahma bull to win that event. Then he laid off for one week to let the bone mend.

Rodeo cowboys, unless they are one of the few top winners, and there are only a few, are fortunate to make more than their expenses. They hope to win enough, however, to be eligible for the National Finals. The National Finals Rodeo is held in December each year in Oklahoma City and is cosponsored by the Oklahoma City Chamber of Commerce and the National Cowboy Hall of Fame and Western Heritage Center. This show is the final rodeo of the year, and final totals for championships are not tallied until the competition of the finals is completed. Only the top fifteen money winners in each event participate, and some cowboys are participants in more than one event. There are six events for men: saddle bronc riding; bareback riding; bull riding; calf roping; steer wrestling; and team roping. With fifteen participants in each of the six events, there are only ninety possible competitors who will make it to the NFR. The competitors in the lower positions have won only a few thousand dollars during the regular season. The yearly winnings in each event, exclusive of team roping, which is much lower, usually vary from eight thousand dollars to twenty-five thousand dollars (before expenses). To qualify for the All-Around Cowboy Championship, a cowboy must win in two events. In addition, in order to make a good living a cowboy usually must enter more than one event.

The terminology of the arena includes such phrases as *hazer, piggin' string, day-money,* and *hooey* to mention only a few. A *hazer* is the cowboy who rides as a guide alongside a steer that is to be wrestled; he prevents the steer from turning away from the cowboy who is sliding onto the steer. A *piggin' string* is a rope, usually six feet in length and lightweight, that is used to tie three legs of the calf that has been roped. *Day-money* is the money won from each complete go-round of contestants in an event. Large shows may have as many as seven times around or heads of stock for each cowboy in each event. The largest total day-money wins the event and the additional championship money. *Hooey* is a half-hitch "tie" around the calf's or steer's legs to finish the cowboy's tie; a *tie* is two wraps of the piggin' string around three legs of the calf and then a hooey around two legs. A *twister* is a cowboy, usually in riding events. *Rank* means tough and hard to handle.

Superstitions of the rodeo cowboy include "accidents happen in threes," "hats tossed on a bed in the presence of a rider who is scheduled to contest that day is considered an omen of the worst luck," "a yellow shirt should be shunned," and "if he drops a glove while mounted, he must get down and pick it up—if someone hands it to him he will have an accident and will have to be waited on."

Today rodeos are primarily for men, but in the past women were competitors in all events, no matter how rough. When the rodeo was a part of the Wild West show, girls such as Lucille Muhall thrilled the audiences with riding and roping skills that excelled the abilities of many cowboys. The word *cowgirl* is claimed to have been coined for her alone.

The most colorful era for the rodeo cowgirl was from 1910 to approximately 1930. During this time such cowgirls as "Prairie Lillie" Allen, Fox Wilson, Bertha Blanchet, and "Prairie Rose" Henderson (who in 1901 was the first woman to enter the bronc riding at the Cheyenne show) became well-known and respected rodeo cowgirls. Some married the cowboys who followed the rodeo circuit. Kitty Canutt, wife of the great cowboy Yakima Canutt, had a diamond set in her right front tooth. It is said that when she and Yakima ran out of money, they would remove the diamond and hock it. When their winnings allowed, they would have the diamond re-set in the tooth.

The event for cowgirls that is popular today and a good money event is barrel racing. Barrel racing is a timed event with each girl competing against the stopwatch. The horse is raced in a cloverleaf pattern around three barrels placed in the arena; the fastest time wins. The national championship is determined by competition at the National Finals Rodeo, where, as in the other events, the top fifteen money winners compete. To win between three thousand dollars and ten thousand dollars usually assures a place in the NFR. The other events, especially at RCA shows, are closed to women but a show with no cowgirls making an appearance in some capacity would be dull. For self-protection, the cowgirls organized in 1948 the Girls' Rodeo Association and still stage a few all-cowgirl shows each year.

Other figures vital to the rodeo are the announcer, judges, timekeepers, and producers. The announcer provides the dialog when the action slows down and keeps the spectators alert to where the action is about to take place. The ability to handle a crowd and to work with the cowboys determines the success and popularity of the announcer. "Fog-Horn" Clancy was the most popular announcer before the introduction of the public-address system. In recent years the most popular announcer has been Clem McSpadden. Judges are not obvious to spectators, but they are the men who determine the winners. In riding events there are two judges: one awards points for the horse's performance and the other awards points for the cowboy's ride. Their decision is based on personal judgment. The roping and steer-wrestling events also use two judges, or flagmen. One watches to see if the calf or steer gets a head start; if not, the cowboy is penalized ten seconds for breaking the barrier. The flagman also starts the cowboy's time when he leaves the chute. The other flagman drops the flag to stop the clock when the tie is finished or the steer has been wrestled down; then he indicates if the cowboy qualifies or is to be disqualified due to some error or accident in competition. The timekeepers are at work in each event. They time the riding events so that the cowboy is judged on the correct amount of riding time, and they clock all other events—roping, barrel racing, and bulldogging. The producers provide the livestock for the rodeos. They constantly work at finding and developing strong, healthy animals for competition and take care of the many behind-the-scenes problems of rodeo production. Each of these men is as much a part of the color and action of the rodeo as is the contestant, and each job has its unusual, interesting character.

The rodeo is the wildest, roughest, and most colorful sport in America. It carries the traditions of an industry and of the world of entertainment. It has the thrills and excitement of man pitted against nature, not man against man. Its top winners make good money, but the average contestant does well if he breaks even. Each year men lose their lives in the arena. Death in the arena makes no choice between champion and loser. It is the "suicide" circuit.

A most important characteristic of the rodeo cowboy is his feeling of independence: no sponsors, no guarantee, and no salary. A man is a rodeo cowboy on his own ability to win and to stay in competition. He answers and reports to no one.

When a cowboy misses his tie or loop or does not make his ride, the announcer always says, "He came a long distance, paid his own way, and all that he will take home is your appreciation." Then the applause, excitement, desire to try or gamble "one more time," and friends will lure the rodeo cowboy to the next show.

See Frederick "Foghorn" Clancy, *My Fifty Years in Rodeo* (1952); M. S. Robertson, *Rodeo: Standard Guide to the Cowboy Sport* (1961); and Clifford P. Westermeier, *Man, Beast, Dust* (1947). Of a variety of periodicals, those most useful for current activities are *Hoofs and Horns; Newsletter of the Rodeo Historical Society; Rodeo Sports News;* and *The Western Horseman.* On individual performers, see Thelma Crosby, *Bob Crosby* (1966); Willard H. Porter, *13 Flat* (1967); and Cleo Tom Terry, *The Rawhide Tree* (1957).—G. L.

Rogers, John Rankin (1838-1901). Washington Populist politician. Rogers was born in Maine, where he acquired a rudimentary education; he then studied pharmacy in Boston. Over a twenty-year period he worked as a druggist, farmer, and teacher in Mississippi, Illinois, and Maine. In 1876 he settled in Harvey County, Kansas, where he was active as an Independent and helped organize the Farmers' Alliance. He began his career as a journalist in 1887 when he organized the *Kansas Commoner,* an influential farmer-labor reform newspaper. Before he removed to Puyallup, Washington, in 1889, Rogers was a key leader in the Kansas organizational movement that created the first state People's party in Kansas.

In Washington Rogers established himself in the real estate and mercantile business; undoubtedly he was highly instrumental in transporting the zeal of the Kansas reform movement to the new far-western state. An impressive figure with a magnificent speaking voice, he emerged quickly as the leading Washington Populist.

Representing the Golden Age variety of Populism described by historian Richard Hofstadter, Rogers, from the outset a firm believer in gradual change and fusion of reform elements, was elected governor of Washington in 1896 on a coalition ticket. His administration was such that he won reelection in 1900 by a sizable vote while the remainder of the offices went to Republicans.

See David B. Griffiths, "Far-Western Populist Thought: A Comparative Study of John R. Rogers and Davis H. Waite," *Pacific Northwest Quarterly* (October 1969).—O. G. C.

Rogers, Will[iam Penn Adair] (1879-1935). Humorist, entertainer, and writer. Born on a ranch near Oologah, Cherokee Nation, Indian Territory (present-day Oklahoma), the son of a prominent mixed-blood Cherokee couple, Rogers grew up experiencing the freedom of roping and riding on the range. He attended six schools, including four in the Cherokee Nation, and was an average, although easily bored, student. Despite his later reputation for poor grammar and spelling—a Rogers trademark—he was a literate, well-read man.

In 1898 Rogers went to Texas to work as a cowhand but soon returned home to manage the family ranch. In 1902 he traveled to Argentina to work as a gaucho and a few months later joined Texas Jack's Wild West Show in South Africa, where he was billed as "The Cherokee Kid." In 1903 he toured Australia and New Zealand with the Wirth Brothers Circus, and in 1904 he returned to the United States, joined the Mulhall Wild West Show, and became a vaudeville performer. By this time he had perfected his riding and trick-roping act, which together with his southwestern drawl and wit—another Rogers trademark—made him a star attraction. For more than a decade he worked the vaudeville circuit and in 1916 was billed as a Ziegfeld Follies star attraction. By then, short, pungent comments about newsworthy topics had become the heart of his act. Soon he began combining stage appearances with motion-picture acting.

In 1919 Rogers published his first book, *The Peace Conference*. During the 1920s his popularity with the nation and the world created a demand for lecture tours, radio broadcasts, newspaper and magazine articles, the popular "daily telegrams," and more movies and books. No matter what medium of communication was utilized, the Will Rogers personality and touch remained obvious and dominant.

In 1929 he starred in his first talking movie, *They Had to See Paris*, and his reputation grew. He starred in over fifteen movies. His writing continued at an awesome rate; in all he wrote seven books, an autobiographical manuscript, nearly three thousand "daily telegrams," over one thousand newspaper articles, fifty-eight magazine articles, and literally hundreds of other items.

Most important of all Rogers' talents was his ability to remain current at all times; this ability, together with the Rogers wit, provided laughter and hope for Americans during one of their most trying times, the Great Depression. His concern for his fellow man was expressed through numerous benefits to raise money for hurricane victims in Florida, flood victims in Mississippi, drought victims in the Southwest, earthquake victims in Nicaragua, and many more similar causes.

In 1935 Rogers, long an aviation enthusiast, set out with a fellow Oklahoman, Wiley Post, on a flight to the Orient. On August 15 the plane developed engine trouble near Point Barrow, Alaska, and crashed, killing both men.

Throughout his career Rogers maintained the old family ranch near Oologah and another near Santa Monica, California, both of which have been made into state parks. A third memorial is located in Claremore, Oklahoma.

See William Brown, *Imagemaker: Will Rogers and the American Dream* (1970); Donald Day, *Will Rogers* (1962); Will Rogers, *Autobiography*, ed. by Donald Day (1949); and Betty Rogers, *Will Rogers: His Wife's Story* (1941).—G. L.

Rogers, William Allen (1854-1931). Cartoonist and illustrator. Born in Springfield, Ohio, Rogers at sixteen years of age went to work as an engraver for a firm in Cincinnati and in 1877 joined the staff of *Harper's Weekly*. His first important assignment with *Harper's* was in 1878, when he was sent to cover the visit of President Hayes to the Minnesota State Fair in St. Paul. While in Minnesota, Rogers ventured farther westward, spent some time in Bismarck, then the western terminus of the Northern Pacific Railroad, and visited the nearby Standing Rock Indian agency, where he made a number of sketches of the Sioux in that vicinity. Returning to Bismarck by stage, he traveled by rail to Fargo, North Dakota, and by steamer down the Red River to Fort Garry near present-day Winnipeg. The following year *Harper's* sent Rogers on an excursion to Colorado and New Mexico via the new Santa Fe Railroad out of Kansas City, during which he sketched many scenes of mining life and produced a number of drawings of cowboys and cattle ranching activities. Sometime before 1890 he made another trip to Fargo to observe the industry of the wheat farmers occupying the old buffalo ranges and in 1893 went to Cripple Creek, Colorado, and again to Santa Fe. In 1898-99 he made yet another western tour from Omaha, Nebraska, where he had been sent by *Harper's* to cover the Trans-Mississippi Exposition, continuing on to Oregon and California, and returning to the East by way of Arizona, Texas, and Colorado. The resulting illustrations were considered to be among his best. After about 1900 Rogers devoted himself to cartooning and published an autobiography, *A World Worth While* (1922).

See Robert Taft, *Artists and Illustrators of the Old West, 1850-1900* (1953).—D. C. H.

Rollins, Philip Ashton (1869-1950). Collector of western Americana. Rollins was born in Somersworth, New Hampshire, the son of a prominent railroad financier and insurance executive. When he was five years old, he was entrusted to the famous scout and mountain man Jim Bridger for four months of "tutoring." Later, as a teen-ager, he rode on two occasions with trail herds from Texas to Montana. Such experiences were indeed unique for a Yankee lad raised in luxurious surroundings, but the six months spent on the Dakota reservation of the Cheyenne Indians was even more so.

Rollins received his B.A. degree in American history from Princeton University when he was twenty and his M.A. three years later. He then studied law at Columbia University and was admitted to the New York bar in 1895. Meanwhile, he visited the West regularly and be-

gan assembling his famous library on western Americana and memorabilia. He and his wife, the former Beulah
Brewster Pack, continued their collecting activities for
more than four decades, using their expert knowledge
and appreciation of western lore and their more than
adequate financial resources.

He also developed an interest in writing and in 1922
published his first book, *The Cowboy, His Characteristics,
His Equipment, and His Part in the Development of the West*.
He wrote four other books about cowboys; perhaps the
best known of which was *Jinglebob: A True Story of a Real
Cowboy* (1927). His other published works included four
or five articles for popular magazines and a similar
number of edited narratives, including the journal of
Robert Stuart telling of his overland trip eastward from
the far western fur-trading post of Astoria in 1812-13
(1935).

In 1945 Rollins turned over his valuable collection of
more than three thousand volumes of original manuscripts, guidebooks, maps, printed narratives, and rare
imprints relating to the trans-Mississippi frontier to
Princeton University.—W. E. H.

Rölvagg, O[le] E[dvart] (1876-1931). Novelist. Rölvaag was born in Norway in a small fishing village in the
province Helgeland. His family were fishermen, and he
was trained to follow the sea. He attended school only a
few weeks each year, and when he was fourteen his
father withdrew him entirely, but young Rölvaag read
voraciously on his own. Rölvaag gradually became disillusioned with the fisherman's life, and after a terrible
storm in 1893 that devastated the fishing fleet and from
which he escaped only by a miracle, he wrote to an uncle
who had previously emigrated to the United States asking that he advance the money for a ticket to America. In
1896 Rölvaag, turning down the command of a new
fishing vessel, emigrated and went to work on his uncle's
farm in South Dakota. Though his experiences there
were to form the basis of his famous *Giants in the Earth*
(1926; translated into English, 1927) and its not-so-well-
known sequel, *Peder Victorious* (1928; translated into
English, 1929), Rölvaag worked on the farm for only
three years. In 1899 he entered Augustana College in
Canton, South Dakota, and in 1901 St. Olaf College in
Northfield, Minnesota. After graduation from St. Olaf,
Rölvaag traveled to Norway for a year of graduate study
at the University of Oslo. Upon his return to America in
1906 he joined the faculty of St. Olaf College, where he
remained until his death.

Giants in the Earth, on which Rölvaag's contemporary
reputation almost entirely depends, is the story of the
first Norwegian emigrants to the Dakota Territory. It
tells of the hardships of emigration, of the various
natural perils that the settlers had to overcome, and,
most important, of the psychological threats of loneliness and isolation to the founders of the infant settlements. Rölvaag's unique treatment of the conventional
theme of pioneering hardships may most easily be measured by comparing *Giants in the Earth* with other treatments of closely analogous themes, such as *The Moccasin
Ranch* (1909) by Hamlin Garland, *My Antonia* (1918) by
Willa Cather, *Toilers of the Hills* (1928) by Vardis Fisher.
Unlike these and other more traditionally American
fictional studies of pioneering, *Giants in the Earth* and
Peder Victorious are not at bottom realistically conceived.
As the ominous biblical title of the first indicates,

Rölvaag's prairie serves primarily as a symbolic background against which the inner strengths and weaknesses of his human characters may be shown in bold relief.
Although American in subject, *Giants in the Earth*, with
its psychological orientation, really owes more to a
Norwegian than an American literary tradition.
—J. K. F.

Roman Catholic church. The Roman Catholic
church functioned on a series of frontiers that later
converged to form the United States West. To some of
them she imparted a distinctive flavor; in others her
brief presence during an exploratory and missionary
phase soon gave way to an influx of alien settlers. Sometimes the church persisted in an underground subculture scarcely heeded by the new Establishment, as
among the Mexicans of the Southwest or the Canadian
ex-*voyageur* families of the Northwest. Often she grew
on several levels at a given point—as an Irish immigrant
mass, a French old-settler group, a German farming
community, a network of Indian missions (see ROMAN
CATHOLIC MISSIONARIES), or an assimilated American variety scattered in professional, political, military, or
other spheres. From San Francisco to Portland or Butte,
from St. Louis to Kansas City or Fargo or Santa Fe, each
locality so differed from the others, its reactions and
sometimes its kaleidoscopic evolution so varied, as to
defy neat classfication. The Catholic miner in California
or Montana, the scion of long-established aristocracy in
St. Louis, the Italian vintner or fisherman, the Irish
railroad worker or entrepreneur, the Colorado cattleman or Mississippi riverboat captain did have their faith
in common; but this could be divisive in its cultural
forms, priority of values, and manners of expression.

The spirit of the West lodged in Catholics as it did in
all settlers. There was even a kind of Catholic West. The
settlers became proud of the Catholic antecedents and
heroes they shared with the general populace. Spanish
and French names defined the West. Santa Fe, San
Diego, the Alamo, or the tip of the northwestern coast at
Juan de Fuca Strait bespoke a civilized antiquity long
predating American independence. Dozens of California and Arizona towns recognized their origins in ancient Catholic missions. Four Roman Catholic laymen
and three priests (Eusebio KINO, Jacques MARQUETTE,
and Junípero SERRA) from three western states were
represented in the National Hall of Statuary, a number
equaling that of the more established eastern Catholics.
Even the Mormons pictured Pierre DE SMET on their
Salt Lake monument for his kindly help in designating
Deseret. Catholic national heroes abound, a number of
them converts, such as Kit Carson, Jim Bowie, and (on
his deathbed) "Buffalo Bill" Cody. The "Father of the
Oregon Country," John McLoughlin, and the first governor of California, Peter Burnett, early became
Catholics. General Thomas Meagher, the first acting
governor of Montana Territory; General Shields, the
first governor of Oregon Territory; and Captain John
Mullan, who built the overland military road linking
both oceans via the headwaters of the Columbia and the
Missouri in the 1850s, had always been devoutly so.
Colorful criminals had their Catholic connections.
James Casey, the most notable victim of the San Francisco Vigilantes, rested in a Catholic graveyard amid more
respectable co-religionists; Doc Holliday flirted with
Catholicism and may have died shriven; and Sister Blan-

dina made improbable friends of Billy the Kid and his gang. Catholic cavalry units by the dozen charged Catholic Indians by the hundreds, while armies of Catholic Irish laid rails, punched cows, filled gold and silver boomtowns, and lent both backbone to, and occasion for, the law-and-order movements.

As early as 1841, when parochial prejudices boiled in the East, Archbishop Samuel Eccleston's pastoral letter could remark how "the prairies of the West are dotted with Catholic temples," though in Virginia "Catholicism is scarcely known." To those immigrant Catholic multitudes fortunate enough not to lodge in the eastern ghettoes, the West was a promised land of freedom.

the pastoral structure. Church has multiple meanings—lay, clerical, or ideological—most of them embodied in a range of institutions such as parishes, settlement combines, orders, fraternal organizations, schools, religious papers, hospitals, and myriad groups working within their own separate traditions. Their appearance of efficiency becomes, on closer inspection, the codified confusion of life. But the most visible and documented aspect was the pastoral church—the bishop with his immediate helpers, the priests; his coordinate workers, the nuns and male orders; and the penumbra of lay personnel inserted into the properly episcopal pastorate. This all served as guide, symbol, and point of union for the more massive popular movements, where ultimate effectiveness lay. The school, hall, obligatory Mass, hospital, fund drive, picnic, retreat, fraternal order, or sodality served as focal points for the human dynamics of the whole diocesan body.

The pastoral structure is easily mapped. As a missionary area matured, it became a diocese, usually by progressing through one or more of three embryonic stages: administrative adjunct to a frontier diocese, prefecture apostolic under the mother church in Rome, and vicariate apostolic or inchoate diocese under a bishop. The new diocese (named after a city) lost its underdeveloped hinterlands, which in turn became vicariates, named after a territory; conversely, a vicariate or diocese could suffer progressive amputation as new dioceses were carved out of it. Several dioceses (or even a vast vicariate suddenly broken into dioceses) coagulated into a metropolitan province under its archbishop. Each vicariate or diocese was relatively autonomous, controlling its own parish units and institutions. All would assemble periodically for either a cooperative provincial or a national-plenary council, for common concerns and for uniformity in essentials.

Since the American church was officially missionary or underdeveloped throughout the nineteenth century, Rome intervened more commonly, especially through its Propagation *(Propaganda)* ministry, while European dioceses and orders volunteered men and money. Before 1920 the United States church deployed 70 male orders and 200 female, most of them represented in the West. To start the western church during the United States era, European churches sent distinguished sons— the Spaniard Joseph ALEMANY for California's bishopric, the French-Canadian François BLANCHET for the Pacific Northwest, the French Jean Baptiste LAMY and a few years later Jean Baptiste SALPOINTE for the Southwest, and the French Louis DUBOURG and John Miège or the Italian Joseph Rosati for the church of the Great Plains.

Before the American takeover, the Southwest had begun to outgrow its mission period as a fringe of New Spain, and California had just passed into the diocesan stage. But the national clergy had mostly withdrawn, and their institutions lay collapsed. The same held true for the Louisiana Purchase area, as it went from France to Spain to France to the United States. Quebec expansion reached the Oregon coast in time to transmogrify into an American province and anticipate Catholic settlement. When Bishop Charles Carroll presided over the birth of the first American diocese in 1784, which included all the United States, with 25 priests and 25,000 Catholics, only Quebec's Pierre Gibault at Vincennes remained permanently working in the trans-Allegheny West. Since American control now ran to the Mississippi and the Canadian border (though Rome settled the ecclesiastical jurisdiction only in 1791), Carroll sent Pierre de la Valinière as vicar-general in 1786.

Some remarkable priests followed. The Benedictine Pierre Didier chaplained a settlement project; Admiral François Grasse's chaplain, Charles Whelan, served a tour of duty in the wilds; *émigrés* from the French Revolution fanned out to Vincennes, Kaskaskia, and by 1796, Detroit. The exile Gabriel Richard labored throughout Michigan (1798-1832), becoming delegate to Congress, cofounder of the state university, ecumenist, and publisher of America's first Catholic newspaper. The Russian prince Demetrius Gallitzin spent forty years and a fortune as "Apostle of the Alleghenies" in his Catholic colonies of western Pennsylvania from 1799. But Kentucky was the focus. Here Stephen BADIN, the first priest ordained in the United States, arrived in 1793 to bear the central burden for a quarter century. From 1805 he was helped and succeeded by Charles Nerinckx. Transient auxiliaries included Trappist monks who first came in 1805 and stayed permanently in 1848. Consequently the first western diocese was Bardstown (1808), where Benedict FLAGET presided over Kentucky-Tennessee with responsibility also for the Northwest Territory.

trans-Mississippi West. America's all-encompassing Baltimore diocese was reorganized as a province in 1808, commanding four suffragan dioceses, eighty churches, seventy priests, and seventy thousand Roman Catholics. Its horizons had leaped dramatically when the Louisiana Purchase doubled American territory. Under Carroll's administrative control, Louis Dubourg took over the vacant Spanish-French diocese of New Orleans, residing awhile half way upriver at strategic St. Louis, with an eye on the new West. By 1821 the Dominican Edward Fenwick headed an Ohio diocese in the Old Northwest, and from 1826 Joseph Rosati (from 1843 Peter Kenrick) ruled the vast trans-Mississippi West from his new diocese of St. Louis. As the West became populated dioceses multiplied like rabbits, notably Detroit and the Michigan-into-the-Dakotas area under the German ex-cavalryman Frederick Rese (1833), Indiana's Vincennes under the eminent Parisian physician-turned-priest Simon Bruté (1834), and Iowa's Dubuque under Matthias Loras (1837), each a remarkable leader. By 1840 the American Catholic church had ordered its half-million community into seventeen dioceses with eight in the West. Between 1845 and 1848 the expansionist spirit of manifest destiny added an imperial sweep larger than the Louisiana Territory, to the

Pacific. Beyond the first tier of trans-Mississippi states, each area destined to be a state, or already a state, had evolved into one diocese apiece by 1900. California, Texas, and Kansas, however, had three dioceses each. Nebraska had two. Only Oklahoma and Brownsville, Texas, remained as vicariates apostolic. After 1900 American dioceses proliferated, numbering more than a hundred before 1920.

In the most bizarre episode of structuring the Catholic church, the missionary François Blanchet persuaded Rome to convert the Pacific Northwest region, then a howling wilderness with practically no population, into a galaxy of dioceses grandiloquently organized as the second province of the United States. By 1853 Blanchet's Oregon City (Portland) diocese covered the bottom half of the province from ocean to Rockies, with his brother's Nesqually (Seattle) diocese taking the top. These soon diminished in area to modern Oregon and Washington, the rest becoming Idaho vicariate in 1868 and, after losing western Montana, Boise diocese in 1893. Texas, a prefecture apostolic in 1838, became first a vicariate in 1841 under John Odin, then Galveston diocese from 1847; it gave birth in turn to San Antonio diocese and Brownsville vicariate in 1874 and Dallas diocese in 1890.

The Southwest, finally cleared of claims held by Mexico's bishop of Durango but in deplorable spiritual and clerical condition, was taken in hand as a vicariate apostolic by Bishop Jean Lamy in 1850. It became diocese of Santa Fe in 1853, losing Arizona as vicariate in 1885 and as Tucson diocese in 1897. California broke from Baja California under Alemany in 1850, splitting into a province under San Francisco archdiocese in 1853, with Monterey-Los Angeles in the south as suffragan and the gold country as appendage (vicariate in 1860, diocese of Grass Valley or Sacramento in 1868).

The remainder of the West comprised the vicariate apostolic of Indian Territory under Miège, running east from the crest of the Rockies but excluding the first tier of trans-Mississippi states, and down from Canada into Utah-Colorado-Oklahoma. Vicariates serially detached large masses from it. Kansas broke off in 1850, becoming Leavenworth (later Kansas City) diocese in 1877, then losing Wichita and Concordia dioceses in 1887. Nebraska fell away in 1859, becoming Omaha diocese in 1885, with a twin Lincoln diocese in 1887, and losing both Montana and Wyoming as the dioceses of Helena (1884) and of Cheyenne (1887). Colorado-Utah set up independently under Joseph Macheboeuf in 1868, losing Utah to San Francisco in 1871 (vicariate in 1886 and Salt Lake diocese in 1891) and becoming Denver diocese in 1887. The Dakotas comprised a vicariate in 1879 and split into Fargo and Sioux Falls dioceses in 1889. Oklahoma, last fragment of the grand Indian vicariate, began life anew as a prefecture in 1876, rising to a vicariate in 1887. Thus the 1880s saw a rush of western dioceses—especially those of Cheyenne, Denver, Fargo, Helena, and Sioux Falls for their respective states. As other states came of age in the 1890s, another surge followed in Boise, Dallas, Salt Lake City, and Tucson dioceses.

Further trans-Mississippi provinces consolidated these entities, making in all more than thirty dioceses: Portland (1846), St. Louis (1847), New Orleans (1850), San Francisco (1853), Santa Fe (1875), St. Paul, Min-

nesota (1888), and Dubuque (1893). Brash Texas and Arkansas fell into the orbit of cultivated New Orleans. By the end of the Civil War, sixty religious weeklies had appeared in American dioceses, including Portland's *Sentinel* (1870) and San Francisco's lay-conducted *Monitor* (1858). The country deployed eight orders of men and twenty of women in teaching and counted twenty-nine permanently flourishing colleges; frontier colleges included Notre Dame (1842), St. Louis (1818), Santa Clara (1851), and San Francisco (1855). By 1920, when America's 6,500 parochial schools housed 1.75 million pupils, with 1,500 high schools and 114 colleges, nearly half the 22 universities lay in the trans-Mississippi West with 4 more close by. All these points of contact sited the interrelation of prelates, priests, and nuns with the community. Often such institutions served the non-Catholic community as well. There were many clerical troublemakers, vagabonds, and scalawags in this varied scene and equally plentiful priests of great cultivation, but little has been written about them.

life, told in numbers. The clerical jurisdictions and subculture, so often the substance of "church history," gain their meaning from the needs of the whole Catholic community, to whom they respond. Between 1820 and 1900, as floods of immigrants poured in, the general American populace increased seven and one half times from 9 million to 76 million, but the Catholics needing care increased nearly sixty times! The tiny church of 50,000 in 1800, with fifty priests in two dioceses, nearly doubled by 1810 and again by 1820; it numbered 318,000 by 1830, then doubled in the next decade and again in the 1850s. It held 3 million in 1860 with two thousand priests, 4.5 million in 1870, 6.25 million in 1880, nearly 9 million in 1890, and over 12 million by 1900 with some twelve thousand priests in eighty-two dioceses. Time and again a western region followed the same pattern. A bishop on horseback, disposing of a ludicrously small band of priests, would scatter churches broadcast; carpenter a Gothic cathedral; introduce such orders of priests, monks, friars, contemplatives, brothers, and especially nuns as he could borrow; open a network of schools and (too often) a college; launch a Catholic paper perhaps; hold diocesan synods; organize a chancery; dedicate hospitals, asylums, a seminary, homes for the aged, and other eleemosynary institutions; increase yet again the number of parish centers; and barely keep pace.

Statistics for 1876 show 250,000 Catholics in the St. Louis diocese, with 201 churches, 23 academies, 25 schools, 5 asylums, and 4 hospitals. The northern California-Utah area had 121 priests, 93 churches, 4 colleges, 6 academies, 35 parish schools, 4 asylums, 5 hospitals, and 120,000 Catholics. The other two dioceses of California together held 71 priests, 66 churches with 111 chapels or stations, 4 colleges, 12 academies, 8 parish schools, a hospital, 3 asylums, and 48,000 Catholics. The Southwest, combining the Santa Fe diocese and the vicariates of Arizona and Colorado, reported 170,000 Catholics, 80 priests, 90 churches with 170 chapels, a hospital, 3 academies, a college and 5 schools. The Pacific Northwest, from ocean to Rockies' crest, totaled 31,500 Catholics, 3 hospitals, 3 asylums, 11 academies, 6 parish schools, and 3 colleges; its 51 priests probably included the Indian mission network. The Galveston-Brownsville-San Antonio complex had 95,000 Catholics, 80 churches plus extra chapels, 4 colleges, 20 parish schools, 21 academies, 2 asylums, and 2 hospitals. The Nebraska vicariate, including Wyoming and most of Montana, counted 12,000 Catholics, 20 priests, 20 churches, 56 chapels, 11 parish schools, 3 academies, an asylum, and a hospital. The smaller Kansas vicariate held 40,000 Catholics, 59 priests, 78 churches, and 14 parish schools.

Excluding St. Louis and the more settled first tier of trans-Mississippi states, as well as the sparse Dakotas, these entities included most of the West in 1876 and showed a respectable percentage of the total number of Catholic institutions: 1,600 parish schools, 96 hospitals, 214 asylums, 63 colleges, 557 academies, 5,000 clergy, 5,000 churches, and 5,000 chapels. At the time, Catholics in this geographical half of the country totaled only some 600,000 out of more than 5,600,000 American coreligionists. All these figures soared in the next decade. Around 1885 a diocese-by-diocese history of the American church recorded these typical figures: Portland diocese or the state of Oregon, 43 priests, 50 churches, 2 colleges, 2 seminaries, 13 academies, 9 schools, 2 asylums, 154 nuns, and 17,000 Catholics; San Francisco, 177 priests, 93 churches plus 104 chapels, 6 colleges, 22 academies, 29 schools, 4 hospitals, 5 asylums, and 200,000 Catholics; Santa Fe or the larger part of New Mexico, where Lamy rode horseback 4,000 miles on a single visitation, 54 priests plus missionaries, 36 churches plus 213 chapels, 6 academies, a seminary, a college, a hospital, an asylum, 9 convents, and a mixed population of 111,000 Spanish-speakers, 12,000 unassimilated Indians, and 3,000 others. Utah Territory and vicariate, with only 5,000 Catholics, supported 3 hospitals and a college; Wyoming, with 2,000 Catholics, managed 4 schools and 54 churches or chapels for its 6 priests plus missionaries; Colorado's 50,000 Catholics boasted a college, asylum, 9 academies, and 18 schools, with 64 priests; Arizona's 30,000 had only 16 priests and few institutions yet. Sacramento's 25,000 supported 2 colleges, 8 academies, 3 asylums, and 40 priests; Nebraska's 54,000 had 76 priests and 200 nuns, a college, and 4 academies; South Dakota's 80,000 counted 130 churches plus 94 chapels and 24 schools.

Statistics vary somewhat in nearly simultaneous reports, but the picture reveals such variety as to discourage generalizations, even if one leaves out of account the very different non-Catholic religious ambience of regions and localities. In Texas, Brownsville's 45,000 Catholics were mostly Spanish-speaking with their own devotional patterns, while San Antonio's 60,000 with 3 colleges, 3 academies, 29 schools, a seminary, 2 asylums, and 150 churches or chapels represented a more cosmopolitan and developed situation. In comparison, the three dioceses of settled Kansas with nearly 100,000 Catholics of more northerly origins, 11 hospitals or eleemosynary institutions, 3 colleges, 13 academies, and 200 priests comprised a different world.

Comparative populations by state and Roman Catholicity may suggest the relative impact of Catholics by 1910, when the West still wore its older face. Arizona counted 28,500 Catholics in a population of 204,300; Arkansas, 23,000 out of 1,574,000; California, 391,000 of 2,377,000; Colorado, 105,000 of 799,000; Idaho, 16,000 of 325,000; Iowa, 261,600 of 2,225,000; Kansas, 120,000 of 1,691,000; Louisiana, 583,000 of 1,656,000; Minnesota, 323,000 of 2,075,000; Missouri, 455,000 of 3,293,000; Montana, 85,000 of 376,000; Nebraska, 130,700 of 1,192,000; Nevada, 11,500 of 82,000; New Mexico, 160,570 of 327,000; North Dakota, 93,800 of 577,000; Oklahoma, 36,900 of 1,657,000; Oregon, 61,000 of 672,000; South Dakota, 78,000 of 584,000; Texas, 300,900 of 3,897,000; Utah, 8,000 of 373,000; Washington, 90,000 of 1,142,000; and Wyoming, 12,000 of 98,000. Percentages serve less usefully, since one region was almost deserted in comparison with another. But in 1964 a much rearranged West, reporting Catholics by diocese, gave Arizona's two dioceses as 25 percent and 24 percent of the general population; Arkansas, 3 percent; California's seven as 16, 16, 18, 19, 19, 26, and 37 percent; Colorado's two as 17 and 27 percent; Idaho as 7 percent; Iowa's four as 12, 15, 19, and 22 percent; the Kansas four as 11, 14, 17, and 17 percent; Louisiana's two as 8 and 56 percent; Minnesota's six as 18, 21, 25, 26, 28, and 39 percent; Missouri's four as 4, 10, 11, and 29 percent; Montana's two as 21 and 25 percent; Nebraska's three as 11, 17, and 28 percent; Nevada as 21 percent; New Mexico's odd pattern as totaling 43 percent; North Dakota's two as 24 percent and 30 percent; Oklahoma, 3 percent; Oregon's two as 8 and 12 percent; South Dakota's two as 18 and 22 percent; the Texas eight as ranging across 5, 6, 8, 15, 18, 28, 38, and 58 percent; Utah, 5 percent; Washington's three as 12, 13, and 14 percent; and Wyoming, 15 percent.

laity: the unexamined church. The idea that the layman was passive is an optical illusion, caused by excessive focus on clerical concerns and institutions. In fact, the layman supported his church psychologically and financially in the West, kept the faith amid the distractions and trials of daily life, catechized his children, subscribed to religious journals, underwrote the schools, enrolled in the sodalities, flocked to novenas and revivalistic "missions," applauded church victories, opened ecumenical doors before the clergy knew the word, made charities possible by stupendous generosity, and brought the qualities of Roman Catholic life to the immediate attention of non-Roman Catholic neighbors. His local priest was a symbol of the community, so that the laity set a high standard of conduct for him and were personally pained when he failed them.

The layman lived in a church whose practices and style were rooted in the old-country cultures. Yet his Europeanized church contrived to be distinctly American. From the distant view, it seems that harmony reigns and the saints stand plain. Closer up, it becomes discouragingly clear that scoundrels abound, scandals happen, and heroes are mainly ordinary men who rise to an occasion without losing their unattractive qualities. That world seems much the same as now; yet the stage *was* different and the sense of expectancy was different.

In its woolier phase the West challenged a man's faith; he coped or he drifted away, though an ethnic identification might anchor the weakling. Thus Blanchet remarked how the ubiquitous French-Canadian *voyageurs* he served turned either devout or degenerate. Until the decades settled the western locale into seemly ruts, the sense of new beginnings and voluntary cooperation drew the parishioner closer to the relatively rare clergy, a tendency strengthened by the occasional whiff of outside bigotry and not diminished by inevitable internal quarrels. Catholic bigotry in turn proved insulative and stimulating. It was a part of the pushing assertiveness in an open environment where everyone rather enjoyed a good fight. The oddly nonvirulent polemic of the western regions, full-throated but somehow bloodless, deserves study. Catholicism reinforced both the West's individualistic and its communitarian orientations. The individual had to support his minority religion, take some responsible role or stance, and justify his oddness to neighbors. But he naturally formed part of a supportive sub-community, experiencing a small-town relationship with his Mass-going colleagues. He was much less embattled than eastern or even certain midwestern fellows, since he did not live in an antipathetic society long established. In Butte, Cheyenne, Denver, St. Louis, Sacramento, Tucson, or Santa Fe (though perhaps not Portland), the air differed from that of Boston, New York, or Philadelphia.

Roman Catholicism in the West often displayed the virtues and flaws of its ambience—pragmatic, generous, open, able to survive and eventually transcend ethnic feuds, optimistic, activist, the manipulator and despoiler of nature. It also partook of the ethnic qualities or social prejudices of its times and places, producing Catholic leaders of the Chinese-Must-Go and vigilante movements, as well as defenders of the Indian and the exploited laborer. The western Catholic shared with many Americans a reverence for education, paradoxically combined with a disinclination for its demanding research scholarship and creative underpinnings. A broad cultural base was lacking. The imported clerical scholar of early days, however, often lent a note of distinction that was absent in the general run of American schoolmen who immediately succeeded him. Frequently the European missionary on a frontier, graced with medical and architectural training, as was Anthony RAVALLI, or publishing in several languages, as did De Smet, seemed to pioneers a paragon of intellectuality. Bishops such as Alemany, Blanchet, Lamy and Miège gave their sees a continental flavor. The Far West's Jesuits came under the direction and staffing of northern Italy. The liturgical inheritance and age-old traditions served as a counterweight against the stark western sense of beginnings.

To assess the properly western aspects, however, one must leave the clerical subculture and study the lay communities. For can one generalize about Catholicism in regions as diverse as Mediterranean California, Mormon Utah, the Mexican-American Rio Grande, North Dakota where the majority of Catholics were German-speakers from Russia, Minnesota with a complicated Germanic-Scandinavian flavor, dry-farming Nebraska, or cattle Colorado?

the immigrant church reappraised. To reappraise the Roman Catholic church in the West, each eastern theme that burdens it demands restudy in its western context. Consider the cliché that depicts the nineteenth-century American church as largely the creation of Irish peasants, in the shape of Irish prelates, clergy, and immigrant floods. They created the activist, Philistine, relentlessly Americanizing church of the laboring classes. Is the assumption true for the West? Immigrants did form the West, but everyone there was a new arrival. Western immigrants did include large bodies of Irish, but not to the same extent as the East nor with the same meaning. In 1870, three of ten westerners were foreign; in California the Irish numbered one in four. At the very

moment when Italian, German, and Slavic waves washed over the West while the Irish wave subsided, the Irish were in position to inherit the clerical posts. What reality underlay such appearances? General data, in the absence of sophisticated immigration history, merely point up the problem. From 1820 to 1900, some 2.25 million Irish Catholics entered America, 1.25 million German, .5 million Austrian Empire, .5 million Italian, .33 million Polish, and a million French-speaking. The pace varied. From 1815 to 1866, Irish Catholic immigrants numbered 1.5 million, Germans .5 million and French 140,000, while domestic conversion added 100,000 Americans. From 1870 to 1900 the Irish Catholic arrivals dropped to 520,000, while Germans rose to 686,000 and Austrian Empire peoples to 366,000. From 1880 to 1900, Polish Catholics immigrated to a total of nearly 300,000 and Canadians to 500,000. The distribution throughout the West and into influential positions such as the religious orders, has not yet been charted, though the German and Polish impact on the Midwest is obvious and though a Canadian government report in 1873 estimated 150,000 recent French-Canadian immigrants in the Midwest alone.

Schemes to start specifically Roman Catholic colonies of immigrants in the West had enjoyed some success from 1815 onward, backed by such men as Bishop Mattias Loras of Iowa and Joseph Crétin of Minnesota, culminating in the Buffalo convention of T. D. McGee in 1856. An older West saw the settlement project of the Russian prince Father Gallitzin, helped by the king of Holland and other friends. The trans-Mississippi West became a colonizing target by the 1830s. An organized movement in the 1880s centering on Minnesota, Nebraska, and Arkansas realized limited success. Some 30,000 went to western states in such religious movements, not to mention the ethnic colonies that were only reflexively religious.

The mix among churchmen followed its own formula. Around 1820 the fifty-two priests throughout America divided as fourteen French, twelve Americans, eleven Irish, seven Belgians, four English, three Germans, and one Italian. Of some two dozen bishops in 1830, seven were French, seven Irish, and six of other origin. Of the thirty-two bishops assembled for the 1852 national council, nine were American, eight French-speaking, and eight Irish. In the forty-three dioceses in the seven provinces of 1866, two-thirds of the bishops were foreign—ten French, three French-Canadian, four Belgian, eight German, and six from five other nations, with fifteen of the twenty-five Americans coming from Irish backgrounds. How did this translate in terms of the West? Beyond the first tier of trans-Mississippi states the foreign hand was heavier until 1880. There was but one American as diocesan (Anthony Pellicer) and one as vicar-apostolic (Dominic Manucy). Seven of those sixteen dynamic bishops building the new churches were French-speaking. Three were from Spain and two from Germany; one was Irish, two American; two Irish held the Nebraska vicariate. The 1880s added three French, two Belgians, and two Germans, but was balanced now by seven Irish. The last decade balanced four Irish and four to six American-Irish newcomers against four Belgians, two French, two Spaniards, one German, and one Swiss.

If the majority of priests in America by 1875 were

Irish, as a contemporary historian reckoned, with four hundred of them sharing nineteen names and O'Reilly leading the parade, and if 4 million of the 6.5 million Catholics then were Irish or of Irish descent, how true was this of the West? These statistics certainly do not reflect some of the Wests some of the time. Of the twenty-seven male orders than working in America, only the Dominicans and Holy Cross priests CLEARLY reveal an Irish majority. Of the twenty-three main orders among the forty-four orders of nuns already in the United States, the Irish were a majority in only four with something over a third of the membership. Of these mixed-origin groups, in orders either of men or women, who worked the West? And even if Irish clergy or nuns laid a heavy impress on the western church, did the dominant non-Irish western leaders channel those energies in ways differing from the East? The Jesuit missionaries establishing the church in the Pacific Northwest interior began in 1841 as three Belgians, one French, one Italian, one German, and one Dutch, soon joined by three Italians, two Belgians, one Dutch, one Swiss, one Irish, and one Maltese. Peering closely from another vantage, we see that by 1876 only one western state appears on a list of eight states with the highest population of Irish. This is California, which barely makes last place with 54,000, just enough to stave off the rising Chinese. California was then forty percent foreign, with its Italian population alone rising from 5,000 in 1870 to 60,000 in 1905 and soon becoming the largest foreign stock in the state. Since California attracted many Catholic ethnic groups including the most Negro Catholics in the Far West, the usual interpretations of Irish preponderance call at least for qualification. Elsewhere, of the eight states with highest German immigration, no less than three lay in the trans-Mississippi West.

In America as a whole, the Catholic church of the nineteenth century was urban, immigrant, and an intruder. But this fact has little meaning for San Francisco, which by 1906 was less than fifteen percent Protestant and by 1910 was sixty-eight percent foreign or first-generation. In New Mexico by the turn of the century Mexicans were half the foreign population, and Italians came second. The clichés and assumptions that have been applied to the entire American Catholic church because they have some validity in the East are very misleading for the West. There the assimilation of immigrant groups was swifter, their urbanization was quite different and sometimes much less than that of the easterners, and their foreign handicap was to some extent shared by their mobile American neighbors.

The best source of statistics on Roman Catholic institutions is *Sadlier's Catholic Directory and Almanac,* 61 vols. (1833-96). Information on bishops and other eminent men, dioceses, technical terms, and special topics can be found in the *New Catholic Encyclopedia* (1967). Among general articles in that book, see especially John Tracy Ellis, "United States of America," with the works cited there.—R. I. B.

Roman Catholic missionaries. By 1900 perhaps a third of United States Indians were Roman Catholic, a far higher proportion than among whites. Percentages of Indian Catholics have varied wildly from region to region during the country's development, and whole mission populations have disappeared, as in California

and Kansas. A list of missions would be misleading. Some failed; others half-succeeded or prospered briefly or recovered in erratic cycles; many controlled the Catholics in a dozen neighboring tribes unnamed in mission titles. With or without a mission, most tribes held at least a few Catholics. Wholly pagan tribes, far from any mission, fell under a vast penumbra of influence, some chiefs proudly wearing copper crosses and even during wars welcoming the priest. The "Black-robe" (originally a Jesuit but eventually any Roman Catholic priest) was a dramatically spiritual figure, without family or possessions, and differed from his white contemporaries in dress and in purpose. He commanded respectful cooperation from the greatest non-Roman Catholic leaders, such as Sitting Bull, Kamiakin, Chief Joseph, Little Dog, and Red Cloud.

If mapping the missions is difficult, listing mission contributions to the West is a more elusive task. In places as different as California, New Mexico, and Montana they inaugurated a region's stock and artisan life, introduced agricultural products and methods, and formed the nucleus for cities. No body of men matches the missioners' record as explorers of the West; they also performed such unrecognized services as helping the railroad explorations and the Mullan Road. Their linguistic and ethnological findings form a treasure. From the seventy-three volumes of Jesuit *Relations* to the voluminous works of Pierre DE SMET, they promoted interest and respect for the Indian and preserved the spiritual history of a hundred tribes. They inaugurated medical and educational services as a matter of routine; many a frontier white had his bones set or his child schooled at the local mission. Their work for peace would require volumes. At the height of Sitting Bull's 1868 war, only De Smet could ride through 350 miles of hostile territory into the war camp of the confederated Sioux nations near the Powder River, and against all probability contrive a peace for the government. Living in both worlds, the priests, brothers, and Lady Black-robes, or nuns (such as Rose Philippine DUCHESNE) comprised a universal bridge between Indian and white. Settlers, politicians, and soldiers often aided their work, increasing its humanitarian impact in both directions. Many of the Indian-built edifices left behind—from the California chain of missions and the ALAMO and SAN XAVIER DEL BAC missions of the Southwest, to the imposing baroque Coeur d'Alene edifice erected without nails or proper tools in the Idaho wilderness—still contribute a unique nostalgic beauty.

Evangelization of the Indian in the West, from the sixteenth to the beginning of the twentieth century, surpassed in difficulty the conversion of Europe a millennium or more earlier. The scale of operations was staggering; the Oregon country alone equaled in land area France, Germany, Italy, and Spain combined. Dispersed in this hardly accessible vastness lived some 125 loosely aggregated "tribes" speaking 56 mutually unintelligible languages. A recent classification system lists for all of North America 221 mutually unintelligible languages. Most tribes existed in very small units, usually moving about so as to make sustained contact impossible, while the concept of settling down revolted them. Political structures varied greatly, generally affording no handle for controlling the group. Socioeconomic and cultural differences defied easy analysis and prohibited any single approach. Not only complexity and space, but time itself worked against the United States missioner. Single individuals such as the Iroquois François Saxa, who traveled 2,000 miles from the inaccessible Northwest as part of the Flathead Delegation seeking priests in St. Louis in 1835, lived through the entire span of trans-Mississippi Catholic missions, saw the Northern Pacific Railroad thunder by his door, and died as a respected Montana cattleman in 1919. His career reflects the change in culture from which the Indians suffered. If the process of conversion, involving a sustained psychological transformation, had its normal difficulties, these circumstances rendered it formidable. Inadequate resources compounded the problem. A burgeoning flock of whites—increasing from under 200,000 in 1825 to 1.5 million in 1850, then to nearly 6.25 million by 1880 and over 12 million before 1900—distracted the infant church from Indian ventures. The church deployed her handful of clerics, largely foreign volunteers, with priority for these white birds-in-the-hand, rather than abandoning present Catholics for a merely potential Indian group that totaled only 330,000 in 1837 and (despite the enormous far western Indian population added ten years later) less than 250,000 by 1900.

Resources nonetheless went steadily to this mission field and Indian souls always remained a target. A stubborn array of missionaries, content to be nameless, buried themselves in their Indian apostolates despite appalling recurrence of external adversities—removal and reservations, maniacal intertribal warfare, serial wars with the whites, gold rushes, influx of settlement upon unprepared tribes, corrosive racism, white diseases which devastated, and whiskey which demoralized. Whole tribes diminished at a genocidal rate, as though cut down by scythes, and some nearly disappeared. Through it all the few missioners insinuated themselves into tribe after tribe, mastered each dialect and set of cultural idiosyncrasies, devised some pattern for maintaining contact with far-flung units, altered tribal folkways sufficiently to support the Christian essentials, provided the education required to survive in a white ambience, and then revised their whole program as kaleidoscopic change dictated and tried to cope against the cultural disintegration and despairing apathy that fastened upon the Indian as the prevailing white civilization eventually destroyed initiative.

In addition to the missionaries, there were many heroic Indian Catholic laymen and women who stand neglected in the peripheral shadow of the clerics and institutions—patriarchs such as the Flathead chiefs Happy Man (Victor) and Little Claw of Grizzly (Charlo); Christian warriors such as the Pend d'Oreille head chief, No Horses (Alexander); strong promoters of the faith such as the head chief of the central Sioux, Man Who Strikes the Ree (Pananapapi); stubborn peacemakers such as the Coeur d'Alene Seltis; devout women leaders such as Seltis' colleague Sighouin, or Sister Mary Two-Beard and her heroic band of Sioux nuns on the Cuban battlefields; and a roll call of Catholic chiefs from Seattle of the Dwamish to POKAGON of the Potawatomi to Blackbird of the Ottawa.

The American West comprised a single section of the larger European-world mission front in the nineteenth century—one of the greatest mission eras in history. Popular literacy, new communications, imperial expansion, the Romantic movement, and the renaissance of religious enthusiasm after the Napoleonic era fueled the enthusiasm of high and low. Europe sent its money and sons to the Indian frontier as to a dozen other fields; her orders shifted personnel here as to a correlative war zone. Thus the western missions reflected European vicissitudes, enjoyed an international staff, drew money from such pious organizations as the Propagation de la Foi of Paris and Lyons, the Austrian Leopoldinen Stiftung, and the Bavarian Ludwig-Missionsverein. French and Italian clergy bulked large in the work, though Belgians, Swiss-Germans, troops of Irish and even Indian nuns, and every group from Slovenes to Mexicans contributed distinguished representatives. European anti-clerical pressures sporadically made priests available to the missions; European Catholic self-confidence and sophistication preserved the effort from log-cabin parochialism. And though the missions suffered their share of eccentric, lazy, and scandalous or merely peasant clerics, the average missioner stood out among whites of the early West by education, talent, and general cultivation. Much of the Indians' spiritual story during the 1800s reflects European movements, echoes with European devotions and conventions, and still lies hidden away in European archives.

A concomitant of European influence was the widespread preeminence of French Canada; her langauge and frontiersmen infiltrated the Great Plains and Far Northwest, increasing even during the early nineteenth century and amounting to an immigration movement of many thousand onto or near the tribal scene. François BLANCHET, De Smet, and others testify to this universal preparatory work done especially by the fur trade *voyageurs,* though they acknowledge a whole class of them to be scoundrels. Robillard pre-instructed the Okanagon tribes; Berland, the Flatbow; Pambrun, the lower Columbia, while counterparts influenced such tribes as the Potawatomi and Sioux. Catholic Iroquois roamed the Far Northwest before 1800 and soon formed a third of the Hudson's Bay Company's fur employees. La Mousse, with his twenty-four Iroquois moving from Montreal into the Flathead country in 1816, provides one example of this Indian proselytizing presence, the messianic "Shining Shirt" another. The French-speaking American missionaries with their "French religion" thus found many Indians prepared. Nor were the tribes passive cooperators. From Michigan to Oregon they frequently took the initiative, sending envoys for priests. For twenty years Pananapapi of the Yankton Sioux, who had been refused baptism by De Smet in 1844, reiterated his pleas and prepared his tribe until accepted. Sitting Bull and his chiefs, Little Dog of the Blackfoot Piegan, a council of thirty Shoshoni, the Cheyenne chiefs, and many others requested Blackrobes. The motives of many Indians were mixed at the start. Some superstitiously wanted stronger "medicine," but multitudes persevered in Christian life responsibly. In the person of the Delaware-Comanche Indian Jesuit James BOUCHARD, the tribes turned the tables and for decades helped evangelize whites of the early West.

The United States missions—philanthropic and private rather than religio-governmental, like the Spanish and French missions—lacked resources and protection to attempt an interlocking program of settlement. A nuclear center at some strategic point and itinerant visitation with eventually a modest church-*cum*-school replaced the regimented systems of California or the looser mission-church progression in the Pueblo country. Along the Mississippi River and especially in the Far Northwest and Rockies, Jesuits did experiment with the form of voluntary, educative commune called a Reduction. They respected native cultures insofar as they were compatible with essential Christian commitment and with survival in an increasingly white environment. Their basic principle of "accommodation," reflected to a lesser degree in some other Roman Catholic missions, counseled assimilation to native language and culture, minimal adaptation of Indians to white ways, and naturalizing a society to Christianity rather than "civilizing" or westernizing it. They did not hesitate to transform economic or behavioral patterns where necessity demanded, though the change was always in terms of Indian psychology.

The memory of the successful fur-economy missions of New France and especially the utopian agricultural Indian state of the Paraguay Reductions haunted the American efforts. But whereas the Spanish mission operated as a transitional stage toward a townsman-citizen future (a kind of government project for "developing" underdeveloped nations) and whereas the French government encouraged the essentially transient fur missions for its own economic and military advantage, nineteenth-century Americans considered the Paraguay and New France stages an ideal and end unto themselves, innocently mutating them into an effective new methodology. The more ambitious centers acted as models and service stations for wandering units. They boasted an Indian farming settlement, a range of buildings perhaps encased in a fort, and a handsome church. Resident families from the host tribe and from a dozen unlikely neighboring tribes transformed a center into a wilderness oasis. A concourse of all available Roman Catholics and many pagans flocked here for the pageantry and festivities of recurrent religious feasts. Daily routine emphasized liturgical solemnities, Indian services and rhetoric, training in manual and agricultural skills, a militia for defense, and sometimes a press. Awards, musical bands, organized hunts, games, and even puppetry had their roles.

Like the older missions, the United States effort tried to be universal and continuing, its horizon comprising all tribes. Direction was multiple. The Propaganda Fidei at Rome oversaw the range of activity, and American national councils encouraged the enterprise. But the brunt fell partly on the frontier bishops for their respective neighborhoods, usually by recourse to a spare cleric or part-time effort, and especially on the variety of international, semiautonomous orders, each with its own traditions, resources, and hierarchy of superiors. Benedictines, Dominicans, Franciscans (including branches like Capuchins and Recollects), Oblates, Sulpicians, the newly restored Jesuits, and others sent in priests. Unlike the earlier Franco-Hispanic work, improvisation and circumstance tended to prevail.

the borderlands of New France and New Spain. By locale and effect, the abortive borderland missions link directly with the American West. From the sixteenth to the nineteenth centuries, their blood and incredible endurance won Indian acceptance of the Blackrobe image. Some tribes, wandering or removed westward, carried seeds of the faith; as late as 1879 Ponziglione found this situation among displaced Cherokee and Creek on the Great Plains. From Columbus and Cartier onward, conversion had comprised a concomitant motive of Spanish and French empire builders. Coronado's Franciscan friars of 1540 in the Southwest, Menéndez's lay instructors in Florida a quarter century later, and the Jesuit movement from 1611 down the St. Lawrence in Canada began the epic. Before 1776, from California to New York, Indian tribes had murdered eighty-four clerics. Isaac JOGUES died in New York after terrible tortures; the earliest, Juan de Padilla, fell in central Kansas in 1540. Disease and hardship claimed many more. Eventually the mission networks flanked the incipient Anglo-American entity all along its southern and northern borders and hemmed it in along the west from Detroit past Vincennes to New Orleans. Within these borders, French missioners had converted tribes in Maine and upper New York and labored widely in the trans-Allegheny country. Capuchin, Franciscan, Sulpician, diocesan "Seminary," and especially Jesuit missions radiated in all directions, along the Indian trade and water lanes, hampered by continual colonial and tribal wars but living in symbiosis with French military power. Even the largest contingent, the Jesuits, numbered only fifty around 1750.

After the Huron and Algonquian confederations and the Five Nations of the Iroquois were converted, the main thrust went through the Neutral Indians around the Great Lakes region into the Michigan-Wisconsin-Minnesota area and simultaneously south into the Iowa-Illinois-Indiana country. Claude Jean Allouez, for example, evangelized Indians by the tens of thousands. Following the pioneering of the Jesuit Jacques MARQUETTE in 1673, nomadic and reunion missions began to line either bank of the Mississippi through Oklahoma and Arkansas to the Gulf of Mexico, fanning out in the South. Sheer dimension tended to swallow the few priests. Though not many tribes of the older West or along the margins of the trans-Mississippi West escaped their influence, the movement tended to result in a few solid centers and many weak or ephemeral outposts. Brandy, tribal wars, and Jesuit suppression (1764 in France but more effectively, by papal or universal suppression, 1773) dealt the enterprise awful blows. But the mortal wound came when the Hundred Years War against England, which so harrassed the missions, culminated disastrously in 1763 with France's exclusion from the New World. Still, on the eve of the American Revolution the Ottawa mission on the western Great Lakes alone counted twenty thousand Indians from more than twenty nations. In the Illinois country, Pierre Gibault's influence with Indians and French was able to swing that area to Colonel George Rogers Clark and the American cause against England. The French, including three hundred Jesuits in all, had wrestled with a roll call of tribes belonging then or later to the West—the Arkansas, Caddo, Chickasaw, Choctaw, Cree, Fox, Illinois, Kickapoo, Menomini, Miami, Missouri, Natchez, Ojibwa, Ottawa, Pawnee, Potawatomi, Sauk, Sioux, Winnebago, Yazoo, and a dozen other tribes assimilated to these groups. In the end, however, few areas of permanent conversion survived the departure of France, west and south of the St. Lawrence, though traces remained among the Indiana Potawatomi, Illinois Kaskaskia, Michigan Ottawa and Ojibwa, and an unnumbered diaspora of isolated faithful. If the French effort cannot bear comparison with Spain's, it does stand in its own right as a prodigious achievement. Reinforced by Canadian voyageurs, the tribal West never lost the French imprint. A lifetime later, Blackrobes needed no introduction.

Spanish establishments, more solid and comprehensive, formed a moving frontier. The catechetical *encomienda* system, with its six million Indians, gave way in frontier zones after 1573 to the protective, transitional mission, designed to evolve into a Hispanic town. It varied, according to resources, from sophisticated commune to simple church center. The historian Herbert Bolton calculates that the Jesuits alone, in Latin and North America, baptized at least two million Indians in their missions; around 1750 Jesuits cared for some 700,000, the Franciscans for over 200,000. By 1800, thirty out of forty-one Latin American bishops were Indians or halfbreeds. In the borderlands or United States sector, the Southeast by 1634 counted 30,000 Indians around forty-four centers under thirty-five missionaries; in 1763, ruined by border fighting, the region fell to the English. North from Mexico, a triple thrust carried into the Southwest, by sea to California, and more feebly into Texas. The New Mexico region had 60,000 of the culturally advanced Pueblo in thirty missions and thirty stations under fifty Franciscans until 1680, when the medicine man Popé's nativist rebellion shattered the system beyond more than fractional recovery (see NEW MEXICO MISSIONS). From 1692, it peaked again by 1750-76, with 18,000 Indians in twenty missions. But a variety of factors led to stagnation and then to decline. The legendary Eusebio Francesco KINO—explorer, cartographer, cattle king, and "Apostle of Arizona"—founded twenty-four missions including Tucson's San Xavier del Bac, traveled thousands of miles in forty expeditions, and by 1711 had personally baptized 4,500 Pima and Papago. The promise soon dimmed, however, under the impact of varied misfortunes.

Texas missions such as the ALAMO show a spotty record, but by 1760 they had gathered 15,000 converts from dozens of tribes. The fierce Navaho-Apache-Comanche barrier, penetrated but never broken, the distance and lack of manpower, the compromising accompaniment of white settlement, the rebellions, intramural quarrels, political exploitation, rooted native cults, anti-acculturation resentment, Jesuit suppression by the Spanish crown in 1767, and all the turmoil and governmental scattering of tribes culminating in Mexican independence, with mass flight of missioners refusing the anti-Spanish oath, help explain the southwestern religious collapse on the eve of America's takeover. California's shortlived but imposing twenty-one Franciscan missions, begun in 1769 by Junípero SERRA along 600 miles from San Diego to just north of San Francisco, served by 1830 more than 30,000 Catholic Indians in an empire of irrigated ranches and orchards boasting three quarters of a million head of stock. They soon ended by Mexican confiscation in 1834, epidemic diseases, and genocide by gold miners.

The colonialist implications and arbitrary regimentation of all these church-state schools of Spanish citizenship and religion disquiet the modern American, who sometimes exaggerates these elements and discounts the real share of Indian control, or misapprehends the nature of Europe's unitary societies. From the sixteenth to the nineteenth centuries the Spaniards, aided by Germans and other national groups in the orders, had set up their missions—parochial as well as communal, ephemeral or solid—from San Francisco Bay on the Pacific to Chesapeake Bay on the Virginia coast, and made contact with almost every tribe there from Apache to Zuñi. Sporadic efforts penetrated north as far as Nebraska, encountering the French counterthrust. The solid march of missions, mutating into parishes with Hispanicized citizens as the frontier advanced, helped create a mixed white-Indian people. Its cutting-edge, from the Golden Gate to East Texas, finally crumbled and corrupted just before the American advance swept over it.

United States beginnings: Far Northwest to 1785. The republic's embryonic Roman Catholic church, under its first bishop Charles Carroll, amounted to little more than a large tribe itself—twenty-five thousand in a total population of nearly four million. Still emerging from colonial penal laws and restrictions, it managed an apostolate to neighboring Indians often by using exile-priests from revolutionary France, such as François Ciquard in Maine. Beyond the Alleghenies—where the Quebec diocese had held the field, largely with infrequent transients—Carroll despatched Jean Rivet and Pierre Janin to years of disappointing effort in the Illinois country. Soon a few men such as Benedict FLAGET in Vincennes, Michel Levadoux in Kaskaskia, and Gabriel Richard in Detroit (who interested three presidents in his Plan for Indian Education) joined in to carry the work into the early nineteenth century, often by stopgap visitation to salvage earlier French achievement. In the 1830s the Slovenes Frederic BARAGA and Francis Pierz, and from 1845 Ignatius Mrak, ranged with great success among the Ojibwa and Ottawa, by 1840 boasting nine small schools. The *émigré* Stephen BADIN and the German Frederick Rese (one of Gethard von Blücher's dragoons at Waterloo) went in the 1820s to the Potawatomi. Joseph Crétin and the Dominicans Samuel Mazzuchelli and Theodore Van den Broek were from the 1830s among the Iowa-Michigan-Wisconsin tribes. They worked successfully among the Menomini but ultimately failed with the Winnebago. In the embryonic Kentucky church, Badin and Charles Nerinckx did not neglect their Indians. Modern Canada's westward missions prepared for the American, both by penetrating United States areas and by converting Indians who ignored the white man's boundary line. Severe Dumoulin in the 1820s and George Belcourt in the 1830s visited those bands in North Dakota accessible from Quebec's Red River settlement.

The Louisiana Purchase of 1803 thrust upon the infant church responsibility over a world of trans-Mississippi tribes—under the New Orleans prelate rather than Quebec's, but from 1826 under the new St. Louis diocese. The American government's "voluntary" removal of nearly all Indian tribes, dumping them across the river into this presumably waste territory from 1830, dictated the immediate critical zone. Mexican War and Oregon country acquisitions in 1845-48 soon added the Far West, Southwest, and Pacific Northwest tribes. Louis DUBOURG of New Orleans secured a dozen of the newly restored Jesuits under the quirky Charles Van Quickenborne, who opened a shortlived Indian school near St. Louis (1824-30). The Jesuits unsuccessfully experimented with missions among the Kansas Kickapoo (1836-39), the Iowa Potawatomi (1838-41), and the Kansas Miami (1839-41), receiving from the American bishops main responsibility for the missions of the West. Their gratifyingly successful missions among the Kansas Potawatomi (1837-67) and the mixed-blood Osage (1847-67) led to forays such as De Smet's to the Yankton Sioux in 1839. Arapaho, Cheyenne, and a dozen distant tribes were commonly visited, while the missionaries circulated among Cherokee, Delaware, Kansa, Oto, Ponca, Quapaw, Seneca, Shawnee, and other tribes accessible in the mixed neighborhood. The breakup of reservations dissolved these projects thirty years later. Meanwhile Quebec's François Blanchet opened a second front on the Oregon-Washington coast in 1838, informally mixed with general pastoral concerns but effective.

Many tribes pleaded for priests, the most spectacular example being the four Flathead Delegations from 1831 to 1839. The first delgation communicated only by the Catholic Sign of the Cross; the others, representing half a dozen tribes, were led by French-speaking Catholic Iroquois. De Smet, hard upon a reconnaissance tour in 1840, exuberantly sowed missions among Montana's Flathead, Idaho's Coeur d'Alene, and Washington's Okanagon, Kalispel, Pend d'Oreille, and Kettle, with a roving appointment to the Blackfoot. No man of any mission period enjoyed the rapport that De Smet had with the wide Indian world. An idol of the northwestern and Plains tribes, De Smet commanded the devotion of pagan tribes who hated whites, yet he was more a publicist and financier than a working missioner. He lived among a hundred tribes, from Absaroka to Zingomene, brought a hundred priests and a million francs to the West, won a major's rank in the army as he stopped or forestalled general wars, baptized thousands of children in most of the Plains tribes, published prodigiously in several languages, traveled more than 200,000 miles, strangled to death an attacking bear, and charmed popes, politicians, generals, and rulers. His first trip to the Rockies, for example, turned into a triumphal tour as he preached to the Cheyenne, various tribes of Sioux, Crow, Blackfoot, Bannock, Mandan, Snake, Nez Percé, and a dozen other peoples.

De Smet's northwestern chain never quite stabilized; fluctuating manpower, punitive closure, false starts, wars, and gold rushes caused it to contract, expand, or reorganize. It reported nine units in 1847, deflated to two when California's gold population drained away priests, and recovered to eighteen by 1863. The basic four or five settlements did prosper, however, especially after weathering the crisis-ridden 1850s. They absorbed the short-lived Oblate mission in the Yakima-Cayuse country and moved out across the Plains, adding new missions such as those among the Nez Percé and the Blackfoot.

Men such as Joseph CATALDO, Adrian HOECKEN, Joseph JOSET, Nicolas POINT, and Anthony RAVALLI did Homeric work. By 1875 the chain embraced 7,000 Indians, unevenly distributed among most of the plateau and mountain tribes, plus many Plains converts. They were served by some twenty priests, twenty brothers,

and dozens of nuns. The Flathead Confederacy accounted for 2,000, the Columbia tribes of the northwestern plateau, 2,000, Yakima, 500; and Spokan, 300, with a couple of hundred apiece for southern Okanagon, Kutenai, and Nez Percé. Each mission, though centering on one configuration of tribes, served an extensive territory around it. The Kettle center ministered to other tribes as far as 150 or even 350 miles away at this time, while the Yakima center's main effort lay within a range of 200 by 60 miles, involving fourteen tribes. From the beginning moreover, Catholics from less hospitable tribes gathered at the center for festivities or religious exercises and sometimes came to live there. Besides these Jesuit groups, diocesan missioners such as Adrian Croquet accumulated more than 800 Umatilla and Walla Walla, and 400 Snake. Oblates added 2,000 from the Puget Sound tribes, while there were some 20,000 Catholic Indians in British Columbia. Schools, farms, large churches, and orders of nuns contributed to the sometimes imposing appearance of a frontier settlement.

Midwest, Southwest, and Far West to 1875. By 1875, what had developed outside the venturesome Northwest? In the first tier of trans-Mississippi states, Baraga, Pierz, and others continued their work in the North, but white settlement was displacing the tribes. The second tier of states, with the adjoining third tier as far as the Rockies' crest, became the Indian vicariate under Bishop John Miège, but the advent of settlers, cattle, and railroads soon altered the vicariate's priorities. The Jesuit missions persisted here among the removed tribes in Kansas, until the 1867 Indian withdrawal. When Indian Territory in present-day Oklahoma was becoming a chaotic dumping ground for removed tribes, Jesuits from the Kansas Osage mission visited the removed Catholic Choctaw and Potawatomi but permanent operations had to await the arrival of the French Benedictine Isidore Robot in the mid-1870s. The Civil War disrupted the Osage mission, with four hundred joining one regiment of the Union army and others fighting for the Confederacy; stripped of their lands, this Catholic tribe too retreated to Oklahoma by 1870.

On the Northern Plains, two centuries of continuing Catholic contact with the Sioux began to show results. The layman fur magnate Manuel Lisa exercised deep influence over the central (Yankton) and western (Teton) groups from 1807 on; soon Christian Hoecken in 1837 and De Smet in 1839 began visiting both. Hoecken's death in 1851 ended plans for a permanent mission, but De Smet gave this apostolate his main attention on tours from 1850 to 1870. The Quebec priest Augustin Ravoux undertook occasional visits. When the government chose thirty-eight warriors to hang, as reprisal for the Minnesota massacres of 1862, thirty-three of them turned to Ravoux for baptism.

The third or mountain tier, though under the Indian vicariate, reacted rather as fringes of the northwestern or southwestern mission patterns during this period. In the conquered Southwest, Bishop Jean Baptiste LAMY came down the Santa Fe Trail in 1850 to find five thousand nominally Catholic Pueblos without priests. He applied his meager resources in that long-civilized region to the undifferentiated Catholics, but his clergy, usually French or Belgian, learned the Indian dialects and gave attention to unassimilated tribes. Jesuits revived the old mission at Bac, welcomed by the Papago and Pima. California's Indians, dispersed and disappearing, were in a hopeless state and serious work came late and slowly. Pastors in mining or settlement areas of the Far West grappled at the local level, gleaning Indian souls. The ex-miner and future bishop Patrick Manogue converted Indians far and wide among such Nevada tribes as the Paiute, leaving a wake of baptized Pats and Mikes.

convergence: 1875-1900. In the quarter-century before 1900 the Roman Catholic population lurched from five to twelve million, devouring the pioneer church's personnel and all the foreign priests or nuns she could attract. The widely cast mission activity, despite bright spots, stretched thin and superficial. Except for the Northwest, it was institutionally inferior to the combined Protestant work. Catholic Indians, according to an ambitious listing by tribes and agencies in 1873, came to 106,911 out of a total of all Indians reckoned by census as some 278,000. The multiple efforts at the grass-roots level were converging, however, and in the Northwest a systematic development had laid firm foundations. On the Indian side, the grim progress of the separate-reservations theory, the final desperate wars culminating with the Custer episode in 1876, the imminent extinction of the buffalo, and the obvious shift of balance toward a white-settled West shook the Indians' way of life and opened many to the help and options offered by Blackrobes. The increase of Catholic individuals in disaspora tribes fortified the formal mission advance. A surge of interest among the now more stabilized and numerous Catholics, new sources of funding, and growing manpower contributed. Katherine DREXEL built and supported fourteen Indian schools in eight western states and then structured her continuing philanthropies by founding a congregation of nuns for the Indian and Negro apostolates.

Above all, Grant's PEACE POLICY marshaled vigorous Roman Catholic reaction. Catholics saw the policy both as a brutal attempt to Americanize the tribes under pressure and as a devious transfer of eighty thousand Catholic Indians to Protestant mission-agencies under the pretense of surrendering all agencies to the various religious denominations according to a quota. But the program did subsidize Indian education and led to some sixty Catholic Indian schools by 1900, mostly boarding establishments, from southern California to Montana and over the Southwest and Plains to the Great Lakes, housing four thousand pupils. By allowing Catholics a mere eight missions instead of thirty-eight, it also occasioned in 1874 the creation in Washington, D.C., of the Bureau of Catholic Indian Missions, with its *Annals*. The bureau publicized Catholic Indian grievances, defended their constitutional rights, lobbied for help, and in general promoted a coordinated nationwide effort. John BROUILLET captained its pioneer years.

In 1875 the formal mission effort of 25 priests served 25,000 Indians directly, with 7 schools and 55 chapels. By 1900 there were 140 priests and more than 300 nuns, with 50,000 direct subjects at 175 churches and some 60 schools, and with concomitant increase of auxiliary and part-time aid.

The Jesuit network in the Northwest strengthened its units, added more, absorbed struggling peripheral efforts, and entered fresh fields. Centers flourished among the Yakima, Nez Percé, Umatilla, Spokan, Kettle, and the various tribes by now called the Flathead Confederacy. In Montana alone in 1890 the missionary Lawrence PALLADINO counted nine missions and stations, with 7,000 Catholics out of 10,000 Indians (a thousand in nine schools) served by eighteen priests, twenty other clergy, and seventy-four nuns. The Blackfoot mission, after visits in the 1840s and 1850s and false starts in the 1860s, began in 1874; the Assiniboin-Gros Ventre mission, in 1885; the Cheyenne, in 1884 after years of begging for priests, though whites forced its closure in 1897; and the Crow, after many vicissitudes, finally in 1887. The Arapaho mission previously under New York and then Missouri Jesuits from 1884, became in 1891 part of the Northwest network.

The Swiss Benedictine abbot Martin Marty, arriving in time to help pacify the Sioux in the aftermath of the Custer war, became the preeminent "Apostle of the Sioux." By 1900 a fourth of the Sioux were Catholic. They published a Catholic monthly in their language and established an order of Red Sisters, whose nuns had such lovely names as Sister Aloysia Black-Eyes and Sister Anthony Cloud-Robe. By 1960 Sioux Catholics totaled eighteen thousand. Benedictine monks also went to the Arikara and Gros Ventre. In the Oklahoma melange Robot, as prefect-apostolic, deployed his Benedictines and other clergy among the Catholic Indians. Schools multiplied, but Catholicism never won more than a tenth of that territory's Indians or penetrated deeply beyond its Catholic tribes. At the northeast corner, Minnesota-Wisconsin missions took on new life.

Though the Southwest harvest had to await the twentieth century, promising foundations were laid among the Navaho, Pima, and Papago of Arizona, and the Mescalero Apache in New Mexico. A faint dawn brightened the nearly extinct California bands, as the Mexican Franciscan Luciano Osuna, for example, sought them out. Less than three thousand soon clustered in some thirty reservations in the South, nearly all Catholic, plus a few hundred fragments of the extinct northern majority served by two Franciscan missions.

There had been no time, or perhaps inclination, in the nineteenth century to form a native clergy. Two ill-fated seminarians did go to Rome in 1832, and the Delaware warrior-convert James Bouchard became in 1855 the first United States Indian priest. By 1910, careful statistics set the total number of Catholic Indians under mission care in the United States at 110,711 served by 138 priests plus 391 nuns, in 197 churches, with 72 schools for 6,240 pupils. American census figures listed total Indian population as 237,000 in 1900; 265,000 in 1910; and 244,000 in 1920. The twentieth century, with its own story and setbacks, raised the numbers by 1968 to nearly 140,000 Catholics plus 25,000 living off reservations, in 403 churches under 253 priests, with 53 schools serving 8,696 pupils. Since general statistics for the continental states rose (including descendants) to 350,000 in 1950 and over 600,000 in 1968 (about half under direct government care), comparative religious percentages today require interpretation. By 1900, however, most tribal groups had known some contact with Catholicism; perhaps two-thirds had escaped the net.

Inevitably a survey touches achievements and glosses over bitter quarrels, lost opportunities, scandals, and bumbling, leaving a human dimension unrecorded.

The uncoordinated efforts of missionaries in an episodic Indian world, where circumstance constantly dictated new strategies to meet new crises in every region, prohibit a coherent and complete narrative in brief form or even a mapping of alternate successes and failures. Quite aside from notions of success, the very intrusion of missionaries among the harassed Indians, increasingly isolated in pockets of land and doomed to choose *Götterdämmerung* or loss of identity, seems to some a mischievous factor of the problem itself. By Christian logic, white or Indian, the objection was irrelevant; the prize of salvation belonged to all. But even at the sociological level, the missionary softened the shock of imposed white culture, defended Indian rights, brought educational and medical advantages, offered pride of place as fellow Christians to counter the westerners' contempt, saved many lives as peacemaker, became a bridge to the white world, and consoled and advised in a compassionately personal way. Where the government was manipulative or destructive, the mission was preservative.

On the spiritual plane, one might too easily dismiss the missions as a failure in their overall impact. Institutionally the missions were indeed too thinly spread, too superficially rooted, and at a number of levels ineffective. But it is also true that countless thousands of Indians enjoyed a Christian light and dimension in their life, sometimes to a degree that awed the missionary. Thousands more, clinging to paganism or even hating the white man's Christianity, received incalculable material and spiritual benefits during this death of a people. The nineteenth-century missionary story thus becomes a rescue operation, a shifting of tactics to gain the greatest good for as many as could be reached in each tragic reorientation of the Indian world. Institutional failure, paradoxically, was the price for human success.

For an overview from 1500 to 1800, see John Tracy Ellis, *Catholics in Colonial America* (1965), with works cited; and to 1850 the dated classic, John Gilmary Shea, *History of the Catholic Missions Among the Indian Tribes of the United States, 1529-1854* (1899). For the Far Northwest and Jesuits generally, see Robert Ignatius Burns, *Jesuits and the Indian Wars of the Northwest* (1966), with works cited. See also the diocesan histories cited by dioceses (cities) in the *New Catholic Encyclopedia* (1967). —R. I. B.

Roman Nose (?-1868). Cheyenne leader. Although some sources indicate that Roman Nose was a chief of the Crooked Lance soldier society, historian George Bird Grinnell asserts that this distinguished warrior was not a chief. Assured of protection in battle by the strong "medicine" of his war bonnet, Roman Nose rose to prominence in the wars of the 1860s against the whites. Embittered by Colonel John M. Chivington's Sand Creek Massacre of Black Kettle's Cheyenne in 1864, he not only participated in many of the raids and conflicts of the Cheyenne-Arapaho War of 1864-65 but also remained hostile after the formal conclusion of the war.

Roman Nose met in council with General Winfield Scott Hancock at Fort Larned in the spring of 1867, but he was mistrustful and belligerent, and Hancock by his equally belligerent attitude probably lost any chance of coaxing the war leader into joining the Cheyenne peace faction. With the collapse of the council, Roman Nose, Tall Bull, and other prominent Cheyenne returned to the open plains. Roman Nose soon reappeared as one of the leaders of a combined force of Cheyenne and Kiowa that mauled Captain G. A. Armes' cavalry command near Prairie Dog Creek, Kansas, in August 1867.

When the Indian Peace Commission of 1867 invited the Cheyenne to the council at Medicine Lodge Creek in October, Roman Nose hesitantly participated in preliminary discussions. Suspicious of the white men's intentions, he refused to take part in the council itself, and he was one of the few prominent Cheyenne who did not sign the Treaty of Medicine Lodge. The treaty failed to stop hostilities, however, and Roman Nose was soon joined by other dissidents. In September 1868 he was among the Cheyenne who besieged Major George A. Forsyth's command at Beecher's Island. Shortly before riding off against Forsyth, Roman Nose accidentally broke his war bonnet's "medicine" and had no time to perform purification rites. True to his premonition, he was mortally wounded on the first day of the battle, September 17, 1868.

Aspects of Roman Nose's career are well presented in Donald J. Berthrong, *The Southern Cheyennes* (1963); and George Bird Grinnell, *The Fighting Cheyennes* (1915).—J. T. K.

Roosevelt, Nicholas J. See RIVERMEN.

Roosevelt, Theodore (1858-1919). Politician, historian, and conservationist. In August 1884 Roosevelt established himself on two ranches in the Badlands of Dakota Territory and wrote his friends in the East that he intended to make ranching "my regular business." "The statesman of the past," he told Henry Cabot Lodge, "has been merged, I fear for good, into the cowboy of the present." In the face of Roosevelt's later career, this determination may seem fanciful, for by 1886 the rancher had abandoned the West and was running for mayor of New York City. Roosevelt's celebrated tendency to exaggerate and dramatize his actions invites one to see his three years in Dakota as a gay interlude of outdoorsmanship, not unlike the ventures of several of his Harvard classmates in the Wyoming cattle industry in the 1880s.

The minimal importance of Roosevelt's Dakota years in terms of his later career should nevertheless not lead one to the conclusion that he intended his life on the ranch to be a temporary immersion in the wilderness. Roosevelt's trek to Dakota in 1884 was a retreat from painful memories and vanished hopes. In February of that year his wife of four years had died in childbirth; twelve hours after her death his mother died. By July his political ambitions appeared dashed by the presidential nomination of James G. Blaine, whose candidacy he had bitterly opposed. To Roosevelt these disasters were undoubtedly devastating. From his youth he had been acutely conscious of the values and traditions of his family. His marriage to Alice Hathaway Lee and his determination to study law and enter public service were closely aligned with the perpetuation of his heritage. Between 1881 and 1884 he had twice been elected to the New York State Assembly and had begun construction on a home for his family in Oyster Bay, Long Island. His wife's death, with the poignant legacies of his infant daughter and the half-completed property at Sagamore Hill, cast a long shadow on his future plans. In the fall of 1884 he wrote friends in Dakota renouncing any future political ambitions, noting that "he would never become reconciled to his loss nor expect to find happiness again" and stating that his baby girl would be better off without him.

The Dakota years were thus not conceived as any lark. "Nowhere," Roosevelt wrote in 1884, "does a man feel more lonely than when riding over the far-reaching, seemingly never-ending plains; and after a man has lived a little while on or near them, their very vastness and loneliness and their melancholy monotony have a strong fascination for him . . . nowhere else does one seem so far off from mankind." Roosevelt's first response to the West was that of the distraught prodigal, finding his sorrows reinforced by the severity of an alien environment. His first impressions of Dakota permanently shaped his image of the West: he saw "an abode of iron desolation," "an iron age that the old civilized world has long passed by." The "grim harshness" of the West shaped the destinies of its inhabitants: the lines on the faces of Roosevelt's cowboy companions told "of dangers quietly fronted and hardships uncomplainingly endured."

The effect of this environment on its inhabitants was regarded by Roosevelt as extremely beneficial. His excursions during the summers of 1870-72 to Maine and New York's Adirondack Mountains and, four years later, his boxing lessons at Harvard left him with a firm belief in the rehabilitative aspects of physical exercise. An asthmatic boy had built himself up through dogged self-punishment; a sorrowing man could perhaps find solace in immersion in the rugged outdoors. Roosevelt's frame of mind upon entering Dakota necessitated his finding the West a severe physical test and demonstrating to himself that he could survive it. As such, the episodes from his Dakota years that remained foremost in his consciousness were those in which he mastered a physically taxing situation. The West was a wild, hard land that fostered "the qualities of hardihood, self-reliance, and resolution needed for groping with [its] surroundings."

Three incidents were closely connected with Roosevelt's campaign to immerse himself in his new environment. The first was his celebrated fight with the Mingusville bully, which is reported in his autobiography. Prior to the incident with the bully, Roosevelt had been relatively unsuccessful in overcoming his reputation as a tenderfoot. A reporter from the Pittsburgh *Dispatch,* upon meeting Roosevelt on his way to Dakota in 1885, found him a "pale, slim young man with a thin piping voice . . . who looks the typical New York dude"; while one historian of Roosevelt's Badlands years claims that he was initially "considered something of a joke" by his new neighbors. In April 1885, however, Roosevelt's stock rose after he had successfully defended himself against the tauntings of a "shabby individual" in a hotel in Mingusville. In response to the bully's hazing, Roosevelt, as he tells it, "struck quick and hard with my right just to one side of the point of his jaw," knocking his adversary to the floor, where he hit his head on the corner of the bar. "If he had moved I was about to drop on his ribs with my knees," Roosevelt noted, "but he was senseless. . . . When my assailant came to, he went down to the station and left on a freight."

The news of Roosevelt's triumph spread rapidly, and Dakotans began to reevaluate the newcomer; a year later, the former dude added to his new stature by tracking down a group of desperadoes who had stolen a boat from one of his ranches. In the course of his search for the boat, Roosevelt navigated an ice-ridden stream, battled his way through Sioux country with his captives aboard, and eventually hired a prairie schooner to transport the thieves fifteen miles overland to the nearest town. When he arrived with the thieves in tow an eyewitness called him "the most bedraggled figure I'd ever seen." But for Roosevelt the admiration of his contemporaries was well worth the suffering. "Think we have all got our names pretty well up by this scrape," one of his ranch hands noted after the incident. "Don't think we'll have anything more stolen from us."

A final fond memory of the Badlands was Roosevelt's hunting expedition in Montana in the fall of 1886. On this trip he conquered some personal doubts about his ability with a rifle by shooting a mountain goat at a range of a quarter of a mile. He insisted on having a picture taken of himself with the goat, and later distributed it among his eastern friends. By the close of the trip Roosevelt's guide, who had previously felt him to be "too much of a dude to make any hit with me," had concluded that "he was a Westerner at heart and had the makings of a real man."

After three years in Dakota Roosevelt had regained the self-confidence and sense of balance his dark years in the East had momentarily disturbed. Upon leaving his ranches in 1886 he returned to New York City and a political career. He lost a mayoralty campaign in the city that year, but in 1889, after supporting Benjamin Harrison for president, he was made a civil service commissioner. This was the first of a long line of offices. Roosevelt became president of the New York City board of police commissioners in 1895; in 1896 he became an assistant secretary of the navy under President McKinley. The outbreak of the Spanish-American War in 1898 and Roosevelt's resignation from the navy department allowed him to garner fame by joining and commanding the ROUGH RIDERS, volunteer cavalrymen from the western states. On his return to New York, he capitalized on the popularity of the Rough Riders by running successfully for governor of New York in 1898. Next came a nomination as vice president for President McKinley's second term in 1900. Upon election Roosevelt feared that he had come to a political dead end, but when McKinley was assassinated in 1901 he suddenly became president.

As president Roosevelt pursued active policies in both domestic and foreign affairs, the most noteworthy of which were unrelated to his western experience. Desiring a canal across the Isthmus of Panama, he intervened in Colombia to help insurrectionists establish the breakaway state of Panama. Later, when asked to justify his handling of the affair, Roosevelt said, "I took the canal zone and let Congress debate, and while the debate goes on the canal does also." His jingoism in Latin America has negatively influenced Roosevelt's historical reputation. But there were other dimensions to his foreign policy, as illustrated by the Nobel Peace Prize he received for negotiating a settlement between Japan and Russia in 1905.

In domestic affairs Roosevelt took an active part in the trustbusting fights of the Progressive period. His first administration attempted to bring about the dissolution of the Northern Securities Company through a suit in the Supreme Court for conspiracy in restraint of trade, and was temporarily successful. In 1906 a Roosevelt-sponsored bill, the Hepburn Act, gave the Interstate Commerce Commission some additional power to regulate railroads. He also backed the Food and Drug Act, which was the first legislation to establish quality standards in the content and processing of foods.

In some instances Roosevelt's interest in the outdoors translated itself into social policies. He and Gifford Pinchot, his chief of the Forest Service, were early conservationists, although to them "conservation" meant the efficient use of land and could be equated with reclamation. Roosevelt approved the Newlands Act of 1902, which sought to irrigate western lands through the proceeds of public land sales. In 1903 he established the Public Lands Commission, which suggested that land in the public domain be studied and classified instead of sold at random. In 1905 Roosevelt took steps toward a coherent land policy by bringing together such functions as tree farming and mapping under the Forest Service (then known as the Bureau of Forestry). Two years later he added 16 million acres to the national forest system. He convened conservation congresses in 1908 and 1909 and, in general, was the first president to be concerned with preserving the West as well as developing it. For him, the preservation of the wilderness and the maintenance of the sport of wildlife hunting engendered qualities of manliness and self-reliance. It was always his hope to bring the individualism that he had found in the West back East, for it was in the West and in the history of western settlement that he felt were preserved the most truly American values and strengths of character.

Roosevelt wrote many books and articles on the West: *Hunting Trips of a Ranchman* (1885); *Thomas Hart Benton* (1886); *Ranch Life and the Hunting Trail* (1888); *The Wilderness Hunter* (1893); and a multi-volume frontier history, *The Winning of the West* (1889-1896). All of these illustrate the degree to which Roosevelt identified himself with his subject. Hunting in Dakota came to symbolize "the free, self-reliant, adventurous life"; the chase cultivated a "vigorous manliness"; the men who settled the West were "dauntless, restless backwoods folk . . . impelled mainly by sheer love of adventure"; their leaders, such as Daniel Boone, James Robertson, and George Rogers Clark, were "self-reliant" and "masterful," with "invincible courage," "far-sighted daring," and "indomitable energy." The same characteristics were seen in whole communities: In *The Winning of the West,* a history of the settlement of Ohio and Kentucky, he attributed to the settlers "the fundamental virtues of hardihood and manliness." "The West," he wrote, ". . . was the work of a whole people, of whom each man was impelled mainly by sheer love of adventure; it was the outcome of the ceaseless strivings of all the dauntless, restless backwoods folk." Along with the novels of his friends Owen Wister and Frederic Remington, Roosevelt's works helped shape the popular impression of the West at the turn of the century.

Today the Theodore Roosevelt National Memorial Park in North Dakota embraces the area of his two ranches.

There are many biographies of Roosevelt. Those dealing with his Dakota years include Herman Hagedorn, *Roosevelt in the Badlands* (1921); Carleton Putname,

Theodore Roosevelt: The Formative Years (1958); G. Edward White, *The Eastern Establishment and the Western Experience* (1968); and Jack Willis, *Roosevelt in the Rough* (1931).—G. E. W.

Rosario. See NUESTRA SENORA DEL ESPRITU SANTO DE ZUNIGA.

Rose, Edward (?-1832-33). Interpreter and Crow leader. Rose was the son of a white trader and a Cherokee mother who was part Negro. Rose first gained notoriety as a member of a gang of Mississippi River pirates who operated near New Orleans, and it seems possible that he was actually fleeing the law when he joined Manuel Lisa's fur-trading expedition up the Missouri in 1807 (the date of Rose's appearance on the Missouri, according to some authorities, was 1809). When Lisa returned to St. Louis after the Missouri expedition, Rose remained with the Crow Indians, learned their language, and became one of their leaders, if not an actual chieftan. In 1811 Wilson Price Hunt and his party of Astorians hired Rose to guide them through Crow country as they made their way to the Pacific, but Hunt became so convinced that the fierce-looking Rose intended to lead them into a trap that he dispensed with his services as soon as possible.

Sometime between 1820 and 1823 Rose left the Crow to live with the Arikara tribes on the Missouri. Having also learned their language, he was hired as an interpreter by General William H. Ashley to accompany his ill-fated expedition of 1823. When Ashley's party stopped to trade for horses with the Arikara in June 1823, Rose warned Ashley that the Indians intended to attack his men. Rose's warning went unheeded, and when the Indians did attack, Ashley's party suffered heavy losses. Later in the summer Rose served as an interpreter, with the rank of ensign, in Colonel Henry Leavenworth's punitive expedition against the Arikara. Rose was so trusted by both sides that he alone carried messages back and forth between the Indian and white camps, and he fully merited Leavenworth's later characterization of him as "a brave and enterprising man."

Rose's knowledge of Crow territory and his ability to speak the Crow language and to bargain for horses persuaded Ashley to send him with Jedediah Smith as a guide when Smith struck out overland for the mountains in September 1823. Although Smith is credited with forging a new trail via the Black Hills to the northern trapping grounds and of liberating the fur trade from the river system, it was Rose who knew the country and who more than once saved the party from disaster. Rose served with Smith until 1825 when he became an interpreter for General Henry Atkinson and Major Benjamin O'Fallon as they led a treaty-making military expedition up the Missouri that year.

Rose himself then returned to live with the Crow, among whom his fierce temper and his acts of bravado made him a legend in his own time. Bernard De Voto described him as a man of "steel nerves and nine lives," and Rose looked the part, for his forehead was marked with a vivid scar and his nose was so badly slashed the Indians called him Nez Coupé ("Cut Nose"). His reputation for fearlessness was further enhanced when he attacked a Blackfoot stronghold singlehandedly and killed five men, a deed that also merited him the name Five Scalps. His later exploits are difficult to distinguish from those of Jim Beckwourth, another half-breed who joined the Crow nation in 1828 and who also became a leader. In boasting of his own accomplishments in various Indian wars in his autobiography, *The Life and Adventures of James P. Beckwourth* (1856), it appears that Beckwourth appropriated some of Rose's deeds for himself.

In the past, authorities have differed as to the time and manner of Rose's death, but Dale Morgan asserts that Rose, Hugh Glass, and a third mountain man named Menard were killed and scalped by a band of Arikara on the frozen Yellowstone River in the winter of 1832-33. A site called Rose's Grave is located on the Milk River some nine miles west of the Yellowstone.

No systematic record of Rose's activities exists, but numerous contemporaries spoke of him. Some facts may be gleaned from Zenas Leonard, *Narrative of Adventures* (1955), edited by John C. Ewers; Washington Irving, *Astoria* (1836); and Hiram M. Chittenden, *A History of the American Fur Trade in the Far West* (1902). More up-to-date accounts of Rose's life may be found in Dale Morgan, *Jedediah Smith and the Opening of the West* (1953). A brief but highly laudable biography is Harold W. Felton, *Edward Rose, Negro Trail Blazer* (1967). —G. B. D.

Rosebud, battle of the (June 17, 1876). The battle of the Rosebud pitched General George Crook's force of about twelve hundred infantrymen, cavalrymen, and Indian scouts against a rougly equal number of Sioux and Cheyenne warriors. The battle, fought near the present town of Kirby, Big Horn County, Montana, was a strategic victory for the Indians. Crook's command was one of three columns that were to converge on hostile Indians in the Big Horn country. His column had marched north from Fort Fetterman on the North Platte River in Wyoming as General John Gibbon's column marched east from Fort Ellis in Montana Territory, and as General Alfred H. Terry's force—including General George A. Custer's Seventh Cavalry—marched west from Fort Abraham Lincoln on the Missouri River in the Dakota Territory. Crook had hoped to surprise an Indian village he believed was somewhere on the Rosebud River; however, he had been watched for several days by the Cheyenne and Sioux, who were probably on their way to the large encampment on the Little Big Horn. The battle began at eight thirty in the morning with an attack on Crook's Crow scouts by Sioux from Crazy Horse's war party. The general attempted to form a traditional line of battle, but the broken terrain around the Rosebud made that formation difficult and the battle dissolved into several smaller, hard-fought conflicts. The rescue, in the midst of the fighting, of Cheyenne Chief Comes in Sight by his sister gave the battle its Cheyenne name, "where the girl saved her brother." The combat raged on until the middle of the afternoon, when the Indians—either tired of fighting or hoping to lure Crook's battered command into an ambush— withdrew from the field. Crook, who had already been on the defensive for several hours, was content to go into camp on the battleground.

Crook at first attempted to advertise the battle as a victory, but even as he did so he reversed his line of march and rejoined his supply column at Goose Creek, where he remained for almost eight weeks, resting his troops, treating his wounded and awaiting reinforcements. The Indians, emboldened by their victory, were

free to join their tribesmen on the LITTLE BIG HORN, where they would soon encounter Custer.

The battle of the Rosebud and Crook's part in the summer campaign are treated in John G. Bourke, *On the Border with Crook* (1891); and Martin F. Schmitt, *General George Crook: His Autobiography* (1946). J. W. Vaughn, *With Crook at the Rosebud* (1956), gives a detailed analysis of the battle, while the Indian viewpoint is represented in George Bird Grinnell, *The Fighting Cheyennes* (1915).—J. T. K.

Rosewater, Edward (1841-1906). Nebraska journalist and politician. A native of Bukowan, Bohemia, Rosewater and his parents emigrated to Cleveland, Ohio, in 1854. Four years later Rosewater began a career as a telegrapher and during the Civil War served in that capacity as a civilian with the Union forces. In 1863 he moved to Omaha, Nebraska, where in subsequent years he managed the telegraph offices of the Atlantic and Pacific and Great Western companies.

As he became more familiar with news-gathering, he also developed an interest in politics and in 1870 was elected as a Republican to the Nebraska House of Representatives. In January 1871, amid charges that the state's first governor, David Butler, had misused public funds, Rosewater offered a resolution requesting Butler to account for the disposition of money collected from the United States government for school purposes. The governor's failure to render an adequate explanation led to his indictment, conviction, and removal from office. Rosewater also secured the passage of a bill providing for an elective school board for the city of Omaha. Since this statute required ratification by the Omaha electorate, Rosewater began the publication of a sheet known as the *Bee* as a means of promoting voter approval. The *Bee* won public favor and, following an affirmative vote on the school bill, Rosewater developed the small periodical into one of the region's most important daily newspapers.

Although Rosewater never held public office after his own term in the legislature, he was immersed in politics, and the *Bee* carried his views across Nebraska. A maverick Republican, he often denounced the power of the Union Pacific Railroad in the political and economic life of Nebraska and was a critic of the protective tariff. At a time when Omaha's business leaders were fighting labor organizations, Rosewater supported the working man. In 1890 he campaigned vigorously against a constitutional amendment providing for prohibition, and on election day the "wets" proved triumphant. Rosewater had no use for the Populist free silver doctrine, yet he was in other respects sympathetic toward the People's party. In 1894 he proclaimed that Thomas J. Majors, the Republican nominee for governor, was "a pliant tool of the railroads" and immediately resigned as G.O.P. national committeeman. He then cast his support behind Silas A. Holcomb, the Populist candidate for governor, and was influential in bringing about Holcomb's Democratic nomination and ultimate election. In 1901 and 1906, after having returned to the Republican party, he vainly sought nomination for the United States Senate.

As a result of his outspoken views, Rosewater and the *Daily Bee* made many friends and no small number of enemies. In addition to his political efforts, Rosewater was a stanch promoter of the development of Omaha. In

1898 he played an important role in bringing about the highly successful Trans-Mississippi and International Exposition held in that city. Following his death, the *Bee* remained in the Rosewater family until 1920, and in 1927 it was consolidated with the Omaha *Daily News.* The *Bee-News* ceased publication in 1937.

See Ronald M. Gephart, "Politicians, Soldiers and Strikes: The Reorganization of the Nebraska Militia and the Omaha Strike of 1882," *Nebraska History* (June 1966); Addison E. Sheldon, *Nebraska: The Land and the People,* vol. I (1931); and Ruth Moore Stanley, "Newspaper Comment on Jay Gould and the State Republican Convention of 1876," *Nebraska History* (June 1966). —H. A. D.

Ross, Alexander (1783-1856). Fur trader. Ross was born in Nairnshire, Scotland, and appears to have received a good education before migrating to Canada in 1804. He served as clerk on the Astor maritime expedition to the Pacific Coast in 1810. After Astor abandoned his effort to capture the Pacific Coast fur trade and sold Fort Astoria to the British, Ross joined the North West Company as a trader in 1814. In 1818 he went up the Columbia River as far as the Snake River and established Fort Nez Perces (sic), which he ran until 1823. After the Hudson's Bay Company absorbed the North West Company in 1821, Ross was put in charge of Flathead Post near Flathead Lake in western Montana. He led the company's Snake River expedition in 1823-24, exploring into present-day southern Idaho. Ross, however, allowed Jedediah Smith and a small party of American trappers to visit Flathead House after Smith had rescued Ross's Iroquois trappers from an Indian attack. Realizing that the American trappers would use the visit to inform themselves about the country, Hudson's Bay officials decided that Ross's tolerance of the Americans was unwise and replaced him with Peter Skene Ogden in 1825. Ross was retired to the company's Red River settlement.

Ross published two excellent accounts of the Northwestern fur trade: *Adventures of the First Settlers on the Oregon or Columbia River* (1849) and *The Fur Hunters of the Far West* (2 vols., 1855), which constitute important scources for early Oregon history and have been reprinted in several new editions. In 1856 his *The Red River Settlement, Its Rise, Progress and Present State* appeared.

Besides biographical accounts in later editions of his works, see George B. Grinnell, *Behond the Old Frontier: Adventures of Indian Fighting, Hunters, and Fur Traders* (1919).—G. B. D.

Ross, Charles Benjamin (1876-1946). Idaho politician. Ross grew up on a Boise valley farm near Roswell, and commenced his political career in 1914 when he was elected as a Democrat in a Republican county, to the first of three terms as Canyon County commissioner. Then as an Idaho State Farm Bureau organizer, the major farmers' organization, he lectured and made friends all over Idaho. Settling in Pocatello, he put in six years (1924-30) as mayor prior to winning election in 1930 as governor of Idaho. In 1931 he managed to persuade a factionally divided Republican legislature to restore the state direct primary (which had been repealed in 1919 to thwart the progressive Nonpartisan League), and before Ross was through he had pushed through a series of measures establishing Idaho's modern tax structure

(income tax, gasoline tax, and sales tax, with the property tax minimized). A sales tax referendum in 1936 suspended that revenue device, though, until 1965, when the state finally got bold enough to try it again.

As governor during the Great Depression Ross had to maintain emergency relief programs and other state-level features of President Franklin D. Roosevelt's New Deal. He worked out some humanitarian tax and debt moratorium protections, particularly for farmers who had faced severe economic depression since 1920 and who had fallen into total economic disaster after 1930.

An independent leader who opposed his party organization, Ross ran into Democratic factional difficulties before the end of his last term as governor, and fared badly in his campaign in 1936 to replace the equally independent Republican William E. Borah in the United States Senate. In 1938 Ross won the Democratic nomination for a fourth term as governor, but went into political retirement after he lost the election. Before these setbacks he had made a considerable impact upon Idaho during the depression, and he is numbered among Idaho's influential governors.

Michael P. Malone, *C. Ben Ross and the New Deal in Idaho* (1970), interprets Ross's career in the context of state and national development.—M. W.

Ross, John (1790-1866). Cherokee chief. Ross was born in Rossville, Georgia, the son of a Scottish trader among the Cherokee and an Indian woman who was three-fourths white. He was educated by a tutor and attended briefly an academy in Kingston, Tennessee. He inherited from his mother the status of Indian and married Quatie, nearly a full blood. After earlier public service with the Cherokee tribe he became president of the National Council, 1819-26. He was principal chief from 1828 until the "shot gun removal" of the Cherokee from their eastern home in the Appalachians in 1839. In Indian Territory he was chosen principal chief of the united eastern and western Cherokee, an office he held until his death on a mission to Washington, D.C.

Ross was a competent planter and well educated, having accumulated a small library. In 1827 he took the lead in drafting a constitution modeled on that of the United States, and it was accepted by the tribe. He supported Christianity and education and dreamed of a Cherokee state in the Union. In spite of the inevitability of castastrophe implicit in the Removal Act of 1830, the outcome of the CHEROKEE NATION v. STATE OF GEORGIA, President Andrew Jackson's failure to act on the decision of the Supreme Court in WORCESTER v. STATE OF GEORGIA, and the forcible seizure by Georgia of Cherokee lands, Ross refused to counsel his people to go west. He even withheld from them facts that would have permitted them to make their own judgment.

Ross's position in the tribe derived from his ability as an administrator. In writing and speaking he used a simple, factual style quite different from the metaphorical and emotional language of the greatest of the Cherokee orators, John Ridge. In his vision of a Cherokee state under its own constitution, Ross was a forerunner of the twentieth-century reformers who established the right of tribes to organize politically under constitutions written by themselves and to enjoy under the laws of the states and of the federal government a measure of cultural and political autonomy.

See Rachel C. Eaton, *John Ross and the Cherokee Indians*

(1921); and Grace Steele Woodward, *The Cherokees* (1963).—R. H. G.

Rough Riders. The term "Rough Rider" is permanently fixed in the popular mind as synonymous with Theodore Roosevelt, and one summons up an image of the dashing Teddy, his blue-and-white polka-dot bandana flapping from his campaign hat, charging up San Juan Hill on a sweaty mount, saber flashing in the sun. That the hill Teddy and his men charged up was actually Kettle Hill is a minor point and does not diminish the fact that the Rough Riders are forever symbolized in the stumpy, myopic whirlwind of Sagamore Hill. It was said, with at least some accuracy, that Roosevelt "charged up San Juan Hill and straight into the White House."

Although the history of the Rough Riders actually began on April 25, 1898, the day the United States declared war against Spain, the burning issue of Cuban independence and the mysterious explosion that sank the United States battleship *Maine* in Havana harbor the previous February had given rise to the early formation of volunteer units ready to offer their services for the war everyone knew was a certainty. Moreover, many weeks before war was declared, Under Secretary of the Navy Theodore Roosevelt had announced his intention of resigning to take part in the fighting. Secretary of War Russell Alger offered Roosevelt a colonelcy of volunteers, but Roosevelt wisely demurred in favor of his friend (and President William McKinley's physician) Leonard WOOD.

On April 11, President McKinley asked Congress for authorization to use military force to secure the independence of Cuba. Two weeks later, on the same day war was declared, Secretary Alger wrote Arizona's territorial governor Myron McCord a key letter in the Rough Rider genesis: "The President directs that Capt. Leonard Wood of the U.S. Army be authorized to raise a regiment of cowboys as mounted riflemen, and to be its Colonel, and has named Hon. Theodore Roosevelt as Lt. Colonel. All other officers will come from the vicinity where the troops are raised. What can you do for them?"

The Volunteer Bill of April 22, 1898, which authorized the raising of the regiment of western volunteers Alger referred to, was amended before its passage. The new bill authorized "the Secretary of War to organize companies, troops, battalions or regiments, not to exceed 3,000 men." Thus, Secretary Alger decided to form three regiments of volunteer cavalry to come from the states and territories of the West where, as Theodore Roosevelt later wrote, "the feeling for war was strongest."

Colonel Wood's First United States Volunteer Cavalry Regiment was to be organized in the Arizona, New Mexico, Oklahoma, and Indian territories, the Second regiment in Wyoming, and the Third in the Dakotas. The Second and Third regiments languished at Panama Park (Jacksonville, Florida) and Camp Thomas (Chickamauga, Georgia) throughout the Cuban fighting. Only the first, the Rough Riders, and then only a part of it, saw action in the Santiago campaign.

Colonel Wood's regiment began taking shape in early May when the volunteers began arriving in San Antonio. The Oklahoma troopers were raised by Captain Robert D. Huston, a lawyer from Guthrie, who formed his command by selecting the six best men from each militia company in the territory. The largest single contingent of the "First" was that from New Mexico Territory, 340 men commanded by Major Henry Hersey, territorial adjutant general. The Indian Territory contingent of 170 men was commanded by Lieutenant Allyn Capron, on detached service from the Seventh Cavalry. The Arizona Territory troopers, 203 officers and men commanded by Major Alexander O. BRODIE, claimed the first man to enlist for the war, Captain William Owen "Buckey" O'NEILL (later killed by a Mauser bullet before the assault on Kettle Hill), and also the distinction of being the first to arrive (on May 7) at the Rough Riders' training camp at Riverside Park, San Antonio, Texas.

The War Department's raising of the regimental quota for cavalry volunteers to one thousand men enabled the westerners to be mixed with an assortment of "easterners," organized by Roosevelt's friend Guy Murchie of Harvard University. "We drew recruits from Harvard, Yale, Princeton, and many another college," Roosevelt wrote, "from clubs like the Somerset, of Boston, and Knickerbocker of New York; and from among the men who belonged to neither club nor college, but in whose veins the blood stirred with the same impulse which once sent the Vikings oversea."

On May 9 these "dudes," "Fifth Avenue boys," "la de dah boys," and "swells," as the crusty territorial cowboys, prospectors, hunters, and range riders variously called them, began arriving in San Antonio (many with expensive luggage and hatboxes) and were scattered into several troops, the remainder forming a special unit of their own, under the command of Captain Micah Jenkins of South Carolina.

Roosevelt, like his newspaperman friend Dick Davis, never tired of singing the praises of this strange commingling of drawling cowpokes and clipped-toned New Englanders. "All—Easterners and Westerners, Northerners and Southerners, officers and men, cowboys and college graduates," Roosevelt wrote, "wherever they came from, and whatever their social position—possessed in common the traits of hardihood and a thirst for adventure. They were to a man born adventurers, in the old sense of the word."

On May 17, the Rough Riders were officially mustered in, the regiment consisting of three squadrons of four troops each: the Arizona squadron (including three troops from Arizona and one from Oklahoma); the New Mexico squadron (all from New Mexico); and the third squadron (comprised of superfluous troopers removed from the New Mexico squadron, plus a number of others from various other contingents).

It was during the San Antonio days that the regiment became popularly known as the "Rough Riders," although the term had been used as early as April 21, when a Tucson newspaper quoted Governor McCord as referring to "Col. Brodie's regiment of Arizona Rough Riders." The name, with such periodic variations as "Teddy's Terrors," "Teddy's Terriers," and the "Cowboy Cavalry," stuck. At first, Roosevelt himself tried to disclaim it, but it so quickly became a part of the language that he used it himself as the title of his popular book on the Cuban campaign.

The interlude of "training" in San Antonio was brief (one month) and consisted principally of endless horseback drills on the sunbaked prairie grounds, and occasional firing practice using the Norwegian-designed

Krag-Jorgensen bolt-action, breech-loading rifle and new smokeless powder. These weapons Roosevelt had badgered from the War Department for his troopers before leaving Washington.

That the troopers survived the enervating heat of the San Antonio prairies was due largely to the new light-weight khaki uniforms that were another of Roosevelt's "cumshaw" appropriations. The scratchy blue woolen tunics and heavy drill trousers worn by the Regulars, like the slimy and tainted canned beef rations, were among the many scandalous episodes of the war.

The Rough Riders' most popular pastimes during their stay in the Alamo City were the drinking of beer and the listening to the band concerts of "Professor" Carl Beck. The ubiquitous bandmaster was noted for his rousing renditions of such 1898 favorites as "There'll Be a Hot Time in the Old Town Tonight," "Ta-ra-ra-boom-de-ay," "Goodbye, Dolly Gray," and "La Paloma." "Hot Time" became the semiofficial Rough Rider anthem.

The regiment traveled by train from San Antonio to Tampa, Florida, and there joined the Regulars of the V Corps under the command of Major General William R. Shafter, a gouty, 300-pound, honest and brave (though plodding) veteran of the Civil War and Indian campaigns. More immediately, Wood's troopers fell under the peppery, "hell-for-leather" division leadership of Brigadier General Joseph "Fightin' Joe" Wheeler, the diminutive, white-bearded Confederate army veteran and United States congressman who had been placed in command of all cavalry units in the Corps.

Tampa was a chaotic anthill of activity. Its single-track railroad was overtaxed and freight cars loaded with provisions and matériel were backed up along it for miles; the stench of rotting meat filled the humid air and attracted swarms of mosquitoes and greenbottle flies; the palmetto-grown sand-dune camps were littered with a bedlam of tents, equipment, piled packing crates, horse and mule remudas and attendant saddles, harness and gear. Marching, drilling, milling soldiers, stevedores, newsmen, government officials, and civilian gawkers were everywhere.

The lunatic asylum atmosphere that was to prevail through the landing on the Cuban coast held true on the Tampa quay. Disembarking from the area on June 7, the available transport ships that were supposed to take twenty-five thousand men to Cuba had room for only seventeen thousand. Consequently, the decision was made that each cavalry regiment would embark only eight of its twelve troops. Of the Rough Rider regiment, four troops were left in Tampa under the command of Major Hersey of New Mexico. Moreover, all packtrains were detached from the cavalry units and left in Florida. The Rough Riders thus became to the Regular Army men, "Wood's Weary Walkers."

The foreshortened "First" traveled to Cuba on the transport *Yucatan*. Roosevelt wrote angrily, "The soldiers are jammed together like animals . . . we are in a sewer . . . stinking of rot and putrefaction." The ship reached the jetty at Daiquiri, a squalid coastal village on the southeastern shore of Cuba, on June 22. The landing was a hectic, poorly organized, play-it-by-ear affair in which horses and mules were thrown overboard to swim for shore. Richard Harding Davis, one of the several famous newspaper men who attached themselves to the Rough Rider regiment, watched the Daiquiri land-

ing and noted, "God takes care of drunkards, sailors and the United States."

The next day the Rough Riders marched to Siboney, a yellow-fever pesthole about fifteen miles east of Santiago de Cuba (the objective of the campaign), where the base camp of operations was set up and where further disembarking of troops was proceeding.

On the morning of June 24, led by General Wheeler, the Rough Riders, along with approximately one thousand other men from the regular cavalry, met the rearguard of some fifteen hundred fleeing Spanish soldiers at the crossroads called Las Gúasimas, a few miles from Siboney on the road to Santiago. In a brief skirmish, consisting mainly of sniper fire, sixteen Americans were killed and fifty-two wounded, of which eight of the dead and thirty-four of the wounded were Rough Riders.

Early on July 1, General Henry W. Lawton, commanding a force of more than six thousand men (nearly half of Shafter's command), began the attack on the entrenchments and fortifications around El Caney, a small village dominated by a stone church, which was used by the Spanish as a fort on the eastern perimeter of Santiago. As the attack began, the Rough Riders (now commanded by Colonel Roosevelt since Wood had been promoted to brigade commander) were moved into position in a sunken lane below Kettle Hill, one of a series of strategic hills making up the San Juan ridge complex that ringed Santiago.

After sustaining several casualties in the continuous hail of sniper fire from the breastworks above them, the Rough Riders, with Roosevelt riding his horse Little Texas, took Kettle Hill early in the afternoon and dug in to observe and support the remaining fighting along the ridge complex, particularly on San Juan Hill to the front and left of Kettle.

With the spectacularly successful help of a Gatling-gun detachment commanded by Lieutenant John H. Parker, the Sixth and Sixteenth Infantry (later reinforced by units returning from the El Caney engagement, including the Tenth [Negro] Cavalry under Lieutenant John J. PERSHING), San Juan Hill and its blockhouse fell to the Americans in the late afternoon of July 1. The Rough Rider losses in the San Juan battle, which continued sporadically on July 2, were fifteen men killed and seventy-six wounded.

Sixteen days later, after negotiations with the Spanish military commanders at Santiago, the city surrendered. On August 12 the war ended, three and a half months after it had begun.

After the withdrawal of the V Corps from Cuba on August 8 (more than 4,000 men were on sick report, shaking with malaria, dysentery, and typhoid fever; 514 had died of disease in Cuba), Shafter's army assembled at the recuperation camp at Montauk Point, New York, along with the troopers who had remained in Tampa and other camps during the fighting. There, back on their horses for the final ceremonies, the Rough Riders were mustered out, drawing to a close a singular episode in American military history.

Seven years later, on April 7, 1905, President Theodore Roosevelt returned to San Antonio for a reunion of his Rough Riders and, speaking in front of the Alamo, said: "We had men of inherited wealth and men who all their lives long had earned each day's bread by that day's toil. We had men of every grade socially; men who worked with their heads; men who worked with their hands; men of all the types that our country produces; but each of them glad to get in on his worth as a man only, and content to be judged purely by what he could show himself to be."

Of the several books on the First U.S. Volunteer Cavalry Regiment, Theodore Roosevelt, *The Rough Riders* (1899), is indispensable. See also Edward Marshall, *The Story of the Rough Riders* (1899), for a view by the New York *Journal* correspondent who was gravely wounded at Las Gúasimas; and Charles Herner, *The Arizona Rough Riders* (1970), which contains valuable information on the entire regiment, with emphasis on the Arizona volunteers. The only book published that deals with the Second and Third Volunteer Cavalry regiments is Clifford B. Westermeier, *Who Rush to Glory* (1968). The most thorough accounts of the entire Cuban expedition are the extraordinary three-volume work, *The Campaign of Santiago de Cuba* (1907), by Herbert H. Sargent and *Roosevelt's Rough Riders* (1971), by Virgil C. Jones.—D. L. W.

Royce, Josiah (1855-1916). Philosopher and historian. Royce was born in Grass Valley, California, where his parents had a small store; they had emigrated from England as children and had gone overland to California in 1849. Royce attended public schools in San Francisco and the University of California, where he graduated in 1875; he later acknowledged his intellectual indebtedness to Joseph Le Conte, the geologist. After a year in Germany, at Leipzig and Göttingen, he entered Johns Hopkins University, taking the doctorate in 1878. Failing to find a position in philosophy, he taught English composition at California from 1878 to 1882, when he accepted a temporary instructorship at Harvard. He taught at Harvard for the rest of his life, returning to California only for visits.

Known primarily for developing a system of absolute idealism, rivaling the pragmatic systems of his friends William James and Charles Sanders Peirce, Royce was a scholar of extraordinary energy and versatility, making substantial contributions to mathematical logic, social psychology, and the psychology of perception. In 1883 he began to work on a history of California for the American Commonwealth series, called *California, from the Conquest in 1846 to the Second Vigilance Committee in San Francisco: A Study of American Character* (1886). In it he concentrated on the development of social institutions, analyzing Captain John C. Frémont's actions in the Bear Flag revolt and the conquest of California, the development of government in the mining camps and in San Francisco, and controversies over titles to land as tests of morality and social responsibility. The work is at once a careful examination of detailed evidence on specific events and a case study in social ethics. Royce also urged his mother to write her memoirs, later published as *A Frontier Lady; Recollections of the Gold Rush and Early California,* by Sarah (Bayliss) Royce, edited by Ralph H. Gabriel (1932). He published several articles and introductions to documents (1885-91) on the history of early American California, in some of them further examining Frémont's defense of himself. His one novel, *The Feud of Oakfield Creek, A Novel of California Life* (1887), which is concerned with conflicts over titles to land, is a parable of social and psychological

principles that Royce explored historically in *California.*

Although Royce wrote no more history after about 1891, he turned from time to time to California and his experiences there for examples of social relationships that figured in his philosophies of loyalty and community. Frederick Jackson Turner quoted one of Royce's essays on provincialism in developing his own theme of sections in American history, but whereas Royce occasionally went as far as Turner in arguing geographical influences on traits and institutions—and his affection for California and the scenes of his youth is unmistakable— his views of the experiences of pioneering are much more pessimistic than Turner's. Royce emphasized the rootlessness of the pioneer, his lack of social responsibility, and his needs for community and provincialism (a concept to which Royce attached special importance) as psychological and social anchors against the socially disintegrating and depersonalizing experiences of migration and modern national development.

At the time of publication, Royce's *California* drew sharp criticism from western reviewers, who objected to his severe judgments of the pioneers and to his concentrating on moral issues while entirely omitting conventional description of adventure, romance, and heroism. Later historians more generally recognized the soundness of his research, which he had done primarily in documents in the Bancroft Library and in newspapers; his analysis of Frémont's claim to have had secret instructions is a classic in historical criticism. He also anticipated later concern among western historians as well as sociologists with associational behavior and such themes as race prejudice.

The introduction by John Clendenning to *The Letters of Josiah Royce* (1970) is the best recent biographical sketch. See the "Annotated Bibliography of the Published Works of Josiah Royce" in *The Basic Writings of Josiah Royce* (1969), ed. by John J. McDermott; the introductions by Clendenning to Royce, *The Feud of Oakfield Creek* (1970), and by Earl Pomeroy to Royce, *California* (1970). See also Pomeroy, "Josiah Royce, Historian in Quest of Community," *Pacific Historical Review* (February 1971). Royce's papers are at Harvard University.—E. P.

Ruef, Abraham (1864-1936). Political boss of San Francisco, California. Ruef was born there two years after his moderately wealthy Jewish parents had emigrated from France. He was a brilliant and precocious student at the University of California in Berkeley, from which he was graduated at the age of eighteen with high honors. Taking his degree at the university's Hastings College of Law in San Francisco in 1886, he entered city politics as an idealistic, young Republican reformer, but the conditions of machine rule in the heyday of the Southern Pacific Railroad's control of California soon destroyed his faith in the possibilities of reform and he became a cynical opportunist. In 1901, when the Union Labor party of San Francisco was created, Ruef gained control of it and secured the election of his friend Eugene E. Schmitz, president of the musicians' union, as the party's candidate for mayor. In 1905 the entire Union Labor ticket for the board of supervisors was elected, and this gave Ruef almost complete control of the consolidated city and county government. The San Francisco graft prosecution, led by special assistant district attorney Francis J. Heney, his assistant Hiram W.

Johnson, and detective William J. Burns, revealed that Ruef had received huge attorney's fees from public utility corporations and had bribed most of the supervisors with part of the money. He was convicted of bribery in 1908 and was in San Quentin penitentiary from 1911 to 1915, when he was released on parole, partly through the efforts of Fremont Older, editor of the San Francisco *Bulletin,* who had helped to initiate the prosecution.

Ruef's memoirs, "The Road I Traveled; an Autobiographic Account of My Career from University to Prison, with an Intimate Recital of the Corrupt Alliance between Big Business and Politics in San Francisco," were published serially in the *Bulletin,* April-September, 1912. See also Walton Bean, *Boss Ruef's San Francisco* (1952).—W. B.

Russell, Charles Marion (1864-1926). Painter, sculptor, and illustrator. Russell was born in St. Louis. He is said to have drawn pictures and modeled in wax as a child. At the age of sixteen he was sent by his parents to Montana under the guardianship of a sheepman from whom he soon parted. Working for some time as a cowboy in the West, he continued to sketch, spending his summers on the open range and his winters in various frontier towns, where he often painted pictures in exchange for food or lodging. He reportedly developed at this time the habit of carrying about in his pocket modeling clay with which he fashioned small figures in his leisure moments, in later years casting such sculptures in bronze. In 1896 Russell married Nancy Cooper, under whose influence and direction he developed from an itinerant cowboy into an artist who painted pictures for a living. By 1920 he had achieved financial success and made frequent trips to New York, where he painted for such patrons as Malcomb MacKay and Dr. Phillip G. Cole. Russell seldom used models for his pictures or sculpture and took pride in the accuracy of his memory for the details depicted in his scenes of cowboy and Indian life in the Far West. Although professional critics in the East ignored or panned his work, he found a ready market for his pictures. For more than a quarter of a century Russell worked hard to produce an exhaustive record of the Old West as he had known it before the advent of barbed wire, the automobile, and the airplane.

Russell seems never to have received any formal art training or even to have expressed an interest in the aesthetics of art. Totally preoccupied with his western subjects, he seldom varied from that theme. He maintained a studio for a brief period in Pasadena, California, and in 1924 or 1925 made a trip to Europe. Not really happy away from his adopted state of Montana, however, he returned to Great Falls and the scenes of his youth, where he continued to paint until his death.

The majority of Russell's existing works document his early life as a cowboy, although in later years he turned to the portrayal of the American Indian and to the depiction of historical episodes relative to the exploration and settlement of the western frontier. One of the largest collections of his work, owned by Dr. Phillip G. Cole of Tarrytown, New York, was purchased in 1944 by Tulsa oilman Thomas Gilcrease, and is today on permanent exhibition in the galleries of the Gilcrease Institute of American History and Art, Tulsa, Oklahoma. Other notable collections are at the Stark Museum of Art, Orange, Texas; the Montana State Historical Society in Helena; the Whitney Gallery of Western Art

in the BUFFALO BILL HISTORICAL CENTER, Cody, Wyoming; and the Amon Carter Museum of Western Art, Fort Worth, Texas. Frederic G. RENNER is a consultant to a number of these collections. A volume of Russell's illustrated letters appeared in 1929 under the title *Good Medicine*. With an introduction by Will Rogers and biographical notes by Nancy C. Russell, this edition is today a valued collector's item.

See Ramon F. Adams and Homer E. Britzman, *Charles M. Russell, the Cowboy Artist: a Biography* (1948); Harold McCracken, *The Charles M. Russell Book* (1957); and Paul Rossi and David C. Hunt, *The Art of the Old West* (1971).—D. C. H.

Russell, Hub[bard] Searles (1885-1963). California cattleman. Russell was born in Newbury Park, California. Huge grazing herds of whiteface cattle spread across the lush pasturelands of the Russell family's Conejo Ranch in Ventura County, where Russell grew up. He and his brothers took over the operation of the ranch until it was sold. The Russell brothers then leased ranches in Arizona and other parts of California. In 1939 Russell himself bought forty-five thousand acres of land known as the Cuyama Ranch in Santa Barbara County, California; when his brothers joined him in the ranch ownership, all their other ranch operations were terminated. When oil was discovered on the Cuyama Ranch in 1950, promising new wealth for the family, Russell is supposed to have remarked, "Now I am going to have the kind of cattle I have always wanted."

Russell was active in both the California and American National Cattleman's associations up to the time of his death. From 1948 to 1957 he was a Western Cattle Producer representative on the National Livestock and Meat Board and was one of the organizers of a cooperative marketing association, which he managed for a time. He was also active in California politics and supported candidates who agreed with his own beliefs in the free enterprise system, the right of the cattlemen to rule his own domain, and beneficial legislation for cattlemen.—H. R. L.

Russell, Osborne (1814-1892). Mountain man, pioneer judge, memoirist and businessman. Russell became a fur trapper almost by accident. Born in Bowdoinham, Maine, he ran away to sea at sixteen but found the life of a sailor so unpleasant that he took a job with the North West Trapping and Trading Company, which operated in the area of present-day Wisconsin and Minnesota. In 1834 he joined Nathaniel Wyeth's second expedition to Oregon as an employee of Wyeth's Columbia River Fishing and Trading Company. He was at the famour fur-trading rendezvous of 1834, at which Rocky Mountain Fur Company officials broke their promise to buy Wyeth's trade goods that year. Furious at their refusal, Wyeth exclaimed that he would "roll a stone" into the company's garden that they could never remove. To make good his threat, Wyeth promptly built the important trading post of Fort Hall on the Snake River, and left Robert Evans, Russell, and a handful of men to run it during the winter of 1834-35.

Russell's life as a trapper in the northern reaches of the fur regions over the next nine years was packed with adventure. His initiation into the trade, a successful hunt in the Cache valley in the spring of 1835, was followed by a fall trip to the Tetons and Jackson Hole country, south of Yellowstone. The unwise leadership of Joseph Gale, punctuated by the deaths of fellow trappers and the desertion of others, might have resulted in death to all from Indian raids. But fortunately Osborne's party was joined by an experienced group of mountain men, including James Bridger, Kit Carson, and Joseph Meek, just before a major Blackfoot attack occurred. Subsequently he experienced other Blackfoot attacks, had his horse shot from under him, and was robbed by the Crow.

Disgust with Wyeth's firm led Russell to work for the Rocky Mountain Fur Company and then for the American Fur Company until 1838. Russell then became a free trapper in the vicinity of Fort Hall until 1842. During the summer of that year, however, Russell, who was an avid reader and devoted journal-keeper, was persuaded that he had lived a life of sin and must reform. His conversion coincided with the appearance at Fort Hall of Elijah White's wagon train en route to Oregon, which Russell joined. In Oregon Russell lost an eye in an accident. While recuperating, he trained himself to be a lawyer and was appointed judge by Oregon's provisional government in 1843. A year later he served on the executive committee that governed the province. When Oregon became a territory in 1848, he was elected to the legislative assembly.

Oregonians liked Russell for his rational qualities, his integrity, and his sense of fair play. These same qualities probably motivated him to write his journal in the form of a short book in 1846, after he reportedly became distressed at the inaccurate picture of a fur trapper's life portrayed in James Ohio Pattie's *Narrative* (1833). Although Russell's fine *Journal of a Trapper: or, Nine Years in the Rocky Mountains, 1834-1843* remained unpublished until 1914, it is one of the most valuable accounts of the mountain man in existence. It also expresses the same appreciation of the wilderness that Francis Parkman and, later, John Muir were to develop.

In 1848 Russell went to the California gold fields. Because of his legal experience, he was drafted quickly as a judge for some of the vigilante trials held in Placerville. Remaining in California for the rest of his life as a miner and merchant, Russell's initial business success was marred by a defaulting partner, who left him saddled with debts. He died a bachelor in Placerville, having lived a full and significant life on three western frontiers.

See Aubry L. Haines, *Osborne Russell's Journal of a Trapper* (1955).—G. B. D.

Russell, William Hepburn (1812-1872). Freighter and promoter of the Pony Express. Russell was born in Burlington, Vermont. At sixteen years of age he was employed as a store clerk in Liberty, Missouri, and two years later was working with the Aull Brothers, who had merchandising and business interests in both Richmond and Lexington, Missouri. In June 1835 he married Harriet Elliot Warder. He formed a partnership in 1838 known as Allen, Russell and Company to operate a retail store in Lexington, and shortly thereafter he met his future partner, William B. Waddell, when both men were promoting the First Lexington Addition Company in 1840. The store business failed in 1845, partly because Russell was spending much of his time in performing the duties of public office, serving as postmaster of Lexington (1841-45) and as treasurer of Lafayette County (1840-55). Throughout this period he formed

various and sundry partnerships to engage in enterprise, among which was another store operated under the name of Bullard & Russell. This firm in association with others sent a wagon train of merchandise to Santa Fe in 1847 and another in 1848. In 1850 Russell formed a partnership with James Brown and John S. Jones, known as Brown, Russell & Company, which dispatched a freight train of 135 wagons to Santa Fe loaded with military supplies from Fort Leavenworth. Upon Brown's death, the firm name was changed to Jones & Russell and continued in the business of military freighting.

In 1852 Russell joined William B. Waddell as partner in the mercantile business, and they likewise began transporting military supplies to Santa Fe. Two years later Alexander Majors joined the group when RUSSELL, MAJORS AND WADDELL formed a partnership. Freighting operations expanded rapidly and Russell, a promoter by nature, entered the stagecoach business (see CENTRAL OVERLAND CALIFORNIA AND PIKE'S PEAK EXPRESS). He finally persuaded his partners to join him in this endeavor and the PONY EXPRESS.

Russell's promotions made him famous. He was constantly in the public eye, but his days of glory were brief. To obtain funds for his overexpanded transportation activities, he became involved in the greatest financial scandal of the period. Unable to meet the financial obligations of Russell, Majors and Waddell, he prevailed upon John B. Floyd, the secretary of war, to issue drafts, or acceptances, on the War Department in anticipation of payment for previous or future services. These were used as security for Indian Trust Fund bonds, held in the Interior Department, taken by Russell and used as security for needed cash. Russell's financial affairs went from bad to worse; he could not repay the loans to reclaim the bonds, and the whole affair became public. As a result of a congressional investigation, Secretary Floyd was forced to resign and Russell was indicted. Although Russell's trial was delayed, or diverted, by the coming of the Civil War and legal technicalities, his complicated transportation empire collapsed in 1862 and he was bankrupt. He attempted to engage in several speculative enterprises in New York, none of which succeeded, prior to his death in 1872.

See Arthur Chapman, *The Pony Express* (1932); Raymond W. Settle and Mary L. Settle, *War Drums and Wagon Wheels* (1966) and *Saddles and Spurs: The Pony Express Saga* (1955); and Henry Pickering Walker, *The Wagonmasters* (1966).—W. T. J.

Russell, Majors and Waddell. Freighting partnership. At the end of the Mexican War (1848), the United States established an army supply depot at Santa Fe from which six additional army posts in the New Mexico Territory were to be supplied. Trains supervised by army personnel in 1846 and 1847 were inefficiently organized and costly because of waste, so the War Department resolved to award contracts for the transportation of military supplies to experienced civilian freighters. The first contract was given to James H. Brown, who formed a partnership with William H. RUSSELL. In 1854 the quartermaster general decided to abandon the old practice of awarding a separate contract for each consignment every year in favor of making a contract for supplying all the posts in the West and Southwest for a two-year period. To handle this large assignment, the partnership of Russell, Majors and Waddell was formed. The talents of the three men complemented each other: Alexander MAJORS, a trader on the Santa Fe Trail, had the field experience, Russell the financial and promotional connections, and William B. WADDELL a knowledge about business and trade. The firm attempted to establish a monopoly in the freighting business by handling large government contracts as well as extensive civilian merchandise. From their headquarters at Leavenworth, Kansas, they contracted in 1857 to deliver up to five million pounds of military stores to the forts and depots in Kansas, New Mexico, and Utah.

Upon the outbreak of the Mormon War in 1857, the quartermaster at Fort Leavenworth notified Russell, Majors and Waddell that the army required the shipment of two and a half million pounds of supplies to Salt Lake City, an amount that would make their total for the year greatly in excess of the maximum specified in the contract. Rather than refuse and thereby jeopardize their position as the prime army contractors in the West, the firm undertook the assignment in hopes of future reimbursement. In doing so, they found it necessary to pay inflated prices for wagons, oxen, and train outfits, amounting to more than $240,000, to put fourteen wagon trains on the road. The Mormons, as an aspect of their defense, attempted to destroy the United States Army's supply line by burning the freight wagons and driving off the oxen. Russell, Majors and Waddell lost equipment and supplies valued at $319,000. The government also delayed in paying the firm a similar amount for the services of the previous year over and above their contract. In 1858 Russell, Majors and Waddell agreed to haul ten million pounds of freight, twice as much as the initial contract of the previous year, to Utah at a price of $1.30 for every hundred pounds carried one hundred miles in summer, and $4.00 for the same distance in winter. If additional tonnage up to five million pounds needed to be shipped, the rate would be increased twenty-five percent because the company would again need to purchase additional oxen and wagons.

In spite of continuous expansion since 1855, Russell, Majors and Waddell were embarrassed because of buying on credit. Russell requested the secretary of war, John B. Floyd, for permission to issue drafts, known as acceptances, on the War Department for anticipated payments and earnings. The freighting firm's financial difficulties were further complicated by a decision to enter the express business by organizing what was eventually called the CENTRAL OVERLAND CALIFORNIA AND PIKE'S PEAK EXPRESS and the PONY EXPRESS. Early in

1860 a financial crisis was precipitated when Russell was unable to meet obligations. To protect the acceptances about to be protested, he procured through a friend in the Interior Department Indian Trust Fund Bonds to serve as collateral for additional loans. Being called upon by the lenders to put up additional collateral, Russell again went to the Interior Department and was provided with more bonds amounting to $870,000. When this misuse of the bonds in the Indian Trust Fund was disclosed, President James Buchanan called a special meeting of the cabinet at which the secretary of the interior was instructed to order the arrest of Russell and his accomplice. This turn of events meant one further step toward financial ruin for the firm of Russell, Majors and Waddell, which had already been near bankruptcy and eventually failed in 1862.

See Raymond W. Settle and Mary L. Settle, *War Drums and Wagon Wheels: The Story of Russell, Majors and Waddell* (1966); and Henry Pickering Walker, *The Wagonmasters* (1966).—W. T. J.

Russian-American Company. See ALASKA.

Ryan, John Dennis (1864-1933). Montana businessman. Ryan was born in the copper region of Michigan, where his father was a leader in the industry. In 1900 the younger Ryan went to Butte, Montana, where he knew Marcus Daly well. Daly named him a trustee of his estate just before he died. By 1903 Ryan had succeeded to Daly's former positions of president of the Anaconda Copper Mining Company and director of the Amalgamated Copper Company, of which he became president in 1909. He greatly strengthened his companies in 1906 when he patiently negotiated the purchase of Frederick Augustus Heinze's interests. He thus resolved the "war of the copper kings" by succeeding one and buying out another. He continued the tradition of being a staunch Democrat, but he did not wish political office for himself and he exerted political influence quietly and skillfully.

In 1912 he created the Montana Power Company by merging several small local companies, and in 1913 he secured the profitable contract to electrify the CHICAGO, MILWAUKEE, ST. PAUL AND PACIFIC RAILROAD across the Rocky Mountains. Early in World War I Ryan became director of the Military Relief Department of the American Red Cross and perfected a highly efficient organization. In May 1918 he became director of the Bureau of Aircraft Production; in August this bureau and that of the Aircraft Board were consolidated under him as second assistant secretary of war and director of Air Services.

See Isaac F. Marcosson, *Anaconda* (1957).—M. G. B.

S

Sacagawea (c. 1790-1812 or 1884) Shoshoni interpreter and guide for the Lewis and Clark expedition. Except for that period recorded by Lewis and Clark in their journals, the details of Sacagawea's life are elusive and often controverted. Her father was a Shoshoni chieftain, but in 1800, when about ten years of age, she was captured by a party of Hidatsa near the Three Forks of the Missouri. Subsequently she and another captive girl were purchased and taken to wife by Toussaint CHARBONNEAU a Canadian then living among the Hidatsa. The explorers Lewis and Clark found Charbonneau at Fort Mandan in the winter of 1804-05 and engaged him as interpreter for their expedition, with the specific understanding that Sacagawea be allowed to accompany the party. Eight weeks before the expedition departed from Fort Mandan, she gave birth to her first child, a son named Jean Baptiste CHARBONNEAU and called Pomp or Pompey by William Clark. This infant she carried on a cradleboard when the party headed upriver in early April 1805.

One of her most important services on the expedition was acknowledged by Captain Clark in his *Official Journals:* "The wife of Shabono [Charbonneau] our interpreter we find reconciles all the Indians, as to our friendly intentions—a woman with a party of men is a token of peace." More important perhaps was her role in establishing cordial relations with the Shoshoni, from whom the party needed to secure horses in order to make their way from the Missouri headwaters to the tributaries of the Snake and Columbia rivers. After Captain Lewis first contacted a Shoshoni party, Sacagawea arrived to find the band led by Cameahwait, an elder brother who had taken her father's place upon the old chief's death. Moved deeply with both joy and grief, as Lewis's description makes clear, the young woman still aided the expedition in securing horses and other supplies from her brother's camp, then bade Cameahwait farewell as she dutifully accompanied her husband and the explorers on toward the Pacific.

When the expedition returned eastward, Charbonneau, his wife and his son went only so far as the Hidatsa town at the mouth of the Knife River, where the interpreter took his discharge. At that point the historic Sacagawea passes from view, and the student is left to select as authentic one of two women whose respective claims have been argued with both force and logic. According to one view, she accompanied Charbonneau to St. Louis about 1809, then two years later left her son with Clark and returned upriver with her husband, only to fall victim to a "a putrid fever" at Fort Manuel late in 1812. According to the alternate view, she lived for some time among the Comanche and later returned to her own people on the Wind River Reservation, where she

died in 1884. Faced with a certain weight of evidence on both sides of the dispute, scholarship may still render to both a Scot's verdict: not proven.

The fullest account, contending for the authenticity of the Wyoming Sacagawea, is Grace R. Hebard, *Sacajawea* (1957). The opposing evidence is best summarized in Harold P. Howard, *Sacajawea* (1971). —K. N. O.

Sacramento, California. The site of Sacramento was chosen in 1839 by John Augustus SUTTER, who located his famous trading post and fort at the junction of the American and Sacramento rivers. The river gave him access to the interior valley system and passage to the sea through the delta and into the San Francisco Bay; additionally, the site was conveniently located on what became the trail across the Sierra Nevada pass from the East. With the discovery of gold, the location became even more attractive as a strategic distribution point for men and supplies to the mother lode country. But Sutter benefited as little from his propitious site selection as from the precious metal itself, which brought him nothing but agony and ruin. The town, conceived as a waterfront extention of Sutter's Fort, was laid out with Sutter's cooperation in 1848, but that winter's sale of lots quickly got out of hand, and by spring Sutter was confronted with what he considered a squatter's city on his property, competing with his hitherto mercantile monopoly. Sacramento grew at a fantastic pace, expanding from two shacks in January 1849 to over three hundred canvas buildings by August. Sutter's Fort was quickly out of competition and was out of business by mid-1850.

Sacramento was one of three cities that operated as middle links in a commercial chain supplying the mines. San Francisco was the entrepôt for most of the equipment and supplies. From the bay, this material flowed into the Central Valley along the river artery to Sacramento or its sister cities, Marysville (supplying the mining towns of the far North) and Stockton (from which the mines at the southern end of the lode were supplied). Because of its location at the junction of the valley river system, its juxtaposition near the heart of the mother lode, and its function as a terminus of the Overland Trail, however, Sacramento held a competitive edge and grew at a more rapid pace. From Sacramento and the other river supply cities, men and goods traveled inland to the mining towns, the last stop on the way to the camps themselves. The entire system of distribution sprang up almost overnight.

Taking another clue from Sutter's operation, farmers moved into the fertile valley during the gold-rush years, producing grain, vegetables, and fruit, which flowed downriver in abundance to the expanding market in Sacramento. Floods like those of 1851, which swept the valley and nearly destroyed the city, underlined the necessity for water control, which was begun in the late 1850s. Land reclamation and irrigation projects further expanded the valley's agricultural potential, and by the late 1850s agriculture began to offset the diminishing importance of the mining economy that had spawned the city. The choice of Sacramento as the site for California's capital in 1854 and its selection as the terminus of the continental railroad, completed in 1869, signaled the beginning of Sacramento's new era as the heart of one of the world's richest agricultural districts.

See Julian Dana, *The Sacramento: River of Gold* (1939); and Rodman W. Paul, *California Gold* (1967).—J. F.

Sacramento River. The Sacramento carries almost a third of California's runoff toward the sea. Carried along by the water are flecks of golden sand derived from the mother-lode country of the Sierra Nevada foothills, where the forty-niners made their fortunes.

The source of the Sacramento lies in a small lake on the slopes of Mount Eddy in the Klamath Mountain range. It first flows eastward for 12 miles, turns southward for 370 miles, and mingles with the waters of the San Joaquin in the delta region before emptying into Suisun Bay, the eastern arm of San Francisco Bay. The Sacramento runoff averages over 22 million acre-feet, appreciably more than the mighty Colorado River. Many tributaries that drain the Cascade and Sierra Nevada ranges contribute to its flow. Among the most significant are the McCloud, Pit, Feather, Yuba, Bear, and American rivers. Between the city of Redding and its mouth the river drains the great valley named after it and provides irrigation water for lands along its banks and for the arid San Joaquin Valley farther south.

The stream lies in a region of Mediterranean climate with abundant winter rain and snow and summer drought. Peak flows are related to the melting of winter snow in the spring of the year, but disastrous floods have occurred in the winter season when unusually warm winter rains have melted an early snowpack. Elevations in its drainage area vary from the summit of Mount Shasta, 14,161 feet above sea level, to points in the delta section that lie below sea level, so that temperature conditions vary appreciably. In the Sacramento Valley mild winters and hot summers are experienced. In winter, tule fogs smother the valley floor for weeks on end. Because of the wide range of topographic and climatic conditions, the river boasts a varied landscape. In the north the Sacramento and its major tributaries, the Pit and the McCloud, cross rugged brush and tree-covered country. The Pit, which drains northeastern California, has entrenched itself in the Modoc plateau, the southwestern edge of the great Columbia lava plateau. Where its eastern tributaries flow out of the upland areas of the Sierra Nevada, they are marked by spectacular canyons. One of them in particular, the Feather River Canyon, is well known by transcontinental travelers who have ridden the Western Pacific Railroad. These streams rise in alpine meadows and pass through transition zones that include lodgepole pine, fir, spruce, and pine forests before reaching the oak woodland and chaparral zones that mark the edge of the oak woodland-grass-covered valley floor.

The river was first explored by white men in 1817 when a party of Spanish soldiers under Captain Luis Arguello maneuvered a raft upstream. Before that,

Spanish horsemen had been thwarted in their attempts to penetrate the maze of swampy islands that make up the delta section of the Sacramento and San Joaquin rivers. It was not until the Spanish discovered that they could cross the Golden Gate on rafts and ride around the north end of San Francisco Bay that the Sacramento Valley was explored to any great extent. The river was known as the Rio de San Francisco during much of the Spanish-Mexican period of occupation. However, the explorer Gabriel Moraga had given the name El Rio de los Sacramentos to one of its main branches, the present-day Feather River. In time, European and American settlers applied the name Sacramento to the river as a whole.

The first of these non-Spanish settlers, John Augustus Sutter, a former Swiss army officer, settled at the confluence of the American and Sacramento rivers on August 12, 1839. He soon acquired land grants extending for considerable distances along the rivers, and his fort at New Helvetia became the focal point of new migrants entering the valley from the east. The voyage up river of a forty-foot schooner he had purchased from the Russians at Fort Ross marked the first commercial navigation of the stream.

The discovery of gold at the mill John Marshall had erected in partnership with Sutter sparked the migration of thousands of people into the basin of the Sacramento. Marshall made his discovery on January 24, 1848. By 1850 twenty-eight steamers and sixty or more boats and ships powered by sail and oars were operating on the Sacramento as far upstream as Marysville and Red Bluff.

During the first years of mining activity the stream channels were modified only slightly by men using pans or shovels and small sluice boxes. After 1852, however, when hydraulic mining and dredging activities began in earnest, tons of silt and sand clogged the stream beds creating sandbars, killing the fish, and making boat traffic along the Sacramento difficult, if not impossible. By the time that legislation banning hydraulic mining was passed in 1884, navigation had become limited to shallow-draft craft only, and most of the tributary streams had built their beds above the levels of the intervening basins. The last of the river passenger boats went out of existence in 1941, but today pleasure craft make extensive use of the waterways extending through the valley, and ocean-going vessels reach Sacramento via a thirty-foot ship canal.

Miners had early diverted mountain streams to provide water for their activities in the foothill zone, and these dams and diversion canals were soon taken over by bonanza grain farmers who converted the Sacramento into one of the world's greatest wheat-growing areas in the latter part of the nineteenth century. Not until 1945, however, when Shasta Dam was completed as part of the Bureau of Reclamation's Central Valley project, was the Sacramento brought under control. Designed principally for flood control and water conservation, the dam is also used to generate electricity for the northern part of the state. Pacific Gas and Electricity, the principal purveyor of electricity in northern California, has likewise constructed many dams on tributaries of the Sacramento. Only recently, the state of California has completed the major unit in the California Water Project, Oroville Dam, on the Feather River. Water from the Sacramento is now used to flood rice fields along its banks, to grow cotton and other field crops in the San Joaquin, and to satisfy the thirst of millions of residents of southern California. It truly is the lifeblood of the state.

For map, see CALIFORNIA.

See California Division of Water Resources, *The Sacramento River Basin* (1934); California Department of Water Resources, *The California Water Plan* (1957); S. T. Harding, *Water in California* (1960); and Lawrence R. McDonnell, ed., *Rivers of California* (1962).—R. W. D.

saddles. The "cow saddle," "range saddle," or, as it is best known, the "western stock saddle" has long been asociated with cowboy lore and the West. Although saddles have been used throughout the world since ancient times, the western saddle was designed and adapted to the specific needs of the range cattle industry. The saddle served as the cowboy's workbench by day and his pillow by night. The old song "On a ten-dollar horse and a forty-dollar saddle" was not without truth, for cowboys often spent large sums on fine saddles. In the Old West no worse thing could be said of a man than that he had "sold his saddle," which implied that he had betrayed a trust or done something to earn the contempt of his fellows.

Today's western saddles are the result of an evolution from the Mexican *silla de campo* or vaquero saddle, adapted from an earlier model of Persian design brought to Spain by the Moors and introduced into the New World by the conquistadors. Over the years this Spanish war saddle went through a variety of changes,

A Denver saddle dating from 1875. The leather roll lashed behind the horn is a "bucking roll," which helped a cowboy stay in the saddle on a bucking animal. (Colorado State Museum)

with numerous regional variations, in an attempt to develop a saddle suitable for range work.

A modern saddle consists of approximately fifty-nine separate leather pieces carefully fitted over a wooden frame or "tree." Older trees were of one piece, constructed from hardwoods and occasionally inlaid with various colored woods and highly polished "like a fine piece of furniture." Modern trees are made of several pieces of softwood, usually pine or spruce, and covered with wet rawhide, which shrinks as it dries to form a tight, hard surface.

The tree dictates the size and style of saddle. Sizing is determined by the fork, which is measured across the front or back from the extreme outside edges, and the seat, which is measured from the top of the inside edge of the cantle to the back of the fork. Thus a 14-14½ saddle would have a 14-inch fork and a 14½-inch seat. Trees often have colorful or descriptive names such as Visalia, Franzier, Ellenburg, or Little Roper, but most modern trees are variations of one of four basic designs. The "roper" has a low horn and minimum swell with a low cantle for freedom of movement and ease in dismounting; the "bronc buster" has a high pommel and swell with a low horn and high cantle, while the "all purpose," the most popular style, is designed with medium swell and moderate cantle and horn and can be used for all around range work and pleasure riding. Usually built on a modified Ellenburg tree, the "Association" saddle (built to specifications of the Rodeo Association of America) is a variation of the "roper." It has a medium-height cantle, a small, round skirt, and is ³⁄₄ rigged, with the flank rig set somewhat farther back than usual. Although intended for bronc riding, the saddle is sometimes used by riders for roping and ranch work.

The other parts of the saddle include: the fork or swell, the horn or pommel, cantle, skirts, jockeys, stirrup leathers and fenders, cinches, and the stirrup assembly.

The "fork," or front portion of the saddle, may be of several types. Early western saddles had a very narrow straight fork, but during the late nineteenth century bronc riders began tying slickers or other padding across the fork to act as a bumper and leg hold. This innovation led to the "swell fork," which incorporated the bronc riders' padding into the construction of the saddle. The most extreme were the "bear trap" forks, which often were twenty inches wide and deeply undercut. Since it was virtually impossible to be thrown from one, the bear trap was popular with amateur cowboys and riders, but old hands would not ride them, for to have done so would have ruined a man's reputation as a "clean sitter."

The fork terminates in the "horn," or "pommel." Horns vary considerably in height and shape from the long slender horn, often terminating in a carved figure, to the short, thick neck and flat pommel called the "Mexican dinner plate." Steel horns made an appearance about 1880 and after that metal horns and forks, made in one piece and riveted to the tree, became increasingly popular. Metal horns are usually wrapped with rawhide or leather, but parade and show saddles often feature elaborately worked gold or silver, which is inset with precious stones.

The conquistadors' saddles often had a high, bare wooden cantle, but the vaqueros soon modified this design in order to provide both comfort and support for the rider. Today the "cantle," or "backbow," is generally concave, sometimes padded, and varies considerably in shape, height, and slope. A favorite style, the "Cheyenne roll," features a leather flange or rim extending over the cantle board.

Covering the saddle frame are several layers of leather designed to protect both horse and rider. Spanish coverings consisting of *bastos, camiseta,* and *mochila,* are represented in modern saddles by the "skirts" and "jockeys." On vaquero saddles these coverings were detachable, but now they are an integral part of the construction and few riders today would recognize a saddle without them. About 1870 the mochila ("mocheer" in cowboy lingo) gave way to a large, permanent covering known as the "Mother Hubbard." Then, during the 1880s, the full Mother Hubbard was replaced with separate sheepskin-lined skirts and jockeys. At first each jockey was a separate piece fastened to the saddle with screws and short ties or "strings." Later, jockeys were constructed of one piece and stitched to the skirts. Most early saddles had narrow stirrup leathers without *rosaderos,* or "fenders," but later the leathers were widened and fenders added. The size of the skirts and fenders varies according to the purposes and whims of the rider, but most California and West Coast hands prefer small rounded skirts, patterned after the Spanish *bastos,* while Texas and Plains cowboys favor larger, square skirts, sometimes with an *anquero,* or rump, covering added.

There are two principal types of "rigging" or "cinch," arrangements, which are identified by the region where they are used. The "California" or "single-rigged" saddle evolved directly from the vaquero model and has only one cinch, usually placed directly under the pommel. For roping operations the cinch is moved under the stirrup leathers, and the saddle is then known as a "centerfire rig." Locations of the cinch between the original and center position are identified as $5/8$, $3/4$, or $7/8$ rigs. The single cinch is satisfactory for the vaquero, who throws a long rope and then secures it with a quick turn, or "dally," around the saddle horn, but most Texas and Plains cowboys prefer to use a shorter rope tied to the saddle horn. This roping method places more strain on the saddle, and "tie-fast" men prefer a "Texas," "double," or "square-rigged" saddle with a cinch at both front and back, again in various positions. Added to the rigging are *latigos,* long leather straps passed through the cinch, and rigging rings that hold the cinch tight.

Stirrups have changed with the saddle. The Spaniards used both metal and wooden stirrups, and various adaptations of early models have been popular through the years. The most widely used stirrup today is the "Visalia," made of wood bound with metal strips and covered with leather. A *tapadero,* or "tap," is often added to the stirrup assembly as a protective device.

Old-time saddlemakers often added extra touches of their own invention, and many saddles were known by the names of their makers. Shops like those operated by the Collins brothers at Fort Laramie, Heiser at Denver, Frazier and Gallup at Pueblo, Myres at El Paso, Hamley at Portland, and Main and Winchester at San Francisco, to name a few, were known throughout the West. Although most working saddles are of plain design, Anglo cowmen have inherited the Mexican's love for ornately decorated saddles, and elaborately "stamped" (carved) gear remains popular. Some show saddles carry thousands of dollars' worth of gold, silver, and gems, but even the simplest working rig usually has a few silver conchos or other decorative touches.

Necessity or individual whim dictates the additional equipment used in conjunction with the saddle. Some sort of "bridle," or "hackamore," and a good saddle blanket are essential, while a "breast strap," "martingale," or other accouterments may also be used.

In addition to the many innovations and adaptations made from time to time in the western stock saddle, other saddles were also used in the West. Just when sidesaddles came into use for women riders is still a matter of dispute. Although they may have been in use on the Continent as early as the twelfth century, they did not become popular in England until late Elizabethan times. The first sidesaddles were little more than a simple pad equipped with a cinch, crupper, and breast collar. Later a stirrup or a long wooden footboard was added. By the nineteenth century the ladies insisted upon a number of modifications to make the sidesaddle more comfortable for long rides. Sidesaddles were now built on trees, usually with wide sidebars forming a fork and low pommel. American ladies, particularly in the West, favored a high cantle and pommel, and these saddles lacked only the offside stirrup and skirt to make them a regular astride rig. Another popular innovation was the addition of another horn, called a leaping horn, for the left knee so that women riders could join their menfolk in cross-country hunts and in jumping competitions.

During the eighteenth and nineteenth centuries, convention forced most ladies to use sidesaddles, but after 1900 many women gave up these clumsy rigs for the more secure and comfortable astride saddles of their menfolk.

The army used various models of the cavalry saddle, including the Grimsley, Van Dorn, and the famous McClellan. Although not so light or as small as "eastern" saddles, contemptuously termed "postage stamps" or "pimple pads" by westerners, the cavalry saddle was unsuitable for range work and never achieved much popularity outside army posts.

More important, and often neglected in histories of western saddlery, is the packsaddle, or *aparejo.* The packsaddle came in many different shapes and styles, but the most popular was patterned on a Mexican model, which may have been of Arabian origin. After 1866 the aparejo became standard army equipment in rough western terrain, and like the stock saddle played a vital role in the "taming of the West."

See Emmett Essin, "Mules, Packs and Packtrains," *Southwestern Historical Quarterly* (July 1970); Sandra L. Myres, *S. D. Myres: Saddlemaker* (1961); and Glenn Vernam, *Man on Horseback* (1964), which gives a complete history of saddles and saddle-making.—S. L. M.

safety valve theory. George Henry Evans, a labor leader and editor of the *Working Man's Advocate* in the 1830s and early 1840s, argued that it was a natural right of man to own a piece of land for his subsistence and declared that the public lands should be opened freely to all who would take up farming on them. Free land in the West, he maintained, would siphon off unemployed or discontented laborers from eastern cities who were trying to improve their lot by strikes. A better and a safer method of alleviating social unrest would be available if free land were granted. The public lands as free homesteads could "carry off our superabundant labor to the salubrious and fertile West," he wrote. This was the safety valve theory. In the *Working Man's Advocate* and other journals of labor opinion, Evans gave wide publicity to his free-land agrarian doctrine and attacked what he called land monopoly, that is, the large ownerships of land in New York and the speculative purchases of public land being made in 1835 and 1836 in the West. To prevent further accumulations of land in the hands of the few, Evans advocated strict limitations upon the amount of public land individuals could acquire, the reservation of public lands for actual farm makers, and inalienable titles.

Horace Greeley, his chief convert, accepted the safety valve theory, urged the unemployed to go West, and threw the weight of his influential New York *Tribune* in behalf of free land and reserving the public lands for settlers. His influence was important in convincing Republican leaders to accept the theory and to pass the Homestead Act in 1862, with its free-land feature. From that time into the twentieth century the safety valve theory was commonly accepted, and political leaders, boasting of what they and their party had done for the common man, never hesitated to point to the Homestead Act as a boon to the workingman and the farm maker in the West.

In formulating his influential thesis on the role of the frontier West in American history (see FRONTIER THEORY), Frederick Jackson TURNER recognized that the existence of free land in the West meant an "escape" for easterners. The school of frontier historians who followed Turner accepted and elaborated the safety valve theory and for a generation made it a basic feature of their writing and teaching. Then came the inevitable reexamination which turned up little or no evidence to support it. Emigration to the West and indeed to the United States from abroad tended to shrink in periods of depression and unemployment in industrial centers. Workingmen, whether skilled or unskilled, had no knowledge of farming operations, lacked the necessary capital, or even funds to move to the West, for rarely were they able to amass savings. The bulk of the western land seekers were from older farming areas or were peasants attracted from Germany or Sweden by the opportunity of actually owning a farm, which was something they could never hope for in their own country. One historian, Fred A. Shannon, called the results of his investigation "A Post-Mortem on the Labor-Safety-Valve Theory." Recently historians have suggested that the West, by creating new markets as well as market goods, and by providing a field for investment and speculation, helped develop the economy and thus acted as a stimulant if not as a "safety valve."

See Ray A. Billington, *America's Frontier Heritage* (1966); and Helene Sarah Zahler, *Eastern Workingmen and National Land Policy, 1829-1862* (1941).—P. W. G.

St. Clair, Arthur (1736-1818). Soldier and politician. Born in Caithness County, Scotland, St. Clair came to North America as an ensign in Lord Jeffery Amherst's army in 1758. He participated in the captures of Louisburg, Quebec, and Montreal during the French and Indian War. In 1760 he married Phoebe Bayard of Boston, who was related to the prominent Bowdoin family. She bore him seven children. Through his wife he came into a large inheritance which, combined with his own savings, provided enough wealth to establish him as a gentleman farmer. He resigned his army commission in 1762 and moved with his wife to the Ligonier valley of Pennsylvania. His initial purchase of four hundred acres of land was gradually increased through purchase and military bounties until he owned about fifteen thousand acres in Pennsylvania and Ohio. He was appointed a local justice and surveyor for Cumberland County in 1770 and also a member of the governor's council. As new counties were created in the area he received similar appointments in Bedford County and then Westmoreland County. Thus he gained invaluable experience in the operation of local frontier government. In 1773 he represented the Pennsylvania courts in disputes with Virginia over jurisdiction in southwestern Pennsylvania.

With the outbreak of the American Revolution, St. Clair volunteered his services to the Continental army, and Congress commissioned him a colonel in December 1775. The next May he joined the American army in Canada and took part in the retreat to Crown Point and Fort Ticonderoga. He spent a short time at Fort Ticonderoga and then received orders to join General George Washington in New Jersey. At this time, August 1776, he was commissioned brigadier general. He served on Washington's staff and had an active regimental command during the withdrawal across New Jersey and the Christmas Eve attack on Trenton. In January the army went into winter quarters at Morristown. At the request of Washington he was promoted to major general and made adjutant general for the headquarters staff.

In June 1777 he took command of Fort Ticonderoga. During the previous winter the fort had not been fully repaired and the number of troops had declined through illness and desertion. Congress and General Washington expected that the British would feint toward the fort but make their major thrust farther east. The levies requested from the New England states to reinforce the fort did not arrive, and St. Clair had to defend the inadequate fort with about twenty-two hundred men. In early July General John Burgoyne moved his British troops against Fort Ticonderoga and occupied the heights commanding the fort. St. Clair, rather than lose all of his men, chose to evacuate the fort in light of the superior British army. On July 5 the evacuation began and the army retreated rapidly to Fort Edward, where they joined forces with General Philip Schuyler. The retreat continued to the mouth of the Mohawk River. Following the battle of Bennington, the Americans took the offensive and in September forced Burgoyne to surrender at Saratoga. Generals St. Clair and Schuyler had been relieved of command after Bennington and ordered to headquarters. Members of Congress charged both men with negligence in evacuating Fort Ticonderoga. St. Clair requested a court-martial, which was finally held in April 1778, and he and Schuyler were acquitted.

Meanwhile St. Clair had served on Washington's staff at Valley Forge. When General Benedict Arnold defected, St. Clair took temporary command of West Point and served on the jury that convicted Major John André of being a spy. When Washington moved south in the summer of 1781, St. Clair remained in Philadelphia marshaling supplies and men. He later helped clear North Carolina of British and in 1783 helped muster out the army and settle accounts.

Returning home in 1783 he discovered that he was almost bankrupt, and devoted his time to recouping his losses. On November 2, 1785, he took a seat in the Continental Congress as a member from Pennsylvania and a year later was elected president of Congress. In October Congress named him governor of the new Northwest Territory.

He arrived in Marietta in summer 1788 to organize the first territorial government in the history of the United States. As governor, St. Clair endeavored to meet the needs of the residents. His natural inclination toward the Federalist party was strengthened by his political connections, most of whom were New England Federalists and members of the Ohio Company of Associates. Yet St. Clair did not force partisan politics down the throats of the territorial residents. For the most part he attempted to keep the territory at peace with the Indians and to encourage expansion in population. He traveled across the territory regularly to handle governmental matters for all residents. An early political problem developed over the interpretation of the clause in the Northwest Ordinance of 1787 that provided that the governor and judges "shall adopt and publish . . . such laws of the original States, . . . as may be . . . best suited to the circumstances of the district. . . ." Judge John Cleves Symmes, a land speculator, and the other judges argued that the legislature could alter laws of the states to suit the needs of the territory, while the governor insisted that they could only adopt individual laws of the states verbatim. The split between Governor St. Clair and Judge Symmes widened partly over the judge's land schemes and partly over administrative problems from which subsequent territories also suffered. This split was a major cause of the rise of political parties within the territory.

As superintendent of Indian affairs, St. Clair secured several Indian treaties but was unable to keep the Indians from harassing the settlers. In late summer 1791, he led an army against the Indians and suffered a major defeat. This defeat did not increase his popularity.

The traditional picture of St. Clair as an autocratic tyrant was drawn by his political opposition who wished to discredit his work and obtain statehood. St. Clair did not misgovern but became caught between two land-speculating groups concerned with the location of state boundaries, which would affect the value of their lands. St. Clair attempted to maintain a middle ground without success. The election of William Henry Harrison as territorial delegate in 1798 brought the political factions in the territory into alignment with the national political parties, and St. Clair openly supported Federalist policies. With the Federalists he opposed statehood in 1802-03. In November 1802 President Thomas Jefferson removed him from office and St. Clair retired to his home in Pennsylvania. He attempted to collect monies owing him from the federal government for personal debts incurred for military expenses during the Revolution and the Indian campaign of 1791, but forfeited all of his property in 1810 to pay these debts. St. Clair died in poverty.

Most of his correspondence has been collected in Wil-

liam H. Smith's *The Life and Public Services of Arthur St. Clair*, 2 vols. (1882).—J. T. B.

St. Joseph, Missouri. Established in the summer of 1826 as a trading post by Joseph Robidoux III, St. Joseph stood on the Missouri River at the entrance to the Platte country, an area that both the remaining Indians of the region and the land-hungry settlers of Missouri desired. After ten years of tug of war, the Indian claims were extinguished and the territory added to the state of Missouri on June 7, 1836.

Thereafter St. Joseph grew rapidly and by the late 1840s began to challenge Independence, Westport, and other towns along the border as a popular rendezvous for wagon trains going west. More than two thousand wagons crossed the Missouri River there in the spring of 1849. The local paper reported that a building boom was in progress. Emigrant demands for meat led to the raising of large numbers of hogs in the area and the development of a local meat-packing industry, which continued to play an important role in the town's economy until the 1960s.

By the time of the Civil War, St. Joseph had become Missouri's second city, with a population of 8,932. The completion of the Hannibal and St. Joseph Railroad in February 1859 strengthened its position and added to the attractiveness of the town as a jumping-off place for western emigrants. As the first railroad to be completed across Missouri, it siphoned off a great deal of the Missouri River traffic, and, through its links with other lines, carried a lot of trade past St. Louis and into Chicago. St. Joseph became the critical transfer point.

The railroad also played a major role in the selection of St. Joseph as the eastern terminus for the pony express that operated briefly in 1860-61 to facilitate rapid communication with California. In the decade after the Civil War, St. Joseph yielded her position of dominance on the western border to Kansas City, in part because of the latter's closer proximity to the cattle trails and the ability of its boosters to establish a tie into the Hannibal and St. Joseph Railroad east of its river rival. The failure to bridge the Missouri River at St. Joseph until 1873 further handicapped the town, as did discriminatory freight rates that continued until the 1880s.

Good descriptions of St. Joseph's several roles may be found in David D. March, *The History of Missouri*, 4 vols. (1967). The story of the impact of the Hannibal and St. Joseph Railroad is well told in Richard C. Overton, *Burlington West* (1941).—W. E. P.

St. Paul. See TWIN CITIES, MINNESOTA.

St. Vrain, Ceran De Hault De Lassus de (1802-1870). Fur trapper and merchant. St. Vrain was born in St. Louis County, Missouri. He became a clerk for Bernard Pratte and Company and entered the New Mexico trade in 1824 as the partner of François Guerin. Between 1826 and 1828 he was clerk to Sylvestre Pratte. Subsequently he sent out expeditions from his headquarters in Taos and from Santa Fe and also trapped in the field himself. By 1832 he formed a partnership with Charles Bent to form BENT, ST. VRAIN, AND COMPANY. In 1834 they built the famous BENT'S FORT ten miles above the mouth of the Purgatoire River. Other forts were also built on the South Platte and the Canadian rivers. Bent's Fort became a headquarters for the military, trappers, and Indians of the Southwest. So dominant was its influence that it ruined the supply system in the Colorado

Rockies established by the Robidoux brothers, and it held back the encroachments of Fort Laramie from the north.

St. Vrain was a large, genial, outgoing man. Contemporaries called him a gentleman, and he appears to have been a popular figure in both Mexican and American circles. St. Vrain became a Mexican citizen not only for business purposes but to be eligible for the vast land grants that were being awarded by Governor Manuel Armijo. By the time Americans occupied New Mexico, he and other Americans had acquired large tracts of land. After Charles Bent's murder during the Taos rebellion of 1847, St. Vrain became a partner of William Bent but abandoned the partnership by 1850. He continued his realty investments and became an investor in milling, railroads, banking, and publishing. He was also a politician, supporting the party wishing to obtain territorial status for New Mexico after the area was acquired from Mexico in 1848, but he never won public office. He died at Mora, New Mexico, where he had moved from Taos in 1855.

See LeRoy R. Hafen, ed., *The Mountain Men and the Fur Trade of the Far West*, vol. V (1968); and David Lavender, *Bent's Fort* (1954).—G. B. D.

Salinas River. The Salinas, the upside-down river, is the third longest river in California and the largest subterranean stream in America. It appears at the surface only at specific places along its course and at times of high-water flow. Its name is derived from the salt marshes near its mouth and from the alkali crust that appears along its bed in places. It has been known by several other names—Santa Delfina, San Antonio, and Rio de Monterey.

Western tributaries of the Salinas have their sources in the moderately well watered oak woodlands that cover the Santa Lucia range; the eastern tributaries rise on the somewhat more arid western slopes of the Mount Diablo range. The Estrella River is the first important tributary to join it from the east, but soon the Nacimiento and San Antonio rivers contribute their flows. The last two tributaries of any significance are the Arroyo Seco and San Lorenzo Creek. With most of its flow below the surface, the valley of the Salinas presents a tranquil appearance as the river flows northwestward for 170 miles from the middle of San Luis Obispo County to empty into Monterey Bay. Green and sometimes golden leaves of cottonwoods mark its course after the stream descends from the oak-grass woodland that covers the slopes of the Coast Ranges, in which the Salinas originates.

Much of the stream's significance is historical, for this was the route Portola and Serra followed on their first journey of exploration northward from San Diego in search of Monterey Bay in 1769. The mouth of the river had been visited a century and a half earlier by exploring parties arriving by sea, most notably by Vizcaino. With the establishment of the Franciscan mission chain and the presidios and pueblos of the Spanish in 1769, traffic along the Salinas increased appreciably. French, British, and American traders arrived in their ships seeking cattle hides and otter fur, while inland trappers from Hudson's Bay Company and mountain men from the American frontier sought beaver pelts as they scoured the streams of western America.

The Spanish presidio at Monterey held the seat of government for all of California, and the adjacent lands of the Salinas valley provided attractive grazing lands for cattle. Today the Salinas valley is still a major thoroughfare for travelers between San Francisco and Los Angeles. Dams on the tributaries of the Salinas regulate its flow and conserve water for the abundant crops of vegetables, fruits, and hay produced on its fertile soils. The valley is today better known as the salad bowl of the nation, for more than half the lettuce crop comes from here.

For map, see CALIFORNIA.

See California Department of Water Resources, *The California Water Plan* (1957); S. T. Harding, *Water in California* (1960); and Lawrence R. McDonnell, ed., *Rivers of California* (1962).—R. W. D.

Salish Indians. See FLATHEAD INDIANS.

Salish language. See INDIAN LANGUAGES: *Salish*.

saloon. The word *saloon* was in use as early as 1841 and became general after the Civil War. The western saloon was an outgrowth of the TAVERNS AND HOTELS of the colonial and early nineteenth-century periods, which combined the lodging and drinking functions in a single establishment. Typical was a barroom in the Green Tree Tavern in Chicago, 1835. This room served as a combination drinking room and common lounging room. The bar was used not only for serving drinks but as a registry counter for the tavern's guest rooms. The emergence of the saloon as a business devoted to drinking alone stemmed from the alteration of midwestern state laws in the 1830s and 1840s to allow for the licensing of barrooms without transient facilities.

In the eighteenth century drinking was freely indulged in, but excessive tippling was taboo. After 1800 attitudes toward drinking became more relaxed and drunkenness common. The change was probably related to the decline in social controls associated with swift continental frontier expansion, for on the frontier hard drinking flourished, especially among the lonely and frustrated single men in the mining and cow-town saloons. Well before the Civil War drinking had gained the center of the social rituals of the hearty, male-dominated frontier society. As the British visitor Frederick Marryat noted in his *Diary in America* (1839): "there is an unceasing pouring out and amalgamation of alcohol and other compounds, from morning to late at night. To drink with a friend when you meet him is good fellowship, to drink with a stranger is politeness and a proof of wishing to be better acquainted. . . . Americans can fix nothing without a drink. If you meet, you drink; if you part, you drink; if you make acquaintance, you drink; if you close a bargain, you drink; they quarrel in their drink, and they make it up with a drink. They drink because it is hot; they drink because it is cold. If successful in elections they drink and rejoice; if not they drink and swear. . . ." Smoking and drinking, too, were characteristic of the early midwestern barrooms. So highly masculine were they that in time separate ladies' parlors became fixtures in the taverns and hotels.

Western drinking was often ugly and violent (Wild Bill Hickok and John Wesley Hardin both died in saloon shootings), but even after respectable women came to the West in significant numbers, the saloon retained its crucial social role as an informal men's club, with steady drinking during the week and heavy drinking on Saturday and Sunday when work in the mines and fields and on the range came to a halt. Aside from tippling and the attraction of the ever-present free-lunch counter, saloon hours were whiled away in gambling and in making sexual liaisons with dance-hall girls and prostitutes.

The saloon life of San Francisco was vibrant and continuous from the tough, degenerate groggeries of the gold-rush era to the onset of prohibition. (For example, the Boar's Head drew its name from its special attraction: sexual activity between a woman and a boar.) Alcoholic consumption in the city reached a peak in 1890 when men besieged 3,117 licensed, legal drinking places (one for every ninety-six inhabitants) when not illicitly slaking their thirst in 2,000 "blind tigers" (illegal saloons). Down to the time of San Francisco's calamitous earthquake and fire of 1906, the city's tough waterfront district, the Barbary Coast, boasted such internationally famed saloons as the Balboa, Foam, Bowhead, Grizzly Bear, and Sverdrup's as well as the unsavory, dangerous Cowboy's Rest and Whale.

Typical of thousands upon thousands of saloons was Martin and Horton's unpretentious but popular place in San Francisco, which possessed merely a long bar, bare tables, and a sawdust-covered floor. Drinks at the low prices of one bit (12 ½ cents) for whiskey and 10 cents for beer were obtainable. Mixed drinks such as the julep of early Midwest origin or the Pisco Punch (a creation of noted San Francisco bartender Duncan Nichol) were imbibed, but straight whiskey (along with beer) was the universal favorite. Late nineteenth-century localities throughout the West also had their favorite saloons, among them the celebrated Bull's Head of the wild cow town Abilene, Kansas, and the Gold Room of raucous Cheyenne, Wyoming. A little-known but significant saloon was the Brahma Bull and Red Hot Bar of the small Texas town of Richmond, whose tough, hard-drinking patrons savagely beat David Nation in 1889 and caused a revulsion in his wife, Carry. This incident led to Carry Nation's bar-smashing crusade in Kansas (to which the Nations moved after David's beating) in the early 1900s—a prohibition drive whose blows sounded the death knell of the old-time western saloon.

See Herbert Asbury, *The Barbary Coast: An Informal History of the San Francisco Underworld* (1933); Allan M. Winkler, "Drinking on the American Frontier," *Quarterly Journal of Studies on Alcohol*, vol. 29 (1968); and Paton Yoder, *Taverns and Travelers: Inns of the Early Midwest* (1969).—R. M. B.

Salpointe, Jean Baptiste (1825-1898). Catholic bishop. Father Salpointe was born in St. Maurice, Puy-de-Dôme, France, attended Clermont Seminary in his native country, and was ordained in December 1851. Responding to the call for assistance from Jean Baptiste Lamy, bishop of the diocese of Santa Fe, Salpointe arrived in the United States in 1859 and was assigned to the parish at Mora, New Mexico. In 1866 he was sent as Lamy's vicar general to reestablish the Catholic work in Arizona. Salpointe solicited help from prominent businessmen in Tuson, constructed a church, and organized parishes in Tucson and Yuma. Two years later Arizona was designated a separate vicariate, with Salpointe the first vicar. Additional priests were sent to aid him, and his ecclesiastical jurisdiction was extended east across southern New Mexico to the El Paso vicinity. Under his supervision, the Sisters of St. Joseph opened

schools in Tucson and Yuma and began a small hospital in Prescott. With funds from the Interior Department, Salpointe ran an Indian school at San Xavier Mission for three years. An amiable, practical man with great administrative ability, he raised sufficient funds from railroad, county, and private sources to open St. Mary's Hospital in Tucson in 1880. When called in 1884 to Santa Fe as coadjutor to Archbishop Lamy, Salpointe left behind flourishing churches in the major towns throughout Arizona, a hospital and orphanage in Tucson, and many new parishes. The following year he was elevated to the position of archbishop of Santa Fe, succeeding Lamy. At his retirement in 1894, Salpointe returned to Tucson. His *Soldiers of the Cross* was published posthumously.

See Sister Edward Mary Zerwekh, "John Baptist Salpointe, 1825-1894," *New Mexico Historical Review* (January, April, July 1962).—H. P. H.

Salt Lake City, Utah. At approximately 4,200 feet above sea level, Salt Lake City is in a large valley encompassed by mountains of the Wasatch and Oquirrh ranges, whose peaks rise more than 7,000 feet from the valley floor. Outside the city is the Great Salt Lake, a remnant of prehistoric LAKE BONNEVILLE. The broad avenues, spacious parks, and verdant gardens of the city belie the fact that the valley was considered by many of its early visitors to be a wasteland. Although the valley of the Great Salt Lake was known to the fur trappers of the 1820s, was included in the explorations of Captain Bonneville and John C. Frémont, and was traversed by several wagon companies in the 1840s, the valley continued to be devoid of settlement until the arrival of the Mormons in July 1847.

Naming their new settlement Great Salt Lake City (in 1868 the "Great" was dropped), the Mormons, under the direction of Brigham Young, immediately began to give their city a distinctive organization. Mountain man Jim Bridger allegedly told Young that the valley was sterile, but the Mormons began to irrigate and plant crops from their first arrival. Using a plan originally devised in 1833 by Joseph Smith for his model "City of Zion," Young laid out the city with streets 88 feet wide, running north, south, east, and west. Each block comprised ten acres, and Young designated one of these blocks to the north of the valley as the "Temple Block," where a grand temple would one day be erected.

The Temple Block was then used as the center point for a coordinate system of street designations. The streets bordering Temple Block (now called Temple Square) were named respectively North Temple, South Temple, East Temple, and West Temple. The streets emanating from Temple Block were progressively named according to their separation and direction from the center block. Therefore, streets to the south of South Temple were named First South, Second South, Third South, etc., and streets extending along the other three points of the compass were respectively designated First North, First East, First West, etc. As the population of the city grew, the blocks in residential areas were subdivided into smaller units and the streets received more conventional names. Nonetheless, Young's city-planning is very evident throughout most of Salt Lake City.

Salt Lake City has always been the center of Utah's population and of its rule. As governor of the territory,

A view of Salt Lake City in 1853, looking south. (Library of Congress)

Young in 1851 designated a hamlet as the capital and named it Fillmore after the president. This gesture to the United States government was hardly realistic, since Fillmore was hundreds of miles distant from the center of population at Salt Lake City. In 1857, the capital reverted officially to Salt Lake City. Although Young evacuated the city during the "Utah War" (1857-59) and threatened to burn it to the ground, compromises prevented such a drastic end to the settlement, and the populace returned to their homes.

Having been founded originally as the capital of the Mormon theocracy, it was inevitable that the question of religion would influence the municipal structure of Salt Lake City. The first five mayors (1851-84) were members of the Council of Fifty of the LDS church and kingdom, and the other two mayors who served to 1890 also had consultations with members of that parapolitical, but subterranean, body. Although the Council of Fifty was itself a well-guarded secret, it was still obvious to the growing non-Mormon population in Salt Lake City that municipal government was controlled by the LDS church. Therefore an anti-church party, the Liberal party, was organized in 1870 by William GODBE, an excommunicated Mormon. As a result of the disfranchisement of polygamists and the disruption of Mormon hegemony in the 1880s, the Liberal party gained control of Salt Lake City's government in February 1890 and maintained control until the party dissolved itself in December 1893 as a result of LDS concessions on polygamy and political domination. Another anti-Mormon party, the American party, controlled the

municipal government from 1906 to 1911, as a result of the revival of old religious conflicts caused by the investigation of Mormon Senator Reed SMOOT. After this time, however, Salt Lake municipal government reflected the secular pluralism typical of the general pattern throughout the nation.

The economic situation of Salt Lake City has varied during its history. During its first two years Salt Lake City was dogged by hunger, inadequate housing, and a precarious economy. This marginal existence was dramatically altered by the rush of gold-miners, of whom an estimated ten to fifteen thousand passed through the city in 1849 en route to California. An equal number went by way of Salt Lake City in 1850. Prices of scarce commodities desired by prospectors skyrocketed, and Young specifically urged the Mormons to sell supplies to prospectors at inflated prices. Moreover, the Mormons were able to buy materials unwanted by the prospectors at practically nothing. The forty-niners provided employment for Salt Lake City's tradesmen and strengthened the community's merchandising economy. The gold rush made Salt Lake City a prosperous community and ended suggestions that settlement be abandoned.

The arrival of the railroad in 1869 enhanced mining and merchandising within the state, making many of the city's prominent merchants and mine-owners immensely wealthy by territorial standards. Industry did not really develop in Utah until World War II, when the depressed economy of the state and especially of Salt Lake City experienced tremendous growth.

The development of the Bingham Copper Mine (see COPPER MINING) and of the missile industry has continued a trend of economic growth within the city. However, neither Utah nor Salt Lake City was able to absorb into the economy all of the highly educated populace of the state, which is certainly one factor in the decline of the population of Salt Lake City and the Salt Lake valley between 1960 and 1970. In 1970 the population of the city stood at 176,793, more than 10,000 less than the previous census.

Despite migration to areas of better and more plentiful job opportunities, Salt Lake City is an increasingly popular tourist center. Part of this is due to evidences of the city's unique Mormon past: the six-spired LDS temple of granite: the adjacent Tabernacle, with its amazing acoustics; and the nearby residences of Brigham Young and his wives and children. In addition, Salt Lake City has become a ski center, with four ski resorts within fifteen minutes of the city.—D. M. Q.

salt licks. Kentucky and central Tennessee contained many salt licks. These licks resulted from an upward seepage of chemical brines through fissures from the Ordovician formation. Herbivorous animals gathered at these places to satisfy their need for salt, and in turn these areas became favorite hunting spots for Indians and backwoodsmen. Three or four of the more famous ones were the Big Bone Lick on the Ohio River, the Lower Blue Licks on the Licking River, Bullitts Lick in present-day Bullitt County, Kentucky, and the Elk Lick in middle Tennessee on the Cumberland River. The Lower Blue Licks was the scene, on August 19, 1782, of one of the bloodiest encounters in the early West between Indians and settlers. Salt licks are also found in Ohio, Michigan, and Illinois.

See Thomas D. Clark, "Salt: A Factor in the Settlement of Kentucky," *Filson Club History Quarterly*, vol. 12 (1938); Arthur M. Miller, *The Geology of Kentucky* (1919); and Samuel M. Wilson, *Battle of the Blue Licks, August 19, 1782* (1927).—T. D. C.

Salton Sea. See IMPERIAL VALLEY AND THE SALTON SEA.

San Andreas fault. See PHYSIOGRAPHY OF THE UNITED STATES.

San Antonio, Texas. On April 25, 1718, Martín de Alarcón, recently named governor of Texas, arrived on the banks of the San Antonio River in company with seventy-two soldiers and civilians, and that day construction began on presidio San Antonio de Béxar. An accompanying Franciscan missionary, Father Antonio de San Buenaventura de Olivares, soon opened Mission San Antonio de Valero (whose chapel, the ALAMO, later would become famous). Crops were planted by the civilians, and by December work had begun on irrigation ditches to ensure good crops each year.

Originally San Antonio was intended as a way station between northern Mexico and the capital of the pro-

Salt Lake City's Temple Square in 1889; in the background are (left to right) the Assembly Hall, the Tabernacle, and the Temple. (Utah State Historical Society)

vince, which at that time was Los Adaes, near present Robeline, Louisiana. (Not until 1773 did San Antonio officially become the capital.) When fifteen families from the Canary Islands arrived in 1731, the city was conceded the status of a villa, which meant it had the right to self-government. By 1810 the city numbered 2,500 residents.

After Mexican independence was achieved in 1821, San Antonio was the residence of the lieutenant governor for the combined state of Coahuila y Texas. Therefore, when the Texas revolution began in 1835, Texan troops marched there and in a battle on December 5-10 attacked and defeated the Mexican garrison. Some of these Texans remained at San Antonio to die in the Alamo when Mexican dictator Antonio López de Santa Anna laid siege to it from February 23 to March 6, 1836.

After Texas achieved its independence, San Antonio never again was the capital, but it remained the largest city in the republic and state for many years. From its founding San Antonio had been a military center, and so it remained as an American city. In 1845 a quartermaster depot was established in the Alamo, and four years later it became the headquarters for the 8th Military District (Texas). Fort Sam Houston, opened in 1879, was the largest military establishment in the United States by the turn of the twentieth century. With the coming of World Wars I and II, San Antonio became a major center for training army pilots; major fields included Kelly, Randolph, Brooks, and Lackland. Today it still is a major air force center, for located there are the Air Training Command, the Aerospace Medical Division, and the School of Aerospace Medicine. During World War II, San Antonio's military population alone totaled more than 100,000.

The city early became a center for cattlemen. The construction of the Galveston, Harrisburg, and San Antonio Railroad, opened in 1877, allowed it to become a shipping point for cattle. In addition, the city became the site for many breweries, for the manufacture of aviation items, for food processing, and for banking for South Texas, while its two junior colleges and five colleges and universities draw students from a wide region.

The population of San Antonio stood at 53,321 in 1900 and boomed to 654,153 by 1970. With a greater metropolitan population of 864,014, it is the third largest city in Texas. Because the city has retained much of its Latin charm, it always has drawn a healthy tourist trade, while its mild climate attracts many winter visitors. In 1968 the local citizens attracted tens of thousands of visitors by celebrating the 250th anniversary of the founding of the city with a HemisFair, which included an international exposition, a new convention center, and a cleaned and beautified downtown area.

See Albert Curtis, *Fabulous San Antonio* (1955); and Charles Ramsdell, *San Antonio: A Historical and Pictorial Guide* (1959).—O. B. F.

San Antonio de Padua. Spanish Franciscan mission. Established on July 14, 1771, in the remote beauty of the Santa Lucía Mountains, this third mission in the Franciscans' chain remains one of the most beautiful. Because of the mechanical ingenuity of one of its first padres, Father Sitjar, the mission acquired a complex and effective irrigation system. With the help of plentiful water San Antonio was both an agricultural and a spiritual success almost from the beginning.

In 1779 construction began on an adobe church to replace the little wooden one that had served for six years. The new church was well appointed, and at the time, considered the most impressive one in all of California. But as the mission continued to prosper, even this place of worship became too small, and the ambitious successors to Father Sitjar decided in 1810 to begin construction of the church that is seen today. The nave at San Antonio, like that at San Luís Obispo, was built a dozen feet behind the vaulted brick narthex, a beautifully balanced piece of architecture composed of three arched entryways surmounted by two square bell towers and a smoothly curved gable. The interior, the entry to which has an unusual vaulted ceiling, is otherwise simple and dignified, measuring 200 feet by 40 feet. In 1832 one American traveler, Alfred Robinson, described this tranquil mission as being "in perfect order: the Indians cleanly and well dressed; the apartments tidy; the workshops, granaries and storehouses comfortable and in good keeping." But so relentlessly did San Antonio decline following the secularization of the California missions in 1834 that by 1838 it had only 270 Indians in residence (down from its high point of 1,296 in 1805) and was in a state of disarray.

Father Doroteo Ambrís, a Mexican Indian ordained as a priest at Santa Bárbara, looked after the mission ruins until his death in 1882. Thereafter, they were almost completely neglected. It was only in 1948 that restoration was seriously begun. San Antonio is now essentially restored, enabling the visitor to see it in the rustic setting that once was common to all the missions of California.

For a history of the mission, see Kurt Baer, *Architecture of the California Missions* (1958); and John A. Berger, *The Franciscan Missions of California* (1941). —R. S.

San Antonio de Valero. See ALAMO.

San Buenaventura. Spanish Franciscan mission. Although Father Junípero Serra wanted to found a mission in the Santa Barbara Channel area soon after he arrived in Alta California in 1769, he was unable to do so until March 31, 1782, when he founded his ninth and last mission, San Buenaventura. For over a decade Serra's plans were held back by an insufficient number of troops to guard the mission and a lack of funds, but both problems were overcome when Governor Felipe de Neve lent his support to the mission. In its early years, San Buenaventura was like most other California missions in that it generally failed to attract the Indians. The fathers slowly built up the establishment, erecting buildings and planting crops. In 1792 a fire destroyed much of the mission, but by the following year, when it was visited by Captain George Vancouver, reconstruction was well under way. Vancouver remarked that nowhere else had he found gardens with the "quantity, quality and variety" to be found at San Buenaventura, thus identifying one of the hallmarks of the "Mission by the Sea." The mission also became famous for its fine pasturage and large herds of cattle. Like all other missions in California, San Buenaventura was as important an economic center as it was a religious one.

A stone church was built and dedicated in 1809 but seriously damaged in the earthquake of 1812; it was rebuilt by 1818. In 1819 a group of Mohave Indians intending to trade at the mission started a fight in which ten Mohave, two soldiers, and a mission Indian were killed. The possibility of similar raids kept San Buenaventura and nearby missions in a constant state of alert until secularization in 1834. In 1845 the mission became a parish church. Now contained within the environs of Ventura, California, the pleasant cream-textured and red-trimmed façade has remained the same since mission days. Unfortunately, the interior of the church was disastrously "restored and modernized" in 1893, but this damage was repaired insofar as it could be in 1957.

For a history of the mission, see Zephyrin Engelhardt, *San Buenaventura, The Mission by the Sea* (1930); and Rexford Newcomb, *The Old Mission Churches and Historic Houses of California* (1925).—R. S.

San Carlos Borromeo. Spanish Franciscan mission. On June 3, 1770, at Monterey Bay Father Junípero Serra founded San Carlos Borromeo, the second California mission. It was to be Father Serra's headquarters and was first erected near Monterey's presidio for the safety that soldiers could provide. The following year, however, Father Serra moved the mission site, to escape the interference of the military, which had become more trouble than it was worth. The new mission, variously called San Carlos Borromeo del Carmelo, San Carlos de Monterey, and Carmel Mission, was in a more secluded spot in Rio Carmelo valley. The original church by the presidio became known as La Capilla Reál de Monterey because the royal governors residing there used it for worship. In 1774 San Carlos Borromeo's temporary structures began to be replaced by adobe buildings. The general layout of the mission was that which later became typical of other California missions: the various mission buildings enclosed a patio on four sides, in a style reaching back to Moorish Spain. On August 28, 1784, Father Serra died peacefully in his quarters and was buried at San Carlos next to his lifelong friend and helper, Father Juan Crespi, in the adobe church Serra had built and worshipped in for twenty years. He was succeeded as mission president by Father Fermín de Lasuén, who, like Father Serra, left San Diego to make his headquarters at San Carlos Borromeo. When the French traveler Jean Lapérouse visited the mission in 1786, he described the church in which Lasuén conducted services as being "very neat, although covered with straw; it is dedicated to Saint Charles, and ornamented with fairly good paintings, copied from Italian originals." Fine as the adobe church was, Father Lasuén had plans for a better one, and so, in 1793, construction of the stone church for which the mission is noted today was begun on the site of the older structure. Its façade is a very pleasing example of California mission architecture. Built of light brown sandstone, it has an arched doorway in the center surmounted by a star window. On either side of the arch are square towers, the belfry in the left one being among the most handsome in California. The interior of the church is unadorned but is dramatized by a wooden tunnel vault divided into four bays by Doric pilasters. A small side chapel and irregular octagonal baptistry under the bell tower are two of the many architectural features unique to San Carlos Borromeo. Unfortunately, beauty alone was not enough to help the mission succeed with Indians. Like neighboring Soledad Mission, it was located in a sparsely settled region. At its high point in 1795 it had only 876 neophytes in residence. When Father Lasuén died in 1803, his successor, Estévan Tapis, moved mission headquarters to Santa Bárbara, thereby depriving San Carlos Borromeo of its administrative importance. An epidemic in that same year killed over ninety Indians and many others fled to escape the disease. From that time onward San Carlos Borromeo declined. Two years after the mission's secularization in 1834, its buildings were almost completely in ruins. The sturdy church lasted longer than most, but even its roof collapsed in 1852. Restoration began in 1884 through the work of Father Angelo Casanova and continued intermittently until completed in the 1950s.

For a history of the mission, see Zephyrin Engelhardt, *Mission San Carlos Borromeo (Carmelo), The Father of the Missions* (1934); and Rexford Newcomb, *The Old Mission Churches and Historic Houses of California* (1925). —R. S.

Sand Creek Massacre (1864). Gunfire shattered the stillness on the morning of November 29, 1864, as the Third Colorado Volunteers under Colonel John CHIVINGTON attacked the sleeping Cheyenne reservation on Sand Creek. The Indians had believed themselves to be in custody and under the protection of the army, but Chivington planned a surprise attack and gave instructions that no prisoners were to be taken. As the soldiers swept into the camp, others cut out the horse herd. Carbine and howitzer fire caused the Indians to flee as best they could, but bitter fighting occurred in places. For the remainder of the day the troopers scoured the area, slaughtering the living and mutilating, often sexually, the dead. When the bloody affair was over some two hundred or more Indians (mostly women and children) were dead, and the volunteers soon displayed their scalps and severed genitals before cheering crowds in Denver. Retaliation by the Cheyenne, however, was swift and destructive. Julesburg, Colorado, was sacked on two occasions, travel across the Plains to Denver was halted, and angry Cheyenne participated in the fighting on the Plains in 1865.

News of the massacre and the mutilation of men, women, and children caused a wave of condemnation, and investigations were conducted by the Committee on the Conduct of the War, a joint congressional committee, and the military. Although Chivington escaped punishment because he had left the army, he was condemned by the investigating bodies.

See Stan Hoig, *The Sand Creek Massacre* (1963). —R. N. E.

Sanders, Wilbur Fisk (1834-1905). Montana politician. Born in New York, Sanders went to Ohio in 1854, where he studied law with his uncle, Sidney Edgerton. In 1856 he was admitted to the bar and went into partnership with his uncle. When the Civil War broke out Sanders joined the Union army; ill health forced his withdrawal in August 1862. When his uncle was named chief justice of Idaho Territory in 1863, Sanders accompanied him to the mining camp of Bannack, which later became the first capital of Montana. Here in a country ridden with bandits and murderers Sanders assisted in organizing the Vigilantes, who effectively curtailed the lawlessness. He then was a leader in the movement to secure territorial status for Montana and served in the territorial legislature for six years. He was defeated for the office of territorial delegate to Congress four times, but when Montana achieved statehood in 1889, Sanders was one of its first United States senators. The "Mr. Republican" of Montana as long as he lived, Sanders' early unbending Unionist position and later opposition to the Populism and free-silver movements caused the loss of political support which his cogent reasoning and superb oratory could not overcome. He was an organizer of the Montana Bar Association and a founder and the president for some thirty years of the Montana Historical Society.

See Helen F. Sanders, *A History of Montana,* Vol. I (1913); and *Progressive Men of the State of Montana* (1901).—M. G. B.

San Diego de Alcalá. Spanish Franciscan mission. The irst of the twenty-one Alta California missions and the starting point for El Camino Real (the King's Highway), San Diego was begun by mission president Father Junípero Serra on July 16, 1769, scarcely two weeks after he arrived on foot at San Diego Bay. That day he raised a large wooden cross at the site selected for the chapel, sang a high mass of dedication, and preached a sermon on the importance of the work to be done there. It took hard and patient labor to make the mission a success. The wary Indians were not anxious to be converted and at first would not come near the Spaniards. Father Serra finally attracted the Indians to his mission by handing out trinkets and gifts. The fascinated Indians saw nothing wrong in taking these on their own initiative and so, on August 15, raided the mission. Several of them were killed by soldiers from the adjoining presidio. Relations improved after the Indians at San Diego realized that their weapons were no match for the Spaniards' guns. But troubles were not over. In August 1774 an uncertain water supply and difficulties with the soldiers forced the missionaries to move from a hill in what is now Old Town, San Diego, about six miles up the San Diego River to a spot now generally called Mission Valley. In the following year the new mission was attacked in a major Indian revolt. A number of Spaniards were killed, including Father Luís Jayme. By 1777, however, the burned-out buildings had been repaired and a new church of adobe with a thatched roof erected.

As the fathers learned more about the people among whom they worked, San Diego slowly increased in prosperity and peacefulness. After surviving a near-famine in 1773 and 1774 (which also caused great suffering at Carmel Mission), the missionaries at San Diego learned how to grow food in southern California's dry climate. In 1795 work began at San Diego on what were the first irrigation dam and water ditches in California. The mission also contained an almost self-sufficient collection of barns, shops, and orchards.

In all mission activities at San Diego, as at other missions, the Franciscan padres directed the labors of their Indian converts. The standard workweek consisted of five to six days and the workday, of six to eight hours. The physical demands on the Indians were not great, but the mental strains were severe, for the Indians' previous life-style had not accustomed them to the continual labor of cultivation. But the advantages of a constant food supply, of clothing, and of a generally higher standard of living attracted Indians to San Diego, so that as early as 1797 the mission had a population of 1,405 neophytes.

As the mission prospered, its guardians, Fathers José Bernardo Sánchez and Fernando Martín, realized the need to build a larger church than the simple one that had been finished in 1780. They spent five years constructing the new edifice and dedicated it in 1813. That church, which survives, is simple in design. Its most interesting features are its façade, which has a softly curved pediment, and a picturesque bell tower with five bells. Once this building was finished, the missionaries at San Diego attempted to broaden their field of work by founding two submissions, the *asistencias* of Santa Ysâbel some fifty miles east and Santa Monica a few miles east in the El Cajon valley. The resident convert population of San Diego, including the *asistencias,* reached its highest point in 1824, with 1,829 Indians. But although the missionaries did not believe their work was finished, the government of Mexico, which had won independence from Spain in 1821, wanted to be rid of them because of their Spanish affiliations and clericalism. In 1834 the mission was secularized; almost immediately it was plundered by the secular authorities and their cronies. Governor José Manuel Micheltorena returned it to the Franciscans in 1843 but could not return the lands and equipment necessary to keep it running. It was sold by Governor Pío Pico in June 1846 but shortly thereafter was commandeered by John C. Frémont as a barracks for American troops. After fifteen years of being thus used, it was returned to the Roman Catholic church in 1862. Almost seventy years later, in 1931, restoration of the mission began.

For a history of the mission, see John A. Berger, *The Franciscan Missions of California* (1941); and Zephyrin Engelhardt, *San Diego, Mother of the Missions* (1920). —R. S.

Sandoz, Mari (1907-1966). Historian. Sandoz was born in Sheridan County, Nebraska. She attended the University of Nebraska irregularly from 1922 to 1930; she left without a degree but was awarded an honorary Doctor of Letters degree from that institution in 1950. For a time a rural schoolteacher in Nebraska, she drifted into editorial work, historical research, and free-lance writing.

Although Sandoz tried her hand at fiction—her novel *Slogum House* (1937) is a fictionalized portrait of the Nebraska of her youth—her real gift is for historical writing. The biography *Crazy Horse* (1942), *These Were the Sioux* (1951), and *Cheyenne Autumn* (1953) are some of her studies of Indian history; *The Buffalo Hunters* (1954) and *The Beaver Men* (1954), of the pioneers. Her best book is her first, the biography of her father, *Old Jules* (1935). It received the *Atlantic Monthly* prize for the most distinguished book of nonfiction published in that year. *Old Jules* is a superb study of the frontier experience. Sandoz resisted the temptation to write a saccharine "official" biography of her father, and the book clearly delineates not only the rewards of pioneering a new country but the tremendous sacrifices demanded of the early settlers by the harsh environment of the Great Plains.—J. K. F.

sand painting. Sand painting forms a basic part of the ritual religious ceremonial life of the Navaho and Pueblo Indians, and, to a lesser extent, the Apache and other Indians. Although sand paintings are considered by some modern aficionados as an art form because they are frequently strikingly beautiful in color and design, the traditional sand painting pattern is fully prescribed,

A Navaho sand painting. (Library of Congress)

with little variation allowed the painter. Patterns have been handed down in memory for generations, from one singer or chanter (the so-called medicine man) and his assistants to their successors.

Sand paintings are formed on either a bed of sand or buckskin spread on the ground. The pattern, or design, is made from pulverized minerals and charcoal, crushed flowers, leaves, pollen or cornmeal, and colored sands. Colors used in sand paintings are many, but white, blue, yellow, and black (which have symbolic associations with the cardinal directions) are always included.

The method of preparing the sand painting is itself a ritual, from the procurement of the sand to the ultimate disposition of the painting. The Hopi, when gathering the sand, takes some meal and two feather-strings to the sand hill. Before filling his blanket with sand, he holds the feather-strings and meal to his lips, mutters a prayer, and places the feather-strings and meal on the sand hill.

Among the Pueblo peoples, sand paintings are made on the floor of a ceremonial chamber, or *kiva,* adjacent to the altar. Among the Navaho, a sand painting is made in the *hogan* (or infrequently out of doors) in which the ceremony will be performed. The hogan may be an ordinary dwelling from which all unnecessary furnishings have been removed, or it may be a specially built structure, called a "medicine hogan."

The floor is swept, then a blanket of valley or brown sand is sifted onto the floor in the shape of the outer margins that will form the design and to a depth of up to three inches. This basic layer of sand is smoothed and made ready for the painting. Generally the singer

(medicine man) directs the pattern. His assistants actually perform the work. All the colored sands that will be used to construct the design have been placed in small vessels. The artists proceed with the design by pouring bits of the colored sand from between thumb and index finger. Because the design, once executed, must not be disturbed until after the ceremony, painters work from the center outward. Errors, if made, are not rubbed out, but covered over with the neutral sand of the background.

Sand paintings, because of their supernatural power, must be eradicated once the ceremony has been performed. In the Zuñi whipping ceremony to exorcise evil, sand from the sand painting is rubbed upon a child, thus transferring the magic to the youngster and effectively erasing the painting. A similar procedure is employed by the Zía, except that all present are rubbed with the material from the painting. The Navaho, at the completion of treatment during a curing ceremony, destroy the painting bit by bit in the order that it was made, sweep up the sand, and deposit it outside the hogan.

See TL'AH HASTIIN.

See C. I. Alexander, *An Introduction to Navaho Sandpainting* (1971); Clyde Kluckhohn and Dorthea Leighton, *The Navaho* (1962); Franc J. Newcomb, *Hosteen Klah* (1964); Elsie C. Parsons, *Pueblo Indian Religion* (1939); Gladys A. Reichard, *Navajo Medicine Man* (1939), and "Distinctive Features of Navajo Religion," *Southwestern Journal of Anthropology* (1945); Steven Tremper, "The Museum of Navaho Ceremonial Art— A Place for Understanding," *New Mexico Journal for*

Social Studies (April 1972); Ruth Underhill, *Red Man's Religion* (1965); and Leland C. Wyman, *Navaho Sandpainting: The Huckel Collection* (1971).—B. P. D. and M. L.

San Fernando Rey de España. Spanish Franciscan mission. San Fernando, the seventeenth mission in Alta California and the last of four founded in 1797 (on September 8) by Father Fermín de Lasuén, was situated upon the lands of Rancho Encino, one of the first land grants in California. Apparently its owner made little protest. By 1804 the mission included nearly a thousand Indians and was a supply center to the surrounding region for goods such as tallow, shoes, hides, lentils, pomegranates, olives, and wine (reportedly as much as two thousand gallons were produced annually).

Architecturally, San Fernando is not as interesting as other missions in the area. The original church was completed in 1806 but was seriously damaged by earthquake in 1812. The present church probably dates from 1818 and is of adobe. San Fernando's grand reception room, or *sala,* was the largest in California. After secularization in 1834, San Fernando was used off and on by the California governors as a military headquarters. After Americans came to California, the mission house was used for many years to room ranch hands and store grain. Restoration was completed in 1950. The mission is located west of the city of San Fernando on San Fernando Mission Boulevard.

For a history of the mission, see Zephyrin Engelhardt, *San Fernando Rey, the Mission of the Valley* (1927); and Francis J. Weber, *Mission San Fernando* (1968).—R. S.

San Francisco, California. history. The city named for St. Francis of Assisi was founded as a Spanish presidio and mission by the second expedition of Captain Juan Bautista de Anza in the summer and early autumn of 1776. Anza himself had already left for Mexico. Lieutenant José Moraga was in charge of the 193 settlers, mostly soldiers and their families. The port was founded in 1835 under the name of Yerba Buena, on a cove south of Telegraph Hill. William A. Richardson, an English deserter from a whaler, was in charge of the port under the authority of the Mexican governor José Figueroa, and Richardson erected the first building, described by Richard Henry Dana as "a shanty of rough boards." In 1846 the waterfront was named Montgomery Street after the captain of the U.S.S. *Portsmouth,* which anchored there and took possession of California for the United States on July 9. It is a significant commentary on the history of California under Spain and Mexico that the San Francisco district then had fewer people than it had at its founding seventy years before. When the ship *Brooklyn* arrived on July 31, 1846, bringing Samuel Brannan and his party of about two hundred Mormons, the local population was nearly tripled. Early in 1847 Lieutenant Washington Bartlett of the *Portsmouth,* by his authority as alcalde, changed the name of Yerba Buena to San Francisco.

The gold rush boomed San Francisco's population to 20,000 in 1850 and 36,000 in 1852. The city, built largely of wood and canvas, was repeatedly devastated by fires, and rose from the ashes so often that a phoenix was placed on its official seal. The crime rate was high and there was suspicion that criminals had started some of the conflagrations to facilitate looting. This idea played a part in the founding of the Committee of Vigilance in 1851. Five years later the committee was revived on a larger scale, and ruled the city with a private army for nearly three months. After finally disbanding, its leaders organized a People's Reform party, which won all the offices of the newly consolidated city and county in the elections of November 1856 and controlled the local government for ten years afterward.

As the writer Bayard Taylor put it, San Francisco had telescoped half a century's growth into one year—1849—and within five years was a financial rival of New York and a cultural rival of Boston. Its per capita wealth, though unevenly distributed, was the highest in the nation. San Francisco was a rich, cosmopolitan, and literate community. There was a remarkable flourishing of literature and particularly of journalism from such writers as Bayard Taylor and John Shertze Hittell. In 1859 San Francisco had twelve daily newspapers, among them the *Alta,* the *Bulletin,* the *Call,* and the *Herald.* The *Chronicle* was founded as the *Daily Dramatic Chronicle* in 1865 by the brothers Charles and M. H. de Young.

The labor movement began to achieve substantial power in the 1880s. The thousands of Chinese laborers who had built the Central Pacific Railroad in the 1860s were largely concentrated in San Francisco in later years, and the concern felt about competition from Chinese workers gave a strong impetus to the growth of all-white unions, especially the workingmen's party of Denis Kearney. By the turn of the century San Francisco was the most effectively unionized city in the United States. In 1901, when the Democratic administration of Mayor James D. Phelan broke a teamsters' strike by assigning policemen to protect scab drivers, a Union Labor party of San Francisco was formed in protest. Abe Ruef, a clever Republican lawyer and politician, opportunistically gained control of the party and eventually of the city by securing the nomination and election of his friend Eugene E. Schmitz, president of the musicians' union, as mayor. In 1906 Fremont Older, editor of the *Bulletin,* brought about the launching of a graft prosecution led by special prosecutor Francis J. Heney and detective William J. Burns. In the longest and most searching investigation of political graft in American history, Schmitz was convicted of extortion and Ruef of bribery, and several executives of the city's main public utility corporations were indicted and their systematic practice of bribery exposed.

The great earthquake in the early morning of April 18, 1906, and the ensuing three days of fire killed 452 people and destroyed most of the city. This was a turning point in the history of San Francisco's growth and its predominance in the state. Before the earthquake a fourth of the population of California lived in "the city," but its potential growth was limited by the small land area—a mere thumbnail seven miles square at the tip of a peninsula. Yet the magnificent bay, with its beautiful bridges built in the 1930s, was an ideal location, and so, after the earthquake, towns sprouted around the bay. They eventually surpassed San Francisco in population growth but made it the heart of one of the world's great metropolitan areas.—W. B.

today. San Francisco's natural setting destined it for uniqueness. Standing on the city's peninsula—about forty-nine square miles and composed of forty-two hills —one looks out onto one of the world's most magnificent harbors. It faces the Orient, thus making the city an

Nob Hill and the Fairmount Hotel rise above the ruins of Chinatown following the great San Francisco earthquake of 1906. (Library of Congress)

international port and trading center. Foreigners return to their native lands telling others that San Francisco is the most charming metropolis in the United States. Its location also gives the city an unusual climate. Even though California may be sweltering in a summer heat wave, the city is cool and frequently foggy. The hot interior pulls ocean winds through the Golden Gate, leaving San Francisco moist; yet furious gusts may dissipate local mistiness. In the course of one day residents can experience widespread degrees of temperature and air movements—from brilliant sunlight to a gray, cold briskness.

The California gold rush made San Francisco a quickly growing metropolis and California's first city. The new cosmopolitan culture was nourished by thousands of foreigners, among them the artists Edward Vischer and Charles Christian Nahl. Writers Mark Twain, Bret Harte, and lesser known local colorists gave wide publicity to the city, as did the theatrical performers Edwin Booth and Lola Montez and the opera divas Nellie Melba, Adelina Patti, and Luisa Tetrazzini. In 1906 the great tenor Enrico Caruso was in the Palace Hotel on the night of the earthquake and fire. Today the city still encourages an atmosphere in which cosmopolitanism may flourish; it is significant that the United Nations was launched there in 1945. Residents who choose to live within the city are generally tolerant of deviations in styles of living, as well as of its "oddball" residents, including the beatniks of the 1950s and the hippies of the 1960s.

San Francisco's position as the cultural capital of California remained unchallenged until the 1950s, when Los Angeles began to be a serious rival. The M. H. de Young Memorial Museum in Golden Gate Park was the leading art gallery on the Pacific Coast. The San Francisco Opera Company, founded in 1923, is the second oldest continuing opera company in the United States, after New York's Metropolitan, and in quality ranks with the companies in New York and Chicago (see OPERA).

San Franciscans revere their past. They continue to live in row houses along the rims of hills, in spite of the complexities of parking cars on steep inclines and carrying packages up them. (Early surveyors gave the town a street plan suited to a level area, and so it has lateral streets, some of which wend perpendicularly up and down.) Bay windows of all varieties (one of the city's characteristics) coax into the homes every ray of sunshine that pierces through the fog. Future redevelopment plans do not call for large-scale clearing of existing residences. Wrecking crews continue to spare numerous "gingerbread" Victorian row houses that homeowners have modernized, although city planning has also featured construction of new high-rise apartments. The identifying symbol of San Francisco—the cable car—also remains more than serviceable. For reasons of economy and practicality San Francisco should have retired these hulks to a museum long ago, yet voters have kept them in service.

Although they cherish the city's older charms, San Franciscans are progressive in dealing with the complexities of modern times. The creation in the 1930s of the two bridges that span sections of the bay was, in its time, a daring feat of engineering. San Francisco's answer to traffic congestion has, paradoxically, been to stop freeway construction. In the mid-1960s a "freeway revolt" led to suspension of construction on the Embarcadero Freeway. The city also struggled to keep the state's Panhandle Freeway out of Golden Gate Park. Critics averred that the narcissism and celebration of self-satisfied citizens formed a barrier to future planning. San Francisco voters also rejected construction of auto parking facilities in favor of "mini-parks."

Unlike Los Angeles, which repeatedly votes down rapid-transit reforms, San Francisco is constructing a vast underground transport network. In 1962 the supposedly tradition-bound San Franciscans adopted an $800 million Bay Area Rapid Transit System, known as BART. This electrified rail system will eventually connect all the cities of the eastern bay area. Tunnels under the bay will link them with subway stations on the peninsula.

The waterfront originally lay six blocks inland from the existing bay, but mud silted up the dock area in the early days. A seawall, begun in 1878 and made of rock blasted off the face of Telegraph Hill, made possible the present deep-water docks and allowed for land to be filled in for commercial development. At the heart of the waterfront is the Ferry Building, which separates the odd- and even-numbered piers. Before the bay bridges were constructed, the building was an entry point for persons reaching San Francisco via the ferry from across the bay. Today it is the World Trade Center.

Tourism now vies with commerce as the central attraction of San Francisco's waterfront Embarcadero. Located on its northernmost section is the Maritime Museum, a ship-like structure. Nearby Ghirardelli Square features specialty shops, cafés, and an old-fashioned ice cream parlor housed in a former chocolate factory. Instead of tearing down this obsolete manufactury (built in 1878), developers have remodeled the existing structure. The same sort of planning characterized renovation of the sprawling old red brick Del Monte Cannery, located nearby. Like Ghirardelli Square, it was converted into shops, markets, restaurants, and picture galleries to suit all tastes. Fishermen's Wharf, a tourist attraction for more than fifty years, still

serves as an anchorage for the local fishing fleet, but each year new restaurants, souvenir shops, and seafood stands crop up. Maritime authenticity is retained aboard the *Balclutha,* an eighty-year-old square-rigged veteran of the Pacific trade. City planners are turning their attention to the forty-two piers that stretch southward from Fishermen's Wharf.

Between the waterfront and the downtown civic zone are two key areas whose residents have clung to their own culture—the Italian colony on North Beach and the Chinese ghetto that surrounds Grant Street (see CHINATOWNS). North Beach, however, has been partially transformed into a mecca for hippies and is also filled with topless "Go-Go" cabarets and bars.

Redevelopment of downtown San Francisco makes the area ring with the thump of the pile driver and the grating sounds of bulldozers. Because "the only way to go is up," more plans are underway for taller buildings. Connecting malls and green plazas are planned to extend over much of the old business sections. Most traffic will flow underground through the BART system.

A number of critics believe that the city should not be allowed to grow any larger. The Greater San Francisco Chamber of Commerce, however, is anxious for new hotels to be built. The Yerba Buena Convention Center and Sports Arena, located south of Market Street near the shopping center, was built to attract visitors. Convention visitors need more hotel rooms, and their sustained spending for food, drink, and sight-seeing encourages continued expansion. All areas of the city will be affected by the convention center, including Union Square, the heart of the shopping district since the Civil War. Fine hotels and department stores face the square, many of which continue to be remodeled. Montgomery Street, center of the financial district and called the "Wall Street of the West," began its current expansion with the development of Zellerbach Plaza. There, workers from adjacent office buildings can lunch in an open area surrounded by greenery, running water, pebbles, and stone artifacts at the base of a tall skyscraper. The effect is both Occidental and Oriental. The Japanese Trade and Cultural Center is another new complex that gives one a sense of Oriental values, by the use of formal gardens and shrubbery in the midst of a mall.

Not everything worth seeing is crowded into the northeast corner of the city. Roads around the peninsula offer vistas of rocky beaches pounded by a cold surf along the ocean front. Near the 1,700-acre Army Presidio (a fortified post since 1776) is the Palace of Fine Arts, built during the Panama-Pacific Exposition of 1905, and rebuilt as a cultural center. In 1967 the federal government declared the old fort under Golden Gate Bridge a national monument, to be refurbished as a recreational site. Golden Gate Park, near the center of the city, embraces five square miles of walks, ponds, museums, buildings used for botanical research, a Japanese tea garden, and long stretches of grass where people can picnic. The world's largest man-made park, it also includes greenhouses, the M. H. de Young Memorial Museum, and the Fleishacker Zoo. Adjacent to it is Lake Merced, alongside the Parkmerced residential development.

In November 1970 agreements were made between federal and state authorities and the city to ensure that trees, vistas, and open spaces would be preserved for future beneficial utilization. Campaigning for these mutual understandings were conservationists who headed off earlier proposals to construct office and school buildings as well as apartments on released army sites along the peninsula. Most San Franciscans would like future planning to take this kind of long-range view.

See Julia Altrocchi, *The Spectacular San Franciscans* (1949); T. A. Barry and B. A. Patten, *Men and Memories of San Francisco* (1873); William M. Camp, *San Francisco, Port of Gold* (1947); Amelia R. Neville, *Fantastic City* (1932); Helen Throop Purdy, *San Francisco As It Was* (1912); and Theodore Treutlein, *San Francisco Bay, Discovery and Colonization, 1769-1776* (1968).—A. R.

San Francisco de Asís. Spanish Franciscan mission. Named after St. Francis of Assisi, founder of the Franciscan order but more commonly known as Dolores Mission—after the stream by which is was located—to avoid confusion with San Francisco Solano Mission, this mission was founded on October 9, 1776, under the direction of Father Francisco Palóu. "After having blessed the site, set up the Holy Cross, and made a procession in honor of our Father San Francisco," wrote Palóu, "I sang the first High Mass and preached, taking as the theme the life of our Father San Francisco, our Patron Saint." Dolores Mission had troubles from its inception, as suggested by Palóu's observation that on the occasion described "only the heathen did not enjoy themselves on this happy day." The mission had the bay's large Indian population to draw upon, but its cold and foggy surroundings were unattractive and the sandy soil around it was not conducive to agriculture. Even as experienced a missionary as Palóu had difficulty in persuading members of surrounding tribes to come to the mission. Nor did affairs ever really improve. In 1806, for example, a measles epidemic (only the worst of many) killed 236 Indians in two months. No wonder San Francisco de Asís Mission had more runaways than any other mission. The manifest problems with the mission's site led the Franciscans to found San Rafael Arcángel as an *asistencia* of San Francisco de Asís. With this help, the mission reached its highest population of 1,801 in 1821, but only 1,076 Indians actually lived on the mission site.

A more lasting achievement than the gathering of Indians was Father Palóu's construction of a mission church. This adobe structure was begun in 1782. Whether that church survives today cannot be determined for want of building records between 1782 and 1794. But the edifice seen today, whether Palóu's or a second structure, was completed by 1810 when two side-altars of carved wood were installed in it. Following secularization in 1834, the mission buildings, including the church, deteriorated rapidly. When the forty-niners rushed west to find gold, they used the mission to house taverns, hotels, and the like. In the 1860s the church's adobe walls were covered with boards to preserve them. And in 1916 the church, which had survived the 1906 earthquake shaken but standing, was carefully restored. It is located today near the intersection of Sixteenth and Dolores streets in San Francisco.

For a history of the mission, see John A. Berger, *The Franciscan Missions of California* (1941); and Zephyrin Engelhardt, *San Francisco or Mission Dolores* (1924). — R. S.

San Francisco de la Espada. Spanish mission. San Francisco de la Espada, one of five Franciscan missions founded in San Antonio, Texas, in 1731, actually began its existence as the oldest mission in East Texas, under the name of SAN FRANCISCO DE LOS TEJAS, which first stood on the Neches River in 1690. But the constant threat of the French in neighboring Louisiana to the Tejas and other missions in East Texas, and the refusal of the natives to live at the missions, persuaded Spanish authorities to allow the Tejas mission and San José los Nazonis and NUESTRA SENORA DE LA PURISIMA CONCEPCION DE ACUNA to be relocated on the San Antonio River where San Antonio de Valero (the ALAMO) and SAN JOSE Y SAN MIGUEL DE AGUAYO were already flourishing. The move really represented the abandonment of one mission and the beginning of a new one, a fact symbolized in the change of the mission's name.

The new mission began as a small church located five miles southeast of the present city of San Antonio. In 1745, however, the original building was replaced with a more enduring structure of stone and mortar. Faced with the problem of securing water in a location where the San Antonio River bank was steep, the fathers at Espada built an aqueduct two miles long to bring water from upriver. It has been called the only true Spanish aqueduct built within the boundaries of the United States.

Espada managed to attract some 230 Indians, many of them from the Pacaos tribe, but its very existence was threatened by Apache raids in 1736-37 and by a virulent smallpox and measles epidemic in 1739 that devastated all the San Antonio missions. While Espada prospered during the years 1740-80, it was never as large or as important as the other four missions in the vicinity; indeed, when most of the mission lands were turned over to the Indians in 1794 there were only twenty-five Indians still living at the mission. After secularization Espada deteriorated rapidly and suffered from the intrigues of opposing forces in Mexico's struggle for her independence during the years 1810-21, for the Mexican forces tended to be anticlerical while the loyalists defended the church establishment. Thus, Mexican independence meant that government support for missions had ended. During the Mexican years Espada was little more than a campsite for travelers on their way to San Antonio. After mission properties were returned to the Roman Catholic church by the Republic of Texas in 1841, Espada survived largely because of the efforts of the Reverend Francis Bouchu, who kept the mission in repair during the latter half of the nineteenth century.

Today Espada consists of a simple cruciform stone church whose façade has an open gable with bells and a carved doorway. The mission has a thick-walled tower with portholes for firearms. The nearby military barracks have been renovated and serve as a school for neighborhood children.

See James Wakefield Burke, *Missions of Old Texas* (1971); Carlos E. Castañeda, *Our Catholic Heritage in Texas*, vols. II-III (1936-38); *Texas, A Guide to the Lone Star State* (1940); and Dorman H. Winfrey et al., *Six Missions of Texas* (1965).—H. R. L.

San Francisco de los Neches. See SAN FRANCISCO DE LOS TEJAS.

San Francisco de los Tejas. Spanish mission. Also known as San Francisco de los Neches, this, the first of six Spanish missions in East Texas, was founded in June 1690 by Father Damién Massanet and a small group of fellow Franciscans who had accompanied Captain Alonso de León and a detachment of soldiers sent from Coahuila Province to occupy the region. Massanet located the mission near present-day Weches, Texas, in Houston County.

Although some sixteen missions had already been founded along the Rio Grande by 1684, the real history of missions in Texas began in that year when the Spanish learned that the Frenchman Sieur de LA SALLE had landed on Matagorda Bay and had built Fort St. Louis there. Greatly alarmed at what seemed to be a French invasion of territory claimed by Spain, the Spanish sent several expeditions into Texas between 1685 and 1687 to locate La Salle and his men. When they finally found Fort St. Louis, it was in ruins, La Salle was dead, and his men had scattered. Nevertheless, La Salle's attempt goaded the Spanish into moving their first line of defense from the Rio Grande to East Texas.

As its name implies, San Francisco de los Tejas served the Tejas Indians, one of several tribes of the Hasinai family who, along with certain Caddo tribes, lived in the region of the Sabinas, Angelina, and Neches rivers. Early visitors had given favorable reports of the local Indians, even to the point of claiming that they were nearly as advanced as the Aztecs. The Indians themselves already seemed destined to be Christians, for they declared they had been visited by a mysterious "Lady in Blue," which led the excited fathers to wonder if the Virgin of Guadalupe had appeared to them (see NEW MEXICO MISSIONS).

In 1691, when the region was organized as a province and given a government, it, too, took the name Tejas. During the first year it appears that at least one other mission, Santísimo Nombre de María, was founded in the area. But in 1691 disease struck the Indians at the missions and the soldiers' abuse of the Indian women destroyed amicable relations. These events, coupled with bad weather and lack of supplies, so discouraged the missionaries that in 1693 they abandoned East Texas.

In 1716 renewed French activity along the Louisiana-Texas border led the Spanish to send Captain Domingo Ramón to hold the area militarily and to reestablish the Tejas mission on a new site with the name San Francisco de los Neches. Five others were also founded. La Purísima Concepción de los Ainai, near which Ramón built a presidio; Nuestra Señora de Guadalupe de los Nacogdoches, near Douglas, Texas; and San José de los Nazonis, near Cushing, Texas, all lay between the Sabinas and Angelina rivers. Ramón daringly located San Miguel de Linares, which ministered to the Adai tribe, so far east that it was actually in Louisiana, near the modern town of Robeline. The fifth mission, Nuestra Señora de los Dolores de los Ais, was founded near San Augustine, Texas. This time the guiding force behind the missions was Father Antonio Margil de Jesús, a Zacatecan Franciscan who is one of the true founders of Texas, although the actual running of the Tejas mission was handled by Father Isidro Félix de Espinosa and Francisco Hidalgo.

Once again the affairs of Europe affected the fortunes of the Tejas and other missions when France and Spain went to war in 1719. French forces in Louisiana used the war as an excuse to drive the missionaries and soldiers from the area, and it was not until 1721 that the Marqués de Aguayo was able to reoccupy East Texas. This time the Spanish were determined to stay. The Tejas mission was reopened under its new name, and the others were revived as well. A presidio was located close to the Louisiana border at Los Adaes, a tiny settlement that also served as the provincial capital of Texas during 1721-72. Even so, the East Texas missions never really prospered, despite the devoted efforts of dozens of capable and devoted Franciscan friars. The missions continued, for the most part, to be little more than communities of log huts and brush shelters that were moved from time to time in an unending search for a truly hospitable site. The local Indians resisted complete acculturation and frequently wandered away. A visitor to the area in 1768 described the Ais Indians as still "decadent" and wedded to pagan dances.

An admission of partial failure came in 1731 when the Neches, Nazonis, and Concepción missions were moved to the banks of the San Antonio River where Missions San Antonio de Valero (better known as the ALAMO) and SAN JOSE Y SAN MIGUEL DE AGUAYO were already located. To avoid confusion the Tejas mission was renamed SAN FRANCISCO DE LA ESPADA, and San Jose de los Nazonis became SAN JUAN CAPISTRANO, while the new Concepción was sometimes called NUESTRA SEÑORA DE LA PURISIMA CONCEPCION DE ACUNA. Perhaps as many as one thousand neophytes accompanied the missionaries to San Antonio, a move that suggests that they had made some impact on the East Texas Indians.

The three remaining East Texas missions, Dolores, Linares, and Guadalupe, continued to be more important as Spanish bastions against French encroachment than they were centers for conversion. The founding of Nuestra Señora de la Luz Mission at the mouth of the Trinity River in 1754, for example, was really in response to increasing French influence over the Orcoquiza Indians there. When France ceded Louisiana to Spain in 1763 at the end of the Seven Years' War, even the strategic need for the missions disappeared, and by 1773 they, too, had become moribund, although a temporary mission was established at Nacogdoches in 1775 to subdue the troublesome Orcoquiza, Bidai, and Tejas tribes. Although deprived of a base of operations, individual missionaries continued to work in the area until 1834, when the last Franciscan there, Father Diaz de León, was killed by an unknown assailant. A restored version of the Tejas mission can be seen in Weches Park, Texas.

See John Francis Bannon, *The Spanish Borderlands Frontier, 1513-1821* (1970); James Wakefield Burke, *Missions of Old Texas* (1971); Carlos E. Castañeda, *Our Catholic Heritage in Texas,* vols. I and II (1936-38); and Walter F. McCaleb, *The Spanish Missions of Texas* (1954).—H. R. L.

San Francisco Solano. Spanish Franciscan mission. San Francisco Solano, the last of the California missions, was begun on July 4, 1823, when Father José Altimira dedicated a site to which he intended to move San Francisco de Asís Mission. Although he had received the approval of Governor Argüello to move all the activities of both San Francisco de Asís and its *asistencia,* San Rafael Arcángel, to a sunnier climate north of San Pablo Bay, Father Altimira neglected to inform his superior, the mission president, Father Vicente Sarría. Father Sarría, furious at what he saw as the scheming of a

Mexican governor to usurp Franciscan religious authority, at first refused to allow the abandonment of Old San Francisco or the establishment of New San Francisco, as Father Altimira then referred to the two. But he was forced to compromise; he accepted the accomplished fact that a new mission existed by allowing Father Altimira to keep his post, renamed San Francisco Solano, while maintaining San Francisco de Asís where it was and elevating San Rafael to full mission status on its own. (San Francisco Solano also came to be popularly called Sonoma Mission after the valley in which it was located.)

The mission, having come into being after Mexican independence, did not receive as much attention as some of its predecessors. Father Altimira completed a simple adobe church in 1824, similar in style to that at San Miguel Arcángel. In 1828 the church and other mission buildings were burned in an Indian attack, and Father Altimira was driven away. Under his successor, Father Buenaventura Fortuni, Solano reached its maximum population of 996 in 1832. It might have increased in size after that, but for its abrupt termination in 1834 because of secularization. As was the case elsewhere, Solano quickly fell to ruins. The only person to give it any attention was Mariano Vallejo, an influential rancher who founded the town of Sonoma on the mission site. When Altimira's church became unusable, Vallejo had a small chapel built (sometime after 1840) to serve the town in its place. This chapel and the mission's old monastery wing were purchased for the state of California by William Randolph Hearst in 1903 and restored.

For a history of the mission, see John A. Berger, *The Franciscan Missions of California* (1941); and Rexford Newcomb, *The Old Mission Churches and Historic Houses of California* (1925).—R. S.

San Francisco Xavier de Horcasitas. See SAN XAVIER RIVER MISSIONS.

San Gabriel Arcángel. Spanish Franciscan mission. The fourth of the Alta California missions, San Gabriel Arcángel was dedicated by Father Junípero Serra on September 8, 1771, at a spot near what is now Rio Hondo. It was moved a short distance to its present site in 1775. The early years of the mission were discouraging ones. Crops were scanty, supplies from Mexico did not always arrive when needed, and soldiers assigned to the mission caused trouble with the Indians. Conditions improved after 1775 when San Gabriel served as an important military center for the route from Mexico over which Juan Bautista de Anza brought new colonists to the province. Because of population growth around San Gabriel, the Pueblo de Nuestra Señora la Reina de los Angeles, California's second town, was founded seven miles away in 1782.

At the beginning of the nineteenth century, San Gabriel was the most prosperous mission of the California chain, because of its famous large orchards, fine wines, and brandy. During the 1820s a thousand Indians tended to the mission harvests. All the early buildings at the permanent site were of adobe. The present church, made of brick and stone, was begun in 1791 and completed in 1805. Its fortresslike appearance was influenced by the cathedral at Cordova, Spain, birthplace of San Gabriel's architect, Father Antonio Cruzado. Originally the church possessed a vaulted roof supported by

The belfry of Mission San Gabriel Arcángel.

the heavy buttresses still seen along its walls today, but the roof suffered from cracks from the start, was damaged by an earthquake in 1803, and was torn down in 1807. The stone vault was replaced by a flat tiled roof whose original wooden beams are now concealed by a painted ceiling. In 1834 the mission was secularized along with others. In the 1850s it was returned to the Roman Catholic church and used as a parish church until 1908, when it was given to the Claretian fathers. The bell tower at San Gabriel is one of the most frequently pictured symbols of the California missions. The present church includes the mission's original hammered-copper baptismal font and a series of paintings, both made by Indians.

For a history of the mission, see John A. Berger, *The Franciscan Missions of California* (1947); and Zephyrin Engelhardt, *San Gabriel Mission and the Beginnings of Los Angeles* (1927).—R. S.

San Ildefonso. See SAN XAVIER RIVER MISSIONS.

San Ildefonso, Treaty of (1800). Cession of Louisiana back to France. One day after the plenipotentiaries of the United States signed the Treaty of Mortefontaine ending the undeclared naval war between the United States and France, the French and Spanish on October 1, 1800, affixed their signatures and seals to the Treaty of San Ildefonso, a secret engagement by which Louisiana was to return to France. Had the government of the First Consul, Napoleon Bonaparte, been able to establish French rule in Louisiana, the American West, as we now know it, would have become the French West. It was necessary for the French government to conclude a second treaty with the Spanish, the Godoy-Lucien

Bonaparte treaty of March 21, 1801, which set out details of the prospective exchange of Louisiana for a Spanish kingdom in Italy. The young son-in-law of the king and queen of Spain, Louis, the titular prince of Parma, was to receive Tuscany as a sovereign kingdom, to become known as the kingdom of Etruria, with Florence as its capital. Louis died, however, and the kingdom never materialized. Spain pressed for the return of Louisiana, but to no avail.

The chief importance of the Treaty of San Ildefonso was that rumors and then confirmation of its existence, including the actual text of the Godoy-Bonaparte treaty, arrived in Washington in 1801-02 and prompted President Thomas Jefferson to make a bid for the "island" of New Orleans and the Floridas, which resulted in his obtaining all of Louisiana. A definition of the territory of Louisiana appeared in the Louisiana Purchase Treaty of 1803 that came bodily out of the Treaty of San Ildefonso and was to cause much trouble because of its ambiguity: "Louisiana with the same extent that is now in the hands of Spain, and that it had when France possessed it, and such as it should be after the treaties subsequently entered into between Spain and other States." The question of whether the Louisiana Purchase ("The same extent") included the Floridas and Texas was to be an important one when the United States sought to annex those areas.

See E. Wilson Lyon, *Louisiana in French Diplomacy: 1759-1804* (1934).—R. H. F.

San Jacinto, battle of (1836). Texas revolution. Just four days after they declared the independence of Texas from Mexico on March 2, 1836, the delegates to the convention meeting at Washington-on-the-Brazos named Sam Houston commander-in-chief of the Texan army. Immediately the former governor of Tennessee and congressman from that state departed to take command in the field. Arriving at Gonzales on March 11, he found 374 ill-clad and poorly equipped men, most of them raw recruits with no military experience, many without guns, others without ammunition, and only two days' rations on hand.

Houston's immediate intent was to hasten to the relief of the Alamo, then under siege by Antonio López de Santa Anna, self-proclaimed dictator of Mexico. Two days after his arrival, however, scouts returned with confirmation of the bloody Mexican victory at San Antonio—and with word that Santa Anna and his army were moving eastward to pacify the rebellious province. Houston thereupon ordered a series of retreats that took him eastward to the Colorado River, thence to San Felipe on the Brazos River; then, turning north at that point, he moved his army to Groce's Ferry, arriving there on March 31 to encamp for twelve days. This maneuvering was done during the wettest weather seen in Texas for years.

After the fall of the Alamo, Santa Anna concluded that he had broken resistance in Texas. Rashly he split his army into small detachments, personally leading one part eastward. He crossed the Brazos on April 15, four days later burned the town of Harrisburg, and then hurried on to New Washington in a vain attempt to capture the provisional government of the newly proclaimed Republic of Texas. Failing that, he pointed his troops toward the village of Lynchburg.

Houston was meanwhile trying to organize, train, and equip his inadequate force, seek recruits, contend with frequent desertions, and, simultaneously, face the curses of his officers and government for inactivity. His troops wanted to fight the Mexicans, not drill, while Texas president David G. Burnet and Secretary of War Thomas J. Rusk were urging Houston to halt his retreating, make a stand, and contest Santa Anna for mastery of Texas.

Houston left Groce's Ferry on April 11 after receiving the "Twin Sisters," two six-pound cannon, a gift from the people of Cincinnati, but again he ordered a retreat to the east. Some of his troops thereupon deserted to assist their families in abandoning Texas, for many settlers, fearing Mexican retribution, fled wildly toward the safety of Louisiana in what became known as the "Runaway Scrape." The soldiers who stayed talked about deposing Houston, electing another commander, and going in search of the Mexicans. However, Houston knew exactly where Santa Anna was, for his scouts sent extremely accurate information to the Texan commander. On April 17 he ordered the column to turn south rather than continue on the road toward Louisiana. The order meant fighting, and a cheer went up among the soldiers. The following day at White Oak Bayou, he learned that the Mexicans were nearby on the banks of the San Jacinto River. On April 19 he ordered the 248 sick and ineffective troops left behind with the baggage; then he and Secretary of War Rusk made speeches to the soldiers, urging them to remember the massacres at the Alamo and at Goliad.

On April 20 the Texans arrived at the confluence of Buffalo Bayou and the San Jacinto River, as did the Mexican army that afternoon. The two sides exchanged artillery fire, whereupon Sidney Sherman and a detachment of Texan cavalry attempted unsuccessfully to capture the Mexican cannon. That night Houston allowed his men to eat a hot meal and sleep, while Santa Anna kept his men alert and building a breastwork from their baggage. Early on the morning of April 21, while the Texans ate a hearty breakfast, the sleepy Mexicans were joined by about 500 troops commanded by General Martín Pérfecto de Cós; these men had made a forced march and also were tired. Santa Anna, with some 1,400 soldiers in his camp as opposed to Houston's 783, felt secure and ordered his men to rest, leaving few guards on duty. The Texan commander meanwhile had sent Erastus "Deaf" Smith to burn Vince's Bridge, over which any additional reinforcements might join Santa Anna; the destruction of this bridge meant the hour of confrontation had arrive c, for no one could escape.

After a council with his officers had produced no major decision, Houston called his troops into formation at 3:30 P.M. Quietly the Texans crossed the two hundred yards separating them from the enemy, their advance screened by a rise in the ground and by trees. Suddenly an improvised Texan band of drum and bugle burst forth with a popular tune of the day, "Will You Come to the Bower I Have Shaded For You," while the Twin Sisters belched forth shot, nails, and broken horseshoes. To the cry of "Remember the Alamo! Remember Goliad!" the Texans stormed into the Mexican position, the cavalry on the right and the infantry on the left. Briefly a few Mexican offiers attempted to rally their soldiers, then broke and fled. The rout became a slaughter that stopped only at nightfall and then resumed during the next two days.

The battle of San Jacinto had lasted just eighteen minutes, but it guaranteed the independence of Texas. A count afterward showed 630 Mexicans dead and 730 captured, among them Santa Anna himself, along with a large supply of weapons, provisions, horses and mules, and $12,000 in silver. Texan losses amounted to two killed and some thirty wounded, six of them mortally; Houston had been shot in the ankle during the affray. The captured Santa Anna, fearing execution at the hands of his captors, quickly signed an order for all Mexican troops to withdraw south of the Rio Grande.

Never again did Mexico seriously challenge the independence of the Lone Star Republic. The battle of San Jacinto therefore brought a change in ownership of a million square miles of territory. This land eventually became American when Texas joined the Union on December 29, 1845.

See Llerena Friend, *Sam Houston: The Great Designer* (1954), and Amelia Williams and Eugene C. Barker, *The Writings of Sam Houston,* 8 vols. (1938-43).—O. B. F.

San Joaquin River. The San Joaquin, one of the two major river systems in California, drains the southern part of the great Central Valley of California. Named for Saint Joachim, the river rises at elevations above 11,000 feet in the Sierra Nevada southeast of Yosemite National Park. It is formed by the juncture of a number of headwater streams and flows south-westward for about 125 miles before reaching the foothills of the Central Valley, where its waters are now impounded behind Friant Dam. From this point northeast of Fresno, California, the San Joaquin turns west and then northwest, receiving the waters of several tributaries that flow out of the Sierra Nevada. The most important are the Fresno, Chowchilla, Merced, Tuolumne, Stanislaus, Calaveras, and Mokelumne rivers.

The basin of the San Joaquin occupies 32,000 square miles or one fifth of the entire state, and the river flows almost 300 miles through mountains and valleys before entering the delta region, where its waters mingle with those of the Sacramento River. In the basin about ninety percent of the precipitation falls from November to April, much of it in the form of snow. Thus, its peak season of runoff extends from spring into summer as the snow line retreats up the slopes of the mountains.

The river was first seen by Father Crespi on March 30, 1772, and was named the San Francisco by him. It was later visited by Gabriel Moraga in 1805 or 1806 and renamed the San Joaquin, although parts of it were known by other names for a time thereafter. The valley was not visited often or used to any great extent by the Spaniards or Mexicans, and the gold rush left it relatively untouched. (Gold discoveries of any significance occurred only on its northern tributaries and in the mother lode country of the Sacramento.) The greatest spur to development of the region was the building of the Southern Pacific line southward in the 1870s. This opened the land up for settlement and made it possible to ship livestock and grain to market. However, it was not until the monopoly held by the Southern Pacific was broken in the late 1880s by the building of the Santa Fe that the area really began to prosper. Oil was discovered early and added to the general prosperity.

The San Joaquin's many tributary streams were developed to irrigate farmlands. Completion in 1933 of a deep-water canal (thirty-three feet) to Stockton on the San Joaquin meant that the valley had an ocean port from which its products could be shipped. The invention of deep-well pumps at about this time also opened up vast areas for the production of cotton. Finally, the Central Valley project was authorized in the late 1930s to control the flow of the San Joaquin and to bring Sacramento River water southward into the basin of the San Joaquin. Today oil and agriculture dominate the economy of the valley, but outfitting recreationists bound for the Sierra Nevada is also important.

For map, see CALIFORNIA.

See California Department of Water Resources, *The California Water Plan* (1957); California Division of Water Resources, *The San Joaquin River Basin* (1934); S. T. Harding, *Water in California* (1960); and Lawrence R. McDonnell, ed., *Rivers of California* (1962).—R. W. D.

San José de Guadalupe. Spanish Franciscan mission. Impetus for establishing San José came from an Alta California governor, Diego Borica, who hoped that a strategically located Spanish settlement in the interior valleys south of San Francisco Bay would make the whole area easier to defend from hostile Indian tribes. The Franciscans were happy to comply with the government's wishes, and so Father Fermín de Lasuén founded their fourteenth California mission on June 11, 1797.

For over twenty years San José was virtually a military post, with the soldiers connected to it making constant forays against Indians in the region. Father Buenaventura Fortuni, who was in charge of the mission from 1806 to 1826, was equally practiced at saying mass and firing muskets. Although the fighting never ended, the mission gradually grew as nearby Indian tribes became pacified by Spanish firepower. San José reached its maximum size, with a population of 1,886, in 1831, well after most other missions had gone into decline. In 1833 it was transferred from the Spanish to the Mexican Franciscans (Zacatecans), who continued to run it well for as long as possible in the anticlericalism sweeping across California.

San José became the last mission to be secularized when Father José María Rubio turned over its management to José Vallejo (brother of Mariano Vallejo) on November 29, 1836. Being so close to the settlements at San Francisco and San José, the mission was rapidly picked clean. Its return to the Roman Catholic church in 1858 did not halt its decline, however. The church, which was a simple structure built of adobe, lasted until 1868. In the middle of a priest's efforts to modernize it in that year by removing thick buttresses from its walls, an earthquake brought the unsupported walls down. In its place a new wooden church of Norman architecture was built on what remained of the tiled floor of the adobe church. The only building from the mission period that survives is part of the monastery, which houses a museum and a chapel.

For a history of the mission, see Kurt Baer, *Architecture of the California Missions* (1958); and Francis Florence McCarthy, *The History of Mission San José California, 1797-1835* (1958).—R. S.

San José de los Nazonis. See SAN FRANCISCO DE LOS TEJAS.

San José y San Miguel de Aguayo. Spanish mission. San José y San Miguel, which was founded on the San

Antonio River within the city limits of present-day San Antonio, Texas, in 1719, has been aptly called the "Queen of the Texas Missions," for it was the largest and most beautiful of those built within the state's borders.

San José y San Miguel owes its founding to one of the most remarkable figures in the history of Spanish Texas—Father Antonio Margil de Jesús, who came to the province from the Franciscan college at Zacatecas, Mexico. Often called "the Apostle of Texas," Margil had been instrumental in reviving the moribund East Texas missions in 1716 and was serving there when war broke out between the French and the Spanish in 1719. After French forces in Louisiana drove the Spanish missionaries and soldiers from the region, the Marqués de Aguayo was ordered to recapture the area, to establish new missions and presidios, and to improve the defenses of the province generally. The strategy also called for strengthening San Antonio de Valero mission (the ALAMO) and the presidio of San Antonio de Béjar, which was the halfway station between the Rio Grande settlements and East Texas. At this point Margil proposed building a second mission at the San Antonio presidio to be run by the Zacatecan Franciscans. Father Antonio de San Buenaventura de Olivares, the Querétaran Franciscan who was in charge of the Valero mission, understandably objected to a new mission so near to his own, but Margil gave the excuse that the new one would serve several Indian tribes who were unfriendly to the Indians already at Valero. Margil won the support of the wealthy and influential Marqués de Aguayo for his project, however, and even used the name of his patron's home district in the name of the new mission when it was dedicated in 1720.

Located on the east bank of the San Antonio River less than six miles southeast of Valero mission, San José y San Miguel, unlike so many Texas missions, soon became a prosperous, self-supporting community. In 1739 a smallpox and measles epidemic killed many of the Indians there, but the fathers found new recruits and moved the original mission to the west bank of the river, to what they hoped would be a more hospitable site. To speed the conversion of the Coahuiltecan Indians of Texas, Margil himself compiled a dictionary of Indian dialects.

Between 1740 and 1780, San José y San Miguel's prosperity was at its height. Of the five missions eventually established in the San Antonio area (the others being San Antonio de Valero, NUESTRA SEÑORA DE LA PURISIMA CONCEPCION DE ACUNA, SAN FRANCISCO DE LA ESPADA, and SAN JUAN CAPISTRANO), it boasted the largest number of Indian converts. Its fertile fields produced enough corn, beans, and sugarcane to supply NUESTRA SEÑORA DEL ESPIRITU SANTO DE ZUNIGA Mission on the coast as well as local markets. Indian men grew cotton, which their wives and daughters spun and wove into cloth. Father Gaspar de Solís, who visited the missions in 1768, found 350 Indians there speaking Spanish and attending church school. Indian cowboys and shepherds tended herds of one thousand cattle and three thousand sheep without white supervision. When they were not farming, working as carpenters and tailors, or quarrying the soft tufa stone for the new mission buildings the men were also organized to fight raiding Apaches. In 1744 the original adobe church

and, later, other buildings were replaced with larger stone structures.

When the Marqués de Rubí called at San José y San Miguel in 1767 on an inspection tour of the northern frontier, he called the mission "opulent." Nearly a decade later Juan Agustín Morfi described it as being the most easily defended of all Texas outposts because of its high, fortresslike walls.

Visitors in the 1780s were confronted with a handsome set of stone buildings that combined Gothic, Moorish, and Romanesque architectural styles in ways both pleasing and functional. Aqueducts brought water into the mission for bathing pools as well as for ordinary use. Its granary walls were supported by graceful arches, and the apartments of the Indians seemed comfortable. San José y San Miguel's most famous architectural features, however, were the richly decorated façade of the stone church (begun in 1768 and completed in 1782) and an elaborate, graceful rose window in the sacristy. Both are thought to have been the work of Pedro Huisar, a talented sculptor who made full use of the soft tufa stone from a nearby quarry to beautify the church. Persistent legends suggest that Huisar's rose window, and, indeed, all his work, expressed his love for a Spanish girl who died before she could join him in the New World.

After 1768 the Spanish government began to press for the secularization of those missions that had converted and Hispanized local Indians. Secularization was also avidly supported by local officials and settlers in San Antonio, for they were in frequent conflict with the missionaries. The independent and outspoken Canary Islanders who had formed the first civilian colony in San Antonio in 1731 complained that the missions flooded the market with produce and would not let the colonists use the Indians as a source of labor. They also coveted the fertile lands controlled by the mission. By 1794 the lands had been awarded to Indian families and the herds had been dispersed, but the mission continued to function as a religious institution until 1824. During the decade before Mexican independence was achieved in 1821 the mission's importance declined precipitately. Abandoned by the 1830s, it was used at different times as barracks for the armies of both Mexico and the Republic of Texas. After the Mexican War, outlaws made it a meeting place. By 1850 the mission had fallen into ruins, and in 1874 its dome collapsed. While various Roman Catholic orders tried to restore the church and use its buildings, it was not until 1928, when the bell tower fell, that full restoration was undertaken. Declared a National Historic Site in 1941, exactly one hundred years after the Republic of Texas had returned the property to the Catholic church, San José y San Miguel is now maintained by federal, state, and private funds. The restored mission buildings are a part of San José Mission State Park.

See John Francis Bannon, *The Spanish Borderlands Frontier, 1513-1821* (1970); James Wakefield Burke, *Missions of Old Texas* (1971); Carlos E. Castañeda, *Our Catholic Heritage in Texas*, vols. II-III (1936-38); Marion A. Habig, *San Antonio's Mission San José* (1968); and Walter F. McCaleb, *Spanish Missions of Texas* (1954). —H. R. L.

San Juan Bautista. Spanish Franciscan mission. On June 24, 1797, Father Fermín de Lasuén founded the fifteenth California mission on a site overlooking the valley of the San Benito River. San Juan Bautista, named after St. John the Baptist, prospered from the start. Crops were plentiful and the surrounding Indians relatively peaceful. Most mission buildings, including a simple church, had been built within five years of the mission's establishment. Construction on the present church began in 1803 and was completed in 1812. It originally had a huge interior, with a nave bounded by two side aisles, the only such floor plan in the mission system. However, the church was too large for its role, and so, to make the structure secure against earthquakes, the side aisles were walled off from the nave except for their first two bays, giving San Juan Bautista's interior a cruciform appearance. Various furnishings, including an ornate reredos, were completed by 1818.

By this time, San Juan Bautista was being directed by two famous Spanish priests, Fathers Felipe Arroyo de la Cuesta and Estévan Tapis. Father Cuesta had come to the mission in 1808. Mastering thirteen Indian dialects, he became an accomplished linguist at San Juan and in 1815 completed an eighty-five-page Indian vocabulary of great scholarly value. Father Tapis retired to San Juan in 1815, after serving as mission president for nine years. His musical talents gave the mission a widely admired Indian choir. Under leadership of these two men, the mission reached a population of 1,248 in 1823. Father Tapis was buried at the mission in 1825, while Father Cuesta turned over his post to the Zacatecans (Mexican Franciscans) in 1833.

Although the mission was secularized in 1835, the church continued to be used for parish services under Father Antonio Anzar, a Zacatecan who served there from 1833 to 1854. After Father Anzar's departure, the mission was preserved by various resident priests. It weathered—not without some damage—its severest test, the earthquake of 1906. The mission today looks almost exactly as it did over a century and a half ago.

For a history, see John A. Berger, *The Franciscan Missions of California* (1941); and Zephyrin Engelhardt, *Mission San Juan Bautista* (1931).—R. S.

San Juan Capistrano (California). Spanish Franciscan mission. This, the seventh California mission to be founded, survives largely as a most impressive set of ruins. It was originally begun by Father Fermín de Lasuén in October 1775, but the Indian uprising at San Diego Mission that November caused the new establishment at San Juan Capistrano to be abandoned until Father Junípero Serra refounded it on All Saint's Day (November 1) of 1776. The mission grew slowly and not without hardships such as drought, sickness, and famines. The small adobe church, begun in 1777, is the oldest surviving building in California and the only one left in which Father Serra celebrated mass. The majestic stone cruciform church, 146 feet long by 26 feet wide, with walls over four feet thick, and crowned by seven domes, was built in the years 1797 to 1806. But it was destroyed six years later in the earthquake of December 8, 1812, when the tower fell in on worshippers during the first mass of the day. Further damage was done to the ruins in the 1860s when some of the remaining domes in the ceiling were blown down with gunpowder in a misguided attempt to rebuild the structure in adobe. Today several of the buildings surrounding the mission patio have been restored and an ornate Spanish baroque reredos has been installed in place of the original altar in Father Serra's chapel. The mission is sometimes referred to as the Swallows Mission because of the flocks of swallows that return to it each spring and always, the story has it, on St. Joseph's Day (March 19). Located in the town of San Juan Capistrano, it has become a major tourist attraction.

For a history of the mission, see John A. Berger, *The Franciscan Missions of California* (1941); and Zephyrin Engelhardt, *San Juan Capistrano Mission* (1922).—R. S.

San Juan Capistrano (Texas). Spanish mission. San Juan Capistrano was one of three missions that the Querétaran Franciscans established on the San Antonio River in 1731. The history of Capistrano actually began in East Texas in 1716 when the Spanish planted six missions in the region of the Sabinas, Angelina, and Neches rivers. One of these, San José de los Nazonis, located near present-day Cushing, Texas, to serve the Nazonis Indians, never prospered. It was abandoned between 1719 and 1721, when the French in Louisiana drove the Spanish from the area. The mission was reestablished in 1721, but ten years later Spanish authorities allowed the Nazonis, SAN FRANCISCO DE LOS TEJAS, and NUESTRA SENORA DE LA PURISIMA CONCEPCION DE ACUNA MISSIONS to move west to the banks of the San Antonio River where two missions, San Antonio de Valero (the ALAMO) and SAN JOSE Y SAN MIGUEL DE AGUAYO were already located. In order to avoid a confusion in names, San José de los Nazonis was renamed San Juan Capistrano. In effect the mission, located seven miles east of the center of San Antonio, was a new one, for it now served Indians speaking Coahuiltecan languages and especially those of the Tolujac tribes.

While all five San Antonio missions experienced a period of great success between 1740 and 1780, San Juan Capistrano was at its height during the 1760s. Like its neighbors San Juan Capistrano trained Indian recruits in Christian doctrine twice a day; the men were also taught to farm and to herd cattle and sheep, and the women, to weave. Capistrano's growth was hampered, unfortunately, by the fact that it was situated in a lowland humid area. It was also dependent on an aqueduct for irrigation water. The result was that Capistrano, along with SAN FRANCISCO DE LA ESPADA, was destined to be one of the least important of the five missions in the San Antonio area. It began to decline as early as 1780, and when the mission was secularized in 1794 and its lands and herds were turned over to the Indians, only a few still remained there to benefit from the act. The mission buildings soon fell into ruins.

Unlike its neighbor, San José y San Miguel, San Juan Capistrano's church was never decorated with ornate carvings. Instead, it reflected plain Moorish and Romanesque designs. Rebuilt in 1907 the chapel is different from the surrounding missions in that it features a pointed gable and its bells are in open apertures above the entrance. The remains of the original mission are substantial enough to give the visitor an accurate impression of the living quarters, workrooms, granaries, and religious buildings that made up a Texas mission.

See James Wakefield Burke, *Missions of Old Texas* (1971); Carlos E. Castañeda, *Our Catholic Heritage in Texas*, vol. III (1938); Marion A. Habig, *San Antonio's Mission San José* (1968); *Texas, A Guide to the Lone Star*

State (1940); and Dorman H. Winfrey et al., *Six Missions of Texas* (1965).—H. R. L.

San Lorenzo, Treaty of (1795). Establishment of the boundary of the United States with the Spanish Floridas. It was perhaps natural that in seeking to secure commercial rights for the European nations during the 1790s the United States would discover that the Spanish government was vulnerable to pressure because of its New World possessions—far more so than the British government. The Spanish government could not possibly defend its North American possessions in the event that the American government chose to take them. This vulnerability, together with a change in Spain's allies from England to France during the then-raging European war (and fear that the Americans would ally with the English and take the Spanish Floridas), produced the Treaty of San Lorenzo, often called Pinckney's Treaty, signed on October 27, 1795. At this time the Spanish held present-day Florida, a strip of land (known as West Florida) along the Gulf Coast to New Orleans, and the entire Louisiana territory, not to mention California, Mexico, and the lands to the south.

The Spanish had found themselves in straits with the French, who were worsting them in the European war that had begun in 1793. The Spanish desired to change sides, returning to an alliance with their ancient partner France despite the new regime in that country. To be sure, the British, then allied with the Spanish, were not going to be happy about losing an ally and gaining an enemy; the Spanish in turn were worried that Jay's Treaty, signed with Great Britain in 1794, might contain a secret article allying the United States with Britain for the purpose of despoiling Spain's New World possessions.

For the Americans the result was a marvelous treaty. Among its provisions, the San Lorenzo treaty recognized the boundary of the United States set forth in the Treaty of Paris of 1783 with Britain: to the south, the thirty-first parallel; to the west, the Mississippi. The Spanish conceded the right of navigation on the great river and a permission (the Americans claimed it was a right) for deposit of goods passing down the river for transshipment to oceangoing vessels. The treaty granted the deposit at New Orleans for a term of three years and agreed to continue it or provide another equal establishment elsewhere on the river. The apparently arbitrary withdrawal of the permission of deposit by the local intendant in 1802 was one of the factors leading to the Louisiana Purchase.

See Samuel Flagg Bemis, *Pinckney's Treaty,* rev. ed. (1960); and Arthur P. Whitaker, *The Spanish-American Frontier: 1783-1795* (1927).—R. H. F.

San Luís Obispo de Tolosa. Spanish Franciscan mission. While on his way south to procure food for the hunger-ridden missions and settlements around Monterey, Father Junípero Serra stopped in La Cañada de Los Osos (Valley of the Bears) long enough to found San Luís Obispo on September 1, 1772. Although the bears after which the valley had been named were soon hunted out for food, the mission had less success in the more difficult work of hunting Indian souls: at its height in 1804 it had only 832 neophytes. The mission became better known for the activities of its guardian, Father Luís Antonio Martínez, a man of fierce individualism and caustic wit. Under his guidance (1798-1830) the

mission became materially very prosperous for a time. But after years of fighting the civil government Father Martínez was banished from California in 1830 upon charges of smuggling and treason. The mission he left behind could not avoid the general decline that set in at all California missions after Mexican independence. The last Franciscan father left San Luís Obispo in 1841. Four years later its rundown property, once valued at $70,000, was sold by Governor Pío Pico at auction for a paltry $510. The mission was returned to the Roman Catholic church by the United States in 1859 and its chapel has since served as a parish church. Architecturally it is pleasing but undistinguished, with an unadorned façade. Of historical interest, however, is the fact that it was at San Luís Obispo that the burned-clay tile roofs now associated with the California mission style were first used. Hostile Indians set fire to San Luís Obispo's originally thatched reed roofs on a number of occasions. Around 1790 the anxious padres hit upon the idea of using rounded fireproof clay tiles instead of thatch; it was such a success that the practice rapidly spread to other missions. Although in bad repair for a time and then subjected to thoughtless restoration that covered over its distinctive features, the mission now looks much as it did in the days of New Spain.

For a history, of the mission, see Zephyrin Engelhardt, *Mission San Luís Obispo in the Valley of the Bears* (1933); and Rexford Newcomb, *The Old Mission Churches and Historic Houses of California* (1925).—R. S.

San Luís Rey de Francia. Spanish Franciscan mission. San Luís Rey, the eighteenth and one of the most beautiful of the Spanish missions in Alta California, was founded by Father Fermín de Lasuén on June 13, 1798. It was dedicated to St. Louis the Crusader (king of France from 1236 to 1270). The mission flourished from the very beginning under the able and kind hands of Father Antonio Peyri, its guardian for thirty-four years. By the year 1800 this priest had converted more than three hundred Indians. As soon as he could, Father Peyri undertook an extensive building program. He completed a temporary chapel by the end of 1798. Within five years a church, four granaries, quarters for Indian men and women, and a spacious patio had been completed. In 1810 the mission's extensive farming operations in the Pala Valley necessitated the construction of an additional granary there. In 1815 Father Peyri founded the *asistencia* of San Antonio de Pala near the villages of the Pala and Palatingwa Indians at the foot of Palomar Mountain.

San Antonio de Pala, Father Peyri's submission, was as successful in its own right as were many independent missions. By 1818 it had a population of over a thousand converts and had earned its rank as the most famous California *asistencia*. The buildings there were of simply styled adobe, but San Antonio de Pala's well-proportioned detached bell tower gives the complex its architectural distinction. In 1903 a reservation was laid out around the *asistencia;* the church is still in use.

Not surprisingly, the man who supervised San Antonio de Pala had even more impressive plans for his own mission. In 1811 Father Peyri laid the foundations of the church for which the mission is known today. With the exception of San Juan Capistrano's now-ruined place of worship, the structure that Father Peyri built was the most beautiful in all of Spanish California.

Although the left tower lacks a belfry, indicating that Father Peyri's plans for the church were not completed, the combination of brick façade, bell tower, and an adjoining cemetery wall give a sense of majesty befitting the king after which the mission was named. The church, completed in 1815, was one of two in California built with a cruciform design and the only one left to have a dome over the crossing.

Another of the mission's unusual features was its large octagonal mortuary chapel, with an intricately carved altar whose likes were to be found nowhere else in California at the time. Altogether, San Luís Rey was a remarkable sight. A wide and convenient stairway that led to the mission orchard put one French visitor in mind "of the conservatory of citrus fruits at Versailles."

Under Father Peyri the mission reached its highest population—almost 2,900 neophytes, including those at San Antonio de Pala—in 1826, far and away the largest number resident at any California mission in a given year.

Legend has it that when Father Peyri retired in 1832, he had to leave in secrecy to prevent demonstrations among his grieving Indian congregation. But like any other mission, San Luís Rey was secularized in 1834. In 1843 Governor Micheltorena returned the mission to the Franciscans, but it was unable to recover. Restoration was begun in 1893 when a group of Franciscan seminarians arrived. Today the Franciscan order still uses the mission facilities, located four miles east of Oceanside, California.

For a history of the mission, see Zephyrin Engelhardt *San Luís Rey Mission* (1921); and Rexford Newcomb, *The Old Mission Churches and Historic Houses of California* (1925) .—R. S.

San Miguel Arcángel. Spanish Franciscan mission. San Miguel Arcángel was the third mission founded by Father Fermín de Lasuén in 1797 (on July 25) and the sixteenth started since Father Junípero Serra's arrival in Alta California. It more or less quietly followed the pattern of uneventful success and slow decline that characterized many other California missions. Large numbers of sheep were raised by the Franciscans at San Miguel, and large numbers of Indians were converted. The banner year for the mission was 1814, when it had 1,096 neophytes in residence. It was secularized by the Mexican government on July 14, 1836. After the American conquest, the mission buildings, located as they were on a main route between San Francisco and Los Angeles, a few miles north of Paso Robles, were put to various uses that the Spanish fathers would not have approved of; for example, a saloon occupied San Miguel's reception rooms in the 1860s and 1870s.

Restoration was begun in 1886 and was completed after the mission was returned to the Franciscans in 1928. The church is of simple design, with a long nave and an unadorned façade. The interior walls are decorated with mural paintings executed by the Indians who once resided at the mission. Although described by one author as "wholly lacking in natural inspiration," these book-copied murals are the best-preserved examples of those visual designs intended by the Spanish padres to attract California's native inhabitants to Christianity.

For a history of the mission, see Kurt Baer, *Architecture of the California Missions* (1958); and Zephyrin Engelhardt, *San Miguel Arcángel, The Mission on the Highway* (1929).—R. S.

San Rafael Arcángel. Spanish Franciscan mission. San Rafael originally began on December 14, 1817 as an *asistencia* for San Francisco de Asís Mission. Father Luís Gil, its first guardian, believed that the sunny location of the *asistencia* would assist the recuperation of the many Indians who became ill at San Francisco de Asís Mission. In 1818 a church and mission house were erected for San Rafael. San Rafael's church was similar in style to the simple architecture of San Miguel Arcángel Mission, its only distinguishing feature being a star-shaped window in the façade patterned after that of San Carlos Borromeo. The customary mission quadrangle was never completed at San Rafael. It became a full mission in 1823 when Gil's successor, Father Juan Amorós, vigorously protested the plans for its abandonment being made by Father José Altimira (see SAN FRANCISCO SOLANO). San Rafael reached its highest population, 1,140 Indians in residence, under Father Amorós in 1828. A year after his death in 1832, the mission was turned over to the Mexican Franciscans. San Rafael had the misfortune of being placed in charge of Father José Mercado, who thoroughly disrupted it before being recalled by Father Francisco García Diego, his superior. The mission was secularized in 1834 and became an Indian village, after which time its neglected buildings slowly disintegrated. In 1870 the ruins of the mission were cleared away to make room for a parish church. A replica of the chapel has since been placed on the original site.

For a history of the mission see Kurt Baer, *Architecture of the California Missions* (1958); and John A. Berger, *The Franciscan Missions of California* (1941).—R. S.

San Rafael Ranch. The San Rafael Ranch, a Spanish land grant on the Mexican border east of Nogales, Arizona, came into prominence after 1882 when Colin and Brewster Cameron bought it from R. R. Richardson. They paid $150,000 for 152,000 acres within poorly defined boundaries, creating problems among neighboring cattlemen and squatters. After continuous litigation, Colin finally received a clear title to four leagues, about one fourth of the land claimed for the ranch.

He improved the ranch and became a progressive Hereford breeder and leader in the Arizona cattle industry. In 1903 Cameron sold the ranch for $1,500,000 to bon vivant Colonel William Greene, who owned mines and ranches near Cananea, Mexico. By 1909 Greene transferred his top ranch-manager, Tom Heady, from the Cananea cattle company to operate the San Rafael Ranch. Heady ran the spread for thirty-eight years, improved it immensely, and personally became one of the state's greatest Hereford breeders.

See Nancy Pierce et al., *Arizonac—Men of the Range* (1969); Roscoe Wilson, *Pioneer and Well-Known Cattlemen of Arizona*, vol. I (1951); and Jay J. Wagoner, *Arizona Territory 1863-1912* (1970).—B. W. A.

San Sabá. Spanish mission. San Sabá, founded in 1757 on the San Sabá River, near present-day Menard, Texas, was the most ambitious effort of the Franciscan missionaries to reach and convert the Apache tribes of Texas. During the 1740s the Comanche and their allies, the Wichita, both traditional enemies of the Apache, began to press the Apache from the north, after having already displaced them from the Texas Panhandle in the eighteenth century. Reluctantly some of the easternmost Apache tribes and the Lipan Apache of West Texas began to drift toward an alliance of sorts with the Spanish, whom they had previously viewed as mortal enemies.

Spanish authorities encouraged this shift, while missionaries advocated missions for the Apache. In 1753 and again in 1755 officials sent expeditions to the San Sabá River region to hunt for a site for a mission. Meanwhile, various Franciscans, among them Father Mariano Francisco de los Dolores y Viana, who had been the driving force behind the founding of the SAN XAVIER RIVER MISSIONS, pressed for Apache missions in central Texas, while others advocated missions for the Lipan Apache on the Nueces and Rio Grande watersheds. Government support for the San Sabá project was not really forthcoming until rumors of a rich silver strike on the Llano River began to circulate and prospectors began to penetrate the region. This development and the willingness of Don Pedro de los Terreros, a wealthy philanthropist, to donate a large sum of money for a mission at San Sabá finally led authorities to act.

In 1757 Colonel Diego Ortiz Parilla led a military-religious expedition to the San Sabá, where he established the presidio of San Luis de las Amarillas on the north bank, while the friars, headed by Father Alonso Giraldo de Terreros, a cousin of San Sabá's benefactor, began the mission on the south bank. The strategic importance of the little colony, which was considered a halfway station between San Antonio and Santa Fe, was reflected in the size of Parilla's garrison of one hundred soldiers, the largest in Texas.

Despite the enormous amount of expense and energy that went into the founding of San Sabá, it was a total failure. The friars and the soldiers were in constant conflict with one another, for Parilla and other officers had doubts that an Apache mission could succeed. The Apache themselves, fearing both the diseases that had so often decimated mission Indians and attacks by the Comanche, refused to come to the mission. In essence, San Sabá remained a mission without Indians. By the summer of 1757 at least one friar had already returned to the Rio Grande settlements convinced that the mission was a failure. Then in March 1758 an estimated two thousand Comanche Indians and their allies swept down on the mission, killed Father Terreros, several mission workers, and several soldiers and destroyed the mission. The foremost authority on San Sabá, Robert S. Weddle, states that the event marked the beginning of Comanche-white warfare in Texas, a conflict that was not to end until the Red River Indian Wars of 1870-75 finally brought the Comanche onto reservations.

News of the destruction of San Sabá and of serious attacks on the presidio itself greatly upset Spanish officials in the border provinces, who feared that the Plains Indians might become bold enough to attack the San Antonio and Rio Grande settlements. Believing that a massive counterattack was necessary, they ordered Parilla to lead an expedition of nearly six hundred men north from San Antonio to punish the Indians. In the summer of 1759 a force made up of soldiers from several presidios, Tlascalan and mission Indians, and 134 friendly Apache warriors proceeded to San Sabá and then continued north. Near a fork of the Brazos River they attacked a camp of the unsuspecting Tonkawa,

killing some fifty-five Indians and taking nearly one hundred and fifty prisoners. Parilla then marched northeastward to the Red River, where he encountered Comanche, Wichita, and other tribes in a stockaded fort near present-day Ringgold, Texas. In the fighting the Spanish were repulsed, nineteen of them were killed, and another fourteen of them were wounded. Retreating to San Sabá, Parilla grimly reported to his superiors what was to be one of the major defeats in the history of New Spain's northern border.

The Spanish held on to San Sabá until 1768, when the garrison retreated to the Lipan Apache missions on the Nueces River, but even that outpost was abandoned in 1771.

San Sabá's original presidio buildings were made of wood, but in 1761 they were replaced by an imposing stone fortress, which, after falling into ruins, has been partially restored. San Sabá was a turning point both in the history of Texas missions and in the history of Spain's relations with the Plains Indians.

See John Francis Bannon, *The Spanish Borderlands Frontier, 1513-1821* (1971); and Robert S. Weddle, *The San Sabá Mission: Spanish Pivot in Texas* (1964) and *San Juan Bautista: Gateway to Spanish Texas* (1968).—H. R. L.

Santa Bárbara. Spanish Franciscan mission. Santa Bárbara, the tenth California mission and the first founded by Father Fermín de Lasuén, is located on a beautiful site at the foot of the Santa Ynéz Mountains. The mission, founded December 4, 1786, was a large one, with some 250 Indians housed in a mission village and an extensive water works. It remains one of the best preserved missions because it was used after the mission period as the see of California's first bishop, Francisco García Diego, and later as a college for Franciscan novitiates. The present, impressive sandstone church was begun after an earthquake in 1812 seriously damaged the earlier adobe building. The design was thought out by Father Antonio Ripoll, who combined an angular classic Roman front with the softly curved belfries and flowing arches of the Spanish colonial style. While this architectural mixture has had its critics, Santa Bárbara has more frequently been praised as the "Queen of the Missions."

The mission has been through many trials. In 1824 its converts joined an Indian uprising that had started at Santa Inés Mission and drove out the fathers and a contingent of soldiers before fleeing to the hills. It had not recovered when secularized in 1834. Mission buildings and lands were sold in 1846 by California's Governor Pío Pico. The Franciscans returned in 1853 and from then on tried to keep it in good repair. An earthquake in 1925 caused the collapse of the east tower, requiring massive repairs. Then in 1950 both the east and west towers began to crack because of disintegration of the church's foundations. The entire façade and its twin towers were torn down and rebuilt. The church was rededicated on December 4, 1953. Today the mission and its handsome grounds are a major tourist attraction. A museum there contains many objects preserved from old mission days.

For a history of the mission, see Zephyrin Engelhardt, *Santa Barbara, Queen of the Missions* (1923).—R. S.

Santa Clara de Asís. Spanish Franciscan mission. Founded by Father Tomás de la Peña on January 12, 1777, Santa Clara, the eighth Franciscan mission in Alta

California, soon became the most prosperous. The original site was on a flood plain, so the mission was moved to higher ground between 1780 and 1782. The surrounding farmlands were exceedingly fertile, and the Indians, originally hostile (as were those at nearby San José de Guadalupe), were won over by Fathers Magín Catalá and José Viader, who came to Santa Clara in 1794 and 1796, respectively. Both men remained for over thirty years. Under them the mission reached its maximum population of 1,464 in 1827, while over the length of its service it recorded over 8,600 Indian converts, more than any other of California's Franciscan missions. In February 1833 Father Viader ceded Santa Clara to Father Francisco García Diego, superior of the Zacatecan Franciscans and later first Roman Catholic bishop of California. In 1835 Father Diego returned to Mexico, hoping to influence the government at Mexico City to prevent further civil interference with the missions. He was succeeded at Santa Clara by Father Rafael Jesus de Moreno, who was forced to preside over the mission's secularization in 1836. This meant the end of Santa Clara as a center for converting Indians, but the church retained a certain prestige because it was often frequented by California notables such as Governor Juan Bautista Alvarado and the Castro family. In 1843 Governor José Manuel Micheltorena returned the mission to the Mexican Franciscans, but it was put under the control of Father José Mercado, a fiery and often drunken troublemaker who was forcibly returned to Mexico in 1844. The mission never recovered from his misrule. Father José Reál took his place, having to sell and rent much of the mission property in 1846 to pay off debts and maintain himself. He left California to return to Mexico in 1851, being succeeded by Father John Nobili, a representative of the Jesuit order to whom Santa Clara was ceded to establish a college to train English-speaking priests for the newly arriving Americans. The old mission church became the center of the new Santa Clara College (renamed the University of Santa Clara in 1911) and would have been preserved along with other venerable California churches but for a series of fires, the last of which completely ruined it in 1926. A rebuilt church was dedicated in 1929. It has a façade similar to that of the old mission church.

For a history of the mission see see John A. Berger, *The Franciscan Missions of California* (1941); and Rexford Newcomb, *The Old Mission Churches and Historic Houses of California* (1925).—R. S.

Santa Cruz. Spanish Franciscan mission. Founded on August 28, 1791, by Father Fermín de Lasuén on the north side of Monterey Bay opposite San Carlos Borromeo, the Mission of the Holy Cross was the twelfth and smallest of the California missions, reaching its maximum population of 523 in 1796. The Spanish and Indians at Santa Cruz did not get along from the beginning. Large numbers of neophytes ran away because of punishments they received and had to be brought back by force. Then Governor Diego Borica founded Branciforte, the third California pueblo, across the Lorenzo River from the mission on July 24, 1797. The citizenry got along even worse with the Indians than did the Franciscans, who from then on were in continual struggle with the town's civil government. In 1812 Father Andrés Quintana, who had thrashed Indians with a whip too often for his own good, was murdered in bed

by nine of his charges. As early as 1805 such troubles brought forth suggestions that the Franciscans abandon Santa Cruz. But the mission managed to hold on until August 22, 1834, when it was among the first to be secularized. Within thirty years, no traces remained of its weatherbeaten ruins. In 1931 a replica of the mission church modeled on an 1854 painting was opened in the town of Santa Cruz.

For a history of the mission, see Kurt Baer, *Architecture of the California Missions* (1958); and H. A. van Coenen Torchiana, *Story of the Mission Santa Cruz* (1933).—R. S.

Santa Fe, New Mexico. New Mexico's capital was founded in 1610 by the Spanish governor Don Pedro de Peralta, acting under orders of the viceroy in Mexico City. It was situated, according to Spanish municipal law, with an eye toward "cleanliness and stability," on the banks of the Santa Fe River, a small tributary of the Rio Grande, at the foot of the Sangre de Cristo Mountains. The name *Santa Fe*, meaning "Holy Faith," was probably borrowed from the city of Santa Fe in southern Spain. In 1823 St. Francis was made municipal patron and the town's official designation became La Villa de Santa Fe de San Francisco de Assisi.

The first Spaniards under Peralta's direction laid out a plaza, distributed lots to citizens, and began the construction of official buildings, including the PALACE OF THE GOVERNORS, a *cabildo*, or town council hall, and a church. Most of the work on these projects was performed by conscripted Pueblo Indian labor. Within time a defensive wall was raised, and a suburb called the Barrio de Analco appeared on the east bank of the Santa Fe River. This barrio sheltered the Indian servants who had accompanied the Spaniards from central Mexico, and it was for them that San Miguel Chapel, sometimes referred to as the oldest church in the United States, was originally built.

Throughout the seventeenth century Santa Fe remained the only formally organized municipality in the province of New Mexico. Its Spanish population in 1630 numbered a mere 250, only about 50 of whom were able to bear arms. Because of the remoteness of the community, there was little luxury available to Santa Fe citizens. The arrival of a supply caravan every three years bringing news, goods, and new faces offered one of the few breaks in the monotony of life on this frontier.

In the summer of 1680, Santa Fe was swept up in the general conflagration of the Pueblo revolt. Beginning on August 10 the Pueblo Indians, provoked by a prolonged assault on their religion and culture, began to massacre the Spanish rural population and pillage the countryside. On August 15 Santa Fe was besieged, forcing the entire populace to take refuge in the royal buildings surrounding the Governor's Palace. After profaning the churches, the Indian armies set fire to most of the city and cut off the Spaniards' water supply. Governor Antonio de Otermín and the survivors finally broke through enemy lines on August 21 and escaped southward. With the expulsion of Santa Fe's residents, Indians occupied the city and soon converted the ruins of the Governor's Palace into a pueblo. Here they were encountered by General Diego de VARGAS, who led a reconquering army northward from El Paso in 1692. The Pueblo had to be dislodged by force, but once the city was made safe the Spaniards began to rebuild all that had been destroyed in the revolt.

During the eighteenth century Santa Fe grew and prospered as large numbers of colonists from Mexico augmented its population. Government officials, soldiers, clergymen, and a few *hacendados,* who maintained town houses in the capital, composed the upper class. Below were the bulk of the citizenry made up of artisans, tradesmen, and small farmers whose fields enveloped the community and extended several miles downriver. Indians also constituted a significant portion of the population: a few descendants of Mexican Indian servants, some Pueblo, and large numbers of Plains Indians (termed *genízaros)* who had been captured or bought as children and raised in Spanish households. A few Negroes had come with the earliest colonists and by late colonial times the census showed several hundred mulattoes in the capital. The total population by the opening of the nineteenth century was approximately twenty-five hundred.

In 1807 Lieutenant Zebulon M. Pike, while exploring the headwaters of the Arkansas and Red rivers, strayed into Spanish New Mexico and was escorted to Santa Fe. With its rambling adobe structures, which he likened from a distance to flat-bottomed boats on the Ohio River, the town left him singularly unimpressed, but his description of what he had seen, published in 1811, aroused the interest of his fellow countrymen. However, since Spain would countenance no intrusion into her colony, those who crossed the Plains hoping to find profit in trading or trapping usually found a home in the Santa Fe jail. With independence from Spain in 1821, this policy was reversed by the new republican government in Mexico, and Yankee traders, blazing the Santa Fe trail from Missouri, were warmly welcomed in New Mexico's capital. The infusion of money and goods stimulated the somnolent economy and the influx of foreigners brought new ideas and altered Santa Fe's social complexion.

In 1837 the town was shaken briefly by a popular uprising that resulted in the death of Governor Albino Pérez and other political figures, but the revolt was swiftly put down by Manuel Armijo, who dominated provincial affairs thereafter until the Mexican War. When General Stephen Watts Kearny invaded New Mexico in mid-1846, Governor Armijo made some pretense of rallying defenses before finally abandoning his office and fleeing to Mexico. In a virtually bloodless conquest, Kearny occupied Santa Fe, established a military government, and began construction of Fort Marcy on a hill behind the Governor's Palace. An observer of these events, young Susan Shelby Magoffin, wife of the prominent trader Samuel Magoffin, wrote confidently in her diary: "Though Gen. Kearny has come in and taken entire possession, seated himself in the former Governor's chair, raised the American flag, and holds Santa Fe as part of the United States, still he has not molested the habits, religion &c. of the people, who so far are well pleased with their truly republican governor."

Probably the Santa Feans were not all that pleased with the imposition of alien rule, but the more astute among the old regime moved to ingratiate themselves with the Americans and win a place in the new political order. They had to compete, however, with many newcomers from the United States—especially young lawyers eager to carve out a future for themselves in New Mexico. A formal territorial government was organized in 1850 and a succession of governors presided in Santa Fe until invasion of the capital by a Confederate army under General H. H. Sibley early in 1862. With the defeat of the southerners shortly afterward at Apache Canyon, Santa Fe was restored to Union hands.

In 1851 Jean Baptiste Lamy became the first Roman Catholic bishop of Santa Fe (later elevated to archbishop). Spiritual affairs had long been in decline owing to the remoteness of the Mexican bishop at Durango, upon whom New Mexico had been dependent, and Lamy encountered some opposition in attempting to institute reforms. Nevertheless, he placed the Catholic church in good order and in Santa Fe introduced the Sisters of Loretto and the Christian Brothers, who opened much needed educational institutions. Other signs of progress were the coming of a military telegraph line in 1869 and the arrival of the Santa Fe Railroad in 1880.

In the post-Civil War period a group of republican politicians and businessmen gained a stranglehold on territorial politics and through their nebulous "Santa Fe Ring" controlled elections, the territorial legislature and courts, and most Washington appointments. One purpose of the ring was to acquire possession of old Spanish and Mexican land grants (see MAXWELL LAND GRANT COMPANY), although its exploitation extended to mining, ranching, and railroads. General Lew Wallace, who became territorial executive in 1878 and is remembered for his authorship of *Ben Hur,* found his hands tied when he tried to buck the Santa Fe Ring and resigned in frustration in 1881. A series of murders and assassinations in 1891, including an attempt on the life of Thomas Benton Catron, boss of the ring, and the slaying of a former sheriff, Francisco Chávez, characterized the turbulence the capital experienced at the end of the nineteenth century. By 1912, when ceremonies on the historic old plaza celebrated New Mexico's admission to statehood, Santa Fe had already begun to shed her frontier garb and assume a more mature and stable mien.

Santa Fe of the twentieth century has remained proudly conscious of her rich and vital heritage. About 1915 revival of the Spanish-Indian building tradition began. Soon artists established a colony in an older section of the city, and archaeologists were attracted by the extensive prehistoric sites in the surrounding country. In 1926 a group of interested citizens formed the Old Santa Fe Association, which to this day works to preserve the city's "ancient landmarks, historical structures, and traditions . . . which are the priceless assets and heritage of old Santa Fe." And appropriately, the initial organizational meeting of the Western History Association convened in Santa Fe in the fall of 1961. Thus New Mexico's capital remains unique in character among American cities. Its distinctive ADOBE ARCHITECTURE, numerous museums such as the MUSEUM OF NEW MEXICO and the Museum of Navaho Ceremonial Art (see TL'AH HASTIIN), and the associations of its citizenry, such as the Caballeros de Vargas, which strives to preserve historical tradition, all assure that the past will not be forgotten.

The standard text on the history of Santa Fe continues to be Ralph Emerson Twitchell, *Old Santa Fe* (1925;

repr. 1963). Of special interest is Oliver La Farge, *Santa Fe: The Autobiography of a Southwestern Town* (1959), which covers the territorial years.—M. Sɪ.

Santa Fe and Chihuahua Trail. The commercial thoroughfare that developed after 1821 between the Missouri settlements and Santa Fe, New Mexico, became known as the Santa Fe Trail. At Santa Fe, New Mexico's capital, it joined with the historic Chihuahua Trail, the province's lifeline to the Mexican settlements below El Paso. The Chihuahua road actually formed the northernmost segment of the old colonial Camino Real, or Royal Road, that linked Spanish New Mexico with the viceregal capital at Mexico City. From 1598 when Juan de Oñate, New Mexico's founder, extended the Camino Real to the upper Rio Grande to the time of Mexican independence in 1821, wagon caravans and mule trains traversed this highway bringing supplies needed by colonists and missionaries, and carrying the raw products of the frontier—buffalo hides, jerked meat, salt, piñon nuts, and Indian slaves—to be sold in the mining towns of Chihuahua.

From Santa Fe, main terminus of the Camino Real, the route led south along the Rio Grande through Bernalillo, Albuquerque, and Peralta to a point below present Socorro, where the river arches to the west, and the trail struck out across the ninety-mile stretch of desert called the Jornada del Muerto, or Deadman's March. Below this waterless waste, the Chihuahua route rejoined the river and continued on to El Paso del Norte and thence south across the sand dunes of Médanos to the cities of Chihuahua, Durango, Zacatecas, San Juan de los Lagos, Querétaro, and Mexico, a distance of sixteen hundred miles. Owing to danger from Indian raiders in later colonial times, a large convoy of wagons usually collected in Santa Fe each autumn and proceeded to the southern markets under soldier escort. The travelers might number five hundred and the number of sheep and cattle driven in the wake of the cavalcade, several thousand. These annual caravans, called by the Spaniards *conductas,* were the prototype of the wagon trains that streamed down the Santa Fe Trail in the nineteenth century. By 1803 goods imported from Chihuahua to New Mexico were valued at more than $100,000. But the province's exports were averaging much less than this figure, so that the small merchant group in Santa Fe was constantly in debt and the general populace suffered a perpetual shortage of manufactured goods.

With independence from Spain in 1821, the republican government of Mexico decreed that the Camino Real be known henceforth as the Camino Constitucional, or Constitutional Highway. In popular usage, however, it continued to be called the Royal Road and was so known to Santa Fe residents well into the twentieth century. More significantly, the new government relaxed the old controls by which Spain had excluded all foreigners from her frontier territories. The few American traders venturing into the Southwest prior to 1820 had been imprisoned and their property confiscated by Spanish officials. When William BECKNELL, a Missouri Indian trader, encountered a company of Mexican soldiers on the southern Plains in the autumn of 1821, he learned that Mexico had become independent and that his kind could now expect a warm reception in Santa Fe. Hastening on to the capital, he disposed of his small

stock of trade goods at an enormous profit and by January 1822 was back in Franklin, Missouri, displaying bags of Mexican silver coin. The summer of the same year he returned to Santa Fe with three well-provisioned wagons, this time pioneering a route across the Cimarron Desert and avoiding the precipitous Raton Pass over which his mule train had passed earlier. For his work in opening and marking out the trail, Becknell has been remembered as the "Father of the Santa Fe Trade." The GLENN-FOWLER EXPEDITION of 1821-22 also pioneered a trail to Santa Fe.

By 1824 a brisk commerce over the Santa Fe Trail was well established, the American traders realizing in that year gross receipts of $190,000. At the same time Indians, particularly Comanche and Kiowa, began to loom as a serious threat to the security of the caravans. Emphasizing the growing economic importance of the trade and the need for protection, Missouri Senator Thomas Hart Benton engaged the attention of Congress and by March 1825 won a bill authorizing an official survey to define the road and a $20,000 appropriation to treat with the Indians for a right of way. For a while beginning in 1828, military escorts afforded security to wagon trains crossing the plains, but this ended in 1830 with congressional economy, and the traders were obliged to protect themselves.

Initially, Franklin, Missouri, was the jump-off for Santa Fe; but by 1830 Independence, a hundred miles farther west, was the chief outfitting point. The way led across well-watered prairies westward to Council Grove. Beyond Pawnee Rock, a conspicuous sandstone landmark, the trail forded the ARKANSAS RIVER, and those taking the popular Cimarron Cutoff proceeded across sixty dry miles to the Cimarron River. In succession, the caravans then passed the Rabbit Ears, the Round Mound, the Canadian River, and finally reached San Miguel del Vado on the Pecos River, the first substantial town in New Mexican territory. From here it was a trip of several days to Santa Fe over Glorieta Pass. An alternate route from the Arkansas River, which avoided the Cimarron Desert and was less exposed to Indian danger but longer and more difficult for wagons, was the Mountain Branch. It ran westward to Bent's Fort near modern La Junta, Colorado, and then dropped into New Mexico over Raton Pass, rejoining the Cimarron trail at the Mora River. Bent's Fort, completed in 1832 by Charles and William Bent and Céran St. Vrain, dominated the Indian and fur trade of the southern Plains, and its thick adobe walls, invulnerable to Indian assault, offered a haven for travelers bound for Santa Fe.

In *Commerce of the Prairies* (1844), the classic account of the trails, Josiah GREGG has preserved in vivid detail the mode of organization for caravans, the techniques of handling mule trains, and a large measure of the spirit that animated those who braved the rigors of prairie travel. Witnessing the departure from Independence, Gregg wrote, "Each teamster vies with his fellows who shall be soonest ready; and it is a matter of boastful pride to be the first to cry out—'All's set!' The charioteer, as he smacks his whip, feels a bounding elasticity of soul within him, which he finds it impossible to restrain."

At Council Grove, the final rendezvous for those joining a caravan, the company was set in strict order with the captain assigning places, appointing lieutenants, and designating members of the night guard. Once in motion the mule- or ox-drawn prairie schooners, usually Pittsburgh-made Conestogas, covered ten to fifteen miles a day. With night camp, the wagons were drawn into a square to provide an enclosure for the animals and a fortification against Indian attack. The trek from the Missouri settlements to New Mexico generally lasted two to three months for the eight hundred miles, although the return trip with a light load might take half as long. The high point of any journey was the arrival in Santa Fe. The Mexican populace flooded the streets to welcome the traders, and the wagon drivers, self-consciously bedecked in "their choicest Sunday suit," vied with one another to crack the loudest whip.

Emphasis on the many-faceted aspects of the Santa Fe trade has tended to obscure the equally significant growth of commerce southward over the Chihuahua Trail. The markets in New Mexico were limited owing to the scarcity of hard currency, but in Chihuahua, Durango, Aguascalientes, and other mining communities the opportunities appeared boundless. Thus by the late 1830s, more than half the goods brought by the Yankee merchants were funneled through Santa Fe and on south. Neglected also has been the role played by Mexican businessmen in this commerce. As early as 1825 an enterprising trader from Chihuahua and another from Sonora journeyed to the United States with a pack train of five hundred horses and mules, although in later years others who came from the south found it convenient to acquire a stock of goods in Santa Fe where there was a ready supply. A substantial number of leading New Mexicans also entered the trade, operating stores, traveling to Independence and beyond for merchandise, and sending their sons to be educated in the United States. One such was Antonio José Chávez, a prominent trader, who on his way to Missouri was foully murdered by border ruffians near the Little Arkansas River in 1843.

The regulation and taxing of Santa Fe trade by the Mexican government was arbitrary and oppressive. Customhouses existed at San Miguel del Vado in the east and Taos in the north, but the real port of entry was Santa Fe itself. Here the tariff imposts (derechos de arancel) were supposed to be levied, but many traders heading for Chihuahua avoided them by transferring their merchandise to mules in eastern New Mexico and slipping past the capital on little-used trails. For a time Governor Manuel Armijo established a tarriff of his own, exacting five hundred dollars per wagon, irrespective of size. This prompted traders to use larger vehicles and stock goods of greater value and modest size and weight. Because of graft in the collection and handling of tariff receipts, only a small amount of what was owing ever found its way into the national treasury.

By 1840 the Mexican government, growing nervous over continued Anglo-American penetration along its northern frontier, began to look askance at the Missouri traffic. The abortive Texan-Santa Fe expedition of 1841, an attempt by the Republic of Texas to conquer New Mexico, did nothing to ease apprehension, and a series of laws to restrict the activities of foreigners had little effect. That fears were justified was proven in the summer of 1846, when General Stephen Watts Kearny, with the outbreak of the Mexican War, marched into Santa Fe and claimed the province for the United States. The Santa Fe Trail now entered a new phase as the old

Mexican tariffs vanished, the army began construction of forts to protect travelers, and stagecoach and mail service was inaugurated. The volume of business over the trail increased prodigiously as freighters hurried to supply the government and private companies with contract goods. By 1855 trade was valued at $5 million. Heaviest traffic was borne by the road during the California gold rush and later during the Civil War years, when New Mexico was a major theater of conflict in the West. By the late 1860s rails were pointing toward the Rio Grande, but it was not until 1878 that the Santa Fe Railroad surmounted Raton Pass. Two years later when tracks reached Lamy, the station for the New Mexican capital, the Santa Fe Trail ceased to exist. At a few points along the route, ruts riven deep in the prairie sod remain as a monument to the oldest and most colorful of America's far western roads.

The most complete study of the Chihuahua and Santa Fe trails is Max L. Moorhead, *New Mexico's Royal Road* (1958). An older account, R. L. Duffus, *The Santa Fe Trail* (1931), remains useful. Josiah Gregg, *Commerce of the Prairies* has appeared in numerous editions, the most recent one being in 1954. Two other recent significant books are Jack D. Rittenhouse, *The Santa Fe Trail, A Historical Bibliography* (1971); and Morris F. Taylor, *First Mail West, Stagecoach Lines on the Santa Fe Trail* (1971).—M. Si.

Santa Fe Ring. See MAXWELL LAND GRANT COMPANY.

Santa Inés, Virgin y Martyr. Spanish Franciscan mission. Santa Inés, the nineteenth in the chain of Alta California missions, was founded on September 17, 1804, by Father Estévan Tapis. It reached its greatest population in 1816, with 760 Indians in residence, who were employed in tending the mission herd of some twelve thousand cattle. Thereafter the mission steadily declined until secularization. The mission was located to the east of the coastal mountains. The Indians of the area were unhappy with their treatment by Spanish soldiers and revolted on Feburary 21, 1824. The revolt at Santa Inés spread to two other missions, La Purísima Concepción and Santa Bárbara, but eventually was quieted by the Franciscan fathers. After secularization the mission lands went untended except for a brief period in 1844 when a seminary college founded by Bishop García Diego occupied a portion of the lands. The mission was abandoned in 1850, and from then until 1904 the buildings were left to disintegrate. Restoration has been completed, and the attractive mission, which is modeled on San Gabriel Mission, serves as a parish church in the popular tourist town of Solvang.

For a history of the mission, see John A. Berger, *The Franciscan Missions of California* (1941); and Zephyrin Engelhardt, *Mission Santa Inés, Virgen y Martir* (1932). —R. S.

Santee, Ross (1888-1965). Writer, artist, and historian. Born in Iowa, Santee spent his childhood there and in Moline, Illinois. In 1910, after attending Chicago's Art Institute for four years, he decided to be a cartoonist and went to New York. He sold a few cartoons, but found the work neither satisfying nor financially rewarding. While there, however, he made a lasting friendship with another artist, Thomas Benton. With Benton's encouragement, young Santee put aside his institute teachings ("imitate the successful artists . . .") and began developing an original style. He was to become one of the finest black-and-white illustrators of his day.

In 1915, fed up with New York, he went to Arizona, where he became a cowboy, beginning as a horse wrangler (the lowest rung on the cowboy ladder). In 1919 he returned to the institute to study under artist George Bellows. The artist encouraged Santee to try again in New York. He did, but only on a part-time basis, splitting his time between ranch work in Arizona and selling his art in New York.

His writing career began almost by accident. His first story, written with the urging of the *Boy's Life* editor, related an incident on the range that "once I started, almost wrote itself." The story led to invitations to submit illustrated articles and stories to *Leslie's Weekly* and *Century* magazines; his career was launched.

In 1922 he exhibited his etchings in New York. He then pulled his *Century* stories together in *Men and Horses* (1926), which with its sketches and drawings provides an outstanding record of Arizona cowboys and cow horses. His next book, *Cowboy* (1928), was described by cow-country historian J. Frank Dobie as ". . . the best story of the making of a cowboy yet written. . . ." Unlike most of his books, which were largely autobiographical, *Cowboy* was a fictionalized biography of his friend Shorty Caroway, the Texas tenderfoot kid who became an expert Arizona cowboy. *Cowboy* was followed by a number of equally entertaining and informative accounts: *The Pooch* (1931, reissued as *Spike* in 1934), about a cowpuncher's dog; *Sleepy Black* (1933), a cow-horse story equally revealing about the horse's owners; and *The Bar X Golf Course* (1933), a rollicking tale of a three-hundred-mile-long golf course. Santee also illustrated some sixty books for other authors and frequently contributed drawings to such magazines as *Arizona Highways.*

As the state supervisor for the federal writers' project in Arizona in 1936, Santee was largely responsible for *Arizona, A State Guide* (1941), one of the best in the American Guide Series, and helped in the preparation of *Wyoming* and *Colorado.*

Quite late in life, Santee began using color. He sold his first completed oil when he was past seventy. But it was not as an artist or illustrator that Santee won the plaudits of critics; it was the books that he wrote, and illustrated, that brought him lasting fame.

See Jeff C. Dykes, "Ross Santee: A Tentative Bibliographic Check List," *American Book Collector* (Summer 1966); and Neal B. Houston, *Ross Santee,* Southwest Writers Series No. 18 (1968).—J. C. D.

San Xavier del Bac. Spanish mission. San Xavier del Bac, located on five acres in the middle of the Papago's San Xavier Reservation near Tucson, Arizona, has been acclaimed the most beautiful example of Spanish colonial architecture in the United States and one of the Southwest's greatest active churches. The present structure of fired brick was built between 1779 or 1780 and 1797 by Franciscan friars Juan Bautista Velderrain and Juan Bautista Llorens and is the last of three churches known to have been built on the site. It is famed for its unfinished bell tower, barrel vaults, and white, gleaming dome rising abruptly from its desert surroundings.

Bac, when first visited by the Jesuit priest Eusebio KINO in 1692, was a Piman Indian village, the largest in New Spain. Father Kino christened the place and in

The entrance of San Xavier del Bac. (Library of Congress)

1700 began construction of a church destined never to be completed. Sometime after 1732 a mission finally was built. Some twenty-five years later it was replaced by a long, rectangular, sun-dried adobe church built by Father Alonso Espinosa, another Jesuit. That church remained until the present edifice was completed in 1797. Although the church itself was without resident priests for short periods of time during the nineteenth century, the village was never abandoned by the Piman. In 1913 the Franciscans again took charge.

In addition to being an active mission church, serving the Papago on the reservation, San Xavier is a registered United States national landmark visited by thousands of tourists annually. In 1972 Pima County, Arizona, created a "historic sites zone" on county lands beyond the reservation to protect the church from dense population encroachment.

Although damaged by an earthquake in 1887, the mission remains essentially as it was in 1797 except for the addition of living quarters and a few coats of white paint.

See Bernard L. Fontana, "Biography of a Desert Church: The Story of Mission San Xavier del Bac," *Smoke Signal,* no. 3 (1963).—B. L. F.

San Xavier River missions. Spanish missions. In 1746 the Querétaran Franciscans received permission to found new missions in central Texas, northeast of San Antonio, on a stream that was then called the San Xavier River (now the San Gabriel River), near present-day Rockdale. The first of the missions, San Francisco Xavier de Horcasitas, was founded in 1748 by Father Mariano Francisco de los Dolores y Viana, who for many years had been agitating for a new chain of missions to convert the Tonkawa, Atakapa, and Karankawa tribes whose lands bordered on Apache and Comanche territory; this was to be the first step toward the conversion of the hostile Plains Indians. A year later Missions San Ildefonso and Nuestra Señora de la Candelaria were founded nearby; the presidio of San Xavier was built there in 1750—but not put into full operation until 1751—to protect the missions. Christian Indians from San Antonio and the Rio Grande missions were sent to San Xavier to assist the fathers in their work.

Nearly five hundred Indians settled at the three missions, but unfortunately disease and drought plagued them from the outset and decimated their numbers. Even more distressing was the abuse of the Indian women by the presidio soldiers and the hatred that grew up between Felipe Rábago y Terán, the presidio captain, and the Franciscan fathers. The conflicts became so intense that in 1752 Father José de Ganzábal and a soldier whose wife had been Rábago's mistress were murdered at Candelaria mission. A disaffected Coco Indian was blamed for the crime, but soldiers appear to have done the killing at the behest of Rábago. The captain was removed from his post, but the investigation that followed failed to convict him of the crime.

In 1755 both civil and religious authorities agreed that the drought-stricken San Xavier location was untenable and moved the missions to the San Marcos River. By 1757, however, even the new site was being abandoned, undoubtedly so that all energies could be devoted to establishing a new mission for the Apache on the San Sabá River (see SAN SABA).

Meanwhile Rábago not only escaped punishment but served at the San Sabá presidio in 1760 and in 1762 was assigned to guard the short-lived Nuestra Señora de la Candelaria mission near Montell for the Apache on the Nueces River. But Candelaria and a second mission, San Lorenzo, near Camp Wood, eventually failed and appear to have been abandoned by 1771. Similar heroic efforts to establish missions for the Apache along the Rio Grande also met with scant success. The attempts at the San Xavier, San Sabá, Nueces, and Rio Grande missions between 1748 and 1762 mark the last effort to expand the mission system in Texas. Not only did the San Xavier missions fail, but the resources and herds needed to start them put a serious strain on, and hampered the operations of, the other Texas missions.

See Herbert E. Bolton, *Texas in the Middle Eighteenth Century* (1915); James Wakefield Burke, *Missions of Old Texas* (1971); Carlos E. Castañeda, *Our Catholic Heritage in Texas,* vol. III (1938); and Robert S. Weddle, *San Juan Bautista: Gateway to Spanish Texas* (1968).—H. R. L.

Sapir, Edward (1884-1939). Linguist. Sapir was one of the pioneers in the study of Indian languages spoken in the West. Born in Germany, he came to America with his parents at the age of five. He graduated in 1904 from Columbia College, where he had been a student of anthropologist Franz Boas.

While holding various positions at the universities of California and Pennsylvania and in the Geological Survey of Canada in Ottawa, he followed his graduate study of the Takelma langauge of Oregon with important publications on the Southern Paiute, Nootka, Sarcee, Wishram, Yana, Wiyot, Yurok, Kutenai, Haida, and Navaho. He worked on the relationships of these languages to their larger families and simultaneously published a number of articles describing in general the cultures of the Indians of western Canada. Sapir spent his later years teaching at the University of Chicago and Yale University.

See Ruth Benedict, "Edward Sapir," *American Anthropologist,* vol. 41, no. 3 (1939).—B. L. F.

Sappington, John (1776-1856). Frontier physician. Sappington was born in Maryland and while still a young boy moved with his family to Tennessee. There he studied medicine with his father and later practiced with him at Nashville. After a brief independent practice at Franklin, Tennessee, he sought to further his medical knowledge through study at the University of Pennsylvania.

In 1817 Sappington moved to Howard County on the Missouri frontier, but after two years he relocated near Arrow Rock in Saline County, where his home, Fox Castle, became a popular rendezvous for the political leaders of the state. In his frontier practice Sappington had had experience with the treatment of malaria, a prevalent fever of the West and South, and in the 1820s he led the way in prescribing the use of quinine (recently isolated from Peruvian bark) as an antidote for this disease.

Since other doctors were slow to accept his findings on the new drug's value, Sappington decided to manufacture his own "Anti-Fever Pills" with a quinine base. More than a million boxes were distributed in the 1830s and 1840s with tremendous benefit to malaria sufferers. In Arrow Rock the Methodist Church bells rang every evening to remind the citizens that it was time to take their daily fever pill.

In 1844 Sappington wrote and published his *Theory and Treatment of Fevers,* expounding his theories on the treatment of malaria and detailing his method for producing his pills. These medical discoveries placed Sappington far ahead of his time.

More detailed accounts may be found in Thomas B. Hall, "John Sappington, M.D., (1776-1856), *Missouri Historical Review* (January 1930); and Robert Z. Terry, "Dr. John Sappington, Pioneer in the Use of Quinine in the Mississippi Valley," *Proceedings of Tercentennary Celebration of Cinchona* (1931).—W. E. P.

Sargent, Winthrop (1753-1823). Territorial administrator and planter. Sargent was one of the first men to serve in more than one United States territory. His career represents the beginning of a territorial bureaucracy. Born in Gloucester, Massachusetts, Sargent graduated from Harvard College and served in the army during the American Revolution. By 1786 he was surveying the Seven Ranges in the Northwest Territory for the government, and probably looking for good land for himself at the same time. This same year he attended the organizational meeting of the Ohio Company of Associates, made up of Massachusetts speculators who elected him secretary of the company, and he went with the company's agent, the Reverend Manasseh Cutler, to New York to negotiate a land purchase from Congress.

Following adoption of the Northwest Ordinance in 1787 and the Ohio Company's land purchase, Congress appointed Sargent secretary of the Northwest Territory in October 1787. He traveled to Marietta with Governor Arthur St. Clair in summer 1788 to help establish the first territorial government. Throughout the 1790s he was secretary of the territory and the governor's aide on Indian campaigns. In 1798 President John Adams appointed Sargent governor of the newly created Mississippi Territory.

In Natchez, Sargent walked into political factionalism that had developed following the prospect of United States occupation and that was encouraged by the personality of Andrew Ellicott, one of the United States commissioners who had arrived in 1795. Sargent sided with Ellicott. In 1800 Narsworthy Hunter proceeded to Philadelphia with complaints about the governor. The next year a congressional committee under William C. C. Claiborne found no reason to prosecute or punish Govenor Sargent but observed that certain "irregularities originated from incorrect and misconceived opinions." Following adoption of the report, Congress approved second-stage government for Mississippi Territory and President Thomas Jefferson did not renew Sargent's appointment. He then retired to his plantation outside Natchez where he specialized in raising cattle and cotton.—J. T. B.

Sasquatch. The North American counterpart of the Yeti, or Abominable Snowman, is best known by the names Sasquatch ("Wild Man of the Woods"), given him by the Salish Indians of southwestern British Columbia, and Bigfoot, given him because of the size of the footprints attributed to him. He also appears in American lore as the Jersey Devil of New Jersey's pine woods, as the Fouke River Monster in Arkansas, and as Momo in Missouri. Sasquatch is generally described as a hairy humanoid standing about eight feet tall that gives off a foul smell and can emit a high-pitched cry.

Evidence of the existence of a man-beast is limited to tracks, visual sightings, and photographs, all of which have generally been met with either skepticism or accusations of hoax. Over 750 sets of footprints, some measuring up to twenty-four inches in length and eight inches in width, have been discovered in North America since David Thompson first discovered a set in Canada in 1811. It is in fact a set of tracks that offers the most convincing evidence of Sasquatch's existence: the tracks of the so-called Bossburg Cripple, of Bossburg, Washington, are those of a creature with a club foot, the distortions of which could have been forged only by someone with a highly sophisticated knowledge of anatomy.

The most noteworthy photographic evidence is a twenty-foot-long sequence of color film taken by Roger Patterson at Bluff Creek, California, in 1967, that purports to show a Bigfoot at a range of a few yards. Unlike the ape and the bear, with which Sasquatch has been compared, this female Bigfoot had pendulous breasts and moved in a distinctly human manner. The film has, however, stirred controversy rather than put it to rest.

Boris Porshnev, a member of the Soviet Academy of Science, compared data on Sasquatch and his Russian counterpart, the Almas, and concluded that a branch of Neanderthals survive in various parts of the world. Some scientists concur, but disbelievers are in the major-

ity. Real or not, Sasquatch will survive in lore, if only because he has become a creature of commercial exploitation in the Bigfoot country of northern California and southern Oregon.

See Michael Grumley, *There Are Giants in the Earth* (1974); Don Hunter, *Sasquatch* (1973); and John Napier, *Bigfoot: The Yeti and Sasquatch in Myth and Reality* (1973).—J. T.

Satanta (Set-taint-te, "White Bear"), (c. 1830-1878). Kiowa warrior. A leading chief in the 1860s and 1870s and renowned as a warrior and orator, Satanta signed the Kiowa treaties negotiated in 1865 and 1867. In tribal politics he was allied with conservatives, who resisted the government's efforts to force them to abandon their life of warrior nomads.

Between 1868 and 1871 Satanta participated in several attacks on whites, leading to his arrest in 1871. Taken to Texas for trial, he was sentenced to be hanged, but the sentence was later commuted to life imprisonment. In August 1873 Satanta was paroled, but during the Red River War (1874-75) he was once more belligerent. On October 24, 1874, Satanta surrendered at the Cheyenne Agency and was returned to the Texas penitentiary. He committed suicide, according to official statements, by jumping from a window of the prison hospital.

See Mildred P. Mayhall, *The Kiowas* (1962).—W. T. H.

Sauk Indians. See IOWA.

scalping. Among all war practices and forms of trophy-hunting, the taking of scalps or scalp locks is most firmly associated in the popular imagination with American Indian warfare. The picture of a tawny warrior waving aloft a fresh scalp, the victim's blood still reddening his knife blade, has become a fixed part of America's image of the Indian as a brutal savage. Against this stereotyped view, it has been strongly protested that scalping was not practiced at all by American native peoples prior to the coming of Europeans. A stereotype of another sort, this latter contention is disproved by the least acquaintance with early European accounts of native societies throughout the eastern woodlands. Jacques Cartier in 1535, Hernando de Soto in 1540, Tristán de Luna in 1559, René Goulaine de Laudonnière in 1564, and, among others, Lescarbot, John Smith, and Samuel de Champlain in the early decades of the seventeenth century all provide authentic reports of scalping practices that long antedated white contact. At the same time it is clear that scalping was by no means a universal practice among native American societies. Few Indian peoples of the American West took scalps before the custom was introduced during the late seventeenth and eighteenth centuries, and then the traditional ritual aspects of scalping as a war practice were often subordinated to scalp-hunting for bounties paid by white authorities.

Prior to white contact, the taking of enemy heads was a more common and apparently more ancient warpractice among American native peoples. Scalping seems to have derived from this older practice, for just as head trophies represented the whole person of the slain enemy, so in turn the scalp was meant to represent the head. At the time of earliest white contact scalping was most prevalent among the Tunica and the Muskogean of the Southeast, although the custom was generally followed by many Algonquian and Iroquoian peoples of the eastern woodlands. Ritual scalping also was part of the war complex of such separate and ethnically diverse peoples as the Tlingit of the Northwest coast, the Salishan of the western interior plateau, and the Yuman of the lower Colorado basin, among others.

Great variations in native scalping techniques, as well as in the ceremonial significance of the act, have been reported. In some cases the whole skin of the upper head, including the ears, was carefully removed. In other cases a tonsure effect was achieved by cutting away a large area on the crown of the head. A speedier method, practiced most widely after the arrival of Europeans, was to take only a scalp lock by making one slash in front, then popping the trophy from the skull by a sharp tug upon the victim's hair.

The practice of scalping spread widely across the continent as a consequence of native contact with Europeans. Many reasons can be suggested. Technically, scalping became easier with the introduction of steel knives and tomahawks. Intertribal warfare, frequently encouraged and aided by Euro-American officials, increased in magnitude and intensity, giving greater occasion for the taking of scalps as war trophies. In the American West, the example set by white frontiersmen and eastern Indians helped to popularize the practice. But above all, scalping became more widespread as a result of the payment of scalp bounties by the white colonial governments and later by agencies of the Mexican and United States governments as a means to encourage the annihilation of hostile Indian groups. Although many peoples renowned as fierce warriors, such as the Apache, never did adopt scalping as a customary war trait, by the nineteenth century scalps were honored war-trophies among virtually all of the Plains tribes. Even so, the taking of heads was still considered among many Plains peoples an act that offered the greater insult to the victim and his tribesmen.

Basic research on scalping first appeared in English in Georg Friedrici, "Scalping in America," *Smithsonian Institution Annual Report for 1906* (1907). Other important sources include G. Nadeau, "Indian Scalping Techniques in Different Tribes," *Ciba Symposia*, vol. 5 (1944); and G. K. Neumann, "Evidence for the Antiquity of Scalping from Central Illinois," *American Antiquity*, vol. 5 (1940).—K. N. O.

Schaefer, Jack Warner (1907-   ). Journalist and writer. A native of Ohio, Schaefer was educated at Oberlin College and Columbia University. In 1930 he joined the United Press as a reporter. In 1931 he was appointed assistant director of education at the Connecticut State Reformatory, a post he held for seven years. These duties did not preclude his journalistic interests, however, for he continued his news work with the New Haven *Journal-Courier,* becoming its editor in 1939. From 1942 until 1944 he was an editorial writer for the *Baltimore Sun,* and from 1944 until 1948 an associate editor of the Norfolk *Virginia Pilot.* In 1949 he became the editor of the *Shoreliner.*

While he was with the *Shoreliner,* he published his first novel, *Shane* (1949). The story of a range drifter with a fast gun and a love of justice, it became an immediate success and was later made into the well-known motion picture. After the publication of *Shane,* Schaefer wrote constantly—*First Blood* (1953); *The Pioneers* (1954); *The Kean Land and Other Stories* (1959), one of the best collections of western stories by a single author; and *The Great Endurance Horse Race* (1963), a historical narrative. In addition, he published many short stories, which many critics believe to be even superior to his novels.—J. C. D.

Schafer, Joseph (1867-1941). Historian. Born on a farm near Muscoda, Wisconsin, Schafer was not able to enroll in college until 1887, when he entered Dakota Normal School at Madison in Dakota Territory. After graduating in 1890, he taught in Wisconsin high schools for two years before entering the University of Wisconsin in Madison to complete his undergraduate education. He then taught history at State Normal School in Valley City, North Dakota, for the next four years. In 1898 he returned to Wisconsin to study with Frederick Jackson Turner and became one of his most devoted disciples.

While completing his graduate work, he embarked in 1900 on a college teaching career at the University of Oregon, where he remained until 1920. At that time he accepted appointment as the superintendent of the Wisconsin State Historical Society in Madison, a position he held until his death.

Schafer, a productive historian, was concerned with the development of a variety of topics in western history within the confines of the Turner theories. His first monograph, *The Origin of the System of Land Grants for Education* (1902), traced the impact of the frontier on American education. His move to Oregon awakened his interest in the local history of the region and several publications reflected this concern, including *A History of the Pacific Northwest* (1905), *The Pacific Slope and Alaska* (1905), and a pamphlet, *The Acquisition of Oregon Territory* (1908).

His return to Wisconsin led him to shift his interests once more. In addition to his superintendent duties, he also became editor of the Wisconsin Domesday Book series—a series encompassing intensive studies of local areas in Wisconsin—which he himself considered to be his most significant contribution to historical scholarship. In addition to encouraging other authors in this project, he turned much of his attention to Wisconsin history. From his pen came *A History of Agriculture in Wisconsin* (1922), *Four Wisconsin Counties, Prairie and Forest* (1927), *Carl Schurz—Militant Liberal* (1930), The *Wisconsin Lead Region* (1932), and *The Winnebago-Horicon Basin* (1937). In 1936 he also delivered a series of lectures at the University of London that were subsequently published as *The Social History of American Agriculture* (1936).

One of the most prominent historians of his era, Schafer was active in the Mississippi Valley Historical Association.—G. D. N.

Scheiber, Harry A. (1935-   ). Historian. Scheiber was born in New York City and educated at Columbia University, where he studied history under the direction of Paul W. Gates, a leading authority on United States land policies. In 1960 he began teaching at Dartmouth College in Hanover, New Hampshire, and in 1971 joined the history department at the University of California at San Diego.

Scheiber's interests focused on the nineteenth-century Northwest, especially its economic development. His first book, *The Ohio Canal Era, 1815-1860* (1968), was a careful analysis of the role of Ohio's state government in the promotion and construction of canals within the state. He also published numerous articles on detailed aspects of the subject. In 1970 he edited a collection of essays by various scholars about the Old Northwest.—G. D. N.

Schoolcraft, Henry Rowe (1793-1864). Geologist, Indian administrator, explorer, and ethnologist. Schoolcraft was born in Albany County, New York, the son of a glass-factory superintendent. He went to Union and Middlebury colleges where he studied chemistry and mineralogy, and taught himself Hebrew, German, French, and geology. In 1817-18 he made his first trip to the West, visiting Missouri and Arkansas to make a geological and mineralogical reconnaissance. In 1820 he served as geologist under the territorial governor of Michigan, Lewis Cass, exploring the Lake Superior copper region. He was secretary of the Cass commission that in 1821 concluded a treaty with the Chippewa, Ottawa, and Potawatomi, by which these tribes lost the peninsula of Michigan south of the Grand River.

In 1822 Schoolcraft became an Indian agent on the northwest frontier, with headquarters first at Sault Ste. Marie and subsequently at Michilimackinac. Marriage to a European-educated granddaughter of a Chippewa man set his life's course. He published a grammar of the Algonquian language; discovered that Lake Itasca was the source of the Mississippi River; negotiated a cession of sixteen million acres of land from the tribes of the upper Great Lakes in 1836; and served as acting superintendent of Indian Affairs for the northern department.

In 1841 Schoolcraft moved to New York City and shortly afterward he toured parts of Europe, Canada, and the United States, lecturing on Indians and Indian antiquities. In 1845 he was appointed by New York State to make a census of the Six Nations (Iroquois) tribes in that state.

In 1847 his dream of more than a decade came to pass when Congress commissioned him to compile what was to be his greatest work, the six-volume *Historical and Statistical Information Respecting the History, Condition, and Prospects of the Indian Tribes of the United States* (1851-57). Although Schoolcraft wrote personally of the tribes with which he was familiar, he sent a 348-entry questionnaire to Indian Office employees, travelers, missionaries, traders, scholars, and to virtually everyone who might be expected to have reliable information concerning Indians. The result was a compilation of the state of knowledge in the mid-nineteenth century concerning tribes from Maine to California, including all major groups of the trans-Mississippi West. An index prepared by Frances S. Nichols was published in 1954 as *Bulletin of the Bureau of American Ethnology*, no. 152.

See Chase S. Osborn and Stellanova Osborn, *Schoolcraft, Longfellow, Hiawatha* (1942).—B. L. F.

Schreiner, Charles (1838-1927). Texas cattleman. Born in Riquewihr, France, Schreiner immigrated with his parents to Texas in 1852. At age seventeen he entered a frontier ranger company, remaining with the battalion for one year. After the death of his mother, he engaged in small-scale cattle-raising. In 1857 he moved his operations from Bexar to Kerr County. When the Civil War was declared, he enlisted as a volunteer in Captain S. G. Newton's company at San Antonio, participating in the battles of Jenkins' Ferry and many other engagements.

By 1874 Schreiner was back in the cattle business and sending herds of eighteen hundred to twenty-five hundred cattle up the trail to Kansas. During the 1880s he and some other Texas cattlemen leased the grazing rights on part of the Kiowa and Comanche reservations. Schreiner recalled that "we paid the chiefs for the lease, but they spent the money and forgot to give an account to the tribesmen. When the cattle went on the reservation, the Indians set up a complaint about the trespassing and we produced our leases. Soon trouble began. General Sheridan investigated the trouble, and told us the only way that an uprising could be prevented was to remove our cattle from the range. We had put 13,000 beef steers on the land, and gathered only 1,027 head. This broke several of the men who were associated with me but the mercantile business pulled me through the disaster."

At the peak of his career as a landowner Schreiner held title to more than one-half million acres of land in Kerr and adjoining counties and in other sections of Texas.—H. R. L.

Schreyvogel, Charles (1861-1912). Painter. Born in New York City, Schreyvogel sold newspapers as a youth and worked as an office boy for a New York firm before moving with his parents to Hoboken, New Jersey, henceforth his home. Except for a temporary apprenticeship with a lithographer, he concentrated on drawing and painting, earning some money by giving lessons. In 1887 he was enabled to go abroad for serious study with financial assistance from H. August Schwabe, president of the Newark Art League. After three years in Munich, he returned to the United States an accomplished draftsman and colorist.

Advised to seek employment in the West for the sake of his health, Schreyvogel began to work and save money toward that end. Meanwhile, the manager of "Buffalo Bill" Cody's famed Wild West show gave him permission to use the Indian and cowboy performers with that company as models for his sketches. Colonel Cody likewise encouraged the artist to work on western subjects, and in 1893 Schreyvogel made his first trip west to the Ute reservation in southwestern Colorado. Upon his return to the East, Schreyvogel determined to devote his efforts to the portrayal of the army man in the West.

Schreyvogel won the admiration of a group of friends in the lithographic trade, but his paintings o, western action did not sell. He tried his hand at portraiture, miniatures, glass painting, and lithography, realizing only a limited success. At the suggestion of a friend, he offered one of his cavalry pictures, entitled *My Bunkie,* to the National Academy of Design in New York for its annual judging and exhibition in 1900. To his amazement it won the highest award in the show, and Schreyvogel found himself catapulted from obscurity to fame virtually overnight.

There followed a dozen years in which he enjoyed the admiration of critics and buyers alike, highlighted by an invitation to the White House, at which time President Theodore Roosevelt issued a permit allowing the artist to visit any military post or Indian reservation in the United States in pursuit of his work. With poverty and disappointment behind him, he gave his whole attention to the creation of a series of paintings depicting western riders in action. As unexpectedly as he had come to

Attack at Dawn by Charles Schreyvogel. (Thomas Gilcrease Institute)

public notice, however, he died a few days following his fiftieth birthday, the victim of blood poisoning.

Almost all of Schreyvogel's pictures were painted upon large canvases, and he did not produce the volume of work characteristic of some of his contemporaries. One of the largest collections of his pictures is owned by the Thomas Gilcrease Institute of American History and Art in Tulsa, Oklahoma, purchased originally from the estate of Dr. Phillip G. Cole, Tarrytown, New York. Other important collections of Schreyvogel's works may be seen in the National Cowboy Hall of Fame in Oklahoma City and the Whitney Gallery of Western Art, Cody, Wyoming.

See Paul Rossi and David C. Hunt, *The Art of the Old West* (1971); and Robert Taft, *Artists and Illustrators of the Old West, 1850-1900* (1953).—D. C. H.

Schurz, Carl (1829-1906). Conservationist. Born and educated in Germany, Schurz participated in the revolutionary movement of 1848 until forced to flee to Switzerland. In 1852 he immigrated to the United States and became a journalist. When the Civil War began, he joined the Union army and participated in several major battles. After the war Schurz resumed his journalistic career in St. Louis. Liberal and reform-minded, he was elected to the United States Senate from Missouri in 1868. He did not run for reelection, but in 1877 Presi-

dent Rutherford B. Hayes appointed Schurz secretary of the interior. In that post for four years, Schurz's primary concern was management of the nation's forests. Acquainted with European methods of scientific forestry, Schurz was shocked at the cut-out-and-get-out philosophy that ruled American lumbering. Questioning the myth of inexhaustibility, Schurz criticized Americans for their wastefulness. "The rapidity with which this country is being stripped of its forests," he wrote in his annual report for 1877, "must alarm every thinking man." In twenty years, Schurz predicted, there would be a timber shortage and a consequent decline of national prosperity.

As a remedial measure Schurz proposed tightening and enforcing regulations governing lumbering on federal lands. With the notorious TIMBER AND STONE ACT (1878) in mind, he advised against selling any more of the public domain to private parties. The federal government, Schurz argued, should retain title to the land and strictly control any private use. This system was a guarantee "that no large areas be entirely stripped of their timber, so as not to prevent the natural renewal of the forest." In this idea were the seeds of the United States Forest Service and the national forests. Schurz's later years were devoted to writing, editing, and political reform. During his time he stood as one of the few exceptions to the rule of federal indifference to conservation.

References include Claude M. Fuess, *Carl Schurz, Reformer* (1932); and Adolf E. Zucker, *The Forty-eighters: Political Refugees of the German Revolution of 1848* (1950).—R. N.

Scotch-Irish. The Scotch-Irish were, after the English, the second largest ethnic group in the American colonies and have traditionally been characterized as archetypical rough-and-ready pioneers and frontiersmen. The term "Scotch-Irish" was not native to them and did not come into general use until after 1850, when it was employed to distinguish them from the Irish Catholics who were coming into the United States in great numbers.

The Scotch-Irish had their origin in early seventeenth-century attempts of British monarchs to subdue the wild tribes of Ireland. Under the sponsorship of James I, Scottish lowlanders, predominantly Presbyterian, were encouraged to move to the Irish "kingdom" of Ulster, where they obtained farms. Despite bloody resistance from the displaced Irish, and the wilderness character of the land, the opportunity was attractive to the Scots and throughout the century immigration to Ireland continued. Freed from the restrictions of ancient Scottish feudalism, the Ulster Scots became fiercely independent. Conflict developed between them and absentee English landlords, and over economic sanctions against the growing Ulster wool industry. This, coupled with resentment of anti-Presbyterian laws, forced tax-support of the Anglican church, and four years of severe drought, led to mass emigrations from the north of Ireland to America beginning about 1715.

The first Scotch-Irish migrants were drawn to New England by the strict Calvinist reputation of that region, but by 1725 they were almost completely diverted elsewhere. The New England Puritans did not welcome large groups of outsiders. There was very little ungranted land available in New England, even for the low-level subsistence farming of which the Ulstermen were capable; nor could the region's economy support a large indentured-servant population, which was the immigrant's only alternative to farming. The middle colonies, however, particularly Pennsylvania, had an abundance of potentially fertile backcountry and were the stronghold of the indentured-labor system. Between 1700 and 1775 an estimated 200,000 Scotch-Irish came to the colonies, and approximately seventy percent entered through Philadelphia and other Delaware River ports. Of the remainder, most landed at New York or, after 1750, entered the Carolina Piedmont through Charleston. Though continuous, the migration had five peaks, which reflected periods of economic depression in Ireland. These were in 1717-18, 1725-29, 1740-41, 1754-55, and 1771-75. During the 1750s influx, Pennsylvania alone received as many as 10,000 a year. To the sparsely populated colonies such numbers were unsettling and disrupted the orderly pattern of settlement that administrators had laid out.

The vast majority of Scotch-Irish immigrants were farmers, although at least half of the total migration had to enter the colonies as indentured servants. As soon as most were able, they left the settled seaboard region and moved to the frontier border, where they found an environment very similar to the Ireland their grandfathers had settled. The Scotch-Irish first concentrated in the Cumberland valley of Pennsylvania west of Harrisburg during the 1720s. The Pennsylvania proprietors had welcomed—even solicited—Scotch-Irish immigration, but their attitude changed when it became clear that the poverty-stricken new arrivals had little patience with proper forms of land patents or quitrents and cared not at all for Indian claims to unceded lands. The Scotch-Irish made plain their feeling that "it was against the laws of God and nature, that so much land be idle, while so many Christians wanted it to labor on, and to raise their bread." When officials went into the back-country to take payments and rents they were usually laughed at, and attempts to evict squatters were futile, often occasioning brawls and bloodshed. Relations between eastern Pennsylvania and the western settlements became notorious for their unharmoniousness.

With each successive wave of migration and the natural increase in their numbers, the Scotch-Irish pushed farther into the frontier, following the natural line of the great valley of the Appalachians southwestward into the backcountry of adjoining colonies. The first effective Scotch-Irish settlements were begun in Virginia in 1732, North Carolina in 1740, and South Carolina in 1760. In each colony the story was generally the same. The pioneers spread throughout the forests, cleared what land they chose, fought bloody skirmishes with Indian occupants, and cared little for the claims of seaboard governments for jurisdiction or administration. When the colonial governments returned this disregard in the form of imbalanced representation, overtaxation, and failure to provide what the frontiersmen believed adequate defense measures against Indian depredations, the Scotch-Irish were not loath to take violent action, as evidenced by the march of the "Paxton Boys" in Pennsylvania (1763) and the Carolina Regulator movement of 1768-71.

Isolated in the backwoods, the Scotch-Irish evolved a folk society and customary law of their own, and most of the classic American pioneerisms, from husking bee and corn whiskey to turkey shoot and shivaree, are associated with their life-style. The settlers of the backcountry were not all Scotch-Irish, however. Large numbers of German farmers were entering the colonies at the same time and expanding in the same pattern. Throughout the frontier their settlements grew up side by side with the Scotch-Irish. The two peoples had little to do with each other, except feud, because of the language barrier and differing folkways. And while German families were more respectful of legalities and tended to stay in a place once settled, many Scotch-Irish were continually on the move. The modern American image of the typical frontiersman as a hard-fighting, hard-drinking, quick-tempered roamer, always anxious to pull up stakes and move on to the next valley, is a reflection of those characteristics that colonial observers and writers called uniquely Scotch-Irish.

During the years of conflict with the French and Indians, the frontierspeople bore the brunt of attacks, and the Scotch-Irish acquired a reputation for effectiveness and cruelty in forest warfare. Their bitter hatred of the Indian was probably not a manifestation of the same kind of racial arrogance that characterized the more civilized parts of the colonies, however. The Scotch-Irish hatred was for an enemy who was accepted on his own terms and fought on his own grounds and with his own methods. The scalps of Indians were as common a trophy in pioneer cabins as were the scalps of whites in Indian lodges. After the French and Indian War, the Scotch-Irish were in the vanguard of settlement that crossed the Appalachians in defiance of the Proclamation of 1763 and took up lands in the Kentucky and Tennessee country. There their numbers diffused and ceased to be identifiable as a coherent ethnic bloc, although large numbers of pioneers from Scotch-Irish backgrounds continued in the forefront of westward expansion throughout the nation's history.

The Scotch-Irish contributed more to American culture than just a cutting edge for frontier advancement and an adventuresome mythology of frontier life. During the period of the American Revolution, Scotch-Irish people were almost entirely pro-independence, and they have been called America's first political radicals. The establishment of a firm Presbyterian church in America and the educational institutions associated with it was a by-product of the Scotch-Irish migrations, although many Scotch-Irish deserted it for the more back-woodsy Baptists and Methodists. More important was Scotch-Irish impact in shaping the pattern of rural settlement and land use. The characteristic single-family farm with woodland outfields, located away from town and with the family home located on it, is a Scotch-Irish inheritance. So are the thousands of rural crossroads villages that grew up to service the surrounding farms, as opposed to the centralized New England town system of agricultural advancement. The typical Scotch-Irish belief in the right of landownership through possession and use, as given statutory embodiment in the Homestead Act of 1862, has become one of this nation's most cherished traditions.

I. C. C. Graham, *Colonists From Scotland: Emigration to North America, 1707-1783* (1956), is the best survey of Scotch-Irish migration and settlement and should be read along with J. G. Leyburn, *The Scotch-Irish: A Social History* (1962). R. J. Dickson, *Ulster Migration to Colonial America* (1966), is a detailed statistical analysis of the demography of the migration from the departure from Ireland to the arrival in America. See also C. K. Bolton, *Scotch-Irish Pioneers in Ulster and America* (1910); H. J. Ford, *The Scotch-Irish in America* (1915); and E. R. R. Green, ed., *Essays in Scotch-Irish History* (1969). — P. R. M.

Scott, Thomas Alexander (1823-1881). Railroad builder and executive. The seventh of eleven children of a Franklin County, Pennsylvania, tavern keeper, Scott became station agent at Duncansville for the Pennsylvania Railroad in 1850, before the road had been completed to Pittsburgh. By 1860 he was first vice-president in charge of all operations. As an army officer during the Civil War he planned and supervised the first large-scale movement of an entire army by rail. In 1870 Scott became president of the Pennsylvania Company, a new subsidiary operating all of the lines west of Pittsburgh and, upon the death of J. Edgar Thomson in 1874, succeeded to the presidency of the parent company.

So well organized was the Pennsylvania Railroad, which had numbered young Andrew Carnegie among its division superintendents, that Scott had long since begun to give most of his attention to expansion plans. A true transcontinental, Atlantic-to-Pacific railroad was

his dream, and the TEXAS AND PACIFIC RAILROAD, planned to run, with connections, from the Pennsylvania's western terminus at St. Louis to the California coast, was to be its realization. After the Credit Mobilier scandal, however, Congress shut off all further land-grant aid to western railroads, and in west Texas Scott ran into a stonewall in the form of Collis P. HUNTINGTON and the SOUTHERN PACIFIC. The Texas and Pacific never got farther west than a point on the Southern Pacific a few miles east of El Paso, Texas.

His ambitions disappointed and his health failing, Scott retired in 1880. A charming, widely read man, his temperament and bearing belied the stereotype of the nineteenth-century railroad tycoon.

The authorized history of the Pennsylvania Railroad, George H. Burgess and Miles C. Kennedy, *Centennial History of the Pennsylvania Railroad Co.* (1949), contains a good summary of Scott's career in the East. Julius Grodinsky, *Transcontinental Railroad Strategy, 1869-1893* (1949) is a highly perceptive account of his western project.—A. M.

Scott, Winfield (1786-1866). Soldier and presidential candidate. Born near Petersburg, Virginia, Scott attended William and Mary College, was admitted to the bar, and became a militia officer. Commissioned a captain of light artillery in the regular army in 1808, he began his military career on the Louisiana frontier. During the War of 1812, Scott attained the rank of brigadier general and won fame in the battles at Chippewa and Lundy's Lane. Congress and the state of Virginia voted him medals, and he was brevetted a major general. In 1815 Scott was appointed a departmental commander and wrote and published his *Rules and Regulations for the Field Exercise and Maneuvers of Infantry*, which was a standard work until the Civil War. He not only was a brave soldier, brilliant strategist, and able administrator, but also a tactful and responsible diplomat. He was a personal emissary of President Andrew Jackson to South Carolina during the nullification controversy, prosecuted the Seminole War in Florida, guarded the Canadian frontier during the Patriot War, and supervised the removal of the Cherokee Indians from the South. In 1841 Scott became commanding general of the army.

When war was declared on Mexico in 1846, Scott helped raise an army and drew up invasion plans, but because of his Whig politics was denied a field command by the Democratic administration. In 1847 he was finally authorized to strike at the heart of Mexico (see MEXICAN WAR).

A large, impressive man, Scott wore glittering uniforms and was nicknamed "Old Fuss and Feathers" by his troops. Acclaimed a national hero, Scott in 1852 was voted the rank of lieutenant general and ran unsuccessfully on the Whig ticket for president. As the Civil War loomed, Scott, as commanding general, urged President James Buchanan and Secretary of War James B. Floyd to grant him authority to send troops and arms to reinforce the federal forts in the South. In the spring of 1861 he organized the defense of Washington, D.C., and was retired in October 1861, after which he settled at West Point, where he died. Scott was one of the ablest soldiers the nation has ever produced.

See Charles E. Elliott, *Winfield Scott: The Soldier and the Man* (1937).—H. P. H.

Scrugham, James G. (1880-1945). Nevada politician and engineer. Born in Lexington, Kentucky, Scrugham went to Nevada in 1903 to join the College of Engineering of the University of Nevada. He served as dean of that college from 1914 to 1917. In the latter year he was granted a leave of absence to become state engineer, which position he held for four years. In 1922 he was elected governor of Nevada as a Democrat and served one term. His popularity was not enough to stem the tide of rising Republicanism within the state and he was defeated in 1926. He became editor and publisher of the *Nevada State Journal* in 1927 and held that post until 1932 when he was elected to serve as congressman from Nevada. He was reelected to that position four times and in 1942 was elected to the United States Senate to complete the unexpired term of Key Pittman, who had died shortly after his election in 1940. Scrugham is the only person in the history of the state to serve as governor, congressman, and United States senator.

Some of Scrugham's official papers are in the Nevada State Archives. See James G. Scrugham, ed., *Nevada: A Narrative of the Conquest of a Frontier Land*, 3 vols., (1935).—R. R. E.

Seattle, Washington. In 1852, when the history of Seattle begins, there were scattered clearings in many spots along the shores of Puget Sound. The traditional date for Seattle's founding, however, is November 1852, when a small number of Americans landed from the schooner *Exact* in what is now West Seattle. The optimistic settlers named the barren sandpit where they went ashore "New York, Alki," which in the jargon of the locality means "New York, someday." The place of their landing is still called Alki Point.

Within a few months the settlers realized that their dwelling site was not suited to permanent settlement, and accordingly they accepted an offer of land from Dr. David Maynard, who promised part o‖ his donation claim on Elliott Bay, five miles northeast of Alki, as the location for a permanent townsite. A few remained at Alki, but the rest moved to Seattle, the new village, named after Seathl, the local Indian headman and a friend of Maynard.

The main attractions of Seattle were the existence of a tremendous forest on the bluff in back of the village; a millsite; and a man willing to invest in a sawmill to take advantage of the California market. Henry M. Yesler built his mill, which was the main source of employment for the men of the community. The logs were "skidded" to the mill by a long chute, known as the skid road. In time this log chute became the main street of Seattle and was still called the skid road. Eventually the business center moved north, and the old part of town became a haven for derelict men and disreputable businesses. The name remained, and subsequently this frontier term has been used to describe a badly deteriorated business section of any American city.

Animosity between the Indians and the settlers who took their lands broke into open warfare in 1855-56 along Puget Sound. Indians from the White River valley to the south attacked Seattle in January 1856. The whites were convinced that the cause of Indian anger was the policies of the territorial governor, Isaac Ingalls Stevens. Accordingly, Seattle's citizens attempted to frustrate the governor by ignoring his proclamation of martial law and by trying to rescue the Nisqualli Indian

Leschi, who had been condemned to death by a military tribunal for murdering a white man. Stevens retaliated by removing Seattle Judge Edward Lander from office after he had found Stevens guilty of contempt of court for suspending civil law. The governor also secured the dishonorable discharge of all the "Seattle Volunteers," for their insubordination. This pioneer attitude of nonconformity toward authority may still be found among some Seattle citizens.

Throughout the entire West during the mining and logging days of the middle nineteenth century there was a serious shortage of marriageable young women. In 1865, therefore, the youthful president of the University of Washington, Asa Mercer, proposed to remedy this situation by inducing hundreds of "widows and orphans" of the Civil War to move to the Northwest. His main concern was that they be female and between the ages of seventeen and twenty-five. He actually did bring a "cargo of brides" to the Northwest, but not as many reached Seattle as he had promised his backers. The disappointed Seattle single men who were unable to find wives after financing Mercer's scheme virtually forced him from the community.

During the 1870s Seattle had high hopes of becoming the terminus of a transcontinental railroad, but to its disappointment the Northern Pacific Railroad chose Tacoma, Washington, instead. The subsequent rivalry between Seattle and the Northern Pacific continued to influence state politics for the following fifty years. For example, in 1885 a labor dispute involving employees of the Northern Pacific caused a mob of Seattle citizens to expel Chinese strikebreakers in what are called the "anti-Chinese riots." In another action, Seattle politicians successfully prevented Northern Pacific promoters from changing the name of Mount Rainier to Mount Tacoma.

By the end of the 1880s Seattle began to grow more rapidly. Although a fire almost completely destroyed the town's flimsy buildings in 1889, determined citizens such as Judge Thomas BURKE rebuilt within a few months. Washington became a state in November of that year, and James J. HILL announced plans to make Seattle the terminus of the Great Northern Railroad. Hill and Joshua GREEN actively cultivated trade with Japan, and Seattle was the major port for this commerce. Through Hill's local representative, Judge Burke, Seattle, as well as other communities along the Great Northern mainline, increased rapidly in population.

The prosperity inspired by the railroad activity was shattered by the depression of 1893, and Seattle's economy did not recover until gold was discovered in the Yukon in 1897. Seattle became the main outlet for the northern gold fields and, as a result of publicity put out by Erastus BRAINERD and the Seattle Commercial Club, it grew from forty thousand to almost two hundred thousand in less than a dozen years. In addition, the successful Alaska gold-seekers returned "outside" to Seattle in order to spend their money, and Seattle soon became a wide-open city, furnishing entertainment for all kinds of fun-seekers around the clock, every day of the week. The more conservative citizens were horrified at the vice that flourished along the old skid road.

Much of the thrust for Progressive-era reform, such

as the 1909 blue laws or the constitutional amendment permitting public officials to be recalled from office, was the result of the scandals associated with Seattle's public officials and the open-town tradition of a seaport connected to Alaska. On the other hand, the city took considerable pride in its growth and prosperity. It celebrated the decade of gold-related excitement in the Alaska-Yukon-Pacific Exposition of 1909.

By the beginning of World War I, Seattle was a major city. Roland H. Thomson, city engineer, successfully completed a project in which millions of tons of earth from high hills near the city center was removed and dumped into Elliott Bay, creating new waterfront facilities and potential business sites.

With the growth of industrialism during World War I came a rising tide of labor unrest and social protest that verged on radicalism. After the war, in 1919, the city became the first large center in America to have a general strike. The INDUSTRIAL WORKERS OF THE WORLD (I.W.W.) were active in agitating for union hiring halls and better living conditions for workers in the nearby forests. In addition, grievances of shipyard workers whose wages were reduced in the face of sharply increasing costs of living received much publicity, and for three days Seattle was paralyzed when its entire labor force struck in sympathy. As a result of such radical activity, the 1920s in Seattle was a period of reaction against the labor movement, although at the same time Dave Beck was able to build the local teamsters union into a national political and labor power.

The Great Depression of 1929-40 hit Seattle hard, with unemployment at a staggeringly high level. Factories closed, soup kitchens opened, and thousands of unemployed men lived on the local garbage dump, which they named with obvious irony "Hooverville." Slowly Seattle, like the nation, began the long road back as social and economic experimentation at state and national levels began to take effect. One of the more successful experiments during the depression was done by the BOEING AIRPLANE COMPANY, founded by William E. Boeing. The company designed and built a number of all-metal, multiengined airplanes that proved highly successful. When World War II came, Boeing was ready to build thousands of aircraft. A leader in a war-based economy, it brought unprecedented growth and prosperity once again to Seattle.

When the war ended, the boom continued, as Boeing furnished leadership not only in jet-powered passenger and military aircraft, but also in other aspects of the AEROSPACE INDUSTRY. For a time during the 1960s more than 100,000 workers were employed in the Seattle area by this one corporation. Too much depended on the continued prosperity of one industry and one corporation, however. The cutback in government contracts in 1970 and the cancellation of the supersonic transport planes in 1971 reduced production and employment by nearly two-thirds, and once again depressionlike conditions existed in volatile Seattle. By 1973 the economy had improved dramatically. Seattle was once more relatively prosperous, aided by a tremendous burst of construction in the central business area and at the airport and by a restoration project in the pioneer district of the city.

See Robert L. Friedham, *The Seattle General Strike* (1964); Dorothy O. Johansen and Charles M. Gates,

Empire of the Columbia (1967); Murray Morgan, *Skid Road: An Informal Portrait of Seattle* (1951); Robert C. Nesbit, *He Built Seattle* (1961); Harvey O'Conner, *Revolution in Seattle* (1964); and Grant H. Redford, *That Man Thomson* (1950).—K. A. M.

Second Awakening. See REVIVALISM.

Sellers, Isaiah. See RIVERMEN.

Selman, John Henry (1839-1896). Outlaw and lawman. Selman was born in Arkansas and lived there until his large family moved to Grayson County, Texas, in 1858. When his father died, he became head of the family until December 1861, when he joined the Confederate army. His undistinguished career as a soldier ended with his desertion in 1863. He fled southwest to Fort Davis with his family. Early in 1864 he enlisted in the Texas State Militia. When the war was over, Selman married and moved to New Mexico for a short while and then returned to Texas and cattle raising near Fort Griffin. That was a turning point in Selman's life, for he soon fell under the influence of John Larn and the Fort Griffin Vigilance Committee. Larn and Selman were responsible for the lynching of more than twenty men before Larn was killed and Selman took the high road west.

He next turned up in New Mexico during the LINCOLN COUNTY WAR, where he became the leader of a gang of outlaws known as Selman's Scouts. Most of the gang had previously ridden with Jesse Evans in support of the Murphy-Dolan faction in the Lincoln County troubles. Selman himself was not directly involved as a partisan in the Lincoln County War. But after the conflict was climaxed in July 1878 by the death of Alexander McSween, leader of one of the factions, the Evans gang broke up and gradually came under the influence of Selman. Taking advantage of continuing violence and the absence of effective law enforcement, the gang launched a series of thefts, burnings, and killings. Then Lew Wallace became governor of New Mexico and issued an amnesty to both factions in the war. Selman's Scouts were not included, of course, because of the obvious criminal character of their operations; this increased the heat on Selman's gang. The final blow to Selman's New Mexico activities came when he fell victim to smallpox. In 1880 he was arrested and returned to Texas for crimes committed there.

He was soon released and in the 1880s showed up in El Paso, where he was a deputy sheriff and a constable. At El Paso he shot and killed Bass Outlaw, a former Texas Ranger and a generally reprehensible character. But Selman made enemies in El Paso as well. One of them was John Wesley Hardin, the famous Texas outlaw, who had come to El Paso after serving a lengthy prison sentence. The dispute between them grew out of the plight of an outlaw named Martin Morose, who retained Hardin as an attorney. When Hardin started living with Morose's wife, animosities resulted, and in June 1895 Morose was killed on the Mexican Central Railway bridge between El Paso and Juarez by lawmen, including George Scarborough and Jeff Milton. It was whispered around El Paso that Hardin had been involved in the killing. Thereafter, Hardin and Mrs. Morose continued their liaison, although the relationship became increasingly stormy (both were notorious drinkers). Some accounts say that when John Selman, Jr., old John's son, arrested Mrs. Morose, Hardin took offense and threatened the Selmans' lives. If that is true, and John Selman testified that it was, there was no outward appearance of animosity between them when, in August 1895, Selman stepped through the door of the Acme Saloon and shot John Wesley Hardin dead.

The Hardin shooting is the act for which Selman is generally remembered. He was charged with murder, but the trial ended with a hung jury in February 1896. The case was rescheduled for the next term of court, but John Selman was never retried. In April 1896 a drunken Selman walked into an alley with Deputy United States Marshal George Scarborough and was shot four times. The evidence suggests that he was murdered for comments he had made about Scarborough, although Scarborough claimed that Selman threatened to kill him. A witness testified at Scarborough's trial that he had found Selman's gun loaded and cocked in the alley. In any case, Scarborough was acquitted.

The Hardin and Selman deaths were probably related. Local citizens in a position to know always held that Hardin was killed because of the Morose shooting. They held that Morose was killed at the instigation of Hardin by a group that included Selman, Scarborough, and Milton. According to this version of the story, Selman killed Hardin because Hardin would not divide the money he had taken from Morose's body. Selman allegedly believed that Hardin did share the money with Scarborough and said so around town, sparking the argument that led to his death.

See Leon C. Metz, *John Selman: Texas Gunfighter* (1966).—G. L. R.

Seltzer, Olaf Carl (1877-1957). Painter and illustrator. Born in Copenhagen, Denmark, Seltzer showed remarkable talent in art as a youth and was admitted to an art institute in his native city at the age of twelve. Following the death of his father, he traveled with his mother to the United States in 1892 and settled in Great Falls, Montana, where he worked briefly as a ranch hand and was apprenticed as a machinist with the Great Northern Railroad. During this time he continued to sketch Indians, wild game, and various frontier characters, his productivity largely confined to pen and ink or pencil. In 1897 he met Charles M. Russell and thereafter spent a great deal of time with the elder artist at his studio or traveling about the countryside on sketching trips. Seltzer and Russell remained friends until Russell's death in 1926, following which Seltzer visited New York City and assumed several commissions for pictures from western art collectors. During the 1930s he worked almost exclusively for Dr. Phillip Gillett Cole of Tarrytown, New York, on a series of miniature oils documenting events in Montana history. Back in Great Falls, he continued to produce other series for Cole, some based upon earlier ideas outlined by Russell and almost all illustrative of characters or events in the history of the Old West. During World War II, Seltzer worked again as a machinist at the Great Falls Iron Works and taught lathe operation at a local high school.

During his lifetime Seltzer's work was exhibited in New York City, Chicago, Seattle, and Great Falls. He also painted a mural for the Masonic Lodge in Helena, Montana, and produced some pictures based upon Oriental and South American themes. The largest collection of his work, numbering in excess of 250 pieces, is owned by the Thomas Gilcrease Institute of American

Mission Priest *by O. C. Seltzer. (Thomas Gilcrease Institute)*

History and Art, Tulsa, Oklahoma, whose founder purchased them from the estate of Phillip Cole in 1944.

See Paul Rossi and David C. Hunt, *The Art of the Old West* (1971).—D. C. H.

Seminole Indians. See FIVE CIVILIZED TRIBES.

Seminole Wars (1816-1818, 1835-1847). In 1818 General Andrew Jackson entered Florida in command of American forces sent to allay disturbances along the old Creek frontier. The provocation of this so-called war were the aggressive activities of British and Spanish traders and the sanctuary the Indians gave to runaway black slaves from the border plantations (see NEGROES ON THE FRONTIER). The conflict in this area had grown in intensity since 1814. United States troops seeking fugitive slaves had destroyed "Fort Negro" on the Apalachicola River in 1816, and the Seminole and the blacks retaliated with raids on settlements. Jackson's campaign was to create both a serious diplomatic situation, because East Florida was still Spanish territory, and also a domestic political issue. These facts, however, had little bearing on Jackson's immediate activities. He and his troops chased the Seminole and their black allies into the swamps, fought in skirmishes, and became involved with the traders of the area. The most famous international incidents of this campaign were the hanging of the British traders Arbuthnot and Ambrister. The first Seminole War may have been an important fact in bringing about the conclusion of the ADAMS-ONIS TREATY of 1819. Jackson's raiding resulted in the burning of Indian villages west of the Suwannee River.

The first war failed to bring peace with the Seminole. Between 1820 and 1835 there were intermittent raids, and the constant friction along the swampy frontier of Florida Territory required the maintenance of armed protection in the region. The United States government refused Jackson's recommendation that the disgruntled Creek refugees from the Creek War of 1813-14 be removed from Florida. The causes of the second Seminole War were almost as numerous as the contacts between whites and Indians. Treacherous acts were committed on both sides.

Between 1835 and 1842 the war went on with considerable vigor. The Indians were led by clever people, the most important being OSCEOLA. More than a thousand Indian warriors and five to ten thousand American soldiers, sailors, and marines were engaged along the southern border. Brigadier General Thomas Sidney JESUP was in overall command of the United States troops, and by the end of 1836 he had achieved almost no appreciable results in his efforts to corner the Indians. On the other hand, the Seminole proved themselves a genuine threat. On December 28, 1835, Osceola and his braves slew 110 men of Brevet Major Langhorne Dade's command, and with them 5 white Indian agents.

The army was not able to make much headway, and public pressure led the military to adopt questionable tactics. United States'troops, and General Jesup in particular, did not cover themselves with glory in the flag of truce treachery, which resulted in the taking of Osceola on May 15, 1837. General Zachary Taylor took over as tactical commander in 1837 and began building a series of forts across the middle of Florida and into the boggy depths of the Kissimmee River and Lake Okeechobee. By systematically advancing against the Seminole and by taking a heavy toll of their forces by attrition, this phase of the war was eventually brought to a close, but not without the occurrence of several bloody incidents and attacks upon outlying plantations and the ambushing of supply trains.

The back of Seminole resistance was broken by the capture of Osceola and surrender of Jumper, a war leader of Yamasee descent, along with large numbers of their people. The Seminole War was not ended until 1843, but there were still constant outbreaks and border skirmishes until 1857. About three thousand troops were lost in the war, and the cost approximated $30 million. About four thousand Indians were moved west of the Mississippi. In 1857 the United States government made a cash settlement with Chief Billy Bowlegs and moved all but about 150 Seminoles from Florida to the western Indian Territory. Seminole descendants in Florida still pride themselves that their people could not be beaten and never surrendered, but instead had to be bought off by an exhausted white government.

See John Bemrose, *Reminiscences of the Second Seminole War*, ed. by John K. Mahon (1966); Holman Hamilton, *Zachary Taylor, Soldier of the Republic* (1941); Woodburne Potter, *The War in Florida* (1836); and Harry Errald Stafford, *The Early Inhabitants of the Americas* (1959). —T. D. C.

Seneca Indians. See IROQUOIS CONFEDERACY.

Sequoia and Kings Canyon national parks. Sequoia and Kings Canyon national parks adjoin each other in the southern reaches of California's Sierra Nevada mountain range. Indian tribes roamed through this area for hundreds of years: the Western Mono (Monache), the Tübatulabal, and the Owens valley Paiute lived in this part of the Sierra. White men drove them out in the 1850s and 1860s. The sequoia trees, the soaring redwoods that characterize this region, were discovered by Joseph R. Walker in 1833. The first white man to see the redwoods of the Giant Forest (in Sequoia National Park) was Hale Tharp, a cattleman and homesteader who was guided to the trees in 1858 by friendly Indians. In 1860 he and his stepson, John Swanson, explored much of the territory now included in the park. Beginning in 1861, Tharp pastured horses and a few cattle in the vicinity of the Giant Forest, living in a hollow redwood log that is still on display in the park. In 1873-75, John Muir explored the General Grant Grove and the Kings Canyon area, writing about his experiences and publicizing the big trees. The area was systematically explored for the first time by a survey expedition led by William H. Brewer in 1864.

Gold was discovered in the Kern River in 1854 and in Inyo County, to the east of the sequoia groves, in 1859. Prospectors swarmed through the region, but the mining boom was short-lived and caused little damage to the scenic terrain. Sheep-grazing and lumbering were more destructive. Many sequoia trees, including some of the finest specimens, were felled by commercial logging operations. But because most of the groves were inaccessible and the trees splintered when felled, redwood lumbering was seldom profitable. This fact undoubtedly saved the trees that are now in the park. The Kaweah Colony, a communitarian group, laid claim to the Giant Forest under the Timber and Stone Act, hoping to build a railroad into the area and develop its natural resources. These plans died aborning, but they received considerable publicity.

Public demand to preserve the big trees of the Kings and Kern watersheds began in the 1870s and accelerated as commercial operations of various kinds seemed to threaten them. George W. Stewart, the publisher and editor of the Visalia (Calif.) *Delta*, headed the drive in the 1880s that led to the establishment of Sequoia National Park on September 25, 1890. About a week later, Congress passed additional legislation setting aside General Grant National Park in the same region. The army administered these parks as a combined unit until World War I. The National Park Service has had jurisdiction over Sequoia National Park since 1916. General Grant National Park was later consolidated with Sequoia.

Kings Canyon National Park, which brought Mount Whitney and the beautiful Kings Canyon country into the park system, was established on March 4, 1940, after more than twenty years of tough political battling. Hydroelectric power developers, irrigationists, and sportsmen had opposed plans to make this area a national park. Secretary of the Interior Harold L. Ickes took a leading part in the final drive for congressional action to establish the park. He pledged that the area, which was essentially an extension of Sequoia National Park, would be administered as a primitive area, with a minimum of roads and public facilities.

The Sequoia-Kings Canyon region is one of remarkable beauty and diversity. It contains splendid redwood groves, spectacular gorges, Mount Whitney (14,495 feet), and the most rugged wilderness area in the south-

The Cherokee alphabet, devised by Sequoyah. (Library of Congress)

ern Sierra Nevada. Sequoia National Park includes 386,551 acres; Kings Canyon contains 454,650 acres. The parks may be entered via Visalia, California. —D. C. S.

Sequoyah (c. 1770-1843). Inventor of the Cherokee syllabary. Born in the Overhill Cherokee town of Tuskegee, near Fort Loudon on the Tennessee River, Sequoyah was beyond reasonable doubt the son of the Virginia trader, explorer, and soldier Nathaniel Gist.

Known by his Indian name as a youth, he later used his father's last name, which he understood to be Guess, and assumed the first name of George. He was reared by his mother, Wurteh, sister of the Cherokee chieftain Onitositah (Old Tassel). Although unschooled and never versed in English, Sequoyah demonstrated throughout his life an inquiring intelligence, practical genius, and reflective spirit that marked him as a man of great mental power.

As a young man, partially lamed by disease, he trained himself in the silversmith's art. He served with Cherokee volunteers under Andrew Jackson during the Creek campaign of 1813-14. In 1815 he married. Three years later, after having signed a removal treaty negotiated under questionable circumstances, he joined the first large Cherokee migration west and took up a small farm in present-day Pope County, Arkansas.

In Arkansas Sequoyah completed the work upon which rests his principal fame. According to later accounts, he had begun his efforts to devise a written form for the Cherokee language about 1809, speculating upon the mystery of the white man's "talking leaves." Slowly he worked on the problem, encountering skepticism and ridicule, until he hit upon the plan of providing a separate written character for each syllable in the spoken tongue. This plan he perfected by 1821, when he introduced a syllabary of eighty-six characters that could be mastered in a week or less. Once he secured the official endorsement of the Cherokee leadership on an eastern visit in 1821-22, Sequoyah's syllabary almost immediately came into wide popular use. In the words of one contemporary chronicler, "the whole nation became an academy for the study of the system."

The General Council of the Cherokee Nation, through arrangement with the American Board of Foreign Missions, purchased the first printing press in the Cherokee language in 1828. On this press a newspaper entitled the *Cherokee Phoenix* was brought out at New Echota that year, under the original editorship of Elias Boudinot. Although this press was subsequently seized by Georgia state authorities. publication of a Cherokee newspaper and other works were resumed in the 1840s after the nation's forced removal to the West.

Although he continued to live in humble circumstances, Sequoyah gathered honor for his accomplishment during the last decades of his life, and his prominence brought him again into public affairs. In 1828 he journeyed to Washington, D.C., a member of an Arkansas Cherokee treaty delegation, where he was acclaimed by national officials and had his portrait painted by Charles Bird King. The following year, in consequence of the 1828 relocation treaty, he moved again to a permanent home near Sallisaw in modern Sequoyah County, Oklahoma. When the remaining eastern Cherokee arrived in that country over the "trail of tears" in 1839, he joined efforts to soothe the strong rancor between various tribal factions. The Cherokee Act of Union, July 12, 1839, establishing one united government, bore his signature as "President of the Western Cherokee."

Sequoyah was guided to the last by an ambition to aid his people. In 1842, though not in good health, he set out with a son and another companion to find a Cherokee band that had earlier migrated to Mexico. After a long and trying journey they discovered their tribesmen living in a small town south of Matamoros. Sequoyah, enfeebled by disease, sent back the younger two men, and there among the Mexican Cherokee he died.

The Cherokee Nation first honored Sequoyah by striking a special medal for him in 1825, and in 1841 the Cherokee National Council voted him an allowance and special annuity. The state of Oklahoma placed his statue in the national capitol, and his farmstead is an Oklahoma state historical shrine. Among other tributes, his memory is also perpetuated in the genus name *Sequoia* for the California redwood trees.

The basic account is Grant Foreman's *Sequoyah* (1938), though additional details will be found in Grace Steele Woodward's *The Cherokees* (1963). A fanciful account of Sequoyah, based on spurious evidence and false assertions, appears in Traveller Bird, *Tell Them They Lie: The Sequoyah Myth* (1971).—K. N. O.

Serra, Junípero (1713-1784). Roman Catholic missionary. Serra was a native of the island of Majorca. After becoming a Franciscan in 1730, he taught philosophy at the university on that island. But he gave up this prestige and a promising future in 1749 to labor among the Indians of the New World. For Serra, martyrdom was the true "gold of the Indies." He worked for nine years with the Pame Indians in eastern Mexico and, in 1768, after serving as a circuit missionary, was made president of the Baja California missions.

Spain's General José de Gálvez, after surveying Baja California, planned an expedition to occupy Alta California. Religious supervision of that party was entrusted to the Franciscan order headed by Father Serra. Its military command was given to Gaspar de Portolá. In the inception and carrying out this plan for the occupation of California, Serra was figuratively at the right hand of Gálvez.

Serra's zeal brushed aside obstacles that would have stopped lesser men. One of the worst of them was his own frail health, aggravated by a lame leg, from which he suffered nearly all of his life. Public mortification of the flesh (such as flogging himself with a chain, beating his breast with a stone, and burning his body with candles) further damaged his health. When he set out on the 1769 expedition, he was so weak that it was necessary for two men to lift him into the saddle of his mule; but when his friend Father Francisco Palóu expressed discouragement at the sight, Serra gently rebuked him and insisted that with the aid of God he would reach Alta California and there raise the cross.

In addition to occupying the ports of San Diego and Monterey, Portolá and Serra hoped, in 1769, to establish other missions in Alta California. Church ornaments and sacred vessels did not constitute all of Serra's cargo, however. He also brought along flower and vegetable seeds from both the Old World and the New. These were to become the basis of Alta California's future mission gardens. Father Serra also arranged for the two land expeditions to take a herd of two hundred cattle from the northernmost mission of the Baja California peninsula.

On July 16, 1769, Serra founded SAN DIEGO DE ALCALA, the mission whose church was the first within the present state of California. Soon thereafter he joined Portolá on a northern expedition in search of the great landlocked harbor that Sebastián Vizcaíno had earlier described. Instead, they discovered San Francisco Bay. At tiny Carmel Bay, on their return to San Diego, the group set up a cross near the shore, with a letter buried at its base; if future ships should come into the vicinity they would thereby be informed that Portolá's expedition had been there. Success in locating Monterey Bay came after a second trip northward. On June 3, 1770, beneath the very oak tree where the Vizcaíno expedition had held religious services in 1602, Father Serra conducted a solemn mass. Amid the ringing of bells and salvos of artillery, he thus founded the second mission in Alta California and dedicated it to SAN CARLOS BOR-ROMEO. For convenience in obtaining wood and water, the mission was later removed to the little bay of Carmel, about four miles from Monterey. Carmel became Serra's headquarters until the end of his life.

Serra personally founded nine of California's string of twenty-one Franciscan missions, which ran from San Diego to Sonoma. These establishments were separated by about a day's travel on horseback—some thirty miles apart. El Camino Real, or the King's Highway, of modern tourist literature, was then scarcely more than a dusty path, the only trail from mission to mission. For Serra, teaching and introducing agricultural methods to Indians was a discouraging task. He pleaded for increased economic support of his work at the missions and for greater power in dealing with the military presidios. He also argued for an overland line of communication and supply from Mexico. His suggestions ultimately led to colonizing expeditions (including that of Juan Bautista de Anza) designed to support Spain's California colony.

In spite of his poor health and advanced age, Serra labored vigorously for his missions until his death at San Carlos Mission in Carmel, where he is buried. His friend, Father Palóu, wrote an extensive and enthusiastic biography of Serra that has helped to augment his stature in the history of the West. His statue in the National Statuary Hall in Washington, D.C., represents California. In recent years repeated attempts have been made to elevate Father Serra to sainthood in the Roman Catholic church.

See Maynard J. Geiger, *The Life and Times of Junípero Serra*, 2 vols. (1959).—A. R.

Sevier, Ambrose Hundley (1801-1848). Arkansas politician. Sevier was a Tennessean who settled in Arkansas Territory in 1821. A relative of the politically powerful Conway brothers, a son-in-law of federal judge Benjamin Johnson (whose brother Richard Mentor Johnson was vice president under Van Buren), and a skilled stump speaker, Sevier was elected delegate to Congress in 1827 in place of Henry Conway, who had been killed in a duel. He served until 1836, when he became Arkansas's first senator. He supported Van Buren's fiscal measures, Polk's expansionist program, and resigned in 1848 at Polk's request to go to Mexico to conclude negotiations with Mexico, a successful mission. He was defeated in a bid for reelection to the Senate that autumn. Ill from his rigorous trip to Mexico, he died a month later at his plantation in Chicot County. —W. L. B.

Sevier, John (1745-1815). Land speculator and Tennessee politician. Sevier, of French-English extraction, was born near the present town of New Market, Virginia. He was a precocious lad who at the age of sixteen married Sarah Hawkins and entered actively upon a career of merchandising and land speculation. He laid out the town of New Market, sold town lots, and operated a tavern. Between 1771 and 1772 he became interested in the lands on the Holston River in the rising Watauga settlements. In 1771 he·was elected to what came to be the WATAUGA ASSOCIATION, but he did not move to the settlements until 1772. Almost from the start of his move to the Watauga settlements, Sevier became an active leader.

John Sevier, as portrayed by Charles Willson Peale. (North Carolina Department of Archives and History)

Between 1776 and 1785 Sevier was a rampant Indian fighter, having fought in more than thirty battles against the Cherokee. In the battle of KINGS MOUNTAIN (1780) he was at the head of the "Men from the Holston," and shared with Isaac Shelby and William Campbell the honors of being a hero. Sevier, however, was more interested in politics and land speculation than in military glory. Because of his great interest in land speculation, Sevier allowed himself to be drawn into the SPANISH CONSPIRACY of the late 1780s. He hoped by gaining the favor of the Spanish official Esteban Miró to be able to establish a settlement about Muscle Shoals on the Tennessee River. He served as governor of the state of FRANKLIN and six terms as governor of Tennessee, was elected to four terms in Congress, and was one of the major figures in forming the state of Tennessee. In politics he was a Federalist, opposing the course of action taken by North Carolina in the ratification of the United States Constitution.

Sevier found himself in a long-drawn-out feud with Andrew JACKSON, which was rooted in Tennessee politics and land issues. His last important political expressions were in favor of the War of 1812. Sevier died in a tent deep in the Creek country of Alabama, where the magnetism of land had drawn him.

Sevier left behind him an extensive record of frontier activities. There is the highly romanticized story of his rescue of Catherine Sherrill in an Indian attack upon the fort at Watauga in 1777. This story, or most of it, overstates the facts. He did marry "Bonny Kate," however, and she supported him in his frontier activities. They had a large family of children (eighteen in all) with whom "Nolichucky Jack" was jovial and kind. To his friends and associates he appeared carefree, oblivious to danger, and able to endure the rough and tumble of the woods, the political debate, and the great gamble for land. In his running dispute with Jackson, Sevier demonstrated how vigorously he could deal with a political foe by use of any means at hand.

See Thomas Perkins Abernethy, *From Frontier to Plantation in Tennessee: A Study in Frontier Democracy* (1967); Carl S. Driver, *John Sevier, Pioneer of the Old Southwest* (1932); and J. G. M. Ramsey, *The Annals of Tennessee,* (1853).—T. D. C.

Shafroth, John Franklin (1854-1922). Colorado politician. Shafroth was born in Fayette, Missouri, of Swiss-German parentage. He earned a bachelor's degree at the University of Michigan in 1875 and was admitted to the bar a year later. He came to Denver in 1879, where he became a prominent lawyer and civil servant. He served as Denver city attorney from 1887 to 1891 and was a member of the United States House of Representatives from 1895 to 1904. In the House he championed woman suffrage and advocated the unlimited coinage of silver. With Henry M. Teller and others he helped found the Silver Republican party, which supported Democrat and silver spokesman William Jennings Bryan in the election of 1896. Endorsed by a fusion of Silver Republicans, Democrats, and Populists in the elections of 1896 and 1898, Shafroth later joined the Democratic party. He resigned his seat in 1904 after he determined that fraud had been committed by the Democrats in the contested 1902 election, in which he ran for the House. Shafroth subsequently served two terms as Democratic governor of Colorado, from 1909 to 1913, during which time a number of progressive reforms, such as a direct primary law, initiative, and referendum, were enacted. From 1913 to 1919 he represented Colorado in the United States Senate, where he supported President Woodrow Wilson's policies. Defeated for reelection in 1918, he completed his public service as administrator of the War Materials Relief Act.

E. K. MacColl has treated Shafroth's years as governor in "John Franklin Shafroth, Reform Governor of Colorado, 1909-1913," *Colorado Magazine* (January 1952). Biographical sketches are in James Baker and LeRoy R. Hafen, eds., *History of Colorado*, vol. V (1927); and Jerome Smiley, *Semi-Centennial History of the State of Colorado,* vol. II (1913).—M. B.

Shakers. Out of revivals in Manchester, England, conducted by refugee French Camisards in 1747, came a small pentecostal group called Shaking Quakers or Shakers. The name derived from the physical responses characteristic of their emotion-charged form of public worship. Ann Lee (1736-1784), illiterate daughter of a Manchester blacksmith, joined the movement in 1758. A mystical experience while in prison for "profanation of the sabbath" caused her to be accepted as the prophetess of the Shakers. She, with a small group of followers, came to New York City in 1774. After two years of working at washing and ironing in the city, "Mother" Ann moved to a property that more affluent members of her group had purchased at Niskeyuna (later Watervliet) near Albany, New York. There Mother Ann continued to have visions and revelations concerning the conduct of the "Church."

In the summer of 1779 a highly emotional revival among New Light Baptists in the frontier towns of New Lebanon, New York, and Hancock, Massachusetts, persuaded the participants that the second coming of Christ was at hand. In the following spring, after the excitement had sputtered out, two disillusioned New Light leaders struck out for the West in search of new fortunes. They paused by chance at Niskeyuna and fell under the spell of Mother Ann. The meeting led to the later appearance at Niskeyuna of a Baptist delegation from New Lebanon. The Americanization of the Shaker movement had begun. In 1787, four years after the death of Mother Ann, the first Shaker society was founded at New Lebanon. The second came quickly at Watervliet. Before her death Mother Ann, who had become known as a faith healer, had traveled in Massachusetts and Connecticut making disciples. The New Lebanon Society sent three of them to Kentucky at the time of the camp meeting revivals, which reached their climax in the years from 1800 to 1802. This outthrust resulted in the founding of five Shaker communities in Kentucky, Ohio, and Indiana.

Each Shaker "family," which lived and worked together as a communal group, was made up of men, women, and adopted children and numbered from thirty to ninety persons. Shakers did not condemn marriage but declared their celibate and communal societies, withdrawn from the world, to be the expression of Christ's Kingdom on the earth. The Shakers worshiped a Father-Mother God. They called themselves "The United Society of Believers in Christ's Second Appearing" or, more simply, "The Millennial Church." In Jesus the male principle of Christ had appeared on earth. In the person of Ann Lee the female principle of Christ, the "second coming," moved among men and prepared the way for the emergence of the Kingdom. The Shaker worship consisted of marching, dancing, hymn singing, and "speaking with tongues." The members of the sect wrote their own hymns and devised the routines of their marches and dances. "We believed," said the Shaker Covenant of 1795, "that we were debtors to God in relation to each other, and all men, to improve our time and Talents in this Life in that manner in which be most useful."

Agriculture provided the economic base of the first Shaker families. Later the Shakers developed handicrafts and in time their furniture achieved fame for its quality and design. Between 1787 and 1794 the Shakers established eleven communities in New York and New England, one being on the northern frontier in New Hampshire. Shaker evangelists preached beside those of the Presbyterians, Methodists, and Baptists at the spectacular Cane Ridge camp meeting in Kentucky in 1801. In the nineteenth century the Shakers created seven communities in Ohio, Kentucky, and Indiana. The movement reached its zenith in the 1850s, when the sect numbered some six thousand adherents. A century later Shakerism was approaching extinction. Even so, the Shakers had the longest history of successful operation of any of the communal societies that appeared in the United States.

See E. D. Andrews, *The People Called Shakers: A Search for the Perfect Society* (1953).—R. H. G.

Shambaugh, Benjamin Franklin (1871-1940). Political scientist and historian. Shambaugh was born at Elvira, Iowa, and received his bachelor and master of arts degrees from the University of Iowa. In 1895 he earned a doctorate in political science from the University of Pennsylvania and did further graduate study in Germany. Shambaugh then returned to Iowa to accept a professorship in political science at the University of Iowa; a short time later he was named head of the department. He spent the remainder of his life in Iowa serving in the dual role as head of the political science department and superintendent and editor of the state historical society of Iowa.

During the more than forty years that Shambaugh was head of his department, he played an active national role within his academic discipline. He was a founding member of the American Political Science Association and was elected its president in 1930. He was on the committee that established the *American Political Science Review* and was one of the founders of the Mississippi Valley Historical Association.

Shambaugh believed deeply in the relevance of studies in state and local history, and his scholarly work engendered interest in and respect for these fields of history. Under his skillful guidance, the state historical society was reorganized and developed into a research society that achieved a national reputation. Shambaugh edited many works while serving as editor of the historical society; included are the *Iowa Biographical Series* (1907-39); *Iowa Economic History Series* (1910-28); and *Iowa Applied History Series* (1912-30). He wrote several books of which *The Old Stone Capitol Remembers* (1939) was the most popular. Upon his recommendations the society began publication of the *Iowa Journal of History and Politics* in 1903 and *The Palimpsest* in 1920.

Shambaugh's interests and activities are related in the memorial publication *Benjamin Franklin Shambaugh, as Iowa Remembers Him* (1941).—D. S.

Sharkey, William Lewis (1793-1873). Mississippi judge and politician. Born in East Tennessee, Sharkey moved at an early age to the Old Natchez District in Mississippi. Although he opposed the principle of an elective judiciary, claiming that the judges should be above the whims and caprices of the people, he was elected to the first High Court of Errors and Appeals, formed under Mississippi's constitution of 1832. His colleagues on this court selected him for chief justice, an office he held continuously until his retirement from the court in 1851.

During the 1850s Sharkey fought constantly against the secessionists and served briefly as consul-general in Cuba. Under an act of the legislature, he was appointed a member of a three-man committee to revise, digest, and codify the laws of the state. As Mississippi's most outstanding Whig, he took no part in either the state or Confederate governments during the Civil War.

On June 13, 1865, President Andrew Johnson appointed Sharkey provisional governor of Mississippi. The facts that in 1863 he had taken the oath of allegiance to the United States and that he came from East Tennessee, Johnson's birthplace, made him a likely choice. Also, he had been one of the most active anti-secessionists in Mississippi before 1861. He was given the difficult task of executing President Johnson's plan of reconstruction. He had the support of pre-Civil War Union Whigs as well as conservatives who feared for their lives and property if crimes and disorders continued; too, they preferred a reconstruction plan to

military rule. But the state government established under Sharkey's supervision and according to President Johnson's instructions was rejected by Congress in December 1865. Thus Sharkey never became United States senator, the post he had been elected to by the legislature in 1865.

See William C. Harris, *Presidential Reconstruction in Mississippi* (1967); and John R. Skates, Jr., *History of the Mississippi Supreme Court, 1817-1948* (1973).—J. E. G.

Sharp, Joseph Henry (1859-1953). Painter. Sharp was born in Bridgeport, Ohio. Enrolled at the McMicken School of Design in Cincinnati, Ohio, at the age of fourteen, he spent the next several years in the pursuit of his art studies, traveling periodically to Europe to advance his education. In 1883 he made his first trip into the American West, passing by way of Santa Fe, New Mexico, and Tucson, Arizona, to the West Coast. Impressed by the western country in general and its aboriginal inhabitants in particular, Sharp made many studies of Indian life and thereafter was in the West whenever the opportunity presented itself. He returned to Europe in 1886 and by 1892 was an instructor at the Cincinnati Art Museum, where he taught life drawing during the winter months for the next ten years. He visited Taos, New Mexico, for the first time in 1893 and was back again in Paris from 1894 to 1896. During this time he became acquainted with two other American students, Bert Phillips and Ernest Blumenschein, who with Sharp later formed what came to be known as the Taos Society of Artists at the beginning of the twentieth century. Sharp exhibited in the Paris Exposition of 1900 and attracted considerable notice for his Indian subjects. Shortly thereafter, the federal government commissioned him to paint a series of Indian life studies for its permanent collection at the Smithsonian Institution.

Sharp's first studio in the West was an old sheep herder's wagon set up on the site of the Custer battlefield in Montana. In 1901 President Theodore Roosevelt built him a cabin near the Crow agency in this same vicinity. Here Sharp spent a number of months for the next few seasons painting Indian scenes and portraits. One of the more important series produced at this time involved the painting of the portraits of more than two hundred warriors reputed to have taken part in the Custer defeat at the Little Big Horn in 1876.

In 1902 Sharp resigned his post at the Cincinnati Academy and began touring all through the western states. He spent several months each year in and around Taos but did not settle there permanently until 1909, when he acquired a studio across the street from the old Kit Carson residence. Although he considered Taos his home from that time, Sharp did a great deal of traveling abroad, making extended trips to the Orient and to Hawaii, where he executed a number of landscapes and still lifes. During the last few years of his life he maintained a winter home in Pasadena, California, where he died.

Sharp is remembered chiefly as the founder of the Taos art colony and for his paintings of Indian culture, which have earned him the respect of historians and ethnologists alike. Sharp's approach to art was based upon direct observation. He took great care with the portrayal of particulars and was fond of using strong color to produce contrast or dramatic effect. A realist in style, he was a romanticist in concept.

Sharp is represented by collections in the Bureau of Ethnology of the Smithsonian Institution, Washington, D.C.; the Thomas Gilcrease Institute of American History and Art, Tulsa, Oklahoma; Woolaroc Museum, Bartlesville, Oklahoma; the Stark Museum of Art, Orange, Texas; the department of anthropology, University of California at Berkeley; Fine Arts Museum, Santa Fe, New Mexico; and the Cincinnati Art Museum, Cincinnati, Ohio.

See Mabel Dodge Luhan, *Taos and Its Artists* (1947); and Robert Taft, *Artists and Illustrators of the Old West, 1850-1900* (1953).—D. C. H.

Shawnee Indians. The Shawnee were an Algonquian tribe that apparently migrated from the North into the Cumberland River valley of Tennessee not long before the white man's arrival. The tribe consisted of many subdivisions that moved from Tennessee at different times and in different directions during the late seventeenth and eighteenth centuries. Some went to Georgia and Alabama, but most settled in eastern Pennsylvania and New York and in southeastern Ohio between 1678 and 1730. The eastern bands attached themselves to the English interest, but colonial encroachments on their lands drove them westward about 1750 to join their kinsmen on the upper Ohio.

From this time onward they were the most constant and active opponents of the English and Americans in this part of the continent. Under CORNSTALK they sided with the French in 1754 and raided frontier settlements in Pennsylvania. They continued to do so sporadically after the French had been expelled (1763), taking part in LORD DUNMORE'S WAR of 1774 and fighting American armies that invaded their territory in the 1780s and 1790s. In 1795 they were forced to surrender their lands on the Miami River of southwestern Ohio, some retiring to northern Ohio and Indiana and others moving to Missouri. In 1811 under TECUMSEH and TENSKWATAWA, they resisted the whites once more and were defeated in the battle of TIPPECANOE. They sided with the British in the War of 1812, which produced their final defeat. Between 1825 and 1845 most of the Ohio and Missouri Shawnee moved to Kansas and later to Oklahoma, where they became incorporated largely into other tribes.

The Shawnee were a numerous people, but their fragmentation has made population estimates extremely difficult. They numbered at least three thousand in 1650 and perhaps half that number since the eighteenth century.

See F. W. Hodge, *Handbook of American Indians North of Mexico*, 2 vols. (1907-10); A. P. Nasatir, *Before Lewis and Clark* (1952); and Glenn Tucker, *Tecumseh: Vision of Glory* (1956).—A. W. T.

Shawnee Prophet. See TENSKWATAWA.

sheep ranching. Sheep ranching got its start in the United States in 1598 when Juan de Oñate and a group of colonizers drove a herd of approximately one thousand ewes and rams into New Mexico. In time it became the principal industry of the BASQUES in all the northern Spanish provinces in the New World. Along with cattle and goats, sheep remained the chief economic support of the far-flung missions that extended from San Francisco to San Antonio. Even so, quality gradually deteriorated by 1800, until one animal could produce no more than two pounds of wool annu-

ally. The most common breed in the Southwest before the arrival of the Anglo-Americans was the Chaurro, a lean and gaunt creature who was resistant to many diseases and capable of subsisting on semidesert plants. Unfortunately, its flesh was tough and stringy.

Spanish missionaries encouraged sheep ranching among the southwestern Indians, and the Navaho adjusted especially well to the industry. As Anglo-Americans drifted in they found the idea of herding sheep degrading, refused to eat the mutton, and generally treated the Mexican and Indian herders with contempt. Thus, as late as 1900 some two dozen native New Mexican families controlled four fifths of the sheep in the entire territory.

Meanwhile, the American Merino was introduced into the Southwest from Kentucky in 1859 and was soon crossbred with the Chaurro. The result was a heavier animal capable of producing four pounds of wool each year, hardy enough to withstand the rigors of the climate, yet tender enough to eat. During the next several decades new strains were introduced, including the Cotswold, Southdown, Shropshire, Lincoln, and Rambouillet. Improved flavor of the meat, increased annual wool clip per animal, and the demand for choice lambs on the eastern markets contributed to the expansion of sheep raising throughout the trans-Mississippi West.

Soon after the discovery of gold in California, Miguel Otero and Antonio JoséLuna drove a flock of approximately twenty-five thousand sheep from New Mexico into the San Joaquin valley. Following this successful example, Kit Carson, Lucien Maxwell, "Uncle Dick" Wootton, and other Anglo-Americans delivered thousands of sheep from the Santa Fe area to the mining camps of the Sierra Nevada. Most of the half-million head driven from New Mexico during the decade of the 1850s followed trails along the Gila River through present Arizona, or along a more northerly route via present Las Vegas and the Mojave Desert. Various trails across Utah and Nevada were infrequently used but offered limited supplies of good water.

Sheep were brought to other areas of the West before the Civil War, but mostly for breeding rather than for food supply. A sizable industry already had shifted from New England to Ohio, Indiana, Michigan, and Illinois by the 1840s. During the same decade immigrants moving into Oregon Territory brought improved varieties of rams and ewes to supplement the approximately six thousand head introduced earlier by the Hudson's Bay Company. Mormon determination for self-sufficiency likewise contributed to the development of a sheep industry throughout the Great Basin.

Following the Civil War the western livestock industry expanded rapidly beyond its regional orientation. The postwar years, which witnessed the opening of the famous cattle trails from Texas to Kansas railheads, was also a period during which sheep trails spread throughout the West. They generally followed ill-defined paths along east-west lines rather than the well-defined routes northward from Texas that characterized the cattle industry. Although Pacific Coast stockmen continued to import superior strains, by the 1880s they were shipping more lambs and ewes eastward than they were importing. As the virgin pasture lands received ever-increasing flocks from California, Oregon, and Texas, midwestern ranchers and farmers likewise began to take advantage of the nutritious grasslands of the Rocky Mountains and Great Plains.

Improvements in transportation helped augment the spread of the sheep industry throughout the vast region beyond the Mississippi. Wherever railroads crossed the frontier, they facilitated the shipment of mutton and wool. With eastern markets more readily accessible, sheepmen increased production and thus further undermined a rapidly declining business in the older states. At the same time railroads gradually replaced the overland sheep trails. Few of them were still being used by the end of the nineteenth century, except those that ran from pastures and ranches to the loading pens.

Western sheep ranching during the 1880s lent itself to the same kind of get-rich-quick schemes that troubled the cattle industry. Private investors, railroad companies, and fledgling town builders distributed pamphlets praising the suitability of certain range lands for sheep production. Such propaganda enticed herders from worn-out lands in the East as well as capital from Europe. James Brisbin, a leading proponent of the American cattle business, admitted in 1880 that sheep ranching represented a more lucrative investment than either horse or cattle production.

Because sheep had to be more closely supervised than cattle, investors escaped some of the economic disaster that accompanied the harsh winters of 1886-88 on the northern Plains. President Grover Cleveland's elimination of the protective tariff on wool in 1894, however, brought the boom period of the industry to a dramatic halt. Faced with foreign competition, wool producers in Idaho, Wyoming, and Montana especially suffered financial losses until the policy was reversed by the protective Dingley Tariff of 1897.

Cattle ranchers objected strongly at first to the incursion of sheep and argued that they cropped the grass too short and ruined the water holes for the cattle. They also held deep-seated prejudices against the Basque and Mexican shepherds, and relations between cattlemen and sheepmen frequently resulted in bloody confrontations. The GRAHAM-TEWKSBURY FEUD began in the Tonto Basin of Arizona in 1887 and by the time it ended five years later approximately thirty men had been killed, including every male member of the Graham family. During the same period in Wyoming, cowboys on one occasion drove more than ten thousand sheep into the mountains, where they subsequently were destroyed by wolves. Another group drove twelve thousand sheep plunging to their death over a cliff.

Sheep ranchers eventually gained the advantage over cattlemen, primarily because prices for mutton and wool remained fairly stable in comparison to those for beef. In addition, sheep were more prolific than cattle and could exist on sparsely covered rangelands and withstand extremes of climate. By 1900 many who had previously ridiculed the animals were engaging in the industry, which then involved more than thirty million sheep in the various western states and territories.

Throughout many parts of the West today the production of sheep far exceeds that of cattle. This is especially true in New Mexico, Arizona, Utah, Idaho, Nevada, and in the vast Edwards Plateau region of western Texas. Colorado, Wyoming, and Montana also produce substantial quantities of wool and mutton. In these and other sections where blizzards and predatory animals are common, it is necessary to maintain smaller flocks and to provide shelter pens. Such care increases the cost of production but also increases the quality of the wool and mutton.

Westerners have been reluctant to break with traditional Spanish practices, particularly in sections where government lands and open range still exist. Work on the larger operations originally was divided among four types of employees. The lowest in rank was the *pastor*, assisted by one or more dogs, who kept watch over a flock of 1,000 to 1,500 sheep. Supervising two or three *pastores* was a *vaquero*, who selected the watering places and the areas to be grazed for the day. A *caporal* had charge of several *vaqueros*, and a *major-domo* supervised the *caporales* and accepted responsibility for the entire activity. This system has changed very little in many parts of the West during the past century or more.

In regions such as the Edwards Plateau in Texas, where the ranches are fenced into several pastures, the work today is done by cowboys. They patrol the fences on horseback or in pick-up trucks, repair windmills, doctor the diseased animals, and watch for signs of predatory animals. The "marking" (castration) of the lambs is generally supervised by the owner, but the shearing is always done by highly skilled, itinerant crews with mechanical equipment.

Despite the numerous parallels between the life of a cowboy and that of a sheepherder, the latter has not won much esteem in history or folklore. Yet both shared a life of frequent isolation, attacks by Indians or rustlers, and constant struggles with the natural elements. Perhaps the sheepherder is less glorified because he originally was forced to abandon the horse and to conduct most of his duties on foot. Novelists ignored him but transformed the cowboy's image into that of a romantic knight on horseback. Robbed of praise and nobility, the sheepman has practically become a forgotten entity in popular conception of the American West.

The sheep industry is still important, especially in the mountains and arid regions and on the Indian reservations. Low wages and loneliness makes it difficult to hire dependable shepherds, and many ranchers use Mexican "wetbacks." Dogs are still important and more often than not the shepherd carries a transistor radio, sleeps and eats in a pick-up camper, and receives his supplies by jeep, airplane, or helicopter. Impressive as these operations appear, many sheep are raised throughout the West in small herds. The owner performs much of the work himself and does not depend exclusively for his living upon the production of wool and mutton.

See Charles W. Towne and Edward N. Wentworth, *Shepherd's Empire* (1945); and Edward N. Wentworth, *America's Sheep Trails* (1948).—W. E. H.

Shelby, Isaac (1750-1826). Kentucky politician and soldier. Shelby was born near North Mountain in Frederick County, Virginia, to Evan and Laetitia Cox Shelby. As a youth Shelby worked in Virginia and what is now Tennessee as a deputy sheriff and surveyor. He was one of the first surveyors for the Transylvania Company of Kentucky.

Shelby's long and honorable military career began before the American Revolution, during General Andrew Lewis' Indian campaign of 1774. His services during the War of Independence brought him national fame and the thanks of the Continental Congress. In

July 1780, upon hearing of the fall of Charleston, he raised a force of volunteers for Colonel Charles McDowell. In August of that same year, following the news of Gates's disastrous defeat at Camden, he cooperated with Colonel John Sevier and others in the campaign that led to the battle of KINGS MOUNTAIN, October 8, 1780. Shelby was also credited with the plan of battle that resulted in the victory at Cowpens, January 17, 1781.

Early in 1783, after serving two terms in the North Carolina Assembly, Shelby moved to Lincoln County, Kentucky, then part of the western region of Virginia. That same year he married Susanna Hart, by whom he had eleven children. In Kentucky Shelby served as high sheriff of Lincoln County and attended the four conventions (1784, 1787, 1788, 1789) that led to independent statehood. During the convention of 1792 he helped frame the Kentucky constitution and was elected governor in May by an almost unanimous vote.

As Kentucky's first governor, Shelby faced a series of unprecedented problems, particularly that posed by Spanish unwillingness to relinquish control of the Mississippi River. In dealing with the situation he followed a moderate course that frustrated speculators and political opportunists alike. On one occasion, only the exercise of great firmness prevented the declaration of open warfare against the Spanish by the angry residents of the state. During his tenure of office, the Kentucky militia participated in General Anthony Wayne's Indian campaigns in the Northwest Territory. After a successful term, Shelby declined reelction in 1796 and retired to his home for the next fifteen years.

With the approach of war with Great Britain in 1812, Shelby came out of retirement and was elected for a second four-year term as governor. He personally led four thousand Kentucky volunteers north to join General William Henry Harrison's Northwest expedition, which decisively defeated the British at the battle of the THAMES, October 5, 1813. Shelby was appointed secretary of war by President Monroe in March 1817 but declined the position because of age. The following year he performed his final public service, concluding a treaty with the Chickasaw Indians for the purchase of their lands in western Tennessee.

Throughout his career, Shelby proved himself repeatedly to be a courageous, resourceful, and intelligent leader. So great was his reputation that at his death he was mourned along with Adams and Jefferson as one of the greatest patriots of the American Revolution.

See Archibald Henderson, "Isaac Shelby, Revolutionary Patriot and Border Hero," *North Carolina Booklet,* vols. 16 (1917) and 17 (1918); and Shelby Manuscripts, Library of Congress.—E. H. S.

Sheridan, Philip Henry (1831-1888). Soldier. Sheridan was born in New York and reared in Ohio. He was graduated in 1853 from West Point, thirty-fourth in a class of forty-nine, and served in Texas, California, and the Northwest. His rapid advancement during the Civil War was based on his record in Tennessee and Virginia, and he attracted attention for his role at Chattanooga, Cedar Run, and Petersburg. Following the war he was sent to the Division of the Gulf, and his moral and material support to the Republicans in Mexico helped bring the collapse of Maximilian's regime in that country. His harsh rule as commander of the Fifth Military District (Texas and Louisiana) inspired the hatred of southerners and a charge of "absolute tyranny" from President Andrew Johnson, who relieved him of command.

In August 1867, immediately following his six-month period of command in the South, Sheridan went to the Department of the Missouri and added the innovation of a winter campaign to Plains warfare, in the battle of the WASHITA. Sheridan's philosophy was to advance in force into the heart of the country of the Kiowa, Comanche, and Southern Cheyenne when not expected. His multicolumn campaign brought temporary peace with these tribes. In 1869 he was promoted to lieutenant general and moved on to command the Division of the Missouri, which embraced the entire Plains region.

A forceful commander who felt less sympathy for the Indians than did some other officers, Sheridan believed that military control of the reservations was essential and that Indians should be punished for misdeeds. Sheridan is occasionally accused of saying, "The only good Indians I ever saw were dead" (the apparent source of the aphorism "The only good Indian is a dead Indian"), but it is unlikely that the comment, any more than the sentiment, originated with Sheridan. He was, in any case, an able administrator and directed and coordinated the large campaigns against the southern Plains tribes in 1874-75 and against the Sioux in 1876-77.

Sheridan became commander-in-chief of the army in 1883 and was promoted to general in 1888.

See Carl C. Rister, *Border Command: General Phil Sheridan in the West* (1944). The Philip H. Sheridan Papers are in the Library of Congress.—R. N. E.

Sherman, William Tecumseh (1820-1891). Soldier. Sherman was born in Ohio and was graduated from West Point in 1840, sixth in his class. He saw little action in the Mexican War and resigned from the army in 1853 to go into banking and then law with little success. He was superintendent of a military college in Louisiana before rejoining the Union army in 1861. He came into his own at Shiloh; his Atlanta campaign and march through Georgia are the best-known aspects of his Civil War career.

From 1866 to 1869 Sherman commanded the Division of the Missouri, which embraced the Plains country. He protected the lines of travel, especially railroads then under construction, and arranged the defenses in this region while the army was being reduced. Sherman was critical of the Bureau of Indian Affairs and favored the transfer of Indian management to the Department of War, and as a member of the peace commission of 1867 he influenced its final report. Sherman believed that atrocities commited by Indians justified punishment and that the Indians must be placed on reservations and forced to remain there. He put his philosophy into effect in the RED RIVER WAR. When secretaries of war John Rawlins and W. W. Belknap attempted to limit Sherman's power and authority as general of the army (1869-84), he felt powerless and humiliated and thus moved his headquarters from Washington, D.C., to St. Louis from 1874 to 1876. Nevertheless, until his retirement in 1884, Lieutenant General Sherman continued to influence military policies in the West. He refused offers to run for president and died in New York.

See Robert G. Athearn, *William Tecumseh Sherman*

Luke Short (rear center) is surrounded by the rest of the "Dodge City Peace Commissioners": (left to right) Charles Bassett, W. H. Harris, Wyatt Earp, L. McLean, Bat Masterson, and Neal Brown. (National Archives)

and the Settlement of the West (1956). The Sherman papers are in the Library of Congress.—R. N. E.

Short, Luke L. (1854-1893). Gambler and gunman. Short was two years old when his parents left Mississippi for Texas. He grew up in northeast Texas in an area exposed to Comanche and Kiowa raiders. In 1870 he headed north to Kansas as a cowhand, and for the next five years drifted about Kansas peddling whiskey and learning the gambler's trade. In 1876 he opened a trading post in northern Nebraska near the Dakota line and dispensed whiskey to the Sioux, a crime for which he was reportedly arrested some time between 1876 and 1878. He escaped military arrest en route to Omaha, it is said. What happened next is obscure. He may have visited Denver for a time, but he was back in Nebraska by the fall of 1878, apparently without fear of military arrest since he served briefly as a scout for the army against Dull Knife's Cheyenne. Afterward he left Nebraska for Leadville, Colorado, and a new way of life.

From that point on, Short's future and fortunes were tied to the pasteboards. He soon turned up in Dodge City, Kansas, where he worked as a gambler at the Long Branch Saloon and acquired a taste for fancy clothes. In 1881 he followed his friends, Wyatt Earp and Bat Masterson, to Tombstone, Arizona, where he worked as a dealer in the Oriental Saloon. In February 1881 he quarreled with a gambler named Charlie Storms over a card game. Bat Masterson prevented immediate gunplay, but Storms accosted Short later the same day, and Short killed him in the fight that followed. He was subsequently exonerated of criminal intent at a formal hearing, but the shooting was enough to make him leave Tombstone and return to his old haunts at Dodge City.

He took his old job at the Long Branch Saloon in August 1882, and early in 1883 bought an interest in the business. But times were changing. Prohibiton was coming to Kansas, if not to Dodge City, and a reform element had already emerged in opposition to an older political group composed largely of saloonkeepers and gamblers known locally as the Gang. By friendship with men like James H. "Dog" Kelley, Bat Masterson, and W. H. Harris, his partner in the Long Branch, Short was associated with the Gang. The "reform" mayor, A. B. Webster, pushed through a series of ordinances designed to regulate saloons and dance halls. While many applauded the new moral code, others quickly pointed out that the laws were not fairly enforced. After all, many of the reformers, including Mayor Webster, were saloonkeepers, and Webster's chief business rivals were Harris and Short.

In the spring of 1883 the reform faction won the local elections again with Lawrence E. Deger, Webster's handpicked successor, defeating W. H. Harris, Short's partner, for the office of mayor. Within two weeks after Deger's election ordinances against prostitution and vagrancy were passed, and it soon became apparent that there were personal as well as political motives behind the ordinances. The first attempts to enforce the ordinances were directed against the Long Branch. Had the laws been fairly enforced, nothing would probably have come of it, but by singling out Luke Short's establishment, Webster, Deger, and company sparked the Dodge City War.

Late in April 1883, three girl "singers" who worked at the Long Branch were arrested for violation of the ordinance against prostitution. Short and Harris were infuriated, not because they thought the women were innocent but because other women of similar occupation were employed in the saloons of ex-Mayor Webster and his associates. Luke took to the streets in a rage, ran into L. C. Hartman, the officer who arrested the prostitutes at the Long Branch, and exchanged shots with him. In his haste to depart Hartman tripped and fell. Short thought he had killed the lawman and retreated to the safety of a nearby saloon. Later that night he was arrested on charges filed by Hartman and then released on bond. When word reached Luke that the reform element was organizing a vigilante group, he swore he would resist them. Learning of this, Deger had Short and six others arrested, escorted to the depot, and put on a train.

Luke headed for Kansas City and then Topeka, where he laid his case before the governor and the newspapers. There followed a profusion of correspondence between Topeka and Dodge City. The governor was bombarded with petitions and telegrams from both sides. The governor refused to send troops to defend Dodge City and listened patiently to both sides. When it became apparent that the governor would not interfere, Luke made his move to reestablish himself. He contacted Bat Masterson and Wyatt Earp and planned his strategy with them. By that time the governor was so confused he sent the adjutant general to Dodge for a first-hand report. The Dodge City group were watching the trains from the east, so Earp, Doc Holliday, Rowdy Joe Lowe, Shotgun Collins, and others began to drift into town. Early in June, escorted by Masterson and Earp, Short returned to Dodge. Faced with formidable fire power, the reformers compromised, and Luke was again a first-class citizen of Dodge City. In high spirits, Short, Harris, Earp, Masterson, and others posed for a photograph that has always been identified as the Dodge City Peace Commission.

Short had won, but things were not the same after that. In November he and Harris put the Long Branch up for sale, and Short left Dodge for Fort Worth, Texas, where he acquired an interest in the White Elephant Saloon. In February 1887 he shot and killed "Long-haired Jim" Courtright, a detective and former lawman who demanded protection money from local saloon-keepers. Short lived quietly after that. In 1890 he was wounded in one last gunfight, an affair without fatal results for either Luke or his assailant, a gambler named Charles Wright. Shortly after he recovered, he became ill and went to Geuda Springs, Kansas, for treatment and died there.

William R. Cox, *Luke Short and His Era* (1961) is the only biography. Also helpful are Robert R. Dykstra, *The Cattle Towns* (1968); Nyle M. Miller and Joseph W. Snell, *Why the West Was Wild* (1963); and Dale T. Schoenberger, *The Gunfighters* (1972).—G. L. R.

Shortridge, Eli C. D. (1819-1098). North Dakota politician. In 1892 Shortridge became governor of North Dakota on the Independent-Populist ticket, which promised to attack the corporate control of North Dakota. A Larimore farmer and a long-time member of the Farmers' Alliance, Shortridge advocated a state-owned terminal elevator and railroad legislation to improve the position of Dakota farmers.

The state legislature wasted most of the time in haggling over the election of a senator for the state. The documents containing Shortridge's major reforms, passed on the last day of the session, were mysteriously lost or stolen before they reached the governor's desk. Unfortunately Shortridge's term in office coincided with the Panic of 1893, and the ensuing depression nearly bankrupted the state treasury. The forces that had merged to elect Shortridge in 1892 split apart in 1894, ending any hope of political reform. —D. J. T.

Shoshoni Indians . The Shoshoni, who lived mostly in central Wyoming and southern Idaho in the nineteenth century, were the rear guard of the extensive Uto-Aztecan migration from Asia that began about two thousand years ago. About 1700 the Shoshoni occupied a strip of land east of the Rocky Mountains from the Bow River in Alberta southward into central Wyoming. They also held all of the upper Missouri drainage in southwestern Montana, all of southern Idaho, some of which they shared with the Bannock, and northern Utah. Several small hunting bands, entirely separate from the larger bands, ranged through the high desert plateau of northern Nevada (see INDIANS OF THE GREAT BASIN). This widely scattered people, several thousand in all, were united only by a common language.

About 1690 the Shoshoni along the Bear River in northern Utah and in the upper Snake River country in southeastern Idaho secured horses from the Spanish settlements of New Mexico with the help of the intervening Navaho and Ute. On their good rangelands the Shoshoni raised large horse herds, supplying animals to their brethren across the continental divide on the upper Missouri, then to the bands east of the Rocky Mountains as far north as Alberta. They also supplied horses, often unwillingly, to all their neighbors from the Columbia Basin tribes to the northwest, the Flathead and Blackfoot to the north and the Crow to the east. At about the time that the Shoshoni secured their first horses, large herds of buffalo crossed from the upper Yellowstone valley into the upper Missouri and on over the continental divide into the Snake River country. This combination of buffalo and horses brought the Shoshoni more food and in time allowed them to raise larger families. The small hunting bands on the high desert had neither horses nor buffalo and so remained destitute.

A smallpox epidemic in 1781 wiped out most of the Shoshoni in southern Alberta and northern Montana. The Blackfoot savagely attacked the survivors and by 1800 had driven them from all of the Montana plains. At that time the Shoshoni were collected in four bands, one of which held the Boise and Payette valleys in southwestern Idaho and depended on ocean run salmon for their staple food. The Lemhi Shoshoni, a smaller band, lived on the upper Salmon River and also depended on salmon for most of their food, although they killed some buffalo. The largest band, the Northern Shoshoni, with their neighbors, the Bannock, usually hunted and camped in the Idaho Falls-Pocatello area. They had no salmon and depended on the buffalo herds for their food, as did the fourth band, the Wind River Shoshoni, across the continental divide in central Wyoming.

One of the best known of all the Shoshoni was a woman, SACAGAWEA, of the Lemhi band, who traveled with the Lewis and Clark expedition, the first white men to visit Shoshoni country. When Lewis and Clark met Sacagawea's people on the upper Salmon River, she rendered them valuable aid as an interpreter and was instrumental in securing horses to carry the expedition's baggage and supplies across the mountains.

Fur traders reached the Shoshoni on the upper Snake River in 1810, and in 1812 set up a small trading post at the mouth of the Boise River, only to have it destroyed and the garrison killed by the tribe. During the next thirty years only a few incidents marred the relations between the fur men and the Shoshoni. A second post at the mouth of the Boise River, built in 1819, was later rebuilt as Fort Boise and endured until 1853. A second post, Fort Hall, on the upper Snake River at the mouth of the Portneuf River, was built in 1834 but was never profitable, for the Shoshoni were poor trappers and seldom had anything to trade. Instead, fur brigades each year trapped their streams for beaver.

The yearly rendezvous of trappers was held in Shoshoni country in one or another of the high mountain valleys on the headwaters of the Snake, Green, or Wind rivers. The presence of large numbers of mountain men and bands of Nez Percé and Flathead coming in to trade gave the Shoshoni some protection against the Blackfoot, who raided each year deep into Idaho. When the Blackfoot were seriously weakened by the smallpox epidemic of 1837, they finally ceased their raids west of the mountains. Freedom from their old enemies allowed the Shoshoni to hunt once again in the Three Forks country until the buffalo there were all killed. They then followed the dwindling herds eastward, until by 1870 their chief hunting grounds were north of the Yellowstone River just east of the Crazy Mountains.

When the covered wagon trains began to roll through Shoshoni lands in 1843, they brought new troubles. The whites killed Shoshoni game, pastured off their grass, and often took potshots at stray Indians. Shoshoni retaliated with many attacks on the livestock, usually intent on stealing horses and cattle. Sometimes a train was ambushed and suffered serious losses in people killed and wagons plundered. A few small trains were wiped out completely. The Shoshoni also drove out a Mormon colony that was established at Fort Lemhi in 1854. The Indians made no direct attack on the buildings, but by constantly harassing the herds and trampling the crops they forced the settlers to withdraw.

In 1863 the Shoshoni finally drew some drastic reprisals from the whites. The Indians had been resentful ever since the little colony of Franklin was established in 1860 just north of the Idaho border on the Bear River in one of the Shoshoni winter camping grounds. They vented their displeasure on travelers along the Oregon Trail and attacked the overla rd mail coaches. They also paraded the street of Franklin uttering threats against the people. As the problem became acute, Colonel Patrick Connor was sent with a force of California volunteers to Salt Lake City in the fall of 1862 to subdue the Indians.

He readied his 250 soldiers and waited for a northern blizzard to hide his movements from the Shoshoni scouts. By a forced march at night in the storm, he surprised the Indians in their camp on the right bank of the Bear River a few miles above Franklin soon after daybreak on a cold January morning in 1863. The Indians fought well in defense of their families, killing 23 soldiers and wounding 44 more. In addition, 73 soldiers had to be treated for frozen toes and feet. Connor put the Shoshoni losses at about 224, but a Mormon civilian who counted the bodies the next day reported a total of about 400 dead, at least two-thirds of them women and children.

Three hundred miles to the west around the new mining camps in the Boise Basin and the Owyhee mountains, volunteer groups reported killing another 124 Shoshoni in several attacks during the winter of 1863-64. These drastic measures by Connor's troops and the volunteers kept the trail from Wyoming to Oregon free from major attacks after that.

A federal treaty with the Shoshoni in 1868, together with a supplementary agreement in 1873, established a reservation around Fort Hall, but some of the restless young men slipped away from the reservation in 1878 to join the Bannock forces under Chief Buffalo Horn in his brief campaign called the Bannock War.

The Wind River Shoshoni in central Wyoming escaped many of the difficulties that beset their kinsmen to the west. Their land was guarded on the west by the complex of rugged ridges along the continental divide and on the east by the lofty, massive Big Horn Mountains. The Crow occupied their whole northern frontier, while the Arapaho held the land to the south. In their homeland the Shoshoni escaped the attacks from the Blackfoot and Sioux that affected their neighbors, and few white men, except the fur trappers and traders, passed along their trails. The Shoshoni had ready access to trade goods at the yearly rendezvous until 1840 and from trading posts along the Oregon Trail after that.

During the period of Indian wars, 1866-80, the Wind River Shoshoni held aloof from the fighting. None of the trouble reached their lands, and their peaceful conduct and goodwill toward the whites were constantly encouraged by their great leader, Chief WASHAKI. They did join in the Ghost Dance movement for a time, in 1889-90.

When white settlers began encroaching on Shoshoni lands, the federal government drastically reduced the reservation, paying the tribe a small sum. As the result of oil discoveries in the 1920s, the land increased greatly in value and the Shoshoni finally secured the consent of Congress to file their claims for more money in the federal courts. The obvious injustices presented by the Indians earned them an award of more than $30 million in 1935 after a lengthy court hearing. This Shoshoni case was a major reason for the passage of the important Indian Claims Commission Act of 1946, which has been a great help to other tribes that had suffered the loss of lands under similar circumstances.

See D. L. Crowder, *Tendoy, Chief of the Lemhis* (1969); Edward Dorn, *The Shoshoneans: The People of the Basin-Plateau* (1966); R. H. Lowrie, *The Northern Shoshone* (1909); D. B. Shimkin, *Wind River Shoshone Ethnography* (1947); and Virginia Cole Trenholm and Maurine Carley, *The Shoshonis, Sentinels of the Rockies* (1964).—F. H.

Shoulders, James. See RODEO.

Shoup, George Laird (1836-1904). Idaho politician. Originally from Kittanning, Pennsylvania, Shoup became a stock raiser in Galesburg, Illinois, before joining the gold rush to Pikes Peak, Colorado, in 1859. He became a merchant in Denver and saw military service with the Colorado volunteers during the Civil War. His cavalry, in fact, was engaged in John M. Chivington's massacre of Cheyenne Indians living under a flag of truce at Sand Creek, on November 29, 1864. That same year, Shoup had served as a member of Colorado's constitutional convention.

Moving to the Northwest in 1866, he opened stores in Virginia City, Montana, and in Salmon, Idaho. In 1867 he settled permanently in Salmon, where he kept up a large cattle business along with his mercantile pursuits. Continuing his political career, he was one of the original Lemhi County commissioners in 1869, was chosen county superintendent of schools in 1872, and was elected twice to the legislature as a Republican. Moving to the national scene, he served on the Republican National Committee from 1880 to 1884 and again in 1888. He also went to great personal effort to publicize Idaho, and arranged at his own expense an Idaho exhibit at the New Orleans exposition of 1884 and 1885. Offered the Republican nomination for Congress in 1886, he declined. But when his Idaho associates wanted him to become governor in 1889, he assented.

As governor, Shoup completed arrangements for the Idaho constitutional convention to assemble in the summer of 1889 and worked effectively to have Idaho admitted as a state. He consented to serve a month in 1890 as Idaho's first state governor with assurance of election to the United States Senate on December 18. There he served two terms, although he lost political influence in Idaho after he chose not to become a Silver Republican in 1896. (His McKinley Republican faction, which also favored the silver standard, managed to elect only one member in the entire legislature that year.) However, he and Senator William E. Borah became the two Idaho leaders honored in Statuary Hall in the national Capitol.—M. W.

showboat. See TRANSPORTATION ON THE MISSISSIPPI RIVER SYSTEM.

Shreve, Henry M. See RIVERMEN.

Sibley, Henry Hastings (1811-1891). Minnesota politician and soldier. Born in Detroit, Sibley began his career as a fur trader with the American Fur Company. In 1834 he was put in charge of the company's operations on the upper Mississippi. His headquarters were at Mendota, across the Minnesota River at Fort Snelling. There he built his now-famous stone house. In 1848 he was elected congressional delegate by the settlers in the Minnesota country to go to Washington and secure the organization of a territory, which he did. He was instrumental in bringing about land-ceding treaties of 1851 with the Sioux. In a close election in 1857, he defeated Alexander Ramsey, Minnesota's first territorial governor, to become the state's first governor.

In 1862 Ramsey, now governor, called upon Sibley to command the state militia during the MINNESOTA UPRISING. Sibley's forces defeated those of Little Crow at Wood Lake on September 23, 1862, thus ending the Sioux war in Minnesota. For this service he was named a brigadier general by President Lincoln. During the summers of 1863 and 1864 Sibley led military expeditions into Dakota Territory to put down the remaining Sioux. Thereafter he retired from public service but remained active in a variety of roles. Prominent in St. Paul business affairs as president of the St. Paul Gas Light Company, he was also president of the St. Paul chamber of commerce, chairman of the board of regents of the University of Minnesota, and president of the Minnesota Historical Society.

See Theodore C. Blegen, ed., *The Unfinished Autobiography of Henry H. Sibley together with a selection of hitherto unpublished letters, from the thirties.* (1932). —R. W. F.

Sieber, Al[bert] (1844-1907). Army scout. Sieber was born in Germany and moved to Lancaster, Pennsylvania, where he grew up. A Union soldier, he was twice wounded during the battle of Gettysburg.

Sieber's western rambles took him eventually to the booming mining area around Prescott, Arizona. Mastering the Apache and Mexican languages, he was chosen by the army to be chief of Indian scouts and was stationed at the San Carlos Indian Reservation. He held the position from 1870 to 1890, serving under generals George Crook, O. O. Howard, and Nelson A. Miles. Most of Sieber's scouts were Apache and included Apache Kid, who deserted and became a killer in Mexico and the United States.

Historian Frank C. Lockwood wrote that Sieber "possessed elements of tenderness and nobility, of honor and generosity that endeared him to both savage and white man." Indians referred to him as a "crazy old gray head" whose word was as good as gold. Sieber could also be grumpy, a quality that his aide, Tom Horn, attributed, in part, to aches from twenty-nine gun, arrow, and knife wounds and from arthritis.

In 1907 Sieber was supervising a gang of Apache constructing a road near the Roosevelt Dam on the Salt River. He was killed there in a rockslide. Near the site of his death is a large rock monument built in memory of Arizona's most famous scout.

See A. McKinney Griffith, *Mickey Free: Manhunter* (1969); Tom Horn, *Life of Tom Horn* (1904; repr. 1964); Frank C. Lockwood, *Al Sieber, Man of Blood and Iron: More Arizona Characters* (1942); and Dan L. Trapp, *Al Sieber, Chief of Scouts* (1964).—B. W. A.

Sierra Club. Conservationist organization. The Sierra Club was founded in 1892 by a group of Californians who loved the mountains of their home state. John MUIR became the leading spirit and first president of the club. Its initial interest was wilderness outings in the Sierra and the protection of Yosemite National Park. Between 1908 and 1913 the Sierra Club led an unsuccessful effort to prevent Yosemite's Hetch Hetchy Valley from being damned. The city of San Francisco wanted Hetch Hetchy as a reservoir and eventually received authorization. Determined to prevent similar invasion of national parks and wilderness, the Sierra Club gave aggressive leadership to the aesthetic wing of the American conservation movement. Recent victories have included the defense of Dinosaur National Monument from a proposed dam at Echo Park, the establishment of the National Wilderness Preservation System, and the creation of the Redwoods National Park. With a membership of more than one hundred thousand in all fifty states, the Sierra Club has a national reputation for militancy in the cause of environmental quality. In the late 1960s the club helped block the construction of two dams in the Grand Canyon. By-products of the controversy were revocation of the club's tax-exempt status by the Internal Revenue Service and the respect of millions of citizens. Still, many Americans know the Sierra Club best for its lavishly illustrated books about wilderness.

The early history of the Sierra Club is given detailed treatment in Holway R. Jones, *John Muir and the Sierra Club* (1965). Roderick Nash, *Wilderness and the American Mind* (1967), describes the club's involvement in wilderness controversies. Additional information and a fine library may be found at the club's main office in San Francisco.—R. N.

Sierra Nevada. See PHYSIOGRAPHY OF THE UNITED STATES.

silver issue. Should silver, with gold, be used as backing for United States currency? The silver issue emerged in the mid-1870s and became the key issue in the ELECTION OF 1896. Actually the United States did not formally commit itself to the gold standard until 1900, but, in effect, the nation had been on the gold standard since 1879, as a result of silver's demonetization and the implementation of the Resumption of Specie Payment Act. Gold enjoyed a preferential position and the dollar also appreciated significantly in value throughout the period (the extent of the relationship between these two situations is an interesting but moot point). This much is clear: the ideal monetary situation would maintain a stable dollar—that is, a dollar that would retain a reasonably constant exchange value and one that neither appreciated nor depreciated in a significant manner. Ardent silver advocates contended that silver would bring about a stable-dollar situation; gold-standard advocates believed that just the opposite would be the result.

For a number of reasons, the whole issue is defiant of simple explanation. Since the great debate about silver, the preferential position of gold has been discontinued; it was sacrificed during the Great Depression of the 1930s and happily without the dreadful results prophesized by its partisans in the 1890s. This is not to suggest that the domestic and foreign monetary conditions in the two periods were the same; nor is it to suggest that a triumph for the silverites would have ushered in the millennium. It is to say, however, that both sides, the "goldbugs" and the "silverites," exaggerated the significance of the gold-versus-silver question and in their debates obscured the thought of a number

of individuals, in the camp of the financiers themselves and among the critics of the financiers, who viewed the monetary needs of the nation in far more realistic terms.

The issue had its roots intricately entangled in the controversial and far-reaching post-Civil War economic revolution. The dispute ultimately involved the whole question of what money was, how its value should be determined, and what the role of government should be in determining its value and quantity. Throughout American history there had been advocates of paper money backed merely by the credit of the government. The Civil War greenbacks (see GREENBACK PARTY) were money of this kind until 1879, when the Treasury assumed responsibility for redeeming them in coin upon demand. At that point they became, literally, "as good as gold." In the face of an ever-increasing deflationary situation, certain economic reformers viewed the resumption of specie payment as unwarranted. The influential business community, supported by orthodox fiscal thought, however, insisted that true money was "hard money," which had intrinsic value and was acceptable in international exchange.

Until 1873, the government sanctioned a bimetallic standard. The United States mints coined both silver and gold into dollars when bullion was presented. Before the Civil War the ratio between them had been set by law at sixteen to one—that is, sixteen ounces of silver were recognized as equal in value to one ounce of gold, and the weight of a dollar in either metal was fixed accordingly. Because of its relative scarcity, silver was slightly undervalued at sixteen to one and was not carried to the mints for coinage. In 1873, in routine fashion, Congress then dropped the silver dollar from the list of coins, an act soon to be excoriated as the "Crime of '73." Only a few key governmental leaders were aware of the timeliness of this action—timely because, between 1861 and 1873, silver output had increased, while at the same time gold production had entered a period of relative and absolute decline. Beginning in 1871 the major European financial powers, one after another, had also abandoned silver coinage. By 1874, as a result of vanishing governmental markets and the steadily declining silver price, it became profitable to sell silver at the legal ratio for coinage purposes; but at that point it was no longer possible. Recent research has revealed that there was an element of "gold standard malice aforethought" in these actions, but not nearly as great as the determined opponents of a tight-money policy later contended.

Silver producers would have profited if the "free and unlimited" coinage of silver at the ratio of sixteen to one had remained in effect, and debt-burdened farmers and some small businessmen of the West and South also envisaged advantages to themselves in the anticipated increase in the amount of circulating money—a prospect that was aggravated by a significant decline in the per capita circulation throughout the period. As a result, from the middle 1870s to the middle 1890s, free silver assumed a prominent position in the list of reform demands, ultimately becoming the key issue of the 1896 campaign.

By 1890, bimetallists had won several sops—halfway measures that satisfied neither the silver-mining interests nor the opponents of a "tight-money" policy. These measures came with the passage of the Bland-Allison

This 1896 Washington Post *cartoon, critical of partisans on both sides of the silver question, bore the caption:* As it was written, "Issachar is a strong ass that stoopeth down between two burdens."—Gen. XLIX:14. *(Library of Congress)*

Act of 1878 (see Richard P. BLAND) and the Silver Purchase Act of 1890. The former act made provision for neither the free (sixteen to one) nor the unlimited coinage of silver; the latter virtually provided for the unlimited purchase of the domestic output, but at the current low market price, and not at sixteen to one. Accordingly, the slumping price of silver in a glutted world and domestic market was not stemmed and the deflationary spiral likewise was not reversed.

Yet the silver agitation might never have become a major issue had it not been for the combination of circumstances that were set in motion by the 1892 elections. The new Populist party (see POPULISM), despite an impressive showing, was confronted with the fact that it had virtually no following in the East or in the ranks of labor, and that its comprehensive radical program had not been embraced by significant numbers of voters; its national ticket had in fact been most successful in the silver stronghold of the West. Fusion with one or the other of the old parties on the basis of the money question became a practical necessity, despite the fact that the silver issue badly distorted the true Populist position on the money question. As events would have it, the election of a Democratic president and Congress ultimately intensified this move. Grover Cleveland was on

record as intent upon repealing the 1890 silver act, and after he was saddled with the depression that began in 1893 he called a special session of Congress for that purpose. In fact, his shortsighted focus upon the Silver Purchase Act as the cause of the depression and its repeal as the cure assisted mightily in undermining the Populist movement as a radical movement and in making silver a far more important issue than it deserved to be. In seeking and winning a repeal of the act, Cleveland divided his party along sectional lines; and in the South and West, where silver sentiment knew no party bounds, the tendency of the disenchanted to seek common ground on that one issue was greatly exacerbated. The end result was an even greater polarization of the nation along sectional and rural-versus-urban lines; a repudiation of Cleveland's leadership by his own party and a declaration of Democratic support for silver; and the nomination of the Nebraska silverite William Jennings BRYAN for president in 1896 by both Democrats and Populists.

By this time, the market price of silver had fallen to about thirty-two to one. If government policy had been altered so as to open its mints to the unlimited purchase of silver at sixteen to one internationally, the result would have been an indefinite and *perhaps* disastrous inflation; on the other hand, bimetallism, implemented nationally, might have produced a salutary devaluation in the midst of a severe depression. In the unfavorable political climate of the middle 1890s, however, the mere mention of such a course created an emotional fervor detrimental to reasoned consideration of the question.

The symbolism of silver suggests its significance and explains its defeat. Reformers, especially westerners and southerners, saw reflected in it their hopes for a better society, founded upon governmental concern for the welfare of all. This applies even though free silver would not have had nearly as great an effect as was claimed. Yet insofar as free silver symbolized a commitment for governmental intervention in the economy for the purpose of achieving a stable dollar, it symbolized the quest for greater reforms. Conversely, free silver epitomized all that was detestable to the business-creditor interests of the day. It controverted conventional economic standards by redefining the "proper role" of government, and, given the international commitment to the gold standard, it threatened isolation for the United States from the European financial center.

The silver issue, of course, suffered defeat with William Jennings Bryan in 1896, but the question of a need for a more flexible monetary system, which was at the heart of the great silver crusade, remained a live issue. Ironically, new gold discoveries and new extraction processes provided temporarily for some expansion in the gold supply, and with that came temporary relief for the monetary system—a curious turn of events that undermined, yet proved, at one and the same time, the silverites' contention that the monetary system was inflexible.

See Davis R. Dewey, *Financial History of the United States* (1956); Milton Friedman and Anna J. Schwartz, *Monetary History of the United States, 1867-1960* (1963); and Paul W. Glad, *McKinley, Bryan, and the People* (1964).—O. G. C.

Silver King, Arizona. Ghost town. Silver King, in Pinal County, was built around the fabulously wealthy Silver King Mine, which was discovered in 1875. This mine produced an estimated $17 million in silver and supported not only Silver King but also the nearby town of Pinal. The area boomed until 1888 when the mine's production slowed, but Silver King and Pinal managed to survive until the turn of the century. Today little is left of the towns except for the ghostly remains of a few old buildings.

See Nell Murbarger, *Ghosts of the Adobe Walls* (1964); Duane Smith, *Rocky Mountain Mining Camps* (1967); and Muriel S. Wolle, *The Bonanza Trail* (1953). —R. B. W.

Silver Plume, Colorado. Ghost town. Silver Plume, located fifty-four miles west of Denver, was a prosperous silver- and lead-mining town throughout the last quarter of the nineteenth century. The town was named after the first pay ore, which was in the form of leaf silver and shaped in the form of a feather. Silver Plume was founded in 1870 following the discovery of a rich vein of silver in the surrounding mountains, but the town was not formally incorporated until 1880.

Silver Plume suffered severely from the usual hazards of mining town existence—fire and avalanche. In 1884 fire destroyed nearly all the town's business district, and

the avalanche of 1899 killed twenty people and caused heavy damage to mining property.

Railroad connections to the town arrived in 1882 via the famous Loop to Plume, a winding four-mile stretch of track linking Silver Plume with Georgetown. Geography texts of the nineteenth century placed the Loop alongside the Grand Canyon and Niagara Falls as one of the wonders of America. The tracks were torn out in 1939, and today Silver Plume is a sleepy little village. Several of the town's early buildings remain, and a local museum maintains a tie with its heyday.

See Robert L. Brown, *Ghost Towns of the Colorado Rockies* (1968); and Muriel S. Wolle, *The Bonanza Trail* (1953).—R. B. W.

Silver Reef, Utah. Ghost town. Today one of the bleakest of ghost towns, Silver Reef was once a prosperous silver-mining town. Located in the southwestern corner of Utah, the mines around Silver Reef disproved the geological theory that silver could not occur in sandstone. The town was born in the early 1870s, reached its peak between 1877 and 1880, and slowly died around the turn of the century. During this time $10,500,000 worth of silver was extracted from the sandstone. Today only a few buildings remain, the most notable being the Wells Fargo Bank.

See Nell Murbarger, *Ghosts of the Glory Trail* (1956); Duane Smith, *Rocky Mountain Mining Camps* (1967); and Muriel S. Wolle, *The Bonanza Trail* (1953). —R. B. W.

silver rushes. See GOLD AND SILVER RUSHES.

silverwork, southwestern Indian. Today, Indian silverwork is an intrinsic part of the Southwest's economy. Navaho and Pueblo Indian smiths work at their craft in the bench-shops of New Mexico and Arizona cities, as well as in their own hogans and pueblos. These pieces are handmade and not one is perfect or exactly like another. Greater skill has come with finer tools, better techniques, and high standards.

A wide variety of styles exist, although the different Indian peoples are now employing each other's techniques. Generally speaking, Navaho work is simple with emphasis upon the beauty of the silver itself. The Navaho are noted for their handsome sand-cast bracelets, guards for bow and arrows, belt buckles, rings, and lustrous hollow silver beads. Their use of turquoise is spare.

Zuñi Pueblo jewelry is so eleborately studded with turquoise that the silver is secondary. They cut and polished stone and shell for hundreds of years before the Spanish came, making disk beads and fine turquoise mosaic. At present, the inlay and channel work employs turquoise, coral, jet, gleaming colored shells, and semiprecious stones.

The work of the Hopi Pueblo Indians of northeastern Arizona is distinguished by the use of silver overlay. This technique employs two sheets of silver. The design is cut from one and laid upon the other, then the two pieces are "sweated" together. The back portion is turned black with a chemical, and the finished article appears to have been carved from one piece of silver.

Santo Domingo Pueblo, known for its remarkably fine shell necklaces, works in some of the above-mentioned styles and turns out jewelry in brass as well as in silver.

Historically, the Navaho and some of the Pueblo Indians learned blacksmithing from Spanish-Americans as early as the 1850s, but silversmithing came later and as an offshoot of this knowledge.

In 1864 the Navaho were driven to Fort Sumner, New Mexico, to be incarcerated for four years by the United States military. While there, they were given coils of brass and copper from which they made bracelets and ring bits. When they went home in 1868, a number of them took up silversmithing. Because they had to make, dig for, and scrounge everything they needed, they began with very crude tools. Prehistoric pottery sherds picked up in ancient pueblo ruins were used as crucibles because, unlike their own wares, the sherds were so well fired and durable that they easily withstood the heat of juniper coals and the draft of crude bellows. Ingot molds were chiseled out of slabs of sandstone. Anvils were fashioned from short lengths of railroad rail. Bolts and other bits of scrap metal were made into simple tools. The smiths laboriously cut dies in scrap metal. These designs, stamped on the silverwork, are those that appear on Mexican leatherwork.

American silver dollars were melted into ingots and arduously hammered into workable flat pieces from which the smiths fashioned bridle mountings and other horse trappings, bracelets, rings, buttons, and, now and then, tobacco canteens and gunpowder measures bought by soldiers stationed in Navaho country.

A Navaho mother-in-law may wear small bells on her sash so that her son-in-law can hear her coming and make himself scarce. These little bells and other small ornaments were made from American quarters. (Today, silver dimes with a button loop soldered on the back decorate the sleeves and bodices of Navaho blouses and shirts.) Later, when laws were enforced to prevent the melting or disfigurement of American coinage, they used Mexican *pesos*, which had a higher silver content and, because of their softness, were easier to melt. Now the Indians use silver in slugs, sheets, and wire.

Soft volcanic pumice or tuff was and is used for sand-cast molds. After the top of a slab is smoothly ground, a design is carefully tooled in it to the right depth. Channels are carved into which the molten silver will flow to fill the design, and the mold is smoked to help the silver pass freely over the surface. A flat piece of smoked tuff is laid on top and wired into place. The silver is then poured into the mold. If the mold is not warm enough, or the silver not hot enough, the mold will break and the whole process must be repeated. When pieces come out successfully they must be carefully filed and polished.

Mexican trouser ornaments included a silver pomegranate blossom shape, which came to Mexico through Spain from Moorish Africa. The Navaho changed these into the squash blossom with which they were familiar and used them between silver beads as pendants in necklaces. Suspended at the base of these necklaces was a crescent shape known as a *naja*. The naja appeared in the middle of Spanish silver-mounted bridles, and supposedly dates back to the Moorish period. It is generally regarded as a fertility symbol.

Until the railroad came to the Southwest in the late 1890s, the various Indians made silver and turquoise jewelry for trade and sale among themselves. With the coming of the tourist, the traders and curio companies ordered lighter weight silver in forms never before dreamed of: spoons, cuff links, salt dishes, boxes, tie bars, and a multitude of other tiems ever changing with fad and fashion. The designs they ordered stamped into jewelry were also unknown before—the trader's notion of the tourist's idea of what Indian design *should* look like. The average tourist believed that every mark on a given piece should "mean something," and the traders obligingly made up "legends" to account for the "symbols." The Indians laughed and everyone was happy.

Today an almost infinite, and unusually tasteful, variety of shapes and forms and sizes of silver jewelry may be chosen for everyone from the discerning collector to the man, woman, or child who simply wants a charming ornament.

See John Adair, *The Navajo and Pueblo Silversmiths* (1944); Margery Bedinger, *Indian Silver* (1973); Bertha P. Dutton, *Indians of the Southwest* (1965); W. Ben Hunt, *Indian Silversmithing* (1960); Harry P. Mera, *Indian Silverwork of the Southwest* (1959); Arthur Woodward, *Navajo Silver* (1938); and Margaret Wright, *Hopi Silver* (1972).—B. P. D. and M. L.

Simpson, Jerry (1842-1905). Kansas Populist politician. Simpson was perhaps the most popular and renowned of the Populist leaders. An extraordinary wit and a genuine sense of humor brought him immediately to the public's attention during the 1890 congressional campaign when he turned to his advantage the opposition's sarcastic and false accusation that he wore no socks. Known thereafter as either "Sockless Jerry" or the "Sockless Socrates of the Plains," he became a highly influential Populist spokesman and served three terms in Congress (1890, 1892, and 1896). Almost always portrayed by the opposition as an ignorant country bumpkin, Simpson was actually a shrewd and capable politician. Although a poor writer, he had read widely and at times amazed his congressional opponents, who were naive enough to believe their own caricature. Had it not been for his Canadian birth, Simpson undoubtedly would have been a serious contender for the presidential nomination.

His background was unique for a congressman. For more than twenty years, after leaving his boyhood home in New York at the age of fourteen, he sailed the Great Lakes as cook, sailor, mate, and captain, with service in the Union army the only interruption. In the 1870s he gave up his sailor life for a wife and family and the lure of the West. In 1878, after a few years in Indiana, he moved to Kansas, where he ultimately acquired a ranch in the southwestern part of the state near Medicine Lodge. Years before his move to Kansas he had left the Republican party in disgust to fight for reform as a Henry George "single-taxer" within the ranks of the Greenback and Union Labor parties. In light of Simpson's third-party record before 1890, his nomination as the Populist candidate for Congress that year was no great anomaly, but his election was something of a surprise. He became a skilled Populist campaigner and congressman. However, several years after his defeat in the 1898 election, his health failing him and Populism no longer a viable force, Simpson sold his Kansas ranch and attempted a new start in New Mexico Territory. On a return visit to Kansas in 1905, shortly before his death in Wichita, he was told repeatedly by old opponents how the Progressive spirit was bringing the whole state around to the earlier excoriated Populist position. The ever-sardonic Simpson replied: "You are the conservative businessmen of the state, and doubtless all wisdom is lodged with you, but you are just learning now what the farmers . . . knew fourteen years ago."

See O. Gene Clanton, *Kansas Populism: Ideas and Men* (1969).—O. G. C.

Siouan language. See INDIAN LANGUAGES: *Siouan.*

Siouan tribes, Southern. Archaeologists indicate that the Southern Siouan Indians, or Dhegiha language group—the Osage, Ponca, Omaha, Kansa, and Quapaw tribes—were early inhabitants of the southern Atlantic seaboard who migrated to the trans-Mississippi region via the Ohio valley long before the United States was founded. Later, as residents of the future states of Missouri, Kansas, and Nebraska, most of them also became identified as "Lower Missouri Sioux." However, the Southern and Lower Sioux differed, not only chronologically and geographically, but in the latter group's exclusion of the Quapaw and inclusion of tribes with different linguistic and historical backgrounds.

The Southern Sioux had much in common as a people and in their relations with whites. In terms of population, all but the Osage belonged to small tribes. As of 1830, for example, there were only about 500 Quapaw, 600 Ponca, 900 Omaha, and 1,700 Kansa, whereas the Osage population was approximately 5,000. These tribes all lived in more or less permanent villages, comprised of multifamily, earth-covered lodges or, as in the case of the Quapaw, bark-covered houses. While circumstances permitted, they all hunted buffalo and other game and also did some farming to supplement their diet. At least until the 1860s, all except the Quapaw were almost continuously involved in hostilities with neighboring tribes.

Yet, in their many contacts with Caucasians, including French and Spanish explorers, trappers, and traders, who occupied Louisiana Territory before it was purchased by the United States, the Southern Sioux usually avoided warfare. A temporary, though significant departure from this disposition occurred during the Civil War, when the Confederacy pressed the Osage into service against the Union and forced the Quapaw to take sides in the fighting or flee their homes. Otherwise, these tribes were not only peaceful but cooperative, for each of them signed and generally observed at least three treaties with the federal government before 1865. Under these agreements, they all ceded vast amounts of land and accepted living on reservations, which concentrated the Ponca in northern Nebraska, the Omaha in northeastern Nebraska, the Kansa in central Kansas, the Osage in southeastern Kansas, and the Quapaw in northeastern Indian Territory. Moreover, in the 1870s, the United States pressured the Ponca, Osage, and Kansa into further one-sided negotiations and forcibly removed them to Indian Territory without encountering violent resistance.

In their dealings with whites, however, each of the Southern Sioux tribes also had historical peculiarities. The more populous and powerful Osage, distinguished by their band affiliations as Great and Little Osage, were particularly influential in the settlement of the central and southern Plains. While the Louisiana region was under Spanish control, they lived in the present state of Missouri, where competing French and Spanish traders divided their loyalties. In 1802 some of the pro-French Osage were induced to move to present northeast Oklahoma. But their initial stay there was only temporary,

for despite the intervention of American agents and missionaries, they feuded so constantly with native and incoming eastern tribes that the United States compelled them to rejoin their Missouri brethren on a Kansas reservation in the 1830s. Subsequent white expansion, plus the tribe's unfortunate alliance with the South in the 1860s, led to their final removal to what is now Osage County, Oklahoma, in 1872. Soon afterward many of them died of physical privations, but eventually the effective utilization of grazing contracts, trust funds, and oil and gas proceeds made the Osage the wealthiest Indians in America.

The less numerous Ponca also attained a special, but unfortunate, place in the annals of Indian-white relations. They did little to shape the preliminary international maneuvers and American policies affecting the area reserved to them in Nebraska Territory in 1858. But their later misfortunes—the cession of their Niobrara River lands to the hostile Sioux in 1868; their compulsory and costly removal to Indian Territory in 1877; and the ensuing arrest of Standing Bear's hapless band for attempting to return to Nebraska—received national attention in the 1880s. In fact, the plight of the Ponca was so convincingly presented in court, in Congress, and in publications by Indian rights advocates, such as Helen Hunt Jackson, that the government paid them an indemnity and allowed some of them to acquire permanent homesteads in Nebraska.

Meanwhile, the fate of the Kansa was an extreme example of the disastrous effects of white aggrandizement upon the Southern Sioux. They still numbered about 1,700 when assigned to a 250,000-acre reservation near the Neosho River in Kansas in 1850. But because of disease, the loss of game, and a later removal to Indian Territory, only 533 survivors reached their final reservation on the Arkansas River in 1873. Furthermore, food shortages, unhealthful conditions, and their own resistance to reform reduced the Kansa population to only 194 in 1889 before the remnant began to make economic and social adjustments that promoted their gradual recovery.

Finally, the uniqueness of the interracial experiences of the Omaha and Quapaw was at least partly manifested by the decisions the government made with respect to their lands. The Omahas, on one hand, were not exempted from the exploitation, loss of independence, and cultural disruption that affected their relatives, but they did escape mass removal to Indian Territory by satisfactorily complying with the demands of white authorities. Thus, as late as 1930, more than 1,100 Omaha remained on the Nebraska reservation assigned to their tribe in 1854. On the other hand, the Quapaw were repeatedly dispossessed of areas they claimed in Arkansas, Louisiana, and Indian Territory before the Civil War and were not permanently located in Ottawa County, Oklahoma, until after Appomattox. In the 1890s, however, they had the distinction of being permitted to plan and implement their own land allotment program.

In general, the literature on Indian affairs gives less attention to the amenable Southern Sioux than to other, more warlike tribes. Nevertheless, an examination of their mutual and separate relationships with the white community offers some significant insights into the nature and persistence of the Indian problem.

Tribal histories have been published on three of the five Southern Siouan tribes. John J. Mathews, *The Osages* (1961), is a detailed, but sparsely footnoted, work that uses oral accounts and a variety of primary sources in bringing some aspects of the Osage story up to the mid-twentieth century. James H. Howard, *The Ponca Tribe* (1965), is the most complete work available on the Ponca, and it gives attention to the culture and customs as well as the history of that tribe. A prominent episode in Ponca history, the Standing Bear trial of 1879, is analyzed in James T. King, " 'A Better Way': Gen. George Crook and the Ponca Indians," *Nebraska History* (Fall 1969). William E. Unrau, *The Kansa Indians, A History of the Wind People, 1673-1873* (1971), is a well-written, scholarly treatment of Kansa developments from earliest white contacts to the time of their settlement in Indian Territory. Unrau has also published two informative articles: "United States 'Diplomacy' with the Dhegiha-Siouan Kansa, 1815-1825," *Kansas Quarterly* (Fall 1971), and "The Council Grove Merchants and the Kansa Indians, 1855-1870," *Kansas Historical Quarterly* (Autumn 1968). Some aspects of Omaha history are cited in Alice C. Fletcher and Francis La Fleshe, *The Omaha Tribe* (1911), but this publication is largely ethnological in focus. All of the Southern Siouans are discussed in concise essays in Muriel H. Wright, *A Guide to the Indian Tribes of Oklahoma* (1951). Each tribe is also covered in Frederick W. Hodge, ed., *Handbook of American Indians North of Mexico,* 2 vols. (1907-11) and in the annual reports of the commissioner of Indian affairs.
—H. G. W.

Sioux Falls, South Dakota. A treaty between the Sioux Indians and the United States government in 1851 opened up the area around present-day Sioux Falls for settlement. The town was placed at the falls of the Big Sioux River—hence its name. The first successful white occupation of the area occurred in 1857, when pioneers purchased land from the land company of Dubuque, Iowa, and the Dakota Land Company of St. Paul, Minnesota. The population in 1858 was twenty-five, only two of whom were women.

Sioux Falls grew rapidly as rail lines pushed westward. By 1888 five different railroad lines had built tracks through the town. In 1880 the town's population was 2,164. A decade later it had grown to 10,177. The 1970 census showed its population to be 72,488.—D. J. T.

Sioux (Dakota) Indians. The peoples commonly known as the Sioux, members of the largest and most powerful group in the Siouan language family, have been most conspicuous in American history and legend. The name "Sioux" is a French corruption of the Ojibwa term *nadowe-is-iw,* meaning "adder" or "enemy." The Sioux called themselves *Ocheti Sakowin* ("seven council fires") or, more commonly, used one of several dialectical variations of the term *dah-kota* ("alliance of friends"), which in the anglicized form "Dakota" is today generally used by scholars and the Indians themselves.

The Sioux are commonly remembered as a fiercely warlike people who fanatically resisted white expansion into western Minnesota and the Northern Plains from about 1850 to 1880. Hence they are often associated with such militant chiefs as Little Crow, Sitting Bull, Crazy Horse, and Red Cloud and with violent events such as the Minnesota Uprising, the Custer massacre at

the Little Big Horn, and the Wounded Knee Massacre. However, the history of Sioux-white relations is much more complex than these references imply, for the Sioux varied considerably in their way of life and disposition toward the United States.

The Sioux originated from the prehistoric Siouan population which is believed to have occupied the lower Ohio and middle Mississippi valleys. This population was dispersed by as yet undetermined causes, and fragments scattered in several directions. The ancestral Dakota moved northward and occupied parts of Wisconsin and most of northern Minnesota by the sixteenth and seventeenth centuries, during which time they are considered to have been divided into seven tribal groups. In the mid-1600s they were first contacted by French explorers and missionaries, and at about the same time began to drift southwestward toward the Plains due to pressure from the adjacent Ojibwa on the east and the depletion of food in their territory. In the process of migration, which continued for two centuries, the sevenfold division of the tribes coalesced into three regional groupings, although the tribes retained their traditional names. These three groupings developed distinct but mutually intelligible dialects, and became known to whites as Santee, comprising the Mdewakanton, Wahpekute, Wahpeton, and Sisseton tribes; the Yankton, comprising the Yankton and Yanktonai; and the Teton. Even after the three divisions developed different cultural characteristics associated with the regions they inhabited, they remained linked and continued to think of themselves as one people.

The Santee and Yankton generally receive only limited attention in the literature on Indian affairs, largely because most of their constituents were submissive wards of the government after the Civil War. Yet they comprised about half of the Sioux population, dominated Sioux relations with the white community before 1850, participated in key developments in the 1860s, and significantly influenced the evolution of Indian policies in later years. The Santee were sedentary village farmers who lived in the trans-Mississippi region of southern Minnesota during the early nineteenth century. They met American traders and settlers with general amiability, peacefully acknowledging the extension of United States jurisdiction. As white farmers moved into the Minnesota country the Santee were gradually required to cede portions of their land through a series of treaties, until by 1860 they were restricted to reserves along the upper Minnesota River. Corrupt administration of the government Indian agencies and the arrogant attitudes of the settlers finally led to an outbreak of violence in 1862, when a large number of Santee, mainly Mdewakanton and Wahpekute led by LITTLE CROW, killed over seven hundred whites in the MINNESOTA UPRISING. An army of white militia mounted a harsh campaign of reprisal, several of the warrior leaders were tried and hanged, and nearly all the Santee, hostile or not, were expelled from Minnesota. Later, under treaties signed in 1867, all but a few were assigned to the Santee Reservation in Nebraska, the Sisseton Reservation in South Dakota, or Devil's Lake Reservation in North Dakota.

Meanwhile, a majority of the more populous, semisedentary Yankton group which resided between the Missouri River and Minnesota, were peaceful and

In the Black Hills of South Dakota the Sioux entombed their dead in coffins atop scaffolds. (Library of Congress)

cooperative in their contacts with whites. Culturally, they were intermediary between the primarily agricultural Santee and the buffalo-hunting Teton, although closer in most matters to the latter. After 1859 most of the Yankton quietly attempted to raise crops on a small reservation on the Missouri, just north of Nebraska. Some of the Yanktonai tribe, though, were persistent and unruly nomads. After signing a treaty in 1865, the Lower Yanktonai moved to Crow Creek Reservation in South Dakota, but many of the Upper Yanktonai did not settle on reservations, farther up the Missouri, until the 1870s. By the twentieth century a growing percentage of the Santee and Yankton groups had acquired individual land allotments and citizenship, were farming, raising stock, or leasing their property, and were at least superficially assimilating the white man's social institutions. Still, for most of them, the search for a new cultural stability and economic well-being had only begun.

What the overall picture of the Sioux is the fact that scholars and casual observers have been especially fascinated by the belligerent, wandering, buffalo-hunting Teton, the seventh of the major Sioux tribes, who repeatedly defied the power of the United States in the post-Civil War era. About fifteen thousand strong in 1850, the Teton tribe incorporated seven subdivisions, the Hunkpapa, Two-Kettle, Sans-Arc, Blackfoot, Miniconjou, Oglala, and Brulé, of which the last

two were larger and more formidable than many contemporary whole tribes.

The cultural complex of the Teton is considered to be archetypical of the Plains Indians as a group. Approximately eighty percent of their subsistence economy was based on hunting buffalo. Each subdivision comprised several kinship bands, which would gather in the late spring for a communal hunt and the performance of their primary religious ritual, the SUN DANCE. Then the bands would separate for the duration of the year, roaming their favorite hunting grounds and making a winter camp in some sheltered stream bottom. During the winter, buffalo robes were prepared for trade at the white posts along the Missouri and Platte rivers. The political structure of the Teton was loosely organized; leadership was limited to band level, and both the civil chiefs and war leaders wielded authority only through a consensus of respect. There were no tribal chiefs until the last stages of the wars against the whites, although overall leaders were appointed for collective actions such as the communal hunt. Social organization was based on kinship affiliation; small extended families were the living unit, and sororal polygamy was widely practiced. Descent was bilateral, and individual residence could be either patrilocal or matrilocal as preference and economic conditions warranted. There was evidently no clan structure, but there was a series of age-graded (though not successive) men's societies to which each male would belong. Religion was almost entirely individual-oriented, and directed at the acquisition by each individual of supernatural aid, which would guide his conduct in domestic life and warfare. War was the recognized occupation of men, and success according to its rules of honor and bravery was the accepted way to status and respect among the people.

In the early nineteenth century, while extending their control over the country encompassed by the Platte valley, the upper Missouri and Yellowstone rivers, and the eastern slopes of the Rockies, these former inhabitants of the upper Midwest seldom met or caused trouble for whites. But in the 1840s they grew increasingly restive over the mounting emigration and military activity along the Platte. The government thus cajoled some of their chiefs into signing the Treaty of Fort LARAMIE (1851), also known as the Treaty of Horse Creek, promising them annuities in return for their peaceful avoidance of specified roads and installations. The influence of this bribery is debatable, but the western Sioux were relatively quiet for the next twelve years, except for those involved in the GRATTAN MASSACRE and its aftermath in 1854-55. In that turn of events, Brulé and Oglala warriors wiped out a thirty-man military detachment that made an unwarranted attack on their camp near Fort Laramie, then withdrew from the area, but were again attacked and decisively defeated by the expedition of William S. HARNEY.

The first extensive warfare on the part of the Teton began in 1864 and continued sporadically for about four years. Although some of them remained passive or even conciliatory throughout this period, the increasing invasion of their hunting grounds in eastern Wyoming, plus the disquieting news of the Minnesota outbreak and the slaughter of scores of Cheyenne by Colorado militiamen in 1864 in the Sand Creek Massacre, strengthened and aroused the hostile element. Aided by Cheyenne and Arapaho allies, war parties of up to two thousand struck civilians and troops at scattered points northwest and east of Fort Laramie. The army responded with the POWDER RIVER INDIAN EXPEDITION in 1865. Some of the bloodiest fighting occurred along the Bozeman Trail to Montana, where the Indians killed approximately 260 whites in the last six months of 1866, including brevet Lieutenant Colonel W. J. Fetterman and his entire command of eighty men (see FETTERMAN MASSACRE). This brought public demands for retaliation, but instead, Congress called for an all-out effort to negotiate a settlement with the Sioux and other warring tribes. It took the peacemakers until late 1868 to complete a treaty with the Teton, primarily because the influential Oglala war leader, RED CLOUD, refused to sign until the army abandoned its Bozeman forts. Even then, some of the hostiles remained unreconciled. But the Indian peace commission announced that it had pacified the Sioux and assigned them to a reservation on the western half of present-day South Dakota, with hunting privileges in the Powder River country.

Between 1868 and 1876, in keeping with its PEACE POLICY, the Indian Bureau attempted to teach the Teton Sioux to live like white men at several agencies on or near their reservation. But the results were limited by numerous problems. Poor agency locations, ineffective and corrupt administrators, inadequate supplies, natural disasters (such as grasshopper plagues and floods),

and unscrupulous white neighbors were only a few of the deterrents to progress. Some of the agencies were also plagued by hundreds of roving "nonprogressives" who occasionally came in to demand handouts or to raid the agency storehouses and herds. Furthermore, by 1875 Sioux leaders, both on and off the reservation, were becoming anxious about the discovery of gold in the Black Hills. Their rejection of a lease proposal and the army's tacit refusal to keep trespassers out of the gold fields set the Sioux and the United States on another collision course.

At least one dramatic event of the "Sioux War" of 1876-77, the battle of the LITTLE BIG HORN, is common knowledge. But some of the developments preceding and following Custer's "last stand" are sometimes overlooked. It should be noted that the government precipitated a military showdown by authorizing the army to go into the Powder River country to round up the followers of SITTING BULL, CRAZY HORSE, GALL, and other hostiles who refused an arbitrary order to go to the agencies in the midst of the winter of 1875-76. Rather than forcing the independent Sioux to obey orders, the army's initial assaults actually galvanized the resistance of the Oglala, Miniconjou, Sans-Arc, and Hunkpapa Teton and their Cheyenne and eastern Sioux allies. Their combined strength was first unveiled on June 17, when one of the columns of troops sent to converge on the Little Big Horn River incurred modest losses in a brief encounter with a large war party near ROSEBUD. Then, eight days later, Custer led his 211-man command in their fatal charge on a camp of at least 2,500 well-armed warriors. The Indians, however, did not have long to celebrate their great victory, for by fall, many had been subdued by massive military operations. AMERICAN HORSE was killed in the battle of SLIM BUTTES in September. Perhaps four thousand hostiles, including Crazy Horse, remained at large and were hit hard in winter campaigns before surrendering at the Red Cloud and Spotted Tail agencies in the spring of 1877. A few others followed Sitting Bull into Canada and did not give up until 1881.

Although the conquest of the recalcitrant Sioux removed a primary obstacle to the government's work among the Teton, the road to their acculturation was neither easy nor short. The Agreement of 1876, which satisfied the white expansionists' demands for the cession of the Black Hills, required the Teton youngsters to attend classes and the able-bodied adults to work in exchange for schools, vocational training, and temporary subsistence. But various circumstances caused a relaxation of these requirements, and despite some change in appearance and involvement in ranching, freighting, and agency employment, many of the Indians remained wedded to the past. Indeed, a significant number not only clung to such traditions as the sun dance, but eagerly adopted the GHOST DANCE religion that swept the Sioux nation in 1889-90. The report that an Indian messiah had come to destroy the white man and restore the buffalo inspired some of the disaffected Sioux to take to the Bad Lands and threaten war. This led to the last major conflict in Indian history, highlighted by the WOUNDED KNEE MASSACRE near Pine Ridge Agency on December 29, 1890. In that tragic affair more than two hundred Sioux men, women, and children were killed by impetuous troops.

After the 1890s, Sioux-white animosity gradually subsided, and the Sioux learned to resign themselves to being a disadvantaged minority in a conformity-conscious American society. Although they eventually lost much of their land, through allotments and cessions, they still retain six large reservations in the Dakotas, where they occupy a cultural limbo that is not quite Indian and not quite white.

The Sioux have been the subject of many excellent historical works, only a few of which are cited here. While light on documentation, George E. Hyde's trilogy—*Red Cloud's Folk* (1937), *A Sioux Chronicle* (1956), and *Spotted Tail's Folk* (1961)—are widely regarded as classics. The first traces the history of the Oglala from early times to 1878; the second examines the experiences of the Teton between 1876 and 1891; and the third carries the story of the Brulé up to the 1880s. Other well-written, scholarly works on the Sioux have been published in recent years. Robert Utley, *The Last Days of the Sioux Nation* (1963), is a balanced and exacting treatment of the conditions of the Sioux before and after the battle of Wounded Knee. James C. Olson, *Red Cloud and the Sioux Problem* (1965), is an outstanding analysis of the life of the famous chief Red Cloud and the fate of his people. Roy W. Meyer, *History of the Santee Sioux* (1967), is a painstaking chronicle of the history of some of the smaller and less notorious Sioux bands, with noteworthy observations on their circumstances in the twentieth century. Royal Hassrick, *The Sioux* (1964), is a detailed description of traditional Teton culture. Finally, many specific aspects of the Sioux heritage are also cited in Frederick W. Hodge, ed., *Handbook of American Indians North of Mexico*, 2 vols. (1907-11), and in the annual reports of the commissioner of Indian affairs.—H. G. W.

Sioux Uprising. See MINNESOTA UPRISING.

Sire, Joseph A. See RIVERMEN.

Siringo, Charles A. (1855-1928). Cowboy and historian. Siringo was born in Matagorda County, Texas, and began his cowboy career working on Shanghai Pierce's Rancho Grande in 1871.

At the age of thirty, he wrote *A Texas Cowboy, or, Fifteen Years on the Hurricane Deck of a Spanish Cow Pony* (1885), the first autobiography of a cowboy. In the book, Siringo describes himself as "an old stove-up cow puncher who has spent almost twenty years on the great Western cattle ranges." It was an immediate success, the first edition selling out within the year. The second edition, published a year later, included an addenda of thirty-one pages that tells "how to get rich and go broke in the cattle business." So popular was *A Texas Cowboy* that it ran through printing after printing; Siringo claimed that it sold over a million copies. Although range historian J. Frank Dobie called Siringo's figure a bit high, he did state that "no record of cowboy life has supplanted his . . . chronicle" and that it was "the most-read non-fiction book on cowboy life."

Siringo was a storekeeper in Caldwell, Kansas, when his first book was issued. After that he spent the next two decades with Pinkerton's National Detective Agency, where he lived through the Coeur d'Alene, Idaho, labor riots of 1892 (his testimony aided in the conviction of eighteen union leaders for dynamiting mines and murder), hunted moonshiners in the Appalachians, and chased Butch Cassidy's Wild Bunch. Leaving Pinker-

ton, he spent some time as a peace officer in New Mexico but devoted most of his effort to writing about his many experiences.

Among his many books were *The Cowboy Detective* (1912), one of two books recounting his Pinkerton experiences; *A Lone Star Cowboy* (1919), *A History of "Billy the Kid"* (1920); and *Riata and Spurs* (1927), which was reprinted in 1931 with the material on his Pinkerton experiences deleted and accounts of bad men substituted.

Siringo is described as being "a small wiry man, cold and steady as a rock" and "as being born without fear." Dobie put it well when he said that "no other cowboy ever talked about himself so much in print; few had so much to talk about."—J. C. D.

Sitka, Alaska. The town of Sitka, home of the Sitka-kwon of the Tlingit Indians, is located on the western side of Baranof Island in the Alexander Archipelago of southeastern Alaska (57°03′N, 135°20′W). Captain Aleksei Chirikov, of Vitus Bering's expedition, made a landfall near the site in July 1741. When a party went ashore to explore but failed to report, a second boat, Chirikov's last one, was sent to investigate. It too disappeared, and the Russian navigator weighed anchor. Despite this tragic beginning, the area saw the flags of Spain, England, France, and the United States before the end of the century. In 1799 the chief manager of the new Russian-American Company, Aleksandr Baranov, who resented the competition of fur traders from other nations, organized a huge flotilla of bidarkas manned by Aleuts and escorted by two larger vessels, for the purpose of settling the Alaskan Panhandle. Mikailovsk, or Redoubt St. Michael, was established six miles north of present-day Sitka. In June 1802, Tlingit warriors captured the new fort; some survivors were taken aboard English and American trading ships in the bay. Outraged by the Indian success, Baranov in 1803 regained the post with the help of the Russian naval frigate *Neva*, commanded by Yurii Lisianskii. The town was relocated at its present site and named Novo Arkhangelsk but continued to be popularly known by the Indian name Sitka. As headquarters of the Russian-American Company it became an outpost of European civilization in the Far West, when Seattle was Indian country and San Francisco only a tiny mission and presidio. The town boasted a large residence for the company manager, barracks, two churches, a school, a foundry, a flour mill, a sawmill, a hospital, a shipyard, and a surprisingly active social life.

The formal transfer of Alaska from Russia to the United States took place in Sitka on October 18, 1867. Attempts to organize a new civil government were short-lived, leaving the United States Army in control until the troops were withdrawn in 1877. Two years later the town again surfaced in the nation's press. As a consequence of Indian disturbances stimulated by a vile homemade liquor called hoochinoo, residents requested American military protection. When their pleas went unanswered, they petitioned the British at Victoria, Canada. H.M.S. *Osprey* sped north; it was relieved by a United States man-of-war. The navy lingered until passage by Congress of Alaska's first Organic Act of 1884. Sitka received some of its income serving as the country's capital; it was also a center of trade and tourism. Some mineral prospecting expeditions were dispatched from Sitka during the period. One led to the discovery of gold at Juneau, and that city became the territory's capital in 1900 despite opposition from Governor John Green BRADY, whose home town was Sitka. Fishing and expenditures by governmental agencies were important sources of income in the next few decades. After World War II, a Japanese lumber firm built a mill nearby and began to log the surrounding forests, providing a brace to the town's precarious economic existence. The population of Sitka remained more or less stable at about one thousand from 1890 through 1930; the figure was double that in the censuses of 1940 and 1950 and triple in 1960 and 1970.

See Clarence L. Andrews, *Sitka* (1945); H. H. Bancroft, *History of Alaska* (1886); Hector Chevigny, *Russian America* (1965); and Morgan B. Sherwood, "Ardent Spirits: Hooch and the *Osprey* Affair at Sitka," *Journal of the West* (July 1965).—M. B. S.

Sitting Bull (Tatanka Iyotake) (c.1831-1890). Leading chief and holy man of the Teton Sioux (Dakota). Perhaps the most famous of all American Indians, Sitting Bull was born near the Grand River in present-day South Dakota. He was of the Hunkpapa subtribe, the northernmost division of the Teton. Sitting Bull gained his first war honors at age fourteen in a fight against the Crow. Acquiring a reputation for utter fearlessness, he became leader of the Strong Heart warrior society about 1856. His followers attributed his war success to the strength of his visions, and Sitting Bull himself believed his power came from a complete accord with the mystical force of the universe.

Sitting Bull. (Museum of the American Indian)

During the 1840s and 1850s, while the southern Teton divisions were involved in hostilities in the Platte River country stemming from white migration along the Oregon-California Trail, Sitting Bull had little contact with whites except for traders. His people were occupied in extending their hunting grounds westward into the Yellowstone and Powder River country by warring with the Shoshoni, Assiniboin, and Crow. It was not until 1863 and 1864, when generals Henry Sibley and Alfred Sully moved against the Sioux in the aftermath of the Santee's Minesota Uprising of 1862, that Sitting Bull became involved in fighting against whites. He was involved in small skirmishes with Sibley's force in the summer of 1863 and helped to defend the Teton camp that Sully successfully attacked at Killdeer Mountain on July 28, 1864. Exactly a year later Sitting Bull led a large war party that laid siege to Fort Rice, and in September 1865 his warriors were instrumental in the rout of Cole and Walker's Powder River march. Sitting Bull had little to do, however, with the so-called Red Cloud War of 1866-67, which centered around Fort Phil Kearny. During that time the Hunkpapa bands were hunting on the Yellowstone.

Sitting Bull was from his youth an uncompromising enemy of the whites. This was not due to any specific personal experience with white men but was rather a manifestation of his complete devotion to the traditional customs and virtues of his own race. A total ethnocentrist, he felt that contact with the whites could only pervert and weaken the strength of Teton culture. His observations of the treachery and brutality displayed by the whites who began to press in on the Sioux country, and the accompanying degeneration of large numbers of Indians through drunkenness and disease, only rein-

forced his attitude. In 1868 a portion of the southern Teton Sioux, including the war leader Red Cloud, made peace with the whites in exchange for a large reservation surrounding the Black Hills. The unreconciled remainder of the tribe realized that the crisis of survival was approaching and determined to choose a man to act as head chief of all the Teton, a position that had never before been part of their practice. The traditional independence and individualism of their manner of warfare had to be changed to a system of centralized leadership, and Sitting Bull was selected as the only head man who could command the necessary respect. With the aid of leading warriors such as Crazy Horse, Gall, and the elder American Horse, Sitting Bull strove to instill a spirit of discipline and unity into the Sioux.

In 1874 the discovery of gold in the Black Hills brought miners swarming into the Sioux reservation, and the government in 1875 ordered all the tribe to come in to agencies near the White River. When no response was forthcoming from Sitting Bull's nomadic bands, an army campaign was mounted against them in the spring of 1876. A great number of Sioux, Cheyenne, and Arapaho (estimates run as high as eleven thousand) had gathered with Sitting Bull in the vicinity of the Rosebud and Little Big Horn rivers to discuss the white threat. After much fasting, Sitting Bull experienced a vision of dead soldiers falling like rain into the Indian camp. Soon after, warriors led by Crazy Horse defeated General George Crook's command in the battle of the Rosebud (June 17), and on June 25 Lieutenant Colonel George A. Custer and five troops of the Seventh Cavalry were annihilated at the Little Big Horn when they tried to attack the great encampment. During these battles

Sitting Bull took no active part in the fighting, having surrendered that pleasure when he assumed the head chieftaincy.

Worried that their great victories would provoke massive retaliation by the whites, the Indians scattered into small bands, which were picked off singly by the army during the following year. Sitting Bull and his immediate followers withdrew to Canada, but the Canadian government would not acknowledge responsibility for them. Faced with starvation, they returned to the United States, and Sitting Bull surrendered at Fort Buford on July 19, 1881. After a period of confinement, he was assigned to the Standing Rock Agency in 1883. For a time during 1885 he traveled with Buffalo Bill's Wild West show, displaying arrogant amusement at the cheers and jeers of fickle white crowds. Returning to the reservation, Sitting Bull maintained his power over his people while white agents attempted to ignore his preeminent status, but he could only vainly oppose the continual reduction of tribal lands and erosion of Sioux culture. When the Indians' discontent boiled over during the Ghost Dance movement of 1890, agent James McLaughlin feared that the old warrior might lead another war and sent some of his handpicked Indian police to Sitting Bull's cabin on Grand River to arrest him. After a sharp fight in the early dawn of December 15, Sitting Bull, his teenaged son, and six of his loyal bodyguard were dead. Six policemen were also killed; the remainder reported that the chief had resisted arrest. Sitting Bull's body was taken to agency headquarters and buried in quicklime.

Sitting Bull was a vast enigma to the whites of his era, and his subsequent reputation has reflected their puzzlement. His talents were greater than most Americans were willing to attribute to a mere savage, and so he was both denigrated and rationalized. Some chroniclers denied that he was a warrior and claimed he was a coward and beggar, cruel, and small-minded. Others seriously put forth that he had been secretly schooled at West Point and had even taught there incognito. R. D. Clark's spurious *The Works of Sitting Bull* (1878) portrayed him as a college graduate and a poet in Greek, Latin, and French. Among his own people he was admired as a loving father and a brave defender, always affable in manner, devoutly religious, and a prophet with much honor.

Of the many books that deal in whole or in part with Sitting Bull, Stanley Vestal, *Sitting Bull: Champion of the Sioux* (rev. ed., 1957), is the most detailed biography, although frankly admiring. James McLaughlin, *My Friend the Indian* (1910), is also interesting, although it's a thinly veiled attempt to justify his conduct at the time of Sitting Bull's death. Joe De Barth, *Life and Adventures of Frank Grouard* (1894), sheds light on Sitting Bull's character. See also R. M. Utley, *The Last Days of the Sioux Nation* (1963).—P. R. M.

Skitswish Indians. See COEUR D'ALENE INDIANS.

Slaughter, John (1841-1922). Cattleman. John Slaughter, born in the Republic of Texas, was a member of a prominent ranch family. He journeyed to Arizona in the late 1860s and in 1884 bought the famous San Bernardino land grant. The Mexican government had granted these sixty-five thousand acres to Ignacio Perez in 1822. Slaughter soon thereafter began grazing cattle on both sides of the international border. In 1886 he

formed a partnership with a famous trail driver and rancher, George W. Lang. These two men operated a profitable ranching enterprise until 1890, when the partnership was dissolved. Slaughter also owned a packinghouse in Los Angeles that provided substantial profit. He entered law enforcement in 1886 when he became sheriff of Cochise County, Arizona. He retired in 1890, but was appointed honorary deputy sheriff of the county, a position he held until his death in 1922. —J. A. S.

Slidell, John (1793-1871). Louisiana politician. Born in New York City, Slidell migrated to New Orleans in the early 1820s, where he became an enthusiastic Jacksonian. His political efforts won him appointment in 1829 as federal attorney for the eastern district of Louisiana, a position from which he was ousted when he alienated Martin Gordon, boss of the Jacksonian faction in the state. After long political obscurity, he returned to prominence as Democratic congressman from Louisiana (1843-45). President Polk sent him as United States minister to Mexico in 1845, hoping to reconcile that government to American annexation of Texas, but he was refused recognition and the Mexican War erupted. In the 1850s Slidell completely dominated Democratic politics in Louisiana, was in great measure responsible for the election of President Buchanan in 1856, and became the reputed power behind the throne in the Buchanan administration.

Despite a previous posture against the southern radicals, in 1861 he threw in his lot with the Confederacy, was appointed commissioner to France, and became the center of a diplomatic crisis surrounding his seizure with James M. Mason in the Trent Affair. The two were taken from the British mail packet *Trent* on November 8, 1861, by Captain Charles Wilkes of the U.S.S. *San Jacinto* and returned to the United States. British public opinion was so aroused by this affront that there was serious danger of war, but release of the agents by Secretary of State William E. Seward and acknowledgment that their seizure had been illegal, reduced tensions. Slidell's efforts to win French recognition of the Confederacy proved fruitless because of Napoleon III's refusal to act independently of Great Britain. Never reconciled to southern defeat, Slidell refused to ask for clemency at the end of the war. He died in England.

See Louis M. Sears, *John Slidell* (1925).—J. G. T.

Slim Buttes, battle of (1876). Indian war. In the aftermath of the Custer disaster at the Little Big Horn on June 25, 1876, generals George S. Crook and Alfred Terry launched a campaign from the Rosebud valley in pursuit of the scattering Sioux and Cheyenne Indians. Crook's command split off from Terry's and followed a trail leading first eastward into the Dakota badlands and then south toward the Black Hills. The army's rations gave out and Crook ordered Captain Anson Mills with 150 men to hurry ahead to Deadwood and obtain supplies. On September 8, Mills's scouts reported an Indian village just ahead in the ravines of Slim Buttes (near present-day Reva, South Dakota). This was the Brulé-Sioux band of the elder American Horse (known also as Iron Shield). Approaching the village under cover of fog and rain at dawn of the ninth, Mills's force surprised the Sioux and drove them from their camp up into the rocks. Both sides sent runners for reinforcements, and when Crook's command approached the Buttes about midmorning, it was attacked by a war party from Sitting Bull's Hunkpapa Sioux camp. The Hunkpapa were unable to break through the army to relieve the surrounded Brulé, but in the confusion most of American Horse's people were able to scatter and escape. Their chief, however, had been seriously wounded in the abdomen and surrendered with some relatives near nightfall, coming out to greet his captors with his right hand while holding his intestines in his left. Despite the efforts of the army surgeons, he died about midnight.

The soldiers destroyed or confiscated thirty-seven lodges and abundant winter supplies and recovered one of Custer's guidons and other equipment taken at the battle of the Little Big Horn. Similar attacks on other isolated villages by various army patrols during the following winter effectively crushed all possibility of further united resistence by the Sioux and Cheyenne and brought an end to the era of Indian war on the northern Plains.

See Dee Brown, *Bury My Heart at Wounded Knee* (1971); J. W. Vaughn, *Indian Fights: New Facts on Seven Encounters* (1966); and Stanley Vestal, *Sitting Bull: Champion of the Sioux* (rev. ed. 1957).—P. R. M.

Smith, Dan (1865-1934). Illustrator. Born in Greenland of Danish parents, Smith came as a boy to the United States and at the age of fourteen went to Copenhagen to study at the Public Arts Institute. Upon returning to America, he received further training at the Pennsylvania Academy of the Fine Arts and eventually joined the art staff of *Leslie's Illustrated Newspaper* as an illustrator about 1890. His first western pictures were published by *Leslie's* as early as 1891 and continued to appear through 1897, based upon at least one, if not several, western trips. His first were pictorial records of activities at the Pine Ridge Indian agency in South Dakota, and the next series was based on a trip to New Mexico in 1891, which may have been an extension of the South Dakota tour. Several sets of illustrations credited to Dan Smith and picturing the opening of Oklahoma Territory to white settlement also were published in *Leslie's*, probably redrawn from photographs. After about 1897, Smith directed his activities into other channels, serving once more as a pictorial reporter during the Spanish-American War.

See Robert Taft, *Artists and Illustrators of the Old West, 1850-1900.* (1953).—D. C. H.

Smith, Henry Nash (1906-   ). Historian and literary critic. Smith spent most of his life in an academic environment. Born in Dallas, Texas, he received his B.A. degree from Southern Methodist University in 1925 and his Ph.D degree from Harvard in 1940. He taught at Southern Methodist University (1927-41), the University of Texas (1941-47), the University of Minnesota (1947-53), and the University of California at Berkeley.

To specialists in American literature, Smith is probably best known for his work on Mark Twain. He edited *Mark Twain of the Enterprise* (1957) and *Mark Twain, San Francisco Correspondent* (1957) and was co-editor of the *Mark Twain-Howells Letters* (1960). His biographical and critical studies of Twain include *Mark Twain: The Development of a Writer* (1962) and *Mark Twain's Fable of Progress* (1964).

To western Americana buffs, however, Smith's reputation rests largely on *Virgin Land: The American West as Symbol and Myth* (1950), a study of the West with only peripheral reference to Twain. This enormously complex study attempts to relate the actual West to the symbols and myths that, from the very beginning of the American experience, surrounded it. Smith traced the development of the notion of the "passage to India" into the idea of "manifest destiny" and the native American sense of mission; he chronicled the development of the frontier hero from James Fenimore Cooper's Leatherstocking through the various transmutations of the dime novel; and he discussed the ramifications of the mystical notion of America as "the garden of the world."

Virgin Land is an excellent example of a type of history that has been too rarely attempted in the study of the American West. The preponderance has been anecdotal. Biographies of colorful characters—gunfighters, frontier judges, cavalry officers, Indians—abound. Careful studies of railroads, rivers, trails, and of the men who made or explored them also fill libraries. And yet few thoughtful observers of the American West have taken the time to ask just what it all means. This question Smith tried to answer.—J. K. F.

Smith, Jedediah S. (1799-1831). Fur trader and explorer. Smith was born in Bainbridge, New York, the son of New England parents. After serving as a clerk on a Lake Erie vessel in his early teens, Smith went to St. Louis. In 1822 he participated in the first expedition that William H. ASHLEY led up the Missouri. A year later when Ashley's second party was attacked by the Arikara, Smith was one of those engaged in fighting the Indians. Under orders from Ashley he then launched out from Fort Kiowa as a leader of an overland party to the Black Hills, where he was savagely mauled by a grizzly bear. The party moved westward and wintered at the site of modern Dubois, Wyoming. From the Indians they learned of an easy pass through the Rockies, and thus they rediscovered the SOUTH PASS (first discovered by returning Astorians) as they sought to find a way to return to the summer fur-trade rendezvous. Smith's discovery was of incalculable value, for it meant that an easy route along the Platte and Sweetwater rivers to the Rocky Mountain hunting grounds could be used instead of the Missouri. It also meant that wagons, and therefore settlers, might more easily go to Oregon or California by a central route.

In October 1824 he met the Hudson's Bay Company Snake country expedition, commanded by Alexander Ross, and saved the lives of the Iroquois trappers in that party, which he accompanied north to the Hudson's Bay Company fort, Flathead Post. He prepared an able report of Ashley's Canadian rivals on this reconnaissance. In late 1825 he became a partner of Ashley and the leader of his field parties. In the rendezvous of 1826 Smith, David E. Jackson, and William L. Sublette bought out Ashley. That fall he began his greatest exploring expedition from Cache Lake to the Southwest to discover new trapping grounds. His route ran to the Great Salt Lake and then southward onto the Colorado Plateau, and along the Colorado river to the Mojave Desert. The expedition then crossed westward to California, arriving at San Gabriel, the first American party to go overland through the Southwest. It marched northward through the San Joaquin valley and then tried to cross eastward over the mountains via the American River. Eventually Smith and two companions reached Ebbetts Pass and embarked across the Great Basin. After nearly dying of thirst, the three men reached the rendezvous on July 3, 1827, the first ever to cross the Sierras eastward and to traverse the Great Basin.

Soon Smith took another party into the field and retraced much of his previous route to San Gabriel, but this time the Mohave Indians, having recently been beaten by Sylvestre Pratte and his trappers, attacked Smith's party and killed ten of his men. When he reached San Gabriel, the Mexican officials of California greeted the arrival of this Anglo with suspicion. Eventually Smith was able to go by ship to San Francisco and to join the men whom he had left in the San Joaquin valley. His party then marched northward to modern Oregon, where the party was massacred on the Umpqua River on July 13, 1828. Of the eighteen men in the party only Smith and three others escaped death at the hands of the Indians. The remnant fled to Fort Vancouver, where Dr. John McLoughlin of the Hudson's Bay Company welcomed them, and later recovered their furs from the Indians. By 1828 Smith reached the summer fur-trading rendezvous after traveling through the territory of the Hudson's Bay Company. In that year and the next he led two more hunting parties through present-day Wyoming and Montana. In 1830 he reported skillfully to the secretary of war about the British strength in the Oregon country and the Northwest.

Smith determined to retire to the mercantile business in 1830 but was persuaded to enter the Santa Fe trade by taking a supply of goods to the New Mexican capital. En route Smith rode ahead of his party and even his good friend Thomas Fitzpatrick to find a water hole. While alone he was discovered by Comanche on the Cimarron River and killed in 1831. Smith was one of the nation's most important trapper-explorers, and in his travels he filled in many of the missing pieces of western geography and demonstrated that feasible routes existed across the West to northern and southern California and to Oregon. By making the riches of California and the Oregon country seem available for American settlement and American sovereignty, he was a major agent for the advocates of westward expansion. Smith's accomplishments were not fully appreciated, however, until modern scholars compiled a full record of his remarkable explorations and his role in opening the West. It would be a mistake to view Smith as a rough-and-ready frontiersman in buckskin. He was a deeply religious person and a literate and civilized gentleman whom even those giants of the trade, Ashley, Fitzpatrick, and William Sublette, respected and admired.

See William H. Goetzmann, *Exploration and Empire* (1966); Dale L. Morgan, *Jedediah Smith and the Opening of the West* (1953); Alson Jesse Smith, *Men Against the Mountains: Jedediah Smith and the Southwest Expedition of 1826-1829* (1965).—G. B. D.

Smith, Jerome H. (1861-1942). Cartoonist, illustrator, and painter. Born in Pleasant Valley, Illinois, Smith at eighteen years of age made his way to Leadville, Colorado, and drifted about the West for a time before returning to Chicago in 1884 to attend art school. His first cartoons appeared in *The Rambler*, a Chicago weekly, following which he landed a position on the art staff of *Judge*. Cartoons with his signature frequently were seen in that publication between 1887 and 1891. In 1889 Smith was sent to the Northwest on assignment by *Leslie's Illustrated Newspaper*, at that time a *Judge* publication

recently acquired by Russell B. Harrison, publisher of the *Daily Journal* in Helena, Montana. A forthcoming *Leslie's* issue on Montana with pictures failed to materialize, but a series of western illustrations, many of them Smith's, were published. After 1890 Smith traveled widely in the West from Texas to British Columbia and visited California and the Dakotas, where he made his living at mining, herding cattle, freighting, and stage driving. He also may have spent two years abroad in Paris before finally settling in British Columbia, where he began to paint in oils. Most of Smith's later works depict aspects of former western experiences, some of his pictures being reproduced in lithograph. Until the end of his life he recreated the West of an earlier day.

See Robert Taft, *Artists and Illustrators of the Old West, 1850-1900* (1953).—D. C. H.

Smith, Joseph, Jr. (1805-1844). Founder of Mormon church. Perhaps the most charismatic and controversial religious leader of nineteenth-century America, Smith was born in Sharon, Vermont. His family, though both poor and obscure, gave to Smith a heritage of religious devotion, inquiry, and mysticism that resulted in an extraordinary conversion experience while he was still a youth. Putting this experience into writing for the first time in 1832, young Smith revealed the extent of his early religious awakening.

> At about the age of twelve years my mind became seriously impressed with regard to the all-important concerns for the welfare of my immortal soul, which led me to searching the Scriptures, believing as I was taught that they contained the word of God. . . . Thus from the age of twelve years to fifteen I pondered many things in my heart concerning the situation of the world of mankind, the contentions and divisions, the wickedness and abominations, and the darkness which pervaded the minds of mankind. My mind became exceedingly distressed, for I became convicted of my sins and by searching the Scriptures I found that mankind did not come unto the Lord but that they had apostatised from the true and living faith. And there was no society or denomination that built upon the Gospel of Jesus Christ as recorded in the New Testament. And I felt to mourn for my own sins and for the sins of the world. . . . Therefore I cried unto the Lord for mercy, for there was none else to whom I could go and obtain mercy. And the Lord heard my cry in the wilderness. And while in the attitude of calling upon the Lord in the 16th year of my age a pillar of light above the brightness of the sun at noon day came down from above and rested upon me, and I was filled with the spirit of God, and the Lord opened the heavens upon me, and I saw the Lord and he spake unto me saying, "Joseph my son, thy sins are forgiven thee. Go thy way, walk in my statutes, and keep my commandments."

In subsequent accounts of this experience, Smith indicated that it had occurred in the spring of 1820 (his fifteenth year) and that both God the Father and Jesus Christ had appeared to him on this occasion.

This modern-day epiphany allegedly occurred near the Smith farm at Manchester, New York, part of an area described as the "burned-over district" because of the tumultuous religious revivalism in that region. Smith's experience, however, was no ephemeral plunge into religious ecstasy. After being ridiculed for accepting the reality of this experience, Smith submerged his visionary experience into his private consciousness. Three years later he allegedly was visited by the angel Moroni. The angel informed Smith that it was his task to translate an ancient history written upon metal plates by pre-Columbian inhabitants of the Western Hemisphere. Between 1823 and 1827, Smith claimed, he made annual visits to the hill where the plates were buried, in order to receive instruction that would prepare him for his role as a modern prophet of God.

Claiming to have received the ancient records in 1827, Smith created a local sensation in 1829 when his plans to publish a new volume of Scripture became known to the public. During that year three men reported that Moroni had appeared to them and had shown them the plates. Eight other men also testified that Smith had allowed them to see and handle the plates. In 1829 Smith and his scribe, Oliver Cowdery, were allegedly given special authority (priesthood) by John the Baptist and by the ancient apostles Peter, James, and John.

After publishing the Book of Mormon in March 1830, Smith organized a church on April 6, 1830. On that occasion he dictated a revelation that designated him "a seer, a translator, a prophet, and apostle of Jesus Christ." From that time forward Smith's career and increasing claims of revelation and authority were met with rage, derision, or wonderment, but seldom with indifference.

Because he had been rebuffed by some associates at the first disclosure of his youthful visions, he first sought converts within his own family, and it was to his immediate family, near relatives, and acquaintances that Smith turned for much of the leadership of the new church. He also chose men of recognized ability with whom he shared no close family ties. Prominent among these leaders was Sidney Rigdon, an imposing orator and minister who had originally been associated with Alexander Campbell, early leader of the Campbellites (Disciples of Christ). Rigdon became Smith's first counselor. After the church moved to Nauvoo, Illinois, in 1839, William Law, a Canadian merchant, became second counselor. Included among the apostles were John Taylor, former Methodist minister from Canada; the educated and intelligent Pratt brothers (Parley and Orson); and the indomitable and tireless Brigham Young and Heber C. Kimball.

Smith's intense effort to achieve unified leadership through familial and other ties was occasioned by the internal stresses of the church. Membership grew phenomenally, but apostasy was a continued threat that followed every revelatory innovation. Scores apostatized when he announced a vision that dispensed with the conventional concept of heaven and hell. When he incorporated economic leadership within his prophetic role and when the banking institution he founded in Kirtland, Ohio, failed during the national Panic of 1837, hundreds became disaffected. Others left the faith during the bloody persecutions he and his people endured in Missouri as a result of his millenarian aspirations to make Missouri the eventual inheritance of the saints. At Nauvoo, Illinois, Smith's secret introduction of plural marriage as a doctrine and practice alienated many. In

the spring of 1844, his announcement as a candidate for the presidency of the United States caused still others to falter in their devotion to him. Throughout all these stresses and crises, however, the vast majority of the Latter-day Saints remained loyal and devoted to Smith and the church he had organized in 1830. By the time of his death in 1844, there were approximately 35,000 Latter-day Saints.

As a religious leader Smith had a remarkable influence on people. He inspired, awed, and permanently impressed the thousands who joined the church during his lifetime. This influence was not limited to his followers but included such unlikely persons as the men who guarded him while he languished in prison during the darkest period of the Missouri sojourn of the church. When Smith, in chains, rebuked them for their blasphemy and malicious boasting of murder and rape, the armed guards cowered before him. Even Josiah Quincy, the urbane mayor of Boston, was so awed by Smith during a brief visit to Nauvoo, that decades later Quincy strongly praised him in print. An enigma to his age and to many of his most devoted followers, Smith seemed to personify the power, awesomeness, and spiritual canniness characteristic of the ancient prophets he emulated.

There are limits, however, to the historical significance of such extraordinary charisma. It is the catalog of Smith's accomplishments that continues to intrigue his biographers and inspire his followers more than a century after he was murdered by a mob at the Carthage jail on June 27, 1844. The Book of Mormon, longer than the New Testament and rich with a variety of writing styles, historical crises, personalities, and doctrinal treatises, stands as a formidable document whether one regards it as inspired translation of an historical record or as a work of imaginative literature. In addition, his revelatory writings include a portion of the Mosaic revelation absent from Genesis and an autobiographical record of Abraham allegedly translated from papyrus scrolls discovered in Egypt and purchased by Smith. (Both are published in the Salt Lake City edition of the *Pearl of Great Price*, 1851.) He produced an ambitious but incomplete revision of the Authorized Version of the Bible (published in Independence, Missouri, by the Reorganized Church). More than a hundred of Smith's written revelations received between 1823 and 1843 have been collected as the *Doctrine and Covenants* (1835). As a writer, Smith is revealed by extant letters, particularly those written during his imprisonment in Missouri, to have possessed a lyric sensitivity that belies his lack of formal education and literary training. His sermons also indicate the diversity of his metaphysical probings.

Beyond the realm of the written and spoken word, Smith's activities were equally diverse. He personally directed the erection of two imposing temples, one at Kirtland and one at Nauvoo, and became the city planner for Nauvoo, which incorporated farsighted urban design for a city that grew to a population of more than ten thousand in five years. In 1841 the governor of Illinois appointed Smith the lieutenant general of the Nauvoo Legion, the largest city militia in the state, and from 1842 until his death Smith was the mayor of the burgeoning metropolis of Nauvoo. He began campaigning for the presidency of the United States shortly before his death at the hands of a mob.

In 1827 Smith married Emma Hale (1804-79), who bore him eight children: Alva (1828-28), Thaddeus (1831-31), Louisa (1831-31), Joseph (1832-1914), Frederick G. W. (1836-62), Alexander H. (1838-1909), Don C. (1840-41), and David H. (1844-1904). In addition, Smith and his wife adopted two infant children at the time their own twins died in 1831. There is also evidence that Smith was ceremonially "sealed" to a number of other women, but there is no conclusive evidence that any children were born to these unions.

See LATTER-DAY SAINTS.

See May Audentia Smith Anderson, *Ancestry and Posterity of Joseph Smith and Emma Hale* (1929); Richard Anderson, *Joseph Smith's New England Heritage* (1971); Milton V. Backman, Jr., *Joseph Smith's First Vision* (1971); Fawn Brodie, *No Man Knows My History* (1946); John Henry Evans, *Joseph Smith, An American Prophet* (1933); B. H. Roberts, ed., *History of the Church of Jesus Christ of Latter-day Saints: Period I, History of Joseph Smith,* 6 vols. (1901ff.); and Lucy Smith, *Biographical Sketches of Joseph Smith, the Prophet* (1853).—D. M. Q.

Smith, Joseph Fielding (1838-1918). Mormon leader. Nephew of the prophet Joseph Smith, Joseph Fielding Smith went to Utah with his mother, a widow of Hyrum Smith, the fellow martyr of Joseph Smith. In 1854, he left for a mission to Hawaii, returning in 1857. During the "Utah War" period, he served as sergeant-at-arms for the legislative council and in 1860 departed for a proselyting mission to Great Britain. Only a year after his return in 1863, he served another mission to Hawaii. Following his return from Hawaii, Brigham Young ordained Smith an apostle in 1866 and made him a special counselor until there was a vacancy in the Quorum of the Twelve Apostles the following year. As an apostle, he also served in the territorial house of representatives (1865-74), and then left for Great Britain, presiding over the proselyting work there. In 1880 he became second counselor to Mormon president John Taylor and also returned to the territorial legislature. He was second counselor to Taylor, Wilford Woodruff, and Lorenzo Snow from 1880 to 1901. At the death of Snow he became president of the Latter-day Saint church (1901-18).

Smith was president during a difficult transitional period of Mormon history. Eager to continue the trend of LDS acceptance in the American community, he had to discountenance practices and institutions that invited further conflict, such as polygamy and theocratic political control in Utah. When the investigation into Mormon senator Reed Smoot (1904-07) made it apparent that such recidivism must end, President Smith sought to suppress those tendencies. In 1904 he issued a so-called Second Manifesto prohibiting polygamous marriages, in 1906 two recalcitrant apostles resigned from the Quorum, in 1907 he issued a statement disavowing any church attempts to foster polygamy or political-economic domination, and in 1910 he inaugurated a program of systematically investigating and excommunicating persistent violators of the church ruling on new polygamous marriages. Having authorized the construction of temples outside the United States and having begun a vigorous effort at obtaining an international acceptance for the Mormon church, Smith exemplified the characteristics for which twentieth-century Mormonism was to become famous.

See Andrew Jenson, *Latter-day Saint Biographical Encyclopedia* (1901).—L. J. A.

Smith, Thomas James (1830?-1870). Lawman. Smith's early life is a blur of conjecture, supposition, and fact, but he was apparently born in New York City of Irish parents. New York's city records for that period are sparse, and Smith's name is not easy to trace. T. C. Henry, an early mayor of Abilene, Kansas, during Smith's tenure as marshal there, provides most of the information known about him. He believed that Smith was a New York policeman for a time before heading west in the 1850s and that Smith was seriously wounded in 1857 during the slaughter of more than a hundred helpless emigrants by Indians and their Mormon leaders in the Mountain Meadows massacre. There are accounts of his presence in Utah and Nevada and reports of his work with freighting outfits out of Iowa and Nebraska. He is first picked up with some certainty hauling supplies for the construction of western railroads. By 1868, he was employed by Cheesborough and McGee, a firm with a grading contract with the Union Pacific Railroad. In November of that year Smith gained his first real notoriety as a leader of the "Bear River Riot."

Bear River was a railhead about forty miles west of Green River, Wyoming, that had more than its share of the criminal element. The town also had a crusading newspaper called the *Frontier Index,* edited by an itinerant newspaperman named Leigh Freeman. Freeman conducted a one-man campaign against lawlessness in Bear River and was instrumental in organizing a vigilante group that eventually hanged three of the rougher element. In the midst of the excitement a group of Cheesborough and McGee employees descended on the town, got themselves very drunk, and caused such a disturbance that three of them were arrested. The next day, incited by the inflammatory statements of the *Index,* the railroad gang marched on the town. Tom Smith was their leader. First, the graders destroyed the *Index* office in a vain search for Freeman. Next, they marched on the town and attempted to burn down the jail to secure the release of the prisoners. From that point on accounts differ, but it seems clear that the townspeople barricaded themselves in a store. Some say that a parley was held that ended when Smith shot a man named Nuckles and sparked a general fight. Other accounts maintain that the local citizens opened fire on the graders. At any rate, a gun battle ensued that left several men dead. Eventually troops from Fort Bridger arrived and many of the rioters, including Smith (who was seriously wounded in the melee), were arrested.

Henry and others have lauded Smith for his actions at Bear River. The circumstances of the fight are confused at best, but it should be pointed out that many of the eyewitnesses saw nothing heroic in his actions and regarded him as a ruffian. Nevertheless, Bear River gave Smith a nickname, and his reputation for courage and coolness won him the marshal's job at end-of-track as the Union Pacific proceeded west. In 1869 he was marshal at Kit Carson, Colorado. William M. Breakenridge, himself a pioneer lawman in Arizona, met Smith there and called him "the bravest man I ever had the pleasure of meeting."

Somehow the Bear River incident seems out of character with the rest of Smith's career. He was a tall, strikingly handsome man when he rode into Abilene the next year and applied for the position of marshal. Indeed, he seemed so mild-mannered and gentle that Mayor Henry turned him down. But when conditions in Abilene worsened, the mayor wired Smith at Kit Carson and hired him. Smith put the lid on Abilene, enforced the ordinances against guns, gained the respect of the Texas cowhands, and did it all without the use of firearms. Tom Smith quieted Abilene with his forceful manner and backed his decisions with his fists. He wore two guns as he patrolled the city streets on his horse, but he never used them in Abilene, a strange contrast to the image of Tom Smith blazing away in a fury at Bear River.

But it was a brief reprieve for Abilene. On November 2, 1870, as a favor to the local sheriff, Smith rode out to arrest a farmer for murder. In the scuffle that followed, Smith was nearly decapitated with an ax. So died a man whose motto and style was "Anybody can bring in a dead man."

See T. C. Henry, "Thomas James Smith of Abilene," *Kansas Historical Collections* (1905-06); and Nyle H. Miller and Joseph W. Snell, *Why the West was Wild* (1963).
—G. L. R.

Smith, Jackson and Sublette. See FUR TRADE: *in the United States.*

Smoot, Reed (1862-1941). Utah politician. Born in Salt Lake City and reared in Provo, Utah, Smoot attended the local schools, enrolled at the University of Utah briefly, and graduated from Brigham Young Academy. He managed the Provo cooperative general store, served a two-year proselyting mission to England, and upon his return managed the Provo Woolen Mills. He was president of the Provo Commercial Bank and a director of Zion's Co-operative Mercantile Institution, Deseret National Bank, and Deseret Savings Bank. He also held mining interests in Utah.

Smoot was made an apostle in the Mormon church in 1900, and three years later elected to the Senate of the United States as a Republican. He was seated but not permitted to function pending an investigation of the Mormon religion and his obligations as an apostle. Many senators felt that his leadership in the Latter-day Saint church was incompatible with the allegiance he would have to swear as a senator. Less than the required two thirds felt there was cause to expel him, and Smoot was finally seated in 1907. He served in the Senate continuously for thirty years. Smoot's victory indicated that American pluralism had developed sufficiently to accommodate even leaders of unpopular religions within the governmental framework.

Smoot was interested in tariff and taxation and became chairman of the Senate Finance Committee. He advocated business, conservation, and mining development in the West and was responsible for the creation of Zion and Bryce national parks in Utah. An advocate of high protective tariffs, he was co-sponsor of the Hawley-Smoot Tariff Act of 1929.

See Milton R. Merrill, *Reed Smoot, Utah Politician* (1953).

Smythe, William Ellsworth (1861-1922). Leader of the irrigation movement. Smythe was born in Worcester, Massachusetts, and inherited the New Englander's concern for social problems. Following the example set by his hero, Horace Greeley, Smythe decided to become a journalist at the age of sixteen. After becoming a seasoned newspaperman on the Boston *Herald,* he heeded the advice of Greeley and went west in 1888 to become editor and publisher of the Kearney (Nebraska) *Expositor.* The searing drought of 1890 led him to promote the cause of irrigation through the columns of the Omaha *Bee.* With his typical fervor, he said he was taking up the "cross of a new crusade," and a crusade it soon became.

Though an easterner, Smythe was well equipped to propagandize for the "conquest of arid America" through irrigation. Hitherto, the foremost spokesman for irrigation, John Wesley Powell, director of the U.S. Geological Survey, had voiced the need and won congressional backing for irrigation surveys but had run afoul of western resistance to reserving irrigable lands from private entry. In April 1891 Smythe launched a national movement with the publication of the journal *Irrigation Age.* The first National Irrigation Congress, held at Salt Lake City in July 1891, was attended by several hundred delegates from most of the seventeen arid states and territories. They adopted a resolution favoring cession of federal lands in aid of irrigation and established a continuing organization with Smythe as secretary and later as chairman. *Irrigation Age,* with circulation bounding to ten thousand in the first year, was accepted as the voice of the movement and discussed engineering, bond sales, and irrigation farming, as well as the more ethereal sketchings of a new society. Smythe always linked colonization with irrigation. Until he severed his ties with the journal in 1895, his editorials painted in rosy hues his dreams for the desert fulfillment of the American homestead ideal, where colonies of settlers could live in democratic equality and economic security.

When the second congress met at Los Angeles, the Panic of 1893 had eroded some of the support of western capital. A minor rift developed when Powell and Frederick Newell of the Geological Survey presented a more realistic portrayal of the limits of western reclamation. Subsequent congresses shifted their demands from cession of public lands for private development to actual construction of reclamation projects by the federal government. By that time (1897), Smythe had turned to practical colonizing experience. The national campaign forged ahead under the leadership of George Maxwell, Francis Newlands, and others.

Smythe continued to be the foremost popularizer of the reclamation theme on the national scene even while savoring the vicissitudes of sagebrush colony life in Idaho and California. A series of articles and his book *The Conquest of Arid America* (1900) described in attractive terms the accomplishments of garden communities reclaimed from the desert, such as Greeley, Colorado, the Mormon colonies, and Riverside, California. A most significant revision of this volume, now a classic in conservation history, was published in 1905 and carried a full progress report on Reclamation Service projects.

When Smythe moved to California again, to join the staff of the San Diego *Union* in 1900, he participated in Elwood Mead's Irrigation Institutions survey in California, which demonstrated the need for water law reform in the Golden State, and campaigned for this legislation. When special economic interests obtruded, he ran unsuccessfully for Congress from the San Diego district in

1902. He then contributed to "The 20th Century West" department in the distinctive southern California periodical *Land of Sunshine,* edited by the outspoken Charles Lummis. His *Constructive Democracy* (1905) was a prescription for social justice with Square Deal connotations in the device of federally chartered corporations. Civic leaders in San Diego funded his next project, *History of San Diego* (1907), which has evoked praise over the years for its definitive and literary character. His last published work, *City Homes on Country Lanes* (1921), came at the end of his experience as promoter and resident of several Little Lander colonies in California during the years 1907 to 1918 and is a promotional essay for future colonies. This movement spawned the magazine *Little Lands in America* and also prompted his appointment in the Department of the Interior to plan the abortive soldiers' homestead program. At the time of his death he was in the midst of a campaign to raise funds for suburban workingmen's colonies in the East.

While in his later years Smythe hazarded his talents and energies in bringing western man into communion with the "new earth," he is little remembered today for his advancement of the back-to-the-land movement. His lasting reputation must rest with his inauguration and championship of the national reclamation movement.

There is no biography of Smythe. The best recent sketch of his life is found in Lawrence B. Lee, "Introduction to the 1969 Edition" of William E. Smythe, *The Conquest of Arid America* (1969). For Smythe's Nebraska years and the inception of the irrigation movement, see Martin E. Carlson, "William E. Smythe: Irrigation Crusader," *Journal of the West* (January 1968). Smythe's contributions to Charles Lummis' journal, *Out West,* is appraised in Edwin Bingham, *Charles F. Lummis: Editor of the South-West* (1955). A scholarly portrayal of Smythe's Little Lander program is found in Henry S. Anderson, "The Little Landers' Colonies: A Unique Agricultural Experiment in California," *Agricultural History* (October 1931).—L. B. L.

Snake River. The Snake River, principal tributary of the Columbia, was discovered by members of the Lewis and Clark expedition on their way to the Pacific in 1805 and was the route they followed to reach the main stream of the Columbia. The Snake River basin occupies 109,000 square miles of land in Wyoming, Idaho, Oregon, and Washington. This represents about forty-two percent of the total area of the Columbia Basin. The average annual flow of the Snake is 37 million acre-feet, which represents about one fifth the annual flow of the Columbia.

The main stream has its source in Yellowstone National Park and flows through the Jackson Hole country of Wyoming. It then turns and flows south and west into Idaho and thence northwest to its juncture with Henrys Fork, its principal headwater tributary. The combined rivers then make a big arc through the Snake River plain, flowing southwest, then west, and finally northwest before tumbling into the Grand Canyon of the Snake, one of the world's deepest gorges. Its average depth is about 5,500 feet but its maximum depths reach almost 8,000 feet. The gorge, created by the Snake cutting through the Rockies, extends for about 125 miles along the Idaho-Oregon boundary line. Along the way the Snake receives the waters of its largest tributary,

the Salmon, and the waters of the Clearwater before turning west to enter the Columbia River.

The Snake and its tributaries rise among humid snow-covered mountain peaks, but much of their courses lie across the semiarid Columbia Plateau, described by one of the first topographic engineers to see it as "an almost waterless, lifeless region. . . . It is a desolation where even the most hopeful can find nothing in its future prospects to cheer." Fortunately, this young army officer proved to be a poor forecaster and did not visualize the use of the abundant water resources of the Snake for irrigating farmlands. Anyone following the belt of verdant green across Idaho today cannot visualize the landscape as seen by early explorers.

On reaching the Snake basin, Lewis and Clark first explored the Salmon River drainage and then traveled down the Clearwater, made boats near Orofino, Idaho, and floated on the Snake to the Columbia in the fall months of 1805. Their party was soon followed by American and Canadian trappers, one of whom, Andrew Henry, erected Fort Henry in 1810 on a tributary of the Snake near present-day St. Anthony, Idaho. This was the first of a number of trading posts erected on the river in the early part of the nineteenth century. Perhaps the most important of these was Fort Hall, which became the rendezvous point for traders and trappers and later for immigrants moving along the Oregon Trail to the Willamette valley.

Acquisition of Oregon Territory in 1846 by the United States opened the territory for settlement, but it was not until the 1860s that permanent settlement became possible. Hostile Indians had defeated earlier attempts of the pioneers to settle in the Snake River basin. The discovery of gold in 1862 near Boise brought large numbers of miners into the area from California and Oregon. At the same time Mormons had begun to move northward out of Utah to take up farmland under provisions of the Homestead Act. By 1864 regular passenger and mail service connected Snake River communities with Salt Lake City; The Dalles, Oregon; and Walla Walla, Washington. The completion of the Northern Pacific Railroad and a branch of the Union Pacific in 1881 made it possible to travel east or west out of the region.

Following the passage of the Reclamation Act in 1902, several projects to develop the irrigation potential of the Snake were authorized by Congress, and the future of the Snake River basin was assured. However, controversy over the development of the tremendous water resources of the middle portion of the Snake and its tributary, the Salmon, continues. Whether to preserve portions of these streams as "wild rivers" or to develop their tremendous water resources to generate badly needed electrical energy remains a major question of debate between conservationists and developers.

See Boyd Norton, *Snake Wilderness* (1972).—R. W. D.

Snow, Eliza Roxey (1804-1887). Mormon poet and suffragette. Born in Becket, Massachusetts, and a sister of Mormon president Lorenzo Snow, Eliza was still a baby when her family moved to Ohio in 1806. Originally Baptists, the Snows became Mormons in 1835. Eliza had achieved relative success as a poet prior to joining the Mormon church and continued to write significant poetry after becoming a member of that faith. Latter-day Saint (LDS) theology dominated her poetry, but on

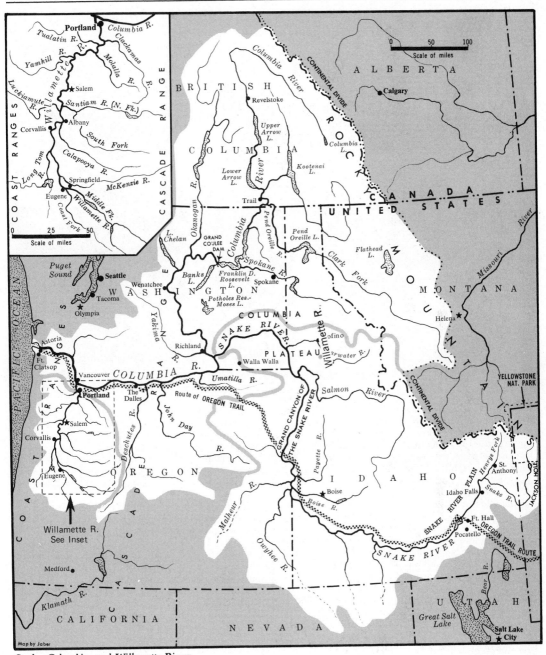

Snake, Columbia, and Willamette Rivers

occasion she wrote secular poems. A few of her poems were put to music and still form part of the LDS hymnal, the most famous of which is "O My Father."

Living in Mormon communities, Snow taught at a girls school in Kirtland, Ohio, and was secretary to the Women's Relief Society in Nauvoo, Illinois. While at Nauvoo, she became a plural wife of Joseph Smith, president and prophet of the LDS church. Joining the second group of Saints who crossed the Plains in 1847,

she served as a Relief Society leader in Utah and was its presiding officer from 1867 to 1887. She married Brigham Young in 1849, but bore him no children. In 1872 she accompanied a tour to the Holy Land. Late in life, in 1882, she accepted the presidency of the new Deseret Hospital.

See Andrew Jenson, *Latter-day Saint Biographical Encyclopedia* (1901).—L. J. A.

sod house. As settlers moved onto the prairie, they

A pioneer family poses in front of its sod house built into the side of a hill, while a cow grazes on the "roof." (Library of Congress)

had to build sod houses because the treeless land did not provide the raw material for numerous log houses, the traditional abode of pioneers. They were first built in Kansas in the 1850s, but the more typical sod house was built in the post-Civil War period. In the prewar sod house, the walls, but not the roof, were of sod.

Often, the first home that a pioneer would construct was a combination of a dugout and a sod house, built into the side of a hill or ravine. Sod houses on the prairie were of many shapes and sizes. Most had only one room; a few contained several. A large sod house was sixteen feet wide and twenty feet long. To construct the typical one-room house, approximately half an acre of ground was needed. The ground was plowed and the sod bricks were carefully cut from the furrows. Each brick was about three feet long and several inches thick. The bricks were then carried to the building site and laid as clay bricks are. Frames for a door and windows (the average house had one small window) were set into the walls and the sod laid around them. Cracks were filled with dirt or clay, and occasionally the walls were reinforced with hickory stems driven into them. The financial status of a pioneer was revealed by the roof of his sod house. The poorer the settler, the cruder his roof. Brush for sheeting was placed on rafters, followed by a layer of prairie grass and finally one of sod. If a settler could afford lumber and tar paper, these items replaced the brush and prairie grass layers, but the final covering was still of sod. Sod bricks for the roof were not as thick and were generally placed so that the grass side was down.

The interior of sod houses also varied according to the financial standing of its owner. Some walls were finished off with plaster, while others were simply smoothed down with a spade. Two small rooms were often created by hanging a room divider, quilt, or rag carpet. Window and door closings could be made of several materials, ranging from buffalo robes and blankets to wood and glass panes. Furniture was often nothing more than nail kegs and soap boxes for chairs and a dry-goods box for a table.

Life in a sod house could be troublesome and even hazardous, especially during a heavy rain. Few sod roofs were leak-proof, and several days were required for a roof to dry out. Occasionally roofs caved in because of their water-soaked weight or the rafters sank into the walls. Space-consuming posts had to be placed inside the house to prevent such calamities.

Even when the sun shone, dirt and grass fell like rain drops from the roof. To combat this nuisance cheese-cloth was hung under the rafters to catch the fallout. An umbrella was often indispensable, for it could be held over the cook and stove during a rainfall to keep the food dry or held over a sick member of the family to protect the patient from falling debris in houses without roof linings of cheesecloth.

Despite these drawbacks, sod houses were cool during summer and warm in the winter months. The houses were sturdy and were rarely blown over. Also, they could not be totally destroyed by prairie fire. As an added precaution fireplaces were usually made of sod. Six or seven years was the life expectancy of a sod house.

When a settler prospered, he usually built a frame house. The livestock were then moved into the vacated sod house from their cruder dugout or shelter of sod.

Sod was also used to build fences, windbreaks, and out-buildings. Thus, the prairie supplied the pioneer not only with a livelihood but also with shelter and protection for himself, his family, livestock, and fowl.

See Everett Dick, *The Sod-House Frontier, 1854-1890*
—D. J. T.

Sonnichsen, Charles Leland (1901-   ). Teacher and historian. Sonnichsen was born in Iowa and educated at the University of Minnesota and Harvard University. In 1927 he began two years of teaching at Carnegie Institute. In 1931 he moved to the University of Texas at El Paso, where in 1933 he became chairman of the English department and in 1960 was appointed dean of the graduate school.

Shortly after Sonnichsen moved to El Paso, he became interested in the legends and lore of the border country and in the literature of the West. Over the years, he slowly amassed a sizable collection of western fiction and historical works.

Not surprisingly, it was not long before he began producing his own books, which, with the exception of an anthology, *The Southwest in Life and Literature* (1952), deal with the history of the old Southwest. His first, *Billy King's Tombstone* (1942), was quickly followed by *Roy Bean: Law West of the Pecos* (1943), the best book on that legendary character. Before Sonnichsen had finished, he had completed at least a dozen books, including: *Cowboys and Cattle Kings* (1950), an account of the modern cowboy; *I'll Die Before I'll Run* (1951), on Texas feuds; *The Mescalero Apaches* (1958), a notable contribution to Apache history; and *Pass of the North* (1968), an impressive history of four centuries on the Rio Grande and the twin cities El Paso and Juarez. In addition to his books, Sonnichsen contributed numerous articles and book reviews to magazines and journals.

Sonnichsen was a member of the Western Writers of America, the American Folklore Society, and the Society of American Historians.—J. C. D.

Sonoma Mission. See SAN FRANCISCO SOLANO.

Sonora, California. Mining town. Sonora, the "queen of the southern mines," yielded more than $40 million in gold from its rivers, creeks, and gulches between 1848 and 1860. The town was the site of the Big Bonanza, often called the "richest single-pocket mine ever discovered in California." Founded by Mexicans from the state of Sonora, the town was large, rich, and violent. Much of the history of the region surrounding Sonora, such as the story of the "ghost of Sonora," Joaquin MURIETA, found its way into the stories of Mark Twain and Bret Harte. Some of the old buildings still remain scattered throughout modern Sonora, a thriving city in the center of a mining, lumbering, and orchard country.

See Remi Nadeau, *Ghost Towns and Mining Camps of California* (1965); and Muriel S. Wolle, *The Bonanza Trail* (1953). See also Robert G. Ferris, ed., *Prospector, Cowhand, and Sodbuster* (1967).—R. B. W.

Sonoran Desert. See VEGETATION: *deserts*.

Sorenson, Elias. See GREAT LAKES, MEN OF THE.

South Carolina, settlement of. In 1663 Charles II granted a charter to eight English courtiers for the vast territory south of Virginia called Carolina. The idea for a Carolina proprietorship was first advanced by Sir John Colleton, a royalist who had lived in Barbados during Cromwell's reign. Colleton and his influential associates regarded their charter as a reward for loyal service to

the Stuarts and as a means of recouping their personal fortunes. The king appears to have modeled his grant largely upon an earlier charter that had been awarded to Lord Baltimore of Maryland. The eight Carolina proprietors received full seignorial privileges, although their charter authorized a legislative assembly of freeholders. It was clear, however, that sovereignty over the decisions of government and the distribution of land lay with the proprietors sitting as a palatine court in London.

The Carolina proprietors were intent on keeping their expenses as low as possible. Earlier colonial ventures had demonstrated the dangers as well as the costs of sending unseasoned Englishmen to America. Colleton and his friends, therefore, tried to attract settlers from New England, Virginia, and Barbados by offering large grants of free land. To promote interest in their project, the proprietors issued two documents, "A Declaration and Proposals to All That Will Plant in Carolina" (1663) and "The Concessions and Agreements" (1665). These statements promised colonists political freedom, religious toleration, and liberal headrights (grants of free land). In 1664 a group of Barbadians established a promising community on the Cape Fear River in present-day North Carolina. The next year a second settlement was started at Port Royal, but by 1667 both of these attempts had failed. The proprietors had not been willing to spend anything on the New World, and they received nothing in return.

After these failures most of the proprietors were willing to give up on Carolina, but Sir Anthony Ashley Cooper, soon to become the earl of Shaftesbury, was not so easily discouraged. This energetic politician convinced his fellow proprietors that successful colonization cost money, and in a matter of months he had pooled more than three thousand pounds. Late in 1669 ships carrying settlers and supplies for a new community at Port Royal departed from England, and although these colonists soon had to relocate twenty-five miles up the Ashley River, their arrival marked the beginning of permanent settlement in South Carolina. In 1669 Shaftesbury, with the assistance of his secretary, John Locke, drafted the Fundamental Constitutions of Carolina. Many historians have ridiculed the cumbersome provisions of this document as unsuited to the conditions of the New World, but only a few have bothered to examine Shaftesbury's aims. He drew heavily upon the ideas of James Harrington (1611-77), one of England's most influential political theorists. The goal of the Fundamental Constitutions was the creation of an economic and political balance between the various classes of society. Two fifths of the land in Carolina was to be granted to a hereditary nobility that bore such strange titles as "landgrave" and "cacique." The proprietors planned to distribute the remaining acreage among small freeholders. The constitutions allowed both groups a voice in the colony's government. For thirty years the proprietors attempted to persuade the Carolina "parliament" to ratify the Fundamental Constitutions, but the settlers rejected it on every occasion, preferring to move and plant wherever they pleased. And that is exactly what they did.

As Barbadian, French, and Scottish immigrants flooded into the colony during the seventeenth century, settlement tended to follow the course of rivers and creeks, rather than a prescribed gridlike pattern. Indian trade was always an important part of the Carolina economy, but it was not until the 1690s that large rice plantations began to appear along the Ashley and Cooper rivers. As time passed, moreover, planters became increasingly reliant upon slave labor, and in 1708 there were as many blacks as whites in the colony. Almost all goods flowed through Charles Town (later Charleston), which, after its founding in 1680, became the center of trade for the entire region. Merchants carried foodstuffs to Barbados, which were exchanged for ginger and sugar. These products in turn were taken to England where the colonial merchants picked up manufactured items that they sold in South Carolina.

The city of Charles Town dominated the colony's social and political development. It was there that the courts and the legislature met; it was there that the merchant-planter elite conducted its business. Because of Charles Town's unique position in the colony's life, South Carolina never established a system of county government comparable to that of Virginia and Maryland. In the 1760s the lack of local government became intolerable to the frontier settlers, who called themselves Regulators, and they demanded the same justice and political representation as that enjoyed by the Tidewater population.

The political history of South Carolina before the mid-1730s is a story of confusion frequently bordering on anarchy. As early as 1670 a group of wealthy Barbadian immigrants known as the Goose Creek faction gained control of the Carolina "parliament." These men dominated the Indian trade and carried on a flourishing, but illegal, business with various pirates. They resisted the proprietors' attempts to collect quitrents or to pass the Fundamental Constitutions into law. On their part, the proprietors tried, but failed, to reduce the influence of the Goose Creek faction. Their appointed governor, James Colleton (1686-90), once had to declare martial law to keep order. When Seth Sothel, a Carolina proprietor by right of purchase, arrived in Charles Town in 1690, the Goose Creek men arrested Colleton and declared Sothel the governor. But Sothel's arbitrary behavior won him few friends and he, too, was soon out of power. During the 1690s the proprietors and their enemies began to work out their differences, but the peace was shattered in 1704 when the proprietors' overzealous governor sponsored legislation excluding non-Anglicans from public office. The Barbadians, most of whom belonged to the Church of England, supported the bill. But Protestant dissenters, who made up a large part of South Carolina's population, complained bitterly of the injustice that had been done to them.

Throughout the entire colonial period, local Indian tribes—often goaded by Spanish or French agents—threatened the security of South Carolina's frontier. In 1715 the YAMASEE INDIANS and Creek Indians, angered by the behavior of certain white traders, attacked the outlying settlements and drove the colonists back toward Charles Town. This uprising, called the Yamasee War (1715-16), had wide political ramifications. English authorities came to realize the strategic importance of South Carolina in the imperial struggle with France and Spain for control of the North American continent. The colonists' poor showing also revealed the proprietors'

inability to provide an adequate defense for the region. The people of South Carolina begged the mother country for aid, and in 1719 they took the government into their own hands. A revolutionary body dismissed the last proprietary governor and invited England to make South Carolina a royal colony. The first royal governor arrived in 1721, but it was not until 1729 that the English exchequer compensated the proprietors for the land they had lost.

Royal government did not heal the colony's deep political divisions. During the 1720s there were violent fights in South Carolina over the merits of paper currency. By the 1740s, however, it was clear that the character of politics had begun to change, and factions no longer appealed directly to the people. M. Eugene Sirmans has explained, "The outstanding feature of South Carolina from 1743 to 1763 was the threefold struggle for power among the governor, council, and Commons House of Assembly, with the victory going to the Commons House."

The fullest account of colonial South Carolina is M. Eugene Sirmans, *Colonial South Carolina, A Political History, 1663-1763* (1966), but Charles M. Andrews, *The Colonial Period of American History* (1937), and Wesley Frank Craven, *The Southern Colonies in the Seventeenth Century, 1607-1689* (1949), contain excellent chapters on the founding.—T. H. B.

South Dakota. The decade after 1889, when DAKOTA TERRITORY was divided into two states, was marked by the heyday of the range-cattle industry and development of rural radicalism in the form of the Populist party in South Dakota. Although the winter of 1886-87 had taken a heavy toll among cattle herds, reorganization of the cattle industry brought an extension of the business in South Dakota. More than fifty outfits continued to operate on the public domain, despite the end of open-range ranching. By the advent of World War I, however, with an influx of small farmers, most of the large outfits had sold out. The population in the cattle areas of western South Dakota tripled between 1910 and 1920. Declining prices and the end of the range spelled doom to the range-cattle industry.

At the same time, farmers were organizing in an attempt to improve their lot. As prices for crops fell in the 1880s, an undercurrent of unrest broke forth with the organization of the Farmers' Alliance. After statehood, the Independent party was formed and became a significant political force during the 1890s. In the legislature of 1891, Independents succeeded in electing James Henderson KYLE to the state senate. Although unable to gain full control of the legislature, South Dakota Populists elected Andrew Lee as governor in 1897 and 1898. The defection of Senator Richard Franklin PETTIGREW from the Republicans to the Populists substantially aided the Independent cause. Although plagued by economic adversity, the Lee administration effected such reforms as the initiative and referendum. Even with the Republican control of the statehouse after 1900, progressives in the party, led by Coe Isaac CRAWFORD, ushered in an age of reform with the defeat of Alfred Beard Kittredge's stalwart machine. The years before World War I were marked by such reforms as antilobbying legislation, a direct-primary law, creation of a food-and-drug commission and a telephone commission, free textbooks, and a maximum railroad rate law. A second wave of progressivism came after Peter NORBECK was elected governor in 1916. Norbeck's program included a rural credits plan, state hail insurance, a state coal mine, state-owned terminal elevators, and the acquisition of waterpower sites.

Although World War I brought new-found prosperity to South Dakotans, postwar deflation made its impact felt throughout the 1920s. By 1925, 175 state banks had failed, and throughout the decade farm prices declined. With a floundering rural credit system and allegations of corruption, the Democrats elected in 1926 their first governor—William J. Bulow.

By the 1930s the signs of economic distress were overwhelming. During the 1920s real estate values had decreased fifty-eight percent, while the average value of farmland had declined from $71.39 per acre in 1920 to $35.24 in 1930 and $18.65 by 1935. For the only time in the state's history, the Democrats swept all state offices in 1932, with the election of Tom Berry as governor. Yet, neither Democrats nor Republicans could defeat the dust storms and low farm prices.

World War II brought the return of good times, and the years following it were prosperous and conservative. Cash income from crops and livestock, exclusive of government payments, neared the half billion figure in 1946 and continued to exceed it each year until 1955. In 1947 average income per farm was $7,600. Farm tenancy dropped from fifty-three percent in 1940 to twenty-nine percent by 1954. Both the number of mortgaged farms and mortgage indebtedness decreased sharply during the 1940s and 1950s. Rural electrification brightened farm life, while improved roads and the increasing availability of automobiles lessened the isolation of rural living.

Conservatism in politics was marked by Republican ascendency. In 1946 South Dakotans overwhelmingly supported an antilabor constitutional amendment establishing the "right to work." Postwar legislatures outlawed the closed shop, made picketing illegal, and permitted labor unions to be sued. The two-party system returned with the election of Democrats George McGovern to a seat in Congress in 1956 and Ralph Herseth to the governorship in 1958.

When South Dakota became a state, its population was 328,808; by 1930 the figure had reached its high of 692,849. During the Great Depression it declined seven percent and slowly gained after 1940 at less than four percent a decade. The Indian population increased at a more rapid rate, from 16,384 in 1920 to about 35,000 in 1970. During the years since World War II, Indian migration to the cities has left only about 6,000 on the reservations.

In 1890 thirty-three percent of the white population was foreign-born; by 1940 only one in ten had been born in a foreign country. Most of the immigrant population came from western Europe, with the Germans comprising the largest ethnic group. The largest religious group —fifteen percent of the population—was the Lutheran; thirteen percent were Roman Catholic.

Half of all South Dakotans still live on farms or in small rural communities. By the 1960s nine out of every ten acres of land were farmland. Farms, however, became larger after the war; the average farm in 1935 was 439 acres, but by 1960 it had increased to 804 acres. Although the cities increased in population and the

value of manufactured products increased dramatically from $19.6 million in 1939 to well over $100 million by the 1960s, South Dakota remains one of the nation's most rural states.

See Herbert S. Schell, *History of South Dakota* (1961). —D. J. T.

Southern Pacific Railroad. The Southern Pacific Railroad is intimately involved in the history of CALIFORNIA. The "Espee," which runs from New Orleans to California, originated in a decision made in 1870 by the "Big Four" (Collis P. HUNTINGTON, Charles CROCKER, Leland STANFORD, and Mark HOPKINS) not to get out of the railroad business once the CENTRAL PACIFIC had been completed, but to remain and develop the western end of their railroad empire.

In 1871 the group acquired the California Pacific, the Central Pacific's vital link from Sacramento to San Francisco, and began building south through the San Joaquin valley. The Southern Pacific Railroad proper had been chartered in 1865 to build direct from San Francisco to San Diego. The Huntington interests, which took control in 1870, began to build southeast to San Bernardino rather than to San Diego. Mojave and Los Angeles were reached in 1876, and by 1883 the line had been pushed eastward to Needles, California, where the Santa Fe Railroad was headed off for a time.

By 1877 the Southern Pacific controlled eighty-five percent of all railroad mileage in California and extended as far east as Yuma, Arizona. Then there occurred the confrontation with ambitious Thomas A. SCOTT, who was trying desperately to push his Texas and Pacific Railroad westward through El Paso to the coast. In an incredible burst of energy and financial daring, Huntington drove the Southern Pacific eastward, linking up with the Santa Fe at Deming, New Mexico, in 1881 to form the nation's second transcontinental railroad and reaching El Paso before Scott, whose project had been handicapped by the hard times and the Credit Mobilier scandal of the 1870s. Shortly thereafter the Southern Pacific gained control of a number of railroads that gave it direct access to New Orleans.

Huntington and his associates made huge profits, notwithstanding the magnitude of the risks and the service they performed for California. Shrewd construction financing, whereby companies controlled by them built the road for cash and stock in the road, assured them large equities in the burgeoning railroad, but it was almost twenty years before the real value of their holdings was assured. As late as 1884, for example, when all of the holdings outside the Central Pacific were reorganized into the present Southern Pacific Railroad Company, the securities of the Central Pacific were still much better known and more marketable in New York than those of the more prosperous Southern Pacific. Perhaps no railroad, except for the Pennsylvania, has ever dominated the life of a single state so thoroughly and acrimoniously as the Southern Pacific.

Because it reached into every phase of the Golden State's prosperous agricultural economy via its many branches and was determined to charge steep rates forced upon it by the existence of water competition, the Southern Pacific earned the nickname "the Octopus." Resentment of such power in the hands of one company was responsible for the emergence of strong commission regulation in California in 1880. The extent of the

Southern Pacific's influence, however, is reflected in the fact that more than one of the commissioners almost inevitably proceeded to adopt a solicitous attitude toward the Southern Pacific's fate under regulation. The interference of the Southern Pacific in California politics is the chief charge brought against it by historians. Southern Pacific historian Stuart Daggett concluded that the actual amount of money the railroad spent in influencing politicians was very small. The heat generated, however, was intense. In addition to the first commissioners, some of whom were clearly taking bribes, Huntington did not scruple to buy state legislators whenever necessary, revealing his contempt for that breed in his famous letters to an associate, later given to the press after a falling out between the two men. "If you have to pay money to have the right thing done," he declared, "it is only just and fair to do it." The Southern Pacific paid the lawmakers and the farmers paid the railroad; the press never lacked for antirailroad grist for its mill; and California acquired in amazingly short order one of the finest railroad systems in the nation. Through rates from the East to the Pacific Coast have always been dominated by the existence of cheap ocean transportation, a situation intensified by the opening of the Panama Canal to commercial shipping. As early as 1874 the Southern Pacific had a steamship affiliate; it eventually controlled the powerful Pacific Mail Steamship Company. Because the Pacific Coast was within easy reach of the East via water, rail rates between New York and the Pacific Coast were much lower than rates to the "intermountain area" around Denver and Salt Lake City, for example, which lacked cheap alternatives. Short-haul local rates from San Francisco to rail points only a hundred miles or so inland seemed high when contrasted with the low rates from New York to San Francisco. Thus, the Southern Pacific's competitive situation in California was one of the main irritants in the lengthy controversy over long- versus short-haul rate discrimination that continued well into the twentieth century.

Another sore point was the Southern Pacific's tendency to favor transcontinental routing via its southern lines, which gave it the haul all the way to New Orleans, over routing via the Central Pacific, which it controlled but which extended only as far east as the junction with the Union Pacific at Ogden, Utah. This anomalous situation (the Central Pacific should long since have been transferred to the Union Pacific) was corrected during the years after 1900 when Union Pacific head Edward H. HARRIMAN acquired a controlling interest in the Southern Pacific-Central Pacific at Huntington's death. Harriman, in fact, had a master plan for controlling the entire railroad situation in the West, south of James J. Hill's empire to the north, but the dream ended with his death in 1909 and the Supreme Court's decision in 1913 that the Union Pacific would have to divest itself of the Southern Pacific.

Since 1913 the Southern Pacific, still retaining its Central Pacific line, has grown progressively stronger. Thoroughly rebuilt, as were most arterial railroad lines in the United States in the two decades before World War I, it is now one of the most modern, efficient, and profitable railroads in the world. Rapid growth of the Gulf and southwestern areas since World War II has further strengthened its position; the "Sunset route" from New Orleans to California, once one of the riskiest

undertakings in the history of American railroad enterprise, is today the most intensively utilized single-track route in the world.

The best history of the Southern Pacific, although it ends with the World War I period, is still Stuart Daggett, *Chapters on the History of the Southern Pacific* (1922; repr. 1966).—A. M.

South Pass. Located on the Continental Divide in the Central Rockies (Fremont County, Wyoming) is South Pass, the most famous gateway to the Far West in American history. Just as Cumberland Gap was the means of access to Kentucky and the first American West in the eighteenth century, so South Pass served California and Oregon in the nineteenth. "Stand at the South Pass in the Rockies a century later," wrote Frederick Jackson Turner, "and see the same procession with wider intervals between." From 1824 to the coming of the Union Pacific Railroad, hundreds of thousands of emigrants crossed it on their way to the Far West.

Although its name suggests a dramatic gap in the Rocky Mountain barrier, South Pass is actually a saddle between the southern extremes of the Wind River Range and the Antelope Hills to the south. Far from appearing distinctive, it is a broad, high plain, twenty miles wide, which rises almost imperceptibly from the Wyoming Basin to a height of 7,550 feet above sea level. After travelers ascending the Sweetwater River portion of the OREGON TRAIL had viewed Devil's Gate, the river's narrow canyon, which was dominated by three-hundred-foot cliffs, the pass was inevitably a disappointment. William T. Newby, an Oregon migrant in 1843, wrote that "if you dident now it was the mountain you wouldent now it from any other plane." But twelve miles beyond the origins of the Sweetwater, the travelers saw the waters of Pacific Spring flowing westward and realized that they had crossed the Continental Divide. From there they could go in a southerly direction to Fort Bridger before continuing on to Oregon or California; or they could use Sublette's Cutoff, which led to the Bear River valley and on to Fort Hall, Idaho, from whence they could turn toward Oregon or take the trail to California.

South Pass was first discovered in October 1812 by Robert Stuart and a party of Astorians who were returning overland from the Pacific Coast. Stuart's discovery remained unknown, however, until the spring of 1824 when friendly Crow Indians told Jedediah Smith and a party of trappers (which included James Clyman and Thomas Fitzpatrick) of the route around the southern end of the Wind River Mountains. Thus, while he was not the first white man to cross the South Pass, Smith made the first effective discovery. Its value to fur trappers and to potential settlers was immediately apparent. One could now bring supplies to the trappers along the Platte, North Platte, Laramie, and Sweetwater rivers—soon to be the route of the Oregon Trail—and avoid the dangerous roundabout trip up the Missouri and overland to the Green. William H. Ashley himself used the route to bring goods to the 1825 rendezvous. Trappers also used the pass to get from the Green River on the western slope of the Rockies to the eastern side and then north to the Yellowstone and the Missouri.

As early as 1826 Ashley told Missouri newspaper reporters that South Pass was a "broad and easy way to the Pacific coast." An 1830 report by Smith and his partners to the secretary of war argued that Oregon could be reached by way of the South Pass. Two years later Captain B. L. E. Bonneville brought the first wagons through the pass and thus demonstrated the feasibility of wagon trains of settlers reaching Oregon and California. In 1836 Eliza Spalding and Narcissa Whitman, wives of Oregon missionaries, were the first American women to cross the pass. Between 1841 and 1853, the pass was used by 150,000 persons on their way west, among whom were the Mormon settlers of Utah and the California gold seekers of 1849.

When wagon trains of emigrants began to move toward Oregon in the late 1830s and the early 1840s, the government sent John C. Frémont to explore the area in 1843, although his expedition added little to existing knowledge. Two years later Colonel Stephen W. Kearny took five companies of United States Dragoons all the way to South Pass to overawe the Indians with a show of force and thus keep the Oregon Trail open. While the government resisted public pressure to keep soldiers stationed on the trail, it did authorize a Pacific road program to remove obstacles, improve the roadbed, and find a more direct route west from South Pass to Fort Hall. In 1858 an energetic engineer, Frederick W. Lander, cut a new emigrant road, suitable for wagons and draft animals, from South Pass to Fort Piney and on to Fort Hall. By 1860 other engineers had improved the road all the way to California, but other efforts during the 1850s to make South Pass part of wagon routes running from Fort Ridgely, Minnesota, to the Pacific Northwest or from South Pass north to the Missouri were never really completed.

Many public leaders thought that the first transcontinental railroad would run through the South Pass, but in 1849-50 Captain Howard Stansbury's government expedition, guided by Jim Bridger, found a more southerly route through Bridger's Pass and Cheyenne Pass; this came to be used by the Overland Stage, the Pony Express, and the Union Pacific. Even today no railroad crosses the historic pass. A brief gold strike on the Sweetwater in 1870 led to the establishment of South Pass City, but finds were so meager that the miners soon drifted elsewhere. Thereafter, the once busy thoroughfare was replaced by other routes.

See Donald McKay Frost, "General Ashley and the Overland Trail," Amer. Antiquarian Soc., *Proceedings, 1944* (1946); William H. Goetzmann, *Exploration and Empire* (1966); W. T. Jackson, *Wagon Roads West* (1965); Dale L. Morgan, *Jedediah Smith and the Opening of the West* (1953); and Marshall Sprague, *The Great Gates: The Story of the Rocky Mountain Passes* (1964).—H. R. L.

Southwest Territory. In 1784 North Carolina proposed to cede to the United States its holdings of territory west of the Appalachian Mountains, but the cession was not accepted by Congress until August 7, 1789. At that date there was established in the "Territory South of the River Ohio" a political organization similar to that established in the 1787 NORTHWEST ORDINANCE for the Northwest Territory. William BLOUNT was appointed territorial governor, and he proceeded to organize territorial offices in the three major areas of TENNESSEE.

The background of the organization of the Southwest Territory involved three major incidents. When North Carolina threatened to cede her western holdings there were positive reactions of a political nature in Tennes-

see, and an attempt was made to organize the independent state of FRANKLIN from the eastern counties. Westerners in general were highly disturbed about the proposed Jay Treaty, which would have shut them off from free use of the Mississippi River, and by the agitation caused by the SPANISH CONSPIRACY, in which some political leaders contemplated swearing allegiance to the Spanish crown. A third issue was raised by a combination of ravenous land speculators and the dissatisfaction of the Cherokee, Creek, Chickasaw, and Choctaw Indians (see FIVE CIVILIZED TRIBES). All of these factors played a part in the eventual formation of the states of Kentucky and Tennessee.

Knoxville was ultimately chosen as the seat of the government of the Southwest Territory, and Blount appointed court and militia officials in the various settled areas. One of his most important accomplishments was the negotiation of the Treaty of Holston, made on July 21, 1791. Under the terms of this treaty the Cherokee placed themselves under the protection of the United States, and the boundaries of potential white settlement were widened.

Blount was faced with exceedingly difficult problems because his territory bordered on four states, and to the south were the hunting grounds of four Indian nations. On top of these problems, Spanish agents stirred trouble, and American land speculators were active. Internally there was political friction among John Sevier, James Robertson, and a host of other land speculators. It was necessary for the government of the Southwest Territory to maintain a system of forts both to protect against Indian raids and to prevent the violations of treaty agreements. Blount also had to raise a force of 332 men to support General St. Clair's campaign against the Miami Indian villages.

The Southwest Territory was the first to send an elected delegate, James WHITE, to Congress. On June 1, 1796, Tennessee was admitted to the Union, ending the need for federal territorial government.

See Thomas Perkins Abernethy, *From Frontier to Plantation in Tennessee* (1932); Carl S. Driver, *John Sevier, Pioneer of the Old Southwest* (1932); William Masterson, *William Blount* (1954); and J. G. M. Ramsey, *The Annals of Tennessee* (1853).—T. D. C.

Spalding, Henry Harmon (1803-1874). Oregon missionary and pioneer. Born out of wedlock in Wheeler, New York, to an uncaring mother, neglected by his foster father, and jilted by his sweetheart Narcissa Prentiss who later married Marcus WHITMAN, Spalding was embittered before he entered upon missionary work in the Pacific Northwest in 1836. In that year he traveled to the Oregon country with his wife, Eliza Hart, and the Whitmans and William Gray. Setting up his mission at Lapwai near present Lewiston, Idaho, in the heart of Nez Percé country, Spalding began the arduous task of converting the Indians. Though limited in imagination and not always understanding, Spalding was persevering, as indeed he had to be. The Indians were quick to discover his limitations and weaknesses while the fellow missionaries undercut his efforts by denouncing him to the board in Boston, and by ridiculing him in front o : his charges. Complaints made by Whitman and Gray along with the acid commentaries of Asa Smith, a missionary arrival of 1838, induced the board to dismiss Spalding in 1840. When the board's decision arrived in

Oregon two years later and tempers and circumstances had altered, Whitmen went east and secured a reversal of the board's decision.

After the Whitman massacre in 1847, Spalding left Lapwai for the Willamette valley, where he became a farmer. While in the valley he was made commissioner of schools and in 1851 he served as Indian agent. He returned to Lapwai in 1862. The Whitman incident, terrible in itself, was preceded by a growing Catholic missionary effort among the Nez Percé. Spalding, along with other Catholic-hating clergymen, lost no time linking both events. He spent considerable effort building a case against the Catholics generally and in making them appear responsible for the massacre in particular. In the process Whitman was elevated to martyrdom and his trip to the East in 1842 became a legend, embellished to include a stop at Washington, D.C., where Whitman allegedly induced President John Tyler to wrest Oregon from Britain's grasp.

The Spalding papers include collections at Washington State University Library, Pullman; the Penrose Memorial Library, Whitman College, Walla Walla, Washington; and at the Beinecke Library, Yale University. See also Clifford M. Drury, *Henry Harmon Spalding* (1936) and *Marcus and Narcissa Whitman and the Opening of Old Oregon* (1973); and Alvin M. Josephy, Jr., *The Nez Percé Indians and the Opening of the Northwest* (1965). —R. J. L.

Spanish-Americans. See CHICANO LIBERATION MOVEMENT; and MEXICAN-AMERICANS.

Spanish-American War. See ROUGH RIDERS.

Spanish conspiracy. The Spanish conspiracy involved the possibility that western settlers would withdraw from the union of states and swear allegiance to the Spanish crown for three basic reasons. The Indian menace to the Southwest was highly disturbing to settlers in eastern Tennessee, along the Cumberland River, and in central and southern Georgia; land speculators were anxious to gain control over as much land as possible, with or without congressional protection; and the proposed Jay Treaty of 1785 threatened to close the Mississippi River to trade by American boatmen for twenty-five years. This conspiracy involved a host of westerners, among them James WILKINSON, Harry Innis, George Muter, John SEVIER, James ROBERTSON, and, no doubt, William BLOUNT. Its basic appeals were the opening of the river to unhindered trade, the granting of large blocks of lands in Spanish territory, and advantages in the Indian trade.

Dr. James White of North Carolina had advanced this idea to the Spanish minister Gardoqui in Philadelphia, and there can be little doubt that in 1787 Wilkinson broached the same idea to Governor Miró in New Orleans. The Tennesseeans made their argument even more convincing when they named their western district in honor of the Spanish governor. Kentuckians were in the process between 1785 and 1792 of separating the western counties from Virginia and forming an independent state. Disappointments over the proposed Jay Treaty and the rising production of agricultural produce made the issue of closing the Mississippi an especially explosive one. Wilkinson added further pressure to keep that river open by his successful venture downstream in 1787 with two flatboatloads of produce, which he sold at high prices.

Despite the activities of Wilkinson and the Tennesseans, the Spanish conspiracy did not have an appreciable effect beyond being an explosive issue in local politics. Wilkinson was roundly defeated in the Kentucky separation conventions, but Sevier and his cohorts survived their mistakes in Tennessee. The plot or conspiracy had almost no practical effects on the more extended history of the West.

See Thomas M. Green, *The Spanish Conspiracy* (1891); Thomas R. Hay and M. R. Werner, *The Admirable Trumpeter* (1941); W. H. Masterson, *William Blount* (1954); Royal O. Shreve, *The Finished Scoundrel* (1933); and Arthur P. Whitaker, *The Spanish-American Frontier, 1783-1795* (1927), and *The Mississippi Question, 1795-1803* (1934).—T. D. C.

Spanish language in the Southwest. Spoken in the five-state region of Texas, New Mexico, Colorado, Arizona, and California, Spanish has shown remarkable persistence despite predictions of its demise under overwhelming pressure from English. A main reason has been the stable bilingualism marking the area, in contrast to the transitory bilingualism typical of speakers of such "immigrant" languages as Polish, Italian, and Yiddish in the New World. Another factor aiding this continued bilingualism has been the divergent culture and life styles of the Mexican-Americans, or Hispanos, and the Anglos (actually a portmanteau term for most non-Mexican-Americans).

Two main periods are to be noted in the history of Southwest Spanish. Lasting until approximately World War I, the first period was characterized by the considerable prestige enjoyed by Spanish language and culture, with active social contacts and intermarriage between Anglo and Hispano families. The lexical borrowings by English occurred mostly during this time, when ranch and frontier terms were adopted; they are now fully integrated into English (e.g., *corral, rodeo,* and *buckaroo,* the last from the Spanish *vaquero*). The next period coincided with the beginning of the Mexican Revolution, which brought numerous refugees to the Southwest. But more important ·for linguistics, economic impoverishment has continued to send thousands of Mexican citizens, mostly from rural backgrounds, north of the border. The prestige of Spanish has decreased, although contacts have continued between Anglos and Hispanos of more affluent status.

At the same time, throughout the period of westward expansion English-speaking settlers were compelled to acquire a working knowledge of Spanish and often of an Indian language—perhaps Navaho, Zuñi, or Yaqui. This type of bilingualism and trilingualism is, however, disappearing as the children and grandchildren of these old-timers pass away.

Estimates of the number of Mexican-Americans in the Southwest are as high as ten million, although few of them can truly be considered balanced bilinguals, able to cope almost equally well in both Spanish and English. As a matter of fact, until the recent movement for recognition of Mexican-American civil rights and a greater respect for their culture and language, only a small minority received as much formal training in Spanish as in English.

From the linguistic point of view, it is necessary to distinguish two main varieties of Southwest Spanish. First of all, there is the northern New Mexico southern Colorado dialect, more or less directly descended from the speech of the sixteenth- and seventeenth-century conquistadores who used the "Golden Age Spanish" of the period. Like the English of the isolated residents of Appalachia, this dialect exhibits a number of archaic features, some of them familiar to students of the earlier Spanish. It also has the epenthetic, or added, *-e* after a final *-l* or *-r*: *Isabele, hablare*. Throughout the rest of the Southwest, a koine called General Southwest Spanish, a term proposed by a linguist in 1969, is used. It is basically a variety of Mexican Spanish, distinguished by strong consonantism (especially persistence of stops in medial and final positions—or in the interior and at the end of words, respectively), Mexican intonational patterns (the result of Nahuatl and Maya influence), and heavy lexical and grammatical interference from English. Except with intellectual and puristically inclined speakers, code-switching—or changing languages—even in mid-sentence, is the rule rather than the exception.

Another noteworthy aspect of Southwest Spanish has been the influence of Pachuco, originally the slang of zoot-suiters who attracted attention during World War II when they moved to Los Angeles. Actually Pachuco represents lexical innovations and borrowings from nonstandard Spanish of Mexico and other parts of the Spanish-speaking world—in the traditional underworld slang *germanía* of Spain, American English, and apparently Gypsy elements with some special intonational patterns. By now, however, much of the "code" aspect of Pachuco has disappeared because many of its terms (e.g., *cantón* for "house," *frajo* for "cigarette," and *ranfla* for "car") are used in informal spoken styles by the younger generation.

It is important to point out, however, that in any linguistic area or speech community rigid and uniform use of one monolithic form of standard language is a fiction. Hence, the Southwest has Mexican-Americans who speak elegant standard educated Mexican Spanish, and —in a fairly wide spectrum—others who speak it as a "bilingual dialect" (Einar Haugen's term to denote heavy interference and mixing from another language), while still others employ a street variety generously interlarded with Pachuco terms.

Scholars are becoming increasingly interested in the study of Southwest Spanish, not only as a regional dialect or dialects, but also as a social dialect. This has been encouraged by sociolinguistic approaches to black and Appalachian English, in which both linguistic and socioeconomic features tend to show significant correlations. At the same time social attitudes have come in for examination, since many of the speakers of Southwest Spanish regard it pejoratively as "Tex-Mex," "border lingo," "pocho," or "Spanglish." However, Southwest Spanish is acquiring new prestige, in part because of the movement toward bilingual education and the passing of the Bilingual Education Act and in part because of increased respect for the cultures and types of speech of minorities. Language educators, nevertheless, tend to feel that courses in Spanish in the Southwest should attempt to acquaint Mexican-Americans and other students both with Southwest Spanish and a more formal variety of standard Spanish of the Latin American type. The proximity of Mexico, which serves as a sociolinguistic-cultural matrix, has helped to prevent creolization of Spanish in the Southwest and to ensure its use in the future.

See George C. Barker, *Pachuco: An American Spanish Argot and Its Social Functions in Tucson, Arizona,* University of Arizona Bulletin No. 21 (1950); Einar Haugen, *Bilingualism in the Americas; a Bibliography and Research Guide,* Publications of the American Dialect Society No. 26 (1956); and Jacob Ornstein, "Language Varieties Along the U.S.-Mexican Border," Cambridge University Press *Proceedings* (Spring 1971).—J. O.

Spanish rule in the Mississippi valley. See MISSISSIPPI VALLEY: *French and Spanish periods.*

Spicer, Edward Holland (1906-   ). Anthropologist. Born in Chittenham, Pennsylvania, Spicer received a bachelor's degree in anthropology in 1932 at the University of Arizona, and the following year wrote a master's thesis based on his study of the black-on-gray pottery culture as exemplified in King's Ruin near Prescott, Arizona. With funds from the Civil Works Administration, Spicer then investigated the Tuzigoot Ruins near Clarkdale. His interest turning toward cultural anthropology, he made a study of the Yaqui living in the Pascua village in Tucson, received a doctorate at the University of Chicago in 1939, and joined the faculty at the University of Arizona. During World War II, Spicer was community analyst at the Japanese-American camp at Poston, Arizona, worked with the War Relocation Authority in Washington, D. C., and with four others published *Impounded People: Japanese-Americans in the Relocation Centers* (1969). After returning to the University of Arizona in 1946, Spicer was vitally concerned with the process of cultural adjustment. He edited *Human Problems in Technological Change* (1952), published *Potam* (1954), a study of a Yaqui village in Sonora, and edited the *American Anthropologist* (1960-62). In his *Cycles of Conquest* (1962), Spicer interpreted the European impact on the Indian cultures of the Southwest. He showed how southwestern peoples have managed to retain their sense of identity and how the Spanish and American institutions for civilizing the Indians have actually enslaved them.—H. P. H.

Spokane Indians. The Spokane tribe, about six hundred people of Salish stock, lived along the Spokane River below Spokane Falls in northeastern Washington, the upper limit of the salmon run. They subsisted chiefly on salmon, supplemented by roots, berries, and game. About 1750 they secured horses from the Nez Percé but made no great use of them. For many years the wolves killed off a large part of their colt crop, so that they had a difficult time raising enough animals for their own needs until they killed off most of the wolves with the help of white trappers.

The flat river bottom at the mouth of the Little Spokane River became an important trading site for the area, with visitors from tribes as distant as the Nez Percé in the Clearwater valley and the Flathead from western Montana. On this spot the Northwest Company established a fur trading post, Spokane House, in 1809.

In 1825 Chief Illim-Spokanee's son, later baptized Spokane Garry by the whites, was taken to the Red River Settlement near Lake Winnipeg to be trained as a missionary to his people. He returned to the tribe in 1829 and had some initial success in teaching his people a little reading and how to build log houses and raise some crops, especially potatoes. His work was supplemented by Protestant missionaries who arrived in 1838 and by the Catholic missionaries among the Coeur d'Alene to the east.

When the Columbia Basin was overrun by men prospecting for gold in the 1850s, friction developed between the intruders and the various tribes whose lands were invaded, with some incidents just to the north of the Spokane around Fort Colville. In May 1858 Colonel Edward J. Steptoe marched north with a force of dragoons to overawe the restless Indians who had united under the leadership of the Coeur d'Alene. They gave Steptoe a sound beating, chasing him out of the country. Some of the Spokane joined in this fighting.

In August 1858 Colonel George H. Wright led a punitive force of four hundred men armed with new long-range rifled muskets into Spokane country, defeating the combined Indian forces at Four Lakes and at Spokane Plains. He captured 850 horses belonging to the Spokane and as a punishment for the tribe's hostile acts, and as a warning to the other tribes, had all of the herd shot. The pile of whitened bones remained a landmark along the Spokane River for many years.

Later the Spokane were given part of their lands north of the Spokane River as a reservation, where they still live.

See R. I. Burns, *The Jesuits in the Indian Wars of the Northwest* (1963); Thomas E. Jessett, *Chief Spokane Garry* (1960); and Dorothy Johansen and Charles M. Gates, *Empire of the Columbia* (1957).—F. H.

sports and pastimes. For the isolated pioneer, sports were diversions from the boredom of unending physical toil and potent anodynes against gnawing doubts about the future. They were often a last resort against sheer desperation.

Very few frontier sports and pastimes lacked the direct human competitiveness that so befitted the frontier. One such sport was the bull-and-bear fight of Hispanic California, although it must be confessed that roping a grizzly bear and manhandling him into *la carreta,* the two-wheeled cart that was the staple vehicle of the area, involved human skill and a modicum of unfettered danger. Roping and transporting a wild range bull was only slightly less hazardous. A stout adobe-and-rock corral made the arena in many cases; in others the main street of the sleepy settlement was blocked off by barricades of rocks, brush, and people while the two combatants had at it. Although the bear might be chained to a stout post to equalize the odds, or have one forepaw tied back against the leg, the bloody event rarely was in doubt—the bear usually won. Witnessing one of these encounters allegedly provided Horace Greeley with the symbols that he later applied to the embattled denizens of New York's Wall Street.

Other nonhuman contests included dog fights, some by prearrangement after the English fashion with a proper pit, handlers, and rules of conducting the encounter; others stemmed from chance encounters and often involved the canines' owners before the scrimmage was done. Cockfights, with razor-sharp steel "gaffs" affixed to the cock's own spurs, were fought under rigid rules and regulations. Cockfights still go on in various sections of the country, albeit illegally, and today, as of yore, the old plantation jingle still applies:

Dey's somet'ings square an' dey's somet'ings round
But little gamecocks ain't sol' by de poun'.
Dey's weighed by dey san' an' dey pluck and dey grit
An' de number o'dead dat dey leave in de pit.

Just when and where horse racing began in the English colonies is unknown, but it seems safe to say that it was imported with the colonists who first settled the southern seaboard colonies. This was a logical extension of the fact that the horse provided the basic, nonhuman energy source. From these early colonial races, often held in the short and dusty, or muddy, street of the local center of trade and commerce, the term "quarter-(mile)horse" worked its way into the frontier's language and thence into prominence in the light-horse cult of today's affluent society. Then as now, the owner, bettor, rider, and spectator found an expansion and an extension of self through competitive horseflesh.

Lotteries, both public and private, were popular, and wagers were won and lost on virtually every event the frontier called sport. This was as it should have been, because the frontier was itself the greatest gamble of them all. "Homesteading is where the government bets you a quarter-section (160 acres) that you starve to death before you prove up on it." Games of chance with cards and dice—faro. brag, euchre, poker, keno, monte, chuck-a-luck, and others—epitomized the masculine frontier (see GAMBLING).

One frontier sport was really a skill necessary to survival: marksmanship with a short or long gun that often meant the difference between life and death, between meat on the fire and moccasin soup. Using the long "Kentucky rifle," developed in Pennsylvania, a man who could "bark" a squirrel, having the ball strike so near the animal that it fell stunned and untouched to the ground, was esteemed more highly than he who brought home his squirrels neatly decapitated by one shot each. When "shooting for a beeve," using six-inch square targets at fifteen rods, the winner was the one whose ball struck nearest the center. His prize was the hide; the meat and tallow going to lesser scores. Some "turkey shoots" tethered the bird at two hundred yards and any fatal ball brought home the fowl; others, more refined perhaps, buried the bird with only its head and snakelike neck protruding, which made chance an accessory of accuracy. Even today a growing number of cultists have taken up the muzzle-loading flintlocks and percussion-cap weapons of their forebears for target use.

Another frontier diversion was telling the "tall tale." The legends of Paul Bunyan, for example, be they folklore or media fakelore, had their genesis in this frontier art form. Frontier humor was rooted solidly in the inescapable fact that the frontier itself was hyperbole compounded. The man who could spin a bigger "windy" than his fellows was esteemed for his social utility, as was the man who could "sing down" his fellows by the extent of his repertoire, not the excellence or even loudness of his voice. The practical joke, the quintessence of boyish animality, was a favorite frontier trick. If it could take advantage of its victim's foibles or characteristics for its success, so much the better. That it might cause physical pain while providing the anticipated acute embarrassment was no barrier to its perpetration. As the cowboy artist Charles M. Russell once noted tersely, "Laugh kills lonesome."

In Tombstone, Arizona, in 1885 the local people amused themselves with the bloody sport of cockfighting. (Arizona Historical Society)

Most frontier sports and pastimes were really harder work in the guise of play and were the products of an isolated, self-sufficient, socially independent, and strenuously competitive society. The agricultural frontier, which comprised the major segment of our frontier experience, produced plowing contests and team-pulling contests. Its exigencies forced the hard-twisted frontier individualists, male and female alike, into cooperative work-play contests. There were haying bees with scythe-and-cradle, where the womenfolk did the raking. There were threshing bees, and flax-scutching bees, and husking bees; and in the latter, the finders of the few red-kerneled ears got certain "bussing" perquisites. And there were quilting bees that made a feminine oasis in a predominantly masculine society.

There were house-raisings, with the "warming" as the climax, and barn-raisings, with dancing on the new-laid floor all redolent of fresh-worked wood. The noisy "shivaree" was an integral part of frontier weddings, a contest to keep the newly wed from bed as long as possible. At all these, raw whiskey flowed and great meals were eaten, and there was competition on the distaff side to see which household could set the biggest and most varied table.

The log drives of the lumber camps produced birling contests, where two men, one at each end of a water-borne log, endeavored to spin the log with such speed, or to reverse its rotation with such quickness, that the opponent got a watery bath. And in town, when the drive was done or the woods shut down by inclement

weather, a truly "catty" birler would get an empty beer or whiskey keg and demonstrate his prowess on his surrogate log. Sawing and chopping contests were also examples of where logging skills became forms of diversion and relaxation. Efforts to make these skills a spectator sport today have had small success save in a few Pacific Coast communities, where logging still is an integral part of everyday life.

Rock-drilling contests against time and special blocks of Colorado granite, where obtainable, gave the aristocrats of the hard-rock camps a chance to demonstrate their expertise before a knowledgeable audience. There were "singlejack" contests, where one man swung a four-pound hammer against steel he held himself, and there were "doublejack" contests, with the "striker" wielding an eight-pound hammer and the "holder" turning the drill steel a quarter-turn between each blow so the steel would not bind in the hole: And there were even three-man teams, two strikers and a holder, where the two hammers rose and fell in a rhythmic fifty or more strokes a minute.

The necessities of winter transportation brought skis to the higher reaches of California's mother lode mining camps, and competitive events, using "snow skates" ten feet and more in length, made their debut there during the 1850s. These "snow skates" had a toe binding only. A long "balance" pole, which could be straddled for braking purposes, was the only other piece of equipment necessary to attain clocked speeds exceeding sixty miles per hour. Each contestant made his own "dope," the equivalent of today's waxes, and guarded his secret jealously.

As the scattered newcomers eventually coalesced into straggling settlements, their early sports were augmented by more social forms. Spelling bees were educational. Political rallies and religious "camp" meetings partook as much of social relaxation as they did of either political enlightenment or salvation. Social relaxation, as well as some psychotherapy, was abetted with the visits of the patent-medicine salesman, peddling Seneca Oil or equally effective nostrums from the end-gate of his wagon. And there was the hoot and the glee of community sings.

When the frontier reached the Great Plains, there were community rabbit drives that released deep tensions in their club-wielding climaxes. Englishmen involved in the speculative frenzy of the open-range cattle industry seem to have introduced coyote-coursing, with imported greyhounds, to the Plains. (Today men use helicopters to hunt down these and other predators against livestock.) Every crossroads hamlet had its champion foot-racer, wrestler, and rough-and-tumble fighter. Contests between community champions were notable civic events.

Many of these community sports went the way of the isolation that spawned them, as urbanization, jet propulsion, and electronic communications completed what the railroad, the telegraph, and the nickelodeon began. With one exception, the RODEO, mechanization and industrialization long since obliterated the frontier's work-derived play-contests. Interestingly enough, the rodeo comes from the frontier's last reflex spasm, the brief heyday—no more than thirty years—of the unfenced, open-range cattle industry.—W. H. H.

Spur Ranch. In 1878 Jim Hall trailed 1,900 head of cattle from the Gulf Coast and turned them loose along the Caprock, an area of West Texas. Thus began what became the 439,972-acre Spur Ranch. The ranch was sold in 1882, yet through a succession of owners the ranch continued to grow. It was owned briefly by Scottish investors, the Espuela Land and Cattle Company, and then was bought in 1906 by S. M. Swenson and Son, one of the oldest and wealthiest ranching and investment companies in Texas. Although much of the land eventually was sold to settlers, the ranch continued to operate until 1942 when the Swensons and the John J. Emery family, then the sole owners of the remaining portion of the ranch, divided their property. The Emery portion was sold, and the remaining part was acquired by the SMS Ranches.

See William C. Holden, *The Espuela Land and Cattle Company* (1970).—J. A. S.

spurs. See COWBOY CLOTHING.

squatter club. See CLAIM ASSOCIATION.

stagecoach. Of all the symbols associated with the American West, few have been as enduring or celebrated as the stagecoach. The art of coaching in the United States received its impetus from the spread of settlers westward in the years following the American Revolution, reached a peak during the heyday of western development from 1850 to 1870, then declined as the railroad gradually replaced horse-drawn transportation as the foremost carrier of passengers and mail.

Though stagecoaching had been prevalent in England for some hundred and fifty years prior to the Revolution, the first long-distance line in the United States did not begin operating until 1785, when coaches successfully linked New York City with Albany. Coaching was not a means of transportation readily adaptable to American conditions. Roads were poor, facilities unavailable, and the expense of running a large stage line prohibitive. Furthermore, the heavy, cumbersome English coach of the period proved to be particularly ill-suited to the task of opening up a rugged and mostly undeveloped frontier.

The disadvantages of the British coach centered around the steel springs of its suspension system. These springs, if strong enough to support a heavily loaded vehicle over the potholes and impedimenta of an American road, proved to be so rigid that they threw the passengers from their seats or jarred them unmercifully throughout the trip. More flexible springs only brought home the shortcomings of backwoods roads with bone-crushing force. The lateral rigidity of the springs could actually capsize a coach on sharp curves, while a broken spring would of course leave the passengers stranded in the middle of nowhere.

Such disadvantages led to the development of a new, peculiarly American type of stagecoach in the years following the Revolution. The Yankee coachmakers' first innovation was the substitution of leather thoroughbraces for steel springs in the suspension. A heavy undercarriage was mounted on the axles in the same manner as for a freight wagon. At the four corners of this frame iron standards about a foot high were mounted and securely braced. To the top of the pair of standards on each side was shackled a six- or eight-ply belt of the thickest steer-hide leather, about four inches wide, forming a cradle upon which the body of the coach was suspended. The thoroughbraces functioned as shock absorbers for the team as well as the passengers, allowing the coach body to sway fore and aft as well as sideways—"a function of such importance to the Western staging world," according to historian George Hugh Banning, "that we may hazard the contention that an empire once rocked and perhaps depended upon thoroughbraces."

American coachmakers likewise modified the superstructure of their vehicles to take advantage of the improved suspension system. The egg-shaped, bulging coach body of the early nineteenth century lowered the center of gravity and combined strength and durability with a relatively light construction.

The history of the stagecoach in America is inseparably linked with the Abbot-Downing Company, established by Lewis Downing at Concord, New Hampshire, in 1813. Downing and his assistant, J. Stephen Abbot, built their first Concord coach in 1826; by mid-century their products were the envy of every stage driver in America and were being exported to half a dozen countries throughout the world. Abbot brought a continual stream of design improvements to the partnership. Lewis Downing was a driving perfectionist convinced that the finest quality product depended upon skilled craftsmanship and the use of flawless materials. Together they produced a vehicle that became a household synonym for perfection.

In building the Concord coach, Abbot and Downing improved upon the then prevalent American design. To keep the center of gravity equidistant between the

The ability of this lightweight coach to travel the worst of roads earned it the name "mud wagon." (Library of Congress)

wheels, they built the lower third of the body in the form of a modified oval with curved panels at the sides, but with the ends widened enough to allow seating for three passengers. The walls of the coach, though curved out slightly, lost most of their distinctive egg-shaped appearance. The top bulged just enough to insure quick drainage and was surrounded by a stout iron railing, providing space for several hundred pounds of express or three extra passengers. A platform at the rear for additional baggage was supported by straps attached to the corners of the roof, and was enclosed in black oiled leather to form a weatherproof boot. The driver's seat was raised to within two feet of the roof to improve visibility and handling. Valuables were usually carried in a locked strongbox under the seat.

The completed Concord coach weighed close to 2,500 pounds and retailed for $1,050. The coach body stood eight feet six inches above the ground, the rear wheels five feet one inch, and the front wheels three feet ten inches. Nine passengers could sit in reasonable comfort on the three interior seats provided, two at the front and back facing each other and one in the middle facing forward. Two additional passengers, the most distinguished or the prettiest, might join the driver on his lofty perch.

Abbot and Downing spared no expense in making each Concord coach a perfect creation. Small-dimension, straight-grained white ash, steamed pliable and bent to the exact curve required before being kiln-dried to insure toughness, formed the framework of the body. The side panels of poplar were steamed into shape and dried on templates, then hand tooled to fit snugly into the framework. In an era when wagon wheels frequently warped or buckled from shoddy construction, the Concord's running gear was the sturdiest and most reliable that could possibly be produced. Hand-forged Norway iron provided the axle bars, tires, standards, brake rods, fittings, and collars for the wheel hubs; the rest of the running gear was manufactured from straight-grained ash or white oak lumber, seasoned and sun-warped for at least three years. Expert carpenters shaped each wheel spoke to the exact weight and measurement of every other, then mortised them to the hub so accurately that a man could not pull them apart with his hands. The fellies, or wheel rims, were band-sawed; balanced in weight, width, and thickness; then mortised to the spokes by hand and covered with a three-eighths-inch-thick tire of Norway iron. So perfect was the wheel-making process that no bolts or screws were needed in the construction.

As if this painstaking craftsmanship were not enough, every Concord coach left the factory as a rolling work of art. Multiple coats of paint (red, blue, yellow, or green) were applied to the body, rubbed down with pumice, and covered with two coats of spar varnish for polish. Artists then decorated the exterior with ornate scrollwork and gold leaf. A landscape was usually painted on each door. The steps and top railing were shiny black, the running gear yellow with fine red pinstriping on the spokes.

Driving a Concord coach was a skill as fully developed as the manufacture of the vehicle itself. In contrast to the British, who hitched their six-horse teams snugly to the coach pole and eliminated any untidy slackness in the harness, American drivers allowed the breast straps and traces to dangle loosely, and did away with horse collars altogether. The resulting arrangement left the coach pole free to swing sideways if the front wheels hit an obstacle, thus minimizing unnecessary stress and pull on the harness. The reinsman, often called the whip or jehu, held the reins of the leaders (the team farthest from the wheels) between the fore and middle fingers of each hand, those for the swing, or middle, team between the middle and third fingers, and those for the wheelers between the third and little fingers. The ends of the "off," or right-hand, reins dangled from the heel of the right hand, but the ends of the "near" reins were looped up over the left thumb before being allowed to hang. The driver manipulated each rein by "climbing," alternately gathering it in with the fingers, or letting it slip out the desired amount. Delicate adjustments of the rein length, combined with a judicious use of the foot brake and the whip, let the reinsman control all six horses independently and with apparent effortlessness.

The first stage line west of the Missouri was apparently Oregon's "Telegraph Line," established by one S. H. L. Meek in 1846. With the discovery of gold in California two years later, efficient cross-country mail and passenger service became a necessity. In 1857 the government awarded its first mail contract to the (Southern) OVERLAND MAIL COMPANY, owned by John BUTTERFIELD. Butterfield's coaches covered the distance between St. Louis and Los Angeles in twenty-four hours and thirty minutes. In the years before the completion of the transcontinental railroad in 1869, stagecoach franchises proliferated, the most famous being the Pioneer Line, the celebrated (Central) Overland Mail and Express Company (originally called the CENTRAL OVERLAND CALIFORNIA AND PIKE'S PEAK EXPRESS), owned by Ben HOLLADAY, and the immortal WELLS, FARGO & CO. Even after the coming of the railroad, numerous gold strikes at isolated points in the West gave the Concord a second lease on life.

The Abbot-Downing Company declined as the need for horse-drawn transportation diminished. By the turn of the century it had diversified into ambulances, gun carriages, and circus and specialty wagons. Later, with the advent of the automobile, it turned to the manufacture of truck bodies and the assembling of truck and fire engines. But the high standards and hand craftsmanship that had created the Concord coach were anachronistic in an age of mass production and standardization. In 1920 the company that had revolutionized commercial transport in the United States ceased production. With it went the vehicle that had served, as *Harper's Weekly* put it in 1874, as "the advance guard of civilization in the far West." (See also BRIGHAM YOUNG EXPRESS AND CARRYING CO.; George CHORPENNING; William G. FARGO; and Henry WELLS.)

See Captain William Banning and George Hugh Banning, *Six Horses* (1930); Edwin G. Burgum, "The Concord Coach," *Colorado Magazine,* vol. 16 (1939); S. Blackwell Duncan, "The Legendary Concords," *American West,* vol. 8 (1971); George Estes, *The Stagecoach* (1925); Ralph Moody, *Stagecoach West* (1967); and Oscar Osburn Winther, *Express and Stagecoach Days in California* (1936).—E. H. S.

Stanford, Leland (1824-1893). Railroad builder and

The "Wells Fargo" was the most sophisticated of the Concord coaches. (Wells Fargo Bank History Room)

Leland Stanford. (Southern Pacific)

politician. Stanford was one of the "Big Four" (the others were Charles Crocker, Mark Hopkins, and Collis P. Huntington) who built the CENTRAL PACIFIC and SOUTHERN PACIFIC. He was born in Watervliet, New York. After reading law in Albany, New York, he emigrated with his wife to the new town of Port Washington, Wisconsin. The town failed to prosper, and so the Stanfords, attracted by the success of his merchant brothers in Sacramento, California, went west in 1852. He was soon attracted to politics and in 1861 became governor in time to help keep California in the Union.

Far from brilliant, Stanford recognized, nevertheless, the value of a transcontinental railroad, and the faith his fellow promoters of the Central Pacific Railroad placed in his political influence was fully justified. Stanford successfully lobbied for several legislative acts that smoothed the way for the railroad, and although he contributed hardly anything to the actual building and management of the project, he was president of the Central Pacific from 1863 until his death and of its sister railroad, the Southern Pacific, until 1890. By then his relations with Huntington, chief of the Big Four, had declined; instead of supporting Huntington's man for the United States Senate in 1885, Stanford had claimed the office for himself.

His slender talents constantly diluted by a wide variety of interests in farming, horse breeding, art collecting, and European travel and by declining health, he made no mark as senator, even though the first federal railroad regulation act was passed during his tenure.

When the Stanfords' only son died of typhoid in Florence, Italy, at the age of fifteen, the couple resolved to perpetuate his memory. The result was Stanford University, which opened in 1891. Two years later Stanford's widow fought successfully to save the university in the face of the 1890s depression that coincided with her husband's death.

George T. Clark, *Leland Stanford* (1931), is as objective as most "official" biographies. Not much is added by Norman E. Tutorow, *Leland Stanford, Man of Many Careers* (1971).—A. M.

Stanley, John Mix (1814-1872). Painter and landscape draftsman. Born in Canandaigua, New York, Stanley began painting professionally at about twenty years of age. He made his living from about 1835 to 1839 as an itinerant artist in and around Detroit, Fort Snelling, Minnesota, and Chicago, traveled widely in the west on his own and with a number of government expeditions, and was one of the first to make practical use of the daguerreotype for documentary purposes. In 1842 he accompanied a friend on a trip to what is now Oklahoma, arriving at Fort Gibson in the fall of the year and establishing a studio he later moved to nearby Tahlequah, then the seat of the Cherokee national government. He was one of the few white men to attend the Grand Council of all the tribes in that region, called by Cherokee chief John Ross in 1843, and that same year accompanied P. M. Butler, agent to the Cherokee, to another council held near the headwaters of the Red River along the present Oklahoma-Texas border.

In 1845 Stanley was in Cincinnati, where he joined a wagon train bound for Santa Fe under the leadership of Colonel S. C. Owen. Owen's party reached Santa Fe in August 1846, at about the same time that Colonel Stephen Kearny's troops arrived to take over the city from the Mexican government following the United States declaration of war with Mexico. Kearny organized an expedition to California at this time and added Stanley to his scientific staff as artist for the proposed campaign. Stanley was involved in fighting near San Diego, and a number of his sketches later illustrated Kearny's published reports. Afterward, Stanley traveled to Oregon and in 1848 sailed for Hawaii, where he stayed for more than a year.

Returning to the United States in 1849, Stanley spent the next two years exhibiting his portraits and western scenes throughout the East. In 1852 he exhibited at the Smithsonian Institution in Washington, D.C., and with Captain Seth Eastman's encouragement succeeded in bringing his pictures to the attention of the Senate Committee on Indian Affairs, which recommended their purchase for the sum of $19,200. A bill to this effect failed to pass in 1853. While in Washington, Stanley was selected to accompany Isaac Stevens on a government-sponsored railroad survey to the Pacific in 1853-54. The reports of this expedition, along with others, were published by Congress between 1855 and 1861, illustrated throughout with lithographs, a great many of which were credited to Stanley.

Stanley was a graphic realist, although he produced a number of rather romantically conceived scenes of Indian life. His portraits are essentially descriptive, rather than interpretive. He employed color to great effect, and some of his few remaining canvases suggest a dramatic flair. He had no formal training.

Few of Stanley's original western paintings remain today. Those exhibited at the Smithsonian were for the most part destroyed in a fire on January 24, 1865. A large canvas depicting the Grand Council at Tahlequah survives at the Smithsonian and a few portraits and random scenes executed during Stanley's sojourn in Indian Territory are included in the collections of the Thomas Gilcrease Institute of American History and Art, Tulsa, Oklahoma. A collection of sixteen paintings are owned by the Stark Foundation, Orange, Texas. The artist's portraits of Hawaiian King Kamehameha III and his queen are in the Bernice P. Bishop Museum, Honolulu.

See Bernard DeVoto, *Across the Wide Missouri* (1947); and Robert Taft, *Artists and Illustrators of the Old West, 1850-1900* (1953).—D. C. H.

Stark, Henry Jacob Lutcher (1887-1965). Philanthropist and art collector. Born in Orange, Texas, Stark graduated from the University of Texas in 1910 and then managed extensive lumbering and investment enterprises. Known nationally for his philanthropies to education, he was for twenty-four years a member of the board of regents of the University of Texas at Austin. As a private collector, he assembled a large inventory of paintings, sculptures, and other items of importance to American art and natural history. Stark traveled widely, acquiring much of his collection in the 1940s and 1950s during frequent visits to New Mexico and Colorado, where he owned a ranch. Also interested in conservation, he created in Orange in the 1940s a botanical garden and wild bird park that for years constituted a regional attraction.

With his wife he established the Nelda C. and H. J. Lutcher Stark Foundation in 1961, in part to support the creation in Orange of a museum to house his art collection, which also includes unique examples of American porcelain, crystal, and glass. Among its documentaries on the western frontier are works by George Catlin, Alfred Jacob Miller, Thomas Moran, John Mix Stanley, and more than two hundred paintings by Canadian artist Paul Kane. Of further interest are many sculptures by Frederic Remington and Charles M. Russell, and what is probably the largest single collection of paintings by artists active in and around Taos, New Mexico, during the first half of the twentieth century. In addition to the construction of an art museum, the Stark Foundation restored the home of Stark's parents to house other treasures accumulated over the past seventy years by the Stark family. A gift of some 12,000 printed volumes was made to the University of Texas library in 1938 by Stark's mother, a collector in her own right. —D. C. H.

Starr, Belle (1848-1889). Outlaw. Belle Starr was born Myra Belle Shirley on a farm near Carthage, Missouri. Her father, John Shirley, later became an innkeeper in Carthage, and Belle attended the Carthage Female Academy, whose curriculum included Greek, Latin, and Hebrew.

The Kansas-Missouri border troubles of the 1850s, which grew out of the issue of whether Kansas was to be a slave or a free territory, disrupted the elder Shirley's business and later led to the death of Belle's brother in a border raid; the family therefore moved to Scyrene, Texas, about ten miles east of Dallas. In 1866 Belle met Cole Younger, the theatrical member of the James-Younger band, who probably fathered her first child, Pearl. Their romance was short-lived, but Cole Younger is said to have dominated Belle's affections for the rest of her life (see YOUNGER BROTHERS).

Belle certainly did not pine over Cole; within a year she had joined forces with another outlaw, Jim Reed, and traveled to California with him when his notoriety as a bank and train robber made migration advisable. In California, Belle bore Reed a son, Edward. By 1869, Belle and Reed were back in the Dallas area stealing horses, cattle, or money whenever the opportunity arose. Dressing in velvet skirts and plumed hats and riding her mare, Venus, Belle took up the role of "bandit queen." In 1874, Reed was killed by a member of his own gang; Belle left her children with her mother and went to that portion of the Indian Territory occupied by the Five Civilized Tribes in present-day eastern Oklahoma. Operating in the region west of Fort Smith, Arkansas, and east of Eufaula, Oklahoma, she led her own band of cattle and horse thieves. She stayed for a time with an Indian named Blue Duck but later settled down in a common-law marriage with a Cherokee named Sam Starr at a spot called Younger's Bend near Briartown, Oklahoma, on the Canadian River.

In 1883 Belle and Sam were indicted on a charge of horse theft. Belle was thus the first female ever tried for a major crime in "Hanging Judge" Isaac Parker's Arkansas court. She and her husband were both convicted and served five months in the federal prison at Detroit.

Unreformed, the Starrs returned from prison and took up their earlier careers. In 1886 Sam was killed in a gunfight. As usual, Belle did not waste time mourning: a young Creek Indian, Jim July, soon became her companion. But he, too, was soon in trouble with the law and in July 1889 was summoned to Fort Smith to face larceny charges. Belle accompanied him part of the way but turned back before reaching Fort Smith. While on her way home, she was shot from behind and killed. Jim July blamed a neighbor named Watson; others blamed Belle's own son, Ed Reed, but no one was ever convicted for the murder.

Belle Starr ranks with Cattle Kate Watson and Calamity Jane as one of the most extraordinary women in the history of the West. Even so, most of the legends about Belle stem from sensational newspaper and dime-novel accounts of her as a bandit queen. A hack writer for Richard K. Fox's dime-biographies described Belle with typical eloquence and dishonesty when he wrote: "Of all women of the Cleopatra type, since the days of the Egyptian queen herself, the universe has produced none more remarkable than Belle Starr, the Bandit Queen, more amorous than Anthony's mistress, more relentless than Pharaoh's daughter; and braver than

Joan of Arc." Belle's own description is probably more reliable: "I regard myself," she said shortly before her death, "as a woman who has seen much of life."

See James D. Horan and Paul Sann, *Pictorial History of the Wild West* (1954); and Burton Rascoe, *Belle Starr* (1941).—P. L. N.

steamboat. See TRANSPORTATION ON THE MISSISSIPPI RIVER SYSTEM.

Steffens, [Joseph] Lincoln (1866-1936). Writer. Steffens was born in San Francisco. His father, Joseph, became a partner in a paint and oil business in Sacramento. In 1887 the family moved into a house that the elder Steffens sold in 1903 to the state, which made it the governor's mansion. Lincoln attended the University of California, receiving a Ph.B. degree in 1889; he then studied in Europe. Returning to the United States, he was a reporter on the New York *Evening Post,* 1892-97, and city editor of the New York *Commercial Advertiser,* 1897-1901. In 1901 he moved to *McClure's Magazine* as managing editor but worked instead as a reporter, concentrating on the articles on city and state governments that were published in *The Shame of the Cities* (1904), *The Struggle for Self-Government* (1906), and *Upbuilders* (1909). In the fall of 1906 he left *McClure's* and with Ida Tarbell, Finley Peter Dunne, William Allen White, and Ray Stannard Baker took over the *American Magazine*; he sold his interest to his colleagues early in 1908. After going to Boston, at the invitation of Edward A. Filene and the Good Government Association, to make a one-year study of the city, he occupied himself with lecturing and free-lance writing.

From his early days at *McClure's* Steffens became increasingly interested in politics as a participant as well as reporter. Having become interested in the single-tax theory while interviewing Mayor Tom L. Johnson of Cleveland in 1903, he became in 1909 a member of the Joseph Fels Commission of America, which subsidized movements for the single tax, and a member of the national committee of the National Single Tax League in 1917. He became an active partisan and collaborator with various reformers on whom he had reported, especially of Judge Ben Lindsey of Denver, Francis J. Heney of San Francisco, and Senator Robert M. La Follette. Although he spent most of his life in the East and abroad, Steffens always considered himself a Californian. His absorbing interest in California affairs was epitomized by his description of himself as a central figure in the trials of James B. and John J. McNamara for bombing the Los Angeles *Times* in 1910, and of Clarence Darrow, their attorney, for attempting to bribe a juror. Losing interest in American politics as the demand for his articles and lectures declined, he went to Europe in 1914, to Mexico in 1914 and 1915-16, to Russia in 1917, and again to Russia with William C. Bullitt, then attached to the American peace commission, for the United States government in March 1919.

In 1924 he married Ella Winter, who after his death married Donald Ogden Stewart in 1939. Returning to the United States in 1927, to his native California, he bought a house at Carmel and became an elder statesman in leftist literary circles. His *Autobiography* (1931) brought him a new reputation as a social philosopher and new friends, including fellow admirers of the Soviet Union and Paul C. Smith, editor of the San Francisco *Chronicle* and friend of Herbert Hoover. He continued to write columns for local newspapers after a heart attack in December 1933, which left him bedridden. Responding to an offer of nomination for United States senator by the Communist party in 1934, he declined to join the party.

The articles that Steffens wrote between about 1906 and 1908 on Lindsey, Rudolph Spreckels, William S. U'Ren, and other western leaders are standard sources on them. Historians of California have felt less confidence in his versions of events in Los Angeles in 1910-12; Louis Adamic, in *Dynamite* (1931) and *My America, 1928-1938* (1938), claimed they were seriously inaccurate.

The *Autobiography* (1931) is indispensable. It is, however, unreliable for details such as dates, and contemporary records often do not sustain its picture of Steffens' detachment from the reform movements that he investigated as a reporter. See also Ella Winter and Granville Hicks, eds., *The Letters of Lincoln Steffens,* 2 vols. (1938), *The World of Lincoln Steffens* (1962); and introductions to reprints of *The Shame of the Cities* (1957) and *Upbuilders* (1968). The only biography is Justin Kaplan, *Lincoln Steffens* (1974). Columbia University Library has unpublished correspondence, including long letters from political friends in Colorado, Oregon, and California.—E. P.

Stegner, Wallace (1909-   ). Historian and novelist. Born in Lake Mills, Iowa, Stegner was educated at the University of Utah and the University of Iowa, where he received a Ph.D. degree in 1935. From 1933 until 1945 he was an instructor of English at various colleges and in 1945 became professor of English at Stanford University.

A prolific writer, his books include historical and descriptive studies of the West: *Mormon Country* (1942), *Beyond the Hundredth Meridian: John Wesley Powell and the Second Opening of the West* (1954), *The Gathering of Zion: The Story of the Mormon Trail* (1964), and *The Sound of Mountain Water* (1969), among others. He also wrote short stories and other fiction, notably his famous novel *The Big Rock Candy Mountain* (1943). His novel *Angel of Repose* (1971) won a Pulitzer Prize.

As a historian, Stegner had a gift for re-creation of the past, making it eminently believable through his depiction of its confusions and uncertainties. Unlike many western historians, who often see the past as pointing unerringly toward the present, Stegner emphasized its contradictory qualities. He made the point that "the past" is something of a meaningless phrase; since when "the past" existed it was "the present," with all of the present's confusion. This is nowhere more evident than in his studies of the Mormons, a group that has generally been badly handled both by its own historians and by critical outsiders. Stegner is one of the few to have written of the Mormons as people, possessed of very human virtues and vices, rather than as either archangels or archfiends.

His gift for seeing people as people rather than as walking statements of some favorite philosophical idea is also basic to his best fiction. In *The Big Rock Candy Mountain* his characters successfully escape the Freudian stereotypes into which a less able writer would have transformed them, as well as the Marxist categories in which many other writers would try to make them fit. The novel, in common with other fine writing in the western idiom, is a study of the ironies of change. Its hero, Bo Mason, is a pioneer born too late, a frontier character cast adrift in a world that has run out of new frontiers.—J. K. F.

Steinbeck, John (1902-1968). Novelist. Steinbeck was born in Salinas, California. After graduation from the Salinas high school in 1918 he matriculated at Stanford University in 1919, but left without receiving a degree. Until he was able to make a living from his writing he supported himself by odd jobs. His writing soon became financially remunerative, however, as well as critically favored. He received the Pulitzer Prize for literature in 1940 and the Nobel Prize in 1962.

With few exceptions, notably *The Moon Is Down* (1942), Steinbeck's work is set in the California where he grew up. Monterey, near Salinas, is the setting for his humorous trilogy *Tortilla Flat* (1935), *Cannery Row* (1945), and *Sweet Thursday* (1954). Southward, in the vicinity of Soledad, is the locale for *Of Mice and Men* (1937). Northward lies the Torgas valley, scene of *In Dubious Battle* (1936), in one sense a preliminary version of his perhaps best-known novel, *The Grapes of Wrath* (1939), itself set in the San Joaquin valley to the east. The stories in *The Red Pony* (1937) and *The Long Valley* (1938) are placed in the same geographical area, as is *East of Eden* (1952).

The remarkable success of *The Grapes of Wrath,* coupled with Steinbeck's many nonfictional statements to the effect that his work is totally partisan in nature, enlisted in the aid of the laboring man, has worked somewhat to the detriment of his literary reputation. Critics in the 1940s expected a thematic sequel to *The Grapes of Wrath,* and when none was forthcoming they accused Steinbeck of backing away from those social issues which, in the dark days of the Great Depression, were often assumed to offer the only possible themes for serious literature. Today, with all of his literary career before us, a different assessment seems more just. For Steinbeck was, *par excellence,* a storyteller, closer to Mark Twain and the tradition of often bitter folk humor than to John Dos Passos, James T. Farrell, and the tradition of the proletarian novel. In all his stories, even his proletarian ones, the authorial voice is close to the "once upon a time" of his avowedly parabolic tales, such as *The Pearl* (1947) and *The Short Reign of Pippin IV* (1957). In many ways *Travels with Charley* (1962) is a fitting summation to Steinbeck's literary career. Superficially an account of an American journey Steinbeck made with a dog, the book is in fact a sober study of the strengths and weaknesses of the American character. It is remarkably similar to Mark Twain's similar studies in *The Innocents Abroad* (1869) and *Roughing It* (1872).

See John Fontenrose, *John Steinbeck: An Introduction and Interpretation* (1963); Warren French, *John Steinbeck* (1961); Tetsumaro Hayashi, *John Steinbeck: A Concise Bibliography* (1967); and H. T. Moore, *The Novels of John Steinbeck* (1939).—J. K. F.

Stetson hat. See COWBOY CLOTHING.

Steunenberg, Frank (1861-1905). Idaho politician and businessman. A native of Keokuk, Iowa, Steunenberg was educated at Iowa State College of Agriculture in Ames. In Knoxville, Iowa, he became a printer and then worked as a compositor on the Des Moines *Register.* Returning to Knoxville in 1884, he published the Knoxville *Express* with his brother until the end of 1886. Then he and his brother took over the Caldwell *Tribune* in Idaho at the beginning of 1887 and published it until 1893.

A Democrat, Steunenberg became a delegate to the Idaho constitutional convention in 1889 and was elected in 1890 to the House of Representatives. At the head of a fusion ticket of Democrats, Silver Republicans, and Populists, he was chosen governor in 1896 and was reelected in 1898 by Democrats and Silver Republicans. Strife between sheep and cattlemen (focused on the trial of Diamondfield Jack Davis, accused by mistake of shooting two sheepherders in 1896) created a major problem that lasted through both of Steunenberg's terms of office. Labor trouble between the WESTERN FEDERATION OF MINERS and the mine owners in the Coeur d'Alene mining region (see IDAHO) plagued the last two years of Steunenberg's administration; after the Bunker Hill and Sullivan concentrator at Wardner was blown up on April 29, 1899, the mines remained under martial law until after Steunenberg retired from office.

After his retirement, Steunenberg had important sheep, lumber, and banking interests. He was instrumental in establishing the lumber company that expanded to become Boise Cascade. His assassination by bomb at his home in Caldwell was carried out by Harry Orchard (alias for Albert E. Horsley); it created a national sensation and led to the celebrated trial of William D. Haywood for conspiracy to the assassination. Haywood was acquitted, but Harry Orchard served a life sentence in the penitentiary.—M. W.

Stevens, Isaac Ingalls (1818-1862). Washington politician. Stevens was born in Andover, Massachusetts. He enrolled at West Point and received his commission to the army engineers in 1839. After serving in the Mexican War in 1846-47, he was appointed Indian agent for Washington Territory, chief of the Northern Pacific Railroad survey, and in 1853 governor of Washington Territory by his friend President Franklin Pierce. While governor he negotiated a series of seven treaties with the Indian tribes from both eastern and western Washington that almost immediately resulted in conflicts between him and citizens of SEATTLE and bloodshed between natives and settlers (see YAKIMA INDIANS). The legal issues over conflicts between Indian fishing rights and state conservation laws raised by the treaties have remained unresolved for more than a century.

On the national scene, Stevens was elected territorial delegate to Congress in 1857 and delegate to the Democratic party convention in Charleston in 1860. During the Civil War he was commissioned a brigadier general and later a major general in the Union army, at which time he appointed his son, Hazard Stevens, to serve on his staff. He was killed at the battle of Chantilly, Virginia.

See Joseph T. Hazard, *Companion of Adventure* (1952); Donald W. Meinig, "Isaac Stevens: Practical Geographer of the Early Northwest," *Geographical Review* (October 1955); and Hazard Stevens, *The Life of Isaac Ingalls Stevens,* 2 vols. (1900).—K. A. M.

Stevenson, Edward Augustus (1831-1895). Idaho politician. A native of New York, Stevenson resided in Michigan before making the long trip west at the age of eighteen to join the California gold rush. Going into politics at an early age, he entered the California legislature when he was only twenty-two and served four terms.

Stevenson came to Boise Basin, Idaho, in 1863, and acquired important mining interests near Grimes' Pass. There he kept up his political career by serving in the Idaho legislature intermittently from 1866 to 1876. He also worked in a term as Boise County commissioner, beginning in 1872. Moving to Payette valley in 1882, he identified himself with Idaho's growing agricultural interests.

During Grover Cleveland's first presidential term, Stevenson became territorial governor, serving from 1885 to 1889. When Congress belatedly decided to annex North Idaho to Washington in 1887, Stevenson managed to induce Cleveland not to approve the measure. Idaho thus was saved at the last moment, and Stevenson then assumed a position of leadership in Idaho's movement to become a state. When the legislature failed to get around to calling a constitutional convention in 1889, he summoned one on his own initiative as governor. And even after George Laird Shoup had succeeded him as governor in May 1889, Stevenson continued to work effectively for Idaho admission, which was finally accomplished in 1890.

Taking over a Boise Basin stage line after Idaho became a state, Stevenson won the Democratic nomination for governor in 1894. The Democrats had no chance that year, though, and he did not live long enough to try again in 1896, when a fusion of the pro-silver forces transformed Idaho's political structure.—M. W.

Stevenson, Matilda Coxe (1850-1915). Ethnologist. One of the most colorful fieldworkers in southwestern ethnology, Stevenson was in the grande dame tradition. Born in Texas, her family moved to Washington, D.C., and she attended a female seminary, Miss Anable's School, in Philadelphia. In 1872 "Tilly" married James Stevenson, a geologist. Seven years later she, her husband, Frank Hamilton Cushing, and J. K. Hillers went on an anthropological trip to Zuñi, New Mexico. Her ethnological career now begun, Mrs. Stevenson set to work learning the ways of Zuñi women and conducting a one-woman campaign to introduce the pueblo to the use of soap. She selected as her co-worker in the cleanliness campaign a male transvestite, a Zuñi man more than six feet tall, whose psychological and social makeup was completely feminine. Before long, following the example set by the transvestite, innumerable Zuñi villagers began regularly laundering their clothes.

In 1881 Stevenson's work was extended to the Hopi Indians of Arizona. From then until her husband's death in 1888 she continued fieldwork among these two groups, and in 1890-91 she visited the Sia Indians of New Mexico. She was able to view esoteric rites and religious paraphernalia normally closed to outsiders partly because of the respect that some Zuñi had for her, partly through bribery, and partly—with the Sia and Hopi—through sheer bravado. Many of her antics in insisting on what she deemed to be her inalienable right to move among Indians as she chose may be at least partly responsible for hostility directed toward anthropologists by many Pueblo Indians today.

Stevenson spent her declining years seeking solace in alcohol and living near San Ildefonso, New Mexico, but she continued her researches until her death. She was regarded by local Indians and others as a curious relic of the past and was nicknamed "Big Bottom" by the Tewa peoples of San Ildefonso. Nonetheless, her death marked the passing of a woman who had left future generations of Pueblo Indians and non-Indians alike an incredible legacy of published material on what was then a passing way of life. *The Sia* (1894) and especially *The Zuñi Indians* (1904) will stand forever as enlightened descriptions of western cultural scenes now gone.

See W. H. Holmes, "In Memoriam, Matilda Coxe Stevenson," *American Anthropologist,* vol. 18 (1916); and Nancy O. Lurie, "Woman in Early American Anthropology," in June Helm, ed., *Pioneers of American Anthropology* (1966)—B. L. F.

Stewart, William Morris (1827-1909). Lawyer and Nevada politician. Stewart was born in Galen, New York, attended Farmington Academy in Ohio, and taught high school mathematics in his native state. After a brief stay at Yale, he moved to California in 1850. Modest success as a gold-seeker financed the study of law, and he soon developed expertise in mining litigation. He also pursued a political career as a district attorney in 1853 and acting attorney general a year later.

Silver discoveries in Nevada in 1859 lured Stewart out of California, and he plunged into the turbulent economic life of the Comstock Lode. He remained active politically and served in the territorial legislature and the constitutional convention in 1863. When Nevada entered the Union in 1864, he was elected to the Senate as a Republican. During two terms he took part in radical Reconstruction, helped write the Fifteenth Amendment, and supported the impeachment of Andrew Johnson. In a moment of inattention he voted for the coinage legislation that later won notoriety as the alleged "Crime of '73."

Leaving the Senate in 1875, Stewart practiced law in California on behalf of such clients as Collis P. Huntington. The railroad magnate later called him "one of the men who had no special need of being looked after, as the right thing was always done by him." He resumed his Nevada residence in 1886, and with the help of the Southern Pacific railroad, again won a Senate seat.

Stewart represented the parochial interests of his state energetically for eighteen years. He helped to defeat the Federal Elections bill in 1891 to assist the cause of silver, he protected Nevada's corrupt election practices, and prevented aid to Negroes. As sentiment for the silver standard and the unlimited coinage of silver reached feverish proportions among Nevadans, he left the Republicans in 1892, joined the local Silver party, and advocated bimetallism in speeches, private letters, and his own newspaper, the *Silver Knight-Watchman.* He endorsed William Jennings Bryan in 1896 and successfully urged fusion of Democrats and Populists.

William McKinley's election left Stewart almost powerless in Washington, and his popularity ebbed away. Railroad money secured his reelection as a silverite in 1899, but his return to the Republican fold in 1900 led to his retirement from public office at the end of his term. Aside from the years as a mining lawyer, his career is noteworthy largely for its length. Unlike champions of silver from outside Nevada, no concern with social problems motivated Stewart's commitment to the cause. His political opportunism, deference to railroads, and myopic view of national issues did much to give Nevada a reputation as a "rotten borough" and to cast doubt on western politics in general.

See the Stewart Papers, Nevada Historical Society, Reno; George R. Brown, ed., *Reminiscences of Senator William Morris Stewart* (1908); and H. E. Glass, *Silver and Politics in Nevada, 1892-1902* (1969).—L. L. G.

Stockton, Robert Field (1795-1866). Naval officer and politician. Stockton was born in Princeton, New Jersey, graduated from the College of New Jersey (Princeton), and served as a naval officer during the War of 1812. Transferred to the Mediterranean, he engaged in the war with Algiers. After the war he and his father-in-law were instrumental in building the Princeton canal. Later he became interested in naval architecture and fostered the construction of the steamship *Princeton*, of which he was commander when one of the guns exploded and killed several cabinet members. In July 1846, with the outbreak of the Mexican War, Stockton arrived at Monterey, California, and succeeded Commodore John D. Sloat as commander of the American forces in California. He collected an army, which included Captain John C. Frémont and his contingent, captured Los Angeles in mid-August, and proclaimed California a United States territory and himself governor. A month later, however, the Mexicans retook all the southern coastal towns except San Diego. In late December, with General Stephen Watts Kearny, who had recently arrived from New Mexico, Stockton marched from San Diego and on January 8 and 9, 1847, drove General Andreas Pico's forces from the field near Los Angeles and entered the city with flags flying and a band playing. When Pico attempted to parley, Stockton brushed him aside; so the Mexican general met Frémont at nearby Cahuenga and concluded an armistice. Stockton appointed Frémont to succeed him as governor and by October had returned to Washington. In 1850 he resigned from the navy.

As a Democratic senator from New Jersey, 1851-53, Stockton encouraged internal improvements. He himself helped build the Perth Amboy railroad and held a controlling interest in the line. He attended the Peace Conference in Washington in February 1861 and died at Princeton.

See Samuel J. Bayard, *A Sketch of the Life of Commodore Robert F. Stockton* (1856).—H. P. H.

Stone, Barton W. See DISCIPLES OF CHRIST.

Stone, Willard (1916-   ). Sculptor. Stone was born in Oktaha near Muskogee, Oklahoma, and credited his career as an artist to the influence of the late Oklahoma historian Grant Foreman, who, after seeing some of Stone's work exhibited at the Muskogee and Okmulgee state fairs in 1935, encouraged the artist to enroll at Bacone College, where he came under the supervision of Acee Blue Eagle and Woodrow Crumbo, noted American Indian painters. Himself a quarter Cherokee, Stone continued at Bacone from about 1935 to 1939, after which he married and attempted to support himself at various jobs. For a period of three years he worked under the sponsorship of Thomas Gilcrease of Tulsa, Oklahoma, during which time he produced some of his most characteristic pieces, primarily abstract or interpretive in style. He later worked as a designer for the Ernest Wieman Iron Works and the Douglas Aircraft facility in Tulsa. He gained wide recognition and exhibited nationally, his primary subjects being taken directly from nature. His most popular works are animal and Indian figures executed at his studio near Locust Grove, Oklahoma. Several pieces of an allegorical nature relating to the advent of the atomic age are in the collection of the Thomas Gilcrease Institute of American History and Art, Tulsa, Oklahoma. They are among the few of his works based upon a modern theme. Other of Stone's sculptures are scattered in private collections or are displayed at the Cherokee National Historical Society near Tahlequah, Oklahoma, and the Five Civilized Tribes Museum at Muskogee.

See Jeanne O. Snodgrass, *American Indian Painters: A Biographical Dictionary* (1968).—D. C. H.

Stoudenmire, Dallas (1845-1882). Texas lawman. Stoudenmire was a big, angry lawman who drank too much and shot too fast. From Alabama, he twice enlisted in the Confederate army only to be discharged for being under age. In 1864 he enlisted again and served until the end of the Civil War, after which he went to Texas, riding with the Texas Rangers in 1874. Afterward, he wandered through Texas trying his hand at various jobs and building a reputation as a tough and honest man until April 1881, when he settled in El Paso to be its marshal. He did such a good job—although resorting to violence more than once—that the citizens presented him with a gold-headed cane in recognition of his services. But Stoudenmire made powerful enemies in the process, notably the three Manning brothers, James, Frank, and George Felix.

George Felix Manning, a physician known as Doc, was the leader of the brothers in their saloon and ranching interests. By the time Stoudenmire became marshal, the Mannings were well established in El Paso. They enjoyed a dubious reputation, and evidence strongly suggested that they were involved in rustling activities in Mexico. In the spring of 1881, two Mexicans were killed by associates of the Mannings, and a large party of Mexicans descended on El Paso. They asked Gus Krempkau, a quiet and honest constable, to help them recover the bodies of the dead men. Krempkau agreed, but at the inquest that followed tensions were so high that it was quickly closed. After the Mexicans left, a George Campbell taunted Krempkau for helping them, and John Hale, a partner of the Mannings, ran into the street and shot Krempkau at close range. At the sound of gunfire, Stoudenmire rushed to the scene where he killed Hale, Campbell, and an innocent bystander.

It was the death of Campbell that really caused Stoudenmire's trouble. Several persons had heard Campbell exclaim that he did not want to fight just before Stoudenmire shot him, but it is probable that Stoudenmire did not hear him in the melee. He saw only a man with a gun and shot him. But the Mannings persuaded the whiskey-besotted ex-marshal, Bill Johnson, to assassinate Stoudenmire. Three days later, Johnson fired at Stoudenmire with a shotgun and Stoudenmire killed him. At that moment, Stoudenmire was fired on by other assailants. He charged them and was wounded by a ricocheting bullet, but the hidden gunmen escaped. Suspicions were directed at the Mannings. Stoudenmire kept a tight rein on El Paso after that, but in February 1882, Stoudenmire's brother-in-law, Doc Cummings, was killed by Jim Manning. Although it appeared that Cummings provoked the fight, Stoudenmire brooded over the killing and drank heavily. His life was threatened. Murders increased. The town was increasingly uneasy. Stoudenmire became increasingly obnoxious. In April 1882 a truce was literally signed between the Mannings and Stoudenmire, but that did not last long. In May, Stoudenmire resigned as marshal. His boasting, brooding, and drinking had finally brought him to open conflict with the city fathers. He was appointed a deputy United States marshal in July 1882, but his hatred for the Mannings continued to dominate his mind. On the afternoon of September 18, 1882, Stoudenmire was killed in a gunfight with Doc and Jim Manning.

See Leon C. Metz, *Dallas Stoudenmire: El Paso Marshal* (1969).—G. L. R.

Strahorn, Robert Edmond (1852-1944). Journalist, railroad publicist, and builder. Strahorn was one of the rare individuals who knew almost all areas of the West intimately. As correspondent for the *Rocky Mountain News* of Denver, he accompanied Brigadier General George Crook's forces during the Sioux War of 1876-77, participating in an attack on a Powder River village in March 1876, the battle of the Rosebud, and the Slim Buttes battle.

Upon writing *The Hand-Book of Wyoming* in 1877, Strahorn was offered a position as the first director of the literary bureau of the Union Pacific. During the next twelve years he wrote for the railroad many guidebooks publicizing the West, among them *To the Rockies and Beyond, Enchanted Land or an October Ramble in Yellowstone National Park,* and *Where Rolls the Oregon.* His first wife, Carrie Adell Strahorn, accompanied him on the extensive travels in which he gathered materials for the guidebooks and wrote an important western travel book of her own, *Fifteen Thousand Miles by Stage* (1911).

From 1883 to 1890 Strahorn managed the Oregon and Idaho Land Improvement Company, a Union Pacific affiliate, which was engaged in building towns and irrigation projects. After living in Boston for eight years as a broker, Strahorn returned to the West, making his home in Spokane, Washington. There, from 1898 to 1925, he built the North Coast Railway, the Spokane Union Terminal, and the Portland, Eugene & Eastern Railway.

Discussions of Strahorn's work are in Oliver Knight, "Robert E. Strahorn: Propagandist for the West," *Pacific Northwest Quarterly* (January 1968), and *Following the Indian Wars* (1960).—O. K.

Strang, James Jesse (1813-1856). Religious leader and founder of the Strangites. James Jesse Strang was born in Cayuga County, New York, to Clement and Abigail James Strang. Though sickly as a child, Strang possessed from his earliest years a profound love of learning and a conviction that he was destined for some high and unusual calling. Through his marriage in 1836 to Mary Perce, sister-in-law of an ardent Mormon, he acquired an intimate connection with the Church of Latter-day Saints. He was baptized by Joseph Smith himself at Nauvoo, Illinois, in February 1844 and soon rose to the position of elder. After Smith's death in Illinois in 1844, Strang produced a letter in which the Mormon leader allegedly revealed his approaching martyrdom and appointed Strang as his successor. His attempts to assume the leadership of the church were defeated, however, by the rival factions of Sidney Rigdon and Brigham Young.

Following a Messianic vision on September 1, 1845, Strang dug up three inscribed brass plates at Voree, near the White River, between Racine and Walworth counties, Wisconsin. The subsequent translation and publication of these "Voree plates" enabled Strang to set up his own Mormon community at Voree in 1846. Further heavenly revelations directed him to explore Beaver Island at the northern end of Lake Michigan. Here he established a second Strangite community in 1847 which attracted a steady stream of immigrants and supplanted Voree by the spring of 1850.

A commanding figure and powerful orator, Strang exercised strict spiritual and temporal control over his Beaver Island community. Deciding that the Kingdom of God on Earth had been established, he crowned himself on July 8, 1850, and renamed the settlement the Kingdom of Saint James. Shortly afterward followed the publication of *The Book of the Law of the Lord,* a translation of eighteen additional brass plates, withheld from the Children of Israel, which Strang had discovered in 1849. The volume stressed absolutism and isolation from the world as the keys to the Strangite religion. The king was the supreme master in every sphere of human thought and action. He collected tithes, declared the law and commandments, and executed punishment on transgressors. Gambling, alcohol, and narcotics were prohibited, but polygamy permitted, a provision introduced largely to explain the four additional wives which Strang had accumulated after 1848.

Strang's arbitrary rule and authoritarian personality, which became more pronounced during his later years, eventually led to his death and the destruction of his community. From the beginning, continuous gentile persecution from the nearby island of Mackinac had forced the Strangites to maintain a militaristic posture toward the outside world. On June 16, 1856, two malcontents in the community shot Strang and escaped through the connivance of officers on board the U.S.S. *Michigan.* Mortally wounded, Strang was removed by steamer to the home of his first wife's parents at Voree, where he died on July 9. Within a week of the assassination, a drunken mob from Mackinac wrecked the Kingdom of Saint James and scattered the inhabitants, effectively ending the Strangite church as well.

See Milo M. Quaife, *The Kingdom of Saint James* (1930); O. W. Riegel, *Crown of Glory: The Life of James J. Strang* (1935); James J. Strang, *The Diary of James J. Strang,* Mark A. Strang, ed. (1961), *The Book of the Law of the Lord* (1856?) and *The Diamond: Being the Law of Prophetic Succession* (1848).—E. H. S.

Streeter, Thomas W. See COLLECTORS AND COLLECTIONS OF WESTERN AMERICANA.

Stuart, Granville (1834-1918). Montana pioneer. Stuart was born in Clarksburg, now West Virginia. During his childhood Stuart's family pioneered on the Illinois and Iowa frontiers. In 1849 his father joined the California gold rush, and in 1852 Granville and his brother John also went to the gold fields. Finding little luck as prospectors, the two brothers started back east in 1857. Near Salt Lake they were alarmed by inflated reports of Mormon hostility and so turned north, crossing into present Montana. While waiting for the Mormon situation to abate before resuming their journey, the Stuarts did some informal prospecting and on May 2, 1858, found gold in the Deer Lodge valley near present Goldcreek. Gold had earlier been located in the area, but the news of the Stuarts' find started the rush to Montana in 1862, and they are credited with discovery.

Granville Stuart for several years followed the rush to the various Montana mining camps without much success and finally settled in Deer Lodge in 1867. He opened a store and lumberyard and took a leading part in community affairs. Stuart was elected to the territorial council in 1871 and 1883, serving as its president, and was elected to the lower house in 1876 and 1879. Stuart was a leader of the 1884 Montana vigilante movement, which was to become the most notorious in American history: it took the lives of thirty-five horse and cattle thieves. He increased his business interests and pioneered in the Montana range cattle industry, but like many overstocked ranchers was driven out of that business by the market collapse and severe winter of 1886-87. Appointed United States minister to Uruguay and Paraguay by President Cleveland in 1894, he occupied that post until 1899, when he retired to Montana.

Although informally educated, Stuart was by nature philosophic and an avid reader. He kept extensive journals during his life and enlivened them with excellent sketches, which are evocative of the styles of Karl Bodmer and Alfred Jacob Miller. Stuart's reminiscences were published posthumously as *Forty Years on the Frontier* and are a vivid and valuable source on information about the gold rush era and early Montana history.

See M. G. Burlingame, *The Montana Frontier* (1942); and Granville Stuart, *Forty Years on the Frontier*, ed. P. C. Phillips (1925) and *Diary and Sketchbook of a Journey,* introduction by Carl Dentzel (1963).—P. R. M.

Stuart, John (1718-1784). Businessman and Indian agent. Stuart was born in Inverness, Scotland. After receiving a grammar school education, he was sent on a business mission to London. From that city he went to Spain on an adventure he was not to forget. In 1740 Stuart accompanied Captain John Anson on a marauding venture against the Spanish galleons in the New World. He went as clerk and agent victualler. Anson circumnavigated the globe in what was financially a successful voyage, but from the standpoint of naval personnel was a major disaster. He returned to England with only 135 men out of a complement of 1,939. Stuart was promoted to the rank of captain's clerk, a position that gave him high confidence.

From 1743 to 1748 Stuart lived in London. In the latter year he sailed for South Carolina, landing in Charleston as a partner of the trading company of Stuart and Reid. This firm, however, suffered reverses, and it was necessary for Stuart to return to England the next year. In 1750 he was back in Charleston, where he became an active political, commercial, and social figure of the city for the next quarter of a century.

About 1761 Stuart became Indian superintendent of the British southern colonial district, a position he held until 1779. He was an active participant in numerous Indian treaty conferences, the most important of which were Hard Labor, Lochaber, and the Augusta Congress. During the twelve years before the American Revolution Stuart prospered from the Indian trade in Georgia, Florida, and South Carolina. He became especially friendly with the Cherokee and had extensive dealings with the Creek, Choctaw, Chickasaw, and Catawba. He

was said to have had a son of part-Cherokee blood named Oonotata, known to whites as "Bushyhead."

At the outset of the revolution Stuart undertook to keep the western Indians friendly to the British, an act that eventually forced him to depart for England. When Stuart's property was confiscated by South Carolina during the revolution, it became necessary for the British government to grant his family a substantial subsidy.

See John R. Alden, *John Stuart and the Southern Colonial Frontier,* (1944); Philip M. Hamer, "John Stuart's Indian Policy During the Early Months of the American Revolution," *Mississippi Valley Historical Review,* vol. 17 (1930); and David D. Wallace, *The History of South Carolina,* 4 vols. (1934).—T. D. C.

Sublette brothers. Fur traders and mountain men. The five members of the Sublette family who were associated with the fur trade were born in Kentucky, the sons of Philip A. and Isabella Whitley Sublette. Sometime during the period 1816-17 the Sublette family migrated to Missouri Territory, where Philip kept a tavern in present-day St. Charles. By 1822, however, both parents had died.

William Lewis (1799-1845), the eldest, and various relatives assumed the responsibility for raising the younger children. In the spring of 1823 William joined General William Ashley's second fur-trading expedition up the Missouri, but it met with disaster when the Arikara Indians attacked the party, killed several men, wounded others, and seized some of Ashley's supplies. William, having escaped injury, joined Colonel Henry Leavenworth's makeshift military expedition of soldiers and trappers that was sent to chastise the Indians and to recover stolen property. The Leavenworth expedition did not fully succeed at its task, but its presence allowed Ashley to resume operations. That fall William joined a small party of Ashley's trappers, led by Jedediah Smith, on an untried overland trek to the Rockies to hunt and trap. By breaking away from the usual river routes and by traveling overland on horseback, the Smith party blazed new trails and opened up the northern Rockies to the fur trade. William was with Smith when South Pass was rediscovered in the following year, a find that enabled trappers to reach the yet unexploited Green River region.

In 1826 William, now a seasoned mountain man, joined Smith and David E. Jackson in purchasing Ashley's fur firm. In 1830 he was the first trader to take wagons to the northern Rockies; but in that same year he sold out to the Rocky Mountain Fur Company, a newly organized firm among whose partners were the famous mountain men Jim Bridger, Thomas Fitzpatrick, and Milton Sublette, William's own brother. In 1831 he began profitable operations in the Santa Fe trade, but he continued to play a major role in the fur business. After 1830 he was successively a partner of Jackson and of Robert Campbell and became the economic overlord (although not a member) of the ROCKY MOUNTAIN FUR COMPANY, for he was the major source of supplies purchased by the trappers at their annual summer fur-trading rendezvous in the mountains. In 1832 he was wounded at the battle of Pierre's Hole. In partnership with Robert Campbell, William built Fort Laramie in eastern Wyoming in 1834 but soon lost control of it to the American Fur Company.

In 1836 William left the mountains to enter the mercantile business in St. Louis and to become a gentleman farmer. He maintained a race track, hotel, and watering place on his country estate at nearby Sulphur Springs, which his sister, Sophronia, helped manage. He continued to assist his brothers in various enterprises, but his own interests turned to politics. He supported Thomas Hart Benton and the local Democratic party and served as an elector from Missouri in the 1844 presidential election. That same year William ended a life of bachelorhood when he married Frances Hereford. By then, however, he was ill with tuberculosis. While on his way east to recuperate at Cape May, New Jersey, he suddenly grew worse and died in a Pittsburgh hotel.

Milton Green (1801-1837) began his career in the southwestern fur trade when he joined the Gila River expedition of Ewing YOUNG in 1826. When Governor Manuel Armijo of New Mexico seized the expedition's pelts on flimsy legal charges, Milton, who was a large, heavily muscled man, defied authorities and escaped with his share of the skins. In 1827-28 he was on the Pratte-St. Vrain expedition into the northern Rockies. In 1830 he was one of the five partners who formed the Rocky Mountain Fur Company. Thereafter, he had numerous daring adventures, which led a reporter to call him the "Thunderbolt of the Rockies." He fought in the battle of Pierre's Hole (1832) and married the Shoshoni Indian beauty Mountain Lamb. In 1832 he guided Nathaniel Wyeth, the Boston ice merchant turned fur trader, and a small party through hostile Blackfoot country to Oregon. In 1833 Milton agreed to accept his annual supplies from Wyeth but could not fulfill this contract when Wyeth appeared with the goods at the rendezvous of 1834. When the Rocky Mountain Fur Company was dissolved that year, Milton continued in partnership with Thomas Fitzpatrick and James Bridger, two of the original members of the company. Milton's left leg had to be amputated in 1835—he was probably suffering from bone cancer—and he died two years later at Fort Laramie.

Andrew Whitley (1808?-1853) began to work for his brother William about 1827. He accompanied him on various journeys to the Rockies and to Santa Fe. Like William and Milton he participated in the battle of Pierre's Hole. In 1835 he formed a partnership with Louis Vasquez based at Fort Vasquez, the first trading post constructed on the South Platte River. After the firm failed in 1841, he worked for William again, served as a guide, and commanded a company in the Mexican War. He moved in 1849 to California, where he was involved in mining, local politics, and market hunting. He was killed by a grizzly bear in December 1853. As was the case with the other Sublette brothers, Andrew's travels were motivated in part by a desperate effort to overcome tuberculosis, a disease that plagued the entire family.

Pinckney W. (1812?-1828) was taken to the mountains for his health but was killed in Blackfoot country. Rumors persisted that somehow he had survived and had lived quietly in the wilderness until 1864, but later official investigations failed to turn up convincing evidence that this was the case.

Solomon Perry (1816?-1857) ran an outfitting store in Independence, Missouri, in 1836 (an endeavor backed by his brother William's money) that served traders on the Santa Fe Trail as well as Oregon immigrants. A genial but restless man, he traveled in many parts of the West, visited Santa Fe, and trapped and traded in partnership with his brother Andrew between 1839 and 1842, although Andrew was still in partnership with Louis Vasquez during part of that time. Later, Solomon traveled over parts of the Oregon Trail, sojourned at Fort Laramie, visited Taos, and in 1845 journeyed to California, where he met Colonel John Sutter. In the spring of 1846 he helped Joseph R. WALKER drive horses from southern California over Cajon Pass up to Fort Bridger. Eventually he returned to St. Louis, and there, in 1849, he married William's widow, Frances Hereford Sublette. But death claimed Solomon and his wife in 1857 and their only surviving child soon thereafter, marking the demise of the entire Sublette family and its immediate heirs. The bulk of an impressive estate built on furs and trade went to the Hereford family.

See Dale L. Morgan and Eleanor T. Harris, eds., *Rocky Mountain Journals of William Marshall Anderson* (1967); Doyce B. Nunis, Jr., *Andrew Sublette, Rocky Mountain Prince, 1808-1853* (1960); John E. Sunder, *Bill Sublette, Mountain Man* (1959), *The Fur Trade on the Upper Missouri, 1840-1865* (1965), and "Solomon Perry Sublette: Mountain Man of the Forties," *New Mexico Historical Review*, vol. 36 (January 1961). The Sublette Family Papers, 1819-60, are located in the Missouri Historical Society, St. Louis.—G. B. D.

suffrage. See WOMAN SUFFRAGE.

Sullivan-Clinton Campaign (1779). American military expedition against the New York Iroquois. Except for the Oneida and Tuscarora, who remained neutral, the Iroquois tribes sided overwhelmingly with the British at the outbreak of the American Revolution. Under such leaders as the Mohawk Joseph BRANT and in company with Tory settlers, they repeatedly raided the New York and Pennsylvania frontiers, perpetrating the Wyoming and Cherry Valley massacres of 1778, among others.

To retaliate and to prevent further attacks, General George Washington authorized a multiple invasion of the Iroquois country in 1779. One force moved up the Mohawk valley to destroy the Onondaga village near present-day Syracuse, New York, in April. The main body, about forty-five hundred men under generals John Sullivan and James Clinton, marched northward from Tioga (Athens, Pennsylvania) late in August. After pushing aside a small Indian and Tory force near modern Elmira, the army split into smaller detachments which marched at will through the Seneca and Cayuga country, destroying villages and food supplies. In the space of a month forty towns were burned, along with 160,000 bushels of corn and other supplies, before the army returned to Pennsylvania. Meanwhile a third and smaller force under Colonel Daniel Brodhead moved north from Pittsburgh and burned several villages along the upper Allegheny River.

The Iroquois lacked the numbers and firepower to contest these invasions successfully; they also lacked any tradition of European battlefield warfare. As in the French invasions of their territory a century earlier, they wisely retreated. Their casualties were minimal, but destruction of their homes, food supplies, and morale was very great. One purpose of the campaign had been to capture Indian hostages with which to buy peace along the frontier. In this it failed, and the border raids continued. But at the end of the revolutionary war many Iroquois fled to Canada; the remainder lost most of their lands in New York and ceased any longer to be a military factor in North America.

See A. C. Flick, *The Sullivan-Clinton Campaign in 1779* (1929); Dale Van Every, *A Company of Heroes* (1962); and C. P. Whittemore, *A General of the Revolution: John Sullivan of New Hampshire* (1961).—A. W. T.

Sully, Alfred (1820-1879). Soldier. Sully, the son of painter Thomas Sully, was born in Philadelphia and graduated thirty-fourth in his class from West Point in 1841. He served in the Mexican War, participated in the Seminole War and Oregon's Rogue River War in 1853, and was on the northern Plains with Colonel William Selby Harney in 1856. During the Civil War he participated in the peninsula campaign and other battles in Virginia until 1863, when he was sent to the Department of the Northwest to lead an expedition up the Missouri River against the Sioux. Although Sully with about 1,800 men was unable to join with General Henry H. Sibley's 3,000 men, who had marched from Minnesota and defeated the Sioux in several skirmishes, he did defeat the Sioux at Whitestone Hill, killing an estimated 300 Indians and capturing 250 women and children. In 1864 Sully established Fort Rice on the upper Missouri and marched with 2,200 men against the Sioux west of the river, defeating them at Killdeer Mountain. The campaigns of 1863 and 1864 were the largest expeditions sent against the Plains tribes to date and marked a significant expansion of warfare with the Sioux.

In September 1868 Sully moved against the Southern Cheyenne south of the Arkansas River with little success, while in November he briefly participated in Philip H. Sheridan's winter campaign before being relieved by Lieutenant Colonel George A. Custer. In 1869 Sully was superintendent of Indian affairs for Montana and was involved in the dispute over the Marias Massacre by Colonel E. M. Baker.

Sully made many sketches of his experiences, painting primarily in watercolors, and his views of western forts are of historical as well as artistic interest. They are scattered widely in various collections.—R. N. E.

Summerhayes, Martha (1846-1911). Memoirist. A reminiscing army wife and New England blueblood, Summerhayes wrote *Vanishing Arizona, Recollections of the Army Life* (1908), an astonishing story about the western frontier (1874-78) from a cultivated woman's viewpoint. Married to Second Lieutenant John W. Summerhayes, she followed him over dusty leagues from one army camp to another in Arizona, California, and Texas. The young couple had a short assignment at Fort D. A. Russell at Cheyenne, Wyoming, before taking the train to California, where they sailed to Port Isabel at the mouth of the Colorado River. From there they boarded a river steamer and nearly cooked in the summer heat before docking at Fort Mojave. Then they took a long, jolting journey by mule-drawn wagon train to Fort Whipple and Fort Apache in Arizona Territory. Her initiation into rough camp life was a shocker to a properly brought-up young lady. Learning to tolerate the rustic army cooking and the succulent profanity that teamsters laid on tempermental mules, took a bit of doing. Summerhayes' description of her trip from Fort Apache, where a son was born, to Holbrook, with

threatening Apache all around, is written with the full drama of her frenzied experience.—B. W. A.

Sumner, Edwin Vose (1797-1863). Soldier. Sumner, born in Boston, Massachusetts, entered the army as a second lieutenant in 1819 and spent most of his career as a cavalry officer on the frontier. Serving with Winfield Scott in the Mexican War as commanding officer of the Regiment of Mounted Riflemen, Sumner received brevets for the battles of Cerro Gordo, where he was wounded, and Molino del Rey. He was known as "Bull" Sumner because a musket ball allegedly had bounced off his head.

In 1851 he was appointed to the Ninth Military Department (New Mexico), where he developed a defense system for the territory that endured without basic change for forty years. In August Sumner established Fort Defiance and marched into Canyon de Chelly against the Navaho with little success. The Santa Fe *Gazette* reported, "He went, and saw, and left." Under Sumner civil-military relations in New Mexico broke down as the aggressive soldier engaged in a running feud with the citizens and with governors James S. Calhoun and William Carr Lane. Sumner did not like the region or the people, and they reciprocated. Getting involved in territorial politics, he was determined that neither the governor nor the Bureau of Indian Affairs would interfere with his plan for subduing the Indians. The feud was climaxed when Sumner recommended that New Mexico be abandoned by the United States.

Sumner was commander of Fort Leavenworth during the civil disturbances in Kansas and in 1857 led a two-pronged expedition against the Cheyenne, defeating them on the Solomon River. In 1858 he commanded the Department of the West, and during the Civil War he fought in the peninsular campaign and at Antietam, Fair Oaks, and Fredericksburg. Sumner was a major general at the time of his death.—R. N. E.

sun dance. Indian ceremony. The sun dance was the most conspicuous religious ceremony of the Plains Indians in the nineteenth century and is probably the most famous of American Indian rites. The name "sun dance" is actually a misnomer, stemming from the Dakota term *wiwanyag wachipi* ("sun-gazing-dance"). Among other tribes it was known as the "thirsting dance," or else named for the characteristic enclosure where it was held. Its functional justification varied from tribe to tribe, but generally it was intended as a ceremony of tribal unity by which the whole people, through the actions of the selected participants, demonstrated to the supernaturals their deservingness of abundance of food and resistance of human enemies. It was neither a rite of sun worship nor a rite of manhood initiation, as some observers interpreted its self-torture aspect to imply.

The most elaborate forms of the ritual were practiced by the Arapaho, Cheyenne, and Oglala. It may have originated with the Arapaho-Cheyenne from practices they observed among the early Missouri River tribes. From this center the sun dance diffused throughout the Plains, involving sedentary as well as nomadic peoples. Because the ceremony was specifically oriented to the exigencies of the Plains environment, with its emphasis on endurance of heat, prayers against drought, and buffalo symbolism, it was easily adopted by tribes of widely differing cultural heritage. By 1900 it was practiced by twenty-six tribes. Among all there was a general uniformity of ceremonial regalia and behavior, although the mythological and organizational ideas behind it varied according to each tribe's cosmology.

The sun dance was generally annual, usually in June or July, and was connected with the communal spring hunts. It was the only ritual practiced by the Plains tribes wherein the entire political unit acted as a ceremonial unit. Women were prohibited from participation, though not observation, and some tribes reserved associated ritual tasks, such as the cutting of the center pole, for their performance.

The ceremony began with an individual's vision or vow of personal sacrifice for the good of his people. A qualified group, usually shamans or those who had previously participated in the rite, would then manage the procedure. The principal dancer (he with the initial vow ot vision), along with others with similar vows, underwent purification, rehearsals, and preparation in a preliminary lodge. Scouts were sent to locate an appropriate tree for the center pole, and it was felled as if it were an enemy. The trimmed pole was ceremonially carried to an already prepared circular enclosure and formally raised in place. Affixed to the pole's top fork were symbolic objects representing bountiful game, tribal power bundles (religious artifacts connecting the tribe to the creator), or killed enemies. Horizontal poles were then placed from the top of the outside wall to the center pole. An altar centering around a buffalo skull was constructed opposite the east-facing entrance, completing the ceremonial enclosure.

The dancers entered in procession. Each would then spring, without actually jumping, from flatfoot to tiptoe, while blowing bone whistles and staring at the sun or other ritual objects. The dancers were barefoot, painted white, and wore kilts, wristlets, anklets, and head wreaths, all of sage or rabbit's fur. The ceremony lasted a week and the actual dance four days, during which the dancers fasted and abstained from water. Those who had so vowed performed the self-torture in the final days. Skewers were passed through chest or back muscles and attached to heavy weights or to the center pole by leather thongs. The dancer tugged against them until unconscious or the skewers tore loose. In some tribes the dancer was suspended from overhead beams. The wounds resulting from this practice were usually tended so as to leave obvious scars, which were prized as marks of character and courage.

The torture was not essential to the sun dance except among the Oglala, and in all cases it required a preliminary public vow. The principal dancer was never tortured. Among most tribes the self-torture was infrequent, and the Kiowa and Ute forbade it entirely. This aspect of the sun dance evidently evolved separately from the rest of the ritual and was incorporated from Siouan practices of self-mortification to induce visions. Its significance in the ceremony was as an expression of individual sacrifice for common good, the Plains peoples' ultimate ethic. White missionaries and federal officials regarded the practice as a horrible heathen cruelty, and in 1904 the government outlawed the sun dance along with most of the rest of Indian religious practices. Many tribes, however, continued benign forms of the ceremony, usually disguised as parts of Fourth of July celebrations, and in recent years some tribes have attempted to revive the sun dance in its original form and meaning.

Clark Wissler, ed., *Sun Dance of the Plains Indians,* American Museum of Natural History Anthropological Papers, vol. XVI (1921), is a collection of studies of the sun dance among several tribes and an analysis of its development and diffusion. See also J. E. Brown, ed., *The Sacred Pipe: Black Elk's Account of the Seven Rites of the Oglala Sioux* (1953).—P. R. M.

Sundance Kid. See Butch CASSIDY.

Sun Valley, Idaho. Located ninety-three miles east of Boise in south-central Idaho, Sun Valley was an inconspicuous little village before the Union Pacific Railroad developed it into an attractive recreation area in 1936. Today Sun Valley is an internationally famous winter resort and an almost equally popular summer vacation site. As of 1970 its native population was a mere 317.

Sun Valley is situated south of the Sawtooth Range between two national forests. The area lies at an altitude of six thousand feet and features beautiful scenery, as well as excellent facilities for skiing, year-round ice-skating, hiking, riding, hunting, and fishing. During the winter a number of notable sporting events are held at Sun Valley.—R. B. W.

Superior Upland. See PHYSIOGRAPHY OF THE UNITED STATES.

Susquehanna [Susquehannock] Indians. The Susquehanna were an Iroquois tribe, or perhaps confederacy, related to but distinct from the Iroquois proper of New York. They lived in the valley of the Susquehanna River in central Pennsylvania at the time of the white man's arrival and may have numbered six thousand persons. The tribe played an important part in seventeenth-century frontier history, yet had little direct contact with the European colonists; hence, comparatively little is known of it today. The Susquehanna were a warlike people who, for a time, more than held their own against the Iroquois and were able to defeat and displace weaker tribes of Pennsylvania, Maryland, and Virginia. For a generation or more they were the chief suppliers of peltry to the Dutch, Swedes, and English on the Delaware and Chesapeake. Their incursions on other tribes as well as on frontiersmen farther south led to hostilities in Maryland and Virginia and helped to precipitate Bacon's Rebellion in Virginia in 1675-76. These incursions apparently resulted from a bitterly contested war with the Iroquois, in which the Susquehanna were driven southward and then totally defeated by them in 1676. The tribe was scattered, some assimilating with the Iroquois in New York and others remaining in Pennsylvania under the name of Conestoga. Most of the latter were massacred by whites—the so-called Paxton Boys—in 1763.

See E. A. Benson, *The Story of the Susquehannocks* (1958); F. W. Hodge, ed., *Handbook of American Indians North of Mexico,* 2 vols. (1907-10); and H. A. McCord, "The Susquehannock Indians in West Virginia, 1630-1677," *West Virginia History,* vol. 13 (1952).—A. W. T.

Sutro, Adolph Heinrich (1830-1898). Mining engineer and businessman. A Prussian-born emigrant, Sutro came to California's gold fields in 1851, where he established himself as a successful merchant. In 1860 he followed the mining frontier to Nevada and there developed a successful process for extracting silver from tailings. He also conceived an ingenious tunneling plan for mining the Comstock Lode: a shaft cut through four miles of Mount Davidson would provide ventilation, drainage, and easy extraction of ore. But for nearly ten years Sutro was blocked by other capitalists who feared his control of the lode. Finally, with the backing of European capital, he was able to complete the shaft in 1878, selling out the next year at a fantastic profit.

During the next two decades Sutro became the most powerful landowner in San Francisco and was mayor of the city from 1894 to 1896.

See Robert E. Stewart, Jr., and Mary F. Stewart, *Adolph Sutro: A Biography* (1962).—J. F.

Sutter, John Augustus (1803-1880). Colonizer of the Sacramento valley. Sutter (born John Augustus Suter) was a German Swiss who left Berne for America in 1834 in flight from his debts and an unhappy marriage. Traveling by way of New York, St. Louis, Santa Fe, Oregon, and Honolulu, he arrived in Mexican California in July 1839. The wide open spaces of the Sacramento valley offered the degree of freedom that his dreams and ambitions required. Governor Juan Bautista Alvarado granted him eleven square leagues, or nearly fifty thousand acres, in the valley and authorized him "to represent in the Establishment of New Helvetia all the laws of the country, to function as political authority and dispenser of justice, in order to prevent the robberies commited by adventurers from the United States, to stop the invasion of savage Indians and the hunting and trapping by companies from the Columbia." The capital of Sutter's colony of New Helvetia was Sutter's Fort, built near what is now the city of Sacramento. The fort was a large quadrangular structure built of adobe. It was 330 feet long and less than 200 feet wide with walls 18 feet high. When the Russians abandoned Fort Ross in 1841 Sutter purchased its implements, livestock, and cannon, primarily with an unsecured note that he never paid. New Helvetia prospered far beyond most California *ranchos* probably because Sutter diversified his operation to include trapping and agriculture as well as cattle-raising.

From 1841 to 1848 Sutter's Fort was a focal point for the increasing flow of covered wagons bringing settlers from the United States. Profiting from their trade, Sutter encouraged their passage and heartily endorsed the American conquest, for his rising power had made him a feared and mistrusted figure among the Mexicans. On January 24, 1848, his carpenter James Wilson Marshall found some bright metal in the stream beneath a mill he was building at Coloma, and Sutter, after reading the relevant articles in the *American Encyclopedia*, pronounced it to be gold. The secret soon leaked out, and the subsequent gold rush was Sutter's ruin. His workers abandoned him for the gold fields and squatters and miners living in SACRAMENTO overran his lands, dispersed and slaughtered his herds, and destroyed fields. By 1852 New Helvetia had been destroyed, and Sutter spent his remaining years in Washington, D. C., petitioning the government for compensation. The Supreme Court finally disallowed his land claims.

Sutter's Fort has been restored and is now a state historical monument.

Sutter's Own Story, as told to Hubert Howe Bancroft, was edited by Erwin G. Gudde (1936). Good secondary works are Richard Dillon, *Fool's Gold* (1967); Oscar Lewis, *Sutter's Fort: Gateway to the Gold Fields* (1966); and

James P. Zollinger, *Sutter: The Man and His Empire* (1939).—W. B.

Sutter's Fort. See John Augustus SUTTER.

Swan, Alexander Hamilton (1831-1905). Wyoming cattle king. Swan was born in Pennsylvania, of Scottish and Welsh ancestry. While still a young man, he moved to Ohio and Iowa, where he spent fourteen years in stock raising and merchandising. In 1873 he organized the Swan Brothers Cattle Company with brothers Thomas and Henry and a nephew, Will R. Swan (one of eight large companies in the intermountain region with which Swan would be identified during his career). He soon became widely known for his ability to appraise cattle and as a shrewd, but honorable, businessman. In 1880 Swan pulled out of Swan Brothers and with his nephew launched the Ell Seven Cattle Company. Then in 1883, operating in conjunction with a syndicate holding $3,750,000 in Scottish capital, Swan started the Swan Land and Cattle Company, Ltd. At one time the huge company owned or controlled 600,000 acres reaching west from Ogallala, Nebraska, to Fort Steele, Wyoming, and stretching south from the Union Pacific tracks to the Platte River. The firm is reputed to have purchased a half million acres in alternate sections from the Union Pacific. Within five years the company's holding had a value of fifty million dollars. Swan also had a large farm in Iowa, fed cattle at two points in Nebraska, and in 1879 joined W. A. Paxton and John W. Spratlen to build the Transfer Stockyards at Council Bluffs, Iowa. He helped construct the Union Stockyards at Omaha and, with the purchase of two thousand acres, founded South Omaha in 1883.

During the 1880s Swan became a major figure in the political and economic life of Wyoming. He was chairman of the Laramie County board of commissioners and served on the territorial council. His role in that body was all the more powerful since he was also one of the founders of the powerful Wyoming Stock Growers' Association (first called the Stock Association of Laramie County).

After years of enjoying great success and a reputation throughout the nation, Swan came upon difficult times; in one movement of 17,000 head of two-year-old Texas steers he lost 15,800 head to disease and most of the rest to bad weather and Indians. Already hurt by falling cattle prices and by Swan's extravagance, the famous company was wiped out by the blizzard of 1886-87, when heavy snow and freezing weather reduced Swan's herd from 113,000 to 57,000. In May 1887 the nearly legendary company went into receivership: a symbolic end to the era of open-range cattle kings. Swan's own fortune was wiped out in the bankruptcy proceedings.

After reorganization John Clay took over the management of the Swan Land and Cattle Company and ran it on a reduced basis. In 1904 the firm turned to sheep ranching and operated until 1947. A private firm still operates a portion of the vast properties that once bore Swan's name. The ranch headquarters, built in 1876, may still be seen at Chugwater in southeastern Wyoming.

See Robert H. Burns et al., *Wyoming's Pioneer Ranches* (1955); John Clay, *My Life on the Range* (1924); and Alfred Sorenson, *The Story of Omaha* (1923).—H. R. L.

Swisshelm, Jane Grey (1815-1884). Minnesota editor and crusader for civil rights. Swisshelm was born near

James Marshall standing in front of Sutter's mill (1852). (Wells Fargo Bank)

Pittsburgh, Pennsylvania. Arriving in St. Cloud, Minnesota, in 1857, she became editor of the St. Cloud *Visitor* the same year. As editor she advertised the frontier territory in which she lived and advised settlers on how to supply their needs. To help free women from the fashionable hoop skirt, she reported that Empress Eugénie of France had appeared "without a crinoline." Card playing, she declared, was "gambling." Dancing the quadrille was permissible but the waltz was improper, for it "requires the encircling of the waist by supporting arms."

She spoke her mind on every subject and was fearless in her battle for any who needed a champion—women, blacks, and soldiers. She was best known for her crusade against slavery. During her editorship Swisshelm was hanged in effigy and sued for libel. Fellow townsmen in St. Cloud once tried to silence her by destroying her printing press. But she installed new equipment and continued to crusade until 1863, when she returned to the East and served as nurse to Union soldiers in Washington, D.C.

See Arthur J. Larsen, ed., *Crusader and Feminist: Letters of Jane Grey Swisshelm, 1858-1865* (1934).—R. W. F.

Sycamore Shoals, Treaty of (1775). This treaty between the ambitious Transylvania Land Company and the Cherokee Indians involved a transfer of the lands comprising that part of Kentucky south of the Kentucky River and that part of Tennessee north of the big bend of the Cumberland River. Master negotiator of this tremendous land bargain was Richard Henderson, head of the Transylvanians, who wanted to set up a colony beyond Cumberland Gap. The Indians accepted in exchange for their lands, which they may have held only tenuously, a pile of trade goods worth approximately £10,000. These had been inspected before delivery from Fayetteville, North Carolina, by representatives of the Indians. At Sycamore Shoals, in the Holston River in eastern Tennessee, the Indians again had an opportunity to examine the trade goods.

Chief Oconostota, head of the Cherokee, sent messages to his people to gather for negotiation of a treaty early in 1775. The assembled Indians were only partially informed as to the purpose of the gathering. By March a large number of Cherokee had assembled, and by the middle of the month negotiations were under way. On March 17 an agreement was reached by which the Indians would relinquish their claims to the territory described above.

In accordance with Henderson's grandiose plans for colonization, he dispatched Daniel Boone and a party to blaze a trail through the wilderness to the south bank of the Kentucky River before the treaty was completed. There they were to locate Fortress Boonesboro.

The making of the Treaty of Sycamore Shoals was not an entirely harmonious affair. Younger chiefs protested that the elders had virtually given away their lands. Among them was the son of the Cherokee chief, Attakullakulla, named DRAGGING CANOE, who gave the overhill lands the name "Dark and Bloody Ground." These unyielding Indians went on to fight the Transyl-

vanians as if the treaty had not been made at all. In addition, the agreement was technically illegal as it was a private transaction and clearly violated the British Proclamation of 1763 forbidding trans-Appalachian settlement. In reality the Transylvania Company was only paying lip service to legality and would have carried on settlement in defiance of government and Indians even without a treaty.

See Archibald Henderson, *The Conquest of the Old Southwest* (1920); William Stewart Lester, *The Transylvania Colony* (1935); and J. G. M. Ramsey, *The Annals of Tennessee* (1853).—T. D. C.

T

Tabor, Horace Austin Warner (1830-1899). Colorado mining magnate. Tabor was born in Orleans County, Vermont, and spent his early years on the family farm. He joined his brother, a stonecutter, in Quincy, Massachusetts, learning the trade from him and later striking out on his own. He went to Kansas in 1855, where he was elected to the legislature on the Free-Soil ticket. Returning briefly to New England, he married Augusta Pierce in 1857. Hearing of the Pikes Peak gold rush in Colorado, Tabor, his wife, and their infant son set out for the gold fields, arriving in Denver in 1859. In 1860 the Tabors journeyed to the headwaters of the Arkansas at California Gulch, Colorado. There Tabor met some success in mining and opened stores in Buckskin Joe and Oro City. In the late 1870s silver-bearing ore was discovered in the vicinity, setting off the Leadville rush. Tabor grubstaked two needy prospectors who discovered the Little Pittsburg mine, bringing Tabor one-third of the find. His career as Colorado's greatest "bonanza king" was thus begun. Additional mining enterprises prospered, making Tabor a millionaire several times over. He built lavish opera houses in Leadville and Denver and erected the Tabor Block in Denver, the city's first substantial "skyscraper." He also served as Leadville's mayor, was lieutenant governor of Colorado (1879-83), and completed an unexpired term in the United States Senate in 1883. Divorcing his first wife, he married a beautiful young blonde divorcee, Elizabeth McCourt Doe (Baby Doe), by whom he had two daughters.

Although money poured in from Tabor's mines during the 1880s, unwise investments in paper railroads and worthless mines in Mexico and South America depleted his fortune. The crash of 1893 and the repeal of the Sherman Silver Purchase Act, following decreased production of his mines, left Tabor bankrupt. Friends secured the position of Denver postmaster for him in 1898, and he was serving in this post at the time of his death. Following Tabor's advice to "hold on to the Matchless," Baby Doe returned to Leadville, where she lived out her last years in poverty in a shack behind the

Matchless Mine, dying in 1935. The romantic and tragic story of Horace, Augusta, and Baby Doe Tabor has been recounted in numerous books and was the subject of the American opera *The Ballad of Baby Doe* by Douglas Moore, which had its world premiere in Central City in 1956.

See Duane A. Smith, *Horace Tabor: His Life and the Legend* (1973).—M. B.

Taliaferro, Lawrence (pronounced "Tol-i-ver") (1794-1871). Indian agent. Taliaferro was Indian agent at Fort Snelling, between 1819 and 1839, making him the foremost civil official on the upper reaches of the Mississippi for two decades. Personally selected for the post by President James Monroe, Taliaferro, a member of an old Virginia family of Italian ancestry, was reappointed by John Quincy Adams, Andrew Jackson, and Martin Van Buren. Originally, his jurisdiction included the Sioux and Ojibwa.

His career is remarkable for the confidence he inspired in the Indian people he served. His twenty years were marked by absolute truthfulness in his dealings with the tribes, steadfast opposition to the liquor traffic fostered by white fur traders, an appreciation of Indian culture, and a determined role as peacemaker between the feuding tribes and as a champion of Indian rights at treaty parleys. At a time when the Indian tribes on the upper Mississippi were increasingly vulnerable to the white man's invasion of their lands, his role was exceedingly difficult. Though his commission was renewed five times, he resigned discouraged and disillusioned. Traders evaded the laws he enforced and undermined some of his influence, feuds between the tribes accelerated in the 1830s, and his attempt to turn the Indian to agriculture failed. Furthermore, the federal government frequently shifted policies he diligently tried to interpret to the Indians, split off the Ojibwa from his domain in 1827, and often delayed shipments of goods needed on the remote frontier.

In a priceless diary, Taliaferro recorded his experiences over two decades—day-by-day occurrences, primeval scenes, councils, solemn orations by Indian lead-

Horace Tabor and his Baby Doe. (State Historical Society of Colorado)

ers, his replies, weather conditions, visits from dignitaries, and many problems that made his position in the end discouraging. The spirit of the man is reflected in a speech to the Sioux midway in his service. He praised the Indian leaders of the past—"the old branches which have fallen from the Trunk of the old oak of your Nation." He urged the Sioux to abstain from war, and he alluded to American power: "Your Great Father has had much to do with war—but his heart is changed for peace." He counseled the Indians to follow that "good example" as one that would please not only the "Great Father" but also the "Great Spirit." With peace, he told them, "You will see your children growing up around you and your wives smiling as you approach from your day's hunt."

Taliaferro's importance rests on his personal integrity in an era characterized by low standards in the administration of Indian affairs and on his faithful recording of two decades of frontier history. One of Taliaferro's slaves, Harriet Robinson, married Dred Scott, who lived at Fort Snelling from 1836 to 1838.

See Willoughby M. Babcock, "Major Lawrence Taliaferro, Indian Agent," *Mississippi Valley Historical Review* (December 1924).—R. W. F.

Tall Bull (c.1815-1869). Chief of the Dog Soldiers, a Cheyenne warrior society. The most prominent of several distinguished Cheyenne who bore the same name, Tall Bull by 1860 had led the Dog Soldiers in intertribal warfare for about two decades. He participated in the Cheyenne-Arapaho War of 1864-65, but was among those who refused to sign the Treaty of the Little Arkansas (1865). With Roman Nose and others, he met in council with General Winfield Scott Hancock at Fort Larned, Kansas (April 1867), but the general's belliger-

ence led the Indians to break off negotiations. Although Tall Bull at last joined other Cheyenne and Sioux leaders in signing the Treaty of Medicine Lodge Creek (October 1867), the treaty arrangements soon broke down, and the chief figured prominently in new Plains warfare. He fought the Kaw in Kansas in May 1868 and was with Roman Nose in the battle of Beecher's Island, Colorado, in September. In October Tall Bull and his Dog Soldiers mauled Colonel W. B. Royall's cavalry command and skillfully dodged pursuits by both Royall and his superior, General Eugene A. Carr. The chief soon led his band south, where they opposed General Philip H. Sheridan's forces in the winter campaign against the Southern Plains Indians. Refusing to surrender after the battle of the Washita, Tall Bull and his people returned to the North in the spring of 1869 and located in the Republican River area. When General Carr destroyed a large Cheyenne and Sioux encampment near Beaver Creek, Kansas, Tall Bull retaliated with a series of raids along the Kansas frontier, which in turn prompted the formation of Carr's Republican River Expedition to clear the region of hostile Indians. After a long pursuit, Carr surprised and destroyed the Dog Soldiers' village in the battle of Summit Springs, Colorado, on July 11, 1869. Tall Bull died in the battle, and the influence of the Dog Soldiers was shattered.

Both Donald J. Berthrong, *The Southern Cheyennes* (1963), and George Bird Grinnell, *The Fighting Cheyennes* (1915), provide good general coverage of Tall Bull's career.—J. T. K.

Talmage, James E. (1862-1933). Educator and Mormon theologian. Born in Berkshire, England, Talmage received his early education in England and in 1874 was diocesan prize scholar. Migrating to Provo, Utah, in 1876, he studied at Brigham Young Academy and at age seventeen began to teach Latin and English.

Desiring advanced training in science, in 1882 Talmage enrolled at Lehigh University in Pennsylvania to study chemistry and geology and completed four years of school in one year. After doing advanced work at Johns Hopkins University, he was summoned home to work at Brigham Young Academy, where he was professor of geology and chemistry from 1884 to 1888. During those years he was also a city councilor, an alderman, a justice of the peace, and a member of Brigham Young Academy's board of directors. From 1888 to 1893 he was president and professor of the Latter-day Saint College in Salt Lake City, and introduced there the first classes in domestic science and agricultural chemistry in the mountain West. Talmage was placed in charge of the Mormon church's Deseret Museum in 1891 and was president of the University of Utah from 1894 to 1897. In 1897 he visited St. Petersburg, Russia, as a delegate of the Royal Society of Edinburgh to the International Geological Congress. In 1907 he retired from his professorship to put his geological knowledge to practical use.

Talmage's membership in learned societies is impressive. He was a fellow of the Royal Microscopical Society of London and the Royal Scottish Geographical Society of Edinburgh and belonged to various other geographical societies as well as the American Association for the Advancement of Science and the Philosophical Society of Great Britain. His books of science include *First Book of Nature* (1888), *Domestic Science* (1891), *The Great Salt Lake—Past and Present* (1900), and *Tables for Blow Pipe Determination of Minerals* (1899).

Talmage was also a Mormon scholar. In 1906 he testified in the Senate investigation of apostle and Senator Reed Smoot, providing a synthesis and clarification of the contradictory testimony that had been given concerning the precepts of the Mormon church. He became an apostle in the Latter-day Saint church in 1911 and from that time dedicated himself to preaching, teaching, and writing for the church. His skillful logic was devoted to explaining and defending Mormonism, and his knowledge and stature as a scholar was responsible for much of England's new attitude toward the Latter-day Saints in the 1920s. His books include *The Book of Mormon, An Account of Its Origin* (1899), *The Articles of Faith* (1899), *The Great Apostasy* (1909), *The House of the Lord* (1912), *The Story of Mormonism* (1907), *The Vitality of Mormonism* (1917), and *Jesus the Christ* (1915). Talmage also researched and organized the notes and cross-references in the Book of Mormon, *Pearl of Great Price*, and *Doctrine and Covenants*.

See John R. Talmage, *The Talmage Story, Life of James E. Talmage—Educator, Scientist, Apostle* (1972).—L. J. A.

Tanner, John (1780-?1846). The "White Indian." The life of Tanner is one of the most tragically fascinating stories of Indian captivity in frontier history. He was born in Kentucky, the son of a pioneering clergyman. At age nine he was kidnapped by a band of Shawnee who were seeking to replace a dead son. Soon after his capture he was adopted by an Ottawa woman who took him to the Ojibwa country west of Lake Superior, where for the next thirty years he lived as a member of the Ojibwa tribe. During that time he became an Indian in every way, so completely that he forgot his own name and could no longer speak English. He made two Ojib-

wa marriages and had several children, but always retained a hunger to return to find his own people and to be a white man. In 1819 Tanner returned to Kentucky and Ohio and succeeded in locating several relatives, including his brother, who had been searching for him. Soon after he went back to the Ojibwa to recover his children by both his Indian wives, but after several years of passing back and forth between white and Indian settlements, was able to bring only two daughters and his second wife to Mackinac, Michigan, where he enrolled them in school. In 1828 Tanner finally settled at Sault Ste. Marie, finding employment as interpreter for the United States Indian agent James Schoolcraft.

Though Tanner tried desperately to adjust to white society, he found it impossible. He was a man lost between two worlds. His Indian friends had come to distrust him when his white inclinations were revealed, and his first Indian wife even tried to have him killed. His deeply rooted Indian traits likewise made him suspect to the whites. In 1830 his oldest daughter was taken from him by legislative edict, and soon afterward her Indian mother left him for good and returned to her people. Tanner's inner confusion of heritages was never resolved, and his later years were lonely and bitter. The people of his adopted white town held him in alternate contempt and awe, and even his few friends feared violence from him. In the early 1840s, in a final attempt to gain acceptance, he married a white woman. They had one child, but the woman left him because of what to her were intolerable living conditions. During the summer of 1846 Schoolcraft was murdered, and Tanner was automatically suspected of the act. At the height of the furor, he disappeared from Sault Ste. Marie without a trace. Troops with bloodhounds were put on his trail, but no trace was ever found, and the time and place of his death are still unknown. Years afterward, an army officer admitted to having killed Schoolcraft in a dispute over a woman.

During the 1820s, soon after Tanner's first return from the Indians, Dr. Edwin James, the chronicler of Major Stephen Long's explorations, took down Tanner's narrative of his experiences and had it published in 1830. This work is remarkable for the lucidity and straightforwardness of Tanner's account. It is by far the best and most useful of all the many Indian captivity narratives and holds insights for the historian, ethnologist, and psychologist as well as the general reader.

See Frederick Drimmer, ed., *Scalps and Tomahawks* (1961); Edwin James, ed., *A Narrative of the Captivity and Adventures of John Tanner,* introduction by Noel Loomis (1956); and R. H. Pearce, "The Significance of the Captivity Narrative," *American Literature* (March 1947). —P. R. M.

tariff policy. Before the rise of the Republican party the West was ambivalent on the tariff question and had no clearly defined position. There were outright protectionists like Henry Clay and most Whigs, and there were out-and-out free traders like Robert J. Walker and many Democrats. Others conceded that infant industries needed protection for a time and were willing to make concessions, but still preferred to keep tariff rates down. In Kentucky, Missouri, and Ohio, producers of flax, hemp, and wool wanted protection for linen and linseed oil, rope and bagging, raw wool and woolen cloth. Kentucky was the third-ranking state in the production of hemp and flax in 1840 and first in 1850, Missouri being second in both years. Ohio was second in the production of wool and third in the number of sheep in 1840 and first in both in 1850. Hemp and flax ranked next in importance after tobacco with Kentuckians, who had a double reason to be satisfied with the tariff stand of Henry Clay, their favorite son. But for Clay protection was only one part of his AMERICAN SYSTEM, by which he planned to build up the nation's economy. He considered it essential for the nation to have diversified industries—protected by high tariffs if necessary—but he also wanted internal improvements to facilitate the flow of interstate commerce and a sound banking and currency system maintained by a powerful national bank.

Western states whose farmers were dependent on the wool, flax, and hemp they raised looked favorably on protection and frequently voted in the Whig column. This was notably true of Tennessee and Kentucky, which voted in presidential elections for the protectionist party five and six times respectively between 1832 and 1852, and Ohio, which so voted three times during that period. Missouri, on the other hand, notwithstanding its hemp, flax, and sheep industries, voted only once for the protectionist candidate. Senator John Tipton of Indiana, a strong Jacksonian when Andrew Jackson was moving toward lower tariffs, favored raising the rates on china and porcelain when he heard that an Englishman had established a plant in Indiana to make these products. Likewise he favored protection on wines and liquors and mackinaw blankets in the hope that they might be produced in his state.

By 1830 leaders in the Democratic party were moving toward free trade or for a revenue-producing tariff. They were successful in lowering rates in 1832, 1846, and 1857. Maps showing the distribution of votes in the House of Representatives on the tariffs of 1828, 1832, 1846, and 1857 in Paullin's and Wright's *Atlas of the Historical Geography of the United States* illustrate the increasing commitment of the Democratic party to free trade, particularly in the South. In 1857 representatives from the southern states voted solidly—exclusive of absentees—for further reductions in the tariff. The average rates were carried back to the level of 1816. Clay was then dead and his state had moved over to a low-tariff stand.

The western position on protection was not as clear. The Tariff of Abominations of 1828, with rates so high that even many protectionists doubted its wisdom, received the solid support of Ohio, Indiana, and Illinois, while the compromise tariff act of 1832 again had the solid support of the same states, plus Missouri and Tennessee and parts of Kentucky. The West was generally in favor of the reform Walker Tariff of 1846, but in 1857 there was much support for protection as is shown by the votes against the low tariff that year. Old parties were disintegrating and the newly organized Republican party, which opposed further extension of slavery into the territories, was proving very attractive to former Whigs, to antislavery Democrats, and especially to the Scandinavian and German settlers. Protection, which the party espoused from its outset, did not go well with some of these converts to Republicanism, but they preferred it because of its stand on other issues. They disliked the opposition of the proslavery Democrats to free land, public aid to agricultural colleges, and the admission of new territories to the Union as free states.

Meantime, new industries were rising to prominence in the West that would ultimately call for protection (see ELECTION OF 1888). Flour milling, soon to be largely centered in the Twin Cities; the lumber industry in the northern lake states; salt mining in Michigan; the mining of copper, iron ore, and other minerals; the oil and gas industry; the production of agricultural machines in Chicago, Rock Island, Milwaukee, and Racine; and the meat-packing industry in Chicago, Kansas City, and Omaha—all were to ask for protection and to add their support to the demands of sheep raisers, the cattle and dairy industry, the beet-sugar farmers of the irrigated lands of the Far West, the cane-sugar growers of Louisiana, and the fruit producers in behalf of protection. Again, the maps in Paullin and Wright show how congressmen strove to gain protection for goods produced in their districts and increasingly voted for protection. On the Dingley Tariff Act of 1897, the Payne-Aldrich Tariff Act of 1909, the Fordney-McCumber Act of 1922, and the Hawley-Smoot Act of 1930, representatives of western states with some exceptions voted for protection; the downward revision of the Underwood-Simmons Tariff of 1913 they opposed. It was not by accident that the last two protectionist measures took the names of members of Congress from North Dakota, Michigan, Utah, and Oregon.

See Frank W. Taussig, *Tariff History of the United States* (1923).—P. W. G.

Tavernier, Jules (1844-1889). Painter and illustrator. Born in France, Tavernier came to the United States in 1871 following brief service in the Franco-Prussian War and soon found employment as an illustrator in New York City with *Graphic* and *Harper's Weekly* magazines. With an associate named Paul Frenzeny, Tavernier was commissioned in 1873 to make a series of sketches of a trip from the Atlantic to the Pacific as a part of a promotional campaign by *Harper's. Harper's* made much of this tour and published illustrations by both Tavernier and Frenzeny between the years 1873 and 1876.

Frenzeny was a Frenchman who had served with the French cavalry in Mexico and had worked in New York City only a few years before the arrival of Tavernier. Both men remained in California for a period of time, Frenzeny for about five years and Tavernier for nearly the remainder of his life. Both were elected to the Bohemian Club of that city in 1874 and enjoyed reputations as eccentrics. Tavernier went to Hawaii in 1884 and died in Honolulu of acute alcoholism. Often in debt, he died in poverty. Frenzeny returned to New York, and continued to work for *Harper's* and other newspaper or magazine publishers. (For picture, see page 1158.)

See Robert Taft, *Artists and Illustrators of the Old West, 1850-1900* (1953).—D. C. H.

taverns and hotels. By the time white settlers had crossed into the trans-Appalachian West shortly after the American Revolution, the public house offering lodging and meals was an established institution. But the name of this institution varied and changed with the times. When English settlers in Virginia and New England first opened public houses, the term used was "ordinaries"—not taverns or inns. The term prevailed throughout the colonies until sometime after the turn of the eighteenth century. In Virginia ordinaries, the price for room and board was a single fee, which could be

Indian Camp at Sunrise *by Jules Tavernier. (Thomas Gilcrease Institute)*

considered the origin of the American plan. By the end of the colonial period, public houses had become known as taverns, and their dining rooms were called ordinaries. Since "tavern" sounded more sophisticated than "ordinary," towns adopted the new terminology more quickly than the countryside. And, in fact, the taverns did become more commodious than the old ordinary, furnishing better food and drink. The taverns—and their colonial predecessors—were never a carbon copy of the English inn, despite such allegations by many writers. They represented a unique American hybrid.

When the process of settling the West began, the public house, like many other institutions, did not spring up fully evolved on the new frontier. It developed from crude origins. At first, wayfarers stopped at the most convenient cabin, seeking bed and board for the night. Hospitality was generally a trait of frontier folk. Sometimes money changed hands, but more often it did not. Even if no charges were made, the householder was not always the gracious host, as Moses Austin (father of Stephen F.) related in connection with his effort to get lodging at a cabin near Cumberland Gap on a dark, snowy evening in 1796. "They absulutely refus.d me, saying, that we could go to a Hous six miles Down the Valley. Finding moderate words would not answer I plainly told Mr. Yancy that I should not go any further, and that stay I would. Old Mrs. Yancy had much to say about the liberties some Men take, and I replied by observing the Humanity of Others, and so ended our dispute." Austin's boldness gained him a bed for the night!

The physical difference between private cabins and the commercial tavern was most often a matter of degree, not kind. Early taverns in the tramontane West closely resembled rude log cabins. A one-room tavern sometimes measured only twelve feet square and was constructed by the same pattern as the log cabin. If the tavern had a loft for storage or sleeping, its ceiling usually was only high enough to accommodate a standing man. If the tavern were new, the floor might still be earthen, but most landlords aspired to at least a puncheon floor. When sawmills entered the area, planks replaced the unfinished puncheons. Depending on the host's prosperity, he would have either proper doors and windows or blankets covering the openings. The easiest addition to such a tavern was simply to build an adjacent cabin of similar or larger proportions and provide a covered passageway between them. If business was good, the owner made improvements quickly, such as enlarging the tavern and partitioning off a dining room and bar. An example of a tavern that began as a commercial venture was Eben Peck's, constructed in Madison, Wisconsin, in 1837. It consisted of two cabins, approximately twenty-four by twenty feet each. Within a year the connecting passage had been framed in, creating a dining room. A lean-to provided servants' quarters, although servants were often unavailable.

As a social institution the tavern played an important part in the developing West. In addition to providing for travelers, taverns offered a meeting place where locals could gather to chat, drink, and play games. This aspect became more important as the SALOON, a bar without transient facilities, became more common. Besides being a place to socialize, the tavern was a listening post for men in commerce and the professions, especially lawyers. The tavern was also the home for some. Newly married couples and single persons sometimes lived at taverns for considerable periods, and some even raised families there.

Taverns often had regular traveling customers, such as drovers, stage drivers, and teamsters. If they liked a house, they would patronize it regularly as they made their rounds. Such clients usually were good bar customers, although they frequently carried their own bedrolls and spread them on the floor of the dining room, thus saving the fee for a bed. By far the largest number of travelers, however, were those making a one-time stop. An appreciable number of foreigners stayed at taverns and hotels in the West, as their voluminous travel accounts testify. Their reactions to their accommodations and tavern society naturally varied with the individual traveler, but most spoke of the democratic or leveling aspect of eating at the "table d'hôte," and hardly any refrained from disdainful comments about Americans' proclivity for spitting tobacco juice anywhere and everywhere. Among the typical native American travelers who stayed at taverns were federal officials, civilian and military, land agents, itinerant preachers (who often were put up free—especially if they could conduct a service), acting troupes, and the great throng participating in the westward movement. Of course, the last group usually slept in the open during seasonable weather, for few could afford the luxury of paying for room and board. Even so, enough of them patronized taverns to comprise the largest segment of guests.

With this social mixture, and because of the fairly primitive physical facilities, guests enjoyed little privacy—either at board or bed. Anyone's conversation was fair game for the eavesdropper, and third parties were likely to respond to a private conversation. If the intervention were protested, the third party might retort that "this is a free country" and swear profusely. Because of the scarcity of bed space, travelers were expected to sleep two to a bed—at least. This meant that the foreign aristocrat would be forced to share a bed with his servant. Often total strangers were assigned to the same bed; on a few occasions, men and women who were complete strangers occupied the same bed. Since it was customary to sleep fully clothed (minus footwear) and since there were usually several beds to a room, this kind of arrangement did not necessarily promote promiscuity.

The food and drink of western taverns was usually simple and unimaginative. Patrons commented on poorly prepared and unbalanced offerings at the board. Pork was the staple meat, because it was cheap and could be easily cured and stored. Beef ran a poor second and was usually tough. About the only fresh meat was poultry, and fish was served only by those taverns near a stream or lake. Most of the bread was made with cornmeal. If fried, it was johnnycake; if baked, corn bread; if boiled, spoon bread or mush. Fresh vegetables were uncommon. While such a diet was probably unpalatable and definitely hard to digest, it did furnish sustenance—except when the pork and butter were rancid, which was not uncommon.

If cornmeal furnished the staff of life in dining rooms of taverns and hotels throughout the West, the most common drink was whiskey. Before the safety of local water supplies could be ascertained, whiskey offered a safe compromise. The alcoholic content was sure to kill any germs, and the only danger lay in the fusel oil content of moonshine whiskey. But tavern records do not report the latter as any significant danger. Whiskey was popular because Americans were accustomed to it, and it was cheap and easy to manufacture. Corn was plentiful and the distillation process simple. Consequently, corn liquor was literally the western *aqua vitae*.

Taverns served cider and brandy as well, but they offered whiskey weak competition. Bartenders could provide a variety of mixed drinks, such as juleps, flips, cherry bounce, toddies, slings, and cider royal.

Possibly one reason for the great consumption of whiskey was that it could make one oblivious of the uncomfortable bed. The earliest bedsteads were made of heavy shingles nailed over a frame. Their hardness varied little from that of the floor, but a tick or mattress filled with feathers, corn husks, or straw provided some softness, as well as ample vermin. Later rope beds allowed more comfort for the body's contours. Teamsters, who did not expect fancy accommodations, usually carried bedrolls made out of carpet with ticking on one side. Even less fancy was the Tucson bed, where one lay on one's stomach, "covering *that* with his back." Usually taverners provided no sheets and rarely had enough blankets. By the time an institution furnished regular linen service, it had evolved from tavern into hotel.

Primitive conditions existed on each new frontier. As taverns and hotels were gaining maturity east of the Mississippi, those in the newer regions west of the river were yet crude. They also provided opportunity for criminals. Rogues and swindlers occasionally lurked near main-traveled roads to cheat and rob wayfarers. On the road from Fort Scott to Independence, Kansas, the Bender family operated a tavern from 1871 to 1875. Unsuspecting guests, lured by the advertisement of food and lodging, were robbed and sometimes murdered. The Benders dispatched at least nine patrons at the tavern. Their operation was reminiscent of Colonel Fluger's tavern near Cairo, Illinois. While the colonel's wife, "Pluggy," charmed the guests, he stole their goods.

After gold was discovered in California, stagecoach and wagon routes stretched across the trans-Mississippi West to the gold fields. Taverns sprang up on these routes to provide for the needs of the adventurous souls responding to the lure of the mines. These establishments, often called stations, trading posts, or road ranches, served as general stores, restaurants, bars, hotels, and post offices. Richard F. Burton, the celebrated scholar who visited Salt Lake City and wrote *City of the Saints* (1861), described a station four hundred miles west of St. Joseph, Missouri, as similar to a Parsi's shop in India, stocking supplies from needles to champagne. Champagne was not so popular as rotgut, which sold for $10 a gallon. Even more lucrative for the road ranchers was selling fodder and trading draft animals. They would trade one healthy ox for two road-weary ones, which they would then turn out to graze and later resell profitably. The experience of road ranchers proved that cattle could survive on the native grasses of the Great Plains—information of value to later cattlemen. These entrepreneurs also bartered with Indians and sold pelts to travelers. But since their relations with Indians were not always peaceful, many road ranches were surrounded by palisades for protection.

Proprietors were crude individuals often leading a precarious existence. Their speech, dress, and manners were generally as primitive as their establishments. One army wife, forced to spend the night at a road ranch, was awakened by wildcats jumping into her room through an uncovered window. Another soldier's spouse found herself sharing a hovel with fifteen men. Despite execrable food, potent liquor, and filthy sleeping accommodations, some road ranches acquiesced to civilization by providing combs, brushes, mirrors, and toothbrushes—all strung together for general use.

An unusual kind of public house was the prairie monitor, or dugout, protected against Indian attacks by being built underground and connected to stables by a subterranean passage. Dugway, one hundred miles west of Salt Lake City, was the most famous. For $1 travelers could buy black coffee, rough bread, and rancid bacon.

As the trans-Mississippi West became more settled, one of the hallmarks of civilization was the emergence of notable hotels. On February 1, 1859, Texas' finest hotel opened in San Antonio. William A. Menger, a German cooper who in 1855 began a brewery in the city, built the hotel near the Alamo and modestly named it for himself. It was celebrated for fine food and drink, parties, and famous guests. Among them were two Civil War generals, Philip H. Sheridan and U. S. Grant, and a Spanish-American War lieutenant colonel, Theodore Roosevelt. In fact, he recruited some Rough Riders at the Menger bar. Literary lights on the guest list included William Sydney Porter and Sidney Lanier. Richard King of the King Ranch was such an habitué of the Menger that he died there and had his funeral service in the parlor.

In San Francisco crude hotels mushroomed during the gold rush, as primitive as any on earlier frontiers—and far more expensive. When it became evident that prosperity had come to stay, hotelmen began building permanent and elaborate structures. The most notable was the Palace, opened in 1875 at a cost of $6 million. Built by William C. Ralston, the Palace had 755 rooms, every second one with a private bath. Among all the splendid and showy features of the Palace, its glass-roofed Palm Court commanded most attention. Five balconies rose above the floor where carriages delivered guests. In later years, the entrance was shifted to the street and the Palm Court became a restaurant, bedecked—as the name indicates—with potted palms, other tropical greenery, and statues. It is still a memorable experience to dine in this ornate setting. The first manager, Warren Leland, was the first San Francisco hotelman to hire Negro employees. His Negro staff included 150 waiters and 40 maids. When the hotel opened on October 2, 1875, the first guest was Leland Stanford, one of the "big four" of the Central Pacific Railroad and governor of California. The guest list of the Palace through the years sounds like a roll call of the great and near-great of the world. President Warren G. Harding died there from an undiagnosed digestive ailment in 1923. Although the original Palace was a victim of the 1906 earthquake, it was rebuilt on the same site. Today it operates as a member of the Sheraton chain.

Crowning Nob Hill in San Francisco are two hotels also associated with the affluence gold brought to California. One, the Mark Hopkins, is named for another member of the "big four." Hopkins, realizing that more money was to be made from selling provisions to miners than from mining, became storekeeper for the gold rush, thereby amassing a fortune. The hotel is a proper monument to his memory. Its highest story, encased on all sides by glass and offering a view of the entire bay area, is one of the world's most famous bars, the Top of the Mark. In recent years, however, the Top of the Mark has been eclipsed by an even higher and

more spectacular saloon across the street atop the Fairmont Hotel. For years the two hotels vied in gentility, but the Fairmont now easily takes the prize as a tourist attraction. Access to the Fairmont's glass-walled cocktail lounge is via an elevator with transparent sides. The elevator shaft is outside the building, so as the elevator ascends hundreds of feet, occupants get a breathtaking view of the city.

California has long been noted for its resorts, such as the Hotel del Coronado of San Diego. Built by Elisha S. Babcock, Jr., who came to southern California as a health-seeker, the Del Coronado featured numerous turrets, balconies, galleries, and verandas. Open-air sleeping porches appealed to those wanting to take the fresh ocean breezes. The 750-room hotel opened as a year-round resort in February 1888, scoring a complete success. Guests were overwhelmed with the hotel's provisions for their comfort and recreation. Each room had a wall safe; and each suite, a fireplace. Seventeen and a half acres of carpeting covered the floors of the hotel, which was built around an inner court that admitted health-giving sunlight. For diversion, a darkroom for photographers, four bowling alleys, and thirty billiard tables were provided. Those who wanted ice could use the De Coppet absorption machine, which took only fifteen hours to produce it. Thomas A. Edison came to the Del Coronado to supervise the installation of the West's largest incandescent light plant, which furnished power for 2,500 bulbs. The ten-thousand-square-foot dining room seated one thousand, and its thirty-three-foot ceiling had no interior support. The hotel remains as gracious and inviting as ever, reminiscent of a more leisurely era.

In Denver the hotel with the longest tradition and richest association with mining and cattle barons is the Brown Palace. Situated in the center of the city, it was once the hub of its social life. Perhaps the most historic incident associated with the hotel was the outbreak of the 1911 nationalist revolution in China. On the day the revolution erupted, the Brown Palace guest register showed the name of Sun Yat-sen.

Closely associated with the economic development of the Southwest has been the Santa Fe railroad. This line had the vision to let Fred Harvey try his hand at providing good food for travelers, up to that time a rarity. In the process of making the fare on the Santa Fe line the best in the country, Harvey built some important hotels in the West. Among his fifteen hotels were those in Trinidad, Las Animas, and La Junta, Colorado; Hutchinson, and Dodge City, Kansas; and Las Vegas, New Mexico. As famous as the food—"Meals by Fred Harvey"—were the waitresses, known as "Harvey girls." These hotel waitresses lived under a strict regimen. A matron saw that they were in their rooms by 10 P.M. and went to prayer meetings on Wednesday nights. This was balanced by the Friday night dance, no doubt appealing to the single, 18- to 30-year-old women. To be employed by Harvey, one had to be pretty, of good character, and willing to stay unmarried and work for a year. Harvey did not enforce the last provision, however. In keeping with the standards prescribed for waitresses, dining room patrons were expected to comport themselves decorously. Men without coats would not be served, although they could be shunted to the lunch counter or furnished a black coat. This accommodation between exterior gentility and western custom may still be observed at Dallas' renowned specialty store, Neiman-Marcus. Its posh restaurant, the Zodiac Room, does not admit coatless men but furnishes coats at no cost to the rich ranchers and oilmen who show up unaware of the city's expectations.

One of the West's most famous and picturesque hotels is La Fonda in Santa Fe, New Mexico. Reflecting Spanish colonial architecture, the hotel has rich textures of heavy beams and adobe. A large interior court illuminates long hallways lined with chairs where guests can relax and visit. Rooms are furnished in traditional Spanish decor, with heavy wooden beds and dressers elaborately carved and decorated. Though the accommodations are not modern, they evoke the atmosphere of a fine hacienda during the nineteenth century, when Spain and Mexico controlled this trading center that bustled when caravans arrived from the overland trail. The exterior lines of the hotel blend well with those of the sixteenth-century palace of the governors across the square. Appropriately, the Western History Association held its first conference (1961) in La Fonda, "the inn at the end of the trail." (See TOURIST TRAVEL.)

For the best treatment of taverns on the trans-Appalachian frontier, see Paton Yoder, *Taverns and Travelers: Inns of the Early Midwest* (1969). Richard A. Van Orman, *A Room for the Night: Hotels of the Old West* (1966), covers the later period in the Far West.—W. R.

Taylor, Bayard (1825-1878). Journalist. In 1849, when Horace Greeley needed a correspondent to cover the fast-breaking gold-rush story for his New York *Tribune*, he turned to young Bayard Taylor, fresh from his first literary triumph, a book on his European travels. Taylor arrived in San Francisco in August 1849 and sent back reports of that bustling city, gold-rush towns, the diggings, the constitutional convention, and California's society and people. After his return east, the reports of his five-month visit were revised and published in 1850 as *Eldorado; or Adventures in the Path of Empire.* It was an immediate and sustained success that increased public interest in California and helped make Taylor's reputation as the foremost travel writer of Victorian America. Taylor's account gives an exciting, colorful view of the tumultuous gold-rush scene.

See Bayard Taylor, *Eldorado; or Adventures in the Path of Empire,* introduction by Robert Glass Cleland (1949).—J. F.

Taylor, John (1808-1887). Mormon leader. Born in Westmoreland, England, Taylor migrated with his parents to Canada in 1832, and served for a time as a Methodist and Irvingite minister. He was converted to Mormonism in 1836 and elevated to the apostleship in 1838. An active and effective missionary, Taylor possessed considerable literary skill. He was editor of two Mormon periodicals, *Times and Seasons* (1841-44) and *The Mormon* (1852). While a missionary in Europe in 1849-50, he supervised the translation of the Book of Mormon into French and German.

Taylor was with Joseph Smith, first prophet of the Mormons, when the latter was assassinated in 1844. Taylor himself sustained several wounds at that time and escaped death when a ball struck his pocket watch. He led a group from the Missouri valley to the Salt Lake valley in 1847, served in the territorial legislature (1857-76), and was elected territorial superintendent of

schools in 1877. Upon the death of Brigham Young in 1877, Taylor became president of the Quorum of the Twelve Apostles and in 1880 was sustained as president of the Mormon church. That year, the church's first "jubilee," he forgave the poor their debts to the church's Perpetual Emigrating Fund and activated a program of wealth redistribution. Antipolygamy legislation by the federal government in the 1880s forced Taylor to abandon, to a degree, his plural families. He died in Salt Lake City while "in hiding for his faith."

See Andrew Jenson, *Latter-day Saint Biographical Encyclopedia* (1901).—L. J. A.

Taylor, Zachary (1784-1850). Soldier and twelfth president of the United States. Born in Montebello, Virginia, Taylor grew up on a plantation in Kentucky. He was appointed a first lieutenant in the Seventh Infantry in 1808 and served in Louisiana. During the War of 1812 he was transferred to Indiana Territory and gained recognition for repulsing a large force of Indians while commanding Fort Harrison. After the hostilities ceased, Taylor commanded at various posts in the upper Mississippi valley, and in 1837 in Florida defeated a Seminole force at Lake Okeechobee. In July 1845 Taylor sailed from New Orleans with one thousand five hundred men and built a camp on the Nueces River near Corpus Christi, Texas, where he held his force in readiness for further orders. In the early spring of 1846 he advanced into the disputed area between the Nueces and the Rio Grande, and on April 25 was attacked by Mexican troops. Congress promptly declared war (see MEXICAN WAR).

Although a poor military strategist, Taylor quickly became a popular figure, acquiring the sobriquet "Old Rough-and-Ready." A short, stout man who wore civilian dress in the field, he was unpretentious in speech and manner. He emerged a national hero from the war and in November returned to the United States to campaign on the Whig ticket. A year later he was elected the twelfth president. Unused to politics, he was soon at loggerheads with most members of Congress after he urged immediate statehood for California and New Mexico as a solution to the crisis over the Mexican cession. In July 1850, after attending a public outing to lay the cornerstone of the Washington Monument, Taylor suffered an attack of recurring cholera and died.

See Brainerd Dyer, *Zachary Taylor* (1946).—H. P. H.

Taylor Museum. The Taylor Museum, established as a department of the Colorado Springs Fine Arts Center, is devoted to the arts of various cultures with focus on the American Southwest and Latin America.

The museum boasts an extraordinary collection of New Mexican *santos,* the old carved and painted wooden saints expressive of Spanish-American religious folk art; extensive holdings of southwestern Indian basketry, textiles, pottery, and decorative arts; and examples of primitive art from around the world. There is a permanent gallery of western American art housing, among other items: the Honnen collection, featuring thirty-three bronze figures by Charles M. Russell; John Frederick Huckel's collection of Navaho sand painting reproductions; and paintings and sculpture by such renowned artists as John Singer Sargent, John Sloan, Georgia O'Keeffe, Albert Bierstadt, Walt Kuhn, Peter Hurd, and Harry Bertoia.

Each summer the public is given an opportunity to

view the museum's New Mexico santo collection. One summer special entitled *Arroyo Hondo, the Folk Art of a New Mexican Village,* was assembled by Harry Garnett between 1936 and 1960. The works were created originally for the village church, a private chapel, and two *moradas,* the meetinghouses of the Penitent brothers. The display spanned the nineteenth century and included the work of the famous *santeros* José Aragon, Juan Miguel Herrera, and a third unknown Spanish-American carver of religious figures.

See E. Boyd, *Saints and Saintmakers* (1946); Robert Shalkop, *Wooden Saints* (1967); Mitchell A. Wilder, *Santos* (1943); and Mitchell A. Wilder and Edgar Breitenbach, *Santos—The Religious Folk Art of New Mexico* (1943).—B. P. D. and M. L.

Teapot Dome scandal. See Albert Bacon FALL.

Tecumseh (c.1768-1813). Shawnee Indian leader and warrior. Tecumseh is believed to have been born near Springfield, Ohio, and was the older brother of TENSKWATAWA, the Shawnee Prophet. In his youth Tecumseh attained distinction as a warrior fighting against Kentuckians who were pushing across the Ohio River. His father and two older brothers were killed in this struggle, and when the Indians were forced to give up most of the Ohio country after the battle of Fallen Timbers (1794) and the Treaty of Greenville (1795), Tecumseh became forever an implacable enemy of Americans. Testimony from his white enemies nevertheless indicates he opposed captive torture and other cruelties practiced by all during these wars, and that his word was trusted on both sides of the frontier.

In 1805 Tecumseh and Tenskwatawa began actively to spread the idea of a united Indian people, and in 1808 they and many of their followers moved to the mouth of the Tippecanoe River in present Indiana, where their village became known as the Prophet's Town. Tenskwatawa had by then already become renowned for his mystical powers, and for several years Tecumseh was known to whites only as the Prophet's brother. From their base on the Tippecanoe, Tecumseh journeyed among the tribes of the Old Northwest and into the Deep South, pleading the need for Indian unity to prevent continued usurpation of their lands and livelihood. He argued that cession of Indian lands was valid only when freely consented to by all tribes assembled, because the land was common to all. He sought to strengthen the moral resistance of the Indians to the degeneracy of white influences, to renew adherence to traditional values, and to persuade the tribes to live by their own resources and reject dependence on white traders. The Shawnee, Potawatomi, Kickapoo, Winnebago, Menomini, Ottawa, and Wyandot responded quickly to his call. Peace chiefs of many other tribes were deserted by their best warriors. Prophet's Town became a mecca where Indians from as far away as Minnesota and Florida gathered to hear a new hope.

It is probably impossible to completely separate the roles and relative importance of Tecumseh and the Prophet in forming the confederacy for which they both labored. To portray the Prophet as the priest and Tecumseh as the statesman, as some observers have, is certainly not accurate, for the Indians of that time made no such separation between religion and the rest of life. But neither was Tecumseh the mere apostle of his brother. It is probable, however, that Tecumseh's

dream of a grand Indian alliance took form from the spirit of unity engendered in the tribes by the Prophet's mystic revivalism, and that this religious aura gave the confederacy much of its short-lived strength. Surely Tecumseh's stature as moral exemplar of the Indian's own best virtues was as important to his success as his prowess as warrior and orator, and he often referred to himself in unmistakably supernatural terms. In any case, after 1808 Tecumseh increasingly overshadowed the Prophet as leader of the Indian resistance.

Tecumseh's nemesis was Governor William Henry Harrison of Indiana Territory, whose ceaseless land-grabbing in the name of the United States had extorted 33 million acres in cessions from small tribes and cowed chiefs from 1803 to 1809. In a series of stormy councils at Vincennes, Tecumseh confronted Harrison with accusations of fraud and bad faith, culminating with the famous incident of 1810 when, to demonstrate the fate of the Indian, Tecumseh crowded Harrison off a bench on which both had been sitting. Harrison was so disturbed that he began urging the elimination of this new "Indian menace" and claiming the British were responsible for Tecumseh's hostility to the United States. Tecumseh did go to Canada in 1810 to solicit support, but the British had no wish to hasten a war with Americans while their European front was struggling against Napoleon. They accordingly urged Tecumseh to avoid any violence, and the Canadian governor general even warned the United States government of Tecumseh's warlike intent. Recognizing the need to depend on his own resources, Tecumseh in 1811 again journeyed to the southern tribes to try to strengthen the bonds of Indian unity. Taking advantage of his absence, Harrison moved against Prophet's Town and goaded the indecisive Tenskwatawa into a confrontation at the battle of TIPPECANOE on November 7. Though the fight was closely balanced, the Indians retreated from the field and the army burned their village. The Prophet's prestige was destroyed, nearly all the Indians' stored supplies were lost, and their main fighting force was scattered. Tecumseh was embittered and enraged. He broke forever with his brother, and his vengeful warriors attacked settler outposts across the frontier throughout the following winter. Harrison's march had only brought on the Indian war he said he would prevent.

When the War of 1812 broke out, Tecumseh and his adherents joined the British army, where he was commissioned a brigadier general. He was active in the capture of Detroit, rallied many Indians to the British cause, and fought at Fort Meigs, Brownstown, and Fort Stephenson. Although Tecumseh had never fully trusted the British or counted on their support, he knew that their victory was the last chance for his vision to be realized. When Perry's triumph on Lake Erie cut the British line of supply and compelled General Proctor to abandon Detroit and withdraw eastward, Tecumseh's last hopes vanished. Reluctantly he covered Proctor's retreat as far as Moraviantown, where he persuaded the British commander to stand and fight. There, at the battle of the Thames (October 5, 1813), Tecumseh fell while urging his warriors never to give up their struggle.

That Tecumseh was a native American genius there is little doubt. All who came in contact with him testified to his magnetic presence, mental superiority, and incredible leadership qualities. In the history of the American Indian, he occupies a place of honor along with Chief Joseph, Crazy Horse, and many others, who because of their personal character, integrity, and devotion to native values became the leaders of their people in the time of ultimate crisis.

See Freeman Cleaves, *Old Tippecanoe: William Henry Harrison and His Time* (1939); Reginald Horsman, "British Indian Policy in the Northwest, 1807-1817," *Mississippi Valley Historical Review*, vol. 45 (1968); J. M. Oskison, *Tecumseh and His Times* (1938); and Glenn Tucker, *Tecumseh: Vision of Glory* (1956).—P. R. M.

telegraph. The electromagnetic telegraph, perfected by Samuel F. B. Morse in 1844, was recognized by the early 1850s as a means of bridging the great distances in the trans-Mississippi West. Congress refused to assume the responsibility for utilizing the patent but left its development to private enterprise. Only a small amount of capital was needed to construct a telegraph line, and with methodless enthusiasm promoters organized local companies both in California and Missouri with grandiose schemes for establishing a monopoly. In 1853 the California State Telegraph Company was established to connect San Francisco with the communities of San Jose, Stockton, Sacramento, and Marysville. The next year the Alta Telegraph Company started construction eastward from Sacramento to the California towns of Placerville, Auburn, Grass Valley, and Nevada City. San Francisco and Sacramento newspaper editors gave publicity and financial support to the building of a telegraph line southward through the San Joaquin valley to obtain the news brought overland by the mail stagecoaches after 1858. By October 1860, San Francisco and Los Angeles had been connected by telegraph. Meanwhile, the California legislature in 1859 had pledged $6,000 a year to the first telegraph company that would connect the state with the East. Legislation was also passed to subsidize a second line by $4,000 in anticipation of technical problems, severe weather conditions, or Indian raids that might put one line temporarily out of service.

Similar construction efforts were taking place in Missouri. One company established a line from St. Louis to Kansas City by way of Booneville in 1858 by following the banks of the Missouri River and utilizing the trees in stringing the wire. Another group of promoters attempted to build along the route of the Overland Mail Company line, starting simultaneously from Memphis and Los Angeles. A scheme was also seriously considered to lay a cable along the bottom of the Canadian River to connect Fort Smith, Arkansas, with Santa Fe, New Mexico.

On June 16, 1860, Congress passed the Pacific Telegraph Act authorizing $40,000 a year for ten years to any company constructing a telegraph from the western boundary of the state of Missouri to San Francisco, with the provision that the government was to have priority in the use of the line to transmit government messages without cost. Jeptha H. Wade consolidated the chaotic telegraph industry of California into the Overland Telegraph Company, with a capital of $1,250,000. This company, under the superintendency of James Gamble, was to push a line east from Carson City, Nevada, along the Pony Express route, into Salt Lake City. The Missouri and Western Telegraph Company already operated a telegraph service between St. Louis and Omaha. The

Western Union Telegraph Company established the Pacific Telegraph Company to start construction westward from Omaha up the Platte River via Fort Kearny to Fort Laramie. Hiram Sibley, president of the company, named Edward Creighton construction superintendent. Creighton spent the summer of 1860 in the West surveying the route and mustering regional support. He decided to string the telegraph wires along the emigrant trail from Fort Laramie through the South Pass, since the citizens of Denver refused to buy $20,000 in company stock to subsidize construction into their community.

Throughout the period of construction the Pony Express bridged the gap between the terminals of the telegraph. Construction problems appeared to be almost overwhelming. Wiring and glass insulators installed on the western section had to be sent by sea from the East to San Francisco around South America and then freighted eastward across the Sierra Nevada to the sparsely settled areas of the Great Basin. The procurement, delivery, and distribution of poles across the treeless Plains was a tremendous undertaking. In addition to supply problems, Indians interfered with construction crews and occasionally destroyed the wires in spite of efforts to maintain their goodwill. The Mormons, fearful of losing their isolation, proved uncooperative in providing needed supplies and workers. With dispatch and remarkable energy, however, Creighton and Gamble overcame all obstacles and the wires were joined in Salt Lake City on October 24, 1861, much earlier than expected. Stephen J. Field, chief justice of California, dispatched the first message to Abraham Lincoln, noting that the telegraph had bound the East with the West, thereby insuring the loyalty of the Pacific Slope to the Union in the years of civil conflict.

Robert L. Thompson, *Wiring a Continent: The History of the Telegraph Industry in the United States, 1832-1866* (1947), is the only reliable book dealing with the subject.—W. T. J.

television. See RADIO AND TELEVISION, WESTERNS ON.

Teller, Henry Moore (1830-1914). Colorado politician. Born in Allegany County, New York, Teller taught at rural schools and did manual labor to finance an education at academies in nearby Alfred and Rushford. In his mid-twenties he began to study law, and after admission to the bar in 1858, he moved to Illinois. The persuasion of a friend led him to settle in the territory of Colorado three years later. Sympathy with the antislavery cause had already made him a confirmed Republican.

Teller spent the next fifteen years in the lucrative practice of mining law in Central City, was intermittently active in territorial politics, and won a reputation as the "best known public speaker in the Territory." In 1876 he capitalized on these pursuits to win a Senate seat over divided opposition from the southern part of the state. During his first term he vigorously supported the western positions on Indian legislation, territorial autonomy, and land policy. President Chester A. Arthur named him secretary of the interior in 1882, a post from which he again spoke for the needs of the West as he saw them.

Returning to the Senate in 1885, Teller became progressively more concerned with the silver issue over the next decade. Since the issue concerned the federal government's unlimited purchase of silver as a backing for the currency, the Colorado mining economy was tied to the fate of the white metal. Teller sacrificed the voting rights of the Negro and joined regional colleagues in killing the Federal Elections bill in 1891 in favor of monetary legislation. He fought repeal of the Sherman Silver Purchase Act in 1893 and attempted generally to convince fellow Republicans of the merits of silver. Teller left the party in 1896 when the national convention endorsed the gold standard. "As a bimetallist," he told the unfriendly delegates, "I must renounce my allegiance to my party." He had a brief boom for the Democratic presidential nomination, but the party preferred William Jennings Bryan. After the silver cause lost, Teller went back to the Senate for twelve years.

His most noteworthy achievement was the Teller Amendment, which pledged the United States to an independent Cuba in 1898. A states' rights Democrat after 1901, he returned to his earlier advocacy of western interests until his retirement. Teller was always more of an orator than a legislator. Able to articulate the felt needs of his constituents, he produced a series of set speeches rather than a record of legislative accomplishment.

See the Teller Papers, Colorado State Historical Society; and Elmer Ellis, *Henry Moore Teller, Defender of the West* (1941).—L. L. G.

"ten-gallon" hat. See COWBOY CLOTHING.

Tennessee, settlement of. The recorded history of Tennessee dates from the latter half of the seventeenth century, when Gabriel ARTHUR and James NEEDHAM appeared in the upper Tennessee River valley. To the west along the Mississippi at approximately the same date came French visitors, including Robert, Sieur de LA SALLE and Martin Chartier. This happened, however, almost a century before Indian traders and long hunters penetrated the great valley beyond the Blue Ridges and the Smoky Mountains. Among the early arrivals were Daniel BOONE, John FINLEY, Elisha Walden, and William Bean.

Within the decade 1765-75 there were numerous long hunters and settlers, including Bean, James Smith, Gaspar Mansker, William Cuthbirth, John SEVIER, James ROBERTSON, and Evan Shelby. Earliest settlements were made at Bean Station and along the Watauga River. (See WATAUGA ASSOCIATION and HOLSTON RIVER SETTLEMENTS.) Before the advent of settlement, Indians had ceded land in the treaties of HARD LABOR (1768) and LOCHABER (1770). The influx of settlers was fairly large after 1772. Many of the settlers had come from North Carolina and were fleeing in the aftermath of the Regulator uprising against taxation at Hillsboro in 1771, but there is not sustainable evidence that they themselves were Regulators.

In the winter of 1774-75 there was considerable excitement over the negotiations between the Transylvania Company officials, led by Richard HENDERSON, and the Cherokee chiefs in the making of the Treaty of SYCAMORE SHOALS. This treaty, while yielding a tremendous grant of land beyond Cumberland Gap, was to prove another irritant to many of the Cherokee of the Tennessee valley, and Indian war followed closely upon its completion. Isolated though they were, the East Tennessee, or Watauga, settlers were scarcely given

time to build their cabins and open their first corn patches before they were caught up in a series of border struggles. The first of these was LORD DUNMORE'S WAR (1794), in which Tennesseans fought under the commands of William Lewis and Evan Shelby at Point Pleasant on the Ohio. By 1775 the border was disturbed by the approaching American Revolution and instances of Indian resistance, some of which bore the earmarks of having been stimulated by British agents.

Between 1775 and 1781 East Tennessee experienced a period of extensive terrorism caused by constant conflict with the Cherokee on both sides of the mountains. Tennesseans followed Isaac SHELBY and John Sevier into battle against the British at KINGS MOUNTAIN, fought with them against the Indians, and stood ready to give assistance to the infant settlements beyond Cumberland Gap in Kentucky.

A major attraction of the Tennessee country was land. Speculators were engaged in land-hunting in at least three major areas, including the territory about the headstreams of the Tennessee River system, about the fall line of the river at Muscle Shoals, about the great bend of the Cumberland, and along the Mississippi. All the major pioneers, such as Evan Shelby, Sevier, Robertson, Bean, John Donelson, William BLOUNT, and Andrew JACKSON, were involved in land speculation. Speculation was, in fact, a central theme in early Tennessee history and led to an early expansion of settlements as far west as the Cumberland valley and south to the shoals. It also helped to shape the political development of Tennessee. As the western territory emerged into statehood, Tennessee was composed of three distinct geographical sections, East, Middle, and West.

Politically, early Tennessee was under the authority of North Carolina from the outbreak of the American Revolution, when the western settlements petitioned to be taken under the protection of North Carolina. Administratively the western settlements were governed under the laws of the quasi-independent District of Washington, later to become Washington County. In 1779 plans were made to survey the line that separated western North Carolina from southwest Virginia, thus giving geographical identity to Tennessee settlements. Between 1778 and 1796 land-grabbing and speculation shaped the pattern of settlement both in East and Middle Tennessee and encouraged an active interest in politics and in Indian relationships.

In 1779-80 settlers under the leadership of Robertson, John Donelson, Stockley Donelson, George Freeland, and others started settlements in the big bend of the Cumberland River. This western advance quickly resulted in the multiplication of the number of small settlements in the Cumberland-Tennessee drainage area and the creation at an early date of Davidson, Tennessee, and Sumner counties. In 1789 the Middle area was formed into a separate administrative unit (Mero District), named for the intendant and governor of New Orleans, Esteban Miró. Provisions were made to connect East and Middle Tennessee by the location and opening of an emigrant trail or road.

The most significant political development in Tennessee prior to the organization of the state was the creation of the state of FRANKLIN. An assembly for this purpose was brought together in Jonesboro in August 1784, and provisions were made for the immediate creation of an independent state. Prior to this, North Carolina ceded early in 1784 its western lands to Congress and then withdrew its cession. Promoters of the new state went ahead anyway with their plans of drafting a constitution and creating an administrative organization that eventually differed little from that of the mother state. From the outset, however, there was disagreement over the nature of the Franklin government and constitution. Major forces were divided in their loyalties, and in the end the delegates adopted a modified version of the North Carolina Constitution instead of the original document that had been prepared. By 1789 controversy and internal political bickering and land-speculating rivalries had defeated the creation of the new state. One of the main sources of difficulty was friction between the officials of Franklin and those of North Carolina.

By the time of the failure of the State of Franklin, major changes had occurred in both the West and in the Confederation of States. To begin with, the NORTHWEST ORDINANCE of 1787 established patterns of land survey and administration in the public domain. In the latter year the Constitutional Convention at Philadelphia prepared the way for the nationalization of many of Tennessee's problems. Indian disturbances, Spanish activities and conspiracy, and speculator rivalries forced the Tennessee country into a new situation. On August 7, 1789, Congress created the SOUTHWEST TERRITORY, and a year later William Blount received his commission as territorial governor. Aside from the creation of an administrative organization, one of Blount's first tasks was that of reaching an agreement with the Cherokee over territorial boundaries and problems. In 1791 at White's Fort, Governor Blount met with the Cherokee representatives and drafted the Treaty of Holston, which essentially was a reaffirmation of the terms of the Treaty of Hopewell, drafted in 1785 by representatives of the State of Franklin and the Cherokee. This latter agreement established a boundary along the divide of the ridge between the Little River and the Little Tennessee River, and ceded to the whites lands south of the French Broad and Holston rivers and east of the ridge. In turn, the Indians were to receive remuneration in an unspecified amount. The Holston treaty specified a thousand dollars a year, which President Washington ordered to be increased to fifteen hundred dollars.

During the earliest formative years the Southwest Territory was troubled by difficulties of communication amongst its several areas, other political handicaps, constant friction with the Indians, and the SPANISH CONSPIRACY. By 1795 the constant flow of immigrants into the region had increased to numbers that seemed to justify the beginning of the organization of an independent state. It elected James WHITE to Congress. On July 11, 1795, the Southwest territorial assembly authorized an enumeration of the inhabitants of the territory. William Blount announced that the results of this census indicated there were 66,650 free persons and 10,613 slaves. The vote to organize the new state was highly sectional in nature, with the voters in the less populous Cumberland settlements opposing the proposition. On November 29, 1795, Blount ordered the meeting of a convention to take place in Knoxville on January 11, 1796. This assembly was in session until the end of February. The document it produced was largely an adaptation of that of North Carolina. A section forbade ministers and priests seats in the general assembly. A bill of rights of thirty-one sections was written into the document, with the thirty-first section guaranteeing land preemption rights to the people residing south of the Holston and French Broad rivers between Big Pigeon River and the Tennessee River. The state government was organized on March 29, 1796, with Sevier as first governor. Blount and William Cocke were nominated United States senators, and Andrew Jackson was a member of the first state legislature. On June 1, 1796, Tennessee was admitted to the Union as the second state to be created on the western frontier.

See Thomas Perkins Abernethy, *From Frontier to Plantation in Tennessee* (1932); Carl S. Driver, *John Sevier, Pioneer of the Old Southwest* (1932); Philip M. Hamer, ed., *Tennessee: A History, 1673-1932*, 4 vols. (1933); John Haywood, *The Civil and Political History of the State of Tennessee* (1891); William Masterson, *William Blount* (1954); J. G. M. Ramsey, *The Annals of Tennessee* (1853); and Samuel Cole Williams, *History of the Lost State of Franklin*, rev. ed. (1933).—T. D. C.

Tenskwatawa, called the **Shawnee Prophet** (c. 1778-c.1837). Shawnee mystic and holy man. Tenskwatawa was probably born near Springfield, Ohio, and was the younger brother of TECUMSEH. During his childhood the Shawnee and other tribes of the Old Northwest were left demoralized and leaderless after their defeats at the battle of Fallen Timbers (1794) and the forced Treaty of Greenville (1795). Cut off from ancestral homelands and pressed upon by white culture, the Indians turned inward toward spiritual beliefs for strength. As a youth Tenskwatawa was a dissolute, drunken idler and loud-mouthed braggart. He put out one of his own eyes in a hunting accident, though this episode is not connected with his drinking. In 1805, however, after observing the meetings of the white Shaker religious sect, he underwent a powerful religious experience and vision that completely transformed his character. Proclaiming himself a prophet (which then became the white man's denigrating epithet for him), he and Tecumseh began calling for Indian unity in the face of white encroachment. The Prophet preached a return to primitive folkways, a revival of community ownership of property, an end to intertribal warfare, and the rejection of all things white, particularly liquor. Like the teachings of other Indian messiahs, such as Smohalla and Wovoka, the Prophet's Code was an amalgam of racial antagonism, white Christian influence, and traditional native rituals and precepts.

Hearing in 1806 of Tenskwatawa's growing influence, Indiana territorial governor William Henry Harrison wrote to the Indians that "if he really is a prophet let him cause the sun to stand still, the moon to change its course." The Prophet immediately predicted the total eclipse of the sun, which occurred on June 16, leaving Harrison fuming and drawing thousands of Indians from as far away as Saskatchewan to the new religion.

In 1808 Tenskwatawa and his brother moved from Ohio to the Tippecanoe River in Indiana, founding the village called Prophet's Town. After that time the Prophet was increasingly overshadowed by the organizational genius of the charismatic Tecumseh, although Tenskwatawa's supernatural reputation was essential to the emerging Indian confederacy's strength. In 1811 Tecumseh journeyed south, leaving the Prophet with instructions to avoid at all cost any premature confrontation with the whites. Lacking his brother's control over the hotheaded young warriors, and perhaps seeking to reestablish his preeminence, Tenskwatawa allowed himself to be drawn into the battle of TIPPECANOE on November 11. Throughout the fight he stayed in the rear, making magic and promising that the soldiers would break and run. They did not, the Indians were defeated, and the Prophet's prestige was destroyed forever. Spurned by the enraged Tecumseh, Tenskwatawa removed to Canada. Although he took no part in the War of 1812, the British government granted him a small pension after that conflict as recognition of his brother's participation. In 1826, a bitter old man, he returned to the United States and lived in Wyandotte County, Kansas, where George Catlin painted his portrait in 1832.

Tenskwatawa's magic had proved a false hope to his people. Still, the Old Northwest border situation had been closely balanced in 1811, and if he had been able to supplement his early successes with only a little of the military judgment possessed by Tecumseh, the history of the American frontier might have been quite different.

See Freeman Cleaves, *Old Tippecanoe: William Henry Harrison and His Time* (1939); Benjamin Drake, *The Life of Tecumseh and His Brother the Prophet* (1841); James Mooney, *The Ghost Dance Religion*, Bureau of American Ethnology Fourteenth Annual Report (1896); and Glenn Tucker, *Tecumseh: Vision of Glory* (1956). —P. R. M.

Territorial Papers of the United States. A United States government project that publishes government records relating to former United States territories that have entered the Union. The volumes of selected, annotated federal records are arranged chronologically in the order of the establishment of the territories, with one or more volumes for each territory. The publication in 1975 of the second of two volumes devoted to Wisconsin Territory brought the number of volumes to 28. In conjunction with the appearance of the first of the Wisconsin volumes (Volume XXVII, 1969) there was issued National Archives Microcopy No. 236, consisting of 122 rolls of microfilm that reproduced virtually everything in the National Archives relating to Wisconsin Territory but without annotation, index, or other editorial paraphernalia. Similar microfilm publications are planned for later territories, along with the continuing series of volumes.

The project began in the United States Department of State in 1931 and has been sponsored since 1950 by the National Archives and Records Service of the General Services Administration. The criteria for selecting records for the volumes were determined by the original editor, Clarence E. CARTER, and are continued by his successor, John Porter BLOOM. The main objective is to illustrate the administrative history of the territories through original sources. Such a collection of material illuminates one of the most important American contributions to the art of government: a system whereby lesser governmental jurisdictions—territories or "colonies"—are supervised while being prepared for ultimate full political equality with the states. The project is one of the oldest continuing government-sponsored historical documentary publication series, and is unique as to type.

The project is often traced back to the publication in 1911 by the Carnegie Institution of David W. Parker's *Calendar of Papers in Washington Archives Relating to the Territories of the United States.* The calendar was incomplete, and seven midwestern state historical societies collaborated soon afterward to employ Newton D. Mereness to list on cards all government documents he could locate relating to the early history of the upper Mississippi and Great Lakes regions. The Mereness Calendar was also incomplete, but it whetted the appetite of historians of the Midwest and other regions. It also made clear the vast problems of locating, identifying, transcribing, verifying, collating, and listing federal records and then annotating and indexing them for publication.

The Territorial Papers project in substantially its present form originated with an act of Congress signed March 3, 1925, known as the Ralston Act from its sponsor, Senator Samuel M. Ralston of Indiana. The act made the first provision for copying and editing documents in federal archives. Later enactments authorized their publication, which was undertaken with the appointment of Carter as editor.—J. P. B.

territorial system. The United States system of territorial government was established in the 1780s and elaborated over many decades. In a limited way it still flourishes. It was formulated out of the experience of the original thirteen colonies-turned-states. With independence in 1783 they found themselves, collectively through Congress, in a relationship with the settlements along the Ohio River similar to that which the British government had had with the American colonies. A revolution in the West might result if Congress mishandled its responsibility, just as the colonies had revolted against the rule of the British crown.

The territorial, or land, ordinances of 1784 and 1785 were the earliest formal responses to this problem. The former, drafted by Thomas JEFFERSON, provided that, when sufficient population developed, boundaries would be established to create perhaps sixteen small territories, eventually to be states, in the territory northwest of the Ohio River. Jefferson proposed that an increasing measure of self-government be allowed the inhabitants and that fanciful names such as Polypotamia and Pelisipia be attached to the future states. This ordinance was a nullity because land titles in the West were largely unsettled and there were few inhabitants. Finally the Ordinance of 1787, or NORTHWEST ORDINANCE, superseded it.

The 1785 land ordinance, on the other hand, was far from ineffective. It established the system of land sale, based on rectilinear survey of sections (one mile square) and townships (thirty-six sections, with one reserved for educational purposes). This ordinance, also, was the result largely of the leadership of Jefferson, who was disenchanted with colonial surveying practices, which resulted in many disputes and much unsalable wasteland. The new system was attractive to Congress in part because it opened the way to the sale of immense tracts at auctions, which would benefit the desperately anemic United States Treasury.

The Northwest Ordinance successfully provided for governance of the Northwest Territory throughout the evolution of five new states, which looked toward admission to the Union on a basis of equality with the original thirteen. The system called for presidential appointment of a governor, a secretary, and three judges, who together adopted from existing states all necessary laws and administered them. The first stage was passed when the population of a territory grew to include five thousand adult white male voters, who then gained authority to elect the lower house of a territorial legislature; the upper house was appointed by the president. The two houses together elected a nonvoting delegate to represent the territory in Congress. When the total population had climbed to sixty thousand, the territory could apply for admission as a state. The promise of statehood and certain declarations of citizen freedoms and rights were set apart as "articles of compact between the original states and the people and states in the said territory," to be forever "unalterable, unless by common consent." With these enactments the basic framework of the American system was erected, to be revised gradually through the years as a result of practical experience and a changing political climate.

In the OLD NORTHWEST, under direct provisions of the Northwest Ordinance, the first territorial officials were appointed in 1788. Governor Arthur ST. CLAIR initiated territorial government in Marietta in October, and administrative precedents were established during his tenure. One thorny issue was the question of whether the first legislature (i.e., the governor, secretary, and judges) was to adopt laws from the states unchanged to apply in the territory or modify them to fit local conditions better. This was resolved in favor of the exercise of greater freedom, and laws were, in effect, enacted from the first stage of government, although not without arduous public and private debate. Territorial governors beginning with St. Clair were simultaneously superintendents of Indian affairs for their territories; St. Clair conducted several ineffectual campaigns against Indians. By 1798 the population had increased to the point where the elected legislature was provided; two years later INDIANA Territory was established; it included all of the Northwest Territory except the present state of Ohio; in 1803 Ohio was admitted into the Union.

In the "Territory South of the River Ohio," the provisions of the Northwest Ordinance were adopted verbatim except that slavery was permitted. Kentucky won statehood without going through territoryhood, but the region ceded by North Carolina, to become the state of TENNESSEE, was subjected to the American territorial system. Created in 1790 with William Blount as governor, the SOUTHWEST TERRITORY was the first to send an elected delegate—James WHITE—to the United States House of Representatives. There he established precedents that are still being observed. As delegate, he led the struggle for statehood, attained in 1796, thereby fixing the usual procedures for this legal transition: (1) Congress passes an enabling act, directing the governor to take a census and call an election for a constitutional convention; (2) following ratification of the proposed state constitution by popular vote, elections for state offices take place; (3) Congress passes on the new constitution; (4) Congress passes and the president signs an act of admission, and the new state's congressional delegation is seated.

Until close to the end of the nineteenth century all United States territories were on the North American mainland and passed through nearly identical phases of political development. The Department of State supervised their government until 1873, when the Department of the Interior was given this responsibility. Only Texas and California, of the trans-Mississippi states, lacked a period of tutelage under one or both of these departments. The broadening of the qualifications for suffrage was one of the changes that was reflected in territorial government over the years, as it was in the nation at large. The first, undemocratic stage of government, as prescribed in the Northwest Ordinance, was dropped in 1817 when Alabama Territory was created with a legislative body elected at the same time. This was the unexceptional rule for mainland territories after 1836, when Wisconsin Territory was established. Popular election of the delegates to Congress (from Mississippi and Indiana) and to the territorial legislature (in Indiana) came as early as 1809. Some significant obstacles to realization of fully representative territorial government lasted throughout this period, however, including presidential appointment of governors, secretaries, and judges; the veto exercised by the governor over acts of the territorial legislature; and indeed his power to prorogue and dissolve an unsatisfactory legislative body. Congress retained the ultimate legislative supremacy, but in practice it rarely assumed the initiative and was often responsive to the petitions and memorials generated in great numbers by territorial citizens and their spokesmen.

Federal support was sought and obtained for land surveys and sales, roads, postal service, river and harbor improvement, and of course protection from Indians. The governor continued to bear a multiple responsibility, being superintendent of Indian affairs in his territory and militia commander as well as civil governor. He had to cooperate, or at least work, with numerous officials over whom he could exercise no authority, including especially those of the United States Army, Post Office, and General Land Office. Given the usual preoccupation of Congress and the president with affairs nearer at hand, it is remarkable that the system did not produce more conflict and schism than it actually did. The potent and almost universal force was that, even though the governors, judges, et al., were frequently outsiders, they rapidly developed local attachments and economic interests that led them to seek local popularity. Successful territorial officeholders often carried their jobs over into the period of statehood and sought new, wider bases of power, such as the United States Senate.

The objective of the entire territorial system was to elevate western "colonies," or territories, into states that would enjoy absolute legal parity with the original states. Perhaps no serious consideration was given to Alaska's attaining statehood when it was purchased in 1867, but both Alaska and Hawaii followed the normal territorial route to statehood.

A new factor entered the American territorial system in 1898 with United States assumption of sovereignty over islands in the Caribbean Sea and Pacific Ocean, which were not expected to be incorporated into the union of states. Upon their acquisition Puerto Rico, Guam, American Samoa, the Philippine Islands, and later the Virgin Islands fell into the new category of unincorporated territories whose distinction included: that provisions of the United States Constitution did not automatically extend over them, that tariffs could be levied on their goods imported into the United States, and that they were not expected ever to become states. The Foraker Act of 1900, which established civil government in Puerto Rico, extended only "applicable laws of the United States" and not the broad provisions of the Constitution, and instead of providing for a territorial delegate to sit in Congress it called for a resident commissioner to represent Puerto Rico before the House of Representatives. The distinction was clearly brought out in Senate debate in 1900, and again two years later in the Act to Provide Civil Government to the Philippine Islands. The United States Supreme Court formalized the concept of dividing territories into the two categories, incorporated and unincorporated, in its decision in 1901 in the case of *Downes* v. *Bidwell.* Hawaii and Alaska were specifically placed on an incorporated basis by organic acts of 1900 and 1912. (A territory is called "organized" only after Congress has enacted organic legislation defining its form of government, which may be incorporated or unincorporated.)

Resident commissioners came to enjoy exactly the same privileges and duties as delegates in the United States House of Representatives, but this was not required. The uncertainties that bear upon the status of unincorporated United States territories or possessions are complex but are suggested, for example, by the facts that the Philippine Islands was given full independence in 1946; that the Virgin Islands and Guam have never been authorized to have either delegates or resident commissioners, although they elect their governors and possess a considerable degree of autonomy in local government; that Puerto Rico as a self-governing commonwealth since 1952 has enjoyed a unique status within the American orbit; that the United States at one time reported to the United Nations on governmental affairs in Panama as if it were a territorial possession; and that American Samoa (limited self-government since 1960), the Trust Territory of the Pacific Islands (elected territorial legislature since 1965), the Ryukyu Islands, and a scattering of other inhabited and uninhabited places have been governed under varied assertions of authority, with local inhabitants having limited but expanding opportunities to practice self-government.

See John Porter Bloom, ed., *The American Territorial System,* National Archives Conferences, vol. 5 (1973). —J. P. B. and J. T. B.

Terry, Alfred Howe (1827-1890). Soldier. Terry was born in Hartford, Connecticut, and trained for the law. In 1860, while clerk of the Superior Court of New Haven County, he raised a regiment of volunteers of which he became colonel. In the course of the Civil War he won a distinguished reputation, his most outstanding exploit being the capture of Fort Fisher, North Carolina, in January 1865, a post that Benjamin F. Butler had previously failed to capture. Terry came out of the war a brigadier general in the regular army and in 1866 was assigned to command the Department of Dakota. In 1869 he was transferred to the Department of the South, where the Ku Klux Klan and other kindred organizations were causing trouble, but in 1872 he was ordered back to Dakota.

It was while Terry was department commander of Dakota that the Yellowstone expeditions of 1872 and 1873 explored that stream and the northern survey, marking the boundary between the United States and Canada, was completed. An accurate survey of the northern boundary line was needed because of the necessity of fixing responsibility for Indian raids, depredations of outlaws, and so forth, and also so that, as the region was settled, the settlers would know if they were residents of the United States or Canada. In 1873, when the Seventh Cavalry was ordered to Terry's department, he became involved in a controversy with the cavalry's leader, George Armstrong CUSTER, over Custer's exploration of the Black Hills. In 1876 came the Sioux War, highlighted by the battle of the LITTLE BIG HORN. In securing permission for Custer to go on this campaign in command of his regiment, General Terry showed a magnanimous and forgiving spirit, and after the disaster, for which he received considerable unmerited criticism, Terry again preferred to accept the criticism in silence rather than engage in a public controversy that would tarnish the reputation of the dead. The next year, troops in his department were active against both the Sioux and the Nez Percé Indians and finally subjugated the Sioux.

General Terry was in command of the Department of Dakota at the time of the court of inquiry into the conduct of Major Marcus A. Reno at the battle of the Little Big Horn. The court raised more questions than it solved. As department commander he also ordered the two courts-martial of Major Reno, the second of which resulted in that officer being dismissed from the service of the United States. It also stirred up considerable controversy, some of which persists to this day.

Because of his judicial background and temperament, General Terry was often selected for membership on army and Indian commissions. In 1867 he was a member of a committee to treat with the Plains Indians, and in 1872 served as president of the board to choose a small-arms system for the army. The board, on which Major Reno also served, received considerable criticism after the Little Big Horn disaster. In 1875, Terry was a member of the Allison Committee, which attempted, without success, to purchase the Black Hills from the Sioux. He was also a member of the commission that attempted to negotiate in 1877 with Sitting Bull, still resisting the white man's invasion. As the commanding general of the Department of Dakota, he naturally played a considerable part in preparing the way for the construction of the northern transcontinental railroads.

After the close of the Civil War Terry was one of the few volunteer officers remaining in the army to reach general rank. In 1886 he was promoted to major general and in the same year was appointed to the command of the Military Division of the Missouri. Two years later he was retired, at his own request, for disability.

Almost every volume dealing with the Indian wars on the northern Plains has considerable material dealing with General Terry. In 1896, Colonel Robert Patterson Hughes, who was Terry's brother-in-law and had been his chief of staff during the campaign that culminated at the Little Big Horn, published "The Campaign Against the Sioux," in the *Journal of the Military Institution of the United States,* vol. 18, in which he claimed that Custer had violated orders. This article was reprinted as an appendix to Colonel William A. Graham, *Story of the Little Big Horn* (1941). As would be expected, there are many references to General Terry in the columns of the *Army and Navy Journal.*—E. I. S.

Texas. Called by some observers a state of mind as well as a state of the Union, Texas is a land of geographical contrast. Its citizens long have been famed for their attachment to and bragging about this region of coastal plains, pine forests, cacti-clad deserts, high plains, and rugged mountains, all of which stretch across 267,339 square miles. Ranging from sea level along the Gulf of Mexico to an altitude of 8,751 feet in the Davis Mountains, the land receives fifty inches and more of rainfall each year along its border with Louisiana but less than ten inches annually in the semiarid western portion of the state.

Indians came to the region fifteen thousand years ago, and perhaps earlier, and were influenced by the geography much as would be the white settlers of a later date. In the east lived an agricultural people, a Caddoan-speaking confederacy of tribes known as the Hasinai; one of these, the Tejas (or Texas), would leave their name to the region. To the southwest, along the Rio Grande valley, were the Coahuiltecan; because their homeland was barren, they subsisted as hunters and gatherers. Along the Gulf Coast were the Karankawa, who were fishermen and beachcombers—and reportedly given to cannibalism. West of the timberline and north of the Rio Grande valley were the Plains Indians, nomadic hunters of buffalo who lived in skin tepees and who starved or feasted depending on the fortunes of the hunt.

The years of sole Indian ownership of Texas came to an end in 1519. At the orders of the governor of Jamaica, Alonso Alvarez de Piñeda that year sailed from the tip of Florida around the Gulf Coast to Tampico, Mexico, on an expedition of mapping and reconnaissance. He stopped briefly at the mouth of the Rio Grande, which he called the River of Palms, to inspect inland. Nine years later some eighty survivors of an expedition to Florida, trying to reach Mexico by means of crude barges they had made, were cast ashore on the coast of Texas, probably at Galveston Island. Only fifteen of them survived that first winter, and they were forced into slavery. Six years passed before one of them, Alvar Núñez Cabeza de Vaca, could mature plans for escape. In company with three other survivors, he set out walking and eighteen months later found Spaniards at Culiacán in northwestern Mexico.

Taken before the viceroy of New Spain (as Mexico then was called), Cabeza de Vaca told that he had seen no evidence of great wealth, but that he had heard of the Seven Cities of Cíbola somewhere to the north. This rumor led to the expedition in 1540 of Francisco Vásquez de Coronado, which in the spring and summer of the following year crossed the Panhandle of Texas in a fruitless search for mineral wealth. In 1542 survivors of the expedition of Hernando de Soto, led by Luís de Moscoso, penetrated Texas from Arkansas looking for a way to New Spain. They found no gold, no silver, and no precious stones—only Indians who fought for their meager supplies for food. Therefore the region once again was left to its native owners.

In 1601, following the colonization of New Mexico three years earlier, Governor Juan de Oñate traced Coronado's footsteps across the Texas Panhandle in search of the Seven Cities of Cíbola or the legendary Gran Quivira, but he found neither. Other explorers came from New Mexico into West Texas: in 1629 and 1632 Father Juan de Salas attempted to convert the Indians living in the vicinity of present San Angelo; in 1650 captains Hernando Martín and Diego del Castillo led soldiers to the same area and, finding fresh-water pearls, inspired a return visit four years later by Captain Diego de Guadalajara; and in 1683-84 Captain Juan Domínguez de Mendoza and Father Nicolás López visited the area yet again. Moreover, in 1681, after Spainards had been driven from present-day New Mexico by the Pueblo uprising the previous year, some of the Indian refugees, who refused to give up Christianity, were settled near present El Paso at a mission named Corpus Christi de Isleta.

Spanish interest in Texas suddenly shifted from the west to the southeast in 1685 when René Robert Cavelier, Sieur de La Salle, attempted to settle his ill-fated Fort St. Louis at Matagorda Bay. Captain Alonso de León finally found the ruins of this settlement in 1688 and the following year returned to destroy all traces of it to prevent any French claim to the region. Moreover, Spanish officials decreed that a mission should be erected in the area to watch for any new French intrusion. Father Damián Massanet, a Franciscan missionary, opened San Francisco de los Tejas in 1690 on the banks of the Trinity River, but three years later the effort was abandoned when the Indians proved unfriendly.

Spaniards returned to Texas two decades later because of a renewed French settlement in the Gulf Coast region. In 1714 Louis Juchereau de St. Denis, a French trader, crossed from Louisiana to northern Mexico in an attempt to open trade, and Spanish officials reacted by ordering the resettlement of Texas. On June 20, 1716, Captain Domingo Ramón arrived at the site of San Francisco de los Tejas to reopen it, and in East Texas and western Louisiana he constructed three other missions and a presidio. Two years later a mission and presidio were built at SAN ANTONIO, which was to serve as a way station to the missions in East Texas; however, San Antonio soon became the principal Spanish settlement in Texas, and to it in 1731 came civilian colonists from the Canary Islands. Other settlements in Texas included La Bahía del Espíritu Santo (the present Goliad) and Nacogdoches.

Texas became a quiet backwater of the Spanish colonial empire, with ranching and farming the principal occupations of the civilians. East Texas was abandoned in 1773, following the transfer of Louisiana to Spain at the end of the Seven Years' War, but settlers illegally returned to Nacogdoches in 1779. By 1810, when the Mexican Revolution began, the population stood at only some four thousand Christians.

Father Miguel Hidalgo's call of September 16, 1810, for expulsion of all Spaniards from Mexico led to disturbances in Texas. On January 22 the following year a retired army captain, Juan Bautista de las Casas, briefly took command of the province, only to be ousted on March 2. Then in August 1812 an adventurer, Bernardo Gutiérrez de Lara, brought an army to the province, captured all the major cities, and declared the Republic of Texas in March 1813. By August, however, he was driven from Texas by a Spanish army. Pirates claiming to be part of the Mexican navy infested Galveston Island—Luís Aury and Jean Laffite the most notorious of them. And in 1819, after the United States and Spain had concluded the Adams-Onís Treaty establishing the present boundary between Louisiana and Texas, Dr. James Long and an army of Americans, angry that Texas had been given to Spain, invaded and captured Nacogdoches, only to be driven out within months of proclaiming another Republic of Texas. In 1821 Long returned and captured La Bahía only to learn that Mexico had achieved its independence.

In December 1820, only months before Mexico freed itself from Spain, Moses AUSTIN arrived in San Antonio with a bold scheme of colonization. He had lived in Missouri while it yet was a Spanish possession, had mined lead there, and had been wealthy until the Panic of 1819 bankrupted him. Hoping to regain his fortune by colonizing three hundred Anglo families in Texas, he won approval for this scheme on January 17, 1821, but died on his return trip to the United States. His son, Stephen F. AUSTIN, fell heir to the project. Learning of Mexican independence, young Austin journeyed to Mexico City and there not only had his project reapproved but also gave advice to those drafting the Mexican constitution of 1824. This document joined Texas to Coahuila to form one state in the new republic, and it included a clause approving further colonization contracts. In 1825 the state of Coahuila y Texas passed legislation that under the EMPRESARIO SYSTEM gave generous land grants to colonists (more than 4,600 acres to most of them).

Austin, along with other colonizers, brought approximately twenty-five thousand people to Texas in the next decade, most of them Anglos. These "Mexican" citizens retained their own language, formed schools, and traded with the United States. Mexicans grew alarmed at these practices and in 1830 tried to end immigration from the United States, increase taxes, and establish military garrisons. Then in 1835 Antonio López de Santa Anna, the president of Mexico, overthrew the constitution of 1824, proclaimed himself dictator, decreed martial law, and attempted to disarm the Texans. On October 2 that year the Texans resisted, and war began.

On November 3, at the "Consultation," held at San Felipe de Austin, the Texans declared that they were fighting for restoration of the constitution of 1824, not for independence, and on December 5-10 they defeated the Mexican troops at San Antonio, thereby ending Mexican military presence in the province. On February 23, 1836, Santa Anna arrived at San Antonio at the head of an army estimated at five thousand men. There he trapped approximately 187 Texans at the ALAMO. Led by David Crockett, James BOWIE, and William B. Travis, the defenders held their fort until it was overrun on March 6. All died, taking with them 1,200 to 1,600 of the enemy. Later that month James W. Fannin and some three hundred men were captured during the battle of GOLIAD, and on March 27 they were executed.

While these events were taking place, another convention was being held by the Texans. Meeting at Washington-on-the-Brazos on March 1, 1836, these men the following day voted a declaration of independence, and in a few days elected Sam HOUSTON commander-in-

chief of the army, drafted a constitution, and named an interim government that included David G. BURNET as president and Lorenzo de Zavala as vice-president. Houston took command of the Texan army, trained it briefly, and on April 21 decisively defeated Santa Anna and his army at the battle of SAN JACINTO, thereby winning the independence of Texas.

In the fall of 1836 Sam Houston was elected president of the Republic of Texas, and the voters indicated their desire for annexation to the United States. Houston sought this, but Congress refused at the urging of abolitionists who charged that the Texas revolution was a "slaveocracy conspiracy" by southerners. Houston did gain American recognition of the republic in 1837, and in his two-year administration sought peace with the Indians and with Mexico. His successor, Mirabeau B. LAMAR, attempted to get loans from European powers and expand westward to the Pacific, and sent Albert Sidney JOHNSTON to expel all Indians from Texas. Lamar did secure diplomatic recognition of the republic from England, France, Belgium, the Netherlands, and several Germanic states, but he got no loans, angered the Mexicans, started a lasting war with the Comanche, and brought runaway inflation of the currency. Houston, in office again (1841-44), and his successor, Dr. Anson Jones (1844-46), worked to pacify the Indians, but mainly they concentrated on securing American annexation of Texas. On December 29, 1845, President James K. Polk signed the proclamation making Texas a state (see TEXAS, ANNEXATION OF).

War with Mexico followed in 1846. Texans happily joined and fought; even Governor J. Pinckney Henderson took a leave of absence to serve. Immediately afterward the state legislators attempted to organize into counties that portion of New Mexico (east of the Rio Grande) which Texas claimed, but they were not allowed to do so by American soldiers there. The result of this quarrel was the COMPROMISE OF 1850, in which Texas received both its present boundary and compensation amounting to $10 million with which it paid its public debt stemming from its days as a republic.

In the following fifteen years Texas prospered mightily, its population jumping from 135,000 to 604,000. The economy was based mainly on farming, with slavery an accepted feature in the state, and gradually the line of settlement moved westward. Transportation was difficult, however, for each county was responsible for its own roads, and only a few miles of railroad track were laid.

The opening of the Civil War brought crisis to Texas, for Governor Sam Houston, elected in 1859 after serving in the United States Senate from 1846 to 1858, stood staunchly for the Union. A secession convention led by Aran Milo ROBERTS voted 166 to 8 in favor of withdrawing from the Union, a decision subsequently ratified by popular vote, but Houston refused to take the oath of allegiance to the Confederacy and was removed from office. Texas was not a major theater in the CIVIL WAR, although it did supply men and military supplies used elsewhere in the South. All federal posts in Texas were captured easily at the outbreak of the conflict and were held until the end of the war. Galveston was occupied by northern troops at the end of 1862 but was retaken by Confederates on January 1, 1863. Other federal attempts to land in Texas were thwarted with the exception of Brownsville, which fell into Union hands late in 1863. In the spring of 1864 General Nathaniel P. Banks attempted an invasion of East Texas from Louisiana by way of the Red River, but was driven off with heavy losses. The last battle of the Civil War was fought at Palmito Ranch in the Rio Grande valley on May 12-13, 1865, with a Texan victory, but on June 19 that year the Emancipation Proclamation was made effective in the state.

Reconstruction cost Texas heavily. In 1860 it had been ninth among the states in per capita wealth, but in 1880, following the end of Reconstruction, it stood thirty-sixth in per capita wealth. Immediately following the collapse of the Confederacy, Andrew J. Hamilton, a former congressman from Texas and a Unionist, became governor; under the guidance of Hamilton and John H. REAGAN, Texas moved quickly to meet the requirements of presidential Reconstruction. However, in 1867 the Radical Republicans in Congress declared that Texas could not yet be readmitted to the Union and imposed military rule. Soon the stable element in Texas was replaced with radicals, and disorder became common. A convention of these radicals drafted a new constitution in 1869, and the following year the Radical Republicans readmitted Texas to the Union under the leadership of Governor Edmund J. Davis and a band of carpetbag-scalawag Republicans. Under them the public debt mounted, lawlessness was rampant, and corruption rife.

The excesses of Reconstruction alienated most Texans, and in 1873, when Richard Coke, a former Confederate captain, was elected governor, residents felt they at last had regained control of their government. Following his inauguration in 1874, Coke called a new constitutional convention, which then drafted the constitution of 1876. This was a long document that severely restricted the powers of the government, provided for short terms of office and low salaries, and stipulated economy at all levels of government. Moreover, the Reconstruction period caused local voters to identify strongly with the Democratic party and to elect former Confederates to almost all state offices for the next thirty years.

In the decade following Reconstruction a major problem was restoring law and order. Frontier region that it was, Texas attracted a sizable lawless element which was augmented by Reconstruction. During this period resistance to Radical-appointed law officers had become a sign of southern manhood (see the careers of King FISHER, William LONGLEY, James MILLER, John Wesley HARDIN, and Benjamin THOMPSON). TEXAS RANGERS led by Leander H. MCNELLY patroled the western portion of the state and imposed a semilegal justice that did restore order, while Dallas STOUDENMIRE in El Paso and other peace officers were able to quiet their particular districts.

At the same time the exploding population was moving westward rapidly. From 604,000 residents in 1860, Texas increased to 3,048,710 by 1900, which made it sixth among the states. Many of these new citizens chose to settle in the western portion of the states, which had been opened by the killing of the buffalo and the removal of the Indians.

The number of buffalo on the Southern Plains in 1865 was estimated at seven million and constituted an indispensable part of the Indians' way of life. Mass destruction of them began when eastern tanners discovered that buffalo hides could be turned into excellent leather. Between 1872 and 1878 the southern herd was virtually exterminated by parties of hunters; in 1873 alone the Atchison, Topeka and Santa Fe Railroad shipped 754,529 hides to market. This slaughter at once angered the Indians of the region—and made certain their eventual conquest. The last great campaign against them was the RED RIVER WAR in 1874-75 when soldiers led by Colonel Ranald S. Mackenzie broke the spirit of the Comanche by attacking their winter homes during the battle of PALO DURO CANYON. All soon surrendered and were placed on a reservation in the Indian Territory.

The slaughter of the buffalo and the removal of the Indians opened vast areas of West Texas to settlement, and the legislature hastened the process by setting the price of land ridiculously low or else by giving it away. More than 30 million acres were deeded free to the several railroads building in the state, and in 1879 the legislature provided for the sale of lands set aside to benefit public education at one dollar per acre—and for the sale of the unreserved public domain at only fifty cents per acre. Four years later the price for all the public domain was fixed at one dollar per acre, thereby forcing the railroads to sell their holdings at the same price.

Onto this land swarmed cattlemen, spurred by the low cost of producing beef and the high price paid for it on northern markets (see CATTLE INDUSTRY). At the end of the Civil War an estimated five million Longhorn cattle were running wild in South Texas. They could be had free by anyone who would round them up, or they could be purchased for four dollars a head; yet in northern cities, industrial workers needing meat had pushed the price of cattle to forty dollars a head. To connect the four-dollar steer with the forty-dollar market, Texans began the great trail drives. Between 1865 and 1886 Texas cattle were driven to the railhead towns of Sedalia, Missouri; Abilene and Dodge City, Kansas; and Ogallala, Nebraska. Other Texans drove cattle as far north as Montana and westward into Arizona and New Mexico to stock the ranges in those regions, and going with them were Texas COWBOYS, who spread Spanish methods of handling cattle from horseback. Some of the better known Texas cattlemen were Samuel Burk BURNETT, Charles GOODNIGHT of the JA RANCH, Mifflin KENEDY, Richard KING of the KING RANCH, Oliver LOVING, John T. LYTLE, Charles SCHREINER, and Daniel WAGGONER.

So much money was made from the open-range cattle industry that British and Scots investors poured millions of dollars into Texas ranches—for example, the MATADOR RANCH—while American corporations likewise bought vast tracts of land on which to raise cattle; for example, in 1881 a Chicago corporation paid $3 million (used to rebuild the capitol which had burned) for 3 million acres of land in the Texas Panhandle (this became the XIT RANCH). The introduction of barbed wire in the 1870s and the harsh winter of 1886 brought the open-range era to a close; thereafter ranchers began the scientific breeding of cattle and the modern ranching industry.

The era of traildriving cattle to market ended also

because of the construction of railroads. In 1861 Texas had only 492 miles of track, and little was built during the Reconstruction period. However, the constitution of 1876 provided for giving sixteen sections of land to any company laying a mile of track, and construction boomed. The major lines in Texas were the TEXAS AND PACIFIC; the Southern Pacific; the Missouri, Kansas, and Texas (Katy); and the Fort Worth and Denver. In 1877 more miles of track were laid in Texas than in any other state, and the following year construction in Texas amounted to more than was built in the rest of the nation combined. By 1890 Texas had more miles of railroad track than any other state.

Because of the inexpensive land and the availability of transportation, farmers soon swarmed into West Texas in the wake of the cattlemen, each trying to raise a family on a quarter-section. In the process these farmers developed new crops and new plant varieties, made increased use of machinery, and pioneered new techniques of settlement (such as the SOD HOUSE) and new methods of farming (especially DRY FARMING). During this period the sodbusters gradually shifted from subsistence farming to a cash-crop approach, especially to COTTON PRODUCTION. Starting out as owner-operators, the settlers were then forced to mortgage their land to secure more machinery and to pay their debts in years of drought, and they were caught in the great farm depression of the 1880s. Therefore by late that decade tenant farming was on the rise, and Texas farmers were joining the Populist movement in growing numbers.

The unrest among farmers was matched by discontent among urban dwellers and brought reform in the election of 1890 when James Stephen HOGG became governor on a platform calling for regulation of monopolies and railroads. During his two administrations (1890-94) a Texas Railroad Commission was established with authority to set rates; later this commisssion would be given the task of regulating oil production in the Lone Star State, thereby becoming extremely influential.

As Texas entered the twentieth century, the economy still was based primarily on agriculture. Cotton prices were high, citrus growing in the Rio Grande valley was beginning, the High Plains had been opened to farming, packing plants were opened in Fort Worth to process Texas beef, and wheat, corn, and lumber were commanding high prices. Suddenly, on January 10, 1901, came the discovery of astonishing amounts of oil at Spindletop Field near Beaumont by Anthony B. Lucas, and the economy of Texas was irrevocably changed. Other major fields soon were opened: Petrolia in 1906, Electra in 1911, Burkburnett in 1913, Mexia in 1921, the East Texas Field in 1930, and many, many others. The Texas Company (Texaco), Humble Oil Company (Exxon), Gulf Oil Corporation, and the Magnolia Petroleum Company (Mobil) were formed to refine and market various products from the production. Refineries were built to process the crude oil, and at Houston, along the ship channel to the Gulf of Mexico, petrochemical plants were erected to produce a wide range of products. The OIL INDUSTRY in turn attracted yet more industry, cities grew, and the population shifted from a rural to an urban concentration. Between 1900 and 1940 the population almost doubled, reaching 6,414,824, and by 1970 had almost doubled again by

totaling 11,196,730. By the late 1940s the voters in the cities outnumbered those in the country; by 1970 eight out of every ten Texans lived in just 41 of the 254 counties.

These changes forced politics in the Lone Star State into new channels, although the Democratic party continued to dominate in the new century. Populists and Prohibitionists were a strong force until 1918, when the state ratified the Eighteenth Amendment to the Constitution (fathered by Texas senator Morris Sheppard). Twice, however, the Democratic party regulars saw outsiders capture the leadership of their organization. James E. "Pa" FERGUSON captured the governor's office in 1914 by appealing to farmers, but in 1917, after gaining reelection, he was impeached, largely because of his quarrel with the University of Texas. In the next twenty-one years he or his wife, Mariam "Ma" Ferguson, were on the ballot in almost every election—and Mrs. Ferguson twice was elected governor herself (1924 and 1932). In 1938 W. "Pappy" Lee O'Daniel, marketer of Hillbilly Flour and a radio personality, won the Democratic nomination without a runoff in a field of fourteen candidates for the governorship.

Other politicians of note in the twentieth century included Colonel E. M. House, adviser to President Woodrow Wilson; Sam Rayburn, speaker of the House of Representatives in Washington for many years; John N. Garner, vice-president from 1932 to 1940; Lyndon B. Johnson, president of the United States from 1963 to 1968; John B. Connally, Democratic governor of Texas from 1963 to 1969 and, after publicly becoming a Republican, a growing force in that party; and John G. Tower, a Republican elected to the United States Senate in 1961 and a widely known conservative.

The depression of the 1930s produced a sharp downturn in business in Texas, followed by the prosperity of World War II, when tens of thousands of troops trained in the Lone Star State. After the war the economy of Texas surged ahead on a wide front, especially in petroleum, petrochemicals, natural gas, manufacturing, and light industry. The National Aeronautics and Space Administration (NASA) located its headquarters near HOUSTON, while federal agencies, including many military installations, have brought additional income. Houston surged past the one million mark in population, while DALLAS and FORT WORTH increasingly grew together to form yet another major metropolitan complex.

Accompanying this growth have been the attendant problems of air and water pollution, urban blight, racial conflict, and a rising crime rate. Moreover, with the rapid influx of population from other states, Texas has lost much of its regional flavor. Yet the pioneer heritage can still be observed in the rural parts of the state.

See also MEXICAN-AMERICANS.

See Seymour V. Connor, *Texas: A History* (1971); Rupert N. Richardson et al., *Texas: The Lone Star State* (1970); *Texas: A Guide to the Lone Star State*, a WPA writers project (1969); and Walter P. Webb, ed., *Handbook of Texas*, 2 vols. (1952).—O. B. F.

Texas, annexation of. Desire for the annexation of Texas went back at least to the time of the Louisiana Purchase in 1803. In fact, for a quarter of a century and more before Jefferson's fortunate bargain there had

been a feeling of "our rising empire," a belief that the
United States—as successor to the titles under the colonial charters that had granted lands from sea to sea—
would itself reach from the Atlantic to the Pacific. Jefferson was not sanguine about the amount of time that
would be necessary to settle so vast a country and
thought that it might require a hundred generations. As
late as 1819, John Quincy Adams was seeking to press
his Spanish adversary, Luis de Onís, for as much territory as possible but found no support in the Monroe
cabinet for Texas at that time; even General Andrew
Jackson deemed possession of the Floridas much more
important than Texas. Within two years of the Adams-
Onís Treaty a flood of settlers began to cross the Sabine
under the aegis of Stephen F. AUSTIN, and by the end of
the 1820s Texas was virtually an American province
within Mexican suzerainty. By the time of the Texas
revolution of 1835-36 the Americans in Texas outnumbered the Mexicans ten to one.

The American government began in the 1820s to
make offers to Mexico to purchase Texas. President
Adams sought through Secretary of State Henry CLAY
to obtain the territory, albeit for the paltry price of a
million dollars and although Clay was ambivalent on the
issue. Clay argued quaintly with the Mexicans that if
they sold Texas to the United States the capital of Mexico would be situated nearer the center of the country.
President Jackson turned to a sharper diplomacy, and
his minister to Mexico City, Colonel Anthony Butler
(whom Jackson at one point denominated a "scamp"),
made persistent efforts to acquire Texas. He even proposed to Jackson that he bribe members of the Mexican
Congress, explaining, "I can assure you Sir that bribery
is not only common and familiar in all ranks and classes,
but familiarly and freely spoken of." Jackson, to his
credit, refrained from bribery, and when the opportunity came to annex Texas after the revolution he refrained
from that too, for he feared the effect of annexation
upon the slavery question, uneasily adjourned by the
Compromise of 1820. His successor, Martin Van Buren,
continued the Jacksonian policy, to the distress of the
Texans, who were forced to become an independent
country.

At last, however, the issue of annexation became so
popular that the government in Washington had to do
something about it. After the death of President William
Henry Harrison, the Virginian John Tyler succeeded to
the presidency, and when he came under the spell of
Secretary of State John C. Calhoun in 1844, he eagerly
sponsored a treaty of annexation. The Calhoun treaty
failed, not because of antislavery or proslavery agitation
but because the Senate split along partisan lines, with
southern Whigs voting against the treaty. There followed the presidential election of 1844, an election that
many students later would describe as turning on a
question of foreign affairs—the annexation of Texas. It
was a confused contest, as are most contests for the
American presidency, but the newly elected president,
James K. Polk, interpreted his victory as a mandate
requiring annexation. Meanwhile, Tyler, still in office,
arranged for and signed a joint congressional resolution
for annexing Texas on March 1, 1845. There followed a
period of weeks during which the Texans resolved formally upon joining the Union. Meanwhile the Mexican
minister in Washington, who had warned the govern-

ment that Mexico would consider annexation an act of
war, asked for and received his passport.

See E. C. Barker, *Mexico and Texas: 1821-1835* (1928);
William C. Binkley, *The Texan Revolution* (1952);
Frederick Merk, *Slavery and the Annexation of Texas*
(1972); David M. Pletcher, *The Diplomacy of Annexation:
Texas, Oregon, and the Mexican War* (1973); and Justin H.
Smith, *The Annexation of Texas* (1911).—R. H. F.

Texas and Pacific Railroad. The Texas and Pacific
Railroad connects Texarkana, Arkansas-Texas, with El
Paso in the west and Houston and San Antonio in the
south, via Dallas and Fort Worth. The line still maintains
the appearance of an independent railroad (in deference to the laws of Texas), although it has been an
integral part of the MISSOURI PACIFIC system since Jay
Gould gained control in 1882.

Chartered in 1857 to build twenty-three miles from
Swanson's Landing on Caddo Lake to Marshall in east-
central Texas, it made little progress until Thomas A.
SCOTT took it over and sought to make it a transcontinental extension of the Pennsylvania Railroad. Scott's
plans foundered with the Panic of 1873 and the Credit
Mobilier scandal of the same year. Collis P. HUNTING-
TON and the SOUTHERN PACIFIC reached El Paso from
the west before the Texas and Pacific in 1881, and
shortly thereafter Scott's leadership passed to Gould.

There is no history of the Texas and Pacific Railroad,
although Julius Grodinsky, *Transcontinental Railroad
Strategy* (1962) is a superb account of Scott's struggles
with Huntington and the federal government.—A. M.

Texas fever. Cattle disease. For many years cattlemen
in the West feared Texas fever (also called cattle tick
fever or red water fever), a disease in cattle characterized by high fever, red corpuscle destruction, enlarged spleen, and engorged liver. The disease frequently resulted in the animal's death.

The disease first came to the widespread attention of
cattlemen as the result of the movement of Texas cattle
northward across Missouri in the 1850s. For while the
disease caused only sickness in Texas cattle, it killed
northern cattle. To prevent the spread of the disease in
the northern Plains, several states passed quarantine
laws, and by 1886 these laws had made the free transit of
cattle difficult if not impossible. These quarantine laws
were a contributing factor in the death of the old open-
range cattle industry.

In 1890 Dr. Theobald Smith and Dr. F. L. Kelborne of
the Department of Agriculture linked the transmission
of the disease with infestations of cattle ticks, which were
later found to transmit the causative organism, *Babesa
bigemina*. It was found that the tick could be effectively
controlled by cattle-dipping. Study of this phenomenon
pointed the way to the solution of similar problems of
other diseases transmitted by parasites—including malaria, yellow fever, typhus, and Rocky Mountain spotted
fever.

See Edward E. Dale, *The Range Cattle Industry* (1960);
and John T. Schlebecker, *Cattle Raising on the Plains,
1900-1961* (1963).—R. B. W.

Texas Rangers. An organization of commissioned
state law-enforcement officers founded in the days of
the Texas revolution against Mexico and headquartered
in Austin. As early as 1826, in a meeting with Texas
colonist Stephen F. Austin, representatives from several
areas agreed to keep "twenty to thirty Rangers in service

all the time." The Rangers gained firmer status in 1835 when the Consultation (a body of fifty-eight Texans who met to determine what attitude and actions to adopt toward the regime established in Mexico by Antonio López de Santa Anna) approved a resolution creating a corps of Texas Rangers to be stationed on the Indian frontier in small scattered detachments.

The first group of Rangers consisted of "twenty-five Rangers whose business shall be to range and guard the frontier between the Brazos and Trinity rivers." Shortly the jurisdiction of the Rangers was extended westward to the Guadalupe River. The Rangers were an irregular body, mounted, but furnishing their own horses and arms; they had no surgeon, no flag, nor any of the other paraphernalia of a regular army or a state militia. Originally the Rangers were supposed to scout for, and defend against, Indians and—in the words of Acting Governor James W. Robinson—"the less merciful spear and ruthless sword of the descendants of Cortez, and his modern Goths and Vandals" (Mexicans, to be specific).

From 1836 to 1845 the Rangers played an important role in the defense of the Republic of Texas. Protecting settlers from Mexican raiders on the southwest and Plains Indians on the west and northwest, small bands of well-mounted and well-armed Rangers patrolled vast areas on the frontier. In 1840 the Rangers were prominent in victories over the Comanche in the Council House and the Plum Creek fights.

During this period Ranger leaders such as Ben McCulloch, W. A. A. "Big Foot" Wallace, and John Coffee Hays gained prominence. Hays was selected to organize and command a regiment of Rangers that served with Generals Zachary Taylor and Winfield Scott in the war with Mexico that erupted after Texas' entry into the Union in 1845.

Following the Civil War and Reconstruction, the organization was revived to help bring order to a lawless Texas frontier. Between 1874 and 1890 the Rangers, including such men as Leander McNelly, established an impressive record in pursuit, capture, and elimination of Indian raiders, outlaws, cattle thieves, bandit gangs, train and stage robbers, murderers, and feudists. Among those brought to justice by the Rangers in this period were such notorious outlaws as Sam Bass, King Fisher, and John Wesley Hardin.

Since 1890 the Rangers have maintained their tradi-·tion of swift and efficient law enforcement. Today each of the sixty-two Rangers is a highly trained criminal investigator, making use of the latest technological methods and the most modern equipment. However, when the situation demands, Texas Rangers still go into the brush on horseback in pursuit of wanted men.

In recent years the Rangers have often been criticized for preferring law and order to justice, especially in their treatment of chicanos. In the 1972 Texas gubernatorial race one candidate ran a strong though unsuccessful runoff campaign on a plank calling for abolition of the Rangers.

See Walter Prescott Webb, *The Texas Rangers: A Century of Frontier Defense* (1934; repr. 1965).—J. B. F.

Thames, battle of the (1813). The western division of the United States militia forces that fought in the battle of the Thames on October 5, 1813, was under the command of General William Henry Harrison, who succeeded General James Winchester to that post. Follow-

ing the horrible debacle of Frenchtown on the Raisin in January of that year, in which British forces massacred Harrison's, Harrison gathered substantial reinforcements from Ohio, Kentucky, and Indiana and concentrated them about the Maumee Rapids, fifteen miles from the shore of Lake Erie. Early in May the Americans at Fort Meigs were placed under light siege by British General Henry Proctor, but he veered off to attack Fort Stephenson, which was under the command of George Croghan, a nephew of George Rogers Clark. The cocky Croghan held his fort and left Proctor partially defeated.

The success of Fort Stephenson was a turning point in the Northwest campaign. By the latter part of September, Harrison's command was greatly enlarged and strengthened by the arrival of Kentucky militiamen commanded by Governor Isaac Shelby, Richard M. Johnson, William Whitley, and General Green Clay. On September 10, Oliver Hazard Perry's miniature fleet had defeated the British in a naval engagement in Put-in-Bay, thus removing heavy pressure from the land forces. Harrison, however, was faced with the difficult problem of moving his army of five thousand men from Put-in-Bay to Bass Island, and then past Detroit. Ahead of his advance, General Proctor and Tecumseh were withdrawing slowly into Canada. On September 28 Harrison began his major drive toward Fort Malden and the River Raisin. The American army reached the scene of the Raisin massacre and saw there some of the skeletons of the troops slaughtered earlier that year. Richard M. Johnson and his mounted riflemen entered Detroit, and then crossed the river to act as scouts ahead of Harrison's forces.

The Americans learned from a British deserter that Proctor was encamped about fifteen miles up the Thames River with approximately seven hundred regulars and twelve hundred Indians. By daybreak, October 3, the Americans were advancing up the winding stream from the mouth of the river at Lake St. Clair. By nightfall they had advanced ten miles, and in early dawn the following day began a forced drive to overtake the enemy. The first contact came at noon on October 4, at the forks of the Thames, and by this time the Americans were in position to engage the British and Indians in full force. Early in the morning of October 5, Richard M. Johnson and Major Suggett with a party of spies came in sight of the British at Moraviantown. Tecumseh had persuaded the vacillating Proctor to stand and fight, threatening to take his Indians and leave otherwise.

The terrain along the Thames was a difficult one over which to deploy troops, especially because of the serpentine nature of the streams. Although both Proctor and Harrison suffered from this fact, Proctor was at a greater disadvantage. He had discarded his artillery and had placed his troops badly in the woods along the river. The main fighting in the battle of the Thames occurred at dawn. In the fighting Richard M. Johnson led a spectacular mounted charge (known afterward as the "Forlorn Hope") into the bush to draw the fire of Tecumseh's braves and succeeded in breaking the British lines. Tecumseh was killed early in the fight and this broke the back of Indian resistance; the fight against the Indians lasted a little over half an hour. Proctor's troops fired only two volleys before they surrendered. Proctor himself had fled the field in a coach as soon as the fight began, tossing away his luggage to gain speed.

The battle of the Thames was of minor military significance, but it had far greater political meaning because it destroyed British and Indian resistance in the Northwest. Like other frontier engagements, this one generated a generous crop of heroes who used their participation in the battle of the Thames to good political advantage in later years.

See Dorothy Burne Goebel, *William Henry Harrison: A Political Biography* (1926); Leland W. Meyer, *Life and Times of Colonel Richard M. Johnson . . . of Kentucky* (1932); and Bennett H. Young, *The Battle of the Thames* (1903).—T. D. C.

theater. Almost as soon as white settlers crossed the Appalachian Mountains—shortly after the American Revolution—theater began in the West. During the next century the westward movement, as it surged to the Pacific Ocean and then filled in various areas bypassed in the quest for quick wealth, carried along the cultural baggage of Anglo-American pioneers. Despite Puritan strictures against playacting, the theater was a popular form of entertainment on most of the frontier. When theaters served communities still in the frontier stage of development, they usually reflected the artistic or commercial interests of such exporting theatrical centers as New York, Philadelphia, New Orleans, and Charleston. Only after the frontier passed did drama in the trans-Appalachian West lose its derivative, imitative quality and begin to make its own contributions to American culture.

New Orleans claims title to the first professional theater in the West, just as it boasts the first opera produced in America. Since both date from the 1790s, when French was the city's major language, they obviously reflected Gallic rather than Anglo-American tastes. After Louisiana became American in 1803, New Orleans continued as an artistic center, exporting drama and opera to other parts of the country. Kentucky, the initial trans-Appalachian area to be settled, had the first English-speaking theater. In the early 1790s, there were amateur performances in Washington and Lexington, Kentucky, the latter involving students at Transylvania University. By 1810 the professional theater had played in Louisville, Frankfort, and Lexington; but with the importation of Samuel Drake's troupe of actors from Albany, New York, in 1815, the drama truly took root in western soil. En route to Kentucky, this company stopped in Pittsburgh and gave that city its first professional season, from August until November. They played Frankfort from December until March and then spent ten weeks in Louisville. That these small towns (Louisville numbering only three thousand) supported seasons of such length testified to their active interest in theater.

One of the players, Noah M. Ludlow, persuaded other actors to leave Drake's troupe and form their own in 1817. With a fair amount of success they played the river towns—Nashville, Cincinnati, Natchez, and New Orleans. Their stop at Natchez was the first professional drama for that city, and their four-month season (December 1817 to April 1818) at the St. Philip Street Theater in New Orleans gave the Crescent City its first English-language drama. Despite hostility toward English

speakers, the city reacted favorably toward Ludlow's productions.

Amateur drama began in St. Louis in 1815, with the courthouse serving as the theater. Three years later a small professional company, led by Mr. and Mrs. William A. Turner, English actors, played six months for the two thousand inhabitants of the town. The interest the Turners kindled resulted in the building of a theater by the citizens in 1819. The following year Ludlow's traveling players ensconced themselves there. Hard upon their heels came their parent company, headed by Samuel Drake. Drake's superior troupe forced Ludlow to join forces, but in 1824 Ludlow formed another company to tour Tennessee and Alabama. While in Alabama, he built Mobile's first playhouse.

For three years before forming this company, Ludlow was associated with one of the great names in New Orleans' theatrical history, James H. Caldwell. Caldwell built two of the finest theaters the city had seen: the Camp Street Theater (1824), the first structure in the city to be lighted by gas, and the St. Charles Street Theater (1835), the largest in the country at the time, accommodating between four and five thousand. Caldwell thought himself responsible for providing entertainment for the English-speaking population of New Orleans, who were still resented by the Creoles. He did this by presenting plays and operas in English, as well as importing Italian opera troupes. The Anglo-Americans may not have understood Italian, but at least it was not the French of their detractors! Caldwell held center stage in New Orleans' theatrical life until his retirement in 1843.

While New Orleans had attained the status of a mature artistic metropolis, Chicago was still a sprawling village. In 1833 it experienced its first professional theater when some actors performed in the dining room of the Sauganash Hotel. This practice of presenting plays in large rooms of hotels, above stores and saloons, or on other improvised stages was common until towns attained sufficient maturity to build playhouses as such. John B. Rice erected Chicago's first theater in 1847.

Among the famous theatrical personalities who toured the western circuit in the early days were the celebrated Irish actor Tyrone Power; George Vandenhoff; J. B. Buckstone; Charlotte Cushman; Fanny Fitzwilliam; Charles Kean and his wife, Ellen Tree Kean; William C. Macready; Mr. and Mrs. George P. Farren; Julia Dean, granddaughter of Samuel Drake; and Joseph Jefferson II.

After the Mexican War added a vast new domain to the United States in 1848, the frontier immediately leapt to the Pacific. As American troops occupied military posts once held by Mexicans, they gave California its first experience with English-speaking theater. These plays and minstrel shows probably did little to elevate the cultural level of the Far West frontier, but they demonstrated that the theater was an accustomed part of American life. In California, as at isolated army posts throughout the West, soldiers were so eager for entertainment that they usually took the female parts, although they doubtless had more difficulty creating the illusion of femininity than did the boy-players of Shakespeare's stage.

Appropriately, California's first English-language drama was Benjamin Webster's *The Golden Farmer*, presented at Sonoma in 1847. With the gold rush in 1849, professional theater arrived in California. Sacramento claimed the first structure designed specifically as a playhouse, the Eagle Theater. Its first production on October 18, 1849, was *The Bandit Chief; or, the Forest Spectre.* Costing $75,000 and seating only four hundred, the crude frame building reflected the inflated conditions of the time. The theater lacked ventilation and elevation. Rain would flood the floor, and the rising Sacramento River often made the audience perch atop the benches. This first playhouse lasted only two and a half months, and the building was used for other purposes.

However flimsy and short-lived the playhouses, professional drama had come to California to stay. In San Francisco and nearby mining camps, an eager and affluent audience proved a magnet for actors and producers. One of the first entrepreneurs to capitalize on San Francisco's boom was Thomas Maguire, who built the Jenny Lind Theater—although she never set foot in California. Shakespeare and Sheridan held great attraction for the miners. Maguire imported Junius Brutus Booth to act and manage his theater in 1852. Booth brought along his nineteen-year-old son Edwin, who developed his art by playing a great variety of roles in the West. The 1850s also saw the famous rivalry for popularity between entertainers Lola MONTEZ and Caroline Chapman in San Francisco, as well as the emergence of Lotta Crabtree. As a child Crabtree toured the crude mining camps of northern California, returning to San Francisco in 1859 as a star of variety shows. She then spent a few years in New York, developing her acting talent, and in 1869 triumphantly returned to San Francisco's new California Theater, built by William C. Ralston.

When the Mormon settlement around the Great Salt Lake became part of the United States after the Mexican War, the western frontier gained not only a religious but a theatrical citadel. While in Nauvoo, Illinois, in the early 1840s, the Latter-day Saints had a theater and staged elaborate pageants. As soon as they gained the bare necessities around Salt Lake, they revived drama as a wholesome form of entertainment and recreation. In 1850 the Deseret Dramatic Association outfitted a crude structure as a theater, calling it the Old Bowery. A more commodious playhouse, Bowring's Theater, was built in 1859. There the Latter-day Saints presented such standard works as the Kotzebue-Sheridan *Pizarro* and Shakespeare's *Othello.* Brigham Young decided that the Saints should have a first-class theater and work began in July 1861. When finished in March 1862, the Salt Lake Theater was the best in the West. Costing $100,000 and built along Doric lines, it seated 1,500. Young ascertained that if actors were treated with respect—were given good facilities—their image would be elevated in the public's mind. This was necessary if the theater was to be reformed. Also, good facilities would attract first-rate artists. To encourage the development of drama as wholesome entertainment, he put his daughters on the stage.

Julia Dean arrived in Salt Lake City by stagecoach from California in 1865 to play Camille. She brought an entire company with her, including George B. Waldron as Armond. The Saints were so taken with Dean and Waldron that they engaged them immediately for the entire season at the Salt Lake Theater. The remainder of Dean's company carried on in an improvised theater but could not compete with its stars in popularity. Dean stayed for a year, presenting her repertory of modern and classic plays. For decades great actors delighted in playing Salt Lake, for the audiences were knowledgeable and the theater one of the best in the nation. A great favorite was Maude Adams, a native of Salt Lake City, who was to become inseparably linked with the role of Peter Pan.

In contrast to the substantial theaters and productions of San Francisco and Salt Lake City, most of the mining towns and cow towns were content with far less—both in the way of buildings and presentations. Most of the structures were called opera houses, although little if any opera was ever heard in them. The frontier communities thought that an opera house automatically bestowed class and status. Although Virginia City, Nevada, had the Piper Opera House (also built by Thomas Maguire) and Deadwood, Dakota, had its Gem Theater, most of the mining town theaters were adjuncts of saloons, such as the Bird Cage in Tombstone, Arizona. These frontier theaters, whether improvised or permanent, provided entertainment—often of amazingly high quality—for lonely, well-heeled men. Miners probably clutched at any form of entertainment and were willing to take the classics along with variety shows just to have some diversion. But the fact that quality entertainment proved popular season after season indicates that the classics communicated with diverse audiences. Shakespeare was produced wherever players went, and the tragedies proved most popular. Gilbert and Sullivan's *The Mikado* ran for 130 nights at the Gem in Deadwood. David Belasco acted in Virginia City for two years (1872-74), and Edwin Booth came to maturity as an actor on the frontier. Hardly any frontier theater missed the spectacle of Adah Isaacs Menken, strapped half-naked to the back of a raging stallion, in her famous vehicle *Mazeppa.*

By the 1830s American playwrights were dealing with the frontier character and experience. The main figure in James K. Paulding's *The Lion of the West* (1831) was Nimrod Wildfire. This "yellow flower of the forest" and "human cataract for Kentucky" was full of bluster and tall tales. T. B. De Walden's *Kit the Arkansas Traveler* (1870) celebrated the rugged character of pioneers in the trans-Mississippi West. *Davy Crockett* (1872), by Frank H. Murdoch, glorified the great Tennessee hunter and congressman. The play was immensely popular throughout the country, with Frank Mayo making the part his own, much as Joseph Jefferson III did with Rip Van Winkle. Bret Harte and Mark Twain collaborated on *Ah Sin* (1877), the drama of a Chinaman in San Francisco. The cast of characters included miners, and the script evoked local color. Joaquin Miller treated the theme of Mormon vengeance in *The Danites of the Sierras* (1877), a play popular for years.

An obvious link between the western theater of frontier times and the present is the Central City Opera House. Built during the mining bonanza of Colorado in 1878, the theater featured most of the great players of the period. With the collapse of silver, the theater closed and Central City became a ghost town. Despite the fact that 1932 was not a particularly propitious time, drama lovers in Denver and the surrounding area reopened

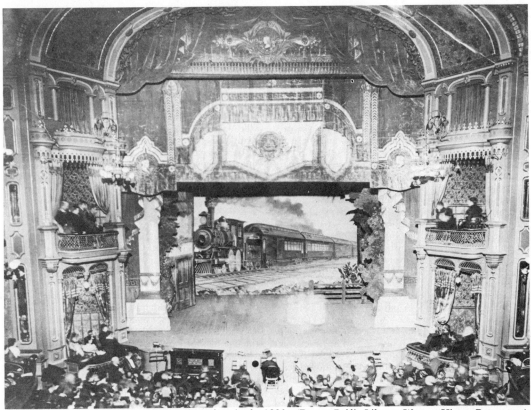

The Salt Lake Theater, built in 1861, is shown here in the 1890s. (Denver Public Library, Western History Department)

the opera house with *Camille*, starring Lillian Gish. Following summers saw such productions as *The Merry Widow*, with Gladys Swarthout and Richard Bonelli; *Othello*, with Walter Huston; *A Doll's House*, with Ruth Gordon; and Mae West's *Diamond Lil*. In recent years, the theater—true to its name—has presented more opera than plays.

When Hollywood was the center of the motion-picture industry, the legitimate theater in the surrounding area benefited. Actors not immediately employed in films often kept their skills intact by working, both as players and teachers, in such theaters as the Pasadena Playhouse.

Among the most creative forces in the American theater have been university experimental dramatic groups. The University of Washington pioneered in 1940 with the first theater built specifically for arena productions, a style that has been copied extensively by commercial and other academic theaters. Another notable theatrical offering of the West Coast is the summer Shakespeare festival at Ashland, Oregon.

In the central part of the country, both Houston and Dallas have made notable contributions to the theater. The Alley Theater in Houston, directed by Nina Vance, has mounted arena productions for more than two decades. They have reflected the typical fare of the American theater—experimental plays, Broadway offerings, and the classics. During the 1940s and 1950s the Margo

Jones Theater of Dallas was among the most creative forces in the field of drama. Miss Jones actively sought new playwriting talent and presented the premieres of *Inherit the Wind*, by Jerome Lawrence and Robert E. Lee, and *Summer and Smoke*, by Tennessee Williams. Shortly after her death, the theater folded. In 1959 the Dallas Theater Center, the only theater designed by Frank Lloyd Wright, opened with Paul Baker as director. One of the most exciting repertory theaters today lies on the western banks of the Mississippi—the Tyrone Guthrie Theater in Minneapolis. Guided by imaginative directors, this company presents drama of high quality. Such a theater preserves the true vitality of the American stage, since it is not limited by the financial strictures incumbent upon Broadway productions.

The most comprehensive survey is Glenn Hughes, *A History of the American Theater, 1700-1950* (1951). Barnard Hewitt, *Theatre U.S.A., 1668-1957* (1959), combines narrative with documents. James H. Dormon, Jr., *Theater in the Ante Bellum South, 1815-1861* (1967), is an exemplary monograph.—W. R.

Thompson, Benjamin F. (1842-1884). Gambler and gunman. Born in England, Thompson was raised in Austin, Texas, where he attended school and worked as an apprentice for a local newspaper. In 1858 he wounded a Negro youth in a petty quarrel. The courts, pressed to take action against Thompson by local citizens, convicted him of aggravated assault. Thompson had served a short jail sentence and paid a part of his fine when the governor intervened on his behalf and secured his release. Two years later he quit Austin for New Orleans and a job as a typesetter. He was soon attracted to the more exciting world of the gambler, and there are dramatic, but apparently apocryphal, stories of shooting incidents involving him.

Thompson served in the Confederate army during the Civil War. His career was undistinguished, although he appears to have fought his comrades in gray with great frequency. His record during the war was frequently marked with personal quarrels, and there are reports of several shootings. Along with other Confederate expatriates, Thompson then became a mercenary in the army of Maximilian, emperor of Mexico and puppet of France's Louis Napoleon. By the time Thompson left Mexico a few jumps ahead of supporters of revolutionary leader Benito Juarez, his reputation as a mankiller was well established.

In 1868 Ben helped his brother Billy escape from Texas to Indian Territory after Billy killed a man in a brothel. It was the first of several efforts in Billy's behalf. Later the same year Ben killed his wife's brother and was sent to prison. He was pardoned in 1870 and, upon his release, moved to Abilene, Kansas, where he operated the Bull's Head Saloon in partnership with Phil Coe during Abilene's heyday as a cow town. In 1871 Coe was killed in a gunfight by Wild Bill Hickok. Ben was out of town at the time visiting his family, and he never went back to Abilene. The following year he joined Billy in Ellsworth, Kansas, where he gambled and enjoyed great popularity among the Texas cattlemen who frequented the town. There, in 1873, the Thompson brothers became involved in a conflict with a local policeman named "Happy Jack" Morco. When Morco intervened in one of their gambling disputes, a violent confrontation seemed inevitable, and Sheriff Chauncey B. Whitney attempted to placate Ben and Billy. He appeared to be successful in smoothing the incident over, but as he walked across the street with the Thompsons, drunken Billy suddenly shot him as Ben watched helplessly. Once again Ben came to Billy's rescue. Backed by a large group of Texas cowboys, Ben completely cowed the police force until Billy was safely out of town. By the time Billy stood trial for murder in 1877, the years had softened the memory and blurred the evidence. It cost Ben a lot of money, but Billy was acquitted.

Ben shifted his operations to Wichita briefly and spent most of the 1870s in and out of Dodge City. In 1879 he and Bat Masterson were among the gunmen hired by the Santa Fe Railroad in the right-of-way war for Royal Gorge. When that adventure was over, Thompson gambled in various Colorado mining camps and returned to Austin in time to run, unsuccessfully, for marshal. With money earned while working for the Santa Fe Railroad, he invested in a chain of gambling houses in Texas and grew prosperous. In 1880 he ran for marshal of Austin again, and this time he was elected.

Thompson was an efficient marshal, but in August 1882 he resigned as a result of a gunfight that proved to be his ultimate undoing.

In 1880 he had incurred the bitter enmity of a trio of San Antonio gamblers, Joseph C. Foster, Jack Harris, and William H. Simms, in a quarrel over a gambling debt Thompson allegedly owed Foster. In 1882, while visiting San Antonio, Thompson killed Harris in a gunfight that was directly connected to the quarrel. The death of Harris deepened the hatred between Thompson and Foster. In March 1884, Thompson met John King Fisher, a noted Texas gunfighter, in Austin, and the two men began drinking heavily. Fisher was going home to Uvalde County, and he persuaded Thompson to ride as far as San Antonio with him. Somehow news of their coming reached Foster and Simms at the Vaudeville Variety Theatre. Both Thompson and Fisher were drunk when their train arrived in San Antonio, and Fisher apparently decided to become peacemaker in the quarrel between Thompson and Foster. Fisher persuaded Thompson to go to the Vaudeville. There they confronted Foster and Simms in a tense, angry exchange, followed by an outburst of gunfire. Thompson and Fisher were killed, shot down by hidden accomplices of Foster and Simms.

See Floyd B. Streeter, *Ben Thompson: Man with a Gun* (1957). An older account, written by a friend of Thompson, is William M. Walton, *Life and Adventures of Ben Thompson* (1884).—G. L. R.

Thompson, David (1770-1857). Fur trader, surveyor, and explorer. Thompson, who has been called one of the greatest practical land geographers of all time, was born in Westminster, England, of pious Welsh parents. Although trained in mathematics at a London school, at the age of fourteen Thompson was apprenticed to the Hudson's Bay Company and sent to Canada. The short, serious, pug-nosed youth picked up the rudiments of astronomy from a company surveyor, while pursuing a vigorous career of trading, surveying, mapmaking, and journal keeping.

While still in his teens Thompson mapped the vast regions west and southwest of his base on Hudson's Bay. He was one of the first whites to deal with the Piegan, Blackfoot, and other Indian tribes living in the borderlands between Montana and Canada and may have supplied some tribes with their first firearms. His journal record of interviews with these and other Indian tribes constitutes the first sure knowledge we have of their lifeways. In 1797 Thompson left the Hudson's Bay Company to work for the North West Company until his retirement from the field in 1812. During this time he crossed the Rocky Mountains via the Saskatchewan River, explored the Columbia River from its source to its mouth, arriving there just after the Americans built Fort Astoria. He himself established the first fur posts in present-day Idaho and western Montana. On other expeditions he ranged as far south as the Mandan villages on the Missouri and east to survey most of the shoreline of Lake Superior. Among his other accomplishments he demonstrated the relations of the streams of the central Canadian plains to the Missouri River.

From 1817 to 1827 he was a member of the British Boundary Commission, which marked the border between Canada and the United States from the St. Lawrence to the Lake of the Woods. Though Thompson's career was largely devoted to the expansion of the Canadian fur trade, his explorations affected the history of the Oregon country by strengthening Britain's claim to the Pacific Northwest.

In 1812 Thompson and his half-breed wife and family settled in Montreal. There he produced a huge map of the western country but was unable to get it published. He also kept a journal, but it, too, remained unpublished until this century. Family troubles eventually dissipated his small fortune; illness and age virtually blinded him, and he died in obscure poverty at the age of eighty-seven.

Thompson's achievements were rediscovered in the 1880s by Joseph B. Tyrell, who found the valuable map and journal while engaged in a geological survey of Canada. He soon realized that the celebrated geographer Aaron Arrowsmith of London had used Thompson's findings (sent in by the Hudson's Bay Company) to draw his own map of North America without giving Thompson credit. Some of Thompson's discoveries were on the Arrowsmith map, which Jefferson used to plan the Lewis and Clark expedition.

In 1916 Tyrell edited and published *David Thompson's Narrative of His Explorations in Western America, 1784-1812,* which is also to be found in Richard Glover, ed., *David Thompson's Narrative, 1784-1812* (1962). —G. B. D.

Thompson, Jacob (1810-1885). Mississippi politician. Born in North Carolina, Thompson graduated from the University of North Carolina at Chapel Hill and remained there for eighteen months as a tutor. In 1835 he moved to Pontotoc, Mississippi, a booming town in the heart of lands that had belonged to the Chickasaw Indians until they had been forced to leave in 1832 to make way for white settlement. He established a very successful law practice there chiefly concerned with land titles and conveyances, purchased some cheap and fertile land in the vicinity of Oxford, Mississippi, and married the daughter of a wealthy planter of the area. Thompson extended his holdings and soon became a wealthy planter. Unlike most southerners who were wealthy in 1860, Thompson was able to retain his property through the era of the war and Reconstruction. His wealth at the time of his death has been estimated to have been more than $500,000.

Thompson became one of the leaders of the newly created counties in northern Mississippi and served six terms (1839-51) in the House of Representatives, where he was active on the Public Lands and Indian Affairs committees. Because he was an active leader of the states' rights wing of the Democratic party in the 1850s, President James Buchanan appointed him secretary of the interior in 1857. He seems to have had considerable influence over Buchanan. He resigned from the cabinet on January 8, 1861, after the *Star of the West* had been sent to Fort Sumter.

During the Civil War Thompson served in the Confederate army until the fall of Vicksburg, was elected to the state legislature in 1863, and became a secret agent of the Confederacy in Canada in 1864. He did not return to the United States until 1868, when he settled in Memphis, Tennessee.

See William C. Davis, "The Conduct of 'Mr. Thompson'," *Civil War Times Illustrated* (1970).—J. E. G.

Thoreau, Henry David (1817-1862). Writer and naturalist. The ideas of Thoreau underlie many subsequent American interpretations of the significance of nature. A Transcendentalist, Thoreau believed that the natural world symbolizes, or reflects, spiritual truths and moral laws. From July 4, 1845, to September 6, 1847, Thoreau lived in a cabin of his own making at Walden Pond near Concord, Massachusetts. The experiment, which later became the basis for Thoreau's best-known book, *Walden* (1854), was intended to shed light on the possibility of finding an optimum balance between nature and civilization. "I would not," he explained, "have . . . every part of a man cultivated, any more than I would have every acre of earth."

Wildness, Thoreau felt, is both a physical and intellectual tonic that braces civilization. It possesses a fertilizing vitality that civilized men need for strength and creativity. This idea influenced Thoreau's thinking about the American West. Using the concept of the West chiefly as a metaphor (Thoreau rarely left New England), he declared that "eastward I go only by force; but westward I go free. . . . I must walk toward Oregon, and not toward Europe. And that is the way the nation is moving, and I may say that mankind progresses from east to west." For Thoreau the East was history, and the West, the future: "The West of which I speak is but another name for the Wild; and what I have been preparing to say is, that in Wildness is the preservation of the World."

Sherman Paul, *The Shores of America: Thoreau's Inward Exploration* (1959), is the best of many books on Thoreau. See Roderick Nash, *Wilderness and the American Mind* (1967), for a discussion of Thoreau's attitude toward wilderness.—R. N.

Thorpe, Thomas Bangs (1815-1878). Short-story writer and painter. Thorpe, the most versatile of the humorists of the Old Southwest, was actually born in Massachusetts and spent most of his early life in Albany and New York City. In 1834 he matriculated at Wesleyan University in Middletown, Connecticut, but ill health forced him to withdraw in 1836. For reasons of health, he went south in the winter of 1836-37, taking up residence in Louisiana. He remained there until 1854, when he moved back to New York. He lived in New York City until his death except for a brief interval between 1862 and 1864, when he returned temporarily to Louisiana with the Union army.

During his adolescence in New York City Thorpe had determined to become a painter, apprenticing himself to the American artist John Quidor. He exhibited at the American Academy in 1833, but he was never successful as an artist, and, though he painted desultorily for the remainder of his life, he turned increasingly to writing and newspaper work. His first story, "Tim Owen, the Bee-Hunter," appeared in 1839, and its success encouraged him to continue his literary career. His most famous story, "The Big Bear of Arkansas," appeared in 1841, and it is for this tale that he is primarily remembered today. The story is ostensibly a hunting story, a tall tale told by a backwoodsman about his pursuit of a gigantic bear. The tale soon escapes from this conventional mold, however, to develop into an almost archetypal hunting story in which the pursuit takes on mythical attributes and the bear itself—which the backwoodsman refers to as a "devil"—becomes a type of supernatural evil.

Thorpe briefly accompanied Zachary Taylor's army in the Mexican War and wrote two accounts of this conflict, *Our Army on the Rio Grande* (1846) and *Our Army at Monterey* (1847). These were accompanied by *The Taylor Anecdote Book* (1848), a collection of Mexican War stories that were put to good use by the Whigs in

Taylor's successful campaign for president. Thorpe also wrote *The Master's House* (1854), an interesting novel of southern life. It is not ultimately successful, however, partly because of Thorpe's own ambiguity toward the South and partly because his talent really lay in shorter forms. He wrote extensively for periodicals, and these shorter sketches fall broadly into four not totally separable categories: sentimental nature pictures; anecdotes of southern life and character; hunting stories; and humorous tall tales. It is for his hunting stories and tall tales that he is best remembered. A representative sampling of his shorter work may be found in his two collections, *The Mysteries of the Backwoods* (1846) and *The Hive of "The Bee-Hunter"* (1854).

See Milton Rickels, *Thomas Bangs Thorpe, Humorist of the Old Southwest* (1962); and Willard Thorpe, *American Humorists* (1964).—J. K. F.

Thwaites, Reuben Gold (1853-1913). Historian. A biographical essay on Thwaites, published a few months after his death, described him as "one of the most industrious and lovable historians of Western America." The adjective "lovable" can be taken on faith, but "industrious" is well substantiated by the record. However, more than industriousness is required to edit and write 183 volumes in a short lifetime; the word "genius" might be more apt, even though he never produced a single volume that would give him rank with historians of the order of Thucydides, Gibbon, Ranke, or Parkman. Among his edited works are seventy-three volumes of *Jesuit Relations* (1896-1901), thirty-two volumes of *Early Western Travels* (1904-07), and eight volumes of the *Original Journals of the Lewis and Clark Expedition* (1904-07). He also edited ten volumes for the Wisconsin Historical Commission and twenty-six volumes of Wisconsin Historical Society *Proceedings*. He was author of fifteen biographies, monographs, and texts on American history.

Thwaites was born a few months after the inauguration of President Franklin Pierce to parents who only recently had migrated from England to Dorchester, Massachusetts. The family soon moved to a farm in Wisconsin, and by his twentieth birthday the future historian had already acquired the equivalent of a college education, taught school, and worked on the staff of the Oshkosh *Times*. One year later he enrolled at Yale University to study English literature and history and to work part-time as a newspaper correspondent.

Returning home in 1876, Thwaites became managing editor of the *Wisconsin State Journal* in Madison. There his interest in history drew him frequently to the rooms of the State Historical Society and into friendship with Lyman C. Draper. In 1886 he succeeded Draper as secretary of the society and quickly applied efficient and advanced business methods to the management of the library and museum. His approach to editing manuscripts resembled an assembly-line technique, although he personally selected and edited the material for the documentary works and wrote and rewrote the drafts of his books. He also employed professional bibliographers and translators as assistants and emphasized specialization among his staff.

Thwaites enjoyed the out-of-doors, field trips in search of manuscripts to add to the famous Draper Collection, public speaking, and the companionship of

Frederick Jackson Turner and other scholarly and public figures. His interests were catholic and his organizing abilities enormous. Aside from the numerous local historical societies, museums, and community libraries he launched throughout Wisconsin, he also founded on a national scale what is presently known as the American Association for State and Local History.

See Clarence W. Alvord, "A Critical Analysis of the Work of Reuben Gold Thwaites," *Proceedings* of the Mississippi Valley Historical Association (1913-14); and Clifford L. Lord, "Reuben Gold Thwaites, 1853-1913," *Arizona and the West* (Spring 1967).—W. E. H.

Tijerina, Reies [Lopez] (1926-   ). Chicano rural leader. The son of a sharecropper, Tijerina was born near Fall City, Texas, one of ten children. His mother died when he was six years old, and the family then turned to migrant labor. Tijerina began working in the fields at the age of seven. For five years the family migrated to Michigan, spending winters around San Antonio. During this period Tijerina spent short times in about twenty rural schools that were segregated and close to migrant camps.

As a child, Tijerina was a deeply religious Catholic. At age eighteen he enrolled at the Assembly of God Bible Institute in Ysleta, Texas; but, although he spent three years there, he did not graduate. After leaving the Bible Institute, Tijerina married Mary Escobar, who had been a fellow student. An evangelist around Santa Fe, New Mexico, he was known for his persuasive oratory and fiery rhetoric. In 1947 Tijerina walked from Illinois to Texas to demonstrate his religious commitment. A Pentecostal preacher during this time, his ministerial credentials were revoked in 1950. Nonetheless, he continued preaching without a denomination or congregation. While traveling through the Southwest, Louisiana, Michigan, and New York, he published several sermons and biblical commentaries under the title *Hallera Fe en la Tierra?* Increasingly concerned with political and social justice, Tijerina in the 1950s turned away from his religious vocation. By the end of the decade, he was a committed activist, concerned with the century-old question of the Spanish and Mexican land grants in New Mexico.

Tijerina in the early 1950s bought 160 acres in the Arizona desert, where he started a settlement called Valle de Paz. Inhabited primarily by workers in the nearby cotton fields, the community was disbanded after prolonged harassment from the citizens of nearby Pete's Corner. On March 19, 1957, Tijerina was charged with two counts of grand theft, which he successfully evaded by exceeding Arizona's statute of limitations. During this time—he termed himself a "fugitive"—he hid in Texas and then went to Mexico in 1958-59 to investigate titles and other documents concerning the New Mexico land grants. He returned to Mexico to continue his search in 1960. The same year, he drove from Texas to New Mexico with seven carloads of his followers to settle. He lived in Albuquerque and worked as a janitor until late 1962, organizing without publicity a new movement. The movement was organized formally on February 2, 1963, when Tijerina and thirty-seven of his followers voted to incorporate as the Alianza Federal de Mercedes (Federal Alliance of Land Grants). The Alianza sought to restore granted land—presumably protected under the Treaty of Guadalupe Hidalgo—to the heirs of the original grantees.

Adapting his "Pentecostal" rhetoric to the new cause, Tijerina sought funds, national recognition, and federal support for the Alianza. He traveled to Washington to meet with Attorney General Robert Kennedy and by 1964 had received the endorsement of congressmen Henry B. Gonzalez and Edward R. Roybal and Senator Joseph M. Montoya for an investigation into the legal rights of heirs of land grants.

By the time of the third annual meeting of the Alianza in September 1965, the Alianza claimed fourteen thousand followers. In mid-1966 Tijerina led a sixty-mile protest march from Albuquerque to Santa Fe, where he presented his arguments to Governor Jack Campbell. To generate moral support and to gain prominence for the Alianza, Tijerina sought to align himself with black organizations and leaders across the country; in 1967, at the fifth annual convention of the Alianza, urban black and Chicano leaders were present to support the rural land-grant movement. Shortly thereafter, Tijerina's legal problems began anew. In October he was arraigned on charges stemming from the "occupation" of the Echo Amphitheater in Rio Arriba County, for assaulting forest rangers, and for damaging federal property. Tijerina claimed that this national campground was part of the nineteenth-century land grant of San Joaquin del Rio de Chama.

After meeting with the new governor of New Mexico, David Cargo, whose election was attributed partly to the support of rural, north-central New Mexico, Tijerina focused his land-grant campaign on the Tierra Amarilla grant of 1832. On May 14, 1967, during a rally in Tierra Amarilla, Tijerina formed a governing council consisting of heirs of the grant. As a legal maneuver, Tijerina resigned as president of the Alianza, which was officially disbanded and reorganized as the Alianza de Pueblos Libres (Confederation of Free City States). After the arrest of several Alianza members on June 4, the highly publicized raid of the Tierra Amarilla Court House occurred. Tijerina allegedly took part, and a week-long search for him involving the governor, National Guard, and state police was begun. In November 1968, representing himself during his trial for kidnapping, false imprisonment, and assault of the jail, Tijerina maintained that the raid had been a "justified citizen's arrest" that had been planned to be carried out nonviolently. He was acquitted of all three charges but was convicted in the spring of 1969 for his attempted "citizen's arrest" of Governor Cargo and Chief Justice of the Supreme Court Warren Burger.

In 1968, after meeting with Martin Luther King, Jr., Tijerina became the southwestern coordinator for King's multiracial Poor People's Campaign. But in Washington, in May 1968, he charged that blacks had taken over the campaign, discriminating against Chicanos. Nonetheless, his actions in New Mexico had gained him the respect of many militant blacks as well as such Chicanos as "Corky" Gonzales. Conversely, he had confused and distressed many middle-class Spanish-Americans in New Mexico, who thought the legal question of the land grants had been settled many years earlier. Tijerina considered himself a leader of the "new breed," which for a time he called "Indo-Hispano" to suggest their mixed Spanish and Indian cultural heritage. He envisioned a role for the brown race in mediating the conflicts between white and black.

Peter Nabokov was a witness to the public and some private events surrounding the Tierra Amarilla raid and wrote a sympathetic account of it in *Tijerina and the Court House Raid* (1969). A recorded interview with Tijerina is reported in *New Republic* (July 1968), by George W. Grayson, Jr.—J. R. V.

Tilghman, William Matthew, Jr. (1854-1924). Lawman. "Uncle Billy" Tilghman's career as a lawman in Kansas and Oklahoma spanned more than four decades and won him a reputation as a fair and honest man, one of the best of the old-time lawmen. He was born in Fort Dodge, Iowa, but he grew up near Atchison, Kansas. In 1870 he ventured west to the real frontier for the first time, and for the next several years he worked as a buffalo hunter. In 1874 he fell in with a disreputable crowd that included such notable frontier scalawags as Hurricane Bill Martin and Dutch Henry Borne. It was a wild spring and summer, stealing horses from the Indians and trading with them as well. That summer the activities of men like Martin helped to set off an Indian uprising, in which young Tilghman had several close calls. He broke loose from the Martin crowd and returned to Dodge City, the headquarters of the hide-hunters. There Charlie Bassett, Ford County's sheriff, hired him as a deputy, a position he held only briefly. Later he opened a saloon in Dodge City. In 1878 he was arrested for participation in a train robbery, but he was exonerated. Scarcely two months later he was arrested again, this time for horse-stealing, but again he was absolved.

From this shaky beginning, Bill Tilghman built a reputation for honesty and respectability in Dodge. He served as deputy sheriff of Ford County and marshal of Dodge City from 1884 to 1886. During 1888 and 1889, Tilghman was involved in the county-seat wars that plagued Kansas, most notably in the dispute between Cimarron and Ingalls, in which he was in the posse that forcibly removed county records from Cimarron.

When Oklahoma was opened in April 1889, Tilghman was among the first arrivals. Oklahoma provided a new beginning for him, and he made the most of it. At Guthrie he served briefly as a lawman in 1889, but he soon established a claim near Chandler. In 1891 he was commissioned a deputy United States marshal and held that position until 1912. When the Cherokee Strip was opened up in 1893, Tilghman was placed in charge of the little town of Perry. He stayed on as chief of police of Perry until 1894, when he resumed active duty as a federal deputy. In that capacity he faced the worst of the Oklahoma outlaws. Along with Chris Madsen and Heck Thomas (the trio became known as "the Three Guardsmen"), Tilghman was assigned to capture the gang of Bill Doolin. In 1896, Tilghman single-handedly captured Doolin at Eureka Springs, Arkansas. But Tilghman also had the reputation for treating even the worst criminals fairly. He was instrumental in securing the parole of Bill Raidler, one of the Doolin gang, and every prisoner in his custody was secure.

In 1898 two innocent Indian youths were lynched by a mob for the rape and murder of a white woman. Tilghman not only arrested the members of the mob, but also secured convictions and prison sentences for eight of them. It was the first recorded instance of such convictions and won national acclaim from bar associations and antilynching forces. Tilghman then went after the rapist-murderer and captured him.

Tilghman was elected sheriff of Lincoln County, Oklahoma, in 1900 and served until 1904. In 1905 he was sent on a special mission into Mexico by President Theodore Roosevelt to arrest a fugitive. He was elected to the state legislature as a senator in 1910 and served one term. From 1911 to 1913 he was chief of police of Oklahoma City. In 1915, Tilghman made a movie about the territorial days entitled *The Passing of the Oklahoma Outlaws* and toured the country with it for several years. He was an old man by then, but he was still called on from time to time to meet special law enforcement needs.

In 1924, at the age of seventy-one and against the advice of his wife and friends, he accepted the position of city marshal of Cromwell, Oklahoma. There, on November 1, 1924, Bill Tilghman was murdered by a drunken prohibition agent named Wiley Lynn. Lynn apparently hated Tilghman because Tilghman refused to look the other way regarding bootlegging operations. On the night Tilghman was shot, Lynn was very drunk; and when the old marshal tried to arrest him, Lynn shot him twice.

See Nyle H. Miller and Joseph W. Snell, *Why the West Was Wild* (1963); and Zoe A. Tilghman, *Marshal of the Last Frontier* (1949).—G. L. R.

Tillamook Indians. See INDIANS OF THE NORTHWEST COAST.

Timber and Stone Act (1878). Some of the laws that transferred the public domain to private ownership were well intentioned but subsequently abused by land grabbers and resource exploiters. The Timber and Stone Act of June 3, 1878, falls into this category. Under the act, any citizen, and some categories of aliens, were permitted to buy up to 160 acres of public land for $2.50 per acre. It applied only to lands "unfit for cultivation" and was valuable chiefly for stone and timber in Washington, Oregon, Nevada, and California. In theory the act was intended to be utilized by individual settlers, but in practice it was an invitation to corruption. Timber companies and land speculators quickly discovered that they could hire "dummy" entrymen to file for the 160 acres, which then became part of sprawling domains. As federal enforcement officers seemingly looked the other way, more than three million acres of the West's choicest timberland were concentrated in the hands of a few giant companies.

The standard account of the management and mismanagement of public domain is Roy M. Robbins, *Our Landed Heritage: The Public Domain, 1776-1936* (1942). —R. N.

Timber Culture Act (1873). The Timber Culture Act of March 13, 1873, was an effort to make the Homestead Act of 1862 more suitable to the western environment. Under the homestead legislation, the title to 160 acres of the public domain was available to any adult who paid a ten dollar fee and occupied the land in question for five years. Farmers in the relatively arid West, however, found 160 acres an awkward unit. If they irrigated, they needed much less land. Ranching, in contrast, required much more. The Timber Culture Act was designed to help the rancher by allowing a homesteader to apply for an extra 160 acres, which would become his property provided he planted trees on at least forty acres of it

within four years. In 1878 the minimum tree-growing requirement was reduced to ten acres in yet another attempt to help the homesteader. In all, more than sixty-five thousand individuals acquired approximately ten million acres under the law. Of dubious conservation value, it nonetheless helped extend the idea of land stewardship when it was in its infancy. The act was repealed in 1891.

The standard history is Roy M. Robbins, *Our Landed Heritage: The Public Domain, 1776-1936* (1942).—R. N.

Tippecanoe, battle of (1811). The battle of Tippecanoe grew out of the forced acquisitions of Indian lands in the Wabash valley by treaties, most of them negotiated by William Henry Harrison. In August 1810 Indian leader Tecumseh informed Harrison that he was displeased with the Treaty of Fort Wayne, which he claimed was made unfairly by a handful of chiefs who had no right to dispose of the lands. In late 1810 and during the spring and summer of 1811, there was unrest among the Shawnee in the Wabash valley, and Harrison and his neighbors were concerned. Tecumseh, however, had no intention of fighting as long as the whites stayed out of the disputed territory. In July he visited Harrison at Vincennes with the news that he was going to visit the southern tribes, and that he expected peace to continue in his absence. Harrison felt that this was a golden opportunity to crush the Indians while they were without effective leadership, since Tecumseh's brother the Prophet would not be able to keep the warriors from attacking if an army entered their country. Acting on orders which only gave him the authority to survey the Fort Wayne treaty lands, Harrison marched a combined force of a thousand regulars and militia up the Wabash toward the Indians' stronghold village of Prophet's Town. Though he was actually trespassing on unceded Indian land, on November 6 his forces had advanced to the outskirts of the village and were camped on the bluff above Tippecanoe River. Although Harrison fully expected, indeed hoped, that the Indians would attack, and ordered his troops to sleep with their arms, he was in an exposed position and failed to mount an adequate night guard.

The Prophet was convinced by the warriors to make an attack, and spent the night making magic to guarantee the whites would cower or flee when struck. In the early dawn of November 7, when the battle began, the soldiers were caught off guard and the fight was a near thing. The troops were nearly overrun in the first moments, but rallied and beat off three assaults. An Indian assassination team penetrated the white defenses to kill Harrison, but got another officer who had mistakenly mounted Harrison's distinctive gray horse in the confusion. When the whites' determination became apparent, the Indians lost faith in the Prophet's magic and deserted the field. The battle lasted for two hours, during which 188 whites were killed or wounded. Indian losses were between 25 and 35 killed. Harrison's margin of victory was indeed a slender one, but he did take possession of Prophet's Town on November 8. There he destroyed a large store of supplies. In the aftermath of the battle the dispersed Indians attacked white outposts across the frontier, and the general Indian war broke out that Harrison had claimed his march would prevent. To justify his conduct to critics, Harrison and the veterans of the battle mounted a speechmaking and newspaper campaign of vindication, which elevated the battle to the status of legend and carried Harrison eventually to the White House.

See Reed Beard, *The Battle of Tippecanoe* (1889); Dorothy Burne Goebel, *William Henry Harrison: A Political Biography* (1926); and Glenn Tucker, *Tecumseh, Vision of Glory* (1956).—T. D. C.

Tl'ah Hastiin (1867-1937). Navaho singer, or medicine man, and sand painter. At birth, probably in the vicinity of Indian Wells, Arizona, Tl'ah possessed certain physical characteristics that, according to the Navaho, gave him unusual powers. Because he was left-handed (the meaning of the Navaho word *tl'ah*), he was thought to possess great magic. Moreover, it is said that he was a hermaphrodite, a condition thought by the Navaho to confer good luck and wealth upon the person himself and his family. These persons are believed also to excel at weaving and at curing ceremonies.

As Tl'ah grew older he was called Big Left-Handed and later Old Big Left-Handed. Anglo-Americans had difficulty pronouncing the "tl" sound and anglicized his name to *Claw* or *Klah*. *Hastiin*, literally a mature male person, or *hosteen*, signifies a gentleman, a man of esteem.

As a singer Tl'ah had learned the ceremonial curing chants and the SAND PAINTING that went with them, including all the different forms necessary to perform the nine-day *yeibichei*. This feat took twenty-six years. Tl'ah settled in western New Mexico, where, in 1919, he began to weave his intricate sand painting designs into tapestries. Although converting the patterns into permanent form was a strict taboo, no evil was wrought upon Tl'ah because "he was magic." It is said that he had completed twenty-five different designs before his death, and that his nieces, whom he had taught, completed as many more.

Franc Johnson Newcomb and her husband, Arthur, who had built a trading post in western New Mexico, met Tl'ah and became friends. Franc Newcomb, especially, was intensely interested in the artistry and mythology of the sand paintings, or "dry paintings" (made with colored sands, ground minerals, and charcoal), that the singer and his assistants made during ceremonials she attended. She observed how the paintings were made and made sketches of them. Appreciating her efforts, Tl'ah ensured that her recordings were accurate. When other medicine men objected to her sketching, Tl'ah held a sing for her, which dispensed with any further criticism. Through the years, she reproduced hundreds of the sand paintings, one for each chant of a particular ceremony, and wrote down their meanings.

Others became fascinated with her collections. One, a wealthy Bostonian named Mary Cabot Wheelwright, visited the Newcombs and was introduced to Tl'ah. Tl'ah mentioned that he was going to give a sing, a yeibichei, and asked Wheelwright to attend. From then on, her promotion of Tl'ah and his ceremonial works became a major life undertaking.

Concerned about preserving Tl'ah's knowledge and ceremonial accouterments, Newcomb conceived the idea of a permanent depository for Tl'ah's possessions. Plans for a museum were discussed with Wheelwright and Tl'ah, who saw the wisdom of preserving his chants, ceremonies, and sacred things. Unfortunately, Beaal

Begay, whom Tl'ah had painstakingly trained as his understudy, teaching him the ceremonial chants and sand paintings, had died in 1931, leaving Tl'ah with no successor to carry on the ceremonies and to care for his vast collection of ceremonial articles.

A good friend of the three, William Penhallow Henderson, an artist and builder, joined in the plans, providing drawings for a great structure. This became the Museum of Navaho Ceremonial Art in Santa Fe, New Mexico.

For the original structure, a "symbolic hogan" was envisioned by the artist-architect. Henderson fashioned the building as an exhibit in itself in order to perpetuate the spirit of a Navaho ceremonial hogan, or chamber, in which ritualistic practices are conducted. The building was constructed not as a precise replica, but rather on a scale in keeping with the spirit of the hogan.

Symbolically, a ceremonial, or medicine, hogan represents the emergence of man from nonliving to life. The long, projecting entrance of the old Navaho hogans typifies this emergence and represents a "going down" before a "coming up." The museum's entryway bespeaks the same ascent from the lower worlds to the present world of the Navaho, here portrayed as a large chamber, or hogan. Inside the chamber an octagonal room, a beautifully cribbed roof of selected timbers, was raised to a lofty height in order to provide a sympathetic background for the exhibit of sand paintings.

The program undertaken within this building is devoted to the preservation of Navaho culture. As an integral part of preserving all possible elements of Navaho life, plans included the housing of collections of ceremonial and general ethnological materials: recordings of their chants, myths, and legends; reproductions of sand paintings; accouterments of the medicine men; dance paraphernalia and daily attire; photographs; descriptions of rituals; examples of all arts and industries; and pertinent comparative items, Pueblo, Apache, et al., that are useful in interpreting Navaho culture.

As soon as the building was erected, collections of valuable materials began to arrive. Tl'ah saw it all in the fall of 1936. After his death, many more of Tl'ah's possessions came to the museum, which was dedicated privately by twenty-one Navaho Indians in November 1937 and opened to the public in 1938.

Other Indian artists have transferred sand painting designs to different media subsequent to Tl'ah's tapestries. But probably none have been as faithful in executing the complete design because of their overriding fear of the supernatural.

See Franc J. Newcomb, *Hosteen Klah: Navaho Medicine Man and Sand Painter* (1964); Steven Tremper, "The Museum of Navaho Ceremonial Art—A Place for Understanding," *New Mexico Journal for Social Studies* (April 1972); and Leland C. Wyman, "Big Lefthanded, Pioneer Navaho Artist," *Plateau* (Summer 1967). —B. P. D. and M. L.

Tlingit Indians. See INDIANS OF THE NORTHWEST COAST.

Tobin, John W. See RIVERMEN.

Tocqueville, Alexis de (1805-1859). French writer. The French nobleman Tocqueville traveled throughout the United States and the western territories in 1831-32. He was one of the first foreign visitors to comment extensively upon the frontier experience and its meaning for American society. In his *De la Démocratie en Amérique* (1835-40), Tocqueville sought to demonstrate how popular government and egalitarian attitudes affected the social system of a nation. His conclusions, probably preconceived, were that *démocratie* (properly translated as "equality," not "democracy") would probably lead to the disappearance of class divisions and the emergence of a tyranny of the majority, which would severely restrict individual freedoms. In America, he believed, this fate might be avoided, partly because of the existence of the vast western territories.

Tocqueville and his traveling companion, Gustave de Beaumont, visited several areas of the West. In Michigan and the upper Great Lakes they found what still remained much a wilderness, where the fur trade and accompanying degeneration of the Indian continued, and where white settlement was mainly a few scattered, rude pioneer farms. In the Ohio valley Tocqueville visited Cincinnati and encountered the prodigious social and economic growth and confusion that marked young statehood. And traveling down the Mississippi to New Orleans, the pair were in the main artery of the burgeoning commerce of the West.

Most important, Tocqueville saw the West as one of the means by which the United States would probably avoid mob tyranny, which he believed democratic societies tended to develop. The great expanse of open lands would decentralize the government and population, draw off excess population from cities, and keep the poor content with at least the hope of new opportunities in the West. This influence would last a century or two, he felt, at least until the wilderness was filled up. After that his prognosis was pessimistic, and he wondered if such an extended diffusion of population might not cause the ties of union to dissolve. He observed a sequential modification of cultural heritage and institutional practices as the frontier moved west, remarking that "the new States of the West stand in the same relation to the older States of the Union as these last stand to Europe." Yet Tocqueville noted that most pioneers viewed their rustic states as entirely temporary and fully intended to re-create the society with which they were familiar as soon as possible. Civilization, it appeared, did not have to grow from scratch in its new environment; it was transplanted full-grown. Of the Indian Tocqueville had little to say, except to note that when not corrupted by degenerate whites the Indian appeared to resemble closely the "noble savage," a concept current among the French intelligentsia of that time. In this Tocqueville was seeing not what was, but what he wished.

There are elements of contradiction in Tocqueville's ideas, as there have been in all explanations of the West's meaning for American development. In retrospect he seems to have missed some obvious considerations, such as the role of western commerce in tying the nation closer together. Still, most of his insights were penetrating and through the immense popularity in the United States of his book, Tocqueville's ideas about the frontier left a lasting mark on American thought and clearly foreshadowed the theories of Frederick Jackson TURNER.

See E. T. Gargan, *De Tocqueville* (1965); J. P. Mayer, *Alexis de Tocqueville: A Biographical Study in Political Science* (1960); George W. Pierson, *Tocqueville and Beaumont in America* (1938); and Alexis de Tocqueville, *Democracy in America*, ed. P. Bradley, 2 vols. (1945). —P. R. M.

Todd, John Blair Smith (?-1884). Dakota Territory promoter. Todd, a native of Springfield, Illinois, with his partner, Daniel Marsh Frost, established in 1855 a general store at Sioux City, Iowa, from which they conducted Indian trading. Todd played a significant role in the creation of Dakota Territory, organizing petitioners and lobbying in Washington for the establishment of a territory. He had been instrumental in the negotiations of a treaty with the Yankton Indians in 1858. Under the terms of the treaty Todd and Frost were allowed to enter Indian lands to trade goods and establish townsites. His lobbying was successful and in 1861 Congress created the territory. Todd, a cousin of Mrs. Abraham Lincoln, was elected territorial delegate to Congress in 1861 but was defeated in 1863. Todd speculated in land and was instrumental in having Yankton established as the territorial capital.—D. J. T.

Tolowa Indians. See INDIANS OF THE NORTHWEST COAST.

Tombstone, Arizona. In 1877 in the San Pedro valley, about seventy miles southeast of Tucson, Edward L. Schieffelin discovered rich silver outcroppings and, with his brother Al and Richard Gird founded the Tombstone Mining District. Within a short time eastern money poured in to develop the mines. In 1880-81 the Schieffelin brothers and Gird sold out for princely sums and left Arizona. By 1881 Tombstone boasted a population of about ten thousand and had been incorporated and made the seat of the newly created Cochise County. At this time it was also a center base for gamblers, outlaws, and their hangers-on—including William C. BROCIUS, Doc HOLLIDAY, Frank LESLIE, John RINGO, Luke L. SHORT, and, most famous of all, the EARP BROTHERS. John H. SLAUGHTER, a rancher and civic leader, and the *Epitaph* and other local newspapers were instrumental in promoting civic growth and in ridding the town of outlaws. (Lawlessness was so rampant that in May 1882 President Chester A. Arthur threatened the town with martial law.) The boom conditions soon ended, however, when miners struck underground water; production faltered, and in the early 1890s most of the mines closed. By 1893, Tombstone had produced $22,860,390; sporadic operations later would net another $13,678,191. After 1900 the Development Company of America sank a shaft, lowered the water, and reopened some of the mines, and the El Paso and Southwestern completed a railroad from Fairbank on the San Pedro to Tombstone. However, by 1911 all production had stopped, and in 1929 the county seat was moved to Bisbee. In 1970 the town population was only about twelve hundred people, but its colorful past, the presence of museums, and the restoration of the O. K. Corral and other sites have attracted so many tourists that the town continues to be "too tough to die."

See Charles H. Dunning and Edward Peplow, Jr., *Rock to Riches* (1959); and Odie B. Faulk, *Tombstone: Myth and Reality* (1972).—H. P. H.

Tomlinson, George A. See GREAT LAKES, MEN OF THE.

Tonopah, Nevada. Mining town. Tonopah lies in the heart of one of the richest mining areas in the West. Although the town is still active, its greatest days were in the early years of the twentieth century. In 1902 the town attained a population of twenty thousand and the area continued to boom until 1913, when the productions of the mines began to decrease. The town is still the biggest mining town in the Nevada desert and has produced over $500 million in ores. Many of the buildings from the town's early days still stand.

See Nell Murbarger, *Ghosts of the Glory Trail* (1956); and Muriel S. Wolle, *The Bonanza Trail* (1953). —R. B. W.

Tonti [Tonty], Henri de (1650?-1704). Explorer and aide of La Salle. Tonti was an Italian soldier in the service of the French. He had lost his right hand in battle and wore a metal one usually covered with a glove. In 1678 he joined La Salle and with him reached the mouth of the Mississippi in April 1682. He also managed Forts Crèvecoeur and St. Louis on the Illinois. Tonti returned to the Gulf in an unsuccessful search for La Salle's colony of St. Louis of Texas and established the settlement of Aux Arcs (Arkansas Fort) on his return upstream. He later extended his interests to the lower Mississippi, where he died near present Mobile.

See Louise Phelps Kellogg, ed., *Early Narratives of the Northwest, 1634-1699* (1917).—R. A. B.

Tonto Basin War. See GRAHAM-TEWKSBURY FEUD.

Toole, K. Ross (1920-   ). Historian. Toole was born in Missoula, Montana. After naval service during World War II, he studied history at the University of Montana and the University of California at Los Angeles, where he worked with John Caughey, a well-known western historian.

While still engaged in graduate studies, Toole directed the historical work for the Montana Historical Society from 1951 to 1957, where he did much to bolster acquisition of manuscript holdings. In addition, he served as editor of the *Montana Magazine of History* from 1951 to 1955 and as a regional editor until 1969. During this period he was also a regional editor for *American Heritage* (1954-56). In 1958 he joined the Museum of the City of New York, where he remained for two years.

In 1960 he returned to the West and became associated with the Museum of New Mexico in Santa Fe. In 1963 he returned to his native Montana to become president of the J-J Ranch Company. Two years later he was appointed Hammond Professor of History at the University of Montana.

Toole wrote primarily about the history of Montana, co-authoring *History of Montana* (1957) and in 1958 editing a collection of historical essays concerning Montana and the Northwest. In 1959 appeared his most important work, *Montana: an Uncommon Land,* a sprightly interpretive history of the state. Critics found the book to be one of the best in the field.—G. D. N.

Topographical Engineers, Corps of. The leading official explorers of the West in the nineteenth century. The need for men trained in geographic and topographic techniques was recognized as early as 1777 when General Washington appointed Robert Erskine as geographer and surveyor with the Continental Army. Such an office existed to the end of the American Revolution. In 1785 Thomas Hutchins, as an official geographer of the new nation, ran the first "Seven Ranges," a strip six miles wide divided into townships six miles square, under the provisions of the Land Ordinance of 1785. Official surveying activities declined, however,

and not until March 3, 1813, was the Topographical Bureau established in the army. When the War of 1812 ended, the group, which never numbered more than sixteen, was reduced to two; then, as the years went by, the Topographical Bureau increased its personnel to ten or more. The early career of Stephen H. LONG, when he not only led explorations but made a number of reconnaissances of routes, is typical of this organization's services.

In 1829 John James ABERT, a West Point graduate, became head of the Topographical Bureau. To this shrewd politician and capable engineer belongs the credit for the change from a small bureau to the Corps of Topographical Engineers. It was established in 1838, as distinct from but equal to the Corps of Engineers. Abert recruited his small professional staff from top members of the graduating classes of West Point (sixty-four of the seventy-two officers in the corps were West Point men), and he built up an *esprit* that was at least partly based upon improved promotional opportunities.

The contributions of the dedicated men to this short-lived unit were enormous. Those of John C. FREMONT are very well known, but of note also were the explorations, surveys, and subsequent reports of expeditions conducted by William H. EMORY, Amiel Weeks Whipple, Andrew A. Humphreys, John N. Macomb, Howard Stansbury, Lorenzo Sitgreaves, John W. Gunnison, William F. Raynolds (see RAYNOLDS EXPEDITION), Gouverneur K. WARREN, Joseph C. Ives, James W. Abert, and others. Accompanying many of their expeditions were scientists, whose extensive reports were embodied in the official publications of the corps, and artists (see ARTISTS OF THE WESTERN SURVEYS).

The Topographical Engineers did valuable services in geodetic mapping of the Great Lakes and rivers in the Mississippi Basin, extended their operations westward with Frémont, and did extensive reconnaissance work in connection with the Mexican War. The corps was active in the survey of the Southwest boundary and of all the domain acquired from Mexico (see BOUNDARY COMMISSIONS), as well as in the Oregon country after the settlement of 1846. It did liege service in the activities of the TRANSCONTINENTAL RAILROAD SURVEYS, 1853-55, and it aided in the routing of military wagon roads and NATIONAL ROADS in the West. Although its prestige waned after 1855, the corps continued its activities in the Far West. The explorations of Lieutenant Joseph Christmas Ives and Captain John Macomb in the Southwest, of Captain James A. Simpson across the Great Basin, of Warren in the Sioux country, and of Lieutenant John G. Parke along the forty-ninth parallel constitute its principal explorations during its last years.

The Corps of Topographical Engineers came to an end on March 3, 1863, when by legislation it was again merged with the Corps of Engineers.

The outstanding work on the subject is William H. Goetzmann, *Army Exploration in the American West* (1959). For information about their maps, see Carl I. Wheat, *Mapping the Trans-Mississippi West,* 5 vols. in 6 (1957-63).—R. A. B.

tourist travel. Tourism in the West, in the sense of travel for pleasure or culture, developed chiefly after the Civil War. Before the 1870s western resorts were modest, serving nearby resident vacationers and hardy adventurers who visited natural curiosities such as the Yosemite Valley. When Governor Alexander Spotswood of Virginia and William Byrd led groups of their friends on western trips, pleasure was incidental to business; normally when gentlemen traveled for pleasure, it was for the sake of diversion at the mineral springs during the malarial season, or for visits with friends and relatives. The price of riding by stagecoach over American distances was too high to pay to see scenery and cities that did not seem culturally significant. By the 1830s, when steamboats were ascending the Missouri, travel to the frontier in reasonable comfort was possible, and some Americans could afford it.

A few wealthy adventurers went west for sport, commonly using trading or military posts as their bases. The most conspicuous were foreigners, such as Maximilian of Wied-Neuwied, who spent the winter of 1833-34 at Fort Clark on the Missouri River in the Mandan country, Sir William G. Drummond Stewart, who met Nathaniel Wyeth on the way to Oregon in 1834, and Sir George Gore, who engaged fur trader Jim Bridger as a guide on a hunting trip that he made in the upper Missouri valley in 1894-97.

The voyage of Richard Henry Dana to California in 1835 and the journey of Francis Parkman along the Oregon Trail in 1846 represented the occasional practice of rich men sending their sons on sea voyages and expeditions to the fur-trading country for their health rather than to an industry or a common pastime.

The closest approach to tourist travel as a popular and organized activity was the California gold rush, in that the forty-niners were more interested in sightseeing and adventure incidental to seeking their fortunes than in becoming settlers; the mines and the new city of San Francisco had quickly become as famous as the cultural monuments of Europe (see TAVERNS AND HOTELS). A few celebrated visitors submitted to the overland stage trip to the mines and Salt Lake City, especially writers, such as Horace Greeley in 1859, Richard Burton in 1860, and Samuel Bowles in 1865.

The railroads built after the Civil War promoted tourist travel in order to attract settlers. By 1881 organized tours were operating from Boston to California. Apart from hunters, the early tourists who went by train to the Far West were predominantly middle-aged and prosperous; often consumptives or refugees from eastern winters outnumbered vacationers. Excursion rates and low-priced tourist-sleeper accommodations in the later 1880s widened the market, which expanded still more after national organizations began holding conventions in the West in the 1890s and after the fairs at Portland in 1905, Seattle in 1909, San Francisco in 1915, and San Diego in 1915-17.

Owners of some railroads developed resorts to draw wealthy tourists. Manitou, established near COLORADO SPRINGS in 1871, and the Hotel Del Monte, built near Monterey in 1880, quickly became watering places for the fashionable summer and winter traffic. The builder of the Raymond—southern California's first major tourist hotel, completed in 1886—was the son of a New England railroad magnate who organized the first transcontinental tours. Such deluxe hotels as these and the Hotel del Coronado, built in 1886 off San Diego, dominated their environs and made little concession to local tradition, importing architecture and staffs alike from the East. Their patrons were predominantly from the East and Midwest, except those of the Del Monte,

which also served San Francisco society. Many became residents of nearby communities.

Dude ranches made their appearance about the same time, serving an equally affluent eastern clientele, which was generally younger than the invalids and, at first, exclusively male. Howard Eaton founded the first commercial dude ranch in Dakota territory in 1881. Shortly thereafter Sheridan, Wyoming, became the center of the industry, initially catering to sportsmen too prudent or not rich enough to go into the cattle business.

As the western urban population grew and railroads extended branch lines, more modest resorts developed for regional clientele. Pacific Grove, established in 1875 near Monterey, was a Methodist conference campground before the railroad took control; many lesser spas began as railroad-controlled townsites, Chautauqua summer camps, and amusement parks on interurban electric lines.

Growing interest in the national parks in the early twentieth century led to the parks' first substantial resort hotels, though often the boarding-house and barrack-type accommodations remained. The first, El Tovar, was built at the Grand Canyon in 1905 after the Santa Fe railroad completed a spur to the rim of the canyon in 1901; it was one of the first resorts designed in regional style. At Yosemite Park concessionaires built cabins and floored tents in 1899 to serve tourists before opening the first deluxe hotel in 1927; by the time the National Park Service began to reduce overnight accommodations in the 1960s, tourist facilities dominated the floor of the valley.

Tourists, meanwhile, scattered more widely, as they discovered the desert and the gold-rush country. Artists had begun to gather around Taos before 1900; it became fashionable during the 1920s. Dude ranches soon abounded in both New Mexico and Arizona, even well outside cattle country. By the 1940s mining towns, such as Virginia City, Nevada, were capitalizing on their pasts.

Widespread use of automobiles for long-distance travel from the 1920s on coincided with these new interests in the desert, the Indian country of the Southwest, and the mountains and wilderness beyond the most celebrated resorts and national curiosities. The heaviest tourist season in California became summer rather than winter. Following the opening of the national parks to automobiles in 1913, visitors increased enormously: from 199,000 in 1910 to 920,000 in 1920; and from 2,775,000 in 1930 to 42,519,000 in 1969. By the 1920s visitors to national forests far outnumbered those to parks.

Resort hotels began to lose their longterm patrons in the 1920s, as vacationers adopted automobiles, and during the Depression, as they turned to cheaper accommodations. Tourist cabins for motorists (in Arizona as early as 1901) and motels (at San Luis Obispo, California, in 1925) drained off some of the traffic; public camping facilities (at Denver in 1915) were becoming increasingly popular.

Beginning in the 1930s and increasingly during and after World War II resort communities near large cities and military installations began to fill up with commuters and pensioners seeking permanent housing. As residents replaced vacationers in such places, new and more specialized resorts appeared, catering to more transient clienteles, such as Disneyland in 1955.

During and after the 1930s increasing interest in winter sports and boating stimulated the development of mountain and desert resorts. Sun Valley, developed by the Union Pacific Railroad in 1936 near Ketchum, Idaho, was the first major western ski resort; skiing came more slowly to Aspen, Colorado, originally built as a mining camp in 1879-80, beginning in the winter of 1936-37—though before the lectures and concerts associated with the Aspen Institute for Humanistic Studies.

Artificial lakes, behind the new dams, supported many small resorts, especially after 1945, that catered to swimmers, yachtsmen, and water-skiers. The largest western resort development, however, was at Las Vegas, Nevada, a construction camp first for the Los Angeles-Salt Lake Railroad from 1903 until 1905. It developed in the 1940s more for gambling and divorcing than for boating; by 1960 it was the largest city in Nevada and the only major western resort dominated by hotels.

Smaller and more exclusive desert resorts catered to more specialized clienteles: golfers, the obese, alcoholics, and sufferers from respiratory ailments—more commonly allergies than tuberculosis by the mid-twentieth century.

See Robert G. Athearn, *Westward the Briton* (1953), for observations on British sportsmen in the Rockies; John E. Baur, *The Health Seekers of Southern California, 1870-1900* (1959); Hans Huth, *Nature and the American: Three Centuries of Changing Attitudes* (1957), which emphasizes aesthetic values; Earl Pomeroy, *In Search of the Golden West: The Tourist in Western America* (1957); and Paton Yoder, *Taverns and Travelers: Inns of the Early Midwest* (1969), a description of the wayside inns that steam transportation displaced.—E. P.

Townley, Arthur Charles (1880-1959). North Dakota political organizer. Townley was born in Minnesota and at age twenty-seven began farming in the extreme western part of North Dakota, near Beach. After going bankrupt, he turned to socialism and joined the North Dakota Socialist party in 1913, serving as organizer for the western counties. He used his talents to create the Nonpartisan League (see AGRARIAN MOVEMENTS). Its program called for state ownership of terminal elevators, flour mills, packing houses, and cold-storage plants. By 1918 the Socialist party was dead in North Dakota, for most socialists had joined in the organization of the Nonpartisan League.

First political successes came in the 1916 primary, when league candidates won over regular Republicans. By the end of 1917 Townley had organized parties in thirteen states under the name of the National Nonpartisan League. By 1918 there were 188,365 paid members, mostly in the Dakotas, Montana, and Minnesota, with a staff of five hundred speakers and organizers. The national organization headed by Townley called for such things as democratic world government, full employment, public works for the unemployed, national ownership of public transportation and communication, a steeply graduated income and inheritance tax, repeal of wartime laws limiting civil rights, and women's suffrage. The league's first national victory came in a special election of 1917, when John M. Baer was elected to the House of Representatives from North Dakota. It

then swept to victory in 1918, capturing all state offices in North Dakota except the superintendent of public instruction and controlling both houses of the legislature.

The league-dominated government in North Dakota brought into being such things as a state-owned mill and elevator and a state-owned bank. League Governor Lynn J. FRAZIER was elected in 1920, but the voters of North Dakota recalled him from office in 1921 along with William Lemke, the attorney general, and John N. Hagen, commissioner of agriculture. This marked the end of league power in North Dakota.

In November 1921 Townley began serving a sentence of ninety days for conspiring to discourage enlistments during the war, and in 1922 he resigned as president of the Nonpartisan League. He returned from political oblivion in the early 1950s to run for the U.S. Senate in North Dakota on a third-party ticket, but his showing was a far-distant third. He died in an automobile accident.

On the Nonpartisan League, see Robert L. Morlan, *Political Prairie Fire* (1955).—D. J. T.

transcontinental railroad surveys (1853-1854). A series of surveys conducted by the army in search of a feasible route to the Pacific. To break the sectional deadlock over a transcontinental railroad route, it was suggested that scientists and engineers run surveys and their recommendations be honored by Congress, although it was bitterly partisan. However, the fact that Secretary of War Jefferson Davis, a southerner, would administer the surveys made the whole plan suspect. The choices of the four routes to be surveyed (really reconnoitered) was also purely political.

The northern survey, under the direction of Isaac I. Stevens, worked from St. Paul west to Puget Sound. Lieutenant George B. McClellan meanwhile explored the Cascade Range for passes. The second survey pushed west along the thirty-eighth parallel, under the direction of Captain John W. Gunnison. The third survey, under Lieutenant Amiel W. Whipple, advanced along the thirty-fifth parallel, west from Fort Smith, Arkansas. The fourth survey ran along the thirty-second parallel, west from Fort Washita under Captain John Pope, and east from Fort Yuma led by Lieutenant John G. Parke. Minor reconnaissances were also carried out for a route between Oregon and California and in search of passes in the southern Sierra. The forty-first parallel route, approximating that of the first transcontinental railroad, was not included, apparently because it had been explored in previous years.

Stevens, who was governor of Washington Territory, enthusiastically recommended the northern route. Since some of his own party disagreed, the legislature of the territory hired Frederick W. Lander to run another survey down to South Pass, where he suggested that one branch of a transcontinental line should advance to San Francisco while another should progress northwest toward Puget Sound. Captain Gunnison got through the San Juan Mountains of southwest Colorado but was murdered by Indians along Utah's Sevier River. Lieutenant E. G. Beckwith assumed command and found a route through Weber Canyon in the Uinta Mountains, and then crossed the Great Basin and discovered two feasible passes over the northern Sierra. Lieutenant Whipple successfully surveyed along the thirty-fifth parallel, much of which had been explored before. Finally, Lieutenant Parke and Captain Pope filed enthusiastic reports of the thirty-second-parallel route.

In 1855 a preliminary report was issued recommending the thirty-second-parallel route, but neither that route nor any other was used until after the Civil War. The final reports came off the presses between 1856 and 1861. They included not only the reports of the commanding officers but illustrations (see ARTISTS OF THE WESTERN SURVEYS) and extensive sections by leading scientists in the fields of soil, climate, botany, geology, and zoology. As for the net value of the surveys, they added to the geographic and scientific knowledge of the West. Ultimately, the general routes of four of the five transcontinental railways were those first recommended by the Pacific railroad surveyors.

See George Leslie Albright, "Official Exploration for Pacific Railroads, 1853–1855" (1921); William H. Goetzmann, *Army Exploration in the American West* (1959); and *The Pacific Railroad Reports* (1855-61).—R. A. B.

Transcontinental Treaty. See ADAMS-ONIS TREATY.

transportation, overland. The war with Mexico and resulting cession of land in 1848 added a territorial domain to the United States two and a half times the size of France. Simultaneous with the signing of the treaty, gold was discovered in California, followed within a decade by additional mineral discoveries in Nevada and Colorado. Miners lived in isolated islands of settlement scattered far and wide throughout the mountain West. United States military posts located strategically to observe the actions of western Indian tribes and to protect the white man were equally isolated. Following the Mexican War, the number of outposts had been increased along the overland trails, near the active mining districts, and particularly in the greater Southwest acquired from Mexico. Residents on the mining and military frontier insisted upon the improvement of transportation and communication in hope of receiving news from family and friends as well as information on public affairs, and also in hope of reducing the price of commodities. A program of government subsidy was called for, and the United States responded favorably because of a concern for the spirit of separatism and independence that pervaded many sections of the West. During the 1850s Congress granted a series of subsidies to aid the delivery of mails and freight, and in the next decade to construct telegraph lines and railroads. Providing overland communication and transportation also became a favorite field of investment for entrepreneurs, who were certain that their ventures would be partially underwritten by the government.

Contracts were made in 1847 to provide a mail service between New York and San Francisco. Letters were carried by the UNITED STATES MAIL STEAMSHIP COMPANY to Panama, transported across the Isthmus, and picked up by the PACIFIC MAIL STEAMSHIP COMPANY. Operations actually began in 1849, simultaneous with the gold rush to California. By 1851 the monthly service was increased to semimonthly, with a government payment of $724,350 a year; postage rates were simultaneously reduced from forty cents a half-ounce to six cents. Passenger fares averaged $500 between New York and San Francisco. The steamship companies made sizable profits, and Cornelius Vanderbilt established the Acces-

sory Transit Company along the Nicaraguan route in an attempt to share the business. In 1853 his employees seized control of the company and joined forces with the United States and Pacific companies to pay him a subsidy to keep out of the business for a few years. A railroad was constructed across the Isthmus of Panama in 1855, placing that route in a preferable position, and immediately postage rates were increased to ten cents. The United States also attempted to develop a mail service through the Isthmus of Tehuantepec, obtaining the right of transit from Mexico in 1853. Five years later a mail contract for $250,000, including a stipulation that a wagon road be built, was granted on this route but the service was not satisfactory.

The high cost and excessive time for delivery by the ocean routes led to demands from westerners for an overland route. Pioneer mail carriers attempted to bridge the gap. A monthly mail service was provided by the BRIGHAM YOUNG EXPRESS & CARRYING CO. between Independence, Missouri, and Salt Lake City. From there another line carried it on to California by light wagon or pack horse. A military express ran between Independence and Santa Fe along the Santa Fe Trail. A monthly mail also was delivered from San Antonio to El Paso and on to San Diego. These four pioneer lines were far from satisfactory. The government subsidy was so low that adequate, regular service could not be maintained. There were no way stations along the route, and Indian depredations resulted in losses both to contractors and passengers.

George CHORPENNING, contractor on the California-Salt Lake City route, told of his difficulties in an official *Statement* seeking additional compensation from the United States government. Like John C. Frémont a few years earlier, his men had to beat down the snow in the Sierra Nevada with wooden mauls to make a trail that would support their animals. At times during the winter of 1852 they could not conquer the snow barrier, and on one occasion a party that did so experienced frightful suffering when their horses and mules were frozen to death in the Goose Creek mountains of Utah. Strapping their mail pouches on their backs, they trudged on foot for two hundred miles to Salt Lake City, surviving on mule meat until it gave out. For the last six days of their fifty-three-day journey they were without food. Such experiences convinced mail contractors that in the winter months it was best to follow the Old Spanish Trail, or Jedediah Smith route, from Salt Lake to Los Angeles and send the mail by steamer from San Pedro north to the Golden Gate, thus bridging the gap between the termini of their mail contract. Meanwhile, men like "Snowshoe Thompson" established lasting reputations for fortitude in crossing the Sierra even in the most inclement weather to maintain mail and express connections between California and Nevada. Summer brought Indian attacks. Absalom Woodward, Chorpenning's partner, and his entire party were murdered by Indians who then stole their animals and supplies. In spite of deeds of valor and personal sacrifice, mail deliveries to California remained uncertain and isolated, homesick miners grew more resentful.

Western pressures on the government reached a climax in 1856 when a petition from California, bearing seventy-five thousand signatures, the largest on record, was laid before Congress. The response was twofold: the

Madame Canutson, a female freighter, held her own in the male-dominated trade in the 1880s. (Library of Congress)

establishment of a federal program for construction and improvement of wagon roads, and the authorization of an overland mail service. Congress created the Pacific Wagon Road Office and appropriated funds to shorten and improve the emigrant route from Fort Kearny, via South Pass, to Honey Lake on the California border; to survey a feeder line from the Minnesota frontier to the South Pass; and to improve the road from El Paso to Fort Yuma, Arizona, and from Albuquerque to Needles, California. With the exception of this last route along the thirty-fifth parallel, the assignment was taken away from the Topographical Engineers of the United States Army, the traditional government road builders, and placed in the hands of civilian contractors, most of whom had been operators of mail services. The program was administered by the Interior Department.

On the route left under its jurisdiction, the army experimented with camel transport. In 1857 Jefferson Davis, secretary of war, had requested and obtained an appropriation of $30,000 from Congress to purchase camels. He seized the opportunity to combine the "Camel Corps" experiment with the road-building assignment. When the camels arrived in Santa Fe and Albuquerque, having been driven overland from Texas ports on the Gulf of Mexico, residents thought a circus had come to town. To the annoyance of teamsters, mules were frightened by the camels on the road and bolted. The experiment, considered unsuccessful, was abandoned.

Congress also approved in 1857 an annual subsidy of $600,000 for a mail service from the Mississippi River to San Francisco, stipulating that delivery must be guaranteed within twenty-five days. Directors of the various express companies pooled their financial resources and talents to organize the OVERLAND MAIL COMPANY, and

the Post Office Department selected a route from St. Louis or Memphis through Fort Smith, across Texas to El Paso, on to Fort Yuma, and north to San Francisco. The trail eventually came to be known as the Butterfield Trail, in honor of John BUTTERFIELD, who was chosen by his fellow board members as the company's first president. Butterfield also had a flair for dramatic action that attracted the attention of western news reporters. This semicircular route, dubbed the "ox-bow route" and twenty-eight hundred miles in length, was reportedly chosen because of the advantages of its terrain and climate, but many claimed its location reflected the influence of southern politicians.

The construction of stations at eight- to twenty-five-mile intervals along the route (including an occasional blacksmith shop and stables), the contracting for supplies of hay and digging wells for a water supply in arid regions, and the employment of station-keepers who could fight off an Indian attack if necessary and stage drivers as adept at handling a gun as the reins required the organizational genius often attributed to entrepreneurs in the West. Waterman L. Ormsby, a reporter for the New York *Herald*, was the sole passenger on the first trip westward for its entire length of twenty-four days. Butterfield, who had placed the first mail bags on the baggage car of the train in St. Louis and accompanied them on the initial leg of the journey to Tipton, was also on hand to take charge of the first mail packets arriving from San Francisco.

Many people preferred to entrust their letters, business papers, and small packages to express companies rather than government mail carriers. The major cities in the United States were connected by express companies early in the nineteenth century, and when they began carrying letters for less than United States postage, their business boomed. Partnerships in the express business were fluid, but by 1850 two major companies had emerged: ADAMS EXPRESS COMPANY and American Express Company, the latter representing a merger of the interests of Wells and Company, Butterfield and Wasson, and Livingston, Fargo and Company. The discovery of gold in California provided a new field of operations for the express companies. Hundreds of small enterprises came into existence to deliver letters, newspapers, and packages on horseback, by pack mule, wagon, and eventually STAGECOACH. Larger companies, such as Adams and Company and WELLS, FARGO & CO., assumed supremacy in the express business in California, which they soon extended throughout the western states. As the postal service developed, the express companies concentrated more on the collection of gold dust, the delivery of treasure and prized packages, and banking activities. Throughout the West, stagecoaches carried the United States mail under contract; letters, papers, and packages entrusted to the express companies for delivery; and passengers.

One method of transporting the mails, which enjoyed a reputation far outdistancing its duration and financial success, was the famous PONY EXPRESS. For twenty months, beginning in April 1860 and ending in November 1861, young men, from fifteen to twenty-two years of age and weighing no more than one hundred and twenty-five pounds, made one hundred-mile "runs" alone on horseback carrying mail. Among their accomplishments was demonstrating that lone riders could get the mail across the desert region and over the Rocky and Sierra mountains in winter as well as spring. They also filled the gap in the delivery of transcontinental telegraph messages until the wires were finally linked between the East and West in Salt Lake City on October 24, 1861. The government contract for carrying the mails by pony officially ended on this date, but the ponies were on the road for an additional month. President Lincoln's first inaugural address was delivered to Sacramento, California, by Pony Express rider.

Less picturesque than the stagecoach, the freight wagon (or PRAIRIE SCHOONER) that delivered supplies to the isolated military posts and mining camps was of equal importance. Supply wagons moved along the Santa Fe Trail as early as 1822 and were still serving as feeders for the railroads as late as 1880. The business was conducted both by individuals and by large companies. The economy of the Midwest, particularly that of the Missouri River towns, was bolstered and stabilized by the business. Entrepreneurs, wagon masters, and teamsters operated lines headed westward to Santa Fe, Salt Lake City, Denver, and the Montana gold fields. Freight was carried in covered wagons drawn usually by oxen, but occasionally by mules; a typical train included twenty-five wagons carrying from three to five tons of freight in each. As early as 1855 the hauling of merchandise to Utah, for example, employed 304 wagons and 3,210 oxen.

The partnership of RUSSELL, MAJORS AND WADDELL was the largest and best known freighting firm in the West. Employed to haul supplies to Utah for the United States Army in 1858, this company used 3,500 wagons, 40,000 oxen, 1,000 mules, and more than 4,000 men. Ben HOLLADAY claimed to have operated 20,000 wagons with 150,000 animals at one time (see HOLLADAY'S STAGECOACH LINES).

Alexander MAJORS in his *Seventy Years on the Frontier* (1893) remembered that oxen

proved to be the cheapest and most reliable teams for long trips, where they had to live upon the grass. This was invariably the case. They did good daily work, gathered their own living, and if properly driven would travel two thousand miles in a season, or during the months from April to November. . . . However, the distance traveled depended much upon the skill of the wagonmasters who had them in charge. For if the master was not skilled in handling the animals and men, they could not make anything like good headway and success. To make everything work expeditiously, thorough discipline was required, each man performing his duty and being in the place assigned him without confusion or delay. I remember once of timing my teamsters when they commenced to yoke their teams after the cattle had been driven into their corral and allowed to stand long enough to become quiet. I gave the word to the men to commence yoking, and held my watch in my hand while they did so, and in sixteen minutes from the time they commenced, each man had yoked six pairs of oxen and had them hitched to their wagons ready to move.

In 1858 Russell, Majors and Waddell alone contracted with the government to deliver up to fifteen million pounds. Each year prior to the completion of the transcontinental railroad the amounts carried by the freighters increased; by 1865 an estimated 125 million pounds of merchandise was being transported in a single year by all the freighting outfits. Without this service, the United States Army would have found it impossible to protect the frontier, and many mining districts in the West could not have survived. At the same time, the cost of delivery, based upon weight and distance, was largely responsible for the high cost of living.

See also CENTRAL OVERLAND CALIFORNIA AND PIKE'S PEAK EXPRESS.

LeRoy R. Hafen, *The Overland Mail, 1849-1869* (1926), is the classic study of the political and administrative history of the subject. W. Turrentine Jackson, *Wagon Roads West* (1965) surveys the role of the federal government in improving roads and trails between 1849 and 1869. Ralph Moody, *Stagecoach West* (1967), the only attempt at a comprehensive treatment of the subject of stagecoaches, is valuable but must be used with discretion. Raymond W. Settle and Mary L. Settle have presented the history of the freighting firm Russell, Majors and Waddell in *War Drums and Wagon Wheels* (1966). Henry Pickering Walker, *The Wagonmasters* (1966), has expanded the study of freighting, noting the economic impact of the many companies involved. The most recent survey of the entire subject of overland transportation will be found in Oscar O. Winther, *The Transportation Frontier: The Trans-Mississippi West, 1865-1890* (1964).—W. T. J.

transportation on the Colorado River. Waterless wastelands and Apache and Mohave angry at white encroachment on their lands nearly stifled overland traffic through Arizona until railroads were constructed in the 1880s. Too, overland transportation was expensive. It cost, for example, the intolerable sum of $75 to haul freight by team and wagon 175 miles from Port Isabel, California, to Yuma, Arizona. Thus, prior to the coming of the railroads, most of the passengers and commerce for southeastern California, Arizona, and southwestern Utah came in by boat, starting in 1851. Seagoing vessels from harbors on the California coast and Panama sailed up the gulf of lower California to the Colorado River delta town of Port Isabel, where loads were lightered onto shallow-draft, wheel-powered steamers or barges for the trip up the silty river current. The first river cargoes were loaded onto flat barges and pulled with ropes by manpower to Yuma. Yuma was the first major river port. More northern landings were at Ehrenburg, Fort Mojave, Hardyville, and finally Callville, a Mormon hamlet, near the mouth of the Virgin River, the head of navigation. Callville was the debarking point for the Utah trade. Cargo barges first landed there in 1866.

Besides civilian passengers and military personnel, upstream vessels carried mining and army equipment, food, clothing, and other merchandise. Downstream cargos included hides, wool, furs, products from mines, passengers, and troops.

Each river port served a distinct trade territory. Commerce moved in all directions from Yuma. Goods were transported to and from Ehrenburg to Wickenburg, and Hardyville was the river depot for Prescott.

Two of the well-known barges were the *Black Crook* and *White Fawn*. Some of the famous steamboats were called *Yuma*, *Colorado*, *Uncle Sam*, *Cacopah*, *Mojave*, *General Jessup*, *Esmerelda*, *Vina Tilden*, and *Explorer*. Lieutenant Joseph Ives commanded the *Explorer* while studying navigation opportunities on the Colorado. Ives's steamer was bested by Captain George A. Johnson's *General Jessup*, which made the first perilous trip to the head of Black Canyon. A 104-foot sidewheeler of seventy horsepower, the *General Jessup* carried as much as sixty tons of cargo on water only two feet deep.

Riverboating required almost clairvoyant navigators skilled in dodging submerged rocks and shifting sandbars. Eventually, most of the steamers either sank when boilers exploded or foundered after jamming hidden rocks. Another hazard was the occasional bore formed at the river mouth when tidal waves drove foaming, turbulent currents up the narrowing river channel. A destructive bore could smash its way as far as thirty-five miles upstream until its latent force was exhausted against the powerful seabound river current.

Today, numerous dams and diversions have reduced river flow near Yuma to a sluggish trickle, too small for canoes.

See Frederick S. Dellenbaugh, *The Romance of the Colorado River* (1902); George H. Denby, *Denby's Report on Opening the Colorado River, 1850-1851* (1969); Martha Summerhayes, *Vanished Arizona* (1939); and Frank Waters, *The Colorado* (1946).—B. W. A.

transportation on the Great Lakes. Nature gave to North America a chain of inland seas unique in the geography of the earth. With their St. Lawrence River gateway, the linked Great Lakes—Ontario, Erie, Huron, Michigan, and Superior—extend for two thousand miles into the heart of the continent, providing a transportation route through a realm of rich resources. During the past three centuries fish and furs, grain and lumber, copper, limestone, and iron ore have come down the lakes in an unending commerce. Indian nations roamed the lake-bordered country and coasted the shores in bark canoes. They lived in the land like foxes, leaving it unchanged. But men from Europe made it a commercial and industrial heartland (see GREAT LAKES, MEN OF THE).

The French entered the Great Lakes by the Ottawa River, which led westward from Montreal; they called it La Grande Rivière, a name contradicted by some forty laborious portages. The lower lakes form a sprawling V between Montreal and the Straits of Mackinac. Barred in the south by the thunderous Falls of Niagara and the hostile Iroquois, the French cut across the top of the V. After hundreds of miles of wilderness travel they came out at the North Channel of Lake Huron. Governor Samuel de Champlain sent men to live among the Indians and to explore the country (see EXPLORATION, FRENCH). By 1620 young Etienne Brulé had traveled with Huron hunters through Georgian Bay, the North Channel, and up the St. Marys River to the foot of Lake Superior. In 1634 Jean Nicolet with seven Huron paddlers breasted unknown waters beyond the Mackinac strait. Crossing Lake Michigan, Nicolet expected to land on the shores of China; he donned a robe of embroidered damask as proper garb for a meeting with Oriental princes. Instead, he landed on the forest shore of Green Bay and found half-naked Winnebago savages.

The French explorers, and the priests and fur traders who followed them, traveled by bark canoe, the masterpiece of the Algonquian tribes. Over a cage of cedar ribs leathery birchbark was sewn with wiry spruce roots; the seams were caulked with pine pitch. This light, strong, buoyant craft, propelled by cedar paddles, carried Father René Ménard and Father Claude Allouez to pioneer missions on Lake Superior. In 1673 it took Father Jacques Marquette and Louis Jolliet across Lake Michigan and, by way of the Fox and Wisconsin rivers, to their discovery of the Mississippi.

With the fur trade the canoe became the lakes' first vessel of commerce. Through bays and rivers passed the *canot du nord*, sixteen feet long, manned by five or six paddlers. As trade grew the craft was enlarged. The *canot du maître*, thirty feet long and five feet wide, paddled by a dozen singing voyageurs, carried two tons of cargo. Westward went boxes of Indian trade goods; back to Montreal came bales of peltry. Riding rocky rivers and skirting jagged shores, a canoe lasted but two seasons.

With the discovery of Lake Erie in 1669 (the last of the Great Lakes to be discovered by white men) a southern route was open to the French. The explorer-merchant René Robert Cavelier, Sieur de La Salle first recognized that the lakes could be a chain of trade routes into the heart of America. In 1678-79, just above Niagara Falls, he built the *Griffin*, a two-masted brig able to carry forty-five tons, the first rigged vessel on the lakes. In 1679 it made a smooth run over Lake Erie and a stormy voyage up Lake Huron. Crossing Lake Michigan to Green Bay, it loaded a cargo of peltry. While La Salle and some of his men canoed southward on Lake Michigan, the *Griffin* headed back to Niagara. Soon after its sailing a storm lashed the northern waters, and the *Griffin* was lost. It would be a hundred years before another decked vessel would sail the lakes.

Meanwhile the fur trade outgrew the bark canoe.

Traders developed the *bateau* and the Mackinaw boat for use in open water. Built of red cedar, the *bateau* had a flat bottom and pointed ends. The Mackinaw boat, commonly made of oak planks, was broader and blunter. Both craft were fitted with mast and sail. In a fair wind a Mackinaw boat, with twenty men and ten tons of cargo, could travel sixty miles a day.

With the nineteenth century came the beginning of the Great Lakes' sailing fleets. The twenty-five-ton schooner *Surprise*, built in Buffalo, New York, in 1804, and the forty-five-ton *Zephyr*, launched in 1808 from Cleveland, Ohio, carried merchandise between pioneer ports on Lake Erie. As settlement spread westward, larger vessels served a growing trade in grain and lumber. There were a variety of rigs—sloops, schooners, barques, and brigs—but by mid-century schooners outnumbered all the rest. The fore-and-aft rigged schooners had three advantages over square-rigged vessels: they required a smaller crew, they could sail closer into the wind, and at the wharf their booms swung clear of the hatches to facilitate cargo-handling. Leaning in the wind or towing through the rivers, the schooners had graceful lines and gracious names: *Sea Flower, Moonlight, Hesperus, Wanderer, Evening Star,* and *Lady of the Lake.* Many of them were run by owner-captains.

As channels and harbors were improved the schooners grew larger. In 1883 the new four-master *Golden Age* carried three thousand tons of coal from Buffalo to Chicago. At Saginaw on Lake Huron and Muskegon on Lake Michigan scores of schooners loaded lumber for the building of the midland cities. The lumber trade crested in the 1880s, when the wind-borne fleet reached its peak. In those years nearly two thousand sailing vessels whitened the lakes. The grain trade from Chicago and Milwaukee to Buffalo and the iron ore commerce from Lake Superior to Lake Erie harbors involved voyages of two to three weeks. A problem for the sailing vessels was the navigating of the connecting river channels. In the Detroit, St. Clair, and St. Marys rivers steam tugs had to tow the tall-masted schooners, as many as six in a line, to open water, where they could ride the wind again.

Two small steamboats had been built on Lake Ontario soon after the War of 1812, but the Niagara escarpment barricaded them from the other lakes. The first steamer on Lake Erie was the side-wheel *Walk-in-the-Water*, launched near Buffalo in 1818. Under Captain Job Fish, a steamboat man from the Hudson, this vessel carried merchandise and up to twenty-nine passengers between Buffalo and Detroit. In 1820 Captain Fish took his steamer through the Straits of Mackinac to Green Bay on Lake Michigan. The *Walk-in-the-Water* was wrecked near Buffalo in an autumn gale in 1821. It was replaced by the *Superior*, with other steamers soon to follow.

For pioneer settlers, the way to the West was by water. There was no railroad to Chicago until 1852. When the Erie Canal was opened in 1825 throngs of immigrants at Buffalo boarded steamboats for Detroit, Saginaw, Milwaukee, and Chicago. With the surge of settlement came larger steamers; the 254-foot *Empire,* launched at Cleveland in 1844, was for a few years the largest steamship in the world. In 1845 steamers departed from Buffalo three times weekly; five years later there were three sailings every day during the navigation season. (With rivers and harbors frozen, the lake trade was halted

from December to April.) These steamers, with propellers replacing the old paddle wheels, carried passengers and package freight, while sailing vessels hauled the bulk cargo of the lakes.

With the twenty-foot drop of the St. Marys Falls, Lake Superior was cut off from the lower lakes. But discovery of copper and iron ore in upper Michigan brought life to the northern wilderness. In the 1840s a dozen schooners and steamers were laboriously hauled over the mile-long portage road at Sault Ste. Marie and launched onto Lake Superior. In 1853 work began on a ship canal, which was opened in 1855. During the first year 193 vessel passages went through the tandem locks, and within half a century the number grew to 20,000.

During the 1880s steam freighters were replacing the sailing vessels as bulk carriers. The change from sail to steam brought a change from personal ownership to company operation. Steamships meant investment on a new scale, and the larger investment required coordinated management. Vessel names reflect the change—from the poetic *Moonlight* and *Evening Star* to the workaday *Charles W. Wetmore* and *Samuel Mather,* the names of the corporation men.

Mining in the pioneer Marquette range on Lake Superior was followed by discovery and development of other iron ore districts. By 1880 the port of Marquette was rivaled by Escanaba on Lake Michigan, where freighters were loading ore from the mines of the Menominee Range. West of the Menominee prospectors discovered a third range, the Gogebic; by 1890 it was shipping nearly three million tons a season from the port of Ashland on Lake Superior. The Mesabi ("Giant") Range, north of Duluth, Minnesota, developed with giant strides: there was one producing mine in 1892, nine in 1893, and eleven in 1894. By 1905 it was shipping more than all the other districts combined. In 1910 a hundred Mesabi locations produced nearly thirty million tons of ore. From open-pit mines railroads brought the heavy rust-colored rock down to Duluth, at the head of Lake Superior. Here freighters were loaded at lofty ore docks. An ever-growing tonnage went down to the blast furnaces of Ohio and Pennsylvania.

Increased commerce called for larger freighters, which required deepened harbors and river channels and successively enlarged locks on the Soo Canal at the foot of Lake Superior. For the bulk trade, wooden hulls gave way to iron, iron hulls to steel. In 1882 the Globe Iron Works in Cleveland built the *Onoko*, the first iron-hulled freighter designed for the ore trade. This vessel had continuous hatches over a single cavernous hold, with engines aft and navigation quarters forward. It set the design for future Great Lakes freighters. For a decade the *Onoko*, 282 feet long and carrying three thousand tons of cargo, was the marvel of the lakes. But in 1895 came the first 400-footers, and by 1900 there were freighters 500 feet long with a capacity of five thousand tons. During the twentieth century they grew to leviathan proportions, approaching 1,000 feet in length and carrying nearly fifty thousand tons of cargo.

A unique vessel on the lakes was the "whaleback" freighter of the 1890s. Invented by Captain Alexander McDougall, it had rounded sides and a bulbous bow, with forward and after cabins stilted on steel stanchions over the tubular hull. The first of these vessels was

The Missouri River steamboat De Smet *in the 1860s at Fort Benton, Montana, the head of navigation. (Montana Historical Society, Helena)*

loaded with iron ore at Two Harbors, Minnesota, in 1888. During the next eight years forty more were built at Duluth on Lake Superior. Many of them were barges, without their own propulsion. A whaleback steamer commonly towed two or three whaleback barges, a ponderous procession passing smoothly through rough seas. But the "pig boats," as sailors called them, were unhandy at the docks, and their narrow hatches hampered discharge of cargo. Thus, no new whalebacks were built after 1898. McDougall's fleet included one whaleback passenger steamer, the *Christopher Columbus.* In 1893 this widely publicized vessel ferried five thousand World's Fair visitors between downtown Chicago and the World's Columbian Exposition in Jackson Park.

Passenger steamers served the Great Lake ports well into the twentieth century, until automobile travel put them out of business. But for the bulk trade in coal, grain, limestone, and iron ore, land transport still cannot equal the economy and efficiency of lake transportation. The Lake Superior region has a virtually unlimited resource of low-grade ore that can be concentrated into iron ore pellets to supply the steel industry, and the Great Plains states and provinces yield grain harvests that help to feed the world. Today more than 100 million tons of cargo annually move over the Great Lakes.

See Walter Havighurst, *The Long Ships Passing: The Story of the Great Lakes* (1942); and J. B. Mansfield, *History of the Great Lakes,* 2 vols. (1899). On the individual lakes, see Harlan Hatcher, *Lake Erie* (1945); Fred Landon, *Lake Huron* (1944); Grace Lee Nute, *Lake Superior* (1944); Arthur Pound, *Lake Ontario* (1945); and Milo Quaife, *Lake Michigan* (1944).—W. H.

transportation on the Mississippi River system. Two centuries ago the West began at the crest of the Appalachian Mountains. Westward from the Alleghenies flowed the Ohio River, in line with the march of America. It led to the Mississippi in the great central valley, as did the Missouri River flowing southeastward from the far-off Rocky Mountains. The Ohio, Mississippi, and Missouri rivers, the chief features of a midcontinental drainage system, total nearly six thousand miles of navigable waterway. They were the routes of national expansion.

In colonial times the Ohio River was the road of exploration, migration, and a rude frontier commerce. Its first vessel was the Indian canoe, hollowed out of a poplar log. This craft carried La Salle on his exploration in 1669-70 as far west as present Louisville; a hundred years later it brought young George Rogers Clark into the Old Northwest, which he would win for the new American nation. During the American Revolution and the Indian wars the Ohio, flowing a thousand miles from Fort Pitt to the Mississippi, was a military road. In flatboats and keelboats it freighted men and material for the winning of the West. Already it was carrying a varied frontier commerce.

In Pittsburgh in the 1790s emigrant families exchanged a jolting wagon for a swaying flatboat. Thirty-five dollars would buy an oblong flat-bottomed craft with a shedlike shelter for its people and an open deck for horses and cattle. Commonly called a broadhorn, it had a pair of long steering oars set in timber crotches. To one Yankee traveler, the broadhorn was "a species of ark, very nearly resembling a New England pig-stye." Horses munched at a hay mound and hens scratched at their feet. On the shed roof a woman might rock a cradle as her husband leaned on the steering oar, while the tireless river took them toward the future. The flatboat was a one-way craft. At journey's end its timbers were broken up for building lumber.

Freight wagons came from Philadelphia and Baltimore to Pittsburgh. On the river landings cargo was transferred to flatboats for the interior country. Pittsburgh RIVERMEN made seasonal trips to Cincinnati and Louisville, and to New Orleans, a voyage of fifty days. They returned on foot, tramping the Natchez Trace through Nashville, Lexington, and Maysville on the upper Ohio. These men saw the valley settlements growing with a migration from all the eastern states and from the countries of Europe. The common greeting, reported the French traveler François Michaux, was " 'What part of the world do you come from?'—as if those immense and fertile regions were to be the asylum common to all the inhabitants of the globe."

More durable than the flatboat was the keelboat, used for military transport and for early commerce through-out the vast Mississippi valley. Up to eighty feet long and twelve feet wide, it had a sharp keel, a shaped hull, rounded bow and stern, and a roofed cargo hold and crew's cabin. It was commonly fitted with mast and sail. The keelboat voyaged downstream and up, an easy trip followed by a hard one.

The first two decades of the nineteenth century were the age of keelboat commerce. Flour, salt, iron, bricks, and barrel staves went west and south on the rivers. Molasses, sugar, coffee, lead, and hides came back upstream. A standard keelboat carried three hundred barrels of freight, a back-breaking load to propel against the river current. From runways at each side, a line of sweating men pushed the boat upstream, lifting and setting their poles to the cry of the steersman. In swift water the boat hugged the riverbank, while the men pulled on willow branches. Where it was too deep for this "bushwhacking," boatmen swam ashore with a towline. Scrambling through mud and thickets, a dozen men hauled fifty tons through deep water. Then they resumed the treadmill toil with their poles. It was a rugged way to earn eighty cents a day—if that. Said an Irishman who was working his passage in a keelboat, "Faith, if it wasn't for the name of riding, I'd sooner walk."

By 1815 there were some three thousand boatmen in three hundred keelboats on the rivers. When two boats met the men shouted information, banter, and curses until the rival craft was past. Each boat had a signal horn of varying pitch and volume. On misty mornings and

The levee at St. Paul in 1859. (Library of Congress)

moonlit nights their mellow notes made the first music on the river.

After 1820 keelboats continued to serve the side rivers while steamboats carried a growing commerce on the main stream. The boatman's horn gave way to the steamer's bell, and setting poles were replaced by churning paddle wheels. But the keelboat men lived on in river lore. Like Paul Bunyan of the woods and Buffalo Bill of the plains, Mike Fink, the burly king of the rivermen, became a folk hero and a frontier myth.

Historians have reflected on the fortuitous invention of the steamboat at the very time when multitudes of people were migrating to western lands. The Ohio-Mississippi waterway, two thousand miles long, was an inevitable highway for the steamboat. Within three years of Fulton's first steam navigation of the Hudson in 1807, a steamboat was taking shape on the riverbank at Pittsburgh. Named for its destination, the *New Orleans* was an impressive craft: 138 feet long, 26 feet wide, with a main deck cabin surmounted by a boxy pilothouse. It had a tall smokestack, two masts with schooner sails, and a pair of big side wheels. Late in 1811, after the autumn rains, it headed westward. After waiting at Louisville for high water to run the falls, it arrived at New Orleans on January 12, 1812. This pioneer vessel did not return to the Ohio. It remained on the lower Mississippi, running between New Orleans and Natchez until it was snagged near Baton Rouge on a summer night in 1814.

Other steamboats followed. By 1815 the *Enterprise* and the *Aetna* ran profitably in the Louisville-New Orleans trade. In 1816 at Brownsville on the Monongahela, fifty miles above Pittsburgh, Henry M. Shreve launched the *Washington.* This 400-ton, two-decked, sternwheel steamer had a shallow, flat-bottomed hull to ride the river currents and rub over the shoals. Its main deck housed a high-pressure engine; above it was a cabin deck with a pilothouse framed by two tall chimneys. This vessel set the pattern for all future steamboats on the western rivers.

The *Washington* voyaged down to New Orleans late in 1816. In the spring of 1817 it made a historic run upstream against the April current, with full cargo, reaching Louisville on the twenty-fifth day out of New Orleans. This trip convinced the public that stream navigation had mastered the willful rivers. Now the boatyards of Pittsburgh and Cincinnati clamored with building. By 1820 some sixty steamboats were churning the Ohio and the Mississippi. The number reached 740 by 1850, the peak year of steamboat commerce. Louisville, at the Falls of the Ohio, was the early center of steamboat trade; from Louisville's wharves regular service ran up to Pittsburgh and down to New Orleans. In the 1840s Cincinnati developed the leading steamboat business, but with westward expansion St. Louis forged ahead. In the 1850s trade between Cincinnati and New Orleans declined while commerce between St. Louis and the South was growing. In years just prior to the Civil War, steamboats were lined for twenty blocks along the St. Louis levee.

In the 1850s the western rivers carried three million people annually. Steamboat travel was both luxurious and squalid. The stately four-deckers, white as a wedding cake, had floral carpets, inlaid furniture, and oil paintings on the stateroom doors. They provided a

The interior of the steamer J. M. White *represented the ultimate in luxury among riverboats. (Library of Congress)*

nursery, a barber shop, gaming rooms, and a gleaming bar. Their cabin passengers sat down to five-course dinners with orchestra music. But most of the travelers were deck passengers who never saw the splendors of the grand salon. Immigrants, woodsmen, and pioneer farmers, they were crowded among livestock and cargo on the lower deck, cooked their porridge on the boiler flues, drank river water, and slept on bales and boxes. Living close to the engines and the waterline, they were the first victims of explosion and collision. The one inducement of deck passage was economy. A decker could travel some five hundred miles for a dollar—one fifth the fare for cabin passengers.

Along with settlement and commerce the rivers brought entertainment to frontier communities. The first showboat, a roofed barge carried by the river current, floated from Pittsburgh to New Orleans in 1831, presenting music, melodrama, and farce to mud-stained farmers and woodsmen at river landings. They paid admission with apples, potatoes, eggs, and bacon more often than with cash. In 1836 came the *Steamboat Theater*. It could move both upstream and down, and it worked side rivers as well as the Ohio and the Mississippi.

The 1850s, the peak decade of steamboat traffic, saw many kinds of entertainment on the rivers—musical troupes, medicine shows, menageries, minstrel shows, and circuses. The biggest of the circus boats, the white and gold *Floating Circus Palace,* could seat a thousand people; it was towed by a sidewheel steamer that provided quarters for its performers. While steamboat commerce ebbed at the end of the century, the showboats held on. Showboating then changed from a simple, grass-roots entertainment to burlesqued melodrama. In river cities people came to laugh at the old-time stage hits. But nostalgia was in their laughter, and magic lingered in the music of the steam calliope.

Steamboat service on the upper Mississippi began in 1823, when the small stern-wheeler *Virginia* labored up the river past army posts and Indian camps to Fort Snelling at the mouth of the Minnesota River. During the next two decades a lively trade developed between St. Louis and the lead mines of southwestern Wisconsin. A surge of settlement in the 1840s brought a growing steamboat commerce to the head of navigation. In 1858 more than a thousand steamboat arrivals were recorded at St. Paul.

Log rafts came down the upper Mississippi from the northern woods. For thirty years it was a silent commerce, the huge slow islands floating past with only the clatter of the cook's iron kettle and the cry of the steersman. At journey's end—at the sawmills of Burlington, Muscatine, New Madison, and St. Louis—the raftsmen shaved their beards, slicked down their hair, and went ashore with money in their pockets. In riverfront saloons the dance-girls sang: "There ain't no cub as cute as him,/Dandy-handy Raftsman Jim." After the Civil War rafting was done by steamboat. Powerful boats with big stern wheels pushed acres of timber around the river bends. Log rafting peaked in the 1880s, when more than a hundred raft boats brought lumber down the Mississippi. By 1900 the pine lands were depleted, however, and rafting was mostly a memory.

A few miles above St. Louis the Missouri River pours its muddy flood into the Mississippi. The longest river on the continent, the Missouri flows about 2,500 miles south from the Bitterroot Range of Montana. In the 1820s an irregular steamboat commerce went as far south on the Mississippi as Council Bluffs, 660 miles from the Missouri mouth. For thirty years keelboats had carried the fur trade, toiling upstream with trade goods

and swirling down with baled peltry. In 1830 the American Fur Company built at Louisville the 144-ton *Yellowstone,* a sturdy steamboat with a roomy cargo deck and an upraised wheelhouse from which a pilot could scan the snag-studded river. In spring 1832 this vessel churned north to the company's big post of Fort Union at the mouth of the Yellowstone River. It was a marvel to the Indians and traders there.

The far western migration, at first to Oregon and Utah and then to the goldfields of California, made a busy steamboat trade on the lower Missouri. In the 1850s some fifty boats ran regularly from St. Louis to Independence, St. Joseph, and Council Bluffs, all stagecoach terminals for the long trek overland. Through the busy lower Missouri also passed some shallow-draft "mountain boats," bound for remoter places. Riding the hump of spring water from melting mountain snow, they carried troops, trade goods, and military supplies to posts on the upper Missouri. In 1859 the stern-wheeler *Chippewa* went 2,200 miles up the river, discharging cargo a few miles short of Fort Benton. In 1860 two steamers, *Chippewa* and *Key West,* made it all the way to the fort. These vessels lived off the land, their hunters seeking game while the crew chopped fuelwood from the river rack heaps.

Discovery of gold in Montana made Fort Benton a busy landing. In 1867 seventy-one steamers cleared St. Louis for the mountains. With cabin fare at $300 and freight at 12½ cents a pound, it was a profitable trade. By clearing $50,000 on the Fort Benton run, a steamboat could pay for itself in a single trip. It was also hazardous. With the menace of snags, shoals, and boiler explosion, the average life of an upper Missouri boat was three years. In 1870 the Northern Pacific Railway began construction and by 1885 it had carried off the steamboat trade on the Missouri.

During the Civil War the lower Mississippi was block-

A flatboat on the Mississippi (1898). (Library of Congress)

aded and main-stream traffic halted. After the war some lavish boats were launched—the *Great Republic*, the new *Natchez*, and the palatial *J. M. White*. But railroad engines were whistling from the riverbank and trains clattered past the steamboats. By 1886 Memphis was shipping four times as much cotton by rail as by river. On the *J. M. White* the roustabouts sang: "Oh shovel up de furnace/Till smoke put out de stars;/We's gwine along de river/Like we's bound to beat de cars." But the cars had already won the race of speed and profit. A few packets hung on into the twentieth century, but the steamboat age was past. The modern bulk commerce on the rivers was moved by diesel towboats and barges.

In 1882 Mark Twain, revisiting the river after an absence of twenty years, wrote: "Mississippi steamboating was born about 1812; at the end of thirty years it had grown to mighty proportions; and in less than thirty more it was dead. A strangely short life for so majestic a creature."

See Samuel L. Clemens [Mark Twain], *Life on the Mississippi* (1883); Walter Havighurst, *Voices on the River* (1964); Joseph Mills Hanson, *The Conquest of the Missouri* (1946); Louis C. Hunter, *Steamboats on the Western Rivers* (1949); and George Byron Merrick, *Old Times on the Upper Mississippi* (1909).—W. H.

Transylvania Company. See Richard HENDERSON and the Treaty of SYCAMORE SHOALS.

Transylvania Seminary. Transylvania Seminary was chartered by the Virginia general assembly in May 1780. The act creating the seminary donated the escheated lands of Tories Robert McKenzie, Alexander McKee, and Henry Collins, who owned eight thousand acres of land distributed in Fayette and Jefferson counties, Kentucky. Administration of this land was vested in a board of thirteen trustees, and the list of their names is almost a roll call of the prominent early settlers of Kentucky. The board was instructed to proceed with the organization of a seminary and to begin the processes of educating the youth of the Kentucky frontier. A first meeting of the board was called at Crow's Station in Boyle County, November 1783. Only a part of the board, now expanded to twenty-one trustees, attended, and little was accomplished except to effect the most elementary organization.

Not until 1784 were classes taught, and then for only one year by the Reverend James Mitchell. The board was unable to secure another teacher after 1785, and the seminary all but disappeared. Report after report of the secretary indicated little or no interest on the part of the board of trustees. In 1788 Transylvania Seminary was moved from Crow's Station to Lexington, which was growing into a cultural center. Here it became no more than another grammar school academy. In 1794 James Moore, the first Episcopal minister in Kentucky, was elected the first president of Transylvania and immediately became involved in a sectarian row. Transylvania was divided in this dispute and was not drawn together again until 1796. In 1799 the seminary was organized into a university, giving instruction in the liberal arts, medicine, law, and theology. Between 1800 and 1830 the Transylvania Medical School was one of the three or four important institutions of its kind in the country. The university itself experienced its golden age during the decade by 1817-27, when the New England Unitarian minister Horace Holley was president. Bick-

ering, sectarianism, poverty, and anti-intellectualism, however, wrecked the school. It never fulfilled its mission of becoming an important western public university.

See W. W. Jennings, *Transylvania, Pioneer University of the West* (1955); Rebecca Smith Lee, *Mary Austin Holley: A Biography* (1962); Robert Peter and Johanna Peter, *Transylvania University* (1896); and Nils Henry Sonne, *Liberal Kentucky, 1780-1828* (1939).—T. D. C.

trappers. During the colonial period the French operated officially through a monopolistic system that relied on the Indians to do the actual trapping (see FUR TRADE: *in the colonies*). However, the illegal white fur trappers—the *coureurs de bois*—bulked large in the total trade until the Treaty of Paris (1763). The English colonial trappers were both private individuals and company employees, as were those of Spain. Following independence, United States trappers were not only private individuals and fur company employees, but also—like Daniel Boone—employees of land-speculating companies as the frontier moved through the Ohio valley to the Old Northwest and the Old Southwest on to the banks of the Mississippi. In Canada both the North West Company and the Hudson's Bay Company used primarily *engagés*, employees who were paid regular salaries. This was also the method used by the Missouri River traders until the innovations introduced by William H. ASHLEY, who decided in the early 1820s to combine Donald Mackenzie's concept of mobile brigades with that of an annual rendezvous rather than a permanent trading post (see FUR TRADE: *in the United States*). Ashley was the first in the Rockies to rely heavily on the colorful free trapper or mountain man, who sold his furs to the highest bidder.

The free trapper in the Rockies and elsewhere was both an enterprising businessman who desired to make enough money to retire to civilization and one of the freest individuals to reside in the American republic. His freedom was precarious though, for the trapper was always menaced by grizzly bears, storms, and Indians throughout his sometimes brief life.

George Frederick Ruxton, who had many opportunities to observe these free men, recorded his impressions in his *Adventures in Mexico and the Rocky Mountains* (1849). The trapper started out on a hunt with all the necessary equipment:

... two or three horses or mules—one for saddle, the others for packs—and six traps, which are carried in a bag of leather called a *trap-sack*. Ammunition, a few pounds of tobacco, dressed deer-skins for moccasins, &c., are carried in a wallet of dressed buffalo-skin, called a possible-sack. [His costume consisted of] a hunting-shirt of dressed buckskin, ornamented with long fringes; pantaloons of the same material, and decorated with porcupine-quills and long fringes down the outside of the leg. A flexible felt hat and moccasins clothe his extremities. Over his left shoulder and under his right arm hang his powder-horn and bullet-pouch, in which he carries his balls, flint and steel, and odds and ends of all kinds. Round the waist is a belt, in which is stuck a large butcher-knife in a sheath of buffalo-hide, made fast to the belt by a chain or guard of steel; which also supports a little buckskin case containing a whetstone. A tomahawk is also often added; and, of course, a long heavy rifle is part and parcel of his equipment.

Dressed so, he left his cabin or Indian village and moved into the mountains, where he followed creeks and streams looking for signs of beaver. When he found a fresh one, he set the trap in the animal's run, hid it under the water, attached it by a chain to a stick driven in the bank or to a tree, and baited it with "medicine," a substance obtained from the animal's scrotum. The animal, attracted by the smell, would put his leg into the trap, becoming a "gone beaver." Each morning the hunter checked the traps. Captured animals were skinned and brought back to camp, where the skins were then stretched over a frame, dried, and scraped, then folded into a square (fur turned inward), bundled up with ten or twenty other skins, and tied—ready for transport. The distances covered in a three-month spring or fall hunt by the competitive brigades and other groups during the 1830s were enormous—often over a thousand miles of rugged trails and dangerous rivers. Every day the trappers had to pitch shelter, cut firewood, look for food, and care for their livestock.

In the summer the trapper came to the rendezvous to mingle with company trappers, traders, and Indians in the annual exchange of goods for fur. For his laborious work he usually obtained about $130 per year, which he dissipated in buying liquor and other goods from the traders and in gambling. The fall hunt then followed, until the trapper was forced into winter quarters. Then the routine was often broken when the trappers regaled one another with stories and reading in the "Rocky Mountain College." The routine always began again as soon as the ice melted.

The trappers were far more than components of an economic enterprise. As explorers, they opened the entire region beyond the Mississippi. Later, some, like Thomas FITZPATRICK were guides to government explorers, such as John Frémont, and to settler and missionary trains; one of the hardiest of the mountain men, Caleb GREENWOOD, led the first wagon train across the Sierra at age eighty-one. They corrupted the Indians. They became an ineradicable part of American folklore, romanticized by journalists, novelists, and painters as children of nature—wild, free, unafraid, often reverting to the Indian level as colorful primitives. (Some trappers and mountain men, such as Jim BECKWOURTH, James BAKER, Edward ROSE, and William S. WILLIAMS, actually lived with Indians.)

The trappers' era was brilliant but brief; by 1840 the decline of beaver by overtrapping had sealed its fate. But trapping continued, principally in the Great Lakes region, mainly as a sideline of farmers and lumbermen. In fact, the fur trade sustained itself until the depression of the 1930s.

See Ray A. Billington, *Far Western Frontier* (1956); Robert Glass Cleland, *This Reckless Breed of Men: The Trappers and Fur Traders of the Southwest* (1950); William H. Goetzmann, *Exploration and Empire* (1966); and LeRoy R. Hafen, ed., *The Mountain Men and the Fur Trade of the Far West,* 9 vols. (1965-72).—G. B. D.

travelers' guidebooks. See EMIGRANTS' GUIDEBOOKS.

Tryon's Line (1767). Tryon's Line was part of the boundary laid off between the English colonies and the trans-Appalachian Indian hunting grounds, according to the requirements of the Proclamation of 1763, which prohibited white settlement west of the Appalachians. After South Carolina completed the survey of its portion of the line in 1766, North Carolina governor William Tryon met with representatives of the Cherokee and agreed upon the location of his colony's western boundary. Tryon appointed John Rutherford, Robert Palmer, and John Frohock as commissioners to survey the line in company with representatives of the Cherokee, which was accomplished in June 1767. Beginning at the end of the South Carolina boundary on Reedy River (a northern tributary of the Saluda), Tryon's Line ran northwesterly to a marked oak atop Tryon's Mountain, and thence northeasterly to Chiswell's Mines (present-day Austinville, Virginia). The line, like the rest of the Indian boundary, had little effect in stopping the westward push of settlement.

See J. R. Alden, *John Stuart and the Southern Colonial Frontier, 1754-1775* (1944).—P. R. M.

Tsimshian Indians. See INDIANS OF THE NORTHWEST COAST.

Tubac, Arizona. Following the Pima revolt in 1751, the Spanish government constructed the presidio San Ignacio de Tubac on the Santa Cruz River near the present international border, and within a decade more than three hundred settlers were living in the vicinity. Irrigated farms were started and mines discovered in the neighboring mountains. In 1775 from Tubac, Captain Juan Bautista de Anza led colonists west to San Francisco Bay, and the garrison was moved north to Tucson. Only a few families remained at Tubac. By 1820 the Mexican government designated the Santa Cruz valley a *partido* (unorganized county) with Tubac the political seat, and it attempted to establish a military colony there. Following the Gadsden Purchase in 1853, the Sonora Exploring and Mining Company occupied Tubac and opened silver mines. In February 1860 the New Mexico legislature created Arizona County with Tubac the county seat, but the following year Tubac was again abandoned and never completely revived. After the Civil War a few of the old families returned and several ranches sprang up in the vicinity. In 1958 the first state park in Arizona was located on the presidio grounds.

See Henry F. Dobyns, "Tubac Through Four Centuries" (1959), a typescript in the Arizona State Museum, Tucson.—H. P. H.

Tucson, Arizona. Spain founded the presidio of San Agustín del Tucson on the east bank of the Santa Cruz River in December 1775. Named after the Papago village across the river at the base of Chuck Son ("blackbase") mountain, the site had been visited by Jesuit missionaries as early as the 1690s. Although suffering severe Apache attacks, Tucson by 1800 grew into a town, with Spanish families building homes near the presidial walls. After the Gadsden Purchase in 1853, which added southern Arizona to the Union, Tucson shared in the prosperity generated by the Sonora Exploring and Mining Company when it opened silver mines in the valley. However, the outbreak of the Civil War caused the mines to close, the garrisons in Arizona to leave, and all regular land transportation to cease. In February 1862 the Confederates occupied Tucson but withdrew when a Union army from California arrived in May. In 1864 Tucson was incorporated and Bill Oury (see OURY

BROTHERS) became mayor. It was designated the seat of Pima County and served as the territorial capital from 1867 to 1877. With the Tombstone and Bisbee mineral discoveries, Tucson entered a boom. The Southern Pacific Railroad arrived in 1880 and subsequently built extensive railroad shops, and the University of Arizona opened its doors in 1885. The Twin Buttes and Silver Bell mines buoyed up the local economy at the turn of the century, as did federal spending in World War I. In the 1920s Tucson became a mecca for health-seekers and tourists, and by 1970 it had a population of 258,000.

See Bernice Cosulich, *Tucson* (1953).—H. P. H.

Tumacácori. Spanish mission. San Cayetano de Tumacácori, as it was first known, was one of three Arizona missions founded by Father Eusebio KINO, the energetic "Padre on Horseback." It began as a *visita,* or outpost of the GUEVAVI mission in 1697. Tumacácori was then a Pima Indian village of some forty families located on the Santa Cruz River, eighteen miles north of Guevavi and about forty miles south of the site of SAN XAVIER DEL BAC. Tumacácori's early history remains fragmentary, but Kino himself reported that the Indians provided three brush shelters for him and Father Juan María Salvatierra (one for saying mass, one for cooking, and one for sleeping) in 1691 when they passed through on a historic tour of the Pimería Alta. By 1695 Kino had provided the Indians with a herd of sheep and goats and two years later ordered cattle driven a hundred miles overland from Sonora to lay the foundation for a mission cattle ranch at Tumacácori. Overshadowed by Guevavi and by Bac, which was in a more heavily populated area, Tumacácori faced an uncertain future. It was often without a resident priest and was abandoned during the Pima rebellion of 1751, during which the fathers fled to safety in Sonora and the missions were looted. In 1752 the Spanish government established a presidio at Tubac, less than five miles from Tumacácori. Some three hundred families soon settled at the presidio, and so Tumacácori became busily engaged in serving the religious needs of the presidio's soldiers, colonists, and Indians.

After the Jesuits were expelled from the New World mission in 1767, by order of Charles III of Spain, Franciscans from Querétaro, Mexico, took over the Arizona missions. At the same time, the entire defense system of the northern border was revamped. Guevavi, less protected from Apache raiders than Tumacácori, began to decline. By 1773 Tumacácori had replaced it as the head mission and had its own visitas. At some point the name of the mission was changed to San José de Tumacácori, while one of the neighboring villages took the name San Cayetano. It would be misleading to suggest that all was well, however, for Tumacácori was also subject to Apache raids. Father Bartholomé Ximeno complained in 1773 that the resident Indian population consisted of less than thirty families, while the mission herd, which once numbered two thousand, had been reduced to forty-six head of cattle. Two years later the commander at Tubac reported that the Apache had carried off everything from Tumacácori.

Tumacácori never enjoyed the peace and prosperity of the California missions, even though it was surrounded by rich farmlands and had an excellent irrigation system. In addition to grain fields, the fathers had a vineyard and lush productive gardens. Important visitors stopped there; in 1775 when Juan Bautista de ANZA led a group of pioneers overland to settle the Bay of San Francisco region, Father Thomas Eixarch, one of its priests, joined Father Garcés of Bac to start a new mission and colony at Yuma on the Colorado River. The Franciscans and the Indians built a large adobe church between 1790 and 1822, which were years of peak activity at the mission as they were at Bac and in California. The church was never really completed, but in 1822 it was occupied and used until Apache raids forced both the Indians and the fathers to abandon the mission completely around 1840. The mission began to fall into ruins, but since 1908, when it was designated a national monument, efforts have been made to preserve it from further deterioration.

Tumacácori confronts the visitor with a mixture of styles, partly primitive and partly baroque. The main doorway is in the shape of a wide Roman arch; the façade is decorated by two tiers of columns and is topped by a rounded wall of half-moon shape, perhaps inspired by Moorish designs. The church itself had a flat roof supported by wooden beams, which collapsed many years ago, but the dome over the altar still stands. Roman arches penetrate the upper story of the unfinished belfry, but the base is such a primitive, massive, and fortresslike quadrangle of adobe that it stands in stark contrast to the more delicate façade of the church. A modern museum nearby depicts the history of the mission and of the region.

See Herbert E. Bolton, *Rim of Christendom: A Biography of Eusebio Kino, Pacific Coast Pioneer* (1939); Earl Jackson, *Tumacácori's Yesterdays,* U.S. Department of the Interior, National Park Service, Southwest National Monuments, no. 6 (1951); Frank C. Lockwood, *Story of the Spanish Missions of the Middle Southwest* (1934); and Fay Jackson Smith, John L. Kessell, and Francis J. Fox, *Father Kino in Arizona* (1966).—H. R. L.

tundra. See VEGETATION: *mountains.*

Tunstall, John. See LINCOLN COUNTY WAR.

Turner, Frederick Jackson (1861-1932). Historian and educator. Turner was born in Portage, Wisconsin. His father, a newspaper editor and local political leader who extolled the virtues of self-sufficiency, exerted a strong influence on young Turner. After graduating from Portage High School, he enrolled at the University of Wisconsin at Madison. Here he came under the influence of William F. Allen, an able teacher who urged his students to adopt the more scientific methods of historical investigation then used in German universities. Allen also passed on to Turner his own conviction that social institutions are formed in part by the powerful forces and evolutionary changes underlying historical events. Following his graduation from the university in 1884, Turner worked briefly as a newspaper correspondent but returned to complete his master's degree under Allen, writing his thesis on the Wisconsin fur trade. In 1888 he entered Johns Hopkins University for doctoral study under Herbert Baxter Adams. Turner's doctoral dissertation, *The Character and Influence of the Indian Trade in Wisconsin* (1891), reflected the teachings of both Allen and Adams in that the fur-trading post was portrayed as a historic institution on the frontiers of Anglo-American civilization. Appointed assistant professor of history at Madison in 1889, Turner, an agreeable colleague and talented teacher, became a faculty leader in dealings with a conservative board of regents. He taught at Wisconsin until 1910, the year of his election to the presidency of the American Historical Association and his move to Harvard University. He retired from teaching in 1924 and, following a temporary residence in Madison, accepted the post of research associate at the Henry E. Huntington Library in 1927, where he spent his last years in writing and research.

Turner's essay "The Significance of the Frontier in American History," setting forth the influential FRONTIER THEORY, was read at the 1893 meeting of the American Historical Association in Chicago. Variations of the frontier theory are set forth in Turner's two books of published essays, *The Frontier in American History* (1920) and *The Significance of Sections in American History* (1932), the latter of which was awarded the Pulitzer Prize. An earlier book, *The Rise of the New West, 1819-1829* (1906), and his last volume, *The United States, 1830-1850* (1935), traced the history of the United States through epochs of frontier and sectional development. The volumes *Significance of Sections* and *The United States, 1830-1850* were published posthumously.

In all his teachings and writings Turner stressed the interrelationships of political, economic, and social history. In his frontier theory he spotlighted the powerful influence that the availability of land and other frontier conditions had on the growth of American society as pioneer settlements went through a process of social evolution. Turner's theory of sections, based on the idea of multiple causation, showed that there were numerous forces behind the federation of sections that comprised the American nation.

A short biography of Turner appears in *America's Great Frontiers and Sections*, Wilbur R. Jacobs, ed. (1969), but a full account of his professional life, including a selection of his correspondence, is in Jacobs, *The Historical World of Frederick Jackson Turner* (1968). Carl Becker, "Frederick Jackson Turner," in *American Masters of Social Science*, Howard W. Odum, ed. (1927), portrays Turner as a teacher. Ray A. Billington, "Why Some Historians Rarely Write History: A Case Study of Frederick Jackson Turner," *Mississippi Valley Historical Review* (1963), reveals Turner's difficulties as a writer. See also Billington, *Frederick Jackson Turner: Historian, Scholar, Teacher* (1973).—W. R. J.

Turner, James Milton (1840-1915). Black leader and diplomat. Turner was born a slave in St. Louis County, Missouri. His father had been brought from Virginia in the early 1830s by one Benjamin Tillman, who subsequently taught him the art of veterinary medicine. The elder Turner managed to save enough to buy his own freedom and then by a ruse reduce the price of his wife to four hundred dollars. Her owner threw her four-year-old son into the bargain for an extra fifty dollars.

When he grew old enough, young Turner was put to work as an office boy at various St. Louis businesses. He also attended a "tallow candle school," instituted secretly for Negroes by a group of Catholic nuns. At age fourteen his father sent him to Oberlin College. Returning to St. Louis in 1859, Turner secured a job with the St. Louis and Iron Mountain Railroad, and when its president, Madison Miller, entered Union service in May 1861, Turner went with him as his body servant. He saw action at Wilson's Creek and received a hip injury at

Shiloh, which left him with a limp for the rest of his life. Following his recovery, Turner returned to St. Louis and spent the rest of the war assisting fugitive slaves in their flight to Illinois and freedom.

After the war Turner became the secretary of the Missouri Equal Rights League, an organization established by blacks and white Radical politicians to secure Negro suffrage. Through his ties with Miller, Turner had direct access to the new Radical administration of Governor Thomas C. Fletcher, his ex-employer's brother-in-law. In April 1866 he became the teacher of the first public school for blacks in Missouri at Kansas City. He also became interested in promoting the recently established Lincoln Institute for Negroes at Jefferson City and was instrumental in securing for it the support of Radical politicians and an annual state appropriation.

When the blacks finally secured suffrage under the Fifteenth Amendment, Turner took the lead in assuring them representation at the Radical state convention of 1870. In the Liberal Republican split of that year he remained loyal to the Radicals, and in the aftermath of their defeat President Grant rewarded him with the appointment as minister resident and consul general to Liberia. He thus became the first black to serve in the diplomatic corps. Turner continued in this capacity until May 1878 and upon his return to the United States was widely recognized as a leading spokesman for his race.

In the 1880s Turner became interested in the claims of freedmen among the Cherokee, Choctaw, and Chickasaw of Oklahoma to their nations' just share of congressional allotments. These he pushed in the courts with considerable success. Thereafter he divided his time between business interests in St. Louis and the Indian Territory.

A complete narrative may be found in Irving Dilliard, "James Milton Turner, a Little Known Benefactor of His Race," *Journal of Negro History* (October 1934). Turner's role in post-Civil War Missouri is traced in William E. Parrish, *Missouri Under Radical Rule, 1865-1870* (1965). Useful interviews with Turner are in the *St. Louis Post-Dispatch*, March 6, 1893, and July 9, 1911. —W. E. P.

Tuscarora Indians. The Tuscarora Indians were a confederation of three Iroquoian tribes, numbering approximately five thousand members, who inhabited eastern North Carolina between the Roanoke and Cape Fear rivers during the late seventeenth and early eighteenth centuries. The length of their occupancy of the region prior to the advent of English exploration and settlement is undetermined, but they had lived previously farther north in close association with the Iroquois of New York. Little is known of the details of their culture during the period of white colonization, but it was generally very similar to that of the Iroquois and became more so in later years.

Their first contacts with the colonists were amiable, but as the whites revealed their racial arrogance by appropriating land without any form of purchase and by seizing large numbers of Indian women and children and selling them as slaves in other colonies, the Tuscarora attitude hardened into enmity. After several unsuccessful attempts to get the governments of some of these colonies to intercede in the slave traffic on their behalf, the Tuscarora were forced to resist with violence. In September 1711 a group of warriors captured John Lawson, the surveyor general of North Carolina, and tried and executed him as a criminal by tribal law. Immediately afterward, a large portion of the Tuscarora, led by Chief Hencock and aided by warriors from some adjoining tribes, attacked and killed about 130 colonists at the Trent and Pamlico rivers on September 22. South Carolina responded to North Carolina's plight by sending a Colonel Barnwell with a force of colonists and friendly Indians to attack the Tuscarora. During January 1712 Barnwell destroyed one Tuscarora town and besieged Chief Hencock's village, forcing the Indians to accept terms of peace. While marching back to South Carolina, however, Barnwell became dissatisfied by North Carolina's failure to reward him in what he felt was a sufficient manner, and so broke his own treaty by capturing several Indians which he sold as slaves. The outraged Tuscarora again rose in arms, and again South Carolina dispatched a force of militia and friendly Indians (primarily Catawba), led by Colonel James Moore. On March 22-23, 1713, Moore stormed the palisaded Tuscarora town of Neoheroka and inflicted nearly a thousand casualties. Soon after, the Tuscarora began to abandon their homes and migrate north to rejoin their Iroquois kinsmen. On this northward trek they were beset by difficulties caused by Indians of Siouan and Algonquian related tribes. The movement was not com plete until the early nineteenth century, but the bulk of the Tuscarora was in New York by 1722, when they were sponsored by the Oneida and granted coordinate rights in the IROQUOIS CONFEDERACY, forming the sixth group of the cluster of nations. There is some doubt, however, that this is entirely so, since the term "Six Nations" had been used prior to the arrival of the Tuscarora. In subsequent years Tuscarora history merged with that of the Iroquois, and particularly the Oneida subdivision.

See Samuel G. Drake, *The Aboriginal Races of North America* (1880); F. W. Hodge, ed., *Handbook of American Indians North of Mexico*, 2 vols. (1907-10); and Harry Errald Stafford, *The Early Inhabitants of the Americas* (1959).—T. D. C.

Twain, Mark. Pen name of **Samuel Langhorne Clemens** (1835-1910). Novelist, short-story writer, and lecturer. Twain was born in the small town of Florida, Missouri, and from 1839 to 1853 lived in Hannibal, Missouri, which he was later to depict in much of his fiction. There his father died in 1847, leaving the family little but the vague hope of financial success, based upon the unlikely eventuality that a tract of land that the family owned in Tennessee would, in some future land boom, appreciate fantastically in value.

Twain was apprenticed as a printer and in 1853-54 traveled to St. Louis and then to New York and Philadelphia. Not much is known of this *Wanderjahr* in the East, but on it Twain apparently picked up the restlessness that was never afterward to leave him. In 1856 he seriously considered the wild scheme of going to South America, to make his fortune by collecting cocoa along the Amazon, supporting himself in the meantime by the fees he would receive from letters he planned to write to a Keokuk, Iowa, newspaper. Though this grandiose plan came to nothing, Twain did apprentice himself as a river pilot on the Mississippi the following year (see RIVERMEN). However, he gave up piloting as well in

1861 to travel west as confidential secretary to his brother Orion, a newly appointed secretary to the territorial governor of Nevada. In Nevada Twain became first an unsuccessful, though enthusiastic, prospector and then, in 1862, a reporter in Virginia City, where his articles appeared under the name of Mark Twain. In 1864 he went to California, where he met Bret Harte, with whom he later collaborated on the drama *Ah Sin* (1877). In 1865 his story "The Celebrated Jumping Frog of Calaveras County" appeared in the New York *Saturday Press*, and on the strength of this slender connection with the literary world a California newspaper sent Twain to the Sandwich Islands as a roving journalist. Later he went to the Mediterranean and the Holy Land, a trip that was reported in *The Innocents Abroad* (1869). This book gave Twain not only a national reputation but a good bit of money as well, enabling him to marry, in 1870, Olivia Langdon. From 1869 to 1871 Twain worked in Buffalo, New York, as a writer for the Buffalo *Express*. Later he moved to Hartford, and then to Redding, Connecticut. When one of his financial speculations, in the publishing house of Charles L. Webster & Co., turned out disastrously after a promising beginning, Twain was left with a considerable amount of personal debts. (Twain's speculations were never happy, and the fate of this company prefigures his even more unsuccessful involvement with the Paige typesetting machine, a linotype-like printing device.) To clear his debts Twain turned again to writing. *Roughing It* appeared in 1872, followed by his first novel, a collaboration with Charles Dudley Warner entitled *The Gilded Age* (1873), and then *Old Times on the Mississippi* (1875), *The Adventures of Tom Sawyer* (1876), *A Tramp Abroad* (1880), *Life on the Mississippi* (1883), *The Adventures of Huckleberry Finn* (1884), *A Connecticut Yankee in King Arthur's Court* (1889), and *The Tragedy of Pudd'nhead Wilson* (1894). By 1898 Twain had paid off his debts, partly from the proceeds of his books and partly from the profits of an enormously successful round-the-world lecture tour begun in 1895.

Strangely enough, however, 1898 was the year of Twain's darkest pessimism. In conjunction with the humorous side of his character, Twain had always had a pessimistic strain, as evidenced by the three books written in 1898, *The Man that Corrupted Hadleyburg* (1900), *What Is Man?* (1906), and *The Mysterious Stranger* (1916). His beloved wife died in 1904, and his daughter, Jean, in 1909. Twain himself died in 1910, fulfilling his half-humorous prediction that since his birth had coincided with the appearance of Halley's comet his death would come when the comet again appeared.

It is somewhat misleading to refer to Twain loosely as a western writer without defining one's terms rather carefully. Missouri, Twain's birthplace, was certainly not the frontier West by any stretch of definition in 1835. Indeed, Twain spent only slightly longer than five years on or near the frontier. Moreover, much discussion of Twain's "southwestern humor" had overemphasized its western elements by an unthinking confusion between rural, provincial life and purely western life. While it is undoubtedly fair to speak of Twain as outside the genteel literary tradition of Brahmin New England, it is inexact to speak of him as an expression of a peculiarly "western" sensitivity, divorced from the tradition of American rural writing. Indeed, *Roughing It* was his only major work to be written specifically about the West, and though it must be ranked as one of the best of the manifold quasiautobiographical travel books about frontier experiences, it is an exception both in theme and subject matter to Twain's ordinary material. It is worth noting that the presentation of *Roughing It* presumes an eastern, rather than a western, sensitivity; the various adventures that Twain encounters, the anecdotes he tells, in short all the manifold experiences he undergoes, are selected as significant on the basis of their oddity and picturesqueness to eastern eyes. As the reporter in *Roughing It,* Twain's stance is that of an easterner, something of a dude, who is amused and bewildered by the western life he finds about him.

Most of Twain's writing that concerns itself with roughly contemporary society is, in theme and setting, Mississippi valley writing, perhaps more southern than western, but more middle western than either. Though in books like *The Prince and the Pauper* (1882), *A Connecticut Yankee in King Arthur's Court,* and *The Mysterious Stranger* Twain forsakes the real world for imaginative fairylands, he instinctively sets his stories in the Mississippi valley of his boyhood when he writes of the world he knows. Another quasitravel book, *Life on the Mississippi,* indicates far more than does *Roughing It* Twain's basic literary world.

Nonetheless, the common definition of Twain as a western writer is accurate if taken in the negative sense that, whatever his writing may be, it is not eastern. Indeed, Twain refused to be cowed by the genteel literary standards of Brahmin "fine writing." He may be compared with Walt Whitman—a poet with whom he has almost nothing else in common—in that both tried to sound a "barbaric yawp" against the confining standards of a too-precious "correct" literary taste.

In this sense, the meaning and significance of Twain's "westernism" is his discovery of a viable way to present folk themes in "polite" literary form. One of his earliest and best stories, "The Celebrated Jumping Frog of Calaveras County," which is based upon an actual anecdote Twain had heard while in California, is a tall story of a type already familiar to anecdotalists about the frontier. Twain's contribution to this already venerable form is to imply ironic depth by pointing out what eastern raconteurs of the quaint western anecdote fail to see: the real butt of the tall story is not the foolish teller but the gullible listener. The teller of the story of the celebrated jumping frog may look like a fool, but he turns out to be smart enough to feed an eastern dude an incredible whopper not only about how a frog named Daniel Webster can pick flies off a bar at command, but how this frog is beaten in a jumping contest by chicanery, when he is fed so full of buckshot that he can't move. In his later writing Twain became even more of a master of the apparently simple statement that conceals biting sarcasm. Who, for example, is really the butt of Huckleberry Finn's apparently innocuous remark that "If you notice, most folks don't go to church only when they've got to; but a hog is different"?

Though critics have long pointed out that in the process of revision many picturesque dialect forms have been cut out of much of Twain's writing (it used to be fashionable to blame his wife's censorship for diluting Twain's colorful prose, but it is now generally agreed

that her influence has been overemphasized), the fact still remains that his work, when it appeared, was startlingly innovative, equally free of the mannered style of the "cultivated" eastern magazines and the condescending and artificial "Wa-al, I swan!" dialect of the local colorists. Ernest Hemingway, in praising *Huckleberry Finn* as the one book from which all American literature descends, probably was speaking of its style. Like Hemingway, Twain wrote in a style that, though apparently simple and straightforward, is actually complex and ambiguous in its implications.

Twain's significance as a western writer, then, is far more than as a writer of stories in some trans-Mississippi idiom. He gave at once an insight into how the apparently uncouth westerner could criticize the pretensions of allegedly "genteel" writing, and a demonstration of the fact—now almost a commonplace—that the language of common speech is a literary language of uncommon power.

See Bernard De Voto, *Mark Twain's America* (1932), *Mark Twain in Eruption* (1940), and *Mark Twain at Work* (1942); William Dean Howells, *My Mark Twain* (1910); Albert Bigelow Paine, *Mark Twain: A Biography* (1912); Roger B. Saloman, *Twain and the Image of History* (1961); Henry Nash Smith, *Mark Twain: The Development of a Writer* (1962); Albert E. Stone, *The Innocent Eye* (1961); and Dixon Wector, *Sam Clemens of Hannibal* (1952).—J. K. F.

Twin Cities, Minnesota. The Twin Cities of St. Paul and Minneapolis, Minnesota's largest metropolitan center, owe their existence to the Mississippi River. St. Paul, located at the head of practical navigation on the river, became a popular port of call for steamboats in the 1840s. The city got its name from Father Lucien Galtier, who built there a log chapel dedicated to Saint Paul in the late fall of 1841. When Minnesota Territory was created in 1849, the bustling commercial town became the capital city. Through St. Paul moved hundreds of immigrants heading for outlying farmlands. Many of the farmers and merchants in the small towns that grew up among them bought supplies in St. Paul and shipped produce to the city. St. Paul thus became the leading commercial center in the state. When, in the 1860s, railroads came to Minnesota, St. Paul became the headquarters of railroads leading to Lake Superior, to southern Minnesota, and to connections with eastern systems (see BURLINGTON NORTHERN RAILROAD and CHICAGO, MILWAUKEE, ST. PAUL AND PACIFIC RAILROAD.) Before the city was thirty years old it could and did boast that it was the railroad and political capital of Minnesota, and the commercial emporium of the Northwest.

St. Paul early overshadowed Mendota and Fort Snelling, sites evoking memories of frontier Minnesota. Another historic spot, nine miles upstream from St. Paul, had a more enduring fame. The Falls of St. Anthony, known to white men since its discovery by Father Hennepin in 1680, attracted settlers too. Since the land at the falls on the west bank of the river was a part of the Fort Snelling military reservation, the pioneers built homes on the east bank. They named their town St. Anthony, in honor of the falls. In the early 1850s, when the military reservation was reduced and the land on the west bank was opened to settlement, a second town grew up at the falls. Called Minneapolis, it was linked to its sister city St.

Anthony by a beautiful suspension bridge. In 1872 the two towns united under the name Minneapolis, joining forces to become the largest city in Minnesota.

Minneapolis took its life from the falls. The cataract generated power for sawmills and the flour-milling industry which was supplied by the vast acreage of spring wheat in the Red River valley and Dakotas. Minneapolis quickly became known for its manufacturers throughout the nation. The city had commercial ambitions, too. Competing with St. Paul for railroads and the trade of the Northwest, Minneapolis became a wholesaling as well as a manufacturing center. Although each of the two cities predicted that it would some day absorb the other, both prospered.

Today St. Paul and Minneapolis are nonidentical twins—similar in economy and urban growth, yet differing in social and political traditions. St. Paul attracted a mix of immigrants, but the German and Irish predominated. It also became the Catholic ecclesiastical and educational center of the upper Midwest. The older of the Twin Cities, it tended to look east, adopting a conservative style of life. It was dubbed "the Boston of the Middle West." Minneapolis started later but grew faster. As the decades passed it became the larger city by a wide margin. More metropolitan than its sister city, it carved out its economic future from the vast resources of the Minnesota forests and the Great Plains states to the northwest. Its sawmills and flour mills were built on the timber and wheat fields that fed its burgeoning early industries. Like St. Paul, it attracted a variety of peoples. Scandinavians, however, were the largest group, and they shaped the city's traditions. Minneapolis became the Lutheran center of the United States as well as the home of the state's only major university. Its cultural endowments are considerable, with two important art centers and the Tyrone Guthrie Theater. Its "regional" position was further fortified as it became the financial and communications center of the upper Midwest.

See Carol Brink, *The Twin Cities* (1961); and Lucile M. Kane, "Rivalry for a River: The Twin Cities and the Mississippi," in Rhoda R. Gilman and June D. Holmquist, eds., *Selections from "Minnesota History": A Fiftieth Anniversary Anthology* (1965).—R. W. F.

Twitchell, Ralph Emerson (1859-1925). Historian and New Mexico politician. Named for the illustrious philosopher of Concord, Twitchell was born in Ann Arbor, Michigan. He was educated in the public schools of Missouri and received an L.L.B. from the University of Michigan in 1882. Attracted to New Mexico by the investment opportunities in railroads and mining and the immense possibilities for self-enrichment in the complicated litigation over Spanish and Mexican land titles, Twitchell arrived in Las Vegas in 1882, where he found employment in the law office of the popular Henry Waldo, the influential solicitor for the Atchison, Topeka and Santa Fe Railroad. This opportunity led to a lifelong association with the Sante Fe Railroad, which continued despite Twitchell's involvement in numerous public service capacities.

Twitchell's political career began when he became district attorney for the First Judicial District in 1889. In 1897 Miguel A. Otero, the first native governor of the Territory of New Mexico, appointed him judge-advocate of the territorial militia with the rank of colonel, a title he bore proudly for the rest of his life. Twitchell became mayor of Santa Fe in 1900, a particular honor because he so dearly loved the rich history and traditions of the ancient city. In the early 1920s, while serving as president of the Santa Fe Chamber of Commerce, he initiated a revival of the old Spanish fiesta commemorating the reconquest of New Mexico by Don Diego de Vargas in 1692, the pageantry of which is still enjoyed by Santa Feans and an increasing number of tourists.

But Twitchell is best remembered for his prodigious writings in New Mexico history from Spanish times through the territorial period. Nine hefty volumes plus many articles and pamphlets are credited to him. His first book was *History of the Military Occupation of the Territory of New Mexico, 1846-1851* (1909). Although containing many invaluable biographical sketches, it was a synthesis of work done by earlier historians of the American occupation of New Mexico. Always sensitive to criticism and self-conscious about his lack of historical training, Twitchell strove to do much better in his *Leading Facts of New Mexican History*, a five-volume work published between 1911 and 1917. Volume II, a chronology of the Mexican and territorial periods, suffered like the first volume from a lack of balance, particularly in its assessment of those territorial leaders who belonged to the controversial group of political manipulators and speculators in Spanish and Mexican land grants, the Santa Fe Ring, of which Twitchell himself was a member. Although Twitchell was hesitant to criticize members of the ring and especially reluctant to praise its opponents, his second volume of *Leading Facts* is, nevertheless, a storehouse of information and a natural starting point for anyone wishing to do serious research on the territorial period.

In 1913 Twitchell founded the historical quarterly *Old Santa Fe*, which was later displaced by the *New Mexico Historical Review*. In 1914 he published the first of a two-volume work entitled *The Spanish Archives of New Mexico*, in which he described the land title documents in the Department of the Interior. Twitchell had a possessive attitude toward the Spanish Archives, resisting the removal of many of the items in the collection to the Library of Congress in 1903. On May 12, 1892, he actually saved the treasured records from destruction when he rushed into the capitol building at night to rescue them from a fire.

Closely associated with the Museum of New Mexico, the School of American Research, and the Historical Society of New Mexico, Twitchell left an impressive amount of historical writings, some of which have become classics about the Southwest.

For an excellent biographical sketch of Twitchell and an analysis of his writings, see Myra Ellen Jenkins, "A Dedication to the Memory of Ralph Emerson Twitchell, 1859-1925," *Arizona and the West*. (1966).—R. W. L.

U

Udall family. Arizona pioneers.

David King (1851-1938), a Mormon bishop and entrepreneur, was born in St. Louis, Missouri. He worked as a freighter and farmer at Kanab, Utah, spent two years in England as a Mormon missionary, and in 1880 arrived in Arizona to preside as Mormon bishop over the St. Johns ward. Established in 1873 on the Little Colorado River, St. Johns was predominantly a Mexican town when the Mormons located a colony there in 1879, purchasing land from an early settler, Solomon Barth. Under Udall's supervision, irrigation ditches were built, a school established, a sawmill and gristmill erected, and the Arizona Cooperative Mercantile Institution organized. Udall held the local mail and express contracts from 1881 to 1918, was involved in the construction of seven water reservoirs, and established the Nebo Electric and Power Company. Vying against a Gentile "St. Johns Ring," he was convicted of perjury after swearing as a witness to prove a homestead patent for Miles P. Romney and was sent to the Detroit House of Correction. At this time also, Udall was indicted for polygamy, having married a second wife in 1882. He was pardoned by President Grover Cleveland, and the polygamy charge was dropped, since the second wife was then living in Utah. In 1887 with other Mormon leaders, Udall went to Washington, D.C., to settle the problem of land rights claimed by the Aztec Land and Cattle Company. Elevated to the presidency of the newly formed St. Johns Stake, Udall in 1898 was elected from Apache County to the territorial council. When the Arizona Temple in Mesa was completed in 1927, he was appointed the first president.

Levi Stewart (1891-1958), a public official and judge and son of David King Udall, received a law degree at the University of Arizona and became president of the St. Johns Stake in 1922. He served as Apache County attorney, superior court judge, and state supreme court justice from 1947 to 1958. Of Levi's brothers, John H. was mayor of Phoenix, Don T. was a superior court judge, and Jesse A. was a state supreme court judge. Levi Udall's sons, Stewart L. and Morris K., reached national political offices.

Stewart (1920-   ) received a law degree from the University of Arizona in 1948, was congressman from the Second District, 1957-61, and secretary of the interior, 1961-69, under presidents John F. Kennedy and Lyndon B. Johnson. During his term of office Udall dramatized the need for federal legislation to preserve the remaining wilderness areas in the United States and Alaska.

Morris (1922-   ) graduated with a University of Arizona law degree in 1949, was Pima County attorney, a founder of the Bank of Tucson, and succeeded his brother as congressman in 1961, a position he still holds.

See David King Udall and Pearl Udall Nelson, *Arizona Pioneer Mormon, David King Udall, History and His Family, 1851-1938* (1959).—H. P. H.

Ulloa, Antonio de (1716-1795). Mathematician, geographer, and astronomer and first Spanish governor of Louisiana. Before coming to Louisiana, Ulloa had distinguished himself in scientific explorations in Peru (1736-44), which had resulted in an account of the people and the region called *A Voyage to South America* (Spanish edition, 1748; English edition, 1758). To this scientific and literary accomplishment he added new fame by founding an astronomical observatory and a mineralogical laboratory, which made him one of the most widely known of European scholars. These honors were no recommendation to French Louisianians, however, who were determined to frustrate execution of the Treaty of Paris of 1763, by which they had been transferred to Spain. Delay in arrival of Spanish authorities in New Orleans deepened this resolve, and when Ulloa finally arrived to take up his post of governor in 1766, he faced not only general antagonism but the refusal of French troops to shift their services to Spain. With few soldiers or civil servants of his own, Ulloa refrained from public transfer of authority to the Spanish crown, preferring to execute his orders through Captain Philippe Aubry, acting governor under the old French sovereignty. This bizarre arrangement, together with his attempts to confine Louisiana commerce to a few select Spanish ports, his refusal to accept responsibility for the full payment of promissory notes issued to Louisiana colonials by the government of France, and his unfortunate shyness combined with arrogance, led to an uprising against him by the leaders of the Superior Council, the still-operative organ of the French colonial system. This "Revolution of 1768" forced Ulloa to flee to Havana, a refugee from what has been called the first American revolt against European colonialism.

See J. Preston Moore, "Antonio de Ulloa," *Louisiana History,* vol. 8 (1967).—J. G. T.

Union Pacific Railroad. The Union Pacific Railroad, the eastern half of the first American transcontinental railroad, embraces in its inception, construction, decline, and rebirth, much of the history of the West. After ten years of agitation by a number of far-sighted people, most notably Asa WHITNEY, Congress authorized in 1853 surveys of five routes from the Missouri River to the Pacific (see RAILROADS). After more than a decade in which the North and South failed to agree upon a route or a method of subsidizing construction, Congress, under the weight of military necessity, finally authorized a railroad to be built along the forty-second parallel: the shortest, most central, and in general the most obvious selection. The Pacific Railroad Act of 1862 authorized a substantial land grant, in line with a precedent and procedure established in the original land grants to mid-western railroads in the early 1850s, and a "subsidy" in the form of United States bonds in the amount of $16,000 per mile of completed road. (The railroad was expected to raise construction funds by selling the bonds for whatever they would bring—which turned out to be far less than 100 cents on a dollar of face value—and at maturity, was to repay to the United States government the full face value of the bonds plus interest accumulated over the thirty-year term of the bonds.)

Investor response to this far-from-munificent offer was almost zero. Except for a small investment by Thomas C. DURANT, a promoter who would never have gained a foothold in a more favored enterprise, no risk capital was forthcoming for a project that held out so little promise of profit. Congress therefore passed the more liberal Pacific Railroad Act of 1864, which doubled the size of the land grant and made the government bonds a second lien (instead of a first) upon the assets of the road, so that the Union Pacific could issue its own first-mortgage bonds in the open capital market—to the extent that there was such a market in 1864.

Durant and his associates formed the Credit Mobilier, named for an investment trust that had effectively mobilized capital for construction of French railroads in the 1850s, and the first few miles were built. Inevitably, however, the prestige and power of eastern capitalism were necessary. Although he would live to regret bitterly his desire "to connect my name conspicuously with the greatest public work of this century," Oakes AMES, scion of a Boston family that had made a fortune in the shovel manufacturing business, became the heart and brain of the enterprise.

Construction progressed rapidly from 1865 onward at an overall average of more than a mile a day, a record achieved entirely with picks, shovels, and mule-drawn scoops in the hands of sweating, swearing Irishmen. Persons of mid-Victorian sensibilities who visited the work camps strung along the track from the railhead to the supply depots further back were shocked by what they saw. The all-male society, composed of the roughest class of day laborer, which crept across prairies, deserts, and finally the mountains in a swirl of fighting, boozing, swearing, and—when possible—whoring, was to such observers a "hell on wheels" (see WYOMING). Trouble was never far off. Each man was expected to double as a soldier as Indian attacks became more frequent.

Toward the end there was bitter rivalry between the Union Pacific and the CENTRAL PACIFIC, which was creeping eastward. The Union Pacific's Irishmen showed their contempt for the Central Pacific's Chinese laborers by cheering lustily on several occasions when mysterious dynamite explosions blew up teams of Orientals. When similar incidents began to happen to the Irishmen, the inscrutable Chinese showed no emotion, but the explosions ceased. Meanwhile the men worked twelve- and sometimes fifteen-hour days, hustling to keep the line graded ahead of the mountains of ties, rails, and hardware that poured irregularly over the just-completed road, every ton of which had had to be transported from the East over the spindly new rail-

roads of the Midwest. Only such men as General Grenville M. DODGE, equally at home in the dignified political and financial councils of the East and among the brawling mass of workmen, could keep such an enterprise moving toward its objective.

Finally, on May 10, 1869, at Promontory Point, Utah, five miles west of Ogden and over a thousand miles from its starting point, the Union Pacific met its western counterpart, the Central Pacific, in a golden-spike-laying ceremony which ranks with the signing of the Declaration of Independence in American history.

The fledgling Pacific railroads were making progress toward establishing themselves as viable business enterprises when the CREDIT MOBILIER scandal struck in 1873. Oakes Ames, it was revealed, though a paragon of honesty and a member of Congress, had "sold" 160 shares of Union Pacific stock to congressmen, "where they will do the most good to us." The astronomical profits subsequent congressional investigations accused the Pacific railroad builders of making have been demonstrated to be sheer nonsense, but the political heat generated by Ames's indiscretion never cooled. Witnessing the close call such high-class politicians as James A. Garfield experienced in the ensuing clamor, lesser statesmen sought eagerly for a means to shrive the government of any guilt in the Pacific railroad affair. Their answer to the Credit Mobilier was the Thurman Act of 1878, which required that the greater part of Union Pacific's operating profits, after payment of dividends, be immobilized in a sinking fund to guarantee payment of the government's subsidy bonds with interest when they came due in the 1880s. Funds that might have been used to build feeder lines were unavailable. The result was to stunt the economic and physical development of the Union Pacific, which began nowhere and ended nowhere—"an apple tree without a limb," as chief builder Sidney DILLON had called it.

Two vastly different men tried to build the Union Pacific into a viable enterprise within the governmental restraints. Jay GOULD, who acquired control in the early 1870s, made life miserable for railroad executives in the Midwest who had sought to stabilize the railroad business through the highly successful "Iowa pool." Realizing that the government's insistence that he "pro rate" (divide eastbound freight delivered by the Union Pacific at its terminal) with all other roads at Omaha deprived Union Pacific of even a modicum of bargaining power in determining through rates, Gould acquired the decrepit Kansas Pacific, which duplicated the Union Pacific through Kansas as far as Denver, and gave the Union Pacific an independent gateway to the East through Kansas City. Gould merged the Kansas Pacific with the Union Pacific. He almost welded the latter into a true transcontinental by grasping the Missouri Pacific and the Wabash, but the sharp recession of 1884-85 caused Gould to relax his grip on most of these properties. Realizing that their main problem was relations with a quixotic federal government, the directors persuaded Charles Francis ADAMS, Jr., scion of the Massachusetts family and a leading authority on railroads' obligations to the public, to take the presidency. After what he called the most frustrating six years of his life, Adams admitted failure. Gould, through his lieutenant, Sidney Dillon, who was president from 1890 to his death in 1892, reasserted his authority, but there was little hope left for the Union Pacific, which was starved for traffic, bound hand and foot by the Thurman Act, and faced millions of dollars of debt which would mature in a few years. Bankruptcy was declared in 1893.

If the Union Pacific was to be reborn an independent enterprise in the midst of the 1890s depression, it would have to be through an act of faith by one who could see a profitable investment in the badly rundown, still incomplete system, which could have been entirely rebuilt for less than it owed the government. One such person emerged: Edward H. HARRIMAN, who foresaw more clearly than anyone else the great wave of prosperity that would follow the depression. Pledging the credit of the Illinois Central, a rich midwestern road that Harriman had helped bring to perfection in the 1880s, and with the cooperation of Jacob Schiff's firm of Kuhn, Loeb and Company, Harriman accomplished the gigantic refinancing. Applying a combination of talent and hard work, which was as common in America's *belle epoque* from 1898 to 1917 as it is rare today, Harriman and his associates rebuilt the Union Pacific into one of the strongest, most efficient, and most profitable railroads in the United States, and so it remains to this day.

Harriman's grand plan was to make the Union Pacific the chief arbiter of railroad affairs in all of the West outside the territory of the Hill lines, and the western trunk of a true transcontinental railroad with either the New York Central or the Baltimore and Ohio as the eastern extension. To this end he recovered for the Union Pacific the Oregon Short Line Railroad, the one extension to the Pacific Coast that the "apple tree" had managed to grow, and built the southwestern extension from Salt Lake City to Los Angeles. He had gained control of the SOUTHERN PACIFIC after the death of Central Pacific's Collis P. Huntington, and was about to sweep the Santa Fe into his "community of interests," when he died in 1909. In 1913 the Supreme Court found the Southern Pacific holdings to be in violation of the Sherman Anti-Trust Act of 1890, and the Southern Pacific was reconstituted as an independent railroad, taking with it the old Central Pacific line from Ogden to San Francisco, which should long since have been merged with the Union Pacific. Although these "Harriman lines," as they were once called, have since been operated in a primly independent manner in deference to the antitrust laws, the harmonious relations Harriman established have seldom been ruffled. By the 1970s, although the Union Pacific was still a strong, independent property, the industry-wide problems of rising wages and subsidized competition caused grave concern for the future.

The best general sources remain Nelson Trottman, *History of the Union Pacific; a Financial and Economic Survey* (1923), a no-nonsense study; and Robert G. Athearn, *Union Pacific Country* (1971), an outstanding account of the heartbreaking efforts to build the Union Pacific into a viable enterprise before 1895. Those who still believe that the government "subsidy" was a blessing to the Union Pacific will ignore Athearn's book at their peril, while those who still cling to the legend of the huge profits of the Credit Mobilier ought to look into Robert W. Fogel, *The Union Pacific Railroad: A Case in Premature Enterprise* (1960).—A. M.

United Order of Enoch (1870s). Mormon system of community cooperatives. Communal or cooperative liv-

ing, motivated by the traditions of Apostolic Christianity, was first introduced to the Mormons by Joseph Smith in Ohio and Missouri in 1831. Failing in Ohio and Missouri, the Mormons attempted to revive the communitarian spirit in the form of the United Order of Enoch in Utah in 1874. A community cooperative was organized in each Mormon settlement in that year. The usual arrangement was for each resident Mormon to donate to the order his economic property and subject his labor to the direction of an elected board of management. Some orders went further and agreed upon equal wages, regardless of their labor assignment, and ate together in a community dining hall. The most famous and long-lasting of these was at Orderville, Utah, 1875-85. The communitarian tradition is one of the oldest and most influential aspects of the Mormon heritage.

See Leonard J. Arrington, *Great Basin Kingdom* (1958).

United States Indian policy. See INDIAN POWER MOVEMENT; and INDIAN-WHITE RELATIONS: *United States Indian policy.*

United States Mail Steamship Company. The United States Mail Steamship Company was incorporated under New York State law in 1848 to provide mail and passenger service between the Atlantic states and the Isthmus of Panama, the first sector of the route to California. The company was apparently slow in initiating the construction of vessels to meet the increased flow of travel after the discovery of gold. In January 1851 this company and the PACIFIC MAIL STEAMSHIP COMPANY, both holding a mail contract to deliver from Panama to San Francisco, came to an agreement for the duration of the mail contracts they held. The United States Mail company sold its four steamers on the Pacific to the Pacific Mail company. Both agreed to encourage the sale of through tickets and the carrying of through freight, with sixty-four percent of the freight income going to the Pacific company and thirty-six percent to the United States company. They agreed to not engage in any competition with each other. This agreement dividing the steamship business between New York and San Francisco lasted until the end of the mail contracts in 1859. At the termination of this contract, the United States Mail Steamship Company withdrew from the trade, and Cornelius Vanderbilt obtained the new mail contract rather than let the Pacific Mail Steamship Company establish a through service.

The United States Mail Steamship Company was more interested in profits than building a reputation for excellent service. The company was notorious for its failure to procure a sufficient number of steamers; their ships were often in need of repair and had to be withdrawn from service, thereby disrupting schedules. However, only one major disaster occurred during eleven years of company operation, the loss of the *Central America* in a hurricane on September 12, 1857, when 433 lives were lost. The company was not a financial success, dividends were erratically paid and were never more than ten percent per year, and the stock consistently sold on the market below par. The company never enjoyed the public confidence comparable to the Pacific Mail Steamship Company. Food service and accommodations, as well as security measures, were a constant source of complaint. At the time of the construction of the Panama Railroad in 1855, the town of Aspinwall replaced Chagres as the terminal point of the voyage by United States mail steamers. The company constructed a dock for the exclusive use of its steamers. Although the service and financial administration of this company left much to be desired, it had performed a major service for a decade in transporting passengers, freight, and mail on the initial portion of the ocean journey to the West, when the overland route was time-consuming and difficult.

See John H. Kemble, *The Panama Route, 1848-1869* (1943).—W. T. J.

universities. See EDUCATION, HIGHER.

uranium mining. Uranium, a radioactive material, was first mined commercially in the western United States in the early twentieth century. Radium and vanadium ores mined at that time were used only for radioactive research in American and European laboratories, and so the mining was done on a small scale. The discovery of pitchblende in the Belgian Congo in the 1920s made the low-grade western mines uneconomical, and activity practically ceased. With the coming of the atomic age and the subsequent arms race, however, the United States had an immediate need for high-grade uranium.

Before the Korean War the United States was forced to buy ninety percent of its radioactive materials from Canada and the Belgian Congo. New uranium discoveries on the Colorado Plateau, a geographical area that encompasses 100,000 square miles around the Four-Corners area of Utah, Colorado, New Mexico, and Arizona, brought renewed life to the mining of radioactive materials in the West. Before 1948 there had been only three uranium mines unearthed in the sandstone and mudstone of the plateau's desert reaches. Between 1948 and 1955 twelve large ore deposits were found, and the government was finally assured a native supply. By 1955 there were about eight hundred mines producing high-grade ore in the area, and the mining, reduction, and refractory processes had evolved into a $100 million-a-year operation.

The most exciting aspect of the uranium saga, outside of the scientific discoveries, was the exploration and development of the western lodes. Reminiscent of nineteenth-century rushes, prospectors dispersed throughout the Southwest desert area in search of riches. They filed 309,380 claims between 1946 and 1959 in four Utah counties alone. The legends and stories that accompany those who struck it rich are not numerous but are characterized by the same bombast and excitement of the earlier mining era. Charles A. Steen, prospector extraordinary, lived on next to nothing, feeding his infant son a weak tea and sugar solution, while he sank his drills into "Steen's Folly." Eventually the Mi Vida Mine, located near Moab, Utah, and controlled by Steen's Utex Development Company, was valued at $60 million. Another mine, the Delta, owned by Vernon Pick, was sold for $9 million. In 1955, well drillers uncovered huge uranium deposits on claims near Ambrosia Lake, New Mexico.

Radioactive materials were not all discovered by geologists, nor were they all found on the Colorado Plateau. Garth Thornburg, a dentist, and his brother Vance developed the Blue Rock Mine in Arizona. More recently, huge discoveries were made in Wyoming, out-side the plateau, and may prove to be richer than those already in production in the Four-Corners area.

Most of the productive finds were made by drilling deep into the abundant sandstone formation and then sampling the cores with a Geiger counter. Today prospecting in this manner continues, but sensitive scintillometers in airplanes have also proven effective in the discovery of radioactive minerals.

Another interesting aspect of this relatively new western industry was the development of Salt Lake City as the Wall Street of uranium stocks. The men who started it sold "penny shares." Jay Walters sold his first penny stock in a restaurant. The restaurant owner also began to sell the shares and soon was a broker dealing exclusively in uranium. With the entrance of the large mining companies into the field of rare and trace elements, the demand for claims and mining companies boomed; some penny stock became worth many dollars.

The mining of high-grade ores ranged up to four hundred tons a day at Steen's mine and thirty tons a day at the Happy Jack. Consequently, mining districts also became the milling and reduction centers necessary for obtaining uranium concentrates. The federal government, because of its involvement, operated a concentrator at Monticello, Utah, for a time, but sold out in 1959. Today, all the mills are owned by large, private mining companies that have had previous experience in the other mineral industries of the West. About thirty plants reduce uranium ores from about five hundred mines. There are also about thirty buying stations in the West, all of which are functionaries of the Atomic Energy Commission.

In the interests of the country's security and to prevent vital uranium from finding its way into other hands, United States Executive Order 9613 was issued in 1945. This stated that all radioactive minerals in the United States and the territory of Alaska would be withdrawn from the commercial market and reserved for government usage. Public lands with radioactive materials were not for sale, and individuals needed a permit to use the land. In 1946 another executive order, number 9701, revoked this land restriction but retained the federal government's right to prospect, mine, and remove fissionable materials, including thorium, uranium, and elements higher on the periodic table. The Atomic Energy Act of 1946 limited ownership of source materials to the Atomic Energy Commission and required that private enterprise be licensed by the commission before it could buy or use radioactive materials. Because the United States government was the only party that could own uranium and plutonium, uranium's commercial usage was small prior to 1953, and by 1959 uranium's usage had increased only slightly in free enterprise. Only in the 1960s has a notable commercial industry developed, and this against the intransigence of the Atomic Energy Commission.

The government contracted at an early date to buy uranium from western mines and from those in Canada and Africa. It stipulated that this guaranteed buying program would continue until 1962. Cutbacks, however, occurred at a much earlier date, and Canadian and African concentrates were not sought for many years before 1962. Part of the reason for this cutback was spiraling costs. The AEC had set a price of thirty-one dollars a ton for high-grade uranium ores, but this was much too low to meet the production costs involved. Another reason was overproduction. In 1956, $46.5 million worth of radioactive material was produced, an increase of more than five times the amount of material produced in 1952. The industry was growing fast, and unchecked growth and competition was actually hurting the fledgling enterprise. This surge brought warnings that too much ore was being mined. These arguments came, in part, from commercial interests that hoped that uranium would be permitted to find its own price in a free market. Finally, in 1957, the AEC announced that it would freeze the buying of uranium ores. The commission would continue to buy ore on established contracts, but would not enter into any new ones. The government had fifteen thousand tons of uranium concentrate stockpiled, enough for military and power needs. The freeze brought about a decrease in prospecting activity, and by 1959 and 1960 a slack in the mining and reduction of ores was noticeable. In 1966, however, uranium was put on the free market, boosting a once sagging need for the West's fissionable metals.

Uranium mining in the West has been especially important because it has centered around sparsely populated desert areas that once had little value besides ranching and tourism. With the demand for commercial uranium growing despite government controls and cutbacks, the industry's future seems secure. Deposits are limited—in fact, they have been steadily dwindling—but if large mining companies continue to invest in uranium, old latent discoveries as well as new deposits will undoubtedly be developed.

See *Mineral Yearbook,* 1945 to the present.—L. J. A.

Utah. The history of Utah's early inhabitants predates the present culture by several millennia. Archaeologists have discovered artifacts of a desert nomadic culture that existed about 10,000 B.C. About A.D. 300 another culture developed, the Anasazi ("the ancient ones"), which flourished southward from the San Juan, Colorado, and Virgin River regions. At this same time the Sevier Frémont (in western Utah) and Frémont (in eastern Utah) cultures developed north of the Anasazi. These were sedentary and agricultural peoples, the Anasazi being the most highly developed culture of the three. The Anasazi became increasingly advanced through several stages, attaining its peak in the Classic Pueblo period (c. 1050-c. 1300). At the end of this period there was a rapid decline or exodus of these cultures, and the inhabitants of the greater Utah area reverted to a nomadic life.

The arrival of the Spanish in the Americas during the sixteenth century brought neither change nor exploration to the Utah region for centuries. An exploring party sent by Coronado may have touched upon Utah's southern extremes in 1540-41, but it was not until 1776 that Europeans explored the area of present Utah. In search of a shorter route to Monterey, California, an exploring party from Santa Fe under the direction of the Franciscan fathers Francísco Atanasio Dominguez and Silvestre Vélez de Escalante penetrated as far as present Utah valley in central Utah, and then moved southward. They failed to see the Great Salt Lake, although they received reports about it from their native guides. They returned southward to Santa Fe without continuing on to Monterey. The Spanish Trail, a horse and cattle trail between Santa Fe and Los Angeles, later arched upward through Utah and maintained a transient Spanish presence in Utah until 1848.

While the Spanish and later the Mexicans maintained technical control over the territory of present Utah, fur trappers entered the Utah region. The first were British trappers employed by the Hudson's Bay Company. Peter Skene Ogden made the deepest penetration, traveling as far south as present Mountain Green (near Ogden) in 1825 and as far west in Utah as Lucin before moving into Nevada in 1828-29. Despite a joint-occupation agreement between the British and the Americans, the Utah region remained largely in the control of American trappers.

John Jacob Astor was the first American to send trappers into the area, and they explored South Pass as early as 1821. William Ashley took a group of mountain men into the region in 1824, and they agreed to meet each other the following year in what was the first of seventeen fur rendezvous. Four of them were held in northern Utah. Following a rendezvous in 1826, Jedediah S. Smith made a trapping and exploring odyssey that took him straight southward through central Utah, and then southwest out of Utah and on to southern California. Among Smith's fellow mountain men were Jim Bridger, Tom Fitzpatrick, Milton and William Sublette, Etienne Provost, and David Jackson.

As fur trapping declined, a series of private forts or trading posts sprang up in Utah. Fort Buenaventura was built by Miles Goodyear in 1846, near present Ogden. Fort Robidoux (1837), Fort Kit Carson (1834), Fort Davy Crockett (1834), and Fort Bridger (1841) were also established in the eastern mountains of Utah. These trading posts provided the first Anglo settlements in Utah.

Coinciding with these semipermanent settlements were the travels of government explorers. Benjamin Lewis Eulalie de Bonneville sent his chief explorer, Joseph Reddeford Walker, on an expedition to California (1832-33), resulting in a map indicating that the area of present Utah was a large basin with internal drainage only. This map was first published in 1837 in Washington Irving's *The Rocky Mountains*. Almost a decade after Walker's explorations, John C. Frémont led three of his five official expeditions into the present borders of Utah (1843, 1845, and 1853), naming the "Great Basin" and publishing an account of his first explorations in 1845. This book was an important guide to the Mormons in their move to the Great Basin two years later.

Prior to the arrival of the Mormons in 1847, several different groups crossed Utah on their way to California and Oregon. They included the John Bartleson-John Bidwell train (1841) and the Lansford W. Hastings train (1842). In 1846 three other wagon trains were successful in crossing the area to the Pacific Coast. They were the parties of Edwin Bryant, George W. Harlan, and Samuel C. Lienhard. In July 1847 the first Mormons entered the Salt Lake valley following portions of these trails (see MORMON TRAIL).

When the Mormons, or LATTER-DAY SAINTS (LDS), moved into the mountain valleys of Utah in 1847, the territory still was in technical control of Mexico. By the Treaty of Guadalupe Hidalgo (1848), the area became a United States possession as a spoil of the Mexican War. The Mormons, perhaps through fear of Indian attacks and certainly with thoughts of empire, founded the provisional State of DESERET in 1849, and sent John M. BERNHISEL to Congress to seek admission into the Union. Their petition for statehood was rejected, but Congress, after reducing the vast Mormon state, gave Utah territorial status. In 1851 the territory was organized and Brigham YOUNG was appointed governor. The capital of the new territory was named Fillmore in honor of President Millard Fillmore. The remoteness of Fillmore from Utah's early population centers rendered it impractical, however, and SALT LAKE CITY assumed the role of capital in 1856.

Following the initial settlement of Utah in 1847, a large portion of the territory was settled through a dual system of colonization sponsored by the LDS church. First there was the "Inner Cordon" of settlements, stretching roughly north and south-southwest of Salt Lake City. Such settlements as OGDEN, LOGAN, PROVO, Fillmore, and Cedar City were established on the cordon during this period. Farther from the centralized Inner Cordon was the "Outer Cordon" of settlements, which comprised Fort Lemhi, Idaho; forts Bridger and Supply, Wyoming; Elk Mountain Mission, Moab, Utah; Carson Valley and Las Vegas, Nevada; and San Bernardino, California, founded by Charles C. RICH. These colonies grew until the fears of Mormon domination in the Great Basin led to the "Utah War" of 1857-58 (see LATTER-DAY SAINTS: *Brigham Young Period*). As a consequence of that threatened conflict, the Outer Cordon colonies were abandoned.

With respect to the relations with the ten thousand or more native Americans in Utah, the Mormon settlers demonstrated a success uncharacteristic of the settlers of the rest of the West. Brigham Young, as superintendent of Indian affairs (1852-57), advocated a policy of coexistence ("it is better to feed them than fight them") so successful that the Indians themselves classed the Mormon settlers of Utah and the Americans ("Mericats") as two distinct groups. Inevitably, however, there were occasions when animosity between individual Indians and Mormon settlers escalated into general conflicts between the two groups, as in the Walker War (1853-54) against the Ute Chief WALKARA and the Blackhawk War (1865-68). As early as 1855, Young sent agricultural missionaries among the Indian tribes of the Great Basin, with instructions to live among them, teach them the arts of husbandry, and build peaceful relationships. Most famous of these emissaries was Jacob Hamblin, whom Brigham Young ordained "an Apostle to the Lamanites" (Indians). After the federal government established reservations in Utah, the Mormons continued to proselyte the Indians in an effort to aid them to attain independence within the American community. A notable accomplishment of this effort was the Washakie Farm in northern Utah, which was established by the LDS church in 1876 as a self-sufficient cooperative farm to enable some four hundred Shoshoni Indians to attain economic independence.

Federal suspicion concerning Utah rose throughout the Civil War, since the federal government was aware that most Utahans were neutral, though not secessionist. The Mormon position was a carry-over of the ill-feeling generated by the Utah War experience. The Mormons regarded the Civil War as God's justice being wreaked upon the nation. To protect the overland mail and keep watch on the Mormons, the federal government sent seven hundred troops to FORT DOUGLAS outside of Salt Lake City in 1862. Led by Patrick E. CONNOR, their main accomplishment was to develop mineral prospecting in ALTA, OPHIR, SILVER REEF, and Bingham.

Free from the ravages of civil war, Utah experienced expansion during the 1860s. Other settlements within the Inner Cordon area of Utah were established. The Pony Express dashed across Utah's desert regions in 1860, only to be made obsolete by the transcontinental telegraph a year later. The Union Pacific and Central Pacific laid rails to the borders of Utah Territory, where the construction work was aided and executed primarily by local residents. The Golden Spike driven at Promontory Summit, near Ogden, in 1869, marked the end of Utah's isolation and brought the inevitable need for Utah to conform its social and political patterns to national norms.

Because Utah's early settlers concentrated on the development of agriculture, mining did not become important until the completion of the transcontinental railroad in 1869. Dominated at first by non-Mormon miners and investors, the mining industry immediately boomed. Several silver mines, such as the EMMA MINE, brought enormous wealth to a few investors. Hit hard by the national panics of 1873 and the 1890s, the mining industry virtually collapsed with the crash of 1929, leaving Utah's primary mining enterprise COPPER MINING. The Bingham copper mine began open-pit operations in 1906 and in the twentieth century produced approximately one third of the nation's output of copper.

During the two decades following the construction of the railroad through Utah the federal government enacted repressive legislation that disrupted political and social life in Utah (see LATTER-DAY SAINTS: *conflict with the nation*). A number of laws were directed at forcing the Mormon church to end Mormon economic and political domination of the territory and to discontinue POLYGAMY; to this end, easterners promoted WOMAN SUFFRAGE in Utah. (Originally almost exclusively Mormon, Utah's population of 145,000 in 1880 was eighty-three percent Mormon.) Once the church had brought itself into alignment with the national system, Utah was granted statehood in 1896. This entrance came long after the "requirements for statehood" had been met and after five unsuccessful efforts by the territory for statehood (1856, 1862, 1872, 1882, and 1887). The exclusion of polygamist Brigham H. ROBERTS from the United States House of Representatives in 1900 and the attempted expulsion of Mormon apostle Reed SMOOT from the Senate indicated lingering suspicions of Utah. The failure to unseat Smoot in 1907, however, signaled the final end of Utah's conflicts with the nation.

Shortly after statehood, Utah had the opportunity to demonstrate its allegiance to the nation. When the United States became involved in a war with Spain in 1898, Utah responded to the call with 425 volunteers within a week. Among those from Utah who distinguished themselves during this conflict was Major Richard W. Young, Brigham's grandson, who participated in the battle of Manila and twenty-five other military engagements of the Spanish-American War and subsequent Philippine hostilities. Far different from Utah's virtual neutrality during the Civil War, Utah's generally enthusiastic support in the Spanish conflict was indicative of its desire to be accepted by the national community.

In the twentieth century, Utah became involved in the national trend of Progressivism. Utah had passed legislation in 1894 setting an eight-hour work day, which was upheld by the United States Supreme Court in 1898. National distrust of trusts and monopolies became a local issue. One side of this reforming zeal manifested itself along the lines of the nineteenth-century religious conflict in Utah, when the American party was established in Utah in 1904. An outgrowth of the investigation into Senator Smoot, the American party combined the national Progressive trends with an animus against the Mormon church. The American party charged the LDS church with controlling the political and economic life of Utah and through the Salt Lake *Tribune* attacked the church and vilified LDS leaders. This bizarre combination of Progressivism and anti-Mormonism controlled Salt Lake City municipal government for several years and exercised influence in state politics until its final demise in 1911. But the Progressive movement in Utah continued with legislation improving the working conditions in the mines, setting minimum wages for women, setting up workmen's compensation, establishing standards for food production and inspection, and in 1917 establishing the initiative and referendum. In the same year, prohibition was established in Utah. The election of 1916 of Utah's first non-Mormon governor, Simon Bamberger (a Jew), suggests the degree to which Utah had been assimilated into the national community.

During World War I, more than twenty-one thousand Utahans entered the military, being the principal component of the "Wild West Division," which distinguished itself at St.-Mihiel and at the Argonne. In the Liberty Bond drive, Utah exceeded its quota of $61 million by almost twenty percent. In addition, Utahans purchased almost $80 million of War Savings Stamps.

The decade following World War I was one of general economic decline. There was a postwar boom in mining and manufacturing, but agriculture was crippled by drought and poor markets. Rural areas were depopulated by migration to the urban centers of Utah and to metropolitan areas on the West Coast. At a time when the rest of the nation was experiencing marked prosperity, Utah's economy remained in a semidepressed condition.

Part of Utah's response to this situation was a heightened investment in education, sponsored by Governor George Henry DERN. Utah had always stressed education, and the added emphasis put Utah far in advance of most of the nation in the proportion of its personal income devoted to education. Particularly noteworthy was the growth of higher education. The University of Utah (1850) became noted for its colleges of mining and medicine, Utah State University (1889) for its colleges of agriculture and forestry, and Brigham Young University (1875) for its college of education. Utah's heavy investment in education improved the bargaining power and earning potential of the many young people who left Utah for areas offering more diverse and plentiful professional opportunities.

In 1928 came the end of an era in Utah s cultural history, when the Salt Lake Theater was razed in order to construct an office building. Under Brigham Young's direction the Salt Lake Theater had been constructed

and opened to the public in 1862. At its completion, it was the largest building in the Great Basin and soon became known as "The Cathedral in the Desert" (see THEATER).

When the crash of 1929 ended the nation's short-lived prosperity, Utah's already grim economic condition worsened. The state's mainstay, the mining industry, collapsed and Utah's already depressed agricultural economy reeled. In the early 1930s more than twenty percent of the population was on relief. The exodus from the state continued, increasing the concentrations of former Utahans on the Atlantic and Pacific coasts. Utah's high birthrate and economic inability to absorb the increased population inevitably led to problems of far longer duration than the Depression.

As with the nation at large, the 1930s witnessed repeated efforts in Utah to lift the economy. A number of locally sponsored self-help efforts were incapable of reversing the economic decline. Aside from direct welfare assistance, such New Deal programs as the Works Projects Administration provided jobs and security for many Utah residents. Not the least of the WPA's contributions to Utah was the Federal Writers' Project, which assisted in the preservation and transcription of diaries and reminiscences relating to Utah's pioneer and territorial periods. As an effort to supplement (or supplant) New Deal economic aid to Utah's largely LDS populace, the LDS church also instituted the Church Welfare Plan in 1936, which developed into a sophisticated and practical program of relief and self-help. All these efforts notwithstanding, the effects of depression in Utah were not really alleviated until the war economy of the 1940s brought prosperity to most of the nation.

The war brought industrialization to Utah and reversed the trend of economic decline. Under the auspices of the War Production Board, the $200 million Geneva Steel Plant was established near Provo, and sixteen other manufacturing plants were similarly established in the state. This federally financed industry brought tremendous economic growth to the state, almost doubling total employment, increasing the manufacturing employment by 120 percent, and nearly trebling total personal income in the state. The prominence of the federal government in Utah economy during these years presaged its later role as the largest employer in the state.

Also established during the war was the Central Utah Relocation Center (known as "Topaz") near Delta. In physical appearance Topaz, with its barbed wire, barracks, and armed guards, differed little from the prisoner-of-war camps established by the belligerents of World War II. It was one of ten such camps established by authority of the federal government to relocate the Japanese-American residents of the Pacific Coast. The advisability of relocation was debatable at the time, and from present perspective seems an unwarranted manifestation of underlying suspicions and prejudices that antedated Pearl Harbor. Acquainted with the problems of prejudice and persecution in their own state history, Utahans have in Topaz a reminder of the dangers of xenophobia, nativism, and war hysteria.

Although more than sixty thousand persons left Utah between 1920 and 1940, the overall improvement of Utah's economy as a result of wartime industrialization reversed that trend, resulting in a net migration into the state. In 1948, after more than a decade of disputes between the seven states involved, there was a mutually agreeable allocation of the Colorado River waters, which increased Utah's potential in agriculture and industry. This development was followed in 1956 by the Colorado River Storage Project, which included Flaming Gorge Dam on the Great River. In 1951 the University of Utah led the nation in one facet of cultural development by establishing the first school of ballet at an American university.

In an unexpected revival of the prospecting boom of the previous decade, uranium was discovered in the deserts of Utah in 1952, igniting a "uranium fever" that made many men millionaires overnight (see URANIUM MINING). In addition, the missile industry was introduced into Utah in 1956. The federal government soon became the largest single employer in the state, and manufacturing entered a period of rapid growth. By 1970 the state's population had exceeded one million, of which one third lived in Salt Lake City. Utah was seventy-four percent Mormon.

A survey of Utah's history may be found in an excellent school text, S. George Ellsworth, *Utah's Heritage* (1972), and in Leonard J. Arrington, *Great Basin Kingdom* (1958). The political history up to the time of statehood is summarized in Howard R. Lamar, *The Far Southwest, 1846-1912: A Territorial History* (1966), while Gustave O. Larson, *The "Americanization" of Utah* (1971), takes the polygamy and statehood fight up into the first years of the twentieth century. Articles on aspects of Utah's history are in *Utah Historical Quarterly,* published by the Utah State Historical Society.—L. J. A.

Utah expedition. See LATTER-DAY SAINTS: *Brigham Young Period.*

Utah War. See LATTER-DAY SAINTS: *Brigham Young period.*

Ute Indians. The Ute, of Uto-Aztecan stock, came southward through Utah along the eastern side of the Great Salt Lake and occupied the upper drainage of the Colorado River in western Colorado and the valley of the Green River in eastern Utah. About four thousand of them lived in several small villages along the streams. They had small garden plots where they raised corn and some vegetables, which they supplemented with wild berries, fruits, seeds, nuts, and game from the mountains to the east. Their crops saved them from starvation, but their food supply was no more than barely adequate. Each village had its own chief, and the various villages were on friendly terms with one another, although they made no attempt until historic times to unite into larger bands.

The Ute traded with the Navaho to the south and thus secured horses, possibly as early as 1650. As their horse herds increased, they became seminomadic, opening trails across the Rocky Mountains to the Plains country of eastern Colorado to hunt buffalo. There the more numerous and hostile Comanche effectively barred them from permanently occupying any of the buffalo country.

In the early nineteenth century the Ute Indians earned a reputation as skilled horse thieves. They operated on a large scale, with the rancheros of California as their chosen target. The most noted of the thieves was Chief WALKARA, who teamed up with Pegleg Smith, a mountain man, for a series of daring raids, with their biggest haul estimated at three thousand head. Many of these stolen horses were driven across the desert to Ute country, then taken south to market at Santa Fe and swapped for guns, ammunition, and trade goods.

When the Mormons first came to the Great Salt Lake area in 1847, the whites and Indians soon established friendly relations. The Ute were allowed to camp near the little settlements but some of the Ute hunters could not resist killing a cow or a sheep from the Mormon herds for food now and then. By 1849 the settlers put an end to such depredations by raising an armed force that killed twenty-seven Ute and drove the rest from the vicinity of the settlements across the mountains to the southeast.

The Ute, away from any of the early important travel routes, lived peacefully on their lands, unmolested by the whites until the great mining rushes of the 1860s brought 100,000 whites into the Colorado mountains within a two-year period. A new Ute leader, Chief Ouray, at the age of twenty-seven took over the leadership of the Uncompahgre, then the largest of the Ute bands. He visited the mining camps and soon realized that the whites were too numerous and powerful for his tribe to fight successfully. With the national government hampered in its western affairs by the Civil War, Ouray in 1863 obtained a very favorable treaty that gave his people sixteen million acres of land in western Colorado for their permanent reservation. Later, at the insistence of the miners, four million acres of this land in the southern Colorado mountains, which included rich new mining strikes, were purchased from the Ute for a token payment.

In the 1870s the Ute pattern of living was one in which several bands roamed freely about their vast holdings, hunting and gathering wild plants for food. They also sent a strong band of hunters each year across the mountains to the east to hunt buffalo, avoiding the hostile Comanche as best they could. They took great pride in owning many more horses than they could use. When Indian troubles throughout the West induced the Indian Bureau to settle all the roving tribes on reservations, an agent was sent to the Ute to teach them how to live in houses and to farm some of their land, thus encouraging them to quit their nomadic life. In 1878 the bureau sent in a new agent, Nathan Meeker, to the White River Agency in western Colorado to implement the new program.

Meeker, an intelligent, sympathetic man, tried to adjust his charges to the new pattern of living, but the Ute resisted strongly. They hated to give up their buffalo hunting, not realizing that the buffalo herds had already been destroyed. They also refused to sell any of their surplus horses so that the rangelands could be used to graze cattle and sheep.

When Meeker reached a showdown with his charges in the fall of 1879, he followed orders from his superiors and sent for a force of cavalry to assist him in coercing the Indians. The Ute responded to the news of the approach of troops by killing Meeker and six of his assistants. Then on September 29, 1879, they attacked the approaching cavalry column, killing fourteen and wounding forty-three. The army officials responded by ordering an overwhelming force to stamp out the resistance in short order, but Chief Ouray managed to arrange a truce before new fighting broke out. When he died the next year the tribe suffered from a lack of effective leadership.

To punish the small hostile Ute band that had fought at White River, federal officials seized the entire tribal holdings, then about twelve million acres, and confined the whole tribe on two small reservations on much poorer land just across the state line in Utah.

In the summer of 1906 about four hundred Ute, chiefly from the White River band, packed up their gear and trekked several hundred miles to the northeast, crossing the Rocky Mountains and reaching the Sioux reservation at Pine Ridge, South Dakota. They created a great deal of excitement among the white settlers along the way, who feared depredations and possible attacks. After much discussion, forty-five of the band were persuaded to return peacefully to Utah. When the rest continued their stubborn resistance, they were placed on leased land on the Cheyenne River reservation, where they stayed a year. They did not like their new home and in 1908 asked to be returned to Utah.

When Congress passed the Indian Claims Commission Act in 1946, the Ute tribe filed claims for the loss of their sixteen million acres of land, taken without adequate payment. Within four years they had won an award of $31.7 million in a settlement that encouraged several other tribes to file similar claims.

See Robert Emmitt, *The Last War Trail* (1954); Wilson Rockwell, *The Utes: A Forgotten People* (1956); and Marshall Sprague, *Massacre: The Tragedy at White River* (1957).—F. H.

Utley, Robert M. (1929-   ). Historian. Utley was born in Bauxite, Arkansas. He was educated at Purdue University and Indiana University, where he studied history and worked with Oscar Winther, a well-known frontier historian.

Much of Utley's career was spent in government service. While serving in the army in 1952-56, he became historian for the Joint Chiefs of Staff in the Department of Defense. In 1957 he joined the National Park Service and moved to Santa Fe, New Mexico, where he worked on a national survey of historical sites and buildings in the Southwest. In 1962 he became a regional historian and in 1964 chief historian.

Utley's historical activities were varied. In his work with the survey he played an important role in arousing interest in the preservation of historical sites in the Southwest and in developing methods for their maintenance. At the same time he was active in numerous professional organizations. In 1967 he was elected president of the Western History Association (until that time the youngest man to be accorded this honor). Throughout his career in the park service he continued to be an active writer. His conclusions regarding some of the controversies surrounding the defeat of General George A. Custer appeared in *Custer and the Great Controversy* (1962). His *The Last Days of the Sioux Nation* (1963), based on extensive research and reflecting mature judgment, was hailed by some critics as a definitive work on the subject. In 1964 he edited the memoirs of General Richard H. Pratt, *Battlefield and Classroom: Four Decades with the American Indian.* Utley then delved deeper into the military history of the western frontier and by 1967 produced a comprehensive book, *Frontiersmen in Blue: the United States Army and the Indian, 1848-1865,* which quickly became one of the standard works

in the field and did much to clarify military relationships between the Untied States Army and western Indian tribes in the nineteenth century.—G. D. N.

Uto-Aztecan language. See INDIAN LANGUAGES: *Uto-Aztecan.*

utopian colonies. The American frontier offered utopian colonies an opportunity for cheap land and potential freedom from interference. The first floodtime of such communitarian efforts, the half-century before the Civil War, coincided with the nation's most expansive frontier period. Such communities are grouped here as religious-mystical, Christian socialist, secular, and modern communes.

religious utopias. Religious utopias based on elements of autocracy and mysticism have usually followed leaders like Mother Ann Lee of the SHAKERS or Father George Rapp, whose new revelations and insights gave them unquestionable authority. Taking a cue from the Old Testament's community covenant, the new truth instituted a communal brotherhood of shared life and property. In theory, the spirit imbued every heart and every product. Shaker furniture, Rappite whiskey, or Fountain Grove wine not only did well in the market and gave the makers a sense of joy in the production, but also embodied the mystical essence of the brotherhood. It was the autocrat, however, who determined how the communal spirit would be achieved. These groups were often offshoots of German Pietism. In general they have been the most enduring of American colonies; the Shakers lived communally for nearly two hundred years. (See also LATTER-DAY SAINTS.)

The Rappites under George Rapp (1757-1847) formed the Harmony Society. Pietist and celibate, the group gathered near Pittsburgh, Pennsylvania, from 1804 to 1814. It then moved to Harmony, Indiana (1814-24), and Economy, Pennsylvania (1825-1905).

The Society of Separatists of Zoar, also Pietist, was founded by Joseph Bäumler (1778-1853). It was celibate only to 1850. The Zoarites lived in Zoar, Ohio, from 1817 to 1898.

The Hutterian Brethren moved from Canada to South Dakota in 1874. By 1963, 142 colonies were established in the northwestern United States and western Canada.

Bethel and Aurora colonies were founded by William Keil (1812-77). Members lived in Bethel, Missouri (1844-80), and Aurora, Oregon (1855-81).

Fountain Grove, the colony for the Brotherhood of the New Life, was founded by Thomas Lake Harris (1823-1906). Mystical and Swedenborgian, Fountain Grove was first located in Brocton, New York (1868-75), then near Santa Rosa, California (1875-1900).

The Theosophical Community, built by Katherine Tingley (1847-1929) was an offshoot of the Theosophical Society founded in 1875 in New York by Helena Blavatsky (1831-91). Mystical and humanitarian, Tingley's group lived at Point Loma, San Diego, California, from 1897 to the early 1930s.

Christian socialist colonies. Christian socialist colonies tended to be community-oriented rather than autocratic. Inasmuch as the New Testament was the focus, Christ replaced the earthly patriach. At Amana, Iowa, for example, the leaders were little more than normal officials, with the social goals more primary than personal charisma. Christian Metz was a strong voice in this group, yet the institutions of his colony relegated his personality to a less important position than that of Mother Ann Lee or George Rapp. The New Testament injunction to love and help thy neighbor was grafted to the Old Testament concept of the covenanted community. The result became a society in which the means of production were controlled by the people for the good of the brotherhood. Class distinctions were minimized in the analysis of economic problems both within and without the colony. The strength of the Christian socialist position lay in its belief that it was implementing the long communal tradition in Christianity; its weakness was a relative lack of zeal. Occasionally, as in Amana and Oneida, New York, dissolution of the colony was followed by a secular corporate reorganization based on stock ownership.

Hopedale, founded by Adin Ballou (1803-90), was a community of Christian reformers. It was located in Milford, Massachusetts, from 1841 to 1856. In its later years a branch opened in Minnesota.

The Amana Society of True Inspiration was Pietist and founded by Christian Metz (1794-1867) and Barbara Heinemann (1795-1883). It was located near Buffalo, New York (1843-55), and Amana, Iowa (1855-1932). Thereafter it was a joint-stock corporation. (See AMANA COLONIES.)

Bishop Hill, in Bishop Hill, Illinois, from 1846 to 1862, was composed of Swedish unorthodox Lutherans. Its founder was Eric Janson (1808-50).

The Altruria colony followed the ideas of William D. Howells' *A Traveler from Altruria* (1894). The colony, founded by the Christian socialist Edward B. Payne near Santa Rosa, California, lasted only a year, 1894-95.

secular colonies. Secular colonies have embraced the socialist vision of shared ownership, but any element of deity is subsumed in the economic and social brotherhood of man. Life in these communes was usually based on abolition of private holdings, except for small items; widespread democratic participation in decision-making; equal distribution of labor according to plans laid out by the group; methods of mutual criticism to minimize interpersonal conflicts; and generally, but not always, traditional monogamy. In the early nineteenth century most secular groups emerged as protests against competition, the profit motive, and other destructive elements in industrial capitalism. Thus Robert Owen's community in New Harmony, Indiana, and the dozens of Fourierist colonies from Massachusetts to Texas reflected unhappiness with factory conditions as they were developing in Europe and America.

Marx and Engels later pointed out that these utopias were unaware of the basic conflict between the worker and the entrepreneur, and Marxism remained generally aloof from the communal dream. Nevertheless some colonies, often outgrowths of labor movements, did follow Marxist principles. But Icaria in Iowa or Llano in California, though they were socialist, were more interested in building a model community than in wider social revolution.

Secular communities were more numerous than the religious groups, but individual experiments averaged fewer members and lasted for shorter periods of time. In any given period members often moved from one colony to another. For example, Josiah Warren began his multi-communitarian career at New Harmony, and

Bronson Alcott started his own community to remedy the defects of Brook Farm. Hopefully, each model would in time provide the necessary evidence for a reformation of the predominant culture.

The external society, however, far from being converted, proved hostile to communitarian ideals. Such hostility was an important cause of decline. In addition, internal disruption, schisms, and disagreements were endemic and far more prevalent than in religious groups.

New Harmony followed the socialism of its founder, Robert Owen (1771-1858). It was on the former site of the Rappite community in the Wabash valley, Indiana (1825-28). There were nine satellite communities, including one in Wisconsin before 1843.

Josiah Warren (1798-1874), an anarchist, founded three colonies during his lifetime. Equity, Ohio, was "a cooperative industrial village" lasting from 1835 to 1846. Utopia, Ohio (1846-50), was built upon a former Fourierist site. Modern Times, New York (1851 to the early 1860s), closed the cycle.

Fourierist communities, inspired by Albert Brisbane (1809-90), who had carried Charles Fourier's ideas across the Atlantic, mainly grew in eastern states. Western manifestations of Fourierism were the Wisconsin Phalanx (1844-50), now Kenosha, Wisconsin, and Réunion, Texas, started by Victor Considérant (1808-93) in 1855.

Icaria was a reflection of the doctrines of Etienne Cabet in his *Voyage en Icarie* (1840). Beginning in Texas in 1848, the colony moved to Nauvoo, Illinois (1849-60) with a branch in Cheltenham, Missouri, after 1858. It gathered in Corning, Iowa, from 1860 to 1898, and had an important offshoot in California (1881-86).

Kaweah Cooperative Commonwealth (1885-91), under the leadership of Burnette G. Haskell (1857-1907), stemmed from socialist labor movements in San Francisco. Its lands included portions of the future Sequoia National Park.

Topolobampo (1886-94) in the state of Sinaloa, Mexico, followed the ideas of Albert K. Owen (1847-1916). Thousands of westerners bought its joint-stock shares, available to sympathizers not living at the colony.

Equality (1895-1903), more properly the Brotherhood of the Cooperative Commonwealth, was led by Theodor Hertzka (1845-1924). It overlooked Puget Sound, Washington.

The Llano Cooperative Colony grew from groups of socialists and labor unions under the leadership of Job Harriman (1861-1925) after his unsuccessful campaign for mayor of Los Angeles. They built a large settlement in the Antelope valley between 1914 and 1917. In part because of water shortages, they moved to Louisiana, near Leesville, where they persisted until 1935.

Another socialist utopia, the Nevada Cooperative Colony, was led by C. V. Eggleston near Fallon from 1916 to 1919.

modern communes. Heirs of the long tradition of communalism, present communes are the result of the peculiar tensions of the mid-twentieth century. There are probably as many as four hundred in the West today with concentrations in northern California, southern Oregon, and the Santa Fe-Taos region in New Mexico. We are witnessing a time of utopian experimentation of greater magnitude than any period since pre-Civil War

America. Orientations now express at least as wide a range of interests as those of the past, including Christianity, Oriental mysticism, arts and crafts, farming, and even urban revolutionary activism. Most colonies involve a blending of several of these interests. Their life-styles in such matters as sex, drugs, work, responsibility, and authority vary between the traditionally communal and the intentionally anarchistic. In general, however, they represent flights from bureaucratic and highly organized society and therefore are less structured than their earlier counterparts.

Morning Star was founded by Lou Gottlieb in 1966 in Occidental, California. Its organization has been unstructured with a "back to nature" theme. A portion of the group moved to Morning Star East (Taos, New Mexico) in 1969.

A similar orientation toward the land underlay William Wheeler's founding of Wheeler Ranch in 1967. It, too, is located near Occidental, California.

The philosophy of B. F. Skinner's *Walden II* guides Twin Oaks. It has been situated in Louisa, Virginia, since its founding in 1967.

Hog Farm is renowned for feeding the crowds at rock festivals from psychedelically painted buses. It moved in 1965 from its two-year-old home base in a canyon near Los Angeles to Llano, New Mexico.

Belief in Oriental mysticism and astrology lay behind the founding of New Buffalo. It is located near Taos, New Mexico, and was organized by George Robinson in 1967.

Lama, at San Cristobal, New Mexico, has become highly mystical. Steve Durkee and Richard Alpert (Baba Ram Dass) have, at various times, been its prime movers.

Camp Joy Farm grew from an organic gardening project at the Santa Cruz campus of the University of California. Early in 1971 Jim and Beth Nelson led a group, which later grew to twelve, to four acres near Boulder Creek, California. Biodynamics and organic gardening have been the focus of their communal life.

See Arthur Bestor, *Backwoods Utopias* (1950); Robert V. Hine, *California's Utopian Colonies* (1966); Robert Houriet, *Getting Back Together* (1971); and Laurence Veysey, *The Communal Experience* (1973).—R. V. H.

V

Valley and Ridge Province. See PHYSIOGRAPHY OF THE UNITED STATES.

Vanderburgh, William H. (1798?-1832). Fur trader. Vanderburgh was born in Vincennes, Indiana, whence his father, a judge of the supreme court of Indiana Territory, had moved from New York State. Vanderburgh attended the United States Military Academy in 1813 but never graduated. He moved to Missouri, where he became a trader with the Missouri Fur Company; after that firm failed in 1825, he worked for the American Fur Company. In an effort to find out where the independent mountain men trapped, Kenneth McKenzie, who ran the Upper Missouri Outfit for the American Fur Company, ordered Vanderburgh and Andrew Drips to follow James Bridger and Thomas Fitzpatrick on their hunts. Indignant that such methods were being used, Bridger and Fitzpatrick at first tried to escape their followers, and when that failed they lured Vanderburgh and his party into hostile Blackfoot country, where Vanderburgh was killed by the Indians.

See LeRoy R. Hafen, ed., *The Mountain Men and the Fur Trade of the Far West*, vol. I (1965); and Paul C. Phillips, "William Henry Vanderburgh, Fur Trader," *Mississippi Valley Historical Review*, vol. 30 (December 1943).—G. B. D.

Van Devanter, Willis (1859-1941). Jurist. Van Devanter was born and brought up in Indiana, graduated from Asbury (Depauw) University and the Cincinnati Law School, and then in 1884 followed to Cheyenne his brother-in-law, John W. Lacey, who had just been appointed chief justice of Wyoming Territory's supreme

court. Five years later Van Devanter was himself appointed chief justice of the territorial supreme court. The combination of his brother-in-law's prestige, his own ability, and his close identification with Francis E. Warren, Wyoming's outstanding political leader, assured rapid upward mobility.

Returning to private practice after Wyoming achieved statehood in 1890, Van Devanter obtained legal retainers from the Union Pacific Railway and several major cattle companies and served them all as efficiently as he did Senator Warren and the Republican party. As chairman of the Republican State Committee and member of the Republican National Committee, he helped Warren build a political machine rarely matched in the West.

His legal work in Wyoming included two especially noteworthy victories. In 1893 he won dismissal of the case against those cattlemen who killed rustlers in the Johnson County War; and in 1896, arguing before the United States Supreme Court, he won a case that circumscribed Indian big-game hunting rights.

Senator Warren rewarded Van Devanter for his faithful service by engineering a series of appointments: assistant United States attorney general (1897-1903); United States circuit judge (1903-10); and associate justice of the United States Supreme Court (1910-37). To snare these appointments Warren employed exceptional persistence and resourcefulness such as Van Devanter himself and very few others possessed.

On the Supreme Court bench Van Devanter continued the ardent defense of property rights and big business. He distinguished himself in the 1930s as a leading foe of New Deal legislation. He wasted no words in the few opinions he wrote. Among his opinions are ones denying the power of a state to fix the weight of bread, invalidating a West Virginia natural resources control law, and denying the power of the federal government to tax the salaries of judges.

See Lewis L. Gould, *Wyoming, A Political History, 1868-1896* (1968); and M. Paul Holsinger, "Willis Van Devanter: Wyoming Leader, 1884-1897," *Annals of Wyoming* (October 1965) and "The Appointment of Supreme Court Justice Van Devanter: A Study of Political Preferment," *American Journal of Legal History* (October 1968).—T. A. L.

Van Every, Dale (1896-   ). Historian and novelist. Van Every was born in Levering, Michigan, and educated at Stanford University. In 1920 he began his career as a journalist, working as an editor for United Press in New York and Washington, D.C. In 1929 he returned to the Pacific Coast and settled in Hollywood, where he became a writer and producer of motion pictures.

Van Every's career as a western writer began with the publication of *Westward the River* in 1945. During the next twenty-five years more than thirteen western novels and narratives flowed from his facile pen. One of his early successful novels was *The Shining Mountains* (1948), about the Lewis and Clark expedition and pioneer life west of the Mississippi River in the early nineteenth century. The work was characterized by Van Every's extraordinary eye for detail and his intimate knowledge about frontier and Indian customs. Three years later, in *The Captive Witch,* he dealt with the opening of the West in 1779 and the activities of George Rogers Clark on the Kentucky frontier. In another novel, *The Voyagers* (1957), he attempted to re-create life on the frontier in the 1780s in the Ohio River valley and New Orleans. Van Every was a master in recapturing and conveying the life and times of the frontier.

In the following decade he embarked on a comprehensive history of the westward movement of pioneers, focusing his attention on outstanding individuals. Four volumes contained fruits of his labors. The first, *Forth to the Wilderness* (1962), was followed in the next year by *A Company of Heroes* and *Ark of Empire*. The fourth volume, *The Final Challenge* (1964), dealing with the years between 1804 and 1848, captured the spirit of frontiersmen much better than many other books and was compared to Theodore Roosevelt's *Winning of the West.*

Van Every's narrative skills, insight into the Old West, and understanding of the impact of the frontier on the American national character together constitute a major contribution to western history.—G. D. N.

Varennes, Pierre Gaultier de. See Pierre Gaultier de Varennes, Sieur de La Verendrye.

Vargas, Diego [José] de (1643-1704). Reconqueror of New Mexico. Vargas was called by one of his comtemporaries a "latter-day Fernán Cortés," while historians generally have ranked him among the great heroic figures who promoted Spain's interest in the northern borderlands. In 1673 Vargas was sent from his native Spain as a special courier of the king to carry royal dispatches to the viceroy in Mexico City. He seems never to have revisited his homeland or seen again a wife and daughter he left there. He occupied several minor government posts in Mexico prior to his appointment as governor and captain general of New Mexico in 1688. His noble blood linking him to some of the leading families in Spain and America must have singled him out for preference, since his career to this point was colorless.

The governorship of New Mexico at this moment in history was scarcely a desirable office. The Pueblo Indians in 1680 had risen in rebellion, slain twenty-one missionaries and several hundred colonists, and had forced the withdrawal of the Spaniards southward to the El Paso district. From this center several futile attempts had been made to recover the province, and here the surviving colonists resided in exile, waiting the day when they could reclaim their old homes.

In February 1691 Vargas took up his duties at El Paso. He planned to organize an expedition to reconquer New Mexico without delay, but uprisings by Indians along the Chihuahua-Sonora frontier distracted him until August 1692, when he started north with a small army. On his initial foray into New Mexico, Vargas to his surprise found the Pueblo in a conciliatory mood— several of their most bellicose leaders had died, the nomadic tribes were pressing them hard, and civil war had caused hardship among many villages. As a result he received the peaceful submission of practically the entire province. But when he returned the following year, 1693, with several hundred colonists, he met resistance and was obliged to do battle with Indians living in the ruins of Santa Fe and others at San Ildefonso and Cochiti. The peace Vargas imposed broke down in 1696 when several pueblos rebelled, killing five missionaries and twenty-one other Spaniards. But this too was suppressed by stern measures, and thereafter the village Indians remained reconciled to alien rule.

In 1697 Don Pedro Cubero succeeded Vargas as governor in Santa Fe and promptly arrested him on a series of charges leveled by the *cabildo* (town council). So remote was New Mexico from the viceregal capital that the aging reconqueror suffered almost three years' imprisonment before he could get an appeal through to Mexico City. In the intervening years he had been awarded the title of marquis for distinguished service to the crown in consummating the reconquest. Subsequent investigation exonerated Vargas of all charges of misconduct, and he was restored to the governorship of New Mexico in 1703. The following year he died while campaigning against the Apache, and his body was conveyed to Santa Fe for burial in the parish church.

Vargas' activities on the southwestern frontier are treated in two works by J. Manuel Espinosa: *First Expedition of Vargas into New Mexico, 1692* (1940); and *Crusaders of the Rio Grande* (1942).—M. Si.

Vasquez, Louis (1798-1868). Fur trapper and trader. Vasquez entered the fur trade so early that long before he reached middle age he was called "Old Vasquez." His career is closely interwoven with those of William and Andrew Sublette (see the Sublette brothers), and James Bridger, who were his lifetime friends. Born in St. Louis, Missouri, the son of a Spanish father and a French-Canadian mother, Vasquez has sometimes been mistakenly called a Mexican trader. Whether he was on Ashley's famous Missouri River fur expedition of 1822 is unclear, but in 1823 Vasquez was granted a license to trade with the Pawnee Indians. Later he joined William Ashley's Rocky Mountain outfit and trapped in the Green River and Salt Lake regions of Utah until the 1830s.

Determined to "make money or die," a phrase Louis once used in a letter to his brother, Benito, he tried all phases of the frontier trade. In 1833 he helped Robert Campbell bring trade goods to the Green River rendezvous; for the next two years he stayed in the mountains, where he traded successfully with the Crow Indians. In 1835 he secured an Indian trader's license and in partnership with Andrew Sublette built an adobe post, Fort Vasquez, on the South Platte a few miles north of present-day Denver. Obviously Vasquez had chosen his site well, for within two years three competing posts, Forts Lupton, Jackson, and St. Vrain, were erected nearby. Always anxious to increase his efficiency and thereby his profits, Vasquez successfully sent a Mackinaw boat of furs down the South Platte and main channel of the Platte to St. Louis. The difficulties encountered discouraged use of the route, however. He hauled supplies over the Santa Fe Trail to Bent's Fort and then northward to his post over a route Pikes Peakers were to use twenty years later. During his years at Fort Bridger, Wyoming, he rushed his furs to Fort Laramie each spring with such dispatch that the supplies he bought with them were on the shelves of his post before the overland trains reached him in the middle of summer.

Vasquez sold his South Platte post in 1840 or 1841 and in partnership with Jim Bridger established the famous overland way station, Fort Bridger, on Black's Fork of the Green River near South Pass. From 1842 to 1855 he and Bridger traded with the Shoshoni and Ute and supplied overland pioneers with fresh horses, cattle, and oxen. In 1849 Vasquez also opened a store in Salt Lake City. By 1855, however, he and his Kentucky-born wife, whom he had married in 1846 and brought to Fort Bridger to live, were ready to leave the mountains. He sold his interest in the fort to the Mormons for four thousand dollars, and, after living in St. Louis for a time, the couple settled permanently in the outfitting town of Westport, Missouri—a choice undoubtedly affected by the fact that the Sublette and Bridger families lived nearby. Vasquez's interest in frontier trade never flagged, and it is likely that he helped Pike Vasquez, a nephew, establish one of the first stores in the gold-rush town of Denver in 1859.

Besides being a good businessman, Vasquez appears to have been liked and respected by Indians, Mormons, and competing traders alike. While his contemporaries protrayed him as an almost legendary mountain man, they also noted that the dark-haired, portly but finely-boned Vasquez was a genial and affectionate gentleman, full of merriment and with a taste for novels.

Vasquez's letters and papers are housed in the Missouri Historical Society. See LeRoy R. Hafen, ed., *The Mountain Men and the Fur Trade of the Far West,* vol. II (1965); and Dale L. Morgan and Eleanor T. Harris, eds., *Rocky Mountain Journals of William Marshall Anderson* (1967).—G. B. D.

Vásquez, Tiburcio (1835-1875). Bandit. Vásquez was born in Monterey County, California. Not much is known of his youth except that he received an elementary education that enabled him to read and write En-

glish. When he was sixteen, he and some Mexican friends attended a dance at which an Anglo sheriff was killed in a fight. One of the Mexicans involved was later hanged. Fearing that he would be unjustly inplicated, Vásquez fled and embarked on a life of crime. He soon became the most notorious bandit in the state.

Beginning in late 1856 and continuing through most of 1857, Vásquez pursued a career of cattle- and horse-stealing, stagecoach robbery, murder, and pillaging; his victims were usually Anglos. Because Mexican peasant society in California was caught in a period of cultural disintegration brought on by the American conquest of the Southwest, Vásquez came to be viewed by Mexicans as a man who did not submit to Anglo oppression and as a champion of the poor. The Mexican population gave him support and respect, which undoubtedly contributed to his success: they provided him with shelter, food, weapons and ammunition, horses, and information about the location of the local sheriff or posse. Coupled with his knowledge of the back mountain trails, his superb horsemanship, and his cunning, their support enabled him to live as long as he did during those violent years.

Vásquez was first captured in 1857 and sentenced to five years in San Quentin for horse-stealing. Two years later he escaped but was again captured and returned to prison until his release in 1863. During the late 1860s he was in and out of jail many times. The frequency with which he was caught is an indication of the massive efforts made by the local authorities to apprehend him and, more important, of their fear of Vásquez's revolutionary potential. By the early 1870s this "quasi-bandit revolutionary" had organized a gang that terrorized California from Monterey to Los Angeles. During the summer of 1873, the governor offered a reward of one thousand dollars for the capture of Vásquez, dead or alive. By January 1874 the reward had been increased to three thousand dollars for him alive and two thousand for him dead.

Vásquez's end came as a result of one of his amorous flings, which were many, and the betrayal by one of his own men. He got in trouble with Abdon Leiva, who caught his wife and Vásquez together. Leiva later gave himself up to the sheriff and told him of the location of one of Vásquez's hideouts. On the night of May 14, 1874, the famous bandit was captured near Los Angeles. He was transferred to the jail in San Jose, where thousands of people visited him, most of them women. After a speedy trial Vásquez was found guilty of murder and, on March 19, 1875, was hanged in San Jose. Vásquez sought to justify his way of life in these words: "A spirit of hatred and revenge took possession of me. I had numerous fights in defense of what I believed to be my rights and those of my countrymen. I believed we were being unjustly deprived of the social rights that belonged to us."

See Pedro Castillo and Alberto Camarillo, eds., *Furia y Muerte: Los Bandidos Chicanos* (1973); and Ernest May, "Tiburcio Vásquez," *Historical Society of Southern California Quarterly,* vol. 29 (1947).—P. C.

vegetation. As first seen by men of European descent, the West was a land of great variety, diversity, and quantity. A recent potential natural vegetation map of the United States lists 155 categories of vegetation communities, more than 80 of which lie west of the Mississippi. These include ten general types of biological communities or ecosystems: tundra; grassland; warm and cold deserts; broad-sclerophyll woodland; deciduous forests; and four coniferous forests, boreal, subalpine, montane, and Pacific coastal. The distribution of each type is closely tied to the environment in ways that are not yet understood in detail.

Whether a particular species or an entire vegetation community prevails, survives, or disappears in one location depends on a complex interaction of many environmental factors, including sunlight, temperature, precipitation, wind, fire, physical and chemical properties of the soil, as well as geological conditions (see PHYSIOGRAPHY OF THE UNITED STATES). Biological factors also control the distribution of vegetation through the effects of herbivorous and parasitic organisms, competition, and the vegetational history of a site—whether it is a site recently vegetated or recently subjected to catastrophe. Each species has its own set of requirements for environmental conditions; each can survive only within a certain range of climate and soil.

These requirements determine a geographic range for each species, and as a species approaches the limit of its range, it survives in those locations that have the most advantageous soil or climatic characteristics. A species limited by its requirement for water in a drier region may survive in the wetter areas, along rivers, for example, but not grow elsewhere.

Although vegetation communities are often referred to by the names of their most conspicuous or most important species, each community is a dynamic system, changing and responding to variations in the environment. Even the earliest explorers did not see a land of static and uniform vegetation; they saw vegetation subject to the effects of the Indians and to many natural catastrophes and pressures, such as fire, drought, disease, and grazing. One of the major properties of such communities, and one which would have given variety and diversity to the scenery over which the early explorers traveled, is succession. This is the process of establishment (primary succession) or reestablishment (secondary succession) of vegetation.

Different species are adapted and therefore characteristic of different stages of succession. Not only do different species become dominant as succession progresses, but often the "life forms," the shapes and sizes, of the characteristic species change. For example, lichens and mosses cling to bare rock surfaces. Then as the rock crumbles and vegetation decays, shrubs and low trees grow on newly formed soil.

Because of the high mountains of the West, the general distribution of vegetation is along two striking patterns, latitudinal and longitudinal, although the specific distribution in any one locale is complicated by local geological, soil, and microclimatic conditions. The amount of rainfall changes dramatically as one travels from the West Coast to the Mississippi, and this has a major effect on the vegetation. With the predominant movement of weather systems from west to east, the West Coast and Rocky Mountain ranges act as a "rain shadow," cooling the air masses moving up and over them, condensing the water vapor, and causing rain on the mountains. Extreme precipitation occurs in the Olympics in Washington, where annual rainfall reaches 150 inches; in the rain shadow east of the Cascades

annual precipitation falls to as little as 8 inches. Similarly, annual rainfall reaches as much as 80 inches in the mountains of California, dropping to as little as 12 inches in Reno, Nevada. The rate increases again in the Rockies. Less than one hundred miles west of Denver the annual precipitation in the mountains is 40 inches; in the plains one hundred miles east of Denver precipitation is 12 to 16 inches. The rainfall then increases steadily as one travels east: 20 inches per year at Dodge City; 28 inches near Lincoln, Nebraska; 36 inches east of Kansas City.

Temperature and length of growing season change with latitude, elevation, and topography. Where the ground is relatively level and elevation is constant, average temperatures and growing-season length decrease consistently from south to north. The average daily January minimum temperature is approximately forty degrees near San Antonio, Texas; thirty-five at Fort Worth; twenty at Dodge City, Kansas; fifteen at Lincoln, Nebraska; less than five at Huron, South Dakota; and below zero at Fargo, North Dakota. Where elevation and topography vary, average temperatures and growing-season length change in a complex way with aspect, slope, elevation, latitude, and with the shadowing of one slope by others. All of these affect the vegetation. North- and south- facing slopes can present different environments and have different distributions of vegetation.

Soils are influenced by the underlying bedrock, meteorological conditions, and vegetation. In areas of great precipitation minerals are leached from the upper layers of the soil. Where vegetation is luxuriant, a heavily organic layer develops near the surface.

Of course man has had many effects on the distribution of vegetation in the West. Livestock raising dates back to about the sixteenth century in the Southwest. Some effects of man, like the changing of much of the prairie into farmland, is obvious even to the most casual traveler. But other effects are more subtle and incompletely understood or recognized. Only a relatively few studies of these more subtle effects of man on the landscape have been made.

prairies. The prairie or the grasslands originally covered more land area in North America than did any other ecosystem, lying primarily in one vast continuous section extending west from Indiana to the woodlands on the slopes of the Rocky Mountains and the deserts of the Southwest, and south from Saskatchewan and Alberta, Canada, to Texas, but also including the Palouse area of Washington and the great valley of California.

The amount of rainfall played an important role in determining the original extent of the prairie, since grasses generally can survive with less precipitation than trees. Because water stress in plants is affected by the warmth of the climate as well as the precipitation (the warmer the climate the more water is required), dry hot summers are particularly important in the predominance of grasses over trees. Grazing and fire also can play an important role, and periodic fires seem to make the difference between prairie and forest in wetter areas and prairie and shrubland in drier ones. Before European settlement the grassland boundary may have been moved eastward by repeated fires set by the Indians. The eastern transition from prairie to forest occurred in Texas in areas with annual precipitation of thirty to forty inches and farther north in areas with twenty to twenty-five inches.

The prairie comprises many species of grasses in a variety of combinations, generally classified into three major types—the tall-grass prairie, mixed-grass prairie, and short-grass prairie.

The tall-grass prairie, occurring in areas of the greatest rainfall, requires soil moisture available to a depth of two feet in the growing season. Bunch grasses more than six feet tall grow in this prairie. The major species of this area includes tall grasses such as porcupine grass (*Stipa spartea*), big bluestem (*Andropogon gerardi*), and yellow Indian grass (*Sorghastrum nutans*); medium grasses such as little bluestem (*Andropogon scoparius*) and side oats grama (*Bouteloua curtipendula*); and short grasses such as blue grama (*B. gracilis*) and hairy grama (*B. hirsuta*).

Which of these dominate depends on the topography. Many other herbaceous species, often called forbs, also play important roles, and at certain times of the year their conspicuous flowers suggest to the casual viewer that they predominate. Members of the daisy family and pea family are particularly important.

Forbs, grasses, and sedges (grasslike plants of the genus *Carex*) combined in presettlement times to produce a productive and, to early travelers, a pretty scene. According to Francis Parkman near Fort Leavenworth in 1847,

> The scenery needed no foreign aid. Nature had done enough for it; and the alternation of rich green prairies and groves that stood in clusters, or lined the banks of the numerous little streams had all the softened and polished beauty of a region that has been for centuries under the hand of man. At that early season, too, it was in the height of its freshness. The woods were flushed with the red buds of the maple; there were frequent flowering shrubs unknown in the east; and the green swells of the prairie were thickly studded with blossoms.

Among the more conspicuous composites of the prairies are blanket flowers (*Gaillardia* spp.) and butter-weeds (*Senecio* spp.), which flower in the spring; sunflowers (*Helianthus* spp.) and coneflowers (*Rudbeckia* spp. and *Ratibida* spp.), flowering in midsummer; and the goldenrods (*Solidago* spp.) and asters (*Aster* spp.), flowing in late summer and fall. One of the major trees along drainages is the cottonwood (*Populus deltoides* var. *occidentalis*). In the north, where moisture conditions are more favorable, a dwarf oak (*Quercus macrocarpa* var. *depressa*) occurs.

At the eastern edge of the prairies in presettlement times, patches of forest occurred along streams, while the grasslands occupied the ridgetops. As the climate has changed since the passing of the last glaciation, so has the extent of the prairie. Several thousand years ago the prairie extended as far east as Ohio, where there are still fragments of prairie and prairie soils.

The original short-grass prairie occupied the drier areas east of the Rocky Mountains, in "buffalo country." The buffalo themselves may have played an important role in determining the extent of this prairie. Some recent studies suggest that without extensive grazing, now done by cattle, this type of prairie would disappear. In this area, rainfall is commonly ten to fifteen inches a

year and irregular. The major species of grasses, which are characteristically only a few inches high, vary from north to south. In the north, blue grama, or little grama, grass and buffalo grass (*Buchloë dactyloides*) dominate, although needle-and-thread grass (*Stipa comata*), western wheatgrass (*Agropyron smithii*), and red three-awn (*Aristida longiseta*) are important in some areas. In the south several species of grama grass and red three-awn dominate.

The mixed-grass prairie forms a strip between the tall- and short-grass prairie, extending from Texas through western Oklahoma, Kansas, Nebraska, central South Dakota and North Dakota to Saskatchewan. The major species of this area include blue grama, hairy grama, and little bluestem. In the north June grass (*Koeleria cristata*), porcupine grass, and needle-and-thread are also important, while elsewhere buffalo grass is an important species.

Before settlement the transitions from tall- to mixed- or mixed- to short-grass prairie were gradual; within the transitions local combinations of species were different on drier exposed rises than on wetter protected swales. But the decrease in rainfall as one traveled westward toward the Rocky Mountains produced clearly visible changes in the vegetation as seen by frontiersmen. According to Josiah Gregg, writing in 1831,

> Thus far, many of the prairies have a fine and productive appearance, though the Neosho River (or Council Grove) seems to form the western boundary of the truly rich and beautiful country of the border. Up to that point the prairies are similar to those of Missouri, the soil equally exuberant and fertile; while all the country that lies beyond is of a far more barren character—vegetation of every kind is more stinted—the gay flowers more scarce, and the scanty timber of a very inferior quality, indeed, the streams, from Council Grove westward, are lined with very little else than cottonwood, barely interspaced here and there with an occasional elm or hackberry.

To the traveler on horseback the prairie did sometimes give an impression of immense uniformity. "This tract of country may truly be styled the grand 'prairie ocean,'" wrote Gregg, viewing the area between the Arkansas and Cimarron rivers, "for not a single landmark is to be seen for more than forty miles—scarcely a visible eminence by which to direct one's course. All is as level as the sea, and the compass was our surest, as well as principal, guide." But the prairie was generally more variable, and the vegetation not always as uniform as it appeared to Gregg. The transitions between prairie and forest and between prairie and desert were gradual and broken. Along the eastern edge of the prairie, peninsulas and islands of forests extended into the grasslands. Some were relics of cooler, wetter climates that existed long ago at the end of the last period of glaciation; others followed drainages or wet swales. Devil's Canyon in Oklahoma still holds a relic stand of sugar maple whose continuous range lies more than one hundred miles to the east and that is otherwise surrounded by prairie.

Before settlement, cottonwood occurred along most of the larger drainages. Parkman described them in *The Oregon Trail:*

On our left was barren prairie, stretching to the horizon; on our right, a deep gulf, with Laramie Creek at the bottom. We found ourselves at length at the edge of a steep descent; a narrow valley, with long rank grass and scattered trees stretching before us for a mile or more along the course of the stream. Reaching the farther end, we stopped and encamped. A huge old cottonwood spread its branches horizontally over our tent. Laramie Creek, circling before our camp, half enclosed us; it swept along the bottom of a line of tall white cliffs that looked down on us from the farther bank. There were dense copses on our right; the cliffs, too, were half hidden by bushes, though behind us a few cottonwood trees, dotting the green prairie, alone impeded the view, and friend or enemy could be discerned in that direction at a mile's distance.

In the north, where moisture conditions are more favorable, a dwarf bur oak occurred naturally. And the prairie did in other places have a look of great diversity, as in Parkman's view of the prairie near Fort Leavenworth:

The path, a rather dubious and uncertain one, led us along the ridge of high bluffs that border the Missouri, and, by looking to the right or to the left, we could enjoy a strong contrast of scenery. On the left, stretched the prairie, rising into swells and undulations, thickly sprinkled with groves, or gracefully expanding into wide grassy basins, of miles in extent, while its curvatures, swelling against the horizon, were often surmounted by lines of sunny woods; a scene to which the freshness of the season and the peculiar mellowness of the atmosphere gave additional softness. Below us, on the right, was a tract of ragged and broken woods. We could look down on the tops of the trees, some living and some dead; some erect, others leaning at every angle, and others piled in masses together by the passage of a hurricane. Beyond their extreme verge the turbid waters of the Missouri were discernible through boughs, rolling powerfully along at the foot of the wood declivities on its farther bank.

mountains. Because of their wide range of elevation, latitude, and topography, the western mountains create a diversity of vegetation habitats. In general, however, there are four principal community types: foothill woodlands at the base of the mountains; montane forest; subalpine forest; and alpine tundra.

The appearance of the Rockies was succinctly described in 1943 by the ecologist R. F. Daubenmire:

On approaching the Rocky Mountains, even the most casual observer cannot fail to be impressed by the sudden change in vegetation where the forest-covered mountain slopes rise abruptly from the unforested basal plain. On ascending the mountain slopes, the forest types observed in the foothills may be seen to give way in rapid succession to other types, each of which in turn predominates only within a particular elevational zone. Near the summits of the higher prominences is only low-growing vegetation of still a different type. To the discriminating eye these

changes in the morphology of the vegetation are accompanied by practically complete changes in the species of herbs, shrubs and trees from one altitude to another.

Daubenmire describes this zonation as being "essentially homogeneous from the Black Hills of South Dakota westward to the divide of the Cascades and the eastern foothills of the Sierras and from the latitude of northern Alberta to the southern end of the Sierra Madres of northern Mexico."

Species composition of a specific community as well as the elevation at which the transition occurs from one community type to another varies with latitude and other environmental factors. The lower types disappear at the northern limits of the mountains; each type is found at increasingly higher elevation as one moves south. Because of the west-to-east movement of the weather patterns and the higher precipitation on western slopes, western and eastern slopes are frequently strikingly different. Northern and southern slopes also show great differences, particularly where slopes are steep.

Sunlight is as much as twenty percent brighter on the top of the highest mountain than at the base; the light is bluer and has more ultraviolet rays; bright clear days are mixed with cold cloudy ones. Temperatures decrease approximately 3.6°F per one thousand feet of elevation in the summer; the date of the last spring frost is delayed about two weeks per thousand feet in Arizona; the date of the first fall frost also becomes earlier as one moves upward. The frost-free period in the lowest-elevation forest of the Arizona mountains is 139 to 185 days; at upper timberline in this area it is 101 to 113 days. And occasional frosts have been recorded throughout the summer in the alpine zone.

The direction of a slope affects the local microclimate greatly. A slope of only one degree toward the north has temperatures similar to a level surface seventy miles farther north. North slopes have shorter growing seasons, but suffer less summer desiccation. At higher elevations the length of the snow-free period affects what vegetation can survive; alpine herbs can survive with a few weeks free of snow. At lower elevations lack of moisture seems important in setting the lower limit of trees on the Rockies' slopes.

The continental divide separates the Rockies into a west slope and an east slope; the west slope is wetter than the east and the vegetation somewhat different. The vegetation of the Rockies also changes north to south. In the southern Rocky Mountains, the lowest-elevational woodlands are called oak-aspen mahogany and are composed of low trees (less than thirty-five feet tall), called "broad-leaved scrub," that grow in dense clumps or widely separated individual plants, interspaced with prairie or desert vegetation.

South of Denver, a variety of oaks predominate, such as the Gambel Oak (*Quercus gambelii*) and Emory oak (*Q. emoryi*). North of Denver, mountain mahogany (*Cercocarpus montanus*) predominates, along with sumac (*Rhus trilobata*), antelope brush (*Purshia tridentata*), Apache plume (*Fallugia paradoxa*), and various species of serviceberry (*Amelanchier*) and *Symphoricarpos*.

Lying above the oak-mahogany in the southern and central Rockies and forming the lowest woodland in the north until it disappears in Canada is the juniper-piñon woodland, the lowest-elevation conifer forest of the Rockies. Juniper-piñon woodlands are comprised of widely spaced trees less than thirty feet high. Principal species are Mexican piñon (*Pinus cembroides*), which occurs in several varieties, and a number of species of juniper including Rocky Mountain juniper (*Juniperus scopulorum*), Utah juniper (*J. osteosperma*), one-seeded juniper (*J. monosperma*), western juniper (*J. occidentalis*), and alligator juniper (*J. deppeana*). Among the trees grow a variety of grasses, including grama, bluestem, and porcupine, and occasional shrubs typical of lower elevations, including mountain mahogany, antelope brush, and sagebrush (*Artemisia tridentata*). These shrubs increase in importance when the woodland is overgrazed or subject to frequent fires. Juniper-piñon is very important in the Great Basin, where it is the only vegetation type on many of the lower ranges.

On the east slope of the Rockies, juniper-piñon extends from Mexico to Fort Collins, Colorado. Northward, junipers grow without piñon. On the west slope, the forest continues into southern Alberta.

Douglas fir (*Pseudotsuga menziesii*) and ponderosa pine (*Pinus ponderosa*) dominate the montane forests of the Rockies. Douglas fir is at higher elevations, the pine at lower ones. Douglas fir has a moderately broad crown, while the spruce and true fir are spirelike. In the southern and central Rockies, white fir (*Abies concolor*) and Colorado blue spruce (*Picea pungens*) are found often among the Douglas fir, particularly along streams. In Canada, and especially along the east slope, white spruce (*Picea glauca*) grows with the fir; in the north, particularly in the west, grand fir (*Abies grandis*) occurs with Douglas fir. An old Douglas fir stand is very dense and little grows beneath the trees. Ponderosa pine forests are savannalike at their lower border, where they fade into the grasslands. At upper elevations, ponderosa pine woodlands are composed of rounded crowns of open-spaced trees that readily distinguish this type from the dense Douglas fir stands. In the southern Rockies, the trees in the pondersa pine zone cover only one quarter of the surface, the rest is excellent pasture of perennial grasses including fescue (*Festuca*), wheatgrass, bluegrass (*Poa*), and muhly (*Muhlenbergia*). Old trees have bright yellow in their plated bark and are known as yellow pines; younger trees, called blackjack or bull pines, have dark gray bark. Fires are common, and old trees are fire-resistant. Where frequent, such fires spread slowly, burning only grasses, tree litter, and small seedlings. Where the zone is overgrazed or heavily logged, the pine is often replaced by dense shrubs such as ceanothus and mountain mahogany.

The ponderosa pine forests were viewed in 1857 in northern Arizona by a Lieutenant Edward Beale, who wrote, "It is the most beautiful region I ever remember to have seen in any part of the world. A vast forest of gigantic pines, intersected frequently with open glades, sprinkled all over with mountains, meadows, and wide savannas, and covered with the richest grasses, was traversed by our party for many days."

These forests were apparently much more open and parklike in the mid-nineteenth century than they are today. Joseph Rothrock, a botanist with the Wheeler survey, described the area south of Gallup, New Mexico, in 1875:

Gaining the summit a thousand feet above Fort Wingate, we were at an altitude of about 8000 feet above the sea, a fine, open, park-like region with a large growth of yellow pine (pinus ponderosa) and fir covering the hillsides. A diversified herbaceous vegetation was out in the most brilliant colors, beautifying alike the woods and open grounds. . . . Good forage was abundant. In the area there are now dense thickets of pine saplings and almost no herbaceous ground cover.

There is also evidence that the watersheds have deteriorated since presettlement conditions. For example, gullies were once apparently rare in forested areas such as along the Kaibab Plateau. In this area according to Clarence Dutton in 1887, "every ravine is as smooth as a lawn and carpeted with a rich turf of mountain grass, richly decked with flowers of rare beauty and luxuriance." Concerning this change, Aldo Leopold has written:

All the old settlers agree that the bottoms of Blue River were, at the time of settlement in about 1885, stirrup-high in gramma grass, and covered with groves of mixed hardwoods and pine. The banks were lined with willows and abundant with trout. . . . About 1900, fifteen years after settlement, floods began to cut an ever-widening channel.

Some of the change in the forest was probably caused by overgrazing, which destroyed the grasses and exposed the mineral soil, facilitating the establishment of pine seeds. But the most important change was apparently the elimination of fire. According to the ecologist C. F. Cooper, light surface fires, caused by Indians or lightning, were a regular occurrence and acted to thin vegetation and remove excess fuel in pine forests. The present emphasis on fire prevention and the introduction of cattle, which remove flammable grasses, have all but eliminated natural fires and have induced marked changes in the vegetation.

As is characteristic of many mountain ranges, spruce and fir dominate the upper reaches of forests in the subalpine zone in the Rocky Mountains. Alpine fir (*Abies lasiocarpa*) is the most important of this genus. In the north the major spruce is Engelmann spruce (*Picea engelmanni*); in the south it is Colorado blue spruce. Mountain hemlock (*Tsuga mertensiana*) occurs in Montana and northern Idaho; farther north near the transition to the northern conifer forest, white spruce is found.

Successional stages following a fire in this zone include stands of lodgepole pine (*Pinus contorta* var. *murrayana*), aspen (*Populus tremuloides*), and Douglas fir, except in the south, where lodgepole pine is absent. On moist sites, aspen is more important than the pine.

On the wetter west slope of the Rockies, mosses and herbaceous flowering plants flourish under the trees; on the drier eastern slope, the ground below the trees is sparsely covered by dwarf species of blueberry (*Vaccinium*).

Near the timberline occur species that cannot compete with the spruce and fir in the rest of the subalpine zone, including bristlecone pine (*Pinus aristata*), noteworthy because of its longevity (individuals of this species have been found to be more than three thousand years old). Limber pine (*P. flexilis*), whitebark pine (*P. albicaulis*), and alpine larch (*Larix lyallii*) also occur in this transitional area. As one approaches the timberline, the trees thin out and, near their upper limit, take on a low, twisted, distorted matlike form called *Krummholz*.

Above the treeline occurs the alpine tundra, a zone of low, often mat-forming plants, adapted to the severe climate and short growing seasons of the summits. In 1823 Dr. Edwin James described the vegetation near the summit of Pikes Peak:

> A little above the point where the timber disappears entirely, commences a region of astonishing beauty, and of great interest on account of its productions; the intervals of soil are sometimes extensive, and are covered with a carpet of low but brilliantly flowering alpine plants. Most of these have either matted procumbent stems, or such as including the flower, rarely rise more than an inch in height. In many of them, the flower is the most conspicuous and the largest part of the plant, and in all, the colouring is astonishingly brilliant.

This scene was all the more striking because the mountain from below had appeared to James to have "its lower half thinly clad with pines, junipers, and other evergreen trees; the upper half a naked conic pile of yellowish rocks, surmounted here and there with broad patches of snow."

This was the tundra, "islands in a sea of forest," composed of low, matlike forms of vegetation, including lichens, sedges, and species often related to, if not the same as, those of the arctic tundra. Approximately 350 species occur in the alpine tundra, 250 of which are not found in other zones of the Rockies. One of the distinctive characteristics of these endemic alpine tundra species is their ability to withstand heavy frost during periods of flowering and active growth. The elevation of the timberline increases from north to south as far as latitudes approximately 30 degrees north; for latitudes below this the timberline seems to decline gradually. The timberline occurs near six thousand feet in Canada and near twelve thousand feet in the San Francisco Mountains of Arizona.

Almost all alpine vegetation is perennial; plants are dwarf, bearing relatively large fruits and flowers on relatively small stems. Near the mountaintops, soil formation occurs extremely slowly, and much of the terrain is covered by angular boulders on which grow crustose lichens. In the crevices between boulders grow a few plants, including mountain sorrel (*Oxyria digyna*), columbine (*Aquiligia* spp), and sibbaldia (*Sibbaldia procumbens*).

Elsewhere, on the gravelly, coarse soil of fell-fields, grow mat or cushion plants, including moss campion (*Silene acaulis*) and sandwort (*Arenaria sajanensis*). Finally, "alpine meadows" develop on the most favorable accumulations of soil. These are densely vegetated with grasses, sedges, and forbs, including bluegrass, alpine Timothy (*Phleum alpinum*), hair grass (*Deschampsia caespitosa*), spiked trisetum (*Trisetum spicatum*), *Agrostis* spp., *Festuca* spp., *Polygonum viviparum*, *Potentilla* spp., *Sieversia turbinata*, *Trifolium* spp., and *Pedicularis parryi*.

Arising out of the Great Plains, the Black Hills are ecologically related to the Rockies, and have a mixture of eastern, western, and northern vegetation. For example, ash, birch, elm, hackberry, and bur oak from eastern forests occur here. White spruce (*Piccea glauca* var. *albertiana*), found on the east slope of the Rockies, dominates the upper elevations of the Black Hills, which reach seven thousand feet. Paper birch (*Betula papyrifera*) of the northern conifer forest also grows at these elevations. Ponderosa pine is the most important tree at lower elevations.

The woodland of the Black Hills is generally scrubby in appearance, reminiscent of the oak-mahogany woodland of the Rockies. And so it looked in 1846 to Parkman, who saw it as "crags and rocks, a black and sullen brook that gurgled with a hollow voice deep among the crevices, a wood of mossy distorted trees and prostrate trunks flung down by ages and storms, scattered among the rocks, or damming the foaming waters of the brook."

Pacific Northwest. The most densely forested area of the United States lies in western Washington and northwest Oregon. Here trees grow rapidly, and the major species are long-lived (many living more than five hundred years) and large (usually 150 to 230 feet high). These trees have never ceased to impress travelers, as in this 1841 description of the yet unsettled area near Mount Rainier by the botanist William Dunlop Brakenridge:

> Our route across the range lay somewhat to the north of Mt. R where the finest timber exists that I ever beheld. For several days our route lay through dense forests of Spruce the stems so straight and clean that it was seldom you could find a branch closer than 150 feet to the ground. . . . Many of the Spruce stems which lay prostrate were so stout that when on horseback we could not see over them. On the decayed bark of such seedlings of the Spruce vegetated freely, forcing their roots through the bark, over the body of the trunk till the[y] reached the ground so that when said trunk became entirely decayed the roots of the young trees became robust [and] formed a sort of archway, under which we occasionally rode.

Originally, a forest extended almost continuously from the coast eastward to the timberline; today eighty-two percent of this area is forest, almost 30 million acres. Much of this area is now composed of second-growth forests that have followed clearing, logging, and fires.

This region is divided into four vegetation zones: the coastal Sitka spruce (*Picea sitchensis*) zone, the western hemlock (*Tsuga heterophylla*) zone, the white fir (*Abies amabilis*) zone, and the mountain hemlock zone.

There is a wide variety of soils, resulting from complex land forms, geological history, and climate. The steep slopes of the mountains prevent development of mature soils. In many areas ash from volcanic eruptions has had a profound influence on the soil and the vegetation.

Moisture, not only as rain, but also as fog, plays an important role in determining the ranges of vegetation communities, and a general east-west patterning of the communities can be distinguished. The climate of the Pacific coastal forest of the Northwest is mild and wet; rainfall is 80 to 120 inches per year. Fog drip condensation in tree crowns can add an additional twenty-five percent to the precipitation.

Sitka spruce dominates the Pacific Northwest forests along the coast, where dense fogs occur. This is part of a coastal forest that occurs all along the West Coast to Alaska. To the south, in California, the redwood (*Sequoia sempervirens*) grows in similar habitats, from the Chetco River in Oregon, just north of the California border, south to Monterey County. It is rarely found more than twenty or thirty miles inland or above 3,000 feet. In northern California it forms pure stands along ravines and the sides of streams. Its relative, the *Sequoia gigantea*, grows at elevations of 5,000 to 8,400 feet in the western slopes of the Sierra Nevada in California.

The western hemlock zone lies in the lowlands east of the coastal forests, extending over the greatest land area of the four types. Within it are extensive stands of Douglas fir and western red cedar (*Thuja plicata*), mixed with western hemlock.

The white fir zone occurs on the western slopes of the Cascades from elevations of 3,000 to 4,500 feet in Oregon and 900 to 4,000 feet in northern Washington. This vegetation type is also found in the Olympic Mountains. Important species of this type include western hemlock, noble fir (*Abies procera*), Douglas fir, western red cedar, and western white pine (*Pinus monticola*). Douglas fir and red alder (*Alnus rubra*) are important pioneer species characteristic of areas clear-cut or burned.

The subalpine mountain hemlock zone is the highest elevation forest of the west slopes of the Cascades and of the Olympics. Important tree species of these elevations are mountain hemlock, subalpine fir, lodgepole pine, and white fir.

A striking effect of geology on vegetation occurs in the Northwest, where there are areas of serpentine rocks that are low in calcium and high in magnesium, chromium, and nickel. In some areas, such as the Siskiyou Mountains, serpentine and nonserpentine soils are juxtaposed, and the vegetation on them differs strikingly. For example, below six thousand feet, sepentine areas are vegetated sparsely by grasses and scattered individuals of Jeffrey pine (*Pinus jeffreyi*), in contrast to surrounding forests, which today typically are much denser stands of Douglas fir, sugar pine (*Pinus lambertiana*), and the incense cedar (*Libocedrus decurrens*). Serpentine soils also occur in the Wenatchee Mountains, near Mount Baker, and in the San Juan Islands. Serpentine soils—and their characteristically striking effect on the vegetation—also occur in the Sierra Nevada foothills area of California.

deserts. These are four major deserts of the United States: the Great Basin, a cold desert, and the Mojave, Sonoran, and Chihauhuan deserts, all of them warm. The deserts extend from southeast Oregon and southern Idaho through the Great Basin, which includes most of Nevada and Utah; to southern California and western Arizona; into the Lower California peninsula; and through Sonora. The continuity of the desert is interrupted by uplands in eastern Arizona and western New Mexico. The environmental factors controlling vegetation are summarized by the ecologist Henry J. Oosting:

Climatic differences, associated with latitude and altitude, are accompanied by differences in species and life forms. Locally, the physical differences in topog-

raphy, exposure, and soils produce distinct vegetational variations. Finally there are numerous undrained depressions into which the water of winter rains flows and upon evaporation, deposits the silts and clays it has transported as well as salts of various kinds. The resulting mud flats (playas) in themselves constitute a special habitat with associated species, but the nature and concentration of salts in the soil is even more effective in controlling the communities there.

Desert communities are simple; approximately sixty percent of the desert communities have four to twelve dominant major plant species, and ten percent have only two or three.

The Great Basin lies primarily above four thousand feet elevation, where week-long periods of freezing weather are frequent in winter. Rainfall is four to eight inches per year at lower elevations and as much as thirteen inches at higher elevations. Sagebrush and shad scale (*Atriplex confertifolia*), generally two to four feet tall and rarely more than seven feet, dominate simple uniform stands twenty to sixty miles in extent in the valleys. Sagebrush communities dominate higher elevations in the north; shad scale dominates the lower elevations in the south. At higher elevations, six thousand to twelve thousand feet, the Utah juniper is characteristic. Sagebrush originally dominated almost all the land now farmed in Nevada and Utah. The uniformity of the vegetation has seemed monotonous even to some of the most careful observers of this region.

In general, salt plays an important role in the distribution of the vegetation. Where the salt concentration is greatest, no plants may grow. Samphire (*Salicornia* spp.) or iodine bush (*Allenrolfea occidentalis*) dominate the most salty yet vegetated areas. In intermediate areas shad scale and greasewood (*Sarcobatus vermiculatus*) or gray molly (*Kochia americana*) dominate. Where sagebrush is dominant it is so on areas of minimum salt.

The Mojave Desert lies almost entirely in California. In its simplicity it is like the Great Basin. Here too soil texture and salt content are important in determining local variations in the vegetation.

The Joshua tree (*Yucca brevifolia*) dominates the upper edges of the desert; below and in drier areas, the creosote bush (*Larrea divaricata*) and bur sage (*Franseria dumosa*) are most important. Other common species are sagebrush, shortspine horsebrush (*Tetradymia spinosa*), and narrow-leaf goldenbush (*Aplopappus linearifolius* var. *interior* and *Acamptopappus sphaerocephalus*).

The Sonoran Desert lies in the lowlands below three thousand feet around the upper Gulf of California, extending from Baja California and the Colorado Desert of California into southwestern Arizona and the western half of Sonora. At the lower elevations rainfall is slight—in places two to four inches per year—and irregular. The ecologist Forrest Shreve mentions an area in Baja California that had gone four years without rain. Rainfall increases with elevation and with distance away from the gulf, reaching twelve to fourteen inches per year. The low elevations are primarily quite level plains, dominated by creosote bush and bur sage, also important in the Mojave Desert. Distinctive vegetation of the Sonoran lies in the upper bajadas and the lower mountain slopes, where one finds columnar and arborescent cacti, such as *Carnegiea gigantea*—which is known as

The dread Jornada del Muerto in southeastern New Mexico. (National Archives)

organ-pipe, or saguaro, cacti and is Arizona's state flower—and staghorn cholla (*Opuntia versicolor*). These make up approximately half of the vegetation. The large barrel cactus (*Ferocactus wislizeni*) as well as evergreen and deciduous shrubs and a few trees occur among the cacti.

The Chihuahuan Desert extends from Mexico into parts of New Mexico and western Texas adjacent to the Rio Grande and into the lower valley of the Pecos River. Mountain ranges and limestone hills interrupt plains and undrained basins. Most of the Chihuahuan Desert lies above four thousand feet, and desert plants are found as high as eighty-five hundred feet. Rainfall is as low as three inches per year in some of the lower basins, reaching twelve to sixteen inches at higher elevations. Most of the rainfall occurs in the summer, from June to September, producing a growing season that is longer and more reliable for vegetation than that of the other desert areas. The major kinds of plants are shrubs and semishrubs, including creosote bush, ocotillo (*Fouquieria splendens*), and mesquite (*Prosopis chilensis*), but the scenery is striking because of plants of unusual shape and size, such as the century plant (*Agave*) and yucca, as well as leafless, green-stemmed trees, columnar cacti, and one species with six-foot linear leaves, *Dasylirion longissimum*.

In the Southwest the various vegetation communities are juxtaposed in transitional areas, giving variety to the scene, as described in 1858 by one Mr. Reid:

The bottoms in places, are several miles wide and highly fertile. Cotton-wood and musquite [sic], of good size, are abundant in them. The valley, tableland and mountain sides here, as elsewhere in the [Gadsden] Purchase, are covered with a luxuriant coating of grama grass . . . [we] drove fifteen miles to the Ranchos do los Calabasa. . . . If you will portray in

your imagination a bottom covered with tall, golden colored grass . . . divided by a meandering stream a dozen yards wide and as many inches deep, this shaded by cotton-woods, willows and musquites . . . you will have a view of Calabasas.

The kind of extensive changes that have taken place in the vegetation of the Southwest is illustrated by the desert grasslands that include areas of eastern New Mexico and western Texas. Parts of this area, once extensive grasslands, are now mesquite woodland. For example, an area of southeastern Arizona, which in 1958 was dense mesquite woodland where it was not cultivated, was described in 1854 as "a level patch of green, resembling a luxuriant meadow, some eight or ten miles long, by one broad."

broad-sclerophyll woodlands. These are the broad-sclerophyll forest and the chaparral, or shrub land. Both are composed of plants with sclerophyllous (that is, tough and thick) evergreen leaves, and both are best developed in the coastal ranges of southern California, although they extend into southern Oregon. Some of the species of these two communities occur on the east slopes of the Sierra and in the desert woodland zones of the Rocky Mountains. The sclerophyll communities dominate in mild-temperature regions with long, dry summers and wet winters. They occur in areas of not less than ten or more than thirty inches rainfall a year. Where rainfall is less than ten inches, desert occurs; where more than thirty, conifer forests are found.

The chaparral occurs over a greater area than the broad-sclerophyll forest; the chaparral dominates the southern part of the region, and the sclerophyll forest dominates the northern portion. However, in almost any part of this area, the two types occur in alternating patches. The major trees of the forest are species of oaks (*Quercus agrifolia, Q. chrysolepis,* and *Q. Wislizenii*), tan oak (*Lithocarpus densiflorus*), California laurel (*Umbellularia californica*), Pacific madrona (*Arbutus menziesii*), Golden Chinquapin (*Castanopsis chrysophylla*), and Pacific bayberry (*Myrica californica*). The major species of the chaparral are chamiso (*Adenostoma fasciculatum*) and various species of manzanita (*Arctostaphylos*), but there are approximately forty species that grow in a variety of combinations, producing low and dense thickets.

Fire, which favors chaparral over sclerophyll forests, plays an important role in the chaparral, for the dense thickets burn readily in the long dry summers when fires are frequent. Following fires that are not too frequent or too severe, the chaparral shrubs sprout abundantly; if the fires are too frequent, grasses may replace the shrubs. Chaparral returns to its original condition in about ten years. Few stands seem to last more than thirty years without a fire; and in one study twenty-five years was a characteristic age for such stands.

A more detailed description of the vegetation zones in the West is in Henry J. Oosting, *The Study of Plant Communities* (1956). A detailed map of vegetation is in A. W. Kuchler, *Potential Natural Vegetation of the Conterminous United States,* American Geographical Society Special Publication 36 (1964). See also H. L. Bauer, "Moisture Relations in the Chaparral of the Santa Monica Mountains, California," *Ecology Monograph* (1936); D. F. Cooper, "Changes in Vegetation, Structure, and Growth of Southwestern Pine Forests Since White Settlement," *Ecology Monograph* (1960); R. F. Daubenmire, "Ecologic Plant Geography of the Pacific Northwest," *Madroño* (1969), and "Vegetation Zonation in the Rocky Mountains," *Botany Review* (1943); and R. H. Humphrey, "The Desert Grassland," *Botany Review* (1958). An interesting discussion of grasslands is focused in J. C. Malin's *The Grasslands of North America* (1967). —D. B. B.

Veniaminov, Ioann (1797-1879). Alaska missionary. Veniaminov was a large man with a mind and spirit to match his stature. He became the outstanding churchman of Russian America, an early scholar of Alaska, and one of its major personalities. Veniaminov was born Ivan Popov in Anginskoe, Siberia. His precocity was soon recognized. At the age of nine he entered the Irkutsk theological seminary of the Russian church; while there, he took the name of the late bishop of Irkutsk. Veniaminov married at a young age, became a deacon, and in 1821 was ordained a priest. A request from the Alaskan Russian-American Company for a priest was answered by Father Veniaminov in 1824; he was twenty-seven when he arrived with his family at Unalaska in the Aleutian Islands. A church and parish house were quickly raised, and Veniaminov began to study the Aleutian-Fox dialect. A school he founded taught the dialect with a dictionary, grammar, and primer prepared by the industrious priest. His success in spreading literacy among the talented Aleut people was as remarkable as his record of conversions, and his writings on the ethnology and natural history of the country have been praised by modern scholars.

After ten years in Unalaska heading its sprawling diocese, Veniaminov moved his headquarters to Sitka where he repeated his Unalaska successes but on a still larger scale. Sir Edward Belcher described him at age forty-one as "a very formidable, athletic man . . . standing in his boots about six feet three inches; quite hercu-

lean and very clever. . . ." Between 1838 and 1841 he visited Russia and Siberia, returning as Innokentii (Innocent), bishop of Kamchatka, the Kuriles, and the Aleutian Islands. Bishop Innokentii's new duties took him to the widely scattered Russian posts in Alaska, where new schools and missions were established. In 1846 he consecrated St. Michael's Cathedral in Sitka; the clock on the belfry was made by Veniaminov. He also made barrel organs, one of which he delivered himself to a Franciscan mission in California. In 1850 he was elevated to the archbishopric of Yakutsk, in Siberia, and in 1868 he became head of the Russian church as the metropolitan of Moscow and Kolomna.

See Hector Chevigny, *Russian America* (1965); A. P. Kashevaroff, "Ivan Veniaminov . . . His Life and Work in Alaska, drawn from His Biography in the Russian," *Alaska Magazine* (February-April 1927); Helen A. Shenitz, "Alaska's 'Good Father,' " in Morgan B. Sherwood, ed., *Alaska and Its History* (1967); and Ioann Veniaminov, "The Condition of the Orthodox Church in Russian America," trans. and ed. by Robert Nichols and Robert Croskey, *Pacific Northwest Quarterly* (April 1972).—M. B. S.

Vermont, settlement of. Vermont was the child of controversy. The trouble began in 1749 when Governor Benning Wentworth of New Hampshire first granted land to land speculators west of the Connecticut River. The governor justified his actions by explaining that New Hampshire's boundary was a line twenty miles east of the Hudson River; but New York authorities quickly pointed out that in 1664 the English crown had given the disputed territory to them, and they asked Wentworth to recall his grants. The governor paid no attention to this request, and by 1764 he had conveyed nearly three million acres to speculators who had no interest in personally settling the area. In 1764 the English Privy Council declared that New Hampshire had acted illegally, since the entire region had always belonged to New York.

After the council's judgment New York began to award acreage to its own speculators, the "Yorkers." Unfortunately, much of this land had already been granted by New Hampshire. Two groups within the area, now called simply the "Grants," resisted New York. The "Yankee" speculators, who held titles from New Hampshire, demanded that New York recognize their prior claims to the land. The settlers—most of whom had come from Connecticut—were afraid that New York would collect high quitrents, charge unfair fees for confirming land titles, and deny them representation in the legislature. Then in 1767 the Privy Council ordered that, until "the King's pleasure shall be known," New York should stop issuing grants that conflicted with those made earlier by New Hampshire. This unexpected move, totally inconsistent with the council's previous decision, threw the entire region into confusion, for no one knew which titles were valid.

Two clever speculators, Ethan and Ira Allen, arrived in the "Grants" in 1772. They purchased as many New Hampshire land grants as they could afford and established the Onion River Land Company. The Allens realized that their holdings would be worthless unless the New York titles were invalidated. For that end they organized the Green Mountain Boys, a vigilante group that harassed the Yorkers of the area. At first, the Allens only wanted to force New York to accept the legality of the New Hampshire grants, but they soon began to advocate complete independence for the region. One historian has written of the Allens, "It appears quite clear that there was a distinct correlation between the political democracy which they championed and their more immediate economic objectives."

In 1777 a convention at Windsor declared Vermont an independent state. To the Allens' surprise, however, the Continental Congress seemed unwilling to support Vermont's separation from New York, and in 1779 Ethan explained bitterly, "We are in the fullest sense as unwilling to be under the jurisdiction of New York as we can conceive America would be to revert back under the Power of Great Britain. . . ."

Vermont remained neutral during most of the American Revolution, and at one point the state's leaders even held secret talks (the Haldimand Negotiations) with England to see if that nation would guarantee the area's independence. After the war, the Allens continued to resist any move to become part of the new American government. But in 1790 other men took political control over Vermont and agreed to pay New York for its claims. This deal opened the way to statehood in 1791.

See Matt Bushnell Jones, *Vermont in the Making 1750-1777* (1939); and Chilton Williamson, *Vermont in Quandary: 1763-1825* (1949).—T. H. B.

Vestal, Stanley (1887-1957). Writer and teacher. Known to his friends and colleagues as Walter Campbell, Vestal devoted most of his adult life to writing about the West. His father died soon after Vestal's birth at Severy, Kansas, and one year later his mother married James Robert Campbell. He took his stepfather's surname but later wrote under his original name in memory of the father he never knew. The Campbell family settled at Guthrie, Oklahoma, a few years after the "run of 1889" and the initial opening of the territory to white settlement. The boy spent his summers at an uncle's farm near Watonga, across the river from a Cheyenne reservation. From the Indians he learned a love of hunting and swimming and acquired a lifelong admiration for their way of life.

He graduated in 1908 from Southwestern State Normal School at Weatherford, Oklahoma, where, at the time, his stepfather was president. From there Vestal went to Oxford University as the state's first Rhodes Scholar, eventually taking a B.A. and M.A. with honors in English literature. However, he remained spiritually attached to the frontier and maintained a large collection of guns, bowie knives, and bows and arrows. He kept a tepee in the backyard of his home and to the end of his life considered it more comfortable in winter than a regular house. A broad-brimmed hat, fringed buckskin jacket, and Indian moccasins were as much a part of his wardrobe as the familiar Oxford blazer that he cherished.

After a short period of teaching in Kentucky, Vestal joined the faculty of the University of Oklahoma in 1915 as an instructor in English and began sharpening his skills as a writer on topics of his native region. Soon after marrying Isabel Jones, he sailed for France during World War I as a captain in the United States Army Field Artillery. He returned to the University of Oklahoma in 1919 where he continued teaching and writing for the rest of his life. As a typical westerner of his time and place, he remained an "old-fashioned patriot" and a staunch believer in "rugged individualism." But his basic philosophy of life perhaps was reflected in his statement: "Research and writing on the Old West, the fur trade, and Indian wars have been my pleasure; my job has been to teach others to write."

During an active career of approximately forty years, Vestal produced more than twenty books and several dozen articles. His best-known works include *Kit Carson: The Happy Warrior of the Old West* (1928); *Sitting Bull: Champion of the Sioux* (1932); *Warpath and Council Fire: The Plains Indians' Struggle for Survival in War and in Diplomacy* (1948); and *Queen of Cowtowns: Dodge City* (1952). His influence as a teacher and director of professional writing courses at the University of Oklahoma perhaps remains his most lasting contribution to southwestern literature and to the frontier he loved. He is buried with the Sioux warriors—some of whom he knew and all of whom he respected—in the National Cemetery at Custer Battlefield National Monument in southeastern Montana.—W. E. H.

Vial, Pedro [Pierre] (c. 1746-1814). Explorer. Of the early life of Vial little is known beyond that he was a native of Lyons, France, and that by the early 1770s he was on the Missouri River. The governor of Louisiana in 1779 referred to him as a gunsmith who "usually lives among the savage nations, for whom he repairs their arms." By 1786, when his name first assumed prominence, Vial was intimately acquainted with numerous southwestern tribes and languages. This was probably the reason why Governor Domingo Cabello of Texas commissioned him to seek out a road from San Antonio to Santa Fe, New Mexico, there being no direct overland communication between these two provincial capitals.

Vial pressed northward from central Texas to the Red River and thence traveled in a westerly direction through Comanche camps to Santa Fe, which he reached on May 26, 1787. This feat established his reputation as a pathfinder, and he next was sent by the governor of New Mexico to explore a route to Natchitoches, Louisiana. This accomplished, he returned to Santa Fe via San Antonio, having covered twenty-five hundred miles. In 1792 he again took the trail from Santa Fe, this time to St. Louis. After a harrowing captivity among the Kansas Indians he reached it. Much of his journey paralleled the Santa Fe Trail, which would not be marked out for another quarter century. Vial evidently made other long-distance trips about which little is known. His last years were spent in Santa Fe, from which he often accompanied Spanish expeditions to the southern plains in the capacity of interpreter and guide. Since Vial's explorations were little publicized, many Anglo-American pioneers who later ventured over the paths he had trod must have believed themselves to be the first white men to visit these remote corners of the Southwest.

Noel M. Loomis and Abraham P. Nasatir, *Pedro Vial and the Roads to Santa Fe* (1967), contains Vial's journals in translation. Consult also Carlos E. Castaneda, *Our Catholic Heritage in Texas*, vol. V (1936-58).—M. Si.

Victor, Frances Fuller (1826-1902). Writer. Although born in Rome township, New York, and active in New York's literary life in the mid-nineteenth century, Victor was identified with the West during most of her life, having migrated to the Pacific Coast in 1863. She achieved her greatest fame as the author of historical and descriptive works about Oregon and California. Her most enduring book is *The River of the West* (1870), in which she combined her history of Oregon with the life and adventures of Joseph L. Meek (as related to her by the mountain man himself).

Frances Fuller completed her education in the Wooster Female Seminary in Ohio, and in May 1841 her first published poem appeared in the Wooster *Democrat*. By 1846 she was living with her family in Monroeville, Ohio, where she and her talented sister, Metta Victoria, gained increasing fame as writers. In 1848 the "Sisters of the West" were named regular contributors to the elite New York *Home Journal* and went to New York City to live. Summoned home by the death of their father, they established a new family home in Ypsilanti, Michigan, in 1850, accepted editorial positions with *The Monthly Hesperian* in Detroit, and published their collected *Poems of Sentiment and Imagination* (1851).

In June 1853 Fuller married Jackson Barritt, but the couple separated in 1856. By 1859 she had returned to New York to be near Metta, now the wife of Orville J. Victor. There she resumed her literary life, publishing among other things two Beadle dime novels about Nebraska (1862), where she and her husband had lived in 1855. She also renewed her acquaintance with Orville Victor's younger brother, Henry, an engineer in the navy. After the death of Henry's wife in 1861, Frances divorced Jackson Barritt and in May 1862 married Henry Victor.

In March 1863 the Victors sailed for Acapulco, where he joined his Pacific Squadron ship. She proceeded on to San Francisco to win a literary reputation in California with her gay, witty "Florence Fane" columns in the *Golden Era* between 1863 and 1864. In that year her husband resigned from the navy and settled in Portland, Oregon, where she joined him. Ever the journalist, she set forth in the spring of 1865 on the first of her many journeys by steamboat and stagecoach to see the Oregon country and to collect reminiscences and historical materials from surviving pioneers, one of her great services to Oregon history. Because of financial and other difficulties, the Victors separated in 1868. In November 1875 Henry was among the 250 passengers lost in the wreck of the steamship *Pacific* off the coast of Washington.

The pattern of Victor's life between 1868 and 1878, as she struggled to earn a living as a free-lance writer, was one of almost constant travel in Oregon and Washington and between Portland and San Francisco. During this decade she published *The River of the West* (1870); *All Over Oregon and Washington* (1872); *Women's War with Whiskey; or, Crusading in Portland* (1874); *Eleven Years in the Rocky Mountains and Life on the Frontier* (1877); and *The New Penelope and Other Stories and Poems* (1877). She also contributed to the *Overland Monthly; The West Shore*, an illustrated monthly published in Portland (1875-92); the Portland *Oregonian;* the San Francisco *Call Bulletin;* and the *New Northwest*, a women's rights and literary newspaper published in Portland (1871-87) by Abigail Scott Duniway.

In 1878 Hubert Howe Bancroft offered Victor a position in his library to work on his projected histories of the Pacific states. Besides writing Bancroft's *History of Oregon*, she is generally credited with writing for Bancroft the *History of Washington, Idaho and Montana;* the *History of Nevada, Colorado and Wyoming*, except for the first two chapters on Nevada; the political and railroad chapters in the *History of California*, volumes 6 and 7; the account of the Modoc War in *California Inter Pocula;* a chapter on the Oregon question in the *History of the Northwest Coast*, volume 2; and nearly a volume of railway history for the *Chronicles of the Builders of the Commonwealth*.

Victor returned to her travels in the Pacific Northwest in 1889. In 1891 she published *Atlantis Arisen* (an expanded, updated revision of *All Over Oregon and Washington*), and the next year the Oregon secretary of state commissioned her to write the *Early Indian Wars of Oregon* (1894). The book completed, she returned to San Francisco to eke out a precarious living by potboiler writing. During these six difficult years she was receiving increased recognition for her historical writing, especially for her work on Marcus Whitman, the Methodist missionary killed by Indians. Among the first to deny publicly the "Whitman legend," she published "Did Dr. Whitman Save Oregon?" in *The Californian* (September 1880) and reiterated her stand in Bancroft's *History of Oregon*. In June 1900 Victor was elected an honorary member of the Oregon Historical Society. At the time, she was visiting in Portland, probably trying to sell copies of her last work, *Poems* (1900).

Victor never returned to San Francisco because she became ill and ran out of funds. For the remainder of her life she lived in Portland, writing articles for the *Oregon Historical Quarterly*, enthusiastically helping to plan the Lewis and Clark exposition to be held in Portland in 1905, and completing a revision of her *The River of the West*.

Among the many biographical references on Frances Fuller Victor are John W. Caughey, *Hubert Howe Bancroft: Historian of the West* (1946); Hazel E. Mills, "The Emergence of Frances Fuller Victor—Historian," *Oregon Historical Quarterly* (December 1961), and "Frances Fuller Victor," *Arizona and the West* (summer 1970); and Alfred Powers, *History of Oregon Literature* (1935). —H. E. M.

Victorio (1809?-1880). Indian chief. Victorio was perhaps the best-known leader of the Eastern Chiricahua Apache (also called Warm Springs, or Mimbreño, Apache. Born in New Mexico, probably in the Black Range area, he lived during a period of general hostility between the APACHE INDIANS and their Spanish, Mexican, and Anglo enemies.

Victorio's name comes into view in the 1850s when he and a group of followers joined NANA and GERONIMO on a vengeance raid into Mexico. He may have been with MANGAS COLORADO when the latter was wounded at the battle in Apache Pass in 1862. When Mangas was killed in 1863, Victorio put together his own group of warriors comprised of Eastern Chiricahua as well as Mescalero. They raided throughout the countryside, but in 1865 they agreed to settle down if they could be given a reservation. John G. BOURKE reported that since September 1869, they had been peacefully camped near Fort Craig, New Mexico, waiting for their reservation to be established. The place was at Ojo Caliente, or Warm Springs. In 1877 Victorio and his people, according to Bourke, "were peremptorily deprived of their little fields and driven away from the crops, half-ripened, and ordered to tramp to San Carlos."

The New Mexico Indians had no use for the Hell's Forty Acres that was San Carlos and its 110 degree summer heat, and so, when in September of 1877 Pionsenay, an Apache who had been raiding in Mexico, told Victorio of his great successes there, the Warm Springs people were off. Victorio soon returned to Warm Springs, and in 1878 the army came to bring him back to San Carlos; but he fled once more—this time for good. With more than 150 fighting men to back him, he killed shepherds, stole army horses, ambushed troops, ran off with settlers' mules and livestock, and pillaged in Chihuahua.

By 1879 Victorio had entrenched himself and a large number of followers south of the Rio Grande in Mexico. From his Chihuahua refuge he raided with impunity on both sides of the border. On October 14, 1880, however, American and Mexican troops tracked him and his band down near the Tres Castillos mountains in Chihuahua south of El Paso, Texas. The Mexicans sent the Americans away and then killed all but about seventeen of the Apache. One account says that Victorio—who may have been the greatest of Apache military strategists—was killed by another Indian, a Tarahumara scout in the employ of the Mexican troops. The Apache belief is that he took his own life. Either way, his death served to inspire the vengeance of Nana and other Chiricahua Apache.

See Eve Ball, *In the Days of Victorio* (1970); F. Stanley, *The Apaches of New Mexico, 1540-1940* (1962); and Dan L. Thrapp, *The Conquest of Apacheria* (1967). —B. L. F.

vigilantism. The taking of the law into one's own hands through the instrument of some type of extralegal committee has been part of the American experience since colonial days. It has taken various forms, ranging from unorganized mobs to quasi-military groups and operating under such names as Regulators, Moderators, Minutemen, and White Caps. Other groups, including the Ku Klux Klan, have incorporated vigilante functions into their activities. Although generally a rural phenomenon, some of the most notorious manifestations of vigilantism have occurred in the cities.

Large-scale vigilante movements came into being shortly before the American Revolution when committees came together to establish LAW AND ORDER and administer "justice" in areas where courts and law officers were either nonexistent, corrupt, or incapable of dealing with the problems at hand. According to Richard Brown, a leading authority on the subject, the practice was much cheaper and more efficient than the cumbersome and complex system of courts, juries, attorneys, and jails. And by the nineteenth century it had become "the lazy way, the careless way, the cheap way by which Americans often dealt with the problem of disorder."

Vigilantism frequently appeared as a rebellion against too much law or unpopular laws; for example, abolitionists in Meigs County, Ohio, organized extralegal groups in the 1820s to protect fugitive slaves. But in the backcountry regions and on the western frontier where little or no legal government existed, it was usually a response to lawlessness and reached its highest expression in the nineteenth century in the form of hundreds of local

organizations. Closely associated with it was the administration of justice by "lynch law," which sometimes proved a lesser evil than complete lawlessness. This was especially true when the frontier advanced so rapidly that organized government failed to keep pace with it. In most of the early mining and cattle towns, there were no jails in which to incarcerate an accused criminal, nor did the residents have the patience for a long, drawn-out trial. Thus, the victim generally was given a quick trial and, if found guilty, was banished, flogged, or hanged. Some individuals suffered for crimes they did not commit, but the rude system of *ad hoc* government did prove remarkably efficient.

The difficulty with vigilantism, no matter how successful, is that it knows no bounds. Men accustomed to taking the law into their own hands will continue to do so long after regular judicial processes are established. The historian Hubert Howe Bancroft observed that during the gold-rush days in California the most trivial incident sometimes would determine whether a culprit would be whipped or hanged. "While multitudes of minor offenders suffered capital punishment, no more could be inflicted upon the worst criminal. Lynching for cattle stealing obtained throughout the whole country, and even around San Francisco Bay, as late as 1855. A criminal affair was often made a sort of pastime, which might be prolonged or shortened according to the appetite of the crowd, or the time at their disposal."

An early manifestation of vigilantism took place in the backcountry of South Carolina when an outbreak of lawlessness followed a war between the militia and the Cherokee Indians. Since the poorer settlers who were uprooted by the war maintained small respect for authority, the property holders determined to discipline them accordingly. Thus, the Regulator movement that subsequently developed in 1767 was led by men of property and standing who took the law into their own hands and promptly executed several of the troublemakers. Such extreme violence practiced against the despised and feared settlers alarmed other conservatives, who then organized themselves as the Moderators. The latter were soon in control of the situation and generally substituted the lash for the noose. By the time of the American Revolution a noticeable degree of law and order had been restored, but no member of either vigilante group was ever tried for illegal or lawless acts committed in the name of justice.

Regulator and Moderator organizations sprang up on the frontier during the decade of the 1840s. The most extensive ones occurred in eastern Texas (1840-44), southwestern Missouri (1842-44), and southern Illinois (1846-50). The East Texas movement arose in Shelby County in the piney-wood area bordering Louisiana as an honest and straightforward attack on rings of corrupt county officials, counterfeiters, horse thieves, and common murderers. The original leader, Charles W. Jackson, was a steamboat operator with a dubious reputation. When Jackson fell victim to an assassin's bullet, leadership passed to a much more nefarious individual named Watt Moorman. The Regulators soon degenerated to the level of the undesirables they were seeking to get rid of.

The extreme measures employed by the East Texas Regulators gave rise to a countermovement, the Moderators, in 1841. But criminal elements were present in both groups, and so, dissension on both sides led to war within a war. Eventually every individual in the county was forced to choose sides, often with neighbors or relatives pitted against one another. By 1844 the Moderator movement had rid itself of some of its criminal elements and was on the verge of a war to the finish with the Regulators. Sam Houston, president of the Republic of Texas, may have prevented wholesale slaughter when he sent in the militia, and the Mexican War, which followed a short time later, temporarily diverted hatred and energies elsewhere. In all, some eighteen men were bushwhacked or murdered outright during the four-year period, dozens more were severely wounded or crippled for life, and bitter feuds and hatred endured for another half century.

Although virtually every town and coastal city in California had its own committee in the 1850s, San Francisco was unique in that the local vigilantes gave each accused man a formal and fair trial. They also worked with the established police courts. The San Francisco vigilance committees of 1851 and 1856 included among their participants such prominent citizens as Samuel Brannan, William T. Coleman, and Leland Stanford, later to serve as governor and senator of California. When a condemned man was due to be hanged, the hills swarmed with human beings. "They seemed to cluster like bees on a tree branch," an English observer wrote, "and for the purpose of seeing a criminal convulsed and writhing in the agonies of violent death! This desire seemed to pervade all classes of Americans in the city." In California, vigilantes frequently buried a victim with one end of a rope still around his neck and the other trailing out the head of the grave to serve as a warning to others.

Support from prominent individuals also characterized the Montana vigilantes of the early 1860s who brought to justice the notorious gang led by Henry PLUMMER. Among the participants were Colonel Wilbur Fisk Sanders, who later became one of Montana's first United States senators; Nathaniel Pitt Langford, father of Yellowstone National Park; and Nelson Story, an important rancher and businessman. A later Montana vigilante committee was formed in 1884, following a dramatic increase in cattle rustling. Granville STUART, head of the local cattlemen's association and later United States minister to Uruguay, led the movement. Some thirty-five deaths have been attributed to the affair. A young rancher in nearby Dakota Territory named Theodore Roosevelt was among those who sympathized with the harsh action taken by the Montana cattlemen. Eight years later another antirustler and antihomesteader movement in Wyoming culminated in the famous JOHNSON COUNTY WAR. Vigilante groups sometimes organized to track down the homicidal maniacs that roamed the state, the most notorious of the thousands of criminals at large during the period being John Wesley Hardin.

Another form of vigilantism in the West was the White Cap movement, which originated in rural southern Indiana in 1887 and also spread briefly throughout the eastern half of the United States. Its general direction was toward the disciplining by flogging of drunks, prostitutes, shiftless characters, and so-called immoral men who failed to support their families. Although it was normally aimed at "white trash," in certain localities it had an anti-Negro or anti-Mexican bias. In New Mexico the name was also taken by a group of Mexican laborers who protested against discrimination and land enclosure. White Capping more closely resembled the Ku Klux Klan than any other vigilante group and may be viewed as a link between the first Klan, which operated during Reconstruction, and the second Klan, organized in 1915. It survived into the twentieth century and remained essentially a rural, local movement.

A noticeable decline in the incidence of vigilantism set in near the close of the nineteenth century, but vigilante movements never disappeared completely. Periods of stress or fear have witnessed a resurgence of vigilante action down to the present. But whereas the lawlessness of the frontier gave some justification to vigilantism as a socializing force, and as such gained the support of many prominent individuals, latter-day vigilantism has tended to be a wholly unjustified attempt by small, relatively homogeneous communities to rid themselves of what they consider "foreign" elements, whether racial, ethnic, religious, or political.

See Hubert H. Bancroft, *Popular Tribunals* (1887); Richard Maxwell Brown, *American Violence* (1970); Hugh Davis Graham and Ted Robert Gurr, *Violence in America* (1969); W. Eugene Hollon, *Frontier Violence: Another Look* (1974); Matt S. Meier and Feliciano Rivera, *The Chicanos: A History of Mexican Americans* (1972). —W. E. H.

Villard, Henry (1835-1900). Journalist and railroad promoter. Villard was born Ferdinand Heinrich Gustav Hilgard in Speyer, Rheinish, Bavaria, where his father was a supreme court judge. Villard was deeply influenced by the revolution of 1848, which his father deplored, and in 1853, although still in the university, decided to emigrate to America. Within five years he had learned English well enough to become correspondent for the New York *Staats-Zeitung*, in time to report the Lincoln-Douglas debates. His reports from the Pikes Peak country of Colorado, which included a guidebook, were a valuable service to the thousands joining the gold rush. In 1861, after reporting on the presidential campaign, Villard became a war correspondent. In 1864 he began operating his own news bureau in the United States and Europe, and in 1868 he became secretary of the American Social Science Association. In the next three years he studied railroad promotion and finance.

In 1871, while traveling in Europe for his health, he met and became the American representative for a group of investors in American railroads. His work in reorganizing their interests in the Pacific Northwest led to his appointment as receiver of the Kansas Pacific Railroad. A rich man by 1879, Villard undertook construction of the Oregon Railway and Navigation Company on the south bank of the Columbia River from Portland to a junction with the Northern Pacific, then pushing westward. To raise funds with which to buy control of the Northern Pacific, which had spurned his offer to carry its traffic to Portland, Villard organized a "blind pool" into which investors, on the strength of his reputation alone, poured $8 million.

Then Villard's luck ran out. Always a better financier than builder, he failed to control costs in building the last sections of the Northern Pacific Railroad, and an unmanageable debt, piled atop substantial personal losses in the New York, West Shore and Buffalo Railroad venture, forced his resignation in 1884. Reportedly bailed out by German investors, Villard stayed on the board of the Northern Pacific until the depression of the 1890s; it remained for others to straighten out the tangled web of railroad interests in the Pacific Northwest (see BURLINGTON NORTHERN RAILROAD).

Villard was a benevolent monopolist with a keen eye for public relations, whose operations, although just as sensational as many another financier's, did not blacken his name. A lifelong ardent supporter of equal rights for minorities, Villard married the only daughter of abolitionist William Lloyd Garrison, a lady who continued to press her husband's reformist ideas for nearly thirty years after his death.

The Memoirs of Henry Villard, 2 vols. (1904; repr. 1969), is a valuable source. J. B. Hedges, *Henry Villard and the Railways of the Northwest* (1930), is enthusiastic but scholarly.—A. M.

Virginia, settlement of. The story of Virginia properly begins with Sir Walter Raleigh (1552-1618), a talented courtier who commissioned two captains in 1584 to reconnoiter the American coast. These captains brought back such glowing reports that Raleigh diplomatically named the region Virginia in honor of Queen Elizabeth. Raleigh and the famous geographer Richard Hakluyt hoped that the English government would help underwrite the costs of colonization, but no monies were forthcoming. In 1585 an expedition under the command of Sir Richard Grenville established a small settlement at Roanoke near the present North Carolina-Virginia boundary. Raleigh may well have planned to use the colony as a base for raids against Spanish shipping in the Caribbean. Whatever his motives the colonists returned home unexpectedly, and a second group, known as the lost colony, disappeared in 1587. Despite these failures Raleigh's efforts had helped gather valuable information about the New World.

Early in the seventeenth century prospects for colonization brightened, and a group of London merchants, called the Virginia Company of London (the London Company), prepared to exploit America for whatever riches it might offer. In 1606 the king granted them a charter for the territory lying roughly between Cape Fear and the Hudson River. The company quickly dispatched an expedition with instructions to construct a fort on one of the large rivers flowing into the Chesapeake Bay. The adventurers selected an easily defensible site on a peninsula in the James River. This settlement, named Jamestown, was situated on low, marshy ground. Although the colonists realized that the site might be dangerous to their health, they argued that the military advantages would outweigh such drawbacks. However, Jamestown was soon overcome by the most fatal of New World diseases—apathy. The colony was governed by a group of councillors who spent more time fighting among themselves than planting crops. Faced with starvation, sickness, and hostile Indians, many men simply lost the will to live. Captain John Smith (1580-1631) watched the growing dissension and idleness with disgust. In 1608 he became president of the ruling council and through the force of his own personality instituted a tough new regime. His orders were clear: no work, no food. Historians have sometimes doubted Smith's veracity about his own political

role, but there can be no question that he saved early Jamestown from disaster.

The London Company tried to correct some of its mistakes. First, the merchants replaced the factious council with "one able and absolute Governor" empowered to make all laws for the colonists. And second, under a new royal charter issued in 1609, they transformed the company into a joint-stock venture. Anyone willing to invest £12 10s. received a share in the Virginia profits, which were to be distributed at the end of seven years. The person chiefly responsible for these changes was Sir Thomas Smith (1558-1625), the company's treasurer and one of the ablest businessmen of his day. The company launched a major appeal for money and colonists. The promotional literature described Virginia as a place where "gold is more plentifull . . . than copper is with us." But the merchants' most effective argument was patriotism, not self-enrichment. They convinced the public that Virginia was a national enterprise and that "the eyes of all Europe are looking upon our endeavours." Well over a thousand people risked their money in the project and another six hundred agreed to settle in Virginia. The company leaders later complained that these colonists were a poor lot: "gallants to escape evil destinies . . . lascivious sons, masters of bad servants and wives of ill husbands." No doubt these people—most of whom died within a few years—were bitterly disappointed when they saw the primitive conditions in Jamestown.

The ambitious plans of 1609 came to nothing. A hurricane struck the main fleet, destroying vital supplies. Most of the unprepared colonists who straggled into Jamestown soon died, for as Captain John Smith explained, "Though there be fish in the sea, fouls in the air and beasts in the woods, their bounds are so large, they so wild, and we so weak and ignorant, we cannot much trouble them." News of the suffering in Virginia dampened public enthusiasm for the project, and the company found it impossible to collect its debts, let alone sell new shares. The entire enterprise would probably have folded had not governors Thomas Gates and Thomas Dale established strict military discipline within the colony, forcing unwilling settlers to work. Nevertheless, in 1616—the year of the profit division—the company had nothing to show for its troubles but land.

In 1618 a large group of stockholders, led by Sir Edwin Sandys (1578-1644), proposed four major changes that they thought would make Virginia profitable. First, they spelled out the conditions under which private individuals could obtain land within the colony. A "headright" of fifty acres was promised to any man paying the transportation costs to America either of himself or some other person. Second, the reformers relaxed the military discipline instituted under Governor Dale. Third, Sandys' group hoped to stimulate settlement by allowing the colonists a voice in their government. In an important decision that led to the founding of the House of Burgesses, the company declared that "no orders of our Court afterwarde shall binde [the] colony unles they bee ratified in like manner in their generall Assembly." In 1619 the first representative body in America gathered at Jamestown. The fourth reform called for a balanced economy in Virginia. As early as 1617 an official in Jamestown complained that he found "the market-place, and streets, and all other spare places planted with Tobacco." Sandys wanted the colonists to produce wine, glass, iron, and other items easily sold in England.

Sandys would have had difficulty putting his economic program into effect under the best of conditions. But conditions were not good. The company was divided into factions that seemed more intent on embarrassing Sandys than in making the colony a success. Moreover, he never possessed the amount of money that his ambitious plans required. The final blow came in 1622, when the local Indians attempted to drive the colonists out of Virginia. The war, coupled with disease, took an appalling toll. Under Sandys' leadership, the company sent almost four thousand new settlers to America, and yet in 1623 only 1,300 people were left alive. An investigation by English officials concluded that the bankrupt London Company had handled Virginia affairs irresponsibly. In 1624 the province became a royal colony under the direction of a governor appointed by the king.

One colonial historian has explained that "the history of tobacco is the history of Jamestown and of Virginia. No one staple or resource ever played a more significant role in the history of any state or nation." John Rolfe (1585-1622), husband of Pocahontas, cultivated the first tobacco crop in the colony. The settlers quickly saw that this weed might bring prosperity, but it took a while before they developed a leaf able to rival that of their Spanish competitors. The cultivation of tobacco required more than thirty-six separate and tedious operations before it could be shipped to market. The colony's reliance on a single crop created many economic problems. Overproduction, poor quality, and commercial conditions beyond the planters' control caused the price to fluctuate greatly. Moreover, the Virginians were at the mercy of their London agents, since any spoilage occurring in England came out of the planters' profits.

The concentration on tobacco influenced the entire character of Virginia society. The planters recognized that tobacco exhausted their soil within a few seasons. Fresh land was therefore in constant demand. Most of the farmers cultivated only part of their holdings in any given year, setting aside unused acreage for future use. Because of the large size of plantations and because of the continuous search for new, undeveloped land, towns were rare in Virginia. One visitor reported that "the inhabitants do not live close together and the country is not settled in villages, because every twenty or thirty years new ground must be broken." It was essential that plantations be located near waterways so that the heavy hogsheads loaded with tobacco could be easily transported to market. As the years passed, Virginians moved to the north and the west—toward large rivers such as the Rappahannock and the Potomac, which flowed into the Chesapeake Bay. Raising tobacco required a sizable, but not necessarily a skilled labor force. As the historian Lewis C. Gray has explained, the experience of the early colonists demonstrated how difficult it was to maintain order when all the workers were equal or had a personal stake in the agricultural operations. In the first decades of the seventeenth century, the successful planters relied on indentured servants who bound themselves to a planter for a stated number of years in exchange for the cost of transportation to

America. But by the 1660s large numbers of African slaves had begun to replace the indentured servants as field laborers.

After 1624 a governor and council were appointed to rule Virginia. Following the dissolution of the London Company, however, no provision was made for continuing the House of Burgesses. On several occasions over the next decade the king called assemblies to discuss specific problems in the tobacco trade or in Indian relations. But the colonists did not regard these meetings as isolated events, and the legislators convened even when the crown had not summoned them. In 1639 the king recognized what was already obvious—the House of Burgesses, elected by the freemen, had become a permanent and indispensable part of colonial government. Its members came from the local unit of government in Virginia, the county court. They were a body of men known as justices of the peace who were appointed by the governor. The county courts usually comprised the wealthiest planters of the area, and the governor seldom selected justices who had not already been nominated by the other members of the court. Almost all the men who were elected Burgesses had previously served on the county courts. As Virginia expanded, new counties were formed, and there is little evidence, even in the eighteenth century, of east-west tension over inequitable political representation.

During the early years of settlement the Virginians managed to keep a strained peace with the Indians. John Rolfe's marriage in 1614 to Pocahontas, daughter of a powerful Powhatan chief, helped bring about more friendly relations. But in 1622 the Indians, led by OPEKACANOUGH, tried unsuccessfully to exterminate the Englishmen. The Indians did not attack again in force until 1644, and by that time the Virginians were better able to defend themselves. According to historian Charles M. Andrews, the arrival of Governor William Berkeley in 1641 marked an important turning point in Virginia history. "The time of experimentation was over and there began an era of adaptation to English needs and influences which was to continue to the end of the century."

See also BACON'S REBELLION.

See Charles M. Andrews, *The Colonial Period of American History,* vol. I (1933); Bernard Bailyn, "Politics and Social Structure in Virginia," in James M. Smith, ed., *Seventeenth-Century America* (1959); Wesley Frank Craven, *Dissolution of the Virginia Company* (1932), and *The Southern Colonies in the Seventeenth Century* (1949); Lewis C. Gray, *History of Agriculture in the Southern United States to 1860,* 2 vols. (1941); Perry Miller, "Early Literature of Virginia," *William and Mary Quarterly,* vols. 5 (1948) and 6 (1949); Richard L. Morton, *Colonial Virginia,* 2 vols. (1960); and E. G. Swem, ed., Jamestown 350th Anniversary Historical Booklets (1957). —T. H. B.

Virginia City, Montana. Ghost town. Virginia City sprang up in the early summer of 1863 following the discovery of gold in nearby Alder Gulch by a party of prospectors from Bannack led by Bill Fairweather. Within a few weeks, an estimated ten thousand miners were camped in the area, and in the first year of mining the sands of Alder Gulch yielded $10 million in gold dust. Incorporated in January 1864, Virginia City continued to grow and one year later supplanted Bannack as the territorial capital, a distinction the town held until 1876.

During its early years, Virginia City was plagued by a band of highwaymen and murderers who robbed the miners of their gold and were said to have killed 190 men in one six-month period of terrorism. In order to combat these renegades, a group of citizens from Virginia City and Bannack formed a vigilante committee. Within a year they brought the outlaws to justice, hanging twenty-one of them. Most notable of the executed was Henry PLUMMER, leader of the gang, who had used his position as sheriff of Virginia City and Bannack to good advantage.

By 1870 the placers had played out, and the city's population declined to 2,555. However, Virginia City managed to stay alive as a business center by serving the nearby mining and ranching areas. Today the town is a popular tourist attraction and one of the best preserved and restored ghost towns in the West. Among its more prominent features are the state's first newspaper office, a general store and a pharamacy equipped to handle the customer of 1875, the Wells Fargo Express Office, and the Bale of Hay Saloon. West of Virginia City are the more "ghostly" ruins of Nevada City on Alder Gulch, from which $70 million in gold was washed.

See Nathaniel P. Langford, *Vigilante Days and Ways* (1890); Virginia R. Towle, *Vigilante Woman* (1966); and Muriel S. Wolle, *The Bonanza Trail* (1953).—R. B. W.

Virginia City, Nevada. Ghost town. Virginia City sprang up in the summer and fall of 1859 as a result of the discovery of the Comstock Lode (see NEVADA) in June of that year. Legend has it that the city received its name when "Old Virginny" (James Finney or Fennimore) fell to the ground, breaking his bottle of whiskey and using the remaining liquid to christen the area "Virginia." Officially it received its name from a miners' district meeting there in September 1859. The Comstock Lode was so big and so rich that its major city soon became an important political, financial, and social hub,

not only for Nevada but for the entire West. No town or city in Nevada, before or since, had equaled its importance in the history of the far western states. Although estimates indicated that the city's population grew to more than 30,000 people, the highest official census figure was 10,917, in 1870. The town began declining after 1878; in 1960 the census reported only 515 people in Virginia City. In recent years the city has become a major tourist attraction, bringing thousands of people to western Nevada from May through October.

The best early views of the town are those given in Mark Twain, *Roughing It* (1872), and J. Ross Browne, *A Peep at Washoe and Washoe Revisited* (1959). Dan De Quille, *History of the Big Bonanza* (1896) is a standard reference. The chapter on the Comstock Lode in Rodman Paul, *Mining Frontiers of the Far West* (1963), is a brief, but superb, account.—R. R. E.

Voigt, Andrew (1867-1939). North Dakota rancher. Born in Saxony, Germany, Voigt came to the northern half of Dakota Territory as a young man. With borrowed money, he began to ranch in an area now inundated by the Garrison Dam. Aided by his wife and hardworking family, Voight eventually built up a large and profitable ranching unit west of Elbowoods, North Dakota, on which he raised Hereford cattle, Percheron horses, and sheep. The Voigt ranch was seen as a model of private enterprise in the Dakotas.

Voigt's energy and business acumen never conflicted with his deeply religious and altruistic nature. Hungry cowboys and Indians dubbed his ranch "Headquarters for Hospitality." He donated beef and mutton to the Indian mission at Elbowood and undoubtedly earned the Indian sobriquet "Andrew, Big Heart White Man Can't Say No," given him by Crows Heart, a Sioux.

After his death his sons continued to operate ranches in various parts of western North Dakota. The senior Voigt's accomplishments were honored with his nomination in 1962 to the National Cowboy Hall of Fame.—H. R. L.

voyageur. See FUR TRADE: *in the United States.*

W

Waddell, William Bradford (1807-1872). Businessman. Waddell was born in Fauquier County, Virginia, and moved with his family to Mason County, Kentucky, as a boy of eight. In 1824 Waddell went to Galena, Illinois, to work in the lead mines for a short period before moving to St. Louis, where he gained experience as a clerk in a general store. Returning to Mason County, he resumed his career as a storekeeper in the town of Washington. In January 1829 he married Susan Byram and went into business on his own in Mayslick, Kentucky. He moved to Lexington, Missouri, in 1835, opened a general merchandise store and commission business, and became involved in the town's affairs.

Among other things, he organized the Lexington First Addition Company, the Lexington Fire and Marine Insurance Company, the Lexington Female Collegiate Institute, and formed a partnership known as Morehead, Waddell & Co., which engaged in various promotions, chiefly real estate. William H. Russell later purchased Morehead's interest and the firm name became Russell and Waddell.

Among his other business promotions, Waddell became interested in railroads, helping to organize and serve on the board of directors of both the Lexington & Booneville and the Lexington & Davies County railroads in 1853. The next year he and Russell formed a partnership with Alexander Majors, RUSSELL, MAJORS AND WADDELL, to enter the freighting business. Upon the failure of that firm in 1862, Waddell encountered severe financial losses and did not attempt to engage in business activity again. He had a reputation as a cautious businessman and unsuccessfully tried to restrain his partners from overextending their financial obligations.

See Arthur Chapman, *The Pony Express* (1932); Raymond W. Settle and Mary L. Settle, *War Drums and Wagon Wheels* (1966) and *Saddles and Spurs: The Pony Express Saga* (1955); and Henry Pickering Walker, *The Wagonmasters* (1966).—W. T. J.

Waggoner, Daniel (1828-1902). Texas cattleman and developer. Born in Tennessee, Waggoner went to Hopkins County, Texas, with his parents in 1848. His earlier life was spent learning the cattle business and trading from his father. Although uneducated in the formal sense, young Waggoner soon acquired a vast knowledge of men, horses, and cattle. At twenty-one Waggoner went to Wise County when it was wild and unsettled. His own stake—accumulated through work and trading— was 242 head of cattle, 6 horses, and a male Negro slave. Locating originally near Decatur, he later bought a ranch and some two hundred cattle from George Isbell in the western part of Wise County. This holding was enlarged until the Waggoner brand was the best known and widest used in that cattle area.

Waggoner encountered all the troubles of his times: Indian raids, white rustlers, bad weather, and an erratic market. But through his knowledge and skill, he was able to increase his holdings to a half-million leased acres and thousands of fee acres in the Texas and Oklahoma panhandles. The cattle herds grew to thousands, with an estimated money value between five million and seven million dollars at the time of his death.

Waggoner branched out from ranching into many other activities, always taking a leading role in the business and cultural development of his region.—H. R. L.

Wagner, Henry Raup. See COLLECTORS AND COLLECTIONS OF WESTERN AMERICANA.

Waite, Davis Hanson (1825-1901). Newspaperman and Colorado politician. Waite was born in Jamestown, New York. After a period of reading law he moved to Wisconsin at the age of twenty-five, where he engaged in merchandising and was elected to the legislature in 1856. He subsequently moved to Missouri and Pennsylvania before returning to Jamestown, where he edited the *Chautauqua Democrat* and became proprietor of the *Jamestown Journal*. In 1876 he moved to Kansas and was elected to the Kansas legislature in 1878. He came to Leadville, Colorado, in 1879 and moved two years later to Aspen, where he practiced law, worked on two newspapers in an editorial capacity, and was the first superintendent of schools for Pitkin County.

In his political views Waite was first a Democrat, then a Republican, and later joined the Populist movement. In 1891 he founded the Populist *Aspen Union Era* and the next year was elected the first and only Populist governor of Colorado. His two-year term was marred by violence in the Cripple Creek mining district and by a conflict with the Denver fire and police board known as the "City Hall War." He earned the nickname "Bloody Bridles Waite" when, in a speech to the Colorado State Silver League Convention in July 1893, he spoke of the war "against oppression and tyranny to preserve

the liberties of man," concluding that "it is better, infinitely better, that blood should flow to the horses' bridles, rather than our national liberties should be destroyed." During Governor Waite's term, in 1893, Colorado became the second state to grant woman suffrage (the first to do so by vote of the male populace). The next year Waite was defeated in his bid for reelection, and he believed he had been undermined by the very women in whom he had had so much faith. "Female suffrage I hope will hereafter be opposed by all Populists," he wrote Populist reformer Ignatius Donnelly after the election. A few years later he returned to Aspen, where he died. Waite was always sympathetic to labor, especially during the Cripple Creek strike, and six years after his death the Western Federation of Miners dedicated a granite memorial at his grave in the Aspen cemetery.

No full-scale biography of Waite has been published, but there are several pertinent articles in *Colorado Magazine:* Leon W. Fuller, "A Populist Newspaper of the Nineties" (May 1932); John R. Morris, "The Women and Governor Waite" (Winter 1967); and Helen Cannon, "First Ladies of Colorado: Celia O. Crane Waite" (Spring 1969).—M. B.

Walkara (c. 1808-1855). Ute chief. Walkara was perhaps the best known and most powerful Indian leader in the Great Basin region between 1830 and 1855. His rise to power through a combination of physical prowess, trade cunning, daring raids on California horse herds, and accommodation with whites suggest a man of unusual complexity and ability.

Walkara, or "Walker" as the whites usually called him, was born in a Timpanogos village on Spanish Fork River in present-day Utah. Surmounting the petty quarrels and blood feuds that perpetually divided and weakened his people, Walkara appears to have organized a band of mounted raiders and fighters from several tribes, among them the Paiute and the Shoshoni, although the latter were traditional enemies of the Ute. Through them he mastered several Indian dialects to which he later added a command of Spanish and a limited ability in English.

By exacting a ruthless loyalty from his followers and tribute from weaker tribes, Walkara was soon a powerful figure in the entire region south of Utah Lake all the way to the Mexican border. In the 1830s he and his band, aided by two mountain men, Thomas "Pegleg" Smith and Jim Beckwourth, slipped through Cajon Pass into southern California to raid outlying ranches. His greatest success came in 1839-40, when his bands divided, each under a brother or devoted lieutenant, and struck simultaneously at many ranches. The raiders succeeded in carrying over three thousand horses back to Utah. This technique, used in New Mexico and even Chihuahua, gave Walkara a fearsome reputation for ubiquity and led Californians to call him "the greatest horse thief in history." Walkara also raided Digger and Paiute villages for Indian women and children, whom he sold as slaves to the New Mexicans, and for years exacted a toll of stock and goods from parties moving over the Old Spanish Trail between New Mexico and California.

When the Mormons settled Utah in 1847, Walkara and his less violent half brother, Chief Sowiette, responded favorably to Brigham Young's policy of accommodation with the local tribes. Walkara traded with the

Saints, though he still sent horses to Fort Bridger for sale to Overland migrants.

Whites who met Walkara at the height of his power described him as an imperious, handsome, tall Indian with a hawklike nose. A vain person, he wore both American clothes and Indian finery. His well-disciplined cavalry was gaudily dressed, and its horses were so decorated with silver-encrusted bridles and metal decorations that they tinkled and flashed in the sun as they walked. Walkara also impressed whites with the number of wives he kept and by his persistent but unsuccessful desire to add a Mormon wife or two to his household. Trappers found him a willing supplier of squaws for their beds.

American occupation of California and the Southwest and Young's assiduous cultivation of Walkara eventually proved to be the chief's undoing. After 1847 United States troops guarded the Cajon Pass to California, and Mormons soon ended the slave traffic to New Mexico. Walkara himself was converted to Mormonism and was baptized as a "brother-in-the-faith" at Manti in 1850. Outmaneuvered by the Saints, his people weakened by a measles epidemic, and his horse herd dwindling, Walkara became so frustrated that when an Indian-white altercation at Springville left several of his tribesmen dead or wounded, he retaliated in the so-called Walker War of 1853. The Mormons defended their villages and stock so well, however, and took such a toll of Walkara's warriors that the chief agreed to a peace. Hemmed in by the whites and with all his major sources of power gone, Walkara died shortly thereafter. Appropriately, fifteen horses were slaughtered at his grave site as a tribute to the once-powerful chief.

See Paul Bailey, *Walkara, Hawk of the Mountains* (1954); Gustive O. Larsen, "Walkara, Ute Chief," in L. R. Hafen, ed., *The Mountain Men and the Fur Trade of the Far West,* vol. II (1965); and Conway B. Sonne, *The World of Walkara* (1962).—H. R. L.

Walker, James (1819-1889). Painter. Walker was brought to New York City from England as a child and continued to make his home there for most of his life. As a young man he spent a winter in New Orleans and was in Mexico City at the outbreak of the Mexican War. Escaping to the American lines, Walker served as an interpreter with the army and remained with it during its occupation of Mexico City. He returned to New York City in 1848 and, following a subsequent visit to South America, established an art studio in 1859. Except for brief periods spent in Washington, D.C., he maintained his New York studio until 1884, at which time he went to San Francisco to execute a large French battle scene for a private gallery in that city. Most of his surviving work show battle scenes with a cast of thousands, among the most prominent being *The Battle of Gettysburg, Battle of Lookout Mountain,* commissioned by Civil War general Joseph Hooker, and *The Battle of Chapultepec* at the Capitol in Washington. Several paintings by Walker depicting the activities of the Mexican *vaquero* are included in the collection of the Thomas Gilcrease Institute of American History and Art in Tulsa, Oklahoma, and are indicative of the artist's interest in the costume and other details associated with the life of the Spanish-American cowboy.

See Robert Taft, *Artists and Illustrators of the Old West, 1850-1900* (1953).—D. C. H.

Walker, Joseph R. (1798-1876). Fur trader and explorer. Walker was born in Tennessee. He raised stock at Fort Osage, Missouri, before going into the Santa Fe trade in 1820. He joined Captain Benjamin Bonneville's expedition in 1832, serving as a guide, a trapper, and (possibly) an investor. He commanded Bonneville's party of 1833-34, which departed from the fur-trapping rendezvous of 1833 at Green River for California, presumably in search of horses and supplies but probably to explore for beaver and to see if a westward-flowing river ran from Great Salt Lake. The party traveled to the Great Salt Lake; followed the Humboldt River to the Humboldt Sink, where it defeated a party of Digger Indians; made its way along the Sierra Nevada to Walker Lake; and went through a pass to the Yosemite region. Walker and his party were probably the first Americans to see Yosemite Valley. Walker spent the winter in the San Joaquin valley and then returned to the rendezvous at Bear River by crossing the Sierra Nevada at Walker Pass and taking the Humboldt-Salt Lake route. His expedition cut out the trail to California for later emigrants and helped establish American interest in the Pacific Coast.

Walker trapped for the American Fur Company from 1835 to 1839. He later trapped and guided emigrant parties to California and guided John C. Frémont on portions of his second and third expeditions. When gold was discovered in California, Walker was one of the first to reach the mines. He decided to settle in California and during 1849 established a ranch in Monterey, but he later moved to Contra Costa County. In 1861-62 he led an expedition to Arizona, where he discovered gold near present-day Prescott.

Although a man of limited education, Walker was one of the most intelligent men to explore the West. His ability to command and his remarkable knowledge of western geography make him one of the most impressive figures in American westward expansion.

The lure of the West affected Walker's brothers as well. His brother Joel P. Walker led one of the first emigrant parties to Oregon in 1840. His brother John died at the Alamo during the Texan war for independence. Another, Samuel S. Walker, died while migrating to California, and a fourth, Isaac, was killed in Arizona.

See Daniel E. Conner, *J. R. Walker and the Arizona Adventure* (1956), edited by Donald J. Berthrong and Odessa Davenport; William H. Goetzmann, *Exploration and Empire* (1966); LeRoy R. Hafen, ed., *The Mountain Men and the Fur Trade of the Far West,* vol. V (1968); and Douglas S. Watson, *West Wind: The Life of Joseph Reddeford Walker* (1934).—G. B. D.

Walker, Robert John (1801-1869). Mississippi lawyer and politician. Born in Pennsylvania, Walker entered the political arena in the 1820s as a supporter of Andrew Jackson. By 1826 he had migrated to Natchez, Mississippi, where he distinguished himself as a lawyer. His flourishing law practice and his friendships enabled him to amass sufficient capital to invest heavily in the purchase of sugar and cotton plantations, slaves, and land to hold for speculative purposes.

Although by 1834 Walker was the recognized leader and foremost orator of the Jackson party in Mississippi, he had held no political office. In 1836, however, he succeeded George Poindexter to the United States Senate. From this point to 1849 he was the single most powerful political figure in Mississippi—first as the elected senator and then as President James K. Polk's secretary of the treasury.

Like most Mississippians, Walker was an ardent expansionist in the 1840s. But his decision to cast his lot with the Union rather than the secessionists cost him popularity in the state. When Walker left Polk's cabinet in 1849, he made no attempt to resume participation in state politics. Until 1857 he lived as a private citizen in Washington, D.C., attending to his extensive speculative interests. During this time he may have also had his eye on the presidency. In 1857 President James Buchanan appointed him tentative governor of Kansas. During the Civil War he was appointed United States financial agent to Europe.

See William E. Dodd, *Robert J. Walker, Imperialist* (1914); and James P. Shenton, *Robert John Walker: A Politician from Jackson to Lincoln* (1961).—J. E. G.

Walker, Tillie (1929-   ). Mandan and Hidatsa specialist in Indian education. Walker was born in Elbowoods, North Dakota. After receiving her education in business administration at the Haskell Institute in Kansas and the University of Nebraska, she took a job with the American Indian Program of the American Friends Service Committee in Philadelphia. Her work with the committee that sponsored summer workshops for Indian college students and with the Indian Rights Association made her a logical choice for director of a new private scholarship agency for Indian students.

In 1960 the Association on American Indian Affairs, the Episcopal church, and the Congregational church (now United Church of Christ) pooled their funds to begin a nationwide service for Indian college students that offered scholarship aid, counseling, and referrals to other government and private funds for which a student might be eligible. As the director of United Scholarship Service (U.S.S.) for American Indian and Spanish-American Students, Walker expanded the program to include aid and counseling to students in public and private secondary and graduate schools. Because most of their students attended private institutions, U.S.S. worked to get matching grants from the schools. The program continued to expand, despite the fact that the Association on American Indian Affairs withdrew its support after two or three years. Under Walker's direction, U.S.S. was often able to continue aiding students with "C" averages, on the premise that the school situation might be alien to the Indian student, but that he could adjust in time; even if he didn't, it was best that he stay in school if he wanted to.

With less foundation money available around 1969, U.S.S. cut back its program of direct aid. But the groundwork of a national Indian student movement had been firmly laid. When the National Indian Youth Council was formed in 1960, U.S.S.'s lists of recipients and applicants were used for recruitment.

Walker was an active participant in the takeover of a Bureau of Indian Affairs office in Littleton, Colorado, in March 1970, to protest the bureau's policies. She was a vice president at large of the National Council of Churches, the first Indian to hold that position.—C. C.

Walker, William (1800-1874). Wyandot chief. Born in Michigan of a white father who had been adopted into the Wyandot tribe and a mother who was one quarter Indian, Walker became one of the chiefs of his tribe in 1824 upon the death of his father. His formal education was completed at the academy at Kenyon College, where he was proficient in languages. He served Michigan's territorial governor, Lewis Cass, as private secretary, but most of his life was devoted to the interests of North American Indians in general and his own tribe in particular.

The Wyandot, located in northern Ohio, was one of the last tribes to undergo removal. Under Walker's leadership in 1831, a Wyandot exploring delegation recommended against removal. Walker, while visiting in General William Clark's St. Louis residence, was impressed by Indians from the far Northwest who were seeking knowledge of the religion of the white man. Walker later wrote a letter about this experience to a New York acquaintance who used it to set into motion the Protestant missionary movement to the Oregon country.

In 1842 the Wyandot agreed to relocation in Indian country, just west of the Missouri border at the mouth of the Kansas River. There on his farm Walker spent most of his remaining years. He was an ardent Democrat and was elected provisional governor of Nebraska Territory in 1853, in a prematurely formed territorial government embracing the region that became the Kansas and Nebraska territories the following year. After moving to that area, he became a slave-owner and strongly opposed the "free-state" and abolition movements in territorial Kansas, but he also opposed secession. He was a recognized authority on Indian lore and supplied Henry Rowe Schoolcraft and other writers with material that they used in their historical accounts of Indians.

There are miscellaneous Walker papers at the Kansas State Historical Society. In 1899 William E. Connelley edited *The Provisional Government of Nebraska and the Journals of William Walker.*—H. E. S.

Walking Purchase (1737). Indian treaty. In 1686 the Delaware Indians conveyed to William Penn of Pennsylvania a deed granting white settlers a tract at the forks of the Lehigh and Delaware rivers extending "back into the woods as far as man can go in one day and a half." For half a century this deed was not called into question, until frontier expansion up the Delaware River in the 1730s began to meet resistance from the Indians living above the forks. Pennsylvania proprietor Thomas Penn and provincial secretary James Logan then began pressuring the Delaware Indians for a new release of the deed. The Indians refused, claiming that the vaguely worded grant applied only to land below the forks. But by means of thinly veiled threats, Penn and Logan in August 1737 secured the Delaware's consent to a retracing of the tract.

Three young athletes were hired as walkers, and the route was cleared of brush and obstacles. At dawn on September 19, beginning near the Wrightsville meeting house at the head line of the 1686 deed, the walkers moved out in a northwesterly direction toward the mountains. The Indians acting as observers fell out from exhaustion, and when the final walker collapsed at noon of the second day he has crossed the Kittatinny ridge into the Poconos, a distance of 66.5 miles. From this point Penn and Logan ordered the line run back to the Delaware River—not to the river's closest point, but at right angles to the line of the walk. The tract thus embraced more than 1,200 square miles and included all or part of the present Pennsylvania counties of

Bucks, Carbon, Northhampton, Monroe, and Pike. The Delaware objected bitterly to such chicanery, but the Pennsylvanians, by judicious bribery, persuaded the Iroquois to order the vassal Delaware off the land. Many Delaware then joined the French and made war against the colony, and the acrimony was not finally settled until 1762, when Pennsylvania bought off the Delaware sachems for £400.

See F. B. Tolles, *James Logan and the Culture of Provincial Pennsylvania* (1957).—P. R. M.

Wallace, Henry Agard (1888-1965). Agriculturist and vice president of the United States. Born in Adair County, Iowa, Wallace graduated from Iowa State College (now Iowa State University) at Ames in 1910. He inherited his grandfather's and father's profound interest in agriculture and as a teen-ager began conducting experiments with seed corn. His research in genetics continued throughout his lifetime, and in 1924 he developed a hybrid seed corn for commercial use. The Wallace family established the Pioneer Hi-Bred Corn Company to market the product. The company later experimented with hybrid chickens, and established the Hy-Line Poultry Farms.

Wallace's agrarian interests were also reflected in his editorship of the family farm journal, *Wallaces' Farmer*, started in 1895 by his grandfather, uncle, and father, Henry Cantwell Wallace. He maintained the journal's reputation as a leading national agricultural publication during his editorship from 1924 to 1933. Wallace stressed the superiority of agrarian life and worked to improve the farmers' economic status.

In 1933 President Franklin D. Roosevelt appointed Wallace secretary of agriculture. Wallace's ideas of production regulation were embodied in the first Agricultural Adjustment Act. He served as secretary of agriculture until 1940 when Roosevelt selected him to be his vice-presidential running mate. Following his term as vice president, Wallace was appointed secretary of commerce in 1945. He resigned the post in less than a year because of administrative disagreements with President Harry S. Truman.

Continuing his national political career, Wallace ran unsuccessfully as presidential candidate for the Progressive party in 1948. This move severely discredited Wallace because of support from Communists and Communist sympathizers, and many of his critics portrayed him as an apologist for Russia and Communism. Following the election Wallace returned to his home in South Salem, New York, where he continued his genetic experiments until his death.

The most recent biographies on Wallace are companion works: Edward L. Schapsmeier and Frederick H. Schapsmeier, *Henry A. Wallace of Iowa: The Agrarian Years, 1910-1940* (1968), and *Prophet in Politics: Henry A. Wallace and the War Years* (1971). Russell Lord, *The Wallaces of Iowa* (1947), covers three generations of the Wallace family. Wallace himself wrote many books and pamphlets, among them *Agricultural Prices* (1920), *Correlation and Machine Calculation* (1925), and *The American Choice: A Foreign and Domestic Policy for Now* (1940).—D. S.

Wallace, Henry Cantwell (1866-1924). Agriculturist. Born in Rock Island, Illinois, Wallace moved with his family to a farm in Winterset, Iowa, when his father, a Presbyterian minister, switched to farming. The father soon expanded his farm operations and became well known throughout the state for his agricultural interests.

Young Wallace attended Iowa State Agricultural College (now Iowa State University) at Ames for two years but left in 1887 to operate one of his father's farms near Orient. He later returned to Ames and following his graduation in 1892 accepted an assistant professorship in the agricultural department. In 1893 Wallace and C. F. Curtiss began publishing *The Farm and Dairy*. Wallace's father joined him and together they purchased Curtiss' interest, incorporating the earlier publication into a semimonthly, *Wallaces' Farm and Dairy*. Publication headquarters were moved to Des Moines and the Wallaces' subsequent publication, *Wallaces' Farmer*, quickly became a leading weekly farm journal.

Wallace was active in midwestern and national agricultural circles for many years. For seventeen years he was secretary of the Cornbelt Meat Producers Association, which represented the midwestern livestock feeders' interests. Through these and other activities, he became recognized as a leader in national farmers' movements.

In 1921 President Warren G. Harding appointed Wallace secretary of agriculture. Wallace recognized the farmers' problem as one of overproduction; he urged them to voluntarily limit production and requested that the government form an export corporation to alleviate the farm surplus. During his tenure in Washington, he was instrumental in establishing the Bureau of Agricultural Economics and the Bureau of Home Economics within his department. Wallace was also a champion of conservation. He was the father of Henry Agard Wallace.

The most recent book on the Wallace family is Edward L. Schapsmeier and Frederick H. Schapsmeier, *Henry A. Wallace of Iowa: The Agrarian Years, 1910-1940* (1968). Although focusing on Henry Agard, the authors also include pertinent information on Henry Cantwell Wallace. Russell Lord, *The Wallaces of Iowa* (1947), covers three generations of the family.—D. S.

wapiti. See ELK, AMERICAN.

Ward, Eber Brock. See GREAT LAKES, MEN OF THE.

war hawks. The war hawks were a small group of young and intensely nationalistic Republican congressmen who in 1811 and 1812 demanded war with England and an American invasion of Canada. Primarily from the South and new western states, the group included John C. Calhoun of South Carolina, Felix Grundy of Tennessee, and Richard M. Johnson and Henry CLAY of Kentucky. The last was elected Speaker of the House in 1811. Though these men were the most vocal in demanding war, they alone could not pass a declaration of war in Congress; the final vote required the support of eastern Republicans, particularly those from Pennsylvania.

The motives of the war hawks, men who came from areas least affected by the maritime issues that preceded the War of 1812, have been a subject of controversy among historians. Some have argued that these westerners were driven by hunger for land and therefore wanted to annex Canada to the north and Florida to the south. Others insist that fear of Indian attacks motivated the war hawks. Westerners wanted to stop the British in Canada from arming Indians against them, while southerners wanted to do the same to the Spanish in Florida. Some maintain that westerners blamed the British Orders in Council and seizure of American ships for a decline in crop prices; they wanted war to stop this disruption and improve prices. Most recently, historians have cited the nationalism of the war hawks, not their concrete interests. According to this school, the war hawks viewed British maritime policy—impressment and seizure of ships—as a violation of American rights and national sovereignty. War and especially an attack on Canada were the simplest ways to vindicate American national honor and force England to recognize the United States as truly independent. Undoubtedly, some combination of these interpretations most accurately portrays the motives of this group.

For the land-hunger thesis, see Louis M. Hacker, "Western Land Hunger and the War of 1812," *Mississippi Valley Historical Review,* vol. 10 (1924). Julius Pratt, *Expansionists of 1812* (1925), challenges this thesis and argues that fear of Indians, not a desire for land, motivated the war hawks. The importance of a depression in western crop prices is stressed in George R. Taylor, "Agrarian Discontent in the Mississippi Valley Preceding the War of 1812," *Journal of Political Economy,* vol. 39 (1931). The best examples of those stressing a defense of national honor are Bradford Perkins, *Prologue to War: England and the United States, 1805-1812* (1961); and Norman K. Risjord, "1812: Conservatives, War Hawks, and the Nation's Honor," *William and Mary Quarterly,* 3rd ser., vol. 18 (1961).—M. F. H.

Warner's Ranch (California). John Trumbull Warner, an Anglo emigrant from Connecticut who came to California in 1831, acquired Rancho Valle de San José in 1844 and converted it to a mercantile trading establishment serving the southern trail to California. During the gold rush Warner's Ranch became a famous trading post and rest stop for thousands of forty-niners traveling from Tucson over the Gila Trail. Later, in the 1850s, the ranch became a stop on the Butterfield Overland Stage route.

During the late 1850s Warner lost control of his ranch properties because of conflicting land claims. John Raine, a California cattle baron, bought the property and turned it into a vast ranch.

Two adobe structures dating back to 1849 and 1858 stand as survivals of the ranching period. Long known for its hot springs, it is now a guest ranch and health spa.

See Ralph P. Bieber, ed., *Southern Trail to California in 1849* (1937); and Lorrin L. Morrison, *Warner: The Man and His Ranch* (1962).—J. F.

War of 1812. The history of the War of 1812 involves almost as many cross currents as that of the nation itself in the first quarter of the nineteenth century. It was a war of diverse causes, and its history was to be shrouded in sectional politics and issues. Before the struggle was ended, many old military and political personalities were slated for oblivion, and a greater number of new ones arose to the status of regional and national importance. Perhaps it is simpler to discuss the War of 1812 in terms of the expanding western frontier. Despite the generous amount of differences of opinion and controversey among historians, it appears on the face of the record that there was clearly a high degree of expansionist influence in the West. This was manifested in the frontier attitude toward land and the Indian barriers to

white settlement in the Northwest and the South, an attitude of which the Indians were fully aware. The presence of the British about the Great Lakes and upper Wabash-Lake Erie frontier was disturbing to the Americans, and so were the background issues pertaining to the diplomatic maneuvers between the Americans and Spanish in the lower Mississippi valley and the Gulf coastal area.

In the Wabash valley of Indiana Territory the land-grabbing activities and treaty-making of William Henry HARRISON and expansion of settlement onto Indian lands created pressures. In fact the frontier in this region had never settled down to full peace after the Harmar-St. Clair-Wayne campaigns against the Indians and the drafting of the Treaty of Greenville in 1795.

In Kentucky and Tennessee westerners were stirred to considerable fervor by the WAR HAWKS. Henry Clay, Richard M. Johnson, and Felix Grundy were key figures. In Indiana Territory Harrison was a major figure in the shaping of public opinion west of the Ohio. From 1805, when he was a member of the Kentucky general assembly, to 1812, Henry CLAY actively agitated opposition to Britain and strongly advocated American territorial expansion. He was active in creating public pressures to acquire vast frontier additions in Canada and Florida. Some of his activities and utterances viewed from the perspective of history seem almost ridiculous, but nevertheless they were effective in accomplishing their purposes. Diplomatic and economic issues created by the orders in council and Napoleonic decrees and the Embargo and Nonintercourse acts cramped western economics. Western tempers were raised by the *Chesapeake-Leopard* affair, when a British frigate fired upon a U.S. naval vessel and forcibly seized four sailors in 1807. The main impetus for the immediate outbreak of the war in the West, however, was created by independent Indian activities along the Wabash River.

The efforts of the Shawnee leader TECUMSEH and his brother TENSKWATAWA to create an Indian confederation, north and south, threatened the peace of the frontier. Too, a rising population pressure of over a million individuals in 1810 helped to force settlement on Indian lands in Indiana Territory. The mode of acquiring claims to this territory was irritating to the Indians, and became increasingly so as Indians were killed in border incidents along the treaty boundaries. On November 7, 1811, the conflict of interest between Indian and settler resulted in the battle of TIPPECANOE on the upper Wabash. To all intents and purposes, this was the opening of the War of 1812 in the West.

Between the convening of the Twelfth Congress on November 4, 1811, and the formal declaration of war on June 18, 1812, there was a tremendous amount of intensive debating of issues both in Congress and the public press. The war hawks were diligent in their chauvinistic campaign, using several arguments, including the annexation of British and Spanish territories. Thus, after June 1812, the West was faced with several frightening realities. First was the problem of raising and training the militia forces of which the war hawks had so glibly boasted; second, securing arms and other war materials was a burdensome undertaking; and third, procuring food and clothing in sufficient quantities for troops in the field taxed productive and transportation facilities. There were few trained officers and the seasoned commanders available were not young. On May 25, 1812, nearly a month before war was declared, General William Hull, a veteran of the American Revolution, arrived in Dayton, Ohio, to take command of the left flank of the United States Army. Between that date and July 5, Hull's command battled woods, heat, humidity, and black flies to cross the great swamp of northwestern Ohio and northeastern Indians on its way to Detroit.

General Hull was uninformed as to the declaration of war until he reached Frenchtown. On July 12 he began his advance against Fort Malden and Amherstburg beyond the Detroit River. A show of considerable strength on the part of the Canadians under the command of Governor Isaac Brock and Colonel Henry Proctor, however, forced Hull to fall back to Fort Detroit. Proctor followed up his advantage and appeared before that place with a good striking force of Indians and Canadians. Hull lost his nerve and surrendered the fort. Two other commands failed, one at Fort Dearborn on Lake Michigan commanded by Captain Nathan Heald, and General Samuel Hopkins' Kentucky militiamen, which was sent out to strike the Indians in central Illinois. The militia of the western states, so vociferous in their war rhetoric, didn't care for fighting. Hopkins' force became mutinous and unmanageable five days after it was mustered.

East of Detroit, General Stephen Van Rensselaer and General Henry Dearborn were engaged in skirmishes along the St. Lawrence and the Niagara rivers. Dearborn was unable to attack Montreal as ordered because his army refused to follow him. He reported his lack of action as due to a tactical armistice. Van Rensselaer failed to cross the Niagara and strike the British, partly because of a fiasco on October 10, when Brigadier General Alexander "Apocalypse" Smythe, Colonel Solomon Van Rensselaer, and a Lieutenant Sims did not cross over to the Canadian shore from Black Rock and Buffalo because Smythe decided halfway across the river that God had deserted them.

These failures were open refutations of the politicians' irresponsible boasts. The Americans now faced a monumental challenge. A dispute of mild proportions arose as to whether Brigadier General James Winchester or William Henry Harrison would command in the Northwest. Militiamen chose Harrison. The autumn of 1812 saw an attempt to restore the American forces in the area about Detroit. Militiamen concentrated their forces in the old Fort Wayne-Fort Defiance-Maumee-Auglaize area. Unhappily for Harrison, British naval forces operating on Lake Erie under the command of Captain Barclay made a bold strike a risky business. Harrison, however, believed an attack could be accomplished in the dead of winter. This move resulted in a stinging defeat and holocaust at Frenchtown and along the river Raisin on January 22, 1813.

The massacre at Frenchtown and the Raisin had an even more shocking effect on the West than the surrender of Detroit. During the spring and summer of 1813 a frantic recruiting and training campaign went on in Ohio, Kentucky, and Indiana. Supplies were gathered and transported through an assembly depot near Cincinnati. Governor Isaac Shelby left the executive office in Frankfort, Kentucky, for the field, and with him went Congressman Richard M. Johnson and his brother James, General Green Clay, and Colonel William Whit-

ley. The tide in the Northwest turned on September 10, 1813, when Oliver Hazard Perry defeated Captain Barclay's lake fleet. Harrison's army could now press against Proctor and the Indians without fear of being cut off by gunboats. On October 5, the Americans defeated the British and Canadians, killed Tecumseh, and routed the Indians in the battle of the THAMES.

At the outset of the war General James Wilkinson was in command on the lower Mississippi and around the Gulf to Mobile. Soon after February 1813, the Spanish withdrew from Mobile Bay, and the Alabama estuary was left in American hands. In Nashville, Tennessee, in the autumn of 1812 Andrew JACKSON mustered the Tennessee Volunteers with the thought of fighting the Canadians along the St. Lawrence-Niagara frontier. Instead the War Department requested Governor Willie Blount (half brother of William Blount) to send 1,500 militiamen to strengthen Wilkinson's command at New Orleans. On December 10, the volunteers assembled at the Cumberland River, and by January 7, 1813, 2,070 men were ready to march or float south. Wilkinson halted the Tennesseans at Natchez, and Jackson marched them back to Nashville, where they were mustered out of service, but not for long.

On August 30, 1813, there occurred a bloody massacre at Form Mims on the Alabama River in which approximately a thousand Creek warriors killed over five hundred whites. News of this bloody incident reached Nashville, where the Tennessee legislature authorized Governor Blount to raise an army of around forty-five hundred men to march into the Alabama woods against the Creek. Jackson was suffering from wounds inflicted on a shoulder in a gun duel with Thomas Hart Benton and his brother Jesse Benton. By October, however, he had marched his army into central Alabama and had established it in hastily constructed frontier posts. Fighting a series of skirmishes, the Tennesseans cornered the Creek in the HORSESHOE BEND of the Tallapoosa River, where on March 27, 1814, the Indians were virtually annihilated. This defeat of the Creek was a somewhat empty victory for the Americans because they had already served the British by holding a large force of militiamen at bay for a considerable period. (On the war in the South, see NEGROES ON THE FRONTIER.)

Jackson was rewarded with a commission as major-general in the regular army and given command of the Seventh Military District.

After a fairly successful foray into Pensacola, Florida, he responded to an appeal from the people of New Orleans to held defend them against attack by the British armada, which was headed in that direction. On November 22, 1814, Jackson split his forces, sending a large body of troops to Mobile under the command of Brigadier General James Winchester. By December 1 Jackson and the other division of his army were in New Orleans, and General John Coffee, commander of the Tennessee volunteer cavalry and a close personal friend of Jackson, was in Baton Rouge. Between that date and January 8, 1815, General Jackson faced the problem of carefully reconnoitering the difficult terrain of the Lake Borgne-Lake Pontchartrain area and of surveying the Mississippi shore southward. American victory at the battle of NEW ORLEANS ended the fighting in the War of 1812.

This conflict had an enormous influence on the West in nearly every aspect of life. Its economic impact alone was tremendous. No influence, however, was greater than the making of a fabulous legend of heroism and victory. A veritable army of popular heroes emerged from the war, and they were not willing to let the people forget them in the future. There came three future presidents of the United States, a host of senators and congressmen, and almost innumerable lesser political figures. How many fundamental international issues the war settled still remains a historically moot question.

See Francis F. Beirne, *The War of 1812* (1949); Harry L. Coles, *The War of 1812* (1965); Reginald Horsman, *The War of 1812* (1969); Robert McNutt McElroy, *Kentucky in the Nation's History* (1909); Leland W. Meyer, *Life and Times of Colonel Richard M. Johnson . . . of Kentucky* (1932); Julius W. Pratt, *Expansionists of 1812* (1925); and Glenn Tucker, *Poltroons and Patriots*, 2 vols. (1954).—T. D. C.

Warre, Henry James (1819-1898). British soldier and topographical artist. Sir Henry is remembered chiefly for his illustrations of the Pacific Northwest, done while serving as a captain with the military in that region. In 1845-46 he made an official reconnaissance of Oregon Territory for the British government, making numerous scenic sketches of the area. They were later engraved and published under the title *Skteches in North America and the Oregon Territory* (1848). The originals for these now reside with the American Antiquarian Society in Worcester, Massachusetts.—D. C. H.

Warren, Francis E[mroy] (1844-1929). Businessman and Wyoming politician. A native of Hinsdale, Massachusetts, where he attended Hinsdale Academy, Warren moved to the West after distinguished service in the Civil War. He settled in Cheyenne, Wyoming, in 1868 and, over the next fifteen years, constructed an economic base that included the Warren Mercantile Company, the Warren Land and Livestock Company, and extensive landholdings in the territory. His success as a sheep-raiser prompted a later Senate colleague to dub him "the greatest shepherd since Abraham." His natural ambition and fervent Republicanism led him into territorial politics, and he rose through subsidiary offices to appointment as governor in early 1885. During two gubernatorial terms between 1885 and 1890, Warren campaigned for railroads, public buildings, and federal subsidies in a manner that characterized his entire public career.

After Wyoming's admission to the Union in 1890, the voters chose Warren governor, but he resigned when the legislature elected him to the Senate weeks later. Identification with the unpopular Johnson County range war of 1892 between large Wyoming cattle ranchers and settlers in the northern part of the state cost him his seat at the end of his two-year term in 1893. A depression, predictable Democratic mistakes, and a smoothly functioning party organization enabled him to regain his place in Washington in 1895. Warren remained a senator until his death thirty-four years later.

In state politics, Warren built a personal machine that rested on efficient distribution of patronage, the abilities of loyal aides, such as future Supreme Court Justice Willis Van Devanter, and a tireless concern with the fortunes of the Wyoming economy. The senator saw the federal government as the indispensable prop of local enterprise in the arid West, and he used his power to insure that Wyoming would receive its share of appropriations. Believing that politicians should "never hunt ducks with a brass band," Warren emphasized quiet persistence and unending effort as the means to success with such subjects as reclamation projects and favored military posts, such as Fort D. A. Russell near Cheyenne.

Seniority made Warren a figure of substantial influence in the Senate. From the chairmanship of the Military Affairs and Appropriations committees, he made sure that his state was rarely slighted. He kept a careful eye on the progress of political friends and on the career of his son-in-law John J. Pershing. Equally solicitous about the tariff on wool and hides, Warren always advocated proteciton as one basis of Wyoming's prosperity and played a large role in the shaping of the Dingley and Payne-Aldrich tariffs in the Progressive era. Similarly, he was an intellectual leader of the anti-conservation forces in Congress in the same period. Warren had scant national impact over his long years in politics, but on the local scene, he demonstrated how an efficient public official might exploit the intimate financial connection between Washington and the West to benefit both his state and his own career.

See the Francis E. Warren Papers, University of Wyoming; Willis Van Devanter Papers, Library of Congress; and Lewis L. Gould, *Wyoming:A Political History, 1868-1896* (1968).—L. L. G.

Warren, Gouverneur Kemble (1830-1882). Army officer and topographical engineer. Major General Warren, who graduated second in his class at West Point in 1850, went directly into the Corps of Topographical Engineers. His services in the West began with his collaboration with Captain A. A. Humphreys in compiling the maps and reports of the Pacific railroad surveys. Until 1859 he was active in mapping Dakota and Nebraska territories. His outstanding contribution was the overall map of the trans-Mississippi West, which he compiled from the knowledge gained by the Pacific railroad surveys.

See William H. Goetzmann, *Army Exploration in the American West* (1959); and E. G. Taylor, *Gouverneur Kemble Warren* (1932). For Warren's maps, see Carl I. Wheat, *Mapping the Trans-Mississippi West*, vol. IV (1960).—R. A. B.

Washakie (1804?-1900). Chief of the eastern Shoshoni. Washakie was head of the Shoshoni band from 1843 until his death. Although he fought courageously against his Indian foes, the Arapaho, Crow, and Sioux, Washakie decided early that the interests of his relatively weak band would best be served by a friendly posture toward the whites. Because of his friendly disposition, travelers along the overland trails in Wyoming west of South Pass normally were undisturbed. When the Mormons came to settle near by, they too found Washakie generally honorable in his dealings with them.

Tall and powerfully built, of commanding presence and exceptional character, Washakie enforced discipline about as well as any Indian chief could. Even so, many members of his band broke with him and raided the trails in the years 1859 to 1862. Some of these defectors died at the hands of Colonel Patrick E. Connor's men in the battle of Bear River in January 1863, after which there was less questioning of Washakie's authority. Under his leadership, the eastern Shoshoni agreed to a treaty at Fort Bridger on July 2, 1863, in which they promised not to molest travelers on the trails and received in return promises of $10,000 in goods each year for twenty years.

A second treaty of Fort Bridger was negotiated July 3, 1868, by which Washakie and his people accepted a permanent home on the Wind River Reservation northeast of South Pass.

In 1876 Washakie led two hundred of his braves east of the Big Horn Mountains intending to join General George Crook in a campaign against the Sioux. He arrived too late to participate in the battle of the Rosebud, and, like Crook, had no part in the battle of the Little Big Horn, which followed. Washakie returned to his reservation when General Crook in August 1876 moved into Montana in pursuit of the scattered Sioux forces.

In March 1878 federal agents persuaded Washakie to share temporarily his Wind River Reservation with a thousand northern Arapaho. Much to Washakie's chagrin the joint occupancy became permanent. Eventually, long after their great chief's death, the Shoshoni received compensation from the government for their hospitality to the Arapaho.

Many testimonials survive from credible white contemporaries who praised Washakie's sterling character, oratory, and exceptional leadership qualities.

See Grace Raymond Hebard, *Washakie* (1930); and Virginia Cole Trenholm, and Maurine Carley, *The Shoshonis: Sentinels of the Rockies* (1964).—T. A. L.

Washington, George (1732-1799). Planter, land speculator, soldier, and first president of the United States. Washington was born in Westmoreland County, Virginia, the first son of the second marriage of his father, Augustine Washington. He received an informal education at home, part of the time at Mount Vernon, the estate inherited by his older half brother, Lawrence.

It was Washington's contribution to the birth of the republic to command the military effort of the American Revolution and to recognize the continental dimensions of the nation that emerged from it. As an English colonial leading the Virginia Militia against the French, as a land speculator and promoter of frontier settlement, and as the first president of the United States, his appreciation of the critical linkage between the settled East and the undeveloped Ohio and Mississippi valleys never faltered. This awareness was a natural product of his environment. Born into the Virginia aristocracy, he early gained that absorbing interest in land and lateral movement, which was characteristic of the gentry of the Old Dominion. Before his death he had acquired not only the Mount Vernon estate on the Potomac but also some sixty thousand acres west of the mountains in present-day Pennsylvania, West Virginia, Kentucky, and Ohio. His sustained and intimate acquaintance with the West, the specific direction of his involvement, and the political implications of that orientation made Washington a major figure in the development of the Old West.

Washington made a number of trips to the West, the first in 1748 when he was just sixteen as a surveyor in the Shenandoah Valley to help lay out lands in the Fairfax grant. He had by then been tutored in the practical arts, such as arithmetic, geometry, and map-making—disciplines that framed his superior surveying skill. Since he was exceptionally tall and robust, and one of the finest horsemen of his day, it is not surprising that Washington was attracted to the wilderness. (Further, the Washington and Fairfax families had recently been connected through the marriage of Lawrence, his older half brother, with Anne Fairfax. Anne was the daughter of William Fairfax, both cousin and agent of Lord Fairfax who had vast land claims in northern Virginia.) In the company of rodmen and chainmen, as well as his fast friend George William Fairfax, the young Washington gained an apprenticeship in surveying and a taste of frontier life.

Washington kept the first of a number of journals of western travels during this trip. His journals are matter-of-fact accounts that reveal greater interest in the depth of a river passage than in its aesthetic qualities. Nor do they suggest that Washington held those characteristic late-eighteenth-century visions of the Indian as a noble savage or of the frontiersman as the virtuous yeoman. Encountering a band of warriors who carried a scalp, he found their war dance "comical." A migrating group of Pennsylvania Germans who could not respond to the English language he characterized "as Ignorant a Set of People as the Indians." His distaste for squatters became equal to his application in securing valid legal title to lands in which he had an interest. Throughout his long involvement in the West there ran an unbroken thread reflecting the concerns of a hardheaded businessman. On this very trip he made the down payment on a 550-acre tract in Frederick County. But if Washington's perception of the West and its inhabitants was informed more by calculation than romance, he treated Indian chiefs with whom he would shortly negotiate with dignity and respect. Much later, as president, he would urge that "the mild principles of religion and philanthropy" guide, whenever possible, United States policy toward the western tribes.

In late 1753 Washington was commissioned a major in the Virginia Militia and ordered by Governor Robert Dinwiddie to undertake a most delicate errand to Fort Le Boeuf on the headwaters of French Creek near Lake Erie. The complexity of his task may be appreciated from the fact that while his primary duty was to convey a message from Governor Dinwiddie warning the French to cease building forts and settlements around the headwaters of the Ohio, he was also acting less overtly to emphasize Virginia's claim to the region and as an agent of the Ohio Company. (The Ohio Company, organized in 1747, was the first of the great land companies. Its membership included many prominent Virginians, notably the Washingtons and Governor Dinwiddie himself. Lawrence Washington had been its president and probably would have led this expedition had he not died the previous year.) The conflicting interests converging in this region were so closely related as to have dangerous potential. Not only did the British and the French disagree about ownership of the Ohio valley, but conflicting claims existed between Virginia and Pennsylvania over the latter's western boundary and between Pennsylvania traders and the Ohio Company over privileges in the area. Too often disregarded, or manipulated, were Indian rights to this hitherto rich hunting ground of the Delaware, Shawnee, and Seneca—tribes that acknowledged allegiance to the powerful Iroquois. It was Washington's responsibility to warn off the French, improve relations with the Indians, give additional emphasis to the Virginia claim, and to prepare for settlements on the Ohio by the Ohio Company whose grant was contingent, in part, on establishing settlements within seven years.

He carried off the mission with some skill but limited success. The conveyance of Dinwiddie's demand to the commander at Fort Le Boeuf, Legardeur de St. Pierre, did not cause the French to evacuate. Moreover, St. Pierre cleverly refused to accept the "Speech-Belt," a symbol of a rupture of peaceful relations, presented (somewhat reluctantly at Washington's insistence) by Tamacharisson, the Seneca chief. Washington was successful, however, in retaining the loyalty of Tamacharisson, often called the "Half-Chief" because of his allegiance to the Iroquois. Washington also succeeded in locating suitable places for settlement and fortifications. Twice he narrowly missed losing his life during the hair-raising and arduous trip back with exhausted horses, in the midst of snow and ice, and in the presence of some hostile Indians. In company with Christopher Gist (a frontier trader and Ohio Company agent) and a French Indian, Washington made a short-cut through the forest on foot. When crossing the ice-choked Allegheny on a raft, he fell into the water and saved himself by catching hold of one of the raft logs. The raft became jammed in the ice, and they spent the night on an island, finally making their way to the shore over the ice the next day. The Indian, who was acting as guide, misdirected them toward the northeast, and after a disagreement fired his gun at Gist and Washington at a range of fifteen paces. Gist recorded in his diary, "I would have killed him; but the Major would not suffer me to. . . ." Washington reached Williamsburg on January 16 and became the center of attention in the colonial capital. Indeed, his journal was published throughout the colonies and in England.

Washington's trip provided Dinwiddie with specific intelligence about French operations in the Ohio headwaters—the forts, men, armament, and supplies—which Dinwiddie hoped would prompt the Virginia Assembly to take action against the enemy. Although the burgesses proved dilatory and suspicious, an appropriation of £10,000 was allowed. The governor used this and a promise of 200,000 acres of bounty land in the West to recruit volunteers for an expedition to clear out the French. Volunteers were disappointingly slow to materialize, and support from adjoining colonies, suspicious of Virginian expansionism, was negligible. Nonetheless, within three months Washington headed back to the Ohio River with two companies of volunteers, some 160 men in all, with instructions to oust the French with force if need be.

For this more aggressive excursion of 1754, which in effect started the Great War for Empire, Washington had no combat experience and little, if any, training in drilling troops. The air was filled with rumors of heavy French concentrations to the west and of defections among the Indian allies of the British. The first was confirmed to some extent by news that the French were building Fort Duquesne at the forks of the Ohio, but the Half-Chief joined Washington and assured him that a strike against the French would rally the Ohio Indians to the British standard. After a victorious skirmish involving unnecessary bloodshed with a small party of French under the young ensign de Jumonville, Washington fell back to GREAT MEADOWS to build the famous Fort Necessity. It was not long before an overwhelming force of French and Indians appeared under the command of Coulon de Villiers, Jumonville's brother. Washington surrendered on July 4 after a day's engagement on terms that allowed the English to evacuate. In the articles of capitulation, drawn up in French, Washington unwittingly admitted the "assassination" of Jumonville, thus tainting an already unsuccessful expedition. In his dispatches Villiers explained the release of Washington and his men on the ground that England and France were not formally at war. Yet actual war had begun, as Voltaire noted when he commented, "A volley fired by a young Virginian in the backwoods of America set the world on fire."

Dinwiddie, intent upon retaliation, was supported by the British crown with a sizable force of more than a thousand regular soldiers under Major General Edward Braddock, who arrived in the colonies in April 1755. As a consequence, the colonial militia was placed in a decidedly inferior position. Informed that as a Virginia colonel he would have to accept orders from a regular captain, Washington found his pride (admittedly readily available) and resigned.

The subsequent disastrous campaign, which resulted in the death of Braddock and a significant portion of his army, is well known. Washington went along as an aide-de-camp. Reinforced with provincials, chiefly Virginians who tested Braddock's penchant for discipline, the column was riddled by an inferior number of well-concealed French and Indians on July 9 some ten miles short of Fort Duquesne. Of three Virginia companies only thirty men survived. Washington escaped unscathed, though with "four Bullets through my Coat and two Horses shot under me." Helping to lead the remnants of the expedition in a semblance of an orderly retreat, Washington gained repute at home and respect from the British and French alike. During the formal phase of the Seven Years' War that followed, Washington served as commander-in-chief of all forces raised in Virginia, both in defense of the frontier—much harassed during the early years—and with General John Forbes in the drive on Fort Duquesne.

Having fought in defense of British interests in the West, Washington was poised to participate in its development. There were essentially two aspects of his activity, which reached a peak by 1770: the acquisition of land and the development of the Potomac River as the chief means of access to the rising western population. Even before the Treaty of Paris conveyed New France to England, Washington and a group of Virginian associates, notably his half brother John Augustine and the brothers Richard Henry and Arthur Lee, framed a land scheme of grandiose proportions. Organized as the Mississippi Company in 1760, they petitioned the crown for 2.5 million acres along the Mississippi River north and south of its juncture with the Ohio. This project, along with other comparable speculations that were to lead to a welter of conflicting claims (all of which foundered with the Revolution), was placed in limbo by the Proclamation of 1763 prohibiting settlement west of the Alleghenies. Incessant pressure from many highly influential speculators, however, resulted in the removal of the line westward in the treaties of Hard Labor and Fort Stanwix in 1768. The result was an intensification of colonization plans on both sides of the Atlantic. In the midst of this frenetic speculative activity Washington joined Richard Henry Lee (as brother Arthur lobbied in England) in an unsuccessful effort to comit the Vriginia Assembly to the improvement of the navigation of the Potomac River. He did, however, secure authorization from the Virginia Council to survey lands along the Ohio north of the Great Kanawha River, pursuant to the military warrants of 200,000 acres made by Dinwiddie for the volunteers of the Virginia regiment who had fought in the French and Indian War in 1754.

Washington made a personal inspection of the land in the late fall of 1770, journeying to Fort Pitt, down the Ohio and up the Great Kanwha. It was on this trip, undertaken on his own behalf and that of his soldier associates, that Washington decided where to locate his major western investments, which were patented under subsequent surveys. He has been criticized by some historians for having engrossed as much as thirty thousand acres of the best bottomlands along the Kanawha and the Ohio to the disadvantage of his fellow veterans. Clearly, he violated the Virginia law stipulating that a tract of land must be no more than three times as long as it was deep when staking his claim along the Kanawha. It may be said, however, that this was a regulation frequently disregarded at the time, and that Washington's associates would have had less chance of securing the land without his weight behind the enterprise.

Washington was a colonizer as well as a speculator. Worried that his claims might be challenged if left unsettled, he advertised abroad for settlers to whom he offered full civil and religious liberties. He purchased "parcels" of indentured servants and gave minute instructions to his agents in the West regarding their labor and sustenance. Hardly had his colonization efforts been launched, however, than they had to be abandoned as a consequence of Indian hostilities culminating in Lord Dunmore's War and, more importantly, Washington's own involvement in the American Revolution in Virginia, in the First Continental Congress, and as leader of the Continental Army from 1775 to 1783. During these years his attention was directed not toward the West but toward the battle regions from Boston to Yorktown.

No sooner had he retired to Mount Vernon, however, than he "found it indispensably necessary to visit my Landed property West of the Apalachean Mountains." This laconic entry at the opening of his journal of the trip to the Youghiogheny River in September 1784 makes the journey seem simply a business trip. Nor was Washington inattentive to the collection of rents from tenants, the operation of his mill in Perryopolis, Pennsylvania, the surveying of lands, and the expulsion of squatting intruders.

Yet Washington's range of vision encompassed more than his own properties—or put somewhat differently, his personal concerns were uniquely congruent with the economic development of Virginia and the need for political coherence in the loosely joined Confederation. The constant attention he paid on this trip to terrain and the navigability of rivers, such as the Cheat and Youghiogheny as connecting links between the Potomac and the Ohio, indicates continued interest in the navigation project. Just a week after his return he wrote to Governor Benjamin Harrison of Virginia urging that the Assembly sponsor improvement of the Potomac access, pointing out that Virginia had a special opportunity to gather in the trade of the rapidly populating West. He stressed that the Spanish had prohibited American trade down the Mississippi and the British had refused to evacuate the posts in the Northwest (thereby inhibiting the press of New Yorkers into the interior). The Assembly responded by authorizing the Potomac Improvement Company, which was capitalized at $200,000 and later endorsed by Maryland following the Mount Vernon Conference of 1785. Washington naturally became its president.

The cooperation between Virginia and Maryland at Mount Vernon was an expression of the larger range of Washington's thinking. In his letter to Harrison he stressed that "the flanks and rear of the United States are possessed by other powers, and formidable ones too"; and that it was necessary to "apply the cement of interest, to bind all parts of the Union together by indissoluble bonds, especially that part of it, which lies immediately west of us, with the middle States." He urged the legislators to recognize what he had observed—that the people of the West stood as "upon a pivot; the touch of a feather would turn them any way." Implicit throughout his message was the assumption that the Potomac would form an important sinew of union.

Washington's hopes for the Potomac avenue to the West, however, were ultimately frustrated by the shift early in the nineteenth century from the use of river transportation to canals (an eventuality Washington anticipated by investing in lands along the Mohawk with George Clinton and by warning the Virginians of the enterprising New Yorkers). The Virginians were partially gratified during his presidency, however, when the national capital was located on the Potomac River, close to his Mount Vernon estate and the city of Alexandria, which he hoped would become a commercial center for western trade. No man's influence was more decisive in the location of this "seat of empire," a phrase that symbolizes Washington's perception of the role of the Potomac as a link with the West.

Neither the passage of the Constitution nor the inauguration of Washington as president eliminated the problem of restiveness among the western population, nor were the policies of his administration uniformly palatable to those peoples. Yet by the end of his second term in office much had been accomplished to provide the national coherence he had sought. By treaty and force the Northwest frontier was made reasonably secure from Indian attack with Anthony Wayne's victory at the battle of Fallen Timbers in 1794. At the same time Washington's proclamation against the potentially disruptive colonization plans of James O'Fallon and the Yazoo Company in the lower Mississippi prevented what might have been a serious war in the Southwest. His handling of Edmond Genêt helped curb that volatile French minister's attempts to take advantage of separatist and expansionist tendencies in the West. By supporting the highly unpopular Jay's Treaty, he was instrumental in bringing about the final evacuation of the British from the Northwest posts. Before he retired from the presidency, he also had the satisfaction of signing the Treaty of San Lorenzo, negotiated by Thomas Pinckney in 1795, which set the boundary between the United States and Spanish Florida and provided for American commerce on the Mississippi.

Washington's influence on western development begs comparison with that of Thomas JEFFERSON, his fellow Virginian and leader of the opposition party that emerged during his administration, and the president under whom the Louisiana Purchase was effected. The work of both men was in many ways complementary. (While Washington was promoting navigation of the Potomac, Jefferson was framing the important land ordinance of 1784.) Yet there were basic differences between their perceptions of the West and its relationship to the emerging American nation. Jefferson saw in the West a yeoman democracy that might rejuvenate a nation tainted by commercialism and aristocracy. Washington, on the other hand, while more personally involved in western promotion, was chary of the social and political consequences of unregulated expansion. His response in 1794 to the rebellion of irate farmers in western Pennsylvania over the whiskey excise was that of a magisterial Federalist who deplored and suppressed the tax resisters: "if the Laws are to be so trampled upon . . . there is an end put, at one stroke, to republican government; and nothing but anarchy and confusion is to be expected thereafter. . . ." But if Washington saw the West as a danger to the Republic, his accomplishments in an earlier and different set of circumstances helped make possible Jefferson's different view of the West as a nutriment of republicanism.

Washington's extensive involvement in the West is reflected in historical literature, particularly Archer B. Hulbert, *Washington and the West* (1905); Roy B. Cook, *Washington's Western Lands* (1930); and Charles Ambler, *George Washington and the West* (1936), the best book of the three. For Washington's interest in the Potomac, a convenient documentary collection is available in Grace L. Nute, ed., "Washington and the Potomac; Manuscripts of the Minnesota Historical Society," *American Historical Review*, vol. 28. Another useful documentary collection is Hugh Cleland, ed., *George Washington in the Ohio Valley* (1955).—H. J. H.

Washington. Archaeological evidence from present-day Washington's prehistory indicates that human migration began moving southward through the Okanogan and Columbia valleys as long as eleven thousand years ago, with the ancestors of modern Indians appearing in the area about one thousand years ago. The Indians had domesticated animals, shaped stone and bone tools, and nomadic living habits, which enabled them to adjust well to their environment. While the Indians of eastern Washington maintained a precarious existence, the coastal Indians enjoyed a higher standard of living because abundant seafood was available. They also developed a genuinely superior artistic style of woven designs and wood carving.

The history of contact between white men and Indians has its roots in legend. Sir Francis Drake made a doubtful claim of having reached 48 degrees north in 1577. A Greek navigator, sailing under the assumed Spanish name of Juan de Fuca, claimed to have discovered a strait in 1592 that extended from the Pacific to the Atlantic oceans. The first clearly documented voyages to the Washington coast were those of the Spanish explorers Juan Pérez, Bruno Heceta, and Juan Bodega y Quadra, who sailed along the coast between 1774 and 1776. Captain James Cook of Great Britain sighted headlands on the Washington coast in 1778. Each of these men was searching for the legendary Northwest Passage, an all-water route that would connect East and West. Instead of such a route, however, they found a multitude of inlets and islands, swarming with fur-bearing animals whose pelts could be sold for huge profits in the markets of Europe and China.

A steady parade of ships and crews came to exploit the fur resources. Free-lance traders from England, Russia, and the United States traded with the Indians, in spite of Spanish claims to control the trade of the north Pacific. Spanish interest in the area was virtually eliminated in 1790 by the diplomatic settlement between Spain and England of the Nootka Sound incident brought on by Spanish attempts to enforce their claims to monopoly trading rights. By this settlement, England was then able to move in the region north of the forty-second parallel without interference from other European powers. Captain George Vancouver, who represented England at Nootka during the settlement talks, was thus able to explore, map, and name the rivers, bays, and inlets of the Northwest.

While Vancouver explored the coast and other English traders and geographers explored the interior, President Jefferson dispatched Meriwether Lewis and William Clark to report on the plants, animals, and inhabitants of the Columbia valley and the north central plains. This expedition reached the Pacific Ocean in the fall of 1805 and returned in 1806 to report its findings to the nation.

Eventually American fur-trading companies established posts at the mouths of the major streams south of the Fraser River system. The associates of John Jacob ASTOR built posts near the mouths of the Columbia, Snake, Okanogan, and Spokane rivers. Immediately their rivals, the British-controlled North West Company of Montreal, built forts at the same locations, until the region north of the Columbia and Snake was blanketed by commercial operations, working through independent trappers, fur brigades, forts, and occasional ships. The War of 1812 ruined the American enterprise, however, and for ten years the North West Company carried on without competition.

By 1821, however, scandalous competition between this company and the more powerful HUDSON'S BAY COMPANY led to a forced merger of the two British corporations. The new, consolidated Hudson's Bay Company established its headquarters for the entire Pacific Northwest at Fort Vancouver on the north bank of the Columbia River opposite the mouth of the Willamette. The company built additional inland posts and also encouraged agriculture around these posts to reduce expenses for feeding the employees. Eventually a subsidiary company, the Puget Sound Agricultural Company, took over the farming activities.

Occasionally Americans intruded into the gigantic Hudson's Bay Company fur preserve during the late 1820s and 1830s. Many of them were missionaries trying to Christianize the local Indians. Around their mission stations grew the first small communities of American citizens (see OREGON). One such community was destroyed when in November 1847 CAYUSE INDIANS murdered the adult male members of a mission established by Marcus WHITMAN at Waiilatpu, near present Walla Walla, Washington. Other American settlements began to grow in the Cowlitz River valley and the Puget Sound basin. Expressing the prevailing philosophy of manifest destiny, these settlers insisted that the Hudson's Bay employees and the Indians both be eliminated and that the area should belong to the United States.

Pending formal British-American agreements about government for the area, the settlers set up a provisional government for the entire Northwest in 1843. In 1846 the two nations signed a treaty whereby the Americans would govern south of the forty-ninth parallel, excluding Vancouver Island, and the British would control lands to the north.

That part of Oregon Territory now controlled by the United States was much too large and sparsely inhabited to be administered efficiently from the Willamette valley. Accordingly, Americans living north of the Columbia River, such as George Washington BUSH of Olympia, asked Congress to divide Oregon, and on May 2, 1853, Congress established Washington Territory with Isaac Ingalls STEVENS as governor. At this time almost all Americans in Washington were living on the west side of the Cascade range.

For thirty years the population grew slowly. More settlers left for the gold fields of California, Idaho, and British Columbia than remained. The white settlers' desire for lands occupied and belonging to Indians led to a brief war in the middle 1850s between the whites and the Indians, whose brilliant leader, KAMIAKIN of the YAKIMA INDIANS, proved a worthy antagonist to Stevens and the settler volunteers. This war also discouraged immigration. The Civil War scarcely affected the remote Northwest, but gold discoveries in eastern parts of the territory resulted in the creation of Montana and Idaho territories, reducing Washington to its present boundaries and area of 68,192 square miles, of which 1,529 are inland waters. The water boundary between the Straits of Georgia and Juan de Fuca became De-Haro's channel west of the San Juan Islands, after an arbitration settlement had been referred to the emperor of Germany in 1872.

At the end of the Civil War Washington Territory, like the nation itself, underwent significant shifts as the nation moved into the urban-industrial period. Migration to Washington increased and people led by Thomas BURKE began to demand better communications with the eastern and southern markets. Such a connection was finally attained in 1883, when the Northern Pacific Railroad completed its line through Montana, giving Washington its first direct rail connection with the eastern states. More people moved into the territory, claiming homesteads by the thousands of acres. In 1889 Congress admitted Washington, along with the other states through which the Northern Pacific ran, as the forty-second state.

Statehood produced a short-lived economic boom in Washington. The expansion of agriculture and silver discoveries in northern Idaho were mainly responsible for it. The panic of 1893, however, caused silver mines to close, homesteaders to abandon their claims, and lumber mills to end production. The railroads, which had taken credit for prosperity, were compelled to share the blame for the hard times. Political unrest caused by depression aided the Populist party to carry the state in 1896, and John R. ROGERS was elected governor.

Gold discoveries in the Yukon in 1897 brightened the economic outlook dramatically. Almost at once gold turned Seattle from a quiet, depression-ridden seaport to a howling madhouse of men and women fighting for passage to Alaska. Seattle's rapid growth was aided by a tremendous and successful publicity campaign originated by Erastus BRAINERD of the Seattle Commercial Club. While Seattle experienced the most spectacular growth, all of western Washington increased in population. The gold rush even helped eastern Washington farmers to sell produce. Political turmoil almost vanished, and conservatives returned to control of state government. Population of the state more than doubled in a decade. Western Washington celebrated this gold-based prosperity in a giant fair, the Alaska-Yukon-Pacific Exposition of 1909.

The pressures of sudden population increase, the social stresses resulting from immigration of non-English groups, and widespread corruption in public and private business dealings, combined with the prevailing spirit of progressivism, fostered among others by newspaperman Rufus WOODS, led to reform legislation. In 1904 and 1905 voters supported measures to regulate railroad rate-making powers. They adopted state constitutional amendments designed to allow more widespread participation of ordinary citizens in government. These amendments provided for direct primary elections, initiative, referendum, recall of public officials, and WOMAN SUFFRAGE. Reformists also supported measures presumed to make the population more virtuous, such as pure food and drug laws, the imposition of "blue laws" to improve the physical and moral environment, and the prohibition of alcoholic beverages.

There were other citizens who rejected a reform of the social order in favor of more revolutionary techniques. Such a group as the INDUSTRIAL WORKERS OF THE WORLD (I.W.W.) involved itself in attempts to unionize timber workers into "One Big Union" in order to destroy the capitalistic order. They held parades without permits and took part in "free-speech" campaigns in 1909-13.

In 1917 the United States entered World War I, and for a short time the economy of the state boomed. Airplane manufacturers scoured the forests for materials to build military aircraft. Shipbuilding eclipsed even the furious activity of the late 1890s. Government-supported prices for agriculture vastly increased farm prosperity.

With the end of World War I, however, the ending of federal price supports and consequent sharp drop in agricultural income affected both the economy and the attitudes of people. On the one hand, labor unrest grew, culminating in the SEATTLE general strike of 1919. But many thought that the activities of the I.W.W. and other groups involved with the strike were subversive. Reform no longer attracted political support for candidates or measures. Widespread unemployment, a result of the army's demobilization, led many citizens to demand restrictions on European immigration and the total exclusion of Japanese immigration. There was widespread support for the Ku Klux Klan. The 1920s, though prosperous in some parts of the nation, were years of deep distress in Washington. Population during this decade remained almost static in numbers and kinds of people.

The Great Depression of the 1930s made an already bad situation worse. Agriculture, already in trouble, was prostrated. Lumber production dropped and thousands of men were unemployed. Many mills were never reopened. After 1935, however, the federal government poured millions of dollars into the economy of the state. Much of the money was used to construct a series of multipurpose hydroelectric and irrigation dams along the Columbia River, especially that promoted by Rufus Woods at Grand Coulee. The first production of cheap electrical power began in 1937 after the completion of Bonneville Dam. This made possible a light-metals industry in the Vancouver and Spokane areas.

When World War II involved the United States, federal expenditures in Washington for war production were even greater than they were during the depression. In addition to the dams on the Columbia, shipyards in Seattle and Tacoma, naval repair facilities in Bremerton, military training bases, and aircraft production at Seattle's BOEING AIRPLANE COMPANY poured several billions of dollars into the economy. During the war, atomic reactors and plutonium plants were built in the Richland-Hanford area to develop new kinds of energy for bombs. Unemployment vanished. Immigration was more than encouraged; restless farmers from the Midwest and ethnic minority groups were recruited to move to the Northwest to satisfy the demand for laborers.

At the war's end, both agriculture and lumbering were relatively less important than they had been. The irrigation of the Columbia Basin from the reservoir behind Grand Coulee Dam added to the numbers of farmers, but heavy manufacturing, especially that related to aluminum production and the construction of Boeing-built, jet-propelled aircraft, employed the major group of workers. Eventually, almost ten percent of Washington's working force were working in some activity related to the aerospace program, and hundreds of thousands of others were dependent on this industry for their work in service or related activities. The industry was well protected by Henry Martin Jackson, a Democrat who began his fifth term in the Senate in 1976. While civic and business leaders realized the danger of so much dependence on one kind of manufacturing, not enough had been accomplished toward diversification when the expected decline in aerospace activity occurred in 1969. Accordingly, in some parts of Washington unemployment approached the proportion reached only during the great depressions of the previous one hundred years. The problems were further accentuated by the desire of many citizens to increase the quality of life for all Americans, including those of minority ethnic and racial groups. Warren Grant Magnuson, a Democrat first elected to the Senate in 1944, promoted legislation for public health and to insure civil rights for minority groups. For his sponsorship of laws to protect people from unethical or illegal marketing practices, Magnuson is known as the "father of the consumer movement."

No one can predict the future of the state. It ranks high in potential for recreation, and tourism will possibly become a major source of employment. Three national parks—Rainier, Olympic, and North Cas-cade—two national monuments—Fort Vancouver and the Whitman Mission—one national historic site, an excellent system of state parks, hundreds of miles of lake and saltwater shorelands, and spectacular mountain scenery already attract thousands of visitors annually. The distance of the state from major American and world markets will continue to be a negative factor. Cheap electrical power, the tradition of light-metals production combined with aircraft manufacturing, and above all the timber that has made Washington the Evergreen State should prove advantageous for those who live in the Northwest.

See Dorothy O. Johansen and Charles M. Gates, *Empire of the Columbia: A History of the Pacific Northwest* (1967); Edmond S. Meany, *History of the State of Washington* (1924); Murray Morgan, *The Northwest Corner: The Pacific Northwest, Its Past and Present* (1962); and Oscar O. Winther, *The Great Northwest: A History* (1950). —K. A. M.

Washita, battle of (November 17, 1868). After widespread and vicious Indian raids in Kansas during the summer of 1868, Major General Philip Sheridan decided on a winter campaign that would end the Indians' usual pattern of summer war and winter peace in his Military Department of the Missouri. To force Cheyenne and Arapaho to move onto a reservation in the vicinity of Fort Cobb, Indian Territory, he organized three columns to flush and engage them and drive them toward northwestern Indian Territory. The main force, operating from a newly established base camp known as Camp Supply (now Fort Supply, Oklahoma), was expected to do the principal fighting. On November 23, 1868, Lieutenant Colonel George Armstrong Custer led the Seventh Cavalry from Camp Supply in a snowstorm to search for the Indian village. When scouts found a large village near present Cheyenne, Oklahoma, Custer ordered that four columns were to attack from as many directions as possible at dawn on November 27.

That this village was actually on reservation soil and had been guaranteed safety by the commander at Fort Cobb made no difference to Custer. With the regimental band playing "Garry Owen," the Seventh Cavalry charged at dawn. Surprised warriors fled from their lodges to fight from ravines and underbrush. Within ten minutes, the troops had captured the entire Cheyenne village, but it turned out to be the village of Black Kettle, a peaceful chief, whom they killed during the fighting. Seeing additional warriors approach, Custer discovered that he had struck not one but part of a chain of villages stretching along the Washita. Soon, oncoming warriors from the Cheyenne and other tribes outnumbered him. Rather than risk an all-out assault on the other villages, Custer feinted toward the villages to lure the warriors away from him and then withdrew under cover of darkness.

In the meantime, Major Joel Elliott and eighteen men had ridden out to engage the Indians and had not yet returned. Because Custer did not search for them before leaving and because they later were found to have been annihilated, the Elliott incident became a festering sore within the regiment, causing some of the officers to despise Custer.

Undecisive, as many Indian battles were, the battle of the Washita nevertheless helped to persuade the

Cheyenne to move onto the reservation; the move was virtually assured by the campaign's final blow, the defeat of the Cheyenne Dog Soldiers under Tall Bull by Major Eugene Carr at Summit Springs, Colorado, on July 11, 1869.

Contemporary accounts were written by DeBenneville Randolph Keim, a correspondent for the New York *Herald*, in *Sheridan's Troopers on the Borders* (1870), and George Armstrong Custer, *My Life on the Plains* (1952). An older, secondary account, Charles J. Brill, *Conquest of the Southern Plains* (1938), is biased in favor of the Indians and highly critical of Custer. A book of the same generation, *Custer's Indian Battles* (1936), by Charles Francis Bates, is highly sympathetic toward Custer. More recent studies are Donald J. Berthrong, *The Southern Cheyennes* (1963); and William H. Leckie, *Military Conquest of the Southern Plains* (1963).—O. K.

Washo Indians. See INDIANS OF THE GREAT BASIN.

Watauga Association. Virginia settlers had moved by 1768 close to the boundaries of the Cherokee hunting grounds in the upper Holston and Clinch river valleys; in fact, in some places they had crossed the boundaries. With the negotiation of the Treaty of HARD LABOR in October 1768, this country in present-day Tennessee was opened to further settler activities. Here the established pattern of westward expansion was revealed. There first appeared on the scene parties of long hunters who prowled through the country. Early in January 1769, three scattered settlements were begun, and within the next eighteen months numerous hunters and settlers had entered the complex of the upper river valleys (see HOLSTON RIVER SETTLEMENTS). Both Virginia and North Carolina fed this stream of emigrants crossing the mountains, with such names as James ROBERTSON, John SEVIER, William Bean, Jacob Brown, John Carter, and George Russell becoming prominent in the settlements.

In 1772 the Watauga, or upper Tennessee, settlers formed an association based upon a written code or a series of articles that declared their divine rights to govern themselves. The Watauga Association was to be administered by five commissioners (eventually increased to thirteen) appointed by a majority vote of the settlers. The commissioners were authorized to settle disputes and to attend to other matters that pertained to the common good. Carter became the leader of the association, and Robertson and Sevier were members of the commission. This association played an important role in drawing the Watauga settlers together in a common defense of their settlement, and in establishing the foundations of a rule of law on this island of frontier settlements. It may even be said that the Watauga Association was the beginning of the political organization that eventually led to the creation of the state of Tennessee itself.

See Carl S. Driver, *John Sevier, Pioneer of the Old Southwest* (1932); Samuel Kercheval, *History of the Valley of Virginia* (1902); and J. G. M. Ramsey, *The Annals of Tennessee* (1853).—T. D. C.

Waters, Frank (1902–). Historian and novelist. Waters was born in Colorado and attended Colorado College from 1921 to 1924. He left school without a degree, worked at various jobs, and ultimately became a writer, settling in Taos, New Mexico.

For convenience, Waters' work may be divided into two groups. The lesser known part comprises his careful historical and descriptive studies of the West, notably *Masked Gods: Navaho and Pueblo Ceremonialism* (1950), *Book of the Hopi* (1963), and *The Colorado* (1963). He is best known for his fictional work, notably *The Dust within the Rock* (1940), *People of the Valley* (1941), and, probably his most widely read work, *The Man Who Killed the Deer* (1942).

Waters' basic fictional theme is the search for and acceptance of the mystical meaning of life, which exists beneath, but partially independent of, social forms. Of the hero of *The Dust within the Rock* Waters remarked that "he wanted life, the rich and secret flow. Not the frozen form." The remark could almost stand as a general thematic statement of Waters' best work. His heroes are often caught between two cultures, neither of which they totally belong to. Trapped by change in a world where old values are eroded and new ones not yet strong enough to live by, Waters' heroes must discover for themselves the meaning of life independent of its imperfect forms.—J. K. F.

Watie, Stand (1806-1871). Cherokee politician and soldier. Watie was born in the old Cherokee Nation near Rome, Georgia, of mixed Indian-white parents. His name was derived form the Cherokee word *takertawker*, meaning "immovable" or "to stand firm." Until he was twelve years old, he spoke only Cherokee. He studied at Brainerd, a Moravian mission school situated on the Georgia-Tennessee border, where he developed a talent for writing persuasive political tracts and cogent letters. His brother Buck (Elias Boudinot) was the founder and editor of the *Cherokee Phoenix*, a bilingual newspaper that contained columns printed in Cherokee, using Sequoyah's syllabary, and in English.

Watie was a member of the mixed-blood elite who, in the face of intense settler pressure, favored removal to the West. As such, he signed the controversial Treaty of NEW ECHOTA (1835), which surrendered the Cherokee's eastern homeland and obligated the tribe to move to the West. In Indian Territory Watie established a thriving plantation on Spavinaw Creek, became a prosperous slaveowner, and served as the leader of the mixed-blood faction in the Cherokee Nation. In 1861 he used his influence to associate the Cherokee Nation with the Confederacy and organized a regiment of cavalry, the First Cherokee Mounted Rifles. Watie conducted operations against Union positions in Missouri, Kansas, Arkansas, and northern Indian Territory. His daring cavalry raids included the capture of a steamer on the Arkansas River and the Cabin Creek raid, which wiped out a vast Union supply column. Watie was elevated to the rank of brigadier general in 1864. He tendered his sword to Union commissioners at Doaksville in the Choctaw Nation on June 23, 1865, the last Confederate general to surrender.

During the Reconstruction era, Watie worked at rehabilitating the Cherokee Nation from the ravages of war and recouping his personal fortune. One of his most lasting contributions was his effort to permanently congeal ancient tribal factions into a unified political community.

See M. W. Anderson, *Life of General Stand Watie* (1915), and E. E. Dale, *Cherokee Cavaliers* (1939). —A. M. G.

Watson, Ella. See CATTLE KATE.

Waud, Alfred R. (1828-1891). Illustrator and correspondent. Born in London, Waud came to the United States about 1858 and almost immediately became a staff artist with *Harper's Weekly.* During the Civil War he was one of this magazine's most prolific illustrators and afterward was sent on an assignment through the South to depict the results of that conflict. Making his way down the Ohio and Mississippi rivers, Waud produced views of Cincinnati, Louisville, and Nashville, and later crossed into Louisiana and Texas to make a pictorial exploration of the Southwest. He later executed a sketch entitled *A Drove of Texas Cattle Crossing a Stream,* the first of its kind ever to appear in the national illustrated press. It is thought that he made at least one more trip into the West in 1872. He contributed many illustrations to *Picturesque America,* edited by William Cullen Bryant and published in two volumes that same year. After about 1882, Waud's activity was restricted owing to ill health.

A brother, William, also was an artist for *Leslie's Illustrated Newspaper* and *Harper's Weekly.* Born in England and trained as an architect, he probably came to the United States with Alfred Waud.

See Robert Taft, *Artists and Illustrators of the Old West, 1850-1900* (1953).—D. C. H.

Wayne, Anthony (1745-1796). Soldier. General Wayne, known as "Mad Anthony" because of his impetuous battle tactics, was born in Waynesboro, Pennsylvania, of a prominent family of the region. The young Wayne was given home instruction in the classics and was then sent to an academy in Philadelphia, although no record can be found of his enrollment there. The lad's interests were in the outdoors world, and even in early youth he indicated a military leaning. Like his famous contemporary George Washington, Wayne took up surveying as a vocation and was active in this profession in the backcountry of Pennsylvania. In 1765 he was employed by Benjamin Franklin and a group of associates to survey two large tracts of land in Nova Scotia and to plant on them settlements. Wayne was successful in accomplishing both tasks, but changing times and growing tensions with England brought the latter effort to a quick end.

In 1766 Wayne returned to Pennsylvania, married, and returned to Nova Scotia, but only for a brief time. In the years between 1768 and 1775, he spent a fairly quiet time in Waynesboro, Pennsylvania, as a gentleman farmer, interesting himself deeply in the revolutionary stirrings of the latter years. In 1776 he was elected colonel of the Fourth Battalion in the continental services.

Wayne saw extensive service in the campaigns of the American Revolution. He went with his regiment to reinforce John Sullivan and Benedict Arnold in their fruitless Canada expedition. He engaged in fighting at Three Rivers and fell back to Ticonderoga, where he was placed in command of the fort during the winter of 1776-77. In February 1777, Wayne was promoted to the rank of brigadier general and was transferred to Morristown, New Jersey, where he was active in the campaigns of Brandywine, Germantown, and Valley Forge. Subsequently Wayne took part in the battles of Monmouth and Stony Point in the East. In New York State he was beset by all the problems arising from lack of supplies and dissension in the ranks, complicated by Benedict

Arnold's treasonous acts, which he helped to counteract.

When fighting shifted into the South early in the spring of 1781, Wayne was instructed to move his Pennsylvanians into Virginia, and before Yorktown he commanded two battalions of Pennsylvanians and one of Virginians in cooperation with General Lafayette. Following the battle of Yorktown, Wayne moved southward to aid General Nathanael Greene and to patrol the Georgia Indian frontier. The latter experience was to stand him in good stead in campaigning against the Indians north of the Ohio River. Wayne returned to civil life in 1783 and during the next decade served as a member of several Pennsylvania governmental bodies, including the constitutional ratification convention.

Wayne's big moment of glory on the frontier came in April 1792, when President Washington, facing a crisis with Britain (see JAY'S TREATY), chose him to command western troops in the campaign against the Indians in the Northwest Territory. In this campaign he demonstrated genuine leadership capacity, not only conducting a successful recruiting and training program, but also conducting a careful scouting activity. As Wayne advanced from the Ohio toward the Great Lakes frontier, he established outposts and prepared his rear for maneuvering if necessary. His planning paid big dividends in the battle of FALLEN TIMBERS on August 20, 1794, when the back of Indian resistance was broken. The following year was spent in planning for the execution of the Treaty of GREENVILLE, which was consumated on August 3, 1795. General Wayne survived the treaty-making little more than a year. He died in the western military post at Presque Isle (present-day Erie, Pennsylvania).

See Richard C. Knopf, *Anthony Wayne, A Name in Arms* (1960); Samuel Whitaker Pennypacker, *Anthony Wayne* (1908); John Hyde Preston, *A Gentleman Rebel* (1930); John R. Spears, *Anthony Wayne, Sometimes Called "Mad Anthony"* (1903); and Charles Janeway Stillé, *Major-General Anthony Wayne and the Pennsylvania Line in the Continental Army* (1893).—T. D. C.

W-Bar Ranch. Established in 1883 in Wibaux County fifteen miles northeast of Wibaux by the wealthy Frenchman Pierre Wibaux, this became one of Montana's largest ranches. Wibaux survived the disastrous winter of 1886-87 and shortly thereafter purchased remnants of cattle herds from men forced out of business. During the 1890s his was one of the biggest ranches in the United States. He maintained sixty-five thousand head of stock on a gigantic ranch that reached from eastern Montana to western North Dakota. Wibaux turned to mining in the twentieth century, but the ranch was still in operation in the 1960s.—J. A. S.

Weaver, James Baird (1833-1912). Iowa third-party politician. Although best known as the Populist candidate for president in 1892, Weaver's most important political activities and contributions came before the Populist era. Frontier Ohio was his birthplace; however, while he was quite young, his pioneering parents settled in Iowa. Weaver experienced a poverty-stricken farm boyhood on these frontiers but was obviously not driven to complacency. He was determined to overcome adversity. Joining the California gold rush he drove ox teams and later, by means of a loan acquired at a high rate of interest, financed his way through law school in Cincinnati. A frontier Democrat from birth, he early converted to the free-soil cause and from 1857 on was an active Iowa Republican. At the outbreak of the Civil War he entered the army as a first lieutenant. In May 1864, his enlistment expired, Colonel Weaver returned to Iowa and to the legal profession, where he witnessed the war's end and was brevetted brigadier general of volunteers shortly before Appomattox for his exceptional record.

From 1865 to 1875, Weaver actively engaged in Republican politics and was gradually alienated from the party in the process. In 1866 he was elected district attorney, but was unsuccessful thereafter in several attempts to win his party's nomination for state and congressional offices, despite apparent popularity among the rank-and-file members. Weaver's district was Democratic and he was an ardent prohibitionist. This particular combination probably explains, as much as anything, his failures to gain the party's nomination. His anticorporation stand and his position on the financial question undoubtedly figured in his failure also, as perhaps did some political duplicity employed by party bosses. After 1875, in any case, Weaver developed even stronger reservations about his party's financial policies, and in 1877 he pointed to these as his major reason for disassociating himself from the Republican party. Thereafter, with Democratic help, Weaver was elected to Congress as a Greenbacker in 1878, 1884, and 1886. He quickly became the most noted and articulate spokesman for the Greenback-Labor cause, and, in the ensuing decade, no one struggled more effectively or more persistently for the party's program. Although he actively supported Greenbackism in its entirety, his major concern was financial reform, not just free silver but a complete and badly needed overhaul of the entire system.

His terms in Congress put him on the scene at a time when some critical and little-understood issues were debated. He had much of substance to say about these issues; he could be witty, often perceptive, at times prophetic, and occasionally he combined all three traits. The last was most effectively demonstrated in 1887 when Congress was debating the Interstate Commerce Act. Weaver, an early champion of a federal commission, voted against the act because he believed it had been purposely rendered "obscure and unintelligible." The "hand of Talleyrand," he insisted, had been at work.

Suppose the great Lawgiver had constructed the Ten Commandments with the same uncertainty. Suppose he had said: "Thou shalt not steal; thou shalt not bear false witness; thou shalt not covet—contemporaneously or under substantially similar circumstances and conditions"; or suppose, at the conclusion of the decalogue the following provision had been added: "Provided, however, that upon application to the high priest or ecclesiastical commissioner appointed under the provision of this act persons so designated may be authorized to cheat, steal, bear false witness, or covet, and said commission may from time to time prescribe the extent to which said persons may be relieved from any or all of said commandments." Under such circumstances would not the world have been without moral law from Moses to Cullom and from Mount Sinai to Pike's Peak?

In 1880 Weaver's obvious talents won him the presidential nomination of the Greenback-Labor party. He waged a losing but impressive campaign. Having remained active throughout the 1880s, he quite naturally affiliated with and maintained a leadership position in the Populist party during the 1890s and was its presidential nominee in 1892. For a party that was almost devoid of figures of national prominence, Weaver was a logical and worthy choice. With this seasoned campaigner at the helm, it became the first minor party since the Civil War to break into the electoral column. After the defeat of 1892, Weaver became an influential advocate of fusion with the Democratic party on the basis of the financial question, foreseeing in the move the first real opportunity to alter the financial policies of the national government. Gradually, Weaver, along with many other Populists, became a part of what he believed was a rejuvenated Democratic party. An old yet still vigorous reformer at his death, he believed that Woodrow Wilson's brand of Democratic politics had thoroughly vindicated his life struggle.

See Fred Emeroy Haynes, *James Baird Weaver* (1919).—O. G. C.

Weaverville, California. Ghost town. Weaverville still retains the atmosphere and flavor of the California gold-mining camps of the 1850s. First settled in 1849, when John Weaver discovered gold on Weaver Creek, Weaverville grew rapidly and by 1852 was the capital of the Coast Range diggings. The camp thrived for several decades as a gold camp and transportation center for the northwestern mines. Today it is a quaint museumpiece built around a number of brick and adobe buildings that date from the late 1850s. The town features one of the oldest newspapers in California, a historical museum, and a Chinese Joss House, built in 1864 as a place of worship for several thousand Chinese who worked the nearby gold mines.

See Remi Nadeau, *Ghost Towns and Mining Camps of California* (1965).—R. B. W.

Webb, Walter Prescott (1888-1963). Historian and writer. Born on a farm in Panola County, Texas, Webb eventually settled on the marginal plains of Stephens County. With perhaps less than five years of formal precollege education, he began teaching in one-room country schools. In 1915 he was graduated from the University of Texas. Three years later he joined the university's history department, where, except for visiting professorships, he remained for the rest of his life.

In 1931 Webb published his *The Great Plains*, winner of the Loubat Prize for the best book over a five-year period. In it he argues that Frederick Jackson Turner's West was not the West men actually encountered when they arrived on the Great Plains, having left behind such necessities as axes, water, and long-barreled rifles. Instead, they had to adapt to a world of scant water, short grass, and mounted Indians, perfecting such innovations as the revolver, windmill, and barbed wire to overcome the deficiencies in their new environment. Challenged by historian Fred A. Shannon that his book was not good history, Webb retorted that he looked upon it as art not history, and, therefore, freed from the more detailed demands of history. In the 1950s a national panel of historians chose the book as the most significant historical work by a living author. Frequently hailed as a historian of the Turnerian school, Webb always denied the association, pointing out that he never met Turner and that he purposely refrained from reading his work until he had completed *The Great Plains*, as he wanted that work to be his own and influenced as little as possible by Turner.

Webb's *The Great Frontier* (1952), winner of the 1952 Texas Institute of Letters award, advanced the thesis that Columbus and his explorer-successors came out of a static economic situation in western Europe, threw the two basic ingredients of land and capital out of balance with labor, and touched off a boom whose influence made possible the development of modern free capitalistic democracy. In the twentieth century these ingredients returned to a stable relationship with labor, ending the centuries of boom psychology. Webb attributed the economic, intellectual, and political dislocations of the present century to the fact that boom conditions no longer pertained and that, therefore, the chief element producing constitutional democracy had disappeared. The twentieth century has been a time of searching, testing, and adjusting to a new set of conditions. Webb's thesis was attacked by members of several academic disciplines, particularly historians dealing with Russia east of the Urals. Webb, who believed this work to be superior to his earlier one, argued that several centuries would have to pass before the validity of his thesis could be measured.

He also wrote *The Texas Rangers* (1935), a definitive but overly detailed account, and *Divided We Stand* (1937), which supposedly influenced President Franklin D. Roosevelt's perception of economic necessities of the South. Webb, who considered himself more a writer than historian, also wrote a number of fiction pieces, for which he used a pseudonym, as well as several articles for popular magazines, including *Harper's* and *Reader's Digest*. Despite his somewhat cosmic pretensions in later years, Webb is still regarded mainly as a historian of the West.

His plans for a Ford Foundation-supported television series on American civilization were ended with his death in an auto accident near Austin, although the series was completed by another University of Texas professor. Webb served as director of the Texas State Historical Association, where he conceived the *Handbook of Texas*, the association's first book-publication program, and the "Texas Collection" section of the *Southwestern Historical Quarterly*. He was a charter member and the second fellow of the Texas Institute of Letters, a fellow of the Texas State Historical Association, a member of the Philosophical Society of Texas, and president of the Mississippi Valley Historical Association (1954-55) and of the American Historical Association (1957-58). He was the recipient of two Guggenheim fellowships, various university research grants, honorary degrees from the University of Chicago, Southern Methodist University, and Oxford University, and awards from the American Council of Learned Societies as well as the federal Bureau of Reclamation for distinguished service to conservation. Always concerned with water problems, Webb also served as special adviser to Senate Majority Leader and later Vice-President Lyndon B. Johnson. He was Harmsworth Professor at Harvard (1942-43) and Harkness Professor at the University of London (1938). His Great Frontier thesis was the sole topic under examination at the 1958 meeting of the Second International Congress of Historians of the United States and Mexico.

See Walter Rundell, Jr., "Walter Prescott Webb: Product of Environment," *Arizona and the West* (Spring 1963).—J. B. F.

Weber, John H. (1799-1859). Fur trader. Weber was born in Denmark but ran away to sea and eventually came to the United States. An early associate of Andrew Henry and William H. Ashley, he joined the latter in the fur business in 1822, probably as a partner. In 1824-25 he led an Ashley expedition that may have discovered the Great Salt Lake, although James Bridger, a member of his party, is usually credited with the first sighting. Shortly thereafter, he left the fur trade for civilization. Contemporaries describe Weber as a man of commanding presence and moody temperament.

See Dale L. Morgan and Eleanor T. Harris, eds., *The Rocky Mountain Journals of William Marshall Anderson* (1967).—G. B. D.

Webster-Ashburton Treaty (1842). Settlement of the Maine boundary. The Webster-Ashburton Treaty of August 9, 1842, concluded at Washington between Secretary of State Daniel Webster and the British plenipotentiary, Lord Ashburton, ended an argument over the northeast boundary between the United States and Canada, which had continued since the Treaty of Paris of 1783. The latter treaty had used the best map of its day, Mitchell's Map of North America, but the Mitchell map contained some guesswork in the area of the present-day northern boundary of the state of Maine, and the boundary at once became uncertain. The north-south gap between British and American claims spread out over 7,697,280 acres. A mixed commission under Jay's Treaty of 1794 established that a river then called the Schoodiac was in truth the St. Croix mentioned in the Treaty of Paris, but beyond running the boundary up the Schoodiac to its source the commission failed. The remainder of the northeast boundary, up around the hump of present-day Maine and New Hampshire and almost straight westward across the top of Vermont and New York to the St. Lawrence River, remained in dispute.

A clause in the Treaty of Ghent of 1814 provided for another mixed commission, which failed, but it also provided that in case of disagreement the two parties should submit their dispute to the arbitration of a friendly sovereign. The king of the Netherlands in 1831 made an award that was not an arbitration but a splitting of the difference (an arbitrator must choose between two contentions, and not make his own arrangement). After this error President Jackson chose to submit the matter to Congress, knowing that Congress would turn the award down. There followed an increasingly dangerous era in the dispute during the 1830s, in the course of which Americans discovered the fertile Aroostook valley and fought the "Roostook War" with the Canadians. Matters reached such an impasse that General Winfield Scott had to go up to Maine to halt the hostilities.

At last the boundary dispute came in 1842 into the hands of Daniel Webster, secretary of state. Webster had no feeling for the territory in dispute, but may have had some feeling for funds, which clearly passed from the hands of his diplomatic opposite, Ashburton, into the hands of some Americans through the agency of Webster's friend Professor Jared Sparks of Harvard. Webster then managed to find maps to support the British position in the dispute, and Sparks took the maps up to Boston and Augusta to convince the authorities in those two places that it would be best to make an accommodation with the British. (Sparks had to consult with officials in Boston because when Maine split off from Massachusetts in 1820, Masssachusetts was to receive half the proceeds from any sale of Maine's public lands.) In the treaty Webster gave the British 893 more square miles than they would have received under the award of the king of the Netherlands. The treaty, incidentally, provided also for separate British and American squadrons to stand off the African coast and prevent the African slave trade. After Webster concluded his treaty, it turned out that there were several maps in existence, at least one of which was available in the John Jay papers in the United States, that proved the correctness of the most extensive American claims in Maine.

See Samuel Flagg Bemis, *John Quincy Adams and the Foundations of American Foreign Policy* (1949); A. B. Corey, *The Crisis of 1830-1842 in Canadian-American Relations* (1941); and W. D. Jones, *Lord Aberdeen and the Americas* (1958).—R. H. F.

Weiser, [Johann] Conrad (1696-1760). Indian diplomat. Weiser was born in the village of Afstaedt near Herrenberg, Germany. He was reared by a stern father and was deeply religious. In his fourteenth year he came to America with his father and seven brothers and sisters and moved toward the frontier. In 1713 Chief Quagnant of the Iroquois Six Nations visited in the Weiser home, and young Conrad went with him to live for eight months with the Indians. Perhaps Weiser was more tempted by the opportunity to get away from a termagant stepmother than by the prospect of adventure with tribesmen of the Six Nations.

The visit with the Indians was the beginning of a half-century of activity as an Indian interpreter and diplomat. Weiser was an apt pupil and he quickly deserted his unhappy home for life in an Indian village near Schoharie, New York. From there he went south to Pennsylvania. Gossip had it that his wife, whom he married in 1720, was a Mohawk maiden, but his biographer denies this on the basis of deductive logic rather than historical fact.

From 1731 on, Weiser served on innumerable occasions as a trusted interpreter of both whites and Indians. He was present at many councils between the Six Nations and the governors of Pennsylvania, Maryland, and Virginia. In 1737 he was instrumental in conning the Delaware Indians out of twelve hundred square miles of land through the notorious "Walking Purchase." In 1741 he was appointed a justice of the peace in Lancaster, County, Pennsylvania, and was an Indian agent for the province. He was associated for a time with the Moravian missionary David Zeisberger and accompanied Count Zinzendorf on a preaching mission to the Indian frontier.

Weiser was an active participant in events leading up to the calling of the Lancaster Conference of 1744. In the conference itself, which led to the treaty agreement of June 22, he acted as interpreter and helped to distribute the governors' presents and otherwise cultivate the goodwill of the Indians. In future years, he performed many missions to the Indians along the western frontier and about the headwaters of the Ohio.

At the outbreak of the French and Indian War Weiser was appointed a colonel of militia in 1755, but by that time his health was too poor to permit him to accept the honor. For the next five years Weiser was too weak to be active, even though these were years of stirring activity in the western woods. He died at his home in Reading, Pennsylvania, from an attack of cholera.

See C. Z. Weiser, *The Life of (John) Conrad Weiser, the German Pioneer, Patriot, and Patron of Two Races*, abridg. ed. (1899); and Conrad Weiser, *Journal of a Tour to the Ohio, August 11 to October 2, 1748*, ed. by Reuben Gold Thwaites, Early Western Travels series, vol. I (1904). —T. D. C.

Weitzel, Godfrey. See GREAT LAKES, MEN OF THE.

Wellman, Paul I. (1898-1966). Novelist and historian. Wellman was born in Enid, Oklahoma, but spent ten years of his childhood in Angola (Portuguese West Africa). In 1918 he received a B.A. from Fairmount College, now the University of Wichita, and he lived in Wichita until 1936. From 1919 to 1936 he worked for Wichita newspapers. During this time Wellman began writing both factual accounts of and fiction about western life and history, and he continued his writing during his employment, from 1936 to 1944, with the Kansas City *Star*. In 1944 he moved to Los Angeles, where he lived until his death. There he first became a screenwriter, but shortly gave that up in order to devote his time exclusively to western writing.

Wellman was one of the few recent authors in the western tradition to make a reputation both as a narrative historian and as a writer of fiction. His *Death on Horseback* (1947), a history of the Indian wars of the Great Plains put together from his earlier *Death on the Prairie* (1934) and *Death in the Desert* (1935), and his history of the cattle industry, *The Trampling Herd* (1939), together with his account of the early explorations of the Southwest, *Glory, God and Gold* (1954), earned him a considerable reputation as a chronicler of Great Plains history. Indeed, the fact that Wellman was so deeply versed in western history explains the compelling quality of his fiction, which reads as though it were sober fact even though it often is not. Wellman was fond of writing a fictional account that is true to the probabilities of western history, even though it cannot in actuality be documented; he wrote history at one remove from fact. Hence his *Broncho Apache* (1936) is a fictional attempt to write the life of Massai, a semilegendary Apache about whose actual life almost nothing is known, and his *The Comancheros* (1952) is a fictional history of a group of mysterious white renegades of whom little is remembered except for the fact of their trading with the Comanche and stirring up Indian unrest in Texas in the 1840s. *The Bowl of Brass* (1944)—the first in chronology of Wellman's novels about Jericho, a fictional Kansas town—is true to the facts of corrupt politics in the boomtowns of the Great Plains, and his *Jubal Troop* (1939) is a kind of fictional travelogue through the West of 1880-1910. The hero of this novel is consecutively a cowboy, a rancher, a trader with Mexican *bandidos*, and an oil magnate. Wellman's profound knowledge of western history enabled him to tell the hero's story as factual biography, even though it is totally fictional. This very real ability to create a western world that is profoundly true in essence though fictional in its particulars made Wellman one of the very best historical novelists writing within the western tradition.—J. K. F.

Wells, Henry (1805-1878). Businessman. Wells was born at Thetford, Vermont, the son of a Presbyterian minister. In 1814 the family moved to central New York, where he attended school and worked on a farm near Fayette. Thrown upon his own resources at sixteen, he was apprenticed to a tanning and shoemaking firm in Palmyra. He married Sarah Daggett; Sarah died in October 1859, and two years later Wells took a second wife, Mary Prentice of Boston.

In 1836 Wells turned to transportation for a living and worked with companies operating on the Erie Canal and the Great Lakes and then with railroad lines in Pennsylvania. At that time, the express business had not begun. William F. Harnden, its originator, employed Wells as his agent in Albany for the express business between there and New York City. Within two years, Wells formed a partnership with George E. Pomeroy and Crawford Livingston to operate between Albany and Buffalo and assumed the responsibility for serving as the messenger, making a weekly trip via railroads and stages. Wells carried letters for six cents each or one dollar for twenty, while the United States Post Office charged two to four times as much. With another partner, James W. Hale, he offered a through service from Bangor, Maine, via Boston to New York. Public support of his services forced the United States to pass legislation in 1845 authorizing five-cent postage.

In 1844 Wells formed with William G. Fargo a partnership known as the Western Express, and extended his business first to Detroit and later to Cincinnati, Chicago, and St. Louis. He sold his interest in this western business in 1846 and moved from Buffalo to New York to supervise the expansion of service overseas to London and Paris. By 1850 competition on the important route between Albany and Buffalo was so keen that a merger of three companies—Wells and Company; Butterfield and Wasson; and Livingston, Fargo and Company—was made under the name of the American Express Company. Wells served as president for eighteen years.

In 1852 Wells was instrumental in organizing another joint stock company, WELLS, FARGO & CO. to enter the express and banking business in California. Edwin B. Morgan, Wells's neighbor in Aurora, New York, was named president. This West Coast firm had phenomenal success in the express and banking business, establishing its dominance in California by 1855 and a virtual monopoly in western express by 1860. Through the purchase of the Pioneer Stage Company and investment in the Overland Mail Company, Wells, Fargo & Co. gradually became interested in nearly all aspects of western communication and transportation by 1866. With the completion of the transcontinental railroad in 1869 Wells Fargo's stagecoach operations were quickly brought to a close, but its express business expanded with the development of the West and ultimately was extended to the East Coast. East of the Missouri River, the Merchants Union Express Company challenged the dominance of the American Express Company and in 1868 a merger was negotiated, the American Merchants' Union Company, at which time Wells retired from the presidency, having made a fortune.

The remaining years of Wells's life were spent in extensive travels and in supporting favorite charities. He invested in the First National Bank of Aurora and in the Cayuga Lake Railroad, serving as president of both. In 1868 he founded Wells Seminary for young ladies, now known as Wells College. Throughout his life, Wells had suffered from a speech impediment, and he became interested in various methods for alleviating stammering, establishing schools in several cities for children thus afflicted. He died in Glasgow, Scotland.

See Alvin F. Harlow, *Old Waybills* (1934); Edward Hungerford, *Wells Fargo: Advancing the American Frontier* (1949); and A. L. Stimson, *History of the Express Business* (1881).—W. T. J.

Wells, Merle W. (1918-   ). Historian. Born in Lethbridge, Alberta, Canada, Wells attended the College of Idaho and then pursued graduate studies at the University of California under the direction of John D. Hicks, a well-known western historian and follower of Frederick Jackson Turner. In 1942 Wells began teaching history at the College of Idaho and, after interrupting his teaching for further graduate training, in 1950 joined Alliance College for six years. He then became a consultant until 1959, when he was appointed historian and archivist for the Idaho State Historical Society. After 1965 he also held an appointment in the history department of Boise State College.

Wells contributed much to our knowledge of Idaho history. With Merrill D. Beal, he wrote *History of Idaho* (1959) and various articles in historical journals that dealt with the creation of Idaho Territory, anti-Mormon sentiment in late nineteenth-century Idaho, and the impact of the Nonpartisan League in Idaho after World War I. His studies of mining in Idaho culminated in *Rush to Idaho* (1961) and *Gold Camps and Silver Cities* (1963). He also compiled *Idaho: Student's Guide to Localized History* (1965).

Wells's major contributions to western history were to improve the systematic collection of historical sources for Idaho history and, through his own research, to develop and clarify various aspects of the history of the state.—G. D. N.

Wells, Fargo & Co. Freighting and banking company. Wells, Fargo & Co. was established as a joint stock association in New York during March 1852 by a group of experienced eastern expressmen, among them Henry WELLS and William G. FARGO, to take advantage of express, banking, and other business opportunities in California. Within two months the company had completed its organization whereby mails, papers, packages, and freight of all description could be conveyed between the eastern seaboard and San Francisco, thence to and from the mining camps in California. Business got under way in California in July 1852. The company quickly established a network of express lines by purchasing numerous smaller express services, some of which operated their own stages, and contracting with other organizations to transport packages entrusted to Wells Fargo. Upon the failure of Adams and Company of California in 1855, Wells, Fargo & Co. attained supremacy in the express field (see ADAMS EXPRESS COMPANY). At this time the company operated 55 offices scattered throughout the mining districts, and the number was steadily increased to 147 by 1860, when the company had attained a monopoly of the express business.

From the outset, Wells, Fargo & Co. was engaged not only in express services but also in banking. Significant profits were made from the traffic in gold dust. Pony express riders dispatched to the gold camps could buy dust at fifteen or sixteen dollars an ounce and sell it at the United States mint for eighteen dollars. The company became involved in general banking, receiving money on deposit, making collections, extending credit on various bases, issuing bills of exchange in favor of payees in eastern cities to whom the customers in the mining camp wished to remit, and taking the responsibility for the execution, recording, and delivery of important business documents. In the California banking crisis of 1855, the company sustained sizable loan losses but nevertheless weathered the storm that caused the failure of most of its banking competitors, and the company emerged with greatly enhanced position and prestige. In addition to the banking headquarters in San Francisco, branches were established in Sacramento, Stockton, and Marysville, California.

Stagecoaches were employed by the company in forwarding gold dust, business papers, and express. Louis McLane, general manager of Wells, Fargo & Co. in California after 1855, organized a partnership known as Louis McLane & Co. that owned the Pioneer Stage Company operating between Sacramento and Carson City and Virginia City, Nevada. The Pioneer Stage Company also had a contract to deliver the overland mail on this western sector of the route after 1861. In December 1864 Wells, Fargo & Co. purchased the Pioneer Stage Company for $175,000 and thenceforth became directly engaged in stagecoach operations in addition to its express and banking business. Besides the extensive stagecoach operations for mails, express, and passengers on the trans-Sierra route, Wells, Fargo & Co. operated between 1864 and 1868 a "fast freight service" (soon changed to a "fast freight and passenger service") from the western Nevada mining camps to the railhead at Latrobe, California.

From the time Wells, Fargo & Co. entered the express business in California the company never hesitated to send a rider on horseback to deliver or pick up an important message, treasure, or package. Several routes were regularly run by pony express riders in Placer County in 1852. Between 1861 and 1865, in four different periods, the company operated a pony express service on the trans-Sierra route to assist businessmen who were interested in speed, particularly on those occasions when stage and rail communication was uncertain during the winter.

Wells, Fargo & Co. also had a financial interest in the OVERLAND MAIL COMPANY from its beginning in 1857. An interlocking directorate between the two companies existed, and Wells, Fargo & Co. served as banker, advancing the necessary funds to outfit the western end of the route from El Paso, Texas, to San Francisco, and otherwise extending general credit, both secured and unsecured. Before 1861, when the mail service was moved to the central route and run on a daily basis, Wells, Fargo & Co.'s financial stake in the enterprises was so great that it directed policy and controlled personnel. The company obtained an exclusive privilege to handle all express service west of Salt Lake City on the overland route. Moreover, the 1861 overland mail contract provided for the continuation of the trans-Missouri Pony Express on the central route, for the first time with government subsidy. Wells, Fargo & Co. assumed responsibility for administering and advertising this service during the last third of its existence.

In 1866 a grand consolidation of all the major express and stagecoach lines west of the Missouri was negotiated whereby Ben Holladay sold out his extensive interests. The Overland Mail Company, the Pioneer Stage Company, and several express companies merged into a corporation under the name and control of Wells, Fargo & Co. At this point a stagecoach department comparable to those in the express business and banking was established in the company. Communication and transportation services were maintained by Wells, Fargo & Co. between the terminals of the Central Pacific Railroad in California and western Nevada and of the Union Pacific Railroad in eastern Nevada and Utah Territory. This service continued until all sections of the two lines were completed and joined in 1869. The company also operated branch stage lines to carry mail, express, and passengers to and from the railroad into Idaho and Montana and into the mining camps of Nevada, Utah, and Colorado.

In California, Wells, Fargo & Co., through the Pioneer Stage Company, had purchased the route of the California Stage Company from the railhead of the Central Pacific into Virginia City. As noted, stagecoach connections were maintained over the crest of the Sierra Nevada as some crews built eastward and other railroad gangs constructed westward from Reno. In March 1867 Wells, Fargo & Co. officials decided to place the company name on all the stagecoaches operating on the Nevada-California route, replacing the Pioneer Stage Company name, and thus make them comparable in appearance to the new Concord stagecoaches that had been purchased for service in the Great Basin and Rocky Mountain region. These stagecoaches bearing the Wells Fargo name ran on both routes to the north and south of Lake Tahoe.

Completion of the transcontinental railroad in 1869, three years earlier than anticipated, necessitated a reorganization of the express business. Meanwhile, Wells, Fargo & Co. had been a highly successful enterprise earning sizable profits for its owners; furthermore, they were able to meet the problems of retrenchment and liquidation of stage-line equipment.

Three books on Wells, Fargo & Co. are available: Lucius Beebe and Charles Clegg, *U.S. West: The Saga of Wells Fargo* (1949) a popular and sympathetic illustrated presentation; Edward Hungerford, *Wells Fargo: Advancing the American Frontier* (1949), a readable account dealing with well-known episodes; and Noel M. Loomis, *Wells Fargo: An Illustrated History* (1968), more recent but of minimal historical value. Oscar O. Winther, *Express and Stagecoach Days in California* (1936), is a pioneering, scholarly investigation. The most recent interpretation using new documentation will be found in W. Turrentine Jackson, "A New Look at Wells Fargo, Stagecoaches, and the Pony Express," *California Historical Society Quarterly* (December 1966), and "Wells Fargo Stagecoach Lines Across the Sierra," in the same journal.—W. T. J.

Welsh, Herbert (1851-1941). Humanitarian. Welsh

was the grandson of John Welsh, a wealthy Philadelphia merchant and minister to England. He graduated from the University of Pennsylvania in 1871, studied art in Paris for two years, and then returned to Philadelphia, where he immediately took up a succession of cultural and humanitarian interests while living on the family fortune.

Welsh soon focused his attention on Indian affairs, and in December 1882 brought some prominent residents of Philadelphia together to form the INDIAN RIGHTS ASSOCIATION. For the next thirty-four years he served it as corresponding secretary, for eleven years thereafter as president, and until his death as president emeritus. The structure of the association allowed Welsh almost total control over its operations, which, in turn, gave him an unrivaled position of leadership within the larger humanitarian movement devoted to Indian affairs.

Welsh was in full accord with the theory of assimilating the Indian into American life, then current among the humanitarians, and he was convinced that the goal would indeed be accomplished with the proper laws and perfected administration of them. This could be insured only by an informed and aroused public. Under his leadership, therefore, the Indian Rights Association concentrated on investigating and publicizing conditions on the reservations.

It was this somewhat limited program that hampered the association's effectiveness in the 1890s. Welsh was instrumental in rallying support for the DAWES SEVERALTY ACT in 1887, but thereafter persisted in the belief that it was the final solution to the Indian problem. He viewed the difficulties encountered by the allotment policy in the 1890s simply as evidence of corrupt administration, and concentrated the whole effort of his association behind the plan to introduce civil service rules into the Indian Service. Once this had been done he believed that time alone would accomplish the assimilation of the Indian, and he turned his attention more and more to other interests, such as the reform of municipal government.

Although his greater vision of a vigorous and self-sufficient Indian citizenry never materialized, in part because of the inadequacy of his own work, Welsh made a significant contribution in arousing public interest, long dormant, in the plight of the Indian, and his investigations of frauds on the reservations doubtless improved the lot of many tribes.—E. A. G.

West, Oswald (1873-1960). Oregon politician. West, Democratic governor of Oregon from 1911 to 1915, championed the "Oregon System" (see OREGON), conservation, and penal reform. Consolidating the gains of his Democratic predecessor, Governor George Chamberlain (1903-09), West brought new strength to the governor's office. Republican legislators, long accustomed to little interference and less direction from the executive branch, found themselves forced to pass far-reaching prison reform legislation and other measures or face the governor's veto and his "resort to the people" via the Oregon System. West vetoed sixty-three bills in 1911 alone.

West came to the governorship with a strong record as a reformer. Appointed state land agent (1903) by Governor Chamberlain, for whom he had campaigned, West initiated a number of changes of which the overall

effect was to reduce the bureaucratic distance between the sale of lands and the purchaser, thus eliminating go-betweens and illegal fees. He uncovered a land "steal" involving the state's Republican senator, John H. Mitchell, which brought President Theodore Roosevelt's special prosecutor, Francis J. Heney, to Oregon. Mitchell was convicted. In 1907 West accepted a four-year appointment with the Oregon Railroad Commission, where his zeal for reform extended to disguising himself as a cowboy to investigate shipping affairs firsthand. As governor he was equally persevering. He once sent his personal secretary to a mining town, Copperfield in Wallowa County, where lawlessness and immorality flourished and had the town closed down by executive declaration.

In 1917 West ran for United States senator against George McNary, whom he had appointed to the Oregon Supreme Court four years before. West, running with the poorly organized Democratic party, lost the election.

An articulate and talented storyteller, West made contributions to the *Oregon Historical Quarterly* that are guides to parts of Oregon's history and to his own. —R. J. L.

West, Walter Richard (1912-   ). Cheyenne artist. Born in Darlington, Oklahoma, West is best known for a series of paintings illustrating the New Testament in Plains Indian settings, but he also did wood sculpture and ceramics and made Indian flutes. He was the first Indian to receive both a bachelor of fine arts and a master of fine arts degree from the University of Oklahoma. An art teacher at Phoenix (Arizona) Indian School when World War II began, West enlisted in the navy as painter, third class! After the war he returned to Phoenix and was then appointed art director at Bacone College in Oklahoma, one of his alma maters, where he taught for many years.

West's art has been exhibited internationally and at the Smithsonian Institution and the Philbrook Art Center. He won the Waite Phillips trophy and many other jury awards. He illustrated several books.—C. C.

Westermeier, Clifford P. (1910-   ). Historian. Westermeier was born in Buffalo, New York. Interested in art as a child, he studied art and art history at the University of Buffalo. In 1935 he began teaching at the Buffalo School of Fine Arts, where he remained for the next nine years, also serving as a lecturer at the University of Buffalo. Meanwhile, he continued graduate studies in history at the University of Colorado. In 1946 he began his career as a historian, teaching at St. Louis University for two years, Loretto Heights College in the Denver area for three years, and the University of Arkansas, where he remained for the next fourteen years. In 1964 he returned to the West and became a member of the history staff at the University of Colorado.

While studying under Henry D. Abbott at the University of Buffalo, Westermeier became interested in the cattle industry. This interest was intensified when he went to Colorado, where western historian Colin B. Goodykoontz taught. Meanwhile, during his travels through the West he made numerous sketches and paintings of the inhabitants and the scenery, and while acquainting himself with his subjects, Westermeier found himself more and more immersed in the history of the region and some of its distinctive characteristics, such as cowboys and the cattle industry.

This interest in cattle was reflected in his writing. He wrote *Man, Beast, and Dust: The Story of the Rodeo* and *Trailing the Cowboy* in 1958 and published a number of articles on the cowboy's role in the cattle industry.

Utilizing his early training in art, Westermeier edited a collection of striking photographs concerning the early history of Colorado, *Colorado's First Portrait: The Nineteenth-Century Scene* (1970.

Westermeier's contribution to western history has been to add interesting details to the existing knowledge about the cattle industry and nineteenth-century Colorado.—G. D. N.

Western Apache Indians. See APACHE INDIANS.

Westerners, The. A unique international fellowship of "pro" and "buff" devotees of the lore and history of the American West—in complete agreement with Lord Bryce's observation that "the West is the most American part of America." The organization has nearly a hundred local units in North America and Western Europe. Each is autonomous and is usually known as a Corral, but their "brands" are registered by "the home ranch," at Tucson, Arizona, called Westerners International. Westerners helped to start the scholarly Western Historical Association at Santa Fe in 1961, with which it maintains a close relationship.

Corrals are as paradoxical as a platypus. All are oriented to the American West. They revel in history but are not historical societies. They are as informal as a Lions Club at noon feeding-time, yet they are not a service club, and they meet at night. In "cow culture" jargon, a Corral is a bunch of males mostly—although some admit selected "sidesaddlers"—who meet monthly, usually, to chat and chomp and after a scholarly speech to praise, haze, and even "spook" their speaker. Westerners take their West seriously but never grimly. They ride with an easy rein.

Some regional cults resemble Minerva, who sprang from Jupiter's computered brow clothed, armed, nubile. Not The Westerners. They have a doglegged descent that began in Stockholm in 1937 when a wandering writer and ex-professor named Leland D. Case vibrated with approval at the outdoor museum called Skansen. It had been a pivotal factor in Sweden's cultural and economic renaissance. He sensed psychological consanguinity between this indigenous Swedish creativity and the Emersonian self-reliance of the pioneers of the upper Missouri River valley who were badgered in those "dirty thirties" by grasshoppers and overdue mortgages. America's "Middle Border" was what Hamlin Garland had dubbed this region, and the name was borrowed for the Friends of the Middle Border, which in 1939 started a Skansen-like social-history museum and art gallery at Mitchell, South Dakota, on the campus of Dakota Wesleyan University.

Garland himself gave it his blessing. Others also serving on its board of directors or as advisers included novelist Stewart Edward White; Nebraska's poet laureate, John Neihardt; Mount Rushmore's sculptor, Gutzon Borglum; "Ash Can School" artist John Sloan; and historian James Truslow Adams, chancellor of the American Academy of Arts and Letters, who characterized the project as "a fine example of democracy at work, of what I have called 'the American Dream.' "

Of all Middle Borderlanders, none was more pleased with the museum-gallery in South Dakota than those who had left the area and were living elsewhere. In Chicago, the nostalgia of these émigrés was peculiarly acute and articulate. When one former "Black Hiller" was advised by ear-weary friends to return, his answer was prompt and complete: "Wish I could! But I'm just an ordinary guy and have to make a living. Out there they're too smart for me!"

From such interest was born a Chicago chapter of Friends of the Middle Border. By functional fission and through the energetic effort of journalists Case and Elmo Scott Watson, Chicago soon had a group of western history buffs calling themselves the first Corral of Westerners. Its organizational meeting on Feburary 25, 1944, drew fourteen men whose vocations ranged from artist to editor, elevator mechanic to steel corporation vice president. The speaker was Clarence Paine of Beloit, Wisconsin, a college librarian who presented "a short but unlearned treatise on Calamity Jane."

The Westerners spurned such organizational impedimenta as a constitution with bylaws, preferring Old Traditions—which, they vouchsafed, could be adopted at the drop of a sombrero or the clank of a spur. Minutes of previous meetings need not be read, they decided, certainly not if tucked away handily in the mimeographed *Brand Book*. The tooth of time has nibbled, however, and now Corrals frequently incorporate and boast of printed periodicals—but they didn't start with such foolish foofaraw.

The Chicago Corral maintained its umbilical tie with Friends of the Middle Border a few years, but separation was accelerated when a second Westerner unit started at Denver in 1945. Interest was generated spontaneously, it seemed, as new Corrals came on fast—in St. Louis, Los Angeles, New York, Tucson, Laramie, and South Dakota's Black Hills. In 1954 the movement leaped the Atlantic to London, and overseas units have since been established in France, Germany, and Sweden. Recently North American interest in The Westerners has overflowed the United States into Canada and Mexico.

Why? Perhaps conservationist-author Emerson Hough sensed the rationale when he exclaimed, "The Frontier! There is no word in the English language more stirring, more intimate, or more beloved." For the frontier is more than a historical phenomenon of the Rockies running from Alaska into Mexico. Derived from Latin *frons*, "forehead," it holds the concept of free men challenged by new conditions—facing the future thoughtfully and boldly. In Germany a psychiatrist links it to the Teutonic quest for *Lebensraum*, but a Paris Westerner explained his fascination with the American Indian by a continuing French interest in the "noble savage" of Jean Jacques Rousseau.

But such philosophizing fades when Westerners meet. Typically, they see history in terms of biography. They would not fault Sir Max Beerbohm's aphorism that "Extraordinary saints grow faint to posterity, whilst quite ordinary sinners pass vividly down the ages."

The half-savage and rank-smelling beaver-trapping ilk of Jedediah Smith, first American to cross overland to California (1826), get attention; so do such military men as George Armstrong Custer and their adversaries, *les Indiens*. California Corrals keep green the memories of the 1849 gold rush which, they occasionally remind themselves, has been cited for sheer historic drama as second only to the Crusades. Southwestern Corrals are fascinated by the *conquistadores*. Westerners at Nashville have been known to ponder upon Tennessee characters who emigrated to Texas and, so 'twas said, thereby raised the cultural, moral, and social level of both states. The badman and his nemesis, the lawman, personalized by such worthies as Big Nose George, Black Bart, Wild Bill Hickok, and Buffalo Bill Cody, hold endless possibilities for roundup programs.

Top-scoring popularity ratings go to the cowboy, however. The lush heraldry of the open range, with the creak of straining leather and the clank of spurs, has elicited nomenclature with all the creative exuberance celebrated by H. L. Mencken as typically American. The Los Angeles Corral, for example, backs up its topman, the Sheriff, with a Registrar of Marks & Brands, Round-up Foreman, Keeper of the Chips, Trail Boss, Daguerreotype Wrangler, and "Rep" (for Representative). Washington's Potomac Corral has a Chuck Wrangler, Range Rider, Faro Dealer, and His Honor the Judge. The Yale Corral at New Haven sports an Honorary Calamity Jane!

Westerner nomenclature, it may be well said, carries the aroma of corral and cuspidor. And with it goes joshing of the Lincolnesque stripe. Pedants might be surprised that Plato said it, but no Westerner would fault his aphorism that "Unmitigated seriousness is always out of place in human affairs." Merry moments mingle with the serious. When the late raconteur J. Frank Dobie howdied with Tucson Westerners, he puffed on his bulldog pipe with delight when named "Chief Grand Exalted Coyote—with the right to howl whenever you come to town!" The Potomac Corral warmed ninety-year-old Senator Carl Hayden with a canvas painted by Westerner Bill Loechel, depicting him as a young Arizona sheriff. He was dubbed "Westerner of the Century."

As naturally as a steer munching buffalo grass, Westerners have enriched literature on the West. The *Buckskin Bulletin* is issued by Westerners International at its headquarters at Tucson, Arizona. Several Corrals publish speeches in periodicals inspired by Chicago's *Brand Book*, edited by scholar and encyclopedist Don Russell. Corrals in Abilene, Denver, San Diego, Stockton, Tucson, Los Angeles, and other cities issue hardbound volumes. Westerners are so prolific with periodicals and books that Dr. Llerena Friend of the University of Texas library whimsically lamented that "a book wrangler who wished to round up all of them would have to sell his saddle."

If the world is going cowboy-minded, the reasons include The Westerners along with western books and movies and TV "oaters." The hired man on horseback—to use Eugene Manlove Rhodes's term—is beginning to eclipse Uncle Sam as the folk symbol for America, and this The Westerners would also approve. They even quote journalist François Pasqualini, who, in a dispatch from La Camargue, where France has its own cattle country, declared that *le cowboy* "is the United States's best ambassador at large."—L. D. C.

Western Federation of Miners. Labor union. Founded in 1893, the Western Federation of Miners (WFM) was a product of the warfare between capital and labor that shook the western mining industry in the late nineteenth century. The event that led to the union's creation was the violent confrontation in 1892 between a local miners' union and a mine operators' association in the Coeur d'Alene mining district of northern Idaho. Miners were killed, a company-guard barracks was dynamited, and mills and mines were captured by strikers. The strike was broken only with the intervention of federal and state troops, who concentrated the unionists in an oppressive "bullpen."

In reaction to the Coeur d'Alene defeat, representatives from local miners' unions throughout the West met in 1893 in Butte, Montana, long a center of militant unionism, to found the WFM. Fumbling leadership by men of the Butte miners' union was in a few years' time supplanted by an aggressive new president, Edward Boyce, who served from 1896 to 1902. After the turn of the century Charles A. Moyer, as president, and William D. HAYWOOD, as secretary, emerged as the dominant figures in the union. Immediately after its founding the WFM became a major factor in the western industrial and class warfare from which it sprang. The new union was soon embroiled in strikes in Cripple Creek and Leadville, Colorado (1894), in the Coeur d'Alene area again, and in Telluride, Colorado (1901). Violence escalated in the Coeur d'Alene trouble spot in 1899 as the WFM's drive against the large Bunker Hill and Sullivan silver-mine complex resulted in the destruction of the company's concentrator at Wardner, Idaho. Again federal troops were sent in. Strikers were locked in the hated bullpens, and military occupation of the district continued until 1901.

Despite the repeated violence in the Coeur d'Alene region, the cockpit of the WFM's struggle against the mine owners was in Colorado, where a massive vendetta flamed in 1903-04. It began with a WFM strike in Colorado City, which extended to Cripple Creek (see CRIPPLE CREEK STRIKE). Eventually a campaign of mine owners, state authorities, and a vigilante-type citizens' alliance subdued the WFM with what has been called the most systematic use of violence by management in American labor history.

Following the crushing defeat in Colorado, the WFM attempted to recoup its fortunes by joining a transcendent radical union, the INDUSTRIAL WORKERS OF THE WORLD (IWW), in whose founding in Chicago in 1905 the WFM took a leading role. In 1905 former Idaho governor Frank Steunenberg, who had taken certain antiunion actions in the Coeur d'Alene troubles, was assassinated. Harry Orchard admitted to planting the bomb that killed Steunenberg and implicated WFM officials Haywood and Moyer and a WFM ally, George Pettibone, all of whom went on trial in 1907. After a sensational defense by the famous Chicago lawyer Clarence Darrow, the three men won a notable acquittal. But behind the solid front presented at the trial, internal tensions were building in the WFM. A widening chasm between the increasingly radical Haywood and a more conservatively minded group headed by Moyer led to the victory of the Moyer faction. The following decade of shifts and setbacks left the WFM in a seriously weakened state. In 1907 the WFM left the IWW (which thereafter claimed the energies of Haywood), and in 1911 it returned to the American Federation of Labor (AFL), to which it had briefly belonged in 1896-97. On the strike front, losing campaigns in Goldfield, Nevada

(1907), and the upper Michigan copper district (1913) were followed by a costly conflict with the Butte miners' union (1913-14). In 1916 the WFM changed its name to the International Union of Mine, Mill, and Smelter Workers and dropped the concept of class struggle from its preamble in favor of an emphasis upon better hours, wages, and working conditions. Although eclipsed by the bravura of "Big Bill" Haywood, the WFM had an important leader in the colorless but dogged Charles A. Moyer, who served as president from 1902 to 1926. The evolution in Moyer's outlook mirrored the union's development from its violent, radical formative years, to moderate middle age, to post-World War I dormancy.

Section 7(a) of the National Industrial Recovery Act (1933) encouraged labor union organizing activity and the mine, mill, and smelter workers' union revived throughout the West. The resurgence was exemplified when the gigantic Anaconda Copper Mining Company of Montana recognized the union after a long strike. In time the union went into the newly formed Congress of Industrial Organizations (CIO), 1937-38, along with other industrial unions. Controversy returned after World War II with charges of Communist domination. The union was ousted from the CIO and was regarded with hostility by the federal government. With the warning of Communist influence, the renamed International Union of Mine Workers of America has survived in the West as a vigorous independent union.

See Irving Bernstein, *Turbulent Years: A History of the American Worker: 1933-1941* (1970); Vernon H. Jensen, *Heritage of Conflict: Labor Relations in the Nonferrous Metals Industry up to 1930* (1968); and Philip Taft and Philip Ross, "American Labor Violence: Its Causes, Character, and Outcome," in Hugh D. Graham and Ted R. Gurr, eds., *The History of Violence in America* (1969).—R. M. B.

Western Pacific Railroad. The Western Pacific Railroad, which operates about nineteen hundred miles between Salt Lake City and San Francisco and within the state of California, was incorporated in 1903 to fulfill George Gould's dream of a single transcontinental railroad. Always intimately connected with the DENVER AND RIO GRANDE WESTERN RAILROAD, upon which it depended for connections to the East, the Western Pacific did not become a self-supporting railroad until after its reorganization in 1916.

Today the road forms the western portion of an important transcontinental route, with the Denver and Rio Grande and the Burlington (now part of the Burlington Northern), and operates the "Inside Gateway" route from the Pacific Northwest to southern California in conjunction with the Burlington Northern. In receivership during the Depression, the Western Pacific was revitalized by the prosperity of World War II. Since the war considerable progress was made, though rising costs once again placed its future in doubt.

The essential facts about the Western Pacific are covered in Robert G. Athearn, *Rebel of the Rockies: A History of the Denver and Rio Grande Western Railroad* (1962).—A. M.

West Florida. See EAST AND WEST FLORIDA QUESTION.

Westo Indians. The Westo Indians occupied the interior coastal region of Georgia and the lower Carolinas at the time of first English settlement, about 1670. Their population in that period has been estimated at about 1,600. Ranging from their center of power on the Savannah River, the Westo terrorized the smaller tribes from Port Royal to Kayawah, and fear of them facilitated the founding of Charles Town by ensuring the friendship of the coast Indians. After sporadic hostilities, Henry Woodward, the colonial proprietor's agent for Indian trade, in 1674 formed a trading alliance with the Westo, which until 1680 was the cornerstone of the South Carolina Indian system. Well supplied with arms, the Westo nevertheless continued to prey upon the small tribes with whom the English also traded, and out of this situation grew the Westo war of 1680-81. The colonists engaged a band of eastern Shawnee to expel the Westo from the area, and after sharp and bloody fighting the Shawnee succeeded. The remnants of the defeated Westo drifted west and were eventually incorporated into the lower Creek villages on the Ocmulgee and Chattahoochee rivers, sharing the later fate of that tribe.

There is debate among ethnologists over the tribal identity of the Westo. Swanton and Speck have argued convincingly that the Westo were an eastern subtribe of the Yuchi Indians. Others believe they were not Yuchi, but were instead identical to the Rickahockan Indians of Virginia and possibly the southernmost offshoot of the Iroquoian stock.

See Verner Crane, "An Historical Note on the Westo Indians," *American Anthropologist*, vol. 20 (1918), and *The Southern Colonial Frontier* (1928); F. G. Speck, *Ethnology of the Yuchi Indians* (1909); and J. R. Swanton, "Identity of the Westo Indians," *American Anthropologist*, vol. 21 (1921).—P. R. M.

Westport Landing, Missouri. Important center on the Missouri River for transshipment of goods along the SANTA FE AND CHIHUAHUA TRAIL. Westport Landing was founded in the early 1830s on the site of present-day Kansas City, Missouri, by François Chouteau as a trading post for the American Fur Company. In 1833 John C. McCoy established the town of Westport four miles south of Chouteau's outpost, and the two settlements joined hands in exploiting the Santa Fe trade. Supplies were unloaded from steamboats at Westport Landing and hauled to Westport for shipment west. The history of Westport is intertwined with that of the neighboring town of Kansas City, which annexed the smaller community in 1899.

After 1833 Westport Landing succeeded Independence, Missouri, as a center for the Santa Fe trade between the Mississippi valley and New Mexico. It was the loading point for the ox and mule caravans which rolled across the prairie carrying goods for New Mexicans, who were starved for manufactured items and had the gold, silver, and furs to pay for them. Later, Westport also served as a jumping-off point for the overland trails used by settlers moving west, though it was secondary in importance to Independence and St. Joseph, Missouri.

During the flight of the Mormons to Utah in the 1840s Westport was an important collection point. Mormon agents in the East sent overseas immigrants to Westport Landing, where they were provided with teams and wagons for the trip to Utah.

When gold was discovered in California and Colorado, the town found itself the embarkation point for a different breed of men. Thousands of miners awaiting the spring thaw and the trip west were jammed into boardinghouses and hotel rooms in Westport.

Storekeepers took advantage of the situation and inflated their prices mercilessly. Many a miner left his life savings on the town's grocery counters and gambling tables.

The Civil War hurt Westport's trade over the Rocky Mountains and with New Mexico, and after the war, with the growth of railroads, the town was unable to regain the virtual monopoly of the route it enjoyed in the antebellum period. Nonetheless Westport remained a capital of trade to the Southwest until it became part of Kansas City.

See Ray Billington, *The Far Western Frontier* (1956); and Josiah Gregg, *Commerce of the Prairies* (1958).
—R. B. W.

West Virginia, settlement of. "It was a pleasing tho' dreadful sight to see the mountains and Hills as if piled one upon another," wrote the first Englishman in 1671 to record his impressions of western Virginia. Later generations of frontiersmen confronted the Appalachian wilderness with the same mixed feelings of awe and aversion. Consequently most of them passed around or through the present limits of West Virginia in favor of more attractive lands farther west. Those pioneers who braved the mountain frontier established narrow ribbons of settlement along the present Virginia-West Virginia border and planted outposts in the valleys of the Ohio River and its major tributaries, the Monongahela and Great Kanawha. Despite recurrent Indian attacks and the Proclamation of 1763, the major points of later population concentration in West Virginia were occupied between 1730 and 1776. The victory of Andrew LEWIS and his frontier militia at Point Pleasant (1774) ended Indian warfare in the border settlements, but the Ohio valley remained open to attack until the battle of Fallen Timbers (1794).

Two relatively distinct regions developed from these initial settlements. One lay east of the Allegheny Front, a physiographic boundary running parallel to but some twenty to sixty miles west of West Virginia's eastern border. It occupied a series of highland valleys that, except for their smaller size and greater altitude, resembled the central Valley of Virginia, whose social and economic conditions the West Virginia valleys eventually reproduced. The other region lay northwest in bottomlands and foothills along the western rivers and matured in the company of eastern Ohio and western Pennsylvania. The differences between these two regions were important, but so were the similarities. Both contained native-Virginian populations of English, German, and Scotch-Irish descent, the majority of them small farmers and herdsmen, although large farms and slaveholding were more common in the east, as were manufacturing and (after 1850) coal mining in the northwest. Both regions harbored divisions of interest, loyalty, and principle that would produce in each a genuine civil war in 1861, although, again, Confederates predominated in one, Unionists in the other. Moreover, while the two regions were divided by the mountain barriers in their midst, they were also united by the enduring circumstances of the mountain frontier.

Between the eastern and northwestern settlements in western Virginia, and penetrating deep within each of them, lay a wildly beautiful "interior" consisting of the peaks of the Allegheny Mountains and the rugged heartland of the Appalachian Plateau. Avoided by the earliest settlers, this territory was gradually occupied after 1800 by their descendants and by small numbers of latecomers from eastern Virginia, New England, and Europe, who established a "domestic economy" based on subsistence farming and the harvest of forest products. In remote highland districts, frontier characteristics of isolation, privation, and "backwardness" persisted throughout the nineteenth century. During the antebellum decades these conditions were present to some extent everywhere in western Virginia save in the most populous districts along the Ohio and Potomac. Thus, internal differences were defined less by prominent ecological features than by subtler variations in the quality and accessibility of land and by the interpenetration of people who, as the sayings go, "live[d] on the bottom and look[ed] down on the people on top" with those who "raise[d] corn on the hillside and the devil in the valley."

Long before railroads and extractive industries penetrated the interior, the mountain frontier provided the basis of western Virginia's political economy. At the center of temptation for the ambitious and the powerful were millions of acres of wilderness land. The American Revolution eliminated the more extravagant claims of colonial land speculators, but post-revolutionary speculation remained centered among influential eastern merchants and politicians. From the 1780s, however, a trend was evident whereby resident lawyers, surveyors, and public officials deputed by eastern authorities or speculators to supervise the land alienation process began to acquire significant amounts of the land themselves. Western lawyers were further benefited during the early nineteenth century by a growing volume of litigation deriving from uncertain land titles and overlapping claims. Of special importance was reform legislation adopted between 1831 and 1846. It invalidated many earlier claims for nonpayment of taxes and shifted the point of sale of delinquent land from Richmond to the chancery courts of the western counties involved. Writing of the involvement of western lawyers and public officials in land speculation, one local historian noted that "there is no evidence of sharp practices. . . . The old deeds show that the sales of forfeited lands at the Courthouse were always well-advertised." But the isolation of most western districts, plus low literacy rates, poor roads, and limited newspaper circulation and postal service, ensured a minimum of competition at the advertised sales. Equally important, these factors placed a political premium on the itinerant nature of the lawyers' profession, which brought them into frequent personal contact with backwoods constituents, made them the principal bearers of political information and influence and the centers of attention at the sociable quarterly court days.

In these circumstances, there developed in western Virginia a local politico-economic elite whose central figures were circuit-riding lawyers specializing in land litigation and speculation and providing political linkages between the isolated mountain settlements. The oligarchical political institutions of antebellum Virginia tended to make the elite's advantages cumulative and hereditary. Local offices, which until 1851 were appointive and open to nonresidents, provided sinecures for impecunious relatives and training posts for younger ones. The most successful lawyers developed regional influence, extending outward through the interior from courthouse towns such as Clarksburg, Weston, Parkersburg, Charleston, and Lewisburg, and competed with one another for judgeships and seats in the legislature and in Congress. Even after 1851, the *viva voce* method of voting preserved habits of political deference to local notables, while of course the lawyers retained the prerogatives of bar and bench.

With the exception of Philip Doddridge and John S. Carlile, the outstanding leaders of western Virginia—the George JACKSON FAMILY, Charles James Faulkner, Jonathan M. Bennett, George W. Summers, Samuel Price, and Benjamin Smith—were lawyers whose family connections and acreage belied the egalitarian rhetoric of western politics. In this context the recurrent sectional conflict between western and eastern Virginia over such issues as taxation, legislative apportionment, internal improvements, and suffrage restrictions appears to have been as much a struggle for local autonomy for the western elite as a clash between frontier democrats and plantation oligarchs. Two developments of the 1850s—constitutional reforms in 1851, which compromised some sectional issues and provided for the eventual settlement of the key apportionment question, and the reorganization of Virginia politics across earlier sectional and party lines under the leadership of Governor Henry A. Wise—moderated sectional antagonism except among a small number of northwestern spokesmen, such as Carlile and Francis G. PIERPONT. Hence many prominent western leaders followed Virginia into the Confederacy, a decision endorsed by an estimated 35 percent of those westerners who voted in the secession referendum of May 23, 1861. Those leaders who did not "go South" tended to oppose the movement for West Virginia statehood. The separatist leaders, Carlile and Pierpont, in turn repudiated "the Court House cliques" and "leading politicians, both of the East and of the West" and found supporters in 1861 among the farmers, businessmen, and editors of the northwest. The West Virginia Constitution of 1863 sought to trim the power of the antebellum elite by providing for universal education, the township form of local government, a reorganized judiciary, the secret ballot, annual elections, and other democratic controls.

While it derived from earlier sectional conflicts, the statehood movement was thus a movement of new men and, more particularly, of a new political culture emerging in the manufacturing, mining, and commercial farming districts of northwestern Virginia, one that relied upon a literate electorate mobilized by means of modern communications and the techniques of mass political organization. Methodist and other evangelical preachers, another itinerant group with wide contacts, joined in assaulting the older politics of parochialism and deference, carrying the statehood and antislavery messages into the backwoods districts. But separatism was centered in the economically advanced northwestern districts, where citizens responded to universalistic appeals to democracy and nationalism. On this basis, and with the support of federal troops and authorities, the "statemakers" successfully brought West Virginia into the Union on June 20, 1863, as the thirty-fifth state. Otherwise their achievements were remarkably transient.

Rather unwisely, the statemakers ignored Carlile's original proposal for a small state confined to northwestern Virginia and, for complicated political, military, and economic reasons, incorporated into West Virginia wide areas of the interior and eastern regions where Confederate sentiment predominated. When the racial policies of wartime and Reconstruction alienated a significant minority of northwestern Unionists, the founding fathers found themselves confronting a hostile political majority in their own state. The election of 1870 and the constitutional convention of 1872 marked the antebellum leadership's return to power. The convention, meeting in the southern village of Charleston in preference to "ironhearted" Wheeling, discarded the "Yankeefied" institutions of 1863 in favor of Virginian models and restored a modified form of oral voting. The constitution of 1872 became known as "The Lawyers' Constitution" among its critics, who suggested that its land title provisions were "gotten up to make litigation the principal business in West Virginia." While this may not have been the intended result, the new provisions entailed further confusion in land and tax policies and facilitated, under the supervision of "distinguished land attorneys," the eventual transfer of titles and mineral rights from small owners to mining and lumber corporations.

The political culture of old Virginia, modified under the circumstances of the mountain frontier, persisted in parts of West Virginia through the end of the nineteenth century. Gradually the advance of railroads, towns, and modern communications eroded the old culture and fostered the growth of modern political organizations throughout the state. These were no longer led by men like the statemakers, however, but by representatives of the new extractive industries. By 1900 a quartet of big industrialists—Stephen B. ELKINS, Henry G. Davis, Johnson N. CAMDEN, and Nathan B. Scott—had reorganized West Virginia politics in a manner that was aptly described as a bipartisan "merger" operated by and for the state's largest industrial firms and railroads. The new regime continued the antebellum policies of low taxation for the benefit of vested property interests, further neglected educational and other public facilities, and encouraged the extraction of fuels and raw materials with a minimum of local investment and a maximum of environmental destruction. The political economy of West Virginia remained oligarchical and colonial and its social and economic development no less at variance with national standards than had been the case in antebellum times. The "arrested frontier" of modern "Appalachia" is one of the results.

The above account differs substantially in emphasis from other treatments of early West Virginia history. Otis K. Rice, *The Allegheny Frontier: West Virginia Beginnings, 1730-1830* (1970), offers important insights into the role of land speculation and stresses the frontier roots of modern "Appalachia." Charles H. Ambler, *Sectionalism in Virginia from 1776 to 1861* (1910), is a classic account of sectional politics by a gifted student of Frederick Jackson Turner. Richard O. Curry, *A House Divided: Statehood Politics and the Copperhead Movement* (1964), is a revisionist work that, although it avoids sociological and economic analyses, affronts traditionalists by its emphasis on political differences within the Unionist camp. Three valuable compilations of documents are C. H. Ambler, F. H. Atwood, and W. B. Mathews, eds., *Debates and Proceedings of the First Constitutional Convention of West Virginia*, 3 vols. (1939); Elizabeth Cometti and Festus P. Summers, *The Thirty-fifth State: A Documentary History of West Virginia* (1966); and Virgil A. Lewis, ed., *How West Virginia Was Made* (1909).—J. A. W.

wheat production. Since the early colonial days wheat has been a major product of American farms in terms of acreage devoted to the crop, its marketability and value, and importance as an export. Most colonies encouraged the raising of wheat, even to the extent of giving bounties for it, but some areas of the northern colonies were ill-adapted to its growth. Wheat was less easy to grow in the pioneering stage of farm making when the land was being cleared of the forest cover because it could not be sown around stumps as corn could. Also, wheat was more difficult to prepare for human consumption than corn if a gristmill was not nearby. By 1770 wheat, wheat flour, and bread constituted one fifth of the total exports of the colonies. The most important wheat-growing districts were the limestone areas of southeastern Pennsylvania and the Piedmont of Virginia.

During the National Period (1783-1860) wheat continued to be produced in these areas and in the Genesee valley of New York; by 1839, Ohio, and by 1859, Illinois, Indiana, and Wisconsin had become major producers. New York farmers had erred in sowing wheat on the same land year after year until their fields had become infested with the Hessian fly, the chinch bug, and other parasites, and the yield had so decreased as to make cultivation no longer feasible except in a rotation scheme. Furthermore, grain raised on the cheaper and richer land of the Middle West was coming into the East by way of the canals and was underselling the New York product. Pennsylvania farmers, who followed the best practices of their day—rotating their crops, housing their stock, and utilizing animal manures—continued until late in the century to be major producers of wheat.

Wheat's great advantage was that it brought a higher price in relation to its weight than other grains. Thus it was worthwhile to transport the grain considerable distances overland. Though corn, which always brought a lower price, was easier to start on new land, it was wheat the farmer tried to raise because it was always in demand and was a good cash crop or one that brought fair returns in a barter economy. Much of the land on which farmers tried to grow wheat, as they moved into Ohio, Indiana, and Illinois in the years after 1820, was better adapted to corn, but since there was generally a surplus of corn it brought in little profit and in the farm-making stage a cash crop was needed. From 1839 on the farmers of the Old Northwest struggled and frequently succeeded in raising good crops of wheat. By 1859 the wheat country was definitely west of the Appalachians, the chief producers being Illinois, Indiana, Wisconsin, and Ohio. Gradually, when there were very small yields or near failures caused by weather, diseases, or parasites, midwestern farmers turned to corn.

Meantime, the primitive methods of preparing the soil, sowing, harvesting, cleaning, storing, marketing, milling, and shipping wheat were going through profound changes that relieved the farmer of some of his hardest labor and made it possible for him to sow larger

acreages. He was, however, dependent on hired labor in the harvest season. At the opening of the nineteenth century it was said that the method of raising wheat had not changed much since the time of Christ. Plowing was done with crude wooden implements which barely touched the surface of the land; sowing was by hand; reaping with the sickle, scythe, or cradle; threshing with a flail or with oxen treading out the grain; and winnowing by tossing the grain and chaff in the air to rid it of weed seeds and dirt. Finally, if the grain was not ground in a nearby gristmill for local consumption, it was hauled in great wagons to market. By mid-century the soil was being plowed with cast-iron or steel plows which could bite deeply into the earth, seed was more carefully selected, drills were being experimented with, and the reaper was coming into use—especially in the new centers of wheat production (Cyrus McCormick had moved his reaper manufacturing plant to Chicago in 1847). Railroads were penetrating the wheat country and shortening the long-distance hauls; huge elevators were being erected in Chicago, Buffalo, and other centers to store the grain; wheat was being graded and premium prices paid for the top quality; flour mills with equipment superior to the old gristmills were doing much of the milling; midwestern flour was not only selling throughout the country but was finding expanding markets abroad and was becoming second only to cotton among the agricultural items in American exports. The horse-powered thresher was soon displaced by the steam-powered thresher; then came the self-binder followed by the twine binder on the reaper; and finally, the twentieth century introduced the tractor-drawn combine, which both harvested and threshed the grain.

Specialization in wheat production with greater dependence upon the new equipment made larger farm units necessary. The newly opened areas of central and western Kansas and Nebraska, and the Red River valley of Minnesota and Dakota, were taken up by wheat farmers in the last decades of the nineteenth century. The huge *ranchos* of California and the bonanza farms of Dakota Territory, with their thousands of acres in single farm units, their many hired hands, large herds of horses, and steam-driven threshers, were operated on a scale not generally seen in the United States except on the plantations of the South. Minnesota, North Dakota, and Kansas became the leading wheat-producing states and Minneapolis the flour-milling center of the United States. The building of transcontinental railroads—particularly the Northern Pacific, which was finished in 1883, and the Great Northern, completed a decade later, and their numerous branches—pushed the wheat frontier still farther west. Huge areas of public and railroad lands came to the attention of immigrants from northern Europe and settlers from the Granger states, where land prices had reached such heights as to make it almost impossible for a man to gain ownership of a tract of land over a full lifetime of application.

Settlers approaching the drier portion of the Great Plains after the humid lands were gone had to adapt their farming operations by carefully conserving the moisture in the soil through processes of dust mulching, letting the land lie fallow in alternate years, and firmly packing the seed. DRY FARMING called for larger farm units and Congress responded in 1904, 1909, and 1916 by allowing 320- and 640-acre homesteads to farm makers. Dry farming in World War I aided materially in meeting the heavy wartime demands for wheat. It also contributed to the dust storms of the 1930s and to complex marketing problems.

Soft winter wheat (autumn planted)—where the winter season was not too severe—was commonly preferred to spring wheat (spring planted) because it yielded a larger crop and matured before the hottest summer weather. However, as settlement moved toward the ninety-ninth meridian into arid lands, the common varieties of winter wheat were found less satisfactory. Mennonites from southern Russia brought with them a hard winter wheat which proved strong and thrifty, more productive, and better adapted to the searing winds and pests that ravaged Kansas in particularly bad years. The kernels of the new variety, known as Red Turkey, and of the new strains of hard spring wheat being developed in the Dakotas forced changes in flour milling to utilize more of the glutinous cells and eliminate the oily germ in the process of gradual reduction of the berry. New strains of hard spring wheat made Dakota wheat and flour equal or superior to the winter wheat produced in Kansas.

Plant breeding to develop varieties of wheat resistant to disease, parasites, drought, and severe winters, yet with strong stems and grain suitable for milling, has been practiced in the laboratories and fields for years with marked success. Yet it was not until 1945 that experiments in crossbreeding wheat varieties began to produce results as spectacular as those achieved with hybrid corn. By crossing Japanese Norin 10, a short or dwarf, stout stemmed wheat with normal-sized berries, with other varieties and then making extensive selections from the crosses, new varieties of wheat were developed—such as Gaines and Nugaines—which, as one writer said, "triggered a revolution in wheat culture which has reached around the world." The "green revolution," as it has been called, has been taking place all over the world. New high-yielding strains of rice as well as of wheat, replacing old varieties, make it possible for countries like India, Pakistan, and Mexico— previously highly dependent on imports of wheat—to come nearer to self-sufficiency in these important items.

The green revolution has increased the average yield of wheat in the United States from 17 bushels per acre for the years 1946-50 to 26.2 bushels per acre for the years 1965-67. Surpluses of wheat and falling prices have resulted, but these problems had existed long before the green revolution and were not more devastating in their effect than they had been in the decades of the 1920s and 1930s. Wheat farmers appealed for government support to aid in storing and marketing their surpluses as proposed in the McNary-Haugen bills, but not until 1929 with the adoption of the Agricultural Marketing Act was any political action taken to affect prices of surplus agricultural commodities and it was an outright failure. In 1933, under the Agricultural Adjustment Act, the process of reversing the downward spiral of farm prices was begun through inducements to limit production. Even this act was not altogether successful, because agricultural scientists were developing new strains of wheat and agronomists were arriving at a better understanding of soil management which, together, made possible increased yields per acre. Continued surpluses of major farm staples led to the estab-

lishment of the Commodity Credit Corporation, which advanced money on, and stored, the surpluses until they could be sold, and to the "soil bank" plan of 1956 whereby an average of 17.9 million acres during the period 1956-65 were withdrawn from the production of grains of which there was a surplus. These devices, and the allotment plan, with its reduction of acreage in basic crops, have kept the problem of surplus wheat and cotton constantly before Congress. The green revolution, with its accompanying mechanization in planting and harvesting, which is depriving great numbers of peasants in India and Pakistan of employment in agriculture—and for whom there is no other work—has its counterpart in the United States in the hundreds of thousands of farmers who are no longer needed because of consolidation of farms and the extensive spread of corporate farming.

Today wheat is raised in appreciable quantities in nearly every state, though its greatest concentration is in the tier of states extending from Texas to North Dakota, where forty-five percent of the nation's crop is produced. Kansas leads with eighteen percent, North Dakota is second with eleven percent, and Oklahoma is third with eight percent.

See Mary Wilma M. Hargreaves, *Dry Farming in the Northern Great Plains, 1900-1925* (1957); and United States Department of Agriculture, *Yearbook*.—P. W. G.

Wheeler, George Montague (1842-1905). Army engineer and surveyor. Lieutenant (later Captain) Wheeler was the head of the army's United States Geographical Surveys West of the One-Hundredth Meridian. This project crystallized in 1872—although Wheeler had been surveying since 1867—and lasted until the creation of the United States Geological Survey in 1879. Wheeler's survey was the army's reply to the Hayden, King, and Powell surveys, which the army considered as imposters and as preempting duties that traditionally belonged to the army engineers. (Hayden and Powell were under the Interior Department, and King held civilian status with the Corps of Engineers.)

Wheeler was born in Hopkinton, Massachusetts, attended West Point, and graduated sixth in the class of 1866. He began his career as engineer and surveyor of Point Lobos in the San Francisco Bay area, but by 1871, with the rank of first lieutenant, he was evolving an ambitious army survey plan. The emphasis was to be on the production of useful topographical maps for army purposes, although scientific work could be accomplished also. From 1872 until the consolidation of the several surveys into the United States Geological Survey in 1879, Wheeler led his survey parties into the American West, mapping much of California, Nevada, and present Arizona, New Mexico, and Colorado. If the plan had been allowed to proceed, the army would have presented the American people by 1900 with a useful map of the American West. It is interesting to note that the United States Geological Survey has not yet completed the task.

Wheeler's health broke after the destruction of his survey, and his later career consisted in little more than a completion of some of his survey reports. He died in New York City.

See *Report Upon United States Geographical Surveys West of the One-Hundredth Meridian*, 7 vols. (1875-89); and

Richard A. Bartlett, *Great Surveys of the American West* (1962).—R. A. B.

Wherry, Kenneth Spicer (1892-1951). Nebraska politician. A native of Liberty, Nebraska, Wherry graduated from the University of Nebraska in 1914. After military service during World War I, he returned to his home in Pawnee City, Nebraska, where he became in succession an automobile dealer, furniture store owner, mortician, lawyer, and farmer. In 1928 he was elected as a Republican to the state senate and in two terms established a reputation as a Progressive, largely as a result of his efforts in behalf of depositors who had lost their savings in the failure of state-chartered banks.

In the mid-1930s Wherry became sharply critical of the farm policies of the Franklin D. Roosevelt administration, arguing that the New Deal was of little benefit to the Nebraska farmer. As Republican state chairman in 1940 he mounted an aggressive campaign that did much to bring an end to a decade of Democratic control of Nebraska politics, and he easily won the Republican nomination for United States senator in 1942. He defeated his Democratic opponent, Omaha broadcaster Foster May, and the veteran incumbent, George W. Norris, who very belatedly decided not to retire and ran as an independent. Senator Norris had run with the endorsement of President Roosevelt, but rural discontent with the military draft of farm labor, the belief in some localities that not enough war industries had been established in Nebraska, and a split Democratic vote helped produce this Republican triumph.

Wherry soon won notice in Washington as the champion of the interests of rural and small-town mid-America. One of the most vigorous foes of the Roosevelt administration, he waged a constant and successful fight against the Office of Price Administration, contending that the policies of that wartime agency were working unnecessary hardships upon farmers and small businessmen. Later, he fought President Harry S. Truman's farm program on grounds that it was too laden with government regulations and opposed the reinstitution of controls upon agricultural prices during the Korean War. In a more positive expression of the interests of Nebraska, Wherry in 1949 secured the enactment of a military housing program bearing his name, thus enabling Omaha to retain the headquarters of the Strategic Air Command of the United States Air Force, which had been tentatively located south of the city.

Wherry feared that the expanding role of government in the economy was leading the nation toward socialism, but he often criticized big-business policies as well, which he felt were intended to destroy the small entrepreneur. Ironically, Wherry's belief that rural America was subject to improper external economic control was similar to the thinking of such famous Nebraskans as William Jennings Bryan and George W. Norris, who had espoused progressive or liberal solutions to the problems of their state and region.

Wherry's doctrinaire conservatism often placed him at odds with moderate and liberal eastern Republicans. Yet his dynamism and frankness made him one of the most colorful figures in Washington and Nebraska during his time.

See Harl A. Dalstrom, " 'Remote Bigness' as a Theme in Nebraska Politics: The Case of Kenneth S. Wherry," *North Dakota Quarterly* (Summer 1970).—H. A. D.

Whig party. In contrast to the Democrats, the Whigs took an unfavorable position on most issues of concern to the West. While vigorous advocates of the federal internal improvements desired by that section, the Whigs were generally opposed to the quick and cheap disposal of public lands and were always hostile to territorial acquisition, especially forceful acquisition.

If Democrats championed manifest destiny, Whigs consistently opposed continental expansion. Commercial growth always interested them, and they were anxious to acquire San Francisco or some other Pacific port to facilitate Asian trade. But they united against the immediate annexation of Texas, though southern Whigs probably desired it eventually. Whigs opposed the all-Oregon movement. They denounced the Mexican War and the very idea of a cession of any territory to the United States because of it. Whigs sponsored the "no territory" cry in Congress in response to Democratic demands for all of Mexico.

Several factors explained this hostility to expansionism. One historian has suggested that it derived from Federalist dismay at Jefferson's triumph in the Louisiana Purchase. More important, Whigs believed in a homogeneous nation with national authority over a limited area. Expansion to the Pacific, argued Daniel Webster and other Whigs, would make the United States too large and heterogeneous to be a manageable republic. Here they echoed a cry of the opponents of the Constitution in the 1780s. In the 1840s both Whigs and Democrats had a sense of American mission to serve as a beacon and defender of liberty, a bastion of democracy protected by a republican form of government. Democrats wanted to spread the realm of liberty by increasing the physical size of the nation, but Whigs hoped to advance liberty by making the United States an example of a successful republic. They wanted to strengthen, develop, and purify the nation, not expend energy expanding and diffusing it. Territorial acquisition, thought Webster and other Whigs, endangered national unity and marred the moral example the American republic offered the world.

There were also pragmatic reasons for Whig opposition to expansion. Since Texas annexation and Mexican cession also involved slavery extension, and since the slavery issue could split their party, Whigs simply opposed any extension to avoid that issue and preserve party harmony. The "no territories" formula of the Mexican War was a Whig attempt to dodge the explosive Wilmot Proviso issue, which prohibited slavery in territory ceded by Mexico. President Zachary Taylor's later plan not to organize territories won from Mexico until they applied for statehood was a somewhat similar effort to maintain Whig unity by avoiding the problem of slavery in the territories.

On the question of the disposal of public lands, most Whigs were interested in revenue, not settlement. Therefore, they opposed graduation (the lowering of the minimum price of land the longer it went unsold on the market) and preemption (giving squatters first chance to buy the land on which they had settled), though their position fluctuated in the 1830s and 1840s. Whigs attempted to win western support with internal improvements, not land policy. However, such Whigs as Webster, who constantly wooed western support for his presidential aspirations by trying to win reciprocal trade agreements and pointing out the advantage of high tariffs to the West, firmly believed that settlement, not revenue, was the purpose of public lands. Between 1837 and 1840, he strongly favored preemption, graduation, and the donation of land to actual settlers, even though these positions were diametrically opposed to those of other New Englanders. In those years, however, he supported the scheme favored by Henry Clay and other Whigs—distribution of the proceeds of land sales to the states rather than the reduction of their price. Westerners and Democrats opposed this plan, and in order to get a Distribution Act passed in 1841, Clay against his wishes supported the Preemption Act of 1841, which established permanent preemption. Actual settlers could squat on 160 acres of public domain and when that land was opened for settlement they would have the first chance to buy it. Such concessions won enough support for the Whigs to pass the distribution act that year, but because of another provision, distribution was suspended in 1842 when the tariff was raised.

After the Compromise of 1850 internal improvements probably most interested the West. While Whigs were generally more favorable to railroad grants and rivers and harbors improvements in Congress than were Democrats, party alignments disintegrated in the early 1850s and Whigs voted according to section—East, West, or South—not party. In the late 1850s, when the Republicans combined the active internal improvements position of the Whigs with the cheap land policies of the Democrats, the Republicans won support from both parties in the Northwest and were thus stronger there than the Whigs had ever been.

See ELECTIONS OF 1836-1852.

Superb analyses of the Whig position on expansion can be found in Harry V. Jaffa, *Crisis of the House Divided: An Interpretation of the Issues in the Lincoln-Douglas Debates* (1959); and Frederick Merk, *Manifest Destiny and Mission in American History: A Reinterpretation* (1963). Glyndon G. Van Deusen, *The Jacksonian Era, 1828-1848* (1959), contains a competent treatment of Whig land policies. Whig cohesion in Congress is analyzed in Thomas B. Alexander, *Sectional Stress and Party Strength* (1967). On Webster's relation with the West, see Peter J. Parish, "Daniel Webster, New England, and the West," *Journal of American History*, vol. 54 (1967).
—M. F. H.

Whiskey Rebellion (July-November 1794). An uprising of southwestern Pennsylvania frontiersmen against the whiskey tax. Antigovernment sentiment in the four southwestern Pennsylvania counties of Allegheny, Washington, Fayette, and Westmoreland had festered since the passage of the excise law of 1791, which provided for the taxation of the region's most profitable product, rye whiskey. Grain-growing farmers and small whiskey distillers united in opposition to the tax. Sporadic acts of violence against the collection of the excise, 1791-93, gave way in the summer of 1794 to large-scale noncompliance. The rebellion erupted in July 1974, when legal processes against distillers who refused to pay the tax were blocked. In following weeks the home of the regional inspector of the excise, General John Neville, was burned, a threatening march on Pittsburgh occurred, acts of violence broke out, and large numbers of settlers remained defiant, even though a motion to comply on the excise was carried at a general meeting.

The rank-and-file members of the Whiskey Rebellion were more radical than the leadership. Most aggressive of the top leaders was David Bradford, who fled to Spanish land in present Mississippi when the movement collapsed. Albert Gallatin acted as a spokesman but gave no lead to the violent dissidents. Hugh Henry Brackenridge, a prominent Pittsburgh attorney and writer, played an ambiguous part—participating, so he claimed, to skew the movement away from violence and treason. John Holcroft (the original, apparently, of "Tom the Tinker," the anonymous prototype of the violent members of the insurgency) was typical of the intractable middle-level leadership.

By the fall of 1794 President Washington, strongly urged on by treasury secretary Alexander Hamilton, had concluded that, even though resistance to the excise was waning, only a military occupation would bring the area to full obedience. To this end Washington sent into the disaffected counties in November 1794 an army of thirteen thousand federalized militia commanded by Governor Henry Lee of Virginia. Bolstering Lee was Hamilton himself, in effect the real leader of the force. Twenty insurgents were rounded up and sent to Philadelphia for trial, but all were eventually freed. With this, the rebellion and its suppression sputtered to a close.

Nationally, the episode led to increased support for the Federalist party. In southwestern Pennsylvania the small distillers languished, not so much because of collection of the excise (which was repealed in 1802) but because of the insurmountable competition of the local large distillers.

The Whiskey Rebellion was typical of later frontier dissident movements in two senses: as an alignment of the agrarian frontier against the commercially dominated old settled area and as an example within the frontier itself of liberal/radical *versus* conservative factionalism.

See Leland D. Baldwin, *Whiskey Rebels: The Story of a Frontier Uprising* (1939).—R. M. B.

White, James (1749-1809). Territorial politician, lawyer, and physician. Born in Philadelphia, White attended college in France. He received degrees in law and medicine from the University of Pennsylvania and practiced both professions intermittently throughout his life. During the Revolution, he migrated to North Carolina, eventually settling in the western part of the state. In 1784 White was elected to the lower house of the North Carolina assembly, and the assembly elected him a member of the United States Congress the following year. He served conscientiously until October 1786, when Congress appointed him superintendent for Indian affairs for the Southern District. During his two years in this office he expanded his connections with North Carolina land speculators, particularly Governor Richard Carswell and William Blount. He also discussed the problems of the frontier with the Spanish minister, Don Diego de Gardoqui. Following his resignation from office in 1788, he entered the service of Gardoqui in order to encourage the people of the West to leave the United States and join the Spanish colonies. In this work he visited important men in settlements west of the mountains. He presented the American conditions for secession to the Spanish governor at New Orleans, but no firm agreement was made. In 1789 he was again elected to the North Carolina lower house, where he was active in legislative work. As a member of the ratifying convention in North Carolina he voted for the United States Constitution.

With the creation of the Southwest Territory in 1790, White severed his relationship with the Spanish and became actively involved in territorial affairs as a political colleague of Governor Blount. When the first territorial legislature met in 1794 he was a leader for the administration forces. His loyalty was rewarded with election to Congress as the first territorial delegate in the United States.

Because the widely known and respected Dr. White was the first delegate, Congress established more generous precedents affecting the role and prerogatives of future territorial delegates than might have been expected. His status was that of a member of the House of Representatives with all privileges except that of voting on the floor. He sat and voted on select committees and served as chairman. Pay, privileges, and immunities were the same as those of regular members.

After working with Congress to secure for the Southwest Territory statehood as Tennessee, White returned to Tennessee and continued his law and medical practices. In 1798 he led a group of emigrants to Mississippi Territory but he stayed only a year. He then moved on to St. Martin Parish, Orleans Territory. In 1804 the governor appointed him a local judge, a position he held until his death.—J. T. B.

White, Peter. See GREAT LAKES, MEN OF THE.

White, Stewart Edward (1873-1946). Novelist. White was born in Grand Rapids, Michigan. He was privately educated until he was sixteen, at which time he entered public high school in Grand Rapids. Upon graduation he entered the University of Michigan, from which he received a B.A. in 1895 and after which he went to Columbia University to study law. At Columbia he came under the influence of Brander Matthews, the famed writing teacher, who encouraged him to submit some of his classwork for publication. When it was accepted White decided upon a literary rather than a legal career and spent the remainder of his life in writing and travel. In later life he moved to California, making his residence in Burlingame.

It is slightly misleading to consider White purely as a western writer. He was rather a writer of adventure stories, many of which are set in the American West. He wrote western fiction before it had become clearly separated as a genre from other tales of outdoor adventure, and such books as *The Claim Jumpers* (1901), *The Westerners* (1901), and *Arizona Nights* (1907) were important at the time for establishing the new genre of western fiction as something distinct from, albeit related to, other outdoor tales.

White's early literary preferences, he mentioned in later life, were for history and historical fiction, and much of his own writing clearly reflects this early bias. His four loosely sequential novels about Andy Burnett—*The Long Rifle* (1932), *Ranchero* (1933), *Folded Hills* (1934), and *Stampede* (1942)—are clearly historical; indeed, *The Long Rifle*, probably his best western novel, is almost a fictional history of the early years of the American fur trade, and in his afterword to the

volume White attests to the book's historical accuracy. Critics as well have praised White's fidelity to detail and to historical fact; at his best he wrote fiction that is carefully particularized without being limited by the anecdotalism of too-faithful adherence to minutiae.
—J. K. F.

White, William Allen (1868-1944). Kansas newspaper editor and author. Born in Emporia, Kansas, White grew up in nearby El Dorado, where his father was a physician and his mother ran a hotel. An only child of middle-aged parents, White was provided with an appreciation of literary and cultural excellence. He attended the College of Emporia and the University of Kansas but did not graduate.

After a newspaper apprenticeship in El Dorado, Lawrence, and Kansas City, White bought the Emporia *Gazette* in 1895 and within ten years his paper was the most influential in town. His bristling editorial "What's the Matter with Kansas?"—a severe indictment of the 1896 Democratic-Populist fusion ticket—was reprinted nationally and his books began to gain widespread attention. White wrote twenty-two books: one of poetry, nine of fiction, and twelve of nonfiction, including biography.

White's ardent Republicanism led to an acquaintance with a number of presidents; Theodore Roosevelt was his favorite, although he wrote one biography of Woodrow Wilson and two of Calvin Coolidge. In 1912 when Roosevelt ran for president as the Progressive party candidate, White bolted the Republican party to support him. White soon returned to the G.O.P. but left again in 1924 when he ran as an Independent for governor of Kansas. Defeated, he returned to his party and endeavored to make his progressive opinions felt.

White's influence in Kansas was phenomenal. Kansans read his pungent newspaper comments, and while not always agreeing, they were impressed. He gained a national reputation through his editorials, which made him a spokesman for the grass roots, and through his service with national groups—one of them was the Book-of-the-Month Club selection committee and another was the Committee to Defend America by Aiding the Allies, of which he was chairman before World War II. Although he never held an elective public office, he was considered the state's "senator at large." Numerous memorials to White have been erected throughout Kansas.

Information is found in White's *Autobiography* (1946) and in *Selected Letters of William Allen White, 1899-1943* (1947), edited by Walter Johnson. See also Johnson, *William Allen White's America* (1947); and Everett Rich, *William Allen White* (1941).—H. E. S.

White Hills, Arizona. Ghost town. White Hills, in the northwest corner of Arizona, was a booming silver town of the 1890s. The mineral deposits of the White Hills were long known to the Indians of the area, who dug red oxide for face paint; but the secret location of these mines was long withheld from the greedy white men who combed the area. In 1892, however, the secret was finally revealed, and the rush to White Hills was on.

The town flourished until 1898, under the direction of the White Hills Mining Company headed by promoter R. T. Root and railroad magnate D. H. Moffat, both of Colorado. By 1900, however, production had dropped a great deal, and White Hills's population began to drift away. Today the town is a ghost, the battered false fronts of its dilapidated buildings a grim reminder of a promoter's fallen dream.

See Nell Murbarger, *Ghosts of the Adobe Walls* (1964); and Muriel S. Wolle, *The Bonanza Trail* (1953). —R. B. W.

white-Indian relations. See INDIAN-WHITE RELATIONS.

White Oaks, New Mexico. Ghost town. White Oaks, in Lincoln County, was founded in 1879 following the discovery of gold in nearby Baxter Gulch. This strike, which became the North Homestake mine, was followed by several others, and White Oaks remained prosperous until the early years of the twentieth century. Mining was the town's only resource, however, and when the railroad bypassed White Oaks in favor of nearby Carrizozo the town began its slow decline. Today the town is a fairly well preserved reminder of its past glories, complete with a Victorian mansion and a large brick schoolhouse. One of the town's unforgettable characters was a lady gambler named Madame Varnish.

See Ralph Looney, *Haunted Highways: The Ghost Towns of New Mexico* (1968); Duane Smith, *Rocky Mountain Mining Camps* (1967); and Muriel S. Wolle, *The Bonanza Trail* (1953).—R. B. W.

White Pine, Nevada. See GOLD AND SILVER RUSHES.

Whitman, Marcus (1802-1847). Oregon missionary, pioneer, and physician. Whitman received his degree from the medical college at Fairfield, New York, in 1832. After four years as a doctor in Canada, Whitman returned to New York, where he continued his practice and became an elder of the Presbyterian church. In 1835 he toured the Pacific Northwest with Samuel Parker, seeking a suitable location for a religious mission. Upon his return east, he married Narcissa Prentiss. In February 1836 he left for Oregon as a lay member of the first missionary group sent by the American Board of Commissioners for Foreign Missions, accompanied by Henry Harmon Spalding and William H. Gray. Mrs. Spalding and Mrs. Whitman were the first white women to cross the Rocky Mountains. Whitman established his mission to the Cayuse Indians east of the Hudson's Bay Company fort at Walla Walla, in spite of advice that the Cayuse were dangerous.

After six years of bitter quarrels and rivalries among themselves, the Oregon missionaries received word in 1842 from the American Board of Commissioners for Foreign Missions that the Whitman and Spalding missions were to be abandoned. Whitman rode east to convince the board not to take such action. The board relented and Whitman returned in 1843 in company with the first large immigration bound for the Oregon country. His mission at Waiilatpu in the Walla Walla valley became an important way station for Oregon pioneers during the next few years. Many sick immigrants visited his mission for medical treatment, and their diseases infected Indians living nearby.

Whitman's methods, involving a radical and precipitate break with Indian culture, and the fact that Indians were dying of white men's diseases, did much to ignite Indian hatred, and in 1847 the CAYUSE INDIANS massacred Whitman, his wife, and twelve others. A courageous person and zealous missionary, however, he did win the respect of immigrants and mountain men.

Because of the legend created in part by Gray, Spalding, and others, the collected materials about and by Whitman are relatively out of proportion to his importance. Manuscripts and letters are in the San Francisco Theological Seminary Library, San Anselmo, California; at the Beinecke Library, Yale University; the Oregon Historical Society, Portland; the Washington State University Library, Pullman; and the Penrose Memorial Library, Whitman College, Walla Walla, Washington. Secondary sources are Clifford M. Drury, *Marcus Whitman, M.D., Pioneer and Martyr* (1937) and *Marcus and Narcissa Whitman and the Opening of Old Oregon* (1973); and Alvin M. Josephy, Jr., *The Nez Percé Indians and the Opening of the Northwest* (1965).—R. J. L.

Whitman, Royal. See CAMP GRANT MASSACRE.

Whitney, Asa (1797-1872). Merchant and railroad promoter. The son of a prosperous farmer of North Groton, Connecticut, Whitney moved to New York about 1817, where he learned the dry-goods business. After traveling in Europe for some years as a buyer for American merchants, he founded his own firm in New York. Wiped out by the Panic of 1837, he went to China for fifteen months as agent for several firms. There he amassed large profits that enabled him to spend the rest of his life promoting RAILROADS, which had become the center of his interests.

His dealings between the Orient and America had convinced him that a railroad from Chicago to the Pacific Coast was the missing, vital link in the lucrative CHINA TRADE. Pressing Congress in 1844 to charter such a road through the South Pass of the Rocky Mountains, Whitney suggested that the enormous cost of the project could be defrayed through the sale of fertile lands along the route. Although he waged a speaking campaign and an intensive newspaper publicity effort, Whitney faced massive indifference, his own motives becoming the object of suspicion. He spent seven years in promoting the project, during which time he personally inspected the first eight hundred miles of the proposed route. But neither Congress nor Great Britain, which he approached on behalf of Canada, responded.

In 1852 he retired to an estate near Washington, D.C., where he died of typhoid fever three years after completion of the first transcontinental railroad.

Like Theodore D. Judah of the Central Pacific, Whitney is remembered today only by specialists. His ideas survive, however, in his proposal to Congress, printed as House Executive Document 72, 28th Congress, 2nd Session (1844). See also M. L. Brown, "Asa Whitney and His Pacific Railroad Publicity Campaign," *Mississippi Valley Historical Review* (September 1933); and N. H. Loomis, "Asa Whitney, Father of Pacific Railroads," *Proceedings of the Mississippi Valley Historical Association*, vol. VI (1913).—A. M.

Whitney Gallery of Western Art. See BUFFALO BILL HISTORICAL CENTER.

Wichita, Kansas. See CATTLE TOWNS.

Wier, Jeanne E. (1870-1950). Historian. Born at Grinnell, Iowa, Wier received a B.A. degree from Stanford University. She began teaching at the University of Nevada in 1899 as an assistant professor of history. She became head of the department in 1901 and held that post until her retirement in 1940. She was granted an honorary LL.D. degree by the University of Nevada in 1924. In 1904 she founded the Nevada Historical Society and was responsible for collecting the materials that became the society's library and museum. She held the post of secretary and then director of the society until her death in Reno. She was vice president of the Pacific Coast branch of the American Historical Association in 1915-16 and held numerous other offices with state and local history and community organizations.—R. R. E.

Wild Bunch. See Butch CASSIDY.

Wilder, Laura Ingalls (1867-1957). Author of books for children. Wilder was born in Lake Pepin, Wisconsin. In her early childhood, her family seldom remained in one place for more than two years, but in 1879, the Ingalls settled permanently in De Smet, Dakota Territory. In 1885, Laura married Almanzo Wilder, a homesteading farmer in De Smet; nine years later the Wilders established their permanent home, Rocky Ridge Farm, in Mansfield, Missouri. There Laura Wilder wrote for local newspapers the column "As a Farm Woman Thinks."

Nostalgic after the deaths of her parents and older sister, Wilder wrote *The Little House in the Big Woods* (1932), a largely autobiographical narrative of her family's life in Wisconsin. Its success prompted seven more books: *Farmer Boy* (1933), on her husband's youth in upstate New York; *The Little House on the Prairie* (1935), on her brief stay in Missouri from 1869 to 1871; *On the Banks of Plum Creek* (1937), on her stay in Walnut Grove, Minnesota, from 1874 to 1876; *By the Shores of Silver Lake* (1939), on her first home in Dakota; *The Long Winter* (1940), on the difficult winter of 1880 in Dakota; and *Little Town on the Prairie* (1941) and *These Happy Golden Years* (1943), both on the years before her marriage in De Smet.

See Donald Zochert, *Laura* (1976).—P. L. N.

wilderness. Wilderness is a quality, able to evoke happiness or fearfulness, as well as a physical characteristic of a portion of the earth. Usually an area devoid of visible human influence is considered "wild." Such a definition would encompass the entire New World at the time of its first settlement by Europeans, for in their minds the Indians who occupied the land supported rather than detracted from its wild quality.

When America began to be settled, wilderness was the prime adversary—a dark and fearful environment that civilization and Christianity had to conquer and transform. This attitude, fed by utilitarianism and the profit urge, rode west with frontiersmen and persists into the present. It equates the elimination of wilderness with progress. The pioneers at Massachusetts Bay in 1630 and Prudhoe Bay (the site of the Alaskan oil strike) in 1970 were alike in their hostility toward wild country.

Against this background of bias against wilderness, a counter movement of appreciation gradually developed (see CONSERVATION MOVEMENT). Among the first Americans to recognize the value of wild country for its own sake were botanists, ornithologists, and other naturalists who found it replete with exciting discoveries. In time America's national pride became linked to its possession of spectacular wilderness scenery. The Romantic movement—with its celebration of nature, the noble savage, and the solitary life—also worked toward an appreciation of nature. Of course the Romantic enthusiasts of wilderness were invariably the products of refined, urban situations. For them wilderness was a delightful novelty, and this circumstance does much to explain the difference between their attitude and that of pioneers who lived in close proximity to the wild.

Henry David THOREAU in the 1850s was the first American to express a sophisticated philosophy of wilderness appreciation. John MUIR, who with others founded the SIERRA CLUB in 1892, followed Thoreau's ideas closely. Muir's crusade for wilderness appreciation benefited from a growing cult of the primitive in American society (witness the popularity in the early twentieth century of Jack London's *The Call of the Wild* and the Tarzan sagas of Edgar Rice Burroughs). By this time increasing numbers of Americans found themselves civilized enough to appreciate wilderness. Muir marshaled them in defense of the national parks, particularly Yosemite in California. Aldo LEOPOLD gave them a better rationale with his brilliant writings in the 1920s and 1930s, and Robert Marshall's Wilderness Society (1935) provided organization.

Wilderness gained popularity in the twentieth century at a rate inversely proportional to its presence in the United States. A succession of political victories for wilderness preservation marked its rise in public esteem. The first occurred in 1956 when preservationists completed a successful defense of Dinosaur National Monument, which was threatened with flooding by a proposed dam at Echo Park. The creation by act of Congress of the National Wilderness Preservation System (1964), the defeat of plans to dam the Colorado River in the Grand Canyon (1968), and the salvation of Florida's Everglades from a jetport (1969) marked the highlights of the wilderness movement.

The final irony in the history of the American wilderness is that its increased popularity may ultimately prove its undoing. Having made such remarkable gains in the public's estimation in the twentieth century, wild country could well be loved out of existence in the next. The problem is that wilderness values are so fragile that when subjected to heavy recreational usage they disappear. Man, by definition, is alien to wilderness, and even the most careful camper leaves the marks of his passage on the land. And when securing a campsite becomes the subject of competition among several parties (or if quotas have to be established to limit the number of users and their length of stay), wilderness is no longer wild. Already the most popular wildernesses, such as the High Sierra, the Grand Canyon, and the North Cascades, are crowded during the peak vacation months. For more than a century wilderness advocates labored for just such a goal. They reasoned that preserving wild places depended on persuading Americans to appreciate them. Their success is the source of their gravest present challenge.

The standard source is Roderick Nash, *Wilderness and the American Mind* (1967). Its bibliography will lead to other pertinent published and unpublished material. —R. N.

Wilderness Road. The Wilderness Road extended technically across Kentucky from Cumberland Gap to Boonesboro on the south bank of the Kentucky River, and from the Hazel Patch to Louisville at the Falls of the Ohio. It was, however, an extension of the Great Valley Road, which ran from Wadkin's Ferry on the Potomac to the Watauga valley in the neighborhood of present-day Kingsport, Tennessee. Parts of this road were outlined by Indian and game trails. Long hunters prior to 1775 had come this way in penetrating the Kentucky country. On March 10, 1775, after it became apparent that the

Treaty of Sycamore Shoals would be negotiated with the Cherokee, whereby they would cede land to white settlers, Daniel Boone led a party of eight to blaze the trail from Sycamore Shoals on the Holston River to the Kentucky River. In years to come hundreds of thousands of emigrants to the West passed through Cumberland Gap and over the Wilderness Road to Kentucky and the Ohio valley.

The road forked at the Hazel Patch, now in Laurel County, Kentucky, with the west branch going to Logan's Fort, to Harrod's Town (later called Harrodsburg), and thence to the Falls of the Ohio. In time the road was extended from Boonesboro by way of Winchester and Lexington to Maysville on the Ohio. From 1775 to date, this road has been a main connecting link between the Ohio, Tennessee, and Virginia valleys.

See Robert L. Kincaid, *The Wilderness Road* (1947); William Stewart Lester, *The Transylvania Colony* (1935); William Allen Pusey, *The Wilderness Road to Kentucky* (1921); and Thomas Speed, *The Wilderness Road* (1886).—T. D. C.

wildlife. The trans-Mississippi West possesses a variety of wildlife habitats. Diversity is the result of a number of interrelated factors, including precipitation, topography, the effects of glaciation, fire, and, often, animal life itself (see PHYSIOGRAPHY OF THE UNITED STATES and VEGETATION). The mosaic of wildlife habitats in the West has provided ample opportunity for isolation and the development of genetic differences between animal populations.

When Columbus landed, North American fauna, rich and varied though it was, comprised only a remnant of that existing several thousand years before. In those early days such large mammals as camels, wild horses, giant bison, immense ground sloths, and even beavers of super size existed, along with other herbivores and predatory animals. They are known to us through their fossil remains. Although their disappearance remains a mystery, there is conjecture that early Americans may have had a hand in their demise.

According to a recent National Academy of Sciences study, chaired by Sanford S. Atwood, "the disappearance of this megafauna has not been satisfactorily explained, but it was in progress during the period of roughly 12,000-5,000 B.C., when early men were numerous and active. Well-developed hunting cultures were widely distributed across the continent . . . and finely crafted projectile points were being used against mammoths, bison, and lesser beasts."

When the white men arrived, they found the Great Plains dominated by the bison, or BUFFALO. Associated with the grazing bison was the PRONGHORN antelope, a peculiarly American animal. Wapiti, now often referred to as the American ELK, were also found in abundance on the richer prairies, and bighorn sheep were numerous on the steep grasslands of the mountains and the badlands (those regions along the Missouri River deeply sculptured by erosion).

The typical big-game animals of the forest were whitetailed and mule DEER, and, in the Far West, the black-tail. These deer, browsers that ate shrubby vegetation, as well as elk, benefited from forest fires, which increased their food supplies. Other northern mammals existing from Canada south to the northern Rockies were the caribou, wintering in the ancient, high-altitude forests

of the northern Rockies and eating the arboreal lichens with which they were encrusted; the moose, making good use of the willow bottoms associated with old beaver-workings; and the mountain goat, found in the alpine regions of the northern Rockies and Cascades.

Characteristic carnivores of the West during this period were the WOLF, its smaller relative the coyote, the cougar or MOUNTAIN LION, and the GRIZZLY BEAR. Omnivorous black bears also were abundant.

The impact of European settlement on the eastern coast of North America was indirect. With the development of the fur trade came an increased demand for pelts and the introduction of firearms. With the pressures of settlement against the Indians in the East, westward displacements began. With Spanish exploration in the Gulf states, the HORSE was introduced. These developments changed the relations of the Indian tribes to one another and to wildlife populations. The bison could now be pursued and killed with relative ease, and whole tribes shifted from a mixed farming-hunting economy to one in which hunting was the major food source, and bison the major prey. The initial impact of trade, firearms, horse, and population pressure was followed shortly by the arrival in the West of European man himself. (Interestingly, the Spanish settlers, who really only settled in the far Southwest and California, had only a local impact on the wildlife through the grazing of their livestock; they did not pursue wildlife to any important extent—unlike the Yankee hunters.)

Shortly after the Louisiana Purchase in 1803, Lewis and Clark set forth from St. Louis on the exploratory trek to the mouth of the Columbia River. For the next half-century there was always some money to be made in furs, the most valuable and accessible being the BEAVER of the mountain streams and the sea otter of the coastal Paci¸ic Ocean. Both were wiped out over large parts of their range, not to be brought back for a century or more. Less vulnerable fur-bearers, such as mink, river otter, wolverine, marten, fisher, bobcat, and lynx, were better able to stand up under the heavy pressure.

Meanwhile various expeditions had gone West to locate the best railroad routes, and by the 1850s, when the railroad reached the Mississippi, the stage was set for a half-century of virtually unbridled commercial exploitation of wildlife populations. As the railroads were extended from the Mississippi westward, the laborers were fed bison, elk, sheep, and other game, shot by professional hunters. Rapid advances made in firearms at this time led to more efficient weapons, the replacement of the muzzle-loader with the breech-loader and the single-shot with the repeater.

With the completion of a transcontinental railroad link in 1869, the professional hunters (their ranks augmented with restless Civil War veterans) could ship their bison hides, and later meat, by rail. There was no attempt to regulate the ensuing slaughter; in some quarters the end of the bison was even considered a necessary prerequisite to the "solution of the Indian problem."

With the gold rush professional hunters began operating around every mining camp—without any legal restraint. And with mass production of quantities of cheap, effective firearms, the professional hunter—the "market hunter"—could easily obtain equipment. By the same token, every miner and settler could be well armed, prepared at any time to shoot whatever game seemed worth a cartridge.

Although the western states and territories established laws to protect wild animals from intense, year-round hunting, most were not enforced until the turn of the century. Consequently, hunting pressure soon either reduced most big-game populations, particularly those with especially valuable pelts to small remnants or wiped them out altogether. Among the animals to suffer near-extirpation during this period was the trumpeter swan, a huge white bird that nested on western lakes and had palatable meat. Even its feathered skin was an item of trade in the trapping days.

It was soon evident that no degree of remoteness or difficulty of access to its habitat could completely protect an animal hunted by determined and well-armed men. Only complete protection from hunting would suffice. Early efforts had proven unenforceable. With the establishment of Yellowstone National Park in 1872, there emerged another approach to protection: the creation of refuges or sanctuaries within which no hunting was allowed. This proved practicable, since such areas could be patrolled. The wapiti, extirpated over most of its range in the West, survived in Yellowstone, and, in spite of continual poaching, the herds there increased, eventually providing a surplus from which depleted ranges throughout the West could be restocked.

Although hunting caused the most dramatic decreases in big game, other forces were also at work during the last half of the nineteenth century. Livestock herds that were building up on the Plains and taken high into the mountains during the summer took over the former range of both the bison and the pronghorn. Domestic sheep appeared in large numbers on the ranges of bighorn sheep, competing for food and probably bringing new diseases. And in the rich river-bottoms the former haunts of the wapiti were cleared for agriculture.

On the shortgrass prairies and the sagebrush flats, where it was too dry for farming, the livestock herds were plagued by wolves, which had found the transition from bison to cattle an easy step. Wolves were shot on sight, and dead cattle were laced with strychnine to poison them. Professional wolfers dug out dens and trapped adults. Only the warier wolves survived—living on livestock.

Some notion of the attitudes toward the wolf, the prince of predators, and toward predators in general is conveyed by the words of a prominent conservationist, William Hornaday, after the turn of the century: "We now come to . . . wild species that are everywhere so destructive to valuable property that they deserve to be destroyed, and concerning which there is no dispute. At the head of the list of evil-doers stands the big *Gray Wolf* . . . strong of limb and jaw, a master of cunning and the acme of cruelty . . . wherever found, the proper course with a wild gray wolf is to kill it as quickly as possible . . ." This antipathy for predators was based partly on a concern for the protection of domestic livestock, and partly on a concern for the continued survival of wild species.

Not all changes during this period were disadvantageous for wildlife. The increase in mining demanded mine-props, which required lumbering. Wholesale logging, in turn, was followed by widespread fires. Fires, by

encouraging shrubs at the expense of trees, provided more habitat for deer and wapiti—and less, in the northern Rockies, for caribou.

In the more arable lands of tall-grass prairie the earliest settlements, with their fields of grain, provided the prairie-chicken and, farther west, the sharp-tailed grouse with superior winter food. Prairie-chicken and grouse populations boomed. Soon another sort of market hunter, the bird-shooter, appeared, using the new repeating shotguns, with the newly invented choke-bore, to fill barrels with prairie-chickens and waterfowl for the city markets.

Seed-eating birds, such as quail and mourning dove, had their food supplies increased by heavy livestock-grazing. Grazing reduced the grasses and permitted the growth of weedy herbs, heavy seed-producers.

The first reaction to the wholesale slaughter of wild animals was to attempt protection. When Yellowstone National Park was created, it was closed officially to hunting (although enforcement was difficult initially; hunters were harassed rather than punished). Beginning in the 1870s thought began to be given to reserving some of the western public lands for timber and water production. Gradually at first and later more rapidly the forest reserves were withdrawn from the public domain.

Taking a broader view of the 1850-1900 period, one sees many manifestations of the same phenomenon: an effort by well-educated, well-to-do urbanites from the East Coast (some transplanted to California) to impose conservation ideas derived from Europe on "The West," that is, on the frontiersmen and ranchers, who thought of themselves as taming the wilderness. Many of the eastern elite were sportsmen, Teddy Roosevelt being the prime example. The BOONE AND CROCKETT CLUB was formed to promote conservation legislation, but the local people would not stand for such things. However, the idea that a national park would be a game refuge was acceptable enough.

Another East Coast conservation group formed the American Ornithologists Union, which in the 1880s prepared a model bill for bird protection and a child's pledge, widely circulated in the schools, that urged people not to wear feathers or molest birds. These moves helped pave the way for later successful attempts in bird conservation.

Around the turn of the century a compromise between the protection and use of wild animals evolved: The national parks were closed to all hunting (the elk in Yellowstone immediately began to increase), while the national forests remained open. Then the various states hit upon the plan of charging a license fee for hunting and fishing, creating for the first time revenue for enforcement of the regulations for conserving wildlife populations. Typical big-game conservation regulations of this time were protecting females from hunters, forbidding hunting during winter and spring, limiting the number that each hunter could shoot annually, and waging war on predators.

The state conservation agencies, dependent for their income on the sale of fishing and hunting licenses, were responsive to the interests of sportsmen and concentrated their attention on the game species, rather than on the nongame species. These conservation agencies paid bounties on supposed enemies of game and regulated the kill of game. Later they acquired lands for game increase and began operating state farms to re-store game numbers and introduce new game species. Today nongame species are receiving more attention than previously from state governments. Although most birds are under federal protection, most mammals are resident within a state's boundaries, but they have not been given protection, until quite recently, unless they were game or fur-bearing species. (Up until only a few years ago there were hardly any western states employing biologists to gather information on nongame species. Deer biologists, water-fowl biologists, upland game-bird biologists were employed by the dozen.)

Enforcement was not immediate or complete. As late as 1915 five hundred elk were killed illegally in Yellowstone National Park—for their canine teeth, in demand for watch fobs. But the enforcement of regulations had an increasingly salutary effect on those resident wildlife species for which suitable habitat remained, notably the pronghorn, elk, and deer. In contrast, the once-abundant bighorn sheep persisted only in scattered remnants, the caribou were virtually gone, and the bison survived largely in special fenced refuges.

Migratory birds posed a special problem. The basic law placed the custodianship of wildlife populations under state administration. But ducks and geese, like most other birds, passed seasonally from state to state, north and south across the nation, and commercial hunters and sportsmen shot them during their passages in spring and fall. Seasons and bag limits were too liberal for continued population maintenance. Federal control was needed, but the mechanism through which it could be achieved was not developed until 1916. The Migratory Bird Treaty between the United States and Canada did away with shooting and commercialization, incidentally providing blanket protection for a host of migratory birds that previously had gone unrecognized in law.

During the early twentieth century federal legislative efforts were aimed primarily at bird protection. In 1903 President Theodore Roosevelt established national wildlife refuges that gradually were developed into a nationwide system. In 1913 the Federal Tariff Act and the Weeks-McLean bill were enacted. The former banned importation of bird skins (for hats); the latter imposed federal control over the conservation of migratory birds. (The Weeks-McLean bill was probably unconstitutional; it was superseded in 1918 by the passage of the act which ratified the Migratory Bird Treaty.)

The war against the wolves was taken over by the federal government. Federal predator-control agents were hunting down the last of the Plains wolves in 1918-20. They then turned their attention to lesser predators, notably the coyote (which was destructive to sheep), JACKRABBIT, and especially the PRAIRIE DOG (which was thought to compete with livestock for pasture). Gradually, federal involvement came to cover other points of impact between wildlife and man's interests: crop protection, public health, and protection of species threatened with extinction.

At the same time the states maintained their interest in game species, attempting to control the predators of game through the ineffective device of bounty payments or, on occasion, employing professional predator-control agents.

Conservation philosophy during this period formed

two branches, epitomized by John MUIR and Gifford PINCHOT. The two men personally parted ways in the late 1890s, when Pinchot supported sheep-grazing in the forest reserves in keeping with his philosophy of wise use. Muir, in contrast, believed that natural areas should be completely protected for the restoration of the human spirit. While Pinchot's philosophies strongly influenced the United States Forest Service, where later they were to take the form of "multiple use" administration, there were men within the Forest Service who also recognized the less tangible values of wild lands. One of the most thoughtful and articulate was Aldo LEOPOLD, who went fresh from Yale University to New Mexico in 1919. He became an advocate of a state of primitiveness, or wilderness, as a desirable objective on some public lands, a point of view that would have been congenial to Muir.

During the 1930s and 1940s deer all over the West increased rapidly as enforcement of protective regulations became increasingly effective. (Fewer people violated the regulations without being caught, and people in general tended to abide by the regulations. Those who did violate the law and were caught received more severe punishments.) With more and more die-offs occurring during hard winters, it became increasingly clear that in the semiarid climate of most of the West the growth of the plants eaten by deer is slow and excessive use by deer could weaken and kill the forage. That this also was true for livestock had been noted by an earlier generation. Protection of female deer now was replaced by the concept of balancing deer numbers to their food supply. During the 1940s and 1950s this concept was promulgated with a measure of success throughout most of the West. The patterns of management developed for deer worked for elk and pronghorn as well. The caribou, never numerous, were virtually gone by this time, having been reduced first by hunting and then by destruction of the "old growth," or mature, forests, their essential habitat. Moose built up within the limited ranges available to them, mainly high valleys in the northern Rockies.

Of all the original wildlife habitats of the West, the forested mountains and the semiarid grazing lands were least changed during the twentieth century, and their wildlife populations with few exceptions have recovered well from the excessive hunting pressure of settlement days. Herbivorous animals even have a tendency to increase to the point of damaging their own habitats. This was observed for the mule deer of the Kaibab as early as 1924, when there was the first mass starvation on depleted ranges. More recently, there have been widespread attempts to control big-game numbers by hunting. Even in national parks, where sport hunting is forbidden, there have been some efforts to control big-game numbers (by trapping or shooting) to avoid range damage. However, the management of deer and elk populations for preservation of their habitats has been only partly successful, largely due to man's natural reluctance to apply a heavy measure of control.

The lands suitable for farming have shown a different pattern. The tall-grass prairie regions, once rich in game, were hunted heavily and, more important, were cultivated more and more intensively. In its early stages, cultivation does not disturb the original populations much and opens the way for new species. But prolonged development in farmland tends to one direction, a more efficient production of crops—at the expense of all else. Great strides in this direction have been taken since the West was settled. The horse was replaced around the turn of the century by the steam tractor, and then by the internal-combustion engine. This freed thousands of acres from the production of horse-feed, permitted a farmer to cultivate a larger number of acres, and provided power to remove physical impediments to cultivation.

The principal impediment to cultivation, especially in the northern parts of the tall-grass prairie, was the interrupted drainage left by the receding glacier of ten thousand years ago. A multitude of marshes, sloughs, and potholes dotted the country, providing a rich habitat for marsh birds, waterfowl, mink, and muskrat, and on slightly higher ground, for the wildlife of the grassland. Because the wetlands were worth more to the farmer drained, drainage proceeded as fast as machinery could be developed and capital raised. The federal government helped with advice and financial incentives. The consequent decline of the wetlands was paralleled by the decline of associated native wildlife.

For a time the introduction of the ring-necked pheasant provided something of a replacement. This pheasant, brought from China to Oregon in the 1880s and able to survive wherever grain-farming was practiced outside of the humid Southeast, prospered and became the main gamebird of the central and northern tall-grass prairie states, the irrigated interior valleys, the dryland wheatfields, and the irrigated ricefields. But as grain-farming has become more efficient, cover has declined, and so have pheasant populations. Similarly shifts in crops from grains to livestock pasture have lowered pheasant food production, and hence pheasant numbers.

A number of other species have been introduced in the West, some deliberately and some not. The Hungarian (gray) partridge of Europe is well established among the northern wheatfields, the chukar partridge is widespread through arid grazing-lands, and, in the Southwest, Indian and African antelope have been successfully introduced, along with the Barbary sheep of North Africa, and a number of Asian game-birds. The most abundant accidentally introduced bird is the European starling, which eats fruit and grains and nests in tree-holes.

Ecological changes accompanying the spread of agriculture have had positive as well as negative effects on wildlife populations. A few species of birds, including the native red-winged blackbird, early-migrating, grain-eating ducks like the pintail, and the introduced starling, flourish with grain-farming and can cause severe local damage. Alleviation of this problem, as well as the local control of other pest situations involving wildlife, is a major responsibility of the United States Department of the Interior's Fish and Wildlife Service.

Water is significant when commercial developments in the West are considered. Western waters arise in the mountains and flow out into regions that are often dry. The banks of such rivers are typically rich in wildlife, since they provide water, cover, and green vegetation at seasons when these are otherwise in short supply. Some western rivers originally ended in lakes with no outlets or spread over sun-warmed shallows, and the high evap-oration rate in those hot, dry regions caused a progressive alkalinity of these waters (as the salts were left behind as the water evaporated). An archetypal example is the Great Salt Lake of Utah. Since alkaline waters are a boon to plant and animal life up to a point, these interior western wetlands were great concentration areas for migrating waterfowl. But under certain conditions, including warm water, alkalinity, and decaying organic matter, bacteria produce a toxin that the ducks drink with their water, and from time to time vast numbers of these birds died from a malady first known as "western duck sickness" and now identified as botulism. When water levels are controlled, botulism losses can be reduced. Unfortunately, competition for water exists through much of the West, and some large waterfowl areas are used for irrigation-water wasteways; the entering flow is often irregular and often overly rich in dissolved fertilizers and pesticides.

In the early days the rivers of the West that flowed into the Pacific were full of salmon and steelhead trout migrating upstream to spawn. When man began to dam these rivers for irrigation and the generation of electricity (with the encouragement of the federal government and private enterprise), the fish runs were reduced and the river-bottoms deeply inundated (see FISHERIES: *the West*). Because of damming, the Columbia River is now largely a series of lakes useful to waterfowl as resting places. Those waterfowl species able to feed in the newly established irrigated grainfields of the Columbia Basin, such as the mallard and Canada goose, have built up substantial over-wintering populations there.

At the turn of the century the aim of conservation was preservation; in the 1930s it was wise economic use. Dryland farming in the boom years of the 1920s had been followed by the dust bowl of the 1930s, and men had been forced to search for ways to use the land without destroying it. The drought of the early years dramatized the need for soil and water (including wildlife habitat) conservation; President Franklin D. Roosevelt's administration developed the governmental machinery to meet this need more effectively.

In 1934 a federal waterfowl-hunting license, the Duck Stamp, was created to provide funds for waterfowl refuges. The same year the Taylor Grazing Act closed the remaining public domain to homesteading and opened the way for the ultimate creation of the Bureau of Land Management (in 1946); one of the bureau's major objectives is wildlife conservation. In 1935 the Soil Conservation Service was established to help farmers initiate better soil conservation practices; the SCS also included wildlife conservation among its farm-planning objectives. In 1937 a federal tax on sporting arms and ammunition (authorized by the Pittman-Robertson bill) provided funds to the states for wildlife restoration. And in 1940 the United States Fish and Wildlife Service was established within the Interior Department to absorb the fish-and-wildlife responsibilities formerly vested in the departments of commerce and agriculture.

Throughout the 1930s there was a steady expansion of irrigation projects in the West. The introduction of water changed wildlife habitat, providing new living opportunities for such wildlife species as the ring-necked pheasant and numerous marshland birds. Unfortunately for wildlife, the increasingly efficient agricultural use of irrigation water has resulted in less and less "wastage" and correspondingly fewer benefits to wildlife.

A third wave of conservation focuses on the quality of life and is characterized by the emergence of the "preservationists" as an increasingly strong political force. Led by the SIERRA CLUB, which won its first major contest (Echo Park) in 1955, this "environmentalist" group is concerned with the quality of the human environment in the face of an expanding industrial culture.

Wild animals have become important indicators of environmental quality. Predators, so recently persecuted, are increasingly protected (see BURRO, WILD, and HORSE, WILD). The cougar, for example, has recently received protection as a game species in most western states. Species threatened with extinction are of special concern. Of these the bison is in good condition and the trumpeter swan is out of danger. The whooping crane is only slowly increasing, the California condor continues to decline, and the black-footed ferret is now extremely rare. The sea otter, once hunted toward extinction, is being reintroduced. But new victims appear: peregrine falcons, brown pelicans, even ospreys and bald eagles, are apparently being poisoned by residues of pesticides such as DDT.

Industry and the accompaniments of industry, transportation, power, and waste, are growing in the trans-Mississippi West. Also growing, even faster, is the third wave of conservation. The steady increase in the proportion of the electorate living in coastal cities, which thinks of the West largely as a place to relax and vacation, has provided politically active environmentalists with a strong base of support. Often these efforts run counter to utilitarian developments; the Echo Park controversy, for example, was whether or not a portion of Dinosaur National Monument should be dammed for hydropower and irrigation purposes.

In the United States wildlife, like scenery, is often considered a free benefit. One consequence of the American Revolution was that ownership of wildlife was vested among the citizens of each state, in common. Hunting was essentially free, and even private property was protected only by weak trespass-laws. The private landowner, managing his lands for commercial purposes, has no financial reason to take wildlife into account. Consequently, the more intensive the land management, the less place there is for wildlife. So private agricultural lands have become poorer and poorer places for wild animals. On less intensively managed private lands, such as grazing and forest lands, habitat remains for wildlife. And public lands, widespread throughout the West, generally are managed with wildlife well-being as one objective.

The hunting of wild animals was part of the western tradition from the start. As needs for control became evident, the hunters were taxed (through the sale of licenses) to provide funds for enforcement. As additional needs emerged—for state game-ranges, biological investigations, and the like—funds were increased largely by raising license fees and by taxing sporting arms and ammunition. Even on the federal level a waterfowl hunting license provided funds for the acquisition of wetlands for refuges. Since the turn of the century to the present day, then, the sportsman has been the source of most financial support for wildlife conservation, and

on the whole the conservation efforts have not been in vain.

However, much still remains to be done. The position of wildlife on private lands needs to be improved, though not to the detriment of the landowner. Threatened species which are still dwindling need to be restored. Conflicts between animals and man's crops need to be resolved. Contamination of animal habitat must be reversed. And as broader and broader segments of the public grow in awareness of the needs of wild animals, the financial support for wildlife conservation should flow not only from the sportsmen, but from society as a whole.

See Durwood L. Allen, *Our Wildlife Legacy* (1954); Stanford S. Atwood, chm., *Land Uses and Wildlife Resources* (1970); Raymond F. Dasman, *Wildlife Biology* (1964); Frank Graham, Jr., *Man's Dominion—The Story of Conservation in America* (1971); William T. Hornaday, *Wildlife Conservation in Theory and Practice* (1914); Peter Matthiessen, *Wildlife in America* (1959); and James B. Trefethen, *Crusade for Wildlife* (1961).—R. D. T.

Wild West show. An exhibition illustrating scenes and events characteristic of the frontier West. The Wild West show was a popular form of outdoor entertainment from 1883 to 1938. Its origin and development closely paralleled those of the rodeo, a competitive sport in which the contestants pay entrance fees and receive prize money but no pay. Most rodeos include exhibition acts, and a traveling rodeo in which the competitors are hired employees differs little except in name from the traditional Wild West show.

"Buffalo Bill" CODY is generally accepted as the originator of the Wild West show type of entertainment, although he was not the first showman to exploit the romantic appeal of the frontier West. P. T. BARNUM staged Indian dances, a "Grand Buffalo Hunt" in Hoboken, New Jersey, in 1843, and in 1860 was partner of James Capen "Grizzly" Adams in his California Menagerie. Tyler's Indian Exhibition toured with circuses in 1855-56. "Wild Bill" HICKOK was featured in a buffalo hunt in Niagara Falls in 1872. Contests of cowboy skills were held at cattle roundups as early as 1847 and became a feature of Fourth of July celebrations in such cow towns as Deer Trail, Colorado, in 1869 and Cheyenne, Wyoming, in 1872. A thousand contestants entered an "Old Glory Blowout" staged by Cody in North Platte, Nebraska, in 1882. In partnership with Dr. William Frank Carver, "Evil Spirit of the Plains," Cody opened Buffalo Bill's Wild West in Omaha in 1883.

Cody had behind him a notable record as an army scout in Indian campaigns and ten years' experience in stage melodramas about the West. He was also a hero of DIME NOVELS. He had a faculty for dramatizing his own experiences, and the show put together in 1883 set the pattern. It included a demonstration of the Pony Express, an attack on the Deadwood stagecoach, bucking broncos, roping and riding wild steers, horse races, shooting by Doc Carver, Buffalo Bill himself, and Captain A. H. Bogardus (called champion pigeon shot of America), and a spectacle introducing buffalo, elk, deer, mountain sheep, mustangs, and Longhorns. William Levi "Buck" Taylor, "King of the Cowboys," became the first fictional cowboy hero in dime novels written by Prentiss Ingraham. Johnny Baker became a famous

Buffalo Bill's troupe brought the Wild West to London's Olympia Stadium in 1903. (Library of Congress)

marksman as "The Cow-Boy Kid." Major Frank North of the Pawnee Scouts enrolled Indians in the show, with Pawnee Bill (Gordon William Lillie) as interpreter.

Cody and Carver parted after the first season, and Carver started his own Wild West show with Captain Jack Crawford, the "Poet Scout." Buffalo Bill's Wild West played the Cotton Exposition in New Orleans during the winter of 1884-85 and there acquired perhaps the greatest personality developed in Wild West shows, Annie OAKLEY, known as "Little Sure Shot." Sitting Bull was with the show in 1885 and toured Canada. In 1887 Cody and his partner, Nate Salsbury, took Buffalo Bill's Wild West to London for Queen Victoria's Golden Jubilee, where it proved a big success. At one performance the Deadwood coach had as passengers four kings and the Prince of Wales, with Buffalo Bill driving. A European tour, opening in Paris in 1889, left a lasting impression of the romantic aspects of the American frontier. The show returned to America for the World's Columbian Exposition in Chicago in 1893, where it scored the most successful season in outdoor show business.

Meanwhile Cody's success spawned imitation. Adam Forepaugh added Wild West acts and a spectacle of Custer's Last Fight to his all-feature show, 1887-89, employing Bogardus and Carver. Carver took a Wild America show to Europe in 1889 and later to Australia. Pawnee Bill's Historic Wild West got its start in 1888 and toured Europe in 1894. Buck Taylor, Kennedy Brothers, and Kemp Sisters were other Wild West shows of the 1890s. In the opening years of the twentieth century there were large numbers of small shows with such colorful names as Broncho Ben, Buckskin Ben, Buckskin Bill, Cherokee Ed, Dickey's Circle D, Indian

Bill, Kit Carson's Buffalo Ranch, Lone Star May, Texas Bill, and Tiger Bill.

Colonel Frederic T. Cummins staged an Indian Congress at the world's fairs in Omaha (1898-99), Buffalo (1901), and St. Louis (1904), touring it in Europe as Cummins' Wild West and Indian Congress (1907-11). The Jamestown Exposition of 1907 was a springboard for Miller Bros. 101 Ranch Real Wild West, which became one of the biggest shows.

Salsbury died in 1902 and James A. Bailey of Barnum & Bailey circus fame entered the management of Buffalo Bill's Wild West. He billed it for extensive tours of the United States, including one-day stands—in 1895 the show played 131 stands in 190 days—and returned it to Europe in 1902 for a tour that lasted until 1906. Meanwhile Bailey died, leaving Cody in a financial tangle. Cody and his expert press relations manager, Major John M. Burke, had avoided using the word "show" in their advertising; it was billed as an "exhibition" and particularly scorned any connotation of "circus." A merger was made under the title Buffalo Bill's Wild West and Pawnee Bill's Far East, the "Far East" including elephants. This show was on the road from 1909 to 1913, with many "farewell appearances" by Buffalo Bill. It also had imitators. Cummins joined Vernon C. Seavers in the Young Buffalo Wild West and Col. Fred Cummins Far East Combined, with which Annie Oakley traveled for three seasons. Even Miller Bros. 101 Ranch added "Great Far East" to its billing.

The "Two Bills" show failed in 1913, and Buffalo Bill toured two years with the Sells-Floto Circus and then joined Miller Bros. for his final season in 1916. Although he died in 1917, the show went on the road under the Buffalo Bill name, with Jess Willard, heavyweight champion, featured. At the end of that war year Wild West shows ended, at least temporarily.

In the early 1920s there was an upsurge in the popularity of the RODEO, little known under that name previously. Of course, many a "rodeo" was a Wild West show under another name. Miller Bros. 101 Ranch Real Wild West came back successfully in 1925. Bill Pickett, the Negro cowboy who invented bulldogging, was one of its stars. Others were Ezra Meeker of Oregon Trail fame, Tad Lucas, champion woman rider of rodeo fame, and "Suicide Ted" Elder, who rode standing on two horses in a leap over an automobile. The show failed in 1931, but Zack T. Miller, the surviving brother, kept trying with small shows until his death in 1952.

The Wild West as a concert or after-show of a circus or a combined circus and Wild West was common in the 1930s, starring such personalities as Tom Mix, Ken Maynard, Jack Hoxie, and the "Lone Ranger." Colonel Tim McCoy headed the after-show for Ringling Bros.-Barnum & Bailey and in 1938 staged Colonel Tim McCoy's Real Wild West and Rough ˙Riders of the World. This was the last big Wild West, but it failed within a month. McCoy continued trouping with small shows, but the great days of the outdoor Wild West were over. Rodeo, its successor, remained a thriving spectacle.

The Wild West show dramatized the American West as a place of romance and glamor to people throughout the world. It introduced the cowboy hero, and the western of fiction, film, and television was its offspring.

Don Russell, *The Wild West: A History of the Wild West Shows* (1970), gives details and background and has a checklist of 116 shows.—D. R.

Wilkes expedition (1838-1842). A worldwide naval exploring expedition. In August 1838 a naval squadron under the command of Lieutenant Charles Wilkes set out from Norfolk, Virginia, on a voyage of exploration and surveying. In the three years and ten months of its existence the expedition confirmed that Antarctica was a continent and made such excellent charts of certain islands in the south and central Pacific that they were used by naval and marine units in World War II. Then, in April 1841, Wilkes arrived off the coast of Oregon. One of his vessels, the *Peacock*, was lost trying to cross the sandbar at the mouth of the Columbia, though all hands were saved.

In the following months contingents of the expedition explored all the way up the Columbia to the mouth of the Snake River, and others pushed through the Juan de Fuca Strait into Puget Sound. Grays Harbor on the Olympic peninsula was investigated. Wilkes also sent Lieutenant George F. Emmons with a party down the Willamette and on south through dangerous Indian country to the Sacramento River and Sutter's Fort. Mission San Jose and the Franciscan Mission of Santa Clara were also visited. From Yerba Buena (known as San Francisco after 1848), this contingent rejoined the other units of the expedition and returned to New York in June 1842.

The Wilkes expedition never received the credit that was its due. There was ceaseless antagonism to Wilkes, because he was appointed over other officers who were considered by many to be better qualified and more deserving. Moreover, his character, while assuring success in terms of fulfillment of the mission, was of a kind

that irritated people. The fame of the expedition was further dampened by several courts-martial, including one in which Wilkes was the defendant. Yet the scientific achievements were impressive. James Dwight Dana and Titian Ramsay Peale were but two of several outstanding scientists who accompanied the squadron.

As for the Northwest, Wilkes sensed its importance for an expanding America and spent more time there, ordering more extensive surveys than he was charged to do. The loss of the *Peacock* prompted him to advocate American possession north to 54°40' on the grounds that better harbors were to be found there. In his *Narrative . . .* he suggested that a great state would emerge in the Northwest, free from Mexico and making use of San Francisco Bay and ports within the Juan de Fuca Strait to carry on trade with the Pacific world.

See Harvey H. Bartlett, "The Report of the Wilkes Expedition and the Work of the Specialists in Science," in *Proceedings of the American Philosophical Society* (1940); Daniel C. Haskell, *The United States Exploring Expedition . . . and Its Publications 1844-1875* (1942); David B. Tyler, *The Wilkes Expedition* (1968); and Charles Wilkes, *Narrative of the United States Exploring Expedition* (1844-45).—R. A. B.

Wilkeson, Samuel. See GREAT LAKES, MEN OF THE.

Wilkinson, James (1757-1825). Soldier, land speculator, and politician. Wilkinson was born in the fertile community of Calvert County, Maryland. When he was seventeen he was sent to medical school in Philadelphia, and in this city he first came into association with the military establishment. He prepared himself for the practice of medicine, however, and actually returned to Maryland in 1775 to open a doctor's office, but excitement over the outbreak of the American Revolution led him into the army. He served under General George Washington's command in Boston at Bunker Hill, under General Nathanael Greene in New York, and was present on the Lachine, Quebec, campaign with Benedict Arnold. Later Wilkinson participated in the New Jersey campaigns. He rose to the rank of brigadier general and was placed in charge of the clothing division of the commissary department as clothier general in 1779. This latter position opened numerous economic opportunities to Wilkinson, and he was able to avail himself of the advantages. Too, his marriage to Ann Biddle of Philadelphia did not handicap him either socially or politically.

After the end of the revolutionary war and a brief plunge into politics, Wilkinson turned to the West and Kentucky in 1783 to engage in land and mercantile speculation, entering large blocks of land in the neighborhood of the Falls of the Ohio and on the Kentucky River near Frankfort. He successfully mixed land speculation with local politics. In this period Kentuckians were beginning to grow restless under Virginia restrictions, and after 1784 there followed nine conventions seeking separation of the western territory. Settling in Lexington, Wilkinson soon became a prominent figure. By 1787 he was prepared to begin a profitable trade in western products down the river to New Orleans. He established warehouses at Frankfort and had large flatboats built to navigate the western rivers.

Because of illness Wilkinson was unable to attend the convention at Danville in 1785, but he was elected a delegate in 1786 and was present in the fourth, fifth, and sixth conventions. A charge, perhaps groundless and no more than rumor, was made that he wished to thwart the career of George Rogers Clark and to monopolize use of the Mississippi. In April 1787 Wilkinson set out with a boatload of Kentucky country produce for the New Orleans market. Although no historian can ever fully reconstruct his conversations and dealings with the downriver Spanish officials, his memorial to the authorities did gain him a favored position in the river trade, but forever tarnished his reputation as having been guilty of near treasonous intrigue (see SPANISH CONSPIRACY). Whatever his agreement with the Spanish, Wilkinson's trade monopoly and political maueuvers failed. Nevertheless, there is considerable incriminatory historical evidence against Wilkinson.

In 1792 Wilkinson was appointed commander of western military affairs to be stationed at Fort Washington on the Ohio with the rank of lieutenant colonel. This appointment came immediately on the heels of General Arthur St. Clair's miserable defeat in the Miami valley. Washington, however, passed over Wilkinson and selected Anthony Wayne to the post of command in the Northwest Indian campaign. There seems not to have been any animus toward Wilkinson, and he took part in the campaign and was present at the battle of Fallen Timbers (1794). Nevertheless, Wayne was suspicious of Wilkinson and notified Timothy Pickering, newly appointed secretary of war, of his doubts.

There was little doubt in 1794 that Wilkinson had renewed his intrigues with the Spanish. In time, these activities were to involve several westerners, including George Rogers Clark. There has survived sufficient evidence in these later manipulations to convict the general of highly irregular conduct, if not open treason. Nevertheless, Wilkinson was confirmed as the commanding head of the United States army early in March 1797. As such, he had charge of administering enforcement of the terms of the Treaty of San Lorenzo, which threw him into constant contact with the Spanish of Louisiana. During the years 1797-1801 he was active all across the sprawling western frontier as commanding general, and upon the inauguration of Thomas Jefferson as president sought to improve his social and political lot in Washington.

Wilkinson returned to the Mississippi valley in 1802 and became an active figure in the lower river country during the period when negotiations were under way for the purchase of Louisiana. He proposed to march against New Orleans and was ordered to invade the Choctaw nation. He went as far as Pensacola, Florida, in his general survey of the southern country. When the Spanish surrendered Louisiana to the French and then the French in turn handed it over to the United States on December 18, 1803, Wilkinson was present with a small command of American soldiers (see LEWIS AND CLARK EXPEDITION).

In the spring of 1805 the United States Senate confirmed Wilkinson's appointment as governor of Upper Louisiana. During these years he became deeply involved in the BURR CONSPIRACY, in which incriminating correspondence, often in code, passed back and forth between Wilkinson and Burr. On October 21 and 22, 1806, Wilkinson informed President Jefferson about the conspiracy, which he said extended from New York throughout the West, and announced his plans to meet

it. In this year he moved to Natchez and New Orleans, where he negotiated the famous Neutral Ground Treaty between the United States and Spain pertaining to the territory along the Sabine River. In the subsequent trial of Aaron Burr in Richmond, Virginia, before John Marshall in 1808, Daniel Clark and Wilkinson were seriously embarrassed, if not actually convicted of duplicity. Daniel Clark further embarrassed the general with the publication of his book *Proofs of the Corruption of General James Wilkinson* (1809).

The opening months of the War of 1812 found Wilkinson once again in a position of heavy military responsibility as commander of the western army. He was not, however, to emerge from this struggle a military hero. Failing health and friction with his fellow officers, especially General Wade Hampton over the St. Lawrence campaign, brought Wilkinson's military career to an undistinguished end. He refused a sinecure offered him by James Madison as superintendent of Indian affairs. Wilkinson spent much of his time after 1815 writing his memoirs and trying to recoup his fortune on a Mississippi cotton plantation. Failing at the latter he sought a large grant of land in Mexican territory. During an extended stay in Mexico City he contracted chronic diarrhea and died, far removed from the scenes of his famous activities.

See Thomas Perkins Abernethy, *The Burr Conspiracy* (1954); Thomas M. Green, *The Spanish Conspiracy* (1891); Thomas R. Hay and M. R. Werner, *The Admirable Trumpeter* (1941); Royal O. Shreve, *The Finished Scoundrel* (1933); and James Wilkinson, *Memoirs of My Own Times*, 3 vols. (1816).—T. D. C.

Willamette River. The Willamette River flows in a broad structural valley that constitutes the heartland of Oregon. The Willamette and its tributaries drain an area of about 11,200 square miles lying south of the Columbia River and bounded on the east by the Cascade Range and on the west by the Coast Range. Most of the major tributaries rise among mountains of the Cascade Range, which reach elevations of 10,000 feet and are snow-covered during much of the year. The important tributaries entering from the east are the Middle Fork, McKenzie, Calapooya, Santiam, Molalla, and Clackamas rivers. Western tributaries are the Long Tom, Luckiamute, Yamhill, and Tualatin rivers.

Streamflow from the basin is about twenty-six million acre-feet annually—about twice that of the Colorado River. The large flow is accounted for by the fact that precipitation over the entire basin averages sixty-three inches, sixty percent of which occurs from November through February in the form of snow in the mountains and rain on the valley floor.

The first white men to visit the Willamette valley were members of the Lewis and Clark expedition, who described it in 1806 as "the only desirable situation for settlement on the western side of the Rocky Mountains, and being naturally fertile, would, if properly cultivated, afford subsistence for 40,000 or 50,000 souls." (Today most Oregonians do live in the valley, which, in fact, provides most of Oregon's good arable land.) Lewis and Clark were followed by Canadian fur trappers associated with the Hudson's Bay Company. They trapped in the headwater streams and set up a trading post, Fort Vancouver, on the Columbia opposite the mouth of the Willamette River. In 1828 Jedediah Smith, in one of his epic journeys through the West, passed through the valley and wintered at Fort Vancouver.

The first settlers were retired French trappers who had been given land and supplies by the Hudson's Bay Company. They were the nucleus of the settlement that existed in the valley when Protestant ministers arrived in 1834 to work among the Indians of Oregon Territory. In the following years a number of other settlers, both British and Americans, came to the valley, but it was not until 1843 that a flood of migrants passed over the Oregon Trail to the valley of the Willamette. In 1840 there had only been 120 farms with 3,000 head of cattle and 2,500 horses in the entire territory. By 1845 there were more than five thousand Americans in the valley alone, and with the settlement of the boundary dispute with Great Britain many more settlers migrated to the area.

Had it not been for the discovery of gold in California in 1848, Oregon Territory might have achieved a large population sooner than it did. But the gold discovery not only diverted people southward off the Oregon Trail but also drew people from Oregon to the mines of California. And later, when the lands of Washington and eastern Oregon were opened to settlement, many pioneers came from the Willamette valley.

Nevertheless the population continued to increase and the people to prosper in the relatively mild climate of the region. Economy continued to be based on agriculture and forestry. Portland, at the mouth of the Willamette, grew to be the major port on the Columbia and an important processing and distribution center. Eugene and Corvallis, with their universities, are mainly supply centers for the farmlands around them. The whole valley area is surrounded by verdant forests and sparkling streams that attract large numbers of summer visitors from other parts of the nation. Tourism has become an important industry.

For map, see SNAKE RIVER.—R. W. D.

Williams, Isaac. See CHINO RANCHO.

Williams, William S.. (1787–1849). Mountain man and guide. Williams was born in Rutherford County, North Carolina, but grew up in Missouri. Williams, who "got religion" while in his teens, was an itinerant Baptist preacher for a time before becoming a trapper and trader with the Osage Indians (1813–1825). It is said that during this time he married into the tribe. When Joseph C. Brown conducted a government survey across Osage lands as part of a project to mark the Santa Fe Trail, Williams served as an interpreter for the party. He then became a Rocky Mountain free trapper and by 1832 had gone as far north as the Yellowstone River. In 1833, while on the Green River, he joined Joseph R. Walker's California expedition to buy horses and supplies. As a member of that party he was one of the first Americans to see the Yosemite Valley. Upon his return from California he lived among the Ute Indians. After a sojourn at Bent's Fort he returned east to Kansas and Missouri to visit relatives in 1841. It seems probable that he was also in search of a sponsor for a new expedition, for when he arrived at the Green River trapping grounds in 1842, he was accompanied by young William T. Hamilton, whose father had financed the expedition as part of an agreement to take young Hamilton to the mountains for his health.

In 1843 Williams swung through the West from Bent's Fort to the Columbia River and back to Santa Fe. He served as a guide in John C. Frémont's third expedition but then decided to live with the Ute. In 1848 he took Ute furs to Taos for sale but spent the proceeds on a wild spree. He then joined an expedition against New Mexican Ute and Apache late in 1848. In the fighting he was seriously wounded by the Ute, who undoubtedly had marked him for death because of his treachery.

Much against his better judgment Williams agreed to serve as a guide on Frémont's disastrous fourth expedition, which sought to find a favorable railroad route through the southern Rockies in the dead of winter. When eleven men were killed by freezing weather and deep snow, Frémont blamed Williams for the tragedy. When he and a pack train went back to the mountains to recover Frémont's supplies, Williams and Dr. Benjamin Kern were killed by the Ute Indians in revenge for their losses to American dragoons who had just attacked them.

Williams, who was "Bill" or "Old Bill" to his contemporaries, came close to epitomizing the independent, self-sufficient, taciturn mountain man. A tall, gaunt, pockmarked man with red hair, he was, in Albert Pike's words, "all muscle and sinew" and commanded respect. He worked with Kit Carson and Uncle Dick Wootton and hunted buffalo on the Plains with Captain William Drummond Stewart. It seems likely that he never lost his deep religious convictions. It is reputed that while on a visit to the Hopi villages, he tried to explain Christianity to that fiercely independent tribe.

See Alpheus G. Favour, *Old Bill Williams, Mountain Man* (1936), and William T. Hamilton, *My Sixty Years on the Plains* (1960), with an introduction by Donald J. Berthrong.—G. B. D.

Wills, Robert. See MUSIC, WESTERN.

Wilmot Proviso (1846). Introduced into the House of Representatives on August 8, 1846, as an amendment to an appropriations bill, the Wilmot Proviso prohibited slavery forever in any territory to be ceded by Mexico to the United States as a result of a treaty between the two nations, which were then at war. In both 1846 and 1847 some form of the proviso passed the House, only to die in the Senate. It remained a source of sectional conflict until the Compromise of 1850, and its main principle—congressional prohibition of slavery from western territories—provided the Republican party with its fundamental program in the 1850s.

Political factionalism as much as antislavery sentiment caused the introduction of the proviso by David Wilmot, a Democratic congressman from northern Pennsylvania. By 1846 many Democrats were disillusioned with the administration of James K. Polk. Northwestern Democrats were angry at his veto of a rivers and harbors bill and his failure to acquire all of Oregon Territory as promised in the expansionist Democratic platform of 1844. The faction of the party headed by Martin Van Buren, which drew most of its strength from the Northeast, was angry that it had lost the presidential nomination in 1844 and control of the national party to a coalition of northwestern and southern Democrats bent on territorial expansion. But the wings of that coalition differed on the question of slavery extension; southerners expected slavery to go into any territories won in the war with Mexico, while northwestern Democrats were interested in sheer territorial expansion, not slavery.

Wilmot, a member of the Van Buren faction, introduced his amendment to split up this expansionist coalition by showing that southern Democrats wanted expansion only if slavery extension was included. The hope was that southern opposition to the proviso would drive northwestern Democrats into the arms of the Van Buren element and thus strip the southerners of their control of the Democratic party. Historians, therefore, interpret the northern Democratic votes for the proviso as protest votes against the Polk administration as much as expressions of antislavery sentiment.

By linking the slavery question to territorial expansion, the Wilmot Proviso increased sectional hostility both in Congress and among the public at large. The proviso turned what had been a party issue in Congress into a sectional issue. Normally, the national parties took unified, if opposing, positions on the question of territorial acquisition; Democrats strongly advocated it and Whigs staunchly opposed it. The introduction of the slavery issue into this debate destroyed these clear-cut partisan lines. In their place emerged sectional lines in which northern Whigs and Democrats opposed southern Whigs and Democrats. These bitter sectional divisions forced both national parties to avoid the issue in the presidential ELECTION OF 1848 and thereby led to the formation of the Free-Soil party, which was dedicated to prohibition of slavery from the territories.

The intense sectional hostility in Congress reflected equally virulent sentiment in both the North and the South. The legislature of every northern state but one supported the Wilmot Proviso, while southern legislatures condemned it. Historians disagree over the meaning of and reasons for this popular excitement over the proviso. The "revisionist" historians have maintained that slavery expansion was an unreal issue, since it was economically unfeasible to take slaves west of Texas, and they blame the popular response on agitators and politicians who stirred up the public. Other historians have asserted that the slavery extension issue aroused so much furor because it was a symbol of a more fundamental and more important sectional division over the morality of slavery. In fact, the strong and hostile sentiment espoused in both sections reveals that the issue of slavery expansion into distant territories was itself an important and explosive issue to many people in the 1840s. Northerners saw the proviso as a way to prevent the spread of the slave power into new territories, which could possibly become slave states. Stopping the growth of the political power of southern slaveholders in Congress would prevent the subjugation of the North by the South. In addition, many northerners who were prejudiced against Negroes wanted to stop the spread of slavery primarily to preserve the territories for white men. On the other hand, even though southerners had no immediate plans to take slaves west of Texas, they viewed the Wilmot Proviso as a negation of southern equality in the nation because it denied southerners the right to advance their institutions into common territories on an equal basis with those of northerners. To southerners, the constitutional right to advance slavery was a fundamental issue on which they had to take a stand. Viewing southern opposition to the Wilmot Proviso, one could well anticipate the southern reaction to the election as president of the nominee of a party that adamantly denied such a right.

Absolutely the best account of the Wilmot Proviso and the reaction to it is Chaplain W. Morrison, *Democratic Politics and Sectionalism: The Wilmot Proviso Controversy* (1967). Also helpful is Avery Craven, *The Coming of the Civil War* (1957).—M. F. H.

Wilson, Jack. See GHOST DANCE.

Wilson, James (1835-1920). Agriculturalist and Iowa politician. Born in Ayrshire, Scotland, Wilson migrated with his family to the United States in 1851. They lived in Connecticut for several years and then moved west to a farm in Tama County, Iowa. Wilson attended public school in Iowa and also Iowa College (now Grinnell College) for two years.

Wilson's life in Iowa was varied but always related to agriculture. His political activities consisted of three terms in the Iowa House of Representatives, where he held the speakership for two years, and three terms in the national Congress. In Washington Wilson was given the nickname "Tama Jim" to distinguish him from James Falconer Wilson, a senator from Iowa. Returning to Iowa in 1885, Wilson resumed his farming pursuits and wrote a weekly farm column for several Iowa publications, including the *Iowa Homestead*. In 1891 he accepted a professorship of agriculture at Iowa State Agricultural College and Model Farm (now Iowa State University of Science and Technology) at Ames, where he also directed the Experiment Station.

At sixty-one Wilson embarked on the greatest challenge of his career when President William McKinley appointed him secretary of agriculture. He held the position for sixteen years, being reappointed by Theodore Roosevelt and William Howard Taft. Wilson believed the future of agriculture lay in science and education, and under his direction the department expanded in these areas. During his long tenure Wilson greatly expanded the scope of his department by establishing nationwide agricultural experiment stations, initiating farm demonstration work in southern states, and starting agricultural and home economics cooperative extension work. Wilson aided the passage of extensive legislation that helped the farmers in their fight against insects and plant and animal diseases. He also strongly promoted experimentation with new methods of farming.

See E. V. Wilcox's biography *Tama Jim* (1930). Wilson's main achievements as secretary of agriculture are reviewed in A. E. Winship, *Fifty Famous Farmers* (1924).—D. S.

Wimar, Charles or **Carl Ferdinand** (1828-1862). Painter. Wimar was born near present-day Bonn, West Germany, and came to the United States at the age of fifteen to settle with his parents in St. Louis, Missouri. He received his first instruction in art from Leon Pomarede, local sign painter, muralist, and panoramist, who himself had come from France to America in 1830. Pomarede earlier had collaborated with Henry Lewis on a panorama of the Mississippi valley and in 1849 undertook to make one of his own. With the young Wimar as his assistant, he journeyed upriver to the Falls of St. Anthony and back again, and upon completion of his ambitious project exhibited his *Panorama of the Mississippi River and Indian Life* in New Orleans. This was later destroyed by fire in Newark, New Jersey.

Wimar left Pomarede in 1851 to open a painting shop in St. Louis, abandoning this line of work the following year when the opportunity to go abroad to study presented itself. He spent four years in Düsseldorf under the supervision of Emanuel Leutze, returning again to St. Louis in 1856, and in 1858 made his first trip up the Missouri River to forts Clark and Union. Thereafter he devoted himself to the painting of Indians and buffalo-hunting scenes on the Great Plains, making at least two additional excursions to the headwaters of the Missouri in search of material. Wimar was one of the founders of the Western Academy of Art in 1859. In 1861 he married and that same year received a commission to execute a series of mural decorations in the rotunda of the St. Louis courthouse. He had barely completed this assignment when he died of consumption at the age of thirty-four. Although Wimar's murals were restored in 1888, they have not survived the years and are lost to posterity.

See Robert Taft, *Artists and Illustrators of the Old West, 1850-1900* (1953).—D. C. H.

Winchester rifle. See GUNS.

Wingfield, George (1876-1959). Nevada mineowner, politician, and banker. Wingfield was born on a farm near Fort Smith, Arkansas. His first contact with Nevada came when he was employed to help drive a herd of cattle from west of Lakeview, Oregon, to Winnemucca, Nevada, in 1896. In 1901 he followed the rush to the mining boom at Tonopah in southern Nevada and within a short time had gained control of the gambling concession at the Tonopah Club. From gambling he moved to mine investment at Tonopah and Goldfield. In November 1906, with George Nixon, he formed the Goldfield Consolidated Mines Company and from that time forward controlled the destiny of the community. When the Goldfield boom began to lessen, Wingfield turned to Reno and a new career in banking and real estate, buying the Golden and Riverside hotels and establishing a chain of twelve banks in western and northern Nevada. From about 1916 until 1935 Wingfield was the most powerful political figure in the state, maintaining his influence through a bipartisan machine. He refused an appointment to the United States Senate in 1912 and refused a "draft" for the governorship in 1926. The only elective office he held was that of member of the University of Nevada Board of Regents, serving from 1928 until 1938. He was forced into bankruptcy in 1935 after his chain of banks failed, listing assets of $10,504 and liabilities of $3,098,715.13. He began a financial comeback in 1936, repurchasing the Golden and Riverside hotels and with Noble Getchell began operation of the Getchell gold mine. The University of Nevada conferred an honorary degree of Doctor of Mining Economics on Wingfield in 1957. He continued to be active in Republican politics until his death, although he never regained his former political influence.

See Gilman M. Ostrander, *Nevada: The Great Rotten Borough, 1859-1964* (1966). The Wingfield papers, since 1968 at the Nevada Historical Society Library in Reno, are restricted for fifty years from that date. —R. R. E.

Winnebago Indians. The Winnebago Indians are a Siouan tribe that formerly inhabited east-central Wisconsin, centering around Green Bay. They have no tradition of migration to that region, but they probably settled it during the general prehistoric movement of Siouan peoples westward from the lower Ohio valley. The Winnebago were of close cultural and linguistic similarity to the Central Siouan Oto, Iowa, and Missouri tribes to the west, and may have been the parent stock of those peoples and possibly the Mandan. By not following the Siouan movement farther westward, the Winnebago became surrounded by Algonquian tribes that appeared in the Midwest in late prehistoric and early historic times. The Winnebago managed to maintain friendly accord with these neighbors, particularly the Sauk and Fox and Menomini, and when the Potawatomi, Kickapoo, and Miami were driven from Michigan and Ohio in the 1650s by the Iroquois, the Winnebago freely permitted them to settle in their territory. They really had little choice, for the Winnebago were disease-weakened and numerically inferior (3,800 in 1650) to the Angonquians, and the alternatives to friendship were extinction or eviction. As the Algonquian interlopers moved back into the Ohio country in the eighteenth century, the Winnebago extended their territory southwest toward the lower Wisconsin and Rock rivers. Their population in 1750 had increased to about 5,000.

Winnebago culture was basically similar to the central Siouan pattern, but there was a heavy overlay of acquired characteristics from the Algonquian neighbors, particularly in its artifacts and art. Winnebago social organization was based on two exogamous phratries, comprising four and eight patrilineal clans. The clans and phratries were hierarchically ranked and determined an individual's social status. Each clan had lineage chiefs. Tribal chieftaincy was the hereditary property of the leading clan. The chief was peacekeeper and conciliator of internal disputes. His lodge was an inviolate sanctuary for any who entered, and he alone of all Winnebago could not participate in war. The chief of the leading clan of the lower phratry was tribal war leader and head policeman. Winnebago religion contained many Algonquian-borrowed ceremonials, but their underlying beliefs were classically Siouan. They lived predominantly in woodlands, dwelled in permanent bark-house villages, and cultivated fields of corn, beans, and squash. Hunting, however, was the main source of subsistence, and communal spring journeys to the buffalo country were important annual events.

The Winnebago's first white contact was with French explorers in 1634, and they maintained continuously peaceful trading relations with French Canada until the British triumph in 1763. With the passing of French dominion from the Lakes region, the Winnebago became steadfast allies of the British, and most of the tribe was neutral during Pontiac's Rebellion (1763-64) against harsh British Indian policy. They joined with Tecumseh's confederacy against the Americans and fought for the British during the War of 1812. After the peace of 1815 they attempted nonviolent resistance to white-settler migration into their homeland by charging tolls at river crossings and demanding what amounted to rent payments for land used by whites, but were compelled to cede much of their territory in the Treaty of Prairie du Chien in 1825. In 1827 their discontent boiled over in an uprising in southern Wisconsin known as the Winnebago War, but by a judicious show of force, Governor Lewis Cass convinced the Winnebago of the futility of military opposition to the United States, and the war was ended before serious losses occurred on either side. Some portions of the tribe allied clandestinely with the Sauk and Fox during the Black Hawk War (1832). This conflict led to the forced cession of the entirety of Winnebago lands east of the Mississippi by 1837 and their placement on a small reservation in eastern Iowa.

Weakened by an epidemic of smallpox in 1836, the Winnebago were unable to further resist any policy that the whites devised for them. During the middle years of the nineteenth century they were herded from one location to another by an indecisive and indifferent government. In 1840 they were forcibly removed from eastern Iowa and placed in the western Iowa Neutral Ground. Transferred to Minnesota in 1846, they were first located north of the Minnesota River, then moved to Long Prairie reserve in 1848. Continually shrinking in numbers (from 4,500 to 2,500 between 1843 and 1852) from disease and hunger, they had to be kept on the reservation by force. In 1853 the remaining Winnebago were moved to Crow River, and then in 1856 to Blue Earth Reservation. They were just beginning to make progress toward establishing productive agriculture there when the Sioux Uprising of 1862 broke out and the white population of Minnesota demanded their removal. They were then taken to Crow Creek Reservation in South Dakota, but when extinction from more disease and starvation became imminent, the 1,200 survivors escaped the troops detailed to guard them and fled to the Omaha Reservation in Nebraska for help. There the government allotted them a tract in 1865 and finally permitted them to remain in one place. Some of the Winnebago have since reacquired land in Wisconsin, and a few families managed to remain at various locations during the removals. In the 1960s there were small Winnebago reservations in Nebraska and Wisconsin, and their population in 1962 was reported as 967.

See F. W. Hodge, ed., *Handbook of American Indians North of Mexico*, 2 vols. (1907-10); P. V. Lawson, "The Winnebago Tribe," *Wisconsin Archeologist*, vol. 6 (1907); and Paul Radin, *The Winnebago Tribe* (1923) and "The Influence of Whites on Winnebago Culture," *Proceedings* of the State Historical Society of Wisconsin (1913).—P. R. M.

Winther, Oscar Osborn (1903-1970). Historian. The son of Danish immigrants, Winther was born in Weeping Water, Nebraska. In 1912 the Winthers and their six sons moved to Eugene, Oregon, where young Winther attended high school and the state university. As a youth, he learned the meaning of hard work and responsibility, for his family operated a large dairy farm. However, judging from his lively sense of humor and natural ability to develop lasting friendships, these formative years must have been happy ones.

Winther's interest in history began in high school and by 1925 he had graduated from the University of Oregon with a major in that subject. He accepted a position a few months later at a local high school as basketball coach and teacher of history, geography, and biology. In 1926 he entered Harvard University and earned an M.A. in American history.

Back on the West Coast, he had a succession of assistantships, a scholarship, and finally an instructorship while working toward a Ph.D. degree at Stanford University, which he received in 1934. The following year he worked in San Francisco as assistant curator of the Wells, Fargo & Co. history collection, and then returned to Stanford as an instructor. By now he was thoroughly committed to western history, in part through the influence of Edgar Eugene Robinson, under whom he had written his dissertation, "The Express and Coach Business in California, 1848-1860." The Stanford University Press eventually published the study in book form. The year 1937 was significant in Winther's life; he married Mary Galey and accepted a position as assistant professor of western history at Indiana University. He remained at that institution for the next thirty-three years and by the time of his death he had established himself as a foremost authority on the West.

Winther received fellowships from several institutions and foundations and was a visiting professor at a number of universities throughout the United States and Europe. He held a variety of administrative positions at Indiana and was managing editor of the *Mississippi Valley Historical Review* and the *Journal of American History* (1963-66). Among his dozen major publications on the West are *The Great Northwest* (1947); *The Old Oregon Country* (1950); *A Classified Bibliography of the Periodical Literature of the Trans-Mississippi West, 1811-1957* (1961); and *The Transportation Frontier, 1865-1890* (1964). In recognition of his contributions to scholarship and teaching, the Indiana board of regents in 1965 conferred upon him the distinguished title of University Professor.—W. E. H.

Wisconsin. The Wisconsin frontier period began with the discovery by French explorers in 1634. In the southern half of the state it closed before the Civil War, but in the northern half of the state, originally covered with a great pine forest, the pioneer period lasted down to World War I. The first frontier line to cross Wisconsin was in 1840, though settlement of the mining area began around 1825, and the last line drawn was in 1880.

The discovery and exploration of Wisconsin grew out of the establishment of the French fur trade in the St. Lawrence valley. Samuel de Champlain was eager to expand the fur trade with the Indians by exchanging European goods (guns, knives, needles, and axes). He also wanted to find a way to China via the "Western Sea," which Indian lore said was not far away. The first known explorer to arrive in Wisconsin was young Jean Nicolet. Whether he landed on the south shore of Green Bay or ascended the Fox River to Lake Winnebago is not known, though it is commonly assumed that Green Bay was the place where he first met the "People of the Western Sea." Wearing a "grand robe of China damask, all strewn with flowers and birds of many colors" and carrying "thunder in both hands," he expected to meet an oriental emperor. He found instead the Winnebago Indians, who called him "wonderful man" and feasted him with beavers. Thus reported one of the Jesuit fathers whose records, known as *Jesuit Relations*, constitute the principal source of information about the French in the "Upper Country." Though Nicolet reported that the Wisconsin tribes were eager to welcome French traders, the Iroquois of New York and Canada, armed with Dutch guns, drove traders from the St. Lawrence and harried many tribes westward. It was not until 1658 that two French adventurers, Pierre Esprit Radisson and Médard Chouart Groseilliers, followed the tribes westward to the Lake Superior region.

Though their enormous harvest of furs was seized, their success further increased French interest in that area west of Sault Ste. Marie. Between 1665 and 1670, Nicolas Perrot officially established the fur trade in Wisconsin, built posts on the Mississippi River, and made peace among the warring tribes. Everywhere the Indians welcomed him as "one of the chief spirits, since thou useth iron; it is for thee to rule and protect all men . . ."

The Fox-Wisconsin waterway connecting Lake Michigan with the Mississippi River was first traversed by Jacques Marquette and Louis Jolliet in 1673. Seeking the Mississippi River and the "China Sea," they left Mackinac Island, Michigan, May 17, 1673, in birchbark canoes, supplied with smoked meat and Indian corn. From Green Bay, they ascended the Fox River and were warned by the Menomini Indians to go no farther, since there were people ahead who showed no mercy to strangers and the river was filled with monsters and "even a demon" who "swallowed up all who ventured to approach him . . ." Portaging into the Wisconsin River, they went down to the Mississippi without injury. They recorded for the first time the Indian word *Meskousing*, from which Wisconsin got its name. (Whether it means "gathering of waters" or something else has never been resolved.) The water connection between the Mississippi system and Lake Superior, by way of the St. Croix and Brûle rivers, was discovered by Daniel Greysolon, Sieur Duluth, in 1683. Other French explorers and missionaries traversed the intertwined river-lake system in subsequent years.

When the French surrendered their empire to the British in 1763, they left behind a small settlement of fifty families in Green Bay who followed the tribes in the winter for trading purposes, made maple syrup in the spring, and enjoyed feast days the year around. There were also a few French settlers at Prairie du Chien and an unknown number of half-breeds who lived among the various tribes. One of these of mixed race was Charles LANGLADE of Green Bay, often called the "father of Wisconsin." Another was Michel St. Cyr, who lived with his Winnebago wife and four children in a twelve-by-twelve-foot log cabin where the state capitol is today. There he sold whiskey and meals to travelers. His pot-pies were famous, and when asked what was in them, he always replied "Muskrat."

When the British took over the French possessions, they rebuilt the post at Green Bay and renamed it Fort Edward Augustus. Their fur traders took over the Indian trade. No civil government was established, though the Quebec Act of 1774 presumably applied to the whole region. The coming of Jonathan CARVER to the upper Mississippi in 1766-67 produced the first book about the region written in English, *Travels in the Interior of North America* (1778). In the preface to the third edition (1781), Dr. John C. Lettsom stated that Carver had in his possession a deed to most of northwestern Wisconsin signed by two "chiefs of the Naudowessies" (Dakota Sioux). This grant to Carver, "a chief under the most mighty and potent George the Third," was claimed by his legal wife and family in America and his common-law wife and two children in London, who sold it to speculators. "Carver's Deed" was never recognized by the British or United States governments. Deeds made of skin have shown up over the

years, one of which is now in River Falls, Wisconsin. Historians, however, regard the Carver deeds as fraudulent.

British influence among the Indians was never as great as the French influence had been. Though the Jay Treaty of 1795 excluded British traders from the region, it was not until 1815 that their influence ended. In the War of 1812, Wisconsin Indians led by British traders captured the post at Prairie du Chien as well as at Chicago and Michilimackinac.

The first permanent settlements after the French and British era were made around 1825 near lead deposits in the region where Wisconsin, Illinois, and Iowa meet. The presence of lead had been known to the Indians long before the first Frenchman, Perrot, employed them to extract it in the 1660s. Julian Dubuque, another French trader, had a Spanish license and the consent of the Indians to mine lead there in 1788, after which the reputation of the "Spanish Mines" spread through the Mississippi valley. The finding of a huge nugget in 1819 so large, said a pioneer, "that a whole band of Indians was required to move it," contributed to this growing reputation. Emigrants began to come to the region in numbers, flowing into the area below the Wisconsin River. The Wisconsin settlers increased from 200 in 1825 to 10,000 four years later. By 1840, Wisconsin produced one half of the lead used in the nation, and mining towns with such quaint names as Black Jack, Burlesqueburgh, and Swindler's Ridge dotted the area. Miners located their claims by seeking depressions left by early Indian mines, using divining rods or forked twigs that presumably turned down over veins of lead, or trading a bottle of whiskey for a tip on an Indian "secret mine." Mineral Point became the center of the mining district, and Shake Rag Street the center of Mineral Point. Wives signaled dinnertime to the miners on the hill by running a rag up a stick, and the street carries the name of Shake Rag to this day. A hotel served meals in one room and sold liquor and had free beds in another. Many a miner went to bed alone only to wake up later finding he shared his bed with several customers. The jail, made of unhewn logs, was high enough for a man to stand up unless he was six feet tall. One lanky miner escaped by lifting the corner of the jail and crawling out. In another town, Dodgeville, one miner challenged another to a duel, chose rocks as weapons at forty feet, then told his adversary to go to the bottom of a pit forty feet down and fire away. This incident made a laughing stock of dueling, though most of the miners were from southern states where the code *duello* still prevailed.

According to undocumented lore, the practice of some miners ascending the rivers to the mines in the spring and going back in the fall, as fish do at spawning time, accounts for the name of "Sucker" given to the people of Illinois. The name of "Badger" given to Wisconsin people is said to have come, not from the badger itself, but from the miners' habit of living in caves and digging holes in the hillsides. The southern immigrants to the mines gave the region its flavor. Missouri provided Wisconsin with its first territorial governor, Henry Dodge. However, it was the Cornish miners who came after 1835 who left such visible marks as stone cottages and meat pies (pastries), still in evidence in southwestern Wisconsin.

Prior to the coming of settlers to the mining district, the Sauk and Fox had relinquished their claim to the area below the Wisconsin River. Boundaries among the various tribes were established in 1825. Two years later Chief Red Bird of the Winnebago, motivated by settlers' behavior around Prairie du Chien and rumors that troops had turned over two of the tribes to be killed by the Chippewa, murdered Registre Gagnier and Solomon Lipcap in a revenge killing, and other Winnebago attacked supply boats on the Mississippi River. The "Winnebago Uprising" of 1827 came to a dramatic end when the proud chief, dressed in white deerskin and wearing preserved red birds as epaulettes, surrendered to the troops and was imprisoned in Prairie du Chien, where he died a year later. In 1832 Sauk chief Black Hawk, whose village had been moved across the Mississippi into Iowa, returned to his old village on the Rock River with his entire band of 400 warriors and 900 women and children, ostensibly to plant their corn. Pursued by the Illinois militia, Wisconsin volunteers under Dodge, and United States army units up the Rock and down the Wisconsin to the Mississippi, Black Hawk's band was largely destroyed and the chief captured. While imprisoned he dictated his *Autobiography*, and simply said, "I loved my towns, my cornfields and the home of my people. I fought for it." Abraham Lincoln took part in this war with the Illinois militia, and legend has it that his horse was stolen by Indians.

The BLACK HAWK WAR might well have been averted had not ambitious politicians used the occasion to win reputations by military actions. However, it did end military action in Wisconsin as a means of opening up the land to settlers. In 1833 Indian title to all lands below the historic Fox-Wisconsin water route across Wisconsin was extinguished. The western half of the state was ceded by the Chippewa, Winnebago, and Sioux tribes in 1837, and in 1842 the Chippewa ceded most of their lands in northern Wisconsin. The Menomini and Chippewa accepted reservations in 1854. The Winnebago were removed to Nebraska, but many of them returned to their ancestral homes along the Wisconsin River, where they live today. After the cessions of 1833, the way was open for the white settlement of southern Wisconsin.

An army officer at Green Bay reported in 1827 that the land along Lake Michigan was nothing but a swamp and "entirely uninhabitable." However, the publicity given the Black Hawk War in the nation's newspapers and the signing of the Indian treaties focused attention upon the new frontier now open. Southern Wisconsin was a land of "oak openings" where a farm could be established without much land-clearing, where timber was available for building houses and for fuel, where hay grew abundantly in marshes, and where springs provided drinking water and refrigeration for milk and butter. Rivers provided power for gristmills and sawmills, and lakes contained fish and waterfowl. Armed with the folk knowledge that soil which produces hardwood trees will produce crops, the pioneers began their invasion in 1835, settling close to water transportation on Lake Michigan and Rock River as long as the land was available. Since the land in the southeastern area was not yet for sale under the federal land acts, settlers squatted on their plots and formed clubs to protect their claims from speculators when offered for sale later.

The southeastern frontier was settled largely by "Old American" stock who came west from New York or New England by covered wagon or Great Lakes steamboat. The German immigration began about 1840, coming to Milwaukee, Sheboygan, and Manitowoc on Lake Michigan, and fanning westward and northward where the land was cheaper because it was more heavily wooded. The census of 1850 showed a population of 305,391 in Wisconsin, of whom 198,000 were American-born, 98,000 being from New York. Foreign-born from the British Isles numbered 47,000, and the non-English-speaking, mostly German, were 57,000 in number. The Norwegian immigration began about the same time in the south-central region and moved northward and westward through the state.

The Wisconsin frontier was attractive to nineteenth-century reformers who founded at least a dozen Utopian communities in the 1840s. Ceresco, a settlement based on the communal teaching of Robert Fourier, was established by Yankee emigrants at Ripon. Voree, founded by James Strang, a disgruntled Mormon leader, first existed in southern Wisconsin at Burlington, then moved to Beaver Island in Lake Michigan, where it became the polygamous Kingdom of St. James. There were numerous group settlements, such as the English potters at Portage and the Swiss at New Glarus.

The frontier moved northward until around 1860, when it came to rest against the great pine forest that covered much of the northern half of the state. The frontier line of 1880 ran through northern Wisconsin, but the cutover region of brush and stumps was not settled as long as prairie lands were available farther west.

Originally included in the old Northwest Territory, Wisconsin became a part of Indiana Territory in 1800, and in 1805 Governor William Henry Harrison appointed justices of peace to bring law and order to the settlements at Prairie du Chien and Green Bay. Charles Reaume, a British subject at Green Bay, had been previously commissioned because he could read and write "a little." He was careful not to hand down decisions against fur traders who might appeal them. One pioneer said that a "bottle of spirits" was the best witness to be presented in Judge Reaume's court. In one case, he decided that the plaintiff and defendant were both wrong and ordered one to deliver a load of hay to his home, the other to bring him a load of wood. In a seduction case, he ordered the seducer to purchase a calico dress for the lady and two for the baby, and to pay the cost of splitting a thousand rails for the judge. Though Wisconsin became a part of Illinois Territory in 1809, there were no significant changes in internal government, but when it became a part of Michigan in 1818, three counties (Michilimackinac, Brown, and Crawford) was created and the laws of Michigan loosely extended over them. Governor Lewis Cass explored the region by canoe in 1820 and three years later appointed a young lawyer, James DOTY, to be judge of the territory west of Lake Michigan. Federal troops had occupied Fort Crawford at Prairie du Chien and Fort Howard at Green Bay in 1816, and Fort Winnebago was built at Portage in 1828, creating a permanent Indian frontier across the territory.

It was at Fort Howard that Dr. William Beaumont made the first studies in human digestion. When he served there in 1822, a French-Canadian *voyageur*, Alexis St. Martin, suffered a gunshot wound in the stomach. A flap covering the opening never healed, permitting Dr. Beaumont to insert food suspended on a string. He observed the effect of gastric juices upon it and in 1833 published the first book on the subject. (See DOCTORS.)

The Territory of Wisconsin was established in 1836, and because of the rapidly growing settlement was immediately authorized to elect a council and house of representatives. Henry DODGE, a Democrat, was appointed governor and Henry W. Jones the territorial delegate to Congress. The boundaries between Illinois and Michigan were the same as the present, but the territory included Iowa, Minnesota, South Dakota, and most of North Dakota to the west. The first legislature met at Belmont, a mining town not yet ready for such honors. As described by one legislator, "The accommodations of Belmont were most miserable, there being but a single boarding house. The whole of the Brown [county] delegation lodged in one room, about fifteen by twenty feet, and our lobby friends lived with us. Our beds were all full, and the floor well-spread with blankets and over-coats . . ." It was not expected that this legislature would locate the site of the permanent capital, but through gifts of lots to the governor's son, fifteen or twenty of the legislators, and the clerks of the two houses, Doty influenced the decision to make Madison, the townsite he had laid out in 1829, the capital of the territory. When the first meeting of the legislature was held in the incomplete capitol building, the lower floor was occupied by a drove of hogs. When the debate became too oratorical, one member would "take a long pole, go at the hogs, and stir them up; when they would raise a young pandemonium for noise and confusion the speaker's voice would become completely drowned, and he would be compelled to stop . . ."

Agitation for statehood began immediately. The three territorial governors (Dodge, 1836-41, 1845-48; Doty, 1841-44; Nathaniel P. Tallmadge, 1844-45) gave official support to the movement, but the voters turned down statehood resolutions four times prior to 1844, fearing the tax burden if the federal government withdrew. Boundaries established in the enabling act of 1846 were also controversial. The exclusion of the upper peninsula of Michigan and the placing of the northwest boundary on the St. Croix River rather than the Mississippi was a thorn in the flesh to many people. When the first constitutional convention began October 5, 1846, the 125 members, many of whom were emigrants from New York, used the New York constitution as a model. They provided for election of judges, prohibited banks of issue, made farmsteads under forty acres and town property worth under $1,000 exempt from seizure for debt, gave women the right to hold property, and provided for a referendum on suffrage for free Negroes. Conservative Whigs and Democrats voted against adoption 20,121 to 14,119 because of its radical features. The second convention omitted the homestead exemption, Negro suffrage, and the right of women to hold property but provided for a referendum on banks and, at the urging of Michael FRANK, established a public education system. This was adopted 16,417 to 6,174, and Wisconsin was admitted as the thirtieth state on May 29, 1848.

Wisconsin's frontier did not really end with statehood. The northern thrust of settlement skirted the upper half of the state, since it was covered with an enormous stand of conifers mixed with hardwoods that stretched across the upper parts of Michigan, Wisconsin, and Minnesota. One sixth of all the white pine in the nation grew by the Chippewa River and its tributaries. Described as a "vast, imperial domain" having less than 31,000 inhabitants in 1860, it was not an inviting land for farmers. This explains why Minnesota had 59,000 settlers from Wisconsin in 1860, Iowa had 42,000, and Kansas, Nebraska, and the Dakotas combined had 78,000. However, in the generation after 1890 when the Census Bureau announced the closing of the American frontier, the pine had been cut and the cutover area of stumps and brush was being rapidly settled by thousands of farmers who cleared land and built homes.

The removal of the great forest was done between the Civil War and World War I. The pioneers of southern Wisconsin (1825-60) had built their homes with hardwood trees, such as oak, from the native stands on the hillsides, sawed into lumber at small mills powered by water on the numerous streams. The hunger for good building lumber (pine) caused a number of early settlers to set up sawmills on the rivers in the northern pine forests, sometimes in violation of Indian rights. The Mormons built their tabernacle at Nauvoo, Illinois, with pine lumber cut on the Black River, a tributary of the Mississippi. The rivers of Wisconsin that tapped the great forest flowed into the Mississippi (St. Croix, Chippewa, Black, Wisconsin), Lake Michigan (Menominee, Peshtigo, Oconto, Fox, and Wolf, indirectly), or Lake Superior (Brûle, St. Louis, Montreal, and lesser streams). Since pine logs float and hardwoods do not, this harvest could be moved to market by water before the building of the railroads between 1874 and 1900. Lumber camps rose along the rivers and their numerous tributaries, and lumberjacks, many directly from Europe or Canada, felled the trees with crosscut saws all winter long and floated them down the rivers in the spring. Sawmills were built along the rivers all the way down to St. Louis, and villages and cities developed around the sawmills. The saying about "Hurley, Hayward, and Hell" being the same had meaning when the lumberjacks came into town. As one said, after a winter in the woods, they wanted more than coffee and cream; they wanted something that came in bottles and corsets. The lumberjacks took up farms behind the cutting crews and converted stump land into farms. When the last drives were made—down the Chippewa in 1917 and the St. Croix in 1912—the scattered stands of hardwoods were hauled to the mills by small railroads.

When it became apparent around 1890 that the lumberjack frontier would not last many more years, an effort was made to encourage settlement by farmers. The State Board of Immigration was organized in 1895, and Dean William A. Henry of the College of Agriculture wrote *Northern Wisconsin, a Handbook for the Homeseeker*, which was published by the legislature for wide distribution. At least 300 colonization companies were set up by lumber interests, railroads, and real estate speculators, of which 185 had offices in Wisconsin. They sent agents to American cities and Europe, recruiting settlers for the cutover frontier. For example, the American Colonization Company, formed in 1917, bought 50,000 acres and built the model town of Ojibwa. Log houses and barns on each 40-acre plot were provided, and the company sponsored stump-pulling contests. The company's pamphlet invited city workers thus: "Come to Sunny Sawyer County / There's a future here for you / Mother Nature's always smiling / And the skies are rarest blue." The Weyerhaeuser Company hoped to sell one million acres to Polish, Finnish, and other immigrants who were willing to convert stump land into crop land. The James L. Gates Company owned 800,000 acres at one time.

Cutover farms increased rapidly up to World War I. Stump-pullers and dynamite helped solve the problem of pine stumps, which could last 100 years without decay; extension agents promoted sheep to eat the brush and to grow potatoes for a cash crop; the colonization companies offered generous credit. Log cabins spread over the "New North." By 1920 the population of the twenty-six counties was 703,000, more than one fourth of the total number of people in Wisconsin, and one of the cutover counties, Marathon, had the largest rural population in the state. In this county 31,000 were Germans, 19,000 were Norwegians, 15,000 were Swedish, 13,000 were Poles, 10,000 were Canadians, 5,000 were Finns, and 2,000 were Danes. As the cutover frontier passed, Hayward, Hurley, and other lumber-mill towns remained. They had not yet lost all of their frontier character.

See Robert F. Fries, *Empire in Pine* (1951); Arlan Helgeson, *Farms in the Cutover* (1962); Lucille Kane, "Settling the Wisconsin Cutovers," *Wisconsin Magazine of History*, vol. 40 (1956-57); Louise P. Kellogg, *The French Regime in Wisconsin and the Northwest* (1925), and *The British Regime in Wisconsin and the Northwest* (1935); William F. Raney, *Wisconsin* (1940); Joseph Schafer, *The Wisconsin Lead Region* (1932); and Alice E. Smith, *The History of Wisconsin*, vol. I (1973).—W. D. W.

Wissler, Clark (1870-1947). Anthropologist. Wissler was born in Wayne County, Indiana. Having received his Ph.D. at Columbia in 1901, he joined the staff of the American Museum of Natural History, remaining there from 1902 to 1924, when he moved to Yale.

Wissler's published efforts concerning Blackfoot, Sioux, and other Plains Indians, as well as his pioneering research on the effects of the introduction of the horse among Plains Indians, continue to be basic works on these subjects. For nearly three decades after its first appearance in 1917, his *The American Indian* was the standard college textbook and the source most often turned to by anyone seeking general information. The book represents his work with the Blackfoot and Siouan tribes of Montana between 1902 and 1905. Wissler was also one of the principal formulators and the most successful popularizer of the culture-area concept for native North America.

See George P. Murdock, "Clark Wissler, 1870-1947," *American Anthropologist*, vol. 50, no. 2 (1948).—B. L. F.

Wister, Owen (1860-1938). Novelist. Wister was born in Germantown, Pennsylvania, the son of a successful physician. His family was well to do and interested in cultural activities. As a child Wister spent some time abroad with his parents, briefly attending boarding school in Switzerland and England. Most of his schooling, however, was in the United States. While at Harvard, from which he was graduated *summa cum laude* in 1882, he met Theodore Roosevelt, and their friendship lasted until Roosevelt's death. Wister dedicated his novel *The Virginian* (1902) to Roosevelt and later wrote an intimate portrait of the man in *Roosevelt: The Story of a Friendship, 1880-1919* (1930).

After college Wister decided upon a musical career and went to Paris to study composition, but failing health forced him to return to America and in 1885, on medical advice, he followed Roosevelt to the West. He spent the summer of 1885 on a ranch near Buffalo, Wyoming—a locality that reappears constantly in his western writing—and by autumn found his health sufficiently improved to enter Harvard law school, from which he was graduated in 1888. During his law school years and briefly thereafter he spent his summers in Wyoming, and there he stored up the impressions, anecdotes, and character sketches he used in his later writing. *Red Men and White*, a collection of short stories, appeared in 1896, followed by *Lin McLean* (1898), *The Jimmyjohn Boss* (1900), and *The Virginian*.

The Virginian became a sensation almost overnight, and its popularity has continued. By 1938 it had sold more than one and a half million copies; it was made into a successful Broadway play, produced four times as a motion picture, and, most recently, used as the inspiration for a television series. The Virginian's remark to Trampas, the villain of the story—"When you call me that, smile!"—is probably the best-known line of all western fiction, and the lingering notoriety of this notorious remark points up the immense influence of *The Virginian* on later westerns.

After *The Virginian* Wister wrote no more western novels, though he did collect some of his earlier stories in *Members of the Family* (1911). For the remainder of his life he lived in the East. He died at his summer home in North Kingston, Rhode Island, of a cerebral hemorrhage. Fittingly, in the following year a peak in Grand Teton National Park, Wyoming, was named for him.

Though much of Wister's fiction deals with western themes, he is most widely remembered for *The Virginian*, the novel that firmly established the form for later fictional studies of the American West. Wister's Virginian, the hero, is the first and in many ways the best visualized cowboy hero, a figure later to become a ubiquitous literary character in western fiction. The plot, which tells of the Virginian's courtship of Molly Stark, an eastern visitor to the West, is also familiar to readers of later westerns. Many of what became the staples of later western fiction—the "mail-order bride," the laconic tall-storytelling hero, and, most significantly, the gunfight between the hero and the villain—are clearly sketched in this novel as well.

Critics of Wister have traced many of the defects of *The Virginian*, and of later western fiction, to the fact that Wister was not a native westerner. Consequently, it is alleged, he did not write about western life itself but rather succeeded in creating a method of handling western themes in terms of a successful literary escape, which totally destroyed the possibilities of western fiction as a vehicle for serious literature. Though it is true that *The Virginian* is cast within the framework of an easterner's impressions of western life, it does not necessarily follow that this turns the novel into sentimentalized escape. The strength of *The Virginian* is not that it gives an accurate description of the facts of western life, which it obviously does not, but that it gives stature to the later theme of the dude who goes west and learns to come to terms with the totally different life he finds on the frontier. Hence, though the novel is not true to the peculiarities of western life, it is true to a larger American attitude toward the presence of the West itself and to its importance to the country at large. The dude has become a fascinating figure to the American, who sees in this character something of himself—a new man, perpetually faced with the problem of interpreting a new environment that seems at first impression to make no sense.

Most interesting to the student of Wister's western writing is Fanny Kemble Wister's edition of *Owen Wister Out West: His Journals and Letters* (1958); see also Ben H. Vorpahl, *My Dear Wister: The Frederic Remington-Owen Wister Letters* (1972).—J. K. F.

Wobblies. See INDUSTRIAL WORKERS OF THE WORLD.

wolf. The wolf (*Canis lupus*) is the largest wild member of the dog family, which includes the jackals, hunting dogs, foxes, and raccoon-dogs. Although its range is circumpolar, it has now been extirpated from most of western Europe and from America south of the United States-Canadian border except for a few wilderness areas in northern Minnesota, northern Idaho-Montana, Louisiana, and northwestern Mexico.

The gray wolf (also called timber wolf and lobo) measures 42 to 54 inches from nose to tail-tip and as much as 38 inches in shoulder height; the weight ranges from 60 to 175 pounds. Most timber wolves are gray sprinkled with black, but individuals may be tawny or black, and wolves of the Arctic coast and islands are white the year round. The wolf can be confused with the smaller coyote (sometimes called prairie or brush wolf) but it is much larger and the head is "coarser" with shorter, more rounded ears and a heavier, blunter muzzle. The red wolf (*Canis niger*) tends to be tawnier, smaller, and more slender than the gray wolf, but larger than the coyote. In frontier days it was limited to the south, from Florida to Texas; now it is found only in Texas and Louisiana. Some scientists believe that it is a variety of the gray wolf.

Intelligent and social, wolves have strong attachments for their associates. Family-size and larger groups (as many as twenty-five but usually only six to eight individuals) hunt cooperatively. Having great endurance and considerable tactical skill, such packs have little trouble bringing down animals as large as deer and pronghorns, especially when deep snow hampers the prey. Larger mammals—elk or wapiti, caribou, and moose—are more difficult to run down and overpower, and most of the big game killed by wolves are weak, crippled, or otherwise subnormal. Economical hunters, they normally bury all surplus meat for storage.

Contrary to former belief, wolves are somewhat promiscuous. However, the male routinely brings food in his jaws, or predigested, to his current mate when she is nursing her litter of four to seven pups. When about five months old, the young accompany their parents on hunts; by the time they are two years old, they are physically and sexually mature, and may survive another eight years. Wild wolves are subject to numerous parasites from ticks to flukes and roundworms; to diseases including rabies, distemper, and arthritis; and occasionally to broken bones and other injuries from the flailing hoofs of their prey.

Indians regarded wolves as they did other members of the animal community—"spiritual brothers" of the plains and mountains; a source of food, clothing, and bedding; and even as competitors. At times, Indians camouflaged themselves with wolf hides when approaching enemies or game (particularly buffalo). Northern Indians crossbred wolves with their dogs to haul sleds and travois.

On the other hand, white frontiersmen despised wolves as great nuisances that filled the night with horrendous howls, killed tethered animals, and robbed sleeping campers. "Cowardly, deceitful, and merciless!" Fur trappers ate the meat only in dire necessity, but they sold the skins to some extent. The fur, although thick and durable, brought only $1.40 to $3.50 throughout the 1800s.

Many white men feared the wolf but the only proven attack on a person in North America was undoubtedly made by a rabid animal. As cattle ranches increased, some wolves killed hundreds of stock and cost the stockmen thousands of dollars. Marauders like "Three Toes," old "Peg Leg," and the "Gray Ghost" became so crafty that it took years to catch them.

The ancient Indian methods of capture (deadfalls, pits, snares, and stomach piercers) were succeeded by the white men's dogs, traps, and poison campaigns. The use of strychnine by professional "wolfers" wiped out all wolves except in remote, rugged wildernesses in a few western states. Now that the wolf has become extremely rare, it is beginning to be appreciated as a fascinating species worthy of a permanent place in nature.

See L. David Mech, *The Wolf: The Ecology and Behavior of an Endangered Species* (1970); Russell J. Rutter and Douglas H. Pimlott, *The World of the Wolf* (1968); and Stanley P. Young and Edward A. Goldman, *The Wolves of North America* (1944).—V. H. C.

Wolfskill, William (1798-1866). Fur trader and California pioneer. Wolfskill's parents followed Daniel Boone's Wilderness Road into Kentucky, where William was born. By age fourteen he had mastered the long Kentucky rifle and when twenty-three was skilled in frontier hunting, farming, planting, and raising livestock. By then fur companies, based in St. Louis, were outfitting their western expeditions, and he decided to explore the Southwest and California.

In 1822 Wolfskill went over the Santa Fe Trail with Captain William Becknell's trading expedition and later joined Ewing Young in fur trapping and trading enterprises. He met and worked with the greats of the fur trade, including Charles and William Bent, William Sublette, Ceran St. Vrain, and Kit Carson. Gathering a group of trailwise men in 1830, he went over the Old Spanish Trail to California to join Ewing Young. Other pioneers had marched over this famous trail, but Wolfskill was the first to demonstrate it could be used for pack trains. And by bringing fine New Mexican blankets to California to be traded for superior mules needed in New Mexico, Wolfskill's party initiated a flourishing trade between the two provinces. Within a few months after his arrival in February 1831 other parties appeared with blankets for sale.

One of the first Americans to make California his home, Wolfskill pioneered a number of farming projects after 1836. He started citrus production and cooperated in enormous grape-growing and wine-making ventures. He bought ranches and engaged in a substantial beef-producing operation in southern California. His privately financed school for his own children and those of neighbors was the first American educational attempt in the state.

Wolfskill's widespread accomplishments and benefactions drew such broad acclaim that most California histories recognize his influence on the economic, political, and cultural life of California. See, specifically, Iris Higby Wilson, *William Wolfskill, 1798-1866—Frontier Trapper to California* (1965).—B. W. A.

woman suffrage. When Sacagawea accompanied her husband to the Pacific in 1805 she set a precedent for Marie Dorion in 1811-12 and several missionary wives in the 1830s. Thereafter, more and more women made their way to the Rocky Mountains and the Pacific Coast.

For many years amenities and opportunities for female companionship varied remarkably from one state or territory to another in the Far West. In some communities there were many women living much as women did in the East, while elsewhere there were very few, and conditions were primitive. For instance, California in 1870 had a total population of 560,247 with more women over twenty-one (99,688) than all other states and territories in the western third of the United States combined. In 1870 Idaho and Montana had 8 men over twenty-one for every woman over twenty-one; Wyoming had 6; Nevada, 5; Arizona, 4; Washington, 2.6; Colorado, 2.3; California, 2.28; and Oregon, 2; while New Mexico and Utah had almost as many women as men.

When eastern suffragists who were assembled in convention at Seneca Falls, New York, in 1848 issued their ringing *Declaration of Sentiments*, no echoes were reported in the West. Just six years thereafter, however, a woman suffrage bill was introduced in the legislature of Washington Territory. Four Whigs and four Democrats in the lower house voted for the measure, while nine Democrats voted against it. There is no record of any public agitation preceding the introduction of the bill, although it is assumed that the wife of Arthur A. Denny, "father of Seattle," who sponsored the bill, had privately expressed her approval.

Promotion of woman suffrage had been expanding in the East and Midwest for twenty years before the first agitation for it made its appearance in the West in the form of a lecture by Laura DeForce Gordon in San Francisco in February 1868. Soon after completion of the first transcontinental railway in the following year, suffragists Anna Dickinson and Redelia Bates made lecture tours to Denver and Cheyenne and all the way to the coast. Soon the National Woman Suffrage Association and the American Woman Suffrage Association, both organized in 1869, sent their representatives westward. Copies of woman suffrage journals, *The Revolution* and *The Woman's Journal*, before long carried eastern ideas to women in the West. Also, among the men and women who were settling the West, there were many who brought with them some sympathy for the woman suffrage arguments they had heard or read in the East. Private correspondence provided other links.

Most of the country's promotion of woman suffrage occurred in the East where, generally speaking, the most talented and experienced suffragists resided—Susan B. Anthony, Elizabeth Cady Stanton, Lucy Stone, Henry B. Blackwell, and Colonel Thomas Wentworth Higginson. In just about every form of promotional activity, eastern suffragists outdid the westerners. Nevertheless, significant legislation granting suffrage to women came first in the West, much to the surprise of easterners. Before anything comparable happened in the East, women were granted suffrage in Wyoming Territory in 1869, Utah Territory in 1870, Washington Territory in 1883, the state of Wyoming in 1890, the state of Colorado in 1893, and the states of Utah and Idaho in 1896. Thus the only four woman suffrage states in the country in 1896 lay in a cluster in the mountain West.

The suffrage map of 1914 makes the contrast between East and West even more striking. In 1914 all states from the Rocky Mountains on west, except for New Mexico, had woman suffrage; no state did east of the Rockies, except Kansas. Why after twenty years of strenuous efforts in the East did results first come half a continent away, where agitation was virtually unknown? And why did all victories in the next forty years likewise occur in the West, far from the better organized and better supported eastern campaigns?

Many explanations have been offered to account for the leadership of western lawmakers. Among them are:

Men in the West were rewarding the women for their role in pioneering, their hardihood and endurance, their working beside their husbands, and their full partnership in state-building.

Western men were more chivalrous.

The West was more egalitarian than the East.

The scarcity of women enhanced their value and made men more appreciative of them.

Conservative married men in the West were doubling their vote in order to strengthen their position in relation to the numerous transient bachelors.

Populists and Progressives, more numerous in the West than in the East, favored woman suffrage.

Before the appropriate explanation can be selected, a review of developments is necessary. In the years 1869 to 1871 virtually every legislature in the East, North, and West took up the subject of woman suffrage. Out of all the states and territories whose legislatures considered the question during the period, only Wyoming Territory and Utah Territory actually brought suffrage into fruition. Why did they do it?

One reason is that in a territory women could be granted suffrage by a simple majority vote of the legislature with the approval of the governor, whereas in a state, such as Oregon, California, and Nevada, a constitutional amendment was required, which involved a two-thirds vote of the legislature and a majority vote of the electors. A second special reason must be considered. Sparks thrown out by *The New York Times* and an Indiana congressman, George Washington Julian, gave impetus to western action. The *Times* in 1867 proposed in an editorial that Congress give the ballot to women in Utah. The *Times* thought that, given the ballot, the women of Utah would soon outlaw polygamy. Then in 1868 Congressman Julian introduced a bill to give women the right to vote in all the territories. Hearings in 1869 brought testimony maintaining that woman suffrage would destroy polygamy in Utah and would attract women to the other territories. Before long, however, Julian thought better of it and decided that Brigham Young had so much influence in Utah that female suffrage would not eliminate plural marriage. So the matter was dropped, but not before there had been considerable publicity and opportunity for some of the western pioneers to weigh the possibility that woman suffrage might attract women to a land much in need of femininity. This interesting possibility turned out to be a very important factor in Wyoming Territory, where there were only one thousand women over twenty-one among six thousand men.

Two men played major roles on the Wyoming stage in 1869. One, William H. Bright, who was in his mid-forties, was much devoted to his attractive wife, twenty years his junior and desirous of the right to vote. The other major role was played by Edward M. Lee, a thirty-two-year-old bachelor and secretary of the territory. In 1867 he had introduced a woman suffrage bill in the Connecticut legislature and yielded to no one as a champion of woman suffrage. Bright introduced the bill in Wyoming with the explanation that it was just and that his wife and mother had as much right to the ballot as Negroes did. Arguments based solely on justice would have fallen short, but more persuasive reasons for action were brought to bear. Legislators went along mainly because they thought it would provide a lot of free advertising for the territory and would attract women to it. A few went along more or less for the fun of it, thinking it a good joke, and supposing that it might embarrass the Republican governor, who was mistakenly thought to be opposed. The evidence is abundant, however, that it was mainly the "chamber of commerce" argument, free advertising, that prompted the legislators, all of whom were Democrats, to adopt the measure. It received the approval of Governor John A. Campbell on December 10, 1869.

Two months later, in February 1870, Utah followed close on the heels of Wyoming. After *The New York Times* and Julian had decided that female voters would not terminate polygamy, the Mormans took up the suffrage idea with other purposes in mind. There were eighteen thousand men over twenty-one and seventeen thousand women over twenty-one in Utah. To give women the right to vote, it was calculated, would lessen hostility in Congress and would show critics that Mormon women were not slaves, but contented and loyal followers of Brigham Young and the priesthood. There was possibly also a desire to bolster the strength of the Mormon leadership against non-Mormons, mostly single men, who were coming into the territory. These Gentiles were in 1870 so few that they were a long way from becoming a serious threat, but they might become such in time.

Utah's delegate to Congress had welcomed Julian's bill. After it was discarded, the Utah delegate encouraged Brigham Young to act in the matter, which he did by passing the word to key men in the all-Mormon legislature. Secret discussion led to unanimous passage of an act giving women the right to vote but omitting the officeholding privilege that the Wyoming act included.

Though neighbors, Wyoming and Utah were remarkably unlike socially and spiritually. Obviously, Utah adopted woman suffrage not because Wyoming had done so or for free advertising, but for its own special reasons. But Wyoming and Utah were alike in that neither had any suffrage society, any political partisanship in their one-party legislatures, or any visible indication that the women wanted the franchise. The women in both territories were handed the right to vote, and in the case of Wyoming the right to hold office, "on a platter."

Had the "chamber of commerce" argument been employed in Washington Territory's legislature when it was considering the vote for women in November 1869, or in Idaho's legislature when a bill lost by a tie vote in the lower house in 1871, there might have been a quartet instead of a pair of territories at the head of the woman suffrage parade. The chances were not so good in the other four territories. There were too many Mexican-Americans and too much Roman Catholic influence in New Mexico and Arizona to permit suffrage extension there. On the other hand, the Montana legislature might have acted favorably had chance sent Bright and Lee there instead of to Wyoming.

In Colorado Territory in 1870, proponents encountered strong opposition reminiscent of that which usually greeted suffrage proposals in other parts of the country. Friend and foe engaged in full-dress legislative debate in Denver. Endorsement by a Republican governor hurt more than it helped, since the legislature was controlled by Democrats. There was extensive newspaper coverage, petitions from suffragists, letters to the editor, and public discussion. Opposition mounted, with the result that the lower house voted 15 to 10 against the proposal after the upper house had voted 7 to 6 for it.

Seven years later, in 1877, after Colorado had become a state, there was a statewide referendum in which 14,000 "no" votes were cast against 6,600 "yes" votes. Susan B. Anthony and other eastern suffragists had toured the state in behalf of the proposal, but Mexican-Americans in the southern counties voted nine to one against it, and a negative vote resulted in every other county except one.

Meanwhile the West's outstanding suffragist, Abigail Scott Duniway, had begun a long, spectacular career in the Northwest. Bent on attaining self-realization on the one hand and rights for women on the other, she published a woman's rights journal, *The New Northwest*, in Portland, Oregon, from 1871 to 1887. She put some of her five sons to work setting type while she lectured in Oregon and Washington and later Idaho, selling subscriptions and picking up news for her journal. In an 1871 editorial she declared that "one half of the women are over-taxed and underpaid . . . while the other half are frivolous, idle and expensive." Having lived on an Oregon farm for nine years while raising stair-step children, she recalled her own experience when she wrote that farmers' wives were intolerably lonesome and were worked to death.

Although many men and women agitated persistently for woman suffrage in Washington Territory, some of them doing so before Duniway became active in 1871, she played a leading role in winning suffrage there in 1883. Four years later a court ruling deprived the women of Washington of the ballot at about the same time that the women of Utah were disfranchised by an act of Congress, which was a scatter-gun attack on polygamy. For a few years thereafter woman suffrage survived only in Wyoming Territory and the state of Wyoming (1890).

After an active campaign and with help from the East, the women won the ballot in Colorado in 1893. This was the first victory in a statewide referendum. Populists, who briefly ruled Colorado, favored suffrage extension. So did labor unions, the Farmers' Alliance, a well-organized Women's Christian Temperance Union (WCTU), the press, and most of the Protestant clergy.

After Mormon leaders had withdrawn their public endorsement of plural marriage in 1890, Utah achieved statehood in 1896 with woman suffrage in its constitution. As in Wyoming, the people of Utah had learned to appreciate woman suffrage in the 1870s and 1880s before Congress deprived them of it in 1887. Later, in 1896, Idaho became the fourth suffrage state through constitutional amendment. Idaho's victory is attributable to encouragement from the three adjoining states where women had the ballot, the long-term impact of Duniway's enterprise, the leadership of an outstanding Boise newspaper publisher, work by a small but earnest suffrage association, and assistance from gifted eastern suffragists. In the Idaho drive all four political parties were persuaded to adopt suffrage planks.

Patently the woman suffrage story varied quite remarkably in the four states of the mountain West, where early victories were won. None of the six explanations listed above is very satisfactory for what happened in Wyoming and Utah, although something can be said for the idea that conservative married men were trying to strengthen their position in relation to the many transient bachelors. In the case of Wyoming it is true that, once woman suffrage had been adopted for advertising purposes, the more stable men rallied to the standard and prevented repeal. The territory's second legislature in 1871 voted for repeal and lacked only one vote to override the governor's veto. Whereas the 1869 legislature had been entirely Democratic, a few Republicans infiltrated in 1871, just enough to block repeal. The Democrats now wanted repeal because the female voters had tried to close saloons on Sunday and had voted Republican. The division, however, was not between married men and bachelors. Most of the legislators were bachelors, and bachelors were on both sides of the debate. Three of the four votes that blocked repeal were cast by bachelors.

In the case of Utah, Brigham Young was no doubt a conservative married man who favored power for himself and his kind in Utah, but he was already in complete control, and the threat from transients was but a small cloud on the horizon. Young seems to have been motivated more by a desire to counteract allegations popular in the East that women in Utah were virtual slaves. Probably also he recognized the merit of the justice argument, although there had been little public promotion of that idea in the territory.

The six explanations are more useful in accounting for what happened in Colorado and Idaho. Populism was an important factor in Colorado, while the conservative married man theme has some applicability in Idaho. Otherwise, the six explanations are dubious. Generalizations about chivalry and egalitarianism are not susceptible to proof. Certainly many examples of unchivalric treatment of women can be found in the nineteenth-century West. And egalitarianism and democracy are subject to question in light of the treatment accorded Chinese and blacks and the persistence of male monopolies in every phase of politics except voting.

As to women gaining recognition because they worked beside their men, women probably worked beside their men less in the West than they did in other parts of the country. Wives of pioneer farmers are thought to have worked beside their husbands, but farmers were relatively scarce in the West. The Farmers' Alliance in Colorado and the Grange in Washington and Oregon backed woman suffrage, but in general leaders in the movement came from cities and towns, where middle-class women could find time for club activity and where professional men, merchants, and editors provided know-how, advice, and legislative leadership, with or without prodding from the women.

It is sometimes said that the suffrage movement evolved from an argument based on justice to one on expediency around the turn of the century. This trend is noticeable in the formal statements of suffrage leaders, but in lectures, letters to the editor, and appeals to legislators expediency was prominent in the West from the outset. In 1871 Abigail Scott Duniway accompanied Susan B. Anthony as her business agent on a long lecture tour through Oregon and Washington and learned much from that nonpareil advocate. She heard Anthony argue from justice, but she also heard her promise the Washington legislature that if the women were given the vote "she could promise them the most gratifying of results—the immigration of a large number of good women to the Territory. The ballot is the key that unlocks the door to knowledge, to equal wages, to honor, to prosperity." And she heard Anthony promise in another lecture that if women were admitted to the franchise, wars would cease.

At the beginning of an address before the Washington Woman Suffrage Association in 1873 Duniway said she would put aside the justice argument and discuss political expediency, "the only argument which would have weight with politicians."

The free-advertising argument, which had captivated Wyoming legislators, appeared in other places. In 1900 campaign leaflets promised Oregon voters that "Equal Suffrage will be worth tens of thousands of dollars as a free advertisement for the state in all parts of the Union." And in 1910 Governor Brady of Idaho, when asked what was the greatest thing that woman suffrage had done for Idaho, said, "It has advertised the State more than any other feature . . . it still focuses attention upon us and brings inquiries from all over the world." No doubt Wyoming, Colorado, Utah, and Idaho got lots of free publicity, but whether any significant migration resulted is questionable. Easterners who were annoyed by suffragists would say, "Why don't you move to the Rocky Mountains?" The usual reply was: "We prefer to stay and fight for our rights where we are."

The WCTU, which had a greater membership than suffrage associations did in the West, was regarded with ambivalence by the suffragists. WCTU members who joined the suffrage movement mainly to accomplish prohibition repelled more male voters than they attracted. They sometimes delayed suffrage victory, and there was much quarreling between prohibition-oriented and suffrage-oriented women. Duniway occupied one storm center. She gave highest priority to suffrage, believed in temperance through education rather than prohibition, blamed the WCTU for suffrage defeats, and sometimes advocated a "still hunt," by which she meant stalking legislators with a minimum of public agitation, lest the powerful liquor interests become alarmed and mount a devastating counterattack. Tension between the suffrage and prohibition people was chronic in Oregon, Washington, and California. Also, friction occurred between national and local promoters over such matters as the fees and expenses collected by national organizers and guest lecturers, eastern ignorance about local conditions, and the distribution of credit for victories and blame for defeats. From 1896 to 1910, when fourteen years passed without a victory, frustration was compounded for the activists.

A flood of testimonials and other evidence from the four original suffrage states established that there was general satisfaction with the results, but also made it clear that woman suffrage would not bring nearly as much change as enthusiasts had promised. In particular, a few naïve women who ran for office other than that of county superintendent of schools learned that except in very rare cases few voters, male or female, wanted them in political office.

Then in a well-organized campaign in 1910 the suffragists won back in Washington what had been lost in the courts in 1887, and an even more impressive campaign in 1911 brought victory in California after more than forty years of discouragement. Leadership had come mainly from San Francisco and Los Angeles. San Francisco voters were strongly opposed, as they had been for a long time, but the rest of the state prevailed.

Success in Washington and California exhilarated suffragists everywhere. Other state victories followed quickly, first in the West, then in the East, until woman suffrage became nationwide with the Nineteenth Amendment in 1920.

It must be conceded that Susan B. Anthony's conclusion, that the greatest obstacle had been "the indifference, the inertia, the apathy of women," was just as applicable in the West as in the East. Even in California, where so many of the West's women were, the State Equal Rights Association had only 996 dues-paying members (fifty cents a year) in 1911.

Ironically, by 1900 virtually all the rights that pioneer suffragists had called for had been conceded except for suffrage. The married woman had won the right to do business on her separate account, to hold separate property, to will it, and to share in the control of her children. The age of consent had been raised from ten or twelve to sixteen or eighteen, coeducation had been provided in all western state universities the day they opened (except in California, where there was a one-year delay), many job opportunities had come, and differences in pay for equal work had been reduced.

Western priority in the adoption of woman suffrage did not mean that women in the West would enjoy greater participation in politics indefinitely. In modern times they generally lick the envelopes and do the telephoning while the men monopolize elective offices and dominate policy-making. Two thirds of the states have sent women to Congress, but Wyoming and Colorado have never done so, and Utah and Idaho have sent only one each. Nor do western women get elected more often to state legislatures or executive positions in state government. Wyoming had three women in its 1971 legislature; Idaho, four; Utah, five; and Colorado, six. In recent years all state legislatures have had an average of

six. Thus, the West may be said to have relinquished the leadership position it held for so many years in the woman's rights movement.

Useful references include Susan B. Anthony et al., eds., *The History of Woman Suffrage*, 6 vols. (1887-1922); Eleanor Flexner, *Century of Struggle* (1959); Alan P. Grimes, *The Puritan Ethic and Woman Suffrage* (1967); Leo Kanowitz, *Women and the Law* (1969); Aileen S. Kraditor, *The Ideas of the Woman Suffrage Movement, 1890-1920* (1965); and William L. O'Neill, *Everyone Was Brave* (1969).—T. A. L.

Wood, Abraham (1608?-?). Soldier and explorer. Wood was born at an unspecified place and is of unknown ancestry. The place and condition of his death are also unknown.

In 1645 the Virginia general assembly provided for further expansion up the western rivers toward the Piedmont forests by ordering the erection of a series of forts to protect settlers against Indian attacks. In all, there were to be four forts. Fort Henry was established in 1746 at the falls of the Appomattox and was placed in the command of Captain Abraham Wood and forty-five men. In return for his services Wood was to be granted a tract of six hundred acres of land. In later years the site of Fort Henry was to become Petersburg.

At the fall lines of two of Virginia's rivers Wood gained eminence as a trader, landowner, politician, soldier, and explorer. He encouraged many others to go on long exploring expeditions into the unknown western Virginia country, among them James NEEDHAM and Gabriel ARTHUR. In 1652 he himself secured permission from the assembly to explore areas "where no English have ever been and discovered." In 1671 he was made a major general, and that same year he sent out an exploring expedition under Thomas Batts and Robert Fallam. This pair, after a long and arduous journey, of which they kept a good journal, were the first Englishmen to cross over into the watershed area of the Ohio. On September 13, 1671, they were in the New River valley. General Wood had to his credit the most extensive explorations, performed personally or by persons under his command, of any Englishman at the time of his mysterious death.

See Clarence W. Alvord and Lee Bidgood, *The First Explorations of the Trans-Allegheny Region by the Virginians, 1650-1674* (1912); and W. E. Connelley and E. M. Coulter, *History of Kentucky*, vol. I (1922).—T. D. C.

Wood, Charles Erskine Scott (1852-1944). Writer and attorney. Wood was born in Erie, Pennsylvania, where his father was a naval surgeon attached to the Great Lakes squadron. Graduating from the United States Military Academy in 1874, he was assigned to frontier duty, explored Alaska in 1876, and participated in the Nez Percé campaign, recording Chief Joseph's well-known surrender speech at Bear Paw Mountain, Montana Territory, in October 1877. In 1884 he resigned his commission and set up a law practice in Portland, Oregon.

Wood's interests in literature and art (he sketched and painted throughout most of his life and served as an arbitrator of artistic tastes in Portland for years) took him increasingly into a political and social radicalism that he called "philosophical anarchism." His anarchism derived from nonviolent thinkers, such as Proudhon, Thoreau, and Jefferson. A staunch libertarian, he decried intrusion of the state into citizens' personal lives. Although he defended anarchist Emma Goldman's right to free speech when she was in Portland in 1913, he did not believe in what is called "anarchism of the deed," violence against people and property.

While fulminating against the system that sustained him, Wood built a lucrative practice in maritime and corporation law. In 1918, as agent for an international banking concern, he negotiated the sale of the Willamette Valley and Cascade Mountain Wagon Road Company to the Louis Hall railroad interests and received a one-million-dollar commission. Setting up trust funds for his family, Wood left Portland in 1919 in the company of a young poet and woman suffragist, Sara Bard Field, and after a short European tour the two built a house on a hill in Los Gatos, California, where they lived and wrote until his death.

Wood is best known for a series of satiric dialogs that appeared between 1915 and 1917 in *The Masses*, a radical New York monthly. Later the pieces were published along with new dialogs as *Heavenly Discourse* (1927). The dialogs are set in heaven, with God (the author in thin disguise), Jesus, Satan, Saint Peter, Rabelais, Mark Twain, Teddy Roosevelt, Anthony Comstock, Billy Sunday, Joan of Arc, Margaret Fuller, and others discoursing on sundry topics, including censorship, birth control, militarism, and fundamentalism.

The bulk of his writing, however, was in and of the West. Wood himself looked upon a long poem set in the high desert of southeastern Oregon as his best work. *Poet in the Desert* (1915) was cast in the form of a dialog between an abstraction, Truth, and the Poet, who enters the desert to seek the remedy for a sick society. The strength of the poem lies less in its ideological message than in the sections that evoke the desert's stark, dramatic beauty, and it is such passages that invariably appear in anthologies in which Wood is represented. From the time he first marched across Oregon in 1875 as a young army officer the region remained a theme throughout his long life: He sought to capture it on canvas and in bursts of verse, such as those collected in his *Poems from the Ranges* (1929). He used the eastern Oregon wilderness as an escape from business pressures, and the land rewarded him financially as well as spiritually. In *A Book of Tales* (1901) Wood gathered a number of legends of Indians of the Pacific Northwest, and his friendship with Chief Joseph led him to arrange for his eldest son, Erskine, to spend a summer with Joseph and his people in western Washington.

For more than a decade Wood was a major contributor to *Pacific Monthly*, a regional literary and promotional monthly that enjoyed a modest national circulation.

Wood spent most of his life on the Pacific Slope, first in Oregon and then in California. He was an arresting and unconventional figure, a transplant from the East who became more western than most native sons, and who somehow managed to hold in effective equilibrium artistic and literary talent, radical social and political views, and substantial business and legal skills.

Sara Bard Field Wood's edition of her husband's *Collected Poems* (1955) has a perceptive biographical sketch of Wood. See also Edwin R. Bingham's "Oregon's Romantic Rebels: John Reed and Charles Erskine Scott Wood," *Pacific Northwest Quarterly* (July 1959) and

"Experiment in Launching a Biography: Three Vignettes of Charles Erskine Scott Wood," *Huntington Library Quarterly* (May 1972).—E. R. B.

Wood, Leonard (1860-1927). Surgeon, soldier, and consul. Mark Sullivan, the great newspaperman and historian of the McKinley, Roosevelt, and Wilson eras, settled on the word "bigness" to describe Leonard Wood—bigness of personality, character, dedication, honesty, and foresight: "He was the type to whom, when they have sincerity, average men instinctively pay deference."

Wood was born in Winchester, New Hampshire, and spent his childhood on the Massachusetts coast. Despite financial hardships, he entered Harvard Medical School and received his M.D. degree in 1884. He spent a brief period in private practice in Boston before seeking a commission in the Army Medical Corps.

In Arizona Territory, first as a contract surgeon, then as an assistant surgeon with the Fourth United States Cavalry, Wood plunged into the Apache campaigns and won a Medal of Honor for carrying in May 1885 dispatches on a one-hundred-mile trip through country teeming with hostile Indians.

In 1891 Wood was promoted to captain. In 1895 he was assigned to Washington, D.C., where President and Mrs. William McKinley became his principal patients. It was during his Washington tour of duty that Wood met Theodore Roosevelt, the two men drawn together over the flaming issue of Cuban independence.

When war was declared against Spain in April 1898, Wood became colonel of the First United States Volunteer Cavalry Regiment—the ROUGH RIDERS—with Roosevelt named his second in command. Under the overall division leadership of Brigadier General Joseph "Fightin' Joe" Wheeler, Wood led the Rough Riders in the first clash on Cuban soil, the battle of Las Guásimas, on June 24, 1898. He was then promoted to the command of a cavalry brigade prior to the July 1 San Juan action.

When the war ended, Wood was appointed military governor of Cuba. A physically strong and enduring man, he brought order, justice, and sanitation and public-works programs to the island. By 1901 "Wood's war on the mosquito," a war carried on by Wood, Dr. Walter Reed, and others against the yellow fever epidemic, had eliminated the plague from the country.

In 1903 Wood was sent to the Philippines as governor of Moro Province, Mindanao, and the adjacent islands. With a combination of shrewdness, reason, persuasion, and, when necessary, ruthlessness against Moro institutions, he pacified the bloodstained province and instituted reforms and prosperity. In August 1903 he was promoted to major general, Regular Army. After commanding the Philippine division of the army for two years, Wood returned to the United States.

In the spring of 1910 he was appointed chief of staff, supporting the doctrine of the cadre army and "preparedness," which was to make America ready for any national emergency. When the war in Europe broke out in 1914, Wood organized the first Plattsburg training camps in which volunteers paid for their own food, equipment, and expenses, an innovation that brought him into conflict with the Wilson administration. Wood was an exemplar of preparedness and in public speeches and writings made serious charges about the unpreparedness of America in its army and military in general. This, of course, reflected badly on Woodrow Wilson's government, particularly since Wilson was erecting a façade of neutrality in the early part of World War I. Wood, furthermore, regarded Wilson as "a spineless rabbit" and made no attempt to conceal it. When the United States entered World War I in 1917, Wood was passed over for commander-in-chief of the American Expeditionary Force (A.E.F.) in favor of Major General John J. Pershing.

In 1918 Wood began actively seeking the Republican nomination for the presidency, bringing a large following with him to the Chicago convention in 1920. Warren G. Harding, winning the nomination and the election, subsequently sent Wood on a special mission to the Philippines, where he worked once again to restore economic stability to the islands.

In 1927 Wood's health, already having deteriorated in the tropics, reached a crisis when a tumor in his skull recurred, paralyzing the left side of his body. He returned to the United States for surgical treatment of the tumor and died on August 7, 1927, as a result of the operation.

Historian Mark Sullivan, who knew Wood well, said of him: ". . . the main concern of his life was America, a highminded, calm, steady-burning zeal that the country should be well-managed, that strong ideals should be held before it, and that the people should be at once stimulated and disciplined to follow the ideals."

The exhaustive, two-volume study by Hermann Hagedorn, *Leonard Wood, a Biography* (1931), is the standard work. See also Mark Sullivan's *Our Times: The United States 1900-1925* (1933), vols. V and VI, for another valuable view of Wood's remarkable career. —D. L. W.

Woodruff, Wilford (1807-1898). Mormon leader. Born in Farmington, Connecticut, Woodruff converted to Mormonism in 1832 and served as a proselyting missionary in England and America throughout much of his life. Not an orator, he conveyed an impression of honesty and sincerity, and during an eight-month period in England he converted 1,800 persons to Mormonism. In between his frequent missionary activities, Woodruff became business manager in 1842 for the Nauvoo *Times and Seasons*, became a member of the senate of the provisional State of Deseret in 1850, and was the official historian for the church. His own private journal was so meticulously kept that it has been a vital source for the history of the Latter-day Saint church from its inception to the end of the nineteenth century. Sustained as president of the Quorum of the Twelve Apostles in 1880, Woodruff became president of the church in April 1889. Having had limited experience in the multileveled political and economic activities of the church, Woodruff relied heavily upon the support of his two counselors, George Q. Cannon and Joseph F. Smith.

Woodruff is most noted for his 1890 Manifesto proclaiming an end to polygamy and a virtual end to federal-Utah hostilities. To him, however, must be given the larger credit of having begun the Mormon church's withdrawal from all phases of its previous domination of the social, political, and economic life of the territory.

See Matthias F. Cowley, ed., *Wilford Woodruff, Fourth President of the Church of Jesus Christ of Latter-day Saints,* *History of His Life and Labors as Recorded in His Daily Journals* (1909).—L. J. A.

Woodruff, William Edward (1795-1885). Arkansas journalist. Woodruff was a New Yorker who, in 1819, brought a press to Arkansas Post, the territorial capital, and founded the *Arkansas Gazette*, the oldest newspaper west of the Mississippi River. He moved his paper to Little Rock, the new capital, in 1821. Until 1830 Woodruff's was the only newspaper in Arkansas. He finally sold the *Gazette* in 1843 to the Whigs. He had broken with the powerful Democratic Conway-Sevier-Johnson clique, but, still a Democrat, founded the *Arkansas Democrat* in 1846 to secure the election of Chester Ashley to the United States Senate. Repurchasing the *Gazette* in 1850, he consolidated it with the *Democrat*. In 1853 he sold the paper and retired.—W. L. B.

Woods, Rufus (1878-1950). Washington newspaper editor. Woods was born in Surprise, Nebraska. He received a bachelor of laws degree from the University of Nebraska in 1903 and became editor of two small newspapers in Wenatchee, Washington. From 1907 until his death he was editor and publisher of the Wenatchee *Daily World*.

Woods was also active in the political life of Washington. He helped form the Progressive party of Washington, serving as its chairman, and promoted the political career of Progressive Senator Miles Poindexter. Interested in Washington's economic life as well, in July 1918 he proposed building a dam on the Columbia River at Grand Coulee to produce electricity and irrigation for central Washington. The lake behind Chief Joseph Dam was named Rufus Woods Lake in his honor.

See Bruce Mitchell, *Flowing Water* (1967) and *The Story of Rufus Woods and the Development of Central Washington* (1965); and Fred Smith, *Rufus Woods of Wenatchee* (1948).—K. A. M.

Wool, John Ellis (1784-1869). Soldier. Wool was born in Newburgh, New York, ran a store in Troy, and served in the militia. At the outbreak of the War of 1812, he was commissioned a captain in the Thirteenth Infantry and won national acclaim for his daring in the battles at Queenstown and Plattsburg. Appointed an army inspector general in 1816, Wool championed the modernizing of the artillery and ordnance branches and urged the establishment of training schools. During the 1830s as a brigadier general, he visited Europe as a military observer, performed with skill and tact the thankless task of rounding up the Cherokee for removal west, and policed the Vermont frontier during the Patriot War in Canada. In 1841 Wool, a small, spare man with urbane manners, succeeded to the command of the eastern military division and became a top-ranking general in the army.

When war was declared on Mexico in 1846, Wool supervised the mustering of volunteers in the Ohio and Mississippi valleys, then in the fall marched from San Antonio, Texas, with thirty-four hundred men to conquer Chihuahua. Crossing the Rio Grande into Coahuila, he found it impossible to enter Chihuahua with wheeled vehicles and swung east to Saltillo to join Zachary Taylor's army. On February 22, 1847, on Wool's advice, Taylor concentrated the American forces near Buena Vista to meet an attack by General Santa Anna. The next morning, while Taylor was at Saltillo,

Wool received the full shock of the Mexican legions and was in desperate straits when Taylor rushed additional troops into the line to save the day. Santa Anna withdrew that evening. Brevetted a major general, Wool commanded the occupation forces in northeastern Mexico from November 1847 until July 1848.

Resuming peacetime duties, Wool was transferred in 1854 to the Department of the Pacific, where he curbed filibustering in California and ended an Indian war in the Oregon-Washington country. At the outbreak of the Civil War, he was commanding all the United States troops east of the Mississippi. During the war, Wool commanded at Fortress Monroe, Virginia, and headed an amphibious force that captured Norfolk. He then served in Maryland and finally in New York City, retiring in August 1863. Wool died at Troy.

See Francis P. Baylies, *A Narrative of Major General Wool's Campaign . . . in 1846, 1847, and 1848* (1851); and "Democratic Candidate for the Presidency—[John E. Wool]," *American Whig Review* (April 1852). —H. P. H.

Wootton, Richens Lacy (1816-1893). Fur trapper, Indian fighter, and Colorado pioneer. Born in Mecklenburg County, Virginia, Wootton moved with his family to Kentucky and then lived with a relative on a Mississippi cotton plantation.

At the age of twenty Wootton went west to work for Bent and St. Vrain's fur company. During 1836-37 he traded with the Sioux and Pawnee and in 1837 joined a party of free trappers to hunt beaver in the Colorado Rockies. In 1838 Wootton and a party of older trappers went on a remarkable two-year hunt that took them over much of the Far West. After traveling up the Arkansas River to its headwaters, they crossed the Rockies to trap along the Green River and then moved on to the Big Horn and the Yellowstone. Turning westward, they followed the Snake and Columbia rivers down to Fort Vancouver, where they sold their furs to the Hudson's Bay Company. From Oregon they moved south through California all the way to Los Angeles before turning east to trap the Gila and the Colorado. After crossing Utah and the Rockies, they arrived back at Bent's Fort in 1840.

Wootton spent the remainder of his life engaging in any frontier enterprise that would bring a profit. For a time he was a pioneer rancher near Pueblo, Colorado, where he is supposed to have corralled buffalo cows with calves for the purpose of raising tame buffalo for eastern zoos and circuses. He traded with the Ute and was one of the few to deal successfully in the buffalo-robe trade with the Comanche.

Despite the profits he made from the Indian trade, he hated them and was often described as a great Indian fighter, second only to Kit Carson. Like Carson, he appears to have been quick but calm and cautious in battle. In his first years as a trader he and his men claimed to have killed thirteen Pawnee braves in one encounter and twenty Snake Indians in another. He told of other lethal encounters and once shot a Mexican who had annoyed him. When he learned of the Taos Rebellion of 1847, he hurried south to assist Colonel Sterling Price, in command of American troops at Santa Fe, in suppressing the Indian rebels. He then joined Colonel A. W. Doniphan at the battle of Sacramento in Chihuahua (February 28, 1847). There he was probably a scout and messenger rather than an active soldier, for

it is was he who brought the news of Doniphan's victory over the Mexicans back to Santa Fe. In 1848 he acted as a guide for Colonel Edward Newby's military campaign against the Navaho.

That year Wootton also moved to Taos and married a French-Canadian, the first of his four wives. In 1852 Wootton drove nine thousand sheep to California to sell to the gold-rush immigrants and returned with a herd of mules. (His accomplishment antedated a similar drive by Kit Carson and Lucien Maxwell in 1853.) It is said that Wootton and his partners made more than forty thousand dollars from this enterprise. After the death of his first wife Wootton settled near Pueblo, where he ranched, ran a blacksmith shop, and freighted goods from Missouri to New Mexico. At one point he lived at Fort Barclay near Fort Union, but when he learned of the Pikes Peak gold discoveries, he established a trading post in Denver and later ran a saloon and hotel there. Upon the outbreak of the Civil War he sold the business and returned to the vicinity of Pueblo, where he developed a farm, a move perhaps prompted by the fact that he was a southern sympathizer in unionist Denver.

As an expert on freighting and fast express, Wootton liked to bet on races and on the time it took a wagon train to cross the Plains. Not surprisingly, he and a partner built a badly needed toll road and bridges at the point where the mountainous section of the Santa Fe Trail passes over Raton Pass into New Mexico. Opened in 1866, the twenty-seven-mile road and the inn, which Wootton operated at the crest, brought him a profit until 1879, when the Atchison, Topeka and Santa Fe took over the right-of-way—but not before Wootton had exacted a lifelong pension from the railroad to compensate for his business loss.

Like Kit Carson and Jim Baker, Wootton lived so long that he became a legend in his own time. He was known as a genial and helpful man by the thousands of people who used his toll road, and his exploits were published in exaggerated form by reporters seeking sensational news of the old frontier for their eastern readers. And while many came to see the tall, muscular, well-built Virginian as a frontier Lochinvar because of his four wives, or as a rough mountain man because of his fights with Indians, neither picture was really accurate. Rather he was a shrewd frontier entrepreneur whom the Denver *Republican* called "the pioneer of Colorado pioneers."

H. L. Conard, *Uncle Dick Wootton* (1890), is valuable in that it is based on personal interviews with the old frontiersman. His life is summarized in H. L. Carter, "Richens Lacy Wootton," in L. R. Hafen, ed., *The Mountain Men and the Fur Trade of the Far West*, vol. III (1966).—H. R. L.

Worcester v. State of Georgia (1832). *Worcester v. State of Georgia* was a suit brought before the United States Supreme Court in which laws of Georgia persecutory of the Cherokee Indian Nation were successfully challenged. The suit came one year after the unsuccessful CHEROKEE NATION V. STATE OF GEORGIA. Samuel A. Worcester had gone to the Cherokee Nation in 1825 as a missionary, supported by the American Board of Commissioners for Foreign Missions of Boston. He established his mission in Cherokee territory located within the boundaries of Georgia, and identified himself with the cause of the Cherokee determined to retain their lands and their independence. In December 1828, significantly after the news of the election of Andrew Jackson to the presidency, an act of Georgia extended the authority of the state over all Cherokee territory within its boundaries. By a law of 1830, Georgia required that no white man could reside in the Cherokee country unless he took an oath of allegiance to the state and applied for and received a license from the governor. Georgia authorities jailed Worcester for refusing to comply with the law, and Worcester took his case to the Supreme Court.

William Wirt served as counsel, as he had in the earlier case, but this time he brought suit under Section 25 of the Judiciary Act of 1789. This law provided that the Supreme Court had jurisdiction in cases in which the validity of United States treaties and the validity of state statutes were brought into question. The Court granted jurisdiction over the suit on the grounds that Worcester's conviction had brought both into question.

This time the Court found that treaties signed between the United States and the Cherokee Nation recognized the Indians' right to self-government and the obligation of the United States to protect that right. As well, laws of the United States were to treat the Indians "as nations, respect their rights, and manifest a firm purpose to afford that protection which treaties stipulate." Further, the treaties and national laws provided that all political intercourse with the Indians was to be carried on exclusively by the federal government, and the Georgia laws interfered forcibly with the relations between the two. The Cherokee Nation was characterized as a "distinct community, occupying its own territory . . . , in which the laws of Georgia can have no force." Chief Justice John Marshall, in the opinion of the Court, asserted that "the acts of Georgia are repugnant to the Constitution, laws and treaties of the United States."

But Georgia defied the decision and Worcester remained in jail until the governor issued a pardon. President Jackson undertook no action to enforce the Court's decision, and by 1838 nearly all the Cherokee were on their way across the Mississippi along the "trail of tears."—R. H. G.

Work, John (c. 1792-1861). Fur trader. Work kept valuable journals of his long career as a fur trader for the Hudson's Bay Company; his accounts of three expeditions while a fur brigade leader (1830-33) in the Oregon country are the best known. From them one can reconstruct the adventurous life of a brigade, with its hierarchy of officers, its brightly dressed French-Canadian trappers, and the entourage of Indian wives and Indian hunters.

Born in County Donegal, Ireland, with the surname "Wark," Work appears to have Anglicized his name when he came to the Hudson's Bay region in 1814 as a steward for the Hudson's Bay Company. After the merger of the Hudson's Bay Company with the North West Company, Work was sent to the Columbia River in 1823—the year he began his journals—with a party of men that included the able leader and trapper Peter Skene Ogden. Over the next seven years Work served at Spokane House and Fort George (formerly the American post Astoria), traded with the Flathead, and explored the Fraser River with the result that the company was able to establish a better route (via the Cowlitz portage) between the Columbia and Fort Nisqually. He also

helped construct Fort Colville, the successor to Spokane House.

In 1830 the company named Work to succeed Ogden as the leader of the Snake River fur brigades and to continue American penetration into Oregon by trapping out the interior. On his first expedition he traveled eastward from Walla Walla to the Salmon River and then southwest to the Humboldt before returning to his base via the John Day River.

His second expedition took him into western Montana near the present site of Missoula and into dangerous Blackfoot territory near the headwaters of the Missouri. There Work found he was in active competition with the American trappers, and after several of his men were killed in attack by three hundred Blackfoot warriors, he retreated to the Salmon River to trade with the Snake tribes. Though his catch was disappointing, he had succeeded in making the region unprofitable for the Americans.

Work's third expedition took him south from Walla Walla along the John Day River to the Sacramento valley of California. This time his party was plagued by illness, an Indian attack, and by the fact that the area had already been heavily trapped by other Hudson's Bay Company parties. Still, Work's journal gives us welcome information about the terrain, the Mexican settlements on San Francisco Bay, and the Russians at Fort Ross. Tired of the exhausting life of a brigade leader and prolonged absences from his Spokane Indian wife and their children, Work gladly accepted the job as factor at Fort Simpson. This involved him in the coastal fur trade until 1846, when he replaced Dr. John McLoughlin as chief factor in the Pacific Northwest. By now Work was a dignified, portly official. When he and his family moved to Victoria, Vancouver Island, in 1853, he promoted farming, developed large landholdings, and served in the provincial legislature from that year until his death.

See William S. Lewis and Paul C. Phillips, eds., *The Journal of John Work* (1923); and Alice Bay Maloney, ed., *Fur Brigade to the Bonaventura* (1945).—H. R. L.

Worrall, Henry (1825-1902). Illustrator. Born in Liverpool, England, Worrall immigrated to the United States with his family in 1835. His boyhood was spent in Buffalo, New York, and Cincinnati, Ohio, and late in the 1860s he moved to Kansas, where he became known as a portraitist, musician, lecturer, and public figure in Topeka circles. There is no record of his having had any formal art training, but as a pictorial recorder of life in the West he was an occasional contributor to *Harper's Weekly, Leslie's Illustrated Newspaper*, and other publications. He is perhaps best remembered today for his illustrations appearing in two books on western history: Isaac McCoy's *Historic Sketches of the Cattle Trade* (1874) and W. E. Webb's *Buffalo Land* (1872). Worrall also made a number of sketches and paintings that never were published or exhibited.—D. C. H.

Wounded Knee Massacre (1890). On December 29, 1890, the Seventh Cavalry under Colonel James Forsyth was attempting to disarm the Miniconjou Sioux under Big Foot, who were camped on Wounded Knee Creek on the Pine Ridge Reservation in South Dakota. Having heard of the killing of Sitting Bull a week earlier, the Indians were reluctant to comply, and firing broke out. Witnesses, white and Indian alike, violently disagree on which side fired first. In the midst of the confusion,

The day after the battle of Wounded Knee the field was littered with the frozen corpses of Indians. (Library of Congress)

bitter hand-to-hand fighting took place before the Indians broke through the surrounding troops and exposed themselves to the rapid-firing Hotchkiss guns. Scattered fire fights occurred in the village and nearby ravines before the conflict ended. The Indians suffered 146 known dead (including 44 women and 18 children) and 51 known wounded. The army had 25 killed and 39 wounded. The campaign brought the concentration of 3,500 troops in the vicinity of Pine Ridge and ended with more than 350 deaths and a total expense of nearly $1.2 million.

The Wounded Knee Massacre ended the long history of the Indian wars. It, as well as the many other conflicts, was the result of a complex chain of events that included the destruction of the Indians' old way of life, the failure of Congress to meet its obligations to them, and the appointment of unskilled Indian agents. Specifically, the spread of the Ghost Dance religion and the death of Sitting Bull contributed to the Sioux's final psychological and military defeat at Wounded Knee.

The battle was particularly tragic. It is unlikely that the Indians precipitated the fight, since Big Foot's band was surrounded by well-armed soldiers and artillery. Cooler heads and wiser officials probably could have prevented the crisis from developing. And finally, many lives were lost. Historians have charged the soldiers with brutality, citing, among other reasons, that they were from Custer's Seventh Cavalry and thus wanted revenge. Robert Utley has defended the soldiers and has explained the loss of life by the positions of the troops and the bitterness of the hand-to-hand fighting.

See Dee Brown, *Bury My Heart at Wounded Knee* (1971); James Mooney, *The Ghost Dance Religion and the Sioux Outbreak of 1890* (1896); and Robert Utley, *The Last Days of the Sioux Nation* (1963).—R. N. E.

Wovoka. See Ghost Dance.

Wright, William. See Dan DeQuille.

Wyandot Indians. See Huron Indians.

Wyeth, Nathaniel J. (1802-1856). Fur trader. Born near Cambridge, Massachusetts, Wyeth spent the majority of his life in the Boston ice business, but he is better known for his five-year effort to establish a fur-trading company on the Columbia River.

Wyeth became interested in Oregon through conversations with his fellow townsman Hall Jackson Kelley, a booster of American settlement in the Pacific Northwest. When Kelley organized an Oregon immigrant party in the spring of 1832, Wyeth enthusiastically participated in Kelley's colonization scheme. Wyeth's business sense also led him to plan for an Oregon trading company to go out with Kelley's colonists, but when he saw Kelley's project begin to disintegrate through poor planning, Wyeth determined to carry out his business plans by himself.

Wyeth's expedition was to be in two parts. He arranged to have the ship *Sultana* voyage to the Columbia River around Cape Horn. Meanwhile, he would lead a group of men overland to Oregon, hunting and trapping on the way. When he met the ship, he would be able to sell its cargo at a profit and return to Boston with the furs.

Wyeth's overland journey was beset by difficulties that caused seven of his men to leave him at Pierre's Hole (in present-day Wyoming). The remaining eighteen followed Wyeth to Fort Vancouver, having only average success trapping beaver. Upon arriving, they discovered that the *Sultana* had been shipwrecked in the South Pacific. This bad luck forced Wyeth to return home empty-handed in 1833. On the overland trek east, he made an agreement with Milton Sublette and Thomas Fitzpatrick to supply the Rocky Mountain Fur Company with goods at the 1834 fur-trading rendezvous. Arriving in Boston armed with this contract, he discovered that his cousin, John B. Wyeth, among those who left the party at Pierre's Hole, had published a book that criticized Wyeth's leadership ability and tried to discourage any future western projects. Wyeth dismissed *Oregon, or a Short History of a Long Journey* as one of the "little lies told for gain."

Over the winter, he organized the Columbia River Fishing and Trading Company to operate from a base on the Columbia River and send wares back east by ship rather than overland. He believed his scheme would be so efficient compared to other fur-trading operations that he would be able to take over the entire trade. Hoping that he could establish trade relations with the Hudson's Bay Company, he confined his fur trapping to the region south of the Columbia. He also planned to pack salmon for Boston markets, but both schemes failed. Then, when Wyeth reached the 1834 rendezvous with his goods, Fitzpatrick refused to buy them. Furious at the treatment he had received, Wyeth declared, "I will roll a stone into your garden that you will never be able to get out." Forthwith Wyeth built Fort Hall on the Snake River, from which he hoped to conduct his own fur trade and cut into the territory of Fitzpatrick's firm. When he reached Fort Vancouver, he discovered that his ship, the *May Dacre*, which had been scheduled to arrive on the Columbia early in the summer for the salmon run, had been damaged by lightning and forced to stop for three months at Valparaíso, Chile, while it was repaired. The ship arrived too late to catch any salmon, and Wyeth tried to save the situation by sending it to Hawaii with timber. When the boat returned in April 1835, Wyeth hoped his luck had turned and so had his men prepare for the 1835 salmon catch. But by September he still had only half a cargo and found the Hudson's Bay Company post at Fort Boise competing seriously with his fur-trading operations at Fort Hall. Out of capital and unable to see a profit in the future, Wyeth accepted the fact that his venture had failed. He returned to Boston in 1836 and sold Fort Hall to the Hudson's Bay Company.

On his second expedition west he was accompanied by the naturalists Thomas Nuttall and John K. Townsend, as well as Jason Lee's missionary party. Townsend later published *Narrative of a Journey Across the Rocky Mountains to the Columbia River*, while Lee's mission became the magnet that attracted American settlement to the Willamette valley. Although forced out of the western trade himself, Wyeth had stirred public and private interest in the Oregon country by establishing a trail there and by bringing the first American missionaries and scientists to the region.

The best source on Wyeth is *The Correspondence and Journals of Captain Nathaniel J. Wyeth*, edited by F. G. Young (1899). Reuben Gold Thwaites, *Early Western Travels*, vol. XXI (1905), contains the accounts of John B. Wyeth and John K. Townsend. A good summary of Wyeth's trips is in LeRoy R. Hafen, ed., *The Mountain Men and the Fur Trade of the Far West*, vol. V (1968). A briefer account is in William H. Goetzmann, *Exploration and Empire* (1966).—G. B. D.

Wyoming. "Who pastures high will feed on slender fare / Austere and tough and brief." So reflected the modern poet Wilson O. Clough as he scanned the Wyoming landscape from the continental divide. And so much have thought most of the first visitors when confronted by vast expanses of sagebrush and jagged mountain ranges.

Very few of the westbound homemakers who traveled along the Oregon, Mormon, and California trails in the 1840s and 1850s seriously considered settling in the region that later became Wyoming. In the 1860s, however, construction of the UNION PACIFIC RAILROAD brought people who did tarry. Cheyenne was laid out in July 1867, four months ahead of the tracklayers. Living in tents and shanties, the pioneers agreed on the need for a provisional city government. They borrowed Denver's city ordinances and elected a mayor and council. To the west, other clusters of pioneers formed provisional governments as they waited for the RAILROADS.

Observers applied the name "hell-on-wheels" to the throng that followed the railway construction gangs across what was then southwestern Dakota Territory. Lacking enthusiasm for the task of governing the disorderly newcomers, the Dakota legislature, without a dissenting vote, petitioned Congress to divide their domain so as to make a new territory out of the western part. Between that area and the eastern part of the territory were Indian lands, and there was no direct line of communication. Congress assembled Wyoming from parts of Dakota, Idaho, and Utah territories. On July 25, 1868, President Andrew Johnson signed the organic act that gave Wyoming Territory the same boundaries that the state would later receive.

President Johnson immediately nominated a set of territorial officials, but since he was at odds with Congress, he could not get Senate approval. Wyoming was disorganized, if not turbulent, until another set of officials, named by President U. S. Grant, arrived in May 1869. In the interval there had been occasional exercise of authority by Dakota Territory, the Union Pacific, the federal army, provisional city governments, and vigilance committees. Grant's appointees found that before they could take charge the worst law-and-order problems had already moved on into Utah with the construction camps.

Wyoming probably had close to 20,000 people in the summer of 1868, but the federal census takers found only 9,118 in 1870, not counting the Indians who roamed over most of the territory away from the railroad towns. For several years thereafter the territory's development was distressingly slow. The altitude and aridity discouraged agriculture. Precious metals were scarce, although they were abundant beyond the territorial borders to the south, west, and north. Except to fuel Union Pacific locomotives, there was little market for the vast low-grade coal beds. Railroads had not yet penetrated into the north.

The principal employers in the 1870s were the army and the Union Pacific, but by themselves they could not support more than a few thousand people. President Grant in 1872 favored dismemberment of the territory and distribution of its parts to Colorado, Utah, Idaho, and Montana. Although such action could have been justified, a wait-and-see policy was adopted instead. In the next few years just enough progress occurred to insure survival. A series of relatively mild winters encouraged expansion of the livestock industry at the same time that confinement of Indian tribes on reservations opened a vast grazing area north of the Platte River and east of the Big Horn Mountains. Also, Cheyenne prospered for a few years as the principal supply base for gold miners in Dakota's Black Hills. These developments enabled the population to grow to 20,789 by 1880.

There was some talk in the territory about statehood as soon as President Johnson signed the organic act in 1868. Such talk disappeared in the troubled 1870s but revived with the rapid expansion of the open-range cattle industry in the early 1880s. With such ranchers as Alexander H. SWAN, William C. IRVINE, John Benjamin KENDRICK, and John CLAY leading the way, cattle increased from 300,000 in 1880 to 1.5 million in 1885. Governor William Hale reported in 1883 that the cattle industry composed ninety percent of all economic activity in the territory. The four-hundred-member Wyoming Stock Growers' Association in the mid-1880s certainly had political clout; it was not unusual to have half or more of the legislative seats occupied by members of the association, and favorable legislation could usually be arranged. Notably, the 1884 legislature passed the Maverick Law, which gave the association full control of roundups and strictly limited livestock branding except on the official roundups. Not everyone could get into the association, and to operate outside of it was dangerous.

Representatives of the association in testimony before the United States Public Lands Commission in 1879 voiced solid opposition to a proposal that occupants of the public lands, who were paying nothing for such use, take title by paying five cents an acre. At the moment, free use without the need to pay taxes looked better, but a few years later they found the free range overcrowded and their profits dwindling. Besides, open-range methods, without provision for water and supplementary feed, proved costly when severe winters returned after several years' absence. In particular, the winter of 1886-87 delivered a stunning setback to the territory's one-crop economy.

Meanwhile, the territory's political leaders, Francis E. WARREN and Joseph Maull CAREY, had made up their minds to seek statehood. Warren governed the territory, 1885-86 and 1889-90, while his ally Carey served as delegate to Congress, 1885-90. Realistic economic analysis following the collapse of the cattle industry in 1887 might have persuaded less aggressive politicians to shelve temporarily their drive for statehood. Instead, Warren and Carey redoubled their efforts, calculating that statehood would bring a more favorable climate for economic recovery. Warren headed the drive at home; Carey in Washington.

Unable to get an enabling act in 1889, which would allow the territory to set up the machinery preparatory for statehood, Governor Warren moved ahead without one. He arranged for a convention, which patched together a long constitution in just twenty-five working days. The document was copied for the most part from the constitutions recently made in North and South Dakota, Montana, and Idaho.

Wyoming voters' allegiance had been unpredictable in earlier years, but they appeared in the late 1880s to be settling down in the Republican groove, a convenient coincidence since the G.O.P. had returned to power in Washington. Carey's astute handling of the final drive helped achieve statehood in 1890. His later assertion—that Speaker Thomas Reed of the House of Representatives told him that without his (Carey's) work "Wyoming would not have been a state for twenty years to come"—is plausible.

Floored by the devastating winter of 1886-87, the cattlemen would not stay down. They began to modify their open-range methods and successfully withstood the onslaught of assorted enemies. Thieves harassed them until they reacted violently. Failing to get justice in the courts, they took the law into their own hands in what has become known as the JOHNSON COUNTY WAR. Although in this instance their vigilante activity fizzled and drew sharp criticism, rustling declined thereafter, permitting cattlemen to boast that they had won the "war."

Another major threat to the cattle industry arose in the form of sheep, which were moved onto the public lands in increasing numbers until there were six million at times between 1902 and 1910, when there were fewer than one million cattle. The cattlemen insisted that prior use of public land gave them rights, but sheepmen replied that no legal rights accrued merely from prior use and that the public grazing lands were open to all. As in the Johnson County War, small groups of cattlemen took extralegal action. Between 1897 and 1909 their nocturnal assaults brought death to fifteen men and a boy and to perhaps ten thousand sheep before arrests and convictions ended the slaughter and the cattlemen resigned themselves to sharing the range. In the long run, however, the cattlemen were able to strengthen their dominance in the partnership.

Next came dry farmers to homestead much of the range in the eastern counties. They encountered disheartening opposition from drought, wind, grasshoppers, and short growing seasons, as well as from the graziers. After encouraging dry farmers for several years, the state university experiment station's *Farm Bulletin* advised in August 1913: "Some land has been taken up which might better go back to cattle and sheep." Meanwhile some of the cattlemen had made fraudulent land entries and had put up illegal fences. The United States attorney for Wyoming told an Interior Department special agent: "inasmuch as three-fourths of the public domain has been proved up by perjury, let them have it; that the paying of taxes is enough punishment for the deed, and what the State needs is . . . land on the tax rolls." Land laws unsuited to the semiarid West partly explained the prevalence of fraud. For many ranchers it took scheming and perjury to assemble the five thousand or more acres needed for a sound ranch operation.

During World War I high grain and land prices brought a homesteading spree in which townspeople and newcomers from out of state joined native ranchers and farmers. More than twenty-one thousand homestead entries were made in Wyoming in the two peak years of 1920 and 1921. However, people who were already on the land in 1919 sooner or later acquired most of the new homesteads. Although private ownership of land doubled in the 1920s to forty percent of the state's total area, the number of farm and ranch units increased only from 15,748 to 16,011.

Gradually a pattern emerged. Cattle, sheep, and big game (antelope, mule deer, and elk) rather than dry farmers and irrigators would occupy virtually all the state's surface outside of national parks. In 1934 the

Taylor Grazing Act and the complementary Executive Order 6910 ended homesteading except on small reclamation projects, leaving the federal government permanently in control of one half of the land surface. In the 1960s roughly sixty-five percent of the state's annual cash agricultural income of $200 million or less came from cattle, twenty percent from crops, and fifteen percent from sheep.

Agriculture ceased to be Wyoming's most important industry after World War II as mineral production came to the fore. Since earliest times there had been widespread prospecting for minerals, with some significant discoveries. The Union Pacific mined its immense reserves of low-grade bituminous coal for eighty years. In the 1950s it terminated this activity when it dieselized its locomotives. The Colorado Fuel and Iron Company mined iron ore at Sunrise in Platte County ever since 1900. The Encampment area in Carbon County produced copper in the first decade of the twentieth century. United States Steel in the 1950s began tapping iron ore deposits in South Pass. It was petroleum, however, that would dominate the minerals picture. The fur trader Captain Bonneville reported seeing a "great tar spring" just east of South Pass in 1832. Other oil seeps attracted interest thereafter until some of them were dug out to increase the flow in the 1870s. Drilling of wells began in the 1880s, and the great Salt Creek Field became a producer in 1890. Exploration and discoveries spread, until by 1970 all but two of the twenty-three counties had oil-producing wells.

Remoteness from markets caused known oil fields to lie undeveloped for many years. World War I needs, however, stimulated drilling and production, but again in the 1920s and 1930s more favorably located producers in other states monopolized the markets. World War II gave renewed impetus to the industry, and this time there was no postwar loss of markets. Instead, output rose fourfold from 35 million barrels in 1945 to more than 140 million barrels in 1970. Beginning in the 1960s Wyoming ranked fifth in production of oil among the states of the Union. In terms of cash value of product, oil was the most lucrative industry, with annual output being worth more than $400 million. This was more than the combined value of the second and third industries, livestock-agriculture and tourism. Most of the crude oil, however, was piped out of the state for refining, so that once the exploration, well drilling, and pipeline construction had been completed few workers were employed in the industry. Production of natural gas rose as fast as that of oil, and it too was mostly piped out of the state.

Other minerals, particularly uranium and trona, gained prominence in the postwar years. The state led all others in trona output, and ranked first or second in production of uranium yellowcake. The total cash value of uranium and trona was nevertheless small in comparison with that of petroleum. Strip mining of coal became popular for fueling steam-power generating plants in several states of the Middle West as well as in Wyoming.

Total mineral production in 1970 was worth $700 million, and petroleum was worth more than $400 million while the cash value of the cattle industry's product remained little more than $100 million.

Although well behind minerals in value, the fastest growing major industry after World War II was tourism, as automobiles brought hordes of visitors to parks, national forests, and fishing and hunting areas. Nineteenth-century sportsmen such as William Drummond Stewart and George Gore and occasional remittance men and dudes were the precursors of millions of recreation-seekers. When tourists first arrived in force in the 1920s they supplied much-needed stimulation to a faltering economy. Restaurants, souvenir shops, "cottage camps," filling stations, and garages offered new employment opportunities.

In 1970 about 2.3 million tourists crowded Yellowstone National Park and more than 3 million visitors flowed through Grand Teton National Park. The economic importance of game and fish increased tremendously, as many people were employed in supplying the needs of out-of-state sportsmen. Conservation problems multiplied. Out-of-state deer-hunting licenses, for example, had to be cut from seventy-five thousand in 1970 to fifty thousand in 1971. Resident fishermen, hunters, and ranchers complained about too many intruders from out of state, and natives had to schedule their visits to Yellowstone Park early or late to avoid the crowds of July and August.

Despite persistent promotion the manufacturing industry lagged. The state ranked last among the fifty states, with about seven thousand employed in manufacturing in 1970, which was less than the number so employed in the 1920s. Wyoming's undeserved reputation for exceedingly long, cold winters constituted the major obstacle to industrialization, and there were other limiting factors. Some natives had never wanted special promotion of industrialization. With increasing pressure from conservationists, educators, and persons associated with the tourist industry, environmental and aesthetic considerations gained attention in the 1960s. No longer could developers of raw materials or other industrialists expect a green light, a clear track, and accolades right and left even at a chamber of commerce annual dinner.

Included in the state's economic "mix" was the federal government's substantial contribution in the form of grants-in-aid, salaries, and military construction contracts. The state exported crude oil, natural gas, coal, electricity, cattle, sheep, wool, wheat, iron-ore pellets, trona, and uranium yellowcake, and imported all kinds of manufactured goods, transportation, communications, insurance, meat, milk, fruits, and vegetables. Since modern mechanized raw materials production required only a small work force, and absentee owners of the state's wealth took part of what was collected for exports, paying for the imports became a vexing problem. The federal government made up the difference, as it sometimes spent more in the state than it took out in taxes.

Wyoming's state government has been cautious, conservative, slow to innovate, and relatively free from corruption. Most of the time the voters have chosen Republicans for state and local offices, although they have sent almost as many Democrats, such as John Benjamin Kendrick and Joseph Christopher O'MAHONEY, as Republicans to the Senate and have usually favored the winners in presidential contests. From territorial days until he died in 1929, Francis E. Warren, an old guard Republican governor and senator, and his ally, the judge Willis

Van Devanter, had extraordinary influence on politics and government. Another influential conservative Republican was Frank Wheeler Mondell.

The nickname "Equality State," which is just about as popular as "Cowboy State," denotes early leadership in woman suffrage. Wyoming Territory in 1869 was the first political unit anywhere in the world to give women full rights to vote and hold office; Esther Morris was appointed a judge by the governor. In 1890 Wyoming became the first state with full suffrage rights for women. Despite this, women have been no more prominent in state politics and government than elsewhere. Election of a woman governor in 1924, another "first," was a case of widow's succession. When Governor William B. Ross died halfway through his four-year term, Nellie Tayloe Ross was elected to fill out the term. Not until 1910 was a woman elected to the legislature, and no more than five women have ever served in that body at one time. Indeed, male dominance has normally been conspicuous, partly because men much outnumbered the women until World War II.

No third party has ever won many adherents. One exception was in 1912, when Theodore Roosevelt, running as an independent, won 9,000 votes to 14,000 for Taft and 15,000 for Wilson. Third-party legislators have been virtually nonexistent except in 1893, when five Populists held the balance of power between embattled Republicans and Democrats. Populism and Progressivism touched Wyoming more lightly than they did neighboring states because Wyoming had no silver, few crop farmers, few liberals, and only a few cities and those small. Beyond wanting the direct primary and popular election of senators, relatively few Wyoming people felt much reform spirit during the Progressive period.

Wyoming's cattlemen, sheepmen, farmers, developers of oil, gas, coal, and other minerals, and small-business people have usually wanted as little government as possible. Not until 1969 did the legislature adopt an oil and gas severance tax and a law requiring restoration of land surface after exploration or mining activity. Federal ownership of land has been a major source of a states' rights controversy, as exemplified by the Carey Act and its promotor, Wyoming engineer Elwood Mead. The federal government has often been charged with interfering with economic development by "locking up" natural resources and collecting excessive user fees and with overregulation and "bureaucratic" bungling. In 1970 the federal government still owned forty-eight percent of the surface rights and seventy-two percent of the mineral rights in the state, owing in part to the unattractiveness of the area before the public domain was closed to private entry.

In the Great Depression, Wyoming was the last state to ask for or to receive federal aid for the needy. Thereafter federal grants requiring matching were watched warily. State officials usually preferred to postpone acceptance of new programs until other states had tested them. They felt that some programs were unnecessary in a state with so few people. One state official declared that to impose on Wyoming all the programs appropriate for New York or California was "like putting a workhorse harness on a Shetland pony."

The constitution with which the state entered the Union in 1890 still served in 1970, although some thirty amendments had been adopted. In 1933, made desperate by shrinking revenue, the legislature considered but finally rejected drastic reduction in the number of counties and school districts and the substitution of a small unicameral legislature for the traditional two-house body (consisting of sixty-one representatives and thirty senators in 1971). In keeping with the principle that the less government, the better, the legislature meets only forty days every other year except for rare special sessions.

In the 1960s rural influence in the legislature declined noticeably, owing in part to federal court-imposed reapportionment of the upper house in 1965. For a time oil and mining interests, prospering as never before, appeared ready to take over the leadership position long held by cattlemen, but there were enough cross-currents among seven or eight influential interests to prevent dominance by any one.

Ninety-eight percent of Wyoming's 332,416 people are white, the other two percent consisting of four thousand Arapaho and Shoshoni Indians, two thousand blacks, and a few Japanese and Chinese. The educational level is high; illiteracy, rare. Among the whites are more than twenty thousand Hispanos (locally known as Mexicans), who constitute the largest minority group.

Less than one fourth of the people were foreign-born at the time of statehood (1890), and the fraction declined thereafter until it was negligible in 1970. In the territorial period, newcomers gave their birthplaces as New York, Pennsylvania, Ohio, Illinois, Great Britain, Ireland, and Germany, in that order. Thereafter the Midwest forged to the front. Iowa led the states in contributing people to Wyoming in 1910, and after that Nebraska did so. Willa Cather once wrote that crop failures and depression in Nebraska in the 1890s "winnowed out the settlers with a purpose from the drifting malcontents who are ever seeking a land where man does not live by the sweat of his brow. The slack farmer moved on." Phyllis Winkelman, director of education, Nebraska State Historical Society, later wrote: "Many of the scoundrels moved on as the frontier moved westward and left behind a pretty solid citizenry." These generalizations have no more validity than the one preferred in Wyoming: "The cowards never started and the weak died by the way."

The percentage of transients has always been high. Seasonal workers in tourism and agriculture, and oilmen from Texas and Oklahoma, came and went. As late as 1950 only thirty-eight percent of the residents were natives. In the 1940s more people moved out than moved in, as California and Colorado became powerful magnets. Employment dropped in agriculture, rail transportation, and coal mining. So many moved out of the state during the 1960s (39,000) that the population was only 2,350 greater in 1970 (332,416) than in 1960. Most of the people lived in cities and towns, with only 40,000 residing on the nine thousand ranches and farms in 1970. Major cities were the capital, Cheyenne, and the "oil capital," Casper. Each had about 40,000 people in 1970, while Laramie had 23,000, Rock Springs, 12,000, and Sheridan, 11,000.

Church membership percentages have always been low in comparison with states of the Midwest. A Laramie editor complained in 1881 that not one in ten was a "church goer." When asked about their lack of interest, individuals explained that there was no church of their denomination or that they did not expect to stay long. The superintendent of the Wyoming mission of the Methodist Church reported in 1897 that the sparse population made it impossible to reach some people and that many teen-agers had never seen a minister of the gospel. As more midwesterners came, especially women, to join what had been a largely male population, the contrast with the Midwest diminished but did not disappear entirely. Roman Catholics made up perhaps eighteen percent of the population and Mormons, six percent. Most of the Mormons were concentrated in the western part of the state.

Two extensive studies published in 1931 in *The American Mercury* and in 1969 in *State Government Administration* ranked the states of the Union according to such criteria as wealth, education, culture, health, public order, status of the individual, equality, economic growth, technology change, and living conditions. Averaging the results, Wyoming was ranked thirtieth in the 1931 study and twenty-fourth in the 1969 study, very close in both cases to the middle of the list of states. Nevertheless, perhaps because they were so few, people who had lived for more than twenty years in Wyoming tended to exhibit remarkable state pride and loyalty. They seemed reluctant to admit that any other place in the world could compare with Wyoming.

See Lewis L. Gould, *Wyoming: A Political History, 1868-1896* (1968); T. A. Larson, *History of Wyoming* (1965); and WPA Writers Project, *Wyoming: A Guide to Its History, Highways, and People* (1941).—T. A. L.

Wyoming Basin. See PHYSIOGRAPHY OF THE UNITED STATES: *Rocky Mountains*.

X

XIT Ranch. Perhaps the largest ranch in the world at its peak, the XIT Ranch (also referred to as the Capitol Freehold Ranch or the Capitol Syndicate Ranch) encompassed 3 million acres in the Texas Panhandle. In 1879 the Texas legislature appropriated 3,050,000 acres for sale to finance the surveying of the land and for the construction of a state capitol in Austin, Texas. A Chicago syndicate was formed to contract with the state for building a magnificent statehouse. The first stone was laid in 1885, and the building was completed in 1888. As work progressed, the Chicago group received title to parts of the land. Ultimately it obtained 3 million acres and organized a huge ranching enterprise covering parts of nine counties. Divided into seven divisions, the ranch was run in a businesslike manner. At one point the ranch had 160,000 head of cattle, 150 cowboys, and more than 1,000 horses in the company remuda. The ranch also owned a grazing range in Montana, to which about 12,000 head of cattle were driven each summer for fattening. Between 1904 and 1922 the ranch sold all but a million acres, because of the high price of land and the declining cattle prices. Finally, by 1950, all but 20,000 acres had been sold. Since then, this also has been sold to smaller farmers and ranchers.

See J. Evetts Haley, *The XIT Ranch of Texas and the Early Days of the Llano Estacado* (1929).—J. A. S.

Y

Yadkin valley. The Yadkin valley extends from the confluence of the Yadkin River with the upper Pee Dee near Boonville, North Carolina, to the Appalachian highlands. This fairly broad valley, sweeping up from the central Piedmont to the Blue Ridge ranges, formed an open trough for westward-moving settlers. By 1746 six families had settled in this valley, and by 1770 there was a constant inflow of Scotch-Irish, German, Scottish Highlander, Welsh, and English immigrants. It was to this valley that the Boone family emigrated from Pennsylvania.

Many of the men of the Yadkin valley became long hunters and went hunting and exploring far beyond the Blue Ridge. From this region prior to the American Revolution came a steady flow of deer skins, cattle hides, cornmeal, wheat, flour, hemp, herbs, and cattle on foot. In 1774 a thousand head of cattle were driven from Wachovia to Philadelphia. As the HOLSTON RIVER SETTLEMENTS and Kentucky settlements were opened, many Yadkin settlers moved on through Cumberland Gap to the Ohio valley. The Yadkin settlements formed a backwoods base for penetrating the greater western frontier.

See John Bakeless, *Daniel Boone, Master of the Wilder-*

ness (1939); J. H. Clewell, *History of Wachovia in North Carolina* (1902); and Hugh T. Lefler and Albert R. Newsome, *North Carolina: The History of a Southern State*, rev. ed. (1963).—T. D. C.

Yakima Indians. The Yakima were the largest of the Shahaptian tribes in the Columbia Basin and had come up the Columbia River with the early migration. They were so scattered in small fishing villages along the Yakima River and the right bank of the Columbia that there is no firm agreement on just how many of these small groups should be included in the tribe. The core villages were located at the good fishing sites near Union Gap and Wapato on the Yakima River. The Yakima language, except for some slight differences in pronunciation, was the same as that of the Nez Percé and Palouse. Ocean run salmon furnished their staple food, supplemented with roots, berries, and game. They lived in large houses built with heavy timber frames and covered with reed mats.

The several Yakima villages had no tribal organization, but were held together by a common language, culture, and living area. Each village had a chief, or head man, whose slight authority did not extend to any other village. A chief with a reputation as a warrior, however, had respect from the other villages and could control a war party composed of men from his own and other villages.

The Yakima secured their first horses from the Nez Percé and Cayuse about 1735 and in a few years became important horse raisers. A complex of timbered ridges with broad summits stretched from Mount Adams off to the east for about a hundred miles. Most of the timber consisted of open stands of yellow pine, while a heavy growth of grass covered most of the area. Blessed with nutritious grasses, plenty of shade, and many good streams, this great pastureland, covering several thousand square miles, was known later as Horse Heaven.

The Yakima soon learned to ride and became a tribe of horsemen. The bands roamed over the country several months each year, but they still had to keep their fishing sites and harvest the annual salmon run. They went to the large Indian fishing and trading center at The Dalles, where they traded horses and deer and elk skins for shells and trinkets from the coast and for supplies of salmon oil and some dried salmon. Then they went northeastward to the Spokane Falls trading center and traded off more horses and some of the coast items for goods from the mountains and plains to the east, including buffalo robes and war bonnets.

Yakima bands joined with other Columbia Basin bands and crossed the mountains to hunt buffalo in Montana. Within a few years they adopted many customs of the Plains culture, such as the tepee. It was a fine portable lodge, much superior to their own small lodges covered with reed mats, which they had used when traveling. With its covering of tanned skins, the tepee was well adapted to the arid climate of the Yakima homeland.

When the fur traders came to the Columbia Basin in the early nineteenth century they found the Yakima rather hard to deal with at times. In 1815 Alexander Ross went to the large Yakima encampment to buy horses for his trading operations and escaped serious trouble by a very narrow margin. In 1817, when Donald

Mackenzie went to the mouth of the Walla Walla River to establish Fort Nez Percé, often called Fort Walla Walla, he was surrounded by about two thousand hostile Indians, led by the Yakima, who threatened him with violence and demanded many presents and a yearly rent for the land for his proposed post. Mackenzie forted up on a sandbar in the Columbia and waited out his opposition, for the Indians had neither the supplies nor the organization to sustain such a force in the field for any length of time. Also, Mackenzie was skilled in Indian diplomacy and calmed the chiefs with his presentation of the benefits such a post would bring to the tribes.

The Yakima had little contact with the whites except for a few fur traders for the next thirty-five years, until General Isaac Stevens arrived in 1853 as the governor of the newly created Washington Territory. Stevens had orders to hold council meetings with all the tribes in the area and to assign them to reservations of their own choosing, centered around their permanent village sites. Federal officials believed that if each tribe marked out the land it claimed, there would be a great deal of land left that no tribe claimed. Also, several of the tribes had suffered severe losses from disease and might willingly surrender some of their land. In addition, Stevens wanted the Indians to allow the whites to cross Indian lands on recognized trails.

Stevens held a great treaty council in the valley of the Walla Walla in May and June 1855, at which leaders of the several tribes, including the Yakima, agreed to accept certain reservations and surrender all claims to the lands outside the reservation boundaries. They also agreed that the whites could have roads across their lands. In return, the federal government was to pay each tribe a large amount of trade goods each year.

The new treaties caused trouble from the first. Many of the small villages near the Yakima lands denied that the Yakima leader, Chief KAMIAKIN, a noted warrior and a powerful personality, had any power or authority to sign for them. Also, the Indians expected the treaty payments to start that summer, but no payments could be made until the United States Senate ratified the treaties and appropriated the necessary funds.

Stevens disregarded the protests of the various small bands and declared that Chief Kamiakin did have the authority to sign for them. Then he went across the Rockies to talk with the Blackfoot. During his absence many prospectors bound for the new gold discoveries in British Columbia insisted that the new treaties gave them the right to cross Indian lands. A few prospectors were killed on the trails by young Indian men patrolling the valley. This set off a period of disturbances and sporadic fighting called the Yakima War, which lasted from September 1855 to November 1856.

Indian agent A. J. Bolen, well liked by the Yakima, went north from The Dalles to investigate the reported killings and on the return trip was killed because he had threatened to return with soldiers. Major Granville O. Haller then marched from The Dalles with a hundred men and a howitzer to investigate further. On October 8, 1855, after skirmishing for two days with about five hundred Indians, Haller buried his howitzer, burned his baggage and supplies, and retreated. Five of his men were killed and seventeen were wounded.

In November Major Gabriel Rains, the commander at The Dalles, led a force of regular soldiers and several companies of volunteers, seven hundred men in all, into the Yakima valley. After a brief skirmish the Yakima scattered and hid out in remote valleys and Rains returned to his post.

During this same period, Lieutenant Colonel James K. Kelly of the Oregon volunteers had marched up the Walla Walla valley and had a running skirmish with a large force of Walla Walla, Umatilla, and Cayuse from December 7 to 10. During the fighting the volunteers killed the famous Chief Peo Peo Mox Mox, of the Walla Walla, and five of his men. The Indians had all come into camp on invitation, under a flag of truce, and had been seized as hostages.

During the entire period of the Yakima War Governor Stevens and General John E. Wool, commander of the Department of the Pacific, were engaged in a petty personal squabble that prevented efficient cooperation between the regular troops and the volunteers, who often behaved in disgraceful fashion toward peaceful Indians.

In 1856 the volunteers in the Walla Walla valley were commanded by Colonel Thomas R. Cornelius. Their continued presence there and their conduct kept the Indians angry. In March Cornelius led his men north across the Snake River into Palouse country, then west across the Columbia and up the Yakima, where he had a brief encounter with the Indians. He then returned to The Dalles.

While he was away, an Indian force staged a surprise attack on the people working at the Cascades portage, thirty-five miles down the Columbia from The Dalles, and killed fifteen people.

Colonel George H. Wright, the new commander at The Dalles, marched north to Yakima country in April in an attempt to hold a council meeting with the dissident chiefs. After six weeks of talks in which no decisions were reached, Wright rounded up five hundred Indians from various bands and escorted them to the new Warm Springs Reservation on the Deschutes River in Oregon.

In July a force of volunteers under Colonel B. F. Shaw, which Governor Stevens had kept in the Walla Walla valley, marched across the Blue Mountains to the Grand Ronde valley to attack a peaceful camp of Walla Walla and Cayuse families that had very few warriors to protect it. Against such a camp the volunteers could and did dash about, killing anyone they could catch. They made no count of the many dead, but destroyed the tepees, baggage, and food supplies; five volunteers were killed and four wounded.

Peace finally came to the Columbia Basin after Colonel Wright induced Governor Stevens to withdraw all the volunteers. Once the Indians felt secure, they were willing to stop all resistance and the war slowed to a halt in November 1856.

The Yakima were restless during the Coeur d'Alene War in 1858, but only a few young men joined the hostiles. They flocked to the "Dreamer" movement in the 1860s. When the Nez Percé War broke out in 1877, General O. O. Howard feared that the Yakima would join the hostiles, but they remained on their reservation. A number of Yakima warriors, however, joined Chief Buffalo Horn when he called for men to help him fight the Bannock War in 1878. With Buffalo Horn's death, the fighting force soon disbanded and the Yakima returned stealthily to their homes.

As white settlers flocked into the Columbia Basin, federal officials bought large portions of the Yakima reservation for irrigation projects, which have since made the Yakima valley a highly productive area.

When a series of large dams were built on the Columbia River in the period 1938-70, the structures cut down on the salmon runs to the Yakima River and the backwater from the dams flooded good fishing spots along the Columbia River, especially the great fisheries at Celilo Falls. In a series of treaties the Yakima tribe was paid several million dollars for these losses.

The Yakima tribal council paid some of this money directly to the individual tribesmen and put the rest into a tribal fund for improving the reservation. The council has built three longhouses that are social halls suitable for public meetings, Indian dances, and basketball. The young people are encouraged to engage in sports and to learn Indian dances. Also, promising young people who are interested in college educations receive grants for each term successfully completed.

See R. I. Burns, *The Jesuits in the Indian Wars of the Northwest* (1963); Thelma Kimmel, *The Fort Simcoe Story* (1954); and A. J. Splawn, *Ka-mi-akin: The Last Hero of the Yakimas* (1917).—F. H.

Yakima War. See YAKIMA INDIANS.

Yamasee Indians. The Yamasee Indians were a Muskogean people who were occupying the country centering around the junction of the Ocmulgee and Oconee rivers in Georgia and extending into northern Florida when Spanish explorers entered that region in the sixteenth century. Nearly nothing is known of their prehistory or of the form of their aboriginal culture. They were of darker complexion than surrounding tribes and of good physical form. John Bartram, the famous botanist, said that the Creek called the Yamasee women "daughters of the sun." The Spanish established missions among them about 1590, and they were under Spanish jurisdiction until 1684-85 when, in response to an attempt to transport large numbers of them to the West Indies as slaves, the Yamasee attacked and destroyed a number of mission settlements and withdrew northward to the lower Savannah River region of English South Carolina. At this time they numbered about 1,200 people.

For several years they got along well with the English, who regarded them as a beneficial buffer against the Spanish, and Yamasee warriors aided the colonists' campaign against the Tuscarora in 1711-13. By 1715, however, dissatisfaction with corrupt English trading practices and encroachment on the lands guaranteed them by South Carolina led the Yamasee to organize against the colonists an uprising which included nearly all the Indians from Cape Fear to St. Augustine and some of the neighboring backcountry tribes as well. In the ensuing "Yamasee War" the Indians killed all the traders among them and perhaps three hundred settlers along the frontier. An expedition of militia and friendly tribes, mounted by Governor Craven of South Carolina, defeated the Yamasee in April 1715 at Sadkeche village on the Combahee River and impelled them to retrace their migration path southward to the swamps of Florida. Some fragments of the tribe dispersed and were absorbed by the Creek and Catawba, and the other allies of the Yamasee were brought to terms during the following year.

Until the acquisition of Florida by Britain, the surviving tribal group of Yamasee was considered an ally of Spain, and Yamasee raids continued into Georgia and South Carolina. They also warred with the expanding Seminole peoples, which depleted Yamasee numbers until they were overwhelmed and generally merged with the Seminole by 1800. The Oklawaha band of Seminole is considered to have descended from the Yamasee, and two leading warriors of the Seminole War (1816-41), Jumper and Alligator, were identified as "Yemassee" by General T. S. Jesup when they surrendered at Fort Dade in 1837. After that date no separate identification of the Yamasee is possible.

See Samuel G. Drake, *The Aboriginal Races of North America* (1880); Thomas L. McKenny and James Hall, *The Indian Tribes of North America*, 2 vols. (1933-34); and John L. Stoutenburgh, Jr., *Dictionary of the American Indian* (1960).—T. D. C.

Yankton, South Dakota. Yankton, one of the earliest white settlements in Dakota Territory, took its name from the Yankton Indians, who were a subtribe of the Teton Sioux and who ceded the land to the United States government in 1858. The name itself came from the Sioux *E-hank-ton-wan,* meaning "end village." The first white inhabitants of the region were involved in fur trading. There were enough pioneers by 1861 to justify the creation of Dakota Territory, and in the following year Yankton was chosen the territorial capital. Although a small village when compared to most state or territorial capitals, Yankton soon developed a national reputation as a lively political center, full of ambitious politicians, fiercely partisan newspapers, and vigorous mercantile firms.

As the uppermost town on the Missouri River in the 1860s and 1870s, Yankton supplied army posts and Indian reservations. Like most frontier towns it went through a series of boom-and-bust cycles. When war broke out between the Minnesota Sioux and white settlers in 1862, Yankton's future seemed dim; ultimately, the Indian scare and the Civil War discouraged settlers from coming to Dakota for five years. A land boom between 1868 and 1873 benefited the town, but so desperate were the Yankton businessmen to gain an edge on surrounding towns that they persuaded Yankton County to float bonds to build a railroad. The coming of the Dakota Southern Railroad in January 1873 helped offset the depression brought on by the national panic of that year, and a second land boom developed between 1873 and 1878. When the Black Hills gold rush began in 1876, Yankton merchants and steamboat lines reaped enormous benefits.

In the spring thaw of 1881 the Missouri overflowed its banks and swept away part of the town and many of the nearby settlements and ruined the town's steamboat industry. The removal of the capital in 1883 to Bismarck and the completion of other lines to the Missouri that bypassed Yankton meant the end of its dominance as a supply town. Thereafter Yankton's growth was slow.

The completion of an automobile bridge across the Missouri to Nebraska in 1924 aided its economy, but the town was hard hit by the Depression of the 1930s and did not recover until World War II. In 1957 the Gavins Point Dam, part of the Missouri flood-control system, was built near Yankton. The dam created a large reservoir, Lewis and Clark Lake, which has since become a major attraction for tourists and fishermen and a boon to the city. Noted for its civic pride and its determination to grow, Yankton was named the "All-America City" by the National Municipal League in 1958.

See Robert F. Karolevitz, *Yankton: A Pioneer Past* (1972).—D. J. T.

Yazoo land grant. See LAND COMPANIES.

Yell, Archibald (1797-1847). Arkansas politician and soldier. Born in North Carolina, Yell migrated to Tennessee, served under Andrew Jackson at New Orleans during the War of 1812 and in Florida against the Seminole Indians, and moved to Arkansas Territory in 1835, where he became a federal judge. A popular figure, he was the state's first representative in Congress (1836-39) and became its second governor in 1840. He resigned the governorship in 1844 to return to Congress. A life-long friend of President James K. Polk, Yell in 1845 went to Texas on a special mission of investigation connected with annexation. He led Arkansas's volunteers in the Mexican War and was killed at Buena Vista.—W. L. B.

Yellowstone National Park. Yellowstone National Park, the oldest and largest of the national parks, straddles Wyoming, Montana, and Idaho, most of it being in Wyoming. It was established by Congress on March 1, 1872. The legislation, which reserved 2,221,773 acres from the public domain, gave the area unique protection from commercial exploitation. The Yellowstone Act of 1872 stated categorically that the land was being set aside as a public "pleasuring-ground" for the "preservation, from injury or spoilation, of all timber, mineral deposits, natural curiosities, or wonders within . . . and their retention in their natural condition." The establishment of Yellowstone set the precedent for all of the national parks that were to follow. The concept of reserving lands from the public domain for use as parks and to preserve unique examples of natural beauty was a distinctly American idea. Many other nations later set up parks modeled after the national park system in the United States. The Yellowstone Act of 1872 therefore had great historical significance.

Yellowstone was known to the Indians for hundreds of years before the white man visited the region. Native tribes made their homes in the area and used it as hunting and fishing grounds. John Colter was the first white man to view the region. He passed through the Yellowstone area in 1807 after leaving the Lewis and Clark expedition on its return trip from the Pacific. Hunters and trappers occasionally ventured into the area before the Civil War, but not much was known about it until the 1860s. The Folsom-Cook expedition explored it in 1869; the Washburn-Langford-Doane expedition made a detailed exploration of the area in 1870. In 1871, the Hayden expedition also covered the Yellowstone. Pictures by William H. Jackson, the pioneer photographer of the West, and the paintings of Thomas Moran, both of whom were with the Hayden party, helped publicize the Yellowstone. Congress acted to preserve the region partly because of the visual proof these men provided of Yellowstone's incredible bubbling pots, lakes, canyons, and waterfalls.

Cornelius Hedges, a member of the Washburn-Langford-Doane expedition, has often been credited with originating the "national park idea." The story of

Hedges sitting by a campfire in Yellowstone in 1870, persuading his colleagues to work for the establishment of a national park in the region instead of exploiting it for private gain, has improved with the telling, and historians have now largely discredited the tale.

Yellowstone was administered by the army engineers from 1872 until the National Park Service took over in 1919. They gave the park generally adequate protection over the years. Its road system was designed and built by General Hiram M. Chittenden, a well-known engineer. These roads, though now modernized, have been only slightly extended, so that much of the park is still a magnificent wilderness preserve.

The first civilian superintendent of the park was Horace M. Albright, who held the position from 1919 to 1929. During these years Yellowstone was the crown jewel of the national park system, internationally renowned for its geysers and beautiful scenery. In the 1920s in Yellowstone, Albright established the administrative pattern that was later applied to all of the large parks in the national park system. Warren G. Harding, Calvin Coolidge, and Herbert Hoover, as well as dignitaries from around the world, came to Yellowstone in the 1920s.

The park has retained much of its luster in the years since the 1920s. Tourists by the thousands watch Old Faithful erupt. Lake Yellowstone, the Grand Canyon of the park, and Mammoth Hot Springs are still major attractions. Relatively few of the visitors to the park get into the backcountry, however, where the forests are magnificent and the valleys practically untouched by civilization. The park is one of the great wildlife sanctuaries in the United States; grizzly and black bear, deer, moose, elk, beaver, wolves, mountain lions, and buffalo thrive in its inaccessible regions. More than two hundred species of birds inhabit the park.—D. C. S.

Yosemite National Park. Yosemite National Park, located on the western slope of California's Sierra Nevada range, was named after the Indians who originally inhabited the area. They called Yosemite Valley "Ahwahnee"—the place of the deep grass. The Joseph R. Walker expedition in 1833 passed close to the valley and may have seen it. Undoubtedly, some of the early gold prospectors viewed it but left no confirming records. James Savage, an Indian trader who operated a trading post on the south fork of the Merced River about fifteen miles below the valley, led the first party of white men into the valley in 1851. His objective was to punish the Indians who, after considerable provocation, had burned three trading posts in the region. The Indians were soon driven out of the valley. James M. Hutchings brought the first party of tourists into Yosemite in 1855 and subsequently publicized its magnificent scenery in articles in the Mariposa *Gazette*, the *California Magazine*, and elsewhere. Almost from the beginning, the valley was a mecca for travelers and tourists. On June 30, 1864, Congress granted the Yosemite Valley and the nearby Mariposa Grove of redwoods to the state of California as a public park.

California pledged to protect Yosemite's extraordinary beauty, but John Muir, who saw Yosemite Valley for the first time in 1868, was not sure this would be sufficient protection. His writing and political campaigning led to the establishment on October 1, 1890, of Yosemite National Park, a doughnut-shaped preserve that surrounded the valley. Muir then led a drive, which culminated in 1906, to persuade California to re-cede the valley to the federal government for inclusion in the national park. Muir founded the Sierra Club to provide organized backing for these and other conservation ventures.

One of the most famous conservation controversies—the so-called Hetch Hetchy steal—involved both Muir and Yosemite National Park. Hetch Hetchy was a magnificent ice-carved gorge in Yosemite park, almost as beautiful as Yosemite Valley itself. About 1900, the city of San Francisco, searching for a domestic water supply, asked for permission to build a reservoir in Hetch Hetchy Valley. Muir was aghast at this plan, and he mounted a nationwide campaign to block the proposed reservoir. The fight over Hetch Hetchy raged for more than ten years. In 1913 Congress finally granted permission for the reservoir to be constructed, thus ending the first great conservation battle of the twentieth century. In future years, preservationists and national park supporters often invoked the memory of the Hetch Hetchy steal to remind conservationists that constant vigilance would be necessary to keep the national parks inviolate.

The best-known feature of Yosemite National Park is, of course, Yosemite Valley, whose combination of granite cliffs, lofty waterfalls, verdant meadows, clear streams, and spreading trees makes it captivating and quite unforgettable. But the park contains vast stretches of scenic wilderness, uncut by roads and unmarred by the crowds that congregate in the valley. There are also remarkable groves of *Sequoia gigantea* and sugar pines. Tuolumne Meadows (8,500 feet) is the hub of a magnificent network of high country trails. The park encompasses 761,320 acres. It may be entered through Merced, California, on the west or via the scenic Tioga Road, which begins at Lee Vining, California, to the east of the park.—D. C. S.

Young, Brigham (1801-1877). Mormon leader. Born in Whittingham, Vermont, the ninth of eleven children, Young was poorly educated but practical and industrious. A carpenter, painter, and glazier, he was in business for himself at the age of sixteen. Although moralistic and with tendencies toward piety, he attached himself to no religion until he was twenty-one, at which time he joined the Methodist church. In 1824 he moved with his first wife, Miriam Works, to western New York. There, in 1830 or 1831, he happened to see a copy of the Book of Mormon, was converted, and was baptized into the Mormon church in 1832. That same year he met Joseph Smith and was sent on a proselyting mission to Canada. He moved to the Mormon community of Kirtland, Ohio, in 1833. By this time a widower, he married his second wife, Mary Ann Angell, in 1834. He was involved in Zion's Camp, the march in 1834 to wrest control of Jackson County, Missouri, from the anti-Mormon mob that had driven the Mormons out.

Designated an apostle in 1835, Young spent the next few years traveling as a missionary in the summers and practicing his trades in the winters. He served a mission to the eastern states in 1836-37 and another to New York in late 1837. When the failure of the church's bank in Kirtland caused a schismatic crisis in 1837, he stood stalwartly behind the Mormon prophet, Joseph Smith. With others he moved from Ohio to Far West, Missouri, in 1838. Upon the expulsion of the Mormons from

Missouri later in the year, he helped organize the move to Nauvoo, Illinois. While on a proselyting mission to England in 1840-41, he became impressed with the poverty of the working class there and later instituted steps to assist thousands of them to migrate to Mormon communities in the American Far West.

Upon his return to Illinois in 1841, Young was called to be president of the Quorum of the Twelve Apostles. For a time he helped with the building of Nauvoo, but by July 1843 he was headed east on yet another mission, this time to raise funds for the Nauvoo temple and for the Nauvoo House, a hotel. He was in the East when Joseph Smith was killed in 1844.

Returning to Nauvoo, Young served as head of the church in his capacity as president of the Quorum of the Twelve Apostles. Although he worked diligently to complete the picturesque Nauvoo temple, Young nonetheless realized that the Mormons had no future in Illinois. Under pressure but with some advance planning, approximately sixteen thousand Mormons left Illinois, beginning in February 1846. They settled temporarily on Indian lands in Council Bluffs, Iowa, and Winter Quarters, Nebraska. Under Young's urging, in 1846 some five hundred Mormon men volunteered for military duty during the Mexican War, which helped finance the trek to the Salt Lake valley in 1847. Traveling on the MORMON TRAIL, Young led an advance company to the Rocky Mountains, which arrived in the Salt Lake valley on July 24, 1847, at which time, it has been reported, Young declared, "This is the place." What lay before them was a huge desert, but under Young's direction the Mormons set to work irrigating and planting seed. Young returned to Winter Quarters in December 1847, where he was named president and prophet of the church. This act was sustained by the Saints in Salt Lake City the following year.

As the first governor and superintendent of Indian affairs of Utah Territory (1851-58), Young functioned primarily through a theocracy (see LATTER-DAY SAINTS: *Brigham Young period*). With his removal as governor (1858), the coming of federal troops (1858 and 1862), the completion of the transcontinental railroad (1869), and the increasing numbers of non-Mormons in the territory, Young's theocratic practices frequently had to be modified. Relations with the federal government and with other Americans were exacerbated by Mormon economic exclusion and polygamy. The nation pressured Utah to conform to national norms. Specifically, laws were passed to eliminate the practice of plural marriage, church domination of government, and church economic programs. Having married more than twenty wives (and having fathered fifty-seven children), Young himself was tried for bigamy in 1871 but was not convicted.

Always a builder, Young started four temples during his administration. He assisted in founding the University of Deseret (later University of Utah) in Salt Lake City in 1850, Brigham Young Academy (now Brigham Young University) in Provo in 1876, and Brigham Young College in Logan in 1877. He sent pioneers throughout the West and established more than 350 communities. Young advocated home industry and self-sufficiency and abhorred the unsteady and unruly elements sometimes associated with western mining. The Latter-day Saints did, however, embark on ventures in coal, iron, lead, and gold mining. Young also undertook construction projects on the transcontinental telegraph (1861) and on the transcontinental railroad (1868-69). Stemming from these enterprises, he constructed branch railroads and telegraph systems for the benefit of the Mormon people. He devoted the last decade of his life to building economic solidarity among the Mormons though the establishment of ZION'S CO-OPERATIVE MERCANTILE INSTITUTION, industrial cooperatives, and the UNITED ORDER OF ENOCH.

Young was an indefatigable leader and gave several thousand sermons during his ministry, most of which have been published. The sermons are a mixture of theology, instruction in practical living, exhortation, and explanations of policies. He died of peritonitis following an acute attack of appendicitis.

See Susa Young Gates and L. E. Widtsoe, *The Life Story of Brigham Young* (1931); Stanley P. Hirshson, *The Lion of the Lord* (1969); Milton R. Hunter, *Brigham Young: The Colonizer* (1945); Dean C. Jessee, ed., *Letters of Brigham Young to His Sons* (1974); Preston Nibley, *Brigham Young: The Man and His Work* (1936); M. R. Werner, *Brigham Young* (1925); and Ray B. West, Jr., *Kingdom of the Saints* (1957).—L. J. A.

Young, Ewing (1792?-1841). Fur trader and Oregon pioneer. Young almost ranks with Jedediah Smith in the range of his travels and the success of his enterprises. Young was one of the first Americans to trap in the Southwest and to reach California overland by the Gila River route across southern Arizona. He was also one of the first to send California horses eastward to New Mexico and to drive cattle northward from California to Oregon, where he finally settled in 1834.

Pioneering must have been in Young's blood. Born in eastern Tennessee, he was the third generation of his family to live on the frontier. By January 1822 Young had moved to Chariton, Missouri, where he joined a friend to farm; by then he was also skilled as a carpenter and cabinetmaker. Before the year was out, he sold his land and purchased a stock of goods to take to Santa Fe in William Becknell's second expedition to New Mexico. Once in the Southwest, Young trapped on the Pecos and other New Mexico rivers with his friend William Wolfskill. During the 1820s he made several trips to St. Louis, where he exchanged his furs and New Mexican mules and horses for more goods. At one time he and Wolfskill operated a store in Taos.

Young's deserved reputation as a true leader of men and a shrewd trader and businessman began in the winter of 1826-27 when he led a large band of trappers southwestward through the area of the Santa Rita copper mines on the headwaters of the Gila River, to hunt in the little-known region of the Salt and Gila river valleys. It was on this trip that Young's outfit encountered the remains of a trapping party that had been ambushed by Papago. Two of the three known survivors, James Ohio Pattie and Michel Robidoux, explained their plight to Young, who retaliated with such force that the Papago left his men alone as they trapped to the mouth of the Gila and along the lower Colorado before returning to New Mexico. Although Pattie, in his famous *Personal Narrative*, states that the trappers traveled northward along the Colorado into Utah, turned eastward in the vicinity of Longs Peak, and eventually moved south to Taos along the eastern slope, the evidence suggests that

Young and his party returned east by the Gila route to New Mexico. There Young's pelts were promptly confiscated by the incoming governor, Manuel Armijo, on a flimsy legal pretext, and Young himself was jailed for hunting without the proper license.

On his second major hunt, Young was more circumspect: he obtained an American passport from Secretary of State Henry Clay and applied for Mexican citizenship, although there is no evidence that he was ever naturalized. He and his party left Taos in August 1829, ostensibly to trap in the central Rockies; but once out of sight of Mexican officials, they returned to the Salt and Gila valleys. Young then sent half his party back with furs; he and the remainder of his party, which included the youthful Kit Carson, went on to California via the Mohave River and Cajon Pass to Mission San Gabriel Arcángel near Los Angeles. From there they traveled to the San Joaquin River to hunt beaver. On this trip Young ran into a competing fur brigade led by Peter Skene Ogden of the Hudson's Bay Company, who had also been sent to exploit the region.

Young sold his pelts to a sea captain on the California shore, bought horses and mules for the New Mexican and Missouri markets, and on his return again trapped in southern Arizona before finally reaching Taos in April 1831. Meanwhile, Wolfskill had departed over the Old Spanish Trail to California with a pack train of blankets and goods to be traded for mules and horses needed by New Mexicans. This bright prospect of double profits led Young, in partnership with David Waldo and David Jackson, to repeat the scheme. This time Jackson returned with the herds while Young trapped the San Joaquin again. But the horse and mule trade proved less profitable than expected, and for a time Young turned to the sea-otter trade. He and his men were taken out in boats to the coastal islands of southern California or to the feeding grounds of the otters, where they shot the otters with their rifles. This venture, too, proved to be less than profitable and once again he turned to trapping beaver in the San Joaquin. He also trapped and explored in northern California only to find that Hudson's Bay Company brigades under John Work and Michael La Framboise had stripped the region. Young then trapped along the Gila before returning to California, presumably to settle there.

In 1834 Young met Hall J. Kelley, the Oregon promoter, who persuaded him to migrate to Oregon with a large stock of horses; but his arrival there was marred by the fact that California officials had incorrectly notified Dr. John McLoughlin, the powerful Hudson's Bay factor at Fort Vancouver, that Young's herd had been stolen from California ranches. Ostracized by McLoughlin, who refused to sell him supplies and clothing, Young had a difficult time surviving, but he did found a ranch in the Chehalem valley, begin to raise wheat, and—in partnership with other American immigrants—build a gristmill and a sawmill. In 1837, visiting Lieutenant W. A. Slacum of the United States Navy assisted Young and the American settlers in forming a company to bring badly needed herds of cattle from California overland to the Willamette valley. Young's success at this task—which provided Oregon with nearly seven hundred head of cattle—as well as in his wheat and lumber businesses, established him as a major economic figure in early Oregon history.

When his success was tragically cut short by his death in 1841, he left no will. Ironically it was the problem of disposing of his intestate property in a land with no legal authority that brought the American settlers in Oregon together to establish a provisional government. (Like so many other mountain men Young had formed a common-law alliance with a Taos girl, and it was their son, Joaquin, who eventually came to Oregon to claim his father's estate; the courts awarded him only about $4,000.)

Young's accomplishments suggest that even if Jedediah Smith, Joseph R. Walker, or someone else had not found the central routes to California during the 1820s and 1830s, men of Young's intelligence and acumen would soon have taken their place as the trailblazers to California. As it was, Young's career dramatized the accessibility of California from New Mexico via the Gila route and the Old Spanish Trail. His successful movement of stock over great distances antedated the famous long cattle drives of the 1870s and the 1880s by almost thirty years, and his role in forwarding the American settlement of Oregon was of crucial importance. Like so many western pioneers, Young defies easy analysis. Although he spent most of his life on the frontier, the tall, quiet-spoken Young appears to have been literate and was an excellent businessman. He was notably kind and helpful to his fellow Americans and yet was seen as a troublemaker by New Mexican authorities, and his dealings with Indians were always characterized by hostility and often needless killing.

See L. R. Hafen, *The Mountain Men and the Fur Trade of the Far West*, vol. II (1965); Kenneth L. Holmes, *Ewing Young, Master Trapper* (1967); and David J. Weber, *The Taos Trappers: The Fur Trade in the Far Southwest, 1540-1846* (1971).—H. R. L.

Young, Mahonri Macintosh (1877-1957). Sculptor. Born in Salt Lake City and a grandson of Brigham Young, Young studied art in Salt Lake City, New York, Paris, and Italy. His sculpture, usually in bronze, falls into two categories. The first depicts peoples of the western frontier, usually cowboys, pioneer settlers, Indians, and mountain men. His work included several well-known Indian sculptures for the American Museum of Natural History in New York City. He also did large statues of Brigham Young, which are located in Washington, D.C., and on the campus of Brigham Young University in Provo, Utah. The seagull monument on Temple Square in Salt Lake City is one of his creations. Young was extremely sympathetic to the labor movement, and his second group of sculpture deals with workmen and men of action. Most notable among these are *Stevedore* (1904), *Driller* (1915), and *Beat Him to the Punch* (1932). His etchings have a strong emphasis on cities and urban life.—L. J. A.

Younger brothers. Outlaws. Of all the desperate men of western outlawry, the Younger brothers are numbered among the most ruthless and resourceful. Legend places them in the shadow of America's Robin Hood, Jesse James, with Cole Younger as Jesse's Little John. Cole, who disliked Jesse, resented this, and his feeling is sustained by a record as bloody and devoid of respect for law and life as that compiled by Jesse James.

Thomas Coleman ("Cole") Younger (1844-1916) was the oldest of Henry Washington Younger's four outlaw sons, the others being John (1846-74), James (1850-

Bob Younger in 1889. (National Archives)

1902), and Robert (1853-89). The Younger boys came from a respectable family of some stature in the vicinity of Lee's Summit, Missouri. Cole even went to school. His schoolmaster was Stephen B. Elkins, later a United States senator from West Virginia. He also attended a school in Harrisonville, Missouri, known as the Academy.

But those were terrible times in Missouri, especially for impressionable children. The Younger boys were witnesses to the bloody border skirmishes between Kansans and Missourians long before the South seceded in 1861. Henry Younger was a Union man, but when the Civil War began, Cole joined the Confederate state guard and fought at Carthage in July 1861. In October he joined QUANTRILL'S RAIDERS and a month later killed his first man. Quantrill's vicious guerrillas soon built an appalling record of atrocities, and Cole Younger was in the thick of them, particularly after his father was murdered by Union sympathizers in July 1862.

In August, Cole received a commission as a lieutenant in the regular Confederate service. He served as a spy and distinguished himself at the battle of Lone Jack on August 16, 1862, by distributing ammunition under heavy federal fire with great danger to himself. He also saved the life of a Union officer who had been captured and prevented a young Confederate soldier from riding into a Union trap. A few months later he intervened to prevent the execution of Stephen B. Elkins, his former teacher.

So far Cole Younger was just a soldier with a reputation for bravery and leadership. But then he was accused of murdering a man in Kansas. Cole eluded capture, but on Christmas 1862 he killed a man who recog-

nized him in a Kansas City saloon. A reward was offered for his capture. By August 1863, Cole had rejoined Quantrill, who had been outlawed even by the Confederacy, and in the same month Cole participated in Quantrill's raid on Lawrence, Kansas, one of the most inexcusable atrocities of the war. Afterward, the guerrillas scattered, and Cole went into hiding.

During this time, Jim and John Younger reportedly killed four Union soldiers who were looking for Cole at Six Mile Church near Harrisonville. The situation grew so bad that Cole fled Missouri and reported to General Benjamin McCulloch in Texas. He was assigned to duty running down southern planters who were trading cotton to the Union. He was, as always, efficient and ruthless. Later he led a raid into Arkansas. That winter he also met Myra Belle Shirley, who later became the notorious Belle STARR.

In May 1864 Cole rode with George S. Jackson to Colorado on an expedition to destroy western telegraph lines and then was sent to Mexico. Early in 1865 he was ordered to Canada to receive two ships for the Confederate navy. He was en route to Canada by way of California when the war ended.

Cole reached Missouri in the fall of 1865. He learned of Quantrill's inglorious demise at the hands of Union guerrillas and of Jim's apprenticeship in mayhem with Quantrill. Still, Cole and Jim, fresh from war and dying, might have settled down like most of the others who rode in the border wars, but they did not. Cole had scarcely arrived home when an unsolved murder from prewar days was blamed on him, and he was forced into hiding again. Early in 1866, through his friend Frank James, Cole met Jesse JAMES. It was the beginning of a fateful relationship.

On February 13, 1866, twelve men, among them Jesse James and Cole Younger, robbed the bank at Liberty, Missouri, and killed a student. Afterward, Cole went to Texas, where he renewed his acquaintance with Belle Shirley. For the next couple of years Cole visited Belle periodically, and in 1867 Belle bore a child, whom she named Pearl Younger.

The Youngers, the Jameses, and their associates continued to rob banks. Jim Younger joined Cole and Jesse after the Russellville, Kentucky, bank robbery in May 1868, but none of them was clearly identified until the Gallatin, Missouri, bank job late in 1869. About this time, John Younger, who had killed a man in Texas, joined his brothers. By then banking interests had retained the Pinkerton Detective Agency to break up the gang. A grim conflict between the detectives and the outlaws followed, but the James and Younger boys grew even bolder. In April 1872 Bob Younger was one of three men who robbed the box office at the Kansas City fairgrounds. Now all of the Youngers were together.

The next summer the gang tried its hand at train robbery at Adair, Iowa. Their success spurred them to still greater depredations and strengthened the resolve of the Pinkertons. Early in March 1874 two detectives and a Missouri sheriff were confronted by John and Jim Younger. One of the agents and the sheriff were killed and the third man fled, but not before John Younger had been killed. In reprisal the outlaws taunted authorities with more murders and robberies. In 1875, public opinion turned against the Pinkertons after a tragic explosion attributed to them crippled Jesse

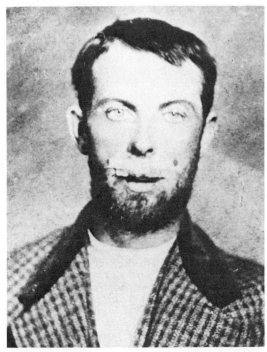

Jim Younger at the time of his trial (1876); he had been shot through the upper jaw. (National Archives)

James's mother and killed his half brother. That year the Youngers were inactive until December, when they robbed a train at Muncie, Kansas. By the end of the year they were in Dallas, Texas, playing the role of respectable citizens and chuckling over a then new book by John T. Appler called *The Guerillas of the West; or, The Life, Character and Daring Exploits of the Younger Brothers*. It was a curious mixture of reasonably accurate information and fanciful tales. Appler's little book was widely read and, in time, became the source of many falsehoods about Cole and his brothers. Unfortunately for Cole, the stories were accepted, and later, when Cole was trying to get out of the Minnesota State Prison, Appler's book was used to deny him pardon. The most damaging story involved Cole in the purported execution of fifteen Union prisoners. According to the story, Cole was told that a new Enfield rifle would shoot a mile. He purportedly replied that if that were true, one bullet ought to kill ten men; then he lined up the prisoners, one behind the other, and fired until he had killed them all. If Cole had known the impact of that story upon readers, he might not have thought the book was so funny.

In May 1876 the Youngers and Frank and Jesse James robbed a stage between Austin and San Antonio and, in July, a bank at Otterville, Missouri. They then confidently planned to rob the bank at Northfield, Minnesota, but when they made the attempt on September 7, 1876, the citizenry of Northfield turned the robbery into a death trap for the outlaws. Two Northfield citizens died that day, but two of the outlaws were also killed. The rest of the gang was badly shot up. Jim Younger's jaw was nearly shot away, Bob's elbow was

shattered, Cole was wounded in the shoulder. The Minnesota farmers pursued them into the swamps, where the gang split up. Jesse James urged Cole to abandon the badly wounded Jim Younger because he was slowing the escape. When Cole refused, he and Jesse argued violently and the James brothers abandoned the Youngers. Jesse and Frank eluded capture, while the Youngers were cornered at Hanska Slough and forced to surrender after losing another of their companions to the posse's marksmanship.

The Youngers pleaded guilty to robbery and murder and were sentenced to life in prison. The story of the Youngers would have ended there if it had not been for a man named Warren C. Bronaugh. In 1882 he visited Cole at the Minnesota State Penitentiary. Bronaugh explained that he was the soldier whose life Cole had saved at the battle of Lone Jack and promised Cole that he would get him out of prison. Popular opinion was against pardon, but Bronaugh was persistent. Year after year he worked for a pardon, enlisting the aid of men like Major Emory Foster and Stephen B. Elkins, who were also indebted to Cole. In 1889 Bob Younger died in prison; he had been weak since the Northfield raid, and his condition became hopeless when he contracted tuberculosis. Finally, Bronaugh's efforts paid off: in 1901, Cole and Jim received conditional pardons, but they were not permitted to leave Minnesota. A combination of ill health and the reluctance of people to hire him, drove Jim into despondency. Sick and bitter, he became a recluse in his hotel room, refusing to see anyone. Finally, in utter despair, he put a pistol to his head and killed himself. Ironically, Cole had taken a job selling tombstones.

Because of Bronaugh's continued efforts, Cole was granted a full pardon in 1903. He returned to Missouri, where he was a celebrity, and there renewed his acquaintance with Frank James. The two of them organized a Wild West show and toured with it for a while. After Frank quit the show, Cole continued to work with carnivals for several years, but he was getting old. He retired to his home at Lee's Summit, where he joined a church and lived quietly until his death.

See Homer Croy, *Last of the Great Outlaws* (1956). The story of Warren C. Bronaugh's efforts to secure the pardon of the Youngers is told in his book, *The Youngers' Fight for Freedom* (1906). Cole told his own story in an autobiography entitled *The Story of Cole Younger* (1903). The Northfield raid is covered in Dallas Cantrell, *Youngers' Fatal Blunder: Northfield, Minnesota* (1973). —G. L. R.

Yreka, California. Ghost town. Yreka was the capital of the Klamath River gold-mining region in the extreme northern part of California. Gold was discovered in the area in 1851, but by the 1880s the placers were drying up. Yreka, however, has survived as a commercial and recreation center. Some of the old buildings still remain, and an interesting exhibit of gold samples is on display at the County Courthouse. Other ghost towns in the area are Greenhorn, Hawkinsville, Humbug City, Sawyer's Bar, and High Grade.

See Remi Nadeau, *Ghost Towns and Mining Camps of California* (1965).—R. B. W.

Yuchi Indians. The Yuchi Indians were a semisedentary hunting and agricultural people whose earliest known habitat (c. 1550) was the highlands of eastern

Tennessee, centering around the Hiwassee River. Their language constituted a distinct linguistic stock, the Uchean, which had some structural resemblances to both Siouan and Muskogean. The Yuchi were not a unified tribe, being divided into independent village-bands with individual identity designations and organization. They were first noted by de Soto in 1540, and in 1567 suffered severe losses in encounters with units of Juan Pardo's expedition. The Yuchi bands apparently dispersed after these episodes and took up a migratory existence, wandering throughout the Southeast and Midwest.

The Rickohockan Indians of Virginia mentioned by John Lederer in 1670 were probably Yuchi, as were almost certainly the Hogologe of Georgia, and most ethnologists believe that the Westo Indians who warred against the Carolina colonists and their Indian allies in 1681 were a Yuchi group. A Yuchi village was encountered in 1682 by La Salle near his Fort St. Louis (present Utica, Illinois). The majority of the Yuchi people, however, evidently became allied with the Creek villages on the Chattahoochee and Talapoosa rivers by 1800 and were a major portion of the population of the Creek Confederacy. Some Yuchi bands were also absorbed by the Cherokee and Shawnee, and at least one Yuchi village joined with the Seminole peoples about 1810. Undoubtedly many of the small southeastern Indian groups that were designated by whites as separate tribes were in fact Yuchi bands, but these were early overwhelmed by the white population advance and have long since vanished from the historical record.

Those Yuchi who allied with larger tribes shared their hosts' fate, generally moving with them to the Oklahoma Indian Territory during the great removals of the 1830s. The identifiable Yuchi population has been estimated at about 3,000 in 1650, declining to 1,100 by 1830, and to 216 in the 1930 census. The Yuchi were not granted independent tribal status by the United States government and have had no individual reservation, although those remaining with the Creek settled in one body in the northwest part of the old Creek Nation in Creek County, Oklahoma, where some of their descendents still live.

See C. T. Foreman, "The Yuchi: Children of the Sun," *Chronicles of Oklahoma*, vol. 37 (1959-60); F. G. Speck, *Ethnology of the Yuchi Indians* (1909); and J. R. Swanton, *The Indian Tribes of North America* (1952). —P. R. M.

Yulee, David Levy (1810-1886). Florida politician and railroad builder. Born on St. Thomas in the West Indies to Jewish parents, an English mother and a Moroccan father of Portuguese extraction, Yulee (whose original name was David Levy) resided there until 1819. In that year his father sent him to Norfolk, Virginia, for his formal education. In 1829 he went to work on one of his father's plantations in Alachua County, Florida. Brief service as a deputy clerk in the county court interested him in the law, and in 1832 he settled in St. Augustine to study with Judge Robert Raymond Reid. At this time the young man broke with his father and launched on an individualistic course that carried him from his father's faith to Christianity. In 1845 he changed his name to Yulee.

Yulee's introduction to politics came with his election to the Florida territorial legislature in 1837. In 1838 he was elected to the state constitutional convention. He was an ardent member of its anti-bank faction and participated in the formation of the Florida Democratic party at the close of the convention. He went as territorial delegate to Congress in 1841, and after the admission of Florida to the Union in 1845 was elected a United States senator, serving until 1851. In 1855 he was returned to the Senate, serving until his resignation following Florida's secession in 1861. He was a leader of the movement that culminated in the Nashville Southern Convention of 1850 and advocated secession in that year.

Between his two Senate terms he was active in plans for an Atlantic to Gulf railroad, which he incorporated in 1853 with himself as president. Both state and federal land grants were secured and the bond issues of the corporation were guaranteed by the state. In 1855 actual construction of the proposed line from Fernandina was begun. By March 1861 the line was completed to Cedar Key on the Gulf Coast. The road operated under Yulee until 1866 when financial difficulties caused the state to take possession. During the war the railroad and planting had been Yulee's chief interests, but the war brought destruction to the line's Gulf and Atlantic terminals and many miles of rail were torn up. During 1865-66 Yulee was imprisoned for a time with other southern leaders at Fort Pulaski, Georgia. Since the resources Yulee was able to muster after Confederate defeat were inadequate for rebuilding the line, the state had seized it and sold it to its creditors. Yulee continued his association with the road as vice president and by 1869 the reorganized railroad had been rebuilt and its debt retired. Yulee and his new partners turned then to Europe for new capital in order to improve and expand the facilities, acquiring $1 million in the Netherlands in 1872. The road did not prosper, however, and Yulee's attempts to build a Tampa Bay branch were not immediately productive. In 1880 the new creditors forced a reorganization, which led in 1881 to complete control of the corporation by English capitalists led by Sir Edward Reed. Although Yulee continued to sit on the board of directors until his death, his influence waned. In 1881 he moved to Washington.

The principal collection of the Yulee papers is in the P. K. Yonge Library of Florida History at the University of Florida.—H. J. D.

Yuma, Arizona. Located at the junction of the Colorado and Gila rivers, Yuma was named after the Yuma (*fumo*, "smoke") Indians, whom the Spaniards here found building bonfires in the vicinity in 1540. By 1779 the junction was an important crossing on the road from Sonora to California, and Spain planted a mission settlement on the California side; however, two years later, the local Indians massacred the inhabitants. In 1849 the United States Army founded Fort Yuma on the old mission site to protect travelers bound for California, and the Colorado Steam Navigation Company began operating steamers on the river. In 1854 Charles D. Poston and Herman Ehrenberg surveyed a townsite on the Arizona shore; by 1862 it was called Arizona City. An army depot and wagon shop were built. In 1871 the seat for Yuma County was moved from La Paz to Arizona City, the town was incorporated, and in 1873 the name was changed to Yuma. Within a decade the territorial prison was located there and the Southern Pacific Railroad had arrived—and built east through

Tucson to El Paso. After 1900 Laguna Dam was constructed upriver, and water was channeled south to the Imperial (California) and Yuma valleys. A mild land boom followed and an extensive irrigation system developed. Military installations built during World War II added to the economic stability of the town. The population in 1970 was 28,835 people.

See Robert Wizniki, *A History of Yuma and the Territorial Prison* (1968).—H. P. H.

Yuma (Quechan) Indians. The Quechan Indians, more popularly known as the Yuma Indians, are one of several Yuman-speaking tribal groups who live along the Colorado River in Arizona and California. Their linguistic relatives include the Cocopa, Mohave, Walapai, and Havasupai along the river; the mountain-dwelling Yavapai; the Maricopa of the Gila River; and the Halchidhoma of the Salt River.

Historically the Yuma are famous for having controlled the Yuma crossing of the Colorado River. First contacted by non-Indians in 1540 when Hernando de Alarcón sailed up the river in a vain attempt to make contact with Francisco Vásquez de CORONADO, they found themselves in the path of the Spanish empire in its surge to open an overland route to California. In 1604 Don Juan de ONATE, the governor of New Mexico, trekked all the way from his capital to the Quechan country and the mouth of the Colorado River, claiming all for New Spain. But the claims lay dormant until the late seventeenth century when there was renewed interest in tying Alta California firmly to the realms of the Spanish crown—an interest that led in 1775 to the overland journey to California by Juan Bautista de ANZA and a group of Spanish colonists.

In 1780 the Spaniards established two settlements among the Yuma, near the junction of the Gila and Colorado rivers. Missionaries, soldiers, and settlers lived in these communities, each of which was half mission and half colony, an arrangement that ultimately led to their dramatic downfall. The missionaries were unable to control the excesses of the soldiers with respect to the latter's treatment of the Indians; the settlers appropriated Indian lands. The Yuma, like the Spaniards, were farmers who relied on water from the river and on crops planted in fields adjacent to it for their subsistence. Spanish troops, moreover, helped themselves to Yuma stores of food when they needed them.

On July 17, 1781, the Yuma decided to rid themselves of their oppressors. Then, and in the next two days, they killed four Franciscan friars, thirty-one soldiers, and twenty settlers. All attempts by Spaniards to place settlements among the Yuma came forever to an end. Just as the Pueblo in New Mexico had revolted in 1680, so had these doughty Indian warriors in 1781. But unlike what happened in New Mexico, there was to be no Spanish reconquest.

By the 1840s, as the "manifest destiny" of the United States began to make itself felt in the Southwest, the crossing of the Gila River at Yuma came into increasing use by Anglo-Americans. The army of General Stephen W. KEARNY, en route from Santa Fe to southern California in 1846 during the Mexican War, crossed the river near Yuma, and the gold rush of 1849 saw a veritable flood of non-Indian passersby. The Yuma took advantage of the situation by charging travelers to raft them over the river, but in August 1849 the first of many non-Indian ferries was built to do the job instead. United States troops were stationed at the Yuma crossing in 1850, and in spite of some hostilities between the Yuma and Anglos then and after, by the time the Gadsden Purchase and the acquisition of Yuma by the United States became law in 1854, the Indians had been militarily subdued.

The Fort Yuma Indian reservation, now 9,141 acres, was set aside for the Yuma in 1884. Individual Yuma also own 480 acres of trust land on the Arizona side of the river. The tribe was organized in 1936 under the Indian Reorganization Act and has its own chairman and council. Leasing, governmental employment, wage labor, and welfare account for most of its modern income. The tribe operates a small museum and arts-and-crafts center on the reservation. The Yuma do fine beadwork and are attempting to revive their age-old crafts of pottery making and basketry. Today there are about a thousand Yuma, who live in California and Arizona, possibly three thousand fewer than there were in the early 1700s. But they have not relinquished their post at the Yuma crossing, and it is likely they will continue, as they have in the past, to be witnesses to the parade of history marching by them.

See Jack D. Forbes, *Warriors of the Colorado* (1960); C. Daryll Forde, *Ethnography of the Yuma Indians* (1931); and Douglas D. Martin, *Yuma Crossing* (1954).—B. L. F.

Z

Zane's Trace. Zane's Trace was a direct land connection between the two major Ohio River points of Wheeling, West Virginia, and Maysville, Kentucky. Crossing the shoulder of eastern Ohio, this road shortened the distance of travel as compared with the great elbow of the Ohio River. The trace was located after 1796 by Ebenezer Zane. Zane's survey was not in fact an original

one, because he followed the old Mingo Trail from Wheeling to the Muskingum River, and roughly an Indian path to the Scioto River. From Chillicothe, Ohio, on the Scioto the trace cut overland, following rather closely the Ohio River, to the great Limestone, or Maysville, crossing of that stream. Ferries and inns were established at the major crossings, and in time the three major towns of Zanesville, Lancaster, and Chillicothe came into being. Zane's Trace was in fact an extension of the Limestone or Maysville Road, which led up from central Kentucky to the Ohio. Because of this, it became a direct overland link for flatboatmen returning to Ohio from New Orleans and for the heavy amount of land travel between the West and Philadelphia, Baltimore, and Washington.

See Beverly Bond, *The Foundations of Ohio* (1941); and R. C. Buley, *The Old Northwest Pioneer Period, 1815-1840*, vol. I (1950).—T. D. C.

Zion National Park. Zion National Park is located in southwestern Utah. The park, which contains 147,035 acres, is highlighted by deep canyons cut through the Kolob Terrace (of Navaho sandstone) and by the brilliant colors of the exposed rock formations. Some of the canyons are exceedingly narrow, with almost perpendicular walls. Angels Landing, the Temple of Sinawava, and the Great White Throne are some of the best-known rock formations in Zion Canyon. They rise about three thousand feet above the floor of the canyon.

The area was first settled by Mormon ranchers and farmers. Some of its scenic canyons were reserved by presidential proclamation in 1909 as the Mukuntuweap National Monument. The monument was enlarged in 1918 and established as a national park on November 19, 1919. Horace M. Albright, the assistant director of the National Park Service, was largely responsible for the establishment of the park. He had visited the area in 1918 and was convinced that the scenery was national park caliber. The park originally focused on Zion Canyon, but it was enlarged in 1956 and 1960 to include the wild Canyons of the Kolobs.—D. C. S.

Zion's Co-operative Mercantile Institution. Mormon cooperative. With the coming of the transcontinental railroad to Utah Territory in 1869, Brigham Young organized Zion's Co-operative Mercantile Institution (ZCMI) in Salt Lake City to handle all the wholesale trade of the Mormons. ZCMI was formed out of a department store owned by Mormon William JENNINGS. Under the ZCMI's leadership, cooperative general retail stores were established in some 150 Mormon settlements. Mormons were expected to give exclusive patronage to these local Mormon-controlled institutions. As a means of underlining the religious role of ZCMI in coordinating the business affairs of the Mormons, signs inscribed with "Holiness to the Lord" were hung over the doors of its various outlets. ZCMI was a profitable enterprise and its earnings helped the Mormon church, which was the principal stockholder.

Cooperative local stores drifted into the hands of a few private owners during the anti-Mormon prosecutions of the 1880s, and virtually all semblance of "cooperation" ended by the time of the depression of 1893. By that time Mormon exclusivism in trade had ended. ZCMI became essentially a Salt Lake City mercantile store with a few retail branches in the surrounding area. The Mormon church continued to hold a controlling interest in ZCMI and has retained that control to the present.

See Leonard J. Arrington, *Great Basin Kingdom* (1958).—L. J. A.

Zogbaum, Rufus Fairchild (1849-1925). Illustrator. Zogbaum was born in Charleston, South Carolina, and from 1878 to 1879 studied at the Art Students League in New York City. After a trip to Paris in 1880, he traveled to the West to record life in the army. He may have made several trips to Montana and is known to have visited the Darlington Indian Agency near Fort Reno, Indian Territory, in 1888. Some of his western illustrations appeared in *Harper's Weekly* from about 1885 to 1889, and several of his travel journals were published, at least in part, as articles in various periodicals. In about 1895, Zogbaum began illustrating western fiction. He also illustrated factual articles on the West, particularly its military aspect. Few of Zogbaum's original works have survived the years.—D. C. H.